# THE OFFICIAL

## 2010 PRICE GUIDE TO

# BASEBALL CARDS

## DR. JAMES BECKETT

### THIRTIETH EDITION

**House of Collectibles**
New York

P9-AOE-723

Copyright © 2010 by James Beckett III

All rights reserved. Published in the United States by House of Collectibles, an imprint of The Random House Information Group, a division of Random House, Inc., New York, and in Canada by Random House of Canada Limited, Toronto.

House of Collectibles and colophon
are trademarks of Random House, Inc.

Random House is a registered trademark of Random House, Inc.
Please address inquiries about electronic licensing of any products for use
on a network, in software, or on CD-ROM to the
Subsidiary Rights Department, Random House Information Group,
fax 212-572-6003.

This book is available for special discounts for bulk purchases for sales promotions or premiums. Special editions, including personalized covers, excerpts of existing books, and corporate imprints, can be created in large quantities for special needs. For more information, write to Random House, Inc., Special Markets/Premium Sales, 1745 Broadway, MD 6-2, New York, NY 10019 or e-mail specialmarkets@randomhouse.com

www.randomhouse.com

Manufactured in the United States of America

ISSN: 1062-7138

ISBN: 978-0-375-72336-0

10 9 8 7 6 5 4 3 2 1

Thirtieth Edition: May 2010

# Table of Contents

## About the Author

Jim Beckett, the leading authority on sports card values in the United States, maintains a wide range of activities in the world of sports. He possesses one of the finest collections of sports cards and autographs in the world, has made numerous appearances on radio and television, and has been frequently cited in many national publications. He was awarded the first "Special Achievement Award" for Contributions to the Hobby by the National Sports Collectors Convention in 1980, the "Jock Jaspersen Award" for Hobby Dedication in 1983, and the "Buck Barker, Spirit of the Hobby" award in 1991.

Dr. Beckett is the author of *Beckett Baseball Card Price Guide*, *The Official Price Guide to Baseball Cards*, *Price Guide to Baseball Collectibles*, *The Sport Americana Baseball Memorabilia and Autograph Price Guide*, *Beckett Almanac of Baseball Cards and Collectibles*, *Beckett Football Card Price Guide*, *The Official Price Guide to Football Cards*, *Beckett Hockey Card Price Guide*, *The Official Price Guide to Hockey Cards*, *Beckett Basketball Card Price Guide*, *The Official Price Guide to Basketball Cards*, *The Beckett Basketball Card Alphabetical Checklist*, *The Beckett Basketball Card Alphabetical Checklist*, and *The Beckett Football Card Alphabetical Checklist*. In addition, he is the founder, publisher, and editor of *Beckett Baseball*, *Beckett Basketball*, *Beckett Football*, *Beckett Hockey*, *Beckett Sports Cards Monthly*, and *Beckett Racing*.

Jim Beckett received his Ph.D. in Statistics from Southern Methodist University in 1975. Prior to starting Beckett Publications in 1984, Dr. Beckett served as an Associate Professor of Statistics at Bowling Green State University and as a vice president of a consulting firm in Dallas, Texas.

## How to Use This Book

Isn't it great? Every year this book gets better with all the new sets coming out. But even more exciting is that every year there are more options in collecting the cards we love so much. This edition has been enhanced and expanded from the previous edition. The cards you collect — who appears on them, what they look like, where they are from, and (most important to most of you) what their current values are — are enumerated within. Many of the features contained in the other *Beckett Price Guides* have been incorporated into this volume since condition grading, terminology, and many other aspects of collecting are common to the card hobby in general. We hope you find the book both interesting and useful in your collecting pursuits.

*The Beckett Guide* has been successful where other attempts have failed because it is complete, current, and valid. This price guide contains not just one, but three prices by condition for all the baseball cards listed. The prices were added to the card lists just prior to printing and reflect not the author's opinions or desires but the going retail prices for each card, based on the marketplace (sports memorabilia conventions and shows, sports card shops, hobby papers, current mail-order catalogs, local club meetings, auction results, and other firsthand reportings of actually realized prices).

What is the best price guide available on the market today? Of course, card sellers prefer the price guide with the highest prices, while card buyers naturally prefer the one with the lowest prices. Accuracy, however, is the true test. Use the price guide trusted by more collectors and dealers than all the others combined. Look for the Beckett® name. I won't put my name on anything I won't stake my reputation on. Not the lowest and not the highest — but the most accurate, with integrity.

To facilitate your use of this book, read the complete introductory section on the following pages before going to the pricing pages. Every collectible field has its own terminology; we've tried to capture most of these terms and definitions in our glossary. Please read carefully the section on grading and the condition of your cards, as you cannot determine which price column is appropriate for a given card without first knowing its condition.

Welcome to the world of baseball cards.

# How to Collect

Each collection is personal and reflects the individuality of its owner. There are no set rules on how to collect cards. Since card collecting is a hobby or leisure pastime, what you collect, how much you collect, and how much time and money you spend collecting are entirely up to you. The funds you have available for collecting and your own personal taste should determine how you collect. Information and ideas presented here are intended to help you get the most enjoyment from this hobby.

It is impossible to collect every card ever produced. Therefore, beginners as well as intermediate and advanced collectors usually specialize in some way. One of the reasons this hobby is popular is that individual collectors can define and tailor their collecting methods to match their own tastes. To give you some idea of the various approaches to collecting, we will list some of the more popular areas of specialization.

Many collectors select complete sets from particular years. For example, they may concentrate on assembling complete sets from all the years since their birth or since they became avid sports fans. They may try to collect a card for every player during that specified period of time.

Many others wish to acquire only certain players. Usually such players are the superstars of the sport, but occasionally collectors will specialize in all the cards of players who attended a particular college or came from a certain town. Some collectors are interested in only the first cards or Rookie Cards of certain players. A handy guide for collectors interested in pursuing the hobby this way is *The Sport Americana Baseball Card Alphabetical Checklist.*

Another fun way to collect cards is by team. Most fans have a favorite team, and it is natural for that loyalty to be translated into a desire for cards of the players on that favorite team. For most of the recent years, team sets (all the cards from a given team for that year) are readily available at a reasonable price. *The Sport Americana Team Baseball Card Checklist* will open up this field to the collector.

## Obtaining Cards

Several avenues are open to card collectors. Cards still can be purchased in the traditional way: by the pack at the local candy, grocery, drug, or major discount store.

But there are also thousands of card shops across the country that specialize in selling cards individually or by the pack, box, or set. Another alternative is the thousands of card shows held each month around the country, which feature anywhere from 8 to 800 tables of sports cards and memorabilia for sale.

For many years, it has been possible to purchase complete sets of baseball cards through mail-order advertisers in traditional sports media publications, such as the *Sporting News, Baseball Digest,* and *Street & Smith* yearbooks. These sets also are advertised in the card collecting periodicals. Many collectors will begin by subscribing to at least one of the hobby periodicals, all with good up-to-date information. In fact, subscription offers can be found in the advertising section of this book.

Most serious card collectors obtain old (and new) cards from one or more of several main sources: (1) trading or buying from other collectors or dealers; (2) responding to sale or auction ads in the hobby publications; (3) buying at a local hobby store; (4) attending sports collectibles shows or conventions; and (5) purchasing cards over the Internet.

We advise that you try all five methods since each has its own distinct advantages: (1) trading is a great way to make new friends; (2) hobby periodicals help you keep up with what's going on in the hobby (including when and where the conventions are happening); (3) stores provide the opportunity to enjoy personalized service and consider a great diversity of material in a relaxed sports-oriented atmosphere; (4) shows allow you to choose from multiple dealers and thousands of cards under one roof in a competitive situation; and (5) the Internet allows one to purchase cards in a convenient manner from almost anywhere in the world.

## Preserving Your Cards

Cards are fragile. They must be handled properly in order to retain their value. Careless handling can easily result in creased or bent cards. It is, however, not recommended that tweezers or tongs be used to pick up your cards since such utensils might mar or indent card surfaces and thus reduce those cards conditions and values.

In general, your cards should be handled directly as little as possible. This is sometimes easier to say than to do.

Although there are still many who use custom boxes, storage trays, or even shoe boxes, plastic sheets are the preferred method of many collectors for storing cards.

A collection stored in plastic pages in a three-ring album allows you to view your collection at any time without the need to touch the cards themselves. Cards can also be kept in single holders (of various types and thicknesses) designed for the enjoyment of each card individually.

For a large collection, some collectors may use a combination of the above methods. When purchasing plastic sheets for your cards, be sure that you find the pocket size that fits the cards snugly. Don´t put your 1951 Bowman in a sheet designed to fit 1981 Topps.

Most hobby and collectibles shops and virtually all collectors´ conventions will have these plastic pages available in quantity for the various sizes offered, or you can purchase them directly from the advertisers in this book.

Also, remember that pocket size isn´t the only factor to consider when looking for plastic sheets. Other factors such as safety, economy, appearance, availability, or personal preference also may influence which types of sheets a collector may want to buy.

Damp, sunny, and/or hot conditions — no, this is not a weather forecast — are three elements to avoid in extremes if you are interested in preserving your collection. Too much (or too little) humidity can cause the gradual deterioration of a card. Direct, bright sun (or fluorescent light) over time will bleach out the color of a card. Extreme heat accelerates the decomposition of the card. On the other hand, many cards have lasted more than 75 years without much scientific intervention. So be cautious, even if the above factors typically present a problem only when present in the extreme. It never hurts to be prudent.

## Collecting vs. Investing

Collecting individual players and collecting complete sets are both popular vehicles for investment and speculation.

Most investors and speculators stock up on complete sets or on quantities of players they think have good investment potential.

There is obviously no guarantee in this book, or anywhere else for that matter, that cards will outperform the stock market or other investment alternatives in the future. After all, baseball cards do not pay quarterly dividends and cards cannot be sold at their "current values" as easily as stocks or bonds.

Nevertheless, investors have noticed a favorable long-term trend in the past performance of baseball and other sports collectibles, and certain cards and sets have outperformed just about any other investment in some years.

Many hobbyists maintain that the best investment is and always will be the building of a collection, which traditionally has held up better than outright speculation.

Some of the obvious questions are: Which cards? When to buy? When to sell? The best investment you can make is in your own education.

The more you know about your collection and the hobby, the more informed the decisions you will be able to make. We´re not selling investment tips. We´re selling information about the current value of baseball cards. It´s up to you to use that information to your best advantage.

# Terminology

Each hobby has its own language to describe its area of interest. The nomenclature traditionally used for trading cards is derived from the American Card Catalog,

published in 1960 by Nostalgia Press. That catalog, written by Jefferson Burdick (who is called the "Father of Card Collecting" for his pioneering work), uses letter and number designations for each separate set of cards. The letter used in the ACC designation refers to the generic type of card. While both sport and nonsport issues are classified in the ACC, we shall confine ourselves to the sport issues. The following list defines the letters and their meanings as used by the American Card Catalog.

**(none) or N** - 19th Century U.S. Tobacco.

**B** - Blankets.

**D** - Bakery Inserts Including Bread.

**E** - Early Candy and Gum.

**F** - Food Inserts.

**H** - Advertising.

**M** - Periodicals.

**PC** - Postcards.

**R** - Candy and Gum since 1930.

**T** - Tobacco.

Following the letter prefix and an optional hyphen are one-, two-, or three-digit numbers, R(-)999. These typically represent the company or entity issuing the cards. In several cases, the ACC number is extended by an additional hyphen and another one- or two-digit numerical suffix. For example, the 1957 Topps regular-series baseball card issue carries an ACC designation of R414-11. The "R" indicates a Candy or Gum card produced since 1930. The "414" is the ACC designation for Topps Chewing Gum baseball card issues, and the "11" is the ACC designation for the 1957 regular issue (Topps' eleventh baseball set). Like other traditional methods of identification, this system provides order to the process of cataloging cards; however, most serious collectors learn the ACC designation of the popular sets by repetition and familiarity, rather than by attempting to "figure out" what they might or should be. From 1948 forward, collectors and dealers commonly refer to all sets by their year, maker, type of issue, and any other distinguishing characteristic. For example, such a characteristic could be an unusual issue or one of several regular issues put out by a specific maker in a single year. Regional issues are usually referred to by year, maker, and sometimes by title or theme of the set.

# Glossary/Legend

Our glossary defines terms used in the card collecting hobby and in this book. Many of these terms are also common to other types of sports memorabilia collecting. Some terms may have several meanings depending on use and context.

**ACETATE**—A transparent plastic.

**AS**—All-Star card. A card portraying an All-Star Player of the previous year that says "All-Star" on its face.

**ATG**—All-Time Great card.

**ATL**—All-Time Leaders card.

**AU(TO)**—Autographed card.

**AW**—Award Winner.

**BB**—Building Blocks.

**BC**—Bonus Card.

**BF**—Bright Futures.

**BL**—Blue Letters.

**BNR**—Banner Season.

**BOX CARD**—Card issued on a box (e.g., 1987 Topps Box Bottoms).

**BRICK**—A group of 50 or more cards having common characteristics that is intended to be bought, sold, or traded as a unit.

**CABINETS**—Popular and highly valuable photographs on thick card stock produced in the 19th and early 20th centuries.

**CC**—Curtain Call.

**CG**—Cornerstones of the Game.

**CHECKLIST**—A list of the cards contained in a particular set. The list is always in numerical order if the cards are numbered. Some unnumbered sets are artificially numbered in alphabetical order, by team and alphabetically within the team, or by uniform number for convenience.

**CL**—Checklist card. A card that lists in order the cards and players in the set or series. Older checklist cards in Mint condition that have not been marked are very desirable and command premiums.

**CO**—Coach.

**COMM**—Commissioner.

**COMMON CARD**—The typical card of any set; it has no premium value accruing from subject matter, numerical scarcity, popular demand, or anomaly.

**CONVENTION**—A gathering of dealers and collectors at a single location for the purpose of buying, selling, and trading sports memorabilia items. Conventions are open to the public and sometimes feature autograph guests, door prizes, contests, seminars, etc. They are frequently referred to simply as "shows."

**COOP**—Cooperstown.

**COR**—Corrected card.

**CP**—Changing Places.

**CT**—Cooperstown.

**CY**—Cy Young Award.

**DD**—Decade of Dominance.

**DEALER**—A person who engages in buying, selling, and trading sports collectibles or supplies. A dealer may also be a collector, but as a dealer, his main goal is to earn a profit.

**DIE-CUT**—A card with part of its stock partially cut, allowing one or more parts to be folded or removed. After removal or appropriate folding, the remaining part of the card can frequently be made to stand up.

**DK**—Diamond King.

**DL**—Division Leaders.

**DP**—Double Print (a card that was printed in double the quantity compared to the other cards in the same series) or a Draft Pick card.

**DT**—Dream Team.

**DUFEX**—A method of card manufacturing technology patented by Pinnacle Brands, Inc. It involves a refractive quality to a card with a foil coating.

**ERA**—Earned Run Average.

**ERR**—Error card. A card with erroneous information, spelling, or depiction on either side of the card. Most errors are not corrected by the producing card company.

**FC**—Fan Club.

**FDP**—First or First-Round Draft Pick.

**FF**—Future Foundation.

**FOIL**—Foil embossed stamp on card.

**FOLD**—Foldout.

**FP**—Franchise Player.

**FR**—Franchise.

**FS**—Father/son card.

**FS**—Future Star.

**FUN**—Fun cards.

**FY**—First Year.

**GL**—Green Letters.

**GLOSS**—A card with luster; a shiny finish as in a card with UV coating.

**HG**—Heroes of the Game.

**HH**—Hometown Heroes.

**HIGH NUMBER**—The cards in the last series of numbers in a year in which such higher-numbered cards were printed or distributed in significantly lesser amounts than the lower-numbered cards. The high-number designation refers to a scarcity of the high-numbered cards. Not all years have high numbers in terms of this definition.

**HL**—Highlight card.

**HOF**—Hall of Fame, or a card that portrays a Hall of Famer (HOFer).

**HOLOGRAM**—A three-dimensional photographic image.

**HOR**—Horizontal pose on card as opposed to the standard vertical orientation found on most cards.

**IA**—In Action card.

**IF**—Infielder.

**INSERT**—A card of a different type or any other sports collectible (typically a poster or sticker) contained and sold in the same package along with a card or cards of a major set. An insert card is either unnumbered or not numbered in the same sequence as the major set. Sometimes the inserts are randomly distributed and are not found in every pack.

**INTERACTIVE**—A concept that involves collector participation.

**IRT**—International Road Trip.

**ISSUE**—Synonymous with set, but usually used in conjunction with a manufacturer, e.g., a Topps issue.

**JSY**—Jersey.

**KM**—K-Men.

**LHP**—Left-handed Pitcher.

**LL**—League Leaders or large letters on card.

**LUM**—Lumberjack.

**MAJOR SET**—A set produced by a national manufacturer of cards containing a large number of cards. Usually 100 or more different cards constitute a major set.

**MB**—Master Blasters.

**MEM**—Memorial card. For example, the 1990 Donruss and Topps Bart Giamatti cards.

**METALLIC**—A glossy design method that enhances card features.

**MG**—Manager.

**MI**—Maximum Impact.

**MINI**—A small card; for example, a 1975 Topps card of identical design but smaller dimensions than the regular Topps issue of 1975.

**ML**—Major League.

**MM**—Memorable Moments.

**MULTI-PLAYER CARD**—A single card depicting two or more players (but not a team card).

**MVP**—Most Valuable Player.

**NAU**—No autograph on card.

**NG**—Next Game.

**NH**—No-Hitter.

**NNOF**—No name on front.

**NOF**—Name on front.

**NOTCHING**—The grooving of the card, usually caused by fingernails, rubber bands, or bumping card edges against other objects.

**NT**—Now and Then.

**NV**—Novato.

**OF**—Outfield or Outfielder.

**OLY**—Olympics Card.

**P**—Pitcher or Pitching pose.

**P1**—First Printing.

**P2**—Second Printing.

**P3**—Third Printing.

**PACKS**—A means by which cards are issued in terms of pack type (wax, cello, foil, rack, etc.) and channel of distribution (hobby, retail, etc.).

**PARALLEL**— A card that is similar in design to its counterpart from a basic set but that has a distinguishing quality.

**PF**—Profiles.

**PG**—Postseason Glory.

**PLASTIC SHEET**—A clear, plastic page that is punched for insertion into a binder (with standard three-ring spacing) containing pockets for displaying cards. Many different styles of sheets exist with pockets of varying sizes to hold the many differing card formats. Also called a display sheet or storage sheet.

**PLATINUM**—A metallic element used in the process of creating a glossy card.

**PP**—Power Passion.

**PR**—Printed name on back.

**PREMIUM**—A card, sometimes on photographic stock, that is purchased or obtained in conjunction with, or redemption for, another card or product. The premium is not packaged in the same unit as the primary item.

**PRES**—President.

**PRISMATIC/PRISM**—A glossy or bright design that refracts or disperses light.

**PS**—Pace Setters.

**PT**—Power Tools.

**PUZZLE CARD**—A card whose back contains a part of a picture which, when joined correctly with other puzzle cards, forms the completed picture.

**PUZZLE PIECE**—A die-cut piece designed to interlock with similar pieces (e.g., early 1980s Donruss).

**PVC**—Polyvinyl chloride, a substance used to make many of the popular card display protective sheets. Non-PVC sheets are considered preferable for long-term storage of cards by many.

**RARE**—A card or series of cards of very limited availability. Unfortunately, "rare" is a subjective term frequently used indiscriminately to hype value. "Rare" cards are harder to obtain than "scarce" cards.

**RB**—Record Breaker.

**RC**—Rookie Card.

**REDEMPTION**—A program established by multiple card manufacturers that allows collectors to mail in a special card (usually a random insert) in return for special cards, sets, or other prizes not available through conventional channels.

**REFRACTOR**—A card that features a design element that enhances (distorts) its color/appearance through deflecting light.

**REV NEG**—Reversed or flopped photo side of the card. This is a major type of error card, but only some are corrected.

**RHP**—Right-handed Pitcher.

**RHW**—Rookie Home Whites.

**RIF**—Rifleman.

**RPM**—Rookie Premiere Materials.

**RR**—Rated Rookie.

**ROO**—Rookie.

**ROY**—Rookie of the Year.

**RP**—Relief Pitcher.

**RTC**—Rookie True Colors.

**SA**—Super Action card.

**SASE**—Self-Addressed, Stamped Envelope.

**SB**—Scrapbook.

**SB**—Stolen Bases.

**SCARCE**—A card or series of cards of limited availability. This subjective term is sometimes used indiscriminately to hype value. "Scarce" cards are not as difficult to obtain as "rare" cards.

**SCR**—Script name on back.

**SD**—San Diego Padres.

**SEMI-HIGH**—A card from the next-to-last series of a sequentially issued set. It has more value than an average card and generally less value than a high number. A card is not called a semi-high unless the next-to-last series in which it exists has an additional premium attached to it.

**SERIES**—The entire set of cards issued by a particular producer in a particular year; e.g., the 1971 Topps series. Also, within a particular set, series can refer to a group of (consecutively numbered) cards printed at the same time, e.g., the first series of the 1957 Topps issue (#1 through #88).

**SET**—One each of the entire run of cards of the same type produced by a particular manufacturer during a single year. In other words, if you have a complete set of 1976 Topps, then you have every card from #1 up to and including #660; i.e., all the different cards that were produced.

**SF**—Starflics.

**SH**—Season Highlight.

**SHEEN**—Brightness or luster emitted by card.

**SKIP-NUMBERED**—A set that has many unissued card numbers between the lowest number in the set and the highest number in the set, e.g., the 1948 Leaf baseball set contains ninety-eight cards skip-numbered from #1 to #168. A major set in which a few numbers were not printed is not considered to be skip-numbered.

**SP**—Single or Short Print (a card that was printed in lesser quantity compared to the other cards in the same series; see also DP and TP).

**SPECIAL CARD**—A card that portrays something other than a single player or team, for example, a card that portrays the previous year's statistical leaders or the results from the previous year's World Series.

**SS**—Shortstop.

**STANDARD SIZE**—Most modern sports cards measure 2-1/2 by 3-1/2 inches. Exceptions are noted in card descriptions throughout this book.

**STAR CARD**—A card that portrays a player of some repute, usually determined by his ability, but sometimes referring to sheer popularity.

**STOCK**—The cardboard or paper on which the card is printed.

**SUPERIMPOSED**—Affixed on top of something; i.e., a player photo over a solid background.

**SUPERSTAR CARD**—A card that portrays a superstar, e.g., a Hall of Famer or player with strong Hall of Fame potential.

**TC**—Team Checklist.

**TEAM CARD**—A card that depicts an entire team.

**THREE-DIMENSIONAL (3D)**—A visual image that provides an illusion of depth and perspective.

**TOPICAL**—A subset or group of cards that have a common theme (e.g., MVP award winners).

**TP**—Triple Print (a card that was printed in triple the quantity compared to the other cards in the same series).

**TR**—Trade reference on card.

**TRANSPARENT**—Clear, see-through.

**UDCA**—Upper Deck Classic Alumni.

**UER**—Uncorrected Error.

**UMP**—Umpire.

**USA**—Team USA.

**UV**—Ultraviolet, a glossy coating used in producing cards.

**VAR**—Variation card. One of two or more cards from the same series with the same number (or player with identical pose if the series is unnumbered) differing from one another by some aspect, the different feature stemming from the printing or stock of the card. This can be caused when the manufacturer of the cards notices an error in one or more of the cards, makes the changes, and then resumes the print run. In this case there will be two versions or variations of the same card. Sometimes one of the variations is relatively scarce.

**VERT**—Vertical pose on card.

**WAS**—Washington National League (1974 Topps).

**WC**—What's the Call?

**WL**—White letters on front.

**WS**—World Series card.

**YL**—Yellow letters on front.

**YT**—Yellow team name on front.

**\***—to denote multi-sport sets.

# Understanding Card Values

## Determining Value

Why are some cards more valuable than others? Obviously, the economic laws of supply and demand are applicable to card collecting just as they are to any other field where a commodity is bought, sold, or traded in a free, unregulated market.

Supply (the number of cards available on the market) is less than the total number of cards originally produced since attrition diminishes that original quantity. Each year a percentage of cards is typically thrown away, destroyed, or otherwise lost to collectors. This percentage is much, much smaller today than it was in the past because more and more people have become increasingly aware of the value of their cards.

For those who collect only Mint condition cards, the supply of older cards can be quite small indeed. Until recently, collectors were not so conscious of the need to preserve the condition of their cards. For this reason, it is difficult to know exactly how many 1953 Topps are currently available, Mint or otherwise. It is generally accepted that there are fewer 1953 Topps available than 1963, 1973, or 1983 Topps cards. If demand were equal for each of these sets, the law of supply and demand would increase the price for the least available sets. Demand, however, is never equal for all sets, so price correlations can be complicated. The demand for a card is influenced by many factors. These include: (1) the age of the card; (2) the number of cards printed; (3) the player(s) portrayed on the card; (4) the attractiveness and popularity of the set; and (5) the physical condition of the card.

In general, (1) the older the card, (2) the fewer the number of the cards printed, (3) the more famous, popular, and talented the player, (4) the more attractive and popular the set, and (5) the better the condition of the card, the higher the value of the card will be. There are exceptions to all but one of these factors: the condition of the card. Given two cards similar in all respects except condition, the one in the best condition will always be valued higher.

While those guidelines help to establish the value of a card, the countless exceptions and peculiarities make any simple, direct mathematical formula to determine card values impossible.

## Regional Variation

Since the market varies from region to region, prices may be higher. This is known as a regional premium. How significant the premium is — and if there is any premium at all — depends on the local popularity of the team and the player.

The largest regional premiums usually do not apply to superstars, who often are so well known nationwide that the prices of their key cards are too high for local dealers to realize a premium.

Lesser stars often command the strongest premiums. Their popularity is concentrated in their home regions, creating local demand that greatly exceeds overall demand.

Regional premiums can apply to popular retired players and sometimes can be found in the areas where the players grew up or starred in college.

A regional discount is the converse of a regional premium. Regional discounts occur when a player has been so popular in his region for so long that local collectors and dealers have accumulated quantities of his key cards. The abundant supply may make the cards available in that area at the lowest prices anywhere.

## Set Prices

A somewhat paradoxical situation exists regarding the price of a complete set versus the combined cost of the individual cards in the set. In nearly every case, the sum of the prices for the individual cards is higher than the cost for the complete set. This is especially true of cards from the last few years. The reasons for this apparent anomaly stem from the habits of collectors and from the carrying costs to dealers. Today, each card in a set normally is produced in the same quantity as all other cards in its set.

Many collectors pick up only stars, superstars, and particular teams. As a result, the dealer is left with a shortage of certain player cards and an abundance of others. He therefore incurs an expense in simply "carrying" these less desirable cards in stock. On the other hand, if he sells a complete set, he gets rid of large numbers of cards at one time. For this reason, he generally is willing to receive less money for a complete set. By doing this, he recovers all of his costs and also makes a profit.

The disparity between the price of the complete set and the sum of the prices of the individual cards also has been influenced by the fact that some of the major manufacturers now are pre-collating card sets. Since "pulling" individual cards from the sets involves a specific type of labor (and cost), the singles or star card market is not affected significantly by pre-collation.

Set prices also do not include rare card varieties, unless specifically stated. Of course, the prices for sets do include one example of each type for the given set, but this is the least expensive variety.

## Scarce Series

Scarce series occur because cards issued before 1974 were made available to the public each year in several series of finite numbers of cards, rather than all cards of the set being available for purchase at one time. At some point during the year, usually toward the end of the baseball season, interest in current year baseball cards waned. Consequently, the manufacturers produced smaller numbers of these later-series cards.

Nearly all nationwide issues from post–World War II manufacturers (1948 to 1973) exhibit these series variations. In the past, Topps, for example, may have issued series consisting of many different numbers of cards, including 55, 66, 80, 88, and others. Recently, Topps has settled on what is now its standard sheet size of 132 cards, six of which constitute its 792-card set.

While the number of cards within a given series is usually the same as the number of cards on one printed sheet, this is not always the case. For example, Bowman used 36 cards on its standard printed sheets, but in 1948 substituted 12 cards during later print runs of that year's baseball cards. Twelve of the cards from the initial sheet of 36 cards were removed and replaced by 12 different cards, giving, in effect, a first series of 36 cards and a second series of 12 new cards. This replacement produced a scarcity of 24 cards — the 12 cards removed from the original sheet and the 12 new cards added to the sheet. A full sheet of 1948 Bowman cards (second printing) shows that card numbers 37 through 48 have replaced 12 of the cards on the first printing sheet.

The Topps Company also has created scarcities and/or excesses of certain cards in many of its sets. Topps, however, has most frequently gone the other direction by double printing some of the cards. Double printing causes an abundance of cards of the players who are on the same sheet more than one time. During the years 1978 to 1981, Topps double printed 66 cards out of its large 726-card set. The Topps practice of double printing cards in earlier years is the most logical explanation for the known scarcities of particular cards in some of these Topps sets.

From 1988 through 1990, Donruss short printed and double printed certain cards in its major sets. Ostensibly this was because of its addition of bonus team MVP cards in its regular-issue wax packs.

We are always looking for information about or photographs of printing sheets of cards for research. Each year, we try to update the hobby's knowledge of distribution anomalies. Please let us know at the address in this book if you have firsthand knowledge that would be helpful in this pursuit.

# Grading Your Cards

Each hobby — stamps, coins, comic books, record collecting, etc. — has its own close up grading terminology. Collectors of sports cards are no exception. The one invariable criterion for determining the value of a card is its condition: The better the condition of the card, the more valuable it is. Condition grading, however, is subjective. Individual card dealers and collectors differ in the strictness of their grading, but the stated condition of a card should be determined without regard to whether it is being bought or sold.

No allowance is made for age. A 1952 card is judged by the same standards as a 1992 card. But there are specific sets and cards that are condition-sensitive (marked with "!" in the Price Guide) because of their border color, consistently poor centering, etc. Such cards and sets sometimes command premiums above the listed percentages in Mint condition.

### Centering

Current centering terminology uses numbers representing the percentage of border on either side of the main design. Obviously, centering is diminished in importance for borderless cards such as Stadium Club.

**Slightly Off-Center (60/40):** A slightly off-center card is one that, upon close inspection, is found to have one border bigger than the opposite border. This degree once was offensive only to purists, but now some hobbyists try to avoid cards that are anything other than perfectly centered.

**Off-Center (70/30):** An off-center card has one border that is noticeably more than twice as wide as the opposite border.

**Badly Off-Center (80/20 or worse):** A badly off-center card has virtually no border on one side of the card.

**Miscut:** A miscut card actually shows part of the adjacent card in its larger border and consequently a corresponding amount of its card is cut off.

### Corner Wear

Corner wear is the most scrutinized grading criteria in the hobby. These are the major categories of corner wear:

**Corner with a slight touch of wear:** The corner still is sharp, but there is a slight touch of wear showing. On a dark-bordered card, this shows as a dot of white.

**Fuzzy corner:** The corner still comes to a point, but the point has just begun to fray. A slightly "dinged" corner is considered the same as a fuzzy corner.

**Slightly rounded corner:** The fraying of the corner has increased to where there is only a hint of a point. Mild layering may be evident. A "dinged" corner is considered the same as a slightly rounded corner.

**Rounded corner**: The point is completely gone. Some layering is noticeable.

**Badly rounded corner**: The corner is completely round and rough. Severe layering is evident.

### Creases

A third common defect is the crease. The degree of creasing in a card is difficult to show in a drawing or picture. On giving the specific condition of an expensive card for sale, the seller should note any creases additionally. Creases can be categorized as to severity according to the following scale:

**Light Crease**: A light crease is a crease that is barely noticeable upon close inspection. In fact, when cards are in plastic sheets or holders, a light crease may not be seen (until the card is taken out of the holder). A light crease on the front is much more serious than a light crease on the card back only.

**Medium Crease**: A medium crease is noticeable when held and studied at arm's length by the naked eye, but does not overly detract from the appearance of the card. It is an obvious crease, but not one that breaks the picture surface of the card.

**Heavy Crease**: A heavy crease is one that has torn or broken through the card's picture surface; i.e., puts a tear in the photo surface.

### Alterations

**Deceptive Trimming**: This occurs when someone alters the card in order (1) to shave off edge wear, (2) to improve the sharpness of the corners, or (3) to improve centering — obviously the objective is to falsely increase the perceived value of the card to an unsuspecting buyer. The shrinkage usually is evident only if the trimmed card is compared to an adjacent full-size card or if the trimmed card is itself measured.

**Obvious Trimming**: Obvious trimming is noticeable and unfortunate. It is usually performed by noncollectors who give no thought to the present or future value of their cards.

**Deceptively Retouched Borders**: This occurs when the borders (especially on those cards with dark borders) are touched up on the edges and corners with magic marker or crayons of appropriate color in order to make the card appear Mint.

### Categorization of Defects—Miscellaneous Flaws

The following are common minor flaws that, depending on severity, lower a card's condition by one to four grades and often render it no better than Excellent-Mint: bubbles (lumps in surface), gum and wax stains, diamond cutting (slanted borders), notching, off-centered backs, paper wrinkles, scratched-off cartoons or puzzles on back, rubber band marks, scratches, surface impressions, and warping.

The following are common serious flaws that, depending on severity, lower a card's condition at least four grades and often render it no better than Good: chemical or sun fading, erasure marks, mildew, miscutting (severe off-centering), holes, bleached or retouched borders, tape marks, tears, trimming, water or coffee stains, and writing.

## Condition Guide

### Grades

**Mint (Mt)**—A card with no flaws or wear. The card has four perfect corners, 60/40 or better centering from top to bottom and from left to right, original gloss, smooth edges, and original color borders. A Mint card does not have print spots or color or focus imperfections.

**Near Mint-Mint (NrMt-Mt)**—A card with one minor flaw. Any one of the following would lower a Mint card to Near Mint-Mint: one corner with a slight touch of wear, barely noticeable print spots, or color or focus imperfections. The card must have

60/40 or better centering in both directions, original gloss, smooth edges, and original color borders.

**Near Mint (NrMt)**—A card with one minor flaw. Any one of the following would lower a Mint card to Near Mint: one fuzzy corner or two to four corners with slight touches of wear, 70/30 to 60/40 centering, slightly rough edges, minor print spots, color or focus imperfections. The card must have original gloss and original color borders.

**Excellent-Mint (ExMt)**—A card with two or three fuzzy, but not rounded, corners and centering no worse than 80/20. The card may have no more than two of the following: slightly rough edges, very slightly discolored borders, minor print spots, color or focus imperfections. The card must have original gloss.

**Excellent (Ex)**—A card with four fuzzy but definitely not rounded corners and centering no worse than 80/20. The card may have a small amount of original gloss lost, rough edges, slightly discolored borders, and minor print spots or color or focus imperfections.

**Very Good (Vg)**—A card that has been handled but not abused: slightly rounded corners with slight layering, slight notching on edges, a significant amount of gloss lost from the surface (but no scuffing) and moderate discoloration of borders. The card may have a few light creases.

**Good (G), Fair (F), Poor (P)**—A well-worn, mishandled, or abused card: badly rounded and layered corners, scuffing, most or all original gloss missing, seriously discolored borders, moderate or heavy creases, and one or more serious flaws. The grade of Good, Fair, or Poor depends on the severity of wear and flaws. Good, Fair, and Poor cards generally are used only as fillers.

The most widely used grades are defined above. Obviously, many cards will not perfectly fit one of the definitions.

Therefore, categories between the major grades known as in-between grades are used, such as Good to Very Good (G-Vg), Very Good to Excellent (VgEx), and Excellent-Mint to Near Mint (ExMt-NrMt). Such grades indicate a card with all qualities of the lower category but with at least a few qualities of the higher category.

Beckett Baseball Card Price Guide lists each card and set in two grades, with the middle grade valued at about 40%–45% of the top grade.

The value of cards that fall between the listed columns can also be calculated using a percentage of the top grade. For example, a card that falls between the top and middle grades (Ex, ExMt, or NrMt in most cases) will generally be valued at anywhere from 50%–90% of the top grade.

Similarly, a card that falls between the middle and bottom grades (G-Vg, Vg, or VgEx in most cases) will generally be valued at anywhere from 20%–40% of the top grade.

There are also cases where cards are in better condition than the top grade or worse than the bottom grade. Cards that grade worse than the lowest grade are generally valued at 5%–10% of the top grade.

When a card exceeds the top grade by one — such as NrMt-Mt when the top grade is NrMt, or Mint when the top grade is NrMt-Mt — a premium of up to 50% is possible, with 10%–20% the usual norm.

When a card exceeds the top grade by two — such as Mint when the top grade is NrMt, or NrMt-Mt when the top grade is ExMt — a premium of 25%–50% is the usual norm. But certain condition-sensitive cards or sets, particularly those from the pre-war era, can bring premiums of up to 100% or even more.

Unopened packs, boxes, and factory-collated sets are considered Mint in their unknown (and presumed perfect) state. Once opened, however, each card can be graded (and valued) in its own right by taking into account any defects that may be present in spite of the fact that the card has never been handled.

# Selling Your Cards

Just about every collector sells or will sell cards eventually. Someday you may be interested in selling your duplicates or maybe even your whole collection. You may sell to other collectors, friends, or dealers. You may even sell cards you purchased from a certain dealer back to that same dealer. In any event, it helps to know some of the mechanics of the typical transaction between buyer and seller.

Dealers will buy cards in order to resell them to other collectors who are interested in the cards. Dealers will always pay a higher percentage for items that (in their opinion) can be resold quickly, and a much lower percentage for those items that are perceived as having low demand and hence are slow moving. In either case, dealers must buy at a price that allows for the expense of doing business and a margin for profit.

If you have cards for sale, the best advice we can give is that you get several offers for your cards — either from card shops or at a card show — and take the best offer, all things considered. Note, the "best" offer may not be the one for the highest amount. And remember, if a dealer really wants your cards, he won't let you get away without making his best competitive offer. Another alternative is to place your cards in an auction as one or several lots.

Many people think nothing of going into a department store and paying $15 for an item of clothing for which the store paid $5. But if you were selling your $15 card to a dealer and he offered you $5 for it, you might consider his markup unreasonable. To complete the analogy: Most department stores (and card dealers) that consistently pay $10 for $15 items eventually go out of business. An exception is when the dealer has lined up a willing buyer for the item(s) you are attempting to sell, or if the cards are so hot that it's likely he'll have to hold the cards for just a short period of time.

In those cases, an offer of up to 75% of book value still will allow the dealer to make a reasonable profit considering the short time he will need to hold the merchandise. In general, however, most cards and collections will bring offers in the range of 25%–50% of retail price. Also consider that most material from the last five to ten years is plentiful. If that's what you're selling, don't be surprised if your best offer is well below that range.

## Interesting Notes

The first card numerically of an issue is the single card most likely to obtain excessive wear.

Consequently, you typically will find the price on the #1 card (in NrMt or Mint condition) somewhat higher than might otherwise be the case.

Similarly, but to a lesser extent (because normally the less important, reverse side of the card is the one exposed), the last card numerically in an issue also is prone to abnormal wear. This extra wear and tear occurs because the first and last cards are exposed to the elements (human element included) more than any of the other cards. They are generally end cards in any brick formations and are subject to rubber bandings, stackings on wet surfaces, and like activities.

Sports cards have no intrinsic value. The value of a card, like the value of other collectibles, can be determined only by you and your enjoyment in viewing and possessing these cardboard treasures.

Remember, the buyer ultimately determines the price of each baseball card. You are the determining price factor because you have the ability to say "No" to the price of any card by not exchanging your hard-earned money for a given issue. When the cost of a trading card exceeds the enjoyment you will receive from it, your answer should be "No." We assess and report the prices. You set them!

We are always interested in receiving the price input of collectors and dealers. We happily credit major contributors.

We welcome your opinions, since your contributions assist us in ensuring a better guide each year.

If you would like to join our survey list for the next editions of this book and others authored by Dr. Beckett, please send your name and address to Dr. James Beckett, 15850 Dallas Parkway, Dallas, TX 75248.

## History of Baseball Cards

Today's version of the baseball card, with its colorful and oftentimes high-tech front and back, is a far cry from its earliest predecessors. The issue remains cloudy as to which was the very first baseball card ever produced, but the institution of base-

## *Centering*

**Well-centered**

**Slightly Off-centered**

**Off-centered**

**Badly Off-centered**

**Miscut**

ball cards dates from the latter half of the 19th century, more than 100 years ago. Early issues, generally printed on heavy cardboard, were of poor quality, with photographs, drawings, and printing far short of today's standards.

Goodwin & Co., of New York, makers of Gypsy Queen, Old Judge, and other cigarette brands, is considered by many to be the first issuer of baseball and other sports cards. Its issues, predominantly sized 1-1/2 by 2-1/2 inches, generally consisted of photographs of baseball players, boxers, wrestlers, and other subjects mounted on stiff cardboard. More than 2,000 different photos of baseball players alone have been identified. These "Old Judges," a collective name commonly used for the Goodwin & Co. cards, were issued from 1886 to 1890 and are treasured parts of many collections today.

Among the other cigarette companies that issued baseball cards still attracting attention today are Allen & Ginter, D. Buchner & Co. (Gold Coin Chewing Tobacco), and P. H. Mayo & Brother. Cards from the first two companies bear colored line drawings, while the Mayos are sepia photographs on black cardboard. In addition to the small-size cards from this era, several tobacco companies issued cabinet-size baseball cards. These "cabinets" were considerably larger than the small cards, usually about 4-1/4 by 6-1/2 inches, and were printed on heavy stock. Goodwin & Co.'s Old Judge cabinets and the National Tobacco Works' "Newsboy" baseball photos are two that remain popular today.

By 1895, the American Tobacco Company began to dominate its competition. They discontinued baseball card inserts in their cigarette packages (actually slide boxes in those days). The lack of competition in the cigarette market had made these inserts unnecessary. This marked the end of the first era of baseball cards. At the dawn of the 20th century, few baseball cards were being issued. But once again, it was the cigarette companies, particularly, the American Tobacco Company, followed to a lesser extent by the candy and gum makers that revived the practice of including baseball cards with their products. The bulk of these cards, identified in the American Card Catalog (designated hereafter as ACC) as T or E cards for 20th century "Tobacco" or "Early Candy and Gum" issues, respectively, were released from 1909 to 1915.

This romantic and popular era of baseball card collecting produced many desirable items. The most outstanding is the fabled T-206 Honus Wagner card. Other perennial favorites among collectors are the T-206 Eddie Plank card, and the T-206 Magee error card. The former was once the second most valuable card and only recently relinquished that position to a more distinctive and aesthetically pleasing Napoleon Lajoie card from the 1933–34 Goudey Gum series. The latter misspells the player's name as "Magie", the most famous and most valuable blooper card.

The ingenuity and distinctiveness of this era has yet to be surpassed. Highlights include:

- The T-202 Hassan triple-folders, one of the best looking and the most distinctive cards ever issued;
- The durable T-201 Mecca double-folders, one of the first sets with players' records on the reverse;
- The T-3 Turkey Reds, the hobby's most popular cabinet card;
- The E-145 Cracker Jacks, the only major set containing Federal League player cards; and
- The T-204 Ramlys, with their distinctive black-and-white oval photos and ornate gold borders.

These are but a few of the varieties issued during this period.

## Increasing Popularity

While the American Tobacco Company dominated the field, several other tobacco companies, as well as clothing manufacturers, newspapers and periodicals, game makers, and companies whose identities remain anonymous, also issued cards during this period. In fact, the Collins-McCarthy Candy Company, makers of Zeenuts Pacific Coast League baseball cards, issued cards yearly from 1911 to 1938. Its record for continuous annual card production has been exceeded only by the Topps Chewing Gum Company. The era of the tobacco card issues closed with the onset of World War I, with the exception of the Red Man chewing tobacco sets produced from 1952 to 1955.

## Corner Wear

The partial cards here have been photographed at 300%. This was done in order to magnify each card's corner wear to such a degree that differences could be shown on a printed page.

The 1962 Topps Mickey Mantle card definitely has a rounded corner. Some may say that this card is badly rounded, but that is a judgment call.

The 1962 Topps Hank Aaron card has a slightly rounded corner. Note that there is definite corner wear evident by the fraying and that the corner no longer sports a sharp point.

The 1962 Topps Gil Hodges card has corner wear; it is slightly better than the Aaron card above. Nevertheless, some collectors might classify this Hodges corner as slightly rounded.

The 1962 Topps Manager's Dream card showing Mantle and Mays has slight corner wear. This is not a fuzzy corner as very slight wear is noticeable on the card's photo surface.

The 1962 Topps Don Mossi card has very slight corner wear such that it might be called a fuzzy corner. A close look at the original card shows the corner is not perfect, but almost. However, note that the issue of corner wear is somewhat academic with respect to this card. As you can plainly see, the heavy crease going across his name breaks through the photo surface.

The next flurry of card issues came in the roaring and prosperous 1920s, the era of the E card. The caramel companies (National Caramel, American Caramel, York Caramel) were the leading distributors of these E cards. In addition, the strip card, a continuous strip with several cards divided by dotted lines or other sectioning features, flourished during this time. While the E cards and the strip cards generally are considered less imaginative than the T cards or the recent candy and gum issues, they still are pursued by many advanced collectors.

Another significant event of the 1920s was the introduction of the arcade card. Taking its designation from its issuer, the Exhibit Supply Company of Chicago, it is usually known as the "Exhibit" card. Once a trademark of the penny arcades, amusement parks, and county fairs across the country, Exhibit machines dispensed nearly postcard-size photos on thick stock for one penny. These picture cards bore likenesses of a favorite cowboy, actor, actress, or baseball player. Exhibit Supply and its associated companies produced baseball cards during a longer time span, although discontinuous, than any other manufacturer. Its first cards appeared in 1921, while its last issue was in 1966. In 1979, the Exhibit Supply Company was bought and somewhat revived by a collector/dealer who has since reprinted Exhibit photos of the past.

If the T card period, from 1909 to 1915, can be designated the "Golden Age" of baseball card collecting, then perhaps the "Silver Age" commenced with the introduction of the Big League Gum series of 239 cards in 1933 (a 240th card was added in 1934). These are the forerunners of today's baseball gum cards, and the Goudey Gum Company of Boston is responsible for their success. This era spanned the period from the Depression days of 1933 to America's formal involvement in World War II in 1941.

Goudey's attractive designs, with full-color line drawings on thick card stock, greatly influenced other cards being issued at that time. As a result, the most attractive and popular vintage cards in history were produced in this "Silver Age." The 1933 Goudey Big League Gum series also owes its popularity to the more than forty Hall of Fame players in the set. These include four cards of Babe Ruth and two of Lou Gehrig. Goudey's reign continued in 1934, when it issued a 96-card set in color, together with the single remaining card from the 1933 series, #106, the Napoleon Lajoie card.

In addition to Goudey, several other bubblegum manufacturers issued baseball cards during this era. DeLong Gum Company issued an extremely attractive set in 1933. National Chicle Company's 192-card "Batter-Up" series of 1934-36 became the largest die-cut set in card history. In addition, that company offered the popular "Diamond Stars" series during the same period. Other popular sets included the "Tattoo Orbit" set of sixty color cards issued in 1933 and Gum Products' 75-card "Double Play" set, featuring sepia depictions of two players per card.

In 1939, Gum Inc., which later became Bowman Gum, replaced Goudey Gum as the leading baseball card producer. In 1939 and the following year, it issued two important sets of black-and-white cards. In 1939, its "Play Ball America" set consisted of 162 cards. The larger, 240-card "Play Ball" set of 1940 still is considered by many to be the most attractive black-and-white cards ever produced. That firm introduced its only color set in 1941, consisting of 72 cards titled "Play Ball Sports Hall of Fame." Many of these were colored repeats of poses from the black-and-white 1940 series.

In addition to regular gum cards, many manufacturers distributed premium issues during the 1930s. These premiums were printed on paper or photographic stock, rather than card stock. They were much larger than the regular cards and were sold for a penny across the counter with gum (which was packaged separately from the premium). They often were redeemed at the store or through the mail in exchange for the wrappers of previously purchased gum cards, like proof-of-purchase box-top premiums today. The gum premiums are scarcer than the card issues of the 1930s, and in most cases, no manufacturer's name is present.

World War II brought an end to this popular era of card collecting when paper and rubber shortages curtailed the production of bubblegum baseball cards. They were resurrected again in 1948 by the Bowman Gum Company (the direct descendent of Gum Inc.). This marked the beginning of the modern era of card collecting.

In 1948, Bowman Gum issued a 48-card set in black and white consisting of one card and one slab of gum in every 1-cent pack. That same year, the Leaf Gum Company also issued a set of cards. Although rather poor in quality, these cards were issued in color. A squabble over the rights to use players' pictures developed between Bowman and Leaf. Eventually Leaf dropped out of the card market, but not before it had left a lasting heritage to the hobby by issuing some of the rarest cards now in existence. Leaf's baseball card series of 1948-49 contained 98 cards, skip numbered to #168 (not all numbers were printed). Of these 98 cards, 49 are relatively plentiful; the other 49, however, are rare and quite valuable.

Bowman continued its production of cards in 1949 with a color series of 240 cards. Because there are many scarce "high numbers," this series remains the most difficult Bowman regular issue to complete. Although the set was printed in color and commands great interest due to its scarcity, it is considered aesthetically inferior to the Goudey and National Chicle issues of the 1930s. In addition to the regular issue of 1949, Bowman also produced a set of 36 Pacific Coast League players. Although this was not a regular issue, it still is prized by collectors. In fact, it has become the most valuable Bowman series.

In 1950 (representing Bowman's one-year monopoly of the baseball card market), the company began a string of top-quality cards that continued until its demise in 1955. The 1950 series was itself something of an oddity because the low numbers, rather than the traditional high numbers, were the more difficult cards to obtain.

The year 1951 marked the beginning of the most competitive and perhaps the highest quality period of baseball card production. In that year, Topps Chewing Gum Company of Brooklyn entered the market. Topps' 1951 series consisted of two sets of 52 cards each, one set with red backs and the other with blue backs. In addition, Topps also issued 31 insert cards, three of which remain the rarest Topps cards ("Current All-Stars" Konstanty, Roberts, and Stanky). The 1951 Topps cards were unattractive and paled in comparison to the 1951 Bowman issues. They were successful, however, and Topps has continued to produce cards ever since.

## Intensified Competition

Topps issued a larger and more attractive card set in 1952. This larger size became standard for the next five years. (Bowman followed with larger-size baseball cards in 1953.) This 1952 Topps set has become, like the 1933 Goudey series and the T-206 white border series, the classic set of its era. The 407-card set is a collector's dream of scarcities, rarities, errors, and variations. It also contains the first Topps issues of Mickey Mantle and Willie Mays.

As with Bowman and Leaf in the late 1940s, competition over player rights arose. Ensuing court battles occurred between Topps and Bowman. The market split due to stiff competition, and in January 1956, Topps bought out Bowman. (Topps, using the Bowman name, resurrected Bowman as a label in 1989.) Topps remained essentially unchallenged as the primary producer of baseball cards through 1980. So, the story of major baseball card sets from 1956 through 1980 is by and large the story of Topps' issues. Notable exceptions include the small sets produced by Fleer Gum in 1959, 1960, 1961, and 1963, and the Kellogg's Cereal and Hostess Cakes baseball cards issued to promote their products.

A court decision in 1980 paved the way for two other large gum companies to enter (or reenter, in Fleer's case) the baseball card arena. Fleer, which had last made photo cards in 1963, and the Donruss Company (then a division of General Mills) secured rights to produce baseball cards of current players, thus breaking Topps' monopoly. Each company issued major card sets in 1981 with bubblegum products.

Then a higher court decision in that year overturned the lower court ruling against Topps. It appeared that Topps had regained its sole position as a producer of baseball cards. Undaunted by the revocation ruling, Fleer and Donruss continued to issue cards in 1982 but without bubblegum or any other edible product. Fleer issued its current player baseball cards with "team logo stickers," while Donruss issued its cards with a piece of a baseball jigsaw puzzle.

**Sharing the Pie**

Since 1981, these three major baseball card producers all have thrived, sharing relatively equal recognition. Each has steadily increased its involvement in terms of numbers of issues per year. To the delight of collectors, their competition has generated novel, and in some cases exceptional, issues of current Major League Baseball players. Collectors also eagerly accepted the debut efforts of Score (1988) and Upper Deck (1989). These five companies were about to embark on a wild ride through the 1990s.

Upper Deck's successful entry into the market turned out to be very important. The company's card stock, photography, packaging, and marketing gave baseball cards a new standard for quality and began the "premium card" trend that continues today. The second premium baseball card set to be issued was the 1990 Leaf set, named for and issued by the parent company of Donruss. To gauge the significance of the premium card trend, one need only note that two of the most valuable post-1986 regular-issue cards in the hobby are the 1989 Upper Deck Ken Griffey Jr. and 1990 Leaf Frank Thomas Rookie Cards.

The impressive debut of Leaf in 1990 was followed by those of Studio, Ultra, and Stadium Club in 1991. Of those, Stadium Club with its dramatic borderless photos and uncoated card fronts made the biggest impact. In 1992, Bowman and Pinnacle joined the premium fray. In 1992, Donruss and Fleer abandoned the traditional 50-cent pack market and instead produced premium sets comparable to (and presumably designed to compete against) Upper Deck's set. Those moves, combined with the almost instantaneous spread of premium cards to the other major team sports cards, serve as strong indicators that premium cards were here to stay. Bowman had been a lower-level product from 1989 to 1991.

In 1993, Fleer, Topps, and Upper Deck produced the first "super premium" cards with Flair, Finest, and SP, respectively. The success of all three products was an indication the baseball card market was headed toward even higher price levels, and that turned out to be the case in 1994 with the introduction of Bowman's Best (a Topps hybrid of prospect-oriented Bowman and the superpremium Finest) and Leaf Limited. Other 1994 debuts included Upper Deck's entry-level Collector's Choice and Pinnacle's hobby-only Select.

Overall, inserts continued to dominate the hobby scene. Specifically, the parallel chase cards introduced in 1992 with Topps Gold became the latest major hobby trend. Topps Gold was followed by 1993 Finest Refractors (at the time the scarcest insert ever produced and still a landmark set) and the one-per-box Stadium Club First Day Issue.

Of course, the biggest on-field news of 1994 was the owner-provoked players' strike that halted the season prematurely. While the baseball card hobby suffered noticeably from the strike, there was no catastrophic market crash as some had feared. However, the strike drastically slowed down a market that was both strong and growing and contributed to a serious hobby contraction that continues to this day.

By 1995, parallel insert sets were commonplace and had taken on a new complexion: the most popular ones were those that had announced (or at least suspected) print runs of 500 or less, such as Finest Refractors and Select Artist's Proofs.

This trend continued in 1996, with several parallel inserts that were printed in quantities of 250 or less, such as Finest Gold Refractors, Fleer Circa Rave, Studio Silver Press Proofs, and three of the six Select Certified parallels. It could be argued that the high price tags on these extremely limited parallel cards (many exceeded the $1,000 plateau) were driving many single-player collectors to frustration, and even completely out of the hobby. At the same time, average pack prices soared while average number of cards per pack dropped, making the baseball card hobby increasingly expensive.

On the positive side, two trends from 1996 clearly brought in new collectors: Topps' Mickey Mantle retrospective inserts in both series of Topps and Stadium Club and Leaf's Signature Series, which included one certified autograph per pack. Although the Mantle craze following his passing seemed to be a short-term phenomenon, the inclusion of autographs in packs seemed to have more long-term significance.

In 1997 the print runs in selected sets got even lower. Both Fleer/SkyBox and Pinnacle brands issued cards of which only one exists.

The growth in popularity of autographs also continued. Many products had autographed cards in their packs. A very positive trend was a return to basics. Many collectors bought Rookie Cards, as they understood that concept, and worked on finishing sets.

There was also an increase in international players collecting. Hideo Nomo was incredibly popular in Japan while Chan Ho Park was in demand in Korea. This bodes well for international growth in the hobby.

Clearly, 1998 was a year of rebirth and growth for the hobby. The big boost came from the home run chase being conducted by Mark McGwire and Sammy Sosa, as well as the continued brilliance of stalwarts like Ken Griffey Jr. and Roger Clemens. The baseball card hobby received a great deal of positive publicity from the renewed interest in the game.

Rookie Cards of the key players of 1998 made significant gains in value as the hobby once again turned to Rookie Cards as the collectible of choice. Also, cards professionally graded by companies such as PSA and SGC were becoming more heavily traded in both older and newer material.

In addition, the Internet and various services such as eBay contributed to the strong growth in collecting interest over the year.

There were downsides in 1998, though. Pinnacle Brands folded, leaving a legacy of innovation and promotions not seen by other companies. In addition, there still was the problem of collectors being frustrated by the extremely short printed cards of their favorite players, making set completion almost impossible.

During 1998, Pacific received a full baseball license and added many innovations to the card market. Their 1998 OnLine set is the most comprehensive set issued in the last five years and many veteran collectors applauded Pacific's continuing attempts to get as many players as possible into their sets.

In the last couple of years, card companies have been printing specific subsets (usually young players or Rookie Cards) in shorter supply than the regular cards. This is not in every set, but in many sets produced since 1998.

In 1999, many of the trends of the last couple of years continued to gain strength. Buying, selling, and trading cards over the Internet became a dominant factor in the secondary market. Beckett Media LP began its own Marketplace, offering collectors a chance to search across inventory from many of the finest dealers nationwide in one comprehensive on-line database; eBay continued to flourish, while many other parties began to reap the benefits of the burgeoning online auction market. The Barry Halper collection was auctioned off, bringing many museum quality items to the market and giving the older memorabilia market a significant boost as many treasures were made available to collectors.

Also, the boom in Internet trading created a perfect fit for professionally graded cards, as buyers and sellers traded cards sight unseen with the confidence established by a third-party grader.

From a field of almost a dozen contenders, three companies emerged in 1999 to dominate the field of professional grading, BGS (Beckett Grading Services), PSA (Professional Sports Authenticator), and SGC (Sportscard Guaranty L.L.C.). In 1999 these companies made dramatic expansions in on-site grading and submissions at card shows throughout the nation. In response to the widespread acceptance of graded cards, the line of monthly Beckett Price Guides each added a separate section within the price guide area for professionally graded cards.

Similar to 1998, four licensed manufacturers (Fleer/SkyBox, Pacific, Topps, and Upper Deck) produced slightly more than fifty different products for 1999.

Perhaps the biggest hit of the 1999 card season was created by Topps. Card #220 within the basic issue first series 1999 Topps brand featured Home Run King Mark McGwire in 70 variations, one for each homer he slugged in 1998, and many collectors went after the whole set. Continuing a legacy as strong as the Yankees, the basic Topps issue was one of the most popular sets released in 1999.

Closely trailing the Topps McGwire promotion was Upper Deck's dynamic A Piece of History bat card promotion. The card that kicked off the frenzy was the Babe Ruth A Piece of History distributed in 1999 Upper Deck series 1 packs. Upper Deck actually purchased a cracked game-used Babe Ruth bat for $24,000 and proceeded

to cut it up into approximately 350 to 400 chips of wood to create the now famous Ruth bat card. The card instantly created polar opposites of opinion among hobbyists. Traditional collectors howled at the sacrilegious act of destroying such a historic piece of memorabilia, while more open-minded collectors jumped at the opportunity to chase such an important card. The Ruth card was followed up by the cross-brand "500 Club" bat card promotion, whereby UD produced bat cards from every major league ballplayer who hit 500 or more home runs in his career (except for Mark McGwire, who hit his 500th in the midst of the 1999 season and promptly stated that he did not support Upper Deck's promotion).

More memorabilia cards than ever were offered to collectors in 1999 as Fleer/SkyBox kicked up their efforts to match the standards set by Upper Deck in previous years. Batting gloves, hats, and shoes joined the typical bats and jerseys as pieces of game-used equipment to be featured on trading cards. Sets like E-X Century Authen-Kicks and Fleer Mystique Feel the Game typified the new offerings.

Topps only dabbled with memorabilia cards in 1999, but continued to offer some of the hottest autographed inserts, highlighted by the Topps Stars Rookie Reprint Autographs and the Topps Nolan Ryan Autographs.

Pacific made a clear decision to steer free of memorabilia and autograph inserts, instead focusing on offering collectors a wide selection of beautifully designed insert and parallel cards. Those themes worked beautifully with their established presence for making comprehensive sets, providing collectors with the necessary challenge to pursue regional stars and a favorite team in addition to the typical superstars.·

An astounding total of 264 players made their first appearance on a major league licensed trading card in 1999. What may go down as the deepest class of Rookie Cards of all time features a cornucopia of talented youngsters led by Rick Ankiel, Josh Beckett, Pat Burrell, Josh Hamilton, Eric Munson, Corey Patterson, and Alfonso Soriano.

As in years past, Topps continued to provide collectors with a fistful of Rookie Cards within their Bowman, Bowman Chrome, and Bowman's Best brands. In a trend established in 1998 by Fleer when they released their Fleer Update set (fueled largely by a J. D. Drew Rookie Card), hobbyists enjoyed a bevy of late-season sets chock full of RC's. Fleer/SkyBox made an all-out effort by stuffing more than 100 Rookie Cards into their 1999 Fleer Update set. Topps produced their first boxed Traded set since 1994. Each 1999 Topps Traded set contained 1 of 75 different cards autographed by a rookie prospect. Considering how much wider the selection of Rookie Cards became in 1999, it's amazing to see that so few of these RC's were serial numbered. When one looks at the success established with serial, numbered Rookie Cards in the basketball and football card markets with brands like SP Authentic and SPx Finite, one can only scratch his head when realizing that Fleer Mystique was the only brand to offer baseball collectors serial numbered RC's. Thus, it's not surprising to see that despite having twenty-five different Rookie Cards issued in 1999, Pat Burrell's Fleer Mystique RC (#'d of 2,999) had been established as his "best" RC by year's end.

Youngsters weren't the only players in the limelight in 1999 as retired stars and Hall of Famers were featured on more cards than any other year during the 1990s. Upper Deck's Century Legends brand, featuring the top fifty active and top fifty retired players of the decade as chosen by the Sporting News was a runaway hit.

Perhaps the most popular insert set of the year, outpacing all of the dazzling high-dollar memorabilia cards, was Topps Gallery Heritage. Utilizing the design and painting style of artist Gerry Dvorak from the classic 1953 Topps set, these modern masterpieces proved that insert cards can still be a hot commodity in the secondary market, albeit assuming they're well conceived and well made, an unfortunate rarity these days.

The spate of basic issue sets with short-printed subsets continued across many brands in 1999. In reaction to many frustrated dealers and collectors struggling to complete these sets, Fleer/SkyBox created dual versions of each prospect card for the 1999 SkyBox Premium set, an action shot was short-printed and a posed shot was seeded at the same rate as other basic issue cards. The idea was well received by collectors but enjoyed a surprisingly short-lived period of active trading in the secondary market.

The year 2000 was marked by several major developments that would continue shaping the future of our hobby. First off, Pacific decided to forfeit their baseball card license on January 1st, 2000, in an effort to more sharply focus their production expenditures into football and hockey.

In a separate development, Wizards of the Coast (primarily known for their non-sport gaming cards) was granted a license to produce baseball trading cards and debuted their MLB Showdown brand. The cards proved to be quite successful in that they were collected as a set by veteran collectors and played as a game by children (and some adults) both inside and outside of the typical collecting community.

By year's end, Fleer fazed out their SkyBox and Flair brand names in an effort to take full advantage of the historic significance and brand recognition of their flagship Fleer sets issued sporadically during the late 1950s –1970s and consistently from 1981 to the present.

Almost sixty brands of MLB-licensed cards, issued by five manufacturers, were produced in 2000. In addition, Just Minors and Team Best produced a variety of attractive minor league products. Most shop owners continued to generate their income primarily through the sales of packs and boxes of new product, and, as in years past, they had to make careful decisions as to what to keep in stock for customers and what to pass up for fear of a low sell through.

Vintage (or retro-themed) sets dominated the market highlighted by Fleer Greats of the Game, Upper Deck Yankees Legends, and the run of 3,000 hit club and Joe DiMaggio game-used cards issued by Fleer and Upper Deck. In 2001, Topps Heritage (mimicking the style of the classic '52 Topps cards), Upper Deck Vintage (in an homage to '63 Topps baseball), and the return of Topps Archives (after a six-year hiatus) added fuel to the fire.

Using the vintage-theme to tap into a base of wealthy consumers, Upper Deck rolled out their line of Master Collection products (which debuted in basketball a year prior with a Michael Jordan set). Both the Yankees Master Collection and Brooklyn Dodgers Master Collection sets carried initial SRP's of $4,000 or more, marking the most expensive "factory set" of all time. Each of these sets was serial numbered (500 Yankees and 250 Dodgers), came in a stylish wood box and contained an assortment of game-used and autograph cards from legends of days gone by.

Game-used memorabilia cards became more abundant in all products to the point where a few early 2001 releases (2001 Pacific Private Stock and 2001 SP Game Bat Edition both carrying SRP's in the $15 to $20 range) included them at a rate of one per pack. Both products enjoyed a dynamic sell through and proved to be very popular in the secondary market. The result, however, on the secondary market values of game-used memorabilia cards has been dramatic. An Alex Rodriguez or Ken Griffey Jr. game bat or game jersey card that sold for $200+ in 1999 could be had for as little as $25 to $50 in early 2001.

Patch cards (a swatch of jersey that contains part of a multicolored patch) really caught on by year's end as the market formalized premium values on these cards. Upper Deck was the first to create separate "super-premium" jersey Patch inserts within 2000 Upper Deck 1 and 2000 Upper Deck Game Jersey Edition (aka series 2). Pacific followed suit with their Game Gear patch subset within the invincible brand.

By early 2001, Major League Baseball Properties had gotten involved with the trading card autograph and memorabilia programs. From 2001 on, all MLB-licensed trading cards produced by the manufacturers that involved an autograph or game-used memorabilia item had to have the procurement of the item witnessed by a representative of Andersen Consulting, a firm hired by MLB to oversee this historic program. Never before had the league and manufacturers made such an effort to offer autographed or game-used memorabilia trading cards of such authentic provenance.

Short-printed subset cards, a trend started in 1999, continued to be a common element in most basic sets. The trend, however, evolved to the point where these short prints were now being serial numbered, autographed by the player, or incorporating an element of game-used material onto the card. The result was higher values on the key singles, but lower odds of actually finding a good RC in a pack. By year's end, a general sentiment of frustration over not being able to pull good Rookie Cards

from a box was beginning to be heard more and more often from collectors.

Rookie Cards incorporating game-used material debuted at year's end in 2000 Black Diamond Rookie Edition. Also, Rookie Cards signed by the player, introduced within the basketball and football card markets in 1999 (with Upper Deck's SPx brand), made their baseball debut in 2000 SPx. Serial-numbered Rookie Cards grew in total usage, but shrank in print run numbers as production figures reached an all-time low of 999 copies for a basic issue RC within the 2000 Pacific Omega set.

Year-end boxed sets, a trend brought back from a four-year hiatus by Fleer in 1998 with its Fleer Update set, continued to expand as Topps issued its Bowman Draft Picks and Bowman Chrome Draft Picks sets to cap the now single-series accompanying standard Bowman and Bowman Chrome products.

Fleer broke new ground by blending a 1980s "old-school" concept with some postmodern angles in their 2000 Fleer Glossy boxed set. Harkening back to the run of Glossy parallel factory sets produced from 1987 to 1989, the 2000 Fleer Glossy set included a parallel version of the complete 400-card basic 2000 Fleer set. In addition, 50 new cards (card #'s 401-450, each serial numbered to 1,000 copies) featuring a selection of prospects and rookies were created. Each Glossy factory set contained 5 of the 50 new cards, making it a real challenge to complete the Glossy set.

In a first of its kind for the baseball market, Upper Deck issued a product in December 2000 called Rookie Update that incorporated new cards for three separate popular brands (SP Authentic, SPx, and UD Pros and Prospects) into each pack of cards.

Upper Deck came to terms with Major League Baseball for a license to produce cards featuring members of past and present Team USA squads (bringing back a run of cards last seen in 1993 Topps Traded). That allowed Upper Deck the opportunity to radically expand their production of "true" Rookie Cards in year-end 2000 products, adding a spate of cards featuring heroes from the Olympics in Sydney, Australia, like Ben Sheets. Not surprisingly, the number of prospects making their Rookie Card debut in 2000 sets jumped from about 280 players in 1999 to slightly more than 350 players in 2000.

The influence of sports card dealers and collectors from the Far East (and most noticeably Japan) continued to grow in 2000 as stateside buying approached frenzied levels over scarce Hideo Nomo and Kazuhiro Sasaki cards. A much-traveled starter these days, Nomo's first-ever certified autograph card (issued within the Fleer Mystique Fresh Ink insert set) was the hottest card in the hobby for two months (initially trading for as much as $600-$800).

Not all trends were met with success this year. In particular, low-end products geared towards the youth audience (like 2000 Impact by Fleer) were roundly ignored. The hobby still faces a tough road ahead to keep new waves of collectors involved from generation to generation. Part of the Catch-22 with creating affordable brands catered to youths is that the same customers are most interested in the high-end, expensive material.

Also, Upper Deck's PowerDeck product faced an indifferent audience for a second year in a row, as collectors and even general sports enthusiasts outside the hobby failed to get excited over the CD-ROM cards. More success was met by UD's e-Card insert program, whereby collectors who pulled an e-Card from a pack of UD cards had to go to UD's Website and check the serial number printed on the card to see whether it could evolve into an autograph, game jersey, or game jersey autograph exchange.

The Internet continued to have profound ramifications on shaping the destiny of sports card collecting. By 2000, nearly every dealer (and hard-core collector) was buying or selling cards to some degree in online auctions. Auction sales had become so prolific that they were now having a strong effect on the secondary market sales levels of trading cards in arenas entirely outside of cyberspace, like shops, shows, and mail order.

The eBay site continued to dominate the online auction action, introducing what appears to be a popular "Buy It Now" option to their already established auction format. The Pit.com opened in mid-year with their concept of buying and selling a portfolio of professionally graded sports cards through their Web site. The concept is based almost exactly upon the methodology used for buying and selling stocks

through a brokerage house, with daily ebbs and flows in posted buy and sell prices on your inventory.

Beckett.com made radical improvements to their Marketplace search engines and expanded their inventory of sports cards to the point where they were providing both a wider and deeper selection of trading cards than any site on the Internet. In addition, a company-wide effort to provide daily news content on their site (coupled with a weekly newsletter sent to over 400,000 collectors) began at year's end, and the hobby has reaped the benefits ever since.

As the 2001 season approached, hobbyists waited with bated breath for seven-time Japanese batting champ Ichiro Suzuki to make his debut in the Seattle Mariner's outfield. And what a stunning debut it was. Ichiro led the league in hitting, led the Mariners to their best record ever, and walked off with the A.L. Rookie of the Year and Most Valuable Player awards. Upper Deck obtained the exclusive rights to produce his autograph cards and they hit a grand slam in midsummer by releasing his SPx Rookie Card, featuring a game jersey swatch and a cut signature autograph. In a year studded with notable cards, this one was likely the most memorable.

In the National League, 37-year-old San Francisco Giants superstar Barry Bonds captivated the nation by bashing a jaw-dropping 73 home runs, shattering Mark McGwire's 1998 single-season home run record.

Cardinals' rookie Albert Pujols emerged out of the low minor leagues to become an instant hobby superstar and walk away with N.L. Rookie of the Year honors.

The year 2001 was a tumultuous one for sports cards. Topps started the year off with a bang by celebrating their 50th anniversary producing baseball cards. Pacific forfeited its license to make baseball cards after an eight-year run to focus on football and hockey cards. Playoff, a company based out of Grand Prairie, Texas, that had earned its stripes by producing football cards in the late 1990s, purchased the rights to the much-hallowed Donruss corporate name and became a formal MLB licensee in the spring of 2001. Their entrance into the baseball card market heralded the return of benchmark brands like Donruss, Donruss Signature, and Leaf.

Competition was fiercer than ever among the four primary licensees (Donruss-Playoff, Fleer, Topps, and Upper Deck) as they cranked out almost 80 different products over the course of 2001.

Of all these, likely the most historically important product, Upper Deck Prospect Premieres, was widely overlooked upon release. In a bold move, Upper Deck created a set of 102 prospects, none of which had played a day in the majors. Each player was pictured, however, in the major league uniforms of their parent ballclubs and signed to individual contracts. Because no active major leaguers were featured, Upper Deck did not have to include licensing rights from the MLB Players Association, though they did get licensing from Major League Properties. The industry had never seen a major release featuring active ballplayers marketed to the mainstream audience that lacked licensing from the MLBPA. Because of its lack of historical predecessors and a mixed reception from collectors, the cards were tagged by Beckett Baseball Card Monthly as XRC's (or Extended Rookie Cards), a term that had not been used since 1989.

UD's Prospect Premieres was the first major effort by a manufacturer to level the playing field between Topps and everyone else in that Topps has exclusive rights from the MLBPA to include minor leaguers in their basic brands.

Rookie Cards continued to fascinate collectors, especially in a year with talents like Ichiro and Albert Pujols. The number of players featured on Rookie Cards in 2001 ballooned to an almost absurd figure of 505.

Exchange cards became more prevalent than ever, as manufacturers expanded their use from autograph cards that didn't get returned in time for pack out to slots within basic sets left open in brands released early in the year to fill in with late-season rookie call-ups.

Certified autograph cards remained a huge player in how brands were structured, but the quality of the players suffered greatly as autograph fees continued to spiral out of control. Signatures from superstars like Barry Bonds and Derek Jeter were now being featured on cards with minuscule print runs of 25 or 50 copies while unknown (and often aging and talentless) prospects signed their serial-numbered Rookies Cards by the hundred count.

More serial-numbered Rookie Cards were produced than ever before, but the quantities produced kept sinking lower and lower as companies tried to create secondary market value by simply limiting supply, a dangerous move to say the least. Donruss-Playoff produced the scarcest Rookie Cards of the year, a handful of Game Base cards (including Ichiro) each serial #'d to a scant 100 copies, within their Leaf Limited set.

After a six-month delay, Topps released their much awaited e-Topps program, a product sold entirely on their Web site whereby trading is conducted in a similar fashion to the buying and selling of stocks, in September.

Several products incorporated non-card memorabilia such as signed caps, bobbing head dolls, and signed baseballs, with mixed results.

Memorabilia cards continued their slide into mediocrity as the number of cards featuring various bits and pieces of balls, bases, bats, jerseys, pants, shoes, seats, and whatever else could be dreamt up continued to be offered to consumers, who found the cards less appealing with each passing month. To battle consumer apathy, companies often started to offer combination memorabilia cards featuring notable teammates or several pieces of equipment from a notable star.

Retro-themed cards continued to grow in popularity, and some of the innovations seen in these sets were remarkable. Of particular note was Upper Deck's SP Legendary Cuts Autographs set, featuring 84 deceased players. The set required UD to purchase more than 3,300 autograph cuts, which were then incorporated into a windowpane card design. The result was the first certified autograph cards for legends like Roger Maris, Satchell Paige, and Jackie Robinson. Also, Topps Tribute, released at year's end and carrying a hefty $40 per pack suggested retail was widely hailed as one of the most beautiful retro-themed cards ever designed, with their crystal-board fronts encasing full-color, razor-sharp photos.

Pack prices continued to escalate, but surprisingly, the public did not balk as long as they delivered value. The most notable high-end product to hit the market in 2001 was Upper Deck Ultimate Collection with a suggested retail of $100 per pack.

September 11th, 2001, is a day that will go down as one of the most devastating in the history of the United States of America. The game of baseball and the hobby of collecting sports cards were rightfully cast aside as the nation mourned the tragic loss of lives in New York, Pennsylvania, and Washington, D.C. America's economy tumbled as airline traveling ground to a near halt and threats of anthrax crippled the mail system. An economy threatening to slip into recession at the beginning of the year dove headlong into it. The sports card market, along with many other industries, felt the hit for several months. Slowly, Americans looked to move past the grief and the sports card industry, steeped in American nostalgia, provided an ideal retreat for many.

The Arizona Diamondbacks beat the New York Yankees in one of the finest World Series ever played, a much-needed diversion for a grief-stricken nation and a calling card for the dramatic power and glory of our National Pastime.

2002 was a relatively quiet one for baseball cards. Dodger's rookie pitcher Kazuhisa Ishii got off to a blazing first half start and his cards carried many releases through to the All-Star break. Ishii stumbled badly in the second half and no notable rookies were in place to pick up market interest. Cubs hurler Mark Prior created a stir, and his 2001 Rookie Cards were red hot at mid-season. For the second straight season, Barry Bonds was the most dominant star in our sport. His early cards continued to outpace all others in volume trading and professional grading submissions.

The number of players featured on Rookie Cards (or Extended Rookie Cards) reached an all-time high of 524 in 2002 as the manufacturers continued to push the envelope toward more immediate coverage of the current year draft. Though few collectors took notice at the time of release, Upper Deck's incorporation of collegiate Team USA athletes into several year-end brands may take hold and grow into a more prominent position in our industry for collegiate ballplayers. The results of these trends, however, are cards that feature a lot of talented youngsters whom most collectors, unfortunately, have never heard of and won't see in a major league uniform for several years.

To make up for the void in excitement generated by rookies and prospects, the manufacturers made some interesting innovations in product distribution and brand

development. In general, base sets got noticeably bigger (including Upper Deck's 1,182-card 40-Man brand and Topps 990-card Topps Total brand). In addition, brands like Topps 206, Leaf Rookies and Stars, and Fleer Fall Classics started to incorporate variations of the base cards directly into the basic issue set (different images, switched out teams, etc.).

One of the bigger surprise hits of the year was the aforementioned Topps 206 brand, which borrowed design elements and set composition from the legendary T-206 tobacco set. Other brands continued to successfully mine from cards and eras long since passed.

Donruss continued to push the creative envelope by incorporating 8½" by 11" framed signature pieces directly into boxes of their Playoff Absolute brand. After a four-year hiatus, Fleer brought back their eponymous "Fleer" name brand with a 540-card set. Donruss introduced their wildly successful Diamond Kings brand, which featured a 150-card painted set. Fleer's Box Score brand was also a popular debut utilizing a unique box-inside-a-box distribution concept. Popular brands like SP Legendary Cuts, Leaf Certified, Topps Heritage, and Topps Tribute all received warm welcomes for their follow-ups to their successes achieved the prior year.

The 2004 season continued to bring us again a growing number of sets with price points ranging from $1.29 to $150. There were also many new heroes during the 2003 season as players such as Josh Beckett, Miguel Cabrera, and Dontrelle Willis of the World Champion Florida Marlins were very strong sellers.

Hideki Matsui, who was the most anticipated rookie for the 2003 season, had a very fine year for the American League Champion Yankees but did not draw the same interest from collectors as Ichiro Suzuki did during the 2001 season.

The 2005 season was most notable for the departure of both Fleer and Donruss/Playoff from the ranks of major manufacturers. One of the issues in recent years has been the staggering amount of sets as well as the complexities of those sets. With some direction from the licensors, the baseball card market was reduced and a maximum of 40 products are expected to be released during the 2006 calendar year.

Despite the struggles the sport of baseball has endured; in recent years, the baseball card market has stepped back to the forefront of the card-collecting hobby, outpacing football, basketball, hockey, golf, and motor sports in volume dollars. As the hobby of collecting baseball cards evolves, we continue to face a market that is blessed with bold creativity and superlative quality; and also challenged with the need to reach new consumers both in mass retail and in cyberspace to continue its growth.

# Additional Reading

Each year Beckett Media LP produces comprehensive annual price guides for several sports: *Beckett Baseball Card Price Guide, Beckett Basketball Card Price Guide, Beckett Football Card Price Guide, Beckett Hockey Card Price Guide, Beckett Racing Price Guide,* and a line of *Beckett Alphabetical Checklists* books have been released as well. The aim of these annual guides is to provide information and accurate pricing on a wide array of sports cards, ranging from main issues by the major card manufacturers to various regional, promotional, and food issues. Alphabetical checklist books are published to assist the collector in identifying all the cards of any particular player. The seasoned collector will find these tools valuable sources of information that will enable him to pursue his hobby interests.

In addition, abridged editions of the *Beckett Price Guides* have been published for each of these major sports as part of the House of Collectibles series: *The Official Price Guide to Baseball Cards, The Official Price Guide to Football Cards,* and *The Official Price Guide to Basketball Cards.* Published in a convenient mass-market paperback format, these price guides provide information and accurate pricing on all the main issues by the major card manufacturers.

# Prices in This Guide

Prices found in this guide reflect current retail rates just prior to the printing of this book. They do not reflect the FOR SALE prices of the author, the publisher, the distributors, the advertisers, or any card dealers associated with this guide. No one is obligated in any way to buy, sell, or trade his or her cards based on these prices. The price listings were compiled by the author from actual buy/sell transactions at sports conventions, sports card shops, buy/sell advertisements in the hobby papers, for sale prices from dealer catalogs and price lists, and discussions with leading hobbyists in the United States and Canada. All prices are in U.S. dollars.

# Acknowledgments

A great deal of diligence, hard work, and dedicated effort went into this year's volume. However, the high standards to which we hold ourselves could not have been met without the expert input and generous amount of time contributed by many people. Our sincere thanks are extended to each and every one of you.

A complete list of these invaluable contributors appears after the **Price Guide** section.

## 1948 Bowman

| | | |
|---|---|---|
| ❑ COMPLETE SET (48) | 3000.00 | 5000.00 |
| ❑ COMMON CARD (1-36) | 10.00 | 20.00 |
| ❑ COMMON CARD (37-48) | 15.00 | 30.00 |
| ❑ WRAPPER (5-CENT) | 600.00 | 700.00 |
| ❑ WRAPPER (1-CENT) | | |
| ❑ 1 Bob Elliott RC | 75.00 | 125.00 |
| ❑ 2 Ewell Blackwell RC | 35.00 | 60.00 |
| ❑ 3 Ralph Kiner RC | 150.00 | 250.00 |
| ❑ 4 Johnny Mize RC | 75.00 | 125.00 |
| ❑ 5 Bob Feller RC | 150.00 | 250.00 |
| ❑ 6 Yogi Berra RC | 500.00 | 800.00 |
| ❑ 7 Pete Reiser SP RC | 75.00 | 125.00 |
| ❑ 8 Phil Rizzuto SP RC | 200.00 | 350.00 |
| ❑ 9 Walker Cooper RC | 10.00 | 20.00 |
| ❑ 10 Buddy Rosar RC | 10.00 | 20.00 |
| ❑ 11 Johnny Lindell RC | 12.50 | 25.00 |
| ❑ 12 Johnny Sain RC | 50.00 | 80.00 |
| ❑ 13 Willard Marshall SP RC | 20.00 | 40.00 |
| ❑ 14 Allie Reynolds RC | 35.00 | 60.00 |
| ❑ 15 Eddie Joost | 10.00 | 20.00 |
| ❑ 16 Jack Lohrke SP RC | 20.00 | 40.00 |
| ❑ 17 Enos Slaughter RC | 60.00 | 100.00 |
| ❑ 18 Warren Spahn RC | 175.00 | 300.00 |
| ❑ 19 Tommy Henrich | 35.00 | 60.00 |
| ❑ 20 Buddy Kerr SP RC | 20.00 | 40.00 |
| ❑ 21 Ferris Fain RC | 20.00 | 40.00 |
| ❑ 22 Floyd Bevens SP RC | 30.00 | 50.00 |
| ❑ 23 Larry Jansen RC | 12.50 | 25.00 |
| ❑ 24 Dutch Leonard SP | 20.00 | 40.00 |
| ❑ 25 Barney McCosky | 10.00 | 20.00 |
| ❑ 26 Frank Shea SP RC | 30.00 | 50.00 |
| ❑ 27 Sid Gordon RC | 12.50 | 25.00 |
| ❑ 28 Emil Verban SP RC | 20.00 | 40.00 |
| ❑ 29 Joe Page SP RC | 50.00 | 80.00 |
| ❑ 30 Whitey Lockman SP RC | 30.00 | 50.00 |
| ❑ 31 Bill McCahan RC | 10.00 | 20.00 |
| ❑ 32 Bill Rigney RC | 10.00 | 20.00 |
| ❑ 33 Bill Johnson RC | 12.50 | 25.00 |
| ❑ 34 Sheldon Jones SP RC | 20.00 | 40.00 |
| ❑ 35 Snuffy Stirnweiss RC | 20.00 | 40.00 |
| ❑ 36 Stan Musial RC | 500.00 | 800.00 |
| ❑ 37 Clint Hartung RC | 15.00 | 30.00 |
| ❑ 38 Red Schoendienst RC | 125.00 | 200.00 |
| ❑ 39 Augie Galan RC | 15.00 | 30.00 |
| ❑ 40 Marty Marion RC | 35.00 | 60.00 |
| ❑ 41 Rex Barney RC | 35.00 | 60.00 |
| ❑ 42 Ray Poat RC | 15.00 | 30.00 |
| ❑ 43 Bruce Edwards RC | 20.00 | 40.00 |
| ❑ 44 Johnny Wyrostek RC | 15.00 | 30.00 |
| ❑ 45 Hank Sauer RC | 35.00 | 60.00 |
| ❑ 46 Herman Wehmeier RC | 15.00 | 30.00 |
| ❑ 47 Bobby Thomson RC | 60.00 | 100.00 |
| ❑ 48 Dave Koslo RC | 50.00 | 80.00 |

## 1949 Bowman

| | | |
|---|---|---|
| ❑ COMP. MASTER SET (252) | 10000.00 | 16000.00 |
| ❑ COMPLETE SET (240) | 10000.00 | 15000.00 |
| ❑ COMMON CARD (1-144) | 7.50 | 15.00 |

| | | |
|---|---|---|
| ❑ COMMON CARD (145-240) | 30.00 | 50.00 |
| ❑ WRAPPER (1-CENT,Rd,Wh,Bl) | | |
| ❑ WRAPPER (5-CENT, GR.) | 200.00 | 250.00 |
| ❑ WRAPPER (5-CENT, BL.) | 150.00 | 200.00 |
| ❑ 1 Vern Bickford RC | 75.00 | 125.00 |
| ❑ 2 Whitey Lockman | 20.00 | 40.00 |
| ❑ 3 Bob Porterfield RC | 7.50 | 15.00 |
| ❑ 4A Jerry Priddy NNOF RC | 7.50 | 15.00 |
| ❑ 4B Jerry Priddy NOF | 20.00 | 40.00 |
| ❑ 5 Hank Sauer | 20.00 | 40.00 |
| ❑ 6 Phil Cavarretta RC | 20.00 | 40.00 |
| ❑ 7 Joe Dobson RC | 7.50 | 15.00 |
| ❑ 8 Murry Dickson RC | 7.50 | 15.00 |
| ❑ 9 Ferris Fain | 20.00 | 40.00 |
| ❑ 10 Ted Gray RC | 7.50 | 15.00 |
| ❑ 11 Lou Boudreau MG RC | 50.00 | 80.00 |
| ❑ 12 Cass Michaels RC | 7.50 | 15.00 |
| ❑ 13 Bob Chesnes RC | 7.50 | 15.00 |
| ❑ 14 Curt Simmons RC | 20.00 | 40.00 |
| ❑ 15 Ned Garver RC | 7.50 | 15.00 |
| ❑ 16 Al Kozar RC | 7.50 | 15.00 |
| ❑ 17 Earl Torgeson RC | 7.50 | 15.00 |
| ❑ 18 Bobby Thomson | 20.00 | 40.00 |
| ❑ 19 Bobby Brown RC | 35.00 | 60.00 |
| ❑ 20 Gene Hermanski RC | 7.50 | 15.00 |
| ❑ 21 Frank Baumholtz RC | 12.50 | 25.00 |
| ❑ 22 Peanuts Lowrey RC | 7.50 | 15.00 |
| ❑ 23 Bobby Doerr | 50.00 | 80.00 |
| ❑ 24 Stan Musial | 350.00 | 600.00 |
| ❑ 25 Carl Scheib RC | 7.50 | 15.00 |
| ❑ 26 George Kell RC | 50.00 | 80.00 |
| ❑ 27 Bob Feller | 200.00 | 300.00 |
| ❑ 28 Don Kolloway RC | 7.50 | 15.00 |
| ❑ 29 Ralph Kiner | 75.00 | 125.00 |
| ❑ 30 Andy Seminick | 20.00 | 40.00 |
| ❑ 31 Dick Kokos RC | 7.50 | 15.00 |
| ❑ 32 Eddie Yost RC | 35.00 | 60.00 |
| ❑ 33 Warren Spahn | 125.00 | 200.00 |
| ❑ 34 Dave Koslo | 7.50 | 15.00 |
| ❑ 35 Vic Raschi RC | 35.00 | 60.00 |
| ❑ 36 Pee Wee Reese | 125.00 | 200.00 |
| ❑ 37 Johnny Wyrostek | 7.50 | 15.00 |
| ❑ 38 Emil Verban | 7.50 | 15.00 |
| ❑ 39 Billy Goodman RC | 12.50 | 25.00 |
| ❑ 40 George Munger RC | 7.50 | 15.00 |
| ❑ 41 Lou Brissie RC | 7.50 | 15.00 |
| ❑ 42 Hoot Evers RC | 7.50 | 15.00 |
| ❑ 43 Dale Mitchell RC | 20.00 | 40.00 |
| ❑ 44 Dave Philley RC | 7.50 | 15.00 |
| ❑ 45 Wally Westlake RC | 7.50 | 15.00 |
| ❑ 46 Robin Roberts RC | 150.00 | 250.00 |
| ❑ 47 Johnny Sain | 35.00 | 60.00 |
| ❑ 48 Willard Marshall | 7.50 | 15.00 |
| ❑ 49 Frank Shea | 12.50 | 25.00 |
| ❑ 50 Jackie Robinson RC | 900.00 | 1500.00 |
| ❑ 51 Herman Wehmeier | 7.50 | 15.00 |
| ❑ 52 Johnny Schmitz RC | 7.50 | 15.00 |
| ❑ 53 Jack Kramer RC | 7.50 | 15.00 |
| ❑ 54 Marty Marion | 35.00 | 60.00 |
| ❑ 55 Eddie Joost | 7.50 | 15.00 |
| ❑ 56 Pat Mullin RC | 7.50 | 15.00 |
| ❑ 57 Gene Bearden RC | 7.50 | 15.00 |
| ❑ 58 Bob Elliott | 20.00 | 40.00 |
| ❑ 59 Jack Lohrke | 7.50 | 15.00 |
| ❑ 60 Yogi Berra | 175.00 | 300.00 |
| ❑ 61 Rex Barney | 20.00 | 40.00 |
| ❑ 62 Grady Hatton RC | 7.50 | 15.00 |
| ❑ 63 Andy Pafko RC | 20.00 | 40.00 |
| ❑ 64 Dom DiMaggio RC | 35.00 | 60.00 |
| ❑ 65 Enos Slaughter | 50.00 | 80.00 |
| ❑ 66 Elmer Valo RC | 7.50 | 15.00 |
| ❑ 67 Alvin Dark RC | 20.00 | 40.00 |
| ❑ 68 Sheldon Jones | 7.50 | 15.00 |
| ❑ 69 Tommy Henrich | 20.00 | 40.00 |
| ❑ 70 Carl Furillo RC | 90.00 | 150.00 |
| ❑ 71 Vern Stephens RC | 7.50 | 15.00 |
| ❑ 72 Tommy Holmes RC | 20.00 | 40.00 |
| ❑ 73 Billy Cox RC | 20.00 | 40.00 |
| ❑ 74 Tom McBride RC | 7.50 | 15.00 |
| ❑ 75 Eddie Mayo RC | 7.50 | 15.00 |
| ❑ 76 Bill Nicholson RC | 12.50 | 25.00 |
| ❑ 77 Ernie Bonham RC | 7.50 | 15.00 |
| ❑ 78A Sam Zoldak NNOF RC | 7.50 | 15.00 |
| ❑ 78B Sam Zoldak NOF | 30.00 | 50.00 |
| ❑ 79 Ron Northey RC | 7.50 | 15.00 |
| ❑ 80 Bill McCahan | 7.50 | 15.00 |
| ❑ 81 Virgil Stallcup RC | 7.50 | 15.00 |
| ❑ 82 Joe Page | 35.00 | 60.00 |

| | | |
|---|---|---|
| ❑ 83A Bob Scheffing NNOF RC | 7.50 | 15.00 |
| ❑ 83B Bob Scheffing NOF | 30.00 | 50.00 |
| ❑ 84 Roy Campanella RC | 500.00 | 800.00 |
| ❑ 85A Johnny Mize NNOF | 60.00 | 100.00 |
| ❑ 85B Johnny Mize NOF | 90.00 | 150.00 |
| ❑ 86 Johnny Pesky RC | 35.00 | 60.00 |
| ❑ 87 Randy Gumpert RC | 7.50 | 15.00 |
| ❑ 88A Bill Salkeld NNOF RC | 7.50 | 15.00 |
| ❑ 88B Bill Salkeld NOF | 30.00 | 50.00 |
| ❑ 89 Mizell Platt RC | 7.50 | 15.00 |
| ❑ 90 Gil Coan RC | 7.50 | 15.00 |
| ❑ 91 Dick Wakefield RC | 7.50 | 15.00 |
| ❑ 92 Willie Jones RC | 20.00 | 40.00 |
| ❑ 93 Ed Stevens RC | 7.50 | 15.00 |
| ❑ 94 Mickey Vernon RC | 20.00 | 40.00 |
| ❑ 95 Howie Pollet RC | 7.50 | 15.00 |
| ❑ 96 Taft Wright | 7.50 | 15.00 |
| ❑ 97 Danny Litwhiler RC | 7.50 | 15.00 |
| ❑ 98A Phil Rizzuto NNOF | 125.00 | 200.00 |
| ❑ 98B Phil Rizzuto NOF | 150.00 | 250.00 |
| ❑ 99 Frank Gustine RC | 7.50 | 15.00 |
| ❑ 100 Gil Hodges RC | 150.00 | 250.00 |
| ❑ 101 Sid Gordon | 7.50 | 15.00 |
| ❑ 102 Stan Spence RC | 7.50 | 15.00 |
| ❑ 103 Joe Tipton RC | 7.50 | 15.00 |
| ❑ 104 Eddie Stanky RC | 20.00 | 40.00 |
| ❑ 105 Bill Kennedy RC | 7.50 | 15.00 |
| ❑ 106 Jake Early RC | 7.50 | 15.00 |
| ❑ 107 Eddie Lake RC | 7.50 | 15.00 |
| ❑ 108 Ken Heintzelman RC | 7.50 | 15.00 |
| ❑ 109A Ed Fitzgerald SCR RC | 7.50 | 15.00 |
| ❑ 109B Ed Fitzgerald PR | 35.00 | 60.00 |
| ❑ 110 Early Wynn RC | 90.00 | 150.00 |
| ❑ 111 Red Schoendienst | 60.00 | 100.00 |
| ❑ 112 Sam Chapman | 20.00 | 40.00 |
| ❑ 113 Ray LaManno RC | 7.50 | 15.00 |
| ❑ 114 Allie Reynolds | 35.00 | 60.00 |
| ❑ 115 Dutch Leonard | 7.50 | 15.00 |
| ❑ 116 Joe Hatten RC | 7.50 | 15.00 |
| ❑ 117 Walker Cooper | 7.50 | 15.00 |
| ❑ 118 Sam Mele RC | 7.50 | 15.00 |
| ❑ 119 Floyd Baker RC | 7.50 | 15.00 |
| ❑ 120 Cliff Fannin RC | 7.50 | 15.00 |
| ❑ 121 Mark Christman RC | 7.50 | 15.00 |
| ❑ 122 George Vico RC | 7.50 | 15.00 |
| ❑ 123 Johnny Blatnik | 7.50 | 15.00 |
| ❑ 124A D.Murtaugh SCR RC | 20.00 | 40.00 |
| ❑ 124B D.Murtaugh PR | 35.00 | 60.00 |
| ❑ 125 Ken Keltner RC | 12.50 | 25.00 |
| ❑ 126A Al Brazle SCR RC | 7.50 | 15.00 |
| ❑ 126B Al Brazle PR | 35.00 | 60.00 |
| ❑ 127A Hank Majeski SCR RC | 7.50 | 15.00 |
| ❑ 127B Hank Majeski PR | 35.00 | 60.00 |
| ❑ 128 Johnny VanderMeer | 20.00 | 40.00 |
| ❑ 129 Bill Johnson | 20.00 | 40.00 |
| ❑ 130 Harry Walker RC | 7.50 | 15.00 |
| ❑ 131 Paul Lehner RC | 7.50 | 15.00 |
| ❑ 132A Al Evans SCR RC | 7.50 | 15.00 |
| ❑ 132B Al Evans PR | 35.00 | 60.00 |
| ❑ 133 Aaron Robinson RC | 7.50 | 15.00 |
| ❑ 134 Hank Borowy RC | 7.50 | 15.00 |
| ❑ 135 Stan Rojek RC | 7.50 | 15.00 |
| ❑ 136 Hank Edwards RC | 7.50 | 15.00 |
| ❑ 137 Ted Wilks RC | 7.50 | 15.00 |
| ❑ 138 Buddy Rosar | 7.50 | 15.00 |
| ❑ 139 Hank Arft RC | 7.50 | 15.00 |
| ❑ 140 Ray Scarborough RC | 7.50 | 15.00 |
| ❑ 141 Tony Lupien RC | 7.50 | 15.00 |
| ❑ 142 Eddie Waitkus RC | 20.00 | 40.00 |
| ❑ 143A Bob Dillinger SCR RC | 12.50 | 25.00 |
| ❑ 143B Bob Dillinger PR | 35.00 | 60.00 |
| ❑ 144 Mickey Haefner RC | 7.50 | 15.00 |
| ❑ 145 Sylvester Donnelly RC | 30.00 | 50.00 |
| ❑ 146 Mike McCormick RC | 30.00 | 50.00 |
| ❑ 147 Bert Singleton RC | 30.00 | 50.00 |
| ❑ 148 Bob Swift RC | 30.00 | 50.00 |
| ❑ 149 Roy Partee RC | 30.00 | 50.00 |
| ❑ 150 Allie Clark RC | 30.00 | 50.00 |
| ❑ 151 Mickey Harris RC | 30.00 | 50.00 |
| ❑ 152 Clarence Maddern RC | 30.00 | 50.00 |
| ❑ 153 Phil Masi RC | 30.00 | 50.00 |
| ❑ 154 Clint Hartung | 35.00 | 60.00 |
| ❑ 155 Mickey Guerra RC | 30.00 | 50.00 |
| ❑ 156 Al Zarilla RC | 30.00 | 50.00 |
| ❑ 157 Walt Masterson RC | 30.00 | 50.00 |
| ❑ 158 Harry Brecheen RC | 35.00 | 60.00 |
| ❑ 159 Glen Moulder RC | 30.00 | 50.00 |
| ❑ 160 Jim Blackburn RC | 30.00 | 50.00 |

|  |  | | |
|---|------|------|------|
| 161 | Jocko Thompson RC | 30.00 | 50.00 |
| 162 | Preacher Roe RC | 75.00 | 125.00 |
| 163 | Clyde McCullough RC | 30.00 | 50.00 |
| 164 | Vic Wertz RC | 50.00 | 80.00 |
| 165 | Snuffy Stirnweiss | 50.00 | 80.00 |
| 166 | Mike Tresh RC | 30.00 | 50.00 |
| 167 | Babe Martin RC | 30.00 | 50.00 |
| 168 | Doyle Lade RC | 30.00 | 50.00 |
| 169 | Jeff Heath RC | 35.00 | 60.00 |
| 170 | Bill Rigney | 35.00 | 60.00 |
| 171 | Dick Fowler RC | 30.00 | 50.00 |
| 172 | Eddie Pellagrini RC | 30.00 | 50.00 |
| 173 | Eddie Stewart RC | 30.00 | 50.00 |
| 174 | Terry Moore RC | 50.00 | 80.00 |
| 175 | Luke Appling | 90.00 | 150.00 |
| 176 | Ken Raffensberger RC | 30.00 | 50.00 |
| 177 | Stan Lopata RC | 35.00 | 60.00 |
| 178 | Tom Brown RC | 35.00 | 60.00 |
| 179 | Hugh Casey | 50.00 | 80.00 |
| 180 | Connie Berry | 30.00 | 50.00 |
| 181 | Gus Niarhos RC | 30.00 | 50.00 |
| 182 | Hal Peck RC | 30.00 | 50.00 |
| 183 | Lou Stringer RC | 30.00 | 50.00 |
| 184 | Bob Chipman RC | 30.00 | 50.00 |
| 185 | Pete Reiser | 50.00 | 80.00 |
| 186 | Buddy Kerr | 30.00 | 50.00 |
| 187 | Phil Marchildon RC | 30.00 | 50.00 |
| 188 | Karl Drews RC | 30.00 | 50.00 |
| 189 | Earl Wooten RC | 30.00 | 50.00 |
| 190 | Jim Hearn RC | 30.00 | 50.00 |
| 191 | Joe Haynes RC | 30.00 | 50.00 |
| 192 | Harry Gumbert RC | 30.00 | 50.00 |
| 193 | Ken Trinkle RC | 30.00 | 50.00 |
| 194 | Ralph Branca RC | 60.00 | 100.00 |
| 195 | Eddie Bockman RC | 30.00 | 50.00 |
| 196 | Fred Hutchinson RC | 35.00 | 60.00 |
| 197 | Johnny Lindell | 35.00 | 60.00 |
| 198 | Steve Gromek RC | 30.00 | 50.00 |
| 199 | Tex Hughson RC | 30.00 | 50.00 |
| 200 | Jess Dobernic RC | 30.00 | 50.00 |
| 201 | Sibby Sisti RC | 30.00 | 50.00 |
| 202 | Larry Jansen RC | 35.00 | 60.00 |
| 203 | Barney McCosky RC | 30.00 | 50.00 |
| 204 | Bob Savage RC | 30.00 | 50.00 |
| 205 | Dick Sisler RC | 35.00 | 60.00 |
| 206 | Bruce Edwards RC | 30.00 | 50.00 |
| 207 | Johnny Hopp RC | 30.00 | 50.00 |
| 208 | Dizzy Trout | 35.00 | 60.00 |
| 209 | Charlie Keller | 50.00 | 80.00 |
| 210 | Joe Gordon RC | 50.00 | 80.00 |
| 211 | Boo Ferriss RC | 30.00 | 50.00 |
| 212 | Ralph Hamner RC | 30.00 | 50.00 |
| 213 | Red Barrett RC | 30.00 | 50.00 |
| 214 | Richie Ashburn RC | 350.00 | 600.00 |
| 215 | Kirby Higbe | 30.00 | 50.00 |
| 216 | Schoolboy Rowe | 35.00 | 60.00 |
| 217 | Marino Pieretti RC | 30.00 | 50.00 |
| 218 | Dick Kryhoski RC | 30.00 | 50.00 |
| 219 | Virgil Trucks RC | 35.00 | 60.00 |
| 220 | Johnny McCarthy | 30.00 | 50.00 |
| 221 | Bob Muncrief RC | 30.00 | 50.00 |
| 222 | Alex Kellner RC | 30.00 | 50.00 |
| 223 | Bobby Holman RC | 30.00 | 50.00 |
| 224 | Satchel Paige RC | 1000.00 | 1500.00 |
| 225 | Jerry Coleman RC | 50.00 | 80.00 |
| 226 | Duke Snider RC | 600.00 | 1000.00 |
| 227 | Fritz Ostermueller RC | 30.00 | 50.00 |
| 228 | Jackie Mayo RC | 30.00 | 50.00 |
| 229 | Ed Lopat RC | 90.00 | 150.00 |
| 230 | Augie Galan | 35.00 | 60.00 |
| 231 | Earl Johnson RC | 30.00 | 50.00 |
| 232 | George McQuinn | 35.00 | 60.00 |
| 233 | Larry Doby RC | 175.00 | 300.00 |
| 234 | Rip Sewell RC | 30.00 | 50.00 |
| 235 | Jim Russell RC | 30.00 | 50.00 |
| 236 | Fred Sanford RC | 30.00 | 50.00 |
| 237 | Monte Kennedy RC | 30.00 | 50.00 |
| 238 | Bob Lemon RC | 125.00 | 200.00 |
| 239 | Frank McCormick | 30.00 | 50.00 |
| 240 | Babe Young UER | 60.00 | 100.00 |

## 1950 Bowman

|  |  | | |
|---|------|------|------|
| | COMPLETE SET (252) | 6000.00 | 8500.00 |
| | COMMON CARD (1-72) | 30.00 | 50.00 |
| | COMMON CARD (73-252) | 7.50 | 15.00 |
| | WRAPPER (1-CENT) | 200.00 | 250.00 |
| | WRAPPER (5-CENT) | 200.00 | 250.00 |
| 1 | Mel Parnell RC | 90.00 | 150.00 |
| 2 | Vern Stephens | 35.00 | 60.00 |
| 3 | Dom DiMaggio | 50.00 | 80.00 |
| 4 | Gus Zernial RC | 35.00 | 60.00 |
| 5 | Bob Kuzava RC | 30.00 | 50.00 |
| 6 | Bob Feller | 175.00 | 300.00 |
| 7 | Jim Hegan | 35.00 | 60.00 |
| 8 | George Kell | 50.00 | 80.00 |
| 9 | Vic Wertz | 35.00 | 60.00 |
| 10 | Tommy Henrich | 50.00 | 80.00 |
| 11 | Phil Rizzuto | 175.00 | 300.00 |
| 12 | Joe Page | 50.00 | 80.00 |
| 13 | Ferris Fain | 35.00 | 60.00 |
| 14 | Alex Kellner | 30.00 | 50.00 |
| 15 | Al Kozar | 30.00 | 50.00 |
| 16 | Roy Sievers RC | 50.00 | 80.00 |
| 17 | Sid Hudson | 30.00 | 50.00 |
| 18 | Eddie Robinson RC | 30.00 | 50.00 |
| 19 | Warren Spahn | 175.00 | 300.00 |
| 20 | Bob Elliott | 35.00 | 60.00 |
| 21 | Pee Wee Reese | 175.00 | 300.00 |
| 22 | Jackie Robinson | 700.00 | 1200.00 |
| 23 | Don Newcombe RC | 90.00 | 150.00 |
| 24 | Johnny Schmitz | 30.00 | 50.00 |
| 25 | Hank Sauer | 35.00 | 60.00 |
| 26 | Grady Hatton | 30.00 | 50.00 |
| 27 | Herman Wehmeier | 30.00 | 50.00 |
| 28 | Bobby Thomson | 50.00 | 80.00 |
| 29 | Eddie Stanky | 35.00 | 60.00 |
| 30 | Eddie Waitkus | 35.00 | 60.00 |
| 31 | Del Ennis | 50.00 | 80.00 |
| 32 | Robin Roberts | 90.00 | 150.00 |
| 33 | Ralph Kiner | 60.00 | 100.00 |
| 34 | Murry Dickson | 30.00 | 50.00 |
| 35 | Enos Slaughter | 60.00 | 100.00 |
| 36 | Eddie Kazak RC | 35.00 | 60.00 |
| 37 | Luke Appling | 50.00 | 80.00 |
| 38 | Bill Wight RC | 30.00 | 50.00 |
| 39 | Larry Doby | 60.00 | 100.00 |
| 40 | Bob Lemon | 50.00 | 80.00 |
| 41 | Hoot Evers | 30.00 | 50.00 |
| 42 | Art Houtteman RC | 30.00 | 50.00 |
| 43 | Bobby Doerr | 50.00 | 80.00 |
| 44 | Joe Dobson RC | 30.00 | 50.00 |
| 45 | Al Zarilla | 30.00 | 50.00 |
| 46 | Yogi Berra | 250.00 | 400.00 |
| 47 | Jerry Coleman | 50.00 | 80.00 |
| 48 | Lou Brissie RC | 35.00 | 60.00 |
| 49 | Elmer Valo | 30.00 | 50.00 |
| 50 | Dick Kokos | 30.00 | 50.00 |
| 51 | Ned Garver | 35.00 | 60.00 |
| 52 | Sam Mele | 30.00 | 50.00 |
| 53 | Clyde Vollmer RC | 30.00 | 50.00 |
| 54 | Gil Coan | 30.00 | 50.00 |
| 55 | Buddy Kerr | 30.00 | 50.00 |
| 56 | Del Crandall RC | 35.00 | 60.00 |
| 57 | Vern Bickford | 30.00 | 50.00 |
| 58 | Carl Furillo | 50.00 | 80.00 |
| 59 | Ralph Branca | 50.00 | 80.00 |
| 60 | Andy Pafko | 35.00 | 60.00 |
| 61 | Bob Rush RC | 30.00 | 50.00 |
| 62 | Ted Kluszewski | 75.00 | 125.00 |
| 63 | Ewell Blackwell | 35.00 | 60.00 |
| 64 | Alvin Dark | 35.00 | 60.00 |
| 65 | Dave Koslo | 30.00 | 50.00 |
| 66 | Larry Jansen | 35.00 | 60.00 |
| 67 | Willie Jones | 30.00 | 50.00 |
| 68 | Curt Simmons | 35.00 | 60.00 |
| 69 | Wally Westlake | 30.00 | 50.00 |

|  |  | | |
|---|------|------|------|
| 70 | Bob Chesnes | 30.00 | 50.00 |
| 71 | Red Schoendienst | 50.00 | 80.00 |
| 72 | Howie Pollet | 30.00 | 50.00 |
| 73 | Willard Marshall | 7.50 | 15.00 |
| 74 | Johnny Antonelli RC | 35.00 | 60.00 |
| 75 | Roy Campanella | 175.00 | 300.00 |
| 76 | Rex Barney | 20.00 | 40.00 |
| 77 | Duke Snider | 175.00 | 300.00 |
| 78 | Mickey Owen | 12.50 | 25.00 |
| 79 | Johnny VanderMeer | 20.00 | 40.00 |
| 80 | Howard Fox RC | 7.50 | 15.00 |
| 81 | Ron Northey | 7.50 | 15.00 |
| 82 | Whitey Lockman | 12.50 | 25.00 |
| 83 | Sheldon Jones | 7.50 | 15.00 |
| 84 | Richie Ashburn | 75.00 | 125.00 |
| 85 | Ken Heintzelman | 7.50 | 15.00 |
| 86 | Stan Rojek | 7.50 | 15.00 |
| 87 | Bill Werle RC | 7.50 | 15.00 |
| 88 | Marty Marion | 20.00 | 40.00 |
| 89 | George Munger | 7.50 | 15.00 |
| 90 | Harry Brecheen | 20.00 | 40.00 |
| 91 | Cass Michaels | 7.50 | 15.00 |
| 92 | Hank Majeski | 7.50 | 15.00 |
| 93 | Gene Bearden | 20.00 | 40.00 |
| 94 | Lou Boudreau MG | 35.00 | 60.00 |
| 95 | Aaron Robinson | 7.50 | 15.00 |
| 96 | Virgil Trucks | 12.50 | 25.00 |
| 97 | Maurice McDermott RC | 7.50 | 15.00 |
| 98 | Ted Williams | 600.00 | 1000.00 |
| 99 | Billy Goodman | 12.50 | 25.00 |
| 100 | Vic Raschi | 35.00 | 60.00 |
| 101 | Bobby Brown | 35.00 | 60.00 |
| 102 | Billy Johnson | 12.50 | 25.00 |
| 103 | Eddie Joost | 7.50 | 15.00 |
| 104 | Sam Chapman | 7.50 | 15.00 |
| 105 | Bob Dillinger | 7.50 | 15.00 |
| 106 | Cliff Fannin | 7.50 | 15.00 |
| 107 | Sam Dente RC | 7.50 | 15.00 |
| 108 | Ray Scarborough | 7.50 | 15.00 |
| 109 | Sid Gordon | 7.50 | 15.00 |
| 110 | Tommy Holmes | 12.50 | 25.00 |
| 111 | Walker Cooper | 7.50 | 15.00 |
| 112 | Gil Hodges | 75.00 | 125.00 |
| 113 | Gene Hermanski | 7.50 | 15.00 |
| 114 | Wayne Terwilliger RC | 7.50 | 15.00 |
| 115 | Roy Smalley | 7.50 | 15.00 |
| 116 | Virgil Stallcup | 7.50 | 15.00 |
| 117 | Bill Rigney | 7.50 | 15.00 |
| 118 | Clint Hartung | 7.50 | 15.00 |
| 119 | Dick Sisler | 12.50 | 25.00 |
| 120 | John Thompson | 7.50 | 15.00 |
| 121 | Andy Seminick | 12.50 | 25.00 |
| 122 | Johnny Hopp | 12.50 | 25.00 |
| 123 | Dino Restelli RC | 7.50 | 15.00 |
| 124 | Clyde McCullough | 7.50 | 15.00 |
| 125 | Del Rice RC | 7.50 | 15.00 |
| 126 | Al Brazle | 7.50 | 15.00 |
| 127 | Dave Philley | 7.50 | 15.00 |
| 128 | Phil Masi | 7.50 | 15.00 |
| 129 | Joe Gordon | 12.50 | 25.00 |
| 130 | Dale Mitchell | 12.50 | 25.00 |
| 131 | Steve Gromek | 7.50 | 15.00 |
| 132 | Mickey Vernon | 12.50 | 25.00 |
| 133 | Don Kolloway | 7.50 | 15.00 |
| 134 | Paul Trout | 7.50 | 15.00 |
| 135 | Pat Mullin | 7.50 | 15.00 |
| 136 | Buddy Rosar | 7.50 | 15.00 |
| 137 | Johnny Pesky | 12.50 | 25.00 |
| 138 | Allie Reynolds | 35.00 | 60.00 |
| 139 | Johnny Mize | 50.00 | 80.00 |
| 140 | Pete Suder RC | 7.50 | 15.00 |
| 141 | Joe Coleman RC | 12.50 | 25.00 |
| 142 | Sherman Lollar RC | 20.00 | 40.00 |
| 143 | Eddie Stewart | 7.50 | 15.00 |
| 144 | Al Evans | 7.50 | 15.00 |
| 145 | Jack Graham RC | 7.50 | 15.00 |
| 146 | Floyd Baker | 7.50 | 15.00 |
| 147 | Mike Garcia RC | 20.00 | 40.00 |
| 148 | Early Wynn | 50.00 | 80.00 |
| 149 | Bob Swift | 7.50 | 15.00 |
| 150 | George Vico | 7.50 | 15.00 |
| 151 | Fred Hutchinson | 12.50 | 25.00 |
| 152 | Ellis Kinder RC | 7.50 | 15.00 |
| 153 | Walt Masterson | 7.50 | 15.00 |
| 154 | Gus Niarhos | 7.50 | 15.00 |
| 155 | Frank Shea | 12.50 | 25.00 |
| 156 | Fred Sanford | 12.50 | 25.00 |
| 157 | Mike Guerra | 7.50 | 15.00 |

| | | |
|---|---|---|
| ❏ 158 Paul Lehner | 7.50 | 15.00 |
| ❏ 159 Joe Tipton | 7.50 | 15.00 |
| ❏ 160 Mickey Harris | 7.50 | 15.00 |
| ❏ 161 Sherry Robertson RC | 7.50 | 15.00 |
| ❏ 162 Eddie Yost | 12.50 | 25.00 |
| ❏ 163 Earl Torgeson | 7.50 | 15.00 |
| ❏ 164 Sibby Sisti | 7.50 | 15.00 |
| ❏ 165 Bruce Edwards | 7.50 | 15.00 |
| ❏ 166 Joe Hatton | 7.50 | 15.00 |
| ❏ 167 Preacher Roe | 35.00 | 60.00 |
| ❏ 168 Bob Scheffing | 7.50 | 15.00 |
| ❏ 169 Hank Edwards | 7.50 | 15.00 |
| ❏ 170 Dutch Leonard | 7.50 | 15.00 |
| ❏ 171 Harry Gumbert | 7.50 | 15.00 |
| ❏ 172 Peanuts Lowrey | 7.50 | 15.00 |
| ❏ 173 Lloyd Merriman RC | 7.50 | 15.00 |
| ❏ 174 Hank Thompson RC | 20.00 | 40.00 |
| ❏ 175 Monte Kennedy | 7.50 | 15.00 |
| ❏ 176 Sylvester Donnelly | 7.50 | 15.00 |
| ❏ 177 Hank Borowy | 7.50 | 15.00 |
| ❏ 178 Ed Fitzgerald | 7.50 | 15.00 |
| ❏ 179 Chuck Diering RC | 7.50 | 15.00 |
| ❏ 180 Harry Walker | 12.50 | 25.00 |
| ❏ 181 Marino Pieretti | 7.50 | 15.00 |
| ❏ 182 Sam Zoldak | 7.50 | 15.00 |
| ❏ 183 Mickey Haefner | 7.50 | 15.00 |
| ❏ 184 Randy Gumpert | 7.50 | 15.00 |
| ❏ 185 Howie Judson RC | 7.50 | 15.00 |
| ❏ 186 Ken Keltner | 12.50 | 25.00 |
| ❏ 187 Lou Stringer | 7.50 | 15.00 |
| ❏ 188 Earl Johnson | 7.50 | 15.00 |
| ❏ 189 Owen Friend RC | 7.50 | 15.00 |
| ❏ 190 Ken Wood RC | 7.50 | 15.00 |
| ❏ 191 Dick Starr RC | 7.50 | 15.00 |
| ❏ 192 Bob Chipman | 7.50 | 15.00 |
| ❏ 193 Pete Reiser | 20.00 | 40.00 |
| ❏ 194 Billy Cox | 35.00 | 60.00 |
| ❏ 195 Phil Cavarretta | 20.00 | 40.00 |
| ❏ 196 Doyle Lade | 7.50 | 15.00 |
| ❏ 197 Johnny Wyrostek | 7.50 | 15.00 |
| ❏ 198 Danny Litwhiler | 7.50 | 15.00 |
| ❏ 199 Jack Kramer | 7.50 | 15.00 |
| ❏ 200 Kirby Higbe | 12.50 | 25.00 |
| ❏ 201 Pete Castiglione RC | 7.50 | 15.00 |
| ❏ 202 Cliff Chambers RC | 7.50 | 15.00 |
| ❏ 203 Danny Murtaugh | 12.50 | 25.00 |
| ❏ 204 Granny Hamner | 20.00 | 40.00 |
| ❏ 205 Mike Goliat RC | 7.50 | 15.00 |
| ❏ 206 Stan Lopata | 12.50 | 25.00 |
| ❏ 207 Max Lanier RC | 7.50 | 15.00 |
| ❏ 208 Jim Hearn | 7.50 | 15.00 |
| ❏ 209 Johnny Lindell | 7.50 | 15.00 |
| ❏ 210 Ted Gray | 7.50 | 15.00 |
| ❏ 211 Charlie Keller | 20.00 | 40.00 |
| ❏ 212 Jerry Priddy | 7.50 | 15.00 |
| ❏ 213 Carl Scheib | 7.50 | 15.00 |
| ❏ 214 Dick Fowler | 7.50 | 15.00 |
| ❏ 215 Ed Lopat | 35.00 | 60.00 |
| ❏ 216 Bob Porterfield | 12.50 | 25.00 |
| ❏ 217 Casey Stengel MG | 75.00 | 125.00 |
| ❏ 218 Cliff Mapes RC | 12.50 | 25.00 |
| ❏ 219 Hank Bauer RC | 60.00 | 100.00 |
| ❏ 220 Leo Durocher MG | 35.00 | 60.00 |
| ❏ 221 Don Mueller RC | 20.00 | 40.00 |
| ❏ 222 Bobby Morgan RC | 7.50 | 15.00 |
| ❏ 223 Jim Russell | 7.50 | 15.00 |
| ❏ 224 Jack Banta RC | 7.50 | 15.00 |
| ❏ 225 Eddie Sawyer MG RC | 12.50 | 25.00 |
| ❏ 226 Jim Konstanty RC | 35.00 | 60.00 |
| ❏ 227 Bob Miller RC | 12.50 | 25.00 |
| ❏ 228 Bill Nicholson | 12.50 | 25.00 |
| ❏ 229 Frankie Frisch MG | 35.00 | 60.00 |
| ❏ 230 Bill Serena RC | 7.50 | 15.00 |
| ❏ 231 Preston Ward RC | 7.50 | 15.00 |
| ❏ 232 Al Rosen RC | 35.00 | 60.00 |
| ❏ 233 Allie Clark | 7.50 | 15.00 |
| ❏ 234 Bobby Shantz RC | 35.00 | 60.00 |
| ❏ 235 Harold Gilbert RC | 7.50 | 15.00 |
| ❏ 236 Bob Cain RC | 7.50 | 15.00 |
| ❏ 237 Bill Salkeld | 7.50 | 15.00 |
| ❏ 238 Nippy Jones RC | 7.50 | 15.00 |
| ❏ 239 Bill Howerton RC | 7.50 | 15.00 |
| ❏ 240 Eddie Lake | 7.50 | 15.00 |
| ❏ 241 Neil Berry RC | 7.50 | 15.00 |
| ❏ 242 Dick Kryhoski | 7.50 | 15.00 |
| ❏ 243 Johnny Groth RC | 7.50 | 15.00 |
| ❏ 244 Dale Coogan RC | 7.50 | 15.00 |
| ❏ 245 Al Papai RC | 7.50 | 15.00 |

| | | |
|---|---|---|
| ❏ 246 Walt Dropo RC | 20.00 | 40.00 |
| ❏ 247 Irv Noren RC | 12.50 | 25.00 |
| ❏ 248 Sam Jethroe RC | 35.00 | 60.00 |
| ❏ 249 Snuffy Stirnweiss | 12.50 | 25.00 |
| ❏ 250 Ray Coleman RC | 7.50 | 15.00 |
| ❏ 251 Les Moss RC | 7.50 | 15.00 |
| ❏ 252 Billy DeMars RC | 35.00 | 60.00 |

## 1951 Bowman

| | | |
|---|---|---|
| ❏ COMPLETE SET (324) | 15000.00 | 20000.00 |
| ❏ COMMON CARD (1-252) | 10.00 | 20.00 |
| ❏ COMMON CARD (253-324) | 30.00 | 50.00 |
| ❏ WRAPPER (1-CENT) | 150.00 | 200.00 |
| ❏ WRAPPER (5-CENT) | 200.00 | 250.00 |
| ❏ 1 Whitey Ford RC | 1500.00 | 2500.00 |
| ❏ 2 Yogi Berra | 250.00 | 400.00 |
| ❏ 3 Robin Roberts | 60.00 | 100.00 |
| ❏ 4 Del Ennis | 12.50 | 25.00 |
| ❏ 5 Dale Mitchell | 12.50 | 25.00 |
| ❏ 6 Don Newcombe | 35.00 | 60.00 |
| ❏ 7 Gil Hodges | 75.00 | 125.00 |
| ❏ 8 Paul Lehner | 10.00 | 20.00 |
| ❏ 9 Sam Chapman | 10.00 | 20.00 |
| ❏ 10 Red Schoendienst | 35.00 | 60.00 |
| ❏ 11 George Munger | 10.00 | 20.00 |
| ❏ 12 Hank Majeski | 10.00 | 20.00 |
| ❏ 13 Eddie Stanky | 12.50 | 25.00 |
| ❏ 14 Alvin Dark | 20.00 | 40.00 |
| ❏ 15 Johnny Pesky | 12.50 | 25.00 |
| ❏ 16 Maurice McDermott | 10.00 | 20.00 |
| ❏ 17 Pete Castiglione | 10.00 | 20.00 |
| ❏ 18 Gil Coan | 10.00 | 20.00 |
| ❏ 19 Sid Gordon | 10.00 | 20.00 |
| ❏ 20 Del Crandall UER | 12.50 | 25.00 |
| ❏ 21 Snuffy Stirnweiss | 12.50 | 25.00 |
| ❏ 22 Hank Sauer | 12.50 | 25.00 |
| ❏ 23 Hoot Evers | 10.00 | 20.00 |
| ❏ 24 Ewell Blackwell | 20.00 | 40.00 |
| ❏ 25 Vic Raschi | 35.00 | 60.00 |
| ❏ 26 Phil Rizzuto | 90.00 | 150.00 |
| ❏ 27 Jim Konstanty | 12.50 | 25.00 |
| ❏ 28 Eddie Waitkus | 10.00 | 20.00 |
| ❏ 29 Allie Clark | 10.00 | 20.00 |
| ❏ 30 Bob Feller | 75.00 | 125.00 |
| ❏ 31 Roy Campanella | 175.00 | 300.00 |
| ❏ 32 Duke Snider | 150.00 | 250.00 |
| ❏ 33 Bob Hooper RC | 10.00 | 20.00 |
| ❏ 34 Marty Marion MG | 20.00 | 40.00 |
| ❏ 35 Al Zarilla | 10.00 | 20.00 |
| ❏ 36 Joe Dobson | 10.00 | 20.00 |
| ❏ 37 Whitey Lockman | 20.00 | 40.00 |
| ❏ 38 Al Evans | 10.00 | 20.00 |
| ❏ 39 Ray Scarborough | 10.00 | 20.00 |
| ❏ 40 Gus Bell RC | 35.00 | 60.00 |
| ❏ 41 Eddie Yost | 12.50 | 25.00 |
| ❏ 42 Vern Bickford | 10.00 | 20.00 |
| ❏ 43 Billy DeMars | 10.00 | 20.00 |
| ❏ 44 Roy Smalley | 10.00 | 20.00 |
| ❏ 45 Art Houtteman | 10.00 | 20.00 |
| ❏ 46 George Kell UER | 35.00 | 60.00 |
| ❏ 47 Grady Hatton | 10.00 | 20.00 |
| ❏ 48 Ken Raffensberger | 10.00 | 20.00 |
| ❏ 49 Jerry Coleman | 12.50 | 25.00 |
| ❏ 50 Johnny Mize | 50.00 | 80.00 |
| ❏ 51 Andy Seminick | 10.00 | 20.00 |
| ❏ 52 Dick Sisler | 20.00 | 40.00 |
| ❏ 53 Bob Lemon | 35.00 | 60.00 |
| ❏ 54 Ray Boone RC | 20.00 | 40.00 |
| ❏ 55 Gene Hermanski | 10.00 | 20.00 |
| ❏ 56 Ralph Branca | 35.00 | 60.00 |
| ❏ 57 Alex Kellner | 10.00 | 20.00 |
| ❏ 58 Enos Slaughter | 35.00 | 60.00 |
| ❏ 59 Randy Gumpert | 10.00 | 20.00 |
| ❏ 60 Chico Carrasquel RC | 35.00 | 60.00 |

| | | |
|---|---|---|
| ❏ 61 Jim Hearn | 12.50 | 25.00 |
| ❏ 62 Lou Boudreau MG | 35.00 | 60.00 |
| ❏ 63 Bob Dillinger | 10.00 | 20.00 |
| ❏ 64 Bill Werle | 10.00 | 20.00 |
| ❏ 65 Mickey Vernon | 20.00 | 40.00 |
| ❏ 66 Bob Elliott | 12.50 | 25.00 |
| ❏ 67 Roy Sievers | 12.50 | 25.00 |
| ❏ 68 Dick Kokos | 10.00 | 20.00 |
| ❏ 69 Johnny Schmitz | 10.00 | 20.00 |
| ❏ 70 Ron Northey | 10.00 | 20.00 |
| ❏ 71 Jerry Priddy | 10.00 | 20.00 |
| ❏ 72 Lloyd Merriman | 10.00 | 20.00 |
| ❏ 73 Tommy Byrne RC | 10.00 | 20.00 |
| ❏ 74 Billy Johnson | 12.50 | 25.00 |
| ❏ 75 Russ Meyer RC | 12.50 | 25.00 |
| ❏ 76 Stan Lopata | 12.50 | 25.00 |
| ❏ 77 Mike Goliat | 10.00 | 20.00 |
| ❏ 78 Early Wynn | 35.00 | 60.00 |
| ❏ 79 Jim Hegan | 12.50 | 25.00 |
| ❏ 80 Pee Wee Reese | 125.00 | 200.00 |
| ❏ 81 Carl Furillo | 35.00 | 60.00 |
| ❏ 82 Joe Tipton | 10.00 | 20.00 |
| ❏ 83 Carl Scheib | 10.00 | 20.00 |
| ❏ 84 Barney McCosky | 10.00 | 20.00 |
| ❏ 85 Eddie Kazak | 10.00 | 20.00 |
| ❏ 86 Harry Brecheen | 12.50 | 25.00 |
| ❏ 87 Floyd Baker | 10.00 | 20.00 |
| ❏ 88 Eddie Robinson | 10.00 | 20.00 |
| ❏ 89 Hank Thompson | 12.50 | 25.00 |
| ❏ 90 Dave Koslo | 10.00 | 20.00 |
| ❏ 91 Clyde Vollmer | 10.00 | 20.00 |
| ❏ 92 Vern Stephens | 12.50 | 25.00 |
| ❏ 93 Danny O'Connell RC | 10.00 | 20.00 |
| ❏ 94 Clyde McCullough | 10.00 | 20.00 |
| ❏ 95 Sherry Robertson | 10.00 | 20.00 |
| ❏ 96 Sandy Consuegra RC | 10.00 | 20.00 |
| ❏ 97 Bob Kuzava | 10.00 | 20.00 |
| ❏ 98 Willard Marshall | 10.00 | 20.00 |
| ❏ 99 Earl Torgeson | 10.00 | 20.00 |
| ❏ 100 Sherm Lollar | 12.50 | 25.00 |
| ❏ 101 Owen Friend | 10.00 | 20.00 |
| ❏ 102 Dutch Leonard | 10.00 | 20.00 |
| ❏ 103 Andy Pafko | 20.00 | 40.00 |
| ❏ 104 Virgil Trucks | 12.50 | 25.00 |
| ❏ 105 Don Kolloway | 10.00 | 20.00 |
| ❏ 106 Pat Mullin | 10.00 | 20.00 |
| ❏ 107 Johnny Wyrostek | 10.00 | 20.00 |
| ❏ 108 Virgil Stallcup | 10.00 | 20.00 |
| ❏ 109 Allie Reynolds | 35.00 | 60.00 |
| ❏ 110 Bobby Brown | 20.00 | 40.00 |
| ❏ 111 Curt Simmons | 12.50 | 25.00 |
| ❏ 112 Willie Jones | 10.00 | 20.00 |
| ❏ 113 Bill Nicholson | 10.00 | 20.00 |
| ❏ 114 Sam Zoldak | 10.00 | 20.00 |
| ❏ 115 Steve Gromek | 10.00 | 20.00 |
| ❏ 116 Bruce Edwards | 10.00 | 20.00 |
| ❏ 117 Eddie Miksis RC | 10.00 | 20.00 |
| ❏ 118 Preacher Roe | 35.00 | 60.00 |
| ❏ 119 Eddie Joost | 10.00 | 20.00 |
| ❏ 120 Joe Coleman | 12.50 | 25.00 |
| ❏ 121 Gerry Staley RC | 10.00 | 20.00 |
| ❏ 122 Joe Garagiola RC | 60.00 | 100.00 |
| ❏ 123 Howie Judson | 10.00 | 20.00 |
| ❏ 124 Gus Niarhos | 10.00 | 20.00 |
| ❏ 125 Bill Rigney | 12.50 | 25.00 |
| ❏ 126 Bobby Thomson | 35.00 | 60.00 |
| ❏ 127 Sal Maglie RC | 35.00 | 60.00 |
| ❏ 128 Ellis Kinder | 10.00 | 20.00 |
| ❏ 129 Matt Batts | 10.00 | 20.00 |
| ❏ 130 Tom Saffell RC | 10.00 | 20.00 |
| ❏ 131 Cliff Chambers | 10.00 | 20.00 |
| ❏ 132 Cass Michaels | 10.00 | 20.00 |
| ❏ 133 Sam Dente | 10.00 | 20.00 |
| ❏ 134 Warren Spahn | 90.00 | 150.00 |
| ❏ 135 Walker Cooper | 10.00 | 20.00 |
| ❏ 136 Ray Coleman | 10.00 | 20.00 |
| ❏ 137 Dick Starr | 10.00 | 20.00 |
| ❏ 138 Phil Cavarretta | 12.50 | 25.00 |
| ❏ 139 Doyle Lade | 10.00 | 20.00 |
| ❏ 140 Eddie Lake | 10.00 | 20.00 |
| ❏ 141 Fred Hutchinson | 12.50 | 25.00 |
| ❏ 142 Aaron Robinson | 10.00 | 20.00 |
| ❏ 143 Ted Kluszewski | 50.00 | 80.00 |
| ❏ 144 Herman Wehmeier | 10.00 | 20.00 |
| ❏ 145 Fred Sanford | 12.50 | 25.00 |
| ❏ 146 Johnny Hopp | 12.50 | 25.00 |
| ❏ 147 Ken Heintzelman | 10.00 | 20.00 |
| ❏ 148 Granny Hamner | 10.00 | 20.00 |

|  |  | | |
|---|---|---|---|
| 149 | Bubba Church RC | 10.00 | 20.00 |
| 150 | Mike Garcia | 12.50 | 25.00 |
| 151 | Larry Doby | 35.00 | 60.00 |
| 152 | Cal Abrams RC | 10.00 | 20.00 |
| 153 | Rex Barney | 12.50 | 25.00 |
| 154 | Pete Suder | 10.00 | 20.00 |
| 155 | Lou Brissie | 10.00 | 20.00 |
| 156 | Del Rice | 10.00 | 20.00 |
| 157 | Al Brazle | 10.00 | 20.00 |
| 158 | Chuck Diering | 10.00 | 20.00 |
| 159 | Eddie Stewart | 10.00 | 20.00 |
| 160 | Phil Masi | 10.00 | 20.00 |
| 161 | Wes Westrum RC | 10.00 | 20.00 |
| 162 | Larry Jansen | 12.50 | 25.00 |
| 163 | Monte Kennedy | 10.00 | 20.00 |
| 164 | Bill Wight | 10.00 | 20.00 |
| 165 | Ted Williams UER | 500.00 | 800.00 |
| 166 | Stan Rojek | 10.00 | 20.00 |
| 167 | Murry Dickson | 10.00 | 20.00 |
| 168 | Sam Mele | 10.00 | 20.00 |
| 169 | Sid Hudson | 10.00 | 20.00 |
| 170 | Sibby Sisti | 10.00 | 20.00 |
| 171 | Buddy Kerr | 10.00 | 20.00 |
| 172 | Ned Garver | 10.00 | 20.00 |
| 173 | Hank Arft | 10.00 | 20.00 |
| 174 | Mickey Owen | 12.50 | 25.00 |
| 175 | Wayne Terwilliger | 10.00 | 20.00 |
| 176 | Vic Wertz | 20.00 | 40.00 |
| 177 | Charlie Keller | 12.50 | 25.00 |
| 178 | Ted Gray | 10.00 | 20.00 |
| 179 | Danny Litwhiler | 10.00 | 20.00 |
| 180 | Howie Fox | 10.00 | 20.00 |
| 181 | Casey Stengel MG | 50.00 | 80.00 |
| 182 | Tom Ferrick | 10.00 | 20.00 |
| 183 | Hank Bauer | 35.00 | 60.00 |
| 184 | Eddie Sawyer MG | 20.00 | 40.00 |
| 185 | Jimmy Bloodworth | 10.00 | 20.00 |
| 186 | Richie Ashburn | 60.00 | 100.00 |
| 187 | Al Rosen | 20.00 | 40.00 |
| 188 | Bobby Avila RC | 12.50 | 25.00 |
| 189 | Erv Palica RC | 10.00 | 20.00 |
| 190 | Joe Hatten | 10.00 | 20.00 |
| 191 | Billy Hitchcock RC | 10.00 | 20.00 |
| 192 | Hank Wyse RC | 10.00 | 20.00 |
| 193 | Ted Wilks | 10.00 | 20.00 |
| 194 | Peanuts Lowrey | 10.00 | 20.00 |
| 195 | Paul Richards MG | 12.50 | 25.00 |
| 196 | Billy Pierce RC | 35.00 | 60.00 |
| 197 | Bob Cain | 10.00 | 20.00 |
| 198 | Monte Irvin RC | 75.00 | 125.00 |
| 199 | Sheldon Jones | 10.00 | 20.00 |
| 200 | Jack Kramer | 10.00 | 20.00 |
| 201 | Steve O'Neill MG RC | 10.00 | 20.00 |
| 202 | Mike Garcia | 10.00 | 20.00 |
| 203 | Vern Law RC | 35.00 | 60.00 |
| 204 | Vic Lombardi RC | 10.00 | 20.00 |
| 205 | Mickey Grasso RC | 10.00 | 20.00 |
| 206 | Conrado Marrero RC | 10.00 | 20.00 |
| 207 | Billy Southworth MG RC | 10.00 | 20.00 |
| 208 | Blix Donnelly | 10.00 | 20.00 |
| 209 | Ken Wood | 10.00 | 20.00 |
| 210 | Les Moss | 10.00 | 20.00 |
| 211 | Hal Jeffcoat RC | 10.00 | 20.00 |
| 212 | Bob Rush | 10.00 | 20.00 |
| 213 | Neil Berry | 10.00 | 20.00 |
| 214 | Bob Swift | 10.00 | 20.00 |
| 215 | Ken Peterson | 10.00 | 20.00 |
| 216 | Connie Ryan RC | 10.00 | 20.00 |
| 217 | Joe Page | 12.50 | 25.00 |
| 218 | Ed Lopat | 35.00 | 60.00 |
| 219 | Gene Woodling RC | 30.00 | 50.00 |
| 220 | Bob Miller | 10.00 | 20.00 |
| 221 | Dick Whitman RC | 10.00 | 20.00 |
| 222 | Thurman Tucker RC | 10.00 | 20.00 |
| 223 | Johnny VanderMeer | 20.00 | 40.00 |
| 224 | Billy Cox | 12.50 | 25.00 |
| 225 | Dan Bankhead RC | 10.00 | 20.00 |
| 226 | Jimmie Dykes MG | 10.00 | 20.00 |
| 227 | Bobby Shantz UER | 12.50 | 25.00 |
| 228 | Cloyd Boyer RC | 12.50 | 25.00 |
| 229 | Bill Howerton | 10.00 | 20.00 |
| 230 | Max Lanier | 10.00 | 20.00 |
| 231 | Luis Aloma RC | 10.00 | 20.00 |
| 232 | Nellie Fox RC | 150.00 | 250.00 |
| 233 | Leo Durocher MG | 35.00 | 60.00 |
| 234 | Clint Hartung | 12.50 | 25.00 |
| 235 | Jack Lohrke | 10.00 | 20.00 |
| 236 | Buddy Rosar | 10.00 | 20.00 |
| 237 | Billy Goodman | 12.50 | 25.00 |
| 238 | Pete Reiser | 20.00 | 40.00 |
| 239 | Bill MacDonald RC | 10.00 | 20.00 |
| 240 | Joe Haynes | 10.00 | 20.00 |
| 241 | Irv Noren | 12.50 | 25.00 |
| 242 | Sam Jethroe | 12.50 | 25.00 |
| 243 | Johnny Antonelli | 12.50 | 25.00 |
| 244 | Cliff Fannin | 10.00 | 20.00 |
| 245 | John Berardino RC | 35.00 | 60.00 |
| 246 | Bill Serena | 10.00 | 20.00 |
| 247 | Bob Ramazzotti RC | 10.00 | 20.00 |
| 248 | Johnny Klippstein RC | 10.00 | 20.00 |
| 249 | Johnny Groth | 10.00 | 20.00 |
| 250 | Hank Borowy | 10.00 | 20.00 |
| 251 | Willard Ramsdell RC | 10.00 | 20.00 |
| 252 | Dixie Howell RC | 10.00 | 20.00 |
| 253 | Mickey Mantle | 5000.00 | 8000.00 |
| 254 | Jackie Jensen RC | 60.00 | 100.00 |
| 255 | Milo Candini RC | 30.00 | 50.00 |
| 256 | Ken Silvestri RC | 30.00 | 50.00 |
| 257 | Birdie Tebbetts RC | 35.00 | 60.00 |
| 258 | Luke Easter RC | 35.00 | 60.00 |
| 259 | Chuck Dressen MG | 35.00 | 60.00 |
| 260 | Carl Erskine RC | 60.00 | 100.00 |
| 261 | Wally Moses | 35.00 | 60.00 |
| 262 | Gus Zernial | 30.00 | 50.00 |
| 263 | Howie Pollet | 30.00 | 50.00 |
| 264 | Don Richmond | 30.00 | 50.00 |
| 265 | Steve Bilko RC | 30.00 | 50.00 |
| 266 | Harry Dorish RC | 30.00 | 50.00 |
| 267 | Ken Holcombe RC | 30.00 | 50.00 |
| 268 | Don Mueller | 35.00 | 60.00 |
| 269 | Ray Noble RC | 30.00 | 50.00 |
| 270 | Willard Nixon RC | 30.00 | 50.00 |
| 271 | Tommy Wright RC | 30.00 | 50.00 |
| 272 | Billy Meyer MG RC | 30.00 | 50.00 |
| 273 | Danny Murtaugh | 35.00 | 60.00 |
| 274 | George Metkovich RC | 30.00 | 50.00 |
| 275 | Bucky Harris MG | 50.00 | 80.00 |
| 276 | Frank Quinn RC | 30.00 | 50.00 |
| 277 | Roy Hartsfield RC | 30.00 | 50.00 |
| 278 | Norman Roy RC | 30.00 | 50.00 |
| 279 | Jim Delsing RC | 30.00 | 50.00 |
| 280 | Frank Overmire | 30.00 | 50.00 |
| 281 | Al Widmar RC | 30.00 | 50.00 |
| 282 | Frankie Frisch MG | 60.00 | 100.00 |
| 283 | Walt Dubiel RC | 30.00 | 50.00 |
| 284 | Gene Bearden | 35.00 | 60.00 |
| 285 | Johnny Lipon RC | 30.00 | 50.00 |
| 286 | Bob Usher RC | 30.00 | 50.00 |
| 287 | Jim Blackburn | 30.00 | 50.00 |
| 288 | Bobby Adams | 30.00 | 50.00 |
| 289 | Cliff Mapes | 35.00 | 60.00 |
| 290 | Bill Dickey CO | 90.00 | 150.00 |
| 291 | Tommy Henrich CO | 50.00 | 80.00 |
| 292 | Eddie Pellagrini | 30.00 | 50.00 |
| 293 | Ken Johnson RC | 30.00 | 50.00 |
| 294 | Jocko Thompson | 30.00 | 50.00 |
| 295 | Al Lopez MG RC | 75.00 | 125.00 |
| 296 | Bob Kennedy RC | 35.00 | 60.00 |
| 297 | Dave Philley | 30.00 | 50.00 |
| 298 | Joe Astroth RC | 30.00 | 50.00 |
| 299 | Clyde King RC | 30.00 | 50.00 |
| 300 | Hal Rice RC | 30.00 | 50.00 |
| 301 | Tommy Glaviano RC | 30.00 | 50.00 |
| 302 | Jim Busby RC | 30.00 | 50.00 |
| 303 | Marv Rotblatt RC | 30.00 | 50.00 |
| 304 | Al Gettell RC | 30.00 | 50.00 |
| 305 | Willie Mays RC | 1800.00 | 2500.00 |
| 306 | Jimmy Piersall RC | 75.00 | 125.00 |
| 307 | Walt Masterson | 30.00 | 50.00 |
| 308 | Ted Beard RC | 30.00 | 50.00 |
| 309 | Mel Queen RC | 30.00 | 50.00 |
| 310 | Erv Dusak | 30.00 | 50.00 |
| 311 | Mickey Harris | 30.00 | 50.00 |
| 312 | Gene Mauch RC | 35.00 | 60.00 |
| 313 | Ray Mueller RC | 30.00 | 50.00 |
| 314 | Johnny Sain | 50.00 | 80.00 |
| 315 | Zack Taylor MG | 30.00 | 50.00 |
| 316 | Duane Pillette RC | 30.00 | 50.00 |
| 317 | Smoky Burgess RC | 50.00 | 80.00 |
| 318 | Warren Hacker RC | 30.00 | 50.00 |
| 319 | Red Rolfe MG | 35.00 | 60.00 |
| 320 | Hal White RC | 30.00 | 50.00 |
| 321 | Earl Johnson | 30.00 | 50.00 |
| 322 | Luke Sewell RC | 35.00 | 60.00 |
| 323 | Joe Adcock RC | 50.00 | 80.00 |
| 324 | Johnny Pramesa RC | 75.00 | 125.00 |

## 1952 Bowman

| | | | |
|---|---|---|---|
| COMPLETE SET (252) | | 5500.00 | 8500.00 |
| COMMON CARD (1-216) | | 7.50 | 15.00 |
| COMMON CARD (217-252) | | 35.00 | 60.00 |
| WRAPPER (1-CENT) | | 150.00 | 200.00 |
| WRAPPER (5-CENT) | | 75.00 | 100.00 |
| 1 | Yogi Berra | 350.00 | 600.00 |
| 2 | Bobby Thomson | 20.00 | 40.00 |
| 3 | Fred Hutchinson | 12.50 | 25.00 |
| 4 | Robin Roberts | 50.00 | 80.00 |
| 5 | Minnie Minoso RC | 75.00 | 125.00 |
| 6 | Virgil Stallcup | 7.50 | 15.00 |
| 7 | Mike Garcia | 12.50 | 25.00 |
| 8 | Pee Wee Reese | 90.00 | 150.00 |
| 9 | Vern Stephens | 12.50 | 25.00 |
| 10 | Bob Hooper | 7.50 | 15.00 |
| 11 | Ralph Kiner | 35.00 | 60.00 |
| 12 | Max Surkont RC | 7.50 | 15.00 |
| 13 | Cliff Mapes | 7.50 | 15.00 |
| 14 | Cliff Chambers | 7.50 | 15.00 |
| 15 | Sam Mele | 7.50 | 15.00 |
| 16 | Turk Lown RC | 7.50 | 15.00 |
| 17 | Ed Lopat | 20.00 | 40.00 |
| 18 | Don Mueller | 12.50 | 25.00 |
| 19 | Bob Cain | 7.50 | 15.00 |
| 20 | Willie Jones | 7.50 | 15.00 |
| 21 | Nellie Fox | 60.00 | 100.00 |
| 22 | Willard Ramsdell | 7.50 | 15.00 |
| 23 | Bob Lemon | 35.00 | 60.00 |
| 24 | Carl Furillo | 20.00 | 40.00 |
| 25 | Mickey McDermott | 7.50 | 15.00 |
| 26 | Eddie Joost | 7.50 | 15.00 |
| 27 | Joe Garagiola | 20.00 | 40.00 |
| 28 | Roy Hartsfield | 7.50 | 15.00 |
| 29 | Ned Garver | 7.50 | 15.00 |
| 30 | Red Schoendienst | 35.00 | 60.00 |
| 31 | Eddie Yost | 12.50 | 25.00 |
| 32 | Eddie Miksis | 7.50 | 15.00 |
| 33 | Gil McDougald RC | 50.00 | 80.00 |
| 34 | Alvin Dark | 12.50 | 25.00 |
| 35 | Granny Hamner | 7.50 | 15.00 |
| 36 | Cass Michaels | 7.50 | 15.00 |
| 37 | Vic Raschi | 12.50 | 25.00 |
| 38 | Whitey Lockman | 7.50 | 15.00 |
| 39 | Vic Wertz | 12.50 | 25.00 |
| 40 | Bubba Church | 7.50 | 15.00 |
| 41 | Chico Carrasquel | 12.50 | 25.00 |
| 42 | Johnny Wyrostek | 7.50 | 15.00 |
| 43 | Bob Feller | 90.00 | 150.00 |
| 44 | Roy Campanella | 150.00 | 250.00 |
| 45 | Johnny Pesky | 12.50 | 25.00 |
| 46 | Carl Scheib | 7.50 | 15.00 |
| 47 | Pete Castiglione | 7.50 | 15.00 |
| 48 | Vern Bickford | 7.50 | 15.00 |
| 49 | Jim Hearn | 7.50 | 15.00 |
| 50 | Gerry Staley | 7.50 | 15.00 |
| 51 | Gil Coan | 7.50 | 15.00 |
| 52 | Phil Rizzuto | 90.00 | 150.00 |
| 53 | Richie Ashburn | 75.00 | 125.00 |
| 54 | Billy Pierce | 12.50 | 25.00 |
| 55 | Ken Raffensberger | 7.50 | 15.00 |
| 56 | Clyde King | 12.50 | 25.00 |
| 57 | Clyde Vollmer | 7.50 | 15.00 |
| 58 | Hank Majeski | 7.50 | 15.00 |
| 59 | Murry Dickson | 7.50 | 15.00 |
| 60 | Sid Gordon | 7.50 | 15.00 |
| 61 | Tommy Byrne | 7.50 | 15.00 |
| 62 | Joe Presko RC | 7.50 | 15.00 |
| 63 | Irv Noren | 7.50 | 15.00 |
| 64 | Roy Smalley | 7.50 | 15.00 |
| 65 | Hank Bauer | 20.00 | 40.00 |
| 66 | Sal Maglie | 12.50 | 25.00 |
| 67 | Johnny Groth | 7.50 | 15.00 |

|  |  | | |
|---|--------|------|------|
| 68 | Jim Busby | 7.50 | 15.00 |
| 69 | Joe Adcock | 12.50 | 25.00 |
| 70 | Carl Erskine | 20.00 | 40.00 |
| 71 | Vern Law | 7.50 | 15.00 |
| 72 | Earl Torgeson | 7.50 | 15.00 |
| 73 | Jerry Coleman | 12.50 | 25.00 |
| 74 | Wes Westrum | 12.50 | 25.00 |
| 75 | George Kell | 35.00 | 60.00 |
| 76 | Del Ennis | 12.50 | 25.00 |
| 77 | Eddie Robinson | 7.50 | 15.00 |
| 78 | Lloyd Merriman | 7.50 | 15.00 |
| 79 | Lou Brissie | 7.50 | 15.00 |
| 80 | Gil Hodges | 60.00 | 100.00 |
| 81 | Billy Goodman | 12.50 | 25.00 |
| 82 | Gus Zernial | 12.50 | 25.00 |
| 83 | Howie Pollet | 7.50 | 15.00 |
| 84 | Sam Jethroe | 12.50 | 25.00 |
| 85 | Marty Marion CO | 12.50 | 25.00 |
| 86 | Cal Abrams | 7.50 | 15.00 |
| 87 | Mickey Vernon | 12.50 | 25.00 |
| 88 | Bruce Edwards | 7.50 | 15.00 |
| 89 | Billy Hitchcock | 7.50 | 15.00 |
| 90 | Larry Jensen | 12.50 | 25.00 |
| 91 | Don Kolloway | 7.50 | 15.00 |
| 92 | Eddie Waitkus | 12.50 | 25.00 |
| 93 | Paul Richards MG | 12.50 | 25.00 |
| 94 | Luke Sewell MG | 12.50 | 25.00 |
| 95 | Luke Easter | 12.50 | 25.00 |
| 96 | Ralph Branca | 12.50 | 25.00 |
| 97 | Willard Marshall | 7.50 | 15.00 |
| 98 | Jimmie Dykes MG | 12.50 | 25.00 |
| 99 | Clyde McCullough | 7.50 | 15.00 |
| 100 | Sibby Sisti | 7.50 | 15.00 |
| 101 | Mickey Mantle | 1500.00 | 2500.00 |
| 102 | Peanuts Lowrey | 7.50 | 15.00 |
| 103 | Joe Haynes | 7.50 | 15.00 |
| 104 | Hal Jeffcoat | 7.50 | 15.00 |
| 105 | Bobby Brown | 12.50 | 25.00 |
| 106 | Randy Gumpert | 7.50 | 15.00 |
| 107 | Del Rice | 7.50 | 15.00 |
| 108 | George Metkovich | 7.50 | 15.00 |
| 109 | Tom Morgan RC | 7.50 | 15.00 |
| 110 | Max Lanier | 7.50 | 15.00 |
| 111 | Hoot Evers | 7.50 | 15.00 |
| 112 | Smoky Burgess | 12.50 | 25.00 |
| 113 | Al Zarilla | 7.50 | 15.00 |
| 114 | Frank Hiller RC | 7.50 | 15.00 |
| 115 | Larry Doby | 35.00 | 60.00 |
| 116 | Duke Snider | 125.00 | 200.00 |
| 117 | Bill Wight | 7.50 | 15.00 |
| 118 | Ray Murray RC | 7.50 | 15.00 |
| 119 | Bill Howerton | 7.50 | 15.00 |
| 120 | Chet Nichols RC | 7.50 | 15.00 |
| 121 | Al Corwin RC | 7.50 | 15.00 |
| 122 | Billy Johnson | 7.50 | 15.00 |
| 123 | Sid Hudson | 7.50 | 15.00 |
| 124 | Birdie Tebbetts | 7.50 | 15.00 |
| 125 | Howie Fox | 7.50 | 15.00 |
| 126 | Phil Cavarretta | 12.50 | 25.00 |
| 127 | Dick Sisler | 7.50 | 15.00 |
| 128 | Don Newcombe | 35.00 | 60.00 |
| 129 | Gus Niarhos | 7.50 | 15.00 |
| 130 | Allie Clark | 7.50 | 15.00 |
| 131 | Bob Swift | 7.50 | 15.00 |
| 132 | Dave Cole RC | 7.50 | 15.00 |
| 133 | Dick Kryhoski | 7.50 | 15.00 |
| 134 | Al Brazle | 7.50 | 15.00 |
| 135 | Mickey Harris | 7.50 | 15.00 |
| 136 | Gene Hermanski | 7.50 | 15.00 |
| 137 | Stan Rojek | 7.50 | 15.00 |
| 138 | Ted Wilks | 7.50 | 15.00 |
| 139 | Jerry Priddy | 7.50 | 15.00 |
| 140 | Ray Scarborough | 7.50 | 15.00 |
| 141 | Hank Edwards | 7.50 | 15.00 |
| 142 | Early Wynn | 35.00 | 60.00 |
| 143 | Sandy Consuegra | 7.50 | 15.00 |
| 144 | Joe Hatton | 7.50 | 15.00 |
| 145 | Johnny Mize | 35.00 | 60.00 |
| 146 | Leo Durocher MG | 35.00 | 60.00 |
| 147 | Marlin Stuart RC | 7.50 | 15.00 |
| 148 | Ken Heintzelman | 7.50 | 15.00 |
| 149 | Howie Judson | 7.50 | 15.00 |
| 150 | Herman Wehmeier | 7.50 | 15.00 |
| 151 | Al Rosen | 12.50 | 25.00 |
| 152 | Billy Cox | 12.50 | 25.00 |
| 153 | Fred Hatfield RC | 7.50 | 15.00 |
| 154 | Ferris Fain | 12.50 | 25.00 |
| 155 | Billy Meyer MG | 7.50 | 15.00 |
| 156 | Warren Spahn | 75.00 | 125.00 |
| 157 | Jim Delsing | 7.50 | 15.00 |
| 158 | Bucky Harris MG | 20.00 | 40.00 |
| 159 | Dutch Leonard | 7.50 | 15.00 |
| 160 | Eddie Stanky | 12.50 | 25.00 |
| 161 | Jackie Jensen | 20.00 | 40.00 |
| 162 | Monte Irvin | 35.00 | 60.00 |
| 163 | Johnny Lipon | 7.50 | 15.00 |
| 164 | Connie Ryan | 7.50 | 15.00 |
| 165 | Saul Rogovin RC | 7.50 | 15.00 |
| 166 | Bobby Adams | 7.50 | 15.00 |
| 167 | Bobby Avila | 12.50 | 25.00 |
| 168 | Preacher Roe | 12.50 | 25.00 |
| 169 | Walt Dropo | 12.50 | 25.00 |
| 170 | Joe Astroth | 7.50 | 15.00 |
| 171 | Mel Queen | 7.50 | 15.00 |
| 172 | Ebba St.Claire RC | 7.50 | 15.00 |
| 173 | Gene Bearden | 7.50 | 15.00 |
| 174 | Mickey Grasso | 7.50 | 15.00 |
| 175 | Randy Jackson RC | 7.50 | 15.00 |
| 176 | Harry Brecheen | 12.50 | 25.00 |
| 177 | Gene Woodling | 12.50 | 25.00 |
| 178 | Dave Williams RC | 12.50 | 25.00 |
| 179 | Pete Suder | 7.50 | 15.00 |
| 180 | Ed Fitzgerald | 7.50 | 15.00 |
| 181 | Joe Collins RC | 12.50 | 25.00 |
| 182 | Dave Koslo | 7.50 | 15.00 |
| 183 | Pat Mullin | 7.50 | 15.00 |
| 184 | Curt Simmons | 12.50 | 25.00 |
| 185 | Eddie Stewart | 7.50 | 15.00 |
| 186 | Frank Smith RC | 7.50 | 15.00 |
| 187 | Jim Hegan | 12.50 | 25.00 |
| 188 | Chuck Dressen MG | 12.50 | 25.00 |
| 189 | Jimmy Piersall | 12.50 | 25.00 |
| 190 | Dick Fowler | 7.50 | 15.00 |
| 191 | Bob Friend RC | 20.00 | 40.00 |
| 192 | John Cusick RC | 7.50 | 15.00 |
| 193 | Bobby Young RC | 7.50 | 15.00 |
| 194 | Bob Porterfield | 7.50 | 15.00 |
| 195 | Frank Baumholtz | 7.50 | 15.00 |
| 196 | Stan Musial | 300.00 | 500.00 |
| 197 | Charlie Silvera RC | 7.50 | 15.00 |
| 198 | Chuck Diering | 7.50 | 15.00 |
| 199 | Ted Gray | 7.50 | 15.00 |
| 200 | Ken Silvestri | 7.50 | 15.00 |
| 201 | Ray Coleman | 7.50 | 15.00 |
| 202 | Harry Perkowski RC | 7.50 | 15.00 |
| 203 | Steve Gromek | 7.50 | 15.00 |
| 204 | Andy Pafko | 12.50 | 25.00 |
| 205 | Walt Masterson | 7.50 | 15.00 |
| 206 | Elmer Valo | 7.50 | 15.00 |
| 207 | George Strickland RC | 7.50 | 15.00 |
| 208 | Walker Cooper | 7.50 | 15.00 |
| 209 | Dick Littlefield RC | 7.50 | 15.00 |
| 210 | Archie Wilson RC | 7.50 | 15.00 |
| 211 | Paul Minner RC | 7.50 | 15.00 |
| 212 | Solly Hemus RC | 7.50 | 15.00 |
| 213 | Monte Kennedy | 7.50 | 15.00 |
| 214 | Ray Boone | 7.50 | 15.00 |
| 215 | Sheldon Jones | 7.50 | 15.00 |
| 216 | Matt Batts | 7.50 | 15.00 |
| 217 | Casey Stengel MG | 90.00 | 150.00 |
| 218 | Willie Mays | 900.00 | 1500.00 |
| 219 | Neil Berry | 35.00 | 60.00 |
| 220 | Russ Meyer | 35.00 | 60.00 |
| 221 | Lou Kretlow RC | 35.00 | 60.00 |
| 222 | Dixie Howell | 35.00 | 60.00 |
| 223 | Harry Simpson RC | 35.00 | 60.00 |
| 224 | Johnny Schmitz | 35.00 | 60.00 |
| 225 | Del Wilber RC | 35.00 | 60.00 |
| 226 | Alex Kellner | 35.00 | 60.00 |
| 227 | Clyde Sukeforth CO RC | 35.00 | 60.00 |
| 228 | Bob Chipman | 35.00 | 60.00 |
| 229 | Hank Arft | 35.00 | 60.00 |
| 230 | Frank Shea | 35.00 | 60.00 |
| 231 | Dee Fondy RC | 35.00 | 60.00 |
| 232 | Enos Slaughter | 75.00 | 100.00 |
| 233 | Bob Kuzava | 35.00 | 60.00 |
| 234 | Fred Fitzsimmons CO | 35.00 | 60.00 |
| 235 | Steve Souchock RC | 35.00 | 60.00 |
| 236 | Tommy Brown | 35.00 | 60.00 |
| 237 | Sherm Lollar | 35.00 | 60.00 |
| 238 | Roy McMillan RC | 35.00 | 60.00 |
| 239 | Dale Mitchell | 35.00 | 60.00 |
| 240 | Billy Loes RC | 35.00 | 60.00 |
| 241 | Mel Parnell | 35.00 | 60.00 |
| 242 | Everett Kell RC | 35.00 | 60.00 |
| 243 | George Munger | 35.00 | 60.00 |
| 244 | Lew Burdette RC | 50.00 | 80.00 |
| 245 | George Schmees RC | 35.00 | 60.00 |
| 246 | Jerry Snyder RC | 35.00 | 60.00 |
| 247 | Johnny Pramesa | 35.00 | 60.00 |
| 248 | Bill Werle Full Name | 35.00 | 60.00 |
| 248A | Bill Werle No W | 35.00 | 60.00 |
| 249 | Hank Thompson | 35.00 | 60.00 |
| 250 | Ike Delock RC | 35.00 | 60.00 |
| 251 | Jack Lohrke | 35.00 | 60.00 |
| 252 | Frank Crosetti CO | 75.00 | 125.00 |

## 1953 Bowman Black and White

|  |  | | |
|---|--------|------|------|
| | COMPLETE SET (64) | 2000.00 | 3000.00 |
| | WRAPPER (1-CENT) | 300.00 | 350.00 |
| 1 | Gus Bell | 75.00 | 125.00 |
| 2 | Willard Nixon | 25.00 | 40.00 |
| 3 | Bill Rigney | 25.00 | 40.00 |
| 4 | Pat Mullin | 25.00 | 40.00 |
| 5 | Dee Fondy | 25.00 | 40.00 |
| 6 | Ray Murray | 25.00 | 40.00 |
| 7 | Andy Seminick | 25.00 | 40.00 |
| 8 | Pete Suder | 25.00 | 40.00 |
| 9 | Walt Masterson | 25.00 | 40.00 |
| 10 | Dick Sisler | 35.00 | 60.00 |
| 11 | Dick Gernert | 25.00 | 40.00 |
| 12 | Randy Jackson | 25.00 | 40.00 |
| 13 | Joe Tipton | 25.00 | 40.00 |
| 14 | Bill Nicholson | 35.00 | 60.00 |
| 15 | Johnny Mize | 75.00 | 125.00 |
| 16 | Stu Miller RC | 35.00 | 60.00 |
| 17 | Virgil Trucks | 25.00 | 40.00 |
| 18 | Billy Hoeft | 25.00 | 40.00 |
| 19 | Paul LaPalme | 25.00 | 40.00 |
| 20 | Eddie Robinson | 25.00 | 40.00 |
| 21 | Clarence Podbielan | 25.00 | 40.00 |
| 22 | Matt Batts | 25.00 | 40.00 |
| 23 | Wilmer Mizell | 35.00 | 60.00 |
| 24 | Del Wilber | 25.00 | 40.00 |
| 25 | Johnny Sain | 50.00 | 80.00 |
| 26 | Preacher Roe | 50.00 | 80.00 |
| 27 | Bob Lemon | 100.00 | 175.00 |
| 28 | Hoyt Wilhelm | 75.00 | 125.00 |
| 29 | Sid Hudson | 25.00 | 40.00 |
| 30 | Walker Cooper | 25.00 | 40.00 |
| 31 | Gene Woodling | 50.00 | 80.00 |
| 32 | Rocky Bridges | 25.00 | 40.00 |
| 33 | Bob Kuzava | 25.00 | 40.00 |
| 34 | Ebba St.Claire | 25.00 | 40.00 |
| 35 | Johnny Wyrostek | 25.00 | 40.00 |
| 36 | Jimmy Piersall | 50.00 | 80.00 |
| 37 | Hal Jeffcoat | 25.00 | 40.00 |
| 38 | Dave Cole | 25.00 | 40.00 |
| 39 | Casey Stengel MG | 200.00 | 350.00 |
| 40 | Larry Jensen | 35.00 | 60.00 |
| 41 | Bob Ramazzotti | 25.00 | 40.00 |
| 42 | Howie Judson | 25.00 | 40.00 |
| 43 | Hal Bevan ERR RC | 25.00 | 40.00 |
| 43A | Hal Bevan COR | 25.00 | 40.00 |
| 44 | Jim Delsing | 25.00 | 40.00 |
| 45 | Irv Noren | 35.00 | 60.00 |
| 46 | Bucky Harris MG | 50.00 | 80.00 |
| 47 | Jack Lohrke | 25.00 | 40.00 |
| 48 | Steve Ridzik RC | 25.00 | 40.00 |
| 49 | Floyd Baker | 25.00 | 40.00 |
| 50 | Dutch Leonard | 25.00 | 40.00 |
| 51 | Lew Burdette | 50.00 | 80.00 |
| 52 | Ralph Branca | 35.00 | 60.00 |
| 53 | Morrie Martin | 25.00 | 40.00 |
| 54 | Bill Miller | 25.00 | 40.00 |
| 55 | Don Johnson | 25.00 | 40.00 |
| 56 | Roy Smalley | 25.00 | 40.00 |
| 57 | Andy Pafko | 35.00 | 60.00 |
| 58 | Jim Konstanty | 35.00 | 60.00 |

| | | |
|---|---|---|
| ❏ 59 Duane Pillette | 25.00 | 40.00 |
| ❏ 60 Billy Cox | 50.00 | 80.00 |
| ❏ 61 Tom Gorman RC | 25.00 | 40.00 |
| ❏ 62 Keith Thomas RC | 25.00 | 40.00 |
| ❏ 63 Steve Gromek | 25.00 | 40.00 |
| ❏ 64 Andy Hansen | 50.00 | 80.00 |

## 1953 Bowman Color

| | | |
|---|---|---|
| ❏ COMPLETE SET (160) | 9000.00 | 15000.00 |
| ❏ COMMON CARD (1-112) | 20.00 | 40.00 |
| ❏ COMMON CARD (113-128) | 50.00 | 80.00 |
| ❏ COMMON CARD (129-160) | 45.00 | 75.00 |
| ❏ WRAPPER (1-CENT) | 300.00 | 400.00 |
| ❏ WRAPPER (5-CENT) | 250.00 | 300.00 |
| ❏ 1 Davey Williams | 100.00 | 175.00 |
| ❏ 2 Vic Wertz | 30.00 | 50.00 |
| ❏ 3 Sam Jethroe | 30.00 | 50.00 |
| ❏ 4 Art Houtteman | 20.00 | 40.00 |
| ❏ 5 Sid Gordon | 20.00 | 40.00 |
| ❏ 6 Joe Ginsberg | 20.00 | 40.00 |
| ❏ 7 Harry Chiti RC | 20.00 | 40.00 |
| ❏ 8 Al Rosen | 30.00 | 50.00 |
| ❏ 9 Phil Rizzuto | 150.00 | 225.00 |
| ❏ 10 Richie Ashburn | 90.00 | 150.00 |
| ❏ 11 Bobby Shantz | 30.00 | 50.00 |
| ❏ 12 Carl Erskine | 35.00 | 60.00 |
| ❏ 13 Gus Zernial | 30.00 | 50.00 |
| ❏ 14 Billy Loes | 30.00 | 50.00 |
| ❏ 15 Jim Busby | 20.00 | 40.00 |
| ❏ 16 Bob Friend | 30.00 | 50.00 |
| ❏ 17 Gerry Staley | 20.00 | 40.00 |
| ❏ 18 Nellie Fox | 90.00 | 150.00 |
| ❏ 19 Alvin Dark | 30.00 | 50.00 |
| ❏ 20 Don Lenhardt | 20.00 | 40.00 |
| ❏ 21 Joe Garagiola | 35.00 | 60.00 |
| ❏ 22 Bob Porterfield | 20.00 | 40.00 |
| ❏ 23 Herman Wehmeier | 20.00 | 40.00 |
| ❏ 24 Jackie Jensen | 35.00 | 60.00 |
| ❏ 25 Hoot Evers | 20.00 | 40.00 |
| ❏ 26 Roy McMillan | 30.00 | 50.00 |
| ❏ 27 Vic Raschi | 35.00 | 60.00 |
| ❏ 28 Smoky Burgess | 30.00 | 50.00 |
| ❏ 29 Bobby Avila | 30.00 | 50.00 |
| ❏ 30 Phil Cavarretta | 30.00 | 50.00 |
| ❏ 31 Jimmy Dykes MG | 30.00 | 50.00 |
| ❏ 32 Stan Musial | 350.00 | 600.00 |
| ❏ 33 Pee Wee Reese | 500.00 | 1000.00 |
| ❏ 34 Gil Coan | 20.00 | 40.00 |
| ❏ 35 Maurice McDermott | 20.00 | 40.00 |
| ❏ 36 Minnie Minoso | 50.00 | 80.00 |
| ❏ 37 Jim Wilson | 20.00 | 40.00 |
| ❏ 38 Harry Byrd RC | 20.00 | 40.00 |
| ❏ 39 Paul Richards MG | 30.00 | 50.00 |
| ❏ 40 Larry Doby | 60.00 | 100.00 |
| ❏ 41 Sammy White | 20.00 | 40.00 |
| ❏ 42 Tommy Brown | 20.00 | 40.00 |
| ❏ 43 Mike Garcia | 30.00 | 50.00 |
| ❏ 44 Bauer/Berra/Mantle | 500.00 | 800.00 |
| ❏ 45 Walt Dropo | 30.00 | 50.00 |
| ❏ 46 Roy Campanella | 200.00 | 350.00 |
| ❏ 47 Ned Garver | 20.00 | 40.00 |
| ❏ 48 Hank Sauer | 30.00 | 50.00 |
| ❏ 49 Eddie Stanky MG | 30.00 | 50.00 |
| ❏ 50 Lou Kretlow | 20.00 | 40.00 |
| ❏ 51 Monte Irvin | 50.00 | 80.00 |
| ❏ 52 Marty Marion MG | 30.00 | 50.00 |
| ❏ 53 Del Rice | 20.00 | 40.00 |
| ❏ 54 Chico Carrasquel | 20.00 | 40.00 |
| ❏ 55 Leo Durocher MG | 50.00 | 80.00 |
| ❏ 56 Bob Cain | 20.00 | 40.00 |
| ❏ 57 Lou Boudreau MG | 50.00 | 80.00 |
| ❏ 58 Willard Marshall | 20.00 | 40.00 |
| ❏ 59 Mickey Mantle | 1200.00 | 2000.00 |
| ❏ 60 Granny Hamner | 20.00 | 40.00 |

| | | |
|---|---|---|
| ❏ 61 George Kell | 50.00 | 80.00 |
| ❏ 62 Ted Kluszewski | 60.00 | 100.00 |
| ❏ 63 Gil McDougald | 50.00 | 80.00 |
| ❏ 64 Curt Simmons | 30.00 | 50.00 |
| ❏ 65 Robin Roberts | 75.00 | 125.00 |
| ❏ 66 Mel Parnell | 30.00 | 50.00 |
| ❏ 67 Mel Clark RC | 20.00 | 40.00 |
| ❏ 68 Allie Reynolds | 35.00 | 60.00 |
| ❏ 69 Charlie Grimm MG | 30.00 | 50.00 |
| ❏ 70 Clint Courtney RC | 20.00 | 40.00 |
| ❏ 71 Paul Minner | 20.00 | 40.00 |
| ❏ 72 Ted Gray | 20.00 | 40.00 |
| ❏ 73 Billy Pierce | 30.00 | 50.00 |
| ❏ 74 Don Mueller | 30.00 | 50.00 |
| ❏ 75 Saul Rogovin | 20.00 | 40.00 |
| ❏ 76 Jim Hearn | 20.00 | 40.00 |
| ❏ 77 Mickey Grasso | 20.00 | 40.00 |
| ❏ 78 Carl Furillo | 35.00 | 60.00 |
| ❏ 79 Ray Boone | 30.00 | 50.00 |
| ❏ 80 Ralph Kiner | 60.00 | 100.00 |
| ❏ 81 Enos Slaughter | 60.00 | 100.00 |
| ❏ 82 Joe Astroth | 20.00 | 40.00 |
| ❏ 83 Jack Daniels RC | 20.00 | 40.00 |
| ❏ 84 Hank Bauer | 35.00 | 60.00 |
| ❏ 85 Solly Hemus | 20.00 | 40.00 |
| ❏ 86 Harry Simpson | 20.00 | 40.00 |
| ❏ 87 Harry Perkowski | 20.00 | 40.00 |
| ❏ 88 Joe Dobson | 20.00 | 40.00 |
| ❏ 89 Sandy Consuegra | 20.00 | 40.00 |
| ❏ 90 Joe Nuxhall | 30.00 | 50.00 |
| ❏ 91 Steve Souchock | 20.00 | 40.00 |
| ❏ 92 Gil Hodges | 175.00 | 300.00 |
| ❏ 93 P.Rizzuto/B.Martin | 175.00 | 300.00 |
| ❏ 94 Bob Addis | 20.00 | 40.00 |
| ❏ 95 Wally Moses CO | 30.00 | 50.00 |
| ❏ 96 Sal Maglie | 30.00 | 50.00 |
| ❏ 97 Eddie Mathews | 200.00 | 350.00 |
| ❏ 98 Hector Rodriguez RC | 20.00 | 40.00 |
| ❏ 99 Warren Spahn | 200.00 | 350.00 |
| ❏ 100 Bill Wight | 20.00 | 40.00 |
| ❏ 101 Red Schoendienst | 50.00 | 80.00 |
| ❏ 102 Jim Hegan | 30.00 | 50.00 |
| ❏ 103 Del Ennis | 30.00 | 50.00 |
| ❏ 104 Luke Easter | 30.00 | 50.00 |
| ❏ 105 Eddie Joost | 20.00 | 40.00 |
| ❏ 106 Ken Raffensberger | 20.00 | 40.00 |
| ❏ 107 Alex Kellner | 20.00 | 40.00 |
| ❏ 108 Bobby Adams | 20.00 | 40.00 |
| ❏ 109 Ken Wood | 20.00 | 40.00 |
| ❏ 110 Bob Rush | 20.00 | 40.00 |
| ❏ 111 Jim Dyck RC | 20.00 | 40.00 |
| ❏ 112 Toby Atwell | 20.00 | 40.00 |
| ❏ 113 Karl Drews | 50.00 | 80.00 |
| ❏ 114 Bob Feller | 350.00 | 500.00 |
| ❏ 115 Cloyd Boyer | 50.00 | 80.00 |
| ❏ 116 Eddie Yost | 50.00 | 80.00 |
| ❏ 117 Duke Snider | 350.00 | 600.00 |
| ❏ 118 Billy Martin | 250.00 | 400.00 |
| ❏ 119 Dale Mitchell | 60.00 | 100.00 |
| ❏ 120 Marlin Stuart | 50.00 | 80.00 |
| ❏ 121 Yogi Berra | 500.00 | 800.00 |
| ❏ 122 Bill Serena | 50.00 | 80.00 |
| ❏ 123 Johnny Lipon | 50.00 | 80.00 |
| ❏ 124 Chuck Dressen MG | 60.00 | 100.00 |
| ❏ 125 Fred Hatfield | 50.00 | 80.00 |
| ❏ 126 Al Corwin | 50.00 | 80.00 |
| ❏ 127 Dick Kryhoski | 50.00 | 80.00 |
| ❏ 128 Whitey Lockman | 60.00 | 100.00 |
| ❏ 129 Russ Meyer | 45.00 | 75.00 |
| ❏ 130 Cass Michaels | 45.00 | 75.00 |
| ❏ 131 Connie Ryan | 45.00 | 75.00 |
| ❏ 132 Fred Hutchinson | 60.00 | 90.00 |
| ❏ 133 Willie Jones | 45.00 | 75.00 |
| ❏ 134 Johnny Pesky | 60.00 | 90.00 |
| ❏ 135 Bobby Morgan | 45.00 | 75.00 |
| ❏ 136 Jim Brideweser RC | 45.00 | 75.00 |
| ❏ 137 Sam Dente | 45.00 | 75.00 |
| ❏ 138 Bubba Church | 45.00 | 75.00 |
| ❏ 139 Pete Runnels | 60.00 | 90.00 |
| ❏ 140 Al Brazle | 45.00 | 75.00 |
| ❏ 141 Frank Shea | 45.00 | 75.00 |
| ❏ 142 Larry Miggins RC | 45.00 | 75.00 |
| ❏ 143 Al Lopez MG | 70.00 | 110.00 |
| ❏ 144 Warren Hacker | 45.00 | 75.00 |
| ❏ 145 George Shuba | 60.00 | 90.00 |
| ❏ 146 Early Wynn | 125.00 | 200.00 |
| ❏ 147 Clem Koshorek | 45.00 | 75.00 |
| ❏ 148 Billy Goodman | 60.00 | 90.00 |

| | | |
|---|---|---|
| ❏ 149 Al Corwin | 45.00 | 75.00 |
| ❏ 150 Carl Scheib | 45.00 | 75.00 |
| ❏ 151 Joe Adcock | 70.00 | 110.00 |
| ❏ 152 Clyde Vollmer | 45.00 | 75.00 |
| ❏ 153 Whitey Ford | 500.00 | 800.00 |
| ❏ 154 Turk Lown | 45.00 | 75.00 |
| ❏ 155 Allie Clark | 45.00 | 75.00 |
| ❏ 156 Max Surkont | 45.00 | 75.00 |
| ❏ 157 Sherm Lollar | 60.00 | 90.00 |
| ❏ 158 Howard Fox | 45.00 | 75.00 |
| ❏ 159 Mickey Vernon UER | 60.00 | 90.00 |
| ❏ 160 Cal Abrams | 300.00 | 500.00 |

## 1954 Bowman

| | | |
|---|---|---|
| ❏ COMPLETE SET (224) | 2500.00 | 4000.00 |
| ❏ WRAP.(1-CENT, DATED) | 100.00 | 150.00 |
| ❏ WRAP.(1-CENT, UNDAT) | 150.00 | 200.00 |
| ❏ WRAP.(5-CENT, DATED) | 100.00 | 150.00 |
| ❏ WRAP.(5-CENT, UNDAT) | 50.00 | 60.00 |
| ❏ 1 Phil Rizzuto | 100.00 | 175.00 |
| ❏ 2 Jackie Jensen | 15.00 | 30.00 |
| ❏ 3 Marion Fricano | 6.00 | 12.00 |
| ❏ 4 Bob Hooper | 6.00 | 12.00 |
| ❏ 5 Billy Hunter | 6.00 | 12.00 |
| ❏ 6 Nellie Fox | 50.00 | 80.00 |
| ❏ 7 Walt Dropo | 10.00 | 20.00 |
| ❏ 8 Jim Busby | 6.00 | 12.00 |
| ❏ 9 Dave Williams | 6.00 | 12.00 |
| ❏ 10 Carl Erskine | 10.00 | 20.00 |
| ❏ 11 Sid Gordon | 6.00 | 12.00 |
| ❏ 12A Roy McMillan 551/1290 At Bat | 10.00 | 20.00 |
| ❏ 12B Roy McMillan 557/1265 At Bat | 6.00 | 12.00 |
| ❏ 13 Paul Minner | 6.00 | 12.00 |
| ❏ 14 Gerry Staley | 6.00 | 12.00 |
| ❏ 15 Richie Ashburn | 50.00 | 80.00 |
| ❏ 16 Jim Wilson | 6.00 | 12.00 |
| ❏ 17 Tom Gorman | 6.00 | 12.00 |
| ❏ 18 Hoot Evers | 6.00 | 12.00 |
| ❏ 19 Bobby Shantz | 10.00 | 20.00 |
| ❏ 20 Art Houtteman | 6.00 | 12.00 |
| ❏ 21 Vic Wertz | 6.00 | 12.00 |
| ❏ 22A Sam Mele 213/1661 Putouts | 6.00 | 12.00 |
| ❏ 22B Sam Mele 217/1665 Putouts | 6.00 | 12.00 |
| ❏ 23 Harvey Kuenn RC | 15.00 | 30.00 |
| ❏ 24 Bob Porterfield | 6.00 | 12.00 |
| ❏ 25A Wes Westrum 1.000/.987 Fielding Avg. | 10.00 | 20.00 |
| ❏ 25B Wes Westrum .982/.986 Fielding Avg. | 10.00 | 20.00 |
| ❏ 26A Billy Cox 1.000/.960 Fielding Avg. | 10.00 | 20.00 |
| ❏ 26B Billy Cox .972/.960 Fielding Avg. | 10.00 | 20.00 |
| ❏ 27 Dick Cole RC | 6.00 | 12.00 |
| ❏ 28A Jim Greengrass Birthplace Addison, NJ | 6.00 | 12.00 |
| ❏ 28B Jim Greengrass Birthplace Addison, NY | 6.00 | 12.00 |
| ❏ 29 Johnny Klippstein | 6.00 | 12.00 |
| ❏ 30 Del Rice | 6.00 | 12.00 |
| ❏ 31 Smoky Burgess | 10.00 | 20.00 |
| ❏ 32 Del Crandall | 10.00 | 20.00 |
| ❏ 33A Vic Raschi No Trade | 10.00 | 20.00 |
| ❏ 33B Vic Raschi Traded to St.Louis | 15.00 | 30.00 |
| ❏ 34 Sammy White | 6.00 | 12.00 |
| ❏ 35A Eddie Joost Quiz Answer is 8 | 6.00 | 12.00 |
| ❏ 35B Eddie Joost Quiz Answer is 33 | 6.00 | 12.00 |
| ❏ 36 George Strickland | 6.00 | 12.00 |
| ❏ 37 Dick Kokos | 6.00 | 12.00 |
| ❏ 38A Minnie Minoso .895/.961 Fielding Avg. | 15.00 | 30.00 |
| ❏ 38B Minnie Minoso .963/.963 Fielding Avg. | 15.00 | 30.00 |
| ❏ 39 Ned Garver | 6.00 | 12.00 |
| ❏ 40 Gil Coan | 6.00 | 12.00 |
| ❏ 41A Alvin Dark .986/960 Fielding Avg. | 10.00 | 20.00 |
| ❏ 41B Alvin Dark .968/.960 Fielding Avg. | 10.00 | 20.00 |
| ❏ 42 Billy Loes | 10.00 | 20.00 |
| ❏ 43A Bob Friend 20 Shutouts in Quiz | 10.00 | 20.00 |
| ❏ 43B Bob Friend 16 Shutouts in Quiz | 10.00 | 20.00 |

| | | |
|---|---|---|
| 44 Harry Perkowski | 6.00 | 12.00 |
| 45 Ralph Kiner | 25.00 | 50.00 |
| 46 Rip Repulski | 6.00 | 12.00 |
| 47A Granny Hamner .970/.953 Fielding Avg. | 6.00 | 12.00 |
| 47B Granny Hamner .953/.951 Fielding Avg. | 6.00 | 12.00 |
| 48 Jack Dittmer | 6.00 | 12.00 |
| 49 Harry Byrd | 6.00 | 12.00 |
| 50 George Kell | 25.00 | 50.00 |
| 51 Alex Kellner | 6.00 | 12.00 |
| 52 Joe Ginsberg | 6.00 | 12.00 |
| 53A Don Lenhardt .969/.984 Fielding Avg. | 6.00 | 12.00 |
| 53B Don Lenhardt .966/.983 Fielding Avg. | 6.00 | 12.00 |
| 54 Chico Carrasquel | 6.00 | 12.00 |
| 55 Jim Delsing | 6.00 | 12.00 |
| 56 Maurice McDermott | 6.00 | 12.00 |
| 57 Hoyt Wilhelm | 25.00 | 50.00 |
| 58 Pee Wee Reese | 50.00 | 80.00 |
| 59 Bob Schultz | 6.00 | 12.00 |
| 60 Fred Baczewski RC | 6.00 | 12.00 |
| 61A Eddie Miksis .954/.962 Fielding Avg. | 6.00 | 12.00 |
| 61B Eddie Miksis .954/.961 Fielding Avg. | 6.00 | 12.00 |
| 62 Enos Slaughter | 25.00 | 50.00 |
| 63 Earl Torgeson | 6.00 | 12.00 |
| 64 Eddie Mathews | 50.00 | 80.00 |
| 65 Mickey Mantle | 900.00 | 1500.00 |
| 66A Ted Williams | 1800.00 | 3000.00 |
| 66B Jimmy Piersall | 50.00 | 80.00 |
| 67A Carl Scheib .306 Pct. Two Lines under Bio | 6.00 | 12.00 |
| 67B Carl Scheib .306 Pct. One Line under Bio | 6.00 | 12.00 |
| 67C Carl Scheib .300 Pct. | 6.00 | 12.00 |
| 68 Bobby Avila | 10.00 | 20.00 |
| 69 Clint Courtney | 6.00 | 12.00 |
| 70 Willard Marshall | 6.00 | 12.00 |
| 71 Ted Gray | 6.00 | 12.00 |
| 72 Eddie Yost | 10.00 | 20.00 |
| 73 Don Mueller | 6.00 | 20.00 |
| 74 Jim Gilliam | 15.00 | 30.00 |
| 75 Max Surkont | 6.00 | 12.00 |
| 76 Joe Nuxhall | 10.00 | 20.00 |
| 77 Bob Rush | 6.00 | 12.00 |
| 78 Sal Yvars | 6.00 | 12.00 |
| 79 Curt Simmons | 10.00 | 20.00 |
| 80A Johnny Logan 106 Runs | 6.00 | 12.00 |
| 80B Johnny Logan 100 Runs | 6.00 | 12.00 |
| 81A Jerry Coleman 1.000/.975 Fielding Avg. | 6.00 | 12.00 |
| 81B Jerry Coleman .952/.975 Fielding Avg. | 10.00 | 20.00 |
| 82A Bill Goodman .965/.986 Fielding Avg. | 10.00 | 20.00 |
| 82B Bill Goodman .972/.985 Fielding Avg. | 10.00 | 20.00 |
| 83 Ray Murray | 6.00 | 12.00 |
| 84 Larry Doby | 25.00 | 50.00 |
| 85A Jim Dyck .926/.956 Fielding Avg. | 6.00 | 12.00 |
| 85B Jim Dyck .947/.960 Fielding Avg. | 6.00 | 12.00 |
| 86 Harry Dorish | 6.00 | 12.00 |
| 87 Don Lund | 6.00 | 12.00 |
| 88 Tom Umphlett RC | 6.00 | 12.00 |
| 89 Willie Mays | 300.00 | 500.00 |
| 90 Roy Campanella | 90.00 | 150.00 |
| 91 Cal Abrams | 6.00 | 12.00 |
| 92 Ken Raffensberger | 6.00 | 12.00 |
| 93A Bill Serena .983/.966 Fielding Avg. | 6.00 | 12.00 |
| 93B Bill Serena .977/.966 Fielding Avg. | 6.00 | 12.00 |
| 94A Solly Hemus 476/1343 Assists | 6.00 | 12.00 |
| 94B Solly Hemus 477/1343 Assists | 6.00 | 12.00 |
| 95 Robin Roberts | 25.00 | 50.00 |
| 96 Joe Adcock | 10.00 | 20.00 |
| 97 Gil McDougald | 10.00 | 20.00 |
| 98 Ellis Kinder | 6.00 | 12.00 |
| 99A Peter Suder .985/.974 Fielding Avg. | 6.00 | 12.00 |
| 99B Peter Suder .978/.974 Fielding Avg. | 6.00 | 12.00 |
| 100 Mike Garcia | 10.00 | 20.00 |
| 101 Don Larsen RC | 50.00 | 80.00 |
| 102 Billy Pierce | 10.00 | 20.00 |
| 103A Stephen Souchock 144/1192 Putouts | 6.00 | 12.00 |
| 103B Stephen Souchock 147/1195 Putouts | 6.00 | 12.00 |
| 104 Frank Shea | 6.00 | 12.00 |
| 105A Sal Maglie Quiz Answer is 8 | 10.00 | 20.00 |
| 105B Sal Maglie Quiz Answer is 1904 | 10.00 | 20.00 |
| 106 Clem Labine | 10.00 | 20.00 |
| 107 Paul LaPalme | 6.00 | 12.00 |
| 108 Bobby Adams | 6.00 | 12.00 |
| 109 Roy Smalley | 6.00 | 12.00 |
| 110 Red Schoendienst | 25.00 | 50.00 |
| 111 Murry Dickson | 6.00 | 12.00 |
| 112 Andy Pafko | 10.00 | 20.00 |
| 113 Allie Reynolds | 10.00 | 20.00 |
| 114 Willard Nixon | 6.00 | 12.00 |
| 115 Don Bollweg | 6.00 | 12.00 |
| 116 Luke Easter | 10.00 | 20.00 |
| 117 Dick Kryhoski | 6.00 | 12.00 |
| 118 Bob Boyd | 6.00 | 12.00 |
| 119 Fred Hatfield | 6.00 | 12.00 |
| 120 Mel Hoderlein RC | 6.00 | 12.00 |
| 121 Ray Katt RC | 6.00 | 12.00 |
| 122 Carl Furillo | 15.00 | 30.00 |
| 123 Toby Atwell | 6.00 | 12.00 |
| 124A Gus Bell 15/27 Errors | 10.00 | 20.00 |
| 124B Gus Bell 11/26 Errors | 10.00 | 20.00 |
| 125 Warren Hacker | 6.00 | 12.00 |
| 126 Cliff Chambers | 6.00 | 12.00 |
| 127 Del Ennis | 10.00 | 20.00 |
| 128 Ebba St.Claire | 6.00 | 12.00 |
| 129 Hank Bauer | 15.00 | 30.00 |
| 130 Milt Bolling | 6.00 | 12.00 |
| 131 Joe Astroth | 6.00 | 12.00 |
| 132 Bob Feller | 50.00 | 80.00 |
| 133 Duane Pillette | 6.00 | 12.00 |
| 134 Luis Aloma | 6.00 | 12.00 |
| 135 Johnny Pesky | 10.00 | 20.00 |
| 136 Clyde Vollmer | 6.00 | 12.00 |
| 137 Al Corwin | 6.00 | 12.00 |
| 138A Gil Hodges .993/.991 Fielding Avg. | 50.00 | 80.00 |
| 138B Gil Hodges .992/.991 Fielding Avg. | 50.00 | 80.00 |
| 139A Preston Ward .961/.992 Fielding Avg. | 6.00 | 12.00 |
| 139B Preston Ward .990/.992 Fielding Avg. | 6.00 | 12.00 |
| 140A Saul Rogovin 7-12 W-L 2 Strikeouts | 6.00 | 12.00 |
| 140B Saul Rogovin 7-12 W-L 62 Strikeouts | 6.00 | 12.00 |
| 140C Saul Rogovin 8-12 W-L | 6.00 | 12.00 |
| 141 Joe Garagiola | 15.00 | 30.00 |
| 142 Al Brazle | 6.00 | 12.00 |
| 143 Willie Jones | 6.00 | 12.00 |
| 144 Ernie Johnson RC | 15.00 | 30.00 |
| 145A Billy Martin .985/.983 Fielding Avg. | 50.00 | 80.00 |
| 145B Billy Martin .983/.982 Fielding Avg. | 50.00 | 80.00 |
| 146 Dick Gernert | 6.00 | 12.00 |
| 147 Joe DeMaestri | 6.00 | 12.00 |
| 148 Dale Mitchell | 10.00 | 20.00 |
| 149 Bob Young | 6.00 | 12.00 |
| 150 Cass Michaels | 6.00 | 12.00 |
| 151 Pat Mullin | 6.00 | 12.00 |
| 152 Mickey Vernon | 10.00 | 20.00 |
| 153A Whitey Lockman 100/331 Assists | 10.00 | 20.00 |
| 153B Whitey Lockman 102/333 Assists | 10.00 | 20.00 |
| 154 Don Newcombe | 15.00 | 30.00 |
| 155 Frank Thomas RC | 6.00 | 12.00 |
| 156A Rocky Bridges 320/467 Assists | 6.00 | 12.00 |
| 156B Rocky Bridges 328/475 Assists | 6.00 | 12.00 |
| 157 Turk Lown | 6.00 | 12.00 |
| 158 Stu Miller | 6.00 | 12.00 |
| 159 Johnny Lindell | 6.00 | 12.00 |
| 160 Danny O'Connell | 6.00 | 12.00 |
| 161 Yogi Berra | 100.00 | 175.00 |
| 162 Ted Lepcio | 6.00 | 12.00 |
| 163A Dave Philley No Trade 152 Games | 10.00 | 20.00 |
| 163B Dave Philley Traded to Cleveland 152 Games | 15.00 | 30.00 |
| 163C Dave Philley Traded to Cleveland 157 Games | 15.00 | 30.00 |
| 164 Early Wynn | 25.00 | 50.00 |
| 165 Johnny Groth | 6.00 | 12.00 |
| 166 Sandy Consuegra | 6.00 | 12.00 |
| 167 Billy Hoeft | 6.00 | 12.00 |
| 168 Ed Fitzgerald | 6.00 | 12.00 |
| 169 Larry Jansen | 6.00 | 12.00 |
| 170 Duke Snider | 150.00 | 250.00 |
| 171 Carlos Bernier | 6.00 | 12.00 |
| 172 Andy Seminick | 6.00 | 12.00 |
| 173 Dee Fondy | 6.00 | 12.00 |
| 174A Pete Castiglione .966/.959 Fielding Avg. | 6.00 | 12.00 |
| 174B Pete Castiglione .970/.959 Fielding Avg. | 6.00 | 12.00 |
| 175 Mel Clark | 6.00 | 12.00 |
| 176 Vern Bickford | 6.00 | 12.00 |
| 177 Whitey Ford | 60.00 | 100.00 |
| 178 Del Wilber | 6.00 | 12.00 |
| 179A Morris Martin 44 ERA | 6.00 | 12.00 |
| 179B Morris Martin 4.44 ERA | 6.00 | 12.00 |
| 180 Joe Tipton | 6.00 | 12.00 |
| 181 Les Moss | 6.00 | 12.00 |
| 182 Sherm Lollar | 10.00 | 20.00 |
| 183 Matt Batts | 6.00 | 12.00 |
| 184 Mickey Grasso | 6.00 | 12.00 |
| 185A Daryl Spencer .941/.944 Fielding Avg. RC | 6.00 | 12.00 |
| 185B Daryl Spencer .933/.936 Fielding Avg. | 6.00 | 12.00 |
| 186 Russ Meyer | 6.00 | 12.00 |
| 187 Vern Law | 10.00 | 20.00 |
| 188 Frank Smith | 6.00 | 12.00 |
| 189 Randy Jackson | 6.00 | 12.00 |
| 190 Joe Presko | 6.00 | 12.00 |
| 191 Karl Drews | 6.00 | 12.00 |
| 192 Lew Burdette | 10.00 | 20.00 |
| 193 Eddie Robinson | 6.00 | 12.00 |
| 194 Sid Hudson | 6.00 | 12.00 |
| 195 Bob Cain | 6.00 | 12.00 |
| 196 Bob Lemon | 25.00 | 50.00 |
| 197 Lou Kretlow | 6.00 | 12.00 |
| 198 Virgil Trucks | 6.00 | 12.00 |
| 199 Steve Gromek | 6.00 | 12.00 |
| 200 Conrado Marrero | 6.00 | 12.00 |
| 201 Bobby Thomson | 15.00 | 30.00 |
| 202 George Shuba | 10.00 | 20.00 |
| 203 Vic Janowicz | 10.00 | 20.00 |
| 204 Jack Collum RC | 6.00 | 12.00 |
| 205 Hal Jeffcoat | 6.00 | 12.00 |
| 206 Steve Bilko | 6.00 | 12.00 |
| 207 Stan Lopata | 6.00 | 12.00 |
| 208 Johnny Antonelli | 10.00 | 20.00 |
| 209 Gene Woodling UER Reversed Photo | 6.00 | 12.00 |
| 210 Jimmy Piersall | 15.00 | 30.00 |
| 211 Al Robertson RC | 6.00 | 12.00 |
| 212A Owen Friend .964/.957 Fielding Avg. | 6.00 | 12.00 |
| 212B Owen Friend .967/.958 Fielding Avg. | 6.00 | 12.00 |
| 213 Dick Littlefield | 6.00 | 12.00 |
| 214 Ferris Fain | 10.00 | 20.00 |
| 215 Johnny Bucha | 6.00 | 12.00 |
| 216A Jerry Snyder .988/.988 Fielding Avg. | 6.00 | 12.00 |
| 216B Jerry Snyder .968/.968 Fielding Avg. | 6.00 | 12.00 |
| 217A Henry Thompson .956/.951 Fielding Avg. | 10.00 | 20.00 |
| 217B Henry Thompson .958/.952 Fielding Avg. | 10.00 | 20.00 |
| 218 Preacher Roe | 10.00 | 20.00 |
| 219 Hal Rice | 6.00 | 12.00 |
| 220 Hobie Landrith RC | 6.00 | 12.00 |
| 221 Frank Baumholtz | 6.00 | 12.00 |
| 222 Memo Luna RC | 6.00 | 12.00 |
| 223 Steve Ridzik | 6.00 | 12.00 |
| 224 Bill Bruton | 25.00 | 50.00 |

## 1955 Bowman

| | | |
|---|---|---|
| COMPLETE SET (320) | 3500.00 | 6000.00 |
| COMMON CARD (1-96) | 6.00 | 12.00 |
| COM. CARD (97-224) | 5.00 | 10.00 |
| COM. CARD (225-320) | 7.50 | 15.00 |
| COM. UMPIRE (225-320) | 18.00 | 30.00 |
| WRAPPER (1-CENT) | 50.00 | 60.00 |
| WRAPPER (5-CENT) | 50.00 | 60.00 |
| 1 Hoyt Wilhelm | 60.00 | 100.00 |
| 2 Alvin Dark | 7.50 | 15.00 |
| 3 Joe Coleman | 7.50 | 15.00 |
| 4 Eddie Waitkus | 7.50 | 15.00 |
| 5 Jim Robertson | 6.00 | 12.00 |
| 6 Pete Suder | 6.00 | 12.00 |
| 7 Gene Baker RC | 6.00 | 12.00 |
| 8 Warren Hacker | 6.00 | 12.00 |
| 9 Gil McDougald | 10.00 | 20.00 |
| 10 Phil Rizzuto | 75.00 | 125.00 |
| 11 Bill Bruton | 7.50 | 15.00 |
| 12 Andy Pafko | 7.50 | 15.00 |
| 13 Clyde Vollmer | 6.00 | 12.00 |
| 14 Gus Keriazakos RC | 6.00 | 12.00 |
| 15 Frank Sullivan RC | 6.00 | 12.00 |
| 16 Jimmy Piersall | 10.00 | 20.00 |
| 17 Del Ennis | 7.50 | 15.00 |
| 18 Stan Lopata | 6.00 | 12.00 |
| 19 Bobby Avila | 7.50 | 15.00 |

|  | | |
|---|---|---|
| 20 Al Smith | 7.50 | 15.00 |
| 21 Don Hoak | 6.00 | 12.00 |
| 22 Roy Campanella | 75.00 | 125.00 |
| 23 Al Kaline | 90.00 | 150.00 |
| 24 Al Aber | 6.00 | 12.00 |
| 25 Minnie Minoso | 15.00 | 30.00 |
| 26 Virgil Trucks | 7.50 | 15.00 |
| 27 Preston Ward | 6.00 | 12.00 |
| 28 Dick Cole | 6.00 | 12.00 |
| 29 Red Schoendienst | 15.00 | 30.00 |
| 30 Bill Sarni | 6.00 | 12.00 |
| 31 Johnny Temple RC | 7.50 | 15.00 |
| 32 Wally Post | 7.50 | 15.00 |
| 33 Nellie Fox | 30.00 | 50.00 |
| 34 Clint Courtney | 6.00 | 12.00 |
| 35 Bill Tuttle RC | 6.00 | 12.00 |
| 36 Wayne Belardi RC | 6.00 | 12.00 |
| 37 Pee Wee Reese | 60.00 | 100.00 |
| 38 Early Wynn | 15.00 | 30.00 |
| 39 Bob Darnell RC | 7.50 | 15.00 |
| 40 Vic Wertz | 7.50 | 15.00 |
| 41 Mel Clark | 6.00 | 12.00 |
| 42 Bob Greenwood RC | 6.00 | 12.00 |
| 43 Bob Buhl | 7.50 | 15.00 |
| 44 Danny O'Connell | 6.00 | 12.00 |
| 45 Tom Umphlett | 6.00 | 12.00 |
| 46 Mickey Vernon | 7.50 | 15.00 |
| 47 Sammy White | 6.00 | 12.00 |
| 48A Milt Bolling ERR | 10.00 | 20.00 |
| 48B Milt Bolling COR | 10.00 | 20.00 |
| 49 Jim Greengrass | 6.00 | 12.00 |
| 50 Hobie Landrith | 6.00 | 12.00 |
| 51 Elvin Tappe RC | 6.00 | 12.00 |
| 52 Hal Rice | 6.00 | 12.00 |
| 53 Alex Kellner | 6.00 | 12.00 |
| 54 Don Bollweg | 6.00 | 12.00 |
| 55 Cal Abrams | 6.00 | 12.00 |
| 56 Billy Cox | 7.50 | 15.00 |
| 57 Bob Friend | 7.50 | 15.00 |
| 58 Frank Thomas | 7.50 | 15.00 |
| 59 Whitey Ford | 60.00 | 100.00 |
| 60 Enos Slaughter | 15.00 | 30.00 |
| 61 Paul LaPalme | 6.00 | 12.00 |
| 62 Royce Lint RC | 6.00 | 12.00 |
| 63 Irv Noren | 7.50 | 15.00 |
| 64 Curt Simmons | 7.50 | 15.00 |
| 65 Don Zimmer RC | 10.00 | 20.00 |
| 66 George Shuba | 10.00 | 20.00 |
| 67 Don Larsen | 10.00 | 20.00 |
| 68 Elston Howard RC | 50.00 | 80.00 |
| 69 Billy Hunter | 6.00 | 12.00 |
| 70 Lew Burdette | 10.00 | 20.00 |
| 71 Dave Jolly | 6.00 | 12.00 |
| 72 Chet Nichols | 6.00 | 12.00 |
| 73 Eddie Yost | 7.50 | 15.00 |
| 74 Jerry Snyder | 6.00 | 12.00 |
| 75 Brooks Lawrence RC | 6.00 | 12.00 |
| 76 Tom Poholsky | 6.00 | 12.00 |
| 77 Jim McDonald RC | 6.00 | 12.00 |
| 78 Gil Coan | 6.00 | 12.00 |
| 79 Willie Miranda | 6.00 | 12.00 |
| 80 Lou Limmer | 6.00 | 12.00 |
| 81 Bobby Morgan | 6.00 | 12.00 |
| 82 Lee Walls RC | 6.00 | 12.00 |
| 83 Max Surkont | 6.00 | 12.00 |
| 84 George Freese RC | 6.00 | 12.00 |
| 85 Cass Michaels | 6.00 | 12.00 |
| 86 Ted Gray | 6.00 | 12.00 |
| 87 Randy Jackson | 6.00 | 12.00 |
| 88 Steve Bilko | 6.00 | 12.00 |
| 89 Lou Boudreau MG | 15.00 | 30.00 |
| 90 Art RC | 6.00 | 12.00 |
| 91 Dick Marlowe RC | 6.00 | 12.00 |
| 92 George Zuverink | 6.00 | 12.00 |
| 93 Andy Seminick | 6.00 | 12.00 |
| 94 Hank Thompson | 7.50 | 15.00 |
| 95 Sal Maglie | 7.50 | 15.00 |
| 96 Ray Narleski RC | 6.00 | 12.00 |
| 97 Johnny Podres | 15.00 | 30.00 |
| 98 Jim Gilliam | 10.00 | 20.00 |
| 99 Jerry Coleman | 7.50 | 15.00 |
| 100 Tom Morgan | 5.00 | 10.00 |
| 101A Don Johnson ERR | 10.00 | 20.00 |
| 101B Don Johnson COR | 10.00 | 20.00 |
| 102 Bobby Thomson | 7.50 | 15.00 |
| 103 Eddie Mathews | 50.00 | 80.00 |
| 104 Bob Porterfield | 5.00 | 10.00 |
| 105 Johnny Schmitz | 5.00 | 10.00 |
| 106 Del Rice | 5.00 | 10.00 |
| 107 Solly Hemus | 5.00 | 10.00 |
| 108 Lou Kretlow | 5.00 | 10.00 |
| 109 Vern Stephens | 7.50 | 15.00 |
| 110 Bob Miller | 5.00 | 10.00 |
| 111 Steve Ridzik | 5.00 | 10.00 |
| 112 Granny Hamner | 5.00 | 10.00 |
| 113 Bob Hall RC | 5.00 | 10.00 |
| 114 Vic Janowicz | 5.00 | 10.00 |
| 115 Roger Bowman RC | 5.00 | 10.00 |
| 116 Sandy Consuegra | 5.00 | 10.00 |
| 117 Johnny Groth | 5.00 | 10.00 |
| 118 Bobby Adams | 5.00 | 10.00 |
| 119 Joe Astroth | 5.00 | 10.00 |
| 120 Ed Burtschy RC | 5.00 | 10.00 |
| 121 Rufus Crawford RC | 5.00 | 10.00 |
| 122 Al Corwin | 5.00 | 10.00 |
| 123 Marv Grissom RC | 5.00 | 10.00 |
| 124 Johnny Antonelli | 7.50 | 15.00 |
| 125 Paul Giel RC | 7.50 | 15.00 |
| 126 Billy Goodman | 7.50 | 15.00 |
| 127 Hank Majeski | 5.00 | 10.00 |
| 128 Mike Garcia | 7.50 | 15.00 |
| 129 Hal Naragon RC | 5.00 | 10.00 |
| 130 Richie Ashburn | 30.00 | 50.00 |
| 131 Willard Marshall | 5.00 | 10.00 |
| 132A Harvey Kueen ERR | 30.00 | 50.00 |
| 132B Harvey Kuenn COR | 15.00 | 30.00 |
| 133 Charles King RC | 5.00 | 10.00 |
| 134 Bob Feller | 50.00 | 80.00 |
| 135 Lloyd Merriman | 5.00 | 10.00 |
| 136 Rocky Bridges | 5.00 | 10.00 |
| 137 Bob Talbot | 5.00 | 10.00 |
| 138 Davey Williams | 7.50 | 15.00 |
| 139 W.Shantz/B.Shantz | 7.50 | 15.00 |
| 140 Bobby Shantz | 7.50 | 15.00 |
| 141 Wes Westrum | 7.50 | 15.00 |
| 142 Rudy Regalado RC | 5.00 | 10.00 |
| 143 Don Newcombe | 15.00 | 30.00 |
| 144 Art Houtteman | 5.00 | 10.00 |
| 145 Bob Nieman RC | 5.00 | 10.00 |
| 146 Don Liddle | 5.00 | 10.00 |
| 147 Sam Mele | 5.00 | 10.00 |
| 148 Bob Chakales | 5.00 | 10.00 |
| 149 Cloyd Boyer | 5.00 | 10.00 |
| 150 Billy Klaus RC | 5.00 | 10.00 |
| 151 Jim Brideweser | 5.00 | 10.00 |
| 152 Johnny Klippstein | 5.00 | 10.00 |
| 153 Eddie Robinson | 5.00 | 10.00 |
| 154 Frank Lary RC | 7.50 | 15.00 |
| 155 Gerry Staley | 5.00 | 10.00 |
| 156 Jim Hughes | 7.50 | 15.00 |
| 157A Ernie Johnson ERR | 10.00 | 20.00 |
| 157B Ernie Johnson COR | 10.00 | 20.00 |
| 158 Gil Hodges | 30.00 | 50.00 |
| 159 Harry Byrd | 5.00 | 10.00 |
| 160 Bill Skowron | 10.00 | 20.00 |
| 161 Matt Batts | 5.00 | 10.00 |
| 162 Charlie Maxwell | 5.00 | 10.00 |
| 163 Sid Gordon | 5.00 | 10.00 |
| 164 Toby Atwell | 5.00 | 10.00 |
| 165 Maurice McDermott | 5.00 | 10.00 |
| 166 Jim Busby | 5.00 | 10.00 |
| 167 Bob Grim RC | 10.00 | 20.00 |
| 168 Yogi Berra | 75.00 | 125.00 |
| 169 Carl Furillo | 15.00 | 30.00 |
| 170 Carl Erskine | 10.00 | 20.00 |
| 171 Robin Roberts | 30.00 | 50.00 |
| 172 Willie Jones | 5.00 | 10.00 |
| 173 Chico Carrasquel | 5.00 | 10.00 |
| 174 Sherm Lollar | 7.50 | 15.00 |
| 175 Wilmer Shantz RC | 5.00 | 10.00 |
| 176 Joe DeMaestri | 5.00 | 10.00 |
| 177 Willard Nixon | 5.00 | 10.00 |
| 178 Tom Brewer RC | 5.00 | 10.00 |
| 179 Hank Aaron | 150.00 | 250.00 |
| 180 Johnny Logan | 7.50 | 15.00 |
| 181 Eddie Miksis | 5.00 | 10.00 |
| 182 Bob Rush | 5.00 | 10.00 |
| 183 Ray Katt | 5.00 | 10.00 |
| 184 Willie Mays | 150.00 | 250.00 |
| 185 Vic Raschi | 7.50 | 15.00 |
| 186 Alex Grammas | 5.00 | 10.00 |
| 187 Fred Hatfield | 5.00 | 10.00 |
| 188 Ned Garver | 5.00 | 10.00 |
| 189 Jack Collum | 5.00 | 10.00 |
| 190 Fred Baczewski | 5.00 | 10.00 |
| 191 Bob Lemon | 15.00 | 30.00 |
| 192 George Strickland | 5.00 | 10.00 |
| 193 Howie Judson | 5.00 | 10.00 |
| 194 Joe Nuxhall | 7.50 | 15.00 |
| 195A Erv Palica | 7.50 | 15.00 |
| 195B Erv Palica TR | 20.00 | 40.00 |
| 196 Russ Meyer | 7.50 | 15.00 |
| 197 Ralph Kiner | 15.00 | 30.00 |
| 198 Dave Pope RC | 5.00 | 10.00 |
| 199 Vern Law | 7.50 | 15.00 |
| 200 Dick Littlefield | 5.00 | 10.00 |
| 201 Allie Reynolds | 10.00 | 20.00 |
| 202 Mickey Mantle UER | 500.00 | 800.00 |
| 203 Steve Gromek | 5.00 | 10.00 |
| 204A Frank Bolling ERR | 10.00 | 20.00 |
| 204B Frank Bolling COR | 10.00 | 20.00 |
| 205 Rip Repulski | 5.00 | 10.00 |
| 206 Ralph Beard RC | 5.00 | 10.00 |
| 207 Frank Shea | 5.00 | 10.00 |
| 208 Ed Fitzgerald | 5.00 | 10.00 |
| 209 Smoky Burgess | 7.50 | 15.00 |
| 210 Earl Torgeson | 5.00 | 10.00 |
| 211 Sonny Dixon RC | 5.00 | 10.00 |
| 212 Jack Dittmer | 5.00 | 10.00 |
| 213 George Kell | 15.00 | 30.00 |
| 214 Billy Pierce | 7.50 | 15.00 |
| 215 Bob Kuzava | 5.00 | 10.00 |
| 216 Preacher Roe | 10.00 | 20.00 |
| 217 Del Crandall | 7.50 | 15.00 |
| 218 Joe Adcock | 7.50 | 15.00 |
| 219 Whitey Lockman | 7.50 | 15.00 |
| 220 Jim Hearn | 5.00 | 10.00 |
| 221 Hector Brown | 5.00 | 10.00 |
| 222 Russ Kemmerer RC | 5.00 | 10.00 |
| 223 Hal Jeffcoat | 5.00 | 10.00 |
| 224 Dee Fondy | 5.00 | 10.00 |
| 225 Paul Richards MG | 7.50 | 15.00 |
| 226 Bill McKinley UMP | 18.00 | 30.00 |
| 227 Frank Baumholtz | 7.50 | 15.00 |
| 228 John Phillips RC | 7.50 | 15.00 |
| 229 Jim Brosnan RC | 10.00 | 20.00 |
| 230 Al Brazle | 7.50 | 15.00 |
| 231 Jim Konstanty | 10.00 | 20.00 |
| 232 Birdie Tebbetts MG | 10.00 | 20.00 |
| 233 Bill Serena | 7.50 | 15.00 |
| 234 Dick Bartell CO | 10.00 | 20.00 |
| 235 Joe Paparella UMP | 18.00 | 30.00 |
| 236 Murry Dickson | 7.50 | 15.00 |
| 237 Johnny Wyrostek | 7.50 | 15.00 |
| 238 Eddie Stanky MG | 10.00 | 20.00 |
| 239 Edwin Rommel UMP | 20.00 | 40.00 |
| 240 Billy Loes | 10.00 | 20.00 |
| 241 Johnny Pesky | 10.00 | 20.00 |
| 242 Ernie Banks | 200.00 | 350.00 |
| 243 Gus Bell | 10.00 | 20.00 |
| 244 Duane Pillette | 7.50 | 15.00 |
| 245 Bill Miller | 7.50 | 15.00 |
| 246 Hank Bauer | 15.00 | 30.00 |
| 247 Dutch Leonard CO | 7.50 | 15.00 |
| 248 Harry Dorish | 7.50 | 15.00 |
| 249 Billy Gardner RC | 10.00 | 20.00 |
| 250 Larry Napp UMP | 18.00 | 30.00 |
| 251 Stan Jok | 7.50 | 15.00 |
| 252 Roy Smalley | 7.50 | 15.00 |
| 253 Jim Wilson | 7.50 | 15.00 |
| 254 Bennett Flowers RC | 7.50 | 15.00 |
| 255 Pete Runnels | 10.00 | 20.00 |
| 256 Owen Friend | 7.50 | 15.00 |
| 257 Tom Alston RC | 7.50 | 15.00 |
| 258 John Stevens UMP | 18.00 | 30.00 |
| 259 Don Mossi RC | 15.00 | 30.00 |
| 260 Edwin Hurley UMP | 18.00 | 30.00 |
| 261 Walt Moryn RC | 7.50 | 15.00 |
| 262 Jim Lemon FBC | 7.50 | 15.00 |
| 263 Eddie Joost | 7.50 | 15.00 |
| 264 Bill Henry RC | 7.50 | 15.00 |
| 265 Al Barlick UMP | 50.00 | 80.00 |
| 266 Mike Fornieles | 7.50 | 15.00 |
| 267 J.Honochick UMP | 50.00 | 80.00 |
| 268 Roy Lee Hawes RC | 7.50 | 15.00 |
| 269 Joe Amalfitano RC | 10.00 | 20.00 |
| 270 Chico Fernandez RC | 10.00 | 20.00 |
| 271 Bob Hooper | 7.50 | 15.00 |
| 272 John Flaherty UMP | 18.00 | 30.00 |
| 273 Bubba Church | 7.50 | 15.00 |
| 274 Jim Delsing | 7.50 | 15.00 |
| 275 William Grieve UMP | 18.00 | 30.00 |
| 276 Ike Delock | 7.50 | 15.00 |
| 277 Ed Runge UMP | 18.00 | 30.00 |

|  |  | | |
|---|---|---|---|
| 278 | Charlie Neal RC | 20.00 | 40.00 |
| 279 | Hank Soar UMP | 20.00 | 40.00 |
| 280 | Clyde McCullough | 7.50 | 15.00 |
| 281 | Charles Berry UMP | 20.00 | 40.00 |
| 282 | Phil Cavarretta MG | 10.00 | 20.00 |
| 283 | Nestor Chylak UMP | 50.00 | 80.00 |
| 284 | Bill Jackowski UMP | 18.00 | 30.00 |
| 285 | Walt Dropo | 10.00 | 20.00 |
| 286 | Frank Secory UMP | 18.00 | 30.00 |
| 287 | Ron Mrozinski RC | 7.50 | 15.00 |
| 288 | Dick Smith RC | 7.50 | 15.00 |
| 289 | Arthur Gore UMP | 18.00 | 30.00 |
| 290 | Hershell Freeman RC | 7.50 | 15.00 |
| 291 | Frank Dascoli UMP | 18.00 | 30.00 |
| 292 | Marv Blaylock RC | 7.50 | 15.00 |
| 293 | Thomas Gorman CO | 20.00 | 40.00 |
| 294 | Wally Moses CO | 7.50 | 15.00 |
| 295 | Lee Ballantant UMP | 18.00 | 30.00 |
| 296 | Bill Virdon RC | 15.00 | 30.00 |
| 297 | Dusty Boggess UMP | 18.00 | 30.00 |
| 298 | Charlie Grimm | 10.00 | 20.00 |
| 299 | Lon Warneke UMP | 20.00 | 40.00 |
| 300 | Tommy Byrne | 10.00 | 20.00 |
| 301 | William Engeln UMP | 18.00 | 30.00 |
| 302 | Frank Malzone RC | 15.00 | 30.00 |
| 303 | Jocko Conlan UMP | 50.00 | 80.00 |
| 304 | Harry Chiti | 7.50 | 15.00 |
| 305 | Frank Umont UMP | 18.00 | 30.00 |
| 306 | Bob Cerv | 10.00 | 20.00 |
| 307 | Babe Pinelli UMP | 20.00 | 40.00 |
| 308 | Al Lopez MG | 30.00 | 50.00 |
| 309 | Hal Dixon UMP | 18.00 | 30.00 |
| 310 | Ken Lehman RC | 7.50 | 15.00 |
| 311 | Lawrence Goetz UMP | 18.00 | 30.00 |
| 312 | Bill Wight | 7.50 | 15.00 |
| 313 | Augie Donatelli UMP | 30.00 | 50.00 |
| 314 | Dale Mitchell | 10.00 | 20.00 |
| 315 | Cal Hubbard UMP | 50.00 | 80.00 |
| 316 | Marion Fricano | 7.50 | 15.00 |
| 317 | William Summers UMP | 10.00 | 20.00 |
| 318 | Sid Hudson | 7.50 | 15.00 |
| 319 | Al Schroll RC | 7.50 | 15.00 |
| 320 | George Susce RC | 30.00 | 50.00 |

## 1989 Bowman

|  |  | | |
|---|---|---|---|
| | COMPLETE SET (484) | 10.00 | 25.00 |
| | COMP.FACT.SET (484) | 10.00 | 25.00 |
| 1 | Oswald Peraza | .01 | .05 |
| 2 | Brian Holton | .01 | .05 |
| 3 | Jose Bautista RC | .02 | .10 |
| 4 | Pete Harnisch RC | .08 | .25 |
| 5 | Dave Schmidt | .01 | .05 |
| 6 | Gregg Olson RC | .08 | .25 |
| 7 | Jeff Ballard | .01 | .05 |
| 8 | Bob Melvin | .01 | .05 |
| 9 | Cal Ripken | .30 | .75 |
| 10 | Randy Milligan | .01 | .05 |
| 11 | Juan Bell RC | .02 | .10 |
| 12 | Billy Ripken | .01 | .05 |
| 13 | Jim Traber | .01 | .05 |
| 14 | Pete Stanicek | .01 | .05 |
| 15 | Steve Finley RC | .30 | .75 |
| 16 | Larry Sheets | .01 | .05 |
| 17 | Phil Bradley | .01 | .05 |
| 18 | Brady Anderson RC | .15 | .40 |
| 19 | Lee Smith | .02 | .10 |
| 20 | Tom Fischer | .01 | .05 |
| 21 | Mike Boddicker | .01 | .05 |
| 22 | Rob Murphy | .01 | .05 |
| 23 | Wes Gardner | .01 | .05 |
| 24 | John Dopson | .01 | .05 |
| 25 | Bob Stanley | .01 | .05 |
| 26 | Roger Clemens | .40 | 1.00 |
| 27 | Rich Gedman | .01 | .05 |
| 28 | Marty Barrett | .01 | .05 |
| 29 | Luis Rivera | .01 | .05 |
| 30 | Jody Reed | .01 | .05 |
| 31 | Nick Esasky | .01 | .05 |
| 32 | Wade Boggs | .05 | .15 |
| 33 | Jim Rice | .02 | .10 |
| 34 | Mike Greenwell | .01 | .05 |
| 35 | Dwight Evans | .05 | .15 |
| 36 | Ellis Burks | .02 | .10 |
| 37 | Chuck Finley | .02 | .10 |
| 38 | Kirk McCaskill | .01 | .05 |
| 39 | Jim Abbott RC | .40 | 1.00 |
| 40 | Bryan Harvey RC * | .08 | .25 |
| 41 | Bert Blyleven | .02 | .10 |
| 42 | Mike Witt | .01 | .05 |
| 43 | Bob McClure | .01 | .05 |
| 44 | Bill Schroeder | .01 | .05 |
| 45 | Lance Parrish | .02 | .10 |
| 46 | Dick Schofield | .01 | .05 |
| 47 | Wally Joyner | .02 | .10 |
| 48 | Jack Howell | .01 | .05 |
| 49 | Johnny Ray | .01 | .05 |
| 50 | Chili Davis | .02 | .10 |
| 51 | Tony Armas | .02 | .10 |
| 52 | Claudell Washington | .01 | .05 |
| 53 | Brian Downing | .02 | .10 |
| 54 | Devon White | .01 | .05 |
| 55 | Bobby Thigpen | .01 | .05 |
| 56 | Bill Long | .01 | .05 |
| 57 | Jerry Reuss | .01 | .05 |
| 58 | Shawn Hillegas | .01 | .05 |
| 59 | Melido Perez | .01 | .05 |
| 60 | Jeff Bittiger | .01 | .05 |
| 61 | Jack McDowell | .02 | .10 |
| 62 | Carlton Fisk | .05 | .15 |
| 63 | Steve Lyons | .01 | .05 |
| 64 | Ozzie Guillen | .02 | .10 |
| 65 | Robin Ventura RC | .30 | .75 |
| 66 | Fred Manrique | .01 | .05 |
| 67 | Dan Pasqua | .01 | .05 |
| 68 | Ivan Calderon | .01 | .05 |
| 69 | Ron Kittle | .01 | .05 |
| 70 | Daryl Boston | .01 | .05 |
| 71 | Dave Gallagher | .01 | .05 |
| 72 | Harold Baines | .02 | .10 |
| 73 | Charles Nagy RC | .08 | .25 |
| 74 | John Farrell | .01 | .05 |
| 75 | Kevin Wickander | .01 | .05 |
| 76 | Greg Swindell | .01 | .05 |
| 77 | Mike Walker | .01 | .05 |
| 78 | Doug Jones | .01 | .05 |
| 79 | Rich Yett | .01 | .05 |
| 80 | Tom Candiotti | .01 | .05 |
| 81 | Jesse Orosco | .01 | .05 |
| 82 | Bud Black | .01 | .05 |
| 83 | Andy Allanson | .01 | .05 |
| 84 | Pete O'Brien | .01 | .05 |
| 85 | Jerry Browne | .01 | .05 |
| 86 | Brook Jacoby | .01 | .05 |
| 87 | Mark Lewis RC | .08 | .25 |
| 88 | Luis Aguayo | .01 | .05 |
| 89 | Cory Snyder | .01 | .05 |
| 90 | Oddibe McDowell | .01 | .05 |
| 91 | Joe Carter | .02 | .10 |
| 92 | Frank Tanana | .02 | .10 |
| 93 | Jack Morris | .02 | .10 |
| 94 | Doyle Alexander | .01 | .05 |
| 95 | Steve Searcy | .01 | .05 |
| 96 | Randy Bockus | .01 | .05 |
| 97 | Jeff M. Robinson | .01 | .05 |
| 98 | Mike Henneman | .01 | .05 |
| 99 | Paul Gibson | .01 | .05 |
| 100 | Frank Williams | .01 | .05 |
| 101 | Matt Nokes | .01 | .05 |
| 102 | Rico Brogna RC | .15 | .40 |
| 103 | Lou Whitaker | .02 | .10 |
| 104 | Al Pedrique | .01 | .05 |
| 105 | Alan Trammell | .02 | .10 |
| 106 | Chris Brown | .01 | .05 |
| 107 | Pat Sheridan | .01 | .05 |
| 108 | Chet Lemon | .02 | .10 |
| 109 | Keith Moreland | .01 | .05 |
| 110 | Mel Stottlemyre Jr. | .01 | .05 |
| 111 | Bret Saberhagen | .02 | .10 |
| 112 | Floyd Bannister | .01 | .05 |
| 113 | Jeff Montgomery | .01 | .05 |
| 114 | Steve Farr | .01 | .05 |
| 115 | Tom Gordon UER RC | .15 | .40 |
| 116 | Charlie Leibrandt | .01 | .05 |
| 117 | Mark Gubicza | .01 | .05 |
| 118 | Mike Macfarlane RC * | .08 | .25 |
| 119 | Bob Boone | .02 | .10 |
| 120 | Kurt Stillwell | .01 | .05 |
| 121 | George Brett | .25 | .60 |
| 122 | Frank White | .02 | .10 |
| 123 | Kevin Seitzer | .01 | .05 |
| 124 | Willie Wilson | .02 | .10 |
| 125 | Pat Tabler | .01 | .05 |
| 126 | Bo Jackson | .08 | .25 |
| 127 | Hugh Walker RC | .02 | .10 |
| 128 | Danny Tartabull | .02 | .10 |
| 129 | Teddy Higuera | .01 | .05 |
| 130 | Don August | .01 | .05 |
| 131 | Juan Nieves | .01 | .05 |
| 132 | Mike Birkbeck | .01 | .05 |
| 133 | Dan Plesac | .01 | .05 |
| 134 | Chris Bosio | .01 | .05 |
| 135 | Bill Wegman | .01 | .05 |
| 136 | Chuck Crim | .01 | .05 |
| 137 | B.J. Surhoff | .02 | .10 |
| 138 | Joey Meyer | .01 | .05 |
| 139 | Dale Sveum | .01 | .05 |
| 140 | Paul Molitor | .02 | .10 |
| 141 | Jim Gantner | .01 | .05 |
| 142 | Gary Sheffield RC | .60 | 1.50 |
| 143 | Greg Brock | .01 | .05 |
| 144 | Robin Yount | .15 | .40 |
| 145 | Glenn Braggs | .01 | .05 |
| 146 | Rob Deer | .01 | .05 |
| 147 | Fred Toliver | .01 | .05 |
| 148 | Jeff Reardon | .02 | .10 |
| 149 | Allan Anderson | .01 | .05 |
| 150 | Frank Viola | .02 | .10 |
| 151 | Shane Rawley | .01 | .05 |
| 152 | Juan Berenguer | .01 | .05 |
| 153 | Johnny Ard | .01 | .05 |
| 154 | Tim Laudner | .01 | .05 |
| 155 | Brian Harper | .01 | .05 |
| 156 | Al Newman | .01 | .05 |
| 157 | Kent Hrbek | .02 | .10 |
| 158 | Gary Gaetti | .02 | .10 |
| 159 | Wally Backman | .01 | .05 |
| 160 | Gene Larkin | .01 | .05 |
| 161 | Greg Gagne | .01 | .05 |
| 162 | Kirby Puckett | .08 | .25 |
| 163 | Dan Gladden | .01 | .05 |
| 164 | Randy Bush | .01 | .05 |
| 165 | Dave LaPoint | .01 | .05 |
| 166 | Andy Hawkins | .01 | .05 |
| 167 | Dave Righetti | .02 | .10 |
| 168 | Lance McCullers | .01 | .05 |
| 169 | Jimmy Jones | .01 | .05 |
| 170 | Al Leiter | .08 | .25 |
| 171 | John Candelaria | .01 | .05 |
| 172 | Don Slaught | .01 | .05 |
| 173 | Jamie Quirk | .01 | .05 |
| 174 | Rafael Santana | .01 | .05 |
| 175 | Mike Pagliarulo | .01 | .05 |
| 176 | Don Mattingly | .25 | .60 |
| 177 | Ken Phelps | .01 | .05 |
| 178 | Steve Sax | .02 | .10 |
| 179 | Dave Winfield | .02 | .10 |
| 180 | Stan Jefferson | .01 | .05 |
| 181 | Rickey Henderson | .08 | .25 |
| 182 | Bob Brower | .01 | .05 |
| 183 | Roberto Kelly | .02 | .10 |
| 184 | Curt Young | .01 | .05 |
| 185 | Gene Nelson | .01 | .05 |
| 186 | Bob Welch | .02 | .10 |
| 187 | Rick Honeycutt | .01 | .05 |
| 188 | Dave Stewart | .02 | .10 |
| 189 | Mike Moore | .01 | .05 |
| 190 | Dennis Eckersley | .05 | .15 |
| 191 | Eric Plunk | .01 | .05 |
| 192 | Storm Davis | .01 | .05 |
| 193 | Terry Steinbach | .02 | .10 |
| 194 | Ron Hassey | .01 | .05 |
| 195 | Stan Royer RC | .02 | .10 |
| 196 | Walt Weiss | .01 | .05 |
| 197 | Mark McGwire | .40 | 1.00 |
| 198 | Carney Lansford | .02 | .10 |
| 199 | Glenn Hubbard | .01 | .05 |
| 200 | Dave Henderson | .01 | .05 |
| 201 | Jose Canseco | .08 | .25 |
| 202 | Dave Parker | .02 | .10 |
| 203 | Scott Bankhead | .01 | .05 |

|  |  | | |  |  | | |  |  | | |
|---|--------|---|---|---|--------|---|---|---|--------|---|---|
| 204 | Tom Niedenfuer | .01 | .05 | 292 | Curt Wilkerson | .01 | .05 | 380 | Keith Miller | .01 | .05 |
| 205 | Mark Langston | .01 | .05 | 293 | Vance Law | .01 | .05 | 381 | Gregg Jefferies | .01 | .05 |
| 206 | Erik Hanson RC | .08 | .25 | 294 | Shawon Dunston | .01 | .05 | 382 | Tim Teufel | .01 | .05 |
| 207 | Mike Jackson | .01 | .05 | 295 | Jerome Walton RC | .08 | .25 | 383 | Kevin Elster | .01 | .05 |
| 208 | Dave Valle | .01 | .05 | 296 | Mitch Webster | .01 | .05 | 384 | Dave Magadan | .01 | .05 |
| 209 | Scott Bradley | .01 | .05 | 297 | Dwight Smith RC | .08 | .25 | 385 | Keith Hernandez | .02 | .10 |
| 210 | Harold Reynolds | .02 | .10 | 298 | Andre Dawson | .02 | .10 | 386 | Mookie Wilson | .02 | .10 |
| 211 | Tino Martinez RC | .75 | 2.00 | 299 | Jeff Sellers | .01 | .05 | 387 | Darryl Strawberry | .02 | .10 |
| 212 | Rich Renteria | .01 | .05 | 300 | Jose Rijo | .02 | .10 | 388 | Kevin McReynolds | .01 | .05 |
| 213 | Rey Quinones | .01 | .05 | 301 | John Franco | .02 | .10 | 389 | Mark Carreon | .01 | .05 |
| 214 | Jim Presley | .01 | .05 | 302 | Rick Mahler | .01 | .05 | 390 | Jeff Parrett | .01 | .05 |
| 215 | Alvin Davis | .01 | .05 | 303 | Ron Robinson | .01 | .05 | 391 | Mike Maddux | .01 | .05 |
| 216 | Edgar Martinez | .08 | .25 | 304 | Danny Jackson | .01 | .05 | 392 | Don Carman | .01 | .05 |
| 217 | Darnell Coles | .01 | .05 | 305 | Rob Dibble RC | .15 | .40 | 393 | Bruce Ruffin | .01 | .05 |
| 218 | Jeffrey Leonard | .01 | .05 | 306 | Tom Browning | .01 | .05 | 394 | Ken Howell | .01 | .05 |
| 219 | Jay Buhner | .02 | .10 | 307 | Bo Diaz | .01 | .05 | 395 | Steve Bedrosian | .01 | .05 |
| 220 | Ken Griffey Jr. RC | 2.50 | 6.00 | 308 | Manny Trillo | .01 | .05 | 396 | Floyd Youmans | .01 | .05 |
| 221 | Drew Hall | .01 | .05 | 309 | Chris Sabo RC * | .15 | .40 | 397 | Larry McWilliams | .01 | .05 |
| 222 | Bobby Witt | .01 | .05 | 310 | Ron Oester | .01 | .05 | 398 | Pat Combs RC * | .02 | .10 |
| 223 | Jamie Moyer | .02 | .10 | 311 | Barry Larkin | .05 | .15 | 399 | Steve Lake | .01 | .05 |
| 224 | Charlie Hough | .02 | .10 | 312 | Todd Benzinger | .01 | .05 | 400 | Dickie Thon | .01 | .05 |
| 225 | Nolan Ryan | .40 | 1.00 | 313 | Paul O'Neill | .05 | .15 | 401 | Ricky Jordan RC * | .08 | .25 |
| 226 | Jeff Russell | .01 | .05 | 314 | Kal Daniels | .01 | .05 | 402 | Mike Schmidt | .20 | .50 |
| 227 | Jim Sundberg | .02 | .10 | 315 | Joel Youngblood | .01 | .05 | 403 | Tom Herr | .01 | .05 |
| 228 | Julio Franco | .02 | .10 | 316 | Eric Davis | .02 | .10 | 404 | Chris James | .01 | .05 |
| 229 | Buddy Bell | .02 | .10 | 317 | Dave Smith | .01 | .05 | 405 | Juan Samuel | .01 | .05 |
| 230 | Scott Fletcher | .01 | .05 | 318 | Mark Portugal | .01 | .05 | 406 | Von Hayes | .01 | .05 |
| 231 | Jeff Kunkel | .01 | .05 | 319 | Brian Meyer | .01 | .05 | 407 | Ron Jones | .02 | .10 |
| 232 | Steve Buechele | .01 | .05 | 320 | Jim Deshaies | .01 | .05 | 408 | Curt Ford | .01 | .05 |
| 233 | Monty Fariss | .01 | .05 | 321 | Juan Agosto | .01 | .05 | 409 | Bob Walk | .01 | .05 |
| 234 | Rick Leach | .01 | .05 | 322 | Mike Scott | .02 | .10 | 410 | Jeff D. Robinson | .01 | .05 |
| 235 | Ruben Sierra | .02 | .10 | 323 | Rick Rhoden | .01 | .05 | 411 | Jim Gott | .01 | .05 |
| 236 | Cecil Espy | .01 | .05 | 324 | Jim Clancy | .01 | .05 | 412 | Scott Medvin | .01 | .05 |
| 237 | Rafael Palmeiro | .08 | .25 | 325 | Larry Andersen | .01 | .05 | 413 | John Smiley | .01 | .05 |
| 238 | Pete Incaviglia | .01 | .05 | 326 | Alex Trevino | .01 | .05 | 414 | Bob Kipper | .01 | .05 |
| 239 | Dave Slieb | .02 | .10 | 327 | Alan Ashby | .01 | .05 | 415 | Brian Fisher | .01 | .05 |
| 240 | Jeff Musselman | .01 | .05 | 328 | Craig Reynolds | .01 | .05 | 416 | Doug Drabek | .01 | .05 |
| 241 | Mike Flanagan | .01 | .05 | 329 | Bill Doran | .01 | .05 | 417 | Mike LaValliere | .01 | .05 |
| 242 | Todd Stottlemyre | .01 | .05 | 330 | Rafael Ramirez | .01 | .05 | 418 | Ken Oberkfell | .01 | .05 |
| 243 | Jimmy Key | .01 | .05 | 331 | Glenn Davis | .01 | .05 | 419 | Sid Bream | .01 | .05 |
| 244 | Tony Castillo RC | .02 | .10 | 332 | Willie Ansley RC | .02 | .10 | 420 | Austin Manahan RC | .01 | .05 |
| 245 | Alex Sanchez RC | .01 | .05 | 333 | Gerald Young | .01 | .05 | 421 | Jose Lind | .01 | .05 |
| 246 | Tom Henke | .01 | .05 | 334 | Cameron Drew | .01 | .05 | 422 | Bobby Bonilla | .02 | .10 |
| 247 | John Cerutti | .01 | .05 | 335 | Jay Howell | .01 | .05 | 423 | Glenn Wilson | .01 | .05 |
| 248 | Ernie Whitt | .01 | .05 | 336 | Tim Belcher | .01 | .05 | 424 | Andy Van Slyke | .05 | .15 |
| 249 | Bob Brenly | .01 | .05 | 337 | Fernando Valenzuela | .02 | .10 | 425 | Gary Redus | .01 | .05 |
| 250 | Rance Mulliniks | .01 | .05 | 338 | Ricky Horton | .01 | .05 | 426 | Barry Bonds | .60 | 1.50 |
| 251 | Kelly Gruber | .01 | .05 | 339 | Tim Leary | .01 | .05 | 427 | Don Heinkel | .01 | .05 |
| 252 | Ed Sprague RC | .08 | .25 | 340 | Bill Bene | .01 | .05 | 428 | Ken Dayley | .01 | .05 |
| 253 | Fred McGriff | .05 | .15 | 341 | Orel Hershiser | .02 | .10 | 429 | Todd Worrell | .01 | .05 |
| 254 | Tony Fernandez | .01 | .05 | 342 | Mike Scioscia | .01 | .05 | 430 | Brad DuVall | .01 | .05 |
| 255 | Tom Lawless | .01 | .05 | 343 | Rick Dempsey | .01 | .05 | 431 | Jose DeLeon | .01 | .05 |
| 256 | George Bell | .02 | .10 | 344 | Willie Randolph | .02 | .10 | 432 | Joe Magrane | .01 | .05 |
| 257 | Jesse Barfield | .02 | .10 | 345 | Alfredo Griffin | .01 | .05 | 433 | John Ericks | .01 | .05 |
| 258 | Roberto Alomar w/Dad | .05 | .15 | 346 | Eddie Murray | .08 | .25 | 434 | Frank DiPino | .01 | .05 |
| 259 | Ken Griffey Sr./Jr. | .40 | 1.00 | 347 | Mickey Hatcher | .01 | .05 | 435 | Tony Pena | .01 | .05 |
| 260 | Cal Ripken Sr./Jr. | .08 | .25 | 348 | Mike Sharperson | .01 | .05 | 436 | Ozzie Smith | .15 | .40 |
| 261 | M.Stottlemyre Jr./Sr. | .01 | .05 | 349 | John Shelby | .01 | .05 | 437 | Terry Pendleton | .02 | .10 |
| 262 | Zane Smith | .01 | .05 | 350 | Mike Marshall | .01 | .05 | 438 | Jose Oquendo | .01 | .05 |
| 263 | Charlie Puleo | .01 | .05 | 351 | Kirk Gibson | .02 | .10 | 439 | Tim Jones | .01 | .05 |
| 264 | Derek Lilliquist RC | .02 | .10 | 352 | Mike Davis | .01 | .05 | 440 | Pedro Guerrero | .02 | .10 |
| 265 | Paul Assenmacher | .01 | .05 | 353 | Bryn Smith | .01 | .05 | 441 | Milt Thompson | .01 | .05 |
| 266 | John Smoltz RC | .60 | 1.50 | 354 | Pascual Perez | .01 | .05 | 442 | Willie McGee | .02 | .10 |
| 267 | Tom Glavine | .08 | .25 | 355 | Kevin Gross | .01 | .05 | 443 | Vince Coleman | .01 | .05 |
| 268 | Steve Avery RC | .08 | .25 | 356 | Andy McGaffigan | .01 | .05 | 444 | Tom Brunansky | .01 | .05 |
| 269 | Pete Smith | .01 | .05 | 357 | Brian Holman RC | .02 | .10 | 445 | Walt Terrell | .01 | .05 |
| 270 | Jody Davis | .01 | .05 | 358 | Dave Wainhouse RC | .02 | .10 | 446 | Eric Show | .01 | .05 |
| 271 | Bruce Benedict | .01 | .05 | 359 | Dennis Martinez | .02 | .10 | 447 | Mark Davis | .01 | .05 |
| 272 | Andres Thomas | .01 | .05 | 360 | Tim Burke | .01 | .05 | 448 | Andy Benes RC | .15 | .40 |
| 273 | Gerald Perry | .01 | .05 | 361 | Nelson Santovenia | .01 | .05 | 449 | Ed Whitson | .01 | .05 |
| 274 | Ron Gant | .02 | .10 | 362 | Tim Wallach | .01 | .05 | 450 | Dennis Rasmussen | .01 | .05 |
| 275 | Darrell Evans | .02 | .10 | 363 | Spike Owen | .01 | .05 | 451 | Bruce Hurst | .01 | .05 |
| 276 | Dale Murphy | .05 | .15 | 364 | Rex Hudler | .01 | .05 | 452 | Pat Clements | .01 | .05 |
| 277 | Dion James | .01 | .05 | 365 | Andres Galarraga | .02 | .10 | 453 | Benito Santiago | .02 | .10 |
| 278 | Lonnie Smith | .01 | .05 | 366 | Otis Nixon | .02 | .10 | 454 | Sandy Alomar Jr. RC | .15 | .40 |
| 279 | Geronimo Berroa | .01 | .05 | 367 | Hubie Brooks | .01 | .05 | 455 | Garry Templeton | .02 | .10 |
| 280 | Steve Wilson RC | .02 | .10 | 368 | Mike Aldrete | .01 | .05 | 456 | Jack Clark | .02 | .10 |
| 281 | Rick Sutcliffe | .02 | .10 | 369 | Tim Raines | .02 | .10 | 457 | Tim Flannery | .01 | .05 |
| 282 | Kevin Coffman | .01 | .05 | 370 | Dave Martinez | .01 | .05 | 458 | Roberto Alomar | .08 | .25 |
| 283 | Mitch Williams | .01 | .05 | 371 | Bob Ojeda | .01 | .05 | 459 | Carmelo Martinez | .01 | .05 |
| 284 | Greg Maddux | .20 | .50 | 372 | Ron Darling | .02 | .10 | 460 | John Kruk | .02 | .10 |
| 285 | Paul Kilgus | .01 | .05 | 373 | Wally Whitehurst RC | .02 | .10 | 461 | Tony Gwynn | .10 | .25 |
| 286 | Mike Harkey RC | .02 | .10 | 374 | Randy Myers | .02 | .10 | 462 | Jerald Clark RC | .02 | .10 |
| 287 | Lloyd McClendon | .01 | .05 | 375 | David Cone | .02 | .10 | 463 | Don Robinson | .01 | .05 |
| 288 | Damon Berryhill | .01 | .05 | 376 | Dwight Gooden | .02 | .10 | 464 | Craig Lefferts | .01 | .05 |
| 289 | Ty Griffin | .01 | .05 | 377 | Sid Fernandez | .01 | .05 | 465 | Kelly Downs | .01 | .05 |
| 290 | Ryne Sandberg | .15 | .40 | 378 | Dave Proctor | .01 | .05 | 466 | Rick Reuschel | .02 | .10 |
| 291 | Mark Grace | .08 | .25 | 379 | Gary Carter | .02 | .10 | 467 | Scott Garrelts | .01 | .05 |

|  | | |
|---|---|---|
| 468 Wil Tejada | .01 | .05 |
| 469 Kirt Manwaring | .01 | .05 |
| 470 Terry Kennedy | .01 | .05 |
| 471 Jose Uribe | .01 | .05 |
| 472 Royce Clayton RC | .15 | .40 |
| 473 Robby Thompson | .01 | .05 |
| 474 Kevin Mitchell | .02 | .10 |
| 475 Ernie Riles | .01 | .05 |
| 476 Will Clark | .05 | .15 |
| 477 Donell Nixon | .01 | .05 |
| 478 Candy Maldonado | .01 | .05 |
| 479 Tracy Jones | .01 | .05 |
| 480 Brett Butler | .02 | .10 |
| 481 Checklist 1-121 | .01 | .05 |
| 482 Checklist 122-242 | .01 | .05 |
| 483 Checklist 243-363 | .01 | .05 |
| 484 Checklist 364-484 | .01 | .05 |

## 1990 Bowman

| | | |
|---|---|---|
| COMPLETE SET (528) | 10.00 | 25.00 |
| COMP.FACT.SET (528) | 10.00 | 25.00 |
| 1 Tommy Greene RC | .02 | .10 |
| 2 Tom Glavine | .05 | .15 |
| 3 Andy Nezelek | .01 | .05 |
| 4 Mike Stanton RC | .08 | .25 |
| 5 Rick Luecken RC | .01 | .05 |
| 6 Kent Mercker RC | .08 | .25 |
| 7 Derek Lilliquist | .01 | .05 |
| 8 Charlie Leibrandt | .01 | .05 |
| 9 Steve Avery | .01 | .05 |
| 10 John Smoltz | .08 | .25 |
| 11 Mark Lemke | .01 | .05 |
| 12 Lonnie Smith | .01 | .05 |
| 13 Oddibe McDowell | .01 | .05 |
| 14 Tyler Houston RC | .08 | .25 |
| 15 Jeff Blauser | .01 | .05 |
| 16 Ernie Whitt | .01 | .05 |
| 17 Alexis Infante | .01 | .05 |
| 18 Jim Presley | .01 | .05 |
| 19 Dale Murphy | .05 | .15 |
| 20 Nick Esasky | .01 | .05 |
| 21 Rick Sutcliffe | .02 | .10 |
| 22 Mike Bielecki | .01 | .05 |
| 23 Steve Wilson | .01 | .05 |
| 24 Kevin Blankenship | .01 | .05 |
| 25 Mitch Williams | .01 | .05 |
| 26 Dean Wilkins RC | .01 | .05 |
| 27 Greg Maddux | .15 | .40 |
| 28 Mike Harkey | .01 | .05 |
| 29 Mark Grace | .05 | .15 |
| 30 Ryne Sandberg | .15 | .40 |
| 31 Greg Smith RC | .01 | .05 |
| 32 Dwight Smith | .01 | .05 |
| 33 Damon Berryhill | .01 | .05 |
| 34 Earl Cunningham UER RC | .02 | .10 |
| 35 Jerome Walton | .01 | .05 |
| 36 Lloyd McClendon | .01 | .05 |
| 37 Ty Griffin | .01 | .05 |
| 38 Shawon Dunston | .01 | .05 |
| 39 Andre Dawson | .02 | .10 |
| 40 Luis Salazar | .01 | .05 |
| 41 Tim Layana RC | .01 | .05 |
| 42 Rob Dibble | .02 | .10 |
| 43 Tom Browning | .01 | .05 |
| 44 Danny Jackson | .01 | .05 |
| 45 Jose Rijo | .01 | .05 |
| 46 Scott Scudder | .01 | .05 |
| 47 Randy Myers UER (Career ERA .274, should be 2.74) | .02 | .10 |
| 48 Brian Lane RC | .02 | .10 |
| 49 Paul O'Neill | .05 | .15 |
| 50 Barry Larkin | .05 | .15 |
| 51 Reggie Jefferson RC | .08 | .25 |

| | | |
|---|---|---|
| 52 Jeff Branson RC | .02 | .10 |
| 53 Chris Sabo | .01 | .05 |
| 54 Joe Oliver | .01 | .05 |
| 55 Todd Benzinger | .01 | .05 |
| 56 Rolando Roomes | .01 | .05 |
| 57 Hal Morris | .01 | .05 |
| 58 Eric Davis | .02 | .10 |
| 59 Scott Bryant RC | .01 | .05 |
| 60 Ken Griffey Sr. | .01 | .05 |
| 61 Darryl Kile RC | .20 | .50 |
| 62 Dave Smith | .01 | .05 |
| 63 Mark Portugal | .01 | .05 |
| 64 Jeff Juden RC | .02 | .10 |
| 65 Bill Gullickson | .01 | .05 |
| 66 Danny Darwin | .01 | .05 |
| 67 Larry Andersen | .01 | .05 |
| 68 Jose Cano RC | .01 | .05 |
| 69 Dan Schatzeder | .01 | .05 |
| 70 Jim Deshaies | .01 | .05 |
| 71 Mike Scott | .01 | .05 |
| 72 Gerald Young | .01 | .05 |
| 73 Ken Caminiti | .02 | .10 |
| 74 Ken Oberkfell | .01 | .05 |
| 75 Dave Rohde RC | .01 | .05 |
| 76 Bill Doran | .01 | .05 |
| 77 Andujar Cedeno RC | .02 | .10 |
| 78 Craig Biggio | .08 | .25 |
| 79 Karl Rhodes RC | .08 | .25 |
| 80 Glenn Davis | .01 | .05 |
| 81 Eric Anthony RC | .02 | .10 |
| 82 John Wetteland | .08 | .25 |
| 83 Jay Howell | .01 | .05 |
| 84 Orel Hershiser | .02 | .10 |
| 85 Tim Belcher | .01 | .05 |
| 86 Kiki Jones RC | .05 | .15 |
| 87 Mike Hartley RC | .01 | .05 |
| 88 Ramon Martinez | .01 | .05 |
| 89 Mike Scioscia | .01 | .05 |
| 90 Willie Randolph | .02 | .10 |
| 91 Juan Samuel | .01 | .05 |
| 92 Jose Offerman RC | .08 | .25 |
| 93 Dave Hansen RC | .08 | .25 |
| 94 Jeff Hamilton | .01 | .05 |
| 95 Alfredo Griffin | .01 | .05 |
| 96 Tom Goodwin RC | .08 | .25 |
| 97 Kirk Gibson | .02 | .10 |
| 98 Jose Vizcaino RC | .08 | .25 |
| 99 Kal Daniels | .01 | .05 |
| 100 Hubie Brooks | .01 | .05 |
| 101 Eddie Murray | .08 | .25 |
| 102 Dennis Boyd | .01 | .05 |
| 103 Tim Burke | .01 | .05 |
| 104 Bill Sampen RC | .01 | .05 |
| 105 Brett Gideon | .01 | .05 |
| 106 Mark Gardner RC | .02 | .10 |
| 107 Howard Farmer RC | .01 | .05 |
| 108 Mel Rojas RC | .02 | .10 |
| 109 Kevin Gross | .01 | .05 |
| 110 Dave Schmidt | .01 | .05 |
| 111 Dennis Martinez | .02 | .10 |
| 112 Jerry Goff RC | .01 | .05 |
| 113 Andres Galarraga | .02 | .10 |
| 114 Tim Wallach | .01 | .05 |
| 115 Marquis Grissom RC | .20 | .50 |
| 116 Spike Owen | .01 | .05 |
| 117 Larry Walker RC | .40 | 1.00 |
| 118 Tim Raines | .08 | .25 |
| 119 Delino DeShields RC | .08 | .25 |
| 120 Tom Foley | .01 | .05 |
| 121 Dave Martinez | .01 | .05 |
| 122 Frank Viola UER (Career ERA .384 should be 3.84) | .01 | .05 |
| 123 Julio Valera RC | .01 | .05 |
| 124 Alejandro Pena | .01 | .05 |
| 125 David Cone | .02 | .10 |
| 126 Dwight Gooden | .02 | .10 |
| 127 Kevin D. Brown RC | .01 | .05 |
| 128 John Franco | .01 | .05 |
| 129 Terry Bross RC | .01 | .05 |
| 130 Blaine Beatty RC | .01 | .05 |
| 131 Sid Fernandez | .01 | .05 |
| 132 Mike Marshall | .01 | .05 |
| 133 Howard Johnson | .02 | .10 |
| 134 Jaime Roseboro RC | .01 | .05 |
| 135 Alan Zinter RC | .02 | .10 |
| 136 Keith Miller | .01 | .05 |
| 137 Kevin Elster | .01 | .05 |

| | | |
|---|---|---|
| 138 Kevin McReynolds | .01 | .05 |
| 139 Barry Lyons | .01 | .05 |
| 140 Gregg Jefferies | .02 | .10 |
| 141 Darryl Strawberry | .02 | .10 |
| 142 Todd Hundley RC | .08 | .25 |
| 143 Scott Service | .01 | .05 |
| 144 Chuck Malone RC | .01 | .05 |
| 145 Steve Ontiveros | .01 | .05 |
| 146 Roger McDowell | .01 | .05 |
| 147 Ken Howell | .01 | .05 |
| 148 Pat Combs | .01 | .05 |
| 149 Jeff Parrett | .01 | .05 |
| 150 Chuck McElroy RC | .02 | .10 |
| 151 Jason Grimsley RC | .02 | .10 |
| 152 Len Dykstra | .02 | .10 |
| 153 Mickey Morandini RC | .08 | .25 |
| 154 John Kruk | .02 | .10 |
| 155 Dickie Thon | .01 | .05 |
| 156 Ricky Jordan | .01 | .05 |
| 157 Jeff Jackson RC | .02 | .10 |
| 158 Darren Daulton | .02 | .10 |
| 159 Tom Herr | .01 | .05 |
| 160 Von Hayes | .01 | .05 |
| 161 Dave Hollins RC | .08 | .25 |
| 162 Carmelo Martinez | .01 | .05 |
| 163 Bob Walk | .01 | .05 |
| 164 Doug Drabek | .02 | .10 |
| 165 Walt Terrell | .01 | .05 |
| 166 Bill Landrum | .01 | .05 |
| 167 Scott Ruskin RC | .01 | .05 |
| 168 Bob Patterson | .01 | .05 |
| 169 Bobby Bonilla | .02 | .10 |
| 170 Jose Lind | .01 | .05 |
| 171 Andy Van Slyke | .05 | .15 |
| 172 Mike LaValliere | .01 | .05 |
| 173 Willie Greene RC | .02 | .10 |
| 174 Jay Bell | .02 | .10 |
| 175 Sid Bream | .01 | .05 |
| 176 Tom Prince | .01 | .05 |
| 177 Wally Backman | .01 | .05 |
| 178 Moises Alou RC | .30 | .75 |
| 179 Steve Carter | .01 | .05 |
| 180 Gary Redus | .01 | .05 |
| 181 Barry Bonds | .40 | 1.00 |
| 182 Don Slaught UER (Card back shows headings for a | .01 | .05 |
| 183 Joe Magrane | .01 | .05 |
| 184 Bryn Smith | .01 | .05 |
| 185 Todd Worrell | .01 | .05 |
| 186 Jose DeLeon | .01 | .05 |
| 187 Frank DiPino | .01 | .05 |
| 188 John Tudor | .01 | .05 |
| 189 Howard Hilton RC | .01 | .05 |
| 190 John Ericks RC | .01 | .05 |
| 191 Ken Dayley | .01 | .05 |
| 192 Ray Lankford RC | .20 | .50 |
| 193 Todd Zeile | .02 | .10 |
| 194 Willie McGee | .02 | .10 |
| 195 Ozzie Smith | .15 | .40 |
| 196 Milt Thompson | .01 | .05 |
| 197 Terry Pendleton | .02 | .10 |
| 198 Vince Coleman | .02 | .10 |
| 199 Paul Coleman RC | .01 | .05 |
| 200 Jose Oquendo | .01 | .05 |
| 201 Pedro Guerrero | .02 | .10 |
| 202 Tom Brunansky | .01 | .05 |
| 203 Roger Smithberg RC | .01 | .05 |
| 204 Eddie Whitson | .01 | .05 |
| 205 Dennis Rasmussen | .01 | .05 |
| 206 Craig Lefferts | .01 | .05 |
| 207 Andy Benes | .02 | .10 |
| 208 Bruce Hurst | .01 | .05 |
| 209 Eric Show | .01 | .05 |
| 210 Rafael Valdez RC | .01 | .05 |
| 211 Joey Cora | .02 | .10 |
| 212 Thomas Howard | .01 | .05 |
| 213 Rob Nelson | .01 | .05 |
| 214 Jack Clark | .02 | .10 |
| 215 Garry Templeton | .01 | .05 |
| 216 Fred Lynn | .02 | .10 |
| 217 Tony Gwynn | .10 | .30 |
| 218 Benito Santiago | .02 | .10 |
| 219 Mike Pagliarulo | .01 | .05 |
| 220 Joe Carter | .02 | .10 |
| 221 Roberto Alomar | .05 | .15 |
| 222 Bip Roberts | .01 | .05 |
| 223 Rick Reuschel | .01 | .05 |

|  | | |
|---|---|---|
| 224 Russ Swan RC | .01 | .05 |
| 225 Eric Gunderson RC | .01 | .05 |
| 226 Steve Bedrosian | .01 | .05 |
| 227 Mike Remlinger RC | .01 | .05 |
| 228 Scott Garrelts | .01 | .05 |
| 229 Ernie Camacho | .01 | .05 |
| 230 Andres Santana RC | .02 | .10 |
| 231 Will Clark | .05 | .15 |
| 232 Kevin Mitchell | .01 | .05 |
| 233 Robby Thompson | .01 | .05 |
| 234 Bill Bathe | .01 | .05 |
| 235 Tony Perezchica | .01 | .05 |
| 236 Gary Carter | .02 | .10 |
| 237 Brett Butler | .02 | .10 |
| 238 Matt Williams | .02 | .10 |
| 239 Ernie Riles | .01 | .05 |
| 240 Kevin Bass | .01 | .05 |
| 241 Terry Kennedy | .01 | .05 |
| 242 Steve Hosey RC | .02 | .10 |
| 243 Ben McDonald RC | .08 | .25 |
| 244 Jeff Ballard | .01 | .05 |
| 245 Joe Price | .01 | .05 |
| 246 Curt Schilling | .40 | 1.00 |
| 247 Pete Harnisch | .01 | .05 |
| 248 Mark Williamson | .01 | .05 |
| 249 Gregg Olson | .02 | .10 |
| 250 Chris Myers | .01 | .05 |
| 251A David Segui ERR | .20 | .50 |
| 251B David Segui COR RC | .20 | .50 |
| 252 Joe Orsulak | .01 | .05 |
| 253 Craig Worthington | .01 | .05 |
| 254 Mickey Tettleton | .01 | .05 |
| 255 Cal Ripken | .30 | .75 |
| 256 Bill Ripken | .01 | .05 |
| 257 Randy Milligan | .01 | .05 |
| 258 Brady Anderson | .02 | .10 |
| 259 Chris Hoiles RC | .08 | .25 |
| 260 Mike Devereaux | .01 | .05 |
| 261 Phil Bradley | .01 | .05 |
| 262 Leo Gomez RC | .02 | .10 |
| 263 Lee Smith | .02 | .10 |
| 264 Mike Rochford | .01 | .05 |
| 265 Jeff Reardon | .02 | .10 |
| 266 Wes Gardner | .01 | .05 |
| 267 Mike Boddicker | .01 | .05 |
| 268 Roger Clemens | .40 | 1.00 |
| 269 Rob Murphy | .01 | .05 |
| 270 Mickey Pina RC | .01 | .05 |
| 271 Tony Pena | .01 | .05 |
| 272 Jody Reed | .01 | .05 |
| 273 Kevin Romine | .01 | .05 |
| 274 Mike Greenwell | .01 | .05 |
| 275 Mo Vaughn RC | .40 | 1.00 |
| 226 Danny Heep | .01 | .05 |
| 277 Scott Cooper RC | .02 | .10 |
| 278 Greg Blosser RC | .02 | .10 |
| 279 Dwight Evans UER | .01 | .05 |
| (* by 1990 Team Breakdown) | | |
| 280 Ellis Burks | .05 | .15 |
| 281 Wade Boggs | .05 | .15 |
| 282 Marty Barrett | .01 | .05 |
| 283 Kirk McCaskill | .01 | .05 |
| 284 Mark Langston | .01 | .05 |
| 285 Bert Blyleven | .02 | .10 |
| 286 Mike Fetters RC | .08 | .25 |
| 287 Kyle Abbott RC | .01 | .05 |
| 288 Jim Abbott | .05 | .15 |
| 289 Chuck Finley | .02 | .10 |
| 290 Gary DiSarcina RC | .08 | .25 |
| 291 Dick Schofield | .01 | .05 |
| 292 Devon White | .02 | .10 |
| 293 Bobby Rose | .01 | .05 |
| 294 Brian Downing | .01 | .05 |
| 295 Lance Parrish | .01 | .05 |
| 296 Jack Howell | .01 | .05 |
| 297 Claudell Washington | .01 | .05 |
| 298 John Orton RC | .02 | .10 |
| 299 Wally Joyner | .02 | .10 |
| 300 Lee Stevens | .02 | .10 |
| 301 Chili Davis | .02 | .10 |
| 302 Johnny Ray | .01 | .05 |
| 303 Greg Hibbard RC | .02 | .10 |
| 304 Eric King | .01 | .05 |
| 305 Jack McDowell | .05 | .15 |
| 306 Bobby Thigpen | .01 | .05 |
| 307 Adam Peterson | .01 | .05 |
| 308 Scott Radinsky RC | .08 | .25 |
| 309 Wayne Edwards RC | .01 | .05 |
| 310 Melido Perez | .01 | .05 |
| 311 Robin Ventura | .08 | .25 |
| 312 Sammy Sosa RC | 1.25 | 3.00 |
| 313 Dan Pasqua | .01 | .05 |
| 314 Carlton Fisk | .05 | .15 |
| 315 Ozzie Guillen | .02 | .10 |
| 316 Ivan Calderon | .01 | .05 |
| 317 Daryl Boston | .01 | .05 |
| 318 Craig Grebeck RC | .08 | .25 |
| 319 Scott Fletcher | .01 | .05 |
| 320 Frank Thomas RC | .75 | 2.00 |
| 321 Steve Lyons | .01 | .05 |
| 322 Carlos Martinez | .01 | .05 |
| 323 Joe Skalski | .01 | .05 |
| 324 Tom Candiotti | .01 | .05 |
| 325 Greg Swindell | .01 | .05 |
| 326 Steve Olin RC | .08 | .25 |
| 327 Kevin Wickander | .01 | .05 |
| 328 Doug Jones | .01 | .05 |
| 329 Jeff Shaw | .01 | .05 |
| 330 Kevin Bearse RC | .01 | .05 |
| 331 Dion James | .01 | .05 |
| 332 Jerry Browne | .01 | .05 |
| 333 Albert Belle | .08 | .25 |
| 334 Felix Fermin | .01 | .05 |
| 335 Candy Maldonado | .01 | .05 |
| 336 Cory Snyder | .01 | .05 |
| 337 Sandy Alomar Jr. | .02 | .10 |
| 338 Mark Lewis | .01 | .05 |
| 339 Carlos Baerga RC | .08 | .25 |
| 340 Chris James | .01 | .05 |
| 341 Brook Jacoby | .01 | .05 |
| 342 Keith Hernandez | .02 | .10 |
| 343 Frank Tanana | .01 | .05 |
| 344 Scott Aldred RC | .02 | .10 |
| 345 Mike Henneman | .01 | .05 |
| 346 Steve Wapnick RC | .01 | .05 |
| 347 Greg Gohr RC | .02 | .10 |
| 348 Eric Stone RC | .01 | .05 |
| 349 Brian DuBois RC | .01 | .05 |
| 350 Kevin Ritz RC | .01 | .05 |
| 351 Rico Brogna | .08 | .25 |
| 352 Mike Heath | .01 | .05 |
| 353 Alan Trammell | .02 | .10 |
| 354 Chet Lemon | .01 | .05 |
| 355 Dave Bergman | .01 | .05 |
| 356 Lou Whitaker | .02 | .10 |
| 357 Cecil Fielder UER | .02 | .10 |
| 358 Milt Cuyler RC | .02 | .10 |
| 359 Tony Phillips | .01 | .05 |
| 360 Travis Fryman RC | .20 | .50 |
| 361 Ed Romero | .01 | .05 |
| 362 Lloyd Moseby | .01 | .05 |
| 363 Mark Gubicza | .01 | .05 |
| 364 Bret Saberhagen | .02 | .10 |
| 365 Tom Gordon | .02 | .10 |
| 366 Steve Farr | .01 | .05 |
| 367 Kevin Appier | .02 | .10 |
| 368 Storm Davis | .01 | .05 |
| 369 Mark Davis | .01 | .05 |
| 370 Jeff Montgomery | .02 | .10 |
| 371 Frank White | .02 | .10 |
| 372 Brent Mayne RC | .08 | .25 |
| 373 Bob Boone | .02 | .10 |
| 374 Jim Eisenreich | .01 | .05 |
| 375 Danny Tartabull | .01 | .05 |
| 376 Kurt Stillwell | .01 | .05 |
| 377 Bill Pecota | .01 | .05 |
| 378 Bo Jackson | .08 | .25 |
| 379 Bob Hamelin RC | .08 | .25 |
| 380 Kevin Seitzer | .01 | .05 |
| 381 Rey Palacios | .01 | .05 |
| 382 George Brett | .25 | .60 |
| 383 Gerald Perry | .01 | .05 |
| 384 Teddy Higuera | .01 | .05 |
| 385 Tom Filer | .01 | .05 |
| 386 Dan Plesac | .01 | .05 |
| 387 Cal Eldred RC | .08 | .25 |
| 388 Jaime Navarro | .01 | .05 |
| 389 Chris Bosio | .01 | .05 |
| 390 Randy Veres | .01 | .05 |
| 391 Gary Sheffield | .08 | .25 |
| 392 George Canale RC | .01 | .05 |
| 393 B.J. Surhoff | .02 | .10 |
| 394 Tim McIntosh RC | .01 | .05 |
| 395 Greg Brock | .01 | .05 |
| 396 Greg Vaughn | .01 | .05 |
| 397 Darryl Hamilton | .01 | .05 |
| 398 Dave Parker | .02 | .10 |
| 399 Paul Molitor | .02 | .10 |
| 400 Jim Gantner | .01 | .05 |
| 401 Rob Deer | .01 | .05 |
| 402 Billy Spiers | .01 | .05 |
| 403 Glenn Braggs | .01 | .05 |
| 404 Robin Yount | .15 | .40 |
| 405 Rick Aguilera | .02 | .10 |
| 406 Johnny Ard | .01 | .05 |
| 407 Kevin Tapani RC | .08 | .25 |
| 408 Park Pittman RC | .01 | .05 |
| 409 Allan Anderson | .01 | .05 |
| 410 Juan Berenguer | .01 | .05 |
| 411 Willie Banks RC | .02 | .10 |
| 412 Rich Yett | .01 | .05 |
| 413 Dave West | .01 | .05 |
| 414 Greg Gagne | .01 | .05 |
| 415 Chuck Knoblauch RC | .20 | .50 |
| 416 Randy Bush | .01 | .05 |
| 417 Gary Gaetti | .02 | .10 |
| 418 Kent Hrbek | .02 | .10 |
| 419 Al Newman | .01 | .05 |
| 420 Danny Gladden | .01 | .05 |
| 421 Paul Sorrento RC | .08 | .25 |
| 422 Derek Parks RC | .02 | .10 |
| 423 Scott Leius RC | .02 | .10 |
| 424 Kirby Puckett | .08 | .25 |
| 425 Willie Smith | .01 | .05 |
| 426 Dave Righetti | .01 | .05 |
| 427 Jeff D. Robinson | .01 | .05 |
| 428 Alan Mills RC | .02 | .10 |
| 429 Tim Leary | .01 | .05 |
| 430 Pascual Perez | .01 | .05 |
| 431 Alvaro Espinoza | .01 | .05 |
| 432 Dave Winfield | .02 | .10 |
| 433 Jesse Barfield | .01 | .05 |
| 434 Randy Velarde | .01 | .05 |
| 435 Rick Cerone | .01 | .05 |
| 436 Steve Balboni | .01 | .05 |
| 437 Mel Hall | .01 | .05 |
| 438 Bob Geren | .01 | .05 |
| 439 Bernie Williams RC | .60 | 1.50 |
| 440 Kevin Maas RC | .08 | .25 |
| 441 Mike Blowers RC | .02 | .10 |
| 442 Steve Sax | .01 | .05 |
| 443 Don Mattingly | .25 | .60 |
| 444 Roberto Kelly | .05 | .15 |
| 445 Mike Moore | .01 | .05 |
| 446 Reggie Harris RC | .01 | .05 |
| 447 Scott Sanderson | .01 | .05 |
| 448 Dave Otto | .01 | .05 |
| 449 Dave Stewart | .02 | .10 |
| 450 Rick Honeycutt | .01 | .05 |
| 451 Dennis Eckersley | .02 | .10 |
| 452 Carney Lansford | .02 | .10 |
| 453 Scott Hemond RC | .02 | .10 |
| 454 Mark McGwire | .40 | 1.00 |
| 455 Felix Jose | .01 | .05 |
| 456 Terry Steinbach | .01 | .05 |
| 457 Rickey Henderson | .08 | .25 |
| 458 Dave Henderson | .01 | .05 |
| 459 Mike Gallego | .01 | .05 |
| 460 Jose Canseco | .05 | .15 |
| 461 Walt Weiss | .01 | .05 |
| 462 Ken Phelps | .01 | .05 |
| 463 Darren Lewis RC | .02 | .10 |
| 464 Ron Hassey | .01 | .05 |
| 465 Roger Salkeld RC | .01 | .05 |
| 466 Scott Bankhead | .01 | .05 |
| 467 Keith Comstock | .01 | .05 |
| 468 Randy Johnson | .20 | .50 |
| 469 Erik Hanson | .01 | .05 |
| 470 Mike Schooler | .01 | .05 |
| 471 Gary Eave RC | .01 | .05 |
| 472 Jeffrey Leonard | .01 | .05 |
| 473 Dave Valle | .01 | .05 |
| 474 Omar Vizquel | .08 | .25 |
| 475 Pete O'Brien | .01 | .05 |
| 476 Henry Cotto | .01 | .05 |
| 477 Jay Buhner | .02 | .10 |
| 478 Harold Reynolds | .02 | .10 |
| 479 Alvin Davis | .01 | .05 |
| 480 Darnell Coles | .01 | .05 |
| 481 Ken Griffey Jr. | .30 | .75 |
| 482 Greg Briley | .01 | .05 |
| 483 Scott Bradley | .01 | .05 |
| 484 Tino Martinez | .20 | .50 |

| | | |
|---|---|---|
| 485 Jeff Russell | .01 | .05 |
| 486 Nolan Ryan | .40 | 1.00 |
| 487 Robb Nen RC | .20 | .50 |
| 488 Kevin Brown | .02 | .10 |
| 489 Brian Bohanon RC | .02 | .10 |
| 490 Ruben Sierra | .02 | .10 |
| 491 Pete Incaviglia | .01 | .05 |
| 492 Juan Gonzalez RC | .40 | 1.00 |
| 493 Steve Buechele | .01 | .05 |
| 494 Scott Coolbaugh | .01 | .05 |
| 495 Geno Petralli | .01 | .05 |
| 496 Rafael Palmeiro | .05 | .15 |
| 497 Julio Franco | .02 | .10 |
| 498 Gary Pettis | .01 | .05 |
| 499 Donald Harris RC | .01 | .05 |
| 500 Monty Fariss | .01 | .05 |
| 501 Harold Baines | .02 | .10 |
| 502 Cecil Espy | .01 | .05 |
| 503 Jack Daugherty RC | .01 | .05 |
| 504 Willie Blair RC | .02 | .10 |
| 505 Dave Stieb | .02 | .10 |
| 506 Tom Henke | .01 | .05 |
| 507 John Cerutti | .01 | .05 |
| 508 Paul Kilgus | .01 | .05 |
| 509 Jimmy Key | .02 | .10 |
| 510 John Olerud RC | .40 | 1.00 |
| 511 Ed Sprague | .02 | .10 |
| 512 Manuel Lee | .01 | .05 |
| 513 Fred McGriff | .08 | .25 |
| 514 Glenallen Hill | .01 | .05 |
| 515 George Bell | .05 | .15 |
| 516 Mookie Wilson | .02 | .10 |
| 517 Luis Sojo RC | .08 | .25 |
| 518 Nelson Liriano | .01 | .05 |
| 519 Kelly Gruber | .01 | .05 |
| 520 Greg Myers | .01 | .05 |
| 521 Pat Borders | .01 | .05 |
| 522 Junior Felix | .01 | .05 |
| 523 Eddie Zosky RC | .02 | .10 |
| 524 Tony Fernandez | .01 | .05 |
| 525 Checklist 1-132 UER | | |
| (No copyright mark | | |
| on the ba | .01 | .05 |
| 526 Checklist 133-264 | .01 | .05 |
| 527 Checklist 265-396 | .01 | .05 |
| 528 Checklist 397-528 | .01 | .05 |

## 1991 Bowman

| | | |
|---|---|---|
| COMPLETE SET (704) | 15.00 | 40.00 |
| COMP.FACT.SET (704) | 15.00 | 40.00 |
| 1 Rod Carew I | .05 | .15 |
| 2 Rod Carew II | .05 | .15 |
| 3 Rod Carew III | .05 | .15 |
| 4 Rod Carew IV | .05 | .15 |
| 5 Rod Carew V | .05 | .15 |
| 6 Willie Fraser | .01 | .05 |
| 7 John Olerud | .02 | .10 |
| 8 William Suero RC | .01 | .05 |
| 9 Roberto Alomar | .05 | .15 |
| 10 Todd Stottlemyre | .01 | .05 |
| 11 Joe Carter | .02 | .10 |
| 12 Steve Karsay RC | .20 | .50 |
| 13 Mark Whiten | .05 | .15 |
| 14 Pat Borders | .01 | .05 |
| 15 Mike Timlin RC | .20 | .50 |
| 16 Tom Henke | .01 | .05 |
| 17 Eddie Zosky | .05 | .15 |
| 18 Kelly Gruber | .01 | .05 |
| 19 Jimmy Key | .02 | .10 |
| 20 Jerry Schunk RC | .05 | .15 |
| 21 Manuel Lee | .01 | .05 |
| 22 Dave Stieb | .01 | .05 |
| 23 Pat Hentgen RC | .20 | .50 |
| 24 Glenallen Hill | .01 | .05 |

| | | |
|---|---|---|
| 25 Rene Gonzales | .01 | .05 |
| 26 Ed Sprague | .01 | .05 |
| 27 Ken Dayley | .01 | .05 |
| 28 Pat Tabler | .01 | .05 |
| 29 Denis Boucher RC | .05 | .15 |
| 30 Devon White | .02 | .10 |
| 31 Dante Bichette | .02 | .10 |
| 32 Paul Molitor | .01 | .05 |
| 33 Greg Vaughn | .01 | .05 |
| 34 Dan Plesac | .01 | .05 |
| 35 Chris George RC | .05 | .15 |
| 36 Tim McIntosh | .01 | .05 |
| 37 Franklin Stubbs | .01 | .05 |
| 38 Bo Dodson RC | .05 | .15 |
| 39 Ron Robinson | .01 | .05 |
| 40 Ed Nunez | .01 | .05 |
| 41 Greg Brock | .01 | .05 |
| 42 Jaime Navarro | .01 | .05 |
| 43 Chris Bosio | .01 | .05 |
| 44 B.J. Surhoff | .02 | .10 |
| 45 Chris Johnson RC | .01 | .05 |
| 46 Willie Randolph | .02 | .10 |
| 47 Narciso Elvira RC | .01 | .05 |
| 48 Jim Gantner | .01 | .05 |
| 49 Kevin Brown | .01 | .05 |
| 50 Julio Machado RC | .01 | .05 |
| 51 Chuck Crim | .01 | .05 |
| 52 Gary Sheffield | .02 | .10 |
| 53 Angel Miranda RC | .05 | .15 |
| 54 Ted Higuera | .01 | .05 |
| 55 Robin Yount | .15 | .40 |
| 56 Cal Eldred | .05 | .15 |
| 57 Sandy Alomar Jr. | .01 | .05 |
| 58 Greg Swindell | .01 | .05 |
| 59 Brook Jacoby | .01 | .05 |
| 60 Efrain Valdez RC | .01 | .05 |
| 61 Ever Magallanes RC | .01 | .05 |
| 62 Tom Candiotti | .01 | .05 |
| 63 Eric King | .01 | .05 |
| 64 Alex Cole | .01 | .05 |
| 65 Charles Nagy | .01 | .05 |
| 66 Mitch Webster | .01 | .05 |
| 67 Chris James | .01 | .05 |
| 68 Jim Thome RC | 1.50 | 4.00 |
| 69 Carlos Baerga | .01 | .05 |
| 70 Mark Lewis | .01 | .05 |
| 71 Jerry Browne | .01 | .05 |
| 72 Jesse Orosco | .01 | .05 |
| 73 Mike Huff | .01 | .05 |
| 74 Jose Escobar RC | .01 | .05 |
| 75 Jeff Manto | .01 | .05 |
| 76 Turner Ward RC | .05 | .15 |
| 77 Doug Jones | .01 | .05 |
| 78 Bruce Egloff RC | .01 | .05 |
| 79 Tim Costo RC | .05 | .15 |
| 80 Beau Allred | .01 | .05 |
| 81 Albert Belle | .02 | .10 |
| 82 John Farrell | .01 | .05 |
| 83 Glenn Davis | .01 | .05 |
| 84 Joe Orsulak | .01 | .05 |
| 85 Mark Williamson | .01 | .05 |
| 86 Ben McDonald | .01 | .05 |
| 87 Billy Ripken | .01 | .05 |
| 88 Leo Gomez | .02 | .10 |
| 89 Bob Melvin | .01 | .05 |
| 90 Jeff M. Robinson | .01 | .05 |
| 91 Jose Mesa | .01 | .05 |
| 92 Gregg Olson | .01 | .05 |
| 93 Mike Devereaux | .01 | .05 |
| 94 Luis Mercedes RC | .05 | .15 |
| 95 Arthur Rhodes RC | .20 | .50 |
| 96 Juan Bell | .01 | .05 |
| 97 Mike Mussina RC | 1.50 | 4.00 |
| 98 Jeff Ballard | .01 | .05 |
| 99 Chris Hoiles | .01 | .05 |
| 100 Brady Anderson | .02 | .10 |
| 101 Bob Milacki | .01 | .05 |
| 102 David Segui | .01 | .05 |
| 103 Dwight Evans | .05 | .15 |
| 104 Cal Ripken | .30 | .75 |
| 105 Mike Linskey RC | .05 | .15 |
| 106 Jeff Tackett RC | .05 | .15 |
| 107 Jeff Reardon | .02 | .10 |
| 108 Dana Kiecker | .01 | .05 |
| 109 Ellis Burks | .02 | .10 |
| 110 Dave Owen | .01 | .05 |
| 111 Danny Darwin | .01 | .05 |
| 112 Mo Vaughn | .02 | .10 |

| | | |
|---|---|---|
| 113 Jeff McNeely RC | .05 | .15 |
| 114 Tom Bolton | .01 | .05 |
| 115 Greg Blosser | .01 | .05 |
| 116 Mike Greenwell | .01 | .05 |
| 117 Phil Plantier RC | .05 | .15 |
| 118 Roger Clemens | .30 | .75 |
| 119 John Marzano | .01 | .05 |
| 120 Jody Reed | .01 | .05 |
| 121 Scott Taylor RC | .05 | .15 |
| 122 Jack Clark | .02 | .10 |
| 123 Derek Livernois RC | .01 | .05 |
| 124 Tony Pena | .01 | .05 |
| 125 Tom Brunansky | .01 | .05 |
| 126 Carlos Quintana | .01 | .05 |
| 127 Tim Naehring | .01 | .05 |
| 128 Matt Young | .01 | .05 |
| 129 Wade Boggs | .05 | .15 |
| 130 Kevin Morton RC | .05 | .15 |
| 131 Pete Incaviglia | .01 | .05 |
| 132 Rob Deer | .01 | .05 |
| 133 Bill Gullickson | .01 | .05 |
| 134 Rico Brogna | .01 | .05 |
| 135 Lloyd Moseby | .01 | .05 |
| 136 Cecil Fielder | .02 | .10 |
| 137 Tony Phillips | .01 | .05 |
| 138 Mark Leiter RC | .05 | .15 |
| 139 John Cerutti | .01 | .05 |
| 140 Mickey Tettleton | .01 | .05 |
| 141 Milt Cuyler | .05 | .15 |
| 142 Greg Gohr | .01 | .05 |
| 143 Tony Bernazard | .01 | .05 |
| 144 Dan Gakeler RC | .01 | .05 |
| 145 Travis Fryman | .02 | .10 |
| 146 Dan Petry | .01 | .05 |
| 147 Scott Aldred | .01 | .05 |
| 148 John DeSilva RC | .01 | .05 |
| 149 Rusty Meacham RC | .05 | .15 |
| 150 Lou Whitaker | .02 | .10 |
| 151 Dave Haas RC | .01 | .05 |
| 152 Luis de los Santos | .01 | .05 |
| 153 Ivan Cruz RC | .01 | .05 |
| 154 Alan Trammell | .02 | .10 |
| 155 Pat Kelly RC | .05 | .15 |
| 156 Carl Everett RC | .60 | 1.50 |
| 157 Greg Cadaret | .01 | .05 |
| 158 Kevin Maas | .01 | .05 |
| 159 Jeff Johnson RC | .01 | .05 |
| 160 Willie Smith | .01 | .05 |
| 161 Gerald Williams RC | .20 | .50 |
| 162 Mike Humphreys RC | .05 | .15 |
| 163 Alvaro Espinoza | .01 | .05 |
| 164 Matt Nokes | .01 | .05 |
| 165 Wade Taylor RC | .01 | .05 |
| 166 Roberto Kelly | .01 | .05 |
| 167 John Habyan | .01 | .05 |
| 168 Steve Farr | .01 | .05 |
| 169 Jesse Barfield | .01 | .05 |
| 170 Steve Sax | .01 | .05 |
| 171 Jim Leyritz | .01 | .05 |
| 172 Robert Eenhoorn RC | .08 | .25 |
| 173 Bernie Williams | .08 | .25 |
| 174 Scott Lusader | .01 | .05 |
| 175 Torey Lovullo | .01 | .05 |
| 176 Chuck Cary | .01 | .05 |
| 177 Scott Sanderson | .01 | .05 |
| 178 Don Mattingly | .25 | .60 |
| 179 Mel Hall | .01 | .05 |
| 180 Jason Johnson | .08 | .25 |
| 181 Hensley Meulens | .01 | .05 |
| 182 Jose Offerman | .01 | .05 |
| 183 Jeff Bagwell RC | 1.25 | 3.00 |
| 184 Jeff Conine RC | .40 | 1.00 |
| 185 Henry Rodriguez RC | .20 | .50 |
| 186 Jimmy Reese CO | .02 | .10 |
| 187 Kyle Abbott | .01 | .05 |
| 188 Lance Parrish | .02 | .10 |
| 189 Rafael Montalvo RC | .01 | .05 |
| 190 Floyd Bannister | .01 | .05 |
| 191 Dick Schofield | .01 | .05 |
| 192 Scott Lewis RC | .01 | .05 |
| 193 Jeff D. Robinson | .01 | .05 |
| 194 Kent Anderson | .01 | .05 |
| 195 Wally Joyner | .02 | .10 |
| 196 Chuck Finley | .01 | .05 |
| 197 Luis Sojo | .01 | .05 |
| 198 Jeff Richardson RC | .01 | .05 |
| 199 Dave Parker | .02 | .10 |
| 200 Jim Abbott | .05 | .15 |

|  |  | | |
|---|---|---|---|
| 201 | Junior Felix | .01 | .05 |
| 202 | Mark Langston | .01 | .05 |
| 203 | Tim Salmon RC | .60 | 1.50 |
| 204 | Cliff Young | .01 | .05 |
| 205 | Scott Bailes | .01 | .05 |
| 206 | Bobby Rose | .01 | .05 |
| 207 | Gary Gaetti | .02 | .10 |
| 208 | Ruben Amaro RC | .05 | .15 |
| 209 | Luis Polonia | .01 | .05 |
| 210 | Dave Winfield | .02 | .10 |
| 211 | Bryan Harvey | .01 | .05 |
| 212 | Mike Moore | .01 | .05 |
| 213 | Rickey Henderson | .08 | .25 |
| 214 | Steve Chitren RC | .01 | .05 |
| 215 | Bob Welch | .01 | .05 |
| 216 | Terry Steinbach | .01 | .05 |
| 217 | Earnest Riles | .01 | .05 |
| 218 | Todd Van Poppel RC | .20 | .50 |
| 219 | Mike Gallego | .01 | .05 |
| 220 | Curt Young | .01 | .05 |
| 221 | Todd Burns | .01 | .05 |
| 222 | Vance Law | .01 | .05 |
| 223 | Eric Show | .01 | .05 |
| 224 | Don Peters RC | .05 | .15 |
| 225 | Dave Stewart | .02 | .10 |
| 226 | Dave Henderson | .01 | .05 |
| 227 | Jose Canseco | .05 | .15 |
| 228 | Walt Weiss | .01 | .05 |
| 229 | Dann Howitt | .01 | .05 |
| 230 | Willie Wilson | .01 | .05 |
| 231 | Harold Baines | .02 | .10 |
| 232 | Scott Hemond | .01 | .05 |
| 233 | Joe Slusarski RC | .01 | .05 |
| 234 | Mark McGwire | .30 | .75 |
| 235 | Kirk Dressendorfer RC | .05 | .15 |
| 236 | Craig Paquette RC | .20 | .50 |
| 237 | Dennis Eckersley | .05 | .15 |
| 238 | Dana Allison RC | .01 | .05 |
| 239 | Scott Bradley | .01 | .05 |
| 240 | Brian Holman | .01 | .05 |
| 241 | Mike Schooler | .01 | .05 |
| 242 | Rich DeLucia RC | .05 | .15 |
| 243 | Edgar Martinez | .05 | .15 |
| 244 | Henry Cotto | .01 | .05 |
| 245 | Omar Vizquel | .05 | .15 |
| 246 | Ken Griffey Jr. | .20 | .50 |
| 247 | Jay Buhner | .02 | .10 |
| 248 | Bill Krueger | .01 | .05 |
| 249 | Dave Fleming RC | .05 | .15 |
| 250 | Patrick Lennon RC | .05 | .15 |
| 251 | Dave Valle | .01 | .05 |
| 252 | Harold Reynolds | .02 | .10 |
| 253 | Randy Johnson | .10 | .30 |
| 254 | Scott Bankhead | .01 | .05 |
| 255 | Ken Griffey Sr. UER 246 | .01 | .05 |
| 256 | Greg Briley | .01 | .05 |
| 257 | Tino Martinez | .08 | .25 |
| 258 | Alvin Davis | .01 | .05 |
| 259 | Pete O'Brien | .01 | .05 |
| 260 | Erik Hanson | .01 | .05 |
| 261 | Bret Boone RC | .50 | 1.50 |
| 262 | Roger Salkeld | .05 | .15 |
| 263 | Dave Burba RC | .20 | .50 |
| 264 | Kerry Woodson RC | .05 | .15 |
| 265 | Julio Franco | .02 | .10 |
| 266 | Dan Peltier RC | .05 | .15 |
| 267 | Jeff Russell | .01 | .05 |
| 268 | Steve Buechele | .01 | .05 |
| 269 | Donald Harris | .01 | .05 |
| 270 | Robb Nen | .05 | .15 |
| 271 | Rich Gossage | .02 | .10 |
| 272 | Ivan Rodriguez RC | 1.50 | 4.00 |
| 273 | Jeff Huson | .01 | .05 |
| 274 | Kevin Brown | .02 | .10 |
| 275 | Dan Smith RC | .05 | .15 |
| 276 | Gary Pettis | .01 | .05 |
| 277 | Jack Daugherty | .01 | .05 |
| 278 | Mike Jeffcoat | .01 | .05 |
| 279 | Brad Amsberg | .01 | .05 |
| 280 | Nolan Ryan | .40 | 1.00 |
| 281 | Eric McCray RC | .01 | .05 |
| 282 | Scott Chiamparino | .01 | .05 |
| 283 | Ruben Sierra | .02 | .10 |
| 284 | Geno Petralli | .01 | .05 |
| 285 | Monty Fariss | .01 | .05 |
| 286 | Rafael Palmeiro | .05 | .15 |
| 287 | Bobby Witt | .01 | .05 |
| 288 | Dean Palmer UER | .02 | .10 |
| 289 | Tony Scruggs RC | .01 | .05 |
| 290 | Kenny Rogers | .02 | .10 |
| 291 | Bret Saberhagen | .02 | .10 |
| 292 | Brian McRae RC | .20 | .50 |
| 293 | Storm Davis | .01 | .05 |
| 294 | Danny Tartabull | .01 | .05 |
| 295 | David Howard RC | .01 | .05 |
| 296 | Mike Boddicker | .01 | .05 |
| 297 | Joel Johnston RC | .05 | .15 |
| 298 | Tim Spehr RC | .01 | .05 |
| 299 | Hector Wagner RC | .01 | .05 |
| 300 | George Brett | .25 | .60 |
| 301 | Mike Macfarlane | .01 | .05 |
| 302 | Kirk Gibson | .02 | .10 |
| 303 | Harvey Pulliam RC | .05 | .15 |
| 304 | Jim Eisenreich | .01 | .05 |
| 305 | Kevin Seitzer | .01 | .05 |
| 306 | Mark Davis | .01 | .05 |
| 307 | Kurt Stillwell | .01 | .05 |
| 308 | Jeff Montgomery | .01 | .05 |
| 309 | Kevin Appier | .02 | .10 |
| 310 | Bob Hamelin | .01 | .05 |
| 311 | Tom Gordon | .01 | .05 |
| 312 | Kerwin Moore RC | .05 | .15 |
| 313 | Hugh Walker | .01 | .05 |
| 314 | Terry Shumpert | .01 | .05 |
| 315 | Warren Cromartie | .01 | .05 |
| 316 | Gary Thurman | .01 | .05 |
| 317 | Steve Bedrosian | .01 | .05 |
| 318 | Danny Gladden | .01 | .05 |
| 319 | Jack Morris | .02 | .10 |
| 320 | Kirby Puckett | .08 | .25 |
| 321 | Kent Hrbek | .02 | .10 |
| 322 | Kevin Tapani | .01 | .05 |
| 323 | Denny Neagle RC | .20 | .50 |
| 324 | Rich Garces RC | .05 | .15 |
| 325 | Larry Casian RC | .05 | .15 |
| 326 | Shane Mack | .01 | .05 |
| 327 | Allan Anderson | .01 | .05 |
| 328 | Junior Ortiz | .01 | .05 |
| 329 | Paul Abbott RC | .05 | .15 |
| 330 | Chuck Knoblauch | .02 | .10 |
| 331 | Chili Davis | .01 | .05 |
| 332 | Todd Ritchie RC | .20 | .50 |
| 333 | Brian Harper | .01 | .05 |
| 334 | Rick Aguilera | .02 | .10 |
| 335 | Scott Erickson | .01 | .05 |
| 336 | Pedro Munoz RC | .05 | .15 |
| 337 | Scott Leius | .01 | .05 |
| 338 | Greg Gagne | .01 | .05 |
| 339 | Mike Pagliarulo | .01 | .05 |
| 340 | Terry Leach | .01 | .05 |
| 341 | Willie Banks | .01 | .05 |
| 342 | Bobby Thigpen | .01 | .05 |
| 343 | Roberto Hernandez RC | .20 | .50 |
| 344 | Melido Perez | .01 | .05 |
| 345 | Carlton Fisk | .05 | .15 |
| 346 | Norberto Martin RC | .01 | .05 |
| 347 | Johnny Ruffin RC | .05 | .15 |
| 348 | Jeff Carter | .01 | .05 |
| 349 | Lance Johnson | .01 | .05 |
| 350 | Sammy Sosa | .08 | .25 |
| 351 | Alex Fernandez | .01 | .05 |
| 352 | Jack McDowell | .01 | .05 |
| 353 | Bob Wickman RC | .60 | 1.50 |
| 354 | Wilson Alvarez | .01 | .05 |
| 355 | Charlie Hough | .02 | .10 |
| 356 | Ozzie Guillen | .01 | .05 |
| 357 | Cory Snyder | .01 | .05 |
| 358 | Robin Ventura | .02 | .10 |
| 359 | Scott Fletcher | .01 | .05 |
| 360 | Cesar Bernhardt RC | .01 | .05 |
| 361 | Dan Pasqua | .01 | .05 |
| 362 | Tim Raines | .02 | .10 |
| 363 | Brian Drahman RC | .01 | .05 |
| 364 | Wayne Edwards | .01 | .05 |
| 365 | Scott Radinsky | .01 | .05 |
| 366 | Frank Thomas | .08 | .25 |
| 367 | Cecil Fielder SLUG | .05 | .15 |
| 368 | Julio Franco SLUG | .01 | .05 |
| 369 | Kelly Gruber SLUG | .01 | .05 |
| 370 | Alan Trammell SLUG | .02 | .10 |
| 371 | Rickey Henderson SLUG | .05 | .15 |
| 372 | Jose Canseco SLUG | .02 | .10 |
| 373 | Ellis Burks SLUG | .01 | .05 |
| 374 | Lance Parrish SLUG | .01 | .05 |
| 375 | Dave Parker SLUG | .02 | .10 |
| 376 | Eddie Murray SLUG | .05 | .15 |
| 377 | Ryne Sandberg SLUG | .08 | .25 |
| 378 | Matt Williams SLUG | .01 | .05 |
| 379 | Barry Larkin SLUG | .02 | .10 |
| 380 | Barry Bonds SLUG | .20 | .50 |
| 381 | Bobby Bonilla SLUG | .01 | .05 |
| 382 | Darryl Strawberry SLUG | .01 | .05 |
| 383 | Benny Santiago SLUG | .01 | .05 |
| 384 | Don Robinson SLUG | .01 | .05 |
| 385 | Paul Coleman | .01 | .05 |
| 386 | Milt Thompson | .01 | .05 |
| 387 | Lee Smith | .02 | .10 |
| 388 | Ray Lankford | .02 | .10 |
| 389 | Tom Pagnozzi | .01 | .05 |
| 390 | Ken Hill | .01 | .05 |
| 391 | Jamie Moyer | .02 | .10 |
| 392 | Greg Carmona RC | .01 | .05 |
| 393 | John Ericks | .01 | .05 |
| 394 | Bob Tewksbury | .01 | .05 |
| 395 | Jose Oquendo | .01 | .05 |
| 396 | Rheal Cormier RC | .05 | .15 |
| 397 | Mike Milchin RC | .01 | .05 |
| 398 | Ozzie Smith | .15 | .40 |
| 399 | Aaron Holbert RC | .05 | .15 |
| 400 | Jose DeLeon | .01 | .05 |
| 401 | Felix Jose | .01 | .05 |
| 402 | Juan Agosto | .01 | .05 |
| 403 | Pedro Guerrero | .02 | .10 |
| 404 | Todd Zeile | .01 | .05 |
| 405 | Gerald Perry | .01 | .05 |
| 406 | Donovan Osborne UER RC | .05 | .15 |
| 407 | Bryn Smith | .01 | .05 |
| 408 | Bernard Gilkey | .01 | .05 |
| 409 | Rex Hudler | .01 | .05 |
| 410 | Thomson/Branca FOIL | .08 | .25 |
| 411 | Lance Dickson RC | .05 | .15 |
| 412 | Danny Jackson | .01 | .05 |
| 413 | Jerome Walton | .01 | .05 |
| 414 | Sean Cheetham RC | .01 | .05 |
| 415 | Joe Girardi | .01 | .05 |
| 416 | Ryne Sandberg | .15 | .40 |
| 417 | Mike Harkey | .01 | .05 |
| 418 | George Bell | .01 | .05 |
| 419 | Rick Wilkins RC | .05 | .15 |
| 420 | Earl Cunningham | .05 | .15 |
| 421 | Heathcliff Slocumb RC | .05 | .15 |
| 422 | Mike Bielecki | .01 | .05 |
| 423 | Jessie Hollins RC | .05 | .15 |
| 424 | Shawon Dunston | .01 | .05 |
| 425 | Dave Smith | .01 | .05 |
| 426 | Greg Maddux | .15 | .40 |
| 427 | Jose Vizcaino | .01 | .05 |
| 428 | Luis Salazar | .01 | .05 |
| 429 | Andre Dawson | .02 | .10 |
| 430 | Rick Sutcliffe | .01 | .05 |
| 431 | Paul Assenmacher | .01 | .05 |
| 432 | Erik Pappas RC | .01 | .05 |
| 433 | Mark Grace | .05 | .15 |
| 434 | Dennis Martinez | .02 | .10 |
| 435 | Marquis Grissom | .02 | .10 |
| 436 | Wil Cordero RC | .20 | .50 |
| 437 | Tim Wallach | .01 | .05 |
| 438 | Brian Barnes RC | .01 | .05 |
| 439 | Barry Jones | .01 | .05 |
| 440 | Ivan Calderon | .01 | .05 |
| 441 | Stan Spencer RC | .01 | .05 |
| 442 | Larry Walker | .08 | .25 |
| 443 | Chris Haney RC | .05 | .15 |
| 444 | Hector Rivera RC | .01 | .05 |
| 445 | Delino DeShields | .02 | .10 |
| 446 | Andres Galarraga | .02 | .10 |
| 447 | Gilberto Reyes | .01 | .05 |
| 448 | Willie Greene | .01 | .05 |
| 449 | Greg Colbrunn RC | .20 | .50 |
| 450 | Rondell White RC | .40 | 1.00 |
| 451 | Steve Frey | .01 | .05 |
| 452 | Shane Andrews RC | .05 | .15 |
| 453 | Mike Fitzgerald | .01 | .05 |
| 454 | Spike Owen | .01 | .05 |
| 455 | Dave Martinez | .01 | .05 |
| 456 | Dennis Boyd | .01 | .05 |
| 457 | Eric Bullock | .01 | .05 |
| 458 | Reid Cornelius RC | .05 | .15 |
| 459 | Chris Nabholz | .01 | .05 |
| 460 | David Cone | .02 | .10 |
| 461 | Hubie Brooks | .01 | .05 |
| 462 | Sid Fernandez | .01 | .05 |
| 463 | Doug Simons RC | .05 | .15 |
| 464 | Howard Johnson | .01 | .05 |

|  |  | | |
|---|--------|-----|-----|
| 465 | Chris Donnels RC | .01 | .05 |
| 466 | Anthony Young RC | .05 | .15 |
| 467 | Todd Hundley RC | .01 | .05 |
| 468 | Rick Cerone | .01 | .05 |
| 469 | Kevin Elster | .01 | .05 |
| 470 | Wally Whitehurst | .01 | .05 |
| 471 | Vince Coleman | .01 | .05 |
| 472 | Dwight Gooden | .02 | .10 |
| 473 | Charlie O'Brien | .01 | .05 |
| 474 | Jeromy Burnitz RC | .40 | 1.00 |
| 475 | John Franco | .02 | .10 |
| 476 | Daryl Boston | .01 | .05 |
| 477 | Frank Viola | .02 | .10 |
| 478 | D.J. Dozier | .01 | .05 |
| 479 | Kevin McReynolds | .01 | .05 |
| 480 | Tom Herr | .01 | .05 |
| 481 | Gregg Jefferies | .01 | .05 |
| 482 | Pete Schourek RC | .05 | .15 |
| 483 | Ron Darling | .01 | .05 |
| 484 | Dave Magadan | .01 | .05 |
| 485 | Andy Ashby RC | .20 | .50 |
| 486 | Dale Murphy | .05 | .15 |
| 487 | Von Hayes | .01 | .05 |
| 488 | Kim Batiste RC | .05 | .15 |
| 489 | Tony Longmire RC | .05 | .15 |
| 490 | Wally Backman | .01 | .05 |
| 491 | Jeff Jackson | .01 | .05 |
| 492 | Mickey Morandini | .01 | .05 |
| 493 | Darrel Akerfelds | .01 | .05 |
| 494 | Ricky Jordan | .01 | .05 |
| 495 | Randy Ready | .01 | .05 |
| 496 | Darrin Fletcher | .01 | .05 |
| 497 | Chuck Malone | .01 | .05 |
| 498 | Pat Combs | .01 | .05 |
| 499 | Dickie Thon | .01 | .05 |
| 500 | Roger McDowell | .01 | .05 |
| 501 | Len Dykstra | .02 | .10 |
| 502 | Joe Boever | .02 | .10 |
| 503 | John Kruk | .02 | .10 |
| 504 | Terry Mulholland | .01 | .05 |
| 505 | Wes Chamberlain RC | .05 | .15 |
| 506 | Mike Lieberthal RC | .40 | 1.00 |
| 507 | Darren Daulton | .02 | .10 |
| 508 | Charlie Hayes | .01 | .05 |
| 509 | John Smiley | .01 | .05 |
| 510 | Gary Varsho | .01 | .05 |
| 511 | Curt Wilkerson | .01 | .05 |
| 512 | Orlando Merced RC | .05 | .15 |
| 513 | Barry Bonds | .40 | 1.00 |
| 514 | Mike LaValliere | .01 | .05 |
| 515 | Doug Drabek | .02 | .10 |
| 516 | Gary Redus | .01 | .05 |
| 517 | William Pennyfeather RC | .05 | .15 |
| 518 | Randy Tomlin RC | .05 | .15 |
| 519 | Mike Zimmerman RC | .05 | .15 |
| 520 | Jeff King | .01 | .05 |
| 521 | Kurt Miller RC | .05 | .15 |
| 522 | Jay Bell | .02 | .10 |
| 523 | Bill Landrum | .01 | .05 |
| 524 | Zane Smith | .01 | .05 |
| 525 | Bobby Bonilla | .02 | .10 |
| 526 | Bob Walk | .01 | .05 |
| 527 | Austin Manahan | .01 | .05 |
| 528 | Joe Ausanio RC | .05 | .15 |
| 529 | Andy Van Slyke | .05 | .15 |
| 530 | Jose Lind | .01 | .05 |
| 531 | Carlos Garcia RC | .05 | .15 |
| 532 | Don Slaught | .01 | .05 |
| 533 | Gen.Colin Powell | .20 | .50 |
| 534 | Frank Bolick RC | .05 | .15 |
| 535 | Gary Scott RC | .01 | .05 |
| 536 | Nikco Riesgo RC | .01 | .05 |
| 537 | Reggie Sanders RC | .60 | 1.50 |
| 538 | Tim Howard RC | .05 | .15 |
| 539 | Ryan Bowen RC | .01 | .05 |
| 540 | Eric Anthony | .01 | .05 |
| 541 | Jim Deshaies | .01 | .05 |
| 542 | Tom Nevers RC | .02 | .10 |
| 543 | Ken Caminiti | .02 | .10 |
| 544 | Karl Rhodes | .01 | .05 |
| 545 | Xavier Hernandez | .01 | .05 |
| 546 | Mike Scott | .01 | .05 |
| 547 | Jeff Juden | .01 | .05 |
| 548 | Darryl Kile | .02 | .10 |
| 549 | Willie Ansley | .01 | .05 |
| 550 | Luis Gonzalez RC | .60 | 1.50 |
| 551 | Mike Simms RC | .01 | .05 |
| 552 | Mark Portugal | .01 | .05 |
| 553 | Jimmy Jones | .01 | .05 |
| 554 | Jim Clancy | .01 | .05 |
| 555 | Pete Harnisch | .01 | .05 |
| 556 | Craig Biggio | .05 | .15 |
| 557 | Eric Yelding | .01 | .05 |
| 558 | Dave Rohde | .01 | .05 |
| 559 | Casey Candaele | .01 | .05 |
| 560 | Curt Schilling | .04 | .15 |
| 561 | Steve Finley | .02 | .10 |
| 562 | Javier Ortiz | .01 | .05 |
| 563 | Andujar Cedeno | .01 | .05 |
| 564 | Rafael Ramirez | .01 | .05 |
| 565 | Kenny Lofton RC | .60 | 1.50 |
| 566 | Steve Avery | .05 | .15 |
| 567 | Lonnie Smith | .01 | .05 |
| 568 | Keith Mercker | .01 | .05 |
| 569 | Chipper Jones RC | 2.50 | 6.00 |
| 570 | Terry Pendleton | .02 | .10 |
| 571 | Otis Nixon | .01 | .05 |
| 572 | Juan Berenguer | .01 | .05 |
| 573 | Charlie Leibrandt | .01 | .05 |
| 574 | David Justice | .02 | .10 |
| 575 | Keith Mitchell RC | .05 | .15 |
| 576 | Tom Glavine | .05 | .15 |
| 577 | Greg Olson | .01 | .05 |
| 578 | Rafael Belliard | .01 | .05 |
| 579 | Ben Rivera RC | .05 | .15 |
| 580 | John Smoltz | .05 | .15 |
| 581 | Tyler Houston | .01 | .05 |
| 582 | Mark Wohlers RC | .20 | .50 |
| 583 | Ron Gant | .02 | .10 |
| 584 | Ramon Caraballo RC | .01 | .05 |
| 585 | Sid Bream | .01 | .05 |
| 586 | Jeff Treadway | .01 | .05 |
| 587 | Javy Lopez RC | 1.25 | 3.00 |
| 588 | Deion Sanders | .05 | .15 |
| 589 | Mike Heath | .01 | .05 |
| 590 | Ryan Klesko RC | .40 | 1.00 |
| 591 | Bob Ojeda | .01 | .05 |
| 592 | Alfredo Griffin | .01 | .05 |
| 593 | Raul Mondesi RC | .40 | 1.00 |
| 594 | Greg Smith | .01 | .05 |
| 595 | Orel Hershiser | .02 | .10 |
| 596 | Juan Samuel | .01 | .05 |
| 597 | Brett Butler | .02 | .10 |
| 598 | Gary Carter | .02 | .10 |
| 599 | Stan Javier | .01 | .05 |
| 600 | Kal Daniels | .01 | .05 |
| 601 | Jamie McAndrew RC | .05 | .15 |
| 602 | Mike Sharperson | .01 | .05 |
| 603 | Jay Howell | .01 | .05 |
| 604 | Eric Karros RC | .60 | 1.50 |
| 605 | Tim Belcher | .01 | .05 |
| 606 | Dan Opperman RC | .01 | .05 |
| 607 | Lenny Harris | .01 | .05 |
| 608 | Tom Goodwin | .01 | .05 |
| 609 | Darryl Strawberry | .02 | .10 |
| 610 | Ramon Martinez | .01 | .05 |
| 611 | Kevin Gross | .01 | .05 |
| 612 | Zakany Shinall RC | .01 | .05 |
| 613 | Mike Scioscia | .01 | .05 |
| 614 | Eddie Murray | .08 | .25 |
| 615 | Ronnie Walden RC | .05 | .15 |
| 616 | Will Clark | .05 | .15 |
| 617 | Adam Hyzdu RC | .20 | .50 |
| 618 | Matt Williams | .02 | .10 |
| 619 | Don Robinson | .01 | .05 |
| 620 | Jeff Brantley | .01 | .05 |
| 621 | Greg Litton | .01 | .05 |
| 622 | Steve Decker RC | .01 | .05 |
| 623 | Robby Thompson | .01 | .05 |
| 624 | Mark Leonard RC | .01 | .05 |
| 625 | Kevin Bass | .01 | .05 |
| 626 | Scott Garrelts | .01 | .05 |
| 627 | Jose Uribe | .01 | .05 |
| 628 | Eric Gunderson | .01 | .05 |
| 629 | Steve Hosey | .01 | .05 |
| 630 | Trevor Wilson | .01 | .05 |
| 631 | Terry Kennedy | .01 | .05 |
| 632 | Dave Righetti | .02 | .10 |
| 633 | Kelly Downs | .01 | .05 |
| 634 | Johnny Ard | .01 | .05 |
| 635 | Eric Christopherson RC | .05 | .15 |
| 636 | Kevin Mitchell | .02 | .10 |
| 637 | John Burkett | .01 | .05 |
| 638 | Kevin Rogers RC | .05 | .15 |
| 639 | Bud Black | .01 | .05 |
| 640 | Willie McGee | .02 | .10 |
| 641 | Royce Clayton | .01 | .05 |
| 642 | Tony Fernandez | .01 | .05 |
| 643 | Ricky Bones RC | .05 | .15 |
| 644 | Thomas Howard | .01 | .05 |
| 645 | Dave Staton RC | .05 | .15 |
| 646 | Jim Presley | .01 | .05 |
| 647 | Tony Gwynn | .10 | .30 |
| 648 | Marty Barrett | .01 | .05 |
| 649 | Scott Coolbaugh | .01 | .05 |
| 650 | Craig Lefferts | .01 | .05 |
| 651 | Eddie Whitson | .01 | .05 |
| 652 | Oscar Azocar | .01 | .05 |
| 653 | Wes Gardner | .01 | .05 |
| 654 | Bip Roberts | .01 | .05 |
| 655 | Robbie Beckett RC | .05 | .15 |
| 656 | Benito Santiago | .02 | .10 |
| 657 | Greg W.Harris | .01 | .05 |
| 658 | Jerald Clark | .01 | .05 |
| 659 | Fred McGriff | .05 | .15 |
| 660 | Larry Andersen | .01 | .05 |
| 661 | Bruce Hurst | .01 | .05 |
| 662 | Steve Martin GRR RC | .05 | .15 |
| 663 | Rafael Valdez | .01 | .05 |
| 664 | Paul Faries RC | .01 | .05 |
| 665 | Andy Benes | .05 | .15 |
| 666 | Randy Myers | .01 | .05 |
| 667 | Rob Dibble | .02 | .10 |
| 668 | Glenn Sutko RC | .01 | .05 |
| 669 | Glenn Braggs | .01 | .05 |
| 670 | Billy Hatcher | .01 | .05 |
| 671 | Joe Oliver | .01 | .05 |
| 672 | Freddie Benavides RC | .05 | .15 |
| 673 | Barry Larkin | .05 | .15 |
| 674 | Chris Sabo | .01 | .05 |
| 675 | Mariano Duncan | .01 | .05 |
| 676 | Chris Jones RC | .01 | .05 |
| 677 | Gino Minutelli RC | .01 | .05 |
| 678 | Reggie Jefferson | .01 | .05 |
| 679 | Jack Armstrong | .01 | .05 |
| 680 | Chris Hammond | .01 | .05 |
| 681 | Jose Rijo | .01 | .05 |
| 682 | Bill Doran | .01 | .05 |
| 683 | Terry Lee RC | .01 | .05 |
| 684 | Tom Browning | .01 | .05 |
| 685 | Paul O'Neill | .05 | .15 |
| 686 | Eric Davis | .02 | .10 |
| 687 | Dan Wilson RC | .20 | .50 |
| 688 | Ted Power | .01 | .05 |
| 689 | Tim Layana | .01 | .05 |
| 690 | Norm Charlton | .01 | .05 |
| 691 | Hal Morris | .01 | .05 |
| 692 | Rickey Henderson RB | .05 | .15 |
| 693 | Sam Militello RC | .05 | .15 |
| 694 | Matt Mieske RC | .05 | .15 |
| 695 | Paul Russo RC | .05 | .15 |
| 696 | Domingo Mota MVP | .01 | .05 |
| 697 | Todd Guggiana RC | .05 | .15 |
| 698 | Marc Newfield RC | .05 | .15 |
| 699 | Checklist 1-122 | .01 | .05 |
| 700 | Checklist 123-244 | .01 | .05 |
| 701 | Checklist 245-366 | .01 | .05 |
| 702 | Checklist 367-471 | .01 | .05 |
| 703 | Checklist 472-593 | .01 | .05 |
| 704 | Checklist 594-704 | .01 | .05 |

## 1992 Bowman

| | | | |
|---|---|-----|------|
| | COMPLETE SET (705) | 75.00 | 150.00 |
| 1 | Ivan Rodriguez | .50 | 1.25 |
| 2 | Kirk McCaskill | .20 | .50 |
| 3 | Scott Livingstone | .20 | .50 |
| 4 | Salomon Torres RC | .20 | .50 |
| 5 | Carlos Hernandez | .20 | .50 |
| 6 | Dave Hollins | .20 | .50 |
| 7 | Scott Fletcher | .20 | .50 |

|  |  | | |
|---|---|---|---|
| 8 | Jorge Fabregas RC | .20 | .50 |
| 9 | Andujar Cedeno | .20 | .50 |
| 10 | Howard Johnson | .20 | .50 |
| 11 | Trevor Hoffman RC | 4.00 | 10.00 |
| 12 | Roberto Kelly | .20 | .50 |
| 13 | Gregg Jefferies | .20 | .50 |
| 14 | Marquis Grissom | .20 | .50 |
| 15 | Mike Ignasiak | .20 | .50 |
| 16 | Jack Morris | .20 | .50 |
| 17 | William Pennyfeather | .20 | .50 |
| 18 | Todd Stottlemyre | .20 | .50 |
| 19 | Chito Martinez | .20 | .50 |
| 20 | Roberto Alomar | .30 | .75 |
| 21 | Sam Militello | .20 | .50 |
| 22 | Hector Fajardo RC | .20 | .50 |
| 23 | Paul Quantrill RC | .20 | .50 |
| 24 | Chuck Knoblauch | .20 | .50 |
| 25 | Reggie Jefferson | .20 | .50 |
| 26 | Jeremy McGarity RC | .20 | .50 |
| 27 | Jerome Walton | .20 | .50 |
| 28 | Chipper Jones | 5.00 | 12.00 |
| 29 | Brian Barber RC | .20 | .50 |
| 30 | Ron Darling | .20 | .50 |
| 31 | Roberto Petagine RC | .20 | .50 |
| 32 | Chuck Finley | .20 | .50 |
| 33 | Edgar Martinez | .30 | .75 |
| 34 | Napoleon Robinson | .20 | .50 |
| 35 | Andy Van Slyke | .30 | .75 |
| 36 | Bobby Thigpen | .20 | .50 |
| 37 | Travis Fryman | .20 | .50 |
| 38 | Eric Christopherson | .20 | .50 |
| 39 | Terry Mulholland | .20 | .50 |
| 40 | Darryl Strawberry | .20 | .50 |
| 41 | Manny Alexander RC | .20 | .50 |
| 42 | Tracy Sanders RC | .20 | .50 |
| 43 | Pete Incaviglia | .20 | .50 |
| 44 | Kim Batiste | .20 | .50 |
| 45 | Frank Rodriguez | .20 | .50 |
| 46 | Greg Swindell | .20 | .50 |
| 47 | Delino DeShields | .20 | .50 |
| 48 | John Ericks | .20 | .50 |
| 49 | Franklin Stubbs | .20 | .50 |
| 50 | Tony Gwynn | .60 | 1.50 |
| 51 | Clifton Garrett RC | .20 | .50 |
| 52 | Mike Gardella | .20 | .50 |
| 53 | Scott Erickson | .20 | .50 |
| 54 | Gary Caraballo RC | .20 | .50 |
| 55 | Jose Oliva RC | .20 | .50 |
| 56 | Brook Fordyce | .20 | .50 |
| 57 | Mark Whiten | .20 | .50 |
| 58 | Joe Slusarski | .20 | .50 |
| 59 | J.R. Phillips RC | .20 | .50 |
| 60 | Barry Bonds | 1.50 | 4.00 |
| 61 | Bob Milacki | .20 | .50 |
| 62 | Keith Mitchell | .20 | .50 |
| 63 | Angel Miranda | .20 | .50 |
| 64 | Raul Mondesi | .20 | .50 |
| 65 | Brian Koelling RC | .20 | .50 |
| 66 | Brian McRae | .20 | .50 |
| 67 | John Patterson RC | .20 | .50 |
| 68 | John Wetteland | .20 | .50 |
| 69 | Wilson Alvarez | .20 | .50 |
| 70 | Wade Boggs | .30 | .75 |
| 71 | Darryl Ratliff RC | .20 | .50 |
| 72 | Jeff Jackson | .20 | .50 |
| 73 | Jeremy Hernandez RC | .20 | .50 |
| 74 | Darryl Hamilton | .20 | .50 |
| 75 | Rafael Belliard | .20 | .50 |
| 76 | Rick Tricek RC | .20 | .50 |
| 77 | Felipe Crespo RC | .20 | .50 |
| 78 | Carney Lansford | .20 | .50 |
| 79 | Ryan Long RC | .20 | .50 |
| 80 | Kirby Puckett | .50 | 1.25 |
| 81 | Earl Cunningham | .20 | .50 |
| 82 | Pedro Martinez | 4.00 | 10.00 |
| 83 | Scott Hatteberg RC | .40 | 1.00 |
| 84 | Juan Gonzalez | .30 | .75 |
| 85 | Robert Nutting RC | .20 | .50 |
| 86 | Pokey Reese RC | .40 | 1.00 |
| 87 | Dave Silvestri | .20 | .50 |
| 88 | Scott Ruffcorn RC | .20 | .50 |
| 89 | Rick Aguilera | .20 | .50 |
| 90 | Cecil Fielder | .20 | .50 |
| 91 | Kirk Dressendorfer | .20 | .50 |
| 92 | Jerry DiPoto RC | .20 | .50 |
| 93 | Mike Felder | .20 | .50 |
| 94 | Craig Paquette | .20 | .50 |
| 95 | Elvin Paulino RC | .20 | .50 |
| 96 | Donovan Osborne | .20 | .50 |
| 97 | Hubie Brooks | .20 | .50 |
| 98 | Derek Lowe RC | 1.50 | 4.00 |
| 99 | David Zancanaro | .20 | .50 |
| 100 | Ken Griffey Jr. | .75 | 2.00 |
| 101 | Todd Hundley | .20 | .50 |
| 102 | Mike Trombley RC | .20 | .50 |
| 103 | Ricky Gutierrez RC | .40 | 1.00 |
| 104 | Braulio Castillo | .20 | .50 |
| 105 | Craig Lefferts | .20 | .50 |
| 106 | Rick Sutcliffe | .20 | .50 |
| 107 | Dean Palmer | .20 | .50 |
| 108 | Henry Rodriguez | .20 | .50 |
| 109 | Mark Clark RC | .40 | 1.00 |
| 110 | Kenny Lofton | .30 | .75 |
| 111 | Mark Carreon | .20 | .50 |
| 112 | J.T. Bruett | .20 | .50 |
| 113 | Gerald Williams | .20 | .50 |
| 114 | Frank Thomas | .50 | 1.25 |
| 115 | Kevin Reimer | .20 | .50 |
| 116 | Sammy Sosa | .50 | 1.25 |
| 117 | Mickey Tettleton | .20 | .50 |
| 118 | Reggie Sanders | .20 | .50 |
| 119 | Trevor Wilson | .20 | .50 |
| 120 | Cliff Brantley | .20 | .50 |
| 121 | Spike Owen | .20 | .50 |
| 122 | Jeff Montgomery | .20 | .50 |
| 123 | Alex Sutherland | .20 | .50 |
| 124 | Brian Taylor RC | .40 | 1.00 |
| 125 | Brian Williams RC | .20 | .50 |
| 126 | Kevin Seitzer | .20 | .50 |
| 127 | Carlos Delgado RC | 4.00 | 10.00 |
| 128 | Gary Scott | .20 | .50 |
| 129 | Scott Cooper | .20 | .50 |
| 130 | Domingo Jean RC | .20 | .50 |
| 131 | Pat Mahomes RC | .40 | 1.00 |
| 132 | Mike Boddicker | .20 | .50 |
| 133 | Roberto Hernandez | .20 | .50 |
| 134 | Dave Valle | .20 | .50 |
| 135 | Kurt Stillwell | .20 | .50 |
| 136 | Brad Pennington RC | .20 | .50 |
| 137 | Jermaine Swinton RC | .20 | .50 |
| 138 | Ryan Hawblitzel RC | .20 | .50 |
| 139 | Tito Navarro RC | .20 | .50 |
| 140 | Sandy Alomar Jr. | .20 | .50 |
| 141 | Todd Benzinger | .20 | .50 |
| 142 | Danny Jackson | .20 | .50 |
| 143 | Melvin Nieves RC | .20 | .50 |
| 144 | Jim Campanis | .20 | .50 |
| 145 | Luis Gonzalez | .20 | .50 |
| 146 | Dave Doorneweerd RC | .20 | .50 |
| 147 | Charlie Hayes | .20 | .50 |
| 148 | Greg Maddux | .75 | 2.00 |
| 149 | Brian Harper | .20 | .50 |
| 150 | Brent Miller RC | .20 | .50 |
| 151 | Shawn Estes RC | .40 | 1.00 |
| 152 | Mike Williams RC | .20 | .50 |
| 153 | Charlie Hough | .20 | .50 |
| 154 | Randy Myers | .20 | .50 |
| 155 | Kevin Young RC | .40 | 1.00 |
| 156 | Rick Wilkins | .20 | .50 |
| 157 | Terry Shumpert | .20 | .50 |
| 158 | Steve Karsay | .20 | .50 |
| 159 | Gary DiSarcina | .20 | .50 |
| 160 | Deion Sanders | .30 | .75 |
| 161 | Tom Browning | .20 | .50 |
| 162 | Dickie Thon | .20 | .50 |
| 163 | Luis Mercedes | .20 | .50 |
| 164 | Riccardo Ingram | .20 | .50 |
| 165 | Tavo Alvarez RC | .20 | .50 |
| 166 | Rickey Henderson | .50 | 1.25 |
| 167 | Jaime Navarro | .20 | .50 |
| 168 | Billy Ashley RC | .20 | .50 |
| 169 | Phil Dauphin RC | .20 | .50 |
| 170 | Ivan Cruz | .20 | .50 |
| 171 | Harold Baines | .20 | .50 |
| 172 | Bryan Harvey | .20 | .50 |
| 173 | Alex Cole | .20 | .50 |
| 174 | Curtis Shaw RC | .20 | .50 |
| 175 | Matt Williams | .20 | .50 |
| 176 | Felix Jose | .20 | .50 |
| 177 | Sam Horn | .20 | .50 |
| 178 | Randy Johnson | .50 | 1.25 |
| 179 | Ivan Calderon | .20 | .50 |
| 180 | Steve Avery | .20 | .50 |
| 181 | William Suero | .20 | .50 |
| 182 | Bill Swift | .20 | .50 |
| 183 | Howard Battle RC | .20 | .50 |
| 184 | Ruben Amaro | .20 | .50 |
| 185 | Jim Abbott | .30 | .75 |
| 186 | Mike Fitzgerald | .20 | .50 |
| 187 | Bruce Hurst | .20 | .50 |
| 188 | Jeff Juden | .20 | .50 |
| 189 | Jeromy Burnitz | .20 | .50 |
| 190 | Dave Burba | .20 | .50 |
| 191 | Kevin Brown | .20 | .50 |
| 192 | Patrick Lennon | .20 | .50 |
| 193 | Jeff McNeely | .20 | .50 |
| 194 | Wil Cordero | .20 | .50 |
| 195 | Chili Davis | .20 | .50 |
| 196 | Milt Cuyler | .20 | .50 |
| 197 | Von Hayes | .20 | .50 |
| 198 | Todd Revenig RC | .20 | .50 |
| 199 | Joel Johnston | .20 | .50 |
| 200 | Jeff Bagwell | .50 | 1.25 |
| 201 | Alex Fernandez | .20 | .50 |
| 202 | Todd Jones RC | 1.00 | 2.50 |
| 203 | Charles Nagy | .20 | .50 |
| 204 | Tim Raines | .20 | .50 |
| 205 | Kevin Maas | .20 | .50 |
| 206 | Julio Franco | .20 | .50 |
| 207 | Randy Velarde | .20 | .50 |
| 208 | Lance Johnson | .20 | .50 |
| 209 | Scott Leius | .20 | .50 |
| 210 | Derek Lee | .20 | .50 |
| 211 | Joe Sondrini RC | .20 | .50 |
| 212 | Royce Clayton | .20 | .50 |
| 213 | Chris George | .20 | .50 |
| 214 | Gary Sheffield | .20 | .50 |
| 215 | Mark Gubicza | .20 | .50 |
| 216 | Mike Moore | .20 | .50 |
| 217 | Rick Huisman RC | .20 | .50 |
| 218 | Jeff Russell | .20 | .50 |
| 219 | D.J. Dozier | .20 | .50 |
| 220 | Dave Martinez | .20 | .50 |
| 221 | Alan Newman RC | .20 | .50 |
| 222 | Nolan Ryan | 1.50 | 4.00 |
| 223 | Teddy Higuera | .20 | .50 |
| 224 | Damon Buford RC | .20 | .50 |
| 225 | Ruben Sierra | .20 | .50 |
| 226 | Tom Nevers | .20 | .50 |
| 227 | Tommy Greene | .20 | .50 |
| 228 | Nigel Wilson RC | .20 | .50 |
| 229 | John DeSilva | .20 | .50 |
| 230 | Bobby Witt | .20 | .50 |
| 231 | Greg Cadaret | .20 | .50 |
| 232 | John Vander Wal RC | .40 | 1.00 |
| 233 | Jack Clark | .20 | .50 |
| 234 | Bill Doran | .20 | .50 |
| 235 | Bobby Bonilla | .20 | .50 |
| 236 | Steve Olin | .20 | .50 |
| 237 | Derek Bell | .20 | .50 |
| 238 | David Cone | .20 | .50 |
| 239 | Victor Cole | .20 | .50 |
| 240 | Rod Bolton RC | .20 | .50 |
| 241 | Tom Pagnozzi | .20 | .50 |
| 242 | Rob Dibble | .20 | .50 |
| 243 | Michael Carter RC | .20 | .50 |
| 244 | Don Peters | .20 | .50 |
| 245 | Mike LaValliere | .20 | .50 |
| 246 | Joe Perona RC | .20 | .50 |
| 247 | Mitch Williams | .20 | .50 |
| 248 | Jay Buhner | .20 | .50 |
| 249 | Andy Benes | .20 | .50 |
| 250 | Alex Ochoa RC | .20 | .50 |
| 251 | Greg Blosser | .20 | .50 |
| 252 | Jack Armstrong | .20 | .50 |
| 253 | Juan Samuel | .20 | .50 |
| 254 | Terry Pendleton | .20 | .50 |
| 255 | Ramon Martinez | .20 | .50 |
| 256 | Rico Brogna | .20 | .50 |
| 257 | John Smiley | .20 | .50 |
| 258 | Carl Everett RC | .30 | .75 |
| 259 | Tim Salmon | .30 | .75 |
| 260 | Will Clark | .30 | .75 |
| 261 | Ugueth Urbina RC | .40 | 1.00 |
| 262 | Jason Wood RC | .20 | .50 |
| 263 | Dave Magadan | .20 | .50 |
| 264 | Dante Bichette | .20 | .50 |
| 265 | Jose DeLeon | .20 | .50 |
| 266 | Mike Neill RC | .40 | 1.00 |
| 267 | Paul O'Neill | .20 | .50 |
| 268 | Anthony Young | .20 | .50 |
| 269 | Greg W. Harris | .20 | .50 |
| 270 | Todd Van Poppel | .20 | .50 |
| 271 | Pedro Castellano RC | .20 | .50 |

| □ | # | Player | Price | Price |
|---|---|--------|------:|------:|
| □ | 272 | Tony Phillips | .20 | .50 |
| □ | 273 | Mike Gallego | .20 | .50 |
| □ | 274 | Steve Cooke RC | .20 | .50 |
| □ | 275 | Robin Ventura | .20 | .50 |
| □ | 276 | Kevin Mitchell | .20 | .50 |
| □ | 277 | Doug Linton RC | .20 | .50 |
| □ | 278 | Robert Eenhoorn RC | .20 | .50 |
| □ | 279 | Gabe White RC | .20 | .50 |
| □ | 280 | Dave Stewart | .20 | .50 |
| □ | 281 | Mo Sanford | .20 | .50 |
| □ | 282 | Greg Perschke | .20 | .50 |
| □ | 283 | Kevin Flora RC | .20 | .50 |
| □ | 284 | Jeff Williams RC | .40 | 1.00 |
| □ | 285 | Keith Miller | .20 | .50 |
| □ | 286 | Andy Ashby | .20 | .50 |
| □ | 287 | Doug Dascenzo | .20 | .50 |
| □ | 288 | Eric Karros | .20 | .50 |
| □ | 289 | Glenn Murray RC | .20 | .50 |
| □ | 290 | Troy Percival RC | 1.25 | 3.00 |
| □ | 291 | Orlando Merced | .20 | .50 |
| □ | 292 | Peter Hoy | .20 | .50 |
| □ | 293 | Tony Fernandez | .20 | .50 |
| □ | 294 | Juan Guzman | .20 | .50 |
| □ | 295 | Jesse Barfield | .20 | .50 |
| □ | 296 | Sid Fernandez | .20 | .50 |
| □ | 297 | Scott Cepicky | .20 | .50 |
| □ | 298 | Garret Anderson RC | 2.00 | 5.00 |
| □ | 299 | Cal Eldred | .20 | .50 |
| □ | 300 | Ryne Sandberg | 1.00 | 2.50 |
| □ | 301 | Jim Gantner | .20 | .50 |
| □ | 302 | Mariano Rivera RC | 10.00 | 25.00 |
| □ | 303 | Ron Lockett RC | .20 | .50 |
| □ | 304 | Jose Offerman | .20 | .50 |
| □ | 305 | Dennis Martinez | .20 | .50 |
| □ | 306 | Luis Ortiz RC | .20 | .50 |
| □ | 307 | David Howard | .20 | .50 |
| □ | 308 | Russ Springer RC | .40 | 1.00 |
| □ | 309 | Chris Howard | .20 | .50 |
| □ | 310 | Kyle Abbott | .20 | .50 |
| □ | 311 | Aaron Sele RC | .40 | 1.00 |
| □ | 312 | David Justice | .20 | .50 |
| □ | 313 | Pete O'Brien | .20 | .50 |
| □ | 314 | Greg Hansell RC | .20 | .50 |
| □ | 315 | Dave Winfield | .20 | .50 |
| □ | 316 | Lance Dickson | .20 | .50 |
| □ | 317 | Eric King | .20 | .50 |
| □ | 318 | Vaughn Eshelman RC | .20 | .50 |
| □ | 319 | Tim Belcher | .20 | .50 |
| □ | 320 | Andres Galarraga | .20 | .50 |
| □ | 321 | Scott Bullett RC | .20 | .50 |
| □ | 322 | Doug Strange | .20 | .50 |
| □ | 323 | Jerald Clark | .20 | .50 |
| □ | 324 | Dave Righetti | .20 | .50 |
| □ | 325 | Greg Hibbard | .20 | .50 |
| □ | 326 | Eric Hillman RC | .20 | .50 |
| □ | 327 | Shane Reynolds RC | .40 | 1.00 |
| □ | 328 | Chris Hammond | .20 | .50 |
| □ | 329 | Albert Belle | .20 | .50 |
| □ | 330 | Rich Becker RC | .20 | .50 |
| □ | 331 | Ed Williams | .20 | .50 |
| □ | 332 | Donald Harris | .20 | .50 |
| □ | 333 | Dave Smith | .20 | .50 |
| □ | 334 | Steve Fireovid | .20 | .50 |
| □ | 335 | Steve Buechele | .20 | .50 |
| □ | 336 | Mike Schooler | .20 | .50 |
| □ | 337 | Kevin McReynolds | .20 | .50 |
| □ | 338 | Hensley Meulens | .20 | .50 |
| □ | 339 | Benji Gil RC | .40 | 1.00 |
| □ | 340 | Don Mattingly | 1.25 | 3.00 |
| □ | 341 | Alvin Davis | .20 | .50 |
| □ | 342 | Alan Mills | .20 | .50 |
| □ | 343 | Kelly Downs | .20 | .50 |
| □ | 344 | Leo Gomez | .20 | .50 |
| □ | 345 | Tarrik Brock RC | .20 | .50 |
| □ | 346 | Ryan Turner RC | .20 | .50 |
| □ | 347 | John Smoltz | .30 | .75 |
| □ | 348 | Bill Sampen | .20 | .50 |
| □ | 349 | Paul Byrd RC | 1.25 | 3.00 |
| □ | 350 | Mike Bordick | .20 | .50 |
| □ | 351 | Jose Lind | .20 | .50 |
| □ | 352 | David Wells | .20 | .50 |
| □ | 353 | Barry Larkin | .30 | .75 |
| □ | 354 | Bruce Ruffin | .20 | .50 |
| □ | 355 | Luis Rivera | .20 | .50 |
| □ | 356 | Sid Bream | .20 | .50 |
| □ | 357 | Julian Vasquez RC | .20 | .50 |
| □ | 358 | Jason Bere RC | .40 | 1.00 |
| □ | 359 | Ben McDonald | .20 | .50 |
| □ | 360 | Scott Stahoviak RC | .20 | .50 |
| □ | 361 | Kirt Manwaring | .20 | .50 |
| □ | 362 | Jeff Johnson | .20 | .50 |
| □ | 363 | Rob Deer | .20 | .50 |
| □ | 364 | Tony Pena | .20 | .50 |
| □ | 365 | Melido Perez | .20 | .50 |
| □ | 366 | Clay Parker | .20 | .50 |
| □ | 367 | Dale Sveum | .20 | .50 |
| □ | 368 | Mike Scioscia | .20 | .50 |
| □ | 369 | Roger Salkeld | .20 | .50 |
| □ | 370 | Mike Stanley | .20 | .50 |
| □ | 371 | Jack McDowell | .20 | .50 |
| □ | 372 | Tim Wallach | .20 | .50 |
| □ | 373 | Billy Ripken | .20 | .50 |
| □ | 374 | Mike Christopher | .20 | .50 |
| □ | 375 | Paul Molitor | .20 | .50 |
| □ | 376 | Dave Stieb | .20 | .50 |
| □ | 377 | Pedro Guerrero | .20 | .50 |
| □ | 378 | Russ Swan | .20 | .50 |
| □ | 379 | Bob Ojeda | .20 | .50 |
| □ | 380 | Donn Pall | .20 | .50 |
| □ | 381 | Eddie Zosky | .20 | .50 |
| □ | 382 | Darnell Coles | .20 | .50 |
| □ | 383 | Tom Smith RC | .20 | .50 |
| □ | 384 | Mark McGwire | 1.25 | 3.00 |
| □ | 385 | Gary Carter | .20 | .50 |
| □ | 386 | Rich Amaral RC | .20 | .50 |
| □ | 387 | Alan Embree RC | .40 | 1.00 |
| □ | 388 | Jonathan Hurst RC | .20 | .50 |
| □ | 389 | Bobby Jones RC | .40 | 1.00 |
| □ | 390 | Rico Rossy | .20 | .50 |
| □ | 391 | Dan Smith | .20 | .50 |
| □ | 392 | Terry Steinbach | .20 | .50 |
| □ | 393 | Jon Farrell RC | .20 | .50 |
| □ | 394 | Dave Anderson | .20 | .50 |
| □ | 395 | Benny Santiago | .20 | .50 |
| □ | 396 | Mark Wohlers | .20 | .50 |
| □ | 397 | Mo Vaughn | .20 | .50 |
| □ | 398 | Randy Kramer | .20 | .50 |
| □ | 399 | John Jaha RC | .40 | 1.00 |
| □ | 400 | Cal Ripken | 1.50 | 4.00 |
| □ | 401 | Ryan Bowen | .20 | .50 |
| □ | 402 | Tim McIntosh | .20 | .50 |
| □ | 403 | Bernard Gilkey | .20 | .50 |
| □ | 404 | Junior Felix | .20 | .50 |
| □ | 405 | Cris Colon RC | .20 | .50 |
| □ | 406 | Marc Newfield | .20 | .50 |
| □ | 407 | Bernie Williams | .30 | .75 |
| □ | 408 | Jay Howell | .20 | .50 |
| □ | 409 | Zane Smith | .20 | .50 |
| □ | 410 | Jeff Shaw | .20 | .50 |
| □ | 411 | Kerry Woodson | .20 | .50 |
| □ | 412 | Wes Chamberlain | .20 | .50 |
| □ | 413 | Dave Milicki RC | .40 | 1.00 |
| □ | 414 | Benny Distefano | .20 | .50 |
| □ | 415 | Kevin Rogers | .20 | .50 |
| □ | 416 | Tim Naehring | .20 | .50 |
| □ | 417 | Clemente Nunez RC | .20 | .50 |
| □ | 418 | Luis Sojo | .20 | .50 |
| □ | 419 | Kevin Flitz | .20 | .50 |
| □ | 420 | Omar Olivares | .20 | .50 |
| □ | 421 | Manuel Lee | .20 | .50 |
| □ | 422 | Julio Valera | .20 | .50 |
| □ | 423 | Omar Vizquel | .30 | .75 |
| □ | 424 | Darren Burton RC | .20 | .50 |
| □ | 425 | Mel Hall | .20 | .50 |
| □ | 426 | Dennis Powell | .20 | .50 |
| □ | 427 | Lee Stevens | .20 | .50 |
| □ | 428 | Glenn Davis | .20 | .50 |
| □ | 429 | Willie Greene | .20 | .50 |
| □ | 430 | Kevin Wickander | .20 | .50 |
| □ | 431 | Dennis Eckersley | .20 | .50 |
| □ | 432 | Joe Orsulak | .20 | .50 |
| □ | 433 | Eddie Murray | .50 | 1.25 |
| □ | 434 | Matt Stairs RC | .40 | 1.00 |
| □ | 435 | Wally Joyner | .20 | .50 |
| □ | 436 | Rondell White | .20 | .50 |
| □ | 437 | Rob Maurer | .20 | .50 |
| □ | 438 | Joe Redfield | .20 | .50 |
| □ | 439 | Mark Lewis | .20 | .50 |
| □ | 440 | Darren Daulton | .20 | .50 |
| □ | 441 | Mike Henneman | .20 | .50 |
| □ | 442 | John Cangelosi | .20 | .50 |
| □ | 443 | Vincent Moore RC | .20 | .50 |
| □ | 444 | John Wehner | .20 | .50 |
| □ | 445 | Kent Hrbek | .20 | .50 |
| □ | 446 | Mark McLemore | .20 | .50 |
| □ | 447 | Bill Wegman | .20 | .50 |
| □ | 448 | Robby Thompson | .20 | .50 |
| □ | 449 | Mark Anthony RC | .20 | .50 |
| □ | 450 | Archi Cianfrocco RC | .20 | .50 |
| □ | 451 | Johnny Ruffin | .20 | .50 |
| □ | 452 | Javy Lopez | .75 | 2.00 |
| □ | 453 | Greg Gohr | .20 | .50 |
| □ | 454 | Tim Scott | .20 | .50 |
| □ | 455 | Stan Belinda | .20 | .50 |
| □ | 456 | Darrin Jackson | .20 | .50 |
| □ | 457 | Chris Gardner | .20 | .50 |
| □ | 458 | Esteban Beltre | .20 | .50 |
| □ | 459 | Phil Plantier | .20 | .50 |
| □ | 460 | Jim Thome | 3.00 | 8.00 |
| □ | 461 | Mike Piazza RC | 8.00 | 20.00 |
| □ | 462 | Matt Sinatro | .20 | .50 |
| □ | 463 | Scott Servais | .20 | .50 |
| □ | 464 | Brian Jordan RC | .75 | 2.00 |
| □ | 465 | Doug Drabek | .20 | .50 |
| □ | 466 | Carl Willis | .20 | .50 |
| □ | 467 | Bret Barberie | .20 | .50 |
| □ | 468 | Hal Morris | .20 | .50 |
| □ | 469 | Steve Sax | .20 | .50 |
| □ | 470 | Jerry Willard | .20 | .50 |
| □ | 471 | Dan Wilson | .20 | .50 |
| □ | 472 | Chris Hoiles | .20 | .50 |
| □ | 473 | Rheal Cormier | .20 | .50 |
| □ | 474 | John Morris | .20 | .50 |
| □ | 475 | Jeff Reardon | .20 | .50 |
| □ | 476 | Mark Leiter | .20 | .50 |
| □ | 477 | Tom Gordon | .20 | .50 |
| □ | 478 | Kent Bottenfield RC | .40 | 1.00 |
| □ | 479 | Gene Larkin | .20 | .50 |
| □ | 480 | Dwight Gooden | .20 | .50 |
| □ | 481 | B.J. Surhoff | .20 | .50 |
| □ | 482 | Andy Stankiewicz | .20 | .50 |
| □ | 483 | Tino Martinez | .30 | .75 |
| □ | 484 | Craig Biggio | .30 | .75 |
| □ | 485 | Denny Neagle | .20 | .50 |
| □ | 486 | Rusty Meacham | .20 | .50 |
| □ | 487 | Kal Daniels | .20 | .50 |
| □ | 488 | Dave Henderson | .20 | .50 |
| □ | 489 | Tim Costo | .20 | .50 |
| □ | 490 | Doug Davis | .20 | .50 |
| □ | 491 | Frank Viola | .20 | .50 |
| □ | 492 | Cory Snyder | .20 | .50 |
| □ | 493 | Chris Martin | .20 | .50 |
| □ | 494 | Dion James | .20 | .50 |
| □ | 495 | Randy Tomlin | .20 | .50 |
| □ | 496 | Greg Vaughn | .20 | .50 |
| □ | 497 | Dennis Cook | .20 | .50 |
| □ | 498 | Rosario Rodriguez | .20 | .50 |
| □ | 499 | Dave Staton | .20 | .50 |
| □ | 500 | George Brett | 1.25 | 3.00 |
| □ | 501 | Brian Barnes | .20 | .50 |
| □ | 502 | Butch Henry RC | .20 | .50 |
| □ | 503 | Harold Reynolds | .20 | .50 |
| □ | 504 | David Nied RC | .20 | .50 |
| □ | 505 | Lee Smith | .20 | .50 |
| □ | 506 | Steve Chitren | .20 | .50 |
| □ | 507 | Ken Hill | .20 | .50 |
| □ | 508 | Robbie Beckett | .20 | .50 |
| □ | 509 | Troy Afenir | .20 | .50 |
| □ | 510 | Kelly Gruber | .20 | .50 |
| □ | 511 | Bret Boone | .30 | .75 |
| □ | 512 | Jeff Branson | .20 | .50 |
| □ | 513 | Mike Jackson | .20 | .50 |
| □ | 514 | Pete Harnisch | .20 | .50 |
| □ | 515 | Chad Kreuter | .20 | .50 |
| □ | 516 | Joe Vitko RC | .20 | .50 |
| □ | 517 | Orel Hershiser | .20 | .50 |
| □ | 518 | John Doherty RC | .20 | .50 |
| □ | 519 | Jay Bell | .20 | .50 |
| □ | 520 | Mark Langston | .20 | .50 |
| □ | 521 | Dann Howitt | .20 | .50 |
| □ | 522 | Bobby Reed RC | .20 | .50 |
| □ | 523 | Bobby Munoz RC | .20 | .50 |
| □ | 524 | Todd Ritchie | .20 | .50 |
| □ | 525 | Rip Roberts | .20 | .50 |
| □ | 526 | Pat Listach RC | .40 | 1.00 |
| □ | 527 | Scott Brosius RC | .75 | 2.00 |
| □ | 528 | John Roper RC | .20 | .50 |
| □ | 529 | Phil Hiatt RC | .20 | .50 |
| □ | 530 | Denny Walling | .20 | .50 |
| □ | 531 | Carlos Baerga | .20 | .50 |
| □ | 532 | Manny Ramirez RC | 5.00 | 12.00 |
| □ | 533 | Pat Clements UER | .20 | .50 |
| □ | 534 | Ron Gant | .20 | .50 |
| □ | 535 | Pat Kelly | .20 | .50 |

| | | | |
|---|---|---|---|
| ☐ 536 Bill Spiers | .20 | .50 |
| ☐ 537 Darren Reed | .20 | .50 |
| ☐ 538 Ken Caminiti | .20 | .50 |
| ☐ 539 Butch Huskey RC | .20 | .50 |
| ☐ 540 Matt Nokes | .20 | .50 |
| ☐ 541 John Kruk | .20 | .50 |
| ☐ 542 John Jaha FOIL | .20 | .50 |
| ☐ 543 Justin Thompson RC | .20 | .50 |
| ☐ 544 Steve Hosey | .20 | .50 |
| ☐ 545 Joe Kmak | .20 | .50 |
| ☐ 546 John Franco | .20 | .50 |
| ☐ 547 Devon White | .20 | .50 |
| ☐ 548 Elston Hansen FOIL SP RC | .20 | .50 |
| ☐ 549 Ryan Klesko | .20 | .50 |
| ☐ 550 Danny Tartabull | .20 | .50 |
| ☐ 551 Frank Thomas FOIL | .50 | 1.25 |
| ☐ 552 Kevin Tapani | .20 | .50 |
| ☐ 553 Willie Banks | .20 | .50 |
| ☐ 554 B.J.Wallace FOIL RC | .20 | .50 |
| ☐ 555 Orlando Miller RC | .20 | .50 |
| ☐ 556 Mark Smith RC | .20 | .50 |
| ☐ 557 Tim Wallach FOIL | .20 | .50 |
| ☐ 558 Bill Gullickson | .20 | .50 |
| ☐ 559 Derek Bell FOIL | .20 | .50 |
| ☐ 560 Joe Randa FOIL RC | 1.25 | 3.00 |
| ☐ 561 Frank Seminara RC | .20 | .50 |
| ☐ 562 Mark Gardner | .20 | .50 |
| ☐ 563 Rick Greene FOIL RC | .20 | .50 |
| ☐ 564 Gary Gaetti | .20 | .50 |
| ☐ 565 Ozzie Guillen | .20 | .50 |
| ☐ 566 Charles Nagy FOIL | .20 | .50 |
| ☐ 567 Mike Milchin | .20 | .50 |
| ☐ 568 Ben Shelton RC | .20 | .50 |
| ☐ 569 Chris Roberts FOIL | .20 | .50 |
| ☐ 570 Ellis Burks | .20 | .50 |
| ☐ 571 Scott Scudder | .20 | .50 |
| ☐ 572 Jim Abbott FOIL | .30 | .75 |
| ☐ 573 Joe Carter | .30 | .75 |
| ☐ 574 Steve Finley | .20 | .50 |
| ☐ 575 Jim Olander FOIL | .20 | .50 |
| ☐ 576 Carlos Garcia | .20 | .50 |
| ☐ 577 Gregg Olson | .20 | .50 |
| ☐ 578 Greg Swindell FOIL | .20 | .50 |
| ☐ 579 Matt Williams FOIL | .20 | .50 |
| ☐ 580 Mark Grace | .30 | .75 |
| ☐ 581 Howard House FOIL RC | .20 | .50 |
| ☐ 582 Luis Polonia | .20 | .50 |
| ☐ 583 Erik Hanson | .20 | .50 |
| ☐ 584 Salomon Torres FOIL | .20 | .50 |
| ☐ 585 Carlton Fisk | .30 | .75 |
| ☐ 586 Bret Saberhagen | .20 | .50 |
| ☐ 587 Chad McConnell FOIL RC | .20 | .50 |
| ☐ 588 Jimmy Key | .20 | .50 |
| ☐ 589 Mike Macfarlane | .20 | .50 |
| ☐ 590 Barry Bonds FOIL | 1.50 | 4.00 |
| ☐ 591 Jamie McAndrew | .20 | .50 |
| ☐ 592 Shane Mack | .20 | .50 |
| ☐ 593 Kerwin Moore | .20 | .50 |
| ☐ 594 Joe Oliver | .20 | .50 |
| ☐ 595 Chris Sabo | .20 | .50 |
| ☐ 596 Alex Gonzalez RC | .40 | 1.00 |
| ☐ 597 Brett Butler | .20 | .50 |
| ☐ 598 Mark Hutton RC | .20 | .50 |
| ☐ 599 Andy Benes FOIL | .20 | .50 |
| ☐ 600 Jose Canseco | .30 | .75 |
| ☐ 601 Darryl Kile | .20 | .50 |
| ☐ 602 Matt Stairs FOIL | .20 | .50 |
| ☐ 603 Rob Butler FOIL RC | .20 | .50 |
| ☐ 604 Willie McGee | .20 | .50 |
| ☐ 605 Jack McDowell FOIL | .20 | .50 |
| ☐ 606 Tom Candiotti | .20 | .50 |
| ☐ 607 Ed Martel RC | .20 | .50 |
| ☐ 608 Matt Mieske FOIL | .20 | .50 |
| ☐ 609 Darrin Fletcher | .20 | .50 |
| ☐ 610 Rafael Palmeiro | .30 | .75 |
| ☐ 611 Bill Swift FOIL | .20 | .50 |
| ☐ 612 Mike Mussina | .50 | 1.25 |
| ☐ 613 Vince Coleman | .20 | .50 |
| ☐ 614 Scott Cepicky COR | .20 | .50 |
| ☐ 614A Scott Cepicky FOIL UER | .20 | .50 |
| ☐ 615 Mike Greenwell | .20 | .50 |
| ☐ 616 Kevin McGehee RC | .20 | .50 |
| ☐ 617 Jeffrey Hammonds FOIL | .20 | .50 |
| ☐ 618 Scott Taylor | .20 | .50 |
| ☐ 619 Dave Otto | .20 | .50 |
| ☐ 620 Mark McGwire FOIL | 1.25 | 3.00 |
| ☐ 621 Kevin Tatar RC | .20 | .50 |
| ☐ 622 Steve Farr | .20 | .50 |

| | | | |
|---|---|---|---|
| ☐ 623 Ryan Klesko FOIL | .20 | .50 |
| ☐ 624 Dave Fleming | .20 | .50 |
| ☐ 625 Andre Dawson | .20 | .50 |
| ☐ 626 Tino Martinez FOIL SP | .30 | .75 |
| ☐ 627 Chad Curtis RC | .40 | 1.00 |
| ☐ 628 Mickey Morandini | .20 | .50 |
| ☐ 629 Gregg Olson FOIL SP | .20 | .50 |
| ☐ 630 Lou Whitaker | .20 | .50 |
| ☐ 631 Arthur Rhodes | .20 | .50 |
| ☐ 632 Brandon Wilson RC | .20 | .50 |
| ☐ 633 Lance Jennings RC | .20 | .50 |
| ☐ 634 Allen Watson RC | .20 | .50 |
| ☐ 635 Len Dykstra | .20 | .50 |
| ☐ 636 Joe Girardi | .20 | .50 |
| ☐ 637 Kiki Hernandez FOIL RC | .20 | .50 |
| ☐ 638 Mike Hampton RC | .75 | 2.00 |
| ☐ 639 Al Osuna | .20 | .50 |
| ☐ 640 Kevin Appier | .20 | .50 |
| ☐ 641 Rick Helling FOIL | .20 | .50 |
| ☐ 642 Jody Reed | .20 | .50 |
| ☐ 643 Ray Lankford | .20 | .50 |
| ☐ 644 John Olerud | .20 | .50 |
| ☐ 645 Paul Molitor FOIL | .20 | .50 |
| ☐ 646 Pat Borders | .20 | .50 |
| ☐ 647 Mike Morgan | .20 | .50 |
| ☐ 648 Larry Walker | .30 | .75 |
| ☐ 649 Pedro Castellano FOIL | .20 | .50 |
| ☐ 650 Fred McGriff | .30 | .75 |
| ☐ 651 Walt Weiss | .20 | .50 |
| ☐ 652 Calvin Murray FOIL RC | .40 | 1.00 |
| ☐ 653 Dave Nilsson | .20 | .50 |
| ☐ 654 Greg Pirkl RC | .20 | .50 |
| ☐ 655 Robin Ventura FOIL | .20 | .50 |
| ☐ 656 Mark Portugal | .20 | .50 |
| ☐ 657 Roger McDowell | .20 | .50 |
| ☐ 658 Rick Hirtensteiner FOIL RC | .20 | .50 |
| ☐ 659 Glenallen Hill | .20 | .50 |
| ☐ 660 Greg Gagne | .20 | .50 |
| ☐ 661 Charles Johnson FOIL | .20 | .50 |
| ☐ 662 Brian Hunter | .20 | .50 |
| ☐ 663 Mark Lemke | .20 | .50 |
| ☐ 664 Tim Belcher FOIL SP | .20 | .50 |
| ☐ 665 Rich DeLucia | .20 | .50 |
| ☐ 666 Bob Walk | .20 | .50 |
| ☐ 667 Joe Carter FOIL | .20 | .50 |
| ☐ 668 Jose Guzman | .20 | .50 |
| ☐ 669 Otis Nixon | .20 | .50 |
| ☐ 670 Phil Nevin FOIL | .20 | .50 |
| ☐ 671 Eric Davis | .20 | .50 |
| ☐ 672 Damion Easley RC | .40 | 1.00 |
| ☐ 673 Will Clark FOIL | .30 | .75 |
| ☐ 674 Mark Kiefer RC | .20 | .50 |
| ☐ 675 Ozzie Smith | .75 | 2.00 |
| ☐ 676 Manny Ramirez FOIL | 3.00 | 8.00 |
| ☐ 677 Gregg Olson | .20 | .50 |
| ☐ 678 Cliff Floyd RC | 1.25 | 3.00 |
| ☐ 679 Duane Singleton RC | .20 | .50 |
| ☐ 680 Jose Rijo | .20 | .50 |
| ☐ 681 Willie Randolph | .20 | .50 |
| ☐ 682 Michael Tucker FOIL RC | .40 | 1.00 |
| ☐ 683 Darren Lewis | .20 | .50 |
| ☐ 684 Dale Murphy | .30 | .75 |
| ☐ 685 Mike Pagliarulo | .20 | .50 |
| ☐ 686 Paul Miller RC | .20 | .50 |
| ☐ 687 Mike Robertson RC | .20 | .50 |
| ☐ 688 Mike Devereaux | .20 | .50 |
| ☐ 689 Pedro Astacio RC | .40 | 1.00 |
| ☐ 690 Alan Trammell | .20 | .50 |
| ☐ 691 Roger Clemens | 1.00 | 2.50 |
| ☐ 692 Bud Black | .20 | .50 |
| ☐ 693 Turk Wendell RC | .40 | 1.00 |
| ☐ 694 Barry Larkin FOIL | .30 | .75 |
| ☐ 695 Todd Zeile | .20 | .50 |
| ☐ 696 Pat Hentgen | .20 | .50 |
| ☐ 697 Eddie Taubensee RC | .40 | 1.00 |
| ☐ 698 Guillermo Velasquez RC | .20 | .50 |
| ☐ 699 Tom Glavine | .30 | .75 |
| ☐ 700 Robin Yount | .75 | 2.00 |
| ☐ 701 Checklist 1-141 | .20 | .50 |
| ☐ 702 Checklist 142-282 | .20 | .50 |
| ☐ 703 Checklist 283-423 | .20 | .50 |
| ☐ 704 Checklist 424-564 | .20 | .50 |
| ☐ 705 Checklist 565-705 | .20 | .50 |

## 1993 Bowman

| | | | |
|---|---|---|---|
| ☐ COMPLETE SET (708) | 15.00 | 40.00 |
| ☐ 1 Glenn Davis | .05 | .15 |
| ☐ 2 Hector Roa RC | .08 | .25 |
| ☐ 3 Ken Ryan RC | .08 | .25 |
| ☐ 4 Derek Wallace RC | .08 | .25 |
| ☐ 5 Jorge Fabregas | .05 | .15 |
| ☐ 6 Joe Oliver | .05 | .15 |
| ☐ 7 Brandon Wilson | .05 | .15 |
| ☐ 8 Mark Thompson RC | .08 | .25 |
| ☐ 9 Tracy Sanders | .05 | .15 |
| ☐ 10 Rich Renteria | .05 | .15 |
| ☐ 11 Lou Whitaker | .10 | .30 |
| ☐ 12 Brian L. Hunter RC | .20 | .50 |
| ☐ 13 Joe Vitiello | .05 | .15 |
| ☐ 14 Eric Karros | .10 | .30 |
| ☐ 15 Joe Kmak | .05 | .15 |
| ☐ 16 Tavo Alvarez | .05 | .15 |
| ☐ 17 Steve Dunn RC | .08 | .25 |
| ☐ 18 Tony Fernandez | .05 | .15 |
| ☐ 19 Melido Perez | .05 | .15 |
| ☐ 20 Mike Lieberthal | .10 | .30 |
| ☐ 21 Terry Steinbach | .05 | .15 |
| ☐ 22 Stan Belinda | .05 | .15 |
| ☐ 23 Jay Buhner | .10 | .30 |
| ☐ 24 Allen Watson | .05 | .15 |
| ☐ 25 Daryl Henderson RC | .08 | .25 |
| ☐ 26 Ray McDavid RC | .08 | .25 |
| ☐ 27 Shawn Green | .40 | 1.00 |
| ☐ 28 Bud Black | .05 | .15 |
| ☐ 29 Sherman Obando RC | .08 | .25 |
| ☐ 30 Mike Hostetler RC | .08 | .25 |
| ☐ 31 Nate Minchey RC | .08 | .25 |
| ☐ 32 Randy Myers | .05 | .15 |
| ☐ 33 Brian Grebeck | .05 | .15 |
| ☐ 34 John Roper | .05 | .15 |
| ☐ 35 Larry Thomas | .05 | .15 |
| ☐ 36 Alex Cole | .05 | .15 |
| ☐ 37 Tom Kramer RC | .08 | .25 |
| ☐ 38 Matt Whisenant RC | .08 | .25 |
| ☐ 39 Chris Gomez RC | .20 | .50 |
| ☐ 40 Luis Gonzalez | .10 | .30 |
| ☐ 41 Kevin Appier | .08 | .25 |
| ☐ 42 Omar Daal RC | .10 | .30 |
| ☐ 43 Duane Singleton | .05 | .15 |
| ☐ 44 Bill Risley | .05 | .15 |
| ☐ 45 Pat Meares RC | .20 | .50 |
| ☐ 46 Butch Huskey | .05 | .15 |
| ☐ 47 Bobby Munoz | .05 | .15 |
| ☐ 48 Juan Bell | .05 | .15 |
| ☐ 49 Scott Lydy RC | .08 | .25 |
| ☐ 50 Dennis Moeller | .05 | .15 |
| ☐ 51 Marc Newfield | .08 | .25 |
| ☐ 52 Tripp Cromer RC | .08 | .25 |
| ☐ 53 Kurt Miller | .05 | .15 |
| ☐ 54 Jim Pena | .05 | .15 |
| ☐ 55 Juan Guzman | .10 | .30 |
| ☐ 56 Matt Williams | .10 | .30 |
| ☐ 57 Harold Reynolds | .10 | .30 |
| ☐ 58 Donnie Elliott RC | .08 | .25 |
| ☐ 59 Jon Shave RC | .08 | .25 |
| ☐ 60 Kevin Roberson RC | .08 | .25 |
| ☐ 61 Hilly Hathaway RC | .05 | .15 |
| ☐ 62 Jose Rijo | .05 | .15 |
| ☐ 63 Kerry Taylor RC | .05 | .15 |
| ☐ 64 Ryan Hawblitzel | .05 | .15 |
| ☐ 65 Glenallen Hill | .05 | .15 |
| ☐ 66 Ramon D. Martinez RC | .08 | .25 |
| ☐ 67 Travis Fryman | .10 | .30 |
| ☐ 68 Tom Nevers | .05 | .15 |
| ☐ 69 Phil Hiatt | .05 | .15 |
| ☐ 70 Tim Wallach | .05 | .15 |
| ☐ 71 B.J. Surhoff | .10 | .30 |

|  |  | | |
|---|---|---|---|
| 72 | Rondell White | .10 | .30 |
| 73 | Denny Hocking RC | .20 | .50 |
| 74 | Mike Oquist RC | .08 | .25 |
| 75 | Paul O'Neill | .20 | .50 |
| 76 | Willie Banks | .05 | .15 |
| 77 | Bob Welch | .05 | .15 |
| 78 | Jose Sandoval RC | .08 | .25 |
| 79 | Bill Haselman | .05 | .15 |
| 80 | Rheal Cormier | .05 | .15 |
| 81 | Dean Palmer | .10 | .30 |
| 82 | Pat Gomez RC | .08 | .25 |
| 83 | Steve Karsay | .08 | .25 |
| 84 | Carl Hanselman RC | .08 | .25 |
| 85 | T.R. Lewis RC | .08 | .25 |
| 86 | Chipper Jones | .30 | .75 |
| 87 | Scott Hatteberg | .05 | .15 |
| 88 | Greg Hibbard | .05 | .15 |
| 89 | Lance Painter RC | .08 | .25 |
| 90 | Chad Mottola RC | .20 | .50 |
| 91 | Jason Bere | .05 | .15 |
| 92 | Dante Bichette | .10 | .30 |
| 93 | Sandy Alomar Jr. | .05 | .15 |
| 94 | Carl Everett | .10 | .30 |
| 95 | Danny Bautista RC | .20 | .50 |
| 96 | Steve Finley | .10 | .30 |
| 97 | David Cone | .10 | .30 |
| 98 | Todd Hollandsworth | .05 | .15 |
| 99 | Matt Mieske | .05 | .15 |
| 100 | Larry Walker | .10 | .30 |
| 101 | Shane Mack | .05 | .15 |
| 102 | Aaron Ledesma RC | .08 | .25 |
| 103 | Andy Pettitte RC | 3.00 | 8.00 |
| 104 | Kevin Stocker | .05 | .15 |
| 105 | Mike Mohler RC | .08 | .25 |
| 106 | Tony Menendez | .05 | .15 |
| 107 | Derek Lowe | .10 | .30 |
| 108 | Basil Shabazz | .05 | .15 |
| 109 | Dan Smith | .05 | .15 |
| 110 | Scott Sanders RC | .20 | .50 |
| 111 | Todd Stottlemyre | .08 | .25 |
| 112 | Benji Simonton RC | .08 | .25 |
| 113 | Rick Sutcliffe | .10 | .30 |
| 114 | Lee Heath RC | .08 | .25 |
| 115 | Jeff Russell | .05 | .15 |
| 116 | Dave Stevens RC | .08 | .25 |
| 117 | Mark Holzemer RC | .08 | .25 |
| 118 | Tim Belcher | .05 | .15 |
| 119 | Bobby Thigpen | .05 | .15 |
| 120 | Roger Bailey RC | .08 | .25 |
| 121 | Tony Mitchell RC | .08 | .25 |
| 122 | Junior Felix | .05 | .15 |
| 123 | Rich Robertson RC | .08 | .25 |
| 124 | Andy Cook RC | .08 | .25 |
| 125 | Brian Bevil RC | .08 | .25 |
| 126 | Darryl Strawberry | .10 | .30 |
| 127 | Cal Eldred | .05 | .15 |
| 128 | Cliff Floyd | .10 | .30 |
| 129 | Alan Newman RC | .05 | .15 |
| 130 | Howard Johnson | .05 | .15 |
| 131 | Jim Abbott | .20 | .50 |
| 132 | Chad McConnell | .05 | .15 |
| 133 | Miguel Jimenez RC | .08 | .25 |
| 134 | Brett Backlund RC | .08 | .25 |
| 135 | John Cummings RC | .08 | .25 |
| 136 | Brian Barber | .05 | .15 |
| 137 | Rafael Palmeiro | .20 | .50 |
| 138 | Tim Worrell RC | .08 | .25 |
| 139 | Jose Pett RC | .08 | .25 |
| 140 | Barry Bonds | .75 | 2.00 |
| 141 | Damon Buford | .05 | .15 |
| 142 | Jeff Blauser | .05 | .15 |
| 143 | Frankie Rodriguez | .05 | .15 |
| 144 | Mike Morgan | .05 | .15 |
| 145 | Gary DiSarcina | .05 | .15 |
| 146 | Pokey Reese | .05 | .15 |
| 147 | Johnny Ruffin RC | .05 | .15 |
| 148 | David Nied | .05 | .15 |
| 149 | Charles Nagy | .05 | .15 |
| 150 | Mike Myers RC | .08 | .25 |
| 151 | Kenny Carlyle RC | .08 | .25 |
| 152 | Eric Anthony | .05 | .15 |
| 153 | Jose Lind | .05 | .15 |
| 154 | Pedro Martinez | .60 | 1.50 |
| 155 | Mark Kiefer | .05 | .15 |
| 156 | Tim Laker RC | .08 | .25 |
| 157 | Pat Mahomes | .05 | .15 |
| 158 | Bobby Bonilla | .10 | .30 |
| 159 | Domingo Jean | .05 | .15 |
| 160 | Darren Daulton | .10 | .30 |
| 161 | Mark McGwire | .75 | 2.00 |
| 162 | Jason Kendall RC | .75 | 2.00 |
| 163 | Desi Relaford | .05 | .15 |
| 164 | Ozzie Canseco | .05 | .15 |
| 165 | Rick Helling | .05 | .15 |
| 166 | Steve Pegues RC | .08 | .25 |
| 167 | Paul Molitor | .10 | .30 |
| 168 | Larry Carter RC | .05 | .15 |
| 169 | Arthur Rhodes | .05 | .15 |
| 170 | Damon Hollins RC | .20 | .50 |
| 171 | Frank Viola | .05 | .15 |
| 172 | Steve Trachsel RC | .40 | 1.00 |
| 173 | J.T.Snow RC | .40 | 1.00 |
| 174 | Keith Gordon RC | .08 | .25 |
| 175 | Carlton Fisk | .20 | .50 |
| 176 | Jason Bates RC | .08 | .25 |
| 177 | Mike Crosby RC | .08 | .25 |
| 178 | Benny Santiago | .10 | .30 |
| 179 | Mike Moore | .05 | .15 |
| 180 | Jeff Juden | .05 | .15 |
| 181 | Darren Burton | .08 | .25 |
| 182 | Todd Williams RC | .20 | .50 |
| 183 | John Jaha | .05 | .15 |
| 184 | Mike Lansing RC | .20 | .50 |
| 185 | Pedro Grifol RC | .08 | .25 |
| 186 | Vince Coleman | .05 | .15 |
| 187 | Pat Kelly | .05 | .15 |
| 188 | Clemente Alvarez RC | .08 | .25 |
| 189 | Ron Darling | .05 | .15 |
| 190 | Orlando Merced | .05 | .15 |
| 191 | Chris Bosio | .05 | .15 |
| 192 | Steve Dixon RC | .08 | .25 |
| 193 | Doug Dascenzo | .05 | .15 |
| 194 | Ray Holbert RC | .08 | .25 |
| 195 | Howard Battle | .08 | .25 |
| 196 | Willie McGee | .10 | .30 |
| 197 | John O'Donoghue RC | .08 | .25 |
| 198 | Steve Avery | .05 | .15 |
| 199 | Greg Blosser | .05 | .15 |
| 200 | Ryne Sandberg | .50 | 1.25 |
| 201 | Joe Grahe | .05 | .15 |
| 202 | Dan Wilson | .10 | .30 |
| 203 | Domingo Martinez RC | .08 | .25 |
| 204 | Andres Galarraga | .10 | .30 |
| 205 | Jamie Taylor RC | .08 | .25 |
| 206 | Darrell Whitmore RC | .08 | .25 |
| 207 | Ben Blomdahl RC | .08 | .25 |
| 208 | Doug Drabek | .05 | .15 |
| 209 | Keith Miller | .05 | .15 |
| 210 | Billy Ashley | .08 | .25 |
| 211 | Mike Farrell RC | .08 | .25 |
| 212 | John Wetteland | .10 | .30 |
| 213 | Randy Tomlin | .05 | .15 |
| 214 | Sid Fernandez | .05 | .15 |
| 215 | Quilvio Veras RC | .20 | .50 |
| 216 | Dave Hollins | .05 | .15 |
| 217 | Mike Neill | .05 | .15 |
| 218 | Andy Van Slyke | .20 | .50 |
| 219 | Bret Boone | .10 | .30 |
| 220 | Tom Pagnozzi | .05 | .15 |
| 221 | Mike Welch RC | .08 | .25 |
| 222 | Frank Seminara | .05 | .15 |
| 223 | Ron Villone | .08 | .25 |
| 224 | D.J.Thielen RC | .08 | .25 |
| 225 | Cal Ripken | 1.00 | 2.50 |
| 226 | Pedro Borbon Jr. RC | .08 | .25 |
| 227 | Carlos Quintana | .05 | .15 |
| 228 | Tommy Shields | .05 | .15 |
| 229 | Tim Salmon | .20 | .50 |
| 230 | John Smiley | .05 | .15 |
| 231 | Ellis Burks | .10 | .30 |
| 232 | Pedro Castellano | .05 | .15 |
| 233 | Paul Byrd | .10 | .30 |
| 234 | Bryan Harvey | .05 | .15 |
| 235 | Scott Livingstone | .05 | .15 |
| 236 | James Mouton RC | .08 | .25 |
| 237 | Joe Randa | .10 | .30 |
| 238 | Pedro Astacio | .05 | .15 |
| 239 | Darryl Hamilton | .05 | .15 |
| 240 | Joey Eischen RC | .08 | .25 |
| 241 | Edgar Herrera RC | .08 | .25 |
| 242 | Dwight Gooden | .10 | .30 |
| 243 | Sam Militello | .05 | .15 |
| 244 | Ron Blazier RC | .08 | .25 |
| 245 | Ruben Sierra | .10 | .30 |
| 246 | Al Martin | .05 | .15 |
| 247 | Mike Felder | .05 | .15 |
| 248 | Bob Tewksbury | .05 | .15 |
| 249 | Craig Lefferts | .05 | .15 |
| 250 | Luis Lopez RC | .08 | .25 |
| 251 | Devon White | .10 | .30 |
| 252 | Will Clark | .20 | .50 |
| 253 | Mark Smith | .05 | .15 |
| 254 | Terry Pendleton | .10 | .30 |
| 255 | Aaron Sele | .05 | .15 |
| 256 | Jose Viera RC | .08 | .25 |
| 257 | Damion Easley | .05 | .15 |
| 258 | Rod Lofton RC | .08 | .25 |
| 259 | Chris Snopek RC | .08 | .25 |
| 260 | Quinton McCracken RC | .20 | .50 |
| 261 | Mike Matthews RC | .08 | .25 |
| 262 | Hector Carrasco RC | .08 | .25 |
| 263 | Rick Greene | .05 | .15 |
| 264 | Chris Hall RC | .08 | .25 |
| 265 | George Brett | .75 | 2.00 |
| 266 | Rick Gorecki RC | .08 | .25 |
| 267 | Francisco Gamez RC | .08 | .25 |
| 268 | Marquis Grissom | .10 | .30 |
| 269 | Kevin Tapani UER | .05 | .15 |
| 270 | Ryan Thompson | .05 | .15 |
| 271 | Gerald Williams | .05 | .15 |
| 272 | Paul Fletcher RC | .08 | .25 |
| 273 | Lance Blankenship | .05 | .15 |
| 274 | Marty Neff RC | .08 | .25 |
| 275 | Shawn Estes | .05 | .15 |
| 276 | Rene Arocha RC | .20 | .50 |
| 277 | Scott Eyre RC | .08 | .25 |
| 278 | Phil Plantier | .05 | .15 |
| 279 | Paul Spoljaric RC | .08 | .25 |
| 280 | Chris Gambs | .05 | .15 |
| 281 | Harold Baines | .10 | .30 |
| 282 | Jose Oliva | .05 | .15 |
| 283 | Matt Whiteside RC | .08 | .25 |
| 284 | Brant Brown RC | .20 | .50 |
| 285 | Russ Springer | .05 | .15 |
| 286 | Chris Sabo | .05 | .15 |
| 287 | Ozzie Guillen | .10 | .30 |
| 288 | Marcus Moore RC | .08 | .25 |
| 289 | Chad Ogea | .05 | .15 |
| 290 | Walt Weiss | .05 | .15 |
| 291 | Brian Edmondson | .05 | .15 |
| 292 | Jimmy Gonzalez | .05 | .15 |
| 293 | Danny Miceli RC | .20 | .50 |
| 294 | Jose Offerman | .05 | .15 |
| 295 | Greg Vaughn | .05 | .15 |
| 296 | Frank Bolick | .05 | .15 |
| 297 | Mike Maksudian RC | .08 | .25 |
| 298 | John Franco | .10 | .30 |
| 299 | Danny Tartabull | .05 | .15 |
| 300 | Len Dykstra | .10 | .30 |
| 301 | Bobby Witt | .05 | .15 |
| 302 | Trey Beamon RC | .08 | .25 |
| 303 | Tino Martinez | .20 | .50 |
| 304 | Aaron Holbert | .05 | .15 |
| 305 | Juan Gonzalez | .10 | .30 |
| 306 | Billy Hall RC | .08 | .25 |
| 307 | Duane Ward | .05 | .15 |
| 308 | Rod Beck | .05 | .15 |
| 309 | Jose Mercedes RC | .08 | .25 |
| 310 | Otis Nixon | .05 | .15 |
| 311 | Gettys Glaze RC | .08 | .25 |
| 312 | Candy Maldonado | .05 | .15 |
| 313 | Chad Curtis | .05 | .15 |
| 314 | Tim Costo | .05 | .15 |
| 315 | Mike Robertson | .05 | .15 |
| 316 | Nigel Wilson | .05 | .15 |
| 317 | Greg McMichael RC | .20 | .50 |
| 318 | Scott Pose RC | .08 | .25 |
| 319 | Ivan Cruz | .05 | .15 |
| 320 | Greg Swindell | .05 | .15 |
| 321 | Kevin McReynolds | .05 | .15 |
| 322 | Tom Candiotti | .05 | .15 |
| 323 | Rob Wishnevski RC | .08 | .25 |
| 324 | Ken Hill | .05 | .15 |
| 325 | Kirby Puckett | .30 | .75 |
| 326 | Tim Bogar RC | .08 | .25 |
| 327 | Mariano Rivera | 1.00 | 2.50 |
| 328 | Mitch Williams | .05 | .15 |
| 329 | Craig Paquette | .05 | .15 |
| 330 | Jay Bell | .10 | .30 |
| 331 | Jose Martinez RC | .08 | .25 |
| 332 | Rob Deer | .05 | .15 |
| 333 | Brook Fordyce | .05 | .15 |
| 334 | Matt Nokes | .05 | .15 |
| 335 | Derek Lee | .05 | .15 |

|  | | |  | | |  | | |
|---|---|---|---|---|---|---|---|---|
| 336 Paul Ellis RC | .08 | .25 | 424 Delino DeShields | .05 | .15 | 512 Gene Schall | .05 | .15 |
| 337 Desi Wilson RC | .08 | .25 | 425 Scott Erickson | .05 | .15 | 513 Curtis Shaw | .05 | .15 |
| 338 Roberto Alomar | .20 | .50 | 426 Jeff Kent | .30 | .75 | 514 Steve Cooke | .05 | .15 |
| 339 Jim Tatum FOIL RC | .08 | .25 | 427 Jimmy Key | .10 | .30 | 515 Edgar Martinez | .20 | .50 |
| 340 J.T. Snow FOIL | .40 | 1.00 | 428 Mickey Morandini | .05 | .15 | 516 Mike Milchin | .05 | .15 |
| 341 Tim Salmon FOIL | .20 | .50 | 429 Marcos Armas RC | .08 | .25 | 517 Billy Ripken | .05 | .15 |
| 342 Russ Davis FOIL RC | .20 | .50 | 430 Don Slaught | .05 | .15 | 518 Andy Benes | .05 | .15 |
| 343 Javy Lopez FOIL | .20 | .50 | 431 Randy Johnson | .30 | .75 | 519 Juan de la Rosa RC | .08 | .25 |
| 344 Troy O'Leary FOIL RC | .20 | .50 | 432 Omar Olivares | .05 | .15 | 520 John Burkett | .05 | .15 |
| 345 Marty Cordova FOIL RC | .20 | .50 | 433 Charlie Leibrandt | .05 | .15 | 521 Alex Ochoa | .05 | .15 |
| 346 Bubba Smith RC FOIL | .08 | .25 | 434 Kurt Stillwell | .05 | .15 | 522 Tony Tarasco RC | .20 | .50 |
| 347 Chipper Jones FOIL | .30 | .75 | 435 Scott Brow RC | .08 | .25 | 523 Luis Ortiz | .05 | .15 |
| 348 Jessie Hollins FOIL | .05 | .15 | 436 Robby Thompson | .05 | .15 | 524 Rick Wilkins | .05 | .15 |
| 349 Willie Greene FOIL | .05 | .15 | 437 Ben McDonald | .05 | .15 | 525 Chris Turner RC | .08 | .25 |
| 350 Mark Thompson FOIL | .05 | .15 | 438 Deion Sanders | .20 | .50 | 526 Rob Dibble | .10 | .30 |
| 351 Nigel Wilson FOIL | .05 | .15 | 439 Tony Pena | .05 | .15 | 527 Jack McDowell | .05 | .15 |
| 352 Todd Jones FOIL | .10 | .30 | 440 Mark Grace | .20 | .50 | 528 Daryl Boston | .05 | .15 |
| 353 Raul Mondesi FOIL | .10 | .30 | 441 Eduardo Perez | .05 | .15 | 529 Bill Wertz RC | .08 | .25 |
| 354 Cliff Floyd FOIL | .10 | .30 | 442 Tim Pugh RC | .08 | .25 | 530 Charlie Hough | .10 | .30 |
| 355 Bobby Jones FOIL | .10 | .30 | 443 Scott Ruffcorn | .05 | .15 | 531 Sean Bergman | .05 | .15 |
| 356 Kevin Stocker FOIL | .05 | .15 | 444 Jay Gainer RC | .08 | .25 | 532 Doug Jones | .05 | .15 |
| 357 Midre Cummings FOIL | .05 | .15 | 445 Albert Belle | .20 | .50 | 533 Jeff Montgomery | .05 | .15 |
| 358 Allen Watson FOIL | .05 | .15 | 446 Bret Barberie | .05 | .15 | 534 Roger Cadeno RC | .20 | .50 |
| 359 Ray McDavid FOIL | .05 | .15 | 447 Justin Mashore | .05 | .15 | 535 Robin Yount | .50 | 1.25 |
| 360 Steve Hosey FOIL | .05 | .15 | 448 Pete Harnisch | .05 | .15 | 536 Mo Vaughn | .10 | .30 |
| 361 Brad Pennington FOIL | .05 | .15 | 449 Greg Gagne | .05 | .15 | 537 Brian Harper | .05 | .15 |
| 362 Frankie Rodriquez FOIL | .05 | .15 | 450 Eric Davis | .10 | .30 | 538 Juan Castillo RC | .05 | .15 |
| 363 Troy Percival FOIL | .20 | .50 | 451 Dave Mlicki | .05 | .15 | 539 Steve Farr | .05 | .15 |
| 364 Jason Bere FOIL | .05 | .15 | 452 Moises Alou | .10 | .30 | 540 John Kruk | .10 | .30 |
| 365 Manny Ramirez FOIL | .50 | 1.25 | 453 Rick Aguilera | .05 | .15 | 541 Troy Neel | .05 | .15 |
| 366 Justin Thompson FOIL | .05 | .15 | 454 Eddie Murray | .30 | .75 | 542 Danny Clybum RC | .08 | .25 |
| 367 Joe Vitiello FOIL | .05 | .15 | 455 Bob Wickman | .05 | .15 | 543 Jim Converse RC | .08 | .25 |
| 368 Tyrone Hill FOIL | .05 | .15 | 456 Wes Chamberlain | .05 | .15 | 544 Gregg Jefferies | .05 | .15 |
| 369 David McCarty FOIL | .05 | .15 | 457 Brent Gates | .05 | .15 | 545 Jose Canseco | .20 | .50 |
| 370 Brien Taylor FOIL | .05 | .15 | 458 Paul Wagner | .05 | .15 | 546 Julio Bruno RC | .08 | .25 |
| 371 Todd Van Poppel FOIL | .05 | .15 | 459 Mike Hampton | .10 | .30 | 547 Rob Butler | .05 | .15 |
| 372 Marc Newfield FOIL | .05 | .15 | 460 Ozzie Smith | .50 | 1.25 | 548 Royce Clayton | .05 | .15 |
| 373 Terrell Lowery FOIL RC | .20 | .50 | 461 Tom Henke | .05 | .15 | 549 Chris Hoiles | .05 | .15 |
| 374 Alex Gonzalez FOIL | .05 | .15 | 462 Ricky Gutierrez | .05 | .15 | 550 Greg Maddux | .50 | 1.25 |
| 375 Ken Griffey Jr. | .50 | 1.25 | 463 Jack Morris | .10 | .30 | 551 Joe Ciccarella RC | .08 | .25 |
| 376 Donovan Osborne | .05 | .15 | 464 Joel Chimelis | .05 | .15 | 552 Ozzie Timmons | .05 | .15 |
| 377 Ritchie Moody RC | .08 | .25 | 465 Gregg Olson | .05 | .15 | 553 Chili Davis | .10 | .30 |
| 378 Shane Andrews | .05 | .15 | 466 Javy Lopez | .20 | .50 | 554 Brian Koelling | .05 | .15 |
| 379 Carlos Delgado | .30 | .75 | 467 Scott Cooper | .05 | .15 | 555 Frank Thomas | .30 | .75 |
| 380 Bill Swift | .05 | .15 | 468 Willie Wilson | .05 | .15 | 556 Vinny Castilla | .30 | .75 |
| 381 Leo Gomez | .05 | .15 | 469 Mark Langston | .05 | .15 | 557 Reggie Jefferson | .05 | .15 |
| 382 Ron Gant | .10 | .30 | 470 Barry Larkin | .20 | .50 | 558 Rob Natal | .05 | .15 |
| 383 Scott Fletcher | .05 | .15 | 471 Rod Bolton | .05 | .15 | 559 Mike Henneman | .05 | .15 |
| 384 Matt Walbeck RC | .20 | .50 | 472 Freddie Benavides | .05 | .15 | 560 Craig Biggio | .20 | .50 |
| 385 Chuck Finley | .05 | .15 | 473 Ken Ramos RC | .08 | .25 | 561 Billy Brewer | .05 | .15 |
| 386 Kevin Mitchell | .05 | .15 | 474 Chuck Carr | .05 | .15 | 562 Dan Melendez | .05 | .15 |
| 387 Wilson Alvarez UER | .05 | .15 | 475 Cecil Fielder | .10 | .30 | 563 Kenny Felder RC | .08 | .25 |
| 388 John Burke RC | .08 | .25 | 476 Eddie Taubensee | .05 | .15 | 564 Miguel Batista RC | .40 | 1.00 |
| 389 Alan Embree | .05 | .15 | 477 Chris Eddy RC | .08 | .25 | 565 Dave Winfield | .10 | .30 |
| 390 Trevor Hoffman | .30 | .75 | 478 Greg Hansell | .05 | .15 | 566 Al Shirley | .05 | .15 |
| 391 Alan Trammell | .10 | .30 | 479 Kevin Reimer | .05 | .15 | 567 Robert Eenhoorn | .05 | .15 |
| 392 Todd Jones | .10 | .30 | 480 Dennis Martinez | .10 | .30 | 568 Mike Williams | .05 | .15 |
| 393 Felix Jose | .05 | .15 | 481 Chuck Knoblauch | .10 | .30 | 569 Tanyon Sturtze RC | .08 | .25 |
| 394 Orel Hershiser | .10 | .30 | 482 Mike Draper | .05 | .15 | 570 Tim Wakefield | .30 | .75 |
| 395 Pat Listach | .05 | .15 | 483 Spike Owen | .05 | .15 | 571 Greg Pirkl | .05 | .15 |
| 396 Gabe White | .05 | .15 | 484 Terry Mulholland | .05 | .15 | 572 Sean Lowe RC | .08 | .25 |
| 397 Dan Serafini RC | .08 | .25 | 485 Dennis Eckersley | .10 | .30 | 573 Terry Burrows RC | .08 | .25 |
| 398 Todd Hundley | .05 | .15 | 486 Blas Minor | .05 | .15 | 574 Kevin Higgins | .05 | .15 |
| 399 Wade Boggs | .20 | .50 | 487 Dave Fleming | .05 | .15 | 575 Joe Carter | .10 | .30 |
| 400 Tyler Green | .05 | .15 | 488 Dan Cholowsky | .05 | .15 | 576 Kevin Rogers | .05 | .15 |
| 401 Mike Bordick | .05 | .15 | 489 Ivan Rodriguez | .20 | .50 | 577 Manny Alexander | .05 | .15 |
| 402 Scott Bullett | .05 | .15 | 490 Gary Sheffield | .10 | .30 | 578 David Justice | .10 | .30 |
| 403 LaGrande Russell RC | .08 | .25 | 491 Ed Sprague | .05 | .15 | 579 Brian Conroy RC | .08 | .25 |
| 404 Ray Lankford | .10 | .30 | 492 Steve Hosey | .05 | .15 | 580 Jessie Hollins | .05 | .15 |
| 405 Nolan Ryan | 1.25 | 3.00 | 493 Jimmy Haynes RC | .20 | .50 | 581 Ron Watson RC | .08 | .25 |
| 406 Robbie Beckett | .05 | .15 | 494 John Smoltz | .20 | .50 | 582 Bip Roberts | .05 | .15 |
| 407 Brent Bowers RC | .08 | .25 | 495 Andre Dawson | .10 | .30 | 583 Tom Urbani RC | .08 | .25 |
| 408 Adell Davenport RC | .08 | .25 | 496 Rey Sanchez | .05 | .15 | 584 Jason Hutchins RC | .08 | .25 |
| 409 Brady Anderson | .10 | .30 | 497 Ty Van Burkleo | .05 | .15 | 585 Carlos Baerga | .10 | .30 |
| 410 Tom Glavine | .20 | .50 | 498 Bobby Ayala RC | .08 | .25 | 586 Jeff Mutis | .05 | .15 |
| 411 Doug Hecker RC | .08 | .25 | 499 Tim Raines | .10 | .30 | 587 Justin Thompson | .05 | .15 |
| 412 Jose Guzman | .05 | .15 | 500 Charlie Hayes | .05 | .15 | 588 Orlando Miller | .05 | .15 |
| 413 Luis Polonia | .05 | .15 | 501 Paul Sorrento | .05 | .15 | 589 Brian McRae | .05 | .15 |
| 414 Brian Williams | .05 | .15 | 502 Richie Lewis RC | .08 | .25 | 590 Ramon Martinez | .10 | .30 |
| 415 Bo Jackson | .30 | .75 | 503 Jason Pfaff RC | .08 | .25 | 591 Dave Nilsson | .05 | .15 |
| 416 Eric Young | .05 | .15 | 504 Ken Caminiti | .10 | .30 | 592 Jose Vidro RC | .75 | 2.00 |
| 417 Kenny Lofton | .10 | .30 | 505 Mike Macfarlane | .05 | .15 | 593 Rich Becker | .05 | .15 |
| 418 Christos Destrade | .05 | .15 | 506 Jody Reed | .05 | .15 | 594 Preston Stinson RC | .60 | 1.50 |
| 419 Tony Phillips | .05 | .15 | 507 Bobby Hughes RC | .08 | .25 | 595 Don Mattingly | .75 | 2.00 |
| 420 Jeff Bagwell | .20 | .50 | 508 Wil Cordero | .05 | .15 | 596 Tony Longmire | .05 | .15 |
| 421 Mark Gardner | .05 | .15 | 509 George Tsamis RC | .08 | .25 | 597 Kevin Seitzer | .05 | .15 |
| 422 Brett Butler | .10 | .30 | 510 Bret Saberhagen | .10 | .30 | 598 Midre Cummings RC | .08 | .25 |
| 423 Graeme Lloyd RC | .20 | .50 | 511 Derek Jeter RC | 10.00 | 25.00 | 599 Omar Vizquel | .20 | .50 |

| | | |
|---|---|---|
| ☐ 600 Lee Smith | .10 | .30 |
| ☐ 601 David Hulse RC | .08 | .25 |
| ☐ 602 Darrell Sherman RC | .08 | .25 |
| ☐ 603 Alex Gonzalez | .05 | .15 |
| ☐ 604 Geronimo Pena | .05 | .15 |
| ☐ 605 Mike Devereaux | .05 | .15 |
| ☐ 606 Sterling Hitchcock RC | .20 | .50 |
| ☐ 607 Mike Greenwell | .05 | .15 |
| ☐ 608 Steve Buechele | .05 | .15 |
| ☐ 609 Troy Percival | .20 | .50 |
| ☐ 610 Roberto Kelly | .05 | .15 |
| ☐ 611 James Baldwin RC | .05 | .15 |
| ☐ 612 Jerald Clark | .05 | .15 |
| ☐ 613 Albie Lopez RC | .08 | .25 |
| ☐ 614 Dave Magadan | .05 | .15 |
| ☐ 615 Mickey Tettleton | .05 | .15 |
| ☐ 616 Sean Runyan RC | .08 | .25 |
| ☐ 617 Bob Hamelin | .05 | .15 |
| ☐ 618 Raul Mondesi | .10 | .30 |
| ☐ 619 Tyrone Hill | .05 | .15 |
| ☐ 620 Darrin Fletcher | .05 | .15 |
| ☐ 621 Mike Trombley | .05 | .15 |
| ☐ 622 Jeromy Burnitz | .10 | .30 |
| ☐ 623 Bernie Williams | .20 | .50 |
| ☐ 624 Mike Farmer RC | .08 | .25 |
| ☐ 625 Rickey Henderson | .30 | .75 |
| ☐ 626 Carlos Garcia | .05 | .15 |
| ☐ 627 Jeff Darwin RC | .08 | .25 |
| ☐ 628 Todd Zeile | .05 | .15 |
| ☐ 629 Benji Gil | .05 | .15 |
| ☐ 630 Tony Gwynn | .40 | 1.00 |
| ☐ 631 Aaron Small RC | .40 | 1.00 |
| ☐ 632 Joe Rosselli RC | .08 | .25 |
| ☐ 633 Mike Mussina | .20 | .50 |
| ☐ 634 Ryan Klesko | .10 | .30 |
| ☐ 635 Roger Clemens | .60 | 1.50 |
| ☐ 636 Sammy Sosa | .30 | .75 |
| ☐ 637 Orlando Palmeiro RC | .08 | .25 |
| ☐ 638 Willie Greene | .05 | .15 |
| ☐ 639 George Bell | .05 | .15 |
| ☐ 640 Garvin Alston RC | .08 | .25 |
| ☐ 641 Pete Janicki RC | .08 | .25 |
| ☐ 642 Chris Sheff RC | .08 | .25 |
| ☐ 643 Felipe Lira RC | .08 | .25 |
| ☐ 644 Roberto Petagine | .05 | .15 |
| ☐ 645 Wally Joyner | .10 | .30 |
| ☐ 646 Mike Piazza | 1.25 | 3.00 |
| ☐ 647 Jaime Navarro | .05 | .15 |
| ☐ 648 Jeff Hartsock | .05 | .15 |
| ☐ 649 David McCarty | .05 | .15 |
| ☐ 650 Bobby Jones | .10 | .30 |
| ☐ 651 Mark Hutton | .05 | .15 |
| ☐ 652 Kyle Abbott | .05 | .15 |
| ☐ 653 Steve Cox RC | .08 | .25 |
| ☐ 654 Jeff King | .05 | .15 |
| ☐ 655 Norm Charlton | .05 | .15 |
| ☐ 656 Mike Gulan RC | .08 | .25 |
| ☐ 657 Julio Franco | .10 | .30 |
| ☐ 658 Cameron Cairncross RC | .08 | .25 |
| ☐ 659 John Olerud | .10 | .30 |
| ☐ 660 Salomon Torres | .05 | .15 |
| ☐ 661 Brad Pennington | .05 | .15 |
| ☐ 662 Melvin Nieves | .05 | .15 |
| ☐ 663 Ivan Calderon | .05 | .15 |
| ☐ 664 Turk Wendell | .05 | .15 |
| ☐ 665 Chris Pritchett | .05 | .15 |
| ☐ 666 Reggie Sanders | .10 | .30 |
| ☐ 667 Robin Ventura | .05 | .15 |
| ☐ 668 Joe Girardi | .05 | .15 |
| ☐ 669 Manny Ramirez | .50 | 1.25 |
| ☐ 670 Jeff Conine | .05 | .15 |
| ☐ 671 Greg Gohr | .05 | .15 |
| ☐ 672 Anduar Cedeno | .05 | .15 |
| ☐ 673 Les Norman RC | .08 | .25 |
| ☐ 674 Mike James RC | .08 | .25 |
| ☐ 675 Marshall Boze RC | .08 | .25 |
| ☐ 676 B.J. Wallace | .05 | .15 |
| ☐ 677 Kent Hrbek | .10 | .30 |
| ☐ 678 Jack Voigt RC | .08 | .25 |
| ☐ 679 Brien Taylor | .05 | .15 |
| ☐ 680 Curt Schilling | .10 | .30 |
| ☐ 681 Todd Van Poppel | .05 | .15 |
| ☐ 682 Kevin Young | .10 | .30 |
| ☐ 683 Tommy Adams | .05 | .15 |
| ☐ 684 Bernard Gilkey | .05 | .15 |
| ☐ 685 Kevin Brown | .10 | .30 |
| ☐ 686 Fred McGriff | .20 | .50 |
| ☐ 687 Pat Borders | .05 | .15 |

| | | |
|---|---|---|
| ☐ 688 Kirt Manwaring | .05 | .15 |
| ☐ 689 Sid Bream | .05 | .15 |
| ☐ 690 John Valentin | .05 | .15 |
| ☐ 691 Steve Olsen RC | .08 | .25 |
| ☐ 692 Roberto Mejia RC | .08 | .25 |
| ☐ 693 Carlos Delgado RC | .30 | .75 |
| ☐ 694 Steve Gibralter RC | .08 | .25 |
| ☐ 695 Gary Mota FOIL RC | .08 | .25 |
| ☐ 696 Jose Malave FOIL RC | .08 | .25 |
| ☐ 697 Larry Sutton FOIL RC | .08 | .25 |
| ☐ 698 Dan Frye FOIL RC | .08 | .25 |
| ☐ 699 Tim Clark FOIL RC | .08 | .25 |
| ☐ 700 Brian Rupp FOIL RC | .08 | .25 |
| ☐ 701 Felipe/Moises Alou FOIL | .10 | .30 |
| ☐ 702 Barry/Bobby Bonds FOIL | .40 | 1.00 |
| ☐ 703 Ken Griffey Jr./Sr. FOIL | .30 | .75 |
| ☐ 704 Brian/Hal McRae FOIL | .05 | .15 |
| ☐ 705 Checklist 1 | .05 | .15 |
| ☐ 706 Checklist 2 | .05 | .15 |
| ☐ 707 Checklist 3 | .05 | .15 |
| ☐ 708 Checklist 4 | .05 | .15 |

### 1994 Bowman

| | | |
|---|---|---|
| ☐ COMPLETE SET (682) | 30.00 | 60.00 |
| ☐ 1 Joe Carter | .15 | .40 |
| ☐ 2 Marcus Moore | .08 | .25 |
| ☐ 3 Doug Creek RC | .15 | .40 |
| ☐ 4 Pedro Martinez | .40 | 1.00 |
| ☐ 5 Ken Griffey Jr. | .60 | 1.50 |
| ☐ 6 Greg Swindell | .08 | .25 |
| ☐ 7 J.J. Johnson | .15 | .40 |
| ☐ 8 Homer Bush RC | .15 | .40 |
| ☐ 9 Arquimedez Pozo RC | .15 | .40 |
| ☐ 10 Bryan Harvey | .08 | .25 |
| ☐ 11 J.T. Snow | .15 | .40 |
| ☐ 12 Alan Benes RC | .40 | 1.00 |
| ☐ 13 Chad Kreuter | .08 | .25 |
| ☐ 14 Eric Karros | .15 | .40 |
| ☐ 15 Frank Thomas | .40 | 1.00 |
| ☐ 16 Bret Saberhagen | .15 | .40 |
| ☐ 17 Terrell Lowery | .08 | .25 |
| ☐ 18 Rod Bolton | .08 | .25 |
| ☐ 19 Harold Baines | .15 | .40 |
| ☐ 20 Matt Walbeck | .08 | .25 |
| ☐ 21 Tom Glavine | .25 | .60 |
| ☐ 22 Todd Jones | .08 | .25 |
| ☐ 23 Alberto Castillo RC | .15 | .40 |
| ☐ 24 Ruben Sierra | .15 | .40 |
| ☐ 25 Don Mattingly | 1.00 | 2.50 |
| ☐ 26 Mike Morgan | .08 | .25 |
| ☐ 27 Jim Musselwhite RC | .08 | .25 |
| ☐ 28 Matt Brunson RC | .15 | .40 |
| ☐ 29 Adam Meinershagen RC | .15 | .40 |
| ☐ 30 Joe Girardi | .08 | .25 |
| ☐ 31 Shane Halter | .08 | .25 |
| ☐ 32 Jose Paniagua RC | .40 | 1.00 |
| ☐ 33 Paul Perkins RC | .15 | .40 |
| ☐ 34 John Hudek RC | .15 | .40 |
| ☐ 35 Frank Viola | .08 | .25 |
| ☐ 36 David Lamb RC | .15 | .40 |
| ☐ 37 Marshall Boze | .08 | .25 |
| ☐ 38 Jorge Posada RC | 3.00 | 8.00 |
| ☐ 39 Brian Anderson RC | .40 | 1.00 |
| ☐ 40 Mark Whiten | .08 | .25 |
| ☐ 41 Sean Bergman | .08 | .25 |
| ☐ 42 Jose Parra RC | .15 | .40 |
| ☐ 43 Mike Robertson | .08 | .25 |
| ☐ 44 Pete Walker RC | .15 | .40 |
| ☐ 45 Juan Gonzalez | .40 | 1.00 |
| ☐ 46 Cleveland Ladell RC | .15 | .40 |
| ☐ 47 Mark Smith | .08 | .25 |
| ☐ 48 Kevin Jarvis RC UER | .15 | .40 |
| ☐ 49 Amaury Telemaco RC | .15 | .40 |
| ☐ 50 Andy Van Slyke | .25 | .60 |

| | | |
|---|---|---|
| ☐ 51 Rikkert Faneyte RC | .15 | .40 |
| ☐ 52 Curtis Shaw | .08 | .25 |
| ☐ 53 Matt Drews RC | .15 | .40 |
| ☐ 54 Wilson Alvarez | .08 | .25 |
| ☐ 55 Manny Ramirez | .40 | 1.00 |
| ☐ 56 Bobby Munoz | .08 | .25 |
| ☐ 57 Ed Sprague | .08 | .25 |
| ☐ 58 Jamey Wright RC | .40 | 1.00 |
| ☐ 59 Jeff Montgomery | .08 | .25 |
| ☐ 60 Kirk Rueter | .08 | .25 |
| ☐ 61 Edgar Martinez | .25 | .60 |
| ☐ 62 Luis Gonzalez | .15 | .40 |
| ☐ 63 Tim Vanegmond RC | .15 | .40 |
| ☐ 64 Bip Roberts | .08 | .25 |
| ☐ 65 John Jaha | .08 | .25 |
| ☐ 66 Chuck Carr | .08 | .25 |
| ☐ 67 Chuck Finley | .15 | .40 |
| ☐ 68 Aaron Holbert | .08 | .25 |
| ☐ 69 Cecil Fielder | .15 | .40 |
| ☐ 70 Tom Engle RC | .15 | .40 |
| ☐ 71 Ron Karkovice | .08 | .25 |
| ☐ 72 Joe Orsulak | .08 | .25 |
| ☐ 73 Dutch Brumley RC | .15 | .40 |
| ☐ 74 Craig Clayton RC | .15 | .40 |
| ☐ 75 Cal Ripken | 1.25 | 3.00 |
| ☐ 76 Brad Fullmer RC | .40 | 1.00 |
| ☐ 77 Tony Tarasco | .15 | .40 |
| ☐ 78 Terry Farrar RC | .15 | .40 |
| ☐ 79 Matt Williams | .25 | .60 |
| ☐ 80 Rickey Henderson | .40 | 1.00 |
| ☐ 81 Terry Mulholland | .08 | .25 |
| ☐ 82 Sammy Sosa | .40 | 1.00 |
| ☐ 83 Paul Sorrento | .08 | .25 |
| ☐ 84 Pete Incaviglia | .08 | .25 |
| ☐ 85 Darren Hall RC | .15 | .40 |
| ☐ 86 Scott Klingenbeck | .08 | .25 |
| ☐ 87 Dario Perez RC | .15 | .40 |
| ☐ 88 Ugueth Urbina | .25 | .60 |
| ☐ 89 Dave Vanhof RC | .15 | .40 |
| ☐ 90 Domingo Jean | .08 | .25 |
| ☐ 91 Otis Nixon | .08 | .25 |
| ☐ 92 Andres Berumen | .08 | .25 |
| ☐ 93 Jose Valentin | .08 | .25 |
| ☐ 94 Edgar Renteria RC | 2.00 | 5.00 |
| ☐ 95 Chris Turner | .08 | .25 |
| ☐ 96 Ray Lankford | .15 | .40 |
| ☐ 97 Danny Bautista | .08 | .25 |
| ☐ 98 Chan Ho Park RC | .60 | 1.50 |
| ☐ 99 Glenn DiSarcina RC | .15 | .40 |
| ☐ 100 Butch Huskey | .08 | .25 |
| ☐ 101 Ivan Rodriguez | .25 | .60 |
| ☐ 102 Johnny Ruffin | .08 | .25 |
| ☐ 103 Alex Ochoa | .15 | .40 |
| ☐ 104 Torii Hunter RC | 2.00 | 5.00 |
| ☐ 105 Ryan Klesko | .25 | .60 |
| ☐ 106 Jay Bell | .08 | .25 |
| ☐ 107 Kurt Peltzer RC | .15 | .40 |
| ☐ 108 Miguel Jimenez | .08 | .25 |
| ☐ 109 Russ Davis | .08 | .25 |
| ☐ 110 Derek Wallace | .08 | .25 |
| ☐ 111 Keith Lockhart RC | .40 | 1.00 |
| ☐ 112 Mike Lieberthal | .15 | .40 |
| ☐ 113 Dave Stewart | .15 | .40 |
| ☐ 114 Tom Schmidt | .08 | .25 |
| ☐ 115 Brian McRae | .08 | .25 |
| ☐ 116 Moises Alou | .15 | .40 |
| ☐ 117 Dave Fleming | .08 | .25 |
| ☐ 118 Jeff Bagwell | .25 | .60 |
| ☐ 119 Luis Ortiz | .08 | .25 |
| ☐ 120 Tony Gwynn | .50 | 1.25 |
| ☐ 121 Jaime Navarro | .08 | .25 |
| ☐ 122 Benito Santiago | .08 | .25 |
| ☐ 123 Darrell Whitmore | .08 | .25 |
| ☐ 124 John Mabry RC | .40 | 1.00 |
| ☐ 125 Mickey Tettleton | .08 | .25 |
| ☐ 126 Tom Candiotti | .08 | .25 |
| ☐ 127 Tim Raines | .15 | .40 |
| ☐ 128 Bobby Bonilla | .15 | .40 |
| ☐ 129 John Dettmer | .08 | .25 |
| ☐ 130 Hector Carrasco | .08 | .25 |
| ☐ 131 Chris Holles | .08 | .25 |
| ☐ 132 Rick Aguilera | .08 | .25 |
| ☐ 133 David Justice | .15 | .40 |
| ☐ 134 Esteban Loaiza RC | .60 | 1.50 |
| ☐ 135 Barry Bonds | 1.00 | 2.50 |
| ☐ 136 Bob Welch | .08 | .25 |
| ☐ 137 Mike Stanley | .08 | .25 |
| ☐ 138 Roberto Hernandez | .08 | .25 |

|  |  | | |
|---|---|---|---|
| ❏ 139 | Sandy Alomar Jr. | .08 | .25 |
| ❏ 140 | Darren Daulton | .15 | .40 |
| ❏ 141 | Angel Martinez RC | .15 | .40 |
| ❏ 142 | Howard Johnson | .08 | .25 |
| ❏ 143 | Bob Hamelin | .08 | .25 |
| ❏ 144 | J.J.Thobe RC | .15 | .40 |
| ❏ 145 | Roger Salkeld | .08 | .25 |
| ❏ 146 | Orlando Miller | .08 | .25 |
| ❏ 147 | Dmitri Young | .15 | .40 |
| ❏ 148 | Tim Hyers RC | .15 | .40 |
| ❏ 149 | Mark Loretta RC | 2.00 | 5.00 |
| ❏ 150 | Chris Hammond | .08 | .25 |
| ❏ 151 | Joel Moore RC | .15 | .40 |
| ❏ 152 | Todd Zeile | .08 | .25 |
| ❏ 153 | Wil Cordero | .08 | .25 |
| ❏ 154 | Chris Smith | .08 | .25 |
| ❏ 155 | James Baldwin | .08 | .25 |
| ❏ 156 | Edgardo Alfonzo RC | .40 | 1.00 |
| ❏ 157 | Kym Ashworth RC | .15 | .40 |
| ❏ 158 | Paul Bako RC | .15 | .40 |
| ❏ 159 | Rick Krivda RC | .15 | .40 |
| ❏ 160 | Pat Mahomes | .08 | .25 |
| ❏ 161 | Damon Hollins | .08 | .25 |
| ❏ 162 | Felix Martinez RC | .15 | .40 |
| ❏ 163 | Jason Myers RC | .15 | .40 |
| ❏ 164 | Izzy Molina RC | .15 | .40 |
| ❏ 165 | Brien Taylor | .08 | .25 |
| ❏ 166 | Kevin Orie RC | .15 | .40 |
| ❏ 167 | Casey Whitten RC | .15 | .40 |
| ❏ 168 | Tony Longmire | .08 | .25 |
| ❏ 169 | John Olerud | .15 | .40 |
| ❏ 170 | Mark Thompson | .08 | .25 |
| ❏ 171 | Jorge Fabregas | .08 | .25 |
| ❏ 172 | John Wetteland | .08 | .25 |
| ❏ 173 | Dan Wilson | .08 | .25 |
| ❏ 174 | Doug Drabek | .08 | .25 |
| ❏ 175 | Jeff McNeely | .08 | .25 |
| ❏ 176 | Melvin Nieves | .08 | .25 |
| ❏ 177 | Doug Glanville RC | .40 | 1.00 |
| ❏ 178 | Javier De La Hoya RC | .15 | .40 |
| ❏ 179 | Chad Curtis | .08 | .25 |
| ❏ 180 | Brian Barber | .08 | .25 |
| ❏ 181 | Mike Henneman | .08 | .25 |
| ❏ 182 | Jose Offerman | .08 | .25 |
| ❏ 183 | Robert Ellis RC | .15 | .40 |
| ❏ 184 | John Franco | .08 | .25 |
| ❏ 185 | Benji Gil | .08 | .25 |
| ❏ 186 | Hal Morris | .08 | .25 |
| ❏ 187 | Chris Sabo | .08 | .25 |
| ❏ 188 | Blaise Ilsley RC | .15 | .40 |
| ❏ 189 | Steve Avery | .08 | .25 |
| ❏ 190 | Rick White RC | .15 | .40 |
| ❏ 191 | Rod Beck | .08 | .25 |
| ❏ 192 | Mark McGwire UER NNO | 1.00 | 2.50 |
| ❏ 193 | Jim Abbott | .25 | .40 |
| ❏ 194 | Randy Myers | .08 | .25 |
| ❏ 195 | Kenny Lofton | .15 | .40 |
| ❏ 196 | Mariano Duncan | .08 | .25 |
| ❏ 197 | Lee Daniels RC | .15 | .40 |
| ❏ 198 | Armando Reynoso | .08 | .25 |
| ❏ 199 | Joe Randa | .15 | .40 |
| ❏ 200 | Cliff Floyd | .15 | .40 |
| ❏ 201 | Tim Harkrider RC | .15 | .40 |
| ❏ 202 | Kevin Gallaher RC | .15 | .40 |
| ❏ 203 | Scott Cooper | .08 | .25 |
| ❏ 204 | Phil Stidham RC | .15 | .40 |
| ❏ 205 | Jeff D'Amico RC | .15 | .40 |
| ❏ 206 | Matt Whisenant | .08 | .25 |
| ❏ 207 | De Shawn Warren RC | .15 | .40 |
| ❏ 208 | Rene Arocha | .08 | .25 |
| ❏ 209 | Tony Clark RC | .60 | 1.50 |
| ❏ 210 | Jason Jacome RC | .15 | .40 |
| ❏ 211 | Scott Christman RC | .15 | .40 |
| ❏ 212 | Bill Pulsipher RC | .15 | .40 |
| ❏ 213 | Dean Palmer | .08 | .25 |
| ❏ 214 | Chad Mottola | .08 | .25 |
| ❏ 215 | Manny Alexander | .08 | .25 |
| ❏ 216 | Rich Becker | .08 | .25 |
| ❏ 217 | Andre King RC | .15 | .40 |
| ❏ 218 | Carlos Garcia | .08 | .25 |
| ❏ 219 | Ron Pezzoni RC | .15 | .40 |
| ❏ 220 | Steve Karsay | .08 | .25 |
| ❏ 221 | Jose Musset RC | .15 | .40 |
| ❏ 222 | Karl Rhodes | .08 | .25 |
| ❏ 223 | Frank Cimorelli RC | .15 | .40 |
| ❏ 224 | Kevin Jordan RC | .15 | .40 |
| ❏ 225 | Duane Ward | .08 | .25 |
| ❏ 226 | John Burke | .08 | .25 |
| ❏ 227 | Mike Macfarlane | .08 | .25 |
| ❏ 228 | Mike Lansing | .08 | .25 |
| ❏ 229 | Chuck Knoblauch | .15 | .40 |
| ❏ 230 | Ken Caminiti | .08 | .25 |
| ❏ 231 | Gar Finnvold RC | .15 | .40 |
| ❏ 232 | Derek Lee RC | 3.00 | 8.00 |
| ❏ 233 | Brady Anderson | .08 | .25 |
| ❏ 234 | Vic Darensbourg RC | .15 | .40 |
| ❏ 235 | Mark Langston | .08 | .25 |
| ❏ 236 | T.J.Mathews RC | .15 | .40 |
| ❏ 237 | Lou Whitaker | .15 | .40 |
| ❏ 238 | Roger Cedeno | .08 | .25 |
| ❏ 239 | Alex Fernandez | .08 | .25 |
| ❏ 240 | Ryan Thompson | .08 | .25 |
| ❏ 241 | Kerry Lacy RC | .15 | .40 |
| ❏ 242 | Reggie Sanders | .15 | .40 |
| ❏ 243 | Brad Pennington | .08 | .25 |
| ❏ 244 | Bryan Eversgerd RC | .15 | .40 |
| ❏ 245 | Greg Maddux | .60 | 1.50 |
| ❏ 246 | Jason Kendall | .15 | .40 |
| ❏ 247 | J.R. Phillips | .08 | .25 |
| ❏ 248 | Bobby Witt | .08 | .25 |
| ❏ 249 | Paul O'Neill | .25 | .40 |
| ❏ 250 | Ryne Sandberg | .60 | 1.50 |
| ❏ 251 | Charles Nagy | .08 | .25 |
| ❏ 252 | Kevin Stocker | .08 | .25 |
| ❏ 253 | Shawn Green | .40 | 1.00 |
| ❏ 254 | Charlie Hayes | .08 | .25 |
| ❏ 255 | Donnie Elliott | .08 | .25 |
| ❏ 256 | Rob Fitzpatrick RC | .15 | .40 |
| ❏ 257 | Tim Davis | .08 | .25 |
| ❏ 258 | James Mouton | .08 | .25 |
| ❏ 259 | Mike Greenwell | .08 | .25 |
| ❏ 260 | Ray McDavid | .08 | .25 |
| ❏ 261 | Mike Kelly | .08 | .25 |
| ❏ 262 | Andy Larkin RC | .15 | .40 |
| ❏ 263 | Marquis Riley UER | .08 | .25 |
| ❏ 264 | Bob Tewksbury | .08 | .25 |
| ❏ 265 | Brian Edmondson | .08 | .25 |
| ❏ 266 | Eduardo Lantigua RC | .15 | .40 |
| ❏ 267 | Brandon Wilson | .08 | .25 |
| ❏ 268 | Mike Welch | .08 | .25 |
| ❏ 269 | Tom Henke | .08 | .25 |
| ❏ 270 | Pokey Reese | .08 | .25 |
| ❏ 271 | Gregg Zaun RC | .40 | 1.00 |
| ❏ 272 | Todd Ritchie | .08 | .25 |
| ❏ 273 | Javier Lopez | .15 | .40 |
| ❏ 274 | Kevin Young | .08 | .25 |
| ❏ 275 | Kirt Manwaring | .08 | .25 |
| ❏ 276 | Bill Taylor RC | .15 | .40 |
| ❏ 277 | Robert Eenhoorn | .08 | .25 |
| ❏ 278 | Jessie Hollins | .08 | .25 |
| ❏ 279 | Julian Tavarez RC | .40 | 1.00 |
| ❏ 280 | Gene Schall | .08 | .25 |
| ❏ 281 | Paul Molitor | .15 | .40 |
| ❏ 282 | Neifi Perez RC | .40 | 1.00 |
| ❏ 283 | Gregg Gagne | .08 | .25 |
| ❏ 284 | Marquis Grissom | .15 | .40 |
| ❏ 285 | Randy Johnson | .40 | 1.00 |
| ❏ 286 | Pete Harnisch | .08 | .25 |
| ❏ 287 | Joel Bennett RC | .15 | .40 |
| ❏ 288 | Jeff Kent | .08 | .25 |
| ❏ 289 | Darryl Hamilton | .08 | .25 |
| ❏ 290 | Gary Sheffield | .15 | .40 |
| ❏ 291 | Eduardo Perez | .08 | .25 |
| ❏ 292 | Basil Shabazz | .08 | .25 |
| ❏ 293 | Eric Davis | .15 | .40 |
| ❏ 294 | Pedro Astacio | .08 | .25 |
| ❏ 295 | Robin Ventura | .15 | .40 |
| ❏ 296 | Jeff Kent | .25 | .60 |
| ❏ 297 | Rick Helling | .08 | .25 |
| ❏ 298 | Joe Oliver | .08 | .25 |
| ❏ 299 | Lee Smith | .15 | .40 |
| ❏ 300 | Dave Winfield | .15 | .40 |
| ❏ 301 | Deion Sanders | .25 | .60 |
| ❏ 302 | Ravelo Manzanillo RC | .15 | .40 |
| ❏ 303 | Mark Portugal | .08 | .25 |
| ❏ 304 | Brent Gates | .08 | .25 |
| ❏ 305 | Wade Boggs | .25 | .60 |
| ❏ 306 | Rick Wilkins | .08 | .25 |
| ❏ 307 | Carlos Baerga | .08 | .25 |
| ❏ 308 | Curt Schilling | .15 | .40 |
| ❏ 309 | Shannon Stewart | .40 | 1.00 |
| ❏ 310 | Darren Holmes | .08 | .25 |
| ❏ 311 | Robert Toth RC | .15 | .40 |
| ❏ 312 | Gabe White | .08 | .25 |
| ❏ 313 | Mac Suzuki RC | .40 | 1.00 |
| ❏ 314 | Alvin Morman RC | .15 | .40 |
| ❏ 315 | Mo Vaughn | .15 | .40 |
| ❏ 316 | Bryce Florie RC | .15 | .40 |
| ❏ 317 | Gabby Martinez RC | .15 | .40 |
| ❏ 318 | Carl Everett | .15 | .40 |
| ❏ 319 | Kerwin Moore | .08 | .25 |
| ❏ 320 | Tom Pagnozzi | .08 | .25 |
| ❏ 321 | Chris Gomez | .08 | .25 |
| ❏ 322 | Todd Williams | .08 | .25 |
| ❏ 323 | Pat Hentgen | .08 | .25 |
| ❏ 324 | Kirk Presley RC | .15 | .40 |
| ❏ 325 | Kevin Brown | .15 | .40 |
| ❏ 326 | Jason Isringhausen RC | 1.25 | 3.00 |
| ❏ 327 | Rick Forney RC | .15 | .40 |
| ❏ 328 | Carlos Pulido RC | .15 | .40 |
| ❏ 329 | Terrell Wade RC | .15 | .40 |
| ❏ 330 | Al Martin | .08 | .25 |
| ❏ 331 | Dan Carlson RC | .15 | .40 |
| ❏ 332 | Mark Acre RC | .15 | .40 |
| ❏ 333 | Sterling Hitchcock | .08 | .25 |
| ❏ 334 | Jon Ratliff RC | .15 | .40 |
| ❏ 335 | Alex Ramirez RC | .15 | .40 |
| ❏ 336 | Phil Geisler RC | .15 | .40 |
| ❏ 337 | Eddie Zambrano RC | .15 | .40 |
| ❏ 338 | Jim Thome FOIL | .25 | .60 |
| ❏ 339 | James Mouton FOIL | .25 | .60 |
| ❏ 340 | Cliff Floyd FOIL | .15 | .40 |
| ❏ 341 | Carlos Delgado FOIL | .25 | .60 |
| ❏ 342 | Roberto Petagine FOIL | .08 | .25 |
| ❏ 343 | Tim Clark FOIL | .08 | .25 |
| ❏ 344 | Bubba Smith FOIL | .08 | .25 |
| ❏ 345 | Randy Curtis FOIL RC | .08 | .25 |
| ❏ 346 | Joe Biasucci FOIL RC | .15 | .40 |
| ❏ 347 | D.J. Boston FOIL RC | .15 | .40 |
| ❏ 348 | Ruben Rivera FOIL RC | .15 | .40 |
| ❏ 349 | Bryan Link FOIL RC | .08 | .25 |
| ❏ 350 | Mike Bell FOIL RC | .15 | .40 |
| ❏ 351 | Marty Watson FOIL RC | .08 | .25 |
| ❏ 352 | Jason Myers FOIL | .08 | .25 |
| ❏ 353 | Chipper Jones FOIL | .40 | 1.00 |
| ❏ 354 | Brooks Kieschnick FOIL | .15 | .40 |
| ❏ 355 | Pokey Reese FOIL | .08 | .25 |
| ❏ 356 | John Burke FOIL | .08 | .25 |
| ❏ 357 | Kurt Miller FOIL | .08 | .25 |
| ❏ 358 | Orlando Miller FOIL | .08 | .25 |
| ❏ 359 | Todd Hollandsworth FOIL | .08 | .25 |
| ❏ 360 | Rondell White FOIL | .15 | .40 |
| ❏ 361 | Bill Pulsipher FOIL | .08 | .25 |
| ❏ 362 | Tyler Green FOIL | .08 | .25 |
| ❏ 363 | Midre Cummings FOIL | .08 | .25 |
| ❏ 364 | Brian Barber FOIL | .08 | .25 |
| ❏ 365 | Melvin Nieves FOIL | .08 | .25 |
| ❏ 366 | Salomon Torres FOIL | .08 | .25 |
| ❏ 367 | Alex Ochoa FOIL | .08 | .25 |
| ❏ 368 | Frankie Rodriguez FOIL | .08 | .25 |
| ❏ 369 | Brian Anderson FOIL | .15 | .40 |
| ❏ 370 | James Baldwin FOIL | .08 | .25 |
| ❏ 371 | Manny Ramirez FOIL | .40 | 1.00 |
| ❏ 372 | Justin Thompson FOIL | .08 | .25 |
| ❏ 373 | Johnny Damon FOIL | .25 | .60 |
| ❏ 374 | Jeff D'Amico FOIL | .08 | .25 |
| ❏ 375 | Rich Becker FOIL | .08 | .25 |
| ❏ 376 | Derek Jeter FOIL | 1.25 | 3.00 |
| ❏ 377 | Steve Karsay FOIL | .08 | .25 |
| ❏ 378 | Mac Suzuki FOIL | .15 | .40 |
| ❏ 379 | Benji Gil FOIL | .08 | .25 |
| ❏ 380 | Alex Gonzalez FOIL | .15 | .40 |
| ❏ 381 | Jason Bere FOIL | .08 | .25 |
| ❏ 382 | Brett Butler FOIL | .08 | .25 |
| ❏ 383 | Jeff Conine FOIL | .08 | .25 |
| ❏ 384 | Darren Daulton FOIL | .15 | .40 |
| ❏ 385 | Jeff Kent FOIL | .25 | .60 |
| ❏ 386 | Don Mattingly FOIL | 1.00 | 2.50 |
| ❏ 387 | Mike Piazza FOIL | .75 | 2.00 |
| ❏ 388 | Ryne Sandberg FOIL | .60 | 1.50 |
| ❏ 389 | Rich Amaral FOIL | .08 | .25 |
| ❏ 390 | Craig Biggio | .25 | .60 |
| ❏ 391 | Jeff Suppan RC | .75 | 2.00 |
| ❏ 392 | Andy Benes | .08 | .25 |
| ❏ 393 | Cal Eldred | .08 | .25 |
| ❏ 394 | Jeff Conine | .15 | .40 |
| ❏ 395 | Tim Salmon | .25 | .60 |
| ❏ 396 | Ray Suplee RC | .15 | .40 |
| ❏ 397 | Tony Phillips | .08 | .25 |
| ❏ 398 | Ramon Martinez | .15 | .40 |
| ❏ 399 | Julio Franco | .15 | .40 |
| ❏ 400 | Dwight Gooden | .15 | .40 |
| ❏ 401 | Kevin Loman RC | .15 | .40 |
| ❏ 402 | Jose Rijo | .08 | .25 |

|  |  | | |
|---|--------|---|---|
| ❏ 403 | Mike Devereaux | .08 | .25 |
| ❏ 404 | Mike Zolecki RC | .15 | .40 |
| ❏ 405 | Fred McGriff | .25 | .60 |
| ❏ 406 | Danny Clyburn | .08 | .25 |
| ❏ 407 | Robby Thompson | .08 | .25 |
| ❏ 408 | Terry Steinbach | .08 | .25 |
| ❏ 409 | Luis Polonia | .08 | .25 |
| ❏ 410 | Mark Grace | .25 | .60 |
| ❏ 411 | Albert Belle | .15 | .40 |
| ❏ 412 | John Kruk | .15 | .40 |
| ❏ 413 | Scott Spiezio RC | .40 | 1.00 |
| ❏ 414 | Ellis Burks UER | .15 | .40 |
| ❏ 416 | Tim Costo | .08 | .25 |
| ❏ 417 | Marc Newfield | .08 | .25 |
| ❏ 418 | Oscar Henriquez RC | .15 | .40 |
| ❏ 419 | Matt Perisho RC | .15 | .40 |
| ❏ 420 | Julio Bruno | .08 | .25 |
| ❏ 421 | Kenny Felder | .08 | .25 |
| ❏ 422 | Tyler Green | .08 | .25 |
| ❏ 423 | Jim Edmonds | .40 | 1.00 |
| ❏ 424 | Ozzie Smith | .60 | 1.50 |
| ❏ 425 | Rick Greene | .08 | .25 |
| ❏ 426 | Todd Hollandsworth | .08 | .25 |
| ❏ 427 | Eddie Pearson RC | .15 | .40 |
| ❏ 428 | Quilvio Veras | .08 | .25 |
| ❏ 429 | Kenny Rogers | .15 | .40 |
| ❏ 430 | Willie Greene | .08 | .25 |
| ❏ 431 | Vaughn Eshelman | .08 | .25 |
| ❏ 432 | Pat Meares | .08 | .25 |
| ❏ 433 | Jermaine Dye RC | 2.50 | 6.00 |
| ❏ 434 | Steve Cooke | .08 | .25 |
| ❏ 435 | Bill Swift | .08 | .25 |
| ❏ 436 | Fausto Cruz RC | .15 | .40 |
| ❏ 437 | Mark Hutton | .08 | .25 |
| ❏ 438 | Brooks Kieschnick RC | .15 | .40 |
| ❏ 439 | Yorkis Perez | .08 | .25 |
| ❏ 440 | Len Dykstra | .15 | .40 |
| ❏ 441 | Pat Borders | .08 | .25 |
| ❏ 442 | Doug Walls RC | .15 | .40 |
| ❏ 443 | Wally Joyner | .15 | .40 |
| ❏ 444 | Ken Hill | .08 | .25 |
| ❏ 445 | Eric Anthony | .08 | .25 |
| ❏ 446 | Mitch Williams | .08 | .25 |
| ❏ 447 | Cory Bailey RC | .15 | .40 |
| ❏ 448 | Dave Staton | .08 | .25 |
| ❏ 449 | Greg Vaughn | .08 | .25 |
| ❏ 450 | Dave Magadan | .08 | .25 |
| ❏ 451 | Chili Davis | .15 | .40 |
| ❏ 452 | Gerald Santos RC | .15 | .40 |
| ❏ 453 | Joe Perona | .08 | .25 |
| ❏ 454 | Delino DeShields | .08 | .25 |
| ❏ 455 | Jack McDowell | .08 | .25 |
| ❏ 456 | Todd Hundley | .08 | .25 |
| ❏ 457 | Ritchie Moody | .08 | .25 |
| ❏ 458 | Bret Boone | .15 | .40 |
| ❏ 459 | Ben McDonald | .08 | .25 |
| ❏ 460 | Kirby Puckett | .40 | 1.00 |
| ❏ 461 | Gregg Olson | .08 | .25 |
| ❏ 462 | Rich Aude RC | .15 | .40 |
| ❏ 463 | John Burkett | .08 | .25 |
| ❏ 464 | Troy Neel | .08 | .25 |
| ❏ 465 | Jimmy Key | .15 | .40 |
| ❏ 466 | Ozzie Timmons | .08 | .25 |
| ❏ 467 | Eddie Murray | .40 | 1.00 |
| ❏ 468 | Mark Tranberg RC | .15 | .40 |
| ❏ 469 | Alex Gonzalez | .08 | .25 |
| ❏ 470 | David Nied | .08 | .25 |
| ❏ 471 | Barry Larkin | .25 | .60 |
| ❏ 472 | Brian Looney RC | .15 | .40 |
| ❏ 473 | Shawn Estes | .08 | .25 |
| ❏ 474 | A.J.Sager RC | .15 | .40 |
| ❏ 475 | Roger Clemens | .75 | 2.00 |
| ❏ 476 | Vince Moore | .08 | .25 |
| ❏ 477 | Scott Karl RC | .15 | .40 |
| ❏ 478 | Kurt Miller | .08 | .25 |
| ❏ 479 | Garret Anderson | .40 | 1.00 |
| ❏ 480 | Allen Watson | .08 | .25 |
| ❏ 481 | Jose Lima RC | .40 | 1.00 |
| ❏ 482 | Rick Gorecki | .15 | .40 |
| ❏ 483 | Jimmy Hurst RC | .15 | .40 |
| ❏ 484 | Preston Wilson | .15 | .40 |
| ❏ 485 | Will Clark | .25 | .60 |
| ❏ 486 | Mike Ferry RC | .15 | .40 |
| ❏ 487 | Curtis Goodwin RC | .15 | .40 |
| ❏ 488 | Mike Myers | .08 | .25 |
| ❏ 489 | Chipper Jones | .40 | 1.00 |
| ❏ 490 | Jeff King | .08 | .25 |
| ❏ 491 | W.VanLandingham RC | .15 | .40 |
| ❏ 492 | Carlos Reyes RC | .15 | .40 |
| ❏ 493 | Andy Pettitte | .40 | 1.00 |
| ❏ 494 | Brant Brown | .08 | .25 |
| ❏ 495 | Daron Kirkreit | .08 | .25 |
| ❏ 496 | Ricky Bottalico RC | .15 | .40 |
| ❏ 497 | Devon White | .15 | .40 |
| ❏ 498 | Jason Johnson RC | .40 | 1.00 |
| ❏ 499 | Vince Coleman | .15 | .40 |
| ❏ 501 | Bobby Ayala | .08 | .25 |
| ❏ 502 | Steve Finley | .15 | .40 |
| ❏ 503 | Scott Fletcher | .08 | .25 |
| ❏ 504 | Brad Ausmus | .25 | .60 |
| ❏ 505 | Scott Talanoa RC | .15 | .40 |
| ❏ 506 | Orestes Destrade | .08 | .25 |
| ❏ 507 | Gary DiSarcina | .08 | .25 |
| ❏ 508 | Willie Smith RC | .15 | .40 |
| ❏ 509 | Alan Trammell | .15 | .40 |
| ❏ 510 | Mike Piazza | .75 | 2.00 |
| ❏ 511 | Ozzie Guillen | .08 | .25 |
| ❏ 512 | Jeromy Burnitz | .15 | .40 |
| ❏ 513 | Darren Oliver RC | .40 | 1.00 |
| ❏ 514 | Kevin Mitchell | .08 | .25 |
| ❏ 515 | Rafael Palmeiro | .25 | .60 |
| ❏ 516 | David McCarty | .08 | .25 |
| ❏ 517 | Jeff Blauser | .08 | .25 |
| ❏ 518 | Trey Beamon | .08 | .25 |
| ❏ 519 | Royce Clayton | .08 | .25 |
| ❏ 520 | Dennis Eckersley | .15 | .40 |
| ❏ 521 | Bernie Williams | .25 | .60 |
| ❏ 522 | Steve Buechele | .08 | .25 |
| ❏ 523 | Dennis Martinez | .15 | .40 |
| ❏ 524 | Dave Hollins | .08 | .25 |
| ❏ 525 | Joey Hamilton | .08 | .25 |
| ❏ 526 | Andres Galarraga | .15 | .40 |
| ❏ 527 | Jeff Granger | .08 | .25 |
| ❏ 528 | Joey Eischen | .08 | .25 |
| ❏ 529 | Desi Relaford | .08 | .25 |
| ❏ 530 | Roberto Petagine | .08 | .25 |
| ❏ 531 | Andre Dawson | .15 | .40 |
| ❏ 532 | Ray Holbert | .08 | .25 |
| ❏ 533 | Duane Singleton | .08 | .25 |
| ❏ 534 | Kurt Abbott RC | .15 | .40 |
| ❏ 535 | Bo Jackson | .40 | 1.00 |
| ❏ 536 | Gregg Jefferies | .15 | .40 |
| ❏ 537 | David Wayel | .08 | .25 |
| ❏ 538 | Raul Mondesi | .15 | .40 |
| ❏ 539 | Chris Snopek | .08 | .25 |
| ❏ 540 | Brook Fordyce | .08 | .25 |
| ❏ 541 | Ron Frazier RC | .15 | .40 |
| ❏ 542 | Brian Koelling | .08 | .25 |
| ❏ 543 | Jimmy Haynes | .08 | .25 |
| ❏ 544 | Marty Cordova | .08 | .25 |
| ❏ 545 | Jason Green RC | .15 | .40 |
| ❏ 546 | Orlando Merced | .08 | .25 |
| ❏ 547 | Lou Pote RC | .15 | .40 |
| ❏ 548 | Todd Van Poppel | .08 | .25 |
| ❏ 549 | Pat Kelly | .08 | .25 |
| ❏ 550 | Turk Wendell | .08 | .25 |
| ❏ 551 | Herbert Perry RC | .15 | .40 |
| ❏ 552 | Ryan Karp RC | .15 | .40 |
| ❏ 553 | Juan Guzman | .08 | .25 |
| ❏ 554 | Bryan Rekar RC | .15 | .40 |
| ❏ 555 | Kevin Appier | .15 | .40 |
| ❏ 556 | Chris Schwab RC | .15 | .40 |
| ❏ 557 | Jay Buhner | .15 | .40 |
| ❏ 558 | Andujar Cedeno | .08 | .25 |
| ❏ 559 | Ryan McGuire RC | .15 | .40 |
| ❏ 560 | Ricky Gutierrez | .08 | .25 |
| ❏ 561 | Keith Kimsey RC | .15 | .40 |
| ❏ 562 | Tim Clark | .08 | .25 |
| ❏ 563 | Damion Easley | .08 | .25 |
| ❏ 564 | Clint Davis RC | .15 | .40 |
| ❏ 565 | Mike Moore | .08 | .25 |
| ❏ 566 | Orel Hershiser | .15 | .40 |
| ❏ 567 | Jason Bere | .08 | .25 |
| ❏ 568 | Kevin McReynolds | .08 | .25 |
| ❏ 569 | Leland Macon RC | .15 | .40 |
| ❏ 570 | John Courtright RC | .15 | .40 |
| ❏ 571 | Sid Fernandez | .08 | .25 |
| ❏ 572 | Chad Roper | .08 | .25 |
| ❏ 573 | Terry Pendleton | .15 | .40 |
| ❏ 574 | Danny Miceli | .08 | .25 |
| ❏ 575 | Joe Rosselli | .08 | .25 |
| ❏ 576 | Mike Bordick | .08 | .25 |
| ❏ 577 | Danny Tartabull | .08 | .25 |
| ❏ 578 | Jose Guzman | .08 | .25 |
| ❏ 579 | Omar Vizquel | .25 | .60 |
| ❏ 580 | Tommy Greene | .08 | .25 |
| ❏ 581 | Paul Spoljaric | .08 | .25 |
| ❏ 582 | Walt Weiss | .08 | .25 |
| ❏ 583 | Oscar Jimenez RC | .15 | .40 |
| ❏ 584 | Rod Henderson | .08 | .25 |
| ❏ 585 | Derek Lowe | .15 | .40 |
| ❏ 586 | Richard Hidalgo RC | .40 | 1.00 |
| ❏ 587 | Shayne Bennett RC | .15 | .40 |
| ❏ 588 | Tim Belk RC | .15 | .40 |
| ❏ 589 | Matt Mieske | .08 | .25 |
| ❏ 590 | Nigel Wilson | .08 | .25 |
| ❏ 591 | Jeff Knox RC | .15 | .40 |
| ❏ 592 | Bernard Gilkey | .08 | .25 |
| ❏ 593 | David Cone | .15 | .40 |
| ❏ 594 | Paul LoDuca RC | 2.00 | 5.00 |
| ❏ 595 | Scott Ruffcorn | .08 | .25 |
| ❏ 596 | Chris Roberts | .08 | .25 |
| ❏ 597 | Oscar Munoz RC | .15 | .40 |
| ❏ 598 | Scott Sullivan RC | .15 | .40 |
| ❏ 599 | Matt Jarvis RC | .15 | .40 |
| ❏ 600 | Jose Canseco | .25 | .60 |
| ❏ 601 | Tony Graffanino RC | .60 | 1.50 |
| ❏ 602 | Don Slaught | .08 | .25 |
| ❏ 603 | Brett King RC | .15 | .40 |
| ❏ 604 | Jose Herrera RC | .15 | .40 |
| ❏ 605 | Melido Perez | .08 | .25 |
| ❏ 606 | Mike Hubbard RC | .15 | .40 |
| ❏ 607 | Chad Ogea | .08 | .25 |
| ❏ 608 | Wayne Gomes RC | .40 | 1.00 |
| ❏ 609 | Roberto Alomar | .25 | .60 |
| ❏ 610 | Angel Echevarria RC | .15 | .40 |
| ❏ 611 | Jose Lind | .08 | .25 |
| ❏ 612 | Darrin Fletcher | .08 | .25 |
| ❏ 613 | Chris Bosio | .08 | .25 |
| ❏ 614 | Darryl Kile | .15 | .40 |
| ❏ 615 | Frankie Rodriguez | .08 | .25 |
| ❏ 616 | Phil Plantier | .08 | .25 |
| ❏ 617 | Pat Listach | .08 | .25 |
| ❏ 618 | Charlie Hough | .15 | .40 |
| ❏ 619 | Ryan Hancock RC | .15 | .40 |
| ❏ 620 | Darrel Deak RC | .15 | .40 |
| ❏ 621 | Travis Fryman | .15 | .40 |
| ❏ 622 | Brett Butler | .15 | .40 |
| ❏ 623 | Lance Johnson | .08 | .25 |
| ❏ 624 | Pete Smith | .08 | .25 |
| ❏ 625 | James Hurst RC | .15 | .40 |
| ❏ 626 | Roberto Kelly | .08 | .25 |
| ❏ 627 | Mike Mussina | .25 | .60 |
| ❏ 628 | Kevin Tapani | .08 | .25 |
| ❏ 629 | John Smoltz | .25 | .60 |
| ❏ 630 | Midre Cummings | .08 | .25 |
| ❏ 631 | Salomon Torres | .08 | .25 |
| ❏ 632 | Willie Adams | .08 | .25 |
| ❏ 633 | Derek Jeter | 1.25 | 3.00 |
| ❏ 634 | Steve Trachsel | .08 | .25 |
| ❏ 635 | Albie Lopez | .08 | .25 |
| ❏ 636 | Jason Moler | .08 | .25 |
| ❏ 637 | Carlos Delgado | .25 | .60 |
| ❏ 638 | Roberto Mejia | .08 | .25 |
| ❏ 639 | Darren Burton | .08 | .25 |
| ❏ 640 | B.J. Wallace | .08 | .25 |
| ❏ 641 | Brad Clontz RC | .15 | .40 |
| ❏ 642 | Billy Wagner RC | 1.50 | 4.00 |
| ❏ 643 | Aaron Sele | .15 | .40 |
| ❏ 644 | Cameron Cairncross | .08 | .25 |
| ❏ 645 | Brian Harper | .08 | .25 |
| ❏ 646 | Marc Valdes UER NNO | .08 | .25 |
| ❏ 647 | Mark Ratekin | .08 | .25 |
| ❏ 648 | Terry Bradshaw RC | .15 | .40 |
| ❏ 649 | Justin Thompson | .08 | .25 |
| ❏ 650 | Mike Busch RC | .15 | .40 |
| ❏ 651 | Joe Hall RC | .15 | .40 |
| ❏ 652 | Bobby Jones | .08 | .25 |
| ❏ 653 | Kelly Stinnett RC | .40 | 1.00 |
| ❏ 654 | Rod Steph RC | .15 | .40 |
| ❏ 655 | Jay Powell RC | .15 | .40 |
| ❏ 656 | Keith Garagozzo RC | .15 | .40 |
| ❏ 657 | Todd Dunn | .08 | .25 |
| ❏ 658 | Charles Peterson RC | .15 | .40 |
| ❏ 659 | Darren Lewis | .08 | .25 |
| ❏ 660 | John Wasdin RC | .15 | .40 |
| ❏ 661 | Tate Seefried RC | .15 | .40 |
| ❏ 662 | Hector Trinidad RC | .15 | .40 |
| ❏ 663 | John Carter RC | .08 | .25 |
| ❏ 664 | Larry Mitchell | .08 | .25 |
| ❏ 665 | David Catlett RC | .15 | .40 |
| ❏ 666 | Dante Bichette | .15 | .40 |

| | | |
|---|---|---|
| ❏ 667 Felix Jose | .08 | .25 |
| ❏ 668 Rondell White | .15 | .40 |
| ❏ 669 Tino Martinez | .25 | .60 |
| ❏ 670 Brian L. Hunter | .08 | .25 |
| ❏ 671 Jose Malave | .08 | .25 |
| ❏ 672 Archi Cianfrocco | .08 | .25 |
| ❏ 673 Mike Matheny RC | .60 | 1.50 |
| ❏ 674 Bret Barberie | .08 | .25 |
| ❏ 675 Andrew Lorraine RC | .15 | .40 |
| ❏ 676 Brian Jordan | .15 | .40 |
| ❏ 677 Tim Belcher | .08 | .25 |
| ❏ 678 Antonio Osuna RC | .15 | .40 |
| ❏ 679 Checklist | .08 | .25 |
| ❏ 680 Checklist | .08 | .25 |
| ❏ 681 Checklist | .08 | .25 |
| ❏ 682 Checklist | .08 | .25 |

## 1995 Bowman

| | | |
|---|---|---|
| ❏ COMPLETE SET (439) | 90.00 | 150.00 |
| ❏ 1 Billy Wagner | .30 | .75 |
| ❏ 2 Chris Widger | .08 | .25 |
| ❏ 3 Brent Bowers | .08 | .25 |
| ❏ 4 Bob Abreu RC | 3.00 | 8.00 |
| ❏ 5 Lou Collier RC | .40 | 1.00 |
| ❏ 6 Juan Acevedo RC | .20 | .50 |
| ❏ 7 Jason Kelley RC | .20 | .50 |
| ❏ 8 Brian Sackinsky | .08 | .25 |
| ❏ 9 Scott Christman | .08 | .25 |
| ❏ 10 Damon Hollins | .08 | .25 |
| ❏ 11 Willis Otanez RC | .20 | .50 |
| ❏ 12 Jason Ryan RC | .20 | .50 |
| ❏ 13 Jason Giambi | .30 | .75 |
| ❏ 14 Andy Taulbee RC | .20 | .50 |
| ❏ 15 Mark Thompson | .08 | .25 |
| ❏ 16 Hugo Pivaral RC | .20 | .50 |
| ❏ 17 Brien Taylor | .08 | .25 |
| ❏ 18 Antonio Osuna | .08 | .25 |
| ❏ 19 Edgardo Alfonzo | .20 | .50 |
| ❏ 20 Carl Everett | .20 | .50 |
| ❏ 21 Matt Drews | .08 | .25 |
| ❏ 22 Bartolo Colon RC | 1.50 | 4.00 |
| ❏ 23 Andruw Jones RC | 5.00 | 12.00 |
| ❏ 24 Robert Person RC | .40 | 1.00 |
| ❏ 25 Derrek Lee | .50 | 1.25 |
| ❏ 26 John Ambrose RC | .20 | .50 |
| ❏ 27 Eric Knowles RC | .20 | .50 |
| ❏ 28 Chris Roberts | .08 | .25 |
| ❏ 29 Don Wengert | .08 | .25 |
| ❏ 30 Marcus Jensen RC | .40 | 1.00 |
| ❏ 31 Brian Barber | .20 | .50 |
| ❏ 32 Kevin Brown C | .20 | .50 |
| ❏ 33 Benji Gil | .20 | .50 |
| ❏ 34 Mike Hubbard | .20 | .50 |
| ❏ 35 Bart Evans RC | .20 | .50 |
| ❏ 36 Enrique Wilson RC | .20 | .50 |
| ❏ 37 Brian Buchanan RC | .20 | .50 |
| ❏ 38 Ken Ray RC | .20 | .50 |
| ❏ 39 Micah Franklin RC | .20 | .50 |
| ❏ 40 Ricky Otero RC | .20 | .50 |
| ❏ 41 Jason Kendall | .20 | .50 |
| ❏ 42 Jimmy Hurst | .20 | .50 |
| ❏ 43 Jerry Wolak RC | .20 | .50 |
| ❏ 44 Jayson Peterson RC | .20 | .50 |
| ❏ 45 Allen Battle RC | .20 | .50 |
| ❏ 46 Scott Stahoviak | .20 | .50 |
| ❏ 47 Steve Schrenk RC | .20 | .50 |
| ❏ 48 Travis Miller RC | .20 | .50 |
| ❏ 49 Eddie Rios RC | .20 | .50 |
| ❏ 50 Mike Hampton | .20 | .50 |
| ❏ 51 Chad Frontera RC | .20 | .50 |
| ❏ 52 Tom Evans | .08 | .25 |
| ❏ 53 C.J. Nitkowski | .08 | .25 |
| ❏ 54 Clay Caruthers RC | .20 | .50 |
| ❏ 55 Shannon Stewart | .20 | .50 |

| | | |
|---|---|---|
| ❏ 56 Jorge Posada | .50 | 1.25 |
| ❏ 57 Aaron Holbert | .08 | .25 |
| ❏ 58 Harry Berrios RC | .20 | .50 |
| ❏ 59 Steve Rodriguez | .08 | .25 |
| ❏ 60 Shane Andrews | .08 | .25 |
| ❏ 61 Will Cunnane RC | .20 | .50 |
| ❏ 62 Richard Hidalgo | .08 | .25 |
| ❏ 63 Bill Selby RC | .20 | .50 |
| ❏ 64 Jay Cranford RC | .20 | .50 |
| ❏ 65 Jeff Suppan | .20 | .50 |
| ❏ 66 Curtis Goodwin | .08 | .25 |
| ❏ 67 John Thomson RC | .40 | 1.00 |
| ❏ 68 Justin Thompson | .08 | .25 |
| ❏ 69 Troy Percival | .20 | .50 |
| ❏ 70 Matt Wagner RC | .20 | .50 |
| ❏ 71 Terry Bradshaw | .08 | .25 |
| ❏ 72 Greg Hansell | .08 | .25 |
| ❏ 73 John Burke | .08 | .25 |
| ❏ 74 Jeff D'Amico | .08 | .25 |
| ❏ 75 Ernie Young | .08 | .25 |
| ❏ 76 Jason Bates | .08 | .25 |
| ❏ 77 Chris Stynes | .08 | .25 |
| ❏ 78 Cade Gaspar RC | .20 | .50 |
| ❏ 79 Melvin Nieves | .08 | .25 |
| ❏ 80 Rick Gorecki | .08 | .25 |
| ❏ 81 Felix Rodriguez RC | .20 | .50 |
| ❏ 82 Ryan Hancock | .08 | .25 |
| ❏ 83 Chris Carpenter RC | 3.00 | 8.00 |
| ❏ 84 Ray McDavid | .08 | .25 |
| ❏ 85 Chris Wimmer | .08 | .25 |
| ❏ 86 Doug Glanville | .08 | .25 |
| ❏ 87 DeShawn Warren | .08 | .25 |
| ❏ 88 Damian Moss RC | .20 | .50 |
| ❏ 89 Rafael Orellano RC | .20 | .50 |
| ❏ 90 Vladimir Guerrero RC ! | 8.00 | 20.00 |
| ❏ 91 Raul Casanova RC | .20 | .50 |
| ❏ 92 Karim Garcia RC | .20 | .50 |
| ❏ 93 Bryce Florie | .08 | .25 |
| ❏ 94 Kevin Orie | .08 | .25 |
| ❏ 95 Ryan Nye RC | .20 | .50 |
| ❏ 96 Matt Sachse RC | .20 | .50 |
| ❏ 97 Ivan Arteaga RC | .20 | .50 |
| ❏ 98 Glenn Murray | .08 | .25 |
| ❏ 99 Stacy Hollins RC | .20 | .50 |
| ❏ 100 Jim Pittsley | .08 | .25 |
| ❏ 101 Craig Mattson RC | .20 | .50 |
| ❏ 102 Neifi Perez | .08 | .25 |
| ❏ 103 Keith Williams | .08 | .25 |
| ❏ 104 Roger Cedeno | .08 | .25 |
| ❏ 105 Tony Terry RC | .20 | .50 |
| ❏ 106 Jose Malave | .08 | .25 |
| ❏ 107 Joe Rosselli | .08 | .25 |
| ❏ 108 Kevin Jordan | .08 | .25 |
| ❏ 109 Sid Roberson RC | .20 | .50 |
| ❏ 110 Alan Embree | .08 | .25 |
| ❏ 111 Terrell Wade | .08 | .25 |
| ❏ 112 Bob Wolcott | .08 | .25 |
| ❏ 113 Carlos Perez RC | .40 | 1.00 |
| ❏ 114 Mike Bovee RC | .20 | .50 |
| ❏ 115 Tommy Davis RC | .20 | .50 |
| ❏ 116 Jeremey Kendall RC | .20 | .50 |
| ❏ 117 Rich Aude | .08 | .25 |
| ❏ 118 Rick Huisman | .08 | .25 |
| ❏ 119 Tim Belk | .08 | .25 |
| ❏ 120 Edgar Renteria | .20 | .50 |
| ❏ 121 Calvin Maduro RC | .20 | .50 |
| ❏ 122 Jerry Martin RC | .20 | .50 |
| ❏ 123 Ramon Fermin RC | .20 | .50 |
| ❏ 124 Kimera Bartee RC | .20 | .50 |
| ❏ 125 Mark Ferris | .08 | .25 |
| ❏ 126 Frank Rodriguez | .08 | .25 |
| ❏ 127 Bob Higginson RC | .75 | 2.00 |
| ❏ 128 Bret Wagner | .08 | .25 |
| ❏ 129 Edwin Diaz RC | .20 | .50 |
| ❏ 130 Jimmy Haynes | .08 | .25 |
| ❏ 131 Chris Weinke RC QB | .40 | 1.00 |
| ❏ 132 Damian Jackson RC | .20 | .50 |
| ❏ 133 Felix Martinez | .08 | .25 |
| ❏ 134 Edwin Hurtado RC | .20 | .50 |
| ❏ 135 Matt Raleigh RC | .20 | .50 |
| ❏ 136 Paul Wilson | .20 | .50 |
| ❏ 137 Ron Villone | .08 | .25 |
| ❏ 138 Eric Stuckenschneider RC | .20 | .50 |
| ❏ 139 Tate Seefried | .20 | .50 |
| ❏ 140 Rey Ordonez RC | .75 | 2.00 |
| ❏ 141 Eddie Pearson | .08 | .25 |
| ❏ 142 Kevin Gallaher | .08 | .25 |
| ❏ 143 Torii Hunter | .30 | .75 |

| | | |
|---|---|---|
| ❏ 144 Daron Kirkreit | .08 | .25 |
| ❏ 145 Craig Wilson | .08 | .25 |
| ❏ 146 Ugueth Urbina | .08 | .25 |
| ❏ 147 Chris Snopek | .08 | .25 |
| ❏ 148 Kym Ashworth | .08 | .25 |
| ❏ 149 Wayne Gomes | .08 | .25 |
| ❏ 150 Mark Loretta | .20 | .50 |
| ❏ 151 Ramon Morel RC | .20 | .50 |
| ❏ 152 Trot Nixon | .20 | .50 |
| ❏ 153 Desi Relaford | .08 | .25 |
| ❏ 154 Scott Sullivan | .08 | .25 |
| ❏ 155 Marc Barcelo | .08 | .25 |
| ❏ 156 Willie Adams | .08 | .25 |
| ❏ 157 Derrick Gibson RC | .20 | .50 |
| ❏ 158 Brian Meadows RC | .20 | .50 |
| ❏ 159 Julian Tavarez | .08 | .25 |
| ❏ 160 Bryan Rekar | .08 | .25 |
| ❏ 161 Steve Gibralter | .08 | .25 |
| ❏ 162 Esteban Loaiza | .08 | .25 |
| ❏ 163 John Wasdin | .08 | .25 |
| ❏ 164 Kirk Presley | .08 | .25 |
| ❏ 165 Mariano Rivera | .60 | 1.50 |
| ❏ 166 Andy Larkin | .08 | .25 |
| ❏ 167 Sean Whiteside RC | .20 | .50 |
| ❏ 168 Matt Apana RC | .20 | .50 |
| ❏ 169 Shawn Senior RC | .20 | .50 |
| ❏ 170 Scott Gentile | .08 | .25 |
| ❏ 171 Quilvio Veras | .08 | .25 |
| ❏ 172 Eli Marrero RC | .60 | 1.50 |
| ❏ 173 Mendy Lopez RC | .20 | .50 |
| ❏ 174 Homer Bush | .08 | .25 |
| ❏ 175 Brian Stephenson RC | .20 | .50 |
| ❏ 176 Jon Nunnally | .08 | .25 |
| ❏ 177 Jose Herrera | .08 | .25 |
| ❏ 178 Corey Avrard RC | .20 | .50 |
| ❏ 179 David Bell | .20 | .50 |
| ❏ 180 Jason Isringhausen | .20 | .50 |
| ❏ 181 Jamey Wright | .08 | .25 |
| ❏ 182 Lonell Roberts RC | .20 | .50 |
| ❏ 183 Marty Cordova | .20 | .50 |
| ❏ 184 Amaury Telemaco | .08 | .25 |
| ❏ 185 John Mabry | .08 | .25 |
| ❏ 186 Andrew Vessel RC | .20 | .50 |
| ❏ 187 Jim Cole RC | .20 | .50 |
| ❏ 188 Marquis Riley | .08 | .25 |
| ❏ 189 Todd Dunn | .08 | .25 |
| ❏ 190 John Carter | .08 | .25 |
| ❏ 191 Donnie Sadler RC | .40 | 1.00 |
| ❏ 192 Mike Bell | .08 | .25 |
| ❏ 193 Chris Cumberland RC | .20 | .50 |
| ❏ 194 Jason Schmidt | .50 | 1.25 |
| ❏ 195 Matt Brunson | .08 | .25 |
| ❏ 196 James Baldwin | .20 | .50 |
| ❏ 197 Bill Simas RC | .20 | .50 |
| ❏ 198 Gus Gandarillas | .08 | .25 |
| ❏ 199 Mac Suzuki | .08 | .25 |
| ❏ 200 Rick Holifield RC | .20 | .50 |
| ❏ 201 Fernando Lunar RC | .20 | .50 |
| ❏ 202 Kevin Jarvis | .08 | .25 |
| ❏ 203 Everett Stull | .08 | .25 |
| ❏ 204 Steve Wojciechowski | .08 | .25 |
| ❏ 205 Shawn Estes | .08 | .25 |
| ❏ 206 Jermaine Dye | .20 | .50 |
| ❏ 207 Marc Kroon | .08 | .25 |
| ❏ 208 Peter Munro RC | .40 | 1.00 |
| ❏ 209 Pat Watkins | .08 | .25 |
| ❏ 210 Matt Smith | .08 | .25 |
| ❏ 211 Joe Vitiello | .08 | .25 |
| ❏ 212 Gerald Witasick Jr. | .08 | .25 |
| ❏ 213 Freddy Adrian Garcia RC | .20 | .50 |
| ❏ 214 Glenn Dishman RC | .20 | .50 |
| ❏ 215 Jay Canizaro RC | .20 | .50 |
| ❏ 216 Angel Martinez | .08 | .25 |
| ❏ 217 Yamil Benitez RC | .20 | .50 |
| ❏ 218 Fausto Macey RC | .20 | .50 |
| ❏ 219 Eric Owens | .08 | .25 |
| ❏ 220 Checklist | .08 | .25 |
| ❏ 221 Dwayne Hosey FOIL RC | .08 | .25 |
| ❏ 222 Brad Woodall FOIL RC | .08 | .25 |
| ❏ 223 Billy Ashley FOIL | .08 | .25 |
| ❏ 224 Mark Grudzielanek FOIL RC | .75 | 2.00 |
| ❏ 225 Mark Johnson FOIL RC | .08 | .25 |
| ❏ 226 Tim Unroe FOIL RC | .08 | .25 |
| ❏ 227 Todd Greene FOIL | .08 | .25 |
| ❏ 228 Larry Sutton FOIL | .08 | .25 |
| ❏ 229 Derek Jeter FOIL | 1.50 | 4.00 |
| ❏ 230 Sal Fasano FOIL RC | .08 | .25 |
| ❏ 231 Ruben Rivera FOIL | .08 | .25 |

|  |  | | |
|---|---|---|---|
| ❏ 232 | Chris Truby FOIL RC | .20 | .50 |
| ❏ 233 | John Donati FOIL | .20 | .50 |
| ❏ 234 | Decomba Conner FOIL RC | .20 | .50 |
| ❏ 235 | Sergio Nunez FOIL RC | .20 | .50 |
| ❏ 236 | Ray Brown FOIL RC | .20 | .50 |
| ❏ 237 | Juan Melo FOIL RC | .20 | .50 |
| ❏ 238 | Hideo Nomo FOIL RC | 2.00 | 5.00 |
| ❏ 239 | Jaime Bluma RC FOIL | .20 | .50 |
| ❏ 240 | Jay Payton FOIL RC | .75 | 2.00 |
| ❏ 241 | Paul Konerko FOIL | 1.50 | 4.00 |
| ❏ 242 | Scott Elarton FOIL RC | .40 | 1.00 |
| ❏ 243 | Jeff Abbott FOIL RC | .40 | 1.00 |
| ❏ 244 | Jim Brower FOIL RC | .20 | .50 |
| ❏ 245 | Geoff Blum FOIL RC | .75 | 2.00 |
| ❏ 246 | Aaron Boone FOIL RC | .75 | 2.00 |
| ❏ 247 | J.R. Phillips FOIL | .08 | .25 |
| ❏ 248 | Alex Ochoa FOIL | .08 | .25 |
| ❏ 249 | Nomar Garciaparra FOIL | 1.50 | 4.00 |
| ❏ 250 | Garret Anderson FOIL | .20 | .50 |
| ❏ 251 | Ray Durham FOIL | .20 | .50 |
| ❏ 252 | Paul Shuey FOIL | .08 | .25 |
| ❏ 253 | Tony Clark FOIL | .08 | .25 |
| ❏ 254 | Johnny Damon FOIL | .30 | .75 |
| ❏ 255 | Duane Singleton FOIL | .08 | .25 |
| ❏ 256 | LaTroy Hawkins FOIL | .08 | .25 |
| ❏ 257 | Andy Pettitte FOIL | .30 | .75 |
| ❏ 258 | Ben Grieve FOIL | .08 | .25 |
| ❏ 259 | Marc Newfield FOIL | .08 | .25 |
| ❏ 260 | Terrell Lowery FOIL | .08 | .25 |
| ❏ 261 | Shawn Green FOIL | .20 | .50 |
| ❏ 262 | Chipper Jones FOIL | .50 | 1.25 |
| ❏ 263 | Brooks Kieschnick FOIL | .08 | .25 |
| ❏ 264 | Pokey Reese FOIL | .08 | .25 |
| ❏ 265 | Doug Million FOIL | .08 | .25 |
| ❏ 266 | Marc Valdes FOIL | .08 | .25 |
| ❏ 267 | Brian L.Hunter FOIL | .08 | .25 |
| ❏ 268 | Todd Hollandsworth FOIL | .08 | .25 |
| ❏ 269 | Rod Henderson FOIL | .08 | .25 |
| ❏ 270 | Bill Pulsipher FOIL | .08 | .25 |
| ❏ 271 | Scott Rolen FOIL RC | 5.00 | 12.00 |
| ❏ 272 | Trey Beamon FOIL | .08 | .25 |
| ❏ 273 | Alan Benes FOIL | .08 | .25 |
| ❏ 274 | Dustin Hermanson FOIL | .08 | .25 |
| ❏ 275 | Ricky Bottalico | .08 | .25 |
| ❏ 276 | Albert Belle | .20 | .50 |
| ❏ 277 | Deion Sanders | .30 | .75 |
| ❏ 278 | Matt Williams | .20 | .50 |
| ❏ 279 | Jeff Bagwell | .30 | .75 |
| ❏ 280 | Kirby Puckett | .50 | 1.25 |
| ❏ 281 | Dave Hollins | .08 | .25 |
| ❏ 282 | Don Mattingly | 1.25 | 3.00 |
| ❏ 283 | Joey Hamilton | .08 | .25 |
| ❏ 284 | Bobby Bonilla | .20 | .50 |
| ❏ 285 | Moises Alou | .20 | .50 |
| ❏ 286 | Tom Glavine | .30 | .75 |
| ❏ 287 | Brett Butler | .20 | .50 |
| ❏ 288 | Chris Hoiles | .08 | .25 |
| ❏ 289 | Kenny Rogers | .20 | .50 |
| ❏ 290 | Larry Walker | .20 | .50 |
| ❏ 291 | Tim Raines | .20 | .50 |
| ❏ 292 | Kevin Appier | .20 | .50 |
| ❏ 293 | Roger Clemens | 1.00 | 2.50 |
| ❏ 294 | Chuck Carr | .08 | .25 |
| ❏ 295 | Randy Myers | .08 | .25 |
| ❏ 296 | Dave Nilsson | .08 | .25 |
| ❏ 297 | Joe Carter | .20 | .50 |
| ❏ 298 | Chuck Finley | .20 | .50 |
| ❏ 299 | Ray Lankford | .20 | .50 |
| ❏ 300 | Roberto Kelly | .08 | .25 |
| ❏ 301 | Jon Lieber | .08 | .25 |
| ❏ 302 | Travis Fryman | .20 | .50 |
| ❏ 303 | Mark McGwire | 1.25 | 3.00 |
| ❏ 304 | Tony Gwynn | .60 | 1.50 |
| ❏ 305 | Kenny Lofton | .20 | .50 |
| ❏ 306 | Mark Whiten | .08 | .25 |
| ❏ 307 | Doug Drabek | .08 | .25 |
| ❏ 308 | Terry Steinbach | .08 | .25 |
| ❏ 309 | Ryan Klesko | .20 | .50 |
| ❏ 310 | Mike Piazza | .75 | 2.00 |
| ❏ 311 | Ben McDonald | .08 | .25 |
| ❏ 312 | Reggie Sanders | .20 | .50 |
| ❏ 313 | Alex Fernandez | .08 | .25 |
| ❏ 314 | Aaron Sele | .08 | .25 |
| ❏ 315 | Gregg Jefferies | .08 | .25 |
| ❏ 316 | Rickey Henderson | .50 | 1.25 |
| ❏ 317 | Brian Anderson | .08 | .25 |
| ❏ 318 | Jose Valentin | .08 | .25 |
| ❏ 319 | Rod Beck | .08 | .25 |
| ❏ 320 | Marquis Grissom | .20 | .50 |
| ❏ 321 | Ken Griffey Jr. | .75 | 2.00 |
| ❏ 322 | Bret Saberhagen | .20 | .50 |
| ❏ 323 | Juan Gonzalez | .20 | .50 |
| ❏ 324 | Paul Molitor | .20 | .50 |
| ❏ 325 | Gary Sheffield | .20 | .50 |
| ❏ 326 | Darren Daulton | .20 | .50 |
| ❏ 327 | Bill Swift | .08 | .25 |
| ❏ 328 | Brian McRae | .08 | .25 |
| ❏ 329 | Robin Ventura | .20 | .50 |
| ❏ 330 | Lee Smith | .08 | .25 |
| ❏ 331 | Fred McGriff | .30 | .75 |
| ❏ 332 | Delino DeShields | .08 | .25 |
| ❏ 333 | Edgar Martinez | .30 | .75 |
| ❏ 334 | Mike Mussina | .30 | .75 |
| ❏ 335 | Orlando Merced | .08 | .25 |
| ❏ 336 | Carlos Baerga | .08 | .25 |
| ❏ 337 | Wil Cordero | .08 | .25 |
| ❏ 338 | Tom Pagnozzi | .08 | .25 |
| ❏ 339 | Pat Hentgen | .08 | .25 |
| ❏ 340 | Chad Curtis | .08 | .25 |
| ❏ 341 | Darren Lewis | .08 | .25 |
| ❏ 342 | Jeff Kent | .20 | .50 |
| ❏ 343 | Bip Roberts | .08 | .25 |
| ❏ 344 | Ivan Rodriguez | .30 | .75 |
| ❏ 345 | Jeff Montgomery | .08 | .25 |
| ❏ 346 | Hal Morris | .08 | .25 |
| ❏ 347 | Danny Tartabull | .08 | .25 |
| ❏ 348 | Raul Mondesi | .20 | .50 |
| ❏ 349 | Ken Hill | .08 | .25 |
| ❏ 350 | Pedro Martinez | .30 | .75 |
| ❏ 351 | Frank Thomas | .50 | 1.25 |
| ❏ 352 | Manny Ramirez | .30 | .75 |
| ❏ 353 | Tim Salmon | .30 | .75 |
| ❏ 354 | W. VanLandingham | .08 | .25 |
| ❏ 355 | Andres Galarraga | .20 | .50 |
| ❏ 356 | Paul O'Neill | .30 | .75 |
| ❏ 357 | Brady Anderson | .08 | .25 |
| ❏ 358 | Ramon Martinez | .08 | .25 |
| ❏ 359 | John Olerud | .20 | .50 |
| ❏ 360 | Ruben Sierra | .20 | .50 |
| ❏ 361 | Cal Eldred | .08 | .25 |
| ❏ 362 | Jay Buhner | .20 | .50 |
| ❏ 363 | Jay Bell | .20 | .50 |
| ❏ 364 | Wally Joyner | .20 | .50 |
| ❏ 365 | Chuck Knoblauch | .20 | .50 |
| ❏ 366 | Len Dykstra | .20 | .50 |
| ❏ 367 | John Wetteland | .20 | .50 |
| ❏ 368 | Roberto Alomar | .30 | .75 |
| ❏ 369 | Craig Biggio | .20 | .50 |
| ❏ 370 | Ozzie Smith | .75 | 2.00 |
| ❏ 371 | Terry Pendleton | .20 | .50 |
| ❏ 372 | Sammy Sosa | .50 | 1.25 |
| ❏ 373 | Carlos Garcia | .08 | .25 |
| ❏ 374 | Jose Rijo | .08 | .25 |
| ❏ 375 | Chris Gomez | .08 | .25 |
| ❏ 376 | Barry Bonds | 1.25 | 3.00 |
| ❏ 377 | Steve Avery | .08 | .25 |
| ❏ 378 | Rick Wilkins | .08 | .25 |
| ❏ 379 | Pete Harnisch | .08 | .25 |
| ❏ 380 | Dean Palmer | .20 | .50 |
| ❏ 381 | Bob Hamelin | .08 | .25 |
| ❏ 382 | Jason Bere | .08 | .25 |
| ❏ 383 | Jimmy Key | .20 | .50 |
| ❏ 384 | Dante Bichette | .20 | .50 |
| ❏ 385 | Rafael Palmeiro | .30 | .75 |
| ❏ 386 | David Justice | .20 | .50 |
| ❏ 387 | Chili Davis | .08 | .25 |
| ❏ 388 | Mike Greenwell | .08 | .25 |
| ❏ 389 | Todd Zeile | .08 | .25 |
| ❏ 390 | Jeff Conine | .20 | .50 |
| ❏ 391 | Rick Aguilera | .08 | .25 |
| ❏ 392 | Eddie Murray | .50 | 1.25 |
| ❏ 393 | Mike Stanley | .08 | .25 |
| ❏ 394 | Cliff Floyd UER | .20 | .50 |
| ❏ 395 | Randy Johnson | .50 | 1.25 |
| ❏ 396 | David Nied | .08 | .25 |
| ❏ 397 | Devon White | .20 | .50 |
| ❏ 398 | Royce Clayton | .08 | .25 |
| ❏ 399 | Andy Benes | .08 | .25 |
| ❏ 400 | John Hudek | .08 | .25 |
| ❏ 401 | Bobby Jones | .08 | .25 |
| ❏ 402 | Eric Karros | .20 | .50 |
| ❏ 403 | Will Clark | .30 | .75 |
| ❏ 404 | Mark Langston | .08 | .25 |
| ❏ 405 | Kevin Brown | .20 | .50 |
| ❏ 406 | Greg Maddux | .75 | 2.00 |
| ❏ 407 | David Cone | .20 | .50 |
| ❏ 408 | Wade Boggs | .30 | .75 |
| ❏ 409 | Steve Trachsel | .08 | .25 |
| ❏ 410 | Greg Vaughn | .08 | .25 |
| ❏ 411 | Mo Vaughn | .20 | .50 |
| ❏ 412 | Wilson Alvarez | .08 | .25 |
| ❏ 413 | Cal Ripken | 1.50 | 4.00 |
| ❏ 414 | Rico Brogna | .08 | .25 |
| ❏ 415 | Barry Larkin | .30 | .75 |
| ❏ 416 | Cecil Fielder | .20 | .50 |
| ❏ 417 | Jose Canseco | .30 | .75 |
| ❏ 418 | Jack McDowell | .08 | .25 |
| ❏ 419 | Mike Lieberthal | .20 | .50 |
| ❏ 420 | Andrew Lorraine | .08 | .25 |
| ❏ 421 | Rich Becker | .08 | .25 |
| ❏ 422 | Tony Phillips | .08 | .25 |
| ❏ 423 | Scott Ruffcorn | .08 | .25 |
| ❏ 424 | Jeff Granger | .08 | .25 |
| ❏ 425 | Greg Pirkl | .08 | .25 |
| ❏ 426 | Dennis Eckersley | .20 | .50 |
| ❏ 427 | Jose Lima | .08 | .25 |
| ❏ 428 | Russ Davis | .08 | .25 |
| ❏ 429 | Armando Benitez | .08 | .25 |
| ❏ 430 | Alex Gonzalez | .08 | .25 |
| ❏ 431 | Carlos Delgado | .20 | .50 |
| ❏ 432 | Chan Ho Park | .20 | .50 |
| ❏ 433 | Mickey Tettleton | .08 | .25 |
| ❏ 434 | Dave Winfield | .20 | .50 |
| ❏ 435 | John Burkett | .08 | .25 |
| ❏ 436 | Orlando Miller | .08 | .25 |
| ❏ 437 | Rondell White | .20 | .50 |
| ❏ 438 | Jose Oliva | .08 | .25 |
| ❏ 439 | Checklist | .08 | .25 |

## 1996 Bowman

|  |  | | |
|---|---|---|---|
| ❏ | COMPLETE SET (385) | 20.00 | 50.00 |
| ❏ 1 | Cal Ripken | 1.00 | 2.50 |
| ❏ 2 | Ray Durham | .10 | .30 |
| ❏ 3 | Ivan Rodriguez | .20 | .50 |
| ❏ 4 | Fred McGriff | .20 | .50 |
| ❏ 5 | Hideo Nomo | .30 | .75 |
| ❏ 6 | Troy Percival | .10 | .30 |
| ❏ 7 | Moises Alou | .10 | .30 |
| ❏ 8 | Mike Stanley | .10 | .30 |
| ❏ 9 | Jay Buhner | .10 | .30 |
| ❏ 10 | Shawn Green | .10 | .30 |
| ❏ 11 | Ryan Klesko | .10 | .30 |
| ❏ 12 | Andres Galarraga | .10 | .30 |
| ❏ 13 | Dean Palmer | .10 | .30 |
| ❏ 14 | Jeff Conine | .10 | .30 |
| ❏ 15 | Brian L.Hunter | .10 | .30 |
| ❏ 16 | J.T. Snow | .10 | .30 |
| ❏ 17 | Larry Walker | .10 | .30 |
| ❏ 18 | Barry Larkin | .20 | .50 |
| ❏ 19 | Alex Gonzalez | .10 | .30 |
| ❏ 20 | Edgar Martinez | .10 | .30 |
| ❏ 21 | Mo Vaughn | .10 | .30 |
| ❏ 22 | Mark McGwire | .75 | 2.00 |
| ❏ 23 | Jose Canseco | .20 | .50 |
| ❏ 24 | Jack McDowell | .10 | .30 |
| ❏ 25 | Dante Bichette | .10 | .30 |
| ❏ 26 | Wade Boggs | .20 | .50 |
| ❏ 27 | Mike Piazza | .50 | 1.25 |
| ❏ 28 | Ray Lankford | .10 | .30 |
| ❏ 29 | Craig Biggio | .20 | .50 |
| ❏ 30 | Rafael Palmeiro | .10 | .30 |
| ❏ 31 | Ron Gant | .10 | .30 |
| ❏ 32 | Javy Lopez | .10 | .30 |
| ❏ 33 | Brian Jordan | .10 | .30 |
| ❏ 34 | Paul O'Neill | .10 | .30 |
| ❏ 35 | Mark Grace | .20 | .50 |
| ❏ 36 | Matt Williams | .10 | .30 |
| ❏ 37 | Pedro Martinez | .30 | .75 |
| ❏ 38 | Rickey Henderson | .30 | .75 |
| ❏ 39 | Bobby Bonilla | .10 | .30 |

|  |  | | |
|---|---|---|---|
| 40 | Todd Hollandsworth | .10 | .30 |
| 41 | Jim Thome | .20 | .50 |
| 42 | Gary Sheffield | .30 | .75 |
| 43 | Tim Salmon | .20 | .50 |
| 44 | Gregg Jefferies | .10 | .30 |
| 45 | Roberto Alomar | .20 | .50 |
| 46 | Carlos Baerga | .10 | .30 |
| 47 | Mark Grudzielanek | .10 | .30 |
| 48 | Randy Johnson | .30 | .75 |
| 49 | Tino Martinez | .10 | .30 |
| 50 | Robin Ventura | .10 | .30 |
| 51 | Ryne Sandberg | .50 | 1.25 |
| 52 | Jay Bell | .10 | .30 |
| 53 | Jason Schmidt | .20 | .50 |
| 54 | Frank Thomas | .30 | .75 |
| 55 | Kenny Lofton | .10 | .30 |
| 56 | Ariel Prieto | .10 | .30 |
| 57 | David Cone | .10 | .30 |
| 58 | Reggie Sanders | .10 | .30 |
| 59 | Michael Tucker | .10 | .30 |
| 60 | Vinny Castilla | .10 | .30 |
| 61 | Len Dykstra | .10 | .30 |
| 62 | Todd Hundley | .10 | .30 |
| 63 | Brian McRae | .10 | .30 |
| 64 | Dennis Eckersley | .10 | .30 |
| 65 | Rondell White | .10 | .30 |
| 66 | Eric Karros | .10 | .30 |
| 67 | Greg Maddux | .50 | 1.25 |
| 68 | Kevin Appier | .10 | .30 |
| 69 | Eddie Murray | .30 | .75 |
| 70 | John Olerud | .10 | .30 |
| 71 | Tony Gwynn | .40 | 1.00 |
| 72 | David Justice | .10 | .30 |
| 73 | Ken Caminiti | .10 | .30 |
| 74 | Terry Steinbach | .10 | .30 |
| 75 | Alan Benes | .10 | .30 |
| 76 | Chipper Jones | .30 | .75 |
| 77 | Jeff Bagwell | .20 | .50 |
| 78 | Barry Bonds | .75 | 2.00 |
| 79 | Ken Griffey Jr. | .60 | 1.50 |
| 80 | Roger Cedeno | .10 | .30 |
| 81 | Joe Carter | .10 | .30 |
| 82 | Henry Rodriguez | .10 | .30 |
| 83 | Jason Isringhausen | .10 | .30 |
| 84 | Chuck Knoblauch | .10 | .30 |
| 85 | Manny Ramirez | .20 | .50 |
| 86 | Tom Glavine | .20 | .50 |
| 87 | Jeffrey Hammonds | .10 | .30 |
| 88 | Paul Molitor | .10 | .30 |
| 89 | Roger Clemens | .60 | 1.50 |
| 90 | Greg Vaughn | .10 | .30 |
| 91 | Marty Cordova | .10 | .30 |
| 92 | Albert Belle | .10 | .30 |
| 93 | Mike Mussina | .20 | .50 |
| 94 | Garret Anderson | .10 | .30 |
| 95 | Juan Gonzalez | .20 | .50 |
| 96 | John Valentin | .10 | .30 |
| 97 | Jason Giambi | .10 | .30 |
| 98 | Kirby Puckett | .30 | .75 |
| 99 | Jim Edmonds | .10 | .30 |
| 100 | Cecil Fielder | .10 | .30 |
| 101 | Mike Aldrete | .10 | .30 |
| 102 | Marquis Grissom | .10 | .30 |
| 103 | Derek Bell | .10 | .30 |
| 104 | Raul Mondesi | .10 | .30 |
| 105 | Sammy Sosa | .30 | .75 |
| 106 | Travis Fryman | .10 | .30 |
| 107 | Rico Brogna | .10 | .30 |
| 108 | Will Clark | .20 | .50 |
| 109 | Bernie Williams | .20 | .50 |
| 110 | Brady Anderson | .10 | .30 |
| 111 | Torii Hunter | .10 | .30 |
| 112 | Derek Jeter | .75 | 2.00 |
| 113 | Mike Kusiewicz RC | .20 | .50 |
| 114 | Scott Rolen | .30 | .75 |
| 115 | Ramon Castro | .10 | .30 |
| 116 | Jose Guillen RC | 1.25 | 3.00 |
| 117 | Wade Walker RC | .20 | .50 |
| 118 | Shawn Senior | .10 | .30 |
| 119 | Onan Masaoka RC | .40 | 1.00 |
| 120 | Marlon Anderson RC | .40 | 1.00 |
| 121 | Katsuhiro Maeda RC | .40 | 1.00 |
| 122 | Garrett Stephenson RC | .20 | .50 |
| 123 | Butch Huskey | .10 | .30 |
| 124 | D'Angelo Jimenez RC | .40 | 1.00 |
| 125 | Tony Mounce RC | .20 | .50 |
| 126 | Jay Canizaro | .10 | .30 |
| 127 | Juan Melo | .10 | .30 |
| 128 | Steve Gibralter | .10 | .30 |
| 129 | Freddy Adrian Garcia | .10 | .30 |
| 130 | Julio Santana | .10 | .30 |
| 131 | Richard Hidalgo | .10 | .30 |
| 132 | Jermaine Dye | .10 | .30 |
| 133 | Willie Adams | .10 | .30 |
| 134 | Everett Stull | .10 | .30 |
| 135 | Ramon Morel | .10 | .30 |
| 136 | Chan Ho Park | .10 | .30 |
| 137 | Jamey Wright | .10 | .30 |
| 138 | Luis R. Garcia RC | .20 | .50 |
| 139 | Dan Serafini | .10 | .30 |
| 140 | Ryan Dempster RC | .75 | 2.00 |
| 141 | Tate Seefried | .10 | .30 |
| 142 | Jimmy Hurst | .10 | .30 |
| 143 | Travis Miller | .10 | .30 |
| 144 | Curtis Goodwin | .10 | .30 |
| 145 | Rocky Coppinger RC | .20 | .50 |
| 146 | Enrique Wilson | .10 | .30 |
| 147 | Jaime Bluma | .10 | .30 |
| 148 | Andrew Vessel | .10 | .30 |
| 149 | Damian Moss | .10 | .30 |
| 150 | Shawn Gallagher RC | .20 | .50 |
| 151 | Pat Watkins | .10 | .30 |
| 152 | Jose Paniagua | .10 | .30 |
| 153 | Danny Graves | .10 | .30 |
| 154 | Bryon Gainey RC | .20 | .50 |
| 155 | Steve Soderstrom | .10 | .30 |
| 156 | Cliff Brumbaugh RC | .20 | .50 |
| 157 | Eugene Kingsale RC | .20 | .50 |
| 158 | Lou Collier | .10 | .30 |
| 159 | Todd Walker | .20 | .50 |
| 160 | Kris Detmers RC | .20 | .50 |
| 161 | Josh Booty RC | .20 | .50 |
| 162 | Greg Whiteman RC | .20 | .50 |
| 163 | Damian Jackson | .10 | .30 |
| 164 | Tony Clark | .10 | .30 |
| 165 | Jeff D'Amico | .10 | .30 |
| 166 | Johnny Damon | .20 | .50 |
| 167 | Rafael Orellano | .10 | .30 |
| 168 | Ruben Rivera | .10 | .30 |
| 169 | Alex Ochoa | .10 | .30 |
| 170 | Jay Powell | .10 | .30 |
| 171 | Tom Evans | .10 | .30 |
| 172 | Ron Villone | .10 | .30 |
| 173 | Shawn Estes | .10 | .30 |
| 174 | John Wasdin | .10 | .30 |
| 175 | Bill Simas | .10 | .30 |
| 176 | Kevin Brown | .10 | .30 |
| 177 | Shannon Stewart | .10 | .30 |
| 178 | Todd Greene | .10 | .30 |
| 179 | Bob Wolcott | .10 | .30 |
| 180 | Chris Snopek | .10 | .30 |
| 181 | Nomar Garciaparra | .60 | 1.50 |
| 182 | Cameron Smith RC | .20 | .50 |
| 183 | Matt Drews | .10 | .30 |
| 184 | Jimmy Haynes | .10 | .30 |
| 185 | Chris Carpenter | .20 | .50 |
| 186 | Desi Relaford | .10 | .30 |
| 187 | Ben Grieve | .10 | .30 |
| 188 | Mike Bell | .10 | .30 |
| 189 | Luis Castillo RC | .60 | 1.50 |
| 190 | Ugueth Urbina | .10 | .30 |
| 191 | Paul Wilson | .10 | .30 |
| 192 | Andruw Jones | .50 | 1.25 |
| 193 | Wayne Gomes | .10 | .30 |
| 194 | Craig Counsell RC | .60 | 1.50 |
| 195 | Jim Cole | .10 | .30 |
| 196 | Brooks Kieschnick | .10 | .30 |
| 197 | Trey Beamon | .10 | .30 |
| 198 | Marino Santana RC | .20 | .50 |
| 199 | Bob Abreu | .30 | .75 |
| 200 | Pokey Reese | .10 | .30 |
| 201 | Dante Powell | .10 | .30 |
| 202 | George Arias | .10 | .30 |
| 203 | Jorge Velandia RC | .20 | .50 |
| 204 | George Lombard RC | .20 | .50 |
| 205 | Byron Browne RC | .20 | .50 |
| 206 | John Frascatore | .10 | .30 |
| 207 | Terry Adams | .10 | .30 |
| 208 | Wilson Delgado RC | .20 | .50 |
| 209 | Billy McMillon | .10 | .30 |
| 210 | Jeff Abbott | .10 | .30 |
| 211 | Trot Nixon | .20 | .50 |
| 212 | Amaury Telemaco | .10 | .30 |
| 213 | Scott Sullivan | .10 | .30 |
| 214 | Justin Thompson | .10 | .30 |
| 215 | Decomba Conner | .10 | .30 |
| 216 | Ryan McGuire | .10 | .30 |
| 217 | Matt Luke | .10 | .30 |
| 218 | Doug Million | .10 | .30 |
| 219 | Jason Dickson RC | .20 | .50 |
| 220 | Ramon Hernandez RC | .75 | 2.00 |
| 221 | Mark Bellhorn RC | .75 | 2.00 |
| 222 | Eric Ludwick RC | .20 | .50 |
| 223 | Luke Wilcox RC | .20 | .50 |
| 224 | Marty Malloy RC | .20 | .50 |
| 225 | Gary Coffee RC | .20 | .50 |
| 226 | Wendell Magee RC | .20 | .50 |
| 227 | Brett Tomko RC | .40 | 1.00 |
| 228 | Derek Lowe | .20 | .50 |
| 229 | Jose Rosado RC | .20 | .50 |
| 230 | Steve Bourgeois RC | .20 | .50 |
| 231 | Neil Weber RC | .20 | .50 |
| 232 | Jeff Ware | .10 | .30 |
| 233 | Edwin Diaz | .10 | .30 |
| 234 | Greg Norton | .10 | .30 |
| 235 | Aaron Boone | .10 | .30 |
| 236 | Jeff Suppan | .10 | .30 |
| 237 | Bret Wagner | .10 | .30 |
| 238 | Elieser Marrero | .10 | .30 |
| 239 | Will Cunnane | .10 | .30 |
| 240 | Brian Barkley RC | .20 | .50 |
| 241 | Jay Payton | .10 | .30 |
| 242 | Marcus Jensen | .10 | .30 |
| 243 | Ryan Nye | .10 | .30 |
| 244 | Chad Mottola | .10 | .30 |
| 245 | Scott McClain RC | .20 | .50 |
| 246 | Jesse Ibarra RC | .20 | .50 |
| 247 | Mike Darr RC | .20 | .50 |
| 248 | Bobby Estalella RC | .20 | .50 |
| 249 | Michael Barrett | .10 | .30 |
| 250 | Jaime Lopiccolo RC | .20 | .50 |
| 251 | Shane Spencer RC | .40 | 1.00 |
| 252 | Ben Petrick RC | .20 | .50 |
| 253 | Jason Bell RC | .20 | .50 |
| 254 | Arnold Gooch RC | .20 | .50 |
| 255 | T.J. Mathews | .10 | .30 |
| 256 | Jason Ryan | .10 | .30 |
| 257 | Pat Cline RC | .20 | .50 |
| 258 | Rafael Carmona RC | .20 | .50 |
| 259 | Carl Pavano RC | .75 | 2.00 |
| 260 | Ben Davis | .10 | .30 |
| 261 | Matt Lawton RC | .40 | 1.00 |
| 262 | Kevin Sefcik RC | .20 | .50 |
| 263 | Chris Fussell RC | .20 | .50 |
| 264 | Mike Cameron RC | .60 | 1.50 |
| 265 | Marty Janzen RC | .20 | .50 |
| 266 | Livan Hernandez RC | .75 | 2.00 |
| 267 | Raul Ibanez RC | 2.00 | 5.00 |
| 268 | Juan Encarnacion | .10 | .30 |
| 269 | David Yocum RC | .20 | .50 |
| 270 | Jonathan Johnson RC | .20 | .50 |
| 271 | Reggie Taylor | .10 | .30 |
| 272 | Danny Buxbaum RC | .20 | .50 |
| 273 | Jacob Cruz | .10 | .30 |
| 274 | Bobby Morris RC | .20 | .50 |
| 275 | Andy Fox RC | .20 | .50 |
| 276 | Greg Keagle | .10 | .30 |
| 277 | Charles Peterson | .10 | .30 |
| 278 | Derrek Lee | .20 | .50 |
| 279 | Bryant Nelson RC | .20 | .50 |
| 280 | Antone Williamson | .10 | .30 |
| 281 | Scott Elarton | .20 | .50 |
| 282 | Shad Williams RC | .20 | .50 |
| 283 | Rich Hunter RC | .20 | .50 |
| 284 | Chris Sheff | .10 | .30 |
| 285 | Derrick Gibson | .10 | .30 |
| 286 | Felix Rodriguez | .10 | .30 |
| 287 | Brian Banks RC | .20 | .50 |
| 288 | Jason McDonald | .10 | .30 |
| 289 | Glendon Rusch RC | .40 | 1.00 |
| 290 | Gary Rath | .10 | .30 |
| 291 | Peter Munro | .10 | .30 |
| 292 | Tom Fordham | .10 | .30 |
| 293 | Jason Kendall | .10 | .30 |
| 294 | Russ Johnson | .10 | .30 |
| 295 | Joe Long | .10 | .30 |
| 296 | Robert Smith RC | .20 | .50 |
| 297 | Jarrod Washburn RC | .60 | 1.50 |
| 298 | Dave Coggin RC | .20 | .50 |
| 299 | Jeff Yoder RC | .20 | .50 |
| 300 | Jed Hansen RC | .20 | .50 |
| 301 | Matt Morris RC | 1.00 | 2.50 |
| 302 | Josh Bishop RC | .20 | .50 |
| 303 | Dustin Hermanson | .10 | .30 |

| | | |
|---|---|---|
| ☐ 304 Mike Gulan | .10 | .30 |
| ☐ 305 Felipe Crespo | .10 | .30 |
| ☐ 306 Quinton McCracken | .10 | .30 |
| ☐ 307 Jim Bonnici RC | .20 | .50 |
| ☐ 308 Sal Fasano | .10 | .30 |
| ☐ 309 Gabe Alvarez RC | .20 | .50 |
| ☐ 310 Heath Murray RC | .20 | .50 |
| ☐ 311 Javier Valentin RC | .20 | .50 |
| ☐ 312 Bartolo Colon | .30 | .75 |
| ☐ 313 Olmedo Saenz | .10 | .30 |
| ☐ 314 Norm Hutchins RC | .20 | .50 |
| ☐ 315 Chris Holt | .10 | .30 |
| ☐ 316 David Doster RC | .20 | .50 |
| ☐ 317 Robert Person | .10 | .30 |
| ☐ 318 Donne Wall RC | .20 | .50 |
| ☐ 319 Adam Riggs RC | .20 | .50 |
| ☐ 320 Homer Bush | .10 | .30 |
| ☐ 321 Brad Rigby RC | .20 | .50 |
| ☐ 322 Lou Merloni RC | .20 | .50 |
| ☐ 323 Neifi Perez | .20 | .50 |
| ☐ 324 Chris Cumberland | .10 | .30 |
| ☐ 325 Alvie Shepherd RC | .20 | .50 |
| ☐ 326 Jarrod Patterson RC | .20 | .50 |
| ☐ 327 Ray Ricken RC | .20 | .50 |
| ☐ 328 Danny Klassen RC | .20 | .50 |
| ☐ 329 David Miller RC | .20 | .50 |
| ☐ 330 Chad Alexander RC | .20 | .50 |
| ☐ 331 Matt Beaumont | .10 | .30 |
| ☐ 332 Damon Hollins | .10 | .30 |
| ☐ 333 Todd Dunn | .10 | .30 |
| ☐ 334 Mike Sweeney RC | .75 | 2.00 |
| ☐ 335 Richie Sexson | .20 | .50 |
| ☐ 336 Billy Wagner | .10 | .30 |
| ☐ 337 Ron Wright RC | .20 | .50 |
| ☐ 338 Paul Konerko | .30 | .75 |
| ☐ 339 Tommy Phelps RC | .20 | .50 |
| ☐ 340 Karim Garcia | .10 | .30 |
| ☐ 341 Mike Grace RC | .20 | .50 |
| ☐ 342 Russell Branyan RC | .40 | 1.00 |
| ☐ 343 Randy Winn RC | .60 | 1.50 |
| ☐ 344 A.J. Pierzynski RC | 1.50 | 4.00 |
| ☐ 345 Mike Busby RC | .20 | .50 |
| ☐ 346 Matt Beech RC | .20 | .50 |
| ☐ 347 Jose Cepeda RC | .20 | .50 |
| ☐ 348 Brian Stephenson | .10 | .30 |
| ☐ 349 Rey Ordonez | .10 | .30 |
| ☐ 350 Rich Aurilia RC | .40 | 1.00 |
| ☐ 351 Edgard Velazquez RC | .20 | .50 |
| ☐ 352 Raul Casanova | .10 | .30 |
| ☐ 353 Carlos Guillen RC | .75 | 2.00 |
| ☐ 354 Bruce Aven RC | .20 | .50 |
| ☐ 355 Ryan Jones RC | .20 | .50 |
| ☐ 356 Derek Aucoin RC | .20 | .50 |
| ☐ 357 Brian Rose RC | .20 | .50 |
| ☐ 358 Richard Almanzar RC | .20 | .50 |
| ☐ 359 Fletcher Bates RC | .20 | .50 |
| ☐ 360 Russ Ortiz RC | .60 | 1.50 |
| ☐ 361 Wilton Guerrero RC | .20 | .50 |
| ☐ 362 Geoff Jenkins RC | .60 | 1.50 |
| ☐ 363 Pete Janicki | .10 | .30 |
| ☐ 364 Yamil Benitez | .10 | .30 |
| ☐ 365 Aaron Holbert | .10 | .30 |
| ☐ 366 Tim Belk | .10 | .30 |
| ☐ 367 Terrell Wade | .10 | .30 |
| ☐ 368 Terrence Long | .10 | .30 |
| ☐ 369 Brad Fullmer | .10 | .30 |
| ☐ 370 Matt Wagner | .10 | .30 |
| ☐ 371 Craig Wilson RC | .20 | .50 |
| ☐ 372 Mark Loretta | .10 | .30 |
| ☐ 373 Eric Owens | .10 | .30 |
| ☐ 374 Vladimir Guerrero | .60 | 1.50 |
| ☐ 375 Tommy Davis | .10 | .30 |
| ☐ 376 Donnie Sadler | .20 | .50 |
| ☐ 377 Edgar Renteria | .10 | .30 |
| ☐ 378 Todd Helton | .60 | 1.50 |
| ☐ 379 Ralph Milliard RC | .20 | .50 |
| ☐ 380 Darin Blood RC | .20 | .50 |
| ☐ 381 Shayne Bennett | .10 | .30 |
| ☐ 382 Mark Redman | .10 | .30 |
| ☐ 383 Felix Martinez | .10 | .30 |
| ☐ 384 Sean Watkins RC | .20 | .50 |
| ☐ 385 Oscar Henriquez | .10 | .30 |
| ☐ M20 52 Bowman Mantle | 2.00 | 5.00 |
| ☐ NNO Unnumbered Checklists | .10 | .30 |

**1997 Bowman**

| | | |
|---|---|---|
| ☐ COMPLETE SET (441) | 25.00 | 60.00 |
| ☐ COMPLETE SERIES 1 (221) | 12.50 | 30.00 |
| ☐ COMPLETE SERIES 2 (220) | 12.50 | 30.00 |
| ☐ 1 Derek Jeter | .75 | 2.00 |
| ☐ 2 Edgar Renteria | .10 | .30 |
| ☐ 3 Chipper Jones | .30 | .75 |
| ☐ 4 Hideo Nomo | .30 | .75 |
| ☐ 5 Tim Salmon | .20 | .50 |
| ☐ 6 Jason Giambi | .20 | .50 |
| ☐ 7 Robin Ventura | .10 | .30 |
| ☐ 8 Tony Clark | .10 | .30 |
| ☐ 9 Barry Larkin | .20 | .50 |
| ☐ 10 Paul Molitor | .10 | .30 |
| ☐ 11 Bernard Gilkey | .10 | .30 |
| ☐ 12 Jack McDowell | .10 | .30 |
| ☐ 13 Andy Benes | .10 | .30 |
| ☐ 14 Ryan Klesko | .10 | .30 |
| ☐ 15 Mark McGwire | .75 | 2.00 |
| ☐ 16 Ken Griffey Jr. | .50 | 1.25 |
| ☐ 17 Robb Nen | .10 | .30 |
| ☐ 18 Cal Ripken | 1.00 | 2.50 |
| ☐ 19 John Valentin | .10 | .30 |
| ☐ 20 Ricky Bottalico | .10 | .30 |
| ☐ 21 Mike Lansing | .10 | .30 |
| ☐ 22 Ryne Sandberg | .50 | 1.25 |
| ☐ 23 Carlos Delgado | .10 | .30 |
| ☐ 24 Craig Biggio | .20 | .50 |
| ☐ 25 Eric Karros | .10 | .30 |
| ☐ 26 Kevin Appier | .10 | .30 |
| ☐ 27 Mariano Rivera | .30 | .75 |
| ☐ 28 Vinny Castilla | .10 | .30 |
| ☐ 29 Juan Gonzalez | .40 | 1.00 |
| ☐ 30 Al Martin | .10 | .30 |
| ☐ 31 Jeff Cirillo | .10 | .30 |
| ☐ 32 Eddie Murray | .30 | .75 |
| ☐ 33 Ray Lankford | .10 | .30 |
| ☐ 34 Manny Ramirez | .20 | .50 |
| ☐ 35 Roberto Alomar | .20 | .50 |
| ☐ 36 Will Clark | .20 | .50 |
| ☐ 37 Chuck Knoblauch | .20 | .50 |
| ☐ 38 Harold Baines | .10 | .30 |
| ☐ 39 Trevor Hoffman | .10 | .30 |
| ☐ 40 Edgar Martinez | .20 | .50 |
| ☐ 41 Geronimo Berroa | .10 | .30 |
| ☐ 42 Rey Ordonez | .10 | .30 |
| ☐ 43 Mike Stanley | .10 | .30 |
| ☐ 44 Mike Mussina | .20 | .50 |
| ☐ 45 Kevin Brown | .10 | .30 |
| ☐ 46 Dennis Eckersley | .10 | .30 |
| ☐ 47 Henry Rodriguez | .10 | .30 |
| ☐ 48 Tino Martinez | .20 | .50 |
| ☐ 49 Eric Young | .10 | .30 |
| ☐ 50 Bret Boone | .10 | .30 |
| ☐ 51 Raul Mondesi | .10 | .30 |
| ☐ 52 Sammy Sosa | .30 | .75 |
| ☐ 53 John Smoltz | .20 | .50 |
| ☐ 54 Billy Wagner | .10 | .30 |
| ☐ 55 Jeff D'Amico | .10 | .30 |
| ☐ 56 Ken Caminiti | .20 | .50 |
| ☐ 57 Jason Kendall | .10 | .30 |
| ☐ 58 Wade Boggs | .20 | .50 |
| ☐ 59 Andres Galarraga | .20 | .50 |
| ☐ 60 Jeff Brantley | .10 | .30 |
| ☐ 61 Mel Rojas | .10 | .30 |
| ☐ 62 Brian L. Hunter | .10 | .30 |
| ☐ 63 Bobby Bonilla | .10 | .30 |
| ☐ 64 Roger Clemens | .60 | 1.50 |
| ☐ 65 Jeff Kent | .10 | .30 |
| ☐ 66 Matt Williams | .10 | .30 |
| ☐ 67 Albert Belle | .10 | .30 |
| ☐ 68 Jeff King | .10 | .30 |
| ☐ 69 John Wetteland | .10 | .30 |

| | | |
|---|---|---|
| ☐ 70 Deion Sanders | .20 | .50 |
| ☐ 71 Bubba Trammell RC | .25 | .60 |
| ☐ 72 Felix Heredia RC | .15 | .40 |
| ☐ 73 Billy Koch RC | .40 | 1.00 |
| ☐ 74 Sidney Ponson RC | .40 | 1.00 |
| ☐ 75 Ricky Ledee RC | .25 | .60 |
| ☐ 76 Brett Tomko | .10 | .30 |
| ☐ 77 Braden Looper RC | .15 | .40 |
| ☐ 78 Damian Jackson | .10 | .30 |
| ☐ 79 Jason Dickson | .10 | .30 |
| ☐ 80 Chad Green RC | .15 | .40 |
| ☐ 81 R.A. Dickey RC | .15 | .40 |
| ☐ 82 Jeff Liefer | .10 | .30 |
| ☐ 83 Matt Wagner | .10 | .30 |
| ☐ 84 Richard Hidalgo | .10 | .30 |
| ☐ 85 Adam Riggs | .10 | .30 |
| ☐ 86 Robert Smith | .10 | .30 |
| ☐ 87 Chad Hermansen RC | .15 | .40 |
| ☐ 88 Felix Martinez | .10 | .30 |
| ☐ 89 J.J. Johnson | .10 | .30 |
| ☐ 90 Todd Dunwoody | .10 | .30 |
| ☐ 91 Katsuhiro Maeda | .10 | .30 |
| ☐ 92 Darin Erstad | .10 | .30 |
| ☐ 93 Elieser Marrero | .10 | .30 |
| ☐ 94 Bartolo Colon | .10 | .30 |
| ☐ 95 Chris Fussell | .10 | .30 |
| ☐ 96 Ugueth Urbina | .10 | .30 |
| ☐ 97 Josh Paul RC | .15 | .40 |
| ☐ 98 Jaime Bluma | .10 | .30 |
| ☐ 99 Seth Greisinger RC | .15 | .40 |
| ☐ 100 Jose Cruz Jr. RC | .25 | .60 |
| ☐ 101 Todd Dunn | .10 | .30 |
| ☐ 102 Joe Young RC | .15 | .40 |
| ☐ 103 Jonathan Johnson | .10 | .30 |
| ☐ 104 Justin Towle RC | .15 | .40 |
| ☐ 105 Brian Rose | .10 | .30 |
| ☐ 106 Jose Guillen | .10 | .30 |
| ☐ 107 Andruw Jones | .20 | .50 |
| ☐ 108 Mark Kotsay RC | .60 | 1.50 |
| ☐ 109 Wilton Guerrero | .10 | .30 |
| ☐ 110 Jacob Cruz | .10 | .30 |
| ☐ 111 Mike Sweeney | .10 | .30 |
| ☐ 112 Julio Mosquera | .10 | .30 |
| ☐ 113 Matt Morris | .10 | .30 |
| ☐ 114 Wendell Magee | .10 | .30 |
| ☐ 115 John Thomson | .10 | .30 |
| ☐ 116 Javier Valentin | .10 | .30 |
| ☐ 117 Tom Fordham | .10 | .30 |
| ☐ 118 Ruben Rivera | .10 | .30 |
| ☐ 119 Mike Drumright RC | .15 | .40 |
| ☐ 120 Chris Holt | .10 | .30 |
| ☐ 121 Sean Maloney | .10 | .30 |
| ☐ 122 Michael Barrett | .15 | .40 |
| ☐ 123 Tony Saunders RC | .15 | .40 |
| ☐ 124 Kevin Brown C | .10 | .30 |
| ☐ 125 Richard Almanzar | .10 | .30 |
| ☐ 126 Mark Redman | .10 | .30 |
| ☐ 127 Anthony Sanders RC | .15 | .40 |
| ☐ 128 Jeff Abbott | .10 | .30 |
| ☐ 129 Eugene Kingsale | .10 | .30 |
| ☐ 130 Paul Konerko | .20 | .50 |
| ☐ 131 Randall Simon RC | .25 | .60 |
| ☐ 132 Andy Larkin | .10 | .30 |
| ☐ 133 Rafael Medina | .10 | .30 |
| ☐ 134 Mendy Lopez | .10 | .30 |
| ☐ 135 Freddy Adrian Garcia | .10 | .30 |
| ☐ 136 Karim Garcia | .10 | .30 |
| ☐ 137 Larry Rodriguez RC | .15 | .40 |
| ☐ 138 Carlos Guillen | .10 | .30 |
| ☐ 139 Aaron Boone | .10 | .30 |
| ☐ 140 Donnie Sadler | .10 | .30 |
| ☐ 141 Brooks Kieschnick | .10 | .30 |
| ☐ 142 Scott Spiezio | .10 | .30 |
| ☐ 143 Everett Stull | .10 | .30 |
| ☐ 144 Enrique Wilson | .10 | .30 |
| ☐ 145 Milton Bradley RC | .75 | 2.00 |
| ☐ 146 Kevin Orie | .10 | .30 |
| ☐ 147 Derek Wallace | .10 | .30 |
| ☐ 148 Russ Johnson | .10 | .30 |
| ☐ 149 Joe Lagarde RC | .15 | .40 |
| ☐ 150 Luis Castillo | .10 | .30 |
| ☐ 151 Jay Payton | .10 | .30 |
| ☐ 152 Joe Long | .10 | .30 |
| ☐ 153 Livan Hernandez | .10 | .30 |
| ☐ 154 Vladimir Nunez RC | .25 | .60 |
| ☐ 155 Pokey Reese RC | .15 | .40 |
| ☐ 156 George Arias | .10 | .30 |
| ☐ 157 Homer Bush | .10 | .30 |

|  |  | | |
|---|---|---|---|
| 158 | Chris Carpenter UER | .10 | .30 |
| 159 | Eric Milton RC | .25 | .60 |
| 160 | Richie Sexson | .10 | .30 |
| 161 | Carl Pavano | .10 | .30 |
| 162 | Chris Gissell RC | .15 | .40 |
| 163 | Mac Suzuki | .10 | .30 |
| 164 | Pat Cline | .10 | .30 |
| 165 | Ron Wright | .10 | .30 |
| 166 | Dante Powell | .10 | .30 |
| 167 | Mark Bellhorn | .10 | .30 |
| 168 | George Lombard | .10 | .30 |
| 169 | Pee Wee Lopez RC | .15 | .40 |
| 170 | Paul Wilder RC | .15 | .40 |
| 171 | Brad Fullmer | .10 | .30 |
| 172 | Willie Martinez RC | .15 | .40 |
| 173 | Dario Veras RC | .15 | .40 |
| 174 | Dave Coggin | .10 | .30 |
| 175 | Kris Benson RC | .40 | 1.00 |
| 176 | Torii Hunter | .10 | .30 |
| 177 | D.T. Cromer | .10 | .30 |
| 178 | Nelson Figueroa RC | .15 | .40 |
| 179 | Hiram Bocachica RC | .15 | .40 |
| 180 | Shane Monahan | .15 | .40 |
| 181 | Jimmy Anderson RC | .15 | .40 |
| 182 | Juan Melo | .10 | .30 |
| 183 | Pablo Ortega RC | .15 | .40 |
| 184 | Calvin Pickering RC | .15 | .40 |
| 185 | Reggie Taylor | .10 | .30 |
| 186 | Jeff Farnsworth RC | .15 | .40 |
| 187 | Terrence Long | .10 | .30 |
| 188 | Geoff Jenkins | .10 | .30 |
| 189 | Steve Rain RC | .15 | .40 |
| 190 | Nerio Rodriguez RC | .15 | .40 |
| 191 | Derrick Gibson | .15 | .40 |
| 192 | Darin Blood | .10 | .30 |
| 193 | Ben Davis | .10 | .30 |
| 194 | Adrian Beltre RC | 1.25 | 3.00 |
| 195 | Damian Sapp RC UER | .10 | .30 |
| 196 | Kerry Wood RC | 2.00 | 5.00 |
| 197 | Nate Rolison RC | .15 | .40 |
| 198 | Fernando Tatis RC | .15 | .40 |
| 199 | Brad Penny RC | 1.25 | 3.00 |
| 200 | Jake Westbrook RC | .40 | 1.00 |
| 201 | Edwin Diaz | .10 | .30 |
| 202 | Joe Fontenot RC | .25 | .60 |
| 203 | Matt Halloran RC | .15 | .40 |
| 204 | Blake Stein RC | .15 | .40 |
| 205 | Onan Masaoka | .10 | .30 |
| 206 | Ben Petrick | .10 | .30 |
| 207 | Matt Clement RC | .40 | 1.00 |
| 208 | Todd Greene | .10 | .30 |
| 209 | Ray Ricken | .10 | .30 |
| 210 | Eric Chavez RC | 1.50 | 4.00 |
| 211 | Edgard Velazquez | .10 | .30 |
| 212 | Bruce Chen RC | .40 | 1.00 |
| 213 | Danny Patterson | .10 | .30 |
| 214 | Jeff Yoder | .10 | .30 |
| 215 | Luis Ordaz RC | .15 | .40 |
| 216 | Chris Widger | .10 | .30 |
| 217 | Jason Brester | .10 | .30 |
| 218 | Carlton Loewer | .10 | .30 |
| 219 | Chris Reitsma RC | .25 | .60 |
| 220 | Neifi Perez | .10 | .30 |
| 221 | Hideki Irabu RC | .25 | .60 |
| 222 | Ellis Burks | .20 | .50 |
| 223 | Pedro Martinez | .20 | .50 |
| 224 | Kenny Lofton | .30 | .75 |
| 225 | Randy Johnson | .30 | .75 |
| 226 | Terry Steinbach | .10 | .30 |
| 227 | Bernie Williams | .20 | .50 |
| 228 | Dean Palmer | .10 | .30 |
| 229 | Alan Benes | .10 | .30 |
| 230 | Marquis Grissom | .10 | .30 |
| 231 | Gary Sheffield | .10 | .30 |
| 232 | Curt Schilling | .10 | .30 |
| 233 | Reggie Sanders | .10 | .30 |
| 234 | Bobby Higginson | .10 | .30 |
| 235 | Moises Alou | .10 | .30 |
| 236 | Tom Glavine | .20 | .50 |
| 237 | Mark Grace | .20 | .50 |
| 238 | Ramon Martinez | .10 | .30 |
| 239 | Rafael Palmeiro | .10 | .30 |
| 240 | John Olerud | .10 | .30 |
| 241 | Dante Bichette | .10 | .30 |
| 242 | Greg Vaughn | .10 | .30 |
| 243 | Jeff Bagwell | .20 | .50 |
| 244 | Barry Bonds | .75 | 2.00 |
| 245 | Pat Hentgen | .10 | .30 |
| 246 | Jim Thome | .20 | .50 |
| 247 | Jermaine Allensworth | .10 | .30 |
| 248 | Andy Pettitte | .20 | .50 |
| 249 | Jay Bell | .10 | .30 |
| 250 | John Jaha | .10 | .30 |
| 251 | Jim Edmonds | .10 | .30 |
| 252 | Ron Gant | .10 | .30 |
| 253 | David Cone | .10 | .30 |
| 254 | Jose Canseco | .20 | .50 |
| 255 | Jay Buhner | .10 | .30 |
| 256 | Greg Maddux | .50 | 1.25 |
| 257 | Brian McRae | .10 | .30 |
| 258 | Lance Johnson | .10 | .30 |
| 259 | Travis Fryman | .10 | .30 |
| 260 | Paul O'Neill | .20 | .50 |
| 261 | Ivan Rodriguez | .20 | .50 |
| 262 | Gregg Jefferies | .10 | .30 |
| 263 | Fred McGriff | .20 | .50 |
| 264 | Derek Bell | .10 | .30 |
| 265 | Jeff Conine | .10 | .30 |
| 266 | Mike Piazza | .50 | 1.25 |
| 267 | Mark Grudzielanek | .10 | .30 |
| 268 | Brady Anderson | .10 | .30 |
| 269 | Marty Cordova | .10 | .30 |
| 270 | Ray Durham | .10 | .30 |
| 271 | Joe Carter | .10 | .30 |
| 272 | Brian Jordan | .10 | .30 |
| 273 | David Justice | .10 | .30 |
| 274 | Tony Gwynn | .40 | 1.00 |
| 275 | Larry Walker | .10 | .30 |
| 276 | Cecil Fielder | .10 | .30 |
| 277 | Mo Vaughn | .10 | .30 |
| 278 | Alex Fernandez | .10 | .30 |
| 279 | Michael Tucker | .10 | .30 |
| 280 | Jose Valentin | .10 | .30 |
| 281 | Sandy Alomar Jr. | .10 | .30 |
| 282 | Todd Hollandsworth | .10 | .30 |
| 283 | Rico Brogna | .10 | .30 |
| 284 | Rusty Greer | .10 | .30 |
| 285 | Roberto Hernandez | .10 | .30 |
| 286 | Hal Morris | .10 | .30 |
| 287 | Johnny Damon | .20 | .50 |
| 288 | Todd Hundley | .10 | .30 |
| 289 | Rondell White | .10 | .30 |
| 290 | Frank Thomas | .30 | .75 |
| 291 | Don Denbow RC | .15 | .40 |
| 292 | Derrek Lee | .20 | .50 |
| 293 | Todd Walker | .10 | .30 |
| 294 | Scott Rolen | .20 | .50 |
| 295 | Wes Helms | .10 | .30 |
| 296 | Bob Abreu | .20 | .50 |
| 297 | John Patterson RC | .60 | 1.50 |
| 298 | Alex Gonzalez RC | .40 | 1.00 |
| 299 | Grant Roberts RC | .15 | .40 |
| 300 | Jeff Suppan | .10 | .30 |
| 301 | Luke Wilcox | .10 | .30 |
| 302 | Marlon Anderson | .10 | .30 |
| 303 | Ray Brown | .10 | .30 |
| 304 | Mike Caruso RC | .15 | .40 |
| 305 | Sam Marsonek RC | .15 | .40 |
| 306 | Brady Raggio RC | .15 | .40 |
| 307 | Kevin McGlinchy RC | .25 | .60 |
| 308 | Roy Halladay RC | 3.00 | 8.00 |
| 309 | Jeremi Gonzalez RC | .15 | .40 |
| 310 | Aramis Ramirez RC | 1.50 | 4.00 |
| 311 | Dee Brown RC | .15 | .40 |
| 312 | Justin Thompson | .10 | .30 |
| 313 | Jay Tessmer RC | .15 | .40 |
| 314 | Mike Johnson RC | .15 | .40 |
| 315 | Danny Clyburn | .10 | .30 |
| 316 | Bruce Aven | .10 | .30 |
| 317 | Keith Foulke RC | .60 | 1.50 |
| 318 | Jimmy Osting RC | .25 | .60 |
| 319 | Valerio De Los Santos RC | .15 | .40 |
| 320 | Shannon Stewart | .10 | .30 |
| 321 | Willie Adams | .10 | .30 |
| 322 | Larry Barnes RC | .15 | .40 |
| 323 | Mark Johnson RC | .15 | .40 |
| 324 | Chris Stowers RC | .15 | .40 |
| 325 | Brandon Reed | .10 | .30 |
| 326 | Randy Winn | .10 | .30 |
| 327 | Steve Chavez RC | .15 | .40 |
| 328 | Nomar Garciaparra | .60 | 1.50 |
| 329 | Jacque Jones RC | .60 | 1.50 |
| 330 | Chris Clemons | .10 | .30 |
| 331 | Todd Helton | .30 | .75 |
| 332 | Ryan Brannan RC | .15 | .40 |
| 333 | Alex Sanchez RC | .25 | .60 |
| 334 | Arnold Gooch | .10 | .30 |
| 335 | Russell Branyan | .10 | .30 |
| 336 | Daryle Ward | .15 | .40 |
| 337 | John LeRoy RC | .15 | .40 |
| 338 | Steve Cox | .10 | .30 |
| 339 | Kevin Witt | .10 | .30 |
| 340 | Norm Hutchins | .10 | .30 |
| 341 | Gabby Martinez | .10 | .30 |
| 342 | Kris Detmers | .10 | .30 |
| 343 | Mike Villano RC | .15 | .40 |
| 344 | Preston Wilson | .10 | .30 |
| 345 | James Manias RC | .15 | .40 |
| 346 | Deivi Cruz RC | .25 | .60 |
| 347 | Donzell McDonald RC | .15 | .40 |
| 348 | Rod Myers RC | .15 | .40 |
| 349 | Shawn Chacon RC | .40 | 1.00 |
| 350 | Elvin Hernandez RC | .25 | .60 |
| 351 | Orlando Cabrera RC | .60 | 1.50 |
| 352 | Brian Banks | .10 | .30 |
| 353 | Robbie Bell | .15 | .40 |
| 354 | Brad Rigby | .10 | .30 |
| 355 | Scott Elarton | .10 | .30 |
| 356 | Kevin Sweeney RC | .15 | .40 |
| 357 | Steve Soderstrom | .10 | .30 |
| 358 | Ryan Nye | .10 | .30 |
| 359 | Marlon Allen RC | .15 | .40 |
| 360 | Donny Leon RC | .15 | .40 |
| 361 | Garrett Neubart RC | .25 | .60 |
| 362 | Abraham Nunez RC | .25 | .60 |
| 363 | Adam Eaton RC | .40 | 1.00 |
| 364 | Octavio Dotel RC | .25 | .60 |
| 365 | Dean Crow RC | .15 | .40 |
| 366 | Jason Baker RC | .15 | .40 |
| 367 | Sean Casey | .40 | 1.00 |
| 368 | Joe Lawrence RC | .15 | .40 |
| 369 | Adam Johnson RC | .15 | .40 |
| 370 | Scott Schoeneweis RC | .25 | .60 |
| 371 | Gerald Witasick Jr. | .10 | .30 |
| 372 | Ronnie Belliard RC | .50 | 1.25 |
| 373 | Russ Ortiz | .10 | .30 |
| 374 | Robert Stratton RC | .25 | .60 |
| 375 | Bobby Estalella | .10 | .30 |
| 376 | Corey Lee RC | .15 | .40 |
| 377 | Carlos Beltran RC | .75 | 2.00 |
| 378 | Mike Cameron | .10 | .30 |
| 379 | Scott Randall RC | .15 | .40 |
| 380 | Corey Erickson RC | .15 | .40 |
| 381 | Jay Canizaro | .10 | .30 |
| 382 | Kerry Robinson RC | .15 | .40 |
| 383 | Todd Noel RC | .15 | .40 |
| 384 | A.J. Zapp RC | .15 | .40 |
| 385 | Jarrod Washburn | .10 | .30 |
| 386 | Ben Grieve | .10 | .30 |
| 387 | Javier Vazquez RC | .50 | 1.50 |
| 388 | Tony Graffanino | .10 | .30 |
| 389 | Travis Lee RC | .25 | .60 |
| 390 | DaRond Stovall | .10 | .30 |
| 391 | Dennis Reyes RC | .25 | .60 |
| 392 | Danny Buxbaum | .10 | .30 |
| 393 | Marc Lewis RC | .15 | .40 |
| 394 | Kelvim Escobar RC | .40 | 1.00 |
| 395 | Danny Klassen | .10 | .30 |
| 396 | Ken Cloude RC | .15 | .40 |
| 397 | Gabe Alvarez | .10 | .30 |
| 398 | Jaret Wright RC | .75 | 2.00 |
| 399 | Raul Casanova | .10 | .30 |
| 400 | Clayton Bruner RC | .10 | .30 |
| 401 | Jason Marquis RC | .60 | 1.50 |
| 402 | Marc Kroon | .10 | .30 |
| 403 | Jamey Wright | .10 | .30 |
| 404 | Matt Snyder RC | .15 | .40 |
| 405 | Josh Garrett RC | .15 | .40 |
| 406 | Juan Encarnacion | .10 | .30 |
| 407 | Heath Murray | .10 | .30 |
| 408 | Brett Herbison RC | .25 | .60 |
| 409 | Brent Butler RC | .15 | .40 |
| 410 | Danny Peoples RC | .15 | .40 |
| 411 | Miguel Tejada RC | 2.00 | 5.00 |
| 412 | Damian Moss | .10 | .30 |
| 413 | Jim Pittsley | .10 | .30 |
| 414 | Dmitri Young | .10 | .30 |
| 415 | Glendon Rusch | .10 | .30 |
| 416 | Vladimir Guerrero | .30 | .75 |
| 417 | Cole Liniak RC | .25 | .60 |
| 418 | Ramon Hernandez | .10 | .30 |
| 419 | Cliff Politte RC | .10 | .30 |
| 420 | Mel Rosario RC | .15 | .40 |
| 421 | Jorge Carrion RC | .15 | .40 |

|  |  | | |
|---|---|---|---|
| 422 | John Barnes RC | .15 | .40 |
| 423 | Chris Stowe RC | .15 | .40 |
| 424 | Vernon Wells RC | 2.00 | 5.00 |
| 425 | Brett Caradonna RC | .15 | .40 |
| 426 | Scott Hodges RC | .25 | .60 |
| 427 | Jon Garland RC | 1.00 | 2.50 |
| 428 | Nathan Haynes RC | .15 | .40 |
| 429 | Geoff Goetz RC | .15 | .40 |
| 430 | Adam Kennedy RC | .40 | 1.00 |
| 431 | T.J. Tucker RC | .15 | .40 |
| 432 | Aaron Akin RC | .15 | .40 |
| 433 | Jayson Werth RC | .40 | 1.00 |
| 434 | Glenn Davis RC | .15 | .40 |
| 435 | Mark Mangum RC | .15 | .40 |
| 436 | Troy Cameron RC | .15 | .40 |
| 437 | J.J. Davis RC | .15 | .40 |
| 438 | Lance Berkman RC | 4.00 | 10.00 |
| 439 | Jason Standridge RC | .15 | .40 |
| 440 | Jason Dellaero RC | .25 | .60 |
| 441 | Hideki Irabu | .25 | .60 |

## 1998 Bowman

| | | | |
|---|---|---|---|
| COMPLETE SET (441) | | 20.00 | 50.00 |
| COMPLETE SERIES 1 (221) | | 10.00 | 25.00 |
| COMPLETE SERIES 2 (221) | | 10.00 | 25.00 |
| 1 | Nomar Garciaparra | .50 | 1.25 |
| 2 | Scott Rolen | .20 | .50 |
| 3 | Andy Pettitte | .20 | .50 |
| 4 | Ivan Rodriguez | .20 | .50 |
| 5 | Mark McGwire | .75 | 2.00 |
| 6 | Jason Dickson | .10 | .30 |
| 7 | Jose Cruz Jr. | .10 | .30 |
| 8 | Jeff Kent | .10 | .30 |
| 9 | Mike Mussina | .20 | .50 |
| 10 | Jason Kendall | .10 | .30 |
| 11 | Brett Tomko | .10 | .30 |
| 12 | Jeff King | .10 | .30 |
| 13 | Brad Radke | .10 | .30 |
| 14 | Robin Ventura | .10 | .30 |
| 15 | Jeff Bagwell | .20 | .50 |
| 16 | Greg Maddux | .50 | 1.25 |
| 17 | John Jaha | .10 | .30 |
| 18 | Mike Piazza | .50 | 1.25 |
| 19 | Edgar Martinez | .20 | .50 |
| 20 | David Justice | .20 | .50 |
| 21 | Todd Hundley | .10 | .30 |
| 22 | Tony Gwynn | .40 | 1.00 |
| 23 | Larry Walker | .20 | .50 |
| 24 | Bernie Williams | .20 | .50 |
| 25 | Edgar Renteria | .20 | .50 |
| 26 | Rafael Palmeiro | .20 | .50 |
| 27 | Tim Salmon | .20 | .50 |
| 28 | Matt Morris | .10 | .30 |
| 29 | Shawn Estes | .10 | .30 |
| 30 | Vladimir Guerrero | .30 | .75 |
| 31 | Fernando Tatis | .10 | .30 |
| 32 | Justin Thompson | .10 | .30 |
| 33 | Ken Griffey Jr. | .50 | 1.25 |
| 34 | Edgardo Alfonzo | .10 | .30 |
| 35 | Mo Vaughn | .20 | .50 |
| 36 | Marty Cordova | .10 | .30 |
| 37 | Craig Biggio | .20 | .50 |
| 38 | Roger Clemens | .60 | 1.50 |
| 39 | Mark Grace | .20 | .50 |
| 40 | Ken Caminiti | .10 | .30 |
| 41 | Tony Womack | .10 | .30 |
| 42 | Albert Belle | .20 | .50 |
| 43 | Tino Martinez | .20 | .50 |
| 44 | Sandy Alomar Jr. | .10 | .30 |
| 45 | Jeff Cirillo | .10 | .30 |
| 46 | Jason Giambi | .10 | .30 |
| 47 | Darin Erstad | .10 | .30 |
| 48 | Livan Hernandez | .10 | .30 |
| 49 | Mark Grudzielanek | .10 | .30 |
| 50 | Sammy Sosa | .30 | .75 |
| 51 | Curt Schilling | .10 | .30 |
| 52 | Brian Hunter | .10 | .30 |
| 53 | Neifi Perez | .10 | .30 |
| 54 | Todd Walker | .10 | .30 |
| 55 | Jose Guillen | .10 | .30 |
| 56 | Jim Thome | .20 | .50 |
| 57 | Tom Glavine | .20 | .50 |
| 58 | Todd Greene | .10 | .30 |
| 59 | Rondell White | .10 | .30 |
| 60 | Roberto Alomar | .20 | .50 |
| 61 | Tony Clark | .20 | .50 |
| 62 | Vinny Castilla | .10 | .30 |
| 63 | Barry Larkin | .20 | .50 |
| 64 | Hideki Irabu | .10 | .30 |
| 65 | Johnny Damon | .20 | .50 |
| 66 | Juan Gonzalez | .30 | .75 |
| 67 | John Olerud | .10 | .30 |
| 68 | Gary Sheffield | .10 | .30 |
| 69 | Raul Mondesi | .10 | .30 |
| 70 | Chipper Jones | .30 | .75 |
| 71 | David Ortiz | 1.00 | 2.50 |
| 72 | Warren Morris RC | .15 | .40 |
| 73 | Alex Gonzalez | .10 | .30 |
| 74 | Nick Bierbrodt | .10 | .30 |
| 75 | Roy Halladay | .10 | .30 |
| 76 | Danny Buxbaum | .10 | .30 |
| 77 | Adam Kennedy | .10 | .30 |
| 78 | Jared Sandberg | .10 | .30 |
| 79 | Michael Barrett | .10 | .30 |
| 80 | Gil Meche | .25 | .60 |
| 81 | Jayson Werth | .10 | .30 |
| 82 | Abraham Nunez | .10 | .30 |
| 83 | Ben Petrick | .10 | .30 |
| 84 | Brett Caradonna | .10 | .30 |
| 85 | Mike Lowell RC | 1.25 | 3.00 |
| 86 | Clayton Bruner | .10 | .30 |
| 87 | John Curtice RC | .25 | .60 |
| 88 | Bobby Estalella | .10 | .30 |
| 89 | Juan Melo | .10 | .30 |
| 90 | Arnold Gooch | .10 | .30 |
| 91 | Kevin Millwood RC | .60 | 1.50 |
| 92 | Richie Sexson | .10 | .30 |
| 93 | Orlando Cabrera | .10 | .30 |
| 94 | Pat Cline | .10 | .30 |
| 95 | Anthony Sanders | .10 | .30 |
| 96 | Russ Johnson | .10 | .30 |
| 97 | Ben Grieve | .20 | .50 |
| 98 | Kevin McGlinchy | .10 | .30 |
| 99 | Paul Wilder | .10 | .30 |
| 100 | Russ Ortiz | .10 | .30 |
| 101 | Ryan Jackson RC | .15 | .40 |
| 102 | Heath Murray | .10 | .30 |
| 103 | Brian Rose | .10 | .30 |
| 104 | Ryan Radmanovich RC | .15 | .40 |
| 105 | Ricky Ledee | .10 | .30 |
| 106 | Jeff Wallace RC | .15 | .40 |
| 107 | Ryan Minor RC | .15 | .40 |
| 108 | Dennis Reyes | .10 | .30 |
| 109 | James Manias | .10 | .30 |
| 110 | Chris Carpenter | .10 | .30 |
| 111 | Daryle Ward | .10 | .30 |
| 112 | Vernon Wells | .10 | .30 |
| 113 | Chad Green | .10 | .30 |
| 114 | Mike Stoner RC | .15 | .40 |
| 115 | Brad Fullmer | .10 | .30 |
| 116 | Adam Eaton | .10 | .30 |
| 117 | Jeff Liefer | .10 | .30 |
| 118 | Corey Koskie RC | .40 | 1.00 |
| 119 | Todd Helton | .20 | .50 |
| 120 | Jaime Jones RC | .15 | .40 |
| 121 | Mel Rosario | .10 | .30 |
| 122 | Geoff Goetz | .10 | .30 |
| 123 | Adrian Beltre | .10 | .30 |
| 124 | Jason Dellaero | .10 | .30 |
| 125 | Gabe Kapler RC | .40 | 1.00 |
| 126 | Scott Schoenewels | .10 | .30 |
| 127 | Ryan Brannan | .10 | .30 |
| 128 | Aaron Akin | .10 | .30 |
| 129 | Ryan Anderson RC | .15 | .40 |
| 130 | Brad Penny | .10 | .30 |
| 131 | Bruce Chen | .10 | .30 |
| 132 | Eli Marrero | .10 | .30 |
| 133 | Eric Chavez | .10 | .30 |
| 134 | Troy Glaus RC | 1.50 | 4.00 |
| 135 | Troy Cameron | .10 | .30 |
| 136 | Brian Sikorski RC | .15 | .40 |
| 137 | Mike Kinkade RC | .15 | .40 |
| 138 | Braden Looper | .10 | .30 |
| 139 | Mark Mangum | .10 | .30 |
| 140 | Danny Peoples | .10 | .30 |
| 141 | J.J. Davis | .10 | .30 |
| 142 | Ben Davis | .10 | .30 |
| 143 | Jacque Jones | .10 | .30 |
| 144 | Derrick Gibson | .10 | .30 |
| 145 | Bronson Arroyo | .60 | 1.50 |
| 146 | Luis De Los Santos RC | .15 | .40 |
| 147 | Jeff Abbott | .10 | .30 |
| 148 | Mike Cuddyer RC | .60 | 1.50 |
| 149 | Jason Romano | .10 | .30 |
| 150 | Shane Monahan | .10 | .30 |
| 151 | Ntema Ndungidi RC | .15 | .40 |
| 152 | Alex Sanchez | .10 | .30 |
| 153 | Jack Cust RC | .75 | 2.00 |
| 154 | Brent Butler | .10 | .30 |
| 155 | Ramon Hernandez | .10 | .30 |
| 156 | Norm Hutchins | .10 | .30 |
| 157 | Jason Marquis | .10 | .30 |
| 158 | Jacob Cruz | .10 | .30 |
| 159 | Rob Burger RC | .15 | .40 |
| 160 | Dave Coggin | .10 | .30 |
| 161 | Preston Wilson | .10 | .30 |
| 162 | Jason Fitzgerald RC | .15 | .40 |
| 163 | Dan Serafini | .10 | .30 |
| 164 | Peter Munro | .10 | .30 |
| 165 | Trot Nixon | .10 | .30 |
| 166 | Homer Bush | .10 | .30 |
| 167 | Dermal Brown | .10 | .30 |
| 168 | Chad Hermansen | .10 | .30 |
| 169 | Julio Moreno RC | .15 | .40 |
| 170 | John Roskos RC | .15 | .40 |
| 171 | Grant Roberts | .10 | .30 |
| 172 | Ken Cloude | .10 | .30 |
| 173 | Jason Brester | .10 | .30 |
| 174 | Jason Conti | .10 | .30 |
| 175 | Jon Garland | .10 | .30 |
| 176 | Robbie Bell | .10 | .30 |
| 177 | Nathan Haynes | .10 | .30 |
| 178 | Ramon Ortiz RC | .25 | .60 |
| 179 | Shannon Stewart | .10 | .30 |
| 180 | Pablo Ortega | .10 | .30 |
| 181 | Jimmy Rollins RC | 2.50 | 6.00 |
| 182 | Sean Casey | .10 | .30 |
| 183 | Ted Lilly RC | .40 | 1.00 |
| 184 | Chris Enochs RC | .15 | .40 |
| 185 | Maggio Ordonez UER RC | 2.00 | 5.00 |
| 186 | Mike Drumright | .10 | .30 |
| 187 | Aaron Boone | .10 | .30 |
| 188 | Matt Clement | .10 | .30 |
| 189 | Todd Dunwoody | .10 | .30 |
| 190 | Larry Rodriguez | .10 | .30 |
| 191 | Todd Noel | .10 | .30 |
| 192 | Geoff Jenkins | .10 | .30 |
| 193 | George Lombard | .10 | .30 |
| 194 | Lance Berkman | .10 | .30 |
| 195 | Marcus McCain | .10 | .30 |
| 196 | Ryan McGuire | .10 | .30 |
| 197 | Jhensy Sandoval | .10 | .30 |
| 198 | Corey Lee | .10 | .30 |
| 199 | Mario Valdez | .10 | .30 |
| 200 | Robert Fick RC | .25 | .60 |
| 201 | Donnie Sadler | .10 | .30 |
| 202 | Marc Kroon | .10 | .30 |
| 203 | David Miller | .10 | .30 |
| 204 | Jarrod Washburn | .10 | .30 |
| 205 | Miguel Tejada | .30 | .75 |
| 206 | Raul Ibanez | .10 | .30 |
| 207 | John Patterson | .10 | .30 |
| 208 | Calvin Pickering | .10 | .30 |
| 209 | Felix Martinez | .10 | .30 |
| 210 | Mark Redman | .10 | .30 |
| 211 | Scott Elarton | .10 | .30 |
| 212 | Jose Amado RC | .15 | .40 |
| 213 | Kerry Wood | .10 | .30 |
| 214 | Dante Powell | .10 | .30 |
| 215 | Aramis Ramirez | .10 | .30 |
| 216 | A.J. Hinch | .10 | .30 |
| 217 | Dustin Carr RC | .15 | .40 |
| 218 | Mark Kotsay | .10 | .30 |
| 219 | Jason Standridge | .10 | .30 |
| 220 | Luis Ordaz | .10 | .30 |
| 221 | Orlando Hernandez RC | .75 | 2.00 |
| 222 | Cal Ripken | 1.00 | 2.50 |
| 223 | Paul Molitor | .30 | .75 |
| 224 | Derek Jeter | .75 | 2.00 |
| 225 | Barry Bonds | .75 | 2.00 |

|  |  | | |
|---|---|---|---|
| ☐ 226 | Jim Edmonds | .10 | .30 |
| ☐ 227 | John Smoltz | .20 | .50 |
| ☐ 228 | Eric Karros | .10 | .30 |
| ☐ 229 | Ray Lankford | .10 | .30 |
| ☐ 230 | Rey Ordonez | .10 | .30 |
| ☐ 231 | Kenny Lofton | .10 | .30 |
| ☐ 232 | Alex Rodriguez | .50 | 1.25 |
| ☐ 233 | Dante Bichette | .10 | .30 |
| ☐ 234 | Pedro Martinez | .20 | .50 |
| ☐ 235 | Carlos Delgado | .10 | .30 |
| ☐ 236 | Rod Beck | .10 | .30 |
| ☐ 237 | Matt Williams | .10 | .30 |
| ☐ 238 | Charles Johnson | .10 | .30 |
| ☐ 239 | Rico Brogna | .10 | .30 |
| ☐ 240 | Frank Thomas | .30 | .75 |
| ☐ 241 | Paul O'Neill | .20 | .50 |
| ☐ 242 | Jaret Wright | .10 | .30 |
| ☐ 243 | Brant Brown | .10 | .30 |
| ☐ 244 | Ryan Klesko | .10 | .30 |
| ☐ 245 | Chuck Finley | .10 | .30 |
| ☐ 246 | Derek Bell | .10 | .30 |
| ☐ 247 | Delino DeShields | .10 | .30 |
| ☐ 248 | Chan Ho Park | .10 | .30 |
| ☐ 249 | Wade Boggs | .20 | .50 |
| ☐ 250 | Jay Buhner | .10 | .30 |
| ☐ 251 | Butch Huskey | .10 | .30 |
| ☐ 252 | Steve Finley | .10 | .30 |
| ☐ 253 | Will Clark | .20 | .50 |
| ☐ 254 | John Valentin | .10 | .30 |
| ☐ 255 | Bobby Higginson | .10 | .30 |
| ☐ 256 | Darryl Strawberry | .20 | .50 |
| ☐ 257 | Randy Johnson | .30 | .75 |
| ☐ 258 | Al Martin | .10 | .30 |
| ☐ 259 | Travis Fryman | .10 | .30 |
| ☐ 260 | Fred McGriff | .20 | .50 |
| ☐ 261 | Jose Valentin | .10 | .30 |
| ☐ 262 | Andruw Jones | .20 | .50 |
| ☐ 263 | Kenny Rogers | .10 | .30 |
| ☐ 264 | Moises Alou | .10 | .30 |
| ☐ 265 | Denny Neagle | .10 | .30 |
| ☐ 266 | Ugueth Urbina | .10 | .30 |
| ☐ 267 | Derrek Lee | .20 | .50 |
| ☐ 268 | Ellis Burks | .10 | .30 |
| ☐ 269 | Mariano Rivera | .30 | .75 |
| ☐ 270 | Dean Palmer | .10 | .30 |
| ☐ 271 | Eddie Taubensee | .10 | .30 |
| ☐ 272 | Brady Anderson | .10 | .30 |
| ☐ 273 | Brian Giles | .10 | .30 |
| ☐ 274 | Quinton McCracken | .10 | .30 |
| ☐ 275 | Henry Rodriguez | .10 | .30 |
| ☐ 276 | Andres Galarraga | .10 | .30 |
| ☐ 277 | Jose Canseco | .20 | .50 |
| ☐ 278 | David Segui | .10 | .30 |
| ☐ 279 | Bret Saberhagen | .10 | .30 |
| ☐ 280 | Kevin Brown | .20 | .50 |
| ☐ 281 | Chuck Knoblauch | .10 | .30 |
| ☐ 282 | Jeromy Burnitz | .10 | .30 |
| ☐ 283 | Jay Bell | .10 | .30 |
| ☐ 284 | Manny Ramirez | .20 | .50 |
| ☐ 285 | Rick Helling | .10 | .30 |
| ☐ 286 | Francisco Cordova | .10 | .30 |
| ☐ 287 | Bob Abreu | .10 | .30 |
| ☐ 288 | J.T. Snow | .10 | .30 |
| ☐ 289 | Hideo Nomo | .30 | .75 |
| ☐ 290 | Brian Jordan | .10 | .30 |
| ☐ 291 | Javy Lopez | .10 | .30 |
| ☐ 292 | Travis Lee | .10 | .30 |
| ☐ 293 | Russell Branyan | .10 | .30 |
| ☐ 294 | Paul Konerko | .10 | .30 |
| ☐ 295 | Masato Yoshii RC | .25 | .60 |
| ☐ 296 | Kris Benson | .10 | .30 |
| ☐ 297 | Juan Encarnacion | .10 | .30 |
| ☐ 298 | Eric Milton | .10 | .30 |
| ☐ 299 | Mike Caruso | .10 | .30 |
| ☐ 300 | Ricardo Aramboles RC | .15 | .40 |
| ☐ 301 | Bobby Smith | .10 | .30 |
| ☐ 302 | Billy Koch | .10 | .30 |
| ☐ 303 | Richard Hidalgo | .10 | .30 |
| ☐ 304 | Justin Baughman RC | .15 | .40 |
| ☐ 305 | Chris Gissell | .10 | .30 |
| ☐ 306 | Donnie Bridges RC | .15 | .40 |
| ☐ 307 | Nelson Lara RC | .15 | .40 |
| ☐ 308 | Randy Wolf RC | .25 | .60 |
| ☐ 309 | Jason LaRue RC | .25 | .60 |
| ☐ 310 | Jason Gooding RC | .15 | .40 |
| ☐ 311 | Edgard Clemente | .10 | .30 |
| ☐ 312 | Andrew Vessel | .10 | .30 |
| ☐ 313 | Chris Reitsma | .10 | .30 |
| ☐ 314 | Jesus Sanchez RC | .15 | .40 |
| ☐ 315 | Buddy Carlyle RC | .15 | .40 |
| ☐ 316 | Randy Winn | .10 | .30 |
| ☐ 317 | Luis Rivera RC | .15 | .40 |
| ☐ 318 | Marcus Thames RC | 1.00 | 2.50 |
| ☐ 319 | A.J. Pierzynski | .10 | .30 |
| ☐ 320 | Scott Randall | .10 | .30 |
| ☐ 321 | Damian Sapp | .10 | .30 |
| ☐ 322 | Ed Yarnall RC | .15 | .40 |
| ☐ 323 | Luke Allen RC | .15 | .40 |
| ☐ 324 | J.D. Smart | .10 | .30 |
| ☐ 325 | Willie Martinez | .10 | .30 |
| ☐ 326 | Alex Ramirez | .10 | .30 |
| ☐ 327 | Eric DuBose RC | .15 | .40 |
| ☐ 328 | Kevin Witt | .10 | .30 |
| ☐ 329 | Dan McKinley RC | .15 | .40 |
| ☐ 330 | Cliff Politte | .10 | .30 |
| ☐ 331 | Vladimir Nunez | .10 | .30 |
| ☐ 332 | John Halama RC | .15 | .40 |
| ☐ 333 | Nerio Rodriguez | .10 | .30 |
| ☐ 334 | Desi Relaford | .10 | .30 |
| ☐ 335 | Robinson Checo | .10 | .30 |
| ☐ 336 | John Nicholson | .20 | .50 |
| ☐ 337 | Tom LaRosa RC | .15 | .40 |
| ☐ 338 | Kevin Nicholson RC | .15 | .40 |
| ☐ 339 | Javier Vazquez | .10 | .30 |
| ☐ 340 | A.J. Zapp | .10 | .30 |
| ☐ 341 | Tom Evans | .10 | .30 |
| ☐ 342 | Kerry Robinson | .10 | .30 |
| ☐ 343 | Gabe Gonzalez RC | .15 | .40 |
| ☐ 344 | Ralph Milliard | .10 | .30 |
| ☐ 345 | Enrique Wilson | .10 | .30 |
| ☐ 346 | Elvin Hernandez | .10 | .30 |
| ☐ 347 | Mike Lincoln RC | .15 | .40 |
| ☐ 348 | Cesar King RC | .15 | .40 |
| ☐ 349 | Cristian Guzman RC | .25 | .60 |
| ☐ 350 | Donzell McDonald | .10 | .30 |
| ☐ 351 | Jim Parque RC | .15 | .40 |
| ☐ 352 | Mike Saipe RC | .15 | .40 |
| ☐ 353 | Carlos Febles RC | .25 | .60 |
| ☐ 354 | Demell Stenson RC | .15 | .40 |
| ☐ 355 | Mark Osborne RC | .15 | .40 |
| ☐ 356 | Odalis Perez RC | .60 | 1.50 |
| ☐ 357 | Jason Dewey RC | .10 | .30 |
| ☐ 358 | Joe Fontenot | .10 | .30 |
| ☐ 359 | Jason Grilli RC | .15 | .40 |
| ☐ 360 | Kevin Haverbusch RC | .15 | .40 |
| ☐ 361 | Jay Yennaco RC | .15 | .40 |
| ☐ 362 | Brian Buchanan | .10 | .30 |
| ☐ 363 | John Barnes | .10 | .30 |
| ☐ 364 | Chris Fussell | .10 | .30 |
| ☐ 365 | Kevin Gibbs RC | .15 | .40 |
| ☐ 366 | Joe Lawrence | .10 | .30 |
| ☐ 367 | DaRond Stovall | .10 | .30 |
| ☐ 368 | Brian Fuentes RC | .15 | .40 |
| ☐ 369 | Jimmy Anderson | .10 | .30 |
| ☐ 370 | Lariel Gonzalez RC | .15 | .40 |
| ☐ 371 | Scott Williamson RC | .15 | .40 |
| ☐ 372 | Milton Bradley | .10 | .30 |
| ☐ 373 | Jason Halper RC | .15 | .40 |
| ☐ 374 | Brent Billingsley RC | .15 | .40 |
| ☐ 375 | Joe DePastino RC | .15 | .40 |
| ☐ 376 | Jake Westbrook | .10 | .30 |
| ☐ 377 | Octavio Dotel | .10 | .30 |
| ☐ 378 | Jason Williams RC | .15 | .40 |
| ☐ 379 | Julio Ramirez RC | .15 | .40 |
| ☐ 380 | Seth Greisinger | .10 | .30 |
| ☐ 381 | Mike Judd RC | .15 | .40 |
| ☐ 382 | Ben Ford RC | .15 | .40 |
| ☐ 383 | Tom Bennett RC | .15 | .40 |
| ☐ 384 | Adam Butler RC | .15 | .40 |
| ☐ 385 | Wade Miller RC | .40 | 1.00 |
| ☐ 386 | Kyle Peterson RC | .15 | .40 |
| ☐ 387 | Tommy Peterman RC | .15 | .40 |
| ☐ 388 | Onan Masaoka | .10 | .30 |
| ☐ 389 | Jason Rakers RC | .15 | .40 |
| ☐ 390 | Rafael Medina | .10 | .30 |
| ☐ 391 | Luis Lopez RC | .15 | .40 |
| ☐ 392 | Jeff Yoder | .10 | .30 |
| ☐ 393 | Vance Wilson RC | .15 | .40 |
| ☐ 394 | Fernando Seguignol RC | .15 | .40 |
| ☐ 395 | Ron Wright | .10 | .30 |
| ☐ 396 | Ruben Mateo RC | .40 | 1.00 |
| ☐ 397 | Steve Lomasney RC | .25 | .60 |
| ☐ 398 | Damian Jackson | .10 | .30 |
| ☐ 399 | Mike Jerzembeck RC | .15 | .40 |
| ☐ 400 | Luis Rivas RC | .40 | 1.00 |
| ☐ 401 | Kevin Burford RC | .15 | .40 |
| ☐ 402 | Glenn Davis | .10 | .30 |
| ☐ 403 | Robert Luce RC | .15 | .40 |
| ☐ 404 | Cole Liniak | .10 | .30 |
| ☐ 405 | Matt LeCroy RC | .25 | .60 |
| ☐ 406 | Jeremy Giambi RC | .25 | .60 |
| ☐ 407 | Shawn Chacon | .10 | .30 |
| ☐ 408 | Dewayne Wise RC | .15 | .40 |
| ☐ 409 | Steve Woodard | .10 | .30 |
| ☐ 410 | Francisco Cordero RC | .40 | 1.00 |
| ☐ 411 | Damon Minor RC | .15 | .40 |
| ☐ 412 | Lou Collier | .10 | .30 |
| ☐ 413 | Justin Towle | .15 | .40 |
| ☐ 414 | Juan LeBron | .15 | .40 |
| ☐ 415 | Michael Coleman | .10 | .30 |
| ☐ 416 | Felix Rodriguez | .10 | .30 |
| ☐ 417 | Paul Ah Yat RC | .15 | .40 |
| ☐ 418 | Kevin Barker RC | .15 | .40 |
| ☐ 419 | Brian Meadows | .10 | .30 |
| ☐ 420 | Darnell McDonald RC | .15 | .40 |
| ☐ 421 | Matt Kinney RC | .15 | .40 |
| ☐ 422 | Mike Vavrek RC | .15 | .40 |
| ☐ 423 | Courtney Duncan RC | .15 | .40 |
| ☐ 424 | Kevin Millar RC | .60 | 1.50 |
| ☐ 425 | Ruben Rivera | .10 | .30 |
| ☐ 426 | Steve Shoemaker RC | .15 | .40 |
| ☐ 427 | Dan Reichert RC | .15 | .40 |
| ☐ 428 | Carlos Lee RC | 1.25 | 3.00 |
| ☐ 429 | Rod Barajas | .40 | 1.00 |
| ☐ 430 | Pablo Ozuna RC | .25 | .60 |
| ☐ 431 | Todd Belitz RC | .15 | .40 |
| ☐ 432 | Sidney Ponson | .10 | .30 |
| ☐ 433 | Steve Carver RC | .15 | .40 |
| ☐ 434 | Esteban Yan RC | .25 | .60 |
| ☐ 435 | Cedrick Bowers | .10 | .30 |
| ☐ 436 | Marlon Anderson | .10 | .30 |
| ☐ 437 | Carl Pavano | .10 | .30 |
| ☐ 438 | Jae Weong Seo RC | .25 | .60 |
| ☐ 439 | Jose Taveras RC | .15 | .40 |
| ☐ 440 | Matt Anderson RC | .15 | .40 |
| ☐ 441 | Darron Ingram RC | .15 | .40 |
| ☐ NNO | S.Hasegawa '91 REM | 4.00 | 10.00 |
| ☐ NNO | H.Irabu '91 REM | 4.00 | 10.00 |
| ☐ NNO | H.Nomo '91 REM | 10.00 | 25.00 |

**1999 Bowman**

|  |  | | |
|---|---|---|---|
| ☐ COMPLETE SET (440) | | 30.00 | 80.00 |
| ☐ COMPLETE SERIES 1 (220) | | 12.50 | 30.00 |
| ☐ COMPLETE SERIES 2 (220) | | 20.00 | 50.00 |
| ☐ 1 | Ben Grieve | .10 | .30 |
| ☐ 2 | Kerry Wood | .10 | .30 |
| ☐ 3 | Ruben Rivera | .10 | .30 |
| ☐ 4 | Sandy Alomar Jr. | .10 | .30 |
| ☐ 5 | Cal Ripken | 1.00 | 2.50 |
| ☐ 6 | Mark McGwire | .75 | 2.00 |
| ☐ 7 | Vladimir Guerrero | .30 | .75 |
| ☐ 8 | Moises Alou | .10 | .30 |
| ☐ 9 | Jim Edmonds | .10 | .30 |
| ☐ 10 | Greg Maddux | .50 | 1.25 |
| ☐ 11 | Gary Sheffield | .10 | .30 |
| ☐ 12 | John Valentin | .10 | .30 |
| ☐ 13 | Chuck Knoblauch | .10 | .30 |
| ☐ 14 | Tony Clark | .10 | .30 |
| ☐ 15 | Rusty Greer | .10 | .30 |
| ☐ 16 | Al Leiter | .10 | .30 |
| ☐ 17 | Travis Lee | .10 | .30 |
| ☐ 18 | Jose Cruz Jr. | .10 | .30 |
| ☐ 19 | Pedro Martinez | .10 | .50 |
| ☐ 20 | Paul O'Neill | .20 | .50 |
| ☐ 21 | Todd Walker | .10 | .30 |
| ☐ 22 | Vinny Castilla | .10 | .30 |
| ☐ 23 | Barry Larkin | .20 | .50 |
| ☐ 24 | Curt Schilling | .10 | .30 |
| ☐ 25 | Jason Kendall | .10 | .30 |
| ☐ 26 | Scott Erickson | .10 | .30 |

|  |  | | |
|---|---|---|---|
| 27 | Andres Galarraga | .10 | .30 |
| 28 | Jeff Shaw | .10 | .30 |
| 29 | John Olerud | .10 | .30 |
| 30 | Orlando Hernandez | .10 | .30 |
| 31 | Larry Walker | .10 | .30 |
| 32 | Andruw Jones | .20 | .50 |
| 33 | Jeff Cirillo | .10 | .30 |
| 34 | Barry Bonds | .75 | 2.00 |
| 35 | Manny Ramirez | .20 | .50 |
| 36 | Mark Kotsay | .10 | .30 |
| 37 | Ivan Rodriguez | .20 | .50 |
| 38 | Jeff King | .10 | .30 |
| 39 | Brian Hunter | .10 | .30 |
| 40 | Ray Durham | .10 | .30 |
| 41 | Bernie Williams | .20 | .50 |
| 42 | Darin Erstad | .10 | .30 |
| 43 | Chipper Jones | .30 | .75 |
| 44 | Pat Hentgen | .10 | .30 |
| 45 | Eric Young | .10 | .30 |
| 46 | Jarel Wright | .10 | .30 |
| 47 | Juan Guzman | .10 | .30 |
| 48 | Jorge Posada | .20 | .50 |
| 49 | Bobby Higginson | .10 | .30 |
| 50 | Jose Guillen | .10 | .30 |
| 51 | Trevor Hoffman | .10 | .30 |
| 52 | Ken Griffey Jr. | .50 | 1.25 |
| 53 | David Justice | .10 | .30 |
| 54 | Matt Williams | .10 | .30 |
| 55 | Eric Karros | .10 | .30 |
| 56 | Derek Bell | .10 | .30 |
| 57 | Ray Lankford | .10 | .30 |
| 58 | Mariano Rivera | .30 | .75 |
| 59 | Brett Tomko | .10 | .30 |
| 60 | Mike Mussina | .20 | .50 |
| 61 | Kenny Lofton | .10 | .30 |
| 62 | Chuck Finley | .10 | .30 |
| 63 | Alex Gonzalez | .10 | .30 |
| 64 | Mark Grace | .20 | .50 |
| 65 | Raul Mondesi | .10 | .30 |
| 66 | David Cone | .10 | .30 |
| 67 | Brad Fullmer | .10 | .30 |
| 68 | Andy Benes | .10 | .30 |
| 69 | John Smoltz | .20 | .50 |
| 70 | Shane Reynolds | .10 | .30 |
| 71 | Bruce Chen | .10 | .30 |
| 72 | Adam Kennedy | .10 | .30 |
| 73 | Jack Cust | .10 | .30 |
| 74 | Matt Clement | .10 | .30 |
| 75 | Derrick Gibson | .10 | .30 |
| 76 | Darnell McDonald | .10 | .30 |
| 77 | Adam Everett RC | .40 | 1.00 |
| 78 | Ricardo Aramboles | .10 | .30 |
| 79 | Mark Quinn RC | .15 | .40 |
| 80 | Jason Rakers | .10 | .30 |
| 81 | Seth Etherton RC | .15 | .40 |
| 82 | Jeff Urban RC | .25 | .60 |
| 83 | Manny Aybar | .10 | .30 |
| 84 | Mike Nannini RC | .15 | .40 |
| 85 | Onan Masaoka | .10 | .30 |
| 86 | Rod Barajas | .10 | .30 |
| 87 | Mike Frank | .10 | .30 |
| 88 | Scott Randall | .10 | .30 |
| 89 | Justin Bowles RC | .15 | .40 |
| 90 | Chris Haas | .10 | .30 |
| 91 | Arturo McDowell RC | .15 | .40 |
| 92 | Matt Belisle RC | .15 | .40 |
| 93 | Scott Elarton | .10 | .30 |
| 94 | Vernon Wells | .10 | .30 |
| 95 | Pat Cline | .10 | .30 |
| 96 | Ryan Anderson | .10 | .30 |
| 97 | Kevin Barker | .10 | .30 |
| 98 | Ruben Mateo | .10 | .30 |
| 99 | Robert Fick | .10 | .30 |
| 100 | Corey Koskie | .10 | .30 |
| 101 | Ricky Ledee | .10 | .30 |
| 102 | Rick Elder RC | .15 | .40 |
| 103 | Jack Cressend RC | .10 | .30 |
| 104 | Joe Lawrence | .10 | .30 |
| 105 | Mike Lincoln | .10 | .30 |
| 106 | Kit Pellow RC | .15 | .40 |
| 107 | Matt Burch RC | .25 | .60 |
| 108 | Cole Liniak | .10 | .30 |
| 109 | Jason Dewey | .10 | .30 |
| 110 | Cesar King | .10 | .30 |
| 111 | Julio Ramirez | .10 | .30 |
| 112 | Jake Westbrook | .10 | .30 |
| 113 | Eric Valent RC | .25 | .60 |
| 114 | Roosevelt Brown RC | .15 | .40 |
| 115 | Choo Freeman RC | .25 | .60 |
| 116 | Juan Melo | .10 | .30 |
| 117 | Jason Grilli | .10 | .30 |
| 118 | Jared Sandberg | .10 | .30 |
| 119 | Glenn Davis | .10 | .30 |
| 120 | David Riske RC | .15 | .40 |
| 121 | Jacque Jones | .10 | .30 |
| 122 | Corey Lee | .10 | .30 |
| 123 | Michael Barrett | .10 | .30 |
| 124 | Lariel Gonzalez | .10 | .30 |
| 125 | Mitch Meluskey | .10 | .30 |
| 126 | F. Adrian Garcia | .10 | .30 |
| 127 | Tony Torcato RC | .15 | .40 |
| 128 | Jeff Liefer | .10 | .30 |
| 129 | Ntema Ndungidi | .10 | .30 |
| 130 | Andy Brown RC | .15 | .40 |
| 131 | Ryan Mills RC | .15 | .40 |
| 132 | Andy Abad RC | .15 | .40 |
| 133 | Carlos Febles | .10 | .30 |
| 134 | Jason Tyner RC | .15 | .40 |
| 135 | Mark Osborne | .10 | .30 |
| 136 | Phil Norton RC | .15 | .40 |
| 137 | Nathan Haynes | .10 | .30 |
| 138 | Roy Halladay | .10 | .30 |
| 139 | Juan Encarnacion | .10 | .30 |
| 140 | Brad Penny | .10 | .30 |
| 141 | Grant Roberts | .10 | .30 |
| 142 | Aramis Ramirez | .10 | .30 |
| 143 | Cristian Guzman | .10 | .30 |
| 144 | Mamon Tucker RC | .15 | .40 |
| 145 | Ryan Bradley | .10 | .30 |
| 146 | Brian Simmons | .10 | .30 |
| 147 | Dan Reichert | .10 | .30 |
| 148 | Russ Branyan | .10 | .30 |
| 149 | Victor Valencia RC | .20 | .50 |
| 150 | Scott Schoeneweis | .10 | .30 |
| 151 | Sean Spencer RC | .15 | .40 |
| 152 | Odalis Perez | .10 | .30 |
| 153 | Joe Fontenot | .10 | .30 |
| 154 | Milton Bradley | .10 | .30 |
| 155 | Josh McKinley RC | .15 | .40 |
| 156 | Terrence Long | .10 | .30 |
| 157 | Danny Klassen | .10 | .30 |
| 158 | Paul Hoover RC | .25 | .60 |
| 159 | Ron Belliard | .10 | .30 |
| 160 | Armando Rios | .10 | .30 |
| 161 | Ramon Hernandez | .10 | .30 |
| 162 | Jason Conti | .10 | .30 |
| 163 | Chad Hermansen | .10 | .30 |
| 164 | Jason Standridge | .10 | .30 |
| 165 | Jason Dellaero | .10 | .30 |
| 166 | John Curtice | .10 | .30 |
| 167 | Clayton Andrews RC | .15 | .40 |
| 168 | Jeremy Giambi | .10 | .30 |
| 169 | Alex Ramirez | .10 | .30 |
| 170 | Gabe Molina RC | .15 | .40 |
| 171 | Mario Encamacion RC | .15 | .40 |
| 172 | Mike Zywica RC | .15 | .40 |
| 173 | Chip Ambres RC | .15 | .40 |
| 174 | Trot Nixon | .10 | .30 |
| 175 | Pat Burrell RC | 1.25 | 3.00 |
| 176 | Jeff Yoder | .10 | .30 |
| 177 | Chris Jones RC | .15 | .40 |
| 178 | Kevin Witt | .10 | .30 |
| 179 | Keith Luuloa RC | .15 | .40 |
| 180 | Billy Koch | .10 | .30 |
| 181 | Damaso Marte RC | .15 | .40 |
| 182 | Ryan Glynn RC | .15 | .40 |
| 183 | Calvin Pickering | .10 | .30 |
| 184 | Michael Cuddyer | .10 | .30 |
| 185 | Nick Johnson RC | .75 | 2.00 |
| 186 | Doug Mientkiewicz RC | .40 | 1.00 |
| 187 | Nate Comejo RC | .15 | .40 |
| 188 | Octavio Dotel | .10 | .30 |
| 189 | Wes Helms | .10 | .30 |
| 190 | Nelson Lara | .10 | .30 |
| 191 | Chuck Abbott RC | .15 | .40 |
| 192 | Tony Armas Jr. | .10 | .30 |
| 193 | Gil Meche | .10 | .30 |
| 194 | Ben Petrick | .10 | .30 |
| 195 | Chris George RC | .15 | .40 |
| 196 | Scott Hunter RC | .15 | .40 |
| 197 | Ryan Brannan | .10 | .30 |
| 198 | Amaury Garcia RC | .25 | .60 |
| 199 | Chris Gissell | .10 | .30 |
| 200 | Austin Kearns RC | 1.25 | 3.00 |
| 201 | Alex Gonzalez | .10 | .30 |
| 202 | Wade Miller | .10 | .30 |
| 203 | Scott Williamson | .10 | .30 |
| 204 | Chris Enochs | .10 | .30 |
| 205 | Fernando Seguignol | .10 | .30 |
| 206 | Marlon Anderson | .10 | .30 |
| 207 | Todd Sears RC | .15 | .40 |
| 208 | Nate Bump RC | .15 | .40 |
| 209 | J.M. Gold RC | .15 | .40 |
| 210 | Matt LeCroy | .10 | .30 |
| 211 | Alex Hernandez | .10 | .30 |
| 212 | Luis Rivera | .10 | .30 |
| 213 | Troy Cameron | .10 | .30 |
| 214 | Alex Escobar RC | .25 | .60 |
| 215 | Jason LaRue | .10 | .30 |
| 216 | Kyle Peterson | .10 | .30 |
| 217 | Brent Butler | .10 | .30 |
| 218 | Darnell Stenson | .10 | .30 |
| 219 | Adrian Beltre | .10 | .30 |
| 220 | Daryle Ward | .10 | .30 |
| 221 | Jim Thome | .20 | .50 |
| 222 | Cliff Floyd | .10 | .30 |
| 223 | Rickey Henderson | .30 | .75 |
| 224 | Garret Anderson | .10 | .30 |
| 225 | Ken Caminiti | .10 | .30 |
| 226 | Bret Boone | .10 | .30 |
| 227 | Jeromy Burnitz | .10 | .30 |
| 228 | Steve Finley | .10 | .30 |
| 229 | Miguel Tejada | .10 | .30 |
| 230 | Greg Vaughn | .10 | .30 |
| 231 | Jose Offerman | .10 | .30 |
| 232 | Andy Ashby | .10 | .30 |
| 233 | Albert Belle | .10 | .30 |
| 234 | Fernando Tatis | .10 | .30 |
| 235 | Todd Helton | .20 | .50 |
| 236 | Sean Casey | .10 | .30 |
| 237 | Brian Giles | .10 | .30 |
| 238 | Andy Pettitte | .20 | .50 |
| 239 | Fred McGriff | .20 | .50 |
| 240 | Roberto Alomar | .20 | .50 |
| 241 | Edgar Martinez | .10 | .30 |
| 242 | Lee Stevens | .10 | .30 |
| 243 | Shawn Green | .10 | .30 |
| 244 | Ryan Klesko | .10 | .30 |
| 245 | Sammy Sosa | .30 | .75 |
| 246 | Todd Hundley | .10 | .30 |
| 247 | Shannon Stewart | .10 | .30 |
| 248 | Randy Johnson | .30 | .75 |
| 249 | Rondell White | .10 | .30 |
| 250 | Mike Piazza | .50 | 1.25 |
| 251 | Craig Biggio | .20 | .50 |
| 252 | David Wells | .10 | .30 |
| 253 | Brian Jordan | .10 | .30 |
| 254 | Edgar Renteria | .10 | .30 |
| 255 | Bartolo Colon | .10 | .30 |
| 256 | Frank Thomas | .30 | .75 |
| 257 | Will Clark | .20 | .50 |
| 258 | Dean Palmer | .10 | .30 |
| 259 | Dmitri Young | .10 | .30 |
| 260 | Scott Rolen | .20 | .50 |
| 261 | Jeff Kent | .10 | .30 |
| 262 | Dante Bichette | .10 | .30 |
| 263 | Nomar Garciaparra | .50 | 1.25 |
| 264 | Tony Gwynn | .40 | 1.00 |
| 265 | Alex Rodriguez | .50 | 1.25 |
| 266 | Jose Canseco | .20 | .50 |
| 267 | Jason Giambi | .10 | .30 |
| 268 | Jeff Bagwell | .20 | .50 |
| 269 | Carlos Delgado | .10 | .30 |
| 270 | Tom Glavine | .20 | .50 |
| 271 | Eric Davis | .10 | .30 |
| 272 | Edgardo Alfonzo | .10 | .30 |
| 273 | Tim Salmon | .10 | .30 |
| 274 | Johnny Damon | .20 | .50 |
| 275 | Rafael Palmeiro | .20 | .50 |
| 276 | Denny Neagle | .10 | .30 |
| 277 | Neifi Perez | .10 | .30 |
| 278 | Roger Clemens | .60 | 1.50 |
| 279 | Brant Brown | .10 | .30 |
| 280 | Kevin Brown | .20 | .50 |
| 281 | Jay Bell | .10 | .30 |
| 282 | Jay Buhner | .10 | .30 |
| 283 | Matt Lawton | .10 | .30 |
| 284 | Robin Ventura | .10 | .30 |
| 285 | Juan Gonzalez | .30 | .75 |
| 286 | Mo Vaughn | .10 | .30 |
| 287 | Kevin Millwood | .10 | .30 |
| 288 | Tino Martinez | .20 | .50 |
| 289 | Justin Thompson | .10 | .30 |
| 290 | Derek Jeter | .75 | 2.00 |

| | | |
|---|---|---|
| ☐ 291 Ben Davis | .10 | .30 |
| ☐ 292 Mike Lowell | .10 | .30 |
| ☐ 293 Calvin Murray | .10 | .30 |
| ☐ 294 Micah Bowie RC | .15 | .40 |
| ☐ 295 Lance Berkman | .10 | .30 |
| ☐ 296 Jason Marquis | .10 | .30 |
| ☐ 297 Chad Green | .10 | .30 |
| ☐ 298 Dee Brown | .10 | .30 |
| ☐ 299 Jerry Hairston Jr. | .10 | .30 |
| ☐ 300 Gabe Kapler | .10 | .30 |
| ☐ 301 Brent Stentz RC | .25 | .60 |
| ☐ 302 Scott Mullen RC | .15 | .40 |
| ☐ 303 Brandon Reed | .10 | .30 |
| ☐ 304 Shea Hillenbrand RC | .60 | 1.50 |
| ☐ 305 J.D. Closser RC | .25 | .60 |
| ☐ 306 Gary Matthews Jr. | .10 | .30 |
| ☐ 307 Toby Hall RC | .25 | .60 |
| ☐ 308 Jason Phillips RC | .15 | .40 |
| ☐ 309 Jose Macias RC | .15 | .40 |
| ☐ 310 Jung Bong RC | .15 | .40 |
| ☐ 311 Ramon Soler RC | .15 | .40 |
| ☐ 312 Kelly Dransfeldt RC | .10 | .30 |
| ☐ 313 Carlos E. Hernandez RC | .25 | .60 |
| ☐ 314 Kevin Haverbusch | .10 | .30 |
| ☐ 315 Aaron Myette RC | .15 | .40 |
| ☐ 316 Chad Harville RC | .15 | .40 |
| ☐ 317 Kyle Farnsworth RC | .25 | .60 |
| ☐ 318 Gookie Dawkins RC | .15 | .40 |
| ☐ 319 Willie Martinez | .10 | .30 |
| ☐ 320 Carlos Lee | .10 | .30 |
| ☐ 321 Carlos Pena RC | .30 | .75 |
| ☐ 322 Peter Bergeron RC | .15 | .40 |
| ☐ 323 A.J. Burnett RC | .60 | 1.50 |
| ☐ 324 Bucky Jacobsen RC | .25 | .60 |
| ☐ 325 Mo Bruce RC | .15 | .40 |
| ☐ 326 Reggie Taylor | .10 | .30 |
| ☐ 327 Jackie Rexrode | .10 | .30 |
| ☐ 328 Alvin Morrow RC | .15 | .40 |
| ☐ 329 Carlos Beltran | .20 | .50 |
| ☐ 330 Eric Chavez | .10 | .30 |
| ☐ 331 John Patterson | .10 | .30 |
| ☐ 332 Jayson Werth | .10 | .30 |
| ☐ 333 Richie Sexson | .10 | .30 |
| ☐ 334 Randy Wolf | .10 | .30 |
| ☐ 335 Eli Marrero | .10 | .30 |
| ☐ 336 Paul LoDuca | .10 | .30 |
| ☐ 337 J.D Smart | .10 | .30 |
| ☐ 338 Ryan Minor | .10 | .30 |
| ☐ 339 Kris Benson | .10 | .30 |
| ☐ 340 George Lombard | .10 | .30 |
| ☐ 341 Troy Glaus | .20 | .50 |
| ☐ 342 Eddie Yarnall | .10 | .30 |
| ☐ 343 Kip Wells RC | .25 | .60 |
| ☐ 344 C.C. Sabathia RC | 1.00 | 2.50 |
| ☐ 345 Sean Burroughs RC | .40 | 1.00 |
| ☐ 346 Felipe Lopez RC | 1.00 | 2.50 |
| ☐ 347 Ryan Rupe RC | .15 | .40 |
| ☐ 348 Orber Moreno RC | .15 | .40 |
| ☐ 349 Rafael Roque RC | .15 | .40 |
| ☐ 350 Alfonso Soriano RC | 2.50 | 6.00 |
| ☐ 351 Pablo Ozuna | .10 | .30 |
| ☐ 352 Corey Patterson RC | .60 | 1.50 |
| ☐ 353 Braden Looper | .10 | .30 |
| ☐ 354 Robbie Bell | .10 | .30 |
| ☐ 355 Mark Mulder RC | 1.00 | 2.50 |
| ☐ 356 Angel Pena | .10 | .30 |
| ☐ 357 Kevin McGlinchy | .10 | .30 |
| ☐ 358 Michael Restovich RC | .25 | .60 |
| ☐ 359 Eric DuBose | .10 | .30 |
| ☐ 360 Geoff Jenkins | .10 | .30 |
| ☐ 361 Mark Harriger RC | .15 | .40 |
| ☐ 362 Junior Herndon RC | .15 | .40 |
| ☐ 363 Tim Raines Jr. RC | .15 | .40 |
| ☐ 364 Rafael Furcal RC | 1.00 | 2.50 |
| ☐ 365 Marcus Giles RC | .60 | 1.50 |
| ☐ 366 Ted Lilly | .10 | .30 |
| ☐ 367 Jorge Toca RC | .25 | .60 |
| ☐ 368 David Kelton RC | .15 | .40 |
| ☐ 369 Adam Dunn RC | 2.00 | 5.00 |
| ☐ 370 Guillermo Mota RC | .15 | .40 |
| ☐ 371 Brett Laxton RC | .15 | .40 |
| ☐ 372 Travis Harper RC | .25 | .60 |
| ☐ 373 Tom Davey RC | .15 | .40 |
| ☐ 374 Darren Blakely RC | .15 | .40 |
| ☐ 375 Tim Hudson RC | 1.50 | 4.00 |
| ☐ 376 Jason Romano RC | .10 | .30 |
| ☐ 377 Dan Reichert | .10 | .30 |
| ☐ 378 Julio Lugo RC | .40 | 1.00 |

| | | |
|---|---|---|
| ☐ 379 Jose Garcia RC | .15 | .40 |
| ☐ 380 Erubiel Durazo RC | .25 | .60 |
| ☐ 381 Jose Jimenez | .10 | .30 |
| ☐ 382 Chris Fussell | .10 | .30 |
| ☐ 383 Steve Lomasney | .10 | .30 |
| ☐ 384 Juan Pena RC | .25 | .60 |
| ☐ 385 Allen Levrault RC | .15 | .40 |
| ☐ 386 Juan Rivera RC | .60 | 1.50 |
| ☐ 387 Steve Colyer RC | .15 | .40 |
| ☐ 388 Joe Nathan RC | .75 | 2.00 |
| ☐ 389 Ron Walker RC | .15 | .40 |
| ☐ 390 Nick Bierbrodt | .10 | .30 |
| ☐ 391 Luke Prokopec RC | .15 | .40 |
| ☐ 392 Dave Roberts RC | .40 | 1.00 |
| ☐ 393 Mike Darr | .10 | .30 |
| ☐ 394 Abraham Nunez RC | .25 | .60 |
| ☐ 395 Giuseppe Chiaramonte RC | .15 | .40 |
| ☐ 396 Jermaine Van Buren RC | .15 | .40 |
| ☐ 397 Mike Kusiewicz | .10 | .30 |
| ☐ 398 Matt Wise RC | .15 | .40 |
| ☐ 399 Joe McEwing RC | .25 | .60 |
| ☐ 400 Matt Holliday RC | 2.50 | 6.00 |
| ☐ 401 Willi Mo Pena RC | 2.00 | 5.00 |
| ☐ 402 Ruben Quevedo RC | .15 | .40 |
| ☐ 403 Rob Ryan RC | .15 | .40 |
| ☐ 404 Freddy Garcia RC | .60 | 1.50 |
| ☐ 405 Kevin Eberwein RC | .15 | .40 |
| ☐ 406 Jesus Colome RC | .15 | .40 |
| ☐ 407 Chris Singleton | .10 | .30 |
| ☐ 408 Bubba Crosby RC | .40 | 1.00 |
| ☐ 409 Jesus Cordero RC | .15 | .40 |
| ☐ 410 Donny Leon | .10 | .30 |
| ☐ 411 Goefrey Tomlinson RC | .25 | .60 |
| ☐ 412 Jeff Winchester RC | .15 | .40 |
| ☐ 413 Adam Piatt RC | .15 | .40 |
| ☐ 414 Robert Stratton | .10 | .30 |
| ☐ 415 T.J. Tucker | .10 | .30 |
| ☐ 416 Ryan Langerhans RC | .40 | 1.00 |
| ☐ 417 Anthony Shumaker RC | .15 | .40 |
| ☐ 418 Matt Miller RC | .15 | .40 |
| ☐ 419 Doug Clark RC | .15 | .40 |
| ☐ 420 Kory DeHaan RC | .15 | .40 |
| ☐ 421 David Eckstein RC | 1.25 | 3.00 |
| ☐ 422 Brian Cooper RC | .15 | .40 |
| ☐ 423 Brady Clark RC | .60 | 1.50 |
| ☐ 424 Chris Magruder RC | .25 | .60 |
| ☐ 425 Bobby Seay RC | .15 | .40 |
| ☐ 426 Aubrey Huff RC | .75 | 2.00 |
| ☐ 427 Mike Jerzembeck | .10 | .30 |
| ☐ 428 Matt Blank RC | .25 | .60 |
| ☐ 429 Benny Agbayani RC | .25 | .60 |
| ☐ 430 Kevin Beirne RC | .15 | .40 |
| ☐ 431 Josh Hamilton RC | 2.50 | 6.00 |
| ☐ 432 Josh Girdley RC | .15 | .40 |
| ☐ 433 Kyle Snyder RC | .15 | .40 |
| ☐ 434 Mike Paradis RC | .15 | .40 |
| ☐ 435 Jason Jennings RC | .40 | 1.00 |
| ☐ 436 David Walling RC | .15 | .40 |
| ☐ 437 Omar Ortiz RC | .25 | .60 |
| ☐ 438 Jay Gehrke RC | .25 | .60 |
| ☐ 439 Casey Burns RC | .25 | .60 |
| ☐ 440 Carl Crawford RC | 1.50 | 4.00 |

## 2000 Bowman

| | | |
|---|---|---|
| ☐ COMPLETE SET (440) | 25.00 | 60.00 |
| ☐ 1 Vladimir Guerrero | .30 | .75 |
| ☐ 2 Chipper Jones | .30 | .75 |
| ☐ 3 Todd Walker | .10 | .30 |
| ☐ 4 Barry Larkin | .20 | .50 |
| ☐ 5 Bernie Williams | .20 | .50 |
| ☐ 6 Todd Helton | .20 | .50 |
| ☐ 7 Jermaine Dye | .10 | .30 |
| ☐ 8 Brian Giles | .10 | .30 |
| ☐ 9 Freddy Garcia | .10 | .30 |
| ☐ 10 Greg Vaughn | .10 | .30 |
| ☐ 11 Alex Gonzalez | .10 | .30 |
| ☐ 12 Luis Gonzalez | .10 | .30 |
| ☐ 13 Ron Belliard | .10 | .30 |
| ☐ 14 Ben Grieve | .10 | .30 |
| ☐ 15 Carlos Delgado | .10 | .30 |
| ☐ 16 Brian Jordan | .10 | .30 |
| ☐ 17 Fernando Tatis | .10 | .30 |
| ☐ 18 Ryan Rupe | .10 | .30 |
| ☐ 19 Miguel Tejada | .10 | .30 |
| ☐ 20 Mark Grace | .20 | .50 |
| ☐ 21 Kenny Lofton | .10 | .30 |
| ☐ 22 Eric Karros | .10 | .30 |
| ☐ 23 Cliff Floyd | .10 | .30 |
| ☐ 24 John Halama | .10 | .30 |
| ☐ 25 Cristian Guzman | .10 | .30 |
| ☐ 26 Scott Williamson | .10 | .30 |
| ☐ 27 Mike Lieberthal | .10 | .30 |
| ☐ 28 Tim Hudson | .10 | .30 |
| ☐ 29 Warren Morris | .10 | .30 |
| ☐ 30 Pedro Martinez | .20 | .50 |
| ☐ 31 John Smoltz | .20 | .50 |
| ☐ 32 Ray Durham | .10 | .30 |
| ☐ 33 Chad Allen | .10 | .30 |
| ☐ 34 Tony Clark | .10 | .30 |
| ☐ 35 Tino Martinez | .20 | .50 |
| ☐ 36 J.T. Snow | .10 | .30 |
| ☐ 37 Kevin Brown | .10 | .30 |
| ☐ 38 Bartolo Colon | .10 | .30 |
| ☐ 39 Rey Ordonez | .10 | .30 |
| ☐ 40 Jeff Bagwell | .20 | .50 |
| ☐ 41 Ivan Rodriguez | .20 | .50 |
| ☐ 42 Eric Chavez | .10 | .30 |
| ☐ 43 Eric Milton | .10 | .30 |
| ☐ 44 Jose Canseco | .20 | .50 |
| ☐ 45 Shawn Green | .10 | .30 |
| ☐ 46 Rich Aurilia | .10 | .30 |
| ☐ 47 Roberto Alomar | .20 | .50 |
| ☐ 48 Brian Daubach | .10 | .30 |
| ☐ 49 Magglio Ordonez | .10 | .30 |
| ☐ 50 Derek Jeter | .75 | 2.00 |
| ☐ 51 Kris Benson | .10 | .30 |
| ☐ 52 Albert Belle | .10 | .30 |
| ☐ 53 Rondell White | .10 | .30 |
| ☐ 54 Justin Thompson | .10 | .30 |
| ☐ 55 Nomar Garciaparra | .50 | 1.25 |
| ☐ 56 Chuck Finley | .10 | .30 |
| ☐ 57 Omar Vizquel | .20 | .50 |
| ☐ 58 Luis Castillo | .10 | .30 |
| ☐ 59 Richard Hidalgo | .10 | .30 |
| ☐ 60 Barry Bonds | .75 | 2.00 |
| ☐ 61 Craig Biggio | .20 | .50 |
| ☐ 62 Doug Glanville | .10 | .30 |
| ☐ 63 Gabe Kapler | .10 | .30 |
| ☐ 64 Johnny Damon | .20 | .50 |
| ☐ 65 Pokey Reese | .10 | .30 |
| ☐ 66 Andy Pettitte | .20 | .50 |
| ☐ 67 B.J. Surhoff | .10 | .30 |
| ☐ 68 Richie Sexson | .10 | .30 |
| ☐ 69 Javy Lopez | .10 | .30 |
| ☐ 70 Raul Mondesi | .10 | .30 |
| ☐ 71 Darin Erstad | .10 | .30 |
| ☐ 72 Kevin Millwood | .10 | .30 |
| ☐ 73 Ricky Ledee | .10 | .30 |
| ☐ 74 John Olerud | .10 | .30 |
| ☐ 75 Sean Casey | .10 | .30 |
| ☐ 76 Carlos Febles | .10 | .30 |
| ☐ 77 Paul O'Neill | .20 | .50 |
| ☐ 78 Bob Abreu | .10 | .30 |
| ☐ 79 Neifi Perez | .10 | .30 |
| ☐ 80 Tony Gwynn | .40 | 1.00 |
| ☐ 81 Russ Ortiz | .10 | .30 |
| ☐ 82 Matt Williams | .10 | .30 |
| ☐ 83 Chris Carpenter | .10 | .30 |
| ☐ 84 Roger Cedeno | .10 | .30 |
| ☐ 85 Tim Salmon | .20 | .50 |
| ☐ 86 Billy Koch | .10 | .30 |
| ☐ 87 Jeromy Burnitz | .10 | .30 |
| ☐ 88 Edgardo Alfonzo | .10 | .30 |
| ☐ 89 Jay Bell | .10 | .30 |
| ☐ 90 Manny Ramirez | .20 | .50 |
| ☐ 91 Frank Thomas | .30 | .75 |
| ☐ 92 Mike Mussina | .20 | .50 |
| ☐ 93 J.D. Drew | .10 | .30 |
| ☐ 94 Adrian Beltre | .10 | .30 |
| ☐ 95 Alex Rodriguez | .50 | 1.25 |
| ☐ 96 Larry Walker | .10 | .30 |
| ☐ 97 Juan Encarnacion | .10 | .30 |

|  |  | | |
|---|---|---|---|
| ❑ 98 | Mike Sweeney | .10 | .30 |
| ❑ 99 | Rusty Greer | .10 | .30 |
| ❑ 100 | Randy Johnson | .30 | .75 |
| ❑ 101 | Jose Vidro | .10 | .30 |
| ❑ 102 | Preston Wilson | .10 | .30 |
| ❑ 103 | Greg Maddux | .50 | 1.25 |
| ❑ 104 | Jason Giambi | .10 | .30 |
| ❑ 105 | Cal Ripken | 1.00 | 2.50 |
| ❑ 106 | Carlos Beltran | .10 | .30 |
| ❑ 107 | Vinny Castilla | .10 | .30 |
| ❑ 108 | Mariano Rivera | .30 | .75 |
| ❑ 109 | Mo Vaughn | .10 | .30 |
| ❑ 110 | Rafael Palmeiro | .20 | .50 |
| ❑ 111 | Shannon Stewart | .10 | .30 |
| ❑ 112 | Mike Hampton | .10 | .30 |
| ❑ 113 | Joe Nathan | .10 | .30 |
| ❑ 114 | Ben Davis | .10 | .30 |
| ❑ 115 | Andruw Jones | .20 | .50 |
| ❑ 116 | Robin Ventura | .10 | .30 |
| ❑ 117 | Damion Easley | .10 | .30 |
| ❑ 118 | Jeff Cirillo | .10 | .30 |
| ❑ 119 | Kerry Wood | .10 | .30 |
| ❑ 120 | Scott Rolen | .20 | .50 |
| ❑ 121 | Sammy Sosa | .30 | .75 |
| ❑ 122 | Ken Griffey Jr. | .50 | 1.25 |
| ❑ 123 | Shane Reynolds | .10 | .30 |
| ❑ 124 | Troy Glaus | .10 | .30 |
| ❑ 125 | Tom Glavine | .20 | .50 |
| ❑ 126 | Michael Barrett | .10 | .30 |
| ❑ 127 | Al Leiter | .10 | .30 |
| ❑ 128 | Jason Kendall | .10 | .30 |
| ❑ 129 | Roger Clemens | .60 | 1.50 |
| ❑ 130 | Juan Gonzalez | .10 | .30 |
| ❑ 131 | Corey Koskie | .10 | .30 |
| ❑ 132 | Curt Schilling | .10 | .30 |
| ❑ 133 | Mike Piazza | .50 | 1.25 |
| ❑ 134 | Gary Sheffield | .10 | .30 |
| ❑ 135 | Jim Thome | .20 | .50 |
| ❑ 136 | Orlando Hernandez | .10 | .30 |
| ❑ 137 | Ray Lankford | .10 | .30 |
| ❑ 138 | Geoff Jenkins | .10 | .30 |
| ❑ 139 | Jose Lima | .10 | .30 |
| ❑ 140 | Mark McGwire | .75 | 2.00 |
| ❑ 141 | Adam Piatt | .10 | .30 |
| ❑ 142 | Pat Manning RC | .10 | .30 |
| ❑ 143 | Marcos Castillo RC | .10 | .30 |
| ❑ 144 | Lesli Brea RC | .10 | .30 |
| ❑ 145 | Humberto Cota RC | .20 | .50 |
| ❑ 146 | Ben Petrick | .10 | .30 |
| ❑ 147 | Kip Wells | .10 | .30 |
| ❑ 148 | Wily Pena | .10 | .30 |
| ❑ 149 | Chris Wakeland RC | .10 | .30 |
| ❑ 150 | Brad Baker RC | .10 | .30 |
| ❑ 151 | Robbie Morrison RC | .10 | .30 |
| ❑ 152 | Reggie Taylor | .10 | .30 |
| ❑ 153 | Matt Ginter RC | .10 | .30 |
| ❑ 154 | Peter Bergeron | .10 | .30 |
| ❑ 155 | Roosevelt Brown | .10 | .30 |
| ❑ 156 | Matt Cepicky RC | .10 | .30 |
| ❑ 157 | Ramon Castro | .10 | .30 |
| ❑ 158 | Brad Baisley RC | .10 | .30 |
| ❑ 159 | Jeff Goldbach RC | .10 | .30 |
| ❑ 160 | Mitch Meluskey | .10 | .30 |
| ❑ 161 | Chad Harville | .10 | .30 |
| ❑ 162 | Brian Cooper | .10 | .30 |
| ❑ 163 | Marcus Giles | .10 | .30 |
| ❑ 164 | Jim Morris | .30 | .75 |
| ❑ 165 | Geoff Goetz | .10 | .30 |
| ❑ 166 | Bobby Bradley RC | .10 | .30 |
| ❑ 167 | Rob Bell | .10 | .30 |
| ❑ 168 | Joe Crede | .60 | 1.50 |
| ❑ 169 | Michael Restovich | .10 | .30 |
| ❑ 170 | Quincy Foster RC | .10 | .30 |
| ❑ 171 | Enrique Cruz RC | .10 | .30 |
| ❑ 172 | Mark Quinn | .10 | .30 |
| ❑ 173 | Nick Johnson | .10 | .30 |
| ❑ 174 | Jeff Liefer | .10 | .30 |
| ❑ 175 | Kevin Mench RC | .75 | 2.00 |
| ❑ 176 | Steve Lomasney | .10 | .30 |
| ❑ 177 | Jayson Werth | .10 | .30 |
| ❑ 178 | Tim Drew | .10 | .30 |
| ❑ 179 | Chip Ambres | .10 | .30 |
| ❑ 180 | Ryan Anderson | .10 | .30 |
| ❑ 181 | Matt Blank | .10 | .30 |
| ❑ 182 | Giuseppe Chiaramonte | .10 | .30 |
| ❑ 183 | Corey Myers RC | .10 | .30 |
| ❑ 184 | Jeff Yoder | .10 | .30 |
| ❑ 185 | Craig Dingman RC | .10 | .30 |
| ❑ 186 | Jon Hamilton RC | .10 | .30 |
| ❑ 187 | Toby Hall | .10 | .30 |
| ❑ 188 | Russell Branyan | .10 | .30 |
| ❑ 189 | Brian Falkenborg RC | .10 | .30 |
| ❑ 190 | Aaron Harang RC | 1.00 | 2.50 |
| ❑ 191 | Juan Pena | .10 | .30 |
| ❑ 192 | Travis Thompson RC | .10 | .30 |
| ❑ 193 | Alfonso Soriano | .30 | .75 |
| ❑ 194 | Alejandro Diaz RC | .10 | .30 |
| ❑ 195 | Carlos Pena | .10 | .30 |
| ❑ 196 | Kevin Nicholson | .10 | .30 |
| ❑ 197 | Mo Bruce | .10 | .30 |
| ❑ 198 | C.C. Sabathia | .10 | .30 |
| ❑ 199 | Carl Crawford | .10 | .30 |
| ❑ 200 | Rafael Furcal | .10 | .30 |
| ❑ 201 | Andrew Beinbrink RC | .10 | .30 |
| ❑ 202 | Jimmy Osting | .10 | .30 |
| ❑ 203 | Aaron McNeal RC | .10 | .30 |
| ❑ 204 | Brett Laxton | .10 | .30 |
| ❑ 205 | Chris George | .10 | .30 |
| ❑ 206 | Felipe Lopez | .10 | .30 |
| ❑ 207 | Ben Sheets RC | 1.00 | 2.50 |
| ❑ 208 | Mike Meyers RC | .20 | .50 |
| ❑ 209 | Jason Conti | .10 | .30 |
| ❑ 210 | Milton Bradley | .10 | .30 |
| ❑ 211 | Chris Mears RC | .10 | .30 |
| ❑ 212 | Carlos Hernandez RC | .30 | .75 |
| ❑ 213 | Jason Romano | .10 | .30 |
| ❑ 214 | Geofrey Tomlinson | .10 | .30 |
| ❑ 215 | Jimmy Rollins | .10 | .30 |
| ❑ 216 | Pablo Ozuna | .10 | .30 |
| ❑ 217 | Steve Cox | .10 | .30 |
| ❑ 218 | Terrence Long | .10 | .30 |
| ❑ 219 | Jeff DeVanon RC | .20 | .50 |
| ❑ 220 | Rick Ankiel | .10 | .30 |
| ❑ 221 | Jason Standridge | .10 | .30 |
| ❑ 222 | Tony Armas Jr. | .10 | .30 |
| ❑ 223 | Jason Tyner | .10 | .30 |
| ❑ 224 | Ramon Ortiz | .10 | .30 |
| ❑ 225 | Daryle Ward | .10 | .30 |
| ❑ 226 | Enger Veras RC | .10 | .30 |
| ❑ 227 | Chris Jones | .10 | .30 |
| ❑ 228 | Eric Cammack RC | .10 | .30 |
| ❑ 229 | Ruben Mateo | .10 | .30 |
| ❑ 230 | Ken Harvey RC | .20 | .50 |
| ❑ 231 | Jake Westbrook | .10 | .30 |
| ❑ 232 | Rob Purvis RC | .10 | .30 |
| ❑ 233 | Choo Freeman | .10 | .30 |
| ❑ 234 | Aramis Ramirez | .10 | .30 |
| ❑ 235 | A.J. Burnett | .10 | .30 |
| ❑ 236 | Kevin Barker | .10 | .30 |
| ❑ 237 | Chance Caple RC | .10 | .30 |
| ❑ 238 | Jarrod Washburn | .10 | .30 |
| ❑ 239 | Lance Berkman | .10 | .30 |
| ❑ 240 | Michael Wenner RC | .10 | .30 |
| ❑ 241 | Alex Sanchez | .10 | .30 |
| ❑ 242 | Pat Daneker | .10 | .30 |
| ❑ 243 | Grant Roberts | .10 | .30 |
| ❑ 244 | Mark Ellis RC | .20 | .50 |
| ❑ 245 | Donny Leon | .10 | .30 |
| ❑ 246 | David Eckstein | .10 | .30 |
| ❑ 247 | Dicky Gonzalez RC | .10 | .30 |
| ❑ 248 | John Patterson | .10 | .30 |
| ❑ 249 | Chad Green | .10 | .30 |
| ❑ 250 | Scot Shields RC | .10 | .30 |
| ❑ 251 | Troy Cameron | .10 | .30 |
| ❑ 252 | Jose Molina | .10 | .30 |
| ❑ 253 | Rob Pugmire RC | .10 | .30 |
| ❑ 254 | Rick Elder | .10 | .30 |
| ❑ 255 | Sean Burroughs | .10 | .30 |
| ❑ 256 | Josh Kalinowski RC | .10 | .30 |
| ❑ 257 | Matt LeCroy | .10 | .30 |
| ❑ 258 | Alex Graman RC | .10 | .30 |
| ❑ 259 | Tomo Ohka RC | .20 | .50 |
| ❑ 260 | Brady Clark | .10 | .30 |
| ❑ 261 | Rico Washington RC | .10 | .30 |
| ❑ 262 | Gary Matthews Jr. | .10 | .30 |
| ❑ 263 | Matt Wise | .10 | .30 |
| ❑ 264 | Keith Reed RC | .10 | .30 |
| ❑ 265 | Santiago Ramirez RC | .10 | .30 |
| ❑ 266 | Ben Broussard RC | .50 | 1.25 |
| ❑ 267 | Ryan Langerhans | .10 | .30 |
| ❑ 268 | Juan Rivera | .10 | .30 |
| ❑ 269 | Shawn Gallagher | .10 | .30 |
| ❑ 270 | Jorge Toca | .10 | .30 |
| ❑ 271 | Brad Lidge | .20 | .50 |
| ❑ 272 | Leoncio Estrella RC | .10 | .30 |
| ❑ 273 | Ruben Quevedo | .10 | .30 |
| ❑ 274 | Jack Cust | .10 | .30 |
| ❑ 275 | T.J. Tucker | .10 | .30 |
| ❑ 276 | Mike Colangelo | .10 | .30 |
| ❑ 277 | Brian Schneider | .10 | .30 |
| ❑ 278 | Calvin Murray | .10 | .30 |
| ❑ 279 | Josh Girdley | .10 | .30 |
| ❑ 280 | Mike Paradis | .10 | .30 |
| ❑ 281 | Chad Hermansen | .10 | .30 |
| ❑ 282 | Ty Howington RC | .10 | .30 |
| ❑ 283 | Aaron Myette | .10 | .30 |
| ❑ 284 | D'Angelo Jimenez | .10 | .30 |
| ❑ 285 | Dernell Stenson | .10 | .30 |
| ❑ 286 | Jerry Hairston Jr. | .10 | .30 |
| ❑ 287 | Gary Majewski RC | .20 | .50 |
| ❑ 288 | Derrin Ebert | .10 | .30 |
| ❑ 289 | Steve Fish RC | .10 | .30 |
| ❑ 290 | Carlos E. Hernandez | .10 | .30 |
| ❑ 291 | Allen Levrault | .10 | .30 |
| ❑ 292 | Sean McNally RC | .10 | .30 |
| ❑ 293 | Randey Dorame RC | .10 | .30 |
| ❑ 294 | Wes Anderson RC | .10 | .30 |
| ❑ 295 | B.J. Ryan | .10 | .30 |
| ❑ 296 | Alan Webb RC | .10 | .30 |
| ❑ 297 | Brandon Inge RC | .75 | 2.00 |
| ❑ 298 | David Walling | .10 | .30 |
| ❑ 299 | Sun Woo Kim RC | .10 | .30 |
| ❑ 300 | Pat Burrell | .10 | .30 |
| ❑ 301 | Rick Guttormson RC | .10 | .30 |
| ❑ 302 | Gil Meche | .10 | .30 |
| ❑ 303 | Carlos Zambrano RC | 2.00 | 5.00 |
| ❑ 304 | Eric Byrnes UER RC | .20 | .50 |
| ❑ 305 | Robb Quinlan RC | .20 | .50 |
| ❑ 306 | Jackie Rexrode | .10 | .30 |
| ❑ 307 | Nate Bump | .10 | .30 |
| ❑ 308 | Sean DePaula RC | .10 | .30 |
| ❑ 309 | Matt Riley | .10 | .30 |
| ❑ 310 | Ryan Minor | .10 | .30 |
| ❑ 311 | J.J. Davis | .10 | .30 |
| ❑ 312 | Randy Wolf | .10 | .30 |
| ❑ 313 | Jason Jennings | .10 | .30 |
| ❑ 314 | Scott Seabol RC | .10 | .30 |
| ❑ 315 | Doug Davis | .10 | .30 |
| ❑ 316 | Todd Moser RC | .10 | .30 |
| ❑ 317 | Rob Ryan | .10 | .30 |
| ❑ 318 | Bubba Crosby | .10 | .30 |
| ❑ 319 | Lyle Overbay RC | .50 | 1.25 |
| ❑ 320 | Mario Encarnacion | .10 | .30 |
| ❑ 321 | Francisco Rodriguez RC | 1.25 | 3.00 |
| ❑ 322 | Michael Cuddyer | .10 | .30 |
| ❑ 323 | Ed Yarnall | .10 | .30 |
| ❑ 324 | Cesar Saba RC | .10 | .30 |
| ❑ 325 | Gookie Dawkins | .10 | .30 |
| ❑ 326 | Alex Escobar | .10 | .30 |
| ❑ 327 | Julio Zuleta RC | .10 | .30 |
| ❑ 328 | Josh Hamilton | .40 | 1.00 |
| ❑ 329 | Nick Neugebauer RC | .10 | .30 |
| ❑ 330 | Matt Belisle | .10 | .30 |
| ❑ 331 | Kurt Ainsworth RC | .10 | .30 |
| ❑ 332 | Tim Raines Jr. | .10 | .30 |
| ❑ 333 | Eric Munson | .10 | .30 |
| ❑ 334 | Donzell McDonald | .10 | .30 |
| ❑ 335 | Larry Bigbie RC | .30 | .75 |
| ❑ 336 | Matt Watson RC | .10 | .30 |
| ❑ 337 | Aubrey Huff | .10 | .30 |
| ❑ 338 | Julio Ramirez | .10 | .30 |
| ❑ 339 | Jason Grabowski RC | .10 | .30 |
| ❑ 340 | Jon Garland | .10 | .30 |
| ❑ 341 | Austin Kearns | .10 | .30 |
| ❑ 342 | Josh Pressley RC | .10 | .30 |
| ❑ 343 | Miguel Olivo RC | .30 | .75 |
| ❑ 344 | Julio Lugo | .10 | .30 |
| ❑ 345 | Roberto Vaz | .10 | .30 |
| ❑ 346 | Ramon Soler | .10 | .30 |
| ❑ 347 | Brandon Phillips RC | .60 | 1.50 |
| ❑ 348 | Vince Faison RC | .10 | .30 |
| ❑ 349 | Mike Venatro | .10 | .30 |
| ❑ 350 | Rick Asadoorian RC | .20 | .50 |
| ❑ 351 | B.J. Garbe RC | .10 | .30 |
| ❑ 352 | Dan Reichert | .10 | .30 |
| ❑ 353 | Jason Stumm RC | .10 | .30 |
| ❑ 354 | Ruben Salazar RC | .10 | .30 |
| ❑ 355 | Francisco Cordero | .10 | .30 |
| ❑ 356 | Juan Guzman RC | .10 | .30 |
| ❑ 357 | Mike Bacsik RC | .10 | .30 |
| ❑ 358 | Jared Sandberg | .10 | .30 |
| ❑ 359 | Rod Barajas | .10 | .30 |
| ❑ 360 | Junior Brignac RC | .10 | .30 |
| ❑ 361 | J.M. Gold | .10 | .30 |

| | | |
|---|---|---|
| ☐ 362 Octavio Dotel | .10 | .30 |
| ☐ 363 David Kelton | .10 | .30 |
| ☐ 364 Scott Morgan | .10 | .30 |
| ☐ 365 Wascar Serrano RC | .10 | .30 |
| ☐ 366 Wilton Veras | .10 | .30 |
| ☐ 367 Eugene Kingsale | .10 | .30 |
| ☐ 368 Ted Lilly | .10 | .30 |
| ☐ 369 George Lombard | .10 | .30 |
| ☐ 370 Chris Haas | .10 | .30 |
| ☐ 371 Wilton Pena RC | .10 | .30 |
| ☐ 372 Vernon Wells | .10 | .30 |
| ☐ 373 Jason Royer RC | .10 | .30 |
| ☐ 374 Jeff Heaverlo RC | .10 | .30 |
| ☐ 375 Calvin Pickering | .10 | .30 |
| ☐ 376 Mike Lamb | .30 | .75 |
| ☐ 377 Kyle Snyder | .10 | .30 |
| ☐ 378 Javier Cardona RC | .10 | .30 |
| ☐ 379 Aaron Rowand RC | .75 | 2.00 |
| ☐ 380 Dee Brown | .10 | .30 |
| ☐ 381 Brett Myers RC | .60 | 1.50 |
| ☐ 382 Abraham Nunez | .10 | .30 |
| ☐ 383 Eric Valent | .10 | .30 |
| ☐ 384 Jody Gerut RC | .20 | .50 |
| ☐ 385 Adam Dunn | .30 | .75 |
| ☐ 386 Jay Gehrke | .10 | .30 |
| ☐ 387 Omar Ortiz | .10 | .30 |
| ☐ 388 Darnell McDonald | .10 | .30 |
| ☐ 389 Tony Schrager RC | .10 | .30 |
| ☐ 390 J.D. Closser | .10 | .30 |
| ☐ 391 Ben Christensen RC | .10 | .30 |
| ☐ 392 Adam Kennedy | .10 | .30 |
| ☐ 393 Nick Green RC | .10 | .30 |
| ☐ 394 Ramon Hernandez | .10 | .30 |
| ☐ 395 Roy Oswalt RC | 4.00 | 10.00 |
| ☐ 396 Andy Tracy RC | .10 | .30 |
| ☐ 397 Eric Gagne | .30 | .75 |
| ☐ 398 Michael Tejera RC | .10 | .30 |
| ☐ 399 Adam Everett | .10 | .30 |
| ☐ 400 Corey Patterson | .10 | .30 |
| ☐ 401 Gary Knotts RC | .10 | .30 |
| ☐ 402 Ryan Christianson RC | .10 | .30 |
| ☐ 403 Eric Ireland RC | .10 | .30 |
| ☐ 404 Andrew Good RC | .10 | .30 |
| ☐ 405 Brad Penny | .10 | .30 |
| ☐ 406 Jason LaRue | .10 | .30 |
| ☐ 407 Kit Pellow | .10 | .30 |
| ☐ 408 Kevin Beirne | .10 | .30 |
| ☐ 409 Kelly Dransfeldt | .10 | .30 |
| ☐ 410 Jason Grilli | .10 | .30 |
| ☐ 411 Scott Downs RC | .10 | .30 |
| ☐ 412 Jesus Colome | .10 | .30 |
| ☐ 413 John Sneed RC | .10 | .30 |
| ☐ 414 Tony McKnight | .10 | .30 |
| ☐ 415 Luis Rivera | .10 | .30 |
| ☐ 416 Adam Eaton | .10 | .30 |
| ☐ 417 Mike MacDougal RC | .20 | .50 |
| ☐ 418 Mike Nannini | .10 | .30 |
| ☐ 419 Barry Zito RC | 1.50 | 4.00 |
| ☐ 420 DeWayne Wise | .10 | .30 |
| ☐ 421 Jason Dellaero | .10 | .30 |
| ☐ 422 Chad Moeller | .10 | .30 |
| ☐ 423 Jason Marquis | .10 | .30 |
| ☐ 424 Tim Redding RC | .20 | .50 |
| ☐ 425 Mark Mulder | .10 | .30 |
| ☐ 426 Josh Paul | .10 | .30 |
| ☐ 427 Chris Enochs | .10 | .30 |
| ☐ 428 Wilfredo Rodriguez RC | .10 | .30 |
| ☐ 429 Kevin Witt | .10 | .30 |
| ☐ 430 Scott Sobkowiak RC | .10 | .30 |
| ☐ 431 McKay Christensen | .10 | .30 |
| ☐ 432 Jung Bong | .10 | .30 |
| ☐ 433 Keith Evans RC | .10 | .30 |
| ☐ 434 Garry Maddox Jr. RC | .10 | .30 |
| ☐ 435 Ramon Santiago RC | .10 | .30 |
| ☐ 436 Alex Cora | .10 | .30 |
| ☐ 437 Carlos Lee | .10 | .30 |
| ☐ 438 Jason Repko RC | .30 | .30 |
| ☐ 439 Matt Burch | .10 | .30 |
| ☐ 440 Shawn Sonnier RC | .10 | .30 |

## 2000 Bowman Draft

| | | |
|---|---|---|
| ☐ COMP.FACT.SET (111) | 20.00 | 40.00 |
| ☐ COMPLETE SET (110) | 10.00 | 25.00 |
| ☐ 1 Pat Burrell | .10 | .30 |
| ☐ 2 Rafael Furcal | .10 | .30 |
| ☐ 3 Grant Roberts | .10 | .30 |
| ☐ 4 Barry Zito | .60 | 1.50 |
| ☐ 5 Julio Zuleta | .10 | .30 |
| ☐ 6 Mark Mulder | .10 | .30 |
| ☐ 7 Rob Bell | .10 | .30 |
| ☐ 8 Adam Platt | .10 | .30 |
| ☐ 9 Mike Lamb | .25 | .60 |
| ☐ 10 Pablo Ozuna | .10 | .30 |
| ☐ 11 Jason Tyner | .10 | .30 |
| ☐ 12 Jason Marquis | .10 | .30 |
| ☐ 13 Eric Munson | .10 | .30 |
| ☐ 14 Seth Etherton | .10 | .30 |
| ☐ 15 Milton Bradley | .10 | .30 |
| ☐ 16 Nick Green | .10 | .30 |
| ☐ 17 Chin-Feng Chen RC | .25 | .60 |
| ☐ 18 Matt Boone RC | .10 | .30 |
| ☐ 19 Kevin Gregg RC | .10 | .30 |
| ☐ 20 Eddy Garabito RC | .10 | .30 |
| ☐ 21 Aaron Capista RC | .10 | .30 |
| ☐ 22 Esteban German RC | .10 | .30 |
| ☐ 23 Derek Thompson RC | .10 | .30 |
| ☐ 24 Phil Merrell RC | .10 | .30 |
| ☐ 25 Brian O'Connor RC | .10 | .30 |
| ☐ 26 Yamid Haad | .10 | .30 |
| ☐ 27 Hector Mercado RC | .10 | .30 |
| ☐ 28 Jason Woolf RC | .10 | .30 |
| ☐ 29 Eddy Furniss RC | .10 | .30 |
| ☐ 30a Cha Sueng Baek RC | .10 | .30 |
| ☐ 31 Colby Lewis RC | .10 | .30 |
| ☐ 32 Pasqual Coco RC | .10 | .30 |
| ☐ 33 Jorge Cantu RC | 1.00 | 2.50 |
| ☐ 34 Erasmo Ramirez RC | .10 | .30 |
| ☐ 35 Bobby Kielty RC | .15 | .40 |
| ☐ 36 Joaquin Benoit RC | .10 | .30 |
| ☐ 37 Brian Esposito RC | .10 | .30 |
| ☐ 38 Michael Wenner | .10 | .30 |
| ☐ 39 Juan Rincon RC | .10 | .30 |
| ☐ 40 Yorvit Torrealba RC | .25 | 6.00 |
| ☐ 41 Chad Durham RC | .10 | .30 |
| ☐ 42 Jim Mann RC | .10 | .30 |
| ☐ 43 Shane Loux RC | .10 | .30 |
| ☐ 44 Luis Rivas | .10 | .30 |
| ☐ 45 Ken Chenard RC | .10 | .30 |
| ☐ 46 Mike Lockwood RC | .10 | .30 |
| ☐ 47 Yovanny Lara RC | .10 | .30 |
| ☐ 48 Bubba Carpenter RC | .10 | .30 |
| ☐ 49 Ryan Dittfurth RC | .10 | .30 |
| ☐ 50 John Stephens RC | .10 | .30 |
| ☐ 51 Pedro Feliz RC | .40 | 1.00 |
| ☐ 52 Kenny Kelly RC | .10 | .30 |
| ☐ 53 Neil Jenkins RC | .10 | .30 |
| ☐ 54 Mike Glendenning RC | .10 | .30 |
| ☐ 55 Bo Porter | .10 | .30 |
| ☐ 56 Eric Byrnes | .10 | .30 |
| ☐ 57 Tony Alvarez RC | .10 | .30 |
| ☐ 58 Kazuhiro Sasaki RC | .25 | .60 |
| ☐ 59 Chad Durbin RC | .10 | .30 |
| ☐ 60 Mike Bynum RC | .10 | .30 |
| ☐ 61 Travis Wilson RC | .10 | .30 |
| ☐ 62 Jose Leon RC | .10 | .30 |
| ☐ 63 Ryan Vogelsong RC | .10 | .30 |
| ☐ 64 Geraldo Guzman RC | .10 | .30 |
| ☐ 65 Craig Anderson RC | .10 | .30 |
| ☐ 66 Carlos Silva RC | .15 | .40 |
| ☐ 67 Brad Thomas RC | .10 | .30 |
| ☐ 68 Chin-Hui Tsao RC | .75 | 2.00 |
| ☐ 69 Mark Buehrle RC | 3.00 | 8.00 |
| ☐ 70 Juan Salas RC | .10 | .30 |

| | | |
|---|---|---|
| ☐ 71 Denny Abreu RC | .10 | .30 |
| ☐ 72 Keith McDonald RC | .10 | .30 |
| ☐ 73 Chris Richard RC | .10 | .30 |
| ☐ 74 Tomas De la Rosa RC | .10 | .30 |
| ☐ 75 Vicente Padilla RC | .15 | .40 |
| ☐ 76 Justin Brunette RC | .10 | .30 |
| ☐ 77 Scott Linebrink RC | .10 | .30 |
| ☐ 78 Jeff Sparks RC | .10 | .30 |
| ☐ 79 Tike Redman RC | .25 | .60 |
| ☐ 80 John Lackey RC | 1.00 | 2.50 |
| ☐ 81 Joe Strong RC | .10 | .30 |
| ☐ 82 Brian Tollberg RC | .10 | .30 |
| ☐ 83 Steve Sisco RC | .10 | .30 |
| ☐ 84 Chris Clapinski RC | .10 | .30 |
| ☐ 85 Augie Ojeda RC | .10 | .30 |
| ☐ 86 Adrian Gonzalez RC | 1.25 | 3.00 |
| ☐ 87 Mike Stodolka RC | .10 | .30 |
| ☐ 88 Adam Johnson RC | .10 | .30 |
| ☐ 89 Matt Wheatland RC | .10 | .30 |
| ☐ 90 Corey Smith RC | .10 | .30 |
| ☐ 91 Rocco Baldelli RC | .75 | 2.00 |
| ☐ 92 Keith Bucktrot RC | .10 | .30 |
| ☐ 93 Adam Wainwright RC | .75 | 2.00 |
| ☐ 94 Blaine Boyer RC | .10 | .30 |
| ☐ 95 Aaron Herr RC | .15 | .40 |
| ☐ 96 Scott Thorman RC | .40 | 1.00 |
| ☐ 97 Bryan Digby RC | .10 | .30 |
| ☐ 98 Josh Shortslef RC | .20 | .50 |
| ☐ 99 Sean Smith RC | .10 | .30 |
| ☐ 100 Alex Cruz RC | .10 | .30 |
| ☐ 101 Marc Love RC | .10 | .30 |
| ☐ 102 Kevin Lee RC | .10 | .30 |
| ☐ 103 Victor Ramos RC | .10 | .30 |
| ☐ 104 Jason Kaanoi RC | .10 | .30 |
| ☐ 105 Luis Escobar RC | .10 | .30 |
| ☐ 106 Tripper Johnson RC | .10 | .30 |
| ☐ 107 Phil Dumatrait RC | .10 | .30 |
| ☐ 108 Bryan Edwards RC | .10 | .30 |
| ☐ 109 Greg Sizemore RC | 4.00 | 10.00 |
| ☐ 110 Thomas Mitchell RC | .10 | .30 |

## 2001 Bowman

| | | |
|---|---|---|
| ☐ COMPLETE SET (440) | 90.00 | 150.00 |
| ☐ COMMON CARD (1-440) | .10 | .30 |
| ☐ COMMON RC | .15 | .40 |
| ☐ 1 Jason Giambi | .10 | .30 |
| ☐ 2 Rafael Furcal | .10 | .30 |
| ☐ 3 Rick Ankiel | .10 | .30 |
| ☐ 4 Freddy Garcia | .10 | .30 |
| ☐ 5 Maggilo Ordonez | .10 | .30 |
| ☐ 6 Bernie Williams | .20 | .50 |
| ☐ 7 Kenny Lofton | .10 | .30 |
| ☐ 8 Al Leiter | .10 | .30 |
| ☐ 9 Albert Belle | .10 | .30 |
| ☐ 10 Craig Biggio | .20 | .50 |
| ☐ 11 Mark Mulder | .10 | .30 |
| ☐ 12 Carlos Delgado | .10 | .30 |
| ☐ 13 Darin Erstad | .10 | .30 |
| ☐ 14 Richie Sexson | .10 | .30 |
| ☐ 15 Randy Johnson | .30 | .75 |
| ☐ 16 Greg Maddux | .50 | 1.25 |
| ☐ 17 Cliff Floyd | .10 | .30 |
| ☐ 18 Mark Buehrle | .20 | .50 |
| ☐ 19 Chris Singleton | .10 | .30 |
| ☐ 20 Orlando Hernandez | .10 | .30 |
| ☐ 21 Javier Vazquez | .10 | .30 |
| ☐ 22 Jeff Kent | .10 | .30 |
| ☐ 23 Jim Thome | .20 | .50 |
| ☐ 24 John Olerud | .10 | .30 |
| ☐ 25 Jason Kendall | .10 | .30 |
| ☐ 26 Scott Rolen | .20 | .50 |
| ☐ 27 Tony Gwynn | .40 | 1.00 |
| ☐ 28 Edgardo Alfonzo | .10 | .30 |
| ☐ 29 Pokey Reese | .10 | .30 |

|  |  | |  |  | |  |  | |
|---|---|---|---|---|---|---|---|---|
| 30 | Todd Helton | .20 .50 | 118 | Gabe Kapler | .10 .30 | 206 | Adam Wainwright | .25 .60 |
| 31 | Mark Quinn | .10 .30 | 119 | Jeff Cirillo | .10 .30 | 207 | Matt White RC | .25 .60 |
| 32 | Dan Tosca RC | .15 .40 | 120 | Frank Thomas | .30 .75 | 208 | Chin-Feng Chen | .10 .30 |
| 33 | Dean Palmer | .10 .30 | 121 | David Justice | .10 .30 | 209 | Jeff Andra RC | .15 .40 |
| 34 | Jacque Jones | .10 .30 | 122 | Cal Ripken | 1.00 2.50 | 210 | Willie Bloomquist | .10 .30 |
| 35 | Ray Durham | .10 .30 | 123 | Rich Aurilia | .10 .30 | 211 | Wes Anderson | .10 .30 |
| 36 | Rafael Palmeiro | .20 .50 | 124 | Curt Schilling | .10 .30 | 212 | Enrique Cruz | .10 .30 |
| 37 | Carl Everett | .10 .30 | 125 | Barry Zito | .20 .50 | 213 | Jerry Hairston Jr. | .10 .30 |
| 38 | Ryan Dempster | .10 .30 | 126 | Brian Jordan | .10 .30 | 214 | Mike Bynum | .10 .30 |
| 39 | Randy Wolf | .10 .30 | 127 | | .10 .30 | 215 | Brian Hitchcox RC | .15 .40 |
| 40 | Vladimir Guerrero | .30 .75 | 128 | J.T. Snow | .10 .30 | 216 | Ryan Christianson | .10 .30 |
| 41 | Livan Hernandez | .10 .30 | 129 | Kazuhiro Sasaki | .10 .30 | 217 | J.J. Davis | .10 .30 |
| 42 | Mo Vaughn | .10 .30 | 130 | Alex Rodriguez | .50 1.25 | 218 | Jovanny Cedeno | .10 .30 |
| 43 | Shannon Stewart | .10 .30 | 131 | Mariano Rivera | .30 .75 | 219 | Elvin Nina | .10 .30 |
| 44 | Preston Wilson | .10 .30 | 132 | Eric Milton | .10 .30 | 220 | Alex Graman | .10 .30 |
| 45 | Jose Vidro | .10 .30 | 133 | Andy Pettitte | .20 .50 | 221 | Arturo McDowell | .10 .30 |
| 46 | Fred McGriff | .20 .50 | 134 | Scott Elarton | .10 .30 | 222 | Deivis Santos RC | .15 .40 |
| 47 | Kevin Brown | .10 .30 | 135 | Ken Griffey Jr. | .50 1.25 | 223 | Jody Gerut | .10 .30 |
| 48 | Peter Bergeron | .10 .30 | 136 | Bengie Molina | .10 .30 | 224 | Sun Woo Kim | .10 .30 |
| 49 | Miguel Tejada | .10 .30 | 137 | Jeff Bagwell | .20 .50 | 225 | Jimmy Rollins | .10 .30 |
| 50 | Chipper Jones | .30 .75 | 138 | Kevin Millwood | .10 .30 | 226 | Ntema Ndungidi | .10 .30 |
| 51 | Edgar Martinez | .20 .50 | 139 | Tino Martinez | .20 .50 | 227 | Ruben Salazar | .10 .30 |
| 52 | Tony Batista | .10 .30 | 140 | Mark McGwire | .75 2.00 | 228 | Josh Girdley | .10 .30 |
| 53 | Jorge Posada | .20 .50 | 141 | Larry Barnes | .10 .30 | 229 | Carl Crawford | .10 .30 |
| 54 | Ricky Ledee | .10 .30 | 142 | John Buck RC | .40 1.00 | 230 | Luis Montanez RC | .30 .75 |
| 55 | Sammy Sosa | .30 .75 | 143 | Freddie Bynum RC | .15 .40 | 231 | Ramon Carvajal RC | .25 .60 |
| 56 | Steve Cox | .10 .30 | 144 | Abraham Nunez | .10 .30 | 232 | Matt Riley | .10 .30 |
| 57 | Tony Armas Jr. | .10 .30 | 145 | Felix Diaz RC | .15 .40 | 233 | Ben Davis | .10 .30 |
| 58 | Gary Sheffield | .10 .30 | 146 | Horacio Estrada | .10 .30 | 234 | Jason Grabowski | .10 .30 |
| 59 | Bartolo Colon | .10 .30 | 147 | Ben Diggins | .10 .30 | 235 | Chris George | .10 .30 |
| 60 | Pat Burrell | .10 .30 | 148 | Tsuyoshi Shinjo RC | .40 1.00 | 236 | Hank Blalock RC | 2.00 5.00 |
| 61 | Jay Payton | .10 .30 | 149 | Rocco Baldelli | .10 .30 | 237 | Roy Oswalt | .30 .75 |
| 62 | Sean Casey | .10 .30 | 150 | Rod Barajas | .10 .30 | 238 | Eric Reynolds RC | .15 .40 |
| 63 | Larry Walker | .10 .30 | 151 | Luis Terrero | .10 .30 | 239 | Brian Cole | .10 .30 |
| 64 | Mike Mussina | .20 .50 | 152 | Milton Bradley | .10 .30 | 240 | Denny Bautista RC | .40 1.00 |
| 65 | Nomar Garciaparra | .50 1.25 | 153 | Kurt Ainsworth | .10 .30 | 241 | Hector Garcia RC | .15 .40 |
| 66 | Darren Dreifort | .10 .30 | 154 | Russell Branyan | .10 .30 | 242 | Joe Thurston RC | .25 .60 |
| 67 | Richard Hidalgo | .10 .30 | 155 | Ryan Anderson | .10 .30 | 243 | Brad Cresse | .10 .30 |
| 68 | Troy Glaus | .10 .30 | 156 | Mitch Jones RC | .25 .60 | 244 | Corey Patterson | .30 .75 |
| 69 | Ben Grieve | .10 .30 | 157 | Chip Ambres | .10 .30 | 245 | Brett Evert RC | .15 .40 |
| 70 | Jim Edmonds | .10 .30 | 158 | Steve Bennett RC | .15 .40 | 246 | Elpidio Guzman RC | .15 .40 |
| 71 | Raul Mondesi | .10 .30 | 159 | Ivanon Coffie | .10 .30 | 247 | Vernon Wells | .10 .30 |
| 72 | Andruw Jones | .20 .50 | 160 | Sean Burroughs | .10 .30 | 248 | Roberto Miniel RC | .25 .60 |
| 73 | Luis Castillo | .10 .30 | 161 | Keith Bucktrot | .10 .30 | 249 | Brian Bass RC | .15 .40 |
| 74 | Mike Sweeney | .10 .30 | 162 | Tony Alvarez | .10 .30 | 250 | Mark Burnett RC | .25 .60 |
| 75 | Derek Jeter | .75 2.00 | 163 | Joaquin Benoit | .10 .30 | 251 | Juan Silvestre | .10 .30 |
| 76 | Ruben Mateo | .10 .30 | 164 | Rick Asadoorian | .10 .30 | 252 | Pablo Ozuna | .10 .30 |
| 77 | Carlos Lee | .10 .30 | 165 | Ben Broussard | .10 .30 | 253 | Jayson Werth | .10 .30 |
| 78 | Cristian Guzman | .10 .30 | 166 | Ryan Madson RC | .50 1.25 | 254 | Russ Jacobson | .10 .30 |
| 79 | Mike Hampton | .10 .30 | 167 | Dee Brown | .10 .30 | 255 | Chad Hermansen | .10 .30 |
| 80 | J.D. Drew | .10 .30 | 168 | Sergio Contreras RC | .25 .60 | 256 | Travis Hafner RC | 4.00 10.00 |
| 81 | Matt Lawton | .10 .30 | 169 | John Barnes | .10 .30 | 257 | Brad Baker | .10 .30 |
| 82 | Moises Alou | .10 .30 | 170 | Ben Washburn RC | .15 .40 | 258 | Gookie Dawkins | .10 .30 |
| 83 | Terrence Long | .10 .30 | 171 | Erick Almonte RC | .15 .40 | 259 | Michael Cuddyer | .10 .30 |
| 84 | Geoff Jenkins | .10 .30 | 172 | Shawn Fagan RC | .15 .40 | 260 | Mark Buehrle | .20 .50 |
| 85 | Manny Ramirez Sox | .20 .50 | 173 | Gary Johnson RC | .15 .40 | 261 | Ricardo Aramboles | .10 .30 |
| 86 | Johnny Damon | .20 .50 | 174 | Brady Clark | .10 .30 | 262 | Esix Snead RC | .15 .40 |
| 87 | Barry Larkin | .20 .50 | 175 | Grant Roberts | .10 .30 | 263 | Wilson Betemit RC | 1.25 3.00 |
| 88 | Pedro Martinez | .20 .50 | 176 | Tony Torcato | .10 .30 | 264 | Albert Pujols RC | 40.00 80.00 |
| 89 | Juan Gonzalez | .10 .30 | 177 | Ramon Castro | .10 .30 | 265 | Joe Lawrence | .10 .30 |
| 90 | Roger Clemens | .60 1.50 | 178 | Esteban German | .10 .30 | 266 | Ramon Ortiz | .10 .30 |
| 91 | Carlos Beltran | .10 .30 | 179 | Joe Hamer RC | .25 .60 | 267 | Ben Sheets | .20 .50 |
| 92 | Brad Radke | .10 .30 | 180 | Nick Neugebauer | .10 .30 | 268 | Luke Lockwood RC | .25 .60 |
| 93 | Orlando Cabrera | .10 .30 | 181 | Darnell Stenson | .10 .30 | 269 | Toby Hall | .10 .30 |
| 94 | Roberto Alomar | .20 .50 | 182 | Yhency Brazoban RC | .40 1.00 | 270 | Jack Cust | .10 .30 |
| 95 | Barry Bonds | .75 2.00 | 183 | Aaron Myette | .10 .30 | 271 | Pedro Feliz | .10 .30 |
| 96 | Tim Hudson | .10 .30 | 184 | Juan Sosa | .10 .30 | 272 | Noel Devarez RC | .25 .60 |
| 97 | Tom Glavine | .20 .50 | 185 | Brandon Inge | .10 .30 | 273 | Josh Beckett | .20 .50 |
| 98 | Jeromy Burnitz | .10 .30 | 186 | Domingo Guante RC | .15 .40 | 274 | Alex Escobar | .10 .30 |
| 99 | Adrian Beltre | .10 .30 | 187 | Adrian Brown | .10 .30 | 275 | Doug Gredvig RC | .15 .40 |
| 100 | Mike Piazza | .50 1.25 | 188 | Deivi Mendez RC | .15 .40 | 276 | Marcus Giles | .10 .30 |
| 101 | Kerry Wood | .10 .30 | 189 | Luis Matos | .10 .30 | 277 | Jon Rauch | .10 .30 |
| 102 | Steve Finley | .10 .30 | 190 | Pedro Liriano RC | .25 .60 | 278 | Brian Schmitt RC | .15 .40 |
| 103 | Alex Cora | .10 .30 | 191 | Donnie Bridges | .10 .30 | 279 | Seung Song RC | .25 .60 |
| 104 | Bob Abreu | .10 .30 | 192 | Alex Cintron | .10 .30 | 280 | Kevin Mench | .10 .30 |
| 105 | Neifi Perez | .10 .30 | 193 | Jace Brewer | .10 .30 | 281 | Adam Eaton | .10 .30 |
| 106 | Mark Redman | .10 .30 | 194 | Ron Davenport RC | .25 .60 | 282 | Shawn Sonnier | .10 .30 |
| 107 | Paul Konerko | .10 .30 | 195 | Jason Belcher RC | .15 .40 | 283 | Andy Van Hekken RC | .15 .40 |
| 108 | Jermaine Dye | .10 .30 | 196 | Adrian Hernandez RC | .15 .40 | 284 | Aaron Rowand | .10 .30 |
| 109 | Brian Giles | .10 .30 | 197 | Bobby Kielty | .10 .30 | 285 | Tony Blanco RC | .25 .60 |
| 110 | Ivan Rodriguez | .20 .50 | 198 | Reggie Griggs RC | .25 .60 | 286 | Ryan Kohlmeier | .10 .30 |
| 111 | Vinny Castilla | .10 .30 | 199 | Reggie Abercrombie RC | .40 1.00 | 287 | C.C. Sabathia | .10 .30 |
| 112 | Adam Kennedy | .10 .30 | 200 | Troy Farnsworth RC | .25 .60 | 288 | Bubba Crosby | .10 .30 |
| 113 | Eric Chavez | .10 .30 | 201 | Matt Belisle | .10 .30 | 289 | Josh Hamilton | .25 .60 |
| 114 | Billy Koch | .10 .30 | 202 | Miguel Villilo RC | .25 .60 | 290 | Dee Haynes RC | .15 .40 |
| 115 | Shawn Green | .10 .30 | 203 | Adam Everett | .10 .30 | 291 | Jason Marquis | .10 .30 |
| 116 | Matt Williams | .10 .30 | 204 | John Lackey | .10 .30 | 292 | Julio Zuleta | .10 .30 |
| 117 | Greg Vaughn | .10 .30 | 205 | Pasqual Coco | .10 .30 | 293 | Carlos Hernandez | .10 .30 |

|  |  | | |
|---|---|---|---|
| 294 | Matt Lecroy | .10 | .30 |
| 295 | Andy Beal RC | .15 | .40 |
| 296 | Carlos Pena | .10 | .30 |
| 297 | Reggie Taylor | .10 | .30 |
| 298 | Bob Keppel RC | .15 | .40 |
| 299 | Miguel Cabrera | .60 | 1.50 |
| 300 | Ryan Franklin | .10 | .30 |
| 301 | Brandon Phillips | .10 | .30 |
| 302 | Victor Hall RC | .25 | .60 |
| 303 | Tony Pena Jr. | .10 | .30 |
| 304 | Jim Journell RC | .25 | .60 |
| 305 | Cristian Guerrero | .10 | .30 |
| 306 | Miguel Olivo | .10 | .30 |
| 307 | Jin Ho Cho | .10 | .30 |
| 308 | Choo Freeman | .10 | .30 |
| 309 | Danny Borrell RC | .15 | .40 |
| 310 | Doug Mientkiewicz | .10 | .30 |
| 311 | Aaron Herr | .10 | .30 |
| 312 | Keith Ginter | .10 | .30 |
| 313 | Felipe Lopez | .10 | .30 |
| 314 | Jeff Goldbach | .10 | .30 |
| 315 | Travis Harper | .10 | .30 |
| 316 | Paul LoDuca | .10 | .30 |
| 317 | Joe Torres | .10 | .30 |
| 318 | Eric Byrnes | .10 | .30 |
| 319 | George Lombard | .10 | .30 |
| 320 | Dave Krynzel | .10 | .30 |
| 321 | Ben Christensen | .10 | .30 |
| 322 | Aubrey Huff | .10 | .30 |
| 323 | Lyle Overbay | .10 | .30 |
| 324 | Sean McGowan | .10 | .30 |
| 325 | Jeff Heaverlo | .10 | .30 |
| 326 | Timo Perez | .10 | .30 |
| 327 | Octavio Martinez RC | .25 | .60 |
| 328 | Vince Faison | .10 | .30 |
| 329 | David Parrish RC | .15 | .40 |
| 330 | Bobby Bradley | .10 | .30 |
| 331 | Jason Miller RC | .15 | .40 |
| 332 | Corey Spencer RC | .15 | .40 |
| 333 | Craig House | .10 | .30 |
| 334 | Maxim St. Pierre RC | .25 | .60 |
| 335 | Adam Johnson | .10 | .30 |
| 336 | Joe Crede | .30 | .75 |
| 337 | Greg Nash RC | .15 | .40 |
| 338 | Chad Durbin | .10 | .30 |
| 339 | Pat Magness RC | .25 | .60 |
| 340 | Matt Wheatland | .10 | .30 |
| 341 | Julio Lugo | .10 | .30 |
| 342 | Grady Sizemore | .60 | 1.50 |
| 343 | Adrian Gonzalez | .10 | .30 |
| 344 | Tim Raines Jr. | .10 | .30 |
| 345 | Rainier Olmedo RC | .25 | .60 |
| 346 | Phil Dumatrait | .10 | .30 |
| 347 | Brandon Mims RC | .15 | .40 |
| 348 | Jason Jennings | .10 | .30 |
| 349 | Phil Wilson RC | .25 | .60 |
| 350 | Jason Hart | .10 | .30 |
| 351 | Cesar Izturis | .10 | .30 |
| 352 | Matt Butler RC | .25 | .60 |
| 353 | David Kelton | .10 | .30 |
| 354 | Luke Prokopec | .10 | .30 |
| 355 | Corey Smith | .10 | .30 |
| 356 | Joel Pineiro | .25 | .60 |
| 357 | Ken Chenard | .10 | .30 |
| 358 | Keith Reed | .10 | .30 |
| 359 | David Walling | .10 | .30 |
| 360 | Alexis Gomez RC | .15 | .40 |
| 361 | Justin Morneau RC | 4.00 | 10.00 |
| 362 | Josh Fogg RC | .25 | .60 |
| 363 | J.R. House | .10 | .30 |
| 364 | Andy Tracy | .10 | .30 |
| 365 | Kenny Kelly | .10 | .30 |
| 366 | Aaron McNeal | .10 | .30 |
| 367 | Nick Johnson | .10 | .30 |
| 368 | Brian Esposito | .10 | .30 |
| 369 | Charles Frazier RC | .15 | .40 |
| 370 | Scott Heard | .10 | .30 |
| 371 | Pat Strange | .10 | .30 |
| 372 | Mike Meyers | .10 | .30 |
| 373 | Ryan Ludwick RC | 3.00 | 8.00 |
| 374 | Brad Wilkerson | .10 | .30 |
| 375 | Allen Levrault | .10 | .30 |
| 376 | Seth McClung RC | .25 | .60 |
| 377 | Joe Nathan | .10 | .30 |
| 378 | Rafael Soriano RC | .25 | .60 |
| 379 | Chris Richard | .10 | .30 |
| 380 | Jared Sandberg | .10 | .30 |
| 381 | Tike Redman | .10 | .30 |
| 382 | Adam Dunn | .20 | .50 |
| 383 | Jared Abruzzo RC | .15 | .40 |
| 384 | Jason Richardson RC | .15 | .40 |
| 385 | Matt Holliday | .15 | .40 |
| 386 | Darren Cubillan RC | .15 | .40 |
| 387 | Mike Nannini | .10 | .30 |
| 388 | Blake Williams RC | .15 | .40 |
| 389 | Valentino Pascucci RC | .25 | .60 |
| 390 | Jon Garland | .10 | .30 |
| 391 | Josh Pressley | .10 | .30 |
| 392 | Jose Ortiz | .10 | .30 |
| 393 | Ryan Hannaman RC | .25 | .60 |
| 394 | Steve Smyth RC | .25 | .60 |
| 395 | John Patterson | .10 | .30 |
| 396 | Chad Petty RC | .15 | .40 |
| 397 | Jake Peavy UER RC | 2.50 | 6.00 |
| 398 | Onix Mercado RC | .25 | .60 |
| 399 | Jason Romano | .10 | .30 |
| 400 | Luis Torres RC | .25 | .60 |
| 401 | Casey Fossum RC | .15 | .40 |
| 402 | Eduardo Figueroa RC | .15 | .40 |
| 403 | Bryan Barnowski RC | .15 | .40 |
| 404 | Tim Redding | .10 | .30 |
| 405 | Jason Standridge | .10 | .30 |
| 406 | Marvin Seale RC | .25 | .60 |
| 407 | Todd Moser | .10 | .30 |
| 408 | Alex Gordon | .10 | .30 |
| 409 | Steve Smitherman RC | .25 | .60 |
| 410 | Ben Petrick | .10 | .30 |
| 411 | Eric Munson | .10 | .30 |
| 412 | Luis Rivas | .10 | .30 |
| 413 | Matt Ginter | .10 | .30 |
| 414 | Alfonso Soriano | .20 | .50 |
| 415 | Rafael Boitel RC | .15 | .40 |
| 416 | Dany Morban RC | .15 | .40 |
| 417 | Justin Woodrow RC | .25 | .60 |
| 418 | Wilfredo Rodriguez | .10 | .30 |
| 419 | Derrick Van Dusen RC | .15 | .40 |
| 420 | Josh Spoerl RC | .25 | .60 |
| 421 | Juan Pierre | .10 | .30 |
| 422 | J.C. Romero | .10 | .30 |
| 423 | Ed Rogers RC | .10 | .30 |
| 424 | Tomo Ohka | .10 | .30 |
| 425 | Ben Hendrickson RC | .25 | .60 |
| 426 | Carlos Zambrano | .20 | .50 |
| 427 | Brett Myers | .10 | .30 |
| 428 | Scott Seabol | .10 | .30 |
| 429 | Thomas Mitchell | .10 | .30 |
| 430 | Jose Reyes RC | 6.00 | 15.00 |
| 431 | Kip Wells | .10 | .30 |
| 432 | Donzell McDonald | .10 | .30 |
| 433 | Adam Pettyjohn RC | .10 | .30 |
| 434 | Austin Kearns | .10 | .30 |
| 435 | Rico Washington | .10 | .30 |
| 436 | Doug Nickle RC | .10 | .30 |
| 437 | Steve Lomasney | .10 | .30 |
| 438 | Jason Jones RC | .10 | .30 |
| 439 | Bobby Seay | .10 | .30 |
| 440 | Justin Wayne RC | .25 | .60 |
| ROYR | Sasaki/Furcal ROY Jsy | 6.00 | 15.00 |
| NNO | Sean Burroughs Ball/80 | 6.00 | 15.00 |

## 2001 Bowman Draft

| | | | |
|---|---|---|---|
| COMP.FACT.SET (112) | | 30.00 | 60.00 |
| COMPLETE SET (110) | | 20.00 | 50.00 |
| BDP1 | Alfredo Amezaga RC | .10 | .30 |
| BDP2 | Andrew Good | .10 | .30 |
| BDP3 | Kelly Johnson RC | 1.25 | 3.00 |
| BDP4 | Larry Bigbie | .10 | .30 |
| BDP5 | Matt Thompson RC | .15 | .40 |
| BDP6 | Wilton Chavez RC | .15 | .40 |
| BDP7 | Joe Borchard RC | .15 | .40 |
| BDP8 | David Espinosa | .10 | .30 |
| BDP9 | Zach Day RC | .15 | .40 |
| BDP10 | Brad Hawpe RC | 1.00 | 2.50 |
| BDP11 | Nate Cornejo | .10 | .30 |
| BDP12 | Matt Cooper RC | .15 | .40 |
| BDP13 | Brad Lidge | .10 | .30 |
| BDP14 | Angel Berroa RC | .25 | .60 |
| BDP15 | Lamont Matthews RC | .15 | .40 |
| BDP16 | Jose Garcia | .10 | .30 |
| BDP17 | Grant Balfour RC | .10 | .30 |
| BDP18 | Ron Chiavacci RC | .10 | .30 |
| BDP19 | Jae Seo | .10 | .30 |
| BDP20 | Juan Rivera | .10 | .30 |
| BDP21 | D'Angelo Jimenez | .10 | .30 |
| BDP22 | Juan A.Pena RC | .15 | .40 |
| BDP23 | Marlon Byrd RC | .15 | .40 |
| BDP24 | Sean Burnett | .10 | .30 |
| BDP25 | Josh Pearce RC | .15 | .40 |
| BDP26 | Brandon Duckworth RC | .10 | .30 |
| BDP27 | Jack Taschner RC | .10 | .30 |
| BDP28 | Marcus Thames | .10 | .30 |
| BDP29 | Brent Abernathy | .10 | .30 |
| BDP30 | David Elder RC | .10 | .30 |
| BDP31 | Scott Cassidy RC | .15 | .40 |
| BDP32 | Dennis Tankersley RC | .15 | .40 |
| BDP33 | Denny Stark | .10 | .30 |
| BDP34 | Dave Williams RC | .10 | .30 |
| BDP35 | Boof Bonser RC | .10 | .30 |
| BDP36 | Kris Foster RC | .10 | .30 |
| BDP37 | Luis Garcia RC | .15 | .40 |
| BDP38 | Shawn Chacon | .10 | .30 |
| BDP39 | Mike Rivera RC | .15 | .40 |
| BDP40 | Will Smith RC | .15 | .40 |
| BDP41 | Morgan Ensberg RC | .75 | 2.00 |
| BDP42 | Ken Harvey | .10 | .30 |
| BDP43 | Ricardo Rodriguez RC | .15 | .40 |
| BDP44 | Jose Mieses RC | .15 | .40 |
| BDP45 | Luis Maza RC | .10 | .30 |
| BDP46 | Julio Perez RC | .15 | .40 |
| BDP47 | Dustan Mohr RC | .15 | .40 |
| BDP48 | Randy Flores RC | .10 | .30 |
| BDP49 | Covelli Crisp RC | 2.00 | 5.00 |
| BDP50 | Kevin Reese RC | .15 | .40 |
| BDP51 | Brad Thomas UER | .10 | .30 |
| BDP52 | Xavier Nady | .10 | .30 |
| BDP53 | Ryan Vogelsong | .10 | .30 |
| BDP54 | Carlos Silva | .10 | .30 |
| BDP55 | Dan Wright | .10 | .30 |
| BDP56 | Brent Butler | .10 | .30 |
| BDP57 | Brandon Knight RC | .10 | .30 |
| BDP58 | Brian Reith RC | .10 | .30 |
| BDP59 | Mario Valenzuela RC | .15 | .40 |
| BDP60 | Bobby Hill RC | .15 | .40 |
| BDP61 | Rich Rundles RC | .15 | .40 |
| BDP62 | Rick Elder | .10 | .30 |
| BDP63 | J.D. Closser | .10 | .30 |
| BDP64 | Scot Shields | .10 | .30 |
| BDP65 | Miguel Olivo | .10 | .30 |
| BDP66 | Stubby Clapp RC | .10 | .30 |
| BDP67 | Jerome Williams RC | .25 | .60 |
| BDP68 | Jason Lane RC | .25 | .60 |
| BDP69 | Chase Utley RC | 10.00 | 25.00 |
| BDP70 | Erik Bedard RC | 2.00 | 5.00 |
| BDP71 | Alex Herrera UER RC | .10 | .30 |
| BDP72 | Juan Cruz RC | .15 | .40 |
| BDP73 | Billy Martin RC | .10 | .30 |
| BDP74 | Ronnie Merrill RC | .15 | .40 |
| BDP75 | Jason Kinchen RC | .10 | .30 |
| BDP76 | Wilkin Ruan RC | .15 | .40 |
| BDP77 | Cody Ransom RC | .10 | .30 |
| BDP78 | Buds Smith RC | .10 | .30 |
| BDP79 | Wily Mo Pena | .10 | .30 |
| BDP80 | Jeff Nettles RC | .15 | .40 |
| BDP81 | Jamal Strong RC | .15 | .40 |
| BDP82 | Bill Ortega RC | .10 | .30 |
| BDP83 | Mike Bell | .10 | .30 |
| BDP84 | Ichiro Suzuki RC | 4.00 | 10.00 |
| BDP85 | Fernando Rodney RC | .10 | .30 |
| BDP86 | Chris Smith RC | .10 | .30 |
| BDP87 | John VanBenscholen RC | .15 | .40 |
| BDP88 | Bobby Crosby RC | 1.50 | 4.00 |
| BDP89 | Kenny Baugh RC | .10 | .30 |
| BDP90 | Jake Gautreau RC | .10 | .30 |
| BDP91 | Gabe Gross RC | .25 | .60 |
| BDP92 | Kris Honel RC | .10 | .30 |
| BDP93 | Dan Denham RC | .10 | .30 |
| BDP94 | Aaron Heilman RC | .15 | .40 |
| BDP95 | Irvin Guzman RC | 1.50 | 4.00 |
| BDP96 | Mike Jones RC | .25 | .60 |
| BDP97 | John-Ford Griffin RC | .15 | .40 |

|  |  | | |
|---|---|---|---|
| □ BDP98 Macay McBride RC | .40 | 1.00 |
| □ BDP99 John Rheinecker RC | .40 | 1.00 |
| □ BDP100 Bronson Sardinha RC | .10 | .30 |
| □ BDP101 Jason Weintraub RC | .10 | .30 |
| □ BDP102 J.D. Martin RC | .10 | .30 |
| □ BDP103 Jayson Nix RC | .15 | .40 |
| □ BDP104 Noah Lowry RC | 1.00 | 2.50 |
| □ BDP105 Richard Lewis RC | .15 | .40 |
| □ BDP106 Brad Hennessey RC | .25 | .60 |
| □ BDP107 Jeff Mathis RC | .25 | .60 |
| □ BDP108 Jon Skaggs RC | .15 | .40 |
| □ BDP109 Justin Pope RC | .15 | .40 |
| □ BDP110 Josh Burrus RC | .15 | .40 |

## 2002 Bowman

| | | | |
|---|---|---|---|
| □ COMPLETE SET (440) | 40.00 | 80.00 |
| □ COMMON CARD (1-110) | .10 | .30 |
| □ COMMON CARD (111-440) | .10 | .30 |
| □ 1 Adam Dunn | .10 | .30 |
| □ 2 Derek Jeter | .75 | 2.00 |
| □ 3 Alex Rodriguez | .50 | 1.25 |
| □ 4 Miguel Tejada | .10 | .30 |
| □ 5 Nomar Garciaparra | .50 | 1.25 |
| □ 6 Toby Hall | .10 | .30 |
| □ 7 Brandon Duckworth | .10 | .30 |
| □ 8 Paul LoDuca | .10 | .30 |
| □ 9 Brian Giles | .10 | .30 |
| □ 10 C.C. Sabathia | .10 | .30 |
| □ 11 Curt Schilling | .10 | .30 |
| □ 12 Tsuyoshi Shinjo | .10 | .30 |
| □ 13 Ramon Hernandez | .10 | .30 |
| □ 14 Jose Cruz Jr. | .10 | .30 |
| □ 15 Albert Pujols | .60 | 1.50 |
| □ 16 Joe Mays | .10 | .30 |
| □ 17 Javy Lopez | .10 | .30 |
| □ 18 J.T. Snow | .10 | .30 |
| □ 19 David Segui | .10 | .30 |
| □ 20 Jorge Posada | .20 | .50 |
| □ 21 Doug Mientkiewicz | .10 | .30 |
| □ 22 Jerry Hairston Jr. | .10 | .30 |
| □ 23 Bernie Williams | .20 | .50 |
| □ 24 Mike Sweeney | .10 | .30 |
| □ 25 Jason Giambi | .10 | .30 |
| □ 26 Ryan Dempster | .10 | .30 |
| □ 27 Ryan Klesko | .10 | .30 |
| □ 28 Mark Quinn | .10 | .30 |
| □ 29 Jeff Kent | .10 | .30 |
| □ 30 Eric Chavez | .10 | .30 |
| □ 31 Adrian Beltre | .10 | .30 |
| □ 32 Andruw Jones | .20 | .50 |
| □ 33 Alfonso Soriano | .10 | .30 |
| □ 34 Aramis Ramirez | .10 | .30 |
| □ 35 Greg Maddux | .50 | 1.25 |
| □ 36 Andy Pettitte | .20 | .50 |
| □ 37 Bartolo Colon | .10 | .30 |
| □ 38 Ben Sheets | .10 | .30 |
| □ 39 Bobby Higginson | .10 | .30 |
| □ 40 Ivan Rodriguez | .20 | .50 |
| □ 41 Brad Penny | .10 | .30 |
| □ 42 Carlos Lee | .10 | .30 |
| □ 43 Damion Easley | .10 | .30 |
| □ 44 Preston Wilson | .10 | .30 |
| □ 45 Jeff Bagwell | .20 | .50 |
| □ 46 Eric Milton | .10 | .30 |
| □ 47 Rafael Palmeiro | .10 | .30 |
| □ 48 Gary Sheffield | .10 | .30 |
| □ 49 J.D. Drew | .10 | .30 |
| □ 50 Jim Thome | .20 | .50 |
| □ 51 Ichiro Suzuki | .60 | 1.50 |
| □ 52 Bud Smith | .10 | .30 |
| □ 53 Chan Ho Park | .10 | .30 |
| □ 54 D'Angelo Jimenez | .10 | .30 |
| □ 55 Ken Griffey Jr. | .50 | 1.25 |
| □ 56 Wade Miller | .10 | .30 |
| □ 57 Vladimir Guerrero | .30 | .75 |
| □ 58 Troy Glaus | .10 | .30 |
| □ 59 Shawn Green | .10 | .30 |
| □ 60 Kerry Wood | .10 | .30 |
| □ 61 Jack Wilson | .10 | .30 |
| □ 62 Kevin Brown | .10 | .30 |
| □ 63 Marcus Giles | .10 | .30 |
| □ 64 Pat Burrell | .10 | .30 |
| □ 65 Larry Walker | .10 | .30 |
| □ 66 Sammy Sosa | .30 | .75 |
| □ 67 Raul Mondesi | .10 | .30 |
| □ 68 Tim Hudson | .10 | .30 |
| □ 69 Lance Berkman | .10 | .30 |
| □ 70 Mike Mussina | .20 | .50 |
| □ 71 Barry Zito | .10 | .30 |
| □ 72 Jimmy Rollins | .10 | .30 |
| □ 73 Barry Bonds | .75 | 2.00 |
| □ 74 Craig Biggio | .20 | .50 |
| □ 75 Todd Helton | .20 | .50 |
| □ 76 Roger Clemens | .60 | 1.50 |
| □ 77 Frank Catalanotto | .10 | .30 |
| □ 78 Josh Towers | .10 | .30 |
| □ 79 Roy Oswalt | .10 | .30 |
| □ 80 Chipper Jones | .30 | .75 |
| □ 81 Cristian Guzman | .10 | .30 |
| □ 82 Darin Erstad | .10 | .30 |
| □ 83 Freddy Garcia | .10 | .30 |
| □ 84 Jason Tyner | .10 | .30 |
| □ 85 Carlos Delgado | .10 | .30 |
| □ 86 Jon Lieber | .10 | .30 |
| □ 87 Juan Pierre | .10 | .30 |
| □ 88 Matt Morris | .10 | .30 |
| □ 89 Phil Nevin | .10 | .30 |
| □ 90 Jim Edmonds | .20 | .50 |
| □ 91 Magglio Ordonez | .10 | .30 |
| □ 92 Mike Hampton | .10 | .30 |
| □ 93 Rafael Furcal | .10 | .30 |
| □ 94 Richie Sexson | .10 | .30 |
| □ 95 Luis Gonzalez | .10 | .30 |
| □ 96 Scott Rolen | .20 | .50 |
| □ 97 Tim Redding | .10 | .30 |
| □ 98 Moises Alou | .10 | .30 |
| □ 99 Jose Vidro | .10 | .30 |
| □ 100 Mike Piazza | .50 | 1.25 |
| □ 101 Pedro Martinez | .30 | .75 |
| □ 102 Geoff Jenkins | .10 | .30 |
| □ 103 Johnny Damon Sox | .20 | .50 |
| □ 104 Mike Cameron | .10 | .30 |
| □ 105 Randy Johnson | .30 | .75 |
| □ 106 David Eckstein | .10 | .30 |
| □ 107 Javier Vazquez | .10 | .30 |
| □ 108 Mark Mulder | .10 | .30 |
| □ 109 Robert Fick | .10 | .30 |
| □ 110 Roberto Alomar | .20 | .50 |
| □ 111 Wilson Betemit | .10 | .30 |
| □ 112 Chris Tritle RC | .10 | .30 |
| □ 113 Ed Rogers | .10 | .30 |
| □ 114 Juan Pena | .10 | .30 |
| □ 115 Josh Beckett | .15 | .40 |
| □ 116 Juan Cruz | .10 | .30 |
| □ 117 Noochie Varner RC | .15 | .40 |
| □ 118 Taylor Buchholz RC | .25 | .60 |
| □ 119 Mike Rivera | .10 | .30 |
| □ 120 Hank Blalock | .25 | .60 |
| □ 121 Hansel Izquierdo RC | .15 | .40 |
| □ 122 Orlando Hudson | .15 | .40 |
| □ 123 Bill Hall | .15 | .40 |
| □ 124 Jose Reyes | .25 | .60 |
| □ 125 Juan Rivera | .10 | .30 |
| □ 126 Eric Valent | .10 | .30 |
| □ 127 Scotty Layfield RC | .15 | .40 |
| □ 128 Austin Kearns | .15 | .40 |
| □ 129 Nic Jackson RC | .15 | .40 |
| □ 130 Chris Baker RC | .15 | .40 |
| □ 131 Chad Qualls RC | .20 | .50 |
| □ 132 Marcus Thames | .10 | .30 |
| □ 133 Nathan Haynes | .10 | .30 |
| □ 134 Brett Evert | .10 | .30 |
| □ 135 Joe Borchard | .10 | .30 |
| □ 136 Ryan Christianson | .10 | .30 |
| □ 137 Josh Hamilton | .25 | .60 |
| □ 138 Corey Patterson | .10 | .30 |
| □ 139 Travis Wilson | .10 | .30 |
| □ 140 Alex Escobar | .10 | .30 |
| □ 141 Alexis Gomez | .10 | .30 |
| □ 142 Nick Johnson | .15 | .40 |
| □ 143 Kenny Kelly | .10 | .30 |
| □ 144 Marlon Byrd | .10 | .30 |
| □ 145 Kory DeHaan | .10 | .30 |
| □ 146 Matt Belisle | .10 | .30 |
| □ 147 Carlos Hernandez | .10 | .30 |
| □ 148 Sean Burroughs | .10 | .30 |
| □ 149 Angel Berroa | .10 | .30 |
| □ 150 Aubrey Huff | .15 | .40 |
| □ 151 Travis Hafner | .15 | .40 |
| □ 152 Brandon Berger | .10 | .30 |
| □ 153 David Krynzel | .10 | .30 |
| □ 154 Ruben Salazar | .10 | .30 |
| □ 155 J.R. House | .10 | .30 |
| □ 156 Juan Silvestre | .10 | .30 |
| □ 157 Dewon Brazelton | .10 | .30 |
| □ 158 Jayson Werth | .10 | .30 |
| □ 159 Larry Barnes | .10 | .30 |
| □ 160 Elvis Pena | .10 | .30 |
| □ 161 Ruben Gotay RC | .20 | .50 |
| □ 162 Tommy Marx RC | .15 | .40 |
| □ 163 John Suomi RC | .15 | .40 |
| □ 164 Javier Colina | .10 | .30 |
| □ 165 Greg Sain RC | .15 | .40 |
| □ 166 Robert Cosby RC | .15 | .40 |
| □ 167 Angel Pagan RC | .20 | .50 |
| □ 168 Ralph Santana RC | .15 | .40 |
| □ 169 Joe Orloski RC | .15 | .40 |
| □ 170 Shayne Wright RC | .15 | .40 |
| □ 171 Jay Caligiuri RC | .15 | .40 |
| □ 172 Greg Montalbano RC | .15 | .40 |
| □ 173 Rich Harden RC | 1.25 | 3.00 |
| □ 174 Rich Thompson RC | .15 | .40 |
| □ 175 Fred Bastardo RC | .15 | .40 |
| □ 176 Alejandro Giron RC | .15 | .40 |
| □ 177 Jesus Medrano RC | .15 | .40 |
| □ 178 Kevin Deaton RC | .15 | .40 |
| □ 179 Mike Rosamond RC | .15 | .40 |
| □ 180 Jon Guzman RC | .15 | .40 |
| □ 181 Gerard Oakes RC | .15 | .40 |
| □ 182 Francisco Cirianno RC | 3.00 | 8.00 |
| □ 183 Matt Allegra RC | .15 | .40 |
| □ 184 Mike Snyder RC | .15 | .40 |
| □ 185 James Shanks RC | .15 | .40 |
| □ 186 Anderson Hernandez RC | .15 | .40 |
| □ 187 Dan Trumble RC | .15 | .40 |
| □ 188 Luis DePaula RC | .15 | .40 |
| □ 189 Randall Shelley RC | .15 | .40 |
| □ 190 Richard Lane RC | .15 | .40 |
| □ 191 Antwon Rollins RC | .15 | .40 |
| □ 192 Ryan Bukvich RC | .15 | .40 |
| □ 193 Derrick Lewis | .10 | .30 |
| □ 194 Eric Miller RC | .15 | .40 |
| □ 195 Justin Schuda RC | .15 | .40 |
| □ 196 Brian West RC | .10 | .30 |
| □ 197 Adam Roller RC | .15 | .40 |
| □ 198 Neal Frendling RC | .15 | .40 |
| □ 199 Jeremy Hill RC | .15 | .40 |
| □ 200 James Barrett RC | .15 | .40 |
| □ 201 Brett Kay RC | .15 | .40 |
| □ 202 Ryan Mottl RC | .15 | .40 |
| □ 203 Brad Nelson RC | .15 | .40 |
| □ 204 Juan M. Gonzalez RC | .15 | .40 |
| □ 205 Curtis Legendre RC | .15 | .40 |
| □ 206 Ronald Acuna RC | .15 | .40 |
| □ 207 Chris Flinn RC | .15 | .40 |
| □ 208 Nick Alvarez RC | .15 | .40 |
| □ 209 Jason Ellison RC | .30 | .75 |
| □ 210 Blake McGinley RC | .15 | .40 |
| □ 211 Dan Phillips RC | .15 | .40 |
| □ 212 Demetrius Heath RC | .15 | .40 |
| □ 213 Eric Brundlett RC | .15 | .40 |
| □ 214 Joe Jannetti RC | .15 | .40 |
| □ 215 Mike Hill RC | .15 | .40 |
| □ 216 Ricardo Cordova RC | .15 | .40 |
| □ 217 Mark Hamilton RC | .15 | .40 |
| □ 218 David Matlox RC | .15 | .40 |
| □ 219 Jose Morban RC | .15 | .40 |
| □ 220 Scott Wiggins RC | .10 | .30 |
| □ 221 Steve Green | .10 | .30 |
| □ 222 Brian Rogers | .10 | .30 |
| □ 223 Chin-Hui Tsao | .15 | .40 |
| □ 224 Kenny Baugh | .10 | .30 |
| □ 225 Nate Teut | .10 | .30 |
| □ 226 Josh Wilson RC | .15 | .40 |
| □ 227 Christian Parker | .10 | .30 |
| □ 228 Tim Raines Jr. | .10 | .30 |
| □ 229 Anastacio Martinez RC | .15 | .40 |
| □ 230 Richard Lewis | .10 | .30 |
| □ 231 Tim Kalita RC | .15 | .40 |
| □ 232 Edwin Almonte | .15 | .40 |

|  |  | | |
|---|--------|---|---|
| 233 | Hee-Seop Choi | .10 | .30 |
| 234 | Ty Howington | .10 | .30 |
| 235 | Victor Alvarez RC | .15 | .40 |
| 236 | Morgan Ensberg | .15 | .40 |
| 237 | Jeff Austin RC | .15 | .40 |
| 238 | Luis Terrero | .10 | .30 |
| 239 | Adam Wainwright | .20 | .50 |
| 240 | Clint Weibl RC | .10 | .30 |
| 241 | Eric Cyr | .10 | .30 |
| 242 | Marlyn Tisdale RC | .15 | .40 |
| 243 | John VanBenschoten | .10 | .30 |
| 244 | Ryan Raburn RC | .15 | .40 |
| 245 | Miguel Cabrera | .60 | 1.50 |
| 246 | Jung Bong | .10 | .30 |
| 247 | Raul Chavez RC | .10 | .30 |
| 248 | Erik Bedard | .15 | .40 |
| 249 | Chris Snelling RC | .25 | .60 |
| 250 | Joe Rogers RC | .15 | .40 |
| 251 | Nate Field RC | .15 | .40 |
| 252 | Matt Herges RC | .10 | .30 |
| 253 | Matt Childers RC | .15 | .40 |
| 254 | Erick Almonte | .10 | .30 |
| 255 | Nick Neugebauer | .10 | .30 |
| 256 | Ron Calloway RC | .15 | .40 |
| 257 | Seung Song | .10 | .30 |
| 258 | Brandon Phillips | .15 | .40 |
| 259 | Cole Barthel RC | .10 | .30 |
| 260 | Jason Lane | .15 | .40 |
| 261 | Jae Seo | .10 | .30 |
| 262 | Randy Flores | .10 | .30 |
| 263 | Scott Chiasson | .10 | .30 |
| 264 | Chase Utley | 1.00 | 2.50 |
| 265 | Tony Alvarez | .10 | .30 |
| 266 | Ben Howard RC | .15 | .40 |
| 267 | Nelson Castro RC | .15 | .40 |
| 268 | Mark Lukasiewicz | .10 | .30 |
| 269 | Eric Glaser RC | .15 | .40 |
| 270 | Rob Henkel RC | .15 | .40 |
| 271 | Jose Valverde RC | .15 | .40 |
| 272 | Ricardo Rodriguez | .10 | .30 |
| 273 | Chris Smith | .10 | .30 |
| 274 | Mark Prior | .25 | .60 |
| 275 | Miguel Olivo | .10 | .30 |
| 276 | Ben Broussard | .10 | .30 |
| 277 | Zach Sorensen | .10 | .30 |
| 278 | Brian Mallette RC | .10 | .30 |
| 279 | Brad Wilkerson | .10 | .30 |
| 280 | Carl Crawford | .15 | .40 |
| 281 | Choe Figgins RC | .60 | 1.50 |
| 282 | Jimmy Alvarez RC | .15 | .40 |
| 283 | Gavin Floyd RC | .40 | 1.00 |
| 284 | Josh Bonifay RC | .15 | .40 |
| 285 | Garrett Guzman RC | .15 | .40 |
| 286 | Blake Williams | .10 | .30 |
| 287 | Matt Holliday | .10 | .30 |
| 288 | Ryan Madson | .10 | .30 |
| 289 | Luis Torres | .10 | .30 |
| 290 | Jeff Verplancke RC | .15 | .40 |
| 291 | Nate Espy RC | .15 | .40 |
| 292 | Jeff Lincoln RC | .10 | .30 |
| 293 | Ryan Snare RC | .15 | .40 |
| 294 | Jose Ortiz | .10 | .30 |
| 295 | Eric Munson | .10 | .30 |
| 296 | Denny Bautista | .10 | .30 |
| 297 | Willy Aybar | .15 | .40 |
| 298 | Kelly Johnson | .25 | .60 |
| 299 | Justin Morneau | .40 | 1.00 |
| 300 | Derrick Van Dusen | .10 | .30 |
| 301 | Chad Petty | .10 | .30 |
| 302 | Mike Restovich | .10 | .30 |
| 303 | Shawn Fagan | .10 | .30 |
| 304 | Yurendell DeCaster RC | .15 | .40 |
| 305 | Justin Wayne | .10 | .30 |
| 306 | Mike Peeples RC | .10 | .30 |
| 307 | Joel Guzman | .40 | 1.00 |
| 308 | Ryan Vogelsong | .10 | .30 |
| 309 | Jorge Padilla RC | .15 | .40 |
| 310 | Grady Sizemore | .40 | 1.00 |
| 311 | Joe Jester RC | .15 | .40 |
| 312 | Jim Journell | .10 | .30 |
| 313 | Bobby Seay | .10 | .30 |
| 314 | Ryan Church RC | .40 | 1.00 |
| 315 | Grant Balfour | .10 | .30 |
| 316 | Mitch Jones | .10 | .30 |
| 317 | Travis Foley RC | .15 | .40 |
| 318 | Bobby Crosby | .40 | 1.00 |
| 319 | Adrian Gonzalez | .10 | .30 |
| 320 | Ronnie Merrill | .10 | .30 |
| 321 | Joel Pineiro | .10 | .30 |
| 322 | John-Ford Griffin | .10 | .30 |
| 323 | Brian Forystek RC | .15 | .40 |
| 324 | Sean Douglass | .10 | .30 |
| 325 | Manny Delcarmen RC | .20 | .50 |
| 326 | Donnie Bridges | .10 | .30 |
| 327 | Jim Kavourias RC | .15 | .40 |
| 328 | Gabe Gross | .10 | .30 |
| 329 | Jon Rauch | .10 | .30 |
| 330 | Bill Ortega | .10 | .30 |
| 331 | Joey Hammond RC | .15 | .40 |
| 332 | Ramon Moreta RC | .15 | .40 |
| 333 | Ron Davenport | .10 | .30 |
| 334 | Brett Myers | .15 | .40 |
| 335 | Carlos Pena | .15 | .40 |
| 336 | Ezequiel Astacio RC | .15 | .40 |
| 337 | Edwin Yan RC | .15 | .40 |
| 338 | Josh Girdley | .10 | .30 |
| 339 | Shaun Boyd | .10 | .30 |
| 340 | Juan Rincon | .10 | .30 |
| 341 | Chris Duffy RC | .20 | .50 |
| 342 | Jason Kinchen | .10 | .30 |
| 343 | Brad Thomas | .10 | .30 |
| 344 | David Kelton | .10 | .30 |
| 345 | Rafael Soriano | .10 | .30 |
| 346 | Colin Young RC | .15 | .40 |
| 347 | Eric Byrnes | .15 | .40 |
| 348 | Chris Narveson RC | .20 | .50 |
| 349 | John Rheinecker | .10 | .30 |
| 350 | Mike Wilson RC | .15 | .40 |
| 351 | Justin Sherrod RC | .15 | .40 |
| 352 | Beni Mendez | .10 | .30 |
| 353 | Wily Mo Pena | .15 | .40 |
| 354 | Brett Roneberg RC | .15 | .40 |
| 355 | Trey Lunsford RC | .15 | .40 |
| 356 | Jimmy Gobble RC | .15 | .40 |
| 357 | Brent Butler | .10 | .30 |
| 358 | Aaron Heilman | .10 | .30 |
| 359 | Wilkin Ruan | .10 | .30 |
| 360 | Brian Wolfe RC | .10 | .30 |
| 361 | Cody Ransom | .10 | .30 |
| 362 | Koyie Hill | .10 | .30 |
| 363 | Scott Cassidy | .10 | .30 |
| 364 | Tony Fontana RC | .15 | .40 |
| 365 | Mark Teixeira | .60 | 1.50 |
| 366 | Doug Sessions RC | .15 | .40 |
| 367 | Victor Hall | .10 | .30 |
| 368 | Josh Cisneros RC | .15 | .40 |
| 369 | Kevin Mench | .10 | .30 |
| 370 | Tike Redman | .10 | .30 |
| 371 | Jeff Heaverlo | .10 | .30 |
| 372 | Carlos Brackley RC | .15 | .40 |
| 373 | Brad Harvey | .10 | .30 |
| 374 | Jesus Colome | .10 | .30 |
| 375 | David Espinosa | .10 | .30 |
| 376 | Jesse Foppert RC | .20 | .50 |
| 377 | Ross Peeples RC | .15 | .40 |
| 378 | Alex Requena RC | .15 | .40 |
| 379 | Joe Mauer RC | 5.00 | 12.00 |
| 380 | Carlos Silva | .10 | .30 |
| 381 | David Wright RC | 6.00 | 15.00 |
| 382 | Craig Kuzmic RC | .15 | .40 |
| 383 | Pete Zamora RC | .15 | .40 |
| 384 | Matt Parker RC | .15 | .40 |
| 385 | Keith Ginter | .10 | .30 |
| 386 | Gary Cates Jr. RC | .15 | .40 |
| 387 | Justin Reid RC | .15 | .40 |
| 388 | Jake Mauer RC | .15 | .40 |
| 389 | Dennis Tankersley | .10 | .30 |
| 390 | Josh Barfield RC | 1.00 | 2.50 |
| 391 | Luis Maza | .10 | .30 |
| 392 | Henry Pichardo RC | .15 | .40 |
| 393 | Michael Floyd RC | .15 | .40 |
| 394 | Clint Nageotte RC | .20 | .50 |
| 395 | Raymond Cabrera RC | .15 | .40 |
| 396 | Mauricio Lara RC | .15 | .40 |
| 397 | Alejandro Cadena RC | .15 | .40 |
| 398 | Jonny Gomes RC | 1.00 | 2.50 |
| 399 | Jason Bulger RC | .15 | .40 |
| 400 | Bobby Jenks RC | .60 | 1.50 |
| 401 | David Gil RC | .15 | .40 |
| 402 | Joel Crump RC | .15 | .40 |
| 403 | Kazuhisa Ishii RC | .30 | .75 |
| 404 | So Taguchi RC | .30 | .75 |
| 405 | Ryan Doumit RC | .25 | .60 |
| 406 | Macay McBride | .10 | .30 |
| 407 | Brandon Claussen | .10 | .30 |
| 408 | Chin-Feng Chen | .15 | .40 |
| 409 | Josh Phelps | .10 | .30 |
| 410 | Freddie Money RC | .20 | .50 |
| 411 | Cliff Bartosh RC | .15 | .40 |
| 412 | Josh Pearce | .10 | .30 |
| 413 | Lyle Overbay | .10 | .30 |
| 414 | Ryan Anderson | .10 | .30 |
| 415 | Terrance Hill RC | .15 | .40 |
| 416 | John Rodriguez RC | .20 | .50 |
| 417 | Richard Stahl | .10 | .30 |
| 418 | Brian Specht | .10 | .30 |
| 419 | Chris Latham RC | .10 | .30 |
| 420 | Carlos Cabrera RC | .15 | .40 |
| 421 | Jose Bautista RC | .40 | 1.00 |
| 422 | Kevin Frederick RC | .15 | .40 |
| 423 | Jerome Williams | .10 | .30 |
| 424 | Napoleon Calzado RC | .15 | .40 |
| 425 | Benito Baez | .10 | .30 |
| 426 | Xavier Nady | .15 | .40 |
| 427 | Jason Botts RC | .25 | .60 |
| 428 | Steve Bechler RC | .15 | .40 |
| 429 | Reed Johnson RC | .40 | 1.00 |
| 430 | Mark Outlaw RC | .15 | .40 |
| 431 | Billy Sylvester | .10 | .30 |
| 432 | Luke Lockwood | .10 | .30 |
| 433 | Jake Peavy | .25 | .60 |
| 434 | Alfredo Amezaga | .10 | .30 |
| 435 | Aaron Cook RC | .15 | .40 |
| 436 | Josh Shaffer RC | .15 | .40 |
| 437 | Dan Wright | .10 | .30 |
| 438 | Ryan Gripp RC | .15 | .40 |
| 439 | Alex Herrera | .10 | .30 |
| 440 | Jason Bay RC | 2.00 | 5.00 |

## 2002 Bowman Draft

| | | | |
|---|---|---|---|
| COMPLETE SET (165) | | 25.00 | 50.00 |
| BDP1 | Clint Everts RC | .20 | .50 |
| BDP2 | Fred Lewis RC | .15 | .40 |
| BDP3 | Jon Broxton RC | .40 | 1.00 |
| BDP4 | Jason Anderson RC | .15 | .40 |
| BDP5 | Mike Eusebio RC | .15 | .40 |
| BDP6 | Zack Greinke RC | 3.00 | 8.00 |
| BDP7 | Joe Blanton RC | .75 | 2.00 |
| BDP8 | Sergio Santos RC | .20 | .50 |
| BDP9 | Carlos Quentin RC | .15 | .40 |
| BDP10 | Delwyn Young RC | .40 | 1.00 |
| BDP11 | Jeremy Hermida RC | 2.00 | 5.00 |
| BDP12 | Dan Ortmeier RC | .20 | .50 |
| BDP13 | Kevin Jepsen RC | .20 | .50 |
| BDP14 | Russ Adams RC | .20 | .50 |
| BDP15 | Mike Nixon RC | .15 | .40 |
| BDP16 | Nick Swisher RC | 2.00 | 5.00 |
| BDP17 | Cole Hamels RC | 5.00 | 12.00 |
| BDP18 | Brian Dopirak RC | .40 | 1.00 |
| BDP19 | James Loney RC | 2.50 | 6.00 |
| BDP20 | Denard Span RC | .75 | 2.00 |
| BDP21 | Billy Petrick RC | .15 | .40 |
| BDP22 | Jared Doyle RC | .15 | .40 |
| BDP23 | Jeff Francoeur RC | 6.00 | 15.00 |
| BDP24 | Nick Bourgeois RC | .15 | .40 |
| BDP25 | Matt Cain RC | 2.50 | 6.00 |
| BDP26 | John McCurdy RC | .15 | .40 |
| BDP27 | Mark Kiger RC | .15 | .40 |
| BDP28 | Bill Murphy RC | .15 | .40 |
| BDP29 | Matt Craig RC | .20 | .50 |
| BDP30 | Mike Megrew RC | .15 | .40 |
| BDP31 | Ben Crockett RC | .15 | .40 |
| BDP32 | Luke Hagerty RC | .15 | .40 |
| BDP33 | Matt Whitney RC | .15 | .40 |
| BDP34 | Dan Meyer RC | .20 | .50 |
| BDP35 | Jeremy Brown RC | .15 | .40 |
| BDP36 | Doug Johnson RC | .15 | .40 |
| BDP37 | Steve Obenchain RC | .15 | .40 |
| BDP38 | Matt Clanton RC | .15 | .40 |
| BDP39 | Mark Teahen RC | .40 | 1.00 |

|  | | |
|---|---|---|
| BDP40 Tom Carrow RC | .15 | .40 |
| BDP41 Micah Schilling RC | .15 | .40 |
| BDP42 Blair Johnson RC | .15 | .40 |
| BDP43 Jason Pridie RC | .15 | .40 |
| BDP44 Joey Votto RC | 1.25 | 3.00 |
| BDP45 Taber Lee RC | .15 | .40 |
| BDP46 Adam Peterson RC | .15 | .40 |
| BDP47 Adam Donachie RC | .15 | .40 |
| BDP48 Josh Murray RC | .15 | .40 |
| BDP49 Brent Clevlen RC | .75 | 2.00 |
| BDP50 Chad Pleiness RC | .15 | .40 |
| BDP51 Zach Hammes RC | .15 | .40 |
| BDP52 Chris Snyder RC | .20 | .50 |
| BDP53 Chris Smith RC | .15 | .40 |
| BDP54 Justin Maureau RC | .15 | .40 |
| BDP55 David Bush RC | .40 | 1.00 |
| BDP56 Tim Gilhooly RC | .15 | .40 |
| BDP57 Blair Barbier RC | .15 | .40 |
| BDP58 Zach Segovia RC | .15 | .40 |
| BDP59 Jeremy Reed RC | .40 | 1.00 |
| BDP60 Matt Pender RC | .15 | .40 |
| BDP61 Eric Thomas RC | .15 | .40 |
| BDP62 Justin Jones RC | .20 | .50 |
| BDP63 Brian Slocum RC | .15 | .40 |
| BDP64 Larry Broadway RC | .15 | .40 |
| BDP65 Bo Flowers RC | .15 | .40 |
| BDP66 Scott White RC | .15 | .40 |
| BDP67 Steve Stanley RC | .15 | .40 |
| BDP68 Alex Merricks RC | .15 | .40 |
| BDP69 Josh Womack RC | .15 | .40 |
| BDP70 Dave Jensen RC | .15 | .40 |
| BDP71 Curtis Granderson RC | 2.00 | 5.00 |
| BDP72 Pat Osborn RC | .15 | .40 |
| BDP73 Nic Carter RC | .15 | .40 |
| BDP74 Mitch Talbot RC | .15 | .40 |
| BDP75 Don Murphy RC | .15 | .40 |
| BDP76 Val Majewski RC | .15 | .40 |
| BDP77 Javy Rodriguez RC | .15 | .40 |
| BDP78 Fernando Pacheco RC | .15 | .40 |
| BDP79 Steve Russell RC | .15 | .40 |
| BDP80 Jon Slack RC | .15 | .40 |
| BDP81 John Baker RC | .15 | .40 |
| BDP82 Aaron Coonrod RC | .15 | .40 |
| BDP83 Josh Johnson RC | 2.00 | 5.00 |
| BDP84 Jake Blalock RC | 2.00 | 5.00 |
| BDP85 Alex Hart RC | .15 | .40 |
| BDP86 Wes Bankston RC | .75 | 2.00 |
| BDP87 Josh Rupe RC | .15 | .40 |
| BDP88 Dan Cevette RC | .15 | .40 |
| BDP89 Kiel Fisher RC | .20 | .50 |
| BDP90 Alan Rick RC | .15 | .40 |
| BDP91 Charlie Morton RC | .15 | .40 |
| BDP92 Chad Spann RC | .15 | .40 |
| BDP93 Kyle Boyer RC | .15 | .40 |
| BDP94 Bob Malek RC | .15 | .40 |
| BDP95 Ryan Rodriguez RC | .15 | .40 |
| BDP96 Jordan Renz RC | .15 | .40 |
| BDP97 Randy Frye RC | .15 | .40 |
| BDP98 Rich Hill RC | 2.00 | 5.00 |
| BDP99 B.J. Upton RC | 2.00 | 5.00 |
| BDP100 Dan Christensen RC | .15 | .40 |
| BDP101 Casey Kotchman RC | .40 | 1.00 |
| BDP102 Eric Good RC | .10 | .30 |
| BDP103 Mike Fontenot RC | .15 | .40 |
| BDP104 John Webb RC | .15 | .40 |
| BDP105 Jason Dubois RC | .20 | .50 |
| BDP106 Ryan Kibler RC | .15 | .40 |
| BDP107 Jhonny Peralta RC | 1.00 | 2.50 |
| BDP108 Kirk Saarloos RC | .15 | .40 |
| BDP109 Rhett Parrott RC | .15 | .40 |
| BDP110 Jason Grove RC | .15 | .40 |
| BDP111 Colt Griffin RC | .15 | .40 |
| BDP112 Dallas McPherson RC | .40 | 1.00 |
| BDP113 Oliver Perez RC | 1.00 | 1.00 |
| BDP114 Marshall McDougall RC | .15 | .40 |
| BDP115 Mike Wood RC | .15 | .40 |
| BDP116 Scott Hairston RC | .20 | .50 |
| BDP117 Jason Simontacchi RC | .15 | .40 |
| BDP118 Taggert Bozied RC | .20 | .50 |
| BDP119 Shelley Duncan RC | 1.25 | 3.00 |
| BDP120 Dontrelle Willis RC | 2.00 | 5.00 |
| BDP121 Sean Burnett RC | .10 | .30 |
| BDP122 Aaron Cook RC | .10 | .30 |
| BDP123 Brett Evert RC | .10 | .30 |
| BDP124 Jimmy Journell RC | .10 | .30 |
| BDP125 Brett Myers RC | .10 | .30 |
| BDP126 Brad Baker RC | .10 | .30 |
| BDP127 Billy Traber RC | .15 | .40 |
| BDP128 Adam Wainwright | .20 | .50 |
| BDP129 Jason Young RC | .10 | .30 |
| BDP130 John Buck | .10 | .30 |
| BDP131 Kevin Cash RC | .15 | .40 |
| BDP132 Jason Stokes RC | .20 | .50 |
| BDP133 Drew Henson | .10 | .30 |
| BDP134 Chad Tracy RC | .40 | 1.00 |
| BDP135 Orlando Hudson | .10 | .30 |
| BDP136 Brandon Phillips | .10 | .30 |
| BDP137 Joe Borchard | .10 | .30 |
| BDP138 Marlon Byrd | .10 | .30 |
| BDP139 Carl Crawford | .10 | .30 |
| BDP140 Michael Restovich | .10 | .30 |
| BDP141 Corey Hart RC | .60 | 1.50 |
| BDP142 Edwin Almonte | .10 | .30 |
| BDP143 Francis Beltran RC | .15 | .40 |
| BDP144 Jorge De La Rosa RC | .15 | .40 |
| BDP145 Gerardo Garcia RC | .15 | .40 |
| BDP146 Franklyn German RC | .15 | .40 |
| BDP147 Francisco Liriano | 1.25 | 3.00 |
| BDP148 Francisco Rodriguez | .10 | .30 |
| BDP149 Ricardo Rodriguez | .10 | .30 |
| BDP150 Seung Song | .10 | .30 |
| BDP151 John Stephens | .10 | .30 |
| BDP152 Justin Huber RC | .30 | .75 |
| BDP153 Victor Martinez | .30 | .75 |
| BDP154 Hee Seop Choi | .30 | .75 |
| BDP155 Justin Momeau | .10 | .30 |
| BDP156 Miguel Cabrera | .50 | 1.25 |
| BDP157 Victor Diaz RC | .30 | .75 |
| BDP158 Jose Reyes | .20 | .50 |
| BDP159 Omar Infante | .10 | .30 |
| BDP160 Angel Berroa | .10 | .30 |
| BDP161 Tony Alvarez | .10 | .30 |
| BDP162 Shin Soo Choo RC | .30 | .75 |
| BDP163 Wily Mo Pena | .10 | .30 |
| BDP164 Andres Torres | .10 | .30 |
| BDP165 Jose Lopez RC | .75 | 2.00 |

**2003 Bowman**

|  | | |
|---|---|---|
| COMPLETE SET (330) | 25.00 | 60.00 |
| COMMON CARD (1-155) | .10 | .30 |
| COMMON CARD (156-330) | .10 | .30 |
| 1 Garret Anderson | .10 | .30 |
| 2 Derek Jeter | .75 | 2.00 |
| 3 Gary Sheffield | .10 | .30 |
| 4 Matt Morris | .10 | .30 |
| 5 Derek Lowe | .10 | .30 |
| 6 Andy Van Hekken | .10 | .30 |
| 7 Sammy Sosa | .30 | .75 |
| 8 Ken Griffey Jr. | .50 | 1.25 |
| 9 Omar Vizquel | .20 | .50 |
| 10 Jorge Posada | .20 | .50 |
| 11 Lance Berkman | .10 | .30 |
| 12 Mike Sweeney | .10 | .30 |
| 13 Adrian Beltre | .10 | .30 |
| 14 Richie Sexson | .10 | .30 |
| 15 A.J. Pierzynski | .10 | .30 |
| 16 Bartolo Colon | .10 | .30 |
| 17 Mike Mussina | .20 | .50 |
| 18 Paul Byrd | .10 | .30 |
| 19 Bobby Abreu | .10 | .30 |
| 20 Miguel Tejada | .10 | .30 |
| 21 Aramis Ramirez | .10 | .30 |
| 22 Edgardo Alfonzo | .10 | .30 |
| 23 Edgar Martinez | .20 | .50 |
| 24 Albert Pujols | .60 | 1.50 |
| 25 Carl Crawford | .10 | .30 |
| 26 Eric Hinske | .10 | .30 |
| 27 Tim Salmon | .20 | .50 |
| 28 Luis Gonzalez | .20 | .50 |
| 29 Jay Gibbons | .10 | .30 |
| 30 John Smoltz | .20 | .50 |
| 31 Tim Wakefield | .10 | .30 |
| 32 Mark Prior | .20 | .50 |
| 33 Magglio Ordonez | .10 | .30 |
| 34 Adam Dunn | .10 | .30 |
| 35 Larry Walker | .10 | .30 |
| 36 Luis Castillo | .10 | .30 |
| 37 Wade Miller | .10 | .30 |
| 38 Carlos Beltran | .10 | .30 |
| 39 Odalis Perez | .10 | .30 |
| 40 Alex Sanchez | .10 | .30 |
| 41 Torii Hunter | .10 | .30 |
| 42 Cliff Floyd | .10 | .30 |
| 43 Andy Pettitte | .20 | .50 |
| 44 Francisco Rodriguez | .10 | .30 |
| 45 Eric Chavez | .10 | .30 |
| 46 Kevin Millwood | .10 | .30 |
| 47 Dennis Tankersley | .10 | .30 |
| 48 Hideo Nomo | .30 | .75 |
| 49 Freddy Garcia | .10 | .30 |
| 50 Randy Johnson | .30 | .75 |
| 51 Aubrey Huff | .10 | .30 |
| 52 Carlos Delgado | .10 | .30 |
| 53 Troy Glaus | .10 | .30 |
| 54 Junior Spivey | .10 | .30 |
| 55 Mike Hampton | .10 | .30 |
| 56 Sidney Ponson | .10 | .30 |
| 57 Aaron Boone | .10 | .30 |
| 58 Kerry Wood | .10 | .30 |
| 59 Runelvys Hernandez | .10 | .30 |
| 60 Nomar Garciaparra | .50 | 1.25 |
| 61 Todd Helton | .20 | .50 |
| 62 Mike Lowell | .10 | .30 |
| 63 Roy Oswalt | .10 | .30 |
| 64 Raul Ibanez | .10 | .30 |
| 65 Brian Jordan | .10 | .30 |
| 66 Geoff Jenkins | .10 | .30 |
| 67 Jermaine Dye | .10 | .30 |
| 68 Tom Glavine | .20 | .50 |
| 69 Bernie Williams | .20 | .50 |
| 70 Vladimir Guerrero | .30 | .75 |
| 71 Mark Mulder | .10 | .30 |
| 72 Jimmy Rollins | .10 | .30 |
| 73 Oliver Perez | .10 | .30 |
| 74 Rich Aurilia | .10 | .30 |
| 75 Joel Pineiro | .10 | .30 |
| 76 J.D. Drew | .10 | .30 |
| 77 Ivan Rodriguez | .20 | .50 |
| 78 Josh Phelps | .10 | .30 |
| 79 Darin Erstad | .10 | .30 |
| 80 Curt Schilling | .10 | .30 |
| 81 Paul Lo Duca | .10 | .30 |
| 82 Marty Cordova | .10 | .30 |
| 83 Manny Ramirez | .20 | .50 |
| 84 Bobby Hill | .10 | .30 |
| 85 Paul Konerko | .10 | .30 |
| 86 Austin Kearns | .10 | .30 |
| 87 Jason Jennings | .10 | .30 |
| 88 Brad Penny | .10 | .30 |
| 89 Jeff Bagwell | .20 | .50 |
| 90 Shawn Green | .10 | .30 |
| 91 Jason Schmidt | .10 | .30 |
| 92 Doug Mientkiewicz | .10 | .30 |
| 93 Jose Vidro | .10 | .30 |
| 94 Bret Boone | .10 | .30 |
| 95 Jason Giambi | .20 | .50 |
| 96 Barry Zito | .10 | .30 |
| 97 Roy Halladay | .10 | .30 |
| 98 Pat Burrell | .10 | .30 |
| 99 Sean Burroughs | .10 | .30 |
| 100 Barry Bonds | .75 | 2.00 |
| 101 Kazuhiro Sasaki | .10 | .30 |
| 102 Fernando Vina | .10 | .30 |
| 103 Chan Ho Park | .10 | .30 |
| 104 Andruw Jones | .20 | .50 |
| 105 Adam Kennedy | .10 | .30 |
| 106 Shea Hillenbrand | .10 | .30 |
| 107 Greg Maddux | .50 | 1.25 |
| 108 Jim Edmonds | .20 | .50 |
| 109 Pedro Martinez | .20 | .50 |
| 110 Moises Alou | .10 | .30 |
| 111 Jeff Weaver | .10 | .30 |
| 112 C.C. Sabathia | .10 | .30 |
| 113 Robert Fick | .10 | .30 |
| 114 A.J. Burnett | .10 | .30 |
| 115 Jeff Kent | .10 | .30 |
| 116 Kevin Brown | .10 | .30 |
| 117 Rafael Furcal | .10 | .30 |
| 118 Cristian Guzman | .10 | .30 |
| 119 Brad Wilkerson | .10 | .30 |

| | | |
|---|---|---|
| ☐ 120 Mike Piazza | .50 | 1.25 |
| ☐ 121 Alfonso Soriano | .10 | .30 |
| ☐ 122 Mark Ellis | .10 | .30 |
| ☐ 123 Vicente Padilla | .10 | .30 |
| ☐ 124 Eric Gagne | .10 | .30 |
| ☐ 125 Ryan Klesko | .10 | .30 |
| ☐ 126 Ichiro Suzuki | .60 | 1.50 |
| ☐ 127 Tony Batista | .10 | .30 |
| ☐ 128 Roberto Alomar | .20 | .50 |
| ☐ 129 Alex Rodriguez | .50 | 1.25 |
| ☐ 130 Jim Thome | .20 | .50 |
| ☐ 131 Jarrod Washburn | .10 | .30 |
| ☐ 132 Orlando Hudson | .10 | .30 |
| ☐ 133 Chipper Jones | .30 | .75 |
| ☐ 134 Rodrigo Lopez | .10 | .30 |
| ☐ 135 Johnny Damon | .20 | .50 |
| ☐ 136 Matt Clement | .10 | .30 |
| ☐ 137 Frank Thomas | .30 | .75 |
| ☐ 138 Ellis Burks | .10 | .30 |
| ☐ 139 Carlos Pena | .10 | .30 |
| ☐ 140 Josh Beckett | .10 | .30 |
| ☐ 141 Joe Randa | .10 | .30 |
| ☐ 142 Brian Giles | .10 | .30 |
| ☐ 143 Kazuhisa Ishii | .10 | .30 |
| ☐ 144 Corey Koskie | .10 | .30 |
| ☐ 145 Orlando Cabrera | .10 | .30 |
| ☐ 146 Mark Buehrle | .10 | .30 |
| ☐ 147 Roger Clemens | .60 | 1.50 |
| ☐ 148 Tim Hudson | .10 | .30 |
| ☐ 149 Randy Wolf | .10 | .30 |
| ☐ 150 Josh Fogg | .10 | .30 |
| ☐ 151 Phil Nevin | .10 | .30 |
| ☐ 152 John Olerud | .10 | .30 |
| ☐ 153 Scott Rolen | .20 | .50 |
| ☐ 154 Joe Kennedy | .10 | .30 |
| ☐ 155 Rafael Palmeiro | .20 | .50 |
| ☐ 156 Chad Hutchinson | .10 | .30 |
| ☐ 157 Quincy Carter XRC | .15 | .40 |
| ☐ 158 Hee Seop Choi | .10 | .30 |
| ☐ 159 Joe Borchard | .10 | .30 |
| ☐ 160 Brandon Phillips | .10 | .30 |
| ☐ 161 Wily Mo Pena | .10 | .30 |
| ☐ 162 Victor Martinez | .20 | .50 |
| ☐ 163 Jason Stokes | .10 | .30 |
| ☐ 164 Ken Harvey | .10 | .30 |
| ☐ 165 Juan Rivera | .10 | .30 |
| ☐ 166 Jose Contreras RC | .60 | 1.50 |
| ☐ 167 Dan Haren RC | .60 | 1.50 |
| ☐ 168 Michel Hernandez RC | .15 | .40 |
| ☐ 169 Eider Torres RC | .15 | .40 |
| ☐ 170 Chris De La Cruz RC | .15 | .40 |
| ☐ 171 Ramon Nivar-Martinez RC | .15 | .40 |
| ☐ 172 Mike Adams RC | .15 | .40 |
| ☐ 173 Justin Ameson RC | .15 | .40 |
| ☐ 174 Jamie Athas RC | .15 | .40 |
| ☐ 175 Dwaine Bacon RC | .15 | .40 |
| ☐ 176 Clint Barmes RC | .40 | 1.00 |
| ☐ 177 B.J. Barns RC | .15 | .40 |
| ☐ 178 Tyler Johnson RC | .15 | .40 |
| ☐ 179 Bobby Basham RC | .15 | .40 |
| ☐ 180 T.J. Bohn RC | .15 | .40 |
| ☐ 181 J.D. Durbin RC | .15 | .40 |
| ☐ 182 Brandon Bowe RC | .15 | .40 |
| ☐ 183 Craig Brazell RC | .15 | .40 |
| ☐ 184 Dusty Brown RC | .15 | .40 |
| ☐ 185 Brian Bruney RC | .20 | .50 |
| ☐ 186 Greg Bruso RC | .15 | .40 |
| ☐ 187 Jaime Bubela RC | .15 | .40 |
| ☐ 188 Bryan Bullington RC | .15 | .40 |
| ☐ 189 Brian Burgamy RC | .15 | .40 |
| ☐ 190 Ery Cabrera RC | .50 | 1.25 |
| ☐ 191 Daniel Cabrera RC | .30 | .75 |
| ☐ 192 Ryan Cameron RC | .15 | .40 |
| ☐ 193 Lance Caraccioli RC | .15 | .40 |
| ☐ 194 David Cash RC | .15 | .40 |
| ☐ 195 Bernie Castro RC | .15 | .40 |
| ☐ 196 Ismael Castro RC | .20 | .50 |
| ☐ 197 Daryl Clark RC | .15 | .40 |
| ☐ 198 Jeff Clark RC | .15 | .40 |
| ☐ 199 Chris Colton RC | .15 | .40 |
| ☐ 200 Dexter Cooper RC | .15 | .40 |
| ☐ 201 Callix Crabbe RC | .20 | .50 |
| ☐ 202 Chien-Ming Wang RC | 2.50 | 6.00 |
| ☐ 203 Eric Crozier RC | .20 | .50 |
| ☐ 204 Nook Logan RC | .20 | .50 |
| ☐ 205 David DeJesus RC | .30 | .75 |
| ☐ 206 Matt DeMarco RC | .15 | .40 |
| ☐ 207 Chris Duncan RC | 1.50 | 4.00 |

| | | |
|---|---|---|
| ☐ 208 Eric Eckenstahler | .10 | .30 |
| ☐ 209 Willie Eyre RC | .15 | .40 |
| ☐ 210 Evel Bastida-Martinez RC | .15 | .40 |
| ☐ 211 Chris Fallon RC | .15 | .40 |
| ☐ 212 Mike Flannery RC | .15 | .40 |
| ☐ 213 Mike O'Keefe RC | .15 | .40 |
| ☐ 214 Ben Francisco RC | .15 | .40 |
| ☐ 215 Kason Gabbard RC | .15 | .40 |
| ☐ 216 Mike Gallo RC | .15 | .40 |
| ☐ 217 Jairo Garcia RC | .20 | .50 |
| ☐ 218 Angel Garcia RC | .20 | .50 |
| ☐ 219 Michael Garciaparra RC | .10 | .30 |
| ☐ 220 Joey Gomes RC | .15 | .40 |
| ☐ 221 Dusty Gomon RC | .20 | .50 |
| ☐ 222 Bryan Grace RC | .15 | .40 |
| ☐ 223 Tyson Graham RC | .15 | .40 |
| ☐ 224 Henry Guerrero RC | .15 | .40 |
| ☐ 225 Franklin Gutierrez RC | .40 | 1.00 |
| ☐ 226 Carlos Guzman RC | .15 | .40 |
| ☐ 227 Mather Hagen RC | .15 | .40 |
| ☐ 228 Josh Hall RC | .15 | .40 |
| ☐ 229 Rob Hammock RC | .15 | .40 |
| ☐ 230 Brendan Harris RC | .20 | .50 |
| ☐ 231 Gary Harris RC | .15 | .40 |
| ☐ 232 Clay Hensley RC | .15 | .40 |
| ☐ 233 Michael Hinckley RC | .20 | .50 |
| ☐ 234 Luis Hodge RC | .15 | .40 |
| ☐ 235 Donnie Hood RC | .20 | .50 |
| ☐ 236 Travis Ishikawa RC | .40 | 1.00 |
| ☐ 237 Edwin Jackson RC | .40 | 1.00 |
| ☐ 238 Ardley Jansen RC | .20 | .50 |
| ☐ 239 Ferenc Jongejan RC | .15 | .40 |
| ☐ 240 Matt Kata RC | .15 | .40 |
| ☐ 241 Kazuhiro Takeoka RC | .15 | .40 |
| ☐ 242 Beau Kemp RC | .15 | .40 |
| ☐ 243 Il Kim RC | .15 | .40 |
| ☐ 244 Brennan King RC | .15 | .40 |
| ☐ 245 Chris Kroski RC | .15 | .40 |
| ☐ 246 Jason Kubel RC | .75 | 2.00 |
| ☐ 247 Pete LaForest RC | .15 | .40 |
| ☐ 248 Wil Ledezma RC | .15 | .40 |
| ☐ 249 Jeremy Bonderman RC | 1.25 | 3.00 |
| ☐ 250 Gonzalo Lopez RC | .15 | .40 |
| ☐ 251 Brian Luderer RC | .15 | .40 |
| ☐ 252 Ruddy Lugo RC | .15 | .40 |
| ☐ 253 Wayne Lydon RC | .15 | .40 |
| ☐ 254 Mark Malaska RC | .15 | .40 |
| ☐ 255 Andy Marte RC | 1.25 | 3.00 |
| ☐ 256 Tyler Martin RC | .15 | .40 |
| ☐ 257 Branden Florence RC | .15 | .40 |
| ☐ 258 Aneudis Mateo RC | .15 | .40 |
| ☐ 259 Derell McCall RC | .15 | .40 |
| ☐ 260 Brian McCann RC | 3.00 | 8.00 |
| ☐ 261 Mike McNutt RC | .15 | .40 |
| ☐ 262 Jacabo Meque RC | .15 | .40 |
| ☐ 263 Derek Michaelis RC | .15 | .40 |
| ☐ 264 Aaron Miles RC | .20 | .50 |
| ☐ 265 Jose Morales RC | .15 | .40 |
| ☐ 266 Dustin Moseley RC | .15 | .40 |
| ☐ 267 Adrian Myers RC | .15 | .40 |
| ☐ 268 Dan Neil RC | .15 | .40 |
| ☐ 269 Jon Nelson RC | .20 | .50 |
| ☐ 270 Mike Neu RC | .15 | .40 |
| ☐ 271 Leigh Neuage RC | .15 | .40 |
| ☐ 272 Wes O'Brien RC | .15 | .40 |
| ☐ 273 Trent Oeltjen RC | .20 | .50 |
| ☐ 274 Tim Olson RC | .15 | .40 |
| ☐ 275 David Pahucki RC | .15 | .40 |
| ☐ 276 Nathan Panther RC | .15 | .40 |
| ☐ 277 Arnie Munoz RC | .15 | .40 |
| ☐ 278 Dave Pember RC | .15 | .40 |
| ☐ 279 Jason Perry RC | .20 | .50 |
| ☐ 280 Matthew Peterson RC | .15 | .40 |
| ☐ 281 Ryan Shealy RC | 1.00 | 2.50 |
| ☐ 282 Jorge Piedra RC | .20 | .50 |
| ☐ 283 Simon Pond RC | .15 | .40 |
| ☐ 284 Aaron Rakers RC | .15 | .40 |
| ☐ 285 Hanley Ramirez RC | 2.50 | 6.00 |
| ☐ 286 Manuel Ramirez RC | .20 | .50 |
| ☐ 287 Kevin Randel RC | .15 | .40 |
| ☐ 288 Darrell Rasner RC | .15 | .40 |
| ☐ 289 Prentice Redman RC | .15 | .40 |
| ☐ 290 Eric Reed RC | .15 | .40 |
| ☐ 291 Wilton Reynolds RC | .15 | .40 |
| ☐ 292 Eric Riggs RC | .20 | .50 |
| ☐ 293 Carlos Rijo RC | .15 | .40 |
| ☐ 294 Rajai Davis RC | .15 | .40 |
| ☐ 295 Aron Weston RC | .15 | .40 |

| | | |
|---|---|---|
| ☐ 296 Arturo Rivas RC | .15 | .40 |
| ☐ 297 Kyle Roat RC | .15 | .40 |
| ☐ 298 Bubba Nelson RC | .20 | .50 |
| ☐ 299 Levi Robinson RC | .15 | .40 |
| ☐ 300 Ray Sadler RC | .15 | .40 |
| ☐ 301 Gary Schneidmiller RC | .15 | .40 |
| ☐ 302 Jon Schuerholz RC | .15 | .40 |
| ☐ 303 Corey Shafer RC | .15 | .40 |
| ☐ 304 Brian Shackelford RC | .15 | .40 |
| ☐ 305 Bill Simon RC | .15 | .40 |
| ☐ 306 Haj Turay RC | .10 | .30 |
| ☐ 307 Sean Smith RC | .20 | .50 |
| ☐ 308 Ryan Spataro RC | .15 | .40 |
| ☐ 309 Jemel Spearman RC | .15 | .40 |
| ☐ 310 Keith Stamler RC | .15 | .40 |
| ☐ 311 Luke Steidlmayer RC | .15 | .40 |
| ☐ 312 Adam Stern RC | .10 | .30 |
| ☐ 313 Jay Sitzman RC | .15 | .40 |
| ☐ 314 Thomari Story-Harden RC | .20 | .50 |
| ☐ 315 Terry Tiffee RC | .15 | .40 |
| ☐ 316 Nick Trzesniak RC | .15 | .40 |
| ☐ 317 Denny Tussen RC | .15 | .40 |
| ☐ 318 Scott Tyler RC | .20 | .50 |
| ☐ 319 Shane Victorino RC | .40 | 1.00 |
| ☐ 320 Doug Waechter RC | .20 | .50 |
| ☐ 321 Brandon Watson RC | .15 | .40 |
| ☐ 322 Todd Wellemeyer RC | .15 | .40 |
| ☐ 323 Eli Whiteside RC | .15 | .40 |
| ☐ 324 Josh Willingham RC | .40 | 1.00 |
| ☐ 325 Travis Wong RC | .20 | .50 |
| ☐ 326 Brian Wright RC | .15 | .40 |
| ☐ 327 Kevin Youkilis RC | 1.25 | 3.00 |
| ☐ 328 Andy Sisco RC | .10 | .30 |
| ☐ 329 Dustin Yount RC | .20 | .50 |
| ☐ 330 Andrew Dominique RC | .15 | .40 |
| ☐ NNO Hinske/Jennings ROY Relic | 6.00 | 15.00 |

## 2003 Bowman Draft

| | | |
|---|---|---|
| ☐ COMPLETE SET (165) | 20.00 | 50.00 |
| ☐ 1 Dontrelle Willis | .30 | .75 |
| ☐ 2 Freddy Sanchez | .10 | .30 |
| ☐ 3 Miguel Cabrera | .30 | .75 |
| ☐ 4 Ryan Ludwick | .10 | .30 |
| ☐ 5 Ty Wigginton | .10 | .30 |
| ☐ 6 Mark Teixeira | .20 | .50 |
| ☐ 7 Trey Hodges | .10 | .30 |
| ☐ 8 Laynce Nix | .10 | .30 |
| ☐ 9 Antonio Perez | .10 | .30 |
| ☐ 10 Jody Gerut | .10 | .30 |
| ☐ 11 Jae Weong Seo | .10 | .30 |
| ☐ 12 Erick Almonte | .10 | .30 |
| ☐ 13 Lyle Overbay | .10 | .30 |
| ☐ 14 Billy Traber | .10 | .30 |
| ☐ 15 Andres Torres | .10 | .30 |
| ☐ 16 Jose Valverde | .10 | .30 |
| ☐ 17 Aaron Heilman | .10 | .30 |
| ☐ 18 Brandon Larson | .10 | .30 |
| ☐ 19 Jung Bong | .10 | .30 |
| ☐ 20 Jesse Foppert | .10 | .30 |
| ☐ 21 Angel Berroa | .10 | .30 |
| ☐ 22 Jeff DaVanon | .10 | .30 |
| ☐ 23 Kurt Ainsworth | .10 | .30 |
| ☐ 24 Brandon Claussen | .10 | .30 |
| ☐ 25 Xavier Nady | .10 | .30 |
| ☐ 26 Travis Hafner | .10 | .30 |
| ☐ 27 Jerome Williams | .10 | .30 |
| ☐ 28 Jose Reyes | .10 | .30 |
| ☐ 29 Sergio Mitre RC | .20 | .50 |
| ☐ 30 Bo Hart RC | .15 | .40 |
| ☐ 31 Adam Miller RC | 1.00 | 2.50 |
| ☐ 32 Brian Finch RC | .15 | .40 |
| ☐ 33 Taylor Mattingly RC | .20 | .50 |
| ☐ 34 Chric Barton RC | 1.00 | 2.50 |
| ☐ 35 Chris Ray RC | .40 | 1.00 |

| ☐ 36 Jarrod Saltalamacchia RC | 3.00 | 8.00 |
|---|---|---|
| ☐ 37 Dennis Dove RC | .20 | .50 |
| ☐ 38 James Houser RC | .20 | .50 |
| ☐ 39 Clint King RC | .20 | .50 |
| ☐ 40 Lou Palmisano RC | .20 | .50 |
| ☐ 41 Dan Moore RC | .15 | .40 |
| ☐ 42 Craig Stansberry RC | .20 | .50 |
| ☐ 43 Jo Jo Reyes RC | .50 | 1.25 |
| ☐ 44 Jake Stevens RC | .20 | .50 |
| ☐ 45 Tom Gorzelanny RC | .50 | 1.25 |
| ☐ 46 Brian Marshall RC | .15 | .40 |
| ☐ 47 Scott Beerer RC | .15 | .40 |
| ☐ 48 Javi Herrera RC | .20 | .50 |
| ☐ 49 Steve LeRud RC | .20 | .50 |
| ☐ 50 Josh Banks RC | .30 | .75 |
| ☐ 51 Jon Papelbon RC | 5.00 | 12.00 |
| ☐ 52 Juan Valdes RC | .20 | .50 |
| ☐ 53 Beau Vaughan RC | .20 | .50 |
| ☐ 54 Matt Chico RC | .20 | .50 |
| ☐ 55 Todd Jennings RC | .20 | .50 |
| ☐ 56 Anthony Gwynn RC | .50 | 1.25 |
| ☐ 57 Matt Harrison RC | .30 | .75 |
| ☐ 58 Aaron Marsden RC | .20 | .50 |
| ☐ 59 Casey Abrams RC | .15 | .40 |
| ☐ 60 Cory Stuart RC | .15 | .40 |
| ☐ 61 Mike Wagner RC | .15 | .40 |
| ☐ 62 Jordan Pratt RC | .20 | .50 |
| ☐ 63 Andre Randolph RC | .20 | .50 |
| ☐ 64 Blake Balkcom RC | .20 | .50 |
| ☐ 65 Josh Muecke RC | .15 | .40 |
| ☐ 66 Jamie D'Antona RC | .30 | .75 |
| ☐ 67 Cole Seifrig RC | .15 | .40 |
| ☐ 68 Josh Anderson RC | .20 | .50 |
| ☐ 69 Matt Lorenzo RC | .20 | .50 |
| ☐ 70 Nate Spears RC | .20 | .50 |
| ☐ 71 Chris Goodman RC | .15 | .40 |
| ☐ 72 Brian McFall RC | .15 | .40 |
| ☐ 73 Billy Hogan RC | .20 | .50 |
| ☐ 74 Jamie Romak RC | .20 | .50 |
| ☐ 75 Jeff Cook RC | .20 | .50 |
| ☐ 76 Brooks McNiven RC | .15 | .40 |
| ☐ 77 Xavier Paul RC | .20 | .50 |
| ☐ 78 Bob Zimmermann RC | .15 | .40 |
| ☐ 79 Mickey Hall RC | .20 | .50 |
| ☐ 80 Shaun Marcum RC | .20 | .50 |
| ☐ 81 Matt Nachreiner RC | .20 | .50 |
| ☐ 82 Chris Kinsey RC | .15 | .40 |
| ☐ 83 Jonathan Fulton RC | .20 | .50 |
| ☐ 84 Edgardo Baez RC | .20 | .50 |
| ☐ 85 Robert Valido RC | .20 | .50 |
| ☐ 86 Kenny Lewis RC | .20 | .50 |
| ☐ 87 Trent Peterson RC | .15 | .40 |
| ☐ 88 Johnny Woodard RC | .20 | .50 |
| ☐ 89 Wes Littleton RC | .20 | .50 |
| ☐ 90 Sean Rodriguez RC | .60 | 1.50 |
| ☐ 91 Kyle Pearson RC | .15 | .40 |
| ☐ 92 Josh Rainwater RC | .20 | .50 |
| ☐ 93 Travis Schlichting RC | .20 | .50 |
| ☐ 94 Tim Battle RC | .30 | .75 |
| ☐ 95 Aaron Hill RC | .60 | 1.50 |
| ☐ 96 Bob McCrory RC | .15 | .40 |
| ☐ 97 Rick Guarno RC | .20 | .50 |
| ☐ 98 Brandon Yarbrough RC | .15 | .40 |
| ☐ 99 Peter Stonard RC | .15 | .40 |
| ☐ 100 Darin Downs RC | .20 | .50 |
| ☐ 101 Matt Bruback RC | .10 | .30 |
| ☐ 102 Danny Garcia RC | .15 | .40 |
| ☐ 103 Cory Stewart RC | .15 | .40 |
| ☐ 104 Ferdin Tejeda RC | .10 | .30 |
| ☐ 105 Kade Johnson RC | .15 | .40 |
| ☐ 106 Andrew Brown RC | .20 | .50 |
| ☐ 107 Aquilino Lopez RC | .15 | .40 |
| ☐ 108 Stephen Randolph RC | .15 | .40 |
| ☐ 109 Dave Matranga RC | .15 | .40 |
| ☐ 110 Dustin McGowan RC | .20 | .50 |
| ☐ 111 Juan Camacho RC | .15 | .40 |
| ☐ 112 Cliff Lee | .10 | .30 |
| ☐ 113 Jeff Duncan RC | .10 | .30 |
| ☐ 114 C.J. Wilson | .10 | .30 |
| ☐ 115 Brandon Roberson RC | .15 | .40 |
| ☐ 116 David Corrente RC | .15 | .40 |
| ☐ 117 Kevin Beavers RC | .15 | .40 |
| ☐ 118 Anthony Webster RC | .20 | .50 |
| ☐ 119 Oscar Villarreal RC | .15 | .40 |
| ☐ 120 Hong-Chih Kuo RC | 1.00 | 2.50 |
| ☐ 121 Josh Barfield RC | .20 | .50 |
| ☐ 122 Denny Bautista RC | .10 | .30 |
| ☐ 123 Chris Burke RC | .50 | 1.25 |

| ☐ 124 Robinson Cano RC | 3.00 | 8.00 |
|---|---|---|
| ☐ 125 Jose Castillo RC | .10 | .30 |
| ☐ 126 Neal Cotts | .10 | .30 |
| ☐ 127 Jorge De La Rosa | .10 | .30 |
| ☐ 128 J.D. Durbin | .15 | .40 |
| ☐ 129 Edwin Encarnacion | .40 | 1.00 |
| ☐ 130 Gavin Floyd | .10 | .30 |
| ☐ 131 Alexis Gomez | .10 | .30 |
| ☐ 132 Edgar Gonzalez RC | .15 | .40 |
| ☐ 133 Khalil Greene | .30 | .75 |
| ☐ 134 Zack Greinke | .10 | .30 |
| ☐ 135 Franklin Gutierrez | .20 | .50 |
| ☐ 136 Rich Harden | .10 | .30 |
| ☐ 137 J.J. Hardy RC | 2.00 | 5.00 |
| ☐ 138 Ryan Howard RC | 6.00 | 15.00 |
| ☐ 139 Justin Huber | .10 | .30 |
| ☐ 140 David Kelton | .10 | .30 |
| ☐ 141 Dave Krynzel | .10 | .30 |
| ☐ 142 Pete LaForest | .15 | .40 |
| ☐ 143 Adam LaRoche | .10 | .30 |
| ☐ 144 Preston Larrison RC | .20 | .50 |
| ☐ 145 John Maine RC | 2.00 | 5.00 |
| ☐ 146 Andy Marte | .50 | 1.25 |
| ☐ 147 Jeff Mathis | .10 | .30 |
| ☐ 148 Joe Mauer | .30 | .75 |
| ☐ 149 Clint Nageotte | .10 | .30 |
| ☐ 150 Chris Narveson | .10 | .30 |
| ☐ 151 Ramon Nivar | .10 | .30 |
| ☐ 152 Felix Pie RC | 2.00 | 5.00 |
| ☐ 153 Guillermo Quiroz RC | .15 | .40 |
| ☐ 154 Rene Reyes | .10 | .30 |
| ☐ 155 Royce Ring | .10 | .30 |
| ☐ 156 Alexis Rios | .40 | 1.00 |
| ☐ 157 Grady Sizemore | .30 | .75 |
| ☐ 158 Stephen Smitherman | .10 | .30 |
| ☐ 159 Seung Song | .10 | .30 |
| ☐ 160 Scott Thorman | .10 | .30 |
| ☐ 161 Chad Tracy | .10 | .30 |
| ☐ 162 Chin-Hui Tsao | .10 | .30 |
| ☐ 163 John VanBenscholen | .10 | .30 |
| ☐ 164 Kevin Youkilis | 1.50 | 4.00 |
| ☐ 165 Chien-Ming Wang | 2.00 | 5.00 |

**2004 Bowman**

| ☐ COMPLETE SET (330) | 40.00 | 80.00 |
|---|---|---|
| ☐ ROY ODDS: 1,829 H, 1,284 HTA, 1:632 R | | |
| ☐ 1 Garret Anderson | .10 | .30 |
| ☐ 2 Larry Walker | .10 | .30 |
| ☐ 3 Derek Jeter | .60 | 1.50 |
| ☐ 4 Curt Schilling | .20 | .50 |
| ☐ 5 Carlos Zambrano | .10 | .30 |
| ☐ 6 Shawn Green | .10 | .30 |
| ☐ 7 Manny Ramirez | .20 | .50 |
| ☐ 8 Randy Johnson | .30 | .75 |
| ☐ 9 Jeremy Bonderman | .10 | .30 |
| ☐ 10 Alfonso Soriano | .20 | .50 |
| ☐ 11 Scott Rolen | .20 | .50 |
| ☐ 12 Kerry Wood | .10 | .30 |
| ☐ 13 Eric Gagne | .10 | .30 |
| ☐ 14 Ryan Klesko | .10 | .30 |
| ☐ 15 Kevin Millar | .10 | .30 |
| ☐ 16 Ty Wigginton | .10 | .30 |
| ☐ 17 David Ortiz | .30 | .75 |
| ☐ 18 Luis Castillo | .10 | .30 |
| ☐ 19 Bernie Williams | .20 | .50 |
| ☐ 20 Edgar Renteria | .10 | .30 |
| ☐ 21 Matt Kata | .10 | .30 |
| ☐ 22 Bartolo Colon | .10 | .30 |
| ☐ 23 Derrek Lee | .20 | .50 |
| ☐ 24 Gary Sheffield | .20 | .50 |
| ☐ 25 Nomar Garciaparra | .50 | 1.25 |
| ☐ 26 Kevin Millwood | .10 | .30 |
| ☐ 27 Corey Patterson | .10 | .30 |
| ☐ 28 Carlos Beltran | .10 | .30 |

| ☐ 29 Mike Lieberthal | .10 | .30 |
|---|---|---|
| ☐ 30 Troy Glaus | .10 | .30 |
| ☐ 31 Preston Wilson | .10 | .30 |
| ☐ 32 Jorge Posada | .20 | .50 |
| ☐ 33 Bo Hart | .10 | .30 |
| ☐ 34 Mark Prior | .20 | .50 |
| ☐ 35 Hideo Nomo | .30 | .75 |
| ☐ 36 Jason Kendall | .10 | .30 |
| ☐ 37 Roger Clemens | .60 | 1.50 |
| ☐ 38 Dmitri Young | .10 | .30 |
| ☐ 39 Jason Giambi | .10 | .30 |
| ☐ 40 Jim Edmonds | .10 | .30 |
| ☐ 41 Ryan Ludwick | .10 | .30 |
| ☐ 42 Brandon Webb | .10 | .30 |
| ☐ 43 Todd Helton | .20 | .50 |
| ☐ 44 Jacque Jones | .10 | .30 |
| ☐ 45 Jamie Moyer | .10 | .30 |
| ☐ 46 Tim Salmon | .20 | .50 |
| ☐ 47 Kelvim Escobar | .10 | .30 |
| ☐ 48 Tony Batista | .10 | .30 |
| ☐ 49 Nick Johnson | .10 | .30 |
| ☐ 50 Jim Thome | .30 | .75 |
| ☐ 51 Casey Blake | .10 | .30 |
| ☐ 52 Trot Nixon | .10 | .30 |
| ☐ 53 Luis Gonzalez | .10 | .30 |
| ☐ 54 Dontrelle Willis | .20 | .50 |
| ☐ 55 Mike Mussina | .20 | .50 |
| ☐ 56 Carl Crawford | .10 | .30 |
| ☐ 57 Mark Buehrle | .10 | .30 |
| ☐ 58 Scott Podsednik | .10 | .30 |
| ☐ 59 Brian Giles | .10 | .30 |
| ☐ 60 Rafael Furcal | .10 | .30 |
| ☐ 61 Miguel Cabrera | .20 | .50 |
| ☐ 62 Rich Harden | .10 | .30 |
| ☐ 63 Mark Teixeira | .20 | .50 |
| ☐ 64 Frank Thomas | .30 | .75 |
| ☐ 65 Johan Santana | .30 | .75 |
| ☐ 66 Jason Schmidt | .10 | .30 |
| ☐ 67 Aramis Ramirez | .10 | .30 |
| ☐ 68 Jose Reyes | .10 | .30 |
| ☐ 69 Magglio Ordonez | .10 | .30 |
| ☐ 70 Mike Sweeney | .10 | .30 |
| ☐ 71 Eric Chavez | .10 | .30 |
| ☐ 72 Rocco Baldelli | .10 | .30 |
| ☐ 73 Sammy Sosa | .30 | .75 |
| ☐ 74 Javy Lopez | .10 | .30 |
| ☐ 75 Roy Oswalt | .10 | .30 |
| ☐ 76 Raul Ibanez | .10 | .30 |
| ☐ 77 Ivan Rodriguez | .20 | .50 |
| ☐ 78 Jerome Williams | .10 | .30 |
| ☐ 79 Carlos Lee | .10 | .30 |
| ☐ 80 Geoff Jenkins | .10 | .30 |
| ☐ 81 Sean Burroughs | .10 | .30 |
| ☐ 82 Marcus Giles | .10 | .30 |
| ☐ 83 Mike Lowell | .10 | .30 |
| ☐ 84 Barry Zito | .10 | .30 |
| ☐ 85 Aubrey Huff | .10 | .30 |
| ☐ 86 Esteban Loaiza | .10 | .30 |
| ☐ 87 Torii Hunter | .20 | .50 |
| ☐ 88 Phil Nevin | .10 | .30 |
| ☐ 89 Andruw Jones | .20 | .50 |
| ☐ 90 Josh Beckett | .10 | .30 |
| ☐ 91 Mark Mulder | .10 | .30 |
| ☐ 92 Hank Blalock | .10 | .30 |
| ☐ 93 Jason Phillips | .10 | .30 |
| ☐ 94 Russ Ortiz | .10 | .30 |
| ☐ 95 Juan Pierre | .10 | .30 |
| ☐ 96 Tom Glavine | .20 | .50 |
| ☐ 97 Gil Meche | .10 | .30 |
| ☐ 98 Ramon Ortiz | .10 | .30 |
| ☐ 99 Richie Sexson | .10 | .30 |
| ☐ 100 Albert Pujols | .60 | 1.50 |
| ☐ 101 Javier Vazquez | .10 | .30 |
| ☐ 102 Johnny Damon | .20 | .50 |
| ☐ 103 Alex Rodriguez Yanks | .50 | 1.25 |
| ☐ 104 Omar Vizquel | .20 | .50 |
| ☐ 105 Chipper Jones | .30 | .75 |
| ☐ 106 Lance Berkman | .10 | .30 |
| ☐ 107 Tim Hudson | .10 | .30 |
| ☐ 108 Carlos Delgado | .10 | .30 |
| ☐ 109 Austin Kearns | .10 | .30 |
| ☐ 110 Orlando Cabrera | .10 | .30 |
| ☐ 111 Edgar Martinez | .10 | .30 |
| ☐ 112 Melvin Mora | .10 | .30 |
| ☐ 113 Jeff Bagwell | .20 | .50 |
| ☐ 114 Marlon Byrd | .10 | .30 |
| ☐ 115 Vernon Wells | .10 | .30 |
| ☐ 116 C.C. Sabathia | .10 | .30 |

|  | | |
|---|---|---|
| ☐ 117 Cliff Floyd | .10 | .30 |
| ☐ 118 Ichiro Suzuki | .60 | 1.50 |
| ☐ 119 Miguel Olivo | .10 | .30 |
| ☐ 120 Mike Piazza | .50 | 1.25 |
| ☐ 121 Adam Dunn | .10 | .30 |
| ☐ 122 Paul Lo Duca | .10 | .30 |
| ☐ 123 Brett Myers | .10 | .30 |
| ☐ 124 Michael Young | .10 | .30 |
| ☐ 125 Sidney Ponson | .10 | .30 |
| ☐ 126 Greg Maddux | .50 | 1.25 |
| ☐ 127 Vladimir Guerrero | .30 | .75 |
| ☐ 128 Miguel Tejada | .10 | .30 |
| ☐ 129 Andy Pettitte | .20 | .50 |
| ☐ 130 Rafael Palmeiro | .20 | .50 |
| ☐ 131 Ken Griffey Jr. | .50 | 1.25 |
| ☐ 132 Shannon Stewart | .10 | .30 |
| ☐ 133 Joel Pineiro | .10 | .30 |
| ☐ 134 Luis Matos | .10 | .30 |
| ☐ 135 Jeff Kent | .10 | .30 |
| ☐ 136 Randy Wolf | .10 | .30 |
| ☐ 137 Chris Woodward | .10 | .30 |
| ☐ 138 Jody Gerut | .10 | .30 |
| ☐ 139 Jose Vidro | .10 | .30 |
| ☐ 140 Bret Boone | .10 | .30 |
| ☐ 141 Bill Mueller | .10 | .30 |
| ☐ 142 Angel Berroa | .10 | .30 |
| ☐ 143 Bobby Abreu | .10 | .30 |
| ☐ 144 Roy Halladay | .10 | .30 |
| ☐ 145 Delmon Young | .20 | .50 |
| ☐ 146 Jonny Gomes | .10 | .30 |
| ☐ 147 Rickie Weeks | .20 | .50 |
| ☐ 148 Edwin Jackson | .10 | .30 |
| ☐ 149 Neal Cotts | .10 | .30 |
| ☐ 150 Jason Bay | .10 | .30 |
| ☐ 151 Khalil Greene | .20 | .50 |
| ☐ 152 Joe Mauer | .30 | .75 |
| ☐ 153 Bobby Jenks | .10 | .30 |
| ☐ 154 Chin-Feng Chen | .10 | .30 |
| ☐ 155 Chien-Ming Wang | .40 | 1.00 |
| ☐ 156 Mickey Hall | .10 | .30 |
| ☐ 157 James Houser | .10 | .30 |
| ☐ 158 Jay Sborz | .10 | .30 |
| ☐ 159 Jonathan Fulton | .10 | .30 |
| ☐ 160 Steven Lerud | .10 | .30 |
| ☐ 161 Grady Sizemore | .30 | .75 |
| ☐ 162 Felix Pie | .20 | .50 |
| ☐ 163 Dustin McGowan | .10 | .30 |
| ☐ 164 Chris Lubanski | .10 | .30 |
| ☐ 165 Tom Gorzelanny | .10 | .30 |
| ☐ 166 Rudy Guillen FY RC | .30 | .75 |
| ☐ 167 Bobby Brownlie FY RC | .40 | 1.00 |
| ☐ 168 Conor Jackson FY RC | 1.25 | 3.00 |
| ☐ 169 Matt Moses FY RC | .40 | 1.00 |
| ☐ 170 Ervin Santana FY RC | .60 | 1.50 |
| ☐ 171 Merkin Valdez FY RC | .20 | .50 |
| ☐ 172 Erick Aybar FY RC | .40 | 1.00 |
| ☐ 173 Brad Sullivan FY RC | .20 | .50 |
| ☐ 174 David Aardsma FY RC | .30 | .75 |
| ☐ 175 Brad Snyder FY RC | .40 | 1.00 |
| ☐ 176 Alberto Callaspo FY RC | .30 | .75 |
| ☐ 177 Brandon Medders FY RC | .15 | .40 |
| ☐ 178 Zach Miner FY RC | .50 | 1.25 |
| ☐ 179 Charlie Zink FY RC | .10 | .30 |
| ☐ 180 Adam Greenberg FY RC | .30 | .75 |
| ☐ 181 Kevin Howard FY RC | .20 | .50 |
| ☐ 182 Wanell Severino FY RC | .10 | .30 |
| ☐ 183 Kevin Kouzmanoff FY RC | .75 | 2.00 |
| ☐ 184 Joel Zumaya FY RC | 2.00 | 5.00 |
| ☐ 185 Skip Schumaker FY RC | .15 | .40 |
| ☐ 186 Nic Ungs FY RC | .15 | .40 |
| ☐ 187 Todd Sell FY RC | .20 | .50 |
| ☐ 188 Brian Stefek FY RC | .10 | .30 |
| ☐ 189 Brock Peterson FY RC | .15 | .40 |
| ☐ 190 Greg Thissen FY RC | .15 | .40 |
| ☐ 191 Frank Brooks FY RC | .15 | .40 |
| ☐ 192 Estee Harris FY RC | .20 | .50 |
| ☐ 193 Chris Mabeus FY RC | .15 | .40 |
| ☐ 194 Dan Giese FY RC | .15 | .40 |
| ☐ 195 Jared Wells FY RC | .15 | .40 |
| ☐ 196 Carlos Sosa FY RC | .15 | .40 |
| ☐ 197 Bobby Madritsch FY | .15 | .40 |
| ☐ 198 Calvin Hayes FY RC | .20 | .50 |
| ☐ 199 Omar Quintanilla FY RC | .20 | .50 |
| ☐ 200 Chris O'Riordan FY RC | .15 | .40 |
| ☐ 201 Tim Hutting FY RC | .10 | .30 |
| ☐ 202 Carlos Quentin FY RC | 1.00 | 2.50 |
| ☐ 203 Brayan Pena FY RC | .15 | .40 |
| ☐ 204 Jeff Salazar FY RC | .40 | 1.00 |
| ☐ 205 David Murphy FY RC | .30 | .75 |
| ☐ 206 Alberto Garcia FY RC | .20 | .50 |
| ☐ 207 Ramon Ramirez FY RC | .15 | .40 |
| ☐ 208 Luis Bolivar FY RC | .20 | .50 |
| ☐ 209 Rodney Choy Foo FY RC | .10 | .30 |
| ☐ 210 Kyle Sleeth FY RC | .20 | .50 |
| ☐ 211 Anthony Acevedo FY RC | .15 | .40 |
| ☐ 212 Chad Santos FY RC | .15 | .40 |
| ☐ 213 Jason Frasor FY RC | .15 | .40 |
| ☐ 214 Jesse Roman FY RC | .10 | .30 |
| ☐ 215 James Tomlin FY RC | .15 | .40 |
| ☐ 216 Josh Labandeira FY RC | .15 | .40 |
| ☐ 217 Joaquin Arias FY RC | .30 | .75 |
| ☐ 218 Don Sutton FY UER RC | .40 | 1.00 |
| ☐ 219 Danny Gonzalez FY RC | .10 | .30 |
| ☐ 220 Javier Guzman FY RC | .20 | .50 |
| ☐ 221 Anthony Lerew FY RC | .30 | .75 |
| ☐ 222 Jon Knott FY RC | .15 | .40 |
| ☐ 223 Jesse English FY RC | .15 | .40 |
| ☐ 224 Felix Hernandez FY RC | 3.00 | 8.00 |
| ☐ 225 Travis Hanson FY RC | .20 | .50 |
| ☐ 226 Jesse Floyd FY RC | .15 | .40 |
| ☐ 227 Nick Gorneault FY RC | .15 | .40 |
| ☐ 228 Craig Ansman FY RC | .15 | .40 |
| ☐ 229 Wardell Starling FY RC | .15 | .40 |
| ☐ 230 Carl Loadenthal FY RC | .20 | .50 |
| ☐ 231 Dave Crouthers FY RC | .10 | .30 |
| ☐ 232 Harvey Garcia FY RC | .10 | .30 |
| ☐ 233 Casey Kopitzke FY RC | .10 | .30 |
| ☐ 234 Ricky Nolasco FY RC | .50 | 1.25 |
| ☐ 235 Miguel Perez FY RC | .15 | .40 |
| ☐ 236 Ryan Mulhern FY RC | .10 | .30 |
| ☐ 237 Chris Aguila FY RC | .15 | .40 |
| ☐ 238 Brooks Conrad FY RC | .20 | .50 |
| ☐ 239 Damaso Espino FY RC | .10 | .30 |
| ☐ 240 Jereme Milons FY RC | .30 | .75 |
| ☐ 241 Luke Hughes FY RC | .10 | .30 |
| ☐ 242 Kory Casto FY RC | .20 | .50 |
| ☐ 243 Jose Valdez FY RC | .15 | .40 |
| ☐ 244 J.T. Stotts FY RC | .10 | .30 |
| ☐ 245 Lee Gwaltney FY RC | .10 | .30 |
| ☐ 246 Yoann Torrealba FY RC | .15 | .40 |
| ☐ 247 Omar Falcon FY RC | .15 | .40 |
| ☐ 248 Jon Coutlangus FY RC | .10 | .30 |
| ☐ 249 George Sherrill FY RC | .15 | .40 |
| ☐ 250 John Santor FY RC | .10 | .30 |
| ☐ 251 Tony Richie FY RC | .15 | .40 |
| ☐ 252 Kevin Richardson FY RC | .10 | .30 |
| ☐ 253 Tim Bittner FY RC | .15 | .40 |
| ☐ 254 Dustin Nippert FY RC | .50 | 1.25 |
| ☐ 255 Jose Capellan FY RC | .20 | .50 |
| ☐ 256 Donald Levinski FY RC | .10 | .30 |
| ☐ 257 Jerome Gamble FY RC | .10 | .30 |
| ☐ 258 Jeff Keppinger FY RC | .75 | 2.00 |
| ☐ 259 Jason Szuminski FY RC | .10 | .30 |
| ☐ 260 Akinori Otsuka FY RC | .15 | .40 |
| ☐ 261 Ryan Budde FY RC | .15 | .40 |
| ☐ 262 Shingo Takatsu FY RC | .30 | .75 |
| ☐ 263 Jeff Allison FY RC | .15 | .40 |
| ☐ 264 Hector Gimenez FY RC | .10 | .30 |
| ☐ 265 Tim Frend FY RC | .15 | .40 |
| ☐ 266 Tom Farmer FY RC | .15 | .40 |
| ☐ 267 Shawn Hill FY RC | .15 | .40 |
| ☐ 268 Lastings Milledge FY RC | 2.00 | 5.00 |
| ☐ 269 Scott Proctor FY RC | .20 | .50 |
| ☐ 270 Jorge Mejia FY RC | .15 | .40 |
| ☐ 271 Terry Jones FY RC | .20 | .50 |
| ☐ 272 Zach Duke FY RC | .75 | 2.00 |
| ☐ 273 Tim Stauffer FY RC | .30 | .75 |
| ☐ 274 Luke Anderson FY RC | .10 | .30 |
| ☐ 275 Hunter Brown FY RC | .10 | .30 |
| ☐ 276 Matt Lemanczyk FY RC | .15 | .40 |
| ☐ 277 Fernando Cortez FY RC | .10 | .30 |
| ☐ 278 Vince Perkins FY RC | .20 | .50 |
| ☐ 279 Tommy Murphy FY RC | .15 | .40 |
| ☐ 280 Mike Gosling FY RC | .10 | .30 |
| ☐ 281 Paul Bacot FY RC | .20 | .50 |
| ☐ 282 Matt Capps FY RC | .15 | .40 |
| ☐ 283 Juan Gutierrez FY RC | .15 | .40 |
| ☐ 284 Teodoro Encarnacion FY RC | .20 | .50 |
| ☐ 285 Juan Cedeno FY RC | .15 | .40 |
| ☐ 286 Matt Creighton FY RC | .10 | .30 |
| ☐ 287 Ryan Hankins FY RC | .10 | .30 |
| ☐ 288 Leo Nunez FY RC | .15 | .40 |
| ☐ 289 Dave Wallace FY RC | .15 | .40 |
| ☐ 290 Rob Tejeda FY RC | .30 | .75 |
| ☐ 291 Lincoln Holdzkom FY RC | .15 | .40 |
| ☐ 292 Jason Hirsh FY RC | .60 | 1.50 |
| ☐ 293 Tydus Meadows FY RC | .15 | .40 |
| ☐ 294 Khalid Ballouli FY RC | .10 | .30 |
| ☐ 295 Benji DeQuin FY RC | .10 | .30 |
| ☐ 296 Tyler Davidson FY RC | .60 | 1.50 |
| ☐ 297 Brant Colamarino FY RC | .30 | .75 |
| ☐ 298 Marcus McBeth FY RC | .10 | .30 |
| ☐ 299 Brad Eldred FY RC | .25 | .60 |
| ☐ 300 David Pauley FY RC | .50 | 1.25 |
| ☐ 301 Yadier Molina FY RC | .60 | 1.50 |
| ☐ 302 Chris Shelton FY RC | .50 | 1.25 |
| ☐ 303 Travis Blackley FY RC | .15 | .40 |
| ☐ 304 Jon DeVries FY RC | .15 | .40 |
| ☐ 305 Sheldon Fulse FY RC | .10 | .30 |
| ☐ 306 Vito Chiaravalloti FY RC | .15 | .40 |
| ☐ 307 Warner Madrigal FY RC | .30 | .75 |
| ☐ 308 Reid Gorecki FY RC | .15 | .40 |
| ☐ 309 Sung Jung FY RC | .15 | .40 |
| ☐ 310 Pete Sheir FY RC | .10 | .30 |
| ☐ 311 Michael Mooney FY RC | .15 | .40 |
| ☐ 312 Kenny Perez FY RC | .15 | .40 |
| ☐ 313 Michael Mallory FY RC | .15 | .40 |
| ☐ 314 Ben Himes FY RC | .10 | .30 |
| ☐ 315 Ivan Ochoa FY RC | .15 | .40 |
| ☐ 316 Donald Kelly FY RC | .15 | .40 |
| ☐ 317 Logan Kensing FY RC | .15 | .40 |
| ☐ 318 Kevin Davidson FY RC | .10 | .30 |
| ☐ 319 Brian Pilkington FY RC | .10 | .30 |
| ☐ 320 Alex Romero FY RC | .15 | .40 |
| ☐ 321 Chad Chop FY RC | .15 | .40 |
| ☐ 322 Dioner Navarro FY RC | .30 | .75 |
| ☐ 323 Casey Myers FY RC | .15 | .40 |
| ☐ 324 Mike Rouse FY RC | .15 | .40 |
| ☐ 325 Sergio Silva FY RC | .10 | .30 |
| ☐ 326 J.J. Furmaniak FY RC | .30 | .75 |
| ☐ 327 Brad Vericker FY RC | .15 | .40 |
| ☐ 328 Blake Hawksworth FY RC | .20 | .50 |
| ☐ 329 Brock Jacobsen FY RC | .15 | .40 |
| ☐ 330 Alec Zumwalt FY RC | .10 | .30 |
| ☐ BW Berroa Bat/Willis Jsy ROY | 6.00 | 15.00 |

| | | |
|---|---|---|
| ☐ COMPLETE SET (165) | 15.00 | 40.00 |
| ☐ COMMON CARD (1-165) | .10 | .30 |
| ☐ COMMON RC (1-165) | .10 | .30 |
| ☐ COMMON YR | .10 | .30 |
| ☐ PLATES ODDS 1:559 HOBBY | | |
| ☐ PLATES PRINT RUN 1 SERIAL #'d SET | | |
| ☐ BLACK-CYAN-MAGENTA-YELLOW EXIST | | |
| ☐ NO PLATES PRICING DUE TO SCARCITY | | |
| ☐ 1 Lyle Overbay | .10 | .30 |
| ☐ 2 David Newhan | .10 | .30 |
| ☐ 3 J.R. House | .10 | .30 |
| ☐ 4 Chad Tracy | .10 | .30 |
| ☐ 5 Humberto Quintero | .10 | .30 |
| ☐ 6 Dave Bush | .10 | .30 |
| ☐ 7 Scott Hairston | .10 | .30 |
| ☐ 8 Mike Wood | .10 | .30 |
| ☐ 9 Alexis Rios | .15 | .40 |
| ☐ 10 Sean Burnett | .10 | .30 |
| ☐ 11 Wilson Valdez | .10 | .30 |
| ☐ 12 Lew Ford | .10 | .30 |
| ☐ 13 Freddy Thon RC | .15 | .40 |
| ☐ 14 Zack Greinke | .30 | .75 |
| ☐ 15 Bucky Jacobsen | .10 | .30 |
| ☐ 16 Kevin Youkilis | .30 | .75 |
| ☐ 17 Grady Sizemore | .30 | .75 |
| ☐ 18 Denny Bautista | .10 | .30 |
| ☐ 19 David DeJesus | .15 | .40 |
| ☐ 20 Craig Kotchman | .10 | .30 |
| ☐ 21 David Kelton | .10 | .30 |
| ☐ 22 Charles Thomas RC | .15 | .40 |
| ☐ 23 Kazuhito Tadano RC | .20 | .50 |
| ☐ 24 Justin Leone RC | .10 | .30 |
| ☐ 25 Eduardo Villacis RC | .15 | .40 |

|  | | |
|---|---|---|
| ❏ 26 Brian Dallimore RC | .10 | .30 |
| ❏ 27 Nick Green | .10 | .30 |
| ❏ 28 Sam McConnell RC | .15 | .40 |
| ❏ 29 Brad Halsey RC | .20 | .50 |
| ❏ 30 Roman Colon RC | .10 | .30 |
| ❏ 31 Josh Fields RC | .75 | 2.00 |
| ❏ 32 Cody Bunkelman RC | .20 | .50 |
| ❏ 33 Jay Rainville RC | .50 | 1.25 |
| ❏ 34 Richie Robnett RC | .40 | 1.00 |
| ❏ 35 Jon Poterson RC | .30 | .75 |
| ❏ 36 Huston Street RC | .75 | 2.00 |
| ❏ 37 Erick San Pedro RC | .15 | .40 |
| ❏ 38 Cory Dunlap RC | .50 | 1.25 |
| ❏ 39 Kurt Suzuki RC | .40 | 1.00 |
| ❏ 40 Anthony Swarzak RC | .30 | .75 |
| ❏ 41 Ian Desmond RC | .30 | .75 |
| ❏ 42 Chris Covington RC | .20 | .50 |
| ❏ 43 Christian Garcia RC | .30 | .75 |
| ❏ 44 Gaby Hernandez RC | .50 | 1.25 |
| ❏ 45 Steven Register RC | .15 | .40 |
| ❏ 46 Eduardo Morlan RC | .30 | .75 |
| ❏ 47 Collin Balester RC | .20 | .50 |
| ❏ 48 Nathan Phillips RC | .20 | .50 |
| ❏ 49 Dan Schwartzbauer RC | .20 | .50 |
| ❏ 50 Rafael Gonzalez RC | .15 | .40 |
| ❏ 51 K.C. Herren RC | .30 | .75 |
| ❏ 52 William Susdorf RC | .15 | .40 |
| ❏ 53 Rob Johnson RC | .20 | .50 |
| ❏ 54 Louis Marson RC | .30 | .75 |
| ❏ 55 Joe Koshansky RC | .75 | 2.00 |
| ❏ 56 Jamar Walton RC | .30 | .75 |
| ❏ 57 Mark Lowe RC | .60 | 1.50 |
| ❏ 58 Matt Macri RC | .15 | .40 |
| ❏ 59 Donny Lucy RC | .15 | .40 |
| ❏ 60 Mike Ferris RC | .20 | .50 |
| ❏ 61 Mike Nickeas RC | .20 | .50 |
| ❏ 62 Eric Hurley RC | .40 | 1.00 |
| ❏ 63 Scott Elbert RC | .40 | 1.00 |
| ❏ 64 Blake DeWitt RC | .60 | 1.50 |
| ❏ 65 Danny Putnam RC | .30 | .75 |
| ❏ 66 J.P. Howell RC | .40 | 1.00 |
| ❏ 67 John Wiggins RC | .15 | .40 |
| ❏ 68 Justin Orenduff RC | .30 | .75 |
| ❏ 69 Ray Liotta RC | .50 | 1.25 |
| ❏ 70 Billy Buckner RC | .20 | .50 |
| ❏ 71 Eric Campbell RC | .75 | 2.00 |
| ❏ 72 Olin Wick RC | .30 | .75 |
| ❏ 73 Sean Gamble RC | .30 | .75 |
| ❏ 74 Seth Smith RC | .40 | 1.00 |
| ❏ 75 Wade Davis RC | .60 | 1.50 |
| ❏ 76 Joe Jacobitz RC | .15 | .40 |
| ❏ 77 J.A. Happ RC | .75 | 2.00 |
| ❏ 78 Eric Ridener RC | .15 | .40 |
| ❏ 79 Matt Tuiasosopo RC | .75 | 2.00 |
| ❏ 80 Brad Bergesen RC | .15 | .40 |
| ❏ 81 Javy Guerra RC | .20 | .50 |
| ❏ 82 Buck Shaw RC | .20 | .50 |
| ❏ 83 Paul Janish RC | .30 | .75 |
| ❏ 84 Sean Kazmar RC | .15 | .40 |
| ❏ 85 Josh Johnson RC | .20 | .50 |
| ❏ 86 Angel Salome RC | .50 | 1.25 |
| ❏ 87 Jordan Parraz RC | .30 | .75 |
| ❏ 88 Kelvin Vazquez RC | .15 | .40 |
| ❏ 89 Grant Hansen RC | .15 | .40 |
| ❏ 90 Matt Fox RC | .15 | .40 |
| ❏ 91 Trevor Plouffe RC | .50 | 1.25 |
| ❏ 92 Wes Whisler RC | .15 | .40 |
| ❏ 93 Curtis Thigpen RC | .30 | .75 |
| ❏ 94 Donnie Smith RC | .20 | .50 |
| ❏ 95 Luis Rivera RC | .20 | .50 |
| ❏ 96 Jesse Hoover RC | .20 | .50 |
| ❏ 97 Jason Vargas RC | .60 | 1.50 |
| ❏ 98 Clary Carlsen RC | .15 | .40 |
| ❏ 99 Mark Robinson RC | .15 | .40 |
| ❏ 100 J.C. Holt RC | .20 | .50 |
| ❏ 101 Chad Blackwell RC | .20 | .50 |
| ❏ 102 Daryl Jones RC | .40 | 1.00 |
| ❏ 103 Jonathan Tierce RC | .15 | .40 |
| ❏ 104 Patrick Bryant RC | .15 | .40 |
| ❏ 105 Eddie Prasch RC | .20 | .50 |
| ❏ 106 Mitch Einertson RC | .20 | .50 |
| ❏ 107 Kyle Waldrop RC | .40 | 1.00 |
| ❏ 108 Jeff Marquez RC | .20 | .50 |
| ❏ 109 Zach Jackson RC | .30 | .75 |
| ❏ 110 Josh Wahpepah RC | .15 | .40 |
| ❏ 111 Adam Lind RC | .75 | 2.00 |
| ❏ 112 Kyle Bloom RC | .20 | .50 |
| ❏ 113 Ben Harrison RC | .15 | .40 |
| ❏ 114 Taylor Tankersley RC | .20 | .50 |
| ❏ 115 Steven Jackson RC | .15 | .40 |
| ❏ 116 David Purcey RC | .30 | .75 |
| ❏ 117 Jacob McGee RC | .40 | 1.00 |
| ❏ 118 Lucas Harrell RC | .15 | .40 |
| ❏ 119 Brandon Allen RC | .50 | 1.25 |
| ❏ 120 Van Pope RC | .20 | .50 |
| ❏ 121 Jeff Francis | .10 | .30 |
| ❏ 122 Joe Blanton | .10 | .30 |
| ❏ 123 Wil Ledezma | .10 | .30 |
| ❏ 124 Bryan Bullington | .10 | .30 |
| ❏ 125 Jairo Garcia | .10 | .30 |
| ❏ 126 Matt Cain | .40 | 1.00 |
| ❏ 127 Amie Munoz | .10 | .30 |
| ❏ 128 Clint Everts | .10 | .30 |
| ❏ 129 Jesus Cota | .10 | .30 |
| ❏ 130 Gavin Floyd | .10 | .30 |
| ❏ 131 Edwin Encarnacion | .10 | .30 |
| ❏ 132 Koyie Hill | .10 | .30 |
| ❏ 133 Ruben Gotay | .10 | .30 |
| ❏ 134 Jeff Mathis | .10 | .30 |
| ❏ 135 Andy Marte | .20 | .50 |
| ❏ 136 Dallas McPherson | .10 | .30 |
| ❏ 137 Justin Morneau | .10 | .30 |
| ❏ 138 Rickie Weeks | .20 | .50 |
| ❏ 139 Joel Guzman | .20 | .50 |
| ❏ 140 Shin Soo Choo | .10 | .30 |
| ❏ 141 Yusmeiro Petit RC | .75 | 2.00 |
| ❏ 142 Jorge Cortes RC | .10 | .30 |
| ❏ 143 Val Majewski | .10 | .30 |
| ❏ 144 Felix Pie | .20 | .50 |
| ❏ 145 Aaron Hill | .10 | .30 |
| ❏ 146 Jose Capellan | .10 | .30 |
| ❏ 147 Dioner Navarro | .20 | .50 |
| ❏ 148 Fausto Carmona RC | .30 | .75 |
| ❏ 149 Robinzon Diaz RC | .15 | .40 |
| ❏ 150 Felix Hernandez RC | 1.50 | 4.00 |
| ❏ 151 Andres Blanco RC | .10 | .30 |
| ❏ 152 Jason Kubel | .10 | .30 |
| ❏ 153 Willy Taveras RC | .40 | 1.00 |
| ❏ 154 Merkin Valdez | .20 | .50 |
| ❏ 155 Robinson Cano | .50 | 1.25 |
| ❏ 156 Bill Murphy | .10 | .30 |
| ❏ 157 Chris Burke | .10 | .30 |
| ❏ 158 Kyle Sleeth | .10 | .30 |
| ❏ 159 B.J. Upton | .30 | .75 |
| ❏ 160 Tim Stauffer | .20 | .50 |
| ❏ 161 David Wright | .75 | 2.00 |
| ❏ 162 Conor Jackson | .50 | 1.25 |
| ❏ 163 Brad Thompson RC | .10 | .30 |
| ❏ 164 Delmon Young | .20 | .50 |
| ❏ 165 Jeremy Reed | .10 | .30 |

## 2005 Bowman

| | | |
|---|---|---|
| ❏ COMPLETE SET (330) | 40.00 | 80.00 |
| ❏ COMMON CARD (1-140) | .10 | .30 |
| ❏ COMMON CARD (141-165) | .15 | .40 |
| ❏ COMMON CARD (166-330) | .10 | .30 |
| ❏ PLATE CARDS 1:695 HOBBY, 1:177 HTA | | |
| ❏ PLATE PRINT RUN 1 SET PER COLOR | | |
| ❏ BLACK-CYAN-MAGENTA-YELLOW ISSUED | | |
| ❏ NO PLATE PRICING DUE TO SCARCITY | | |
| ❏ ROY ODDS 1:668 H, 1:248 HTA, 1:1535 R | | |
| ❏ 1 Gavin Floyd | .10 | .30 |
| ❏ 2 Eric Chavez | .10 | .30 |
| ❏ 3 Miguel Tejada | .10 | .30 |
| ❏ 4 Dmitri Young | .10 | .30 |
| ❏ 5 Hank Blalock | .10 | .30 |
| ❏ 6 Kerry Wood | .10 | .30 |
| ❏ 7 Andy Pettitte | .20 | .50 |
| ❏ 8 Pat Burrell | .10 | .30 |
| ❏ 9 Johnny Estrada | .10 | .30 |
| ❏ 10 Frank Thomas | .30 | .75 |
| ❏ 11 Juan Pierre | .10 | .30 |
| ❏ 12 Tom Glavine | .20 | .50 |
| ❏ 13 Lyle Overbay | .10 | .30 |
| ❏ 14 Jim Edmonds | .10 | .30 |
| ❏ 15 Steve Finley | .10 | .30 |
| ❏ 16 Jermaine Dye | .10 | .30 |
| ❏ 17 Omar Vizquel | .20 | .50 |
| ❏ 18 Nick Johnson | .10 | .30 |
| ❏ 19 Brian Giles | .10 | .30 |
| ❏ 20 Justin Morneau | .10 | .30 |
| ❏ 21 Preston Wilson | .10 | .30 |
| ❏ 22 Wily Mo Pena | .10 | .30 |
| ❏ 23 Rafael Palmeiro | .20 | .50 |
| ❏ 24 Scott Kazmir | .10 | .30 |
| ❏ 25 Derek Jeter | .60 | 1.50 |
| ❏ 26 Barry Zito | .10 | .30 |
| ❏ 27 Mike Lowell | .10 | .30 |
| ❏ 28 Jason Bay | .10 | .30 |
| ❏ 29 Ken Harvey | .10 | .30 |
| ❏ 30 Nomar Garciaparra | .30 | .75 |
| ❏ 31 Roy Halladay | .10 | .30 |
| ❏ 32 Todd Helton | .20 | .50 |
| ❏ 33 Mark Kotsay | .10 | .30 |
| ❏ 34 Jake Peavy | .10 | .30 |
| ❏ 35 David Wright | .50 | 1.25 |
| ❏ 36 Dontrelle Willis | .10 | .30 |
| ❏ 37 Marcus Giles | .10 | .30 |
| ❏ 38 Chone Figgins | .10 | .30 |
| ❏ 39 Sidney Ponson | .10 | .30 |
| ❏ 40 Randy Johnson | .30 | .75 |
| ❏ 41 John Smoltz | .20 | .50 |
| ❏ 42 Kevin Millar | .10 | .30 |
| ❏ 43 Mark Teixeira | .20 | .50 |
| ❏ 44 Alex Rios | .10 | .30 |
| ❏ 45 Mike Piazza | .30 | .75 |
| ❏ 46 Victor Martinez | .10 | .30 |
| ❏ 47 Jeff Bagwell | .20 | .50 |
| ❏ 48 Shawn Green | .10 | .30 |
| ❏ 49 Ivan Rodriguez | .20 | .50 |
| ❏ 50 Alex Rodriguez | .50 | 1.25 |
| ❏ 51 Kazuo Matsui | .10 | .30 |
| ❏ 52 Mark Mulder | .10 | .30 |
| ❏ 53 Michael Young | .20 | .50 |
| ❏ 54 Javy Lopez | .10 | .30 |
| ❏ 55 Johnny Damon | .20 | .50 |
| ❏ 56 Jeff Francis | .10 | .30 |
| ❏ 57 Rich Harden | .10 | .30 |
| ❏ 58 Bobby Abreu | .10 | .30 |
| ❏ 59 Mark Loretta | .10 | .30 |
| ❏ 60 Gary Sheffield | .10 | .30 |
| ❏ 61 Jamie Moyer | .10 | .30 |
| ❏ 62 Garret Anderson | .10 | .30 |
| ❏ 63 Vernon Wells | .10 | .30 |
| ❏ 64 Orlando Cabrera | .10 | .30 |
| ❏ 65 Magglio Ordonez | .10 | .30 |
| ❏ 66 Ronnie Belliard | .10 | .30 |
| ❏ 67 Carlos Lee | .10 | .30 |
| ❏ 68 Carl Pavano | .10 | .30 |
| ❏ 69 Jon Lieber | .10 | .30 |
| ❏ 70 Aubrey Huff | .10 | .30 |
| ❏ 71 Rocco Baldelli | .10 | .30 |
| ❏ 72 Jason Schmidt | .10 | .30 |
| ❏ 73 Bernie Williams | .20 | .50 |
| ❏ 74 Hideki Matsui | .50 | 1.25 |
| ❏ 75 Ken Griffey Jr. | .50 | 1.25 |
| ❏ 76 Josh Beckett | .10 | .30 |
| ❏ 77 Mark Buehrle | .10 | .30 |
| ❏ 78 David Ortiz | .30 | .75 |
| ❏ 79 Luis Gonzalez | .10 | .30 |
| ❏ 80 Scott Rolen | .20 | .50 |
| ❏ 81 Joe Mauer | .30 | .75 |
| ❏ 82 Jose Reyes | .10 | .30 |
| ❏ 83 Adam Dunn | .20 | .50 |
| ❏ 84 Greg Maddux | .50 | 1.25 |
| ❏ 85 Bartolo Colon | .10 | .30 |
| ❏ 86 Bret Boone | .10 | .30 |
| ❏ 87 Mike Mussina | .20 | .50 |
| ❏ 88 Ben Sheets | .10 | .30 |
| ❏ 89 Lance Berkman | .10 | .30 |
| ❏ 90 Miguel Cabrera | .30 | .75 |
| ❏ 91 C.C. Sabathia | .10 | .30 |
| ❏ 92 Mike Maroth | .10 | .30 |
| ❏ 93 Andruw Jones | .20 | .50 |
| ❏ 94 Jack Wilson | .10 | .30 |
| ❏ 95 Ichiro Suzuki | .60 | 1.50 |
| ❏ 96 Geoff Jenkins | .10 | .30 |
| ❏ 97 Zack Greinke | .10 | .30 |
| ❏ 98 Jorge Posada | .20 | .50 |
| ❏ 99 Travis Hafner | .10 | .30 |

|  |  | | |
|---|---|---|---|
| 100 | Barry Bonds | .75 | 2.00 |
| 101 | Aaron Rowand | .10 | .30 |
| 102 | Aramis Ramirez | .10 | .30 |
| 103 | Curt Schilling | .20 | .50 |
| 104 | Melvin Mora | .10 | .30 |
| 105 | Albert Pujols | .60 | 1.50 |
| 106 | Austin Kearns | .10 | .30 |
| 107 | Shannon Stewart | .10 | .30 |
| 108 | Carl Crawford | .10 | .30 |
| 109 | Carlos Zambrano | .10 | .30 |
| 110 | Roger Clemens | .50 | 1.25 |
| 111 | Javier Vazquez | .10 | .30 |
| 112 | Randy Wolf | .10 | .30 |
| 113 | Chipper Jones | .30 | .75 |
| 114 | Larry Walker | .20 | .50 |
| 115 | Alfonso Soriano | .10 | .30 |
| 116 | Brad Wilkerson | .10 | .30 |
| 117 | Bobby Crosby | .10 | .30 |
| 118 | Jim Thome | .20 | .50 |
| 119 | Oliver Perez | .10 | .30 |
| 120 | Vladimir Guerrero | .30 | .75 |
| 121 | Roy Oswalt | .10 | .30 |
| 122 | Torii Hunter | .10 | .30 |
| 123 | Rafael Furcal | .10 | .30 |
| 124 | Luis Castillo | .10 | .30 |
| 125 | Carlos Beltran | .10 | .30 |
| 126 | Mike Sweeney | .10 | .30 |
| 127 | Johan Santana | .30 | .75 |
| 128 | Tim Hudson | .10 | .30 |
| 129 | Troy Glaus | .10 | .30 |
| 130 | Manny Ramirez | .20 | .50 |
| 131 | Jeff Kent | .10 | .30 |
| 132 | Jose Vidro | .10 | .30 |
| 133 | Edgar Renteria | .10 | .30 |
| 134 | Russ Ortiz | .10 | .30 |
| 135 | Sammy Sosa | .30 | .75 |
| 136 | Carlos Delgado | .10 | .30 |
| 137 | Richie Sexson | .10 | .30 |
| 138 | Pedro Martinez | .20 | .50 |
| 139 | Adrian Beltre | .10 | .30 |
| 140 | Mark Prior | .20 | .50 |
| 141 | Omar Quintanilla | .15 | .40 |
| 142 | Carlos Quentin | .20 | .50 |
| 143 | Dan Johnson | .20 | .50 |
| 144 | Jake Stevens | .15 | .40 |
| 145 | Nate Schierholtz | .20 | .50 |
| 146 | Neil Walker | .15 | .40 |
| 147 | Bill Bray | .15 | .40 |
| 148 | Taylor Tankersley | .15 | .40 |
| 149 | Trevor Plouffe | .20 | .50 |
| 150 | Felix Hernandez | .75 | 2.00 |
| 151 | Phillip Hughes | .20 | .50 |
| 152 | James Houser | .15 | .40 |
| 153 | David Murphy | .15 | .40 |
| 154 | Ervin Santana | .15 | .40 |
| 155 | Andrew Whitington | .15 | .40 |
| 156 | Chris Lambert | .15 | .40 |
| 157 | Jeremy Sowers | .20 | .50 |
| 158 | Giovanny Gonzalez | .15 | .40 |
| 159 | Blake DeWitt | .20 | .50 |
| 160 | Thomas Diamond | .20 | .50 |
| 161 | Greg Golson | .15 | .40 |
| 162 | David Aardsma | .15 | .40 |
| 163 | Paul Maholm | .15 | .40 |
| 164 | Mark Rogers | .20 | .50 |
| 165 | Homer Bailey | .20 | .50 |
| 166 | Chip Cannon FY RC | .40 | 1.00 |
| 167 | Tony Giarratano FY RC | .20 | .50 |
| 168 | Darren Fenster FY RC | .20 | .50 |
| 169 | Elvys Quezada FY RC | .20 | .50 |
| 170 | Glen Perkins FY RC | .40 | 1.00 |
| 171 | Ian Kinsler FY RC | 1.25 | 3.00 |
| 172 | Mike Bourn FY RC | .40 | 1.00 |
| 173 | Jeremy West FY RC | .30 | .75 |
| 174 | Austin Verlander FY RC | 2.00 | 5.00 |
| 175 | Kevin West FY RC | .20 | .50 |
| 176 | Luis Hernandez FY RC | .20 | .50 |
| 177 | Matt Campbell FY RC | .20 | .50 |
| 178 | Nate McLouth FY RC | .40 | 1.00 |
| 179 | Ryan Goleski FY RC | .30 | .75 |
| 180 | Matthew Lindstrom FY RC | .30 | .75 |
| 181 | Matt DeSalvo FY RC | .30 | .75 |
| 182 | Kole Strayhorn FY RC | .20 | .50 |
| 183 | Jose Vaquedano FY RC | .20 | .50 |
| 184 | James Jurries FY RC | .30 | .75 |
| 185 | Ian Bladergroen FY RC | .30 | .75 |
| 186 | Eric Nielsen FY RC | .20 | .50 |
| 187 | Chris Vines FY RC | .20 | .50 |
| 188 | Chris Denorfia FY RC | .40 | 1.00 |
| 189 | Kevin Melillo FY RC | .40 | 1.00 |
| 190 | Melky Cabrera FY RC | 1.00 | 2.50 |
| 191 | Ryan Sweeney FY RC | .50 | 1.25 |
| 192 | Sean Marshall FY RC | .75 | 2.00 |
| 193 | Andy LaRoche FY RC | 1.50 | 4.00 |
| 194 | Tyler Pelland FY RC | .30 | .75 |
| 195 | Mike Morse FY RC | .25 | .60 |
| 196 | Wes Swackhamer FY RC | .20 | .50 |
| 197 | Wade Robinson FY RC | .20 | .50 |
| 198 | Dan Santin FY RC | .20 | .50 |
| 199 | Steve Doetsch FY RC | .30 | .75 |
| 200 | Shane Costa FY RC | .50 | 1.25 |
| 201 | Scott Mathieson FY RC | .40 | 1.00 |
| 202 | Ben Jones FY RC | .40 | 1.00 |
| 203 | Michael Rogers FY RC | .20 | .50 |
| 204 | Matt Rogelstad FY RC | .20 | .50 |
| 205 | Luis Ramirez FY RC | .20 | .50 |
| 206 | Landon Powell FY RC | .30 | .75 |
| 207 | Erik Cordier FY RC | .20 | .50 |
| 208 | Chris Seddon FY RC | .20 | .50 |
| 209 | Chris Roberson FY RC | .20 | .50 |
| 210 | Thomas Oldham FY RC | .20 | .50 |
| 211 | Dana Eveland FY RC | .20 | .50 |
| 212 | Cody Haerther FY RC | .20 | .50 |
| 213 | Danny Core FY RC | .20 | .50 |
| 214 | Craig Tatum FY RC | .20 | .50 |
| 215 | Elliot Johnson FY RC | .20 | .50 |
| 216 | Ender Chavez FY RC | .20 | .50 |
| 217 | Errol Simonitsch FY RC | .30 | .75 |
| 218 | Matt Van Der Bosch FY RC | .20 | .50 |
| 219 | Eulogio de la Cruz FY RC | .20 | .50 |
| 220 | C.J. Smith FY RC | .20 | .50 |
| 221 | Adam Boeve FY RC | .20 | .50 |
| 222 | Adam Harben FY RC | .30 | .75 |
| 223 | Baltazar Lopez FY RC | .20 | .50 |
| 224 | Russ Martin FY RC | .75 | 2.00 |
| 225 | Brian Bannister FY RC | .40 | 1.00 |
| 226 | Brian Miller FY RC | .20 | .50 |
| 227 | Casey McGehee FY RC | .20 | .50 |
| 228 | Humberto Sanchez FY RC | .75 | 2.00 |
| 229 | Javon Moran FY RC | .20 | .50 |
| 230 | Brandon McCarthy FY RC | .60 | 1.50 |
| 231 | Danny Zell FY RC | .20 | .50 |
| 232 | Jake Postlewait FY RC | .20 | .50 |
| 233 | Juan Tejeda FY RC | .20 | .50 |
| 234 | Keith Ramsey FY RC | .20 | .50 |
| 235 | Lorenzo Scott FY RC | .20 | .50 |
| 236 | Wladimir Balentien FY RC | .40 | 1.00 |
| 237 | Martin Prado FY RC | .20 | .50 |
| 238 | Matt Albers FY RC | .50 | 1.25 |
| 239 | Brian Schweiger FY RC | .20 | .50 |
| 240 | Brian Slavisky FY RC | .20 | .50 |
| 241 | Pat Misch FY RC | .20 | .50 |
| 242 | Pat Osborn FY | .15 | .40 |
| 243 | Ryan Feierabend FY RC | .20 | .50 |
| 244 | Shaun Marcum FY | .15 | .40 |
| 245 | Kevin Collins FY RC | .20 | .50 |
| 246 | Stuart Pomeranz FY RC | .20 | .50 |
| 247 | Tetsu Yolu FY RC | .20 | .50 |
| 248 | Heman Iribarren FY RC | .30 | .75 |
| 249 | Mike Spidale FY RC | .20 | .50 |
| 250 | Tony Americh FY RC | .20 | .50 |
| 251 | Manny Parra FY RC | .50 | 1.25 |
| 252 | Drew Anderson FY RC | .20 | .50 |
| 253 | T.J. Beam FY RC | .40 | 1.00 |
| 254 | Pedro Lopez FY RC | .20 | .50 |
| 255 | Andy Sides FY RC | .20 | .50 |
| 256 | Bear Bay FY RC | .30 | .75 |
| 257 | Matt McCarthy FY RC | .20 | .50 |
| 258 | Daniel Haigwood FY RC | .40 | 1.00 |
| 259 | Brian Sprout FY RC | .40 | 1.00 |
| 260 | Bryan Triplett FY RC | .20 | .50 |
| 261 | Steven Bondurant FY RC | .30 | .75 |
| 262 | Darwinson Salazar FY RC | .20 | .50 |
| 263 | David Shepard FY RC | .20 | .50 |
| 264 | Johan Silva FY RC | .20 | .50 |
| 265 | J.B. Thurmond FY RC | .20 | .50 |
| 266 | Brandon Moorhead FY RC | .20 | .50 |
| 267 | Kyle Nichols FY RC | .30 | .75 |
| 268 | Jonathan Sanchez FY RC | .75 | 2.00 |
| 269 | Mike Esposito FY RC | .20 | .50 |
| 270 | Erik Schindewolf FY RC | .20 | .50 |
| 271 | Peeter Ramos FY RC | .20 | .50 |
| 272 | Juan Senreiso FY RC | .20 | .50 |
| 273 | Matthew Kemp FY RC | 1.50 | 4.00 |
| 274 | Vinny Rottino FY RC | .20 | .50 |
| 275 | Micah Furtado FY RC | .20 | .50 |
| 276 | George Kottaras FY RC | .40 | 1.00 |
| 277 | Billy Butler FY RC | 1.50 | 4.00 |
| 278 | Buck Coats FY RC | .20 | .50 |
| 279 | Kenny Durost FY RC | .20 | .50 |
| 280 | Nick Touchstone FY RC | .20 | .50 |
| 281 | Jerry Owens FY RC | .30 | .75 |
| 282 | Stefan Bailie FY RC | .20 | .50 |
| 283 | Jesse Gutierrez FY RC | .20 | .50 |
| 284 | Chuck Tiffany FY RC | .50 | 1.25 |
| 285 | Brendan Ryan FY RC | .20 | .50 |
| 286 | Hayden Penn FY RC | .40 | 1.00 |
| 287 | Shawn Bowman FY RC | .30 | .75 |
| 288 | Alexander Smit FY RC | .20 | .50 |
| 289 | Micah Schnurstein FY RC | .20 | .50 |
| 290 | Jared Gothreaux FY RC | .20 | .50 |
| 291 | Jair Jurrjens FY RC | .60 | 1.50 |
| 292 | Bobby Livingston FY RC | .20 | .50 |
| 293 | Ryan Speier FY RC | .20 | .50 |
| 294 | Zach Parker FY RC | .20 | .50 |
| 295 | Christian Colonel FY RC | .20 | .50 |
| 296 | Scott Mitchinson FY RC | .20 | .50 |
| 297 | Neil Wilson FY RC | .20 | .50 |
| 298 | Chuck James FY RC | .75 | 2.00 |
| 299 | Heath Totten FY RC | .20 | .50 |
| 300 | Sean Tracey FY RC | .20 | .50 |
| 301 | Ismael Ramirez FY RC | .20 | .50 |
| 302 | Matt Brown FY RC | .20 | .50 |
| 303 | Franklin Morales FY RC | .30 | .75 |
| 304 | Brandon Sing FY RC | .30 | .75 |
| 305 | D.J. Houlton FY RC | .20 | .50 |
| 306 | Jayce Tingler FY RC | .20 | .50 |
| 307 | Mitchell Arnold FY RC | .20 | .50 |
| 308 | Jim Burt FY RC | .20 | .50 |
| 309 | Jason Motte FY RC | .20 | .50 |
| 310 | David Gassner FY RC | .20 | .50 |
| 311 | Andy Santana FY RC | .20 | .50 |
| 312 | Kelvin Pichardo FY RC | .20 | .50 |
| 313 | Carlos Carrasco FY RC | .50 | 1.25 |
| 314 | Willy Mota FY RC | .20 | .50 |
| 315 | Frank Mata FY RC | .20 | .50 |
| 316 | Carlos Gonzalez FY RC | 1.25 | 3.00 |
| 317 | Jeff Niemann FY RC | .40 | 1.00 |
| 318 | Chris B.Young FY RC | 1.00 | 2.50 |
| 319 | Billy Sadler FY RC | .20 | .50 |
| 320 | Ricky Barrett FY RC | .20 | .50 |
| 321 | Ben Harrison FY | .15 | .40 |
| 322 | Steve Nelson FY RC | .20 | .50 |
| 323 | Daryl Thompson FY RC | .20 | .50 |
| 324 | Philip Humber FY RC | .40 | 1.00 |
| 325 | Jeremy Harts FY RC | .20 | .50 |
| 326 | Nick Masset FY RC | .20 | .50 |
| 327 | Mike Rodriguez FY RC | .20 | .50 |
| 328 | Mike Garber FY RC | .20 | .50 |
| 329 | Kargell Bibbe FY RC | .20 | .50 |
| 330 | Ryan Garko FY RC | .60 | 1.50 |
| | CB Bay Bat/Crosby Bat HOY | 6.00 | 15.00 |

## 2005 Bowman Draft

| | | | |
|---|---|---|---|
| COMPLETE SET (165) | | 15.00 | 40.00 |
| COMMON CARD (1-165) | | .10 | .30 |
| COMMON RC | | .10 | .30 |
| COMMON RC YR | | .10 | .30 |
| OVERALL PLATE ODDS 1:826 HOBBY | | | |
| PLATE PRINT RUN 1 SET PER COLOR | | | |
| BLACK-CYAN-MAGENTA-YELLOW ISSUED | | | |
| NO PLATE PRICING DUE TO SCARCITY | | | |
| 1 | Rickie Weeks | .10 | .30 |
| 2 | Kyle Davies | .10 | .30 |
| 3 | Garrett Atkins | .10 | .30 |
| 4 | Chien-Ming Wang | .40 | 1.00 |
| 5 | Dallas McPherson | .10 | .30 |
| 6 | Dan Johnson | .10 | .30 |
| 7 | Andy Sisco | .10 | .30 |
| 8 | Ryan Doumit | .10 | .30 |

|  |  | | |
|---|---|---|---|
| 9 | J.P. Howell | .10 | .30 |
| 10 | Tim Stauffer | .10 | .30 |
| 11 | Willy Taveras | .10 | .30 |
| 12 | Aaron Hill | .10 | .30 |
| 13 | Victor Diaz | .10 | .30 |
| 14 | Wilson Betemit | .10 | .30 |
| 15 | Ervin Santana | .10 | .30 |
| 16 | Mike Morse | .10 | .30 |
| 17 | Yadier Molina | .10 | .30 |
| 18 | Kelly Johnson | .10 | .30 |
| 19 | Clint Barmes | .10 | .30 |
| 20 | Robinson Cano | .20 | .50 |
| 21 | Brad Thompson | .10 | .30 |
| 22 | Jorge Cantu | .10 | .30 |
| 23 | Brad Halsey | .10 | .30 |
| 24 | Lance Niekro | .10 | .30 |
| 25 | D.J. Houlton | .10 | .30 |
| 26 | Ryan Church | .10 | .30 |
| 27 | Hayden Penn | .30 | .75 |
| 28 | Chris Young | .10 | .30 |
| 29 | Chad Orvella RC | .10 | .30 |
| 30 | Mark Teahen | .10 | .30 |
| 31 | Mark McCormick FY RC | .20 | .50 |
| 32 | Jay Bruce FY RC | 3.00 | 8.00 |
| 33 | Beau Jones FY RC | .20 | .50 |
| 34 | Tyler Greene FY RC | .30 | .75 |
| 35 | Zach Ward FY RC | .10 | .30 |
| 36 | Josh Bell FY RC | .30 | .75 |
| 37 | Josh Wall FY RC | .20 | .50 |
| 38 | Nick Webber FY RC | .10 | .30 |
| 39 | Travis Buck FY RC | .40 | 1.00 |
| 40 | Kyle Winters FY RC | .20 | .50 |
| 41 | Mitch Boggs FY RC | .10 | .30 |
| 42 | Tommy Mendoza FY RC | .30 | .75 |
| 43 | Brad Corley FY RC | .20 | .50 |
| 44 | Drew Butera FY RC | .10 | .30 |
| 45 | Ryan Mount FY RC | .30 | .75 |
| 46 | Tyler Herron FY RC | .20 | .50 |
| 47 | Nick Weglarz FY RC | .20 | .50 |
| 48 | Brandon Erbe FY RC | .40 | 1.00 |
| 49 | Cody Allen FY RC | .10 | .30 |
| 50 | Eric Fowler FY RC | .10 | .30 |
| 51 | James Boone FY RC | .20 | .50 |
| 52 | Josh Flores FY RC | .50 | 1.25 |
| 53 | Brandon Monk FY RC | .20 | .50 |
| 54 | Kieron Pope FY RC | .30 | .75 |
| 55 | Kyle Cofield FY RC | .10 | .30 |
| 56 | Brent Lillibridge FY RC | .20 | .50 |
| 57 | Daryl Jones FY RC | .10 | .30 |
| 58 | Eli Iorg FY RC | .20 | .50 |
| 59 | Brett Hayes FY RC | .10 | .30 |
| 60 | Mike Durant FY RC | .30 | .75 |
| 61 | Michael Bowden FY RC | .75 | 2.00 |
| 62 | Paul Kelly FY RC | .20 | .50 |
| 63 | Andrew McCutchen FY RC | 1.00 | 2.50 |
| 64 | Travis Wood FY RC | .40 | 1.00 |
| 65 | Cesar Ramos FY RC | .20 | .50 |
| 66 | Chaz Roe FY RC | .20 | .50 |
| 67 | Matt Torra FY RC | .20 | .50 |
| 68 | Kevin Slowey FY RC | .60 | 1.50 |
| 69 | Trayvon Robinson FY RC | .30 | .75 |
| 70 | Reid Engel FY RC | .10 | .30 |
| 71 | Kris Harvey FY RC | .20 | .50 |
| 72 | Craig Italiano FY RC | .30 | .75 |
| 73 | Matt Maloney FY RC | .40 | 1.00 |
| 74 | Sean West FY RC | .30 | .75 |
| 75 | Henry Sanchez FY RC | .20 | .50 |
| 76 | Scott Blue FY RC | .10 | .30 |
| 77 | Jordan Schafer FY RC | 1.00 | 2.50 |
| 78 | Chris Robinson FY RC | .20 | .50 |
| 79 | Chris Hobdy FY RC | .10 | .30 |
| 80 | Brandon Durden FY RC | .10 | .30 |
| 81 | Clay Buchholz FY RC | 2.50 | 6.00 |
| 82 | Josh Geer FY RC | .10 | .30 |
| 83 | Sam LeCure FY RC | .10 | .30 |
| 84 | Justin Thomas FY RC | .10 | .30 |
| 85 | Brett Gardner FY RC | .20 | .50 |
| 86 | Tommy Manzella FY RC | .10 | .30 |
| 87 | Matt Green FY RC | .10 | .30 |
| 88 | Yunel Escobar FY RC | .75 | 2.00 |
| 89 | Mike Costanzo FY RC | .30 | .75 |
| 90 | Nick Hundley FY RC | .10 | .30 |
| 91 | Zach Simons FY RC | .10 | .30 |
| 92 | Jacob Marceaux FY RC | .10 | .30 |
| 93 | Jed Lowrie FY RC | .20 | .50 |
| 94 | Brandon Snyder FY RC | .40 | 1.00 |
| 95 | Matt Goyen FY RC | .10 | .30 |
| 96 | Jon Egan FY RC | .20 | .50 |
| 97 | Drew Thompson FY RC | .20 | .50 |
| 98 | Bryan Anderson FY RC | .40 | 1.00 |
| 99 | Clayton Richard FY RC | .10 | .30 |
| 100 | Jimmy Shull FY RC | .20 | .50 |
| 101 | Mark Pawelek FY RC | .60 | 1.50 |
| 102 | P.J. Phillips FY RC | .30 | .75 |
| 103 | John Drennen FY RC | .50 | 1.25 |
| 104 | Nolan Reimold FY RC | .50 | 1.25 |
| 105 | Troy Tulowitzki FY RC | 1.50 | 4.00 |
| 106 | Kevin Whelan FY RC | .15 | .40 |
| 107 | Wade Townsend FY RC | .20 | .50 |
| 108 | Micah Owings FY RC | .50 | 1.25 |
| 109 | Ryan Tucker FY RC | .20 | .50 |
| 110 | Jeff Clement FY RC | .60 | 1.50 |
| 111 | Josh Sullivan FY RC | .10 | .30 |
| 112 | Jeff Lyman FY RC | .20 | .50 |
| 113 | Brian Bogusevic FY RC | .10 | .30 |
| 114 | Trevor Bell FY RC | .20 | .50 |
| 115 | Brent Cox FY RC | .20 | .50 |
| 116 | Michael Bilek FY RC | .10 | .30 |
| 117 | Garrett Olson FY RC | .20 | .50 |
| 118 | Steven Johnson FY RC | .10 | .30 |
| 119 | Chase Headley FY RC | .30 | .75 |
| 120 | Daniel Carte FY RC | .20 | .50 |
| 121 | Francisco Liriano PROS | .60 | 1.50 |
| 122 | Fausto Carmona PROS | .10 | .30 |
| 123 | Zach Jackson PROS | .10 | .30 |
| 124 | Adam Loewen PROS | .10 | .30 |
| 125 | Chris Lambert PROS | .10 | .30 |
| 126 | Scott Mathieson FY | .10 | .30 |
| 127 | Paul Maholm PROS | .10 | .30 |
| 128 | Fernando Nieve PROS | .10 | .30 |
| 129 | Justin Verlander PROS | .60 | 1.50 |
| 130 | Yusmeiro Petit PROS | .20 | .50 |
| 131 | Joel Zumaya PROS | .20 | .50 |
| 132 | Merkin Valdez PROS | .10 | .30 |
| 133 | Ryan Garko FY | .10 | .30 |
| 134 | Edison Volquez FY RC | 1.50 | 4.00 |
| 135 | Russ Martin FY | .30 | .75 |
| 136 | Conor Jackson PROS | .10 | .30 |
| 137 | Miguel Montero FY RC | .40 | 1.00 |
| 138 | Josh Barfield PROS | .10 | .30 |
| 139 | Delmon Young PROS | .20 | .50 |
| 140 | Andy LaRoche PROS | .30 | .75 |
| 141 | William Bergolla PROS | .10 | .30 |
| 142 | B.J. Upton PROS | .30 | .75 |
| 143 | Heman Iribarren FY | .10 | .30 |
| 144 | Brandon Wood PROS | .30 | .75 |
| 145 | Jose Bautista PROS | .10 | .30 |
| 146 | Edwin Encarnacion PROS | .30 | .75 |
| 147 | Javier Herrera FY | .30 | .75 |
| 148 | Jeremy Hermida PROS | .30 | .75 |
| 149 | Frank Diaz PROS RC | .10 | .30 |
| 150 | Chris B.Young FY | .40 | 1.00 |
| 151 | Shin-Soo Choo PROS | .10 | .30 |
| 152 | Kevin Thompson PROS RC | .10 | .30 |
| 153 | Hanley Ramirez PROS | .20 | .50 |
| 154 | Lastings Milledge PROS | .30 | .75 |
| 155 | Luis Montanez PROS | .10 | .30 |
| 156 | Justin Huber PROS | .10 | .30 |
| 157 | Zach Duke PROS | .20 | .50 |
| 158 | Jeff Francoeur PROS | .30 | .75 |
| 159 | Melky Cabrera FY | .40 | 1.00 |
| 160 | Bobby Jenks PROS | .10 | .30 |
| 161 | Ian Snell PROS | .10 | .30 |
| 162 | Fernando Cabrera PROS | .10 | .30 |
| 163 | Troy Patton PROS | .20 | .50 |
| 164 | Anthony Lerew PROS | .10 | .30 |
| 165 | Nelson Cruz FY | .75 | 1.50 |

## 2006 Bowman

| | | |
|---|---|---|
| COMP.SET w/o AU's (220) | 15.00 | 40.00 |
| COMP.SET w/PROS (330) | 40.00 | 80.00 |
| COMMON CARD (1-200) | .10 | .30 |

| | | |
|---|---|---|
| SEMISTARS 1-220 | .20 | .50 |
| UNLISTED STARS 1-220 | .30 | .75 |
| COMMON ROOKIE (201-220) | .15 | .40 |
| ROOKIE SEMIS 201-220 | .25 | .60 |
| 219-220 AU ODDS 1:1150 HOBBY, 1:699 HTA | | |
| COMMON AUTO (221-231) | 4.00 | 10.00 |
| 221-231 AU ODDS 1:82 HOBBY, 1:40 HTA | | |
| 1-220 PLATE ODDS 1:588 HOBBY, 1:575 HTA | | |
| 221-231 AU PLATES 1:15,700 H, 1:4100 HTA | | |
| PLATE PRINT RUN 1 SET PER COLOR | | |
| BLACK-CYAN-MAGENTA-YELLOW ISSUED | | |
| NO PLATE PRICING DUE TO SCARCITY | | |

|  |  | | |
|---|---|---|---|
| 1 | Nick Swisher | .12 | .30 |
| 2 | Ted Lilly | .12 | .30 |
| 3 | John Smoltz | .20 | .50 |
| 4 | Lyle Overbay | .12 | .30 |
| 5 | Alfonso Soriano | .12 | .30 |
| 6 | Javier Vazquez | .12 | .30 |
| 7 | Ronnie Belliard | .12 | .30 |
| 8 | Jose Reyes | .30 | .75 |
| 9 | Brian Roberts | .12 | .30 |
| 10 | Curt Schilling | .20 | .50 |
| 11 | Adam Dunn | .12 | .30 |
| 12 | Zack Greinke | .12 | .30 |
| 13 | Carlos Guillen | .12 | .30 |
| 14 | Jon Garland | .12 | .30 |
| 15 | Robinson Cano | .20 | .50 |
| 16 | Chris Burke | .10 | .30 |
| 17 | Barry Zito | .10 | .30 |
| 18 | Russ Adams | .10 | .30 |
| 19 | Chris Capuano | .12 | .30 |
| 20 | Scott Rolen | .20 | .50 |
| 21 | Kerry Wood | .12 | .30 |
| 22 | Scott Kazmir | .20 | .50 |
| 23 | Brandon Webb | .12 | .30 |
| 24 | Jeff Kent | .10 | .30 |
| 25 | Albert Pujols | .60 | 1.50 |
| 26 | C.C. Sabathia | .10 | .30 |
| 27 | Adrian Beltre | .10 | .30 |
| 28 | Brad Wilkerson | .10 | .30 |
| 29 | Randy Wolf | .10 | .30 |
| 30 | Jason Bay | .20 | .50 |
| 31 | Austin Kearns | .10 | .30 |
| 32 | Clint Barmes | .10 | .30 |
| 33 | Mike Sweeney | .10 | .30 |
| 34 | Justin Verlander | .50 | 1.25 |
| 35 | Justin Morneau | .10 | .30 |
| 36 | Scott Podsednik | .10 | .30 |
| 37 | Jason Giambi | .10 | .30 |
| 38 | Steve Finley | .10 | .30 |
| 39 | Morgan Ensberg | .10 | .30 |
| 40 | Eric Chavez | .10 | .30 |
| 41 | Roy Halladay | .20 | .50 |
| 42 | Horacio Ramirez | .10 | .30 |
| 43 | Ben Sheets | .10 | .30 |
| 44 | Chris Carpenter | .10 | .30 |
| 45 | Andruw Jones | .20 | .50 |
| 46 | Carlos Zambrano | .10 | .30 |
| 47 | Jonny Gomes | .10 | .30 |
| 48 | Shawn Green | .10 | .30 |
| 49 | Moises Alou | .10 | .30 |
| 50 | Ichiro Suzuki | .50 | 1.25 |
| 51 | Juan Pierre | .20 | .50 |
| 52 | Grady Sizemore | .20 | .50 |
| 53 | Kazuo Matsui | .10 | .30 |
| 54 | Jose Vidro | .10 | .30 |
| 55 | Jake Peavy | .10 | .30 |
| 56 | Dallas Mcpherson | .10 | .30 |
| 57 | Ryan Howard | .50 | 1.25 |
| 58 | Zach Duke | .10 | .30 |
| 59 | Michael Young | .10 | .30 |
| 60 | Todd Helton | .20 | .50 |
| 61 | David Dejesus | .10 | .30 |
| 62 | Ivan Rodriguez | .20 | .50 |
| 63 | Johan Santana | .20 | .50 |
| 64 | Danny Haren | .10 | .30 |
| 65 | Derek Jeter | .75 | 2.00 |
| 66 | Greg Maddux | .50 | 1.25 |
| 67 | Jorge Cantu | .10 | .30 |
| 68 | Conor Jackson | .10 | .30 |
| 69 | Victor Martinez | .10 | .30 |
| 70 | David Wright | .50 | 1.25 |
| 71 | Ryan Church | .10 | .30 |
| 72 | Khalil Greene | .20 | .50 |
| 73 | Jimmy Rollins | .10 | .30 |
| 74 | Hank Blalock | .10 | .30 |
| 75 | Pedro Martinez | .20 | .50 |
| 76 | Jon Papelbon | .75 | 2.00 |

|  | | |
|---|---|---|
| 77 Felipe Lopez | .10 | .30 |
| 78 Jeff Francis | .10 | .30 |
| 79 Andy Sisco | .10 | .30 |
| 80 Hideki Matsui | .50 | 1.25 |
| 81 Ken Griffey Jr. | .50 | 1.25 |
| 82 Nomar Garciaparra | .30 | .75 |
| 83 Kevin Millwood | .10 | .30 |
| 84 Paul Konerko | .10 | .30 |
| 85 A.J. Burnett | .10 | .30 |
| 86 Mike Piazza | .30 | .75 |
| 87 Brian Giles | .10 | .30 |
| 88 Johnny Damon | .20 | .50 |
| 89 Jim Thome | .20 | .50 |
| 90 Roger Clemens | .60 | 1.50 |
| 91 Aaron Rowand | .10 | .30 |
| 92 Rafael Furcal | .10 | .30 |
| 93 Gary Sheffield | .10 | .30 |
| 94 Mike Cameron | .10 | .30 |
| 95 Carlos Delgado | .10 | .30 |
| 96 Jorge Posada | .20 | .50 |
| 97 Denny Bautista | .10 | .30 |
| 98 Mike Maroth | .10 | .30 |
| 99 Brad Radke | .10 | .30 |
| 100 Alex Rodriguez | .50 | 1.25 |
| 101 Freddy Garcia | .10 | .30 |
| 102 Oliver Perez | .10 | .30 |
| 103 Jon Lieber | .10 | .30 |
| 104 Melvin Mora | .10 | .30 |
| 105 Travis Hafner | .10 | .30 |
| 106 Matt Cain | .20 | .50 |
| 107 Derek Lowe | .10 | .30 |
| 108 Luis Castillo | .10 | .30 |
| 109 Livan Hernandez | .10 | .30 |
| 110 Tadahito Iguchi | .10 | .30 |
| 111 Shawn Chacon | .10 | .30 |
| 112 Frank Thomas | .30 | .75 |
| 113 Josh Beckett | .12 | .30 |
| 114 Aubrey Huff | .10 | .30 |
| 115 Derrek Lee | .10 | .30 |
| 116 Chien-Ming Wang | .30 | .75 |
| 117 Joe Crede | .10 | .30 |
| 118 Torii Hunter | .10 | .30 |
| 119 J.D. Drew | .10 | .30 |
| 120 Troy Glaus | .10 | .30 |
| 121 Sean Casey | .10 | .30 |
| 122 Edgar Renteria | .10 | .30 |
| 123 Craig Wilson | .10 | .30 |
| 124 Adam Eaton | .10 | .30 |
| 125 Jeff Francoeur | .30 | .75 |
| 126 Bruce Chen | .10 | .30 |
| 127 Cliff Floyd | .10 | .30 |
| 128 Jeremy Reed | .10 | .30 |
| 129 Jake Westbrook | .10 | .30 |
| 130 Wily Mo Pena | .10 | .30 |
| 131 Toby Hall | .10 | .30 |
| 132 David Ortiz | .20 | .50 |
| 133 David Eckstein | .10 | .30 |
| 134 Brady Clark | .10 | .30 |
| 135 Marcus Giles | .10 | .30 |
| 136 Aaron Hill | .10 | .30 |
| 137 Mark Kotsay | .10 | .30 |
| 138 Carlos Lee | .10 | .30 |
| 139 Roy Oswalt | .10 | .30 |
| 140 Chone Figgins | .10 | .30 |
| 141 Mike Mussina | .20 | .50 |
| 142 Orlando Hernandez | .10 | .30 |
| 143 Magglio Ordonez | .10 | .30 |
| 144 Jim Edmonds | .20 | .50 |
| 145 Bobby Abreu | .10 | .30 |
| 146 Nick Johnson | .10 | .30 |
| 147 Carlos Beltran | .10 | .30 |
| 148 Jhonny Peralta | .10 | .30 |
| 149 Pedro Feliz | .10 | .30 |
| 150 Miguel Tejada | .10 | .30 |
| 151 Luis Gonzalez | .10 | .30 |
| 152 Carl Crawford | .10 | .30 |
| 153 Yadier Molina | .10 | .30 |
| 154 Rich Harden | .10 | .30 |
| 155 Tim Wakefield | .10 | .30 |
| 156 Rickie Weeks | .10 | .30 |
| 157 Johnny Estrada | .10 | .30 |
| 158 Gustavo Chacin | .10 | .30 |
| 159 Dan Johnson | .10 | .30 |
| 160 Willy Taveras | .10 | .30 |
| 161 Garret Anderson | .10 | .30 |
| 162 Randy Johnson | .30 | .75 |
| 163 Jermaine Dye | .10 | .30 |
| 164 Joe Mauer | .30 | .75 |
| 165 Ervin Santana | .10 | .30 |
| 166 Jeremy Bonderman | .10 | .30 |
| 167 Garrett Atkins | .10 | .30 |
| 168 Warren Ramirez | .20 | .50 |
| 169 Brad Eldred | .10 | .30 |
| 170 Chase Utley | .30 | .75 |
| 171 Mark Loretta | .10 | .30 |
| 172 John Patterson | .10 | .30 |
| 173 Tom Glavine | .20 | .50 |
| 174 Dontrelle Willis | .20 | .50 |
| 175 Mark Teixeira | .20 | .50 |
| 176 Felix Hernandez | .20 | .50 |
| 177 Cliff Lee | .10 | .30 |
| 178 Jason Schmidt | .10 | .30 |
| 179 Chad Tracy | .10 | .30 |
| 180 Rocco Baldelli | .10 | .30 |
| 181 Aramis Ramirez | .10 | .30 |
| 182 Andy Pettitte | .20 | .50 |
| 183 Mark Mulder | .10 | .30 |
| 184 Geoff Jenkins | .10 | .30 |
| 185 Chipper Jones | .30 | .75 |
| 186 Vernon Wells | .10 | .30 |
| 187 Bobby Crosby | .10 | .30 |
| 188 Lance Berkman | .10 | .30 |
| 189 Vladimir Guerrero | .30 | .75 |
| 190 Jose Capellan | .10 | .30 |
| 191 Brad Penny | .10 | .30 |
| 192 Jose Guillen | .10 | .30 |
| 193 Brett Myers | .10 | .30 |
| 194 Miguel Cabrera | .20 | .50 |
| 195 Bartolo Colon | .10 | .30 |
| 196 Craig Biggio | .20 | .50 |
| 197 Tim Hudson | .10 | .30 |
| 198 Mark Prior | .20 | .50 |
| 199 Mark Buehrle | .10 | .30 |
| 200 Barry Bonds | .75 | 2.00 |
| 201 Anderson Hernandez (RC) | .15 | .40 |
| 202 Charlton Jimerson (RC) | .15 | .40 |
| 203 Jeremy Accardo RC | .15 | .40 |
| 204 Hanley Ramirez (RC) | .40 | 1.00 |
| 205 Matt Capps (RC) | .15 | .40 |
| 206 John-Ford Griffin (RC) | .15 | .40 |
| 207 Chuck James (RC) | .25 | .60 |
| 208 Jaime Bubela (RC) | .15 | .40 |
| 209 Mark Woodyard (RC) | .15 | .40 |
| 210 Jason Botts (RC) | .15 | .40 |
| 211 Chris Demaria RC | .15 | .40 |
| 212 Miguel Perez (RC) | .15 | .40 |
| 213 Tom Gorzelanny (RC) | .15 | .40 |
| 214 Adam Wainwright (RC) | .25 | .60 |
| 215 Ryan Garko (RC) | .15 | .40 |
| 216 Jason Bergmann RC | .15 | .40 |
| 217 J.J. Furmaniak (RC) | .15 | .40 |
| 218 Francisco Liriano (RC) | .75 | 2.00 |
| 219 Kenji Johjima RC | .75 | 2.00 |
| 219a Kenji Johjima AU | 30.00 | 60.00 |
| 220 Craig Hansen RC | .60 | 1.50 |
| 220a Craig Hansen AU | 20.00 | 50.00 |
| 221 Ryan Zimmerman AU (RC) | 20.00 | 50.00 |
| 222 Joey Devine AU (RC) | 4.00 | 10.00 |
| 223 Scott Olsen AU (RC) | 4.00 | 10.00 |
| 224 Darrel Rasner AU (RC) | 4.00 | 10.00 |
| 225 Craig Breslow AU RC | 4.00 | 10.00 |
| 226 Reggie Abercrombie AU (RC) | 4.00 | 10.00 |
| 227 Dan Uggla AU (RC) | 6.00 | 15.00 |
| 228 Willie Eyre AU (RC) | .15 | .40 |
| 229 Joel Zumaya AU (RC) | 12.50 | 30.00 |
| 230 Ricky Nolasco AU (RC) | 4.00 | 10.00 |
| 231 Ian Kinsler AU (RC) | 8.00 | 20.00 |

## 2006 Bowman Draft

| | | |
|---|---|---|
| COMPLETE SET (55) | 6.00 | 15.00 |
| COMMON RC (1-55) | .15 | .40 |
| RC SEMIS 1-55 | .25 | .60 |
| RC UNLISTED 1-55 | .40 | 1.00 |

APPX. TWO PER HOBBY/RETAIL PACK
ODDS INFO PROVIDED BY BECKETT
OVERALL PLATE ODDS: 1,990 HOBBY
PLATE PRINT RUN 1 SET PER COLOR
BLACK-CYAN-MAGENTA-YELLOW ISSUED
NO PLATE PRICING DUE TO SCARCITY

|  | | |
|---|---|---|
| 1 Matt Kemp (RC) | .40 | 1.00 |
| 2 Taylor Tankersley (RC) | .15 | .40 |
| 3 Mike Napoli (RC) | .40 | 1.00 |
| 4 Brian Bannister (RC) | .15 | .40 |
| 5 Melky Cabrera (RC) | .25 | .60 |
| 6 Bill Bray (RC) | .15 | .40 |
| 7 Brian Anderson (RC) | .15 | .40 |
| 8 Jered Weaver (RC) | .50 | 1.25 |
| 9 Chris Duncan (RC) | .25 | .60 |
| 10 Boof Bonser (RC) | .25 | .60 |
| 11 Mike Rouse (RC) | .25 | .60 |
| 12 David Pauley (RC) | .15 | .40 |
| 13 Russ Martin (RC) | .25 | .60 |
| 14 Jeremy Sowers (RC) | .15 | .40 |
| 15 Kevin Reese (RC) | .15 | .40 |
| 16 John Rheineclair (RC) | .15 | .40 |
| 17 Tommy Murphy (RC) | .15 | .40 |
| 18 Sean Marshall (RC) | .15 | .40 |
| 19 Jason Kubel (RC) | .15 | .40 |
| 20 Chad Billingsley (RC) | .25 | .60 |
| 21 Kendry Morales (RC) | .40 | 1.00 |
| 22 Jon Lester RC | 1.00 | 2.50 |
| 23 Brandon Fahey RC | .15 | .40 |
| 24 Josh Johnson (RC) | .25 | .60 |
| 25 Kevin Frandsen (RC) | .15 | .40 |
| 26 Casey Janssen RC | .25 | .60 |
| 27 Scott Thorman (RC) | .15 | .40 |
| 28 Scott Mathieson (RC) | .15 | .40 |
| 29 Jeremy Hermida (RC) | .15 | .40 |
| 30 Dustin Nippert (RC) | .15 | .40 |
| 31 Kevin Thompson (RC) | .15 | .40 |
| 32 Bobby Livingston (RC) | .15 | .40 |
| 33 Travis Ishikawa (RC) | .15 | .40 |
| 34 Jeff Mathis (RC) | .15 | .40 |
| 35 Charlie Haeger RC | .25 | .60 |
| 36 Josh Willingham (RC) | .15 | .40 |
| 37 Taylor Buchholz (RC) | .15 | .40 |
| 38 Joel Guzman (RC) | .15 | .40 |
| 39 Zach Jackson (RC) | .15 | .40 |
| 40 Howie Kendrick (RC) | .40 | 1.00 |
| 41 T.J. Beam (RC) | .15 | .40 |
| 42 Ty Taubenheim RC | .25 | .60 |
| 43 Erick Aybar (RC) | .15 | .40 |
| 44 Anibal Sanchez (RC) | .25 | .60 |
| 45 Michael Pelfrey RC | .60 | 1.50 |
| 46 Shawn Hill (RC) | .15 | .40 |
| 47 Chris Roberson (RC) | .15 | .40 |
| 48 Carlos Villanueva RC | .15 | .40 |
| 49 Andre Ethier (RC) | .40 | 1.00 |
| 50 Anthony Reyes (RC) | .25 | .50 |
| 51 Franklin Gutierrez (RC) | .15 | .40 |
| 52 Angel Guzman (RC) | .15 | .40 |
| 53 Michael O'Connor RC | .15 | .40 |
| 54 James Shields RC | .15 | .40 |
| 55 Nate McLouth (RC) | .15 | .40 |

## 2007 Bowman

| | | |
|---|---|---|
| COMP.SET w/o AU's (221) | 20.00 | 50.00 |
| COMMON CARD (1-200) | .12 | .30 |
| COMMON ROOKIE (201-220) | .15 | .40 |
| COMMON AUTO (221-236) | 4.00 | 10.00 |

219/221-236 AU ODDS 1:98 HOBBY, 1:25 HTA
BONDS ODDS 1:51 HTA, 1:610 RETAIL
1-220 PLATE ODDS 1:1468 H, 1:212 HTA
221-231 AU PLATES 1:8200 H, 1:1150 HTA
BONDS PLATE ODDS 1:106,000 HTA
PLATE PRINT RUN 1 SET PER COLOR

❑ BLACK-CYAN-MAGENTA-YELLOW ISSUED
❑ NO PLATE PRICING DUE TO SCARCITY

| | | |
|---|---|---|
| ❑ 1 Hanley Ramirez | .20 | .50 |
| ❑ 2 Justin Verlander | .30 | .75 |
| ❑ 3 Ryan Zimmerman | .30 | .75 |
| ❑ 4 Jered Weaver | .20 | .50 |
| ❑ 5 Stephen Drew | .20 | .50 |
| ❑ 6 Jonathan Papelbon | .30 | .75 |
| ❑ 7 Melky Cabrera | .12 | .30 |
| ❑ 8 Francisco Liriano | .30 | .75 |
| ❑ 9 Prince Fielder | .30 | .75 |
| ❑ 10 Dan Uggla | .20 | .50 |
| ❑ 11 Jeremy Sowers | .12 | .30 |
| ❑ 12 Carlos Quentin | .12 | .30 |
| ❑ 13 Chuck James | .12 | .30 |
| ❑ 14 Andre Ethier | .20 | .50 |
| ❑ 15 Cole Hamels UER | .30 | .75 |
| ❑ 16 Kenji Johjima | .30 | .75 |
| ❑ 17 Chad Billingsley | .12 | .30 |
| ❑ 18 Ian Kinsler | .12 | .30 |
| ❑ 19 Jason Hirsh | .12 | .30 |
| ❑ 20 Nick Markakis | .20 | .50 |
| ❑ 21 Jeremy Hermida | .12 | .30 |
| ❑ 22 Ryan Shealy | .12 | .30 |
| ❑ 23 Scott Olsen | .12 | .30 |
| ❑ 24 Russell Martin | .12 | .30 |
| ❑ 25 Conor Jackson | .12 | .30 |
| ❑ 26 Erik Bedard | .12 | .30 |
| ❑ 27 Brian McCann | .12 | .30 |
| ❑ 28 Michael Barrett | .12 | .30 |
| ❑ 29 Brandon Phillips | .12 | .30 |
| ❑ 30 Garrett Atkins | .12 | .30 |
| ❑ 31 Freddy Garcia | .12 | .30 |
| ❑ 32 Mark Loretta | .12 | .30 |
| ❑ 33 Craig Biggio | .20 | .50 |
| ❑ 34 Jeremy Bonderman | .12 | .30 |
| ❑ 35 Johan Santana | .30 | .75 |
| ❑ 36 Jorge Posada | .20 | .50 |
| ❑ 37 Brian Bannister | .12 | .30 |
| ❑ 38 Carlos Delgado | .12 | .30 |
| ❑ 39 Gary Matthews Jr. | .12 | .30 |
| ❑ 40 Mike Cameron | .12 | .30 |
| ❑ 41 Adrian Beltre | .12 | .30 |
| ❑ 42 Freddy Sanchez | .12 | .30 |
| ❑ 43 Austin Kearns | .12 | .30 |
| ❑ 44 Mark Buehrle | .12 | .30 |
| ❑ 45 Miguel Cabrera | .20 | .50 |
| ❑ 46 Josh Beckett | .20 | .50 |
| ❑ 47 Chone Figgins | .12 | .30 |
| ❑ 48 Edgar Renteria | .12 | .30 |
| ❑ 49 Derek Lowe | .12 | .30 |
| ❑ 50 Ryan Howard | .50 | 1.25 |
| ❑ 51 Shawn Green | .12 | .30 |
| ❑ 52 Jason Giambi | .12 | .30 |
| ❑ 53 Ervin Santana | .12 | .30 |
| ❑ 54 Jack Wilson | .12 | .30 |
| ❑ 55 Roy Oswalt | .12 | .30 |
| ❑ 56 Dan Haren | .12 | .30 |
| ❑ 57 Jose Vidro | .12 | .30 |
| ❑ 58 Kevin Millwood | .12 | .30 |
| ❑ 59 Jim Edmonds | .12 | .30 |
| ❑ 60 Carl Crawford | .12 | .30 |
| ❑ 61 Randy Wolf | .12 | .30 |
| ❑ 62 Paul LoDuca | .12 | .30 |
| ❑ 63 Johnny Estrada | .12 | .30 |
| ❑ 64 Brian Roberts | .12 | .30 |
| ❑ 65 Manny Ramirez | .20 | .50 |
| ❑ 66 Jose Contreras | .12 | .30 |
| ❑ 67 Josh Barfield | .12 | .30 |
| ❑ 68 Juan Pierre | .12 | .30 |
| ❑ 69 David DeJesus | .12 | .30 |
| ❑ 70 Gary Sheffield | .12 | .30 |
| ❑ 71 Jon Lieber | .12 | .30 |
| ❑ 72 Randy Johnson | .30 | .75 |
| ❑ 73 Rickie Weeks | .12 | .30 |
| ❑ 74 Brian Giles | .12 | .30 |
| ❑ 75 Ichiro Suzuki | .50 | 1.25 |
| ❑ 76 Nick Swisher | .12 | .30 |
| ❑ 77 Justin Morneau | .12 | .30 |
| ❑ 78 Scott Kazmir | .12 | .30 |
| ❑ 79 Lyle Overbay | .12 | .30 |
| ❑ 80 Alfonso Soriano | .12 | .30 |
| ❑ 81 Brandon Webb | .12 | .30 |
| ❑ 82 Joe Crede | .12 | .30 |
| ❑ 83 Corey Patterson | .12 | .30 |
| ❑ 84 Kenny Rogers | .12 | .30 |
| ❑ 85 Ken Griffey Jr | .50 | 1.25 |
| ❑ 86 Cliff Lee | .12 | .30 |

| | | |
|---|---|---|
| ❑ 87 Mike Lowell | .12 | .30 |
| ❑ 88 Marcus Giles | .12 | .30 |
| ❑ 89 Orlando Cabrera | .12 | .30 |
| ❑ 90 Derek Jeter | .75 | 2.00 |
| ❑ 91 Josh Johnson | .12 | .30 |
| ❑ 92 Carlos Guillen | .12 | .30 |
| ❑ 93 Bill Hall | .12 | .30 |
| ❑ 94 Michael Cuddyer | .12 | .30 |
| ❑ 95 Miguel Tejada | .12 | .30 |
| ❑ 96 Todd Helton | .20 | .50 |
| ❑ 97 C.C. Sabathia | .12 | .30 |
| ❑ 98 Tadahito Iguchi | .12 | .30 |
| ❑ 99 Jose Reyes | .30 | .75 |
| ❑ 100 David Wright | .50 | 1.25 |
| ❑ 101 Barry Zito | .12 | .30 |
| ❑ 102 Jake Peavy | .12 | .30 |
| ❑ 103 Richie Sexson | .12 | .30 |
| ❑ 104 A.J. Burnett | .12 | .30 |
| ❑ 105 Eric Chavez | .12 | .30 |
| ❑ 106 Jorge Cantu | .12 | .30 |
| ❑ 107 Grady Sizemore | .20 | .50 |
| ❑ 108 Bronson Arroyo | .12 | .30 |
| ❑ 109 Mike Mussina | .20 | .50 |
| ❑ 110 Magglio Ordonez | .12 | .30 |
| ❑ 111 Anibal Sanchez | .12 | .30 |
| ❑ 112 Jeff Francoeur | .30 | .75 |
| ❑ 113 Kevin Youkilis | .12 | .30 |
| ❑ 114 Aubrey Huff | .12 | .30 |
| ❑ 115 Carlos Zambrano | .12 | .30 |
| ❑ 116 Mark Teahen | .12 | .30 |
| ❑ 117 Carlos Silva | .12 | .30 |
| ❑ 118 Pedro Martinez | .20 | .50 |
| ❑ 119 Hideki Matsui | .30 | .75 |
| ❑ 120 Mike Piazza | .30 | .75 |
| ❑ 121 Jason Schmidt | .12 | .30 |
| ❑ 122 Greg Maddux | .50 | 1.25 |
| ❑ 123 Joe Blanton | .12 | .30 |
| ❑ 124 Chris Carpenter | .12 | .30 |
| ❑ 125 David Ortiz | .20 | .50 |
| ❑ 126 Alex Rios | .12 | .30 |
| ❑ 127 Nick Johnson | .12 | .30 |
| ❑ 128 Carlos Lee | .12 | .30 |
| ❑ 129 Pat Burrell | .12 | .30 |
| ❑ 130 Ben Sheets | .12 | .30 |
| ❑ 131 Kazuo Matsui | .12 | .30 |
| ❑ 132 Adam Dunn | .12 | .30 |
| ❑ 133 Jermaine Dye | .12 | .30 |
| ❑ 134 Curt Schilling | .20 | .50 |
| ❑ 135 Chad Tracy | .12 | .30 |
| ❑ 136 Vladimir Guerrero | .30 | .75 |
| ❑ 137 Melvin Mora | .12 | .30 |
| ❑ 138 John Smoltz | .20 | .50 |
| ❑ 139 Craig Monroe | .12 | .30 |
| ❑ 140 Dontrelle Willis | .12 | .30 |
| ❑ 141 Jeff Francis | .12 | .30 |
| ❑ 142 Chipper Jones | .30 | .75 |
| ❑ 143 Frank Thomas | .30 | .75 |
| ❑ 144 Brett Myers | .12 | .30 |
| ❑ 145 Xavier Nady | .12 | .30 |
| ❑ 146 Robinson Cano | .20 | .50 |
| ❑ 147 Jeff Kent | .12 | .30 |
| ❑ 148 Scott Rolen | .20 | .50 |
| ❑ 149 Roy Halladay | .12 | .30 |
| ❑ 150 Joe Mauer | .30 | .75 |
| ❑ 151 Bobby Abreu | .12 | .30 |
| ❑ 152 Matt Cain | .20 | .50 |
| ❑ 153 Hank Blalock | .12 | .30 |
| ❑ 154 Chris Capuano | .12 | .30 |
| ❑ 155 Jake Westbrook | .12 | .30 |
| ❑ 156 Javier Vazquez | .12 | .30 |
| ❑ 157 Garret Anderson | .12 | .30 |
| ❑ 158 Aramis Ramirez | .12 | .30 |
| ❑ 159 Mark Kotsay | .12 | .30 |
| ❑ 160 Matt Kemp | .30 | .75 |
| ❑ 161 Adrian Gonzalez | .12 | .30 |
| ❑ 162 Felix Hernandez | .20 | .50 |
| ❑ 163 David Eckstein | .12 | .30 |
| ❑ 164 Curtis Granderson | .12 | .30 |
| ❑ 165 Paul Konerko | .12 | .30 |
| ❑ 166 Orlando Hudson | .12 | .30 |
| ❑ 167 Tim Hudson | .12 | .30 |
| ❑ 168 J.D. Drew | .12 | .30 |
| ❑ 169 Chien-Ming Wang | .30 | .75 |
| ❑ 170 Jimmy Rollins | .12 | .30 |
| ❑ 171 Matt Morris | .12 | .30 |
| ❑ 172 Raul Ibanez | .20 | .50 |
| ❑ 173 Mark Teixeira | .20 | .50 |
| ❑ 174 Ted Lilly | .12 | .30 |

| | | |
|---|---|---|
| ❑ 175 Albert Pujols | .60 | 1.50 |
| ❑ 176 Carlos Beltran | .12 | .30 |
| ❑ 177 Lance Berkman | .12 | .30 |
| ❑ 178 Ivan Rodriguez | .20 | .50 |
| ❑ 179 Torii Hunter | .12 | .30 |
| ❑ 180 Johnny Damon | .20 | .50 |
| ❑ 181 Chase Utley | .30 | .75 |
| ❑ 182 Jason Bay | .20 | .50 |
| ❑ 183 Jeff Weaver | .12 | .30 |
| ❑ 184 Troy Glaus | .12 | .30 |
| ❑ 185 Rocco Baldelli | .12 | .30 |
| ❑ 186 Rafael Furcal | .12 | .30 |
| ❑ 187 Jim Thome | .20 | .50 |
| ❑ 188 Travis Hafner | .12 | .30 |
| ❑ 189 Matt Holliday | .30 | .75 |
| ❑ 190 Andruw Jones | .20 | .50 |
| ❑ 191 Ramon Hernandez | .12 | .30 |
| ❑ 192 Victor Martinez | .12 | .30 |
| ❑ 193 Aaron Hill | .12 | .30 |
| ❑ 194 Michael Young | .12 | .30 |
| ❑ 195 Vernon Wells | .12 | .30 |
| ❑ 196 Mark Mulder | .12 | .30 |
| ❑ 197 Derrek Lee | .12 | .30 |
| ❑ 198 Tom Glavine | .20 | .50 |
| ❑ 199 Chris Young | .12 | .30 |
| ❑ 200 Alex Rodriguez | .50 | 1.25 |
| ❑ 201 Delmon Young (RC) | .25 | .60 |
| ❑ 202 Alexi Casilla RC | .25 | .60 |
| ❑ 203 Shawn Riggans (RC) | .15 | .40 |
| ❑ 204 Jeff Baker (RC) | .15 | .40 |
| ❑ 205 Hector Gimenez (RC) | .15 | .40 |
| ❑ 206 Ubaldo Jimenez (RC) | .15 | .40 |
| ❑ 207 Adam Lind (RC) | .15 | .40 |
| ❑ 208 Joaquin Arias (RC) | .15 | .40 |
| ❑ 209 David Murphy (RC) | .15 | .40 |
| ❑ 210 Daisuke Matsuzaka RC | 2.00 | 5.00 |
| ❑ 211 Jerry Owens (RC) | .15 | .40 |
| ❑ 212 Ryan Sweeney (RC) | .15 | .40 |
| ❑ 213 Kei Igawa RC | .60 | 1.50 |
| ❑ 214 Fred Lewis (RC) | .25 | .60 |
| ❑ 215 Philip Humber (RC) | .15 | .40 |
| ❑ 216 Kevin Hooper (RC) | .15 | .40 |
| ❑ 217 Jeff Fiorentino (RC) | .15 | .40 |
| ❑ 218 Michael Bourn (RC) | .15 | .40 |
| ❑ 219 Hideki Okajima RC | .75 | 2.00 |
| ❑ 219b H.Okajima English AU | 8.00 | 20.00 |
| ❑ 219c H.Okajima Japan AU | 30.00 | 60.00 |
| ❑ 220 Josh Fields (RC) | .15 | .40 |
| ❑ 221 Andrew Miller AU RC | 10.00 | 25.00 |
| ❑ 222 Troy Tulowitzki AU RC | 12.50 | 30.00 |
| ❑ 223 Ryan Braun AU RC | 10.00 | 25.00 |
| ❑ 224 Oswaldo Navarro AU RC | 4.00 | 10.00 |
| ❑ 225 Philip Humber AU RC | 4.00 | 10.00 |
| ❑ 226 Mitch Maier AU RC | 4.00 | 10.00 |
| ❑ 227 Jerry Owens AU RC | 4.00 | 10.00 |
| ❑ 228 Mike Rabelo AU RC | 4.00 | 10.00 |
| ❑ 229 Delwyn Young AU (RC) | 4.00 | 10.00 |
| ❑ 230 Miguel Montero AU (RC) | 4.00 | 10.00 |
| ❑ 231 Akinori Iwamura AU RC | 8.00 | 20.00 |
| ❑ 232 Matt Lindstrom AU (RC) | 4.00 | 10.00 |
| ❑ 233 Josh Hamilton AU RC | 12.50 | 30.00 |
| ❑ 235 Elijah Dukes AU RC | 6.00 | 15.00 |
| ❑ 236 Sean Henn AU (RC) | 4.00 | 10.00 |
| ❑ 237 Barry Bonds | .60 | 1.50 |

## 2007 Bowman Draft

| | | |
|---|---|---|
| ❑ COMMON RC (1-54) | .15 | .40 |
| ❑ SEE 07 BOWMAN FOR BONDS PRICING | | |
| ❑ OVERALL PLATE ODDS 1:1,294, HOBBY | | |
| ❑ PLATE PRINT RUN 1 SET PER COLOR | | |
| ❑ BLACK-CYAN-MAGENTA-YELLOW ISSUED | | |
| ❑ NO PLATE PRICING DUE TO SCARCITY | | |
| ❑ BDP1 Travis Buck (RC) | .15 | .40 |
| ❑ BDP2 Matt Chico (RC) | .15 | .40 |

|  |  | | |
|---|---|---|---|
| BDP3 | Justin Upton RC | 1.00 | 2.50 |
| BDP4 | Chase Wright RC | .40 | 1.00 |
| BDP5 | Kevin Kouzmanoff (RC) | .15 | .40 |
| BDP6 | John Danks RC | .15 | .40 |
| BDP7 | Alejandro De Aza RC | .25 | .60 |
| BDP8 | Jamie Vermilyea RC | .15 | .40 |
| BDP9 | Jesus Flores RC | .15 | .40 |
| BDP10 | Glen Perkins (RC) | .15 | .40 |
| BDP11 | Tim Lincecum RC | 2.00 | 5.00 |
| BDP12 | Cameron Maybin RC | .75 | 2.00 |
| BDP13 | Brandon Morrow RC | .40 | 1.00 |
| BDP14 | Mike Rabelo RC | .15 | .40 |
| BDP15 | Alex Gordon RC | .60 | 1.50 |
| BDP16 | Zack Segovia (RC) | .15 | .40 |
| BDP17 | Jon Knott (RC) | .15 | .40 |
| BDP18 | Joba Chamberlain RC | .75 | 2.00 |
| BDP19 | Danny Putnam (RC) | .15 | .40 |
| BDP20 | Matt DeSalvo (RC) | .15 | .40 |
| BDP21 | Fred Lewis (RC) | .25 | .60 |
| BDP22 | Sean Gallagher (RC) | .15 | .40 |
| BDP23 | Brandon Wood (RC) | .15 | .40 |
| BDP24 | Dennis Dove (RC) | .15 | .40 |
| BDP25 | Hunter Pence (RC) | .75 | 2.00 |
| BDP26 | Jarrod Saltalamacchia (RC) | .25 | .60 |
| BDP27 | Ben Francisco (RC) | .15 | .40 |
| BDP28 | Doug Slaten RC | .15 | .40 |
| BDP29 | Tony Abreu RC | .40 | 1.00 |
| BDP30 | Billy Butler (RC) | .25 | .60 |
| BDP31 | Jesse Litsch RC | .25 | .60 |
| BDP32 | Nate Schierholtz (RC) | .15 | .40 |
| BDP33 | Jared Burton RC | .15 | .40 |
| BDP34 | Matt Brown RC | .15 | .40 |
| BDP35 | Dallas Braden RC | .25 | .60 |
| BDP36 | Carlos Gomez RC | .25 | .60 |
| BDP37 | Brian Stokes RC | .15 | .40 |
| BDP38 | Kory Casto RC | .15 | .40 |
| BDP39 | Mark McLemore (RC) | .15 | .40 |
| BDP40 | Andy LaRoche RC | .25 | .60 |
| BDP41 | Tyler Clippard (RC) | .25 | .60 |
| BDP42 | Curtis Thigpen (RC) | .15 | .40 |
| BDP43 | Yunel Escobar (RC) | .15 | .40 |
| BDP44 | Andy Sonnanstine RC | .15 | .40 |
| BDP45 | Felix Pie (RC) | .15 | .40 |
| BDP46 | Homer Bailey RC | .25 | .60 |
| BDP47 | Kyle Kendrick RC | .40 | 1.00 |
| BDP48 | Angel Sanchez RC | .15 | .40 |
| BDP49 | Phil Hughes RC | .75 | 2.00 |
| BDP50 | Ryan Braun RC | 1.00 | 2.50 |
| BDP51 | Kevin Slowey RC | .40 | 1.00 |
| BDP52 | Brendan Ryan (RC) | .15 | .40 |
| BDP53 | Yovani Gallardo (RC) | .50 | 1.25 |
| BDP54 | Mark Reynolds RC | 1.00 | 2.50 |

## 2008 Bowman

| | | | |
|---|---|---|---|
| COMP.SET w/o AU's (220) | | 10.00 | 25.00 |
| COMMON CARD (1-200) | | .12 | .30 |
| COMMON ROOKIE (201-220) | | .15 | .40 |
| COMMON AUTO (221-230) | | 4.00 | 10.00 |
| AU RC ODDS 1:233 HOBBY | | | |
| 1-220 PLATE ODDS 1:732 HOBBY | | | |
| 221-231 AU PLATES 1:4700 HOBBY | | | |
| PLATE PRINT RUN 1 SET PER COLOR | | | |
| BLACK-CYAN-MAGENTA-YELLOW ISSUED | | | |
| NO PLATE PRICING DUE TO SCARCITY | | | |
| 1 | Ryan Braun | .40 | 1.00 |
| 2 | David DeJesus | .12 | .30 |
| 3 | Brandon Phillips | .12 | .30 |
| 4 | Mark Teixeira | .20 | .50 |
| 5 | Daisuke Matsuzaka | .40 | 1.00 |
| 6 | Justin Upton | .30 | .75 |
| 7 | Jered Weaver | .12 | .30 |
| 8 | Todd Helton | .20 | .50 |
| 9 | Cameron Maybin | .20 | .50 |
| 10 | Erik Bedard | .12 | .30 |
| 11 | Jason Bay | .20 | .50 |
| 12 | Cole Hamels | .30 | .75 |
| 13 | Bobby Abreu | .12 | .30 |
| 14 | Carlos Zambrano | .12 | .30 |
| 15 | Vladimir Guerrero | .30 | .75 |
| 16 | Joe Blanton | .12 | .30 |
| 17 | Bengie Molina | .12 | .30 |
| 18 | Paul Maholm | .12 | .30 |
| 19 | Adrian Gonzalez | .20 | .50 |
| 20 | Brandon Webb | .20 | .50 |
| 21 | Carl Crawford | .12 | .30 |
| 22 | A.J. Burnett | .12 | .30 |
| 23 | Dmitri Young | .12 | .30 |
| 24 | Jeremy Hermida | .12 | .30 |
| 25 | C.C. Sabathia | .12 | .30 |
| 26 | Adam Dunn | .12 | .30 |
| 27 | Matt Garza | .12 | .30 |
| 28 | Adrian Beltre | .12 | .30 |
| 29 | Kevin Millwood | .12 | .30 |
| 30 | Manny Ramirez | .30 | .75 |
| 31 | Javier Vazquez | .12 | .30 |
| 32 | Carlos Delgado | .12 | .30 |
| 33 | Jason Schmidt | .12 | .30 |
| 34 | Torii Hunter | .20 | .50 |
| 35 | Ivan Rodriguez | .20 | .50 |
| 36 | Nick Markakis | .20 | .50 |
| 37 | Gil Meche | .12 | .30 |
| 38 | Garrett Atkins | .12 | .30 |
| 39 | Fausto Carmona | .12 | .30 |
| 40 | Joe Mauer | .30 | .75 |
| 41 | Tom Glavine | .20 | .50 |
| 42 | Hideki Matsui | .30 | .75 |
| 43 | Scott Rolen | .20 | .50 |
| 44 | Tim Lincecum | .40 | 1.00 |
| 45 | Prince Fielder | .30 | .75 |
| 46 | Ted Lilly | .12 | .30 |
| 47 | Frank Thomas | .30 | .75 |
| 48 | Tom Gorzelanny | .12 | .30 |
| 49 | Lance Berkman | .20 | .50 |
| 50 | David Ortiz | .20 | .50 |
| 51 | Dontrelle Willis | .12 | .30 |
| 52 | Travis Hafner | .12 | .30 |
| 53 | Aaron Harang | .12 | .30 |
| 54 | Chris Young | .12 | .30 |
| 55 | Vernon Wells | .12 | .30 |
| 56 | Francisco Liriano | .20 | .50 |
| 57 | Derek Lee | .12 | .30 |
| 58 | Phil Hughes | .30 | .75 |
| 59 | Melvin Mora | .12 | .30 |
| 60 | Johan Santana | .20 | .50 |
| 61 | Brian McCann | .20 | .50 |
| 62 | Pat Burrell | .12 | .30 |
| 63 | Chris Carpenter | .12 | .30 |
| 64 | Brian Giles | .12 | .30 |
| 65 | Jose Reyes | .20 | .50 |
| 66 | Hanley Ramirez | .30 | .75 |
| 67 | Ubaldo Jimenez | .12 | .30 |
| 68 | Felix Pie | .12 | .30 |
| 69 | Jeremy Bonderman | .12 | .30 |
| 70 | Jimmy Rollins | .20 | .50 |
| 71 | Miguel Tejada | .12 | .30 |
| 72 | Derek Lowe | .12 | .30 |
| 73 | Alex Gordon | .20 | .50 |
| 74 | John Maine | .12 | .30 |
| 75 | Alfonso Soriano | .20 | .50 |
| 76 | Richie Sexson | .12 | .30 |
| 77 | Ben Sheets | .20 | .50 |
| 78 | Hunter Pence | .30 | .75 |
| 79 | Magglio Ordonez | .20 | .50 |
| 80 | Josh Beckett | .20 | .50 |
| 81 | Victor Martinez | .12 | .30 |
| 82 | Mark Buehrle | .12 | .30 |
| 83 | Jason Varitek | .30 | .75 |
| 84 | Chien-Ming Wang | .30 | .75 |
| 85 | Ken Griffey Jr. | .50 | 1.25 |
| 86 | Billy Butler | .12 | .30 |
| 87 | Brad Penny | .12 | .30 |
| 88 | Carlos Beltran | .20 | .50 |
| 89 | Curt Schilling | .20 | .50 |
| 90 | Jorge Posada | .20 | .50 |
| 91 | Andruw Jones | .20 | .50 |
| 92 | Bobby Crosby | .12 | .30 |
| 93 | Freddy Sanchez | .12 | .30 |
| 94 | Barry Zito | .12 | .30 |
| 95 | Miguel Cabrera | .30 | .75 |
| 96 | B.J. Upton | .20 | .50 |
| 97 | Matt Cain | .12 | .30 |
| 98 | Lyle Overbay | .12 | .30 |
| 99 | Austin Kearns | .12 | .30 |
| 100 | Alex Rodriguez | .50 | 1.25 |
| 101 | Rich Harden | .12 | .30 |
| 102 | Justin Morneau | .20 | .50 |
| 103 | Oliver Perez | .12 | .30 |
| 104 | Gary Matthews | .12 | .30 |
| 105 | Matt Holliday | .20 | .50 |
| 106 | Justin Verlander | .20 | .50 |
| 107 | Orlando Cabrera | .12 | .30 |
| 108 | Rich Hill | .12 | .30 |
| 109 | Tim Hudson | .12 | .30 |
| 110 | Ryan Zimmerman | .20 | .50 |
| 111 | Roy Oswalt | .20 | .50 |
| 112 | Nick Swisher | .12 | .30 |
| 113 | Raul Ibanez | .20 | .50 |
| 114 | Kelly Johnson | .12 | .30 |
| 115 | Alex Rios | .20 | .50 |
| 116 | John Lackey | .12 | .30 |
| 117 | Robinson Cano | .20 | .50 |
| 118 | Michael Young | .20 | .50 |
| 119 | Jeff Francis | .12 | .30 |
| 120 | Grady Sizemore | .20 | .50 |
| 121 | Mike Lowell | .20 | .50 |
| 122 | Aramis Ramirez | .12 | .30 |
| 123 | Stephen Drew | .20 | .50 |
| 124 | Yovani Gallardo | .12 | .30 |
| 125 | Chase Utley | .30 | .75 |
| 126 | Dan Haren | .12 | .30 |
| 127 | Jose Vidro | .12 | .30 |
| 128 | Ronnie Belliard | .12 | .30 |
| 129 | Yunel Escobar | .20 | .50 |
| 130 | Greg Maddux | .40 | 1.00 |
| 131 | Garret Anderson | .12 | .30 |
| 132 | Aubrey Huff | .12 | .30 |
| 133 | Paul Konerko | .20 | .50 |
| 134 | Dan Uggla | .20 | .50 |
| 135 | Roy Halladay | .20 | .50 |
| 136 | Andre Ethier | .20 | .50 |
| 137 | Orlando Hernandez | .12 | .30 |
| 138 | Troy Tulowitzki | .30 | .75 |
| 139 | Carlos Guillen | .12 | .30 |
| 140 | Scott Kazmir | .20 | .50 |
| 141 | Aaron Rowand | .12 | .30 |
| 142 | Jim Edmonds | .12 | .30 |
| 143 | Jermaine Dye | .12 | .30 |
| 144 | Orlando Hudson | .12 | .30 |
| 145 | Derrek Lee | .12 | .30 |
| 146 | Travis Buck | .12 | .30 |
| 147 | Zack Greinke | .12 | .30 |
| 148 | Jeff Kent | .12 | .30 |
| 149 | John Smoltz | .30 | .75 |
| 150 | David Wright | .40 | 1.00 |
| 151 | Joba Chamberlain | .40 | 1.00 |
| 152 | Adam LaRoche | .12 | .30 |
| 153 | Kevin Youkilis | .20 | .50 |
| 154 | Troy Glaus | .20 | .50 |
| 155 | Nick Johnson | .12 | .30 |
| 156 | J.J. Hardy | .12 | .30 |
| 157 | Felix Hernandez | .20 | .50 |
| 158 | Khalil Greene | .12 | .30 |
| 159 | Gary Sheffield | .12 | .30 |
| 160 | Albert Pujols | .60 | 1.50 |
| 161 | Chuck James | .12 | .30 |
| 162 | Rocco Baldelli | .12 | .30 |
| 163 | Eric Byrnes | .12 | .30 |
| 164 | Brad Hawpe | .12 | .30 |
| 165 | Delmon Young | .20 | .50 |
| 166 | Chris Young | .12 | .30 |
| 167 | Brian Roberts | .12 | .30 |
| 168 | Russell Martin | .20 | .50 |
| 169 | Hank Blalock | .12 | .30 |
| 170 | Yadier Molina | .12 | .30 |
| 171 | Jeremy Guthrie | .12 | .30 |
| 172 | Chipper Jones | .40 | 1.00 |
| 173 | Johnny Damon | .20 | .50 |
| 174 | Ryan Garko | .12 | .30 |
| 175 | Jake Peavy | .20 | .50 |
| 176 | Chone Figgins | .12 | .30 |
| 177 | Edgar Renteria | .12 | .30 |
| 178 | Jim Thome | .20 | .50 |
| 179 | Carlos Pena | .30 | .75 |
| 180 | Corey Patterson | .12 | .30 |
| 181 | Dustin Pedroia | .40 | 1.00 |
| 182 | Brett Myers | .12 | .30 |
| 183 | Josh Hamilton | .40 | 1.00 |
| 184 | Randy Johnson | .30 | .75 |
| 185 | Ichiro Suzuki | .50 | 1.25 |
| 186 | Aaron Hill | .12 | .30 |

|  |  | | |
|---|---|---|---|
| 187 | Jarrod Saltalamacchia | .12 | .30 |
| 188 | Michael Cuddyer | .12 | .30 |
| 189 | Jeff Francoeur | .20 | .50 |
| 190 | Derek Jeter | .75 | 2.00 |
| 191 | Curtis Granderson | .12 | .30 |
| 192 | James Loney | .20 | .50 |
| 193 | Brian Bannister | .12 | .30 |
| 194 | Carlos Lee | .12 | .30 |
| 195 | Pedro Martinez | .20 | .50 |
| 196 | Asdrubal Cabrera | .12 | .30 |
| 197 | Kenji Johjima | .12 | .30 |
| 198 | Bartolo Colon | .12 | .30 |
| 199 | Jacoby Ellsbury | .50 | 1.25 |
| 200 | Ryan Howard | .40 | 1.00 |
| 201 | Radhames Liz RC | .25 | .60 |
| 202 | Justin Ruggiano RC | .25 | .60 |
| 203 | Lance Broadway (RC) | .15 | .40 |
| 204 | Joey Votto (RC) | .40 | 1.00 |
| 205 | Billy Buckner (RC) | .15 | .40 |
| 206 | Joe Koshansky (RC) | .15 | .40 |
| 207 | Ross Detwiler RC | .40 | 1.00 |
| 208 | Chin-Lung Hu (RC) | .25 | .60 |
| 209 | Luke Hochevar RC | .25 | .60 |
| 210 | Jeff Clement (RC) | .25 | .60 |
| 211 | Troy Patton (RC) | .25 | .60 |
| 212 | Hiroki Kuroda RC | .25 | .60 |
| 213 | Emilio Bonifacio RC | .40 | 1.00 |
| 214 | Armando Galarraga RC | .25 | .60 |
| 215 | Josh Anderson (RC) | .25 | .40 |
| 216 | Nick Blackburn RC | .25 | .60 |
| 217 | Seth Smith (RC) | .15 | .40 |
| 218 | Jonathan Meloan RC | .25 | .60 |
| 219 | Alberto Gonzalez RC | .25 | .60 |
| 220 | Josh Banks (RC) | .15 | .40 |
| 221 | Clay Buchholz AU (RC) | 6.00 | 15.00 |
| 222 | Nyjer Morgan AU (RC) | 4.00 | 10.00 |
| 223 | Brandon Jones AU RC | 4.00 | 10.00 |
| 224 | Sam Fuld AU RC | 4.00 | 10.00 |
| 225 | Daric Barton AU (RC) | 4.00 | 10.00 |
| 226 | Chris Seddon AU RC | 4.00 | 10.00 |
| 227 | J.R. Towles AU RC | 4.00 | 10.00 |
| 228 | Steve Pearce AU RC | 4.00 | 10.00 |
| 229 | Ross Ohlendorf AU RC | 4.00 | 10.00 |
| 230 | Clint Sammons AU (RC) | 4.00 | 10.00 |

## 2009 Bowman

| | | | |
|---|---|---|---|
| | COMP SET w/o AU's (220) | 12.50 | 30.00 |
| | COMMON CARD (1-190) | .12 | .30 |
| | COMMON ROOKIE (66/191-220) | .25 | .60 |
| | COMMON AU (221-230) | 4.00 | 10.00 |
| | PLATE PRINT RUN 1 SET PER COLOR | | |
| | BLACK-CYAN-MAGENTA-YELLOW ISSUED | | |
| | NO PLATE PRICING DUE TO SCARCITY | | |
| 1 | David Wright | .40 | 1.00 |
| 2 | Albert Pujols | .75 | 2.00 |
| 3 | Alex Rodriguez | .50 | 1.25 |
| 4 | Chase Utley | .30 | .75 |
| 5 | Chien-Ming Wang | .30 | .75 |
| 6 | Jimmy Rollins | .20 | .50 |
| 7 | Ken Griffey Jr. | .50 | 1.25 |
| 8 | Manny Ramirez | .30 | .75 |
| 9 | Chipper Jones | .30 | .75 |
| 10 | Ichiro Suzuki | .50 | 1.25 |
| 11 | Justin Morneau | .20 | .50 |
| 12 | Hanley Ramirez | .30 | .75 |
| 13 | Cliff Lee | .20 | .50 |
| 14 | Ryan Howard | .40 | 1.00 |
| 15 | Ian Kinsler | .20 | .50 |
| 16 | Jose Reyes | .30 | .75 |
| 17 | Ted Lilly | .12 | .30 |
| 18 | Miguel Cabrera | .30 | .75 |
| 19 | Nate McLouth | .12 | .30 |
| 20 | Josh Beckett | .20 | .50 |
| 21 | John Lackey | .12 | .30 |
| 22 | David Ortiz | .30 | .75 |
| 23 | Carlos Lee | .12 | .30 |
| 24 | Adam Dunn | .20 | .50 |
| 25 | B.J. Upton | .20 | .50 |
| 26 | Curtis Granderson | .30 | .75 |
| 27 | David DeJesus | .12 | .30 |
| 28 | CC Sabathia | .20 | .50 |
| 29 | Russell Martin | .20 | .50 |
| 30 | Torii Hunter | .20 | .50 |
| 31 | Rich Harden | .12 | .30 |
| 32 | Johnny Damon | .12 | .30 |
| 33 | Cristian Guzman | .12 | .30 |
| 34 | Grady Sizemore | .20 | .50 |
| 35 | Jorge Posada | .20 | .50 |
| 36 | Placido Polanco | .12 | .30 |
| 37 | Ryan Ludwick | .20 | .50 |
| 38 | Dustin Pedroia | .40 | 1.00 |
| 39 | Matt Garza | .12 | .30 |
| 40 | Prince Fielder | .30 | .75 |
| 41 | Rick Ankiel | .20 | .50 |
| 42 | Jonathan Sanchez | .12 | .30 |
| 43 | Erik Bedard | .12 | .30 |
| 44 | Ryan Braun | .40 | 1.00 |
| 45 | Ervin Santana | .12 | .30 |
| 46 | Brian Roberts | .12 | .30 |
| 47 | Mike Jacobs | .12 | .30 |
| 48 | Phil Hughes | .20 | .50 |
| 49 | Justin Masterson | .20 | .50 |
| 50 | Felix Hernandez | .20 | .50 |
| 51 | Stephen Drew | .12 | .30 |
| 52 | Bobby Abreu | .12 | .30 |
| 53 | Jay Bruce | .30 | .75 |
| 54 | Josh Hamilton | .30 | .75 |
| 55 | Garrett Atkins | .12 | .30 |
| 56 | Jacoby Ellsbury | .30 | .75 |
| 57 | Johan Santana | .30 | .75 |
| 58 | James Shields | .12 | .30 |
| 59 | Armando Galarraga | .12 | .30 |
| 60 | Carlos Pena | .20 | .50 |
| 61 | Matt Kemp | .30 | .75 |
| 62 | Joey Votto | .30 | .75 |
| 63 | Raul Ibanez | .20 | .50 |
| 64 | Casey Kotchman | .12 | .30 |
| 65 | Hunter Pence | .20 | .50 |
| 66 | Daniel Murphy RC | .60 | 1.50 |
| 67 | Carlos Beltran | .12 | .30 |
| 68 | Evan Longoria | .50 | 1.25 |
| 69 | Daisuke Matsuzaka | .50 | 1.25 |
| 70 | Cole Hamels | .30 | .75 |
| 71 | Robinson Cano | .20 | .50 |
| 72 | Clayton Kershaw | .30 | .75 |
| 73 | Kenji Johjima | .12 | .30 |
| 74 | Kazuo Matsui | .12 | .30 |
| 75 | Jayson Werth | .12 | .30 |
| 76 | Brian McCann | .20 | .50 |
| 77 | Barry Zito | .12 | .30 |
| 78 | Glen Perkins | .12 | .30 |
| 79 | Jeff Francoeur | .20 | .50 |
| 80 | Derek Jeter | .75 | 2.00 |
| 81 | Ryan Doumit | .12 | .30 |
| 82 | Dan Haren | .12 | .30 |
| 83 | Justin Duchscherer | .12 | .30 |
| 84 | Marlon Byrd | .12 | .30 |
| 85 | Derek Lowe | .12 | .30 |
| 86 | Pat Burrell | .20 | .50 |
| 87 | Jair Jurrjens | .12 | .30 |
| 88 | Zack Greinke | .30 | .75 |
| 89 | Jon Lester | .20 | .50 |
| 90 | Justin Verlander | .20 | .50 |
| 91 | Jorge Cantu | .12 | .30 |
| 92 | John Maine | .12 | .30 |
| 93 | Brad Hawpe | .12 | .30 |
| 94 | Mike Aviles | .12 | .30 |
| 95 | Victor Martinez | .20 | .50 |
| 96 | Ryan Dempster | .12 | .30 |
| 97 | Miguel Tejada | .20 | .50 |
| 98 | Joe Mauer | .30 | .75 |
| 99 | Scott Olsen | .12 | .30 |
| 100 | Tim Lincecum | .40 | 1.00 |
| 101 | Francisco Liriano | .12 | .30 |
| 102 | Chris Iannetta | .12 | .30 |
| 103 | Jamie Moyer | .12 | .30 |
| 104 | Milton Bradley | .12 | .30 |
| 105 | John Lannan | .12 | .30 |
| 106 | Yovani Gallardo | .20 | .50 |
| 107 | Xavier Nady | .12 | .30 |
| 108 | Jermaine Dye | .12 | .30 |
| 109 | Dioner Navarro | .12 | .30 |
| 110 | Joba Chamberlain | .40 | 1.00 |
| 111 | Nelson Cruz | .12 | .30 |
| 112 | Johnny Cueto | .12 | .30 |
| 113 | Adam LaRoche | .12 | .30 |
| 114 | Aaron Rowand | .12 | .30 |
| 115 | Jason Bay | .20 | .50 |
| 116 | Aaron Cook | .12 | .30 |
| 117 | Mark Teixeira | .30 | .75 |
| 118 | Gavin Floyd | .12 | .30 |
| 119 | Magglio Ordonez | .20 | .50 |
| 120 | Rafael Furcal | .12 | .30 |
| 121 | Mark Buehrle | .12 | .30 |
| 122 | Alexi Casilla | .12 | .30 |
| 123 | Scott Kazmir | .20 | .50 |
| 124 | Nick Swisher | .12 | .30 |
| 125 | Carlos Gomez | .12 | .30 |
| 126 | Javier Vazquez | .12 | .30 |
| 127 | Paul Konerko | .12 | .30 |
| 128 | Ronnie Belliard | .12 | .30 |
| 129 | Pat Neshek | .20 | .50 |
| 130 | Josh Johnson | .12 | .30 |
| 131 | Carlos Zambrano | .12 | .30 |
| 132 | Chris Davis | .12 | .30 |
| 133 | Bobby Crosby | .12 | .30 |
| 134 | Alex Gordon | .20 | .50 |
| 135 | Chris Young | .12 | .30 |
| 136 | Carlos Delgado | .12 | .30 |
| 137 | Adam Wainwright | .20 | .50 |
| 138 | Justin Upton | .20 | .50 |
| 139 | Tim Hudson | .12 | .30 |
| 140 | J.D. Drew | .12 | .30 |
| 141 | Adam Lind | .12 | .30 |
| 142 | Mike Lowell | .20 | .50 |
| 143 | Lance Berkman | .20 | .50 |
| 144 | J.J. Hardy | .20 | .50 |
| 145 | A.J. Burnett | .20 | .50 |
| 146 | Jake Peavy | .20 | .50 |
| 147 | Blake DeWitt | .12 | .30 |
| 148 | Matt Holliday | .20 | .50 |
| 149 | Carl Crawford | .20 | .50 |
| 150 | Andre Ethier | .20 | .50 |
| 151 | Howie Kendrick | .12 | .30 |
| 152 | Ryan Zimmerman | .20 | .50 |
| 153 | Troy Tulowitzki | .20 | .50 |
| 154 | Brett Myers | .12 | .30 |
| 155 | Chris Young | .12 | .30 |
| 156 | Jered Weaver | .12 | .30 |
| 157 | Jeff Clement | .12 | .30 |
| 158 | Alex Rios | .12 | .30 |
| 159 | Shane Victorino | .12 | .30 |
| 160 | Jeremy Hermida | .12 | .30 |
| 161 | James Loney | .12 | .30 |
| 162 | Michael Young | .20 | .50 |
| 163 | Aramis Ramirez | .12 | .30 |
| 164 | Geovany Soto | .20 | .50 |
| 165 | Aubrey Huff | .12 | .30 |
| 166 | Delmon Young | .20 | .50 |
| 167 | Vernon Wells | .20 | .50 |
| 168 | Chone Figgins | .12 | .30 |
| 169 | Carlos Quentin | .12 | .30 |
| 170 | Chad Billingsley | .12 | .30 |
| 171 | Matt Cain | .12 | .30 |
| 172 | Derek Lee | .20 | .50 |
| 173 | A.J. Pierzynski | .12 | .30 |
| 174 | Collin Balester | .12 | .30 |
| 175 | Greg Smith | .12 | .30 |
| 176 | Alfonso Soriano | .20 | .50 |
| 177 | Adrian Gonzalez | .20 | .50 |
| 178 | George Sherrill | .12 | .30 |
| 179 | Nick Markakis | .20 | .50 |
| 180 | Brandon Webb | .20 | .50 |
| 181 | Vladimir Guerrero | .30 | .75 |
| 182 | Roy Oswalt | .20 | .50 |
| 183 | Adam Jones | .20 | .50 |
| 184 | Edinson Volquez | .12 | .30 |
| 185 | Yunel Escobar | .12 | .30 |
| 186 | Joe Saunders | .12 | .30 |
| 187 | Yadier Molina | .20 | .50 |
| 188 | Kevin Youkilis | .20 | .50 |
| 189 | Dan Uggla | .12 | .30 |
| 190 | Kosuke Fukudome | .30 | .75 |
| 191 | Matt Antonelli RC | .40 | 1.00 |
| 192 | Jeff Baisley RC | .25 | .60 |
| 193 | Jason Bourgeois (RC) | .25 | .60 |
| 194 | Michael Bowden (RC) | .40 | 1.00 |
| 195 | Andrew Carpenter RC | .40 | 1.00 |
| 196 | Phil Coke RC | .40 | 1.00 |
| 197 | Aaron Cunningham RC | .25 | .60 |
| 198 | Aloides Escobar RC | .40 | 1.00 |
| 199 | Dexter Fowler RC | .40 | 1.00 |
| 200 | Mat Gamel RC | .60 | 1.50 |
| 201 | Josh Geer (RC) | .25 | .60 |
| 202 | Greg Golson (RC) | .25 | .60 |
| 203 | John Jaso RC | .25 | .60 |
| 204 | Kila Ka'aihue (RC) | .40 | 1.00 |
| 205 | George Kottaras RC | .25 | .60 |
| 206 | Lou Marson (RC) | .25 | .60 |
| 207 | Shairon Martis RC | .40 | 1.00 |
| 208 | Juan Miranda RC | .40 | 1.00 |
| 209 | Luke Montz RC | .25 | .60 |
| 210 | Jonathon Niese RC | .40 | 1.00 |
| 211 | Bobby Parnell RC | .40 | 1.00 |

| | | |
|---|---|---|
| ❑ 212 Fernando Perez (RC) | .25 | .60 |
| ❑ 213 David Price RC | .75 | 2.00 |
| ❑ 214 Angel Salome (RC) | .25 | .60 |
| ❑ 215 Gaby Sanchez (RC) | .25 | .60 |
| ❑ 216 Freddy Sandoval (RC) | .25 | .60 |
| ❑ 217 Travis Snider RC | .60 | 1.50 |
| ❑ 218 Will Venable RC | .25 | .60 |
| ❑ 219 Edwin Maysonet RC | .25 | .60 |
| ❑ 220 Josh Outman RC | .40 | 1.00 |
| ❑ 221 Luke Montz AU (RC) | 4.00 | 10.00 |
| ❑ 222 Kila Ka'aihue AU (RC) | 4.00 | 10.00 |
| ❑ 223 Conor Gillaspie AU (RC) | 5.00 | 12.00 |
| ❑ 224 Aaron Cunningham AU (RC) | 4.00 | 10.00 |
| ❑ 225 Mat Gamel AU (RC) | 8.00 | 20.00 |
| ❑ 226 Matt Antonelli AU (RC) | 4.00 | 10.00 |
| ❑ 227 Bobby Parnell AU (RC) | 4.00 | 10.00 |
| ❑ 228 Jose Mijares AU (RC) | 4.00 | 10.00 |
| ❑ 229 Josh Geer AU (RC) | 4.00 | 10.00 |
| ❑ 230 Shairon Martis AU (RC) | 6.00 | 15.00 |

## 2008 Bowman Draft

| | | |
|---|---|---|
| ❑ COMPLETE SET (55) | 10.00 | 25.00 |
| ❑ COMMON CARD (1-55) | .20 | .50 |
| ❑ OVERALL PLATE ODDS 1:750 HOBBY | | |
| ❑ PLATE PRINT RUN 1 SET PER COLOR | | |
| ❑ BLACK-CYAN-MAGENTA-YELLOW ISSUED | | |
| ❑ NO PLATE PRICING DUE TO SCARCITY | | |
| ❑ BDP1 Nick Adenhart (RC) | .20 | .50 |
| ❑ BDP2 Michael Aubrey RC | .30 | .75 |
| ❑ BDP3 Mike Aviles RC | .30 | .75 |
| ❑ BDP4 Burke Badenhop RC | .20 | .50 |
| ❑ BDP5 Wladimir Balentien (RC) | .20 | .50 |
| ❑ BDP6 Collin Balester (RC) | .20 | .50 |
| ❑ BDP7 Josh Banks (RC) | .20 | .50 |
| ❑ BDP8 Wes Bankston (RC) | .20 | .50 |
| ❑ BDP9 Joey Votto RC | .50 | 1.25 |
| ❑ BDP10 Mitch Boggs (RC) | .20 | .50 |
| ❑ BDP11 Jay Bruce (RC) | .75 | 2.00 |
| ❑ BDP12 Chris Carter (RC) | .30 | .75 |
| ❑ BDP13 Justin Christian RC | .30 | .75 |
| ❑ BDP14 Chris Davis RC | .50 | 1.25 |
| ❑ BDP15 Blake DeWitt (RC) | .50 | 1.25 |
| ❑ BDP16 Nick Evans RC | .20 | .50 |
| ❑ BDP17 Jaime Garcia RC | .20 | .50 |
| ❑ BDP18 Brett Gardner (RC) | .50 | 1.25 |
| ❑ BDP19 Carlos Gonzalez (RC) | .20 | .50 |
| ❑ BDP20 Matt Harrison (RC) | .20 | .50 |
| ❑ BDP21 Micah Hoffpauir RC | .60 | 1.50 |
| ❑ BDP22 Nick Hundley (RC) | .20 | .50 |
| ❑ BDP23 Eric Hurley (RC) | .20 | .50 |
| ❑ BDP24 Elliot Johnson (RC) | .20 | .50 |
| ❑ BDP25 Matt Joyce RC | .50 | 1.25 |
| ❑ BDP26 Clayton Kershaw RC | 1.00 | 2.50 |
| ❑ BDP27 Evan Longoria RC | 2.00 | 5.00 |
| ❑ BDP28 Matt Macri (RC) | .20 | .50 |
| ❑ BDP29 Chris Perez RC | .30 | .75 |
| ❑ BDP30 Max Ramirez (RC) | .30 | .75 |
| ❑ BDP31 Greg Reynolds (RC) | .30 | .75 |
| ❑ BDP32 Brooks Conrad (RC) | .20 | .50 |
| ❑ BDP33 Max Scherzer RC | .50 | 1.25 |
| ❑ BDP34 Daryl Thompson (RC) | .20 | .50 |
| ❑ BDP35 Taylor Teagarden RC | .30 | .75 |
| ❑ BDP36 Rich Thompson RC | .20 | .50 |
| ❑ BDP37 Ryan Tucker (RC) | .20 | .50 |
| ❑ BDP38 Jonathan Van Every RC | .20 | .50 |
| ❑ BDP39 Chris Volstad (RC) | .20 | .50 |
| ❑ BDP40 Michael Hollimon (RC) | .20 | .50 |
| ❑ BDP41 Brad Ziegler RC | 1.00 | 2.50 |
| ❑ BDP42 Jamie D'Antona (RC) | .20 | .50 |
| ❑ BDP43 Clayton Richard (RC) | .20 | .50 |
| ❑ BDP44 Edgar Gonzalez (RC) | .20 | .50 |
| ❑ BDP45 Bryan LaHair RC | .20 | .50 |
| ❑ BDP46 Warner Madrigal (RC) | .20 | .50 |
| ❑ BDP47 Reid Brignac (RC) | .30 | .75 |
| ❑ BDP48 David Robertson RC | .30 | .75 |
| ❑ BDP49 Nick Stavinoha RC | .30 | .75 |
| ❑ BDP50 Jai Miller (RC) | .20 | .50 |
| ❑ BDP51 Charlie Morton (RC) | .20 | .50 |
| ❑ BDP52 Brandon Boggs (RC) | .30 | .75 |
| ❑ BDP53 Joe Mather RC | .30 | .75 |
| ❑ BDP54 Gregorio Petit RC | .30 | .75 |
| ❑ BDP55 Jeff Samardzija RC | .60 | 1.50 |

## 1997 Bowman Chrome

| | | |
|---|---|---|
| ❑ COMPLETE SET (300) | 75.00 | 150.00 |
| ❑ 1 Derek Jeter | 1.25 | 3.00 |
| ❑ 2 Chipper Jones | .50 | 1.25 |
| ❑ 3 Hideo Nomo | .50 | 1.25 |
| ❑ 4 Tim Salmon | .30 | .75 |
| ❑ 5 Robin Ventura | .20 | .50 |
| ❑ 6 Tony Clark | .20 | .50 |
| ❑ 7 Barry Larkin | .30 | .75 |
| ❑ 8 Paul Molitor | .20 | .50 |
| ❑ 9 Andy Benes | .20 | .50 |
| ❑ 10 Ryan Klesko | .20 | .50 |
| ❑ 11 Mark McGwire | 1.25 | 3.00 |
| ❑ 12 Ken Griffey Jr. | .75 | 2.00 |
| ❑ 13 Robb Nen | .20 | .50 |
| ❑ 14 Cal Ripken | 1.50 | 4.00 |
| ❑ 15 John Valentin | .20 | .50 |
| ❑ 16 Ricky Bottalico | .20 | .50 |
| ❑ 17 Mike Lansing | .20 | .50 |
| ❑ 18 Ryne Sandberg | .75 | 2.00 |
| ❑ 19 Carlos Delgado | .30 | .75 |
| ❑ 20 Craig Biggio | .30 | .75 |
| ❑ 21 Eric Karros | .20 | .50 |
| ❑ 22 Kevin Appier | .20 | .50 |
| ❑ 23 Mariano Rivera | .50 | 1.25 |
| ❑ 24 Vinny Castilla | .20 | .50 |
| ❑ 25 Juan Gonzalez | .50 | 1.25 |
| ❑ 26 Al Martin | .20 | .50 |
| ❑ 27 Jeff Cirillo | .20 | .50 |
| ❑ 28 Ray Lankford | .20 | .50 |
| ❑ 29 Manny Ramirez | .50 | 1.25 |
| ❑ 30 Roberto Alomar | .30 | .75 |
| ❑ 31 Will Clark | .30 | .75 |
| ❑ 32 Chuck Knoblauch | .20 | .50 |
| ❑ 33 Harold Baines | .20 | .50 |
| ❑ 34 Edgar Martinez | .30 | .75 |
| ❑ 35 Mike Mussina | .30 | .75 |
| ❑ 36 Kevin Brown | .20 | .50 |
| ❑ 37 Dennis Eckersley | .30 | .75 |
| ❑ 38 Tino Martinez | .20 | .50 |
| ❑ 39 Raul Mondesi | .20 | .50 |
| ❑ 40 Sammy Sosa | .50 | 1.25 |
| ❑ 41 John Smoltz | .30 | .75 |
| ❑ 42 Billy Wagner | .20 | .50 |
| ❑ 43 Ken Caminiti | .20 | .50 |
| ❑ 44 Wade Boggs | .30 | .75 |
| ❑ 45 Andres Galarraga | .20 | .50 |
| ❑ 46 Roger Clemens | 1.00 | 2.50 |
| ❑ 47 Matt Williams | .20 | .50 |
| ❑ 48 Albert Belle | .30 | .75 |
| ❑ 49 Jeff King | .20 | .50 |
| ❑ 50 John Wetteland | .20 | .50 |
| ❑ 51 Deion Sanders | .30 | .75 |
| ❑ 52 Ellis Burks | .20 | .50 |
| ❑ 53 Pedro Martinez | .30 | .75 |
| ❑ 54 Kenny Lofton | .30 | .75 |
| ❑ 55 Randy Johnson | .50 | 1.25 |
| ❑ 56 Bernie Williams | .30 | .75 |
| ❑ 57 Marquis Grissom | .20 | .50 |
| ❑ 58 Gary Sheffield | .30 | .75 |
| ❑ 59 Curt Schilling | .30 | .75 |
| ❑ 60 Reggie Sanders | .20 | .50 |
| ❑ 61 Bobby Higginson | .20 | .50 |
| ❑ 62 Moises Alou | .20 | .50 |
| ❑ 63 Tom Glavine | .30 | .75 |
| ❑ 64 Mark Grace | .30 | .75 |
| ❑ 65 Rafael Palmeiro | .30 | .75 |
| ❑ 66 John Olerud | .20 | .50 |
| ❑ 67 Dante Bichette | .20 | .50 |
| ❑ 68 Jeff Bagwell | .30 | .75 |
| ❑ 69 Barry Bonds | 1.25 | 3.00 |
| ❑ 70 Pat Hentgen | .20 | .50 |
| ❑ 71 Jim Thome | .30 | .75 |
| ❑ 72 Andy Pettitte | .30 | .75 |
| ❑ 73 Jay Bell | .20 | .50 |
| ❑ 74 Jim Edmonds | .20 | .50 |
| ❑ 75 Ron Gant | .20 | .50 |
| ❑ 76 David Cone | .20 | .50 |
| ❑ 77 Jose Canseco | .30 | .75 |
| ❑ 78 Jay Buhner | .20 | .50 |
| ❑ 79 Greg Maddux | .75 | 2.00 |
| ❑ 80 Lance Johnson | .20 | .50 |
| ❑ 81 Travis Fryman | .20 | .50 |
| ❑ 82 Paul O'Neill | .30 | .75 |
| ❑ 83 Ivan Rodriguez | .30 | .75 |
| ❑ 84 Fred McGriff | .30 | .75 |
| ❑ 85 Mike Piazza | .75 | 2.00 |
| ❑ 86 Brady Anderson | .20 | .50 |
| ❑ 87 Marty Cordova | .20 | .50 |
| ❑ 88 Joe Carter | .20 | .50 |
| ❑ 89 Brian Jordan | .20 | .50 |
| ❑ 90 David Justice | .20 | .50 |
| ❑ 91 Tony Gwynn | .60 | 1.50 |
| ❑ 92 Larry Walker | .30 | .75 |
| ❑ 93 Mo Vaughn | .20 | .50 |
| ❑ 94 Sandy Alomar Jr. | .20 | .50 |
| ❑ 95 Rusty Greer | .20 | .50 |
| ❑ 96 Roberto Hernandez | .20 | .50 |
| ❑ 97 Hal Morris | .20 | .50 |
| ❑ 98 Todd Hundley | .20 | .50 |
| ❑ 99 Rondell White | .20 | .50 |
| ❑ 100 Frank Thomas | .50 | 1.25 |
| ❑ 101 Bubba Trammell RC | .60 | 1.50 |
| ❑ 102 Sidney Ponson RC | 1.00 | 2.50 |
| ❑ 103 Ricky Ledee RC | .60 | 1.50 |
| ❑ 104 Brett Tomko | .20 | .50 |
| ❑ 105 Braden Looper RC | .40 | 1.00 |
| ❑ 106 Jason Dickson | .20 | .50 |
| ❑ 107 Chad Green RC | .40 | 1.00 |
| ❑ 108 R.A. Dickey RC | .40 | 1.00 |
| ❑ 109 Jeff Liefer | .20 | .50 |
| ❑ 110 Richard Hidalgo | .20 | .50 |
| ❑ 111 Chad Hermansen RC | .40 | 1.00 |
| ❑ 112 Felix Martinez | .20 | .50 |
| ❑ 113 J.J. Johnson | .20 | .50 |
| ❑ 114 Todd Dunwoody | .20 | .50 |
| ❑ 115 Katsuhiro Maeda | .20 | .50 |
| ❑ 116 Darin Erstad | .40 | 1.00 |
| ❑ 117 Eliezer Marrero | .20 | .50 |
| ❑ 118 Bartolo Colon | .20 | .50 |
| ❑ 119 Ugueth Urbina | .20 | .50 |
| ❑ 120 Jaime Bluma | .20 | .50 |
| ❑ 121 Seth Greisinger RC | .40 | 1.00 |
| ❑ 122 Jose Cruz Jr. RC | .60 | 1.50 |
| ❑ 123 Todd Dunn | .20 | .50 |
| ❑ 124 Justin Towle RC | .40 | 1.00 |
| ❑ 125 Brian Rose | .20 | .50 |
| ❑ 126 Jose Guillen | .20 | .50 |
| ❑ 127 Andruw Jones | .30 | .75 |
| ❑ 128 Mark Kotsay RC | 1.50 | 4.00 |
| ❑ 129 Wilton Guerrero | .20 | .50 |
| ❑ 130 Jacob Cruz | .20 | .50 |
| ❑ 131 Mike Sweeney | .20 | .50 |
| ❑ 132 Matt Morris | .20 | .50 |
| ❑ 133 John Thomson | .20 | .50 |
| ❑ 134 Javier Valentin | .20 | .50 |
| ❑ 135 Mike Drumright RC | .40 | 1.00 |
| ❑ 136 Michael Barrett | .40 | 1.00 |
| ❑ 137 Tony Saunders RC | .40 | 1.00 |
| ❑ 138 Kevin Brown | .20 | .50 |
| ❑ 139 Anthony Sanders RC | .40 | 1.00 |
| ❑ 140 Jeff Abbott | .20 | .50 |
| ❑ 141 Eugene Kingsale | .20 | .50 |
| ❑ 142 Paul Konerko | .50 | .75 |
| ❑ 143 Randall Simon RC | .60 | 1.50 |
| ❑ 144 Freddy Adrian Garcia | .20 | .50 |
| ❑ 145 Karim Garcia | .20 | .50 |
| ❑ 146 Carlos Guillen | .20 | .50 |
| ❑ 147 Aaron Boone | .20 | .50 |
| ❑ 148 Donnie Sadler | .20 | .50 |
| ❑ 149 Brooks Kieschnick | .20 | .50 |
| ❑ 150 Scott Spiezio | .20 | .50 |
| ❑ 151 Kevin Orie | .20 | .50 |

|  |  | | |
|---|---|---|---|
| 152 | Russ Johnson | .20 | .50 |
| 153 | Livan Hernandez | .20 | .50 |
| 154 | Vladimir Nunez RC | .40 | 1.00 |
| 155 | Pokey Reese | .20 | .50 |
| 156 | Chris Carpenter | .20 | .50 |
| 157 | Eric Milton RC | .60 | 1.50 |
| 158 | Richie Sexson | .20 | .50 |
| 159 | Carl Pavano | .20 | .50 |
| 160 | Pat Cline | .20 | .50 |
| 161 | Ron Wright | .20 | .50 |
| 162 | Dante Powell | .20 | .50 |
| 163 | Mark Bellhorn | .20 | .50 |
| 164 | George Lombard | .20 | .50 |
| 165 | Paul Wilder RC | .40 | 1.00 |
| 166 | Brad Fullmer | .20 | .50 |
| 167 | Kris Benson RC | 1.00 | 2.50 |
| 168 | Torii Hunter | .20 | .50 |
| 169 | D.T. Cromer RC | .40 | 1.00 |
| 170 | Nelson Figueroa RC | .40 | 1.00 |
| 171 | Hiram Bocachica RC | .40 | 1.00 |
| 172 | Shane Monahan | .20 | .50 |
| 173 | Juan Melo | .20 | .50 |
| 174 | Calvin Pickering RC | .40 | 1.00 |
| 175 | Reggie Taylor | .20 | .50 |
| 176 | Geoff Jenkins | .20 | .50 |
| 177 | Steve Rain RC | .20 | .50 |
| 178 | Nerio Rodriguez RC | .40 | 1.00 |
| 179 | Derrick Gibson | .20 | .50 |
| 180 | Darin Blood | .20 | .50 |
| 181 | Ben Davis | .20 | .50 |
| 182 | Adrian Beltre RC | 3.00 | 8.00 |
| 183 | Kerry Wood RC | 5.00 | 12.00 |
| 184 | Nate Rolison RC | .40 | 1.00 |
| 185 | Fernando Tatis RC | .40 | 1.00 |
| 186 | Jake Westbrook RC | 1.00 | 2.50 |
| 187 | Edwin Diaz | .20 | .50 |
| 188 | Joe Fontenot RC | .40 | 1.00 |
| 189 | Matt Halloran RC | .40 | 1.00 |
| 190 | Matt Clement RC | 1.00 | 2.50 |
| 191 | Todd Greene | .20 | .50 |
| 192 | Eric Chavez RC | 4.00 | 10.00 |
| 193 | Edgard Velazquez | .20 | .50 |
| 194 | Bruce Chen RC | 1.00 | 2.50 |
| 195 | Jason Brester | .20 | .50 |
| 196 | Chris Reitsma RC | .60 | 1.50 |
| 197 | Nelfi Perez | .20 | .50 |
| 198 | Hideki Irabu RC | .60 | 1.50 |
| 199 | Don Denbow RC | .40 | 1.00 |
| 200 | Derrek Lee | .30 | .75 |
| 201 | Todd Walker | .20 | .50 |
| 202 | Scott Rolen | .30 | .75 |
| 203 | Wes Helms | .20 | .50 |
| 204 | Bob Abreu | .30 | .75 |
| 205 | John Patterson RC | 1.50 | 4.00 |
| 206 | Alex Gonzalez RC | 1.00 | 2.50 |
| 207 | Grant Roberts RC | .40 | 1.00 |
| 208 | Jeff Suppan | .20 | .50 |
| 209 | Luke Wilcox | .20 | .50 |
| 210 | Marlon Anderson | .20 | .50 |
| 211 | Mike Caruso RC | .40 | 1.00 |
| 212 | Roy Halladay RC | 6.00 | 15.00 |
| 213 | Jeremi Gonzalez RC | .40 | 1.00 |
| 214 | Aramis Ramirez RC | 4.00 | 10.00 |
| 215 | Dee Brown RC | .40 | 1.00 |
| 216 | Justin Thompson | .20 | .50 |
| 217 | Danny Clyburn | .20 | .50 |
| 218 | Bruce Aven | .20 | .50 |
| 219 | Keith Foulke RC | 1.50 | 4.00 |
| 220 | Shannon Stewart | .20 | .50 |
| 221 | Larry Barnes RC | .40 | 1.00 |
| 222 | Mark Johnson RC | .40 | 1.00 |
| 223 | Randy Winn | .20 | .50 |
| 224 | Nomar Garciaparra | .75 | 2.00 |
| 225 | Jacque Jones RC | 1.50 | 4.00 |
| 226 | Chris Clemons | .20 | .50 |
| 227 | Todd Helton | .50 | 1.25 |
| 228 | Ryan Brannan RC | .40 | 1.00 |
| 229 | Alex Sanchez RC | .60 | 1.50 |
| 230 | Russell Branyan | .40 | 1.00 |
| 231 | Daryle Ward | .40 | 1.00 |
| 232 | Kevin Witt | .20 | .50 |
| 233 | Gabby Martinez | .20 | .50 |
| 234 | Preston Wilson | .20 | .50 |
| 235 | Donzell McDonald RC | .40 | 1.00 |
| 236 | Orlando Cabrera RC | 1.50 | 4.00 |
| 237 | Brian Banks | .20 | .50 |
| 238 | Robbie Bell | .40 | 1.00 |
| 239 | Brad Rigby | .20 | .50 |

|  |  | | |
|---|---|---|---|
| 240 | Scott Elarton | .20 | .50 |
| 241 | Donny Leon RC | .40 | 1.00 |
| 242 | Abraham Nunez RC | .40 | 1.00 |
| 243 | Adam Eaton RC | 1.00 | 2.50 |
| 244 | Octavio Dotel RC | .60 | 1.50 |
| 245 | Sean Casey | 1.00 | 2.50 |
| 246 | Joe Lawrence RC | .40 | 1.00 |
| 247 | Adam Johnson RC | .40 | 1.00 |
| 248 | Ronnie Belliard RC | 1.25 | 3.00 |
| 249 | Bobby Estalella | .20 | .50 |
| 250 | Corey Lee RC | .40 | 1.00 |
| 251 | Mike Cameron | .20 | .50 |
| 252 | Kerry Robinson RC | .40 | 1.00 |
| 253 | A.J. Zapp RC | .40 | 1.00 |
| 254 | Jarrod Washburn | .20 | .50 |
| 255 | Ben Grieve | .20 | .50 |
| 256 | Javier Vazquez RC | 1.50 | 4.00 |
| 257 | Travis Lee RC | .60 | 1.50 |
| 258 | Dennis Reyes RC | .40 | 1.00 |
| 259 | Danny Buxbaum | .20 | .50 |
| 260 | Kelvim Escobar RC | 1.00 | 2.50 |
| 261 | Danny Klassen | .20 | .50 |
| 262 | Ken Cloude RC | .40 | 1.00 |
| 263 | Gabe Alvarez | .20 | .50 |
| 264 | Clayton Bruner RC | .40 | 1.00 |
| 265 | Jason Marquis RC | 1.50 | 4.00 |
| 266 | Jamey Wright | .20 | .50 |
| 267 | Matt Snyder RC | .40 | 1.00 |
| 268 | Josh Garrett RC | .40 | 1.00 |
| 269 | Juan Encarnacion | .20 | .50 |
| 270 | Heath Murray | .20 | .50 |
| 271 | Brent Butler RC | .40 | 1.00 |
| 272 | Danny Peoples RC | .40 | 1.00 |
| 273 | Miguel Tejada RC | 5.00 | 12.00 |
| 274 | Jim Pittsley | .20 | .50 |
| 275 | Dmitri Young | .20 | .50 |
| 276 | Vladimir Guerrero | .50 | 1.25 |
| 277 | Cole Liniak RC | .40 | 1.00 |
| 278 | Ramon Hernandez RC | .20 | .50 |
| 279 | Cliff Politte RC | .40 | 1.00 |
| 280 | Mel Rosario RC | .20 | .50 |
| 281 | Jorge Carrion RC | .40 | 1.00 |
| 282 | John Barnes RC | .40 | 1.00 |
| 283 | Chris Stowe RC | .40 | 1.00 |
| 284 | Vernon Wells RC | 5.00 | 12.00 |
| 285 | Brett Caradonna RC | .40 | 1.00 |
| 286 | Scott Hodges RC | .40 | 1.00 |
| 287 | Jon Garland RC | 2.50 | 6.00 |
| 288 | Nathan Haynes RC | .40 | 1.00 |
| 289 | Geoff Goetz RC | .40 | 1.00 |
| 290 | Adam Kennedy RC | 1.00 | 2.50 |
| 291 | T.J. Tucker RC | .40 | 1.00 |
| 292 | Aaron Akin RC | .40 | 1.00 |
| 293 | Jayson Werth RC | 1.25 | 3.00 |
| 294 | Glenn Davis RC | 1.00 | 2.50 |
| 295 | Mark Mangum RC | .40 | 1.00 |
| 296 | Troy Cameron RC | .40 | 1.00 |
| 297 | J.J. Davis RC | .40 | 1.00 |
| 298 | Lance Berkman RC | 5.00 | 12.00 |
| 299 | Jason Standridge RC | .40 | 1.00 |
| 300 | Jason Dellaero RC | .40 | 1.00 |

## 1998 Bowman Chrome

| | | | |
|---|---|---|---|
| COMPLETE SET (441) | | 60.00 | 160.00 |
| COMPLETE SERIES 1 (221) | | 30.00 | 80.00 |
| COMPLETE SERIES 2 (220) | | 30.00 | 80.00 |
| 1 | Nomar Garciaparra | .75 | 2.00 |
| 2 | Scott Rolen | .30 | .75 |
| 3 | Andy Pettitte | .30 | .75 |
| 4 | Ivan Rodriguez | .30 | .75 |
| 5 | Mark McGwire | 1.25 | 3.00 |
| 6 | Jason Dickson | .20 | .50 |
| 7 | Jose Cruz Jr. | .20 | .50 |
| 8 | Jeff Kent | .20 | .50 |

|  |  | | |
|---|---|---|---|
| 9 | Mike Mussina | .30 | .75 |
| 10 | Jason Kendall | .20 | .50 |
| 11 | Brett Tomko | .20 | .50 |
| 12 | Jeff King | .20 | .50 |
| 13 | Brad Radke | .20 | .50 |
| 14 | Robin Ventura | .20 | .50 |
| 15 | Jeff Bagwell | .30 | .75 |
| 16 | Greg Maddux | .75 | 2.00 |
| 17 | John Jaha | .20 | .50 |
| 18 | Mike Piazza | .75 | 2.00 |
| 19 | Edgar Martinez | .30 | .75 |
| 20 | David Justice | .20 | .50 |
| 21 | Todd Hundley | .20 | .50 |
| 22 | Tony Gwynn | .60 | 1.50 |
| 23 | Larry Walker | .20 | .50 |
| 24 | Bernie Williams | .30 | .75 |
| 25 | Edgar Renteria | .20 | .50 |
| 26 | Rafael Palmeiro | .30 | .75 |
| 27 | Tim Salmon | .30 | .75 |
| 28 | Matt Morris | .20 | .50 |
| 29 | Shawn Estes | .20 | .50 |
| 30 | Vladimir Guerrero | .50 | 1.25 |
| 31 | Fernando Tatis | .20 | .50 |
| 32 | Justin Thompson | .20 | .50 |
| 33 | Ken Griffey Jr. | .75 | 2.00 |
| 34 | Edgardo Alfonzo | .20 | .50 |
| 35 | Mo Vaughn | .20 | .50 |
| 36 | Marty Cordova | .20 | .50 |
| 37 | Craig Biggio | .30 | .75 |
| 38 | Roger Clemens | 1.00 | 2.50 |
| 39 | Mark Grace | .30 | .75 |
| 40 | Ken Caminiti | .20 | .50 |
| 41 | Tony Womack | .20 | .50 |
| 42 | Albert Belle | .20 | .50 |
| 43 | Tino Martinez | .30 | .75 |
| 44 | Sandy Alomar Jr. | .20 | .50 |
| 45 | Jeff Cirillo | .20 | .50 |
| 46 | Jason Giambi | .20 | .50 |
| 47 | Darin Erstad | .20 | .50 |
| 48 | Livan Hernandez | .20 | .50 |
| 49 | Mark Grudzielanek | .20 | .50 |
| 50 | Sammy Sosa | .50 | 1.25 |
| 51 | Curt Schilling | .20 | .50 |
| 52 | Brian Hunter | .20 | .50 |
| 53 | Neifi Perez | .20 | .50 |
| 54 | Todd Walker | .20 | .50 |
| 55 | Jose Guillen | .20 | .50 |
| 56 | Jim Thome | .30 | .75 |
| 57 | Tom Glavine | .30 | .75 |
| 58 | Todd Greene | .20 | .50 |
| 59 | Rondell White | .20 | .50 |
| 60 | Roberto Alomar | .30 | .75 |
| 61 | Tony Clark | .20 | .50 |
| 62 | Vinny Castilla | .20 | .50 |
| 63 | Barry Larkin | .30 | .75 |
| 64 | Hideki Irabu | .20 | .50 |
| 65 | Johnny Damon | .20 | .50 |
| 66 | Juan Gonzalez | .20 | .50 |
| 67 | John Olerud | .20 | .50 |
| 68 | Gary Sheffield | .20 | .50 |
| 69 | Raul Mondesi | .20 | .50 |
| 70 | Chipper Jones | .50 | 1.25 |
| 71 | David Ortiz | 2.50 | 6.00 |
| 72 | Warren Morris RC | .40 | 1.00 |
| 73 | Alex Gonzalez | .20 | .50 |
| 74 | Nick Bierbrodt | .20 | .50 |
| 75 | Roy Halladay | .60 | 1.50 |
| 76 | Danny Buxbaum | .20 | .50 |
| 77 | Adam Kennedy | .20 | .50 |
| 78 | Jared Sandberg | .20 | .50 |
| 79 | Michael Barrett | .20 | .50 |
| 80 | Gil Meche | .60 | 1.50 |
| 81 | Jayson Werth | .20 | .50 |
| 82 | Abraham Nunez | .20 | .50 |
| 83 | Ben Petrick | .20 | .50 |
| 84 | Brett Caradonna | .20 | .50 |
| 85 | Mike Lowell RC | 2.50 | 6.00 |
| 86 | Clay Bruner | .20 | .50 |
| 87 | John Curtice RC | .60 | 1.50 |
| 88 | Bobby Estalella | .20 | .50 |
| 89 | Juan Melo | .20 | .50 |
| 90 | Arnold Gooch | .20 | .50 |
| 91 | Kevin Millwood RC | 1.50 | 4.00 |
| 92 | Richie Sexson | .20 | .50 |
| 93 | Orlando Cabrera | .20 | .50 |
| 94 | Pat Cline | .20 | .50 |
| 95 | Anthony Sanders | .20 | .50 |
| 96 | Russ Johnson | .20 | .50 |

| # | Player | Price 1 | Price 2 |
|---|--------|--------|--------|
| 97 | Ben Grieve | .20 | .50 |
| 98 | Kevin McGlinchy | .20 | .50 |
| 99 | Paul Wilder | .20 | .50 |
| 100 | Russ Ortiz | .20 | .50 |
| 101 | Ryan Jackson RC | .40 | 1.00 |
| 102 | Heath Murray | .20 | .50 |
| 103 | Brian Rose | .20 | .50 |
| 104 | Ryan Radmanovich RC | .40 | 1.00 |
| 105 | Ricky Ledee | .20 | .50 |
| 106 | Jeff Wallace RC | .40 | 1.00 |
| 107 | Ryan Minor RC | .40 | 1.00 |
| 108 | Dennis Reyes | .20 | .50 |
| 109 | James Manias | .20 | .50 |
| 110 | Chris Carpenter | .20 | .50 |
| 111 | Daryle Ward | .20 | .50 |
| 112 | Vernon Wells | .20 | .50 |
| 113 | Chad Green | .20 | .50 |
| 114 | Mike Stoner RC | .40 | 1.00 |
| 115 | Brad Fullmer | .20 | .50 |
| 116 | Adam Eaton | .20 | .50 |
| 117 | Jeff Liefer | .20 | .50 |
| 118 | Corey Koskie RC | 1.00 | 2.50 |
| 119 | Todd Helton | .30 | .75 |
| 120 | Jaime Jones RC | .40 | 1.00 |
| 121 | Mel Rosario | .20 | .50 |
| 122 | Geoff Goetz | .20 | .50 |
| 123 | Adrian Beltre | .20 | .50 |
| 124 | Jason Dellaero | .20 | .50 |
| 125 | Gabe Kapler RC | 1.00 | 2.50 |
| 126 | Scott Schoeneweis | .20 | .50 |
| 127 | Ryan Brannan | .20 | .50 |
| 128 | Aaron Akin | .20 | .50 |
| 129 | Ryan Anderson RC | .40 | 1.00 |
| 130 | Brad Penny | .20 | .50 |
| 131 | Bruce Chen | .20 | .50 |
| 132 | Eli Marrero | .20 | .50 |
| 133 | Eric Chavez | .20 | .50 |
| 134 | Troy Glaus RC | 3.00 | 8.00 |
| 135 | Troy Cameron | .20 | .50 |
| 136 | Brian Sikorski RC | .40 | 1.00 |
| 137 | Mike Kinkade RC | .40 | 1.00 |
| 138 | Braden Looper | .20 | .50 |
| 139 | Mark Mangum | .20 | .50 |
| 140 | Danny Peoples | .20 | .50 |
| 141 | J.J. Davis | .20 | .50 |
| 142 | Ben Davis | .20 | .50 |
| 143 | Jacque Jones | .20 | .50 |
| 144 | Derrick Gibson | .20 | .50 |
| 145 | Bronson Arroyo | 1.50 | 4.00 |
| 146 | Luis De Los Santos RC | .40 | 1.00 |
| 147 | Jeff Abbott | .20 | .50 |
| 148 | Mike Cuddyer RC | 1.50 | 4.00 |
| 149 | Jason Romano | .20 | .50 |
| 150 | Shane Monahan | .20 | .50 |
| 151 | Nlema Ndungidi RC | .40 | 1.00 |
| 152 | Alex Sanchez | .20 | .50 |
| 153 | Jack Cust RC | 3.00 | 8.00 |
| 154 | Brent Butler | .20 | .50 |
| 155 | Ramon Hernandez | .20 | .50 |
| 156 | Norm Hutchins | .20 | .50 |
| 157 | Jason Marquis | .20 | .50 |
| 158 | Jacob Cruz | .20 | .50 |
| 159 | Rob Burger RC | .40 | 1.00 |
| 160 | Dave Coggin | .20 | .50 |
| 161 | Preston Wilson | .20 | .50 |
| 162 | Jason Fitzgerald RC | .40 | 1.00 |
| 163 | Dan Serafini | .20 | .50 |
| 164 | Pete Munro | .20 | .50 |
| 165 | Trot Nixon | .20 | .50 |
| 166 | Homer Bush | .20 | .50 |
| 167 | Dermal Brown | .20 | .50 |
| 168 | Chad Hermansen | .20 | .50 |
| 169 | Julio Moreno RC | .40 | 1.00 |
| 170 | John Roskos RC | .40 | 1.00 |
| 171 | Grant Roberts | .20 | .50 |
| 172 | Ken Cloude | .20 | .50 |
| 173 | Jason Brester | .20 | .50 |
| 174 | Jason Conti | .20 | .50 |
| 175 | Jon Garland | .20 | .50 |
| 176 | Robbie Bell | .20 | .50 |
| 177 | Nathan Haynes | .20 | .50 |
| 178 | Ramon Ortiz RC | .60 | 1.50 |
| 179 | Shannon Stewart | .20 | .50 |
| 180 | Pablo Ortega | .20 | .50 |
| 181 | Jimmy Rollins RC | 4.00 | 10.00 |
| 182 | Sean Casey | .20 | .50 |
| 183 | Ted Lilly RC | 1.00 | 2.50 |
| 184 | Chris Enochs RC | .40 | 1.00 |
| 185 | Magglio Ordonez UER RC | 4.00 | 10.00 |
| 186 | Mike Drumright | .20 | .50 |
| 187 | Aaron Boone | .20 | .50 |
| 188 | Matt Clement | .20 | .50 |
| 189 | Todd Dunwoody | .20 | .50 |
| 190 | Larry Rodriguez | .20 | .50 |
| 191 | Todd Noel | .20 | .50 |
| 192 | Geoff Jenkins | .20 | .50 |
| 193 | George Lombard | .20 | .50 |
| 194 | Lance Berkman | .20 | .50 |
| 195 | Marcus McCain | .20 | .50 |
| 196 | Ryan McGuire | .20 | .50 |
| 197 | Jhensy Sandoval | .20 | .50 |
| 198 | Corey Lee | .20 | .50 |
| 199 | Mario Valdez | .20 | .50 |
| 200 | Robert Fick RC | .60 | 1.50 |
| 201 | Donnie Sadler | .20 | .50 |
| 202 | Marc Kroon | .20 | .50 |
| 203 | David Miller | .20 | .50 |
| 204 | Jarrod Washburn | .20 | .50 |
| 205 | Miguel Tejada | .50 | 1.25 |
| 206 | Raul Ibanez | .20 | .50 |
| 207 | John Patterson | .20 | .50 |
| 208 | Calvin Pickering | .20 | .50 |
| 209 | Felix Martinez | .20 | .50 |
| 210 | Mark Redman | .20 | .50 |
| 211 | Scott Elarton | .20 | .50 |
| 212 | Jose Amado RC | .40 | 1.00 |
| 213 | Kerry Wood | .20 | .50 |
| 214 | Dante Powell | .20 | .50 |
| 215 | Aramis Ramirez | .20 | .50 |
| 216 | A.J. Hinch | .20 | .50 |
| 217 | Dustin Carr RC | .40 | 1.00 |
| 218 | Mark Kotsay | .20 | .50 |
| 219 | Jason Standridge | .20 | .50 |
| 220 | Luis Ordaz | .20 | .50 |
| 221 | Orlando Hernandez RC | 2.00 | 5.00 |
| 222 | Cal Ripken | 1.50 | 4.00 |
| 223 | Paul Molitor | .20 | .50 |
| 224 | Derek Jeter | 1.25 | 3.00 |
| 225 | Barry Bonds | 1.25 | 3.00 |
| 226 | Jim Edmonds | .20 | .50 |
| 227 | John Smoltz | .30 | .75 |
| 228 | Eric Karros | .20 | .50 |
| 229 | Ray Lankford | .20 | .50 |
| 230 | Rey Ordonez | .20 | .50 |
| 231 | Kenny Lofton | .20 | .50 |
| 232 | Alex Rodriguez | .75 | 2.00 |
| 233 | Dante Bichette | .20 | .50 |
| 234 | Pedro Martinez | .30 | .75 |
| 235 | Carlos Delgado | .20 | .50 |
| 236 | Rod Beck | .20 | .50 |
| 237 | Matt Williams | .20 | .50 |
| 238 | Charles Johnson | .20 | .50 |
| 239 | Rico Brogna | .20 | .50 |
| 240 | Frank Thomas | .50 | 1.25 |
| 241 | Paul O'Neill | .30 | .75 |
| 242 | Jaret Wright | .20 | .50 |
| 243 | Brant Brown | .20 | .50 |
| 244 | Ryan Klesko | .20 | .50 |
| 245 | Chuck Finley | .20 | .50 |
| 246 | Derek Bell | .20 | .50 |
| 247 | Delino DeShields | .20 | .50 |
| 248 | Chan Ho Park | .20 | .50 |
| 249 | Wade Boggs | .30 | .75 |
| 250 | Jay Buhner | .20 | .50 |
| 251 | Butch Huskey | .20 | .50 |
| 252 | Steve Finley | .20 | .50 |
| 253 | Will Clark | .30 | .75 |
| 254 | John Valentin | .20 | .50 |
| 255 | Bobby Higginson | .20 | .50 |
| 256 | Darryl Strawberry | .30 | .75 |
| 257 | Randy Johnson | .50 | 1.25 |
| 258 | Al Martin | .20 | .50 |
| 259 | Travis Fryman | .20 | .50 |
| 260 | Fred McGriff | .30 | .75 |
| 261 | Jose Valentin | .20 | .50 |
| 262 | Andruw Jones | .30 | .75 |
| 263 | Kenny Rogers | .20 | .50 |
| 264 | Moises Alou | .20 | .50 |
| 265 | Denny Neagle | .20 | .50 |
| 266 | Ugueth Urbina | .20 | .50 |
| 267 | Derrek Lee | .20 | .50 |
| 268 | Ellis Burks | .20 | .50 |
| 269 | Mariano Rivera | .50 | 1.25 |
| 270 | Dean Palmer | .20 | .50 |
| 271 | Eddie Taubensee | .20 | .50 |
| 272 | Brady Anderson | .20 | .50 |
| 273 | Brian Giles | .20 | .50 |
| 274 | Quinton McCracken | .20 | .50 |
| 275 | Henry Rodriguez | .20 | .50 |
| 276 | Andres Galarraga | .30 | .75 |
| 277 | Jose Canseco | .30 | .75 |
| 278 | David Segui | .20 | .50 |
| 279 | Bret Saberhagen | .20 | .50 |
| 280 | Kevin Brown | .30 | .75 |
| 281 | Chuck Knoblauch | .20 | .50 |
| 282 | Jeromy Burnitz | .20 | .50 |
| 283 | Jay Bell | .20 | .50 |
| 284 | Manny Ramirez | .30 | .75 |
| 285 | Rick Helling | .20 | .50 |
| 286 | Francisco Cordova | .20 | .50 |
| 287 | Bob Abreu | .20 | .50 |
| 288 | J.T. Snow | .20 | .50 |
| 289 | Hideo Nomo | .50 | 1.25 |
| 290 | Brian Jordan | .20 | .50 |
| 291 | Javy Lopez | .20 | .50 |
| 292 | Travis Lee | .20 | .50 |
| 293 | Russell Branyan | .20 | .50 |
| 294 | Paul Konerko | .20 | .50 |
| 295 | Masato Yoshii RC | .60 | 1.50 |
| 296 | Kris Benson | .20 | .50 |
| 297 | Juan Encarnacion | .20 | .50 |
| 298 | Eric Milton | .20 | .50 |
| 299 | Mike Caruso | .20 | .50 |
| 300 | Ricardo Arreboles RC | .40 | 1.00 |
| 301 | Bobby Smith | .20 | .50 |
| 302 | Billy Koch | .20 | .50 |
| 303 | Richard Hidalgo | .20 | .50 |
| 304 | Justin Baughman RC | .40 | 1.00 |
| 305 | Chris Gissell | .20 | .50 |
| 306 | Donnie Bridges RC | .40 | 1.00 |
| 307 | Nelson Lara RC | .40 | 1.00 |
| 308 | Randy Wolf RC | .60 | 1.50 |
| 309 | Jason LaRue RC | .60 | 1.50 |
| 310 | Jason Gooding RC | .40 | 1.00 |
| 311 | Edgard Clemente | .20 | .50 |
| 312 | Andrew Vessel | .20 | .50 |
| 313 | Chris Reitsma | .20 | .50 |
| 314 | Jesus Sanchez RC | .40 | 1.00 |
| 315 | Buddy Carlyle RC | .40 | 1.00 |
| 316 | Randy Winn | .20 | .50 |
| 317 | Luis Rivera RC | .40 | 1.00 |
| 318 | Marcus Thames RC | 2.50 | 6.00 |
| 319 | A.J. Pierzynski | .20 | .50 |
| 320 | Scott Randall | .20 | .50 |
| 321 | Damian Sapp | .20 | .50 |
| 322 | Ed Yarnall RC | .40 | 1.00 |
| 323 | Luke Allen RC | .40 | 1.00 |
| 324 | J.D. Smart | .20 | .50 |
| 325 | Willie Martinez | .20 | .50 |
| 326 | Alex Ramirez | .20 | .50 |
| 327 | Eric DuBose RC | .40 | 1.00 |
| 328 | Kevin Witt | .20 | .50 |
| 329 | Dan McKinley RC | .40 | 1.00 |
| 330 | Cliff Politte | .20 | .50 |
| 331 | Vladimir Nunez | .20 | .50 |
| 332 | John Halama RC | .40 | 1.00 |
| 333 | Nerio Rodriguez | .20 | .50 |
| 334 | Desi Relaford | .20 | .50 |
| 335 | Robinson Checo | .20 | .50 |
| 336 | John Nicholson | .30 | .75 |
| 337 | Tom LaRosa RC | .40 | 1.00 |
| 338 | Kevin Nicholson RC | .40 | 1.00 |
| 339 | Javier Vazquez | .20 | .50 |
| 340 | A.J. Zapp | .20 | .50 |
| 341 | Tom Evans | .20 | .50 |
| 342 | Kerry Robinson | .20 | .50 |
| 343 | Gabe Gonzalez RC | .40 | 1.00 |
| 344 | Ralph Milliard | .20 | .50 |
| 345 | Enrique Wilson | .20 | .50 |
| 346 | Elvin Hernandez | .20 | .50 |
| 347 | Mike Lincoln RC | .40 | 1.00 |
| 348 | Cesar King RC | .40 | 1.00 |
| 349 | Cristian Guzman RC | .60 | 1.50 |
| 350 | Donzell McDonald | .20 | .50 |
| 351 | Jim Parque RC | .40 | 1.00 |
| 352 | Mike Saipe RC | .40 | 1.00 |
| 353 | Carlos Febles RC | .60 | 1.50 |
| 354 | Demell Stenson RC | .40 | 1.00 |
| 355 | Mark Osborne RC | .40 | 1.00 |
| 356 | Odalis Perez RC | 1.50 | 4.00 |
| 357 | Jason Dewey RC | .40 | 1.00 |
| 358 | Joe Fontenot | .20 | .50 |
| 359 | Jason Grilli RC | .40 | 1.00 |
| 360 | Kevin Haverbusch RC | .40 | 1.00 |

| | | |
|---|---|---|
| ❑ 361 Jay Yennaco RC | .40 | 1.00 |
| ❑ 362 Brian Buchanan | .20 | .50 |
| ❑ 363 John Barnes | .20 | .50 |
| ❑ 364 Chris Fussell | .20 | .50 |
| ❑ 365 Kevin Gibbs RC | .40 | 1.00 |
| ❑ 366 Joe Lawrence | .20 | .50 |
| ❑ 367 DaRond Stovall | .20 | .50 |
| ❑ 368 Brian Fuentes RC | .40 | 1.00 |
| ❑ 369 Jimmy Anderson | .20 | .50 |
| ❑ 370 Lariel Gonzalez RC | .40 | 1.00 |
| ❑ 371 Scott Williamson RC | .40 | 1.00 |
| ❑ 372 Milton Bradley RC | .40 | 1.00 |
| ❑ 373 Jason Halper RC | .40 | 1.00 |
| ❑ 374 Brent Billingsley RC | .40 | 1.00 |
| ❑ 375 Joe DePastino RC | .40 | 1.00 |
| ❑ 376 Jake Westbrook | .20 | .50 |
| ❑ 377 Octavio Dotel | .20 | .50 |
| ❑ 378 Jason Williams RC | .40 | 1.00 |
| ❑ 379 Julio Ramirez RC | .40 | 1.00 |
| ❑ 380 Seth Greisinger | .40 | 1.00 |
| ❑ 381 Mike Judd RC | .40 | 1.00 |
| ❑ 382 Ben Ford RC | .40 | 1.00 |
| ❑ 383 Tom Bennett RC | .40 | 1.00 |
| ❑ 384 Adam Butler RC | .40 | 1.00 |
| ❑ 385 Wade Miller RC | 1.00 | 2.50 |
| ❑ 386 Kyle Peterson RC | .40 | 1.00 |
| ❑ 387 Tommy Peterman RC | .40 | 1.00 |
| ❑ 388 Onan Masaoka | .20 | .50 |
| ❑ 389 Jason Rakers RC | .40 | 1.00 |
| ❑ 390 Rafael Medina | .20 | .50 |
| ❑ 391 Luis Lopez RC | .40 | 1.00 |
| ❑ 392 Jeff Yoder | .20 | .50 |
| ❑ 393 Vance Wilson RC | .40 | 1.00 |
| ❑ 394 Fernando Seguignol RC | .40 | 1.00 |
| ❑ 395 Ron Wright | .40 | 1.00 |
| ❑ 396 Ruben Mateo RC | .40 | 1.00 |
| ❑ 397 Steve Lomasney RC | .60 | 1.50 |
| ❑ 398 Damian Jackson | .20 | .50 |
| ❑ 399 Mike Jerzembeck RC | .40 | 1.00 |
| ❑ 400 Luis Rivas RC | 1.00 | 2.50 |
| ❑ 401 Kevin Burford RC | .40 | 1.00 |
| ❑ 402 Glenn Davis | .20 | .50 |
| ❑ 403 Robert Luce RC | .40 | 1.00 |
| ❑ 404 Cole Liniak | .20 | .50 |
| ❑ 405 Matt LeCroy RC | .60 | 1.50 |
| ❑ 406 Jeremy Giambi RC | .60 | 1.50 |
| ❑ 407 Shawn Chacon | .20 | .50 |
| ❑ 408 Dewayne Wise RC | .40 | 1.00 |
| ❑ 409 Steve Woodard | .20 | .50 |
| ❑ 410 Francisco Cordero RC | 1.00 | 2.50 |
| ❑ 411 Damon Minor RC | .40 | 1.00 |
| ❑ 412 Lou Collier | .20 | .50 |
| ❑ 413 Justin Towle | .20 | .50 |
| ❑ 414 Juan LeBron | .20 | .50 |
| ❑ 415 Michael Coleman | .20 | .50 |
| ❑ 416 Felix Rodriguez | .20 | .50 |
| ❑ 417 Paul Ah Yat RC | .40 | 1.00 |
| ❑ 418 Kevin Barker RC | .40 | 1.00 |
| ❑ 419 Brian Meadows | .20 | .50 |
| ❑ 420 Darnell McDonald RC | .40 | 1.00 |
| ❑ 421 Matt Kinney RC | .40 | 1.00 |
| ❑ 422 Mike Vavrek RC | .40 | 1.00 |
| ❑ 423 Courtney Duncan RC | .40 | 1.00 |
| ❑ 424 Kevin Millar RC | 1.50 | 4.00 |
| ❑ 425 Ruben Rivera | .20 | .50 |
| ❑ 426 Steve Shoemaker RC | .40 | 1.00 |
| ❑ 427 Dan Reichert RC | .40 | 1.00 |
| ❑ 428 Carlos Lee RC | 2.50 | 6.00 |
| ❑ 429 Rod Barajas | 1.00 | 2.50 |
| ❑ 430 Pablo Ozuna RC | .60 | 1.50 |
| ❑ 431 Todd Belitz RC | .40 | 1.00 |
| ❑ 432 Sidney Ponson | .20 | .50 |
| ❑ 433 Steve Carver RC | .40 | 1.00 |
| ❑ 434 Esteban Yan RC | .60 | 1.50 |
| ❑ 435 Cedrick Bowers | .20 | .50 |
| ❑ 436 Marlon Anderson | .20 | .50 |
| ❑ 437 Carl Pavano | .20 | .50 |
| ❑ 438 Jae Weong Seo RC | .60 | 1.50 |
| ❑ 439 Jose Taveras RC | .40 | 1.00 |
| ❑ 440 Matt Anderson RC | .40 | 1.00 |
| ❑ 441 Darron Ingram RC | .40 | 1.00 |

## 1999 Bowman Chrome

| | | |
|---|---|---|
| ❑ COMPLETE SET (440) | 100.00 | 200.00 |
| ❑ COMPLETE SERIES 1 (220) | 40.00 | 80.00 |
| ❑ COMPLETE SERIES 2 (220) | 60.00 | 120.00 |
| ❑ 1 Ben Grieve | .20 | .50 |
| ❑ 2 Kerry Wood | .20 | .50 |
| ❑ 3 Ruben Rivera | .20 | .50 |
| ❑ 4 Sandy Alomar Jr. | .20 | .50 |
| ❑ 5 Cal Ripken | 1.50 | 4.00 |
| ❑ 6 Mark McGwire | 1.25 | 3.00 |
| ❑ 7 Vladimir Guerrero | .50 | 1.25 |
| ❑ 8 Moises Alou | .20 | .50 |
| ❑ 9 Jim Edmonds | .20 | .50 |
| ❑ 10 Greg Maddux | .75 | 2.00 |
| ❑ 11 Gary Sheffield | .20 | .50 |
| ❑ 12 John Valentin | .20 | .50 |
| ❑ 13 Chuck Knoblauch | .20 | .50 |
| ❑ 14 Tony Clark | .20 | .50 |
| ❑ 15 Rusty Greer | .20 | .50 |
| ❑ 16 Al Leiter | .20 | .50 |
| ❑ 17 Travis Lee | .20 | .50 |
| ❑ 18 Jose Cruz Jr. | .20 | .50 |
| ❑ 19 Pedro Martinez | .30 | .75 |
| ❑ 20 Paul O'Neill | .30 | .75 |
| ❑ 21 Todd Walker | .20 | .50 |
| ❑ 22 Vinny Castilla | .20 | .50 |
| ❑ 23 Barry Larkin | .30 | .75 |
| ❑ 24 Curt Schilling | .20 | .50 |
| ❑ 25 Jason Kendall | .20 | .50 |
| ❑ 26 Scott Erickson | .20 | .50 |
| ❑ 27 Andres Galarraga | .20 | .50 |
| ❑ 28 Jeff Shaw | .20 | .50 |
| ❑ 29 John Olerud | .20 | .50 |
| ❑ 30 Orlando Hernandez | .20 | .50 |
| ❑ 31 Larry Walker | .20 | .50 |
| ❑ 32 Andruw Jones | .30 | .75 |
| ❑ 33 Jeff Cirillo | .20 | .50 |
| ❑ 34 Barry Bonds | 1.25 | 3.00 |
| ❑ 35 Manny Ramirez | .30 | .75 |
| ❑ 36 Mark Kotsay | .20 | .50 |
| ❑ 37 Ivan Rodriguez | .30 | .75 |
| ❑ 38 Jeff King | .20 | .50 |
| ❑ 39 Brian Hunter | .20 | .50 |
| ❑ 40 Ray Durham | .20 | .50 |
| ❑ 41 Bernie Williams | .30 | .75 |
| ❑ 42 Darin Erstad | .20 | .50 |
| ❑ 43 Chipper Jones | .50 | 1.25 |
| ❑ 44 Pat Hentgen | .20 | .50 |
| ❑ 45 Eric Young | .20 | .50 |
| ❑ 46 Jaret Wright | .20 | .50 |
| ❑ 47 Juan Guzman | .20 | .50 |
| ❑ 48 Jorge Posada | .30 | .75 |
| ❑ 49 Bobby Higginson | .20 | .50 |
| ❑ 50 Jose Guillen | .20 | .50 |
| ❑ 51 Trevor Hoffman | .20 | .50 |
| ❑ 52 Ken Griffey Jr. | .75 | 2.00 |
| ❑ 53 David Justice | .20 | .50 |
| ❑ 54 Matt Williams | .20 | .50 |
| ❑ 55 Eric Karros | .20 | .50 |
| ❑ 56 Derek Bell | .20 | .50 |
| ❑ 57 Ray Lankford | .20 | .50 |
| ❑ 58 Mariano Rivera | .50 | 1.25 |
| ❑ 59 Brett Tomko | .20 | .50 |
| ❑ 60 Mike Mussina | .30 | .75 |
| ❑ 61 Kenny Lofton | .30 | .75 |
| ❑ 62 Chuck Finley | .20 | .50 |
| ❑ 63 Alex Gonzalez | .20 | .50 |
| ❑ 64 Mark Grace | .30 | .75 |
| ❑ 65 Raul Mondesi | .20 | .50 |
| ❑ 66 David Cone | .20 | .50 |
| ❑ 67 Brad Fullmer | .20 | .50 |
| ❑ 68 Andy Benes | .20 | .50 |
| ❑ 69 John Smoltz | .30 | .75 |

| | | |
|---|---|---|
| ❑ 70 Shane Reynolds | .20 | .50 |
| ❑ 71 Bruce Chen | .20 | .50 |
| ❑ 72 Adam Kennedy | .20 | .50 |
| ❑ 73 Jack Cust | .20 | .50 |
| ❑ 74 Matt Clement | .20 | .50 |
| ❑ 75 Derrick Gibson | .20 | .50 |
| ❑ 76 Darnell McDonald | .20 | .50 |
| ❑ 77 Adam Everett RC | 1.00 | 2.50 |
| ❑ 78 Ricardo Aramboles | .20 | .50 |
| ❑ 79 Mark Quinn RC | .40 | 1.00 |
| ❑ 80 Jason Rakers | .20 | .50 |
| ❑ 81 Seth Etherton RC | .40 | 1.00 |
| ❑ 82 Jeff Urban RC | .40 | 1.00 |
| ❑ 83 Manny Aybar | .20 | .50 |
| ❑ 84 Mike Nannini RC | .40 | 1.00 |
| ❑ 85 Onan Masaoka | .20 | .50 |
| ❑ 86 Rod Barajas | .20 | .50 |
| ❑ 87 Mike Frank | .20 | .50 |
| ❑ 88 Scott Randall | .20 | .50 |
| ❑ 89 Justin Bowles RC | .40 | 1.00 |
| ❑ 90 Chris Haas | .20 | .50 |
| ❑ 91 Arturo McDowell RC | .40 | 1.00 |
| ❑ 92 Matt Belisle RC | .40 | 1.00 |
| ❑ 93 Scott Elarton | .20 | .50 |
| ❑ 94 Vernon Wells | .20 | .50 |
| ❑ 95 Pat Cline | .20 | .50 |
| ❑ 96 Ryan Anderson | .20 | .50 |
| ❑ 97 Kevin Barker | .20 | .50 |
| ❑ 98 Ruben Mateo | .20 | .50 |
| ❑ 99 Robert Fick | .20 | .50 |
| ❑ 100 Corey Koskie | .20 | .50 |
| ❑ 101 Ricky Ledee | .20 | .50 |
| ❑ 102 Rick Elder RC | .40 | 1.00 |
| ❑ 103 Jack Cressend RC | .40 | 1.00 |
| ❑ 104 Joe Lawrence | .20 | .50 |
| ❑ 105 Mike Lincoln | .20 | .50 |
| ❑ 106 Kit Pellow RC | .40 | 1.00 |
| ❑ 107 Matt Burch RC | .40 | 1.00 |
| ❑ 108 Cole Liniak | .20 | .50 |
| ❑ 109 Jason Dewey | .20 | .50 |
| ❑ 110 Cesar King | .20 | .50 |
| ❑ 111 Julio Ramirez | .20 | .50 |
| ❑ 112 Jake Westbrook | .20 | .50 |
| ❑ 113 Eric Valent RC | .60 | 1.50 |
| ❑ 114 Roosevelt Brown RC | .40 | 1.00 |
| ❑ 115 Choo Freeman RC | .60 | 1.50 |
| ❑ 116 Juan Melo | .20 | .50 |
| ❑ 117 Jason Grilli | .20 | .50 |
| ❑ 118 Jared Sandberg | .20 | .50 |
| ❑ 119 Glenn Davis | .20 | .50 |
| ❑ 120 David Riske RC | .40 | 1.00 |
| ❑ 121 Jacque Jones | .20 | .50 |
| ❑ 122 Corey Lee | .20 | .50 |
| ❑ 123 Michael Barrett | .20 | .50 |
| ❑ 124 Lariel Gonzalez | .20 | .50 |
| ❑ 125 Mitch Meluskey | .20 | .50 |
| ❑ 126 F.Adrian Garcia | .20 | .50 |
| ❑ 127 Tony Torcado RC | .40 | 1.00 |
| ❑ 128 Jeff Liefer | .20 | .50 |
| ❑ 129 Ntema Ndungidi | .20 | .50 |
| ❑ 130 Andy Brown RC | .40 | 1.00 |
| ❑ 131 Ryan Mills RC | .40 | 1.00 |
| ❑ 132 Andy Abad RC | .40 | 1.00 |
| ❑ 133 Carlos Febles | .20 | .50 |
| ❑ 134 Jason Tyner RC | .40 | 1.00 |
| ❑ 135 Mark Osborne | .20 | .50 |
| ❑ 136 Phil Norton RC | .40 | 1.00 |
| ❑ 137 Nathan Haynes | .20 | .50 |
| ❑ 138 Roy Halladay | .20 | .50 |
| ❑ 139 Juan Encarnacion | .20 | .50 |
| ❑ 140 Brad Penny | .20 | .50 |
| ❑ 141 Grant Roberts | .20 | .50 |
| ❑ 142 Aramis Ramirez | .20 | .50 |
| ❑ 143 Cristian Guzman | .20 | .50 |
| ❑ 144 Mamon Tucker RC | .40 | 1.00 |
| ❑ 145 Ryan Bradley | .20 | .50 |
| ❑ 146 Brian Simmons | .20 | .50 |
| ❑ 147 Dan Reichert | .20 | .50 |
| ❑ 148 Russell Branyan | .20 | .50 |
| ❑ 149 Victor Valencia RC | .40 | 1.00 |
| ❑ 150 Scott Schoeneweis | .20 | .50 |
| ❑ 151 Sean Spencer RC | .40 | 1.00 |
| ❑ 152 Odalis Perez | .20 | .50 |
| ❑ 153 Joe Fontenot | .20 | .50 |
| ❑ 154 Milton Bradley | .20 | .50 |
| ❑ 155 Josh McKinley RC | .40 | 1.00 |
| ❑ 156 Terrence Long | .20 | .50 |
| ❑ 157 Danny Klassen | .20 | .50 |

|  |  | | |
|---|--------|------|------|
| 158 | Paul Hoover RC | .40 | 1.00 |
| 159 | Ron Belliard | .20 | .50 |
| 160 | Armando Rios | .20 | .50 |
| 161 | Ramon Hernandez | .20 | .50 |
| 162 | Jason Conti | .20 | .50 |
| 163 | Chad Hermansen | .20 | .50 |
| 164 | Jason Standridge | .20 | .50 |
| 165 | Jason Dellaero | .20 | .50 |
| 166 | John Curtice | .20 | .50 |
| 167 | Clayton Andrews RC | .40 | 1.00 |
| 168 | Jeremy Giambi | .20 | .50 |
| 169 | Alex Ramirez | .20 | .50 |
| 170 | Gabe Molina RC | .40 | 1.00 |
| 171 | Mario Encarnacion RC | .40 | 1.00 |
| 172 | Mike Zywica RC | .40 | 1.00 |
| 173 | Chip Ambres RC | .40 | 1.00 |
| 174 | Trot Nixon | .20 | .50 |
| 175 | Pat Burrell RC | 3.00 | 8.00 |
| 176 | Jeff Yoder | .20 | .50 |
| 177 | Chris Jones RC | .20 | .50 |
| 178 | Kevin Witt | .20 | .50 |
| 179 | Keith Luuloa RC | .20 | .50 |
| 180 | Billy Koch | .20 | .50 |
| 181 | Damaso Marte RC | .40 | 1.00 |
| 182 | Ryan Glynn RC | .40 | 1.00 |
| 183 | Calvin Pickering | .20 | .50 |
| 184 | Michael Cuddyer | .20 | .50 |
| 185 | Nick Johnson RC | 2.00 | 5.00 |
| 186 | Doug Mientkiewicz RC | 1.00 | 2.50 |
| 187 | Nate Cornejo RC | .40 | 1.00 |
| 188 | Octavio Dotel | .20 | .50 |
| 189 | Wes Helms | .20 | .50 |
| 190 | Nelson Lara | .20 | .50 |
| 191 | Chuck Abbott RC | .40 | 1.00 |
| 192 | Tony Armas Jr. | .20 | .50 |
| 193 | Gil Meche | .20 | .50 |
| 194 | Ben Petrick | .20 | .50 |
| 195 | Chris George RC | .40 | 1.00 |
| 196 | Scott Hunter RC | .40 | 1.00 |
| 197 | Ryan Brannan | .20 | .50 |
| 198 | Amaury Garcia RC | .40 | 1.00 |
| 199 | Chris Gissell | .20 | .50 |
| 200 | Austin Kearns RC | 3.00 | 8.00 |
| 201 | Alex Gonzalez | .20 | .50 |
| 202 | Wade Miller | .20 | .50 |
| 203 | Scott Williamson | .20 | .50 |
| 204 | Chris Enochs | .20 | .50 |
| 205 | Fernando Seguignol | .20 | .50 |
| 206 | Marlon Anderson | .20 | .50 |
| 207 | Todd Sears RC | .40 | 1.00 |
| 208 | Nate Bump RC | .40 | 1.00 |
| 209 | J.M. Gold RC | .40 | 1.00 |
| 210 | Matt LeCroy | .20 | .50 |
| 211 | Alex Hernandez | .20 | .50 |
| 212 | Luis Rivera | .20 | .50 |
| 213 | Troy Cameron | .20 | .50 |
| 214 | Alex Escobar RC | .60 | 1.50 |
| 215 | Jason LaRue | .20 | .50 |
| 216 | Kyle Peterson | .20 | .50 |
| 217 | Brent Butler | .20 | .50 |
| 218 | Dernell Stenson | .20 | .50 |
| 219 | Adrian Beltre | .20 | .50 |
| 220 | Daryle Ward | .20 | .50 |
| 221 | Jim Thome | .30 | .75 |
| 222 | Cliff Floyd | .20 | .50 |
| 223 | Rickey Henderson | .50 | 1.25 |
| 224 | Garret Anderson | .20 | .50 |
| 225 | Ken Caminiti | .20 | .50 |
| 226 | Bret Boone | .20 | .50 |
| 227 | Jeromy Burnitz | .20 | .50 |
| 228 | Steve Finley | .20 | .50 |
| 229 | Miguel Tejada | .40 | 1.00 |
| 230 | Greg Vaughn | .20 | .50 |
| 231 | Jose Offerman | .20 | .50 |
| 232 | Andy Ashby | .20 | .50 |
| 233 | Albert Belle | .30 | .75 |
| 234 | Fernando Tatis | .20 | .50 |
| 235 | Todd Helton | .30 | .75 |
| 236 | Sean Casey | .20 | .50 |
| 237 | Brian Giles | .20 | .50 |
| 238 | Andy Pettitte | .30 | .75 |
| 239 | Fred McGriff | .30 | .75 |
| 240 | Roberto Alomar | .30 | .75 |
| 241 | Edgar Martinez | .20 | .50 |
| 242 | Lee Stevens | .20 | .50 |
| 243 | Shawn Green | .20 | .50 |
| 244 | Ryan Klesko | .20 | .50 |
| 245 | Sammy Sosa | .50 | 1.25 |
| 246 | Todd Hundley | .20 | .50 |
| 247 | Shannon Stewart | .20 | .50 |
| 248 | Randy Johnson | .50 | 1.25 |
| 249 | Rondell White | .20 | .50 |
| 250 | Mike Piazza | .75 | 2.00 |
| 251 | Craig Biggio | .30 | .75 |
| 252 | David Wells | .20 | .50 |
| 253 | Brian Jordan | .20 | .50 |
| 254 | Edgar Renteria | .20 | .50 |
| 255 | Bartolo Colon | .20 | .50 |
| 256 | Frank Thomas | .50 | 1.25 |
| 257 | Will Clark | .30 | .75 |
| 258 | Dean Palmer | .20 | .50 |
| 259 | Dmitri Young | .20 | .50 |
| 260 | Scott Rolen | .30 | .75 |
| 261 | Jeff Kent | .20 | .50 |
| 262 | Dante Bichette | .20 | .50 |
| 263 | Nomar Garciaparra | .75 | 2.00 |
| 264 | Tony Gwynn | .60 | 1.50 |
| 265 | Alex Rodriguez | .75 | 2.00 |
| 266 | Jose Canseco | .30 | .75 |
| 267 | Jason Giambi | .20 | .50 |
| 268 | Jeff Bagwell | .30 | .75 |
| 269 | Carlos Delgado | .20 | .50 |
| 270 | Tom Glavine | .30 | .75 |
| 271 | Eric Davis | .20 | .50 |
| 272 | Edgardo Alfonzo | .20 | .50 |
| 273 | Tim Salmon | .30 | .75 |
| 274 | Johnny Damon | .30 | .75 |
| 275 | Rafael Palmeiro | .30 | .75 |
| 276 | Denny Neagle | .20 | .50 |
| 277 | Neifi Perez | .20 | .50 |
| 278 | Roger Clemens | 1.00 | 2.50 |
| 279 | Brant Brown | .20 | .50 |
| 280 | Kevin Brown | .30 | .75 |
| 281 | Jay Bell | .20 | .50 |
| 282 | Jay Buhner | .20 | .50 |
| 283 | Matt Lawton | .20 | .50 |
| 284 | Robin Ventura | .20 | .50 |
| 285 | Juan Gonzalez | .20 | .50 |
| 286 | Mo Vaughn | .20 | .50 |
| 287 | Kevin Millwood | .30 | .75 |
| 288 | Tino Martinez | .30 | .75 |
| 289 | Justin Thompson | .20 | .50 |
| 290 | Derek Jeter | 1.25 | 3.00 |
| 291 | Ben Davis | .20 | .50 |
| 292 | Mike Lowell | .20 | .50 |
| 293 | Calvin Murray | .20 | .50 |
| 294 | Micah Bowie RC | .40 | 1.00 |
| 295 | Lance Berkman | .20 | .50 |
| 296 | Jason Marquis | .20 | .50 |
| 297 | Chad Green | .20 | .50 |
| 298 | Dee Brown | .20 | .50 |
| 299 | Jerry Hairston Jr. | .20 | .50 |
| 300 | Gabe Kapler | .20 | .50 |
| 301 | Brent Stentz RC | .40 | 1.00 |
| 302 | Scott Mullen RC | .40 | 1.00 |
| 303 | Brandon Reed | .20 | .50 |
| 304 | Shea Hillenbrand RC | 1.50 | 4.00 |
| 305 | J.D. Closser RC | .60 | 1.50 |
| 306 | Gary Matthews Jr. | .20 | .50 |
| 307 | Toby Hall RC | .60 | 1.50 |
| 308 | Jason Phillips RC | .40 | 1.00 |
| 309 | Jose Macias RC | .40 | 1.00 |
| 310 | Jung Bong RC | .40 | 1.00 |
| 311 | Ramon Soler RC | .40 | 1.00 |
| 312 | Kelly Dransfeldt RC | .40 | 1.00 |
| 313 | Carlos E. Hernandez RC | .60 | 1.50 |
| 314 | Kevin Haverbusch | .20 | .50 |
| 315 | Aaron Myette RC | .40 | 1.00 |
| 316 | Chad Harville RC | .40 | 1.00 |
| 317 | Kyle Farnsworth RC | .60 | 1.50 |
| 318 | Gookie Dawkins RC | .60 | 1.50 |
| 319 | Willie Martinez | .20 | .50 |
| 320 | Carlos Lee | .20 | .50 |
| 321 | Carlos Pena RC | 1.25 | 3.00 |
| 322 | Peter Bergeron RC | .40 | 1.00 |
| 323 | A.J. Burnett RC | 1.50 | 4.00 |
| 324 | Bucky Jacobsen RC | .60 | 1.50 |
| 325 | Mo Bruce RC | .40 | 1.00 |
| 326 | Reggie Taylor | .20 | .50 |
| 327 | Jackie Rexrode | .20 | .50 |
| 328 | Alvin Morrow RC | .40 | 1.00 |
| 329 | Carlos Beltran | .30 | .75 |
| 330 | Eric Chavez | .20 | .50 |
| 331 | John Patterson | .20 | .50 |
| 332 | Jayson Werth | .20 | .50 |
| 333 | Richie Sexson | .20 | .50 |
| 334 | Randy Wolf | .20 | .50 |
| 335 | Eli Marrero | .20 | .50 |
| 336 | Paul LoDuca | .20 | .50 |
| 337 | J.D. Smart | .20 | .50 |
| 338 | Ryan Minor | .20 | .50 |
| 339 | Kris Benson | .20 | .50 |
| 340 | George Lombard | .20 | .50 |
| 341 | Troy Glaus | .30 | .75 |
| 342 | Eddie Yarnall | .20 | .50 |
| 343 | Kip Wells RC | .60 | 1.50 |
| 344 | C.C. Sabathia RC | 3.00 | 8.00 |
| 345 | Sean Burroughs RC | 1.00 | 2.50 |
| 346 | Felipe Lopez RC | 2.50 | 6.00 |
| 347 | Ryan Rupe RC | .40 | 1.00 |
| 348 | Orber Moreno RC | .40 | 1.00 |
| 349 | Rafael Roque RC | .40 | 1.00 |
| 350 | Alfonso Soriano RC | 5.00 | 12.00 |
| 351 | Pablo Ozuna | .20 | .50 |
| 352 | Corey Patterson RC | 1.50 | 4.00 |
| 353 | Braden Looper | .20 | .50 |
| 354 | Robbie Bell | .20 | .50 |
| 355 | Mark Mulder RC | 2.50 | 6.00 |
| 356 | Angel Pena | .20 | .50 |
| 357 | Kevin McGlinchy | .20 | .50 |
| 358 | Michael Restovich RC | .60 | 1.50 |
| 359 | Eric DuBose | .20 | .50 |
| 360 | Geoff Jenkins | .20 | .50 |
| 361 | Mark Harriger RC | .40 | 1.00 |
| 362 | Junior Herndon RC | .40 | 1.00 |
| 363 | Tim Raines Jr. RC | .40 | 1.00 |
| 364 | Rafael Furcal RC | 2.50 | 6.00 |
| 365 | Marcus Giles RC | 1.50 | 4.00 |
| 366 | Ted Lilly | .20 | .50 |
| 367 | Jorge Toca RC | .60 | 1.50 |
| 368 | David Kelton RC | .40 | 1.00 |
| 369 | Adam Dunn RC | 5.00 | 12.00 |
| 370 | Guillermo Mota RC | .40 | 1.00 |
| 371 | Brett Laxton RC | .40 | 1.00 |
| 372 | Travis Harper RC | .40 | 1.00 |
| 373 | Tom Davey RC | .40 | 1.00 |
| 374 | Darren Blakely RC | .40 | 1.00 |
| 375 | Tim Hudson RC | 3.00 | 8.00 |
| 376 | Jason Romano | .20 | .50 |
| 377 | Dan Reichert | .20 | .50 |
| 378 | Julio Lugo RC | 1.00 | 2.50 |
| 379 | Jose Garcia RC | .40 | 1.00 |
| 380 | Erubiel Durazo RC | .60 | 1.50 |
| 381 | Jose Jimenez | .20 | .50 |
| 382 | Chris Fussell | .20 | .50 |
| 383 | Steve Lomasney | .20 | .50 |
| 384 | Juan Pena RC | .40 | 1.00 |
| 385 | Allen Levrault RC | .40 | 1.00 |
| 386 | Juan Rivera RC | 1.50 | 4.00 |
| 387 | Steve Colyer RC | .40 | 1.00 |
| 388 | Joe Nathan RC | 2.00 | 5.00 |
| 389 | Ron Walker RC | .40 | 1.00 |
| 390 | Nick Bierbrodt | .20 | .50 |
| 391 | Luke Prokopec RC | .40 | 1.00 |
| 392 | Dave Roberts RC | 1.00 | 2.50 |
| 393 | Mike Darr | .20 | .50 |
| 394 | Abraham Nunez RC | .60 | 1.50 |
| 395 | Giuseppe Chiaramonte RC | .40 | 1.00 |
| 396 | Jermaine Van Buren RC | .40 | 1.00 |
| 397 | Mike Kusiewicz | .20 | .50 |
| 398 | Matt Wise RC | .40 | 1.00 |
| 399 | Joe McEwing RC | .60 | 1.50 |
| 400 | Matt Holliday RC | 5.00 | 12.00 |
| 401 | Willi Mo Pena RC | 5.00 | 12.00 |
| 402 | Ruben Quevedo RC | .40 | 1.00 |
| 403 | Rob Ryan RC | .40 | 1.00 |
| 404 | Freddy Garcia RC | 1.50 | 4.00 |
| 405 | Kevin Eberwein RC | .40 | 1.00 |
| 406 | Jesus Colome RC | .40 | 1.00 |
| 407 | Chris Singleton | .20 | .50 |
| 408 | Bubba Crosby RC | 1.00 | 2.50 |
| 409 | Jesus Cordero RC | .40 | 1.00 |
| 410 | Donny Leon | .20 | .50 |
| 411 | Goefrey Tomlinson RC | .40 | 1.00 |
| 412 | Jeff Winchester RC | .40 | 1.00 |
| 413 | Adam Piatt RC | .40 | 1.00 |
| 414 | Robert Stratton | .20 | .50 |
| 415 | T.J. Tucker | .20 | .50 |
| 416 | Ryan Langerhans RC | 1.00 | 2.50 |
| 417 | Anthony Shumaker RC | .40 | 1.00 |
| 418 | Matt Miller RC | .40 | 1.00 |
| 419 | Doug Clark RC | .40 | 1.00 |
| 420 | Kory DeHaan RC | .40 | 1.00 |
| 421 | David Eckstein RC | 3.00 | 8.00 |

|  |  | | |
|---|---|---|---|
| 422 | Brian Cooper RC | .40 | 1.00 |
| 423 | Brady Clark RC | 1.50 | 4.00 |
| 424 | Chris Magruder RC | .40 | 1.00 |
| 425 | Bobby Seay RC | .40 | 1.00 |
| 426 | Aubrey Huff RC | 2.00 | 5.00 |
| 427 | Mike Jerzembeck RC | .40 | 1.00 |
| 428 | Matt Blank RC | .40 | 1.00 |
| 429 | Benny Agbayani RC | .60 | 1.50 |
| 430 | Kevin Beirne RC | .40 | 1.00 |
| 431 | Josh Hamilton RC | 6.00 | 15.00 |
| 432 | Josh Girdley RC | .40 | 1.00 |
| 433 | Kyle Snyder RC | .40 | 1.00 |
| 434 | Mike Paradis RC | .40 | 1.00 |
| 435 | Jason Jennings RC | 1.00 | 2.50 |
| 436 | David Walling RC | .40 | 1.00 |
| 437 | Omar Ortiz RC | .40 | 1.00 |
| 438 | Jay Gehrke RC | .60 | 1.50 |
| 439 | Casey Burns RC | .40 | 1.00 |
| 440 | Carl Crawford RC | 4.00 | 10.00 |

## 2000 Bowman Chrome

|  |  | | |
|---|---|---|---|
| | COMPLETE SET (440) | 60.00 | 120.00 |
| 1 | Vladimir Guerrero | .50 | 1.25 |
| 2 | Chipper Jones | .50 | 1.25 |
| 3 | Todd Walker | .20 | .50 |
| 4 | Barry Larkin | .20 | .50 |
| 5 | Bernie Williams | .30 | .75 |
| 6 | Todd Helton | .30 | .75 |
| 7 | Jermaine Dye | .20 | .50 |
| 8 | Brian Giles | .20 | .50 |
| 9 | Freddy Garcia | .20 | .50 |
| 10 | Greg Vaughn | .20 | .50 |
| 11 | Alex Gonzalez | .20 | .50 |
| 12 | Luis Gonzalez | .20 | .50 |
| 13 | Ron Belliard | .20 | .50 |
| 14 | Ben Grieve | .20 | .50 |
| 15 | Carlos Delgado | .20 | .50 |
| 16 | Brian Jordan | .20 | .50 |
| 17 | Fernando Tatis | .20 | .50 |
| 18 | Ryan Rupe | .20 | .50 |
| 19 | Miguel Tejada | .20 | .50 |
| 20 | Mark Grace | .30 | .75 |
| 21 | Kenny Lofton | .20 | .50 |
| 22 | Eric Karros | .20 | .50 |
| 23 | Cliff Floyd | .20 | .50 |
| 24 | John Halama | .20 | .50 |
| 25 | Cristian Guzman | .20 | .50 |
| 26 | Scott Williamson | .20 | .50 |
| 27 | Mike Lieberthal | .20 | .50 |
| 28 | Tim Hudson | .30 | .75 |
| 29 | Warren Morris | .20 | .50 |
| 30 | Pedro Martinez | .30 | .75 |
| 31 | John Smoltz | .20 | .50 |
| 32 | Ray Durham | .20 | .50 |
| 33 | Chad Allen | .20 | .50 |
| 34 | Tony Clark | .20 | .50 |
| 35 | Tino Martinez | .30 | .75 |
| 36 | J.T. Snow | .20 | .50 |
| 37 | Kevin Brown | .30 | .75 |
| 38 | Bartolo Colon | .20 | .50 |
| 39 | Rey Ordonez | .20 | .50 |
| 40 | Jeff Bagwell | .30 | .75 |
| 41 | Ivan Rodriguez | .30 | .75 |
| 42 | Eric Chavez | .20 | .50 |
| 43 | Eric Milton | .20 | .50 |
| 44 | Jose Canseco | .30 | .75 |
| 45 | Shawn Green | .20 | .50 |
| 46 | Rich Aurilia | .20 | .50 |
| 47 | Roberto Alomar | .30 | .75 |
| 48 | Brian Daubach | .20 | .50 |
| 49 | Magglio Ordonez | .30 | .75 |
| 50 | Derek Jeter | 1.25 | 3.00 |
| 51 | Kris Benson | .20 | .50 |
| 52 | Albert Belle | .20 | .50 |
| 53 | Rondell White | .20 | .50 |
| 54 | Justin Thompson | .20 | .50 |
| 55 | Nomar Garciaparra | .75 | 2.00 |
| 56 | Chuck Finley | .20 | .50 |
| 57 | Omar Vizquel | .20 | .50 |
| 58 | Luis Castillo | .20 | .50 |
| 59 | Richard Hidalgo | .20 | .50 |
| 60 | Barry Bonds | 1.25 | 3.00 |
| 61 | Craig Biggio | .30 | .75 |
| 62 | Doug Glanville | .20 | .50 |
| 63 | Gabe Kapler | .20 | .50 |
| 64 | Johnny Damon | .30 | .75 |
| 65 | Pokey Reese | .20 | .50 |
| 66 | Andy Pettitte | .30 | .75 |
| 67 | B.J. Surhoff | .20 | .50 |
| 68 | Richie Sexson | .20 | .50 |
| 69 | Javy Lopez | .20 | .50 |
| 70 | Raul Mondesi | .20 | .50 |
| 71 | Darin Erstad | .20 | .50 |
| 72 | Kevin Millwood | .20 | .50 |
| 73 | Ricky Ledee | .20 | .50 |
| 74 | John Olerud | .20 | .50 |
| 75 | Sean Casey | .20 | .50 |
| 76 | Carlos Febles | .20 | .50 |
| 77 | Paul O'Neill | .30 | .75 |
| 78 | Bob Abreu | .20 | .50 |
| 79 | Neifi Perez | .20 | .50 |
| 80 | Tony Gwynn | .60 | 1.50 |
| 81 | Russ Ortiz | .20 | .50 |
| 82 | Matt Williams | .20 | .50 |
| 83 | Chris Carpenter | .20 | .50 |
| 84 | Roger Cedeno | .20 | .50 |
| 85 | Tim Salmon | .30 | .75 |
| 86 | Billy Koch | .20 | .50 |
| 87 | Jeromy Burnitz | .20 | .50 |
| 88 | Edgardo Alfonzo | .20 | .50 |
| 89 | Jay Bell | .20 | .50 |
| 90 | Manny Ramirez | .30 | .75 |
| 91 | Frank Thomas | .50 | 1.25 |
| 92 | Mike Mussina | .30 | .75 |
| 93 | J.D. Drew | .20 | .50 |
| 94 | Adrian Beltre | .20 | .50 |
| 95 | Alex Rodriguez | .75 | 2.00 |
| 96 | Larry Walker | .20 | .50 |
| 97 | Juan Encarnacion | .20 | .50 |
| 98 | Mike Sweeney | .20 | .50 |
| 99 | Rusty Greer | .20 | .50 |
| 100 | Randy Johnson | .50 | 1.25 |
| 101 | Jose Vidro | .20 | .50 |
| 102 | Preston Wilson | .20 | .50 |
| 103 | Greg Maddux | .75 | 2.00 |
| 104 | Jason Giambi | .20 | .50 |
| 105 | Cal Ripken | 1.50 | 4.00 |
| 106 | Carlos Beltran | .20 | .50 |
| 107 | Vinny Castilla | .20 | .50 |
| 108 | Mariano Rivera | .50 | 1.25 |
| 109 | Mo Vaughn | .20 | .50 |
| 110 | Rafael Palmeiro | .30 | .75 |
| 111 | Shannon Stewart | .20 | .50 |
| 112 | Mike Hampton | .20 | .50 |
| 113 | Joe Nathan | .20 | .50 |
| 114 | Ben Davis | .20 | .50 |
| 115 | Andruw Jones | .30 | .75 |
| 116 | Robin Ventura | .20 | .50 |
| 117 | Damion Easley | .20 | .50 |
| 118 | Jeff Cirillo | .20 | .50 |
| 119 | Kerry Wood | .20 | .50 |
| 120 | Scott Rolen | .30 | .75 |
| 121 | Sammy Sosa | .50 | 1.25 |
| 122 | Ken Griffey Jr. | .75 | 2.00 |
| 123 | Shane Reynolds | .20 | .50 |
| 124 | Troy Glaus | .20 | .50 |
| 125 | Tom Glavine | .30 | .75 |
| 126 | Michael Barrett | .20 | .50 |
| 127 | Al Leiter | .20 | .50 |
| 128 | Jason Kendall | .20 | .50 |
| 129 | Roger Clemens | 1.00 | 2.50 |
| 130 | Juan Gonzalez | .30 | .75 |
| 131 | Corey Koskie | .20 | .50 |
| 132 | Curt Schilling | .20 | .50 |
| 133 | Mike Piazza | .75 | 2.00 |
| 134 | Gary Sheffield | .30 | .75 |
| 135 | Jim Thome | .30 | .75 |
| 136 | Orlando Hernandez | .20 | .50 |
| 137 | Ray Lankford | .20 | .50 |
| 138 | Geoff Jenkins | .20 | .50 |
| 139 | Jose Lima | .20 | .50 |
| 140 | Mark McGwire | 1.25 | 3.00 |
| 141 | Adam Platt | .20 | .50 |
| 142 | Pat Manning RC | .30 | .75 |
| 143 | Marcos Castillo RC | .30 | .75 |
| 144 | Lesli Brea RC | .50 | 1.25 |
| 145 | Humberto Cota RC | .50 | 1.25 |
| 146 | Ben Petrick | .20 | .50 |
| 147 | Kip Wells | .20 | .50 |
| 148 | Wily Pena | .20 | .50 |
| 149 | Chris Wakeland RC | .30 | .75 |
| 150 | Brad Baker RC | .30 | .75 |
| 151 | Robbie Morrison RC | .30 | .75 |
| 152 | Reggie Taylor | .20 | .50 |
| 153 | Matt Ginter RC | .30 | .75 |
| 154 | Peter Bergeron | .20 | .50 |
| 155 | Roosevelt Brown | .20 | .50 |
| 156 | Matt Cepicky RC | .30 | .75 |
| 157 | Ramon Castro | .20 | .50 |
| 158 | Brad Baisley RC | .30 | .75 |
| 159 | Jason Hart RC | .30 | .75 |
| 160 | Mitch Meluskey | .20 | .50 |
| 161 | Chad Harville | .20 | .50 |
| 162 | Brian Cooper | .20 | .50 |
| 163 | Marcus Giles | .20 | .50 |
| 164 | Jim Morris | .50 | 1.25 |
| 165 | Geoff Goetz | .20 | .50 |
| 166 | Bobby Bradley RC | .30 | .75 |
| 167 | Rob Bell | .20 | .50 |
| 168 | Joe Crede | 1.00 | 2.50 |
| 169 | Michael Restovich | .20 | .50 |
| 170 | Quincy Foster RC | .30 | .75 |
| 171 | Enrique Cruz RC | .30 | .75 |
| 172 | Mark Quinn | .20 | .50 |
| 173 | Nick Johnson | .20 | .50 |
| 174 | Jeff Liefer | .20 | .50 |
| 175 | Kevin Mench RC | 2.00 | 5.00 |
| 176 | Steve Lomasney | .20 | .50 |
| 177 | Jayson Werth | .20 | .50 |
| 178 | Tim Drew | .20 | .50 |
| 179 | Chip Ambres | .20 | .50 |
| 180 | Ryan Anderson | .20 | .50 |
| 181 | Matt Blank | .20 | .50 |
| 182 | Giuseppe Chiaramonte | .20 | .50 |
| 183 | Corey Myers RC | .30 | .75 |
| 184 | Jeff Yoder | .20 | .50 |
| 185 | Craig Dingman RC | .30 | .75 |
| 186 | Jon Hamilton RC | .30 | .75 |
| 187 | Toby Hall | .20 | .50 |
| 188 | Russell Branyan | .20 | .50 |
| 189 | Brian Falkenborg RC | .30 | .75 |
| 190 | Aaron Harang RC | 2.00 | 5.00 |
| 191 | Juan Pena | .20 | .50 |
| 192 | Chin-Hui Tsao RC | 2.00 | 5.00 |
| 193 | Alfonso Soriano | .50 | 1.25 |
| 194 | Alejandro Diaz RC | .30 | .75 |
| 195 | Carlos Pena | .20 | .50 |
| 196 | Kevin Nicholson | .20 | .50 |
| 197 | Mo Bruce | .20 | .50 |
| 198 | C.C. Sabathia | .20 | .50 |
| 199 | Carl Crawford | .20 | .50 |
| 200 | Rafael Furcal | .20 | .50 |
| 201 | Andrew Beinbrink RC | .30 | .75 |
| 202 | Jimmy Osting | .20 | .50 |
| 203 | Aaron McNeal RC | .30 | .75 |
| 204 | Brett Laxton | .20 | .50 |
| 205 | Chris George | .20 | .50 |
| 206 | Felipe Lopez | .20 | .50 |
| 207 | Sean Sheets RC | 2.50 | 6.00 |
| 208 | Mike Meyers RC | .50 | 1.25 |
| 209 | Jason Conti | .20 | .50 |
| 210 | Milton Bradley | .20 | .50 |
| 211 | Chris Mears RC | .30 | .75 |
| 212 | Carlos Hernandez RC | .50 | 1.25 |
| 213 | Jason Romano | .20 | .50 |
| 214 | Geofrey Tomlinson | .20 | .50 |
| 215 | Jimmy Rollins | .20 | .50 |
| 216 | Pablo Ozuna | .20 | .50 |
| 217 | Steve Cox | .20 | .50 |
| 218 | Terrence Long | .20 | .50 |
| 219 | Jeff DaVanon RC | .50 | 1.25 |
| 220 | Rick Ankiel | .20 | .50 |
| 221 | Jason Standridge | .20 | .50 |
| 222 | Tony Armas Jr. | .20 | .50 |
| 223 | Jason Tyner | .20 | .50 |
| 224 | Ramon Ortiz | .20 | .50 |
| 225 | Daryle Ward | .20 | .50 |
| 226 | Enger Veras RC | .30 | .75 |
| 227 | Chris Jones | .20 | .50 |
| 228 | Eric Cammack RC | .30 | .75 |

| | | | | | | | |
|---|---|---|---|---|---|---|---|
| ☐ 229 Ruben Mateo | .20 | .50 | ☐ 317 Rob Ryan | .20 | .50 | ☐ 405 Brad Penny | .20 | .50 |

| | | | |
|---|---|---|---|
| ☐ 229 Ruben Mateo | .20 | .50 |
| ☐ 230 Ken Harvey RC | .50 | 1.25 |
| ☐ 231 Jake Westbrook | .20 | .50 |
| ☐ 232 Rob Purvis RC | .20 | .75 |
| ☐ 233 Choo Freeman | .20 | .50 |
| ☐ 234 Aramis Ramirez | .20 | .50 |
| ☐ 235 A.J. Burnett | .20 | .50 |
| ☐ 236 Kevin Barker | .20 | .50 |
| ☐ 237 Chance Caple RC | .30 | .75 |
| ☐ 238 Jarrod Washburn | .20 | .50 |
| ☐ 239 Lance Berkman | .20 | .50 |
| ☐ 240 Michael Wenner RC | .20 | .50 |
| ☐ 241 Alex Sanchez | .20 | .50 |
| ☐ 242 Pat Daneker | .20 | .50 |
| ☐ 243 Grant Roberts | .20 | .50 |
| ☐ 244 Mark Ellis RC | .50 | 1.25 |
| ☐ 245 Donny Leon | .20 | .50 |
| ☐ 246 David Eckstein | .20 | .50 |
| ☐ 247 Dicky Gonzalez RC | .30 | .75 |
| ☐ 248 John Patterson | .20 | .50 |
| ☐ 249 Chad Green | .20 | .50 |
| ☐ 250 Scot Shields RC | .30 | .75 |
| ☐ 251 Troy Cameron | .20 | .50 |
| ☐ 252 Jose Molina | .20 | .50 |
| ☐ 253 Rob Pugmire RC | .30 | .75 |
| ☐ 254 Rick Elder | .20 | .50 |
| ☐ 255 Sean Burroughs | .20 | .50 |
| ☐ 256 Josh Kalinowski RC | .30 | .75 |
| ☐ 257 Matt LeCroy | .20 | .50 |
| ☐ 258 Alex Graman RC | .30 | .75 |
| ☐ 259 Juan Silvestre RC | .30 | .75 |
| ☐ 260 Brady Clark | .20 | .50 |
| ☐ 261 Rico Washington RC | .30 | .75 |
| ☐ 262 Gary Matthews Jr. | .20 | .50 |
| ☐ 263 Matt Wise | .20 | .50 |
| ☐ 264 Keith Reed RC | .30 | .75 |
| ☐ 265 Santiago Ramirez RC | .30 | .75 |
| ☐ 266 Ben Broussard RC | 1.25 | 3.00 |
| ☐ 267 Ryan Langerhans | .20 | .50 |
| ☐ 268 Juan Rivera | .20 | .50 |
| ☐ 269 Shawn Gallagher | .20 | .50 |
| ☐ 270 Jorge Toca | .20 | .50 |
| ☐ 271 Brad Lidge | .30 | .75 |
| ☐ 272 Leoncio Estrella RC | .30 | .75 |
| ☐ 273 Ruben Quevedo | .20 | .50 |
| ☐ 274 Jack Cust | .20 | .50 |
| ☐ 275 T.J. Tucker | .20 | .50 |
| ☐ 276 Mike Colangelo | .20 | .50 |
| ☐ 277 Brian Schneider | .20 | .50 |
| ☐ 278 Calvin Murray | .20 | .50 |
| ☐ 279 Josh Girdley | .20 | .50 |
| ☐ 280 Mike Paradis | .20 | .50 |
| ☐ 281 Chad Hermansen | .20 | .50 |
| ☐ 282 Ty Howington RC | .30 | .75 |
| ☐ 283 Aaron Myette | .20 | .50 |
| ☐ 284 D'Angelo Jimenez | .20 | .50 |
| ☐ 285 Dernell Stenson | .20 | .50 |
| ☐ 286 Jerry Hairston Jr. | .20 | .50 |
| ☐ 287 Gary Majewski RC | .50 | 1.25 |
| ☐ 288 Derrin Ebert | .20 | .50 |
| ☐ 289 Steve Fish RC | .30 | .75 |
| ☐ 290 Carlos E. Hernandez | .20 | .50 |
| ☐ 291 Allen Levrault | .20 | .50 |
| ☐ 292 Sean McNally RC | .30 | .75 |
| ☐ 293 Randey Dorame RC | .30 | .75 |
| ☐ 294 Wes Anderson RC | .30 | .75 |
| ☐ 295 B.J. Ryan | .20 | .50 |
| ☐ 296 Alan Webb RC | .30 | .75 |
| ☐ 297 Brandon Inge RC | 2.00 | 5.00 |
| ☐ 298 David Walling | .20 | .50 |
| ☐ 299 Sun Woo Kim RC | .30 | .75 |
| ☐ 300 Pat Burrell | .20 | .50 |
| ☐ 301 Rick Guttormson RC | .30 | .75 |
| ☐ 302 Gil Meche | .20 | .50 |
| ☐ 303 Carlos Zambrano RC | 4.00 | 10.00 |
| ☐ 304 Eric Byrnes UER RC | .40 | 1.00 |
| ☐ 305 Robb Quinlan RC | .50 | 1.25 |
| ☐ 306 Jackie Rexrode | .20 | .50 |
| ☐ 307 Nate Bump | .20 | .50 |
| ☐ 308 Sean DePaula RC | .30 | .75 |
| ☐ 309 Matt Riley | .20 | .50 |
| ☐ 310 Ryan Minor | .20 | .50 |
| ☐ 311 J.J. Davis | .20 | .50 |
| ☐ 312 Randy Wolf | .20 | .50 |
| ☐ 313 Jason Jennings | .20 | .50 |
| ☐ 314 Scott Seabol RC | .30 | .75 |
| ☐ 315 Doug Davis | .20 | .50 |
| ☐ 316 Todd Moser RC | .30 | .75 |

| | | | |
|---|---|---|---|
| ☐ 317 Rob Ryan | .20 | .50 |
| ☐ 318 Bubba Crosby | .20 | .50 |
| ☐ 319 Lyle Overbay RC | 1.25 | 3.00 |
| ☐ 320 Mario Encarnacion | .20 | .50 |
| ☐ 321 Francisco Rodriguez RC | 2.50 | 6.00 |
| ☐ 322 Michael Cuddyer | .20 | .50 |
| ☐ 323 Ed Yarnall | .20 | .50 |
| ☐ 324 Cesar Saba RC | .30 | .75 |
| ☐ 325 Gookie Dawkins | .20 | .50 |
| ☐ 326 Alex Escobar | .20 | .50 |
| ☐ 327 Julio Zuleta RC | .30 | .75 |
| ☐ 328 Josh Hamilton | .60 | 1.50 |
| ☐ 329 Carlos Urquiola RC | .30 | .75 |
| ☐ 330 Matt Belisle | .20 | .50 |
| ☐ 331 Kurt Ainsworth RC | .30 | .75 |
| ☐ 332 Tim Raines Jr. | .20 | .50 |
| ☐ 333 Eric Munson | .20 | .50 |
| ☐ 334 Donzell McDonald | .20 | .50 |
| ☐ 335 Larry Bigbie RC | .75 | 2.00 |
| ☐ 336 Matt Watson RC | .30 | .75 |
| ☐ 337 Aubrey Huff | .20 | .50 |
| ☐ 338 Julio Ramirez | .20 | .50 |
| ☐ 339 Jason Grabowski RC | .30 | .75 |
| ☐ 340 Jon Garland | .20 | .50 |
| ☐ 341 Austin Kearns | .20 | .50 |
| ☐ 342 Josh Pressley RC | .30 | .75 |
| ☐ 343 Miguel Olivo RC | .75 | 2.00 |
| ☐ 344 Julio Lugo | .20 | .50 |
| ☐ 345 Roberto Vaz | .20 | .50 |
| ☐ 346 Ramon Soler | .20 | .50 |
| ☐ 347 Brandon Phillips RC | 1.50 | 4.00 |
| ☐ 348 Vince Faison RC | .30 | .75 |
| ☐ 349 Mike Venafro | .20 | .50 |
| ☐ 350 Rick Asadoorian RC | .50 | 1.25 |
| ☐ 351 B.J. Garbe RC | .30 | .75 |
| ☐ 352 Dan Reichert | .20 | .50 |
| ☐ 353 Jason Stumm RC | .30 | .75 |
| ☐ 354 Ruben Salazar RC | .30 | .75 |
| ☐ 355 Francisco Cordero | .20 | .50 |
| ☐ 356 Juan Guzman RC | .30 | .75 |
| ☐ 357 Mike Bacsik RC | .30 | .75 |
| ☐ 358 Jared Sandberg | .20 | .50 |
| ☐ 359 Rod Barajas | .20 | .50 |
| ☐ 360 Junior Brignac RC | .30 | .75 |
| ☐ 361 J.M. Gold | .20 | .50 |
| ☐ 362 Octavio Dotel | .20 | .50 |
| ☐ 363 David Kelton | .20 | .50 |
| ☐ 364 Scott Morgan | .20 | .50 |
| ☐ 365 Wascar Serrano RC | .30 | .75 |
| ☐ 366 Wilton Veras | .20 | .50 |
| ☐ 367 Eugene Kingsale | .20 | .50 |
| ☐ 368 Ted Lilly | .20 | .50 |
| ☐ 369 George Lombard | .20 | .50 |
| ☐ 370 Chris Haas | .20 | .50 |
| ☐ 371 Wilton Pena RC | .30 | .75 |
| ☐ 372 Vernon Wells | .20 | .50 |
| ☐ 373 Keith Ginter RC | .30 | .75 |
| ☐ 374 Jeff Heaverlo RC | .30 | .75 |
| ☐ 375 Calvin Pickering | .20 | .50 |
| ☐ 376 Mike Lamb RC | .75 | 2.00 |
| ☐ 377 Kyle Snyder | .20 | .50 |
| ☐ 378 Javier Cardona RC | .30 | .75 |
| ☐ 379 Aaron Rowand RC | 2.00 | 5.00 |
| ☐ 380 Dee Brown | .20 | .50 |
| ☐ 381 Brett Myers RC | 1.50 | 4.00 |
| ☐ 382 Abraham Nunez | .20 | .50 |
| ☐ 383 Eric Valent | .20 | .50 |
| ☐ 384 Jody Gerut RC | .50 | 1.25 |
| ☐ 385 Adam Dunn | .50 | 1.25 |
| ☐ 386 Jay Gehrke | .20 | .50 |
| ☐ 387 Omar Ortiz | .20 | .50 |
| ☐ 388 Darnell McDonald | .20 | .50 |
| ☐ 389 Tony Schrager RC | .30 | .75 |
| ☐ 390 J.D. Closser | .20 | .50 |
| ☐ 391 Ben Christensen RC | .30 | .75 |
| ☐ 392 Adam Kennedy | .20 | .50 |
| ☐ 393 Nick Green RC | .30 | .75 |
| ☐ 394 Ramon Hernandez | .20 | .50 |
| ☐ 395 Roy Oswalt RC | 6.00 | 15.00 |
| ☐ 396 Andy Tracy RC | .30 | .75 |
| ☐ 397 Eric Gagne | .50 | 1.25 |
| ☐ 398 Michael Tejera RC | .20 | .50 |
| ☐ 399 Adam Everett | .20 | .50 |
| ☐ 400 Corey Patterson | .20 | .50 |
| ☐ 401 Gary Knotts RC | .20 | .50 |
| ☐ 402 Ryan Christianson RC | .30 | .75 |
| ☐ 403 Eric Ireland RC | .30 | .75 |
| ☐ 404 Andrew Good RC | .30 | .75 |

| | | | |
|---|---|---|---|
| ☐ 405 Brad Penny | .20 | .50 |
| ☐ 406 Jason LaRue | .20 | .50 |
| ☐ 407 Kit Pellow | .20 | .50 |
| ☐ 408 Kevin Beirne | .20 | .50 |
| ☐ 409 Kelly Dransfeldt | .20 | .50 |
| ☐ 410 Jason Grilli | .20 | .50 |
| ☐ 411 Scott Downs RC | .30 | .75 |
| ☐ 412 Jesus Colome | .20 | .50 |
| ☐ 413 John Sneed RC | .30 | .75 |
| ☐ 414 Tony McKnight | .20 | .50 |
| ☐ 415 Luis Rivera | .20 | .50 |
| ☐ 416 Adam Eaton | .20 | .50 |
| ☐ 417 Mike MacDougal RC | .50 | 1.25 |
| ☐ 418 Mike Nannini | .20 | .50 |
| ☐ 419 Barry Zito RC | 4.00 | 10.00 |
| ☐ 420 DeWayne Wise | .20 | .50 |
| ☐ 421 Jason Dellaero | .20 | .50 |
| ☐ 422 Chad Moeller | .20 | .50 |
| ☐ 423 Jason Marquis | .20 | .50 |
| ☐ 424 Tim Redding RC | .50 | 1.25 |
| ☐ 425 Mark Mulder | .20 | .50 |
| ☐ 426 Josh Paul | .20 | .50 |
| ☐ 427 Chris Enochs | .20 | .50 |
| ☐ 428 Wilfredo Rodriguez RC | .30 | .75 |
| ☐ 429 Kevin Witt | .20 | .50 |
| ☐ 430 Scott Sobkowiak RC | .30 | .75 |
| ☐ 431 McKay Christensen | .20 | .50 |
| ☐ 432 Jung Bong | .20 | .50 |
| ☐ 433 Keith Evans RC | .30 | .75 |
| ☐ 434 Garry Maddox Jr. RC | .30 | .75 |
| ☐ 435 Ramon Santiago RC | .30 | .75 |
| ☐ 436 Alex Cora | .20 | .50 |
| ☐ 437 Carlos Lee | .20 | .50 |
| ☐ 438 Jason Repko RC | .75 | 2.00 |
| ☐ 439 Matt Burch | .20 | .50 |
| ☐ 440 Shawn Sonnier RC | .30 | .75 |

## 2000 Bowman Chrome Draft

| | | |
|---|---|---|
| ☐ COMP.FACT.SET (110) | 20.00 | 50.00 |
| ☐ 1 Pat Burrell | .20 | .50 |
| ☐ 2 Rafael Furcal | .20 | .50 |
| ☐ 3 Grant Roberts | .20 | .50 |
| ☐ 4 Barry Zito | 1.50 | 4.00 |
| ☐ 5 Julio Zuleta | .20 | .50 |
| ☐ 6 Mark Mulder | .20 | .50 |
| ☐ 7 Rob Bell | .20 | .50 |
| ☐ 8 Adam Piatt | .20 | .50 |
| ☐ 9 Mike Lamb | .30 | .75 |
| ☐ 10 Pablo Ozuna | .20 | .50 |
| ☐ 11 Jason Tyner | .20 | .50 |
| ☐ 12 Jason Marquis | .20 | .50 |
| ☐ 13 Eric Munson | .20 | .50 |
| ☐ 14 Seth Etherton | .20 | .50 |
| ☐ 15 Milton Bradley | .20 | .50 |
| ☐ 16 Nick Green | .20 | .50 |
| ☐ 17 Chin-Feng Chen RC | .60 | 1.50 |
| ☐ 18 Matt Boone RC | .20 | .50 |
| ☐ 19 Kevin Gregg RC | .20 | .50 |
| ☐ 20 Eddy Garabito RC | .20 | .50 |
| ☐ 21 Aaron Capista RC | .20 | .50 |
| ☐ 22 Esteban German RC | .20 | .50 |
| ☐ 23 Derek Thompson RC | .20 | .50 |
| ☐ 24 Phil Merrell RC | .20 | .50 |
| ☐ 25 Brian O'Connor RC | .20 | .50 |
| ☐ 26 Yamid Haad | .20 | .50 |
| ☐ 27 Hector Mercado RC | .20 | .50 |
| ☐ 28 Jason Woolf RC | .20 | .50 |
| ☐ 29 Eddy Furniss RC | .20 | .50 |
| ☐ 30 Cha Sueng Baek RC | .20 | .50 |
| ☐ 31 Coby Lewis RC | .20 | .50 |
| ☐ 32 Pasqual Coco RC | .20 | .50 |
| ☐ 33 Jorge Cantu RC | 2.00 | 5.00 |
| ☐ 34 Erasmo Ramirez RC | .20 | .50 |

| | | |
|---|---|---|
| ❑ 35 Bobby Kielty RC | .40 | 1.00 |
| ❑ 36 Joaquin Benoit RC | .20 | .50 |
| ❑ 37 Brian Esposito RC | .20 | .50 |
| ❑ 38 Michael Wenner | .20 | .50 |
| ❑ 39 Juan Rincon RC | .20 | .50 |
| ❑ 40 Yorvit Torrealba RC | .40 | 1.00 |
| ❑ 41 Chad Durham RC | .20 | .50 |
| ❑ 42 Jim Mann RC | .20 | .50 |
| ❑ 43 Shane Loux RC | .20 | .50 |
| ❑ 44 Luis Rivas | .20 | .50 |
| ❑ 45 Ken Chenard RC | .20 | .50 |
| ❑ 46 Mike Lockwood RC | .20 | .50 |
| ❑ 47 Yovanny Lara RC | .20 | .50 |
| ❑ 48 Bubba Carpenter RC | .20 | .50 |
| ❑ 49 Ryan Dittfurth RC | .20 | .50 |
| ❑ 50 John Stephens RC | .20 | .50 |
| ❑ 51 Pedro Feliz RC | 1.00 | 2.50 |
| ❑ 52 Kenny Kelly RC | .20 | .50 |
| ❑ 53 Neil Jenkins RC | .20 | .50 |
| ❑ 54 Mike Glendenning RC | .20 | .50 |
| ❑ 55 Bo Porter | .20 | .50 |
| ❑ 56 Eric Byrnes | .20 | .50 |
| ❑ 57 Tony Alvarez RC | .20 | .50 |
| ❑ 58 Kazuhiro Sasaki RC | .60 | 1.50 |
| ❑ 59 Chad Durbin RC | .20 | .50 |
| ❑ 60 Mike Bynum RC | .20 | .50 |
| ❑ 61 Travis Wilson RC | .20 | .50 |
| ❑ 62 Jose Leon RC | .20 | .50 |
| ❑ 63 Ryan Vogelsong RC | .20 | .50 |
| ❑ 64 Geraldo Guzman RC | .20 | .50 |
| ❑ 65 Craig Anderson RC | .20 | .50 |
| ❑ 66 Carlos Silva RC | .40 | 1.00 |
| ❑ 67 Brad Thomas RC | .20 | .50 |
| ❑ 68 Chin-Hui Tsao | .60 | 1.50 |
| ❑ 69 Mark Buehrle RC | 6.00 | 15.00 |
| ❑ 70 Juan Salas RC | .20 | .50 |
| ❑ 71 Denny Abreu RC | .20 | .50 |
| ❑ 72 Keith McDonald RC | .20 | .50 |
| ❑ 73 Chris Richard RC | .20 | .50 |
| ❑ 74 Tomas De la Rosa RC | .20 | .50 |
| ❑ 75 Vicente Padilla RC | .40 | 1.00 |
| ❑ 76 Justin Brunette RC | .20 | .50 |
| ❑ 77 Scott Linebrink RC | .20 | .50 |
| ❑ 78 Jeff Sparks RC | .20 | .50 |
| ❑ 79 Tike Redman RC | .60 | 1.50 |
| ❑ 80 John Lackey RC | 2.00 | 5.00 |
| ❑ 81 Joe Strong RC | .20 | .50 |
| ❑ 82 Brian Tollberg RC | .20 | .50 |
| ❑ 83 Steve Sisco RC | .20 | .50 |
| ❑ 84 Chris Clapinski RC | .20 | .50 |
| ❑ 85 Augie Ojeda RC | .20 | .50 |
| ❑ 86 Adrian Gonzalez RC | 2.50 | 6.00 |
| ❑ 87 Mike Stodolka RC | .20 | .50 |
| ❑ 88 Adam Johnson RC | .20 | .50 |
| ❑ 89 Matt Wheatland RC | .20 | .50 |
| ❑ 90 Corey Smith RC | .20 | .50 |
| ❑ 91 Rocco Baldelli RC | 2.00 | 5.00 |
| ❑ 92 Keith Bucktrot RC | .20 | .50 |
| ❑ 93 Adam Wainwright RC | 1.50 | 4.00 |
| ❑ 94 Blaine Boyer RC | .20 | .50 |
| ❑ 95 Aaron Herr RC | .40 | 1.00 |
| ❑ 96 Scott Thorman RC | 1.00 | 2.50 |
| ❑ 97 Bryan Digby RC | .20 | .50 |
| ❑ 98 Josh Shortslef RC | .20 | .50 |
| ❑ 99 Sean Smith RC | .20 | .50 |
| ❑ 100 Alex Cruz RC | .20 | .50 |
| ❑ 101 Marc Love RC | .20 | .50 |
| ❑ 102 Kevin Lee RC | .20 | .50 |
| ❑ 103 Timo Perez RC | .40 | 1.00 |
| ❑ 104 Alex Cabrera RC | .40 | 1.00 |
| ❑ 105 Shane Heams RC | .20 | .50 |
| ❑ 106 Tripper Johnson RC | .20 | .50 |
| ❑ 107 Brent Abernathy RC | .20 | .50 |
| ❑ 108 John Cotton RC | .20 | .50 |
| ❑ 109 Brad Wilkerson RC | 1.00 | 2.50 |
| ❑ 110 Jon Rauch RC | .20 | .50 |

## 2001 Bowman Chrome

| | | |
|---|---|---|
| ❑ COMP.SET w/o SP's (220) | 20.00 | 50.00 |
| ❑ COMMON (1-110/201-310) | .20 | .50 |
| ❑ COM.REF (111-200/311-330) | 2.00 | 5.00 |
| ❑ COMMON AU REF (331-390) | 20.00 | 50.00 |
| ❑ 1 Jason Giambi | .20 | .50 |
| ❑ 2 Rafael Furcal | .20 | .50 |
| ❑ 3 Bernie Williams | .30 | .75 |
| ❑ 4 Kenny Lofton | .20 | .50 |
| ❑ 5 Al Leiter | .20 | .50 |
| ❑ 6 Albert Belle | .20 | .50 |
| ❑ 7 Craig Biggio | .30 | .75 |
| ❑ 8 Mark Mulder | .20 | .50 |
| ❑ 9 Carlos Delgado | .20 | .50 |
| ❑ 10 Darin Erstad | .20 | .50 |
| ❑ 11 Richie Sexson | .20 | .50 |
| ❑ 12 Randy Johnson | .50 | 1.25 |
| ❑ 13 Greg Maddux | .75 | 2.00 |
| ❑ 14 Orlando Hernandez | .20 | .50 |
| ❑ 15 Javier Vazquez | .20 | .50 |
| ❑ 16 Jeff Kent | .20 | .50 |
| ❑ 17 Jim Thome | .30 | .75 |
| ❑ 18 John Olerud | .20 | .50 |
| ❑ 19 Jason Kendall | .20 | .50 |
| ❑ 20 Scott Rolen | .30 | .75 |
| ❑ 21 Tony Gwynn | .60 | 1.50 |
| ❑ 22 Edgardo Alfonzo | .20 | .50 |
| ❑ 23 Pokey Reese | .20 | .50 |
| ❑ 24 Todd Helton | .30 | .75 |
| ❑ 25 Mark Quinn | .20 | .50 |
| ❑ 26 Dean Palmer | .20 | .50 |
| ❑ 27 Ray Durham | .20 | .50 |
| ❑ 28 Rafael Palmeiro | .30 | .75 |
| ❑ 29 Carl Everett | .20 | .50 |
| ❑ 30 Vladimir Guerrero | .50 | 1.25 |
| ❑ 31 Livan Hernandez | .20 | .50 |
| ❑ 32 Preston Wilson | .20 | .50 |
| ❑ 33 Jose Vidro | .20 | .50 |
| ❑ 34 Fred McGriff | .30 | .75 |
| ❑ 35 Kevin Brown | .20 | .50 |
| ❑ 36 Miguel Tejada | .30 | .75 |
| ❑ 37 Chipper Jones | .50 | 1.25 |
| ❑ 38 Edgar Martinez | .30 | .75 |
| ❑ 39 Tony Batista | .20 | .50 |
| ❑ 40 Jorge Posada | .30 | .75 |
| ❑ 41 Sammy Sosa | .50 | 1.25 |
| ❑ 42 Gary Sheffield | .20 | .50 |
| ❑ 43 Bartolo Colon | .20 | .50 |
| ❑ 44 Pat Burrell | .20 | .50 |
| ❑ 45 Jay Payton | .20 | .50 |
| ❑ 46 Mike Mussina | .30 | .75 |
| ❑ 47 Nomar Garciaparra | .75 | 2.00 |
| ❑ 48 Darren Dreifort | .20 | .50 |
| ❑ 49 Richard Hidalgo | .20 | .50 |
| ❑ 50 Troy Glaus | .20 | .50 |
| ❑ 51 Ben Grieve | .20 | .50 |
| ❑ 52 Jim Edmonds | .30 | .75 |
| ❑ 53 Raul Mondesi | .20 | .50 |
| ❑ 54 Andruw Jones | .30 | .75 |
| ❑ 55 Mike Sweeney | .20 | .50 |
| ❑ 56 Derek Jeter | 1.25 | 3.00 |
| ❑ 57 Ruben Mateo | .20 | .50 |
| ❑ 58 Cristian Guzman | .20 | .50 |
| ❑ 59 Mike Hampton | .20 | .50 |
| ❑ 60 J.D. Drew | .20 | .50 |
| ❑ 61 Matt Lawton | .20 | .50 |
| ❑ 62 Moises Alou | .20 | .50 |
| ❑ 63 Terrence Long | .20 | .50 |
| ❑ 64 Geoff Jenkins | .20 | .50 |
| ❑ 65 Manny Ramirez Sox | .30 | .75 |
| ❑ 66 Johnny Damon | .30 | .75 |
| ❑ 67 Pedro Martinez | .30 | .75 |
| ❑ 68 Juan Gonzalez | .20 | .50 |

| | | |
|---|---|---|
| ❑ 69 Roger Clemens | 1.00 | 2.50 |
| ❑ 70 Carlos Beltran | .20 | .50 |
| ❑ 71 Roberto Alomar | .30 | .75 |
| ❑ 72 Barry Bonds | 1.25 | 3.00 |
| ❑ 73 Tim Hudson | .20 | .50 |
| ❑ 74 Tom Glavine | .30 | .75 |
| ❑ 75 Jeromy Burnitz | .20 | .50 |
| ❑ 76 Adrian Beltre | .20 | .50 |
| ❑ 77 Mike Piazza | .75 | 2.00 |
| ❑ 78 Kerry Wood | .20 | .50 |
| ❑ 79 Steve Finley | .20 | .50 |
| ❑ 80 Bob Abreu | .20 | .50 |
| ❑ 81 Neifi Perez | .20 | .50 |
| ❑ 82 Mark Redman | .20 | .50 |
| ❑ 83 Paul Konerko | .20 | .50 |
| ❑ 84 Jermaine Dye | .20 | .50 |
| ❑ 85 Brian Giles | .20 | .50 |
| ❑ 86 Ivan Rodriguez | .30 | .75 |
| ❑ 87 Adam Kennedy | .20 | .50 |
| ❑ 88 Eric Chavez | .20 | .50 |
| ❑ 89 Billy Koch | .20 | .50 |
| ❑ 90 Shawn Green | .20 | .50 |
| ❑ 91 Matt Williams | .20 | .50 |
| ❑ 92 Greg Vaughn | .20 | .50 |
| ❑ 93 Jeff Cirillo | .20 | .50 |
| ❑ 94 Frank Thomas | .50 | 1.25 |
| ❑ 95 David Justice | .20 | .50 |
| ❑ 96 Cal Ripken | 1.50 | 4.00 |
| ❑ 97 Curt Schilling | .30 | .75 |
| ❑ 98 Barry Zito | .30 | .75 |
| ❑ 99 Brian Jordan | .20 | .50 |
| ❑ 100 Chan Ho Park | .20 | .50 |
| ❑ 101 J.T. Snow | .20 | .50 |
| ❑ 102 Kazuhiro Sasaki | .20 | .50 |
| ❑ 103 Alex Rodriguez | .75 | 2.00 |
| ❑ 104 Mariano Rivera | .50 | 1.25 |
| ❑ 105 Eric Milton | .20 | .50 |
| ❑ 106 Andy Pettitte | .30 | .75 |
| ❑ 107 Ken Griffey Jr. | .75 | 2.00 |
| ❑ 108 Bengie Molina | .20 | .50 |
| ❑ 109 Jeff Bagwell | .30 | .75 |
| ❑ 110 Mark McGwire | 1.25 | 3.00 |
| ❑ 111 Dan Tosca RC | 2.00 | 5.00 |
| ❑ 112 Sergio Contreras RC | 3.00 | 8.00 |
| ❑ 113 Mitch Jones RC | 3.00 | 8.00 |
| ❑ 114 Ramon Carvajal RC | 3.00 | 8.00 |
| ❑ 115 Ryan Madson RC | 4.00 | 10.00 |
| ❑ 116 Hank Blalock RC | 12.50 | 30.00 |
| ❑ 117 Ben Washburn RC | 2.00 | 5.00 |
| ❑ 118 Erick Almonte RC | 2.00 | 5.00 |
| ❑ 119 Shawn Fagan RC | 3.00 | 8.00 |
| ❑ 120 Gary Johnson RC | 2.00 | 5.00 |
| ❑ 121 Brett Evert RC | 2.00 | 5.00 |
| ❑ 122 Joe Hamer RC | 3.00 | 8.00 |
| ❑ 123 Yhency Brazoban RC | 4.00 | 10.00 |
| ❑ 124 Domingo Guante RC | 2.00 | 5.00 |
| ❑ 125 Deivi Mendez RC | 2.00 | 5.00 |
| ❑ 126 Adrian Hernandez RC | 2.00 | 5.00 |
| ❑ 127 Reggie Abercrombie RC | 4.00 | 10.00 |
| ❑ 128 Steve Bennett RC | 2.00 | 5.00 |
| ❑ 129 Matt White RC | 3.00 | 8.00 |
| ❑ 130 Brian Hitchcox RC | 2.00 | 5.00 |
| ❑ 131 Deivis Santos RC | 2.00 | 5.00 |
| ❑ 132 Luis Montanez RC | 4.00 | 10.00 |
| ❑ 133 Eric Reynolds RC | 2.00 | 5.00 |
| ❑ 134 Denny Bautista RC | 4.00 | 10.00 |
| ❑ 135 Hector Garcia RC | 2.00 | 5.00 |
| ❑ 136 Joe Thurston RC | 3.00 | 8.00 |
| ❑ 137 Tsuyoshi Shinjo RC | 4.00 | 10.00 |
| ❑ 138 Elpidio Guzman RC | 2.00 | 5.00 |
| ❑ 139 Brian Bass RC | 2.00 | 5.00 |
| ❑ 140 Mark Burnett RC | 3.00 | 8.00 |
| ❑ 141 Russ Jacobson UER | 2.00 | 5.00 |
| ❑ 142 Travis Hafner RC | 12.50 | 30.00 |
| ❑ 143 Wilson Betemit RC | 6.00 | 15.00 |
| ❑ 144 Luke Lockwood RC | 2.00 | 5.00 |
| ❑ 145 Noel Devarez RC | 3.00 | 8.00 |
| ❑ 146 Doug Gredvig RC | 2.00 | 5.00 |
| ❑ 147 Seung Song RC | 3.00 | 8.00 |
| ❑ 148 Andy Van Hekken RC | 2.00 | 5.00 |
| ❑ 149 Ryan Kohlmeier | 2.00 | 5.00 |
| ❑ 150 Dee Haynes RC | 2.00 | 5.00 |
| ❑ 151 Jim Journell RC | 3.00 | 8.00 |
| ❑ 152 Chad Petty RC | 2.00 | 5.00 |
| ❑ 153 Danny Borrell RC | 2.00 | 5.00 |
| ❑ 154 Dave Krynzel RC | 2.00 | 5.00 |
| ❑ 155 Octavio Martinez RC | 3.00 | 8.00 |
| ❑ 156 David Parrish RC | 2.00 | 5.00 |

|  |  | | |
|---|--------|------|------|
| 157 | Jason Miller RC | 2.00 | 5.00 |
| 158 | Corey Spencer RC | 2.00 | 5.00 |
| 159 | Maxim St. Pierre RC | 3.00 | 8.00 |
| 160 | Pat Magness RC | 3.00 | 8.00 |
| 161 | Ranier Olmedo RC | 3.00 | 8.00 |
| 162 | Brandon Mims RC | 2.00 | 5.00 |
| 163 | Phil Wilson RC | 3.00 | 8.00 |
| 164 | Jose Reyes RC | 30.00 | 60.00 |
| 165 | Matt Butler RC | 3.00 | 8.00 |
| 166 | Joel Pineiro | 3.00 | 8.00 |
| 167 | Ken Chenard | 2.00 | 5.00 |
| 168 | Alexis Gomez RC | 2.00 | 5.00 |
| 169 | Justin Morneau RC | 20.00 | 50.00 |
| 170 | Josh Fogg RC | 3.00 | 8.00 |
| 171 | Charles Frazier RC | 2.00 | 5.00 |
| 172 | Ryan Ludwick RC | 10.00 | 25.00 |
| 173 | Seth McClung RC | 3.00 | 8.00 |
| 174 | Justin Wayne RC | 3.00 | 8.00 |
| 175 | Rafael Soriano RC | 3.00 | 8.00 |
| 176 | Jared Abruzzo RC | 2.00 | 5.00 |
| 177 | Jason Richardson RC | 2.00 | 5.00 |
| 178 | Darwin Cubillan RC | 2.00 | 5.00 |
| 179 | Blake Williams RC | 2.00 | 5.00 |
| 180 | Valentino Pascucci RC | 3.00 | 8.00 |
| 181 | Ryan Hannaman RC | 3.00 | 8.00 |
| 182 | Steve Smyth RC | 3.00 | 8.00 |
| 183 | Jake Peavy RC | 15.00 | 40.00 |
| 184 | Onix Mercado RC | 3.00 | 8.00 |
| 185 | Luis Torres RC | 3.00 | 8.00 |
| 186 | Casey Fossum RC | 2.00 | 5.00 |
| 187 | Eduardo Figueroa RC | 2.00 | 5.00 |
| 188 | Bryan Barnowski RC | 2.00 | 5.00 |
| 189 | Jason Standridge | 2.00 | 5.00 |
| 190 | Marvin Seale RC | 3.00 | 8.00 |
| 191 | Steve Smitherman RC | 3.00 | 8.00 |
| 192 | Rafael Boitel RC | 2.00 | 5.00 |
| 193 | Dany Morban RC | 2.00 | 5.00 |
| 194 | Justin Woodrow RC | 3.00 | 8.00 |
| 195 | Ed Rogers RC | 2.00 | 5.00 |
| 196 | Ben Hendrickson RC | 2.00 | 5.00 |
| 197 | Thomas Mitchell | 2.00 | 5.00 |
| 198 | Adam Pettyjohn RC | 2.00 | 5.00 |
| 199 | Doug Nickle RC | 2.00 | 5.00 |
| 200 | Jason Jones RC | 2.00 | 5.00 |
| 201 | Larry Barnes | .20 | .50 |
| 202 | Ben Diggins | .20 | .50 |
| 203 | Dee Brown | .20 | .50 |
| 204 | Rocco Baldelli | .20 | .50 |
| 205 | Luis Terrero | .20 | .50 |
| 206 | Milton Bradley | .20 | .50 |
| 207 | Kurt Ainsworth | .20 | .50 |
| 208 | Sean Burroughs | .20 | .50 |
| 209 | Rick Asadoorian | .20 | .50 |
| 210 | Ramon Castro | .20 | .50 |
| 211 | Nick Neugebauer | .20 | .50 |
| 212 | Aaron Myette | .20 | .50 |
| 213 | Luis Matos | .20 | .50 |
| 214 | Donnie Bridges | .20 | .50 |
| 215 | Alex Cintron | .20 | .50 |
| 216 | Bobby Kielty | .20 | .50 |
| 217 | Matt Belisle | .20 | .50 |
| 218 | Adam Everett | .20 | .50 |
| 219 | John Lackey | .20 | .50 |
| 220 | Adam Wainwright | .75 | 2.00 |
| 221 | Jerry Hairston Jr. | .20 | .50 |
| 222 | Mike Bynum | .20 | .50 |
| 223 | Ryan Christianson | .20 | .50 |
| 224 | J.J. Davis | .20 | .50 |
| 225 | Alex Graman | .20 | .50 |
| 226 | Abraham Nunez | .20 | .50 |
| 227 | Sun Woo Kim | .20 | .50 |
| 228 | Jimmy Rollins | .20 | .50 |
| 229 | Ruben Salazar | .20 | .50 |
| 230 | Josh Girdley | .20 | .50 |
| 231 | Carl Crawford | .20 | .50 |
| 232 | Ben Davis | .20 | .50 |
| 233 | Jason Grabowski | .20 | .50 |
| 234 | Chris George | .20 | .50 |
| 235 | Roy Oswalt | .50 | 1.25 |
| 236 | Brian Cole | .20 | .50 |
| 237 | Corey Patterson | .20 | .50 |
| 238 | Vernon Wells | .20 | .50 |
| 239 | Brad Baker | .20 | .50 |
| 240 | Gookie Dawkins | .20 | .50 |
| 241 | Michael Cuddyer | .20 | .50 |
| 242 | Ricardo Aramboles | .20 | .50 |
| 243 | Ben Sheets | .30 | .75 |
| 244 | Toby Hall | .20 | .50 |
| 245 | Jack Cust | .20 | .50 |
| 246 | Pedro Feliz | .20 | .50 |
| 247 | Josh Beckett | .30 | .75 |
| 248 | Alex Escobar | .20 | .50 |
| 249 | Marcus Giles | .20 | .50 |
| 250 | Jon Rauch | .20 | .50 |
| 251 | Kevin Mench | .20 | .50 |
| 252 | Shawn Sonnier | .20 | .50 |
| 253 | Aaron Rowand | .20 | .50 |
| 254 | C.C. Sabathia | .20 | .50 |
| 255 | Bubba Crosby | .20 | .50 |
| 256 | Josh Hamilton | .40 | 1.00 |
| 257 | Carlos Hernandez | .20 | .50 |
| 258 | Carlos Pena | .20 | .50 |
| 259 | Miguel Cabrera | 1.50 | 4.00 |
| 260 | Brandon Phillips | .20 | .50 |
| 261 | Tony Pena Jr. | .20 | .50 |
| 262 | Cristian Guerrero | .20 | .50 |
| 263 | Jin Ho Cho | .20 | .50 |
| 264 | Aaron Herr | .20 | .50 |
| 265 | Keith Ginter | .20 | .50 |
| 266 | Felipe Lopez | .20 | .50 |
| 267 | Travis Harper | .20 | .50 |
| 268 | Joe Torres | .20 | .50 |
| 269 | Eric Byrnes | .20 | .50 |
| 270 | Ben Christensen | .20 | .50 |
| 271 | Aubrey Huff | .20 | .50 |
| 272 | Lyle Overbay | .20 | .50 |
| 273 | Vince Faison | .20 | .50 |
| 274 | Bobby Bradley | .20 | .50 |
| 275 | Joe Crede | .50 | 1.25 |
| 276 | Matt Wheatland | .20 | .50 |
| 277 | Grady Sizemore | .75 | 2.00 |
| 278 | Adrian Gonzalez | .20 | .50 |
| 279 | Tim Raines Jr. | .20 | .50 |
| 280 | Phil Dumatrait | .20 | .50 |
| 281 | Jason Hart | .20 | .50 |
| 282 | David Kelton | .20 | .50 |
| 283 | David Walling | .20 | .50 |
| 284 | J.R. House | .20 | .50 |
| 285 | Kenny Kelly | .20 | .50 |
| 286 | Aaron McNeal | .20 | .50 |
| 287 | Nick Johnson | .20 | .50 |
| 288 | Scott Heard | .20 | .50 |
| 289 | Brad Wilkerson | .20 | .50 |
| 290 | Allen Levrault | .20 | .50 |
| 291 | Chris Richard | .20 | .50 |
| 292 | Jared Sandberg | .20 | .50 |
| 293 | Tike Redman | .20 | .50 |
| 294 | Adam Dunn | .30 | .75 |
| 295 | Josh Pressley | .20 | .50 |
| 296 | Jose Ortiz | .20 | .50 |
| 297 | Jason Romano | .20 | .50 |
| 298 | Tim Redding | .20 | .50 |
| 299 | Alex Gordon | .20 | .50 |
| 300 | Ben Petrick | .20 | .50 |
| 301 | Eric Munson | .20 | .50 |
| 302 | Luis Rivas | .20 | .50 |
| 303 | Matt Ginter | .20 | .50 |
| 304 | Alfonso Soriano | .30 | .75 |
| 305 | Wilfredo Rodriguez | .20 | .50 |
| 306 | Brett Myers | .20 | .50 |
| 307 | Scott Seabol | .20 | .50 |
| 308 | Tony Alvarez | .20 | .50 |
| 309 | Donzell McDonald | .20 | .50 |
| 310 | Austin Kearns | .20 | .50 |
| 311 | Will Ohman RC | 3.00 | 8.00 |
| 312 | Ryan Soules RC | 2.00 | 5.00 |
| 313 | Cody Ross RC | 2.00 | 5.00 |
| 314 | Bill Whitecotton RC | 2.00 | 5.00 |
| 315 | Mike Burns RC | 3.00 | 8.00 |
| 316 | Manuel Acosta RC | 2.00 | 5.00 |
| 317 | Lance Niekro RC | 4.00 | 10.00 |
| 318 | Travis Thompson RC | 3.00 | 8.00 |
| 319 | Zach Sorensen RC | 3.00 | 8.00 |
| 320 | Austin Evans RC | 3.00 | 8.00 |
| 321 | Brad Stiles RC | 2.00 | 5.00 |
| 322 | Joe Kennedy RC | 4.00 | 10.00 |
| 323 | Luke Martin RC | 3.00 | 8.00 |
| 324 | Juan Diaz RC | 3.00 | 8.00 |
| 325 | Pat Hallmark RC | 2.00 | 5.00 |
| 326 | Christian Parker RC | 2.00 | 5.00 |
| 327 | Ronny Corona RC | 3.00 | 8.00 |
| 328 | Jermaine Clark RC | 3.00 | 8.00 |
| 329 | Scott Dunn RC | 3.00 | 8.00 |
| 330 | Scott Chiasson RC | 2.00 | 5.00 |
| 331 | Greg Nash AU RC | 20.00 | 50.00 |
| 332 | Brad Cresse AU | 20.00 | 50.00 |
| 333 | John Buck AU RC | 40.00 | 80.00 |
| 334 | Freddie Bynum AU RC | 20.00 | 50.00 |
| 335 | Felix Diaz AU RC | 20.00 | 50.00 |
| 336 | Jason Belcher AU RC | 20.00 | 50.00 |
| 337 | Troy Farnsworth AU RC | 20.00 | 50.00 |
| 338 | Roberto Miniel AU RC | 20.00 | 50.00 |
| 339 | Esix Snead AU RC | 20.00 | 50.00 |
| 340 | Albert Pujols AU RC | 3000.00 | 4000.00 |
| 341 | Jeff Andra AU RC | 20.00 | 50.00 |
| 342 | Victor Hall AU RC | 20.00 | 50.00 |
| 343 | Pedro Liriano AU RC | 20.00 | 50.00 |
| 344 | Andy Beal AU RC | 20.00 | 50.00 |
| 345 | Bob Keppel AU RC | 20.00 | 50.00 |
| 346 | Brian Schmitt AU RC | 20.00 | 50.00 |
| 347 | Ron Davenport AU RC | 90.00 | 150.00 |
| 348 | Tony Blanco AU RC | 20.00 | 50.00 |
| 349 | Reggie Griggs AU RC | 20.00 | 50.00 |
| 350 | Derrick Van Dusen AU RC | 20.00 | 50.00 |
| 351A | Ichiro Suzuki English RC | 60.00 | 100.00 |
| 351B | Ichiro Suzuki AU RC | 60.00 | 100.00 |

## 2002 Bowman Chrome

| | | | |
|---|---|------|------|
| | COMP. RED SET (110) | 15.00 | 40.00 |
| | COMP. BLUE w/o SP's (110) | 15.00 | 40.00 |
| | COMMON RED (1-110) | .20 | .50 |
| | COMMON BLUE (111-383) | .30 | .75 |
| | COMMON AU (324B/384-405) | 4.00 | 10.00 |
| | 324B/384-405 GROUP A AUTO ODDS 1:26 | | |
| | 303-404 GROUP B AUTO ODDS 1:1290 | | |
| | 324B/384-405 OVERALL AUTO ODDS 1:27 | | |
| 1 | Adam Dunn | .20 | .50 |
| 2 | Derek Jeter | 1.25 | 3.00 |
| 3 | Alex Rodriguez | .75 | 2.00 |
| 4 | Miguel Tejada | .20 | .50 |
| 5 | Nomar Garciaparra | .75 | 2.00 |
| 6 | Toby Hall | .20 | .50 |
| 7 | Brandon Duckworth | .20 | .50 |
| 8 | Paul LoDuca | .20 | .50 |
| 9 | Brian Giles | .20 | .50 |
| 10 | C.C. Sabathia | .20 | .50 |
| 11 | Curt Schilling | .30 | .75 |
| 12 | Tsuyoshi Shinjo | .20 | .50 |
| 13 | Ramon Hernandez | .20 | .50 |
| 14 | Jose Cruz Jr. | .20 | .50 |
| 15 | Albert Pujols | 1.00 | 2.50 |
| 16 | Joe Mays | .20 | .50 |
| 17 | Javy Lopez | .20 | .50 |
| 18 | J.T. Snow | .20 | .50 |
| 19 | David Segui | .20 | .50 |
| 20 | Jorge Posada | .30 | .75 |
| 21 | Doug Mientkiewicz | .20 | .50 |
| 22 | Jerry Hairston Jr. | .20 | .50 |
| 23 | Bernie Williams | .30 | .75 |
| 24 | Mike Sweeney | .20 | .50 |
| 25 | Jason Giambi | .30 | .75 |
| 26 | Ryan Dempster | .20 | .50 |
| 27 | Ryan Klesko | .20 | .50 |
| 28 | Mark Quinn | .20 | .50 |
| 29 | Jeff Kent | .20 | .50 |
| 30 | Eric Chavez | .20 | .50 |
| 31 | Adrian Beltre | .20 | .50 |
| 32 | Andruw Jones | .30 | .75 |
| 33 | Alfonso Soriano | .20 | .50 |
| 34 | Aramis Ramirez | .20 | .50 |
| 35 | Greg Maddux | .75 | 2.00 |
| 36 | Andy Pettitte | .30 | .75 |
| 37 | Barry Zito | .20 | .50 |
| 38 | Ben Sheets | .20 | .50 |
| 39 | Bobby Higginson | .20 | .50 |
| 40 | Ivan Rodriguez | .30 | .75 |
| 41 | Brad Penny | .20 | .50 |
| 42 | Carlos Lee | .20 | .50 |
| 43 | Damion Easley | .20 | .50 |
| 44 | Preston Wilson | .20 | .50 |

|  |  | | |
|---|---|---|---|
| ☐ 45 | Jeff Bagwell | .30 | .75 |
| ☐ 46 | Eric Milton | .20 | .50 |
| ☐ 47 | Rafael Palmeiro | .30 | .75 |
| ☐ 48 | Gary Sheffield | .20 | .50 |
| ☐ 49 | J.D. Drew | .20 | .50 |
| ☐ 50 | Jim Thome | .30 | .75 |
| ☐ 51 | Ichiro Suzuki | 1.00 | 2.50 |
| ☐ 52 | Bud Smith | .20 | .50 |
| ☐ 53 | Chan Ho Park | .20 | .50 |
| ☐ 54 | D'Angelo Jimenez | .20 | .50 |
| ☐ 55 | Ken Griffey Jr. | .75 | 2.00 |
| ☐ 56 | Wade Miller | .20 | .50 |
| ☐ 57 | Vladimir Guerrero | .50 | 1.25 |
| ☐ 58 | Troy Glaus | .20 | .50 |
| ☐ 59 | Shawn Green | .20 | .50 |
| ☐ 60 | Kerry Wood | .20 | .50 |
| ☐ 61 | Jack Wilson | .20 | .50 |
| ☐ 62 | Kevin Brown | .20 | .50 |
| ☐ 63 | Marcus Giles | .20 | .50 |
| ☐ 64 | Pat Burrell | .20 | .50 |
| ☐ 65 | Larry Walker | .20 | .50 |
| ☐ 66 | Sammy Sosa | .50 | 1.25 |
| ☐ 67 | Raul Mondesi | .20 | .50 |
| ☐ 68 | Tim Hudson | .20 | .50 |
| ☐ 69 | Lance Berkman | .20 | .50 |
| ☐ 70 | Mike Mussina | .30 | .75 |
| ☐ 71 | Barry Zito | .20 | .50 |
| ☐ 72 | Jimmy Rollins | .20 | .50 |
| ☐ 73 | Barry Bonds | 1.25 | 3.00 |
| ☐ 74 | Craig Biggio | .30 | .75 |
| ☐ 75 | Todd Helton | .30 | .75 |
| ☐ 76 | Roger Clemens | 1.00 | 2.50 |
| ☐ 77 | Frank Catalanotto | .20 | .50 |
| ☐ 78 | Josh Towers | .20 | .50 |
| ☐ 79 | Roy Oswalt | .20 | .50 |
| ☐ 80 | Chipper Jones | .50 | 1.25 |
| ☐ 81 | Cristian Guzman | .20 | .50 |
| ☐ 82 | Darin Erstad | .20 | .50 |
| ☐ 83 | Freddy Garcia | .20 | .50 |
| ☐ 84 | Jason Tyner | .20 | .50 |
| ☐ 85 | Carlos Delgado | .20 | .50 |
| ☐ 86 | Jon Lieber | .20 | .50 |
| ☐ 87 | Juan Pierre | .20 | .50 |
| ☐ 88 | Matt Morris | .20 | .50 |
| ☐ 89 | Phil Nevin | .20 | .50 |
| ☐ 90 | Jim Edmonds | .20 | .50 |
| ☐ 91 | Magglio Ordonez | .20 | .50 |
| ☐ 92 | Mike Hampton | .20 | .50 |
| ☐ 93 | Rafael Furcal | .20 | .50 |
| ☐ 94 | Richie Sexson | .20 | .50 |
| ☐ 95 | Luis Gonzalez | .20 | .50 |
| ☐ 96 | Scott Rolen | .20 | .50 |
| ☐ 97 | Tim Redding | .20 | .50 |
| ☐ 98 | Moises Alou | .20 | .50 |
| ☐ 99 | Jose Vidro | .20 | .50 |
| ☐ 100 | Mike Piazza | .75 | 2.00 |
| ☐ 101 | Pedro Martinez | .30 | .75 |
| ☐ 102 | Geoff Jenkins | .20 | .50 |
| ☐ 103 | Johnny Damon Sox | .20 | .50 |
| ☐ 104 | Mike Cameron | .20 | .50 |
| ☐ 105 | Randy Johnson | .50 | 1.25 |
| ☐ 106 | David Eckstein | .20 | .50 |
| ☐ 107 | Javier Vazquez | .20 | .50 |
| ☐ 108 | Mark Mulder | .20 | .50 |
| ☐ 109 | Robert Fick | .20 | .50 |
| ☐ 110 | Roberto Alomar | .30 | .75 |
| ☐ 111 | Wilson Betemit | .20 | .50 |
| ☐ 112 | Chris Tritle SP RC | 2.00 | 5.00 |
| ☐ 113 | Ed Rogers | .30 | .75 |
| ☐ 114 | Juan Pena | .30 | .75 |
| ☐ 115 | Josh Beckett | .50 | 1.25 |
| ☐ 116 | Juan Cruz | .20 | .50 |
| ☐ 117 | Noochie Varner SP RC | 2.00 | 5.00 |
| ☐ 118 | Blake Williams | .30 | .75 |
| ☐ 119 | Mike Rivera | .30 | .75 |
| ☐ 120 | Hank Blalock | .75 | 2.00 |
| ☐ 121 | Hansel Izquierdo RC | .30 | .75 |
| ☐ 122 | Orlando Hudson | .30 | .75 |
| ☐ 123 | Bill Hall SP | 2.00 | 5.00 |
| ☐ 124 | Jose Reyes | .75 | 2.00 |
| ☐ 125 | Juan Rivera | .30 | .75 |
| ☐ 126 | Eric Valent | .20 | .50 |
| ☐ 127 | Scotty Layfield SP RC | 2.00 | 5.00 |
| ☐ 128 | Austin Kearns | .30 | .75 |
| ☐ 129 | Nic Jackson SP RC | 2.00 | 5.00 |
| ☐ 130 | Scott Chiasson | .30 | .75 |
| ☐ 131 | Chad Qualls SP RC | 3.00 | 8.00 |
| ☐ 132 | Marcus Thames | .20 | .50 |
| ☐ 133 | Nathan Haynes | .30 | .75 |
| ☐ 134 | Joe Borchard | .30 | .75 |
| ☐ 135 | Josh Hamilton | .60 | 1.50 |
| ☐ 136 | Corey Patterson | .30 | .75 |
| ☐ 137 | Travis Wilson | .30 | .75 |
| ☐ 138 | Alex Escobar | .30 | .75 |
| ☐ 139 | Alexis Gomez | .30 | .75 |
| ☐ 140 | Nick Johnson | .50 | 1.25 |
| ☐ 141 | Marlon Byrd | .30 | .75 |
| ☐ 142 | Kory DeHaan | .30 | .75 |
| ☐ 143 | Carlos Hernandez | .30 | .75 |
| ☐ 144 | Sean Burroughs | .30 | .75 |
| ☐ 145 | Angel Berroa | .30 | .75 |
| ☐ 146 | Aubrey Huff | .50 | 1.25 |
| ☐ 147 | Travis Hafner | .50 | 1.25 |
| ☐ 148 | Brandon Berger | .30 | .75 |
| ☐ 149 | J.R. House | .30 | .75 |
| ☐ 150 | Dewon Brazelton | .30 | .75 |
| ☐ 151 | Jayson Werth | .30 | .75 |
| ☐ 152 | Larry Barnes | .30 | .75 |
| ☐ 153 | Ruben Gotay SP RC | 3.00 | 8.00 |
| ☐ 154 | Tommy Marx SP RC | 2.00 | 5.00 |
| ☐ 155 | John Suomi SP RC | 2.00 | 5.00 |
| ☐ 156 | Javier Colina SP | 2.00 | 5.00 |
| ☐ 157 | Greg Sain SP RC | 2.00 | 5.00 |
| ☐ 158 | Robert Cosby SP RC | 2.00 | 5.00 |
| ☐ 159 | Angel Pagan SP RC | 3.00 | 8.00 |
| ☐ 160 | Ralph Santana RC | .50 | 1.25 |
| ☐ 161 | Joe Orloski RC | .50 | 1.25 |
| ☐ 162 | Shayne Wright SP RC | 2.00 | 5.00 |
| ☐ 163 | Jay Caliguiri SP RC | 2.00 | 5.00 |
| ☐ 164 | Greg Montalbano SP RC | 2.00 | 5.00 |
| ☐ 165 | Rich Harden SP RC | 10.00 | 25.00 |
| ☐ 166 | Rich Thompson SP RC | 2.00 | 5.00 |
| ☐ 167 | Fred Bastardo SP RC | 2.00 | 5.00 |
| ☐ 168 | Alejandro Giron SP RC | 2.00 | 5.00 |
| ☐ 169 | Jesus Medrano SP RC | 2.00 | 5.00 |
| ☐ 170 | Kevin Deaton SP RC | 2.00 | 5.00 |
| ☐ 171 | Mike Rosamond RC | .50 | 1.25 |
| ☐ 172 | Jon Guzman SP RC | 2.00 | 5.00 |
| ☐ 173 | Gerard Oakes SP RC | 2.00 | 5.00 |
| ☐ 174 | Francisco Liriano SP RC | 12.50 | 30.00 |
| ☐ 175 | Matt Allegra SP RC | 2.00 | 5.00 |
| ☐ 176 | Mike Snyder SP RC | 2.00 | 5.00 |
| ☐ 177 | James Shanks SP RC | 2.00 | 5.00 |
| ☐ 178 | Anderson Hernandez SP RC | 2.00 | 5.00 |
| ☐ 179 | Dan Trumble SP RC | 2.00 | 5.00 |
| ☐ 180 | Luis DePaula SP RC | 2.00 | 5.00 |
| ☐ 181 | Randall Shelley SP RC | 2.00 | 5.00 |
| ☐ 182 | Richard Lane SP RC | 2.00 | 5.00 |
| ☐ 183 | Antwon Rollins SP RC | 2.00 | 5.00 |
| ☐ 184 | Ryan Bukvich SP RC | 2.00 | 5.00 |
| ☐ 185 | Derrick Lewis SP | 2.00 | 5.00 |
| ☐ 186 | Eric Miller SP RC | 2.00 | 5.00 |
| ☐ 187 | Justin Schuda SP RC | 2.00 | 5.00 |
| ☐ 188 | Brian West SP RC | 2.00 | 5.00 |
| ☐ 189 | Brad Wilkerson | .30 | .75 |
| ☐ 190 | Neal Frendling SP RC | 2.00 | 5.00 |
| ☐ 191 | Jeremy Hill SP RC | 2.00 | 5.00 |
| ☐ 192 | James Barrett SP RC | 2.00 | 5.00 |
| ☐ 193 | Brett Kay SP RC | 2.00 | 5.00 |
| ☐ 194 | Ryan Mottl SP RC | 2.00 | 5.00 |
| ☐ 195 | Brad Nelson SP RC | 2.00 | 5.00 |
| ☐ 196 | Juan M. Gonzalez SP RC | 2.00 | 5.00 |
| ☐ 197 | Curtis Legendre SP RC | 2.00 | 5.00 |
| ☐ 198 | Ronald Acuna SP RC | 2.00 | 5.00 |
| ☐ 199 | Chris Flinn SP RC | 2.00 | 5.00 |
| ☐ 200 | Nick Alvarez SP RC | 2.00 | 5.00 |
| ☐ 201 | Jason Ellison SP RC | 4.00 | 10.00 |
| ☐ 202 | Blake McGinley SP RC | 2.00 | 5.00 |
| ☐ 203 | Dan Phillips SP RC | 2.00 | 5.00 |
| ☐ 204 | Demetrius Heath SP RC | 2.00 | 5.00 |
| ☐ 205 | Eric Bruntlett SP RC | 2.00 | 5.00 |
| ☐ 206 | Joe Jiannetti SP RC | 2.00 | 5.00 |
| ☐ 207 | Mike Hill SP RC | 2.00 | 5.00 |
| ☐ 208 | Ricardo Cordova SP RC | 2.00 | 5.00 |
| ☐ 209 | Mark Hamilton SP RC | 2.00 | 5.00 |
| ☐ 210 | David Mattox SP RC | 2.00 | 5.00 |
| ☐ 211 | Jose Morban SP RC | 2.00 | 5.00 |
| ☐ 212 | Scott Wiggins SP RC | 2.00 | 5.00 |
| ☐ 213 | Steve Green | .30 | .75 |
| ☐ 214 | Brian Rogers SP RC | 2.00 | 5.00 |
| ☐ 215 | Kenny Baugh | .30 | .75 |
| ☐ 216 | Anastacio Martinez SP RC | 2.00 | 5.00 |
| ☐ 217 | Richard Lewis | .30 | .75 |
| ☐ 218 | Tim Kalita SP RC | 2.00 | 5.00 |
| ☐ 219 | Edwin Almonte SP RC | 2.00 | 5.00 |
| ☐ 220 | Hee Seop Choi | 2.00 | 5.00 |
| ☐ 221 | Ty Howington | .30 | .75 |
| ☐ 222 | Victor Alvarez RC | 2.00 | 5.00 |
| ☐ 223 | Morgan Ensberg | .50 | 1.25 |
| ☐ 224 | Jeff Austin SP RC | 2.00 | 5.00 |
| ☐ 225 | Clint Weibl SP RC | 2.00 | 5.00 |
| ☐ 226 | Eric Cyr | .30 | .75 |
| ☐ 227 | Marlyn Tisdale SP RC | 2.00 | 5.00 |
| ☐ 228 | John VanBenschoten | .30 | .75 |
| ☐ 229 | David Krynzel | .30 | .75 |
| ☐ 230 | Raul Chavez SP RC | 2.00 | 5.00 |
| ☐ 231 | Brett Evert | .30 | .75 |
| ☐ 232 | Joe Rogers SP RC | 2.00 | 5.00 |
| ☐ 233 | Adam Wainwright | .50 | 1.25 |
| ☐ 234 | Matt Herges RC | .30 | .75 |
| ☐ 235 | Matt Childers SP RC | 2.00 | 5.00 |
| ☐ 236 | Nick Neugebauer | .30 | .75 |
| ☐ 237 | Cant Crawford | .50 | 1.25 |
| ☐ 238 | Seung Song | .30 | .75 |
| ☐ 239 | Randy Flores | .30 | .75 |
| ☐ 240 | Jason Lane | .50 | 1.25 |
| ☐ 241 | Chase Utley | 4.00 | 10.00 |
| ☐ 242 | Ben Howard SP RC | 2.00 | 5.00 |
| ☐ 243 | Eric Glaser SP RC | 2.00 | 5.00 |
| ☐ 244 | Josh Wilson RC | .50 | 1.25 |
| ☐ 245 | Jose Valverde SP RC | 2.00 | 5.00 |
| ☐ 246 | Chris Smith | .30 | .75 |
| ☐ 247 | Mark Prior | .75 | 2.00 |
| ☐ 248 | Brian Mallette SP RC | 2.00 | 5.00 |
| ☐ 249 | Chone Figgins SP RC | 3.00 | 8.00 |
| ☐ 250 | Jimmy Alvarez SP RC | 2.00 | 5.00 |
| ☐ 251 | Luis Terrero | .30 | .75 |
| ☐ 252 | Josh Bonifay SP RC | 2.00 | 5.00 |
| ☐ 253 | Garrett Guzman SP RC | 2.00 | 5.00 |
| ☐ 254 | Jeff Verplancke SP RC | 2.00 | 5.00 |
| ☐ 255 | Nate Espy SP RC | 2.00 | 5.00 |
| ☐ 256 | Jeff Lincoln SP RC | 2.00 | 5.00 |
| ☐ 257 | Ryan Snare SP RC | 2.00 | 5.00 |
| ☐ 258 | Jose Ortiz | .30 | .75 |
| ☐ 259 | Denny Bautista | .30 | .75 |
| ☐ 260 | Wily Aybar | .30 | .75 |
| ☐ 261 | Kelly Johnson | 1.25 | 3.00 |
| ☐ 262 | Shawn Fagan | .30 | .75 |
| ☐ 263 | Yurendell DeCaster SP RC | 2.00 | 5.00 |
| ☐ 264 | Mike Peeples SP RC | 2.00 | 5.00 |
| ☐ 265 | Jose Guzman | 1.25 | 3.00 |
| ☐ 266 | Ryan Vogelsong | .30 | .75 |
| ☐ 267 | Jorge Padilla SP RC | 2.00 | 5.00 |
| ☐ 268 | Joe Jester SP RC | 2.00 | 5.00 |
| ☐ 269 | Ryan Church SP RC | 4.00 | 10.00 |
| ☐ 270 | Mitch Jones | .30 | .75 |
| ☐ 271 | Travis Foley SP RC | 2.00 | 5.00 |
| ☐ 272 | Bobby Crosby | 1.25 | 3.00 |
| ☐ 273 | Adrian Gonzalez | .30 | .75 |
| ☐ 274 | Ronnie Merrill | .30 | .75 |
| ☐ 275 | Josh Pineiro | .30 | .75 |
| ☐ 276 | John-Ford Griffin | .30 | .75 |
| ☐ 277 | Brian Forystek SP RC | 2.00 | 5.00 |
| ☐ 278 | Sean Douglass | .30 | .75 |
| ☐ 279 | Manny Delcarmen SP RC | 3.00 | 8.00 |
| ☐ 280 | Jim Kavourias SP RC | 2.00 | 5.00 |
| ☐ 281 | Gabe Gross | .30 | .75 |
| ☐ 282 | Bill Ortega | .30 | .75 |
| ☐ 283 | Joey Hammond SP RC | 2.00 | 5.00 |
| ☐ 284 | Brett Myers | .50 | 1.25 |
| ☐ 285 | Carlos Pena | .30 | .75 |
| ☐ 286 | Ezequiel Astacio SP RC | 2.00 | 5.00 |
| ☐ 287 | Edwin Yan SP RC | 2.00 | 5.00 |
| ☐ 288 | Chris Duffy SP RC | 3.00 | 8.00 |
| ☐ 289 | Jason Kinchen | .30 | .75 |
| ☐ 290 | Rafael Soriano | .30 | .75 |
| ☐ 291 | Colin Young RC | 2.00 | 5.00 |
| ☐ 292 | Eric Byrnes | .30 | .75 |
| ☐ 293 | Chris Narveson SP RC | 3.00 | 8.00 |
| ☐ 294 | John Rheinecker | .30 | .75 |
| ☐ 295 | Mike Wilson SP RC | 2.00 | 5.00 |
| ☐ 296 | Justin Sherrod SP RC | 2.00 | 5.00 |
| ☐ 297 | Denni Mendez | .30 | .75 |
| ☐ 298 | Wily Mo Pena | .50 | 1.25 |
| ☐ 299 | Brett Roneberg SP RC | 2.00 | 5.00 |
| ☐ 300 | Trey Lunsford SP RC | 2.00 | 5.00 |
| ☐ 301 | Christian Parker | .30 | .75 |
| ☐ 302 | Brent Butler | .30 | .75 |
| ☐ 303 | Aaron Rowand | .30 | .75 |
| ☐ 304 | Wilkin Ruan | .30 | .75 |
| ☐ 305 | Kenny Kelly | .30 | .75 |
| ☐ 306 | Cody Ransom | .30 | .75 |
| ☐ 307 | Koyie Hill SP | 2.00 | 5.00 |
| ☐ 308 | Tony Fontana SP RC | 2.00 | 5.00 |

| | | |
|---|---|---|
| ☐ 309 Mark Teixeira | 2.00 | 5.00 |
| ☐ 310 Doug Sessions SP RC | 2.00 | 5.00 |
| ☐ 311 Josh Cisneros SP RC | 2.00 | 5.00 |
| ☐ 312 Carlos Brackley SP RC | 2.00 | 5.00 |
| ☐ 313 Tim Raines Jr. | .30 | .75 |
| ☐ 314 Ross Peeples SP RC | 2.00 | 5.00 |
| ☐ 315 Alex Requena SP RC | 2.00 | 5.00 |
| ☐ 316 Chin-Hui Tsao | .50 | 1.25 |
| ☐ 317 Tony Alvarez | .30 | .75 |
| ☐ 318 Craig Kuzmic SP RC | 2.00 | 5.00 |
| ☐ 319 Pete Zamora SP RC | 2.00 | 5.00 |
| ☐ 320 Matt Parker SP RC | 2.00 | 5.00 |
| ☐ 321 Keith Ginter | .30 | .75 |
| ☐ 322 Gary Cates Jr. SP RC | 2.00 | 5.00 |
| ☐ 323 Matt Belisle | .30 | .75 |
| ☐ 324A Ben Broussard | .30 | .75 |
| ☐ 324B Jake Mauer AU RC | 4.00 | 10.00 |
| ☐ 325 Dennis Tankersley | .30 | .75 |
| ☐ 326 Juan Silvestre | .30 | .75 |
| ☐ 327 Henry Pichardo SP RC | 2.00 | 5.00 |
| ☐ 328 Micheal Floyd SP RC | 2.00 | 5.00 |
| ☐ 329 Clint Nageotte SP RC | 3.00 | 8.00 |
| ☐ 330 Raymond Cabrera SP RC | 2.00 | 5.00 |
| ☐ 331 Mauricio Lara SP RC | 2.00 | 5.00 |
| ☐ 332 Alejandro Cadena SP RC | 2.00 | 5.00 |
| ☐ 333 Jonny Gomes SP RC | 6.00 | 15.00 |
| ☐ 334 Jason Bulger SP RC | 2.00 | 5.00 |
| ☐ 335 Nate Teut | .30 | .75 |
| ☐ 336 David Gil SP RC | 2.00 | 5.00 |
| ☐ 337 Joel Crump SP RC | 2.00 | 5.00 |
| ☐ 338 Brandon Phillips | .30 | .75 |
| ☐ 339 Macay McBride | .50 | 1.25 |
| ☐ 340 Brandon Claussen | .30 | .75 |
| ☐ 341 Josh Phelps | .30 | .75 |
| ☐ 342 Freddie Money SP RC | 2.00 | 5.00 |
| ☐ 343 Cliff Bartosh SP RC | 2.00 | 5.00 |
| ☐ 344 Terrance Hill SP RC | 2.00 | 5.00 |
| ☐ 345 John Rodriguez SP RC | 3.00 | 8.00 |
| ☐ 346 Chris Latham SP RC | 2.00 | 5.00 |
| ☐ 347 Carlos Cabrera SP RC | 2.00 | 5.00 |
| ☐ 348 Jose Bautista SP RC | 4.00 | 10.00 |
| ☐ 349 Kevin Frederick SP RC | 2.00 | 5.00 |
| ☐ 350 Jerome Williams | .30 | .75 |
| ☐ 351 Napoleon Calzado SP RC | 2.00 | 5.00 |
| ☐ 352 Benito Baez SP | 2.00 | 5.00 |
| ☐ 353 Xavier Nady | .30 | .75 |
| ☐ 354 Jason Botts SP RC | 3.00 | 8.00 |
| ☐ 355 Steve Bechler SP RC | 2.00 | 5.00 |
| ☐ 356 Reed Johnson SP RC | 4.00 | 10.00 |
| ☐ 357 Mark Outlaw SP RC | 2.00 | 5.00 |
| ☐ 358 Jake Peavy | .75 | 2.00 |
| ☐ 359 Josh Shaffer SP RC | 2.00 | 5.00 |
| ☐ 360 Dan Wright SP | 2.00 | 5.00 |
| ☐ 361 Ryan Gripp SP RC | 2.00 | 5.00 |
| ☐ 362 Nelson Castro SP RC | 2.00 | 5.00 |
| ☐ 363 Jason Bay SP RC | 6.00 | 15.00 |
| ☐ 364 Franklyn German SP RC | 2.00 | 5.00 |
| ☐ 365 Corwin Malone SP RC | 2.00 | 5.00 |
| ☐ 366 Kelly Ramos SP RC | 2.00 | 5.00 |
| ☐ 367 John Ennis SP RC | 2.00 | 5.00 |
| ☐ 368 George Perez SP | 2.00 | 5.00 |
| ☐ 369 Rene Reyes SP RC | 2.00 | 5.00 |
| ☐ 370 Rolando Viera SP RC | 2.00 | 5.00 |
| ☐ 371 Earl Snyder SP RC | 2.00 | 5.00 |
| ☐ 372 Kyle Kane SP RC | 2.00 | 5.00 |
| ☐ 373 Mario Ramos SP RC | 2.00 | 5.00 |
| ☐ 374 Tyler Yates SP RC | 2.00 | 5.00 |
| ☐ 375 Jason Young SP RC | 2.00 | 5.00 |
| ☐ 376 Chris Bootcheck SP RC | 2.00 | 5.00 |
| ☐ 377 Jesus Cota SP RC | 2.00 | 5.00 |
| ☐ 378 Corky Miller SP | 2.00 | 5.00 |
| ☐ 379 Matt Erickson SP RC | 2.00 | 5.00 |
| ☐ 380 Justin Huber SP RC | 4.00 | 10.00 |
| ☐ 381 Felix Escalona SP RC | 2.00 | 5.00 |
| ☐ 382 Kevin Cash SP RC | 2.00 | 5.00 |
| ☐ 383 J.J. Putz SP RC | 3.00 | 8.00 |
| ☐ 384 Chris Snelling AU A RC | 8.00 | 20.00 |
| ☐ 385 David Wright AU A RC | 125.00 | 250.00 |
| ☐ 386 Brian Wolfe AU A RC | 4.00 | 10.00 |
| ☐ 387 Justin Reid AU A RC | 4.00 | 10.00 |
| ☐ 388 Ryan Rabum AU A RC | 4.00 | 10.00 |
| ☐ 390 Josh Barfield AU A RC | 25.00 | 50.00 |
| ☐ 391 Joe Mauer AU A RC | 100.00 | 175.00 |
| ☐ 392 Bobby Jenks AU A RC | 4.00 | 10.00 |
| ☐ 393 Rob Henkel AU A RC | 4.00 | 10.00 |
| ☐ 394 Jimmy Gobble AU A RC | 4.00 | 10.00 |
| ☐ 395 Jesse Foppert AU A RC | 4.00 | 10.00 |
| ☐ 396 Gavin Floyd AU A RC | 6.00 | 15.00 |

| | | |
|---|---|---|
| ☐ 397 Nate Field AU A RC | 4.00 | 10.00 |
| ☐ 398 Ryan Doumit AU A RC | 6.00 | 15.00 |
| ☐ 399 Ron Calloway AU A RC | 4.00 | 10.00 |
| ☐ 401 Adam Roller AU A RC | 4.00 | 10.00 |
| ☐ 402 Cole Barthel AU A RC | 4.00 | 10.00 |
| ☐ 403A Kazuhisa Ishii SP RC | 3.00 | 8.00 |
| ☐ 403A Kazuhisa Ishii AU B | 30.00 | 50.00 |
| ☐ 404 So Taguchi SP RC | 3.00 | 8.00 |
| ☐ 404A So Taguchi AU B | 30.00 | 50.00 |
| ☐ 405 Chris Baker AU A RC | 4.00 | 10.00 |

## 2002 Bowman Chrome Draft

| | | |
|---|---|---|
| ☐ COMPLETE SET (175) | 200.00 | 350.00 |
| ☐ COMP.SET w/o AU's (165) | 135.00 | 200.00 |
| ☐ COMMON CARD (1-165) | .15 | .40 |
| ☐ COMMON CARD (166-175) | 4.00 | 10.00 |
| ☐ 1 Clint Everts RC | .60 | 1.50 |
| ☐ 2 Fred Lewis RC | .40 | 1.00 |
| ☐ 3 Jon Broxton RC | 1.25 | 3.00 |
| ☐ 4 Jeson Anderson RC | .40 | 1.00 |
| ☐ 5 Mike Eusebio RC | .40 | 1.00 |
| ☐ 6 Zack Greinke RC | 5.30 | 12.00 |
| ☐ 7 Joe Blanton RC | 2.00 | 5.00 |
| ☐ 8 Sergio Santos RC | .60 | 1.50 |
| ☐ 9 Jason Cooper RC | .40 | 1.00 |
| ☐ 10 Delwyn Young RC | 1.25 | 3.00 |
| ☐ 11 Jeremy Hermida RC | 5.00 | 12.00 |
| ☐ 12 Dan Ortmeier RC | .60 | 1.50 |
| ☐ 13 Kevin Jepsen RC | .40 | 1.00 |
| ☐ 14 Russ Adams RC | .60 | 1.50 |
| ☐ 15 Mike Nixon RC | .40 | 1.00 |
| ☐ 16 Nick Swisher RC | 6.00 | 15.00 |
| ☐ 17 Cole Hamels RC | 15.00 | 40.00 |
| ☐ 18 Brian Dopirak RC | 1.25 | 3.00 |
| ☐ 19 James Loney RC | 5.00 | 12.00 |
| ☐ 20 Denard Span RC | 1.50 | 4.00 |
| ☐ 21 Billy Petrick RC | .40 | 1.00 |
| ☐ 22 Jared Doyle RC | .40 | 1.00 |
| ☐ 23 Jeff Francoeur RC | 20.00 | 40.00 |
| ☐ 24 Nick Bourgeois RC | .40 | 1.00 |
| ☐ 25 Matt Cain RC | 6.00 | 15.00 |
| ☐ 26 John McCurdy RC | .40 | 1.00 |
| ☐ 27 Mark Kiger RC | .40 | 1.00 |
| ☐ 28 Bill Murphy RC | .40 | 1.00 |
| ☐ 29 Matt Craig RC | .60 | 1.50 |
| ☐ 30 Mike Megrew RC | .40 | 1.00 |
| ☐ 31 Ben Crockett RC | .40 | 1.00 |
| ☐ 32 Luke Hagerty RC | .40 | 1.00 |
| ☐ 33 Matt Whitney RC | .40 | 1.00 |
| ☐ 34 Dan Meyer RC | .60 | 1.50 |
| ☐ 35 Jeremy Brown RC | .40 | 1.00 |
| ☐ 36 Doug Johnson RC | .40 | 1.00 |
| ☐ 37 Steve Obenchain RC | .40 | 1.00 |
| ☐ 38 Matt Clanton RC | .40 | 1.00 |
| ☐ 39 Mark Teahen RC | 1.25 | 3.00 |
| ☐ 40 Tom Carrow RC | .40 | 1.00 |
| ☐ 41 Micah Schilling RC | .40 | 1.00 |
| ☐ 42 Blair Johnson RC | .40 | 1.00 |
| ☐ 43 Jason Pridie RC | .40 | 1.00 |
| ☐ 44 Joey Votto RC | 5.00 | 12.00 |
| ☐ 45 Taber Lee RC | .40 | 1.00 |
| ☐ 46 Adam Peterson RC | .40 | 1.00 |
| ☐ 47 Adam Donachie RC | .40 | 1.00 |
| ☐ 48 Josh Murray RC | .40 | 1.00 |
| ☐ 49 Brent Clevlen RC | 2.50 | 6.00 |
| ☐ 50 Chad Pleiness RC | .40 | 1.00 |
| ☐ 51 Zach Hammes RC | .40 | 1.00 |
| ☐ 52 Chris Snyder RC | .60 | 1.50 |
| ☐ 53 Chris Smith RC | .40 | 1.00 |
| ☐ 54 Justin Maureau RC | .40 | 1.00 |
| ☐ 55 David Bush RC | 1.25 | 3.00 |
| ☐ 56 Tim Gilhooly RC | .40 | 1.00 |
| ☐ 57 Blair Barbier RC | .40 | 1.00 |

| | | |
|---|---|---|
| ☐ 58 Zach Segovia RC | .40 | 1.00 |
| ☐ 59 Jeremy Reed RC | 1.25 | 3.00 |
| ☐ 60 Matt Pender RC | .40 | 1.00 |
| ☐ 61 Eric Thomas RC | .40 | 1.00 |
| ☐ 62 Justin Jones RC | .60 | 1.50 |
| ☐ 63 Brian Slocum RC | .40 | 1.00 |
| ☐ 64 Larry Broadway RC | .40 | 1.00 |
| ☐ 65 Bo Flowers RC | .40 | 1.00 |
| ☐ 66 Scott White RC | .40 | 1.00 |
| ☐ 67 Steve Stanley RC | .40 | 1.00 |
| ☐ 68 Alex Merricks RC | .40 | 1.00 |
| ☐ 69 Josh Womack RC | .40 | 1.00 |
| ☐ 70 Dave Jensen RC | .40 | 1.00 |
| ☐ 71 Curtis Granderson RC | 5.00 | 12.00 |
| ☐ 72 Pat Osborn RC | .40 | 1.00 |
| ☐ 73 Nic Carter RC | .40 | 1.00 |
| ☐ 74 Mitch Talbot RC | .40 | 1.00 |
| ☐ 75 Don Murphy RC | .40 | 1.00 |
| ☐ 76 Val Majewski RC | .40 | 1.00 |
| ☐ 77 Jawy Rodriguez RC | .40 | 1.00 |
| ☐ 78 Fernando Pacheco RC | .40 | 1.00 |
| ☐ 79 Steve Russell RC | .40 | 1.00 |
| ☐ 80 Jon Slack RC | .40 | 1.00 |
| ☐ 81 John Baker RC | .40 | 1.00 |
| ☐ 82 Aaron Coonrod RC | .40 | 1.00 |
| ☐ 83 Josh Johnson RC | 4.00 | 10.00 |
| ☐ 84 Jake Blalock RC | .60 | 1.50 |
| ☐ 85 Alex Hart RC | .40 | 1.00 |
| ☐ 86 Wes Bankston RC | 2.50 | 6.00 |
| ☐ 87 Josh Rupe RC | .40 | 1.00 |
| ☐ 88 Dan Cevette RC | .40 | 1.00 |
| ☐ 89 Kiel Fisher RC | .60 | 1.50 |
| ☐ 90 Alan Rick RC | .40 | 1.00 |
| ☐ 91 Charlie Morton RC | .40 | 1.00 |
| ☐ 92 Chad Spann RC | .40 | 1.00 |
| ☐ 93 Kyle Boyer RC | .40 | 1.00 |
| ☐ 94 Bob Malek RC | .40 | 1.00 |
| ☐ 95 Ryan Rodriguez RC | .40 | 1.00 |
| ☐ 96 Jordan Renz RC | .40 | 1.00 |
| ☐ 97 Randy Frye RC | .40 | 1.00 |
| ☐ 98 Rich Hill RC | 5.00 | 12.00 |
| ☐ 99 B.J. Upton RC | 5.00 | 12.00 |
| ☐ 100 Dan Christensen RC | .40 | 1.00 |
| ☐ 101 Casey Kotchman RC | 2.50 | 6.00 |
| ☐ 102 Eric Good RC | .40 | 1.00 |
| ☐ 103 Mike Fontenot RC | .40 | 1.00 |
| ☐ 104 John Webb RC | .40 | 1.00 |
| ☐ 105 Jason Dubois RC | .60 | 1.50 |
| ☐ 106 Ryan Kibler RC | .40 | 1.00 |
| ☐ 107 Jhonny Peralta RC | 3.00 | 8.00 |
| ☐ 108 Kirk Saarloos RC | .40 | 1.00 |
| ☐ 109 Rhett Parrott RC | .40 | 1.00 |
| ☐ 110 Jason Grove RC | .40 | 1.00 |
| ☐ 111 Colt Griffin RC | .40 | 1.00 |
| ☐ 112 Dallas McPherson RC | 1.25 | 3.00 |
| ☐ 113 Oliver Perez RC | 1.25 | 3.00 |
| ☐ 114 Marshall McDougall RC | .40 | 1.00 |
| ☐ 115 Mike Wood RC | .40 | 1.00 |
| ☐ 116 Scott Hairston RC | .60 | 1.50 |
| ☐ 117 Jason Simontacchi RC | .40 | 1.00 |
| ☐ 118 Taggert Buzzied RC | .60 | 1.50 |
| ☐ 119 Shelley Duncan RC | 4.00 | 10.00 |
| ☐ 120 Dontrelle Willis RC | 6.00 | 15.00 |
| ☐ 121 Sean Burnett | .15 | .40 |
| ☐ 122 Aaron Cook | .25 | .60 |
| ☐ 123 Brett Evert | .15 | .40 |
| ☐ 124 Jimmy Journell | .15 | .40 |
| ☐ 125 Brett Myers | .25 | .60 |
| ☐ 126 Brad Baker | .15 | .40 |
| ☐ 127 Billy Traber RC | .40 | 1.00 |
| ☐ 128 Adam Wainwright | .25 | .60 |
| ☐ 129 Jason Young | .15 | .40 |
| ☐ 130 John Buck | .15 | .40 |
| ☐ 131 Kevin Cash | .40 | 1.00 |
| ☐ 132 Jason Stokes RC | .60 | 1.50 |
| ☐ 133 Drew Henson | .15 | .40 |
| ☐ 134 Chad Tracy RC | 2.00 | 5.00 |
| ☐ 135 Orlando Hudson | .15 | .40 |
| ☐ 136 Brandon Phillips | .15 | .40 |
| ☐ 137 Joe Borchard | .15 | .40 |
| ☐ 138 Marlon Byrd | .15 | .40 |
| ☐ 139 Carl Crawford | .25 | .60 |
| ☐ 140 Michael Restovich | .15 | .40 |
| ☐ 141 Corey Hart RC | 2.00 | 5.00 |
| ☐ 142 Edwin Almonte | .25 | .60 |
| ☐ 143 Francis Beltran RC | .40 | 1.00 |
| ☐ 144 Jorge De La Rosa RC | .40 | 1.00 |
| ☐ 145 Gerardo Garcia RC | .40 | 1.00 |

|  |  | | |
|---|---|---|---|
| 146 | Franklyn German RC | .40 | 1.00 |
| 147 | Francisco Liriano | 4.00 | 10.00 |
| 148 | Francisco Rodriguez | .25 | .60 |
| 149 | Ricardo Rodriguez | .15 | .40 |
| 150 | Seung Song | .15 | .40 |
| 151 | John Stephens | .15 | .40 |
| 152 | Justin Huber RC | 1.00 | 2.50 |
| 153 | Victor Martinez | .60 | 1.50 |
| 154 | Hee Seop Choi | .15 | .40 |
| 155 | Justin Morneau | .25 | .60 |
| 156 | Miguel Cabrera | 1.00 | 2.50 |
| 157 | Victor Diaz RC | 1.00 | 2.50 |
| 158 | Jose Reyes | .40 | 1.00 |
| 159 | Omar Infante | .15 | .40 |
| 160 | Angel Berroa | .15 | .40 |
| 161 | Tony Alvarez | .15 | .40 |
| 162 | Shin Soo Choo RC | 1.00 | 2.50 |
| 163 | Wily Mo Pena | .25 | .60 |
| 164 | Andres Torres | .15 | .40 |
| 165 | Jose Lopez RC | 2.50 | 6.00 |
| 166 | Scott Moore AU RC | 4.00 | 10.00 |
| 167 | Chris Gruler AU RC | 4.00 | 10.00 |
| 168 | Joe Saunders AU RC | 5.00 | 12.00 |
| 169 | Jeff Francis AU RC | 6.00 | 15.00 |
| 170 | Royce Ring AU RC | 4.00 | 10.00 |
| 171 | Greg Miller AU RC | 6.00 | 15.00 |
| 172 | Brandon Weeden AU RC | 4.00 | 10.00 |
| 173 | Drew Meyer AU RC | 4.00 | 10.00 |
| 174 | Khalil Greene AU RC | 30.00 | 60.00 |
| 175 | Mark Schramek AU RC | 4.00 | 10.00 |

## 2003 Bowman Chrome

| | | | |
|---|---|---|---|
| | COMPLETE SET (351) | 300.00 | 500.00 |
| | COMP.SET with AU's (331) | 75.00 | 150.00 |
| | COMMON CARD (1-165) | .20 | .50 |
| | COMMON CARD (166-330) | .20 | .50 |
| | COMMON RC (156-330) | .40 | 1.00 |
| | COMP.SET with AU's INCLUDES 351 MAYS | | |
| | MAYS AU IS NOT PART OF 351-CARD SET | | |
| 1 | Garret Anderson | .20 | .50 |
| 2 | Derek Jeter | 1.25 | 3.00 |
| 3 | Gary Sheffield | .20 | .50 |
| 4 | Matt Morris | .20 | .50 |
| 5 | Derek Lowe | .20 | .50 |
| 6 | Andy Van Hekken | .20 | .50 |
| 7 | Sammy Sosa | .50 | 1.25 |
| 8 | Ken Griffey Jr. | .75 | 2.00 |
| 9 | Omar Vizquel | .30 | .75 |
| 10 | Jorge Posada | .20 | .50 |
| 11 | Lance Berkman | .20 | .50 |
| 12 | Mike Sweeney | .20 | .50 |
| 13 | Adrian Beltre | .20 | .50 |
| 14 | Richie Sexson | .20 | .50 |
| 15 | A.J. Pierzynski | .20 | .50 |
| 16 | Bartolo Colon | .20 | .50 |
| 17 | Mike Mussina | .30 | .75 |
| 18 | Paul Byrd | .20 | .50 |
| 19 | Bobby Abreu | .20 | .50 |
| 20 | Miguel Tejada | .20 | .50 |
| 21 | Aramis Ramirez | .20 | .50 |
| 22 | Edgardo Alfonzo | .20 | .50 |
| 23 | Edgar Martinez | .30 | .75 |
| 24 | Albert Pujols | 1.00 | 2.50 |
| 25 | Carl Crawford | .20 | .50 |
| 26 | Eric Hinske | .20 | .50 |
| 27 | Tim Salmon | .30 | .75 |
| 28 | Luis Gonzalez | .20 | .50 |
| 29 | Jay Gibbons | .20 | .50 |
| 30 | John Smoltz | .20 | .50 |
| 31 | Tim Wakefield | .20 | .50 |
| 32 | Mark Prior | .30 | .75 |
| 33 | Magglio Ordonez | .20 | .50 |
| 34 | Adam Dunn | .20 | .50 |
| 35 | Larry Walker | .20 | .50 |
| 36 | Luis Castillo | .20 | .50 |
| 37 | Wade Miller | .20 | .50 |
| 38 | Carlos Beltran | .20 | .50 |
| 39 | Odalis Perez | .20 | .50 |
| 40 | Alex Sanchez | .20 | .50 |
| 41 | Torii Hunter | .20 | .50 |
| 42 | Cliff Floyd | .20 | .50 |
| 43 | Andy Pettitte | .30 | .75 |
| 44 | Francisco Rodriguez | .20 | .50 |
| 45 | Eric Chavez | .20 | .50 |
| 46 | Kevin Millwood | .20 | .50 |
| 47 | Dennis Tankersley | .20 | .50 |
| 48 | Hideo Nomo | .50 | 1.25 |
| 49 | Freddy Garcia | .20 | .50 |
| 50 | Randy Johnson | .50 | 1.25 |
| 51 | Aubrey Huff | .20 | .50 |
| 52 | Carlos Delgado | .20 | .50 |
| 53 | Troy Glaus | .20 | .50 |
| 54 | Junior Spivey | .20 | .50 |
| 55 | Mike Hampton | .20 | .50 |
| 56 | Sidney Ponson | .20 | .50 |
| 57 | Aaron Boone | .20 | .50 |
| 58 | Kerry Wood | .20 | .50 |
| 59 | Willie Harris | .20 | .50 |
| 60 | Nomar Garciaparra | .75 | 2.00 |
| 61 | Todd Helton | .30 | .75 |
| 62 | Mike Lowell | .20 | .50 |
| 63 | Roy Oswalt | .20 | .50 |
| 64 | Raul Ibanez | .20 | .50 |
| 65 | Brian Jordan | .20 | .50 |
| 66 | Geoff Jenkins | .20 | .50 |
| 67 | Jermaine Dye | .20 | .50 |
| 68 | Tom Glavine | .30 | .75 |
| 69 | Bernie Williams | .30 | .75 |
| 70 | Vladimir Guerrero | .50 | 1.25 |
| 71 | Mark Mulder | .20 | .50 |
| 72 | Jimmy Rollins | .20 | .50 |
| 73 | Oliver Perez | .20 | .50 |
| 74 | Rich Aurilia | .20 | .50 |
| 75 | Joel Pineiro | .20 | .50 |
| 76 | J.D. Drew | .20 | .50 |
| 77 | Ivan Rodriguez | .30 | .75 |
| 78 | Josh Phelps | .20 | .50 |
| 79 | Darin Erstad | .20 | .50 |
| 80 | Curt Schilling | .20 | .50 |
| 81 | Paul Lo Duca | .20 | .50 |
| 82 | Marty Cordova | .20 | .50 |
| 83 | Manny Ramirez | .30 | .75 |
| 84 | Bobby Hill | .20 | .50 |
| 85 | Paul Konerko | .20 | .50 |
| 86 | Austin Kearns | .20 | .50 |
| 87 | Jason Jennings | .20 | .50 |
| 88 | Brad Penny | .20 | .50 |
| 89 | Jeff Bagwell | .30 | .75 |
| 90 | Shawn Green | .20 | .50 |
| 91 | Jason Schmidt | .20 | .50 |
| 92 | Doug Mientkiewicz | .20 | .50 |
| 93 | Jose Vidro | .20 | .50 |
| 94 | Bret Boone | .20 | .50 |
| 95 | Jason Giambi | .20 | .50 |
| 96 | Barry Zito | .20 | .50 |
| 97 | Roy Halladay | .20 | .50 |
| 98 | Pat Burrell | .20 | .50 |
| 99 | Sean Burroughs | .20 | .50 |
| 100 | Barry Bonds | 1.25 | 3.00 |
| 101 | Kazuhiro Sasaki | .20 | .50 |
| 102 | Fernando Vina | .20 | .50 |
| 103 | Chan Ho Park | .20 | .50 |
| 104 | Andruw Jones | .30 | .75 |
| 105 | Adam Kennedy | .20 | .50 |
| 106 | Shea Hillenbrand | .20 | .50 |
| 107 | Greg Maddux | .75 | 2.00 |
| 108 | Jim Edmonds | .20 | .50 |
| 109 | Pedro Martinez | .30 | .75 |
| 110 | Moises Alou | .20 | .50 |
| 111 | Jeff Weaver | .20 | .50 |
| 112 | C.C. Sabathia | .20 | .50 |
| 113 | Robert Fick | .20 | .50 |
| 114 | A.J. Burnett | .20 | .50 |
| 115 | Jeff Kent | .20 | .50 |
| 116 | Kevin Brown | .20 | .50 |
| 117 | Rafael Furcal | .20 | .50 |
| 118 | Cristian Guzman | .20 | .50 |
| 119 | Brad Wilkerson | .20 | .50 |
| 120 | Mike Piazza | .75 | 2.00 |
| 121 | Alfonso Soriano | .20 | .50 |
| 122 | Mark Ellis | .20 | .50 |
| 123 | Vicente Padilla | .20 | .50 |
| 124 | Eric Gagne | .20 | .50 |
| 125 | Ryan Klesko | .20 | .50 |
| 126 | Ichiro Suzuki | 1.00 | 2.50 |
| 127 | Tony Batista | .20 | .50 |
| 128 | Roberto Alomar | .30 | .75 |
| 129 | Alex Rodriguez | .75 | 2.00 |
| 130 | Jim Thome | .30 | .75 |
| 131 | Jarrod Washburn | .20 | .50 |
| 132 | Orlando Hudson | .20 | .50 |
| 133 | Chipper Jones | .50 | 1.25 |
| 134 | Rodrigo Lopez | .20 | .50 |
| 135 | Johnny Damon | .30 | .75 |
| 136 | Matt Clement | .20 | .50 |
| 137 | Frank Thomas | .50 | 1.25 |
| 138 | Ellis Burks | .20 | .50 |
| 139 | Carlos Pena | .20 | .50 |
| 140 | Josh Beckett | .20 | .50 |
| 141 | Joe Randa | .20 | .50 |
| 142 | Brian Giles | .20 | .50 |
| 143 | Kazuhisa Ishii | .20 | .50 |
| 144 | Corey Koskie | .20 | .50 |
| 145 | Orlando Cabrera | .20 | .50 |
| 146 | Mark Buehrle | .20 | .50 |
| 147 | Roger Clemens | 1.00 | 2.50 |
| 148 | Tim Hudson | .20 | .50 |
| 149 | Randy Wolf | .20 | .50 |
| 150 | Josh Fogg | .20 | .50 |
| 151 | Phil Nevin | .20 | .50 |
| 152 | John Olerud | .20 | .50 |
| 153 | Scott Rolen | .30 | .75 |
| 154 | Joe Kennedy | .20 | .50 |
| 155 | Rafael Palmeiro | .30 | .75 |
| 156 | Chad Hutchinson | .20 | .50 |
| 157 | Quincy Carter XRC | .60 | 1.50 |
| 158 | Hee Seop Choi | .60 | 1.50 |
| 159 | Joe Borchard | .20 | .50 |
| 160 | Brandon Phillips | .20 | .50 |
| 161 | Wily Mo Pena | .20 | .50 |
| 162 | Victor Martinez | .30 | .75 |
| 163 | Jason Stokes | .20 | .50 |
| 164 | Ken Harvey | .20 | .50 |
| 165 | Juan Rivera | .20 | .50 |
| 166 | Joe Valentine RC | .60 | 1.50 |
| 167 | Michel Hernandez RC | .60 | 1.50 |
| 168 | Eider Torres RC | .60 | 1.50 |
| 170 | Chris De La Cruz RC | .60 | 1.50 |
| 171 | Ramon Nivar-Martinez RC | .60 | 1.50 |
| 172 | Mike Adams RC | .60 | 1.50 |
| 173 | Justin Arneson RC | .60 | 1.50 |
| 174 | Jamie Athas RC | .60 | 1.50 |
| 175 | Dwaine Bacon RC | .60 | 1.50 |
| 176 | Clint Barmes RC | 1.50 | 4.00 |
| 177 | B.J. Barns RC | .60 | 1.50 |
| 178 | Tyler Johnson RC | .60 | 1.50 |
| 179 | Brandon Webb RC | 6.00 | 15.00 |
| 180 | T.J. Bohn RC | .60 | 1.50 |
| 181 | Ozzie Chavez RC | .60 | 1.50 |
| 182 | Brandon Bowe RC | .60 | 1.50 |
| 183 | Craig Brazell RC | .60 | 1.50 |
| 184 | Dusty Brown RC | .60 | 1.50 |
| 185 | Brian Bruney RC | .75 | 2.00 |
| 186 | Greg Bruso RC | .60 | 1.50 |
| 187 | Jaime Bubela RC | .60 | 1.50 |
| 188 | Matt Diaz RC | 1.25 | 3.00 |
| 189 | Brian Burgamy RC | .60 | 1.50 |
| 190 | Eny Cabreja RC | 2.00 | 5.00 |
| 191 | Daniel Cabrera RC | 1.25 | 3.00 |
| 192 | Ryan Cameron RC | .60 | 1.50 |
| 193 | Lance Caraccioli RC | .60 | 1.50 |
| 194 | David Cash RC | .60 | 1.50 |
| 195 | Bernie Castro RC | .60 | 1.50 |
| 196 | Ismael Castro RC | .75 | 2.00 |
| 197 | Cory Doyne RC | .60 | 1.50 |
| 198 | Jeff Clark RC | .60 | 1.50 |
| 199 | Chris Colton RC | .60 | 1.50 |
| 200 | Dexter Cooper RC | .60 | 1.50 |
| 201 | Callix Crabbe RC | .75 | 2.00 |
| 202 | Chien-Ming Wang RC | 6.00 | 15.00 |
| 203 | Eric Crozier RC | .75 | 2.00 |
| 204 | Nook Logan RC | .75 | 2.00 |
| 205 | David DeJesus RC | 1.25 | 3.00 |
| 206 | Matt DeMarco RC | .60 | 1.50 |
| 207 | Chris Duncan RC | 5.00 | 12.00 |
| 208 | Eric Eckenstahler RC | .60 | 1.50 |
| 209 | Willie Eyre RC | .60 | 1.50 |
| 210 | Evel Bastida-Martinez RC | .60 | 1.50 |
| 211 | Chris Fallon RC | .60 | 1.50 |
| 212 | Mike Flannery RC | .60 | 1.50 |

| | | |
|---|---|---|
| 213 Mike O'Keefe RC | .60 | 1.50 |
| 214 Lew Ford RC | .75 | 2.00 |
| 215 Kason Gabbard RC | .60 | 1.50 |
| 216 Mike Gallo RC | .60 | 1.50 |
| 217 Jairo Garcia RC | .75 | 2.00 |
| 218 Angel Garcia RC | .60 | 1.50 |
| 219 Michael Garciaparra RC | .60 | 1.50 |
| 220 Jeremy Griffiths RC | .60 | 1.50 |
| 221 Dusty Gomon RC | .75 | 2.00 |
| 222 Bryan Grace RC | .60 | 1.50 |
| 223 Tyson Graham RC | .60 | 1.50 |
| 224 Henry Guerrero RC | .60 | 1.50 |
| 225 Franklin Gutierrez RC | 1.50 | 4.00 |
| 226 Carlos Guzman RC | .75 | 2.00 |
| 227 Matthew Hagen RC | .60 | 1.50 |
| 228 Josh Hall RC | .60 | 1.50 |
| 229 Rob Hammock RC | .60 | 1.50 |
| 230 Brendan Harris RC | .75 | 2.00 |
| 231 Gary Harris RC | .60 | 1.50 |
| 232 Clay Hensley RC | .60 | 1.50 |
| 233 Michael Hinckley RC | .60 | 1.50 |
| 234 Luis Hodge RC | .60 | 1.50 |
| 235 Donnie Hood RC | .75 | 2.00 |
| 236 Matt Hensley RC | .60 | 1.50 |
| 237 Edwin Jackson RC | .75 | 2.00 |
| 238 Ardley Jansen RC | .75 | 2.00 |
| 239 Ferenc Jongejan RC | .60 | 1.50 |
| 240 Matt Kata RC | .60 | 1.50 |
| 241 Kazuhiro Takeoka RC | .60 | 1.50 |
| 242 Charlie Manning RC | .60 | 1.50 |
| 243 Il Kim RC | .60 | 1.50 |
| 244 Brennan King RC | .60 | 1.50 |
| 245 Chris Kroski RC | .60 | 1.50 |
| 246 David Martinez RC | .60 | 1.50 |
| 247 Pete LaForest RC | .60 | 1.50 |
| 248 Wil Ledezma RC | .60 | 1.50 |
| 249 Jeremy Bonderman RC | 4.00 | 10.00 |
| 250 Gonzalo Lopez RC | .60 | 1.50 |
| 251 Brian Luderer RC | .60 | 1.50 |
| 252 Ruddy Lugo RC | .60 | 1.50 |
| 253 Wayne Lydon RC | .60 | 1.50 |
| 254 Mark Malaska RC | .60 | 1.50 |
| 255 Andy Marte RC | 4.00 | 10.00 |
| 256 Tyler Martin RC | .60 | 1.50 |
| 257 Branden Florence RC | .60 | 1.50 |
| 258 Aneudis Mateo RC | .60 | 1.50 |
| 259 Derell McCall RC | .60 | 1.50 |
| 260 Elizardo Ramirez RC | .75 | 2.00 |
| 261 Mike McNutt RC | .60 | 1.50 |
| 262 Jacobo Meque RC | .60 | 1.50 |
| 263 Derek Michaelis RC | .60 | 1.50 |
| 264 Aaron Miles RC | .75 | 2.00 |
| 265 Jose Morales RC | .60 | 1.50 |
| 266 Dustin Moseley RC | .60 | 1.50 |
| 267 Adrian Myers RC | .60 | 1.50 |
| 268 Dan Neil RC | .60 | 1.50 |
| 269 Jon Nelson RC | .75 | 2.00 |
| 270 Mike Neu RC | .60 | 1.50 |
| 271 Leigh Neuage RC | .60 | 1.50 |
| 272 Wes O'Brien RC | .60 | 1.50 |
| 273 Trent Oeltjen RC | .75 | 2.00 |
| 274 Tim Olson RC | .60 | 1.50 |
| 275 David Pahucki RC | .60 | 1.50 |
| 276 Nathan Panther RC | .60 | 1.50 |
| 277 Arnie Munoz RC | .60 | 1.50 |
| 278 Dave Pember RC | .60 | 1.50 |
| 279 Jason Perry RC | .75 | 2.00 |
| 280 Matthew Peterson RC | .60 | 1.50 |
| 281 Greg Aquino RC | .60 | 1.50 |
| 282 Jorge Piedra RC | .75 | 2.00 |
| 283 Simon Pond RC | .60 | 1.50 |
| 284 Aaron Rakers RC | .60 | 1.50 |
| 285 Felix Sanchez RC | .60 | 1.50 |
| 286 Manuel Ramirez RC | .75 | 2.00 |
| 287 Kevin Randel RC | .60 | 1.50 |
| 288 Kelly Shoppach RC | 1.25 | 3.00 |
| 289 Prentice Redman RC | .60 | 1.50 |
| 290 Eric Reed RC | .60 | 1.50 |
| 291 Wilton Reynolds RC | .75 | 2.00 |
| 292 Eric Riggs RC | .75 | 2.00 |
| 293 Carlos Rijo RC | .60 | 1.50 |
| 294 Tyler Adamczyk RC | .60 | 1.50 |
| 295 Jon-Mark Sprowl RC | .60 | 1.50 |
| 296 Arturo Rivas RC | .60 | 1.50 |
| 297 Kyle Roat RC | .60 | 1.50 |
| 298 Bubba Nelson RC | .30 | .75 |
| 299 Levi Robinson RC | .60 | 1.50 |
| 300 Ray Sadler RC | .60 | 1.50 |
| 301 Rylan Reed RC | .60 | 1.50 |
| 302 Jon Schuerholz RC | .60 | 1.50 |
| 303 Nobuaki Yoshida RC | .60 | 1.50 |
| 304 Brian Shackelford RC | .60 | 1.50 |
| 305 Bill Simon RC | .60 | 1.50 |
| 306 Haj Turay RC | .40 | 1.00 |
| 307 Sean Smith RC | .75 | 2.00 |
| 308 Ryan Spataro RC | .60 | 1.50 |
| 309 Jemel Spearman RC | .60 | 1.50 |
| 310 Keith Stamler RC | .60 | 1.50 |
| 311 Luke Steidlmayer RC | .60 | 1.50 |
| 312 Adam Stern RC | .40 | 1.00 |
| 313 Jay Sitzman RC | .60 | 1.50 |
| 314 Mike Wodnicki RC | .60 | 1.50 |
| 315 Terry Tiffee RC | .60 | 1.50 |
| 316 Nick Trzesniak RC | .60 | 1.50 |
| 317 Denny Tussen RC | .60 | 1.50 |
| 318 Scott Tyler RC | .75 | 2.00 |
| 319 Shane Victorino RC | 1.50 | 4.00 |
| 320 Doug Waechter RC | .75 | 2.00 |
| 321 Brandon Watson RC | .60 | 1.50 |
| 322 Todd Wellemeyer RC | .60 | 1.50 |
| 323 Eli Whiteside RC | .60 | 1.50 |
| 324 Josh Willingham RC | 1.50 | 4.00 |
| 325 Travis Wong RC | .75 | 2.00 |
| 326 Brian Wright RC | .60 | 1.50 |
| 327 Felix Pie RC | 5.00 | 12.00 |
| 328 Andy Sisco RC | .20 | .50 |
| 329 Dustin Yount RC | .75 | 2.00 |
| 330 Andrew Dominique RC | .60 | 1.50 |
| 331 Brian McCann AU A RC | 20.00 | 50.00 |
| 332 Jose Contreras AU B RC | 30.00 | 60.00 |
| 333 Corey Shafer AU A RC | 4.00 | 10.00 |
| 334 Hanley Ramirez AU A RC | 100.00 | 200.00 |
| 335 Ryan Shealy AU A RC | 4.00 | 10.00 |
| 336 Kevin Youkilis AU A RC | 30.00 | 60.00 |
| 337 Jason Kubel AU A RC | 5.00 | 12.00 |
| 338 Aron Weston AU A RC | 4.00 | 10.00 |
| 338B Rajai Davis AU A ERR | | |
| 339 J.D. Durbin AU A RC | | |
| 340 Gary Schneidmiller AU A RC | 4.00 | 10.00 |
| 341 Travis Ishikawa AU A RC | 4.00 | 10.00 |
| 342 Ben Francisco AU A RC | 4.00 | 10.00 |
| 343 Bobby Basham AU A RC | 4.00 | 10.00 |
| 344 Joey Gomes AU A RC | 4.00 | 10.00 |
| 345 Beau Kemp AU A RC | 4.00 | 10.00 |
| 346 T.Story-Harden AU A RC | 4.00 | 10.00 |
| 347 Daryl Clark AU A RC | 4.00 | 10.00 |
| 348 Bryan Bullington AU A RC | 4.00 | 10.00 |
| 349 Rajai Davis AU A RC | 4.00 | 10.00 |
| 350 Darrell Rasner AU A RC | 4.00 | 10.00 |
| 351 Willie Mays | .75 | 2.00 |
| 351AU Willie Mays AU | 150.00 | 250.00 |

## 2003 Bowman Chrome Draft

| | | |
|---|---|---|
| COMPLETE SET (176) | 400.00 | 550.00 |
| COMP.SET w/o AU's (165) | 50.00 | 100.00 |
| COMMON CARD (1-165) | .15 | .40 |
| COMMON CARD (166-176) | 4.00 | 10.00 |
| 166-176 STATED ODDS 1:41 H/R | | |
| LUBANSKI IS AN SP BY 1000 COPIES | | |
| 1 Dontrelle Willis | .60 | 1.50 |
| 2 Freddy Sanchez | .15 | .40 |
| 3 Miguel Cabrera | .60 | 1.50 |
| 4 Ryan Ludwick | .15 | .40 |
| 5 Ty Wigginton | .15 | .40 |
| 6 Mark Teixeira | .40 | 1.00 |
| 7 Trey Hodges | .15 | .40 |
| 8 Laynce Nix | .25 | .60 |
| 9 Antonio Perez | .15 | .40 |
| 10 Jody Gerut | .15 | .40 |
| 11 Jae Weong Seo | .15 | .40 |
| 12 Erick Almonte | .15 | .40 |
| 13 Lyle Overbay | .15 | .40 |
| 14 Billy Traber | .15 | .40 |
| 15 Andres Torres | .15 | .40 |
| 16 Jose Valverde | .15 | .40 |
| 17 Aaron Heilman | .15 | .40 |
| 18 Brandon Larson | .15 | .40 |
| 19 Jung Bong | .15 | .40 |
| 20 Jesse Foppert | .15 | .40 |
| 21 Angel Berroa | .15 | .40 |
| 22 Jeff DaVanon | .15 | .40 |
| 23 Kurt Ainsworth | .15 | .40 |
| 24 Brandon Claussen | .15 | .40 |
| 25 Xavier Nady | .15 | .40 |
| 26 Travis Hafner | .25 | .60 |
| 27 Jerome Williams | .15 | .40 |
| 28 Jose Reyes | .25 | .60 |
| 29 Sergio Mitre RC | .60 | 1.50 |
| 30 Bo Hart RC | .40 | 1.00 |
| 31 Adam Miller RC | 4.00 | 10.00 |
| 32 Brian Finch RC | .40 | 1.00 |
| 33 Taylor Mattingly RC | .60 | 1.50 |
| 34 Daric Barton RC | 2.50 | 6.00 |
| 35 Chris Ray RC | 1.25 | 3.00 |
| 36 Jarrod Saltalamacchia RC | 6.00 | 15.00 |
| 37 Dennis Dove RC | .60 | 1.50 |
| 38 James Houser RC | .60 | 1.50 |
| 39 Clint King RC | .60 | 1.50 |
| 40 Lou Palmisano RC | .60 | 1.50 |
| 41 Dan Moore RC | .40 | 1.00 |
| 42 Craig Stansberry RC | .60 | 1.50 |
| 43 Jo Jo Reyes RC | 1.25 | 3.00 |
| 44 Jake Stevens RC | .60 | 1.50 |
| 45 Tom Gorzelanny RC | 2.00 | 5.00 |
| 46 Brian Marshall RC | .40 | 1.00 |
| 47 Scott Beerer RC | .40 | 1.00 |
| 48 Javi Herrera RC | .60 | 1.50 |
| 49 Steve LeRud RC | .60 | 1.50 |
| 50 Josh Banks RC | 1.00 | 2.50 |
| 51 Jon Papelbon RC | 6.00 | 15.00 |
| 52 Juan Valdes RC | .60 | 1.50 |
| 53 Beau Vaughan RC | .60 | 1.50 |
| 54 Matt Chico RC | .60 | 1.50 |
| 55 Todd Jennings RC | .60 | 1.50 |
| 56 Anthony Gwynn RC | 1.50 | 4.00 |
| 57 Matt Harrison RC | 1.00 | 2.50 |
| 58 Aaron Marsden RC | .40 | 1.00 |
| 59 Casey Abrams RC | .60 | 1.50 |
| 60 Cory Stuart RC | .40 | 1.00 |
| 61 Mike Wagnes RC | .40 | 1.00 |
| 62 Jordan Pratt RC | .60 | 1.50 |
| 63 Andre Randolph RC | .60 | 1.50 |
| 64 Blake Balkcom RC | .60 | 1.50 |
| 65 Josh Muecke RC | .40 | 1.00 |
| 66 Jamie D'Antona RC | 1.00 | 2.50 |
| 67 Cole Seilfrig RC | .40 | 1.00 |
| 68 Josh Anderson RC | .60 | 1.50 |
| 69 Matt Lorenzo RC | .40 | 1.00 |
| 70 Nate Spears RC | .60 | 1.50 |
| 71 Chris Goodman RC | .40 | 1.00 |
| 72 Brian McFall RC | .60 | 1.50 |
| 73 Billy Hogan RC | .60 | 1.50 |
| 74 Jamie Romak RC | .60 | 1.50 |
| 75 Jeff Cook RC | .50 | 1.50 |
| 76 Brooks McNiven RC | .40 | 1.00 |
| 77 Xavier Paul RC | .60 | 1.50 |
| 78 Bob Zimmerman RC | .40 | 1.00 |
| 79 Mickey Hall RC | .60 | 1.50 |
| 80 Shaun Marcum RC | .60 | 1.50 |
| 81 Matt Nachreiner RC | .60 | 1.50 |
| 82 Chris Kinsey RC | .40 | 1.00 |
| 83 Jonathan Fulton RC | .60 | 1.50 |
| 84 Edgardo Baez RC | .15 | .40 |
| 85 Robert Valido RC | .60 | 1.50 |
| 86 Kenny Lewis RC | .60 | 1.50 |
| 87 Trent Peterson RC | .60 | 1.50 |
| 88 Johnny Woodard RC | .60 | 1.50 |
| 89 Wes Littleton RC | .60 | 1.50 |
| 90 Sean Rodriguez RC | 2.00 | 5.00 |
| 91 Kyle Pearson RC | .60 | 1.50 |
| 92 Josh Rainwater RC | .60 | 1.50 |
| 93 Travis Schlichting RC | .60 | 1.50 |
| 94 Tim Battle RC | 1.00 | 2.50 |
| 95 Aaron Hill RC | 2.00 | 5.00 |
| 96 Bob McCrory RC | .60 | 1.50 |
| 97 Rick Guerno RC | .60 | 1.50 |
| 98 Brandon Yarbrough RC | .60 | 1.50 |
| 99 Peter Stonard RC | .40 | 1.00 |

| | | |
|---|---|---|
| ☐ 100 Darin Downs RC | .60 | 1.50 |
| ☐ 101 Matt Bruback RC | .40 | 1.00 |
| ☐ 102 Danny Garcia RC | .40 | 1.00 |
| ☐ 103 Cory Stewart RC | .40 | 1.00 |
| ☐ 104 Ferdin Tejeda RC | .40 | 1.00 |
| ☐ 105 Kade Johnson RC | .40 | 1.00 |
| ☐ 106 Andrew Brown RC | .60 | 1.50 |
| ☐ 107 Aquilino Lopez RC | .40 | 1.00 |
| ☐ 108 Stephen Randolph RC | .40 | 1.00 |
| ☐ 109 Dave Matranga RC | .40 | 1.00 |
| ☐ 110 Dustin McGowan RC | .60 | 1.50 |
| ☐ 111 Juan Camacho RC | .40 | 1.00 |
| ☐ 112 Cliff Lee | 1.50 | 4.00 |
| ☐ 113 Jeff Duncan RC | .40 | 1.00 |
| ☐ 114 C.J. Wilson | .15 | .40 |
| ☐ 115 Brandon Roberson RC | .40 | 1.00 |
| ☐ 116 David Corrente RC | .40 | 1.00 |
| ☐ 117 Kevin Beavers RC | .40 | 1.00 |
| ☐ 118 Anthony Webster RC | .60 | 1.50 |
| ☐ 119 Oscar Villarreal RC | .40 | 1.00 |
| ☐ 120 Hong-Chih Kuo RC | 3.00 | 8.00 |
| ☐ 121 Josh Barfield | .25 | .60 |
| ☐ 122 Denny Bautista RC | .15 | .40 |
| ☐ 123 Chris Burke RC | 1.50 | 4.00 |
| ☐ 124 Robinson Cano RC | 8.00 | 20.00 |
| ☐ 125 Jose Castillo | .15 | .40 |
| ☐ 126 Neal Cotts | .15 | .40 |
| ☐ 127 Jorge De La Rosa | .15 | .40 |
| ☐ 128 J.D. Durbin | .20 | .50 |
| ☐ 129 Edwin Encarnacion | .75 | 2.00 |
| ☐ 130 Gavin Floyd | .15 | .40 |
| ☐ 131 Alexis Gomez | .15 | .40 |
| ☐ 132 Edgar Gonzalez RC | .40 | 1.00 |
| ☐ 133 Khalil Greene | .60 | 1.50 |
| ☐ 134 Zack Greinke | .25 | .60 |
| ☐ 135 Franklin Gutierrez | .60 | 1.50 |
| ☐ 136 Rich Harden | .40 | 1.00 |
| ☐ 137 J.J. Hardy RC | 4.00 | 10.00 |
| ☐ 138 Ryan Howard RC | 12.50 | 30.00 |
| ☐ 139 Justin Huber | .15 | .40 |
| ☐ 140 David Kelton | .15 | .40 |
| ☐ 141 Dane Krynzel | .15 | .40 |
| ☐ 142 Pete LaForest | .20 | .50 |
| ☐ 143 Adam LaRoche | .15 | .40 |
| ☐ 144 Preston Larrison RC | .40 | 1.00 |
| ☐ 145 John Maine RC | 5.00 | 12.00 |
| ☐ 146 Andy Marte | 1.50 | 4.00 |
| ☐ 147 Jeff Mathis | .15 | .40 |
| ☐ 148 Joe Mauer | .60 | 1.50 |
| ☐ 149 Clint Nageotte | .15 | .40 |
| ☐ 150 Chris Narveson | .15 | .40 |
| ☐ 151 Ramon Nivar | .20 | .50 |
| ☐ 152 Felix Pie | 2.00 | 5.00 |
| ☐ 153 Guillermo Quiroz RC | .40 | 1.00 |
| ☐ 154 Rene Reyes | .15 | .40 |
| ☐ 155 Royce Ring | .15 | .40 |
| ☐ 156 Alexis Rios | 1.25 | 3.00 |
| ☐ 157 Grady Sizemore | .60 | 1.50 |
| ☐ 158 Stephen Smitherman | .15 | .40 |
| ☐ 159 Seung Song | .15 | .40 |
| ☐ 160 Scott Thorman | .15 | .40 |
| ☐ 161 Chad Tracy | .15 | .40 |
| ☐ 162 Chin-Hui Tsao | .25 | .60 |
| ☐ 163 John VanBenschoten | .15 | .40 |
| ☐ 164 Kevin Youkilis | 2.00 | 5.00 |
| ☐ 165 Chien-Ming Wang | 2.50 | 6.00 |
| ☐ 166 Chris Lubanski AU SP RC | 10.00 | 25.00 |
| ☐ 167 Ryan Harvey AU RC | 4.00 | 10.00 |
| ☐ 168 Matt Murton AU RC | 4.00 | 10.00 |
| ☐ 169 Jay Sborz AU RC | 4.00 | 10.00 |
| ☐ 170 Brandon Wood AU RC | 20.00 | 50.00 |
| ☐ 171 Nick Markakis AU RC | 40.00 | 80.00 |
| ☐ 172 Rickie Weeks AU RC | 10.00 | 25.00 |
| ☐ 173 Eric Duncan AU RC | 6.00 | 15.00 |
| ☐ 174 Chad Billingsley AU RC | 20.00 | 50.00 |
| ☐ 175 Ryan Wagner AU RC | 4.00 | 10.00 |
| ☐ 176 Delmon Young AU RC | 30.00 | 60.00 |

## 2004 Bowman Chrome

| | | |
|---|---|---|
| ☐ COMPLETE SET (350) | 250.00 | 400.00 |
| ☐ COMP.SET w/o AU's (330) | 60.00 | 120.00 |
| ☐ COMMON CARD (1-150) | .20 | .50 |
| ☐ COMMON CARD (151-165) | .20 | .50 |
| ☐ COMMON AUTO (331-350) | 4.00 | 10.00 |
| ☐ 331-350 AU'S ARE NOT SERIAL-NUMBERED | | |
| ☐ 331-350 PRINT RUN PROVIDED BY TOPPS | | |
| ☐ 1 Garret Anderson | .20 | .50 |
| ☐ 2 Larry Walker | .20 | .50 |
| ☐ 3 Derek Jeter | 1.00 | 2.50 |
| ☐ 4 Curt Schilling | .30 | .75 |
| ☐ 5 Carlos Zambrano | .20 | .50 |
| ☐ 6 Shawn Green | .20 | .50 |
| ☐ 7 Manny Ramirez | .30 | .75 |
| ☐ 8 Randy Johnson | .50 | 1.25 |
| ☐ 9 Jeremy Bonderman | .20 | .50 |
| ☐ 10 Alfonso Soriano | .20 | .50 |
| ☐ 11 Scott Rolen | .20 | .50 |
| ☐ 12 Kerry Wood | .20 | .50 |
| ☐ 13 Eric Gagne | .20 | .50 |
| ☐ 14 Ryan Klesko | .20 | .50 |
| ☐ 15 Kevin Millar | .20 | .50 |
| ☐ 16 Ty Wigginton | .20 | .50 |
| ☐ 17 David Ortiz | .50 | 1.25 |
| ☐ 18 Luis Castillo | .20 | .50 |
| ☐ 19 Bernie Williams | .30 | .75 |
| ☐ 20 Edgar Renteria | .20 | .50 |
| ☐ 21 Matt Kata | .20 | .50 |
| ☐ 22 Bartolo Colon | .20 | .50 |
| ☐ 23 Derrek Lee | .30 | .75 |
| ☐ 24 Gary Sheffield | .30 | .75 |
| ☐ 25 Nomar Garciaparra | .75 | 2.00 |
| ☐ 26 Kevin Millwood | .20 | .50 |
| ☐ 27 Corey Patterson | .20 | .50 |
| ☐ 28 Carlos Beltran | .20 | .50 |
| ☐ 29 Mike Lieberthal | .20 | .50 |
| ☐ 30 Troy Glaus | .20 | .50 |
| ☐ 31 Preston Wilson | .20 | .50 |
| ☐ 32 Jorge Posada | .30 | .75 |
| ☐ 33 Bo Hart | .20 | .50 |
| ☐ 34 Mark Prior | .30 | .75 |
| ☐ 35 Hideo Nomo | .50 | 1.25 |
| ☐ 36 Jason Kendall | .20 | .50 |
| ☐ 37 Roger Clemens | 1.00 | 2.50 |
| ☐ 38 Dmitri Young | .20 | .50 |
| ☐ 39 Jason Giambi | .20 | .50 |
| ☐ 40 Jim Edmonds | .20 | .50 |
| ☐ 41 Ryan Ludwick | .20 | .50 |
| ☐ 42 Brandon Webb | .20 | .50 |
| ☐ 43 Todd Helton | .30 | .75 |
| ☐ 44 Jacque Jones | .20 | .50 |
| ☐ 45 Jamie Moyer | .20 | .50 |
| ☐ 46 Tim Salmon | .30 | .75 |
| ☐ 47 Kelvim Escobar | .20 | .50 |
| ☐ 48 Tony Batista | .20 | .50 |
| ☐ 49 Nick Johnson | .20 | .50 |
| ☐ 50 Jim Thome | .30 | .75 |
| ☐ 51 Casey Blake | .20 | .50 |
| ☐ 52 Trot Nixon | .20 | .50 |
| ☐ 53 Luis Gonzalez | .30 | .75 |
| ☐ 54 Dontrelle Willis | .30 | .75 |
| ☐ 55 Mike Mussina | .30 | .75 |
| ☐ 56 Carl Crawford | .30 | .75 |
| ☐ 57 Mark Buehrle | .20 | .50 |
| ☐ 58 Scott Podsednik | .20 | .50 |
| ☐ 59 Brian Giles | .20 | .50 |
| ☐ 60 Rafael Furcal | .20 | .50 |
| ☐ 61 Miguel Cabrera | .50 | 1.25 |
| ☐ 62 Mark Teixeira | .30 | .75 |
| ☐ 63 Mark Teixeira | .50 | 1.25 |
| ☐ 64 Frank Thomas | .50 | 1.25 |
| ☐ 65 Johan Santana | .50 | 1.25 |

| | | |
|---|---|---|
| ☐ 66 Jason Schmidt | .20 | .50 |
| ☐ 67 Aramis Ramirez | .20 | .50 |
| ☐ 68 Jose Reyes | .20 | .50 |
| ☐ 69 Magglio Ordonez | .20 | .50 |
| ☐ 70 Mike Sweeney | .20 | .50 |
| ☐ 71 Eric Chavez | .20 | .50 |
| ☐ 72 Rocco Baldelli | .20 | .50 |
| ☐ 73 Sammy Sosa | .50 | 1.25 |
| ☐ 74 Javy Lopez | .20 | .50 |
| ☐ 75 Roy Oswalt | .20 | .50 |
| ☐ 76 Raul Ibanez | .20 | .50 |
| ☐ 77 Ivan Rodriguez | .30 | .75 |
| ☐ 78 Jerome Williams | .20 | .50 |
| ☐ 79 Carlos Lee | .20 | .50 |
| ☐ 80 Geoff Jenkins | .20 | .50 |
| ☐ 81 Sean Burroughs | .20 | .50 |
| ☐ 82 Marcus Giles | .20 | .50 |
| ☐ 83 Mike Lowell | .20 | .50 |
| ☐ 84 Barry Zito | .20 | .50 |
| ☐ 85 Aubrey Huff | .20 | .50 |
| ☐ 86 Esteban Loaiza | .20 | .50 |
| ☐ 87 Torii Hunter | .20 | .50 |
| ☐ 88 Phil Nevin | .20 | .50 |
| ☐ 89 Andruw Jones | .30 | .75 |
| ☐ 90 Josh Beckett | .20 | .50 |
| ☐ 91 Mark Mulder | .20 | .50 |
| ☐ 92 Hank Blalock | .20 | .50 |
| ☐ 93 Jason Phillips | .20 | .50 |
| ☐ 94 Russ Ortiz | .20 | .50 |
| ☐ 95 Juan Pierre | .20 | .50 |
| ☐ 96 Tom Glavine | .30 | .75 |
| ☐ 97 Gil Meche | .20 | .50 |
| ☐ 98 Ramon Ortiz | .20 | .50 |
| ☐ 99 Richie Sexson | .20 | .50 |
| ☐ 100 Albert Pujols | 1.00 | 2.50 |
| ☐ 101 Javier Vazquez | .20 | .50 |
| ☐ 102 Johnny Damon | .30 | .75 |
| ☐ 103 Alex Rodriguez | .75 | 2.00 |
| ☐ 104 Omar Vizquel | .30 | .75 |
| ☐ 105 Chipper Jones | .50 | 1.25 |
| ☐ 106 Lance Berkman | .20 | .50 |
| ☐ 107 Tim Hudson | .20 | .50 |
| ☐ 108 Carlos Delgado | .20 | .50 |
| ☐ 109 Austin Kearns | .20 | .50 |
| ☐ 110 Orlando Cabrera | .20 | .50 |
| ☐ 111 Edgar Martinez | .30 | .75 |
| ☐ 112 Melvin Mora | .20 | .50 |
| ☐ 113 Jeff Bagwell | .30 | .75 |
| ☐ 114 Marlon Byrd | .20 | .50 |
| ☐ 115 Vernon Wells | .20 | .50 |
| ☐ 116 C.C. Sabathia | .20 | .50 |
| ☐ 117 Cliff Floyd | .20 | .50 |
| ☐ 118 Ichiro Suzuki | 1.00 | 2.50 |
| ☐ 119 Miguel Olivo | .20 | .50 |
| ☐ 120 Mike Piazza | .75 | 2.00 |
| ☐ 121 Adam Dunn | .20 | .50 |
| ☐ 122 Paul Lo Duca | .20 | .50 |
| ☐ 123 Brett Myers | .20 | .50 |
| ☐ 124 Michael Young | .20 | .50 |
| ☐ 125 Sidney Ponson | .20 | .50 |
| ☐ 126 Greg Maddux | .75 | 2.00 |
| ☐ 127 Vladimir Guerrero | .50 | 1.25 |
| ☐ 128 Miguel Tejada | .20 | .50 |
| ☐ 129 Andy Pettitte | .30 | .75 |
| ☐ 130 Rafael Palmeiro | .30 | .75 |
| ☐ 131 Ken Griffey Jr. | .75 | 2.00 |
| ☐ 132 Shannon Stewart | .20 | .50 |
| ☐ 133 Joel Pineiro | .20 | .50 |
| ☐ 134 Luis Matos | .20 | .50 |
| ☐ 135 Jeff Kent | .20 | .50 |
| ☐ 136 Randy Wolf | .20 | .50 |
| ☐ 137 Chris Woodward | .20 | .50 |
| ☐ 138 Jody Gerut | .20 | .50 |
| ☐ 139 Jose Vidro | .20 | .50 |
| ☐ 140 Bret Boone | .20 | .50 |
| ☐ 141 Bill Mueller | .20 | .50 |
| ☐ 142 Angel Berroa | .20 | .50 |
| ☐ 143 Bobby Abreu | .20 | .50 |
| ☐ 144 Roy Halladay | .20 | .50 |
| ☐ 145 Delmon Young | .30 | .75 |
| ☐ 146 Jonny Gomes | .20 | .50 |
| ☐ 147 Rickie Weeks | .20 | .50 |
| ☐ 148 Edwin Jackson | .20 | .50 |
| ☐ 149 Neal Cotts | .20 | .50 |
| ☐ 150 Jason Bay | .20 | .50 |
| ☐ 151 Khalil Greene | .40 | 1.00 |
| ☐ 152 Joe Mauer | .50 | 1.25 |
| ☐ 153 Bobby Jenks | .30 | .75 |

|  |  | | |
|---|---|---|---|
| 154 | Chin-Feng Chen | .20 | .50 |
| 155 | Chien-Ming Wang | .75 | 2.00 |
| 156 | Mickey Hall | .20 | .50 |
| 157 | James Houser | .20 | .50 |
| 158 | Jay Sborz | .20 | .50 |
| 159 | Jonathan Fulton | .20 | .50 |
| 160 | Steven Lerud | .20 | .50 |
| 161 | Grady Sizemore | .60 | 1.50 |
| 162 | Felix Pie | .75 | 2.00 |
| 163 | Dustin McGowan | .40 | 1.00 |
| 164 | Chris Lubanski | .30 | .75 |
| 165 | Tom Gorzelanny | .20 | .50 |
| 166 | Rudy Guillen RC | 1.25 | 3.00 |
| 167 | Aarom Baldiris RC | .75 | 2.00 |
| 168 | Conor Jackson RC | 4.00 | 10.00 |
| 169 | Matt Moses RC | 1.50 | 4.00 |
| 170 | Ervin Santana RC | 2.50 | 6.00 |
| 171 | Marvin Valdez RC | .75 | 2.00 |
| 172 | Erick Aybar RC | 1.25 | 3.00 |
| 173 | Brad Sullivan RC | .75 | 2.00 |
| 174 | Joey Gathright RC | 1.50 | 4.00 |
| 175 | Brad Snyder RC | 1.50 | 4.00 |
| 176 | Alberto Callaspo RC | 1.25 | 3.00 |
| 177 | Brandon Medders RC | .60 | 1.50 |
| 178 | Zach Miner RC | 2.00 | 5.00 |
| 179 | Charlie Zink RC | .40 | 1.00 |
| 180 | Adam Greenberg RC | 1.25 | 3.00 |
| 181 | Kevin Howard RC | .75 | 2.00 |
| 182 | Wanell Severino RC | .40 | 1.00 |
| 183 | Chin-Lung Hu RC | 2.00 | 5.00 |
| 184 | Joel Zumaya RC | 5.00 | 12.00 |
| 185 | Skip Schumaker RC | .60 | 1.50 |
| 186 | Nic Ungs RC | .60 | 1.50 |
| 187 | Todd Self RC | .75 | 2.00 |
| 188 | Brian Stavisk RC | .40 | 1.00 |
| 189 | Brock Peterson RC | .60 | 1.50 |
| 190 | Greg Thissen RC | .60 | 1.50 |
| 191 | Frank Brooks RC | .40 | 1.00 |
| 192 | Scott Olsen RC | 2.50 | 6.00 |
| 193 | Chris Mabeus RC | .60 | 1.50 |
| 194 | Dan Giese RC | .60 | 1.50 |
| 195 | Jared Wells RC | .40 | 1.00 |
| 196 | Carlos Sosa RC | .60 | 1.50 |
| 197 | Bobby Madritsch RC | .40 | 1.00 |
| 198 | Calvin Hayes RC | .75 | 2.00 |
| 199 | Omar Quintanilla RC | .75 | 2.00 |
| 200 | Chris O'Riordan RC | .60 | 1.50 |
| 201 | Tim Hutting RC | .40 | 1.00 |
| 202 | Carlos Quentin RC | 4.00 | 10.00 |
| 203 | Brayan Pena RC | .60 | 1.50 |
| 204 | Jeff Salazar RC | 1.50 | 4.00 |
| 205 | David Murphy RC | 1.25 | 3.00 |
| 206 | Alberto Garcia RC | .75 | 2.00 |
| 207 | Ramon Ramirez RC | .60 | 1.50 |
| 208 | Luis Bolivar RC | .60 | 1.50 |
| 209 | Rodney Choy Foo RC | .40 | 1.00 |
| 210 | Fausto Carmona RC | 1.50 | 4.00 |
| 211 | Anthony Acevedo RC | .60 | 1.50 |
| 212 | Chad Santos RC | .60 | 1.50 |
| 213 | Jason Frasor RC | .40 | 1.00 |
| 214 | Jesse Roman RC | .40 | 1.00 |
| 215 | James Tomlin RC | .60 | 1.50 |
| 216 | Josh Labandeira RC | .60 | 1.50 |
| 217 | Ryan Meaux RC | .60 | 1.50 |
| 218 | Don Sutton RC | 1.50 | 4.00 |
| 219 | Danny Gonzalez RC | .40 | 1.00 |
| 220 | Javier Guzman RC | .75 | 2.00 |
| 221 | Anthony Lerew RC | 1.25 | 3.00 |
| 222 | Jon Connolly RC | 1.50 | 4.00 |
| 223 | Jesse English RC | .60 | 1.50 |
| 224 | Hector Made RC | 1.25 | 3.00 |
| 225 | Travis Hanson RC | .75 | 2.00 |
| 226 | Jesse Floyd RC | .60 | 1.50 |
| 227 | Nick Gorneault RC | .75 | 2.00 |
| 228 | Craig Ansman RC | .60 | 1.50 |
| 229 | Paul McAnulty RC | 1.25 | 3.00 |
| 230 | Carl Loadenthal RC | .75 | 2.00 |
| 231 | Dave Crouthers RC | .40 | 1.00 |
| 232 | Harvey Garcia RC | .40 | 1.00 |
| 233 | Casey Kopitzke RC | .40 | 1.00 |
| 234 | Ricky Nolasco RC | 2.00 | 5.00 |
| 235 | Miguel Perez RC | .60 | 1.50 |
| 236 | Ryan Mulhern RC | .60 | 1.50 |
| 237 | Chris Aguila RC | .60 | 1.50 |
| 238 | Brooks Conrad RC | .75 | 2.00 |
| 239 | Damaso Espino RC | .40 | 1.00 |
| 240 | Jereme Milons RC | .75 | 2.00 |
| 241 | Luke Hughes RC | .40 | 1.00 |
| 242 | Kory Casto RC | .75 | 2.00 |
| 243 | Jose Valdez RC | .60 | 1.50 |
| 244 | J.T. Slotts RC | .40 | 1.00 |
| 245 | Lee Gwaltney RC | .40 | 1.00 |
| 246 | Yoann Torrealba RC | .40 | 1.00 |
| 247 | Omar Falcon RC | .60 | 1.50 |
| 248 | Jon Coutlangus RC | .40 | 1.00 |
| 249 | George Sherrill RC | .60 | 1.50 |
| 250 | John Santor RC | .40 | 1.00 |
| 251 | Tony Richie RC | .60 | 1.50 |
| 252 | Kevin Richardson RC | .40 | 1.00 |
| 253 | Tim Bittner RC | .60 | 1.50 |
| 254 | Chris Saenz RC | .60 | 1.50 |
| 255 | Jose Capellan RC | .75 | 2.00 |
| 256 | Donald Levinski RC | .40 | 1.00 |
| 257 | Jerome Gamble RC | .40 | 1.00 |
| 258 | Jeff Keppinger RC | 2.50 | 6.00 |
| 259 | Jason Szuminski RC | .40 | 1.00 |
| 260 | Akinori Otsuka RC | .60 | 1.50 |
| 261 | Ryan Budde RC | .60 | 1.50 |
| 262 | Marland Williams RC | .75 | 2.00 |
| 263 | Jeff Allison RC | .60 | 1.50 |
| 264 | Hector Gimenez RC | .40 | 1.00 |
| 265 | Tim Frend RC | .60 | 1.50 |
| 266 | Shawn Hill RC | .60 | 1.50 |
| 267 | Tom Farmer RC | .60 | 1.50 |
| 268 | Mike Huggins RC | .60 | 1.50 |
| 269 | Scott Proctor RC | .75 | 2.00 |
| 270 | Jorge Mejia RC | .60 | 1.50 |
| 271 | Terry Jones RC | .75 | 2.00 |
| 272 | Zach Duke RC | 3.00 | 8.00 |
| 273 | Jesse Crain RC | 1.25 | 3.00 |
| 274 | Luke Anderson RC | .40 | 1.00 |
| 275 | Hunter Brown RC | .40 | 1.00 |
| 276 | Matt Lamarocca RC | .60 | 1.50 |
| 277 | Fernando Cortez RC | .40 | 1.00 |
| 278 | Vince Perkins RC | .75 | 2.00 |
| 279 | Tommy Murphy RC | .60 | 1.50 |
| 280 | Mike Gosling RC | .40 | 1.00 |
| 281 | Paul Bacot RC | .75 | 2.00 |
| 282 | Matt Capps RC | .60 | 1.50 |
| 283 | Juan Gutierrez RC | .60 | 1.50 |
| 284 | Teodoro Encamacion RC | .75 | 2.00 |
| 285 | Chad Bentz RC | .60 | 1.50 |
| 286 | Kazuo Matsui RC | .75 | 2.00 |
| 287 | Ryan Hankins RC | .40 | 1.00 |
| 288 | Leo Nunez RC | .60 | 1.50 |
| 289 | Dave Wallace RC | .60 | 1.50 |
| 290 | Rob Tejeda RC | 1.25 | 3.00 |
| 291 | Paul Maholm RC | 1.50 | 4.00 |
| 292 | Casey Daigle RC | .60 | 1.50 |
| 293 | Tydus Meadows RC | .40 | 1.00 |
| 294 | Khalid Ballouli RC | .40 | 1.00 |
| 295 | Benji DeQuin RC | .40 | 1.00 |
| 296 | Tyler Davidson RC | .75 | 2.00 |
| 297 | Brant Colamarino RC | .60 | 1.50 |
| 298 | Marcus McBeth RC | .40 | 1.00 |
| 299 | Brad Eldred RC | .75 | 2.00 |
| 300 | David Pauley RC | 2.00 | 5.00 |
| 301 | Yadier Molina RC | 1.50 | 4.00 |
| 302 | Chris Shelton RC | 2.00 | 5.00 |
| 303 | Nyjer Morgan RC | .40 | 1.00 |
| 304 | Jon DeVries RC | .60 | 1.50 |
| 305 | Sheidon Fulse RC | .40 | 1.00 |
| 306 | Vito Chiaravalloti RC | .60 | 1.50 |
| 307 | Warner Madrigal RC | 1.25 | 3.00 |
| 308 | Reid Gorecki RC | .60 | 1.50 |
| 309 | Sung Jung RC | .40 | 1.00 |
| 310 | Pete Shier RC | .40 | 1.00 |
| 311 | Michael Mooney RC | .60 | 1.50 |
| 312 | Kenny Perez RC | .60 | 1.50 |
| 313 | Michael Mallory RC | .40 | 1.00 |
| 314 | Ben Himes RC | .40 | 1.00 |
| 315 | Ivan Ochoa RC | .60 | 1.50 |
| 316 | Donald Kelly RC | .60 | 1.50 |
| 317 | Tom Mastny RC | .60 | 1.50 |
| 318 | Kevin Davidson RC | .40 | 1.00 |
| 319 | Brian Pilkington RC | .75 | 2.00 |
| 320 | Alex Romero RC | .60 | 1.50 |
| 321 | Chad Chop RC | .60 | 1.50 |
| 322 | Kody Kirkland RC | .75 | 2.00 |
| 323 | Casey Myers RC | .40 | 1.00 |
| 324 | Mike Rouse RC | .40 | 1.00 |
| 325 | Sergio Silva RC | .40 | 1.00 |
| 326 | J.J. Furmaniak RC | 1.25 | 3.00 |
| 327 | Brad Vericker RC | .60 | 1.50 |
| 328 | Blake Hawksworth RC | .75 | 2.00 |
| 329 | Brock Jacobsen RC | .40 | 1.00 |
| 330 | Alec Zumwalt RC | .40 | 1.00 |
| 331 | Wardell Starling AU RC | 4.00 | 10.00 |
| 332 | Estee Harris AU RC | 4.00 | 10.00 |
| 333 | Kyle Sleeth AU RC | 4.00 | 10.00 |
| 334 | Dioner Navarro AU RC | 6.00 | 15.00 |
| 335 | Logan Kensing AU RC | 4.00 | 10.00 |
| 336 | Travis Blackley AU RC | 4.00 | 10.00 |
| 337 | Lincoln Holdzkom AU RC | 4.00 | 10.00 |
| 338 | Jason Hirsh AU RC | 10.00 | 25.00 |
| 339 | Juan Cedeno AU RC | 4.00 | 10.00 |
| 340 | Matt Creighton AU RC | 4.00 | 10.00 |
| 341 | Tim Stauffer AU RC | 6.00 | 15.00 |
| 342 | Shingo Takatsu AU RC | 6.00 | 15.00 |
| 343 | Lastings Milledge AU RC | 20.00 | 50.00 |
| 344 | Dustin Nippert AU RC | 4.00 | 10.00 |
| 345 | Felix Hernandez AU RC | 60.00 | 120.00 |
| 346 | Joaquin Arias AU RC | 6.00 | 15.00 |
| 347 | Kevin Kouzmanoff AU RC | 10.00 | 25.00 |
| 348 | B.Brownlie AU RC | 4.00 | 10.00 |
| 349 | David Aardsma AU RC | 4.00 | 10.00 |
| 350 | Jon Knott AU RC | 6.00 | 15.00 |

## 2004 Bowman Chrome Draft

| | | |
|---|---|---|
| COMPLETE SET (175) | 175.00 | 300.00 |
| COMP.SET w/o SP's (165) | 50.00 | 100.00 |
| COMMON CARD (1-165) | .15 | .40 |
| COMMON YR | .15 | .40 |
| 1-165 TWO PER BOWMAN DRAFT PACK | | |
| 166-175 ODDS 1:60 BOWMAN DRAFT HOBBY | | |
| 166-175 ODDS 1:60 BOWMAN DRAFT RETAIL | | |
| 166-175 STATED PRINT RUN 1695 SETS | | |
| 166-175 ARE NOT SERIAL-NUMBERED | | |
| 166-175 PRINT RUN PROVIDED BY TOPPS | | |
| PLATES 1-165 ODDS 1:559 HOBBY | | |
| PLATES 166-175 ODDS 1:18,354 HOBBY | | |
| PLATES PRINT RUN 1 SERIAL #'d SET | | |
| BLACK-CYAN-MAGENTA-YELLOW EXIST | | |
| NO PLATES PRICING DUE TO SCARCITY | | |
| 1 Lyle Overbay | .15 | .40 |
| 2 David Newhan | .15 | .40 |
| 3 J.R. House | .15 | .40 |
| 4 Chad Tracy | .15 | .40 |
| 5 Humberto Quintero | .15 | .40 |
| 6 Dave Bush | .15 | .40 |
| 7 Scott Hairston | .15 | .40 |
| 8 Mike Wood | .15 | .40 |
| 9 Alexis Rios | .25 | .60 |
| 10 Sean Burnett | .15 | .40 |
| 11 Wilson Valdez | .15 | .40 |
| 12 Lew Ford | .15 | .40 |
| 13 Freddy Thon RC | .40 | 1.00 |
| 14 Zack Greinke | .25 | .60 |
| 15 Bucky Jacobsen | .15 | .40 |
| 16 Kevin Youkilis | .15 | .40 |
| 17 Grady Sizemore | .60 | 1.50 |
| 18 Denny Bautista | .15 | .40 |
| 19 David DeJesus | .15 | .40 |
| 20 Casey Kotchman | .25 | .60 |
| 21 David Kelton | .15 | .40 |
| 22 Charles Thomas RC | .40 | 1.00 |
| 23 Kazuhito Tadano RC | .60 | 1.50 |
| 24 Justin Leone RC | .60 | 1.50 |
| 25 Eduardo Villacis RC | .40 | 1.00 |
| 26 Brian Dallimore RC | .40 | 1.00 |
| 27 Nick Green | .15 | .40 |
| 28 Sam McConnell RC | .40 | 1.00 |
| 29 Brad Halsey RC | .60 | 1.50 |
| 30 Roman Colon RC | .40 | 1.00 |
| 31 Josh Fields RC | 2.50 | 6.00 |
| 32 Cody Bunkelman RC | .60 | 1.50 |
| 33 Jay Rainville RC | 1.50 | 4.00 |
| 34 Richie Robnett RC | 1.25 | 3.00 |
| 35 Jon Poterson RC | 1.00 | 2.50 |

| # | Player | Lo | Hi |
|---|--------|-----|------|
| 36 | Huston Street RC | 2.00 | 5.00 |
| 37 | Erick San Pedro RC | .40 | 1.00 |
| 38 | Cory Dunlap RC | 1.25 | 3.00 |
| 39 | Kurt Suzuki RC | 1.25 | 3.00 |
| 40 | Anthony Swarzak RC | 1.00 | 2.50 |
| 41 | Ian Desmond RC | 1.25 | 3.00 |
| 42 | Chris Covington RC | .60 | 1.50 |
| 43 | Christian Garcia RC | 1.00 | 2.50 |
| 44 | Gaby Hernandez RC | 1.50 | 4.00 |
| 45 | Steven Register RC | .40 | 1.00 |
| 46 | Eduardo Morlan RC | 1.25 | 3.00 |
| 47 | Collin Balester RC | .60 | 1.50 |
| 48 | Nathan Phillips RC | .60 | 1.50 |
| 49 | Dan Schwartzbauer RC | .60 | 1.50 |
| 50 | Rafael Gonzalez RC | .40 | 1.00 |
| 51 | K.C. Herren RC | 1.00 | 2.50 |
| 52 | William Susdorf RC | .40 | 1.00 |
| 53 | Rob Johnson RC | .60 | 1.50 |
| 54 | Louis Marson RC | 1.00 | 2.50 |
| 55 | Joe Koshansky RC | 2.50 | 6.00 |
| 56 | Jamar Walton RC | 1.00 | 2.50 |
| 57 | Mark Lowe RC | 2.00 | 5.00 |
| 58 | Matt Macri RC | 1.25 | 3.00 |
| 59 | Donny Lucy RC | .40 | 1.00 |
| 60 | Mike Ferris RC | .60 | 1.50 |
| 61 | Mike Nickeas RC | .60 | 1.50 |
| 62 | Eric Hurley RC | 1.25 | 3.00 |
| 63 | Scott Elbert RC | 1.25 | 3.00 |
| 64 | Blake DeWitt RC | 2.00 | 5.00 |
| 65 | Danny Putnam RC | 1.00 | 2.50 |
| 66 | J.P. Howell RC | 1.25 | 3.00 |
| 67 | John Wiggins RC | .40 | 1.00 |
| 68 | Justin Orenduff RC | 1.00 | 2.50 |
| 69 | Ray Liotta RC | 1.25 | 3.00 |
| 70 | Billy Buckner RC | .60 | 1.50 |
| 71 | Eric Campbell RC | 2.50 | 6.00 |
| 72 | Olin Wick RC | 1.00 | 2.50 |
| 73 | Sean Gamble RC | .60 | 1.50 |
| 74 | Seth Smith RC | 1.25 | 3.00 |
| 75 | Wade Davis RC | 2.00 | 5.00 |
| 76 | Joe Jacobitz RC | .40 | 1.00 |
| 77 | J.A. Happ RC | 1.50 | 4.00 |
| 78 | Eric Ridener RC | .40 | 1.00 |
| 79 | Matt Tuiasosopo RC | 1.50 | 4.00 |
| 80 | Brad Bergesen RC | .40 | 1.00 |
| 81 | Javy Guerra RC | .60 | 1.50 |
| 82 | Buck Shaw RC | .60 | 1.50 |
| 83 | Paul Janish RC | .75 | 2.00 |
| 84 | Sean Kazmar RC | .40 | 1.00 |
| 85 | Josh Johnson RC | .60 | 1.50 |
| 86 | Angel Salome RC | 1.50 | 4.00 |
| 87 | Jordan Parraz RC | 1.00 | 2.50 |
| 88 | Kelvin Vazquez RC | .40 | 1.00 |
| 89 | Grant Hansen RC | .40 | 1.00 |
| 90 | Matt Fox RC | .40 | 1.00 |
| 91 | Trevor Plouffe RC | 1.50 | 4.00 |
| 92 | Wes Whisler RC | .40 | 1.00 |
| 93 | Curtis Thigpen RC | 1.00 | 2.50 |
| 94 | Donnie Smith RC | .60 | 1.50 |
| 95 | Luis Rivera RC | .60 | 1.50 |
| 96 | Jesse Hoover RC | .60 | 1.50 |
| 97 | Jason Vargas RC | 1.50 | 4.00 |
| 98 | Clary Carlsen RC | .40 | 1.00 |
| 99 | Mark Robinson RC | .40 | 1.00 |
| 100 | J.C. Holt RC | .40 | 1.00 |
| 101 | Chad Blackwell RC | .40 | 1.00 |
| 102 | Darryl Jones RC | 1.25 | 3.00 |
| 103 | Jonathan Tierce RC | .40 | 1.00 |
| 104 | Patrick Bryant RC | .40 | 1.00 |
| 105 | Eddie Prasch RC | .60 | 1.50 |
| 106 | Mitch Einertson RC | .75 | 2.00 |
| 107 | Kyle Waldrop RC | 1.25 | 3.00 |
| 108 | Jeff Marquez RC | .60 | 1.50 |
| 109 | Zach Jackson RC | 1.00 | 2.50 |
| 110 | Josh Wahpepah RC | 1.50 | 4.00 |
| 111 | Adam Lind RC | 3.00 | 8.00 |
| 112 | Kyle Bloom RC | .60 | 1.50 |
| 113 | Ben Harrison RC | .40 | 1.00 |
| 114 | Taylor Tankersley RC | .60 | 1.50 |
| 115 | Steven Jackson RC | .40 | 1.00 |
| 116 | David Purcey RC | 1.00 | 2.50 |
| 117 | Jacob McGee RC | 2.00 | 5.00 |
| 118 | Lucas Harrell RC | .40 | 1.00 |
| 119 | Brandon Allen RC | 1.50 | 4.00 |
| 120 | Van Pope RC | .60 | 1.50 |
| 121 | Jeff Francis RC | .25 | .60 |
| 122 | Joe Blanton | .25 | .60 |
| 123 | Wil Ledezma | .15 | .40 |
| 124 | Bryan Bullington | .15 | .40 |
| 125 | Jairo Garcia | .15 | .40 |
| 126 | Matt Cain | .75 | 2.00 |
| 127 | Arnie Munoz | .15 | .40 |
| 128 | Clint Everts | .15 | .40 |
| 129 | Jesus Cota | .15 | .40 |
| 130 | Gavin Floyd | .15 | .40 |
| 131 | Edwin Encamacion | .25 | .60 |
| 132 | Koyie Hill | .15 | .40 |
| 133 | Ruben Gotay | .15 | .40 |
| 134 | Jeff Mathis | .15 | .40 |
| 135 | Andy Marte | .40 | 1.00 |
| 136 | Dallas McPherson | .25 | .60 |
| 137 | Justin Morneau | .25 | .60 |
| 138 | Rickie Weeks | .25 | .60 |
| 139 | Joel Guzman | .40 | 1.00 |
| 140 | Shin Soo Choo | .40 | 1.00 |
| 141 | Yusmeiro Petit RC | 2.00 | 5.00 |
| 142 | Jorge Cortes RC | .15 | .40 |
| 143 | Val Majewski | .15 | .40 |
| 144 | Felix Pie | .40 | 1.00 |
| 145 | Aaron Hill | .15 | .40 |
| 146 | Jose Capellan | .25 | .60 |
| 147 | Dioner Navarro | .40 | 1.00 |
| 148 | Fausto Carmona | .50 | 1.25 |
| 149 | Robinzon Diaz RC | .40 | 1.00 |
| 150 | Felix Hernandez | 4.00 | 10.00 |
| 151 | Andres Blanco RC | .15 | .40 |
| 152 | Jason Kubel | .15 | .40 |
| 153 | Willy Taveras RC | 1.00 | 2.50 |
| 154 | Merkin Valdez | .15 | .40 |
| 155 | Robinson Cano | .60 | 1.50 |
| 156 | Bill Murphy | .15 | .40 |
| 157 | Chris Burke | .25 | .60 |
| 158 | Kyle Sleeth | .15 | .40 |
| 159 | B.J. Upton | .40 | 1.00 |
| 160 | Tim Stauffer | .40 | 1.00 |
| 161 | David Wright | 1.50 | 4.00 |
| 162 | Conor Jackson | 1.50 | 4.00 |
| 163 | Brad Thompson RC | 1.00 | 2.50 |
| 164 | Delmon Young | .40 | 1.00 |
| 165 | Jeremy Reed | .25 | .60 |
| 166 | Matt Bush AU RC | 10.00 | 25.00 |
| 167 | Mark Rogers AU RC | 8.00 | 20.00 |
| 168 | Thomas Diamond AU RC | 6.00 | 15.00 |
| 169 | Greg Golson AU RC | 8.00 | 20.00 |
| 170 | Homer Bailey AU RC | 30.00 | 60.00 |
| 171 | Chris Lambert AU RC | 4.00 | 10.00 |
| 172 | Neil Walker AU RC | 12.50 | 30.00 |
| 173 | Bill Bray AU RC | 4.00 | 10.00 |
| 174 | Philip Hughes AU RC | 40.00 | 80.00 |
| 175 | Gio Gonzalez AU RC | 12.50 | 30.00 |

## 2005 Bowman Chrome

| | | | |
|---|---|---|---|
| COMP.SET w/o AU's (330) | | 60.00 | 120.00 |
| COMMON CARD (1-140) | | .20 | .50 |
| COMMON CARD (141-165) | | .20 | .50 |
| COMMON CARD (166-330) | | .40 | 1.00 |
| COMMON AUTO (331-353) | | 4.00 | 10.00 |
| 1-330 PLATE ODDS 1:779 HOBBY | | | |
| 331-353 AU PLATE ODDS 1:10,996 HOBBY | | | |
| PLATE PRINT RUN 1 SET PER COLOR | | | |
| BLACK-CYAN-MAGENTA-YELLOW ISSUED | | | |
| NO PLATE PRICING DUE TO SCARCITY | | | |
| 1 Gavin Floyd | | .20 | .50 |
| 2 Eric Chavez | | .20 | .50 |
| 3 Miguel Tejada | | .20 | .50 |
| 4 Dmitri Young | | .20 | .50 |
| 5 Hank Blalock | | .20 | .50 |
| 6 Kerry Wood | | .20 | .50 |
| 7 Andy Pettitte | | .30 | .75 |
| 8 Pat Burrell | | .20 | .50 |
| 9 Johnny Estrada | | .20 | .50 |
| 10 Frank Thomas | | .50 | 1.25 |
| 11 Juan Pierre | | .20 | .50 |
| 12 Tom Glavine | | .30 | .75 |
| 13 Lyle Overbay | | .20 | .50 |
| 14 Jim Edmonds | | .20 | .50 |
| 15 Steve Finley | | .20 | .50 |
| 16 Jermaine Dye | | .20 | .50 |
| 17 Omar Vizquel | | .30 | .75 |
| 18 Nick Johnson | | .20 | .50 |
| 19 Brian Giles | | .20 | .50 |
| 20 Justin Morneau | | .20 | .50 |
| 21 Preston Wilson | | .20 | .50 |
| 22 Wily Mo Pena | | .20 | .50 |
| 23 Rafael Palmeiro | | .30 | .75 |
| 24 Scott Kazmir | | .20 | .50 |
| 25 Derek Jeter | | 1.00 | 2.50 |
| 26 Barry Zito | | .20 | .50 |
| 27 Mike Lowell | | .20 | .50 |
| 28 Jason Bay | | .20 | .50 |
| 29 Ken Harvey | | .20 | .50 |
| 30 Nomar Garciaparra | | .50 | 1.25 |
| 31 Roy Halladay | | .20 | .50 |
| 32 Todd Helton | | .30 | .75 |
| 33 Mark Kotsay | | .20 | .50 |
| 34 Jake Peavy | | .20 | .50 |
| 35 David Wright | | .75 | 2.00 |
| 36 Dontrelle Willis | | .20 | .50 |
| 37 Marcus Giles | | .20 | .50 |
| 38 Chone Figgins | | .20 | .50 |
| 39 Sidney Ponson | | .20 | .50 |
| 40 Randy Johnson | | .50 | 1.25 |
| 41 John Smoltz | | .30 | .75 |
| 42 Kevin Millar | | .20 | .50 |
| 43 Mark Teixeira | | .20 | .50 |
| 44 Alex Rios | | .20 | .50 |
| 45 Mike Piazza | | .50 | 1.25 |
| 46 Victor Martinez | | .20 | .50 |
| 47 Jeff Bagwell | | .30 | .75 |
| 48 Shawn Green | | .20 | .50 |
| 49 Ivan Rodriguez | | .30 | .75 |
| 50 Alex Rodriguez | | .75 | 2.00 |
| 51 Kazuo Matsui | | .20 | .50 |
| 52 Mark Mulder | | .20 | .50 |
| 53 Michael Young | | .20 | .50 |
| 54 Javy Lopez | | .20 | .50 |
| 55 Johnny Damon | | .30 | .75 |
| 56 Jeff Francis | | .20 | .50 |
| 57 Rich Harden | | .20 | .50 |
| 58 Bobby Abreu | | .20 | .50 |
| 59 Mark Loretta | | .20 | .50 |
| 60 Gary Sheffield | | .20 | .50 |
| 61 Jamie Moyer | | .20 | .50 |
| 62 Garret Anderson | | .20 | .50 |
| 63 Vernon Wells | | .20 | .50 |
| 64 Orlando Cabrera | | .20 | .50 |
| 65 Magglio Ordonez | | .20 | .50 |
| 66 Ronnie Belliard | | .20 | .50 |
| 67 Carlos Lee | | .20 | .50 |
| 68 Carl Pavano | | .20 | .50 |
| 69 Jon Lieber | | .20 | .50 |
| 70 Aubrey Huff | | .20 | .50 |
| 71 Rocco Baldelli | | .20 | .50 |
| 72 Jason Schmidt | | .20 | .50 |
| 73 Bernie Williams | | .30 | .75 |
| 74 Hideki Matsui | | .75 | 2.00 |
| 75 Ken Griffey Jr. | | .75 | 2.00 |
| 76 Josh Beckett | | .20 | .50 |
| 77 Mark Buehrle | | .20 | .50 |
| 78 David Ortiz | | .50 | 1.25 |
| 79 Luis Gonzalez | | .20 | .50 |
| 80 Scott Rolen | | .30 | .75 |
| 81 Joe Mauer | | .50 | 1.25 |
| 82 Jose Reyes | | .20 | .50 |
| 83 Adam Dunn | | .20 | .50 |
| 84 Greg Maddux | | .75 | 2.00 |
| 85 Bartolo Colon | | .20 | .50 |
| 86 Bret Boone | | .20 | .50 |
| 87 Mike Mussina | | .30 | .75 |
| 88 Ben Sheets | | .20 | .50 |
| 89 Lance Berkman | | .20 | .50 |
| 90 Miguel Cabrera | | .30 | .75 |
| 91 C.C. Sabathia | | .20 | .50 |
| 92 Mike Maroth | | .20 | .50 |
| 93 Andruw Jones | | .30 | .75 |
| 94 Jack Wilson | | .20 | .50 |
| 95 Ichiro Suzuki | | 1.00 | 2.50 |
| 96 Geoff Jenkins | | .20 | .50 |
| 97 Zack Greinke | | .20 | .50 |
| 98 Jorge Posada | | .30 | .75 |

| # | Player | Lo | Hi |
|---|---|---|---|
| 99 | Travis Hafner | .20 | .50 |
| 100 | Barry Bonds | 1.25 | 3.00 |
| 101 | Aaron Rowand | .20 | .50 |
| 102 | Aramis Ramirez | .20 | .50 |
| 103 | Curt Schilling | .30 | .75 |
| 104 | Melvin Mora | .20 | .50 |
| 105 | Albert Pujols | 1.00 | 2.50 |
| 106 | Austin Kearns | .20 | .50 |
| 107 | Shannon Stewart | .20 | .50 |
| 108 | Carl Crawford | .20 | .50 |
| 109 | Carlos Zambrano | .20 | .50 |
| 110 | Roger Clemens | .75 | 2.00 |
| 111 | Javier Vazquez | .20 | .50 |
| 112 | Randy Wolf | .20 | .50 |
| 113 | Chipper Jones | .50 | 1.25 |
| 114 | Larry Walker | .30 | .75 |
| 115 | Alfonso Soriano | .50 | 1.25 |
| 116 | Brad Wilkerson | .20 | .50 |
| 117 | Bobby Crosby | .20 | .50 |
| 118 | Jim Thome | .30 | .75 |
| 119 | Oliver Perez | .20 | .50 |
| 120 | Vladimir Guerrero | .50 | 1.25 |
| 121 | Roy Oswalt | .20 | .50 |
| 122 | Torii Hunter | .20 | .50 |
| 123 | Rafael Furcal | .20 | .50 |
| 124 | Luis Castillo | .20 | .50 |
| 125 | Carlos Beltran | .20 | .50 |
| 126 | Mike Sweeney | .20 | .50 |
| 127 | Johan Santana | .50 | 1.25 |
| 128 | Tim Hudson | .20 | .50 |
| 129 | Troy Glaus | .20 | .50 |
| 130 | Manny Ramirez | .30 | .75 |
| 131 | Jeff Kent | .20 | .50 |
| 132 | Jose Vidro | .20 | .50 |
| 133 | Edgar Renteria | .20 | .50 |
| 134 | Ja Russ Ortiz | .20 | .50 |
| 135 | Sammy Sosa | .50 | 1.25 |
| 136 | Carlos Delgado | .20 | .50 |
| 137 | Richie Sexson | .20 | .50 |
| 138 | Pedro Martinez | .30 | .75 |
| 139 | Adrian Beltre | .20 | .50 |
| 140 | Mark Prior | .30 | .75 |
| 141 | Omar Quintanilla | .20 | .50 |
| 142 | Carlos Quentin | .30 | .75 |
| 143 | Dan Johnson | .20 | .50 |
| 144 | Jake Stevens | .20 | .50 |
| 145 | Nate Schierholtz | .30 | .75 |
| 146 | Neil Walker | .20 | .50 |
| 147 | Bill Bray | .20 | .50 |
| 148 | Taylor Tankersley | .20 | .50 |
| 149 | Trevor Plouffe | .30 | .75 |
| 150 | Felix Hernandez | 2.50 | 6.00 |
| 151 | Philip Hughes | .75 | 2.00 |
| 152 | James Houser | .20 | .50 |
| 153 | David Murphy | .20 | .50 |
| 154 | Ervin Santana | .30 | .75 |
| 155 | Anthony Whittington | .20 | .50 |
| 156 | Chris Lambert | .20 | .50 |
| 157 | Jeremy Sowers | .30 | .75 |
| 158 | Giovanny Gonzalez | .30 | .75 |
| 159 | Blake DeWitt | .30 | .75 |
| 160 | Thomas Diamond | .30 | .75 |
| 161 | Greg Golson | .30 | .75 |
| 162 | David Aardsma | .20 | .50 |
| 163 | Paul Maholm | .20 | .50 |
| 164 | Mark Rogers | .30 | .75 |
| 165 | Homer Bailey | .30 | .75 |
| 166 | Elvin Puello RC | .60 | 1.50 |
| 167 | Tony Giarratano RC | .60 | 1.50 |
| 168 | Darren Fenster RC | .60 | 1.50 |
| 169 | Elvys Quezada RC | .60 | 1.50 |
| 170 | Glen Perkins RC | 1.25 | 3.00 |
| 171 | Ian Kinsler RC | 4.00 | 10.00 |
| 172 | Adam Bostick RC | .60 | 1.50 |
| 173 | Jeremy West RC | .75 | 2.00 |
| 174 | Brett Harper RC | .75 | 2.00 |
| 175 | Kevin West RC | .60 | 1.50 |
| 176 | Luis Hernandez RC | .60 | 1.50 |
| 177 | Matt Campbell RC | .60 | 1.50 |
| 178 | Nate McLouth RC | 1.50 | 4.00 |
| 179 | Ryan Goleski RC | .75 | 2.00 |
| 180 | Matthew Lindstrom RC | .60 | 1.50 |
| 181 | Matt DeSalvo RC | .75 | 2.00 |
| 182 | Kole Strayhorn RC | .60 | 1.50 |
| 183 | Jose Vaquedano RC | .60 | 1.50 |
| 184 | James Jurries RC | .75 | 2.00 |
| 185 | Ian Bladergroen RC | .75 | 2.00 |
| 186 | Kila Kaaihue RC | 1.50 | 4.00 |
| 187 | Luke Scott RC | 2.50 | 6.00 |
| 188 | Chris Denorfia RC | 1.50 | 4.00 |
| 189 | Jai Miller RC | .75 | 2.00 |
| 190 | Melky Cabrera RC | 3.00 | 8.00 |
| 191 | Ryan Sweeney RC | 1.50 | 4.00 |
| 192 | Sean Marshall RC | 2.50 | 6.00 |
| 193 | Erick Abreu RC | 1.25 | 3.00 |
| 194 | Tyler Pelland RC | .75 | 2.00 |
| 195 | Cole Armstrong RC | .60 | 1.50 |
| 196 | John Hudgins RC | .60 | 1.50 |
| 197 | Wade Robinson RC | .60 | 1.50 |
| 198 | Dan Santin RC | .60 | 1.50 |
| 199 | Steve Doetsch RC | .60 | 1.50 |
| 200 | Shane Costa RC | .60 | 1.50 |
| 201 | Scott Mathieson RC | 1.25 | 3.00 |
| 202 | Ben Jones RC | .75 | 2.00 |
| 203 | Michael Rogers RC | .60 | 1.50 |
| 204 | Matt Rogelstad RC | .60 | 1.50 |
| 205 | Luis Ramirez RC | .60 | 1.50 |
| 206 | Landon Powell RC | .75 | 2.00 |
| 207 | Erik Cordier RC | .60 | 1.50 |
| 208 | Chris Seddon RC | .60 | 1.50 |
| 209 | Chris Roberson RC | .60 | 1.50 |
| 210 | Thomas Oldham RC | .60 | 1.50 |
| 211 | Dana Eveland RC | .60 | 1.50 |
| 212 | Cody Haerther RC | .60 | 1.50 |
| 213 | Danny Core RC | .60 | 1.50 |
| 214 | Craig Tatum RC | .60 | 1.50 |
| 215 | Elliot Johnson RC | .60 | 1.50 |
| 216 | Ender Chavez RC | .60 | 1.50 |
| 217 | Errol Simonitsch RC | .75 | 2.00 |
| 218 | Matt Van Der Bosch RC | .60 | 1.50 |
| 219 | Eulogio de la Cruz RC | .60 | 1.50 |
| 220 | Drew Toussaint RC | .60 | 1.50 |
| 221 | Adam Boeve RC | .60 | 1.50 |
| 222 | Adam Harben RC | .75 | 2.00 |
| 223 | Saltazar Lopez RC | .60 | 1.50 |
| 224 | Ruas Martin RC | 2.00 | 5.00 |
| 225 | Brian Bannister RC | 1.50 | 4.00 |
| 226 | Chris Walker RC | .60 | 1.50 |
| 227 | Casey McGehee RC | .60 | 1.50 |
| 228 | Humberto Sanchez RC | 2.50 | 6.00 |
| 229 | Javon Moran RC | .60 | 1.50 |
| 230 | Brandon McCarthy RC | 2.00 | 5.00 |
| 231 | Danny Zell RC | .60 | 1.50 |
| 232 | Kevin Barry RC | .60 | 1.50 |
| 233 | Juan Tejeda RC | .60 | 1.50 |
| 234 | Keith Ramsey RC | .60 | 1.50 |
| 235 | Lorenzo Scott RC | .60 | 1.50 |
| 236 | Jon Barratt RC | .60 | 1.50 |
| 237 | Martin Prado RC | .60 | 1.50 |
| 238 | Matt Albers RC | 1.50 | 4.00 |
| 239 | Brian Schweiger RC | .60 | 1.50 |
| 240 | Raul Tablado RC | .60 | 1.50 |
| 241 | Pat Misch RC | .60 | 1.50 |
| 242 | Pat Osborn RC | .60 | 1.50 |
| 243 | Ryan Feierabend RC | .60 | 1.50 |
| 244 | Shaun Marcum RC | .40 | 1.00 |
| 245 | Kevin Collins RC | .60 | 1.50 |
| 246 | Stuart Pomeranz RC | .60 | 1.50 |
| 247 | Tetsu Yofu RC | .60 | 1.50 |
| 248 | Hernan Iribarren RC | .75 | 2.00 |
| 249 | Mike Spidale RC | .60 | 1.50 |
| 250 | Tony Americh RC | .60 | 1.50 |
| 251 | Manny Parra RC | 2.00 | 5.00 |
| 252 | Drew Anderson RC | .60 | 1.50 |
| 253 | T.J. Beam RC | 1.25 | 3.00 |
| 254 | Claudio Arias RC | .75 | 2.00 |
| 255 | Andy Sides RC | .60 | 1.50 |
| 256 | Bear Bay RC | .75 | 2.00 |
| 257 | Bill McCarthy RC | .60 | 1.50 |
| 258 | Daniel Haigwood RC | 1.25 | 3.00 |
| 259 | Brian Sprout RC | .75 | 2.00 |
| 260 | Bryan Triplett RC | .60 | 1.50 |
| 261 | Steven Bondurant RC | .60 | 1.50 |
| 262 | Darwinson Salazar RC | .60 | 1.50 |
| 263 | David Shepard RC | .60 | 1.50 |
| 264 | Johan Silva RC | .60 | 1.50 |
| 265 | J.B. Thurmond RC | .60 | 1.50 |
| 266 | Brandon Moorhead RC | .60 | 1.50 |
| 267 | Kyle Nichols RC | .75 | 2.00 |
| 268 | Jonathan Sanchez RC | 1.50 | 4.00 |
| 269 | Mike Esposito RC | .60 | 1.50 |
| 270 | Erik Schindewolf RC | .60 | 1.50 |
| 271 | Peeter Ramos RC | .60 | 1.50 |
| 272 | Juan Senreiso RC | .60 | 1.50 |
| 273 | Travis Chick RC | .75 | 2.00 |
| 274 | Vinny Rottino RC | .60 | 1.50 |
| 275 | Micah Furtado RC | .60 | 1.50 |
| 276 | George Kottaras RC | 1.25 | 3.00 |
| 277 | Abel Gomez RC | .75 | 2.00 |
| 278 | Buck Coats RC | .60 | 1.50 |
| 279 | Kenny Durost RC | .60 | 1.50 |
| 280 | Nick Touchstone RC | .60 | 1.50 |
| 281 | Jerry Owens RC | .75 | 2.00 |
| 282 | Stefan Bailie RC | .60 | 1.50 |
| 283 | Jesse Gutierrez RC | .60 | 1.50 |
| 284 | Chuck Tiffany RC | 1.50 | 4.00 |
| 285 | Brendan Ryan RC | .60 | 1.50 |
| 286 | Julio Pimentel RC | .75 | 2.00 |
| 287 | Shawn Bowman RC | .75 | 2.00 |
| 288 | Alexander Smit RC | .60 | 1.50 |
| 289 | Micah Schnurstein RC | .60 | 1.50 |
| 290 | Jared Gothreaux RC | .60 | 1.50 |
| 291 | Jair Jurrjens RC | 1.50 | 4.00 |
| 292 | Bobby Livingston RC | .60 | 1.50 |
| 293 | Ryan Speier RC | .60 | 1.50 |
| 294 | Zach Parker RC | .60 | 1.50 |
| 295 | Christian Colonel RC | .60 | 1.50 |
| 296 | Scott Mitchinson RC | .60 | 1.50 |
| 297 | Neil Wilson RC | .60 | 1.50 |
| 298 | Chuck James RC | 2.50 | 6.00 |
| 299 | Heath Totten RC | .60 | 1.50 |
| 300 | Sean Tracey RC | .60 | 1.50 |
| 301 | Tadahito Iguchi RC | 2.00 | 5.00 |
| 302 | Matt Brown RC | .60 | 1.50 |
| 303 | Franklin Morales RC | 1.25 | 3.00 |
| 304 | Brandon Sing RC | .75 | 2.00 |
| 305 | D.J. Houlton RC | .60 | 1.50 |
| 306 | Jayce Tingler RC | .60 | 1.50 |
| 307 | Mitchell Arnold RC | .60 | 1.50 |
| 308 | Jim Burt RC | .60 | 1.50 |
| 309 | Jason Motte RC | .60 | 1.50 |
| 310 | David Gassner RC | .60 | 1.50 |
| 311 | Andy Santana RC | .60 | 1.50 |
| 312 | Kalvin Pichardo RC | .60 | 1.50 |
| 313 | Carlos Carrasco RC | 2.00 | 5.00 |
| 314 | Willy Mota RC | .60 | 1.50 |
| 315 | Frank Mata RC | .60 | 1.50 |
| 316 | Carlos Gonzalez RC | 2.00 | 5.00 |
| 317 | Jesse Floyd | .40 | 1.00 |
| 318 | Chris B. Young RC | 3.00 | 8.00 |
| 319 | Billy Sadler RC | .60 | 1.50 |
| 320 | Ricky Barrett RC | .60 | 1.50 |
| 321 | Ben Harrison | .60 | 1.50 |
| 322 | Steve Nelson RC | .60 | 1.50 |
| 323 | Daryl Thompson RC | .60 | 1.50 |
| 324 | Davis Romero RC | .60 | 1.50 |
| 325 | Jeremy Harts RC | .60 | 1.50 |
| 326 | Nick Massel RC | .60 | 1.50 |
| 327 | Thomas Pauly RC | .60 | 1.50 |
| 328 | Mike Garber RC | .60 | 1.50 |
| 329 | Kennard Bibbs RC | .60 | 1.50 |
| 330 | Colter Bean RC | .60 | 1.50 |
| 331 | Justin Verlander AU RC | 30.00 | 60.00 |
| 332 | Chip Cannon AU RC | 10.00 | 25.00 |
| 333 | Kevin Melillo AU RC | 6.00 | 15.00 |
| 334 | Jake Postlewait AU RC | 4.00 | 10.00 |
| 335 | Wes Swackhamer AU RC | 4.00 | 10.00 |
| 336 | Mike Rodriguez AU RC | 4.00 | 10.00 |
| 337 | Philip Humber AU RC | 10.00 | 25.00 |
| 338 | Jeff Niemann AU RC | 6.00 | 15.00 |
| 339 | Brian Miller AU RC | 4.00 | 10.00 |
| 340 | Chris Vines AU RC | 4.00 | 10.00 |
| 341 | Andy LaRoche AU RC | 10.00 | 25.00 |
| 342 | Mike Bourn AU RC | 10.00 | 25.00 |
| 343 | Eric Nielsen AU RC | 4.00 | 10.00 |
| 344 | Wladimir Balentien AU RC | 20.00 | 50.00 |
| 345 | Ismael Ramirez AU RC | 4.00 | 10.00 |
| 346 | Pedro Lopez AU RC | 4.00 | 10.00 |
| 347 | Shawn Bowman AU | 6.00 | 15.00 |
| 348 | Hayden Penn AU RC | 10.00 | 25.00 |
| 349 | Matthew Kemp AU RC | 40.00 | 80.00 |
| 350 | Brian Stavisky AU RC | 4.00 | 10.00 |
| 351 | C.J. Smith AU RC | 4.00 | 10.00 |
| 352 | Mike Morse AU RC | 5.00 | 12.00 |
| 353 | Billy Butler AU RC | 40.00 | 80.00 |

## 2005 Bowman Chrome Draft

| | | |
|---|---|---|
| ❑ COMP. SET w/o SP's (165) | 50.00 | 100.00 |
| ❑ COMMON CARD (1-165) | .15 | .40 |
| ❑ COMMON RC | .40 | 1.00 |
| ❑ COMMON RC YR | .15 | .40 |
| ❑ 1-165 TWO PER BOWMAN DRAFT PACK | | |
| ❑ 166-180 GROUP A ODDS 1:671 H, 1:643 R | | |
| ❑ 166-180 GROUP B ODDS 1:69 H, 1:69 R | | |
| ❑ 1-165 PLATE ODDS 1:826 HOBBY | | |
| ❑ 166-180 AU PLATE ODDS 1:18,411 HOBBY | | |
| ❑ PLATE PRINT RUN 1 SET PER COLOR | | |
| ❑ BLACK-CYAN-MAGENTA-YELLOW ISSUED | | |
| ❑ NO PLATE PRICING DUE TO SCARCITY | | |
| ❑ 1 Rickie Weeks | .25 | .60 |
| ❑ 2 Kyle Davies | .15 | .40 |
| ❑ 3 Garrett Atkins | .15 | .40 |
| ❑ 4 Chien-Ming Wang | .75 | 2.00 |
| ❑ 5 Dallas McPherson | .15 | .40 |
| ❑ 6 Dan Johnson | .25 | .60 |
| ❑ 7 Andy Sisco | .15 | .40 |
| ❑ 8 Ryan Doumit | .15 | .40 |
| ❑ 9 J.P. Howell | .15 | .40 |
| ❑ 10 Tim Stauffer | .15 | .40 |
| ❑ 11 Willy Taveras | .25 | .60 |
| ❑ 12 Aaron Hill | .15 | .40 |
| ❑ 13 Victor Diaz | .15 | .40 |
| ❑ 14 Wilson Betemit | .15 | .40 |
| ❑ 15 Ervin Santana | .25 | .60 |
| ❑ 16 Mike Morse | .25 | .60 |
| ❑ 17 Yadier Molina | .25 | .60 |
| ❑ 18 Kelly Johnson | .15 | .40 |
| ❑ 19 Clint Barmes | .25 | .60 |
| ❑ 20 Robinson Cano | .40 | 1.00 |
| ❑ 21 Brad Thompson | .15 | .40 |
| ❑ 22 Jorge Cantu | .25 | .60 |
| ❑ 23 Brad Halsey | .15 | .40 |
| ❑ 24 Lance Niekro | .25 | .60 |
| ❑ 25 D.J. Houlton | .15 | .40 |
| ❑ 26 Ryan Church | .25 | .60 |
| ❑ 27 Hayden Penn | .60 | 1.50 |
| ❑ 28 Chris Young | .25 | .60 |
| ❑ 29 Chad Orvella RC | .40 | 1.00 |
| ❑ 30 Mark Teahen | .40 | 1.00 |
| ❑ 31 Mark McCormick FY RC | .40 | 1.00 |
| ❑ 32 Jay Bruce FY RC | 5.00 | 12.00 |
| ❑ 33 Beau Jones FY RC | 1.00 | 2.50 |
| ❑ 34 Tyler Greene FY RC | 1.00 | 2.50 |
| ❑ 35 Zach Ward FY RC | .40 | 1.00 |
| ❑ 36 Josh Bell FY RC | 1.50 | 4.00 |
| ❑ 37 Josh Wall FY RC | .60 | 1.50 |
| ❑ 38 Nick Walker FY RC | .40 | 1.00 |
| ❑ 39 Travis Buck FY RC | 1.25 | 4.00 |
| ❑ 40 Kyle Winters FY RC | .60 | 1.50 |
| ❑ 41 Mitch Boggs FY RC | .60 | 1.50 |
| ❑ 42 Tommy Mendoza FY RC | 1.00 | 2.50 |
| ❑ 43 Brad Corley FY RC | .60 | 1.50 |
| ❑ 44 Drew Stubbs FY RC | 2.00 | 5.00 |
| ❑ 45 Ryan Mount FY RC | 1.00 | 2.50 |
| ❑ 46 Tyler Herron FY RC | .60 | 1.50 |
| ❑ 47 Nick Weglarz FY RC | 1.00 | 2.50 |
| ❑ 48 Brandon Erbe FY RC | 1.50 | 4.00 |
| ❑ 49 Cody Allen FY RC | .40 | 1.00 |
| ❑ 50 Eric Fowler FY RC | .40 | 1.00 |
| ❑ 51 James Boone FY RC | .60 | 1.50 |
| ❑ 52 Josh Fiore FY RC | 1.50 | 4.00 |
| ❑ 53 Brandon Monk FY RC | .60 | 1.50 |
| ❑ 54 Kieron Pope FY RC | 1.00 | 2.50 |
| ❑ 55 Kyle Cofield FY RC | .60 | 1.50 |
| ❑ 56 Brett Lillibridge FY RC | .60 | 1.50 |
| ❑ 57 Daryl Jones FY RC | .60 | 1.50 |
| ❑ 58 Eli Iorg FY RC | .60 | 1.50 |
| ❑ 59 Brett Hayes FY RC | .40 | 1.00 |

| | | |
|---|---|---|
| ❑ 60 Mike Durant FY RC | 1.25 | 3.00 |
| ❑ 61 Michael Bowden FY RC | 2.00 | 5.00 |
| ❑ 62 Paul Kelly FY RC | .60 | 1.50 |
| ❑ 63 Andrew McCutchen FY RC | 3.00 | 8.00 |
| ❑ 64 Travis Wood FY RC | 1.25 | 3.00 |
| ❑ 65 Cesar Ramos FY RC | .60 | 1.50 |
| ❑ 66 Chaz Roe FY RC | .60 | 1.50 |
| ❑ 67 Matt Torra FY RC | .60 | 1.50 |
| ❑ 68 Kevin Slowey FY RC | 2.50 | 6.00 |
| ❑ 69 Trayvon Robinson FY RC | .60 | 1.50 |
| ❑ 70 Reid Engel FY RC | .40 | 1.00 |
| ❑ 71 Kris Harvey FY RC | .60 | 1.50 |
| ❑ 72 Craig Italiano FY RC | 1.00 | 2.50 |
| ❑ 73 Matt Maloney FY RC | 1.25 | 3.00 |
| ❑ 74 Sean West FY RC | 1.25 | 3.00 |
| ❑ 75 Henry Sanchez FY RC | 1.00 | 2.50 |
| ❑ 76 Scott Blue FY RC | .40 | 1.00 |
| ❑ 77 Jordan Schafer FY RC | 3.00 | 8.00 |
| ❑ 78 Chris Robinson FY RC | .60 | 1.50 |
| ❑ 79 Chris Hobdy FY RC | .40 | 1.00 |
| ❑ 80 Brandon Durden FY RC | .40 | 1.00 |
| ❑ 81 Clay Buchholz FY RC | 6.00 | 15.00 |
| ❑ 82 Josh Geer FY RC | .40 | 1.00 |
| ❑ 83 Sam LeCure FY RC | .40 | 1.00 |
| ❑ 84 Justin Thomas FY RC | .40 | 1.00 |
| ❑ 85 Brett Gardner FY RC | 1.00 | 2.50 |
| ❑ 86 Tommy Manzella FY RC | .40 | 1.00 |
| ❑ 87 Matt Green FY RC | .40 | 1.00 |
| ❑ 88 Yunel Escobar FY RC | 2.00 | 5.00 |
| ❑ 89 Mike Costanzo FY RC | 1.25 | 3.00 |
| ❑ 90 Nick Hundley FY RC | .40 | 1.00 |
| ❑ 91 Zach Simons FY RC | .40 | 1.00 |
| ❑ 92 Jacob Marceaux FY RC | .40 | 1.00 |
| ❑ 93 Brandon Snyder FY RC | 1.25 | 3.00 |
| ❑ 94 Matt Goyen FY RC | .40 | 1.00 |
| ❑ 95 Jon Egan FY RC | .60 | 1.50 |
| ❑ 96 Jon Egan FY RC | .60 | 1.50 |
| ❑ 97 Drew Thompson FY RC | .60 | 1.50 |
| ❑ 98 Bryan Anderson FY RC | 1.50 | 4.00 |
| ❑ 99 Clayton Richard FY RC | .40 | 1.00 |
| ❑ 100 Jimmy Shull FY RC | .60 | 1.50 |
| ❑ 101 Mark Pawelek FY RC | 2.00 | 5.00 |
| ❑ 102 P.J. Phillips FY RC | 1.00 | 2.50 |
| ❑ 103 John Drennen FY RC | 1.50 | 4.00 |
| ❑ 104 Nolan Reimold FY RC | 1.50 | 4.00 |
| ❑ 105 Troy Tulowitzki FY RC | 2.50 | 6.00 |
| ❑ 106 Kevin Whelan FY RC | .50 | 1.25 |
| ❑ 107 Wade Townsend FY RC | .60 | 1.50 |
| ❑ 108 Micah Owings FY RC | 1.00 | 2.50 |
| ❑ 109 Ryan Tucker FY RC | .60 | 1.50 |
| ❑ 110 Jeff Clement FY RC | 3.00 | 8.00 |
| ❑ 111 Josh Sullivan FY RC | .40 | 1.00 |
| ❑ 112 Jeff Lyman FY RC | .60 | 1.50 |
| ❑ 113 Brian Bogusevic FY RC | .40 | 1.00 |
| ❑ 114 Trevor Bell FY RC | .60 | 1.50 |
| ❑ 115 Brent Cox FY RC | .40 | 1.00 |
| ❑ 116 Michael Bilek FY RC | .40 | 1.00 |
| ❑ 117 Garrett Olson FY RC | .60 | 1.50 |
| ❑ 118 Steven Johnson FY RC | .60 | 1.50 |
| ❑ 119 Chase Headley FY RC | 2.00 | 5.00 |
| ❑ 120 Daniel Carte FY RC | .60 | 1.50 |
| ❑ 121 Francisco Liriano PROS | 1.00 | 2.50 |
| ❑ 122 Fausto Carmona PROS | .15 | .40 |
| ❑ 123 Zach Jackson PROS | .40 | 1.00 |
| ❑ 124 Adam Loewen PROS | .15 | .40 |
| ❑ 125 Chris Lambert PROS | .15 | .40 |
| ❑ 126 Scott Mathieson PROS | .25 | .60 |
| ❑ 127 Paul Maholm PROS | .25 | .60 |
| ❑ 128 Fernando Nieve PROS | .15 | .40 |
| ❑ 129 Justin Verlander PROS | 1.50 | 4.00 |
| ❑ 130 Yusmeiro Petit PROS | .40 | 1.00 |
| ❑ 131 Joel Zumaya PROS | .60 | 1.50 |
| ❑ 132 Merkin Valdez PROS | .15 | .40 |
| ❑ 133 Ryan Garko FY RC | 1.50 | 4.00 |
| ❑ 134 Edison Volquez FY RC | 5.00 | 12.00 |
| ❑ 135 Russ Martin FY | .60 | 1.50 |
| ❑ 136 Conor Jackson PROS | .25 | .60 |
| ❑ 137 Miguel Montero FY RC | 1.50 | 4.00 |
| ❑ 138 Josh Barfield PROS | .25 | .60 |
| ❑ 139 Delmon Young PROS | .60 | 1.50 |
| ❑ 140 Andy LaRoche FY | .60 | 1.50 |
| ❑ 141 William Bergolla PROS | .15 | .40 |
| ❑ 142 B.J. Upton PROS | .25 | .60 |
| ❑ 143 Heman Iribarren FY | .40 | 1.00 |
| ❑ 144 Brandon Wood PROS | .50 | 1.25 |
| ❑ 145 Jose Bautista PROS | .15 | .40 |
| ❑ 146 Edwin Encarnacion PROS | .25 | .60 |
| ❑ 147 Javier Herrera FY RC | 1.00 | 2.50 |
| ❑ 148 Jeremy Hermida PROS | .60 | 1.50 |

| | | |
|---|---|---|
| ❑ 149 Frank Diaz PROS RC | .40 | 1.00 |
| ❑ 150 Chris B.Young FY | 1.25 | 3.00 |
| ❑ 151 Shin-Soo Choo PROS | .15 | .40 |
| ❑ 152 Kevin Thompson PROS RC | .40 | 1.00 |
| ❑ 153 Hanley Ramirez PROS | .40 | 1.00 |
| ❑ 154 Lastings Milledge PROS | .25 | .60 |
| ❑ 155 Luis Montanez PROS | .15 | .40 |
| ❑ 156 Justin Huber PROS | .15 | .40 |
| ❑ 157 Zach Duke PROS | .30 | .75 |
| ❑ 158 Jeff Francoeur PROS | .50 | 1.25 |
| ❑ 159 Melky Cabrera FY | 1.25 | 3.00 |
| ❑ 160 Bobby Jenks PROS | .25 | .60 |
| ❑ 161 Ian Snell PROS | .15 | .40 |
| ❑ 162 Fernando Cabrera PROS | .15 | .40 |
| ❑ 163 Troy Patton PROS | .40 | 1.00 |
| ❑ 164 Anthony Lerew PROS | .25 | .60 |
| ❑ 165 Nelson Cruz FY PROS | 2.00 | 5.00 |
| ❑ 166 Stephen Drew AU A RC | 20.00 | 50.00 |
| ❑ 167 Jered Weaver AU A RC | 20.00 | 50.00 |
| ❑ 168 Ryan Braun AU A RC | 100.00 | 175.00 |
| ❑ 169 John Mayberry Jr. AU B RC | 8.00 | 20.00 |
| ❑ 170 Aaron Thompson AU B RC | 6.00 | 15.00 |
| ❑ 171 Cesar Carrillo AU B RC | 10.00 | 25.00 |
| ❑ 172 Jacoby Ellsbury AU A RC | 60.00 | 120.00 |
| ❑ 173 Matt Garza AU B RC | 12.50 | 30.00 |
| ❑ 174 Cliff Pennington AU A RC | 4.00 | 10.00 |
| ❑ 175 Colby Rasmus AU B RC | 40.00 | 80.00 |
| ❑ 176 Chris Volstad AU B RC | 12.50 | 30.00 |
| ❑ 177 Ricky Romero AU B RC | 6.00 | 15.00 |
| ❑ 178 Ryan Zimmerman AU B RC | 30.00 | 60.00 |
| ❑ 179 C.J. Henry AU B RC | 10.00 | 25.00 |
| ❑ 180 Eddy Martinez AU B RC | 6.00 | 15.00 |

## 2006 Bowman Chrome

| | | |
|---|---|---|
| ❑ COMP. SET w/o AU's (220) | 30.00 | 60.00 |
| ❑ COMMON CARD (1-200) | .20 | .50 |
| ❑ COMMON ROOKIE (201-220) | .25 | .60 |
| ❑ 219 AU ODDS 1:2734 HOBBY, 1:6617 RETAIL | | |
| ❑ 221-224 AU ODDS 1:27 HOBBY, 1:65 RETAIL | | |
| ❑ 1-220 PLATE ODDS 1:836 HOBBY | | |
| ❑ 219 AU PLATE ODDS 1:292,536 HOBBY | | |
| ❑ 221-224 AU PLATES ODDS 1:9,000 HOBBY | | |
| ❑ PLATE PRINT RUN 1 SET PER COLOR | | |
| ❑ BLACK-CYAN-MAGENTA-YELLOW ISSUED | | |
| ❑ NO PLATE PRICING DUE TO SCARCITY | | |
| ❑ 1 Nick Swisher | .20 | .50 |
| ❑ 2 Ted Lilly | .20 | .50 |
| ❑ 3 John Smoltz | .30 | .75 |
| ❑ 4 Lyle Overbay | .20 | .50 |
| ❑ 5 Alfonso Soriano | .20 | .50 |
| ❑ 6 Javier Vazquez | .20 | .50 |
| ❑ 7 Ronnie Belliard | .20 | .50 |
| ❑ 8 Jose Reyes | .50 | 1.25 |
| ❑ 9 Brian Roberts | .20 | .50 |
| ❑ 10 Curt Schilling | .30 | .75 |
| ❑ 11 Adam Dunn | .20 | .50 |
| ❑ 12 Zack Greinke | .20 | .50 |
| ❑ 13 Carlos Guillen | .20 | .50 |
| ❑ 14 Jon Garland | .20 | .50 |
| ❑ 15 Robinson Cano | .30 | .75 |
| ❑ 16 Chris Burke | .20 | .50 |
| ❑ 17 Barry Zito | .20 | .50 |
| ❑ 18 Russ Adams | .20 | .50 |
| ❑ 19 Chris Capuano | .20 | .50 |
| ❑ 20 Scott Rolen | .30 | .75 |
| ❑ 21 Kerry Wood | .20 | .50 |
| ❑ 22 Scott Kazmir | .30 | .75 |
| ❑ 23 Brandon Webb | .20 | .50 |
| ❑ 24 Jeff Kent | .20 | .50 |
| ❑ 25 Albert Pujols | 1.00 | 2.50 |
| ❑ 26 C.C. Sabathia | .20 | .50 |
| ❑ 27 Adrian Beltre | .20 | .50 |
| ❑ 28 Brad Wilkerson | .20 | .50 |
| ❑ 29 Randy Wolf | .20 | .50 |

|  |  | | |
|---|---|---|---|
| 30 | Jason Bay | .20 | .50 |
| 31 | Austin Kearns | .20 | .50 |
| 32 | Clint Barmes | .20 | .50 |
| 33 | Mike Sweeney | .20 | .50 |
| 34 | Kevin Youkilis | .20 | .50 |
| 35 | Justin Morneau | .20 | .50 |
| 36 | Scott Podsednik | .20 | .50 |
| 37 | Jason Giambi | .20 | .50 |
| 38 | Steve Finley | .20 | .50 |
| 39 | Morgan Ensberg | .20 | .50 |
| 40 | Eric Chavez | .20 | .50 |
| 41 | Roy Halladay | .20 | .50 |
| 42 | Horacio Ramirez | .20 | .50 |
| 43 | Ben Sheets | .20 | .50 |
| 44 | Chris Carpenter | .20 | .50 |
| 45 | Andruw Jones | .30 | .75 |
| 46 | Carlos Zambrano | .20 | .50 |
| 47 | Jonny Gomes | .20 | .50 |
| 48 | Shawn Green | .20 | .50 |
| 49 | Moises Alou | .20 | .50 |
| 50 | Ichiro Suzuki | .75 | 2.00 |
| 51 | Juan Pierre | .20 | .50 |
| 52 | Grady Sizemore | .30 | .75 |
| 53 | Kazuo Matsui | .20 | .50 |
| 54 | Jose Vidro | .20 | .50 |
| 55 | Jake Peavy | .20 | .50 |
| 56 | Dallas McPherson | .20 | .50 |
| 57 | Ryan Howard | .75 | 2.00 |
| 58 | Zach Duke | .20 | .50 |
| 59 | Michael Young | .20 | .50 |
| 60 | Todd Helton | .30 | .75 |
| 61 | David DeJesus | .20 | .50 |
| 62 | Ivan Rodriguez | .30 | .75 |
| 63 | Johan Santana | .20 | .50 |
| 64 | Danny Haren | .20 | .50 |
| 65 | Derek Jeter | 1.25 | 3.00 |
| 66 | Greg Maddux | .75 | 2.00 |
| 67 | Jorge Cantu | .20 | .50 |
| 68 | J.J. Hardy | .20 | .50 |
| 69 | Victor Martinez | .20 | .50 |
| 70 | David Wright | .75 | 2.00 |
| 71 | Ryan Church | .20 | .50 |
| 72 | Khalil Greene | .30 | .75 |
| 73 | Jimmy Rollins | .20 | .50 |
| 74 | Hank Blalock | .20 | .50 |
| 75 | Pedro Martinez | .30 | .75 |
| 76 | Chris Shelton | .20 | .50 |
| 77 | Felipe Lopez | .20 | .50 |
| 78 | Jeff Francis | .20 | .50 |
| 79 | Andy Sisco | .20 | .50 |
| 80 | Hideki Matsui | .50 | 1.25 |
| 81 | Ken Griffey Jr. | .75 | 2.00 |
| 82 | Nomar Garciaparra | .50 | 1.25 |
| 83 | Kevin Millwood | .20 | .50 |
| 84 | Paul Konerko | .20 | .50 |
| 85 | A.J. Burnett | .20 | .50 |
| 86 | Mike Piazza | .50 | 1.25 |
| 87 | Brian Giles | .20 | .50 |
| 88 | Johnny Damon | .30 | .75 |
| 89 | Jim Thome | .30 | .75 |
| 90 | Roger Clemens | 1.00 | 2.50 |
| 91 | Aaron Rowand | .20 | .50 |
| 92 | Rafael Furcal | .20 | .50 |
| 93 | Gary Sheffield | .20 | .50 |
| 94 | Mike Cameron | .20 | .50 |
| 95 | Carlos Delgado | .20 | .50 |
| 96 | Jorge Posada | .30 | .75 |
| 97 | Denny Bautista | .20 | .50 |
| 98 | Mike Maroth | .20 | .50 |
| 99 | Brad Radke | .20 | .50 |
| 100 | Alex Rodriguez | .75 | 2.00 |
| 101 | Freddy Garcia | .20 | .50 |
| 102 | Oliver Perez | .20 | .50 |
| 103 | Jon Lieber | .20 | .50 |
| 104 | Melvin Mora | .20 | .50 |
| 105 | Travis Hunter | .20 | .50 |
| 106 | Alex Rios | .20 | .50 |
| 107 | Derek Lowe | .20 | .50 |
| 108 | Luis Castillo | .20 | .50 |
| 109 | Livan Hernandez | .20 | .50 |
| 110 | Tadahito Iguchi | .20 | .50 |
| 111 | Shawn Chacon | .20 | .50 |
| 112 | Frank Thomas | .50 | 1.25 |
| 113 | Josh Beckett | .20 | .50 |
| 114 | Aubrey Huff | .20 | .50 |
| 115 | Derek Lee | .20 | .50 |
| 116 | Chien-Ming Wang | .50 | 1.25 |
| 117 | Joe Crede | .20 | .50 |
| 118 | Torii Hunter | .20 | .50 |
| 119 | J.D. Drew | .20 | .50 |
| 120 | Troy Glaus | .20 | .50 |
| 121 | Sean Casey | .20 | .50 |
| 122 | Edgar Renteria | .20 | .50 |
| 123 | Craig Wilson | .20 | .50 |
| 124 | Adam Eaton | .20 | .50 |
| 125 | Jeff Francoeur | .50 | 1.25 |
| 126 | Bruce Chen | .20 | .50 |
| 127 | Cliff Floyd | .20 | .50 |
| 128 | Jeremy Reed | .20 | .50 |
| 129 | Jake Westbrook | .20 | .50 |
| 130 | Wily Mo Pena | .20 | .50 |
| 131 | Toby Hall | .20 | .50 |
| 132 | David Ortiz | .30 | .75 |
| 133 | David Eckstein | .20 | .50 |
| 134 | Brady Clark | .20 | .50 |
| 135 | Marcus Giles | .20 | .50 |
| 136 | Aaron Hill | .20 | .50 |
| 137 | Mark Kotsay | .20 | .50 |
| 138 | Carlos Lee | .20 | .50 |
| 139 | Roy Oswalt | .20 | .50 |
| 140 | Chone Figgins | .20 | .50 |
| 141 | Mike Mussina | .30 | .75 |
| 142 | Orlando Hernandez | .20 | .50 |
| 143 | Magglio Ordonez | .20 | .50 |
| 144 | Jim Edmonds | .30 | .75 |
| 145 | Bobby Abreu | .20 | .50 |
| 146 | Nick Johnson | .20 | .50 |
| 147 | Carlos Beltran | .20 | .50 |
| 148 | Jhonny Peralta | .20 | .50 |
| 149 | Pedro Feliz | .20 | .50 |
| 150 | Miguel Tejada | .20 | .50 |
| 151 | Luis Gonzalez | .20 | .50 |
| 152 | Carl Crawford | .20 | .50 |
| 153 | Yadier Molina | .20 | .50 |
| 154 | Rich Harden | .20 | .50 |
| 155 | Tim Wakefield | .20 | .50 |
| 156 | Rickie Weeks | .20 | .50 |
| 157 | Johnny Estrada | .20 | .50 |
| 158 | Gustavo Chacin | .20 | .50 |
| 159 | Dan Johnson | .20 | .50 |
| 160 | Willy Taveras | .20 | .50 |
| 161 | Garret Anderson | .20 | .50 |
| 162 | Randy Johnson | .50 | 1.25 |
| 163 | Jermaine Dye | .20 | .50 |
| 164 | Joe Mauer | .50 | 1.25 |
| 165 | Ervin Santana | .20 | .50 |
| 166 | Jeremy Bonderman | .20 | .50 |
| 167 | Garrett Atkins | .20 | .50 |
| 168 | Manny Ramirez | .30 | .75 |
| 169 | Brad Eldred | .20 | .50 |
| 170 | Chase Utley | .50 | 1.25 |
| 171 | Mark Loretta | .20 | .50 |
| 172 | John Patterson | .20 | .50 |
| 173 | Tom Glavine | .30 | .75 |
| 174 | Dontrelle Willis | .30 | .75 |
| 175 | Mark Teixeira | .30 | .75 |
| 176 | Felix Hernandez | .30 | .75 |
| 177 | Cliff Lee | .20 | .50 |
| 178 | Jason Schmidt | .20 | .50 |
| 179 | Chad Tracy | .20 | .50 |
| 180 | Rocco Baldelli | .20 | .50 |
| 181 | Aramis Ramirez | .20 | .50 |
| 182 | Andy Pettitte | .30 | .75 |
| 183 | Mark Mulder | .20 | .50 |
| 184 | Geoff Jenkins | .20 | .50 |
| 185 | Chipper Jones | .50 | 1.25 |
| 186 | Vernon Wells | .20 | .50 |
| 187 | Bobby Crosby | .20 | .50 |
| 188 | Lance Berkman | .20 | .50 |
| 189 | Vladimir Guerrero | .50 | 1.25 |
| 190 | Coco Crisp | .20 | .50 |
| 191 | Brad Penny | .20 | .50 |
| 192 | Jose Guillen | .20 | .50 |
| 193 | Brett Myers | .20 | .50 |
| 194 | Miguel Cabrera | .30 | .75 |
| 195 | Bartolo Colon | .20 | .50 |
| 196 | Craig Biggio | .30 | .75 |
| 197 | Tim Hudson | .20 | .50 |
| 198 | Mark Prior | .30 | .75 |
| 199 | Mark Buehrle | .20 | .50 |
| 200 | Barry Bonds | 1.00 | 2.50 |
| 201 | Anderson Hernandez (RC) | .25 | .60 |
| 202 | Jose Capellan (RC) | .25 | .60 |
| 203 | Jeremy Accardo RC | .25 | .60 |
| 204 | Hanley Ramirez (RC) | .60 | 1.50 |
| 205 | Matt Capps (RC) | .25 | .60 |
| 206 | Jonathan Papelbon (RC) | 1.25 | 3.00 |
| 207 | Chuck James (RC) | .40 | 1.00 |
| 208 | Matt Cain (RC) | .40 | 1.00 |
| 209 | Cole Hamels (RC) | 1.00 | 2.50 |
| 210 | Jason Botts (RC) | .25 | .60 |
| 211 | Lastings Milledge (RC) | .40 | 1.00 |
| 212 | Conor Jackson (RC) | .40 | 1.00 |
| 213 | Yusmeiro Petit (RC) | .25 | .60 |
| 214 | Alay Soler RC | .25 | .60 |
| 215 | Willy Aybar (RC) | .25 | .60 |
| 216 | Adam Loewen (RC) | .25 | .60 |
| 217 | Justin Verlander (RC) | 1.00 | 2.50 |
| 218 | Francisco Liriano (RC) | .60 | 1.50 |
| 219 | Kenji Johjima RC | 1.25 | 3.00 |
| 219a | Kenji Johjima AU | 60.00 | 120.00 |
| 220 | Craig Hansen RC | 1.00 | 2.50 |
| 221 | Prince Fielder AU | 20.00 | 50.00 |
| 222 | Josh Barfield AU (RC) | 6.00 | 15.00 |
| 223 | Fausto Carmona AU (RC) | 6.00 | 15.00 |
| 224 | James Loney AU (RC) | 15.00 | 40.00 |

## 2006 Bowman Chrome Draft

| | | |
|---|---|---|
| COMPLETE SET (55) | 15.00 | 40.00 |
| COMMON RC (1-65) | .40 | 1.00 |
| RC SEMIS 1-55 | .60 | 1.50 |
| RC UNLISTED 1-55 | 1.00 | 2.50 |
| APPX. ODDS 1:2 HOBBY, 1:2 RETAIL | | |
| ODDS INFO PROVIDED BY BECKETT | | |
| OVERALL PLATE ODDS 1:990 HOBBY | | |
| PLATE PRINT RUN 1 SET PER COLOR | | |
| BLACK-CYAN-MAGENTA-YELLOW ISSUED | | |
| NO PLATE PRICING DUE TO SCARCITY | | |

|  |  | | |
|---|---|---|---|
| 1 | Matt Kemp RC | 1.00 | 2.50 |
| 2 | Taylor Tankersley RC | .40 | 1.00 |
| 3 | Mike Napoli RC | 1.00 | 2.50 |
| 4 | Brian Bannister (RC) | .40 | 1.00 |
| 5 | Melky Cabrera (RC) | .60 | 1.50 |
| 6 | Bill Bray (RC) | .40 | 1.00 |
| 7 | Brian Anderson (RC) | .40 | 1.00 |
| 8 | Jered Weaver (RC) | 1.25 | 3.00 |
| 9 | Chris Duncan (RC) | .40 | 1.00 |
| 10 | Boof Bonser (RC) | .60 | 1.50 |
| 11 | Mike Rouse (RC) | .40 | 1.00 |
| 12 | David Pauley (RC) | .40 | 1.00 |
| 13 | Russ Martin (RC) | .60 | 1.50 |
| 14 | Jeremy Sowers (RC) | .40 | 1.00 |
| 15 | Kevin Reese (RC) | .40 | 1.00 |
| 16 | John Rheinecker (RC) | .40 | 1.00 |
| 17 | Tommy Murphy (RC) | .40 | 1.00 |
| 18 | Sean Marshall (RC) | .40 | 1.00 |
| 19 | Jason Kubel (RC) | .40 | 1.00 |
| 20 | Chad Billingsley (RC) | .60 | 1.50 |
| 21 | Kendry Morales (RC) | 1.00 | 2.50 |
| 22 | Jon Lester RC | 2.00 | 5.00 |
| 23 | Brandon Fahey RC | .40 | 1.00 |
| 24 | Josh Johnson (RC) | .60 | 1.50 |
| 25 | Kevin Frandsen (RC) | .40 | 1.00 |
| 26 | Casey Janssen RC | .60 | 1.50 |
| 27 | Scott Thorman (RC) | .40 | 1.00 |
| 28 | Scott Mathieson (RC) | .40 | 1.00 |
| 29 | Jeremy Hermida (RC) | .40 | 1.00 |
| 30 | Dustin Nippert (RC) | .40 | 1.00 |
| 31 | Kevin Thompson (RC) | .40 | 1.00 |
| 32 | Bobby Livingston (RC) | .40 | 1.00 |
| 33 | Travis Ishikawa (RC) | .40 | 1.00 |
| 34 | Jeff Mathis (RC) | .40 | 1.00 |
| 35 | Charlie Haeger RC | .60 | 1.50 |
| 36 | Josh Willingham (RC) | .60 | 1.50 |
| 37 | Taylor Buchholz (RC) | .40 | 1.00 |
| 38 | Joel Guzman (RC) | .40 | 1.00 |
| 39 | Zach Jackson (RC) | .40 | 1.00 |
| 40 | Howie Kendrick (RC) | 1.00 | 2.50 |
| 41 | T.J. Beam (RC) | .40 | 1.00 |

| | | |
|---|---|---|
| ☐ 42 Ty Taubenheim RC | .60 | 1.50 |
| ☐ 43 Erick Aybar (RC) | .40 | 1.00 |
| ☐ 44 Anibal Sanchez (RC) | .60 | 1.50 |
| ☐ 45 Michael Pelfrey RC | 3.00 | 8.00 |
| ☐ 46 Shawn Hill (RC) | .40 | 1.00 |
| ☐ 47 Chris Roberson (RC) | .40 | 1.00 |
| ☐ 48 Carlos Villanueva (RC) | .40 | 1.00 |
| ☐ 49 Andre Ethier (RC) | 1.00 | 2.50 |
| ☐ 50 Anthony Reyes (RC) | .60 | 1.50 |
| ☐ 51 Franklin Gutierrez (RC) | .40 | 1.00 |
| ☐ 52 Angel Guzman (RC) | .40 | 1.00 |
| ☐ 53 Michael O'Connor RC | .40 | 1.00 |
| ☐ 54 James Shields RC | .40 | 1.00 |
| ☐ 55 Nate McLouth (RC) | .40 | 1.00 |

## 2007 Bowman Chrome

| | | |
|---|---|---|
| ☐ COMPLETE SET (220) | 30.00 | 60.00 |
| ☐ COMMON CARD (1-190) | .20 | .50 |
| ☐ COMMON ROOKIE (191-220) | .30 | .75 |
| ☐ 1-220 PLATE ODDS 1:1054 HOBBY | | |
| ☐ PLATE PRINT RUN 1 SET PER COLOR | | |
| ☐ BLACK-CYAN-MAGENTA-YELLOW ISSUED | | |
| ☐ NO PLATE PRICING DUE TO SCARCITY | | |
| ☐ 1 Hanley Ramirez | .30 | .75 |
| ☐ 2 Justin Verlander | .50 | 1.25 |
| ☐ 3 Ryan Zimmerman | .50 | 1.25 |
| ☐ 4 Jered Weaver | .30 | .75 |
| ☐ 5 Stephen Drew | .30 | .75 |
| ☐ 6 Jonathan Papelbon | .50 | 1.25 |
| ☐ 7 Melky Cabrera | .20 | .50 |
| ☐ 8 Francisco Liriano | .50 | 1.25 |
| ☐ 9 Prince Fielder | .50 | 1.25 |
| ☐ 10 Dan Uggla | .20 | .50 |
| ☐ 11 Jeremy Sowers | .20 | .50 |
| ☐ 12 Carlos Quentin | .20 | .50 |
| ☐ 13 Chuck James | .20 | .50 |
| ☐ 14 Andre Ethier | .20 | .50 |
| ☐ 15 Cole Hamels | .50 | 1.25 |
| ☐ 16 Kenji Johjima | .50 | 1.25 |
| ☐ 17 Chad Billingsley | .20 | .50 |
| ☐ 18 Ian Kinsler | .20 | .50 |
| ☐ 19 Jason Hirsh | .20 | .50 |
| ☐ 20 Nick Markakis | .30 | .75 |
| ☐ 21 Jeremy Hermida | .20 | .50 |
| ☐ 22 Ryan Shealy | .20 | .50 |
| ☐ 23 Scott Olsen | .20 | .50 |
| ☐ 24 Russell Martin | .20 | .50 |
| ☐ 25 Conor Jackson | .20 | .50 |
| ☐ 26 Erik Bedard | .20 | .50 |
| ☐ 27 Brian McCann | .20 | .50 |
| ☐ 28 Michael Barrett | .20 | .50 |
| ☐ 29 Brandon Phillips | .20 | .50 |
| ☐ 30 Garrett Atkins | .20 | .50 |
| ☐ 31 Freddy Garcia | .20 | .50 |
| ☐ 32 Mark Loretta | .20 | .50 |
| ☐ 33 Craig Biggio | .30 | .75 |
| ☐ 34 Jeremy Bonderman | .20 | .50 |
| ☐ 35 Johan Santana | .50 | 1.25 |
| ☐ 36 Jorge Posada | .30 | .75 |
| ☐ 37 Victor Martinez | .30 | .75 |
| ☐ 38 Carlos Delgado | .20 | .50 |
| ☐ 39 Gary Matthews Jr. | .20 | .50 |
| ☐ 40 Mike Cameron | .20 | .50 |
| ☐ 41 Adrian Beltre | .20 | .50 |
| ☐ 42 Freddy Sanchez | .20 | .50 |
| ☐ 43 Austin Kearns | .20 | .50 |
| ☐ 44 Mark Buehrle | .20 | .50 |
| ☐ 45 Miguel Cabrera | .50 | 1.50 |
| ☐ 46 Josh Beckett | .30 | .75 |
| ☐ 47 Chone Figgins | .20 | .50 |
| ☐ 48 Edgar Renteria | .20 | .50 |
| ☐ 49 Derek Lowe | .20 | .50 |
| ☐ 50 Ryan Howard | .75 | 2.00 |
| ☐ 51 Shawn Green | .20 | .50 |

| | | |
|---|---|---|
| ☐ 52 Jason Giambi | .20 | .50 |
| ☐ 53 Ervin Santana | .20 | .50 |
| ☐ 54 Aaron Hill | .20 | .50 |
| ☐ 55 Roy Oswalt | .20 | .50 |
| ☐ 56 Dan Haren | .20 | .50 |
| ☐ 57 Jose Vidro | .20 | .50 |
| ☐ 58 Kevin Millwood | .20 | .50 |
| ☐ 59 Jim Edmonds | .30 | .75 |
| ☐ 60 Carl Crawford | .20 | .50 |
| ☐ 61 Randy Wolf | .20 | .50 |
| ☐ 62 Paul LoDuca | .20 | .50 |
| ☐ 63 Johnny Estrada | .20 | .50 |
| ☐ 64 Brian Roberts | .20 | .50 |
| ☐ 65 Manny Ramirez | .30 | .75 |
| ☐ 66 Jose Contreras | .20 | .50 |
| ☐ 67 Josh Barfield | .20 | .50 |
| ☐ 68 Juan Pierre | .20 | .50 |
| ☐ 69 David DeJesus | .20 | .50 |
| ☐ 70 Gary Sheffield | .20 | .50 |
| ☐ 71 Michael Young | .20 | .50 |
| ☐ 72 Randy Johnson | .50 | 1.25 |
| ☐ 73 Rickie Weeks | .20 | .50 |
| ☐ 74 Brian Giles | .20 | .50 |
| ☐ 75 Ichiro Suzuki | .75 | 2.00 |
| ☐ 76 Nick Swisher | .20 | .50 |
| ☐ 77 Justin Morneau | .20 | .50 |
| ☐ 78 Scott Kazmir | .30 | .75 |
| ☐ 79 Lyle Overbay | .20 | .50 |
| ☐ 80 Alfonso Soriano | .20 | .50 |
| ☐ 81 Brandon Webb | .20 | .50 |
| ☐ 82 Joe Crede | .20 | .50 |
| ☐ 83 Corey Patterson | .20 | .50 |
| ☐ 84 Kenny Rogers | .20 | .50 |
| ☐ 85 Ken Griffey Jr. | .75 | 2.00 |
| ☐ 86 Cliff Lee | .20 | .50 |
| ☐ 87 Mike Lowell | .20 | .50 |
| ☐ 88 Marcus Giles | .20 | .50 |
| ☐ 89 Orlando Cabrera | .20 | .50 |
| ☐ 90 Derek Jeter | 1.25 | 3.00 |
| ☐ 91 Ramon Hernandez | .20 | .50 |
| ☐ 92 Carlos Guillen | .20 | .50 |
| ☐ 93 Bill Hall | .20 | .50 |
| ☐ 94 Michael Cuddyer | .20 | .50 |
| ☐ 95 Miguel Tejada | .20 | .50 |
| ☐ 96 Todd Helton | .30 | .75 |
| ☐ 97 C.C. Sabathia | .20 | .50 |
| ☐ 98 Tadahito Iguchi | .20 | .50 |
| ☐ 99 Jose Reyes | .50 | 1.25 |
| ☐ 100 David Wright | .75 | 2.00 |
| ☐ 101 Barry Zito | .20 | .50 |
| ☐ 102 Jake Peavy | .20 | .50 |
| ☐ 103 Richie Sexson | .20 | .50 |
| ☐ 104 A.J. Burnett | .20 | .50 |
| ☐ 105 Eric Chavez | .20 | .50 |
| ☐ 106 Vernon Wells | .20 | .50 |
| ☐ 107 Grady Sizemore | .30 | .75 |
| ☐ 108 Bronson Arroyo | .20 | .50 |
| ☐ 109 Mike Mussina | .30 | .75 |
| ☐ 110 Magglio Ordonez | .20 | .50 |
| ☐ 111 Anibal Sanchez | .20 | .50 |
| ☐ 112 Jeff Francoeur | .50 | 1.25 |
| ☐ 113 Kevin Youkilis | .20 | .50 |
| ☐ 114 Aubrey Huff | .20 | .50 |
| ☐ 115 Carlos Zambrano | .20 | .50 |
| ☐ 116 Mark Teahen | .20 | .50 |
| ☐ 117 Mark Mulder | .20 | .50 |
| ☐ 118 Pedro Martinez | .30 | .75 |
| ☐ 119 Hideki Matsui | .50 | 1.25 |
| ☐ 120 Mike Piazza | .50 | 1.25 |
| ☐ 121 Jason Schmidt | .20 | .50 |
| ☐ 122 Greg Maddux | .75 | 2.00 |
| ☐ 123 Joe Blanton | .20 | .50 |
| ☐ 124 Chris Carpenter | .20 | .50 |
| ☐ 125 David Ortiz | .30 | .75 |
| ☐ 126 Alex Rios | .20 | .50 |
| ☐ 127 Nick Johnson | .20 | .50 |
| ☐ 128 Carlos Lee | .20 | .50 |
| ☐ 129 Pat Burrell | .20 | .50 |
| ☐ 130 Ben Sheets | .20 | .50 |
| ☐ 131 Derrek Lee | .20 | .50 |
| ☐ 132 Adam Dunn | .20 | .50 |
| ☐ 133 Jermaine Dye | .20 | .50 |
| ☐ 134 Curt Schilling | .30 | .75 |
| ☐ 135 Chad Tracy | .20 | .50 |
| ☐ 136 Vladimir Guerrero | .50 | 1.25 |
| ☐ 137 Melvin Mora | .20 | .50 |
| ☐ 138 John Smoltz | .30 | .75 |
| ☐ 139 Craig Monroe | .20 | .50 |

| | | |
|---|---|---|
| ☐ 140 Dontrelle Willis | .20 | .50 |
| ☐ 141 Jeff Francis | .20 | .50 |
| ☐ 142 Chipper Jones | .50 | 1.25 |
| ☐ 143 Frank Thomas | .50 | 1.25 |
| ☐ 144 Brett Myers | .20 | .50 |
| ☐ 145 Tom Glavine | .30 | .75 |
| ☐ 146 Robinson Cano | .30 | .75 |
| ☐ 147 Jeff Kent | .20 | .50 |
| ☐ 148 Scott Rolen | .30 | .75 |
| ☐ 149 Roy Halladay | .20 | .50 |
| ☐ 150 Joe Mauer | .50 | 1.25 |
| ☐ 151 Bobby Abreu | .20 | .50 |
| ☐ 152 Matt Cain | .30 | .75 |
| ☐ 153 Hank Blalock | .20 | .50 |
| ☐ 154 Chris Young | .20 | .50 |
| ☐ 155 Jake Westbrook | .20 | .50 |
| ☐ 156 Javier Vazquez | .20 | .50 |
| ☐ 157 Garret Anderson | .20 | .50 |
| ☐ 158 Aramis Ramirez | .20 | .50 |
| ☐ 159 Mark Kotsay | .20 | .50 |
| ☐ 160 Matt Kemp | .50 | 1.25 |
| ☐ 161 Adrian Gonzalez | .20 | .50 |
| ☐ 162 Felix Hernandez | .30 | .75 |
| ☐ 163 David Eckstein | .20 | .50 |
| ☐ 164 Curtis Granderson | .20 | .50 |
| ☐ 165 Paul Konerko | .20 | .50 |
| ☐ 166 Alex Rodriguez | .75 | 2.00 |
| ☐ 167 Tim Hudson | .20 | .50 |
| ☐ 168 J.D. Drew | .20 | .50 |
| ☐ 169 Chien-Ming Wang | .50 | 1.25 |
| ☐ 170 Jimmy Rollins | .20 | .50 |
| ☐ 171 Matt Morris | .20 | .50 |
| ☐ 172 Raul Ibanez | .30 | .75 |
| ☐ 173 Mark Teixeira | .30 | .75 |
| ☐ 174 Ted Lilly | .20 | .50 |
| ☐ 175 Albert Pujols | 1.00 | 2.50 |
| ☐ 176 Carlos Beltran | .20 | .50 |
| ☐ 177 Lance Berkman | .20 | .50 |
| ☐ 178 Ivan Rodriguez | .30 | .75 |
| ☐ 179 Torii Hunter | .20 | .50 |
| ☐ 180 Johnny Damon | .30 | .75 |
| ☐ 181 Chase Utley | .50 | 1.25 |
| ☐ 182 Jason Bay | .20 | .50 |
| ☐ 183 Jeff Weaver | .20 | .50 |
| ☐ 184 Troy Glaus | .20 | .50 |
| ☐ 185 Rocco Baldelli | .20 | .50 |
| ☐ 186 Rafael Furcal | .20 | .50 |
| ☐ 187 Jim Thome | .30 | .75 |
| ☐ 188 Travis Hafner | .20 | .50 |
| ☐ 189 Matt Holliday | .50 | 1.25 |
| ☐ 190 Andruw Jones | .30 | .75 |
| ☐ 191 Andrew Miller RC | 2.00 | 5.00 |
| ☐ 192 Ryan Braun RC | .30 | .75 |
| ☐ 193 Oswaldo Navarro RC | .30 | .75 |
| ☐ 194 Mike Rabelo RC | .30 | .75 |
| ☐ 195 Delwyn Young (RC) | .30 | .75 |
| ☐ 196 Miguel Montero (RC) | .30 | .75 |
| ☐ 197 Matt Lindstrom (RC) | .30 | .75 |
| ☐ 198 Josh Hamilton (RC) | .75 | 2.00 |
| ☐ 199 Elijah Dukes RC | .50 | 1.25 |
| ☐ 200 Sean Henn (RC) | .30 | .75 |
| ☐ 201 Delmon Young (RC) | .50 | 1.25 |
| ☐ 202 Alexi Casilla RC | .50 | 1.25 |
| ☐ 203 Hunter Pence (RC) | 1.50 | 4.00 |
| ☐ 204 Jeff Baker (RC) | .30 | .75 |
| ☐ 205 Hector Gimenez (RC) | .30 | .75 |
| ☐ 206 Ubaldo Jimenez (RC) | .30 | .75 |
| ☐ 207 Adam Lind (RC) | .30 | .75 |
| ☐ 208 Joaquin Arias (RC) | .30 | .75 |
| ☐ 209 David Murphy (RC) | .30 | .75 |
| ☐ 210 Daisuke Matsuzaka RC | 2.50 | 6.00 |
| ☐ 211 Jerry Owens (RC) | .30 | .75 |
| ☐ 212 Ryan Sweeney (RC) | .30 | .75 |
| ☐ 213 Kei Igawa RC | .75 | 2.00 |
| ☐ 214 Mitch Maier RC | .30 | .75 |
| ☐ 215 Philip Humber (RC) | .30 | .75 |
| ☐ 216 Troy Tulowitzki (RC) | .75 | 2.00 |
| ☐ 217 Tim Lincecum RC | 4.00 | 10.00 |
| ☐ 218 Michael Bourn (RC) | .30 | .75 |
| ☐ 219 Hideki Okajima RC | 1.50 | 4.00 |
| ☐ 220 Josh Fields (RC) | .30 | .75 |

### 2007 Bowman Chrome Draft

| | | |
|---|---|---|
| ❑ COMPLETE SET (55) | 15.00 | 40.00 |
| ❑ COMMON RC (1-55) | .25 | .60 |
| ❑ OVERALL PLATE ODDS 1:1294 HOBBY | | |
| ❑ PLATE PRINT RUN 1 SET PER COLOR | | |
| ❑ BLACK-CYAN-MAGENTA-YELLOW ISSUED | | |
| ❑ NO PLATE PRICING DUE TO SCARCITY | | |
| ❑ BDP1 Travis Buck (RC) | .25 | .60 |
| ❑ BDP2 Matt Chico (RC) | .25 | .60 |
| ❑ BDP3 Justin Upton RC | 1.50 | 4.00 |
| ❑ BDP4 Chase Wright (RC) | .60 | 1.50 |
| ❑ BDP5 Kevin Kouzmanoff (RC) | .25 | .60 |
| ❑ BDP6 John Danks RC | .25 | .60 |
| ❑ BDP7 Alejandro De Aza RC | .40 | 1.00 |
| ❑ BDP8 Jamie Vermilyea RC | .25 | .60 |
| ❑ BDP9 Jesus Flores RC | .25 | .60 |
| ❑ BDP10 Glen Perkins (RC) | .25 | .60 |
| ❑ BDP11 Tim Lincecum RC | 3.00 | 8.00 |
| ❑ BDP12 Cameron Maybin RC | 1.25 | 3.00 |
| ❑ BDP13 Brandon Morrow RC | .60 | 1.50 |
| ❑ BDP14 Mike Rabelo RC | .25 | .60 |
| ❑ BDP15 Alex Gordon RC | 1.00 | 2.50 |
| ❑ BDP16 Zack Segovia (RC) | .25 | .60 |
| ❑ BDP17 Jon Knott (RC) | .25 | .60 |
| ❑ BDP18 Joba Chamberlain RC | 1.25 | 3.00 |
| ❑ BDP19 Danny Putnam (RC) | .25 | .60 |
| ❑ BDP20 Matt DeSalvo (RC) | .25 | .60 |
| ❑ BDP21 Fred Lewis (RC) | .40 | 1.00 |
| ❑ BDP22 Sean Gallagher (RC) | .25 | .60 |
| ❑ BDP23 Brandon Wood (RC) | .25 | .60 |
| ❑ BDP24 Dennis Dove (RC) | .25 | .60 |
| ❑ BDP25 Hunter Pence (RC) | 1.25 | 3.00 |
| ❑ BDP26 Jarrod Saltalamacchia (RC) | .40 | 1.00 |
| ❑ BDP27 Ben Francisco (RC) | .25 | .60 |
| ❑ BDP28 Doug Slaten RC | .25 | .60 |
| ❑ BDP29 Tony Abreu RC | .60 | 1.50 |
| ❑ BDP30 Billy Butler (RC) | .40 | 1.00 |
| ❑ BDP31 Jesse Litsch RC | .40 | 1.00 |
| ❑ BDP32 Nate Schierholtz (RC) | .60 | 1.50 |
| ❑ BDP33 Jared Burton RC | .25 | .60 |
| ❑ BDP34 Matt Brown RC | .25 | .60 |
| ❑ BDP35 Dallas Braden RC | .40 | 1.00 |
| ❑ BDP36 Carlos Gomez RC | .40 | 1.00 |
| ❑ BDP37 Brian Stokes (RC) | .25 | .60 |
| ❑ BDP38 Kory Casto (RC) | .25 | .60 |
| ❑ BDP39 Mark McLemore (RC) | .25 | .60 |
| ❑ BDP40 Andy LaRoche (RC) | .40 | 1.00 |
| ❑ BDP41 Tyler Clippard (RC) | .40 | 1.00 |
| ❑ BDP42 Curtis Thigpen (RC) | .25 | .60 |
| ❑ BDP43 Yunel Escobar (RC) | .25 | .60 |
| ❑ BDP44 Andy Sonnanstine RC | .25 | .60 |
| ❑ BDP45 Felix Pie (RC) | .25 | .60 |
| ❑ BDP46 Homer Bailey (RC) | .40 | 1.00 |
| ❑ BDP47 Kyle Kendrick RC | .60 | 1.50 |
| ❑ BDP48 Angel Sanchez (RC) | .25 | .60 |
| ❑ BDP49 Phil Hughes (RC) | 1.25 | 3.00 |
| ❑ BDP50 Ryan Braun (RC) | 1.50 | 4.00 |
| ❑ BDP51 Kevin Slowey (RC) | .60 | 1.50 |
| ❑ BDP52 Brendan Ryan (RC) | .25 | .60 |
| ❑ BDP53 Yovani Gallardo RC | .75 | 2.00 |
| ❑ BDP54 Mark Reynolds RC | 1.50 | 4.00 |
| ❑ 237 Barry Bonds | 1.25 | 3.00 |

### 2008 Bowman Chrome

| | | |
|---|---|---|
| ❑ COMPLETE SET (220) | 15.00 | 40.00 |
| ❑ COMMON CARD (1-190) | .20 | .50 |
| ❑ COMMON ROOKIE (1-220) | .60 | 1.50 |
| ❑ 1 Ryan Braun | .60 | 1.50 |
| ❑ 2 David DeJesus | .20 | .50 |
| ❑ 3 Brandon Phillips | .20 | .50 |
| ❑ 4 Mark Teixeira | .30 | .75 |
| ❑ 5 Daisuke Matsuzaka | .50 | 1.25 |
| ❑ 6 Justin Upton | .50 | 1.25 |
| ❑ 7 Jered Weaver | .20 | .50 |
| ❑ 8 Todd Helton | .30 | .75 |
| ❑ 9 Adam Jones | .20 | .50 |
| ❑ 10 Erik Bedard | .20 | .50 |
| ❑ 11 Jason Bay | .30 | .75 |
| ❑ 12 Cole Hamels | .50 | 1.25 |
| ❑ 13 Bobby Abreu | .20 | .50 |
| ❑ 14 Carlos Zambrano | .20 | .50 |
| ❑ 15 Vladimir Guerrero | .50 | 1.25 |
| ❑ 16 Joe Blanton | .20 | .50 |
| ❑ 17 Paul Maholm | .20 | .50 |
| ❑ 18 Adrian Gonzalez | .30 | .75 |
| ❑ 19 Brandon Webb | .30 | .75 |
| ❑ 20 Carl Crawford | .20 | .50 |
| ❑ 21 A.J. Burnett | .20 | .50 |
| ❑ 22 Dmitri Young | .20 | .50 |
| ❑ 23 Jeremy Hermida | .20 | .50 |
| ❑ 24 C.C. Sabathia | .30 | .75 |
| ❑ 25 Adam Dunn | .20 | .50 |
| ❑ 26 Matt Garza | .20 | .50 |
| ❑ 27 Adrian Beltre | .20 | .50 |
| ❑ 28 Kevin Milwood | .20 | .50 |
| ❑ 29 Manny Ramirez | .50 | 1.25 |
| ❑ 30 Javier Vazquez | .20 | .50 |
| ❑ 31 Carlos Delgado | .20 | .50 |
| ❑ 32 Torii Hunter | .20 | .50 |
| ❑ 33 Ivan Rodriguez | .30 | .75 |
| ❑ 34 Nick Markakis | .30 | .75 |
| ❑ 35 Gil Meche | .20 | .50 |
| ❑ 36 Garrett Atkins | .20 | .50 |
| ❑ 37 Fausto Carmona | .20 | .50 |
| ❑ 38 Joe Mauer | .50 | 1.25 |
| ❑ 39 Tom Glavine | .30 | .75 |
| ❑ 40 Hideki Matsui | .50 | 1.25 |
| ❑ 41 Scott Rolen | .20 | .50 |
| ❑ 42 Tim Lincecum | .60 | 1.50 |
| ❑ 43 Prince Fielder | .20 | .50 |
| ❑ 44 Kazuo Matsui | .20 | .50 |
| ❑ 45 Tom Gorzelanny | .20 | .50 |
| ❑ 46 Lance Berkman | .30 | .75 |
| ❑ 47 David Ortiz | .30 | .75 |
| ❑ 48 Dontrelle Willis | .20 | .50 |
| ❑ 49 Travis Hafner | .20 | .50 |
| ❑ 50 Aaron Harang | .20 | .50 |
| ❑ 51 Chris Young | .20 | .50 |
| ❑ 52 Vernon Wells | .20 | .50 |
| ❑ 53 Francisco Liriano | .30 | .75 |
| ❑ 54 Eric Chavez | .20 | .50 |
| ❑ 55 Phil Hughes | .50 | 1.25 |
| ❑ 56 Melvin Mora | .20 | .50 |
| ❑ 57 Johan Santana | .30 | .75 |
| ❑ 58 Brian McCann | .20 | .50 |
| ❑ 59 Pat Burrell | .20 | .50 |
| ❑ 60 Chris Carpenter | .20 | .50 |
| ❑ 61 Brian Giles | .20 | .50 |
| ❑ 62 Jose Reyes | .30 | .75 |
| ❑ 63 Hanley Ramirez | .50 | 1.25 |
| ❑ 64 Ubaldo Jimenez | .20 | .50 |
| ❑ 65 Felix Pie | .20 | .50 |
| ❑ 66 Jeremy Bonderman | .20 | .50 |
| ❑ 67 Jimmy Rollins | .30 | .75 |
| ❑ 68 Miguel Tejada | .20 | .50 |
| ❑ 69 Derek Lowe | .20 | .50 |
| ❑ 70 Alex Gordon | .30 | .75 |
| ❑ 71 John Maine | .20 | .50 |
| ❑ 72 Alfonso Soriano | .30 | .75 |
| ❑ 73 Ben Sheets | .30 | .75 |
| ❑ 74 Hunter Pence | .50 | 1.25 |
| ❑ 75 Magglio Ordonez | .30 | .75 |
| ❑ 76 Josh Beckett | .30 | .75 |
| ❑ 77 Victor Martinez | .20 | .50 |
| ❑ 78 Mark Buehrle | .20 | .50 |
| ❑ 79 Jason Varitek | .50 | 1.25 |
| ❑ 80 Chien-Ming Wang | .50 | 1.25 |
| ❑ 81 Ken Griffey Jr. | .75 | 2.00 |
| ❑ 82 Billy Butler | .20 | .50 |
| ❑ 83 Brad Penny | .20 | .50 |
| ❑ 84 Carlos Beltran | .20 | .50 |
| ❑ 85 Curt Schilling | .30 | .75 |
| ❑ 86 Jorge Posada | .30 | .75 |
| ❑ 87 Andruw Jones | .20 | .50 |
| ❑ 88 Bobby Crosby | .20 | .50 |
| ❑ 89 Freddy Sanchez | .20 | .50 |
| ❑ 90 Barry Zito | .20 | .50 |
| ❑ 91 Miguel Cabrera | .30 | .75 |
| ❑ 92 B.J. Upton | .30 | .75 |
| ❑ 93 Matt Cain | .20 | .50 |
| ❑ 94 Lyle Overbay | .20 | .50 |
| ❑ 95 Austin Kearns | .20 | .50 |
| ❑ 96 Alex Rodriguez | .75 | 2.00 |
| ❑ 97 Rich Harden | .20 | .50 |
| ❑ 98 Justin Morneau | .30 | .75 |
| ❑ 99 Oliver Perez | .20 | .50 |
| ❑ 100 Gary Matthews | .20 | .50 |
| ❑ 101 Matt Holliday | .30 | .75 |
| ❑ 102 Justin Verlander | .30 | .75 |
| ❑ 103 Orlando Cabrera | .20 | .50 |
| ❑ 104 Rich Hill | .20 | .50 |
| ❑ 105 Tim Hudson | .20 | .50 |
| ❑ 106 Ryan Zimmerman | .30 | .75 |
| ❑ 107 Roy Oswalt | .30 | .75 |
| ❑ 108 Nick Swisher | .30 | .75 |
| ❑ 109 Raul Ibanez | .20 | .50 |
| ❑ 110 Kelly Johnson | .20 | .50 |
| ❑ 111 Alex Rios | .20 | .50 |
| ❑ 112 John Lackey | .20 | .50 |
| ❑ 113 Robinson Cano | .30 | .75 |
| ❑ 114 Michael Young | .20 | .50 |
| ❑ 115 Jeff Francis | .20 | .50 |
| ❑ 116 Grady Sizemore | .30 | .75 |
| ❑ 117 Mike Lowell | .20 | .50 |
| ❑ 118 Aramis Ramirez | .20 | .50 |
| ❑ 119 Stephen Drew | .20 | .50 |
| ❑ 120 Yovani Gallardo | .20 | .50 |
| ❑ 121 Chase Utley | .50 | 1.25 |
| ❑ 122 Dan Haren | .20 | .50 |
| ❑ 123 Yunel Escobar | .20 | .50 |
| ❑ 124 Greg Maddux | .60 | 1.50 |
| ❑ 125 Garret Anderson | .20 | .50 |
| ❑ 126 Aubrey Huff | .20 | .50 |
| ❑ 127 Paul Konerko | .20 | .50 |
| ❑ 128 Dan Uggla | .20 | .50 |
| ❑ 129 Roy Halladay | .30 | .75 |
| ❑ 130 Andre Ethier | .20 | .50 |
| ❑ 131 Orlando Hernandez | .20 | .50 |
| ❑ 132 Troy Tulowitzki | .30 | .75 |
| ❑ 133 Carlos Guillen | .20 | .50 |
| ❑ 134 Scott Kazmir | .30 | .75 |
| ❑ 135 Aaron Rowand | .20 | .50 |
| ❑ 136 Jim Edmonds | .20 | .50 |
| ❑ 137 Jermaine Dye | .20 | .50 |
| ❑ 138 Orlando Hudson | .20 | .50 |
| ❑ 139 Derrek Lee | .30 | .75 |
| ❑ 140 Travis Buck | .20 | .50 |
| ❑ 141 Zack Greinke | .30 | .75 |
| ❑ 142 Jeff Kent | .20 | .50 |
| ❑ 143 John Smoltz | .50 | 1.25 |
| ❑ 144 David Wright | .60 | 1.50 |
| ❑ 145 Joba Chamberlain | .60 | 1.50 |
| ❑ 146 Adam LaRoche | .20 | .50 |
| ❑ 147 Kevin Youkilis | .30 | .75 |
| ❑ 148 Troy Glaus | .20 | .50 |
| ❑ 149 Nick Johnson | .20 | .50 |
| ❑ 150 J.J. Hardy | .20 | .50 |
| ❑ 151 Felix Hernandez | .30 | .75 |
| ❑ 152 Gary Sheffield | .30 | .75 |
| ❑ 153 Albert Pujols | 1.00 | 2.50 |
| ❑ 154 Chuck James | .20 | .50 |
| ❑ 155 Kosuke Fukudome | 4.00 | 10.00 |
| ❑ 155b Kosuke Fukudome Japan | 4.00 | 10.00 |
| ❑ 155c Fukudome No Sig/1600 * | 10.00 | 25.00 |

| # | Player | Lo | Hi |
|---|--------|----|----|
| 156 | Eric Byrnes | .20 | .50 |
| 157 | Brad Hawpe | .20 | .50 |
| 158 | Delmon Young | .30 | .75 |
| 159 | Brian Roberts | .30 | .75 |
| 160 | Russ Martin | .30 | .75 |
| 161 | Hank Blalock | .20 | .50 |
| 162 | Yadier Molina | .30 | .75 |
| 163 | Jeremy Guthrie | .20 | .50 |
| 164 | Chipper Jones | .60 | 1.50 |
| 165 | Johnny Damon | .30 | .75 |
| 166 | Ryan Garko | .20 | .50 |
| 167 | Jake Peavy | .30 | .75 |
| 168 | Chone Figgins | .20 | .50 |
| 169 | Edgar Renteria | .20 | .50 |
| 170 | Jim Thome | .30 | .75 |
| 171 | Carlos Pena | .50 | 1.25 |
| 172 | Dustin Pedroia | .60 | 1.50 |
| 173 | Brett Myers | .20 | .50 |
| 174 | Josh Hamilton | .60 | 1.50 |
| 175 | Randy Johnson | .50 | 1.25 |
| 176 | Ichiro Suzuki | .75 | 2.00 |
| 177 | Aaron Hill | .20 | .50 |
| 178 | Corey Hart | .20 | .50 |
| 179 | Jarrod Saltalamacchia | .20 | .50 |
| 180 | Jeff Francoeur | .30 | .75 |
| 181 | Derek Jeter | 1.25 | 3.00 |
| 182 | Curtis Granderson | .30 | .75 |
| 183 | James Loney | .30 | .75 |
| 184 | Brian Bannister | .20 | .50 |
| 185 | Carlos Lee | .20 | .50 |
| 186 | Pedro Martinez | .30 | .75 |
| 187 | Asdrubal Cabrera | .20 | .50 |
| 188 | Kenji Johjima | .20 | .50 |
| 189 | Jacoby Ellsbury | .75 | 2.00 |
| 190 | Ryan Howard | .60 | 1.50 |
| 191 | Sean Rodriguez (RC) | .60 | 1.50 |
| 192 | Justin Ruggiano (RC) | 1.00 | 2.50 |
| 193 | Jed Lowrie (RC) | 1.50 | 4.00 |
| 194 | Joey Votto (RC) | 1.50 | 4.00 |
| 195 | Denard Span (RC) | 1.00 | 2.50 |
| 196 | Brad Harman RC | 1.00 | 2.50 |
| 197 | Jeff Niemann (RC) | 1.00 | 2.50 |
| 198 | Chin-Lung Hu (RC) | 1.00 | 2.50 |
| 199 | Luke Hochevar RC | 1.00 | 2.50 |
| 200 | German Duran RC | 1.00 | 2.50 |
| 201 | Troy Patton (RC) | .60 | 1.50 |
| 202 | Hiroki Kuroda (RC) | 1.00 | 2.50 |
| 203 | David Purcey (RC) | .60 | 1.50 |
| 204 | Armando Galarraga RC | 1.00 | 2.50 |
| 205 | John Bowker (RC) | .60 | 1.50 |
| 206 | Nick Blackburn RC | 1.00 | 2.50 |
| 207 | Hernan Inbarren (RC) | 1.00 | 2.50 |
| 208 | Greg Smith RC | .60 | 1.50 |
| 209 | Alberto Gonzalez RC | 1.00 | 2.50 |
| 210 | Justin Masterson RC | 3.00 | 8.00 |
| 211 | Brian Barton RC | 1.00 | 2.50 |
| 212 | Robinzon Diaz (RC) | .60 | 1.50 |
| 213 | Clete Thomas RC | 1.00 | 2.50 |
| 214 | Kazuo Fukumori RC | 1.00 | 2.50 |
| 215 | Jayson Nix (RC) | .60 | 1.50 |
| 216 | Evan Longoria RC | 6.00 | 15.00 |
| 217 | Johnny Cueto RC | 1.00 | 2.50 |
| 218 | Matt Tolbert RC | 1.00 | 2.50 |
| 219 | Masahide Kobayashi RC | 1.00 | 2.50 |
| 220 | Callix Crabbe (RC) | .60 | 1.50 |

## 2009 Bowman Chrome

| | | Lo | Hi |
|---|---|----|----|
| | COMPLETE SET (220) | 75.00 | 150.00 |
| | COMMON CARD (1-190) | .20 | .50 |
| | COMMON ROOKIE | | |
| | PRINTING PLATE ODDS 1:538 HOBBY | | |
| | PLATE PRINT RUN 1 SET PER COLOR | | |
| | BLACK-CYAN-MAGENTA-YELLOW ISSUED | | |
| | NO PLATE PRICING DUE TO SCARCITY | | |
| 1 | David Wright | .60 | 1.50 |
| 2 | Albert Pujols | 1.25 | 3.00 |
| 3 | Alex Rodriguez | .75 | 2.00 |
| 4 | Chase Utley | .50 | 1.25 |
| 5 | Chien-Ming Wang | .50 | 1.25 |
| 6 | Jimmy Rollins | .30 | .75 |
| 7 | Ken Griffey Jr. | .75 | 2.00 |
| 8 | Manny Ramirez | .50 | 1.25 |
| 9 | Chipper Jones | .50 | 1.25 |
| 10 | Ichiro Suzuki | .75 | 2.00 |
| 11 | Justin Morneau | .30 | .75 |
| 12 | Hanley Ramirez | .50 | 1.25 |
| 13 | Cliff Lee | .30 | .75 |
| 14 | Ryan Howard | .60 | 1.50 |
| 15 | Ian Kinsler | .30 | .75 |
| 16 | Jose Reyes | .50 | 1.25 |
| 17 | Ted Lilly | .20 | .50 |
| 18 | Miguel Cabrera | .30 | .75 |
| 19 | Nate McLouth | .20 | .50 |
| 20 | Josh Beckett | .30 | .75 |
| 21 | John Lackey | .20 | .50 |
| 22 | David Ortiz | .30 | .75 |
| 23 | Carlos Lee | .20 | .50 |
| 24 | Adam Dunn | .30 | .75 |
| 25 | B.J. Upton | .30 | .75 |
| 26 | Curtis Granderson | .50 | 1.25 |
| 27 | David DeJesus | .20 | .50 |
| 28 | CC Sabathia | .30 | .75 |
| 29 | Russell Martin | .30 | .75 |
| 30 | Torii Hunter | .20 | .50 |
| 31 | Rich Harden | .20 | .50 |
| 32 | Johnny Damon | .30 | .75 |
| 33 | Cristian Guzman | .20 | .50 |
| 34 | Grady Sizemore | .30 | .75 |
| 35 | Jorge Posada | .30 | .75 |
| 36 | Placido Polanco | .20 | .50 |
| 37 | Ryan Ludwick | .30 | .75 |
| 38 | Dustin Pedroia | .60 | 1.50 |
| 39 | Matt Garza | .20 | .50 |
| 40 | Prince Fielder | .50 | 1.25 |
| 41 | Rick Ankiel | .30 | .75 |
| 42 | David Huff RC | .60 | 1.50 |
| 43 | Erik Bedard | .20 | .50 |
| 44 | Ryan Braun | .60 | 1.50 |
| 45 | Ervin Santana | .20 | .50 |
| 46 | Brian Roberts | .20 | .50 |
| 47 | Mike Jacobs | .20 | .50 |
| 48 | Phil Hughes | .30 | .75 |
| 49 | Justin Masterson | .30 | .75 |
| 50 | Felix Hernandez | .30 | .75 |
| 51 | Stephen Drew | .20 | .50 |
| 52 | Bobby Abreu | .20 | .50 |
| 53 | Jay Bruce | .50 | 1.25 |
| 54 | Josh Hamilton | .50 | 1.25 |
| 55 | Garrett Atkins | .20 | .50 |
| 56 | Jacoby Ellsbury | .50 | 1.25 |
| 57 | Johan Santana | .50 | 1.25 |
| 58 | James Shields | .20 | .50 |
| 59 | Sergio Escalona RC | 1.00 | 2.50 |
| 60 | Carlos Pena | .30 | .75 |
| 61 | Matt Kemp | .50 | 1.25 |
| 62 | Joey Votto | .30 | .75 |
| 63 | Raul Ibanez | .20 | .50 |
| 64 | Casey Kotchman | .20 | .50 |
| 65 | Hunter Pence | .30 | .75 |
| 66 | Daniel Murphy RC | 1.50 | 4.00 |
| 67 | Carlos Beltran | .20 | .50 |
| 68 | Evan Longoria | .75 | 2.00 |
| 69 | Daisuke Matsuzaka | .75 | 2.00 |
| 70 | Cole Hamels | .50 | 1.25 |
| 71 | Robinson Cano | .30 | .75 |
| 72 | Clayton Kershaw | .50 | 1.25 |
| 73 | Kenji Johjima | .20 | .50 |
| 74 | Kazuo Matsui | .20 | .50 |
| 75 | Jayson Werth | .20 | .50 |
| 76 | Brian McCann | .30 | .75 |
| 77 | Barry Zito | .20 | .50 |
| 78 | Glen Perkins | .20 | .50 |
| 79 | Jeff Francoeur | .30 | .75 |
| 80 | Derek Jeter | 1.25 | 3.00 |
| 81 | Ryan Doumit | .20 | .50 |
| 82 | Dan Haren | .20 | .50 |
| 83 | Justin Duchscherer | .20 | .50 |
| 84 | Marlon Byrd | .20 | .50 |
| 85 | Derek Lowe | .20 | .50 |
| 86 | Pat Burrell | .30 | .75 |
| 87 | Jair Jurrjens | .30 | .75 |
| 88 | Zack Greinke | .30 | .75 |
| 89 | Jon Lester | .30 | .75 |
| 90 | Jorge Cantu | .20 | .50 |
| 91 | John Maine | .20 | .50 |
| 92 | Brad Hawpe | .20 | .50 |
| 93 | Mike Aviles | .20 | .50 |
| 94 | Victor Martinez | .30 | .75 |
| 95 | Ryan Dempster | .20 | .50 |
| 96 | Miguel Tejada | .20 | .50 |
| 97 | Joe Mauer | .50 | 1.25 |
| 98 | Scott Olsen | .20 | .50 |
| 99 | Tim Lincecum | .60 | 1.50 |
| 100 | Francisco Liriano | .20 | .50 |
| 101 | Chris Iannetta | .20 | .50 |
| 103 | Greg Burke RC | 1.00 | 2.50 |
| 104 | Milton Bradley | .20 | .50 |
| 105 | John Lannan | .20 | .50 |
| 106 | Yovani Gallardo | .20 | .50 |
| 107 | Luke French (RC) | .60 | 1.50 |
| 108 | Jermaine Dye | .20 | .50 |
| 109 | Dioner Navarro | .20 | .50 |
| 110 | Joba Chamberlain | .60 | 1.50 |
| 111 | Nelson Cruz | .20 | .50 |
| 112 | Johnny Cueto | .20 | .50 |
| 113 | Adam LaRoche | .20 | .50 |
| 114 | Aaron Rowand | .20 | .50 |
| 115 | Jason Bay | .30 | .75 |
| 116 | Roy Halladay | .30 | .75 |
| 117 | Mark Teixeira | .50 | 1.25 |
| 118 | Gavin Floyd | .20 | .50 |
| 119 | Magglio Ordonez | .30 | .75 |
| 120 | Rafael Furcal | .20 | .50 |
| 121 | Mark Buehrle | .20 | .50 |
| 122 | Alexi Casilla | .20 | .50 |
| 123 | Scott Kazmir | .30 | .75 |
| 124 | Nick Swisher | .20 | .50 |
| 125 | Carlos Gomez | .20 | .50 |
| 126 | Javier Vazquez | .20 | .50 |
| 127 | Paul Konerko | .20 | .50 |
| 128 | Nolan Reimold (RC) | 1.00 | 2.50 |
| 129 | Gerardo Parra RC | 1.00 | 2.50 |
| 130 | Josh Johnson | .20 | .50 |
| 131 | Carlos Zambrano | .20 | .50 |
| 132 | Chris Davis | .20 | .50 |
| 133 | Bobby Crosby | .20 | .50 |
| 134 | Alex Gordon | .30 | .75 |
| 135 | Chris Young | .20 | .50 |
| 136 | Carlos Delgado | .20 | .50 |
| 137 | Adam Wainwright | .30 | .75 |
| 138 | Justin Upton | .30 | .75 |
| 139 | Chris Coghlan RC | 1.50 | 4.00 |
| 140 | J.D. Drew | .20 | .50 |
| 141 | Adam Lind | .20 | .50 |
| 142 | Mike Lowell | .20 | .50 |
| 143 | Lance Berkman | .30 | .75 |
| 144 | J.J. Hardy | .20 | .50 |
| 145 | A.J. Burnett | .30 | .75 |
| 146 | Jake Peavy | .20 | .50 |
| 147 | Xavier Paul (RC) | 1.00 | 2.50 |
| 148 | Matt Holliday | .30 | .75 |
| 149 | Carl Crawford | .30 | .75 |
| 150 | Andre Ethier | .30 | .75 |
| 151 | Howie Kendrick | .20 | .50 |
| 152 | Ryan Zimmerman | .30 | .75 |
| 153 | Troy Tulowitzki | .30 | .75 |
| 154 | Brett Myers | .20 | .50 |
| 155 | Chris Young | .20 | .50 |
| 156 | Jered Weaver | .20 | .50 |
| 157 | Jeff Clement | .20 | .50 |
| 158 | Alex Rios | .20 | .50 |
| 159 | Shane Victorino | .20 | .50 |
| 160 | Jeremy Hermida | .20 | .50 |
| 161 | James Loney | .30 | .75 |
| 162 | Michael Young | .30 | .75 |
| 163 | Aramis Ramirez | .20 | .50 |
| 164 | Geovany Soto | .30 | .75 |
| 165 | Aubrey Huff | .20 | .50 |
| 166 | Rick Porcello RC | 2.50 | 6.00 |
| 167 | Vernon Wells | .20 | .50 |
| 168 | Chone Figgins | .20 | .50 |
| 169 | Carlos Quentin | .20 | .50 |
| 170 | Chad Billingsley | .20 | .50 |
| 171 | Matt Cain | .20 | .50 |
| 172 | Derek Lee | .30 | .75 |
| 173 | A.J. Pierzynski | .20 | .50 |
| 174 | Daniel Bard RC | .60 | 1.50 |
| 175 | Bobby Scales RC | 1.00 | 2.50 |
| 176 | Alfonso Soriano | .30 | .75 |
| 177 | Adrian Gonzalez | .30 | .75 |
| 178 | Andrew McCutchen (RC) | 1.50 | 4.00 |
| 179 | Nick Markakis | .30 | .75 |
| 180 | Brandon Webb | .30 | .75 |
| 181 | Vladimir Guerrero | .50 | 1.25 |
| 182 | Roy Oswalt | .20 | .50 |
| 183 | Adam Jones | .30 | .75 |
| 184 | Edinson Volquez | .20 | .50 |
| 185 | Gordon Beckham RC | 5.00 | 12.00 |
| 186 | Joe Saunders | .20 | .50 |
| 187 | Yadier Molina | .30 | .75 |
| 188 | Kevin Youkilis | .30 | .75 |
| 189 | Dan Uggla | .20 | .50 |
| 190 | Kosuke Fukudome | .50 | 1.25 |

| | | |
|---|---|---|
| 191 Matt LaPorta RC | 1.50 | 4.00 |
| 192 Trevor Cahill RC | 1.00 | 2.50 |
| 193 Derek Holland RC | 1.50 | 4.00 |
| 194 Michael Bowden (RC) | 1.00 | 2.50 |
| 195 Andrew Carpenter RC | 1.00 | 2.50 |
| 196 Phil Coke RC | 1.00 | 2.50 |
| 197 Graham Taylor RC | 1.00 | 2.50 |
| 198 Alcides Escobar RC | 1.00 | 2.50 |
| 199 Dexter Fowler (RC) | 1.00 | 2.50 |
| 200 Mat Gamel RC | 1.50 | 4.00 |
| 201 Jordan Zimmermann RC | 1.50 | 4.00 |
| 202 Greg Golson (RC) | .60 | 1.50 |
| 203 Andrew Bailey RC | 1.00 | 2.50 |
| 204 David Hernandez RC | 1.00 | 2.50 |
| 205 George Kottaras (RC) | .60 | 1.50 |
| 206 Lou Marson (RC) | .60 | 1.50 |
| 207 Shairon Martis RC | 1.00 | 2.50 |
| 208 Juan Miranda RC | 1.00 | 2.50 |
| 209 Tyler Greene (RC) | .60 | 1.50 |
| 210 Jonathon Niese RC | 1.00 | 2.50 |
| 211 Bobby Parnell RC | 1.00 | 2.50 |
| 212 Colby Rasmus (RC) | 1.00 | 2.50 |
| 213 David Price RC | 2.00 | 5.00 |
| 214 Angel Salome (RC) | .60 | 1.50 |
| 215 Gaby Sanchez RC | .60 | 1.50 |
| 216 Freddy Sandoval (RC) | .60 | 1.50 |
| 217 Travis Snider RC | 1.50 | 4.00 |
| 218 Will Venable RC | .60 | 1.50 |
| 219 Brett Anderson RC | 1.00 | 2.50 |
| 220 Josh Outman RC | 1.00 | 2.50 |

## 2001 Bowman Heritage

| | | |
|---|---|---|
| COMPLETE SET (440) | 125.00 | 200.00 |
| COMP.SET w/o SP's (330) | 20.00 | 50.00 |
| COMMON CARD (1-330) | .15 | .40 |
| COMMON CARD (1-330) | .15 | .40 |
| COMMON CARD (331-440) | .75 | 2.00 |
| 1 Chipper Jones | .40 | 1.00 |
| 2 Pete Harnisch | .15 | .40 |
| 3 Brian Giles | .15 | .40 |
| 4 J.T. Snow | .15 | .40 |
| 5 Bartolo Colon | .15 | .40 |
| 6 Jorge Posada | .25 | .60 |
| 7 Shawn Green | .15 | .40 |
| 8 Derek Jeter | 1.00 | 2.50 |
| 9 Benito Santiago | .15 | .40 |
| 10 Ramon Hernandez | .15 | .40 |
| 11 Bernie Williams | .25 | .60 |
| 12 Greg Maddux | .60 | 1.50 |
| 13 Barry Bonds | 1.00 | 2.50 |
| 14 Roger Clemens | .75 | 2.00 |
| 15 Miguel Tejada | .15 | .40 |
| 16 Pedro Feliz | .15 | .40 |
| 17 Jim Edmonds | .15 | .40 |
| 18 Tom Glavine | .25 | .60 |
| 19 David Justice | .15 | .40 |
| 20 Rich Aurilia | .15 | .40 |
| 21 Jason Giambi | .15 | .40 |
| 22 Orlando Hernandez | .15 | .40 |
| 23 Shawn Estes | .15 | .40 |
| 24 Nelson Figueroa | .15 | .40 |
| 25 Terrence Long | .15 | .40 |
| 26 Mike Mussina | .25 | .60 |
| 27 Eric Davis | .15 | .40 |
| 28 Jimmy Rollins | .25 | .60 |
| 29 Andy Pettitte | .25 | .60 |
| 30 Shawon Dunston | .15 | .40 |
| 31 Tim Hudson | .15 | .40 |
| 32 Jeff Kent | .15 | .40 |
| 33 Scott Brosius | .15 | .40 |
| 34 Livan Hernandez | .15 | .40 |
| 35 Alfonso Soriano | .25 | .60 |
| 36 Mark McGwire | 1.00 | 2.50 |
| 37 Russ Ortiz | .15 | .40 |

| | | |
|---|---|---|
| 38 Fernando Vina | .15 | .40 |
| 39 Ken Griffey Jr. | .60 | 1.50 |
| 40 Edgar Renteria | .15 | .40 |
| 41 Kevin Brown | .15 | .40 |
| 42 Robb Nen | .15 | .40 |
| 43 Paul LoDuca | .15 | .40 |
| 44 Bobby Abreu | .15 | .40 |
| 45 Adam Dunn | .25 | .60 |
| 46 Osvaldo Fernandez | .15 | .40 |
| 47 Marvin Benard | .15 | .40 |
| 48 Mark Gardner | .15 | .40 |
| 49 Alex Rodriguez | .60 | 1.50 |
| 50 Preston Wilson | .15 | .40 |
| 51 Roberto Alomar | .25 | .60 |
| 52 Ben Davis | .15 | .40 |
| 53 Derek Bell | .15 | .40 |
| 54 Ken Caminiti | .15 | .40 |
| 55 Barry Zito | .25 | .60 |
| 56 Scott Rolen | .25 | .60 |
| 57 Geoff Jenkins | .15 | .40 |
| 58 Mike Cameron | .15 | .40 |
| 59 Ben Grieve | .15 | .40 |
| 60 Chuck Knoblauch | .15 | .40 |
| 61 Matt Lawton | .15 | .40 |
| 62 Chan Ho Park | .15 | .40 |
| 63 Lance Berkman | .15 | .40 |
| 64 Carlos Beltran | .15 | .40 |
| 65 Dean Palmer | .15 | .40 |
| 66 Alex Gonzalez | .15 | .40 |
| 67 Larry Walker | .15 | .40 |
| 68 Magglio Ordonez | .15 | .40 |
| 69 Ellis Burks | .15 | .40 |
| 70 Mark Mulder | .15 | .40 |
| 71 Randy Johnson | .40 | 1.00 |
| 72 John Smoltz | .25 | .60 |
| 73 Jerry Hairston Jr. | .15 | .40 |
| 74 Pedro Martinez | .25 | .60 |
| 75 Fred McGriff | .25 | .60 |
| 76 Sean Casey | .15 | .40 |
| 77 C.C. Sabathia | .25 | .60 |
| 78 Todd Helton | .25 | .60 |
| 79 Brad Penny | .15 | .40 |
| 80 Mike Sweeney | .15 | .40 |
| 81 Billy Wagner | .15 | .40 |
| 82 Mark Buehrle | .25 | .60 |
| 83 Cristian Guzman | .15 | .40 |
| 84 Jose Vidro | .15 | .40 |
| 85 Pat Burrell | .15 | .40 |
| 86 Jermaine Dye | .15 | .40 |
| 87 Brandon Inge | .15 | .40 |
| 88 David Wells | .15 | .40 |
| 89 Mike Piazza | .60 | 1.50 |
| 90 Jose Cabrera | .15 | .40 |
| 91 Cliff Floyd | .15 | .40 |
| 92 Matt Morris | .15 | .40 |
| 93 Raul Mondesi | .15 | .40 |
| 94 Joe Kennedy RC | .25 | .60 |
| 95 Jack Wilson RC | .25 | .60 |
| 96 Andruw Jones | .25 | .60 |
| 97 Mariano Rivera | .40 | 1.00 |
| 98 Mike Hampton | .15 | .40 |
| 99 Roger Cedeno | .15 | .40 |
| 100 Jose Cruz | .15 | .40 |
| 101 Mike Lowell | .15 | .40 |
| 102 Pedro Astacio | .15 | .40 |
| 103 Joe Mays | .15 | .40 |
| 104 John Franco | .15 | .40 |
| 105 Tim Redding | .15 | .40 |
| 106 Sandy Alomar Jr. | .15 | .40 |
| 107 Bret Boone | .15 | .40 |
| 108 Josh Towers RC | .25 | .60 |
| 109 Matt Stairs | .15 | .40 |
| 110 Chris Truby | .15 | .40 |
| 111 Jeff Suppan | .15 | .40 |
| 112 J.C. Romero | .15 | .40 |
| 113 Felipe Lopez | .15 | .40 |
| 114 Ben Sheets | .25 | .60 |
| 115 Frank Thomas | .40 | 1.00 |
| 116 A.J. Burnett | .15 | .40 |
| 117 Tony Clark | .15 | .40 |
| 118 Mac Suzuki | .15 | .40 |
| 119 Brad Radke | .15 | .40 |
| 120 Jeff Shaw | .15 | .40 |
| 121 Nick Neugebauer | .15 | .40 |
| 122 Kenny Lofton | .15 | .40 |
| 123 Jacque Jones | .15 | .40 |
| 124 Brent Mayne | .15 | .40 |
| 125 Carlos Hernandez | .15 | .40 |

| | | |
|---|---|---|
| 126 Shane Spencer | .15 | .40 |
| 127 John Lackey | .15 | .40 |
| 128 Sterling Hitchcock | .15 | .40 |
| 129 Darron Dreifort | .15 | .40 |
| 130 Rusty Greer | .15 | .40 |
| 131 Michael Cuddyer | .15 | .40 |
| 132 Tyler Houston | .15 | .40 |
| 133 Chin-Feng Chen | .15 | .40 |
| 134 Ken Harvey | .15 | .40 |
| 135 Marquis Grissom | .15 | .40 |
| 136 Russell Branyan | .15 | .40 |
| 137 Eric Karros | .15 | .40 |
| 138 Josh Beckett | .25 | .60 |
| 139 Todd Zeile | .15 | .40 |
| 140 Corey Koskie | .15 | .40 |
| 141 Steve Sparks | .15 | .40 |
| 142 Bobby Seay | .15 | .40 |
| 143 Tim Raines Jr. | .15 | .40 |
| 144 Julio Zuleta | .15 | .40 |
| 145 Jose Lima | .15 | .40 |
| 146 Dante Bichette | .15 | .40 |
| 147 Randy Keisler | .15 | .40 |
| 148 Brent Butler | .15 | .40 |
| 149 Antonio Alfonseca | .15 | .40 |
| 150 Bryan Rekar | .15 | .40 |
| 151 Jeffrey Hammonds | .15 | .40 |
| 152 Larry Bigbie | .15 | .40 |
| 153 Blake Stein | .15 | .40 |
| 154 Robin Ventura | .15 | .40 |
| 155 Rondell White | .15 | .40 |
| 156 Juan Silvestre | .15 | .40 |
| 157 Marcus Thames | .15 | .40 |
| 158 Sidney Ponson | .15 | .40 |
| 159 Juan A. Pena RC | .15 | .40 |
| 160 C.J. Nitkowski | .15 | .40 |
| 161 Adam Everett | .15 | .40 |
| 162 Eric Munson | .15 | .40 |
| 163 Jason Isringhausen | .15 | .40 |
| 164 Brad Fullmer | .15 | .40 |
| 165 Miguel Olivo | .15 | .40 |
| 166 Fernando Tatis | .15 | .40 |
| 167 Freddy Garcia | .15 | .40 |
| 168 Tom Goodwin | .15 | .40 |
| 169 Armando Benitez | .15 | .40 |
| 170 Paul Konerko | .15 | .40 |
| 171 Jeff Cirillo | .15 | .40 |
| 172 Shane Reynolds | .15 | .40 |
| 173 Kevin Tapani | .15 | .40 |
| 174 Joe Crede | .40 | 1.00 |
| 175 Omar Infante RC | .15 | .40 |
| 176 Jake Peavy RC | 2.00 | 5.00 |
| 177 Corey Patterson | .15 | .40 |
| 178 Mike Penney RC | .15 | .40 |
| 179 Jeromy Burnitz | .15 | .40 |
| 180 David Segui | .15 | .40 |
| 181 Marcus Giles | .15 | .40 |
| 182 Paul O'Neill | .25 | .60 |
| 183 John Olerud | .15 | .40 |
| 184 Andy Benes | .15 | .40 |
| 185 Brad Cresse | .15 | .40 |
| 186 Ricky Ledee | .15 | .40 |
| 187 Allen Levrault UER | .15 | .40 |
| 188 Royce Clayton | .15 | .40 |
| 189 Kelly Johnson RC | 1.25 | 3.00 |
| 190 Quilvio Veras | .15 | .40 |
| 191 Mike Williams | .15 | .40 |
| 192 Jason Lane RC | .25 | .60 |
| 193 Rick Helling | .15 | .40 |
| 194 Tim Wakefield | .15 | .40 |
| 195 James Baldwin | .15 | .40 |
| 196 Cody Ransom RC | .15 | .40 |
| 197 Bobby Kielty | .15 | .40 |
| 198 Bobby Jones | .15 | .40 |
| 199 Steve Cox | .15 | .40 |
| 200 Jamal Strong RC | .15 | .40 |
| 201 Steve Lomasney | .15 | .40 |
| 202 Brian Cardwell RC | .15 | .40 |
| 203 Mike Matheny | .15 | .40 |
| 204 Jeff Randazzo RC | .15 | .40 |
| 205 Aubrey Huff | .15 | .40 |
| 206 Chuck Finley | .15 | .40 |
| 207 Danny Bautista RC | .25 | .60 |
| 208 Terry Mulholland | .15 | .40 |
| 209 Rey Ordonez | .15 | .40 |
| 210 Keith Surkont RC | .15 | .40 |
| 211 Orlando Cabrera | .15 | .40 |
| 212 Juan Encarnacion | .15 | .40 |
| 213 Dustin Hermanson | .15 | .40 |

|  | | |
|---|---|---|
| ☐ 214 Luis Rivas | .15 | .40 |
| ☐ 215 Mark Quinn | .15 | .40 |
| ☐ 216 Randy Velarde | .15 | .40 |
| ☐ 217 Billy Koch | .15 | .40 |
| ☐ 218 Ryan Rupe | .15 | .40 |
| ☐ 219 Keith Ginter | .15 | .40 |
| ☐ 220 Woody Williams | .15 | .40 |
| ☐ 221 Ryan Franklin | .15 | .40 |
| ☐ 222 Aaron Myette | .15 | .40 |
| ☐ 223 Joe Borchard RC | .15 | .40 |
| ☐ 224 Nate Cornejo | .15 | .40 |
| ☐ 225 Julian Tavarez | .15 | .40 |
| ☐ 226 Kevin Millwood | .15 | .40 |
| ☐ 227 Travis Hafner RC | 2.00 | 5.00 |
| ☐ 228 Charles Nagy | .15 | .40 |
| ☐ 229 Mike Lieberthal | .15 | .40 |
| ☐ 230 Jeff Nelson | .15 | .40 |
| ☐ 231 Ryan Dempster | .15 | .40 |
| ☐ 232 Andres Galarraga | .15 | .40 |
| ☐ 233 Chad Durbin | .15 | .40 |
| ☐ 234 Timo Perez | .15 | .40 |
| ☐ 235 Troy O'Leary | .15 | .40 |
| ☐ 236 Kevin Young | .15 | .40 |
| ☐ 237 Gabe Kapler | .15 | .40 |
| ☐ 238 Juan Cruz RC | .15 | .40 |
| ☐ 239 Masato Yoshii | .15 | .40 |
| ☐ 240 Aramis Ramirez | .15 | .40 |
| ☐ 241 Matt Cooper RC | .15 | .40 |
| ☐ 242 Randy Flores RC | .15 | .40 |
| ☐ 243 Rafael Furcal | .15 | .40 |
| ☐ 244 David Eckstein | .15 | .40 |
| ☐ 245 Matt Clement | .15 | .40 |
| ☐ 246 Craig Biggio | .25 | .60 |
| ☐ 247 Rick Reed | .15 | .40 |
| ☐ 248 Jose Macias | .15 | .40 |
| ☐ 249 Alex Escobar | .15 | .40 |
| ☐ 250 Roberto Hernandez | .15 | .40 |
| ☐ 251 Andy Ashby | .15 | .40 |
| ☐ 252 Tony Armas Jr. | .15 | .40 |
| ☐ 253 Jamie Moyer | .15 | .40 |
| ☐ 254 Jason Tyner | .15 | .40 |
| ☐ 255 Charles Kegley RC | .15 | .40 |
| ☐ 256 Jeff Conine | .15 | .40 |
| ☐ 257 Francisco Cordova | .15 | .40 |
| ☐ 258 Ted Lilly | .15 | .40 |
| ☐ 259 Joe Randa | .15 | .40 |
| ☐ 260 Jeff D'Amico | .15 | .40 |
| ☐ 261 Albie Lopez | .15 | .40 |
| ☐ 262 Kevin Appier | .15 | .40 |
| ☐ 263 Richard Hidalgo | .15 | .40 |
| ☐ 264 Omar Daal | .15 | .40 |
| ☐ 265 Ricky Gutierrez | .15 | .40 |
| ☐ 266 John Rocker | .15 | .40 |
| ☐ 267 Ray Lankford | .15 | .40 |
| ☐ 268 Beau Hale RC | .15 | .40 |
| ☐ 269 Tony Blanco RC | .15 | .40 |
| ☐ 270 Derrek Lee UER | .25 | .60 |
| ☐ 271 Jamey Wright | .15 | .40 |
| ☐ 272 Alex Gordon | .15 | .40 |
| ☐ 273 Jeff Weaver | .15 | .40 |
| ☐ 274 Jaret Wright | .15 | .40 |
| ☐ 275 Jose Hernandez | .15 | .40 |
| ☐ 276 Bruce Chen | .15 | .40 |
| ☐ 277 Todd Hollandsworth | .15 | .40 |
| ☐ 278 Wade Miller | .15 | .40 |
| ☐ 279 Luke Prokopec | .15 | .40 |
| ☐ 280 Rafael Soriano RC | .15 | .40 |
| ☐ 281 Damion Easley | .15 | .40 |
| ☐ 282 Darren Oliver | .15 | .40 |
| ☐ 283 Brandon Duckworth RC | .15 | .40 |
| ☐ 284 Aaron Herr | .15 | .40 |
| ☐ 285 Ray Durham | .15 | .40 |
| ☐ 286 Wilmy Caceras RC | .15 | .40 |
| ☐ 287 Ugueth Urbina | .15 | .40 |
| ☐ 288 Scott Seabol | .15 | .40 |
| ☐ 289 Lance Niekro RC | .25 | .60 |
| ☐ 290 Trot Nixon | .15 | .40 |
| ☐ 291 Adam Kennedy | .15 | .40 |
| ☐ 292 Brian Schmitt RC | .15 | .40 |
| ☐ 293 Grant Roberts | .15 | .40 |
| ☐ 294 Benny Agbayani | .15 | .40 |
| ☐ 295 Travis Lee | .15 | .40 |
| ☐ 296 Erick Almonte RC | .15 | .40 |
| ☐ 297 Jim Thome | .25 | .60 |
| ☐ 298 Eric Young | .15 | .40 |
| ☐ 299 Dan Denham RC | .15 | .40 |
| ☐ 300 Boof Bonser RC | .15 | .40 |
| ☐ 301 Denny Neagle | .15 | .40 |

|  | | |
|---|---|---|
| ☐ 302 Kenny Rogers | .15 | .40 |
| ☐ 303 J.D. Closser | .15 | .40 |
| ☐ 304 Chase Utley RC | 4.00 | 10.00 |
| ☐ 305 Rey Sanchez | .15 | .40 |
| ☐ 306 Sean McGowan | .15 | .40 |
| ☐ 307 Justin Pope RC | .15 | .40 |
| ☐ 308 Torii Hunter | .15 | .40 |
| ☐ 309 B.J. Surhoff | .15 | .40 |
| ☐ 310 Aaron Heilman RC | .20 | .50 |
| ☐ 311 Gabe Gross RC | .25 | .60 |
| ☐ 312 Lee Stevens | .15 | .40 |
| ☐ 313 Todd Hundley | .15 | .40 |
| ☐ 314 Macay McBride RC | .40 | 1.00 |
| ☐ 315 Edgar Martinez | .25 | .60 |
| ☐ 316 Omar Vizquel | .25 | .60 |
| ☐ 317 Reggie Sanders | .15 | .40 |
| ☐ 318 John-Ford Griffin RC | .15 | .40 |
| ☐ 319 T.Salmon UER Glaus Photo | .15 | .40 |
| ☐ 320 Pokey Reese | .15 | .40 |
| ☐ 321 Jay Payton | .15 | .40 |
| ☐ 322 Doug Glanville | .15 | .40 |
| ☐ 323 Greg Vaughn | .15 | .40 |
| ☐ 324 Ruben Sierra | .15 | .40 |
| ☐ 325 Kip Wells | .15 | .40 |
| ☐ 326 Carl Everett | .15 | .40 |
| ☐ 327 Garret Anderson | .15 | .40 |
| ☐ 328 Jay Bell | .15 | .40 |
| ☐ 329 Barry Larkin | .25 | .60 |
| ☐ 330 Jeff Mathis RC | .25 | .60 |
| ☐ 331 Adrian Gonzalez SP | .75 | 2.00 |
| ☐ 332 Juan Rivera SP | .75 | 2.00 |
| ☐ 333 Tony Alvarez SP | .75 | 2.00 |
| ☐ 334 Xavier Nady SP | .75 | 2.00 |
| ☐ 335 Josh Hamilton SP | 1.50 | 4.00 |
| ☐ 336 Will Smith SP RC | .75 | 2.00 |
| ☐ 337 Israel Alcantara SP | .75 | 2.00 |
| ☐ 338 Chris George SP | .75 | 2.00 |
| ☐ 339 Sean Burroughs SP | .75 | 2.00 |
| ☐ 340 Jack Cust SP | .75 | 2.00 |
| ☐ 341 Henry Mateo SP RC | .75 | 2.00 |
| ☐ 342 Carlos Pena SP | .75 | 2.00 |
| ☐ 343 J.R. House SP | .75 | 2.00 |
| ☐ 344 Carlos Silva SP | .75 | 2.00 |
| ☐ 345 Mike Rivera SP RC | .75 | 2.00 |
| ☐ 346 Adam Johnson SP | .75 | 2.00 |
| ☐ 347 Scott Heard SP | .75 | 2.00 |
| ☐ 348 Alex Cintron SP | .75 | 2.00 |
| ☐ 349 Miguel Cabrera SP | 3.00 | 8.00 |
| ☐ 350 Nick Johnson SP | .75 | 2.00 |
| ☐ 351 Albert Pujols SP RC | 20.00 | 50.00 |
| ☐ 352 Ichiro Suzuki SP RC | 10.00 | 25.00 |
| ☐ 353 Carlos Delgado SP | .75 | 2.00 |
| ☐ 354 Troy Glaus SP | .75 | 2.00 |
| ☐ 355 Sammy Sosa SP | 1.25 | 3.00 |
| ☐ 356 Ivan Rodriguez SP | 1.25 | 3.00 |
| ☐ 357 Vladimir Guerrero SP | 1.25 | 3.00 |
| ☐ 358 Manny Ramirez Sox SP | 1.25 | 3.00 |
| ☐ 359 Luis Gonzalez SP | .75 | 2.00 |
| ☐ 360 Roy Oswalt SP | 1.25 | 3.00 |
| ☐ 361 Moises Alou SP | .75 | 2.00 |
| ☐ 362 Juan Gonzalez SP | .75 | 2.00 |
| ☐ 363 Tony Gwynn SP | 1.50 | 4.00 |
| ☐ 364 Hideo Nomo SP | 1.25 | 3.00 |
| ☐ 365 Tsuyoshi Shinjo SP | 1.25 | 3.00 |
| ☐ 366 Kazuhiro Sasaki SP | .75 | 2.00 |
| ☐ 367 Cal Ripken SP | 4.00 | 10.00 |
| ☐ 368 Rafael Palmeiro SP | 1.25 | 3.00 |
| ☐ 369 J.D. Drew SP | .75 | 2.00 |
| ☐ 370 Doug Mientkiewicz SP | .75 | 2.00 |
| ☐ 371 Jeff Bagwell SP | 1.25 | 3.00 |
| ☐ 372 Darin Erstad SP | .75 | 2.00 |
| ☐ 373 Tom Gordon SP | .75 | 2.00 |
| ☐ 374 Ben Petrick SP | .75 | 2.00 |
| ☐ 375 Eric Milton SP | .75 | 2.00 |
| ☐ 376 Nomar Garciaparra SP | 2.00 | 5.00 |
| ☐ 377 Julio Lugo SP | .75 | 2.00 |
| ☐ 378 Tino Martinez SP | 1.25 | 3.00 |
| ☐ 379 Javier Vazquez SP | .75 | 2.00 |
| ☐ 380 Jeremy Giambi SP | .75 | 2.00 |
| ☐ 381 Marty Cordova SP | .75 | 2.00 |
| ☐ 382 Adrian Beltre SP | .75 | 2.00 |
| ☐ 383 John Burkett SP | .75 | 2.00 |
| ☐ 384 Aaron Boone SP | .75 | 2.00 |
| ☐ 385 Eric Chavez SP | .75 | 2.00 |
| ☐ 386 Curt Schilling SP | .75 | 2.00 |
| ☐ 387 Cory Lidle UER SP | .75 | 2.00 |
| ☐ 388 Jason Schmidt SP | .75 | 2.00 |
| ☐ 389 Johnny Damon SP | 1.25 | 3.00 |

|  | | |
|---|---|---|
| ☐ 390 Steve Finley SP | .75 | 2.00 |
| ☐ 391 Edgardo Alfonzo SP | .75 | 2.00 |
| ☐ 392 Jose Valentin SP | .75 | 2.00 |
| ☐ 393 Jose Canseco SP | 1.25 | 3.00 |
| ☐ 394 Ryan Klesko SP | .75 | 2.00 |
| ☐ 395 David Cone SP | .75 | 2.00 |
| ☐ 396 Jason Kendall UER SP | .75 | 2.00 |
| ☐ 397 Placido Polanco SP | .75 | 2.00 |
| ☐ 398 Glendon Rusch SP | .75 | 2.00 |
| ☐ 399 Aaron Sele SP | .75 | 2.00 |
| ☐ 400 D'Angelo Jimenez SP | .75 | 2.00 |
| ☐ 401 Mark Grace SP | 1.25 | 3.00 |
| ☐ 402 Al Leiter SP | .75 | 2.00 |
| ☐ 403 Brian Jordan SP | .75 | 2.00 |
| ☐ 404 Phil Nevin SP | .75 | 2.00 |
| ☐ 405 Brent Abernathy SP | .75 | 2.00 |
| ☐ 406 Kerry Wood SP | .75 | 2.00 |
| ☐ 407 Alex Gonzalez SP | .75 | 2.00 |
| ☐ 408 Robert Fick SP | .75 | 2.00 |
| ☐ 409 Dmitri Young UER SP | .75 | 2.00 |
| ☐ 410 Wes Helms SP | .75 | 2.00 |
| ☐ 411 Trevor Hoffman SP | .75 | 2.00 |
| ☐ 412 Rickey Henderson SP | 1.25 | 3.00 |
| ☐ 413 Bobby Higginson SP | .75 | 2.00 |
| ☐ 414 Gary Sheffield SP | .75 | 2.00 |
| ☐ 415 Darryl Kile SP | .75 | 2.00 |
| ☐ 416 Richie Sexson SP | .75 | 2.00 |
| ☐ 417 Frank Menechino SP | .75 | 2.00 |
| ☐ 418 Javy Lopez SP | .75 | 2.00 |
| ☐ 419 Carlos Lee SP | .75 | 2.00 |
| ☐ 420 Jon Lieber SP | .75 | 2.00 |
| ☐ 421 Hank Blalock SP RC | 2.50 | 6.00 |
| ☐ 422 Marlon Byrd SP RC | .75 | 2.00 |
| ☐ 423 Jason Kinchen SP RC | .75 | 2.00 |
| ☐ 424 Morgan Ensberg SP RC | 2.00 | 5.00 |
| ☐ 425 Greg Nash SP RC | .75 | 2.00 |
| ☐ 426 Dennis Tankersley SP RC | .75 | 2.00 |
| ☐ 427 Nate Murphy SP RC | .75 | 2.00 |
| ☐ 428 Chris Smith SP RC | .75 | 2.00 |
| ☐ 429 Jake Gautreau SP RC | .75 | 2.00 |
| ☐ 430 John VanBenschoten SP RC | .75 | 2.00 |
| ☐ 431 Travis Thompson SP RC | .75 | 2.00 |
| ☐ 432 Orlando Hudson SP RC | 1.25 | 3.00 |
| ☐ 433 Jerome Williams SP RC | 1.25 | 3.00 |
| ☐ 434 Kevin Reese SP RC | .75 | 2.00 |
| ☐ 435 Ed Rogers SP RC | .75 | 2.00 |
| ☐ 436 Ryan Jamison SP RC | .75 | 2.00 |
| ☐ 437 Adam Pettyjohn SP RC | .75 | 2.00 |
| ☐ 438 Hee Seop Choi SP | 1.25 | 3.00 |
| ☐ 439 Justin Morneau SP RC | 4.00 | 10.00 |
| ☐ 440 Mitch Jones SP | .75 | 2.00 |

## 2002 Bowman Heritage

|  | | |
|---|---|---|
| ☐ COMP.SET w/o SP's (324) | 25.00 | 50.00 |
| ☐ COMMON CARD (1-439) | .15 | .40 |
| ☐ COMMON SP | .75 | 2.00 |
| ☐ 1 Brent Abernathy | .15 | .40 |
| ☐ 2 Jermaine Dye | .15 | .40 |
| ☐ 3 James Shanks RC | .15 | .40 |
| ☐ 4 Chris Flinn RC | .15 | .40 |
| ☐ 5 Mike Peeples SP RC | .75 | 2.00 |
| ☐ 6 Gary Sheffield | .15 | .40 |
| ☐ 7 Livan Hernandez SP | .75 | 2.00 |
| ☐ 8 Jeff Austin RC | .15 | .40 |
| ☐ 9 Jeremy Giambi | .15 | .40 |
| ☐ 10 Adam Roller RC | .15 | .40 |
| ☐ 11 Sandy Alomar Jr. SP | .75 | 2.00 |
| ☐ 12 Matt Williams SP | .75 | 2.00 |
| ☐ 13 Hee Seop Choi | .15 | .40 |
| ☐ 14 Jose Offerman | .15 | .40 |
| ☐ 15 Robin Ventura | .15 | .40 |
| ☐ 16 Craig Biggio | .25 | .60 |
| ☐ 17 David Wells | .15 | .40 |
| ☐ 18 Rob Henkel RC | .15 | .40 |

|  |  | | |
|---|---|---|---|
| ☐ 19 | Edgar Martinez | .25 | .60 |
| ☐ 20 | Matt Morris SP | .75 | 2.00 |
| ☐ 21 | Jose Valentin | .15 | .40 |
| ☐ 22 | Barry Bonds | 1.00 | 2.50 |
| ☐ 23 | Justin Schuda RC | .15 | .40 |
| ☐ 24 | Josh Phelps | .15 | .40 |
| ☐ 25 | John Rodriguez RC | .20 | .50 |
| ☐ 27 | Aramis Ramirez | .15 | .40 |
| ☐ 28 | Jack Wilson | .15 | .40 |
| ☐ 29 | Roger Clemens | .75 | 2.00 |
| ☐ 30 | Kazuhisa Ishii RC | .20 | .50 |
| ☐ 31 | Carlos Beltran | .15 | .40 |
| ☐ 32 | Drew Henson SP | .75 | 2.00 |
| ☐ 33 | Kevin Young SP | .75 | 2.00 |
| ☐ 34 | Juan Cruz SP | .75 | 2.00 |
| ☐ 35 | Curtis Legendre RC | .15 | .40 |
| ☐ 36 | Jose Morban SP | .15 | .40 |
| ☐ 37 | Ricardo Cordova SP RC | .75 | 2.00 |
| ☐ 38 | Adam Everett | .15 | .40 |
| ☐ 39 | Mark Prior | .25 | .60 |
| ☐ 40 | Jose Bautista RC | .40 | 1.00 |
| ☐ 41 | Travis Foley RC | .15 | .40 |
| ☐ 42 | Kerry Wood | .15 | .40 |
| ☐ 43 | B.J. Surhoff | .15 | .40 |
| ☐ 44 | Moises Alou | .15 | .40 |
| ☐ 45 | Joey Hammond | .15 | .40 |
| ☐ 46 | Eric Bruntlett RC | .15 | .40 |
| ☐ 47 | Carlos Guillen | .15 | .40 |
| ☐ 48 | Joe Crede | .15 | .40 |
| ☐ 49 | Dan Phillips RC | .15 | .40 |
| ☐ 50 | Jason LaRue | .15 | .40 |
| ☐ 51 | Javy Lopez | .15 | .40 |
| ☐ 52 | Larry Bigbie SP | .75 | 2.00 |
| ☐ 53 | Chris Baker RC | .15 | .40 |
| ☐ 54 | Marty Cordova | .15 | .40 |
| ☐ 55 | C.C. Sabathia | .15 | .40 |
| ☐ 56 | Mike Piazza | .60 | 1.50 |
| ☐ 57 | Brian Giles | .15 | .40 |
| ☐ 58 | Mike Bordick SP | .75 | 2.00 |
| ☐ 59 | Tyler Houston SP | .75 | 2.00 |
| ☐ 60 | Gabe Kapler | .15 | .40 |
| ☐ 61 | Ben Broussard | .15 | .40 |
| ☐ 62 | Steve Finley SP | .75 | 2.00 |
| ☐ 63 | Koyie Hill | .15 | .40 |
| ☐ 64 | Jeff D'Amico | .15 | .40 |
| ☐ 65 | Edwin Almonte RC | .15 | .40 |
| ☐ 66 | Pedro Martinez | .25 | .60 |
| ☐ 66B | Nomar Garciaparra 66 | .60 | 1.50 |
| ☐ 67 | Travis Fryman SP | .75 | 2.00 |
| ☐ 68 | Brady Clark SP | .75 | 2.00 |
| ☐ 69 | Reed Johnson SP RC | 1.50 | 4.00 |
| ☐ 70 | Mark Grace SP | 1.25 | 3.00 |
| ☐ 71 | Tony Batista SP | .75 | 2.00 |
| ☐ 72 | Roy Oswalt | .15 | .40 |
| ☐ 73 | Pat Burrell SP | .75 | 2.00 |
| ☐ 74 | Dennis Tankersley | .15 | .40 |
| ☐ 75 | Ramon Ortiz | .15 | .40 |
| ☐ 76 | Neal Frendling SP RC | .75 | 2.00 |
| ☐ 77 | Omar Vizquel SP | 1.25 | 3.00 |
| ☐ 78 | Hideo Nomo | .40 | 1.00 |
| ☐ 79 | Orlando Hernandez SP | .75 | 2.00 |
| ☐ 80 | Andy Pettitte | .25 | .60 |
| ☐ 81 | Cole Barthel RC | .15 | .40 |
| ☐ 82 | Bret Boone | .15 | .40 |
| ☐ 83 | Alfonso Soriano | .15 | .40 |
| ☐ 84 | Brandon Duckworth | .15 | .40 |
| ☐ 85 | Ben Grieve | .15 | .40 |
| ☐ 86 | Mike Rosamond SP RC | .75 | 2.00 |
| ☐ 87 | Luke Prokopec | .15 | .40 |
| ☐ 88 | Chone Figgins RC | .60 | 1.50 |
| ☐ 89 | Rick Ankiel SP | .75 | 2.00 |
| ☐ 90 | David Eckstein | .15 | .40 |
| ☐ 91 | Corey Koskie | .15 | .40 |
| ☐ 92 | David Justice | .15 | .40 |
| ☐ 93 | Jimmy Alvarez RC | .15 | .40 |
| ☐ 94 | Jason Schmidt | .15 | .40 |
| ☐ 95 | Reggie Sanders | .15 | .40 |
| ☐ 96 | Victor Alvarez RC | .15 | .40 |
| ☐ 97 | Brett Roneberg RC | .15 | .40 |
| ☐ 98 | D'Angelo Jimenez | .15 | .40 |
| ☐ 99 | Hank Blalock | .25 | .60 |
| ☐ 100 | Juan Rivera | .15 | .40 |
| ☐ 101 | Mark Buehrle SP | .75 | 2.00 |
| ☐ 102 | Juan Uribe | .15 | .40 |
| ☐ 103 | Royce Clayton SP | .75 | 2.00 |
| ☐ 104 | Brett Kay RC | .15 | .40 |
| ☐ 105 | John Olerud | .15 | .40 |
| ☐ 106 | Richie Sexson | .15 | .40 |
| ☐ 107 | Chipper Jones | .40 | 1.00 |
| ☐ 108 | Adam Dunn | .15 | .40 |
| ☐ 109 | Tim Salmon SP | 1.25 | 3.00 |
| ☐ 110 | Eric Karros | .15 | .40 |
| ☐ 111 | Jose Vidro | .15 | .40 |
| ☐ 112 | Jerry Hairston Jr. | .15 | .40 |
| ☐ 113 | Anastacio Martinez SP | .15 | .40 |
| ☐ 114 | Robert Fick SP | .75 | 2.00 |
| ☐ 115 | Randy Johnson | .40 | 1.00 |
| ☐ 116 | Trot Nixon SP | .75 | 2.00 |
| ☐ 117 | Nick Bierbrodt SP | .75 | 2.00 |
| ☐ 118 | Jim Edmonds | .15 | .40 |
| ☐ 119 | Rafael Palmeiro | .25 | .60 |
| ☐ 120 | Jose Macias | .15 | .40 |
| ☐ 121 | Josh Beckett | .15 | .40 |
| ☐ 122 | Sean Douglass | .15 | .40 |
| ☐ 123 | Jeff Kent | .15 | .40 |
| ☐ 124 | Tim Redding | .15 | .40 |
| ☐ 125 | Xavier Nady | .15 | .40 |
| ☐ 126 | Carl Everett | .15 | .40 |
| ☐ 127 | Joe Randa | .15 | .40 |
| ☐ 128 | Luke Hudson SP | .75 | 2.00 |
| ☐ 129 | Eric Miller RC | .15 | .40 |
| ☐ 130 | Melvin Mora | .15 | .40 |
| ☐ 131 | Adrian Gonzalez | .15 | .40 |
| ☐ 132 | Larry Walker SP | .75 | 2.00 |
| ☐ 133 | Nic Jackson SP RC | .75 | 2.00 |
| ☐ 134 | Mike Lowell SP | .75 | 2.00 |
| ☐ 135 | Jim Thome | .25 | .60 |
| ☐ 136 | Eric Milton | .15 | .40 |
| ☐ 137 | Rich Thompson SP RC | .75 | 2.00 |
| ☐ 138 | Placido Polanco SP | .75 | 2.00 |
| ☐ 139 | Juan Pierre | .15 | .40 |
| ☐ 140 | David Segui | .15 | .40 |
| ☐ 141 | Chuck Finley | .15 | .40 |
| ☐ 142 | Felipe Lopez | .15 | .40 |
| ☐ 143 | Toby Hall | .15 | .40 |
| ☐ 144 | Fred Bastardo RC | .15 | .40 |
| ☐ 145 | Troy Glaus | .15 | .40 |
| ☐ 146 | Todd Helton | .25 | .60 |
| ☐ 147 | Ruben Gotay SP RC | 1.25 | 3.00 |
| ☐ 148 | Darin Erstad | .15 | .40 |
| ☐ 149 | Ryan Grip SP RC | .75 | 2.00 |
| ☐ 150 | Orlando Cabrera | .15 | .40 |
| ☐ 151 | Jason Young RC | .15 | .40 |
| ☐ 152 | Sterling Hitchcock SP | .75 | 2.00 |
| ☐ 153 | Miguel Tejada | .15 | .40 |
| ☐ 154 | Al Leiter | .15 | .40 |
| ☐ 155 | Taylor Buchholz RC | .20 | .50 |
| ☐ 156 | Juan M. Gonzalez RC | .15 | .40 |
| ☐ 157 | Damion Easley | .15 | .40 |
| ☐ 158 | Jimmy Gobble RC | .15 | .40 |
| ☐ 159 | Dennis Ulacia SP RC | .75 | 2.00 |
| ☐ 160 | Shane Reynolds SP | .75 | 2.00 |
| ☐ 161 | Javier Colina | .15 | .40 |
| ☐ 162 | Frank Thomas | .40 | 1.00 |
| ☐ 163 | Chuck Knoblauch | .15 | .40 |
| ☐ 164 | Sean Burroughs | .15 | .40 |
| ☐ 165 | Greg Maddux | .60 | 1.50 |
| ☐ 166 | Jason Ellison RC | .30 | .75 |
| ☐ 167 | Tony Womack | .15 | .40 |
| ☐ 168 | Randall Shelley SP RC | .75 | 2.00 |
| ☐ 169 | Jason Marquis | .15 | .40 |
| ☐ 170 | Brian Jordan | .15 | .40 |
| ☐ 171 | Vicente Padilla | .15 | .40 |
| ☐ 172 | Barry Zito | .15 | .40 |
| ☐ 173 | Matt Allegra SP RC | .75 | 2.00 |
| ☐ 174 | Ralph Santana SP RC | .75 | 2.00 |
| ☐ 175 | Carlos Lee | .15 | .40 |
| ☐ 176 | Richard Hidalgo SP | .75 | 2.00 |
| ☐ 177 | Kevin Deaton RC | .15 | .40 |
| ☐ 178 | Juan Encarnacion | .15 | .40 |
| ☐ 179 | Mark Quinn | .15 | .40 |
| ☐ 180 | Rafael Furcal | .15 | .40 |
| ☐ 181 | G.Anderson UER Figgins | .15 | .40 |
| ☐ 182 | David Wright RC | 6.00 | 15.00 |
| ☐ 183 | Jose Reyes | .25 | .60 |
| ☐ 184 | Mario Ramos SP RC | .75 | 2.00 |
| ☐ 185 | J.D. Drew | .15 | .40 |
| ☐ 186 | Juan Gonzalez | .25 | .60 |
| ☐ 187 | Nick Neugebauer | .15 | .40 |
| ☐ 188 | Alejandro Giron RC | .15 | .40 |
| ☐ 189 | John Burkett | .15 | .40 |
| ☐ 190 | Ben Sheets | .15 | .40 |
| ☐ 191 | Vinny Castilla SP | .75 | 2.00 |
| ☐ 192 | Cory Lidle | .15 | .40 |
| ☐ 193 | Fernando Vina | .15 | .40 |
| ☐ 194 | Russell Branyan SP | .75 | 2.00 |
| ☐ 195 | Ben Davis | .15 | .40 |
| ☐ 196 | Angel Berroa | .15 | .40 |
| ☐ 197 | Alex Gonzalez | .15 | .40 |
| ☐ 198 | Jared Sandberg | .15 | .40 |
| ☐ 199 | Travis Lee SP | .75 | 2.00 |
| ☐ 200 | Luis DePaula SP RC | .75 | 2.00 |
| ☐ 201 | Ramon Hernandez SP | .75 | 2.00 |
| ☐ 202 | Brandon Inge | .15 | .40 |
| ☐ 203 | Aubrey Huff | .15 | .40 |
| ☐ 204 | Mike Rivera | .15 | .40 |
| ☐ 205 | Brad Nelson RC | .15 | .40 |
| ☐ 206 | Colt Griffin SP RC | .75 | 2.00 |
| ☐ 207 | Joel Pineiro | .15 | .40 |
| ☐ 208 | Adam Pettyjohn | .15 | .40 |
| ☐ 209 | Mark Redman | .15 | .40 |
| ☐ 210 | Roberto Alomar SP | 1.25 | 3.00 |
| ☐ 211 | Denny Neagle | .15 | .40 |
| ☐ 212 | Adam Kennedy | .15 | .40 |
| ☐ 213 | Jason Arnold SP RC | .75 | 2.00 |
| ☐ 214 | Jamie Moyer | .15 | .40 |
| ☐ 215 | Aaron Boone | .15 | .40 |
| ☐ 216 | Doug Glanville | .15 | .40 |
| ☐ 217 | Nick Johnson SP | .75 | 2.00 |
| ☐ 218 | Mike Cameron SP | .75 | 2.00 |
| ☐ 219 | Tim Wakefield SP | .75 | 2.00 |
| ☐ 220 | Todd Stottlemyre SP | .75 | 2.00 |
| ☐ 221 | Mo Vaughn SP | .75 | 2.00 |
| ☐ 222 | Vladimir Guerrero | .40 | 1.00 |
| ☐ 223 | Bill Ortega | .15 | .40 |
| ☐ 224 | Kevin Brown | .15 | .40 |
| ☐ 225 | Peter Bergeron SP | .75 | 2.00 |
| ☐ 226 | Shannon Stewart SP | .75 | 2.00 |
| ☐ 227 | Eric Chavez | .15 | .40 |
| ☐ 228 | Clint Weibl RC | .15 | .40 |
| ☐ 229 | Todd Hollandsworth SP | .75 | 2.00 |
| ☐ 230 | Jeff Bagwell | .25 | .60 |
| ☐ 231 | Chad Qualls RC | .20 | .50 |
| ☐ 232 | Ben Howard RC | .15 | .40 |
| ☐ 233 | Rondell White SP | .75 | 2.00 |
| ☐ 234 | Fred McGriff | .25 | .60 |
| ☐ 235 | Steve Cox SP | .75 | 2.00 |
| ☐ 236 | Chris Tritle RC | .15 | .40 |
| ☐ 237 | Eric Valent | .15 | .40 |
| ☐ 238 | Joe Mauer RC | 4.00 | 10.00 |
| ☐ 239 | Shawn Green | .15 | .40 |
| ☐ 240 | Jimmy Rollins | .15 | .40 |
| ☐ 241 | Edgar Renteria | .15 | .40 |
| ☐ 242 | Edwin Yan RC | .15 | .40 |
| ☐ 243 | Noochie Varner RC | .15 | .40 |
| ☐ 244 | Kris Benson SP | .75 | 2.00 |
| ☐ 245 | Mike Hampton | .15 | .40 |
| ☐ 246 | So Taguchi RC | .20 | .50 |
| ☐ 247 | Sammy Sosa | .40 | 1.00 |
| ☐ 248 | Terrence Long | .15 | .40 |
| ☐ 249 | Jason Bay RC | 2.00 | 5.00 |
| ☐ 250 | Kevin Millar SP | .75 | 2.00 |
| ☐ 251 | Albert Pujols | .75 | 2.00 |
| ☐ 252 | Chris Latham RC | .15 | .40 |
| ☐ 253 | Eric Byrnes | .15 | .40 |
| ☐ 254 | Napoleon Calzado SP RC | .75 | 2.00 |
| ☐ 255 | Bobby Higginson | .15 | .40 |
| ☐ 256 | Ben Molina | .15 | .40 |
| ☐ 257 | Toni Hunter SP | .75 | 2.00 |
| ☐ 258 | Jason Giambi | .15 | .40 |
| ☐ 259 | Bartolo Colon | .15 | .40 |
| ☐ 260 | Benito Baez | .15 | .40 |
| ☐ 261 | Ichiro Suzuki | .75 | 2.00 |
| ☐ 262 | Mike Sweeney | .15 | .40 |
| ☐ 263 | Brian West RC | .15 | .40 |
| ☐ 264 | Brad Penny | .15 | .40 |
| ☐ 265 | Kevin Millwood SP | .75 | 2.00 |
| ☐ 266 | Orlando Hudson | .15 | .40 |
| ☐ 267 | Doug Mientkiewicz | .15 | .40 |
| ☐ 268 | Luis Gonzalez SP | .75 | 2.00 |
| ☐ 269 | Jay Caligiuri RC | .15 | .40 |
| ☐ 270 | Nate Cornejo SP | .75 | 2.00 |
| ☐ 271 | Lee Stevens | .15 | .40 |
| ☐ 272 | Eric Hinske | .15 | .40 |
| ☐ 273 | Antwon Rollins RC | .15 | .40 |
| ☐ 274 | Bobby Jenks RC | .60 | 1.50 |
| ☐ 275 | Joe Mays | .15 | .40 |
| ☐ 276 | Josh Shaffer RC | .15 | .40 |
| ☐ 277 | Jonny Gomes RC | 1.00 | 2.50 |
| ☐ 278 | Bernie Williams | .25 | .60 |
| ☐ 279 | Byron Gettis | .15 | .40 |
| ☐ 280 | Carlos Delgado | .15 | .40 |
| ☐ 281 | Raul Mondesi SP | .75 | 2.00 |
| ☐ 282 | Jose Ortiz | .15 | .40 |

|  |  | | |
|---|------|---|---|
| 283 | Cesar Izturis | .15 | .40 |
| 284 | Ryan Dempster SP | .75 | 2.00 |
| 285 | Brian Daubach | .15 | .40 |
| 286 | Hansel Izquierdo RC | .15 | .40 |
| 287 | Mike Lieberthal SP | .75 | 2.00 |
| 288 | Marcus Thames | .15 | .40 |
| 289 | Nomar Garciaparra | .60 | 1.50 |
| 290 | Brad Fullmer | .15 | .40 |
| 291 | Tino Martinez | .25 | .60 |
| 292 | James Barrett RC | .15 | .40 |
| 293 | Jacque Jones | .15 | .40 |
| 294 | Nick Alvarez SP RC | .75 | 2.00 |
| 295 | Jason Grove SP RC | .75 | 2.00 |
| 296 | Mike Wilson SP RC | .75 | 2.00 |
| 297 | J.T. Snow | .15 | .40 |
| 298 | Cliff Floyd | .15 | .40 |
| 299 | Todd Hundley SP | .75 | 2.00 |
| 300 | Tony Clark SP | .75 | 2.00 |
| 301 | Demetrius Heath RC | .15 | .40 |
| 302 | Morgan Ensberg | .15 | .40 |
| 303 | Cristian Guzman | .15 | .40 |
| 304 | Frank Catalanotto | .15 | .40 |
| 305 | Jeff Weaver | .15 | .40 |
| 306 | Tim Hudson | .15 | .40 |
| 307 | Scott Wiggins SP RC | .75 | 2.00 |
| 308 | Shea Hillenbrand SP | .75 | 2.00 |
| 309 | Todd Walker SP | .75 | 2.00 |
| 310 | Tsuyoshi Shinjo | .15 | .40 |
| 311 | Adrian Beltre | .15 | .40 |
| 312 | Craig Kuzmic RC | .15 | .40 |
| 313 | Paul Konerko | .15 | .40 |
| 314 | Scott Hairston RC | .20 | .50 |
| 315 | Chan Ho Park | .15 | .40 |
| 316 | Jorge Posada | .25 | .60 |
| 317 | Chris Snelling RC | .30 | .75 |
| 318 | Keith Foulke | .15 | .40 |
| 319 | John Smoltz | .25 | .60 |
| 320 | Ryan Church SP RC | 1.50 | 4.00 |
| 321 | Mike Mussina | .25 | .60 |
| 322 | Tony Armas Jr. SP | .75 | 2.00 |
| 323 | Craig Counsell | .15 | .40 |
| 324 | Marcus Giles | .15 | .40 |
| 325 | Greg Vaughn | .15 | .40 |
| 326 | Curt Schilling | .15 | .40 |
| 327 | Jeromy Burnitz | .15 | .40 |
| 328 | Eric Byrnes | .15 | .40 |
| 329 | Johnny Damon Sox | .25 | .60 |
| 330 | Michael Floyd SP RC | .75 | 2.00 |
| 331 | Edgardo Alfonzo | .15 | .40 |
| 332 | Jeremy Hill RC | .15 | .40 |
| 333 | Josh Bonifay RC | .15 | .40 |
| 334 | Byung-Hyun Kim | .15 | .40 |
| 335 | Keith Ginter | .15 | .40 |
| 336 | Ronald Acuna SP RC | .75 | 2.00 |
| 337 | Mike Hill SP RC | .75 | 2.00 |
| 338 | Sean Casey | .15 | .40 |
| 339 | Matt Anderson SP | .75 | 2.00 |
| 340 | Dan Wright | .15 | .40 |
| 341 | Ben Petrick | .15 | .40 |
| 342 | Mike Sirotka SP | .75 | 2.00 |
| 343 | Alex Rodriguez | .60 | 1.50 |
| 344 | Einar Diaz | .15 | .40 |
| 345 | Derek Jeter | 1.00 | 2.50 |
| 346 | Jeff Conine | .15 | .40 |
| 347 | Ray Durham SP | .75 | 2.00 |
| 348 | Wilson Betemit SP | .75 | 2.00 |
| 349 | Jeffrey Hammonds | .15 | .40 |
| 350 | Dan Trumble RC | .15 | .40 |
| 351 | Phil Nevin SP | .75 | 2.00 |
| 352 | A.J. Burnett | .15 | .40 |
| 353 | Bill Mueller | .15 | .40 |
| 354 | Charles Nagy | .15 | .40 |
| 355 | Rusty Greer SP | .75 | 2.00 |
| 356 | Jason Botts RC | .20 | .50 |
| 357 | Magglio Ordonez | .15 | .40 |
| 358 | Kevin Appier | .15 | .40 |
| 359 | Brad Radke | .15 | .40 |
| 360 | Chris George | .15 | .40 |
| 361 | Chris Piersoll RC | .15 | .40 |
| 362 | Ivan Rodriguez | .25 | .60 |
| 363 | Jim Kavourias RC | .15 | .40 |
| 364 | Rick Helling SP | .75 | 2.00 |
| 365 | Dean Palmer | .15 | .40 |
| 366 | Rich Aurilia SP | .75 | 2.00 |
| 367 | Ryan Vogelsong | .15 | .40 |
| 368 | Matt Lawton | .15 | .40 |
| 369 | Wade Miller | .15 | .40 |
| 370 | Dustin Hermanson | .15 | .40 |
| 371 | Craig Wilson | .15 | .40 |
| 372 | Todd Zeile SP | .75 | 2.00 |
| 373 | Jon Guzman RC | .15 | .40 |
| 374 | Ellis Burks | .15 | .40 |
| 375 | Robert Cosby SP RC | .75 | 2.00 |
| 376 | Jason Kendall | .15 | .40 |
| 377 | Scott Rolen SP | 1.25 | 3.00 |
| 378 | Andruw Jones | .25 | .60 |
| 379 | Greg Sain RC | .15 | .40 |
| 380 | Paul LoDuca | .15 | .40 |
| 381 | Scotty Layfield RC | .15 | .40 |
| 382 | Tomo ONa | .15 | .40 |
| 383 | Garrett Guzman RC | .15 | .40 |
| 384 | Jack Cust SP | .75 | 2.00 |
| 385 | Shayne Wright RC | .15 | .40 |
| 386 | Derrek Lee | .25 | .60 |
| 387 | Jesus Medrano RC | .15 | .40 |
| 388 | Javier Vazquez | .15 | .40 |
| 389 | Preston Wilson SP | .75 | 2.00 |
| 390 | Gavin Floyd RC | .40 | 1.00 |
| 391 | Sidney Ponson SP | .75 | 2.00 |
| 392 | Jose Hernandez | .15 | .40 |
| 393 | Scott Erickson SP | .75 | 2.00 |
| 394 | Jose Valverde RC | .15 | .40 |
| 395 | Mark Hamilton SP | .75 | 2.00 |
| 396 | Brad Cresse | .15 | .40 |
| 397 | Danny Bautista | .15 | .40 |
| 398 | Ray Lankford SP | .75 | 2.00 |
| 399 | Miguel Batista SP | .75 | 2.00 |
| 400 | Brent Butler | .15 | .40 |
| 401 | Manny Delcarmen SP RC | 1.25 | 3.00 |
| 402 | Kyle Farnsworth SP | .75 | 2.00 |
| 403 | Freddy Garcia | .15 | .40 |
| 404 | Joe Jiannetti RC | .15 | .40 |
| 405 | Josh Barfield RC | 1.00 | 2.50 |
| 406 | Corey Patterson | .15 | .40 |
| 407 | Josh Towers | .15 | .40 |
| 408 | Carlos Pena | .15 | .40 |
| 409 | Jeff Cirillo | .15 | .40 |
| 410 | Jon Lieber | .15 | .40 |
| 411 | Woody Williams SP | .75 | 2.00 |
| 412 | Richard Lane SP RC | .15 | .40 |
| 413 | Alex Gonzalez | .15 | .40 |
| 414 | Wilkin Ruan | .15 | .40 |
| 415 | Geoff Jenkins | .15 | .40 |
| 416 | Carlos Hernandez | .15 | .40 |
| 417 | Matt Clement SP | .75 | 2.00 |
| 418 | Jose Cruz Jr. | .15 | .40 |
| 419 | Jake Mauer RC | .15 | .40 |
| 420 | Matt Childers SP | .15 | .40 |
| 421 | Tom Glavine SP | 1.25 | 3.00 |
| 422 | Ken Griffey Jr. | .60 | 1.50 |
| 423 | Anderson Hernandez RC | .15 | .40 |
| 424 | John Suomi RC | .15 | .40 |
| 425 | Doug Sessions RC | .15 | .40 |
| 426 | Jarel Wright | .15 | .40 |
| 427 | Rolando Viera SP RC | .75 | 2.00 |
| 428 | Aaron Sele | .15 | .40 |
| 429 | Dmitri Young | .15 | .40 |
| 430 | Ryan Klesko | .15 | .40 |
| 431 | Kevin Tapani SP | .75 | 2.00 |
| 432 | Joe Kennedy | .15 | .40 |
| 433 | Austin Kearns | .15 | .40 |
| 434 | Roger Cedeno SP | .75 | 2.00 |
| 435 | Lance Berkman | .15 | .40 |
| 436 | Frank Menechino | .15 | .40 |
| 437 | Brett Myers | .15 | .40 |
| 438 | Bob Abreu | .15 | .40 |
| 439 | Shawn Estes SP | .75 | 2.00 |

## 2003 Bowman Heritage

MARK PRIOR
Pitcher - CUBS

|  |  | | |
|---|------|---|---|
| | COMPLETE SET (300) | 60.00 | 120.00 |
| 1 | Jorge Posada | .25 | .60 |
| 2 | Todd Helton | .25 | .60 |
| 3 | Marcus Giles | .15 | .40 |
| 4 | Eric Chavez | .15 | .40 |
| 5 | Edgar Martinez | .25 | .60 |
| 6 | Luis Gonzalez | .15 | .40 |
| 7 | Corey Patterson | .15 | .40 |
| 8 | Preston Wilson | .15 | .40 |
| 9 | Ryan Klesko | .15 | .40 |
| 10 | Randy Johnson | .40 | 1.00 |
| 11 | Jose Guillen | .15 | .40 |
| 12 | Carlos Lee | .15 | .40 |
| 13 | Steve Finley | .15 | .40 |
| 14 | A.J. Pierzynski | .15 | .40 |
| 15 | Troy Glaus | .15 | .40 |
| 16 | Darin Erstad | .15 | .40 |
| 17 | Moises Alou | .15 | .40 |
| 18 | Torii Hunter | .15 | .40 |
| 19 | Marlon Byrd | .15 | .40 |
| 20 | Mark Prior | .25 | .60 |
| 21 | Shannon Stewart | .15 | .40 |
| 22 | Craig Biggio | .25 | .60 |
| 23 | Johnny Damon | .25 | .60 |
| 24 | Robert Fick | .15 | .40 |
| 25 | Jason Giambi | .25 | .60 |
| 26 | Fernando Vina | .15 | .40 |
| 27 | Aubrey Huff | .15 | .40 |
| 28 | Benito Santiago | .15 | .40 |
| 29 | Jay Gibbons | .15 | .40 |
| 30 | Ken Griffey Jr. | .60 | 1.50 |
| 31 | Rocco Baldelli | .15 | .40 |
| 32 | Pat Burrell | .15 | .40 |
| 33 | A.J. Burnett | .15 | .40 |
| 34 | Omar Vizquel | .25 | .60 |
| 35 | Greg Maddux | .60 | 1.50 |
| 36 | Cliff Floyd | .15 | .40 |
| 37 | C.C. Sabathia | .15 | .40 |
| 38 | Geoff Jenkins | .15 | .40 |
| 39 | Ty Wigginton | .15 | .40 |
| 40 | Jeff Kent | .15 | .40 |
| 41 | Orlando Hudson | .15 | .40 |
| 42 | Edgardo Alfonzo | .15 | .40 |
| 43 | Greg Myers | .15 | .40 |
| 44 | Melvin Mora | .15 | .40 |
| 45 | Sammy Sosa | .40 | 1.00 |
| 46 | Russ Ortiz | .15 | .40 |
| 47 | Josh Beckett | .15 | .40 |
| 48 | David Wells | .15 | .40 |
| 49 | Woody Williams | .15 | .40 |
| 50 | Alex Rodriguez | .60 | 1.50 |
| 51 | Randy Wolf | .15 | .40 |
| 52 | Carlos Beltran | .15 | .40 |
| 53 | Austin Kearns | .15 | .40 |
| 54 | Phil Nixon | .15 | .40 |
| 55 | Ivan Rodriguez | .25 | .60 |
| 56 | Shea Hillenbrand | .15 | .40 |
| 57 | Roberto Alomar | .25 | .60 |
| 58 | John Olerud | .15 | .40 |
| 59 | Michael Young | .25 | .60 |
| 60 | Garret Anderson | .15 | .40 |
| 61 | Mike Lieberthal | .15 | .40 |
| 62 | Adam Dunn | .15 | .40 |
| 63 | Raul Ibanez | .15 | .40 |
| 64 | Kenny Lofton | .15 | .40 |
| 65 | Ichiro Suzuki | .75 | 2.00 |
| 66 | Jarrod Washburn | .15 | .40 |
| 67 | Shawn Chacon | .15 | .40 |
| 68 | Alex Gonzalez | .15 | .40 |
| 69 | Roy Halladay | .15 | .40 |
| 70 | Vladimir Guerrero | .40 | 1.00 |
| 71 | Hee Seop Choi | .15 | .40 |
| 72 | Jody Gerut | .15 | .40 |
| 73 | Ray Durham | .15 | .40 |
| 74 | Mark Teixeira | .25 | .60 |
| 75 | Hank Blalock | .15 | .40 |
| 76 | Jerry Hairston Jr. | .15 | .40 |
| 77 | Erubiel Durazo | .15 | .40 |
| 78 | Frank Catalanotto | .15 | .40 |
| 79 | Jacque Jones | .15 | .40 |
| 80 | Bobby Abreu | .15 | .40 |
| 81 | Mike Hampton | .15 | .40 |
| 82 | Zach Day | .15 | .40 |
| 83 | Jimmy Rollins | .15 | .40 |
| 84 | Joel Pineiro | .15 | .40 |
| 85 | Brett Myers | .15 | .40 |
| 86 | Frank Thomas | .40 | 1.00 |
| 87 | Aramis Ramirez | .15 | .40 |
| 88 | Paul Lo Duca | .15 | .40 |
| 89 | Dmitri Young | .15 | .40 |
| 90 | Brian Giles | .15 | .40 |

| | | | |
|---|---|---|---|
| ☐ 91 Jose Cruz Jr. | .15 | .40 |
| ☐ 92 Derek Lowe | .15 | .40 |
| ☐ 93 Mark Buehrle | .15 | .40 |
| ☐ 94 Wade Miller | .15 | .40 |
| ☐ 95 Derek Jeter | 1.00 | 2.50 |
| ☐ 96 Bret Boone | .15 | .40 |
| ☐ 97 Tony Batista | .15 | .40 |
| ☐ 98 Sean Casey | .15 | .40 |
| ☐ 99 Eric Hinske | .15 | .40 |
| ☐ 100 Albert Pujols | .75 | 2.00 |
| ☐ 101 Runelvys Hernandez | .15 | .40 |
| ☐ 102 Vernon Wells | .15 | .40 |
| ☐ 103 Kerry Wood | .15 | .40 |
| ☐ 104 Lance Berkman | .15 | .40 |
| ☐ 105 Alfonso Soriano | .15 | .40 |
| ☐ 106 Bill Mueller | .15 | .40 |
| ☐ 107 Bartolo Colon | .15 | .40 |
| ☐ 108 Andy Pettitte | .25 | .60 |
| ☐ 109 Rafael Furcal | .15 | .40 |
| ☐ 110 Dontrelle Willis | .40 | 1.00 |
| ☐ 111 Carl Crawford | .15 | .40 |
| ☐ 112 Scott Rolen | .25 | .60 |
| ☐ 113 Chipper Jones | .40 | 1.00 |
| ☐ 114 Magglio Ordonez | .15 | .40 |
| ☐ 115 Bernie Williams | .15 | .40 |
| ☐ 116 Roy Oswalt | .15 | .40 |
| ☐ 117 Kevin Brown | .15 | .40 |
| ☐ 118 Cristian Guzman | .15 | .40 |
| ☐ 119 Kazuhisa Ishii | .15 | .40 |
| ☐ 120 Larry Walker | .15 | .40 |
| ☐ 121 Miguel Tejada | .25 | .60 |
| ☐ 122 Manny Ramirez | .25 | .60 |
| ☐ 123 Mike Mussina | .15 | .40 |
| ☐ 124 Mike Lowell | .15 | .40 |
| ☐ 125 Scott Podsednik | .15 | .40 |
| ☐ 126 Aaron Boone | .15 | .40 |
| ☐ 127 Carlos Delgado | .15 | .40 |
| ☐ 128 Jose Vidro | .15 | .40 |
| ☐ 129 Brad Radke | .15 | .40 |
| ☐ 130 Rafael Palmeiro | .25 | .60 |
| ☐ 131 Mark Mulder | .15 | .40 |
| ☐ 132 Jason Schmidt | .15 | .40 |
| ☐ 133 Gary Sheffield | .15 | .40 |
| ☐ 134 Richie Sexson | .15 | .40 |
| ☐ 135 Barry Zito | .15 | .40 |
| ☐ 136 Tom Glavine | .25 | .60 |
| ☐ 137 Jim Edmonds | .25 | .60 |
| ☐ 138 Andruw Jones | .25 | .60 |
| ☐ 139 Pedro Martinez | .25 | .60 |
| ☐ 140 Curt Schilling | .25 | .60 |
| ☐ 141 Phil Nevin | .15 | .40 |
| ☐ 142 Nomar Garciaparra | .60 | 1.50 |
| ☐ 143 Vicente Padilla | .15 | .40 |
| ☐ 144 Kevin Millwood | .15 | .40 |
| ☐ 145 Shawn Green | .15 | .40 |
| ☐ 146 Jeff Bagwell | .25 | .60 |
| ☐ 147 Hideo Nomo | .40 | 1.00 |
| ☐ 148 Fred McGriff | .25 | .60 |
| ☐ 149 Matt Morris | .15 | .40 |
| ☐ 150 Roger Clemens | .75 | 2.00 |
| ☐ 151 Jerome Williams | .15 | .40 |
| ☐ 152 Orlando Cabrera | .15 | .40 |
| ☐ 153 Tim Hudson | .15 | .40 |
| ☐ 154 Mike Sweeney | .15 | .40 |
| ☐ 155 Jim Thome | .25 | .60 |
| ☐ 156 Rich Aurilia | .15 | .40 |
| ☐ 157 Mike Piazza | .60 | 1.50 |
| ☐ 158 Edgar Renteria | .15 | .40 |
| ☐ 159 Javy Lopez | .15 | .40 |
| ☐ 160 Jamie Moyer | .15 | .40 |
| ☐ 161 Miguel Cabrera DI | .40 | 1.00 |
| ☐ 162 Adam Loewen DI RC | .40 | 1.00 |
| ☐ 163 Jose Reyes DI | .15 | .40 |
| ☐ 164 Zack Greinke DI | .15 | .40 |
| ☐ 165 Gavin Floyd DI | .15 | .40 |
| ☐ 166 Jeremy Guthrie DI | .15 | .40 |
| ☐ 167 Victor Martinez DI | .25 | .60 |
| ☐ 168 Rich Harden DI | .25 | .60 |
| ☐ 169 Joe Mauer DI | .40 | 1.00 |
| ☐ 170 Khalil Greene DI | .40 | 1.00 |
| ☐ 171A Willie Mays | .75 | 2.00 |
| ☐ 171B Willie Mays DI | .75 | 2.00 |
| ☐ 171C Willie Mays KN | .75 | 2.00 |
| ☐ 172A Phil Rizzuto | .25 | .60 |
| ☐ 172B Phil Rizzuto DI | .25 | .60 |
| ☐ 172C Phil Rizzuto KN | .25 | .60 |
| ☐ 173A Al Kaline | .40 | 1.00 |
| ☐ 173B Al Kaline DI | .40 | 1.00 |

| | | |
|---|---|---|
| ☐ 173C Al Kaline KN | .40 | 1.00 |
| ☐ 174A Warren Spahn | .25 | .60 |
| ☐ 174B Warren Spahn DI | .25 | .60 |
| ☐ 174C Warren Spahn KN | .25 | .60 |
| ☐ 175A Jimmy Piersall | .15 | .40 |
| ☐ 175B Jimmy Piersall DI | .15 | .40 |
| ☐ 175C Jimmy Piersall KN | .15 | .40 |
| ☐ 176A Luis Aparicio | .15 | .40 |
| ☐ 176B Luis Aparicio DI | .15 | .40 |
| ☐ 176C Luis Aparicio KN | .15 | .40 |
| ☐ 177A Whitey Ford | .25 | .60 |
| ☐ 177B Whitey Ford DI | .25 | .60 |
| ☐ 177C Whitey Ford KN | .25 | .60 |
| ☐ 178A Harmon Killebrew | .40 | 1.00 |
| ☐ 178B Harmon Killebrew DI | .40 | 1.00 |
| ☐ 178C Harmon Killebrew KN | .40 | 1.00 |
| ☐ 179A Duke Snider | .25 | .60 |
| ☐ 179B Duke Snider DI | .25 | .60 |
| ☐ 179C Duke Snider KN | .25 | .60 |
| ☐ 180A Roberto Clemente | 1.00 | 2.50 |
| ☐ 180B Roberto Clemente DI | 1.00 | 2.50 |
| ☐ 180C Roberto Clemente KN | 1.00 | 2.50 |
| ☐ 181 David Martinez KN RC | .15 | .40 |
| ☐ 182 Felix Pie KN RC | 1.50 | 4.00 |
| ☐ 183 Kevin Correia KN RC | .15 | .40 |
| ☐ 184 Brandon Webb KN RC | 1.00 | 2.50 |
| ☐ 185 Matt Diaz KN RC | .30 | .75 |
| ☐ 186 Lew Ford KN RC | .20 | .50 |
| ☐ 187 Jeremy Griffiths KN RC | .15 | .40 |
| ☐ 188 Matt Hensley KN RC | .15 | .40 |
| ☐ 189 Danny Garcia KN RC | .15 | .40 |
| ☐ 190 Elizardo Ramirez KN RC | .20 | .50 |
| ☐ 191 Greg Aquino KN RC | .15 | .40 |
| ☐ 192 Felix Sanchez KN RC | .15 | .40 |
| ☐ 193 Kelly Shoppach KN RC | .30 | .75 |
| ☐ 194 Bubba Nelson KN RC | .15 | .40 |
| ☐ 195 Mike O'Keefe KN RC | .15 | .40 |
| ☐ 196 Hanley Ramirez KN RC | 1.50 | 4.00 |
| ☐ 197 Todd Wellemeyer KN RC | .15 | .40 |
| ☐ 198 Dustin Moseley KN RC | .15 | .40 |
| ☐ 199 Eric Crozier KN RC | .20 | .50 |
| ☐ 200 Ryan Shealy KN RC | 1.00 | 2.50 |
| ☐ 201 Jeremy Bonderman KN RC | 1.00 | 2.50 |
| ☐ 202 Bo Hart KN RC | .15 | .40 |
| ☐ 203 Dusty Brown KN RC | .15 | .40 |
| ☐ 204 Rob Hammock KN RC | .15 | .40 |
| ☐ 205 Jorge Piedra KN RC | .20 | .50 |
| ☐ 206 Jason Kubel KN RC | .60 | 1.50 |
| ☐ 207 Stephen Randolph KN RC | .15 | .40 |
| ☐ 208 Andy Sisco KN RC | .15 | .40 |
| ☐ 209 Matt Kata KN RC | .15 | .40 |
| ☐ 210 Robinson Cano KN RC | 3.00 | 8.00 |
| ☐ 211 Ben Francisco KN RC | .15 | .40 |
| ☐ 212 Amie Munoz KN RC | .15 | .40 |
| ☐ 213 Ozzie Chavez KN RC | .15 | .40 |
| ☐ 214 Beau Kemp KN RC | .15 | .40 |
| ☐ 215 Travis Wong KN RC | .20 | .50 |
| ☐ 216 Brian McCann KN RC | 2.50 | 6.00 |
| ☐ 217 Aquilino Lopez KN RC | .15 | .40 |
| ☐ 218 Bobby Basham KN RC | .15 | .40 |
| ☐ 219 Tim Olson KN RC | .15 | .40 |
| ☐ 220 Nathan Panther KN RC | .15 | .40 |
| ☐ 221 Wil Ledezma KN RC | .15 | .40 |
| ☐ 222 Josh Willingham KN RC | .40 | 1.00 |
| ☐ 223 David Cash KN RC | .15 | .40 |
| ☐ 224 Oscar Villarreal KN RC | .15 | .40 |
| ☐ 225 Jeff Duncan KN RC | .15 | .40 |
| ☐ 226 Dan Haren KN RC | .40 | 1.00 |
| ☐ 227 Michel Hernandez KN RC | .15 | .40 |
| ☐ 228 Matt Murton KN RC | .75 | 2.00 |
| ☐ 229 Clay Hensley KN RC | .15 | .40 |
| ☐ 230 Tyler Johnson KN RC | .15 | .40 |
| ☐ 231 Tyler Martin KN RC | .15 | .40 |
| ☐ 232 J.D. Durbin KN RC | .15 | .40 |
| ☐ 233 Shane Victorino KN RC | .40 | 1.00 |
| ☐ 234 Rajai Davis KN RC | .15 | .40 |
| ☐ 235 Chien-Ming Wang KN RC | 2.00 | 5.00 |
| ☐ 236 Travis Ishikawa KN RC | .30 | .75 |
| ☐ 237 Eric Eckenstahler KN | .15 | .40 |
| ☐ 238 Dustin McGowan KN RC | .20 | .50 |
| ☐ 239 Prentice Redman KN RC | .15 | .40 |
| ☐ 240 Haj Turay KN RC | .15 | .40 |
| ☐ 241 Matt DeMarco KN RC | .15 | .40 |
| ☐ 242 Lou Palmisano KN RC | .20 | .50 |
| ☐ 243 Eric Reed KN RC | .15 | .40 |
| ☐ 244 Willie Eyre KN RC | .15 | .40 |
| ☐ 245 Fentin Tejeda KN RC | .15 | .40 |
| ☐ 246 Michael Garciaparra KN RC | .15 | .40 |

| | | |
|---|---|---|
| ☐ 247 Michael Hinckley KN RC | .20 | .50 |
| ☐ 248 Brandan Florence KN RC | .15 | .40 |
| ☐ 249 Trent Oeltjen KN RC | .20 | .50 |
| ☐ 250 Mike Neu KN RC | .15 | .40 |
| ☐ 251 Chris Lubanski KN RC | .40 | 1.00 |
| ☐ 252 Brandon Wood KN RC | 4.00 | 10.00 |
| ☐ 253 Delmon Young KN RC | 2.00 | 5.00 |
| ☐ 254 Matt Harrison KN RC | .30 | .75 |
| ☐ 255 Chad Billingsley KN RC | 1.25 | 3.00 |
| ☐ 256 Josh Anderson KN RC | .20 | .50 |
| ☐ 257 Brian McFall KN RC | .15 | .40 |
| ☐ 258 Ryan Wagner KN RC | .15 | .40 |
| ☐ 259 Billy Hogan KN RC | .20 | .50 |
| ☐ 260 Nate Spears KN RC | .20 | .50 |
| ☐ 261 Ryan Harvey KN RC | .75 | 2.00 |
| ☐ 262 Wes Littleton KN RC | .20 | .50 |
| ☐ 263 Xavier Paul KN RC | .20 | .50 |
| ☐ 264 Sean Rodriguez KN RC | .75 | 2.00 |
| ☐ 265 Brian Finch KN RC | .15 | .40 |
| ☐ 266 Josh Hairston KN RC | .20 | .50 |
| ☐ 267 Brian Snyder KN RC | .20 | .50 |
| ☐ 268 Eric Duncan KN RC | .75 | 2.00 |
| ☐ 269 Rickie Weeks KN RC | 1.25 | 3.00 |
| ☐ 270 Tim Battle KN RC | .30 | .75 |
| ☐ 271 Scott Baker KN RC | .15 | .40 |
| ☐ 272 Aaron Hill KN RC | .30 | .75 |
| ☐ 273 Casey Abrams KN RC | .15 | .40 |
| ☐ 274 Jonathan Fulton KN RC | .20 | .50 |
| ☐ 275 Todd Jennings KN RC | .20 | .50 |
| ☐ 276 Jordan Pratt KN RC | .20 | .50 |
| ☐ 277 Tom Gorzelanny KN RC | .50 | 1.25 |
| ☐ 278 Matt Lorenzo KN RC | .15 | .40 |
| ☐ 279 Jarrod Saltalamacchia KN RC | 2.00 | 5.00 |
| ☐ 280 Mike Wagner KN RC | .15 | .40 |

## 2004 Bowman Heritage

| | | |
|---|---|---|
| ☐ COMPLETE SET (351) | 175.00 | 300.00 |
| ☐ COMP.SET w/o SP's (300) | 25.00 | 50.00 |
| ☐ SP STATED ODDS 1:3 HOBBY, 1:3 RETAIL | | |
| ☐ SP's: 2/9/13/21/25/40B/46/48B/50/55/61 | | |
| ☐ SP's: 77/80/87/89/95/100/104/109/127/130 | | |
| ☐ SP's: 132/141/183A/189/204/206/208/210 | | |
| ☐ SP's: 213/216/220/224/228/234/240/243 | | |
| ☐ SP's: 246/249/259/268/270-271/282/291 | | |
| ☐ SP's: 304/318/327/334/342/348 | | |
| ☐ PLATES STATED ODDS 1:240 HOBBY | | |
| ☐ PLATES PRINT RUN 1 #'d SET PER COLOR | | |
| ☐ PLATES: BLACK, CYAN, MAGENTA & YELLOW | | |
| ☐ NO PLATES PRICING DUE TO SCARCITY | | |
| ☐ ROOP BINDER ODDS 1:240 HOBBY | | |
| ☐ ROOP BINDER EXCH.DEADLINE 12/31/05 | | |
| ☐ 1 Tom Glavine | .25 | .60 |
| ☐ 2 Mike Piazza SP | 3.00 | 8.00 |
| ☐ 3 Sidney Ponson | .15 | .40 |
| ☐ 4 Jerry Hairston Jr. | .15 | .40 |
| ☐ 5 Jermaine Dye | .15 | .40 |
| ☐ 6 Bobby Crosby | .15 | .40 |
| ☐ 7 Carlos Zambrano | .15 | .40 |
| ☐ 8 Moises Alou | .15 | .40 |
| ☐ 9 Alex Rodriguez SP | 3.00 | 8.00 |
| ☐ 10 Derek Jeter | .75 | 2.00 |
| ☐ 11 Rafael Furcal | .15 | .40 |
| ☐ 12 J.D. Drew | .15 | .40 |
| ☐ 13 Joe Mauer SP | 2.50 | 6.00 |
| ☐ 14 Brad Radke | .15 | .40 |
| ☐ 15 Johnny Damon | .15 | .40 |
| ☐ 16 Derek Lowe | .15 | .40 |
| ☐ 17 Pat Burrell | .15 | .40 |
| ☐ 18 Mike Lieberthal | .15 | .40 |
| ☐ 19 Cliff Lee | .15 | .40 |
| ☐ 20 Ronnie Belliard | .15 | .40 |
| ☐ 21 Eric Gagne SP | 2.00 | 5.00 |
| ☐ 22 Brad Penny | .15 | .40 |
| ☐ 23 Al Kaline RET | .60 | 1.50 |

|  |  | | |
|---|---|---|---|
| ☐ 24 | Mike Maroth | .15 | .40 |
| ☐ 25 | Magglio Ordonez SP | 2.00 | 5.00 |
| ☐ 26 | Mark Buehrle | .15 | .40 |
| ☐ 27 | Jack Wilson | .15 | .40 |
| ☐ 28 | Oliver Perez | .15 | .40 |
| ☐ 29 | Red Schoendienst RET | .25 | .60 |
| ☐ 30 | Yadier Molina FY RC | .75 | 2.00 |
| ☐ 31 | Ryan Freel | .15 | .40 |
| ☐ 32 | Adam Dunn | .15 | .40 |
| ☐ 33 | Paul Konerko | .15 | .40 |
| ☐ 34 | Esteban Loaiza | .15 | .40 |
| ☐ 35 | Ivan Rodriguez | .25 | .60 |
| ☐ 36 | Carlos Guillen | .15 | .40 |
| ☐ 37 | Adrian Beltre | .15 | .40 |
| ☐ 38 | C.C. Sabathia | .15 | .40 |
| ☐ 39 | Hideo Nomo | .40 | 1.00 |
| ☐ 40A | Victor Martinez | .15 | .40 |
| ☐ 40B | V.Martinez Pedro Stats SP | 2.00 | 5.00 |
| ☐ 41 | Bobby Abreu | .15 | .40 |
| ☐ 42 | Randy Wolf | .15 | .40 |
| ☐ 43 | Johnny Estrada | .15 | .40 |
| ☐ 44 | Russ Ortiz | .15 | .40 |
| ☐ 45 | Kenny Rogers | .15 | .40 |
| ☐ 46 | Hank Blalock SP | 2.00 | 5.00 |
| ☐ 47 | David Ortiz | .40 | 1.00 |
| ☐ 48A | Pedro Martinez | .25 | .60 |
| ☐ 48B | P.Martinez Victor Stats SP | 3.00 | 8.00 |
| ☐ 49 | Austin Kearns | .15 | .40 |
| ☐ 50 | Ken Griffey Jr. SP | 3.00 | 8.00 |
| ☐ 51 | Mark Prior | .25 | .60 |
| ☐ 52 | Kerry Wood | .15 | .40 |
| ☐ 53 | Eric Chavez | .15 | .40 |
| ☐ 54 | Tim Hudson | .15 | .40 |
| ☐ 55 | Rafael Palmeiro SP | 3.00 | 8.00 |
| ☐ 56 | Javy Lopez | .15 | .40 |
| ☐ 57 | Jason Bay | .15 | .40 |
| ☐ 58 | Craig Wilson | .15 | .40 |
| ☐ 59 | Whitey Ford RET | .40 | 1.00 |
| ☐ 60 | Jason Giambi | .25 | .60 |
| ☐ 61 | Scott Rolen SP | 3.00 | 8.00 |
| ☐ 62 | Matt Morris | .15 | .40 |
| ☐ 63 | Javier Vazquez | .15 | .40 |
| ☐ 64 | Jim Thome | .25 | .60 |
| ☐ 65 | Don Zimmer RET | .25 | .60 |
| ☐ 66 | Shawn Green | .15 | .40 |
| ☐ 67 | Don Larsen RET | .40 | 1.00 |
| ☐ 68 | Gary Sheffield | .15 | .40 |
| ☐ 69 | Jorge Posada | .25 | .60 |
| ☐ 70 | Bernie Williams | .25 | .60 |
| ☐ 71 | Chipper Jones | .40 | 1.00 |
| ☐ 72 | Andruw Jones | .25 | .60 |
| ☐ 73 | John Thomson | .15 | .40 |
| ☐ 74 | Jim Edmonds | .15 | .40 |
| ☐ 75 | Albert Pujols | .75 | 2.00 |
| ☐ 76 | Chris Carpenter | .15 | .40 |
| ☐ 77 | Aubrey Huff SP | 2.00 | 5.00 |
| ☐ 78 | Carl Crawford | .15 | .40 |
| ☐ 79 | Victor Zambrano | .15 | .40 |
| ☐ 80 | Alfonso Soriano SP | 2.00 | 5.00 |
| ☐ 81 | Lance Berkman | .15 | .40 |
| ☐ 82 | Mike Sweeney | .15 | .40 |
| ☐ 83 | Ken Harvey | .15 | .40 |
| ☐ 84 | Angel Berroa | .15 | .40 |
| ☐ 85 | A.J. Burnett | .15 | .40 |
| ☐ 86 | Mike Lowell | .15 | .40 |
| ☐ 87 | Miguel Cabrera SP | 3.00 | 8.00 |
| ☐ 88 | Preston Wilson | .15 | .40 |
| ☐ 89 | Todd Helton SP | 3.00 | 8.00 |
| ☐ 90 | Larry Walker Cards | .25 | .60 |
| ☐ 91 | Vladimir Guerrero | .40 | 1.00 |
| ☐ 92 | Garret Anderson | .15 | .40 |
| ☐ 93 | Bartolo Colon | .15 | .40 |
| ☐ 94 | Scott Hairston | .15 | .40 |
| ☐ 95 | Richie Sexson SP | 2.00 | 5.00 |
| ☐ 96 | Sean Casey | .15 | .40 |
| ☐ 97 | John Podres RET | .25 | .60 |
| ☐ 98 | Andy Pettitte | .25 | .60 |
| ☐ 99 | Roy Oswalt | .15 | .40 |
| ☐ 100 | Roger Clemens SP | 3.00 | 8.00 |
| ☐ 101 | Scott Podsednik | .15 | .40 |
| ☐ 102 | Ben Sheets | .15 | .40 |
| ☐ 103 | Lyle Overbay | .15 | .40 |
| ☐ 104 | Nick Johnson SP | 2.00 | 5.00 |
| ☐ 105 | Zach Day | .15 | .40 |
| ☐ 106 | Jose Reyes | .15 | .40 |
| ☐ 107 | Khalil Greene | .25 | .60 |
| ☐ 108 | Sean Burroughs | .15 | .40 |
| ☐ 109 | David Wells SP | 2.00 | 5.00 |
| ☐ 110 | Jason Schmidt | .15 | .40 |
| ☐ 111 | Neifi Perez | .15 | .40 |
| ☐ 112 | Edgar Renteria | .15 | .40 |
| ☐ 113 | Rich Aurilia | .15 | .40 |
| ☐ 114 | Edgar Martinez | .25 | .60 |
| ☐ 115 | Joel Pineiro | .15 | .40 |
| ☐ 116 | Mark Teixeira | .25 | .60 |
| ☐ 117 | Michael Young | .15 | .40 |
| ☐ 118 | Ricardo Rodriguez | .15 | .40 |
| ☐ 119 | Carlos Delgado | .15 | .40 |
| ☐ 120 | Roy Halladay | .15 | .40 |
| ☐ 121 | Jose Guillen | .15 | .40 |
| ☐ 122 | Troy Glaus | .15 | .40 |
| ☐ 123 | Shea Hillenbrand | .15 | .40 |
| ☐ 124 | Luis Gonzalez | .15 | .40 |
| ☐ 125 | Horacio Ramirez | .15 | .40 |
| ☐ 126 | Melvin Mora | .15 | .40 |
| ☐ 127 | Miguel Tejada SP | 2.00 | 5.00 |
| ☐ 128 | Manny Ramirez | .25 | .60 |
| ☐ 129 | Tim Wakefield | .15 | .40 |
| ☐ 130 | Curt Schilling SP | 3.00 | 8.00 |
| ☐ 131 | Aramis Ramirez | .15 | .40 |
| ☐ 132 | Sammy Sosa SP | 3.00 | 8.00 |
| ☐ 133 | Matt Clement | .15 | .40 |
| ☐ 134 | Juan Uribe | .15 | .40 |
| ☐ 135 | Dontrelle Willis | .25 | .60 |
| ☐ 136 | Paul Lo Duca | .15 | .40 |
| ☐ 137 | Juan Pierre | .15 | .40 |
| ☐ 138 | Kevin Brown | .15 | .40 |
| ☐ 139 | B.Giles/M.Giles | .15 | .40 |
| ☐ 140 | Brian Giles | .15 | .40 |
| ☐ 141 | Nomar Garciaparra SP | 3.00 | 8.00 |
| ☐ 142 | Cesar Izturis | .15 | .40 |
| ☐ 143 | Don Newcombe RET | .25 | .60 |
| ☐ 144 | Craig Biggio | .25 | .60 |
| ☐ 145 | Carlos Beltran | .15 | .40 |
| ☐ 146 | Torii Hunter | .15 | .40 |
| ☐ 147 | Livan Hernandez | .15 | .40 |
| ☐ 148 | Cliff Floyd | .15 | .40 |
| ☐ 149 | Barry Zito | .15 | .40 |
| ☐ 150 | Mark Mulder | .15 | .40 |
| ☐ 151 | Rocco Baldelli | .15 | .40 |
| ☐ 152 | Bret Boone | .15 | .40 |
| ☐ 153 | Jamie Moyer | .15 | .40 |
| ☐ 154 | Ichiro Suzuki | .75 | 2.00 |
| ☐ 155 | Brett Myers | .15 | .40 |
| ☐ 156 | Carl Pavano | .15 | .40 |
| ☐ 157 | Josh Beckett | .15 | .40 |
| ☐ 158 | Randy Johnson | .40 | 1.00 |
| ☐ 159 | Trot Nixon | .15 | .40 |
| ☐ 160 | Dmitri Young | .15 | .40 |
| ☐ 161 | Jacque Jones | .15 | .40 |
| ☐ 162 | Lew Ford | .15 | .40 |
| ☐ 163 | Jose Vidro | .15 | .40 |
| ☐ 164 | Mark Kotsay | .15 | .40 |
| ☐ 165 | A.J. Pierzynski | .15 | .40 |
| ☐ 166 | Dewon Brazelton | .15 | .40 |
| ☐ 167 | Jeromy Burnitz | .15 | .40 |
| ☐ 168 | Johan Santana | .40 | 1.00 |
| ☐ 169 | Greg Maddux | .60 | 1.50 |
| ☐ 170 | Carl Erskine RET | .25 | .60 |
| ☐ 171 | Robin Roberts RET | .25 | .60 |
| ☐ 172 | Freddy Garcia | .15 | .40 |
| ☐ 173 | Carlos Lee | .15 | .40 |
| ☐ 174 | Jeff Bagwell | .25 | .60 |
| ☐ 175 | Jeff Kent | .15 | .40 |
| ☐ 176 | Kazuhisa Ishii | .15 | .40 |
| ☐ 177 | Orlando Cabrera | .15 | .40 |
| ☐ 178 | Shannon Stewart | .15 | .40 |
| ☐ 179 | Mike Cameron | .15 | .40 |
| ☐ 180 | Mike Mussina | .25 | .60 |
| ☐ 181 | Frank Thomas | .40 | 1.00 |
| ☐ 182 | Jaret Wright | .15 | .40 |
| ☐ 183A | Alex Gonzalez Marlins SP | 2.00 | 5.00 |
| ☐ 183B | Alex Gonzalez Padres | .15 | .40 |
| ☐ 184 | Matt Lawton | .15 | .40 |
| ☐ 185 | Derrek Lee | .25 | .60 |
| ☐ 186 | Omar Vizquel | .15 | .40 |
| ☐ 187 | Jeremy Bonderman | .15 | .40 |
| ☐ 188 | Jake Westbrook | .15 | .40 |
| ☐ 189 | Zack Greinke SP | 2.00 | 5.00 |
| ☐ 190 | Chad Tracy | .15 | .40 |
| ☐ 191 | Rondell White | .15 | .40 |
| ☐ 192 | Alex Gonzalez | .15 | .40 |
| ☐ 193 | Geoff Jenkins | .15 | .40 |
| ☐ 194 | Ralph Kiner RET | .40 | 1.00 |
| ☐ 195 | Al Leiter | .15 | .40 |
| ☐ 196 | Kevin Millwood | .15 | .40 |
| ☐ 197 | Jason Kendall | .15 | .40 |
| ☐ 198 | Kris Benson | .15 | .40 |
| ☐ 199 | Ryan Klesko | .15 | .40 |
| ☐ 200 | Mark Loretta | .15 | .40 |
| ☐ 201 | Richard Hidalgo | .15 | .40 |
| ☐ 202 | Reed Johnson | .15 | .40 |
| ☐ 203 | Luis Castillo | .15 | .40 |
| ☐ 204 | Jon Zeringue DP SP RC | 2.00 | 5.00 |
| ☐ 205 | Matt Bush DP RC | .15 | .40 |
| ☐ 206 | Kurt Suzuki DP SP RC | 2.50 | 6.00 |
| ☐ 207 | Mark Rogers DP RC | .75 | 2.00 |
| ☐ 208 | Jason Vargas DP SP RC | 2.00 | 5.00 |
| ☐ 209 | Homer Bailey DP RC | 1.50 | 4.00 |
| ☐ 210 | Ray Liotta DP SP RC | 2.00 | 5.00 |
| ☐ 211 | Eric Campbell DP RC | 1.25 | 3.00 |
| ☐ 212 | Thomas Diamond DP RC | 1.00 | 2.50 |
| ☐ 213 | Gaby Hernandez DP SP RC | 3.00 | 8.00 |
| ☐ 214 | Neil Walker DP RC | .75 | 2.00 |
| ☐ 215 | Bill Bray DP RC | .30 | .75 |
| ☐ 216 | Wade Davis DP SP RC | 3.00 | 8.00 |
| ☐ 217 | David Purcey DP RC | .60 | 1.50 |
| ☐ 218 | Scott Elbert DP RC | .75 | 2.00 |
| ☐ 219 | Josh Fields DP RC | 1.50 | 4.00 |
| ☐ 220 | Josh Johnson DP SP RC | 2.00 | 5.00 |
| ☐ 221 | Chris Lambert DP RC | .40 | 1.00 |
| ☐ 222 | Trevor Plouffe DP RC | 1.00 | 2.50 |
| ☐ 223 | Bruce Froemming UMP | .20 | .50 |
| ☐ 224 | Matt Macri DP SP RC | 1.50 | 4.00 |
| ☐ 225 | Greg Golson DP RC | 1.00 | 2.50 |
| ☐ 226 | Philip Hughes DP RC | 4.00 | 10.00 |
| ☐ 227 | Kyle Waldrop DP RC | .75 | 2.00 |
| ☐ 228 | Matt Tuiasosopo DP SP RC | 3.00 | 8.00 |
| ☐ 229 | Richie Robnett DP RC | .75 | 2.00 |
| ☐ 230 | Taylor Tankersley DP RC | .40 | 1.00 |
| ☐ 231 | Blake DeWitt DP RC | 1.25 | 3.00 |
| ☐ 232 | Charlie Relliford UMP | .20 | .50 |
| ☐ 233 | Eric Hurley DP RC | .75 | 2.00 |
| ☐ 234 | Jordan Parraz DP SP RC | 2.00 | 5.00 |
| ☐ 235 | J.P. Howell DP RC | .75 | 2.00 |
| ☐ 236 | Dana DeMuth UMP | .20 | .50 |
| ☐ 237 | Zach Jackson DP RC | .60 | 1.50 |
| ☐ 238 | Justin Orenduff DP RC | .60 | 1.50 |
| ☐ 239 | Brad Thompson FY RC | .30 | .75 |
| ☐ 240 | J.C. Holt DP SP RC | 2.00 | 5.00 |
| ☐ 241 | Matt Fox DP RC | .30 | .75 |
| ☐ 242 | Danny Putnam DP RC | .60 | 1.50 |
| ☐ 243 | Daryl Jones DP SP RC | 2.00 | 5.00 |
| ☐ 244 | Jon Poterson DP RC | .30 | .75 |
| ☐ 245 | Gio Gonzalez DP RC | 1.00 | 2.50 |
| ☐ 246 | Lucas Harrell DP SP RC | 2.00 | 5.00 |
| ☐ 247 | Jerry Crawford UMP | .20 | .50 |
| ☐ 248 | Jay Rainville DP RC | 1.00 | 2.50 |
| ☐ 249 | Donnie Smith DP SP RC | 2.00 | 5.00 |
| ☐ 250 | Huston Street DP RC | 1.25 | 3.00 |
| ☐ 251 | Jeff Marquez DP RC | .40 | 1.00 |
| ☐ 252 | Reid Brignac DP RC | .75 | 2.00 |
| ☐ 253 | Yusmeiro Petit FY RC | .75 | 2.00 |
| ☐ 254 | K.C. Herren DP RC | .60 | 1.50 |
| ☐ 255 | Dale Scott UMP | .20 | .50 |
| ☐ 256 | Erick San Pedro DP RC | .30 | .75 |
| ☐ 257 | Ed Montague UMP | .20 | .50 |
| ☐ 258 | Billy Buckner DP RC | .40 | 1.00 |
| ☐ 259 | Mitch Einertson DP SP RC | 2.00 | 5.00 |
| ☐ 260 | Aarom Baldiris FY RC | .20 | .50 |
| ☐ 261 | Conor Jackson DP RC | 1.25 | 3.00 |
| ☐ 262 | Rick Reed UMP | .20 | .50 |
| ☐ 263 | Ervin Santana FY RC | .75 | 2.00 |
| ☐ 264 | Gerry Davis UMP | .20 | .50 |
| ☐ 265 | Merkin Valdez FY RC | .20 | .50 |
| ☐ 266 | Joey Gathright FY RC | .40 | 1.00 |
| ☐ 267 | Alberto Callaspo FY RC | .30 | .75 |
| ☐ 268 | Carlos Quentin FY SP RC | 4.00 | 10.00 |
| ☐ 269 | Gary Darling UMP | .20 | .50 |
| ☐ 270 | Jeff Salazar FY SP RC | 2.00 | 5.00 |
| ☐ 271 | Akinori Otsuka FY SP RC | 2.00 | 5.00 |
| ☐ 272 | Joe Brinkman UMP | .20 | .50 |
| ☐ 273 | Omar Quintanilla FY RC | .20 | .50 |
| ☐ 274 | Brian Runge UMP | .20 | .50 |
| ☐ 275 | Tom Mastny FY RC | .15 | .40 |
| ☐ 276 | John Hirschbeck UMP | .20 | .50 |
| ☐ 277 | Warner Madrigal FY RC | .30 | .75 |
| ☐ 278 | Joe West UMP | .20 | .50 |
| ☐ 279 | Paul Maholm FY RC | .40 | 1.00 |
| ☐ 280 | Larry Young UMP | .20 | .50 |
| ☐ 281 | Mike Reilly UMP | .20 | .50 |
| ☐ 282 | Kazuo Matsui FY SP RC | 2.00 | 5.00 |
| ☐ 283 | Randy Marsh UMP | .20 | .50 |
| ☐ 284 | Frank Francisco FY RC | .15 | .40 |

| | | |
|---|---|---|
| ❏ 285 Zach Duke FY RC | .75 | 2.00 |
| ❏ 286 Tim McClelland UMP | .20 | .50 |
| ❏ 287 Jesse Crain FY RC | .30 | .75 |
| ❏ 288 Hector Gimenez FY RC | .15 | .40 |
| ❏ 289 Marland Williams FY RC | .20 | .50 |
| ❏ 290 Brian Gorman UMP | .20 | .50 |
| ❏ 291 Jose Capellan FY SP RC | 2.00 | 5.00 |
| ❏ 292 Tim Welke UMP | .20 | .50 |
| ❏ 293 Javier Guzman FY RC | .20 | .50 |
| ❏ 294 Paul McAnulty FY RC | .30 | .75 |
| ❏ 295 Hector Made FY RC | .30 | .75 |
| ❏ 296 Jon Connolly FY RC | .15 | 1.00 |
| ❏ 297 Don Sutton FY RC | .40 | 1.00 |
| ❏ 298 Fausto Carmona FY RC | .75 | 2.00 |
| ❏ 299 Ramon Ramirez FY RC | .15 | .40 |
| ❏ 300 Brad Snyder FY RC | .40 | 1.00 |
| ❏ 301 Chin-Lung Hu FY RC | .50 | 1.25 |
| ❏ 302 Rudy Guillen FY RC | .30 | .75 |
| ❏ 303 Matt Moses FY RC | .40 | 1.00 |
| ❏ 304 Brad Halsey FY SP RC | 2.00 | 5.00 |
| ❏ 305 Erick Aybar FY RC | .40 | 1.00 |
| ❏ 306 Brad Sullivan FY RC | .20 | .50 |
| ❏ 307 Nick Gorneault FY RC | .20 | .50 |
| ❏ 308 Craig Ansman FY RC | .15 | .40 |
| ❏ 309 Ricky Nolasco FY RC | .50 | 1.25 |
| ❏ 310 Luke Hughes FY RC | .15 | .40 |
| ❏ 311 Danny Gonzalez FY RC | .15 | .40 |
| ❏ 312 Josh Labandeira FY RC | .15 | .40 |
| ❏ 313 Donald Levinski FY RC | .15 | .40 |
| ❏ 314 Vince Perkins FY RC | .20 | .50 |
| ❏ 315 Tommy Murphy FY RC | .15 | .40 |
| ❏ 316 Chad Bentz FY RC | .15 | .40 |
| ❏ 317 Chris Shelton FY RC | .75 | 2.00 |
| ❏ 318 Nyjer Morgan FY SP RC | 2.00 | 5.00 |
| ❏ 319 Kody Kirkland FY RC | .20 | .50 |
| ❏ 320 Blake Hawksworth FY RC | .20 | .50 |
| ❏ 321 Alex Romero FY RC | .15 | .40 |
| ❏ 322 Mike Gosling FY RC | .15 | .40 |
| ❏ 323 Ryan Budde FY RC | .15 | .40 |
| ❏ 324 Kevin Howard FY RC | .20 | .50 |
| ❏ 325 Wanell Macia FY RC | .15 | .40 |
| ❏ 326 Travis Blackley FY RC | .15 | .40 |
| ❏ 327 Kazuhito Tadano FY SP RC | 2.00 | 5.00 |
| ❏ 328 Shingo Takatsu FY RC | .30 | .75 |
| ❏ 329 Joaquin Arias FY RC | .30 | .75 |
| ❏ 330 Juan Cedeno FY RC | .15 | .40 |
| ❏ 331 Bobby Brownlie FY RC | .40 | 1.00 |
| ❏ 332 Lastings Milledge FY RC | 2.00 | 5.00 |
| ❏ 333 Estee Harris FY RC | .15 | .40 |
| ❏ 334 Tim Stauffer FY SP RC | 2.00 | 5.00 |
| ❏ 335 Jon Knott FY RC | .15 | .40 |
| ❏ 336 David Aardsma FY RC | .20 | .50 |
| ❏ 337 Wardell Starling FY RC | .15 | .40 |
| ❏ 338 Dioner Navarro FY RC | .30 | .75 |
| ❏ 339 Logan Kensing FY RC | .15 | .40 |
| ❏ 340 Jason Hirsh FY RC | .75 | 2.00 |
| ❏ 341 Matt Creighton FY RC | .15 | .40 |
| ❏ 342 Felix Hernandez FY SP RC | 8.00 | 20.00 |
| ❏ 343 Kyle Sleeth FY RC | .20 | .50 |
| ❏ 344 Dustin Nippert FY RC | .20 | .50 |
| ❏ 345 Anthony Lerew FY RC | .30 | .75 |
| ❏ 346 Chris Saenz FY RC | .15 | .40 |
| ❏ 347 Steve Palermo SUP | .40 | 1.00 |
| ❏ 348 Barry Bonds SP | 6.00 | 15.00 |
| ❏ MJ Roop Binder EXCH | | |

## 2005 Bowman Heritage

| | | |
|---|---|---|
| ❏ COMPLETE SET (350) | 175.00 | 300.00 |
| ❏ COMP.SET w/o SP's (300) | 25.00 | 50.00 |
| ❏ COMMON CARD (1-300) | .15 | .40 |
| ❏ COMMON RC (1-300) | .15 | .40 |
| ❏ COMMON SP (301-350) | 2.00 | 5.00 |
| ❏ COM.SP RC (301-350) | 2.00 | 5.00 |
| ❏ 301-350 SP ODDS 1:3 H, 1:3 R | | |

| | | |
|---|---|---|
| ❏ PLATES STATED ODDS 1:343 HOBBY | | |
| ❏ PLATES PRINT RUN 1 #'d SET PER COLOR | | |
| ❏ PLATES: BLACK, CYAN, MAGENTA & YELLOW | | |
| ❏ NO PLATES PRICING DUE TO SCARCITY | | |
| ❏ ROOP BINDER EXCH ODDS 1:240 H | | |
| ❏ ROOP BINDER EXCH.DEADLINE 12/31/07 | | |
| ❏ 1 Steven White FY RC | .15 | .40 |
| ❏ 2 Jorge Posada | .25 | .60 |
| ❏ 3 Brett Myers | .15 | .40 |
| ❏ 4 Pat Burrell | .15 | .40 |
| ❏ 5 Grady Sizemore | .25 | .60 |
| ❏ 6 Jeff Weaver | .15 | .40 |
| ❏ 7 Jeff Kent | .15 | .40 |
| ❏ 8 Mark Kotsay | .15 | .40 |
| ❏ 9 Nick Swisher | .25 | .60 |
| ❏ 10 Scott Rolen | .25 | .60 |
| ❏ 11 Matt Morris | .15 | .40 |
| ❏ 12 Luis Castillo | .15 | .40 |
| ❏ 13 Pedro Feliz | .15 | .40 |
| ❏ 14 Omar Vizquel | .25 | .60 |
| ❏ 15 Edgar Renteria | .15 | .40 |
| ❏ 16 David Wells | .15 | .40 |
| ❏ 17 Chad Cordero | .15 | .40 |
| ❏ 18 Brad Wilkerson | .15 | .40 |
| ❏ 19 Kelly Johnson | .15 | .40 |
| ❏ 20 Johnny Estrada | .15 | .40 |
| ❏ 21 Brian Roberts | .15 | .40 |
| ❏ 22 Jeromy Burnitz | .15 | .40 |
| ❏ 23 Magglio Ordonez | .15 | .40 |
| ❏ 24 Adam Dunn | .15 | .40 |
| ❏ 25 Randy Johnson | .40 | 1.00 |
| ❏ 26 Derek Jeter | .75 | 2.00 |
| ❏ 27 Jon Lieber | .15 | .40 |
| ❏ 28 Jim Thome | .25 | .60 |
| ❏ 29 Ronnie Belliard | .15 | .40 |
| ❏ 30 Jake Westbrook | .15 | .40 |
| ❏ 31 Bengie Molina | .15 | .40 |
| ❏ 32 J.D. Drew | .15 | .40 |
| ❏ 33 Rich Harden | .15 | .40 |
| ❏ 34 David Eckstein | .15 | .40 |
| ❏ 35 Scott Podsednik | .15 | .40 |
| ❏ 36 Mark Buehrle | .15 | .40 |
| ❏ 37 Barry Bonds | 1.00 | 2.50 |
| ❏ 38 Brian Schneider | .15 | .40 |
| ❏ 39 Tim Wakefield | .15 | .40 |
| ❏ 40 Craig Wilson | .15 | .40 |
| ❏ 41 Jose Vidro | .15 | .40 |
| ❏ 42 Jacque Jones | .15 | .40 |
| ❏ 43 Felix Hernandez | .40 | 1.00 |
| ❏ 44 Nomar Garciaparra | .40 | 1.00 |
| ❏ 45 Neifi Perez | .15 | .40 |
| ❏ 46 Brandon Inge | .15 | .40 |
| ❏ 47 Felipe Lopez | .15 | .40 |
| ❏ 48 Ken Griffey Jr. | .60 | 1.50 |
| ❏ 49 Robinson Cano | .25 | .60 |
| ❏ 50 Jason Giambi | .15 | .40 |
| ❏ 51 Mike Lieberthal | .15 | .40 |
| ❏ 52 Bobby Abreu | .15 | .40 |
| ❏ 53 C.C. Sabathia | .15 | .40 |
| ❏ 54 Aaron Boone | .15 | .40 |
| ❏ 55 Milton Bradley | .15 | .40 |
| ❏ 56 Derek Lowe | .15 | .40 |
| ❏ 57 Barry Zito | .15 | .40 |
| ❏ 58 Jim Edmonds | .15 | .40 |
| ❏ 59 Jon Garland | .15 | .40 |
| ❏ 60 Tadahito Iguchi RC | .60 | 1.50 |
| ❏ 61 Jason Schmidt | .15 | .40 |
| ❏ 62 David Ortiz | .40 | 1.00 |
| ❏ 63 Matt Lawton | .15 | .40 |
| ❏ 64 Zach Duke | .25 | .60 |
| ❏ 65 Gary Sheffield | .15 | .40 |
| ❏ 66 Chipper Jones | .40 | 1.00 |
| ❏ 67 Sammy Sosa | .40 | 1.00 |
| ❏ 68 Rafael Palmeiro | .25 | .60 |
| ❏ 69 Carlos Zambrano | .15 | .40 |
| ❏ 70 Aramis Ramirez | .15 | .40 |
| ❏ 71 Chris Shelton | .15 | .40 |
| ❏ 72 Willy Mo Pena | .15 | .40 |
| ❏ 73 Mike Mussina | .25 | .60 |
| ❏ 74 Chien-Ming Wang | .60 | 1.50 |
| ❏ 75 Randy Wolf | .15 | .40 |
| ❏ 76 Jimmy Rollins | .15 | .40 |
| ❏ 77 Chase Utley | .25 | .60 |
| ❏ 78 Kevin Millwood | .15 | .40 |
| ❏ 79 Victor Martinez | .15 | .40 |
| ❏ 80 Morgan Ensberg | .15 | .40 |
| ❏ 81 Bartolo Colon | .15 | .40 |
| ❏ 82 Bobby Crosby | .15 | .40 |

| | | |
|---|---|---|
| ❏ 83 Dan Johnson | .15 | .40 |
| ❏ 84 Dan Haren | .15 | .40 |
| ❏ 85 Yadier Molina | .15 | .40 |
| ❏ 86 Mark Mulder | .15 | .40 |
| ❏ 87 Russell Branyan | .15 | .40 |
| ❏ 88 Lyle Overbay | .15 | .40 |
| ❏ 89 Edgardo Alfonzo | .15 | .40 |
| ❏ 90 Mike Matheny | .15 | .40 |
| ❏ 91 J.T. Snow | .15 | .40 |
| ❏ 92 Curt Schilling | .25 | .60 |
| ❏ 93 Oliver Perez | .15 | .40 |
| ❏ 94 Mark Redman | .15 | .40 |
| ❏ 95 Esteban Loaiza | .15 | .40 |
| ❏ 96 Livan Hernandez | .15 | .40 |
| ❏ 97 Ryan Church | .15 | .40 |
| ❏ 98 Kyle Davies | .15 | .40 |
| ❏ 99 Mike Hampton | .15 | .40 |
| ❏ 100 Jeff Francoeur | .40 | 1.00 |
| ❏ 101 Javy Lopez | .15 | .40 |
| ❏ 102 Mark Prior | .25 | .60 |
| ❏ 103 Kerry Wood | .15 | .40 |
| ❏ 104 Carlos Guillen | .15 | .40 |
| ❏ 105 Dmitri Young | .15 | .40 |
| ❏ 106 David Wright | .60 | 1.50 |
| ❏ 107 Cliff Floyd | .15 | .40 |
| ❏ 108 Carlos Beltran | .15 | .40 |
| ❏ 109 Melky Cabrera RC | .75 | 2.00 |
| ❏ 110 Carl Pavano | .15 | .40 |
| ❏ 111 Jamie Moyer | .15 | .40 |
| ❏ 112 Joel Pineiro | .15 | .40 |
| ❏ 113 Adrian Beltre | .15 | .40 |
| ❏ 114 Jhonny Peralta | .15 | .40 |
| ❏ 115 Travis Hafner | .15 | .40 |
| ❏ 116 Cesar Izturis | .15 | .40 |
| ❏ 117 Brad Penny | .15 | .40 |
| ❏ 118 Garret Anderson | .15 | .40 |
| ❏ 119 Scott Kazmir | .15 | .40 |
| ❏ 120 Aubrey Huff | .15 | .40 |
| ❏ 121 Larry Walker | .25 | .60 |
| ❏ 122 Albert Pujols | .75 | 2.00 |
| ❏ 123 Paul Konerko | .15 | .40 |
| ❏ 124 Frank Thomas | .40 | 1.00 |
| ❏ 125 Phil Nevin | .15 | .40 |
| ❏ 126 Brian Giles | .15 | .40 |
| ❏ 127 Ramon Hernandez | .15 | .40 |
| ❏ 128 Johnny Damon | .25 | .60 |
| ❏ 129 Trot Nixon | .15 | .40 |
| ❏ 130 Rocco Baldelli | .15 | .40 |
| ❏ 131 Carl Crawford | .15 | .40 |
| ❏ 132 Alfonso Soriano | .15 | .40 |
| ❏ 133 Mark Teixeira | .25 | .60 |
| ❏ 134 Gustavo Chacin | .15 | .40 |
| ❏ 135 Vernon Wells | .15 | .40 |
| ❏ 136 Erik Bedard | .15 | .40 |
| ❏ 137 Daniel Cabrera | .15 | .40 |
| ❏ 138 Michael Barrett | .15 | .40 |
| ❏ 139 Greg Maddux | .60 | 1.50 |
| ❏ 140 Javier Vazquez | .15 | .40 |
| ❏ 141 Chad Tracy | .15 | .40 |
| ❏ 142 Michael Young | .15 | .40 |
| ❏ 143 Kenny Rogers | .15 | .40 |
| ❏ 144 Mike Piazza | .40 | 1.00 |
| ❏ 145 Jose Reyes | .15 | .40 |
| ❏ 146 Geoff Jenkins | .15 | .40 |
| ❏ 147 Carlos Lee | .15 | .40 |
| ❏ 148 Brady Clark | .15 | .40 |
| ❏ 149 Torii Hunter | .15 | .40 |
| ❏ 150 Johan Santana | .40 | 1.00 |
| ❏ 151 Steve Finley | .15 | .40 |
| ❏ 152 Darin Erstad | .15 | .40 |
| ❏ 153 Jake Peavy | .15 | .40 |
| ❏ 154 Xavier Nady | .15 | .40 |
| ❏ 155 Ryan Klesko | .15 | .40 |
| ❏ 156 Ichiro Suzuki | .75 | 2.00 |
| ❏ 157 Richie Sexson | .15 | .40 |
| ❏ 158 Raul Ibanez | .15 | .40 |
| ❏ 159 Freddy Garcia | .15 | .40 |
| ❏ 160 Brad Hawpe | .15 | .40 |
| ❏ 161 Jeff Francis | .15 | .40 |
| ❏ 162 Todd Helton | .25 | .60 |
| ❏ 163 Clint Barmes | .15 | .40 |
| ❏ 164 Rodrigo Lopez | .15 | .40 |
| ❏ 165 Melvin Mora | .15 | .40 |
| ❏ 166 Brandon Webb | .15 | .40 |
| ❏ 167 Shawn Green | .15 | .40 |
| ❏ 168 Moises Alou | .15 | .40 |
| ❏ 169 Matt Clement | .15 | .40 |
| ❏ 170 John Smoltz | .25 | .60 |

| | | |
|---|---|---|
| ❏ 171 Rafael Furcal | .15 | .40 |
| ❏ 172 Jeff Bagwell | .25 | .60 |
| ❏ 173 Roger Clemens | .60 | 1.50 |
| ❏ 174 Dontrelle Willis | .15 | .40 |
| ❏ 175 Paul Lo Duca | .15 | .40 |
| ❏ 176 Zack Greinke | .15 | .40 |
| ❏ 177 David DeJesus | .15 | .40 |
| ❏ 178 Mike Sweeney | .15 | .40 |
| ❏ 179 Ben Sheets | .15 | .40 |
| ❏ 180 Doug Davis | .15 | .40 |
| ❏ 181 Mike Cameron | .15 | .40 |
| ❏ 182 Lance Berkman | .15 | .40 |
| ❏ 183 Craig Biggio | .25 | .60 |
| ❏ 184 Shannon Stewart | .15 | .40 |
| ❏ 185 Joe Mauer | .40 | 1.00 |
| ❏ 186 Justin Morneau | .15 | .40 |
| ❏ 187 Mike Maroth | .15 | .40 |
| ❏ 188 Ivan Rodriguez | .25 | .60 |
| ❏ 189 Luis Gonzalez | .15 | .40 |
| ❏ 190 Troy Glaus | .15 | .40 |
| ❏ 191 Adam Eaton | .15 | .40 |
| ❏ 192 Khalil Greene | .15 | .40 |
| ❏ 193 Mike Lowell | .15 | .40 |
| ❏ 194 Miguel Cabrera | .25 | .60 |
| ❏ 195 Roy Halladay | .15 | .40 |
| ❏ 196 Ted Lilly | .15 | .40 |
| ❏ 197 Alex Rios | .15 | .40 |
| ❏ 198 Josh Beckett | .15 | .40 |
| ❏ 199 A.J. Burnett | .15 | .40 |
| ❏ 200 Juan Pierre | .15 | .40 |
| ❏ 201 Marcus Giles | .15 | .40 |
| ❏ 202 Craig Tatum FY RC | .15 | .40 |
| ❏ 203 Hayden Penn FY RC | .30 | .75 |
| ❏ 204 C.J. Smith FY RC | .15 | .40 |
| ❏ 205 Matt Albers FY RC | .40 | 1.00 |
| ❏ 206 Jared Gothreaux FY RC | .15 | .40 |
| ❏ 207 Mike Rodriguez FY RC | .15 | .40 |
| ❏ 208 Hernan Inbarren FY RC | .20 | .50 |
| ❏ 209 Manny Parra FY RC | .12 | .30 |
| ❏ 210 Kevin Collins FY RC | .15 | .40 |
| ❏ 211 Buck Coats FY RC | .15 | .40 |
| ❏ 212 Jeremy West FY RC | .30 | .75 |
| ❏ 213 Ian Bladergroen FY RC | .20 | .50 |
| ❏ 214 Chuck Tiffany FY RC | .40 | 1.00 |
| ❏ 215 Andy LaRoche FY RC | 1.25 | 3.00 |
| ❏ 216 Frank Diaz FY RC | .15 | .40 |
| ❏ 217 Jai Miller FY RC | .20 | .50 |
| ❏ 218 Tony Giarratano FY RC | .15 | .40 |
| ❏ 219 Danny Zell FY RC | .15 | .40 |
| ❏ 220 Justin Verlander FY RC | 1.50 | 4.00 |
| ❏ 221 Ryan Sweeney FY RC | .40 | 1.00 |
| ❏ 222 Brandon McCarthy FY RC | .50 | 1.25 |
| ❏ 223 Jerry Owens FY RC | .15 | .40 |
| ❏ 224 Glen Perkins FY RC | .30 | .75 |
| ❏ 225 Kevin West FY RC | .15 | .40 |
| ❏ 226 Billy Butler FY RC | 1.50 | 4.00 |
| ❏ 227 Shane Costa FY RC | .15 | .40 |
| ❏ 228 Erik Schindewolf FY RC | .15 | .40 |
| ❏ 229 Miguel Montero FY RC | .50 | 1.25 |
| ❏ 230 Stephen Drew FY RC | 2.00 | 5.00 |
| ❏ 231 Matt DeSalvo FY RC | .20 | .50 |
| ❏ 232 Ben Jones FY RC | .20 | .50 |
| ❏ 233 Bill McCarthy FY RC | .15 | .40 |
| ❏ 234 Chuck James FY RC | .60 | 1.50 |
| ❏ 235 Brandon Sing FY RC | .20 | .50 |
| ❏ 236 Andy Santana FY RC | .15 | .40 |
| ❏ 237 Brendan Ryan FY RC | .15 | .40 |
| ❏ 238 Wes Swackhamer FY RC | .15 | .40 |
| ❏ 239 Jeff Niemann FY RC | .30 | .75 |
| ❏ 240 Ian Kinsler FY RC | 1.50 | 4.00 |
| ❏ 241 Micah Furtado FY RC | .15 | .40 |
| ❏ 242 Ryan Mount FY RC | .30 | .75 |
| ❏ 243 P.J. Phillips FY RC | .30 | .75 |
| ❏ 244 Trevor Bell FY RC | .30 | .75 |
| ❏ 245 Jared Weaver FY RC | 2.00 | 5.00 |
| ❏ 246 Eddy Martinez FY RC | .40 | 1.00 |
| ❏ 247 Brian Bannister FY RC | .30 | .75 |
| ❏ 248 Philip Humber FY RC | .30 | .75 |
| ❏ 249 Michael Rogers FY RC | .15 | .40 |
| ❏ 250 Landon Powell FY RC | .20 | .50 |
| ❏ 251 Kennard Bibbs FY RC | .15 | .40 |
| ❏ 252 Nelson Cruz FY RC | .75 | 2.00 |
| ❏ 253 Paul Kelly FY RC | .20 | .50 |
| ❏ 254 Kevin Slowey FY RC | .50 | 1.25 |
| ❏ 255 Brandon Snyder FY RC | .60 | 1.50 |
| ❏ 256 Nolan Reimold FY RC | .40 | 1.00 |
| ❏ 257 Brian Stavisky FY RC | .15 | .40 |
| ❏ 258 Javier Herrera FY RC | .75 | 2.00 |

| | | |
|---|---|---|
| ❏ 259 Russ Martin FY RC | .50 | 1.25 |
| ❏ 260 Matthew Kemp FY RC | 2.00 | 5.00 |
| ❏ 261 Wade Townsend FY RC | .20 | .50 |
| ❏ 262 Nick Touchstone FY RC | .15 | .40 |
| ❏ 263 Ryan Feierabend FY RC | .15 | .40 |
| ❏ 264 Bobby Livingston FY RC | .15 | .40 |
| ❏ 265 Wladimir Balentien FY RC | .30 | .75 |
| ❏ 266 Kelichi Yabu FY RC | .15 | .40 |
| ❏ 267 Craig Italiano FY RC | .30 | .75 |
| ❏ 268 Ryan Goleski FY RC | .20 | .50 |
| ❏ 269 Ryan Garko FY RC | .50 | 1.25 |
| ❏ 270 Mike Boum FY RC | .15 | .40 |
| ❏ 271 Scott Mathieson FY RC | .30 | .75 |
| ❏ 272 Scott Mitchinson FY RC | .15 | .40 |
| ❏ 273 Tyler Greene FY RC | .30 | .75 |
| ❏ 274 Mark McCormick FY RC | .20 | .50 |
| ❏ 275 Daryl Jones FY RC | .15 | .40 |
| ❏ 276 Travis Chick FY RC | .15 | .40 |
| ❏ 277 Luis Hernandez FY RC | .15 | .40 |
| ❏ 278 Steve Doetsch FY RC | .15 | .40 |
| ❏ 279 Chris Vines FY RC | .15 | .40 |
| ❏ 280 Mike Costanzo FY RC | .50 | 1.25 |
| ❏ 281 Matt Maloney FY RC | .40 | 1.00 |
| ❏ 282 Matt Goyen FY RC | .15 | .40 |
| ❏ 283 Jacob Marceaux FY RC | .15 | .40 |
| ❏ 284 David Gassner FY RC | .15 | .40 |
| ❏ 285 Ricky Barrett FY RC | .15 | .40 |
| ❏ 286 Jon Egan FY RC | .20 | .50 |
| ❏ 287 Scott Blue FY RC | .15 | .40 |
| ❏ 288 Steven Bondurant FY RC | .15 | .40 |
| ❏ 289 Kevin Melillo FY RC | .30 | .75 |
| ❏ 290 Brad Corley FY RC | .20 | .50 |
| ❏ 291 Brent Lillibridge FY RC | .15 | .40 |
| ❏ 292 Mike Morse FY RC | .30 | .75 |
| ❏ 293 Justin Thomas FY RC | .15 | .40 |
| ❏ 294 Nick Webber FY RC | .15 | .40 |
| ❏ 295 Mitch Boggs FY RC | .15 | .40 |
| ❏ 296 Jeff Lyman FY RC | .20 | .50 |
| ❏ 297 Jordan Schafer FY RC | .60 | 1.50 |
| ❏ 298 Ismael Ramirez FY RC | .15 | .40 |
| ❏ 299 Chris B.Young FY RC | .75 | 2.00 |
| ❏ 300 Brian Miller FY RC | .15 | .40 |
| ❏ 301 Jason Bay SP | 2.00 | 5.00 |
| ❏ 302 Tim Hudson SP | 2.00 | 5.00 |
| ❏ 303 Miguel Tejada SP | 2.00 | 5.00 |
| ❏ 304 Jeremy Bonderman SP | 2.00 | 5.00 |
| ❏ 305 Alex Rodriguez SP | 3.00 | 8.00 |
| ❏ 306 Rickie Weeks SP | 2.00 | 5.00 |
| ❏ 307 Manny Ramirez SP | 3.00 | 8.00 |
| ❏ 308 Nick Johnson SP | 2.00 | 5.00 |
| ❏ 309 Andruw Jones SP | 3.00 | 8.00 |
| ❏ 310 Hideki Matsui SP | 2.50 | 6.00 |
| ❏ 311 Jeremy Reed SP | 2.00 | 5.00 |
| ❏ 312 Dallas McPherson SP | 2.00 | 5.00 |
| ❏ 313 Vladimir Guerrero SP | 3.00 | 8.00 |
| ❏ 314 Eric Chavez SP | 2.00 | 5.00 |
| ❏ 315 Chris Carpenter SP | 2.00 | 5.00 |
| ❏ 316 Aaron Hill SP | 2.00 | 5.00 |
| ❏ 317 Derrek Lee SP | 3.00 | 8.00 |
| ❏ 318 Mark Loretta SP | 2.00 | 5.00 |
| ❏ 319 Garrett Atkins SP | 2.00 | 5.00 |
| ❏ 320 Hank Blalock SP | 2.00 | 5.00 |
| ❏ 321 Chris Young SP | 2.00 | 5.00 |
| ❏ 322 Roy Oswalt SP | 2.00 | 5.00 |
| ❏ 323 Carlos Delgado SP | 2.00 | 5.00 |
| ❏ 324 Pedro Martinez SP | 3.00 | 8.00 |
| ❏ 325 Jeff Clement FY SP RC | 4.00 | 10.00 |
| ❏ 326 Jimmy Shull FY SP RC | 2.00 | 5.00 |
| ❏ 327 Daniel Carte FY SP RC | 2.00 | 5.00 |
| ❏ 328 Travis Buck FY SP RC | 2.50 | 6.00 |
| ❏ 329 Chris Volstad FY SP RC | 2.00 | 5.00 |
| ❏ 330 A.McCutchen FY SP RC | 4.00 | 10.00 |
| ❏ 331 Cliff Pennington FY SP RC | 2.00 | 5.00 |
| ❏ 332 John Mayberry Jr. FY SP RC | 2.00 | 5.00 |
| ❏ 333 C.J. Henry FY SP RC | 3.00 | 8.00 |
| ❏ 334 Ricky Romero FY SP RC | 2.00 | 5.00 |
| ❏ 335 Aaron Thompson FY SP RC | 2.00 | 5.00 |
| ❏ 336 Cesar Carrillo FY SP RC | 2.00 | 5.00 |
| ❏ 337 Jacoby Ellsbury FY SP RC | 8.00 | 20.00 |
| ❏ 338 Matt Garza FY SP RC | 3.00 | 8.00 |
| ❏ 339 Colby Rasmus FY SP RC | 5.00 | 12.00 |
| ❏ 340 Ryan Zimmerman FY SP RC | 5.00 | 12.00 |
| ❏ 341 Ryan Braun FY SP RC | 6.00 | 15.00 |
| ❏ 342 Brent Lillibridge FY SP RC | 2.00 | 5.00 |
| ❏ 343 Jay Bruce FY SP RC | 6.00 | 15.00 |
| ❏ 344 Matt Green FY SP RC | 2.00 | 5.00 |
| ❏ 345 Brent Cox FY SP RC | 2.00 | 5.00 |
| ❏ 346 Jed Lowrie FY SP RC | 2.00 | 5.00 |

| | | |
|---|---|---|
| ❏ 347 Beau Jones FY SP RC | 2.00 | 5.00 |
| ❏ 348 Eli Iorg FY SP RC | 2.00 | 5.00 |
| ❏ 349 Chaz Roe FY SP RC | 2.00 | 5.00 |
| ❏ 350 Mickey Mantle | 10.00 | 25.00 |
| ❏ NNO Roop Binder Redemption | 6.00 | 15.00 |

## 2006 Bowman Heritage

| | | |
|---|---|---|
| ❏ COMPLETE SET (300) | 75.00 | 150.00 |
| ❏ COMP.SET w/o SP's (250) | 15.00 | 40.00 |
| ❏ COMMON CARD (1-300) | .15 | .40 |
| ❏ SEMISTARS 1-300 | .25 | .60 |
| ❏ UNLISTED 1-300 | .40 | 1.00 |
| ❏ COMMON RC (1-300) | .15 | .40 |
| ❏ RC UNLISTED 1-300 | .40 | 1.00 |
| ❏ COMMON SP (202-300) | 2.00 | 5.00 |
| ❏ SP SEMIS 202-300 | 3.00 | 8.00 |
| ❏ SP UNL 202-300 | 3.00 | 8.00 |
| ❏ COM.SP RC (202-300) | 2.00 | 5.00 |
| ❏ SP RC SEMI 202-300 | 2.00 | 5.00 |
| ❏ SP RC UNL 202-300 | 2.00 | 5.00 |
| ❏ 202-300 SP ODDS 1:3 H, 1:3 R | | |
| ❏ SP CL: EVEN #s B/WN 202-300 | | |
| ❏ OVERALL PLATE ODDS 1:487 HOBBY | | |
| ❏ PLATE PRINT RUN 1 SET PER COLOR | | |
| ❏ BLACK-CYAN-MAGENTA-YELLOW ISSUED | | |
| ❏ NO PLATE PRICING DUE TO SCARCITY | | |
| ❏ 1 David Wright | .60 | 1.50 |
| ❏ 2 Andruw Jones | .25 | .60 |
| ❏ 3 Ryan Howard | .60 | 1.50 |
| ❏ 4 Jason Bay | .15 | .40 |
| ❏ 5 Paul Konerko | .15 | .40 |
| ❏ 6 Jake Peavy | .15 | .40 |
| ❏ 7 Todd Jones | .15 | .40 |
| ❏ 8 Troy Glaus | .15 | .40 |
| ❏ 9 Rocco Baldelli | .15 | .40 |
| ❏ 10 Rafael Furcal | .15 | .40 |
| ❏ 11 Freddy Sanchez | .15 | .40 |
| ❏ 12 Jermaine Dye | .15 | .40 |
| ❏ 13 A.J. Burnett | .15 | .40 |
| ❏ 14 Michael Cuddyer | .15 | .40 |
| ❏ 15 Barry Zito | .15 | .40 |
| ❏ 16 Chipper Jones | .40 | 1.00 |
| ❏ 17 Paul LoDuca | .15 | .40 |
| ❏ 18 Mark Mulder | .15 | .40 |
| ❏ 19 Raul Ibanez | .15 | .40 |
| ❏ 20 Carlos Delgado | .15 | .40 |
| ❏ 21 Marcus Giles | .15 | .40 |
| ❏ 22 Dan Haren | .15 | .40 |
| ❏ 23 Justin Morneau | .15 | .40 |
| ❏ 24 Livan Hernandez | .15 | .40 |
| ❏ 25 Ken Griffey Jr. | .60 | 1.50 |
| ❏ 26 Aaron Hill | .15 | .40 |
| ❏ 27 Tadahito Iguchi | .15 | .40 |
| ❏ 28 Nate Robertson | .15 | .40 |
| ❏ 29 Kevin Millwood | .15 | .40 |
| ❏ 30 Jim Thome | .25 | .60 |
| ❏ 31 Aubrey Huff | .15 | .40 |
| ❏ 32 Dontrelle Willis | .15 | .40 |
| ❏ 33 Khalil Greene | .15 | .40 |
| ❏ 34 Doug Davis | .15 | .40 |
| ❏ 35 Ivan Rodriguez | .25 | .60 |
| ❏ 36 Rickie Weeks | .15 | .40 |
| ❏ 37 Jhonny Peralta | .15 | .40 |
| ❏ 38 Yadier Molina | .15 | .40 |
| ❏ 39 Eric Chavez | .15 | .40 |
| ❏ 40 Alfonso Soriano | .15 | .40 |
| ❏ 41 Pat Burrell | .15 | .40 |
| ❏ 42 B.J. Ryan | .15 | .40 |
| ❏ 43 Carl Crawford | .15 | .40 |
| ❏ 44 Preston Wilson | .15 | .40 |
| ❏ 45 Jorge Posada | .25 | .60 |
| ❏ 46 Carlos Zambrano | .15 | .40 |
| ❏ 47 Mark Teahen | .15 | .40 |
| ❏ 48 Nick Johnson | .15 | .40 |

|  |  | | |
|---|---|---|---|
| 49 | Mark Kotsay | .15 | .40 |
| 50 | Derek Jeter | 1.00 | 2.50 |
| 51 | Moises Alou | .15 | .40 |
| 52 | Ryan Freel | .15 | .40 |
| 53 | Shannon Stewart | .15 | .40 |
| 54 | Casey Blake | .15 | .40 |
| 55 | Edgar Renteria | .15 | .40 |
| 56 | Frank Thomas | .40 | 1.00 |
| 57 | Ty Wigginton | .15 | .40 |
| 58 | Jeff Kent | .15 | .40 |
| 59 | Chien-Ming Wang | .60 | 1.50 |
| 60 | Josh Beckett | .15 | .40 |
| 61 | Chase Utley | .40 | 1.00 |
| 62 | Gary Matthews | .15 | .40 |
| 63 | Torii Hunter | .15 | .40 |
| 64 | Bobby Jenks | .15 | .40 |
| 65 | Wilson Betemit | .15 | .40 |
| 66 | Jeremy Bonderman | .15 | .40 |
| 67 | Scott Rolen | .25 | .60 |
| 68 | Brad Penny | .15 | .40 |
| 69 | Jacque Jones | .15 | .40 |
| 70 | Jose Reyes | .15 | .40 |
| 71 | Brian Roberts | .15 | .40 |
| 72 | John Smoltz | .25 | .60 |
| 73 | Johnny Estrada | .15 | .40 |
| 74 | Ronnie Belliard | .15 | .40 |
| 75 | Vladimir Guerrero | .40 | 1.00 |
| 76 | A.J. Pierzynski | .15 | .40 |
| 77 | Garrett Atkins | .15 | .40 |
| 78 | Adam LaRoche | .15 | .40 |
| 79 | Mark Loretta | .15 | .40 |
| 80 | Todd Helton | .25 | .60 |
| 81 | Jose Vidro | .15 | .40 |
| 82 | Carlos Guillen | .15 | .40 |
| 83 | Michael Barrett | .15 | .40 |
| 84 | Lyle Overbay | .15 | .40 |
| 85 | Travis Hafner | .15 | .40 |
| 86 | Shea Hillenbrand | .15 | .40 |
| 87 | Julio Lugo | .15 | .40 |
| 88 | Tim Hudson | .15 | .40 |
| 89 | Scott Podsednik | .15 | .40 |
| 90 | Roy Halladay | .15 | .40 |
| 91 | Bartolo Colon | .15 | .40 |
| 92 | Ryan Langerhans | .15 | .40 |
| 93 | Tom Glavine | .25 | .60 |
| 94 | Kenny Rogers | .15 | .40 |
| 95 | Robinson Cano | .25 | .60 |
| 96 | Mark Prior | .15 | .40 |
| 97 | Jason Schmidt | .15 | .40 |
| 98 | Bengie Molina | .15 | .40 |
| 99 | Jon Lieber | .15 | .40 |
| 100 | Alex Rodriguez | .60 | 1.50 |
| 101 | Scott Kazmir | .25 | .60 |
| 102 | Jeff Francoeur | .40 | 1.00 |
| 103 | Chris Carpenter | .15 | .40 |
| 104 | Juan Uribe | .15 | .40 |
| 105 | Mariano Rivera | .40 | 1.00 |
| 106 | Rich Harden | .15 | .40 |
| 107 | Jack Wilson | .15 | .40 |
| 108 | Austin Kearns | .15 | .40 |
| 109 | Marcus Thames | .15 | .40 |
| 110 | Miguel Tejada | .15 | .40 |
| 111 | Chone Figgins | .15 | .40 |
| 112 | Bronson Arroyo | .15 | .40 |
| 113 | Chad Cordero | .15 | .40 |
| 114 | Bill Hall | .15 | .40 |
| 115 | Curt Schilling | .25 | .60 |
| 116 | David Eckstein | .15 | .40 |
| 117 | Ramon Hernandez | .15 | .40 |
| 118 | Eric Byrnes | .15 | .40 |
| 119 | Clint Barmes | .15 | .40 |
| 120 | Bobby Abreu | .15 | .40 |
| 121 | Joe Crede | .15 | .40 |
| 122 | Derek Lowe | .15 | .40 |
| 123 | Jason Marquis | .15 | .40 |
| 124 | Erik Bedard | .15 | .40 |
| 125 | Derek Lee | .15 | .40 |
| 126 | Brian McCann | .15 | .40 |
| 127 | Magglio Ordonez | .15 | .40 |
| 128 | Ben Sheets | .15 | .40 |
| 129 | Brandon Inge | .15 | .40 |
| 130 | Miguel Cabrera | .25 | .60 |
| 131 | Jim Edmonds | .25 | .60 |
| 132 | John Lackey | .15 | .40 |
| 133 | Kevin Mench | .15 | .40 |
| 134 | Adrian Beltre | .15 | .40 |
| 135 | Curtis Granderson | .15 | .40 |
| 136 | Shawn Green | .15 | .40 |
| 137 | Jose Contreras | .15 | .40 |
| 138 | Joe Nathan | .15 | .40 |
| 139 | Bobby Crosby | .15 | .40 |
| 140 | Johnny Damon | .25 | .60 |
| 141 | Brad Hawpe | .15 | .40 |
| 142 | Brandon Phillips | .15 | .40 |
| 143 | Victor Martinez | .15 | .40 |
| 144 | Jimmy Rollins | .15 | .40 |
| 145 | Corey Patterson | .15 | .40 |
| 146 | Grady Sizemore | .25 | .60 |
| 147 | Placido Polanco | .15 | .40 |
| 148 | Mike Lowell | .15 | .40 |
| 149 | Francisco Rodriguez | .15 | .40 |
| 150 | Ichiro Suzuki | .60 | 1.50 |
| 151 | Kris Benson | .15 | .40 |
| 152 | Scott Hatteberg | .15 | .40 |
| 153 | Akinori Otsuka | .15 | .40 |
| 154 | Cesar Izturis | .15 | .40 |
| 155 | Roger Clemens | .75 | 2.00 |
| 156 | Kerry Wood | .15 | .40 |
| 157 | Tom Gordon | .15 | .40 |
| 158 | Sean Casey | .15 | .40 |
| 159 | Jose Lopez | .15 | .40 |
| 160 | Orlando Hernandez | .15 | .40 |
| 161 | Aramis Ramirez | .15 | .40 |
| 162 | J.D. Drew | .15 | .40 |
| 163 | David DeJesus | .15 | .40 |
| 164 | Craig Biggio | .25 | .60 |
| 165 | Brett Myers | .15 | .40 |
| 166 | C.C. Sabathia | .15 | .40 |
| 167 | Zach Duke | .15 | .40 |
| 168 | Luis Castillo | .15 | .40 |
| 169 | Hideki Matsui | .40 | 1.00 |
| 170 | Brian Giles | .15 | .40 |
| 171 | Coco Crisp | .15 | .40 |
| 172 | Richie Sexson | .15 | .40 |
| 173 | Nomar Garciaparra | .40 | 1.00 |
| 174 | Roy Oswalt | .15 | .40 |
| 175 | David Ortiz | .40 | 1.00 |
| 176 | Matt Morris | .15 | .40 |
| 177 | Felipe Lopez | .15 | .40 |
| 178 | Garret Anderson | .15 | .40 |
| 179 | Kevin Youkilis | .15 | .40 |
| 180 | Alex Rios | .15 | .40 |
| 181 | Jon Garland | .15 | .40 |
| 182 | Luis Gonzalez | .15 | .40 |
| 183 | Cliff Floyd | .15 | .40 |
| 184 | Juan Encarnacion | .15 | .40 |
| 185 | Nick Swisher | .15 | .40 |
| 186 | Mike Cameron | .15 | .40 |
| 187 | Jose Castillo | .15 | .40 |
| 188 | Ray Durham | .15 | .40 |
| 189 | Jorge Cantu | .15 | .40 |
| 190 | Andy Pettitte | .15 | .40 |
| 191 | Chad Tracy | .15 | .40 |
| 192 | Adrian Gonzalez | .15 | .40 |
| 193 | Jose Valentin | .15 | .40 |
| 194 | Mark Buehrle | .15 | .40 |
| 195 | Huston Street | .15 | .40 |
| 196 | Chris Capuano | .15 | .40 |
| 197 | Aaron Rowand | .15 | .40 |
| 198 | Billy Wagner | .15 | .40 |
| 199 | Orlando Cabrera | .15 | .40 |
| 200 | Albert Pujols | .75 | 2.00 |
| 201 | Dan Uggla (RC) | .40 | 1.00 |
| 202 | Alay Soler SP RC | 2.00 | 5.00 |
| 203 | Matt Kemp | .25 | .60 |
| 204 | Mike Napoli SP RC | 2.00 | 5.00 |
| 205 | Joel Zumaya (RC) | .40 | 1.00 |
| 206 | Mike Pelfrey SP RC | 3.00 | 8.00 |
| 207 | Ian Kinsler (RC) | .25 | .60 |
| 208 | Josh Willingham SP (RC) | 2.00 | 5.00 |
| 209 | Erick Aybar (RC) | .15 | .40 |
| 210 | Willie Eyre SP (RC) | 2.00 | 5.00 |
| 211 | Kendry Morales (RC) | .25 | .60 |
| 212 | Scott Thorman SP (RC) | 2.00 | 5.00 |
| 213 | Hanley Ramirez (RC) | .40 | 1.00 |
| 214 | Boof Bonser SP (RC) | 2.00 | 5.00 |
| 215 | Anthony Reyes (RC) | .25 | .60 |
| 216 | Justin Huber SP (RC) | 2.00 | 5.00 |
| 217 | Yusmeiro Petit (RC) | .15 | .40 |
| 218 | Jason Bartlett SP (RC) | 2.00 | 5.00 |
| 219 | Shin-Soo Choo (RC) | .25 | .60 |
| 220 | Francisco Liriano SP (RC) | 2.00 | 5.00 |
| 221 | Craig Hansen RC | .60 | 1.50 |
| 222 | Ricky Nolasco SP (RC) | 2.00 | 5.00 |
| 223 | Adam Loewen (RC) | .15 | .40 |
| 224 | Scott Olsen SP (RC) | 2.00 | 5.00 |
| 225 | Cole Hamels (RC) | .40 | 1.00 |
| 226 | Martin Prado SP (RC) | 2.00 | 5.00 |
| 227 | James Loney (RC) | .25 | .60 |
| 228 | Kevin Thompson SP (RC) | 2.00 | 5.00 |
| 229 | Adam Jones RC | .50 | 1.25 |
| 230 | Josh Johnson SP (RC) | 2.00 | 5.00 |
| 231 | Anderson Hernandez (RC) | .15 | .40 |
| 232 | Tony Gwynn Jr. SP (RC) | 2.00 | 5.00 |
| 233 | Casey Janssen RC | .25 | .60 |
| 234 | Taylor Tankersley SP (RC) | 2.00 | 5.00 |
| 235 | Mike Thompson SP (RC) | .15 | .40 |
| 236 | Jeremy Sowers SP (RC) | 2.00 | 5.00 |
| 237 | Anibal Sanchez (RC) | .25 | .60 |
| 238 | Adam Wainwright SP (RC) | 2.00 | 5.00 |
| 239 | Rich Hill (RC) | .15 | .40 |
| 240 | Russ Martin SP (RC) | 2.00 | 5.00 |
| 241 | Joe Inglett RC | .15 | .40 |
| 242 | Tony Pena SP (RC) | 2.00 | 5.00 |
| 243 | Josh Sharpless RC | .15 | .40 |
| 244 | Darrell Rasner SP (RC) | 2.00 | 5.00 |
| 245 | Joe Saunders (RC) | .15 | .40 |
| 246 | Jon Lester SP RC | 2.00 | 5.00 |
| 247 | Jeremy Hermida (RC) | .15 | .40 |
| 248 | Chad Billingsley SP (RC) | 2.00 | 5.00 |
| 249 | Bobby Livingston (RC) | .15 | .40 |
| 250 | Justin Verlander SP (RC) | 2.00 | 5.00 |
| 251 | Mickey Mantle SP | 3.00 | 8.00 |
| 252 | Hank Blalock SP | 2.00 | 5.00 |
| 253 | Manny Ramirez | .25 | .60 |
| 254 | Mike Mussina SP | 3.00 | 8.00 |
| 255 | Greg Maddux | .60 | 1.50 |
| 256 | Jason Giambi SP | 2.00 | 5.00 |
| 257 | Mark Teixeira | .25 | .60 |
| 258 | Carlos Beltran SP | 2.00 | 5.00 |
| 259 | Matt Holliday | .20 | .50 |
| 260 | Pedro Martinez SP | 3.00 | 8.00 |
| 261 | Joe Mauer | .25 | .60 |
| 262 | Melvin Mora SP | 2.00 | 5.00 |
| 263 | Mike Piazza | .40 | 1.00 |
| 264 | B.J. Upton SP | 2.00 | 5.00 |
| 265 | Vernon Wells | .15 | .40 |
| 266 | Gary Sheffield SP | 2.00 | 5.00 |
| 267 | Randy Johnson | .40 | 1.00 |
| 268 | Ryan Zimmerman SP | 2.00 | 5.00 |
| 269 | Lance Berkman | .15 | .40 |
| 270 | Johan Santana SP | 3.00 | 8.00 |
| 271 | Carlos Lee | .15 | .40 |
| 272 | Brandon Webb SP | 2.00 | 5.00 |
| 273 | Adam Dunn | .15 | .40 |
| 274 | Michael Young SP | 2.00 | 5.00 |
| 275 | Barry Bonds | .75 | 2.00 |
| 276 | Jonathan Papelbon SP (RC) | 2.00 | 5.00 |
| 277 | Howie Kendrick (RC) | .40 | 1.00 |
| 278 | Melky Cabrera SP (RC) | 2.00 | 5.00 |
| 279 | Jered Weaver (RC) | .50 | 1.25 |
| 280 | Josh Barfield SP (RC) | 2.00 | 5.00 |
| 281 | Chuck James (RC) | .25 | .60 |
| 282 | Lastings Milledge SP (RC) | 2.00 | 5.00 |
| 283 | Nick Markakis (RC) | .25 | .60 |
| 284 | Jose Capellan SP (RC) | 2.00 | 5.00 |
| 285 | Prince Fielder (RC) | .60 | 1.50 |
| 286 | Jason Botts SP (RC) | 2.00 | 5.00 |
| 287 | Eliezer Alfonzo RC | .15 | .40 |
| 288 | Sean Marshall SP (RC) | 2.00 | 5.00 |
| 289 | Ryan Garko (RC) | .15 | .40 |
| 290 | Stephen Drew SP (RC) | 2.00 | 5.00 |
| 291 | Joel Guzman (RC) | .15 | .40 |
| 292 | Hong-Chih Kuo SP (RC) | 2.00 | 5.00 |
| 293 | Zach Miner (RC) | .15 | .40 |
| 294 | Angel Guzman SP (RC) | 2.00 | 5.00 |
| 295 | Andre Ethier (RC) | .40 | 1.00 |
| 296 | Fausto Carmona SP (RC) | 2.00 | 5.00 |
| 297 | Ronny Paulino (RC) | .15 | .40 |
| 298 | Matt Cain SP (RC) | 2.00 | 5.00 |
| 299 | Carlos Quentin (RC) | .25 | .60 |
| 300 | Kenji Johjima SP RC | 2.00 | 5.00 |

## 2007 Bowman Heritage

| | | |
|---|---|---|
| ☐ COMP.SET w/o SPs (251) | 15.00 | 40.00 |
| ☐ COMMON CARD (1-200) | .15 | .40 |
| ☐ COMMON ROOKIE (201-251) | .20 | .50 |
| ☐ COMMON SP (181-200) | 1.25 | 3.00 |
| ☐ COMMON SP RC (226-250) | 1.50 | 4.00 |
| ☐ SP ODDS 1:3 HOBBY | | |
| ☐ NO SIG CARDS ARE SHORT PRINTS | | |
| ☐ COMP.SET INCLUDES ALL MANTLE VAR. | | |
| ☐ OVERALL PLATE ODDS 1:463 HOBBY | | |
| ☐ PLATE PRINT RUN 1 SET PER COLOR | | |
| ☐ BLACK-CYAN-MAGENTA-YELLOW ISSUED | | |
| ☐ NO PLATE PRICING DUE TO SCARCITY | | |
| ☐ 1 Jeff Francoeur | .40 | 1.00 |
| ☐ 2 Jered Weaver | .25 | .60 |
| ☐ 3 Derrek Lee | .15 | .40 |
| ☐ 4 Todd Helton | .25 | .60 |
| ☐ 5 Shawn Hill | .15 | .40 |
| ☐ 6 Ivan Rodriguez | .25 | .60 |
| ☐ 7 Mickey Mantle | 2.00 | 5.00 |
| ☐ 8 Ramon Hernandez | .15 | .40 |
| ☐ 9 Randy Johnson | .40 | 1.00 |
| ☐ 10 Jermaine Dye | .15 | .40 |
| ☐ 11 Brian Roberts | .15 | .40 |
| ☐ 12 Hank Blalock | .15 | .40 |
| ☐ 13 Chien-Ming Wang | .40 | 1.00 |
| ☐ 14 Mike Lowell | .15 | .40 |
| ☐ 15 Brandon Webb | .15 | .40 |
| ☐ 16 Kelly Johnson | .15 | .40 |
| ☐ 17 Nick Johnson | .15 | .40 |
| ☐ 18 Zach Duke | .15 | .40 |
| ☐ 19 Aaron Hill | .15 | .40 |
| ☐ 20 Miguel Tejada | .15 | .40 |
| ☐ 21 Mark Buehrle | .15 | .40 |
| ☐ 22 Michael Young | .15 | .40 |
| ☐ 23 Carlos Delgado | .15 | .40 |
| ☐ 24 Anibal Sanchez | .15 | .40 |
| ☐ 25 Vladimir Guerrero | .40 | 1.00 |
| ☐ 26 Russell Martin | .15 | .40 |
| ☐ 27 Lance Berkman | .15 | .40 |
| ☐ 28 Bobby Crosby | .15 | .40 |
| ☐ 29 Javier Vazquez | .15 | .40 |
| ☐ 30 Manny Ramirez | .25 | .60 |
| ☐ 31 Rich Hill | .15 | .40 |
| ☐ 32 Mike Sweeney | .15 | .40 |
| ☐ 33 Jeff Kent | .15 | .40 |
| ☐ 34 Noah Lowry | .15 | .40 |
| ☐ 35 Alfonso Soriano | .25 | .60 |
| ☐ 36 Paul Lo Duca | .15 | .40 |
| ☐ 37 J.D. Drew | .15 | .40 |
| ☐ 38 C.C. Sabathia | .15 | .40 |
| ☐ 39 Craig Biggio | .25 | .60 |
| ☐ 40 Adam Dunn | .15 | .40 |
| ☐ 41 Josh Beckett | .25 | .60 |
| ☐ 42 Carlos Guillen | .15 | .40 |
| ☐ 43 Jeff Francis | .15 | .40 |
| ☐ 44 Orlando Hudson | .15 | .40 |
| ☐ 45 Grady Sizemore | .25 | .60 |
| ☐ 46 Jason Jennings | .15 | .40 |
| ☐ 47 Mark Teixeira | .25 | .60 |
| ☐ 48 Freddy Garcia | .15 | .40 |
| ☐ 49 Adrian Gonzalez | .15 | .40 |
| ☐ 50 Albert Pujols | .75 | 2.00 |
| ☐ 51 Tom Glavine | .25 | .60 |
| ☐ 52 J.J. Hardy | .15 | .40 |
| ☐ 53 Bobby Abreu | .15 | .40 |
| ☐ 54 Bartolo Colon | .15 | .40 |
| ☐ 55 Garrett Atkins | .15 | .40 |
| ☐ 56 Moises Alou | .15 | .40 |
| ☐ 57 Cliff Lee | .15 | .40 |
| ☐ 58 Michael Cuddyer | .15 | .40 |
| ☐ 59 Brandon Phillips | .15 | .40 |
| ☐ 60 Jeremy Bonderman | .15 | .40 |
| ☐ 61 Rickie Weeks | .15 | .40 |
| ☐ 62 Chris Carpenter | .15 | .40 |
| ☐ 63 Frank Thomas | .40 | 1.00 |
| ☐ 64 Victor Martinez | .15 | .40 |
| ☐ 65 Dontrelle Willis | .15 | .40 |
| ☐ 66 Jim Thome | .25 | .60 |
| ☐ 67 Aaron Rowand | .15 | .40 |
| ☐ 68 Andy Pettitte | .25 | .60 |
| ☐ 69 Brian McCann | .15 | .40 |
| ☐ 70 Roger Clemens | .60 | 1.50 |
| ☐ 71 Gary Matthews | .15 | .40 |
| ☐ 72 Bronson Arroyo | .15 | .40 |
| ☐ 73 Jeremy Hermida | .15 | .40 |
| ☐ 74 Eric Chavez | .15 | .40 |
| ☐ 75 David Ortiz | .25 | .60 |
| ☐ 76 Stephen Drew | .25 | .60 |
| ☐ 77 Ronnie Belliard | .15 | .40 |
| ☐ 78 James Shields | .15 | .40 |
| ☐ 79 Richie Sexson | .15 | .40 |
| ☐ 80 Johan Santana | .25 | .60 |
| ☐ 81 Orlando Cabrera | .15 | .40 |
| ☐ 82 Aramis Ramirez | .15 | .40 |
| ☐ 83 Greg Maddux | .60 | 1.50 |
| ☐ 84 Reggie Sanders | .15 | .40 |
| ☐ 85 Carlos Zambrano | .15 | .40 |
| ☐ 86 Bengie Molina | .15 | .40 |
| ☐ 87 David DeJesus | .15 | .40 |
| ☐ 88 Adam Wainwright | .25 | .60 |
| ☐ 89 Conor Jackson | .15 | .40 |
| ☐ 90 David Wright | .60 | 1.50 |
| ☐ 91 Ryan Garko | .15 | .40 |
| ☐ 92 Bill Hall | .15 | .40 |
| ☐ 93 Marcus Giles | .15 | .40 |
| ☐ 94 Kenny Rogers | .15 | .40 |
| ☐ 95 Joe Mauer | .40 | 1.00 |
| ☐ 96 Hanley Ramirez | .25 | .60 |
| ☐ 97 Brian Giles | .15 | .40 |
| ☐ 98 Dan Haren | .15 | .40 |
| ☐ 99 Robinson Cano | .25 | .60 |
| ☐ 100 Ryan Howard | .60 | 1.50 |
| ☐ 101 Andruw Jones | .25 | .60 |
| ☐ 102 Aaron Harang | .15 | .40 |
| ☐ 103 Hideki Matsui | .40 | 1.00 |
| ☐ 104 Nick Swisher | .15 | .40 |
| ☐ 105 Pedro Martinez | .25 | .60 |
| ☐ 106 Felipe Lopez | .15 | .40 |
| ☐ 107 Erik Bedard | .15 | .40 |
| ☐ 108 Rafael Furcal | .15 | .40 |
| ☐ 109 Curt Schilling | .25 | .60 |
| ☐ 110 Jose Reyes | .40 | 1.00 |
| ☐ 111 Adam LaRoche | .15 | .40 |
| ☐ 112 Mike Mussina | .25 | .60 |
| ☐ 113 Melvin Mora | .15 | .40 |
| ☐ 114 Zack Greinke | .15 | .40 |
| ☐ 115 Justin Morneau | .15 | .40 |
| ☐ 116 Ervin Santana | .15 | .40 |
| ☐ 117 Ken Griffey Jr. | .60 | 1.50 |
| ☐ 118 David Eckstein | .15 | .40 |
| ☐ 119 Jamie Moyer | .15 | .40 |
| ☐ 120 Jorge Posada | .25 | .60 |
| ☐ 121 Justin Verlander | .40 | 1.00 |
| ☐ 122 Sammy Sosa | .25 | .60 |
| ☐ 123 Jason Schmidt | .15 | .40 |
| ☐ 124 Josh Willingham | .15 | .40 |
| ☐ 125 Roy Oswalt | .15 | .40 |
| ☐ 126 Travis Hafner | .15 | .40 |
| ☐ 127 John Maine | .15 | .40 |
| ☐ 128 Willy Taveras | .15 | .40 |
| ☐ 129 Magglio Ordonez | .15 | .40 |
| ☐ 130 Barry Zito | .15 | .40 |
| ☐ 131 Prince Fielder | .40 | 1.00 |
| ☐ 132 Michael Barrett | .15 | .40 |
| ☐ 133 Livan Hernandez | .15 | .40 |
| ☐ 134 Troy Glaus | .15 | .40 |
| ☐ 135 Rocco Baldelli | .15 | .40 |
| ☐ 136 Jason Giambi | .15 | .40 |
| ☐ 137 Austin Kearns | .15 | .40 |
| ☐ 138 Dan Uggla | .25 | .60 |
| ☐ 139 Pat Burrell | .15 | .40 |
| ☐ 140 Carlos Beltran | .25 | .60 |
| ☐ 141 Carlos Quentin | .15 | .40 |
| ☐ 142 Johnny Estrada | .15 | .40 |
| ☐ 143 Torii Hunter | .25 | .60 |
| ☐ 144 Carlos Lee | .15 | .40 |
| ☐ 145 Mike Piazza | .40 | 1.00 |
| ☐ 146 Mark Teahen | .15 | .40 |
| ☐ 147 Juan Pierre | .15 | .40 |
| ☐ 148 Paul Konerko | .15 | .40 |
| ☐ 149 Freddy Sanchez | .15 | .40 |
| ☐ 150 Derek Jeter | 1.00 | 2.50 |
| ☐ 151 Orlando Hernandez | .15 | .40 |
| ☐ 152 Raul Ibanez | .25 | .60 |
| ☐ 153 John Smoltz | .25 | .60 |
| ☐ 154 Scott Rolen | .25 | .60 |
| ☐ 155 Jimmy Rollins | .25 | .60 |
| ☐ 156 A.J. Burnett | .15 | .40 |
| ☐ 157 Jason Varitek | .40 | 1.00 |
| ☐ 158 Ben Sheets | .15 | .40 |
| ☐ 159 Matt Cain | .25 | .60 |
| ☐ 160 Carl Crawford | .15 | .40 |
| ☐ 161 Jeff Suppan | .15 | .40 |
| ☐ 162 Tadahito Iguchi | .15 | .40 |
| ☐ 163 Kevin Millwood | .15 | .40 |
| ☐ 164 Chris Duncan | .15 | .40 |
| ☐ 165 Rich Harden | .25 | .60 |
| ☐ 166 Joe Crede | .15 | .40 |
| ☐ 167 Chipper Jones | .40 | 1.00 |
| ☐ 168 Gary Sheffield | .25 | .60 |
| ☐ 169 Cole Hamels | .40 | 1.00 |
| ☐ 170 Jason Bay | .25 | .60 |
| ☐ 171 Jhonny Peralta | .15 | .40 |
| ☐ 172 Aubrey Huff | .15 | .40 |
| ☐ 173 Xavier Nady | .15 | .40 |
| ☐ 174 Kazuo Matsui | .15 | .40 |
| ☐ 175 Vernon Wells | .15 | .40 |
| ☐ 176 Johnny Damon | .25 | .60 |
| ☐ 177 Jim Edmonds | .25 | .60 |
| ☐ 178 Jose Vidro | .15 | .40 |
| ☐ 179 Garret Anderson | .15 | .40 |
| ☐ 180 Alex Rios | .15 | .40 |
| ☐ 181a Ichiro Suzuki | .60 | 1.50 |
| ☐ 181b Ichiro Suzuki SP | 3.00 | 8.00 |
| ☐ 182a Jake Peavy | .15 | .40 |
| ☐ 182b Jake Peavy SP | 1.25 | 4.00 |
| ☐ 183a Ian Kinsler | .15 | .40 |
| ☐ 183b Ian Kinsler SP | 1.25 | 4.00 |
| ☐ 184a Tom Gorzelanny | .15 | .40 |
| ☐ 184b Tom Gorzelanny SP | 1.25 | 4.00 |
| ☐ 185a Miguel Cabrera | .25 | .60 |
| ☐ 185b Miguel Cabrera SP | 2.00 | 5.00 |
| ☐ 186a Scott Kazmir | .15 | .40 |
| ☐ 186b Scott Kazmir SP | 2.00 | 5.00 |
| ☐ 187a Matt Holliday | .40 | 1.00 |
| ☐ 187b Matt Holliday SP | 2.00 | 5.00 |
| ☐ 188a Roy Halladay | .15 | .40 |
| ☐ 188b Roy Halladay SP | 1.25 | 4.00 |
| ☐ 189a Ryan Zimmerman | .40 | 1.00 |
| ☐ 189b Ryan Zimmerman SP | 2.00 | 5.00 |
| ☐ 190a Alex Rodriguez | .60 | 1.50 |
| ☐ 190b Alex Rodriguez SP | 3.00 | 8.00 |
| ☐ 191a Kenji Johjima | .15 | .40 |
| ☐ 191b Kenji Johjima SP | 1.25 | 4.00 |
| ☐ 192a Gil Meche | .15 | .40 |
| ☐ 192b Gil Meche SP | 1.25 | 4.00 |
| ☐ 193a Chase Utley | .25 | .60 |
| ☐ 193b Chase Utley SP | 2.00 | 5.00 |
| ☐ 194a Jeremy Sowers | .15 | .40 |
| ☐ 194b Jeremy Sowers SP | 1.25 | 3.00 |
| ☐ 195a John Lackey | .15 | .40 |
| ☐ 195b John Lackey SP | 1.25 | 3.00 |
| ☐ 196a Nick Markakis | .25 | .60 |
| ☐ 196b Nick Markakis SP | 2.00 | 5.00 |
| ☐ 197a Tim Hudson | .15 | .40 |
| ☐ 197b Tim Hudson SP | 1.25 | 3.00 |
| ☐ 198a B.J. Upton | .15 | .40 |
| ☐ 198b B.J. Upton SP | 1.25 | 3.00 |
| ☐ 199a Felix Hernandez | .25 | .60 |
| ☐ 199b Felix Hernandez SP | 2.00 | 5.00 |
| ☐ 200a Barry Bonds | .75 | 2.00 |
| ☐ 200b Barry Bonds SP | 4.00 | 10.00 |
| ☐ 201 Jarrod Saltalamacchia (RC) | .30 | .75 |
| ☐ 202 Tim Lincecum RC | 2.50 | 6.00 |
| ☐ 203 Kory Casto (RC) | .20 | .50 |
| ☐ 204 Sean Henn (RC) | .20 | .50 |
| ☐ 205 Hector Gimenez (RC) | .20 | .50 |
| ☐ 206 Homer Bailey (RC) | .30 | .75 |
| ☐ 207 Yunel Escobar (RC) | .20 | .50 |
| ☐ 208 Matt Lindstrom (RC) | .20 | .50 |
| ☐ 209 Tyler Clippard (RC) | .30 | .75 |
| ☐ 210 Joe Smith RC | .20 | .50 |
| ☐ 211 Tony Abreu RC | .50 | 1.25 |
| ☐ 212 Billy Butler (RC) | .30 | .75 |
| ☐ 213 Gustavo Molina RC | .20 | .50 |
| ☐ 214 Brian Stokes (RC) | .20 | .50 |
| ☐ 215 Kevin Slowey (RC) | .50 | 1.25 |
| ☐ 216 Curtis Thigpen (RC) | .20 | .50 |

| | | |
|---|---|---|
| 217 Carlos Gomez RC | .30 | .75 |
| 218 Rick Vanden Hurk RC | .30 | .75 |
| 219 Michael Boum (RC) | .20 | .50 |
| 220 Jeff Baker (RC) | .20 | .50 |
| 221 Andy LaRoche (RC) | .20 | .50 |
| 222 Andy Sonnanstine (RC) | .20 | .50 |
| 223 Chase Wright RC | .50 | 1.25 |
| 224 Mark Reynolds RC | 1.25 | 3.00 |
| 225 Matt Chico (RC) | .20 | .50 |
| 226a Hunter Pence (RC) | 1.00 | 2.50 |
| 226b Hunter Pence SP | 3.00 | 8.00 |
| 227a John Danks RC | .20 | .50 |
| 227b John Danks SP | 1.50 | 4.00 |
| 228a Elijah Dukes RC | .30 | .75 |
| 228b Elijah Dukes SP | 2.50 | 6.00 |
| 229a Kei Igawa RC | .50 | 1.25 |
| 229b Kei Igawa SP | 2.50 | 6.00 |
| 230a Felix Pie (RC) | .20 | .50 |
| 230b Felix Pie SP | 1.50 | 4.00 |
| 231a Jesus Flores RC | .20 | .50 |
| 231b Jesus Flores SP | 1.50 | 4.00 |
| 232a Dallas Braden RC | .30 | .75 |
| 232b Dallas Braden SP | 2.50 | 6.00 |
| 233a Akinori Iwamura RC | .50 | 1.25 |
| 233b Akinori Iwamura SP | 2.50 | 6.00 |
| 234a Ryan Braun (RC) | 1.25 | 3.00 |
| 234b Ryan Braun SP | 3.00 | 8.00 |
| 235a Alex Gordon RC | .75 | 2.00 |
| 235b Alex Gordon SP | 3.00 | 8.00 |
| 236a Micah Owings (RC) | .20 | .50 |
| 236b Micah Owings SP | 1.50 | 4.00 |
| 237a Kevin Kouzmanoff (RC) | .20 | .50 |
| 237b Kevin Kouzmanoff SP | 1.50 | 4.00 |
| 238a Glen Perkins (RC) | .20 | .50 |
| 238b Glen Perkins SP | 1.50 | 4.00 |
| 239a Danny Putnam (RC) | .20 | .50 |
| 239b Danny Putnam SP | 1.50 | 4.00 |
| 240a Philip Hughes (RC) | 1.00 | 2.50 |
| 240b Philip Hughes SP | 3.00 | 8.00 |
| 241a Ryan Sweeney (RC) | .20 | .50 |
| 241b Ryan Sweeney SP | 1.50 | 4.00 |
| 242a Josh Hamilton (RC) | .50 | 1.25 |
| 242b Josh Hamilton SP | 5.00 | 12.00 |
| 243a Hideki Okajima RC | 1.00 | 2.50 |
| 243b Hideki Okajima SP | 3.00 | 8.00 |
| 244a Adam Lind (RC) | .20 | .50 |
| 244b Adam Lind SP | 1.50 | 4.00 |
| 245a Travis Buck (RC) | .20 | .50 |
| 245b Travis Buck SP | 1.50 | 4.00 |
| 246a Miguel Montero (RC) | .20 | .50 |
| 246b Miguel Montero SP | 1.50 | 4.00 |
| 247a Brandon Morrow RC | .40 | 1.00 |
| 247b Brandon Morrow SP | 2.50 | 6.00 |
| 248a Troy Tulowitzki (RC) | .50 | 1.25 |
| 248b Troy Tulowitzki SP | 2.50 | 6.00 |
| 249a Delmon Young (RC) | .30 | .75 |
| 249b Delmon Young SP | 2.50 | 6.00 |
| 250a Daisuke Matsuzaka RC | 1.50 | 4.00 |
| 250b Daisuke Matsuzaka SP | 4.00 | 10.00 |
| 251 Joba Chamberlain RC | 3.00 | 8.00 |

## 2004 Bowman Sterling

FY ODDS APPX.TWO PER HOBBY PACK
FY AU ODDS APPX.ONE PER HOBBY PACK
AU-GU ODDS APPX.ONE PER HOBBY PACK
AU-GU 1:2 WRAPPER ODDS IS AN ERROR
GU ODDS APPX. 1.5 PER HOBBY PACK
GU 1:2 WRAPPER ODDS IS AN ERROR

| | | |
|---|---|---|
| AB Angel Berroa Bat | 2.00 | 5.00 |
| ABA Aarom Baldiris FY RC | 2.00 | 5.00 |
| AC Alberto Callaspo FY AU RC | 8.00 | 20.00 |
| AD Adam Dunn Bat | 2.00 | 5.00 |
| AER Alex Rodriguez Bat | 6.00 | 15.00 |
| AJ Andruw Jones Jsy | 3.00 | 8.00 |
| AK Austin Kearns Jsy | 2.00 | 5.00 |
| ANR Aramis Ramirez Bat | 2.00 | 5.00 |
| AP Albert Pujols Jsy | 8.00 | 20.00 |
| AR Alex Romero Bat | 3.00 | 8.00 |
| AW Adam Wainwright AU Jsy | 10.00 | 25.00 |
| AWH A.Whittington FY AU | 3.00 | 8.00 |
| AZ Alex Zumwalt FY AU RC | 4.00 | 10.00 |
| BB Brian Bixler AU Jsy RC | 4.00 | 10.00 |
| BBR Bill Bray FY RC | 1.50 | 4.00 |
| BBU Billy Buckner FY RC | 2.00 | 5.00 |
| BC2 Bobby Crosby Jsy | 2.00 | 5.00 |
| BD Blake DeWitt AU Jsy RC | 6.00 | 15.00 |
| BE Brad Eldred FY RC | 2.00 | 5.00 |
| BH B.Hawksworth FY AU RC | 4.00 | 10.00 |
| BT Brad Thompson FY RC | 2.00 | 5.00 |
| BU B.J. Upton AU Bat | 8.00 | 20.00 |
| BW Bernie Williams Jsy | 3.00 | 8.00 |
| CA Chris Aguila FY AU RC | 3.00 | 8.00 |
| CB Craig Biggio Jsy | 3.00 | 8.00 |
| CC Chad Cordero AU Jsy | 6.00 | 15.00 |
| CG Christian Garcia AU Jsy RC | 6.00 | 15.00 |
| CH Chin-Lung Hu FY RC | 6.00 | 15.00 |
| CIB Carlos Beltran Bat | 2.00 | 5.00 |
| CJ Conor Jackson FY AU | 8.00 | 20.00 |
| CL Chris Lubanski AU Bat | 4.00 | 10.00 |
| CLA Chris Lambert FY RC | 2.00 | 5.00 |
| CN Chris Nelson FY RC | 2.00 | 5.00 |
| CQ Carlos Quentin FY AU RC | 8.00 | 20.00 |
| CT Curtis Thigpen FY RC | 2.00 | 5.00 |
| DD David DeJesus AU Jsy | 6.00 | 15.00 |
| DP Danny Putnam AU Jsy RC | 4.00 | 10.00 |
| DPU David Purcey FY RC | 2.00 | 5.00 |
| DW David Wright AU Jsy | 30.00 | 50.00 |
| DWW Dontrelle Willis Jsy | 3.00 | 8.00 |
| DY Delmon Young AU Bat | 12.50 | 30.00 |
| EG Eric Gagne Jsy | 2.00 | 5.00 |
| EH Eric Hurley FY RC | 2.00 | 5.00 |
| ESP Erick San Pedro FY RC | 1.50 | 4.00 |
| FC Fausto Carmona FY RC | 2.00 | 5.00 |
| FG Freddy Guzman FY RC | 1.50 | 4.00 |
| FH Felix Hernandez FY RC | 8.00 | 20.00 |
| FP Felix Pie AU Jsy | 10.00 | 25.00 |
| FT Frank Thomas Bat | 3.00 | 8.00 |
| GG Greg Golson FY RC | 2.00 | 5.00 |
| GH Gaby Hernandez FY RC | 2.00 | 5.00 |
| GIG Gio Gonzalez FY RC | 4.00 | 10.00 |
| GS Gary Sheffield Bat | 2.00 | 5.00 |
| HB Homer Bailey AU Jsy RC | 15.00 | 40.00 |
| HC Hee Seop Choi Bat | 2.00 | 5.00 |
| HG Hector Gimenez FY RC | 2.00 | 5.00 |
| HJB Hank Blalock Bat | 2.00 | 5.00 |
| HM Hector Made FY RC | 2.00 | 5.00 |
| HS Huston Street AU Jsy RC | 10.00 | 25.00 |
| IR Ivan Rodriguez Bat | 3.00 | 8.00 |
| JB Jeff Bagwell Jsy | 3.00 | 8.00 |
| JC Jose Capellan FY RC | 2.00 | 5.00 |
| JCR Jesse Crain FY RC | 2.00 | 5.00 |
| JD Johnny Damon Bat | 3.00 | 8.00 |
| JE Johnny Estrada Bat | 2.00 | 5.00 |
| JFI Josh Fields FY RC | 5.00 | 12.00 |
| JG Joey Gathright FY RC | 2.00 | 5.00 |
| JH Jesse Hoover FY RC | 2.00 | 5.00 |
| JK Jason Kendall Bat | 2.00 | 5.00 |
| JM Jeff Marquez AU Jsy RC | 6.00 | 15.00 |
| JO Justin Orenduff FY RC | 2.00 | 5.00 |
| JP Juan Pierre Bat | 2.00 | 5.00 |
| JPH J.P. Howell FY RC | 2.00 | 5.00 |
| JR Jay Rainville FY AU RC | 4.00 | 10.00 |
| JS Jeremy Sowers FY RC | 15.00 | 30.00 |
| JZ Jon Zeringue FY RC | 2.00 | 5.00 |
| KCH K.C. Herren FY RC | 2.00 | 5.00 |
| KS Kurt Suzuki FY RC | 2.50 | 6.00 |
| KT Kazuhito Tadano FY RC | 2.00 | 5.00 |
| KW Kerry Wood Jsy | 2.00 | 5.00 |
| KWA Kyle Waldrop AU Jsy RC | 6.00 | 15.00 |
| LB Lance Berkman Jsy | 2.00 | 5.00 |
| LC Luis Castillo Jsy | 2.00 | 5.00 |
| LH Linc Holdzkom FY AU RC | 3.00 | 8.00 |
| LN Laynce Nix Bat | 2.00 | 5.00 |
| MA Moises Alou Bat | 2.00 | 5.00 |
| MAM Mark Mulder Jsy | 2.00 | 5.00 |
| MAR Manny Ramirez Bat | 3.00 | 8.00 |
| MB Matt Bush AU Jsy RC | 10.00 | 25.00 |
| MC Miguel Cabrera Bat | 3.00 | 8.00 |
| MCT Mark Teixeira Bat | 3.00 | 8.00 |
| ME Mitch Einertson FY RC | 2.00 | 5.00 |
| MF Mike Ferris FY RC | 2.00 | 5.00 |
| MFO Matt Fox FY RC | 1.50 | 4.00 |
| MJP Mike Piazza Bat | 3.00 | 8.00 |
| MM Matt Moses FY AU RC | 6.00 | 15.00 |
| MMC Matt Macri FY RC | 2.50 | 6.00 |
| MP Mark Prior Jsy | 3.00 | 8.00 |
| MR Mike Rouse FY AU RC | 3.00 | 8.00 |
| MRO Mark Rogers FY RC | 3.00 | 8.00 |
| MT M.Tuiasosopo AU Bat RC | 12.50 | 30.00 |
| MT1 Miguel Tejada Bat | 2.00 | 5.00 |
| MT2 Miguel Tejada Jsy | 2.00 | 5.00 |
| MW Marland Williams FY RC | 2.00 | 5.00 |
| MY Michael Young Bat | 2.00 | 5.00 |
| NJ Nick Johnson Bat | 2.00 | 5.00 |
| NM Nyjer Morgan FY RC | 1.50 | 4.00 |
| NS Nate Schierholtz FY RC | 3.00 | 8.00 |
| NW Neil Walker FY RC | 3.00 | 8.00 |
| OQ Omar Quintanilla FY RC | 2.00 | 5.00 |
| PGM Paul Maholm FY RC | 3.00 | 8.00 |
| PH Philip Hughes FY RC | 10.00 | 25.00 |
| PL Paul LoDuca Bat | 2.00 | 5.00 |
| PR Pokey Reese Bat | 2.00 | 5.00 |
| RB Rocco Baldelli Bat | 2.00 | 5.00 |
| RBR Reid Brignac FY RC | 4.00 | 10.00 |
| RC Robinson Cano AU Jsy | 20.00 | 50.00 |
| RH Ryan Harvey AU Bat | 6.00 | 15.00 |
| RJH Richard Hidalgo Bat | 2.00 | 5.00 |
| RM Ryan Meaux FY AU RC | 3.00 | 8.00 |
| RO Russ Ortiz Jsy | 2.00 | 5.00 |
| RP Rafael Palmeiro Bat | 3.00 | 8.00 |
| SK Scott Kazmir AU Jsy RC | 6.00 | 15.00 |
| SO Scott Olsen AU Jsy RC | 15.00 | 30.00 |
| SS Sammy Sosa Jsy | 3.00 | 8.00 |
| SSM Seth Smith FY RC | 3.00 | 8.00 |
| TD Thomas Diamond FY RC | 3.00 | 8.00 |
| TG Troy Glaus Bat | 2.00 | 5.00 |
| TLH Todd Helton Bat | 3.00 | 8.00 |
| TM Tino Martinez Bat | 3.00 | 8.00 |
| TMG Tom Glavine Jsy | 2.00 | 5.00 |
| TP Trevor Plouffe AU Jsy RC | 6.00 | 15.00 |
| TT T.Tankersley AU Jsy RC | 4.00 | 10.00 |
| VG Vladimir Guerrero Bat | 3.00 | 8.00 |
| VP Vince Perkins FY AU RC | 4.00 | 10.00 |
| YP Yusmeiro Petit FY RC | 4.00 | 10.00 |
| ZD Zack Duke FY RC | 4.00 | 10.00 |
| ZJ Zach Jackson FY RC | 2.00 | 5.00 |

## 2005 Bowman Sterling

| | | |
|---|---|---|
| COMMON CARD | 1.50 | 4.00 |

BASIC CARDS APPX.TWO PER HOBBY PACK
BASIC CARDS APPX.TWO PER RETAIL PACK
AU GROUP A ODDS 1:2 HOBBY
AU GROUP B ODDS 1:3 HOBBY
AU-GU GROUP A ODDS 1:2 H, 1:2 R
AU-GU GROUP B ODDS 1:37 H, 1:37 R
AU-GU GROUP C ODDS 1:11 H, 1:11 R
AU-GU GROUP D ODDS 1:10 H, 1:10 R
AU-GU GROUP E ODDS 1:27 H, 1:27 R
AU-GU GROUP F ODDS 1:13 H, 1:13 R
GU GROUP A ODDS 1:3 H, 1:3 R
GU GROUP B ODDS 1:5 H, 1:5 R
GU GROUP C ODDS 1:6 H, 1:6 R

| | | |
|---|---|---|
| ACL Andy LaRoche B | 3.00 | 8.00 |
| AL Adam Lind AU Bat B | 10.00 | 25.00 |
| AM A.McCutchen AU Jsy D RC | 20.00 | 50.00 |
| AP Albert Pujols Jsy B | 6.00 | 15.00 |
| AR Alex Rodriguez Jsy B UER | 6.00 | 15.00 |
| ARA Aramis Ramirez Bat A | 2.00 | 5.00 |
| AS Alfonso Soriano Bat A | 2.00 | 5.00 |
| AT Aaron Thompson AU A RC | 4.00 | 10.00 |
| BA Brian Anderson RC | 2.50 | 6.00 |
| BB Billy Buckner AU Jsy A | 4.00 | 10.00 |
| BBU Billy Butler RC | 5.00 | 12.00 |
| BC Brent Cox AU Jsy D RC | 6.00 | 15.00 |
| BCR Brad Corley RC | 2.00 | 5.00 |
| BE Brad Eldred AU Jsy C | 4.00 | 10.00 |

| | | |
|---|---|---|
| BH Brett Hayes RC | 1.50 | 4.00 |
| BJ Beau Jones AU Jsy A RC | 8.00 | 20.00 |
| BL B.Livingston AU Jsy A RC | 4.00 | 10.00 |
| BLB Barry Bonds Jsy C | 6.00 | 15.00 |
| BM B.McCarthy AU Jsy A RC | 10.00 | 25.00 |
| BMU Bill Mueller Jsy C | 2.00 | 5.00 |
| BRB Brian Bogusevic RC | 1.50 | 4.00 |
| BS Brandon Sing AU A RC | 4.00 | 10.00 |
| BSN Brandon Snyder RC | 3.00 | 8.00 |
| BZ Barry Zito Uni A | 2.00 | 5.00 |
| CB Carlos Beltran Bat A | 2.00 | 5.00 |
| CBU Clay Buchholz RC | 12.50 | 30.00 |
| CC Cesar Carrillo RC | 2.50 | 6.00 |
| CD Carlos Delgado Jsy A | 2.00 | 5.00 |
| CH C.J. Henry AU B RC | 5.00 | 12.00 |
| CHE Chase Headley RC | 3.00 | 8.00 |
| CI Craig Italiano RC | 2.00 | 5.00 |
| CJ Chuck James RC | 4.00 | 10.00 |
| CLT Chuck Tiffany RC | 2.00 | 5.00 |
| CN Chris Nelson AU Jsy A | 4.00 | 10.00 |
| CP Cliff Pennington AU B RC | 4.00 | 10.00 |
| CPP C.Pignatiello AU Jsy A RC | 4.00 | 10.00 |
| CR Colby Rasmus AU Jsy A RC | 20.00 | 50.00 |
| CRA Cesar Ramos RC | 2.00 | 5.00 |
| CRO Chaz Roe AU Jsy A RC | 6.00 | 15.00 |
| CS C.J. Smith AU Jsy A RC | 4.00 | 10.00 |
| CSU Curt Schilling Jsy C | 3.00 | 8.00 |
| CT Curtis Thigpen AU Jsy A | 4.00 | 10.00 |
| CV Chris Volstad AU B RC | 6.00 | 15.00 |
| DC Dan Carte RC | 2.00 | 5.00 |
| DL Derrek Lee Bat A | 3.00 | 8.00 |
| DO David Ortiz Bat A | 3.00 | 8.00 |
| DP Dustin Pedroia AU Jsy A | 60.00 | 120.00 |
| DT Drew Thompson RC | 2.00 | 5.00 |
| DW Dontrelle Willis Jsy C | 2.00 | 5.00 |
| EC Eric Chavez Uni B | 2.00 | 5.00 |
| EI Eli Iorg AU Jsy C | 6.00 | 15.00 |
| EM Eddy Martinez AU AR RC | 4.00 | 10.00 |
| GK George Kottaras AU A RC | 4.00 | 10.00 |
| GM Greg Maddux Jsy C | 4.00 | 10.00 |
| GO Garrett Olson AU A RC | 6.00 | 15.00 |
| GS Gary Sheffield Bat A | 2.00 | 5.00 |
| HAS Henry Sanchez RC | 2.50 | 6.00 |
| HB Hank Blalock Bat A | 2.00 | 5.00 |
| HI Heman Iribarren RC | 2.00 | 5.00 |
| HM Hideki Matsui AS Jsy C | 4.00 | 10.00 |
| HS Hum Sanchez AU A RC | 8.00 | 20.00 |
| IR Ivan Rodriguez Bat A | 3.00 | 8.00 |
| JB Jay Bruce AU Jsy D RC | 30.00 | 60.00 |
| JBE Josh Beckett Uni A | 2.00 | 5.00 |
| JC Jeff Clement RC | 6.00 | 15.00 |
| JCN John Nelson AU Uni A RC | 4.00 | 10.00 |
| JD Johnny Damon Bat A | 3.00 | 8.00 |
| JDR John Drennen RC | 3.00 | 8.00 |
| JE J.Ellsbury AU Jsy E RC | 50.00 | 100.00 |
| JEG Jon Egan RC | 2.00 | 5.00 |
| JF Josh Fields AU Jsy A | 5.00 | 12.00 |
| JG Josh Geer AU Jsy A RC | 4.00 | 10.00 |
| JGI Josh Gibson Seat C | 6.00 | 15.00 |
| JL Jed Lowrie AU Jsy F RC | 15.00 | 40.00 |
| JLY Jeff Lyman RC | 2.00 | 5.00 |
| JM John Mayberry Jr. AU A RC | 4.00 | 10.00 |
| JMA Jacob Marceaux RC | 1.50 | 4.00 |
| JN Jeff Niemann AU Jsy A RC | 6.00 | 15.00 |
| JO Justin Olson AU Jsy A RC | 4.00 | 10.00 |
| JP Jorge Posada Bat A | 3.00 | 8.00 |
| JPE Jim Edmonds Jsy B | 2.00 | 5.00 |
| JS John Smoltz Jsy A | 3.00 | 8.00 |
| JV J.Verlander AU Jsy A RC | 20.00 | 50.00 |
| JW Josh Wall RC | 2.00 | 5.00 |
| JWE Jered Weaver RC | 6.00 | 15.00 |
| KG Khalil Greene Jsy B | 3.00 | 8.00 |
| KM Kevin Millar Bat A | 2.00 | 5.00 |
| KS Kevin Slowey RC | 6.00 | 15.00 |
| KW Kevin Whelan RC | 2.00 | 5.00 |
| LWJ Chipper Jones Bat A | 3.00 | 8.00 |
| MA Matt Albers AU A RC | 4.00 | 10.00 |
| MAM Matt Maloney RC | 2.50 | 6.00 |
| MB M.Bowden AU Jsy A RC | 20.00 | 50.00 |
| MC Mike Conroy AU Jsy A RC | 4.00 | 10.00 |
| MCA Miguel Cabrera Jsy A | 3.00 | 8.00 |
| MCO Mike Costanzo RC | 3.00 | 8.00 |
| MG Matt Green AU A RC | 3.00 | 8.00 |
| MGA Matt Garza RC | 4.00 | 10.00 |
| MGI Marcus Giles AS Jsy B | 2.00 | 5.00 |
| MM Mark Mulder Uni B | 2.00 | 5.00 |
| MMC Mark McCormick RC | 2.00 | 5.00 |
| MP Mike Piazza Bat A | 3.00 | 8.00 |

| | | |
|---|---|---|
| MPR Mark Prior Jsy B | 3.00 | 8.00 |
| MR Manny Ramirez Bat A | 3.00 | 8.00 |
| MT Miguel Tejada Uni A | 2.00 | 5.00 |
| MTE Mark Teixeira Bat A | 3.00 | 8.00 |
| MTO Matt Torra RC | 2.00 | 5.00 |
| MY Michael Young Bat A | 2.00 | 5.00 |
| NH Nick Hundley RC | 1.50 | 4.00 |
| NR Nolan Reimold RC | 1.50 | 4.00 |
| NW Nick Webber RC | 1.50 | 4.00 |
| PH Phillip Humber AU Jsy A RC | 10.00 | 25.00 |
| PK Paul Kelly RC | 2.00 | 5.00 |
| PL Paul Lo Duca Bat A | 2.00 | 5.00 |
| PM Pedro Martinez Jsy A | 3.00 | 8.00 |
| PP P.J. Phillips RC | 2.00 | 5.00 |
| RB Ryan Braun AU A RC | 50.00 | 100.00 |
| RBE Ronnie Belliard Bat A | 2.00 | 5.00 |
| RF Rafael Furcal Jsy A | 2.00 | 5.00 |
| RM Russ Martin AU Jsy F RC | 10.00 | 25.00 |
| RMO Ryan Mount RC | 2.00 | 5.00 |
| RR Ricky Romero RC | 2.00 | 5.00 |
| RT Raul Tablado AU Jsy A RC | 4.00 | 10.00 |
| RZ Ryan Zimmerman RC | 6.00 | 15.00 |
| SD Stephen Drew RC | 8.00 | 20.00 |
| SE Scott Elbert AU Jsy A | 4.00 | 10.00 |
| SM Steve Marek AU Jsy A RC | 4.00 | 10.00 |
| SR Scott Rolen Jsy B | 3.00 | 8.00 |
| SS Sammy Sosa Bat A | 3.00 | 8.00 |
| SW Steven White AU B RC | 4.00 | 10.00 |
| TB Trevor Bell AU Jsy C RC | 6.00 | 15.00 |
| TBU Travis Buck RC | 3.00 | 8.00 |
| TC Travis Chick AU A RC | 3.00 | 8.00 |
| TG Tyler Greene RC | 2.00 | 5.00 |
| TH Torii Hunter Bat A | 2.00 | 5.00 |
| THE Tyler Herron RC | 2.00 | 5.00 |
| THU Tim Hudson Uni A | 2.00 | 5.00 |
| TI Tadahito Iguchi RC | 2.00 | 5.00 |
| TLH Todd Helton Jsy B | 3.00 | 8.00 |
| TM Tyler Minges AU Jsy A RC | 4.00 | 10.00 |
| TMO Tino Martinez Bat A | 3.00 | 8.00 |
| TN Trot Nixon Bat A | 2.00 | 5.00 |
| TT Troy Tulowitzki RC | 3.00 | 8.00 |
| TW Travis Wood RC | 2.50 | 6.00 |
| VG Vladimir Guerrero Bat A | 3.00 | 8.00 |
| VM Victor Martinez Bat A | 2.00 | 5.00 |
| WT Wade Townsend RC | 2.00 | 5.00 |
| YE Yunel Escobar RC | 6.00 | 15.00 |
| ZS Zach Simons RC | 1.50 | 4.00 |

## 2006 Bowman Sterling

| | | |
|---|---|---|
| COMMON ROOKIE | 1.25 | 3.00 |
| COMMON AU | 3.00 | 8.00 |
| AU GU AUTO ODDS 1:4 HOBBY | | |
| COMMON AU-GU RC | 4.00 | 10.00 |
| AU-GU RC ODDS 1:4 HOBBY | | |
| COMMON GU VET | 2.50 | 6.00 |
| GU VET ODDS 1:4 HOBBY | | |
| OVERALL PLATE ODDS 1:23 BOXES | | |
| PLATE PRINT RUN 1 SET PER COLOR | | |
| BLACK-CYAN-MAGENTA-YELLOW ISSUED | | |
| NO PLATE PRICING DUE TO SCARCITY | | |
| EXCHANGE DEADLINE 12/31/08 | | |
| AD Adam Dunn Jsy | 2.50 | 6.00 |
| AE Andre Ethier AU (RC) | 6.00 | 15.00 |
| AER Alex Rodriguez Bat | 10.00 | 25.00 |
| AJ Andruw Jones Jsy | 3.00 | 8.00 |
| ALR A.Reyes Jsy AU (RC) EXCH | 6.00 | 15.00 |
| ALS Alay Soler RC | 1.25 | 3.00 |
| AP Albert Pujols Jsy | 8.00 | 20.00 |
| AP2 Albert Pujols Bat | 8.00 | 20.00 |
| APS Alfonso Soriano Bat | 4.00 | 10.00 |
| AR Aramis Ramirez Bat UER | 3.00 | 8.00 |
| AS Anibal Sanchez (RC) | 1.50 | 4.00 |
| BA Brian Anderson (RC) | 1.25 | 3.00 |
| BB Brian Bannister (RC) | 1.25 | 3.00 |

| | | |
|---|---|---|
| BL B.Livingston Jsy AU (RC) | 4.00 | 10.00 |
| BLB Barry Bonds Bat | 6.00 | 15.00 |
| BON Boof Bonser RC | 1.50 | 4.00 |
| BR Brian Roberts Jsy | 2.50 | 6.00 |
| BZ Ben Zobrist (RC) | 1.50 | 4.00 |
| CB Carlos Beltran Jsy | 2.50 | 6.00 |
| CB2 Carlos Beltran Bat | 2.50 | 6.00 |
| CC Chris Carpenter Jsy | 2.50 | 6.00 |
| CH Cole Hamels Jsy AU (RC) | 20.00 | 50.00 |
| CHJ Chuck James (RC) | 1.50 | 4.00 |
| CI Chris Iannetta Jsy AU (RC) | 8.00 | 20.00 |
| CJ Conor Jackson (RC) | 1.50 | 4.00 |
| CJJ Casey Janssen RC | 1.50 | 4.00 |
| CQ Carlos Quentin (RC) | 1.50 | 4.00 |
| CRB Chad Billingsley (RC) | 1.50 | 4.00 |
| CRH Craig Hansen RC | 2.00 | 5.00 |
| CS Curt Schilling Jsy | 3.00 | 8.00 |
| DG David Gassner (RC) | 1.25 | 3.00 |
| DO David Ortiz Bat | 4.00 | 10.00 |
| DP David Pauley (RC) | 1.25 | 3.00 |
| DU Dan Uggla (RC) | 3.00 | 8.00 |
| DW David Wright Jsy | 6.00 | 15.00 |
| DWW Dontrelle Willis Jsy | 2.50 | 6.00 |
| EC Eric Chavez Jsy | 2.50 | 6.00 |
| EG Eric Enrique Gonzalez (RC) | 1.25 | 3.00 |
| FG Franklin Gutierrez (RC) | 1.25 | 3.00 |
| FL Francisco Liriano (RC) | 2.50 | 6.00 |
| GS Grady Sizemore Jsy | 4.00 | 10.00 |
| HB Hank Blalock Jsy | 2.50 | 6.00 |
| HK1 Howie Kendrick (RC) | 2.00 | 5.00 |
| HK2 H.Kendrick Jsy AU (RC) EXCH | 8.00 | 20.00 |
| HM Hideki Matsui Bat | 6.00 | 15.00 |
| HP Hayden Penn (RC) | 1.25 | 3.00 |
| HR Hanley Ramirez (RC) | 3.00 | 8.00 |
| IK Ian Kinsler AU (RC) | 12.50 | 30.00 |
| IR Ivan Rodriguez Jsy | 3.00 | 8.00 |
| IS Ichiro Suzuki Jsy | 10.00 | 25.00 |
| JAS Johan Santana Jsy | 4.00 | 10.00 |
| JB J.Bulger Jsy AU (RC) EXCH | 4.00 | 10.00 |
| JBS Jeremy Sowers (RC) | 1.25 | 3.00 |
| JCB Jason Botts AU (RC) | 2.00 | 5.00 |
| JD Joey Devine RC | 1.25 | 3.00 |
| JDD Johnny Damon Bat | 4.00 | 10.00 |
| JHT Jim Thome Bat | 4.00 | 10.00 |
| JI Joe Inglett AU RC | 4.00 | 12.00 |
| JJ Josh Johnson (RC) | 1.50 | 4.00 |
| JK Jeff Karstens RC | 1.50 | 4.00 |
| JL James Loney (RC) | 1.50 | 4.00 |
| JLB Josh Barfield AU (RC) | 3.00 | 8.00 |
| JM Jeff Mathis (RC) | 1.25 | 3.00 |
| JP Jonathan Papelbon (RC) | 3.00 | 8.00 |
| JRH Rich Harden Jsy | 2.50 | 6.00 |
| JS James Shields RC | 1.25 | 3.00 |
| JT Jack Taschner Jsy AU RC | 4.00 | 10.00 |
| JTA Jordan Tata RC | 1.25 | 3.00 |
| JTJ Jon Lester Jsy AU RC | 20.00 | 50.00 |
| JV Justin Verlander (RC) | 3.00 | 8.00 |
| JW Jered Weaver (RC) | 2.50 | 6.00 |
| JZ Joel Zumaya (RC) | 2.00 | 5.00 |
| KF Kevin Frandsen (RC) | 1.25 | 3.00 |
| KJ Kenji Johjima RC | 3.00 | 8.00 |
| KM Kendry Morales (RC) | 1.50 | 4.00 |
| LB Lance Berkman Jsy | 3.00 | 8.00 |
| LM Lastings Milledge AU (RC) | 8.00 | 20.00 |
| LWJ Chipper Jones Jsy | 4.00 | 10.00 |
| MC Miguel Cabrera Jsy | 3.00 | 8.00 |
| MC2 Miguel Cabrera Bat | 3.00 | 8.00 |
| MCC Melky Cabrera (RC) | 1.50 | 4.00 |
| MCM Mickey Mantle Bat | 30.00 | 60.00 |
| MCT Mark Teixeira Bat | 4.00 | 10.00 |
| ME Morgan Ensberg Jsy | 2.50 | 6.00 |
| MJP Mike Piazza Bat | 4.00 | 10.00 |
| MK Matt Kemp (RC) | 4.00 | 10.00 |
| MM Mark Mulder Pants | 2.50 | 6.00 |
| MN Mike Napoli Jsy AU RC EXCH | 6.00 | 15.00 |
| MP Martin Prado Jsy AU (RC) | 8.00 | 20.00 |
| MPF Mike Pelfrey RC | 6.00 | 15.00 |
| MR Manny Ramirez Jsy | 4.00 | 10.00 |
| MR2 Manny Ramirez Bat | 4.00 | 10.00 |
| MS Matt Smith (RC) | 1.50 | 4.00 |
| MT Miguel Tejada Pants | 2.50 | 6.00 |
| NM Nick Markakis (RC) | 4.00 | 10.00 |
| PF Prince Fielder Jsy AU (RC) | 20.00 | 50.00 |
| PK Paul Konerko Bat | 4.00 | 10.00 |
| PM Pedro Martinez Pants | 3.00 | 8.00 |
| RC Robinson Cano Bat | 5.00 | 12.00 |
| RH Ryan Howard AU Jsy | 8.00 | 20.00 |
| RK Ryan Garko (RC) | 1.25 | 3.00 |

|  | | |
|---|---|---|
| ☐ RM Russ Martin (RC) | 1.50 | 4.00 |
| ☐ RN Ricky Nolasco AU (RC) | 3.00 | 8.00 |
| ☐ RP Ronny Paulino Jsy AU (RC) | 6.00 | 15.00 |
| ☐ RZ Ryan Zimmerman AU (RC) | 3.00 | 8.00 |
| ☐ SD Stephen Drew (RC) | 2.00 | 5.00 |
| ☐ SM Scott Mathieson (RC) | 1.25 | 3.00 |
| ☐ SO Scott Olsen (RC) | 1.25 | 3.00 |
| ☐ SR Scott Rolen Pants | 3.00 | 8.00 |
| ☐ ST S.Thoman Jsy AU (RC) EXCH | 5.00 | 12.00 |
| ☐ TGJ Tony Gwynn Jr (RC) | 3.00 | 8.00 |
| ☐ TH Todd Helton Jsy | 3.00 | 8.00 |
| ☐ TT Taylor Tankersley (RC) | 1.25 | 3.00 |
| ☐ VG Vladimir Guerrero Jsy | 3.00 | 8.00 |
| ☐ WA Willy Aybar (RC) | 1.25 | 3.00 |
| ☐ YP Yusmeiro Petit Jsy AU (RC) | 4.00 | 10.00 |
| ☐ ZM Zach Miner AU (RC) | 3.00 | 8.00 |

## 2007 Bowman Sterling

| | | |
|---|---|---|
| ☐ COMMON ROOKIE | 1.00 | 2.50 |
| ☐ COMMON AUTO RC | 3.00 | 8.00 |
| ☐ AU RC AUTO ODDS 1:2 PACKS | | |
| ☐ COMMON GU VET | 2.50 | 6.00 |
| ☐ GU VET GROUP A ODDS 1:5 PACKS | | |
| ☐ GU VET GROUP B ODDS 1:3 PACKS | | |
| ☐ GU VET GROUP C ODDS 1:253 PACKS | | |
| ☐ PRINTING PLATE ODDS 1:29 BOXES | | |
| ☐ PRINTING PLATE AU ODDS 1:41 BOXES | | |
| ☐ PLATE PRINT RUN 1 SET PER COLOR | | |
| ☐ BLACK-CYAN-MAGENTA-YELLOW ISSUED | | |
| ☐ NO PLATE PRICING DUE TO SCARCITY | | |
| ☐ AAL Adam Lind (RC) | 1.00 | 2.50 |
| ☐ AER Alex Rodriguez Bat A | 6.00 | 15.00 |
| ☐ AG Alex Gordon RC | 2.50 | 6.00 |
| ☐ AI Akinori Iwamura RC | 1.50 | 4.00 |
| ☐ AJ Andruw Jones Bat B | 2.50 | 6.00 |
| ☐ AL Andy LaRoche (RC) | 1.00 | 2.50 |
| ☐ AM Andrew Miller RC | 2.50 | 6.00 |
| ☐ AP Albert Pujols Jsy A | 5.00 | 12.00 |
| ☐ AR Alex Rios Jsy B | 2.50 | 6.00 |
| ☐ AS Alfonso Soriano Bat B | 2.50 | 6.00 |
| ☐ ASo Andy Sonnanstine RC | 1.00 | 2.50 |
| ☐ BB Billy Butler (RC) | 1.25 | 3.00 |
| ☐ BF Ben Francisco (RC) | 1.00 | 2.50 |
| ☐ BLB Barry Bonds Pants A | 4.00 | 10.00 |
| ☐ BP Brad Penny Jsy B | 2.50 | 6.00 |
| ☐ BR Brian Roberts Jsy A | 2.50 | 6.00 |
| ☐ BS Brian Stokes (RC) | 2.50 | 6.00 |
| ☐ BU B.J. Upton Bat B | 2.50 | 6.00 |
| ☐ BW Brandon Webb Jsy B | 2.50 | 6.00 |
| ☐ BW Brandon Wood (RC) | 1.00 | 2.50 |
| ☐ CAB Craig Biggio Jsy B | 3.00 | 8.00 |
| ☐ CAG Carlos Guillen Jsy B | 2.50 | 6.00 |
| ☐ CG Carlos Gomez RC | 1.25 | 3.00 |
| ☐ CH Cole Hamels Jsy A | 5.00 | 12.00 |
| ☐ CH Chase Headley AU (RC) | 2.50 | 6.00 |
| ☐ CL Carlos Lee Jsy B | 2.50 | 6.00 |
| ☐ CM Cameron Maybin AU RC | 6.00 | 15.00 |
| ☐ CMS Curt Schilling Jsy B | 2.50 | 6.00 |
| ☐ CT Curtis Thigpen (RC) | 1.00 | 2.50 |
| ☐ DDY Dmitri Young Jsy B | 2.50 | 6.00 |
| ☐ DM Daisuke Matsuzaka RC | 4.00 | 10.00 |
| ☐ DMM David Murphy (RC) | 1.00 | 2.50 |
| ☐ DO David Ortiz Bat B | 3.00 | 8.00 |
| ☐ DP Danny Putnam (RC) | 1.00 | 2.50 |
| ☐ DW David Wright Bat B | 4.00 | 10.00 |
| ☐ DWW Dontrelle Willis Jsy B | 2.50 | 6.00 |
| ☐ DY Delmon Young Jsy | 1.25 | 3.00 |
| ☐ EC Eric Chavez Pants B | 2.50 | 6.00 |
| ☐ FL Fred Lewis (RC) | 1.25 | 3.00 |
| ☐ FP Felix Pie AU (RC) | 3.00 | 8.00 |
| ☐ GO Garrett Olson (RC) | 1.00 | 2.50 |
| ☐ GP Glen Perkins AU (RC) | 3.00 | 8.00 |
| ☐ HB Homer Bailey AU (RC) | 4.00 | 10.00 |
| ☐ HG Hector Gimenez (RC) | 1.00 | 2.50 |

| | | |
|---|---|---|
| ☐ HO Hideki Okajima RC | 2.50 | 6.00 |
| ☐ HP Hunter Pence (RC) | 2.50 | 6.00 |
| ☐ IS Ichiro Suzuki Bat B | 5.00 | 12.00 |
| ☐ JAV Jason Varitek Jsy B | 3.00 | 8.00 |
| ☐ JB Jeff Baker (RC) | 1.00 | 2.50 |
| ☐ JBR Jose Reyes Jsy A | 3.00 | 8.00 |
| ☐ JC1 Joba Chamberlain RC | 5.00 | 12.00 |
| ☐ JC2 Joba Chamberlain AU | 20.00 | 50.00 |
| ☐ JD John Danks AU RC | 4.00 | 10.00 |
| ☐ JDF Josh Fields (RC) | 1.00 | 2.50 |
| ☐ JE Jim Edmonds Jsy B | 3.00 | 8.00 |
| ☐ JE Jacoby Ellsbury (RC) | 5.00 | 12.00 |
| ☐ JF Jesus Flores RC | 1.00 | 2.50 |
| ☐ JH Josh Hamilton AU (RC) | 10.00 | 25.00 |
| ☐ JL Jesse Litsch AU (RC) | 3.00 | 8.00 |
| ☐ JQF Jake Fox RC | 1.25 | 3.00 |
| ☐ JR Jo-Jo Reyes (RC) | 1.00 | 2.50 |
| ☐ JS Johan Santana Jsy A | 3.00 | 8.00 |
| ☐ JS J.Salty AU (RC) | 4.00 | 10.00 |
| ☐ JU Justin Upton AU | 2.50 | 6.00 |
| ☐ JV Justin Verlander Jsy B | 3.00 | 8.00 |
| ☐ KI Kei Igawa RC | 1.50 | 4.00 |
| ☐ KK Kevin Kouzmanoff (RC) | 1.00 | 2.50 |
| ☐ KKS Kurt Suzuki AU (RC) | 3.00 | 8.00 |
| ☐ KRK Kyle Kendrick AU (RC) | 3.00 | 8.00 |
| ☐ KS Kevin Slowey AU (RC) | 6.00 | 15.00 |
| ☐ LB Lance Berkman Jsy A | 2.50 | 6.00 |
| ☐ MAR Manny Ramirez Bat B | 5.00 | 12.00 |
| ☐ MB Michael Bourn (RC) | 1.00 | 2.50 |
| ☐ MC Melky Cabrera Bat B | 2.50 | 6.00 |
| ☐ MC Matt Chico AU (RC) | 3.00 | 8.00 |
| ☐ MCT Mark Teixeira Bat A | 2.50 | 6.00 |
| ☐ MF Mike Fontenot (RC) | 1.00 | 2.50 |
| ☐ MH Matt Holliday Jsy B | 3.00 | 8.00 |
| ☐ MJO Magglio Ordonez Bat B | 2.50 | 6.00 |
| ☐ MK Masumi Kuwata RC | 1.25 | 3.00 |
| ☐ MM Mickey Mantle Jsy C | 40.00 | 80.00 |
| ☐ MM Miguel Montero (RC) | 1.00 | 2.50 |
| ☐ MO Micah Owings (RC) | 1.00 | 2.50 |
| ☐ MP Manny Parra (RC) | 1.00 | 2.50 |
| ☐ MR Mark Reynolds RC | 2.50 | 6.00 |
| ☐ MSM Mark McLemore (RC) | 1.00 | 2.50 |
| ☐ MT Miguel Tejada Pants B | 2.50 | 6.00 |
| ☐ MY Michael Young Jsy B | 2.50 | 6.00 |
| ☐ NG Nick Gomeault AU (RC) | 3.00 | 8.00 |
| ☐ NS Nate Schierholtz AU (RC) | 5.00 | 12.00 |
| ☐ OC Orlando Cabrera Jsy | 2.50 | 6.00 |
| ☐ PF Prince Fielder Jsy A | 3.00 | 8.00 |
| ☐ PH Phil Hughes (RC) | 2.50 | 6.00 |
| ☐ PH Phil Hughes AU (RC) | 6.00 | 15.00 |
| ☐ RB Rocco Baldelli Jsy B | 2.50 | 6.00 |
| ☐ RB Ryan Braun AU (RC) | 20.00 | 50.00 |
| ☐ RC Roger Clemens Jsy B | 4.00 | 10.00 |
| ☐ RJC Robinson Cano Bat B | 4.00 | 10.00 |
| ☐ RJH Ryan Howard Bat A | 4.00 | 10.00 |
| ☐ RS Ryan Sweeney (RC) | 1.00 | 2.50 |
| ☐ RV Rick Vanden Hurk RC | 1.25 | 3.00 |
| ☐ RZ Ryan Zimmerman Bat B | 3.00 | 8.00 |
| ☐ SD Shelley Duncan (RC) | 1.00 | 2.50 |
| ☐ SG Sean Gallagher (RC) | 1.00 | 2.50 |
| ☐ SK Scott Kazmir Jsy B | 2.50 | 6.00 |
| ☐ TA Tony Abreu RC | 1.50 | 4.00 |
| ☐ TB Travis Buck (RC) | 1.00 | 2.50 |
| ☐ TC Tyler Clippard (RC) | 1.25 | 3.00 |
| ☐ TH Tim Hudson Jsy B | 2.50 | 6.00 |
| ☐ TL Tim Lincecum AU AU | 40.00 | 80.00 |
| ☐ TLH Todd Helton Bat A | 2.50 | 6.00 |
| ☐ TM Travis Metcalf RC | 1.00 | 2.50 |
| ☐ TW Tim Wakefield Jsy B | 2.50 | 6.00 |
| ☐ UJ Ubaldo Jimenez (RC) | 1.00 | 2.50 |
| ☐ VG Vladimir Guerrero Jsy A | 2.50 | 6.00 |
| ☐ YE Yunel Escobar (RC) | 1.00 | 2.50 |
| ☐ YG Yovani Gallardo AU (RC) | 6.00 | 15.00 |

## 2008 Bowman Sterling

| | | |
|---|---|---|
| ☐ COMMON GU VET | 2.50 | 6.00 |
| ☐ EXCHANGE DEADLINE 11/30/2010 | | |
| ☐ COMMON RC | 1.00 | 2.50 |
| ☐ COMMON RC VAR | 1.25 | 3.00 |
| ☐ RC VAR ODDS 1:2 BOXES | | |
| ☐ RC VAR PRINT RUN 399 SER.#'d SETS | | |
| ☐ COMMON AU RC | 3.00 | 8.00 |
| ☐ AU RC ODDS 1:3 PACKS | | |
| ☐ PRINTING PLATE ODDS 1:93 PACKS | | |
| ☐ PRINTING PLATE AU ODDS 1:238 PACKS | | |
| ☐ PLATE PRINT RUN 1 SET PER COLOR | | |
| ☐ BLACK-CYAN-MAGENTA-YELLOW ISSUED | | |
| ☐ NO PLATE PRICING DUE TO SCARCITY | | |

| | | |
|---|---|---|
| ☐ AAG Armando Galarraga AU RC | 4.00 | 10.00 |
| ☐ AP Albert Pujols Jsy | 5.00 | 12.00 |
| ☐ AR Alex Rodriguez Jsy | 5.00 | 12.00 |
| ☐ ARA Aramis Ramirez Mem EXCH | 2.50 | 6.00 |
| ☐ ARU Adam Russell AU (RC) | 3.00 | 8.00 |
| ☐ BG Brett Gardner (RC) | 2.50 | 6.00 |
| ☐ BH Brian Horwitz RC | 1.00 | 2.50 |
| ☐ BJ Brandon Jones RC | 2.50 | 6.00 |
| ☐ BJB Brian Bixler AU (RC) | 3.00 | 8.00 |
| ☐ BM Brian McCann Bat | 2.50 | 6.00 |
| ☐ BZ Brad Ziegler RC | 5.00 | 12.00 |
| ☐ CC Carl Crawford Jsy | 2.50 | 6.00 |
| ☐ CD Chris Davis RC | 2.50 | 6.00 |
| ☐ CDB Clay Buchholz (RC) | 2.50 | 6.00 |
| ☐ CEGa Carlos Gonzalez (RC) | 1.00 | 2.50 |
| ☐ CEGb Carlos Gonzalez VAR RC | 1.25 | 3.00 |
| ☐ CG Chris Getz AU RC | 3.00 | 8.00 |
| ☐ CG Curtis Granderson Mem EXCH | 2.50 | 6.00 |
| ☐ CH Cole Hamels Jsy | 3.00 | 8.00 |
| ☐ CJ Chipper Jones Jsy | 3.00 | 8.00 |
| ☐ CKa Clayton Kershaw RC | 5.00 | 12.00 |
| ☐ CKb Clayton Kershaw VAR RC | 6.00 | 15.00 |
| ☐ CLH Chin-Lung Hu (RC) | 1.50 | 4.00 |
| ☐ CM Charlie Morton (RC) | 1.00 | 2.50 |
| ☐ CMT Matt Tolbert RC | 1.00 | 2.50 |
| ☐ CP Chris Perez AU RC | 3.00 | 8.00 |
| ☐ CR Clayton Richard (RC) | 1.00 | 2.50 |
| ☐ CRPa Cliff Pennington (RC) | 1.00 | 2.50 |
| ☐ CRPb Cliff Pennington VAR RC | 1.25 | 3.00 |
| ☐ CU Chase Utley Jsy | 4.00 | 10.00 |
| ☐ CW Chien-Ming Wang Jsy | 4.00 | 10.00 |
| ☐ DB Daric Barton (RC) | 1.00 | 2.50 |
| ☐ DM Daisuke Matsuzaka Jsy | 4.00 | 10.00 |
| ☐ DO David Ortiz Jsy | 3.00 | 8.00 |
| ☐ DP David Purcey (RC) | 1.00 | 2.50 |
| ☐ DW David Wright Bat | 4.00 | 10.00 |
| ☐ DY Delmon Young Jsy | 2.50 | 6.00 |
| ☐ EH Eric Hurley (RC) | 1.00 | 2.50 |
| ☐ EL Evan Longoria AU RC | 30.00 | 60.00 |
| ☐ EV Edinson Volquez Jsy | 2.50 | 6.00 |
| ☐ FC Fausto Carmona Mem EXCH | 3.00 | 8.00 |
| ☐ GB Gregor Blanco (RC) | 1.00 | 2.50 |
| ☐ GD German Duran RC | 1.00 | 2.50 |
| ☐ GR Greg Reynolds (RC) | 1.00 | 2.50 |
| ☐ GS Geovany Soto Jsy | 3.00 | 8.00 |
| ☐ GTS Greg Smith AU RC | 3.00 | 8.00 |
| ☐ HI Hernan Iribarren (RC) | 1.50 | 4.00 |
| ☐ HKa Hiroki Kuroda RC | 1.50 | 4.00 |
| ☐ HKb Hiroki Kuroda VAR SP | 2.00 | 5.00 |
| ☐ HP Hunter Pence Jsy | 3.00 | 8.00 |
| ☐ HR Hanley Ramirez Jsy | 2.50 | 6.00 |
| ☐ IS Ichiro Suzuki Jsy | 6.00 | 15.00 |
| ☐ JABa Jay Bruce (RC) | 4.00 | 10.00 |
| ☐ JABj Jay Bruce VAR SP | 5.00 | 12.00 |
| ☐ JB Josh Banks (RC) | 1.00 | 2.50 |
| ☐ JBC Jeff Clement (RC) | 1.50 | 4.00 |
| ☐ JBR Jose Reyes Jsy | 3.00 | 8.00 |
| ☐ JC Joba Chamberlain Jsy | 5.00 | 12.00 |
| ☐ JCH Justin Christian RC | 1.50 | 4.00 |
| ☐ JCO Johnny Cueto RC | 1.50 | 4.00 |
| ☐ JE Jacoby Ellsbury Jsy | 4.00 | 10.00 |
| ☐ JH Josh Hamilton Jsy | 5.00 | 12.00 |
| ☐ JLa Jed Lowrie (RC) | 2.50 | 6.00 |
| ☐ JLb Jed Lowrie VAR SP | 3.00 | 8.00 |
| ☐ JMR Justin Ruggiano AU RC | 3.00 | 8.00 |
| ☐ JN Jeff Niemann (RC) | 1.00 | 2.50 |
| ☐ JR Jimmy Rollins Jsy | 2.50 | 6.00 |
| ☐ JSa Jeff Samardzija RC | 3.00 | 8.00 |
| ☐ JSb Jeff Samardzija VAR SP | 4.00 | 10.00 |
| ☐ JT J.R. Towles RC | 1.50 | 4.00 |
| ☐ JU Justin Upton Bat | 2.50 | 6.00 |
| ☐ JVa Joey Votto (RC) | 2.50 | 6.00 |
| ☐ JVb Joey Votto VAR SP | 3.00 | 8.00 |
| ☐ KFa Kosuke Fukudome (RC) | 3.00 | 8.00 |
| ☐ KFb Kosuke Fukudome VAR RC | 4.00 | 10.00 |
| ☐ LHb Luke Hochevar RC | 1.50 | 4.00 |
| ☐ MA Manny Aybrey RC | 1.50 | 4.00 |
| ☐ MC Miguel Cabrera Bat | 3.00 | 8.00 |
| ☐ MH Matt Holliday Bat | 2.50 | 6.00 |
| ☐ MJ Matt Joyce RC | 2.50 | 6.00 |
| ☐ MK Masahide Kobayashi RC | 1.50 | 4.00 |
| ☐ MM Mickey Mantle Jsy | 30.00 | 60.00 |
| ☐ MR Manny Ramirez Jsy | 4.00 | 10.00 |
| ☐ MRRa Max Ramirez (RC) | 1.00 | 2.50 |
| ☐ MRRb Max Ramirez VAR SP | 1.25 | 3.00 |
| ☐ MT Mark Teixeira Bat | 3.00 | 8.00 |
| ☐ MTA Miguel Tejada Mem EXCH | 2.50 | 6.00 |
| ☐ MTH Michael Holliman RC | 1.00 | 2.50 |

| | | |
|---|---|---|
| NA Nick Adenhart (RC) | 1.00 | 2.50 |
| NB Nick Blackburn RC | 1.50 | 4.00 |
| NE Nick Evans RC | 1.00 | 2.50 |
| NH Nick Hundley (RC) | 1.00 | 2.50 |
| NLS Nick Stavinoha RC | 1.50 | 4.00 |
| NM Nick Markakis Jsy | 4.00 | 10.00 |
| PF Prince Fielder Jsy | 3.00 | 8.00 |
| RB Ryan Braun Jsy | 4.00 | 10.00 |
| RB Reid Brignac (RC) | 1.50 | 4.00 |
| RH Ryan Howard Jsy | 4.00 | 10.00 |
| RJM Jai Miller (RC) | 1.00 | 2.50 |
| RL Radhames Liz RC | 1.50 | 4.00 |
| RM Russ Martin Bat | 3.00 | 8.00 |
| RT Ryan Tucker (RC) | 1.00 | 2.50 |
| SR Sean Rodriguez (RC) | 1.00 | 2.50 |
| SS Seth Smith AU (RC) | 3.00 | 8.00 |
| TL Tim Lincecum Jsy | 6.00 | 15.00 |
| TT Taylor Teagarden AU RC | 5.00 | 12.00 |
| VG Vladimir Guerrero Jsy | 2.50 | 6.00 |
| VM Victor Martinez Jsy | 2.50 | 6.00 |
| WB Wladimir Balentien RC | 1.00 | 2.50 |
| WCC Chris Carter (RC) | 1.50 | 4.00 |

## 1994 Bowman's Best

| | | |
|---|---|---|
| COMPLETE SET (200) | 15.00 | 40.00 |
| B1 Chipper Jones Jsy | .50 | 1.25 |
| B2 Derek Jeter | 1.50 | 4.00 |
| B3 Ball Pulsipher | .20 | .50 |
| B4 James Baldwin | .08 | .25 |
| B5 Brooks Kieschnick RC | .20 | .50 |
| B6 Justin Thompson | .08 | .25 |
| B7 Midre Cummings | .08 | .25 |
| B8 Joey Hamilton | .08 | .25 |
| B9 Pokey Reese | .08 | .25 |
| B10 Brian Barber | .08 | .25 |
| B11 John Burke | .08 | .25 |
| B12 DeShawn Warren | .08 | .25 |
| B13 Edgardo Alfonzo RC | .40 | 1.00 |
| B14 Eddie Pearson RC | .20 | .50 |
| B15 Jimmy Haynes | .08 | .25 |
| B16 Danny Bautista | .08 | .25 |
| B17 Roger Cedeno | .20 | .50 |
| B18 Jon Lieber | .20 | .50 |
| B19 Billy Wagner RC | 2.00 | 5.00 |
| B20 Tate Seefried RC | .20 | .50 |
| B21 Chad Mottola | .08 | .25 |
| B22 Jose Malave | .08 | .25 |
| B23 Terrell Wade RC | .20 | .50 |
| B24 Shane Andrews | .08 | .25 |
| B25 Chan Ho Park RC | .60 | 1.50 |
| B26 Kirk Presley RC | .20 | .50 |
| B27 Robbie Beckett | .08 | .25 |
| B28 Orlando Miller | .08 | .25 |
| B29 Jorge Posada RC | 4.00 | 10.00 |
| B30 Frankie Rodriguez | .08 | .25 |
| B31 Brian L. Hunter | .08 | .25 |
| B32 Billy Ashley | .20 | .50 |
| B33 Rondell White | .20 | .50 |
| B34 John Roper | .08 | .25 |
| B35 Marc Valdes | .08 | .25 |
| B36 Scott Ruffcorn | .08 | .25 |
| B37 Rod Henderson | .08 | .25 |
| B38 Curtis Goodwin RC | .20 | .50 |
| B39 Russ Davis | .08 | .25 |
| B40 Rick Gorecki | .08 | .25 |
| B41 Johnny Damon | .50 | 1.25 |
| B42 Roberto Petagine | .08 | .25 |
| B43 Chris Snopek | .08 | .25 |
| B44 Mark Acre | .20 | .50 |
| B45 Todd Hollandsworth | .20 | .50 |
| B46 Shawn Green | .50 | 1.25 |
| B47 John Carter RC | .20 | .50 |
| B48 Jim Pittsley RC | .20 | .50 |
| B49 John Wasdin RC | .20 | .50 |

| | | |
|---|---|---|
| B50 D.J. Boston RC | .20 | .50 |
| B51 Tim Clark | .08 | .25 |
| B52 Alex Ochoa | .08 | .25 |
| B53 Chad Roper | .08 | .25 |
| B54 Mike Kelly | .08 | .25 |
| B55 Brad Fullmer RC | .40 | 1.00 |
| B56 Carl Everett | .20 | .50 |
| B57 Tim Belk RC | .20 | .50 |
| B58 Jimmy Hurst RC | .20 | .50 |
| B59 Mac Suzuki RC | .40 | 1.00 |
| B60 Mike Moore | .08 | .25 |
| B61 Alan Benes RC | .20 | .50 |
| B62 Tony Clark RC | .60 | 1.50 |
| B63 Edgar Renteria RC | 2.00 | 5.00 |
| B64 Trey Beamon | .08 | .25 |
| B65 LaTroy Hawkins RC | .40 | 1.00 |
| B66 Wayne Gomes RC | .40 | 1.00 |
| B67 Ray McDavid | .08 | .25 |
| B68 John Dettmer | .08 | .25 |
| B69 Willie Greene | .08 | .25 |
| B70 Dave Stevens | .08 | .25 |
| B71 Kevin Orie RC | .08 | .25 |
| B72 Chad Ogea | .08 | .25 |
| B73 Ben Van Ryn RC | .20 | .50 |
| B74 Kym Ashworth RC | .20 | .50 |
| B75 Dmitri Young | .20 | .50 |
| B76 Herbert Perry RC | .20 | .50 |
| B77 Joey Eischen | .08 | .25 |
| B78 Arquimedez Pozo RC | .20 | .50 |
| B79 Ugueth Urbina | .08 | .25 |
| B80 Keith Williams RC | .20 | .50 |
| B81 John Frascatore RC | .20 | .50 |
| B82 Garey Ingram RC | .20 | .50 |
| B83 Aaron Small | .08 | .25 |
| B84 Olmedo Saenz RC | .20 | .50 |
| B85 Jesus Tavarez RC | .20 | .50 |
| B86 Jose Silva RC | .40 | 1.00 |
| B87 Jay Witasick RC | .20 | .50 |
| B88 Jay Maldonado RC | .20 | .50 |
| B89 Keith Heberling RC | .20 | .50 |
| B90 Rusty Greer RC | .60 | 1.50 |
| R1 Paul Molitor | .20 | .50 |
| R2 Eddie Murray | .50 | 1.25 |
| R3 Ozzie Smith | .75 | 2.00 |
| R4 Rickey Henderson | .50 | 1.25 |
| R5 Lee Smith | .20 | .50 |
| R6 Dave Winfield | .20 | .50 |
| R7 Roberto Alomar | .30 | .75 |
| R8 Matt Williams | .20 | .50 |
| R9 Mark Grace | .30 | .75 |
| R10 Lance Johnson | .08 | .25 |
| R11 Darren Daulton | .20 | .50 |
| R12 Tom Glavine | .30 | .75 |
| R13 Gary Sheffield | .20 | .50 |
| R14 Rod Beck | .08 | .25 |
| R15 Fred McGriff | .20 | .50 |
| R16 Joe Carter | .20 | .50 |
| R17 Dante Bichette | .20 | .50 |
| R18 Danny Tartabull | .08 | .25 |
| R19 Juan Gonzalez | .20 | .50 |
| R20 Steve Avery | .08 | .25 |
| R21 John Wetteland | .20 | .50 |
| R22 Ben McDonald | .08 | .25 |
| R23 Jack McDowell | .08 | .25 |
| R24 Jose Canseco | .20 | .50 |
| R25 Tim Salmon | .30 | .75 |
| R26 Wilson Alvarez | .08 | .25 |
| R27 Gregg Jefferies | .20 | .50 |
| R28 John Burkett | .08 | .25 |
| R29 Greg Vaughn | .20 | .50 |
| R30 Robin Ventura | .20 | .50 |
| R31 Paul O'Neill | .30 | .75 |
| R32 Cecil Fielder | .20 | .50 |
| R33 Kevin Mitchell | .20 | .50 |
| R34 Jeff Conine | .20 | .50 |
| R35 Carlos Baerga | .20 | .50 |
| R36 Greg Maddux | .75 | 2.00 |
| R37 Roger Clemens | 1.00 | 2.50 |
| R38 Deion Sanders | .30 | .75 |
| R39 Delino DeShields | .08 | .25 |
| R40 Ken Griffey Jr. | .75 | 2.00 |
| R41 Albert Belle | .30 | .75 |
| R42 Wade Boggs | .30 | .75 |
| R43 Andres Galarraga | .20 | .50 |
| R44 Aaron Sele | .08 | .25 |
| R45 Don Mattingly | 1.25 | 3.00 |
| R46 David Cone | .20 | .50 |
| R47 Len Dykstra | .20 | .50 |

| | | |
|---|---|---|
| R48 Brett Butler | .20 | .50 |
| R49 Bill Swift | .08 | .25 |
| R50 Bobby Bonilla | .20 | .50 |
| R51 Rafael Palmeiro | .30 | .75 |
| R52 Moises Alou | .20 | .50 |
| R53 Jeff Bagwell | .30 | .75 |
| R54 Mike Mussina | .50 | 1.25 |
| R55 Frank Thomas | .50 | 1.25 |
| R56 Jose Rijo | .08 | .25 |
| R57 Ruben Sierra | .20 | .50 |
| R58 Randy Myers | .08 | .25 |
| R59 Barry Bonds | 1.25 | 3.00 |
| R60 Jimmy Key | .20 | .50 |
| R61 Travis Fryman | .20 | .50 |
| R62 John Olerud | .20 | .50 |
| R63 David Justice | .20 | .50 |
| R64 Ray Lankford | .08 | .25 |
| R65 Bob Tewksbury | .08 | .25 |
| R66 Chuck Carr | .08 | .25 |
| R67 Jay Buhner | .08 | .25 |
| R68 Kenny Lofton | .30 | .75 |
| R69 Marquis Grissom | .20 | .50 |
| R70 Sammy Sosa | .50 | 1.25 |
| R71 Cal Ripken | 1.50 | 4.00 |
| R72 Ellis Burks | .20 | .50 |
| R73 Jeff Montgomery | .08 | .25 |
| R74 Julio Franco | .08 | .25 |
| R75 Kirby Puckett | .50 | 1.25 |
| R76 Larry Walker | .30 | .75 |
| R77 Andy Van Slyke | .20 | .50 |
| R78 Tony Gwynn | .60 | 1.50 |
| R79 Will Clark | .30 | .75 |
| R80 Mo Vaughn | .20 | .50 |
| R81 Mike Piazza | 1.00 | 2.50 |
| R82 James Mouton | .08 | .25 |
| R83 Carlos Delgado | .30 | .75 |
| R84 Ryan Klesko | .20 | .50 |
| R85 Javier Lopez | .20 | .50 |
| R86 Raul Mondesi | .20 | .50 |
| R87 Cliff Floyd | .20 | .50 |
| R88 Manny Ramirez | .50 | 1.25 |
| R89 Hector Carrasco | .08 | .25 |
| R90 Jeff Granger | .08 | .25 |
| X91 F.Thomas/D.Young | .30 | .75 |
| X92 F.McGriff/B.Kieschnick | .20 | .50 |
| X93 M.Williams/S.Andrews | .08 | .25 |
| X94 C.Ripken/K.Orie | .75 | 2.00 |
| X95 D.Jeter/B.Larkin | .75 | 2.00 |
| X96 K.Griffey Jr./J.Damon | .40 | 1.00 |
| X97 B.Bonds/R.White | .60 | 1.50 |
| X98 A.Belle/L.Hurst | .20 | .50 |
| X99 R.Rivera RC/R.Mondesi | .20 | .50 |
| X100 R.Clemens/S.Ruffcom | .50 | 1.25 |
| X101 G.Maddux/J.Wasdin | .50 | 1.25 |
| X102 T.Salmon/C.Mottola | .30 | .75 |
| X103 C.Baerga/A.Pozo | .08 | .25 |
| X104 M.Piazza/B.Hughes | .50 | 1.25 |
| X105 C.Delgado/M.Nieves | .30 | .75 |
| X106 J.Posada/J.Lopez | 1.00 | 2.50 |
| X107 M.Ramirez/J.Malave | .50 | 1.25 |
| X108 C.Jones/T.Fryman | .30 | .75 |
| X109 S.Avery/B.Pulsipher | .20 | .50 |
| X110 J.Olerud/S.Green | .50 | 1.25 |

## 1995 Bowman's Best

| | | |
|---|---|---|
| COMPLETE SET (195) | 125.00 | 250.00 |
| COMMON CARD (B1-R90) | .20 | .50 |
| COMMON CARD (X1-X15) | .20 | .50 |
| B1 Derek Jeter | 1.25 | 3.00 |
| B2 Vladimir Guerrero RC | 15.00 | 40.00 |
| B3 Bob Abreu RC | 5.00 | 12.00 |
| B4 Chan Ho Park | .20 | .50 |
| B5 Paul Wilson | .20 | .50 |
| B6 Chad Ogea | .20 | .50 |

| | | |
|---|---|---|
| B7 Andruw Jones RC | 6.00 | 15.00 |
| B8 Brian Barber | .20 | .50 |
| B9 Andy Larkin | .20 | .50 |
| B10 Richie Sexson RC | 4.00 | 10.00 |
| B11 Everett Stull | .20 | .50 |
| B12 Brooks Kieschnick | .20 | .50 |
| B13 Matt Murray | .20 | .50 |
| B14 John Wasdin | .20 | .50 |
| B15 Shannon Stewart | .20 | .50 |
| B16 Luis Ortiz | .20 | .50 |
| B17 Marc Kroon | .20 | .50 |
| B18 Todd Greene | .20 | .50 |
| B19 Juan Acevedo RC | .40 | 1.00 |
| B20 Tony Clark | .20 | .50 |
| B21 Jermaine Dye | .20 | .50 |
| B22 Derrek Lee | .50 | 1.25 |
| B23 Pat Watkins | .20 | .50 |
| B24 Pokey Reese | .20 | .50 |
| B25 Ben Grieve | .20 | .50 |
| B26 Julio Santana RC | .20 | .50 |
| B27 Felix Rodriguez RC | .40 | 1.00 |
| B28 Paul Konerko | 3.00 | 8.00 |
| B29 Nomar Garciaparra | 2.00 | 5.00 |
| B30 Pat Ahearne RC | .20 | .50 |
| B31 Jason Schmidt | .50 | 1.25 |
| B32 Billy Wagner | .30 | .75 |
| B33 Rey Ordonez RC | 1.25 | 3.00 |
| B34 Curtis Goodwin | .20 | .50 |
| B35 Sergio Nunez RC | .40 | 1.00 |
| B36 Tim Belk | .20 | .50 |
| B37 Scott Elarton RC | .75 | 2.00 |
| B38 Jason Isringhausen | .20 | .50 |
| B39 Trot Nixon | .20 | .50 |
| B40 Sid Roberson RC | .40 | 1.00 |
| B41 Ron Villone | .20 | .50 |
| B42 Ruben Rivera | .20 | .50 |
| B43 Rick Huisman | .20 | .50 |
| B44 Todd Hollandsworth | .20 | .50 |
| B45 Johnny Damon | .30 | .75 |
| B46 Garrel Anderson | .20 | .50 |
| B47 Jeff D'Amico | .20 | .50 |
| B48 Dustin Hermanson | .20 | .50 |
| B49 Juan Encarnacion RC | 1.25 | 3.00 |
| B50 Andy Pettitte | .30 | .75 |
| B51 Chris Stynes | .20 | .50 |
| B52 Troy Percival | .20 | .50 |
| B53 LaTroy Hawkins | .20 | .50 |
| B54 Roger Cedeno | .20 | .50 |
| B55 Alan Benes | .20 | .50 |
| B56 Karim Garcia RC | .40 | 1.00 |
| B57 Andrew Lorraine | .20 | .50 |
| B58 Gary Rath RC | .40 | 1.00 |
| B59 Bret Wagner | .20 | .50 |
| B60 Jeff Suppan | .20 | .50 |
| B61 Bill Pulsipher | .20 | .50 |
| B62 Jay Payton RC | 1.25 | 3.00 |
| B63 Alex Ochoa | .20 | .50 |
| B64 Ugueth Urbina | .20 | .50 |
| B65 Armando Benitez | .20 | .50 |
| B66 George Arias | .20 | .50 |
| B67 Raul Casanova RC | .40 | 1.00 |
| B68 Matt Drews | .20 | .50 |
| B69 Jimmy Haynes | .20 | .50 |
| B70 Jimmy Hurst | .20 | .50 |
| B71 C.J. Nitkowski | .20 | .50 |
| B72 Tommy Davis RC | .40 | 1.00 |
| B73 Bartolo Colon RC | 3.00 | 8.00 |
| B74 Chris Carpenter RC | 5.00 | 12.00 |
| B75 Trey Beamon | .20 | .50 |
| B76 Bryan Rekar | .20 | .50 |
| B77 James Baldwin | .20 | .50 |
| B78 Marc Valdes | .20 | .50 |
| B79 Tom Fordham RC | .40 | 1.00 |
| B80 Marc Newfield | .20 | .50 |
| B81 Angel Martinez | .20 | .50 |
| B82 Brian L. Hunter | .20 | .50 |
| B83 Jose Herrera | .20 | .50 |
| B84 Glenn Dishman RC | .40 | 1.00 |
| B85 Jason Cruz RC | .75 | 2.00 |
| B86 Paul Shuey | .20 | .50 |
| B87 Scott Rolen RC | 8.00 | 20.00 |
| B88 Doug Million | .20 | .50 |
| B89 Desi Relaford | .20 | .50 |
| B90 Michael Tucker | .20 | .50 |
| R1 Randy Johnson | .50 | 1.25 |
| R2 Joe Carter | .20 | .50 |
| R3 Chili Davis | .20 | .50 |
| R4 Moises Alou | .20 | .50 |

| | | |
|---|---|---|
| R5 Gary Sheffield | .20 | .50 |
| R6 Kevin Appier | .20 | .50 |
| R7 Denny Neagle | .20 | .50 |
| R8 Ruben Sierra | .20 | .50 |
| R9 Darren Daulton | .20 | .50 |
| R10 Cal Ripken | 1.50 | 4.00 |
| R11 Bobby Bonilla | .20 | .50 |
| R12 Manny Ramirez | .30 | .75 |
| R13 Barry Bonds | 1.25 | 3.00 |
| R14 Eric Karros | .20 | .50 |
| R15 Greg Maddux | .75 | 2.00 |
| R16 Jeff Bagwell | .30 | .75 |
| R17 Paul Molitor | .20 | .50 |
| R18 Ray Lankford | .20 | .50 |
| R19 Mark Grace | .30 | .75 |
| R20 Kenny Lofton | .20 | .50 |
| R21 Tony Gwynn | .60 | 1.50 |
| R22 Will Clark | .30 | .75 |
| R23 Roger Clemens | 1.00 | 2.50 |
| R24 Dante Bichette | .20 | .50 |
| R25 Barry Larkin | .30 | .75 |
| R26 Wade Boggs | .30 | .75 |
| R27 Kirby Puckett | .50 | 1.25 |
| R28 Cecil Fielder | .20 | .50 |
| R29 Jose Canseco | .30 | .75 |
| R30 Juan Gonzalez | .20 | .50 |
| R31 David Cone | .20 | .50 |
| R32 Craig Biggio | .20 | .50 |
| R33 Tim Salmon | .30 | .75 |
| R34 David Justice | .50 | 1.25 |
| R35 Sammy Sosa | .50 | 1.25 |
| R36 Mike Piazza | .75 | 2.00 |
| R37 Carlos Baerga | .20 | .50 |
| R38 Jeff Conine | .20 | .50 |
| R39 Rafael Palmeiro | .30 | .75 |
| R40 Bret Saberhagen | .20 | .50 |
| R41 Len Dykstra | .20 | .50 |
| R42 Mo Vaughn | .20 | .50 |
| R43 Wally Joyner | .20 | .50 |
| R44 Chuck Knoblauch | .20 | .50 |
| R45 Robin Ventura | .20 | .50 |
| R46 Don Mattingly | 1.25 | 3.00 |
| R47 Dave Hollins | .20 | .50 |
| R48 Andy Benes | .20 | .50 |
| R49 Ken Griffey Jr. | .75 | 2.00 |
| R50 Albert Belle | .20 | .50 |
| R51 Matt Williams | .20 | .50 |
| R52 Rondell White | .20 | .50 |
| R53 Raul Mondesi | .20 | .50 |
| R54 Brian Jordan | .20 | .50 |
| R55 Greg Vaughn | .20 | .50 |
| R56 Fred McGriff | .30 | .75 |
| R57 Roberto Alomar | .30 | .75 |
| R58 Dennis Eckersley | .20 | .50 |
| R59 Lee Smith | .20 | .50 |
| R60 Eddie Murray | .50 | 1.25 |
| R61 Henry Rodgers | .20 | .50 |
| R62 Ron Gant | .20 | .50 |
| R63 Larry Walker | .20 | .50 |
| R64 Chad Curtis | .20 | .50 |
| R65 Frank Thomas | .50 | 1.25 |
| R66 Paul O'Neill | .30 | .75 |
| R67 Kevin Seitzer | .20 | .50 |
| R68 Marquis Grissom | .20 | .50 |
| R69 Mark McGwire | 1.50 | 4.00 |
| R70 Travis Fryman | .20 | .50 |
| R71 Andres Galarraga | .20 | .50 |
| R72 Carlos Perez RC | .75 | 2.00 |
| R73 Tyler Green | .20 | .50 |
| R74 Marty Cordova | .20 | .50 |
| R75 Shawn Green | .20 | .50 |
| R76 Vaughn Eshelman | .20 | .50 |
| R77 John Mabry | .20 | .50 |
| R78 Jason Bates | .20 | .50 |
| R79 Jon Nunnally | .20 | .50 |
| R80 Ray Durham | .20 | .50 |
| R81 Edgardo Alfonzo | .20 | .50 |
| R82 Esteban Loaiza | .20 | .50 |
| R83 Hideo Nomo RC | 3.00 | 8.00 |
| R84 Orlando Miller | .20 | .50 |
| R85 Alex Gonzalez | .20 | .50 |
| R86 Mark Grudzielanek RC | 1.25 | 3.00 |
| R87 Julian Tavarez | .20 | .50 |
| R88 Benji Gil | .20 | .50 |
| R89 Quilvio Veras | .20 | .50 |
| R90 Ricky Bottalico | .20 | .50 |
| X1 B.Davis RC/I.Rodriguez | .60 | 1.50 |
| X2 M.Redman RC/M.Ramirez | .60 | 1.50 |

| | | |
|---|---|---|
| X3 R.Taylor RC/D.Sanders | .60 | 1.50 |
| X4 R.Jaroncyk RC/S.Green | .20 | .50 |
| X5 C.Beltran UER/J.Gonz | 3.00 | 8.00 |
| X6 T.McKnight RC/C.Biggio | .20 | .50 |
| X7 M.Barrett RC/T.Fryman | .60 | 1.50 |
| X8 C.Jenkins RC/M.Vaughn | .20 | .50 |
| X9 R.Rivera/F.Thomas | .50 | 1.25 |
| X10 C.Goodwin/K.Lofton | .20 | .50 |
| X11 B.Hunter/T.Gwynn | .30 | .75 |
| X12 T.Greene/K.Griffey Jr. | .50 | 1.25 |
| X13 A.Garcia/M.Williams | .20 | .50 |
| X14 B.Wagner/R.Johnson | .30 | .75 |
| X15 P.Watkins/J.Bagwell | .30 | .75 |

### 1996 Bowman's Best

| | | |
|---|---|---|
| COMPLETE SET (180) | 15.00 | 40.00 |
| 1 Hideo Nomo | .40 | 1.00 |
| 2 Edgar Martinez | .25 | .60 |
| 3 Cal Ripken | 1.25 | 3.00 |
| 4 Wade Boggs | .25 | .60 |
| 5 Cecil Fielder | .15 | .40 |
| 6 Albert Belle | .15 | .40 |
| 7 Chipper Jones | .40 | 1.00 |
| 8 Ryne Sandberg | .60 | 1.50 |
| 9 Tim Salmon | .25 | .60 |
| 10 Barry Bonds | 1.00 | 2.50 |
| 11 Ken Caminiti | .15 | .40 |
| 12 Ron Gant | .15 | .40 |
| 13 Frank Thomas | .40 | 1.00 |
| 14 Dante Bichette | .15 | .40 |
| 15 Jason Kendall | .15 | .40 |
| 16 Mo Vaughn | .15 | .40 |
| 17 Rey Ordonez | .15 | .40 |
| 18 Henry Rodriguez | .15 | .40 |
| 19 Ryan Klesko | .15 | .40 |
| 20 Jeff Bagwell | .25 | .60 |
| 21 Randy Johnson | .40 | 1.00 |
| 22 Jim Edmonds | .15 | .40 |
| 23 Kenny Lofton | .25 | .60 |
| 24 Andy Pettitte | .25 | .60 |
| 25 Brady Anderson | .15 | .40 |
| 26 Mike Piazza | .60 | 1.50 |
| 27 Greg Vaughn | .15 | .40 |
| 28 Joe Carter | .15 | .40 |
| 29 Jason Giambi | .15 | .40 |
| 30 Ivan Rodriguez | .25 | .60 |
| 31 Jeff Conine | .15 | .40 |
| 32 Rafael Palmeiro | .25 | .60 |
| 33 Roger Clemens UER | .75 | 2.00 |
| 34 Chuck Knoblauch | .15 | .40 |
| 35 Reggie Sanders | .15 | .40 |
| 36 Andres Galarraga | .15 | .40 |
| 37 Paul O'Neill | .25 | .60 |
| 38 Tony Gwynn | .50 | 1.25 |
| 39 Paul Wilson | .15 | .40 |
| 40 Garret Anderson | .15 | .40 |
| 41 David Justice | .15 | .40 |
| 42 Eddie Murray | .40 | 1.00 |
| 43 Mike Grace RC | .20 | .50 |
| 44 Marty Cordova | .15 | .40 |
| 45 Kevin Appier | .15 | .40 |
| 46 Raul Mondesi | .15 | .40 |
| 47 Jim Thome | .25 | .60 |
| 48 Sammy Sosa | .40 | 1.00 |
| 49 Craig Biggio | .25 | .60 |
| 50 Marquis Grissom | .15 | .40 |
| 51 Alan Benes | .15 | .40 |
| 52 Manny Ramirez | .25 | .60 |
| 53 Gary Sheffield | .25 | .60 |
| 54 Mike Mussina | .25 | .60 |
| 55 Robin Ventura | .15 | .40 |
| 56 Johnny Damon | .15 | .40 |
| 57 Jose Canseco | .25 | .60 |
| 58 Juan Gonzalez | .15 | .40 |

|  |  | | |
|---|---|---|---|
| ❑ 59 | Tino Martinez | .25 | .60 |
| ❑ 60 | Brian Hunter | .15 | .40 |
| ❑ 61 | Fred McGriff | .25 | .60 |
| ❑ 62 | Jay Buhner | .15 | .40 |
| ❑ 63 | Carlos Delgado | .15 | .40 |
| ❑ 64 | Moises Alou | .15 | .40 |
| ❑ 65 | Roberto Alomar | .25 | .60 |
| ❑ 66 | Barry Larkin | .25 | .60 |
| ❑ 67 | Vinny Castilla | .15 | .40 |
| ❑ 68 | Ray Durham | .15 | .40 |
| ❑ 69 | Travis Fryman | .15 | .40 |
| ❑ 70 | Jason Isringhausen | .15 | .40 |
| ❑ 71 | Ken Griffey Jr. | .60 | 1.50 |
| ❑ 72 | John Smoltz | .25 | .60 |
| ❑ 73 | Matt Williams | .15 | .40 |
| ❑ 74 | Chan Ho Park | .25 | .60 |
| ❑ 75 | Mark McGwire | 1.25 | 3.00 |
| ❑ 76 | Jeffrey Hammonds | .15 | .40 |
| ❑ 77 | Will Clark | .25 | .60 |
| ❑ 78 | Kirby Puckett | .40 | 1.00 |
| ❑ 79 | Derek Jeter | 1.00 | 2.50 |
| ❑ 80 | Derek Bell | .15 | .40 |
| ❑ 81 | Eric Karros | .15 | .40 |
| ❑ 82 | Len Dykstra | .15 | .40 |
| ❑ 83 | Larry Walker | .15 | .40 |
| ❑ 84 | Mark Grudzielanek | .15 | .40 |
| ❑ 85 | Greg Maddux | .60 | 1.50 |
| ❑ 86 | Carlos Baerga | .15 | .40 |
| ❑ 87 | Paul Molitor | .15 | .40 |
| ❑ 88 | John Valentin | .15 | .40 |
| ❑ 89 | Mark Grace | .25 | .60 |
| ❑ 90 | Ray Lankford | .15 | .40 |
| ❑ 91 | Andruw Jones | .60 | 1.50 |
| ❑ 92 | Nomar Garciaparra | .75 | 2.00 |
| ❑ 93 | Alex Ochoa | .15 | .40 |
| ❑ 94 | Derrick Gibson | .15 | .40 |
| ❑ 95 | Jeff D'Amico | .15 | .40 |
| ❑ 96 | Ruben Rivera | .15 | .40 |
| ❑ 97 | Vladimir Guerrero | .75 | 2.00 |
| ❑ 98 | Pokey Reese | .15 | .40 |
| ❑ 99 | Richard Hidalgo | .15 | .40 |
| ❑ 100 | Bartolo Colon | .40 | 1.00 |
| ❑ 101 | Karim Garcia | .15 | .40 |
| ❑ 102 | Ben Davis | .15 | .40 |
| ❑ 103 | Jay Powell | .15 | .40 |
| ❑ 104 | Chris Snopek | .15 | .40 |
| ❑ 105 | Glendon Rusch RC | .40 | 1.00 |
| ❑ 106 | Enrique Wilson | .15 | .40 |
| ❑ 107 | Antonio Alfonseca RC | .40 | 1.00 |
| ❑ 108 | Wilton Guerrero RC | .20 | .50 |
| ❑ 109 | Jose Guillen RC | 1.50 | 4.00 |
| ❑ 110 | Miguel Mejia RC | .20 | .50 |
| ❑ 111 | Jay Payton | .15 | .40 |
| ❑ 112 | Scott Elarton | .15 | .40 |
| ❑ 113 | Brooks Kieschnick | .15 | .40 |
| ❑ 114 | Dustin Hermanson | .15 | .40 |
| ❑ 115 | Roger Cedeno | .15 | .40 |
| ❑ 116 | Matt Wagner | .15 | .40 |
| ❑ 117 | Lee Daniels | .15 | .40 |
| ❑ 118 | Ben Grieve | .15 | .40 |
| ❑ 119 | Ugueth Urbina | .15 | .40 |
| ❑ 120 | Danny Graves | .15 | .40 |
| ❑ 121 | Dan Donato RC | .20 | .50 |
| ❑ 122 | Matt Ruebel RC | .20 | .50 |
| ❑ 123 | Mark Sievert RC | .20 | .50 |
| ❑ 124 | Chris Stynes | .15 | .40 |
| ❑ 125 | Jeff Abbott | .15 | .40 |
| ❑ 126 | Rocky Coppinger RC | .20 | .50 |
| ❑ 127 | Jermaine Dye | .15 | .40 |
| ❑ 128 | Todd Greene | .15 | .40 |
| ❑ 129 | Chris Carpenter | .15 | .40 |
| ❑ 130 | Edgar Renteria | .15 | .40 |
| ❑ 131 | Matt Drews | .15 | .40 |
| ❑ 132 | Edgard Velazquez RC | .20 | .50 |
| ❑ 133 | Casey Whitten RC | .20 | .50 |
| ❑ 134 | Ryan Jones RC | .20 | .50 |
| ❑ 135 | Todd Walker | .15 | .40 |
| ❑ 136 | Geoff Jenkins RC | .75 | 2.00 |
| ❑ 137 | Matt Morris RC | 1.50 | 4.00 |
| ❑ 138 | Richie Sexson RC | .40 | 1.00 |
| ❑ 139 | Todd Dunwoody RC | .20 | .50 |
| ❑ 140 | Gabe Alvarez RC | .20 | .50 |
| ❑ 141 | J.J. Johnson | .15 | .40 |
| ❑ 142 | Shannon Stewart | .15 | .40 |
| ❑ 143 | Brad Fullmer | .15 | .40 |
| ❑ 144 | Julio Santana | .15 | .40 |
| ❑ 145 | Scott Rolen | .40 | 1.00 |
| ❑ 146 | Amaury Telemaco | .15 | .40 |
| ❑ 147 | Trey Beamon | .15 | .40 |
| ❑ 148 | Billy Wagner | .15 | .40 |
| ❑ 149 | Todd Hollandsworth | .15 | .40 |
| ❑ 150 | Doug Million | .15 | .40 |
| ❑ 151 | Javier Valentin RC | .20 | .50 |
| ❑ 152 | Wes Helms RC | .40 | 1.00 |
| ❑ 153 | Jeff Suppan | .15 | .40 |
| ❑ 154 | Luis Castillo RC | .60 | 1.50 |
| ❑ 155 | Bob Abreu | .40 | 1.00 |
| ❑ 156 | Paul Konerko | .40 | 1.00 |
| ❑ 157 | Jamey Wright | .15 | .40 |
| ❑ 158 | Eddie Pearson | .15 | .40 |
| ❑ 159 | Jimmy Haynes | .15 | .40 |
| ❑ 160 | Derrek Lee | .25 | .60 |
| ❑ 161 | Damian Moss | .15 | .40 |
| ❑ 162 | Carlos Guillen RC | 1.00 | 2.50 |
| ❑ 163 | Chris Fussell RC | .20 | .50 |
| ❑ 164 | Mike Sweeney RC | 1.00 | 2.50 |
| ❑ 165 | Donnie Sadler | .15 | .40 |
| ❑ 166 | Desi Relaford | .15 | .40 |
| ❑ 167 | Steve Gibralter | .15 | .40 |
| ❑ 168 | Neifi Perez | .15 | .40 |
| ❑ 169 | Antone Williamson | .15 | .40 |
| ❑ 170 | Marty Janzen RC | .20 | .50 |
| ❑ 171 | Todd Helton | .75 | 2.00 |
| ❑ 172 | Raul Ibanez RC | 2.50 | 6.00 |
| ❑ 173 | Bill Selby | .15 | .40 |
| ❑ 174 | Shane Monahan RC | .20 | .50 |
| ❑ 175 | Robin Jennings | .15 | .40 |
| ❑ 176 | Bobby Chouinard | .15 | .40 |
| ❑ 177 | Einar Diaz | .15 | .40 |
| ❑ 178 | Jason Thompson RC | .15 | .40 |
| ❑ 179 | Rafael Medina RC | .20 | .50 |
| ❑ 180 | Kevin Orie | .15 | .40 |
| ❑ NNO | 1952 Mantle Atomic Ref. | 4.00 | 10.00 |
| ❑ NNO | 1952 Mantle Refractor | 2.00 | 5.00 |
| ❑ NNO | 1952 Mantle Chrome | 1.00 | 2.50 |

## 1997 Bowman's Best

|  |  | | |
|---|---|---|---|
| ❑ | COMPLETE SET (200) | 15.00 | 40.00 |
| ❑ 1 | Ken Griffey Jr. | .60 | 1.50 |
| ❑ 2 | Cecil Fielder | .15 | .40 |
| ❑ 3 | Albert Belle | .15 | .40 |
| ❑ 4 | Todd Hundley | .15 | .40 |
| ❑ 5 | Mike Piazza | .60 | 1.50 |
| ❑ 6 | Matt Williams | .15 | .40 |
| ❑ 7 | Mo Vaughn | .15 | .40 |
| ❑ 8 | Ryne Sandberg | .40 | 1.00 |
| ❑ 9 | Chipper Jones | .40 | 1.00 |
| ❑ 10 | Edgar Martinez | .25 | .60 |
| ❑ 11 | Kenny Lofton | .15 | .40 |
| ❑ 12 | Ron Gant | .15 | .40 |
| ❑ 13 | Moises Alou | .15 | .40 |
| ❑ 14 | Pat Hentgen | .15 | .40 |
| ❑ 15 | Steve Finley | .15 | .40 |
| ❑ 16 | Mark Grace | .25 | .60 |
| ❑ 17 | Jay Buhner | .15 | .40 |
| ❑ 18 | Jeff Conine | .15 | .40 |
| ❑ 19 | Jim Edmonds | .15 | .40 |
| ❑ 20 | Todd Hollandsworth | .15 | .40 |
| ❑ 21 | Andy Pettitte | .25 | .60 |
| ❑ 22 | Jim Thome | .25 | .60 |
| ❑ 23 | Eric Young | .15 | .40 |
| ❑ 24 | Ray Lankford | .15 | .40 |
| ❑ 25 | Marquis Grissom | .15 | .40 |
| ❑ 26 | Tony Clark | .15 | .40 |
| ❑ 27 | Jermaine Allensworth | .15 | .40 |
| ❑ 28 | Ellis Burks | .15 | .40 |
| ❑ 29 | Tony Gwynn | .50 | 1.25 |
| ❑ 30 | Barry Larkin | .25 | .60 |
| ❑ 31 | John Olerud | .15 | .40 |
| ❑ 32 | Mariano Rivera | .40 | 1.00 |
| ❑ 33 | Paul Molitor | .15 | .40 |
| ❑ 34 | Ken Caminiti | .15 | .40 |
| ❑ 35 | Gary Sheffield | .15 | .40 |
| ❑ 36 | Al Martin | .15 | .40 |
| ❑ 37 | John Valentin | .15 | .40 |
| ❑ 38 | Frank Thomas | .40 | 1.00 |
| ❑ 39 | John Jaha | .15 | .40 |
| ❑ 40 | Greg Maddux | .60 | 1.50 |
| ❑ 41 | Alex Fernandez | .15 | .40 |
| ❑ 42 | Dean Palmer | .15 | .40 |
| ❑ 43 | Bernie Williams | .25 | .60 |
| ❑ 44 | Deion Sanders | .25 | .60 |
| ❑ 45 | Mark McGwire | 1.25 | 3.00 |
| ❑ 46 | Brian Jordan | .15 | .40 |
| ❑ 47 | Bernard Gilkey | .15 | .40 |
| ❑ 48 | Will Clark | .25 | .60 |
| ❑ 49 | Kevin Appier | .15 | .40 |
| ❑ 50 | Tom Glavine | .25 | .60 |
| ❑ 51 | Chuck Knoblauch | .15 | .40 |
| ❑ 52 | Rondell White | .15 | .40 |
| ❑ 53 | Greg Vaughn | .15 | .40 |
| ❑ 54 | Mike Mussina | .25 | .60 |
| ❑ 55 | Brian McRae | .15 | .40 |
| ❑ 56 | Chili Davis | .15 | .40 |
| ❑ 57 | Wade Boggs | .25 | .60 |
| ❑ 58 | Jeff Bagwell | .25 | .60 |
| ❑ 59 | Roberto Alomar | .25 | .60 |
| ❑ 60 | Dennis Eckersley | .15 | .40 |
| ❑ 61 | Ryan Klesko | .15 | .40 |
| ❑ 62 | Manny Ramirez | .25 | .60 |
| ❑ 63 | John Wetteland | .15 | .40 |
| ❑ 64 | Cal Ripken | 1.25 | 3.00 |
| ❑ 65 | Edgar Renteria | .15 | .40 |
| ❑ 66 | Tino Martinez | .15 | .40 |
| ❑ 67 | Larry Walker | .15 | .40 |
| ❑ 68 | Gregg Jefferies | .15 | .40 |
| ❑ 69 | Lance Johnson | .15 | .40 |
| ❑ 70 | Carlos Delgado | .15 | .40 |
| ❑ 71 | Craig Biggio | .25 | .60 |
| ❑ 72 | Jose Canseco | .25 | .60 |
| ❑ 73 | Barry Bonds | 1.00 | 2.50 |
| ❑ 74 | Juan Gonzalez | .15 | .40 |
| ❑ 75 | Eric Karros | .15 | .40 |
| ❑ 76 | Reggie Sanders | .15 | .40 |
| ❑ 77 | Robin Ventura | .15 | .40 |
| ❑ 78 | Hideo Nomo | .40 | 1.00 |
| ❑ 79 | David Justice | .15 | .40 |
| ❑ 80 | Vinny Castilla | .15 | .40 |
| ❑ 81 | Travis Fryman | .15 | .40 |
| ❑ 82 | Derek Jeter | 1.00 | 2.50 |
| ❑ 83 | Sammy Sosa | .40 | 1.00 |
| ❑ 84 | Ivan Rodriguez | .25 | .60 |
| ❑ 85 | Rafael Palmeiro | .25 | .60 |
| ❑ 86 | Roger Clemens | .75 | 2.00 |
| ❑ 87 | Jason Giambi | .15 | .40 |
| ❑ 88 | Andres Galarraga | .15 | .40 |
| ❑ 89 | Jermaine Dye | .15 | .40 |
| ❑ 90 | Joe Carter | .15 | .40 |
| ❑ 91 | Brady Anderson | .15 | .40 |
| ❑ 92 | Derek Bell | .15 | .40 |
| ❑ 93 | Randy Johnson | .40 | 1.00 |
| ❑ 94 | Fred McGriff | .25 | .60 |
| ❑ 95 | John Smoltz | .25 | .60 |
| ❑ 96 | Harold Baines | .15 | .40 |
| ❑ 97 | Paul Mondesi | .15 | .40 |
| ❑ 98 | Tim Salmon | .25 | .60 |
| ❑ 99 | Carlos Baerga | .15 | .40 |
| ❑ 100 | Dante Bichette | .15 | .40 |
| ❑ 101 | Vladimir Guerrero | .40 | 1.00 |
| ❑ 102 | Richard Hidalgo | .15 | .40 |
| ❑ 103 | Paul Konerko | .25 | .60 |
| ❑ 104 | Alex Gonzalez RC | .40 | 1.00 |
| ❑ 105 | Jason Dickson | .15 | .40 |
| ❑ 106 | Jose Rosado | .15 | .40 |
| ❑ 107 | Todd Walker | .15 | .40 |
| ❑ 108 | Seth Greisinger RC | .15 | .40 |
| ❑ 109 | Todd Helton | .40 | 1.00 |
| ❑ 110 | Ben Davis | .15 | .40 |
| ❑ 111 | Bartolo Colon | .15 | .40 |
| ❑ 112 | Elieser Marrero | .15 | .40 |
| ❑ 113 | Jeff D'Amico | .15 | .40 |
| ❑ 114 | Miguel Tejada RC | 1.50 | 4.00 |
| ❑ 115 | Darin Erstad | .15 | .40 |
| ❑ 116 | Kris Benson RC | .40 | 1.00 |
| ❑ 117 | Adrian Beltre RC | 1.25 | 3.00 |
| ❑ 118 | Neifi Perez | .15 | .40 |
| ❑ 119 | Pokey Reese | .15 | .40 |
| ❑ 120 | Carl Pavano | .15 | .40 |
| ❑ 121 | Juan Melo | .15 | .40 |
| ❑ 122 | Kevin McGlinchy RC | .15 | .40 |

**1998 Bowman's Best**

| | | |
|---|---|---|
| ☐ 123 Pat Cline | .15 | .40 |
| ☐ 124 Felix Heredia RC | .15 | .40 |
| ☐ 125 Aaron Boone | .15 | .40 |
| ☐ 126 Glendon Rusch | .15 | .40 |
| ☐ 127 Mike Cameron | .15 | .40 |
| ☐ 128 Justin Thompson | .15 | .40 |
| ☐ 129 Chad Hermansen RC | .15 | .40 |
| ☐ 130 Sidney Ponson RC | .40 | 1.00 |
| ☐ 131 Willie Martinez RC | .15 | .40 |
| ☐ 132 Paul Wilder RC | .15 | .40 |
| ☐ 133 Geoff Jenkins | .15 | .40 |
| ☐ 134 Roy Halladay RC | 2.50 | 6.00 |
| ☐ 135 Carlos Guillen | .15 | .40 |
| ☐ 136 Tony Batista | .15 | .40 |
| ☐ 137 Todd Greene | .15 | .40 |
| ☐ 138 Luis Castillo | .15 | .40 |
| ☐ 139 Jimmy Anderson RC | .15 | .40 |
| ☐ 140 Edgard Velazquez | .15 | .40 |
| ☐ 141 Chris Snopek | .15 | .40 |
| ☐ 142 Ruben Rivera | .15 | .40 |
| ☐ 143 Javier Valentin | .15 | .40 |
| ☐ 144 Brian Rose | .15 | .40 |
| ☐ 145 Fernando Tatis RC | .15 | .40 |
| ☐ 146 Dean Crow RC | .15 | .40 |
| ☐ 147 Karim Garcia | .15 | .40 |
| ☐ 148 Dante Powell | .15 | .40 |
| ☐ 149 Hideki Irabu RC | .25 | .60 |
| ☐ 150 Matt Morris | .15 | .40 |
| ☐ 151 Wes Helms | .15 | .40 |
| ☐ 152 Russ Johnson | .15 | .40 |
| ☐ 153 Jarrod Washburn | .15 | .40 |
| ☐ 154 Kerry Wood RC | 1.50 | 4.00 |
| ☐ 155 Joe Fontenot RC | .15 | .40 |
| ☐ 156 Eugene Kingsale | .15 | .40 |
| ☐ 157 Terrence Long | .15 | .40 |
| ☐ 158 Calvin Maduro | .15 | .40 |
| ☐ 159 Jeff Suppan | .15 | .40 |
| ☐ 160 DaRond Stovall | .15 | .40 |
| ☐ 161 Mark Redman | .15 | .40 |
| ☐ 162 Ken Cloude RC | .15 | .40 |
| ☐ 163 Bobby Estalella | .15 | .40 |
| ☐ 164 Abraham Nunez RC | .15 | .40 |
| ☐ 165 Derrick Gibson | .15 | .40 |
| ☐ 166 Mike Drumright RC | .15 | .40 |
| ☐ 167 Katsuhiro Maeda | .15 | .40 |
| ☐ 168 Jeff Liefer | .15 | .40 |
| ☐ 169 Ben Grieve | .15 | .40 |
| ☐ 170 Bob Abreu | .25 | .60 |
| ☐ 171 Shannon Stewart | .15 | .40 |
| ☐ 172 Braden Looper RC | .30 | .75 |
| ☐ 173 Brant Brown | .15 | .40 |
| ☐ 174 Marlon Anderson | .15 | .40 |
| ☐ 175 Brad Fullmer | .15 | .40 |
| ☐ 176 Carlos Beltran | .75 | 2.00 |
| ☐ 177 Nomar Garciaparra | .60 | 1.50 |
| ☐ 178 Derrek Lee | .25 | .60 |
| ☐ 179 Valerio De Los Santos RC | .15 | .40 |
| ☐ 180 Dmitri Young | .15 | .40 |
| ☐ 181 Jamey Wright | .15 | .40 |
| ☐ 182 Hiram Bocachica RC | .15 | .40 |
| ☐ 183 Wilton Guerrero | .15 | .40 |
| ☐ 184 Chris Carpenter | .15 | .40 |
| ☐ 185 Scott Spiezio | .15 | .40 |
| ☐ 186 Andruw Jones | .25 | .60 |
| ☐ 187 Travis Lee RC | .25 | .60 |
| ☐ 188 Jose Cruz Jr. RC | .25 | .60 |
| ☐ 189 Jose Guillen | .15 | .40 |
| ☐ 190 Jeff Abbott | .15 | .40 |
| ☐ 191 Ricky Ledee RC | .25 | .60 |
| ☐ 192 Mike Sweeney | .15 | .40 |
| ☐ 193 Donnie Sadler | .15 | .40 |
| ☐ 194 Scott Rolen | .15 | .40 |
| ☐ 195 Kevin Orie | .15 | .40 |
| ☐ 196 Jason Conti RC | .15 | .40 |
| ☐ 197 Mark Kotsay RC | .60 | 1.50 |
| ☐ 198 Eric Milton RC | .15 | .40 |
| ☐ 199 Russell Branyan | .15 | .40 |
| ☐ 200 Alex Sanchez RC | .25 | .60 |

| | | |
|---|---|---|
| COMPLETE SET (200) | 15.00 | 40.00 |
| ☐ 1 Mark McGwire | 1.00 | 2.50 |
| ☐ 2 Jeromy Burnitz | .15 | .40 |
| ☐ 3 Barry Bonds | 1.00 | 2.50 |
| ☐ 4 Dante Bichette | .15 | .40 |
| ☐ 5 Chipper Jones | .40 | 1.00 |
| ☐ 6 Frank Thomas | .40 | 1.00 |
| ☐ 7 Kevin Brown | .25 | .60 |
| ☐ 8 Juan Gonzalez | .15 | .40 |
| ☐ 9 Jay Buhner | .15 | .40 |
| ☐ 10 Chuck Knoblauch | .15 | .40 |
| ☐ 11 Cal Ripken | 1.25 | 3.00 |
| ☐ 12 Matt Williams | .15 | .40 |
| ☐ 13 Jim Edmonds | .15 | .40 |
| ☐ 14 Manny Ramirez | .25 | .60 |
| ☐ 15 Tony Clark | .15 | .40 |
| ☐ 16 Mo Vaughn | .15 | .40 |
| ☐ 17 Bernie Williams | .25 | .60 |
| ☐ 18 Scott Rolen | .25 | .60 |
| ☐ 19 Gary Sheffield | .15 | .40 |
| ☐ 20 Albert Belle | .15 | .40 |
| ☐ 21 Mike Piazza | .60 | 1.50 |
| ☐ 22 John Olerud | .15 | .40 |
| ☐ 23 Tony Gwynn | .50 | 1.25 |
| ☐ 24 Jay Bell | .15 | .40 |
| ☐ 25 Jose Cruz Jr. | .25 | .60 |
| ☐ 26 Justin Thompson | .15 | .40 |
| ☐ 27 Ken Griffey Jr. | .60 | 1.50 |
| ☐ 28 Sandy Alomar Jr. | .15 | .40 |
| ☐ 29 Mark Grudzielanek | .15 | .40 |
| ☐ 30 Mark Grace | .25 | .60 |
| ☐ 31 Ron Gant | .15 | .40 |
| ☐ 32 Javy Lopez | .15 | .40 |
| ☐ 33 Jeff Bagwell | .25 | .60 |
| ☐ 34 Fred McGriff | .25 | .60 |
| ☐ 35 Rafael Palmeiro | .25 | .60 |
| ☐ 36 Vinny Castilla | .15 | .40 |
| ☐ 37 Andy Benes | .15 | .40 |
| ☐ 38 Pedro Martinez | .25 | .60 |
| ☐ 39 Andy Pettitte | .25 | .60 |
| ☐ 40 Marty Cordova | .15 | .40 |
| ☐ 41 Rusty Greer | .15 | .40 |
| ☐ 42 Kevin Orie | .15 | .40 |
| ☐ 43 Chan Ho Park | .15 | .40 |
| ☐ 44 Ryan Klesko | .15 | .40 |
| ☐ 45 Alex Rodriguez | .60 | 1.50 |
| ☐ 46 Travis Fryman | .15 | .40 |
| ☐ 47 Jeff King | .15 | .40 |
| ☐ 48 Roger Clemens | .75 | 2.00 |
| ☐ 49 Darin Erstad | .15 | .40 |
| ☐ 50 Brady Anderson | .15 | .40 |
| ☐ 51 Jason Kendall | .15 | .40 |
| ☐ 52 John Valentin | .15 | .40 |
| ☐ 53 Ellis Burks | .15 | .40 |
| ☐ 54 Brian Hunter | .15 | .40 |
| ☐ 55 Paul O'Neill | .25 | .60 |
| ☐ 56 Ken Caminiti | .15 | .40 |
| ☐ 57 David Justice | .25 | .60 |
| ☐ 58 Eric Karros | .15 | .40 |
| ☐ 59 Pat Hentgen | .15 | .40 |
| ☐ 60 Greg Maddux | .60 | 1.50 |
| ☐ 61 Craig Biggio | .25 | .60 |
| ☐ 62 Edgar Martinez | .25 | .60 |
| ☐ 63 Mike Mussina | .25 | .60 |
| ☐ 64 Larry Walker | .25 | .60 |
| ☐ 65 Tino Martinez | .25 | .60 |
| ☐ 66 Jim Thome | .25 | .60 |
| ☐ 67 Tom Glavine | .25 | .60 |
| ☐ 68 Raul Mondesi | .15 | .40 |
| ☐ 69 Marquis Grissom | .15 | .40 |
| ☐ 70 Randy Johnson | .40 | 1.00 |
| ☐ 71 Steve Finley | .15 | .40 |

| | | |
|---|---|---|
| ☐ 72 Jose Guillen | .15 | .40 |
| ☐ 73 Nomar Garciaparra | .60 | 1.50 |
| ☐ 74 Wade Boggs | .25 | .60 |
| ☐ 75 Bobby Higginson | .15 | .40 |
| ☐ 76 Robin Ventura | .15 | .40 |
| ☐ 77 Derek Jeter | 1.00 | 2.50 |
| ☐ 78 Andruw Jones | .25 | .60 |
| ☐ 79 Ray Lankford | .15 | .40 |
| ☐ 80 Vladimir Guerrero | .40 | 1.00 |
| ☐ 81 Kenny Lofton | .15 | .40 |
| ☐ 82 Ivan Rodriguez | .25 | .60 |
| ☐ 83 Neifi Perez | .15 | .40 |
| ☐ 84 John Smoltz | .25 | .60 |
| ☐ 85 Tim Salmon | .25 | .60 |
| ☐ 86 Carlos Delgado | .15 | .40 |
| ☐ 87 Sammy Sosa | .40 | 1.00 |
| ☐ 88 Jaret Wright | .25 | .60 |
| ☐ 89 Roberto Alomar | .25 | .60 |
| ☐ 90 Paul Molitor | .25 | .60 |
| ☐ 91 Dean Palmer | .15 | .40 |
| ☐ 92 Barry Larkin | .25 | .60 |
| ☐ 93 Jason Giambi | .15 | .40 |
| ☐ 94 Curt Schilling | .15 | .40 |
| ☐ 95 Eric Young | .15 | .40 |
| ☐ 96 Denny Neagle | .15 | .40 |
| ☐ 97 Moises Alou | .15 | .40 |
| ☐ 98 Livan Hernandez | .15 | .40 |
| ☐ 99 Todd Hundley | .15 | .40 |
| ☐ 100 Andres Galarraga | .15 | .40 |
| ☐ 101 Travis Lee | .15 | .40 |
| ☐ 102 Lance Berkman | .15 | .40 |
| ☐ 103 Orlando Cabrera | .15 | .40 |
| ☐ 104 Mike Lowell RC | 1.25 | 3.00 |
| ☐ 105 Ben Grieve | .25 | .60 |
| ☐ 106 Jae Weong Seo RC | .25 | .60 |
| ☐ 107 Richie Sexson | .15 | .40 |
| ☐ 108 Eli Marrero | .15 | .40 |
| ☐ 109 Aramis Ramirez | .15 | .40 |
| ☐ 110 Paul Konerko | .15 | .40 |
| ☐ 111 Carl Pavano | .15 | .40 |
| ☐ 112 Brad Fullmer | .15 | .40 |
| ☐ 113 Matt Clement | .15 | .40 |
| ☐ 114 Donzell McDonald | .15 | .40 |
| ☐ 115 Todd Helton | .25 | .60 |
| ☐ 116 Mike Caruso | .15 | .40 |
| ☐ 117 Donnie Sadler | .15 | .40 |
| ☐ 118 Bruce Chen | .15 | .40 |
| ☐ 119 Jarrod Washburn | .15 | .40 |
| ☐ 120 Adrian Beltre | .15 | .40 |
| ☐ 121 Ryan Jackson RC | .15 | .40 |
| ☐ 122 Kevin Millar RC | .60 | 1.50 |
| ☐ 123 Corey Koskie RC | .40 | 1.00 |
| ☐ 124 Dermal Brown | .15 | .40 |
| ☐ 125 Kerry Wood | .15 | .40 |
| ☐ 126 Juan Melo | .15 | .40 |
| ☐ 127 Ramon Hernandez | .15 | .40 |
| ☐ 128 Roy Halladay | .15 | .40 |
| ☐ 129 Ron Wright | .15 | .40 |
| ☐ 130 Darnell McDonald RC | .25 | .60 |
| ☐ 131 Odalis Perez RC | .60 | 1.50 |
| ☐ 132 Alex Cora RC | .25 | .60 |
| ☐ 133 Justin Towle | .15 | .40 |
| ☐ 134 Juan Encarnacion | .15 | .40 |
| ☐ 135 Brian Rose | .15 | .40 |
| ☐ 136 Russell Branyan | .15 | .40 |
| ☐ 137 Cesar King RC | .15 | .40 |
| ☐ 138 Ruben Rivera | .15 | .40 |
| ☐ 139 Ricky Ledee | .15 | .40 |
| ☐ 140 Vernon Wells | .15 | .40 |
| ☐ 141 Luis Rivas RC | .40 | 1.00 |
| ☐ 142 Brent Butler | .15 | .40 |
| ☐ 143 Karim Garcia | .15 | .40 |
| ☐ 144 George Lombard | .15 | .40 |
| ☐ 145 Masato Yoshii RC | .25 | .60 |
| ☐ 146 Braden Looper | .15 | .40 |
| ☐ 147 Alex Sanchez | .15 | .40 |
| ☐ 148 Kris Benson | .15 | .40 |
| ☐ 149 Mark Kotsay | .15 | .40 |
| ☐ 150 Richard Hidalgo | .15 | .40 |
| ☐ 151 Scott Elarton | .15 | .40 |
| ☐ 152 Ryan Minor RC | .15 | .40 |
| ☐ 153 Troy Glaus RC | 1.50 | 4.00 |
| ☐ 154 Carlos Lee RC | 1.25 | 3.00 |
| ☐ 155 Michael Coleman | .15 | .40 |
| ☐ 156 Jason Grilli RC | .15 | .40 |
| ☐ 157 Julio Ramirez RC | .15 | .40 |
| ☐ 158 Randy Wolf RC | .25 | .60 |
| ☐ 159 Ryan Brannan | .15 | .40 |

|  |  | | |
|---|------|---|---|
| ☐ 160 | Edgard Clemente | .15 | .40 |
| ☐ 161 | Miguel Tejada | .40 | 1.00 |
| ☐ 162 | Chad Hermansen | .15 | .40 |
| ☐ 163 | Ryan Anderson RC | .15 | .40 |
| ☐ 164 | Ben Petrick | .15 | .40 |
| ☐ 165 | Alex Gonzalez | .15 | .40 |
| ☐ 166 | Ben Davis | .15 | .40 |
| ☐ 167 | John Patterson | .15 | .40 |
| ☐ 168 | Cliff Politte | .15 | .40 |
| ☐ 169 | Randall Simon | .15 | .40 |
| ☐ 170 | Javier Vazquez | .15 | .40 |
| ☐ 171 | Kevin Witt | .15 | .40 |
| ☐ 172 | Geoff Jenkins | .15 | .40 |
| ☐ 173 | David Ortiz | 1.50 | 4.00 |
| ☐ 174 | Derrick Gibson | .15 | .40 |
| ☐ 175 | Abraham Nunez | .15 | .40 |
| ☐ 176 | A.J. Hinch | .15 | .40 |
| ☐ 177 | Ruben Mateo RC | .15 | .40 |
| ☐ 178 | Magglio Ordonez RC | 2.00 | 5.00 |
| ☐ 179 | Todd Dunwoody | .15 | .40 |
| ☐ 180 | Daryle Ward | .15 | .40 |
| ☐ 181 | Mike Kinkade RC | .15 | .40 |
| ☐ 182 | Willie Martinez | .15 | .40 |
| ☐ 183 | Orlando Hernandez RC | .75 | 2.00 |
| ☐ 184 | Eric Milton | .15 | .40 |
| ☐ 185 | Eric Chavez | .15 | .40 |
| ☐ 186 | Damian Jackson | .15 | .40 |
| ☐ 187 | Jim Parque RC | .25 | .60 |
| ☐ 188 | Dan Reichert RC | .25 | .60 |
| ☐ 189 | Mike Drumright | .15 | .40 |
| ☐ 190 | Todd Walker | .15 | .40 |
| ☐ 191 | Shane Monahan | .15 | .40 |
| ☐ 192 | Derrek Lee | .25 | .60 |
| ☐ 193 | Jeremy Giambi RC | .25 | .60 |
| ☐ 194 | Dan McKinley RC | .15 | .40 |
| ☐ 195 | Tony Armas Jr. RC | .25 | .60 |
| ☐ 196 | Matt Anderson RC | .15 | .40 |
| ☐ 197 | Jim Chamblee RC | .15 | .40 |
| ☐ 198 | Francisco Cordero RC | .40 | 1.00 |
| ☐ 199 | Calvin Pickering | .15 | .40 |
| ☐ 200 | Reggie Taylor | .15 | .40 |

## 1999 Bowman's Best

|  |  | | |
|---|------|---|---|
| ☐ | COMPLETE SET (200) | 15.00 | 40.00 |
| ☐ | COMP.SET w/o SP's (150) | 10.00 | 25.00 |
| ☐ | COMMON CARD (1-150) | .15 | .40 |
| ☐ | COMMON ROOKIE (151-200) | .20 | .50 |
| ☐ 1 | Chipper Jones | .40 | 1.00 |
| ☐ 2 | Brian Jordan | .15 | .40 |
| ☐ 3 | David Justice | .15 | .40 |
| ☐ 4 | Jason Kendall | .15 | .40 |
| ☐ 5 | Mo Vaughn | .15 | .40 |
| ☐ 6 | Jim Edmonds | .15 | .40 |
| ☐ 7 | Wade Boggs | .25 | .60 |
| ☐ 8 | Jeromy Burnitz | .15 | .40 |
| ☐ 9 | Todd Hundley | .15 | .40 |
| ☐ 10 | Rondell White | .15 | .40 |
| ☐ 11 | Cliff Floyd | .15 | .40 |
| ☐ 12 | Sean Casey | .15 | .40 |
| ☐ 13 | Bernie Williams | .25 | .60 |
| ☐ 14 | Dante Bichette | .15 | .40 |
| ☐ 15 | Greg Vaughn | .15 | .40 |
| ☐ 16 | Andres Galarraga | .15 | .40 |
| ☐ 17 | Ray Durham | .15 | .40 |
| ☐ 18 | Jim Thome | .25 | .60 |
| ☐ 19 | Gary Sheffield | .25 | .60 |
| ☐ 20 | Frank Thomas | .40 | 1.00 |
| ☐ 21 | Orlando Hernandez | .25 | .60 |
| ☐ 22 | Ivan Rodriguez | .25 | .60 |
| ☐ 23 | Jose Cruz Jr. | .15 | .40 |
| ☐ 24 | Jason Giambi | .15 | .40 |
| ☐ 25 | Craig Biggio | .25 | .60 |
| ☐ 26 | Kerry Wood | .15 | .40 |
| ☐ 27 | Manny Ramirez | .25 | .60 |
| ☐ 28 | Curt Schilling | .15 | .40 |
| ☐ 29 | Mike Mussina | .25 | .60 |
| ☐ 30 | Tim Salmon | .25 | .60 |
| ☐ 31 | Mike Piazza | .60 | 1.50 |
| ☐ 32 | Roberto Alomar | .25 | .60 |
| ☐ 33 | Larry Walker | .15 | .40 |
| ☐ 34 | Barry Larkin | .25 | .60 |
| ☐ 35 | Nomar Garciaparra | .60 | 1.50 |
| ☐ 36 | Paul O'Neill | .25 | .60 |
| ☐ 37 | Todd Walker | .15 | .40 |
| ☐ 38 | Eric Karros | .15 | .40 |
| ☐ 39 | Brad Fullmer | .15 | .40 |
| ☐ 40 | John Olerud | .15 | .40 |
| ☐ 41 | Todd Helton | .25 | .60 |
| ☐ 42 | Raul Mondesi | .15 | .40 |
| ☐ 43 | Jose Canseco | .25 | .60 |
| ☐ 44 | Matt Williams | .15 | .40 |
| ☐ 45 | Ray Lankford | .15 | .40 |
| ☐ 46 | Carlos Delgado | .15 | .40 |
| ☐ 47 | Darin Erstad | .15 | .40 |
| ☐ 48 | Vladimir Guerrero | .40 | 1.00 |
| ☐ 49 | Robin Ventura | .15 | .40 |
| ☐ 50 | Alex Rodriguez | .60 | 1.50 |
| ☐ 51 | Vinny Castilla | .15 | .40 |
| ☐ 52 | Tony Clark | .15 | .40 |
| ☐ 53 | Pedro Martinez | .25 | .60 |
| ☐ 54 | Rafael Palmeiro | .25 | .60 |
| ☐ 55 | Scott Rolen | .25 | .60 |
| ☐ 56 | Tino Martinez | .25 | .60 |
| ☐ 57 | Tony Gwynn | .50 | 1.25 |
| ☐ 58 | Barry Bonds | 1.00 | 2.50 |
| ☐ 59 | Kenny Lofton | .15 | .40 |
| ☐ 60 | Javy Lopez | .15 | .40 |
| ☐ 61 | Mark Grace | .25 | .60 |
| ☐ 62 | Travis Lee | .15 | .40 |
| ☐ 63 | Kevin Brown | .25 | .60 |
| ☐ 64 | Al Leiter | .15 | .40 |
| ☐ 65 | Albert Belle | .15 | .40 |
| ☐ 66 | Sammy Sosa | .40 | 1.00 |
| ☐ 67 | Greg Maddux | .60 | 1.50 |
| ☐ 68 | Mark Kotsay | .15 | .40 |
| ☐ 69 | Dmitri Young | .15 | .40 |
| ☐ 70 | Mark McGwire | 1.00 | 2.50 |
| ☐ 71 | Juan Gonzalez | .15 | .40 |
| ☐ 72 | Andruw Jones | .25 | .60 |
| ☐ 73 | Derek Jeter | 1.00 | 2.50 |
| ☐ 74 | Randy Johnson | .40 | 1.00 |
| ☐ 75 | Cal Ripken | 1.25 | 3.00 |
| ☐ 76 | Shawn Green | .15 | .40 |
| ☐ 77 | Moises Alou | .15 | .40 |
| ☐ 78 | Tom Glavine | .25 | .60 |
| ☐ 79 | Sandy Alomar Jr. | .15 | .40 |
| ☐ 80 | Ken Griffey Jr. | .60 | 1.50 |
| ☐ 81 | Ryan Klesko | .15 | .40 |
| ☐ 82 | Jeff Bagwell | .25 | .60 |
| ☐ 83 | Ben Grieve | .15 | .40 |
| ☐ 84 | John Smoltz | .25 | .60 |
| ☐ 85 | Roger Clemens | .75 | 2.00 |
| ☐ 86 | Ken Griffey Jr. BP | .40 | 1.00 |
| ☐ 87 | Roger Clemens BP | .40 | 1.00 |
| ☐ 88 | Derek Jeter BP | .50 | 1.25 |
| ☐ 89 | Nomar Garciaparra BP | .30 | .75 |
| ☐ 90 | Mark McGwire BP | .50 | 1.25 |
| ☐ 91 | Sammy Sosa BP | .25 | .60 |
| ☐ 92 | Alex Rodriguez BP | .30 | .75 |
| ☐ 93 | Greg Maddux BP | .30 | .75 |
| ☐ 94 | Vladimir Guerrero BP | .25 | .60 |
| ☐ 95 | Chipper Jones BP | .25 | .60 |
| ☐ 96 | Kerry Wood BP | .15 | .40 |
| ☐ 97 | Ben Grieve BP | .15 | .40 |
| ☐ 98 | Tony Gwynn BP | .25 | .60 |
| ☐ 99 | Juan Gonzalez BP | .15 | .40 |
| ☐ 100 | Mike Piazza BP | .30 | .75 |
| ☐ 101 | Eric Chavez | .15 | .40 |
| ☐ 102 | Billy Koch | .15 | .40 |
| ☐ 103 | Dernell Stenson | .15 | .40 |
| ☐ 104 | Marlon Anderson | .15 | .40 |
| ☐ 105 | Ron Belliard | .15 | .40 |
| ☐ 106 | Bruce Chen | .15 | .40 |
| ☐ 107 | Carlos Beltran | .25 | .60 |
| ☐ 108 | Chad Hermansen | .15 | .40 |
| ☐ 109 | Ryan Anderson | .15 | .40 |
| ☐ 110 | Michael Barrett | .15 | .40 |
| ☐ 111 | Matt Clement | .15 | .40 |
| ☐ 112 | Ben Davis | .15 | .40 |
| ☐ 113 | Calvin Pickering | .15 | .40 |
| ☐ 114 | Brad Penny | .15 | .40 |
| ☐ 115 | Paul Konerko | .15 | .40 |
| ☐ 116 | Alex Gonzalez | .15 | .40 |
| ☐ 117 | George Lombard | .15 | .40 |
| ☐ 118 | John Patterson | .15 | .40 |
| ☐ 119 | Rob Bell | .15 | .40 |
| ☐ 120 | Ruben Mateo | .15 | .40 |
| ☐ 121 | Troy Glaus | .25 | .60 |
| ☐ 122 | Ryan Bradley | .15 | .40 |
| ☐ 123 | Carlos Lee | .15 | .40 |
| ☐ 124 | Gabe Kapler | .15 | .40 |
| ☐ 125 | Ramon Hernandez | .15 | .40 |
| ☐ 126 | Carlos Febles | .15 | .40 |
| ☐ 127 | Mitch Meluskey | .15 | .40 |
| ☐ 128 | Michael Cuddyer | .15 | .40 |
| ☐ 129 | Pablo Ozuna | .15 | .40 |
| ☐ 130 | Jayson Werth | .15 | .40 |
| ☐ 131 | Ricky Ledee | .15 | .40 |
| ☐ 132 | Jeremy Giambi | .15 | .40 |
| ☐ 133 | Danny Klassen | .15 | .40 |
| ☐ 134 | Mark DeRosa | .15 | .40 |
| ☐ 135 | Randy Wolf | .15 | .40 |
| ☐ 136 | Roy Halladay | .15 | .40 |
| ☐ 137 | Derrick Gibson | .15 | .40 |
| ☐ 138 | Ben Petrick | .15 | .40 |
| ☐ 139 | Warren Morris | .15 | .40 |
| ☐ 140 | Lance Berkman | .15 | .40 |
| ☐ 141 | Russell Branyan | .15 | .40 |
| ☐ 142 | Adrian Beltre | .15 | .40 |
| ☐ 143 | Juan Encarnacion | .15 | .40 |
| ☐ 144 | Fernando Seguignol | .15 | .40 |
| ☐ 145 | Corey Koskie | .15 | .40 |
| ☐ 146 | Preston Wilson | .15 | .40 |
| ☐ 147 | Homer Bush | .15 | .40 |
| ☐ 148 | Daryle Ward | .15 | .40 |
| ☐ 149 | Joe McElveng RC | .25 | .60 |
| ☐ 150 | Peter Bergeron RC | .20 | .50 |
| ☐ 151 | Pat Burrell RC | 1.25 | 3.00 |
| ☐ 152 | Choo Freeman RC | .25 | .60 |
| ☐ 153 | Matt Belisle RC | .20 | .50 |
| ☐ 154 | Carlos Pena RC | .30 | .75 |
| ☐ 155 | A.J. Burnett RC | .60 | 1.50 |
| ☐ 156 | Doug Mientkiewicz RC | .40 | 1.00 |
| ☐ 157 | Sean Burroughs RC | .40 | 1.00 |
| ☐ 158 | Mike Zywica RC | .20 | .50 |
| ☐ 159 | Corey Patterson RC | .60 | 1.50 |
| ☐ 160 | Austin Kearns RC | 1.25 | 3.00 |
| ☐ 161 | Chip Ambres RC | .20 | .50 |
| ☐ 162 | Kelly Dransfeldt RC | .20 | .50 |
| ☐ 163 | Mike Nannini RC | .20 | .50 |
| ☐ 164 | Mark Mulder RC | 1.00 | 2.50 |
| ☐ 165 | Jason Tyner RC | .20 | .50 |
| ☐ 166 | Bobby Seay RC | .20 | .50 |
| ☐ 167 | Alex Escobar RC | .25 | .60 |
| ☐ 168 | Nick Johnson RC | .60 | 1.50 |
| ☐ 169 | Alfonso Soriano RC | 3.00 | 8.00 |
| ☐ 170 | Clayton Andrews RC | .20 | .50 |
| ☐ 171 | C.C. Sabathia RC | 1.50 | 4.00 |
| ☐ 172 | Matt Holliday RC | 3.00 | 8.00 |
| ☐ 173 | Brad Lidge RC | 1.50 | 4.00 |
| ☐ 174 | Kit Pellow RC | .20 | .50 |
| ☐ 175 | J.M. Gold RC | .20 | .50 |
| ☐ 176 | Roosevelt Brown RC | .20 | .50 |
| ☐ 177 | Eric Valent RC | .25 | .60 |
| ☐ 178 | Adam Everett RC | .40 | 1.00 |
| ☐ 179 | Jorge Toca RC | .25 | .60 |
| ☐ 180 | Matt Roney RC | .20 | .50 |
| ☐ 181 | Andy Brown RC | .20 | .50 |
| ☐ 182 | Phil Norton RC | .20 | .50 |
| ☐ 183 | Mickey Lopez RC | .20 | .50 |
| ☐ 184 | Chris George RC | .20 | .50 |
| ☐ 185 | Arturo McDowell RC | .20 | .50 |
| ☐ 186 | Jose Fernandez RC | .20 | .50 |
| ☐ 187 | Seth Etherton RC | .20 | .50 |
| ☐ 188 | Josh McKinley RC | .20 | .50 |
| ☐ 189 | Nate Cornejo RC | .20 | .50 |
| ☐ 190 | Giuseppe Chiaramonte RC | .20 | .50 |
| ☐ 191 | Mamon Tucker RC | .20 | .50 |
| ☐ 192 | Ryan Mills RC | .20 | .50 |
| ☐ 193 | Chad Moeller RC | .20 | .50 |
| ☐ 194 | Tony Torcato RC | .20 | .50 |
| ☐ 195 | Jeff Winchester RC | .20 | .50 |
| ☐ 196 | Rick Elder RC | .20 | .50 |
| ☐ 197 | Matt Burch RC | .25 | .60 |
| ☐ 198 | Jeff Urban RC | .25 | .60 |
| ☐ 199 | Chris Jones RC | .20 | .50 |
| ☐ 200 | Masao Kida RC | .25 | .60 |

## 2000 Bowman's Best

NOMAR GARCIAPARRA

| | | |
|---|---|---|
| ☐ COMP.SET w/o RC's (150) | 15.00 | 40.00 |
| ☐ COMMON CARD (1-150) | .15 | .40 |
| ☐ COMMON ROOKIE (151-200) | 2.00 | 5.00 |
| ☐ 1 Nomar Garciaparra | .60 | 1.50 |
| ☐ 2 Chipper Jones | .40 | 1.00 |
| ☐ 3 Tony Clark | .15 | .40 |
| ☐ 4 Bernie Williams | .25 | .60 |
| ☐ 5 Barry Bonds | 1.00 | 2.50 |
| ☐ 6 Jermaine Dye | .15 | .40 |
| ☐ 7 John Olerud | .15 | .40 |
| ☐ 8 Mike Hampton | .15 | .40 |
| ☐ 9 Cal Ripken | 1.25 | 3.00 |
| ☐ 10 Jeff Bagwell | .25 | .60 |
| ☐ 11 Troy Glaus | .15 | .40 |
| ☐ 12 J.D. Drew | .15 | .40 |
| ☐ 13 Jeromy Burnitz | .15 | .40 |
| ☐ 14 Carlos Delgado | .15 | .40 |
| ☐ 15 Shawn Green | .15 | .40 |
| ☐ 16 Kevin Millwood | .15 | .40 |
| ☐ 17 Rondell White | .15 | .40 |
| ☐ 18 Scott Rolen | .25 | .60 |
| ☐ 19 Jeff Cirillo | .15 | .40 |
| ☐ 20 Barry Larkin | .25 | .60 |
| ☐ 21 Brian Giles | .15 | .40 |
| ☐ 22 Roger Clemens | .75 | 2.00 |
| ☐ 23 Manny Ramirez | .25 | .60 |
| ☐ 24 Alex Gonzalez | .15 | .40 |
| ☐ 25 Mark Grace | .15 | .40 |
| ☐ 26 Fernando Tatis | .15 | .40 |
| ☐ 27 Randy Johnson | .40 | 1.00 |
| ☐ 28 Roger Cedeno | .15 | .40 |
| ☐ 29 Brian Jordan | .15 | .40 |
| ☐ 30 Kevin Brown | .15 | .40 |
| ☐ 31 Greg Vaughn | .15 | .40 |
| ☐ 32 Roberto Alomar | .25 | .60 |
| ☐ 33 Larry Walker | .15 | .40 |
| ☐ 34 Rafael Palmeiro | .25 | .60 |
| ☐ 35 Curt Schilling | .15 | .40 |
| ☐ 36 Orlando Hernandez | .15 | .40 |
| ☐ 37 Todd Walker | .15 | .40 |
| ☐ 38 Juan Gonzalez | .15 | .40 |
| ☐ 39 Sean Casey | .15 | .40 |
| ☐ 40 Tony Gwynn | .50 | 1.25 |
| ☐ 41 Albert Belle | .15 | .40 |
| ☐ 42 Gary Sheffield | .15 | .40 |
| ☐ 43 Michael Barrett | .15 | .40 |
| ☐ 44 Preston Wilson | .15 | .40 |
| ☐ 45 Jim Thome | .25 | .60 |
| ☐ 46 Shannon Stewart | .15 | .40 |
| ☐ 47 Mo Vaughn | .15 | .40 |
| ☐ 48 Ben Grieve | .15 | .40 |
| ☐ 49 Adrian Beltre | .15 | .40 |
| ☐ 50 Sammy Sosa | .40 | 1.00 |
| ☐ 51 Bob Abreu | .15 | .40 |
| ☐ 52 Edgardo Alfonzo | .15 | .40 |
| ☐ 53 Carlos Febles | .15 | .40 |
| ☐ 54 Frank Thomas | .40 | 1.00 |
| ☐ 55 Alex Rodriguez | .60 | 1.50 |
| ☐ 56 Cliff Floyd | .15 | .40 |
| ☐ 57 Jose Canseco | .25 | .60 |
| ☐ 58 Erubiel Durazo | .15 | .40 |
| ☐ 59 Tim Hudson | .15 | .40 |
| ☐ 60 Craig Biggio | .25 | .60 |
| ☐ 61 Eric Karros | .15 | .40 |
| ☐ 62 Mike Mussina | .25 | .60 |
| ☐ 63 Robin Ventura | .15 | .40 |
| ☐ 64 Carlos Beltran | .15 | .40 |
| ☐ 65 Pedro Martinez | .25 | .60 |
| ☐ 66 Gabe Kapler | .15 | .40 |
| ☐ 67 Jason Kendall | .15 | .40 |
| ☐ 68 Derek Jeter | 1.00 | 2.50 |
| ☐ 69 Magglio Ordonez | .15 | .40 |
| ☐ 70 Mike Piazza | .60 | 1.50 |
| ☐ 71 Mike Lieberthal | .15 | .40 |
| ☐ 72 Andres Galarraga | .15 | .40 |
| ☐ 73 Raul Mondesi | .15 | .40 |
| ☐ 74 Eric Chavez | .15 | .40 |
| ☐ 75 Greg Maddux | .60 | 1.50 |
| ☐ 76 Matt Williams | .15 | .40 |
| ☐ 77 Kris Benson | .15 | .40 |
| ☐ 78 Ivan Rodriguez | .25 | .60 |
| ☐ 79 Pokey Reese | .15 | .40 |
| ☐ 80 Vladimir Guerrero | .40 | 1.00 |
| ☐ 81 Mark McGwire | 1.00 | 2.50 |
| ☐ 82 Vinny Castilla | .15 | .40 |
| ☐ 83 Todd Helton | .25 | .60 |
| ☐ 84 Andruw Jones | .25 | .60 |
| ☐ 85 Ken Griffey Jr. | .60 | 1.50 |
| ☐ 86 Mark McGwire BP | .50 | 1.25 |
| ☐ 87 Derek Jeter BP | .50 | 1.25 |
| ☐ 88 Chipper Jones BP | .25 | .60 |
| ☐ 89 Nomar Garciaparra BP | .40 | 1.00 |
| ☐ 90 Sammy Sosa BP | .25 | .60 |
| ☐ 91 Cal Ripken BP | .60 | 1.50 |
| ☐ 92 Juan Gonzalez BP | .15 | .40 |
| ☐ 93 Alex Rodriguez BP | .40 | 1.00 |
| ☐ 94 Barry Bonds BP | .50 | 1.25 |
| ☐ 95 Sean Casey BP | .15 | .40 |
| ☐ 96 Vladimir Guerrero BP | .25 | .60 |
| ☐ 97 Mike Piazza BP | .40 | 1.00 |
| ☐ 98 Shawn Green BP | .15 | .40 |
| ☐ 99 Jeff Bagwell BP | .15 | .40 |
| ☐ 100 Ken Griffey Jr. BP | .40 | 1.00 |
| ☐ 101 Rick Ankiel | .15 | .40 |
| ☐ 102 John Patterson | .15 | .40 |
| ☐ 103 David Walling | .15 | .40 |
| ☐ 104 Michael Restovich | .15 | .40 |
| ☐ 105 A.J. Burnett | .15 | .40 |
| ☐ 106 Pablo Ozuna | .15 | .40 |
| ☐ 107 Chad Hermansen | .15 | .40 |
| ☐ 108 Choo Freeman | .15 | .40 |
| ☐ 109 Mark Quinn | .15 | .40 |
| ☐ 110 Corey Patterson | .15 | .40 |
| ☐ 111 Ramon Ortiz | .15 | .40 |
| ☐ 112 Vernon Wells | .15 | .40 |
| ☐ 113 Milton Bradley | .15 | .40 |
| ☐ 114 Gookie Dawkins | .15 | .40 |
| ☐ 115 Sean Burroughs | .15 | .40 |
| ☐ 116 Wily Mo Pena | .15 | .40 |
| ☐ 117 Dee Brown | .15 | .40 |
| ☐ 118 C.C. Sabathia | .15 | .40 |
| ☐ 119 Adam Kennedy | .15 | .40 |
| ☐ 120 Octavio Dotel | .15 | .40 |
| ☐ 121 Kip Wells | .15 | .40 |
| ☐ 122 Ben Petrick | .15 | .40 |
| ☐ 123 Mark Mulder | .15 | .40 |
| ☐ 124 Jason Standridge | .15 | .40 |
| ☐ 125 Adam Piatt | .15 | .40 |
| ☐ 126 Steve Lomasney | .15 | .40 |
| ☐ 127 Jayson Werth | .15 | .40 |
| ☐ 128 Alex Escobar | .15 | .40 |
| ☐ 129 Ryan Anderson | .15 | .40 |
| ☐ 130 Adam Dunn | .40 | 1.00 |
| ☐ 131 Ted Lilly | .15 | .40 |
| ☐ 132 Brad Penny | .15 | .40 |
| ☐ 133 Daryle Ward | .15 | .40 |
| ☐ 134 Eric Munson | .15 | .40 |
| ☐ 135 Nick Johnson | .15 | .40 |
| ☐ 136 Jason Jennings | .15 | .40 |
| ☐ 137 Tim Raines Jr. | .15 | .40 |
| ☐ 138 Ruben Mateo | .15 | .40 |
| ☐ 139 Jack Cust | .15 | .40 |
| ☐ 140 Rafael Furcal | .15 | .40 |
| ☐ 141 Eric Gagne | .40 | 1.00 |
| ☐ 142 Tony Armas Jr. | .15 | .40 |
| ☐ 143 Mike Paradis | .15 | .40 |
| ☐ 144 Peter Bergeron | .15 | .40 |
| ☐ 145 Alfonso Soriano | .40 | 1.00 |
| ☐ 146 Josh Hamilton | .50 | 1.50 |
| ☐ 147 Michael Cuddyer | .15 | .40 |
| ☐ 148 Jay Gehrke | .15 | .40 |
| ☐ 149 Josh Girdley | .15 | .40 |
| ☐ 150 Pat Burrell | .15 | .40 |
| ☐ 151 Brett Myers RC | 5.00 | 12.00 |
| ☐ 152 Scott Seabol RC | 2.00 | 5.00 |
| ☐ 153 Keith Reed RC | 2.00 | 5.00 |
| ☐ 154 Francisco Rodriguez RC | 5.00 | 12.00 |
| ☐ 155 Barry Zito RC | 12.50 | 30.00 |
| ☐ 156 Pat Manning RC | 2.00 | 5.00 |
| ☐ 157 Ben Christensen RC | 2.00 | 5.00 |
| ☐ 158 Corey Myers RC | 2.00 | 5.00 |
| ☐ 159 Wascar Serrano RC | 2.00 | 5.00 |
| ☐ 160 Wes Anderson RC | 2.00 | 5.00 |
| ☐ 161 Andy Tracy RC | 2.00 | 5.00 |
| ☐ 162 Cesar Saba RC | 2.00 | 5.00 |
| ☐ 163 Mike Lamb RC | 3.00 | 8.00 |
| ☐ 164 Bobby Bradley RC | 2.00 | 5.00 |
| ☐ 165 Vince Faison RC | 2.00 | 5.00 |
| ☐ 166 Ty Howington RC | 2.00 | 5.00 |
| ☐ 167 Ken Harvey RC | 2.00 | 5.00 |
| ☐ 168 Josh Kalinowski RC | 2.00 | 5.00 |
| ☐ 169 Ruben Salazar RC | 2.00 | 5.00 |
| ☐ 170 Aaron Rowand RC | 4.00 | 10.00 |
| ☐ 171 Ramon Santiago RC | 2.00 | 5.00 |
| ☐ 172 Scott Sobkowiak RC | 2.00 | 5.00 |
| ☐ 173 Lyle Overbay RC | 3.00 | 8.00 |
| ☐ 174 Rico Washington RC | 2.00 | 5.00 |
| ☐ 175 Rick Asadoorian RC | 2.00 | 5.00 |
| ☐ 176 Matt Ginter RC | 2.00 | 5.00 |
| ☐ 177 Jason Stumm RC | 2.00 | 5.00 |
| ☐ 178 B.J. Garbe RC | 2.00 | 5.00 |
| ☐ 179 Mike MacDougal RC | 2.00 | 5.00 |
| ☐ 180 Ryan Christianson RC | 2.00 | 5.00 |
| ☐ 181 Kurt Ainsworth RC | 2.00 | 5.00 |
| ☐ 182 Brad Baisley RC | 2.00 | 5.00 |
| ☐ 183 Ben Broussard RC | 5.00 | 12.00 |
| ☐ 184 Aaron McNeal RC | 2.00 | 5.00 |
| ☐ 185 John Sneed RC | 2.00 | 5.00 |
| ☐ 186 Junior Brignac RC | 2.00 | 5.00 |
| ☐ 187 Chance Caple RC | 2.00 | 5.00 |
| ☐ 188 Scott Downs RC | 2.00 | 5.00 |
| ☐ 189 Matt Cepicky RC | 2.00 | 5.00 |
| ☐ 190 Chin-Feng Chen RC | 15.00 | 30.00 |
| ☐ 191 Johan Santana RC | 30.00 | 60.00 |
| ☐ 192 Brad Baker RC | 2.00 | 5.00 |
| ☐ 193 Jason Repko RC | 3.00 | 8.00 |
| ☐ 194 Craig Dingman RC | 2.00 | 5.00 |
| ☐ 195 Chris Wakeland RC | 2.00 | 5.00 |
| ☐ 196 Rogelio Arias RC | 2.00 | 5.00 |
| ☐ 197 Luis Matos RC | 2.00 | 5.00 |
| ☐ 198 Rob Ramsay RC | 2.00 | 5.00 |
| ☐ 199 Willie Bloomquist RC | 15.00 | 30.00 |
| ☐ 200 Tony Pena Jr. RC | 2.00 | 5.00 |

## 2001 Bowman's Best

ICHIRO SUZUKI

| | | |
|---|---|---|
| ☐ COMP.SET w/o SP's (150) | 20.00 | 50.00 |
| ☐ COMMON CARD (1-150) | .15 | .40 |
| ☐ COMMON CARD (151-200) | 2.00 | 5.00 |
| ☐ 1 Vladimir Guerrero | .40 | 1.00 |
| ☐ 2 Miguel Tejada | .15 | .40 |
| ☐ 3 Geoff Jenkins | .15 | .40 |
| ☐ 4 Jeff Bagwell | .25 | .60 |
| ☐ 5 Todd Helton | .25 | .60 |
| ☐ 6 Ken Griffey Jr. | .60 | 1.50 |
| ☐ 7 Nomar Garciaparra | .60 | 1.50 |
| ☐ 8 Chipper Jones | .40 | 1.00 |
| ☐ 9 Darin Erstad | .15 | .40 |
| ☐ 10 Frank Thomas | .40 | 1.00 |
| ☐ 11 Jim Thome | .25 | .60 |
| ☐ 12 Preston Wilson | .15 | .40 |
| ☐ 13 Kevin Brown | .15 | .40 |
| ☐ 14 Derek Jeter | 1.00 | 2.50 |
| ☐ 15 Scott Rolen | .25 | .60 |
| ☐ 16 Ryan Klesko | .15 | .40 |
| ☐ 17 Jeff Kent | .15 | .40 |
| ☐ 18 Raul Mondesi | .15 | .40 |
| ☐ 19 Greg Vaughn | .15 | .40 |
| ☐ 20 Bernie Williams | .25 | .60 |
| ☐ 21 Mike Piazza | .60 | 1.50 |
| ☐ 22 Richard Hidalgo | .15 | .40 |
| ☐ 23 Dean Palmer | .15 | .40 |
| ☐ 24 Roberto Alomar | .25 | .60 |
| ☐ 25 Sammy Sosa | .40 | 1.00 |
| ☐ 26 Randy Johnson | .40 | 1.00 |

| | | | |
|---|---|---|---|
| 27 Manny Ramirez Sox | .25 | .60 |
| 28 Roger Clemens | .75 | 2.00 |
| 29 Terrence Long | .15 | .40 |
| 30 Jason Kendall | .15 | .40 |
| 31 Richie Sexson | .15 | .40 |
| 32 David Wells | .15 | .40 |
| 33 Andruw Jones | .25 | .60 |
| 34 Pokey Reese | .15 | .40 |
| 35 Juan Gonzalez | .15 | .40 |
| 36 Carlos Beltran | .15 | .40 |
| 37 Shawn Green | .15 | .40 |
| 38 Mariano Rivera | .40 | 1.00 |
| 39 John Olerud | .15 | .40 |
| 40 Jim Edmonds | .15 | .40 |
| 41 Andres Galarraga | .15 | .40 |
| 42 Carlos Delgado | .15 | .40 |
| 43 Kris Benson | .15 | .40 |
| 44 Andy Pettitte | .25 | .60 |
| 45 Jeff Cirillo | .15 | .40 |
| 46 Magglio Ordonez | .15 | .40 |
| 47 Tom Glavine | .15 | .40 |
| 48 Garret Anderson | .15 | .40 |
| 49 Cal Ripken | 1.25 | 3.00 |
| 50 Pedro Martinez | .25 | .60 |
| 51 Barry Bonds | 1.00 | 2.50 |
| 52 Alex Rodriguez | .60 | 1.50 |
| 53 Ben Grieve | .15 | .40 |
| 54 Edgar Martinez | .25 | .60 |
| 55 Jason Giambi | .15 | .40 |
| 56 Jeremy Burnitz | .15 | .40 |
| 57 Mike Mussina | .25 | .60 |
| 58 Moises Alou | .15 | .40 |
| 59 Sean Casey | .15 | .40 |
| 60 Greg Maddux | .60 | 1.50 |
| 61 Tim Hudson | .15 | .40 |
| 62 Mark McGwire | 1.00 | 2.50 |
| 63 Rafael Palmeiro | .25 | .60 |
| 64 Tony Batista | .15 | .40 |
| 65 Kazuhiro Sasaki | .15 | .40 |
| 66 Jorge Posada | .15 | .40 |
| 67 Johnny Damon | .25 | .60 |
| 68 Brian Giles | .15 | .40 |
| 69 Jose Vidro | .15 | .40 |
| 70 Jermaine Dye | .15 | .40 |
| 71 Craig Biggio | .25 | .60 |
| 72 Larry Walker | .15 | .40 |
| 73 Eric Chavez | .15 | .40 |
| 74 David Segui | .15 | .40 |
| 75 Tim Salmon | .25 | .60 |
| 76 Javy Lopez | .15 | .40 |
| 77 Paul Konerko | .15 | .40 |
| 78 Barry Larkin | .25 | .60 |
| 79 Mike Hampton | .15 | .40 |
| 80 Bobby Higginson | .15 | .40 |
| 81 Mark Mulder | .15 | .40 |
| 82 Pat Burrell | .15 | .40 |
| 83 Kerry Wood | .15 | .40 |
| 84 J.T. Snow | .15 | .40 |
| 85 Ivan Rodriguez | .25 | .60 |
| 86 Edgardo Alfonzo | .15 | .40 |
| 87 Orlando Hernandez | .15 | .40 |
| 88 Gary Sheffield | .15 | .40 |
| 89 Mike Sweeney | .15 | .40 |
| 90 Carlos Lee | .15 | .40 |
| 91 Rafael Furcal | .15 | .40 |
| 92 Troy Glaus | .15 | .40 |
| 93 Bartolo Colon | .15 | .40 |
| 94 Cliff Floyd | .15 | .40 |
| 95 Barry Zito | .25 | .60 |
| 96 J.D. Drew | .15 | .40 |
| 97 Eric Karros | .15 | .40 |
| 98 Jose Valentin | .15 | .40 |
| 99 Ellis Burks | .15 | .40 |
| 100 David Justice | .15 | .40 |
| 101 Larry Barnes | .15 | .40 |
| 102 Rod Barajas | .15 | .40 |
| 103 Tony Pena Jr. | .15 | .40 |
| 104 Jerry Hairston Jr. | .15 | .40 |
| 105 Keith Ginter | .15 | .40 |
| 106 Corey Patterson | .15 | .40 |
| 107 Aaron Rowand | .15 | .40 |
| 108 Miguel Olivo | .15 | .40 |
| 109 Gookie Dawkins | .15 | .40 |
| 110 C.C. Sabathia | .15 | .40 |
| 111 Ben Petrick | .15 | .40 |
| 112 Eric Munson | .15 | .40 |
| 113 Ramon Castro | .15 | .40 |
| 114 Alex Escobar | .15 | .40 |

| | | |
|---|---|---|
| 115 Josh Hamilton | .30 | .75 |
| 116 Jason Marquis | .15 | .40 |
| 117 Ben Davis | .15 | .40 |
| 118 Alex Cintron | .15 | .40 |
| 119 Julio Zuleta | .15 | .40 |
| 120 Ben Broussard | .15 | .40 |
| 121 Adam Everett | .15 | .40 |
| 122 Ramon Carvajal RC | .15 | .40 |
| 123 Felipe Lopez | .15 | .40 |
| 124 Alfonso Soriano | .25 | .60 |
| 125 Jayson Werth | .15 | .40 |
| 126 Donzell McDonald | .15 | .40 |
| 127 Jason Hart | .15 | .40 |
| 128 Joe Crede | .40 | 1.00 |
| 129 Sean Burroughs | .15 | .40 |
| 130 Jack Cust | .15 | .40 |
| 131 Corey Smith | .15 | .40 |
| 132 Adrian Gonzalez | .15 | .40 |
| 133 J.R. House | .15 | .40 |
| 134 Steve Lomasney | .15 | .40 |
| 135 Tim Raines Jr. | .15 | .40 |
| 136 Tony Alvarez | .15 | .40 |
| 137 Doug Mientkiewicz | .15 | .40 |
| 138 Rocco Baldelli | .15 | .40 |
| 139 Jason Romano | .15 | .40 |
| 140 Vernon Wells | .15 | .40 |
| 141 Mike Bynum | .15 | .40 |
| 142 Xavier Nady | .15 | .40 |
| 143 Brad Wilkerson | .15 | .40 |
| 144 Ben Diggins | .15 | .40 |
| 145 Aubrey Huff | .15 | .40 |
| 146 Eric Byrnes | .15 | .40 |
| 147 Alex Gordon | .15 | .40 |
| 148 Roy Oswalt | .40 | 1.00 |
| 149 Brian Esposito | .15 | .40 |
| 150 Scott Seabol | .15 | .40 |
| 151 Erick Almonte RC | 2.00 | 5.00 |
| 152 Gary Johnson RC | 2.00 | 5.00 |
| 153 Pedro Liriano RC | 2.00 | 5.00 |
| 154 Matt White RC | 2.00 | 5.00 |
| 155 Luis Montanez RC | 2.50 | 6.00 |
| 156 Brad Cresse | 2.00 | 5.00 |
| 157 Wilson Betemit RC | 3.00 | 8.00 |
| 158 Octavio Martinez RC | 2.00 | 5.00 |
| 159 Adam Pettyjohn RC | 2.00 | 5.00 |
| 160 Corey Spencer RC | 2.00 | 5.00 |
| 161 Mark Burnett RC | 2.00 | 5.00 |
| 162 Ichiro Suzuki RC | 25.00 | 50.00 |
| 163 Alexis Gomez RC | 2.00 | 5.00 |
| 164 Greg Nash RC | 2.00 | 5.00 |
| 165 Roberto Miniel RC | 2.00 | 5.00 |
| 166 Justin Morneau RC | 12.50 | 30.00 |
| 167 Ben Washburn RC | 2.00 | 5.00 |
| 168 Bob Keppel RC | 2.00 | 5.00 |
| 169 Deivi Mendez RC | 2.00 | 5.00 |
| 170 Tsuyoshi Shinjo RC | 3.00 | 8.00 |
| 171 Jared Abruzzo RC | 2.00 | 5.00 |
| 172 Derrick Van Dusen RC | 2.00 | 5.00 |
| 173 Hee Seop Choi RC | 3.00 | 8.00 |
| 174 Albert Pujols RC | 125.00 | 250.00 |
| 175 Travis Hafner RC | 15.00 | 30.00 |
| 176 Ron Davenport RC | 2.00 | 5.00 |
| 177 Luis Torres RC | 2.00 | 5.00 |
| 178 Jake Peavy RC | 10.00 | 25.00 |
| 179 Elvis Corporan RC | 2.00 | 5.00 |
| 180 Dave Krynzal | 2.00 | 5.00 |
| 181 Tony Blanco RC | 2.00 | 5.00 |
| 182 Elpidio Guzman RC | 2.00 | 5.00 |
| 183 Matt Butler RC | 2.00 | 5.00 |
| 184 Joe Thurston RC | 2.00 | 5.00 |
| 185 Andy Beal RC | 2.00 | 5.00 |
| 186 Kevin Nulton RC | 2.00 | 5.00 |
| 187 Sneidear Santos RC | 2.00 | 5.00 |
| 188 Joe Dillon RC | 2.00 | 5.00 |
| 189 Jeremy Blevins RC | 2.00 | 5.00 |
| 190 Chris Amador RC | 2.00 | 5.00 |
| 191 Mark Hendrickson RC | 2.00 | 5.00 |
| 192 Willy Aybar RC | 2.00 | 5.00 |
| 193 Antoine Cameron RC | 2.00 | 5.00 |
| 194 J.J. Johnson RC | 2.00 | 5.00 |
| 195 Ryan Ketchner RC | 2.00 | 5.00 |
| 196 Bjorn Ivy RC | 2.00 | 5.00 |
| 197 Josh Kroeger RC | 2.00 | 5.00 |
| 198 Ty Wigginton RC | 3.00 | 8.00 |
| 199 Stubby Clapp RC | 2.00 | 5.00 |
| 200 Jerrod Riggan RC | 2.00 | 5.00 |

## 2002 Bowman's Best

| | | |
|---|---|---|
| COMP.SET w/o SP's (90) | 40.00 | 100.00 |
| COMMON CARD (1-90) | .30 | .75 |
| COMMON AUTO A (91-180) | 3.00 | 8.00 |
| AUTO GROUP A ODDS:1:3 | | |
| COMMON AUTO B (91-180) | 4.00 | 10.00 |
| AUTO GROUP B ODDS:1:19 | | |
| COMMON BAT (91-180) | 2.00 | 5.00 |
| 91-180 BAT STATED ODDS 1:5 | | |
| 181 ISHII BAT EXCHANGE ODDS 1:131 | | |
| 1 Josh Beckett | .30 | .75 |
| 2 Derek Jeter | 2.00 | 5.00 |
| 3 Alex Rodriguez | 1.25 | 3.00 |
| 4 Miguel Tejada | .30 | .75 |
| 5 Nomar Garciaparra | 1.25 | 3.00 |
| 6 Aramis Ramirez | .30 | .75 |
| 7 Jeremy Giambi | .30 | .75 |
| 8 Bernie Williams | .50 | 1.25 |
| 9 Juan Pierre | .30 | .75 |
| 10 Chipper Jones | .75 | 2.00 |
| 11 Jimmy Rollins | .30 | .75 |
| 12 Alfonso Soriano | .30 | .75 |
| 13 Mark Prior | .50 | 1.25 |
| 14 Paul Konerko | .30 | .75 |
| 15 Tim Hudson | .30 | .75 |
| 16 Doug Mientkiewicz | .30 | .75 |
| 17 Todd Helton | .50 | 1.25 |
| 18 Moises Alou | .30 | .75 |
| 19 Juan Gonzalez | .30 | .75 |
| 20 Jorge Posada | .50 | 1.25 |
| 21 Jeff Kent | .30 | .75 |
| 22 Roger Clemens | 1.50 | 4.00 |
| 23 Phil Nevin | .30 | .75 |
| 24 Brian Giles | .30 | .75 |
| 25 Carlos Delgado | .30 | .75 |
| 26 Jason Giambi | .50 | 1.25 |
| 27 Vladimir Guerrero | .75 | 2.00 |
| 28 Cliff Floyd | .30 | .75 |
| 29 Shea Hillenbrand | .30 | .75 |
| 30 Ken Griffey Jr. | 1.25 | 3.00 |
| 31 Mike Piazza | 1.25 | 3.00 |
| 32 Carlos Pena | .30 | .75 |
| 33 Larry Walker | .30 | .75 |
| 34 Magglio Ordonez | .30 | .75 |
| 35 Mike Mussina | .50 | 1.25 |
| 36 Andruw Jones | .50 | 1.25 |
| 37 Nick Johnson | .30 | .75 |
| 38 Curt Schilling | .30 | .75 |
| 39 Eric Chavez | .30 | .75 |
| 40 Bartolo Colon | .30 | .75 |
| 41 Eric Hinske | .30 | .75 |
| 42 Sean Burroughs | .75 | 2.00 |
| 43 Randy Johnson | .75 | 2.00 |
| 44 Adam Dunn | .30 | .75 |
| 45 Pedro Martinez | .50 | 1.25 |
| 46 Garret Anderson | .30 | .75 |
| 47 Jim Thome | .50 | 1.25 |
| 48 Gary Sheffield | .30 | .75 |
| 49 Tsuyoshi Shinjo | .30 | .75 |
| 50 Albert Pujols | 1.50 | 4.00 |
| 51 Ichiro Suzuki | 1.50 | 4.00 |
| 52 C.C. Sabathia | .30 | .75 |
| 53 Bobby Abreu | .30 | .75 |
| 54 Ivan Rodriguez | .50 | 1.25 |
| 55 J.D. Drew | .50 | 1.25 |
| 56 Jacque Jones | .30 | .75 |
| 57 Jason Kendall | .30 | .75 |
| 58 Javier Vazquez | .30 | .75 |
| 59 Jeff Bagwell | .50 | 1.25 |
| 60 Greg Maddux | 1.25 | 3.00 |
| 61 Jim Edmonds | .50 | 1.25 |
| 62 Hank Blalock | .50 | 1.25 |
| 63 Jose Vidro | .30 | .75 |

|  |  | | |
|---|---|---|---|
| 64 | Kevin Brown | .30 | .75 |
| 65 | Mark Teixeira | .75 | 2.00 |
| 66 | Sammy Sosa | .75 | 2.00 |
| 67 | Lance Berkman | .30 | .75 |
| 68 | Mark Mulder | .30 | .75 |
| 69 | Marty Cordova | .30 | .75 |
| 70 | Frank Thomas | .75 | 2.00 |
| 71 | Mike Cameron | .30 | .75 |
| 72 | Mike Sweeney | .30 | .75 |
| 73 | Barry Bonds | 2.00 | 5.00 |
| 74 | Troy Glaus | .30 | .75 |
| 75 | Barry Zito | .30 | .75 |
| 76 | Pat Burrell | .30 | .75 |
| 77 | Paul LoDuca | .30 | .75 |
| 78 | Rafael Palmeiro | .50 | 1.25 |
| 79 | Austin Kearns | .30 | .75 |
| 80 | Darin Erstad | .30 | .75 |
| 81 | Richie Sexson | .30 | .75 |
| 82 | Roberto Alomar | .50 | 1.25 |
| 83 | Roy Oswalt | .30 | .75 |
| 84 | Ryan Klesko | .30 | .75 |
| 85 | Luis Gonzalez | .30 | .75 |
| 86 | Scott Rolen | .50 | 1.25 |
| 87 | Shannon Stewart | .30 | .75 |
| 88 | Shawn Green | .30 | .75 |
| 89 | Toby Hall | .30 | .75 |
| 90 | Bret Boone | .30 | .75 |
| 91 | Casey Kotchman Bat RC | 3.00 | 8.00 |
| 92 | Jose Valverde AU A RC | 3.00 | 8.00 |
| 93 | Cole Barthel Bat RC | 2.00 | 5.00 |
| 94 | Brad Nelson AU A RC | 3.00 | 8.00 |
| 95 | Mauricio Lara AU A RC | 3.00 | 8.00 |
| 96 | Ryan Gripp Bat RC | 3.00 | 8.00 |
| 97 | Brian West AU A RC | 3.00 | 8.00 |
| 98 | Chris Piersoll AU B RC | 4.00 | 10.00 |
| 99 | Ryan Church AU A RC | 6.00 | 15.00 |
| 100 | Javier Colina AU A | 3.00 | 8.00 |
| 101 | Juan M. Gonzalez AU A RC | 3.00 | 8.00 |
| 102 | Benito Baez AU A | 3.00 | 8.00 |
| 103 | Mike Hill Bat RC | 2.00 | 5.00 |
| 104 | Jason Grove AU B RC | 4.00 | 10.00 |
| 105 | Koyie Hill AU B | 4.00 | 10.00 |
| 106 | Mark Outlaw AU A RC | 3.00 | 8.00 |
| 107 | Jason Bay Bat RC | 6.00 | 15.00 |
| 108 | Jorge Padilla AU A RC | 3.00 | 8.00 |
| 109 | Pete Zamora AU A RC | 3.00 | 8.00 |
| 110 | Joe Mauer AU A RC | 75.00 | 150.00 |
| 111 | Franklyn German AU A RC | 3.00 | 8.00 |
| 112 | Chris Flinn AU A RC | 3.00 | 8.00 |
| 113 | David Wright Bat RC | 50.00 | 80.00 |
| 114 | Anastacio Martinez AU A RC | 3.00 | 8.00 |
| 115 | Nic Jackson Bat RC | 2.00 | 5.00 |
| 116 | Rene Reyes AU A RC | 3.00 | 8.00 |
| 117 | Colin Young AU A RC | 3.00 | 8.00 |
| 118 | Joe Orloski AU A RC | 3.00 | 8.00 |
| 119 | Mike Wilson AU A RC | 3.00 | 8.00 |
| 120 | Rich Thompson AU A RC | 3.00 | 8.00 |
| 121 | Jake Mauer AU B RC | 4.00 | 10.00 |
| 122 | Mario Ramos AU A RC | 3.00 | 8.00 |
| 123 | Doug Sessions AU B RC | 4.00 | 10.00 |
| 124 | Doug Devore Bat RC | 2.00 | 5.00 |
| 125 | Travis Foley AU A RC | 3.00 | 8.00 |
| 126 | Chris Baker AU A RC | 3.00 | 8.00 |
| 127 | Michael Floyd AU A RC | 3.00 | 8.00 |
| 128 | Josh Barfield Bat RC | 4.00 | 10.00 |
| 129 | Jose Bautista Bat RC | 3.00 | 8.00 |
| 130 | Gavin Floyd AU A RC | 6.00 | 15.00 |
| 131 | Jason Botts Bat RC | 2.00 | 5.00 |
| 132 | Clint Nageotte AU A RC | 4.00 | 10.00 |
| 133 | Jesus Cota AU B RC | 2.00 | 5.00 |
| 134 | Ron Calloway Bat RC | 2.00 | 5.00 |
| 135 | Kevin Cash Bat RC | 2.00 | 5.00 |
| 136 | Jonny Gomes AU B RC | 10.00 | 25.00 |
| 137 | Dennis Ulacia AU A RC | 3.00 | 8.00 |
| 138 | Ryan Snare AU A RC | 3.00 | 8.00 |
| 139 | Kevin Deaton AU A RC | 3.00 | 8.00 |
| 140 | Bobby Jenks AU B RC | 6.00 | 15.00 |
| 141 | Casey Kotchman AU A RC | 6.00 | 15.00 |
| 142 | Adam Walker AU A RC | 3.00 | 8.00 |
| 143 | Mike Gonzalez AU A RC | 3.00 | 8.00 |
| 144 | Ruben Gotay Bat RC | 3.00 | 8.00 |
| 145 | Jason Grove Bat RC | 2.00 | 5.00 |
| 146 | Freddy Sanchez AU B RC | 12.50 | 30.00 |
| 147 | Jason Arnold AU B RC | 4.00 | 10.00 |
| 148 | Scott Hairston AU A RC | 4.00 | 10.00 |
| 149 | Jason St. Clair AU B RC | 4.00 | 10.00 |
| 150 | Chris Tritle Bat RC | 2.00 | 5.00 |
| 151 | Edwin Yan Bat RC | 2.00 | 5.00 |
| 152 | Freddy Sanchez Bat RC | 5.00 | 12.00 |
| 153 | Greg Sain Bat RC | 2.00 | 5.00 |
| 154 | Yurendell De Caster Bat RC | 2.00 | 5.00 |
| 155 | Noochie Varner Bat RC | 2.00 | 5.00 |
| 156 | Nelson Castro AU B RC | 4.00 | 10.00 |
| 157 | Randall Shelley Bat RC | 2.00 | 5.00 |
| 158 | Reed Johnson Bat RC | 3.00 | 8.00 |
| 159 | Ryan Raburn AU A RC | 3.00 | 8.00 |
| 160 | Jose Morban Bat RC | 2.00 | 5.00 |
| 161 | Justin Schuda AU A RC | 3.00 | 8.00 |
| 162 | Henry Pichardo AU A RC | 3.00 | 8.00 |
| 163 | Josh Bard AU A RC | 3.00 | 8.00 |
| 164 | Josh Bonifay AU A RC | 3.00 | 8.00 |
| 165 | Brandon League AU B RC | 4.00 | 10.00 |
| 166 | Jor-Jul DePaula AU A RC | 3.00 | 8.00 |
| 167 | Todd Linden AU B RC | 6.00 | 15.00 |
| 168 | Francisco Liriano AU A RC | 30.00 | 60.00 |
| 169 | Chris Snelling AU A RC | 5.00 | 12.00 |
| 170 | Blake McGinley AU A RC | 3.00 | 8.00 |
| 171 | Cody McKay AU A RC | 3.00 | 8.00 |
| 172 | Jason Stanford AU A RC | 3.00 | 8.00 |
| 173 | Lenny Dinardo AU A RC | 3.00 | 8.00 |
| 174 | Greg Montalbano AU A RC | 3.00 | 8.00 |
| 175 | Earl Snyder AU A RC | 3.00 | 8.00 |
| 176 | Justin Huber AU A RC | 6.00 | 15.00 |
| 177 | Chris Narveson AU A RC | 3.00 | 8.00 |
| 178 | Jon Switzer AU A RC | 3.00 | 8.00 |
| 179 | Ronald Acuna AU A RC | 3.00 | 8.00 |
| 180 | Chris Duffy Bat RC | 3.00 | 8.00 |
| 181 | Kazuhisa Ishii Bat RC | 3.00 | 8.00 |

## 2003 Bowman's Best

|  |  | | |
|---|---|---|---|
| | COMP.SET w/o SP's (50) | 15.00 | 40.00 |
| | COMMON CARD | .40 | 1.00 |
| | COMMON AUTO | 3.00 | 8.00 |
| | COMMON BAT | 1.50 | 4.00 |
| AB | Andrew Brown FY AU RC | 4.00 | 10.00 |
| AK | Austin Kearns | .40 | 1.00 |
| AM | Aneudis Mateo FY AU RC | 3.00 | 8.00 |
| AP | Albert Pujols | 1.25 | 3.00 |
| AR | Alex Rodriguez | 1.00 | 2.50 |
| AS | Alfonso Soriano | .40 | 1.00 |
| AW | Aron Weston FY AU RC | 3.00 | 8.00 |
| BB | Bryan Bullington FY AU RC | 3.00 | 8.00 |
| BC | Bernie Castro FY RC | .40 | 1.00 |
| BFL | Branden Florence FY AU RC | 3.00 | 8.00 |
| BFR | Ben Francisco FY AU RC | 3.00 | 8.00 |
| BH | Brendan Harris FY AU RC | 4.00 | 10.00 |
| BJH | Bo Hart FY RC | .40 | 1.00 |
| BK | Beau Kemp FY AU RC | 3.00 | 8.00 |
| BLB | Barry Bonds | 1.50 | 4.00 |
| BM | Brian McCann FY AU RC | 20.00 | 50.00 |
| BNG | Brian Giles | .40 | 1.00 |
| BWB | Bobby Basham FY AU RC | 3.00 | 8.00 |
| BZ | Barry Zito | .40 | 1.00 |
| CAD | Carlos Duran FY AU RC | 3.00 | 8.00 |
| CDC | Chris De La Cruz FY AU RC | 3.00 | 8.00 |
| CJ | Chipper Jones | .60 | 1.50 |
| CJW | C.J. Wilson FY AU | 3.00 | 8.00 |
| CM | Charlie Manning FY AU RC | 3.00 | 8.00 |
| CMS | Curt Schilling | .40 | 1.00 |
| CSS | Cory Stewart FY AU RC | 3.00 | 8.00 |
| CSS | Corey Shafer FY AU RC | 3.00 | 8.00 |
| CW | Chien-Ming Wang FY RC | 5.00 | 12.00 |
| CWA | Chien-Ming Wang FY AU | 150.00 | 250.00 |
| DAM | Dustin Moseley FY AU RC | 3.00 | 8.00 |
| DC | David Cash FY AU RC | 3.00 | 8.00 |
| DH | Dan Haren FY AU RC | 10.00 | 25.00 |
| DJ | Derek Jeter | 1.50 | 4.00 |
| DM | David Martinez FY AU RC | 3.00 | 8.00 |
| DMM | Dust. McGowan FY AU RC | 4.00 | 10.00 |
| DR | Darrell Rasner FY AU RC | 3.00 | 8.00 |
| DW | Doug Waechter FY AU RC | 3.00 | 8.00 |
| DY | Dustin Yount FY RC | .60 | 1.50 |
| ERA | Elizardo Ramirez FY AU RC | 4.00 | 10.00 |
| ERI | Eric Riggs FY AU RC | 4.00 | 10.00 |
| ET | Eider Torres FY AU RC | 3.00 | 8.00 |
| FP | Felix Pie FY AU RC | 12.50 | 30.00 |
| FS | Felix Sanchez FY AU RC | 3.00 | 8.00 |
| FT | Ferdin Tejeda FY AU RC | 3.00 | 8.00 |
| GA | Greg Aquino FY AU RC | 3.00 | 8.00 |
| GB | Greg Blanco FY AU RC | 3.00 | 8.00 |
| GJA | Garret Anderson | .40 | 1.00 |
| GM | Greg Maddux | 1.00 | 2.50 |
| GS | Gary Schneidmiller FY AU RC | 3.00 | 8.00 |
| HR | Hanley Ramirez FY AU RC | 50.00 | 100.00 |
| HRB | Hanley Ramirez FY Bat | 15.00 | 40.00 |
| HT | Haj Turay FY RC | .40 | 1.00 |
| IS | Ichiro Suzuki | 1.25 | 3.00 |
| JB | Jeremy Bonderman FY RC | 1.50 | 4.00 |
| JC | Jose Contreras FY RC | .60 | 1.50 |
| JFK | Jeff Kent | .40 | 1.00 |
| JG | Joey Gomes FY AU RC | 3.00 | 8.00 |
| JGB | Joey Gomes FY Bat | 1.50 | 4.00 |
| JGG | Jason Giambi | .40 | 1.00 |
| JK | Jason Kubel FY AU RC | 10.00 | 25.00 |
| JKB | Jason Kubel FY Bat | 2.50 | 6.00 |
| JLB | Jaime Bubela FY AU RC | 3.00 | 8.00 |
| JM | Jose Morales FY AU RC | 3.00 | 8.00 |
| JMS | Jon-Mark Sprowl FY RC | .40 | 1.00 |
| JRG | Jeremy Griffiths FY AU RC | 3.00 | 8.00 |
| JT | Jim Thome | .40 | 1.00 |
| JV | Joe Valentine FY AU RC | 3.00 | 8.00 |
| JW | Josh Willingham FY AU RC | 8.00 | 20.00 |
| KBS | Kelly Shoppach FY Bat | 2.00 | 5.00 |
| KG | Ken Griffey Jr. | 1.00 | 2.50 |
| KJ | Kade Johnson FY AU RC | 4.00 | 10.00 |
| KS | Kelly Shoppach FY AU RC | 4.00 | 10.00 |
| KY | Kevin Youkilis FY AU RC | 12.50 | 30.00 |
| KYE | Kevin Youkilis FY Bat | 6.00 | 15.00 |
| LB | Lance Berkman | .40 | 1.00 |
| LF | Lew Ford FY AU RC | 4.00 | 10.00 |
| LFJ | Lew Ford FY Bat | 2.00 | 5.00 |
| LW | Larry Walker | .40 | 1.00 |
| MB | Matt Bruback FY RC | .40 | 1.00 |
| MD | Matt Diaz FY RC | .75 | 2.00 |
| MDA | Matt Diaz FY Bat | 8.00 | 20.00 |
| MDH | Matt Hensley FY AU RC | 3.00 | 8.00 |
| MDM | Mark Malaska FY AU RC | 3.00 | 8.00 |
| MH | Michel Hernandez FY AU RC | 3.00 | 8.00 |
| MHI | Michael Hinckley FY AU RC | 4.00 | 10.00 |
| MJP | Mike Piazza | 1.00 | 2.50 |
| MK | Matt Kata FY AU RC | 3.00 | 8.00 |
| MNH | Matt Hagen FY AU RC | 3.00 | 8.00 |
| MO | Mike O'Keefe FY RC | .40 | 1.00 |
| MOR | Magglio Ordonez | .40 | 1.00 |
| MP | Mark Prior | .40 | 1.00 |
| MM | Manny Ramirez | .40 | 1.00 |
| MS | Mike Sweeney | .40 | 1.00 |
| MT | Miguel Tejada | .40 | 1.00 |
| NG | Nomar Garciaparra | 1.00 | 2.50 |
| NL | Nook Logan FY AU RC | 4.00 | 10.00 |
| OC | Ozzie Chavez FY AU RC | 3.00 | 8.00 |
| PB | Pat Burrell | .40 | 1.00 |
| PL | Pete LaForest FY AU RC | 3.00 | 8.00 |
| PM | Pedro Martinez | .40 | 1.00 |
| PR | Prentice Redman FY AU RC | 3.00 | 8.00 |
| RC | Ryan Cameron FY AU RC | 3.00 | 8.00 |
| RD | Rajai Davis FY AU RC | 3.00 | 8.00 |
| RH | Ryan Howard FY AU RC | 125.00 | 250.00 |
| RHJ | Ryan Howard FY Bat | 20.00 | 50.00 |
| RJ | Randy Johnson | .60 | 1.50 |
| RLD | Rajai Davis FY Bat | 1.50 | 4.00 |
| RM | Ramon Nivar-Martinez FY AU RC | .40 | 1.00 |
| RS | Ryan Shealy FY AU RC | 12.50 | 30.00 |
| RSB | Ryan Shealy FY Bat | 5.00 | 12.00 |
| RWH | Robbie Hammock FY AU RC | 3.00 | 8.00 |
| SG | Shawn Green | .40 | 1.00 |
| SS | Sammy Sosa | .60 | 1.50 |
| ST | Scott Tyler FY AU RC | 4.00 | 10.00 |
| SV | Shane Victorino FY RC | 1.50 | 4.00 |
| TA | Tyler Adamczyk FY AU RC | 3.00 | 8.00 |
| TH | Todd Helton | .40 | 1.00 |
| TI | Travis Ishikawa FY AU RC | 3.00 | 8.00 |
| TJ | Tyler Johnson FY AU RC | 3.00 | 8.00 |
| TJB | T.J. Bohn FY RC | .40 | 1.00 |
| TKH | Torii Hunter | .40 | 1.00 |
| TO | Tim Olson FY AU RC | 3.00 | 8.00 |
| TS | T.Story-Harden FY AU RC | 3.00 | 8.00 |
| TSB | T.Story-Harden FY Bat | 1.50 | 4.00 |
| TT | Terry Tiffee FY RC | .40 | 1.00 |

| | | |
|---|---|---|
| VG Vladimir Guerrero | .60 | 1.50 |
| WE Willie Eyre FY AU RC | 3.00 | 8.00 |
| WL Wil Ledezma FY AU RC | 3.00 | 8.00 |
| WRC Roger Clemens | 1.25 | 3.00 |
| NNO B.Bullington Opened Box AU | 10.00 | 25.00 |
| NNO B.Bullington Sealed Box AU | | |

## 2004 Bowman's Best

| | | |
|---|---|---|
| COMP.SET w/o SP'S (50) | 10.00 | 25.00 |
| COMMON CARD | .40 | 1.00 |
| COMMON RC | .40 | 1.00 |
| ONE AUTO PER HOBBY PACK | | |
| ONE RELIC PER BOX-LOADER PACK | | |
| ONE BOX-LOADER PACK PER HOBBY BOX | | |
| STAUFFER BOX RANDOM IN HOBBY CASES | | |
| OVERALL AU PLATE ODDS 1:391 HOBBY | | |
| AU PLATE PRINT RUN 1 SET PER COLOR | | |
| BLACK-CYAN-MAGENTA-YELLOW ISSUED | | |
| NO AU PLATE PRICING DUE TO SCARCITY | | |
| AER Alex Rodriguez | 1.00 | 2.50 |
| AG Adam Greenberg FY AU RC | 4.00 | 10.00 |
| AL Anthony Lerew FY AU RC | .60 | 1.50 |
| AO Akinori Otsuka FY RC | .40 | 1.00 |
| AP Albert Pujols | 1.25 | 3.00 |
| AS Alfonso Soriano | .40 | 1.00 |
| BB Bobby Brownlie FY AU RC | 4.00 | 10.00 |
| BEM Brandon Medders FY AU RC | 3.00 | 8.00 |
| BG Brian Giles | .40 | 1.00 |
| BMS Brad Snyder FY AU RC | 4.00 | 10.00 |
| BP Brayan Pena FY AU RC | 3.00 | 8.00 |
| BS Brad Sullivan FY AU RC | 4.00 | 10.00 |
| CB Carlos Beltran | .40 | 1.00 |
| CD Carlos Delgado | .40 | 1.00 |
| CJ Conor Jackson FY AU RC | 10.00 | 25.00 |
| CLH Chin-Lung Hu FY RC | 1.00 | 2.50 |
| CMA Craig Ansman FY AU RC | 3.00 | 8.00 |
| CMS Curt Schilling | .40 | 1.00 |
| CZ Charlie Zink FY AU RC | 3.00 | 8.00 |
| DA David Aardsma FY AU RC | 4.00 | 10.00 |
| DC Dave Crouthers FY AU RC | 3.00 | 8.00 |
| DDN Dustin Nippert FY AU RC | 4.00 | 10.00 |
| DG Danny Gonzalez FY RC | .40 | 1.00 |
| DK Donald Kelly FY AU RC | 3.00 | 8.00 |
| DL Donald Lewinski FY AU RC | 4.00 | 10.00 |
| DM David Murphy FY AU RC | 6.00 | 15.00 |
| DN Dioner Navarro FY AU RC | 4.00 | 10.00 |
| DS Don Sutton FY AU | 1.00 | 2.50 |
| EA Erick Aybar FY AU RC | 6.00 | 15.00 |
| EC Eric Chavez | .40 | 1.00 |
| EH Estee Harris FY AU RC | 4.00 | 10.00 |
| ES Ervin Santana FY AU RC | 5.00 | 12.00 |
| FH Felix Hernandez FY AU RC | 20.00 | 50.00 |
| GA Garret Anderson | .40 | 1.00 |
| HB Hank Blalock | .40 | 1.00 |
| HM Hector Made FY RC | .60 | 1.50 |
| IR Ivan Rodriguez | .40 | 1.00 |
| IS Ichiro Suzuki | 1.25 | 3.00 |
| JA Joaquin Arias FY AU RC | 6.00 | 10.00 |
| JAV Jose Vidro | .40 | 1.00 |
| JC Juan Cedeno FY AU RC | 3.00 | 8.00 |
| JDS Jason Scrimsfit | .40 | 1.00 |
| JE Jesse English FY AU RC | 3.00 | 8.00 |
| JGG Jason Giambi | .40 | 1.00 |
| JH Jason Hirsh FY AU RC | 10.00 | 25.00 |
| JJC Jon Connolly FY RC | .75 | 2.00 |
| JK Jon Knott FY AU RC | 3.00 | 8.00 |
| JL Josh Labandeira FY AU RC | 3.00 | 8.00 |
| JLO Javy Lopez | .40 | 1.00 |
| JP Jorge Posada | .40 | 1.00 |
| JRG Joey Gathright FY AU RC | .75 | 2.00 |
| JS Jeff Salazar FY AU RC | 4.00 | 10.00 |
| JSZ Jason Szuminski FY AU RC | 3.00 | 8.00 |
| JT Jim Thome | .40 | 1.00 |
| KCY Kory Casto FY AU RC | 6.00 | 15.00 |

| | | |
|---|---|---|
| KK Kevin Kouzmanoff FY AU RC | 15.00 | 40.00 |
| KM Kazuo Matsui FY Uni RC | 2.00 | 5.00 |
| KRK Kody Kirkland FY Bat RC | 2.00 | 5.00 |
| KS Kyle Sleeth FY RC | .60 | 1.50 |
| KT Kazuhito Tadano FY AU RC | 3.00 | 8.00 |
| LK Logan Kensing FY AU RC | 3.00 | 8.00 |
| LM Lastings Milledge FY AU RC | 12.50 | 30.00 |
| LO Lyle Overbay | .40 | 1.00 |
| LTH Luke Hughes FY AU RC | 3.00 | 8.00 |
| LWJ Chipper Jones | .60 | 1.50 |
| MAR Manny Ramirez | .60 | 1.50 |
| MDC Matt Creighton FY AU RC | 3.00 | 8.00 |
| MG Mike Gosling FY AU RC | .40 | 1.00 |
| MJP Mike Piazza | 1.00 | 2.50 |
| MO Magglio Ordonez | .40 | 1.00 |
| MT Miguel Tejada | .40 | 1.00 |
| MTC Miguel Cabrera | .40 | 1.00 |
| MV Merkin Valdez FY AU RC | 3.00 | 8.00 |
| MWP Mark Prior | .40 | 1.00 |
| MY Michael Young | .40 | 1.00 |
| NAG Nomar Garciaparra | .40 | 2.50 |
| NG Nick Gomeault FY RC | .60 | 1.50 |
| NU Nic Ungs FY AU RC | 3.00 | 8.00 |
| OQ Omar Quintanilla FY AU RC | 4.00 | 10.00 |
| PM Paul Maholm FY AU RC | 4.00 | 10.00 |
| PMM Paul McAnulty FY RC | .60 | 1.50 |
| RB Ryan Budde FY AU RC | 3.00 | 8.00 |
| RC Roger Clemens | 1.25 | 3.00 |
| RG Rudy Guillen FY AU RC | 4.00 | 10.00 |
| RJ Randy Johnson | .60 | 1.50 |
| RN Ricky Nolasco FY AU RC | 8.00 | 20.00 |
| RR Ramon Ramirez FY AU RC | 3.00 | 8.00 |
| RS Richie Sexson | .40 | 1.00 |
| RT Rob Tejeda FY AU RC | 6.00 | 15.00 |
| SH Shawn Hill FY AU RC | 3.00 | 8.00 |
| SR Scott Rolen | .40 | 1.00 |
| SS Sammy Sosa | .60 | 1.50 |
| ST Shingo Takatsu FY Jsy RC | 3.00 | 8.00 |
| TB Travis Blackley FY Jsy RC | 2.00 | 5.00 |
| TD Tyler Davidson FY AU RC | 4.00 | 10.00 |
| TJ Terry Jones FY RC | .60 | 1.50 |
| TJS Tim Stauffer FY AU RC | 4.00 | 10.00 |
| TLH Todd Helton | .40 | 1.00 |
| TOH Travis Hanson FY AU RC | 4.00 | 10.00 |
| TRM Tom Mastny FY AU RC | 3.00 | 8.00 |
| TS Todd Self FY RC | .60 | 1.50 |
| VC Vito Chiaravalloti FY AU RC | 3.00 | 8.00 |
| VG Vladimir Guerrero | .60 | 1.50 |
| WM Warner Madrigal FY RC | .40 | 1.00 |
| WS Wardell Starling FY AU RC | 3.00 | 8.00 |
| YM Yadier Molina FY AU RC | .40 | 1.00 |
| ZD Zach Duke FY AU RC | 8.00 | 20.00 |
| NNO Tim Stauffer AU Box/100 | 10.00 | 25.00 |

## 2005 Bowman's Best

| | | |
|---|---|---|
| COMP.SET w/o SP's (100) | 25.00 | 50.00 |
| COMMON CARD (1-30) | .20 | .50 |
| COMMON CARD (31-100) | .20 | .50 |
| COMMON AU (101-143) | 3.00 | 8.00 |
| OVERALL 1-100 PLATE ODDS 1:345 H | | |
| OVERALL 101-143 AU PLATE ODDS 1:805 H | | |
| PLATE PRINT RUN 1 SET PER COLOR | | |
| BLACK-CYAN-MAGENTA-YELLOW ISSUED | | |
| NO PLATE PRICING DUE TO SCARCITY | | |
| 1 Jose Vidro | .20 | .50 |
| 2 Adam Dunn | .20 | .50 |
| 3 Manny Ramirez | .30 | .75 |
| 4 Miguel Tejada | .20 | .50 |
| 5 Ken Griffey Jr. | .75 | 2.00 |
| 6 Pedro Martinez | .30 | .75 |
| 7 Alex Rodriguez | .75 | 2.00 |
| 8 Ichiro Suzuki | 1.00 | 2.50 |
| 9 Alfonso Soriano | .20 | .50 |
| 10 Brian Giles | .20 | .50 |

| | | |
|---|---|---|
| 11 Roger Clemens | .75 | 2.00 |
| 12 Todd Helton | .30 | .75 |
| 13 Ivan Rodriguez | .30 | .75 |
| 14 David Ortiz | .30 | .75 |
| 15 Sammy Sosa | .50 | 1.25 |
| 16 Chipper Jones | .50 | 1.25 |
| 17 Mark Buehrle | .20 | .50 |
| 18 Miguel Cabrera | .30 | .75 |
| 19 Johan Santana | .50 | 1.25 |
| 20 Randy Johnson | .50 | 1.25 |
| 21 Jim Thome | .30 | .75 |
| 22 Vladimir Guerrero | .50 | 1.25 |
| 23 Dontrelle Willis | .20 | .50 |
| 24 Nomar Garciaparra | .50 | 1.25 |
| 25 Barry Bonds | 1.25 | 3.00 |
| 26 Curt Schilling | .30 | .75 |
| 27 Carlos Beltran | .20 | .50 |
| 28 Albert Pujols | 1.00 | 2.50 |
| 29 Mark Prior | .30 | .75 |
| 30 Derek Jeter | 1.00 | 2.50 |
| 31 Ryan Garko RC | 1.25 | 3.00 |
| 32 Eulogio De La Cruz FY RC | .40 | 1.00 |
| 33 Luke Scott FY RC | 1.25 | 3.00 |
| 34 Shane Costa FY RC | .40 | 1.00 |
| 35 Casey McGehee FY RC | .40 | 1.00 |
| 36 Jered Weaver FY RC | 5.00 | 12.00 |
| 37 Kevin Melillo FY RC | .40 | 1.00 |
| 38 D.J. Houlton FY RC | .40 | 1.00 |
| 39 Brandon Moorhead FY RC | .40 | 1.00 |
| 40 Jerry Owens FY RC | .60 | 1.50 |
| 41 Elliot Johnson FY RC | .40 | 1.00 |
| 42 Kevin West FY RC | .40 | 1.00 |
| 43 Hernan Iribarren FY RC | .60 | 1.50 |
| 44 Miguel Montero FY RC | 2.00 | 5.00 |
| 45 Craig Tatum FY RC | .40 | 1.00 |
| 46 Ryan Sweeney FY RC | 1.00 | 2.50 |
| 47 Micah Furtado FY RC | .40 | 1.00 |
| 48 Cody Haerther FY RC | .40 | 1.00 |
| 49 Erick Abreu FY RC | .75 | 2.00 |
| 50 Chuck Tiffany FY RC | .50 | 1.25 |
| 51 Tadahito Iguchi FY RC | 1.50 | 4.00 |
| 52 Frank Diaz FY RC | .40 | 1.00 |
| 53 Erroll Simonitsch FY RC | .40 | 1.00 |
| 54 Wade Robinson FY RC | .40 | 1.00 |
| 55 Adam Boeve FY RC | .40 | 1.00 |
| 56 Steven Bondurant FY RC | .40 | 1.00 |
| 57 Jason Motte FY RC | .40 | 1.00 |
| 58 Juan Senreiso FY RC | .40 | 1.00 |
| 59 Vinny Rottino FY RC | .40 | 1.00 |
| 60 Jai Miller FY RC | .60 | 1.50 |
| 61 Thomas Pauly FY RC | .40 | 1.00 |
| 62 Tony Giarratano FY RC | .40 | 1.00 |
| 63 Alexander Smit FY RC | .40 | 1.00 |
| 64 Keiichi Yabu FY RC | .40 | 1.00 |
| 65 Brian Bannister FY RC | 1.00 | 2.50 |
| 66 Kennard Bibbs FY RC | .40 | 1.00 |
| 67 Anthony Reyes FY RC | 2.00 | 5.00 |
| 68 Thomas Oldham FY RC | .40 | 1.00 |
| 69 Ben Harrison FY RC | .40 | 1.00 |
| 70 Daryl Thompson FY RC | .40 | 1.00 |
| 71 Kevin Collins FY RC | .40 | 1.00 |
| 72 Wes Swackhamer FY RC | .40 | 1.00 |
| 73 Landon Powell FY RC | .60 | 1.50 |
| 74 Matt Brown FY RC | .40 | 1.00 |
| 75 Russ Martin FY RC | 1.25 | 3.00 |
| 76 Nick Touchstone FY RC | .40 | 1.00 |
| 77 Steven White FY RC | .40 | 1.00 |
| 78 Ian Bladergroen FY RC | .60 | 1.50 |
| 79 Sean Marshall FY RC | 1.50 | 4.00 |
| 80 Nick Masset FY RC | .40 | 1.00 |
| 81 Ryan Goleski FY RC | .40 | 1.00 |
| 82 Matt Campbell FY RC | .40 | 1.00 |
| 83 Manny Parra FY RC | 1.00 | 2.50 |
| 84 Melky Cabrera FY RC | 2.00 | 5.00 |
| 85 Ryan Feierabend FY RC | .40 | 1.00 |
| 86 Nate McLouth FY RC | .60 | 1.50 |
| 87 Glen Perkins FY RC | .75 | 2.00 |
| 88 Kila Kaaihue FY RC | 1.00 | 2.50 |
| 89 Dana Eveland FY RC | .60 | 1.50 |
| 90 Tyler Pelland FY RC | .60 | 1.50 |
| 91 Matt Van Der Bosch FY RC | .40 | 1.00 |
| 92 Andy Santana FY RC | .40 | 1.00 |
| 93 Eric Nielsen FY RC | .40 | 1.00 |
| 94 Brendan Ryan FY RC | .40 | 1.00 |
| 95 Ian Kinsler FY RC | 4.00 | 10.00 |
| 96 Matthew Kemp FY RC | 3.00 | 8.00 |
| 97 Stephen Drew FY RC | 4.00 | 10.00 |
| 98 Peeter Ramos FY RC | .40 | 1.00 |

| | | |
|---|---|---|
| 99 Chris Seddon FY RC | .40 | 1.00 |
| 100 Chuck James FY RC | 1.50 | 4.00 |
| 101 Travis Chick FY AU RC | 4.00 | 10.00 |
| 102 Justin Verlander FY AU RC | 10.00 | 25.00 |
| 103 Billy Butler FY AU RC | 20.00 | 50.00 |
| 104 Chris B.Young FY AU RC | 35.00 | 60.00 |
| 105 Jake Postlewait FY AU RC | 3.00 | 8.00 |
| 106 C.J. Smith FY AU RC | 3.00 | 8.00 |
| 107 Mike Rodriguez FY AU RC | 3.00 | 8.00 |
| 108 Philip Humber FY AU RC | 10.00 | 25.00 |
| 109 Jeff Niemann FY AU RC | 3.00 | 8.00 |
| 110 Brian Miller FY AU RC | 3.00 | 8.00 |
| 111 Chris Vines FY AU RC | 3.00 | 8.00 |
| 112 Andy LaRoche FY AU RC | 12.50 | 30.00 |
| 113 Mike Bourn FY AU RC | 4.00 | 10.00 |
| 114 Wlad Balentein FY AU RC | 12.50 | 30.00 |
| 115 Ismael Ramirez FY AU RC | 3.00 | 8.00 |
| 116 Hayden Penn FY AU RC | 4.00 | 10.00 |
| 117 Pedro Lopez FY AU RC | 3.00 | 8.00 |
| 118 Shawn Bowman FY AU RC | 4.00 | 10.00 |
| 119 Chad Orvella FY AU RC | 3.00 | 8.00 |
| 120 Sean Tracey FY AU RC | 3.00 | 8.00 |
| 121 Bobby Livingston FY AU RC | 3.00 | 8.00 |
| 122 Michael Rogers FY AU RC | 3.00 | 8.00 |
| 123 Willy Mota FY AU RC | 3.00 | 8.00 |
| 124 Bran McCarthy FY AU RC | 10.00 | 25.00 |
| 125 Mike Morse FY AU RC | 3.00 | 8.00 |
| 126 Matt Lindstrom FY AU RC | 3.00 | 8.00 |
| 127 Brian Stavisky FY AU RC | 3.00 | 8.00 |
| 128 Richie Gardner FY AU RC | 3.00 | 8.00 |
| 129 Scott Mitchinson FY AU RC | 3.00 | 8.00 |
| 130 Billy McCarthy FY AU RC | 3.00 | 8.00 |
| 131 Brandon Sing FY AU RC | 4.00 | 10.00 |
| 132 Matt Albers FY AU RC | 4.00 | 10.00 |
| 133 George Kottaras FY AU RC | 4.00 | 10.00 |
| 134 Luis Hernandez FY AU RC | 3.00 | 8.00 |
| 135 Hum Sanchez FY AU RC | 12.50 | 30.00 |
| 136 Buck Coats FY AU RC | 3.00 | 8.00 |
| 137 Jon Barratt FY AU RC | 3.00 | 8.00 |
| 138 Raul Tablado FY AU RC | 3.00 | 8.00 |
| 139 Jake Mullinax FY AU RC | 3.00 | 8.00 |
| 140 Edgar Varela FY AU RC | 3.00 | 8.00 |
| 141 Ryan Garko FY AU | 6.00 | 15.00 |
| 142 Nate McLouth FY AU | 10.00 | 25.00 |
| 143 Shane Costa FY AU | 3.00 | 8.00 |

## 2007 Bowman's Best

| | | |
|---|---|---|
| COMP.SET w/o AU (33) | 6.00 | 15.00 |
| COMMON CARD (1-33) | .20 | .50 |
| COMMON AU VET (23-33) | 6.00 | 15.00 |
| AU VET VAR GROUP A 1:15 PACKS | | |
| AU VET VAR GROUP B 1:122 PACKS | | |
| AU VET VAR GROUP C 1:381 PACKS | | |
| AU VET VAR GROUP D 1:113 PACKS | | |
| COMMON AU VET (34-51) | 3.00 | 8.00 |
| AU VET ODDS 1:2 PACKS | | |
| COMMON RC (52-81) | .40 | 1.00 |
| RC ODDS 1:2 PACKS | | |
| RC PRINT RUN 799 SER.#'D SETS | | |
| GU-RC ODDS 1:35 PACKS | | |
| COMMON AU VAR RC (71-81) | 3.00 | 8.00 |
| AU VAR RC ODDS 1:11 PACKS | | |
| COMMON AU RC (82-99) | 3.00 | 8.00 |
| AU RC ODDS 1:2 PACKS | | |
| PRINTING PLATE ODDS 1:88 PACKS | | |
| PRINTING PLATE AU ODDS 1:173 PACKS | | |
| PRINTING PLATE GU ODDS 1:8945 PACKS | | |
| PLATE PRINT RUN 1 SET PER COLOR | | |
| BLACK-CYAN-MAGENTA-YELLOW ISSUED | | |
| NO PLATE PRICING DUE TO SCARCITY | | |
| 1 Jose Reyes | .50 | 1.25 |
| 2 Derek Jeter | 1.25 | 3.00 |
| 3 Vladimir Guerrero | .50 | 1.25 |
| 4 Ichiro Suzuki | .75 | 2.00 |
| 5 Jason Bay | .30 | .75 |
| 6 Joe Mauer | .50 | 1.25 |
| 7 Alfonso Soriano | .20 | .50 |
| 8 David Ortiz | .30 | .75 |
| 9 Andruw Jones | .30 | .75 |
| 10 Roger Clemens | .75 | 2.00 |
| 11 Grady Sizemore | .30 | .75 |
| 12 Magglio Ordonez | .20 | .50 |
| 13 Carl Crawford | .20 | .50 |
| 14 Chase Utley | .50 | 1.25 |
| 15 Mark Teixeira | .30 | .75 |
| 16 Ryan Zimmerman | .50 | 1.25 |
| 17 Ken Griffey Jr. | .75 | 2.00 |
| 18 Derek Lee | .20 | .50 |
| 19 Barry Bonds | 1.00 | 2.50 |
| 20 Chipper Jones | .50 | 1.25 |
| 21 Vernon Wells | .20 | .50 |
| 22 Manny Ramirez | .30 | .75 |
| 23a Alex Rodriguez | .75 | 2.00 |
| 23b Alex Rodriguez AU A | 60.00 | 120.00 |
| 24a Ryan Howard | .75 | 2.00 |
| 24b Ryan Howard AU B | 20.00 | 50.00 |
| 25a Tom Glavine | .30 | .75 |
| 25b Tom Glavine AU D | 15.00 | 40.00 |
| 26a Gary Sheffield | .20 | .50 |
| 26b Gary Sheffield AU A | 8.00 | 20.00 |
| 27a Miguel Cabrera | .30 | .75 |
| 27b Miguel Cabrera AU B | 8.00 | 20.00 |
| 28a Robinson Cano | .30 | .75 |
| 28b Robinson Cano AU A | 10.00 | 25.00 |
| 29a David Wright | .75 | 2.00 |
| 29b David Wright AU A | 20.00 | 50.00 |
| 30a Jim Thome | .30 | .75 |
| 30b Jim Thome AU A | 10.00 | 25.00 |
| 31a Albert Pujols | 1.00 | 2.50 |
| 31b Albert Pujols AU A | 150.00 | 200.00 |
| 32 Jorge Posada | .30 | .75 |
| 33a Brian McCann | .20 | .50 |
| 33b Brian McCann AU A | 6.00 | 15.00 |
| 34 Josh Barfield AU | 3.00 | 8.00 |
| 35 Melky Cabrera AU | 8.00 | 20.00 |
| 36 Bill Hall AU | 3.00 | 8.00 |
| 37 Cole Hamels AU | 10.00 | 25.00 |
| 38 Adam LaRoche AU | 3.00 | 8.00 |
| 39 Matt Holliday AU | 6.00 | 15.00 |
| 40 Jeremy Hermida AU | 3.00 | 8.00 |
| 41 Jonathan Papelbon AU | 8.00 | 20.00 |
| 42 Hanley Ramirez AU | 8.00 | 20.00 |
| 43 Justin Verlander AU | 8.00 | 20.00 |
| 44 Andre Ethier AU | 4.00 | 10.00 |
| 46 Erik Bedard AU | 5.00 | 12.00 |
| 47 Freddy Sanchez AU | 3.00 | 8.00 |
| 48 Adrian Gonzalez AU | 5.00 | 12.00 |
| 49 Russell Martin AU | 5.00 | 12.00 |
| 50 B.J. Upton AU | 4.00 | 10.00 |
| 51 Prince Fielder AU | 10.00 | 25.00 |
| 52 Tony Abreu RC | 1.00 | 2.50 |
| 53 Ben Francisco (RC) | .40 | 1.00 |
| 54 Billy Butler (RC) | .60 | 1.50 |
| 55 Philip Hughes (RC) | 2.00 | 5.00 |
| 56 Josh Fields (RC) | .40 | 1.00 |
| 57 Carlos Gomez RC | .60 | 1.50 |
| 58 Akinori Iwamura RC | .40 | 1.00 |
| 59 Matt Brown RC | .40 | 1.00 |
| 60 Jesus Flores RC | .40 | 1.00 |
| 61 Mike Fontenot (RC) | .40 | 1.00 |
| 62 Ryan Feierabend (RC) | .40 | 1.00 |
| 63 Miguel Montero (RC) | .40 | 1.00 |
| 64a Daisuke Matsuzaka RC | 3.00 | 8.00 |
| 64b Daisuke Matsuzaka Jsy | 5.00 | 12.00 |
| 66 Kei Igawa RC | 1.00 | 2.50 |
| 66 Shawn Riggans (RC) | .40 | 1.00 |
| 67 Masumi Kuwata RC | 3.00 | 8.00 |
| 68 Kevin Slowey (RC) | 1.00 | 2.50 |
| 69 Josh Hamilton (RC) | 1.00 | 2.50 |
| 70 Curtis Thigpen (RC) | .40 | 1.00 |
| 71a Justin Upton RC | 2.50 | 6.00 |
| 71b Justin Upton RC | 20.00 | 50.00 |
| 72a Delmon Young (RC) | .60 | 1.50 |
| 72b Delmon Young RC | 8.00 | 20.00 |
| 73a Brandon Wood (RC) | .40 | 1.00 |
| 73b Brandon Wood AU | 6.00 | 15.00 |
| 74a Felix Pie AU | .50 | 1.25 |
| 74b Felix Pie AU | 4.00 | 10.00 |
| 75a Alex Gordon RC | 1.50 | 4.00 |
| 75b Alex Gordon AU | 12.50 | 30.00 |
| 76a Mark Reynolds AU | 2.50 | 6.00 |
| 76b Mark Reynolds AU | 12.50 | 30.00 |
| 77a Tyler Clippard (RC) | .60 | 1.50 |
| 77b Tyler Clippard AU | 4.00 | 10.00 |
| 78a Adam Lind (RC) | .40 | 1.00 |
| 78b Adam Lind AU | 3.00 | 8.00 |
| 79a Hunter Pence AU | 2.00 | 5.00 |
| 79b Hunter Pence AU | 20.00 | 50.00 |
| 80 Micah Owings AU | .40 | 1.00 |
| 81a Jarrod Saltalamacchia (RC) | .60 | 1.50 |
| 81b Jarrod Saltalamacchia AU | 6.00 | 15.00 |
| 82 Kevin Kouzmanoff AU (RC) | 3.00 | 8.00 |
| 83 Glen Perkins AU (RC) | 3.00 | 8.00 |
| 84 Michael Bourn AU (RC) | 3.00 | 8.00 |
| 85 Andrew Miller AU RC | 6.00 | 15.00 |
| 86 Fred Lewis AU RC | 3.00 | 8.00 |
| 88 Joba Chamberlain AU RC | 20.00 | 50.00 |
| 89 Hideki Okajima AU RC | 10.00 | 25.00 |
| 90 TroyTulowitzki AU (RC) | 10.00 | 25.00 |
| 91 Ryan Sweeney AU (RC) | 3.00 | 8.00 |
| 92 Matt Lindstrom AU (RC) | 3.00 | 8.00 |
| 93 Tim Lincecum AU RC | 50.00 | 100.00 |
| 94 Homer Bailey AU (RC) | 4.00 | 10.00 |
| 95 Matt DeSalvo AU RC | 3.00 | 8.00 |
| 96 Alejandro De Aza AU RC | 3.00 | 8.00 |
| 97 Ryan Braun AU (RC) | 20.00 | 50.00 |
| 99 Andy LaRoche AU (RC) | 6.00 | 15.00 |

## 1914 Cracker Jack

| | | |
|---|---|---|
| 1 Otto Knabe | 300.00 | 600.00 |
| 2 Frank Baker | 750.00 | 1500.00 |
| 3 Joe Tinker | 1000.00 | 2000.00 |
| 4 Larry Doyle | 200.00 | 400.00 |
| 5 Ward Miller | 200.00 | 400.00 |
| 6 Eddie Plank | 750.00 | 1500.00 |
| 7 Eddie Collins | 750.00 | 1500.00 |
| 8 Rube Oldring | 200.00 | 400.00 |
| 9 Artie Hoffman | 200.00 | 400.00 |
| 10 John McInnis | 200.00 | 400.00 |
| 11 George Stovall | 200.00 | 400.00 |
| 12 Connie Mack MG | 750.00 | 1500.00 |
| 13 Art Wilson | 200.00 | 400.00 |
| 14 Sam Crawford | 750.00 | 1500.00 |
| 15 Reb Russell | 200.00 | 400.00 |
| 16 Howie Camnitz | 200.00 | 400.00 |
| 17 Roger Bresnahan | 750.00 | 1500.00 |
| 18 Johnny Evers | 750.00 | 1500.00 |
| 19 Chief Bender | 750.00 | 1500.00 |
| 20 Cy Faikenberg | 200.00 | 400.00 |
| 21 Heinie Zimmerman | 200.00 | 400.00 |
| 22 Joe Wood | 1250.00 | 2500.00 |
| 23 Charles Comiskey | 750.00 | 1500.00 |
| 24 George Mullen | 200.00 | 400.00 |
| 25 Michael Simon | 200.00 | 400.00 |
| 26 James Scott | 200.00 | 400.00 |
| 27 Bill Carrigan | 200.00 | 400.00 |
| 28 Jack Barry | 200.00 | 400.00 |
| 29 Vean Gregg | 200.00 | 400.00 |
| 30 Ty Cobb | 5000.00 | 10000.00 |
| 31 Heinie Wagner | 200.00 | 400.00 |
| 32 Mordecai Brown | 750.00 | 1500.00 |
| 33 Amos Strunk | 200.00 | 400.00 |
| 34 Ira Thomas | 300.00 | 600.00 |
| 35 Harry Hooper | 750.00 | 1500.00 |
| 36 Ed Walsh | 750.00 | 1500.00 |
| 37 Grover C. Alexander | 2000.00 | 4000.00 |
| 38 Red Dooin | 200.00 | 400.00 |
| 39 Chick Gandil | 750.00 | 1500.00 |
| 40 Jimmy Austin | 200.00 | 400.00 |
| 41 Tommy Leach | 200.00 | 400.00 |
| 42 Al Bridwell | 200.00 | 400.00 |
| 43 Rube Marquard | 750.00 | 1500.00 |
| 44 Jeff (Charles) Tesreau | 200.00 | 400.00 |
| 45 Fred Luderus | 200.00 | 400.00 |
| 46 Bob Groom | 200.00 | 400.00 |
| 47 Josh Devore | 200.00 | 400.00 |

|  |  | | |
|---|---|---|---|
| 48 | Harry Lord | 300.00 | 600.00 |
| 49 | John Miller | 200.00 | 400.00 |
| 50 | John Hummell | 200.00 | 400.00 |
| 51 | Nap Rucker | 200.00 | 400.00 |
| 52 | Zach Wheat | 750.00 | 1500.00 |
| 53 | Otto Miller | 200.00 | 400.00 |
| 54 | Marty O'Toole | 200.00 | 400.00 |
| 55 | Dick Hoblitzel | 200.00 | 400.00 |
| 56 | Clyde Milan | 200.00 | 400.00 |
| 57 | Walter Johnson | 2000.00 | 4000.00 |
| 58 | Wally Schang | 200.00 | 400.00 |
| 59 | Harry Gessler | 200.00 | 400.00 |
| 60 | Rollie Zeider | 300.00 | 600.00 |
| 61 | Ray Schalk | 1000.00 | 2000.00 |
| 62 | Jay Cashion | 300.00 | 600.00 |
| 63 | Babe Adams | 200.00 | 400.00 |
| 64 | Jimmy Archer | 200.00 | 400.00 |
| 65 | Tris Speaker | 750.00 | 1500.00 |
| 66 | Napoleon Lajoie | 1250.00 | 2500.00 |
| 67 | Otis Crandall | 200.00 | 400.00 |
| 68 | Honus Wagner | 4000.00 | 8000.00 |
| 69 | John McGraw | 750.00 | 1500.00 |
| 70 | Fred Clarke | 600.00 | 1200.00 |
| 71 | Chief Meyers | 200.00 | 400.00 |
| 72 | John Boehling | 200.00 | 400.00 |
| 73 | Max Carey | 750.00 | 1500.00 |
| 74 | Frank Owens | 200.00 | 400.00 |
| 75 | Miller Huggins | 600.00 | 1200.00 |
| 76 | Claude Hendrix | 200.00 | 400.00 |
| 77 | Hughie Jennings MG | 750.00 | 1500.00 |
| 78 | Fred Merkle | 200.00 | 400.00 |
| 79 | Ping Bodie | 200.00 | 400.00 |
| 80 | Ed Ruelbach | 200.00 | 400.00 |
| 81 | Jim Delahanty | 200.00 | 400.00 |
| 82 | Gavvy Cravath | 200.00 | 400.00 |
| 83 | Russ Ford | 200.00 | 400.00 |
| 84 | Elmer E. Knetzer | 200.00 | 400.00 |
| 85 | Buck Herzog | 200.00 | 400.00 |
| 86 | Burt Shotton | 200.00 | 400.00 |
| 87 | Forrest Cady | 200.00 | 400.00 |
| 88 | Christy Mathewson | 20000.00 | 50000.00 |
| 89 | Lawrence Cheney | 200.00 | 400.00 |
| 90 | Frank Smith | 200.00 | 400.00 |
| 91 | Roger Peckinpaugh | 200.00 | 400.00 |
| 92 | Al Demaree | 200.00 | 400.00 |
| 93 | Del Pratt | 200.00 | 400.00 |
| 94 | Eddie Cicotte | 750.00 | 1500.00 |
| 95 | Ray Keating | 200.00 | 400.00 |
| 96 | Beals Becker | 200.00 | 400.00 |
| 97 | John (Rube) Benton | 200.00 | 400.00 |
| 98 | Frank LaPorte | 200.00 | 400.00 |
| 99 | Frank Chance | 2000.00 | 4000.00 |
| 100 | Thomas Seaton | 200.00 | 400.00 |
| 101 | Frank Schulte | 200.00 | 400.00 |
| 102 | Ray Fisher | 200.00 | 400.00 |
| 103 | Joe Jackson | 10000.00 | 20000.00 |
| 104 | Vic Saier | 200.00 | 400.00 |
| 105 | James Lavender | 200.00 | 400.00 |
| 106 | Joe Birmingham | 200.00 | 400.00 |
| 107 | Tom Downey | 200.00 | 400.00 |
| 108 | Sherry Magee | 200.00 | 400.00 |
| 109 | Fred Blanding | 200.00 | 400.00 |
| 110 | Bob Bescher | 200.00 | 400.00 |
| 111 | John Callahan | 200.00 | 400.00 |
| 112 | Ed Sweeney | 200.00 | 400.00 |
| 113 | George Suggs | 200.00 | 400.00 |
| 114 | George Moriarity | 200.00 | 400.00 |
| 115 | Addison Brennan | 200.00 | 400.00 |
| 116 | Rollie Zeider | 200.00 | 400.00 |
| 117 | Ted Easterly | 200.00 | 400.00 |
| 118 | Ed Konetchy | 200.00 | 400.00 |
| 119 | George Perring | 200.00 | 400.00 |
| 120 | Mike Doolan | 200.00 | 400.00 |
| 121 | Hub Perdue | 200.00 | 400.00 |
| 122 | Owen Bush | 200.00 | 400.00 |
| 123 | Slim Sallee | 200.00 | 400.00 |
| 124 | Earl Moore | 200.00 | 400.00 |
| 125 | Bert Niehoff | 200.00 | 400.00 |
| 126 | Walter Blair | 200.00 | 400.00 |
| 127 | Butch Schmidt | 200.00 | 400.00 |
| 128 | Steve Evans | 200.00 | 400.00 |
| 129 | Ray Caldwell | 200.00 | 400.00 |
| 130 | Ivy Wingo | 200.00 | 400.00 |
| 131 | Geo. Baumgardner | 200.00 | 400.00 |
| 132 | Les Nunamaker | 200.00 | 400.00 |
| 133 | Branch Rickey MG | 1000.00 | 2000.00 |
| 134 | Armando Marsans | 200.00 | 400.00 |
| 135 | Bill Killefer | 200.00 | 400.00 |
| 136 | Rabbit Maranville | 750.00 | 1500.00 |
| 137 | William Rariden | 200.00 | 400.00 |
| 138 | Hank Gowdy | 200.00 | 400.00 |
| 139 | Rebel Oakes | 200.00 | 400.00 |
| 140 | Danny Murphy | 200.00 | 400.00 |
| 141 | Cy Barger | 200.00 | 400.00 |
| 142 | Eugene Packard | 200.00 | 400.00 |
| 143 | Jake Daubert | 200.00 | 400.00 |
| 144 | James C. Walsh | 200.00 | 400.00 |

## 1915 Cracker Jack

|  |  | | |
|---|---|---|---|
| | COMPLETE SET (176) | 35000.00 | 70000.00 |
| | COMMON CARD (1-144) | 100.00 | 200.00 |
| | COMMON CARD (145-176) | 125.00 | 250.00 |
| 1 | Otto Knabe | 300.00 | 600.00 |
| 2 | Frank Baker | 500.00 | 1000.00 |
| 3 | Joe Tinker | 400.00 | 800.00 |
| 4 | Larry Doyle | 125.00 | 250.00 |
| 5 | Ward Miller | 100.00 | 200.00 |
| 6 | Eddie Plank | 750.00 | 1500.00 |
| 7 | Eddie Collins | 400.00 | 800.00 |
| 8 | Rube Oldring | 100.00 | 200.00 |
| 9 | Artie Hoffman | 100.00 | 200.00 |
| 10 | John McInnis | 100.00 | 200.00 |
| 11 | George Stovall | 100.00 | 200.00 |
| 12 | Connie Mack MG | 400.00 | 800.00 |
| 13 | Art Wilson | 100.00 | 200.00 |
| 14 | Sam Crawford | 400.00 | 800.00 |
| 15 | Reb Russell | 100.00 | 200.00 |
| 16 | Howie Camnitz | 100.00 | 200.00 |
| 17 | Roger Bresnahan | 300.00 | 600.00 |
| 18 | Johnny Evers | 400.00 | 800.00 |
| 19 | Chief Bender | 400.00 | 800.00 |
| 20 | Cy Falkenberg | 100.00 | 200.00 |
| 21 | Heinie Zimmerman | 100.00 | 200.00 |
| 22 | Joe Wood | 500.00 | 1000.00 |
| 23 | Charles Comiskey | 500.00 | 1000.00 |
| 24 | George Mullen | 100.00 | 200.00 |
| 25 | Michael Simon | 100.00 | 200.00 |
| 26 | James Scott | 100.00 | 200.00 |
| 27 | Bill Carrigan | 100.00 | 200.00 |
| 28 | Jack Barry | 125.00 | 250.00 |
| 29 | Vean Gregg | 100.00 | 200.00 |
| 30 | Ty Cobb | 3000.00 | 6000.00 |
| 31 | Heinie Wagner | 100.00 | 200.00 |
| 32 | Mordecai Brown | 500.00 | 1000.00 |
| 33 | Amos Strunk | 100.00 | 200.00 |
| 34 | Ira Thomas | 100.00 | 200.00 |
| 35 | Harry Hooper | 300.00 | 600.00 |
| 36 | Ed Walsh | 400.00 | 800.00 |
| 37 | Grover C. Alexander | 1000.00 | 2000.00 |
| 38 | Red Dooin | 100.00 | 200.00 |
| 39 | Chick Gandil | 400.00 | 800.00 |
| 40 | Jimmy Austin | 125.00 | 250.00 |
| 41 | Tommy Leach | 100.00 | 200.00 |
| 42 | Al Bridwell | 100.00 | 200.00 |
| 43 | Rube Marquard | 300.00 | 600.00 |
| 44 | Jeff (Charles) Tesreau | 100.00 | 200.00 |
| 45 | Fred Luderus | 100.00 | 200.00 |
| 46 | Bob Groom | 100.00 | 200.00 |
| 47 | Josh Devore | 100.00 | 200.00 |
| 48 | John O'Neill | 100.00 | 200.00 |
| 49 | John Miller | 100.00 | 200.00 |
| 50 | John Hummell | 100.00 | 200.00 |
| 51 | Nap Rucker | 100.00 | 200.00 |
| 52 | Zach Wheat | 300.00 | 600.00 |
| 53 | Otto Miller | 100.00 | 200.00 |
| 54 | Marty O'Toole | 100.00 | 200.00 |
| 55 | Dick Hoblitzel | 100.00 | 200.00 |
| 56 | Clyde Milan | 100.00 | 200.00 |
| 57 | Walter Johnson | 1500.00 | 3000.00 |
| 58 | Wally Schang | 100.00 | 200.00 |
| 59 | Harry Gessler | 100.00 | 200.00 |
| 60 | Oscar Dugey | 100.00 | 200.00 |
| 61 | Ray Schalk | 400.00 | 800.00 |
| 62 | Willie Mitchell | 100.00 | 200.00 |
| 63 | Babe Adams | 100.00 | 200.00 |
| 64 | Jimmy Archer | 100.00 | 200.00 |
| 65 | Tris Speaker | 750.00 | 1500.00 |
| 66 | Napoleon Lajoie | 600.00 | 1200.00 |
| 67 | Otis Crandall | 100.00 | 200.00 |
| 68 | Honus Wagner | 3000.00 | 6000.00 |
| 69 | John McGraw MG | 400.00 | 800.00 |
| 70 | Fred Clarke | 300.00 | 600.00 |
| 71 | Chief Meyers | 125.00 | 250.00 |
| 72 | John Boehling | 100.00 | 200.00 |
| 73 | Max Carey | 400.00 | 800.00 |
| 74 | Frank Owens | 100.00 | 200.00 |
| 75 | Miller Huggins | 300.00 | 600.00 |
| 76 | Claude Hendrix | 100.00 | 200.00 |
| 77 | Hughie Jennings MG | 300.00 | 600.00 |
| 78 | Fred Merkle | 100.00 | 200.00 |
| 79 | Ping Bodie | 100.00 | 200.00 |
| 80 | Ed Ruelbach | 100.00 | 200.00 |
| 81 | Jim Delahanty | 100.00 | 200.00 |
| 82 | Gavvy Cravath | 100.00 | 200.00 |
| 83 | Russ Ford | 100.00 | 200.00 |
| 84 | Elmer E. Knetzer | 100.00 | 200.00 |
| 85 | Buck Herzog | 100.00 | 200.00 |
| 86 | Burt Shotton | 100.00 | 200.00 |
| 87 | Forrest Cady | 100.00 | 200.00 |
| 88 | Christy Mathewson | 1750.00 | 3500.00 |
| 89 | Lawrence Cheney | 100.00 | 200.00 |
| 90 | Frank Smith | 100.00 | 200.00 |
| 91 | Roger Peckinpaugh | 100.00 | 200.00 |
| 92 | Al Demaree | 100.00 | 200.00 |
| 93 | Del Pratt | 125.00 | 250.00 |
| 94 | Eddie Cicotte | 450.00 | 900.00 |
| 95 | Ray Keating | 100.00 | 200.00 |
| 96 | Beals Becker | 125.00 | 250.00 |
| 97 | John (Rube) Benton | 100.00 | 200.00 |
| 98 | Frank LaPorte | 100.00 | 200.00 |
| 99 | Hal Chase | 250.00 | 500.00 |
| 100 | Thomas Seaton | 100.00 | 200.00 |
| 101 | Frank Schulte | 100.00 | 200.00 |
| 102 | Ray Fisher | 100.00 | 200.00 |
| 103 | Joe Jackson | 7500.00 | 15000.00 |
| 104 | Vic Saier | 100.00 | 200.00 |
| 105 | James Lavender | 100.00 | 200.00 |
| 106 | Joe Birmingham | 100.00 | 200.00 |
| 107 | Thomas Downey | 100.00 | 200.00 |
| 108 | Sherry Magee | 100.00 | 200.00 |
| 109 | Fred Blanding | 100.00 | 200.00 |
| 110 | Bob Bescher | 100.00 | 200.00 |
| 111 | Herbie Moran | 100.00 | 200.00 |
| 112 | Ed Sweeney | 100.00 | 200.00 |
| 113 | George Suggs | 100.00 | 200.00 |
| 114 | George Moriarity | 100.00 | 200.00 |
| 115 | Addison Brennan | 100.00 | 200.00 |
| 116 | Rollie Zeider | 100.00 | 200.00 |
| 117 | Ted Easterly | 100.00 | 200.00 |
| 118 | Ed Konetchy | 100.00 | 200.00 |
| 119 | George Perring | 100.00 | 200.00 |
| 120 | Mike Doolan | 100.00 | 200.00 |
| 121 | Hub Perdue | 100.00 | 200.00 |
| 122 | Owen Bush | 100.00 | 200.00 |
| 123 | Slim Sallee | 100.00 | 200.00 |
| 124 | Earl Moore | 100.00 | 200.00 |
| 125 | Bert Niehoff | 100.00 | 200.00 |
| 126 | Walter Blair | 100.00 | 200.00 |
| 127 | Butch Schmidt | 100.00 | 200.00 |
| 128 | Steve Evans | 100.00 | 200.00 |
| 129 | Ray Caldwell | 100.00 | 200.00 |
| 130 | Ivy Wingo | 100.00 | 200.00 |
| 131 | Geo. Baumgardner | 100.00 | 200.00 |
| 132 | Les Nunamaker | 100.00 | 200.00 |
| 133 | Branch Rickey MG | 600.00 | 1200.00 |
| 134 | Armando Marsans | 125.00 | 250.00 |
| 135 | William Killefer | 100.00 | 200.00 |
| 136 | Rabbit Maranville | 300.00 | 600.00 |
| 137 | William Rariden | 100.00 | 200.00 |
| 138 | Hank Gowdy | 100.00 | 200.00 |
| 139 | Rebel Oakes | 100.00 | 200.00 |
| 140 | Danny Murphy | 100.00 | 200.00 |
| 141 | Cy Barger | 100.00 | 200.00 |
| 142 | Eugene Packard | 100.00 | 200.00 |
| 143 | Jake Daubert | 100.00 | 200.00 |
| 144 | James C. Walsh | 100.00 | 200.00 |
| 145 | Ted Cather | 125.00 | 250.00 |
| 146 | George Tyler | 125.00 | 250.00 |
| 147 | Lee Magee | 125.00 | 250.00 |
| 148 | Owen Wilson | 125.00 | 250.00 |

| | | |
|---|---|---|
| □ 149 Hal Janvrin | 125.00 | 250.00 |
| □ 150 Doc Johnston | 125.00 | 250.00 |
| □ 151 George Whitted | 125.00 | 250.00 |
| □ 152 George McQuillen | 125.00 | 250.00 |
| □ 153 Bill James | 125.00 | 250.00 |
| □ 154 Dick Rudolph | 125.00 | 250.00 |
| □ 155 Joe Connolly | 125.00 | 250.00 |
| □ 156 Jean Dubuc | 125.00 | 250.00 |
| □ 157 George Kaiserling | 125.00 | 250.00 |
| □ 158 Fritz Maisel | 125.00 | 250.00 |
| □ 159 Heinie Groh | 125.00 | 250.00 |
| □ 160 Benny Kauff | 125.00 | 250.00 |
| □ 161 Edd Roush | 500.00 | 1000.00 |
| □ 162 George Stallings MG | 125.00 | 250.00 |
| □ 163 Bert Whaling | 125.00 | 250.00 |
| □ 164 Bob Shawkey | 125.00 | 250.00 |
| □ 165 Eddie Murphy | 125.00 | 250.00 |
| □ 166 Joe Bush | 125.00 | 250.00 |
| □ 167 Clark Griffith | 300.00 | 600.00 |
| □ 168 Vin Campbell | 125.00 | 250.00 |
| □ 169 Raymond Collins | 125.00 | 250.00 |
| □ 170 Hans Lobert | 125.00 | 250.00 |
| □ 171 Earl Hamilton | 125.00 | 250.00 |
| □ 172 Erskine Mayer | 125.00 | 250.00 |
| □ 173 Tilly Walker | 125.00 | 250.00 |
| □ 174 Robert Veach | 125.00 | 250.00 |
| □ 175 Joseph Benz | 125.00 | 250.00 |
| □ 176 Hippo Vaughn | 300.00 | 600.00 |

## 1981 Donruss

| | | |
|---|---|---|
| □ COMPLETE SET (605) | 20.00 | 50.00 |
| □ 1 Ozzie Smith | 1.25 | 3.00 |
| □ 2 Rollie Fingers | .08 | .25 |
| □ 3 Rick Wise | .02 | .10 |
| □ 4 Gene Richards | .02 | .10 |
| □ 5 Alan Trammell | .20 | .50 |
| □ 6 Tom Brookens | .02 | .10 |
| □ 7A Duffy Dyer P1 | .08 | .25 |
| □ 7B Duffy Dyer P2 | .02 | .10 |
| □ 8 Mark Fidrych | .08 | .25 |
| □ 9 Dave Rozema | .02 | .10 |
| □ 10 Ricky Peters RC | .02 | .10 |
| □ 11 Mike Schmidt | 1.00 | 2.50 |
| □ 12 Willie Stargell | .20 | .50 |
| □ 13 Tim Foli | .02 | .10 |
| □ 14 Manny Sanguillen | .08 | .25 |
| □ 15 Grant Jackson | .02 | .10 |
| □ 16 Eddie Solomon | .02 | .10 |
| □ 17 Omar Moreno | .02 | .10 |
| □ 18 Joe Morgan | .20 | .50 |
| □ 19 Rafael Landestoy | .02 | .10 |
| □ 20 Bruce Bochy | .02 | .10 |
| □ 21 Joe Sambito | .02 | .10 |
| □ 22 Manny Trillo | .02 | .10 |
| □ 23A Dave Smith P1 | .20 | .50 |
| □ 23B Dave Smith P2 RC | .02 | .10 |
| □ 24 Terry Puhl | .02 | .10 |
| □ 25 Bump Wills | .02 | .10 |
| □ 26A John Ellis P1 ERR | .20 | .50 |
| □ 26B John Ellis P2 COR | .08 | .25 |
| □ 27 Jim Kern | .02 | .10 |
| □ 28 Richie Zisk | .02 | .10 |
| □ 29 John Mayberry | .02 | .10 |
| □ 30 Bob Davis | .02 | .10 |
| □ 31 Jackson Todd | .02 | .10 |
| □ 32 Alvis Woods | .02 | .10 |
| □ 33 Steve Carlton | .20 | .50 |
| □ 34 Lee Mazzilli | .08 | .25 |
| □ 35 John Stearns | .02 | .10 |
| □ 36 Roy Lee Jackson RC | .02 | .10 |
| □ 37 Mike Scott | .08 | .25 |
| □ 38 Lamar Johnson | .02 | .10 |
| □ 39 Kevin Bell | .02 | .10 |
| □ 40 Ed Farmer | .02 | .10 |
| □ 41 Ross Baumgarten | .02 | .10 |
| □ 42 Leo Sutherland RC | .02 | .10 |
| □ 43 Dan Meyer | .02 | .10 |
| □ 44 Ron Reed | .02 | .10 |
| □ 45 Mario Mendoza | .02 | .10 |
| □ 46 Rick Honeycutt | .02 | .10 |
| □ 47 Glenn Abbott | .02 | .10 |
| □ 48 Leon Roberts | .02 | .10 |
| □ 49 Rod Carew | .20 | .50 |
| □ 50 Bert Campaneris | .08 | .25 |
| □ 51A Tom Donahue P1 ERR | .08 | .25 |
| □ 51B Tom Donohue P2 RC | .02 | .10 |
| □ 52 Dave Frost | .02 | .10 |
| □ 53 Ed Halicki | .02 | .10 |
| □ 54 Dan Ford | .02 | .10 |
| □ 55 Garry Maddox | .02 | .10 |
| □ 56A Steve Garvey P1 25HR | .08 | .25 |
| □ 56B Steve Garvey P2 21HR | .08 | .25 |
| □ 57 Bill Russell | .08 | .25 |
| □ 58 Don Sutton | .08 | .25 |
| □ 59 Reggie Smith | .08 | .25 |
| □ 60 Rick Monday | .08 | .25 |
| □ 61 Ray Knight | .08 | .25 |
| □ 62 Johnny Bench | .40 | 1.00 |
| □ 63 Mario Soto | .08 | .25 |
| □ 64 Doug Bair | .02 | .10 |
| □ 65 George Foster | .08 | .25 |
| □ 66 Jeff Burroughs | .08 | .25 |
| □ 67 Keith Hernandez | .08 | .25 |
| □ 68 Tom Herr | .02 | .10 |
| □ 69 Bob Forsch | .02 | .10 |
| □ 70 John Fulgham | .02 | .10 |
| □ 71A Bobby Bonds P1 ERR | .40 | 1.00 |
| □ 71B Bobby Bonds P2 COR | .20 | .50 |
| □ 72A Rennie Stennett P1 | .08 | .25 |
| □ 72B Rennie Stennett P2 | .02 | .10 |
| □ 73 Joe Strain | .02 | .10 |
| □ 74 Ed Whitson | .02 | .10 |
| □ 75 Tom Griffin | .02 | .10 |
| □ 76 Billy North | .02 | .10 |
| □ 77 Gene Garber | .02 | .10 |
| □ 78 Mike Hargrove | .02 | .10 |
| □ 79 Dave Rosello | .02 | .10 |
| □ 80 Ron Hassey | .02 | .10 |
| □ 81 Sid Monge | .02 | .10 |
| □ 82A Joe Charboneau P1 | .40 | 1.00 |
| □ 82B Joe Charboneau P2 RC | .40 | 1.00 |
| □ 83 Cecil Cooper | .08 | .25 |
| □ 84 Sal Bando | .08 | .25 |
| □ 85 Moose Haas | .02 | .10 |
| □ 86 Mike Caldwell | .02 | .10 |
| □ 87A Larry Hisle P1 | .08 | .25 |
| □ 87B Larry Hisle P2 | .02 | .10 |
| □ 88 Luis Gomez | .02 | .10 |
| □ 89 Larry Parrish | .02 | .10 |
| □ 90 Gary Carter | .20 | .50 |
| □ 91 Bill Gullickson RC | .20 | .50 |
| □ 92 Fred Norman | .02 | .10 |
| □ 93 Tommy Hutton | .02 | .10 |
| □ 94 Carl Yastrzemski | .60 | 1.50 |
| □ 95 Glenn Hoffman RC | .02 | .10 |
| □ 96 Dennis Eckersley | .20 | .50 |
| □ 97A Tom Burgmeier P1 | .08 | .25 |
| □ 97B Tom Burgmeier P2 | .02 | .10 |
| □ 98 Win Remmerswaal RC | .02 | .10 |
| □ 99 Bob Horner | .08 | .25 |
| □ 100 George Brett | 1.00 | 2.50 |
| □ 101 Dave Chalk | .02 | .10 |
| □ 102 Dennis Leonard | .02 | .10 |
| □ 103 Renie Martin | .02 | .10 |
| □ 104 Amos Otis | .08 | .25 |
| □ 105 Graig Nettles | .08 | .25 |
| □ 106 Eric Soderholm | .02 | .10 |
| □ 107 Tommy John | .08 | .25 |
| □ 108 Tom Underwood | .02 | .10 |
| □ 109 Lou Piniella | .08 | .25 |
| □ 110 Mickey Klutts | .02 | .10 |
| □ 111 Bobby Murcer | .08 | .25 |
| □ 112 Eddie Murray | .60 | 1.50 |
| □ 113 Rick Dempsey | .02 | .10 |
| □ 114 Scott McGregor | .02 | .10 |
| □ 115 Ken Singleton | .08 | .25 |
| □ 116 Gary Roenicke | .02 | .10 |
| □ 117 Dave Revering | .02 | .10 |
| □ 118 Mike Norris | .02 | .10 |
| □ 119 Rickey Henderson | 2.50 | 6.00 |
| □ 120 Mike Heath | .02 | .10 |
| □ 121 Dave Cash | .02 | .10 |
| □ 122 Randy Jones | .08 | .25 |
| □ 123 Eric Rasmussen | .02 | .10 |
| □ 124 Jerry Mumphrey | .02 | .10 |
| □ 125 Richie Hebner | .02 | .10 |
| □ 126 Mark Wagner | .02 | .10 |
| □ 127 Jack Morris | .20 | .50 |
| □ 128 Dan Petry | .02 | .10 |
| □ 129 Bruce Robbins | .02 | .10 |
| □ 130 Champ Summers | .02 | .10 |
| □ 131 Pete Rose | 1.25 | 3.00 |
| □ 131B Pete Rose P2 | .75 | 2.00 |
| □ 132 Willie Stargell | .20 | .50 |
| □ 133 Ed Ott | .02 | .10 |
| □ 134 Jim Bibby | .02 | .10 |
| □ 135 Bert Blyleven | .08 | .25 |
| □ 136 Dave Parker | .08 | .25 |
| □ 137 Bill Robinson | .02 | .10 |
| □ 138 Enos Cabell | .02 | .10 |
| □ 139 Dave Bergman | .02 | .10 |
| □ 140 J.R. Richard | .08 | .25 |
| □ 141 Ken Forsch | .02 | .10 |
| □ 142 Larry Bowa UER | .08 | .25 |
| □ 143 Frank LaCorte UER | .02 | .10 |
| □ 144 Denny Walling | .02 | .10 |
| □ 145 Buddy Bell | .08 | .25 |
| □ 146 Fergie Jenkins | .08 | .25 |
| □ 147 Danny Darwin | .08 | .25 |
| □ 148 John Grubb | .02 | .10 |
| □ 149 Alfredo Griffin | .02 | .10 |
| □ 150 Jerry Garvin | .02 | .10 |
| □ 151 Paul Mirabella RC | .02 | .10 |
| □ 152 Rick Bosetti | .02 | .10 |
| □ 153 Dick Ruthven | .02 | .10 |
| □ 154 Frank Taveras | .02 | .10 |
| □ 155 Craig Swan | .02 | .10 |
| □ 156 Jeff Reardon RC | .40 | 1.00 |
| □ 157 Steve Henderson | .02 | .10 |
| □ 158 Jim Morrison | .02 | .10 |
| □ 159 Glenn Borgmann | .02 | .10 |
| □ 160 LaMarr Hoyt RC | .20 | .50 |
| □ 161 Rich Wortham | .02 | .10 |
| □ 162 Thad Bosley | .02 | .10 |
| □ 163 Julio Cruz | .02 | .10 |
| □ 164A Del Unser P1 | .08 | .25 |
| □ 164B Del Unser P2 | .02 | .10 |
| □ 165 Jim Anderson | .02 | .10 |
| □ 166 Jim Beattie | .02 | .10 |
| □ 167 Shane Rawley | .02 | .10 |
| □ 168 Joe Simpson | .02 | .10 |
| □ 169 Rod Carew | .20 | .50 |
| □ 170 Fred Patek | .02 | .10 |
| □ 171 Frank Tanana | .08 | .25 |
| □ 172 Alfredo Martinez RC | .02 | .10 |
| □ 173 Chris Knapp | .02 | .10 |
| □ 174 Joe Rudi | .08 | .25 |
| □ 175 Greg Luzinski | .08 | .25 |
| □ 176 Steve Garvey | .20 | .50 |
| □ 177 Joe Ferguson | .02 | .10 |
| □ 178 Bob Welch | .08 | .25 |
| □ 179 Dusty Baker | .08 | .25 |
| □ 180 Rudy Law | .02 | .10 |
| □ 181 Dave Concepcion | .08 | .25 |
| □ 182 Johnny Bench | .40 | 1.00 |
| □ 183 Mike LaCoss | .02 | .10 |
| □ 184 Ken Griffey | .08 | .25 |
| □ 185 Dave Collins | .02 | .10 |
| □ 186 Brian Asselstine | .02 | .10 |
| □ 187 Garry Templeton | .08 | .25 |
| □ 188 Mike Phillips | .02 | .10 |
| □ 189 Pete Vuckovich | .02 | .10 |
| □ 190 John Urrea | .02 | .10 |
| □ 191 Tony Scott | .02 | .10 |
| □ 192 Darrell Evans | .08 | .25 |
| □ 193 Milt May | .02 | .10 |
| □ 194 Bob Knepper | .02 | .10 |
| □ 195 Randy Moffitt | .02 | .10 |
| □ 196 Larry Herndon | .02 | .10 |
| □ 197 Rick Camp | .02 | .10 |
| □ 198 Andre Thornton | .08 | .25 |
| □ 199 Tom Veryzer | .02 | .10 |
| □ 200 Gary Alexander | .02 | .10 |
| □ 201 Rick Waits | .02 | .10 |
| □ 202 Rick Manning | .02 | .10 |
| □ 203 Paul Molitor | .40 | 1.00 |
| □ 204 Jim Gantner | .02 | .10 |
| □ 205 Paul Mitchell | .02 | .10 |
| □ 206 Reggie Cleveland | .02 | .10 |
| □ 207 Sixto Lezcano | .02 | .10 |

| Card | Low | High |
|---|---|---|
| ☐ 208 Bruce Benedict | .02 | .10 |
| ☐ 209 Rodney Scott | .02 | .10 |
| ☐ 210 John Tamargo | .02 | .10 |
| ☐ 211 Bill Lee | .08 | .25 |
| ☐ 212 Andre Dawson | .20 | .50 |
| ☐ 213 Rowland Office | .02 | .10 |
| ☐ 214 Carl Yastrzemski | .60 | 1.50 |
| ☐ 215 Jerry Remy | .02 | .10 |
| ☐ 216 Mike Torrez | .02 | .10 |
| ☐ 217 Skip Lockwood | .02 | .10 |
| ☐ 218 Fred Lynn | .08 | .25 |
| ☐ 219 Chris Chambliss | .08 | .25 |
| ☐ 220 Willie Aikens | .02 | .10 |
| ☐ 221 John Wathan | .02 | .10 |
| ☐ 222 Dan Quisenberry | .20 | .50 |
| ☐ 223 Willie Wilson | .08 | .25 |
| ☐ 224 Clint Hurdle | .02 | .10 |
| ☐ 225 Bob Watson | .02 | .10 |
| ☐ 226 Jim Spencer | .02 | .10 |
| ☐ 227 Ron Guidry | .08 | .25 |
| ☐ 228 Reggie Jackson | .40 | 1.00 |
| ☐ 229 Oscar Gamble | .02 | .10 |
| ☐ 230 Jeff Cox RC | .02 | .10 |
| ☐ 231 Luis Tiant | .08 | .25 |
| ☐ 232 Rich Dauer | .02 | .10 |
| ☐ 233 Dan Graham | .02 | .10 |
| ☐ 234 Mike Flanagan | .02 | .10 |
| ☐ 235 John Lowenstein | .02 | .10 |
| ☐ 236 Benny Ayala | .02 | .10 |
| ☐ 237 Wayne Gross | .02 | .10 |
| ☐ 238 Rick Langford | .02 | .10 |
| ☐ 239 Tony Armas | .08 | .25 |
| ☐ 240A Bob Lacy P1 ERR | .20 | .50 |
| ☐ 240B Bob Lacey P2 COR | .08 | .25 |
| ☐ 241 Gene Tenace | .08 | .25 |
| ☐ 242 Bob Shirley | .02 | .10 |
| ☐ 243 Gary Lucas RC | .02 | .10 |
| ☐ 244 Jerry Turner | .02 | .10 |
| ☐ 245 John Wockenfuss | .02 | .10 |
| ☐ 246 Stan Papi | .02 | .10 |
| ☐ 247 Milt Wilcox | .02 | .10 |
| ☐ 248 Dan Schatzeder | .02 | .10 |
| ☐ 249 Steve Kemp | .02 | .10 |
| ☐ 250 Jim Lentine RC | .02 | .10 |
| ☐ 251 Pete Rose | 1.25 | 3.00 |
| ☐ 252 Bill Madlock | .08 | .25 |
| ☐ 253 Dale Berra | .02 | .10 |
| ☐ 254 Kent Tekulve | .02 | .10 |
| ☐ 255 Enrique Romo | .02 | .10 |
| ☐ 256 Mike Easler | .02 | .10 |
| ☐ 257 Chuck Tanner MG | .02 | .10 |
| ☐ 258 Art Howe | .02 | .10 |
| ☐ 259 Alan Ashby | .02 | .10 |
| ☐ 260 Nolan Ryan | 2.00 | 5.00 |
| ☐ 261A Vern Ruhle P1 ERR | .20 | .50 |
| ☐ 261B Vern Ruhle P2 COR | .08 | .25 |
| ☐ 262 Bob Boone | .08 | .25 |
| ☐ 263 Cesar Cedeno | .08 | .25 |
| ☐ 264 Jeff Leonard | .08 | .25 |
| ☐ 265 Pat Putnam | .02 | .10 |
| ☐ 266 Jon Matlack | .02 | .10 |
| ☐ 267 Dave Rajsich | .02 | .10 |
| ☐ 268 Billy Sample | .02 | .10 |
| ☐ 269 Damaso Garcia RC | .08 | .25 |
| ☐ 270 Tom Buskey | .02 | .10 |
| ☐ 271 Joey McLaughlin | .02 | .10 |
| ☐ 272 Barry Bonnell | .02 | .10 |
| ☐ 273 Tug McGraw | .08 | .25 |
| ☐ 274 Mike Jorgensen | .02 | .10 |
| ☐ 275 Pat Zachry | .02 | .10 |
| ☐ 276 Neil Allen | .02 | .10 |
| ☐ 277 Joel Youngblood | .02 | .10 |
| ☐ 278 Greg Pryor | .02 | .10 |
| ☐ 279 Britt Burns RC | .02 | .10 |
| ☐ 280 Rich Dotson RC | .08 | .25 |
| ☐ 281 Chet Lemon | .08 | .25 |
| ☐ 282 Rusty Kuntz RC | .02 | .10 |
| ☐ 283 Ted Cox | .02 | .10 |
| ☐ 284 Sparky Lyle | .08 | .25 |
| ☐ 285 Larry Cox | .02 | .10 |
| ☐ 286 Floyd Bannister | .02 | .10 |
| ☐ 287 Byron McLaughlin | .02 | .10 |
| ☐ 288 Rodney Craig | .02 | .10 |
| ☐ 289 Bobby Grich | .08 | .25 |
| ☐ 290 Dickie Thon | .02 | .10 |
| ☐ 291 Mark Clear | .02 | .10 |
| ☐ 292 Dave Lemanczyk | .02 | .10 |
| ☐ 293 Jason Thompson | .02 | .10 |
| ☐ 294 Rick Miller | .02 | .10 |
| ☐ 295 Lonnie Smith | .08 | .25 |
| ☐ 296 Ron Cey | .08 | .25 |
| ☐ 297 Steve Yeager | .08 | .25 |
| ☐ 298 Bobby Castillo | .02 | .10 |
| ☐ 299 Manny Mota | .08 | .25 |
| ☐ 300 Jay Johnstone | .08 | .25 |
| ☐ 301 Dan Driessen | .02 | .10 |
| ☐ 302 Joe Nolan RC | .02 | .10 |
| ☐ 303 Paul Householder RC | .02 | .10 |
| ☐ 304 Harry Spilman | .02 | .10 |
| ☐ 305 Cesar Geronimo | .02 | .10 |
| ☐ 306A Gary Mathews P1 ERR | .20 | .50 |
| ☐ 306B Gary Matthews P2 COR | .08 | .25 |
| ☐ 307 Ken Reitz | .02 | .10 |
| ☐ 308 Ted Simmons | .08 | .25 |
| ☐ 309 John Littlefield RC | .02 | .10 |
| ☐ 310 George Frazier | .02 | .10 |
| ☐ 311 Dane Iorg | .02 | .10 |
| ☐ 312 Mike Ivie | .02 | .10 |
| ☐ 313 Dennis Littlejohn | .02 | .10 |
| ☐ 314 Gary Lavelle | .02 | .10 |
| ☐ 315 Jack Clark | .08 | .25 |
| ☐ 316 Jim Wohlford | .02 | .10 |
| ☐ 317 Rick Matula | .02 | .10 |
| ☐ 318 Toby Harrah | .08 | .25 |
| ☐ 319A Dwane Kuiper P1 ERR | .08 | .25 |
| ☐ 319B Duane Kuiper P2 COR | .02 | .10 |
| ☐ 320 Len Barker | .08 | .25 |
| ☐ 321 Victor Cruz | .02 | .10 |
| ☐ 322 Dell Alston | .02 | .10 |
| ☐ 323 Robin Yount | .60 | 1.50 |
| ☐ 324 Charlie Moore | .02 | .10 |
| ☐ 325 Lary Sorensen | .02 | .10 |
| ☐ 326A Gorman Thomas P1 | .20 | .50 |
| ☐ 326B Gorman Thomas P2 | .08 | .25 |
| ☐ 327 Bob Rodgers MG | .02 | .10 |
| ☐ 328 Phil Niekro | .08 | .25 |
| ☐ 329 Chris Speier | .02 | .10 |
| ☐ 330A Steve Rodgers P1 | .08 | .25 |
| ☐ 330B Steve Rogers P2 COR | .02 | .10 |
| ☐ 331 Woodie Fryman | .02 | .10 |
| ☐ 332 Warren Cromartie | .02 | .10 |
| ☐ 333 Jerry White | .02 | .10 |
| ☐ 334 Tony Perez | .08 | .25 |
| ☐ 335 Carlton Fisk | .20 | .50 |
| ☐ 336 Dick Drago | .02 | .10 |
| ☐ 337 Steve Renko | .02 | .10 |
| ☐ 338 Jim Rice | .08 | .25 |
| ☐ 339 Jerry Royster | .02 | .10 |
| ☐ 340 Frank White | .08 | .25 |
| ☐ 341 Jamie Quirk | .02 | .10 |
| ☐ 342A Paul Splittorff P1 ERR | .08 | .25 |
| ☐ 342B Paul Splittorff P2 COR | .02 | .10 |
| ☐ 343 Marty Pattin | .02 | .10 |
| ☐ 344 Pete LaCock | .02 | .10 |
| ☐ 345 Willie Randolph | .08 | .25 |
| ☐ 346 Rick Cerone | .02 | .10 |
| ☐ 347 Rich Gossage | .08 | .25 |
| ☐ 348 Reggie Jackson | .40 | 1.00 |
| ☐ 349 Ruppert Jones | .02 | .10 |
| ☐ 350 Dave McKay RC | .02 | .10 |
| ☐ 351 Yogi Berra CO | .40 | 1.00 |
| ☐ 352 Doug DeCinces | .08 | .25 |
| ☐ 353 Jim Palmer | .20 | .50 |
| ☐ 354 Tippy Martinez | .02 | .10 |
| ☐ 355 Al Bumbry | .02 | .10 |
| ☐ 356 Earl Weaver MG | .08 | .25 |
| ☐ 357A Bob Picciolo P1 ERR | .08 | .25 |
| ☐ 357B Rob Picciolo P2 COR | .02 | .10 |
| ☐ 358 Matt Keough | .02 | .10 |
| ☐ 359 Dwayne Murphy | .02 | .10 |
| ☐ 360 Brian Kingman | .02 | .10 |
| ☐ 361 Bill Fahey | .02 | .10 |
| ☐ 362 Steve Mura | .02 | .10 |
| ☐ 363 Dennis Kinney RC | .02 | .10 |
| ☐ 364 Dave Winfield | .20 | .50 |
| ☐ 365 Lou Whitaker | .20 | .50 |
| ☐ 366 Lance Parrish | .08 | .25 |
| ☐ 367 Tim Corcoran | .02 | .10 |
| ☐ 368 Pat Underwood | .02 | .10 |
| ☐ 369 Al Cowens | .02 | .10 |
| ☐ 370 Sparky Anderson MG | .08 | .25 |
| ☐ 371 Pete Rose | 1.25 | 3.00 |
| ☐ 372 Phil Garner | .08 | .25 |
| ☐ 373 Steve Nicosia | .02 | .10 |
| ☐ 374 John Candelaria | .08 | .25 |
| ☐ 375 Don Robinson | .02 | .10 |
| ☐ 376 Lee Lacy | .02 | .10 |
| ☐ 377 John Milner | .02 | .10 |
| ☐ 378 Craig Reynolds | .02 | .10 |
| ☐ 379A Luis Pujols P1 ERR | .08 | .25 |
| ☐ 379B Luis Pujols P2 COR | .02 | .10 |
| ☐ 380 Joe Niekro | .02 | .10 |
| ☐ 381 Joaquin Andujar | .08 | .25 |
| ☐ 382 Keith Moreland RC | .02 | .10 |
| ☐ 383 Jose Cruz | .08 | .25 |
| ☐ 384 Bill Virdon MG | .02 | .10 |
| ☐ 385 Jim Sundberg | .08 | .25 |
| ☐ 386 Doc Medich | .02 | .10 |
| ☐ 387 Al Oliver | .08 | .25 |
| ☐ 388 Jim Norris | .02 | .10 |
| ☐ 389 Bob Bailor | .02 | .10 |
| ☐ 390 Ernie Whitt | .02 | .10 |
| ☐ 391 Otto Velez | .02 | .10 |
| ☐ 392 Roy Howell | .02 | .10 |
| ☐ 393 Bob Walk RC | .20 | .50 |
| ☐ 394 Doug Flynn | .02 | .10 |
| ☐ 395 Pete Falcone | .02 | .10 |
| ☐ 396 Tom Hausman | .02 | .10 |
| ☐ 397 Elliott Maddox | .02 | .10 |
| ☐ 398 Mike Squires | .02 | .10 |
| ☐ 399 Marvis Foley RC | .02 | .10 |
| ☐ 400 Steve Trout | .02 | .10 |
| ☐ 401 Wayne Nordhagen | .02 | .10 |
| ☐ 402 Tony LaRussa MG | .08 | .25 |
| ☐ 403 Bruce Bochte | .08 | .25 |
| ☐ 404 Bake McBride | .08 | .25 |
| ☐ 405 Jerry Narron | .02 | .10 |
| ☐ 406 Rob Dressler | .02 | .10 |
| ☐ 407 Dave Heaverlo | .02 | .10 |
| ☐ 408 Tom Paciorek | .02 | .10 |
| ☐ 409 Carney Lansford | .08 | .25 |
| ☐ 410 Brian Downing | .08 | .25 |
| ☐ 411 Don Aase | .02 | .10 |
| ☐ 412 Jim Barr | .02 | .10 |
| ☐ 413 Don Baylor | .08 | .25 |
| ☐ 414 Jim Fregosi MG | .08 | .25 |
| ☐ 415 Dallas Green MG | .02 | .10 |
| ☐ 416 Dave Lopes | .08 | .25 |
| ☐ 417 Jerry Reuss | .02 | .10 |
| ☐ 418 Rick Sutcliffe | .08 | .25 |
| ☐ 419 Derrel Thomas | .02 | .10 |
| ☐ 420 Tom Lasorda MG | .20 | .50 |
| ☐ 421 Charlie Leibrandt RC | .20 | .50 |
| ☐ 422 Tom Seaver | .40 | 1.00 |
| ☐ 423 Ron Oester | .02 | .10 |
| ☐ 424 Junior Kennedy | .02 | .10 |
| ☐ 425 Tom Seaver | .40 | 1.00 |
| ☐ 426 Bobby Cox MG | .08 | .25 |
| ☐ 427 Leon Durham RC | .20 | .50 |
| ☐ 428 Terry Kennedy | .08 | .25 |
| ☐ 429 Silvio Martinez | .02 | .10 |
| ☐ 430 George Hendrick | .08 | .25 |
| ☐ 431 Red Schoendienst MG | .20 | .50 |
| ☐ 432 Johnnie LeMaster | .02 | .10 |
| ☐ 433 Vida Blue | .08 | .25 |
| ☐ 434 John Montefusco | .02 | .10 |
| ☐ 435 Terry Whitfield | .02 | .10 |
| ☐ 436 Dave Bristol MG | .02 | .10 |
| ☐ 437 Dale Murphy | .20 | .50 |
| ☐ 438 Jerry Dybzinski RC | .02 | .10 |
| ☐ 439 Jorge Orta | .02 | .10 |
| ☐ 440 Wayne Garland | .02 | .10 |
| ☐ 441 Miguel Dilone | .02 | .10 |
| ☐ 442 Dave Garcia MG | .02 | .10 |
| ☐ 443 Don Money | .02 | .10 |
| ☐ 444A Buck Martinez P1 ERR | .08 | .25 |
| ☐ 444B Buck Martinez P2 COR | .02 | .10 |
| ☐ 445 Jerry Augustine | .02 | .10 |
| ☐ 446 Ben Oglivie | .08 | .25 |
| ☐ 447 Jim Slaton | .02 | .10 |
| ☐ 448 Doyle Alexander | .02 | .10 |
| ☐ 449 Tony Bernazard | .02 | .10 |
| ☐ 450 Scott Sanderson | .02 | .10 |
| ☐ 451 David Palmer | .02 | .10 |
| ☐ 452 Stan Bahnsen | .02 | .10 |
| ☐ 453 Dick Williams MG | .02 | .10 |
| ☐ 454 Rick Burleson | .02 | .10 |
| ☐ 455 Gary Allenson | .02 | .10 |
| ☐ 456 Bob Stanley | .02 | .10 |
| ☐ 457A John Tudor ERR | .40 | 1.00 |
| ☐ 457B John Tudor RC | .40 | 1.00 |
| ☐ 458 Dwight Evans | .20 | .50 |
| ☐ 459 Glenn Hubbard | .02 | .10 |
| ☐ 460 U.L. Washington | .02 | .10 |

|  |  | | |
|---|---|---|---|
| 461 | Larry Gura | .02 | .10 |
| 462 | Rich Gale | .02 | .10 |
| 463 | Hal McRae | .08 | .25 |
| 464 | Jim Frey MG RC | .08 | .25 |
| 465 | Bucky Dent | .08 | .25 |
| 466 | Dennis Werth RC | .02 | .10 |
| 467 | Ron Davis | .02 | .10 |
| 468 | Reggie Jackson | .40 | 1.00 |
| 469 | Bobby Brown | .02 | .10 |
| 470 | Mike Davis RC | .20 | .50 |
| 471 | Gaylord Perry | .08 | .25 |
| 472 | Mark Belanger | .02 | .10 |
| 473 | Jim Palmer | .20 | .50 |
| 474 | Sammy Stewart | .02 | .10 |
| 475 | Tim Stoddard | .02 | .10 |
| 476 | Steve Stone | .02 | .10 |
| 477 | Jeff Newman | .02 | .10 |
| 478 | Steve McCatty | .02 | .10 |
| 479 | Billy Martin MG | .20 | .50 |
| 480 | Mitchell Page | .02 | .10 |
| 481 | Steve Carlton CY | .08 | .25 |
| 482 | Bill Buckner | .08 | .25 |
| 483A | Ivan DeJesus P1 ERR | .08 | .25 |
| 483B | Ivan DeJesus P2 COR | .02 | .10 |
| 484 | Cliff Johnson | .02 | .10 |
| 485 | Lenny Randle | .02 | .10 |
| 486 | Larry Milbourne | .02 | .10 |
| 487 | Roy Smalley | .02 | .10 |
| 488 | John Castino | .02 | .10 |
| 489 | Ron Jackson | .02 | .10 |
| 490A | Dave Roberts P1 | .08 | .25 |
| 490B | Dave Roberts P2 | .02 | .10 |
| 491 | George Brett MVP | .60 | 1.50 |
| 492 | Mike Cubbage | .02 | .10 |
| 493 | Rob Wilfong | .02 | .10 |
| 494 | Danny Goodwin | .02 | .10 |
| 495 | Jose Morales | .02 | .10 |
| 496 | Mickey Rivers | .02 | .10 |
| 497 | Mike Edwards | .02 | .10 |
| 498 | Mike Sadek | .02 | .10 |
| 499 | Lenn Sakata | .02 | .10 |
| 500 | Gene Michael MG | .02 | .10 |
| 501 | Dave Roberts | .02 | .10 |
| 502 | Steve Dillard | .02 | .10 |
| 503 | Jim Essian | .02 | .10 |
| 504 | Rance Mulliniks | .02 | .10 |
| 505 | Darrell Porter | .02 | .10 |
| 506 | Joe Torre MG | .08 | .25 |
| 507 | Terry Crowley | .02 | .10 |
| 508 | Bill Travers | .02 | .10 |
| 509 | Nelson Norman | .02 | .10 |
| 510 | Bob McClure | .02 | .10 |
| 511 | Steve Howe RC | .20 | .50 |
| 512 | Dave Rader | .02 | .10 |
| 513 | Mick Kelleher | .02 | .10 |
| 514 | Kiko Garcia | .02 | .10 |
| 515 | Larry Biittner | .02 | .10 |
| 516A | Willie Norwood P1 | .08 | .25 |
| 516B | Willie Norwood P2 | .02 | .10 |
| 517 | Bo Diaz | .02 | .10 |
| 518 | Juan Beniquez | .02 | .10 |
| 519 | Scot Thompson | .02 | .10 |
| 520 | Jim Tracy RC | .40 | 1.00 |
| 521 | Carlos Lezcano RC | .02 | .10 |
| 522 | Joe Amalfitano MG | .02 | .10 |
| 523 | Preston Hanna | .02 | .10 |
| 524A | Ray Burris P1 | .08 | .25 |
| 524B | Ray Burris P2 | .02 | .10 |
| 525 | Broderick Perkins | .02 | .10 |
| 526 | Mickey Hatcher | .02 | .10 |
| 527 | John Goryl MG | .02 | .10 |
| 528 | Dick Davis | .02 | .10 |
| 529 | Butch Wynegar | .02 | .10 |
| 530 | Sal Butera RC | .02 | .10 |
| 531 | Jerry Koosman | .08 | .25 |
| 532A | Geoff Zahn P1 | .08 | .25 |
| 532B | Geoff Zahn P2 | .02 | .10 |
| 533 | Dennis Martinez | .08 | .25 |
| 534 | Gary Thomasson | .02 | .10 |
| 535 | Steve Macko | .02 | .10 |
| 536 | Jim Kaat | .08 | .25 |
| 537 | G.Brett/R.Carew | .60 | 1.50 |
| 538 | Tim Raines RC | 1.00 | 2.50 |
| 539 | Keith Smith | .02 | .10 |
| 540 | Ken Macha | .02 | .10 |
| 541 | Burt Hooton | .02 | .10 |
| 542 | Butch Hobson | .02 | .10 |
| 543 | Bill Stein | .02 | .10 |
| 544 | Dave Stapleton RC | .02 | .10 |
| 545 | Bob Pate RC | .02 | .10 |
| 546 | Doug Corbett RC | .02 | .10 |
| 547 | Darrell Jackson | .02 | .10 |
| 548 | Pete Redfern | .02 | .10 |
| 549 | Roger Erickson | .02 | .10 |
| 550 | Al Hrabosky | .08 | .25 |
| 551 | Dick Tidrow | .02 | .10 |
| 552 | Dave Ford RC | .02 | .10 |
| 553 | Dave Kingman | .08 | .25 |
| 554A | Jerry Martin P1 | .08 | .25 |
| 554B | Jerry Martin P2 | .02 | .10 |
| 555A | Jesus Figueroa P1 | .08 | .25 |
| 555B | Jesus Figueroa P2 RC | .02 | .10 |
| 557 | Don Stanhouse | .02 | .10 |
| 558 | Barry Foote | .02 | .10 |
| 559 | Tim Blackwell | .02 | .10 |
| 560 | Bruce Sutter | .20 | .50 |
| 561 | Rick Reuschel | .08 | .25 |
| 562 | Lynn McGlothen | .02 | .10 |
| 563A | Bob Owchinko P1 | .08 | .25 |
| 563B | Bob Owchinko P2 | .02 | .10 |
| 564 | John Verhoeven | .02 | .10 |
| 565 | Ken Landreaux | .02 | .10 |
| 566A | Glen Adams P1 ERR | .08 | .25 |
| 566B | Glenn Adams P2 COR | .02 | .10 |
| 567 | Hosken Powell | .02 | .10 |
| 568 | Dick Noles | .02 | .10 |
| 569 | Danny Ainge RC | 1.25 | 3.00 |
| 570 | Bobby Mattick MG RC | .02 | .10 |
| 571 | Joe Lefebvre RC | .02 | .10 |
| 572 | Bobby Clark | .02 | .10 |
| 573 | Dennis Lamp | .02 | .10 |
| 574 | Randy Lerch | .02 | .10 |
| 575 | Mookie Wilson RC | 1.25 | 3.00 |
| 576 | Ron LeFlore | .08 | .25 |
| 577 | Jim Dwyer | .02 | .10 |
| 578 | Bill Castro | .02 | .10 |
| 579 | Greg Minton | .02 | .10 |
| 580 | Mark Littell | .02 | .10 |
| 581 | Andy Hassler | .02 | .10 |
| 582 | Dave Stieb | .08 | .25 |
| 583 | Ken Oberkfell | .02 | .10 |
| 584 | Larry Bradford | .02 | .10 |
| 585 | Fred Stanley | .02 | .10 |
| 586 | Bill Caudill | .02 | .10 |
| 587 | Doug Capilla | .02 | .10 |
| 588 | George Riley RC | .02 | .10 |
| 589 | Willie Hernandez | .08 | .25 |
| 590 | Mike Schmidt MVP | 1.00 | 2.50 |
| 591 | Steve Stone CY | .02 | .10 |
| 592 | Rick Sofield | .02 | .10 |
| 593 | Bombo Rivera | .02 | .10 |
| 594 | Gary Ward | .02 | .10 |
| 595A | Dave Edwards P1 | .08 | .25 |
| 595B | Dave Edwards P2 | .02 | .10 |
| 596 | Mike Proly | .02 | .10 |
| 597 | Tommy Boggs | .02 | .10 |
| 598 | Greg Gross | .02 | .10 |
| 599 | Elias Sosa | .02 | .10 |
| 600 | Pat Kelly | .02 | .10 |
| 601A | Checklist 1-120 P1 | .08 | .25 |
| 601B | Checklist 1-120 P2 | .20 | .50 |
| 602 | Checklist 121-240 NNO | .02 | .10 |
| 603A | Checklist 241-360 P1 | .08 | .25 |
| 603B | Checklist 241-360 P2 | .08 | .25 |
| 604A | Checklist 361-480 P1 | .08 | .25 |
| 604B | Checklist 361-480 P2 | .08 | .25 |
| 605A | Checklist 481-600 P1 | .08 | .25 |
| 605B | Checklist 481-600 P2 | .08 | .25 |

**1982 Donruss**

|  |  | | |
|---|---|---|---|
| | COMPLETE SET (660) | 30.00 | 60.00 |
| | COMP.FACT.SET (660) | 30.00 | 60.00 |
| | COMP.RUTH PUZZLE | 5.00 | 10.00 |
| 1 | Pete Rose DK | 1.00 | 2.50 |
| 2 | Gary Carter DK | .07 | .20 |
| 3 | Steve Garvey DK | .07 | .20 |
| 4 | Vida Blue DK | .07 | .20 |
| 5 | Alan Trammell DK | .07 | .20 |
| 5A | Alan Trammel DK ERR | .07 | .20 |
| 6 | Len Barker DK | .02 | .10 |
| 7 | Dwight Evans DK | .15 | .40 |
| 8 | Rod Carew DK | .20 | .50 |
| 9 | George Hendrick DK | .07 | .20 |
| 10 | Phil Niekro DK | .07 | .20 |
| 11 | Richie Zisk DK | .02 | .10 |
| 12 | Dave Parker DK | .07 | .20 |
| 13 | Nolan Ryan DK | 1.50 | 4.00 |
| 14 | Ivan DeJesus DK | .02 | .10 |
| 15 | George Brett DK | .75 | 2.00 |
| 16 | Tom Seaver DK | .15 | .40 |
| 17 | Dave Kingman DK | .07 | .20 |
| 18 | Dave Winfield DK | .20 | .50 |
| 19 | Mike Norris DK | .02 | .10 |
| 20 | Carlton Fisk DK | .15 | .40 |
| 21 | Ozzie Smith DK | .60 | 1.50 |
| 22 | Roy Smalley DK | .02 | .10 |
| 23 | Buddy Bell DK | .07 | .20 |
| 24 | Ken Singleton DK | .02 | .10 |
| 25 | John Mayberry DK | .02 | .10 |
| 26 | Gorman Thomas DK | .07 | .20 |
| 27 | Earl Weaver MG | .07 | .20 |
| 28 | Rollie Fingers | .20 | .50 |
| 29 | Sparky Anderson MG | .07 | .20 |
| 30 | Dennis Eckersley | .15 | .40 |
| 31 | Dave Winfield | .07 | .20 |
| 32 | Burt Hooton | .02 | .10 |
| 33 | Rick Waits | .02 | .10 |
| 34 | George Brett | .75 | 2.00 |
| 35 | Steve McCatty | .02 | .10 |
| 36 | Steve Rogers | .02 | .10 |
| 37 | Bill Stein | .02 | .10 |
| 38 | Steve Renko | .02 | .10 |
| 39 | Mike Squires | .02 | .10 |
| 40 | George Hendrick | .07 | .20 |
| 41 | Bob Knepper | .02 | .10 |
| 42 | Steve Carlton | .15 | .40 |
| 43 | Larry Biittner | .02 | .10 |
| 44 | Chris Welsh | .02 | .10 |
| 45 | Steve Nicosia | .02 | .10 |
| 46 | Jack Clark | .07 | .20 |
| 47 | Chris Chambliss | .07 | .20 |
| 48 | Ivan DeJesus | .02 | .10 |
| 49 | Lee Mazzilli | .02 | .10 |
| 50 | Julio Cruz | .02 | .10 |
| 51 | Pete Redfern | .02 | .10 |
| 52 | Dave Stieb | .07 | .20 |
| 53 | Doug Corbett | .02 | .10 |
| 54 | George Bell RC | .40 | 1.00 |
| 55 | Joe Simpson | .02 | .10 |
| 56 | Rusty Staub | .07 | .20 |
| 57 | Hector Cruz | .02 | .10 |
| 58 | Claudell Washington | .02 | .10 |
| 59 | Enrique Romo | .02 | .10 |
| 60 | Gary Lavelle | .02 | .10 |
| 61 | Tim Flannery | .02 | .10 |
| 62 | Joe Nolan | .02 | .10 |
| 63 | Larry Bowa | .07 | .20 |
| 64 | Sixto Lezcano | .02 | .10 |
| 65 | Joe Sambito | .02 | .10 |
| 66 | Bruce Kison | .02 | .10 |
| 67 | Wayne Nordhagen | .02 | .10 |
| 68 | Woodie Fryman | .02 | .10 |
| 69 | Billy Sample | .02 | .10 |
| 70 | Amos Otis | .07 | .20 |
| 71 | Matt Keough | .02 | .10 |
| 72 | Toby Harrah | .07 | .20 |
| 73 | Dave Righetti RC | .50 | 1.50 |
| 74 | Carl Yastrzemski | .50 | 1.25 |
| 75 | Bob Welch | .07 | .20 |
| 76 | Alan Trammell | .20 | .50 |
| 76A | Alan Trammel ERR | .07 | .20 |
| 77 | Rick Dempsey | .02 | .10 |
| 78 | Paul Molitor | .07 | .20 |
| 79 | Dennis Martinez | .07 | .20 |
| 80 | Jim Slaton | .02 | .10 |
| 81 | Champ Summers | .02 | .10 |
| 82 | Carney Lansford | .07 | .20 |
| 83 | Barry Foote | .02 | .10 |

|  |  | | |
|---|---|---|---|
| 84 | Steve Garvey | .07 | .20 |
| 85 | Rick Manning | .02 | .10 |
| 86 | John Wathan | .02 | .10 |
| 87 | Brian Kingman | .02 | .10 |
| 88 | Andre Dawson | .07 | .20 |
| 89 | Jim Kern | .02 | .10 |
| 90 | Bobby Grich | .07 | .20 |
| 91 | Bob Forsch | .02 | .10 |
| 92 | Art Howe | .02 | .10 |
| 93 | Marty Bystrom | .02 | .10 |
| 94 | Ozzie Smith | .60 | 1.50 |
| 95 | Dave Parker | .07 | .20 |
| 96 | Doyle Alexander | .02 | .10 |
| 97 | Al Hrabosky | .02 | .10 |
| 98 | Frank Taveras | .02 | .10 |
| 99 | Tim Blackwell | .02 | .10 |
| 100 | Floyd Bannister | .02 | .10 |
| 101 | Alfredo Griffin | .02 | .10 |
| 102 | Dave Engle | .02 | .10 |
| 103 | Mario Soto | .07 | .20 |
| 104 | Ross Baumgarten | .02 | .10 |
| 105 | Ken Singleton | .02 | .10 |
| 106 | Ted Simmons | .07 | .20 |
| 107 | Jack Morris | .07 | .20 |
| 108 | Bob Watson | .02 | .10 |
| 109 | Dwight Evans | .15 | .40 |
| 110 | Tom Lasorda MG | .15 | .40 |
| 111 | Bert Blyleven | .07 | .20 |
| 112 | Dan Quisenberry | .02 | .10 |
| 113 | Rickey Henderson | 1.00 | 2.50 |
| 114 | Gary Carter | .07 | .20 |
| 115 | Brian Downing | .02 | .10 |
| 116 | Al Oliver | .07 | .20 |
| 117 | LaMarr Hoyt | .02 | .10 |
| 118 | Cesar Cedeno | .07 | .20 |
| 119 | Keith Moreland | .02 | .10 |
| 120 | Bob Shirley | .02 | .10 |
| 121 | Terry Kennedy | .02 | .10 |
| 122 | Frank Pastore | .02 | .10 |
| 123 | Gene Garber | .02 | .10 |
| 124 | Tony Pena | .07 | .20 |
| 125 | Allen Ripley | .02 | .10 |
| 126 | Randy Martz | .02 | .10 |
| 127 | Richie Zisk | .02 | .10 |
| 128 | Mike Scott | .07 | .20 |
| 129 | Lloyd Moseby | .02 | .10 |
| 130 | Rob Wilfong | .02 | .10 |
| 131 | Tim Stoddard | .02 | .10 |
| 132 | Gorman Thomas | .07 | .20 |
| 133 | Dan Petry | .02 | .10 |
| 134 | Bob Stanley | .02 | .10 |
| 135 | Lou Piniella | .07 | .20 |
| 136 | Pedro Guerrero | .07 | .20 |
| 137 | Len Barker | .02 | .10 |
| 138 | Rich Gale | .02 | .10 |
| 139 | Wayne Gross | .02 | .10 |
| 140 | Tim Wallach RC | .40 | 1.00 |
| 141 | Gene Mauch MG | .02 | .10 |
| 142 | Doc Medich | .02 | .10 |
| 143 | Tony Bernazard | .02 | .10 |
| 144 | Bill Virdon MG | .02 | .10 |
| 145 | John Littlefield | .02 | .10 |
| 146 | Dave Bergman | .02 | .10 |
| 147 | Dick Davis | .02 | .10 |
| 148 | Tom Seaver | .30 | .75 |
| 149 | Matt Sinatro | .02 | .10 |
| 150 | Chuck Tanner MG | .02 | .10 |
| 151 | Leon Durham | .07 | .20 |
| 152 | Gene Tenace | .07 | .20 |
| 153 | Al Bumbry | .02 | .10 |
| 154 | Mark Brouhard | .02 | .10 |
| 155 | Rick Peters | .02 | .10 |
| 156 | Jerry Remy | .02 | .10 |
| 157 | Rick Reuschel | .07 | .20 |
| 158 | Steve Howe | .02 | .10 |
| 159 | Alan Bannister | .02 | .10 |
| 160 | U.L. Washington | .02 | .10 |
| 161 | Rick Langford | .02 | .10 |
| 162 | Bill Gullickson | .02 | .10 |
| 163 | Mark Wagner | .02 | .10 |
| 164 | Geoff Zahn | .02 | .10 |
| 165 | Ron LeFlore | .07 | .20 |
| 166 | Dane Iorg | .02 | .10 |
| 167 | Joe Niekro | .02 | .10 |
| 168 | Pete Rose | 1.00 | 2.50 |
| 169 | Dave Collins | .02 | .10 |
| 170 | Rick Wise | .02 | .10 |
| 171 | Jim Bibby | .02 | .10 |
| 172 | Larry Herndon | .02 | .10 |
| 173 | Bob Horner | .07 | .20 |
| 174 | Steve Dillard | .02 | .10 |
| 175 | Mookie Wilson | .07 | .20 |
| 176 | Dan Meyer | .02 | .10 |
| 177 | Fernando Arroyo | .02 | .10 |
| 178 | Jackson Todd | .02 | .10 |
| 179 | Darrell Jackson | .02 | .10 |
| 180 | Alvis Woods | .02 | .10 |
| 181 | Jim Anderson | .02 | .10 |
| 182 | Dave Kingman | .07 | .20 |
| 183 | Steve Henderson | .02 | .10 |
| 184 | Brian Asselstine | .02 | .10 |
| 185 | Rod Scurry | .02 | .10 |
| 186 | Fred Breining | .02 | .10 |
| 187 | Danny Boone | .02 | .10 |
| 188 | Junior Kennedy | .02 | .10 |
| 189 | Sparky Lyle | .07 | .20 |
| 190 | Whitey Herzog MG | .07 | .20 |
| 191 | Dave Smith | .02 | .10 |
| 192 | Ed Ott | .02 | .10 |
| 193 | Greg Luzinski | .07 | .20 |
| 194 | Bill Lee | .02 | .10 |
| 195 | Don Zimmer MG | .07 | .20 |
| 196 | Hal McRae | .07 | .20 |
| 197 | Mike Norris | .02 | .10 |
| 198 | Duane Kuiper | .02 | .10 |
| 199 | Rick Cerone | .02 | .10 |
| 200 | Jim Rice | .07 | .20 |
| 201 | Steve Yeager | .02 | .10 |
| 202 | Tom Brookens | .02 | .10 |
| 203 | Jose Morales | .02 | .10 |
| 204 | Roy Howell | .02 | .10 |
| 205 | Tippy Martinez | .02 | .10 |
| 206 | Moose Haas | .02 | .10 |
| 207 | Al Cowens | .02 | .10 |
| 208 | Dave Stapleton | .02 | .10 |
| 209 | Bucky Dent | .07 | .20 |
| 210 | Ron Cey | .07 | .20 |
| 211 | Jorge Orta | .02 | .10 |
| 212 | Jamie Quirk | .02 | .10 |
| 213 | Jeff Jones | .02 | .10 |
| 214 | Tim Raines | .15 | .40 |
| 215 | Jon Matlack | .02 | .10 |
| 216 | Rod Carew | .15 | .40 |
| 217 | Jim Kaat | .07 | .20 |
| 218 | Joe Pittman | .02 | .10 |
| 219 | Larry Christenson | .02 | .10 |
| 220 | Juan Bonilla RC | .05 | .15 |
| 221 | Mike Easler | .02 | .10 |
| 222 | Vida Blue | .07 | .20 |
| 223 | Rick Camp | .02 | .10 |
| 224 | Mike Jorgensen | .02 | .10 |
| 225 | Jody Davis | .02 | .10 |
| 226 | Mike Parrott | .02 | .10 |
| 227 | Jim Clancy | .02 | .10 |
| 228 | Hosken Powell | .02 | .10 |
| 229 | Tom Hume | .02 | .10 |
| 230 | Britt Burns | .02 | .10 |
| 231 | Jim Palmer | .07 | .20 |
| 232 | Bob Rodgers MG | .02 | .10 |
| 233 | Milt Wilcox | .02 | .10 |
| 234 | Dave Revering | .02 | .10 |
| 235 | Mike Torrez | .02 | .10 |
| 236 | Robert Castillo | .02 | .10 |
| 237 | Von Hayes RC | .20 | .50 |
| 238 | Renie Martin | .02 | .10 |
| 239 | Dwayne Murphy | .02 | .10 |
| 240 | Rodney Scott | .02 | .10 |
| 241 | Fred Patek | .02 | .10 |
| 242 | Mickey Rivers | .02 | .10 |
| 243 | Steve Trout | .02 | .10 |
| 244 | Jose Cruz | .07 | .20 |
| 245 | Manny Trillo | .02 | .10 |
| 246 | Lary Sorensen | .02 | .10 |
| 247 | Dave Edwards | .02 | .10 |
| 248 | Dan Driessen | .02 | .10 |
| 249 | Tommy Boggs | .02 | .10 |
| 250 | Dale Berra | .02 | .10 |
| 251 | Ed Whitson | .02 | .10 |
| 252 | Lee Smith RC | .75 | 2.00 |
| 253 | Tom Paciorek | .02 | .10 |
| 254 | Pat Zachry | .02 | .10 |
| 255 | Luis Leal | .02 | .10 |
| 256 | John Castino | .02 | .10 |
| 257 | Rich Dauer | .02 | .10 |
| 258 | Cecil Cooper | .07 | .20 |
| 259 | Dave Rozema | .02 | .10 |
| 260 | John Tudor | .07 | .20 |
| 261 | Jerry Mumphrey | .02 | .10 |
| 262 | Jay Johnstone | .02 | .10 |
| 263 | Bo Diaz | .02 | .10 |
| 264 | Dennis Leonard | .02 | .10 |
| 265 | Jim Spencer | .02 | .10 |
| 266 | John Milner | .02 | .10 |
| 267 | Don Aase | .02 | .10 |
| 268 | Jim Sundberg | .07 | .20 |
| 269 | Lamar Johnson | .02 | .10 |
| 270 | Frank LaCorte | .02 | .10 |
| 271 | Barry Evans | .02 | .10 |
| 272 | Enos Cabell | .02 | .10 |
| 273 | Del Unser | .02 | .10 |
| 274 | George Foster | .07 | .20 |
| 275 | Brett Butler RC | .40 | 1.00 |
| 276 | Lee Lacy | .02 | .10 |
| 277 | Ken Reitz | .02 | .10 |
| 278 | Keith Hernandez | .07 | .20 |
| 279 | Doug DeCinces | .07 | .20 |
| 280 | Charlie Moore | .02 | .10 |
| 281 | Lance Parrish | .07 | .20 |
| 282 | Ralph Houk MG | .02 | .10 |
| 283 | Rich Gossage | .07 | .20 |
| 284 | Jerry Reuss | .02 | .10 |
| 285 | Mike Stanton | .02 | .10 |
| 286 | Frank White | .07 | .20 |
| 287 | Bob Owchinko | .02 | .10 |
| 288 | Scott Sanderson | .02 | .10 |
| 289 | Bump Wills | .02 | .10 |
| 290 | Dave Frost | .02 | .10 |
| 291 | Chet Lemon | .07 | .20 |
| 292 | Tito Landrum | .02 | .10 |
| 293 | Vern Ruhle | .02 | .10 |
| 294 | Mike Schmidt | .75 | 2.00 |
| 295 | Sam Mejias | .02 | .10 |
| 296 | Gary Lucas | .02 | .10 |
| 297 | John Candelaria | .02 | .10 |
| 298 | Jerry Martin | .02 | .10 |
| 299 | Dale Murphy | .15 | .40 |
| 300 | Mike Lum | .02 | .10 |
| 301 | Tom Hausman | .02 | .10 |
| 302 | Glenn Abbott | .02 | .10 |
| 303 | Roger Erickson | .02 | .10 |
| 304 | Otto Velez | .02 | .10 |
| 305 | Danny Goodwin | .02 | .10 |
| 306 | John Mayberry | .02 | .10 |
| 307 | Lenny Randle | .02 | .10 |
| 308 | Bob Bailor | .02 | .10 |
| 309 | Jerry Morales | .02 | .10 |
| 310 | Rufino Linares | .02 | .10 |
| 311 | Kent Tekulve | .07 | .20 |
| 312 | Joe Morgan | .07 | .20 |
| 313 | John Urrea | .02 | .10 |
| 314 | Paul Householder | .02 | .10 |
| 315 | Garry Maddox | .02 | .10 |
| 316 | Mike Ramsey | .02 | .10 |
| 317 | Alan Ashby | .02 | .10 |
| 318 | Bob Clark | .02 | .10 |
| 319 | Tony LaRussa MG | .07 | .20 |
| 320 | Charlie Lea | .02 | .10 |
| 321 | Danny Darwin | .02 | .10 |
| 322 | Cesar Geronimo | .02 | .10 |
| 323 | Tom Underwood | .02 | .10 |
| 324 | Andre Thornton | .02 | .10 |
| 325 | Rudy May | .02 | .10 |
| 326 | Frank Tanana | .07 | .20 |
| 327 | Dave Lopes | .07 | .20 |
| 328 | Richie Hebner | .02 | .10 |
| 329 | Mike Flanagan | .02 | .10 |
| 330 | Mike Caldwell | .02 | .10 |
| 331 | Scott McGregor | .02 | .10 |
| 332 | Jerry Augustine | .02 | .10 |
| 333 | Stan Papi | .02 | .10 |
| 334 | Rick Miller | .02 | .10 |
| 335 | Graig Nettles | .07 | .20 |
| 336 | Dusty Baker | .07 | .20 |
| 337 | Dave Garcia MG | .02 | .10 |
| 338 | Larry Gura | .02 | .10 |
| 339 | Cliff Johnson | .02 | .10 |
| 340 | Warren Cromartie | .02 | .10 |
| 341 | Steve Comer | .02 | .10 |
| 342 | Rick Burleson | .02 | .10 |
| 343 | John Martin RC | .05 | .15 |
| 344 | Craig Reynolds | .02 | .10 |
| 345 | Mike Proly | .02 | .10 |
| 346 | Ruppert Jones | .02 | .10 |
| 347 | Omar Moreno | .02 | .10 |

| | | |
|---|---|---|
| 348 Greg Minton | .02 | .10 |
| 349 Rick Mahler | .02 | .10 |
| 350 Alex Trevino | .02 | .10 |
| 351 Mike Krukow | .02 | .10 |
| 352A Shane Rawley ERR (Photo actually Jim Anderson) | .15 | .40 |
| 352B Shane Rawley COR | .02 | .10 |
| 353 Garth Iorg | .02 | .10 |
| 354 Pete Mackanin | .02 | .10 |
| 355 Paul Moskau | .02 | .10 |
| 356 Richard Dotson | .02 | .10 |
| 357 Steve Stone | .02 | .10 |
| 358 Larry Hisle | .02 | .10 |
| 359 Aurelio Lopez | .02 | .10 |
| 360 Oscar Gamble | .02 | .10 |
| 361 Tom Burgmeier | .02 | .10 |
| 362 Terry Forster | .07 | .20 |
| 363 Joe Charboneau | .07 | .20 |
| 364 Ken Brett | .02 | .10 |
| 365 Tony Armas | .07 | .20 |
| 366 Chris Speier | .02 | .10 |
| 367 Fred Lynn | .07 | .20 |
| 368 Buddy Bell | .07 | .20 |
| 369 Jim Essian | .02 | .10 |
| 370 Terry Puhl | .02 | .10 |
| 371 Greg Gross | .02 | .10 |
| 372 Bruce Sutter | .15 | .40 |
| 373 Joe Lefebvre | .02 | .10 |
| 374 Ray Knight | .07 | .20 |
| 375 Bruce Benedict | .02 | .10 |
| 376 Tim Foli | .02 | .10 |
| 377 Al Holland | .02 | .10 |
| 378 Ken Kravec | .02 | .10 |
| 379 Jeff Burroughs | .02 | .10 |
| 380 Pete Falcone | .02 | .10 |
| 381 Ernie Whitt | .02 | .10 |
| 382 Brad Havens | .02 | .10 |
| 383 Terry Crowley | .02 | .10 |
| 384 Don Money | .02 | .10 |
| 385 Dan Schatzeder | .02 | .10 |
| 386 Gary Allenson | .02 | .10 |
| 387 Yogi Berra CO | .30 | .75 |
| 388 Ken Landreaux | .02 | .10 |
| 389 Mike Hargrove | .02 | .10 |
| 390 Darryl Motley | .02 | .10 |
| 391 Dave McKay | .02 | .10 |
| 392 Stan Bahnsen | .02 | .10 |
| 393 Ken Forsch | .02 | .10 |
| 394 Mario Mendoza | .02 | .10 |
| 395 Jim Morrison | .02 | .10 |
| 396 Mike Ivie | .02 | .10 |
| 397 Broderick Perkins | .02 | .10 |
| 398 Darrell Evans | .07 | .20 |
| 399 Ron Reed | .02 | .10 |
| 400 Johnny Bench | .30 | .75 |
| 401 Steve Bedrosian RC | .20 | .50 |
| 402 Bill Robinson | .02 | .10 |
| 403 Bill Buckner | .07 | .20 |
| 404 Ken Oberkfell | .02 | .10 |
| 405 Cal Ripken RC | 10.00 | 25.00 |
| 406 Jim Gantner | .02 | .10 |
| 407 Kirk Gibson | .30 | .75 |
| 408 Tony Perez | .15 | .40 |
| 409 Tommy John | .07 | .20 |
| 410 Dave Stewart RC | .60 | 1.50 |
| 411 Dan Spillner | .02 | .10 |
| 412 Willie Aikens | .02 | .10 |
| 413 Mike Heath | .02 | .10 |
| 414 Ray Burris | .02 | .10 |
| 415 Leon Roberts | .02 | .10 |
| 416 Mike Witt | .20 | .50 |
| 417 Bob Molinaro | .02 | .10 |
| 418 Steve Braun | .02 | .10 |
| 419 Nolan Ryan | 1.50 | 4.00 |
| 420 Tug McGraw | .07 | .20 |
| 421 Dave Concepcion | .07 | .20 |
| 422A Juan Eichelberger ERR (Photo actually Gary Lucas) | .15 | .40 |
| 422B Juan Eichelberger COR | .02 | .10 |
| 423 Rick Rhoden | .02 | .10 |
| 424 Frank Robinson MG | .15 | .40 |
| 425 Eddie Miller | .02 | .10 |
| 426 Bill Caudill | .02 | .10 |
| 427 Doug Flynn | .02 | .10 |
| 428 Larry Andersen UER (Misspelled Anderson on card) | .02 | .10 |
| 429 Al Williams | .02 | .10 |
| 430 Jerry Garvin | .02 | .10 |
| 431 Glenn Adams | .02 | .10 |
| 432 Barry Bonnell | .02 | .10 |
| 433 Jerry Narron | .02 | .10 |
| 434 John Stearns | .02 | .10 |
| 435 Mike Tyson | .02 | .10 |
| 436 Glenn Hubbard | .02 | .10 |
| 437 Eddie Solomon | .02 | .10 |
| 438 Jeff Leonard | .02 | .10 |
| 439 Randy Bass | .20 | .50 |
| 440 Mike LaCoss | .02 | .10 |
| 441 Gary Matthews | .07 | .20 |
| 442 Mark Littell | .02 | .10 |
| 443 Don Sutton | .07 | .20 |
| 444 John Harris | .02 | .10 |
| 445 Vada Pinson CO | .07 | .20 |
| 446 Elias Sosa | .02 | .10 |
| 447 Charlie Hough | .07 | .20 |
| 448 Willie Wilson | .07 | .20 |
| 449 Fred Stanley | .02 | .10 |
| 450 Tom Veryzer | .02 | .10 |
| 451 Ron Davis | .02 | .10 |
| 452 Mark Clear | .02 | .10 |
| 453 Bill Russell | .07 | .20 |
| 454 Lou Whitaker | .07 | .20 |
| 455 Dan Graham | .02 | .10 |
| 456 Reggie Cleveland | .02 | .10 |
| 457 Sammy Stewart | .02 | .10 |
| 458 Pete Vuckovich | .02 | .10 |
| 459 John Wockenfuss | .02 | .10 |
| 460 Glenn Hoffman | .02 | .10 |
| 461 Willie Randolph | .07 | .20 |
| 462 Fernando Valenzuela | .30 | .75 |
| 463 Ron Hassey | .02 | .10 |
| 464 Paul Splittorff | .02 | .10 |
| 465 Rob Picciolo | .02 | .10 |
| 466 Larry Parrish | .02 | .10 |
| 467 Johnny Grubb | .02 | .10 |
| 468 Dan Ford | .02 | .10 |
| 469 Silvio Martinez | .02 | .10 |
| 470 Kiko Garcia | .02 | .10 |
| 471 Bob Boone | .07 | .20 |
| 472 Luis Salazar | .02 | .10 |
| 473 Randy Niemann | .02 | .10 |
| 474 Tom Griffin | .02 | .10 |
| 475 Phil Niekro | .07 | .20 |
| 476 Hubie Brooks | .07 | .20 |
| 477 Dick Tidrow | .02 | .10 |
| 478 Jim Beattie | .02 | .10 |
| 479 Damaso Garcia | .02 | .10 |
| 480 Mickey Hatcher | .02 | .10 |
| 481 Joe Price | .02 | .10 |
| 482 Ed Farmer | .02 | .10 |
| 483 Eddie Murray | .30 | .75 |
| 484 Ben Oglivie | .02 | .10 |
| 485 Kevin Saucier | .02 | .10 |
| 486 Bobby Murcer | .07 | .20 |
| 487 Bill Campbell | .02 | .10 |
| 488 Reggie Smith | .07 | .20 |
| 489 Wayne Garland | .02 | .10 |
| 490 Jim Wright | .02 | .10 |
| 491 Billy Martin MG | .15 | .40 |
| 492 Jim Fanning MG | .02 | .10 |
| 493 Don Baylor | .07 | .20 |
| 494 Rick Honeycutt | .02 | .10 |
| 495 Carlton Fisk | .15 | .40 |
| 496 Denny Walling | .02 | .10 |
| 497 Bake McBride | .02 | .10 |
| 498 Darrell Porter | .02 | .10 |
| 499 Gene Richards | .02 | .10 |
| 500 Ron Oester | .02 | .10 |
| 501 Ken Dayley | .07 | .20 |
| 502 Jason Thompson | .02 | .10 |
| 503 Milt May | .02 | .10 |
| 504 Doug Bird | .02 | .10 |
| 505 Bruce Bochte | .02 | .10 |
| 506 Neil Allen | .02 | .10 |
| 507 Joey McLaughlin | .02 | .10 |
| 508 Butch Wynegar | .02 | .10 |
| 509 Gary Roenicke | .02 | .10 |
| 510 Robin Yount | .50 | 1.25 |
| 511 Dave Tobik | .02 | .10 |
| 512 Rich Gedman | .20 | .50 |
| 513 Gene Nelson | .02 | .10 |
| 514 Rick Monday | .07 | .20 |
| 515 Miguel Dilone | .02 | .10 |
| 516 Clint Hurdle | .02 | .10 |
| 517 Jeff Newman | .02 | .10 |
| 518 Grant Jackson | .02 | .10 |
| 519 Andy Hassler | .02 | .10 |
| 520 Pat Putnam | .02 | .10 |
| 521 Greg Pryor | .02 | .10 |
| 522 Tony Scott | .02 | .10 |
| 523 Steve Mura | .02 | .10 |
| 524 Johnnie LeMaster | .02 | .10 |
| 525 Dick Ruthven | .02 | .10 |
| 526 John McNamara MG | .02 | .10 |
| 527 Larry McWilliams | .02 | .10 |
| 528 Johnny Ray RC | .20 | .50 |
| 529 Pat Tabler | .02 | .10 |
| 530 Tom Herr | .02 | .10 |
| 531A SD Chicken ERR | .40 | 1.00 |
| 531B SD Chicken COR | .40 | 1.00 |
| 532 Sal Butera | .02 | .10 |
| 533 Mike Griffin | .02 | .10 |
| 534 Kelvin Moore | .02 | .10 |
| 535 Reggie Jackson | .15 | .40 |
| 536 Ed Romero | .02 | .10 |
| 537 Derrel Thomas | .02 | .10 |
| 538 Mike O'Berry | .02 | .10 |
| 539 Jack O'Connor | .02 | .10 |
| 540 Bob Ojeda RC | .20 | .50 |
| 541 Roy Lee Jackson | .02 | .10 |
| 542 Lynn Jones | .02 | .10 |
| 543 Gaylord Perry | .07 | .20 |
| 544A Phil Garner ERR (Reverse negative) | .07 | .20 |
| 544B Phil Garner COR | .07 | .20 |
| 545 Garry Templeton | .07 | .20 |
| 546 Rafael Ramirez | .02 | .10 |
| 547 Jeff Reardon | .07 | .20 |
| 548 Ron Guidry | .07 | .20 |
| 549 Tim Laudner | .02 | .10 |
| 550 John Henry Johnson | .02 | .10 |
| 551 Chris Bando | .02 | .10 |
| 552 Bobby Brown | .02 | .10 |
| 553 Larry Bradford | .02 | .10 |
| 554 Scott Fletcher RC | .20 | .50 |
| 555 Jerry Royster | .02 | .10 |
| 556 Shooty Babitt UER (Spelled Babbitt on front) | .02 | .10 |
| 557 Kent Hrbek RC | .40 | 1.00 |
| 558 R.Guidry/T.John | .07 | .20 |
| 559 Mark Bomback | .02 | .10 |
| 560 Julio Valdez | .02 | .10 |
| 561 Buck Martinez | .02 | .10 |
| 562 Mike A. Marshall RC | .20 | .50 |
| 563 Rennie Stennett | .02 | .10 |
| 564 Steve Crawford | .02 | .10 |
| 565 Bob Babcock | .02 | .10 |
| 566 Johnny Podres CO | .07 | .20 |
| 567 Paul Serna | .02 | .10 |
| 568 Harold Baines | .07 | .20 |
| 569 Dave LaRoche | .02 | .10 |
| 570 Lee May | .02 | .10 |
| 571 Gary Ward | .02 | .10 |
| 572 John Denny | .02 | .10 |
| 573 Roy Smalley | .02 | .10 |
| 574 Bob Brenly RC | .40 | 1.00 |
| 575 R.Jackson/D.Winfield | .07 | .20 |
| 576 Luis Pujols | .02 | .10 |
| 577 Butch Hobson | .02 | .10 |
| 578 Harvey Kuenn MG | .02 | .10 |
| 579 Cal Ripken Sr. CO | .07 | .20 |
| 580 Juan Berenguer | .02 | .10 |
| 581 Benny Ayala | .02 | .10 |
| 582 Vance Law | .02 | .10 |
| 583 Rick Leach | .02 | .10 |
| 584 George Frazier | .02 | .10 |
| 585 P.Rose/M.Schmidt | .60 | 1.50 |
| 586 Joe Rudi | .07 | .20 |
| 587 Juan Beniquez | .02 | .10 |
| 588 Luis DeLeon | .02 | .10 |
| 589 Craig Swan | .02 | .10 |
| 590 Dave Chalk | .02 | .10 |
| 591 Billy Gardner MG | .02 | .10 |
| 592 Sal Bando | .07 | .20 |
| 593 Bert Campaneris | .07 | .20 |
| 594 Steve Kemp | .02 | .10 |
| 595A Randy Lerch ERR (Braves) | .15 | .40 |
| 595B Randy Lerch COR | .02 | .10 |

**1983 Donruss**

|  | | |
|---|---|---|
| (Brewers) | .02 | .10 |
| ☐ 596 Bryan Clark RC | .05 | .15 |
| ☐ 597 Dave Ford | .02 | .10 |
| ☐ 598 Mike Scioscia | .07 | .20 |
| ☐ 599 John Lowenstein | .02 | .10 |
| ☐ 600 Rene Lachemann MG | .02 | .10 |
| ☐ 601 Mick Kelleher | .02 | .10 |
| ☐ 602 Ron Jackson | .02 | .10 |
| ☐ 603 Jerry Koosman | .07 | .20 |
| ☐ 604 Dave Goltz | .02 | .10 |
| ☐ 605 Ellis Valentine | .02 | .10 |
| ☐ 606 Lonnie Smith | .02 | .10 |
| ☐ 607 Joaquin Andujar | .07 | .20 |
| ☐ 608 Garry Hancock | .02 | .10 |
| ☐ 609 Jerry Turner | .02 | .10 |
| ☐ 610 Bob Bonner | .02 | .10 |
| ☐ 611 Jim Dwyer | .02 | .10 |
| ☐ 612 Terry Bulling | .02 | .10 |
| ☐ 613 Joel Youngblood | .02 | .10 |
| ☐ 614 Larry Milbourne | .02 | .10 |
| ☐ 615 Gene Roof UER | | |
| (Name on front | | |
| is Phil Roof) | .02 | .10 |
| ☐ 616 Keith Drumwright | .02 | .10 |
| ☐ 617 Dave Rosello | .02 | .10 |
| ☐ 618 Rickey Keeton | .02 | .10 |
| ☐ 619 Dennis Lamp | .02 | .10 |
| ☐ 620 Sid Monge | .02 | .10 |
| ☐ 621 Jerry White | .02 | .10 |
| ☐ 622 Luis Aguayo | .02 | .10 |
| ☐ 623 Jamie Easterly | .02 | .10 |
| ☐ 624 Steve Sax RC | .40 | 1.00 |
| ☐ 625 Dave Roberts | .02 | .10 |
| ☐ 626 Rick Bosetti | .02 | .10 |
| ☐ 627 Terry Francona RC | 1.25 | 3.00 |
| ☐ 628 T.Seaver/J.Bench | .30 | .75 |
| ☐ 629 Paul Mirabella | .02 | .10 |
| ☐ 630 Rance Mullinks | .02 | .10 |
| ☐ 631 Kevin Hickey RC | .05 | .15 |
| ☐ 632 Reid Nichols | .02 | .10 |
| ☐ 633 Dave Geisel | .02 | .10 |
| ☐ 634 Ken Griffey | .07 | .20 |
| ☐ 635 Bob Lemon MG | .15 | .40 |
| ☐ 636 Orlando Sanchez | .02 | .10 |
| ☐ 637 Bill Almon | .02 | .10 |
| ☐ 638 Danny Ainge | .07 | .20 |
| ☐ 639 Willie Stargell | .15 | .40 |
| ☐ 640 Bob Sykes | .02 | .10 |
| ☐ 641 Ed Lynch | .02 | .10 |
| ☐ 642 John Ellis | .02 | .10 |
| ☐ 643 Fergie Jenkins | .07 | .20 |
| ☐ 644 Lenn Sakata | .02 | .10 |
| ☐ 645 Julio Gonzalez | .02 | .10 |
| ☐ 646 Jesse Orosco | .07 | .20 |
| ☐ 647 Jerry Dybzinski | .02 | .10 |
| ☐ 648 Tommy Davis CO | .07 | .20 |
| ☐ 649 Ron Gardenhire RC | .20 | .50 |
| ☐ 650 Felipe Alou CO | .07 | .20 |
| ☐ 651 Harvey Haddix CO | .20 | .50 |
| ☐ 652 Willie Upshaw | .07 | .20 |
| ☐ 653 Bill Madlock | .07 | .20 |
| ☐ 654A DK Checklist 1-26 | | |
| ERR (Unnumbered) | | |
| (With Trammel) | .15 | .40 |
| ☐ 654B DK Checklist 1-26 | | |
| COR (Unnumbered) | | |
| (With Trammel) | .07 | .20 |
| ☐ 655 Checklist 27-130 | | |
| (Unnumbered) | .07 | .20 |
| ☐ 656 Checklist 131-234 | | |
| (Unnumbered) | .07 | .20 |
| ☐ 657 Checklist 235-338 | | |
| (Unnumbered) | .07 | .20 |
| ☐ 658 Checklist 339-442 | | |
| (Unnumbered) | .07 | .20 |
| ☐ 659 Checklist 443-544 | | |
| (Unnumbered) | .07 | .20 |
| ☐ 660 Checklist 545-653 | | |
| (Unnumbered) | .07 | .20 |

|  | | |
|---|---|---|
| ☐ COMPLETE SET (660) | 30.00 | 60.00 |
| ☐ COMP.FACT.SET (660) | 40.00 | 80.00 |
| ☐ COMP.COBB PUZZLE | 2.00 | 5.00 |
| ☐ 1 Fernando Valenzuela DK | .07 | .20 |
| ☐ 2 Rollie Fingers DK | .07 | .20 |
| ☐ 3 Reggie Jackson DK | .15 | .40 |
| ☐ 4 Jim Palmer DK | .07 | .20 |
| ☐ 5 Jack Morris DK | .07 | .20 |
| ☐ 6 George Foster DK | .07 | .20 |
| ☐ 7 Jim Sundberg DK | .07 | .20 |
| ☐ 8 Willie Stargell DK | .15 | .40 |
| ☐ 9 Dave Stieb DK | .07 | .20 |
| ☐ 10 Joe Niekro DK | .02 | .10 |
| ☐ 11 Rickey Henderson DK | .60 | 1.50 |
| ☐ 12 Dale Murphy DK | .15 | .40 |
| ☐ 13 Toby Harrah DK | .07 | .20 |
| ☐ 14 Bill Buckner DK | .07 | .20 |
| ☐ 15 Willie Wilson DK | .07 | .20 |
| ☐ 16 Steve Carlton DK | .15 | .40 |
| ☐ 17 Ron Guidry DK | .07 | .20 |
| ☐ 18 Steve Rogers DK | .07 | .20 |
| ☐ 19 Kent Hrbek DK | .07 | .20 |
| ☐ 20 Keith Hernandez DK | .07 | .20 |
| ☐ 21 Floyd Bannister DK | .02 | .10 |
| ☐ 22 Johnny Bench DK | .30 | .75 |
| ☐ 23 Britt Burns DK | .02 | .10 |
| ☐ 24 Joe Morgan DK | .07 | .20 |
| ☐ 25 Carl Yastrzemski DK | .30 | .75 |
| ☐ 26 Terry Kennedy DK | .02 | .10 |
| ☐ 27 Gary Roenicke | .02 | .10 |
| ☐ 28 Dwight Bernard | .02 | .10 |
| ☐ 29 Pat Underwood | .02 | .10 |
| ☐ 30 Gary Allenson | .02 | .10 |
| ☐ 31 Ron Guidry | .07 | .20 |
| ☐ 32 Burt Hooton | .02 | .10 |
| ☐ 33 Chris Bando | .02 | .10 |
| ☐ 34 Vida Blue | .07 | .20 |
| ☐ 35 Rickey Henderson | .60 | 1.50 |
| ☐ 36 Ray Burris | .02 | .10 |
| ☐ 37 John Butcher | .02 | .10 |
| ☐ 38 Don Aase | .02 | .10 |
| ☐ 39 Jerry Koosman | .07 | .20 |
| ☐ 40 Bruce Sutter | .15 | .40 |
| ☐ 41 Jose Cruz | .07 | .20 |
| ☐ 42 Pete Rose | 1.00 | 2.50 |
| ☐ 43 Cesar Cedeno | .07 | .20 |
| ☐ 44 Floyd Chiffer | .02 | .10 |
| ☐ 45 Larry McWilliams | .02 | .10 |
| ☐ 46 Alan Fowlkes | .02 | .10 |
| ☐ 47 Dale Murphy | .15 | .40 |
| ☐ 48 Doug Bird | .02 | .10 |
| ☐ 49 Hubie Brooks | .07 | .20 |
| ☐ 50 Floyd Bannister | .02 | .10 |
| ☐ 51 Jack O'Connor | .02 | .10 |
| ☐ 52 Steve Senteney | .02 | .10 |
| ☐ 53 Gary Gaetti RC | .40 | 1.00 |
| ☐ 54 Damaso Garcia | .02 | .10 |
| ☐ 55 Gene Nelson | .02 | .10 |
| ☐ 56 Mookie Wilson | .07 | .20 |
| ☐ 57 Allen Ripley | .02 | .10 |
| ☐ 58 Bob Horner | .07 | .20 |
| ☐ 59 Tony Pena | .02 | .10 |
| ☐ 60 Gary Lavelle | .02 | .10 |
| ☐ 61 Tim Lollar | .02 | .10 |
| ☐ 62 Frank Pastore | .02 | .10 |
| ☐ 63 Garry Maddox | .02 | .10 |
| ☐ 64 Bob Forsch | .02 | .10 |
| ☐ 65 Harry Spilman | .02 | .10 |
| ☐ 66 Geoff Zahn | .02 | .10 |
| ☐ 67 Salome Barojas | .02 | .10 |
| ☐ 68 David Palmer | .02 | .10 |
| ☐ 69 Charlie Hough | .07 | .20 |

|  | | |
|---|---|---|
| ☐ 70 Dan Quisenberry | .02 | .10 |
| ☐ 71 Tony Armas | .07 | .20 |
| ☐ 72 Rick Sutcliffe | .07 | .20 |
| ☐ 73 Steve Balboni | .02 | .10 |
| ☐ 74 Jerry Remy | .02 | .10 |
| ☐ 75 Mike Scioscia | .07 | .20 |
| ☐ 76 John Wockenfuss | .02 | .10 |
| ☐ 77 Jim Palmer | .07 | .20 |
| ☐ 78 Rollie Fingers | .07 | .20 |
| ☐ 79 Joe Nolan | .02 | .10 |
| ☐ 80 Pete Vuckovich | .02 | .10 |
| ☐ 81 Rick Leach | .02 | .10 |
| ☐ 82 Rick Miller | .02 | .10 |
| ☐ 83 Graig Nettles | .07 | .20 |
| ☐ 84 Ron Cey | .07 | .20 |
| ☐ 85 Miguel Dilone | .02 | .10 |
| ☐ 86 John Wathan | .02 | .10 |
| ☐ 87 Kelvin Moore | .02 | .10 |
| ☐ 88A Bryn Smith FDC Bym | .07 | .20 |
| ☐ 88B Bryn Smith FDC COR | .15 | .40 |
| ☐ 89 Dave Hostetler | .02 | .10 |
| ☐ 90 Rod Carew | .15 | .40 |
| ☐ 91 Lonnie Smith | .02 | .10 |
| ☐ 92 Bob Knepper | .02 | .10 |
| ☐ 93 Marty Bystrom | .02 | .10 |
| ☐ 94 Chris Welsh | .02 | .10 |
| ☐ 95 Jason Thompson | .02 | .10 |
| ☐ 96 Tom O'Malley | .02 | .10 |
| ☐ 97 Phil Niekro | .07 | .20 |
| ☐ 98 Neil Allen | .02 | .10 |
| ☐ 99 Bill Buckner | .07 | .20 |
| ☐ 100 Ed VandeBerg | .02 | .10 |
| ☐ 101 Jim Clancy | .02 | .10 |
| ☐ 102 Robert Castillo | .02 | .10 |
| ☐ 103 Bruce Berenyi | .02 | .10 |
| ☐ 104 Carlton Fisk | .15 | .40 |
| ☐ 105 Mike Flanagan | .02 | .10 |
| ☐ 106 Cecil Cooper | .07 | .20 |
| ☐ 107 Jack Morris | .07 | .20 |
| ☐ 108 Mike Morgan | .02 | .10 |
| ☐ 109 Luis Aponte | .02 | .10 |
| ☐ 110 Pedro Guerrero | .07 | .20 |
| ☐ 111 Len Barker | .02 | .10 |
| ☐ 112 Willie Wilson | .07 | .20 |
| ☐ 113 Dave Beard | .02 | .10 |
| ☐ 114 Mike Gates | .02 | .10 |
| ☐ 115 Reggie Jackson | .20 | .50 |
| ☐ 116 George Wright RC | .20 | .50 |
| ☐ 117 Vance Law | .02 | .10 |
| ☐ 118 Nolan Ryan | 1.50 | 4.00 |
| ☐ 119 Mike Krukow | .02 | .10 |
| ☐ 120 Ozzie Smith | .50 | 1.25 |
| ☐ 121 Broderick Perkins | .02 | .10 |
| ☐ 122 Tom Seaver | .30 | .75 |
| ☐ 123 Chris Chambliss | .02 | .10 |
| ☐ 124 Chuck Tanner MG | .02 | .10 |
| ☐ 125 Johnnie LeMaster | .02 | .10 |
| ☐ 126 Mel Hall RC | .20 | .50 |
| ☐ 127 Bruce Bochte | .02 | .10 |
| ☐ 128 Charlie Puleo | .02 | .10 |
| ☐ 129 Luis Leal | .02 | .10 |
| ☐ 130 John Pacella | .02 | .10 |
| ☐ 131 Glenn Gulliver | .02 | .10 |
| ☐ 132 Don Money | .02 | .10 |
| ☐ 133 Dave Rozema | .02 | .10 |
| ☐ 134 Bruce Hurst | .02 | .10 |
| ☐ 135 Rudy May | .02 | .10 |
| ☐ 136 Tom Lasorda MG | .15 | .40 |
| ☐ 137 Dan Spillner UER | | |
| (Photo actually | | |
| Ed Whitson) | .02 | .10 |
| ☐ 138 Jerry Martin | .02 | .10 |
| ☐ 139 Mike Norris | .02 | .10 |
| ☐ 140 Al Oliver | .07 | .20 |
| ☐ 141 Daryl Sconiers | .02 | .10 |
| ☐ 142 Lamar Johnson | .02 | .10 |
| ☐ 143 Harold Baines | .07 | .20 |
| ☐ 144 Alan Ashby | .02 | .10 |
| ☐ 145 Garry Templeton | .07 | .20 |
| ☐ 146 Al Holland | .02 | .10 |
| ☐ 147 Bo Diaz | .02 | .10 |
| ☐ 148 Dave Concepcion | .07 | .20 |
| ☐ 149 Rick Camp | .02 | .10 |
| ☐ 150 Jim Morrison | .02 | .10 |
| ☐ 151 Randy Martz | .02 | .10 |
| ☐ 152 Keith Hernandez | .07 | .20 |
| ☐ 153 John Lowenstein | .02 | .10 |
| ☐ 154 Mike Caldwell | .02 | .10 |

|  |  | | |
|---|--------|------|------|
| 155 | Milt Wilcox | .02 | .10 |
| 156 | Rich Gedman | .02 | .10 |
| 157 | Rich Gossage | .07 | .20 |
| 158 | Jerry Reuss | .02 | .10 |
| 159 | Ron Hassey | .02 | .10 |
| 160 | Larry Gura | .02 | .10 |
| 161 | Dwayne Murphy | .02 | .10 |
| 162 | Woodie Fryman | .02 | .10 |
| 163 | Steve Comer | .02 | .10 |
| 164 | Ken Forsch | .02 | .10 |
| 165 | Dennis Lamp | .02 | .10 |
| 166 | David Green RC | .20 | .50 |
| 167 | Terry Puhl | .02 | .10 |
| 168 | Mike Schmidt | .75 | 2.00 |
| 169 | Eddie Milner | .02 | .10 |
| 170 | John Curtis | .02 | .10 |
| 171 | Don Robinson | .02 | .10 |
| 172 | Rich Gale | .02 | .10 |
| 173 | Steve Bedrosian | .07 | .20 |
| 174 | Willie Hernandez | .02 | .10 |
| 175 | Ron Gardenhire | .02 | .10 |
| 176 | Jim Beattie | .02 | .10 |
| 177 | Tim Laudner | .02 | .10 |
| 178 | Buck Martinez | .02 | .10 |
| 179 | Kent Hrbek | .07 | .20 |
| 180 | Alfredo Griffin | .02 | .10 |
| 181 | Larry Andersen | .02 | .10 |
| 182 | Pete Falcone | .02 | .10 |
| 183 | Jody Davis | .02 | .10 |
| 184 | Glenn Hubbard | .02 | .10 |
| 185 | Dale Berra | .02 | .10 |
| 186 | Greg Minton | .02 | .10 |
| 187 | Gary Lucas | .02 | .10 |
| 188 | Dave Van Gorder | .02 | .10 |
| 189 | Bob Demier | .02 | .10 |
| 190 | Willie McGee RC | .60 | 1.50 |
| 191 | Dickie Thon | .02 | .10 |
| 192 | Bob Boone | .07 | .20 |
| 193 | Britt Burns | .02 | .10 |
| 194 | Jeff Reardon | .07 | .20 |
| 195 | Jon Matlack | .02 | .10 |
| 196 | Don Slaught RC | .20 | .50 |
| 197 | Fred Stanley | .02 | .10 |
| 198 | Rick Manning | .02 | .10 |
| 199 | Dave Righetti | .07 | .20 |
| 200 | Dave Stapleton | .02 | .10 |
| 201 | Steve Yeager | .02 | .10 |
| 202 | Enos Cabell | .02 | .10 |
| 203 | Sammy Stewart | .02 | .10 |
| 204 | Moose Haas | .02 | .10 |
| 205 | Lenn Sakata | .02 | .10 |
| 206 | Charlie Moore | .02 | .10 |
| 207 | Alan Trammell | .07 | .20 |
| 208 | Jim Rice | .07 | .20 |
| 209 | Roy Smalley | .02 | .10 |
| 210 | Bill Russell | .07 | .20 |
| 211 | Andre Thornton | .02 | .10 |
| 212 | Willie Aikens | .02 | .10 |
| 213 | Dave McKay | .02 | .10 |
| 214 | Tim Blackwell | .02 | .10 |
| 215 | Buddy Bell | .07 | .20 |
| 216 | Doug DeCinces | .02 | .10 |
| 217 | Tom Herr | .02 | .10 |
| 218 | Frank LaCorte | .02 | .10 |
| 219 | Steve Carlton | .15 | .40 |
| 220 | Terry Kennedy | .02 | .10 |
| 221 | Mike Easler | .02 | .10 |
| 222 | Jack Clark | .07 | .20 |
| 223 | Gene Garber | .02 | .10 |
| 224 | Scott Holman | .02 | .10 |
| 225 | Mike Proly | .02 | .10 |
| 226 | Terry Bulling | .02 | .10 |
| 227 | Jerry Garvin | .02 | .10 |
| 228 | Ron Davis | .02 | .10 |
| 229 | Tom Hume | .02 | .10 |
| 230 | Marc Hill | .02 | .10 |
| 231 | Dennis Martinez | .07 | .20 |
| 232 | Jim Gantner | .02 | .10 |
| 233 | Larry Pashnick | .02 | .10 |
| 234 | Dave Collins | .02 | .10 |
| 235 | Tom Burgmeier | .02 | .10 |
| 236 | Ken Landreaux | .02 | .10 |
| 237 | John Denny | .02 | .10 |
| 238 | Hal McRae | .07 | .20 |
| 239 | Matt Keough | .02 | .10 |
| 240 | Doug Flynn | .02 | .10 |
| 241 | Fred Lynn | .07 | .20 |
| 242 | Billy Sample | .02 | .10 |
| 243 | Tom Paciorek | .02 | .10 |
| 244 | Joe Sambito | .02 | .10 |
| 245 | Sid Monge | .02 | .10 |
| 246 | Ken Oberkfell | .02 | .10 |
| 247 | Joe Pittman UER (Photo actually Juan Eichelberge) | .02 | .10 |
| 248 | Mario Soto | .07 | .20 |
| 249 | Claudell Washington | .02 | .10 |
| 250 | Rick Rhoden | .02 | .10 |
| 251 | Darrell Evans | .07 | .20 |
| 252 | Steve Henderson | .02 | .10 |
| 253 | Manny Castillo | .02 | .10 |
| 254 | Craig Swan | .02 | .10 |
| 255 | Joey McLaughlin | .02 | .10 |
| 256 | Pete Redfern | .02 | .10 |
| 257 | Ken Singleton | .07 | .20 |
| 258 | Robin Yount | .50 | 1.25 |
| 259 | Elias Sosa | .02 | .10 |
| 260 | Bob Ojeda | .07 | .20 |
| 261 | Bobby Murcer | .07 | .20 |
| 262 | Candy Maldonado RC | .20 | .50 |
| 263 | Rick Waits | .02 | .10 |
| 264 | Greg Pryor | .02 | .10 |
| 265 | Bob Owchinko | .02 | .10 |
| 266 | Chris Speier | .02 | .10 |
| 267 | Bruce Kison | .02 | .10 |
| 268 | Mark Wagner | .02 | .10 |
| 269 | Steve Kemp | .02 | .10 |
| 270 | Phil Garner | .07 | .20 |
| 271 | Gene Richards | .02 | .10 |
| 272 | Renie Martin | .02 | .10 |
| 273 | Dave Roberts | .02 | .10 |
| 274 | Dan Driessen | .02 | .10 |
| 275 | Rufino Linares | .02 | .10 |
| 276 | Lee Lacy | .02 | .10 |
| 277 | Ryne Sandberg RC | 4.00 | 10.00 |
| 278 | Darrell Porter | .02 | .10 |
| 279 | Cal Ripken | 2.50 | 6.00 |
| 280 | Jamie Easterly | .02 | .10 |
| 281 | Bill Fahey | .02 | .10 |
| 282 | Glenn Hoffman | .02 | .10 |
| 283 | Willie Randolph | .07 | .20 |
| 284 | Fernando Valenzuela | .07 | .20 |
| 285 | Alan Bannister | .02 | .10 |
| 286 | Paul Splittorff | .02 | .10 |
| 287 | Joe Rudi | .07 | .20 |
| 288 | Bill Gullickson | .02 | .10 |
| 289 | Danny Darwin | .02 | .10 |
| 290 | Andy Hassler | .02 | .10 |
| 291 | Ernesto Escarrega | .02 | .10 |
| 292 | Steve Mura | .02 | .10 |
| 293 | Tony Scott | .02 | .10 |
| 294 | Manny Trillo | .02 | .10 |
| 295 | Greg Harris | .02 | .10 |
| 296 | Luis DeLeon | .02 | .10 |
| 297 | Kent Tekulve | .07 | .20 |
| 298 | Atlee Hammaker | .02 | .10 |
| 299 | Bruce Benedict | .02 | .10 |
| 300 | Fergie Jenkins | .07 | .20 |
| 301 | Dave Kingman | .07 | .20 |
| 302 | Bill Caudill | .02 | .10 |
| 303 | John Castino | .02 | .10 |
| 304 | Ernie Whitt | .02 | .10 |
| 305 | Randy Johnson | .02 | .10 |
| 306 | Garth Iorg | .02 | .10 |
| 307 | Gaylord Perry | .07 | .20 |
| 308 | Ed Lynch | .02 | .10 |
| 309 | Keith Moreland | .02 | .10 |
| 310 | Rafael Ramirez | .02 | .10 |
| 311 | Bill Madlock | .07 | .20 |
| 312 | Milt May | .02 | .10 |
| 313 | John Montefusco | .02 | .10 |
| 314 | Wayne Krenchicki | .02 | .10 |
| 315 | George Vukovich | .02 | .10 |
| 316 | Joaquin Andujar | .07 | .20 |
| 317 | Craig Reynolds | .02 | .10 |
| 318 | Rick Burleson | .02 | .10 |
| 319 | Richard Dotson | .02 | .10 |
| 320 | Steve Rogers | .07 | .20 |
| 321 | Dave Schmidt | .02 | .10 |
| 322 | Bud Black RC | .20 | .50 |
| 323 | Jeff Burroughs | .02 | .10 |
| 324 | Von Hayes | .07 | .20 |
| 325 | Butch Wynegar | .02 | .10 |
| 326 | Carl Yastrzemski | .50 | 1.25 |
| 327 | Ron Roenicke | .02 | .10 |
| 328 | Howard Johnson RC | .40 | 1.00 |
| 329 | Rick Dempsey UER (Posing as a left-handed batte) | | |
| 330A | Jim Slaton (Bio printed black on white) | .02 | .10 |
| 330B | Jim Slaton (Bio printed black on yellow) | .07 | .20 |
| 331 | Benny Ayala | .02 | .10 |
| 332 | Ted Simmons | .07 | .20 |
| 333 | Lou Whitaker | .07 | .20 |
| 334 | Chuck Rainey | .02 | .10 |
| 335 | Lou Piniella | .07 | .20 |
| 336 | Steve Sax | .07 | .20 |
| 337 | Toby Harrah | .07 | .20 |
| 338 | George Brett | .75 | 2.00 |
| 339 | Dave Lopes | .07 | .20 |
| 340 | Gary Carter | .07 | .20 |
| 341 | John Grubb | .02 | .10 |
| 342 | Tim Foli | .02 | .10 |
| 343 | Jim Kaat | .07 | .20 |
| 344 | Mike LaCoss | .02 | .10 |
| 345 | Larry Christenson | .02 | .10 |
| 346 | Juan Bonilla | .02 | .10 |
| 347 | Omar Moreno | .02 | .10 |
| 348 | Chili Davis | .07 | .20 |
| 349 | Tommy Boggs | .02 | .10 |
| 350 | Rusty Staub | .07 | .20 |
| 351 | Bump Wills | .02 | .10 |
| 352 | Rick Sweet | .02 | .10 |
| 353 | Jim Gott RC | .20 | .50 |
| 354 | Terry Felton | .02 | .10 |
| 355 | Jim Kern | .02 | .10 |
| 356 | Bill Almon UER (Expos/Mets in 1983, not Padres/M | .02 | .10 |
| 357 | Tippy Martinez | .02 | .10 |
| 358 | Roy Howell | .02 | .10 |
| 359 | Dan Petry | .07 | .20 |
| 360 | Jerry Mumphrey | .02 | .10 |
| 361 | Mark Clear | .02 | .10 |
| 362 | Mike Marshall | .07 | .20 |
| 363 | Lary Sorensen | .02 | .10 |
| 364 | Amos Otis | .07 | .20 |
| 365 | Rick Langford | .02 | .10 |
| 366 | Brad Mills | .02 | .10 |
| 367 | Brian Downing | .07 | .20 |
| 368 | Mike Richardt | .02 | .10 |
| 369 | Aurelio Rodriguez | .02 | .10 |
| 370 | Dave Smith | .07 | .20 |
| 371 | Tug McGraw | .07 | .20 |
| 372 | Doug Bair | .02 | .10 |
| 373 | Ruppert Jones | .02 | .10 |
| 374 | Alex Trevino | .02 | .10 |
| 375 | Ken Dayley | .02 | .10 |
| 376 | Rod Scurry | .02 | .10 |
| 377 | Bob Brenly | .02 | .10 |
| 378 | Scot Thompson | .02 | .10 |
| 379 | Julio Cruz | .02 | .10 |
| 380 | John Stearns | .02 | .10 |
| 381 | Dale Murray | .02 | .10 |
| 382 | Frank Viola RC | .60 | 1.50 |
| 383 | Al Bumbry | .02 | .10 |
| 384 | Ben Oglivie | .07 | .20 |
| 385 | Dave Tobik | .02 | .10 |
| 386 | Bob Stanley | .02 | .10 |
| 387 | Andre Robertson | .02 | .10 |
| 388 | Jorge Orta | .02 | .10 |
| 389 | Ed Whitson | .02 | .10 |
| 390 | Don Hood | .02 | .10 |
| 391 | Tom Underwood | .02 | .10 |
| 392 | Tim Wallach | .07 | .20 |
| 393 | Steve Renko | .02 | .10 |
| 394 | Mickey Rivers | .07 | .20 |
| 395 | Greg Luzinski | .07 | .20 |
| 396 | Art Howe | .02 | .10 |
| 397 | Alan Wiggins | .02 | .10 |
| 398 | Jim Barr | .02 | .10 |
| 399 | Ivan DeJesus | .02 | .10 |
| 400 | Tom Lawless | .02 | .10 |
| 401 | Bob Walk | .02 | .10 |
| 402 | Jimmy Smith | .02 | .10 |
| 403 | Lee Smith | .15 | .40 |
| 404 | George Hendrick | .07 | .20 |
| 405 | Eddie Murray | .30 | .75 |
| 406 | Marshall Edwards | .02 | .10 |
| 407 | Lance Parrish | .07 | .20 |

|  | | |
|---|---|---|
| 408 Carney Lansford | .07 | .20 |
| 409 Dave Winfield | .07 | .20 |
| 410 Bob Welch | .07 | .20 |
| 411 Larry Milbourne | .02 | .10 |
| 412 Dennis Leonard | .02 | .10 |
| 413 Dan Meyer | .02 | .10 |
| 414 Charlie Lea | .02 | .10 |
| 415 Rick Honeycutt | .02 | .10 |
| 416 Mike Witt | .02 | .10 |
| 417 Steve Trout | .02 | .10 |
| 418 Glenn Brummer | .02 | .10 |
| 419 Denny Walling | .02 | .10 |
| 420 Gary Matthews | .07 | .20 |
| 421 Charlie Leibrandt UER | .02 | .10 |
| (Liebrandt on | | |
| front of car | | |
| 422 Juan Eichelberger UER | | |
| (Photo actually | | |
| Joe Pittma | | |
| 423 Cecilio Guante UER | .02 | .10 |
| (Listed as Matt | | |
| on card) | | |
| 424 Bill Laskey | .02 | .10 |
| 425 Jerry Royster | .02 | .10 |
| 426 Dickie Noles | .02 | .10 |
| 427 George Foster | .07 | .20 |
| 428 Mike Moore RC | .20 | .50 |
| 429 Gary Ward | .02 | .10 |
| 430 Barry Bonnell | .02 | .10 |
| 431 Ron Washington | .02 | .10 |
| 432 Rance Mulliniks | .02 | .10 |
| 433 Mike Stanton | .02 | .10 |
| 434 Jesse Orosco | .02 | .10 |
| 435 Larry Bowa | .07 | .20 |
| 436 Biff Pocoroba | .02 | .10 |
| 437 Johnny Ray | .07 | .20 |
| 438 Joe Morgan | .20 | .50 |
| 439 Eric Show RC | .20 | .50 |
| 440 Larry Biittner | .02 | .10 |
| 441 Greg Gross | .02 | .10 |
| 442 Gene Tenace | .07 | .20 |
| 443 Danny Heep | .02 | .10 |
| 444 Bobby Clark | .02 | .10 |
| 445 Kevin Hickey | .02 | .10 |
| 446 Scott Sanderson | .02 | .10 |
| 447 Frank Tanana | .07 | .20 |
| 448 Cesar Geronimo | .02 | .10 |
| 449 Jimmy Sexton | .02 | .10 |
| 450 Mike Hargrove | .07 | .20 |
| 451 Doyle Alexander | .02 | .10 |
| 452 Dwight Evans | .15 | .40 |
| 453 Terry Forster | .07 | .20 |
| 454 Tom Brookens | .02 | .10 |
| 455 Rich Dauer | .02 | .10 |
| 456 Rob Picciolo | .02 | .10 |
| 457 Terry Crowley | .02 | .10 |
| 458 Ned Yost | .02 | .10 |
| 459 Kirk Gibson | .20 | .50 |
| 460 Reid Nichols | .02 | .10 |
| 461 Oscar Gamble | .02 | .10 |
| 462 Dusty Baker | .07 | .20 |
| 463 Jack Perconte | .02 | .10 |
| 464 Frank White | .07 | .20 |
| 465 Mickey Klutts | .02 | .10 |
| 466 Warren Cromartie | .02 | .10 |
| 467 Larry Parrish | .02 | .10 |
| 468 Bobby Grich | .07 | .20 |
| 469 Dane Iorg | .02 | .10 |
| 470 Joe Niekro | .07 | .20 |
| 471 Ed Farmer | .02 | .10 |
| 472 Tim Flannery | .02 | .10 |
| 473 Dave Parker | .20 | .50 |
| 474 Jeff Leonard | .07 | .20 |
| 475 Al Hrabosky | .02 | .10 |
| 476 Ron Hodges | .02 | .10 |
| 477 Leon Durham | .02 | .10 |
| 478 Jim Essian | .02 | .10 |
| 479 Roy Lee Jackson | .02 | .10 |
| 480 Brad Havens | .02 | .10 |
| 481 Joe Price | .02 | .10 |
| 482 Tony Bernazard | .02 | .10 |
| 483 Scott McGregor | .02 | .10 |
| 484 Paul Molitor | .15 | .40 |
| 485 Mike Ivie | .02 | .10 |
| 486 Ken Griffey | .07 | .20 |
| 487 Dennis Eckersley | .15 | .40 |
| 488 Steve Garvey | .20 | .50 |
| 489 Mike Fischlin | .02 | .10 |
| 490 U.L. Washington | .02 | .10 |
| 491 Steve McCatty | .02 | .10 |
| 492 Roy Johnson | .02 | .10 |
| 493 Don Baylor | .07 | .20 |
| 494 Bobby Johnson | .02 | .10 |
| 495 Mike Squires | .02 | .10 |
| 496 Bert Roberge | .02 | .10 |
| 497 Dick Ruthven | .02 | .10 |
| 498 Tito Landrum | .02 | .10 |
| 499 Sixto Lezcano | .02 | .10 |
| 500 Johnny Bench | .30 | .75 |
| 501 Larry Whisenton | .02 | .10 |
| 502 Manny Sarmiento | .02 | .10 |
| 503 Fred Breining | .02 | .10 |
| 504 Bill Campbell | .02 | .10 |
| 505 Todd Cruz | .02 | .10 |
| 506 Bob Bailor | .02 | .10 |
| 507 Dave Stieb | .07 | .20 |
| 508 Al Williams | .02 | .10 |
| 509 Dan Ford | .02 | .10 |
| 510 Gorman Thomas | .07 | .20 |
| 511 Chet Lemon | .07 | .20 |
| 512 Mike Torrez | .02 | .10 |
| 513 Shane Rawley | .02 | .10 |
| 514 Mark Belanger | .02 | .10 |
| 515 Rodney Craig | .02 | .10 |
| 516 Onix Concepcion | .02 | .10 |
| 517 Mike Heath | .02 | .10 |
| 518 Andre Dawson | .07 | .20 |
| 519 Luis Sanchez | .02 | .10 |
| 520 Terry Bogener | .02 | .10 |
| 521 Rudy Law | .02 | .10 |
| 522 Ray Knight | .07 | .20 |
| 523 Joe Lefebvre | .02 | .10 |
| 524 Jim Wohlford | .02 | .10 |
| 525 Julio Franco RC | 2.50 | 6.00 |
| 526 Ron Oester | .02 | .10 |
| 527 Rick Mahler | .02 | .10 |
| 528 Steve Nicosia | .02 | .10 |
| 529 Junior Kennedy | .02 | .10 |
| 530A Whitey Herzog MG | .07 | .20 |
| (Bio printed | | |
| black on white) | | |
| 530B Whitey Herzog MG | | |
| (Bio printed | | |
| black on yellow) | .07 | .20 |
| 531A Don Sutton | .07 | .20 |
| 531B Don Sutton | .07 | .20 |
| 532 Mark Brouhard | .02 | .10 |
| 533A Sparky Anderson MG | | |
| (Bio printed | | |
| black on white) | .07 | .20 |
| 533B Sparky Anderson MG | | |
| (Bio printed | | |
| black on yellow) | .07 | .20 |
| 534 Roger LaFrancois | .02 | .10 |
| 535 George Frazier | .02 | .10 |
| 536 Tom Niedenfuer | .02 | .10 |
| 537 Ed Glynn | .02 | .10 |
| 538 Lee May | .02 | .10 |
| 539 Bob Kearney | .02 | .10 |
| 540 Tim Raines | .07 | .20 |
| 541 Paul Mirabella | .02 | .10 |
| 542 Luis Tiant | .07 | .20 |
| 543 Ron LeFlore | .07 | .20 |
| 544 Dave LaPoint | .02 | .10 |
| 545 Randy Moffitt | .02 | .10 |
| 546 Luis Aguayo | .02 | .10 |
| 547 Brad Lesley | .05 | .15 |
| 548 Luis Salazar | .02 | .10 |
| 549 John Candelaria | .02 | .10 |
| 550 Dave Bergman | .02 | .10 |
| 551 Bob Watson | .07 | .20 |
| 552 Pat Tabler | .02 | .10 |
| 553 Brent Gaff | .02 | .10 |
| 554 Al Cowens | .02 | .10 |
| 555 Tom Brunansky | .07 | .20 |
| 556 Lloyd Moseby | .02 | .10 |
| 557A Pascual Perez ERR Twins | .75 | 2.00 |
| 557B Pascual Perez COR | | |
| (Braves on proa) | .07 | .20 |
| 558 Willie Upshaw | .02 | .10 |
| 559 Richie Zisk | .02 | .10 |
| 560 Pat Zachry | .02 | .10 |
| 561 Jay Johnstone | .02 | .10 |
| 562 Carlos Diaz RC | .05 | .15 |
| 563 John Tudor | .07 | .20 |
| 564 Frank Robinson MG | .15 | .40 |
| 565 Dave Edwards | .02 | .10 |
| 566 Paul Householder | .02 | .10 |
| 567 Ron Reed | .02 | .10 |
| 568 Mike Ramsey | .02 | .10 |
| 569 Kiko Garcia | .02 | .10 |
| 570 Tommy John | .07 | .20 |
| 571 Tony LaRussa MG | .07 | .20 |
| 572 Joel Youngblood | .02 | .10 |
| 573 Wayne Tolleson | .02 | .10 |
| 574 Keith Creel | .02 | .10 |
| 575 Billy Martin MG | .15 | .40 |
| 576 Jerry Dybzinski | .02 | .10 |
| 577 Rick Cerone | .02 | .10 |
| 578 Tony Perez | .15 | .40 |
| 579 Greg Brock | .02 | .10 |
| 580 Glenn Wilson | .20 | .50 |
| 581 Tim Stoddard | .02 | .10 |
| 582 Bob McClure | .02 | .10 |
| 583 Jim Dwyer | .02 | .10 |
| 584 Ed Romero | .02 | .10 |
| 585 Larry Herndon | .02 | .10 |
| 586 Wade Boggs RC | 4.00 | 10.00 |
| 587 Jay Howell | .02 | .10 |
| 588 Dave Stewart | .07 | .20 |
| 589 Bert Blyleven | .07 | .20 |
| 590 Dick Howser MG | .02 | .10 |
| 591 Wayne Gross | .02 | .10 |
| 592 Terry Francona | .07 | .20 |
| 593 Don Werner | .02 | .10 |
| 594 Bill Stein | .02 | .10 |
| 595 Jesse Barfield | .07 | .20 |
| 596 Bob Molinaro | .02 | .10 |
| 597 Mike Vail | .02 | .10 |
| 598 Tony Gwynn RC | 6.00 | 15.00 |
| 599 Gary Rajsich | .02 | .10 |
| 600 Jerry Ujdur | .02 | .10 |
| 601 Cliff Johnson | .02 | .10 |
| 602 Jerry White | .02 | .10 |
| 603 Bryan Clark | .02 | .10 |
| 604 Joe Ferguson | .02 | .10 |
| 605 Guy Sularz | .02 | .10 |
| 606A Ozzie Virgil | | |
| (Green border | | |
| on photo) | .07 | .20 |
| 606B Ozzie Virgil | | |
| (Orange border | | |
| on photo) | .07 | .20 |
| 607 Terry Harper | .02 | .10 |
| 608 Harvey Kuenn MG | .02 | .10 |
| 609 Jim Sundberg | .07 | .20 |
| 610 Willie Stargell | .15 | .40 |
| 611 Reggie Smith | .07 | .20 |
| 612 Rob Wilfong | .02 | .10 |
| 613 Niekro Brothers | .07 | .20 |
| 614 Lee Elia MG | .02 | .10 |
| 615 Mickey Hatcher | .02 | .10 |
| 616 Jerry Hairston | .02 | .10 |
| 617 John Martin | .02 | .10 |
| 618 Wally Backman | .02 | .10 |
| 619 Storm Davis RC | .20 | .50 |
| 620 Alan Knicely | .02 | .10 |
| 621 John Stuper | .02 | .10 |
| 622 Matt Sinatro | .02 | .10 |
| 623 Geno Petralli | .20 | .50 |
| 624 Duane Walker | .02 | .10 |
| 625 Dick Williams MG | .02 | .10 |
| 626 Pat Corrales MG | .02 | .10 |
| 627 Vern Ruhle | .02 | .10 |
| 628 Joe Torre MG | .07 | .20 |
| 629 Anthony Johnson | .02 | .10 |
| 630 Steve Howe | .02 | .10 |
| 631 Gary Woods | .02 | .10 |
| 632 LaMarr Hoyt | .02 | .10 |
| 633 Steve Swisher | .02 | .10 |
| 634 Terry Leach | .02 | .10 |
| 635 Jeff Newman | .02 | .10 |
| 636 Brett Butler | .07 | .20 |
| 637 Gary Gray | .02 | .10 |
| 638 Lee Mazzilli | .07 | .20 |
| 639A Ron Jackson ERR A's | 8.00 | 20.00 |
| 639B Ron Jackson COR | | |
| (Angels in glove& | | |
| red border | | |
| on | .02 | .10 |
| 639C Ron Jackson COR | | |
| (Angels in glove& | | |
| green border | | |

|  |  |  |
|---|---|---|
|  | .15 | .40 |
| 640 Juan Beniquez | .02 | .10 |
| 641 Dave Rucker | .02 | .10 |
| 642 Luis Pujols | .02 | .10 |
| 643 Rick Monday | .07 | .20 |
| 644 Hosken Powell | .02 | .10 |
| 645 The Chicken | .15 | .40 |
| 646 Dave Engle | .02 | .10 |
| 647 Dick Davis | .02 | .10 |
| 648 F.Robby/V.Blue/J.Morgan | .15 | .40 |
| 649 Al Chambers | .02 | .10 |
| 650 Jesus Vega | .02 | .10 |
| 651 Jeff Jones | .02 | .10 |
| 652 Marvis Foley | .02 | .10 |
| 653 Ty Cobb Puzzle | .30 | .75 |
| 654A Dick Perez/DK CL | .15 | .40 |
| 654B Dick Perez/DK CL | .15 | .40 |
| 655 Checklist 27-130 (Unnumbered) | .02 | .10 |
| 656 Checklist 131-234 (Unnumbered) | .02 | .10 |
| 657 Checklist 235-338 | .02 | .10 |
| 658 Checklist 339-442 (Unnumbered) | .02 | .10 |
| 659 Checklist 443-544 (Unnumbered) | .02 | .10 |
| 660 Checklist 545-653 (Unnumbered) | .02 | .10 |

## 1984 Donruss

|  |  |  |
|---|---|---|
| COMPLETE SET (660) | 70.00 | 120.00 |
| COMP.FACT.SET (658) | 70.00 | 120.00 |
| COMP.SNIDER PUZZLE | 2.00 | 5.00 |
| 1 Robin Yount DK | 1.00 | 2.50 |
| 1A Robin Yount DK ERR | 2.00 | 5.00 |
| 2 Dave Concepcion DK | .08 | .25 |
| 2A Dave Concepcion DK ERR | .30 | .75 |
| 3 Dwayne Murphy DK | .08 | .25 |
| 3A Dwayne Murphy DK ERR | .30 | .75 |
| 4 John Castino DK | .08 | .25 |
| 4A John Castino DK ERR | .30 | .75 |
| 5 Leon Durham DK | .08 | .25 |
| 5A Leon Durham DK ERR | .30 | .75 |
| 6 Rusty Staub DK | .08 | .25 |
| 6A Rusty Staub DK ERR | .30 | .75 |
| 7 Jack Clark DK | .30 | .75 |
| 7A Jack Clark DK ERR | .30 | .75 |
| 8 Dave Dravecky DK | .08 | .25 |
| 8A Dave Dravecky DK ERR | .30 | .75 |
| 9 Al Oliver DK | .08 | .25 |
| 9A Al Oliver DK ERR | .30 | .75 |
| 10 Dave Righetti DK | .30 | .75 |
| 10A Dave Righetti DK ERR | .30 | .75 |
| 11 Hal McRae DK | .08 | .25 |
| 11A Hal McRae DK ERR | .30 | .75 |
| 12 Ray Knight DK | .08 | .25 |
| 12A Ray Knight DK ERR | .30 | .75 |
| 13 Bruce Sutter DK | .60 | 1.50 |
| 13A Bruce Sutter DK ERR | .60 | 1.50 |
| 14 Bob Horner DK | .08 | .25 |
| 14A Bob Horner DK ERR | .30 | .75 |
| 15 Lance Parrish DK | .30 | .75 |
| 15A Lance Parrish DK ERR | .30 | .75 |
| 16 Matt Young DK | .08 | .25 |
| 16A Matt Young DK ERR | .30 | .75 |
| 17 Fred Lynn DK | .08 | .25 |
| 17A Fred Lynn DK ERR | .30 | .75 |
| 18 Ron Kittle DK | .08 | .25 |
| 18A Ron Kittle DK ERR | .08 | .25 |
| 19 Jim Clancy DK | .08 | .25 |
| 19A Jim Clancy DK ERR | .30 | .75 |
| 20 Bill Madlock DK | .08 | .25 |
| 20A Bill Madlock DK ERR | .30 | .75 |
| 21 Larry Parrish DK | .08 | .25 |
| 21A Larry Parrish DK ERR | .08 | .25 |
| 22 Eddie Murray DK | 1.25 | 3.00 |
| 22A Eddie Murray DK ERR | 1.25 | 3.00 |
| 23 Mike Schmidt DK | 2.00 | 5.00 |
| 23A Mike Schmidt DK ERR | 2.00 | 5.00 |
| 24 Pedro Guerrero DK | .30 | .75 |
| 24A Pedro Guerrero DK ERR | .30 | .75 |
| 25 Andre Thornton DK | .08 | .25 |
| 25A Andre Thornton DK ERR | .08 | .25 |
| 26 Wade Boggs DK | 1.25 | 3.00 |
| 26A Wade Boggs DK ERR | 1.25 | 3.00 |
| 27 Joel Skinner RC | .08 | .25 |
| 28 Tommy Dunbar RC | .08 | .25 |
| 29A Mike Stenhouse ERR RC | .08 | .25 |
| 29B Mike Stenhouse COR | 1.25 | 3.00 |
| 30A Ron Darling ERR RC | .75 | 2.00 |
| 30B Ron Darling COR | 1.25 | 3.00 |
| 31 Dion James RC | .08 | .25 |
| 32 Tony Fernandez RC | .75 | 2.00 |
| 33 Angel Salazar RC | .08 | .25 |
| 34 Kevin McReynolds RC | .75 | 2.00 |
| 35 Dick Schofield RC | .40 | 1.00 |
| 36 Brad Komminsk RC | .08 | .25 |
| 37 Tim Teufel RC | .40 | 1.00 |
| 38 Doug Frobel RC | .08 | .25 |
| 39 Greg Gagne RC | .40 | 1.00 |
| 40 Mike Fuentes RC | .08 | .25 |
| 41 Joe Carter RC | 3.00 | 8.00 |
| 42 Mike C. Brown RC | .08 | .25 |
| 43 Mike Jeffcoat RC | .08 | .25 |
| 44 Sid Fernandez RC ! | .75 | 2.00 |
| 45 Brian Dayett RC | .08 | .25 |
| 46 Chris Smith RC | .08 | .25 |
| 47 Eddie Murray | 1.25 | 3.00 |
| 48 Robin Yount | 2.00 | 5.00 |
| 49 Lance Parrish | .60 | 1.50 |
| 50 Jim Rice | .30 | .75 |
| 51 Dave Winfield | .30 | .75 |
| 52 Fernando Valenzuela | .30 | .75 |
| 53 George Brett | 3.00 | 8.00 |
| 54 Rickey Henderson | 2.00 | 5.00 |
| 55 Gary Carter | .30 | .75 |
| 56 Buddy Bell | .30 | .75 |
| 57 Reggie Jackson | .60 | 1.50 |
| 58 Harold Baines | .30 | .75 |
| 59 Ozzie Smith | 2.00 | 5.00 |
| 60 Nolan Ryan | 6.00 | 15.00 |
| 61 Pete Rose | 4.00 | 10.00 |
| 62 Ron Oester | .08 | .25 |
| 63 Steve Garvey | .30 | .75 |
| 64 Jason Thompson | .08 | .25 |
| 65 Jack Clark | .30 | .75 |
| 66 Dale Murphy | .60 | 1.50 |
| 67 Leon Durham | .08 | .25 |
| 68 Darryl Strawberry RC | 3.00 | 8.00 |
| 69 Richie Zisk | .08 | .25 |
| 70 Kent Hrbek | .30 | .75 |
| 71 Dave Stieb | .30 | .75 |
| 72 Ken Schrom | .08 | .25 |
| 73 George Bell | .30 | .75 |
| 74 John Moses | .08 | .25 |
| 75 Ed Lynch | .08 | .25 |
| 76 Chuck Rainey | .08 | .25 |
| 77 Biff Pocoroba | .08 | .25 |
| 78 Cecilio Guante | .08 | .25 |
| 79 Jim Barr | .08 | .25 |
| 80 Kurt Bevacqua | .08 | .25 |
| 81 Tom Foley | .08 | .25 |
| 82 Joe Lefebvre | .08 | .25 |
| 83 Andy Van Slyke RC | 1.50 | 4.00 |
| 84 Bob Lillis MG | .08 | .25 |
| 85 Ricky Adams | .08 | .25 |
| 86 Jerry Hairston | .08 | .25 |
| 87 Bob James | .08 | .25 |
| 88 Joe Altobelli MG | .08 | .25 |
| 89 Ed Romero | .08 | .25 |
| 90 John Grubb | .08 | .25 |
| 91 John Henry Johnson | .08 | .25 |
| 92 Juan Espino | .08 | .25 |
| 93 Candy Maldonado | .08 | .25 |
| 94 Andre Thornton | .08 | .25 |
| 95 Onix Concepcion | .08 | .25 |
| 96 Donnie Hill UER (Listed as P, should be 2B) | .08 | .25 |
| 97 Andre Dawson | .30 | .75 |
| 98 Frank Tanana | .08 | .25 |
| 99 Curt Wilkerson | .08 | .25 |
| 100 Larry Gura | .08 | .25 |
| 101 Dwayne Murphy | .08 | .25 |
| 102 Tom Brennan | .08 | .25 |
| 103 Dave Righetti | .30 | .75 |
| 104 Steve Sax | .30 | .75 |
| 105 Dan Petry | .08 | .25 |
| 106 Cal Ripken | 5.00 | 12.00 |
| 107 Paul Molitor | .30 | .75 |
| 108 Fred Lynn | .30 | .75 |
| 109 Neil Allen | .08 | .25 |
| 110 Joe Niekro | .08 | .25 |
| 111 Steve Carlton | .60 | 1.50 |
| 112 Terry Kennedy | .08 | .25 |
| 113 Bill Madlock | .08 | .25 |
| 114 Chili Davis | .30 | .75 |
| 115 Jim Gantner | .08 | .25 |
| 116 Tom Seaver | 1.25 | 3.00 |
| 117 Bill Buckner | .30 | .75 |
| 118 Bill Caudill | .08 | .25 |
| 119 Jim Clancy | .08 | .25 |
| 120 John Castino | .08 | .25 |
| 121 Dave Concepcion | .08 | .25 |
| 122 Greg Luzinski | .30 | .75 |
| 123 Mike Boddicker | .08 | .25 |
| 124 Pete Ladd | .08 | .25 |
| 125 Juan Berenguer | .08 | .25 |
| 126 John Montefusco | .08 | .25 |
| 127 Ed Jurak | .08 | .25 |
| 128 Tom Niedenfuer | .08 | .25 |
| 129 Bert Blyleven | .30 | .75 |
| 130 Bud Black | .30 | .75 |
| 131 Gorman Heimueller | .08 | .25 |
| 132 Dan Schatzeder | .08 | .25 |
| 133 Ron Jackson | .08 | .25 |
| 134 Tom Henke RC | .75 | 2.00 |
| 135 Kevin Hickey | .08 | .25 |
| 136 Mike Scott | .08 | .25 |
| 137 Bo Diaz | .08 | .25 |
| 138 Glenn Brummer | .08 | .25 |
| 139 Sid Monge | .08 | .25 |
| 140 Rich Gale | .08 | .25 |
| 141 Brett Butler | .30 | .75 |
| 142 Brian Harper RC | .40 | 1.00 |
| 143 John Rabb | .08 | .25 |
| 144 Gary Woods | .08 | .25 |
| 145 Pat Putnam | .08 | .25 |
| 146 Jim Acker | .08 | .25 |
| 147 Mickey Hatcher | .08 | .25 |
| 148 Todd Cruz | .08 | .25 |
| 149 Tom Tellmann | .08 | .25 |
| 150 John Wockenfuss | .08 | .25 |
| 151 Wade Boggs | 3.00 | 8.00 |
| 152 Don Baylor | .30 | .75 |
| 153 Bob Welch | .30 | .75 |
| 154 Alan Bannister | .08 | .25 |
| 155 Willie Aikens | .08 | .25 |
| 156 Jeff Burroughs | .08 | .25 |
| 157 Bryan Little | .08 | .25 |
| 158 Bob Boone | .30 | .75 |
| 159 Dave Hostetler | .08 | .25 |
| 160 Jerry Dybzinski | .08 | .25 |
| 161 Mike Madden | .08 | .25 |
| 162 Luis DeLeon | .08 | .25 |
| 163 Willie Hernandez | .08 | .25 |
| 164 Frank Pastore | .08 | .25 |
| 165 Rick Camp | .08 | .25 |
| 166 Lee Mazzilli | .30 | .75 |
| 167 Scott Thompson | .30 | .75 |
| 168 Bob Forsch | .30 | .75 |
| 169 Mike Flanagan | .08 | .25 |
| 170 Rick Manning | .08 | .25 |
| 171 Chet Lemon | .30 | .75 |
| 172 Jerry Remy | .08 | .25 |
| 173 Ron Guidry | .30 | .75 |
| 174 Pedro Guerrero | .30 | .75 |
| 175 Willie Wilson | .08 | .25 |
| 176 Carney Lansford | .30 | .75 |
| 177 Al Oliver | .30 | .75 |
| 178 Jim Sundberg | .08 | .25 |
| 179 Bobby Grich | .30 | .75 |
| 180 Rich Dotson | .08 | .25 |
| 181 Joaquin Andujar | .08 | .25 |
| 182 Jose Cruz | .30 | .75 |
| 183 Mike Schmidt | 3.00 | 8.00 |
| 184 Gary Redus RC | .40 | 1.00 |
| 185 Garry Templeton | .30 | .75 |
| 186 Tony Pena | .08 | .25 |

|  |  | | |
|---|---|---|---|
| 187 | Greg Minton | .08 | .25 |
| 188 | Phil Niekro | .30 | .75 |
| 189 | Fergie Jenkins | .30 | .75 |
| 190 | Mookie Wilson | .30 | .75 |
| 191 | Jim Beattie | .08 | .25 |
| 192 | Gary Ward | .08 | .25 |
| 193 | Jesse Barfield | .30 | .75 |
| 194 | Pete Filson | .08 | .25 |
| 195 | Roy Lee Jackson | .08 | .25 |
| 196 | Rick Sweet | .08 | .25 |
| 197 | Jesse Orosco | .08 | .25 |
| 198 | Steve Lake | .08 | .25 |
| 199 | Ken Dayley | .08 | .25 |
| 200 | Manny Sarmiento | .08 | .25 |
| 201 | Mark Davis | .08 | .25 |
| 202 | Tim Flannery | .08 | .25 |
| 203 | Bill Scherrer | .08 | .25 |
| 204 | Al Holland | .08 | .25 |
| 205 | Dave Von Ohlen | .08 | .25 |
| 206 | Mike LaCoss | .08 | .25 |
| 207 | Juan Beniquez | .08 | .25 |
| 208 | Juan Agosto | .08 | .25 |
| 209 | Bobby Ramos | .08 | .25 |
| 210 | Al Bumbry | .08 | .25 |
| 211 | Mark Brouhard | .08 | .25 |
| 212 | Howard Bailey | .08 | .25 |
| 213 | Bruce Hurst | .08 | .25 |
| 214 | Bob Shirley | .08 | .25 |
| 215 | Pat Zachry | .08 | .25 |
| 216 | Julio Franco | 1.25 | 3.00 |
| 217 | Mike Armstrong | .08 | .25 |
| 218 | Dave Beard | .08 | .25 |
| 219 | Steve Rogers | .30 | .75 |
| 220 | John Butcher | .08 | .25 |
| 221 | Mike Smithson | .08 | .25 |
| 222 | Frank White | .30 | .75 |
| 223 | Mike Heath | .08 | .25 |
| 224 | Chris Bando | .08 | .25 |
| 225 | Roy Smalley | .08 | .25 |
| 226 | Dusty Baker | .30 | .75 |
| 227 | Lou Whitaker | .30 | .75 |
| 228 | John Lowenstein | .08 | .25 |
| 229 | Ben Oglivie | .08 | .25 |
| 230 | Doug DeCinces | .08 | .25 |
| 231 | Lonnie Smith | .08 | .25 |
| 232 | Ray Knight | .30 | .75 |
| 233 | Gary Matthews | .30 | .75 |
| 234 | Juan Bonilla | .08 | .25 |
| 235 | Rod Scurry | .08 | .25 |
| 236 | Atlee Hammaker | .08 | .25 |
| 237 | Mike Caldwell | .08 | .25 |
| 238 | Keith Hernandez | .30 | .75 |
| 239 | Larry Bowa | .30 | .75 |
| 240 | Tony Bernazard | .08 | .25 |
| 241 | Damaso Garcia | .08 | .25 |
| 242 | Tom Brunansky | .30 | .75 |
| 243 | Dan Driessen | .08 | .25 |
| 244 | Ron Kittle | .30 | .75 |
| 245 | Tim Stoddard | .08 | .25 |
| 246 | Bob L. Gibson RC (Brewers Pitcher) | .08 | .25 |
| 247 | Marty Castillo | .08 | .25 |
| 248 | Don Mattingly RC | 10.00 | 25.00 |
| 249 | Jeff Newman | .08 | .25 |
| 250 | Alejandro Pena RC | .75 | 2.00 |
| 251 | Toby Harrah | .30 | .75 |
| 252 | Cesar Geronimo | .08 | .25 |
| 253 | Tom Underwood | .08 | .25 |
| 254 | Doug Flynn | .08 | .25 |
| 255 | Andy Hassler | .08 | .25 |
| 256 | Odell Jones | .08 | .25 |
| 257 | Rudy Law | .08 | .25 |
| 258 | Harry Spilman | .08 | .25 |
| 259 | Marty Bystrom | .08 | .25 |
| 260 | Dave Rucker | .08 | .25 |
| 261 | Ruppert Jones | .08 | .25 |
| 262 | Jeff R. Jones (Reds OF) | .08 | .25 |
| 263 | Gerald Perry | .40 | 1.00 |
| 264 | Gene Tenace | .30 | .75 |
| 265 | Brad Wellman | .08 | .25 |
| 266 | Dickie Noles | .08 | .25 |
| 267 | Jamie Allen | .08 | .25 |
| 268 | Jim Gott | .08 | .25 |
| 269 | Ron Davis | .08 | .25 |
| 270 | Benny Ayala | .08 | .25 |
| 271 | Ned Yost | .08 | .25 |
| 272 | Dave Rozema | .08 | .25 |
| 273 | Dave Stapleton | .08 | .25 |
| 274 | Lou Piniella | .30 | .75 |
| 275 | Jose Morales | .08 | .25 |
| 276 | Broderick Perkins | .08 | .25 |
| 277 | Butch Davis RC | .08 | .25 |
| 278 | Tony Phillips RC | .75 | 2.00 |
| 279 | Jeff Reardon | .30 | .75 |
| 280 | Ken Forsch | .08 | .25 |
| 281 | Pete O'Brien RC | .40 | 1.00 |
| 282 | Tom Paciorek | .08 | .25 |
| 283 | Frank LaCorte | .08 | .25 |
| 284 | Tim Lollar | .08 | .25 |
| 285 | Greg Gross | .08 | .25 |
| 286 | Alex Trevino | .08 | .25 |
| 287 | Gene Garber | .08 | .25 |
| 288 | Dave Parker | .30 | .75 |
| 289 | Lee Smith | .30 | .75 |
| 290 | Dave LaPoint | .08 | .25 |
| 291 | John Shelby | .08 | .25 |
| 292 | Charlie Moore | .08 | .25 |
| 293 | Alan Trammell | .30 | .75 |
| 294 | Tony Armas | .30 | .75 |
| 295 | Shane Rawley | .08 | .25 |
| 296 | Greg Brock | .08 | .25 |
| 297 | Hal McRae | .30 | .75 |
| 298 | Mike Davis | .08 | .25 |
| 299 | Tim Raines | .30 | .75 |
| 300 | Bucky Dent | .30 | .75 |
| 301 | Tommy John | .30 | .75 |
| 302 | Carlton Fisk | .60 | 1.50 |
| 303 | Darrell Porter | .08 | .25 |
| 304 | Dickie Thon | .08 | .25 |
| 305 | Garry Maddox | .08 | .25 |
| 306 | Cesar Cedeno | .30 | .75 |
| 307 | Gary Lucas | .08 | .25 |
| 308 | Johnny Ray | .08 | .25 |
| 309 | Andy McGaffigan | .08 | .25 |
| 310 | Claudell Washington | .08 | .25 |
| 311 | Ryne Sandberg | 5.00 | 12.00 |
| 312 | George Foster | .30 | .75 |
| 313 | Spike Owen RC | .40 | 1.00 |
| 314 | Gary Gaetti | .60 | 1.50 |
| 315 | Willie Upshaw | .08 | .25 |
| 316 | Al Williams | .08 | .25 |
| 317 | Jorge Orta | .08 | .25 |
| 318 | Orlando Mercado | .08 | .25 |
| 319 | Junior Ortiz | .08 | .25 |
| 320 | Mike Proly | .08 | .25 |
| 321 | Randy Johnson UER (from Twins' '72-'82 stats are) | | |
| 322 | Jim Morrison | .08 | .25 |
| 323 | Max Venable | .08 | .25 |
| 324 | Tony Gwynn | 5.00 | 12.00 |
| 325 | Duane Walker | .08 | .25 |
| 326 | Ozzie Virgil | .08 | .25 |
| 327 | Jeff Lahti | .08 | .25 |
| 328 | Bill Dawley | .08 | .25 |
| 329 | Rob Wilfong | .08 | .25 |
| 330 | Marc Hill | .08 | .25 |
| 331 | Ray Burris | .08 | .25 |
| 332 | Allan Ramirez | .08 | .25 |
| 333 | Chuck Porter | .08 | .25 |
| 334 | Wayne Krenchicki | .08 | .25 |
| 335 | Gary Allenson | .08 | .25 |
| 336 | Bobby Meacham | .08 | .25 |
| 337 | Joe Beckwith | .08 | .25 |
| 338 | Rick Sutcliffe | .30 | .75 |
| 339 | Mark Huismann | .08 | .25 |
| 340 | Tim Conroy | .08 | .25 |
| 341 | Scott Sanderson | .08 | .25 |
| 342 | Larry Biittner | .08 | .25 |
| 343 | Dave Stewart | .30 | .75 |
| 344 | Darryl Motley | .08 | .25 |
| 345 | Chris Codiroli | .08 | .25 |
| 346 | Rich Behenna | .08 | .25 |
| 347 | Andre Robertson | .08 | .25 |
| 348 | Mike Marshall | .30 | .75 |
| 349 | Larry Herndon | .08 | .25 |
| 350 | Rich Dauer | .08 | .25 |
| 351 | Cecil Cooper | .30 | .75 |
| 352 | Rod Carew | .60 | 1.50 |
| 353 | Willie McGee | .30 | .75 |
| 354 | Phil Garner | .08 | .25 |
| 355 | Joe Morgan | .30 | .75 |
| 356 | Luis Salazar | .08 | .25 |
| 357 | John Candelaria | .08 | .25 |
| 358 | Bill Laskey | .08 | .25 |
| 359 | Bob McClure | .08 | .25 |
| 360 | Dave Kingman | .30 | .75 |
| 361 | Ron Cey | .30 | .75 |
| 362 | Matt Young RC | .40 | 1.00 |
| 363 | Lloyd Moseby | .08 | .25 |
| 364 | Frank Viola | .60 | 1.50 |
| 365 | Eddie Milner | .08 | .25 |
| 366 | Floyd Bannister | .08 | .25 |
| 367 | Dan Ford | .08 | .25 |
| 368 | Moose Haas | .08 | .25 |
| 369 | Doug Bair | .08 | .25 |
| 370 | Ray Fontenot | .08 | .25 |
| 371 | Luis Aponte | .08 | .25 |
| 372 | Jack Fimple | .08 | .25 |
| 373 | Neal Heaton | .08 | .25 |
| 374 | Greg Pryor | .08 | .25 |
| 375 | Wayne Gross | .08 | .25 |
| 376 | Charlie Lea | .08 | .25 |
| 377 | Steve Lubratich | .08 | .25 |
| 378 | Jon Matlack | .08 | .25 |
| 379 | Julio Cruz | .08 | .25 |
| 380 | John Mizerock | .08 | .25 |
| 381 | Kevin Gross RC | .40 | 1.00 |
| 382 | Mike Ramsey | .08 | .25 |
| 383 | Doug Gwosdz | .08 | .25 |
| 384 | Kelly Paris | .08 | .25 |
| 385 | Pete Falcone | .08 | .25 |
| 386 | Milt May | .08 | .25 |
| 387 | Fred Breining | .08 | .25 |
| 388 | Craig Lefferts RC | .30 | .75 |
| 389 | Steve Henderson | .08 | .25 |
| 390 | Randy Moffitt | .08 | .25 |
| 391 | Ron Washington | .08 | .25 |
| 392 | Gary Roenicke | .08 | .25 |
| 393 | Tom Candiotti RC | .75 | 2.00 |
| 394 | Larry Pastnick | .08 | .25 |
| 395 | Dwight Evans | .60 | 1.50 |
| 396 | Rich Gossage | .30 | .75 |
| 397 | Derrel Thomas | .08 | .25 |
| 398 | Juan Eichelberger | .08 | .25 |
| 399 | Leon Roberts | .08 | .25 |
| 400 | Dave Lopes | .30 | .75 |
| 401 | Bill Gullickson | .08 | .25 |
| 402 | Geoff Zahn | .08 | .25 |
| 403 | Billy Sample | .08 | .25 |
| 404 | Mike Squires | .08 | .25 |
| 405 | Craig Reynolds | .08 | .25 |
| 406 | Eric Show | .08 | .25 |
| 407 | John Denny | .08 | .25 |
| 408 | Dann Bilardello | .08 | .25 |
| 409 | Bruce Benedict | .08 | .25 |
| 410 | Kent Tekulve | .30 | .75 |
| 411 | Mel Hall | .30 | .75 |
| 412 | John Stuper | .08 | .25 |
| 413 | Rick Dempsey | .30 | .75 |
| 414 | Don Sutton | .30 | .75 |
| 415 | Jack Morris | .30 | .75 |
| 416 | John Tudor | .30 | .75 |
| 417 | Willie Randolph | .30 | .75 |
| 418 | Jerry Reuss | .08 | .25 |
| 419 | Don Slaught | .08 | .25 |
| 420 | Steve McCatty | .08 | .25 |
| 421 | Tim Wallach | .30 | .75 |
| 422 | Larry Parrish | .08 | .25 |
| 423 | Brian Downing | .30 | .75 |
| 424 | Britt Burns | .08 | .25 |
| 425 | David Green | .08 | .25 |
| 426 | Jerry Mumphrey | .08 | .25 |
| 427 | Ivan DeJesus | .08 | .25 |
| 428 | Mario Soto | .30 | .75 |
| 429 | Gene Richards | .08 | .25 |
| 430 | Dale Berra | .08 | .25 |
| 431 | Darrell Evans | .30 | .75 |
| 432 | Glenn Hubbard | .08 | .25 |
| 433 | Jody Davis | .08 | .25 |
| 434 | Danny Heep | .08 | .25 |
| 435 | Edwin Nunez RC | .08 | .25 |
| 436 | Bobby Castillo | .08 | .25 |
| 437 | Ernie Whitt | .08 | .25 |
| 438 | Scott Ullger | .08 | .25 |
| 439 | Doyle Alexander | .08 | .25 |
| 440 | Domingo Ramos | .08 | .25 |
| 441 | Craig Swan | .08 | .25 |
| 442 | Warren Brusstar | .08 | .25 |
| 443 | Len Barker | .08 | .25 |
| 444 | Mike Easler | .08 | .25 |
| 445 | Renie Martin | .08 | .25 |
| 446 | Dennis Rasmussen RC | .40 | 1.00 |

|  | | |
|---|---|---|
| 447 Ted Power | .08 | .25 |
| 448 Charles Hudson | .08 | .25 |
| 449 Danny Cox RC | .08 | .25 |
| 450 Kevin Bass | .08 | .25 |
| 451 Daryl Sconiers | .08 | .25 |
| 452 Scott Fletcher | .08 | .25 |
| 453 Bryn Smith | .08 | .25 |
| 454 Jim Dwyer | .08 | .25 |
| 455 Rob Picciolo | .08 | .25 |
| 456 Enos Cabell | .08 | .25 |
| 457 Dennis Boyd | .30 | .75 |
| 458 Butch Wynegar | .08 | .25 |
| 459 Burt Hooton | .08 | .25 |
| 460 Ron Hassey | .08 | .25 |
| 461 Danny Jackson RC | .40 | 1.00 |
| 462 Bob Kearney | .08 | .25 |
| 463 Terry Francona | .30 | .75 |
| 464 Wayne Tolleson | .08 | .25 |
| 465 Mickey Rivers | .08 | .25 |
| 466 John Wathan | .08 | .25 |
| 467 Bill Almon | .08 | .25 |
| 468 George Vukovich | .08 | .25 |
| 469 Steve Kemp | .08 | .25 |
| 470 Ken Landreaux | .08 | .25 |
| 471 Milt Wilcox | .08 | .25 |
| 472 Tippy Martinez | .08 | .25 |
| 473 Ted Simmons | .30 | .75 |
| 474 Tim Foli | .08 | .25 |
| 475 George Hendrick | .30 | .75 |
| 476 Terry Puhl | .08 | .25 |
| 477 Von Hayes | .08 | .25 |
| 478 Bobby Brown | .08 | .25 |
| 479 Lee Lacy | .08 | .25 |
| 480 Joel Youngblood | .08 | .25 |
| 481 Jim Slaton | .08 | .25 |
| 482 Mike Fitzgerald | .08 | .25 |
| 483 Keith Moreland | .08 | .25 |
| 484 Ron Roenicke | .08 | .25 |
| 485 Luis Leal | .08 | .25 |
| 486 Bryan Oelkers | .08 | .25 |
| 487 Bruce Berenyi | .08 | .25 |
| 488 LaMarr Hoyt | .08 | .25 |
| 489 Joe Nolan | .08 | .25 |
| 490 Marshall Edwards | .08 | .25 |
| 491 Mike Laga | .30 | .75 |
| 492 Rick Cerone | .08 | .25 |
| 493 Rick Miller UER (Listed as Mike on card front) | .08 | .25 |
| 494 Rick Honeycutt | .08 | .25 |
| 495 Mike Hargrove | .08 | .25 |
| 496 Joe Simpson | .08 | .25 |
| 497 Keith Atherton | .08 | .25 |
| 498 Chris Welsh | .08 | .25 |
| 499 Bruce Kison | .08 | .25 |
| 500 Bobby Johnson | .08 | .25 |
| 501 Jerry Koosman | .30 | .75 |
| 502 Frank DiPino | .08 | .25 |
| 503 Tony Perez | .60 | 1.50 |
| 504 Ken Oberkfell | .08 | .25 |
| 505 Mark Thurmond | .08 | .25 |
| 506 Joe Price | .08 | .25 |
| 507 Pascual Perez | .08 | .25 |
| 508 Marvell Wynne | .40 | 1.00 |
| 509 Mike Krukow | .08 | .25 |
| 510 Dick Ruthven | .08 | .25 |
| 511 Al Cowens | .08 | .25 |
| 512 Cliff Johnson | .08 | .25 |
| 513 Randy Bush | .08 | .25 |
| 514 Sammy Stewart | .08 | .25 |
| 515 Bill Schroeder | .08 | .25 |
| 516 Aurelio Lopez | .08 | .25 |
| 517 Mike C. Brown | .30 | .75 |
| 518 Graig Nettles | .30 | .75 |
| 519 Dave Sax | .08 | .25 |
| 520 Jerry Willard | .08 | .25 |
| 521 Paul Splittorff | .08 | .25 |
| 522 Tom Burgmeier | .08 | .25 |
| 523 Chris Speier | .08 | .25 |
| 524 Bobby Clark | .08 | .25 |
| 525 George Wright | .08 | .25 |
| 526 Dennis Lamp | .08 | .25 |
| 527 Tony Scott | .08 | .25 |
| 528 Ed Whitson | .08 | .25 |
| 529 Ron Reed | .08 | .25 |
| 530 Charlie Puleo | .08 | .25 |
| 531 Jerry Royster | .08 | .25 |
| 532 Don Robinson | .08 | .25 |
| 533 Steve Trout | .08 | .25 |
| 534 Bruce Sutter | .60 | 1.50 |
| 535 Bob Homer ! | .30 | .75 |
| 536 Pat Tabler | .08 | .25 |
| 537 Chris Chambliss | .30 | .75 |
| 538 Bob Ojeda | .08 | .25 |
| 539 Alan Ashby | .08 | .25 |
| 540 Jay Johnstone | .08 | .25 |
| 541 Bob Demier | .08 | .25 |
| 542 Brook Jacoby | .40 | 1.00 |
| 543 U.L. Washington | .08 | .25 |
| 544 Danny Darwin | .08 | .25 |
| 545 Kiko Garcia | .08 | .25 |
| 546 Vance Law UER (Listed as P on card front) | .08 | .25 |
| 547 Tug McGraw | .30 | .75 |
| 548 Dave Smith | .08 | .25 |
| 549 Len Matuszek | .08 | .25 |
| 550 Tom Hume | .08 | .25 |
| 551 Dave Dravecky | .08 | .25 |
| 552 Rick Rhoden | .08 | .25 |
| 553 Duane Kuiper | .08 | .25 |
| 554 Rusty Staub | .30 | .75 |
| 555 Bill Campbell | .08 | .25 |
| 556 Mike Torrez | .08 | .25 |
| 557 Dave Henderson | .30 | .75 |
| 558 Len Whitehouse | .08 | .25 |
| 559 Barry Bonnell | .08 | .25 |
| 560 Rick Lysander | .08 | .25 |
| 561 Garth Iorg | .08 | .25 |
| 562 Bryan Clark | .08 | .25 |
| 563 Brian Giles | .08 | .25 |
| 564 Vern Ruhle | .08 | .25 |
| 565 Steve Bedrosian | .08 | .25 |
| 566 Larry McWilliams | .08 | .25 |
| 567 Jeff Leonard UER (Listed as P on card front) | .08 | .25 |
| 568 Alan Wiggins | .08 | .25 |
| 569 Jeff Russell RC | .40 | 1.00 |
| 570 Salome Barojas | .08 | .25 |
| 571 Dane Iorg | .08 | .25 |
| 572 Bob Knepper | .08 | .25 |
| 573 Gary Lavelle | .08 | .25 |
| 574 Gorman Thomas | .30 | .75 |
| 575 Manny Trillo | .08 | .25 |
| 576 Jim Palmer | .30 | .75 |
| 577 Dale Murray | .08 | .25 |
| 578 Tom Brookens | .30 | .75 |
| 579 Rich Gedman | .08 | .25 |
| 580 Bill Doran RC | .40 | 1.00 |
| 581 Steve Yeager | .30 | .75 |
| 582 Dan Spillner | .08 | .25 |
| 583 Dan Quisenberry | .30 | .75 |
| 584 Rance Mulliniks | .08 | .25 |
| 585 Storm Davis | .08 | .25 |
| 586 Dave Schmidt | .08 | .25 |
| 587 Bill Russell | .30 | .75 |
| 588 Pat Sheridan | .08 | .25 |
| 589 Rafael Ramirez UER (A's on front) | .08 | .25 |
| 590 Bud Anderson | .08 | .25 |
| 591 George Frazier | .08 | .25 |
| 592 Lee Tunnell | .08 | .25 |
| 593 Kirk Gibson | 1.25 | 3.00 |
| 594 Scott McGregor | .08 | .25 |
| 595 Bob Bailor | .08 | .25 |
| 596 Tommy Herr | .08 | .25 |
| 597 Luis Sanchez | .08 | .25 |
| 598 Dave Engle | .08 | .25 |
| 599 Craig McMurtry | .08 | .25 |
| 600 Carlos Diaz | .08 | .25 |
| 601 Tom O'Malley | .08 | .25 |
| 602 Nick Esasky | .08 | .25 |
| 603 Ron Hodges | .08 | .25 |
| 604 Ed VandeBerg | .08 | .25 |
| 605 Alfredo Griffin | .08 | .25 |
| 606 Glenn Hoffman | .08 | .25 |
| 607 Hubie Brooks | .08 | .25 |
| 608 Richard Barnes UER (Photo actually Neal Heaton) | .08 | .25 |
| 609 Greg Walker | .40 | 1.00 |
| 610 Ken Singleton | .30 | .75 |
| 611 Mark Clear | .08 | .25 |
| 612 Buck Martinez | .08 | .25 |
| 613 Ken Griffey | .08 | .25 |
| 614 Reid Nichols | .08 | .25 |
| 615 Doug Sisk | .08 | .25 |
| 616 Bob Brenly | .08 | .25 |
| 617 Joey McLaughlin | .08 | .25 |
| 618 Glenn Wilson | .30 | .75 |
| 619 Bob Stoddard | .08 | .25 |
| 620 Lenn Sakata UER (Listed as Len on card front) | .08 | .25 |
| 621 Mike Young RC | .08 | .25 |
| 622 John Stefero | .08 | .25 |
| 623 Carmelo Martinez | .08 | .25 |
| 624 Dave Bergman | .08 | .25 |
| 625 Ozzie Smith/W.McGee | 1.25 | 3.00 |
| 626 Rudy May | .08 | .25 |
| 627 Matt Keough | .08 | .25 |
| 628 Jose DeLeon RC | .40 | 1.00 |
| 629 Jim Essian | .08 | .25 |
| 630 Darnell Coles RC | .40 | 1.00 |
| 631 Mike Warren | .08 | .25 |
| 632 Del Crandall MG | .08 | .25 |
| 633 Dennis Martinez | .30 | .75 |
| 634 Mike Moore | .08 | .25 |
| 635 Lary Sorensen | .08 | .25 |
| 636 Ricky Nelson | .08 | .25 |
| 637 Omar Moreno | .08 | .25 |
| 638 Charlie Hough | .30 | .75 |
| 639 Dennis Eckersley | .60 | 1.50 |
| 640 Walt Terrell | .08 | .25 |
| 641 Denny Walling | .08 | .25 |
| 642 Dave Anderson RC | .08 | .25 |
| 643 Jose Oquendo RC | .40 | 1.00 |
| 644 Bob Stanley | .08 | .25 |
| 645 Dave Geisel | .08 | .25 |
| 646 Scott Garrelts | .08 | .25 |
| 647 Gary Pettis | .08 | .25 |
| 648 Duke Snider Puzzle | .60 | 1.50 |
| 649 Johnnie LeMaster | .08 | .25 |
| 650 Dave Collins | .08 | .25 |
| 651 The Chicken | .60 | 1.50 |
| 652 DK Checklist 1-26 (Unnumbered) | .30 | .75 |
| 653 Checklist 27-130 (Unnumbered) | .08 | .25 |
| 654 Checklist 131-234 (Unnumbered) | .08 | .25 |
| 655 Checklist 235-338 (Unnumbered) | .08 | .25 |
| 656 Checklist 339-442 (Unnumbered) | .08 | .25 |
| 657 Checklist 443-546 (Unnumbered) | .08 | .25 |
| 658 Checklist 547-651 (Unnumbered) | .08 | .25 |
| A G.Perry/R.Fingers SP | 1.00 | 2.50 |
| B J.Bench/C.Yastrzemski SP | 2.00 | 5.00 |

## 1985 Donruss

| | | |
|---|---|---|
| COMPLETE SET (660) | 30.00 | 60.00 |
| COMP.FACT.SET (660) | 50.00 | 100.00 |
| COMP.GEHRIG PUZZLE | 1.50 | 4.00 |
| 1 Ryne Sandberg DK | .50 | 1.25 |
| 2 Doug DeCinces DK | .05 | .15 |
| 3 Richard Dotson DK | .05 | .15 |
| 4 Bert Blyleven DK | .15 | .40 |
| 5 Lou Whitaker DK | .15 | .40 |
| 6 Dan Quisenberry DK | .15 | .40 |
| 7 Don Mattingly DK | 1.00 | 2.50 |
| 8 Carney Lansford DK | .15 | .40 |
| 9 Frank Tanana DK | .15 | .40 |
| 10 Willie Upshaw DK | .05 | .15 |
| 11 Claudell Washington DK | .05 | .15 |
| 12 Mike Marshall DK | .05 | .15 |
| 13 Joaquin Andujar DK | .15 | .40 |

|  | | |
|---|---|---|
| ☐ 14 Cal Ripken DK | 1.00 | 2.50 |
| ☐ 15 Jim Rice DK | .15 | .40 |
| ☐ 16 Don Sutton DK | .15 | .40 |
| ☐ 17 Frank Viola DK | .15 | .40 |
| ☐ 18 Alvin Davis DK | .15 | .40 |
| ☐ 19 Mario Soto DK | .15 | .40 |
| ☐ 20 Jose Cruz DK | .15 | .40 |
| ☐ 21 Charlie Lea DK | .05 | .15 |
| ☐ 22 Jesse Orosco DK | .05 | .15 |
| ☐ 23 Juan Samuel DK | .15 | .40 |
| ☐ 24 Tony Pena DK | .05 | .15 |
| ☐ 25 Tony Gwynn DK | .50 | 1.25 |
| ☐ 26 Bob Brenly DK | .05 | .15 |
| ☐ 27 Danny Tartabull RC | .40 | 1.00 |
| ☐ 28 Mike Bielecki RC | .08 | .25 |
| ☐ 29 Steve Lyons RC | .20 | .50 |
| ☐ 30 Jeff Reed RC | .08 | .25 |
| ☐ 31 Tony Brewer RC | .08 | .25 |
| ☐ 32 John Morris RC | .08 | .25 |
| ☐ 33 Daryl Boston RC | .08 | .25 |
| ☐ 34 Al Pulido RC | .08 | .25 |
| ☐ 35 Steve Kiefer RC | .08 | .25 |
| ☐ 36 Larry Sheets RC | .08 | .25 |
| ☐ 37 Scott Bradley RC | .08 | .25 |
| ☐ 38 Calvin Schiraldi RC | .20 | .50 |
| ☐ 39 Shawon Dunston RC | .40 | 1.00 |
| ☐ 40 Charlie Mitchell RC | .08 | .25 |
| ☐ 41 Billy Hatcher RC | .20 | .50 |
| ☐ 42 Russ Stephans RC | .08 | .25 |
| ☐ 43 Alejandro Sanchez RC | .08 | .25 |
| ☐ 44 Steve Jeltz RC | .08 | .25 |
| ☐ 45 Jim Traber RC | .08 | .25 |
| ☐ 46 Doug Loman RC | .08 | .25 |
| ☐ 47 Eddie Murray | .50 | 1.25 |
| ☐ 48 Robin Yount | .75 | 2.00 |
| ☐ 49 Lance Parrish | .15 | .40 |
| ☐ 50 Jim Rice | .15 | .40 |
| ☐ 51 Dave Winfield | .15 | .40 |
| ☐ 52 Fernando Valenzuela | .15 | .40 |
| ☐ 53 George Brett | 1.25 | 3.00 |
| ☐ 54 Dave Kingman | .15 | .40 |
| ☐ 55 Gary Carter | .15 | .40 |
| ☐ 56 Buddy Bell | .15 | .40 |
| ☐ 57 Reggie Jackson | .30 | .75 |
| ☐ 58 Harold Baines | .15 | .40 |
| ☐ 59 Ozzie Smith | .75 | 2.00 |
| ☐ 60 Nolan Ryan | 2.50 | 6.00 |
| ☐ 61 Mike Schmidt | 1.25 | 3.00 |
| ☐ 62 Dave Parker | .15 | .40 |
| ☐ 63 Tony Gwynn | 1.00 | 2.50 |
| ☐ 64 Tony Pena | .05 | .15 |
| ☐ 65 Jack Clark | .15 | .40 |
| ☐ 66 Dale Murphy | .30 | .75 |
| ☐ 67 Ryne Sandberg | 1.00 | 2.50 |
| ☐ 68 Keith Hernandez | .15 | .40 |
| ☐ 69 Alvin Davis RC* | .20 | .50 |
| ☐ 70 Kent Hrbek | .15 | .40 |
| ☐ 71 Willie Upshaw | .05 | .15 |
| ☐ 72 Dave Engle | .05 | .15 |
| ☐ 73 Alfredo Griffin | .05 | .15 |
| ☐ 74A Jack Perconte (Career Highlights takes four line) | .05 | .15 |
| ☐ 74B Jack Perconte (Career Highlights takes three lin | .05 | .15 |
| ☐ 75 Jesse Orosco | .05 | .15 |
| ☐ 76 Jody Davis | .05 | .15 |
| ☐ 77 Bob Horner | .15 | .40 |
| ☐ 78 Larry McWilliams | .05 | .15 |
| ☐ 79 Joel Youngblood | .05 | .15 |
| ☐ 80 Alan Wiggins | .05 | .15 |
| ☐ 81 Ron Oester | .05 | .15 |
| ☐ 82 Ozzie Virgil | .05 | .15 |
| ☐ 83 Ricky Horton | .05 | .15 |
| ☐ 84 Bill Doran | .05 | .15 |
| ☐ 85 Rod Carew | .30 | .75 |
| ☐ 86 LaMarr Hoyt | .05 | .15 |
| ☐ 87 Tim Wallach | .05 | .15 |
| ☐ 88 Mike Flanagan | .05 | .15 |
| ☐ 89 Jim Sundberg | .15 | .40 |
| ☐ 90 Chet Lemon | .05 | .15 |
| ☐ 91 Bob Stanley | .05 | .15 |
| ☐ 92 Willie Randolph | .15 | .40 |
| ☐ 93 Bill Russell | .15 | .40 |
| ☐ 94 Julio Franco | .15 | .40 |
| ☐ 95 Dan Quisenberry | .05 | .15 |
| ☐ 96 Bill Caudill | .05 | .15 |
| ☐ 97 Bill Gullickson | .05 | .15 |
| ☐ 98 Danny Darwin | .05 | .15 |
| ☐ 99 Curtis Wilkerson | .05 | .15 |
| ☐ 100 Bud Black | .05 | .15 |
| ☐ 101 Tony Phillips | .05 | .15 |
| ☐ 102 Tony Bernazard | .05 | .15 |
| ☐ 103 Jay Howell | .05 | .15 |
| ☐ 104 Burt Hooton | .05 | .15 |
| ☐ 105 Milt Wilcox | .05 | .15 |
| ☐ 106 Rich Dauer | .05 | .15 |
| ☐ 107 Don Sutton | .15 | .40 |
| ☐ 108 Mike Witt | .05 | .15 |
| ☐ 109 Bruce Sutter | .15 | .40 |
| ☐ 110 Enos Cabell | .05 | .15 |
| ☐ 111 John Denny | .05 | .15 |
| ☐ 112 Dave Dravecky | .05 | .15 |
| ☐ 113 Marvell Wynne | .05 | .15 |
| ☐ 114 Johnnie LeMaster | .05 | .15 |
| ☐ 115 Chuck Porter | .05 | .15 |
| ☐ 116 John Gibbons RC | .05 | .15 |
| ☐ 117 Keith Moreland | .05 | .15 |
| ☐ 118 Darnell Coles | .15 | .40 |
| ☐ 119 Dennis Lamp | .05 | .15 |
| ☐ 120 Ron Davis | .05 | .15 |
| ☐ 121 Nick Esasky | .05 | .15 |
| ☐ 122 Vance Law | .05 | .15 |
| ☐ 123 Gary Roenicke | .05 | .15 |
| ☐ 124 Bill Schroeder | .05 | .15 |
| ☐ 125 Dave Rozema | .05 | .15 |
| ☐ 126 Bobby Meacham | .05 | .15 |
| ☐ 127 Marty Barrett | .05 | .15 |
| ☐ 128 R.J. Reynolds | .05 | .15 |
| ☐ 129 Ernie Camacho UER (Photo actually Rich Thompson) | .05 | .15 |
| ☐ 130 Jorge Orta | .05 | .15 |
| ☐ 131 Larry Sorensen | .05 | .15 |
| ☐ 132 Terry Francona | .05 | .15 |
| ☐ 133 Fred Lynn | .15 | .40 |
| ☐ 134 Bob Jones | .05 | .15 |
| ☐ 135 Jerry Hairston | .05 | .15 |
| ☐ 136 Kevin Bass | .05 | .15 |
| ☐ 137 Garry Maddox | .05 | .15 |
| ☐ 138 Dave LaPoint | .05 | .15 |
| ☐ 139 Kevin McReynolds | .15 | .40 |
| ☐ 140 Wayne Krenchicki | .05 | .15 |
| ☐ 141 Rafael Ramirez | .05 | .15 |
| ☐ 142 Rod Scurry | .05 | .15 |
| ☐ 143 Greg Minton | .05 | .15 |
| ☐ 144 Tim Stoddard | .05 | .15 |
| ☐ 145 Steve Henderson | .05 | .15 |
| ☐ 146 George Bell | .15 | .40 |
| ☐ 147 Dave Meier | .05 | .15 |
| ☐ 148 Sammy Stewart | .05 | .15 |
| ☐ 149 Mark Brouhard | .05 | .15 |
| ☐ 150 Larry Herndon | .05 | .15 |
| ☐ 151 Oil Can Boyd | .05 | .15 |
| ☐ 152 Brian Dayett | .05 | .15 |
| ☐ 153 Tom Niedenfuer | .05 | .15 |
| ☐ 154 Brook Jacoby | .05 | .15 |
| ☐ 155 Onix Concepcion | .05 | .15 |
| ☐ 156 Tim Conroy | .05 | .15 |
| ☐ 157 Joe Hesketh | .05 | .15 |
| ☐ 158 Brian Downing | .15 | .40 |
| ☐ 159 Tommy Dunbar | .05 | .15 |
| ☐ 160 Marc Hill | .05 | .15 |
| ☐ 161 Phil Garner | .15 | .40 |
| ☐ 162 Jerry Davis | .05 | .15 |
| ☐ 163 Bill Campbell | .05 | .15 |
| ☐ 164 John Franco RC | .40 | 1.00 |
| ☐ 165 Len Barker | .05 | .15 |
| ☐ 166 Benny Distefano | .05 | .15 |
| ☐ 167 George Frazier | .05 | .15 |
| ☐ 168 Tito Landrum | .05 | .15 |
| ☐ 169 Cal Ripken | 2.00 | 5.00 |
| ☐ 170 Cecil Cooper | .15 | .40 |
| ☐ 171 Alan Trammell | .15 | .40 |
| ☐ 172 Wade Boggs | .50 | 1.25 |
| ☐ 173 Don Baylor | .15 | .40 |
| ☐ 174 Pedro Guerrero | .15 | .40 |
| ☐ 175 Frank White | .15 | .40 |
| ☐ 176 Rickey Henderson | .60 | 1.50 |
| ☐ 177 Charlie Lea | .05 | .15 |
| ☐ 178 Pete O'Brien | .05 | .15 |
| ☐ 179 Doug DeCinces | .05 | .15 |
| ☐ 180 Ron Kittle | .05 | .15 |
| ☐ 181 George Hendrick | .15 | .40 |
| ☐ 182 Joe Niekro | .05 | .15 |
| ☐ 183 Juan Samuel | .05 | .15 |
| ☐ 184 Mario Soto | .15 | .40 |
| ☐ 185 Goose Gossage | .15 | .40 |
| ☐ 186 Johnny Ray | .05 | .15 |
| ☐ 187 Bob Brenly | .05 | .15 |
| ☐ 188 Craig McMurtry | .05 | .15 |
| ☐ 189 Leon Durham | .05 | .15 |
| ☐ 190 Dwight Gooden RC | 1.25 | 3.00 |
| ☐ 191 Barry Bonnell | .05 | .15 |
| ☐ 192 Tim Teufel | .05 | .15 |
| ☐ 193 Dave Stieb | .15 | .40 |
| ☐ 194 Mickey Hatcher | .05 | .15 |
| ☐ 195 Jesse Barfield | .15 | .40 |
| ☐ 196 Al Cowens | .05 | .15 |
| ☐ 197 Hubie Brooks | .15 | .40 |
| ☐ 198 Steve Trout | .05 | .15 |
| ☐ 199 Glenn Hubbard | .05 | .15 |
| ☐ 200 Bill Madlock | .15 | .40 |
| ☐ 201 Jeff D. Robinson | .05 | .15 |
| ☐ 202 Eric Show | .05 | .15 |
| ☐ 203 Dave Concepcion | .15 | .40 |
| ☐ 204 Ivan DeJesus | .05 | .15 |
| ☐ 205 Neil Allen | .05 | .15 |
| ☐ 206 Jerry Mumphrey | .05 | .15 |
| ☐ 207 Mike C. Brown | .05 | .15 |
| ☐ 208 Carlton Fisk | .30 | .75 |
| ☐ 209 Bryn Smith | .05 | .15 |
| ☐ 210 Tippy Martinez | .05 | .15 |
| ☐ 211 Dion James | .05 | .15 |
| ☐ 212 Willie Hernandez | .05 | .15 |
| ☐ 213 Mike Easler | .05 | .15 |
| ☐ 214 Ron Guidry | .15 | .40 |
| ☐ 215 Rick Honeycutt | .05 | .15 |
| ☐ 216 Brett Butler | .15 | .40 |
| ☐ 217 Larry Gura | .05 | .15 |
| ☐ 218 Ray Burris | .05 | .15 |
| ☐ 219 Steve Rogers | .15 | .40 |
| ☐ 220 Frank Tanana UER (Bats Left listed twice on card) | .15 | .40 |
| ☐ 221 Ned Yost | .05 | .15 |
| ☐ 222 Bret Saberhagen RC | .60 | 1.50 |
| ☐ 223 Mike Davis | .05 | .15 |
| ☐ 224 Bert Blyleven | .15 | .40 |
| ☐ 225 Steve Kemp | .05 | .15 |
| ☐ 226 Jerry Reuss | .05 | .15 |
| ☐ 227 Darrell Evans UER (80 homers in 1980) | .15 | .40 |
| ☐ 228 Wayne Gross | .05 | .15 |
| ☐ 229 Jim Gantner | .05 | .15 |
| ☐ 230 Bob Boone | .15 | .40 |
| ☐ 231 Lonnie Smith | .05 | .15 |
| ☐ 232 Frank DiPino | .05 | .15 |
| ☐ 233 Jerry Koosman | .15 | .40 |
| ☐ 234 Graig Nettles | .15 | .40 |
| ☐ 235 John Tudor | .05 | .15 |
| ☐ 236 John Rabb | .05 | .15 |
| ☐ 237 Rick Manning | .05 | .15 |
| ☐ 238 Mike Fitzgerald | .05 | .15 |
| ☐ 239 Gary Matthews | .15 | .40 |
| ☐ 240 Jim Presley | .20 | .50 |
| ☐ 241 Dave Collins | .05 | .15 |
| ☐ 242 Gary Gaetti | .15 | .40 |
| ☐ 243 Dann Bilardello | .05 | .15 |
| ☐ 244 Rudy Law | .05 | .15 |
| ☐ 245 John Lowenstein | .05 | .15 |
| ☐ 246 Tom Tellmann | .05 | .15 |
| ☐ 247 Howard Johnson | .15 | .40 |
| ☐ 248 Ray Fontenot | .05 | .15 |
| ☐ 249 Tony Armas | .15 | .40 |
| ☐ 250 Candy Maldonado | .05 | .15 |
| ☐ 251 Mike Jeffcoat | .05 | .15 |
| ☐ 252 Dane Iorg | .05 | .15 |
| ☐ 253 Bruce Bochte | .05 | .15 |
| ☐ 254 Pete Rose Expos | 1.50 | 4.00 |
| ☐ 255 Don Aase | .05 | .15 |
| ☐ 256 George Wright | .05 | .15 |
| ☐ 257 Britt Burns | .05 | .15 |
| ☐ 258 Mike Scott | .15 | .40 |
| ☐ 259 Len Matuszek | .05 | .15 |
| ☐ 260 Dave Rucker | .05 | .15 |
| ☐ 261 Craig Lefferts | .05 | .15 |
| ☐ 262 Jay Tibbs | .05 | .15 |
| ☐ 263 Bruce Benedict | .05 | .15 |
| ☐ 264 Don Robinson | .05 | .15 |
| ☐ 265 Gary Lavelle | .05 | .15 |
| ☐ 266 Scott Sanderson | .05 | .15 |
| ☐ 267 Matt Young | .05 | .15 |

|  |  | | |
|---|---|---|---|
| 268 | Ernie Whitt | .05 | .15 |
| 269 | Houston Jimenez | .05 | .15 |
| 270 | Ken Dixon | .05 | .15 |
| 271 | Pete Ladd | .05 | .15 |
| 272 | Juan Berenguer | .05 | .15 |
| 273 | Roger Clemens RC | 8.00 | 20.00 |
| 274 | Rick Cerone | .05 | .15 |
| 275 | Dave Anderson | .05 | .15 |
| 276 | George Vukovich | .05 | .15 |
| 277 | Greg Pryor | .05 | .15 |
| 278 | Mike Warren | .05 | .15 |
| 279 | Bob James | .05 | .15 |
| 280 | Bobby Grich | .15 | .40 |
| 281 | Mike Mason RC | .08 | .25 |
| 282 | Ron Reed | .05 | .15 |
| 283 | Alan Ashby | .05 | .15 |
| 284 | Mark Thurmond | .05 | .15 |
| 285 | Joe Lefebvre | .05 | .15 |
| 286 | Ted Power | .05 | .15 |
| 287 | Chris Chambliss | .15 | .40 |
| 288 | Lee Tunnell | .05 | .15 |
| 289 | Rich Bordi | .05 | .15 |
| 290 | Glenn Brummer | .05 | .15 |
| 291 | Mike Boddicker | .05 | .15 |
| 292 | Rollie Fingers | .15 | .40 |
| 293 | Lou Whitaker | .15 | .40 |
| 294 | Dwight Evans | .30 | .75 |
| 295 | Don Mattingly | 2.00 | 5.00 |
| 296 | Mike Marshall | .05 | .15 |
| 297 | Willie Wilson | .15 | .40 |
| 298 | Mike Heath | .05 | .15 |
| 299 | Tim Raines | .15 | .40 |
| 300 | Larry Parrish | .05 | .15 |
| 301 | Geoff Zahn | .05 | .15 |
| 302 | Rich Dotson | .05 | .15 |
| 303 | David Green | .05 | .15 |
| 304 | Jose Cruz | .15 | .40 |
| 305 | Steve Carlton | .15 | .40 |
| 306 | Gary Redus | .05 | .15 |
| 307 | Steve Garvey | .15 | .40 |
| 308 | Jose DeLeon | .05 | .15 |
| 309 | Randy Lerch | .05 | .15 |
| 310 | Claudell Washington | .05 | .15 |
| 311 | Lee Smith | .15 | .40 |
| 312 | Darryl Strawberry | .50 | 1.25 |
| 313 | Jim Beattie | .05 | .15 |
| 314 | John Butcher | .05 | .15 |
| 315 | Damaso Garcia | .05 | .15 |
| 316 | Mike Smithson | .05 | .15 |
| 317 | Luis Leal | .05 | .15 |
| 318 | Ken Phelps | .05 | .15 |
| 319 | Wally Backman | .05 | .15 |
| 320 | Ron Cey | .15 | .40 |
| 321 | Brad Komminsk | .05 | .15 |
| 322 | Jason Thompson | .05 | .15 |
| 323 | Frank Williams | .05 | .15 |
| 324 | Tim Lollar | .05 | .15 |
| 325 | Eric Davis RC | 1.25 | 3.00 |
| 326 | Von Hayes | .05 | .15 |
| 327 | Andy Van Slyke | .30 | .75 |
| 328 | Craig Reynolds | .05 | .15 |
| 329 | Dick Schofield | .05 | .15 |
| 330 | Scott Fletcher | .05 | .15 |
| 331 | Jeff Reardon | .15 | .40 |
| 332 | Rick Dempsey | .05 | .15 |
| 333 | Ben Oglivie | .05 | .15 |
| 334 | Dan Petry | .05 | .15 |
| 335 | Jackie Gutierrez | .05 | .15 |
| 336 | Dave Righetti | .15 | .40 |
| 337 | Alejandro Pena | .05 | .15 |
| 338 | Mel Hall | .15 | .40 |
| 339 | Pat Sheridan | .05 | .15 |
| 340 | Keith Atherton | .05 | .15 |
| 341 | David Palmer | .05 | .15 |
| 342 | Gary Ward | .05 | .15 |
| 343 | Dave Stewart | .15 | .40 |
| 344 | Mark Gubicza RC* | .20 | .50 |
| 345 | Carney Lansford | .15 | .40 |
| 346 | Jerry Willard | .05 | .15 |
| 347 | Ken Griffey | .15 | .40 |
| 348 | Franklin Stubbs | .15 | .40 |
| 349 | Aurelio Lopez | .05 | .15 |
| 350 | Al Bumbry | .05 | .15 |
| 351 | Charlie Moore | .05 | .15 |
| 352 | Luis Sanchez | .05 | .15 |
| 353 | Darrell Porter | .05 | .15 |
| 354 | Bill Dawley | .05 | .15 |
| 355 | Charles Hudson | .05 | .15 |
| 356 | Garry Templeton | .15 | .40 |
| 357 | Cecilio Guante | .05 | .15 |
| 358 | Jeff Leonard | .05 | .15 |
| 359 | Paul Molitor | .15 | .40 |
| 360 | Ron Gardenhire | .05 | .15 |
| 361 | Larry Bowa | .15 | .40 |
| 362 | Bob Kearney | .05 | .15 |
| 363 | Garth Iorg | .05 | .15 |
| 364 | Tom Brunansky | .15 | .40 |
| 365 | Brad Gulden | .05 | .15 |
| 366 | Greg Walker | .05 | .15 |
| 367 | Mike Young | .05 | .15 |
| 368 | Rick Waits | .05 | .15 |
| 369 | Doug Bair | .05 | .15 |
| 370 | Bob Shirley | .05 | .15 |
| 371 | Bob Ojeda | .05 | .15 |
| 372 | Bob Welch | .15 | .40 |
| 373 | Neal Heaton | .05 | .15 |
| 374 | Danny Jackson UER (Photo actually Frank Wills) | | |
| 375 | Donnie Hill | .05 | .15 |
| 376 | Mike Stenhouse | .05 | .15 |
| 377 | Bruce Kison | .05 | .15 |
| 378 | Wayne Tolleson | .05 | .15 |
| 379 | Floyd Bannister | .05 | .15 |
| 380 | Vern Ruhle | .05 | .15 |
| 381 | Tim Corcoran | .05 | .15 |
| 382 | Kurt Kepshire | .05 | .15 |
| 383 | Bobby Brown | .05 | .15 |
| 384 | Dave Van Gorder | .05 | .15 |
| 385 | Rick Mahler | .05 | .15 |
| 386 | Lee Mazzilli | .15 | .40 |
| 387 | Bill Laskey | .05 | .15 |
| 388 | Thad Bosley | .05 | .15 |
| 389 | Al Chambers | .05 | .15 |
| 390 | Tony Fernandez | .15 | .40 |
| 391 | Ron Washington | .05 | .15 |
| 392 | Bill Swaggerty | .05 | .15 |
| 393 | Bob L. Gibson | .05 | .15 |
| 394 | Marty Castillo | .05 | .15 |
| 395 | Steve Crawford | .05 | .15 |
| 396 | Clay Christiansen | .05 | .15 |
| 397 | Bob Bailor | .05 | .15 |
| 398 | Mike Hargrove | .15 | .40 |
| 399 | Charlie Leibrandt | .05 | .15 |
| 400 | Tom Burgmeier | .05 | .15 |
| 401 | Razor Shines | .05 | .15 |
| 402 | Rob Wilfong | .05 | .15 |
| 403 | Tom Henke | .15 | .40 |
| 404 | Al Jones | .05 | .15 |
| 405 | Mike LaCoss | .05 | .15 |
| 406 | Luis DeLeon | .05 | .15 |
| 407 | Greg Gross | .05 | .15 |
| 408 | Tom Hume | .05 | .15 |
| 409 | Rick Camp | .05 | .15 |
| 410 | Milt May | .05 | .15 |
| 411 | Henry Cotto RC | .08 | .25 |
| 412 | David Von Ohlen | .05 | .15 |
| 413 | Scott McGregor | .05 | .15 |
| 414 | Ted Simmons | .15 | .40 |
| 415 | Jack Morris | .15 | .40 |
| 416 | Bill Buckner | .15 | .40 |
| 417 | Butch Wynegar | .05 | .15 |
| 418 | Steve Sax | .15 | .40 |
| 419 | Steve Balboni | .05 | .15 |
| 420 | Dwayne Murphy | .05 | .15 |
| 421 | Andre Dawson | .15 | .40 |
| 422 | Charlie Hough | .15 | .40 |
| 423 | Tommy John | .15 | .40 |
| 424A | Tom Seaver ERR | .30 | .75 |
| 424B | Tom Seaver COR | 4.00 | 10.00 |
| 425 | Tommy Herr | .05 | .15 |
| 426 | Terry Puhl | .05 | .15 |
| 427 | Al Holland | .05 | .15 |
| 428 | Eddie Milner | .05 | .15 |
| 429 | Terry Kennedy | .05 | .15 |
| 430 | John Candelaria | .05 | .15 |
| 431 | Manny Trillo | .05 | .15 |
| 432 | Ken Oberkfell | .05 | .15 |
| 433 | Rick Sutcliffe | .15 | .40 |
| 434 | Ron Darling | .15 | .40 |
| 435 | Spike Owen | .05 | .15 |
| 436 | Frank Viola | .15 | .40 |
| 437 | Lloyd Moseby | .05 | .15 |
| 438 | Kirby Puckett RC | 5.00 | 12.00 |
| 439 | Jim Clancy | .05 | .15 |
| 440 | Mike Moore | .05 | .15 |
| 441 | Doug Sisk | .05 | .15 |
| 442 | Dennis Eckersley | .30 | .75 |
| 443 | Gerald Perry | .05 | .15 |
| 444 | Dale Berra | .05 | .15 |
| 445 | Dusty Baker | .15 | .40 |
| 446 | Ed Whitson | .05 | .15 |
| 447 | Cesar Cedeno | .15 | .40 |
| 448 | Rick Schu | .05 | .15 |
| 449 | Joaquin Andujar | .05 | .15 |
| 450 | Mark Bailey | .05 | .15 |
| 451 | Ron Romanick | .05 | .15 |
| 452 | Julio Cruz | .05 | .15 |
| 453 | Miguel Dilone | .05 | .15 |
| 454 | Storm Davis | .05 | .15 |
| 455 | Jaime Cocanower | .05 | .15 |
| 456 | Barbaro Garbey | .05 | .15 |
| 457 | Rich Gedman | .05 | .15 |
| 458 | Phil Niekro | .15 | .40 |
| 459 | Mike Scioscia | .15 | .40 |
| 460 | Pat Tabler | .05 | .15 |
| 461 | Darryl Motley | .05 | .15 |
| 462 | Chris Codiroli | .05 | .15 |
| 463 | Doug Flynn | .05 | .15 |
| 464 | Billy Sample | .05 | .15 |
| 465 | Mickey Rivers | .05 | .15 |
| 466 | John Wathan | .05 | .15 |
| 467 | Bill Krueger | .05 | .15 |
| 468 | Andre Thornton | .05 | .15 |
| 469 | Rex Hudler | .05 | .15 |
| 470 | Sid Bream RC | .20 | .50 |
| 471 | Kirk Gibson | .15 | .40 |
| 472 | John Shelby | .05 | .15 |
| 473 | Moose Haas | .05 | .15 |
| 474 | Doug Corbett | .05 | .15 |
| 475 | Willie McGee | .15 | .40 |
| 476 | Bob Knepper | .05 | .15 |
| 477 | Kevin Gross | .05 | .15 |
| 478 | Carmelo Martinez | .05 | .15 |
| 479 | Kent Tekulve | .05 | .15 |
| 480 | Chili Davis | .15 | .40 |
| 481 | Bobby Clark | .05 | .15 |
| 482 | Mookie Wilson | .15 | .40 |
| 483 | Dave Owen | .05 | .15 |
| 484 | Ed Nunez | .05 | .15 |
| 485 | Rance Muliniks | .05 | .15 |
| 486 | Ken Schrom | .05 | .15 |
| 487 | Jeff Russell | .05 | .15 |
| 488 | Tom Paciorek | .05 | .15 |
| 489 | Dan Ford | .05 | .15 |
| 490 | Mike Caldwell | .05 | .15 |
| 491 | Scottie Earl | .05 | .15 |
| 492 | Jose Rijo RC | .40 | 1.00 |
| 493 | Bruce Hurst | .15 | .40 |
| 494 | Ken Landreaux | .05 | .15 |
| 495 | Mike Fischlin | .05 | .15 |
| 496 | Don Slaught | .05 | .15 |
| 497 | Steve McCatty | .05 | .15 |
| 498 | Gary Lucas | .05 | .15 |
| 499 | Gary Pettis | .05 | .15 |
| 500 | Marvis Foley | .05 | .15 |
| 501 | Mike Squires | .05 | .15 |
| 502 | Jim Pankovits | .05 | .15 |
| 503 | Luis Aguayo | .05 | .15 |
| 504 | Ralph Citarella | .05 | .15 |
| 505 | Bruce Bochy | .05 | .15 |
| 506 | Bob Owchinko | .05 | .15 |
| 507 | Pascual Perez | .05 | .15 |
| 508 | Lee Lacy | .05 | .15 |
| 509 | Atlee Hammaker | .05 | .15 |
| 510 | Bob Dernier | .05 | .15 |
| 511 | Ed VandeBerg | .05 | .15 |
| 512 | Cliff Johnson | .05 | .15 |
| 513 | Len Whitehouse | .05 | .15 |
| 514 | Dennis Martinez | .15 | .40 |
| 515 | Ed Romero | .05 | .15 |
| 516 | Rusty Kuntz | .05 | .15 |
| 517 | Rick Miller | .05 | .15 |
| 518 | Dennis Rasmussen | .05 | .15 |
| 519 | Steve Yeager | .15 | .40 |
| 520 | Chris Bando | .05 | .15 |
| 521 | U.L. Washington | .05 | .15 |
| 522 | Curt Young | .05 | .15 |
| 523 | Angel Salazar | .05 | .15 |
| 524 | Curt Kaufman | .05 | .15 |
| 525 | Odell Jones | .05 | .15 |
| 526 | Juan Agosto | .05 | .15 |
| 527 | Denny Walling | .05 | .15 |
| 528 | Andy Hawkins | .05 | .15 |

| | | |
|---|---|---|
| 529 Sixto Lezcano | .05 | .15 |
| 530 Skeeter Barnes RC | .08 | .25 |
| 531 Randy Johnson | .05 | .15 |
| 532 Jim Morrison | .05 | .15 |
| 533 Warren Brusstar | .05 | .15 |
| 534A Jeff Pendleton ERR RC | .40 | 1.00 |
| 534B Terry Pendleton COR | .40 | 1.00 |
| 535 Vic Rodriguez | .05 | .15 |
| 536 Bob McClure | .05 | .15 |
| 537 Dave Bergman | .05 | .15 |
| 538 Mark Clear | .05 | .15 |
| 539 Mike Pagliarulo | .05 | .15 |
| 540 Terry Whitfield | .05 | .15 |
| 541 Joe Beckwith | .05 | .15 |
| 542 Jeff Burroughs | .05 | .15 |
| 543 Dan Schatzeder | .05 | .15 |
| 544 Donnie Scott | .05 | .15 |
| 545 Jim Slaton | .05 | .15 |
| 546 Greg Luzinski | .15 | .40 |
| 547 Mark Salas | .05 | .15 |
| 548 Dave Smith | .05 | .15 |
| 549 John Wockenfuss | .05 | .15 |
| 550 Frank Pastore | .05 | .15 |
| 551 Tim Flannery | .05 | .15 |
| 552 Rick Rhoden | .05 | .15 |
| 553 Mark Davis | .05 | .15 |
| 554 Jeff Dedmon | .05 | .15 |
| 555 Gary Woods | .05 | .15 |
| 556 Danny Heep | .05 | .15 |
| 557 Mark Langston RC | .40 | 1.00 |
| 558 Darrell Brown | .05 | .15 |
| 559 Jimmy Key RC | .40 | 1.00 |
| 560 Rick Lysander | .05 | .15 |
| 561 Doyle Alexander | .05 | .15 |
| 562 Mike Stanton | .05 | .15 |
| 563 Sid Fernandez | .15 | .40 |
| 564 Richie Hebner | .05 | .15 |
| 565 Alex Trevino | .05 | .15 |
| 566 Brian Harper | .05 | .15 |
| 567 Dan Gladden RC | .20 | .50 |
| 568 Luis Salazar | .05 | .15 |
| 569 Tom Foley | .05 | .15 |
| 570 Larry Andersen | .05 | .15 |
| 571 Danny Cox | .05 | .15 |
| 572 Joe Sambito | .05 | .15 |
| 573 Juan Beniquez | .05 | .15 |
| 574 Joel Skinner | .05 | .15 |
| 575 Randy St.Claire | .05 | .15 |
| 576 Floyd Rayford | .05 | .15 |
| 577 Roy Howell | .05 | .15 |
| 578 John Grubb | .05 | .15 |
| 579 Ed Jurak | .05 | .15 |
| 580 John Montefusco | .05 | .15 |
| 581 Orel Hershiser RC | 1.25 | 3.00 |
| 582 Tom Waddell | .05 | .15 |
| 583 Mark Huismann | .05 | .15 |
| 584 Joe Morgan | .15 | .40 |
| 585 Jim Wohlford | .05 | .15 |
| 586 Dave Schmidt | .05 | .15 |
| 587 Jeff Kunkel | .05 | .15 |
| 588 Hal McRae | .15 | .40 |
| 589 Bill Almon | .05 | .15 |
| 590 Carmelo Castillo | .05 | .15 |
| 591 Omar Moreno | .05 | .15 |
| 592 Ken Howell | .05 | .15 |
| 593 Tom Brookens | .05 | .15 |
| 594 Joe Nolan | .05 | .15 |
| 595 Willie Lozado | .05 | .15 |
| 596 Tom Nieto | .05 | .15 |
| 597 Walt Terrell | .05 | .15 |
| 598 Al Oliver | .15 | .40 |
| 599 Shane Rawley | .05 | .15 |
| 600 Denny Gonzalez | .05 | .15 |
| 601 Mark Grant | .05 | .15 |
| 602 Mike Armstrong | .05 | .15 |
| 603 George Foster | .15 | .40 |
| 604 Dave Lopes | .15 | .40 |
| 605 Salome Barojas | .05 | .15 |
| 606 Roy Lee Jackson | .05 | .15 |
| 607 Pete Filson | .05 | .15 |
| 608 Duane Walker | .05 | .15 |
| 609 Glenn Wilson | .05 | .15 |
| 610 Rafael Santana | .05 | .15 |
| 611 Roy Smith | .05 | .15 |
| 612 Ruppert Jones | .05 | .15 |
| 613 Joe Cowley | .05 | .15 |
| 614 Al Nipper UER (Photo actually Mike Brown) | .05 | .15 |
| 615 Gene Nelson | .05 | .15 |
| 616 Joe Carter | .50 | 1.25 |
| 617 Ray Knight | .15 | .40 |
| 618 Chuck Rainey | .05 | .15 |
| 619 Dan Driessen | .05 | .15 |
| 620 Daryl Sconiers | .05 | .15 |
| 621 Bill Stein | .05 | .15 |
| 622 Roy Smalley | .05 | .15 |
| 623 Ed Lynch | .05 | .15 |
| 624 Jeff Stone RC | .05 | .15 |
| 625 Bruce Berenyi | .05 | .15 |
| 626 Kelvin Chapman | .05 | .15 |
| 627 Joe Price | .05 | .15 |
| 628 Steve Bedrosian | .05 | .15 |
| 629 Vic Mata | .05 | .15 |
| 630 Mike Krukow | .05 | .15 |
| 631 Phil Bradley | .20 | .50 |
| 632 Jim Gott | .05 | .15 |
| 633 Randy Bush | .05 | .15 |
| 634 Tom Browning RC | .20 | .50 |
| 635 Lou Gehrig Puzzle | .50 | 1.25 |
| 636 Reid Nichols | .05 | .15 |
| 637 Dan Pasqua RC | .20 | .50 |
| 638 German Rivera | .05 | .15 |
| 639 Don Schulze | .05 | .15 |
| 640A Mike Jones (Career Highlights& takes five lines) | .05 | .15 |
| 640B Mike Jones (Career Highlights& takes four lines) | .05 | .15 |
| 641 Pete Rose | 1.50 | 4.00 |
| 642 Wade Rowdon | .05 | .15 |
| 643 Jerry Narron | .05 | .15 |
| 644 Darrell Miller | .05 | .15 |
| 645 Tim Hulett RC | .08 | .25 |
| 646 Andy McGaffigan | .05 | .15 |
| 647 Kurt Bevacqua | .05 | .15 |
| 648 John Russell | .05 | .15 |
| 649 Ron Robinson | .05 | .15 |
| 650 Donnie Moore | .05 | .15 |
| 651A D.Mattingly/D.Winfield YL | .75 | 2.00 |
| 651B D.Mattingly/D.Winfield WL | 2.00 | 5.00 |
| 652 Tim Laudner | .05 | .15 |
| 653 Steve Farr RC | .20 | .50 |
| 654 DK Checklist 1-26 (Unnumbered) | .05 | .15 |
| 655 Checklist 27-130 (Unnumbered) | .05 | .15 |
| 656 Checklist 131-234 (Unnumbered) | .05 | .15 |
| 657 Checklist 235-338 (Unnumbered) | .05 | .15 |
| 658 Checklist 339-442 (Unnumbered) | .05 | .15 |
| 659 Checklist 443-546 (Unnumbered) | .05 | .15 |
| 660 Checklist 547-653 (Unnumbered) | .05 | .15 |

## 1986 Donruss

| | | |
|---|---|---|
| COMPLETE SET (660) | 15.00 | 40.00 |
| COMP.FACT.SET (660) | 15.00 | 40.00 |
| COMP.AARON PUZZLE | .75 | 2.00 |
| 1 Kirk Gibson DK | .08 | .25 |
| 2 Goose Gossage DK | .08 | .25 |
| 3 Willie McGee DK | .08 | .25 |
| 4 George Bell DK | .08 | .25 |
| 5 Tony Armas DK | .08 | .25 |
| 6 Chili Davis DK | .08 | .25 |
| 7 Cecil Cooper DK | .08 | .25 |
| 8 Mike Boddicker DK | .05 | .15 |
| 9 Dave Lopes DK | .08 | .25 |
| 10 Bill Doran DK | .05 | .15 |
| 11 Bret Saberhagen DK | .08 | .25 |
| 12 Brett Butler DK | .08 | .25 |
| 13 Harold Baines DK | .08 | .25 |
| 14 Mike Davis DK | .05 | .15 |
| 15 Tony Perez DK | .20 | .50 |
| 16 Willie Randolph DK | .08 | .25 |
| 17 Bob Boone DK | .08 | .25 |
| 18 Orel Hershiser DK | .20 | .50 |
| 19 Johnny Ray DK | .05 | .15 |
| 20 Gary Ward DK | .05 | .15 |
| 21 Rick Mahler DK | .05 | .15 |
| 22 Phil Bradley DK | .05 | .15 |
| 23 Gary Koosman DK | .08 | .25 |
| 24 Tom Brunansky DK | .05 | .15 |
| 25 Andre Dawson DK | .15 | .40 |
| 26 Dwight Gooden DK | .30 | .75 |
| 27 Kal Daniels RC | .20 | .50 |
| 28 Fred McGriff RC | 3.00 | 8.00 |
| 29 Cory Snyder RC | .05 | .15 |
| 30 Jose Guzman RC | .05 | .15 |
| 31 Ty Gainey RC | .05 | .15 |
| 32 Johnny Abrego RC | .05 | .15 |
| 33A Andres Galarraga RC | .60 | 1.50 |
| 33B Andre's Galarraga RC | .60 | 1.50 |
| 34 Dave Shipanoff RC | .05 | .15 |
| 35 Mark McLemore RC | .40 | 1.00 |
| 36 Marty Clary RC | .05 | .15 |
| 37 Paul O'Neill RC | 1.50 | 4.00 |
| 38 Danny Tartabull | .08 | .25 |
| 39 Jose Canseco RC | 4.00 | 10.00 |
| 40 Juan Nieves RC | .05 | .15 |
| 41 Lance McCullers RC | .05 | .15 |
| 42 Rick Surhoff RC | .05 | .15 |
| 43 Todd Worrell RC | .20 | .50 |
| 44 Bob Kipper RC | .05 | .15 |
| 45 John Habyan RC | .05 | .15 |
| 46 Mike Woodard RC | .05 | .15 |
| 47 Mike Boddicker | .05 | .15 |
| 48 Robin Yount | .50 | 1.25 |
| 49 Lou Whitaker | .08 | .25 |
| 50 Oil Can Boyd | .05 | .15 |
| 51 Rickey Henderson | .30 | .75 |
| 52 Mike Marshall | .05 | .15 |
| 53 George Brett | .75 | 2.00 |
| 54 Dave Kingman | .08 | .25 |
| 55 Hubie Brooks | .05 | .15 |
| 56 Oddibe McDowell | .05 | .15 |
| 57 Doug DeCinces | .05 | .15 |
| 58 Britt Burns | .05 | .15 |
| 59 Ozzie Smith | .50 | 1.25 |
| 60 Jose Cruz | .08 | .25 |
| 61 Mike Schmidt | .75 | 2.00 |
| 62 Pete Rose | 1.00 | 2.50 |
| 63 Steve Garvey | .15 | .40 |
| 64 Tony Pena | .05 | .15 |
| 65 Chili Davis | .05 | .15 |
| 66 Dale Murphy | .20 | .50 |
| 67 Ryne Sandberg | .60 | 1.50 |
| 68 Gary Carter | .08 | .25 |
| 69 Alvin Davis | .05 | .15 |
| 70 Kent Hrbek | .08 | .25 |
| 71 George Bell | .08 | .25 |
| 72 Kirby Puckett | .75 | 2.00 |
| 73 Lloyd Moseby | .05 | .15 |
| 74 Bob Kearney | .05 | .15 |
| 75 Dwight Gooden | .30 | .75 |
| 76 Gary Matthews | .05 | .15 |
| 77 Rick Mahler | .05 | .15 |
| 78 Benny Distefano | .05 | .15 |
| 79 Jeff Leonard | .05 | .15 |
| 80 Kevin McReynolds | .08 | .25 |
| 81 Ron Oester | .05 | .15 |
| 82 John Russell | .05 | .15 |
| 83 Tommy Herr | .05 | .15 |
| 84 Jerry Mumphrey | .05 | .15 |
| 85 Ron Romanick | .05 | .15 |
| 86 Daryl Boston | .05 | .15 |
| 87 Andre Dawson | .08 | .25 |
| 88 Eddie Murray | .30 | .75 |
| 89 Dion James | .05 | .15 |
| 90 Chet Lemon | .08 | .25 |
| 91 Bob Stanley | .05 | .15 |
| 92 Willie Randolph | .08 | .25 |
| 93 Mike Scioscia | .08 | .25 |
| 94 Tom Waddell | .05 | .15 |
| 95 Danny Jackson | .05 | .15 |
| 96 Mike Davis | .05 | .15 |

|  |  | | |
|---|------|----|----|
| 97 | Mike Fitzgerald | .05 | .15 |
| 98 | Gary Ward | .05 | .15 |
| 99 | Pete O'Brien | .05 | .15 |
| * 100 | Bret Saberhagen | .08 | .25 |
| 101 | Alfredo Griffin | .05 | .15 |
| 102 | Brett Butler | .08 | .25 |
| 103 | Ron Guidry | .05 | .15 |
| 104 | Jerry Reuss | .05 | .15 |
| 105 | Jack Morris | .08 | .25 |
| 106 | Rick Dempsey | .05 | .15 |
| 107 | Ray Burris | .05 | .15 |
| 108 | Brian Downing | .05 | .15 |
| 109 | Willie McGee | .08 | .25 |
| 110 | Bill Doran | .05 | .15 |
| 111 | Kent Tekulve | .05 | .15 |
| 112 | Tony Gwynn | .50 | 1.25 |
| 113 | Marvell Wynne | .05 | .15 |
| 114 | David Green | .05 | .15 |
| 115 | Jim Gantner | .05 | .15 |
| 116 | George Foster | .08 | .25 |
| 117 | Steve Trout | .05 | .15 |
| 118 | Mark Langston | .08 | .25 |
| 119 | Tony Fernandez | .05 | .15 |
| 120 | John Butcher | .05 | .15 |
| 121 | Ron Robinson | .05 | .15 |
| 122 | Dan Spillner | .05 | .15 |
| 123 | Mike Young | .05 | .15 |
| 124 | Paul Molitor | .08 | .25 |
| 125 | Kirk Gibson | .08 | .25 |
| 126 | Ken Griffey | .08 | .25 |
| 127 | Tony Armas | .08 | .25 |
| 128 | Mariano Duncan RC | .20 | .50 |
| 129 | Pat Tabler | .05 | .15 |
| 130 | Frank White | .05 | .15 |
| 131 | Carney Lansford | .08 | .25 |
| 132 | Vance Law | .05 | .15 |
| 133 | Dick Schofield | .05 | .15 |
| 134 | Wayne Tolleson | .05 | .15 |
| 135 | Greg Walker | .05 | .15 |
| 136 | Denny Walling | .05 | .15 |
| 137 | Ozzie Virgil | .05 | .15 |
| 138 | Ricky Horton | .05 | .15 |
| 139 | LaMarr Hoyt | .05 | .15 |
| 140 | Wayne Krenchicki | .05 | .15 |
| 141 | Glenn Hubbard | .05 | .15 |
| 142 | Cecilio Guante | .05 | .15 |
| 143 | Mike Krukow | .05 | .15 |
| 144 | Lee Smith | .08 | .25 |
| 145 | Edwin Nunez | .05 | .15 |
| 146 | Dave Stieb | .08 | .25 |
| 147 | Mike Smithson | .05 | .15 |
| 148 | Ken Dixon | .05 | .15 |
| 149 | Danny Darwin | .05 | .15 |
| 150 | Chris Pittaro | .05 | .15 |
| 151 | Bill Buckner | .08 | .25 |
| 152 | Mike Pagliarulo | .05 | .15 |
| 153 | Bill Russell | .05 | .15 |
| 154 | Brook Jacoby | .05 | .15 |
| 155 | Pat Sheridan | .05 | .15 |
| 156 | Mike Gallego RC | .08 | .25 |
| 157 | Jim Wohlford | .05 | .15 |
| 158 | Gary Pettis | .05 | .15 |
| 159 | Toby Harrah | .08 | .25 |
| 160 | Richard Dotson | .05 | .15 |
| 161 | Bob Knepper | .05 | .15 |
| 162 | Dave Dravecky | .05 | .15 |
| 163 | Greg Gross | .05 | .15 |
| 164 | Eric Davis | .30 | .75 |
| 165 | Gerald Perry | .05 | .15 |
| 166 | Rick Rhoden | .05 | .15 |
| 167 | Keith Moreland | .05 | .15 |
| 168 | Jack Clark | .08 | .25 |
| 169 | Storm Davis | .05 | .15 |
| 170 | Cecil Cooper | .08 | .25 |
| 171 | Alan Trammell | .08 | .25 |
| 172 | Roger Clemens | 2.00 | 5.00 |
| 173 | Don Mattingly | 1.00 | 2.50 |
| 174 | Pedro Guerrero | .08 | .25 |
| 175 | Willie Wilson | .08 | .25 |
| 176 | Dwayne Murphy | .05 | .15 |
| 177 | Tim Raines | .08 | .25 |
| 178 | Larry Parrish | .05 | .15 |
| 179 | Mike Witt | .05 | .15 |
| 180 | Harold Baines | .08 | .25 |
| 181 | Vince Coleman UER RC | .40 | 1.00 |
| 182 | Jeff Heathcock | .05 | .15 |
| 183 | Steve Carlton | .08 | .25 |
| 184 | Mario Soto | .08 | .25 |
| 185 | Goose Gossage | .08 | .25 |
| 186 | Johnny Ray | .05 | .15 |
| 187 | Dan Gladden | .05 | .15 |
| 188 | Bob Horner | .08 | .25 |
| 189 | Rick Sutcliffe | .08 | .25 |
| 190 | Keith Hernandez | .06 | .25 |
| 191 | Phil Bradley | .05 | .15 |
| 192 | Tom Brunansky | .05 | .15 |
| 193 | Jesse Barfield | .08 | .25 |
| 194 | Frank Viola | .08 | .25 |
| 195 | Willie Upshaw | .05 | .15 |
| 196 | Jim Beattie | .05 | .15 |
| 197 | Darryl Strawberry | .20 | .50 |
| 198 | Ron Cey | .08 | .25 |
| 199 | Steve Bedrosian | .05 | .15 |
| 200 | Steve Kemp | .05 | .15 |
| 201 | Manny Trillo | .05 | .15 |
| 202 | Garry Templeton | .08 | .25 |
| 203 | Dave Parker | .08 | .25 |
| 204 | John Denny | .05 | .15 |
| 205 | Terry Pendleton | .08 | .25 |
| 206 | Terry Puhl | .05 | .15 |
| 207 | Bobby Grich | .08 | .25 |
| 208 | Ozzie Guillen RC | .75 | 2.00 |
| 209 | Jeff Reardon | .08 | .25 |
| 210 | Cal Ripken | 1.25 | 3.00 |
| 211 | Bill Schroeder | .05 | .15 |
| 212 | Dan Petry | .05 | .15 |
| 213 | Jim Rice | .08 | .25 |
| 214 | Dave Righetti | .08 | .25 |
| 215 | Fernando Valenzuela | .08 | .25 |
| 216 | Julio Franco | .08 | .25 |
| 217 | Darryl Motley | .05 | .15 |
| 218 | Dave Collins | .05 | .15 |
| 219 | Tim Wallach | .08 | .25 |
| 220 | George Wright | .05 | .15 |
| 221 | Tommy Dunbar | .05 | .15 |
| 222 | Steve Balboni | .05 | .15 |
| 223 | Jay Howell | .05 | .15 |
| 224 | Joe Carter | .08 | .25 |
| 225 | Ed Whitson | .05 | .15 |
| 226 | Orel Hershiser | .30 | .75 |
| 227 | Willie Hernandez | .05 | .15 |
| 228 | Lee Lacy | .05 | .15 |
| 229 | Rollie Fingers | .08 | .25 |
| 230 | Bob Boone | .08 | .25 |
| 231 | Joaquin Andujar | .08 | .25 |
| 232 | Craig Reynolds | .05 | .15 |
| 233 | Shane Rawley | .05 | .15 |
| 234 | Eric Show | .05 | .15 |
| 235 | Jose DeLeon | .05 | .15 |
| 236 | Jose Uribe | .05 | .15 |
| 237 | Moose Haas | .05 | .15 |
| 238 | Wally Backman | .05 | .15 |
| 239 | Dennis Eckersley | .20 | .50 |
| 240 | Mike Moore | .05 | .15 |
| 241 | Damaso Garcia | .05 | .15 |
| 242 | Tim Teufel | .05 | .15 |
| 243 | Dave Concepcion | .08 | .25 |
| 244 | Floyd Bannister | .05 | .15 |
| 245 | Fred Lynn | .08 | .25 |
| 246 | Charlie Moore | .05 | .15 |
| 247 | Walt Terrell | .05 | .15 |
| 248 | Dave Winfield | .08 | .25 |
| 249 | Dwight Evans | .20 | .50 |
| 250 | Dennis Powell | .05 | .15 |
| 251 | Andre Thornton | .05 | .15 |
| 252 | Onix Concepcion | .05 | .15 |
| 253 | Mike Heath | .05 | .15 |
| 254A | David Palmer ERR (Position 2B) | .05 | .15 |
| 254B | David Palmer COR (Position P) | .20 | .50 |
| 255 | Donnie Moore | .05 | .15 |
| 256 | Curtis Wilkerson | .05 | .15 |
| 257 | Julio Cruz | .05 | .15 |
| 258 | Nolan Ryan | 1.50 | 4.00 |
| 259 | Jeff Stone | .05 | .15 |
| 260 | John Tudor | .08 | .25 |
| 261 | Mark Thurmond | .05 | .15 |
| 262 | Jay Tibbs | .05 | .15 |
| 263 | Rafael Ramirez | .05 | .15 |
| 264 | Larry McWilliams | .05 | .15 |
| 265 | Mark Davis | .05 | .15 |
| 266 | Bob Dernier | .05 | .15 |
| 267 | Matt Young | .05 | .15 |
| 268 | Jim Clancy | .05 | .15 |
| 269 | Mickey Hatcher | .05 | .15 |
| 270 | Sammy Stewart | .05 | .15 |
| 271 | Bob L. Gibson | .05 | .15 |
| 272 | Nelson Simmons | .05 | .15 |
| 273 | Rich Gedman | .05 | .15 |
| 274 | Butch Wynegar | .05 | .15 |
| 275 | Ken Howell | .05 | .15 |
| 276 | Mel Hall | .05 | .15 |
| 277 | Jim Sundberg | .08 | .25 |
| 278 | Chris Codiroli | .05 | .15 |
| 279 | Herm Winningham | .05 | .15 |
| 280 | Rod Carew | .20 | .50 |
| 281 | Don Slaught | .05 | .15 |
| 282 | Scott Fletcher | .05 | .15 |
| 283 | Bill Dawley | .05 | .15 |
| 284 | Andy Hawkins | .05 | .15 |
| 285 | Glenn Wilson | .05 | .15 |
| 286 | Nick Esasky | .05 | .15 |
| 287 | Claudell Washington | .05 | .15 |
| 288 | Lee Mazzilli | .08 | .25 |
| 289 | Jody Davis | .05 | .15 |
| 290 | Darrell Porter | .05 | .15 |
| 291 | Scott McGregor | .05 | .15 |
| 292 | Ted Simmons | .05 | .15 |
| 293 | Aurelio Lopez | .05 | .15 |
| 294 | Marty Barrett | .05 | .15 |
| 295 | Dale Berra | .05 | .15 |
| 296 | Greg Brock | .05 | .15 |
| 297 | Charlie Leibrandt | .05 | .15 |
| 298 | Bill Krueger | .05 | .15 |
| 299 | Bryn Smith | .05 | .15 |
| 300 | Burt Hooton | .05 | .15 |
| 301 | Stu Cliburn | .05 | .15 |
| 302 | Luis Salazar | .05 | .15 |
| 303 | Ken Dayley | .05 | .15 |
| 304 | Frank DiPino | .05 | .15 |
| 305 | Von Hayes | .05 | .15 |
| 306 | Gary Redus | .05 | .15 |
| 307 | Craig Lefferts | .05 | .15 |
| 308 | Sammy Khalifa | .05 | .15 |
| 309 | Scott Garrelts | .05 | .15 |
| 310 | Rick Cerone | .05 | .15 |
| 311 | Shawon Dunston | .08 | .25 |
| 312 | Howard Johnson | .08 | .25 |
| 313 | Jim Presley | .05 | .15 |
| 314 | Gary Gaetti | .08 | .25 |
| 315 | Luis Leal | .05 | .15 |
| 316 | Mark Salas | .05 | .15 |
| 317 | Bill Caudill | .05 | .15 |
| 318 | Dave Henderson | .08 | .25 |
| 319 | Rafael Santana | .05 | .15 |
| 320 | Leon Durham | .05 | .15 |
| 321 | Bruce Sutter | .08 | .25 |
| 322 | Jason Thompson | .05 | .15 |
| 323 | Bob Brenly | .05 | .15 |
| 324 | Carmelo Martinez | .05 | .15 |
| 325 | Eddie Milner | .05 | .15 |
| 326 | Juan Samuel | .05 | .15 |
| 327 | Tom Nieto | .05 | .15 |
| 328 | Dave Smith | .05 | .15 |
| 329 | Urbano Lugo | .05 | .15 |
| 330 | Joel Skinner | .05 | .15 |
| 331 | Bill Gullickson | .05 | .15 |
| 332 | Floyd Rayford | .05 | .15 |
| 333 | Ben Oglivie | .08 | .25 |
| 334 | Lance Parrish | .08 | .25 |
| 335 | Jackie Gutierrez | .05 | .15 |
| 336 | Dennis Rasmussen | .05 | .15 |
| 337 | Terry Whitfield | .05 | .15 |
| 338 | Neal Heaton | .05 | .15 |
| 339 | Jorge Orta | .05 | .15 |
| 340 | Donnie Hill | .05 | .15 |
| 341 | Joe Hesketh | .05 | .15 |
| 342 | Charlie Hough | .08 | .25 |
| 343 | Dave Rozema | .05 | .15 |
| 344 | Greg Pryor | .05 | .15 |
| 345 | Mickey Tettleton RC | .20 | .50 |
| 346 | George Yukovich | .05 | .15 |
| 347 | Don Baylor | .08 | .25 |
| 348 | Carlos Diaz | .05 | .15 |
| 349 | Barbaro Garbey | .05 | .15 |
| 350 | Larry Sheets | .05 | .15 |
| 351 | Teddy Higuera RC* | .20 | .50 |
| 352 | Juan Beniquez | .05 | .15 |
| 353 | Bob Forsch | .05 | .15 |
| 354 | Mark Bailey | .05 | .15 |
| 355 | Larry Andersen | .05 | .15 |
| 356 | Terry Kennedy | .05 | .15 |
| 357 | Don Robinson | .05 | .15 |

|  |  | | |  |  | | |  |  | | |
|---|---|---|---|---|---|---|---|---|---|---|---|
| 358 | Jim Gott | .05 | .15 | 446 | Jerry Royster | .05 | .15 | 534 | Steve Braun | .05 | .15 |
| 359 | Ernie Riles | .05 | .15 | 447 | Buddy Bell | .08 | .15 | 535 | Wayne Gross | .05 | .15 |
| 360 | John Christensen | .05 | .15 | 448 | Dave Rucker | .05 | .15 | 536 | Ray Searage | .05 | .15 |
| 361 | Ray Fontenot | .05 | .15 | 449 | Ivan DeJesus | .05 | .15 | 537 | Tom Brookens | .05 | .15 |
| 362 | Spike Owen | .05 | .15 | 450 | Jim Pankovits | .05 | .15 | 538 | Al Nipper | .05 | .15 |
| 363 | Jim Acker | .05 | .15 | 451 | Jerry Narron | .05 | .15 | 539 | Billy Sample | .05 | .15 |
| 364 | Ron Davis | .05 | .15 | 452 | Bryan Little | .05 | .15 | 540 | Steve Sax | .08 | .25 |
| 365 | Tom Hume | .05 | .15 | 453 | Gary Lucas | .05 | .15 | 541 | Dan Quisenberry | .05 | .15 |
| 366 | Carlton Fisk | .20 | .50 | 454 | Dennis Martinez | .08 | .25 | 542 | Tony Phillips | .05 | .15 |
| 367 | Nate Snell | .05 | .15 | 455 | Ed Romero | .05 | .15 | 543 | Floyd Youmans | .05 | .15 |
| 368 | Rick Manning | .05 | .15 | 456 | Bob Melvin | .05 | .15 | 544 | Steve Buechele RC | .20 | .50 |
| 369 | Darrell Evans | .08 | .25 | 457 | Glenn Hoffman | .05 | .15 | 545 | Craig Gerber | .05 | .15 |
| 370 | Ron Hassey | .05 | .15 | 458 | Bob Shirley | .05 | .15 | 546 | Joe DeSa | .05 | .15 |
| 371 | Wade Boggs | .20 | .50 | 459 | Bob Welch | .08 | .25 | 547 | Brian Harper | .05 | .15 |
| 372 | Rick Honeycutt | .05 | .15 | 460 | Carmen Castillo | .05 | .15 | 548 | Kevin Bass | .05 | .15 |
| 373 | Chris Bando | .05 | .15 | 461 | Dave Leeper OF | .05 | .15 | 549 | Tom Foley | .05 | .15 |
| 374 | Bud Black | .05 | .15 | 462 | Tim Birtsas | .05 | .15 | 550 | Dave Van Gorder | .05 | .15 |
| 375 | Steve Henderson | .05 | .15 | 463 | Randy St.Claire | .05 | .15 | 551 | Bruce Bochy | .05 | .15 |
| 376 | Charlie Lea | .05 | .15 | 464 | Chris Welsh | .05 | .15 | 552 | R.J. Reynolds | .05 | .15 |
| 377 | Reggie Jackson | .20 | .50 | 465 | Greg Harris | .05 | .15 | 553 | Chris Brown RC | .05 | .15 |
| 378 | Dave Schmidt | .05 | .15 | 466 | Lynn Jones | .05 | .15 | 554 | Bruce Benedict | .05 | .15 |
| 379 | Bob James | .05 | .15 | 467 | Dusty Baker | .08 | .25 | 555 | Warren Brusstar | .05 | .15 |
| 380 | Glenn Davis | .05 | .15 | 468 | Roy Smith | .05 | .15 | 556 | Danny Heep | .05 | .15 |
| 381 | Tim Corcoran | .05 | .15 | 469 | Andre Robertson | .05 | .15 | 557 | Darnell Coles | .05 | .15 |
| 382 | Danny Cox | .05 | .15 | 470 | Ken Landreaux | .05 | .15 | 558 | Greg Gagne | .05 | .15 |
| 383 | Tim Flannery | .05 | .15 | 471 | Dave Bergman | .05 | .15 | 559 | Ernie Whitt | .05 | .15 |
| 384 | Tom Browning | .05 | .15 | 472 | Gary Roenicke | .05 | .15 | 560 | Ron Washington | .05 | .15 |
| 385 | Rick Camp | .05 | .15 | 473 | Pete Vuckovich | .05 | .15 | 561 | Jimmy Key | .08 | .25 |
| 386 | Jim Morrison | .05 | .15 | 474 | Kirk McCaskill RC | .20 | .50 | 562 | Bill Swift | .05 | .15 |
| 387 | Dave LaPoint | .05 | .15 | 475 | Jeff Lahti | .05 | .15 | 563 | Ron Darling | .08 | .25 |
| 388 | Dave Lopes | .08 | .25 | 476 | Mike Scott | .08 | .25 | 564 | Dick Ruthven | .05 | .15 |
| 389 | Al Cowens | .05 | .15 | 477 | Darren Daulton RC | .40 | 1.00 | 565 | Zane Smith | .05 | .15 |
| 390 | Doyle Alexander | .05 | .15 | 478 | Graig Nettles | .08 | .25 | 566 | Sid Bream | .05 | .15 |
| 391 | Tim Laudner | .05 | .15 | 479 | Bill Almon | .05 | .15 | 567A | Joel Youngblood ERR (Position P) | .05 | .15 |
| 392 | Don Aase | .05 | .15 | 480 | Greg Minton | .05 | .15 | 567B | Joel Youngblood COR (Position IF) | .20 | .50 |
| 393 | Jaime Cocanower | .05 | .15 | 481 | Randy Ready | .05 | .15 | 568 | Mario Ramirez | .05 | .15 |
| 394 | Randy O'Neal | .05 | .15 | 482 | Len Dykstra RC | .60 | 1.50 | 569 | Tom Runnells | .05 | .15 |
| 395 | Mike Easler | .05 | .15 | 483 | Thad Bosley | .05 | .15 | 570 | Rick Schu | .05 | .15 |
| 396 | Scott Bradley | .05 | .15 | 484 | Harold Reynolds RC | .60 | 1.50 | 571 | Bill Campbell | .05 | .15 |
| 397 | Tom Niedenfuer | .05 | .15 | 485 | Al Oliver | .08 | .25 | 572 | Dickie Thon | .05 | .15 |
| 398 | Jerry Willard | .05 | .15 | 486 | Roy Smalley | .05 | .15 | 573 | Al Holland | .05 | .15 |
| 399 | Lonnie Smith | .05 | .15 | 487 | John Franco | .08 | .25 | 574 | Reid Nichols | .05 | .15 |
| 400 | Bruce Bochte | .05 | .15 | 488 | Juan Agosto | .05 | .15 | 575 | Bert Roberge | .05 | .15 |
| 401 | Terry Francona | .08 | .25 | 489 | Al Pardo | .05 | .15 | 576 | Mike Flanagan | .05 | .15 |
| 402 | Jim Slaton | .05 | .15 | 490 | Bill Wegman RC | .05 | .15 | 577 | Tim Leary | .05 | .15 |
| 403 | Bill Stein | .05 | .15 | 491 | Frank Tanana | .08 | .25 | 578 | Mike Laga | .05 | .15 |
| 404 | Tim Hulett | .05 | .15 | 492 | Brian Fisher RC | .05 | .15 | 579 | Steve Lyons | .05 | .15 |
| 405 | Alan Ashby | .05 | .15 | 493 | Mark Clear | .05 | .15 | 580 | Phil Niekro | .08 | .25 |
| 406 | Tim Stoddard | .05 | .15 | 494 | Len Matuszek | .05 | .15 | 581 | Gilberto Reyes | .05 | .15 |
| 407 | Garry Maddox | .05 | .15 | 495 | Ramon Romero | .05 | .15 | 582 | Jamie Easterly | .05 | .15 |
| 408 | Ted Power | .05 | .15 | 496 | John Wathan | .05 | .15 | 583 | Mark Gubicza | .05 | .15 |
| 409 | Len Barker | .05 | .15 | 497 | Rob Picciolo | .05 | .15 | 584 | Stan Javier RC | .20 | .50 |
| 410 | Denny Gonzalez | .05 | .15 | 498 | U.L. Washington | .05 | .15 | 585 | Bill Laskey | .05 | .15 |
| 411 | George Frazier | .05 | .15 | 499 | John Candelaria | .05 | .15 | 586 | Jeff Russell | .05 | .15 |
| 412 | Andy Van Slyke | .20 | .50 | 500 | Duane Walker | .05 | .15 | 587 | Dickie Noles | .05 | .15 |
| 413 | Jim Dwyer | .05 | .15 | 501 | Gene Nelson | .05 | .15 | 588 | Steve Farr | .05 | .15 |
| 414 | Paul Householder | .05 | .15 | 502 | John Mizerock | .05 | .15 | 589 | Steve Ontiveros RC | .05 | .15 |
| 415 | Alejandro Sanchez | .05 | .15 | 503 | Luis Aguayo | .05 | .15 | 590 | Mike Hargrove | .05 | .15 |
| 416 | Steve Crawford | .05 | .15 | 504 | Kurt Kepshire | .05 | .15 | 591 | Marty Bystrom | .05 | .15 |
| 417 | Dan Pasqua | .05 | .15 | 505 | Ed Wojna | .05 | .15 | 592 | Franklin Stubbs | .05 | .15 |
| 418 | Enos Cabell | .05 | .15 | 506 | Joe Price | .05 | .15 | 593 | Larry Herndon | .05 | .15 |
| 419 | Mike Jones | .05 | .15 | 507 | Milt Thompson RC | .20 | .50 | 594 | Bill Swaggerty | .05 | .15 |
| 420 | Steve Kiefer | .05 | .15 | 508 | Junior Ortiz | .05 | .15 | 595 | Carlos Ponce | .05 | .15 |
| 421 | Tim Burke | .08 | .25 | 509 | Vida Blue | .08 | .25 | 596 | Pat Perry | .05 | .15 |
| 422 | Mike Mason | .05 | .15 | 510 | Steve Engel | .05 | .15 | 597 | Ray Knight | .08 | .25 |
| 423 | Ruppert Jones | .05 | .15 | 511 | Karl Best | .05 | .15 | 598 | Steve Lombardozzi | .05 | .15 |
| 424 | Jerry Hairston | .05 | .15 | 512 | Cecil Fielder RC | .75 | 2.00 | 599 | Brad Havens | .05 | .15 |
| 425 | Tito Landrum | .05 | .15 | 513 | Frank Eufemia | .05 | .15 | 600 | Pat Clements | .05 | .15 |
| 426 | Jeff Calhoun | .05 | .15 | 514 | Tippy Martinez | .05 | .15 | 601 | Joe Niekro | .05 | .15 |
| 427 | Don Carman | .05 | .15 | 515 | Billy Joe Robidoux | .05 | .15 | 602 | Hank Aaron Puzzle | .30 | .75 |
| 428 | Tony Perez | .20 | .50 | 516 | Bill Scherrer | .05 | .15 | 603 | Dwayne Henry | .05 | .15 |
| 429 | Jerry Davis | .05 | .15 | 517 | Bruce Hurst | .08 | .25 | 604 | Mookie Wilson | .08 | .25 |
| 430 | Bob Walk | .05 | .15 | 518 | Rich Bordi | .05 | .15 | 605 | Buddy Biancalana | .05 | .15 |
| 431 | Brad Wellman | .05 | .15 | 519 | Steve Yeager | .08 | .25 | 606 | Rance Mullinks | .05 | .15 |
| 432 | Terry Forster | .08 | .25 | 520 | Tony Bernazard | .05 | .15 | 607 | Alan Wiggins | .05 | .15 |
| 433 | Billy Hatcher | .05 | .15 | 521 | Hal McRae | .08 | .25 | 608 | Joe Cowley | .05 | .15 |
| 434 | Clint Hurdle | .05 | .15 | 522 | Jose Rijo | .08 | .25 | 609 | Tom Seaver | .20 | .50 |
| 435 | Ivan Calderon RC* | .20 | .50 | 523 | Mitch Webster | .05 | .15 | 609B | Tom Seaver YL | .75 | 2.00 |
| 436 | Pete Filson | .05 | .15 | 524 | Jack Howell | .05 | .15 | 610 | Neil Allen | .05 | .15 |
| 437 | Tom Henke | .08 | .25 | 525 | Alan Bannister | .05 | .15 | 611 | Don Sutton | .08 | .25 |
| 438 | Dave Engle | .05 | .15 | 526 | Ron Kittle | .08 | .25 | 612 | Fred Toliver | .05 | .15 |
| 439 | Tom Filer | .05 | .15 | 527 | Phil Garner | .08 | .25 | 613 | Jay Baller | .05 | .15 |
| 440 | Gorman Thomas | .08 | .25 | 528 | Kurt Bevacqua | .05 | .15 | 614 | Marc Sullivan | .05 | .15 |
| 441 | Rick Aguilera RC | .20 | .50 | 529 | Kevin Gross | .05 | .15 | 615 | John Grubb | .05 | .15 |
| 442 | Scott Sanderson | .05 | .15 | 530 | Bo Diaz | .05 | .15 | 616 | Bruce Kison | .05 | .15 |
| 443 | Jeff Dedmon | .05 | .15 | 531 | Ken Oberkfell | .05 | .15 | 617 | Bill Madlock | .08 | .25 |
| 444 | Joe Orsulak RC* | .20 | .50 | 532 | Rick Reuschel | .08 | .25 | | | | |
| 445 | Atlee Hammaker | .05 | .15 | 533 | Ron Meridith | .05 | .15 | | | | |

|  | | |
|---|---|---|
| 618 Chris Chambliss | .08 | .25 |
| 619 Dave Stewart | .08 | .25 |
| 620 Tim Lollar | .05 | .15 |
| 621 Gary Lavelle | .05 | .15 |
| 622 Charles Hudson | .05 | .15 |
| 623 Joel Davis | .05 | .15 |
| 624 Joe Johnson | .05 | .15 |
| 625 Sid Fernandez | .05 | .15 |
| 626 Dennis Lamp | .05 | .15 |
| 627 Terry Harper | .05 | .15 |
| 628 Jack Lazorko | .05 | .15 |
| 629 Roger McDowell* | .20 | .50 |
| 630 Mark Funderburk | .05 | .15 |
| 631 Ed Lynch | .05 | .15 |
| 632 Rudy Law | .05 | .15 |
| 633 Roger Mason RC | .15 | .40 |
| 634 Mike Felder RC | .05 | .15 |
| 635 Ken Schrom | .05 | .15 |
| 636 Bob Ojeda | .05 | .15 |
| 637 Ed VandeBerg | .05 | .15 |
| 638 Bobby Meacham | .05 | .15 |
| 639 Cliff Johnson | .05 | .15 |
| 640 Garth Iorg | .05 | .15 |
| 641 Dan Driessen | .05 | .15 |
| 642 Mike Brown OF | .05 | .15 |
| 643 John Shelby | .05 | .15 |
| 644 Pete Rose RB | .30 | .75 |
| 645 The Knuckle Brothers | .08 | .25 |
| 646 Jesse Orosco | .05 | .15 |
| 647 Billy Beane RC | .40 | 1.00 |
| 648 Cesar Cedeno | .08 | .25 |
| 649 Bert Blyleven | .08 | .25 |
| 650 Max Venable | .05 | .15 |
| 651 Fleet Feet / Vince Coleman / Willie McGee | .05 | .15 |
| 652 Calvin Schiraldi | .05 | .15 |
| 653 Pete Rose KING | .30 | .75 |
| 654 Diamond Kings CL 1-26 (Unnumbered) | .05 | .15 |
| 655A CL 1: 27-130 (Unnumbered) (45 Beane ERR) | .05 | .15 |
| 655B CL 1: 27-130 (Unnumbered) (45 Habyan COR) | .05 | .15 |
| 656 CL 2: 131-234 (Unnumbered) | .05 | .15 |
| 657 CL 3: 235-338 (Unnumbered) | .05 | .15 |
| 658 CL 4: 339-442 (Unnumbered) | .05 | .15 |
| 659 CL 5: 443-546 (Unnumbered) | .05 | .15 |
| 660 CL 6: 547-653 (Unnumbered) | .05 | .15 |

## 1987 Donruss

|  | | |
|---|---|---|
| COMPLETE SET (660) | 15.00 | 40.00 |
| COMP.FACT.SET (660) | 20.00 | 50.00 |
| COMP.CLEMENTE PUZZLE | .60 | 1.50 |
| 1 Wally Joyner DK | .15 | .40 |
| 2 Roger Clemens DK | .75 | 2.00 |
| 3 Dale Murphy DK | .08 | .25 |
| 4 Darryl Strawberry DK | | |
| 5 Ozzie Smith DK | .25 | .60 |
| 6 Jose Canseco DK | .40 | 1.00 |
| 7 Charlie Hough DK | .05 | .15 |
| 8 Brook Jacoby DK | .02 | .10 |
| 9 Fred Lynn DK | .05 | .15 |
| 10 Rick Rhoden DK | .02 | .10 |
| 11 Chris Brown DK | .02 | .10 |
| 12 Von Hayes DK | .05 | .15 |
| 13 Jack Morris DK | .05 | .15 |
| 14A Kevin McReynolds DK ERR | .15 | .40 |
| 14B Kevin McReynolds DK COR | .02 | .10 |
| 15 George Brett DK | .40 | 1.00 |
| 16 Ted Higuera DK | .02 | .10 |
| 17 Hubie Brooks DK | .02 | .10 |
| 18 Mike Scott DK | .05 | .15 |
| 19 Kirby Puckett DK | .30 | .75 |
| 20 Dave Winfield DK | .05 | .15 |
| 21 Lloyd Moseby DK | .02 | .10 |
| 22A Eric Davis DK ERR | .15 | .40 |
| 22B Eric Davis DK COR | .08 | .25 |
| 23 Jim Presley DK | .02 | .10 |
| 24 Keith Moreland DK | .02 | .10 |
| 25A Greg Walker DK ERR | .15 | .40 |
| 25B Greg Walker DK COR | .08 | .25 |
| 26 Steve Sax DK | .02 | .10 |
| 27 DK Checklist 1-26 | .02 | .10 |
| 28 B.J. Surhoff RC | .25 | .60 |
| 29 Randy Myers RC | .25 | .60 |
| 30 Ken Gerhart RC | .05 | .15 |
| 31 Benito Santiago | .15 | .40 |
| 32 Greg Swindell RC | .15 | .40 |
| 33 Mike Birkbeck RC | .05 | .15 |
| 34 Terry Steinbach RC | .25 | .60 |
| 35 Bo Jackson RC | 2.00 | 5.00 |
| 36 Greg Maddux RC | 4.00 | 10.00 |
| 37 Jim Lindeman RC | .05 | .15 |
| 38 Devon White RC | .25 | .60 |
| 39 Eric Bell RC | .05 | .15 |
| 40 Willie Fraser RC | .05 | .15 |
| 41 Jerry Browne RC | .05 | .15 |
| 42 Chris James RC* | .05 | .15 |
| 43 Rafael Palmeiro RC | 2.00 | 5.00 |
| 44 Pat Dodson RC | .05 | .15 |
| 45 Duane Ward RC* | .15 | .40 |
| 46 Mark McGwire RC | 3.00 | 8.00 |
| 47 Bruce Fields UER RC | .05 | .15 |
| 48 Eddie Murray | .15 | .40 |
| 49 Ted Higuera | .02 | .10 |
| 50 Kirk Gibson | .05 | .15 |
| 51 Oil Can Boyd | .02 | .10 |
| 52 Don Mattingly | .50 | 1.25 |
| 53 Pedro Guerrero | .05 | .15 |
| 54 George Brett | .40 | 1.00 |
| 55 Jose Rijo | .05 | .15 |
| 56 Tim Raines | .05 | .15 |
| 57 Ed Correa | .02 | .10 |
| 58 Mike Witt | .02 | .10 |
| 59 Greg Walker | .02 | .10 |
| 60 Ozzie Smith | .25 | .60 |
| 61 Glenn Davis | .02 | .10 |
| 62 Glenn Wilson | .02 | .10 |
| 63 Tom Browning | .05 | .15 |
| 64 Tony Gwynn | .25 | .60 |
| 65 R.J. Reynolds | .02 | .10 |
| 66 Will Clark RC | .60 | 1.50 |
| 67 Ozzie Virgil | .02 | .10 |
| 68 Rick Sutcliffe | .05 | .15 |
| 69 Gary Carter | .05 | .15 |
| 70 Mike Moore | .02 | .10 |
| 71 Bert Blyleven | .05 | .15 |
| 72 Tony Fernandez | .02 | .10 |
| 73 Kent Hrbek | .05 | .15 |
| 74 Lloyd Moseby | .02 | .10 |
| 75 Alvin Davis | .05 | .15 |
| 76 Keith Hernandez | .05 | .15 |
| 77 Ryne Sandberg | .30 | .75 |
| 78 Dale Murphy | .08 | .25 |
| 79 Sid Bream | .02 | .10 |
| 80 Chris Brown | .02 | .10 |
| 81 Steve Garvey | .05 | .15 |
| 82 Mario Soto | .02 | .10 |
| 83 Shane Rawley | .02 | .10 |
| 84 Willie McGee | .05 | .15 |
| 85 Jose Cruz | .05 | .15 |
| 86 Brian Downing | .05 | .15 |
| 87 Ozzie Guillen | .08 | .25 |
| 88 Hubie Brooks | .02 | .10 |
| 89 Cal Ripken | .60 | 1.50 |
| 90 Juan Nieves | .02 | .10 |
| 91 Lance Parrish | .05 | .15 |
| 92 Jim Rice | .05 | .15 |
| 93 Ron Guidry | .05 | .15 |
| 94 Fernando Valenzuela | .05 | .15 |
| 95 Andy Allanson RC | .02 | .10 |
| 96 Willie Wilson | .05 | .15 |
| 97 Jose Canseco | .40 | 1.00 |
| 98 Jeff Reardon | .05 | .15 |
| 99 Bobby Witt RC | .15 | .40 |
| 100 Checklist 28-133 | .02 | .10 |
| 101 Jose Guzman | .02 | .10 |
| 102 Steve Balboni | .02 | .10 |
| 103 Tony Phillips | .02 | .10 |
| 104 Brook Jacoby | .02 | .10 |
| 105 Dave Winfield | .05 | .15 |
| 106 Orel Hershiser | .08 | .25 |
| 107 Lou Whitaker | .05 | .15 |
| 108 Fred Lynn | .05 | .15 |
| 109 Bill Wegman | .02 | .10 |
| 110 Donnie Moore | .02 | .10 |
| 111 Jack Clark | .05 | .15 |
| 112 Bob Knepper | .02 | .10 |
| 113 Von Hayes | .02 | .10 |
| 114 Big Roberts RC | .15 | .40 |
| 115 Tony Pena | .05 | .15 |
| 116 Scott Garrelts | .02 | .10 |
| 117 Paul Molitor | .05 | .15 |
| 118 Darryl Strawberry | .15 | .40 |
| 119 Shawon Dunston | .02 | .10 |
| 120 Jim Presley | .02 | .10 |
| 121 Jesse Barfield | .05 | .15 |
| 122 Gary Gaetti | .05 | .15 |
| 123 Kurt Stillwell | .02 | .10 |
| 124 Joel Davis | .02 | .10 |
| 125 Mike Boddicker | .02 | .10 |
| 126 Robin Yount | .25 | .60 |
| 127 Alan Trammell | .05 | .15 |
| 128 Dave Righetti | .05 | .15 |
| 129 Dwight Evans | .08 | .25 |
| 130 Mike Scioscia | .05 | .15 |
| 131 Julio Franco | .05 | .15 |
| 132 Bret Saberhagen | .05 | .15 |
| 133 Mike Davis | .02 | .10 |
| 134 Joe Hesketh | .02 | .10 |
| 135 Wally Joyner RC | .25 | .60 |
| 136 Don Slaught | .02 | .10 |
| 137 Daryl Boston | .02 | .10 |
| 138 Nolan Ryan | .75 | 2.00 |
| 139 Mike Schmidt | .40 | 1.00 |
| 140 Tommy Herr | .02 | .10 |
| 141 Garry Templeton | .05 | .15 |
| 142 Kal Daniels | .02 | .10 |
| 143 Billy Sample | .02 | .10 |
| 144 Johnny Ray | .02 | .10 |
| 145 Robby Thompson RC* | .15 | .40 |
| 146 Bob Dernier | .02 | .10 |
| 147 Danny Tartabull | .15 | .40 |
| 148 Ernie Whitt | .02 | .10 |
| 149 Kirby Puckett | .30 | .75 |
| 150 Mike Young | .02 | .10 |
| 151 Ernest Riles | .02 | .10 |
| 152 Frank Tanana | .05 | .15 |
| 153 Rich Gedman | .05 | .15 |
| 154 Willie Randolph | .05 | .15 |
| 155 Bill Madlock | .05 | .15 |
| 156 Joe Carter | .15 | .40 |
| 157 Danny Jackson | .05 | .15 |
| 158 Carney Lansford | .05 | .15 |
| 159 Bryn Smith | .02 | .10 |
| 160 Gary Pettis | .02 | .10 |
| 161 Oddibe McDowell | .02 | .10 |
| 162 John Cangelosi | .02 | .10 |
| 163 Mike Scott | .05 | .15 |
| 164 Eric Show | .02 | .10 |
| 165 Juan Samuel | .05 | .15 |
| 166 Nick Esasky | .02 | .10 |
| 167 Zane Smith | .05 | .15 |
| 168 Mike C. Brown OF | .02 | .10 |
| 169 Keith Moreland | .02 | .10 |
| 170 John Tudor | .05 | .15 |
| 171 Ken Dixon | .02 | .10 |
| 172 Jim Gantner | .05 | .15 |
| 173 Jack Morris | .05 | .15 |
| 174 Bruce Hurst | .05 | .15 |
| 175 Dennis Rasmussen | .02 | .10 |
| 176 Mike Marshall | .05 | .15 |
| 177 Dan Quisenberry | .05 | .15 |
| 178 Eric Plunk | .02 | .10 |
| 179 Tim Wallach | .05 | .15 |
| 180 Steve Buechele | .02 | .10 |
| 181 Don Sutton | .05 | .15 |
| 182 Dave Schmidt | .02 | .10 |
| 183 Terry Pendleton | .15 | .40 |
| 184 Jim Deshaies RC* | .05 | .15 |
| 185 Steve Bedrosian | .02 | .10 |

| | | | | | | | | | | |
|---|---|---|---|---|---|---|---|---|---|---|
| ☐ 186 Pete Rose | .50 | 1.25 | ☐ 274 Rob Deer | .02 | .10 | ☐ 362 Vida Blue | .05 | .15 |
| ☐ 187 Dave Dravecky | .02 | .10 | ☐ 275 Walt Terrell | .02 | .10 | ☐ 363 Cecil Cooper | .05 | .15 |
| ☐ 188 Rick Reuschel | .05 | .15 | ☐ 276 Roger Clemens | .75 | 2.00 | ☐ 364 Bob Ojeda | .02 | .10 |
| ☐ 189 Dan Gladden | .02 | .10 | ☐ 277 Mike Easler | .02 | .10 | ☐ 365 Dennis Eckersley | .08 | .25 |
| ☐ 190 Rick Mahler | .02 | .10 | ☐ 278 Steve Sax | .02 | .10 | ☐ 366 Mike Morgan | .02 | .10 |
| ☐ 191 Thad Bosley | .02 | .10 | ☐ 279 Andre Thornton | .02 | .10 | ☐ 367 Willie Upshaw | .02 | .10 |
| ☐ 192 Ron Darling | .05 | .15 | ☐ 280 Jim Sundberg | .05 | .15 | ☐ 368 Allan Anderson RC | .02 | .10 |
| ☐ 193 Matt Young | .02 | .10 | ☐ 281 Bill Bathe | .02 | .10 | ☐ 369 Bill Gullickson | .02 | .10 |
| ☐ 194 Tom Brunansky | .02 | .10 | ☐ 282 Jay Tibbs | .02 | .10 | ☐ 370 Bobby Thigpen RC | .15 | .40 |
| ☐ 195 Dave Stieb | .05 | .15 | ☐ 283 Dick Schofield | .02 | .10 | ☐ 371 Juan Beniquez | .02 | .10 |
| ☐ 196 Frank Viola | .05 | .15 | ☐ 284 Mike Mason | .02 | .10 | ☐ 372 Charlie Moore | .02 | .10 |
| ☐ 197 Tom Henke | .02 | .10 | ☐ 285 Jerry Hairston | .02 | .10 | ☐ 373 Dan Petry | .02 | .10 |
| ☐ 198 Karl Best | .02 | .10 | ☐ 286 Bill Doran | .02 | .10 | ☐ 374 Rod Scurry | .02 | .10 |
| ☐ 199 Dwight Gooden | .08 | .25 | ☐ 287 Tim Flannery | .02 | .10 | ☐ 375 Tom Seaver | .08 | .25 |
| ☐ 200 Checklist 134-239 | .02 | .10 | ☐ 288 Gary Redus | .02 | .10 | ☐ 376 Ed VandeBerg | .02 | .10 |
| ☐ 201 Steve Trout | .02 | .10 | ☐ 289 John Franco | .05 | .15 | ☐ 377 Tony Bernazard | .02 | .10 |
| ☐ 202 Rafael Ramirez | .02 | .10 | ☐ 290 Paul Assenmacher | .15 | .40 | ☐ 378 Greg Pryor | .02 | .10 |
| ☐ 203 Bob Walk | .02 | .10 | ☐ 291 Joe Orsulak | .02 | .10 | ☐ 379 Dwayne Murphy | .02 | .10 |
| ☐ 204 Roger Mason | .02 | .10 | ☐ 292 Lee Smith | .05 | .15 | ☐ 380 Andy McGaffigan | .02 | .10 |
| ☐ 205 Terry Kennedy | .02 | .10 | ☐ 293 Mike Laga | .02 | .10 | ☐ 381 Kirk McCaskill | .02 | .10 |
| ☐ 206 Ron Oester | .02 | .10 | ☐ 294 Rick Dempsey | .02 | .10 | ☐ 382 Greg Harris | .02 | .10 |
| ☐ 207 John Russell | .02 | .10 | ☐ 295 Mike Felder | .02 | .10 | ☐ 383 Rich Dotson | .02 | .10 |
| ☐ 208 Greg Mathews | .02 | .10 | ☐ 296 Tom Brookens | .02 | .10 | ☐ 384 Craig Reynolds | .02 | .10 |
| ☐ 209 Charlie Kerfeld | .02 | .10 | ☐ 297 Al Nipper | .02 | .10 | ☐ 385 Greg Gross | .02 | .10 |
| ☐ 210 Reggie Jackson | .08 | .25 | ☐ 298 Mike Pagliarulo | .02 | .10 | ☐ 386 Tito Landrum | .02 | .10 |
| ☐ 211 Floyd Bannister | .02 | .10 | ☐ 299 Franklin Stubbs | .02 | .10 | ☐ 387 Craig Lefferts | .02 | .10 |
| ☐ 212 Vance Law | .02 | .10 | ☐ 300 Checklist 240-345 | .02 | .10 | ☐ 388 Dave Parker | .05 | .15 |
| ☐ 213 Rich Bordi | .02 | .10 | ☐ 301 Steve Farr | .02 | .10 | ☐ 389 Bob Horner | .05 | .15 |
| ☐ 214 Dan Plesac | .02 | .10 | ☐ 302 Bill Mooneyham | .02 | .10 | ☐ 390 Pat Clements | .02 | .10 |
| ☐ 215 Dave Collins | .05 | .15 | ☐ 303 Andres Galarraga | .05 | .15 | ☐ 391 Jeff Leonard | .02 | .10 |
| ☐ 216 Bob Stanley | .02 | .10 | ☐ 304 Scott Fletcher | .02 | .10 | ☐ 392 Chris Speier | .02 | .10 |
| ☐ 217 Joe Niekro | .02 | .10 | ☐ 305 Jack Howell | .02 | .10 | ☐ 393 John Moses | .02 | .10 |
| ☐ 218 Tom Niedenfuer | .02 | .10 | ☐ 306 Russ Morman | .02 | .10 | ☐ 394 Garth Iorg | .02 | .10 |
| ☐ 219 Brett Butler | .05 | .15 | ☐ 307 Todd Worrell | .02 | .10 | ☐ 395 Greg Gagne | .02 | .10 |
| ☐ 220 Charlie Leibrandt | .02 | .10 | ☐ 308 Dave Smith | .02 | .10 | ☐ 396 Nate Snell | .02 | .10 |
| ☐ 221 Steve Ontiveros | .02 | .10 | ☐ 309 Jeff Stone | .02 | .10 | ☐ 397 Bryan Clutterbuck | .02 | .10 |
| ☐ 222 Tim Burke | .02 | .10 | ☐ 310 Ron Robinson | .02 | .10 | ☐ 398 Darrell Evans | .05 | .15 |
| ☐ 223 Curtis Wilkerson | .02 | .10 | ☐ 311 Bruce Bochy | .02 | .10 | ☐ 399 Steve Crawford | .02 | .10 |
| ☐ 224 Pete Incaviglia RC * | .15 | .40 | ☐ 312 Jim Winn | .02 | .10 | ☐ 400 Checklist 346-451 | .02 | .10 |
| ☐ 225 Lonnie Smith | .02 | .10 | ☐ 313 Mark Davis | .02 | .10 | ☐ 401 Phil Lombardi | .02 | .10 |
| ☐ 226 Chris Codiroli | .02 | .10 | ☐ 314 Jeff Dedmon | .02 | .10 | ☐ 402 Rick Honeycutt | .02 | .10 |
| ☐ 227 Scott Bailes | .02 | .10 | ☐ 315 Jamie Moyer RC | .40 | 1.00 | ☐ 403 Ken Schrom | .02 | .10 |
| ☐ 228 Rickey Henderson | .15 | .40 | ☐ 316 Wally Backman | .02 | .10 | ☐ 404 Bud Black | .02 | .10 |
| ☐ 229 Ken Howell | .02 | .10 | ☐ 317 Ken Phelps | .02 | .10 | ☐ 405 Donnie Hill | .02 | .10 |
| ☐ 230 Darnell Coles | .02 | .10 | ☐ 318 Steve Lombardozzi | .02 | .10 | ☐ 406 Wayne Krenchicki | .02 | .10 |
| ☐ 231 Don Aase | .02 | .10 | ☐ 319 Rance Mulliniks | .02 | .10 | ☐ 407 Chuck Finley RC | .25 | .60 |
| ☐ 232 Tim Leary | .02 | .10 | ☐ 320 Tim Laudner | .02 | .10 | ☐ 408 Toby Harrah | .05 | .15 |
| ☐ 233 Bob Boone | .05 | .15 | ☐ 321 Mark Eichhorn | .02 | .10 | ☐ 409 Steve Lyons | .02 | .10 |
| ☐ 234 Ricky Horton | .02 | .10 | ☐ 322 Lee Guetterman | .02 | .10 | ☐ 410 Kevin Bass | .02 | .10 |
| ☐ 235 Mark Bailey | .02 | .10 | ☐ 323 Sid Fernandez | .02 | .10 | ☐ 411 Marvell Wynne | .02 | .10 |
| ☐ 236 Kevin Gross | .02 | .10 | ☐ 324 Jerry Mumphrey | .02 | .10 | ☐ 412 Ron Roenicke | .02 | .10 |
| ☐ 237 Lance McCullers | .02 | .10 | ☐ 325 David Palmer | .02 | .10 | ☐ 413 Tracy Jones | .02 | .10 |
| ☐ 238 Cecilio Guante | .02 | .10 | ☐ 326 Bill Almon | .02 | .10 | ☐ 414 Gene Garber | .02 | .10 |
| ☐ 239 Bob Melvin | .02 | .10 | ☐ 327 Candy Maldonado | .02 | .10 | ☐ 415 Mike Bielecki | .02 | .10 |
| ☐ 240 Billy Joe Robidoux | .02 | .10 | ☐ 328 John Kruk RC | .40 | 1.00 | ☐ 416 Frank DiPino | .02 | .10 |
| ☐ 241 Roger McDowell | .02 | .10 | ☐ 329 John Denny | .02 | .10 | ☐ 417 Andy Van Slyke | .08 | .25 |
| ☐ 242 Leon Durham | .02 | .10 | ☐ 330 Milt Thompson | .02 | .10 | ☐ 418 Jim Dwyer | .02 | .10 |
| ☐ 243 Ed Nunez | .02 | .10 | ☐ 331 Mike LaValliere RC * | .15 | .40 | ☐ 419 Ben Oglivie | .05 | .15 |
| ☐ 244 Jimmy Key | .05 | .15 | ☐ 332 Alan Ashby | .02 | .10 | ☐ 420 Dave Bergman | .02 | .10 |
| ☐ 245 Mike Smithson | .02 | .10 | ☐ 333 Doug Corbett | .02 | .10 | ☐ 421 Joe Sambito | .02 | .10 |
| ☐ 246 Bo Diaz | .02 | .10 | ☐ 334 Ron Karkovice RC | .15 | .40 | ☐ 422 Bob Tewksbury RC * | .15 | .40 |
| ☐ 247 Carlton Fisk | .08 | .25 | ☐ 335 Mitch Webster | .02 | .10 | ☐ 423 Len Matuszek | .02 | .10 |
| ☐ 248 Larry Sheets | .02 | .10 | ☐ 336 Lee Lacy | .02 | .10 | ☐ 424 Mike Kingery RC | .05 | .15 |
| ☐ 249 Juan Castillo RC | .05 | .15 | ☐ 337 Glenn Braggs RC | .05 | .15 | ☐ 425 Dave Kingman | .05 | .15 |
| ☐ 250 Eric King | .02 | .10 | ☐ 338 Dwight Lowry | .02 | .10 | ☐ 426 Al Newman RC | .02 | .10 |
| ☐ 251 Doug Drabek RC | .25 | .60 | ☐ 339 Don Baylor | .05 | .15 | ☐ 427 Gary Ward | .02 | .10 |
| ☐ 252 Wade Boggs | .25 | .60 | ☐ 340 Brian Fisher | .02 | .10 | ☐ 428 Ruppert Jones | .02 | .10 |
| ☐ 253 Mariano Duncan | .02 | .10 | ☐ 341 Reggie Williams | .02 | .10 | ☐ 429 Harold Baines | .05 | .15 |
| ☐ 254 Pat Tabler | .02 | .10 | ☐ 342 Tom Candiotti | .02 | .10 | ☐ 430 Pat Perry | .02 | .10 |
| ☐ 255 Frank White | .05 | .15 | ☐ 343 Rudy Law | .02 | .10 | ☐ 431 Terry Puhl | .02 | .10 |
| ☐ 256 Alfredo Griffin | .02 | .10 | ☐ 344 Curt Young | .02 | .10 | ☐ 432 Don Carman | .02 | .10 |
| ☐ 257 Floyd Youmans | .02 | .10 | ☐ 345 Mike Fitzgerald | .02 | .10 | ☐ 433 Eddie Milner | .02 | .10 |
| ☐ 258 Rob Wilfong | .02 | .10 | ☐ 346 Ruben Sierra RC | .40 | 1.00 | ☐ 434 LaMarr Hoyt | .02 | .10 |
| ☐ 259 Pete O'Brien | .02 | .10 | ☐ 347 Mitch Williams RC * | .15 | .40 | ☐ 435 Rick Rhoden | .02 | .10 |
| ☐ 260 Tim Hulett | .02 | .10 | ☐ 348 Jorge Orta | .02 | .10 | ☐ 436 Jose Uribe | .02 | .10 |
| ☐ 261 Dickie Thon | .02 | .10 | ☐ 349 Mickey Tettleton | .02 | .10 | ☐ 437 Ken Oberkfell | .02 | .10 |
| ☐ 262 Darren Daulton | .05 | .15 | ☐ 350 Ernie Camacho | .02 | .10 | ☐ 438 Ron Davis | .02 | .10 |
| ☐ 263 Vince Coleman | .02 | .10 | ☐ 351 Ron Kittle | .02 | .10 | ☐ 439 Jesse Orosco | .02 | .10 |
| ☐ 264 Andy Hawkins | .02 | .10 | ☐ 352 Ken Landreaux | .02 | .10 | ☐ 440 Scott Bradley | .02 | .10 |
| ☐ 265 Eric Davis | .08 | .25 | ☐ 353 Chet Lemon | .05 | .15 | ☐ 441 Randy Bush | .02 | .10 |
| ☐ 266 Andres Thomas | .02 | .10 | ☐ 354 John Shelby | .02 | .10 | ☐ 442 John Cerutti | .02 | .10 |
| ☐ 267 Mike Diaz | .02 | .10 | ☐ 355 Mark Clear | .02 | .10 | ☐ 443 Roy Smalley | .02 | .10 |
| ☐ 268 Chili Davis | .05 | .15 | ☐ 356 Doug DeCinces | .02 | .10 | ☐ 444 Kelly Gruber | .05 | .15 |
| ☐ 269 Jody Davis | .02 | .10 | ☐ 357 Ken Dayley | .02 | .10 | ☐ 445 Bob Kearney | .02 | .10 |
| ☐ 270 Phil Bradley | .02 | .10 | ☐ 358 Phil Garner | .05 | .15 | ☐ 446 Ed Hearn RC | .02 | .10 |
| ☐ 271 George Bell | .05 | .15 | ☐ 359 Steve Jeltz | .02 | .10 | ☐ 447 Scott Sanderson | .02 | .10 |
| ☐ 272 Keith Atherton | .02 | .10 | ☐ 360 Ed Whitson | .02 | .10 | ☐ 448 Bruce Benedict | .02 | .10 |
| ☐ 273 Storm Davis | .02 | .10 | ☐ 361 Barry Bonds RC | 5.00 | 12.00 | ☐ 449 Junior Ortiz | .02 | .10 |

| | | |
|---|---|---|
| ☐ 450 Mike Aldrete | .02 | .10 |
| ☐ 451 Kevin McReynolds | .02 | .10 |
| ☐ 452 Rob Murphy | .02 | .10 |
| ☐ 453 Kent Tekulve | .02 | .10 |
| ☐ 454 Curt Ford | .02 | .10 |
| ☐ 455 Dave Lopes | .05 | .15 |
| ☐ 456 Bob Grich | .05 | .15 |
| ☐ 457 Jose DeLeon | .02 | .10 |
| ☐ 458 Andre Dawson | .05 | .15 |
| ☐ 459 Mike Flanagan | .02 | .10 |
| ☐ 460 Joey Meyer | .05 | .15 |
| ☐ 461 Chuck Cary | .02 | .10 |
| ☐ 462 Bill Buckner | .05 | .15 |
| ☐ 463 Bob Shirley | .02 | .10 |
| ☐ 464 Jeff Hamilton | .02 | .10 |
| ☐ 465 Phil Niekro | .05 | .15 |
| ☐ 466 Mark Gubicza | .02 | .10 |
| ☐ 467 Jerry Willard | .02 | .10 |
| ☐ 468 Bob Sebra | .02 | .10 |
| ☐ 469 Larry Parrish | .02 | .10 |
| ☐ 470 Charlie Hough | .05 | .15 |
| ☐ 471 Hal McRae | .05 | .15 |
| ☐ 472 Dave Leiper | .02 | .10 |
| ☐ 473 Mel Hall | .02 | .10 |
| ☐ 474 Dan Pasqua | .02 | .10 |
| ☐ 475 Bob Welch | .05 | .15 |
| ☐ 476 Johnny Grubb | .02 | .10 |
| ☐ 477 Jim Traber | .02 | .10 |
| ☐ 478 Chris Bosio RC | .15 | .40 |
| ☐ 479 Mark McLemore | .05 | .15 |
| ☐ 480 John Morris | .02 | .10 |
| ☐ 481 Billy Hatcher | .02 | .10 |
| ☐ 482 Dan Schatzeder | .02 | .10 |
| ☐ 483 Rich Gossage | .05 | .15 |
| ☐ 484 Jim Morrison | .02 | .10 |
| ☐ 485 Jim Adduci | .02 | .10 |
| ☐ 486 Mike Heath | .02 | .10 |
| ☐ 487 Mookie Wilson | .05 | .15 |
| ☐ 488 Dave Martinez RC | .15 | .40 |
| ☐ 489 Harold Reynolds | .05 | .15 |
| ☐ 490 Jeff Hearron | .02 | .10 |
| ☐ 491 Mickey Hatcher | .02 | .10 |
| ☐ 492 Barry Larkin RC | .60 | 1.50 |
| ☐ 493 Bob James | .02 | .10 |
| ☐ 494 John Habyan | .02 | .10 |
| ☐ 495 Jim Adduci | .02 | .10 |
| ☐ 496 Mike Heath | .02 | .10 |
| ☐ 497 Tim Stoddard | .02 | .10 |
| ☐ 498 Tony Armas | .05 | .15 |
| ☐ 499 Dennis Powell | .02 | .10 |
| ☐ 500 Checklist 452-557 | .02 | .10 |
| ☐ 501 Chris Bando | .02 | .10 |
| ☐ 502 David Cone RC | .40 | 1.00 |
| ☐ 503 Jay Howell | .02 | .10 |
| ☐ 504 Tom Foley | .02 | .10 |
| ☐ 505 Ray Chadwick | .02 | .10 |
| ☐ 506 Mike Loynd RC | .05 | .15 |
| ☐ 507 Neil Allen | .02 | .10 |
| ☐ 508 Danny Darwin | .02 | .10 |
| ☐ 509 Rick Schu | .02 | .10 |
| ☐ 510 Jose Oquendo | .02 | .10 |
| ☐ 511 Gene Walter | .02 | .10 |
| ☐ 512 Terry McGriff | .02 | .10 |
| ☐ 513 Ken Griffey | .05 | .15 |
| ☐ 514 Benny Distefano | .02 | .10 |
| ☐ 515 Terry Mulholland RC | .15 | .40 |
| ☐ 516 Ed Lynch | .02 | .10 |
| ☐ 517 Bill Swift | .02 | .10 |
| ☐ 518 Manny Lee | .02 | .10 |
| ☐ 519 Andre David | .02 | .10 |
| ☐ 520 Scott McGregor | .02 | .10 |
| ☐ 521 Rick Manning | .02 | .10 |
| ☐ 522 Willie Hernandez | .02 | .10 |
| ☐ 523 Marty Barrett | .02 | .10 |
| ☐ 524 Wayne Tolleson | .02 | .10 |
| ☐ 525 Jose Gonzalez RC | .05 | .15 |
| ☐ 526 Cory Snyder | .05 | .15 |
| ☐ 527 Buddy Biancalana | .02 | .10 |
| ☐ 528 Moose Haas | .02 | .10 |
| ☐ 529 Wilfredo Tejada | .02 | .10 |
| ☐ 530 Stu Cliburn | .02 | .10 |
| ☐ 531 Dale Mohorcic | .02 | .10 |
| ☐ 532 Ron Hassey | .02 | .10 |
| ☐ 533 Ty Gainey | .02 | .10 |
| ☐ 534 Jerry Royster | .02 | .10 |
| ☐ 535 Mike Maddux RC | .15 | .40 |
| ☐ 536 Ted Power | .02 | .10 |
| ☐ 537 Ted Simmons | .05 | .15 |

| | | |
|---|---|---|
| ☐ 538 Rafael Belliard RC | .15 | .40 |
| ☐ 539 Chico Walker | .02 | .10 |
| ☐ 540 Bob Forsch | .02 | .10 |
| ☐ 541 John Stefero | .02 | .10 |
| ☐ 542 Dale Sveum | .02 | .10 |
| ☐ 543 Mark Thurmond | .02 | .10 |
| ☐ 544 Jeff Sellers | .02 | .10 |
| ☐ 545 Joel Skinner | .02 | .10 |
| ☐ 546 Alex Trevino | .02 | .10 |
| ☐ 547 Randy Kutcher | .02 | .10 |
| ☐ 548 Joaquin Andujar | .05 | .15 |
| ☐ 549 Casey Candaele | .02 | .10 |
| ☐ 550 Jeff Russell | .02 | .10 |
| ☐ 551 John Candelaria | .02 | .10 |
| ☐ 552 Joe Cowley | .02 | .10 |
| ☐ 553 Danny Cox | .02 | .10 |
| ☐ 554 Denny Walling | .02 | .10 |
| ☐ 555 Bruce Ruffin RC | .05 | .15 |
| ☐ 556 Buddy Bell | .05 | .15 |
| ☐ 557 Jimmy Jones RC | .02 | .10 |
| ☐ 558 Bobby Bonilla RC | .25 | .60 |
| ☐ 559 Jeff D. Robinson | .02 | .10 |
| ☐ 560 Ed Olwine | .02 | .10 |
| ☐ 561 Glenallen Hill RC | .15 | .40 |
| ☐ 562 Lee Mazzilli | .05 | .15 |
| ☐ 563 Mike G. Brown P | .02 | .10 |
| ☐ 564 George Frazier | .02 | .10 |
| ☐ 565 Mike Sharperson RC | .05 | .15 |
| ☐ 566 Mark Portugal RC * | .15 | .40 |
| ☐ 567 Rick Leach | .02 | .10 |
| ☐ 568 Mark Langston | .02 | .10 |
| ☐ 569 Rafael Santana | .02 | .10 |
| ☐ 570 Manny Trillo | .02 | .10 |
| ☐ 571 Cliff Speck | .02 | .10 |
| ☐ 572 Bob Kipper | .02 | .10 |
| ☐ 573 Kelly Downs RC | .05 | .15 |
| ☐ 574 Randy Asadoor | .02 | .10 |
| ☐ 575 Dave Magadan RC | .15 | .40 |
| ☐ 576 Marvin Freeman RC | .05 | .15 |
| ☐ 577 Jeff Lahti | .02 | .10 |
| ☐ 578 Jeff Calhoun | .02 | .10 |
| ☐ 579 Gus Polidor | .02 | .10 |
| ☐ 580 Gene Nelson | .02 | .10 |
| ☐ 581 Tim Teufel | .02 | .10 |
| ☐ 582 Odell Jones | .02 | .10 |
| ☐ 583 Mark Ryal | .02 | .10 |
| ☐ 584 Randy O'Neal | .02 | .10 |
| ☐ 585 Mike Greenwell RC | .15 | .40 |
| ☐ 586 Ray Knight | .05 | .15 |
| ☐ 587 Ralph Bryant | .02 | .10 |
| ☐ 588 Carmen Castillo | .02 | .10 |
| ☐ 589 Ed Wojna | .02 | .10 |
| ☐ 590 Stan Javier | .02 | .10 |
| ☐ 591 Jeff Musselman | .02 | .10 |
| ☐ 592 Mike Stanley RC | .15 | .40 |
| ☐ 593 Darrell Porter | .02 | .10 |
| ☐ 594 Drew Hall | .02 | .10 |
| ☐ 595 Rob Nelson | .02 | .10 |
| ☐ 596 Bryan Oelkers | .02 | .10 |
| ☐ 597 Scott Nielsen | .02 | .10 |
| ☐ 598 Brian Holton | .02 | .10 |
| ☐ 599 Kevin Mitchell RC * | .25 | .60 |
| ☐ 600 Checklist 558-660 | .02 | .10 |
| ☐ 601 Jackie Gutierrez | .02 | .10 |
| ☐ 602 Barry Jones | .02 | .10 |
| ☐ 603 Jerry Narron | .02 | .10 |
| ☐ 604 Steve Lake | .02 | .10 |
| ☐ 605 Jim Pankovits | .02 | .10 |
| ☐ 606 Ed Romero | .02 | .10 |
| ☐ 607 Dave LaPoint | .02 | .10 |
| ☐ 608 Don Robinson | .02 | .10 |
| ☐ 609 Mike Krukow | .02 | .10 |
| ☐ 610 Dave Valle RC ** | .05 | .15 |
| ☐ 611 Len Dykstra | .05 | .15 |
| ☐ 612 Roberto Clemente PUZ | .20 | .50 |
| ☐ 613 Mike Trujillo | .02 | .10 |
| ☐ 614 Damaso Garcia | .02 | .10 |
| ☐ 615 Neal Heaton | .02 | .10 |
| ☐ 616 Juan Berenguer | .02 | .10 |
| ☐ 617 Steve Carlton | .05 | .15 |
| ☐ 618 Gary Lucas | .02 | .10 |
| ☐ 619 Geno Petralli | .02 | .10 |
| ☐ 620 Rick Aguilera | .02 | .10 |
| ☐ 621 Fred McGriff | .30 | .75 |
| ☐ 622 Dave Henderson | .02 | .10 |
| ☐ 623 Dave Clark RC | .05 | .15 |
| ☐ 624 Angel Salazar | .02 | .10 |
| ☐ 625 Randy Hunt | .02 | .10 |

| | | |
|---|---|---|
| ☐ 626 John Gibbons | .02 | .10 |
| ☐ 627 Kevin Brown RC | .60 | 1.50 |
| ☐ 628 Bill Dawley | .02 | .10 |
| ☐ 629 Aurelio Lopez | .02 | .10 |
| ☐ 630 Charles Hudson | .02 | .10 |
| ☐ 631 Ray Soff | .02 | .10 |
| ☐ 632 Ray Hayward | .02 | .10 |
| ☐ 633 Spike Owen | .02 | .10 |
| ☐ 634 Glenn Hubbard | .02 | .10 |
| ☐ 635 Kevin Elster RC | .15 | .40 |
| ☐ 636 Mike LaCoss | .02 | .10 |
| ☐ 637 Dwayne Henry | .02 | .10 |
| ☐ 638 Rey Quinones | .02 | .10 |
| ☐ 639 Jim Clancy | .02 | .10 |
| ☐ 640 Larry Andersen | .02 | .10 |
| ☐ 641 Calvin Schiraldi | .02 | .10 |
| ☐ 642 Stan Jefferson | .02 | .10 |
| ☐ 643 Marc Sullivan | .02 | .10 |
| ☐ 644 Mark Grant | .02 | .10 |
| ☐ 645 Cliff Johnson | .02 | .10 |
| ☐ 646 Howard Johnson | .05 | .15 |
| ☐ 647 Dave Sax | .02 | .10 |
| ☐ 648 Dave Stewart | .05 | .15 |
| ☐ 649 Danny Heep | .02 | .10 |
| ☐ 650 Joe Johnson | .02 | .10 |
| ☐ 651 Bob Brower | .02 | .10 |
| ☐ 652 Rob Woodward | .02 | .10 |
| ☐ 653 John Mizerock | .02 | .10 |
| ☐ 654 Tim Pyznarski | .02 | .10 |
| ☐ 655 Luis Aquino | .02 | .10 |
| ☐ 656 Mickey Brantley | .02 | .10 |
| ☐ 657 Doyle Alexander | .02 | .10 |
| ☐ 658 Sammy Stewart | .02 | .10 |
| ☐ 659 Jim Acker | .02 | .10 |
| ☐ 660 Pete Ladd | .02 | .10 |

## 1988 Donruss

| | | |
|---|---|---|
| ☐ COMPLETE SET (660) | 4.00 | 10.00 |
| ☐ COMP.FACT.SET (660) | 6.00 | 15.00 |
| ☐ COMMON CARD (1-660) | | .05 |
| ☐ COMMON SP (648-660) | | .05 |
| ☐ 1 Mark McGwire DK | .30 | .75 |
| ☐ 2 Tim Raines DK | .02 | .10 |
| ☐ 3 Benito Santiago DK | .02 | .10 |
| ☐ 4 Alan Trammell DK | .05 | .15 |
| ☐ 5 Danny Tartabull DK | .01 | .05 |
| ☐ 6 Ron Darling DK | .02 | .10 |
| ☐ 7 Paul Molitor DK | .05 | .15 |
| ☐ 8 Devon White DK | .02 | .10 |
| ☐ 9 Andre Dawson DK | .05 | .15 |
| ☐ 10 Julio Franco DK | .01 | .05 |
| ☐ 11 Scott Fletcher DK | .01 | .05 |
| ☐ 12 Tony Fernandez DK | .01 | .05 |
| ☐ 13 Shane Rawley DK | .01 | .05 |
| ☐ 14 Kal Daniels DK | .01 | .05 |
| ☐ 15 Jack Clark DK | .02 | .10 |
| ☐ 16 Dwight Evans DK | .05 | .15 |
| ☐ 17 Tommy John DK | .05 | .15 |
| ☐ 18 Andy Van Slyke DK | .05 | .15 |
| ☐ 19 Gary Gaetti DK | .02 | .10 |
| ☐ 20 Mark Langston DK | .01 | .05 |
| ☐ 21 Will Clark DK | .07 | .20 |
| ☐ 22 Glenn Hubbard DK | .01 | .05 |
| ☐ 23 Billy Hatcher DK | .01 | .05 |
| ☐ 24 Bob Welch DK | .02 | .10 |
| ☐ 25 Ivan Calderon DK | .01 | .05 |
| ☐ 26 Cal Ripken DK | .15 | .40 |
| ☐ DK Checklist 1-26 | .01 | .05 |
| ☐ 28 Mackey Sasser RC | .08 | .25 |
| ☐ 29 Jeff Treadway RC | .08 | .25 |
| ☐ 30 Mike Campbell RR | .01 | .05 |
| ☐ 31 Lance Johnson RR | .08 | .25 |
| ☐ 32 Nelson Liriano RR | .01 | .05 |
| ☐ 33 Shawn Abner RR | .01 | .05 |

|  | | |
|---|---|---|
| 34 Roberto Alomar RC | .75 | 2.00 |
| 35 Shawn Hillegas RR | .01 | .05 |
| 36 Joey Meyer RR | .01 | .05 |
| 37 Kevin Elster RR | .01 | .05 |
| 38 Jose Lind RR | .08 | .25 |
| 39 Kirt Manwaring RC | .08 | .25 |
| 40 Mark Grace RC | .75 | 2.00 |
| 41 Jody Reed RC | .08 | .25 |
| 42 John Farrell RR RC | .02 | .10 |
| 43 Al Leiter RC | .30 | .75 |
| 44 Gary Thurman RR | .01 | .05 |
| 45 Vicente Palacios RR | .01 | .05 |
| 46 Eddie Williams RC | .02 | .10 |
| 47 Jack McDowell RC | .15 | .40 |
| 48 Ken Dixon | .01 | .05 |
| 49 Mike Birkbeck | .01 | .05 |
| 50 Eric King | .01 | .05 |
| 51 Roger Clemens | .40 | 1.00 |
| 52 Pat Clements | .01 | .05 |
| 53 Fernando Valenzuela | .02 | .10 |
| 54 Mark Gubicza | .01 | .05 |
| 55 Jay Howell | .01 | .05 |
| 56 Floyd Youmans | .01 | .05 |
| 57 Ed Correa | .01 | .05 |
| 58 DeWayne Buice | .01 | .05 |
| 59 Jose DeLeon | .01 | .05 |
| 60 Danny Cox | .01 | .05 |
| 61 Nolan Ryan | .40 | 1.00 |
| 62 Steve Bedrosian | .01 | .05 |
| 63 Tom Browning | .01 | .05 |
| 64 Mark Davis | .01 | .05 |
| 65 R.J. Reynolds | .01 | .05 |
| 66 Kevin Mitchell | .02 | .10 |
| 67 Ken Oberkfell | .01 | .05 |
| 68 Rick Sutcliffe | .02 | .10 |
| 69 Dwight Gooden | .02 | .10 |
| 70 Scott Bankhead | .01 | .05 |
| 71 Bert Blyleven | .02 | .10 |
| 72 Jimmy Key | .02 | .10 |
| 73 Les Straker | .01 | .05 |
| 74 Jim Clancy | .01 | .05 |
| 75 Mike Moore | .01 | .05 |
| 76 Ron Darling | .02 | .10 |
| 77 Ed Lynch | .01 | .05 |
| 78 Dale Murphy | .05 | .15 |
| 79 Doug Drabek | .01 | .05 |
| 80 Scott Garrelts | .01 | .05 |
| 81 Ed Whitson | .01 | .05 |
| 82 Rob Murphy | .01 | .05 |
| 83 Shane Rawley | .01 | .05 |
| 84 Greg Mathews | .01 | .05 |
| 85 Jim Deshaies | .01 | .05 |
| 86 Mike Witt | .01 | .05 |
| 87 Donnie Hill | .01 | .05 |
| 88 Jeff Reed | .01 | .05 |
| 89 Mike Boddicker | .01 | .05 |
| 90 Ted Higuera | .01 | .05 |
| 91 Walt Terrell | .01 | .05 |
| 92 Bob Stanley | .01 | .05 |
| 93 Dave Righetti | .02 | .10 |
| 94 Orel Hershiser | .02 | .10 |
| 95 Chris Bando | .01 | .05 |
| 96 Bret Saberhagen | .02 | .10 |
| 97 Curt Young | .01 | .05 |
| 98 Tim Burke | .01 | .05 |
| 99 Charlie Hough | .02 | .10 |
| 100A Checklist 28-137 | .01 | .05 |
| 100B Checklist 28-133 | .01 | .05 |
| 101 Bobby Witt | .01 | .05 |
| 102 George Brett | .20 | .50 |
| 103 Mickey Tettleton | .01 | .05 |
| 104 Scott Bailes | .01 | .05 |
| 105 Mike Pagliarulo | .01 | .05 |
| 106 Mike Scioscia | .02 | .10 |
| 107 Tom Brookens | .01 | .05 |
| 108 Ray Knight | .02 | .10 |
| 109 Dan Plesac | .01 | .05 |
| 110 Wally Joyner | .02 | .10 |
| 111 Bob Forsch | .01 | .05 |
| 112 Mike Scott | .02 | .10 |
| 113 Kevin Gross | .01 | .05 |
| 114 Benito Santiago | .02 | .10 |
| 115 Bob Kipper | .01 | .05 |
| 116 Mike Krukow | .01 | .05 |
| 117 Chris Bosio | .01 | .05 |
| 118 Sid Fernandez | .01 | .05 |
| 119 Jody Davis | .01 | .05 |
| 120 Mike Morgan | .01 | .05 |
| 121 Mark Eichhorn | .01 | .05 |
| 122 Jeff Reardon | .02 | .10 |
| 123 John Franco | .02 | .10 |
| 124 Richard Dotson | .01 | .05 |
| 125 Eric Bell | .01 | .05 |
| 126 Juan Nieves | .01 | .05 |
| 127 Jack Morris | .02 | .10 |
| 128 Rick Rhoden | .01 | .05 |
| 129 Rich Gedman | .01 | .05 |
| 130 Ken Howell | .01 | .05 |
| 131 Brook Jacoby | .01 | .05 |
| 132 Danny Jackson | .01 | .05 |
| 133 Gene Nelson | .01 | .05 |
| 134 Neal Heaton | .01 | .05 |
| 135 Willie Fraser | .01 | .05 |
| 136 Jose Guzman | .01 | .05 |
| 137 Ozzie Guillen | .02 | .10 |
| 138 Bob Knepper | .01 | .05 |
| 139 Mike Jackson RC* | .08 | .25 |
| 140 Joe Magrane RC* | .08 | .25 |
| 141 Jimmy Jones | .01 | .05 |
| 142 Ted Power | .01 | .05 |
| 143 Ozzie Virgil | .01 | .05 |
| 144 Felix Fermin | .01 | .05 |
| 145 Kelly Downs | .01 | .05 |
| 146 Shawon Dunston | .02 | .10 |
| 147 Scott Bradley | .01 | .05 |
| 148 Dave Stieb | .02 | .10 |
| 149 Frank Viola | .02 | .10 |
| 150 Terry Kennedy | .01 | .05 |
| 151 Bill Wegman | .01 | .05 |
| 152 Matt Nokes RC* | .08 | .25 |
| 153 Wade Boggs | .05 | .15 |
| 154 Wayne Tolleson | .01 | .05 |
| 155 Mariano Duncan | .01 | .05 |
| 156 Julio Franco | .02 | .10 |
| 157 Charlie Leibrandt | .01 | .05 |
| 158 Terry Steinbach | .02 | .10 |
| 159 Mike Fitzgerald | .01 | .05 |
| 160 Jack Lazorko | .01 | .05 |
| 161 Mitch Williams | .01 | .05 |
| 162 Greg Walker | .01 | .05 |
| 163 Alan Ashby | .01 | .05 |
| 164 Tony Gwynn | .10 | .30 |
| 165 Bruce Ruffin | .01 | .05 |
| 166 Ron Robinson | .01 | .05 |
| 167 Zane Smith | .01 | .05 |
| 168 Junior Ortiz | .01 | .05 |
| 169 Jamie Moyer | .02 | .10 |
| 170 Tony Pena | .01 | .05 |
| 171 Cal Ripken | .30 | .75 |
| 172 B.J. Surhoff | .02 | .10 |
| 173 Lou Whitaker | .02 | .10 |
| 174 Ellis Burks RC | .15 | .40 |
| 175 Ron Guidry | .02 | .10 |
| 176 Steve Sax | .01 | .05 |
| 177 Danny Tartabull | .02 | .10 |
| 178 Carney Lansford | .02 | .10 |
| 179 Casey Candaele | .01 | .05 |
| 180 Scott Fletcher | .01 | .05 |
| 181 Mark McLemore | .01 | .05 |
| 182 Ivan Calderon | .01 | .05 |
| 183 Jack Clark | .02 | .10 |
| 184 Glenn Davis | .01 | .05 |
| 185 Luis Aguayo | .01 | .05 |
| 186 Bo Diaz | .01 | .05 |
| 187 Stan Jefferson | .01 | .05 |
| 188 Sid Bream | .01 | .05 |
| 189 Bob Brenly | .01 | .05 |
| 190 Dion James | .01 | .05 |
| 191 Leon Durham | .01 | .05 |
| 192 Jesse Orosco | .01 | .05 |
| 193 Alvin Davis | .01 | .05 |
| 194 Gary Gaetti | .02 | .10 |
| 195 Fred McGriff | .07 | .20 |
| 196 Steve Lombardozzi | .01 | .05 |
| 197 Rance Mulliniks | .01 | .05 |
| 198 Rey Quinones | .01 | .05 |
| 199 Gary Carter | .02 | .10 |
| 200A Checklist 138-247 | .01 | .05 |
| 200B Checklist 134-239 | .01 | .05 |
| 201 Keith Moreland | .01 | .05 |
| 202 Ken Griffey | .02 | .10 |
| 203 Tommy Gregg | .01 | .05 |
| 204 Will Clark | .07 | .20 |
| 205 John Kruk | .02 | .10 |
| 206 Buddy Bell | .02 | .10 |
| 207 Von Hayes | .01 | .05 |
| 208 Tommy Herr | .01 | .05 |
| 209 Craig Reynolds | .01 | .05 |
| 210 Gary Pettis | .01 | .05 |
| 211 Harold Baines | .02 | .10 |
| 212 Vance Law | .01 | .05 |
| 213 Ken Gerhart | .01 | .05 |
| 214 Jim Gantner | .01 | .05 |
| 215 Chet Lemon | .02 | .10 |
| 216 Dwight Evans | .05 | .15 |
| 217 Don Mattingly | .25 | .60 |
| 218 Franklin Stubbs | .01 | .05 |
| 219 Pat Tabler | .01 | .05 |
| 220 Bo Jackson | .07 | .20 |
| 221 Tony Phillips | .01 | .05 |
| 222 Tim Wallach | .01 | .05 |
| 223 Ruben Sierra | .02 | .10 |
| 224 Steve Buechele | .01 | .05 |
| 225 Frank White | .02 | .10 |
| 226 Alfredo Griffin | .01 | .05 |
| 227 Greg Swindell | .01 | .05 |
| 228 Willie Randolph | .02 | .10 |
| 229 Mike Marshall | .01 | .05 |
| 230 Alan Trammell | .02 | .10 |
| 231 Eddie Murray | .07 | .20 |
| 232 Dale Sveum | .01 | .05 |
| 233 Dick Schofield | .01 | .05 |
| 234 Jose Oquendo | .01 | .05 |
| 235 Bill Doran | .01 | .05 |
| 236 Milt Thompson | .01 | .05 |
| 237 Marvell Wynne | .01 | .05 |
| 238 Bobby Bonilla | .02 | .10 |
| 239 Chris Speier | .01 | .05 |
| 240 Glenn Braggs | .01 | .05 |
| 241 Wally Backman | .01 | .05 |
| 242 Ryne Sandberg | .15 | .40 |
| 243 Phil Bradley | .01 | .05 |
| 244 Kelly Gruber | .01 | .05 |
| 245 Tom Brunansky | .02 | .10 |
| 246 Ron Oester | .01 | .05 |
| 247 Bobby Thigpen | .01 | .05 |
| 248 Fred Lynn | .02 | .10 |
| 249 Paul Molitor | .02 | .10 |
| 250 Darrell Evans | .02 | .10 |
| 251 Gary Ward | .01 | .05 |
| 252 Bruce Hurst | .01 | .05 |
| 253 Bob Welch | .02 | .10 |
| 254 Joe Carter | .02 | .10 |
| 255 Willie Wilson | .02 | .10 |
| 256 Mark McGwire | .60 | 1.50 |
| 257 Mitch Webster | .01 | .05 |
| 258 Brian Downing | .02 | .10 |
| 259 Mike Stanley | .01 | .05 |
| 260 Carlton Fisk | .05 | .15 |
| 261 Billy Hatcher | .01 | .05 |
| 262 Glenn Wilson | .01 | .05 |
| 263 Ozzie Smith | .10 | .30 |
| 264 Randy Ready | .01 | .05 |
| 265 Kurt Stillwell | .01 | .05 |
| 266 David Palmer | .01 | .05 |
| 267 Mike Diaz | .01 | .05 |
| 268 Bobby Thompson | .01 | .05 |
| 269 Andre Dawson | .02 | .10 |
| 270 Lee Guetterman | .01 | .05 |
| 271 Willie Upshaw | .01 | .05 |
| 272 Randy Bush | .01 | .05 |
| 273 Larry Sheets | .01 | .05 |
| 274 Rob Deer | .02 | .10 |
| 275 Kirk Gibson | .07 | .20 |
| 276 Marty Barrett | .01 | .05 |
| 277 Rickey Henderson | .07 | .20 |
| 278 Pedro Guerrero | .02 | .10 |
| 279 Brett Butler | .02 | .10 |
| 280 Kevin Seitzer | .02 | .10 |
| 281 Mike Davis | .01 | .05 |
| 282 Andres Galarraga | .02 | .10 |
| 283 Devon White | .02 | .10 |
| 284 Pete O'Brien | .01 | .05 |
| 285 Jerry Hairston | .01 | .05 |
| 286 Kevin Bass | .01 | .05 |
| 287 Candelis Martinez | .01 | .05 |
| 288 Juan Samuel | .02 | .10 |
| 289 Kal Daniels | .01 | .05 |
| 290 Albert Hall | .01 | .05 |
| 291 Andy Van Slyke | .05 | .15 |
| 292 Jim Gott | .02 | .10 |
| 293 Vince Coleman | .01 | .05 |
| 294 Tom Niedenfuer | .01 | .05 |
| 295 Robin Yount | .10 | .30 |

|  |  | | |
|---|---|---|---|
| 296 | Jeff M. Robinson | .01 | .05 |
| 297 | Todd Benzinger RC* | .08 | .25 |
| 298 | Dave Winfield | .02 | .10 |
| 299 | Mickey Hatcher | .01 | .05 |
| 300A | Checklist 248-357 | .01 | .05 |
| 300B | Checklist 240-345 | .01 | .05 |
| 301 | Bud Black | .01 | .05 |
| 302 | Jose Canseco | .20 | .50 |
| 303 | Tom Foley | .01 | .05 |
| 304 | Pete Incaviglia | .01 | .05 |
| 305 | Bob Boone | .02 | .10 |
| 306 | Bill Long | .01 | .05 |
| 307 | Willie McGee | .02 | .10 |
| 308 | Ken Caminiti RC | .75 | 2.00 |
| 309 | Darren Daulton | .02 | .10 |
| 310 | Tracy Jones | .01 | .05 |
| 311 | Greg Booker | .01 | .05 |
| 312 | Mike LaValliere | .01 | .05 |
| 313 | Chili Davis | .02 | .10 |
| 314 | Glenn Hubbard | .01 | .05 |
| 315 | Paul Noce | .01 | .05 |
| 316 | Keith Hernandez | .02 | .10 |
| 317 | Mark Langston | .01 | .05 |
| 318 | Keith Atherton | .01 | .05 |
| 319 | Tony Fernandez | .01 | .05 |
| 320 | Kent Hrbek | .02 | .10 |
| 321 | John Cerutti | .01 | .05 |
| 322 | Mike Kingery | .01 | .05 |
| 323 | Dave Magadan | .01 | .05 |
| 324 | Rafael Palmeiro | .15 | .40 |
| 325 | Jeff Dedmon | .01 | .05 |
| 326 | Barry Bonds | .75 | 2.00 |
| 327 | Jeffrey Leonard | .01 | .05 |
| 328 | Tim Flannery | .01 | .05 |
| 329 | Dave Concepcion | .02 | .10 |
| 330 | Mike Schmidt | .20 | .50 |
| 331 | Bill Dawley | .01 | .05 |
| 332 | Larry Andersen | .01 | .05 |
| 333 | Jack Howell | .01 | .05 |
| 334 | Ken Williams | .01 | .05 |
| 335 | Bryn Smith | .01 | .05 |
| 336 | Bill Ripken RC* | .08 | .25 |
| 337 | Greg Brock | .01 | .05 |
| 338 | Mike Heath | .01 | .05 |
| 339 | Mike Greenwell | .01 | .05 |
| 340 | Claudell Washington | .01 | .05 |
| 341 | Jose Gonzalez | .01 | .05 |
| 342 | Mel Hall | .01 | .05 |
| 343 | Jim Eisenreich | .01 | .05 |
| 344 | Tony Bernazard | .01 | .05 |
| 345 | Tim Raines | .02 | .10 |
| 346 | Bob Brower | .01 | .05 |
| 347 | Larry Parrish | .01 | .05 |
| 348 | Thad Bosley | .01 | .05 |
| 349 | Dennis Eckersley | .05 | .15 |
| 350 | Cory Snyder | .01 | .05 |
| 351 | Rick Cerone | .01 | .05 |
| 352 | John Shelby | .01 | .05 |
| 353 | Larry Herndon | .01 | .05 |
| 354 | John Habyan | .01 | .05 |
| 355 | Chuck Crim | .01 | .05 |
| 356 | Gus Polidor | .01 | .05 |
| 357 | Ken Dayley | .01 | .05 |
| 358 | Danny Darwin | .01 | .05 |
| 359 | Lance Parrish | .02 | .10 |
| 360 | James Steels | .01 | .05 |
| 361 | Al Pedrique | .01 | .05 |
| 362 | Mike Aldrete | .01 | .05 |
| 363 | Juan Castillo | .01 | .05 |
| 364 | Len Dykstra | .02 | .10 |
| 365 | Luis Quinones | .01 | .05 |
| 366 | Jim Presley | .01 | .05 |
| 367 | Lloyd Moseby | .01 | .05 |
| 368 | Kirby Puckett | .07 | .20 |
| 369 | Eric Davis | .02 | .10 |
| 370 | Gary Redus | .01 | .05 |
| 371 | Dave Schmidt | .01 | .05 |
| 372 | Mark Clear | .01 | .05 |
| 373 | Dave Bergman | .01 | .05 |
| 374 | Charles Hudson | .01 | .05 |
| 375 | Calvin Schiraldi | .01 | .05 |
| 376 | Alex Trevino | .01 | .05 |
| 377 | Tom Candiotti | .01 | .05 |
| 378 | Steve Farr | .01 | .05 |
| 379 | Mike Gallego | .01 | .05 |
| 380 | Andy McGaffigan | .01 | .05 |
| 381 | Kirk McCaskill | .01 | .05 |
| 382 | Oddibe McDowell | .01 | .05 |
| 383 | Floyd Bannister | .01 | .05 |
| 384 | Denny Walling | .01 | .05 |
| 385 | Don Carman | .01 | .05 |
| 386 | Todd Worrell | .01 | .05 |
| 387 | Eric Show | .01 | .05 |
| 388 | Dave Parker | .02 | .10 |
| 389 | Rick Mahler | .01 | .05 |
| 390 | Mike Dunne | .01 | .05 |
| 391 | Candy Maldonado | .01 | .05 |
| 392 | Bob Dernier | .01 | .05 |
| 393 | Dave Valle | .01 | .05 |
| 394 | Ernie Whitt | .01 | .05 |
| 395 | Juan Berenguer | .01 | .05 |
| 396 | Mike Young | .01 | .05 |
| 397 | Mike Felder | .01 | .05 |
| 398 | Willie Hernandez | .01 | .05 |
| 399 | Jim Rice | .02 | .10 |
| 400A | Checklist 358-467 | .01 | .05 |
| 400B | Checklist 346-451 | .01 | .05 |
| 401 | Tommy John | .02 | .10 |
| 402 | Brian Holton | .01 | .05 |
| 403 | Carmen Castillo | .01 | .05 |
| 404 | Jamie Quirk | .01 | .05 |
| 405 | Dwayne Murphy | .01 | .05 |
| 406 | Jeff Parrett | .01 | .05 |
| 407 | Don Sutton | .02 | .10 |
| 408 | Jerry Browne | .01 | .05 |
| 409 | Jim Winn | .01 | .05 |
| 410 | Dave Smith | .01 | .05 |
| 411 | Shane Mack | .01 | .05 |
| 412 | Greg Gross | .01 | .05 |
| 413 | Nick Esasky | .01 | .05 |
| 414 | Damaso Garcia | .01 | .05 |
| 415 | Brian Fisher | .01 | .05 |
| 416 | Brian Dayett | .01 | .05 |
| 417 | Curt Ford | .01 | .05 |
| 418 | Mark Williamson | .01 | .05 |
| 419 | Bill Schroeder | .01 | .05 |
| 420 | Mike Henneman RC* | .08 | .25 |
| 421 | John Marzano | .01 | .05 |
| 422 | Ron Kittle | .01 | .05 |
| 423 | Matt Young | .01 | .05 |
| 424 | Steve Balboni | .01 | .05 |
| 425 | Luis Polonia RC* | .08 | .25 |
| 426 | Randy St.Claire | .01 | .05 |
| 427 | Greg Harris | .01 | .05 |
| 428 | Johnny Ray | .01 | .05 |
| 429 | Ray Searage | .01 | .05 |
| 430 | Ricky Horton | .01 | .05 |
| 431 | Gerald Young | .01 | .05 |
| 432 | Rick Schu | .01 | .05 |
| 433 | Paul O'Neill | .05 | .15 |
| 434 | Rich Gossage | .02 | .10 |
| 435 | John Cangelosi | .01 | .05 |
| 436 | Mike LaCoss | .01 | .05 |
| 437 | Gerald Perry | .01 | .05 |
| 438 | Dave Martinez | .01 | .05 |
| 439 | Darryl Strawberry | .02 | .10 |
| 440 | John Moses | .01 | .05 |
| 441 | Greg Gagne | .01 | .05 |
| 442 | Jesse Barfield | .02 | .10 |
| 443 | George Frazier | .01 | .05 |
| 444 | Garth Iorg | .01 | .05 |
| 445 | Ed Nunez | .01 | .05 |
| 446 | Rick Aguilera | .01 | .05 |
| 447 | Jerry Mumphrey | .01 | .05 |
| 448 | Rafael Ramirez | .01 | .05 |
| 449 | John Smiley RC* | .08 | .25 |
| 450 | Atlee Hammaker | .01 | .05 |
| 451 | Lance McCullers | .01 | .05 |
| 452 | Guy Hoffman | .01 | .05 |
| 453 | Chris James | .01 | .05 |
| 454 | Terry Pendleton | .02 | .10 |
| 455 | Dave Meads | .01 | .05 |
| 456 | Bill Buckner | .02 | .10 |
| 457 | John Pawlowski | .01 | .05 |
| 458 | Bob Sebra | .01 | .05 |
| 459 | Jim Dwyer | .01 | .05 |
| 460 | Jay Aldrich | .01 | .05 |
| 461 | Frank Tanana | .02 | .10 |
| 462 | Oil Can Boyd | .01 | .05 |
| 463 | Dan Pasqua | .01 | .05 |
| 464 | Tim Crews RC | .08 | .25 |
| 465 | Andy Allanson | .01 | .05 |
| 466 | Bill Pecota RC* | .02 | .10 |
| 467 | Steve Ontiveros | .01 | .05 |
| 468 | Hubie Brooks | .01 | .05 |
| 469 | Paul Kilgus | .01 | .05 |
| 470 | Dale Mohorcic | .01 | .05 |
| 471 | Dan Quisenberry | .01 | .05 |
| 472 | Dave Stewart | .02 | .10 |
| 473 | Dave Clark | .01 | .05 |
| 474 | Joel Skinner | .01 | .05 |
| 475 | Dave Anderson | .01 | .05 |
| 476 | Dan Petry | .01 | .05 |
| 477 | Carl Nichols | .01 | .05 |
| 478 | Ernest Riles | .01 | .05 |
| 479 | George Hendrick | .02 | .10 |
| 480 | John Morris | .01 | .05 |
| 481 | Manny Hernandez | .01 | .05 |
| 482 | Jeff Stone | .01 | .05 |
| 483 | Chris Brown | .01 | .05 |
| 484 | Mike Bielecki | .01 | .05 |
| 485 | Dave Dravecky | .01 | .05 |
| 486 | Rick Manning | .01 | .05 |
| 487 | Bill Almon | .01 | .05 |
| 488 | Jim Sundberg | .02 | .10 |
| 489 | Ken Phelps | .01 | .05 |
| 490 | Tom Henke | .01 | .05 |
| 491 | Dan Gladden | .01 | .05 |
| 492 | Barry Larkin | .05 | .15 |
| 493 | Fred Manrique | .01 | .05 |
| 494 | Mike Griffin | .01 | .05 |
| 495 | Mark Knudson | .01 | .05 |
| 496 | Bill Madlock | .02 | .10 |
| 497 | Tim Stoddard | .01 | .05 |
| 498 | Sam Horn RC | .01 | .05 |
| 499 | Tracy Woodson RC | .02 | .10 |
| 500A | Checklist 468-577 | .01 | .05 |
| 500B | Checklist 452-557 | .01 | .05 |
| 501 | Ken Schrom | .01 | .05 |
| 502 | Angel Salazar | .01 | .05 |
| 503 | Eric Plunk | .01 | .05 |
| 504 | Joe Hesketh | .01 | .05 |
| 505 | Greg Minton | .01 | .05 |
| 506 | Geno Petralli | .01 | .05 |
| 507 | Bob James | .01 | .05 |
| 508 | Robbie Wine | .01 | .05 |
| 509 | Jeff Calhoun | .01 | .05 |
| 510 | Steve Lake | .01 | .05 |
| 511 | Mark Grant | .01 | .05 |
| 512 | Frank Williams | .01 | .05 |
| 513 | Jeff Blauser RC | .08 | .25 |
| 514 | Bob Walk | .01 | .05 |
| 515 | Craig Lefferts | .01 | .05 |
| 516 | Manny Trillo | .01 | .05 |
| 517 | Jerry Reed | .01 | .05 |
| 518 | Rick Leach | .01 | .05 |
| 519 | Mark Davidson | .01 | .05 |
| 520 | Jeff Ballard | .01 | .05 |
| 521 | Dave Stapleton | .01 | .05 |
| 522 | Pat Sheridan | .01 | .05 |
| 523 | Al Nipper | .01 | .05 |
| 524 | Steve Trout | .01 | .05 |
| 525 | Jeff Hamilton | .01 | .05 |
| 526 | Tommy Hinzo | .01 | .05 |
| 527 | Lonnie Smith | .01 | .05 |
| 528 | Greg Cadaret | .01 | .05 |
| 529 | Bob McClure UER (%%Rob– on front) | .01 | .05 |
| 530 | Chuck Finley | .02 | .10 |
| 531 | Jeff Russell | .01 | .05 |
| 532 | Steve Lyons | .01 | .05 |
| 533 | Terry Puhl | .01 | .05 |
| 534 | Eric Nolte | .01 | .05 |
| 535 | Kent Tekulve | .01 | .05 |
| 536 | Pat Pacillo | .01 | .05 |
| 537 | Charlie Puleo | .01 | .05 |
| 538 | Tom Prince | .01 | .05 |
| 539 | Greg Maddux | .40 | 1.00 |
| 540 | Jim Lindeman | .01 | .05 |
| 541 | Pete Stanicek | .01 | .05 |
| 542 | Steve Kiefer | .01 | .05 |
| 543A | Jim Morrison ERR (No decimal before lifetime ave) | .05 | .15 |
| 543B | Jim Morrison COR | .05 | .15 |
| 544 | Spike Owen | .01 | .05 |
| 545 | Jay Buhner RC | .20 | .50 |
| 546 | Mike Devereaux RC | .08 | .25 |
| 547 | Jerry Don Gleaton | .01 | .05 |
| 548 | Jose Rijo | .01 | .05 |
| 549 | Dennis Martinez | .02 | .10 |
| 550 | Mike Loynd | .01 | .05 |
| 551 | Darrell Miller | .01 | .05 |
| 552 | Dave LaPoint | .01 | .05 |

|  |  | | |
|---|------|---|---|
| 553 | John Tudor | .02 | .10 |
| 554 | Rocky Childress | .01 | .05 |
| 555 | Wally Ritchie | .01 | .05 |
| 556 | Terry McGriff | .01 | .05 |
| 557 | Dave Leiper | .01 | .05 |
| 558 | Jeff D. Robinson | .01 | .05 |
| 559 | Jose Uribe | .01 | .05 |
| 560 | Ted Simmons | .02 | .10 |
| 561 | Les Lancaster | .01 | .05 |
| 562 | Keith Miller RC | .08 | .25 |
| 563 | Harold Reynolds | .02 | .10 |
| 564 | Gene Larkin RC* | .08 | .25 |
| 565 | Cecil Fielder | .02 | .10 |
| 566 | Roy Smalley | .01 | .05 |
| 567 | Duane Ward | .01 | .05 |
| 568 | Bill Wilkinson | .01 | .05 |
| 569 | Howard Johnson | .02 | .10 |
| 570 | Frank DiPino | .01 | .05 |
| 571 | Pete Smith RC | .02 | .10 |
| 572 | Darnell Coles | .01 | .05 |
| 573 | Don Robinson | .01 | .05 |
| 574 | Rob Nelson UER (Career 0 RBI& but 1 RBI in '87) | .01 | .05 |
| 575 | Dennis Rasmussen | .01 | .05 |
| 576 | Steve Jeltz UER (Photo actually Juan Samuel; Sam | .01 | .05 |
| 577 | Tom Pagnozzi RC | .01 | .05 |
| 578 | Ty Gainey | .01 | .05 |
| 579 | Gary Lucas | .01 | .05 |
| 580 | Ron Hassey | .01 | .05 |
| 581 | Herm Winningham | .01 | .05 |
| 582 | Rene Gonzales RC | .02 | .10 |
| 583 | Brad Komminsk | .01 | .05 |
| 584 | Doyle Alexander | .01 | .05 |
| 585 | Jeff Sellers | .01 | .05 |
| 586 | Bill Gullickson | .01 | .05 |
| 587 | Tim Belcher | .01 | .05 |
| 588 | Doug Jones RC | .08 | .25 |
| 589 | Melido Perez RC | .08 | .25 |
| 590 | Rick Honeycutt | .01 | .05 |
| 591 | Pascual Perez | .01 | .05 |
| 592 | Curt Wilkerson | .01 | .05 |
| 593 | Steve Howe | .01 | .05 |
| 594 | John Davis | .01 | .05 |
| 595 | Storm Davis | .01 | .05 |
| 596 | Sammy Stewart | .01 | .05 |
| 597 | Neil Allen | .01 | .05 |
| 598 | Alejandro Pena | .01 | .05 |
| 599 | Mark Thurmond | .01 | .05 |
| 600A | Checklist 578-660/BC1-BC26 | .01 | .05 |
| 600B | Checklist 578-660 | .01 | .05 |
| 601 | Jose Mesa RC | .08 | .25 |
| 602 | Don August | .01 | .05 |
| 603 | Terry Leach SP | .02 | .10 |
| 604 | Tom Newell | .01 | .05 |
| 605 | Randall Byers SP | .02 | .10 |
| 606 | Jim Gott | .01 | .05 |
| 607 | Harry Spilman | .01 | .05 |
| 608 | John Candelaria | .01 | .05 |
| 609 | Mike Brumley | .01 | .05 |
| 610 | Mickey Brantley | .01 | .05 |
| 611 | Jose Nunez SP | .02 | .10 |
| 612 | Tom Nieto | .01 | .05 |
| 613 | Rick Reuschel | .02 | .10 |
| 614 | Lee Mazzilli SP | .02 | .10 |
| 615 | Scott Lusader | .01 | .05 |
| 616 | Bobby Meacham | .01 | .05 |
| 617 | Kevin McReynolds SP | .02 | .10 |
| 618 | Gene Garber | .01 | .05 |
| 619 | Barry Lyons SP | .02 | .10 |
| 620 | Randy Myers | .02 | .10 |
| 621 | Donnie Moore | .01 | .05 |
| 622 | Domingo Ramos | .01 | .05 |
| 623 | Ed Romero | .01 | .05 |
| 624 | Greg Myers RC | .08 | .25 |
| 625 | The Ripken Family | .15 | .40 |
| 626 | Pat Perry | .01 | .05 |
| 627 | Andres Thomas SP | .02 | .10 |
| 628 | Matt Williams RC | .30 | .75 |
| 629 | Dave Hengel | .01 | .05 |
| 630 | Jeff Musselman SP | .02 | .10 |
| 631 | Tim Laudner | .01 | .05 |
| 632 | Bob Ojeda SP | .02 | .10 |
| 633 | Rafael Santana | .01 | .05 |
| 634 | Wes Gardner | .01 | .05 |
| 635 | Roberto Kelly SP RC | .08 | .25 |

|  |  | | |
|---|------|---|---|
| 636 | Mike Flanagan SP | .02 | .10 |
| 637 | Jay Bell RC | .15 | .40 |
| 638 | Bob Melvin | .01 | .05 |
| 639 | Damon Berryhill RC | .08 | .25 |
| 640 | David Wells RC | .40 | 1.00 |
| 641 | Stan Musial Puzzle | .07 | .20 |
| 642 | Doug Sisk | .01 | .05 |
| 643 | Keith Hughes | .01 | .05 |
| 644 | Tom Glavine SP | 1.00 | 2.50 |
| 645 | Al Newman | .01 | .05 |
| 646 | Scott Sanderson | .01 | .05 |
| 647 | Scott Terry | .01 | .05 |
| 648 | Tim Teufel SP | .02 | .10 |
| 649 | Garry Templeton SP | .02 | .10 |
| 650 | Manny Lee SP | .02 | .10 |
| 651 | Roger McDowell SP | .02 | .10 |
| 652 | Mookie Wilson SP | .02 | .10 |
| 653 | David Cone | .02 | .10 |
| 654 | Ron Gant RC | .15 | .40 |
| 655 | Joe Price SP | .02 | .10 |
| 656 | George Bell SP | .02 | .10 |
| 657 | Gregg Jefferies SP | .08 | .25 |
| 658 | Todd Stottlemyre SP | .08 | .25 |
| 659 | Geronimo Berroa RC | .08 | .25 |
| 660 | Jerry Royster SP | .02 | .10 |
| XX | Kirby Puckett Blister Pack | .50 | 1.25 |

## 1989 Donruss

|  |  | | |
|---|------|---|---|
| | COMPLETE SET (660) | 10.00 | 25.00 |
| | COMP.FACT.SET (672) | 10.00 | 25.00 |
| 1 | Mike Greenwell DK | .01 | .05 |
| 2 | Bobby Bonilla DK DP | .02 | .10 |
| 3 | Pete Incaviglia DK | .01 | .05 |
| 4 | Chris Sabo DK DP | .02 | .10 |
| 5 | Robin Yount DK | .15 | .40 |
| 6 | Tony Gwynn DK DP | .05 | .15 |
| 7 | Carlton Fisk DK UER | .05 | .15 |
| 8 | Cory Snyder DK | .01 | .05 |
| 9 | David Cone DK UER | .02 | .10 |
| 10 | Kevin Seitzer DK | .01 | .05 |
| 11 | Rick Reuschel DK | .02 | .10 |
| 12 | Johnny Ray DK | .01 | .05 |
| 13 | Dave Schmidt DK | .01 | .05 |
| 14 | Andres Galarraga DK | .02 | .10 |
| 15 | Kirk Gibson DK | .02 | .10 |
| 16 | Fred McGriff DK | .05 | .15 |
| 17 | Mark Grace DK | .08 | .25 |
| 18 | Jeff M. Robinson DK | .01 | .05 |
| 19 | Vince Coleman DK DP | .01 | .05 |
| 20 | Dave Henderson DK | .01 | .05 |
| 21 | Harold Reynolds DK | .01 | .05 |
| 22 | Gerald Perry DK | .01 | .05 |
| 23 | Frank Viola DK | .02 | .10 |
| 24 | Steve Bedrosian DK | .01 | .05 |
| 25 | Glenn Davis DK | .01 | .05 |
| 26 | Don Mattingly DK | .10 | .30 |
| 27 | DK Checklist 1-26 DP | .01 | .05 |
| 28 | Sandy Alomar Jr. DK | .15 | .40 |
| 29 | Steve Searcy RR | .01 | .05 |
| 30 | Cameron Drew RR | .01 | .05 |
| 31 | Gary Sheffield RC | .60 | 1.50 |
| 32 | Erik Hanson RC | .08 | .25 |
| 33 | Ken Griffey Jr. RC | 3.00 | 8.00 |
| 34 | Greg W.Harris RC | .02 | .10 |
| 35 | Gregg Jefferies | .02 | .10 |
| 36 | Luis Medina RR | .01 | .05 |
| 37 | Carlos Quintana RC | .02 | .10 |
| 38 | Felix Jose RC | .15 | .40 |
| 39 | Cris Carpenter RC* | .02 | .10 |
| 40 | Ron Jones RR | .01 | .05 |
| 41 | Dave West RC | .02 | .10 |
| 42 | Randy Johnson RC | .75 | 2.00 |
| 43 | Mike Harkey RC | .02 | .10 |

|  |  | | |
|---|------|---|---|
| 44 | Pete Harnisch RC | .08 | .25 |
| 45 | Tom Gordon RC | .20 | .50 |
| 46 | Gregg Olson DP RC | .08 | .25 |
| 47 | Alex Sanchez RC | .01 | .05 |
| 48 | Ruben Sierra | .02 | .10 |
| 49 | Rafael Palmeiro | .08 | .25 |
| 50 | Ron Gant | .02 | .10 |
| 51 | Cal Ripken | .30 | .75 |
| 52 | Wally Joyner | .02 | .10 |
| 53 | Gary Carter | .02 | .10 |
| 54 | Andy Van Slyke | .05 | .15 |
| 55 | Robin Yount | .15 | .40 |
| 56 | Pete Incaviglia | .01 | .05 |
| 57 | Greg Brock | .01 | .05 |
| 58 | Melido Perez | .01 | .05 |
| 59 | Craig Lefferts | .01 | .05 |
| 60 | Gary Pettis | .01 | .05 |
| 61 | Danny Tartabull | .02 | .10 |
| 62 | Guillermo Hernandez | .01 | .05 |
| 63 | Ozzie Smith | .15 | .40 |
| 64 | Gary Gaetti | .02 | .10 |
| 65 | Mark Davis | .01 | .05 |
| 66 | Lee Smith | .02 | .10 |
| 67 | Dennis Eckersley | .05 | .15 |
| 68 | Wade Boggs | .05 | .15 |
| 69 | Mike Scott | .01 | .05 |
| 70 | Fred McGriff | .05 | .15 |
| 71 | Tom Browning | .01 | .05 |
| 72 | Claudell Washington | .01 | .05 |
| 73 | Mel Hall | .01 | .05 |
| 74 | Don Mattingly | .25 | .60 |
| 75 | Steve Bedrosian | .01 | .05 |
| 76 | Juan Samuel | .01 | .05 |
| 77 | Mike Scioscia | .02 | .10 |
| 78 | Dave Righetti | .02 | .10 |
| 79 | Alfredo Griffin | .01 | .05 |
| 80 | Eric Davis UER (165 games in 1988, should be 135 | .02 | .10 |
| 81 | Juan Berenguer | .01 | .05 |
| 82 | Todd Worrell | .01 | .05 |
| 83 | Joe Carter | .02 | .10 |
| 84 | Steve Sax | .02 | .10 |
| 85 | Frank White | .02 | .10 |
| 86 | John Kruk | .05 | .15 |
| 87 | Rance Mulliniks | .01 | .05 |
| 88 | Alan Ashby | .01 | .05 |
| 89 | Charlie Leibrandt | .01 | .05 |
| 90 | Frank Tanana | .02 | .10 |
| 91 | Jose Canseco | .08 | .25 |
| 92 | Barry Bonds | .60 | 1.50 |
| 93 | Harold Reynolds | .01 | .05 |
| 94 | Mark McLemore | .01 | .05 |
| 95 | Mark McGwire | .40 | 1.00 |
| 96 | Eddie Murray | .08 | .25 |
| 97 | Tim Raines | .02 | .10 |
| 98 | Robby Thompson | .01 | .05 |
| 99 | Kevin McReynolds | .01 | .05 |
| 100 | Checklist 28-137 | .01 | .05 |
| 101 | Carlton Fisk | .05 | .15 |
| 102 | Dave Martinez | .01 | .05 |
| 103 | Glenn Braggs | .01 | .05 |
| 104 | Dale Murphy | .05 | .15 |
| 105 | Ryne Sandberg | .15 | .40 |
| 106 | Dennis Martinez | .02 | .10 |
| 107 | Pete O'Brien | .01 | .05 |
| 108 | Dick Schofield | .01 | .05 |
| 109 | Henry Cotto | .01 | .05 |
| 110 | Mike Marshall | .01 | .05 |
| 111 | Keith Moreland | .01 | .05 |
| 112 | Tom Brunansky | .01 | .05 |
| 113 | Kelly Gruber UER (Wrong birthdate) | .01 | .05 |
| 114 | Brook Jacoby | .01 | .05 |
| 115 | Keith Brown | .01 | .05 |
| 116 | Matt Nokes | .01 | .05 |
| 117 | Keith Hernandez | .02 | .10 |
| 118 | Bob Forsch | .01 | .05 |
| 119 | Bert Blyleven UER | .02 | .10 |
| 120 | Willie Wilson | .02 | .10 |
| 121 | Tommy Gregg | .01 | .05 |
| 122 | Jim Rice | .02 | .10 |
| 123 | Bob Knepper | .01 | .05 |
| 124 | Danny Jackson | .01 | .05 |
| 125 | Eric Plunk | .01 | .05 |
| 126 | Brian Fisher | .01 | .05 |
| 127 | Mike Pagliarulo | .01 | .05 |
| 128 | Tony Gwynn | .10 | .30 |

|  |  | | |
|---|---|---|---|
| ☐ 129 | Lance McCullers | .01 | .05 |
| ☐ 130 | Andres Galarraga | .02 | .10 |
| ☐ 131 | Jose Uribe | .01 | .05 |
| ☐ 132 | Kirk Gibson UER | .02 | .10 |
| ☐ 133 | David Palmer | .01 | .05 |
| ☐ 134 | R.J. Reynolds | .01 | .05 |
| ☐ 135 | Greg Walker | .01 | .05 |
| ☐ 136 | Kirk McCaskill UER (Wrong birthdate) | .01 | .05 |
| ☐ 137 | Shawon Dunston | .01 | .05 |
| ☐ 138 | Andy Allanson | .01 | .05 |
| ☐ 139 | Rob Murphy | .01 | .05 |
| ☐ 140 | Mike Aldrete | .01 | .05 |
| ☐ 141 | Terry Kennedy | .01 | .05 |
| ☐ 142 | Scott Fletcher | .01 | .05 |
| ☐ 143 | Steve Balboni | .01 | .05 |
| ☐ 144 | Bret Saberhagen | .02 | .10 |
| ☐ 145 | Ozzie Virgil | .01 | .05 |
| ☐ 146 | Dale Sveum | .01 | .05 |
| ☐ 147 | Darryl Strawberry | .02 | .10 |
| ☐ 148 | Harold Baines | .02 | .10 |
| ☐ 149 | George Bell | .02 | .10 |
| ☐ 150 | Dave Parker | .02 | .10 |
| ☐ 151 | Bobby Bonilla | .02 | .10 |
| ☐ 152 | Mookie Wilson | .02 | .10 |
| ☐ 153 | Ted Power | .01 | .05 |
| ☐ 154 | Nolan Ryan | .40 | 1.00 |
| ☐ 155 | Jeff Reardon | .02 | .10 |
| ☐ 156 | Tim Wallach | .01 | .05 |
| ☐ 157 | Jamie Moyer | .01 | .05 |
| ☐ 158 | Rich Gossage | .02 | .10 |
| ☐ 159 | Dave Winfield | .02 | .10 |
| ☐ 160 | Von Hayes | .01 | .05 |
| ☐ 161 | Willie McGee | .01 | .05 |
| ☐ 162 | Rich Gedman | .01 | .05 |
| ☐ 163 | Tony Pena | .01 | .05 |
| ☐ 164 | Mike Morgan | .01 | .05 |
| ☐ 165 | Charlie Hough | .02 | .10 |
| ☐ 166 | Mike Stanley | .01 | .05 |
| ☐ 167 | Andre Dawson | .02 | .10 |
| ☐ 168 | Joe Boever | .01 | .05 |
| ☐ 169 | Pete Stanicek | .01 | .05 |
| ☐ 170 | Bob Boone | .02 | .10 |
| ☐ 171 | Ron Darling | .02 | .10 |
| ☐ 172 | Bob Walk | .01 | .05 |
| ☐ 173 | Rob Deer | .01 | .05 |
| ☐ 174 | Steve Buechele | .01 | .05 |
| ☐ 175 | Ted Higuera | .01 | .05 |
| ☐ 176 | Ozzie Guillen | .02 | .10 |
| ☐ 177 | Candy Maldonado | .01 | .05 |
| ☐ 178 | Doyle Alexander | .01 | .05 |
| ☐ 179 | Mark Gubicza | .01 | .05 |
| ☐ 180 | Alan Trammell | .02 | .10 |
| ☐ 181 | Vince Coleman | .01 | .05 |
| ☐ 182 | Kirby Puckett | .08 | .25 |
| ☐ 183 | Chris Brown | .01 | .05 |
| ☐ 184 | Marty Barrett | .01 | .05 |
| ☐ 185 | Stan Javier | .01 | .05 |
| ☐ 186 | Mike Greenwell | .03 | .15 |
| ☐ 187 | Billy Hatcher | .01 | .05 |
| ☐ 188 | Jimmy Key | .02 | .10 |
| ☐ 189 | Nick Esasky | .01 | .05 |
| ☐ 190 | Don Slaught | .01 | .05 |
| ☐ 191 | Cory Snyder | .01 | .05 |
| ☐ 192 | John Candelaria | .01 | .05 |
| ☐ 193 | Mike Schmidt | .20 | .50 |
| ☐ 194 | Kevin Gross | .01 | .05 |
| ☐ 195 | John Tudor | .02 | .10 |
| ☐ 196 | Neil Allen | .01 | .05 |
| ☐ 197 | Orel Hershiser | .02 | .10 |
| ☐ 198 | Kal Daniels | .01 | .05 |
| ☐ 199 | Kent Hrbek | .02 | .10 |
| ☐ 200 | Checklist 138-247 | .01 | .05 |
| ☐ 201 | Joe Magrane | .01 | .05 |
| ☐ 202 | Scott Bailes | .01 | .05 |
| ☐ 203 | Tim Belcher | .01 | .05 |
| ☐ 204 | George Brett | .25 | .60 |
| ☐ 205 | Benito Santiago | .02 | .10 |
| ☐ 206 | Tony Fernandez | .01 | .05 |
| ☐ 207 | Gerald Young | .01 | .05 |
| ☐ 208 | Bo Jackson | .08 | .25 |
| ☐ 209 | Chet Lemon | .02 | .10 |
| ☐ 210 | Storm Davis | .01 | .05 |
| ☐ 211 | Doug Drabek | .01 | .05 |
| ☐ 212 | Mickey Brantley UER (Photo actually Nelson Simmo) | | |
| ☐ 213 | Devon White | .02 | .10 |
| ☐ 214 | Dave Stewart | .02 | .10 |
| ☐ 215 | Dave Schmidt | .01 | .05 |
| ☐ 216 | Bryn Smith | .01 | .05 |
| ☐ 217 | Brett Butler | .02 | .10 |
| ☐ 218 | Bob Ojeda | .01 | .05 |
| ☐ 219 | Steve Rosenberg | .01 | .05 |
| ☐ 220 | Hubie Brooks | .01 | .05 |
| ☐ 221 | B.J. Surhoff | .02 | .10 |
| ☐ 222 | Rick Mahler | .01 | .05 |
| ☐ 223 | Rick Sutcliffe | .02 | .10 |
| ☐ 224 | Neal Heaton | .01 | .05 |
| ☐ 225 | Mitch Williams | .01 | .05 |
| ☐ 226 | Chuck Finley | .02 | .10 |
| ☐ 227 | Mark Langston | .01 | .05 |
| ☐ 228 | Jesse Orosco | .01 | .05 |
| ☐ 229 | Ed Whitson | .01 | .05 |
| ☐ 230 | Terry Pendleton | .02 | .10 |
| ☐ 231 | Lloyd Moseby | .01 | .05 |
| ☐ 232 | Greg Swindell | .01 | .05 |
| ☐ 233 | John Franco | .02 | .10 |
| ☐ 234 | Jack Morris | .02 | .10 |
| ☐ 235 | Howard Johnson | .02 | .10 |
| ☐ 236 | Glenn Davis | .01 | .05 |
| ☐ 237 | Frank Viola | .02 | .10 |
| ☐ 238 | Kevin Seitzer | .01 | .05 |
| ☐ 239 | Gerald Perry | .01 | .05 |
| ☐ 240 | Dwight Evans | .05 | .15 |
| ☐ 241 | Jim Deshaies | .01 | .05 |
| ☐ 242 | Bo Diaz | .01 | .05 |
| ☐ 243 | Carney Lansford | .02 | .10 |
| ☐ 244 | Mike LaValliere | .01 | .05 |
| ☐ 245 | Rickey Henderson | .08 | .25 |
| ☐ 246 | Roberto Alomar | .08 | .25 |
| ☐ 247 | Jimmy Jones | .01 | .05 |
| ☐ 248 | Pascual Perez | .01 | .05 |
| ☐ 249 | Will Clark | .05 | .15 |
| ☐ 250 | Fernando Valenzuela | .02 | .10 |
| ☐ 251 | Shane Rawley | .01 | .05 |
| ☐ 252 | Sid Bream | .01 | .05 |
| ☐ 253 | Steve Lyons | .01 | .05 |
| ☐ 254 | Brian Downing | .02 | .10 |
| ☐ 255 | Mark Grace | .08 | .25 |
| ☐ 256 | Tom Candiotti | .01 | .05 |
| ☐ 257 | Barry Larkin | .05 | .15 |
| ☐ 258 | Mike Krukow | .01 | .05 |
| ☐ 259 | Billy Ripken | .01 | .05 |
| ☐ 260 | Cecilio Guante | .01 | .05 |
| ☐ 261 | Scott Bradley | .01 | .05 |
| ☐ 262 | Floyd Bannister | .01 | .05 |
| ☐ 263 | Pete Smith | .01 | .05 |
| ☐ 264 | Jim Gantner UER (Wrong birthdate) | .01 | .05 |
| ☐ 265 | Roger McDowell | .01 | .05 |
| ☐ 266 | Bobby Thigpen | .01 | .05 |
| ☐ 267 | Jim Clancy | .01 | .05 |
| ☐ 268 | Terry Steinbach | .02 | .10 |
| ☐ 269 | Mike Dunne | .01 | .05 |
| ☐ 270 | Dwight Gooden | .02 | .10 |
| ☐ 271 | Mike Heath | .01 | .05 |
| ☐ 272 | Dave Smith | .01 | .05 |
| ☐ 273 | Keith Atherton | .01 | .05 |
| ☐ 274 | Tim Burke | .01 | .05 |
| ☐ 275 | Damon Berryhill | .01 | .05 |
| ☐ 276 | Vance Law | .01 | .05 |
| ☐ 277 | Rich Dotson | .01 | .05 |
| ☐ 278 | Lance Parrish | .02 | .10 |
| ☐ 279 | Denny Walling | .01 | .05 |
| ☐ 280 | Roger Clemens | .40 | 1.00 |
| ☐ 281 | Greg Mathews | .01 | .05 |
| ☐ 282 | Tom Niedenfuer | .01 | .05 |
| ☐ 283 | Paul Kilgus | .01 | .05 |
| ☐ 284 | Jose Guzman | .01 | .05 |
| ☐ 285 | Calvin Schiraldi | .01 | .05 |
| ☐ 286 | Charlie Puleo UER (Career ERA 4.24& should be 4. | | |
| ☐ 287 | Joe Orsulak | .01 | .05 |
| ☐ 288 | Jack Howell | .01 | .05 |
| ☐ 289 | Kevin Elster | .01 | .05 |
| ☐ 290 | Jose Lind | .01 | .05 |
| ☐ 291 | Paul Molitor | .02 | .10 |
| ☐ 292 | Cecil Espy | .01 | .05 |
| ☐ 293 | Bill Wegman | .01 | .05 |
| ☐ 294 | Dan Pasqua | .01 | .05 |
| ☐ 295 | Scott Garrelts UER (Wrong birthdate) | | |
| ☐ 296 | Walt Terrell | .01 | .05 |
| ☐ 297 | Ed Hearn | .01 | .05 |
| ☐ 298 | Lou Whitaker | .02 | .10 |
| ☐ 299 | Ken Dayley | .01 | .05 |
| ☐ 300 | Checklist 248-357 | .01 | .05 |
| ☐ 301 | Tommy Herr | .01 | .05 |
| ☐ 302 | Mike Brumley | .01 | .05 |
| ☐ 303 | Ellis Burks | .02 | .10 |
| ☐ 304 | Curt Young UER (Wrong birthdate) | .01 | .05 |
| ☐ 305 | Jody Reed | .01 | .05 |
| ☐ 306 | Bill Doran | .01 | .05 |
| ☐ 307 | David Wells | .02 | .10 |
| ☐ 308 | Ron Robinson | .01 | .05 |
| ☐ 309 | Rafael Santana | .01 | .05 |
| ☐ 310 | Julio Franco | .02 | .10 |
| ☐ 311 | Jack Clark | .02 | .10 |
| ☐ 312 | Chris James | .01 | .05 |
| ☐ 313 | Milt Thompson | .01 | .05 |
| ☐ 314 | John Shelby | .01 | .05 |
| ☐ 315 | Al Leiter | .08 | .25 |
| ☐ 316 | Mike Davis | .01 | .05 |
| ☐ 317 | Chris Sabo RC * | .15 | .40 |
| ☐ 318 | Greg Gagne | .01 | .05 |
| ☐ 319 | Jose Oquendo | .01 | .05 |
| ☐ 320 | John Farrell | .01 | .05 |
| ☐ 321 | Franklin Stubbs | .01 | .05 |
| ☐ 322 | Kurt Stillwell | .01 | .05 |
| ☐ 323 | Shawn Abner | .01 | .05 |
| ☐ 324 | Mike Flanagan | .01 | .05 |
| ☐ 325 | Kevin Bass | .01 | .05 |
| ☐ 326 | Pat Tabler | .01 | .05 |
| ☐ 327 | Mike Henneman | .01 | .05 |
| ☐ 328 | Rick Honeycutt | .01 | .05 |
| ☐ 329 | John Smiley | .01 | .05 |
| ☐ 330 | Rey Quinones | .01 | .05 |
| ☐ 331 | Johnny Ray | .01 | .05 |
| ☐ 332 | Bob Welch | .02 | .10 |
| ☐ 333 | Larry Sheets | .01 | .05 |
| ☐ 334 | Jeff Parrett | .01 | .05 |
| ☐ 335 | Rick Reuschel UER (For Don Robinson& should be J | .02 | .10 |
| ☐ 336 | Randy Myers | .02 | .10 |
| ☐ 337 | Ken Williams | .01 | .05 |
| ☐ 338 | Andy McGaffigan | .01 | .05 |
| ☐ 339 | Joey Meyer | .01 | .05 |
| ☐ 340 | Dion James | .01 | .05 |
| ☐ 341 | Les Lancaster | .01 | .05 |
| ☐ 342 | Tom Foley | .01 | .05 |
| ☐ 343 | Geno Petralli | .01 | .05 |
| ☐ 344 | Dan Petry | .01 | .05 |
| ☐ 345 | Alvin Davis | .01 | .05 |
| ☐ 346 | Mickey Hatcher | .01 | .05 |
| ☐ 347 | Marvell Wynne | .01 | .05 |
| ☐ 348 | Danny Cox | .01 | .05 |
| ☐ 349 | Dave Stieb | .02 | .10 |
| ☐ 350 | Jay Bell | .01 | .05 |
| ☐ 351 | Jeff Treadway | .01 | .05 |
| ☐ 352 | Luis Salazar | .01 | .05 |
| ☐ 353 | Len Dykstra | .02 | .10 |
| ☐ 354 | Juan Agosto | .01 | .05 |
| ☐ 355 | Gene Larkin | .01 | .05 |
| ☐ 356 | Steve Farr | .01 | .05 |
| ☐ 357 | Paul Assenmacher | .01 | .05 |
| ☐ 358 | Todd Benzinger | .01 | .05 |
| ☐ 359 | Larry Andersen | .01 | .05 |
| ☐ 360 | Paul O'Neill | .05 | .15 |
| ☐ 361 | Ron Hassey | .01 | .05 |
| ☐ 362 | Jim Gott | .01 | .05 |
| ☐ 363 | Ken Phelps | .01 | .05 |
| ☐ 364 | Tim Flannery | .01 | .05 |
| ☐ 365 | Randy Ready | .01 | .05 |
| ☐ 366 | Nelson Santovenia | .01 | .05 |
| ☐ 367 | Kelly Downs | .01 | .05 |
| ☐ 368 | Danny Heep | .01 | .05 |
| ☐ 369 | Phil Bradley | .01 | .05 |
| ☐ 370 | Jeff D. Robinson | .01 | .05 |
| ☐ 371 | Ivan Calderon | .01 | .05 |
| ☐ 372 | Mike Witt | .01 | .05 |
| ☐ 373 | Greg Maddux | .20 | .50 |
| ☐ 374 | Carmen Castillo | .01 | .05 |
| ☐ 375 | Jose Rijo | .02 | .10 |
| ☐ 376 | Joe Price | .01 | .05 |
| ☐ 377 | Rene Gonzales | .01 | .05 |
| ☐ 378 | Oddibe McDowell | .01 | .05 |
| ☐ 379 | Jim Presley | .01 | .05 |
| ☐ 380 | Brad Wellman | .01 | .05 |
| ☐ 381 | Tom Glavine | .08 | .25 |
| ☐ 382 | Dan Plesac | .01 | .05 |

| # | Name | Price 1 | Price 2 |
|---|------|---------|---------|
| 383 | Wally Backman | .01 | .05 |
| 384 | Dave Gallagher | .01 | .05 |
| 385 | Tom Henke | .01 | .05 |
| 386 | Luis Polonia | .01 | .05 |
| 387 | Junior Ortiz | .01 | .05 |
| 388 | David Cone | .02 | .10 |
| 389 | Dave Bergman | .01 | .05 |
| 390 | Danny Darwin | .01 | .05 |
| 391 | Dan Gladden | .01 | .05 |
| 392 | John Dopson | .01 | .05 |
| 393 | Frank DiPino | .01 | .05 |
| 394 | Al Nipper | .01 | .05 |
| 395 | Willie Randolph | .02 | .10 |
| 396 | Don Carman | .01 | .05 |
| 397 | Scott Terry | .01 | .05 |
| 398 | Rick Cerone | .01 | .05 |
| 399 | Tom Pagnozzi | .01 | .05 |
| 400 | Checklist 358-467 | .01 | .05 |
| 401 | Mickey Tettleton | .01 | .05 |
| 402 | Curtis Wilkerson | .01 | .05 |
| 403 | Jeff Russell | .01 | .05 |
| 404 | Pat Perry | .01 | .05 |
| 405 | Jose Alvarez RC | .02 | .10 |
| 406 | Rick Schu | .01 | .05 |
| 407 | Sherman Corbett | .01 | .05 |
| 408 | Dave Magadan | .01 | .05 |
| 409 | Bob Kipper | .01 | .05 |
| 410 | Don August | .01 | .05 |
| 411 | Bob Brower | .01 | .05 |
| 412 | Chris Bosio | .01 | .05 |
| 413 | Jerry Reuss | .01 | .05 |
| 414 | Atlee Hammaker | .01 | .05 |
| 415 | Jim Walewander | .01 | .05 |
| 416 | Mike Macfarlane RC * | .08 | .25 |
| 417 | Pat Sheridan | .01 | .05 |
| 418 | Pedro Guerrero | .02 | .10 |
| 419 | Allan Anderson | .01 | .05 |
| 420 | Mark Parent | .01 | .05 |
| 421 | Bob Stanley | .01 | .05 |
| 422 | Mike Gallego | .01 | .05 |
| 423 | Bruce Hurst | .01 | .05 |
| 424 | Dave Meads | .01 | .05 |
| 425 | Jesse Barfield | .01 | .05 |
| 426 | Rob Dibble RC | .15 | .40 |
| 427 | Joel Skinner | .01 | .05 |
| 428 | Ron Kittle | .01 | .05 |
| 429 | Rick Rhoden | .01 | .05 |
| 430 | Bob Demier | .01 | .05 |
| 431 | Steve Jeltz | .01 | .05 |
| 432 | Rick Dempsey | .01 | .05 |
| 433 | Roberto Kelly | .01 | .05 |
| 434 | Dave Anderson | .01 | .05 |
| 435 | Herm Winningham | .01 | .05 |
| 436 | Al Newman | .01 | .05 |
| 437 | Jose DeLeon | .01 | .05 |
| 438 | Doug Jones | .01 | .05 |
| 439 | Brian Holton | .01 | .05 |
| 440 | Jeff Montgomery | .01 | .05 |
| 441 | Dickie Thon | .01 | .05 |
| 442 | Cecil Fielder | .02 | .10 |
| 443 | John Fishel | .01 | .05 |
| 444 | Jerry Don Gleaton | .01 | .05 |
| 445 | Paul Gibson | .01 | .05 |
| 446 | Walt Weiss | .01 | .05 |
| 447 | Glenn Wilson | .01 | .05 |
| 448 | Mike Moore | .01 | .05 |
| 449 | Chili Davis | .02 | .10 |
| 450 | Dave Henderson | .01 | .05 |
| 451 | Jose Bautista RC | .02 | .10 |
| 452 | Rex Hudler | .01 | .05 |
| 453 | Bob Brenly | .01 | .05 |
| 454 | Mackey Sasser | .01 | .05 |
| 455 | Daryl Boston | .01 | .05 |
| 456 | Mike R. Fitzgerald | .01 | .05 |
| 457 | Jeffrey Leonard | .01 | .05 |
| 458 | Bruce Sutter | .02 | .10 |
| 459 | Mitch Webster | .01 | .05 |
| 460 | Joe Hesketh | .01 | .05 |
| 461 | Bobby Witt | .01 | .05 |
| 462 | Stu Cliburn | .01 | .05 |
| 463 | Scott Bankhead | .01 | .05 |
| 464 | Ramon Martinez RC | .08 | .25 |
| 465 | Dave Leiper | .01 | .05 |
| 466 | Luis Alicea RC * | .08 | .25 |
| 467 | John Cerutti | .01 | .05 |
| 468 | Ron Washington | .01 | .05 |
| 469 | Jeff Reed | .01 | .05 |
| 470 | Jeff M. Robinson | .01 | .05 |
| 471 | Sid Fernandez | .01 | .05 |
| 472 | Terry Puhl | .01 | .05 |
| 473 | Charlie Lea | .01 | .05 |
| 474 | Israel Sanchez | .01 | .05 |
| 475 | Bruce Benedict | .01 | .05 |
| 476 | Oil Can Boyd | .01 | .05 |
| 477 | Craig Reynolds | .01 | .05 |
| 478 | Frank Williams | .01 | .05 |
| 479 | Greg Cadaret | .01 | .05 |
| 480 | Randy Kramer | .01 | .05 |
| 481 | Dave Eiland | .01 | .05 |
| 482 | Eric Show | .01 | .05 |
| 483 | Garry Templeton | .02 | .10 |
| 484 | Wallace Johnson | .01 | .05 |
| 485 | Kevin Mitchell | .02 | .10 |
| 486 | Tim Crews | .01 | .05 |
| 487 | Mike Maddux | .01 | .05 |
| 488 | Dave LaPoint | .01 | .05 |
| 489 | Fred Manrique | .01 | .05 |
| 490 | Greg Minton | .01 | .05 |
| 491 | Doug Dascenzo UER (Photo actually Damon Berryhill) | .01 | .05 |
| 492 | Willie Upshaw | .01 | .05 |
| 493 | Jack Armstrong RC * | .08 | .25 |
| 494 | Kirt Manwaring | .01 | .05 |
| 495 | Jeff Ballard | .01 | .05 |
| 496 | Jeff Kunkel | .01 | .05 |
| 497 | Mike Campbell | .01 | .05 |
| 498 | Gary Thurman | .01 | .05 |
| 499 | Zane Smith | .01 | .05 |
| 500 | Checklist 468-577 DP | .01 | .05 |
| 501 | Mike Birkbeck | .01 | .05 |
| 502 | Terry Leach | .01 | .05 |
| 503 | Shawn Hillegas | .01 | .05 |
| 504 | Manny Lee | .01 | .05 |
| 505 | Doug Jennings | .01 | .05 |
| 506 | Ken Oberkfell | .01 | .05 |
| 507 | Tim Teufel | .01 | .05 |
| 508 | Tom Brookens | .01 | .05 |
| 509 | Rafael Ramirez | .01 | .05 |
| 510 | Fred Toliver | .01 | .05 |
| 511 | Brian Holman RC * | .02 | .10 |
| 512 | Mike Bielecki | .01 | .05 |
| 513 | Jeff Pico | .01 | .05 |
| 514 | Charles Hudson | .01 | .05 |
| 515 | Bruce Ruffin | .01 | .05 |
| 516 | Larry McWilliams UER (New Richland& should be No) | .01 | .05 |
| 517 | Jeff Sellers | .01 | .05 |
| 518 | John Costello | .01 | .05 |
| 519 | Brady Anderson RC | .15 | .40 |
| 520 | Craig McMurtry | .01 | .05 |
| 521 | Ray Hayward DP | .01 | .05 |
| 522 | Drew Hall DP | .01 | .05 |
| 523 | Mark Lemke DP RC | .15 | .40 |
| 524 | Oswald Peraza DP | .01 | .05 |
| 525 | Bryan Harvey DP RC * | .08 | .25 |
| 526 | Rick Aguilera DP | .01 | .05 |
| 527 | Tom Prince DP | .01 | .05 |
| 528 | Mark Clear DP | .01 | .05 |
| 529 | Jerry Browne DP | .01 | .05 |
| 530 | Juan Castillo DP | .01 | .05 |
| 531 | Jack McDowell DP | .02 | .10 |
| 532 | Chris Speier DP | .01 | .05 |
| 533 | Darrell Evans DP | .02 | .10 |
| 534 | Luis Aquino DP | .01 | .05 |
| 535 | Eric King DP | .01 | .05 |
| 536 | Ken Hill DP RC | .08 | .25 |
| 537 | Randy Bush DP | .01 | .05 |
| 538 | Shane Mack DP | .01 | .05 |
| 539 | Tom Bolton DP | .01 | .05 |
| 540 | Gene Nelson DP | .01 | .05 |
| 541 | Wes Gardner DP | .01 | .05 |
| 542 | Ken Caminiti DP | .05 | .15 |
| 543 | Duane Ward DP | .01 | .05 |
| 544 | Norm Charlton DP RC | .08 | .25 |
| 545 | Hal Morris DP RC | .05 | .15 |
| 546 | Rich Yett DP | .01 | .05 |
| 547 | Hensley Meulens DP RC | .02 | .10 |
| 548 | Greg A. Harris DP | .01 | .05 |
| 549 | Darren Daulton DP | .02 | .10 |
| 550 | Jeff Hamilton DP | .01 | .05 |
| 551 | Luis Aguayo DP | .01 | .05 |
| 552 | Tim Leary DP (Resembles M.Marshall) | .01 | .05 |
| 553 | Ron Oester DP | .01 | .05 |
| 554 | Steve Lombardozzi DP | .01 | .05 |
| 555 | Tim Jones DP | .01 | .05 |
| 556 | Bud Black DP | .01 | .05 |
| 557 | Alejandro Pena DP | .01 | .05 |
| 558 | Jose DeJesus DP | .01 | .05 |
| 559 | Dennis Rasmussen DP | .01 | .05 |
| 560 | Pat Borders DP RC * | .08 | .25 |
| 561 | Craig Biggio RC | 1.25 | 3.00 |
| 562 | Luis DeLosSantos DP | .01 | .05 |
| 563 | Fred Lynn DP | .02 | .10 |
| 564 | Todd Burns DP | .01 | .05 |
| 565 | Felix Fermin DP | .01 | .05 |
| 566 | Darnell Coles DP | .01 | .05 |
| 567 | Willie Fraser DP | .01 | .05 |
| 568 | Glenn Hubbard DP | .01 | .05 |
| 569 | Craig Worthington DP | .01 | .05 |
| 570 | Johnny Paredes DP | .01 | .05 |
| 571 | Don Robinson DP | .01 | .05 |
| 572 | Barry Lyons DP | .01 | .05 |
| 573 | Bill Long DP | .01 | .05 |
| 574 | Tracy Jones DP | .01 | .05 |
| 575 | Juan Nieves DP | .01 | .05 |
| 576 | Andres Thomas DP | .01 | .05 |
| 577 | Rolando Roomes DP | .01 | .05 |
| 578 | Luis Rivera UER DP (Wrong birthdate) | .01 | .05 |
| 579 | Chad Kreuter RC | .08 | .25 |
| 580 | Tony Armas DP | .02 | .10 |
| 581 | Jay Buhner | .02 | .10 |
| 582 | Ricky Horton DP | .01 | .05 |
| 583 | Andy Hawkins DP | .01 | .05 |
| 584 | Sil Campusano | .01 | .05 |
| 585 | Dave Clark | .01 | .05 |
| 586 | Van Snider DP | .01 | .05 |
| 587 | Todd Frohwirth DP | .01 | .05 |
| 588 | Warren Spahn Puzzle DP | .05 | .15 |
| 589 | William Brennan | .01 | .05 |
| 590 | German Gonzalez | .01 | .05 |
| 591 | Ernie Whitt DP | .01 | .05 |
| 592 | Jeff Blauser | .01 | .05 |
| 593 | Spike Owen DP | .01 | .05 |
| 594 | Matt Williams | .08 | .25 |
| 595 | Lloyd McClendon DP | .01 | .05 |
| 596 | Steve Ontiveros | .01 | .05 |
| 597 | Scott Medvin | .01 | .05 |
| 598 | Hipolito Pena DP | .01 | .05 |
| 599 | Jerald Clark DP RC | .02 | .10 |
| 600A | Checklist 578-660 DP | .01 | .05 |
| 600B | Checklist 578-660 DP | .01 | .05 |
| 600C | Checklist 578-660 DP | .01 | .05 |
| 601 | Carmelo Martinez DP | .01 | .05 |
| 602 | Mike LaCoss | .01 | .05 |
| 603 | Mike Devereaux | .01 | .05 |
| 604 | Alex Madrid DP | .01 | .05 |
| 605 | Gary Redus DP | .01 | .05 |
| 606 | Lance Johnson | .01 | .05 |
| 607 | Terry Clark DP | .01 | .05 |
| 608 | Manny Trillo DP | .01 | .05 |
| 609 | Scott Jordan RC | .08 | .25 |
| 610 | Jay Howell DP | .01 | .05 |
| 611 | Francisco Melendez | .01 | .05 |
| 612 | Mike Boddicker | .01 | .05 |
| 613 | Kevin Brown | .08 | .25 |
| 614 | Dave Valle | .01 | .05 |
| 615 | Tim Laudner DP | .01 | .05 |
| 616 | Andy Nezelek UER (Wrong birthdate) | .01 | .05 |
| 617 | Chuck Crim | .01 | .05 |
| 618 | Jack Savage DP | .01 | .05 |
| 619 | Adam Peterson | .01 | .05 |
| 620 | Todd Stottlemyre | .01 | .05 |
| 621 | Lance Blankenship RC | .02 | .10 |
| 622 | Miguel Garcia DP | .01 | .05 |
| 623 | Keith A. Miller DP | .01 | .05 |
| 624 | Ricky Jordan DP RC * | .08 | .25 |
| 625 | Ernest Riles DP | .01 | .05 |
| 626 | John Moses DP | .01 | .05 |
| 627 | Nelson Liriano DP | .01 | .05 |
| 628 | Mike Smithson DP | .01 | .05 |
| 629 | Scott Sanderson | .01 | .05 |
| 630 | Dale Mohorcic | .01 | .05 |
| 631 | Marvin Freeman DP | .01 | .05 |
| 632 | Mike Young DP | .01 | .05 |
| 633 | Dennis Lamp | .01 | .05 |
| 634 | Dante Bichette RC | .15 | .40 |
| 635 | Curt Schilling RC | 1.50 | 4.00 |
| 636 | Scott May DP | .01 | .05 |
| 637 | Mike Schooler | .01 | .05 |

|  |  | | |
|---|------|------|------|
| 638 | Rick Leach | .01 | .05 |
| 639 | Tom Lampkin UER (Throws Left& should be Throws R | .01 | .05 |
| 640 | Brian Meyer | .01 | .05 |
| 641 | Brian Harper | .01 | .05 |
| 642 | John Smoltz RC | .60 | 1.50 |
| 643 | Jose Canseco 40/40 | .08 | .25 |
| 644 | Bill Schroeder | .01 | .05 |
| 645 | Edgar Martinez | .08 | .25 |
| 646 | Dennis Cook RC | .08 | .25 |
| 647 | Barry Jones | .01 | .05 |
| 648 | Orel Hershiser (59 and Counting) | .02 | .10 |
| 649 | Rod Nichols | .01 | .05 |
| 650 | Jody Davis | .01 | .05 |
| 651 | Bob Milacki | .01 | .05 |
| 652 | Mike Jackson | .01 | .05 |
| 653 | Derek Lilliquist RC | .02 | .10 |
| 654 | Paul Mirabella | .01 | .05 |
| 655 | Mike Diaz | .01 | .05 |
| 656 | Jeff Musselman | .01 | .05 |
| 657 | Jerry Reed | .01 | .05 |
| 658 | Kevin Blankenship | .01 | .05 |
| 659 | Wayne Tolleson | .01 | .05 |
| 660 | Eric Hetzel | .01 | .05 |
| BC | Jose Canseco Blister Pack | .75 | 2.00 |

## 1990 Donruss

| | | | |
|---|------|------|------|
| | COMPLETE SET (716) | 6.00 | 15.00 |
| | COMP.FACT.SET (728) | 6.00 | 15.00 |
| | COMP.YAZ PUZZLE | .40 | 1.00 |
| 1 | Bo Jackson DK | .06 | .15 |
| 2 | Dave Sax DK | .01 | .05 |
| 3A | Ruben Sierra DK ERR | .02 | .10 |
| 3B | Ruben Sierra DK COR | .02 | .10 |
| 4 | Ken Griffey Jr. DK | .15 | .40 |
| 5 | Mickey Tettleton DK | .01 | .05 |
| 6 | Dave Stewart DK | .01 | .05 |
| 7 | Jim Deshaies DK DP | .01 | .05 |
| 8 | John Smoltz DK | .08 | .25 |
| 9 | Mike Bielecki DK | .01 | .05 |
| 10A | Brian Downing DK ERR | .05 | .15 |
| 10B | Brian Downing DK COR | .01 | .05 |
| 11 | Kevin Mitchell DK | .01 | .05 |
| 12 | Kelly Gruber DK | .01 | .05 |
| 13 | Joe Magrane DK | .01 | .05 |
| 14 | John Franco DK | .01 | .05 |
| 15 | Ozzie Guillen DK | .02 | .10 |
| 16 | Lou Whitaker DK | .01 | .05 |
| 17 | John Smiley DK | .01 | .05 |
| 18 | Howard Johnson DK | .01 | .05 |
| 19 | Willie Randolph DK | .02 | .10 |
| 20 | Chris Bosio DK | .01 | .05 |
| 21 | Tommy Herr DK DP | .01 | .05 |
| 22 | Dan Gladden DK | .01 | .05 |
| 23 | Ellis Burks DK | .02 | .10 |
| 24 | Pete O'Brien DK | .01 | .05 |
| 25 | Bryn Smith DK | .01 | .05 |
| 26 | Ed Whitson DK DP | .01 | .05 |
| 27 | DK Checklist 1-27 DP (Comments on Perez-Steele) | .01 | .05 |
| 28 | Robin Ventura | .08 | .25 |
| 29 | Todd Zeile | .02 | .10 |
| 30 | Sandy Alomar Jr. | .02 | .10 |
| 31 | Kent Mercker RC | .08 | .25 |
| 32 | Ben McDonald RC | .06 | .20 |
| 33A | Juan Gonzalez RevHg RC | .75 | 2.00 |
| 33B | Juan Gonzalez COR RC | .40 | 1.00 |
| 34 | Eric Anthony RC | .08 | .25 |
| 35 | Mike Fetters RC | .08 | .25 |
| 36 | Marquis Grissom RC | .15 | .40 |

|  |  | | |
|---|------|------|------|
| 37 | Greg Vaughn | .01 | .05 |
| 38 | Brian DuBois RC | .02 | .10 |
| 39 | Steve Avery | .01 | .05 |
| 40 | Mark Gardner RC | .02 | .10 |
| 41 | Andy Benes | .02 | .10 |
| 42 | Delino DeShields RC | .08 | .25 |
| 43 | Scott Coolbaugh RC | .02 | .10 |
| 44 | Pat Combs DP | .01 | .05 |
| 45 | Alex Sanchez DP | .01 | .05 |
| 46 | Kelly Mann DP RC | .02 | .10 |
| 47 | Julio Machado RC | .02 | .10 |
| 48 | Pete Incaviglia | .01 | .05 |
| 49 | Shawon Dunston | .01 | .05 |
| 50 | Jeff Treadway | .01 | .05 |
| 51 | Jeff Ballard | .01 | .05 |
| 52 | Claudell Washington | .01 | .05 |
| 53 | Juan Samuel | .01 | .05 |
| 54 | John Smiley | .01 | .05 |
| 55 | Rob Deer | .01 | .05 |
| 56 | Geno Petralli | .01 | .05 |
| 57 | Chris Bosio | .01 | .05 |
| 58 | Carlton Fisk | .05 | .15 |
| 59 | Kirt Manwaring | .01 | .05 |
| 60 | Chet Lemon | .01 | .05 |
| 61 | Bo Jackson | .08 | .25 |
| 62 | Doyle Alexander | .01 | .05 |
| 63 | Pedro Guerrero | .01 | .05 |
| 64 | Allan Anderson | .01 | .05 |
| 65 | Greg W. Harris | .01 | .05 |
| 66 | Mike Greenwell | .01 | .05 |
| 67 | Walt Weiss | .01 | .05 |
| 68 | Wade Boggs | .05 | .15 |
| 69 | Jim Clancy | .01 | .05 |
| 70 | Junior Felix | .01 | .05 |
| 71 | Barry Larkin | .05 | .15 |
| 72 | Dave LaPoint | .01 | .05 |
| 73 | Joel Skinner | .01 | .05 |
| 74 | Jesse Barfield | .01 | .05 |
| 75 | Tommy Herr | .01 | .05 |
| 76 | Ricky Jordan | .01 | .05 |
| 77 | Eddie Murray | .08 | .25 |
| 78 | Steve Sax | .01 | .05 |
| 79 | Tim Belcher | .01 | .05 |
| 80 | Danny Jackson | .01 | .05 |
| 81 | Kent Hrbek | .02 | .10 |
| 82 | Milt Thompson | .01 | .05 |
| 83 | Brook Jacoby | .01 | .05 |
| 84 | Mike Marshall | .01 | .05 |
| 85 | Kevin Seitzer | .01 | .05 |
| 86 | Tony Gwynn | .10 | .30 |
| 87 | Dave Stieb | .02 | .10 |
| 88 | Dave Smith | .01 | .05 |
| 89 | Bret Saberhagen | .02 | .10 |
| 90 | Alan Trammell | .02 | .10 |
| 91 | Tony Phillips | .01 | .05 |
| 92 | Doug Drabek | .01 | .05 |
| 93 | Jeffrey Leonard | .01 | .05 |
| 94 | Wally Joyner | .02 | .10 |
| 95 | Carney Lansford | .01 | .05 |
| 96 | Cal Ripken | .30 | .75 |
| 97 | Andres Galarraga | .01 | .05 |
| 98 | Kevin Mitchell | .01 | .05 |
| 99 | Howard Johnson | .01 | .05 |
| 100A | Checklist 28-129 | .01 | .05 |
| 100B | Checklist 28-125 | .01 | .05 |
| 101 | Melido Perez | .01 | .05 |
| 102 | Spike Owen | .01 | .05 |
| 103 | Paul Molitor | .02 | .10 |
| 104 | Geronimo Berroa | .01 | .05 |
| 105 | Ryne Sandberg | .15 | .40 |
| 106 | Bryn Smith | .01 | .05 |
| 107 | Steve Buechele | .01 | .05 |
| 108 | Jim Abbott | .05 | .15 |
| 109 | Alvin Davis | .01 | .05 |
| 110 | Lee Smith | .02 | .10 |
| 111 | Roberto Alomar | .05 | .15 |
| 112 | Rick Reuschel | .01 | .05 |
| 113A | Kelly Gruber ERR (Born 2/22) | | |
| 113B | Kelly Gruber COR (Born 2/26; corrected in factor | .01 | .05 |
| 114 | Joe Carter | .02 | .10 |
| 115 | Jose Rijo | .01 | .05 |
| 116 | Greg Minton | .01 | .05 |
| 117 | Bob Ojeda | .01 | .05 |
| 118 | Glenn Davis | .01 | .05 |
| 119 | Jeff Reardon | .02 | .10 |

|  |  | | |
|---|------|------|------|
| 120 | Kurt Stillwell | .01 | .05 |
| 121 | John Smoltz | .08 | .25 |
| 122 | Dwight Evans | .05 | .15 |
| 123 | Eric Yelding RC | .01 | .05 |
| 124 | John Franco | .02 | .10 |
| 125 | Jose Canseco | .05 | .15 |
| 126 | Barry Bonds | .40 | 1.00 |
| 127 | Lee Guetterman | .01 | .05 |
| 128 | Jack Clark | .02 | .10 |
| 129 | Dave Valle | .01 | .05 |
| 130 | Hubie Brooks | .01 | .05 |
| 131 | Ernest Riles | .01 | .05 |
| 132 | Mike Morgan | .01 | .05 |
| 133 | Steve Jeltz | .01 | .05 |
| 134 | Jeff D. Robinson | .01 | .05 |
| 135 | Ozzie Guillen | .02 | .10 |
| 136 | Chili Davis | .02 | .10 |
| 137 | Mitch Webster | .01 | .05 |
| 138 | Jerry Browne | .01 | .05 |
| 139 | Bo Diaz | .01 | .05 |
| 140 | Robby Thompson | .01 | .05 |
| 141 | Craig Worthington | .01 | .05 |
| 142 | Julio Franco | .01 | .05 |
| 143 | Brian Holman | .01 | .05 |
| 144 | George Brett | .25 | .60 |
| 145 | Tom Glavine | .05 | .15 |
| 146 | Robin Yount | .15 | .40 |
| 147 | Gary Carter | .02 | .10 |
| 148 | Ron Kittle | .01 | .05 |
| 149 | Tony Fernandez | .01 | .05 |
| 150 | Dave Stewart | .01 | .05 |
| 151 | Gary Gaetti | .02 | .10 |
| 152 | Kevin Elster | .01 | .05 |
| 153 | Gerald Perry | .01 | .05 |
| 154 | Jesse Orosco | .01 | .05 |
| 155 | Wally Backman | .01 | .05 |
| 156 | Dennis Martinez | .02 | .10 |
| 157 | Rick Sutcliffe | .02 | .10 |
| 158 | Greg Maddux | .15 | .40 |
| 159 | Andy Hawkins | .01 | .05 |
| 160 | John Kruk | .02 | .10 |
| 161 | Jose Oquendo | .01 | .05 |
| 162 | John Dopson | .01 | .05 |
| 163 | Joe Magrane | .01 | .05 |
| 164 | Bill Ripken | .01 | .05 |
| 165 | Fred Manrique | .01 | .05 |
| 166 | Nolan Ryan | .40 | 1.00 |
| 167 | Damon Berryhill | .01 | .05 |
| 168 | Dale Murphy | .05 | .15 |
| 169 | Mickey Tettleton | .01 | .05 |
| 170A | Kirk McCaskill ERR (Born 4/19) | | |
| 170B | Kirk McCaskill COR (Born 4/9; corrected in fact) | .01 | .05 |
| 171 | Dwight Gooden | .02 | .10 |
| 172 | Jose Lind | .01 | .05 |
| 173 | B.J. Surhoff | .02 | .10 |
| 174 | Ruben Sierra | .05 | .15 |
| 175 | Dan Plesac | .01 | .05 |
| 176 | Dan Pasqua | .01 | .05 |
| 177 | Kelly Downs | .01 | .05 |
| 178 | Matt Nokes | .01 | .05 |
| 179 | Luis Aquino | .01 | .05 |
| 180 | Frank Tanana | .01 | .05 |
| 181 | Tony Pena | .01 | .05 |
| 182 | Dan Gladden | .01 | .05 |
| 183 | Bruce Hurst | .01 | .05 |
| 184 | Roger Clemens | .40 | 1.00 |
| 185 | Mark McGwire | .40 | 1.00 |
| 186 | Rob Murphy | .01 | .05 |
| 187 | Jim Deshaies | .01 | .05 |
| 188 | Fred McGriff | .08 | .25 |
| 189 | Rob Dibble | .02 | .10 |
| 190 | Don Mattingly | .25 | .60 |
| 191 | Felix Fermin | .01 | .05 |
| 192 | Roberto Kelly | .05 | .15 |
| 193 | Dennis Cook | .01 | .05 |
| 194 | Darren Daulton | .02 | .10 |
| 195 | Alfredo Griffin | .01 | .05 |
| 196 | Eric Plunk | .01 | .05 |
| 197 | Orel Hershiser | .02 | .10 |
| 198 | Paul O'Neill | .05 | .15 |
| 199 | Randy Bush | .01 | .05 |
| 200A | Checklist 130-231 | .01 | .05 |
| 200B | Checklist 126-223 | .01 | .05 |
| 201 | Ozzie Smith | .15 | .40 |
| 202 | Pete O'Brien | .01 | .05 |

|  |  | | |
|---|--------|----|----|
| 203 | Jay Howell | .01 | .05 |
| 204 | Mark Gubicza | .01 | .05 |
| 205 | Ed Whitson | .01 | .05 |
| 206 | George Bell | .01 | .05 |
| 207 | Mike Scott | .01 | .05 |
| 208 | Charlie Leibrandt | .01 | .05 |
| 209 | Mike Heath | .01 | .05 |
| 210 | Dennis Eckersley | .02 | .10 |
| 211 | Mike LaValliere | .01 | .05 |
| 212 | Darnell Coles | .01 | .05 |
| 213 | Lance Parrish | .01 | .05 |
| 214 | Mike Moore | .01 | .05 |
| 215 | Steve Finley | .02 | .10 |
| 216 | Tim Raines | .02 | .10 |
| 217A | Scott Garrelts ERR (Born 10/20) | .01 | .05 |
| 217B | Scott Garrelts COR (Born 10/30; corrected in fac | .01 | .05 |
| 218 | Kevin McReynolds | .01 | .05 |
| 219 | Dave Gallagher | .01 | .05 |
| 220 | Tim Wallach | .01 | .05 |
| 221 | Chuck Crim | .01 | .05 |
| 222 | Lonnie Smith | .01 | .05 |
| 223 | Andre Dawson | .02 | .10 |
| 224 | Nelson Santovenia | .01 | .05 |
| 225 | Rafael Palmeiro | .05 | .05 |
| 226 | Devon White | .02 | .10 |
| 227 | Harold Reynolds | .02 | .10 |
| 228 | Ellis Burks | .05 | .05 |
| 229 | Mark Parent | .01 | .05 |
| 230 | Will Clark | .05 | .15 |
| 231 | Jimmy Key | .02 | .10 |
| 232 | John Farrell | .01 | .05 |
| 233 | Eric Davis | .02 | .10 |
| 234 | Johnny Ray | .01 | .05 |
| 235 | Darryl Strawberry | .02 | .10 |
| 236 | Bill Doran | .01 | .05 |
| 237 | Greg Gagne | .01 | .05 |
| 238 | Jim Eisenreich | .01 | .05 |
| 239 | Tommy Gregg | .01 | .05 |
| 240 | Marty Barrett | .01 | .05 |
| 241 | Rafael Ramirez | .01 | .05 |
| 242 | Chris Sabo | .01 | .05 |
| 243 | Dave Henderson | .01 | .05 |
| 244 | Andy Van Slyke | .05 | .05 |
| 245 | Alvaro Espinoza | .01 | .05 |
| 246 | Garry Templeton | .01 | .05 |
| 247 | Gene Harris | .01 | .05 |
| 248 | Kevin Gross | .01 | .05 |
| 249 | Brett Butler | .02 | .10 |
| 250 | Willie Randolph | .01 | .05 |
| 251 | Roger McDowell | .01 | .05 |
| 252 | Rafael Belliard | .01 | .05 |
| 253 | Steve Rosenberg | .01 | .05 |
| 254 | Jack Howell | .01 | .05 |
| 255 | Marvell Wynne | .01 | .05 |
| 256 | Tom Candiotti | .01 | .05 |
| 257 | Todd Benzinger | .01 | .05 |
| 258 | Don Robinson | .01 | .05 |
| 259 | Phil Bradley | .01 | .05 |
| 260 | Cecil Espy | .01 | .05 |
| 261 | Scott Bankhead | .01 | .05 |
| 262 | Frank White | .02 | .10 |
| 263 | Andres Thomas | .01 | .05 |
| 264 | Glenn Braggs | .01 | .05 |
| 265 | David Cone | .02 | .10 |
| 266 | Bobby Thigpen | .01 | .05 |
| 267 | Nelson Liriano | .01 | .05 |
| 268 | Terry Steinbach | .01 | .05 |
| 269 | Kirby Puckett | .08 | .25 |
| 270 | Gregg Jefferies | .02 | .10 |
| 271 | Jeff Blauser | .01 | .05 |
| 272 | Cory Snyder | .01 | .05 |
| 273 | Roy Smith | .01 | .05 |
| 274 | Tom Foley | .01 | .05 |
| 275 | Mitch Williams | .01 | .05 |
| 276 | Paul Kilgus | .01 | .05 |
| 277 | Don Slaught | .01 | .05 |
| 278 | Von Hayes | .01 | .05 |
| 279 | Vince Coleman | .02 | .10 |
| 280 | Mike Boddicker | .01 | .05 |
| 281 | Ken Dayley | .01 | .05 |
| 282 | Mike Devereaux | .01 | .05 |
| 283 | Kenny Rogers | .01 | .05 |
| 284 | Jeff Russell | .02 | .10 |
| 285 | Jerome Walton | .01 | .05 |
| 286 | Derek Lilliquist | .01 | .05 |
| 287 | Joe Orsulak | .01 | .05 |
| 288 | Dick Schofield | .01 | .05 |
| 289 | Ron Darling | .01 | .05 |
| 290 | Bobby Bonilla | .02 | .10 |
| 291 | Jim Gantner | .01 | .05 |
| 292 | Bobby Witt | .01 | .05 |
| 293 | Greg Brock | .01 | .05 |
| 294 | Ivan Calderon | .01 | .05 |
| 295 | Steve Bedrosian | .01 | .05 |
| 296 | Mike Henneman | .01 | .05 |
| 297 | Tom Gordon | .02 | .10 |
| 298 | Lou Whitaker | .02 | .10 |
| 299 | Terry Pendleton | .01 | .05 |
| 300A | Checklist 232-333 | .01 | .05 |
| 300B | Checklist 224-321 | .01 | .05 |
| 301 | Juan Berenguer | .01 | .05 |
| 302 | Mark Davis | .01 | .05 |
| 303 | Nick Esasky | .01 | .05 |
| 304 | Rickey Henderson | .08 | .25 |
| 305 | Rick Cerone | .01 | .05 |
| 306 | Craig Biggio | .08 | .25 |
| 307 | Duane Ward | .01 | .05 |
| 308 | Tom Browning | .01 | .05 |
| 309 | Walt Terrell | .01 | .05 |
| 310 | Greg Swindell | .01 | .05 |
| 311 | Dave Righetti | .01 | .05 |
| 312 | Mike Maddux | .01 | .05 |
| 313 | Len Dykstra | .02 | .10 |
| 314 | Jose Gonzalez | .01 | .05 |
| 315 | Steve Balboni | .01 | .05 |
| 316 | Mike Scioscia | .01 | .05 |
| 317 | Ron Oester | .01 | .05 |
| 318 | Gary Wayne | .01 | .05 |
| 319 | Todd Worrell | .01 | .05 |
| 320 | Doug Jones | .01 | .05 |
| 321 | Jeff Hamilton | .01 | .05 |
| 322 | Danny Tartabull | .02 | .10 |
| 323 | Chris James | .01 | .05 |
| 324 | Mike Flanagan | .01 | .05 |
| 325 | Gerald Young | .01 | .05 |
| 326 | Bob Boone | .02 | .10 |
| 327 | Frank Williams | .01 | .05 |
| 328 | Dave Parker | .02 | .10 |
| 329 | Sid Bream | .01 | .05 |
| 330 | Mike Schooler | .01 | .05 |
| 331 | Bert Blyleven | .02 | .10 |
| 332 | Bob Welch | .01 | .05 |
| 333 | Bob Milacki | .01 | .05 |
| 334 | Tim Burke | .01 | .05 |
| 335 | Jose Uribe | .01 | .05 |
| 336 | Randy Myers | .02 | .10 |
| 337 | Eric King | .01 | .05 |
| 338 | Mark Langston | .01 | .05 |
| 339 | Teddy Higuera | .01 | .05 |
| 340 | Oddibe McDowell | .01 | .05 |
| 341 | Lloyd McClendon | .01 | .05 |
| 342 | Pascual Perez | .01 | .05 |
| 343 | Kevin Brown UER (Signed is misspelled as signed) | .02 | .10 |
| 344 | Chuck Finley | .02 | .10 |
| 345 | Erik Hanson | .01 | .05 |
| 346 | Rich Gedman | .01 | .05 |
| 347 | Bip Roberts | .01 | .05 |
| 348 | Matt Williams | .02 | .10 |
| 349 | Tom Henke | .01 | .05 |
| 350 | Brad Komminsk | .01 | .05 |
| 351 | Jeff Reed | .01 | .05 |
| 352 | Brian Downing | .01 | .05 |
| 353 | Frank Viola | .01 | .05 |
| 354 | Terry Puhl | .01 | .05 |
| 355 | Brian Harper | .01 | .05 |
| 356 | Steve Farr | .01 | .05 |
| 357 | Joe Boever | .01 | .05 |
| 358 | Danny Heep | .01 | .05 |
| 359 | Larry Andersen | .01 | .05 |
| 360 | Rolando Roomes | .01 | .05 |
| 361 | Mike Gallego | .01 | .05 |
| 362 | Bob Kipper | .01 | .05 |
| 363 | Clay Parker | .01 | .05 |
| 364 | Mike Pagliarulo | .01 | .05 |
| 365 | Ken Griffey Jr. | .30 | .75 |
| 366 | Rex Hudler | .01 | .05 |
| 367 | Pat Sheridan | .01 | .05 |
| 368 | Kirk Gibson | .02 | .10 |
| 369 | Jeff Parrett | .01 | .05 |
| 370 | Bob Walk | .01 | .05 |
| 371 | Ken Patterson | .01 | .05 |
| 372 | Bryan Harvey | .01 | .05 |
| 373 | Mike Bielecki | .01 | .05 |
| 374 | Tom Magrann RC | .01 | .05 |
| 375 | Rick Mahler | .01 | .05 |
| 376 | Craig Lefferts | .01 | .05 |
| 377 | Gregg Olson | .02 | .10 |
| 378 | Jamie Moyer | .02 | .10 |
| 379 | Randy Johnson | .20 | .50 |
| 380 | Jeff Montgomery | .02 | .10 |
| 381 | Marty Clary | .01 | .05 |
| 382 | Bill Spiers | .01 | .05 |
| 383 | Dave Magadan | .01 | .05 |
| 384 | Greg Hibbard RC | .02 | .10 |
| 385 | Ernie Whitt | .01 | .05 |
| 386 | Rick Honeycutt | .01 | .05 |
| 387 | Dave West | .01 | .05 |
| 388 | Keith Hernandez | .02 | .10 |
| 389 | Jose Alvarez | .01 | .05 |
| 390 | Albert Belle | .08 | .25 |
| 391 | Rick Aguilera | .01 | .05 |
| 392 | Mike Fitzgerald | .01 | .05 |
| 393 | Dwight Smith | .01 | .05 |
| 394 | Steve Wilson | .01 | .05 |
| 395 | Bob Geren | .01 | .05 |
| 396 | Randy Ready | .01 | .05 |
| 397 | Ken Hill | .02 | .10 |
| 398 | Jody Reed | .01 | .05 |
| 399 | Tom Brunansky | .02 | .10 |
| 400A | Checklist 334-435 | .01 | .05 |
| 400B | Checklist 322-419 | .01 | .05 |
| 401 | Rene Gonzales | .01 | .05 |
| 402 | Harold Baines | .02 | .10 |
| 403 | Cecilio Guante | .01 | .05 |
| 404 | Joe Girardi | .05 | .15 |
| 405A | Sergio Valdez ERR RC | .01 | .05 |
| 405B | Sergio Valdez COR RC | .01 | .05 |
| 406 | Mark Williamson | .01 | .05 |
| 407 | Glenn Hoffman | .01 | .05 |
| 408 | Jeff Innis RC | .01 | .05 |
| 409 | Randy Kramer | .01 | .05 |
| 410 | Charlie O'Brien | .01 | .05 |
| 411 | Charlie Hough | .02 | .10 |
| 412 | Gus Polidor | .01 | .05 |
| 413 | Ron Karkovice | .01 | .05 |
| 414 | Trevor Wilson | .01 | .05 |
| 415 | Kevin Ritz RC | .01 | .05 |
| 416 | Gary Thurman | .01 | .05 |
| 417 | Jeff M. Robinson | .01 | .05 |
| 418 | Scott Terry | .01 | .05 |
| 419 | Tim Laudner | .01 | .05 |
| 420 | Dennis Rasmussen | .01 | .05 |
| 421 | Luis Rivera | .01 | .05 |
| 422 | Jim Corsi | .01 | .05 |
| 423 | Dennis Lamp | .01 | .05 |
| 424 | Ken Caminiti | .02 | .10 |
| 425 | David Wells | .02 | .10 |
| 426 | Norm Charlton | .01 | .05 |
| 427 | Deion Sanders | .08 | .25 |
| 428 | Dion James | .01 | .05 |
| 429 | Chuck Cary | .01 | .05 |
| 430 | Ken Howell | .01 | .05 |
| 431 | Steve Lake | .01 | .05 |
| 432 | Kal Daniels | .01 | .05 |
| 433 | Lance McCullers | .01 | .05 |
| 434 | Lenny Harris | .01 | .05 |
| 435 | Scott Scudder | .01 | .05 |
| 436 | Gene Larkin | .01 | .05 |
| 437 | Dan Quisenberry | .01 | .05 |
| 438 | Steve Olin RC | .08 | .25 |
| 439 | Mickey Hatcher | .01 | .05 |
| 440 | Willie Wilson | .01 | .05 |
| 441 | Mark Grant | .01 | .05 |
| 442 | Mookie Wilson | .02 | .10 |
| 443 | Alex Trevino | .01 | .05 |
| 444 | Pat Tabler | .01 | .05 |
| 445 | Dave Bergman | .01 | .05 |
| 446 | Todd Burns | .01 | .05 |
| 447 | R.J. Reynolds | .01 | .05 |
| 448 | Jay Buhner | .02 | .10 |
| 449 | Lee Stevens | .02 | .10 |
| 450 | Ron Hassey | .01 | .05 |
| 451 | Bob Melvin | .01 | .05 |
| 452 | Dave Martinez | .01 | .05 |
| 453 | Greg Litton | .01 | .05 |
| 454 | Mark Carreon | .01 | .05 |
| 455 | Scott Fletcher | .01 | .05 |
| 456 | Otis Nixon | .01 | .05 |
| 457 | Tony Fossas RC | .01 | .05 |

|  |  | | |
|---|---|---|---|
| 458 | John Russell | .01 | .05 |
| 459 | Paul Assenmacher | .01 | .05 |
| 460 | Zane Smith | .01 | .05 |
| 461 | Jack Daugherty RC | .01 | .05 |
| 462 | Rich Monteleone | .01 | .05 |
| 463 | Greg Briley | .01 | .05 |
| 464 | Mike Smithson | .01 | .05 |
| 465 | Benito Santiago | .02 | .10 |
| 466 | Jeff Brantley | .01 | .05 |
| 467 | Jose Nunez | .01 | .05 |
| 468 | Scott Bailes | .01 | .05 |
| 469 | Ken Griffey Sr. | .02 | .10 |
| 470 | Bob McClure | .01 | .05 |
| 471 | Mackey Sasser | .01 | .05 |
| 472 | Glenn Wilson | .01 | .05 |
| 473 | Kevin Tapani RC | .08 | .25 |
| 474 | Bill Buckner | .01 | .05 |
| 475 | Ron Gant | .02 | .10 |
| 476 | Kevin Romine | .01 | .05 |
| 477 | Juan Agosto | .01 | .05 |
| 478 | Herm Winningham | .01 | .05 |
| 479 | Storm Davis | .01 | .05 |
| 480 | Jeff King | .01 | .05 |
| 481 | Kevin Mmahat RC | .01 | .05 |
| 482 | Carmelo Martinez | .01 | .05 |
| 483 | Omar Vizquel | .08 | .25 |
| 484 | Jim Dwyer | .01 | .05 |
| 485 | Bob Knepper | .01 | .05 |
| 486 | Dave Anderson | .01 | .05 |
| 487 | Ron Jones | .01 | .05 |
| 488 | Jay Bell | .02 | .10 |
| 489 | Sammy Sosa RC | 1.00 | 2.50 |
| 490 | Kent Anderson | .01 | .05 |
| 491 | Domingo Ramos | .01 | .05 |
| 492 | Dave Clark | .01 | .05 |
| 493 | Tim Birtsas | .01 | .05 |
| 494 | Ken Oberkfell | .01 | .05 |
| 495 | Larry Sheets | .01 | .05 |
| 496 | Jeff Kunkel | .01 | .05 |
| 497 | Jim Presley | .01 | .05 |
| 498 | Mike Macfarlane | .01 | .05 |
| 499 | Pete Smith | .01 | .05 |
| 500A | Checklist 436-537 DP | .01 | .05 |
| 500B | Checklist 420-517 | .01 | .05 |
| 501 | Gary Sheffield | .08 | .25 |
| 502 | Terry Bross RC | .01 | .05 |
| 503 | Jerry Kutzler RC | .01 | .05 |
| 504 | Lloyd Moseby | .01 | .05 |
| 505 | Curt Young | .01 | .05 |
| 506 | Al Newman | .01 | .05 |
| 507 | Keith Miller | .01 | .05 |
| 508 | Mike Stanton RC | .08 | .25 |
| 509 | Rich Yett | .01 | .05 |
| 510 | Tim Drummond RC | .01 | .05 |
| 511 | Joe Hesketh | .01 | .05 |
| 512 | Rick Wrona | .01 | .05 |
| 513 | Luis Salazar | .01 | .05 |
| 514 | Hal Morris | .01 | .05 |
| 515 | Terry Mulholland | .01 | .05 |
| 516 | John Morris | .01 | .05 |
| 517 | Carlos Quintana | .01 | .05 |
| 518 | Frank DiPino | .01 | .05 |
| 519 | Randy Milligan | .01 | .05 |
| 520 | Chad Kreuter | .01 | .05 |
| 521 | Mike Jeffcoat | .01 | .05 |
| 522 | Mike Harkey | .01 | .05 |
| 523A | Andy Nezelek ERR (Wrong birth year) | .01 | .05 |
| 523B | Andy Nezelek COR (Finally corrected in factory s | .05 | .15 |
| 524 | Dave Schmidt | .01 | .05 |
| 525 | Tony Armas | .01 | .05 |
| 526 | Barry Lyons | .01 | .05 |
| 527 | Rick Reed RC | .08 | .25 |
| 528 | Jerry Reuss | .01 | .05 |
| 529 | Dean Palmer RC | .08 | .25 |
| 530 | Jeff Peterek RC | .01 | .05 |
| 531 | Carlos Martinez | .01 | .05 |
| 532 | Atlee Hammaker | .01 | .05 |
| 533 | Mike Brumley | .01 | .05 |
| 534 | Terry Leach | .01 | .05 |
| 535 | Doug Strange RC | .01 | .05 |
| 536 | Jose DeLeon | .01 | .05 |
| 537 | Shane Rawley | .01 | .05 |
| 538 | Joey Cora | .02 | .10 |
| 539 | Eric Hetzel | .01 | .05 |
| 540 | Gene Nelson | .01 | .05 |
| 541 | Wes Gardner | .01 | .05 |
| 542 | Mark Portugal | .01 | .05 |
| 543 | Al Leiter | .08 | .25 |
| 544 | Jack Armstrong | .01 | .05 |
| 545 | Greg Cadaret | .01 | .05 |
| 546 | Rod Nichols | .01 | .05 |
| 547 | Luis Polonia | .01 | .05 |
| 548 | Charlie Hayes | .01 | .05 |
| 549 | Dickie Thon | .01 | .05 |
| 550 | Tim Crews | .01 | .05 |
| 551 | Dave Winfield | .02 | .10 |
| 552 | Mike Davis | .01 | .05 |
| 553 | Ron Robinson | .01 | .05 |
| 554 | Carmen Castillo | .01 | .05 |
| 555 | John Costello | .01 | .05 |
| 556 | Bud Black | .01 | .05 |
| 557 | Rick Dempsey | .01 | .05 |
| 558 | Jim Acker | .01 | .05 |
| 559 | Eric Show | .01 | .05 |
| 560 | Pat Borders | .01 | .05 |
| 561 | Danny Darwin | .01 | .05 |
| 562 | Rick Luecken RC | .01 | .05 |
| 563 | Edwin Nunez | .01 | .05 |
| 564 | Felix Jose | .01 | .05 |
| 565 | John Cangelosi | .01 | .05 |
| 566 | Bill Swift | .01 | .05 |
| 567 | Bill Schroeder | .01 | .05 |
| 568 | Stan Javier | .01 | .05 |
| 569 | Jim Traber | .01 | .05 |
| 570 | Wallace Johnson | .01 | .05 |
| 571 | Donell Nixon | .01 | .05 |
| 572 | Sid Fernandez | .01 | .05 |
| 573 | Lance Johnson | .01 | .05 |
| 574 | Andy McGaffigan | .01 | .05 |
| 575 | Mark Knudson | .01 | .05 |
| 576 | Tommy Greene RC | .02 | .10 |
| 577 | Mark Grace | .05 | .15 |
| 578 | Larry Walker RC | .40 | 1.00 |
| 579 | Mike Stanley | .01 | .05 |
| 580 | Mike Witt DP | .01 | .05 |
| 581 | Scott Bradley | .01 | .05 |
| 582 | Greg A. Harris | .01 | .05 |
| 583A | Kevin Hickey ERR | .08 | .25 |
| 583B | Kevin Hickey COR | .01 | .05 |
| 584 | Lee Mazzilli | .01 | .05 |
| 585 | Jeff Pico | .01 | .05 |
| 586 | Joe Oliver | .01 | .05 |
| 587 | Willie Fraser DP | .01 | .05 |
| 588 | Carl Yastrzemski Puzzle | .08 | .25 |
| 589 | Kevin Bass DP | .01 | .05 |
| 590 | John Moses DP | .01 | .05 |
| 591 | Tom Pagnozzi DP | .01 | .05 |
| 592 | Tony Castillo DP | .01 | .05 |
| 593 | Jerald Clark DP | .01 | .05 |
| 594 | Dan Schatzeder | .01 | .05 |
| 595 | Luis Quinones DP | .01 | .05 |
| 596 | Pete Harnisch DP | .01 | .05 |
| 597 | Gary Redus | .01 | .05 |
| 598 | Mel Hall | .01 | .05 |
| 599 | Rick Schu | .01 | .05 |
| 600A | Checklist 538-639 | .01 | .05 |
| 600B | Checklist 518-617 | .01 | .05 |
| 601 | Mike Smith DP | .01 | .05 |
| 602 | Terry Kennedy DP | .01 | .05 |
| 603 | Mike Sharperson DP | .01 | .05 |
| 604 | Don Carman DP | .01 | .05 |
| 605 | Jim Gott | .01 | .05 |
| 606 | Donn Pall DP | .01 | .05 |
| 607 | Rance Mulliniks | .01 | .05 |
| 608 | Curt Wilkerson DP | .01 | .05 |
| 609 | Mike Felder DP | .01 | .05 |
| 610 | Guillermo Hernandez DP | .01 | .05 |
| 611 | Candy Maldonado DP | .01 | .05 |
| 612 | Mark Thurmond DP | .01 | .05 |
| 613 | Rick Leach DP | .01 | .05 |
| 614 | Jerry Reed DP | .01 | .05 |
| 615 | Franklin Stubbs | .01 | .05 |
| 616 | Billy Hatcher DP | .01 | .05 |
| 617 | Don August DP | .01 | .05 |
| 618 | Tim Teufel | .01 | .05 |
| 619 | Shawn Hillegas DP | .01 | .05 |
| 620 | Manny Lee | .01 | .05 |
| 621 | Gary Ward DP | .01 | .05 |
| 622 | Mark Guthrie DP RC | .01 | .05 |
| 623 | Jeff Musselman DP | .01 | .05 |
| 624 | Mark Lemke DP | .01 | .05 |
| 625 | Fernando Valenzuela | .02 | .10 |
| 626 | Paul Sorrento DP RC | .08 | .25 |
| 627 | Glenallen Hill DP | .01 | .05 |
| 628 | Les Lancaster DP | .01 | .05 |
| 629 | Vance Law DP | .01 | .05 |
| 630 | Randy Velarde DP | .01 | .05 |
| 631 | Todd Frohwirth DP | .01 | .05 |
| 632 | Willie McGee | .02 | .10 |
| 633 | Dennis Boyd DP | .01 | .05 |
| 634 | Cris Carpenter DP | .01 | .05 |
| 635 | Brian Holton | .01 | .05 |
| 636 | Tracy Jones DP | .01 | .05 |
| 637A | Terry Steinbach AS (Recent Major League Performa | .01 | .05 |
| 637B | Terry Steinbach AS (All-Star Game Performance) | .01 | .05 |
| 638 | Brady Anderson | .02 | .10 |
| 639A | Jack Morris ERR (Card front shows black line cro | .02 | .10 |
| 639B | Jack Morris COR | .02 | .10 |
| 640 | Jaime Navarro | .01 | .05 |
| 641 | Darrin Jackson | .01 | .05 |
| 642 | Mike Dyer RC | .01 | .05 |
| 643 | Mike Schmidt | .20 | .50 |
| 644 | Henry Cotto | .01 | .05 |
| 645 | John Cerutti | .01 | .05 |
| 646 | Francisco Cabrera | .01 | .05 |
| 647 | Scott Sanderson | .01 | .05 |
| 648 | Brian Meyer | .01 | .05 |
| 649 | Ray Searage | .01 | .05 |
| 650A | Bo Jackson AS ERR | .08 | .25 |
| 650B | Bo Jackson AS COR | .08 | .25 |
| 651 | Steve Lyons | .01 | .05 |
| 652 | Mike LaCoss | .01 | .05 |
| 653 | Ted Power | .01 | .05 |
| 654A | Howard Johnson AS (Recent Major League Performan | .01 | .05 |
| 654B | Howard Johnson AS (All-Star Game Performance) | .01 | .05 |
| 655 | Mauro Gozzo RC | .01 | .05 |
| 656 | Mike Blowers RC | .02 | .10 |
| 657 | Paul Gibson | .01 | .05 |
| 658 | Neal Heaton | .01 | .05 |
| 659 | Nolan Ryan 5000K | .20 | .50 |
| 659A | Nolan Ryan 5000K ERR | .60 | 1.50 |
| 660A | H.Baines AS ERR/ERR | .30 | .75 |
| 660B | H.Baines AS ERR/COR | .40 | 1.00 |
| 660C | H.Baines AS COR/ERR | .08 | .25 |
| 660D | Harold Baines AS (Black line behind star on fron | .01 | .05 |
| 661 | Gary Pettis | .01 | .05 |
| 662 | Clint Zavaras RC | .01 | .05 |
| 663A | Rick Reuschel AS (Recent Major League Performanc | .01 | .05 |
| 663B | Rick Reuschel AS (All-Star Game Performance) | .01 | .05 |
| 664 | Alejandro Pena | .01 | .05 |
| 665 | Nolan Ryan KING | .20 | .50 |
| 665A | Nolan Ryan KING ERR | .60 | 1.50 |
| 665C | Nolan Ryan KING NNO | .30 | .75 |
| 666 | Ricky Horton | .01 | .05 |
| 667 | Curt Schilling | .40 | 1.00 |
| 668 | Bill Landrum | .01 | .05 |
| 669 | Todd Stottlemyre | .02 | .10 |
| 670 | Tim Leary | .01 | .05 |
| 671 | John Wetteland | .08 | .25 |
| 672 | Calvin Schiraldi | .01 | .05 |
| 673A | Ruben Sierra AS ERR | .01 | .05 |
| 673B | Ruben Sierra AS COR | .01 | .05 |
| 674A | Pedro Guerrero AS (Recent Major League Performan | .01 | .05 |
| 674B | Pedro Guerrero AS (All-Star Game Performance) | .01 | .05 |
| 675 | Ken Phelps | .01 | .05 |
| 676A | Cal Ripken AS | .15 | .40 |
| 676B | Cal Ripken AS ERR | .30 | .75 |
| 677 | Denny Walling | .01 | .05 |
| 678 | Goose Gossage | .02 | .10 |
| 679 | Gary Mielke RC | .01 | .05 |
| 680 | Bill Bathe | .01 | .05 |

|  |  | | |
|---|---|---|---|
| 681 | Tom Lawless | .01 | .05 |
| 682 | Xavier Hernandez RC | .01 | .05 |
| 683A | Kirby Puckett AS ERR | .05 | .15 |
| 683B | Kirby Puckett AS COR | .05 | .15 |
| 684 | Mariano Duncan | .01 | .05 |
| 685 | Ramon Martinez | .01 | .05 |
| 686 | Tim Jones | .01 | .05 |
| 687 | Tom Filer | .01 | .05 |
| 688 | Steve Lombardozzi | .01 | .05 |
| 689 | Bernie Williams RC | .60 | 1.50 |
| 690 | Chip Hale RC | .01 | .05 |
| 691 | Beau Allred RC | .01 | .05 |
| 692A | Ryne Sandberg AS ERR | .08 | .25 |
| 692B | Ryne Sandberg AS COR | .08 | .25 |
| 693 | Jeff Huson RC | .02 | .10 |
| 694 | Curt Ford | .01 | .05 |
| 695A | Eric Davis AS (Recent League Performance) | .01 | .05 |
| 695B | Eric Davis AS (All-Star Game Performance) | | |
| 696 | Scott Lusader | .01 | .05 |
| 697A | Mark McGwire AS ERR | .20 | .50 |
| 697B | Mark McGwire AS COR | .20 | .50 |
| 698 | Steve Cummings RC | .01 | .05 |
| 699 | George Canale RC | .01 | .05 |
| 700A | Checklist w/out 716 | .08 | .25 |
| 700B | Checklist with 716 | .02 | .10 |
| 700C | Checklist 618-716 | .01 | .05 |
| 701A | Julio Franco AS (Recent Major League Performance) | .01 | .05 |
| 701B | Julio Franco AS (All-Star Game Performance) | | |
| 702 | Dave Wayne Johnson RC | .01 | .05 |
| 703A | Dave Stewart AS ERR | .01 | .05 |
| 703B | Dave Stewart AS COR | .01 | .05 |
| 704 | David Justice RC | .20 | .50 |
| 705 | Tony Gwynn AS | .05 | .15 |
| 705A | Tony Gwynn AS ERR | .05 | .15 |
| 706 | Greg Myers | .01 | .05 |
| 707A | Will Clark AS ERR | .05 | .15 |
| 707B | Will Clark AS COR | .05 | .15 |
| 708A | Benito Santiago AS | .01 | .05 |
| 708B | Benito Santiago AS | .01 | .05 |
| 709 | Larry McWilliams | .01 | .05 |
| 710A | Ozzie Smith AS ML Perf | .08 | .25 |
| 710B | Ozzie Smith AS Perf | .08 | .25 |
| 711 | John Olerud RC | .20 | .50 |
| 712A | Wade Boggs AS ERR | .02 | .10 |
| 712B | Wade Boggs AS COR | .02 | .10 |
| 713 | Gary Eave RC | .01 | .05 |
| 714 | Bob Tewksbury | .01 | .05 |
| 715A | Kevin Mitchell AS (Recent Major League Performan) | .01 | .05 |
| 715B | Kevin Mitchell AS (All-Star Game Performance) | .01 | .05 |
| 716 | Bart Giamatti MEM | .08 | .25 |

### 1991 Donruss

| | | | |
|---|---|---|---|
| COMPLETE SET (770) | | 3.00 | 8.00 |
| COMP.FACT.w/LEAF PREV | | 4.00 | 10.00 |
| COMP.FACT.w/STUDIO PREV | | 4.00 | 10.00 |
| COMP.STARGELL PUZZLE | | .40 | 1.00 |
| 1 | Dave Steib DK | .01 | .05 |
| 2 | Craig Biggio DK | .02 | .10 |
| 3 | Cecil Fielder DK | .01 | .05 |
| 4 | Barry Bonds DK | .20 | .50 |
| 5 | Barry Larkin DK | .02 | .10 |
| 6 | Dave Parker DK | .01 | .05 |

|  |  | | |
|---|---|---|---|
| 7 | Len Dykstra DK | .01 | .05 |
| 8 | Bobby Thigpen DK | .01 | .05 |
| 9 | Roger Clemens DK | .15 | .40 |
| 10 | Ron Gant DK UER | .02 | .10 |
| 11 | Delino DeShields DK | .01 | .05 |
| 12 | Roberto Alomar DK UER | .02 | .10 |
| 13 | Sandy Alomar Jr. DK | .01 | .05 |
| 14 | Ryne Sandberg DK UER | .08 | .25 |
| 15 | Ramon Martinez DK | .01 | .05 |
| 16 | Edgar Martinez DK | .05 | .15 |
| 17 | Dave Magadan DK | .01 | .05 |
| 18 | Matt Williams DK | .01 | .05 |
| 19 | Rafael Palmeiro DK UER | .02 | .10 |
| 20 | Bob Welch DK | .01 | .05 |
| 21 | Dave Righetti DK | .01 | .05 |
| 22 | Brian Harper DK | .01 | .05 |
| 23 | Gregg Olson DK | .01 | .05 |
| 24 | Kurt Stillwell DK | .01 | .05 |
| 25 | Pedro Guerrero DK UER | .01 | .05 |
| 26 | Chuck Finley DK UER | .02 | .10 |
| 27 | DK Checklist 1-27 | .01 | .05 |
| 28 | Tino Martinez RR | .08 | .25 |
| 29 | Mark Lewis RR | .01 | .05 |
| 30 | Bernard Gilkey RR | .01 | .05 |
| 31 | Hensley Meulens RR | .01 | .05 |
| 32 | Derek Bell RR | .02 | .10 |
| 33 | Jose Offerman RR | .01 | .05 |
| 34 | Terry Bross RR | .01 | .05 |
| 35 | Leo Gomez RR | .01 | .05 |
| 36 | Derrick May RR | .01 | .05 |
| 37 | Kevin Morton RR RC | .01 | .05 |
| 38 | Moises Alou RR | .02 | .10 |
| 39 | Julio Valera RR | .01 | .05 |
| 40 | Milt Cuyler RR | .01 | .05 |
| 41 | Phil Plantier RR RC | .08 | .25 |
| 42 | Scott Chiamparino RR | .01 | .05 |
| 43 | Ray Lankford RR | .02 | .10 |
| 44 | Mickey Morandini RR | .01 | .05 |
| 45 | Dave Hansen RR | .01 | .05 |
| 46 | Kevin Belcher RR RC | .01 | .05 |
| 47 | Darrin Fletcher RR | .01 | .05 |
| 48 | Steve Sax AS | .01 | .05 |
| 49 | Ken Griffey Jr. AS | .08 | .25 |
| 50A | Jose Canseco AS ERR | .02 | .10 |
| 50B | Jose Canseco AS COR | .05 | .15 |
| 51 | Sandy Alomar Jr. AS | .01 | .05 |
| 52 | Cal Ripken AS | .15 | .40 |
| 53 | Rickey Henderson AS | .05 | .15 |
| 54 | Bob Welch AS | .01 | .05 |
| 55 | Wade Boggs AS | .02 | .10 |
| 56 | Mark McGwire AS | .15 | .40 |
| 57A | Jack McDowell ERR | .08 | .25 |
| 57B | Jack McDowell COR | .20 | .50 |
| 58 | Jose Lind | .01 | .05 |
| 59 | Alex Fernandez | .01 | .05 |
| 60 | Pat Combs | .01 | .05 |
| 61 | Mike Walker | .01 | .05 |
| 62 | Juan Samuel | .01 | .05 |
| 63 | Mike Blowers UER | .01 | .05 |
| 64 | Mark Guthrie | .01 | .05 |
| 65 | Mark Salas | .01 | .05 |
| 66 | Tim Jones | .01 | .05 |
| 67 | Tim Leary | .01 | .05 |
| 68 | Andres Galarraga | .02 | .10 |
| 69 | Bob Milacki | .01 | .05 |
| 70 | Tim Belcher | .01 | .05 |
| 71 | Todd Zeile | .01 | .05 |
| 72 | Jerome Walton | .01 | .05 |
| 73 | Kevin Seitzer | .01 | .05 |
| 74 | Jerald Clark | .01 | .05 |
| 75 | John Smoltz UER | .05 | .15 |
| 76 | Mike Henneman | .01 | .05 |
| 77 | Ken Griffey Jr. | .20 | .50 |
| 78 | Jim Abbott | .05 | .15 |
| 79 | Gregg Jefferies | .01 | .05 |
| 80 | Kevin Reimer | .01 | .05 |
| 81 | Roger Clemens | .30 | .75 |
| 82 | Mike Fitzgerald | .01 | .05 |
| 83 | Bruce Hurst UER | .01 | .05 |
| 84 | Eric Davis | .02 | .10 |
| 85 | Paul Molitor | .02 | .10 |
| 86 | Will Clark | .05 | .15 |
| 87 | Mike Bielecki | .01 | .05 |
| 88 | Bret Saberhagen | .02 | .10 |
| 89 | Nolan Ryan | .40 | 1.00 |
| 90 | Bobby Thigpen | .01 | .05 |
| 91 | Dickie Thon | .01 | .05 |
| 92 | Duane Ward | .01 | .05 |

|  |  | | |
|---|---|---|---|
| 93 | Luis Polonia | .01 | .05 |
| 94 | Terry Kennedy | .01 | .05 |
| 95 | Kent Hrbek | .02 | .10 |
| 96 | Danny Jackson | .01 | .05 |
| 97 | Sid Fernandez | .01 | .05 |
| 98 | Jimmy Key | .02 | .10 |
| 99 | Franklin Stubbs | .01 | .05 |
| 100 | Checklist 28-103 | .01 | .05 |
| 101 | R.J. Reynolds | .01 | .05 |
| 102 | Dave Stewart | .02 | .10 |
| 103 | Dan Pasqua | .01 | .05 |
| 104 | Dan Plesac | .01 | .05 |
| 105 | Mark McGwire | .30 | .75 |
| 106 | John Farrell | .01 | .05 |
| 107 | Don Mattingly | .25 | .60 |
| 108 | Carlton Fisk | .05 | .15 |
| 109 | Ken Oberkfell | .01 | .05 |
| 110 | Darrel Akerfelds | .01 | .05 |
| 111 | Gregg Olson | .01 | .05 |
| 112 | Mike Scioscia | .01 | .05 |
| 113 | Bryn Smith | .01 | .05 |
| 114 | Bob Geren | .01 | .05 |
| 115 | Tom Candiotti | .01 | .05 |
| 116 | Kevin Tapani | .01 | .05 |
| 117 | Jeff Treadway | .01 | .05 |
| 118 | Alan Trammell | .02 | .10 |
| 119 | Pete O'Brien UER | .01 | .05 |
| 120 | Joel Skinner | .01 | .05 |
| 121 | Mike LaValliere | .01 | .05 |
| 122 | Dwight Evans | .05 | .15 |
| 123 | Jody Reed | .01 | .05 |
| 124 | Lee Guetterman | .01 | .05 |
| 125 | Tim Burke | .01 | .05 |
| 126 | Dave Johnson | .01 | .05 |
| 127 | Fernando Valenzuela UER | .02 | .10 |
| 128 | Jose DeLeon | .01 | .05 |
| 129 | Andre Dawson | .05 | .15 |
| 130 | Gerald Perry | .01 | .05 |
| 131 | Greg W. Harris | .01 | .05 |
| 132 | Tom Glavine | .05 | .15 |
| 133 | Lance McCullers | .01 | .05 |
| 134 | Randy Johnson | .10 | .30 |
| 135 | Lance Parrish AS | .02 | .10 |
| 136 | Mackey Sasser | .01 | .05 |
| 137 | Geno Petralli | .01 | .05 |
| 138 | Dennis Lamp | .01 | .05 |
| 139 | Dennis Martinez | .02 | .10 |
| 140 | Mike Pagliarulo | .01 | .05 |
| 141 | Hal Morris | .05 | .15 |
| 142 | Dave Parker | .02 | .10 |
| 143 | Brett Butler | .02 | .10 |
| 144 | Paul Assenmacher | .01 | .05 |
| 145 | Mark Gubicza | .01 | .05 |
| 146 | Charlie Hough | .01 | .05 |
| 147 | Sammy Sosa | .08 | .25 |
| 148 | Randy Ready | .01 | .05 |
| 149 | Kelly Gruber | .01 | .05 |
| 150 | Devon White | .02 | .10 |
| 151 | Gary Carter | .02 | .10 |
| 152 | Gene Larkin | .01 | .05 |
| 153 | Chris Sabo | .02 | .10 |
| 154 | David Cone | .02 | .10 |
| 155 | Todd Stottlemyre | .01 | .05 |
| 156 | Glenn Wilson | .01 | .05 |
| 157 | Bob Walk | .01 | .05 |
| 158 | Mike Gallego | .01 | .05 |
| 159 | Greg Hibbard | .01 | .05 |
| 160 | Chris Bosio | .01 | .05 |
| 161 | Mike Moore | .01 | .05 |
| 162 | Jerry Browne UER | .01 | .05 |
| 163 | Steve Sax UER | .02 | .10 |
| 164 | Melido Perez | .01 | .05 |
| 165 | Danny Darwin | .01 | .05 |
| 166 | Roger McDowell | .01 | .05 |
| 167 | Bill Ripken | .01 | .05 |
| 168 | Mike Sharperson | .01 | .05 |
| 169 | Lee Smith | .02 | .10 |
| 170 | Matt Nokes | .01 | .05 |
| 171 | Jesse Orosco | .01 | .05 |
| 172 | Rick Aguilera | .02 | .10 |
| 173 | Jim Presley | .01 | .05 |
| 174 | Lou Whitaker | .02 | .10 |
| 175 | Harold Reynolds | .01 | .05 |
| 176 | Brook Jacoby | .01 | .05 |
| 177 | Wally Backman | .01 | .05 |
| 178 | Wade Boggs | .05 | .15 |
| 179 | Chuck Cary UER | .01 | .05 |
| 180 | Tom Foley | .01 | .05 |

|  |  | | |
|---|---|---|---|
| 181 | Pete Harnisch | .01 | .05 |
| 182 | Mike Morgan | .01 | .05 |
| 183 | Bob Tewksbury | .01 | .05 |
| 184 | Joe Girardi | .01 | .05 |
| 185 | Storm Davis | .01 | .05 |
| 186 | Ed Whitson | .01 | .05 |
| 187 | Steve Avery UER | .01 | .05 |
| 188 | Lloyd Moseby | .01 | .05 |
| 189 | Scott Bankhead | .01 | .05 |
| 190 | Mark Langston | .01 | .05 |
| 191 | Kevin McReynolds | .01 | .05 |
| 192 | Julio Franco | .02 | .10 |
| 193 | John Dopson | .01 | .05 |
| 194 | Dennis Boyd | .01 | .05 |
| 195 | Bip Roberts | .01 | .05 |
| 196 | Billy Hatcher | .01 | .05 |
| 197 | Edgar Diaz | .01 | .05 |
| 198 | Greg Litton | .01 | .05 |
| 199 | Mark Grace | .05 | .25 |
| 200 | Checklist 104-179 | .01 | .05 |
| 201 | George Brett | .25 | .60 |
| 202 | Jeff Russell | .01 | .05 |
| 203 | Ivan Calderon | .01 | .05 |
| 204 | Ken Howell | .01 | .05 |
| 205 | Tom Henke | .01 | .05 |
| 206 | Bryan Harvey | .01 | .05 |
| 207 | Steve Bedrosian | .01 | .05 |
| 208 | Al Newman | .01 | .05 |
| 209 | Randy Myers | .01 | .05 |
| 210 | Daryl Boston | .01 | .05 |
| 211 | Manny Lee | .01 | .05 |
| 212 | Dave Smith | .01 | .05 |
| 213 | Don Slaught | .01 | .05 |
| 214 | Walt Weiss | .01 | .05 |
| 215 | Donn Pall | .01 | .05 |
| 216 | Jaime Navarro | .01 | .05 |
| 217 | Willie Randolph | .02 | .10 |
| 218 | Rudy Seanez | .01 | .05 |
| 219 | Jim Leyritz | .01 | .05 |
| 220 | Ron Karkovice | .01 | .05 |
| 221 | Ken Caminiti | .02 | .10 |
| 222 | Von Hayes | .01 | .05 |
| 223 | Cal Ripken | .30 | .75 |
| 224 | Lenny Harris | .01 | .05 |
| 225 | Milt Thompson | .01 | .05 |
| 226 | Alvaro Espinoza | .01 | .05 |
| 227 | Chris James | .01 | .05 |
| 228 | Dan Gladden | .01 | .05 |
| 229 | Jeff Blauser | .01 | .05 |
| 230 | Mike Heath | .01 | .05 |
| 231 | Omar Vizquel | .05 | .15 |
| 232 | Doug Jones | .01 | .05 |
| 233 | Jeff King | .01 | .05 |
| 234 | Luis Rivera | .01 | .05 |
| 235 | Ellis Burks | .02 | .10 |
| 236 | Greg Cadaret | .01 | .05 |
| 237 | Dave Martinez | .01 | .05 |
| 238 | Mark Williamson | .01 | .05 |
| 239 | Stan Javier | .01 | .05 |
| 240 | Ozzie Smith | .15 | .40 |
| 241 | Shawn Boskie | .01 | .05 |
| 242 | Tom Gordon | .01 | .05 |
| 243 | Tony Gwynn | .10 | .30 |
| 244 | Tommy Gregg | .01 | .05 |
| 245 | Jeff M. Robinson | .01 | .05 |
| 246 | Keith Comstock | .01 | .05 |
| 247 | Jack Howell | .01 | .05 |
| 248 | Keith Miller | .01 | .05 |
| 249 | Bobby Witt | .01 | .05 |
| 250 | Rob Murphy UER | .01 | .05 |
| 251 | Spike Owen | .01 | .05 |
| 252 | Garry Templeton | .01 | .05 |
| 253 | Glenn Braggs | .01 | .05 |
| 254 | Ron Robinson | .01 | .05 |
| 255 | Kevin Mitchell | .01 | .05 |
| 256 | Les Lancaster | .01 | .05 |
| 257 | Mel Stottlemyre Jr. | .01 | .05 |
| 258 | Kenny Rogers UER | .02 | .10 |
| 259 | Lance Johnson | .01 | .05 |
| 260 | John Kruk | .02 | .10 |
| 261 | Fred McGriff | .05 | .15 |
| 262 | Dick Schofield | .01 | .05 |
| 263 | Trevor Wilson | .01 | .05 |
| 264 | David West | .01 | .05 |
| 265 | Scott Scudder | .01 | .05 |
| 266 | Dwight Gooden | .02 | .10 |
| 267 | Willie Blair | .01 | .05 |
| 268 | Mark Portugal | .01 | .05 |
| 269 | Doug Drabek | .01 | .05 |
| 270 | Dennis Eckersley | .02 | .10 |
| 271 | Eric King | .01 | .05 |
| 272 | Robin Yount | .15 | .40 |
| 273 | Carney Lansford | .02 | .10 |
| 274 | Carlos Baerga | .01 | .05 |
| 275 | Dave Righetti | .02 | .10 |
| 276 | Scott Fletcher | .01 | .05 |
| 277 | Eric Yelding | .01 | .05 |
| 278 | Charlie Hayes | .01 | .05 |
| 279 | Jeff Ballard | .01 | .05 |
| 280 | Orel Hershiser | .02 | .10 |
| 281 | Jose Oquendo | .01 | .05 |
| 282 | Mike Witt | .01 | .05 |
| 283 | Mitch Webster | .01 | .05 |
| 284 | Greg Gagne | .01 | .05 |
| 285 | Greg Olson | .01 | .05 |
| 286 | Tony Phillips UER | .01 | .05 |
| 287 | Scott Bradley | .01 | .05 |
| 288 | Cory Snyder UER | .01 | .05 |
| 289 | Jay Bell UER | .02 | .10 |
| 290 | Kevin Romine | .01 | .05 |
| 291 | Jeff D. Robinson | .01 | .05 |
| 292 | Steve Frey UER | .01 | .05 |
| 293 | Craig Worthington | .01 | .05 |
| 294 | Tim Crews | .01 | .05 |
| 295 | Joe Magrane | .01 | .05 |
| 296 | Hector Villanueva | .01 | .05 |
| 297 | Terry Shumpert | .01 | .05 |
| 298 | Joe Carter | .02 | .10 |
| 299 | Kent Mercker UER | .01 | .05 |
| 300 | Checklist 180-255 | .01 | .05 |
| 301 | Chet Lemon | .01 | .05 |
| 302 | Mike Schooler | .01 | .05 |
| 303 | Dante Bichette | .02 | .10 |
| 304 | Kevin Elster | .01 | .05 |
| 305 | Jeff Huson | .01 | .05 |
| 306 | Greg A. Harris | .01 | .05 |
| 307 | Marquis Grissom UER | .02 | .10 |
| 308 | Calvin Schiraldi | .01 | .05 |
| 309 | Mariano Duncan | .01 | .05 |
| 310 | Bill Spiers | .01 | .05 |
| 311 | Scott Garrelts | .01 | .05 |
| 312 | Mitch Williams | .01 | .05 |
| 313 | Mike Macfarlane | .01 | .05 |
| 314 | Kevin Brown | .02 | .10 |
| 315 | Robin Ventura | .02 | .10 |
| 316 | Darren Daulton | .02 | .10 |
| 317 | Pat Borders | .01 | .05 |
| 318 | Mark Eichhorn | .01 | .05 |
| 319 | Jeff Brantley | .01 | .05 |
| 320 | Shane Mack | .01 | .05 |
| 321 | Rob Dibble | .02 | .10 |
| 322 | John Franco | .02 | .10 |
| 323 | Junior Felix | .01 | .05 |
| 324 | Casey Candaele | .01 | .05 |
| 325 | Bobby Bonilla | .02 | .10 |
| 326 | Dave Henderson | .01 | .05 |
| 327 | Wayne Edwards | .01 | .05 |
| 328 | Mark Knudson | .01 | .05 |
| 329 | Terry Steinbach | .01 | .05 |
| 330 | Colby Ward UER RC | .01 | .05 |
| 331 | Oscar Azocar | .01 | .05 |
| 332 | Scott Radinsky | .01 | .05 |
| 333 | Eric Anthony | .01 | .05 |
| 334 | Steve Lake | .01 | .05 |
| 335 | Bob Melvin | .01 | .05 |
| 336 | Kal Daniels | .01 | .05 |
| 337 | Tom Pagnozzi | .01 | .05 |
| 338 | Alan Mills | .01 | .05 |
| 339 | Steve Olin | .01 | .05 |
| 340 | Juan Berenguer | .01 | .05 |
| 341 | Francisco Cabrera | .01 | .05 |
| 342 | Dave Bergman | .01 | .05 |
| 343 | Henry Cotto | .01 | .05 |
| 344 | Sergio Valdez | .01 | .05 |
| 345 | Bob Patterson | .01 | .05 |
| 346 | John Marzano | .01 | .05 |
| 347 | Dana Kiecker | .01 | .05 |
| 348 | Dion James | .01 | .05 |
| 349 | Hubie Brooks | .01 | .05 |
| 350 | Bill Landrum | .01 | .05 |
| 351 | Bill Sampen | .01 | .05 |
| 352 | Greg Briley | .01 | .05 |
| 353 | Paul Gibson | .01 | .05 |
| 354 | Dave Eiland | .01 | .05 |
| 355 | Steve Finley | .02 | .10 |
| 356 | Bob Boone | .02 | .10 |
| 357 | Steve Buechele | .01 | .05 |
| 358 | Chris Hoiles FDC | .01 | .05 |
| 359 | Larry Walker | .08 | .25 |
| 360 | Frank DiPino | .01 | .05 |
| 361 | Mark Grant | .01 | .05 |
| 362 | Dave Magadan | .01 | .05 |
| 363 | Robby Thompson | .01 | .05 |
| 364 | Lonnie Smith | .01 | .05 |
| 365 | Steve Farr | .01 | .05 |
| 366 | Dave Valle | .01 | .05 |
| 367 | Tim Naehring | .01 | .05 |
| 368 | Jim Acker | .01 | .05 |
| 369 | Jeff Reardon UER | .02 | .10 |
| 370 | Tim Teufel | .01 | .05 |
| 371 | Juan Gonzalez | .08 | .25 |
| 372 | Luis Salazar | .01 | .05 |
| 373 | Rick Honeycutt | .01 | .05 |
| 374 | Greg Maddux | .15 | .40 |
| 375 | Jose Uribe UER | .01 | .05 |
| 376 | Donnie Hill | .01 | .05 |
| 377 | Don Carman | .01 | .05 |
| 378 | Craig Grebeck | .01 | .05 |
| 379 | Willie Fraser | .01 | .05 |
| 380 | Glenallen Hill | .01 | .05 |
| 381 | Joe Oliver | .01 | .05 |
| 382 | Randy Bush | .01 | .05 |
| 383 | Alex Cole | .01 | .05 |
| 384 | Norm Charlton | .01 | .05 |
| 385 | Gene Nelson | .01 | .05 |
| 386 | Checklist 256-331 | .01 | .05 |
| 387 | Rickey Henderson MVP | .05 | .15 |
| 388 | Lance Parrish MVP | .01 | .05 |
| 389 | Fred McGriff MVP | .02 | .10 |
| 390 | Dave Parker MVP | .01 | .05 |
| 391 | Candy Maldonado MVP | .01 | .05 |
| 392 | Ken Griffey Jr. MVP | .08 | .25 |
| 393 | Gregg Olson MVP | .01 | .05 |
| 394 | Rafael Palmeiro MVP | .02 | .10 |
| 395 | Roger Clemens MVP | .15 | .40 |
| 396 | George Brett MVP | .08 | .25 |
| 397 | Cecil Fielder MVP | .05 | .15 |
| 398 | Brian Harper MVP UER | .01 | .05 |
| 399 | Bobby Thigpen MVP | .01 | .05 |
| 400 | Roberto Kelly MVP UER | .01 | .05 |
| 401 | Danny Darwin MVP | .01 | .05 |
| 402 | David Justice MVP | .05 | .15 |
| 403 | Lee Smith MVP | .01 | .05 |
| 404 | Ryne Sandberg MVP | .08 | .25 |
| 405 | Eddie Murray MVP | .05 | .15 |
| 406 | Tim Wallach MVP | .01 | .05 |
| 407 | Kevin Mitchell MVP | .01 | .05 |
| 408 | Darryl Strawberry MVP | .02 | .10 |
| 409 | Joe Carter MVP | .02 | .10 |
| 410 | Len Dykstra MVP | .01 | .05 |
| 411 | Doug Drabek MVP | .01 | .05 |
| 412 | Chris Sabo MVP | .01 | .05 |
| 413 | Paul Marak RR RC | .01 | .05 |
| 414 | Tim McIntosh RR RC | .01 | .05 |
| 415 | Brian Barnes RR RC | .02 | .10 |
| 416 | Eric Gunderson RR | .01 | .05 |
| 417 | Mike Gardiner RR RC | .01 | .05 |
| 418 | Steve Carter RR | .01 | .05 |
| 419 | Gerald Alexander RR RC | .01 | .05 |
| 420 | Rich Garces RR RC | .02 | .10 |
| 421 | Chuck Knoblauch RR | .10 | .30 |
| 422 | Scott Aldred RR | .01 | .05 |
| 423 | Wes Chamberlain RR RC | .08 | .25 |
| 424 | Lance Dickson RR RC | .02 | .10 |
| 425 | Greg Colbrunn RR RC | .08 | .25 |
| 426 | Rich DeLucia RR UER RC | .01 | .05 |
| 427 | Jeff Conine RR RC | .15 | .40 |
| 428 | Steve Decker RR RC | .05 | .15 |
| 429 | Turner Ward RR RC | .08 | .25 |
| 430 | Mo Vaughn | .02 | .10 |
| 431 | Steve Chitren RR RC | .01 | .05 |
| 432 | Mike Benjamin RR | .01 | .05 |
| 433 | Ryne Sandberg AS | .08 | .25 |
| 434 | Len Dykstra AS | .01 | .05 |
| 435 | Andre Dawson AS | .05 | .15 |
| 436A | Mike Scioscia AS White | .08 | .25 |
| 436B | Mike Scioscia AS Yellow | .08 | .25 |
| 437 | Ozzie Smith AS | .08 | .25 |
| 438 | Kevin Mitchell AS | .01 | .05 |
| 439 | Jack Armstrong AS | .01 | .05 |
| 440 | Chris Sabo AS | .01 | .05 |
| 441 | Will Clark AS | .05 | .15 |
| 442 | Mel Hall | .01 | .05 |
| 443 | Mark Gardner | .01 | .05 |

| Card | Value 1 | Value 2 |
|---|---|---|
| ☐ 444 Mike Devereaux | .01 | .05 |
| ☐ 445 Kirk Gibson | .02 | .10 |
| ☐ 446 Terry Pendleton | .02 | .10 |
| ☐ 447 Mike Harkey | .01 | .05 |
| ☐ 448 Jim Eisenreich | .01 | .05 |
| ☐ 449 Benito Santiago | .02 | .10 |
| ☐ 450 Oddibe McDowell | .01 | .05 |
| ☐ 451 Cecil Fielder | .10 | .20 |
| ☐ 452 Ken Griffey Sr. | .02 | .10 |
| ☐ 453 Bert Blyleven | .02 | .10 |
| ☐ 454 Howard Johnson | .01 | .05 |
| ☐ 455 Monty Fariss UER | .01 | .05 |
| ☐ 456 Tony Pena | .01 | .05 |
| ☐ 457 Tim Raines | .02 | .10 |
| ☐ 458 Dennis Rasmussen | .01 | .05 |
| ☐ 459 Luis Quinones | .01 | .05 |
| ☐ 460 B.J. Surhoff | .02 | .10 |
| ☐ 461 Ernest Riles | .01 | .05 |
| ☐ 462 Rick Sutcliffe | .02 | .10 |
| ☐ 463 Danny Tartabull | .02 | .10 |
| ☐ 464 Pete Incaviglia | .01 | .05 |
| ☐ 465 Carlos Martinez | .01 | .05 |
| ☐ 466 Ricky Jordan | .01 | .05 |
| ☐ 467 John Cerutti | .01 | .05 |
| ☐ 468 Dave Winfield | .02 | .10 |
| ☐ 469 Francisco Oliveras | .01 | .05 |
| ☐ 470 Roy Smith | .01 | .05 |
| ☐ 471 Barry Larkin | .05 | .15 |
| ☐ 472 Ron Darling | .01 | .05 |
| ☐ 473 David Wells | .02 | .10 |
| ☐ 474 Glenn Davis | .01 | .05 |
| ☐ 475 Neal Heaton | .01 | .05 |
| ☐ 476 Ron Hassey | .01 | .05 |
| ☐ 477 Frank Thomas | .08 | .25 |
| ☐ 478 Greg Vaughn | .01 | .05 |
| ☐ 479 Todd Burns | .01 | .05 |
| ☐ 480 Candy Maldonado | .01 | .05 |
| ☐ 481 Dave LaPoint | .01 | .05 |
| ☐ 482 Alvin Davis | .01 | .05 |
| ☐ 483 Mike Scott | .01 | .05 |
| ☐ 484 Dale Murphy | .05 | .15 |
| ☐ 485 Ben McDonald | .05 | .15 |
| ☐ 486 Jay Howell | .01 | .05 |
| ☐ 487 Vince Coleman | .01 | .05 |
| ☐ 488 Alfredo Griffin | .01 | .05 |
| ☐ 489 Sandy Alomar Jr. | .01 | .05 |
| ☐ 490 Kirby Puckett | .08 | .25 |
| ☐ 491 Andres Thomas | .01 | .05 |
| ☐ 492 Jack Morris | .02 | .10 |
| ☐ 493 Matt Young | .01 | .05 |
| ☐ 494 Greg Myers | .01 | .05 |
| ☐ 495 Barry Bonds | .40 | 1.00 |
| ☐ 496 Scott Cooper UER | .01 | .05 |
| ☐ 497 Dan Schatzeder | .01 | .05 |
| ☐ 498 Jesse Barfield | .01 | .05 |
| ☐ 499 Jerry Goff | .01 | .05 |
| ☐ 500 Checklist 332-408 | .01 | .05 |
| ☐ 501 Anthony Telford RC | .05 | .15 |
| ☐ 502 Eddie Murray | .05 | .25 |
| ☐ 503 Omar Olivares RC | .08 | .25 |
| ☐ 504 Ryne Sandberg | .15 | .40 |
| ☐ 505 Jeff Montgomery | .01 | .05 |
| ☐ 506 Mark Parent | .01 | .05 |
| ☐ 507 Ron Gant | .02 | .10 |
| ☐ 508 Frank Tanana | .01 | .05 |
| ☐ 509 Jay Buhner | .02 | .10 |
| ☐ 510 Max Venable | .01 | .05 |
| ☐ 511 Wally Whitehurst | .01 | .05 |
| ☐ 512 Gary Pettis | .01 | .05 |
| ☐ 513 Tom Brunansky | .01 | .05 |
| ☐ 514 Tim Wallach | .01 | .05 |
| ☐ 515 Craig Lefferts | .01 | .05 |
| ☐ 516 Tim Layana | .01 | .05 |
| ☐ 517 Darryl Hamilton | .01 | .05 |
| ☐ 518 Rick Reuschel | .01 | .05 |
| ☐ 519 Steve Wilson | .01 | .05 |
| ☐ 520 Kurt Stillwell | .01 | .05 |
| ☐ 521 Rafael Palmeiro | .05 | .15 |
| ☐ 522 Ken Patterson | .01 | .05 |
| ☐ 523 Len Dykstra | .02 | .10 |
| ☐ 524 Tony Fernandez | .02 | .10 |
| ☐ 525 Kent Anderson | .01 | .05 |
| ☐ 526 Mark Leonard RC | .01 | .05 |
| ☐ 527 Allan Anderson | .01 | .05 |
| ☐ 528 Tom Browning | .01 | .05 |
| ☐ 529 Frank Viola | .02 | .10 |
| ☐ 530 John Olerud | .05 | .10 |
| ☐ 531 Juan Agosto | .01 | .05 |
| ☐ 532 Zane Smith | .01 | .05 |
| ☐ 533 Scott Sanderson | .01 | .05 |
| ☐ 534 Barry Jones | .01 | .05 |
| ☐ 535 Mike Felder | .01 | .05 |
| ☐ 536 Jose Canseco | .05 | .15 |
| ☐ 537 Felix Fermin | .01 | .05 |
| ☐ 538 Roberto Kelly | .01 | .05 |
| ☐ 539 Brian Holman | .01 | .05 |
| ☐ 540 Mark Davidson | .01 | .05 |
| ☐ 541 Terry Mulholland | .01 | .05 |
| ☐ 542 Randy Milligan | .01 | .05 |
| ☐ 543 Jose Gonzalez | .01 | .05 |
| ☐ 544 Craig Wilson RC | .01 | .05 |
| ☐ 545 Mike Hartley | .01 | .05 |
| ☐ 546 Greg Swindell | .01 | .05 |
| ☐ 547 Gary Gaetti | .02 | .10 |
| ☐ 548 David Justice | .08 | .25 |
| ☐ 549 Steve Searcy | .01 | .05 |
| ☐ 550 Erik Hanson | .01 | .05 |
| ☐ 551 Dave Smith | .01 | .05 |
| ☐ 552 Andy Van Slyke | .05 | .15 |
| ☐ 553 Mike Greenwell | .01 | .05 |
| ☐ 554 Kevin Maas | .01 | .05 |
| ☐ 555 Delino DeShields | .05 | .10 |
| ☐ 556 Curt Schilling | .08 | .25 |
| ☐ 557 Ramon Martinez | .05 | .10 |
| ☐ 558 Pedro Guerrero | .02 | .10 |
| ☐ 559 Dwight Smith | .01 | .05 |
| ☐ 560 Mark Davis | .01 | .05 |
| ☐ 561 Shawn Abner | .01 | .05 |
| ☐ 562 Charlie Leibrandt | .01 | .05 |
| ☐ 563 John Shelby | .01 | .05 |
| ☐ 564 Bill Swift | .01 | .05 |
| ☐ 565 Mike Fetters | .01 | .05 |
| ☐ 566 Alejandro Pena | .01 | .05 |
| ☐ 567 Ruben Sierra | .02 | .10 |
| ☐ 568 Carlos Quintana | .01 | .05 |
| ☐ 569 Kevin Gross | .01 | .05 |
| ☐ 570 Derek Lilliquist | .01 | .05 |
| ☐ 571 Jack Armstrong | .01 | .05 |
| ☐ 572 Greg Brock | .01 | .05 |
| ☐ 573 Mike Kingery | .01 | .05 |
| ☐ 574 Greg Smith | .01 | .05 |
| ☐ 575 Brian McRae RC | .08 | .25 |
| ☐ 576 Jack Daugherty | .01 | .05 |
| ☐ 577 Ozzie Guillen | .02 | .10 |
| ☐ 578 Joe Boever | .01 | .05 |
| ☐ 579 Luis Sojo | .01 | .05 |
| ☐ 580 Chili Davis | .02 | .10 |
| ☐ 581 Don Robinson | .01 | .05 |
| ☐ 582 Brian Harper | .01 | .05 |
| ☐ 583 Paul O'Neill | .05 | .15 |
| ☐ 584 Bob Ojeda | .01 | .05 |
| ☐ 585 Mookie Wilson | .02 | .10 |
| ☐ 586 Rafael Ramirez | .01 | .05 |
| ☐ 587 Gary Redus | .01 | .05 |
| ☐ 588 Jamie Quirk | .01 | .05 |
| ☐ 589 Shawn Hillegas | .01 | .05 |
| ☐ 590 Tom Edens RC | .01 | .05 |
| ☐ 591 Joe Klink | .01 | .05 |
| ☐ 592 Charles Nagy | .05 | .15 |
| ☐ 593 Eric Plunk | .01 | .05 |
| ☐ 594 Tracy Jones | .01 | .05 |
| ☐ 595 Craig Biggio | .05 | .15 |
| ☐ 596 Jose DeJesus | .01 | .05 |
| ☐ 597 Mickey Tettleton | .02 | .10 |
| ☐ 598 Chris Gwynn | .01 | .05 |
| ☐ 599 Rex Hudler | .01 | .05 |
| ☐ 600 Checklist 409-506 | .01 | .05 |
| ☐ 601 Jim Gott | .01 | .05 |
| ☐ 602 Jeff Manto | .01 | .05 |
| ☐ 603 Nelson Liriano | .01 | .05 |
| ☐ 604 Mark Lemke | .01 | .05 |
| ☐ 605 Clay Parker | .01 | .05 |
| ☐ 606 Edgar Martinez | .05 | .15 |
| ☐ 607 Mark Whiten | .01 | .05 |
| ☐ 608 Ted Power | .01 | .05 |
| ☐ 609 Tom Bolton | .01 | .05 |
| ☐ 610 Tom Herr | .01 | .05 |
| ☐ 611 Andy Hawkins UER | .01 | .05 |
| ☐ 612 Scott Ruskin | .01 | .05 |
| ☐ 613 Ron Kittle | .01 | .05 |
| ☐ 614 John Wetteland | .02 | .10 |
| ☐ 615 Mike Perez RC | .01 | .05 |
| ☐ 616 Dave Clark | .01 | .05 |
| ☐ 617 Brent Mayne | .01 | .05 |
| ☐ 618 Jack Clark | .02 | .10 |
| ☐ 619 Marvin Freeman | .01 | .05 |
| ☐ 620 Edwin Nunez | .01 | .05 |
| ☐ 621 Russ Swan | .01 | .05 |
| ☐ 622 Johnny Ray | .01 | .05 |
| ☐ 623 Charlie O'Brien | .01 | .05 |
| ☐ 624 Joe Bitker RC | .01 | .05 |
| ☐ 625 Mike Marshall | .01 | .05 |
| ☐ 626 Otis Nixon | .01 | .05 |
| ☐ 627 Andy Benes | .01 | .05 |
| ☐ 628 Ron Oester | .01 | .05 |
| ☐ 629 Ted Higuera | .01 | .05 |
| ☐ 630 Kevin Bass | .01 | .05 |
| ☐ 631 Damon Berryhill | .01 | .05 |
| ☐ 632 Bo Jackson | .08 | .25 |
| ☐ 633 Brad Arnsberg | .01 | .05 |
| ☐ 634 Jerry Willard | .01 | .05 |
| ☐ 635 Tommy Greene | .01 | .05 |
| ☐ 636 Bob MacDonald RC | .05 | .15 |
| ☐ 637 Kirk McCaskill | .01 | .05 |
| ☐ 638 John Burkett | .01 | .05 |
| ☐ 639 Paul Abbott RC | .01 | .05 |
| ☐ 640 Todd Benzinger | .01 | .05 |
| ☐ 641 Todd Hundley | .01 | .05 |
| ☐ 642 George Bell | .01 | .05 |
| ☐ 643 Javier Ortiz | .01 | .05 |
| ☐ 644 Sid Bream | .01 | .05 |
| ☐ 645 Bob Welch | .01 | .05 |
| ☐ 646 Phil Bradley | .01 | .05 |
| ☐ 647 Bill Krueger | .01 | .05 |
| ☐ 648 Rickey Henderson | .08 | .25 |
| ☐ 649 Kevin Wickander | .01 | .05 |
| ☐ 650 Steve Balboni | .01 | .05 |
| ☐ 651 Gene Harris | .01 | .05 |
| ☐ 652 Jim Deshaies | .01 | .05 |
| ☐ 653 Jason Grimsley | .01 | .05 |
| ☐ 654 Joe Orsulak | .01 | .05 |
| ☐ 655 Jim Poole | .01 | .05 |
| ☐ 656 Felix Jose | .01 | .05 |
| ☐ 657 Denis Cook | .01 | .05 |
| ☐ 658 Tom Brookens | .01 | .05 |
| ☐ 659 Junior Ortiz | .01 | .05 |
| ☐ 660 Jeff Parrett | .01 | .05 |
| ☐ 661 Jerry Don Gleaton | .01 | .05 |
| ☐ 662 Brent Knackert | .01 | .05 |
| ☐ 663 Rance Mulliniks | .01 | .05 |
| ☐ 664 John Smiley | .01 | .05 |
| ☐ 665 Larry Andersen | .01 | .05 |
| ☐ 666 Willie McGee | .02 | .10 |
| ☐ 667 Chris Nabholz | .01 | .05 |
| ☐ 668 Brady Anderson | .02 | .10 |
| ☐ 669 Darren Holmes UER RC | .08 | .25 |
| ☐ 670 Ken Hill | .01 | .05 |
| ☐ 671 Gary Varsho | .01 | .05 |
| ☐ 672 Bill Pecota | .01 | .05 |
| ☐ 673 Fred Lynn | .02 | .10 |
| ☐ 674 Kevin D. Brown | .01 | .05 |
| ☐ 675 Dan Petry | .01 | .05 |
| ☐ 676 Mike Jackson | .01 | .05 |
| ☐ 677 Wally Joyner | .02 | .10 |
| ☐ 678 Danny Jackson | .01 | .05 |
| ☐ 679 Bill Haselman RC | .01 | .05 |
| ☐ 680 Mike Boddicker | .01 | .05 |
| ☐ 681 Mel Rojas | .01 | .05 |
| ☐ 682 Roberto Alomar | .05 | .15 |
| ☐ 683 David Justice ROY | .05 | .15 |
| ☐ 684 Chuck Crim | .01 | .05 |
| ☐ 685 Matt Williams | .02 | .10 |
| ☐ 686 Shawon Dunston | .02 | .10 |
| ☐ 687 Jeff Schulz RC | .01 | .05 |
| ☐ 688 John Barfield | .01 | .05 |
| ☐ 689 Gerald Young | .01 | .05 |
| ☐ 690 Luis Gonzalez RC | .20 | .50 |
| ☐ 691 Frank Wills | .01 | .05 |
| ☐ 692 Chuck Finley | .02 | .10 |
| ☐ 693 Sandy Alomar Jr. ROY | .01 | .05 |
| ☐ 694 Tim Drummond | .01 | .05 |
| ☐ 695 Herm Winningham | .01 | .05 |
| ☐ 696 Darryl Strawberry | .02 | .10 |
| ☐ 697 Al Leiter | .02 | .10 |
| ☐ 698 Karl Rhodes | .01 | .05 |
| ☐ 699 Stan Belinda | .01 | .05 |
| ☐ 700 Checklist 507-604 | .01 | .05 |
| ☐ 701 Lance Blankenship | .01 | .05 |
| ☐ 702 Willie Stargell PUZ | .05 | .15 |
| ☐ 703 Jim Gantner | .01 | .05 |
| ☐ 704 Reggie Harris | .01 | .05 |
| ☐ 705 Rob Ducey | .01 | .05 |
| ☐ 706 Tim Hulett | .01 | .05 |
| ☐ 707 Atlee Hammaker | .01 | .05 |

|  | | |
|---|---|---|
| 708 Xavier Hernandez | .01 | .05 |
| 709 Chuck McElroy | .01 | .05 |
| 710 John Mitchell | .01 | .05 |
| 711 Carlos Hernandez | .01 | .05 |
| 712 Geronimo Pena | .01 | .05 |
| 713 Jim Neidlinger RC | .01 | .05 |
| 714 John Orton | .01 | .05 |
| 715 Terry Leach | .01 | .05 |
| 716 Mike Stanton | .01 | .05 |
| 717 Walt Terrell | .01 | .05 |
| 718 Luis Aquino | .01 | .05 |
| 719 Bud Black UER | .01 | .05 |
| 720 Bob Kipper | .01 | .05 |
| 721 Jeff Gray RC | .01 | .05 |
| 722 Jose Rijo | .01 | .05 |
| 723 Curt Young | .01 | .05 |
| 724 Jose Vizcaino | .01 | .05 |
| 725 Randy Tomlin RC | .02 | .10 |
| 726 Junior Noboa | .01 | .05 |
| 727 Bob Welch CY | .01 | .05 |
| 728 Gary Ward | .01 | .05 |
| 729 Rob Deer UER | .01 | .05 |
| 730 David Segui | .01 | .05 |
| 731 Mark Carreon | .01 | .05 |
| 732 Vicente Palacios | .01 | .05 |
| 733 Sam Horn | .01 | .05 |
| 734 Howard Farmer | .01 | .05 |
| 735 Ken Dayley UER | .01 | .05 |
| 736 Kelly Mann | .01 | .05 |
| 737 Joe Grahe RC | .02 | .10 |
| 738 Kelly Downs | .01 | .05 |
| 739 Jimmy Kremers | .01 | .05 |
| 740 Kevin Appier | .02 | .10 |
| 741 Jeff Reed | .01 | .05 |
| 742 Jose Rijo WS | .01 | .05 |
| 743 Dave Rohde | .01 | .05 |
| 744 L.Dykstra/D.Murphy UER | .05 | .15 |
| 745 Paul Sorrento | .01 | .05 |
| 746 Thomas Howard | .01 | .05 |
| 747 Matt Stark RC | .01 | .05 |
| 748 Harold Baines | .02 | .10 |
| 749 Doug Dascenzo | .01 | .05 |
| 750 Doug Drabek CY | .01 | .05 |
| 751 Gary Sheffield | .02 | .10 |
| 752 Terry Lee RC | .01 | .05 |
| 753 Jim Vatcher RC | .01 | .05 |
| 754 Lee Stevens | .01 | .05 |
| 755 Randy Veres | .01 | .05 |
| 756 Bill Doran | .01 | .05 |
| 757 Gary Wayne | .01 | .05 |
| 758 Pedro Munoz RC | .02 | .10 |
| 759 Chris Hammond FDC | .01 | .05 |
| 760 Checklist 605-702 | .01 | .05 |
| 761 Rickey Henderson MVP | .05 | .15 |
| 762 Barry Bonds MVP | .20 | .50 |
| 763 Billy Hatcher WS UER | .01 | .05 |
| 764 Julio Machado | .01 | .05 |
| 765 Jose Mesa | .01 | .05 |
| 766 Willie Randolph WS | .01 | .05 |
| 767 Scott Erickson | .01 | .05 |
| 768 Travis Fryman | .02 | .10 |
| 769 Rich Rodriguez RC | .01 | .05 |
| 770 Checklist 703-770/BC1-BC22 | .01 | .05 |

## 1992 Donruss

| | | |
|---|---|---|
| COMPLETE SET (784) | 4.00 | 10.00 |
| COMP.HOBBY SET (788) | 4.00 | 10.00 |
| COMP.RETAIL SET (788) | 4.00 | 10.00 |
| COMPLETE SERIES 1 (396) | 2.00 | 5.00 |
| COMPLETE SERIES 2 (388) | 2.00 | 5.00 |
| COMP.CAREW PUZZLE | .40 | 1.00 |
| 1 Mark Wohlers RR | .01 | .05 |
| 2 Will Cordero | .01 | .05 |
| 3 Kyle Abbott RR | .01 | .05 |

|  | | |
|---|---|---|
| 4 Dave Nilsson | .01 | .05 |
| 5 Kenny Lofton | .05 | .15 |
| 6 Luis Mercedes RR | .01 | .05 |
| 7 Roger Salkeld RR | .01 | .05 |
| 8 Eddie Zosky RR | .01 | .05 |
| 9 Todd Van Poppel | .01 | .05 |
| 10 Frank Seminara RR RC | .02 | .10 |
| 11 Andy Ashby | .01 | .05 |
| 12 Reggie Jefferson RR | .01 | .05 |
| 13 Ryan Klesko | .02 | .10 |
| 14 Carlos Garcia | .01 | .05 |
| 15 John Ramos RR | .01 | .05 |
| 16 Eric Karros | .01 | .05 |
| 17 Patrick Lennon RR | .01 | .05 |
| 18 Eddie Taubensee RR RC | .08 | .25 |
| 19 Roberto Hernandez RR | .01 | .05 |
| 20 D.J. Dozier RR | .01 | .05 |
| 21 Dave Henderson AS | .01 | .05 |
| 22 Cal Ripken AS | .15 | .40 |
| 23 Wade Boggs AS | .05 | .15 |
| 24 Ken Griffey Jr. AS | .08 | .25 |
| 25 Jack Morris AS | .05 | .15 |
| 26 Danny Tartabull AS | .01 | .05 |
| 27 Cecil Fielder AS | .02 | .10 |
| 28 Roberto Alomar AS | .02 | .10 |
| 29 Sandy Alomar Jr. AS | .01 | .05 |
| 30 Rickey Henderson AS | .05 | .15 |
| 31 Ken Hill | .01 | .05 |
| 32 John Habyan | .01 | .05 |
| 33 Otis Nixon HL | .01 | .05 |
| 34 Tim Wallach | .01 | .05 |
| 35 Cal Ripken | .30 | .75 |
| 36 Gary Carter | .02 | .10 |
| 37 Juan Agosto | .01 | .05 |
| 38 Doug Dascenzo | .01 | .05 |
| 39 Kirk Gibson | .01 | .05 |
| 40 Benito Santiago | .02 | .10 |
| 41 Otis Nixon | .01 | .05 |
| 42 Andy Allanson | .01 | .05 |
| 43 Brian Holman | .01 | .05 |
| 44 Dick Schofield | .01 | .05 |
| 45 Dave Magadan | .01 | .05 |
| 46 Rafael Palmeiro | .05 | .15 |
| 47 Jody Reed | .01 | .05 |
| 48 Ivan Calderon | .01 | .05 |
| 49 Greg W. Harris | .01 | .05 |
| 50 Chris Sabo | .01 | .05 |
| 51 Paul Molitor | .02 | .10 |
| 52 Robby Thompson | .01 | .05 |
| 53 Dave Smith | .01 | .05 |
| 54 Mark Davis | .01 | .05 |
| 55 Kevin Brown | .02 | .10 |
| 56 Donn Pall | .01 | .05 |
| 57 Len Dykstra | .02 | .10 |
| 58 Roberto Alomar | .05 | .15 |
| 59 Jeff D. Robinson | .01 | .05 |
| 60 Willie McGee | .02 | .10 |
| 61 Jay Buhner | .02 | .10 |
| 62 Mike Pagliarulo | .01 | .05 |
| 63 Paul O'Neill | .05 | .15 |
| 64 Hubie Brooks | .01 | .05 |
| 65 Kelly Gruber | .01 | .05 |
| 66 Ken Caminiti | .02 | .10 |
| 67 Gary Redus | .01 | .05 |
| 68 Harold Baines | .02 | .10 |
| 69 Charlie Hough | .01 | .05 |
| 70 B.J. Surhoff | .02 | .10 |
| 71 Walt Weiss | .01 | .05 |
| 72 Shawn Hillegas | .01 | .05 |
| 73 Roberto Kelly | .01 | .05 |
| 74 Jeff Ballard | .01 | .05 |
| 75 Craig Biggio | .05 | .15 |
| 76 Pat Combs | .01 | .05 |
| 77 Jeff M. Robinson | .01 | .05 |
| 78 Tim Belcher | .01 | .05 |
| 79 Cris Carpenter | .01 | .05 |
| 80 Checklist 1-79 | .01 | .05 |
| 81 Steve Avery | .05 | .15 |
| 82 Chris James | .01 | .05 |
| 83 Brian Harper | .01 | .05 |
| 84 Charlie Leibrandt | .01 | .05 |
| 85 Mickey Tettleton | .02 | .10 |
| 86 Pete O'Brien | .01 | .05 |
| 87 Danny Darwin | .01 | .05 |
| 88 Bob Walk | .01 | .05 |
| 89 Jeff Reardon | .02 | .10 |
| 90 Bobby Rose | .01 | .05 |
| 91 Danny Jackson | .01 | .05 |

|  | | |
|---|---|---|
| 92 John Morris | .01 | .05 |
| 93 Bud Black | .01 | .05 |
| 94 Tommy Greene HL | .01 | .05 |
| 95 Rick Aguilera | .02 | .10 |
| 96 Gary Gaetti | .02 | .10 |
| 97 David Cone | .02 | .10 |
| 98 John Olerud | .02 | .10 |
| 99 Joel Skinner | .01 | .05 |
| 100 Jay Bell | .02 | .10 |
| 101 Bob Milacki | .01 | .05 |
| 102 Norm Charlton | .01 | .05 |
| 103 Chuck Crim | .01 | .05 |
| 104 Terry Steinbach | .01 | .05 |
| 105 Juan Samuel | .01 | .05 |
| 106 Steve Howe | .01 | .05 |
| 107 Rafael Belliard | .01 | .05 |
| 108 Joey Cora | .01 | .05 |
| 109 Tommy Greene | .01 | .05 |
| 110 Gregg Olson | .01 | .05 |
| 111 Frank Tanana | .01 | .05 |
| 112 Lee Smith | .02 | .10 |
| 113 Greg A. Harris | .01 | .05 |
| 114 Dwayne Henry | .01 | .05 |
| 115 Chili Davis | .02 | .10 |
| 116 Kent Mercker | .01 | .05 |
| 117 Brian Barnes | .01 | .05 |
| 118 Rich DeLucia | .01 | .05 |
| 119 Andre Dawson | .02 | .10 |
| 120 Carlos Baerga | .05 | .15 |
| 121 Mike LaValliere | .01 | .05 |
| 122 Jeff Gray | .01 | .05 |
| 123 Bruce Hurst | .01 | .05 |
| 124 Alvin Davis | .01 | .05 |
| 125 John Candelaria | .01 | .05 |
| 126 Matt Nokes | .01 | .05 |
| 127 George Bell | .01 | .05 |
| 128 Bret Saberhagen | .02 | .10 |
| 129 Jeff Russell | .01 | .05 |
| 130 Jim Abbott | .05 | .15 |
| 131 Bill Gullickson | .01 | .05 |
| 132 Todd Zeile | .02 | .10 |
| 133 Dave Winfield | .02 | .10 |
| 134 Wally Whitehurst | .01 | .05 |
| 135 Matt Williams | .02 | .10 |
| 136 Tom Browning | .01 | .05 |
| 137 Marquis Grissom | .02 | .10 |
| 138 Erik Hanson | .01 | .05 |
| 139 Rob Dibble | .01 | .05 |
| 140 Don August | .01 | .05 |
| 141 Tom Henke | .01 | .05 |
| 142 Dan Pasqua | .01 | .05 |
| 143 George Brett | .25 | .60 |
| 144 Jerald Clark | .01 | .05 |
| 145 Robin Ventura | .05 | .15 |
| 146 Dale Murphy | .05 | .15 |
| 147 Dennis Eckersley | .02 | .10 |
| 148 Eric Yelding | .01 | .05 |
| 149 Mario Diaz | .01 | .05 |
| 150 Casey Candaele | .01 | .05 |
| 151 Steve Olin | .01 | .05 |
| 152 Luis Salazar | .01 | .05 |
| 153 Kevin Mass | .05 | .15 |
| 154 Nolan Ryan HL | .20 | .50 |
| 155 Barry Jones | .01 | .05 |
| 156 Chris Hoiles | .02 | .10 |
| 157 Bob Ojeda | .01 | .05 |
| 158 Pedro Guerrero | .02 | .10 |
| 159 Paul Assenmacher | .01 | .05 |
| 160 Checklist 80-157 | .01 | .05 |
| 161 Mike Macfarlane | .01 | .05 |
| 162 Craig Lefferts | .01 | .05 |
| 163 Brian Hunter | .01 | .05 |
| 164 Alan Trammell | .02 | .10 |
| 165 Ken Griffey Jr. | .15 | .40 |
| 166 Lance Parrish | .02 | .10 |
| 167 Brian Downing | .01 | .05 |
| 168 John Barfield | .01 | .05 |
| 169 Jack Clark | .02 | .10 |
| 170 Chris Nabholz | .01 | .05 |
| 171 Tim Teufel | .01 | .05 |
| 172 Chris Hammond | .01 | .05 |
| 173 Robin Yount | .15 | .40 |
| 174 Dave Righetti | .02 | .10 |
| 175 Joe Girardi | .01 | .05 |
| 176 Mike Boddicker | .01 | .05 |
| 177 Dean Palmer | .02 | .10 |
| 178 Greg Hibbard | .01 | .05 |
| 179 Randy Ready | .01 | .05 |

|  |  | | |
|-----|--------|-----|-----|
| 180 | Devon White | .02 | .10 |
| 181 | Mark Eichhorn | .01 | .05 |
| 182 | Mike Felder | .01 | .05 |
| 183 | Joe Klink | .01 | .05 |
| 184 | Steve Bedrosian | .01 | .05 |
| 185 | Barry Larkin | .05 | .15 |
| 186 | John Franco | .02 | .10 |
| 187 | Ed Sprague | .01 | .05 |
| 188 | Mark Portugal | .01 | .05 |
| 189 | Jose Lind | .01 | .05 |
| 190 | Bob Welch | .01 | .05 |
| 191 | Alex Fernandez | .01 | .05 |
| 192 | Gary Sheffield | .02 | .10 |
| 193 | Rickey Henderson | .08 | .25 |
| 194 | Rod Nichols | .01 | .05 |
| 195 | Scott Kamieniecki | .01 | .05 |
| 196 | Mike Flanagan | .01 | .05 |
| 197 | Steve Finley | .01 | .05 |
| 198 | Darren Daulton | .02 | .10 |
| 199 | Leo Gomez | .01 | .05 |
| 200 | Mike Morgan | .01 | .05 |
| 201 | Bob Tewksbury | .01 | .05 |
| 202 | Sid Bream | .01 | .05 |
| 203 | Sandy Alomar Jr. | .01 | .05 |
| 204 | Greg Gagne | .01 | .05 |
| 205 | Juan Berenguer | .01 | .05 |
| 206 | Cecil Fielder | .02 | .10 |
| 207 | Randy Johnson | .08 | .25 |
| 208 | Tony Pena | .01 | .05 |
| 209 | Doug Drabek | .01 | .05 |
| 210 | Wade Boggs | .05 | .15 |
| 211 | Bryan Harvey | .01 | .05 |
| 212 | Jose Vizcaino | .01 | .05 |
| 213 | Alonzo Powell | .01 | .05 |
| 214 | Will Clark | .05 | .15 |
| 215 | Rickey Henderson HL | .05 | .15 |
| 216 | Jack Morris | .02 | .10 |
| 217 | Junior Felix | .01 | .05 |
| 218 | Vince Coleman | .01 | .05 |
| 219 | Jimmy Key | .02 | .10 |
| 220 | Alex Cole | .01 | .05 |
| 221 | Bill Landrum | .01 | .05 |
| 222 | Randy Milligan | .01 | .05 |
| 223 | Jose Rijo | .01 | .05 |
| 224 | Greg Vaughn | .01 | .05 |
| 225 | Dave Stewart | .02 | .10 |
| 226 | Lenny Harris | .01 | .05 |
| 227 | Scott Sanderson | .01 | .05 |
| 228 | Jeff Blauser | .01 | .05 |
| 229 | Ozzie Guillen | .02 | .10 |
| 230 | John Kruk | .02 | .10 |
| 231 | Bob Melvin | .01 | .05 |
| 232 | Milt Cuyler | .01 | .05 |
| 233 | Felix Jose | .01 | .05 |
| 234 | Ellis Burks | .02 | .10 |
| 235 | Pete Harnisch | .01 | .05 |
| 236 | Kevin Tapani | .01 | .05 |
| 237 | Terry Pendleton | .02 | .10 |
| 238 | Mark Gardner | .01 | .05 |
| 239 | Harold Reynolds | .01 | .05 |
| 240 | Checklist 158-237 | .02 | .10 |
| 241 | Mike Harkey | .01 | .05 |
| 242 | Felix Fermin | .01 | .05 |
| 243 | Barry Bonds | .40 | 1.00 |
| 244 | Roger Clemens | .20 | .50 |
| 245 | Dennis Rasmussen | .01 | .05 |
| 246 | Jose DeLeon | .01 | .05 |
| 247 | Orel Hershiser | .02 | .10 |
| 248 | Mel Hall | .01 | .05 |
| 249 | Rick Wilkins | .01 | .05 |
| 250 | Tom Gordon | .01 | .05 |
| 251 | Kevin Reimer | .01 | .05 |
| 252 | Luis Polonia | .01 | .05 |
| 253 | Mike Henneman | .01 | .05 |
| 254 | Tom Pagnozzi | .01 | .05 |
| 255 | Chuck Finley | .02 | .10 |
| 256 | Mackey Sasser | .01 | .05 |
| 257 | John Burkett | .01 | .05 |
| 258 | Hal Morris | .01 | .05 |
| 259 | Larry Walker | .05 | .15 |
| 260 | Bill Swift | .01 | .05 |
| 261 | Joe Oliver | .01 | .05 |
| 262 | Julio Machado | .01 | .05 |
| 263 | Todd Stottlemyre | .01 | .05 |
| 264 | Matt Merullo | .01 | .05 |
| 265 | Brent Mayne | .01 | .05 |
| 266 | Thomas Howard | .01 | .05 |
| 267 | Lance Johnson | .01 | .05 |
| 268 | Terry Mulholland | .01 | .05 |
| 269 | Rick Honeycutt | .01 | .05 |
| 270 | Luis Gonzalez | .02 | .10 |
| 271 | Jose Guzman | .01 | .05 |
| 272 | Jimmy Jones | .01 | .05 |
| 273 | Mark Lewis | .01 | .05 |
| 274 | Rene Gonzales | .01 | .05 |
| 275 | Jeff Johnson | .01 | .05 |
| 276 | Dennis Martinez HL | .01 | .05 |
| 277 | Delino DeShields | .05 | .15 |
| 278 | Sam Horn | .01 | .05 |
| 279 | Kevin Gross | .01 | .05 |
| 280 | Jose Oquendo | .01 | .05 |
| 281 | Mark Grace | .05 | .15 |
| 282 | Mark Gubicza | .01 | .05 |
| 283 | Fred McGriff | .05 | .15 |
| 284 | Ron Gant | .02 | .10 |
| 285 | Lou Whitaker | .02 | .10 |
| 286 | Edgar Martinez | .05 | .15 |
| 287 | Ron Tingley | .01 | .05 |
| 288 | Kevin McReynolds | .01 | .05 |
| 289 | Ivan Rodriguez | .08 | .25 |
| 290 | Mike Gardiner | .01 | .05 |
| 291 | Chris Haney | .01 | .05 |
| 292 | Darrin Jackson | .01 | .05 |
| 293 | Bill Doran | .01 | .05 |
| 294 | Ted Higuera | .01 | .05 |
| 295 | Jeff Brantley | .01 | .05 |
| 296 | Les Lancaster | .01 | .05 |
| 297 | Jim Eisenreich | .01 | .05 |
| 298 | Ruben Sierra | .02 | .10 |
| 299 | Scott Radinsky | .01 | .05 |
| 300 | Jose DeJesus | .01 | .05 |
| 301 | Mike Timlin | .01 | .05 |
| 302 | Luis Sojo | .01 | .05 |
| 303 | Kelly Downs | .01 | .05 |
| 304 | Scott Bankhead | .01 | .05 |
| 305 | Pedro Munoz | .01 | .05 |
| 306 | Scott Scudder | .01 | .05 |
| 307 | Kevin Elster | .01 | .05 |
| 308 | Duane Ward | .01 | .05 |
| 309 | Darryl Kile | .02 | .10 |
| 310 | Orlando Merced | .01 | .05 |
| 311 | Dave Henderson | .01 | .05 |
| 312 | Tim Raines | .02 | .10 |
| 313 | Mark Lee | .01 | .05 |
| 314 | Mike Gallego | .01 | .05 |
| 315 | Charles Nagy | .05 | .15 |
| 316 | Jesse Barfield | .01 | .05 |
| 317 | Todd Frohwirth | .01 | .05 |
| 318 | Al Osuna | .01 | .05 |
| 319 | Darrin Fletcher | .01 | .05 |
| 320 | Checklist 238-316 | .02 | .10 |
| 321 | David Segui | .01 | .05 |
| 322 | Stan Javier | .01 | .05 |
| 323 | Bryn Smith | .01 | .05 |
| 324 | Jeff Treadway | .01 | .05 |
| 325 | Mark Whiten | .01 | .05 |
| 326 | Kent Hrbek | .02 | .10 |
| 327 | David Justice | .02 | .10 |
| 328 | Tony Phillips | .01 | .05 |
| 329 | Rob Murphy | .01 | .05 |
| 330 | Kevin Morton | .01 | .05 |
| 331 | John Smiley | .01 | .05 |
| 332 | Luis Rivera | .01 | .05 |
| 333 | Wally Joyner | .02 | .10 |
| 334 | Heathcliff Slocumb | .01 | .05 |
| 335 | Rick Cerone | .01 | .05 |
| 336 | Mike Remlinger | .01 | .05 |
| 337 | Mike Moore | .01 | .05 |
| 338 | Lloyd McClendon | .01 | .05 |
| 339 | Al Newman | .01 | .05 |
| 340 | Kirk McCaskill | .01 | .05 |
| 341 | Howard Johnson | .02 | .10 |
| 342 | Greg Myers | .01 | .05 |
| 343 | Kal Daniels | .01 | .05 |
| 344 | Bernie Williams | .05 | .15 |
| 345 | Shane Mack | .02 | .10 |
| 346 | Gary Thurman | .01 | .05 |
| 347 | Dante Bichette | .02 | .10 |
| 348 | Mark McGwire | .25 | .60 |
| 349 | Ray Lankford | .02 | .10 |
| 350 | Ray Lankford | .02 | .10 |
| 351 | Mike Jeffcoat | .01 | .05 |
| 352 | Jack McDowell | .01 | .05 |
| 353 | Mitch Williams | .01 | .05 |
| 354 | Mike Devereaux | .01 | .05 |
| 355 | Andres Galarraga | .02 | .10 |
| 356 | Henry Cotto | .01 | .05 |
| 357 | Scott Bailes | .01 | .05 |
| 358 | Jeff Bagwell | .08 | .25 |
| 359 | Scott Leius | .01 | .05 |
| 360 | Zane Smith | .01 | .05 |
| 361 | Bill Pecota | .01 | .05 |
| 362 | Tony Fernandez | .01 | .05 |
| 363 | Glenn Braggs | .01 | .05 |
| 364 | Bill Spiers | .01 | .05 |
| 365 | Vicente Palacios | .01 | .05 |
| 366 | Tim Burke | .01 | .05 |
| 367 | Randy Tomlin | .01 | .05 |
| 368 | Kenny Rogers | .02 | .10 |
| 369 | Brett Butler | .02 | .10 |
| 370 | Pat Kelly | .01 | .05 |
| 371 | Bip Roberts | .01 | .05 |
| 372 | Gregg Jefferies | .01 | .05 |
| 373 | Kevin Bass | .01 | .05 |
| 374 | Ron Karkovice | .01 | .05 |
| 375 | Paul Gibson | .01 | .05 |
| 376 | Bernard Gilkey | .01 | .05 |
| 377 | Dave Gallagher | .01 | .05 |
| 378 | Bill Wegman | .01 | .05 |
| 379 | Pat Borders | .01 | .05 |
| 380 | Ed Whitson | .01 | .05 |
| 381 | Gilberto Reyes | .01 | .05 |
| 382 | Russ Swan | .01 | .05 |
| 383 | Andy Van Slyke | .05 | .15 |
| 384 | Wes Chamberlain | .01 | .05 |
| 385 | Steve Chitren | .01 | .05 |
| 386 | Greg Olson | .01 | .05 |
| 387 | Brian McRae | .01 | .05 |
| 388 | Rich Rodriguez | .01 | .05 |
| 389 | Steve Decker | .01 | .05 |
| 390 | Chuck Knoblauch | .02 | .10 |
| 391 | Bobby Witt | .01 | .05 |
| 392 | Eddie Murray | .08 | .25 |
| 393 | Juan Gonzalez | .05 | .15 |
| 394 | Scott Ruskin | .01 | .05 |
| 395 | Jay Howell | .01 | .05 |
| 396 | Checklist 317-396 | .01 | .05 |
| 397 | Royce Clayton RR | .01 | .05 |
| 398 | John Jaha RR RC | .08 | .25 |
| 399 | Dan Wilson RR | .01 | .05 |
| 400 | Archie Corbin | .01 | .05 |
| 401 | Barry Manuel RR | .01 | .05 |
| 402 | Kim Batiste RR | .01 | .05 |
| 403 | Pat Mahomes RR RC | .08 | .25 |
| 404 | Dave Fleming | .01 | .05 |
| 405 | Jeff Juden RR | .01 | .05 |
| 406 | Jim Thome | .08 | .25 |
| 407 | Sam Militello RR | .01 | .05 |
| 408 | Jeff Nelson RR RC | .15 | .40 |
| 409 | Anthony Young | .05 | .15 |
| 410 | Tino Martinez RR | .05 | .15 |
| 411 | Jeff Mutis RR | .01 | .05 |
| 412 | Rey Sanchez RR RC | .08 | .25 |
| 413 | Chris Gardner RR | .01 | .05 |
| 414 | John Vander Wal RR | .01 | .05 |
| 415 | Reggie Sanders | .02 | .10 |
| 416 | Brian Williams RR RC | .02 | .10 |
| 417 | Mo Sanford RR | .01 | .05 |
| 418 | David Weathers RR RC | .15 | .40 |
| 419 | Hector Fajardo RR RC | .02 | .10 |
| 420 | Steve Foster RR | .01 | .05 |
| 421 | Lance Dickson RR | .01 | .05 |
| 422 | Andre Dawson AS | .01 | .05 |
| 423 | Ozzie Smith AS | .08 | .25 |
| 424 | Chris Sabo AS | .01 | .05 |
| 425 | Tony Gwynn AS | .05 | .15 |
| 426 | Tom Glavine AS | .02 | .10 |
| 427 | Bobby Bonilla AS | .02 | .10 |
| 428 | Will Clark AS | .02 | .10 |
| 429 | Ryne Sandberg AS | .08 | .25 |
| 430 | Benito Santiago AS | .01 | .05 |
| 431 | Ivan Calderon AS | .01 | .05 |
| 432 | Ozzie Smith | .15 | .40 |
| 433 | Tim Leary | .01 | .05 |
| 434 | Bret Saberhagen HL | .01 | .05 |
| 435 | Mel Rojas | .01 | .05 |
| 436 | Ben McDonald | .01 | .05 |
| 437 | Tim Crews | .01 | .05 |
| 438 | Rex Hudler | .01 | .05 |
| 439 | Chico Walker | .01 | .05 |
| 440 | Kurt Stillwell | .01 | .05 |
| 441 | Tony Gwynn | .10 | .30 |
| 442 | John Smoltz | .05 | .15 |
| 443 | Lloyd Moseby | .01 | .05 |

|  |  | | |
|---|---|---|---|
| 444 | Mike Schooler | .01 | .05 |
| 445 | Joe Grahe | .01 | .05 |
| 446 | Dwight Gooden | .02 | .10 |
| 447 | Oil Can Boyd | .01 | .05 |
| 448 | John Marzano | .01 | .05 |
| 449 | Bret Barberie | .01 | .05 |
| 450 | Mike Maddux | .01 | .05 |
| 451 | Jeff Reed | .01 | .05 |
| 452 | Dale Sveum | .01 | .05 |
| 453 | Jose Uribe | .01 | .05 |
| 454 | Bob Scanlan | .01 | .05 |
| 455 | Kevin Appier | .02 | .10 |
| 456 | Jeff Huson | .01 | .05 |
| 457 | Ken Patterson | .01 | .05 |
| 458 | Ricky Jordan | .01 | .05 |
| 459 | Tom Candiotti | .01 | .05 |
| 460 | Lee Stevens | .01 | .05 |
| 461 | Rod Beck RC | .08 | .25 |
| 462 | Dave Valle | .01 | .05 |
| 463 | Scott Erickson | .01 | .05 |
| 464 | Chris Jones | .01 | .05 |
| 465 | Mark Carreon | .01 | .05 |
| 466 | Rob Ducey | .01 | .05 |
| 467 | Jim Corsi | .01 | .05 |
| 468 | Jeff King | .01 | .05 |
| 469 | Curt Young | .01 | .05 |
| 470 | Bo Jackson | .08 | .25 |
| 471 | Chris Bosio | .01 | .05 |
| 472 | Jamie Quirk | .01 | .05 |
| 473 | Jesse Orosco | .01 | .05 |
| 474 | Alvaro Espinoza | .01 | .05 |
| 475 | Joe Orsulak | .01 | .05 |
| 476 | Checklist 397-477 | .01 | .05 |
| 477 | Gerald Young | .01 | .05 |
| 478 | Wally Backman | .01 | .05 |
| 479 | Juan Bell | .01 | .05 |
| 480 | Mike Scioscia | .01 | .05 |
| 481 | Omar Olivares | .01 | .05 |
| 482 | Francisco Cabrera | .01 | .05 |
| 483 | Greg Swindell UER (Shown on Indians& but listed) | .01 | .05 |
| 484 | Terry Leach | .01 | .05 |
| 485 | Tommy Gregg | .01 | .05 |
| 486 | Scott Aldred | .01 | .05 |
| 487 | Greg Briley | .01 | .05 |
| 488 | Phil Plantier | .01 | .05 |
| 489 | Curtis Wilkerson | .01 | .05 |
| 490 | Tom Brunansky | .01 | .05 |
| 491 | Mike Fetters | .01 | .05 |
| 492 | Frank Castillo | .01 | .05 |
| 493 | Joe Boever | .01 | .05 |
| 494 | Kirt Manwaring | .01 | .05 |
| 495 | Wilson Alvarez HL | .01 | .05 |
| 496 | Gene Larkin | .01 | .05 |
| 497 | Gary DiSarcina | .01 | .05 |
| 498 | Frank Viola | .02 | .10 |
| 499 | Manuel Lee | .01 | .05 |
| 500 | Albert Belle | .02 | .10 |
| 501 | Stan Belinda | .01 | .05 |
| 502 | Dwight Evans | .05 | .15 |
| 503 | Eric Davis | .02 | .10 |
| 504 | Darren Holmes | .01 | .05 |
| 505 | Mike Bordick | .01 | .05 |
| 506 | Dave Hansen | .01 | .05 |
| 507 | Lee Guetterman | .01 | .05 |
| 508 | Keith Mitchell | .01 | .05 |
| 509 | Melido Perez | .01 | .05 |
| 510 | Dickie Thon | .01 | .05 |
| 511 | Mark Williamson | .01 | .05 |
| 512 | Mark Salas | .01 | .05 |
| 513 | Milt Thompson | .01 | .05 |
| 514 | Mo Vaughn | .02 | .10 |
| 515 | Jim Deshaies | .01 | .05 |
| 516 | Rich Garces | .01 | .05 |
| 517 | Lonnie Smith | .01 | .05 |
| 518 | Spike Owen | .01 | .05 |
| 519 | Tracy Jones | .01 | .05 |
| 520 | Greg Maddux | .15 | .40 |
| 521 | Carlos Martinez | .01 | .05 |
| 522 | Neal Heaton | .01 | .05 |
| 523 | Mike Greenwell | .01 | .05 |
| 524 | Andy Benes | .01 | .05 |
| 525 | Jeff Schaefer UER | .01 | .05 |
| 526 | Mike Sharperson | .01 | .05 |
| 527 | Wade Taylor | .01 | .05 |
| 528 | Jerome Walton | .01 | .05 |
| 529 | Storm Davis | .01 | .05 |
| 530 | Jose Hernandez RC | .08 | .25 |
| 531 | Mark Langston | .01 | .05 |
| 532 | Rob Deer | .01 | .05 |
| 533 | Geronimo Pena | .01 | .05 |
| 534 | Juan Guzman | .01 | .05 |
| 535 | Pete Schourek | .01 | .05 |
| 536 | Todd Benzinger | .01 | .05 |
| 537 | Billy Hatcher | .01 | .05 |
| 538 | Tom Foley | .01 | .05 |
| 539 | Dave Cochrane | .01 | .05 |
| 540 | Mariano Duncan | .01 | .05 |
| 541 | Edwin Nunez | .01 | .05 |
| 542 | Rance Mulliniks | .01 | .05 |
| 543 | Carlton Fisk | .05 | .15 |
| 544 | Luis Aquino | .01 | .05 |
| 545 | Ricky Bones | .01 | .05 |
| 546 | Craig Grebeck | .01 | .05 |
| 547 | Charlie Hayes | .01 | .05 |
| 548 | Jose Canseco | .05 | .15 |
| 549 | Andujar Cedeno | .01 | .05 |
| 550 | Geno Petralli | .01 | .05 |
| 551 | Javier Ortiz | .01 | .05 |
| 552 | Rudy Seanez | .01 | .05 |
| 553 | Rich Gedman | .01 | .05 |
| 554 | Eric Plunk | .01 | .05 |
| 555 | N.Ryan/G.Gossage HL | .15 | .40 |
| 556 | Checklist 478-555 | .01 | .05 |
| 557 | Greg Colbrunn | .01 | .05 |
| 558 | Chito Martinez | .01 | .05 |
| 559 | Darryl Strawberry | .02 | .10 |
| 560 | Luis Alicea | .01 | .05 |
| 561 | Dwight Smith | .01 | .05 |
| 562 | Terry Shumpert | .01 | .05 |
| 563 | Jim Vatcher | .01 | .05 |
| 564 | Deion Sanders | .05 | .15 |
| 565 | Walt Terrell | .01 | .05 |
| 566 | Dave Burba | .01 | .05 |
| 567 | Dave Howard | .01 | .05 |
| 568 | Todd Hundley | .01 | .05 |
| 569 | Jack Daugherty | .01 | .05 |
| 570 | Scott Cooper | .01 | .05 |
| 571 | Bill Sampen | .01 | .05 |
| 572 | Jose Melendez | .01 | .05 |
| 573 | Freddie Benavides | .01 | .05 |
| 574 | Jim Gantner | .01 | .05 |
| 575 | Trevor Wilson | .01 | .05 |
| 576 | Ryne Sandberg | .15 | .40 |
| 577 | Kevin Seitzer | .01 | .05 |
| 578 | Gerald Alexander | .01 | .05 |
| 579 | Mike Huff | .01 | .05 |
| 580 | Von Hayes | .01 | .05 |
| 581 | Derek Bell | .02 | .10 |
| 582 | Mike Stanley | .01 | .05 |
| 583 | Kevin Mitchell | .01 | .05 |
| 584 | Mike Jackson | .01 | .05 |
| 585 | Dan Gladden | .01 | .05 |
| 586 | Ted Power UER (Wrong year given for signing with | .01 | .05 |
| 587 | Jeff Innis | .01 | .05 |
| 588 | Bob MacDonald | .01 | .05 |
| 589 | Jose Tolentino | .01 | .05 |
| 590 | Bob Patterson | .01 | .05 |
| 591 | Scott Brosius RC | .15 | .40 |
| 592 | Frank Thomas | .08 | .25 |
| 593 | Darryl Hamilton | .01 | .05 |
| 594 | Kirk Dressendorfer | .01 | .05 |
| 595 | Jeff Shaw | .01 | .05 |
| 596 | Don Mattingly | .25 | .60 |
| 597 | Glenn Davis | .01 | .05 |
| 598 | Andy Mota | .01 | .05 |
| 599 | Jason Grimsley | .01 | .05 |
| 600 | Jim Poole | .01 | .05 |
| 601 | Jim Gott | .01 | .05 |
| 602 | Stan Royer | .01 | .05 |
| 603 | Marvin Freeman | .01 | .05 |
| 604 | Denis Boucher | .01 | .05 |
| 605 | Denny Neagle | .02 | .10 |
| 606 | Mark Lemke | .01 | .05 |
| 607 | Jerry Don Gleaton | .01 | .05 |
| 608 | Brent Knackert | .01 | .05 |
| 609 | Carlos Quintana | .01 | .05 |
| 610 | Bobby Bonilla | .02 | .10 |
| 611 | Joe Hesketh | .01 | .05 |
| 612 | Daryl Boston | .01 | .05 |
| 613 | Shawon Dunston | .01 | .05 |
| 614 | Danny Cox | .01 | .05 |
| 615 | Darren Lewis | .01 | .05 |
| 616 | Mercker/Pena/Wohlers UER | .01 | .05 |
| 617 | Kirby Puckett | .08 | .25 |
| 618 | Franklin Stubbs | .01 | .05 |
| 619 | Chris Donnels | .01 | .05 |
| 620 | David Wells UER | .02 | .10 |
| 621 | Mike Aldrete | .01 | .05 |
| 622 | Bob Kipper | .01 | .05 |
| 623 | Anthony Telford | .01 | .05 |
| 624 | Randy Myers | .01 | .05 |
| 625 | Willie Randolph | .02 | .10 |
| 626 | Joe Slusarski | .01 | .05 |
| 627 | John Wetteland | .02 | .10 |
| 628 | Greg Cadaret | .01 | .05 |
| 629 | Tom Glavine | .05 | .15 |
| 630 | Wilson Alvarez | .01 | .05 |
| 631 | Wally Ritchie | .01 | .05 |
| 632 | Mike Mussina | .08 | .25 |
| 633 | Mark Leiter | .01 | .05 |
| 634 | Gerald Perry | .01 | .05 |
| 635 | Matt Young | .01 | .05 |
| 636 | Checklist 556-635 | .01 | .05 |
| 637 | Scott Hemond | .01 | .05 |
| 638 | David West | .01 | .05 |
| 639 | Jim Clancy | .01 | .05 |
| 640 | Doug Piatt UER (Not born in 1955 as on card; inc | .01 | .05 |
| 641 | Omar Vizquel | .05 | .15 |
| 642 | Rick Sutcliffe | .02 | .10 |
| 643 | Gienallen Hill | .01 | .05 |
| 644 | Gary Varsho | .01 | .05 |
| 645 | Tony Fossas | .01 | .05 |
| 646 | Jack Howell | .01 | .05 |
| 647 | Jim Campanis | .01 | .05 |
| 648 | Chris Gwynn | .01 | .05 |
| 649 | Jim Leyritz | .01 | .05 |
| 650 | Chuck McElroy | .01 | .05 |
| 651 | Sean Berry | .01 | .05 |
| 652 | Donald Harris | .01 | .05 |
| 653 | Don Slaught | .01 | .05 |
| 654 | Rusty Meacham | .01 | .05 |
| 655 | Scott Terry | .01 | .05 |
| 656 | Ramon Martinez | .01 | .05 |
| 657 | Keith Miller | .01 | .05 |
| 658 | Ramon Garcia | .01 | .05 |
| 659 | Milt Hill | .01 | .05 |
| 660 | Steve Frey | .01 | .05 |
| 661 | Bob McClure | .01 | .05 |
| 662 | Ced Landrum | .01 | .05 |
| 663 | Doug Henry RC | .02 | .10 |
| 664 | Candy Maldonado | .01 | .05 |
| 665 | Carl Willis | .01 | .05 |
| 666 | Jeff Montgomery | .01 | .05 |
| 667 | Craig Shipley | .01 | .05 |
| 668 | Warren Newson | .01 | .05 |
| 669 | Mickey Morandini | .01 | .05 |
| 670 | Brook Jacoby | .01 | .05 |
| 671 | Ryan Bowen | .01 | .05 |
| 672 | Bill Krueger | .01 | .05 |
| 673 | Rob Mallicoat | .01 | .05 |
| 674 | Doug Jones | .01 | .05 |
| 675 | Scott Livingstone | .01 | .05 |
| 676 | Danny Tartabull | .02 | .10 |
| 677 | Joe Carter HL | .05 | .15 |
| 678 | Cecil Espy | .01 | .05 |
| 679 | Randy Velarde | .01 | .05 |
| 680 | Bruce Ruffin | .01 | .05 |
| 681 | Ted Wood | .01 | .05 |
| 682 | Dan Plesac | .01 | .05 |
| 683 | Eric Bullock | .01 | .05 |
| 684 | Junior Ortiz | .01 | .05 |
| 685 | Dave Hollins | .02 | .10 |
| 686 | Dennis Martinez | .02 | .10 |
| 687 | Larry Andersen | .01 | .05 |
| 688 | Doug Simons | .01 | .05 |
| 689 | Tim Spehr | .01 | .05 |
| 690 | Calvin Jones | .01 | .05 |
| 691 | Mark Guthrie | .01 | .05 |
| 692 | Alfredo Griffin | .01 | .05 |
| 693 | Joe Carter | .02 | .10 |
| 694 | Terry Mathews | .01 | .05 |
| 695 | Pascual Perez | .01 | .05 |
| 696 | Gene Nelson | .01 | .05 |
| 697 | Gerald Williams | .01 | .05 |
| 698 | Chris Cron | .01 | .05 |
| 699 | Steve Buechele | .01 | .05 |
| 700 | Paul McClellan | .01 | .05 |
| 701 | Jim Lindeman | .01 | .05 |

| | | |
|---|---|---|
| 702 Francisco Oliveras | .01 | .05 |
| 703 Rob Maurer | .01 | .05 |
| 704 Pat Hentgen | .01 | .05 |
| 705 Jaime Navarro | .01 | .05 |
| 706 Mike Magnante RC | .02 | .10 |
| 707 Nolan Ryan | .40 | 1.00 |
| 708 Bobby Thigpen | .01 | .05 |
| 709 John Cerutti | .01 | .05 |
| 710 Steve Wilson | .01 | .05 |
| 711 Hensley Meulens | .01 | .05 |
| 712 Rheal Cormier | .01 | .05 |
| 713 Scott Bradley | .01 | .05 |
| 714 Mitch Webster | .01 | .05 |
| 715 Roger Mason | .01 | .05 |
| 716 Checklist 636-716 | .01 | .05 |
| 717 Jeff Fassero | .01 | .05 |
| 718 Cal Eldred | .01 | .05 |
| 719 Sid Fernandez | .01 | .05 |
| 720 Bob Zupcic RC | .02 | .10 |
| 721 Jose Offerman | .01 | .05 |
| 722 Cliff Brantley | .01 | .05 |
| 723 Ron Darling | .01 | .05 |
| 724 Dave Stieb | .01 | .05 |
| 725 Hector Villanueva | .01 | .05 |
| 726 Mike Hartley | .01 | .05 |
| 727 Arthur Rhodes | .01 | .05 |
| 728 Randy Bush | .01 | .05 |
| 729 Steve Sax | .01 | .05 |
| 730 Dave Otto | .01 | .05 |
| 731 John Wehner | .01 | .05 |
| 732 Dave Martinez | .01 | .05 |
| 733 Ruben Amaro | .01 | .05 |
| 734 Billy Ripken | .01 | .05 |
| 735 Steve Farr | .01 | .05 |
| 736 Shawn Abner | .01 | .05 |
| 737 Gil Heredia RC | .08 | .25 |
| 738 Ron Jones | .01 | .05 |
| 739 Tony Castillo | .01 | .05 |
| 740 Sammy Sosa | .08 | .25 |
| 741 Julio Franco | .02 | .10 |
| 742 Tim Naehring | .01 | .05 |
| 743 Steve Wapnick | .01 | .05 |
| 744 Craig Wilson | .01 | .05 |
| 745 Darrin Chapin | .01 | .05 |
| 746 Chris George | .01 | .05 |
| 747 Mike Simms | .01 | .05 |
| 748 Rosario Rodriguez | .01 | .05 |
| 749 Skeeter Barnes | .01 | .05 |
| 750 Roger McDowell | .01 | .05 |
| 751 Dann Howitt | .01 | .05 |
| 752 Paul Sorrento | .01 | .05 |
| 753 Braulio Castillo | .01 | .05 |
| 754 Yorkis Perez | .01 | .05 |
| 755 Willie Fraser | .01 | .05 |
| 756 Jeremy Hernandez RC | .02 | .10 |
| 757 Curt Schilling | .05 | .15 |
| 758 Steve Lyons | .01 | .05 |
| 759 Dave Anderson | .01 | .05 |
| 760 Willie Banks | .01 | .05 |
| 761 Mark Leonard | .01 | .05 |
| 762 Jack Armstrong (Listed on Indiana& but shown on | .01 | .05 |
| 763 Scott Servais | .01 | .05 |
| 764 Ray Stephens | .01 | .05 |
| 765 Junior Noboa | .01 | .05 |
| 766 Jim Olander | .01 | .05 |
| 767 Joe Magrane | .01 | .05 |
| 768 Lance Blankenship | .01 | .05 |
| 769 Mike Humphreys | .01 | .05 |
| 770 Jarvis Brown | .01 | .05 |
| 771 Damon Berryhill | .01 | .05 |
| 772 Alejandro Pena | .01 | .05 |
| 773 Jose Mesa | .01 | .05 |
| 774 Gary Cooper | .01 | .05 |
| 775 Carney Lansford | .02 | .10 |
| 776 Mike Bielecki (Shown on Cubs& but listed on Brav | .01 | .05 |
| 777 Charlie O'Brien | .01 | .05 |
| 778 Carlos Hernandez | .01 | .05 |
| 779 Howard Farmer | .01 | .05 |
| 780 Mike Stanton | .01 | .05 |
| 781 Reggie Harris | .01 | .05 |
| 782 Xavier Hernandez | .01 | .05 |
| 783 Bryan Hickerson RC | .02 | .10 |
| 784 Checklist 717-784 and BC1-BC8 | .01 | .05 |

**1993 Donruss**

| | | |
|---|---|---|
| COMPLETE SET (792) | 12.00 | 30.00 |
| COMPLETE SERIES 1 (396) | 6.00 | 15.00 |
| COMPLETE SERIES 2 (396) | 6.00 | 15.00 |
| 1 Craig Lefferts | .02 | .10 |
| 2 Kent Mercker | .02 | .10 |
| 3 Phil Plantier | .02 | .10 |
| 4 Alex Arias | .02 | .10 |
| 5 Julio Valera | .02 | .10 |
| 6 Dan Wilson | .07 | .20 |
| 7 Frank Thomas | .20 | .50 |
| 8 Eric Anthony | .02 | .10 |
| 9 Derek Lilliquist | .02 | .10 |
| 10 Rafael Baumigal | .02 | .10 |
| 11 Manny Alexander | .02 | .10 |
| 12 Bret Barberie | .02 | .10 |
| 13 Mickey Tettleton | .02 | .10 |
| 14 Anthony Young | .02 | .10 |
| 15 Tim Spehr | .02 | .10 |
| 16 Bob Ayrault | .02 | .10 |
| 17 Bill Wegman | .02 | .10 |
| 18 Jay Bell | .07 | .20 |
| 19 Rick Aguilera | .02 | .10 |
| 20 Todd Zeile | .02 | .10 |
| 21 Steve Farr | .02 | .10 |
| 22 Andy Benes | .02 | .10 |
| 23 Lance Blankenship | .02 | .10 |
| 24 Ted Wood | .02 | .10 |
| 25 Omar Vizquel | .10 | .30 |
| 26 Steve Avery | .02 | .10 |
| 27 Brian Bohanon | .02 | .10 |
| 28 Rick Wilkins | .02 | .10 |
| 29 Devon White | .07 | .20 |
| 30 Bobby Ayala RC | .02 | .10 |
| 31 Leo Gomez | .02 | .10 |
| 32 Mike Simms | .02 | .10 |
| 33 Ellis Burks | .07 | .20 |
| 34 Steve Wilson | .02 | .10 |
| 35 Jim Abbott | .10 | .30 |
| 36 Tim Wallach | .02 | .10 |
| 37 Wilson Alvarez | .02 | .10 |
| 38 Daryl Boston | .02 | .10 |
| 39 Sandy Alomar Jr. | .02 | .10 |
| 40 Mitch Williams | .02 | .10 |
| 41 Rico Brogna | .02 | .10 |
| 42 Gary Varsho | .02 | .10 |
| 43 Kevin Appier | .07 | .20 |
| 44 Eric Wedge RC | .07 | .20 |
| 45 Dante Bichette | .07 | .20 |
| 46 Jose Oquendo | .02 | .10 |
| 47 Mike Trombley | .02 | .10 |
| 48 Dan Walters | .02 | .10 |
| 49 Gerald Williams | .07 | .20 |
| 50 Bud Black | .02 | .10 |
| 51 Bobby Witt | .02 | .10 |
| 52 Mark Davis | .02 | .10 |
| 53 Shawn Barton RC | .02 | .10 |
| 54 Paul Assenmacher | .02 | .10 |
| 55 Kevin Reimer | .02 | .10 |
| 56 Billy Ashley | .02 | .10 |
| 57 Chris Sabo | .02 | .10 |
| 58 Billy Ripken | .02 | .10 |
| 59 Scooter Tucker | .02 | .10 |
| 60 ... | | |
| 61 Tim Wakefield | .20 | .50 |
| 62 Mitch Webster | .02 | .10 |
| 63 Jack Clark | .07 | .20 |
| 64 Mark Gardner | .02 | .10 |
| 65 Lee Stevens | .02 | .10 |
| 66 Todd Hundley | .02 | .10 |
| 67 Bobby Thigpen | .02 | .10 |
| 68 Dave Hollins | .07 | .20 |
| 69 Jack Armstrong | .02 | .10 |

| | | |
|---|---|---|
| 70 Alex Cole | .02 | .10 |
| 71 Mark Carreon | .02 | .10 |
| 72 Todd Worrell | .02 | .10 |
| 73 Steve Shifflett | .02 | .10 |
| 74 Jerald Clark | .02 | .10 |
| 75 Paul Molitor | .07 | .20 |
| 76 Larry Carter RC | .02 | .10 |
| 77 Rich Rowland | .02 | .10 |
| 78 Damon Berryhill | .02 | .10 |
| 79 Willie Banks | .02 | .10 |
| 80 Hector Villanueva | .02 | .10 |
| 81 Mike Gallego | .02 | .10 |
| 82 Tim Belcher | .02 | .10 |
| 83 Mike Bordick | .02 | .10 |
| 84 Craig Biggio | .10 | .30 |
| 85 Lance Parrish | .07 | .20 |
| 86 Brett Butler | .07 | .20 |
| 87 Mike Timlin | .02 | .10 |
| 88 Brian Barnes | .02 | .10 |
| 89 Brady Anderson | .07 | .20 |
| 90 D.J. Dozier | .02 | .10 |
| 91 Frank Viola | .07 | .20 |
| 92 Darren Daulton | .07 | .20 |
| 93 Chad Curtis | .07 | .20 |
| 94 Zane Smith | .02 | .10 |
| 95 George Bell | .02 | .10 |
| 96 Rex Hudler | .02 | .10 |
| 97 Mark Whiten | .02 | .10 |
| 98 Tim Teufel | .02 | .10 |
| 99 Kevin Ritz | .02 | .10 |
| 100 Jeff Brantley | .02 | .10 |
| 101 Jeff Conine | .07 | .20 |
| 102 Vinny Castilla | .20 | .50 |
| 103 Greg Vaughn | .02 | .10 |
| 104 Steve Buechele | .02 | .10 |
| 105 Darren Reed | .02 | .10 |
| 106 Bip Roberts | .02 | .10 |
| 107 John Habyan | .02 | .10 |
| 108 Scott Servais | .02 | .10 |
| 109 Walt Weiss | .02 | .10 |
| 110 J.T.Snow RC | .10 | .30 |
| 111 Jay Buhner | .07 | .20 |
| 112 Darryl Strawberry | .07 | .20 |
| 113 Roger Pavlik | .07 | .20 |
| 114 Chris Nabholz | .02 | .10 |
| 115 Pat Borders | .02 | .10 |
| 116 Pat Howell | .02 | .10 |
| 117 Gregg Olson | .02 | .10 |
| 118 Curt Schilling | .07 | .20 |
| 119 Roger Clemens | .40 | 1.00 |
| 120 Victor Cole | .02 | .10 |
| 121 Gary DiSarcina | .02 | .10 |
| 122 Checklist 1-80 Gary Carter and Kirt Manwaring | .02 | .10 |
| 123 Steve Sax | .02 | .10 |
| 124 Chuck Carr | .02 | .10 |
| 125 Mark Lewis | .02 | .10 |
| 126 Tony Gwynn | .25 | .60 |
| 127 Travis Fryman | .07 | .20 |
| 128 Dave Burba | .02 | .10 |
| 129 Wally Joyner | .07 | .20 |
| 130 John Smoltz | .10 | .30 |
| 131 Cal Eldred | .02 | .10 |
| 132 Checklist 81-159 (Roberto Alomar and Devon White) | .07 | .20 |
| 133 Arthur Rhodes | .02 | .10 |
| 134 Jeff Blauser | .02 | .10 |
| 135 Scott Cooper | .02 | .10 |
| 136 Doug Strange | .02 | .10 |
| 137 Luis Sojo | .02 | .10 |
| 138 Jeff Branson | .02 | .10 |
| 139 Alex Fernandez | .07 | .20 |
| 140 Ken Caminiti | .07 | .20 |
| 141 Charles Nagy | .02 | .10 |
| 142 Tom Candiotti | .02 | .10 |
| 143 Willie Greene | .02 | .10 |
| 144 John Vander Wal | .02 | .10 |
| 145 Kurt Knudsen | .02 | .10 |
| 146 John Franco | .07 | .20 |
| 147 Eddie Pierce RC | .02 | .10 |
| 148 Kim Batiste | .02 | .10 |
| 149 Darren Holmes | .02 | .10 |
| 150 Steve Cooke | .02 | .10 |
| 151 Terry Jorgensen | .02 | .10 |
| 152 Mark Clark | .02 | .10 |
| 153 Randy Velarde | .02 | .10 |

|  |  | | |
|---|---|---|---|
| 154 | Greg W. Harris | .02 | .10 |
| 155 | Kevin Campbell | .02 | .10 |
| 156 | John Burkett | .02 | .10 |
| 157 | Kevin Mitchell | .02 | .10 |
| 158 | Deion Sanders | .10 | .30 |
| 159 | Jose Canseco | .10 | .30 |
| 160 | Jeff Hartsock | .02 | .10 |
| 161 | Tom Quinlan RC | .02 | .10 |
| 162 | Tim Pugh RC | .02 | .10 |
| 163 | Glenn Davis | .02 | .10 |
| 164 | Shane Reynolds | .02 | .10 |
| 165 | Jody Reed | .02 | .10 |
| 166 | Mike Sharperson | .02 | .10 |
| 167 | Scott Lewis | .02 | .10 |
| 168 | Dennis Martinez | .07 | .20 |
| 169 | Scott Radinsky | .02 | .10 |
| 170 | Dave Gallagher | .02 | .10 |
| 171 | Jim Thome | .10 | .30 |
| 172 | Terry Mulholland | .02 | .10 |
| 173 | Milt Cuyler | .02 | .10 |
| 174 | Bob Patterson | .02 | .10 |
| 175 | Jeff Montgomery | .02 | .10 |
| 176 | Tim Salmon | .10 | .30 |
| 177 | Franklin Stubbs | .02 | .10 |
| 178 | Donovan Osborne | .02 | .10 |
| 179 | Jeff Reboulet | .02 | .10 |
| 180 | Jeremy Hernandez | .02 | .10 |
| 181 | Charlie Hayes | .02 | .10 |
| 182 | Matt Williams | .07 | .20 |
| 183 | Mike Raczka | .02 | .10 |
| 184 | Francisco Cabrera | .02 | .10 |
| 185 | Rich DeLucia | .02 | .10 |
| 186 | Sammy Sosa | .20 | .50 |
| 187 | Ivan Rodriguez | .10 | .30 |
| 188 | Bret Boone | .07 | .20 |
| 189 | Juan Guzman | .02 | .10 |
| 190 | Tom Browning | .02 | .10 |
| 191 | Randy Milligan | .02 | .10 |
| 192 | Steve Finley | .07 | .20 |
| 193 | John Patterson RR | .02 | .10 |
| 194 | Kip Gross | .02 | .10 |
| 195 | Tony Fossas | .02 | .10 |
| 196 | Ivan Calderon | .02 | .10 |
| 197 | Junior Felix | .02 | .10 |
| 198 | Pete Schourek | .02 | .10 |
| 199 | Craig Grebeck | .02 | .10 |
| 200 | Juan Bell | .02 | .10 |
| 201 | Glenallen Hill | .02 | .10 |
| 202 | Danny Jackson | .02 | .10 |
| 203 | John Kiely | .02 | .10 |
| 204 | Bob Tewksbury | .02 | .10 |
| 205 | Kevin Kosiolski | .02 | .10 |
| 206 | Craig Shipley | .02 | .10 |
| 207 | John Jaha | .02 | .10 |
| 208 | Royce Clayton | .02 | .10 |
| 209 | Mike Piazza | 1.25 | 3.00 |
| 210 | Ron Gant | .07 | .20 |
| 211 | Scott Erickson | .02 | .10 |
| 212 | Doug Dascenzo | .02 | .10 |
| 213 | Andy Stankiewicz | .02 | .10 |
| 214 | Geronimo Berroa | .02 | .10 |
| 215 | Dennis Eckersley | .07 | .20 |
| 216 | Al Osuna | .02 | .10 |
| 217 | Tino Martinez | .10 | .30 |
| 218 | Henry Rodriguez | .02 | .10 |
| 219 | Ed Sprague | .02 | .10 |
| 220 | Ken Hill | .02 | .10 |
| 221 | Chito Martinez | .02 | .10 |
| 222 | Bret Saberhagen | .07 | .20 |
| 223 | Mike Greenwell | .02 | .10 |
| 224 | Mickey Morandini | .02 | .10 |
| 225 | Chuck Finley | .02 | .10 |
| 226 | Denny Neagle | .07 | .20 |
| 227 | Kirk McCaskill | .02 | .10 |
| 228 | Rheal Cormier | .02 | .10 |
| 229 | Paul Sorrento | .02 | .10 |
| 230 | Darrin Jackson | .02 | .10 |
| 231 | Rob Deer | .02 | .10 |
| 232 | Bill Swift | .02 | .10 |
| 233 | Kevin McReynolds | .02 | .10 |
| 234 | Terry Pendleton | .07 | .20 |
| 235 | Dave Nilsson | .02 | .10 |
| 236 | Chuck McElroy | .02 | .10 |
| 237 | Derek Parks | .02 | .10 |
| 238 | Norm Charlton | .02 | .10 |
| 239 | Matt Nokes | .02 | .10 |
| 240 | Juan Guerrero | .02 | .10 |
| 241 | Jeff Parrett | .02 | .10 |
| 242 | Ryan Thompson | .02 | .10 |
| 243 | Dave Fleming | .02 | .10 |
| 244 | Dave Hansen | .02 | .10 |
| 245 | Monty Fariss | .02 | .10 |
| 246 | Archi Cianfrocco | .02 | .10 |
| 247 | Pat Hentgen | .02 | .10 |
| 248 | Bill Pecota | .02 | .10 |
| 249 | Ben McDonald | .02 | .10 |
| 250 | Cliff Brantley | .02 | .10 |
| 251 | John Valentin | .02 | .10 |
| 252 | Jeff King | .02 | .10 |
| 253 | Reggie Williams | .02 | .10 |
| 254 | Checklist 160-238 | .02 | .10 |
| 255 | Ozzie Guillen | .07 | .20 |
| 256 | Mike Perez | .02 | .10 |
| 257 | Thomas Howard | .02 | .10 |
| 258 | Kurt Stillwell | .02 | .10 |
| 259 | Mike Henneman | .02 | .10 |
| 260 | Steve Decker | .02 | .10 |
| 261 | Brent Mayne | .02 | .10 |
| 262 | Otis Nixon | .02 | .10 |
| 263 | Mark Kiefer | .02 | .10 |
| 264 | Checklist 239-317 (Don Mattingly and Mike Bordic) | .10 | .30 |
| 265 | Richie Lewis RC | .02 | .10 |
| 266 | Pat Gomez RC | .02 | .10 |
| 267 | Scott Taylor | .02 | .10 |
| 268 | Shawon Dunston | .02 | .10 |
| 269 | Greg Myers | .02 | .10 |
| 270 | Tim Costo | .02 | .10 |
| 271 | Greg Hibbard | .02 | .10 |
| 272 | Pete Harnisch | .02 | .10 |
| 273 | Dave Mlicki | .02 | .10 |
| 274 | Orel Hershiser | .07 | .20 |
| 275 | Sean Berry RR | .02 | .10 |
| 276 | Doug Simons | .02 | .10 |
| 277 | John Doherty | .02 | .10 |
| 278 | Eddie Murray | .20 | .50 |
| 279 | Chris Haney | .02 | .10 |
| 280 | Stan Javier | .02 | .10 |
| 281 | Jaime Navarro | .02 | .10 |
| 282 | Orlando Merced | .02 | .10 |
| 283 | Kent Hrbek | .07 | .20 |
| 284 | Bernard Gilkey | .02 | .10 |
| 285 | Russ Springer | .02 | .10 |
| 286 | Mike Maddux | .02 | .10 |
| 287 | Eric Fox | .02 | .10 |
| 288 | Mark Leonard | .02 | .10 |
| 289 | Tim Leary | .02 | .10 |
| 290 | Brian Hunter | .02 | .10 |
| 291 | Donald Harris | .02 | .10 |
| 292 | Bob Scanlan | .02 | .10 |
| 293 | Turner Ward | .02 | .10 |
| 294 | Hal Morris | .02 | .10 |
| 295 | Jimmy Poole | .02 | .10 |
| 296 | Doug Jones | .02 | .10 |
| 297 | Tony Pena | .02 | .10 |
| 298 | Ramon Martinez | .02 | .10 |
| 299 | Tim Fortugno | .02 | .10 |
| 300 | Marquis Grissom | .07 | .20 |
| 301 | Lance Johnson | .02 | .10 |
| 302 | Jeff Kent | .20 | .50 |
| 303 | Reggie Jefferson | .02 | .10 |
| 304 | Wes Chamberlain | .02 | .10 |
| 305 | Shawn Hare | .02 | .10 |
| 306 | Mike LaValliere | .02 | .10 |
| 307 | Gregg Jefferies | .07 | .20 |
| 308 | Troy Neel | .02 | .10 |
| 309 | Pat Listach | .02 | .10 |
| 310 | Geronimo Pena | .02 | .10 |
| 311 | Pedro Munoz | .02 | .10 |
| 312 | Guillermo Velasquez | .02 | .10 |
| 313 | Roberto Kelly | .02 | .10 |
| 314 | Mike Jackson | .02 | .10 |
| 315 | Rickey Henderson | .20 | .50 |
| 316 | Mark Lemke | .02 | .10 |
| 317 | Erik Hanson | .02 | .10 |
| 318 | Derrick May | .02 | .10 |
| 319 | Geno Petralli | .02 | .10 |
| 320 | Melvin Nieves | .02 | .10 |
| 321 | Doug Linton | .02 | .10 |
| 322 | Rob Dibble | .07 | .20 |
| 323 | Chris Hoiles | .02 | .10 |
| 324 | Jimmy Jones | .02 | .10 |
| 325 | Dave Staton | .02 | .10 |
| 326 | Pedro Martinez | .40 | 1.00 |
| 327 | Paul Quantrill | .02 | .10 |
| 328 | Greg Colbrunn | .02 | .10 |
| 329 | Hilly Hathaway RC | .02 | .10 |
| 330 | Jeff Innis | .02 | .10 |
| 331 | Ron Karkovice | .02 | .10 |
| 332 | Keith Shepherd RC | .02 | .10 |
| 333 | Alan Embree | .02 | .10 |
| 334 | Paul Wagner | .02 | .10 |
| 335 | Dave Haas | .02 | .10 |
| 336 | Ozzie Canseco | .02 | .10 |
| 337 | Bill Sampen | .02 | .10 |
| 338 | Rich Rodriguez | .02 | .10 |
| 339 | Dean Palmer | .07 | .20 |
| 340 | Greg Litton | .02 | .10 |
| 341 | Jim Tatum RC | .02 | .10 |
| 342 | Todd Haney RC | .02 | .10 |
| 343 | Larry Casian | .02 | .10 |
| 344 | Ryne Sandberg | .30 | .75 |
| 345 | Sterling Hitchcock RC | .07 | .20 |
| 346 | Chris Hammond | .02 | .10 |
| 347 | Vince Horsman | .02 | .10 |
| 348 | Butch Henry | .02 | .10 |
| 349 | Dann Howitt | .02 | .10 |
| 350 | Roger McDowell | .02 | .10 |
| 351 | Jack Morris | .07 | .20 |
| 352 | Bill Krueger | .02 | .10 |
| 353 | Cris Colon | .02 | .10 |
| 354 | Joe Vitko | .02 | .10 |
| 355 | Willie McGee | .07 | .20 |
| 356 | Jay Baller | .02 | .10 |
| 357 | Pat Mahomes | .02 | .10 |
| 358 | Roger Mason | .02 | .10 |
| 359 | Jerry Nielsen | .02 | .10 |
| 360 | Tom Pagnozzi | .02 | .10 |
| 361 | Kevin Baez | .02 | .10 |
| 362 | Tim Scott | .02 | .10 |
| 363 | Domingo Martinez RC | .02 | .10 |
| 364 | Kirt Manwaring | .02 | .10 |
| 365 | Rafael Palmeiro | .10 | .20 |
| 366 | Ray Lankford | .07 | .20 |
| 367 | Tim McIntosh | .02 | .10 |
| 368 | Jessie Hollins | .02 | .10 |
| 369 | Scott Leius | .02 | .10 |
| 370 | Bill Doran | .02 | .10 |
| 371 | Sam Militello | .02 | .10 |
| 372 | Ryan Bowen | .02 | .10 |
| 373 | Dave Henderson | .02 | .10 |
| 374 | Dan Smith | .02 | .10 |
| 375 | Steve Reed RC | .02 | .10 |
| 376 | Jose Offerman | .02 | .10 |
| 377 | Kevin Brown | .02 | .10 |
| 378 | Darrin Fletcher | .02 | .10 |
| 379 | Duane Ward | .02 | .10 |
| 380 | Wayne Kirby | .02 | .10 |
| 381 | Steve Scarsone | .02 | .10 |
| 382 | Mariano Duncan | .02 | .10 |
| 383 | Ken Ryan RC | .02 | .10 |
| 384 | Lloyd McClendon | .02 | .10 |
| 385 | Brian Holman | .02 | .10 |
| 386 | Braulio Castillo | .02 | .10 |
| 387 | Danny Leon | .02 | .10 |
| 388 | Omar Olivares | .02 | .10 |
| 389 | Kevin Wickander | .02 | .10 |
| 390 | Fred McGriff | .10 | .30 |
| 391 | Phil Clark | .02 | .10 |
| 392 | Darren Lewis | .02 | .10 |
| 393 | Phil Hiatt | .02 | .10 |
| 394 | Mike Morgan | .02 | .10 |
| 395 | Shane Mack | .02 | .10 |
| 396 | Checklist 318-396 (Dennis Eckersley and Art Kusn) | .07 | .20 |
| 397 | David Segui | .02 | .10 |
| 398 | Rafael Belliard | .02 | .10 |
| 399 | Tim Naehring | .02 | .10 |
| 400 | Frank Castillo | .02 | .10 |
| 401 | Joe Grahe | .02 | .10 |
| 402 | Reggie Sanders | .07 | .20 |
| 403 | Roberto Hernandez | .02 | .10 |
| 404 | Luis Gonzalez | .02 | .10 |
| 405 | Carlos Baerga | .02 | .10 |
| 406 | Carlos Hernandez | .02 | .10 |
| 407 | Pedro Astacio | .02 | .10 |
| 408 | Mel Rojas | .02 | .10 |
| 409 | Scott Livingstone | .02 | .10 |
| 410 | Chico Walker | .02 | .10 |
| 411 | Brian McRae | .02 | .10 |
| 412 | Ben Rivera | .02 | .10 |
| 413 | Ricky Bones | .02 | .10 |

|  |  | | |
|---|---|---|---|
| 414 | Andy Van Slyke | .10 | .30 |
| 415 | Chuck Knoblauch | .07 | .20 |
| 416 | Luis Alicea | .02 | .10 |
| 417 | Bob Wickman | .02 | .10 |
| 418 | Doug Brocail | .02 | .10 |
| 419 | Scott Brosius | .07 | .20 |
| 420 | Rod Beck | .02 | .10 |
| 421 | Edgar Martinez | .10 | .30 |
| 422 | Ryan Klesko | .07 | .20 |
| 423 | Nolan Ryan | .75 | 2.00 |
| 424 | Rey Sanchez | .02 | .10 |
| 425 | Roberto Alomar | .10 | .30 |
| 426 | Barry Larkin | .10 | .30 |
| 427 | Mike Mussina | .10 | .30 |
| 428 | Jeff Bagwell | .10 | .30 |
| 429 | Mo Vaughn | .07 | .20 |
| 430 | Eric Karros | .07 | .20 |
| 431 | John Orton | .02 | .10 |
| 432 | Wil Cordero | .02 | .10 |
| 433 | Jack McDowell | .02 | .10 |
| 434 | Howard Johnson | .02 | .10 |
| 435 | Albert Belle | .07 | .20 |
| 436 | John Kruk | .07 | .20 |
| 437 | Skeeter Barnes | .02 | .10 |
| 438 | Don Slaught | .02 | .10 |
| 439 | Rusty Meacham | .02 | .10 |
| 440 | Tim Laker RC | .02 | .10 |
| 441 | Robin Yount | .30 | .75 |
| 442 | Brian Jordan | .07 | .20 |
| 443 | Kevin Tapani | .02 | .10 |
| 444 | Gary Sheffield | .07 | .20 |
| 445 | Rich Monteleone | .02 | .10 |
| 446 | Will Clark | .10 | .30 |
| 447 | Jerry Browne | .02 | .10 |
| 448 | Jeff Treadway | .02 | .10 |
| 449 | Mike Schooler | .02 | .10 |
| 450 | Mike Harkey | .02 | .10 |
| 451 | Julio Franco | .07 | .20 |
| 452 | Kevin Young | .07 | .20 |
| 453 | Kelly Gruber | .02 | .10 |
| 454 | Jose Rijo | .02 | .10 |
| 455 | Mike Devereaux | .02 | .10 |
| 456 | Andujar Cedeno | .02 | .10 |
| 457 | Damion Easley RR | .02 | .10 |
| 458 | Kevin Gross | .02 | .10 |
| 459 | Matt Young | .02 | .10 |
| 460 | Matt Stairs | .02 | .10 |
| 461 | Luis Polonia | .02 | .10 |
| 462 | Dwight Gooden | .07 | .20 |
| 463 | Warren Newson | .02 | .10 |
| 464 | Jose DeLeon | .02 | .10 |
| 465 | Jose Mesa | .02 | .10 |
| 466 | Danny Cox | .02 | .10 |
| 467 | Dan Gladden | .02 | .10 |
| 468 | Gerald Perry | .02 | .10 |
| 469 | Mike Boddicker | .02 | .10 |
| 470 | Jeff Gardner | .02 | .10 |
| 471 | Doug Henry | .02 | .10 |
| 472 | Mike Benjamin | .02 | .10 |
| 473 | Dan Peltier | .02 | .10 |
| 474 | Mike Stanton | .02 | .10 |
| 475 | John Smiley | .02 | .10 |
| 476 | Dwight Smith | .02 | .10 |
| 477 | Jim Leyritz | .02 | .10 |
| 478 | Dwayne Henry | .02 | .10 |
| 479 | Mark McGwire | .50 | 1.25 |
| 480 | Pete Incaviglia | .02 | .10 |
| 481 | Dave Cochrane | .02 | .10 |
| 482 | Eric Davis | .07 | .20 |
| 483 | John Olerud | .07 | .20 |
| 484 | Kent Bottenfield | .07 | .20 |
| 485 | Mark McLemore | .02 | .10 |
| 486 | Dave Magadan | .02 | .10 |
| 487 | John Marzano | .02 | .10 |
| 488 | Ruben Amaro | .02 | .10 |
| 489 | Rob Ducey | .02 | .10 |
| 490 | Stan Belinda | .02 | .10 |
| 491 | Dan Pasqua | .02 | .10 |
| 492 | Joe Magrane | .02 | .10 |
| 493 | Brook Jacoby | .02 | .10 |
| 494 | Gene Harris | .02 | .10 |
| 495 | Mark Leiter | .02 | .10 |
| 496 | Bryan Hickerson | .02 | .10 |
| 497 | Tom Gordon | .02 | .10 |
| 498 | Pete Smith | .02 | .10 |
| 499 | Chris Bosio | .02 | .10 |
| 500 | Shawn Boskie | .02 | .10 |
| 501 | Dave West | .02 | .10 |
| 502 | Milt Hill | .02 | .10 |
| 503 | Pat Kelly | .02 | .10 |
| 504 | Joe Boever | .02 | .10 |
| 505 | Terry Steinbach | .02 | .10 |
| 506 | Butch Huskey | .02 | .10 |
| 507 | David Valle | .02 | .10 |
| 508 | Mike Scioscia | .02 | .10 |
| 509 | Kenny Rogers | .07 | .20 |
| 510 | Moises Alou | .07 | .20 |
| 511 | David Wells | .07 | .20 |
| 512 | Mackey Sasser | .02 | .10 |
| 513 | Todd Frohwirth | .02 | .10 |
| 514 | Ricky Jordan | .02 | .10 |
| 515 | Mike Gardiner | .02 | .10 |
| 516 | Gary Redus | .02 | .10 |
| 517 | Gary Gaetti | .07 | .20 |
| 518 | Checklist | .02 | .10 |
| 519 | Carlton Fisk | .10 | .30 |
| 520 | Ozzie Smith | .30 | .75 |
| 521 | Rod Nichols | .02 | .10 |
| 522 | Benito Santiago | .07 | .20 |
| 523 | Bill Gullickson | .02 | .10 |
| 524 | Robby Thompson | .02 | .10 |
| 525 | Mike Macfarlane | .02 | .10 |
| 526 | Sid Bream | .02 | .10 |
| 527 | Darryl Hamilton | .02 | .10 |
| 528 | Checklist | .02 | .10 |
| 529 | Jeff Tackett | .02 | .10 |
| 530 | Greg Olson | .02 | .10 |
| 531 | Bob Zupcic | .02 | .10 |
| 532 | Mark Grace | .10 | .30 |
| 533 | Steve Frey | .02 | .10 |
| 534 | Dave Martinez | .02 | .10 |
| 535 | Robin Ventura | .07 | .20 |
| 536 | Casey Candaele | .02 | .10 |
| 537 | Kenny Lofton | .07 | .20 |
| 538 | Jay Howell | .02 | .10 |
| 539 | Fernando Ramsey RC | .07 | .20 |
| 540 | Larry Walker | .07 | .20 |
| 541 | Cecil Fielder | .07 | .20 |
| 542 | Lee Guetterman | .02 | .10 |
| 543 | Keith Miller | .02 | .10 |
| 544 | Len Dykstra | .07 | .20 |
| 545 | B.J. Surhoff | .02 | .10 |
| 546 | Bob Walk | .02 | .10 |
| 547 | Brian Harper | .02 | .10 |
| 548 | Lee Smith | .07 | .20 |
| 549 | Danny Tartabull | .07 | .20 |
| 550 | Frank Seminara | .02 | .10 |
| 551 | Henry Mercedes | .02 | .10 |
| 552 | Dave Righetti | .02 | .10 |
| 553 | Ken Griffey Jr. | .30 | .75 |
| 554 | Tom Glavine | .10 | .30 |
| 555 | Juan Gonzalez | .07 | .20 |
| 556 | Jim Bullinger | .02 | .10 |
| 557 | Derek Bell | .02 | .10 |
| 558 | Cesar Hernandez | .02 | .10 |
| 559 | Cal Ripken | .60 | 1.50 |
| 560 | Eddie Taubensee | .02 | .10 |
| 561 | John Flaherty | .02 | .10 |
| 562 | Todd Benzinger | .02 | .10 |
| 563 | Hubie Brooks | .02 | .10 |
| 564 | Delino DeShields | .02 | .10 |
| 565 | Tim Raines | .07 | .20 |
| 566 | Sid Fernandez | .02 | .10 |
| 567 | Steve Olin | .02 | .10 |
| 568 | Tommy Greene | .02 | .10 |
| 569 | Buddy Groom | .02 | .10 |
| 570 | Randy Tomlin | .02 | .10 |
| 571 | Hipolito Pichardo | .02 | .10 |
| 572 | Rene Arocha RC | .07 | .20 |
| 573 | Mike Fetters | .02 | .10 |
| 574 | Felix Jose | .02 | .10 |
| 575 | Gene Larkin | .02 | .10 |
| 576 | Bruce Hurst | .02 | .10 |
| 577 | Bernie Williams | .10 | .30 |
| 578 | Trevor Wilson | .02 | .10 |
| 579 | Bob Welch | .02 | .10 |
| 580 | David Justice | .07 | .20 |
| 581 | Randy Johnson | .20 | .50 |
| 582 | Jose Vizcaino | .02 | .10 |
| 583 | Jeff Huson | .02 | .10 |
| 584 | Rob Maurer | .02 | .10 |
| 585 | Todd Stottlemyre | .02 | .10 |
| 586 | Joe Oliver | .02 | .10 |
| 587 | Bob Milacki | .02 | .10 |
| 588 | Rob Murphy | .02 | .10 |
| 589 | Greg Pirkl | .02 | .10 |
| 590 | Lenny Harris | .02 | .10 |
| 591 | Luis Rivera | .02 | .10 |
| 592 | John Wetteland | .07 | .20 |
| 593 | Mark Langston | .02 | .10 |
| 594 | Bobby Bonilla | .07 | .20 |
| 595 | Esteban Beltre | .02 | .10 |
| 596 | Mike Hartley | .02 | .10 |
| 597 | Felix Fermin | .02 | .10 |
| 598 | Carlos Garcia | .02 | .10 |
| 599 | Frank Tanana | .02 | .10 |
| 600 | Pedro Guerrero | .07 | .20 |
| 601 | Terry Shumpert | .02 | .10 |
| 602 | Wally Whitehurst | .02 | .10 |
| 603 | Kevin Seitzer | .02 | .10 |
| 604 | Chris James | .02 | .10 |
| 605 | Greg Gohr | .02 | .10 |
| 606 | Mark Wohlers | .02 | .10 |
| 607 | Kirby Puckett | .30 | .75 |
| 608 | Greg Maddux | .30 | .75 |
| 609 | Don Mattingly | .50 | 1.25 |
| 610 | Greg Cadaret | .02 | .10 |
| 611 | Dave Stewart | .07 | .20 |
| 612 | Mark Portugal | .02 | .10 |
| 613 | Pete O'Brien | .02 | .10 |
| 614 | Bob Ojeda | .02 | .10 |
| 615 | Joe Carter | .07 | .20 |
| 616 | Pete Young | .02 | .10 |
| 617 | Sam Horn | .02 | .10 |
| 618 | Vince Coleman | .02 | .10 |
| 619 | Wade Boggs | .10 | .30 |
| 620 | Todd Pratt RC | .07 | .20 |
| 621 | Ron Tingley | .02 | .10 |
| 622 | Doug Drabek | .02 | .10 |
| 623 | Scott Hemond | .02 | .10 |
| 624 | Tim Jones | .02 | .10 |
| 625 | Dennis Cook | .02 | .10 |
| 626 | Jose Melendez | .02 | .10 |
| 627 | Mike Munoz | .02 | .10 |
| 628 | Jim Pena | .02 | .10 |
| 629 | Gary Thurman | .02 | .10 |
| 630 | Charlie Leibrandt | .02 | .10 |
| 631 | Scott Fletcher | .02 | .10 |
| 632 | Andre Dawson | .07 | .20 |
| 633 | Greg Gagne | .02 | .10 |
| 634 | Greg Swindell | .02 | .10 |
| 635 | Kevin Maas | .02 | .10 |
| 636 | Xavier Hernandez | .02 | .10 |
| 637 | Ruben Sierra | .07 | .20 |
| 638 | Dmitri Young | .07 | .20 |
| 639 | Harold Reynolds | .02 | .10 |
| 640 | Tom Goodwin | .02 | .10 |
| 641 | Todd Burns | .02 | .10 |
| 642 | Jeff Fassero | .02 | .10 |
| 643 | Dave Winfield | .07 | .20 |
| 644 | Willie Randolph | .07 | .20 |
| 645 | Luis Mercedes | .02 | .10 |
| 646 | Dale Murphy | .10 | .30 |
| 647 | Danny Darwin | .02 | .10 |
| 648 | Dennis Moeller | .02 | .10 |
| 649 | Chuck Crim | .02 | .10 |
| 650 | Checklist | .02 | .10 |
| 651 | Shawn Abner | .02 | .10 |
| 652 | Tracy Woodson | .02 | .10 |
| 653 | Scott Scudder | .02 | .10 |
| 654 | Tom Lampkin | .02 | .10 |
| 655 | Alan Trammell | .07 | .20 |
| 656 | Cory Snyder | .02 | .10 |
| 657 | Chris Gwynn | .02 | .10 |
| 658 | Lonnie Smith | .02 | .10 |
| 659 | Jim Austin | .02 | .10 |
| 660 | Rob Picciolo CL | .02 | .10 |
| 661 | Tim Hulett | .02 | .10 |
| 662 | Marvin Freeman | .02 | .10 |
| 663 | Greg A. Harris | .02 | .10 |
| 664 | Heathcliff Slocumb | .02 | .10 |
| 665 | Mike Butcher | .02 | .10 |
| 666 | Steve Foster | .02 | .10 |
| 667 | Donn Pall | .02 | .10 |
| 668 | Darryl Kile | .07 | .20 |
| 669 | Jesse Levis | .02 | .10 |
| 670 | Jim Gott | .02 | .10 |
| 671 | Mark Hutton | .02 | .10 |
| 672 | Brian Drahman | .02 | .10 |
| 673 | Chad Kreuter | .02 | .10 |
| 674 | Tony Fernandez | .07 | .20 |
| 675 | Jose Lind | .02 | .10 |
| 676 | Kyle Abbott | .02 | .10 |
| 677 | Dan Plesac | .02 | .10 |

|  |  | | |
|---|---|---|---|
| 678 | Barry Bonds | .60 | 1.50 |
| 679 | Chili Davis | .07 | .20 |
| 680 | Stan Royer | .02 | .10 |
| 681 | Scott Kamieniecki | .02 | .10 |
| 682 | Carlos Martinez | .02 | .10 |
| 683 | Mike Moore | .02 | .10 |
| 684 | Candy Maldonado | .02 | .10 |
| 685 | Jeff Nelson | .02 | .10 |
| 686 | Lou Whitaker | .07 | .20 |
| 687 | Jose Guzman | .02 | .10 |
| 688 | Manuel Lee | .02 | .10 |
| 689 | Bob MacDonald | .02 | .10 |
| 690 | Scott Bankhead | .02 | .10 |
| 691 | Alan Mills | .02 | .10 |
| 692 | Brian Williams | .02 | .10 |
| 693 | Tom Brunansky | .02 | .10 |
| 694 | Lenny Webster | .02 | .10 |
| 695 | Greg Briley | .02 | .10 |
| 696 | Paul O'Neill | .10 | .30 |
| 697 | Joey Cora | .02 | .10 |
| 698 | Charlie O'Brien | .02 | .10 |
| 699 | Junior Ortiz | .02 | .10 |
| 700 | Ron Darling | .02 | .10 |
| 701 | Tony Phillips | .02 | .10 |
| 702 | William Pennyfeather | .02 | .10 |
| 703 | Mark Gubicza | .02 | .10 |
| 704 | Steve Hosey | .02 | .10 |
| 705 | Henry Cotto | .02 | .10 |
| 706 | David Hulse RC | .02 | .10 |
| 707 | Mike Pagliarulo | .02 | .10 |
| 708 | Dave Stieb | .02 | .10 |
| 709 | Melido Perez | .02 | .10 |
| 710 | Jimmy Key | .07 | .20 |
| 711 | Jeff Russell | .02 | .10 |
| 712 | David Cone | .07 | .20 |
| 713 | Russ Swan | .02 | .10 |
| 714 | Mark Guthrie | .02 | .10 |
| 715 | Checklist | .02 | .10 |
| 716 | Al Martin | .02 | .10 |
| 717 | Randy Knorr | .02 | .10 |
| 718 | Mike Stanley | .02 | .10 |
| 719 | Rick Sutcliffe | .07 | .20 |
| 720 | Terry Leach | .02 | .10 |
| 721 | Chipper Jones | .20 | .50 |
| 722 | Jim Eisenreich | .02 | .10 |
| 723 | Tom Henke | .02 | .10 |
| 724 | Jeff Frye | .02 | .10 |
| 725 | Harold Baines | .07 | .20 |
| 726 | Scott Sanderson | .02 | .10 |
| 727 | Tom Foley | .02 | .10 |
| 728 | Bryan Harvey | .02 | .10 |
| 729 | Tom Edens | .02 | .10 |
| 730 | Eric Young | .02 | .10 |
| 731 | Dave Weathers | .02 | .10 |
| 732 | Spike Owen | .02 | .10 |
| 733 | Scott Aldred | .02 | .10 |
| 734 | Cris Carpenter | .02 | .10 |
| 735 | Dion James | .02 | .10 |
| 736 | Joe Girardi | .02 | .10 |
| 737 | Nigel Wilson | .02 | .10 |
| 738 | Scott Chiamparino | .02 | .10 |
| 739 | Jeff Reardon | .02 | .10 |
| 740 | Willie Blair | .02 | .10 |
| 741 | Jim Corsi | .02 | .10 |
| 742 | Ken Patterson | .02 | .10 |
| 743 | Andy Ashby | .02 | .10 |
| 744 | Rob Natal | .02 | .10 |
| 745 | Kevin Bass | .02 | .10 |
| 746 | Freddie Benavides | .02 | .10 |
| 747 | Chris Donnels | .02 | .10 |
| 748 | Kerry Woodson | .02 | .10 |
| 749 | Calvin Jones | .02 | .10 |
| 750 | Gary Scott | .02 | .10 |
| 751 | Joe Orsulak | .02 | .10 |
| 752 | Armando Reynoso | .02 | .10 |
| 753 | Monty Fariss | .02 | .10 |
| 754 | Billy Hatcher | .02 | .10 |
| 755 | Denis Boucher | .02 | .10 |
| 756 | Walt Weiss | .02 | .10 |
| 757 | Mike Fitzgerald | .02 | .10 |
| 758 | Rudy Seanez | .02 | .10 |
| 759 | Bret Barberie | .02 | .10 |
| 760 | Mo Sanford | .02 | .10 |
| 761 | Pedro Castellano | .02 | .10 |
| 762 | Chuck Carr | .02 | .10 |
| 763 | Steve Howe | .02 | .10 |
| 764 | Andres Galarraga | .07 | .20 |
| 765 | Jeff Conine | .07 | .20 |
| 766 | Ted Power | .02 | .10 |
| 767 | Butch Henry | .02 | .10 |
| 768 | Steve Decker | .02 | .10 |
| 769 | Storm Davis | .02 | .10 |
| 770 | Vinny Castilla | .20 | .50 |
| 771 | Junior Felix | .02 | .10 |
| 772 | Walt Terrell | .02 | .10 |
| 773 | Brad Ausmus | .20 | .50 |
| 774 | Jamie McAndrew | .02 | .10 |
| 775 | Milt Thompson | .02 | .10 |
| 776 | Charlie Hayes | .02 | .10 |
| 777 | Jack Armstrong | .02 | .10 |
| 778 | Dennis Rasmussen | .02 | .10 |
| 779 | Darren Holmes | .02 | .10 |
| 780 | Alex Arias | .02 | .10 |
| 781 | Randy Bush | .02 | .10 |
| 782 | Jerry Lopez | .10 | .30 |
| 783 | Dante Bichette | .07 | .20 |
| 784 | John Johnstone RC | .02 | .10 |
| 785 | Rene Gonzales | .02 | .10 |
| 786 | Alex Cole | .02 | .10 |
| 787 | Jeromy Burnitz | .07 | .20 |
| 788 | Michael Huff | .02 | .10 |
| 789 | Anthony Telford | .02 | .10 |
| 790 | Jerald Clark | .02 | .10 |
| 791 | Joel Johnston | .02 | .10 |
| 792 | David Nied | .02 | .10 |

## 1994 Donruss

|  | | | |
|---|---|---|---|
| | COMPLETE SET (660) | 12.00 | 30.00 |
| | COMPLETE SERIES 1 (330) | 6.00 | 15.00 |
| | COMPLETE SERIES 2 (330) | 6.00 | 15.00 |
| 1 | Nolan Ryan Salute | 1.50 | 4.00 |
| 2 | Mike Piazza | .60 | 1.50 |
| 3 | Moises Alou | .10 | .30 |
| 4 | Ken Griffey Jr. | .50 | 1.25 |
| 5 | Gary Sheffield | .10 | .30 |
| 6 | Roberto Alomar | .20 | .50 |
| 7 | John Kruk | .10 | .30 |
| 8 | Gregg Olson | .05 | .15 |
| 9 | Gregg Jefferies | .05 | .15 |
| 10 | Tony Gwynn | .40 | 1.00 |
| 11 | Chad Curtis | .05 | .15 |
| 12 | Craig Biggio | .20 | .50 |
| 13 | John Burkett | .05 | .15 |
| 14 | Carlos Baerga | .05 | .15 |
| 15 | Robin Yount | .50 | 1.25 |
| 16 | Dennis Eckersley | .10 | .30 |
| 17 | Dwight Gooden | .10 | .30 |
| 18 | Ryne Sandberg | .50 | 1.25 |
| 19 | Rickey Henderson | .30 | .75 |
| 20 | Jack McDowell | .05 | .15 |
| 21 | Jay Bell | .10 | .30 |
| 22 | Kevin Brown | .05 | .15 |
| 23 | Robin Ventura | .10 | .30 |
| 24 | Paul Molitor | .10 | .30 |
| 25 | David Justice | .10 | .30 |
| 26 | Rafael Palmeiro | .20 | .50 |
| 27 | Cecil Fielder | .10 | .30 |
| 28 | Chuck Knoblauch | .10 | .30 |
| 29 | Dave Hollins | .05 | .15 |
| 30 | Jimmy Key | .05 | .15 |
| 31 | Mark Langston | .05 | .15 |
| 32 | Darryl Kile | .10 | .30 |
| 33 | Ruben Sierra | .10 | .30 |
| 34 | Ron Gant | .10 | .30 |
| 35 | Ozzie Smith | .50 | 1.25 |
| 36 | Wade Boggs | .20 | .50 |
| 37 | Marquis Grissom | .10 | .30 |
| 38 | Will Clark | .20 | .50 |
| 39 | Kenny Lofton | .10 | .30 |
| 40 | Cal Ripken | 1.00 | 2.50 |
| 41 | Steve Avery | .05 | .15 |
| 42 | Mo Vaughn | .10 | .30 |
| 43 | Brian McRae | .05 | .15 |
| 44 | Mickey Tettleton | .05 | .15 |
| 45 | Barry Larkin | .20 | .50 |
| 46 | Charlie Hayes | .05 | .15 |
| 47 | Kevin Appier | .10 | .30 |
| 48 | Robby Thompson | .05 | .15 |
| 49 | Juan Gonzalez | .10 | .30 |
| 50 | Paul O'Neill | .05 | .15 |
| 51 | Marcos Armas | .05 | .15 |
| 52 | Mike Butcher | .05 | .15 |
| 53 | Ken Caminiti | .10 | .30 |
| 54 | Pat Borders | .05 | .15 |
| 55 | Pedro Munoz | .05 | .15 |
| 56 | Tim Belcher | .05 | .15 |
| 57 | Paul Assenmacher | .05 | .15 |
| 58 | Damon Berryhill | .05 | .15 |
| 59 | Ricky Bones | .05 | .15 |
| 60 | Rene Arocha | .05 | .15 |
| 61 | Shawn Boskie | .05 | .15 |
| 62 | Pedro Astacio | .05 | .15 |
| 63 | Frank Bolick | .05 | .15 |
| 64 | Bud Black | .05 | .15 |
| 65 | Sandy Alomar Jr. | .05 | .15 |
| 66 | Rich Amaral | .05 | .15 |
| 67 | Luis Aquino | .05 | .15 |
| 68 | Kevin Baez | .05 | .15 |
| 69 | Mike Devereaux | .05 | .15 |
| 70 | Andy Ashby | .05 | .15 |
| 71 | Larry Andersen | .05 | .15 |
| 72 | Steve Cooke | .05 | .15 |
| 73 | Mario Diaz | .05 | .15 |
| 74 | Rob Deer | .05 | .15 |
| 75 | Bobby Ayala | .05 | .15 |
| 76 | Freddie Benavides | .05 | .15 |
| 77 | Stan Belinda | .05 | .15 |
| 78 | John Doherty | .05 | .15 |
| 79 | Willie Banks | .05 | .15 |
| 80 | Spike Owen | .05 | .15 |
| 81 | Mike Bordick | .05 | .15 |
| 82 | Chili Davis | .05 | .15 |
| 83 | Luis Gonzalez | .10 | .30 |
| 84 | Ed Sprague | .05 | .15 |
| 85 | Jeff Reboulet | .05 | .15 |
| 86 | Jason Bere | .05 | .15 |
| 87 | Mark Hutton | .05 | .15 |
| 88 | Jeff Blauser | .05 | .15 |
| 89 | Cal Eldred | .05 | .15 |
| 90 | Bernard Gilkey | .05 | .15 |
| 91 | Frank Castillo | .05 | .15 |
| 92 | Jim Gott | .05 | .15 |
| 93 | Greg Colbrunn | .05 | .15 |
| 94 | Jeff Brantley | .05 | .15 |
| 95 | Jeremy Hernandez | .05 | .15 |
| 96 | Norm Charlton | .05 | .15 |
| 97 | Alex Arias | .05 | .15 |
| 98 | John Franco | .10 | .30 |
| 99 | Chris Hoiles | .05 | .15 |
| 100 | Brad Ausmus | .20 | .50 |
| 101 | Wes Chamberlain | .05 | .15 |
| 102 | Mark Dewey | .05 | .15 |
| 103 | Benji Gil | .05 | .15 |
| 104 | John Dopson | .05 | .15 |
| 105 | John Smiley | .05 | .15 |
| 106 | David Nied | .05 | .15 |
| 107 | George Brett Salute | .75 | 2.00 |
| 108 | Kirk Gibson | .10 | .30 |
| 109 | Larry Casian | .05 | .15 |
| 110 | Ryne Sandberg CL | .30 | .75 |
| 111 | Brent Gates | .05 | .15 |
| 112 | Damion Easley | .05 | .15 |
| 113 | Pete Harnisch | .05 | .15 |
| 114 | Danny Cox | .05 | .15 |
| 115 | Kevin Tapani | .05 | .15 |
| 116 | Roberto Hernandez | .05 | .15 |
| 117 | Domingo Jean | .05 | .15 |
| 118 | Sid Bream | .05 | .15 |
| 119 | Doug Henry | .05 | .15 |
| 120 | Omar Olivares | .05 | .15 |
| 121 | Mike Harkey | .05 | .15 |
| 122 | Carlos Hernandez | .05 | .15 |
| 123 | Jeff Fassero | .05 | .15 |
| 124 | Dave Burba | .05 | .15 |
| 125 | Wayne Kirby | .05 | .15 |
| 126 | John Cummings | .05 | .15 |
| 127 | Bret Barberie | .05 | .15 |
| 128 | Todd Hundley | .05 | .15 |
| 129 | Tim Hulett | .05 | .15 |
| 130 | Phil Clark | .05 | .15 |

|  |  | | |
|---|---|---|---|
| 131 | Danny Jackson | .05 | .15 |
| 132 | Tom Foley | .05 | .15 |
| 133 | Donald Harris | .05 | .15 |
| 134 | Scott Fletcher | .05 | .15 |
| 135 | Johnny Ruffin | .05 | .15 |
| 136 | Jerald Clark | .05 | .15 |
| 137 | Billy Brewer | .05 | .15 |
| 138 | Dan Gladden | .05 | .15 |
| 139 | Eddie Guardado | .10 | .30 |
| 140 | Cal Ripken CL | .30 | .75 |
| 141 | Scott Hemond | .05 | .15 |
| 142 | Steve Frey | .05 | .15 |
| 143 | Xavier Hernandez | .05 | .15 |
| 144 | Mark Eichhorn | .05 | .15 |
| 145 | Ellis Burks | .10 | .30 |
| 146 | Jim Leyritz | .05 | .15 |
| 147 | Mark Lemke | .05 | .15 |
| 148 | Pat Listach | .05 | .15 |
| 149 | Donovan Osborne | .05 | .15 |
| 150 | Glenallen Hill | .05 | .15 |
| 151 | Orel Hershiser | .10 | .30 |
| 152 | Darrin Fletcher | .05 | .15 |
| 153 | Royce Clayton | .05 | .15 |
| 154 | Derek Lilliquist | .05 | .15 |
| 155 | Mike Felder | .05 | .15 |
| 156 | Jeff Conine | .10 | .30 |
| 157 | Ryan Thompson | .05 | .15 |
| 158 | Ben McDonald | .05 | .15 |
| 159 | Ricky Gutierrez | .05 | .15 |
| 160 | Terry Mulholland | .05 | .15 |
| 161 | Carlos Garcia | .05 | .15 |
| 162 | Tom Henke | .05 | .15 |
| 163 | Mike Greenwell | .05 | .15 |
| 164 | Thomas Howard | .05 | .15 |
| 165 | Joe Girardi | .05 | .15 |
| 166 | Hubie Brooks | .05 | .15 |
| 167 | Greg Gohr | .05 | .15 |
| 168 | Chip Hale | .05 | .15 |
| 169 | Rick Honeycutt | .05 | .15 |
| 170 | Hilly Hathaway | .05 | .15 |
| 171 | Todd Jones | .05 | .15 |
| 172 | Tony Fernandez | .05 | .15 |
| 173 | Bo Jackson | .30 | .75 |
| 174 | Bobby Munoz | .05 | .15 |
| 175 | Greg McMichael | .05 | .15 |
| 176 | Graeme Lloyd | .05 | .15 |
| 177 | Tom Pagnozzi | .05 | .15 |
| 178 | Derrick May | .05 | .15 |
| 179 | Pedro Martinez | .30 | .75 |
| 180 | Ken Hill | .05 | .15 |
| 181 | Bryan Hickerson | .05 | .15 |
| 182 | Jose Mesa | .05 | .15 |
| 183 | Dave Fleming | .05 | .15 |
| 184 | Henry Cotto | .05 | .15 |
| 185 | Jeff Kent | .20 | .50 |
| 186 | Mark McLemore | .05 | .15 |
| 187 | Trevor Hoffman | .20 | .50 |
| 188 | Todd Pratt | .05 | .15 |
| 189 | Blas Minor | .05 | .15 |
| 190 | Charlie Leibrandt | .05 | .15 |
| 191 | Tony Pena | .05 | .15 |
| 192 | Larry Luebbers RC | .05 | .15 |
| 193 | Greg W. Harris | .05 | .15 |
| 194 | David Cone | .10 | .30 |
| 195 | Bill Gullickson | .05 | .15 |
| 196 | Brian Harper | .05 | .15 |
| 197 | Steve Karsay | .05 | .15 |
| 198 | Greg Myers | .05 | .15 |
| 199 | Mark Portugal | .05 | .15 |
| 200 | Pat Hentgen | .05 | .15 |
| 201 | Mike LaValliere | .05 | .15 |
| 202 | Mike Stanley | .05 | .15 |
| 203 | Kent Mercker | .05 | .15 |
| 204 | Dave Nilsson | .05 | .15 |
| 205 | Erik Pappas | .05 | .15 |
| 206 | Mike Morgan | .05 | .15 |
| 207 | Roger McDowell | .05 | .15 |
| 208 | Mike Lansing | .05 | .15 |
| 209 | Kirt Manwaring | .05 | .15 |
| 210 | Randy Milligan | .05 | .15 |
| 211 | Erik Hanson | .05 | .15 |
| 212 | Orestes Destrade | .05 | .15 |
| 213 | Mike Maddux | .05 | .15 |
| 214 | Alan Mills | .05 | .15 |
| 215 | Tim Mauser | .05 | .15 |
| 216 | Ben Rivera | .05 | .15 |
| 217 | Don Slaught | .05 | .15 |
| 218 | Bob Patterson | .05 | .15 |
| 219 | Carlos Quintana | .05 | .15 |
| 220 | Tim Raines CL | .05 | .15 |
| 221 | Hal Morris | .05 | .15 |
| 222 | Darren Holmes | .05 | .15 |
| 223 | Chris Gwynn | .05 | .15 |
| 224 | Chad Kreuter | .05 | .15 |
| 225 | Mike Hartley | .05 | .15 |
| 226 | Scott Lydy | .05 | .15 |
| 227 | Eduardo Perez | .05 | .15 |
| 228 | Greg Swindell | .05 | .15 |
| 229 | Al Leiter | .10 | .30 |
| 230 | Scott Radinsky | .05 | .15 |
| 231 | Bob Wickman | .05 | .15 |
| 232 | Otis Nixon | .05 | .15 |
| 233 | Kevin Reimer | .05 | .15 |
| 234 | Geronimo Pena | .05 | .15 |
| 235 | Kevin Roberson | .05 | .15 |
| 236 | Jody Reed | .05 | .15 |
| 237 | Kirk Rueter | .05 | .15 |
| 238 | Willie McGee | .10 | .30 |
| 239 | Charles Nagy | .05 | .15 |
| 240 | Tim Leary | .05 | .15 |
| 241 | Carl Everett | .10 | .30 |
| 242 | Charlie O'Brien | .05 | .15 |
| 243 | Mike Pagliarulo | .05 | .15 |
| 244 | Kerry Taylor | .05 | .15 |
| 245 | Kevin Stocker | .05 | .15 |
| 246 | Joel Johnston | .05 | .15 |
| 247 | Geno Petralli | .05 | .15 |
| 248 | Jeff Russell | .05 | .15 |
| 249 | Joe Oliver | .05 | .15 |
| 250 | Roberto Mejia | .05 | .15 |
| 251 | Chris Haney | .05 | .15 |
| 252 | Bill Krueger | .05 | .15 |
| 253 | Shane Mack | .05 | .15 |
| 254 | Terry Steinbach | .05 | .15 |
| 255 | Luis Polonia | .05 | .15 |
| 256 | Eddie Taubensee | .05 | .15 |
| 257 | Dave Stewart | .10 | .30 |
| 258 | Tim Raines | .05 | .15 |
| 259 | Bernie Williams | .20 | .50 |
| 260 | John Smoltz | .20 | .50 |
| 261 | Kevin Seltzer | .05 | .15 |
| 262 | Bob Tewksbury | .05 | .15 |
| 263 | Bob Scanlan | .05 | .15 |
| 264 | Henry Rodriguez | .05 | .15 |
| 265 | Tim Scott | .05 | .15 |
| 266 | Scott Sanderson | .05 | .15 |
| 267 | Eric Plunk | .05 | .15 |
| 268 | Edgar Martinez | .20 | .50 |
| 269 | Charlie Hough | .10 | .30 |
| 270 | Joe Orsulak | .05 | .15 |
| 271 | Harold Reynolds | .10 | .30 |
| 272 | Tim Teufel | .05 | .15 |
| 273 | Bobby Thigpen | .05 | .15 |
| 274 | Randy Tomlin | .05 | .15 |
| 275 | Gary Redus | .05 | .15 |
| 276 | Ken Ryan | .05 | .15 |
| 277 | Tim Pugh | .05 | .15 |
| 278 | Jayhawk Owens | .05 | .15 |
| 279 | Phil Hiatt | .05 | .15 |
| 280 | Alan Trammell | .10 | .30 |
| 281 | David McCarty | .05 | .15 |
| 282 | Bob Welch | .05 | .15 |
| 283 | J.T. Snow | .10 | .30 |
| 284 | Brian Williams | .05 | .15 |
| 285 | Devon White | .10 | .30 |
| 286 | Steve Sax | .05 | .15 |
| 287 | Tony Tarasco | .05 | .15 |
| 288 | Bill Spiers | .05 | .15 |
| 289 | Allen Watson | .05 | .15 |
| 290 | Rickey Henderson CL | .20 | .50 |
| 291 | Jose Vizcaino | .05 | .15 |
| 292 | Darryl Strawberry | .10 | .30 |
| 293 | John Wetteland | .10 | .30 |
| 294 | Bill Swift | .05 | .15 |
| 295 | Jeff Treadway | .05 | .15 |
| 296 | Tino Martinez | .20 | .50 |
| 297 | Richie Lewis | .05 | .15 |
| 298 | Bret Saberhagen | .10 | .30 |
| 299 | Arthur Rhodes | .05 | .15 |
| 300 | Guillermo Velasquez | .05 | .15 |
| 301 | Milt Thompson | .05 | .15 |
| 302 | Doug Strange | .05 | .15 |
| 303 | Aaron Sele | .05 | .15 |
| 304 | Bip Roberts | .05 | .15 |
| 305 | Bruce Ruffin | .05 | .15 |
| 306 | Jose Lind | .05 | .15 |
| 307 | David Wells | .10 | .30 |
| 308 | Bobby Witt | .05 | .15 |
| 309 | Mark Wohlers | .05 | .15 |
| 310 | B.J. Surhoff | .10 | .30 |
| 311 | Mark Whiten | .05 | .15 |
| 312 | Turk Wendell | .05 | .15 |
| 313 | Raul Mondesi | .10 | .30 |
| 314 | Brian Turang RC | .05 | .15 |
| 315 | Chris Hammond | .05 | .15 |
| 316 | Tim Bogar | .05 | .15 |
| 317 | Brad Pennington | .05 | .15 |
| 318 | Tim Worrell | .05 | .15 |
| 319 | Mitch Williams | .05 | .15 |
| 320 | Rondell White | .10 | .30 |
| 321 | Frank Viola | .10 | .30 |
| 322 | Manny Ramirez | .30 | .75 |
| 323 | Gary Wayne | .05 | .15 |
| 324 | Mike Macfarlane | .05 | .15 |
| 325 | Russ Springer | .05 | .15 |
| 326 | Tim Wallach | .05 | .15 |
| 327 | Salomon Torres | .05 | .15 |
| 328 | Omar Vizquel | .20 | .50 |
| 329 | Andy Tomberlin RC | .05 | .15 |
| 330 | Chris Sabo | .05 | .15 |
| 331 | Mike Mussina | .20 | .50 |
| 332 | Andy Benes | .05 | .15 |
| 333 | Darren Daulton | .10 | .30 |
| 334 | Orlando Merced | .05 | .15 |
| 335 | Mark McGwire | .75 | 2.00 |
| 336 | Dave Winfield | .10 | .30 |
| 337 | Sammy Sosa | .30 | .75 |
| 338 | Eric Karros | .05 | .15 |
| 339 | Greg Vaughn | .05 | .15 |
| 340 | Don Mattingly | .75 | 2.00 |
| 341 | Frank Thomas | .30 | .75 |
| 342 | Fred McGriff | .20 | .50 |
| 343 | Kirby Puckett | .30 | .75 |
| 344 | Roberto Kelly | .05 | .15 |
| 345 | Wally Joyner | .10 | .30 |
| 346 | Andres Galarraga | .10 | .30 |
| 347 | Bobby Bonilla | .10 | .30 |
| 348 | Benito Santiago | .10 | .30 |
| 349 | Barry Bonds | .75 | 2.00 |
| 350 | Delino DeShields | .05 | .15 |
| 351 | Albert Belle | .10 | .30 |
| 352 | Randy Johnson | .30 | .75 |
| 353 | Tim Salmon | .20 | .50 |
| 354 | John Olerud | .10 | .30 |
| 355 | Dean Palmer | .10 | .30 |
| 356 | Roger Clemens | .60 | 1.50 |
| 357 | Jim Abbott | .20 | .50 |
| 358 | Mark Grace | .20 | .50 |
| 359 | Ozzie Guillen | .05 | .15 |
| 360 | Lou Whitaker | .10 | .30 |
| 361 | Jose Rijo | .05 | .15 |
| 362 | Jeff Montgomery | .05 | .15 |
| 363 | Chuck Finley | .10 | .30 |
| 364 | Tom Glavine | .20 | .50 |
| 365 | Jeff Bagwell | .20 | .50 |
| 366 | Joe Carter | .10 | .30 |
| 367 | Ray Lankford | .10 | .30 |
| 368 | Ramon Martinez | .05 | .15 |
| 369 | Jay Buhner | .10 | .30 |
| 370 | Matt Williams | .10 | .30 |
| 371 | Larry Walker | .10 | .30 |
| 372 | Jose Canseco | .20 | .50 |
| 373 | Lenny Dykstra | .10 | .30 |
| 374 | Bryan Harvey | .05 | .15 |
| 375 | Andy Van Slyke | .20 | .50 |
| 376 | Ivan Rodriguez | .20 | .50 |
| 377 | Kevin Mitchell | .05 | .15 |
| 378 | Travis Fryman | .10 | .30 |
| 379 | Duane Ward | .05 | .15 |
| 380 | Greg Maddux | .50 | 1.25 |
| 381 | Scott Servais | .05 | .15 |
| 382 | Greg Olson | .05 | .15 |
| 383 | Rey Sanchez | .05 | .15 |
| 384 | Tom Kramer | .05 | .15 |
| 385 | David Valle | .05 | .15 |
| 386 | Eddie Murray | .30 | .75 |
| 387 | Kevin Higgins | .05 | .15 |
| 388 | Dan Wilson | .05 | .15 |
| 389 | Todd Frohwith | .05 | .15 |
| 390 | Gerald Williams | .05 | .15 |
| 391 | Hipolito Pichardo | .05 | .15 |
| 392 | Pat Meares | .05 | .15 |
| 393 | Luis Lopez | .05 | .15 |
| 394 | Ricky Jordan | .05 | .15 |

|  |  | | |
|---|---|---|---|
| 395 | Bob Walk | .05 | .15 |
| 396 | Sid Fernandez | .05 | .15 |
| 397 | Todd Worrell | .05 | .15 |
| 398 | Darryl Hamilton | .05 | .15 |
| 399 | Randy Myers | .05 | .15 |
| 400 | Rod Brewer | .05 | .15 |
| 401 | Lance Blankenship | .05 | .15 |
| 402 | Steve Finley | .10 | .30 |
| 403 | Phil Leftwich RC | .05 | .15 |
| 404 | Juan Guzman | .05 | .15 |
| 405 | Anthony Young | .05 | .15 |
| 406 | Jeff Gardner | .05 | .15 |
| 407 | Ryan Bowen | .05 | .15 |
| 408 | Fernando Valenzuela | .10 | .30 |
| 409 | David West | .05 | .15 |
| 410 | Kenny Rogers | .10 | .30 |
| 411 | Bob Zupcic | .05 | .15 |
| 412 | Eric Young | .05 | .15 |
| 413 | Bret Boone | .10 | .30 |
| 414 | Danny Tartabull | .05 | .15 |
| 415 | Bob MacDonald | .05 | .15 |
| 416 | Ron Karkovice | .05 | .15 |
| 417 | Scott Cooper | .05 | .15 |
| 418 | Dante Bichette | .10 | .30 |
| 419 | Tripp Cromer | .05 | .15 |
| 420 | Billy Ashley | .05 | .15 |
| 421 | Roger Smithberg | .05 | .15 |
| 422 | Dennis Martinez | .10 | .30 |
| 423 | Mike Blowers | .05 | .15 |
| 424 | Darren Lewis | .05 | .15 |
| 425 | Junior Ortiz | .05 | .15 |
| 426 | Butch Huskey | .05 | .15 |
| 427 | Jimmy Poole | .05 | .15 |
| 428 | Walt Weiss | .05 | .15 |
| 429 | Scott Bankhead | .05 | .15 |
| 430 | Deion Sanders | .20 | .50 |
| 431 | Scott Bullett | .05 | .15 |
| 432 | Jeff Huson | .05 | .15 |
| 433 | Tyler Green | .05 | .15 |
| 434 | Billy Hatcher | .05 | .15 |
| 435 | Bob Hamelin | .05 | .15 |
| 436 | Reggie Sanders | .10 | .30 |
| 437 | Scott Erickson | .05 | .15 |
| 438 | Steve Reed | .05 | .15 |
| 439 | Randy Velarde | .05 | .15 |
| 440 | Tony Gwynn CL | .20 | .50 |
| 441 | Terry Leach | .05 | .15 |
| 442 | Danny Bautista | .05 | .15 |
| 443 | Kent Hrbek | .10 | .30 |
| 444 | Rick Wilkins | .05 | .15 |
| 445 | Tony Phillips | .05 | .15 |
| 446 | Dion James | .05 | .15 |
| 447 | Joey Cora | .05 | .15 |
| 448 | Andre Dawson | .10 | .30 |
| 449 | Pedro Castellano | .05 | .15 |
| 450 | Tom Gordon | .05 | .15 |
| 451 | Rob Dibble | .05 | .15 |
| 452 | Ron Darling | .05 | .15 |
| 453 | Chipper Jones | .30 | .75 |
| 454 | Joe Grahe | .05 | .15 |
| 455 | Domingo Cedeno | .05 | .15 |
| 456 | Tom Edens | .05 | .15 |
| 457 | Mitch Webster | .05 | .15 |
| 458 | Jose Bautista | .05 | .15 |
| 459 | Troy O'Leary | .05 | .15 |
| 460 | Todd Zeile | .05 | .15 |
| 461 | Sean Berry | .05 | .15 |
| 462 | Brad Holman RC | .05 | .15 |
| 463 | Dave Martinez | .05 | .15 |
| 464 | Mark Lewis | .05 | .15 |
| 465 | Paul Carey | .05 | .15 |
| 466 | Jack Armstrong | .05 | .15 |
| 467 | David Telgheder | .05 | .15 |
| 468 | Gene Harris | .05 | .15 |
| 469 | Danny Darwin | .05 | .15 |
| 470 | Kim Batiste | .05 | .15 |
| 471 | Tim Wakefield | .20 | .50 |
| 472 | Craig Lefferts | .05 | .15 |
| 473 | Jacob Brumfield | .05 | .15 |
| 474 | Lance Painter | .05 | .15 |
| 475 | Milt Cuyler | .05 | .15 |
| 476 | Melido Perez | .05 | .15 |
| 477 | Derek Parks | .05 | .15 |
| 478 | Gary DiSarcina | .05 | .15 |
| 479 | Steve Bedrosian | .05 | .15 |
| 480 | Eric Anthony | .05 | .15 |
| 481 | Julio Franco | .10 | .30 |
| 482 | Tommy Greene | .05 | .15 |
| 483 | Pat Kelly | .05 | .15 |
| 484 | Nate Minchey | .05 | .15 |
| 485 | William Pennyfeather | .05 | .15 |
| 486 | Harold Baines | .10 | .30 |
| 487 | Howard Johnson | .05 | .15 |
| 488 | Angel Miranda | .05 | .15 |
| 489 | Scott Sanders | .05 | .15 |
| 490 | Shawon Dunston | .05 | .15 |
| 491 | Mel Rojas | .05 | .15 |
| 492 | Jeff Nelson | .05 | .15 |
| 493 | Archi Cianfrocco | .05 | .15 |
| 494 | Al Martin | .05 | .15 |
| 495 | Mike Gallego | .05 | .15 |
| 496 | Mike Henneman | .05 | .15 |
| 497 | Armando Reynoso | .05 | .15 |
| 498 | Mickey Morandini | .05 | .15 |
| 499 | Rick Renteria | .05 | .15 |
| 500 | Rick Sutcliffe | .10 | .30 |
| 501 | Bobby Jones | .05 | .15 |
| 502 | Gary Gaetti | .10 | .30 |
| 503 | Rick Aguilera | .05 | .15 |
| 504 | Todd Stottlemyre | .05 | .15 |
| 505 | Mike Mohler | .05 | .15 |
| 506 | Mike Stanton | .05 | .15 |
| 507 | Jose Guzman | .05 | .15 |
| 508 | Kevin Rogers | .05 | .15 |
| 509 | Chuck Carr | .05 | .15 |
| 510 | Chris Jones | .05 | .15 |
| 511 | Brent Mayne | .05 | .15 |
| 512 | Greg Harris | .05 | .15 |
| 513 | Dave Henderson | .05 | .15 |
| 514 | Eric Hillman | .05 | .15 |
| 515 | Dan Peltier | .05 | .15 |
| 516 | Craig Shipley | .05 | .15 |
| 517 | John Valentin | .05 | .15 |
| 518 | Wilson Alvarez | .05 | .15 |
| 519 | Andujar Cedeno | .05 | .15 |
| 520 | Troy Neel | .05 | .15 |
| 521 | Tom Candiotti | .05 | .15 |
| 522 | Matt Mieske | .05 | .15 |
| 523 | Jim Thome | .20 | .50 |
| 524 | Lou Frazier | .05 | .15 |
| 525 | Mike Jackson | .05 | .15 |
| 526 | Pedro A. Martinez RC | .05 | .15 |
| 527 | Roger Pavlik | .05 | .15 |
| 528 | Kent Bottenfield | .05 | .15 |
| 529 | Felix Jose | .05 | .15 |
| 530 | Mark Guthrie | .05 | .15 |
| 531 | Steve Farr | .05 | .15 |
| 532 | Craig Paquette | .05 | .15 |
| 533 | Doug Jones | .05 | .15 |
| 534 | Luis Allcea | .05 | .15 |
| 535 | Cory Snyder | .05 | .15 |
| 536 | Paul Sorrento | .05 | .15 |
| 537 | Nigel Wilson | .05 | .15 |
| 538 | Jeff King | .05 | .15 |
| 539 | Willie Greene | .05 | .15 |
| 540 | Kirk McCaskill | .05 | .15 |
| 541 | Al Osuna | .05 | .15 |
| 542 | Greg Hibbard | .05 | .15 |
| 543 | Brett Butler | .10 | .30 |
| 544 | Jose Valentin | .05 | .15 |
| 545 | Wil Cordero | .05 | .15 |
| 546 | Chris Bosio | .05 | .15 |
| 547 | Jamie Moyer | .10 | .30 |
| 548 | Jim Eisenreich | .05 | .15 |
| 549 | Vinny Castilla | .10 | .30 |
| 550 | Dave Winfield CL | .10 | .30 |
| 551 | John Roper | .05 | .15 |
| 552 | Lance Johnson | .05 | .15 |
| 553 | Scott Kamieniecki | .05 | .15 |
| 554 | Mike Moore | .05 | .15 |
| 555 | Steve Buechele | .05 | .15 |
| 556 | Terry Pendleton | .10 | .30 |
| 557 | Todd Van Poppel | .05 | .15 |
| 558 | Rob Butler | .05 | .15 |
| 559 | Zane Smith | .05 | .15 |
| 560 | David Hulse | .05 | .15 |
| 561 | Tim Costo | .05 | .15 |
| 562 | John Habyan | .05 | .15 |
| 563 | Terry Jorgensen | .05 | .15 |
| 564 | Matt Nokes | .05 | .15 |
| 565 | Kevin McReynolds | .05 | .15 |
| 566 | Phil Plantier | .05 | .15 |
| 567 | Chris Turner | .05 | .15 |
| 568 | Carlos Delgado | .20 | .50 |
| 569 | John Jaha | .05 | .15 |
| 570 | Dwight Smith | .05 | .15 |
| 571 | John Vander Wal | .05 | .15 |
| 572 | Trevor Wilson | .05 | .15 |
| 573 | Felix Fermin | .05 | .15 |
| 574 | Marc Newfield | .05 | .15 |
| 575 | Jeromy Burnitz | .10 | .30 |
| 576 | Leo Gomez | .05 | .15 |
| 577 | Curt Schilling | .10 | .30 |
| 578 | Kevin Young | .05 | .15 |
| 579 | Jerry Spradlin RC | .05 | .15 |
| 580 | Curt Leskanic | .05 | .15 |
| 581 | Carl Willis | .05 | .15 |
| 582 | Alex Fernandez | .05 | .15 |
| 583 | Mark Holzemer | .05 | .15 |
| 584 | Domingo Martinez | .05 | .15 |
| 585 | Pete Smith | .05 | .15 |
| 586 | Brian Jordan | .10 | .30 |
| 587 | Kevin Gross | .05 | .15 |
| 588 | J.R. Phillips | .05 | .15 |
| 589 | Chris Nabholz | .05 | .15 |
| 590 | Bill Wertz | .05 | .15 |
| 591 | Derek Bell | .05 | .15 |
| 592 | Brady Anderson | .10 | .30 |
| 593 | Matt Turner | .05 | .15 |
| 594 | Pete Incaviglia | .05 | .15 |
| 595 | Greg Gagne | .05 | .15 |
| 596 | John Flaherty | .05 | .15 |
| 597 | Scott Livingstone | .05 | .15 |
| 598 | Rod Bolton | .05 | .15 |
| 599 | Mike Perez | .05 | .15 |
| 600 | Roger Clemens CL | .30 | .75 |
| 601 | Tony Castillo | .05 | .15 |
| 602 | Henry Mercedes | .05 | .15 |
| 603 | Mike Fetters | .05 | .15 |
| 604 | Rod Beck | .05 | .15 |
| 605 | Damon Buford | .05 | .15 |
| 606 | Matt Whiteside | .05 | .15 |
| 607 | Shawn Green | .30 | .75 |
| 608 | Midre Cummings | .05 | .15 |
| 609 | Jeff McNeely | .05 | .15 |
| 610 | Danny Sheaffer | .05 | .15 |
| 611 | Paul Wagner | .05 | .15 |
| 612 | Torey Lovullo | .05 | .15 |
| 613 | Javier Lopez | .10 | .30 |
| 614 | Mariano Duncan | .05 | .15 |
| 615 | Doug Brocail | .05 | .15 |
| 616 | Dave Hansen | .05 | .15 |
| 617 | Ryan Klesko | .10 | .30 |
| 618 | Eric Davis | .05 | .15 |
| 619 | Scott Ruffcorn | .05 | .15 |
| 620 | Mike Trombley | .05 | .15 |
| 621 | Jaime Navarro | .05 | .15 |
| 622 | Rheal Cormier | .05 | .15 |
| 623 | Jose Offerman | .05 | .15 |
| 624 | David Segui | .05 | .15 |
| 625 | Robb Nen | .10 | .30 |
| 626 | Dave Gallagher | .05 | .15 |
| 627 | Julian Tavarez RC | .10 | .30 |
| 628 | Chris Gomez | .05 | .15 |
| 629 | Jeffrey Hammonds | .05 | .15 |
| 630 | Scott Brosius | .10 | .30 |
| 631 | Willie Blair | .05 | .15 |
| 632 | Doug Drabek | .05 | .15 |
| 633 | Bill Wegman | .05 | .15 |
| 634 | Jeff McKnight | .05 | .15 |
| 635 | Rich Rodriguez | .05 | .15 |
| 636 | Steve Trachsel | .05 | .15 |
| 637 | Buddy Groom | .05 | .15 |
| 638 | Sterling Hitchcock | .05 | .15 |
| 639 | Chuck McElroy | .05 | .15 |
| 640 | Rene Gonzales | .05 | .15 |
| 641 | Dan Plesac | .05 | .15 |
| 642 | Jeff Branson | .05 | .15 |
| 643 | Darrell Whitmore | .05 | .15 |
| 644 | Paul Quantrill | .05 | .15 |
| 645 | Rich Rowland | .05 | .15 |
| 646 | Curtis Pride RC | .10 | .30 |
| 647 | Erik Plantenberg RC | .05 | .15 |
| 648 | Albie Lopez | .05 | .15 |
| 649 | Rich Batchelor RC | .05 | .15 |
| 650 | Lee Smith | .10 | .30 |
| 651 | Cliff Floyd | .10 | .30 |
| 652 | Pete Schourek | .05 | .15 |
| 653 | Reggie Jefferson | .05 | .15 |
| 654 | Bill Haselman | .05 | .15 |
| 655 | Steve Hosey | .05 | .15 |
| 656 | Mark Clark | .05 | .15 |
| 657 | Mark Davis | .05 | .15 |
| 658 | Dave Magadan | .05 | .15 |

| | | | |
|---|---|---|---|
| ❏ 659 Candy Maldonado | .05 | .15 | |
| ❏ 660 Mark Langston CL | .05 | .15 | |

## 1995 Donruss

| | | |
|---|---|---|
| ❏ COMPLETE SET (550) | 12.00 | 30.00 |
| ❏ COMPLETE SERIES 1 (330) | 8.00 | 20.00 |
| ❏ COMPLETE SERIES 2 (220) | 4.00 | 10.00 |
| ❏ 1 David Justice | .10 | .30 |
| ❏ 2 Rene Arocha | .05 | .15 |
| ❏ 3 Sandy Alomar Jr. | .05 | .15 |
| ❏ 4 Luis Lopez | .05 | .15 |
| ❏ 5 Mike Piazza | .50 | 1.25 |
| ❏ 6 Bobby Jones | .05 | .15 |
| ❏ 7 Damion Easley | .05 | .15 |
| ❏ 8 Barry Bonds | .75 | 2.00 |
| ❏ 9 Mike Mussina | .20 | .50 |
| ❏ 10 Kevin Seitzer | .05 | .15 |
| ❏ 11 John Smiley | .05 | .15 |
| ❏ 12 Mark VanLandingham | .05 | .15 |
| ❏ 13 Tom Darling | .05 | .15 |
| ❏ 14 Walt Weiss | .05 | .15 |
| ❏ 15 Mike Lansing | .05 | .15 |
| ❏ 16 Allen Watson | .05 | .15 |
| ❏ 17 Aaron Sele | .05 | .15 |
| ❏ 18 Randy Johnson | .30 | .75 |
| ❏ 19 Dean Palmer | .10 | .30 |
| ❏ 20 Jeff Bagwell | .20 | .50 |
| ❏ 21 Curt Schilling | .10 | .30 |
| ❏ 22 Darrell Whitmore | .05 | .15 |
| ❏ 23 Steve Trachsel | .05 | .15 |
| ❏ 24 Dan Wilson | .05 | .15 |
| ❏ 25 Steve Finley | .05 | .15 |
| ❏ 26 Bret Boone | .10 | .30 |
| ❏ 27 Charles Johnson | .10 | .30 |
| ❏ 28 Mike Stanton | .05 | .15 |
| ❏ 29 Ismael Valdes | .05 | .15 |
| ❏ 30 Salomon Torres | .05 | .15 |
| ❏ 31 Eric Anthony | .05 | .15 |
| ❏ 32 Spike Owen | .05 | .15 |
| ❏ 33 Joey Cora | .05 | .15 |
| ❏ 34 Robert Eenhoorn | .05 | .15 |
| ❏ 35 Rick White | .05 | .15 |
| ❏ 36 Omar Vizquel | .20 | .50 |
| ❏ 37 Carlos Delgado | .10 | .30 |
| ❏ 38 Eddie Williams | .05 | .15 |
| ❏ 39 Shawon Dunston | .05 | .15 |
| ❏ 40 Darrin Fletcher | .05 | .15 |
| ❏ 41 Leo Gomez | .05 | .15 |
| ❏ 42 Juan Gonzalez | .10 | .30 |
| ❏ 43 Luis Alicea | .05 | .15 |
| ❏ 44 Ken Ryan | .05 | .15 |
| ❏ 45 Lou Whitaker | .10 | .30 |
| ❏ 46 Mike Blowers | .05 | .15 |
| ❏ 47 Willie Blair | .05 | .15 |
| ❏ 48 Todd Van Poppel | .05 | .15 |
| ❏ 49 Roberto Alomar | .20 | .50 |
| ❏ 50 Ozzie Smith | .50 | 1.25 |
| ❏ 51 Sterling Hitchcock | .05 | .15 |
| ❏ 52 Mo Vaughn | .10 | .30 |
| ❏ 53 Rick Aguilera | .05 | .15 |
| ❏ 54 Kent Mercker | .05 | .15 |
| ❏ 55 Don Mattingly | .75 | 2.00 |
| ❏ 56 Bob Scanlan | .05 | .15 |
| ❏ 57 Wilson Alvarez | .05 | .15 |
| ❏ 58 Jose Mesa | .05 | .15 |
| ❏ 59 Scott Kamieniecki | .05 | .15 |
| ❏ 60 Todd Jones | .05 | .15 |
| ❏ 61 John Kruk | .10 | .30 |
| ❏ 62 Mike Stanley | .05 | .15 |
| ❏ 63 Tino Martinez | .20 | .50 |
| ❏ 64 Eddie Zambrano | .05 | .15 |
| ❏ 65 Todd Hundley | .05 | .15 |
| ❏ 66 Jamie Moyer | .10 | .30 |
| ❏ 67 Rich Amaral | .05 | .15 |
| ❏ 68 Jose Valentin | .05 | .15 |
| ❏ 69 Alex Gonzalez | .05 | .15 |
| ❏ 70 Kurt Abbott | .05 | .15 |
| ❏ 71 Delino DeShields | .05 | .15 |
| ❏ 72 Brian Anderson | .05 | .15 |
| ❏ 73 John Vander Wal | .05 | .15 |
| ❏ 74 Turner Ward | .05 | .15 |
| ❏ 75 Tim Raines | .10 | .30 |
| ❏ 76 Mark Acre | .05 | .15 |
| ❏ 77 Jose Offerman | .05 | .15 |
| ❏ 78 Jimmy Key | .10 | .30 |
| ❏ 79 Mark Whiten | .05 | .15 |
| ❏ 80 Mark Gubicza | .05 | .15 |
| ❏ 81 Darren Hall | .05 | .15 |
| ❏ 82 Travis Fryman | .10 | .30 |
| ❏ 83 Cal Ripken | 1.00 | 2.50 |
| ❏ 84 Geronimo Berroa | .05 | .15 |
| ❏ 85 Bret Barberie | .05 | .15 |
| ❏ 86 Andy Ashby | .05 | .15 |
| ❏ 87 Steve Avery | .05 | .15 |
| ❏ 88 Rich Becker | .05 | .15 |
| ❏ 89 John Valentin | .05 | .15 |
| ❏ 90 Glenallen Hill | .05 | .15 |
| ❏ 91 Carlos Garcia | .05 | .15 |
| ❏ 92 Dennis Martinez | .10 | .30 |
| ❏ 93 Pat Kelly | .05 | .15 |
| ❏ 94 Orlando Miller | .05 | .15 |
| ❏ 95 Felix Jose | .05 | .15 |
| ❏ 96 Mike Kingery | .05 | .15 |
| ❏ 97 Jeff Kent | .10 | .30 |
| ❏ 98 Pete Incaviglia | .05 | .15 |
| ❏ 99 Chad Curtis | .05 | .15 |
| ❏ 100 Thomas Howard | .05 | .15 |
| ❏ 101 Hector Carrasco | .05 | .15 |
| ❏ 102 Tom Pagnozzi | .05 | .15 |
| ❏ 103 Danny Tartabull | .05 | .15 |
| ❏ 104 Donnie Elliott | .05 | .15 |
| ❏ 105 Danny Jackson | .05 | .15 |
| ❏ 106 Steve Dunn | .05 | .15 |
| ❏ 107 Roger Salkeld | .05 | .15 |
| ❏ 108 Jeff King | .05 | .15 |
| ❏ 109 Cecil Fielder | .10 | .30 |
| ❏ 110 Paul Molitor CL | .10 | .30 |
| ❏ 111 Denny Neagle | .10 | .30 |
| ❏ 112 Troy Neel | .05 | .15 |
| ❏ 113 Rod Beck | .05 | .15 |
| ❏ 114 Alex Rodriguez | .75 | 2.00 |
| ❏ 115 Joey Eischen | .05 | .15 |
| ❏ 116 Tom Candiotti | .05 | .15 |
| ❏ 117 Ray McDavid | .05 | .15 |
| ❏ 118 Vince Coleman | .05 | .15 |
| ❏ 119 Pete Harnisch | .05 | .15 |
| ❏ 120 David Nied | .05 | .15 |
| ❏ 121 Pat Rapp | .05 | .15 |
| ❏ 122 Sammy Sosa | .30 | .75 |
| ❏ 123 Steve Reed | .05 | .15 |
| ❏ 124 Jose Oliva | .05 | .15 |
| ❏ 125 Ricky Bottalico | .05 | .15 |
| ❏ 126 Jose DeLeon | .05 | .15 |
| ❏ 127 Pat Hentgen | .05 | .15 |
| ❏ 128 Will Clark | .20 | .50 |
| ❏ 129 Mark Dewey | .05 | .15 |
| ❏ 130 Greg Vaughn | .05 | .15 |
| ❏ 131 Darren Dreifort | .05 | .15 |
| ❏ 132 Ed Sprague | .05 | .15 |
| ❏ 133 Lee Smith | .10 | .30 |
| ❏ 134 Charles Nagy | .05 | .15 |
| ❏ 135 Phil Plantier | .05 | .15 |
| ❏ 136 Jason Jacome | .05 | .15 |
| ❏ 137 Jose Lima | .05 | .15 |
| ❏ 138 J.R. Phillips | .05 | .15 |
| ❏ 139 J.T. Snow | .10 | .30 |
| ❏ 140 Michael Huff | .05 | .15 |
| ❏ 141 Billy Brewer | .05 | .15 |
| ❏ 142 Jeromy Burnitz | .10 | .30 |
| ❏ 143 Ricky Bones | .05 | .15 |
| ❏ 144 Carlos Rodriguez | .05 | .15 |
| ❏ 145 Luis Gonzalez | .10 | .30 |
| ❏ 146 Mark Lemke | .05 | .15 |
| ❏ 147 Al Martin | .05 | .15 |
| ❏ 148 Mike Bordick | .05 | .15 |
| ❏ 149 Robb Nen | .10 | .30 |
| ❏ 150 Will Cordero | .05 | .15 |
| ❏ 151 Edgar Martinez | .20 | .50 |
| ❏ 152 Gerald Williams | .05 | .15 |
| ❏ 153 Esteban Beltre | .05 | .15 |
| ❏ 154 Mike Moore | .05 | .15 |
| ❏ 155 Mark Langston | .05 | .15 |
| ❏ 156 Mark Clark | .05 | .15 |
| ❏ 157 Bobby Ayala | .05 | .15 |
| ❏ 158 Rick Wilkins | .05 | .15 |
| ❏ 159 Bobby Munoz | .05 | .15 |
| ❏ 160 Brett Butler CL | .05 | .15 |
| ❏ 161 Scott Erickson | .05 | .15 |
| ❏ 162 Paul Molitor | .10 | .30 |
| ❏ 163 Jon Lieber | .05 | .15 |
| ❏ 164 Jason Grimsley | .05 | .15 |
| ❏ 165 Norberto Martin | .05 | .15 |
| ❏ 166 Javier Lopez | .10 | .30 |
| ❏ 167 Brian McRae | .05 | .15 |
| ❏ 168 Gary Sheffield | .10 | .30 |
| ❏ 169 Marcus Moore | .05 | .15 |
| ❏ 170 John Hudek | .05 | .15 |
| ❏ 171 Kelly Stinnett | .05 | .15 |
| ❏ 172 Chris Gomez | .05 | .15 |
| ❏ 173 Rey Sanchez | .05 | .15 |
| ❏ 174 Juan Guzman | .05 | .15 |
| ❏ 175 Chan Ho Park | .10 | .30 |
| ❏ 176 Terry Shumpert | .05 | .15 |
| ❏ 177 Steve Ontiveros | .05 | .15 |
| ❏ 178 Brad Ausmus | .10 | .30 |
| ❏ 179 Tim Davis | .05 | .15 |
| ❏ 180 Billy Ashley | .05 | .15 |
| ❏ 181 Vinny Castilla | .10 | .30 |
| ❏ 182 Bill Spiers | .05 | .15 |
| ❏ 183 Randy Knorr | .05 | .15 |
| ❏ 184 Brian L.Hunter | .05 | .15 |
| ❏ 185 Pat Meares | .05 | .15 |
| ❏ 186 Steve Buechele | .05 | .15 |
| ❏ 187 Kirt Manwaring | .05 | .15 |
| ❏ 188 Tim Naehring | .05 | .15 |
| ❏ 189 Matt Mieske | .05 | .15 |
| ❏ 190 Josias Manzanillo | .05 | .15 |
| ❏ 191 Greg McMichael | .05 | .15 |
| ❏ 192 Chuck Carr | .05 | .15 |
| ❏ 193 Midre Cummings | .05 | .15 |
| ❏ 194 Darryl Strawberry | .10 | .30 |
| ❏ 195 Greg Gagne | .05 | .15 |
| ❏ 196 Steve Cooke | .05 | .15 |
| ❏ 197 Woody Williams | .05 | .15 |
| ❏ 198 Ron Karkovice | .05 | .15 |
| ❏ 199 Phil Leftwich | .05 | .15 |
| ❏ 200 Jim Thome | .20 | .50 |
| ❏ 201 Brady Anderson | .10 | .30 |
| ❏ 202 Pedro A.Martinez | .05 | .15 |
| ❏ 203 Steve Karsay | .05 | .15 |
| ❏ 204 Reggie Sanders | .10 | .30 |
| ❏ 205 Bill Risley | .05 | .15 |
| ❏ 206 Jay Bell | .10 | .30 |
| ❏ 207 Kevin Brown | .10 | .30 |
| ❏ 208 Tim Scott | .05 | .15 |
| ❏ 209 Lenny Dykstra | .10 | .30 |
| ❏ 210 Willie Greene | .05 | .15 |
| ❏ 211 Jim Eisenreich | .05 | .15 |
| ❏ 212 Cliff Floyd | .10 | .30 |
| ❏ 213 Otis Nixon | .05 | .15 |
| ❏ 214 Eduardo Perez | .05 | .15 |
| ❏ 215 Manuel Lee | .05 | .15 |
| ❏ 216 Armando Benitez | .05 | .15 |
| ❏ 217 Dave McCarty | .05 | .15 |
| ❏ 218 Scott Livingstone | .05 | .15 |
| ❏ 219 Chad Kreuter | .05 | .15 |
| ❏ 220 Don Mattingly CL | .40 | 1.00 |
| ❏ 221 Brian Jordan | .10 | .30 |
| ❏ 222 Matt Whiteside | .05 | .15 |
| ❏ 223 Jim Edmonds | .20 | .50 |
| ❏ 224 Tony Gwynn | .40 | 1.00 |
| ❏ 225 Jose Lind | .05 | .15 |
| ❏ 226 Marvin Freeman | .05 | .15 |
| ❏ 227 Ken Hill | .05 | .15 |
| ❏ 228 David Hulse | .05 | .15 |
| ❏ 229 Joe Hesketh | .05 | .15 |
| ❏ 230 Roberto Petagine | .05 | .15 |
| ❏ 231 Jeffrey Hammonds | .10 | .30 |
| ❏ 232 John Jaha | .05 | .15 |
| ❏ 233 John Burkett | .05 | .15 |
| ❏ 234 Hal Morris | .05 | .15 |
| ❏ 235 Tony Castillo | .05 | .15 |
| ❏ 236 Ryan Bowen | .05 | .15 |
| ❏ 237 Wayne Kirby | .05 | .15 |
| ❏ 238 Brent Mayne | .05 | .15 |
| ❏ 239 Jim Bullinger | .05 | .15 |
| ❏ 240 Mike Lieberthal | .10 | .30 |
| ❏ 241 Barry Larkin | .20 | .50 |
| ❏ 242 David Segui | .05 | .15 |
| ❏ 243 Jose Bautista | .05 | .15 |

|  |  | | |
|---|---|---|---|
| 244 | Hector Fajardo | .05 | .15 |
| 245 | Orel Hershiser | .10 | .30 |
| 246 | James Mouton | .05 | .15 |
| 247 | Scott Leius | .05 | .15 |
| 248 | Tom Glavine | .20 | .50 |
| 249 | Danny Bautista | .05 | .15 |
| 250 | Jose Mercedes | .05 | .15 |
| 251 | Marquis Grissom | .10 | .30 |
| 252 | Charlie Hayes | .05 | .15 |
| 253 | Ryan Klesko | .10 | .30 |
| 254 | Vicente Palacios | .05 | .15 |
| 255 | Matias Carrillo | .05 | .15 |
| 256 | Gary DiSarcina | .05 | .15 |
| 257 | Kirk Gibson | .10 | .30 |
| 258 | Garey Ingram | .05 | .15 |
| 259 | Alex Fernandez | .05 | .15 |
| 260 | John Mabry | .05 | .15 |
| 261 | Chris Howard | .05 | .15 |
| 262 | Miguel Jimenez | .05 | .15 |
| 263 | Heathcliff Slocumb | .05 | .15 |
| 264 | Albert Belle | .10 | .30 |
| 265 | Dave Clark | .05 | .15 |
| 266 | Joe Oasulak | .05 | .15 |
| 267 | Joey Hamilton | .05 | .15 |
| 268 | Mark Portugal | .05 | .15 |
| 269 | Kevin Tapani | .05 | .15 |
| 270 | Sid Fernandez | .05 | .15 |
| 271 | Steve Dreyer | .05 | .15 |
| 272 | Denny Hocking | .05 | .15 |
| 273 | Troy O'Leary | .05 | .15 |
| 274 | Milt Cuyler | .05 | .15 |
| 275 | Frank Thomas | .30 | .75 |
| 276 | Jorge Fabregas | .05 | .15 |
| 277 | Mike Gallego | .05 | .15 |
| 278 | Mickey Morandini | .05 | .15 |
| 279 | Roberto Hernandez | .05 | .15 |
| 280 | Henry Rodriguez | .05 | .15 |
| 281 | Garret Anderson | .10 | .30 |
| 282 | Bob Wickman | .05 | .15 |
| 283 | Gar Finnvold | .05 | .15 |
| 284 | Paul O'Neill | .20 | .50 |
| 285 | Royce Clayton | .05 | .15 |
| 286 | Chuck Knoblauch | .10 | .30 |
| 287 | Johnny Ruffin | .05 | .15 |
| 288 | Dave Nilsson | .05 | .15 |
| 289 | David Cone | .10 | .30 |
| 290 | Chuck McElroy | .05 | .15 |
| 291 | Kevin Stocker | .05 | .15 |
| 292 | Jose Rijo | .05 | .15 |
| 293 | Sean Berry | .05 | .15 |
| 294 | Ozzie Guillen | .05 | .15 |
| 295 | Chris Hoiles | .05 | .15 |
| 296 | Kevin Foster | .05 | .15 |
| 297 | Jeff Frye | .05 | .15 |
| 298 | Lance Johnson | .05 | .15 |
| 299 | Mike Kelly | .05 | .15 |
| 300 | Ellis Burks | .10 | .30 |
| 301 | Roberto Kelly | .05 | .15 |
| 302 | Dante Bichette | .10 | .30 |
| 303 | Alvaro Espinoza | .05 | .15 |
| 304 | Alex Cole | .05 | .15 |
| 305 | Rickey Henderson | .30 | .75 |
| 306 | Dave Weathers | .05 | .15 |
| 307 | Shane Reynolds | .05 | .15 |
| 308 | Bobby Bonilla | .10 | .30 |
| 309 | Junior Felix | .05 | .15 |
| 310 | Jeff Fassero | .05 | .15 |
| 311 | Darren Lewis | .05 | .15 |
| 312 | John Doherty | .05 | .15 |
| 313 | Scott Servais | .05 | .15 |
| 314 | Rick Helling | .05 | .15 |
| 315 | Pedro Martinez | .20 | .50 |
| 316 | Wes Chamberlain | .05 | .15 |
| 317 | Bryan Eversgerd | .05 | .15 |
| 318 | Trevor Hoffman | .10 | .30 |
| 319 | John Patterson | .05 | .15 |
| 320 | Matt Walbeck | .05 | .15 |
| 321 | Jeff Montgomery | .05 | .15 |
| 322 | Mel Rojas | .05 | .15 |
| 323 | Eddie Taubensee | .05 | .15 |
| 324 | Ray Lankford | .10 | .30 |
| 325 | Jose Vizcaino | .05 | .15 |
| 326 | Carlos Baerga | .10 | .30 |
| 327 | Jack Voigt | .05 | .15 |
| 328 | Julio Franco | .10 | .30 |
| 329 | Brent Gates | .05 | .15 |
| 330 | Kirby Puckett CL | .20 | .50 |
| 331 | Greg Maddux | .50 | 1.25 |
| 332 | Jason Bere | .05 | .15 |
| 333 | Bill Wegman | .05 | .15 |
| 334 | Tuffy Rhodes | .05 | .15 |
| 335 | Kevin Young | .05 | .15 |
| 336 | Andy Benes | .05 | .15 |
| 337 | Pedro Astacio | .05 | .15 |
| 338 | Reggie Jefferson | .05 | .15 |
| 339 | Tim Belcher | .05 | .15 |
| 340 | Ken Griffey Jr. | .50 | 1.25 |
| 341 | Mariano Duncan | .05 | .15 |
| 342 | Andres Galarraga | .10 | .30 |
| 343 | Rondell White | .10 | .30 |
| 344 | Cory Bailey | .05 | .15 |
| 345 | Bryan Harvey | .05 | .15 |
| 346 | John Franco | .10 | .30 |
| 347 | Greg Swindell | .05 | .15 |
| 348 | David West | .05 | .15 |
| 349 | Fred McGriff | .20 | .50 |
| 350 | Jose Canseco | .20 | .50 |
| 351 | Orlando Merced | .05 | .15 |
| 352 | Rheal Cormier | .05 | .15 |
| 353 | Carlos Pulido | .05 | .15 |
| 354 | Terry Steinbach | .05 | .15 |
| 355 | Wade Boggs | .20 | .50 |
| 356 | B.J. Surhoff | .10 | .30 |
| 357 | Rafael Palmeiro | .20 | .50 |
| 358 | Anthony Young | .05 | .15 |
| 359 | Tom Brunansky | .05 | .15 |
| 360 | Todd Stottlemyre | .05 | .15 |
| 361 | Chris Turner | .05 | .15 |
| 362 | Joe Boever | .05 | .15 |
| 363 | Jeff Blauser | .05 | .15 |
| 364 | Derek Bell | .05 | .15 |
| 365 | Matt Williams | .10 | .30 |
| 366 | Jeremy Hernandez | .05 | .15 |
| 367 | Joe Girardi | .05 | .15 |
| 368 | Mike Devereaux | .05 | .15 |
| 369 | Jim Abbott | .20 | .50 |
| 370 | Manny Ramirez | .20 | .50 |
| 371 | Kenny Lofton | .10 | .30 |
| 372 | Mark Smith | .05 | .15 |
| 373 | Dave Fleming | .05 | .15 |
| 374 | Dave Stewart | .10 | .30 |
| 375 | Roger Pavlik | .05 | .15 |
| 376 | Hipolito Pichardo | .05 | .15 |
| 377 | Bill Taylor | .05 | .15 |
| 378 | Robin Ventura | .10 | .30 |
| 379 | Bernard Gilkey | .05 | .15 |
| 380 | Kirby Puckett | .30 | .75 |
| 381 | Steve Howe | .05 | .15 |
| 382 | Devon White | .10 | .30 |
| 383 | Roberto Mejia | .05 | .15 |
| 384 | Darrin Jackson | .05 | .15 |
| 385 | Mike Morgan | .05 | .15 |
| 386 | Rusty Meacham | .05 | .15 |
| 387 | Bill Swift | .05 | .15 |
| 388 | Lou Frazier | .05 | .15 |
| 389 | Andy Van Slyke | .20 | .50 |
| 390 | Brett Butler | .10 | .30 |
| 391 | Bobby Witt | .05 | .15 |
| 392 | Jeff Conine | .10 | .30 |
| 393 | Tim Hyers | .05 | .15 |
| 394 | Terry Pendleton | .10 | .30 |
| 395 | Ricky Jordan | .05 | .15 |
| 396 | Eric Plunk | .05 | .15 |
| 397 | Melido Perez | .05 | .15 |
| 398 | Darryl Kile | .10 | .30 |
| 399 | Mark McLemore | .05 | .15 |
| 400 | Greg W.Harris | .05 | .15 |
| 401 | Jim Leyritz | .05 | .15 |
| 402 | Doug Strange | .05 | .15 |
| 403 | Tim Salmon | .20 | .50 |
| 404 | Terry Mulholland | .05 | .15 |
| 405 | Robby Thompson | .05 | .15 |
| 406 | Ruben Sierra | .10 | .30 |
| 407 | Tony Phillips | .05 | .15 |
| 408 | Moises Alou | .10 | .30 |
| 409 | Felix Fermin | .05 | .15 |
| 410 | Pat Listach | .05 | .15 |
| 411 | Kevin Bass | .05 | .15 |
| 412 | Ben McDonald | .05 | .15 |
| 413 | Scott Cooper | .05 | .15 |
| 414 | Jody Reed | .05 | .15 |
| 415 | Deion Sanders | .20 | .50 |
| 416 | Ricky Gutierrez | .05 | .15 |
| 417 | Gregg Jefferies | .05 | .15 |
| 418 | Jack McDowell | .05 | .15 |
| 419 | Al Leiter | .10 | .30 |
| 420 | Tony Longmire | .05 | .15 |
| 421 | Paul Wagner | .05 | .15 |
| 422 | Geronimo Pena | .05 | .15 |
| 423 | Ivan Rodriguez | .20 | .50 |
| 424 | Kevin Gross | .05 | .15 |
| 425 | Kirk McCaskill | .05 | .15 |
| 426 | Greg Myers | .05 | .15 |
| 427 | Roger Clemens | .60 | 1.50 |
| 428 | Chris Hammond | .05 | .15 |
| 429 | Randy Myers | .05 | .15 |
| 430 | Roger Mason | .05 | .15 |
| 431 | Bret Saberhagen | .10 | .30 |
| 432 | Jeff Reboulet | .05 | .15 |
| 433 | John Olerud | .10 | .30 |
| 434 | Bill Gullickson | .05 | .15 |
| 435 | Eddie Murray | .30 | .75 |
| 436 | Pedro Munoz | .05 | .15 |
| 437 | Charlie O'Brien | .05 | .15 |
| 438 | Jeff Nelson | .05 | .15 |
| 439 | Mike Macfarlane | .05 | .15 |
| 440 | Don Mattingly CL | .40 | 1.00 |
| 441 | Derrick May | .05 | .15 |
| 442 | John Roper | .05 | .15 |
| 443 | Darryl Hamilton | .05 | .15 |
| 444 | Dan Miceli | .05 | .15 |
| 445 | Tony Eusebio | .05 | .15 |
| 446 | Jerry Browne | .05 | .15 |
| 447 | Wally Joyner | .10 | .30 |
| 448 | Brian Harper | .05 | .15 |
| 449 | Scott Fletcher | .05 | .15 |
| 450 | Bip Roberts | .05 | .15 |
| 451 | Pete Smith | .05 | .15 |
| 452 | Chili Davis | .10 | .30 |
| 453 | Dave Hollins | .05 | .15 |
| 454 | Tony Pena | .05 | .15 |
| 455 | Butch Henry | .05 | .15 |
| 456 | Craig Biggio | .20 | .50 |
| 457 | Zane Smith | .05 | .15 |
| 458 | Ryan Thompson | .05 | .15 |
| 459 | Mike Jackson | .05 | .15 |
| 460 | Mark McGwire | .75 | 2.00 |
| 461 | John Smoltz | .20 | .50 |
| 462 | Steve Scarsone | .05 | .15 |
| 463 | Greg Colbrunn | .05 | .15 |
| 464 | Shawn Green | .10 | .30 |
| 465 | David Wells | .10 | .30 |
| 466 | Jose Newfield | .05 | .15 |
| 467 | Chip Hale | .05 | .15 |
| 468 | Tony Tarasco | .05 | .15 |
| 469 | Kevin Mitchell | .05 | .15 |
| 470 | Billy Hatcher | .05 | .15 |
| 471 | Jay Buhner | .10 | .30 |
| 472 | Ken Caminiti | .10 | .30 |
| 473 | Tom Henke | .05 | .15 |
| 474 | Todd Worrell | .05 | .15 |
| 475 | Mark Eichhorn | .05 | .15 |
| 476 | Bruce Ruffin | .05 | .15 |
| 477 | Chuck Finley | .10 | .30 |
| 478 | Marc Newfield | .05 | .15 |
| 479 | Paul Shuey | .05 | .15 |
| 480 | Bob Tewksbury | .05 | .15 |
| 481 | Ramon J.Martinez | .10 | .30 |
| 482 | Melvin Nieves | .05 | .15 |
| 483 | Todd Zeile | .05 | .15 |
| 484 | Benito Santiago | .10 | .30 |
| 485 | Stan Javier | .05 | .15 |
| 486 | Kirk Rueter | .05 | .15 |
| 487 | Andre Dawson | .10 | .30 |
| 488 | Eric Karros | .10 | .30 |
| 489 | Dave Magadan | .05 | .15 |
| 490 | Joe Carter CL | .05 | .15 |
| 491 | Randy Velarde | .05 | .15 |
| 492 | Larry Walker | .10 | .30 |
| 493 | Cris Carpenter | .05 | .15 |
| 494 | Tom Gordon | .05 | .15 |
| 495 | Dave Burba | .05 | .15 |
| 496 | Darren Bragg | .05 | .15 |
| 497 | Darren Daulton | .10 | .30 |
| 498 | Don Slaught | .05 | .15 |
| 499 | Pat Borders | .05 | .15 |
| 500 | Lenny Harris | .05 | .15 |
| 501 | Joe Ausanio | .05 | .15 |
| 502 | Alan Trammell | .10 | .30 |
| 503 | Mike Felters | .05 | .15 |
| 504 | Scott Ruffcorn | .05 | .15 |
| 505 | Rich Rowland | .05 | .15 |
| 506 | Juan Samuel | .05 | .15 |
| 507 | Bo Jackson | .30 | .75 |

| | | |
|---|---|---|
| ❑ 508 Jeff Branson | .05 | .15 |
| ❑ 509 Bernie Williams | .20 | .50 |
| ❑ 510 Paul Sorrento | .05 | .15 |
| ❑ 511 Dennis Eckersley | .10 | .30 |
| ❑ 512 Pat Mahomes | .05 | .15 |
| ❑ 513 Rusty Greer | .10 | .30 |
| ❑ 514 Luis Polonia | .05 | .15 |
| ❑ 515 Willie Banks | .05 | .15 |
| ❑ 516 John Wetteland | .10 | .30 |
| ❑ 517 Mike LaValliere | .05 | .15 |
| ❑ 518 Tommy Greene | .05 | .15 |
| ❑ 519 Mark Grace | .20 | .50 |
| ❑ 520 Bob Hamelin | .05 | .15 |
| ❑ 521 Scott Sanderson | .05 | .15 |
| ❑ 522 Joe Carter | .10 | .30 |
| ❑ 523 Jeff Brantley | .05 | .15 |
| ❑ 524 Andrew Lorraine | .05 | .15 |
| ❑ 525 Rico Brogna | .05 | .15 |
| ❑ 526 Shane Mack | .05 | .15 |
| ❑ 527 Mark Wohlers | .05 | .15 |
| ❑ 528 Scott Sanders | .05 | .15 |
| ❑ 529 Chris Bosio | .05 | .15 |
| ❑ 530 Andujar Cedeno | .05 | .15* |
| ❑ 531 Kenny Rogers | .10 | .30 |
| ❑ 532 Doug Drabek | .05 | .15 |
| ❑ 533 Curt Leskanic | .05 | .15 |
| ❑ 534 Craig Shipley | .05 | .15 |
| ❑ 535 Craig Grebeck | .05 | .15 |
| ❑ 536 Cal Eldred | .05 | .15 |
| ❑ 537 Mickey Tettleton | .05 | .15 |
| ❑ 538 Harold Baines | .10 | .30 |
| ❑ 539 Tim Wallach | .05 | .15 |
| ❑ 540 Damon Buford | .05 | .15 |
| ❑ 541 Lenny Webster | .05 | .15 |
| ❑ 542 Kevin Appier | .10 | .30 |
| ❑ 543 Raul Mondesi | .10 | .30 |
| ❑ 544 Eric Young | .05 | .15 |
| ❑ 545 Russ Davis | .05 | .15 |
| ❑ 546 Mike Benjamin | .05 | .15 |
| ❑ 547 Mike Greenwell | .05 | .15 |
| ❑ 548 Scott Brosius | .10 | .30 |
| ❑ 549 Brian Dorsett | .05 | .15 |
| ❑ 550 Chili Davis CL | .05 | .15 |

## 1996 Donruss

| | | |
|---|---|---|
| ❑ COMPLETE SET (550) | 16.00 | 40.00 |
| ❑ COMPLETE SERIES 1 (330) | 10.00 | 25.00 |
| ❑ COMPLETE SERIES 2 (220) | 6.00 | 15.00 |
| ❑ 1 Frank Thomas | .30 | .75 |
| ❑ 2 Jason Bates | .10 | .30 |
| ❑ 3 Steve Sparks | .10 | .30 |
| ❑ 4 Scott Servais | .10 | .30 |
| ❑ 5 Angelo Encarnacion RC | .10 | .30 |
| ❑ 6 Scott Sanders | .10 | .30 |
| ❑ 7 Billy Ashley | .10 | .30 |
| ❑ 8 Alex Rodriguez | .60 | 1.50 |
| ❑ 9 Sean Bergman | .10 | .30 |
| ❑ 10 Brad Radke | .10 | .30 |
| ❑ 11 Andy Van Slyke | .20 | .50 |
| ❑ 12 Joe Girardi | .10 | .30 |
| ❑ 13 Mark Grudzielanek | .10 | .30 |
| ❑ 14 Rick Aguilera | .10 | .30 |
| ❑ 15 Randy Veres | .10 | .30 |
| ❑ 16 Tim Bogar | .10 | .30 |
| ❑ 17 Dave Veres | .10 | .30 |
| ❑ 18 Kevin Stocker | .10 | .30 |
| ❑ 19 Marquis Grissom | .20 | .50 |
| ❑ 20 Will Clark | .20 | .50 |
| ❑ 21 Jay Bell | .10 | .30 |
| ❑ 22 Allen Battle | .10 | .30 |
| ❑ 23 Frank Rodriguez | .10 | .30 |
| ❑ 24 Terry Steinbach | .10 | .30 |
| ❑ 25 Gerald Williams | .10 | .30 |
| ❑ 26 Sid Roberson | .10 | .30 |

| | | |
|---|---|---|
| ❑ 27 Greg Zaun | .10 | .30 |
| ❑ 28 Ozzie Timmons | .10 | .30 |
| ❑ 29 Vaughn Eshelman | .10 | .30 |
| ❑ 30 Ed Sprague | .10 | .30 |
| ❑ 31 Gary DiSarcina | .10 | .30 |
| ❑ 32 Joe Boever | .10 | .30 |
| ❑ 33 Steve Avery | .10 | .30 |
| ❑ 34 Brad Ausmus | .10 | .30 |
| ❑ 35 Kirt Manwaring | .10 | .30 |
| ❑ 36 Gary Sheffield | .20 | .50 |
| ❑ 37 Jason Bere | .10 | .30 |
| ❑ 38 Jeff Manto | .10 | .30 |
| ❑ 39 David Cone | .10 | .30 |
| ❑ 40 Manny Ramirez | .20 | .50 |
| ❑ 41 Sandy Alomar Jr. | .10 | .30 |
| ❑ 42 Curtis Goodwin | .10 | .30 |
| ❑ 43 Tino Martinez | .20 | .50 |
| ❑ 44 Woody Williams | .10 | .30 |
| ❑ 45 Dean Palmer | .10 | .30 |
| ❑ 46 Hipolito Pichardo | .10 | .30 |
| ❑ 47 Jason Giambi | .10 | .30 |
| ❑ 48 Lance Johnson | .10 | .30 |
| ❑ 49 Bernard Gilkey | .10 | .30 |
| ❑ 50 Kirby Puckett | .30 | .75 |
| ❑ 51 Tony Fernandez | .10 | .30 |
| ❑ 52 Alex Gonzalez | .10 | .30 |
| ❑ 53 Bret Saberhagen | .10 | .30 |
| ❑ 54 Lyle Mouton | .10 | .30 |
| ❑ 55 Brian McRae | .10 | .30 |
| ❑ 56 Mark Gubicza | .10 | .30 |
| ❑ 57 Sergio Valdez | .10 | .30 |
| ❑ 58 Darrin Fletcher | .10 | .30 |
| ❑ 59 Steve Parris | .10 | .30 |
| ❑ 60 Johnny Damon | .20 | .50 |
| ❑ 61 Rickey Henderson | .30 | .75 |
| ❑ 62 Darrell Whitmore | .10 | .30 |
| ❑ 63 Roberto Petagine | .10 | .30 |
| ❑ 64 Trinidad Hubbard | .10 | .30 |
| ❑ 65 Heathcliff Slocumb | .10 | .30 |
| ❑ 66 Steve Finley | .10 | .30 |
| ❑ 67 Mariano Rivera | .30 | .75 |
| ❑ 68 Brian L.Hunter | .10 | .30 |
| ❑ 69 Jamie Moyer | .10 | .30 |
| ❑ 70 Ellis Burks | .10 | .30 |
| ❑ 71 Pat Kelly | .10 | .30 |
| ❑ 72 Mickey Tettleton | .10 | .30 |
| ❑ 73 Garret Anderson | .10 | .30 |
| ❑ 74 Andy Pettitte | .20 | .50 |
| ❑ 75 Glenallen Hill | .10 | .30 |
| ❑ 76 Brent Gates | .10 | .30 |
| ❑ 77 Lou Whitaker | .10 | .30 |
| ❑ 78 David Segui | .10 | .30 |
| ❑ 79 Dan Wilson | .10 | .30 |
| ❑ 80 Pat Listach | .10 | .30 |
| ❑ 81 Jeff Bagwell | .20 | .50 |
| ❑ 82 Ben McDonald | .10 | .30 |
| ❑ 83 John Valentin | .10 | .30 |
| ❑ 84 John Jaha | .10 | .30 |
| ❑ 85 Pete Schourek | .10 | .30 |
| ❑ 86 Bryce Florie | .10 | .30 |
| ❑ 87 Brian Jordan | .10 | .30 |
| ❑ 88 Ron Karkovice | .10 | .30 |
| ❑ 89 Al Leiter | .10 | .30 |
| ❑ 90 Tony Longmire | .10 | .30 |
| ❑ 91 Nelson Liriano | .10 | .30 |
| ❑ 92 David Bell | .10 | .30 |
| ❑ 93 Kevin Gross | .10 | .30 |
| ❑ 94 Tom Candiotti | .10 | .30 |
| ❑ 95 Dave Martinez | .10 | .30 |
| ❑ 96 Greg Myers | .10 | .30 |
| ❑ 97 Rheal Cormier | .10 | .30 |
| ❑ 98 Chris Hammond | .10 | .30 |
| ❑ 99 Randy Myers | .10 | .30 |
| ❑ 100 Bill Pulsipher | .10 | .30 |
| ❑ 101 Jason Isringhausen | .10 | .30 |
| ❑ 102 Dave Stevens | .10 | .30 |
| ❑ 103 Roberto Alomar | .20 | .50 |
| ❑ 104 Bob Higginson | .10 | .30 |
| ❑ 105 Eddie Murray | .30 | .75 |
| ❑ 106 Matt Walbeck | .10 | .30 |
| ❑ 107 Mark Wohlers | .10 | .30 |
| ❑ 108 Jeff Nelson | .10 | .30 |
| ❑ 109 Tom Goodwin | .10 | .30 |
| ❑ 110 Cal Ripken CL | .50 | 1.25 |
| ❑ 111 Rey Sanchez | .10 | .30 |
| ❑ 112 Hector Carrasco | .10 | .30 |
| ❑ 113 B.J. Surhoff | .10 | .30 |
| ❑ 114 Dan Miceli | .10 | .30 |

| | | |
|---|---|---|
| ❑ 115 Dean Hartgraves | .10 | .30 |
| ❑ 116 John Burkett | .10 | .30 |
| ❑ 117 Gary Gaetti | .10 | .30 |
| ❑ 118 Ricky Bones | .10 | .30 |
| ❑ 119 Mike Macfarlane | .10 | .30 |
| ❑ 120 Bip Roberts | .10 | .30 |
| ❑ 121 Dave Mlicki | .10 | .30 |
| ❑ 122 Chili Davis | .10 | .30 |
| ❑ 123 Mark Whiten | .10 | .30 |
| ❑ 124 Herbert Perry | .10 | .30 |
| ❑ 125 Butch Henry | .10 | .30 |
| ❑ 126 Derek Bell | .10 | .30 |
| ❑ 127 Al Martin | .10 | .30 |
| ❑ 128 John Franco | .10 | .30 |
| ❑ 129 W. VanLandingham | .10 | .30 |
| ❑ 130 Mike Bordick | .10 | .30 |
| ❑ 131 Mike Mordecai | .10 | .30 |
| ❑ 132 Robby Thompson | .10 | .30 |
| ❑ 133 Greg Colbrunn | .10 | .30 |
| ❑ 134 Domingo Cedeno | .10 | .30 |
| ❑ 135 Chad Curtis | .10 | .30 |
| ❑ 136 Jose Hernandez | .10 | .30 |
| ❑ 137 Scott Klingenbeck | .10 | .30 |
| ❑ 138 Ryan Klesko | .10 | .30 |
| ❑ 139 John Smiley | .10 | .30 |
| ❑ 140 Charlie Hayes | .10 | .30 |
| ❑ 141 Jay Buhner | .10 | .30 |
| ❑ 142 Doug Drabek | .10 | .30 |
| ❑ 143 Roger Pavlik | .10 | .30 |
| ❑ 144 Todd Worrell | .10 | .30 |
| ❑ 145 Cal Ripken | 1.00 | 2.50 |
| ❑ 146 Steve Reed | .10 | .30 |
| ❑ 147 Chuck Finley | .10 | .30 |
| ❑ 148 Mike Blowers | .10 | .30 |
| ❑ 149 Orel Hershiser | .10 | .30 |
| ❑ 150 Allen Watson | .10 | .30 |
| ❑ 151 Ramon Martinez | .10 | .30 |
| ❑ 152 Melvin Nieves | .10 | .30 |
| ❑ 153 Tripp Cromer | .10 | .30 |
| ❑ 154 Yorkis Perez | .10 | .30 |
| ❑ 155 Stan Javier | .10 | .30 |
| ❑ 156 Mel Rojas | .10 | .30 |
| ❑ 157 Aaron Sele | .10 | .30 |
| ❑ 158 Eric Karros | .10 | .30 |
| ❑ 159 Robb Nen | .10 | .30 |
| ❑ 160 Raul Mondesi | .10 | .30 |
| ❑ 161 John Wetteland | .10 | .30 |
| ❑ 162 Tim Scott | .10 | .30 |
| ❑ 163 Kenny Rogers | .10 | .30 |
| ❑ 164 Melvin Bunch | .10 | .30 |
| ❑ 165 Rod Beck | .10 | .30 |
| ❑ 166 Andy Benes | .10 | .30 |
| ❑ 167 Lenny Dykstra | .10 | .30 |
| ❑ 168 Orlando Merced | .10 | .30 |
| ❑ 169 Tomas Perez | .10 | .30 |
| ❑ 170 Xavier Hernandez | .10 | .30 |
| ❑ 171 Ruben Sierra | .10 | .30 |
| ❑ 172 Alan Trammell | .10 | .30 |
| ❑ 173 Mike Fetters | .10 | .30 |
| ❑ 174 Wilson Alvarez | .10 | .30 |
| ❑ 175 Erik Hanson | .10 | .30 |
| ❑ 176 Travis Fryman | .10 | .30 |
| ❑ 177 Jim Abbott | .20 | .50 |
| ❑ 178 Bret Boone | .10 | .30 |
| ❑ 179 Sterling Hitchcock | .10 | .30 |
| ❑ 180 Pat Mahomes | .10 | .30 |
| ❑ 181 Mark Acre | .10 | .30 |
| ❑ 182 Charles Nagy | .10 | .30 |
| ❑ 183 Rusty Greer | .10 | .30 |
| ❑ 184 Mike Stanley | .10 | .30 |
| ❑ 185 Jim Bullinger | .10 | .30 |
| ❑ 186 Shane Andrews | .10 | .30 |
| ❑ 187 Brian Keyser | .10 | .30 |
| ❑ 188 Tyler Green | .10 | .30 |
| ❑ 189 Mark Grace | .20 | .50 |
| ❑ 190 Bob Hamelin | .10 | .30 |
| ❑ 191 Luis Ortiz | .10 | .30 |
| ❑ 192 Joe Carter | .10 | .30 |
| ❑ 193 Eddie Taubensee | .10 | .30 |
| ❑ 194 Brian Anderson | .10 | .30 |
| ❑ 195 Edgardo Alfonzo | .10 | .30 |
| ❑ 196 Pedro Munoz | .10 | .30 |
| ❑ 197 David Justice | .10 | .30 |
| ❑ 198 Trevor Hoffman | .10 | .30 |
| ❑ 199 Bobby Ayala | .10 | .30 |
| ❑ 200 Tony Eusebio | .10 | .30 |
| ❑ 201 Jeff Russell | .10 | .30 |
| ❑ 202 Mike Hampton | .10 | .30 |

|  |  | | |
|---|---|---|---|
| ☐ 203 | Walt Weiss | .10 | .30 |
| ☐ 204 | Joey Hamilton | .10 | .30 |
| ☐ 205 | Roberto Hernandez | .10 | .30 |
| ☐ 206 | Greg Vaughn | .10 | .30 |
| ☐ 207 | Felipe Lira | .10 | .30 |
| ☐ 208 | Harold Baines | .10 | .30 |
| ☐ 209 | Tim Wallach | .10 | .30 |
| ☐ 210 | Manny Alexander | .10 | .30 |
| ☐ 211 | Tim Laker | .10 | .30 |
| ☐ 212 | Chris Haney | .10 | .30 |
| ☐ 213 | Brian Maxcy | .10 | .30 |
| ☐ 214 | Eric Young | .10 | .30 |
| ☐ 215 | Darryl Strawberry | .10 | .30 |
| ☐ 216 | Barry Bonds | .75 | 2.00 |
| ☐ 217 | Tim Naehring | .10 | .30 |
| ☐ 218 | Scott Brosius | .10 | .30 |
| ☐ 219 | Reggie Sanders | .10 | .30 |
| ☐ 220 | Eddie Murray CL | .20 | .50 |
| ☐ 221 | Luis Alicea | .10 | .30 |
| ☐ 222 | Albert Belle | .10 | .30 |
| ☐ 223 | Benji Gil | .10 | .30 |
| ☐ 224 | Dante Bichette | .10 | .30 |
| ☐ 225 | Bobby Bonilla | .10 | .30 |
| ☐ 226 | Todd Stottlemyre | .10 | .30 |
| ☐ 227 | Jim Edmonds | .10 | .30 |
| ☐ 228 | Todd Jones | .10 | .30 |
| ☐ 229 | Shawn Green | .10 | .30 |
| ☐ 230 | Javier Lopez | .10 | .30 |
| ☐ 231 | Ariel Prieto | .10 | .30 |
| ☐ 232 | Tony Phillips | .10 | .30 |
| ☐ 233 | James Mouton | .10 | .30 |
| ☐ 234 | Jose Oquendo | .10 | .30 |
| ☐ 235 | Royce Clayton | .10 | .30 |
| ☐ 236 | Chuck Carr | .10 | .30 |
| ☐ 237 | Doug Jones | .10 | .30 |
| ☐ 238 | Mark McLemore | .10 | .30 |
| ☐ 239 | Bill Swift | .10 | .30 |
| ☐ 240 | Scott Leius | .10 | .30 |
| ☐ 241 | Russ Davis | .10 | .30 |
| ☐ 242 | Ray Durham | .10 | .30 |
| ☐ 243 | Matt Mieske | .10 | .30 |
| ☐ 244 | Brent Mayne | .10 | .30 |
| ☐ 245 | Thomas Howard | .10 | .30 |
| ☐ 246 | Troy O'Leary | .10 | .30 |
| ☐ 247 | Jacob Brumfield | .10 | .30 |
| ☐ 248 | Mickey Morandini | .10 | .30 |
| ☐ 249 | Todd Huntley | .10 | .30 |
| ☐ 250 | Chris Bosio | .10 | .30 |
| ☐ 251 | Omar Vizquel | .20 | .50 |
| ☐ 252 | Mike Lansing | .10 | .30 |
| ☐ 253 | John Mabry | .10 | .30 |
| ☐ 254 | Mike Perez | .10 | .30 |
| ☐ 255 | Delino DeShields | .10 | .30 |
| ☐ 256 | Wil Cordero | .10 | .30 |
| ☐ 257 | Mike James | .10 | .30 |
| ☐ 258 | Todd Van Poppel | .10 | .30 |
| ☐ 259 | Joey Cora | .10 | .30 |
| ☐ 260 | Andre Dawson | .10 | .30 |
| ☐ 261 | Jerry DiPoto | .10 | .30 |
| ☐ 262 | Rick Krivda | .10 | .30 |
| ☐ 263 | Glenn Dishman | .10 | .30 |
| ☐ 264 | Mike Mimbs | .10 | .30 |
| ☐ 265 | John Ericks | .10 | .30 |
| ☐ 266 | Jose Canseco | .20 | .50 |
| ☐ 267 | Jeff Branson | .10 | .30 |
| ☐ 268 | Curt Leskanic | .10 | .30 |
| ☐ 269 | Jon Nunnally | .10 | .30 |
| ☐ 270 | Scott Stahoviak | .10 | .30 |
| ☐ 271 | Jeff Montgomery | .10 | .30 |
| ☐ 272 | Hal Morris | .10 | .30 |
| ☐ 273 | Esteban Loaiza | .10 | .30 |
| ☐ 274 | Rico Brogna | .10 | .30 |
| ☐ 275 | Dave Winfield | .10 | .30 |
| ☐ 276 | J.R. Phillips | .10 | .30 |
| ☐ 277 | Todd Zeile | .10 | .30 |
| ☐ 278 | Tom Pagnozzi | .10 | .30 |
| ☐ 279 | Mark Lemke | .10 | .30 |
| ☐ 280 | Dave Magadan | .10 | .30 |
| ☐ 281 | Greg McMichael | .10 | .30 |
| ☐ 282 | Mike Morgan | .10 | .30 |
| ☐ 283 | Moises Alou | .10 | .30 |
| ☐ 284 | Dennis Martinez | .10 | .30 |
| ☐ 285 | Jeff Kent | .10 | .30 |
| ☐ 286 | Mark Johnson | .10 | .30 |
| ☐ 287 | Darren Lewis | .10 | .30 |
| ☐ 288 | Brad Clontz | .10 | .30 |
| ☐ 289 | Chad Fonville | .10 | .30 |
| ☐ 290 | Paul Sorrento | .10 | .30 |
| ☐ 291 | Lee Smith | .10 | .30 |
| ☐ 292 | Tom Glavine | .20 | .50 |
| ☐ 293 | Antonio Osuna | .10 | .30 |
| ☐ 294 | Kevin Foster | .10 | .30 |
| ☐ 295 | Sandy Martinez | .10 | .30 |
| ☐ 296 | Mark Leiter | .10 | .30 |
| ☐ 297 | Julian Tavarez | .10 | .30 |
| ☐ 298 | Mike Kelly | .10 | .30 |
| ☐ 299 | Joe Oliver | .10 | .30 |
| ☐ 300 | John Flaherty | .10 | .30 |
| ☐ 301 | Don Mattingly | .75 | 2.00 |
| ☐ 302 | Pat Meares | .10 | .30 |
| ☐ 303 | John Doherty | .10 | .30 |
| ☐ 304 | Joe Vitiello | .10 | .30 |
| ☐ 305 | Vinny Castilla | .10 | .30 |
| ☐ 306 | Jeff Brantley | .10 | .30 |
| ☐ 307 | Mike Greenwell | .10 | .30 |
| ☐ 308 | Midre Cummings | .10 | .30 |
| ☐ 309 | Curt Schilling | .10 | .30 |
| ☐ 310 | Ken Caminiti | .10 | .30 |
| ☐ 311 | Scott Erickson | .10 | .30 |
| ☐ 312 | Carl Everett | .10 | .30 |
| ☐ 313 | Charles Johnson | .10 | .30 |
| ☐ 314 | Alex Diaz | .10 | .30 |
| ☐ 315 | Jose Mesa | .10 | .30 |
| ☐ 316 | Mark Carreon | .10 | .30 |
| ☐ 317 | Carlos Perez | .10 | .30 |
| ☐ 318 | Ismael Valdes | .10 | .30 |
| ☐ 319 | Frank Castillo | .10 | .30 |
| ☐ 320 | Tom Henke | .10 | .30 |
| ☐ 321 | Spike Owen | .10 | .30 |
| ☐ 322 | Joe Orsulak | .10 | .30 |
| ☐ 323 | Paul Menhart | .10 | .30 |
| ☐ 324 | Pedro Borbon | .10 | .30 |
| ☐ 325 | Paul Molitor CL | .10 | .30 |
| ☐ 326 | Jeff Cirillo | .10 | .30 |
| ☐ 327 | Edwin Hurtado | .10 | .30 |
| ☐ 328 | Orlando Miller | .10 | .30 |
| ☐ 329 | Steve Ontiveros | .10 | .30 |
| ☐ 330 | Kirby Puckett CL | .20 | .50 |
| ☐ 331 | Scott Bullett | .10 | .30 |
| ☐ 332 | Andres Galarraga | .10 | .30 |
| ☐ 333 | Cal Eldred | .10 | .30 |
| ☐ 334 | Sammy Sosa | .30 | .75 |
| ☐ 335 | Don Slaught | .10 | .30 |
| ☐ 336 | Jody Reed | .10 | .30 |
| ☐ 337 | Roger Cedeno | .10 | .30 |
| ☐ 338 | Ken Griffey Jr. | .50 | 1.25 |
| ☐ 339 | Todd Hollandsworth | .10 | .30 |
| ☐ 340 | Mike Trombley | .10 | .30 |
| ☐ 341 | Gregg Jefferies | .10 | .30 |
| ☐ 342 | Larry Walker | .10 | .30 |
| ☐ 343 | Pedro Martinez | .20 | .50 |
| ☐ 344 | Dwayne Hosey | .10 | .30 |
| ☐ 345 | Terry Pendleton | .10 | .30 |
| ☐ 346 | Pete Harnisch | .10 | .30 |
| ☐ 347 | Tony Castillo | .10 | .30 |
| ☐ 348 | Paul Quantrill | .10 | .30 |
| ☐ 349 | Fred McGriff | .20 | .50 |
| ☐ 350 | Ivan Rodriguez | .20 | .50 |
| ☐ 351 | Butch Huskey | .10 | .30 |
| ☐ 352 | Ozzie Smith | .50 | 1.25 |
| ☐ 353 | Marty Cordova | .10 | .30 |
| ☐ 354 | John Wasdin | .10 | .30 |
| ☐ 355 | Wade Boggs | .20 | .50 |
| ☐ 356 | Dave Nilsson | .10 | .30 |
| ☐ 357 | Rafael Palmeiro | .20 | .50 |
| ☐ 358 | Luis Gonzalez | .10 | .30 |
| ☐ 359 | Reggie Jefferson | .10 | .30 |
| ☐ 360 | Carlos Delgado | .10 | .30 |
| ☐ 361 | Orlando Palmeiro | .10 | .30 |
| ☐ 362 | Chris Gomez | .10 | .30 |
| ☐ 363 | John Smoltz | .20 | .50 |
| ☐ 364 | Marc Newfield | .10 | .30 |
| ☐ 365 | Matt Williams | .10 | .30 |
| ☐ 366 | Jesus Tavarez | .10 | .30 |
| ☐ 367 | Bruce Ruffin | .10 | .30 |
| ☐ 368 | Sean Berry | .10 | .30 |
| ☐ 369 | Randy Velarde | .10 | .30 |
| ☐ 370 | Tony Pena | .10 | .30 |
| ☐ 371 | Jim Thome | .20 | .50 |
| ☐ 372 | Jeffrey Hammonds | .10 | .30 |
| ☐ 373 | Bob Wolcott | .10 | .30 |
| ☐ 374 | Juan Guzman | .10 | .30 |
| ☐ 375 | Juan Gonzalez | .30 | .75 |
| ☐ 376 | Michael Tucker | .10 | .30 |
| ☐ 377 | Doug Johns | .10 | .30 |
| ☐ 378 | Mike Cameron RC | .25 | .60 |
| ☐ 379 | Ray Lankford | .10 | .30 |
| ☐ 380 | Jose Parra | .10 | .30 |
| ☐ 381 | Jimmy Key | .10 | .30 |
| ☐ 382 | John Olerud | .10 | .30 |
| ☐ 383 | Kevin Ritz | .10 | .30 |
| ☐ 384 | Tim Raines | .10 | .30 |
| ☐ 385 | Rich Amaral | .10 | .30 |
| ☐ 386 | Keith Lockhart | .10 | .30 |
| ☐ 387 | Steve Scarsone | .10 | .30 |
| ☐ 388 | Cliff Floyd | .10 | .30 |
| ☐ 389 | Rich Aude | .10 | .30 |
| ☐ 390 | Hideo Nomo | .30 | .75 |
| ☐ 391 | Geronimo Berroa | .10 | .30 |
| ☐ 392 | Pat Rapp | .10 | .30 |
| ☐ 393 | Dustin Hermanson | .10 | .30 |
| ☐ 394 | Greg Maddux | .50 | 1.25 |
| ☐ 395 | Darren Daulton | .10 | .30 |
| ☐ 396 | Kenny Lofton | .10 | .30 |
| ☐ 397 | Ruben Rivera | .10 | .30 |
| ☐ 398 | Billy Wagner | .10 | .30 |
| ☐ 399 | Kevin Brown | .10 | .30 |
| ☐ 400 | Mike Kingery | .10 | .30 |
| ☐ 401 | Bernie Williams | .20 | .50 |
| ☐ 402 | Otis Nixon | .10 | .30 |
| ☐ 403 | Damion Easley | .10 | .30 |
| ☐ 404 | Paul O'Neill | .20 | .50 |
| ☐ 405 | Deion Sanders | .20 | .50 |
| ☐ 406 | Dennis Eckersley | .10 | .30 |
| ☐ 407 | Tony Clark | .10 | .30 |
| ☐ 408 | Rondell White | .10 | .30 |
| ☐ 409 | Luis Sojo | .10 | .30 |
| ☐ 410 | David Hulse | .10 | .30 |
| ☐ 411 | Shane Reynolds | .10 | .30 |
| ☐ 412 | Chris Hoiles | .10 | .30 |
| ☐ 413 | Lee Tinsley | .10 | .30 |
| ☐ 414 | Scott Karl | .10 | .30 |
| ☐ 415 | Ron Gant | .10 | .30 |
| ☐ 416 | Brian Johnson | .10 | .30 |
| ☐ 417 | Jose Oliva | .10 | .30 |
| ☐ 418 | Jack McDowell | .10 | .30 |
| ☐ 419 | Paul Molitor | .10 | .30 |
| ☐ 420 | Ricky Bottalico | .10 | .30 |
| ☐ 421 | Paul Wagner | .10 | .30 |
| ☐ 422 | Terry Bradshaw | .10 | .30 |
| ☐ 423 | Bob Tewksbury | .10 | .30 |
| ☐ 424 | Mike Piazza | .50 | 1.25 |
| ☐ 425 | Luis Andujar | .10 | .30 |
| ☐ 426 | Mark Langston | .10 | .30 |
| ☐ 427 | Stan Belinda | .10 | .30 |
| ☐ 428 | Kurt Abbott | .10 | .30 |
| ☐ 429 | Shawon Dunston | .10 | .30 |
| ☐ 430 | Bobby Jones | .10 | .30 |
| ☐ 431 | Jose Vizcaino | .10 | .30 |
| ☐ 432 | Matt Lawton RC | .15 | .40 |
| ☐ 433 | Pat Hentgen | .10 | .30 |
| ☐ 434 | Cecil Fielder | .10 | .30 |
| ☐ 435 | Carlos Baerga | .10 | .30 |
| ☐ 436 | Rich Becker | .10 | .30 |
| ☐ 437 | Chipper Jones | .30 | .75 |
| ☐ 438 | Bill Risley | .10 | .30 |
| ☐ 439 | Kevin Appier | .10 | .30 |
| ☐ 440 | Wade Boggs CL | .10 | .30 |
| ☐ 441 | Jaime Navarro | .10 | .30 |
| ☐ 442 | Barry Larkin | .20 | .50 |
| ☐ 443 | Jose Valentin | .10 | .30 |
| ☐ 444 | Bryan Rekar | .10 | .30 |
| ☐ 445 | Rick Wilkins | .10 | .30 |
| ☐ 446 | Quilvio Veras | .10 | .30 |
| ☐ 447 | Greg Gagne | .10 | .30 |
| ☐ 448 | Mark Kieler | .10 | .30 |
| ☐ 449 | Bobby Witt | .10 | .30 |
| ☐ 450 | Andy Ashby | .10 | .30 |
| ☐ 451 | Alex Ochoa | .10 | .30 |
| ☐ 452 | Jorge Fabregas | .10 | .30 |
| ☐ 453 | Gene Schall | .10 | .30 |
| ☐ 454 | Ken Hill | .10 | .30 |
| ☐ 455 | Tony Tarasco | .10 | .30 |
| ☐ 456 | Donnie Wall | .10 | .30 |
| ☐ 457 | Carlos Garcia | .10 | .30 |
| ☐ 458 | Ryan Thompson | .10 | .30 |
| ☐ 459 | Marvin Benard RC | .15 | .40 |
| ☐ 460 | Jose Herrera | .10 | .30 |
| ☐ 461 | Jeff Blauser | .10 | .30 |
| ☐ 462 | Chris Hook | .10 | .30 |
| ☐ 463 | Jeff Conine | .10 | .30 |
| ☐ 464 | Devon White | .10 | .30 |
| ☐ 465 | Danny Bautista | .10 | .30 |
| ☐ 466 | Steve Trachsel | .10 | .30 |

**1997 Donruss**

|  |  | | |
|---|---|---|---|
| 467 | C.J. Nitkowski | .10 | .30 |
| 468 | Mike Devereaux | .10 | .30 |
| 469 | David Wells | .10 | .30 |
| 470 | Jim Eisenreich | .10 | .30 |
| 471 | Edgar Martinez | .20 | .50 |
| 472 | Craig Biggio | .20 | .50 |
| 473 | Jeff Frye | .10 | .30 |
| 474 | Karim Garcia | .10 | .30 |
| 475 | Jimmy Haynes | .10 | .30 |
| 476 | Darren Holmes | .10 | .30 |
| 477 | Tim Salmon | .20 | .50 |
| 478 | Randy Johnson | .30 | .75 |
| 479 | Eric Plunk | .10 | .30 |
| 480 | Scott Cooper | .10 | .30 |
| 481 | Chan Ho Park | .10 | .30 |
| 482 | Ray McDavid | .10 | .30 |
| 483 | Mark Petkovsek | .10 | .30 |
| 484 | Greg Swindell | .10 | .30 |
| 485 | George Williams | .10 | .30 |
| 486 | Yamil Benitez | .10 | .30 |
| 487 | Tim Wakefield | .10 | .30 |
| 488 | Kevin Tapani | .10 | .30 |
| 489 | Derrick May | .10 | .30 |
| 490 | Ken Griffey Jr. CL | .30 | .75 |
| 491 | Derek Jeter | .75 | 2.00 |
| 492 | Jeff Fassero | .10 | .30 |
| 493 | Benito Santiago | .10 | .30 |
| 494 | Tom Gordon | .10 | .30 |
| 495 | Jamie Brewington RC | .10 | .30 |
| 496 | Vince Coleman | .10 | .30 |
| 497 | Kevin Jordan | .10 | .30 |
| 498 | Jeff King | .10 | .30 |
| 499 | Mike Simms | .10 | .30 |
| 500 | Jose Rijo | .10 | .30 |
| 501 | Denny Neagle | .10 | .30 |
| 502 | Jose Lima | .10 | .30 |
| 503 | Kevin Seitzer | .10 | .30 |
| 504 | Alex Fernandez | .10 | .30 |
| 505 | Mo Vaughn | .10 | .30 |
| 506 | Phil Nevin | .10 | .30 |
| 507 | J.T. Snow | .10 | .30 |
| 508 | Andujar Cedeno | .10 | .30 |
| 509 | Ozzie Guillen | .10 | .30 |
| 510 | Mark Clark | .10 | .30 |
| 511 | Mark McGwire | .75 | 2.00 |
| 512 | Jeff Reboulet | .10 | .30 |
| 513 | Armando Benitez | .10 | .30 |
| 514 | LaTroy Hawkins | .10 | .30 |
| 515 | Brett Butler | .10 | .30 |
| 516 | Tavo Alvarez | .10 | .30 |
| 517 | Chris Snopek | .10 | .30 |
| 518 | Mike Mussina | .20 | .50 |
| 519 | Darryl Kile | .10 | .30 |
| 520 | Wally Joyner | .10 | .30 |
| 521 | Willie McGee | .10 | .30 |
| 522 | Kent Mercker | .10 | .30 |
| 523 | Mike Jackson | .10 | .30 |
| 524 | Troy Percival | .10 | .30 |
| 525 | Tony Gwynn | .40 | 1.00 |
| 526 | Ron Coomer | .10 | .30 |
| 527 | Darryl Hamilton | .10 | .30 |
| 528 | Phil Plantier | .10 | .30 |
| 529 | Norm Charlton | .10 | .30 |
| 530 | Craig Paquette | .10 | .30 |
| 531 | Dave Burba | .10 | .30 |
| 532 | Mike Henneman | .10 | .30 |
| 533 | Terrell Wade | .10 | .30 |
| 534 | Eddie Williams | .10 | .30 |
| 535 | Robin Ventura | .10 | .30 |
| 536 | Chuck Knoblauch | .10 | .30 |
| 537 | Les Norman | .10 | .30 |
| 538 | Brady Anderson | .10 | .30 |
| 539 | Roger Clemens | .60 | 1.50 |
| 540 | Mark Portugal | .10 | .30 |
| 541 | Mike Matheny | .10 | .30 |
| 542 | Jeff Parrett | .10 | .30 |
| 543 | Roberto Kelly | .10 | .30 |
| 544 | Damon Buford | .10 | .30 |
| 545 | Chad Ogea | .10 | .30 |
| 546 | Jose Offerman | .10 | .30 |
| 547 | Brian Barber | .10 | .30 |
| 548 | Danny Tartabull | .10 | .30 |
| 549 | Duane Singleton | .10 | .30 |
| 550 | Tony Gwynn CL | .20 | .50 |

|  |  | | |
|---|---|---|---|
| | COMPLETE SET (450) | 20.00 | 50.00 |
| | COMPLETE SERIES 1 (270) | 10.00 | 25.00 |
| | COMPLETE UPDATE (180) | 10.00 | 25.00 |
| 1 | Juan Gonzalez | .10 | .30 |
| 2 | Jim Edmonds | .10 | .30 |
| 3 | Tony Gwynn | .40 | 1.00 |
| 4 | Andres Galarraga | .10 | .30 |
| 5 | Joe Carter | .10 | .30 |
| 6 | Raul Mondesi | .10 | .30 |
| 7 | Greg Maddux | .50 | 1.25 |
| 8 | Travis Fryman | .10 | .30 |
| 9 | Brian Jordan | .10 | .30 |
| 10 | Henry Rodriguez | .10 | .30 |
| 11 | Manny Ramirez | .20 | .50 |
| 12 | Mark McGwire | .75 | 2.00 |
| 13 | Marc Newfield | .10 | .30 |
| 14 | Craig Biggio | .20 | .50 |
| 15 | Sammy Sosa | .30 | .75 |
| 16 | Brady Anderson | .10 | .30 |
| 17 | Wade Boggs | .20 | .50 |
| 18 | Charles Johnson | .10 | .30 |
| 19 | Matt Williams | .10 | .30 |
| 20 | Denny Neagle | .10 | .30 |
| 21 | Ken Griffey Jr. | .50 | 1.25 |
| 22 | Robin Ventura | .10 | .30 |
| 23 | Barry Larkin | .20 | .50 |
| 24 | Todd Zeile | .10 | .30 |
| 25 | Chuck Knoblauch | .10 | .30 |
| 26 | Todd Hundley | .10 | .30 |
| 27 | Roger Clemens | .60 | 1.50 |
| 28 | Michael Tucker | .10 | .30 |
| 29 | Rondell White | .10 | .30 |
| 30 | Osvaldo Fernandez | .10 | .30 |
| 31 | Ivan Rodriguez | .20 | .50 |
| 32 | Alex Fernandez | .10 | .30 |
| 33 | Jason Isringhausen | .10 | .30 |
| 34 | Chipper Jones | .30 | .75 |
| 35 | Paul O'Neill | .20 | .50 |
| 36 | Hideo Nomo | .30 | .75 |
| 37 | Roberto Alomar | .20 | .50 |
| 38 | Derek Bell | .10 | .30 |
| 39 | Paul Molitor | .10 | .30 |
| 40 | Andy Benes | .10 | .30 |
| 41 | Steve Trachsel | .10 | .30 |
| 42 | J.T. Snow | .10 | .30 |
| 43 | Jason Kendall | .10 | .30 |
| 44 | Alex Rodriguez | .50 | 1.25 |
| 45 | Joey Hamilton | .10 | .30 |
| 46 | Carlos Delgado | .10 | .30 |
| 47 | Jason Giambi | .10 | .30 |
| 48 | Larry Walker | .10 | .30 |
| 49 | Derek Jeter | .75 | 2.00 |
| 50 | Kenny Lofton | .10 | .30 |
| 51 | Devon White | .10 | .30 |
| 52 | Matt Mieske | .10 | .30 |
| 53 | Melvin Nieves | .10 | .30 |
| 54 | Jose Canseco | .20 | .50 |
| 55 | Tino Martinez | .20 | .50 |
| 56 | Rafael Palmeiro | .10 | .30 |
| 57 | Edgardo Alfonzo | .10 | .30 |
| 58 | Jay Buhner | .10 | .30 |
| 59 | Shane Reynolds | .10 | .30 |
| 60 | Steve Finley | .10 | .30 |
| 61 | Bobby Higginson | .10 | .30 |
| 62 | Dean Palmer | .10 | .30 |
| 63 | Terry Pendleton | .10 | .30 |
| 64 | Marquis Grissom | .10 | .30 |
| 65 | Mike Stanley | .10 | .30 |
| 66 | Moises Alou | .10 | .30 |
| 67 | Ray Lankford | .10 | .30 |
| 68 | Marty Cordova | .10 | .30 |
| 69 | John Olerud | .10 | .30 |

|  |  | | |
|---|---|---|---|
| 70 | David Cone | .10 | .30 |
| 71 | Benito Santiago | .10 | .30 |
| 72 | Ryne Sandberg | .50 | 1.25 |
| 73 | Rickey Henderson | .30 | .75 |
| 74 | Roger Cedeno | .10 | .30 |
| 75 | Wilson Alvarez | .10 | .30 |
| 76 | Tim Salmon | .20 | .50 |
| 77 | Orlando Merced | .10 | .30 |
| 78 | Vinny Castilla | .10 | .30 |
| 79 | Ismael Valdes | .10 | .30 |
| 80 | Dante Bichette | .10 | .30 |
| 81 | Kevin Brown | .10 | .30 |
| 82 | Andy Pettitte | .20 | .50 |
| 83 | Scott Stahoviak | .10 | .30 |
| 84 | Mickey Tettleton | .10 | .30 |
| 85 | Jack McDowell | .10 | .30 |
| 86 | Tom Glavine | .20 | .50 |
| 87 | Gregg Jefferies | .10 | .30 |
| 88 | Chili Davis | .10 | .30 |
| 89 | Randy Johnson | .30 | .75 |
| 90 | John Mabry | .10 | .30 |
| 91 | Billy Wagner | .10 | .30 |
| 92 | Jeff Cirillo | .10 | .30 |
| 93 | Trevor Hoffman | .10 | .30 |
| 94 | Juan Guzman | .10 | .30 |
| 95 | Geronimo Berroa | .10 | .30 |
| 96 | Bernard Gilkey | .10 | .30 |
| 97 | Danny Tartabull | .10 | .30 |
| 98 | Johnny Damon | .20 | .50 |
| 99 | Charlie Hayes | .10 | .30 |
| 100 | Reggie Sanders | .10 | .30 |
| 101 | Robby Thompson | .10 | .30 |
| 102 | Bobby Bonilla | .10 | .30 |
| 103 | Reggie Jefferson | .10 | .30 |
| 104 | John Smoltz | .20 | .50 |
| 105 | Jim Thome | .20 | .50 |
| 106 | Ruben Rivera | .10 | .30 |
| 107 | Darren Oliver | .10 | .30 |
| 108 | Mo Vaughn | .10 | .30 |
| 109 | Roger Pavlik | .10 | .30 |
| 110 | Terry Steinbach | .10 | .30 |
| 111 | Jermaine Dye | .10 | .30 |
| 112 | Mark Grudzielanek | .10 | .30 |
| 113 | Rick Aguilera | .10 | .30 |
| 114 | Jamey Wright | .10 | .30 |
| 115 | Eddie Murray | .30 | .75 |
| 116 | Brian L. Hunter | .10 | .30 |
| 117 | Hal Morris | .10 | .30 |
| 118 | Tom Pagnozzi | .10 | .30 |
| 119 | Mike Mussina | .20 | .50 |
| 120 | Mark Grace | .20 | .50 |
| 121 | Cal Ripken | 1.00 | 2.50 |
| 122 | Tom Goodwin | .10 | .30 |
| 123 | Paul Sorrento | .10 | .30 |
| 124 | Jay Bell | .10 | .30 |
| 125 | Todd Hollandsworth | .10 | .30 |
| 126 | Edgar Martinez | .20 | .50 |
| 127 | George Arias | .10 | .30 |
| 128 | Greg Vaughn | .10 | .30 |
| 129 | Roberto Hernandez | .10 | .30 |
| 130 | Delino DeShields | .10 | .30 |
| 131 | Bill Pulsipher | .10 | .30 |
| 132 | Joey Cora | .10 | .30 |
| 133 | Mariano Rivera | .30 | .75 |
| 134 | Mike Piazza | .50 | 1.25 |
| 135 | Carlos Baerga | .10 | .30 |
| 136 | Jose Mesa | .10 | .30 |
| 137 | Will Clark | .20 | .50 |
| 138 | Frank Thomas | .30 | .75 |
| 139 | John Wetteland | .10 | .30 |
| 140 | Shawn Estes | .10 | .30 |
| 141 | Garret Anderson | .10 | .30 |
| 142 | Andre Dawson | .10 | .30 |
| 143 | Eddie Taubensee | .10 | .30 |
| 144 | Ryan Klesko | .10 | .30 |
| 145 | Rocky Coppinger | .10 | .30 |
| 146 | Jeff Bagwell | .20 | .50 |
| 147 | Donovan Osborne | .10 | .30 |
| 148 | Greg Myers | .10 | .30 |
| 149 | Brant Brown | .10 | .30 |
| 150 | Kevin Elster | .10 | .30 |
| 151 | Bob Wells | .10 | .30 |
| 152 | Wally Joyner | .10 | .30 |
| 153 | Rico Brogna | .10 | .30 |
| 154 | Dwight Gooden | .10 | .30 |
| 155 | Jermaine Allensworth | .10 | .30 |
| 156 | Ray Durham | .10 | .30 |
| 157 | Cecil Fielder | .10 | .30 |

|  |  | | |
|---|---|---|---|
| 158 | John Burkett | .10 | .30 |
| 159 | Gary Sheffield | .10 | .30 |
| 160 | Albert Belle | .10 | .30 |
| 161 | Tomas Perez | .10 | .30 |
| 162 | David Doster | .10 | .30 |
| 163 | John Valentin | .10 | .30 |
| 164 | Danny Graves | .10 | .30 |
| 165 | Jose Paniagua | .10 | .30 |
| 166 | Brian Giles RC | .60 | 1.50 |
| 167 | Barry Bonds | .75 | 2.00 |
| 168 | Sterling Hitchcock | .10 | .30 |
| 169 | Bernie Williams | .20 | .50 |
| 170 | Fred McGriff | .20 | .50 |
| 171 | George Williams | .10 | .30 |
| 172 | Amaury Telemaco | .10 | .30 |
| 173 | Ken Caminiti | .10 | .30 |
| 174 | Ron Gant | .10 | .30 |
| 175 | Dave Justice | .10 | .30 |
| 176 | James Baldwin | .10 | .30 |
| 177 | Pat Hentgen | .10 | .30 |
| 178 | Ben McDonald | .10 | .30 |
| 179 | Tim Naehring | .10 | .30 |
| 180 | Jim Eisenreich | .10 | .30 |
| 181 | Ken Hill | .10 | .30 |
| 182 | Paul Wilson | .10 | .30 |
| 183 | Marvin Benard | .10 | .30 |
| 184 | Alan Benes | .10 | .30 |
| 185 | Ellis Burks | .10 | .30 |
| 186 | Scott Servais | .10 | .30 |
| 187 | David Segui | .10 | .30 |
| 188 | Scott Brosius | .10 | .30 |
| 189 | Jose Offerman | .10 | .30 |
| 190 | Eric Davis | .10 | .30 |
| 191 | Brett Butler | .10 | .30 |
| 192 | Curtis Pride | .10 | .30 |
| 193 | Yamil Benitez | .10 | .30 |
| 194 | Chan Ho Park | .10 | .30 |
| 195 | Bret Boone | .10 | .30 |
| 196 | Omar Vizquel | .20 | .50 |
| 197 | Orlando Miller | .10 | .30 |
| 198 | Ramon Martinez | .10 | .30 |
| 199 | Harold Baines | .10 | .30 |
| 200 | Eric Young | .10 | .30 |
| 201 | Fernando Vina | .10 | .30 |
| 202 | Alex Gonzalez | .10 | .30 |
| 203 | Fernando Valenzuela | .10 | .30 |
| 204 | Steve Avery | .10 | .30 |
| 205 | Ernie Young | .10 | .30 |
| 206 | Kevin Appier | .10 | .30 |
| 207 | Randy Myers | .10 | .30 |
| 208 | Jeff Suppan | .10 | .30 |
| 209 | James Mouton | .10 | .30 |
| 210 | Russ Davis | .10 | .30 |
| 211 | Al Martin | .10 | .30 |
| 212 | Troy Percival | .10 | .30 |
| 213 | Al Leiter | .10 | .30 |
| 214 | Dennis Eckersley | .10 | .30 |
| 215 | Mark Johnson | .10 | .30 |
| 216 | Eric Karros | .10 | .30 |
| 217 | Royce Clayton | .10 | .30 |
| 218 | Tony Phillips | .10 | .30 |
| 219 | Tim Wakefield | .10 | .30 |
| 220 | Alan Trammell | .10 | .30 |
| 221 | Eduardo Perez | .10 | .30 |
| 222 | Butch Huskey | .10 | .30 |
| 223 | Tim Belcher | .10 | .30 |
| 224 | Jamie Moyer | .10 | .30 |
| 225 | F.P. Santangelo | .10 | .30 |
| 226 | Rusty Greer | .10 | .30 |
| 227 | Jeff Brantley | .10 | .30 |
| 228 | Mark Langston | .10 | .30 |
| 229 | Ray Montgomery | .10 | .30 |
| 230 | Rich Becker | .10 | .30 |
| 231 | Ozzie Smith | .50 | 1.25 |
| 232 | Rey Ordonez | .10 | .30 |
| 233 | Ricky Otero | .10 | .30 |
| 234 | Mike Cameron | .10 | .30 |
| 235 | Mike Sweeney | .10 | .30 |
| 236 | Mark Lewis | .10 | .30 |
| 237 | Luis Gonzalez | .10 | .30 |
| 238 | Marcus Jensen | .10 | .30 |
| 239 | Ed Sprague | .10 | .30 |
| 240 | Jose Valentin | .10 | .30 |
| 241 | Jeff Frye | .10 | .30 |
| 242 | Charles Nagy | .10 | .30 |
| 243 | Carlos Garcia | .10 | .30 |
| 244 | Mike Hampton | .10 | .30 |
| 245 | B.J. Surhoff | .10 | .30 |
| 246 | Wilton Guerrero | .10 | .30 |
| 247 | Frank Rodriguez | .10 | .30 |
| 248 | Gary Gaetti | .10 | .30 |
| 249 | Lance Johnson | .10 | .30 |
| 250 | Darren Bragg | .10 | .30 |
| 251 | Darryl Hamilton | .10 | .30 |
| 252 | John Jaha | .10 | .30 |
| 253 | Craig Paquette | .10 | .30 |
| 254 | Jaime Navarro | .10 | .30 |
| 255 | Shawon Dunston | .10 | .30 |
| 256 | Mark Loretta | .10 | .30 |
| 257 | Tim Belk | .10 | .30 |
| 258 | Jeff Darwin | .10 | .30 |
| 259 | Ruben Sierra | .10 | .30 |
| 260 | Chuck Finley | .10 | .30 |
| 261 | Darryl Strawberry | .10 | .30 |
| 262 | Shannon Stewart | .10 | .30 |
| 263 | Pedro Martinez | .20 | .50 |
| 264 | Neifi Perez | .10 | .30 |
| 265 | Jeff Conine | .10 | .30 |
| 266 | Orel Hershiser | .10 | .30 |
| 267 | Eddie Murray CL | .20 | .50 |
| 268 | Paul Molitor CL | .10 | .30 |
| 269 | Barry Bonds CL | .40 | 1.00 |
| 270 | Mark McGwire CL | .40 | 1.00 |
| 271 | Matt Williams | .10 | .30 |
| 272 | Todd Zeile | .10 | .30 |
| 273 | Roger Clemens | .60 | 1.50 |
| 274 | Michael Tucker | .10 | .30 |
| 275 | J.T. Snow | .10 | .30 |
| 276 | Kenny Lofton | .10 | .30 |
| 277 | Jose Canseco | .20 | .50 |
| 278 | Marquis Grissom | .10 | .30 |
| 279 | Moises Alou | .10 | .30 |
| 280 | Benito Santiago | .10 | .30 |
| 281 | Willie McGee | .10 | .30 |
| 282 | Chili Davis | .10 | .30 |
| 283 | Ron Coomer | .10 | .30 |
| 284 | Orlando Merced | .10 | .30 |
| 285 | Delino DeShields | .10 | .30 |
| 286 | John Wetteland | .10 | .30 |
| 287 | Darren Daulton | .10 | .30 |
| 288 | Lee Stevens | .10 | .30 |
| 289 | Albert Belle | .10 | .30 |
| 290 | Sterling Hitchcock | .10 | .30 |
| 291 | David Justice | .10 | .30 |
| 292 | Eric Davis | .10 | .30 |
| 293 | Brian Hunter | .10 | .30 |
| 294 | Darryl Hamilton | .10 | .30 |
| 295 | Steve Avery | .10 | .30 |
| 296 | Joe Vitiello | .10 | .30 |
| 297 | Jaime Navarro | .10 | .30 |
| 298 | Eddie Murray | .30 | .75 |
| 299 | Randy Myers | .10 | .30 |
| 300 | Francisco Cordova | .10 | .30 |
| 301 | Javier Lopez | .10 | .30 |
| 302 | Geronimo Berroa | .10 | .30 |
| 303 | Jeffrey Hammonds | .10 | .30 |
| 304 | Deion Sanders | .20 | .50 |
| 305 | Jeff Fassero | .10 | .30 |
| 306 | Curt Schilling | .10 | .30 |
| 307 | Robb Nen | .10 | .30 |
| 308 | Mark McLemore | .10 | .30 |
| 309 | Jimmy Key | .10 | .30 |
| 310 | Quilvio Veras | .10 | .30 |
| 311 | Bip Roberts | .10 | .30 |
| 312 | Esteban Loaiza | .10 | .30 |
| 313 | Andy Ashby | .10 | .30 |
| 314 | Sandy Alomar Jr. | .10 | .30 |
| 315 | Shawn Green | .10 | .30 |
| 316 | Luis Castillo | .10 | .30 |
| 317 | Benji Gil | .10 | .30 |
| 318 | Otis Nixon | .10 | .30 |
| 319 | Aaron Sele | .10 | .30 |
| 320 | Brad Ausmus | .10 | .30 |
| 321 | Troy O'Leary | .10 | .30 |
| 322 | Terrell Wade | .10 | .30 |
| 323 | Jeff King | .10 | .30 |
| 324 | Kevin Seitzer | .10 | .30 |
| 325 | Mark Wohlers | .10 | .30 |
| 326 | Edgar Renteria | .10 | .30 |
| 327 | Dan Wilson | .10 | .30 |
| 328 | Brian McRae | .10 | .30 |
| 329 | Rod Beck | .10 | .30 |
| 330 | Julio Franco | .10 | .30 |
| 331 | Dave Nilsson | .10 | .30 |
| 332 | Glenallen Hill | .10 | .30 |
| 333 | Kevin Elster | .10 | .30 |
| 334 | Joe Girardi | .10 | .30 |
| 335 | David Wells | .10 | .30 |
| 336 | Jeff Blauser | .10 | .30 |
| 337 | Darryl Kile | .10 | .30 |
| 338 | Jeff Kent | .10 | .30 |
| 339 | Jim Leyritz | .10 | .30 |
| 340 | Todd Stottlemyre | .10 | .30 |
| 341 | Tony Clark | .10 | .30 |
| 342 | Chris Hoiles | .10 | .30 |
| 343 | Mike Lieberthal | .10 | .30 |
| 344 | Matt Lawton | .10 | .30 |
| 345 | Alex Ochoa | .10 | .30 |
| 346 | Chris Snopek | .10 | .30 |
| 347 | Rudy Pemberton | .10 | .30 |
| 348 | Eric Owens | .10 | .30 |
| 349 | Joe Randa | .10 | .30 |
| 350 | John Olerud | .10 | .30 |
| 351 | Steve Karsay | .10 | .30 |
| 352 | Mark Whiten | .10 | .30 |
| 353 | Bob Abreu | .20 | .50 |
| 354 | Bartolo Colon | .10 | .30 |
| 355 | Vladimir Guerrero | .30 | .75 |
| 356 | Darin Erstad | .10 | .30 |
| 357 | Scott Rolen | .20 | .50 |
| 358 | Andruw Jones | .20 | .50 |
| 359 | Scott Spiezio | .10 | .30 |
| 360 | Karim Garcia | .10 | .30 |
| 361 | Hideki Irabu RC | .15 | .40 |
| 362 | Nomar Garciaparra | .50 | 1.25 |
| 363 | Dmitri Young | .10 | .30 |
| 364 | Bubba Trammell RC | .15 | .40 |
| 365 | Kevin Orie | .10 | .30 |
| 366 | Jose Rosado | .10 | .30 |
| 367 | Jose Guillen | .10 | .30 |
| 368 | Brooks Kieschnick | .10 | .30 |
| 369 | Pokey Reese | .10 | .30 |
| 370 | Glendon Rusch | .10 | .30 |
| 371 | Jason Dickson | .10 | .30 |
| 372 | Todd Walker | .10 | .30 |
| 373 | Justin Thompson | .10 | .30 |
| 374 | Todd Greene | .10 | .30 |
| 375 | Jeff Suppan | .10 | .30 |
| 376 | Trey Beamon | .10 | .30 |
| 377 | Damon Mashore | .10 | .30 |
| 378 | Wendell Magee | .10 | .30 |
| 379 | Shigetoshi Hasegawa RC | .20 | .50 |
| 380 | Bill Mueller RC | .50 | 1.25 |
| 381 | Chris Widger | .10 | .30 |
| 382 | Tony Graffanino | .10 | .30 |
| 383 | Derrek Lee | .20 | .50 |
| 384 | Brian Moehler RC | .15 | .40 |
| 385 | Quinton McCracken | .10 | .30 |
| 386 | Matt Morris | .10 | .30 |
| 387 | Marvin Benard | .10 | .30 |
| 388 | Deivi Cruz RC | .15 | .40 |
| 389 | Javier Valentin | .10 | .30 |
| 390 | Todd Dunwoody | .10 | .30 |
| 391 | Derrick Gibson | .10 | .30 |
| 392 | Raul Casanova | .10 | .30 |
| 393 | George Arias | .10 | .30 |
| 394 | Tony Womack RC | .15 | .40 |
| 395 | Antone Williamson | .10 | .30 |
| 396 | Jose Cruz Jr. RC | .15 | .40 |
| 397 | Desi Relaford | .10 | .30 |
| 398 | Frank Thomas HIT | .20 | .50 |
| 399 | Ken Griffey Jr. HIT | .30 | .75 |
| 400 | Cal Ripken HIT | .50 | 1.25 |
| 401 | Chipper Jones HIT | .20 | .50 |
| 402 | Mike Piazza HIT | .30 | .75 |
| 403 | Alex Rodriguez HIT | .30 | .75 |
| 404 | Alex Rodriguez HIT | .10 | .30 |
| 405 | Wade Boggs HIT | .10 | .30 |
| 406 | Juan Gonzalez HIT | .10 | .30 |
| 407 | Tony Gwynn HIT | .20 | .50 |
| 408 | Edgar Martinez HIT | .10 | .30 |
| 409 | Jeff Bagwell HIT | .10 | .30 |
| 410 | Larry Walker HIT | .10 | .30 |
| 411 | Kenny Lofton HIT | .10 | .30 |
| 412 | Manny Ramirez HIT | .10 | .30 |
| 413 | Mark Grace HIT | .10 | .30 |
| 414 | Roberto Alomar HIT | .40 | 1.00 |
| 415 | Derek Jeter HIT | .40 | 1.00 |
| 416 | Brady Anderson HIT | .10 | .30 |
| 417 | Paul Molitor HIT | .10 | .30 |
| 418 | Dante Bichette HIT | .10 | .30 |
| 419 | Jim Edmonds HIT | .10 | .30 |
| 420 | Mo Vaughn HIT | .10 | .30 |
| 421 | Barry Bonds HIT | .40 | 1.00 |

| | | |
|---|---|---|
| ☐ 422 Rusty Greer HIT | .10 | .30 |
| ☐ 423 Greg Maddux KING | .30 | .75 |
| ☐ 424 Andy Pettitte KING | .10 | .30 |
| ☐ 425 John Smoltz KING | .10 | .30 |
| ☐ 426 Randy Johnson KING | .20 | .50 |
| ☐ 427 Hideo Nomo KING | .10 | .30 |
| ☐ 428 Roger Clemens KING | .30 | .75 |
| ☐ 429 Tom Glavine KING | .10 | .30 |
| ☐ 430 Pat Hentgen KING | .10 | .30 |
| ☐ 431 Kevin Brown KING | .10 | .30 |
| ☐ 432 Mike Mussina KING | .10 | .30 |
| ☐ 433 Alex Fernandez KING | .10 | .30 |
| ☐ 434 Kevin Appier KING | .10 | .30 |
| ☐ 435 David Cone KING | .10 | .30 |
| ☐ 436 Jeff Fassero KING | .10 | .30 |
| ☐ 437 John Wetteland KING | .10 | .30 |
| ☐ 438 B.Bonds/I.Rodriguez IS | .40 | 1.00 |
| ☐ 439 K.Griffey Jr./A.Galarraga IS | .30 | .75 |
| ☐ 440 F.McGriff/R.Palmeiro IS | .10 | .30 |
| ☐ 441 B.Larkin/J.Thome IS | .20 | .50 |
| ☐ 442 S.Sosa/A.Belle IS | .20 | .50 |
| ☐ 443 B.Williams/T.Hundley IS | .10 | .30 |
| ☐ 444 C.Knoblauch/B.Jordan IS | .10 | .30 |
| ☐ 445 M.Vaughn/J.Conine IS | .10 | .30 |
| ☐ 446 K.Caminiti/J.Giambi IS | .10 | .30 |
| ☐ 447 R.Mondesi/T.Salmon IS | .10 | .30 |
| ☐ 448 Cal Ripken CL | .50 | 1.25 |
| ☐ 449 Greg Maddux CL | .30 | .75 |
| ☐ 450 Ken Griffey Jr. CL | .30 | .75 |

## 1998 Donruss

| | | |
|---|---|---|
| ☐ COMPLETE SET (420) | 20.00 | 50.00 |
| ☐ COMPLETE SERIES 1 (170) | 8.00 | 20.00 |
| ☐ COMPLETE UPDATE (250) | 12.50 | 30.00 |
| ☐ 1 Paul Molitor | .08 | .25 |
| ☐ 2 Juan Gonzalez | .25 | .60 |
| ☐ 3 Darryl Kile | .08 | .25 |
| ☐ 4 Randy Johnson | .25 | .60 |
| ☐ 5 Tom Glavine | .15 | .40 |
| ☐ 6 Pat Hentgen | .08 | .25 |
| ☐ 7 David Justice | .08 | .25 |
| ☐ 8 Kevin Brown | .08 | .25 |
| ☐ 9 Mike Mussina | .15 | .40 |
| ☐ 10 Ken Caminiti | .08 | .25 |
| ☐ 11 Todd Hundley | .08 | .25 |
| ☐ 12 Frank Thomas | .25 | .60 |
| ☐ 13 Ray Lankford | .08 | .25 |
| ☐ 14 Justin Thompson | .08 | .25 |
| ☐ 15 Jason Dickson | .08 | .25 |
| ☐ 16 Kenny Lofton | .08 | .25 |
| ☐ 17 Ivan Rodriguez | .15 | .40 |
| ☐ 18 Pedro Martinez | .15 | .40 |
| ☐ 19 Brady Anderson | .08 | .25 |
| ☐ 20 Barry Larkin | .15 | .40 |
| ☐ 21 Chipper Jones | .25 | .60 |
| ☐ 22 Tony Gwynn | .30 | .75 |
| ☐ 23 Roger Clemens | .50 | 1.25 |
| ☐ 24 Sandy Alomar Jr. | .08 | .25 |
| ☐ 25 Tino Martinez | .15 | .40 |
| ☐ 26 Jeff Bagwell | .15 | .40 |
| ☐ 27 Shawn Estes | .08 | .25 |
| ☐ 28 Ken Griffey Jr. | .40 | 1.00 |
| ☐ 29 Javier Lopez | .08 | .25 |
| ☐ 30 Denny Neagle | .08 | .25 |
| ☐ 31 Mike Piazza | .40 | 1.00 |
| ☐ 32 Andres Galarraga | .08 | .25 |
| ☐ 33 Larry Walker | .08 | .25 |
| ☐ 34 Alex Rodriguez | .40 | 1.00 |
| ☐ 35 Greg Maddux | .40 | 1.00 |
| ☐ 36 Albert Belle | .08 | .25 |
| ☐ 37 Barry Bonds | .60 | 1.50 |
| ☐ 38 Mo Vaughn | .15 | .40 |
| ☐ 39 Kevin Appier | .08 | .25 |
| ☐ 40 Wade Boggs | .15 | .40 |
| ☐ 41 Garret Anderson | .08 | .25 |
| ☐ 42 Jeffrey Hammonds | .08 | .25 |
| ☐ 43 Marquis Grissom | .08 | .25 |
| ☐ 44 Jim Edmonds | .08 | .25 |
| ☐ 45 Brian Jordan | .08 | .25 |
| ☐ 46 Raul Mondesi | .08 | .25 |
| ☐ 47 John Valentin | .08 | .25 |
| ☐ 48 Brad Radke | .08 | .25 |
| ☐ 49 Ismael Valdes | .08 | .25 |
| ☐ 50 Matt Stairs | .08 | .25 |
| ☐ 51 Matt Williams | .08 | .25 |
| ☐ 52 Reggie Jefferson | .08 | .25 |
| ☐ 53 Alan Benes | .08 | .25 |
| ☐ 54 Charles Johnson | .08 | .25 |
| ☐ 55 Chuck Knoblauch | .08 | .25 |
| ☐ 56 Edgar Martinez | .15 | .40 |
| ☐ 57 Nomar Garciaparra | .40 | 1.00 |
| ☐ 58 Craig Biggio | .15 | .40 |
| ☐ 59 Bernie Williams | .15 | .40 |
| ☐ 60 David Cone | .08 | .25 |
| ☐ 61 Cal Ripken | .75 | 2.00 |
| ☐ 62 Mark McGwire | .60 | 1.50 |
| ☐ 63 Roberto Alomar | .15 | .40 |
| ☐ 64 Fred McGriff | .15 | .40 |
| ☐ 65 Eric Karros | .08 | .25 |
| ☐ 66 Robin Ventura | .08 | .25 |
| ☐ 67 Darin Erstad | .08 | .25 |
| ☐ 68 Michael Tucker | .08 | .25 |
| ☐ 69 Jim Thome | .15 | .40 |
| ☐ 70 Mark Grace | .15 | .40 |
| ☐ 71 Lou Collier | .08 | .25 |
| ☐ 72 Karim Garcia | .08 | .25 |
| ☐ 73 Alex Fernandez | .08 | .25 |
| ☐ 74 J.T. Snow | .08 | .25 |
| ☐ 75 Reggie Sanders | .08 | .25 |
| ☐ 76 John Smoltz | .15 | .40 |
| ☐ 77 Tim Salmon | .15 | .40 |
| ☐ 78 Paul O'Neill | .08 | .25 |
| ☐ 79 Vinny Castilla | .08 | .25 |
| ☐ 80 Rafael Palmeiro | .15 | .40 |
| ☐ 81 Jaret Wright | .08 | .25 |
| ☐ 82 Jay Buhner | .08 | .25 |
| ☐ 83 Brett Butler | .08 | .25 |
| ☐ 84 Todd Greene | .08 | .25 |
| ☐ 85 Scott Rolen | .15 | .40 |
| ☐ 86 Sammy Sosa | .25 | .60 |
| ☐ 87 Jason Giambi | .08 | .25 |
| ☐ 88 Carlos Delgado | .08 | .25 |
| ☐ 89 Deion Sanders | .15 | .40 |
| ☐ 90 Wilton Guerrero | .08 | .25 |
| ☐ 91 Andy Pettitte | .15 | .40 |
| ☐ 92 Brian Giles | .08 | .25 |
| ☐ 93 Dmitri Young | .08 | .25 |
| ☐ 94 Ron Coomer | .08 | .25 |
| ☐ 95 Mike Cameron | .08 | .25 |
| ☐ 96 Edgardo Alfonzo | .08 | .25 |
| ☐ 97 Jimmy Key | .08 | .25 |
| ☐ 98 Ryan Klesko | .08 | .25 |
| ☐ 99 Andy Benes | .08 | .25 |
| ☐ 100 Derek Jeter | .60 | 1.50 |
| ☐ 101 Jeff Fassero | .08 | .25 |
| ☐ 102 Neifi Perez | .08 | .25 |
| ☐ 103 Hideo Nomo | .25 | .60 |
| ☐ 104 Andruw Jones | .15 | .40 |
| ☐ 105 Todd Helton | .15 | .40 |
| ☐ 106 Livan Hernandez | .08 | .25 |
| ☐ 107 Brett Tomko | .08 | .25 |
| ☐ 108 Shannon Stewart | .08 | .25 |
| ☐ 109 Bartolo Colon | .08 | .25 |
| ☐ 110 Matt Morris | .08 | .25 |
| ☐ 111 Miguel Tejada | .25 | .60 |
| ☐ 112 Pokey Reese | .08 | .25 |
| ☐ 113 Fernando Tatis | .08 | .25 |
| ☐ 114 Todd Dunwoody | .08 | .25 |
| ☐ 115 Jose Cruz Jr. | .15 | .40 |
| ☐ 116 Chan Ho Park | .15 | .40 |
| ☐ 117 Kevin Young | .08 | .25 |
| ☐ 118 Rickey Henderson | .15 | .40 |
| ☐ 119 Hideki Irabu | .25 | .60 |
| ☐ 120 Francisco Cordova | .08 | .25 |
| ☐ 121 Al Martin | .08 | .25 |
| ☐ 122 Tony Clark | .15 | .40 |
| ☐ 123 Curt Schilling | .15 | .40 |
| ☐ 124 Rusty Greer | .08 | .25 |
| ☐ 125 Jose Canseco | .15 | .40 |
| ☐ 126 Edgar Renteria | .08 | .25 |
| ☐ 127 Todd Walker | .08 | .25 |
| ☐ 128 Wally Joyner | .08 | .25 |
| ☐ 129 Bill Mueller | .08 | .25 |
| ☐ 130 Jose Guillen | .08 | .25 |
| ☐ 131 Manny Ramirez | .15 | .40 |
| ☐ 132 Bobby Higginson | .08 | .25 |
| ☐ 133 Kevin Orie | .08 | .25 |
| ☐ 134 Will Clark | .15 | .40 |
| ☐ 135 Dave Nilsson | .08 | .25 |
| ☐ 136 Jason Kendall | .08 | .25 |
| ☐ 137 Ivan Cruz | .08 | .25 |
| ☐ 138 Gary Sheffield | .15 | .40 |
| ☐ 139 Bubba Trammell | .08 | .25 |
| ☐ 140 Vladimir Guerrero | .25 | .60 |
| ☐ 141 Dennis Reyes | .08 | .25 |
| ☐ 142 Bobby Bonilla | .08 | .25 |
| ☐ 143 Ruben Rivera | .08 | .25 |
| ☐ 144 Ben Grieve | .25 | .60 |
| ☐ 145 Moises Alou | .08 | .25 |
| ☐ 146 Tony Womack | .08 | .25 |
| ☐ 147 Eric Young | .08 | .25 |
| ☐ 148 Paul Konerko | .08 | .25 |
| ☐ 149 Dante Bichette | .08 | .25 |
| ☐ 150 Joe Carter | .08 | .25 |
| ☐ 151 Rondell White | .08 | .25 |
| ☐ 152 Chris Holt | .08 | .25 |
| ☐ 153 Shawn Green | .08 | .25 |
| ☐ 154 Mark Grudzielanek | .08 | .25 |
| ☐ 155 Jermaine Dye | .08 | .25 |
| ☐ 156 Ken Griffey Jr. FC | .25 | .60 |
| ☐ 157 Frank Thomas FC | .15 | .40 |
| ☐ 158 Chipper Jones FC | .15 | .40 |
| ☐ 159 Mike Piazza FC | .25 | .60 |
| ☐ 160 Cal Ripken FC | .40 | 1.00 |
| ☐ 161 Greg Maddux FC | .25 | .60 |
| ☐ 162 Juan Gonzalez FC | .08 | .25 |
| ☐ 163 Alex Rodriguez FC | .25 | .60 |
| ☐ 164 Mark McGwire FC | .30 | .75 |
| ☐ 165 Derek Jeter FC | .30 | .75 |
| ☐ 166 Larry Walker CL | .08 | .25 |
| ☐ 167 Tony Gwynn CL | .15 | .40 |
| ☐ 168 Tino Martinez CL | .08 | .25 |
| ☐ 169 Scott Rolen CL | .08 | .25 |
| ☐ 170 Nomar Garciaparra CL | .25 | .60 |
| ☐ 171 Mike Sweeney | .08 | .25 |
| ☐ 172 Dustin Hermanson | .08 | .25 |
| ☐ 173 Darren Dreifort | .08 | .25 |
| ☐ 174 Ron Gant | .08 | .25 |
| ☐ 175 Todd Hollandsworth | .08 | .25 |
| ☐ 176 John Jaha | .08 | .25 |
| ☐ 177 Kerry Wood | .10 | .30 |
| ☐ 178 Chris Stynes | .08 | .25 |
| ☐ 179 Kevin Orie | .08 | .25 |
| ☐ 180 Derek Bell | .08 | .25 |
| ☐ 181 Darryl Strawberry | .15 | .40 |
| ☐ 182 Damion Easley | .08 | .25 |
| ☐ 183 Jeff Cirillo | .08 | .25 |
| ☐ 184 John Thomson | .08 | .25 |
| ☐ 185 Dan Wilson | .08 | .25 |
| ☐ 186 Jay Bell | .08 | .25 |
| ☐ 187 Bernard Gilkey | .08 | .25 |
| ☐ 188 Marc Valdes | .08 | .25 |
| ☐ 189 Ramon Martinez | .08 | .25 |
| ☐ 190 Charles Nagy | .08 | .25 |
| ☐ 191 Derek Lowe | .08 | .25 |
| ☐ 192 Andy Benes | .08 | .25 |
| ☐ 193 Delino DeShields | .08 | .25 |
| ☐ 194 Ryan Jackson RC | .08 | .25 |
| ☐ 195 Kenny Lofton | .15 | .40 |
| ☐ 196 Chuck Knoblauch | .08 | .25 |
| ☐ 197 Andres Galarraga | .08 | .25 |
| ☐ 198 Jose Canseco | .15 | .40 |
| ☐ 199 John Olerud | .08 | .25 |
| ☐ 200 Lance Johnson | .08 | .25 |
| ☐ 201 Darryl Kile | .08 | .25 |
| ☐ 202 Luis Castillo | .08 | .25 |
| ☐ 203 Joe Carter | .08 | .25 |
| ☐ 204 Dennis Eckersley | .08 | .25 |
| ☐ 205 Steve Finley | .08 | .25 |
| ☐ 206 Esteban Loaiza | .08 | .25 |
| ☐ 207 Ryan Christenson RC | .08 | .25 |
| ☐ 208 Deivi Cruz | .08 | .25 |
| ☐ 209 Mariano Rivera | .25 | .60 |
| ☐ 210 Mike Judd RC | .10 | .30 |
| ☐ 211 Billy Wagner | .08 | .25 |
| ☐ 212 Scott Spiezio | .08 | .25 |
| ☐ 213 Russ Davis | .08 | .25 |
| ☐ 214 Jeff Suppan | .08 | .25 |
| ☐ 215 Doug Glanville | .08 | .25 |
| ☐ 216 Dmitri Young | .08 | .25 |

|  |  | | |
|---|---|---|---|
| ❏ 217 | Rey Ordonez | .08 | .25 |
| ❏ 218 | Cecil Fielder | .08 | .25 |
| ❏ 219 | Masato Yoshii RC | .10 | .30 |
| ❏ 220 | Raul Casanova | .08 | .25 |
| ❏ 221 | Rolando Arrojo RC | .10 | .30 |
| ❏ 222 | Ellis Burks | .08 | .25 |
| ❏ 223 | Butch Huskey | .08 | .25 |
| ❏ 224 | Brian Hunter | .08 | .25 |
| ❏ 225 | Marquis Grissom | .08 | .25 |
| ❏ 226 | Kevin Brown | .15 | .40 |
| ❏ 227 | Joe Randa | .08 | .25 |
| ❏ 228 | Henry Rodriguez | .08 | .25 |
| ❏ 229 | Omar Vizquel | .15 | .40 |
| ❏ 230 | Fred McGriff | .15 | .40 |
| ❏ 231 | Matt Williams | .08 | .25 |
| ❏ 232 | Moises Alou | .08 | .25 |
| ❏ 233 | Travis Fryman | .08 | .25 |
| ❏ 234 | Wade Boggs | .15 | .40 |
| ❏ 235 | Pedro Martinez | .15 | .40 |
| ❏ 236 | Rickey Henderson | .25 | .60 |
| ❏ 237 | Bubba Trammell | .08 | .25 |
| ❏ 238 | Mike Caruso | .08 | .25 |
| ❏ 239 | Wilson Alvarez | .08 | .25 |
| ❏ 240 | Geronimo Berroa | .08 | .25 |
| ❏ 241 | Eric Milton | .08 | .25 |
| ❏ 242 | Scott Erickson | .08 | .25 |
| ❏ 243 | Todd Erdos RC | .08 | .25 |
| ❏ 244 | Bobby Hughes | .08 | .25 |
| ❏ 245 | Dave Hollins | .08 | .25 |
| ❏ 246 | Dean Palmer | .08 | .25 |
| ❏ 247 | Carlos Baerga | .08 | .25 |
| ❏ 248 | Jose Silva | .08 | .25 |
| ❏ 249 | Jose Cabrera RC | .08 | .25 |
| ❏ 250 | Tom Evans | .08 | .25 |
| ❏ 251 | Marty Cordova | .08 | .25 |
| ❏ 252 | Hanley Frias RC | .08 | .25 |
| ❏ 253 | Javier Valentin | .08 | .25 |
| ❏ 254 | Mario Valdez | .08 | .25 |
| ❏ 255 | Joey Cora | .08 | .25 |
| ❏ 256 | Mike Lansing | .08 | .25 |
| ❏ 257 | Jeff Kent | .08 | .25 |
| ❏ 258 | Dave Dellucci RC | .20 | .50 |
| ❏ 259 | Curtis King RC | .08 | .25 |
| ❏ 260 | David Segui | .08 | .25 |
| ❏ 261 | Royce Clayton | .08 | .25 |
| ❏ 262 | Jeff Blauser | .08 | .25 |
| ❏ 263 | Manny Aybar RC | .08 | .25 |
| ❏ 264 | Mike Cather RC | .08 | .25 |
| ❏ 265 | Todd Zeile | .08 | .25 |
| ❏ 266 | Richard Hidalgo | .08 | .25 |
| ❏ 267 | Daron Powell | .08 | .25 |
| ❏ 268 | Mike DeJean RC | .08 | .25 |
| ❏ 269 | Ken Cloude | .08 | .25 |
| ❏ 270 | Danny Klassen | .08 | .25 |
| ❏ 271 | Sean Casey | .08 | .25 |
| ❏ 272 | A.J. Hinch | .08 | .25 |
| ❏ 273 | Rich Butler RC | .08 | .25 |
| ❏ 274 | Ben Ford RC | .08 | .25 |
| ❏ 275 | Billy McMillon | .08 | .25 |
| ❏ 276 | Wilson Delgado | .08 | .25 |
| ❏ 277 | Orlando Cabrera | .08 | .25 |
| ❏ 278 | Geoff Jenkins | .08 | .25 |
| ❏ 279 | Enrique Wilson | .08 | .25 |
| ❏ 280 | Derrek Lee | .15 | .40 |
| ❏ 281 | Marc Pisciotta RC | .08 | .25 |
| ❏ 282 | Abraham Nunez | .08 | .25 |
| ❏ 283 | Aaron Boone | .08 | .25 |
| ❏ 284 | Brad Fullmer | .08 | .25 |
| ❏ 285 | Rob Stanifer RC | .08 | .25 |
| ❏ 286 | Preston Wilson | .08 | .25 |
| ❏ 287 | Greg Norton | .08 | .25 |
| ❏ 288 | Bobby Smith | .08 | .25 |
| ❏ 289 | Josh Booty | .08 | .25 |
| ❏ 290 | Russell Branyan | .08 | .25 |
| ❏ 291 | Jeremi Gonzalez | .08 | .25 |
| ❏ 292 | Michael Coleman | .08 | .25 |
| ❏ 293 | Cliff Politte | .08 | .25 |
| ❏ 294 | Eric Ludwick | .08 | .25 |
| ❏ 295 | Rafael Medina | .08 | .25 |
| ❏ 296 | Jason Varitek | .25 | .60 |
| ❏ 297 | Ron Wright | .08 | .25 |
| ❏ 298 | Mark Kotsay | .08 | .25 |
| ❏ 299 | David Ortiz | .30 | .75 |
| ❏ 300 | Frank Catalanotto RC | .20 | .50 |
| ❏ 301 | Robinson Checo | .08 | .25 |
| ❏ 302 | Kevin Millwood RC | .30 | .75 |
| ❏ 303 | Jacob Cruz | .08 | .25 |
| ❏ 304 | Javier Vazquez | .08 | .25 |

|  |  | | |
|---|---|---|---|
| ❏ 305 | Magglio Ordonez RC | 1.00 | 2.50 |
| ❏ 306 | Kevin Witt | .08 | .25 |
| ❏ 307 | Derrick Gibson | .08 | .25 |
| ❏ 308 | Shane Monahan | .08 | .25 |
| ❏ 309 | Brian Rose | .08 | .25 |
| ❏ 310 | Bobby Estalella | .08 | .25 |
| ❏ 311 | Felix Heredia | .08 | .25 |
| ❏ 312 | Desi Relaford | .08 | .25 |
| ❏ 313 | Esteban Yan RC | .10 | .30 |
| ❏ 314 | Ricky Ledee | .08 | .25 |
| ❏ 315 | Steve Woodard | .08 | .25 |
| ❏ 316 | Pat Watkins | .08 | .25 |
| ❏ 317 | Damian Moss | .08 | .25 |
| ❏ 318 | Bob Abreu | .08 | .25 |
| ❏ 319 | Jeff Abbott | .08 | .25 |
| ❏ 320 | Miguel Cairo | .08 | .25 |
| ❏ 321 | Rigo Beltran RC | .08 | .25 |
| ❏ 322 | Tony Saunders | .08 | .25 |
| ❏ 323 | Randall Simon | .08 | .25 |
| ❏ 324 | Hiram Bocachica | .08 | .25 |
| ❏ 325 | Richie Sexson | .08 | .25 |
| ❏ 326 | Karim Garcia | .08 | .25 |
| ❏ 327 | Mike Lowell RC | .50 | 1.25 |
| ❏ 328 | Pat Cline | .08 | .25 |
| ❏ 329 | Matt Clement | .08 | .25 |
| ❏ 330 | Scott Elarton | .08 | .25 |
| ❏ 331 | Manuel Barrios RC | .08 | .25 |
| ❏ 332 | Bruce Chen | .08 | .25 |
| ❏ 333 | Juan Encarnacion | .08 | .25 |
| ❏ 334 | Travis Lee | .08 | .25 |
| ❏ 335 | Wes Helms | .08 | .25 |
| ❏ 336 | Chad Fox RC | .08 | .25 |
| ❏ 337 | Donnie Sadler | .08 | .25 |
| ❏ 338 | Carlos Mendoza RC | .08 | .25 |
| ❏ 339 | Damian Jackson | .08 | .25 |
| ❏ 340 | Julio Ramirez RC | .08 | .25 |
| ❏ 341 | John Halama RC | .10 | .30 |
| ❏ 342 | Edwin Diaz | .08 | .25 |
| ❏ 343 | Felix Martinez | .08 | .25 |
| ❏ 344 | Eli Marrero | .08 | .25 |
| ❏ 345 | Carl Pavano | .08 | .25 |
| ❏ 346 | Vladimir Guerrero HL | .15 | .40 |
| ❏ 347 | Barry Bonds HL | .30 | .75 |
| ❏ 348 | Darin Erstad HL | .08 | .25 |
| ❏ 349 | Albert Belle HL | .08 | .25 |
| ❏ 350 | Kenny Lofton HL | .08 | .25 |
| ❏ 351 | Mo Vaughn HL | .08 | .25 |
| ❏ 352 | Jose Cruz Jr. HL | .08 | .25 |
| ❏ 353 | Tony Clark HL | .08 | .25 |
| ❏ 354 | Roberto Alomar HL | .08 | .25 |
| ❏ 355 | Manny Ramirez HL | .08 | .25 |
| ❏ 356 | Paul Molitor HL | .08 | .25 |
| ❏ 357 | Jim Thome HL | .08 | .25 |
| ❏ 358 | Tino Martinez HL | .08 | .25 |
| ❏ 359 | Tim Salmon HL | .08 | .25 |
| ❏ 360 | David Justice HL | .08 | .25 |
| ❏ 361 | Raul Mondesi HL | .08 | .25 |
| ❏ 362 | Mark Grace HL | .08 | .25 |
| ❏ 363 | Craig Biggio HL | .08 | .25 |
| ❏ 364 | Larry Walker HL | .08 | .25 |
| ❏ 365 | Mark McGwire HL | .30 | .75 |
| ❏ 366 | Juan Gonzalez HL | .30 | .75 |
| ❏ 367 | Derek Jeter HL | .30 | .75 |
| ❏ 368 | Chipper Jones HL | .15 | .40 |
| ❏ 369 | Frank Thomas HL | .15 | .40 |
| ❏ 370 | Alex Rodriguez HL | .25 | .60 |
| ❏ 371 | Mike Piazza HL | .25 | .60 |
| ❏ 372 | Tony Gwynn HL | .15 | .40 |
| ❏ 373 | Jeff Bagwell HL | .08 | .25 |
| ❏ 374 | Nomar Garciaparra HL | .25 | .60 |
| ❏ 375 | Ken Griffey Jr. HL | .25 | .60 |
| ❏ 376 | Livan Hernandez UN | .08 | .25 |
| ❏ 377 | Chan Ho Park UN | .08 | .25 |
| ❏ 378 | Mike Mussina UN | .08 | .25 |
| ❏ 379 | Andy Pettitte UN | .08 | .25 |
| ❏ 380 | Greg Maddux UN | .25 | .60 |
| ❏ 381 | Hideo Nomo UN | .15 | .40 |
| ❏ 382 | Roger Clemens UN | .25 | .60 |
| ❏ 383 | Randy Johnson UN | .15 | .40 |
| ❏ 384 | Pedro Martinez UN | .15 | .40 |
| ❏ 385 | Jaret Wright UN | .08 | .25 |
| ❏ 386 | Ken Griffey Jr. SG | .25 | .60 |
| ❏ 387 | Todd Helton SG | .08 | .25 |
| ❏ 388 | Paul Konerko SG | .08 | .25 |
| ❏ 389 | Cal Ripken SG | .40 | 1.00 |
| ❏ 390 | Larry Walker SG | .08 | .25 |
| ❏ 391 | Ken Caminiti SG | .08 | .25 |
| ❏ 392 | Jose Guillen SG | .08 | .25 |

|  |  | | |
|---|---|---|---|
| ❏ 393 | Jim Edmonds SG | .08 | .25 |
| ❏ 394 | Barry Larkin SG | .08 | .25 |
| ❏ 395 | Bernie Williams SG | .08 | .25 |
| ❏ 396 | Tony Clark SG | .08 | .25 |
| ❏ 397 | Jose Cruz Jr. SG | .08 | .25 |
| ❏ 398 | Ivan Rodriguez SG | .08 | .25 |
| ❏ 399 | Darin Erstad SG | .08 | .25 |
| ❏ 400 | Scott Rolen SG | .08 | .25 |
| ❏ 401 | Mark McGwire SG | .30 | .75 |
| ❏ 402 | Andruw Jones SG | .08 | .25 |
| ❏ 403 | Juan Gonzalez SG | .08 | .25 |
| ❏ 404 | Derek Jeter SG | .30 | .75 |
| ❏ 405 | Chipper Jones SG | .15 | .40 |
| ❏ 406 | Greg Maddux SG | .25 | .60 |
| ❏ 407 | Frank Thomas SG | .15 | .40 |
| ❏ 408 | Alex Rodriguez SG | .25 | .60 |
| ❏ 409 | Mike Piazza SG | .25 | .60 |
| ❏ 410 | Tony Gwynn SG | .15 | .40 |
| ❏ 411 | Jeff Bagwell SG | .08 | .25 |
| ❏ 412 | Nomar Garciaparra SG | .25 | .60 |
| ❏ 413 | Hideo Nomo SG | .15 | .40 |
| ❏ 414 | Barry Bonds SG | .30 | .75 |
| ❏ 415 | Ben Grieve SG | .08 | .25 |
| ❏ 416 | Barry Bonds CL | .30 | .75 |
| ❏ 417 | Mark McGwire CL | .30 | .75 |
| ❏ 418 | Roger Clemens CL | .25 | .60 |
| ❏ 419 | Livan Hernandez CL | .08 | .25 |
| ❏ 420 | Ken Griffey Jr. CL | .25 | .60 |

## 2001 Donruss

| | | | |
|---|---|---|---|
| ❏ COMP.SET w/o SP's (150) | | 10.00 | 25.00 |
| ❏ COMMON CARD (1-150) | | .10 | .30 |
| ❏ COMMON CARD (151-200) | | 3.00 | 8.00 |
| ❏ COMMON CARD (201-220) | | 1.00 | 2.50 |
| ❏ 1 | Alex Rodriguez | .50 | 1.25 |
| ❏ 2 | Barry Bonds | .75 | 2.00 |
| ❏ 3 | Cal Ripken | 1.00 | 2.50 |
| ❏ 4 | Chipper Jones | .30 | .75 |
| ❏ 5 | Derek Jeter | .75 | 2.00 |
| ❏ 6 | Troy Glaus | .10 | .30 |
| ❏ 7 | Frank Thomas | .30 | .75 |
| ❏ 8 | Greg Maddux | .50 | 1.25 |
| ❏ 9 | Ivan Rodriguez | .20 | .50 |
| ❏ 10 | Jeff Bagwell | .20 | .50 |
| ❏ 11 | Jose Canseco | .20 | .50 |
| ❏ 12 | Todd Helton | .20 | .50 |
| ❏ 13 | Ken Griffey Jr. | .50 | 1.25 |
| ❏ 14 | Manny Ramirez Sox | .20 | .50 |
| ❏ 15 | Mark McGwire | .75 | 2.00 |
| ❏ 16 | Mike Piazza | .50 | 1.25 |
| ❏ 17 | Nomar Garciaparra | .50 | 1.25 |
| ❏ 18 | Pedro Martinez | .20 | .50 |
| ❏ 19 | Randy Johnson | .30 | .75 |
| ❏ 20 | Rick Ankiel | .10 | .30 |
| ❏ 21 | Rickey Henderson | .30 | .75 |
| ❏ 22 | Roger Clemens | .60 | 1.50 |
| ❏ 23 | Sammy Sosa | .30 | .75 |
| ❏ 24 | Tony Gwynn | .40 | 1.00 |
| ❏ 25 | Vladimir Guerrero | .30 | .75 |
| ❏ 26 | Eric Davis | .10 | .30 |
| ❏ 27 | Roberto Alomar | .10 | .30 |
| ❏ 28 | Mark Mulder | .10 | .30 |
| ❏ 29 | Pat Burrell | .10 | .30 |
| ❏ 30 | Harold Baines | .10 | .30 |
| ❏ 31 | Carlos Delgado | .10 | .30 |
| ❏ 32 | J.D. Drew | .10 | .30 |
| ❏ 33 | Jim Edmonds | .10 | .30 |
| ❏ 34 | Darin Erstad | .10 | .30 |
| ❏ 35 | Jason Giambi | .10 | .30 |
| ❏ 36 | Tom Glavine | .20 | .50 |
| ❏ 37 | Juan Gonzalez | .20 | .50 |
| ❏ 38 | Mark Grace | .20 | .50 |
| ❏ 39 | Shawn Green | .10 | .30 |
| ❏ 40 | Tim Hudson | .10 | .30 |

|  |  | | |
|---|--------|------|------|
| 41 | Andruw Jones | .20 | .50 |
| 42 | David Justice | .10 | .30 |
| 43 | Jeff Kent | .10 | .30 |
| 44 | Barry Larkin | .20 | .50 |
| 45 | Pokey Reese | .10 | .30 |
| 46 | Mike Mussina | .20 | .50 |
| 47 | Hideo Nomo | .30 | .75 |
| 48 | Rafael Palmeiro | .20 | .50 |
| 49 | Adam Piatt | .10 | .30 |
| 50 | Scott Rolen | .20 | .50 |
| 51 | Gary Sheffield | .10 | .30 |
| 52 | Bernie Williams | .20 | .50 |
| 53 | Bob Abreu | .10 | .30 |
| 54 | Edgardo Alfonzo | .10 | .30 |
| 55 | Jermaine Clark RC | .10 | .30 |
| 56 | Albert Belle | .10 | .30 |
| 57 | Craig Biggio | .20 | .50 |
| 58 | Andres Galarraga | .10 | .30 |
| 59 | Edgar Martinez | .10 | .30 |
| 60 | Fred McGriff | .20 | .50 |
| 61 | Magglio Ordonez | .20 | .50 |
| 62 | Jim Thome | .20 | .50 |
| 63 | Matt Williams | .10 | .30 |
| 64 | Kerry Wood | .10 | .30 |
| 65 | Moises Alou | .10 | .30 |
| 66 | Brady Anderson | .10 | .30 |
| 67 | Garret Anderson | .10 | .30 |
| 68 | Tony Armas Jr. | .10 | .30 |
| 69 | Tony Batista | .10 | .30 |
| 70 | Jose Cruz Jr. | .10 | .30 |
| 71 | Carlos Beltran | .10 | .30 |
| 72 | Adrian Beltre | .10 | .30 |
| 73 | Kris Benson | .10 | .30 |
| 74 | Lance Berkman | .10 | .30 |
| 75 | Kevin Brown | .10 | .30 |
| 76 | Jay Buhner | .10 | .30 |
| 77 | Jeromy Burnitz | .10 | .30 |
| 78 | Ken Caminiti | .10 | .30 |
| 79 | Sean Casey | .10 | .30 |
| 80 | Luis Castillo | .10 | .30 |
| 81 | Eric Chavez | .10 | .30 |
| 82 | Jeff Cirillo | .10 | .30 |
| 83 | Bartolo Colon | .10 | .30 |
| 84 | David Cone | .10 | .30 |
| 85 | Freddy Garcia | .10 | .30 |
| 86 | Johnny Damon | .20 | .50 |
| 87 | Ray Durham | .10 | .30 |
| 88 | Jermaine Dye | .10 | .30 |
| 89 | Juan Encarnacion | .10 | .30 |
| 90 | Terrence Long | .10 | .30 |
| 91 | Carl Everett | .10 | .30 |
| 92 | Steve Finley | .10 | .30 |
| 93 | Cliff Floyd | .10 | .30 |
| 94 | Brad Fullmer | .10 | .30 |
| 95 | Brian Giles | .10 | .30 |
| 96 | Luis Gonzalez | .10 | .30 |
| 97 | Rusty Greer | .10 | .30 |
| 98 | Jeffrey Hammonds | .10 | .30 |
| 99 | Mike Hampton | .10 | .30 |
| 100 | Orlando Hernandez | .10 | .30 |
| 101 | Richard Hidalgo | .10 | .30 |
| 102 | Geoff Jenkins | .10 | .30 |
| 103 | Jacque Jones | .10 | .30 |
| 104 | Brian Jordan | .10 | .30 |
| 105 | Gabe Kapler | .10 | .30 |
| 106 | Eric Karros | .10 | .30 |
| 107 | Jason Kendall | .10 | .30 |
| 108 | Adam Kennedy | .10 | .30 |
| 109 | Byung-Hyun Kim | .10 | .30 |
| 110 | Ryan Klesko | .10 | .30 |
| 111 | Chuck Knoblauch | .10 | .30 |
| 112 | Paul Konerko | .10 | .30 |
| 113 | Carlos Lee | .10 | .30 |
| 114 | Kenny Lofton | .10 | .30 |
| 115 | Javy Lopez | .10 | .30 |
| 116 | Tino Martinez | .20 | .50 |
| 117 | Ruben Mateo | .10 | .30 |
| 118 | Kevin Millwood | .10 | .30 |
| 119 | Ben Molina | .10 | .30 |
| 120 | Raul Mondesi | .10 | .30 |
| 121 | Trot Nixon | .10 | .30 |
| 122 | John Olerud | .10 | .30 |
| 123 | Paul O'Neill | .20 | .50 |
| 124 | Chan Ho Park | .10 | .30 |
| 125 | Andy Pettitte | .20 | .50 |
| 126 | Jorge Posada | .20 | .50 |
| 127 | Mark Quinn | .10 | .30 |
| 128 | Aramis Ramirez | .10 | .30 |
| 129 | Mariano Rivera | .30 | .75 |
| 130 | Tim Salmon | .20 | .50 |
| 131 | Curt Schilling | .10 | .30 |
| 132 | Richie Sexson | .10 | .30 |
| 133 | John Smoltz | .20 | .50 |
| 134 | J.T. Snow | .10 | .30 |
| 135 | Jay Payton | .10 | .30 |
| 136 | Shannon Stewart | .10 | .30 |
| 137 | B.J. Surhoff | .10 | .30 |
| 138 | Mike Sweeney | .10 | .30 |
| 139 | Fernando Tatis | .10 | .30 |
| 140 | Miguel Tejada | .10 | .30 |
| 141 | Jason Varitek | .30 | .75 |
| 142 | Greg Vaughn | .10 | .30 |
| 143 | Mo Vaughn | .10 | .30 |
| 144 | Robin Ventura | .10 | .30 |
| 145 | Jose Vidro | .10 | .30 |
| 146 | Omar Vizquel | .20 | .50 |
| 147 | Larry Walker | .10 | .30 |
| 148 | David Wells | .10 | .30 |
| 149 | Rondell White | .10 | .30 |
| 150 | Preston Wilson | .10 | .30 |
| 151 | Brent Abernathy RR | 3.00 | 8.00 |
| 152 | Cory Aldridge RR RC | 3.00 | 8.00 |
| 153 | Gene Altman RR | 3.00 | 8.00 |
| 154 | Josh Beckett RR | 4.00 | 10.00 |
| 155 | Wilson Betemit RR RC | 4.00 | 10.00 |
| 156 | Albert Pujols RR/500 RC | 60.00 | 120.00 |
| 157 | Joe Crede RR | 4.00 | 10.00 |
| 158 | Jack Cust RR | 3.00 | 8.00 |
| 159 | Ben Sheets RR/500 | 15.00 | 40.00 |
| 160 | Alex Escobar RR | 3.00 | 8.00 |
| 161 | Adrian Hernandez RR RC | 3.00 | 8.00 |
| 162 | Pedro Feliz RR | 3.00 | 8.00 |
| 163 | Nate Frese RR RC | 3.00 | 8.00 |
| 164 | Carlos Garcia RR RC | 3.00 | 8.00 |
| 165 | Marcus Giles RR | 3.00 | 8.00 |
| 166 | Alexis Gomez RR | 3.00 | 8.00 |
| 167 | Jason Hart RR | 3.00 | 8.00 |
| 168 | Eric Hinske RR RC | 4.00 | 10.00 |
| 169 | Cesar Izturis RR | 3.00 | 8.00 |
| 170 | Nick Johnson RR | 3.00 | 8.00 |
| 171 | Mike Young RR | 4.00 | 10.00 |
| 172 | Brian Lawrence RR RC | 3.00 | 8.00 |
| 173 | Steve Lomasney RR | 3.00 | 8.00 |
| 174 | Nick Maness RR | 3.00 | 8.00 |
| 175 | Jose Mieses RR RC | 3.00 | 8.00 |
| 176 | Greg Miller RR RC | 3.00 | 8.00 |
| 177 | Eric Munson RR | 3.00 | 8.00 |
| 178 | Xavier Nady RR | 3.00 | 8.00 |
| 179 | Blaine Neal RR RC | 3.00 | 8.00 |
| 180 | Abraham Nunez RR | 3.00 | 8.00 |
| 181 | Jose Ortiz RR | 3.00 | 8.00 |
| 182 | Jeremy Owens RR RC | 3.00 | 8.00 |
| 183 | Pablo Ozuna RR | 3.00 | 8.00 |
| 184 | Corey Patterson RR | 3.00 | 8.00 |
| 185 | Carlos Pena RR | 3.00 | 8.00 |
| 186 | Willy Mo Pena RR | 3.00 | 8.00 |
| 187 | Timo Perez RR | 3.00 | 8.00 |
| 188 | Adam Pettyjohn RR RC | 3.00 | 8.00 |
| 189 | Luis Rivas RR | 3.00 | 8.00 |
| 190 | Jackson Melian RR RC | 3.00 | 8.00 |
| 191 | Wilken Ruan RR RC | 3.00 | 8.00 |
| 192 | Duaner Sanchez RR RC | 3.00 | 8.00 |
| 193 | Alfonso Soriano RR | 4.00 | 10.00 |
| 194 | Rafael Soriano RR RC | 3.00 | 8.00 |
| 195 | Ichiro Suzuki RR RC | 30.00 | 60.00 |
| 196 | Billy Sylvester RR RC | 3.00 | 8.00 |
| 197 | Juan Uribe RR RC | 4.00 | 10.00 |
| 198 | Eric Valent RR | 3.00 | 8.00 |
| 199 | Carlos Valderrama RR RC | 3.00 | 8.00 |
| 200 | Matt White RR RC | 3.00 | 8.00 |
| 201 | Alex Rodriguez FC | 2.50 | 6.00 |
| 202 | Barry Bonds FC | 4.00 | 10.00 |
| 203 | Cal Ripken FC | 5.00 | 12.00 |
| 204 | Chipper Jones FC | 1.50 | 4.00 |
| 205 | Derek Jeter FC | 4.00 | 10.00 |
| 206 | Troy Glaus FC | 1.00 | 2.50 |
| 207 | Frank Thomas FC | 1.50 | 4.00 |
| 208 | Greg Maddux FC | 2.50 | 6.00 |
| 209 | Ivan Rodriguez FC | 1.00 | 2.50 |
| 210 | Jeff Bagwell FC | 1.00 | 2.50 |
| 211 | Todd Helton FC | 1.00 | 2.50 |
| 212 | Ken Griffey Jr. FC | 2.50 | 6.00 |
| 213 | Manny Ramirez Sox FC | 1.00 | 2.50 |
| 214 | Mark McGwire FC | 4.00 | 10.00 |
| 215 | Mike Piazza FC | 2.50 | 6.00 |
| 216 | Pedro Martinez FC | 1.00 | 2.50 |
| 217 | Sammy Sosa FC | 1.50 | 4.00 |
| 218 | Tony Gwynn FC | 2.00 | 5.00 |
| 219 | Vladimir Guerrero FC | 1.50 | 4.00 |
| 220 | Nomar Garciaparra FC | 2.50 | 6.00 |
| NNO | BB Best Coupon | .75 | 2.00 |
| NNO | The Rookies Coupon | .20 | .50 |

## 2001 Donruss Rookies

| | | |
|---|------|------|
| COMP.FACT.SET (106) | 60.00 | 100.00 |
| COMP.SET w/o SP's (105) | 40.00 | 80.00 |
| R1 Adam Dunn | .30 | .75 |
| R2 Ryan Drese RC | .30 | .75 |
| R3 Bud Smith RC | .15 | .40 |
| R4 Tsuyoshi Shinjo RC | .30 | .75 |
| R5 Roy Oswalt | .40 | 1.00 |
| R6 Wilmy Caceres RC | .20 | .50 |
| R7 Willie Harris RC | .20 | .50 |
| R8 Andres Torres RC | .15 | .40 |
| R9 Brandon Knight RC | .15 | .40 |
| R10 Horacio Ramirez RC | .30 | .75 |
| R11 Benito Baez RC | .15 | .40 |
| R12 Jeremy Affeldt RC | .20 | .50 |
| R13 Ryan Jensen RC | .20 | .50 |
| R14 Casey Fossum RC | .15 | .40 |
| R15 Ramon Vazquez RC | .20 | .50 |
| R16 Dustan Mohr RC | .15 | .40 |
| R17 Saul Rivera RC | .15 | .40 |
| R18 Zach Day RC | .15 | .40 |
| R19 Erik Hiljus RC | .15 | .40 |
| R20 Cesar Crespo RC | .15 | .40 |
| R21 Wilson Guzman RC | .20 | .50 |
| R22 Travis Hafner RC | 2.00 | 5.00 |
| R23 Grant Balfour RC | .15 | .40 |
| R24 Johnny Estrada RC | .30 | .75 |
| R25 Morgan Ensberg RC | .75 | 2.00 |
| R26 Jack Wilson RC | .30 | .75 |
| R27 Aubrey Huff | .20 | .50 |
| R28 Endy Chavez RC | .20 | .50 |
| R29 Delvin James RC | .15 | .40 |
| R30 Michael Cuddyer | .20 | .50 |
| R31 Jason Michaels RC | .20 | .50 |
| R32 Martin Vargas RC | .20 | .50 |
| R33 Donaldo Mendez RC | .15 | .40 |
| R34 Jorge Julio RC | .20 | .50 |
| R35 Tim Spooneybarger RC | .20 | .50 |
| R36 Kurt Ainsworth | .15 | .40 |
| R37 Josh Fogg RC | .20 | .50 |
| R38 Brian Reith RC | .15 | .40 |
| R39 Rick Bauer RC | .15 | .40 |
| R40 Tim Redding | .15 | .40 |
| R41 Erick Almonte RC | .15 | .40 |
| R42 Juan A.Pena RC | .15 | .40 |
| R43 Ken Harvey | .20 | .50 |
| R44 David Brous RC | .15 | .40 |
| R45 Kevin Olsen RC | .20 | .50 |
| R46 Henry Mateo RC | .15 | .40 |
| R47 Nick Neugebauer | .15 | .40 |
| R48 Mike Penney RC | .15 | .40 |
| R49 Jay Gibbons RC | .30 | .75 |
| R50 Tim Christman RC | .15 | .40 |
| R51 Brandon Duckworth RC | .15 | .40 |
| R52 Brett Jodie RC | .15 | .40 |
| R53 Christian Parker RC | .15 | .40 |
| R54 Carlos Hernandez | .15 | .40 |
| R55 Brandon Larson RC | .15 | .40 |
| R56 Nick Punto RC | .20 | .50 |
| R57 Elpidio Guzman RC | .15 | .40 |
| R58 Joe Beimel RC | .15 | .40 |
| R59 Junior Spivey RC | .30 | .75 |
| R60 Will Ohman RC | .15 | .40 |
| R61 Brandon Lyon RC | .15 | .40 |
| R62 Stubby Clapp RC | .20 | .50 |
| R63 Justin Duchscherer RC | .20 | .50 |
| R64 Jimmy Rollins | .20 | .50 |

|  |  | | |
|---|---|---|---|
| R65 | David Williams RC | .15 | .40 |
| R66 | Craig Monroe RC | 1.00 | 2.50 |
| R67 | Jose Acevedo RC | .15 | .40 |
| R68 | Jason Jennings RC | .15 | .40 |
| R69 | Josh Phelps RC | .15 | .40 |
| R70 | Brian Roberts RC | .75 | 2.00 |
| R71 | Claudio Vargas RC | .15 | .40 |
| R72 | Adam Johnson RC | .15 | .40 |
| R73 | Bart Miadich RC | .15 | .40 |
| R74 | Juan Rivera RC | .15 | .40 |
| R75 | Brad Voyles RC | .15 | .40 |
| R76 | Nate Cornejo RC | .15 | .40 |
| R77 | Juan Moreno RC | .20 | .50 |
| R78 | Brian Rogers RC | .15 | .40 |
| R79 | Ricardo Rodriguez RC | .20 | .50 |
| R80 | Geronimo Gil RC | .15 | .40 |
| R81 | Joe Kennedy RC | .30 | .75 |
| R82 | Kevin Joseph RC | .20 | .50 |
| R83 | Josue Perez RC | .20 | .50 |
| R84 | Victor Zambrano RC | .30 | .75 |
| R85 | Josh Towers RC | .30 | .75 |
| R86 | Mike Rivera RC | .20 | .50 |
| R87 | Mark Prior RC | 2.00 | 5.00 |
| R88 | Juan Cruz RC | .20 | .50 |
| R89 | Dewon Brazelton RC | .20 | .50 |
| R90 | Angel Berroa RC | .30 | .75 |
| R91 | Mark Teixeira RC | 4.00 | 10.00 |
| R92 | Cody Ransom RC | .15 | .40 |
| R93 | Angel Santos RC | .15 | .40 |
| R94 | Corky Miller RC | .15 | .40 |
| R95 | Brandon Berger RC | .15 | .40 |
| R96 | Corey Patterson UPD | .15 | .40 |
| R97 | Albert Pujols UPD | 20.00 | 50.00 |
| R98 | Josh Beckett UPD | .20 | .75 |
| R99 | C.C. Sabathia UPD | .20 | .50 |
| R100 | Alfonso Soriano UPD | .30 | .75 |
| R101 | Ben Sheets UPD | .30 | .75 |
| R102 | Rafael Soriano UPD | .20 | .50 |
| R103 | Wilson Betemit UPD | .75 | 2.00 |
| R104 | Ichiro Suzuki UPD | 5.00 | 12.00 |
| R105 | Jose Ortiz UPD | .15 | .40 |

## 2002 Donruss

|  |  | | |
|---|---|---|---|
| | COMPLETE SET (220) | 60.00 | 150.00 |
| | COMP SET w/o S'PS (150) | 10.00 | 25.00 |
| | COMMON CARD (1-150) | .10 | .30 |
| | COMMON CARD (151-200) | 1.25 | 3.00 |
| | COMMON CARD (201-220) | .60 | 1.50 |
| 1 | Alex Rodriguez | .50 | 1.25 |
| 2 | Barry Bonds | .75 | 2.00 |
| 3 | Derek Jeter | .75 | 2.00 |
| 4 | Robert Fick | .10 | .30 |
| 5 | Juan Pierre | .10 | .30 |
| 6 | Torii Hunter | .10 | .30 |
| 7 | Todd Helton | .20 | .50 |
| 8 | Cal Ripken | 1.00 | 2.50 |
| 9 | Manny Ramirez | .20 | .50 |
| 10 | Johnny Damon | .20 | .50 |
| 11 | Mike Piazza | .50 | 1.25 |
| 12 | Nomar Garciaparra | .50 | 1.25 |
| 13 | Pedro Martinez | .20 | .50 |
| 14 | Brian Giles | .10 | .30 |
| 15 | Albert Pujols | .60 | 1.50 |
| 16 | Roger Clemens | .60 | 1.50 |
| 17 | Sammy Sosa | .30 | .75 |
| 18 | Vladimir Guerrero | .30 | .75 |
| 19 | Tony Gwynn | .40 | 1.00 |
| 20 | Pat Burrell | .10 | .30 |
| 21 | Carlos Delgado | .10 | .30 |
| 22 | Tino Martinez | .10 | .30 |
| 23 | Jim Edmonds | .10 | .30 |
| 24 | Jason Giambi | .20 | .50 |
| 25 | Tom Glavine | .20 | .50 |
| 26 | Mark Grace | .20 | .50 |
| 27 | Tony Armas Jr. | .10 | .30 |
| 28 | Andruw Jones | .20 | .30 |
| 29 | Ben Sheets | .10 | .30 |
| 30 | Jeff Kent | .10 | .30 |
| 31 | Barry Larkin | .20 | .50 |
| 32 | Joe Mays | .10 | .30 |
| 33 | Mike Mussina | .20 | .50 |
| 34 | Hideo Nomo | .30 | .75 |
| 35 | Rafael Palmeiro | .10 | .30 |
| 36 | Scott Brosius | .10 | .30 |
| 37 | Scott Rolen | .20 | .50 |
| 38 | Gary Sheffield | .20 | .50 |
| 39 | Bernie Williams | .20 | .50 |
| 40 | Bob Abreu | .10 | .30 |
| 41 | Edgardo Alfonzo | .10 | .30 |
| 42 | C.C. Sabathia | .10 | .30 |
| 43 | Jeremy Giambi | .10 | .30 |
| 44 | Craig Biggio | .20 | .50 |
| 45 | Andres Galarraga | .10 | .30 |
| 46 | Edgar Martinez | .20 | .50 |
| 47 | Fred McGriff | .20 | .50 |
| 48 | Magglio Ordonez | .20 | .50 |
| 49 | Jim Thome | .20 | .50 |
| 50 | Matt Williams | .10 | .30 |
| 51 | Kerry Wood | .10 | .30 |
| 52 | Moises Alou | .10 | .30 |
| 53 | Brady Anderson | .10 | .30 |
| 54 | Garret Anderson | .10 | .30 |
| 55 | Juan Gonzalez | .20 | .50 |
| 56 | Bret Boone | .10 | .30 |
| 57 | Jose Cruz Jr. | .10 | .30 |
| 58 | Carlos Beltran | .10 | .30 |
| 59 | Adrian Beltre | .10 | .30 |
| 60 | Joe Kennedy | .10 | .30 |
| 61 | Lance Berkman | .20 | .50 |
| 62 | Kevin Brown | .10 | .30 |
| 63 | Tim Hudson | .10 | .30 |
| 64 | Jeromy Burnitz | .10 | .30 |
| 65 | Jarrod Washburn | .10 | .30 |
| 66 | Sean Casey | .10 | .30 |
| 67 | Eric Chavez | .10 | .30 |
| 68 | Bartolo Colon | .10 | .30 |
| 69 | Freddy Garcia | .10 | .30 |
| 70 | Jermaine Dye | .10 | .30 |
| 71 | Terrence Long | .10 | .30 |
| 72 | Cliff Floyd | .10 | .30 |
| 73 | Luis Gonzalez | .10 | .30 |
| 74 | Ichiro Suzuki | .60 | 1.50 |
| 75 | Mike Hampton | .10 | .30 |
| 76 | Richard Hidalgo | .10 | .30 |
| 77 | Geoff Jenkins | .10 | .30 |
| 78 | Gabe Kapler | .10 | .30 |
| 79 | Ken Griffey Jr. | .50 | 1.25 |
| 80 | Jason Kendall | .10 | .30 |
| 81 | Josh Towers | .10 | .30 |
| 82 | Ryan Klesko | .10 | .30 |
| 83 | Paul Konerko | .10 | .30 |
| 84 | Carlos Lee | .10 | .30 |
| 85 | Kenny Lofton | .10 | .30 |
| 86 | Josh Beckett | .10 | .30 |
| 87 | Raul Mondesi | .10 | .30 |
| 88 | Trot Nixon | .10 | .30 |
| 89 | John Olerud | .10 | .30 |
| 90 | Paul O'Neill | .20 | .50 |
| 91 | Chan Ho Park | .10 | .30 |
| 92 | Andy Pettitte | .20 | .50 |
| 93 | Jorge Posada | .10 | .30 |
| 94 | Mark Quinn | .10 | .30 |
| 95 | Aramis Ramirez | .10 | .30 |
| 96 | Curt Schilling | .20 | .50 |
| 97 | Richie Sexson | .10 | .30 |
| 98 | John Smoltz | .20 | .50 |
| 99 | Wilson Betemit | .10 | .30 |
| 100 | Shannon Stewart | .10 | .30 |
| 101 | Alfonso Soriano | .10 | .30 |
| 102 | Mike Sweeney | .10 | .30 |
| 103 | Miguel Tejada | .10 | .30 |
| 104 | Greg Vaughn | .10 | .30 |
| 105 | Robin Ventura | .10 | .30 |
| 106 | Jose Vidro | .10 | .30 |
| 107 | Larry Walker | .10 | .30 |
| 108 | Preston Wilson | .10 | .30 |
| 109 | Corey Patterson | .10 | .30 |
| 110 | Mark Mulder | .10 | .30 |
| 111 | Tony Clark | .10 | .30 |
| 112 | Roy Oswalt | .10 | .30 |
| 113 | Jimmy Rollins | .10 | .30 |
| 114 | Kazuhiro Sasaki | .10 | .30 |
| 115 | Barry Zito | .10 | .30 |
| 116 | Javier Vazquez | .10 | .30 |
| 117 | Mike Cameron | .10 | .30 |
| 118 | Phil Nevin | .10 | .30 |
| 119 | Bud Smith | .10 | .30 |
| 120 | Cristian Guzman | .10 | .30 |
| 121 | Al Leiter | .10 | .30 |
| 122 | Brad Radke | .10 | .30 |
| 123 | Bobby Higginson | .10 | .30 |
| 124 | Robert Person | .10 | .30 |
| 125 | Adam Dunn | .10 | .30 |
| 126 | Ben Grieve | .10 | .30 |
| 127 | Rafael Furcal | .10 | .30 |
| 128 | Jay Gibbons | .10 | .30 |
| 129 | Paul LoDuca | .10 | .30 |
| 130 | Wade Miller | .10 | .30 |
| 131 | Tsuyoshi Shinjo | .10 | .30 |
| 132 | Eric Milton | .10 | .30 |
| 133 | Rickey Henderson | .30 | .75 |
| 134 | Roberto Alomar | .20 | .50 |
| 135 | Darin Erstad | .10 | .30 |
| 136 | J.D. Drew | .10 | .30 |
| 137 | Shawn Green | .10 | .30 |
| 138 | Randy Johnson | .30 | .75 |
| 139 | Austin Kearns | .10 | .30 |
| 140 | Jose Canseco | .30 | .75 |
| 141 | Jeff Bagwell | .20 | .50 |
| 142 | Greg Maddux | .50 | 1.25 |
| 143 | Mark Buehrle | .10 | .30 |
| 144 | Ivan Rodriguez | .20 | .50 |
| 145 | Frank Thomas | .30 | .75 |
| 146 | Rich Aurilia | .10 | .30 |
| 147 | Troy Glaus | .10 | .30 |
| 148 | Ryan Dempster | .10 | .30 |
| 149 | Chipper Jones | .30 | .75 |
| 150 | Matt Morris | .10 | .30 |
| 151 | Marlon Byrd RR | 1.25 | 3.00 |
| 152 | Ben Howard RR | 1.25 | 3.00 |
| 153 | Brandon Backe RR RC | 1.25 | 3.00 |
| 154 | Jorge De La Rosa RR RC | 1.25 | 3.00 |
| 155 | Corky Miller RR | 1.25 | 3.00 |
| 156 | Dennis Tankersley RR | 1.25 | 3.00 |
| 157 | Kyle Kane RR RC | 1.25 | 3.00 |
| 158 | Justin Duchscherer RR | 1.25 | 3.00 |
| 159 | Brian Mallette RR RC | 1.25 | 3.00 |
| 160 | Chris Baker RR RC | 1.25 | 3.00 |
| 161 | Jason Lane RR | 1.25 | 3.00 |
| 162 | Hee Seop Choi RR | 1.25 | 3.00 |
| 163 | Juan Cruz RR | 1.25 | 3.00 |
| 164 | Rodrigo Rosario RR RC | 1.25 | 3.00 |
| 165 | Matt Guerrier RR | 1.25 | 3.00 |
| 166 | Anderson Machado RR RC | 1.25 | 3.00 |
| 167 | Geronimo Gil RR | 1.25 | 3.00 |
| 168 | Dewon Brazelton RR | 1.25 | 3.00 |
| 169 | Mark Prior RR | 1.50 | 4.00 |
| 170 | Bill Hall RR | 1.25 | 3.00 |
| 171 | Jorge Padilla RR RC | 1.25 | 3.00 |
| 172 | Jose Cueto RR | 1.25 | 3.00 |
| 173 | Allan Simpson RR RC | 1.25 | 3.00 |
| 174 | Doug Devore RR RC | 1.25 | 3.00 |
| 175 | Josh Pearce RR | 1.25 | 3.00 |
| 176 | Angel Berroa RR | 1.25 | 3.00 |
| 177 | Steve Bechler RR RC | 1.25 | 3.00 |
| 178 | Antonio Perez RR | 1.25 | 3.00 |
| 179 | Mark Teixeira RR | 1.50 | 4.00 |
| 180 | Erick Almonte RR | 1.25 | 3.00 |
| 181 | Orlando Hudson RR | 1.25 | 3.00 |
| 182 | Michael Rivera RR | 1.25 | 3.00 |
| 183 | Raul Chavez RR RC | 1.25 | 3.00 |
| 184 | Juan Pena RR | 1.25 | 3.00 |
| 185 | Travis Hughes RR RC | 1.25 | 3.00 |
| 186 | Ryan Ludwick RR | 1.25 | 3.00 |
| 187 | Ed Rogers RR | 1.25 | 3.00 |
| 188 | Andy Pratt RR RC | 1.25 | 3.00 |
| 189 | Nick Neugebauer RR | 1.25 | 3.00 |
| 190 | Tom Shearn RR RC | 1.25 | 3.00 |
| 191 | Eric Cyr RR | 1.25 | 3.00 |
| 192 | Victor Martinez RR | 1.50 | 4.00 |
| 193 | Brandon Berger RR | 1.25 | 3.00 |
| 194 | Erik Bedard RR | 1.25 | 3.00 |
| 195 | Fernando Rodney RR | 1.25 | 3.00 |
| 196 | Joe Thurston RR | 1.25 | 3.00 |
| 197 | John Buck RR | 1.25 | 3.00 |
| 198 | Jeff Deardorff RR | 1.25 | 3.00 |
| 199 | Ryan Jamison RR | 1.25 | 3.00 |
| 200 | Alfredo Amezaga RR | 1.25 | 3.00 |
| 201 | Luis Gonzalez FC | .60 | 1.50 |
| 202 | Roger Clemens FC | 2.00 | 5.00 |

| | | |
|---|---|---|
| ❏ 203 Barry Zito FC | .60 | 1.50 |
| ❏ 204 Bud Smith FC | .60 | 1.50 |
| ❏ 205 Magglio Ordonez FC | .60 | 1.50 |
| ❏ 206 Kerry Wood FC | .60 | 1.50 |
| ❏ 207 Freddy Garcia FC | .60 | 1.50 |
| ❏ 208 Adam Dunn FC | .60 | 1.50 |
| ❏ 209 Curt Schilling FC | .60 | 1.50 |
| ❏ 210 Lance Berkman FC | .60 | 1.50 |
| ❏ 211 Rafael Palmeiro FC | .60 | 1.50 |
| ❏ 212 Ichiro Suzuki FC | 2.00 | 5.00 |
| ❏ 213 Bob Abreu FC | .60 | 1.50 |
| ❏ 214 Mark Mulder FC | .60 | 1.50 |
| ❏ 215 Roy Oswalt FC | .60 | 1.50 |
| ❏ 216 Mike Sweeney FC | .60 | 1.50 |
| ❏ 217 Paul LoDuca FC | .60 | 1.50 |
| ❏ 218 Aramis Ramirez FC | .60 | 1.50 |
| ❏ 219 Randy Johnson FC | 1.00 | 2.50 |
| ❏ 220 Albert Pujols FC | 2.00 | 5.00 |

## 2003 Donruss

| | | |
|---|---|---|
| ❏ COMPLETE SET (400) | 25.00 | 50.00 |
| ❏ COMMON CARD (71-400) | .10 | .30 |
| ❏ COMMON CARD (1-20) | .20 | .50 |
| ❏ COMMON CARD (21-70) | .20 | .50 |
| ❏ 1 Vladimir Guerrero DK | .30 | .75 |
| ❏ 2 Derek Jeter DK | .75 | 2.00 |
| ❏ 3 Adam Dunn DK | .20 | .50 |
| ❏ 4 Greg Maddux DK | .50 | 1.25 |
| ❏ 5 Lance Berkman DK | .20 | .50 |
| ❏ 6 Ichiro Suzuki DK | .60 | 1.50 |
| ❏ 7 Mike Piazza DK | .50 | 1.25 |
| ❏ 8 Alex Rodriguez DK | .50 | 1.25 |
| ❏ 9 Tom Glavine DK | .20 | .50 |
| ❏ 10 Randy Johnson DK | .30 | .75 |
| ❏ 11 Nomar Garciaparra DK | .50 | 1.25 |
| ❏ 12 Jason Giambi DK | .20 | .50 |
| ❏ 13 Sammy Sosa DK | .30 | .75 |
| ❏ 14 Barry Zito DK | .20 | .50 |
| ❏ 15 Chipper Jones DK | .30 | .75 |
| ❏ 16 Magglio Ordonez DK | .20 | .50 |
| ❏ 17 Larry Walker DK | .20 | .50 |
| ❏ 18 Alfonso Soriano DK | .20 | .50 |
| ❏ 19 Curt Schilling DK | .20 | .50 |
| ❏ 20 Barry Bonds DK | .75 | 2.00 |
| ❏ 21 Joe Borchard RR | .20 | .50 |
| ❏ 22 Chris Snelling RR | .20 | .50 |
| ❏ 23 Brian Tallet RR | .20 | .50 |
| ❏ 24 Cliff Lee RR | .20 | .50 |
| ❏ 25 Freddy Sanchez RR | .20 | .50 |
| ❏ 26 Chone Figgins RR | .20 | .50 |
| ❏ 27 Kevin Cash RR | .20 | .50 |
| ❏ 28 Josh Bard RR | .20 | .50 |
| ❏ 29 Jeriome Robertson RR | .20 | .50 |
| ❏ 30 Jeremy Hill RR | .20 | .50 |
| ❏ 31 Shane Nance RR | .20 | .50 |
| ❏ 32 Jake Peavy RR | .30 | .75 |
| ❏ 33 Trey Hodges RR | .20 | .50 |
| ❏ 34 Eric Eckenstahler RR | .20 | .50 |
| ❏ 35 Jim Rushford RR | .20 | .50 |
| ❏ 36 Oliver Perez RR | .30 | .75 |
| ❏ 37 Kirk Saarloos RR | .20 | .50 |
| ❏ 38 Hank Blalock RR | .50 | 1.25 |
| ❏ 39 Francisco Rodriguez RR | .50 | 1.25 |
| ❏ 40 Runelvys Hernandez RR | .20 | .50 |
| ❏ 41 Aaron Cook RR | .20 | .50 |
| ❏ 42 Josh Hancock RR | .20 | .50 |
| ❏ 43 P.J. Bevis RR | .20 | .50 |
| ❏ 44 Jon Adkins RR | .20 | .50 |
| ❏ 45 Tim Kalita RR | .20 | .50 |
| ❏ 46 Nelson Castro RR | .20 | .50 |
| ❏ 47 Colin Young RR | .20 | .50 |
| ❏ 48 Adrian Burnside RR | .20 | .50 |
| ❏ 49 Luis Martinez RR | .20 | .50 |
| ❏ 50 Pete Zamora RR | .20 | .50 |

| | | |
|---|---|---|
| ❏ 51 Todd Donovan RR | .20 | .50 |
| ❏ 52 Jeremy Ward RR | .20 | .50 |
| ❏ 53 Wilson Valdez RR | .20 | .50 |
| ❏ 54 Eric Good RR | .20 | .50 |
| ❏ 55 Jeff Baker RR | .20 | .50 |
| ❏ 56 Mitch Wylie RR | .20 | .50 |
| ❏ 57 Ron Calloway RR | .20 | .50 |
| ❏ 58 Jose Valverde RR | .20 | .50 |
| ❏ 59 Jason Davis RR | .20 | .50 |
| ❏ 60 Scotty Layfield RR | .20 | .50 |
| ❏ 61 Matt Thornton RR | .20 | .50 |
| ❏ 62 Adam Walker RR | .20 | .50 |
| ❏ 63 Gustavo Chacin RR | .20 | .50 |
| ❏ 64 Ron Chiavacci RR | .20 | .50 |
| ❏ 65 Wiki Nieves RR | .20 | .50 |
| ❏ 66 Cliff Bartosh RR | .20 | .50 |
| ❏ 67 Mike Gonzalez RR | .20 | .50 |
| ❏ 68 Justin Wayne RR | .20 | .50 |
| ❏ 69 Eric Junge RR | .20 | .50 |
| ❏ 70 Ben Kozlowski RR | .20 | .50 |
| ❏ 71 Darin Erstad | .10 | .30 |
| ❏ 72 Garret Anderson | .10 | .30 |
| ❏ 73 Troy Glaus | .10 | .30 |
| ❏ 74 David Eckstein | .10 | .30 |
| ❏ 75 Adam Kennedy | .10 | .30 |
| ❏ 76 Kevin Appier | .10 | .30 |
| ❏ 77 Jarrod Washburn | .10 | .30 |
| ❏ 78 Scott Spiezio | .10 | .30 |
| ❏ 79 Tim Salmon | .20 | .50 |
| ❏ 80 Ramon Ortiz | .10 | .30 |
| ❏ 81 Bengie Molina | .10 | .30 |
| ❏ 82 Brad Fullmer | .10 | .30 |
| ❏ 83 Troy Percival | .10 | .30 |
| ❏ 84 David Segui | .10 | .30 |
| ❏ 85 Jay Gibbons | .10 | .30 |
| ❏ 86 Tony Batista | .10 | .30 |
| ❏ 87 Scott Erickson | .10 | .30 |
| ❏ 88 Jeff Conine | .10 | .30 |
| ❏ 89 Melvin Mora | .10 | .30 |
| ❏ 90 Buddy Groom | .10 | .30 |
| ❏ 91 Rodrigo Lopez | .10 | .30 |
| ❏ 92 Marty Cordova | .10 | .30 |
| ❏ 93 Geronimo Gil | .10 | .30 |
| ❏ 94 Kenny Lofton | .10 | .30 |
| ❏ 95 Shea Hillenbrand | .10 | .30 |
| ❏ 96 Manny Ramirez | .20 | .50 |
| ❏ 97 Pedro Martinez | .20 | .50 |
| ❏ 98 Nomar Garciaparra | .50 | 1.25 |
| ❏ 99 Rickey Henderson | .30 | .75 |
| ❏ 100 Johnny Damon | .20 | .50 |
| ❏ 101 Trot Nixon | .10 | .30 |
| ❏ 102 Derek Lowe | .10 | .30 |
| ❏ 103 Hee Seop Choi | .10 | .30 |
| ❏ 104 Mark Teixeira | .20 | .50 |
| ❏ 105 Tim Wakefield | .10 | .30 |
| ❏ 106 Jason Varitek | .30 | .75 |
| ❏ 107 Frank Thomas | .30 | .75 |
| ❏ 108 Joe Crede | .10 | .30 |
| ❏ 109 Magglio Ordonez | .20 | .50 |
| ❏ 110 Ray Durham | .10 | .30 |
| ❏ 111 Mark Buehrle | .10 | .30 |
| ❏ 112 Paul Konerko | .10 | .30 |
| ❏ 113 Jose Valentin | .10 | .30 |
| ❏ 114 Carlos Lee | .10 | .30 |
| ❏ 115 Royce Clayton | .10 | .30 |
| ❏ 116 C.C. Sabathia | .10 | .30 |
| ❏ 117 Ellis Burks | .10 | .30 |
| ❏ 118 Omar Vizquel | .10 | .30 |
| ❏ 119 Jim Thome | .20 | .50 |
| ❏ 120 Matt Lawton | .10 | .30 |
| ❏ 121 Travis Fryman | .10 | .30 |
| ❏ 122 Earl Snyder | .10 | .30 |
| ❏ 123 Ricky Gutierrez | .10 | .30 |
| ❏ 124 Einar Diaz | .10 | .30 |
| ❏ 125 Danys Baez | .10 | .30 |
| ❏ 126 Robert Fick | .10 | .30 |
| ❏ 127 Bobby Higginson | .10 | .30 |
| ❏ 128 Steve Sparks | .10 | .30 |
| ❏ 129 Mike Rivera | .10 | .30 |
| ❏ 130 Wendell Magee | .10 | .30 |
| ❏ 131 Randall Simon | .10 | .30 |
| ❏ 132 Carlos Pena | .10 | .30 |
| ❏ 133 Mark Redman | .10 | .30 |
| ❏ 134 Juan Acevedo | .10 | .30 |
| ❏ 135 Mike Sweeney | .10 | .30 |
| ❏ 136 Aaron Guiel | .10 | .30 |
| ❏ 137 Carlos Beltran | .20 | .50 |
| ❏ 138 Joe Randa | .10 | .30 |

| | | |
|---|---|---|
| ❏ 139 Paul Byrd | .10 | .30 |
| ❏ 140 Shawn Sedlacek | .10 | .30 |
| ❏ 141 Raul Ibanez | .10 | .30 |
| ❏ 142 Michael Tucker | .10 | .30 |
| ❏ 143 Torii Hunter | .10 | .30 |
| ❏ 144 Jacque Jones | .10 | .30 |
| ❏ 145 David Ortiz | .30 | .75 |
| ❏ 146 Corey Koskie | .10 | .30 |
| ❏ 147 Brad Radke | .10 | .30 |
| ❏ 148 Doug Mientkiewicz | .10 | .30 |
| ❏ 149 A.J. Pierzynski | .10 | .30 |
| ❏ 150 Dustan Mohr | .10 | .30 |
| ❏ 151 Michael Cuddyer | .10 | .30 |
| ❏ 152 Eddie Guardado | .10 | .30 |
| ❏ 153 Cristian Guzman | .10 | .30 |
| ❏ 154 Derek Jeter | .75 | 2.00 |
| ❏ 155 Bernie Williams | .20 | .50 |
| ❏ 156 Roger Clemens | .60 | 1.50 |
| ❏ 157 Mike Mussina | .20 | .50 |
| ❏ 158 Jorge Posada | .20 | .50 |
| ❏ 159 Alfonso Soriano | .10 | .30 |
| ❏ 160 Jason Giambi | .10 | .30 |
| ❏ 161 Robin Ventura | .10 | .30 |
| ❏ 162 Andy Pettitte | .20 | .50 |
| ❏ 163 David Wells | .10 | .30 |
| ❏ 164 Nick Johnson | .10 | .30 |
| ❏ 165 Jeff Weaver | .10 | .30 |
| ❏ 166 Raul Mondesi | .10 | .30 |
| ❏ 167 Rondell White | .10 | .30 |
| ❏ 168 Tim Hudson | .10 | .30 |
| ❏ 169 Barry Zito | .10 | .30 |
| ❏ 170 Mark Mulder | .10 | .30 |
| ❏ 171 Miguel Tejada | .10 | .30 |
| ❏ 172 Eric Chavez | .10 | .30 |
| ❏ 173 Billy Koch | .10 | .30 |
| ❏ 174 Jermaine Dye | .10 | .30 |
| ❏ 175 Scott Hatteberg | .10 | .30 |
| ❏ 176 Terrence Long | .10 | .30 |
| ❏ 177 David Justice | .10 | .30 |
| ❏ 178 Ramon Hernandez | .10 | .30 |
| ❏ 179 Ted Lilly | .10 | .30 |
| ❏ 180 Ichiro Suzuki | .60 | 1.50 |
| ❏ 181 Edgar Martinez | .20 | .50 |
| ❏ 182 Mike Cameron | .10 | .30 |
| ❏ 183 John Olerud | .10 | .30 |
| ❏ 184 Bret Boone | .10 | .30 |
| ❏ 185 Dan Wilson | .10 | .30 |
| ❏ 186 Freddy Garcia | .10 | .30 |
| ❏ 187 Jamie Moyer | .10 | .30 |
| ❏ 188 Carlos Guillen | .10 | .30 |
| ❏ 189 Ruben Sierra | .10 | .30 |
| ❏ 190 Kazuhiro Sasaki | .10 | .30 |
| ❏ 191 Mark McLemore | .10 | .30 |
| ❏ 192 John Halama | .10 | .30 |
| ❏ 193 Joel Pineiro | .10 | .30 |
| ❏ 194 Jeff Cirillo | .10 | .30 |
| ❏ 195 Rafael Soriano | .10 | .30 |
| ❏ 196 Ben Grieve | .10 | .30 |
| ❏ 197 Aubrey Huff | .10 | .30 |
| ❏ 198 Steve Cox | .10 | .30 |
| ❏ 199 Toby Hall | .10 | .30 |
| ❏ 200 Randy Winn | .10 | .30 |
| ❏ 201 Brent Abernathy | .10 | .30 |
| ❏ 202 Chris Gomez | .10 | .30 |
| ❏ 203 John Flaherty | .10 | .30 |
| ❏ 204 Paul Wilson | .10 | .30 |
| ❏ 205 Chan Ho Park | .10 | .30 |
| ❏ 206 Alex Rodriguez | .50 | 1.25 |
| ❏ 207 Juan Gonzalez | .20 | .50 |
| ❏ 208 Rafael Palmeiro | .20 | .50 |
| ❏ 209 Ivan Rodriguez | .20 | .50 |
| ❏ 210 Rusty Greer | .10 | .30 |
| ❏ 211 Kenny Rogers | .10 | .30 |
| ❏ 212 Ismael Valdes | .10 | .30 |
| ❏ 213 Frank Catalanotto | .10 | .30 |
| ❏ 214 Hank Blalock | .20 | .50 |
| ❏ 215 Michael Young | .20 | .50 |
| ❏ 216 Kevin Mench | .10 | .30 |
| ❏ 217 Herbert Perry | .10 | .30 |
| ❏ 218 Gabe Kapler | .10 | .30 |
| ❏ 219 Carlos Delgado | .10 | .30 |
| ❏ 220 Shannon Stewart | .10 | .30 |
| ❏ 221 Eric Hinske | .10 | .30 |
| ❏ 222 Roy Halladay | .10 | .30 |
| ❏ 223 Felipe Lopez | .10 | .30 |
| ❏ 224 Vernon Wells | .10 | .30 |
| ❏ 225 Josh Phelps | .10 | .30 |
| ❏ 226 Jose Cruz | .10 | .30 |

|  |  | | |
|---|---|---|---|
| ❏ 227 | Curt Schilling | .10 | .30 |
| ❏ 228 | Randy Johnson | .30 | .75 |
| ❏ 229 | Luis Gonzalez | .10 | .30 |
| ❏ 230 | Mark Grace | .20 | .50 |
| ❏ 231 | Junior Spivey | .10 | .30 |
| ❏ 232 | Tony Womack | .10 | .30 |
| ❏ 233 | Matt Williams | .10 | .30 |
| ❏ 234 | Steve Finley | .10 | .30 |
| ❏ 235 | Byung-Hyun Kim | .10 | .30 |
| ❏ 236 | Craig Counsell | .10 | .30 |
| ❏ 237 | Greg Maddux | .50 | 1.25 |
| ❏ 238 | Tom Glavine | .20 | .50 |
| ❏ 239 | John Smoltz | .20 | .50 |
| ❏ 240 | Chipper Jones | .30 | .75 |
| ❏ 241 | Gary Sheffield | .10 | .30 |
| ❏ 242 | Andruw Jones | .20 | .50 |
| ❏ 243 | Vinny Castilla | .10 | .30 |
| ❏ 244 | Damian Moss | .10 | .30 |
| ❏ 245 | Rafael Furcal | .10 | .30 |
| ❏ 246 | Javy Lopez | .10 | .30 |
| ❏ 247 | Kevin Millwood | .10 | .30 |
| ❏ 248 | Kerry Wood | .10 | .30 |
| ❏ 249 | Fred McGriff | .20 | .50 |
| ❏ 250 | Sammy Sosa | .30 | .75 |
| ❏ 251 | Alex Gonzalez | .10 | .30 |
| ❏ 252 | Corey Patterson | .10 | .30 |
| ❏ 253 | Moises Alou | .10 | .30 |
| ❏ 254 | Juan Cruz | .10 | .30 |
| ❏ 255 | Jon Lieber | .10 | .30 |
| ❏ 256 | Matt Clement | .10 | .30 |
| ❏ 257 | Mark Prior | .20 | .50 |
| ❏ 258 | Ken Griffey Jr. | .50 | 1.25 |
| ❏ 259 | Barry Larkin | .10 | .30 |
| ❏ 260 | Adam Dunn | .10 | .30 |
| ❏ 261 | Sean Casey | .10 | .30 |
| ❏ 262 | Jose Rijo | .10 | .30 |
| ❏ 263 | Elmer Dessens | .10 | .30 |
| ❏ 264 | Austin Kearns | .10 | .30 |
| ❏ 265 | Corky Miller | .10 | .30 |
| ❏ 266 | Todd Walker | .10 | .30 |
| ❏ 267 | Chris Reitsma | .10 | .30 |
| ❏ 268 | Ryan Dempster | .10 | .30 |
| ❏ 269 | Aaron Boone | .10 | .30 |
| ❏ 270 | Danny Graves | .10 | .30 |
| ❏ 271 | Brandon Larson | .10 | .30 |
| ❏ 272 | Larry Walker | .10 | .30 |
| ❏ 273 | Todd Helton | .20 | .50 |
| ❏ 274 | Juan Uribe | .10 | .30 |
| ❏ 275 | Juan Pierre | .10 | .30 |
| ❏ 276 | Mike Hampton | .10 | .30 |
| ❏ 277 | Todd Zeile | .10 | .30 |
| ❏ 278 | Todd Hollandsworth | .10 | .30 |
| ❏ 279 | Jason Jennings | .10 | .30 |
| ❏ 280 | Josh Beckett | .10 | .30 |
| ❏ 281 | Mike Lowell | .10 | .30 |
| ❏ 282 | Derrek Lee | .20 | .50 |
| ❏ 283 | A.J. Burnett | .10 | .30 |
| ❏ 284 | Luis Castillo | .10 | .30 |
| ❏ 285 | Tim Raines | .10 | .30 |
| ❏ 286 | Preston Wilson | .10 | .30 |
| ❏ 287 | Juan Encarnacion | .10 | .30 |
| ❏ 288 | Charles Johnson | .10 | .30 |
| ❏ 289 | Jeff Bagwell | .20 | .50 |
| ❏ 290 | Craig Biggio | .20 | .50 |
| ❏ 291 | Lance Berkman | .10 | .30 |
| ❏ 292 | Daryle Ward | .10 | .30 |
| ❏ 293 | Roy Oswalt | .10 | .30 |
| ❏ 294 | Richard Hidalgo | .10 | .30 |
| ❏ 295 | Octavio Dotel | .10 | .30 |
| ❏ 296 | Wade Miller | .10 | .30 |
| ❏ 297 | Julio Lugo | .10 | .30 |
| ❏ 298 | Billy Wagner | .10 | .30 |
| ❏ 299 | Shawn Green | .10 | .30 |
| ❏ 300 | Adrian Beltre | .10 | .30 |
| ❏ 301 | Paul Lo Duca | .10 | .30 |
| ❏ 302 | Eric Karros | .10 | .30 |
| ❏ 303 | Kevin Brown | .10 | .30 |
| ❏ 304 | Hideo Nomo | .30 | .75 |
| ❏ 305 | Odalis Perez | .10 | .30 |
| ❏ 306 | Eric Gagne | .10 | .30 |
| ❏ 307 | Brian Jordan | .10 | .30 |
| ❏ 308 | Cesar Izturis | .10 | .30 |
| ❏ 309 | Mark Grudzielanek | .10 | .30 |
| ❏ 310 | Kazuhisa Ishii | .10 | .30 |
| ❏ 311 | Geoff Jenkins | .10 | .30 |
| ❏ 312 | Richie Sexson | .10 | .30 |
| ❏ 313 | Jose Hernandez | .10 | .30 |
| ❏ 314 | Ben Sheets | .10 | .30 |

|  |  | | |
|---|---|---|---|
| ❏ 315 | Ruben Quevedo | .10 | .30 |
| ❏ 316 | Jeffrey Hammonds | .10 | .30 |
| ❏ 317 | Alex Sanchez | .10 | .30 |
| ❏ 318 | Eric Young | .10 | .30 |
| ❏ 319 | Takahito Nomura | .10 | .30 |
| ❏ 320 | Vladimir Guerrero | .30 | .75 |
| ❏ 321 | Jose Vidro | .10 | .30 |
| ❏ 322 | Orlando Cabrera | .10 | .30 |
| ❏ 323 | Michael Barrett | .10 | .30 |
| ❏ 324 | Javier Vazquez | .10 | .30 |
| ❏ 325 | Tony Armas Jr. | .10 | .30 |
| ❏ 326 | Andres Galarraga | .10 | .30 |
| ❏ 327 | Tomo Ohka | .10 | .30 |
| ❏ 328 | Bartolo Colon | .10 | .30 |
| ❏ 329 | Fernando Tatis | .10 | .30 |
| ❏ 330 | Brad Wilkerson | .10 | .30 |
| ❏ 331 | Masato Yoshii | .10 | .30 |
| ❏ 332 | Mike Piazza | .50 | 1.25 |
| ❏ 333 | Jeromy Burnitz | .10 | .30 |
| ❏ 334 | Roberto Alomar | .20 | .50 |
| ❏ 335 | Mo Vaughn | .10 | .30 |
| ❏ 336 | Al Leiter | .10 | .30 |
| ❏ 337 | Roger Astacio | .10 | .30 |
| ❏ 338 | Edgardo Alfonzo | .10 | .30 |
| ❏ 339 | Armando Benitez | .10 | .30 |
| ❏ 340 | Timo Perez | .10 | .30 |
| ❏ 341 | Jay Payton | .10 | .30 |
| ❏ 342 | Roger Cedeno | .10 | .30 |
| ❏ 343 | Rey Ordonez | .10 | .30 |
| ❏ 344 | Steve Trachsel | .10 | .30 |
| ❏ 345 | Satoru Komiyama | .10 | .30 |
| ❏ 346 | Scott Rolen | .20 | .50 |
| ❏ 347 | Pat Burrell | .10 | .30 |
| ❏ 348 | Bobby Abreu | .10 | .30 |
| ❏ 349 | Mike Lieberthal | .10 | .30 |
| ❏ 350 | Brandon Duckworth | .10 | .30 |
| ❏ 351 | Jimmy Rollins | .10 | .30 |
| ❏ 352 | Marlon Anderson | .10 | .30 |
| ❏ 353 | Travis Lee | .10 | .30 |
| ❏ 354 | Vicente Padilla | .10 | .30 |
| ❏ 355 | Randy Wolf | .10 | .30 |
| ❏ 356 | Jason Kendall | .10 | .30 |
| ❏ 357 | Brian Giles | .10 | .30 |
| ❏ 358 | Aramis Ramirez | .10 | .30 |
| ❏ 359 | Pokey Reese | .10 | .30 |
| ❏ 360 | Kip Wells | .10 | .30 |
| ❏ 361 | Josh Fogg | .10 | .30 |
| ❏ 362 | Mike Williams | .10 | .30 |
| ❏ 363 | Jack Wilson | .10 | .30 |
| ❏ 364 | Kevin Young | .10 | .30 |
| ❏ 365 | Ryan Klesko | .10 | .30 |
| ❏ 366 | Phil Nevin | .10 | .30 |
| ❏ 367 | Brian Lawrence | .10 | .30 |
| ❏ 368 | Mark Kotsay | .10 | .30 |
| ❏ 369 | Brett Tomko | .10 | .30 |
| ❏ 370 | Trevor Hoffman | .10 | .30 |
| ❏ 371 | Deivi Cruz | .10 | .30 |
| ❏ 372 | Bubba Trammell | .10 | .30 |
| ❏ 373 | Sean Burroughs | .10 | .30 |
| ❏ 374 | Barry Bonds | .75 | 2.00 |
| ❏ 375 | Jeff Kent | .10 | .30 |
| ❏ 376 | Rich Aurilia | .10 | .30 |
| ❏ 377 | Tsuyoshi Shinjo | .10 | .30 |
| ❏ 378 | Benito Santiago | .10 | .30 |
| ❏ 379 | Kirk Rueter | .10 | .30 |
| ❏ 380 | Livan Hernandez | .10 | .30 |
| ❏ 381 | Russ Ortiz | .10 | .30 |
| ❏ 382 | David Bell | .10 | .30 |
| ❏ 383 | Jason Schmidt | .10 | .30 |
| ❏ 384 | Hong-Chih Kuo | .10 | .30 |
| ❏ 385 | Reggie Sanders | .10 | .30 |
| ❏ 386 | J.T. Snow | .10 | .30 |
| ❏ 387 | Robb Nen | .10 | .30 |
| ❏ 388 | Ryan Jensen | .10 | .30 |
| ❏ 389 | Jim Edmonds | .10 | .30 |
| ❏ 390 | J.D. Drew | .10 | .30 |
| ❏ 391 | Albert Pujols | .60 | 1.50 |
| ❏ 392 | Fernando Vina | .10 | .30 |
| ❏ 393 | Tino Martinez | .20 | .50 |
| ❏ 394 | Edgar Renteria | .10 | .30 |
| ❏ 395 | Matt Morris | .10 | .30 |
| ❏ 396 | Woody Williams | .10 | .30 |
| ❏ 397 | Jason Isringhausen | .10 | .30 |
| ❏ 398 | Placido Polanco | .10 | .30 |
| ❏ 399 | Eli Marrero | .10 | .30 |
| ❏ 400 | Jason Simontacchi | .10 | .30 |

## 2004 Donruss

|  |  | | |
|---|---|---|---|
| ❏ COMPLETE SET (400) | | 75.00 | 150.00 |
| ❏ COMP.SET w/o SP's (300) | | 10.00 | 25.00 |
| ❏ COMMON CARD (1-370) | | .10 | .30 |
| ❏ COMMON CARD (1-25/371-400) | | .75 | 2.00 |
| ❏ COMMON CARD (26-70) | | .75 | 2.00 |
| 1-70/370-400 RANDOM INSERTS IN PACKS | | | |
| ❏ 1 | Derek Jeter DK | 1.50 | 4.00 |
| ❏ 2 | Greg Maddux DK | 1.25 | 3.00 |
| ❏ 3 | Albert Pujols DK | 1.50 | 4.00 |
| ❏ 4 | Ichiro Suzuki DK | 1.50 | 4.00 |
| ❏ 5 | Alex Rodriguez DK | 1.25 | 3.00 |
| ❏ 6 | Roger Clemens DK | 1.50 | 4.00 |
| ❏ 7 | Andruw Jones DK | .75 | 2.00 |
| ❏ 8 | Barry Bonds DK | 2.00 | 5.00 |
| ❏ 9 | Jeff Bagwell DK | .75 | 2.00 |
| ❏ 10 | Randy Johnson DK | .75 | 2.00 |
| ❏ 11 | Scott Rolen DK | .75 | 2.00 |
| ❏ 12 | Lance Berkman DK | .75 | 2.00 |
| ❏ 13 | Barry Zito DK | .75 | 2.00 |
| ❏ 14 | Manny Ramirez DK | .75 | 2.00 |
| ❏ 15 | Carlos Delgado DK | .75 | 2.00 |
| ❏ 16 | Alfonso Soriano DK | .75 | 2.00 |
| ❏ 17 | Todd Helton DK | .75 | 2.00 |
| ❏ 18 | Mike Mussina DK | .75 | 2.00 |
| ❏ 19 | Austin Kearns DK | .75 | 2.00 |
| ❏ 20 | Nomar Garciaparra DK | 1.25 | 3.00 |
| ❏ 21 | Chipper Jones DK | .75 | 2.00 |
| ❏ 22 | Mark Prior DK | .75 | 2.00 |
| ❏ 23 | Jim Thome DK | .75 | 2.00 |
| ❏ 24 | Vladimir Guerrero DK | .75 | 2.00 |
| ❏ 25 | Pedro Martinez DK | .75 | 2.00 |
| ❏ 26 | Sergio Mitre RR | .75 | 2.00 |
| ❏ 27 | Adam Loewen RR | .75 | 2.00 |
| ❏ 28 | Alfredo Gonzalez RR | .75 | 2.00 |
| ❏ 29 | Miguel Ojeda RR | .75 | 2.00 |
| ❏ 30 | Rosman Garcia RR | .75 | 2.00 |
| ❏ 31 | Arnie Munoz RR | .75 | 2.00 |
| ❏ 32 | Andrew Brown RR | .75 | 2.00 |
| ❏ 33 | Josh Hall RR | .75 | 2.00 |
| ❏ 34 | Josh Stewart RR | .75 | 2.00 |
| ❏ 35 | Clint Barmes RR | 1.25 | 3.00 |
| ❏ 36 | Brandon Webb RR | .75 | 2.00 |
| ❏ 37 | Chien-Ming Wang RR | 3.00 | 8.00 |
| ❏ 38 | Edgar Gonzalez RR | .75 | 2.00 |
| ❏ 39 | Alejandro Machado RR | .75 | 2.00 |
| ❏ 40 | Jeremy Griffiths RR | .75 | 2.00 |
| ❏ 41 | Craig Brazell RR | .75 | 2.00 |
| ❏ 42 | Daniel Cabrera RR | .75 | 2.00 |
| ❏ 43 | Fernando Cabrera RR | .75 | 2.00 |
| ❏ 44 | Termmel Sledge RR | .75 | 2.00 |
| ❏ 45 | Rob Hammock RR | .75 | 2.00 |
| ❏ 46 | Francisco Rosario RR | .75 | 2.00 |
| ❏ 47 | Francisco Cruceta RR | .75 | 2.00 |
| ❏ 48 | Jeff Johnson RR | .75 | 2.00 |
| ❏ 49 | Guillermo Quiroz RR | .75 | 2.00 |
| ❏ 50 | Hong-Chih Kuo RR | 1.25 | 3.00 |
| ❏ 51 | Ian Ferguson RR | .75 | 2.00 |
| ❏ 52 | Tim Olson RR | .75 | 2.00 |
| ❏ 53 | Todd Wellemeyer RR | .75 | 2.00 |
| ❏ 54 | Rich Fischer RR | .75 | 2.00 |
| ❏ 55 | Phil Seibel RR | .75 | 2.00 |
| ❏ 56 | Joe Valentine RR | .75 | 2.00 |
| ❏ 57 | Matt Kata RR | .75 | 2.00 |
| ❏ 58 | Michael Hessman RR | .75 | 2.00 |
| ❏ 59 | Michel Hernandez RR | .75 | 2.00 |
| ❏ 60 | Doug Waechter RR | .75 | 2.00 |
| ❏ 61 | Prentice Redman RR | .75 | 2.00 |
| ❏ 62 | Nook Logan RR | .75 | 2.00 |
| ❏ 63 | Oscar Villarreal RR | .75 | 2.00 |
| ❏ 64 | Pete LaForest RR | .75 | 2.00 |
| ❏ 65 | Matt Bruback RR | .75 | 2.00 |
| ❏ 66 | Dan Haren RR | .75 | 2.00 |

|  |  | | |
|---|---|---|---|
| 67 | Greg Aquino RR | .75 | 2.00 |
| 68 | Lew Ford RR | .75 | 2.00 |
| 69 | Jeff Duncan RR | .75 | 2.00 |
| 70 | Ryan Wagner RR | .75 | 2.00 |
| 71 | Bengie Molina | .10 | .30 |
| 72 | Brad Fullmer | .10 | .30 |
| 73 | Darin Erstad | .10 | .30 |
| 74 | David Eckstein | .10 | .30 |
| 75 | Garret Anderson | .10 | .30 |
| 76 | Jarrod Washburn | .10 | .30 |
| 77 | Kevin Appier | .10 | .30 |
| 78 | Scott Spiezio | .10 | .30 |
| 79 | Tim Salmon | .20 | .50 |
| 80 | Troy Glaus | .10 | .30 |
| 81 | Troy Percival | .10 | .30 |
| 82 | Jason Johnson | .10 | .30 |
| 83 | Jay Gibbons | .10 | .30 |
| 84 | Melvin Mora | .10 | .30 |
| 85 | Sidney Ponson | .10 | .30 |
| 86 | Tony Batista | .10 | .30 |
| 87 | Bill Mueller | .10 | .30 |
| 88 | Byung-Hyun Kim | .10 | .30 |
| 89 | David Ortiz | .30 | .75 |
| 90 | Derek Lowe | .10 | .30 |
| 91 | Johnny Damon | .20 | .50 |
| 92 | Casey Fossum | .10 | .30 |
| 93 | Manny Ramirez | .20 | .50 |
| 94 | Nomar Garciaparra | .50 | 1.25 |
| 95 | Pedro Martinez | .20 | .50 |
| 96 | Todd Walker | .10 | .30 |
| 97 | Trot Nixon | .10 | .30 |
| 98 | Bartolo Colon | .10 | .30 |
| 99 | Carlos Lee | .10 | .30 |
| 100 | D'Angelo Jimenez | .10 | .30 |
| 101 | Esteban Loaiza | .10 | .30 |
| 102 | Frank Thomas | .30 | .75 |
| 103 | Joe Crede | .10 | .30 |
| 104 | Jose Valentin | .10 | .30 |
| 105 | Magglio Ordonez | .10 | .30 |
| 106 | Mark Buehrle | .10 | .30 |
| 107 | Paul Konerko | .10 | .30 |
| 108 | Brandon Phillips | .10 | .30 |
| 109 | C.C Sabathia | .10 | .30 |
| 110 | Ellis Burks | .10 | .30 |
| 111 | Jeremy Guthrie | .10 | .30 |
| 112 | Josh Bard | .10 | .30 |
| 113 | Matt Lawton | .10 | .30 |
| 114 | Milton Bradley | .10 | .30 |
| 115 | Omar Vizquel | .20 | .50 |
| 116 | Travis Hafner | .10 | .30 |
| 117 | Bobby Higginson | .10 | .30 |
| 118 | Carlos Pena | .10 | .30 |
| 119 | Dmitri Young | .10 | .30 |
| 120 | Eric Munson | .10 | .30 |
| 121 | Jeremy Bonderman | .10 | .30 |
| 122 | Nate Cornejo | .10 | .30 |
| 123 | Omar Infante | .10 | .30 |
| 124 | Ramon Santiago | .10 | .30 |
| 125 | Angel Berroa | .10 | .30 |
| 126 | Carlos Beltran | .10 | .30 |
| 127 | Desi Relaford | .10 | .30 |
| 128 | Jeremy Affeldt | .10 | .30 |
| 129 | Joe Randa | .10 | .30 |
| 130 | Ken Harvey | .10 | .30 |
| 131 | Mike MacDougal | .10 | .30 |
| 132 | Michael Tucker | .10 | .30 |
| 133 | Mike Sweeney | .10 | .30 |
| 134 | Raul Ibanez | .10 | .30 |
| 135 | Runelvys Hernandez | .10 | .30 |
| 136 | A.J. Pierzynski | .10 | .30 |
| 137 | Brad Radke | .10 | .30 |
| 138 | Corey Koskie | .10 | .30 |
| 139 | Cristian Guzman | .10 | .30 |
| 140 | Doug Mientkiewicz | .10 | .30 |
| 141 | Dustan Mohr | .10 | .30 |
| 142 | Jacque Jones | .10 | .30 |
| 143 | Kenny Rogers | .10 | .30 |
| 144 | Bobby Kielty | .10 | .30 |
| 145 | Kyle Lohse | .10 | .30 |
| 146 | Luis Rivas | .10 | .30 |
| 147 | Torii Hunter | .10 | .30 |
| 148 | Alfonso Soriano | .10 | .30 |
| 149 | Andy Pettitte | .20 | .50 |
| 150 | Bernie Williams | .10 | .30 |
| 151 | David Wells | .10 | .30 |
| 152 | Derek Jeter | .60 | 1.50 |
| 153 | Hideki Matsui | .50 | 1.25 |
| 154 | Jason Giambi | .10 | .30 |
| 155 | Jorge Posada | .20 | .50 |
| 156 | Jose Contreras | .10 | .30 |
| 157 | Mike Mussina | .20 | .50 |
| 158 | Nick Johnson | .10 | .30 |
| 159 | Robin Ventura | .10 | .30 |
| 160 | Roger Clemens | .60 | 1.50 |
| 161 | Barry Zito | .10 | .30 |
| 162 | Chris Singleton | .10 | .30 |
| 163 | Eric Byrnes | .10 | .30 |
| 164 | Eric Chavez | .10 | .30 |
| 165 | Erubiel Durazo | .10 | .30 |
| 166 | Keith Foulke | .10 | .30 |
| 167 | Mark Ellis | .10 | .30 |
| 168 | Miguel Tejada | .10 | .30 |
| 169 | Mark Mulder | .10 | .30 |
| 170 | Ramon Hernandez | .10 | .30 |
| 171 | Ted Lilly | .10 | .30 |
| 172 | Terrence Long | .10 | .30 |
| 173 | Tim Hudson | .10 | .30 |
| 174 | Bret Boone | .10 | .30 |
| 175 | Carlos Guillen | .10 | .30 |
| 176 | Dan Wilson | .10 | .30 |
| 177 | Edgar Martinez | .20 | .50 |
| 178 | Freddy Garcia | .10 | .30 |
| 179 | Gil Meche | .10 | .30 |
| 180 | Ichiro Suzuki | .60 | 1.50 |
| 181 | Jamie Moyer | .10 | .30 |
| 182 | Joel Pineiro | .10 | .30 |
| 183 | John Olerud | .10 | .30 |
| 184 | Mike Cameron | .10 | .30 |
| 185 | Randy Winn | .10 | .30 |
| 186 | Ryan Franklin | .10 | .30 |
| 187 | Kazuhiro Sasaki | .10 | .30 |
| 188 | Aubrey Huff | .10 | .30 |
| 189 | Carl Crawford | .10 | .30 |
| 190 | Joe Kennedy | .10 | .30 |
| 191 | Marlon Anderson | .10 | .30 |
| 192 | Rey Ordonez | .10 | .30 |
| 193 | Rocco Baldelli | .10 | .30 |
| 194 | Toby Hall | .10 | .30 |
| 195 | Travis Lee | .10 | .30 |
| 196 | Alex Rodriguez | .50 | 1.25 |
| 197 | Carl Everett | .10 | .30 |
| 198 | Chan Ho Park | .10 | .30 |
| 199 | Einar Diaz | .10 | .30 |
| 200 | Hank Blalock | .10 | .30 |
| 201 | Ismael Valdes | .10 | .30 |
| 202 | Juan Gonzalez | .10 | .30 |
| 203 | Mark Teixeira | .20 | .50 |
| 204 | Mike Young | .10 | .30 |
| 205 | Rafael Palmeiro | .20 | .50 |
| 206 | Carlos Delgado | .10 | .30 |
| 207 | Kelvim Escobar | .10 | .30 |
| 208 | Eric Hinske | .10 | .30 |
| 209 | Frank Catalanotto | .10 | .30 |
| 210 | Josh Phelps | .10 | .30 |
| 211 | Orlando Hudson | .10 | .30 |
| 212 | Roy Halladay | .10 | .30 |
| 213 | Shannon Stewart | .10 | .30 |
| 214 | Vernon Wells | .10 | .30 |
| 215 | Carlos Baerga | .10 | .30 |
| 216 | Curt Schilling | .10 | .30 |
| 217 | Junior Spivey | .10 | .30 |
| 218 | Luis Gonzalez | .10 | .30 |
| 219 | Lyle Overbay | .10 | .30 |
| 220 | Mark Grace | .20 | .50 |
| 221 | Matt Williams | .10 | .30 |
| 222 | Randy Johnson | .30 | .75 |
| 223 | Shea Hillenbrand | .10 | .30 |
| 224 | Steve Finley | .10 | .30 |
| 225 | Andruw Jones | .20 | .50 |
| 226 | Chipper Jones | .30 | .75 |
| 227 | Gary Sheffield | .10 | .30 |
| 228 | Greg Maddux | .50 | 1.25 |
| 229 | Javy Lopez | .10 | .30 |
| 230 | John Smoltz | .20 | .50 |
| 231 | Marcus Giles | .10 | .30 |
| 232 | Mike Hampton | .10 | .30 |
| 233 | Rafael Furcal | .10 | .30 |
| 234 | Robert Fick | .10 | .30 |
| 235 | Russ Ortiz | .10 | .30 |
| 236 | Alex Gonzalez | .10 | .30 |
| 237 | Carlos Zambrano | .10 | .30 |
| 238 | Corey Patterson | .10 | .30 |
| 239 | Hee Seop Choi | .10 | .30 |
| 240 | Kerry Wood | .10 | .30 |
| 241 | Mark Bellhorn | .10 | .30 |
| 242 | Mark Prior | .20 | .50 |
| 243 | Moises Alou | .10 | .30 |
| 244 | Sammy Sosa | .30 | .75 |
| 245 | Aaron Boone | .10 | .30 |
| 246 | Adam Dunn | .10 | .30 |
| 247 | Austin Kearns | .10 | .30 |
| 248 | Barry Larkin | .20 | .50 |
| 249 | Felipe Lopez | .10 | .30 |
| 250 | Jose Guillen | .10 | .30 |
| 251 | Ken Griffey Jr. | .50 | 1.25 |
| 252 | Jason LaRue | .10 | .30 |
| 253 | Scott Williamson | .10 | .30 |
| 254 | Sean Casey | .10 | .30 |
| 255 | Shawn Chacon | .10 | .30 |
| 256 | Chris Stynes | .10 | .30 |
| 257 | Jason Jennings | .10 | .30 |
| 258 | Jay Payton | .10 | .30 |
| 259 | Jose Hernandez | .10 | .30 |
| 260 | Larry Walker | .10 | .30 |
| 261 | Preston Wilson | .10 | .30 |
| 262 | Ronnie Belliard | .10 | .30 |
| 263 | Todd Helton | .20 | .50 |
| 264 | A.J. Burnett | .10 | .30 |
| 265 | Alex Gonzalez | .10 | .30 |
| 266 | Brad Penny | .10 | .30 |
| 267 | Derrek Lee | .20 | .50 |
| 268 | Ivan Rodriguez | .20 | .50 |
| 269 | Josh Beckett | .10 | .30 |
| 270 | Juan Encarnacion | .10 | .30 |
| 271 | Juan Pierre | .10 | .30 |
| 272 | Luis Castillo | .10 | .30 |
| 273 | Mike Lowell | .10 | .30 |
| 274 | Todd Hollandsworth | .10 | .30 |
| 275 | Billy Wagner | .10 | .30 |
| 276 | Brad Ausmus | .10 | .30 |
| 277 | Craig Biggio | .20 | .50 |
| 278 | Jeff Bagwell | .20 | .50 |
| 279 | Jeff Kent | .10 | .30 |
| 280 | Lance Berkman | .10 | .30 |
| 281 | Richard Hidalgo | .10 | .30 |
| 282 | Roy Oswalt | .10 | .30 |
| 283 | Wade Miller | .10 | .30 |
| 284 | Adrian Beltre | .10 | .30 |
| 285 | Brian Jordan | .10 | .30 |
| 286 | Cesar Izturis | .10 | .30 |
| 287 | Dave Roberts | .10 | .30 |
| 288 | Eric Gagne | .10 | .30 |
| 289 | Fred McGriff | .20 | .50 |
| 290 | Hideo Nomo | .30 | .75 |
| 291 | Kazuhisa Ishii | .10 | .30 |
| 292 | Kevin Brown | .10 | .30 |
| 293 | Paul Lo Duca | .10 | .30 |
| 294 | Shawn Green | .10 | .30 |
| 295 | Ben Sheets | .10 | .30 |
| 296 | Geoff Jenkins | .10 | .30 |
| 297 | Rey Sanchez | .10 | .30 |
| 298 | Richie Sexson | .10 | .30 |
| 299 | Wes Helms | .10 | .30 |
| 300 | Brad Wilkerson | .10 | .30 |
| 301 | Claudio Vargas | .10 | .30 |
| 302 | Endy Chavez | .10 | .30 |
| 303 | Fernando Tatis | .10 | .30 |
| 304 | Javier Vazquez | .10 | .30 |
| 305 | Jose Vidro | .10 | .30 |
| 306 | Michael Barrett | .10 | .30 |
| 307 | Orlando Cabrera | .10 | .30 |
| 308 | Tony Armas Jr. | .10 | .30 |
| 309 | Vladimir Guerrero | .30 | .75 |
| 310 | Zach Day | .10 | .30 |
| 311 | Al Leiter | .10 | .30 |
| 312 | Cliff Floyd | .10 | .30 |
| 313 | Jae Weong Seo | .10 | .30 |
| 314 | Jeromy Burnitz | .10 | .30 |
| 315 | Mike Piazza | .50 | 1.25 |
| 316 | Mo Vaughn | .10 | .30 |
| 317 | Roberto Alomar | .10 | .30 |
| 318 | Roger Cedeno | .10 | .30 |
| 319 | Tom Glavine | .20 | .50 |
| 320 | Jose Reyes | .10 | .30 |
| 321 | Bobby Abreu | .10 | .30 |
| 322 | Brett Myers | .10 | .30 |
| 323 | David Bell | .10 | .30 |
| 324 | Jim Thome | .20 | .50 |
| 325 | Jimmy Rollins | .10 | .30 |
| 326 | Kevin Millwood | .10 | .30 |
| 327 | Marlon Byrd | .10 | .30 |
| 328 | Mike Lieberthal | .10 | .30 |
| 329 | Pat Burrell | .10 | .30 |
| 330 | Randy Wolf | .20 | .50 |

|  | | |
|---|---|---|
| ❑ 331 Aramis Ramirez | .10 | .30 |
| ❑ 332 Brian Giles | .10 | .30 |
| ❑ 333 Jason Kendall | .10 | .30 |
| ❑ 334 Kenny Lofton | .10 | .30 |
| ❑ 335 Kip Wells | .10 | .30 |
| ❑ 336 Kris Benson | .10 | .30 |
| ❑ 337 Randall Simon | .10 | .30 |
| ❑ 338 Reggie Sanders | .10 | .30 |
| ❑ 339 Albert Pujols | .60 | 1.50 |
| ❑ 340 Edgar Renteria | .10 | .30 |
| ❑ 341 Fernando Vina | .10 | .30 |
| ❑ 342 J.D. Drew | .10 | .30 |
| ❑ 343 Jim Edmonds | .10 | .30 |
| ❑ 344 Matt Morris | .10 | .30 |
| ❑ 345 Mike Matheny | .10 | .30 |
| ❑ 346 Scott Rolen | .20 | .50 |
| ❑ 347 Tino Martinez | .20 | .50 |
| ❑ 348 Woody Williams | .10 | .30 |
| ❑ 349 Brian Lawrence | .10 | .30 |
| ❑ 350 Mark Kotsay | .10 | .30 |
| ❑ 351 Mark Loretta | .10 | .30 |
| ❑ 352 Ramon Vazquez | .10 | .30 |
| ❑ 353 Rondell White | .10 | .30 |
| ❑ 354 Ryan Klesko | .10 | .30 |
| ❑ 355 Sean Burroughs | .10 | .30 |
| ❑ 356 Trevor Hoffman | .10 | .30 |
| ❑ 357 Xavier Nady | .10 | .30 |
| ❑ 358 Andres Galarraga | .10 | .30 |
| ❑ 359 Barry Bonds | .75 | 2.00 |
| ❑ 360 Benito Santiago | .10 | .30 |
| ❑ 361 Deivi Cruz | .10 | .30 |
| ❑ 362 Edgardo Alfonzo | .10 | .30 |
| ❑ 363 J.T. Snow | .10 | .30 |
| ❑ 364 Jason Schmidt | .10 | .30 |
| ❑ 365 Kirk Rueter | .10 | .30 |
| ❑ 366 Kurt Ainsworth | .10 | .30 |
| ❑ 367 Marquis Grissom | .10 | .30 |
| ❑ 368 Ray Durham | .10 | .30 |
| ❑ 369 Rich Aurilia | .10 | .30 |
| ❑ 370 Tim Worrell | .10 | .30 |
| ❑ 371 Troy Glaus TC | .75 | 2.00 |
| ❑ 372 Melvin Mora TC | .75 | 2.00 |
| ❑ 373 Nomar Garciaparra TC | 1.25 | 3.00 |
| ❑ 374 Magglio Ordonez TC | .75 | 2.00 |
| ❑ 375 Omar Vizquel TC | .75 | 2.00 |
| ❑ 376 Dmitri Young TC | .75 | 2.00 |
| ❑ 377 Mike Sweeney TC | .75 | 2.00 |
| ❑ 378 Torii Hunter TC | .75 | 2.00 |
| ❑ 379 Derek Jeter TC | 1.50 | 4.00 |
| ❑ 380 Barry Zito TC | .75 | 2.00 |
| ❑ 381 Ichiro Suzuki TC | 1.50 | 4.00 |
| ❑ 382 Rocco Baldelli TC | .75 | 2.00 |
| ❑ 383 Alex Rodriguez TC | 1.25 | 3.00 |
| ❑ 384 Carlos Delgado TC | .75 | 2.00 |
| ❑ 385 Randy Johnson TC | .75 | 2.00 |
| ❑ 386 Greg Maddux TC | 1.25 | 3.00 |
| ❑ 387 Sammy Sosa TC | .75 | 2.00 |
| ❑ 388 Ken Griffey Jr. TC | 1.25 | 3.00 |
| ❑ 389 Todd Helton TC | .75 | 2.00 |
| ❑ 390 Ivan Rodriguez TC | .75 | 2.00 |
| ❑ 391 Jeff Bagwell TC | .75 | 2.00 |
| ❑ 392 Hideo Nomo TC | .75 | 2.00 |
| ❑ 393 Richie Sexson TC | .75 | 2.00 |
| ❑ 394 Vladimir Guerrero TC | .75 | 2.00 |
| ❑ 395 Mike Piazza TC | 1.25 | 3.00 |
| ❑ 396 Jim Thome TC | .75 | 2.00 |
| ❑ 397 Jason Kendall TC | .75 | 2.00 |
| ❑ 398 Albert Pujols TC | 1.50 | 4.00 |
| ❑ 399 Ryan Klesko TC | .75 | 2.00 |
| ❑ 400 Barry Bonds TC | 2.00 | 5.00 |

**2005 Donruss**

| | | |
|---|---|---|
| ❑ COMPLETE SET (400) | 75.00 | 150.00 |
| ❑ COMP.SET w/o SP's (300) | 10.00 | 25.00 |

|  | | |
|---|---|---|
| ❑ COMMON CARD (71-370) | .10 | .30 |
| ❑ COMMON (1-25/371-400) | .75 | 2.00 |
| ❑ COMMON (26-70) | .75 | 2.00 |
| ❑ 1-25 STATED ODDS 1:6 | | |
| ❑ 26-70 STATED ODDS 1:6 | | |
| ❑ 371-400 STATED ODDS 1:6 | | |
| ❑ 1 Garret Anderson DK | .75 | 2.00 |
| ❑ 2 Vladimir Guerrero DK | .75 | 2.00 |
| ❑ 3 Manny Ramirez DK | .75 | 2.00 |
| ❑ 4 Kerry Wood DK | .75 | 2.00 |
| ❑ 5 Sammy Sosa DK | .75 | 2.00 |
| ❑ 6 Magglio Ordonez DK | .75 | 2.00 |
| ❑ 7 Adam Dunn DK | .75 | 2.00 |
| ❑ 8 Todd Helton DK | .75 | 2.00 |
| ❑ 9 Josh Beckett DK | .75 | 2.00 |
| ❑ 10 Miguel Cabrera DK | .75 | 2.00 |
| ❑ 11 Lance Berkman DK | .75 | 2.00 |
| ❑ 12 Carlos Beltran DK | .75 | 2.00 |
| ❑ 13 Shawn Green DK | .75 | 2.00 |
| ❑ 14 Roger Clemens DK | 1.25 | 3.00 |
| ❑ 15 Mike Piazza DK | 1.25 | 3.00 |
| ❑ 16 Alex Rodriguez DK | 1.25 | 3.00 |
| ❑ 17 Derek Jeter DK | 1.50 | 4.00 |
| ❑ 18 Mark Mulder DK | .75 | 2.00 |
| ❑ 19 Jim Thome DK | .75 | 2.00 |
| ❑ 20 Albert Pujols DK | 1.50 | 4.00 |
| ❑ 21 Scott Rolen DK | .75 | 2.00 |
| ❑ 22 Aubrey Huff DK | .75 | 2.00 |
| ❑ 23 Alfonso Soriano DK | .75 | 2.00 |
| ❑ 24 Hank Blalock DK | .75 | 2.00 |
| ❑ 25 Vernon Wells DK | .75 | 2.00 |
| ❑ 26 Kazuo Matsui RR | 1.25 | 3.00 |
| ❑ 27 B.J. Upton RR | 2.00 | 5.00 |
| ❑ 28 Charles Thomas RR | .75 | 2.00 |
| ❑ 29 Akinori Otsuka RR | .75 | 2.00 |
| ❑ 30 David Aardsma RR | .75 | 2.00 |
| ❑ 31 Travis Blackley RR | .75 | 2.00 |
| ❑ 32 Brad Halsey RR | .75 | 2.00 |
| ❑ 33 David Wright RR | 3.00 | 8.00 |
| ❑ 34 Kazuhito Tadano RR | 1.25 | 3.00 |
| ❑ 35 Casey Kotchman RR | 1.25 | 3.00 |
| ❑ 36 Khalil Greene RR | 2.00 | 5.00 |
| ❑ 37 Adrian Gonzalez RR | .75 | 2.00 |
| ❑ 38 Zack Greinke RR | .75 | 2.00 |
| ❑ 39 Chad Cordero RR | .75 | 2.00 |
| ❑ 40 Scott Kazmir RR | 2.00 | 5.00 |
| ❑ 41 Jeremy Guthrie RR | .75 | 2.00 |
| ❑ 42 Noah Lowry RR | 1.25 | 3.00 |
| ❑ 43 Chase Utley RR | .75 | 2.00 |
| ❑ 44 Billy Traber RR | .75 | 2.00 |
| ❑ 45 Aaron Baldiris RR | .75 | 2.00 |
| ❑ 46 Abe Alvarez RR | .75 | 2.00 |
| ❑ 47 Angel Chavez RR | .75 | 2.00 |
| ❑ 48 Joe Mauer RR | 2.00 | 5.00 |
| ❑ 49 Joey Gathright RR | 1.25 | 3.00 |
| ❑ 50 John Gall RR | .75 | 2.00 |
| ❑ 51 Ronald Belisario RR | .75 | 2.00 |
| ❑ 52 Ryan Wing RR | .75 | 2.00 |
| ❑ 53 Scott Proctor RR | .75 | 2.00 |
| ❑ 54 Yadier Molina RR | 1.25 | 3.00 |
| ❑ 55 Carlos Hines RR | .75 | 2.00 |
| ❑ 56 Frankie Francisco RR | .75 | 2.00 |
| ❑ 57 Graham Koonce RR | .75 | 2.00 |
| ❑ 58 Jake Woods RR | .75 | 2.00 |
| ❑ 59 Jason Bartlett RR | .75 | 2.00 |
| ❑ 60 Mike Rouse RR | .75 | 2.00 |
| ❑ 61 Phil Stockman RR | .75 | 2.00 |
| ❑ 62 Renyel Pinto RR | .75 | 2.00 |
| ❑ 63 Roberto Novoa RR | .75 | 2.00 |
| ❑ 64 Ryan Meaux RR | .75 | 2.00 |
| ❑ 65 Dave Crouthers RR | .75 | 2.00 |
| ❑ 66 Justin Knoedler RR | .75 | 2.00 |
| ❑ 67 Justin Leone RR | .75 | 2.00 |
| ❑ 68 Nick Regilio RR | .75 | 2.00 |
| ❑ 69 Mike Gosling RR | .75 | 2.00 |
| ❑ 70 Omil Joseph RR | .75 | 2.00 |
| ❑ 71 Bartolo Colon | .10 | .30 |
| ❑ 72 Brad Fullmer | .10 | .30 |
| ❑ 73 Chone Figgins | .10 | .30 |
| ❑ 74 Darin Erstad | .10 | .30 |
| ❑ 75 Francisco Rodriguez | .10 | .30 |
| ❑ 76 Garret Anderson | .10 | .30 |
| ❑ 77 Jarrod Washburn | .10 | .30 |
| ❑ 78 John Lackey | .10 | .30 |
| ❑ 79 Jose Guillen | .10 | .30 |
| ❑ 80 Robb Quinlan | .10 | .30 |
| ❑ 81 Tim Salmon | .20 | .50 |
| ❑ 82 Troy Glaus | .10 | .30 |
| ❑ 83 Troy Percival | .10 | .30 |
| ❑ 84 Vladimir Guerrero | .30 | .75 |
| ❑ 85 Brandon Webb | .10 | .30 |
| ❑ 86 Casey Fossum | .10 | .30 |
| ❑ 87 Luis Gonzalez | .10 | .30 |
| ❑ 88 Randy Johnson | .30 | .75 |
| ❑ 89 Richie Sexson | .10 | .30 |
| ❑ 90 Robby Hammock | .10 | .30 |
| ❑ 91 Roberto Alomar | .20 | .50 |
| ❑ 92 Adam LaRoche | .10 | .30 |
| ❑ 93 Andruw Jones | .20 | .50 |
| ❑ 94 Bubba Nelson | .10 | .30 |
| ❑ 95 Chipper Jones | .30 | .75 |
| ❑ 96 J.D. Drew | .10 | .30 |
| ❑ 97 John Smoltz | .20 | .50 |
| ❑ 98 Johnny Estrada | .10 | .30 |
| ❑ 99 Marcus Giles | .10 | .30 |
| ❑ 100 Mike Hampton | .10 | .30 |
| ❑ 101 Nick Green | .10 | .30 |
| ❑ 102 Rafael Furcal | .10 | .30 |
| ❑ 103 Russ Ortiz | .10 | .30 |
| ❑ 104 Adam Loewen | .10 | .30 |
| ❑ 105 Brian Roberts | .10 | .30 |
| ❑ 106 Javy Lopez | .10 | .30 |
| ❑ 107 Jay Gibbons | .10 | .30 |
| ❑ 108 L.Bigbie UER Roberts | .10 | .30 |
| ❑ 109 Luis Matos | .10 | .30 |
| ❑ 110 Melvin Mora | .10 | .30 |
| ❑ 111 Miguel Tejada | .10 | .30 |
| ❑ 112 Rafael Palmeiro | .20 | .50 |
| ❑ 113 Rodrigo Lopez | .10 | .30 |
| ❑ 114 Sidney Ponson | .10 | .30 |
| ❑ 115 Bill Mueller | .10 | .30 |
| ❑ 116 Byung-Hyun Kim | .10 | .30 |
| ❑ 117 Curt Schilling | .20 | .50 |
| ❑ 118 David Ortiz | .30 | .75 |
| ❑ 119 Derek Lowe | .10 | .30 |
| ❑ 120 Doug Mientkiewicz | .10 | .30 |
| ❑ 121 Jason Varitek | .30 | .75 |
| ❑ 122 Johnny Damon | .20 | .50 |
| ❑ 123 Keith Foulke | .10 | .30 |
| ❑ 124 Kevin Youkilis | .10 | .30 |
| ❑ 125 Manny Ramirez | .20 | .50 |
| ❑ 126 Orlando Cabrera | .10 | .30 |
| ❑ 127 Pedro Martinez | .20 | .50 |
| ❑ 128 Trot Nixon | .10 | .30 |
| ❑ 129 Aramis Ramirez | .10 | .30 |
| ❑ 130 Carlos Zambrano | .10 | .30 |
| ❑ 131 Corey Patterson | .10 | .30 |
| ❑ 132 Derrek Lee | .20 | .50 |
| ❑ 133 Greg Maddux | .50 | 1.25 |
| ❑ 134 Kerry Wood | .10 | .30 |
| ❑ 135 Mark Prior | .20 | .50 |
| ❑ 136 Matt Clement | .10 | .30 |
| ❑ 137 Moises Alou | .10 | .30 |
| ❑ 138 Nomar Garciaparra | .30 | .75 |
| ❑ 139 Sammy Sosa | .30 | .75 |
| ❑ 140 Todd Walker | .10 | .30 |
| ❑ 141 Angel Guzman | .10 | .30 |
| ❑ 142 Billy Koch | .10 | .30 |
| ❑ 143 Carlos Lee | .10 | .30 |
| ❑ 144 Frank Thomas | .30 | .75 |
| ❑ 145 Magglio Ordonez | .10 | .30 |
| ❑ 146 Mark Buehrle | .10 | .30 |
| ❑ 147 Paul Konerko | .10 | .30 |
| ❑ 148 Wilson Valdez | .10 | .30 |
| ❑ 149 Adam Dunn | .10 | .30 |
| ❑ 150 Austin Kearns | .10 | .30 |
| ❑ 151 Barry Larkin | .20 | .50 |
| ❑ 152 Benito Santiago | .10 | .30 |
| ❑ 153 Jason LaRue | .10 | .30 |
| ❑ 154 Ken Griffey Jr. | .50 | 1.25 |
| ❑ 155 Ryan Wagner | .10 | .30 |
| ❑ 156 Sean Casey | .10 | .30 |
| ❑ 157 Brandon Phillips | .10 | .30 |
| ❑ 158 Brian Tallet | .10 | .30 |
| ❑ 159 C.C. Sabathia | .10 | .30 |
| ❑ 160 Cliff Lee | .10 | .30 |
| ❑ 161 Jeremy Guthrie | .10 | .30 |
| ❑ 162 Jody Gerut | .10 | .30 |
| ❑ 163 Matt Lawton | .10 | .30 |
| ❑ 164 Omar Vizquel | .20 | .50 |
| ❑ 165 Travis Hafner | .10 | .30 |
| ❑ 166 Victor Martinez | .10 | .30 |
| ❑ 167 Charles Johnson | .10 | .30 |
| ❑ 168 Garrett Atkins | .10 | .30 |
| ❑ 169 Jason Jennings | .10 | .30 |
| ❑ 170 Jay Payton | .10 | .30 |

|  |  | | |
|---|---|---|---|
| ☐ 171 | Jeromy Burnitz | .10 | .30 |
| ☐ 172 | Joe Kennedy | .10 | .30 |
| ☐ 173 | Larry Walker | .20 | .50 |
| ☐ 174 | Preston Wilson | .10 | .30 |
| ☐ 175 | Todd Helton | .20 | .50 |
| ☐ 176 | Vinny Castilla | .10 | .30 |
| ☐ 177 | Bobby Higginson | .10 | .30 |
| ☐ 178 | Brandon Inge | .10 | .30 |
| ☐ 179 | Carlos Guillen | .10 | .30 |
| ☐ 180 | Carlos Pena | .10 | .30 |
| ☐ 181 | Craig Monroe | .10 | .30 |
| ☐ 182 | Dmitri Young | .10 | .30 |
| ☐ 183 | Eric Munson | .10 | .30 |
| ☐ 184 | Fernando Vina | .10 | .30 |
| ☐ 185 | Ivan Rodriguez | .20 | .50 |
| ☐ 186 | Jeremy Bonderman | .10 | .30 |
| ☐ 187 | Rondell White | .10 | .30 |
| ☐ 188 | A.J. Burnett | .10 | .30 |
| ☐ 189 | Dontrelle Willis | .10 | .30 |
| ☐ 190 | Guillermo Mota | .10 | .30 |
| ☐ 191 | Hee Seop Choi | .10 | .30 |
| ☐ 192 | Jeff Conine | .10 | .30 |
| ☐ 193 | Josh Beckett | .10 | .30 |
| ☐ 194 | Juan Encarnacion | .10 | .30 |
| ☐ 195 | Juan Pierre | .10 | .30 |
| ☐ 196 | Luis Castillo | .10 | .30 |
| ☐ 197 | Miguel Cabrera | .20 | .50 |
| ☐ 198 | Mike Lowell | .10 | .30 |
| ☐ 199 | Paul Lo Duca | .10 | .30 |
| ☐ 200 | Andy Pettitte | .20 | .50 |
| ☐ 201 | Brad Ausmus | .10 | .30 |
| ☐ 202 | Carlos Beltran | .10 | .30 |
| ☐ 203 | Chris Burke | .10 | .30 |
| ☐ 204 | Craig Biggio | .20 | .50 |
| ☐ 205 | Jeff Bagwell | .20 | .50 |
| ☐ 206 | Jeff Kent | .10 | .30 |
| ☐ 207 | Lance Berkman | .10 | .30 |
| ☐ 208 | Morgan Ensberg | .10 | .30 |
| ☐ 209 | Octavio Dotel | .10 | .30 |
| ☐ 210 | Roger Clemens | .50 | 1.25 |
| ☐ 211 | Roy Oswalt | .10 | .30 |
| ☐ 212 | Tim Redding | .10 | .30 |
| ☐ 213 | Angel Berroa | .10 | .30 |
| ☐ 214 | Juan Gonzalez | .10 | .30 |
| ☐ 215 | Ken Harvey | .10 | .30 |
| ☐ 216 | Mike Sweeney | .10 | .30 |
| ☐ 217 | Adrian Beltre | .10 | .30 |
| ☐ 218 | Brad Penny | .10 | .30 |
| ☐ 219 | Eric Gagne | .10 | .30 |
| ☐ 220 | Hideo Nomo | .30 | .75 |
| ☐ 221 | Hong-Chih Kuo | .10 | .30 |
| ☐ 222 | Jeff Weaver | .10 | .30 |
| ☐ 223 | Kazuhisa Ishii | .10 | .30 |
| ☐ 224 | Milton Bradley | .10 | .30 |
| ☐ 225 | Shawn Green | .10 | .30 |
| ☐ 226 | Steve Finley | .10 | .30 |
| ☐ 227 | Danny Kolb | .10 | .30 |
| ☐ 228 | Geoff Jenkins | .10 | .30 |
| ☐ 229 | Junior Spivey | .10 | .30 |
| ☐ 230 | Lyle Overbay | .10 | .30 |
| ☐ 231 | Rickie Weeks | .10 | .30 |
| ☐ 232 | Scott Podsednik | .10 | .30 |
| ☐ 233 | Brad Radke | .10 | .30 |
| ☐ 234 | Corey Koskie | .10 | .30 |
| ☐ 235 | Cristian Guzman | .10 | .30 |
| ☐ 236 | Dustan Mohr | .10 | .30 |
| ☐ 237 | Eddie Guardado | .10 | .30 |
| ☐ 238 | J.D. Durbin | .10 | .30 |
| ☐ 239 | Jacque Jones | .10 | .30 |
| ☐ 240 | Joe Nathan | .10 | .30 |
| ☐ 241 | Johan Santana | .30 | .75 |
| ☐ 242 | Lew Ford | .10 | .30 |
| ☐ 243 | Michael Cuddyer | .10 | .30 |
| ☐ 244 | Shannon Stewart | .10 | .30 |
| ☐ 245 | Torii Hunter | .10 | .30 |
| ☐ 246 | Brad Wilkerson | .10 | .30 |
| ☐ 247 | Carl Everett | .10 | .30 |
| ☐ 248 | Jeff Fassero | .10 | .30 |
| ☐ 249 | Jose Vidro | .10 | .30 |
| ☐ 250 | Livan Hernandez | .10 | .30 |
| ☐ 251 | Michael Barrett | .10 | .30 |
| ☐ 252 | Tomy Batista | .10 | .30 |
| ☐ 253 | Zach Day | .10 | .30 |
| ☐ 254 | Al Leiter | .10 | .30 |
| ☐ 255 | Cliff Floyd | .10 | .30 |
| ☐ 256 | Jae Weong Seo | .10 | .30 |
| ☐ 257 | John Olerud | .10 | .30 |
| ☐ 258 | Jose Reyes | .10 | .30 |
| ☐ 259 | Mike Cameron | .10 | .30 |
| ☐ 260 | Mike Piazza | .30 | .75 |
| ☐ 261 | Richard Hidalgo | .10 | .30 |
| ☐ 262 | Tom Glavine | .20 | .50 |
| ☐ 263 | Vance Wilson | .10 | .30 |
| ☐ 264 | Alex Rodriguez | .50 | 1.25 |
| ☐ 265 | Armando Benitez | .10 | .30 |
| ☐ 266 | Bernie Williams | .20 | .50 |
| ☐ 267 | Bubba Crosby | .10 | .30 |
| ☐ 268 | Chien-Ming Wang | .50 | 1.25 |
| ☐ 269 | Derek Jeter | .60 | 1.50 |
| ☐ 270 | Esteban Loaiza | .10 | .30 |
| ☐ 271 | Gary Sheffield | .10 | .30 |
| ☐ 272 | Hideki Matsui | .50 | 1.25 |
| ☐ 273 | Jason Giambi | .10 | .30 |
| ☐ 274 | Javier Vazquez | .10 | .30 |
| ☐ 275 | Jorge Posada | .20 | .50 |
| ☐ 276 | Jose Contreras | .10 | .30 |
| ☐ 277 | Kenny Lofton | .10 | .30 |
| ☐ 278 | Kevin Brown | .10 | .30 |
| ☐ 279 | Mariano Rivera | .30 | .75 |
| ☐ 280 | Mike Mussina | .20 | .50 |
| ☐ 281 | Barry Zito | .10 | .30 |
| ☐ 282 | Bobby Crosby | .10 | .30 |
| ☐ 283 | Eric Byrnes | .10 | .30 |
| ☐ 284 | Eric Chavez | .10 | .30 |
| ☐ 285 | Erubiel Durazo | .10 | .30 |
| ☐ 286 | Jermaine Dye | .10 | .30 |
| ☐ 287 | Mark Kotsay | .10 | .30 |
| ☐ 288 | Mark Mulder | .10 | .30 |
| ☐ 289 | Rich Harden | .10 | .30 |
| ☐ 290 | Tim Hudson | .10 | .30 |
| ☐ 291 | Billy Wagner | .10 | .30 |
| ☐ 292 | Bobby Abreu | .10 | .30 |
| ☐ 293 | Brett Myers | .10 | .30 |
| ☐ 294 | Eric Milton | .10 | .30 |
| ☐ 295 | Jim Thome | .20 | .50 |
| ☐ 296 | Jimmy Rollins | .10 | .30 |
| ☐ 297 | Kevin Millwood | .10 | .30 |
| ☐ 298 | Marlon Byrd | .10 | .30 |
| ☐ 299 | Mike Lieberthal | .10 | .30 |
| ☐ 300 | Pat Burrell | .10 | .30 |
| ☐ 301 | Randy Wolf | .10 | .30 |
| ☐ 302 | Craig Wilson | .10 | .30 |
| ☐ 303 | Jack Wilson | .10 | .30 |
| ☐ 304 | Jacob Cruz | .10 | .30 |
| ☐ 305 | Jason Bay | .10 | .30 |
| ☐ 306 | Jason Kendall | .10 | .30 |
| ☐ 307 | Jose Castillo | .10 | .30 |
| ☐ 308 | Kip Wells | .10 | .30 |
| ☐ 309 | Brian Giles | .10 | .30 |
| ☐ 310 | Brian Lawrence | .10 | .30 |
| ☐ 311 | Chris Oxspring | .10 | .30 |
| ☐ 312 | David Wells | .10 | .30 |
| ☐ 313 | Freddy Guzman | .10 | .30 |
| ☐ 314 | Jake Peavy | .10 | .30 |
| ☐ 315 | Mark Loretta | .10 | .30 |
| ☐ 316 | Ryan Klesko | .10 | .30 |
| ☐ 317 | Sean Burroughs | .10 | .30 |
| ☐ 318 | Trevor Hoffman | .10 | .30 |
| ☐ 319 | Xavier Nady | .10 | .30 |
| ☐ 320 | A.J. Pierzynski | .10 | .30 |
| ☐ 321 | Edgardo Alfonzo | .10 | .30 |
| ☐ 322 | J.T. Snow | .10 | .30 |
| ☐ 323 | Jason Schmidt | .10 | .30 |
| ☐ 324 | Jerome Williams | .10 | .30 |
| ☐ 325 | Kirk Rueter | .10 | .30 |
| ☐ 326 | Bret Boone | .10 | .30 |
| ☐ 327 | Bucky Jacobsen | .10 | .30 |
| ☐ 328 | Edgar Martinez | .20 | .50 |
| ☐ 329 | Freddy Garcia | .10 | .30 |
| ☐ 330 | Ichiro Suzuki | .60 | 1.50 |
| ☐ 331 | Jamie Moyer | .10 | .30 |
| ☐ 332 | Joel Pineiro | .10 | .30 |
| ☐ 333 | Scott Spiezio | .10 | .30 |
| ☐ 334 | Shigetoshi Hasegawa | .10 | .30 |
| ☐ 335 | Albert Pujols | .60 | 1.50 |
| ☐ 336 | Edgar Renteria | .10 | .30 |
| ☐ 337 | Jason Isringhausen | .10 | .30 |
| ☐ 338 | Jim Edmonds | .10 | .30 |
| ☐ 339 | Matt Morris | .10 | .30 |
| ☐ 340 | Mike Matheny | .10 | .30 |
| ☐ 341 | Reggie Sanders | .10 | .30 |
| ☐ 342 | Scott Rolen | .20 | .50 |
| ☐ 343 | Woody Williams | .10 | .30 |
| ☐ 344 | Jeff Suppan | .10 | .30 |
| ☐ 345 | Aubrey Huff | .10 | .30 |
| ☐ 346 | Carl Crawford | .10 | .30 |
| ☐ 347 | Chad Gaudin | .10 | .30 |
| ☐ 348 | Delmon Young | .20 | .50 |
| ☐ 349 | Dewon Brazelton | .10 | .30 |
| ☐ 350 | Jose Cruz Jr. | .10 | .30 |
| ☐ 351 | Rocco Baldelli | .10 | .30 |
| ☐ 352 | Tino Martinez | .20 | .50 |
| ☐ 353 | Toby Hall | .10 | .30 |
| ☐ 354 | Alfonso Soriano | .10 | .30 |
| ☐ 355 | Brian Jordan | .10 | .30 |
| ☐ 356 | Francisco Cordero | .10 | .30 |
| ☐ 357 | Hank Blalock | .10 | .30 |
| ☐ 358 | Kenny Rogers | .10 | .30 |
| ☐ 359 | Kevin Mench | .10 | .30 |
| ☐ 360 | Laynce Nix | .10 | .30 |
| ☐ 361 | Mark Teixeira | .20 | .50 |
| ☐ 362 | Michael Young | .10 | .30 |
| ☐ 363 | Alex S. Gonzalez | .10 | .30 |
| ☐ 364 | Alexis Rios | .10 | .30 |
| ☐ 365 | Carlos Delgado | .10 | .30 |
| ☐ 366 | Eric Hinske | .10 | .30 |
| ☐ 367 | Frank Catalanotto | .10 | .30 |
| ☐ 368 | Josh Phelps | .10 | .30 |
| ☐ 369 | Roy Halladay | .10 | .30 |
| ☐ 370 | Vernon Wells | .10 | .30 |
| ☐ 371 | Vladimir Guerrero TC | .75 | 2.00 |
| ☐ 372 | Randy Johnson TC | .75 | 2.00 |
| ☐ 373 | Chipper Jones TC | .75 | 2.00 |
| ☐ 374 | Miguel Tejada TC | .75 | 2.00 |
| ☐ 375 | Pedro Martinez TC | .75 | 2.00 |
| ☐ 376 | Sammy Sosa TC | .75 | 2.00 |
| ☐ 377 | Frank Thomas TC | .75 | 2.00 |
| ☐ 378 | Ken Griffey Jr. TC | 1.25 | 3.00 |
| ☐ 379 | Victor Martinez TC | .75 | 2.00 |
| ☐ 380 | Todd Helton TC | .75 | 2.00 |
| ☐ 381 | Ivan Rodriguez TC | .75 | 2.00 |
| ☐ 382 | Miguel Cabrera TC | .75 | 2.00 |
| ☐ 383 | Roger Clemens TC | 1.25 | 3.00 |
| ☐ 384 | Ken Harvey TC | .75 | 2.00 |
| ☐ 385 | Eric Gagne TC | .75 | 2.00 |
| ☐ 386 | Lyle Overbay TC | .75 | 2.00 |
| ☐ 387 | Shannon Stewart TC | .75 | 2.00 |
| ☐ 388 | Brad Wilkerson TC | .75 | 2.00 |
| ☐ 389 | Mike Piazza TC | .75 | 2.00 |
| ☐ 390 | Alex Rodriguez TC | 1.25 | 3.00 |
| ☐ 391 | Mark Mulder TC | .75 | 2.00 |
| ☐ 392 | Jim Thome TC | .75 | 2.00 |
| ☐ 393 | Jack Wilson TC | .75 | 2.00 |
| ☐ 394 | Khalil Greene TC | .75 | 2.00 |
| ☐ 395 | Jason Schmidt TC | .75 | 2.00 |
| ☐ 396 | Ichiro Suzuki TC | 1.50 | 4.00 |
| ☐ 397 | Albert Pujols TC | 1.50 | 4.00 |
| ☐ 398 | Rocco Baldelli TC | .75 | 2.00 |
| ☐ 399 | Alfonso Soriano TC | .75 | 2.00 |
| ☐ 400 | Vernon Wells TC | .75 | 2.00 |

## 2003 Donruss Elite Extra Edition

|  |  | | |
|---|---|---|---|
| ☐ 1 | Adam Loewen RC | 2.00 | 5.00 |
| ☐ 2 | Brandon Webb RC | 4.00 | 10.00 |
| ☐ 3 | Chien-Ming Wang RC | 15.00 | 40.00 |
| ☐ 4 | Hong-Chih Kuo RC | 8.00 | 20.00 |
| ☐ 5 | Clint Barmes RC | 2.00 | 5.00 |
| ☐ 6 | Guillermo Quiroz RC | 1.50 | 4.00 |
| ☐ 7 | Edgar Gonzalez RC | 1.50 | 4.00 |
| ☐ 8 | Todd Wellemeyer RC | 2.00 | 5.00 |
| ☐ 9 | Alfredo Gonzalez RC | 1.50 | 4.00 |
| ☐ 10 | Craig Brazell RC | 1.50 | 4.00 |
| ☐ 11 | Tim Olson RC | 1.50 | 4.00 |
| ☐ 12 | Rich Fischer RC | 1.50 | 4.00 |
| ☐ 13 | Daniel Cabrera RC | 2.00 | 5.00 |
| ☐ 14 | Francisco Rosario RC | 1.50 | 4.00 |
| ☐ 15 | Francisco Cruceta RC | 1.50 | 4.00 |
| ☐ 16 | Alejandro Machado RC | 1.50 | 4.00 |
| ☐ 17 | Andrew Brown RC | 2.00 | 5.00 |

| | | |
|---|---|---|
| ☐ 18 Rob Hammock RC | 1.50 | 4.00 |
| ☐ 19 Arnie Munoz RC | 1.50 | 4.00 |
| ☐ 20 Felix Sanchez RC | 1.50 | 4.00 |
| ☐ 21 Nook Logan RC | 2.00 | 5.00 |
| ☐ 22 Cory Stewart RC | 1.50 | 4.00 |
| ☐ 23 Michel Hernandez RC | 1.50 | 4.00 |
| ☐ 24 Rett Johnson RC | 1.50 | 4.00 |
| ☐ 25 Josh Hall RC | 1.50 | 4.00 |
| ☐ 26 Doug Waechter RC | 2.00 | 5.00 |
| ☐ 27 Matt Kata RC | 1.50 | 4.00 |
| ☐ 28 Dan Haren RC | 2.00 | 5.00 |
| ☐ 29 Dontrelle Willis | 2.00 | 5.00 |
| ☐ 30 Ramon Nivar RC | 1.50 | 4.00 |
| ☐ 31 Chad Gaudin RC | 1.50 | 4.00 |
| ☐ 32 Rickie Weeks RC | 4.00 | 10.00 |
| ☐ 33 Ryan Wagner RC | 1.50 | 4.00 |
| ☐ 34 Kevin Correia RC | 1.50 | 4.00 |
| ☐ 35 Bo Hart RC | 1.50 | 4.00 |
| ☐ 36 Oscar Villarreal RC | 1.50 | 4.00 |
| ☐ 37 Josh Willingham RC | 3.00 | 8.00 |
| ☐ 38 Jeff Duncan RC | 1.50 | 4.00 |
| ☐ 39 David DeJesus RC | 2.00 | 5.00 |
| ☐ 40 Dustin McGowan RC | 2.00 | 5.00 |
| ☐ 41 Preston Larrison RC | 1.50 | 4.00 |
| ☐ 42 Kevin Youkilis RC | 3.00 | 8.00 |
| ☐ 43 Bubba Nelson RC | 2.00 | 5.00 |
| ☐ 44 Chris Burke RC | 2.00 | 5.00 |
| ☐ 45 J.D. Durbin RC | 1.50 | 4.00 |
| ☐ 47 Ryan Howard RC | 20.00 | 50.00 |
| ☐ 48 Jason Kubel RC | 2.00 | 5.00 |
| ☐ 49 Brendan Harris RC | 2.00 | 5.00 |
| ☐ 50 Brian Bruney RC | 2.00 | 5.00 |
| ☐ 52 Byron Gettis RC | 1.50 | 4.00 |
| ☐ 53 Edwin Jackson RC | 2.00 | 5.00 |
| ☐ 55 Daniel Garcia RC | 1.50 | 4.00 |
| ☐ 57 Chad Cordero RC | 3.00 | 8.00 |
| ☐ 58 Delmon Young RC | 10.00 | 25.00 |

## 2004 Donruss Elite Extra Edition

| | | |
|---|---|---|
| ☐ COMP.SET w/o SP's (150) | 10.00 | 25.00 |
| ☐ COMMON CARD (1-150) | .10 | .30 |
| ☐ COMMON CARD (206-215) | 1.25 | 3.00 |
| ☐ 206-215 RANDOM INSERTS IN PACKS | | |
| ☐ 206-215 PRINT RUN 1000 SERIAL #'d SETS | | |
| ☐ COMMON NO AU (234-254) | 1.50 | 4.00 |
| ☐ NO AU 234-254 RANDOM IN PACKS | | |
| ☐ NO AU 234-254 PRINT RUN 1000 #'d SETS | | |
| ☐ 216-355 OVERALL AU-GU ODDS 1:4 | | |
| ☐ 216-355 PRINT RUNS B/WN 260-1617 PER | | |
| ☐ DO NOT EXIST: 151-205/232/236-238/240 | | |
| ☐ DO NOT EXIST: 241/245/248-249/251/255 | | |
| ☐ DO NOT EXIST: 274/339 | | |
| ☐ 1 Troy Glaus | .10 | .30 |
| ☐ 2 John Lackey | .10 | .30 |
| ☐ 3 Garret Anderson | .10 | .30 |
| ☐ 4 Francisco Rodriguez | .10 | .30 |
| ☐ 5 Casey Kotchman | .10 | .30 |
| ☐ 6 Jose Guillen | .10 | .30 |
| ☐ 7 Miguel Tejada | .10 | .30 |
| ☐ 8 Rafael Palmeiro | .20 | .50 |
| ☐ 9 Jay Gibbons | .10 | .30 |
| ☐ 10 Melvin Mora | .10 | .30 |
| ☐ 11 Javy Lopez | .10 | .30 |
| ☐ 12 Pedro Martinez | .20 | .50 |
| ☐ 13 Curt Schilling | .20 | .50 |
| ☐ 14 David Ortiz | .30 | .75 |
| ☐ 15 Manny Ramirez | .20 | .50 |
| ☐ 16 Nomar Garciaparra | .50 | 1.25 |
| ☐ 17 Maggio Ordonez | .30 | .75 |
| ☐ 18 Frank Thomas | .30 | .75 |
| ☐ 19 Esteban Loaiza | .10 | .30 |
| ☐ 20 Paul Konerko | .10 | .30 |
| ☐ 21 Mark Buehrle | .10 | .30 |

| | | |
|---|---|---|
| ☐ 22 Jody Gerut | .10 | .30 |
| ☐ 23 Victor Martinez | .10 | .30 |
| ☐ 24 C.C. Sabathia | .10 | .30 |
| ☐ 25 Travis Hafner | .10 | .30 |
| ☐ 26 Cliff Lee | .10 | .30 |
| ☐ 27 Jeremy Bonderman | .10 | .30 |
| ☐ 28 Dallas McPherson | .10 | .30 |
| ☐ 29 Jermaine Dye | .10 | .30 |
| ☐ 30 Carlos Guillen | .10 | .30 |
| ☐ 31 Carlos Beltran | .20 | .50 |
| ☐ 32 Ken Harvey | .10 | .30 |
| ☐ 33 Mike Sweeney | .10 | .30 |
| ☐ 34 Angel Berroa | .10 | .30 |
| ☐ 35 Joe Nathan | .10 | .30 |
| ☐ 36 Johan Santana | .30 | .75 |
| ☐ 37 Jacque Jones | .10 | .30 |
| ☐ 38 Shannon Stewart | .10 | .30 |
| ☐ 39 Torii Hunter | .10 | .30 |
| ☐ 40 Derek Jeter | .60 | 1.50 |
| ☐ 41 Jason Giambi | .10 | .30 |
| ☐ 42 Danny Graves | .10 | .30 |
| ☐ 43 Alfonso Soriano | .10 | .30 |
| ☐ 44 Gary Sheffield | .10 | .30 |
| ☐ 45 Mike Mussina | .20 | .50 |
| ☐ 46 Jorge Posada | .10 | .30 |
| ☐ 47 Hideki Matsui | .50 | 1.25 |
| ☐ 48 Francisco Cordero | .10 | .30 |
| ☐ 49 Javier Vazquez | .10 | .30 |
| ☐ 50 Mariano Rivera | .30 | .75 |
| ☐ 51 Eric Chavez | .10 | .30 |
| ☐ 52 Tim Hudson | .10 | .30 |
| ☐ 53 Mark Mulder | .10 | .30 |
| ☐ 54 Barry Zito | .10 | .30 |
| ☐ 55 Ichiro Suzuki | .60 | 1.50 |
| ☐ 56 Edgar Martinez | .20 | .50 |
| ☐ 57 Bret Boone | .10 | .30 |
| ☐ 58 Lew Ford | .10 | .30 |
| ☐ 59 B.J. Upton | .20 | .50 |
| ☐ 60 Aubrey Huff | .10 | .30 |
| ☐ 61 Rocco Baldelli | .10 | .30 |
| ☐ 62 Carl Crawford | .20 | .50 |
| ☐ 63 Delmon Young | .20 | .50 |
| ☐ 64 Mark Teixeira | .20 | .50 |
| ☐ 65 Hank Blalock | .10 | .30 |
| ☐ 66 Michael Young | .10 | .30 |
| ☐ 67 Alex Rodriguez | .50 | 1.25 |
| ☐ 68 Carlos Delgado | .10 | .30 |
| ☐ 69 Milton Bradley | .10 | .30 |
| ☐ 70 Roy Halladay | .10 | .30 |
| ☐ 71 Vernon Wells | .10 | .30 |
| ☐ 72 Randy Johnson | .30 | .75 |
| ☐ 73 Bobby Crosby | .10 | .30 |
| ☐ 74 Lyle Overbay | .10 | .30 |
| ☐ 75 Luis Gonzalez | .10 | .30 |
| ☐ 76 Steve Finley | .10 | .30 |
| ☐ 77 Chipper Jones | .30 | .75 |
| ☐ 78 Andruw Jones | .20 | .50 |
| ☐ 79 Marcus Giles | .10 | .30 |
| ☐ 80 Rafael Furcal | .10 | .30 |
| ☐ 81 J.D. Drew | .10 | .30 |
| ☐ 82 Sammy Sosa | .30 | .75 |
| ☐ 83 Kerry Wood | .10 | .30 |
| ☐ 84 Mark Prior | .20 | .50 |
| ☐ 85 Derrek Lee | .10 | .30 |
| ☐ 86 Moises Alou | .10 | .30 |
| ☐ 87 Carlos Zambrano | .10 | .30 |
| ☐ 88 Ken Griffey Jr. | .50 | 1.25 |
| ☐ 89 Austin Kearns | .10 | .30 |
| ☐ 90 Adam Dunn | .10 | .30 |
| ☐ 91 Barry Larkin | .20 | .50 |
| ☐ 92 Todd Helton | .10 | .30 |
| ☐ 93 Larry Walker Cards | .10 | .30 |
| ☐ 94 Preston Wilson | .10 | .30 |
| ☐ 95 Sean Casey | .10 | .30 |
| ☐ 96 Luis Castillo | .10 | .30 |
| ☐ 97 Josh Beckett | .10 | .30 |
| ☐ 98 Mike Lowell | .10 | .30 |
| ☐ 99 Miguel Cabrera | .20 | .50 |
| ☐ 100 Brad Penny | .10 | .30 |
| ☐ 101 Dontrelle Willis | .20 | .50 |
| ☐ 102 Andy Pettitte | .20 | .50 |
| ☐ 103 Wade Miller | .10 | .30 |
| ☐ 104 Jeff Bagwell | .20 | .50 |
| ☐ 105 Craig Biggio | .20 | .50 |
| ☐ 106 Lance Berkman | .10 | .30 |
| ☐ 107 Jeff Kent | .10 | .30 |
| ☐ 108 Roy Oswalt | .10 | .30 |
| ☐ 109 Hideo Nomo | .30 | .75 |

| | | |
|---|---|---|
| ☐ 110 Adrian Beltre | .10 | .30 |
| ☐ 111 Paul Lo Duca | .10 | .30 |
| ☐ 112 Shawn Green | .10 | .30 |
| ☐ 113 Roger Clemens | .75 | 2.00 |
| ☐ 114 Eric Gagne | .10 | .30 |
| ☐ 115 Danny Kolb | .10 | .30 |
| ☐ 116 Rickie Weeks | .10 | .30 |
| ☐ 117 Scott Podsednik | .10 | .30 |
| ☐ 118 Livan Hernandez | .10 | .30 |
| ☐ 119 Orlando Cabrera | .10 | .30 |
| ☐ 120 Jose Vidro | .10 | .30 |
| ☐ 121 David Wright | .75 | 2.00 |
| ☐ 122 Tom Glavine | .20 | .50 |
| ☐ 123 Al Leiter | .10 | .30 |
| ☐ 124 Mike Piazza | .50 | 1.25 |
| ☐ 125 Jose Reyes | .10 | .30 |
| ☐ 126 Richard Hidalgo | .10 | .30 |
| ☐ 127 Eric Milton | .10 | .30 |
| ☐ 128 Jim Thome | .20 | .50 |
| ☐ 129 Mike Lieberthal | .10 | .30 |
| ☐ 130 Bobby Abreu | .10 | .30 |
| ☐ 131 Kip Wells | .10 | .30 |
| ☐ 132 Jack Wilson | .10 | .30 |
| ☐ 133 Jason Bay | .10 | .30 |
| ☐ 134 Brian Giles | .10 | .30 |
| ☐ 135 Sean Burroughs | .10 | .30 |
| ☐ 136 Khalil Greene | .20 | .50 |
| ☐ 137 Jake Peavy | .10 | .30 |
| ☐ 138 Jason Schmidt | .10 | .30 |
| ☐ 139 J.T. Snow | .10 | .30 |
| ☐ 140 Craig Wilson | .10 | .30 |
| ☐ 141 Chase Utley | .20 | .50 |
| ☐ 142 Jim Edmonds | .10 | .30 |
| ☐ 143 Albert Pujols | .50 | 1.50 |
| ☐ 144 Edgar Renteria | .10 | .30 |
| ☐ 145 Scott Rolen | .20 | .50 |
| ☐ 146 Matt Morris | .10 | .30 |
| ☐ 147 Ivan Rodriguez | .20 | .50 |
| ☐ 148 Vladimir Guerrero | .30 | .75 |
| ☐ 149 Greg Maddux | .50 | 1.25 |
| ☐ 150 Ben Sheets | .10 | .30 |
| ☐ 206 Will Clark RET | 1.50 | 4.00 |
| ☐ 207 Nolan Ryan RET | 3.00 | 8.00 |
| ☐ 208 Bob Feller RET | 1.25 | 3.00 |
| ☐ 209 Red Schoendienst RET | 1.25 | 3.00 |
| ☐ 210 Brooks Robinson RET | 1.50 | 4.00 |
| ☐ 211 Al Kaline RET | 1.50 | 4.00 |
| ☐ 212 Ozzie Smith RET | 2.00 | 5.00 |
| ☐ 213 Maury Wills RET | 1.25 | 3.00 |
| ☐ 214 Steve Carlton RET | 1.25 | 3.00 |
| ☐ 215 Duke Snider RET | 1.50 | 4.00 |
| ☐ 216 Scott Lewis AU/603 RC | 8.00 | 20.00 |
| ☐ 217 Josh Johnson AU/597 RC | 4.00 | 10.00 |
| ☐ 218 Jeff Fiorentino AU/597 RC | 5.00 | 12.00 |
| ☐ 219 Grant Hansen AU/599 RC | 3.00 | 8.00 |
| ☐ 220 You Gandan AU/603 RC | 30.00 | 50.00 |
| ☐ 221 Eddie Prasch AU/603 RC | 4.00 | 10.00 |
| ☐ 222 Danny Hill AU/603 RC | 3.00 | 8.00 |
| ☐ 223 Chuck Lofgren AU/803 RC | 6.00 | 15.00 |
| ☐ 224 Blake Johnson AU/811 RC | 4.00 | 10.00 |
| ☐ 225 Cory Dunlap AU/599 RC | 6.00 | 15.00 |
| ☐ 226 Carlos Vasquez AU/869 RC | 3.00 | 8.00 |
| ☐ 227 Jesse Crain AU/1000 RC | 3.00 | 8.00 |
| ☐ 228 Yhency Brazoban AU/1000 | 3.00 | 8.00 |
| ☐ 229 Abe Alvarez AU/1000 RC | 4.00 | 10.00 |
| ☐ 230 Scott Kazmir AU/350 RC | 15.00 | 40.00 |
| ☐ 231 J.A. Happ AU/1195 RC | 12.50 | 30.00 |
| ☐ 233 Mark Jecmen AU/1047 RC | 3.00 | 8.00 |
| ☐ 234 Kameron Loe/1000 RC | 2.00 | 5.00 |
| ☐ 235 Ervin Santana/1000 RC | 3.00 | 8.00 |
| ☐ 239 Josh Karp/1000 RC | 1.50 | 4.00 |
| ☐ 242 Alberto Callaspo/1000 RC | 2.00 | 5.00 |
| ☐ 243 Jesse Hoover AU/1191 RC | 4.00 | 10.00 |
| ☐ 246 Just Hoyman AU/1124 RC | 4.00 | 10.00 |
| ☐ 247 Juan Cedeno/1000 RC | 1.50 | 4.00 |
| ☐ 250 Jake Dittler/1000 RC | 1.50 | 4.00 |
| ☐ 252 Ben Zobrist AU/1178 RC | 10.00 | 25.00 |
| ☐ 253 Jeff Salazar/1000 RC | 2.00 | 5.00 |
| ☐ 256 Jor Vasquez AU/1000 RC | 3.00 | 8.00 |
| ☐ 257 Raf Gonzalez AU/603 RC | 3.00 | 8.00 |
| ☐ 258 Andrew Dobies AU/601 RC | 10.00 | 25.00 |
| ☐ 259 Colby Miller AU/997 RC | 3.00 | 8.00 |
| ☐ 260 K.C. Herren AU/735 RC | 3.00 | 8.00 |
| ☐ 261 Ryan Meaux AU/546 RC | 3.00 | 8.00 |
| ☐ 262 Dust Pedroia AU/1114 RC | 50.00 | 100.00 |
| ☐ 263 Fern Nieve AU/1000 RC | 3.00 | 8.00 |
| ☐ 264 Mar Gomez AU/1000 RC | 3.00 | 8.00 |
| ☐ 265 Eric Campbell AU/260 RC | 70.00 | 120.00 |

| | | |
|---|---|---|
| ❑ 266 Billy Killian AU/703 RC | 4.00 | 10.00 |
| ❑ 267 Mike Rouse AU/999 RC | 3.00 | 8.00 |
| ❑ 268 Kyle Bono AU/1203 RC | 3.00 | 8.00 |
| ❑ 269 M.Einertson AU/1047 RC | 6.00 | 15.00 |
| ❑ 270 Scott Proctor AU/1000 RC | 3.00 | 8.00 |
| ❑ 271 Tim Bittner AU/1000 RC | 4.00 | 10.00 |
| ❑ 272 Christian Garcia AU/799 RC | 4.00 | 10.00 |
| ❑ 273 Yadier Molina AU/1000 RC | 6.00 | 15.00 |
| ❑ 274 C.Thomas AU/907 RC | 3.00 | 8.00 |
| ❑ 275 Trey Blackley AU/1000 RC | 3.00 | 8.00 |
| ❑ 276 T.Trowbridge AU/1000 RC | 4.00 | 10.00 |
| ❑ 277 F.Francisco AU/1000 RC | 3.00 | 8.00 |
| ❑ 278 Dion Navarro AU/1000 RC | 3.00 | 8.00 |
| ❑ 279 Joey Gathright AU/1000 RC | 3.00 | 8.00 |
| ❑ 280 Kaz Tadano AU/1000 RC | 4.00 | 10.00 |
| ❑ 281 Matt Bush AU/1100 RC | 6.00 | 15.00 |
| ❑ 282 David Haehnel AU/865 RC | 4.00 | 10.00 |
| ❑ 283 Tommy Hottovy AU/825 RC | 4.00 | 10.00 |
| ❑ 284 Chris Carter AU/973 RC | 5.00 | 12.00 |
| ❑ 285 Mark Rogers AU/578 RC | 6.00 | 15.00 |
| ❑ 286 Jeremy Sowers AU/537 RC | 5.00 | 12.00 |
| ❑ 287 Homer Bailey AU/1571 RC | 15.00 | 40.00 |
| ❑ 288 Mike Butia AU/865 RC | 4.00 | 10.00 |
| ❑ 289 Chris Nelson AU/465 RC | 15.00 | 30.00 |
| ❑ 290 T.Diamond AU/1055 RC | 6.00 | 15.00 |
| ❑ 291 Neil Walker AU/1343 RC | 8.00 | 20.00 |
| ❑ 292 Sean Gamble AU/1229 RC | 3.00 | 8.00 |
| ❑ 293 Bill Bray AU/1073 RC | 3.00 | 8.00 |
| ❑ 294 Reid Brignac AU/522 RC | 30.00 | 60.00 |
| ❑ 295 R.Klosterman AU/865 RC | 3.00 | 8.00 |
| ❑ 296 David Purcey AU/1485 RC | 4.00 | 10.00 |
| ❑ 297 Scott Elbert AU/1617 RC | 8.00 | 20.00 |
| ❑ 298 Josh Fields AU/961 RC | 15.00 | 30.00 |
| ❑ 299 Chris Lambert AU/1954 RC | 4.00 | 10.00 |
| ❑ 300 Trevor Plouffe AU/1329 RC | 6.00 | 15.00 |
| ❑ 301 Greg Golson AU/1334 RC | 4.00 | 10.00 |
| ❑ 302 Josh Baker AU/525 RC | 4.00 | 10.00 |
| ❑ 303 Philip Hughes AU/1485 RC | 20.00 | 50.00 |
| ❑ 304 Matt Macri AU/979 RC | 3.00 | 8.00 |
| ❑ 305 Kyle Waldrop AU/823 RC | 6.00 | 15.00 |
| ❑ 306 Rich Robnett AU/1575 RC | 4.00 | 10.00 |
| ❑ 307 T.Tankersley AU/1073 RC | 4.00 | 10.00 |
| ❑ 308 Blake DeWitt AU/1562 RC | 8.00 | 20.00 |
| ❑ 309 Daryl Jones AU/575 RC | 12.50 | 30.00 |
| ❑ 310 Eric Hurley AU/1021 RC | 10.00 | 25.00 |
| ❑ 311 J.P. Howell AU/1453 RC | 4.00 | 10.00 |
| ❑ 312 Zach Jackson AU/1069 RC | 3.00 | 8.00 |
| ❑ 313 Justin Orenduff AU/473 RC | 12.50 | 30.00 |
| ❑ 314 Tyler Lumsden AU/473 RC | 4.00 | 10.00 |
| ❑ 315 Matt Fox AU/473 RC | 4.00 | 10.00 |
| ❑ 316 Danny Putnam AU/473 RC | 4.00 | 10.00 |
| ❑ 317 Jon Poterson AU/464 RC | 5.00 | 12.00 |
| ❑ 318 Gio Gonzalez AU/473 RC | 10.00 | 25.00 |
| ❑ 319 Jay Rainville AU/823 RC | 4.00 | 10.00 |
| ❑ 320 Huston Street AU/709 RC | 10.00 | 25.00 |
| ❑ 321 Jeff Marquez AU/498 RC | 4.00 | 10.00 |
| ❑ 322 Eric Beattie AU/939 RC | 4.00 | 10.00 |
| ❑ 323 B.Szymanski AU/1497 RC | 4.00 | 10.00 |
| ❑ 324 Seth Smith AU/1065 RC | 4.00 | 10.00 |
| ❑ 325 Rob Johnson AU/790 RC | 4.00 | 10.00 |
| ❑ 326 Wes Whisler AU/473 RC | 4.00 | 10.00 |
| ❑ 327 Billy Buckner AU/673 RC | 4.00 | 10.00 |
| ❑ 328 Jon Zeringue AU/473 RC | 4.00 | 10.00 |
| ❑ 329 Curtis Thigpen AU/673 RC | 12.50 | 30.00 |
| ❑ 330 Donny Lucy AU/673 RC | 3.00 | 8.00 |
| ❑ 331 Mike Ferris AU/558 RC | 4.00 | 10.00 |
| ❑ 332 A.Swarzak AU/370 RC | 10.00 | 25.00 |
| ❑ 333 Jason Jaramillo AU/573 RC | 4.00 | 10.00 |
| ❑ 334 Hunter Pence AU/672 RC | 30.00 | 60.00 |
| ❑ 335 Mike Rozier AU/628 RC | 6.00 | 15.00 |
| ❑ 336 Kurt Suzuki AU/673 RC | 8.00 | 20.00 |
| ❑ 337 Jason Vargas AU/621 RC | 4.00 | 10.00 |
| ❑ 338 Brian Bixler AU/665 RC | 10.00 | 25.00 |
| ❑ 339 Dexter Fowler AU/623 RC | 20.00 | 50.00 |
| ❑ 340 Mark Trumbo AU/1321 RC | 6.00 | 15.00 |
| ❑ 342 Jeff Frazier AU/423 RC | 4.00 | 10.00 |
| ❑ 343 Steve Register AU/673 RC | 3.00 | 8.00 |
| ❑ 344 M.Schlact AU/477 RC | 4.00 | 10.00 |
| ❑ 345 Garrett Mock AU/471 RC | 4.00 | 10.00 |
| ❑ 346 Eric Haberer AU/473 RC | 4.00 | 10.00 |
| ❑ 347 M.Tuiasosopo AU/473 RC | 10.00 | 25.00 |
| ❑ 348 Jason Windsor AU/473 RC | 4.00 | 10.00 |
| ❑ 349 Grant Johnson AU/815 RC | 4.00 | 10.00 |
| ❑ 350 J.C. Holt AU/473 RC | 4.00 | 10.00 |
| ❑ 351 Joe Bauserman AU/472 RC | 4.00 | 10.00 |
| ❑ 352 Jamar Walton AU/481 RC | 4.00 | 10.00 |
| ❑ 353 Eric Patterson AU/1571 RC | 6.00 | 15.00 |
| ❑ 354 Tyler Johnson AU/775 RC | 6.00 | 15.00 |
| ❑ 355 Nick Adenhart AU/653 RC | 10.00 | 25.00 |


## 2007 Donruss Elite
## Extra Edition

| | | |
|---|---|---|
| ❑ COMPLETE SET (142) | | |
| ❑ COMP.SET w/o AU's (92) | 8.00 | 20.00 |
| ❑ COMMON CARD (1-92) | .20 | .50 |
| ❑ COMMON AU (92-142) | 4.00 | 10.00 |
| ❑ OVERALL AUTO/MEM ODDS 1:5 | | |
| ❑ AU PRINT RUNS 374-999 COPIES PER | | |
| ❑ EXCHANGE DEADLINE 07/01/2009 | | |
| ❑ 1 Andrew Brackman | .60 | 1.50 |
| ❑ 2 Austin Gallagher | .20 | .50 |
| ❑ 3 Brett Cecil | .20 | .50 |
| ❑ 4 Darren Barney | .50 | 1.25 |
| ❑ 5 David Price | 2.00 | 5.00 |
| ❑ 6 J. P. Arencibia | .20 | .50 |
| ❑ 7 Josh Donaldson | .20 | .50 |
| ❑ 8 Brandon Hicks | .20 | .50 |
| ❑ 9 Brian Rike | .20 | .50 |
| ❑ 10 Bryan Morris | .20 | .50 |
| ❑ 11 Cale Iorg | .20 | .50 |
| ❑ 12 Casey Weathers | .20 | .50 |
| ❑ 13 Corey Kluber | .20 | .50 |
| ❑ 14 Daniel Moskos | .20 | .50 |
| ❑ 15 Danny Payne | .20 | .50 |
| ❑ 16 David Kopp | .20 | .50 |
| ❑ 17 Dellin Betances | .60 | 1.50 |
| ❑ 18 Derrick Robinson | .20 | .50 |
| ❑ 19 Drew Stubbs | .50 | 1.25 |
| ❑ 20 Eric Eiland | .20 | .50 |
| ❑ 21 Francisco Pena | .20 | .50 |
| ❑ 22 Greg Reynolds | .20 | .50 |
| ❑ 23 Jeff Samardzija | 1.25 | 3.00 |
| ❑ 24 Jess Todd | .20 | .50 |
| ❑ 25 John Tolisano | .20 | .50 |
| ❑ 26 Jordan Zimmerman UER | .50 | 1.25 |
| ❑ 27 Julian Sampson | .20 | .50 |
| ❑ 28 Luke Hochevar | .50 | 1.25 |
| ❑ 29 Mat Latos | .50 | 1.25 |
| ❑ 30 Matt Mangini | .20 | .50 |
| ❑ 31 Matt Spencer | .30 | .75 |
| ❑ 32 Matthew Sweeney | .20 | .50 |
| ❑ 33 Max Scherzer | .75 | 2.00 |
| ❑ 34 Mitch Canham | .20 | .50 |
| ❑ 35 Nick Schmidt | .20 | .50 |
| ❑ 36 Paul Kelly | .20 | .50 |
| ❑ 37 Ryan Pope | .30 | .75 |
| ❑ 38 Sam Runion | .20 | .50 |
| ❑ 39 Steven Souza | .20 | .50 |
| ❑ 40 Travis Mattair | .20 | .50 |
| ❑ 41 Trystan Magnuson | .20 | .50 |
| ❑ 42 Will Middlebrooks | .30 | .75 |
| ❑ 43 Zack Cozart | .20 | .50 |
| ❑ 44 James Adkins | .20 | .50 |
| ❑ 45 Cory Luebke | .20 | .50 |
| ❑ 46 Aaron Poreda | .20 | .50 |
| ❑ 47 Clayton Mortensen | .20 | .50 |
| ❑ 48 Bradley Suttle | .30 | .75 |
| ❑ 49 Tony Butler | .20 | .50 |
| ❑ 50 Zach Britton | .20 | .50 |
| ❑ 51 Scott Cousins | .20 | .50 |
| ❑ 52 Wendell Fairley | .50 | 1.25 |
| ❑ 53 Eric Sogard | .20 | .50 |
| ❑ 54 Jonathan Lucroy | .30 | .75 |
| ❑ 55 Lars Davis | .20 | .50 |
| ❑ 77 Jennie Finch | .50 | 1.25 |
| ❑ 91 Charlie Culberson | .60 | 1.50 |
| ❑ 92 Jacob Smolinski | .20 | .50 |
| ❑ 93 Blake Beaven AU/719 | 6.00 | 15.00 |
| ❑ 94 Brad Chalk AU/613 | 4.00 | 10.00 |
| ❑ 95 Brett Anderson AU/549 | 20.00 | 50.00 |
| ❑ 96 Chris Withrow AU/700 | 4.00 | 10.00 |
| ❑ 97 Clay Fuller AU/674 | 8.00 | 20.00 |
| ❑ 98 Damon Sublett AU/674 | 8.00 | 20.00 |
| ❑ 99 Devin Mesoraco AU/674 | 5.00 | 12.00 |
| ❑ 100 Drew Cumberland AU/744 | 4.00 | 10.00 |
| ❑ 101 Jack McGeary AU/674 | 6.00 | 15.00 |
| ❑ 102 Jake Arrieta AU/949 | 10.00 | 25.00 |
| ❑ 103 James Simmons AU/624 EXCH | 4.00 | 10.00 |
| ❑ 104 Jarrod Parker AU/499 | 15.00 | 40.00 |
| ❑ 105 Jason Dominguez AU/744 | 4.00 | 10.00 |
| ❑ 106 Jason Heyward AU/750 | 40.00 | 80.00 |
| ❑ 107 Joe Savery AU/750 | 8.00 | 20.00 |
| ❑ 108 Jon Gilmore AU/819 | 5.00 | 12.00 |
| ❑ 109 Jordan Walden AU/794 | 12.50 | 30.00 |
| ❑ 110 Josh Smoker AU/719 | 10.00 | 25.00 |
| ❑ 111 Josh Vitters AU/769 | 15.00 | 40.00 |
| ❑ 112 Julio Borbon AU/594 | 8.00 | 20.00 |


| | | |
|---|---|---|
| ❑ 113 Justin Jackson AU/850 | 4.00 | 10.00 |
| ❑ 114 Kellen Kulbacki AU/549 | 5.00 | 12.00 |
| ❑ 115 Kevin Ahrens AU/794 | 8.00 | 20.00 |
| ❑ 116 Kyle Lotzkar AU/611 | 4.00 | 10.00 |
| ❑ 117 Madison Bumgarner AU/794 | 15.00 | 40.00 |
| ❑ 118 Matt Dominguez AU/769 | 10.00 | 25.00 |
| ❑ 119 Matt LaPorta AU/594 | 30.00 | 60.00 |
| ❑ 120 Matt Wieters AU/799 | 90.00 | 150.00 |
| ❑ 121 Michael Burgess AU/672 | 10.00 | 25.00 |
| ❑ 122 Michael Main AU/794 | 5.00 | 12.00 |
| ❑ 123 Mike Moustakas AU/999 | 30.00 | 60.00 |
| ❑ 124 Nathan Vineyard AU/700 | 5.00 | 12.00 |
| ❑ 125 Neil Ramirez AU/774 | 6.00 | 15.00 |
| ❑ 126 Nick Hagadone AU/544 | 6.00 | 15.00 |
| ❑ 127 Pete Kozma AU/719 | 4.00 | 10.00 |
| ❑ 128 Phillippe Aumont AU/674 | 15.00 | 40.00 |
| ❑ 129 Preston Mattingly AU/519 | 10.00 | 25.00 |
| ❑ 130 Mystery EXCH | 40.00 | 80.00 |
| ❑ 131 Ross Detwiler AU/650 | 5.00 | 12.00 |
| ❑ 132 Tim Alderson AU/737 | 8.00 | 20.00 |
| ❑ 133 Todd Frazier AU/774 | 8.00 | 20.00 |
| ❑ 134 Wes Roemer AU/694 | 5.00 | 12.00 |
| ❑ 135 Ben Revere AU/700 | 6.00 | 15.00 |
| ❑ 136 Chris Davis AU/374 EXCH | 60.00 | 120.00 |
| ❑ 138 Bryan Anderson AU/474 EXCH | 4.00 | 10.00 |
| ❑ 141 Austin Jackson AU/794 | 40.00 | 80.00 |
| ❑ 142 Beau Mills AU/624 EXCH | 8.00 | 20.00 |

## 2008 Donruss Elite
## Extra Edition

| | | |
|---|---|---|
| ❑ COMP.SET w/o AU's (100) | 10.00 | 25.00 |
| ❑ COMMON CARD (1-100) | .20 | .50 |
| ❑ COMMON AU (101-200) | 3.00 | 8.00 |
| ❑ RANDOM INSERTS IN PACKS | | |
| ❑ PRINT RUNS 99-1495 | | |
| ❑ EXCH DEADLINE 5/26/2010 | | |
| ❑ 1 Aaron Cunningham | .20 | .50 |
| ❑ 2 Aaron Pribanic | .20 | .50 |
| ❑ 3 Aaron Shafer | .20 | .50 |
| ❑ 4 Adam Mills | .20 | .50 |
| ❑ 5 Adam Moore | .20 | .50 |
| ❑ 6 Beamer Weems | .20 | .50 |
| ❑ 7 Beau Mills | .20 | .50 |
| ❑ 8 Blake Tekotte | .30 | .75 |
| ❑ 9 Bobby Lanigan | .20 | .50 |
| ❑ 10 Brad Hand | .20 | .50 |
| ❑ 11 Brandon Crawford | .30 | .75 |
| ❑ 12 Brandon Waring | .60 | 1.50 |
| ❑ 13 Brent Morel | .20 | .50 |
| ❑ 14 Brett Jacobson | .20 | .50 |
| ❑ 15 Caleb Gindl | .20 | .50 |
| ❑ 16 Carlos Peguero | .30 | .75 |
| ❑ 17 Charlie Blackmon | .20 | .50 |
| ❑ 18 Charlie Furbush | .20 | .50 |
| ❑ 19 Chris Davis | .50 | 1.25 |
| ❑ 20 Chris Valaika | .20 | .50 |
| ❑ 21 Clark Murphy | .30 | .75 |
| ❑ 22 Clayton Cook | .30 | .75 |
| ❑ 23 Cody Adams | .30 | .75 |
| ❑ 24 Cody Satterwhite | .20 | .50 |
| ❑ 25 Cole St. Clair | .20 | .50 |
| ❑ 26 Corey Young | .20 | .50 |
| ❑ 27 Curtis Petersen | .20 | .50 |
| ❑ 28 Daniel Espinosa | .30 | .75 |
| ❑ 29 Dennis Raben | .30 | .75 |
| ❑ 30 Derek Norris | .50 | 1.25 |
| ❑ 31 Tyson Brummett | .20 | .50 |
| ❑ 32 Dusty Coleman | .20 | .50 |
| ❑ 33 Edgar Olmos | .20 | .50 |
| ❑ 34 Engel Beltre | .60 | 1.50 |
| ❑ 35 Eric Beaulac | .20 | .50 |
| ❑ 36 Geison Aguasviva | .20 | .50 |
| ❑ 37 Gerardo Parra | .30 | .75 |
| ❑ 38 Graham Hicks | .30 | .75 |

|  |  | | |
|---|--------|------|------|
| 39 | Greg Halman | .50 | 1.25 |
| 40 | Hector Gomez | .50 | 1.25 |
| 41 | J.D. Alfaro | .20 | .50 |
| 42 | Jack Egbert | .30 | .75 |
| 43 | James Darnell | .20 | .50 |
| 44 | Jay Austin | .20 | .50 |
| 45 | Jeremy Beckham | .30 | .75 |
| 46 | Jeremy Farrell | .20 | .50 |
| 47 | Jeremy Hamilton | .20 | .50 |
| 48 | Jericho Jones | .20 | .50 |
| 49 | Jesse Darcy | .30 | .75 |
| 51 | Jharmdy De Jesus | .20 | .50 |
| 52 | Joba Chamberlain | .60 | 1.50 |
| 53 | Johnny Giavotella | .30 | .75 |
| 54 | Jon Mark Owings | .30 | .75 |
| 55 | Jordan Meaker | .30 | .75 |
| 56 | Jose Duran | .30 | .75 |
| 57 | Josh Harrison | .30 | .75 |
| 58 | Josh Lindblom | .30 | .75 |
| 59 | Josh Reddick | .60 | 1.50 |
| 60 | Juan Carlos Sulbaran | .20 | .50 |
| 61 | Justin Bristow | .20 | .50 |
| 62 | Kenny Gilbert | .20 | .50 |
| 63 | Kirk Nieuwenhuis | .20 | .50 |
| 64 | Kyle Hudson | .20 | .50 |
| 65 | Kyle Russell | .20 | .50 |
| 66 | Kyle Weiland | .50 | 1.25 |
| 67 | L. J. Hoes | .50 | 1.25 |
| 68 | Mark Cohoon | .30 | .75 |
| 69 | Mark Sobolewski | .50 | 1.25 |
| 70 | Matt Gamel | .50 | 1.25 |
| 71 | Matt Harrison | .20 | .50 |
| 72 | Max Ramirez | .30 | .75 |
| 73 | Tony Delmonico | .30 | .75 |
| 74 | Mike Stanton | .60 | 1.50 |
| 75 | Mitch Abeita | .20 | .50 |
| 76 | Neftali Feliz | .75 | 2.00 |
| 77 | Neftali Soto | .30 | .75 |
| 78 | Niko Vasquez | .30 | .75 |
| 79 | Omar Aguilar | .30 | .75 |
| 80 | Petey Paramore | .30 | .75 |
| 81 | Ray Kruml | .20 | .50 |
| 82 | Rolando Gomez | .30 | .75 |
| 83 | Ryan Chaffee | .30 | .75 |
| 84 | Ryan Pressly | .30 | .75 |
| 85 | Sam Freeman | .50 | 1.25 |
| 86 | Sawyer Carroll | .30 | .75 |
| 87 | Scott Green | .20 | .50 |
| 88 | Sean Ratliff | .20 | .50 |
| 89 | Shane Peterson | .30 | .75 |
| 90 | T.J. Steele | .30 | .75 |
| 91 | Tim Federowicz | .30 | .75 |
| 92 | Tyler Chatwood | .30 | .75 |
| 93 | Tyler Cline | .30 | .75 |
| 94 | Tyler Ladendorf | .30 | .75 |
| 95 | Tyler Yockey | .20 | .50 |
| 96 | Wilmer Flores | .75 | 2.00 |
| 97 | Wilson Ramos | .50 | 1.25 |
| 98 | Zach McAllister | .30 | .75 |
| 99 | Zachary Stewart | .20 | .50 |
| 100 | Zeke Spruill | .50 | 1.25 |
| 101 | Adrian Nieto AU/521 | 4.00 | 10.00 |
| 102 | Alan Horne AU/369 | 6.00 | 15.00 |
| 103 | Andrew Cashner AU/685 | 3.00 | 8.00 |
| 104 | Anthony Hewitt AU/920 | 6.00 | 15.00 |
| 105 | Brad Holt AU/432 | 8.00 | 20.00 |
| 106 | Bryan Petersen AU/319 | 3.00 | 8.00 |
| 107 | Bryan Price AU/572 | 4.00 | 10.00 |
| 108 | Bud Norris AU/1095 | 3.00 | 8.00 |
| 109 | Carlos Gutierrez AU/202 | 5.00 | 12.00 |
| 110 | Chase D'Amaud AU/1218 | 4.00 | 10.00 |
| 111 | Chris Johnson AU/99 EXCH | 8.00 | 20.00 |
| 112 | Christian Friedrich AU/402 | 8.00 | 20.00 |
| 113 | Christian Marrero AU/662 | 4.00 | 10.00 |
| 114 | Clayton Conner AU/819 | 3.00 | 8.00 |
| 115 | Cole Rohrbough AU/719 | 4.00 | 10.00 |
| 116 | Collin DeLome AU/819 | 3.00 | 8.00 |
| 117 | Daniel Cortes AU/680 | 3.00 | 8.00 |
| 118 | Daniel Schlereth AU/570 | 3.00 | 8.00 |
| 119 | Danny Almonte AU/821 | 3.00 | 8.00 |
| 120 | Allan Dykstra AU/1069 | 4.00 | 10.00 |
| 121 | Dominic Brown AU/996 | 10.00 | 25.00 |
| 122 | Evan Fredrickson AU/922 | 3.00 | 8.00 |
| 123 | Gordon Beckham AU/710 | 20.00 | 50.00 |
| 124 | Greg Veloz AU/819 | 3.00 | 8.00 |
| 125 | Ike Davis AU/995 | 4.00 | 10.00 |
| 126 | Isaac Galloway AU/1099 | 3.00 | 8.00 |
| 127 | Jacob Jefferies AU/819 | 3.00 | 8.00 |
| 128 | Michael Kohn AU/199 | 3.00 | 8.00 |
| 129 | Jared Goedert AU/819 | 3.00 | 8.00 |
| 130 | Jason Knapp AU/999 | 4.00 | 10.00 |
| 131 | Jhoulys Chacin AU/21 | 4.00 | 10.00 |
| 132 | Jordy Mercer AU/483 | 3.00 | 8.00 |
| 133 | Jorge Bucardo AU/819 | 4.00 | 10.00 |
| 134 | Jose Ceda AU/1470 | 3.00 | 8.00 |
| 135 | Jose Martinez AU/869 | 3.00 | 8.00 |
| 136 | Josh Roenicke AU/829 | 3.00 | 8.00 |
| 137 | Juan Francisco AU/1495 | 4.00 | 10.00 |
| 138 | Justin Parker AU/719 | 3.00 | 8.00 |
| 139 | Kyle Ginley AU/819 | 3.00 | 8.00 |
| 140 | Lance Lynn AU/576 | 6.00 | 15.00 |
| 141 | Logan Forsythe AU/162 | 12.50 | 30.00 |
| 142 | Logan Morrison AU/360 | 15.00 | 40.00 |
| 143 | Logan Schafer AU/793 | 3.00 | 8.00 |
| 144 | Lorenzo Cain AU/817 | 3.00 | 8.00 |
| 145 | Lucas Duda AU/124 | 8.00 | 20.00 |
| 146 | Matt Mitchell AU/719 | 3.00 | 8.00 |
| 147 | Danny Espinosa AU/443 | 3.00 | 8.00 |
| 148 | Michael Taylor AU/720 | 20.00 | 50.00 |
| 149 | Michel Inoa AU/1199 | 6.00 | 15.00 |
| 150 | Mike Montgomery AU/922 | 3.00 | 8.00 |
| 151 | Cord Phelps AU/693 | 5.00 | 12.00 |
| 152 | Pablo Sandoval AU/819 | 40.00 | 80.00 |
| 153 | Quincy Latimore AU/819 | 3.00 | 8.00 |
| 154 | R. J. Seidel AU/819 | 3.00 | 8.00 |
| 155 | Rayner Contreras AU/1349 | 3.00 | 8.00 |
| 156 | Rick Porcello AU/1299 | 20.00 | 50.00 |
| 157 | Robert Hernandez AU/859 | 3.00 | 8.00 |
| 158 | Ryan Kalish AU/1129 | 4.00 | 10.00 |
| 159 | Ryan Perry AU/745 | 4.00 | 10.00 |
| 160 | Shelby Ford AU/819 | 3.00 | 8.00 |
| 161 | Shooter Hunt AU/397 | 8.00 | 20.00 |
| 162 | Tyler Kolodny AU/819 | 4.00 | 10.00 |
| 163 | Tyler Sample AU/819 | 4.00 | 10.00 |
| 164 | Tyson Ross AU/999 | 3.00 | 8.00 |
| 166 | Waldis Joaquin AU/819 | 3.00 | 8.00 |
| 167 | Welington Castillo AU/1319 | 3.00 | 8.00 |
| 168 | Wilin Rosario AU/1099 | 3.00 | 8.00 |
| 169 | Xavier Avery AU/199 | 10.00 | 25.00 |
| 170 | Zach Collier AU/17 | 10.00 | 25.00 |
| 171 | Zach Putnam AU/444 | 3.00 | 8.00 |
| 172 | Anthony Gose AU/819 | 6.00 | 15.00 |
| 173 | Roger Kieschnick AU/569 | 6.00 | 15.00 |
| 174 | Andrew Liebel AU/219 | 5.00 | 12.00 |
| 175 | Tim Murphy AU/244 | 4.00 | 10.00 |
| 176 | Vance Worley AU/219 | 8.00 | 20.00 |
| 177 | Buster Posey AU/934 | 15.00 | 40.00 |
| 178 | Kenn Kasparek AU/694 | 3.00 | 8.00 |
| 179 | J.P. Ramirez AU/719 | 5.00 | 12.00 |
| 180 | Evan Bigley AU/819 | 3.00 | 8.00 |
| 181 | Trey Haley AU/719 | 3.00 | 8.00 |
| 182 | Robbie Grossman AU/719 | 3.00 | 8.00 |
| 183 | Jordan Danks AU/264 EXCH | 12.50 | 30.00 |
| 184 | Brett Hunter AU/269 | 4.00 | 10.00 |
| 185 | Rafael Rodriguez AU/999 | 10.00 | 25.00 |
| 186 | Yeicok Calderon AU/819 | 6.00 | 15.00 |
| 187 | Gustavo Pierre AU/719 | 4.00 | 10.00 |
| 188 | Will Smith AU/719 | 3.00 | 8.00 |
| 189 | Daniel Thomas AU/719 | 3.00 | 8.00 |
| 190 | Carson Blair AU/719 | 3.00 | 8.00 |
| 191 | Chris Hicks AU/719 | 3.00 | 8.00 |
| 192 | Rashun Dixon AU/199 EXCH | 10.00 | 25.00 |
| 193 | Marcus Lemon AU/199 | 5.00 | 12.00 |
| 194 | Kyle Nicholson AU/719 | 3.00 | 8.00 |
| 195 | Mike Cisco AU/719 | 3.00 | 8.00 |
| 196 | Jarek Cunningham AU/719 | 3.00 | 8.00 |
| 197 | Cat Osterman AU/719 | 12.50 | 30.00 |
| 198 | Derrick Rose AU/99 | 60.00 | 120.00 |
| 199 | Michael Beasley AU/99 | 40.00 | 80.00 |
| 200 | O.J. Mayo AU/99 | 40.00 | 80.00 |

## 1993 Finest

|  |  | | |
|---|--------|------|------|
| | COMPLETE SET (199) | 75.00 | 150.00 |
| 1 | David Justice | 1.00 | 2.50 |
| 2 | Lou Whitaker | 1.00 | 2.50 |
| 3 | Bryan Harvey | .60 | 1.50 |
| 4 | Carlos Garcia | .60 | 1.50 |
| 5 | Sid Fernandez | .60 | 1.50 |
| 6 | Brett Butler | 1.00 | 2.50 |
| 7 | Scott Cooper | 1.00 | 2.50 |
| 8 | B.J. Surhoff | 1.00 | 2.50 |
| 9 | Steve Finley | 1.00 | 2.50 |
| 10 | Curt Schilling | 1.00 | 2.50 |
| 11 | Jeff Bagwell | 1.50 | 4.00 |
| 12 | Alex Cole | .60 | 1.50 |
| 13 | John Olerud | 1.00 | 2.50 |
| 14 | John Smiley | .60 | 1.50 |
| 15 | Bip Roberts | .60 | 1.50 |
| 16 | Albert Belle | 1.50 | 4.00 |
| 17 | Duane Ward | .60 | 1.50 |
| 18 | Alan Trammell | 1.00 | 2.50 |
| 19 | Andy Benes | .60 | 1.50 |
| 20 | Reggie Sanders | .60 | 1.50 |
| 21 | Todd Zeile | .60 | 1.50 |
| 22 | Rick Aguilera | .60 | 1.50 |
| 23 | Dave Hollins | .60 | 1.50 |
| 24 | Jose Rijo | .60 | 1.50 |
| 25 | Matt Williams | 1.00 | 2.50 |
| 26 | Sandy Alomar Jr. | .60 | 1.50 |
| 27 | Alex Fernandez | .60 | 1.50 |
| 28 | Ozzie Smith | 4.00 | 10.00 |
| 29 | Ramon Martinez | .60 | 1.50 |
| 30 | Bernie Williams | 1.50 | 4.00 |
| 31 | Gary Sheffield | 1.00 | 2.50 |
| 32 | Eric Karros | 1.00 | 2.50 |
| 33 | Frank Viola | .60 | 1.50 |
| 34 | Kevin Young | 1.00 | 2.50 |
| 35 | Ken Hill | .60 | 1.50 |
| 36 | Tony Fernandez | .60 | 1.50 |
| 37 | Tim Wakefield | 2.50 | 6.00 |
| 38 | John Kruk | 1.00 | 2.50 |
| 39 | Chris Sabo | .60 | 1.50 |
| 40 | Marquis Grissom | 1.00 | 2.50 |
| 41 | Glenn Davis | .60 | 1.50 |
| 42 | Jeff Montgomery | .60 | 1.50 |
| 43 | Kenny Lofton | .60 | 1.50 |
| 44 | John Burkett | .60 | 1.50 |
| 45 | Darryl Hamilton | .60 | 1.50 |
| 46 | Jim Abbott | 1.50 | 4.00 |
| 47 | Ivan Rodriguez | 4.00 | 10.00 |
| 48 | Eric Young | .60 | 1.50 |
| 49 | Mitch Williams | .60 | 1.50 |
| 50 | Harold Reynolds | 1.00 | 2.50 |
| 51 | Brian Harper | .60 | 1.50 |
| 52 | Rafael Palmeiro | 1.50 | 4.00 |
| 53 | Bret Saberhagen | 1.00 | 2.50 |
| 54 | Jeff Conine | .60 | 1.50 |
| 55 | Ivan Calderon | .60 | 1.50 |
| 56 | Juan Guzman | .60 | 1.50 |
| 57 | Carlos Baerga | .60 | 1.50 |
| 58 | Charles Nagy | .60 | 1.50 |
| 59 | Wally Joyner | 1.00 | 2.50 |
| 60 | Charlie Hayes | .60 | 1.50 |
| 61 | Shane Mack | .60 | 1.50 |
| 62 | Pete Harnisch | .60 | 1.50 |
| 63 | George Brett | 6.00 | 15.00 |
| 64 | Lance Johnson | .60 | 1.50 |
| 65 | Ben McDonald | .60 | 1.50 |
| 66 | Bobby Bonilla | .60 | 1.50 |
| 67 | Terry Steinbach | .60 | 1.50 |
| 68 | Ron Gant | 1.00 | 2.50 |
| 69 | Doug Jones | .60 | 1.50 |
| 70 | Paul Molitor | 1.00 | 2.50 |
| 71 | Brady Anderson | 1.00 | 2.50 |
| 72 | Chuck Finley | 1.00 | 2.50 |
| 73 | Mark Grace | 1.50 | 4.00 |
| 74 | Mike Devereaux | .60 | 1.50 |
| 75 | Tony Phillips | .60 | 1.50 |
| 76 | Chuck Knoblauch | 3.00 | 8.00 |
| 77 | Tony Gwynn | 3.00 | 8.00 |
| 78 | Kevin Appier | 1.00 | 2.50 |
| 79 | Sammy Sosa | 2.50 | 6.00 |
| 80 | Mickey Tettleton | .60 | 1.50 |
| 81 | Felix Jose | .60 | 1.50 |
| 82 | Mark Langston | .60 | 1.50 |
| 83 | Gregg Jefferies | .60 | 1.50 |
| 84 | Andre Dawson AS | 1.00 | 2.50 |
| 85 | Greg Maddux AS | 4.00 | 10.00 |
| 86 | Rickey Henderson AS | 2.50 | 6.00 |
| 87 | Tom Glavine AS | 1.50 | 4.00 |

| | | |
|---|---|---|
| 88 Roberto Alomar AS | 1.50 | 4.00 |
| 89 Darryl Strawberry AS | 1.00 | 2.50 |
| 90 Wade Boggs AS | 1.50 | 4.00 |
| 91 Bo Jackson AS | 2.50 | 6.00 |
| 92 Mark McGwire AS | 6.00 | 15.00 |
| 93 Robin Ventura AS | 1.00 | 2.50 |
| 94 Joe Carter AS | 1.00 | 2.50 |
| 95 Lee Smith AS | 1.00 | 2.50 |
| 96 Cal Ripken AS | 8.00 | 20.00 |
| 97 Larry Walker AS | 1.00 | 2.50 |
| 98 Don Mattingly AS | 6.00 | 15.00 |
| 99 Jose Canseco AS | 1.50 | 4.00 |
| 100 Dennis Eckersley AS | 1.00 | 2.50 |
| 101 Terry Pendleton AS | .60 | 1.50 |
| 102 Frank Thomas AS | 2.50 | 6.00 |
| 103 Barry Bonds AS | 6.00 | 15.00 |
| 104 Roger Clemens AS | 5.00 | 12.00 |
| 105 Ryne Sandberg AS | 4.00 | 10.00 |
| 106 Fred McGriff AS | 1.50 | 4.00 |
| 107 Nolan Ryan AS | 10.00 | 25.00 |
| 108 Will Clark AS | 1.50 | 4.00 |
| 109 Pat Listach AS | .60 | 1.50 |
| 110 Ken Griffey Jr. AS | 4.00 | 10.00 |
| 111 Cecil Fielder AS | 1.00 | 2.50 |
| 112 Kirby Puckett AS | 2.50 | 6.00 |
| 113 Dwight Gooden AS | 1.00 | 2.50 |
| 114 Barry Larkin AS | 1.50 | 4.00 |
| 115 David Cone AS | 1.00 | 2.50 |
| 116 Juan Gonzalez AS | 1.00 | 2.50 |
| 117 Kent Hrbek | 1.00 | 2.50 |
| 118 Tim Wallach | .60 | 1.50 |
| 119 Craig Biggio | 1.50 | 4.00 |
| 120 Roberto Kelly | .60 | 1.50 |
| 121 Gregg Olson | .60 | 1.50 |
| 122 Eddie Murray | 2.50 | 6.00 |
| 123 Wil Cordero | .60 | 1.50 |
| 124 Jay Buhner | 1.00 | 2.50 |
| 125 Carlton Fisk | 1.00 | 2.50 |
| 126 Eric Davis | 1.00 | 2.50 |
| 127 Doug Drabek | .60 | 1.50 |
| 128 Ozzie Guillen | 1.00 | 2.50 |
| 129 John Wetteland | 1.00 | 2.50 |
| 130 Andres Galarraga | 1.00 | 2.50 |
| 131 Ken Caminiti | 1.00 | 2.50 |
| 132 Tom Candiotti | .60 | 1.50 |
| 133 Pat Borders | .60 | 1.50 |
| 134 Kevin Brown | 1.00 | 2.50 |
| 135 Travis Fryman | .60 | 1.50 |
| 136 Kevin Mitchell | .60 | 1.50 |
| 137 Greg Swindell | .60 | 1.50 |
| 138 Benito Santiago | 1.00 | 2.50 |
| 139 Reggie Jefferson | .60 | 1.50 |
| 140 Chris Bosio | .60 | 1.50 |
| 141 Deion Sanders | 1.50 | 4.00 |
| 142 Scott Erickson | .60 | 1.50 |
| 143 Howard Johnson | .60 | 1.50 |
| 144 Orestes Destrade | .60 | 1.50 |
| 145 Jose Guzman | .60 | 1.50 |
| 146 Chad Curtis | .60 | 1.50 |
| 147 Cal Eldred | .60 | 1.50 |
| 148 Willie Greene | .60 | 1.50 |
| 149 Tommy Greene | .60 | 1.50 |
| 150 Erik Hanson | .60 | 1.50 |
| 151 Bob Welch | .60 | 1.50 |
| 152 John Jaha | .60 | 1.50 |
| 153 Harold Baines | 1.00 | 2.50 |
| 154 Randy Johnson | 2.50 | 6.00 |
| 155 Al Martin | .60 | 1.50 |
| 156 J.T.Snow RC | 1.50 | 4.00 |
| 157 Mike Mussina | 1.50 | 4.00 |
| 158 Ruben Sierra | 1.00 | 2.50 |
| 159 Dean Palmer | 1.00 | 2.50 |
| 160 Steve Avery | .60 | 1.50 |
| 161 Julio Franco | .60 | 1.50 |
| 162 Dave Winfield | 1.00 | 2.50 |
| 163 Tim Salmon | 1.50 | 4.00 |
| 164 Tom Henke | .60 | 1.50 |
| 165 Mo Vaughn | 1.00 | 2.50 |
| 166 John Smoltz | 1.50 | 4.00 |
| 167 Danny Tartabull | .60 | 1.50 |
| 168 Delino DeShields | 1.00 | 2.50 |
| 169 Charlie Hough | .60 | 1.50 |
| 170 Paul O'Neill | 1.50 | 4.00 |
| 171 Darren Daulton | .60 | 1.50 |
| 172 Jack McDowell | .60 | 1.50 |
| 173 Junior Felix | .60 | 1.50 |
| 174 Jimmy Key | 1.00 | 2.50 |
| 175 George Bell | .60 | 1.50 |

| | | |
|---|---|---|
| 176 Mike Stanton | .60 | 1.50 |
| 177 Len Dykstra | 1.00 | 2.50 |
| 178 Norm Charlton | .60 | 1.50 |
| 179 Eric Anthony | .60 | 1.50 |
| 180 Rob Dibble | 1.00 | 2.50 |
| 181 Otis Nixon | .60 | 1.50 |
| 182 Randy Myers | .60 | 1.50 |
| 183 Tim Raines | 1.00 | 2.50 |
| 184 Orel Hershiser | 1.00 | 2.50 |
| 185 Andy Van Slyke | 1.50 | 4.00 |
| 186 Mike Lansing RC | 1.00 | 2.50 |
| 187 Ray Lankford | 1.00 | 2.50 |
| 188 Mike Morgan | .60 | 1.50 |
| 189 Moises Alou | 1.00 | 2.50 |
| 190 Edgar Martinez | 1.50 | 4.00 |
| 191 John Franco | 1.00 | 2.50 |
| 192 Robin Yount | 4.00 | 10.00 |
| 193 Bob Tewksbury | .60 | 1.50 |
| 194 Jay Bell | 1.00 | 2.50 |
| 195 Luis Gonzalez | 1.00 | 2.50 |
| 196 Dave Fleming | .60 | 1.50 |
| 197 Mike Greenwell | .60 | 1.50 |
| 198 David Nied | .60 | 1.50 |
| 199 Mike Piazza | 6.00 | 15.00 |

## 1994 Finest

| | | |
|---|---|---|
| COMPLETE SET (440) | 50.00 | 120.00 |
| COMPLETE SERIES 1 (220) | 25.00 | 60.00 |
| COMPLETE SERIES 2 (220) | 25.00 | 60.00 |
| 1 Mike Piazza FIN | 2.50 | 6.00 |
| 2 Kevin Stocker FIN | .30 | .75 |
| 3 Greg McMichael FIN | .30 | .75 |
| 4 Jeff Conine FIN | .50 | 1.25 |
| 5 Rene Arocha FIN | .30 | .75 |
| 6 Aaron Sele FIN | .30 | .75 |
| 7 Brent Gates FIN | .30 | .75 |
| 8 Chuck Carr FIN | .30 | .75 |
| 9 Kirk Rueter FIN | .30 | .75 |
| 10 Mike Lansing FIN | .30 | .75 |
| 11 Al Martin FIN | .30 | .75 |
| 12 Jason Bere FIN | .30 | .75 |
| 13 Troy Neel FIN | .30 | .75 |
| 14 Armando Reynoso FIN | .30 | .75 |
| 15 Jeromy Burnitz FIN | .50 | 1.25 |
| 16 Rich Amaral FIN | .30 | .75 |
| 17 David McCarty FIN | .30 | .75 |
| 18 Tim Salmon FIN | .75 | 2.00 |
| 19 Steve Cooke FIN | .30 | .75 |
| 20 Wil Cordero FIN | .30 | .75 |
| 21 Kevin Tapani FIN | .30 | .75 |
| 22 Deion Sanders FIN | .75 | 2.00 |
| 23 Jose Offerman FIN | .30 | .75 |
| 24 Mark Langston FIN | .30 | .75 |
| 25 Ken Hill FIN | .30 | .75 |
| 26 Alex Fernandez FIN | .30 | .75 |
| 27 Jeff Blauser FIN | .30 | .75 |
| 28 Royce Clayton FIN | .30 | .75 |
| 29 Brad Ausmus FIN | .75 | 2.00 |
| 30 Ryan Bowen FIN | .30 | .75 |
| 31 Steve Finley FIN | .50 | 1.25 |
| 32 Charlie Hayes FIN | .30 | .75 |
| 33 Jeff Kent FIN | .75 | 2.00 |
| 34 Mike Henneman FIN | .30 | .75 |
| 35 Andres Galarraga FIN | .50 | 1.25 |
| 36 Wayne Kirby FIN | .30 | .75 |
| 37 Joe Oliver FIN | .30 | .75 |
| 38 Terry Steinbach FIN | .30 | .75 |
| 39 Ryan Thompson FIN | .30 | .75 |
| 40 Luis Alicea FIN | .30 | .75 |
| 41 Randy Velarde FIN | .30 | .75 |
| 42 Bob Tewksbury FIN | .30 | .75 |
| 43 Reggie Sanders FIN | .50 | 1.25 |
| 44 Brian Williams FIN | .30 | .75 |
| 45 Joe Orsulak FIN | .30 | .75 |

| | | |
|---|---|---|
| 46 Jose Lind | .30 | .75 |
| 47 Dave Hollins | .30 | .75 |
| 48 Graeme Lloyd | .30 | .75 |
| 49 Jim Gott | .30 | .75 |
| 50 Andre Dawson | .50 | 1.25 |
| 51 Steve Buechele | .30 | .75 |
| 52 David Cone | .50 | 1.25 |
| 53 Ricky Gutierrez | .30 | .75 |
| 54 Lance Johnson | .30 | .75 |
| 55 Tino Martinez | .75 | 2.00 |
| 56 Phil Hiatt | .30 | .75 |
| 57 Carlos Garcia | .30 | .75 |
| 58 Danny Darwin | .30 | .75 |
| 59 Dante Bichette | .50 | 1.25 |
| 60 Scott Kamieniecki | .30 | .75 |
| 61 Orlando Merced | .30 | .75 |
| 62 Brian McRae | .30 | .75 |
| 63 Pat Kelly | .30 | .75 |
| 64 Tom Henke | .30 | .75 |
| 65 Jeff King | .30 | .75 |
| 66 Mike Mussina | .75 | 2.00 |
| 67 Tim Pugh | .30 | .75 |
| 68 Robby Thompson | .30 | .75 |
| 69 Paul O'Neill | .75 | 2.00 |
| 70 Hal Morris | .30 | .75 |
| 71 Ron Karkovice | .30 | .75 |
| 72 Joe Girardi | .30 | .75 |
| 73 Eduardo Perez | .30 | .75 |
| 74 Raul Mondesi | .50 | 1.25 |
| 75 Mike Gallego | .30 | .75 |
| 76 Mike Stanley | .30 | .75 |
| 77 Kevin Roberson | .30 | .75 |
| 78 Mark McGwire | 3.00 | 8.00 |
| 79 Pat Listach | .30 | .75 |
| 80 Eric Davis | .50 | 1.25 |
| 81 Mike Bordick | .30 | .75 |
| 82 Dwight Gooden | .50 | 1.25 |
| 83 Mike Moore | .30 | .75 |
| 84 Phil Plantier | .30 | .75 |
| 85 Darren Lewis | .30 | .75 |
| 86 Rick Wilkins | .30 | .75 |
| 87 Darryl Strawberry | .50 | 1.25 |
| 88 Bob Dibble | .30 | .75 |
| 89 Greg Vaughn | .50 | 1.25 |
| 90 Jeff Russell | .30 | .75 |
| 91 Mark Lewis | .30 | .75 |
| 92 Gregg Jefferies | .30 | .75 |
| 93 Jose Guzman | .30 | .75 |
| 94 Kevin Rogers | .30 | .75 |
| 95 Mark Lemke | .30 | .75 |
| 96 Mike Morgan | .30 | .75 |
| 97 Andujar Cedeno | .30 | .75 |
| 98 Orel Hershiser | .50 | 1.25 |
| 99 Greg Swindell | .30 | .75 |
| 100 John Smoltz | .75 | 2.00 |
| 101 Pedro A.Martinez RC | .75 | 2.00 |
| 102 Jim Thome | 2.00 | 5.00 |
| 103 David Segui | .30 | .75 |
| 104 Charles Nagy | .30 | .75 |
| 105 Shane Mack | .30 | .75 |
| 106 John Jaha | .30 | .75 |
| 107 Tom Candiotti | .30 | .75 |
| 108 David Wells | .50 | 1.25 |
| 109 Bobby Jones | .30 | .75 |
| 110 Bob Hamelin | .30 | .75 |
| 111 Bernard Gilkey | .30 | .75 |
| 112 Chili Davis | .50 | 1.25 |
| 113 Todd Stottlemyre | .30 | .75 |
| 114 Derek Bell | .30 | .75 |
| 115 Mark McLemore | .30 | .75 |
| 116 Mark Whiten | .30 | .75 |
| 117 Mike Devereaux | .30 | .75 |
| 118 Terry Pendleton | .50 | 1.25 |
| 119 Pat Meares | .30 | .75 |
| 120 Pete Harnisch | .30 | .75 |
| 121 Moises Alou | .50 | 1.25 |
| 122 Jay Buhner | .50 | 1.25 |
| 123 Wes Chamberlain | .30 | .75 |
| 124 Mike Perez | .30 | .75 |
| 125 Devon White | .50 | 1.25 |
| 126 Ivan Rodriguez | .75 | 2.00 |
| 127 Don Slaught | .30 | .75 |
| 128 John Valentin | .30 | .75 |
| 129 Jaime Navarro | .30 | .75 |
| 130 Dave Magadan | .30 | .75 |
| 131 Brady Anderson | .50 | 1.25 |
| 132 Juan Guzman | .30 | .75 |
| 133 John Wetteland | .50 | 1.25 |

|  |  | | |
|---|---|---|---|
| 134 | Dave Stewart | .50 | 1.25 |
| 135 | Scott Servais | .30 | .75 |
| 136 | Ozzie Smith | 2.00 | 5.00 |
| 137 | Darrin Fletcher | .30 | .75 |
| 138 | Jose Mesa | .30 | .75 |
| 139 | Wilson Alvarez | .30 | .75 |
| 140 | Pete Incaviglia | .30 | .75 |
| 141 | Chris Hoiles | .30 | .75 |
| 142 | Darryl Hamilton | .30 | .75 |
| 143 | Chuck Finley | .50 | 1.25 |
| 144 | Archi Cianfrocco | .30 | .75 |
| 145 | Bill Wegman | .30 | .75 |
| 146 | Joey Cora | .30 | .75 |
| 147 | Darrell Whitmore | .30 | .75 |
| 148 | David Hulse | .30 | .75 |
| 149 | Jim Abbott | .75 | 2.00 |
| 150 | Curt Schilling | .50 | 1.25 |
| 151 | Bill Swift | .30 | .75 |
| 152 | Tommy Greene | .30 | .75 |
| 153 | Roberto Mejia | .30 | .75 |
| 154 | Edgar Martinez | .75 | 2.00 |
| 155 | Roger Pavlik | .30 | .75 |
| 156 | Randy Tomlin | .30 | .75 |
| 157 | J.T. Snow | .50 | 1.25 |
| 158 | Bob Welch | .30 | .75 |
| 159 | Alan Trammell | .50 | 1.25 |
| 160 | Ed Sprague | .30 | .75 |
| 161 | Ben McDonald | .30 | .75 |
| 162 | Derrick May | .30 | .75 |
| 163 | Roberto Kelly | .30 | .75 |
| 164 | Bryan Harvey | .30 | .75 |
| 165 | Ron Gant | .50 | 1.25 |
| 166 | Scott Erickson | .30 | .75 |
| 167 | Anthony Young | .30 | .75 |
| 168 | Scott Cooper | .30 | .75 |
| 169 | Rod Beck | .30 | .75 |
| 170 | John Franco | .50 | 1.25 |
| 171 | Gary DiSarcina | .30 | .75 |
| 172 | Dave Fleming | .30 | .75 |
| 173 | Wade Boggs | .75 | 2.00 |
| 174 | Kevin Appier | .50 | 1.25 |
| 175 | Jose Bautista | .30 | .75 |
| 176 | Wally Joyner | .50 | 1.25 |
| 177 | Dean Palmer | .50 | 1.25 |
| 178 | Tony Phillips | .30 | .75 |
| 179 | John Smiley | .30 | .75 |
| 180 | Charlie Hough | .50 | 1.25 |
| 181 | Scott Fletcher | .30 | .75 |
| 182 | Todd Van Poppel | .30 | .75 |
| 183 | Mike Blowers | .30 | .75 |
| 184 | Willie McGee | .50 | 1.25 |
| 185 | Paul Sorrento | .30 | .75 |
| 186 | Eric Young | .30 | .75 |
| 187 | Bret Barberie | .30 | .75 |
| 188 | Manuel Lee | .30 | .75 |
| 189 | Jeff Branson | .30 | .75 |
| 190 | Jim Deshaies | .30 | .75 |
| 191 | Ken Caminiti | .50 | 1.25 |
| 192 | Tim Raines | .50 | 1.25 |
| 193 | Joe Grahe | .30 | .75 |
| 194 | Hipolito Pichardo | .30 | .75 |
| 195 | Denny Neagle | .50 | 1.25 |
| 196 | Jeff Gardner | .30 | .75 |
| 197 | Mike Benjamin | .30 | .75 |
| 198 | Milt Thompson | .30 | .75 |
| 199 | Bruce Ruffin | .30 | .75 |
| 200 | Chris Hammond UER (Back of card has Mariners; sh) | .30 | .75 |
| 201 | Tony Gwynn FIN | 1.50 | 4.00 |
| 202 | Robin Ventura FIN | .50 | 1.25 |
| 203 | Frank Thomas FIN | 1.25 | 3.00 |
| 204 | Kirby Puckett FIN | 1.25 | 3.00 |
| 205 | Roberto Alomar FIN | .75 | 2.00 |
| 206 | Dennis Eckersley FIN | .50 | 1.25 |
| 207 | Joe Carter FIN | .50 | 1.25 |
| 208 | Albert Belle FIN | .50 | 1.25 |
| 209 | Greg Maddux FIN | 2.00 | 5.00 |
| 210 | Ryne Sandberg FIN | 2.00 | 5.00 |
| 211 | Juan Gonzalez FIN | .50 | 1.25 |
| 212 | Jeff Bagwell FIN | .75 | 2.00 |
| 213 | Randy Johnson FIN | 1.25 | 3.00 |
| 214 | Matt Williams FIN | .50 | 1.25 |
| 215 | Dave Winfield FIN | .50 | 1.25 |
| 216 | Larry Walker FIN | .50 | 1.25 |
| 217 | Roger Clemens FIN | 2.50 | 6.00 |
| 218 | Kenny Lofton FIN | .50 | 1.25 |
| 219 | Cecil Fielder FIN | .50 | 1.25 |
| 220 | Darren Daulton FIN | .50 | 1.25 |
| 221 | John Olerud FIN | .50 | 1.25 |
| 222 | Jose Canseco FIN | .75 | 2.00 |
| 223 | Rickey Henderson FIN | 1.25 | 3.00 |
| 224 | Fred McGriff FIN | .75 | 2.00 |
| 225 | Gary Sheffield FIN | .50 | 1.25 |
| 226 | Jack McDowell FIN | .30 | .75 |
| 227 | Rafael Palmeiro FIN | .75 | 2.00 |
| 228 | Travis Fryman FIN | .50 | 1.25 |
| 229 | Marquis Grissom FIN | .50 | 1.25 |
| 230 | Barry Bonds FIN | 3.00 | 8.00 |
| 231 | Carlos Baerga FIN | .30 | .75 |
| 232 | Ken Griffey Jr. FIN | 2.00 | 5.00 |
| 233 | David Justice FIN | .50 | 1.25 |
| 234 | Bobby Bonilla FIN | .50 | 1.25 |
| 235 | Cal Ripken FIN | 4.00 | 10.00 |
| 236 | Sammy Sosa FIN | 1.25 | 3.00 |
| 237 | Len Dykstra FIN | .50 | 1.25 |
| 238 | Will Clark FIN | .75 | 2.00 |
| 239 | Paul Molitor FIN | .50 | 1.25 |
| 240 | Barry Larkin FIN | .75 | 2.00 |
| 241 | Bo Jackson FIN | 1.25 | 3.00 |
| 242 | Mitch Williams FIN | .30 | .75 |
| 243 | Ron Darling FIN | .30 | .75 |
| 244 | Darryl Kile FIN | .50 | 1.25 |
| 245 | Geronimo Berroa | .30 | .75 |
| 246 | Gregg Olson FIN | .30 | .75 |
| 247 | Brian Harper FIN | .30 | .75 |
| 248 | Rheal Cormier FIN | .30 | .75 |
| 249 | Rey Sanchez FIN | .30 | .75 |
| 250 | Jeff Fassero FIN | .30 | .75 |
| 251 | Sandy Alomar Jr. | .30 | .75 |
| 252 | Chris Bosio | .30 | .75 |
| 253 | Andy Stankiewicz | .30 | .75 |
| 254 | Harold Baines | .50 | 1.25 |
| 255 | Andy Ashby | .30 | .75 |
| 256 | Tyler Green | .30 | .75 |
| 257 | Kevin Brown | .50 | 1.25 |
| 258 | Mo Vaughn | .50 | 1.25 |
| 259 | Mike Harkey | .30 | .75 |
| 260 | Dave Henderson | .30 | .75 |
| 261 | Kent Hrbek | .50 | 1.25 |
| 262 | Darrin Jackson | .30 | .75 |
| 263 | Bob Wickman | .30 | .75 |
| 264 | Spike Owen | .30 | .75 |
| 265 | Todd Jones | .30 | .75 |
| 266 | Pat Borders | .30 | .75 |
| 267 | Tom Glavine | .75 | 2.00 |
| 268 | Dave Nilsson | .30 | .75 |
| 269 | Rich Batchelor | .30 | .75 |
| 270 | Delino DeShields | .50 | 1.25 |
| 271 | Felix Fermin | .30 | .75 |
| 272 | Orestes Destrade | .30 | .75 |
| 273 | Mickey Morandini | .30 | .75 |
| 274 | Otis Nixon | .30 | .75 |
| 275 | Ellis Burks | .50 | 1.25 |
| 276 | Greg Gagne | .30 | .75 |
| 277 | John Doherty | .30 | .75 |
| 278 | Julio Franco | .50 | 1.25 |
| 279 | Bernie Williams | .75 | 2.00 |
| 280 | Rick Aguilera | .30 | .75 |
| 281 | Mickey Tettleton | .30 | .75 |
| 282 | David Nied | .30 | .75 |
| 283 | Johnny Ruffin | .30 | .75 |
| 284 | Dan Wilson | .30 | .75 |
| 285 | Omar Vizquel | .75 | 2.00 |
| 286 | Willie Banks | .30 | .75 |
| 287 | Erik Pappas | .30 | .75 |
| 288 | Cal Eldred | .30 | .75 |
| 289 | Bobby Witt | .30 | .75 |
| 290 | Luis Gonzalez | .50 | 1.25 |
| 291 | Greg Pirkl | .30 | .75 |
| 292 | Alex Cole | .30 | .75 |
| 293 | Ricky Bones | .30 | .75 |
| 294 | Denis Boucher | .30 | .75 |
| 295 | John Burkett | .30 | .75 |
| 296 | Steve Trachsel | .30 | .75 |
| 297 | Ricky Jordan | .30 | .75 |
| 298 | Mark Dewey | .30 | .75 |
| 299 | Jimmy Key | .50 | 1.25 |
| 300 | Mike Macfarlane | .30 | .75 |
| 301 | Tim Belcher | .30 | .75 |
| 302 | Carlos Reyes | .30 | .75 |
| 303 | Greg A. Harris | .30 | .75 |
| 304 | Brian Anderson RC | .50 | 1.25 |
| 305 | Terry Mulholland | .30 | .75 |
| 306 | Felix Jose | .30 | .75 |
| 307 | Darren Holmes | .30 | .75 |
| 308 | Jose Rijo | .30 | .75 |
| 309 | Paul Wagner | .30 | .75 |
| 310 | Bob Scanlan | .30 | .75 |
| 311 | Mike Jackson | .30 | .75 |
| 312 | Jose Vizcaino | .30 | .75 |
| 313 | Rob Butler | .30 | .75 |
| 314 | Kevin Seitzer | .30 | .75 |
| 315 | Geronimo Pena | .30 | .75 |
| 316 | Hector Carrasco | .30 | .75 |
| 317 | Eddie Murray | 1.25 | 3.00 |
| 318 | Roger Salkeld | .30 | .75 |
| 319 | Todd Hundley | .30 | .75 |
| 320 | Danny Jackson | .30 | .75 |
| 321 | Kevin Young | .30 | .75 |
| 322 | Mike Greenwell | .50 | 1.25 |
| 323 | Kevin Mitchell | .50 | 1.25 |
| 324 | Chuck Knoblauch | .50 | 1.25 |
| 325 | Danny Tartabull | .50 | 1.25 |
| 326 | Vince Coleman | .30 | .75 |
| 327 | Marvin Freeman | .30 | .75 |
| 328 | Andy Benes | .30 | .75 |
| 329 | Mike Kelly | .30 | .75 |
| 330 | Karl Rhodes | .30 | .75 |
| 331 | Allen Watson | .30 | .75 |
| 332 | Damion Easley | .30 | .75 |
| 333 | Reggie Jefferson | .30 | .75 |
| 334 | Kevin McReynolds | .30 | .75 |
| 335 | Arthur Rhodes | .30 | .75 |
| 336 | Brian Hunter | .30 | .75 |
| 337 | Tom Browning | .30 | .75 |
| 338 | Pedro Munoz | .30 | .75 |
| 339 | Billy Ripken | .30 | .75 |
| 340 | Gene Harris | .30 | .75 |
| 341 | Fernando Vina | .30 | .75 |
| 342 | Sean Berry | .30 | .75 |
| 343 | Pedro Astacio | .30 | .75 |
| 344 | B.J. Surhoff | .50 | 1.25 |
| 345 | Doug Drabek | .30 | .75 |
| 346 | Jody Reed | .30 | .75 |
| 347 | Ray Lankford | .50 | 1.25 |
| 348 | Steve Farr | .30 | .75 |
| 349 | Eric Anthony | .30 | .75 |
| 350 | Pete Smith | .30 | .75 |
| 351 | Lee Smith | .50 | 1.25 |
| 352 | Mariano Duncan | .30 | .75 |
| 353 | Doug Strange | .30 | .75 |
| 354 | Tim Bogar | .30 | .75 |
| 355 | Dave Weathers | .30 | .75 |
| 356 | Eric Karros | .50 | 1.25 |
| 357 | Randy Myers | .30 | .75 |
| 358 | Chad Curtis | .30 | .75 |
| 359 | Steve Avery | .30 | .75 |
| 360 | Brian Jordan | .50 | 1.25 |
| 361 | Tim Wallach | .30 | .75 |
| 362 | Pedro Martinez | 1.25 | 3.00 |
| 363 | Bip Roberts | .30 | .75 |
| 364 | Lou Whitaker | .50 | 1.25 |
| 365 | Luis Polonia | .30 | .75 |
| 366 | Benito Santiago | .50 | 1.25 |
| 367 | Brett Butler | .50 | 1.25 |
| 368 | Shawon Dunston | .30 | .75 |
| 369 | Kelly Stinnett RC | .30 | .75 |
| 370 | Chris Turner | .30 | .75 |
| 371 | Ruben Sierra | .50 | 1.25 |
| 372 | Greg A. Harris | .30 | .75 |
| 373 | Xavier Hernandez | .30 | .75 |
| 374 | Howard Johnson | .30 | .75 |
| 375 | Duane Ward | .30 | .75 |
| 376 | Roberto Hernandez | .30 | .75 |
| 377 | Scott Leius | .30 | .75 |
| 378 | Dave Valle | .30 | .75 |
| 379 | Sid Fernandez | .30 | .75 |
| 380 | Doug Jones | .30 | .75 |
| 381 | Zane Smith | .30 | .75 |
| 382 | Craig Biggio | .75 | 2.00 |
| 383 | Rick White RC | .30 | .75 |
| 384 | Tom Pagnozzi | .30 | .75 |
| 385 | Chris James | .30 | .75 |
| 386 | Bret Boone | .50 | 1.25 |
| 387 | Jeff Montgomery | .30 | .75 |
| 388 | Chad Kreuter | .30 | .75 |
| 389 | Greg Hibbard | .30 | .75 |
| 390 | Mark Grace | .75 | 2.00 |
| 391 | Phil Leftwich RC | .30 | .75 |
| 392 | Don Mattingly | 3.00 | 8.00 |
| 393 | Ozzie Guillen | .50 | 1.25 |
| 394 | Gary Gaetti | .50 | 1.25 |
| 395 | Erik Hanson | .30 | .75 |

|  | | |
|---|---|---|
| 396 Scott Brosius | .50 | 1.25 |
| 397 Tom Gordon | .30 | .75 |
| 398 Bill Gullickson | .30 | .75 |
| 399 Matt Mieske | .30 | .75 |
| 400 Pat Hentgen | .30 | .75 |
| 401 Walt Weiss | .30 | .75 |
| 402 Greg Blosser | .30 | .75 |
| 403 Stan Javier | .30 | .75 |
| 404 Doug Henry | .30 | .75 |
| 405 Ramon Martinez | .30 | .75 |
| 406 Frank Viola | .50 | 1.25 |
| 407 Mike Hampton | .50 | 1.25 |
| 408 Andy Van Slyke | .75 | 2.00 |
| 409 Bobby Ayala | .30 | .75 |
| 410 Todd Zeile | .30 | .75 |
| 411 Jay Bell | .50 | 1.25 |
| 412 Dennis Martinez | .50 | 1.25 |
| 413 Mark Portugal | .30 | .75 |
| 414 Bobby Munoz | .30 | .75 |
| 415 Kirt Manwaring | .30 | .75 |
| 416 John Kruk | .50 | 1.25 |
| 417 Trevor Hoffman | .75 | 2.00 |
| 418 Chris Sabo | .30 | .75 |
| 419 Bret Saberhagen | .50 | 1.25 |
| 420 Chris Nabholz | .30 | .75 |
| 421 James Mouton FIN | .30 | .75 |
| 422 Tony Tarasco FIN | .30 | .75 |
| 423 Carlos Delgado FIN | .75 | 2.00 |
| 424 Rondell White FIN | .75 | 2.00 |
| 425 Javier Lopez FIN | .50 | 1.25 |
| 426 Chan Ho Park FIN RC | .75 | 2.00 |
| 427 Cliff Floyd FIN | .50 | 1.25 |
| 428 Dave Staton FIN | .30 | .75 |
| 429 J.R. Phillips FIN | .30 | .75 |
| 430 Manny Ramirez FIN | 1.25 | 3.00 |
| 431 Kurt Abbott FIN RC | .30 | .75 |
| 432 Melvin Nieves FIN | .30 | .75 |
| 433 Alex Gonzalez FIN | .30 | .75 |
| 434 Rick Helling FIN | .30 | .75 |
| 435 Danny Bautista FIN | .30 | .75 |
| 436 Matt Walbeck FIN | .30 | .75 |
| 437 Ryan Klesko FIN | .50 | 1.25 |
| 438 Steve Karsay FIN | .30 | .75 |
| 439 Salomon Torres FIN | .30 | .75 |
| 440 Scott Ruffcorn FIN | .30 | .75 |

## 1995 Finest

|  | | |
|---|---|---|
| COMPLETE SET (330) | 25.00 | 60.00 |
| COMPLETE SERIES 1 (220) | 20.00 | 50.00 |
| COMPLETE SERIES 2 (110) | 6.00 | 15.00 |
| 1 Raul Mondesi | .40 | 1.00 |
| 2 Kurt Abbott | .20 | .50 |
| 3 Chris Gomez | .20 | .50 |
| 4 Manny Ramirez | .60 | 1.50 |
| 5 Rondell White | .40 | 1.00 |
| 6 William VanLandingham | .20 | .50 |
| 7 Jon Lieber | .20 | .50 |
| 8 Ryan Klesko | .40 | 1.00 |
| 9 John Hudek | .20 | .50 |
| 10 Joey Hamilton | .40 | 1.00 |
| 11 Bob Hamelin | .20 | .50 |
| 12 Brian Anderson | .20 | .50 |
| 13 Mike Lieberthal | .40 | 1.00 |
| 14 Rico Brogna | .20 | .50 |
| 15 Rusty Greer | .40 | 1.00 |
| 16 Carlos Delgado | .40 | 1.00 |
| 17 Jim Edmonds | .60 | 1.50 |
| 18 Steve Trachsel | .20 | .50 |
| 19 Matt Walbeck | .20 | .50 |
| 20 Armando Benitez | .20 | .50 |
| 21 Steve Karsay | .20 | .50 |
| 22 Jose Oliva | .20 | .50 |
| 23 Cliff Floyd | .40 | 1.00 |
| 24 Kevin Foster | .20 | .50 |
| 25 Javier Lopez | .40 | 1.00 |
| 26 Jose Valentin | .20 | .50 |
| 27 James Mouton | .20 | .50 |
| 28 Hector Carrasco | .20 | .50 |
| 29 Orlando Miller | .20 | .50 |
| 30 Garret Anderson | .40 | 1.00 |
| 31 Marvin Freeman | .20 | .50 |
| 32 Brett Butler | .40 | 1.00 |
| 33 Roberto Kelly | .20 | .50 |
| 34 Rod Beck | .20 | .50 |
| 35 Jose Rijo | .20 | .50 |
| 36 Edgar Martinez | .60 | 1.50 |
| 37 Jim Thome | .60 | 1.50 |
| 38 Rick Wilkins | .20 | .50 |
| 39 Wally Joyner | .40 | 1.00 |
| 40 Wil Cordero | .20 | .50 |
| 41 Tommy Greene | .20 | .50 |
| 42 Travis Fryman | .40 | 1.00 |
| 43 Don Slaught | .20 | .50 |
| 44 Brady Anderson | .40 | 1.00 |
| 45 Matt Williams | .40 | 1.00 |
| 46 Rene Arocha | .20 | .50 |
| 47 Rickey Henderson | 1.00 | 2.50 |
| 48 Mike Mussina | .60 | 1.50 |
| 49 Greg McMichael | .20 | .50 |
| 50 Jody Reed | .20 | .50 |
| 51 Tino Martinez | .60 | 1.50 |
| 52 Dave Clark | .20 | .50 |
| 53 John Valentin | .20 | .50 |
| 54 Bret Boone | .40 | 1.00 |
| 55 Walt Weiss | .20 | .50 |
| 56 Kenny Lofton | .60 | 1.50 |
| 57 Scott Leius | .20 | .50 |
| 58 Eric Karros | .40 | 1.00 |
| 59 John Olerud | .40 | 1.00 |
| 60 Chris Hoiles | .20 | .50 |
| 61 Sandy Alomar Jr. | .20 | .50 |
| 62 Tim Wallach | .20 | .50 |
| 63 Cal Eldred | .20 | .50 |
| 64 Tom Glavine | .60 | 1.50 |
| 65 Mark Grace | .60 | 1.50 |
| 66 Rey Sanchez | .20 | .50 |
| 67 Bobby Ayala | .20 | .50 |
| 68 Dante Bichette | .40 | 1.00 |
| 69 Andres Galarraga | .40 | 1.00 |
| 70 Chuck Carr | .20 | .50 |
| 71 Bobby Witt | .20 | .50 |
| 72 Steve Avery | .20 | .50 |
| 73 Bobby Jones | .20 | .50 |
| 74 Delino DeShields | .20 | .50 |
| 75 Kevin Tapani | .20 | .50 |
| 76 Randy Johnson | 1.00 | 2.50 |
| 77 David Nied | .20 | .50 |
| 78 Pat Hentgen | .20 | .50 |
| 79 Tim Salmon | .60 | 1.50 |
| 80 Todd Zeile | .20 | .50 |
| 81 John Wetteland | .40 | 1.00 |
| 82 Albert Belle | .60 | 1.50 |
| 83 Ben McDonald | .40 | 1.00 |
| 84 Bobby Munoz | .20 | .50 |
| 85 Bip Roberts | .20 | .50 |
| 86 Mo Vaughn | .40 | 1.00 |
| 87 Chuck Finley | .40 | 1.00 |
| 88 Chuck Knoblauch | .40 | 1.00 |
| 89 Frank Thomas | 1.00 | 2.50 |
| 90 Danny Tartabull | .20 | .50 |
| 91 Dean Palmer | .40 | 1.00 |
| 92 Len Dykstra | .40 | 1.00 |
| 93 J.R. Phillips | .20 | .50 |
| 94 Tom Candiotti | .20 | .50 |
| 95 Marquis Grissom | .40 | 1.00 |
| 96 Barry Larkin | .60 | 1.50 |
| 97 Bryan Harvey | .20 | .50 |
| 98 David Justice | .60 | 1.50 |
| 99 David Cone | .40 | 1.00 |
| 100 Wade Boggs | .60 | 1.50 |
| 101 Jason Bere | .20 | .50 |
| 102 Hal Morris | .20 | .50 |
| 103 Fred McGriff | .60 | 1.50 |
| 104 Bobby Bonilla | .40 | 1.00 |
| 105 Jay Buhner | .40 | 1.00 |
| 106 Allen Watson | .20 | .50 |
| 107 Mickey Tettleton | .20 | .50 |
| 108 Kevin Appier | .40 | 1.00 |
| 109 Ivan Rodriguez | .60 | 1.50 |
| 110 Carlos Garcia | .20 | .50 |
| 111 Andy Benes | .20 | .50 |
| 112 Eddie Murray | 1.00 | 2.50 |
| 113 Mike Piazza | 1.50 | 4.00 |
| 114 Greg Vaughn | .20 | .50 |
| 115 Paul Molitor | .40 | 1.00 |
| 116 Terry Steinbach | .20 | .50 |
| 117 Jeff Bagwell | .60 | 1.50 |
| 118 Ken Griffey Jr. | 1.50 | 4.00 |
| 119 Gary Sheffield | .40 | 1.00 |
| 120 Cal Ripken | 3.00 | 8.00 |
| 121 Jeff Kent | .40 | 1.00 |
| 122 Jay Bell | .40 | 1.00 |
| 123 Will Clark | .60 | 1.50 |
| 124 Cecil Fielder | .40 | 1.00 |
| 125 Alex Fernandez | .20 | .50 |
| 126 Don Mattingly | 2.50 | 6.00 |
| 127 Reggie Sanders | .40 | 1.00 |
| 128 Moises Alou | .40 | 1.00 |
| 129 Craig Biggio | .60 | 1.50 |
| 130 Eddie Williams | .20 | .50 |
| 131 John Franco | .40 | 1.00 |
| 132 John Kruk | .40 | 1.00 |
| 133 Jeff King | .20 | .50 |
| 134 Royce Clayton | .20 | .50 |
| 135 Doug Drabek | .20 | .50 |
| 136 Ray Lankford | .40 | 1.00 |
| 137 Roberto Alomar | .60 | 1.50 |
| 138 Todd Hundley | .20 | .50 |
| 139 Alex Cole | .20 | .50 |
| 140 Shawon Dunston | .20 | .50 |
| 141 John Roper | .20 | .50 |
| 142 Mark Langston | .20 | .50 |
| 143 Tom Pagnozzi | .20 | .50 |
| 144 Wilson Alvarez | .20 | .50 |
| 145 Scott Cooper | .20 | .50 |
| 146 Kevin Mitchell | .20 | .50 |
| 147 Mark Whiten | .20 | .50 |
| 148 Jeff Conine | .40 | 1.00 |
| 149 Chili Davis | .40 | 1.00 |
| 150 Luis Gonzalez | .20 | .50 |
| 151 Juan Guzman | .20 | .50 |
| 152 Mike Greenwell | .20 | .50 |
| 153 Mike Henneman | .20 | .50 |
| 154 Rick Aguilera | .20 | .50 |
| 155 Dennis Eckersley | .40 | 1.00 |
| 156 Darrin Fletcher | .20 | .50 |
| 157 Darren Lewis | .20 | .50 |
| 158 Juan Gonzalez | .40 | 1.00 |
| 159 Dave Hollins | .20 | .50 |
| 160 Jimmy Key | .40 | 1.00 |
| 161 Roberto Hernandez | .20 | .50 |
| 162 Randy Myers | .20 | .50 |
| 163 Joe Carter | .40 | 1.00 |
| 164 Darren Daulton | .40 | 1.00 |
| 165 Mike Macfarlane | .20 | .50 |
| 166 Bret Saberhagen | .40 | 1.00 |
| 167 Kirby Puckett | 1.00 | 2.50 |
| 168 Lance Johnson | .20 | .50 |
| 169 Mark McGwire | 2.50 | 6.00 |
| 170 Jose Canseco | .60 | 1.50 |
| 171 Mike Stanley | .20 | .50 |
| 172 Lee Smith | .40 | 1.00 |
| 173 Robin Ventura | .40 | 1.00 |
| 174 Greg Gagne | .20 | .50 |
| 175 Brian McRae | .20 | .50 |
| 176 Mike Bordick | .20 | .50 |
| 177 Rafael Palmeiro | .60 | 1.50 |
| 178 Kenny Rogers | .20 | .50 |
| 179 Chad Curtis | .20 | .50 |
| 180 Devon White | .40 | 1.00 |
| 181 Paul O'Neill | .60 | 1.50 |
| 182 Ken Caminiti | .40 | 1.00 |
| 183 Dave Nilsson | .20 | .50 |
| 184 Tim Naehring | .20 | .50 |
| 185 Roger Clemens | 2.00 | 5.00 |
| 186 Otis Nixon | .20 | .50 |
| 187 Tim Raines | .40 | 1.00 |
| 188 Denny Martinez | .20 | .50 |
| 189 Pedro Martinez | .60 | 1.50 |
| 190 Jim Abbott | .60 | 1.50 |
| 191 Ryan Thompson | .20 | .50 |
| 192 Barry Bonds | 2.50 | 6.00 |
| 193 Joe Girardi | .20 | .50 |
| 194 Steve Finley | .40 | 1.00 |
| 195 John Jaha | .20 | .50 |
| 196 Tony Gwynn | 1.25 | 3.00 |
| 197 Sammy Sosa | 1.00 | 2.50 |
| 198 John Burkett | .20 | .50 |
| 199 Carlos Baerga | .20 | .50 |
| 200 Ramon Martinez | .20 | .50 |

|  |  | | |
|---|---|---|---|
| 201 | Aaron Sele | .20 | .50 |
| 202 | Eduardo Perez | .20 | .50 |
| 203 | Alan Trammell | .40 | 1.00 |
| 204 | Orlando Merced | .20 | .50 |
| 205 | Deion Sanders | .60 | 1.50 |
| 206 | Robb Nen | .40 | 1.00 |
| 207 | Jack McDowell | .20 | .50 |
| 208 | Ruben Sierra | .40 | 1.00 |
| 209 | Bernie Williams | .60 | 1.50 |
| 210 | Kevin Seitzer | .20 | .50 |
| 211 | Charles Nagy | .20 | .50 |
| 212 | Tony Phillips | .20 | .50 |
| 213 | Greg Maddux | 1.50 | 4.00 |
| 214 | Jeff Montgomery | .20 | .50 |
| 215 | Larry Walker | .40 | 1.00 |
| 216 | Andy Van Slyke | .60 | 1.50 |
| 217 | Ozzie Smith | 1.50 | 4.00 |
| 218 | Geronimo Pena | .20 | .50 |
| 219 | Gregg Jefferies | .20 | .50 |
| 220 | Lou Whitaker | .40 | 1.00 |
| 221 | Chipper Jones | 1.00 | 2.50 |
| 222 | Benji Gil | .20 | .50 |
| 223 | Tony Phillips | .20 | .50 |
| 224 | Trevor Wilson | .20 | .50 |
| 225 | Tony Tarasco | .20 | .50 |
| 226 | Roberto Petagine | .20 | .50 |
| 227 | Mike Macfarlane | .20 | .50 |
| 228 | Hideo Nomo RC | 4.00 | 10.00 |
| 229 | Mark McLemore | .20 | .50 |
| 230 | Ron Gant | .40 | 1.00 |
| 231 | Andujar Cedeno | .20 | .50 |
| 232 | Michael Mimbs RC | .20 | .50 |
| 233 | Jim Abbott | .60 | 1.50 |
| 234 | Ricky Bones | .20 | .50 |
| 235 | Marty Cordova | .20 | .50 |
| 236 | Mark Johnson RC | .50 | 1.25 |
| 237 | Marquis Grissom | .40 | 1.00 |
| 238 | Tom Henke | .20 | .50 |
| 239 | Terry Pendleton | .40 | 1.00 |
| 240 | John Wetteland | .40 | 1.00 |
| 241 | Lee Smith | .40 | 1.00 |
| 242 | Jaime Navarro | .20 | .50 |
| 243 | Luis Alicea | .20 | .50 |
| 244 | Scott Cooper | .20 | .50 |
| 245 | Gary Gaetti | .40 | 1.00 |
| 246 | Edgardo Alfonzo | .20 | .50 |
| 247 | Brad Clontz | .20 | .50 |
| 248 | Dave Micki | .20 | .50 |
| 249 | Dave Winfield | .40 | 1.00 |
| 250 | Mark Grudzielanek RC | .75 | 2.00 |
| 251 | Alex Gonzalez | .20 | .50 |
| 252 | Kevin Brown | .40 | 1.00 |
| 253 | Esteban Loaiza | .20 | .50 |
| 254 | Vaughn Eshelman | .20 | .50 |
| 255 | Bill Swift | .20 | .50 |
| 256 | Brian McRae | .20 | .50 |
| 257 | Bob Higginson RC | .75 | 2.00 |
| 258 | Jack McDowell | .20 | .50 |
| 259 | Scott Stahoviak | .20 | .50 |
| 260 | Jon Nunnally | .20 | .50 |
| 261 | Charlie Hayes | .20 | .50 |
| 262 | Jacob Brumfield | .20 | .50 |
| 263 | Chad Curtis | .20 | .50 |
| 264 | Heathcliff Slocumb | .20 | .50 |
| 265 | Mark Whiten | .20 | .50 |
| 266 | Mickey Tettleton | .20 | .50 |
| 267 | Jose Mesa | .20 | .50 |
| 268 | Doug Jones | .20 | .50 |
| 269 | Trevor Hoffman | .40 | 1.00 |
| 270 | Paul Sorrento | .20 | .50 |
| 271 | Shane Andrews | .20 | .50 |
| 272 | Brett Butler | .40 | 1.00 |
| 273 | Curtis Goodwin | .20 | .50 |
| 274 | Larry Walker | .40 | 1.00 |
| 275 | Phil Plantier | .20 | .50 |
| 276 | Ken Hill | .20 | .50 |
| 277 | Vinny Castilla | .40 | 1.00 |
| 278 | Billy Ashley | .20 | .50 |
| 279 | Derek Jeter | 2.50 | 6.00 |
| 280 | Bob Tewksbury | .20 | .50 |
| 281 | Jose Offerman | .20 | .50 |
| 282 | Glenallen Hill | .20 | .50 |
| 283 | Tony Fernandez | .20 | .50 |
| 284 | Mike Devereaux | .20 | .50 |
| 285 | John Burkett | .20 | .50 |
| 286 | Geronimo Berroa | .20 | .50 |
| 287 | Quilvio Veras | .20 | .50 |
| 288 | Jason Bates | .20 | .50 |
| 289 | Lee Tinsley | .20 | .50 |
| 290 | Derek Bell | .20 | .50 |
| 291 | Jeff Fassero | .20 | .50 |
| 292 | Ray Durham | .40 | 1.00 |
| 293 | Chad Ogea | .20 | .50 |
| 294 | Bill Pulsipher | .20 | .50 |
| 295 | Phil Nevin | .20 | .50 |
| 296 | Carlos Perez RC | .50 | 1.25 |
| 297 | Roberto Kelly | .20 | .50 |
| 298 | Tim Wakefield | .40 | 1.00 |
| 299 | Jeff Manto | .20 | .50 |
| 300 | Brian L.Hunter | .20 | .50 |
| 301 | C.J. Nitkowski | .20 | .50 |
| 302 | Dustin Hermanson | .20 | .50 |
| 303 | John Mabry | .20 | .50 |
| 304 | Orel Hershiser | .40 | 1.00 |
| 305 | Ron Villone | .20 | .50 |
| 306 | Sean Bergman | .20 | .50 |
| 307 | Tom Goodwin | .20 | .50 |
| 308 | Al Reyes | .20 | .50 |
| 309 | Todd Stottlemyre | .20 | .50 |
| 310 | Rich Becker | .20 | .50 |
| 311 | Joey Cora | .20 | .50 |
| 312 | Ed Sprague | .20 | .50 |
| 313 | John Smoltz | .60 | 1.50 |
| 314 | Frank Castillo | .20 | .50 |
| 315 | Chris Hammond | .20 | .50 |
| 316 | Ismael Valdes | .20 | .50 |
| 317 | Pete Harnisch | .20 | .50 |
| 318 | Bernard Gilkey | .20 | .50 |
| 319 | John Kruk | .40 | 1.00 |
| 320 | Marc Newfield | .20 | .50 |
| 321 | Brian Johnson | .20 | .50 |
| 322 | Mark Portugal | .20 | .50 |
| 323 | David Hulse | .20 | .50 |
| 324 | Luis Ortiz | .20 | .50 |
| 325 | Mike Benjamin | .20 | .50 |
| 326 | Brian Jordan | .40 | 1.00 |
| 327 | Shawn Green | .40 | 1.00 |
| 328 | Joe Oliver | .20 | .50 |
| 329 | Felipe Lira | .20 | .50 |
| 330 | Andre Dawson | .40 | 1.00 |

## 1996 Finest

|  |  | | |
|---|---|---|---|
| | COMP.BRONZE SER.1 (110) | 10.00 | 25.00 |
| | COMP.BRONZE SER.2 (110) | 10.00 | 25.00 |
| | COMMON BRONZE | .20 | .50 |
| | COMMON GOLD | 2.00 | 5.00 |
| | COMMON G RC | 2.00 | 5.00 |
| | COMMON SILVER | 1.00 | 2.50 |
| B5 | Roberto Hernandez B | .20 | .50 |
| B8 | Terry Pendleton B | .20 | .50 |
| B12 | Ken Caminiti B | .20 | .50 |
| B15 | Dan Miceli B | .20 | .50 |
| B16 | Chipper Jones B | .50 | 1.25 |
| B17 | John Wetteland B | .20 | .50 |
| B19 | Tim Naehring B | .20 | .50 |
| B21 | Eddie Murray B | .50 | 1.25 |
| B23 | Kevin Appier B | .20 | .50 |
| B24 | Ken Griffey Jr. B | .75 | 2.00 |
| B26 | Brian McRae B | .20 | .50 |
| B27 | Pedro Martinez B | .30 | .75 |
| B28 | Brian Jordan B | .20 | .50 |
| B29 | Mike Fetters B | .20 | .50 |
| B30 | Carlos Delgado B | .20 | .50 |
| B31 | Shane Reynolds B | .20 | .50 |
| B32 | Terry Steinbach B | .20 | .50 |
| B34 | Mark Leiter B | .20 | .50 |
| B36 | David Segui B | .20 | .50 |
| B40 | Fred McGriff B | .30 | .75 |
| B44 | Glenallen Hill B | .20 | .50 |
| B45 | Brady Anderson B | .20 | .50 |
| B47 | Jim Thome B | .30 | .75 |
| B48 | Frank Thomas B | .50 | 1.25 |
| B49 | Chuck Knoblauch B | .20 | .50 |
| B50 | Len Dykstra B | .20 | .50 |
| B53 | Tom Pagnozzi B | .20 | .50 |
| B55 | Ricky Bones B | .20 | .50 |
| B56 | David Justice B | .20 | .50 |
| B57 | Steve Avery B | .20 | .50 |
| B58 | Robby Thompson B | .20 | .50 |
| B61 | Tony Gwynn B | .60 | 1.50 |
| B63 | Denny Neagle B | .20 | .50 |
| B67 | Robin Ventura B | .20 | .50 |
| B70 | Kevin Seitzer B | .20 | .50 |
| B71 | Ramon Martinez B | .20 | .50 |
| B75 | Brian L.Hunter B | .20 | .50 |
| B76 | Alan Benes B | .20 | .50 |
| B80 | Ozzie Guillen B | .20 | .50 |
| B82 | Benji Gil B | .20 | .50 |
| B85 | Todd Hundley B | .20 | .50 |
| B87 | Pat Hentgen B | .20 | .50 |
| B89 | Chuck Finley B | .20 | .50 |
| B92 | Derek Jeter B | 1.25 | 3.00 |
| B93 | Paul O'Neill B | .30 | .75 |
| B94 | Darrin Fletcher B | .20 | .50 |
| B96 | Delino DeShields B | .20 | .50 |
| B97 | Tim Salmon B | .30 | .75 |
| B98 | John Olerud B | .20 | .50 |
| B101 | Tim Wakefield B | .20 | .50 |
| B103 | Dave Stevens B | .20 | .50 |
| B104 | Orlando Merced B | .20 | .50 |
| B106 | Jay Bell B | .20 | .50 |
| B107 | John Burkett B | .20 | .50 |
| B108 | Chris Hoiles B | .20 | .50 |
| B110 | Dave Nilsson B | .20 | .50 |
| B111 | Rod Beck B | .20 | .50 |
| B113 | Mike Piazza B | .75 | 2.00 |
| B114 | Mark Langston B | .20 | .50 |
| B116 | Rico Brogna B | .20 | .50 |
| B118 | Tom Goodwin B | .20 | .50 |
| B119 | Bryan Rekar B | .20 | .50 |
| B120 | David Cone B | .20 | .50 |
| B122 | Andy Pettitte B | .30 | .75 |
| B123 | Chili Davis B | .20 | .50 |
| B124 | John Smoltz B | .30 | .75 |
| B125 | Heathcliff Slocumb B | .20 | .50 |
| B126 | Dante Bichette B | .20 | .50 |
| B128 | Alex Gonzalez B | .20 | .50 |
| B129 | Jeff Montgomery B | .20 | .50 |
| B131 | Denny Martinez B | .20 | .50 |
| B132 | Mel Rojas B | .20 | .50 |
| B133 | Derek Bell B | .20 | .50 |
| B134 | Trevor Hoffman B | .20 | .50 |
| B136 | Darren Daulton B | .20 | .50 |
| B137 | Pete Schourek B | .20 | .50 |
| B138 | Phil Nevin B | .20 | .50 |
| B139 | Andres Galarraga B | .20 | .50 |
| B140 | Chad Fonville B | .20 | .50 |
| B144 | J.T. Snow B | .20 | .50 |
| B146 | Barry Bonds B | 1.25 | 3.00 |
| B147 | Orel Hershiser B | .20 | .50 |
| B148 | Quilvio Veras B | .20 | .50 |
| B149 | Will Clark B | .30 | .75 |
| B150 | Jose Rijo B | .20 | .50 |
| B152 | Travis Fryman B | .20 | .50 |
| B153 | Alex Fernandez B | .20 | .50 |
| B155 | Wade Boggs B | .30 | .75 |
| B156 | Troy Percival B | .20 | .50 |
| B157 | Moises Alou B | .20 | .50 |
| B158 | Javy Lopez B | .20 | .50 |
| B159 | Jason Giambi B | .20 | .50 |
| B162 | Mark McGwire B | 1.25 | 3.00 |
| B163 | Eric Karros B | .20 | .50 |
| B166 | Mickey Tettleton B | .20 | .50 |
| B167 | Barry Larkin B | .30 | .75 |
| B169 | Ruben Sierra B | .20 | .50 |
| B170 | Bill Swift B | .20 | .50 |
| B172 | Chad Curtis B | .20 | .50 |
| B173 | Dean Palmer B | .20 | .50 |
| B175 | Bobby Bonilla B | .20 | .50 |
| B176 | Greg Colbrunn B | .20 | .50 |
| B177 | Jose Mesa B | .20 | .50 |
| B178 | Mike Greenwell B | .20 | .50 |
| B181 | Doug Drabek B | .20 | .50 |
| B183 | Wilson Alvarez B | .20 | .50 |
| B184 | Marty Cordova B | .20 | .50 |
| B185 | Hal Morris B | .20 | .50 |
| B187 | Carlos Garcia B | .20 | .50 |
| B190 | Marquis Grissom B | .20 | .50 |
| B193 | Will Clark B | .30 | .75 |
| B194 | Paul Molitor B | .20 | .50 |

| □ B195 Kenny Rogers B | .20 | .50 |
|---|---|---|
| □ B196 Reggie Sanders B | .20 | .50 |
| □ B199 Raul Mondesi B | .20 | .50 |
| □ B200 Lance Johnson B | .20 | .50 |
| □ B201 Alvin Morman B | .20 | .50 |
| □ B203 Jack McDowell B | .20 | .50 |
| □ B204 Randy Myers B | .20 | .50 |
| □ B205 Harold Baines B | .20 | .50 |
| □ B206 Marty Cordova B | .20 | .50 |
| □ B207 Rich Hunter B RC | .20 | .50 |
| □ B208 Al Leiter B | .20 | .50 |
| □ B209 Greg Gagne B | .20 | .50 |
| □ B210 Ben McDonald B | .20 | .50 |
| □ B212 Terry Adams B | .20 | .50 |
| □ B213 Paul Sorrento B | .20 | .50 |
| □ B214 Albert Belle B | .20 | .50 |
| □ B215 Mike Blowers B | .20 | .50 |
| □ B216 Jim Edmonds B | .20 | .50 |
| □ B217 Felipe Crespo B | .20 | .50 |
| □ B219 Shawon Dunston B | .20 | .50 |
| □ B220 Jimmy Haynes B | .20 | .50 |
| □ B221 Jose Canseco B | .30 | .75 |
| □ B222 Eric Davis B | .20 | .50 |
| □ B224 Tim Raines B | .20 | .50 |
| □ B225 Tony Phillips B | .20 | .50 |
| □ B226 Charlie Hayes B | .20 | .50 |
| □ B227 Eric Owens B | .20 | .50 |
| □ B228 Roberto Alomar B | .30 | .75 |
| □ B233 Kenny Lofton B | .20 | .50 |
| □ B236 Mark McGwire B | 1.25 | 3.00 |
| □ B237 Jay Buhner B | .20 | .50 |
| □ B238 Craig Biggio B | .30 | .75 |
| □ B240 Barry Bonds B | 1.25 | 3.00 |
| □ B244 Ron Gant B | .20 | .50 |
| □ B245 Paul Wilson B | .20 | .50 |
| □ B246 Todd Hollandsworth B | .20 | .50 |
| □ B247 Todd Zeile B | .20 | .50 |
| □ B248 David Justice B | .20 | .50 |
| □ B250 Moises Alou B | .20 | .50 |
| □ B251 Bob Wolcott B | .20 | .50 |
| □ B252 David Wells B | .20 | .50 |
| □ B253 Juan Gonzalez B | .20 | .50 |
| □ B254 Andres Galarraga B | .20 | .50 |
| □ B255 Dave Hollins B | .20 | .50 |
| □ B257 Sammy Sosa B | .50 | 1.25 |
| □ B258 Ivan Rodriguez B | .30 | .75 |
| □ B259 Bip Roberts B | .20 | .50 |
| □ B260 Tino Martinez B | .30 | .75 |
| □ B262 Mike Stanley B | .20 | .50 |
| □ B264 Butch Huskey B | .20 | .50 |
| □ B265 Jeff Conine B | .20 | .50 |
| □ B267 Mark Grace B | .30 | .75 |
| □ B268 Jason Schmidt B | .20 | .50 |
| □ B269 Otis Nixon B | .20 | .50 |
| □ B271 Kirby Puckett B | .50 | 1.25 |
| □ B273 Andy Benes B | .20 | .50 |
| □ B275 Mike Piazza B | .75 | 2.00 |
| □ B276 Rey Ordonez B | .20 | .50 |
| □ B278 Gary Gaetti B | .20 | .50 |
| □ B280 Robin Ventura B | .20 | .50 |
| □ B281 Cal Ripken B | 1.50 | 4.00 |
| □ B282 Carlos Baerga B | .20 | .50 |
| □ B283 Roger Cedeno B | .20 | .50 |
| □ B285 Terrell Wade B | .20 | .50 |
| □ B286 Kevin Brown B | .20 | .50 |
| □ B287 Rafael Palmeiro B | .30 | .75 |
| □ B288 Mo Vaughn B | .30 | .75 |
| □ B292 Bob Tewksbury B | .20 | .50 |
| □ B297 T.J. Mathews B | .20 | .50 |
| □ B298 Manny Ramirez B | .30 | .75 |
| □ B299 Jeff Bagwell B | .30 | .75 |
| □ B301 Wade Boggs B | .30 | .75 |
| □ B303 Steve Gibralter B | .20 | .50 |
| □ B304 B.J. Surhoff B | .20 | .50 |
| □ B306 Royce Clayton B | .20 | .50 |
| □ B307 Sal Fasano B | .20 | .50 |
| □ B309 Gary Sheffield B | .30 | .75 |
| □ B310 Ken Hill B | .20 | .50 |
| □ B311 Joe Girardi B | .20 | .50 |
| □ B312 Matt Lawton B RC | .20 | .50 |
| □ B314 Julio Franco B | .20 | .50 |
| □ B315 Joe Carter B | .20 | .50 |
| □ B316 Brooks Kieschnick B | .20 | .50 |
| □ B318 Heathcliff Slocumb B | .20 | .50 |
| □ B319 Barry Larkin B | .30 | .75 |
| □ B320 Tony Gwynn B | .60 | 1.50 |
| □ B322 Frank Thomas B | .50 | 1.25 |
| □ B323 Edgar Martinez B | .30 | .75 |

| □ B325 Henry Rodriguez B | .20 | .50 |
|---|---|---|
| □ B326 Marvin Benard B RC | .20 | .50 |
| □ B329 Ugueth Urbina B | .20 | .50 |
| □ B331 Roger Salkeld B | .20 | .50 |
| □ B332 Edgar Renteria B | .20 | .50 |
| □ B333 Ryan Klesko B | .20 | .50 |
| □ B334 Ray Lankford B | .20 | .50 |
| □ B336 Justin Thompson B | .20 | .50 |
| □ B339 Mark Clark B | .20 | .50 |
| □ B340 Ruben Rivera B | .20 | .50 |
| □ B342 Matt Williams B | .20 | .50 |
| □ B343 Francisco Cordova B RC | .20 | .50 |
| □ B344 Cecil Fielder B | .20 | .50 |
| □ B348 Mark Grudzielanek B | .20 | .50 |
| □ B349 Ron Coomer B | .20 | .50 |
| □ B351 Rich Aurilia B RC | .20 | .50 |
| □ B352 Jose Herrera B | .20 | .50 |
| □ B356 Tony Clark B | .20 | .50 |
| □ B358 Dan Naulty B | .20 | .50 |
| □ B359 Checklist B | .20 | .50 |
| □ G4 Marty Cordova G | 2.00 | 5.00 |
| □ G6 Tony Gwynn G | 6.00 | 15.00 |
| □ G9 Albert Belle G | 2.00 | 5.00 |
| □ G18 Kirby Puckett G | 5.00 | 12.00 |
| □ G20 Karim Garcia G | 2.00 | 5.00 |
| □ G25 Cal Ripken G | 15.00 | 40.00 |
| □ G33 Hideo Nomo G | 5.00 | 12.00 |
| □ G39 Ryne Sandberg G | 8.00 | 20.00 |
| □ G42 Jeff Bagwell G | 1.50 | 4.00 |
| □ G51 Jason Isringhausen G | 2.00 | 5.00 |
| □ G64 Mo Vaughn G | 2.00 | 5.00 |
| □ G66 Dante Bichette G | 2.00 | 5.00 |
| □ G74 Mark McGwire G | 12.50 | 30.00 |
| □ G81 Kenny Lofton G | 2.00 | 5.00 |
| □ G83 Jim Edmonds G | 2.00 | 5.00 |
| □ G90 Mike Mussina G | 3.00 | 8.00 |
| □ G100 Jeff Conine G | 2.00 | 5.00 |
| □ G102 Johnny Damon G | 3.00 | 8.00 |
| □ G105 Barry Bonds G | 12.50 | 30.00 |
| □ G117 Jose Canseco G | 3.00 | 8.00 |
| □ G135 Ken Griffey Jr. G | 8.00 | 20.00 |
| □ G141 Chipper Jones G | 5.00 | 12.00 |
| □ G145 Greg Maddux G | 8.00 | 20.00 |
| □ G164 Jay Buhner G | 2.00 | 5.00 |
| □ G186 Frank Thomas G | 5.00 | 12.00 |
| □ G191 Checklist G | 2.00 | 5.00 |
| □ G192 Chipper Jones G | 5.00 | 12.00 |
| □ G197 Roberto Alomar G | 3.00 | 8.00 |
| □ G198 Dennis Eckersley G | 2.00 | 5.00 |
| □ G202 George Arias G | 2.00 | 5.00 |
| □ G232 Hideo Nomo G | 5.00 | 12.00 |
| □ G243 Chris Snopek G | 3.00 | 8.00 |
| □ G249 Tim Salmon G | 3.00 | 8.00 |
| □ G266 Matt Williams G | 2.00 | 5.00 |
| □ G270 Randy Johnson G | 5.00 | 12.00 |
| □ G279 Paul Molitor G | 2.00 | 5.00 |
| □ G290 Cecil Fielder G | 2.00 | 5.00 |
| □ G294 Livan Hernandez G RC | 4.00 | 10.00 |
| □ G300 Marty Janzen G RC | 2.00 | 5.00 |
| □ G308 Ron Gant G | 2.00 | 5.00 |
| □ G321 Ryan Klesko G | 2.00 | 5.00 |
| □ G324 Jermaine Dye G | 2.00 | 5.00 |
| □ G330 Jason Giambi G | 2.00 | 5.00 |
| □ G335 Edgar Martinez G | 3.00 | 8.00 |
| □ G338 Rey Ordonez G | 2.00 | 5.00 |
| □ G347 Sammy Sosa G | 5.00 | 12.00 |
| □ G354 Juan Gonzalez G | 2.00 | 5.00 |
| □ G355 Craig Biggio G | 3.00 | 8.00 |
| □ S1 Greg Maddux S | 4.00 | 10.00 |
| □ S2 Bernie Williams S | 1.50 | 4.00 |
| □ S3 Ivan Rodriguez S | 1.50 | 4.00 |
| □ S7 Barry Larkin S | 1.50 | 4.00 |
| □ S10 Ray Lankford S | 1.00 | 2.50 |
| □ S11 Mike Piazza S | 4.00 | 10.00 |
| □ S13 Larry Walker S | 1.00 | 2.50 |
| □ S14 Matt Williams S | 1.00 | 2.50 |
| □ S22 Tim Salmon S | 1.50 | 4.00 |
| □ S35 Edgar Martinez S | 1.00 | 2.50 |
| □ S37 Gregg Jefferies S | 1.00 | 2.50 |
| □ S38 Bill Pulsipher S | 1.00 | 2.50 |
| □ S41 Shawn Green S | 1.00 | 2.50 |
| □ S43 Jim Abbott S | 1.50 | 4.00 |
| □ S46 Roger Clemens S | 5.00 | 12.00 |
| □ S52 Rondell White S | 1.00 | 2.50 |
| □ S54 Dennis Eckersley S | 1.00 | 2.50 |
| □ S59 Hideo Nomo S | 2.50 | 6.00 |
| □ S60 Gary Sheffield S | 1.00 | 2.50 |
| □ S62 Will Clark S | 1.50 | 4.00 |

| □ S65 Bret Boone S | 1.00 | 2.50 |
|---|---|---|
| □ S68 Rafael Palmeiro S | 1.50 | 4.00 |
| □ S69 Carlos Baerga S | 1.00 | 2.50 |
| □ S72 Tom Glavine S | 1.50 | 4.00 |
| □ S73 Garret Anderson S | 1.00 | 2.50 |
| □ S77 Randy Johnson S | 2.50 | 6.00 |
| □ S78 Jeff King S | 1.00 | 2.50 |
| □ S79 Kirby Puckett S | 2.50 | 6.00 |
| □ S84 Cecil Fielder S | 1.00 | 2.50 |
| □ S86 Reggie Sanders S | 1.00 | 2.50 |
| □ S88 Ryan Klesko S | 1.00 | 2.50 |
| □ S91 John Valentin S | 1.00 | 2.50 |
| □ S95 Manny Ramirez S | 1.50 | 4.00 |
| □ S99 Vinny Castilla S | 1.00 | 2.50 |
| □ S109 Carlos Perez S | 1.00 | 2.50 |
| □ S112 Craig Biggio S | 1.50 | 4.00 |
| □ S115 Juan Gonzalez S | 1.00 | 2.50 |
| □ S121 Ray Durham S | 1.00 | 2.50 |
| □ S127 C.J. Nitkowski S | 1.00 | 2.50 |
| □ S130 Raul Mondesi S | 1.00 | 2.50 |
| □ S142 Lee Smith S | 1.00 | 2.50 |
| □ S143 Joe Carter S | 1.00 | 2.50 |
| □ S151 Mo Vaughn S | 1.00 | 2.50 |
| □ S153 Frank Rodriguez S | 1.00 | 2.50 |
| □ S160 Steve Finley S | 1.00 | 2.50 |
| □ S161 Jeff Bagwell S | 1.50 | 4.00 |
| □ S165 Cal Ripken S | 8.00 | 20.00 |
| □ S168 Lyle Mouton S | 1.00 | 2.50 |
| □ S171 Sammy Sosa S | 2.50 | 6.00 |
| □ S174 John Franco S | 1.00 | 2.50 |
| □ S179 Greg Vaughn S | 1.00 | 2.50 |
| □ S180 Mark Wohlers S | 1.00 | 2.50 |
| □ S182 Paul O'Neill S | 1.50 | 4.00 |
| □ S188 Albert Belle S | 1.00 | 2.50 |
| □ S189 Mark Grace S | 1.50 | 4.00 |
| □ S211 Ernie Young S | 1.00 | 2.50 |
| □ S218 Fred McGriff S | 1.50 | 4.00 |
| □ S223 Kimera Bartee S | 1.00 | 2.50 |
| □ S229 Rickey Henderson S | 2.50 | 6.00 |
| □ S230 Sterling Hitchcock S | 1.00 | 2.50 |
| □ S231 Bernard Gilkey S | 1.00 | 2.50 |
| □ S234 Ryne Sandberg S | 4.00 | 10.00 |
| □ S235 Greg Maddux S | 5.00 | 12.00 |
| □ S239 Todd Stottlemyre S | 1.00 | 2.50 |
| □ S241 Jason Kendall S | 1.00 | 2.50 |
| □ S242 Paul O'Neill S | 1.50 | 4.00 |
| □ S256 Devon White S | 1.00 | 2.50 |
| □ S261 Chuck Knoblauch S | 1.00 | 2.50 |
| □ S263 Wally Joyner S | 1.00 | 2.50 |
| □ S272 Andy Fox S | 1.00 | 2.50 |
| □ S274 Sean Berry S | 1.00 | 2.50 |
| □ S277 Benito Santiago S | 1.00 | 2.50 |
| □ S284 Chad Mottola S | 1.00 | 2.50 |
| □ S289 Dante Bichette S | 1.00 | 2.50 |
| □ S291 Dwight Gooden S | 1.00 | 2.50 |
| □ S293 Kevin Mitchell S | 1.00 | 2.50 |
| □ S295 Russ Davis S | 1.00 | 2.50 |
| □ S296 Chan Ho Park S | 1.00 | 2.50 |
| □ S302 Larry Walker S | 1.00 | 2.50 |
| □ S305 Ken Griffey Jr. S | 4.00 | 10.00 |
| □ S313 Billy Wagner S | 1.00 | 2.50 |
| □ S317 Mike Grace S RC | 1.00 | 2.50 |
| □ S327 Kenny Lofton S | 1.00 | 2.50 |
| □ S328 Derek Bell S | 1.00 | 2.50 |
| □ S337 Gary Sheffield S | 1.00 | 2.50 |
| □ S341 Mark Grace S | 1.50 | 4.00 |
| □ S345 Andres Galarraga S | 1.00 | 2.50 |
| □ S346 Brady Anderson S | 1.00 | 2.50 |
| □ S350 Derek Jeter S | 5.00 | 12.00 |
| □ S353 Jay Buhner S | 1.00 | 2.50 |
| □ S357 Tino Martinez S | 1.50 | 4.00 |

**1997 Finest**

|  |  | | |
|---|------|---|---|
| ❑ | COMP.BRONZE SER.1 (100) | 12.50 | 30.00 |
| ❑ | COMP.BRONZE SER.2 (100) | 12.50 | 30.00 |
| ❑ | COM.BRON.(1-100/176-275) | .20 | .50 |
| ❑ | COMP.SILVER SER.1 (50) | | |
| ❑ | COMP.SILVER SER.2 (50) | | |
| ❑ | COM.SILV.(101-150/276-325) | .75 | 2.00 |
| ❑ | COMP.GOLD SER.1 (25) | | |
| ❑ | COMP.GOLD SER.2 (25) | | |
| ❑ | COM.GOLD (151-175/326-350) | 2.00 | 5.00 |
| ❑ | BICHETTE/JETER BOTH NUMBERED 155 | | |
| ❑ | BICHETTE UER SHOULD BE NUMBER 5 | | |
| ❑ 1 | Barry Bonds B | 1.25 | 3.00 |
| ❑ 2 | Ryne Sandberg B | .75 | 2.00 |
| ❑ 3 | Brian Jordan B | .20 | .50 |
| ❑ 4 | Rocky Coppinger B | .20 | .50 |
| ❑ 5 | Dante Bichette B UER 15 | .20 | .50 |
| ❑ 6 | Al Martin B | .20 | .50 |
| ❑ 7 | Charles Nagy B | .20 | .50 |
| ❑ 8 | Otis Nixon B | .20 | .50 |
| ❑ 9 | Mark Johnson B | .20 | .50 |
| ❑ 10 | Jeff Bagwell B | .30 | .75 |
| ❑ 11 | Ken Hill B | .20 | .50 |
| ❑ 12 | Willie Adams B | .20 | .50 |
| ❑ 13 | Raul Mondesi B | .20 | .50 |
| ❑ 14 | Reggie Sanders B | .20 | .50 |
| ❑ 15 | Derek Jeter B | 1.25 | 3.00 |
| ❑ 16 | Jermaine Dye B | .20 | .50 |
| ❑ 17 | Edgar Renteria B | .20 | .50 |
| ❑ 18 | Travis Fryman B | .20 | .50 |
| ❑ 19 | Roberto Hernandez B | .20 | .50 |
| ❑ 20 | Sammy Sosa B | .50 | 1.25 |
| ❑ 21 | Garret Anderson B | .20 | .50 |
| ❑ 22 | Rey Ordonez B | .20 | .50 |
| ❑ 23 | Glenallen Hill B | .20 | .50 |
| ❑ 24 | Dave Nilsson B | .20 | .50 |
| ❑ 25 | Kevin Brown B | .20 | .50 |
| ❑ 26 | Brian McRae B | .20 | .50 |
| ❑ 27 | Joey Hamilton B | .20 | .50 |
| ❑ 28 | Jamey Wright B | .20 | .50 |
| ❑ 29 | Frank Thomas B | .50 | 1.25 |
| ❑ 30 | Mark McGwire B | 1.25 | 3.00 |
| ❑ 31 | Ramon Martinez B | .20 | .50 |
| ❑ 32 | Jaime Bluma B | .20 | .50 |
| ❑ 33 | Frank Rodriguez B | .20 | .50 |
| ❑ 34 | Andy Benes B | .20 | .50 |
| ❑ 35 | Jay Buhner B | .20 | .50 |
| ❑ 36 | Justin Thompson B | .20 | .50 |
| ❑ 37 | Darin Erstad B | .20 | .50 |
| ❑ 38 | Gregg Jefferies B | .20 | .50 |
| ❑ 39 | Jeff D'Amico B | .20 | .50 |
| ❑ 40 | Pedro Martinez B | .30 | .75 |
| ❑ 41 | Nomar Garciaparra B | .75 | 2.00 |
| ❑ 42 | Jose Valentin B | .20 | .50 |
| ❑ 43 | Pat Hentgen B | .20 | .50 |
| ❑ 44 | Will Clark B | .30 | .75 |
| ❑ 45 | Bernie Williams B | .30 | .75 |
| ❑ 46 | Luis Castillo B | .20 | .50 |
| ❑ 47 | B.J. Surhoff B | .20 | .50 |
| ❑ 48 | Greg Gagne B | .20 | .50 |
| ❑ 49 | Pete Schourek B | .20 | .50 |
| ❑ 50 | Mike Piazza B | .75 | 2.00 |
| ❑ 51 | Dwight Gooden B | .20 | .50 |
| ❑ 52 | Javy Lopez B | .20 | .50 |
| ❑ 53 | Chuck Finley B | .20 | .50 |
| ❑ 54 | James Baldwin B | .20 | .50 |
| ❑ 55 | Jack McDowell B | .20 | .50 |
| ❑ 56 | Royce Clayton B | .20 | .50 |
| ❑ 57 | Carlos Delgado B | .20 | .50 |
| ❑ 58 | Neifi Perez B | .20 | .50 |
| ❑ 59 | Eddie Taubensee B | .20 | .50 |
| ❑ 60 | Rafael Palmeiro B | .30 | .75 |
| ❑ 61 | Marty Cordova B | .20 | .50 |
| ❑ 62 | Wade Boggs B | .30 | .75 |
| ❑ 63 | Rickey Henderson B | .50 | 1.25 |
| ❑ 64 | Mike Hampton B | .20 | .50 |
| ❑ 65 | Troy Percival B | .20 | .50 |
| ❑ 66 | Barry Larkin B | .30 | .75 |
| ❑ 67 | Jermaine Allensworth B | .20 | .50 |
| ❑ 68 | Mark Clark B | .20 | .50 |
| ❑ 69 | Mike Lansing B | .20 | .50 |
| ❑ 70 | Mark Grudzielanek B | .20 | .50 |
| ❑ 71 | Todd Stottlemyre B | .20 | .50 |
| ❑ 72 | Juan Guzman B | .20 | .50 |
| ❑ 73 | John Burkett B | .20 | .50 |
| ❑ 74 | Wilson Alvarez B | .20 | .50 |
| ❑ 75 | Ellis Burks B | .20 | .50 |
| ❑ 76 | Bobby Higginson B | .20 | .50 |
| ❑ 77 | Ricky Bottalico B | .20 | .50 |
| ❑ 78 | Omar Vizquel B | .30 | .75 |
| ❑ 79 | Paul Sorrento B | .20 | .50 |
| ❑ 80 | Denny Neagle B | .20 | .50 |
| ❑ 81 | Roger Pavlik B | .20 | .50 |
| ❑ 82 | Mike Lieberthal B | .20 | .50 |
| ❑ 83 | Devon White B | .20 | .50 |
| ❑ 84 | John Olerud B | .20 | .50 |
| ❑ 85 | Kevin Appier B | .20 | .50 |
| ❑ 86 | Joe Girardi B | .20 | .50 |
| ❑ 87 | Paul O'Neill B | .30 | .75 |
| ❑ 88 | Mike Sweeney B | .20 | .50 |
| ❑ 89 | John Smiley B | .20 | .50 |
| ❑ 90 | Ivan Rodriguez B | .30 | .75 |
| ❑ 91 | Randy Myers B | .20 | .50 |
| ❑ 92 | Bip Roberts B | .20 | .50 |
| ❑ 93 | Jose Mesa B | .20 | .50 |
| ❑ 94 | Paul Wilson B | .20 | .50 |
| ❑ 95 | Mike Mussina B | .30 | .75 |
| ❑ 96 | Ben McDonald B | .20 | .50 |
| ❑ 97 | John Mabry B | .20 | .50 |
| ❑ 98 | Tom Goodwin B | .20 | .50 |
| ❑ 99 | Edgar Martinez B | .30 | .75 |
| ❑ 100 | Andruw Jones B | .30 | .75 |
| ❑ 101 | Jose Canseco B | 1.25 | 3.00 |
| ❑ 102 | Billy Wagner S | .75 | 2.00 |
| ❑ 103 | Dante Bichette S | .75 | 2.00 |
| ❑ 104 | Curt Schilling S | .75 | 2.00 |
| ❑ 105 | Dean Palmer S | .75 | 2.00 |
| ❑ 106 | Larry Walker S | .75 | 2.00 |
| ❑ 107 | Bernie Williams S | 1.25 | 3.00 |
| ❑ 108 | Chipper Jones S | 2.00 | 5.00 |
| ❑ 109 | Gary Sheffield S | .75 | 2.00 |
| ❑ 110 | Randy Johnson S | 2.00 | 5.00 |
| ❑ 111 | Roberto Alomar S | 1.25 | 3.00 |
| ❑ 112 | Todd Walker S | .75 | 2.00 |
| ❑ 113 | Sandy Alomar Jr. S | .75 | 2.00 |
| ❑ 114 | John Jaha S | .75 | 2.00 |
| ❑ 115 | Ken Caminiti S | .75 | 2.00 |
| ❑ 116 | Ryan Klesko S | .75 | 2.00 |
| ❑ 117 | Mariano Rivera S | 2.00 | 5.00 |
| ❑ 118 | Jason Giambi S | .75 | 2.00 |
| ❑ 119 | Lance Johnson S | .75 | 2.00 |
| ❑ 120 | Robin Ventura S | .75 | 2.00 |
| ❑ 121 | Todd Hollandsworth S | .75 | 2.00 |
| ❑ 122 | Johnny Damon S | 1.25 | 3.00 |
| ❑ 123 | William VanLandingham S | .75 | 2.00 |
| ❑ 124 | Jason Kendall S | .75 | 2.00 |
| ❑ 125 | Vinny Castilla S | .75 | 2.00 |
| ❑ 126 | Harold Baines S | .75 | 2.00 |
| ❑ 127 | Joe Carter S | .75 | 2.00 |
| ❑ 128 | Craig Biggio S | 1.25 | 3.00 |
| ❑ 129 | Tony Clark S | .75 | 2.00 |
| ❑ 130 | Ron Gant S | .75 | 2.00 |
| ❑ 131 | David Segui S | .75 | 2.00 |
| ❑ 132 | Steve Trachsel S | .75 | 2.00 |
| ❑ 133 | Scott Rolen S | 1.25 | 3.00 |
| ❑ 134 | Mike Stanley S | .75 | 2.00 |
| ❑ 135 | Cal Ripken S | 6.00 | 15.00 |
| ❑ 136 | John Smoltz S | 1.25 | 3.00 |
| ❑ 137 | Bobby Jones S | .75 | 2.00 |
| ❑ 138 | Manny Ramirez S | 1.25 | 3.00 |
| ❑ 139 | Ken Griffey Jr. S | 3.00 | 8.00 |
| ❑ 140 | Chuck Knoblauch S | .75 | 2.00 |
| ❑ 141 | Mark Grace S | 1.25 | 3.00 |
| ❑ 142 | Chris Snopek S | .75 | 2.00 |
| ❑ 143 | Hideo Nomo S | 2.00 | 5.00 |
| ❑ 144 | Tim Salmon S | 1.25 | 3.00 |
| ❑ 145 | David Cone S | .75 | 2.00 |
| ❑ 146 | Eric Young S | .75 | 2.00 |
| ❑ 147 | Jeff Brantley S | .75 | 2.00 |
| ❑ 148 | Jim Thome S | 1.25 | 3.00 |
| ❑ 149 | Trevor Hoffman S | .75 | 2.00 |
| ❑ 150 | Juan Gonzalez S | .75 | 2.00 |
| ❑ 151 | Mike Piazza G | 8.00 | 20.00 |
| ❑ 152 | Ivan Rodriguez G | 3.00 | 8.00 |
| ❑ 153 | Mo Vaughn G | 2.00 | 5.00 |
| ❑ 154 | Brady Anderson G | 2.00 | 5.00 |
| ❑ 155 | Mark McGwire G | 12.50 | 30.00 |
| ❑ 156 | Rafael Palmeiro G | 3.00 | 8.00 |
| ❑ 157 | Barry Larkin G | 3.00 | 8.00 |
| ❑ 158 | Greg Maddux G | 8.00 | 20.00 |
| ❑ 159 | Jeff Bagwell G | 3.00 | 8.00 |
| ❑ 160 | Frank Thomas G | 8.00 | 20.00 |
| ❑ 161 | Ken Caminiti G | 2.00 | 5.00 |
| ❑ 162 | Andruw Jones G | 3.00 | 8.00 |
| ❑ 163 | Dennis Eckersley G | 2.00 | 5.00 |
| ❑ 164 | Jeff Conine G | 2.00 | 5.00 |
| ❑ 165 | Jim Edmonds G | 2.00 | 5.00 |
| ❑ 166 | Derek Jeter G | 12.50 | 30.00 |
| ❑ 167 | Vladimir Guerrero G | 5.00 | 12.00 |
| ❑ 168 | Sammy Sosa G | 5.00 | 12.00 |
| ❑ 169 | Tony Gwynn G | 6.00 | 15.00 |
| ❑ 170 | Andres Galarraga G | 2.00 | 5.00 |
| ❑ 171 | Todd Hundley G | 2.00 | 5.00 |
| ❑ 172 | Jay Buhner G | 2.00 | 5.00 |
| ❑ 173 | Paul Molitor G | 2.00 | 5.00 |
| ❑ 174 | Kenny Lofton G | 2.00 | 5.00 |
| ❑ 175 | Barry Bonds G | 12.50 | 30.00 |
| ❑ 176 | Gary Sheffield B | .20 | .50 |
| ❑ 177 | Dmitri Young B | .20 | .50 |
| ❑ 178 | Jay Bell B | .20 | .50 |
| ❑ 179 | David Wells B | .20 | .50 |
| ❑ 180 | Walt Weiss B | .20 | .50 |
| ❑ 181 | Paul Molitor B | .20 | .50 |
| ❑ 182 | Jose Guillen B | .20 | .50 |
| ❑ 183 | Al Leiter B | .20 | .50 |
| ❑ 184 | Mike Fetters B | .20 | .50 |
| ❑ 185 | Mark Langston B | .20 | .50 |
| ❑ 186 | Fred McGriff B | .30 | .75 |
| ❑ 187 | Darrin Fletcher B | .20 | .50 |
| ❑ 188 | Brant Brown B | .20 | .50 |
| ❑ 189 | Geronimo Berroa B | .20 | .50 |
| ❑ 190 | Jim Thome B | .30 | .75 |
| ❑ 191 | Jose Vizcaino B | .20 | .50 |
| ❑ 192 | Andy Ashby B | .20 | .50 |
| ❑ 193 | Rusty Greer B | .20 | .50 |
| ❑ 194 | Brian Hunter B | .20 | .50 |
| ❑ 195 | Chris Hoiles B | .20 | .50 |
| ❑ 196 | Orlando Merced B | .20 | .50 |
| ❑ 197 | Brett Butler B | .20 | .50 |
| ❑ 198 | Derek Bell B | .20 | .50 |
| ❑ 199 | Bobby Bonilla B | .20 | .50 |
| ❑ 200 | Alex Ochoa B | .20 | .50 |
| ❑ 201 | Wally Joyner B | .20 | .50 |
| ❑ 202 | Mo Vaughn B | .20 | .50 |
| ❑ 203 | Doug Drabek B | .20 | .50 |
| ❑ 204 | Tino Martinez B | .30 | .75 |
| ❑ 205 | Roberto Alomar B | .30 | .75 |
| ❑ 206 | Brian Giles B RC | 1.25 | 3.00 |
| ❑ 207 | Todd Worrell B | .20 | .50 |
| ❑ 208 | Alan Benes B | .20 | .50 |
| ❑ 209 | Jim Leyritz B | .20 | .50 |
| ❑ 210 | Darryl Hamilton B | .20 | .50 |
| ❑ 211 | Jimmy Key B | .20 | .50 |
| ❑ 212 | Juan Gonzalez B | .20 | .50 |
| ❑ 213 | Vinny Castilla B | .20 | .50 |
| ❑ 214 | Chuck Knoblauch B | .20 | .50 |
| ❑ 215 | Tony Phillips B | .20 | .50 |
| ❑ 216 | Jeff Cirillo B | .20 | .50 |
| ❑ 217 | Carlos Garcia B | .20 | .50 |
| ❑ 218 | Brooks Kieschnick B | .20 | .50 |
| ❑ 219 | Marquis Grissom B | .20 | .50 |
| ❑ 220 | Dan Wilson B | .20 | .50 |
| ❑ 221 | Greg Vaughn B | .20 | .50 |
| ❑ 222 | John Wetteland B | .20 | .50 |
| ❑ 223 | Andres Galarraga B | .20 | .50 |
| ❑ 224 | Ozzie Guillen B | .20 | .50 |
| ❑ 225 | Kevin Elster B | .20 | .50 |
| ❑ 226 | Bernard Gilkey B | .20 | .50 |
| ❑ 227 | Mike Macfarlane B | .20 | .50 |
| ❑ 228 | Heathcliff Slocumb B | .20 | .50 |
| ❑ 229 | Wendell Magee Jr. B | .20 | .50 |
| ❑ 230 | Carlos Baerga B | .20 | .50 |
| ❑ 231 | Kevin Seitzer B | .20 | .50 |
| ❑ 232 | Henry Rodriguez B | .20 | .50 |
| ❑ 233 | Roger Clemens B | 1.00 | 2.50 |
| ❑ 234 | Mark Wohlers B | .20 | .50 |
| ❑ 235 | Eddie Murray B | .50 | 1.25 |
| ❑ 236 | Todd Zeile B | .20 | .50 |
| ❑ 237 | J.T. Snow B | .20 | .50 |
| ❑ 238 | Ken Griffey Jr. B | .75 | 2.00 |
| ❑ 239 | Sterling Hitchcock B | .20 | .50 |
| ❑ 240 | Albert Belle B | .20 | .50 |
| ❑ 241 | Terry Steinbach B | .20 | .50 |
| ❑ 242 | Robb Nen B | .20 | .50 |
| ❑ 243 | Mark McLemore B | .20 | .50 |
| ❑ 244 | Jeff King B | .20 | .50 |
| ❑ 245 | Tony Clark B | .20 | .50 |
| ❑ 246 | Tim Salmon B | .30 | .75 |
| ❑ 247 | Benito Santiago B | .20 | .50 |
| ❑ 248 | Robin Ventura B | .20 | .50 |
| ❑ 249 | Bobba Trammell B RC | .20 | .50 |
| ❑ 250 | Chili Davis B | .20 | .50 |
| ❑ 251 | John Valentin B | .20 | .50 |
| ❑ 252 | Cal Ripken B | 1.50 | 4.00 |
| ❑ 253 | Matt Williams B | .20 | .50 |

|  |  | | |
|---|---|---|---|
| ☐ 254 | Jeff Kent B | .20 | .50 |
| ☐ 255 | Eric Karros B | .20 | .50 |
| ☐ 256 | Ray Lankford B | .20 | .50 |
| ☐ 257 | Ed Sprague B | .20 | .50 |
| ☐ 258 | Shane Reynolds B | .20 | .50 |
| ☐ 259 | Jaime Navarro B | .20 | .50 |
| ☐ 260 | Eric Davis B | .20 | .50 |
| ☐ 261 | Orel Hershiser B | .20 | .50 |
| ☐ 262 | Mark Grace B | .30 | .75 |
| ☐ 263 | Rod Beck B | .20 | .50 |
| ☐ 264 | Ismael Valdes B | .20 | .50 |
| ☐ 265 | Manny Ramirez B | .30 | .75 |
| ☐ 266 | Ken Caminiti B | .20 | .50 |
| ☐ 267 | Tim Naehring B | .20 | .50 |
| ☐ 268 | Jose Rosado B | .20 | .50 |
| ☐ 269 | Greg Colbrunn B | .20 | .50 |
| ☐ 270 | Dean Palmer B | .20 | .50 |
| ☐ 271 | David Justice B | .20 | .50 |
| ☐ 272 | Scott Spiezio B | .20 | .50 |
| ☐ 273 | Chipper Jones B | .50 | 1.25 |
| ☐ 274 | Mel Rojas B | .20 | .50 |
| ☐ 275 | Bartolo Colon B | .20 | .50 |
| ☐ 276 | Darin Erstad S | .75 | 2.00 |
| ☐ 277 | Sammy Sosa S | 2.00 | 5.00 |
| ☐ 278 | Rafael Palmeiro S | 1.25 | 3.00 |
| ☐ 279 | Frank Thomas S | 2.00 | 5.00 |
| ☐ 280 | Ruben Rivera S | .75 | 2.00 |
| ☐ 281 | Hal Morris S | .75 | 2.00 |
| ☐ 282 | Jay Buhner S | .75 | 2.00 |
| ☐ 283 | Kenny Lofton S | .75 | 2.00 |
| ☐ 284 | Jose Canseco S | 1.25 | 3.00 |
| ☐ 285 | Alex Fernandez S | .75 | 2.00 |
| ☐ 286 | Todd Helton S | 2.00 | 5.00 |
| ☐ 287 | Andy Pettitte S | 1.25 | 3.00 |
| ☐ 288 | John Franco S | .75 | 2.00 |
| ☐ 289 | Ivan Rodriguez S | 1.25 | 3.00 |
| ☐ 290 | Ellis Burks S | .75 | 2.00 |
| ☐ 291 | Julio Franco S | .75 | 2.00 |
| ☐ 292 | Mike Piazza S | 3.00 | 8.00 |
| ☐ 293 | Brian Jordan S | .75 | 2.00 |
| ☐ 294 | Greg Maddux S | 3.00 | 8.00 |
| ☐ 295 | Bob Abreu S | 1.25 | 3.00 |
| ☐ 296 | Rondell White S | .75 | 2.00 |
| ☐ 297 | Moises Alou S | .75 | 2.00 |
| ☐ 298 | Tony Gwynn S | 2.50 | 6.00 |
| ☐ 299 | Deion Sanders S | 1.25 | 3.00 |
| ☐ 300 | Jeff Montgomery S | .75 | 2.00 |
| ☐ 301 | Ray Durham S | .75 | 2.00 |
| ☐ 302 | John Wasdin S | .75 | 2.00 |
| ☐ 303 | Ryne Sandberg S | 3.00 | 8.00 |
| ☐ 304 | Delino DeShields S | .75 | 2.00 |
| ☐ 305 | Mark McGwire S | 5.00 | 12.00 |
| ☐ 306 | Andruw Jones S | 1.25 | 3.00 |
| ☐ 307 | Kevin Orie S | .75 | 2.00 |
| ☐ 308 | Matt Williams S | .75 | 2.00 |
| ☐ 309 | Karim Garcia S | .75 | 2.00 |
| ☐ 310 | Derek Jeter S | 5.00 | 12.00 |
| ☐ 311 | Mo Vaughn S | .75 | 2.00 |
| ☐ 312 | Brady Anderson S | .75 | 2.00 |
| ☐ 313 | Barry Bonds S | 5.00 | 12.00 |
| ☐ 314 | Steve Finley S | .75 | 2.00 |
| ☐ 315 | Vladimir Guerrero S | 2.00 | 5.00 |
| ☐ 316 | Matt Morris S | .75 | 2.00 |
| ☐ 317 | Tom Glavine S | 1.25 | 3.00 |
| ☐ 318 | Jeff Bagwell S | 1.25 | 3.00 |
| ☐ 319 | Albert Belle S | .75 | 2.00 |
| ☐ 320 | Hideki Irabu S RC | .75 | 2.00 |
| ☐ 321 | Andres Galarraga S | .75 | 2.00 |
| ☐ 322 | Cecil Fielder S | .75 | 2.00 |
| ☐ 323 | Barry Larkin S | 1.25 | 3.00 |
| ☐ 324 | Todd Hundley S | .75 | 2.00 |
| ☐ 325 | Fred McGriff S | 1.25 | 3.00 |
| ☐ 326 | Gary Sheffield S | 2.00 | 5.00 |
| ☐ 327 | Craig Biggio S | 3.00 | 8.00 |
| ☐ 328 | Raul Mondesi S | 2.00 | 5.00 |
| ☐ 329 | Edgar Martinez G | 3.00 | 8.00 |
| ☐ 330 | Chipper Jones G | 5.00 | 12.00 |
| ☐ 331 | Bernie Williams G | 3.00 | 8.00 |
| ☐ 332 | Juan Gonzalez G | 2.00 | 5.00 |
| ☐ 333 | Ron Gant G | 2.00 | 5.00 |
| ☐ 334 | Cal Ripken G | 15.00 | 40.00 |
| ☐ 335 | Larry Walker G | 2.00 | 5.00 |
| ☐ 336 | Matt Williams G | 2.00 | 5.00 |
| ☐ 337 | Jose Cruz Jr. G RC | 2.00 | 5.00 |
| ☐ 338 | Joe Carter G | 2.00 | 5.00 |
| ☐ 339 | Wilton Guerrero G | 2.00 | 5.00 |
| ☐ 340 | Cecil Fielder G | 2.00 | 5.00 |
| ☐ 341 | Todd Walker G | 2.00 | 5.00 |
| ☐ 342 | Ken Griffey Jr. G | 8.00 | 20.00 |
| ☐ 343 | Ryan Klesko G | 2.00 | 5.00 |
| ☐ 344 | Roger Clemens G | 10.00 | 25.00 |
| ☐ 345 | Hideo Nomo G | 5.00 | 12.00 |
| ☐ 346 | Dante Bichette G | 2.00 | 5.00 |
| ☐ 347 | Albert Belle G | 2.00 | 5.00 |
| ☐ 348 | Randy Johnson G | 5.00 | 12.00 |
| ☐ 349 | Manny Ramirez G | 3.00 | 8.00 |
| ☐ 350 | John Smoltz G | 3.00 | 8.00 |

**1998 Finest**

| | | | |
|---|---|---|---|
| ☐ COMPLETE SET (275) | | 20.00 | 50.00 |
| ☐ COMPLETE SERIES 1 (150) | | 10.00 | 25.00 |
| ☐ COMPLETE SERIES 2 (125) | | 10.00 | 25.00 |
| ☐ 1 | Larry Walker | .15 | .40 |
| ☐ 2 | Andruw Jones | .25 | .60 |
| ☐ 3 | Ramon Martinez | .08 | .25 |
| ☐ 4 | Geronimo Berroa | .08 | .25 |
| ☐ 5 | David Justice | .15 | .40 |
| ☐ 6 | Rusty Greer | .15 | .40 |
| ☐ 7 | Chad Ogea | .08 | .25 |
| ☐ 8 | Tom Goodwin | .08 | .25 |
| ☐ 9 | Tino Martinez | .25 | .60 |
| ☐ 10 | Jose Guillen | .15 | .40 |
| ☐ 11 | Jeffrey Hammonds | .08 | .25 |
| ☐ 12 | Brian McRae | .08 | .25 |
| ☐ 13 | Jeremi Gonzalez | .08 | .25 |
| ☐ 14 | Craig Counsell | .08 | .25 |
| ☐ 15 | Mike Piazza | .60 | 1.50 |
| ☐ 16 | Greg Maddux | .60 | 1.50 |
| ☐ 17 | Todd Greene | .15 | .40 |
| ☐ 18 | Rondell White | .08 | .25 |
| ☐ 19 | Kirk Rueter | .08 | .25 |
| ☐ 20 | Tony Clark | .08 | .25 |
| ☐ 21 | Brad Radke | .15 | .40 |
| ☐ 22 | Jaret Wright | .08 | .25 |
| ☐ 23 | Carlos Delgado | .15 | .40 |
| ☐ 24 | Dustin Hermanson | .08 | .25 |
| ☐ 25 | Gary Sheffield | .15 | .40 |
| ☐ 26 | Jose Canseco | .25 | .60 |
| ☐ 27 | Kevin Young | .08 | .25 |
| ☐ 28 | David Wells | .15 | .40 |
| ☐ 29 | Mariano Rivera | .40 | 1.00 |
| ☐ 30 | Reggie Sanders | .15 | .40 |
| ☐ 31 | Mike Cameron | .08 | .25 |
| ☐ 32 | Bobby Witt | .08 | .25 |
| ☐ 33 | Kevin Orie | .08 | .25 |
| ☐ 34 | Royce Clayton | .08 | .25 |
| ☐ 35 | Edgar Martinez | .25 | .60 |
| ☐ 36 | Neifi Perez | .08 | .25 |
| ☐ 37 | Kevin Appier | .15 | .40 |
| ☐ 38 | Darryl Hamilton | .08 | .25 |
| ☐ 39 | Michael Tucker | .08 | .25 |
| ☐ 40 | Roger Clemens | .75 | 2.00 |
| ☐ 41 | Carl Everett | .15 | .40 |
| ☐ 42 | Mike Sweeney | .15 | .40 |
| ☐ 43 | Pat Meares | .08 | .25 |
| ☐ 44 | Brian Giles | .15 | .40 |
| ☐ 45 | Matt Morris | .15 | .40 |
| ☐ 46 | Jason Dickson | .08 | .25 |
| ☐ 47 | Rich Loiselle RC | .15 | .40 |
| ☐ 48 | Joe Girardi | .08 | .25 |
| ☐ 49 | Steve Trachsel | .08 | .25 |
| ☐ 50 | Ben Grieve | .40 | 1.00 |
| ☐ 51 | Brian Johnson | .08 | .25 |
| ☐ 52 | Hideki Irabu | .25 | .60 |
| ☐ 53 | J.T. Snow | .15 | .40 |
| ☐ 54 | Mike Hampton | .08 | .25 |
| ☐ 55 | Dave Nilsson | .08 | .25 |
| ☐ 56 | Alex Fernandez | .08 | .25 |
| ☐ 57 | Brett Tomko | .08 | .25 |
| ☐ 58 | Wally Joyner | .15 | .40 |
| ☐ 59 | Kelvim Escobar | .08 | .25 |
| ☐ 60 | Roberto Alomar | .25 | .60 |

|  |  | | |
|---|---|---|---|
| ☐ 61 | Todd Jones | .08 | .25 |
| ☐ 62 | Paul O'Neill | .25 | .60 |
| ☐ 63 | Jamie Moyer | .15 | .40 |
| ☐ 64 | Mark Wohlers | .08 | .25 |
| ☐ 65 | Jose Cruz Jr. | .08 | .25 |
| ☐ 66 | Troy Percival | .15 | .40 |
| ☐ 67 | Rick Reed | .08 | .25 |
| ☐ 68 | Will Clark | .25 | .60 |
| ☐ 69 | Jamey Wright | .08 | .25 |
| ☐ 70 | Mike Mussina | .25 | .60 |
| ☐ 71 | David Cone | .15 | .40 |
| ☐ 72 | Ryan Klesko | .15 | .40 |
| ☐ 73 | Scott Hatteberg | .08 | .25 |
| ☐ 74 | James Baldwin | .08 | .25 |
| ☐ 75 | Tony Womack | .08 | .25 |
| ☐ 76 | Carlos Perez | .08 | .25 |
| ☐ 77 | Charles Nagy | .15 | .40 |
| ☐ 78 | Jeromy Burnitz | .15 | .40 |
| ☐ 79 | Shane Reynolds | .08 | .25 |
| ☐ 80 | Cliff Floyd | .15 | .40 |
| ☐ 81 | Jason Kendall | .08 | .25 |
| ☐ 82 | Chad Curtis | .08 | .25 |
| ☐ 83 | Matt Karchner | .08 | .25 |
| ☐ 84 | Ricky Bottalico | .08 | .25 |
| ☐ 85 | Sammy Sosa | .40 | 1.00 |
| ☐ 86 | Javy Lopez | .15 | .40 |
| ☐ 87 | Jeff Kent | .15 | .40 |
| ☐ 88 | Shawn Green | .15 | .40 |
| ☐ 89 | Joey Cora | .08 | .25 |
| ☐ 90 | Tony Gwynn | .50 | 1.25 |
| ☐ 91 | Bob Tewksbury | .08 | .25 |
| ☐ 92 | Derek Jeter | 1.00 | 2.50 |
| ☐ 93 | Eric Davis | .15 | .40 |
| ☐ 94 | Jeff Fassero | .08 | .25 |
| ☐ 95 | Denny Neagle | .08 | .25 |
| ☐ 96 | Ismael Valdes | .08 | .25 |
| ☐ 97 | Tim Salmon | .25 | .60 |
| ☐ 98 | Mark Grudzielanek | .08 | .25 |
| ☐ 99 | Curt Schilling | .15 | .40 |
| ☐ 100 | Ken Griffey Jr. | .60 | 1.50 |
| ☐ 101 | Edgardo Alfonzo | .08 | .25 |
| ☐ 102 | Vinny Castilla | .15 | .40 |
| ☐ 103 | Jose Rosado | .08 | .25 |
| ☐ 104 | Scott Erickson | .08 | .25 |
| ☐ 105 | Alan Benes | .08 | .25 |
| ☐ 106 | Shannon Stewart | .15 | .40 |
| ☐ 107 | Delino DeShields | .08 | .25 |
| ☐ 108 | Mark Loretta | .08 | .25 |
| ☐ 109 | Todd Hundley | .08 | .25 |
| ☐ 110 | Chuck Knoblauch | .25 | .60 |
| ☐ 111 | Todd Helton | .25 | .60 |
| ☐ 112 | F.P. Santangelo | .08 | .25 |
| ☐ 113 | Jeff Cirillo | .08 | .25 |
| ☐ 114 | Omar Vizquel | .15 | .40 |
| ☐ 115 | John Valentin | .08 | .25 |
| ☐ 116 | Damion Easley | .08 | .25 |
| ☐ 117 | Matt Lawton | .08 | .25 |
| ☐ 118 | Jim Thome | .25 | .60 |
| ☐ 119 | Sandy Alomar Jr. | .08 | .25 |
| ☐ 120 | Albert Belle | .15 | .40 |
| ☐ 121 | Chris Stynes | .08 | .25 |
| ☐ 122 | Butch Huskey | .08 | .25 |
| ☐ 123 | Shawn Estes | .08 | .25 |
| ☐ 124 | Terry Adams | .08 | .25 |
| ☐ 125 | Ivan Rodriguez | .25 | .60 |
| ☐ 126 | Ron Gant | .15 | .40 |
| ☐ 127 | John Mabry | .08 | .25 |
| ☐ 128 | Jeff Shaw | .08 | .25 |
| ☐ 129 | Jeff Montgomery | .08 | .25 |
| ☐ 130 | Justin Thompson | .08 | .25 |
| ☐ 131 | Ivan Mesa | .08 | .25 |
| ☐ 132 | Ugueth Urbina | .08 | .25 |
| ☐ 133 | Scott Servais | .08 | .25 |
| ☐ 134 | Troy O'Leary | .08 | .25 |
| ☐ 135 | Cal Ripken | 1.25 | 3.00 |
| ☐ 136 | Quilvio Veras | .08 | .25 |
| ☐ 137 | Pedro Astacio | .08 | .25 |
| ☐ 138 | Willie Greene | .08 | .25 |
| ☐ 139 | Lance Johnson | .08 | .25 |
| ☐ 140 | Nomar Garciaparra | .60 | 1.50 |
| ☐ 141 | Jose Offerman | .08 | .25 |
| ☐ 142 | Scott Rolen | .25 | .60 |
| ☐ 143 | Derek Bell | .08 | .25 |
| ☐ 144 | Johnny Damon | .08 | .25 |
| ☐ 145 | Mark McGwire | 1.00 | 2.50 |
| ☐ 146 | Chan Ho Park | .15 | .40 |
| ☐ 147 | Edgar Renteria | .15 | .40 |
| ☐ 148 | Eric Young | .08 | .25 |

| | | |
|---|---|---|
| ☐ 149 Craig Biggio | .25 | .60 |
| ☐ 150 Checklist (1-150) | .08 | .25 |
| ☐ 151 Frank Thomas | .40 | 1.00 |
| ☐ 152 John Wetteland | .15 | .40 |
| ☐ 153 Mike Lansing | .08 | .25 |
| ☐ 154 Pedro Martinez | .25 | .60 |
| ☐ 155 Rico Brogna | .08 | .25 |
| ☐ 156 Kevin Brown | .25 | .60 |
| ☐ 157 Alex Rodriguez | .60 | 1.50 |
| ☐ 158 Wade Boggs | .25 | .60 |
| ☐ 159 Richard Hidalgo | .08 | .25 |
| ☐ 160 Mark Grace | .25 | .60 |
| ☐ 161 Jose Mesa | .08 | .25 |
| ☐ 162 John Olerud | .15 | .40 |
| ☐ 163 Tim Belcher | .08 | .25 |
| ☐ 164 Chuck Finley | .15 | .40 |
| ☐ 165 Brian Hunter | .08 | .25 |
| ☐ 166 Joe Carter | .15 | .40 |
| ☐ 167 Stan Javier | .08 | .25 |
| ☐ 168 Jay Bell | .15 | .40 |
| ☐ 169 Ray Lankford | .15 | .40 |
| ☐ 170 John Smoltz | .25 | .60 |
| ☐ 171 Ed Sprague | .08 | .25 |
| ☐ 172 Jason Giambi | .15 | .40 |
| ☐ 173 Todd Walker | .08 | .25 |
| ☐ 174 Paul Konerko | .15 | .40 |
| ☐ 175 Rey Ordonez | .15 | .40 |
| ☐ 176 Dante Bichette | .15 | .40 |
| ☐ 177 Bernie Williams | .25 | .60 |
| ☐ 178 Jon Nunnally | .08 | .25 |
| ☐ 179 Rafael Palmeiro | .25 | .60 |
| ☐ 180 Jay Buhner | .15 | .40 |
| ☐ 181 Devon White | .08 | .25 |
| ☐ 182 Jeff D'Amico | .08 | .25 |
| ☐ 183 Walt Weiss | .08 | .25 |
| ☐ 184 Scott Spiezio | .08 | .25 |
| ☐ 185 Moises Alou | .15 | .40 |
| ☐ 186 Carlos Baerga | .08 | .25 |
| ☐ 187 Todd Zeile | .08 | .25 |
| ☐ 188 Gregg Jefferies | .08 | .25 |
| ☐ 189 Mo Vaughn | .25 | .60 |
| ☐ 190 Terry Steinbach | .08 | .25 |
| ☐ 191 Ray Durham | .15 | .40 |
| ☐ 192 Robin Ventura | .15 | .40 |
| ☐ 193 Jeff Reed | .08 | .25 |
| ☐ 194 Ken Caminiti | .15 | .40 |
| ☐ 195 Eric Karros | .15 | .40 |
| ☐ 196 Wilson Alvarez | .08 | .25 |
| ☐ 197 Gary Gaetti | .15 | .40 |
| ☐ 198 Andres Galarraga | .25 | .60 |
| ☐ 199 Alex Gonzalez | .08 | .25 |
| ☐ 200 Garret Anderson | .15 | .40 |
| ☐ 201 Andy Benes | .08 | .25 |
| ☐ 202 Harold Baines | .15 | .40 |
| ☐ 203 Ron Coomer | .08 | .25 |
| ☐ 204 Dean Palmer | .15 | .40 |
| ☐ 205 Reggie Jefferson | .08 | .25 |
| ☐ 206 John Burkett | .08 | .25 |
| ☐ 207 Jermaine Allensworth | .08 | .25 |
| ☐ 208 Bernard Gilkey | .15 | .40 |
| ☐ 209 Jeff Bagwell | .25 | .60 |
| ☐ 210 Kenny Lofton | .25 | .60 |
| ☐ 211 Bobby Jones | .08 | .25 |
| ☐ 212 Bartolo Colon | .15 | .40 |
| ☐ 213 Jim Edmonds | .15 | .40 |
| ☐ 214 Pat Hentgen | .08 | .25 |
| ☐ 215 Matt Williams | .15 | .40 |
| ☐ 216 Bob Abreu | .15 | .40 |
| ☐ 217 Jorge Posada | .25 | .60 |
| ☐ 218 Marty Cordova | .08 | .25 |
| ☐ 219 Ken Hill | .08 | .25 |
| ☐ 220 Steve Finley | .15 | .40 |
| ☐ 221 Jeff King | .08 | .25 |
| ☐ 222 Quinton McCracken | .08 | .25 |
| ☐ 223 Matt Stairs | .08 | .25 |
| ☐ 224 Darin Erstad | .15 | .40 |
| ☐ 225 Fred McGriff | .25 | .60 |
| ☐ 226 Marquis Grissom | .15 | .40 |
| ☐ 227 Doug Glanville | .08 | .25 |
| ☐ 228 Tom Glavine | .25 | .60 |
| ☐ 229 John Franco | .15 | .40 |
| ☐ 230 Darren Bragg | .08 | .25 |
| ☐ 231 Barry Larkin | .25 | .60 |
| ☐ 232 Trevor Hoffman | .15 | .40 |
| ☐ 233 Brady Anderson | .15 | .40 |
| ☐ 234 Al Martin | .08 | .25 |
| ☐ 235 B.J. Surhoff | .15 | .40 |
| ☐ 236 Ellis Burks | .15 | .40 |

| | | |
|---|---|---|
| ☐ 237 Randy Johnson | .40 | 1.00 |
| ☐ 238 Mark Clark | .08 | .25 |
| ☐ 239 Tony Saunders | .08 | .25 |
| ☐ 240 Hideo Nomo | .40 | 1.00 |
| ☐ 241 Brad Fullmer | .08 | .25 |
| ☐ 242 Chipper Jones | .40 | 1.00 |
| ☐ 243 Jose Valentin | .08 | .25 |
| ☐ 244 Manny Ramirez | .25 | .60 |
| ☐ 245 Derek Lee | .25 | .60 |
| ☐ 246 Jimmy Key | .15 | .40 |
| ☐ 247 Tim Naehring | .08 | .25 |
| ☐ 248 Bobby Higginson | .15 | .40 |
| ☐ 249 Charles Johnson | .15 | .40 |
| ☐ 250 Chili Davis | .15 | .40 |
| ☐ 251 Tom Gordon | .08 | .25 |
| ☐ 252 Mike Lieberthal | .15 | .40 |
| ☐ 253 Billy Wagner | .15 | .40 |
| ☐ 254 Juan Guzman | .08 | .25 |
| ☐ 255 Todd Stottlemyre | .15 | .40 |
| ☐ 256 Brian Jordan | .25 | .60 |
| ☐ 257 Barry Bonds | 1.00 | 2.50 |
| ☐ 258 Dan Wilson | .08 | .25 |
| ☐ 259 Paul Molitor | .15 | .40 |
| ☐ 260 Juan Gonzalez | .25 | .60 |
| ☐ 261 Francisco Cordova | .08 | .25 |
| ☐ 262 Cecil Fielder | .15 | .40 |
| ☐ 263 Travis Lee | .08 | .25 |
| ☐ 264 Kevin Tapani | .08 | .25 |
| ☐ 265 Raul Mondesi | .15 | .40 |
| ☐ 266 Travis Fryman | .15 | .40 |
| ☐ 267 Armando Benitez | .08 | .25 |
| ☐ 268 Pokey Reese | .08 | .25 |
| ☐ 269 Rick Aguilera | .08 | .25 |
| ☐ 270 Andy Pettitte | .25 | .60 |
| ☐ 271 Jose Vizcaino | .08 | .25 |
| ☐ 272 Kerry Wood | .20 | .50 |
| ☐ 273 Vladimir Guerrero | .40 | 1.00 |
| ☐ 274 John Smiley | .08 | .25 |
| ☐ 275 Checklist (151-275) | .08 | .25 |

## 1999 Finest

| | | |
|---|---|---|
| ☐ COMPLETE SET (300) | 30.00 | |
| ☐ COMPLETE SERIES 1 (150) | 15.00 | 40.00 |
| ☐ COMPLETE SERIES 2 (150) | 15.00 | 40.00 |
| ☐ COMP.SER.1 w/o SP's (100) | 6.00 | 15.00 |
| ☐ COMP.SER.2 w/o SP's (100) | 6.00 | 15.00 |
| ☐ COMMON (1-100/151-250) | .15 | .40 |
| ☐ COMMON (101-150/251-300) | .20 | .50 |
| ☐ 1 Darin Erstad | .15 | .40 |
| ☐ 2 Javy Lopez | .15 | .40 |
| ☐ 3 Vinny Castilla | .15 | .40 |
| ☐ 4 Jim Thome | .25 | .60 |
| ☐ 5 Tino Martinez | .25 | .60 |
| ☐ 6 Mark Grace | .25 | .60 |
| ☐ 7 Shawn Green | .15 | .40 |
| ☐ 8 Dustin Hermanson | .15 | .40 |
| ☐ 9 Kevin Young | .15 | .40 |
| ☐ 10 Tony Clark | .15 | .40 |
| ☐ 11 Scott Brosius | .15 | .40 |
| ☐ 12 Craig Biggio | .25 | .60 |
| ☐ 13 Brian McRae | .15 | .40 |
| ☐ 14 Chan Ho Park | .15 | .40 |
| ☐ 15 Manny Ramirez | .25 | .60 |
| ☐ 16 Chipper Jones | .40 | 1.00 |
| ☐ 17 Rico Brogna | .15 | .40 |
| ☐ 18 Quinton McCracken | .15 | .40 |
| ☐ 19 J.T. Snow | .15 | .40 |
| ☐ 20 Tony Gwynn | .50 | 1.25 |
| ☐ 21 Juan Guzman | .15 | .40 |
| ☐ 22 John Valentin | .15 | .40 |
| ☐ 23 Rick Helling | .15 | .40 |
| ☐ 24 Sandy Alomar Jr. | .15 | .40 |
| ☐ 25 Frank Thomas | .40 | 1.00 |
| ☐ 26 Jorge Posada | .25 | .60 |

| | | |
|---|---|---|
| ☐ 27 Dmitri Young | .15 | .40 |
| ☐ 28 Rick Reed | .15 | .40 |
| ☐ 29 Kevin Tapani | .15 | .40 |
| ☐ 30 Troy Glaus | .25 | .60 |
| ☐ 31 Kenny Rogers | .15 | .40 |
| ☐ 32 Jeromy Burnitz | .15 | .40 |
| ☐ 33 Mark Grudzielanek | .15 | .40 |
| ☐ 34 Mike Mussina | .25 | .60 |
| ☐ 35 Scott Rolen | .25 | .60 |
| ☐ 36 Neifi Perez | .15 | .40 |
| ☐ 37 Brad Radke | .15 | .40 |
| ☐ 38 Darryl Strawberry | .15 | .40 |
| ☐ 39 Robb Nen | .15 | .40 |
| ☐ 40 Moises Alou | .15 | .40 |
| ☐ 41 Eric Young | .15 | .40 |
| ☐ 42 Livan Hernandez | .15 | .40 |
| ☐ 43 John Wetteland | .15 | .40 |
| ☐ 44 Matt Lawton | .15 | .40 |
| ☐ 45 Ben Grieve | .25 | .60 |
| ☐ 46 Fernando Tatis | .15 | .40 |
| ☐ 47 Travis Fryman | .15 | .40 |
| ☐ 48 David Segui | .15 | .40 |
| ☐ 49 Bob Abreu | .15 | .40 |
| ☐ 50 Nomar Garciaparra | .60 | 1.50 |
| ☐ 51 Paul O'Neill | .25 | .60 |
| ☐ 52 Jeff King | .15 | .40 |
| ☐ 53 Francisco Cordova | .15 | .40 |
| ☐ 54 John Olerud | .15 | .40 |
| ☐ 55 Vladimir Guerrero | .40 | 1.00 |
| ☐ 56 Fernando Vina | .15 | .40 |
| ☐ 57 Shane Reynolds | .15 | .40 |
| ☐ 58 Chuck Finley | .15 | .40 |
| ☐ 59 Rondell White | .15 | .40 |
| ☐ 60 Greg Vaughn | .15 | .40 |
| ☐ 61 Ryan Minor | .15 | .40 |
| ☐ 62 Tom Gordon | .15 | .40 |
| ☐ 63 Damion Easley | .15 | .40 |
| ☐ 64 Ray Durham | .15 | .40 |
| ☐ 65 Orlando Hernandez | .15 | .40 |
| ☐ 66 Bartolo Colon | .15 | .40 |
| ☐ 67 Jaret Wright | .15 | .40 |
| ☐ 68 Royce Clayton | .15 | .40 |
| ☐ 69 Tim Salmon | .25 | .60 |
| ☐ 70 Mark McGwire | 1.00 | 2.50 |
| ☐ 71 Alex Gonzalez | .15 | .40 |
| ☐ 72 Tom Glavine | .25 | .60 |
| ☐ 73 David Justice | .15 | .40 |
| ☐ 74 Omar Vizquel | .15 | .40 |
| ☐ 75 Juan Gonzalez | .40 | 1.00 |
| ☐ 76 Bobby Higginson | .15 | .40 |
| ☐ 77 Todd Walker | .15 | .40 |
| ☐ 78 Dante Bichette | .15 | .40 |
| ☐ 79 Kevin Millwood | .15 | .40 |
| ☐ 80 Roger Clemens | .75 | 2.00 |
| ☐ 81 Kerry Wood | .15 | .40 |
| ☐ 82 Cal Ripken | 1.25 | 3.00 |
| ☐ 83 Jay Bell | .15 | .40 |
| ☐ 84 Barry Bonds | 1.00 | 2.50 |
| ☐ 85 Alex Rodriguez | .60 | 1.50 |
| ☐ 86 Doug Glanville | .15 | .40 |
| ☐ 87 Jason Kendall | .15 | .40 |
| ☐ 88 Sean Casey | .15 | .40 |
| ☐ 89 Aaron Sele | .15 | .40 |
| ☐ 90 Derek Jeter | 1.00 | 2.50 |
| ☐ 91 Andy Ashby | .15 | .40 |
| ☐ 92 Rusty Greer | .15 | .40 |
| ☐ 93 Rod Beck | .15 | .40 |
| ☐ 94 Matt Williams | .15 | .40 |
| ☐ 95 Mike Piazza | .60 | 1.50 |
| ☐ 96 Wally Joyner | .15 | .40 |
| ☐ 97 Barry Larkin | .25 | .60 |
| ☐ 98 Eric Milton | .15 | .40 |
| ☐ 99 Gary Sheffield | .15 | .40 |
| ☐ 100 Greg Maddux | .60 | 1.50 |
| ☐ 101 Ken Griffey Jr. GEM | 1.00 | 2.50 |
| ☐ 102 Frank Thomas GEM | .60 | 1.50 |
| ☐ 103 Nomar Garciaparra GEM | 1.00 | 2.50 |
| ☐ 104 Mark McGwire GEM | 1.50 | 4.00 |
| ☐ 105 Alex Rodriguez GEM | 1.00 | 2.50 |
| ☐ 106 Tony Gwynn GEM | .75 | 2.00 |
| ☐ 107 Juan Gonzalez GEM | .25 | .60 |
| ☐ 108 Jeff Bagwell GEM | .40 | 1.00 |
| ☐ 109 Sammy Sosa GEM | .60 | 1.50 |
| ☐ 110 Vladimir Guerrero GEM | .60 | 1.50 |
| ☐ 111 Roger Clemens GEM | 1.25 | 3.00 |
| ☐ 112 Barry Bonds GEM | 1.50 | 4.00 |
| ☐ 113 Darin Erstad GEM | .25 | .60 |
| ☐ 114 Mike Piazza GEM | 1.00 | 2.50 |

|  |  | | |
|---|------|---|---|
| ❑ 115 | Derek Jeter GEM | 1.50 | 4.00 |
| ❑ 116 | Chipper Jones GEM | .60 | 1.50 |
| ❑ 117 | Larry Walker GEM | .25 | .60 |
| ❑ 118 | Scott Rolen GEM | .40 | 1.00 |
| ❑ 119 | Cal Ripken GEM | 2.00 | 5.00 |
| ❑ 120 | Greg Maddux GEM | 1.00 | 2.50 |
| ❑ 121 | Troy Glaus SENS | .25 | .60 |
| ❑ 122 | Ben Grieve SENS | .20 | .50 |
| ❑ 123 | Ryan Minor SENS | .20 | .50 |
| ❑ 124 | Kerry Wood SENS | .25 | .60 |
| ❑ 125 | Travis Lee SENS | .25 | .60 |
| ❑ 126 | Adrian Beltre SENS | .25 | .60 |
| ❑ 127 | Brad Fullmer SENS | .25 | .60 |
| ❑ 128 | Aramis Ramirez SENS | .25 | .60 |
| ❑ 129 | Eric Chavez SENS | .25 | .60 |
| ❑ 130 | Todd Helton SENS | .40 | 1.00 |
| ❑ 131 | Pat Burrell RC | 1.25 | 3.00 |
| ❑ 132 | Ryan Mills RC | .20 | .50 |
| ❑ 133 | Austin Kearns RC | 1.25 | 3.00 |
| ❑ 134 | Josh McKinley RC | .20 | .50 |
| ❑ 135 | Adam Everett RC | .40 | 1.00 |
| ❑ 136 | Marlon Anderson | .20 | .50 |
| ❑ 137 | Bruce Chen | .20 | .50 |
| ❑ 138 | Matt Clement | .25 | .60 |
| ❑ 139 | Alex Gonzalez | .20 | .50 |
| ❑ 140 | Roy Halladay | .25 | .60 |
| ❑ 141 | Calvin Pickering | .20 | .50 |
| ❑ 142 | Randy Wolf | .20 | .50 |
| ❑ 143 | Ryan Anderson | .20 | .50 |
| ❑ 144 | Ruben Mateo | .25 | .60 |
| ❑ 145 | Alex Escobar RC | .25 | .60 |
| ❑ 146 | Jeremy Giambi | .20 | .50 |
| ❑ 147 | Lance Berkman | .25 | .60 |
| ❑ 148 | Michael Barrett | .20 | .50 |
| ❑ 149 | Preston Wilson | .25 | .60 |
| ❑ 150 | Gabe Kapler | .25 | .60 |
| ❑ 151 | Roger Clemens | .75 | 2.00 |
| ❑ 152 | Jay Buhner | .15 | .40 |
| ❑ 153 | Brad Fullmer | .15 | .40 |
| ❑ 154 | Ray Lankford | .15 | .40 |
| ❑ 155 | Jim Edmonds | .15 | .40 |
| ❑ 156 | Jason Giambi | .15 | .40 |
| ❑ 157 | Bret Boone | .15 | .40 |
| ❑ 158 | Jeff Cirillo | .15 | .40 |
| ❑ 159 | Rickey Henderson | .40 | 1.00 |
| ❑ 160 | Edgar Martinez | .15 | .40 |
| ❑ 161 | Ron Gant | .15 | .40 |
| ❑ 162 | Mark Kotsay | .15 | .40 |
| ❑ 163 | Trevor Hoffman | .15 | .40 |
| ❑ 164 | Jason Schmidt | .15 | .40 |
| ❑ 165 | Brett Tomko | .15 | .40 |
| ❑ 166 | David Ortiz | .40 | 1.00 |
| ❑ 167 | Dean Palmer | .15 | .40 |
| ❑ 168 | Hideki Irabu | .15 | .40 |
| ❑ 169 | Mike Cameron | .15 | .40 |
| ❑ 170 | Pedro Martinez | .25 | .60 |
| ❑ 171 | Tom Goodwin | .15 | .40 |
| ❑ 172 | Brian Hunter | .15 | .40 |
| ❑ 173 | Al Leiter | .15 | .40 |
| ❑ 174 | Charles Johnson | .15 | .40 |
| ❑ 175 | Curt Schilling | .15 | .40 |
| ❑ 176 | Robin Ventura | .15 | .40 |
| ❑ 177 | Travis Lee | .15 | .40 |
| ❑ 178 | Jeff Shaw | .15 | .40 |
| ❑ 179 | Ugueth Urbina | .15 | .40 |
| ❑ 180 | Roberto Alomar | .25 | .60 |
| ❑ 181 | Cliff Floyd | .15 | .40 |
| ❑ 182 | Adrian Beltre | .15 | .40 |
| ❑ 183 | Tony Womack | .15 | .40 |
| ❑ 184 | Brian Jordan | .15 | .40 |
| ❑ 185 | Randy Johnson | .40 | 1.00 |
| ❑ 186 | Mickey Morandini | .15 | .40 |
| ❑ 187 | Todd Hundley | .15 | .40 |
| ❑ 188 | Jose Valentin | .15 | .40 |
| ❑ 189 | Eric Davis | .15 | .40 |
| ❑ 190 | Ken Caminiti | .15 | .40 |
| ❑ 191 | David Wells | .15 | .40 |
| ❑ 192 | Ryan Klesko | .15 | .40 |
| ❑ 193 | Garret Anderson | .15 | .40 |
| ❑ 194 | Eric Karros | .15 | .40 |
| ❑ 195 | Ivan Rodriguez | .25 | .60 |
| ❑ 196 | Aramis Ramirez | .15 | .40 |
| ❑ 197 | Mike Lieberthal | .15 | .40 |
| ❑ 198 | Will Clark | .25 | .60 |
| ❑ 199 | Rey Ordonez | .15 | .40 |
| ❑ 200 | Ken Griffey Jr. | .60 | 1.50 |
| ❑ 201 | Jose Guillen | .15 | .40 |
| ❑ 202 | Scott Erickson | .15 | .40 |
| ❑ 203 | Paul Konerko | .15 | .40 |
| ❑ 204 | Johnny Damon | .25 | .60 |
| ❑ 205 | Larry Walker | .15 | .40 |
| ❑ 206 | Denny Neagle | .15 | .40 |
| ❑ 207 | Jose Offerman | .15 | .40 |
| ❑ 208 | Andy Pettitte | .25 | .60 |
| ❑ 209 | Bobby Jones | .15 | .40 |
| ❑ 210 | Kevin Brown | .25 | .60 |
| ❑ 211 | John Smoltz | .25 | .60 |
| ❑ 212 | Henry Rodriguez | .15 | .40 |
| ❑ 213 | Tim Belcher | .15 | .40 |
| ❑ 214 | Carlos Delgado | .25 | .60 |
| ❑ 215 | Andruw Jones | .25 | .60 |
| ❑ 216 | Andy Benes | .15 | .40 |
| ❑ 217 | Fred McGriff | .25 | .60 |
| ❑ 218 | Edgar Renteria | .15 | .40 |
| ❑ 219 | Miguel Tejada | .15 | .40 |
| ❑ 220 | Bernie Williams | .25 | .60 |
| ❑ 221 | Justin Thompson | .15 | .40 |
| ❑ 222 | Marty Cordova | .15 | .40 |
| ❑ 223 | Delino DeShields | .15 | .40 |
| ❑ 224 | Ellis Burks | .15 | .40 |
| ❑ 225 | Kenny Lofton | .15 | .40 |
| ❑ 226 | Steve Finley | .15 | .40 |
| ❑ 227 | Eric Chavez | .15 | .40 |
| ❑ 228 | Jose Cruz Jr. | .15 | .40 |
| ❑ 229 | Marquis Grissom | .15 | .40 |
| ❑ 230 | Jeff Bagwell | .25 | .60 |
| ❑ 231 | Jose Canseco | .25 | .60 |
| ❑ 232 | Edgardo Alfonzo | .15 | .40 |
| ❑ 233 | Richie Sexson | .15 | .40 |
| ❑ 234 | Jeff Kent | .15 | .40 |
| ❑ 235 | Rafael Palmeiro | .25 | .60 |
| ❑ 236 | David Cone | .15 | .40 |
| ❑ 237 | Gregg Jefferies | .15 | .40 |
| ❑ 238 | Mike Lansing | .15 | .40 |
| ❑ 239 | Mariano Rivera | .15 | .40 |
| ❑ 240 | Albert Belle | .15 | .40 |
| ❑ 241 | Chuck Knoblauch | .15 | .40 |
| ❑ 242 | Derek Bell | .15 | .40 |
| ❑ 243 | Pat Hentgen | .15 | .40 |
| ❑ 244 | Andres Galarraga | .15 | .40 |
| ❑ 245 | Mo Vaughn | .15 | .40 |
| ❑ 246 | Wade Boggs | .25 | .60 |
| ❑ 247 | Devon White | .15 | .40 |
| ❑ 248 | Todd Helton | .25 | .60 |
| ❑ 249 | Raul Mondesi | .15 | .40 |
| ❑ 250 | Sammy Sosa | .40 | 1.00 |
| ❑ 251 | Nomar Garciaparra ST | 1.00 | 2.50 |
| ❑ 252 | Mark McGwire ST | 1.50 | 4.00 |
| ❑ 253 | Alex Rodriguez ST | 1.00 | 2.50 |
| ❑ 254 | Juan Gonzalez ST | .40 | 1.00 |
| ❑ 255 | Vladimir Guerrero ST | .60 | 1.50 |
| ❑ 256 | Ken Griffey Jr. ST | 1.00 | 2.50 |
| ❑ 257 | Mike Piazza ST | 1.00 | 2.50 |
| ❑ 258 | Derek Jeter ST | 1.50 | 4.00 |
| ❑ 259 | Albert Belle ST | .25 | .60 |
| ❑ 260 | Greg Vaughn ST | .20 | .50 |
| ❑ 261 | Sammy Sosa ST | .60 | 1.50 |
| ❑ 262 | Greg Maddux ST | 1.00 | 2.50 |
| ❑ 263 | Frank Thomas ST | .60 | 1.50 |
| ❑ 264 | Mark Grace ST | .40 | 1.00 |
| ❑ 265 | Ivan Rodriguez ST | .40 | 1.00 |
| ❑ 266 | Roger Clemens ST | 1.25 | 3.00 |
| ❑ 267 | Mo Vaughn GM | .40 | 1.00 |
| ❑ 268 | Jim Thome GM | .40 | 1.00 |
| ❑ 269 | Darin Erstad GM | .25 | .60 |
| ❑ 270 | Chipper Jones GM | .60 | 1.50 |
| ❑ 271 | Larry Walker GM | .25 | .60 |
| ❑ 272 | Cal Ripken GM | 2.00 | 5.00 |
| ❑ 273 | Scott Rolen GM | .40 | 1.00 |
| ❑ 274 | Randy Johnson GM | .60 | 1.50 |
| ❑ 275 | Tony Gwynn GM | .75 | 2.00 |
| ❑ 276 | Barry Bonds GM | 1.50 | 4.00 |
| ❑ 277 | Sean Burroughs GM | .40 | 1.00 |
| ❑ 278 | J.M. Gold RC | .20 | .50 |
| ❑ 279 | Carlos Lee | .15 | .40 |
| ❑ 280 | George Lombard | .20 | .50 |
| ❑ 281 | Carlos Beltran | .40 | 1.00 |
| ❑ 282 | Fernando Seguignol | .20 | .50 |
| ❑ 283 | Eric Chavez | .25 | .60 |
| ❑ 284 | Carlos Pena RC | .30 | .75 |
| ❑ 285 | Corey Patterson RC | .60 | 1.50 |
| ❑ 286 | Alfonso Soriano RC | 3.00 | 8.00 |
| ❑ 287 | Nick Johnson RC | .60 | 1.50 |
| ❑ 288 | Jorge Toca RC | .25 | .60 |
| ❑ 289 | A.J. Burnett RC | .60 | 1.50 |
| ❑ 290 | Andy Brown RC | .20 | .50 |
| ❑ 291 | Doug Mientkiewicz RC | .40 | 1.00 |
| ❑ 292 | Bobby Seay RC | .20 | .50 |
| ❑ 293 | Chip Ambres RC | .20 | .50 |
| ❑ 294 | C.C. Sabathia RC | 1.50 | 4.00 |
| ❑ 295 | Choo Freeman RC | .25 | .60 |
| ❑ 296 | Eric Valent RC | .25 | .60 |
| ❑ 297 | Matt Belisle RC | .20 | .50 |
| ❑ 298 | Jason Tyner RC | .20 | .50 |
| ❑ 299 | Masao Kida RC | .25 | .60 |
| ❑ 300 | H.Aaron/M.McGwire | 1.25 | 3.00 |

## 2000 Finest

|  |  | | |
|---|------|---|---|
| ❑ COMP.SERIES 1 w/o SP's (100) | | 10.00 | 25.00 |
| ❑ COMP.SERIES 2 w/o SP's (100) | | 10.00 | 25.00 |
| ❑ COMMON (1-100/147-246) | | .15 | .40 |
| ❑ COMMON ROOKIE (101-120) | | 2.00 | 5.00 |
| ❑ COMMON FEATURES (121-135) | | .60 | 1.50 |
| ❑ COMM.GEM (136-145/277-286) | | .75 | 2.00 |
| ❑ COMMON ROOKIE (247-266) | | 2.00 | 5.00 |
| ❑ COMMON COUNTER (267-276) | | .40 | 1.00 |
| ❑ 1 | Nomar Garciaparra | .60 | 1.50 |
| ❑ 2 | Chipper Jones | .40 | 1.00 |
| ❑ 3 | Enibiel Durazo | .15 | .40 |
| ❑ 4 | Robin Ventura | .25 | .60 |
| ❑ 5 | Garret Anderson | .15 | .40 |
| ❑ 6 | Dean Palmer | .15 | .40 |
| ❑ 7 | Mariano Rivera | .40 | 1.00 |
| ❑ 8 | Rusty Greer | .15 | .40 |
| ❑ 9 | Jim Thome | .25 | .60 |
| ❑ 10 | Jeff Bagwell | .25 | .60 |
| ❑ 11 | Jason Giambi | .15 | .40 |
| ❑ 12 | Jeromy Burnitz | .15 | .40 |
| ❑ 13 | Mark Grace | .25 | .60 |
| ❑ 14 | Russ Ortiz | .15 | .40 |
| ❑ 15 | Kevin Brown | .25 | .60 |
| ❑ 16 | Kevin Millwood | .15 | .40 |
| ❑ 17 | Scott Williamson | .15 | .40 |
| ❑ 18 | Orlando Hernandez | .15 | .40 |
| ❑ 19 | Todd Walker | .15 | .40 |
| ❑ 20 | Carlos Beltran | .15 | .40 |
| ❑ 21 | Ruben Rivera | .15 | .40 |
| ❑ 22 | Curt Schilling | .25 | .60 |
| ❑ 23 | Brian Giles | .15 | .40 |
| ❑ 24 | Eric Karros | .15 | .40 |
| ❑ 25 | Preston Wilson | .15 | .40 |
| ❑ 26 | Al Leiter | .15 | .40 |
| ❑ 27 | Juan Encarnacion | .15 | .40 |
| ❑ 28 | Tim Salmon | .25 | .50 |
| ❑ 29 | B.J. Surhoff | .15 | .40 |
| ❑ 30 | Bernie Williams | .25 | .50 |
| ❑ 31 | Lee Stevens | .15 | .40 |
| ❑ 32 | Pokey Reese | .15 | .40 |
| ❑ 33 | Mike Sweeney | .15 | .40 |
| ❑ 34 | Corey Koskie | .15 | .40 |
| ❑ 35 | Roberto Alomar | .25 | .60 |
| ❑ 36 | Tim Hudson | .15 | .40 |
| ❑ 37 | Tom Glavine | .25 | .60 |
| ❑ 38 | Jeff Kent | .15 | .40 |
| ❑ 39 | Mike Lieberthal | .15 | .40 |
| ❑ 40 | Barry Larkin | .25 | .60 |
| ❑ 41 | Paul O'Neill | .25 | .60 |
| ❑ 42 | Rico Brogna | .15 | .40 |
| ❑ 43 | Brian Daubach | .15 | .40 |
| ❑ 44 | Rich Aurilia | .15 | .40 |
| ❑ 45 | Vladimir Guerrero | .40 | 1.00 |
| ❑ 46 | Luis Castillo | .15 | .40 |
| ❑ 47 | Bartolo Colon | .15 | .40 |
| ❑ 48 | Kevin Appier | .15 | .40 |
| ❑ 49 | Mo Vaughn | .25 | .60 |
| ❑ 50 | Alex Rodriguez | .60 | 1.50 |
| ❑ 51 | Randy Johnson | .40 | 1.00 |
| ❑ 52 | Kris Benson | .15 | .40 |
| ❑ 53 | Tony Clark | .15 | .40 |
| ❑ 54 | Chad Allen | .15 | .40 |

|  |  | | |
|---|------|---|---|
| 55 | Larry Walker | .15 | .40 |
| 56 | Freddy Garcia | .15 | .40 |
| 57 | Paul Konerko | .15 | .40 |
| 58 | Edgardo Alfonzo | .15 | .40 |
| 59 | Brady Anderson | .15 | .40 |
| 60 | Derek Jeter | 1.00 | 2.50 |
| 61 | John Smoltz | .25 | .60 |
| 62 | Doug Glanville | .15 | .40 |
| 63 | Shannon Stewart | .15 | .40 |
| 64 | Greg Maddux | .60 | 1.50 |
| 65 | Mark McGwire | 1.00 | 2.50 |
| 66 | Gary Sheffield | .25 | .60 |
| 67 | Kevin Young | .15 | .40 |
| 68 | Tony Gwynn | .50 | 1.25 |
| 69 | Rey Ordonez | .15 | .40 |
| 70 | Cal Ripken | 1.25 | 3.00 |
| 71 | Todd Helton | .25 | .60 |
| 72 | Brian Jordan | .15 | .40 |
| 73 | Jose Canseco | .25 | .60 |
| 74 | Luis Gonzalez | .15 | .40 |
| 75 | Barry Bonds | 1.00 | 2.50 |
| 76 | Jermaine Dye | .15 | .40 |
| 77 | Jose Offerman | .15 | .40 |
| 78 | Magglio Ordonez | .25 | .60 |
| 79 | Fred Mcgriff | .25 | .60 |
| 80 | Ivan Rodriguez | .25 | .60 |
| 81 | Josh Hamilton | .75 | 2.00 |
| 82 | Vernon Wells | .15 | .40 |
| 83 | Mark Mulder | .15 | .40 |
| 84 | John Patterson | .15 | .40 |
| 85 | Nick Johnson | .15 | .40 |
| 86 | Pablo Ozuna | .15 | .40 |
| 87 | A.J. Burnett | .15 | .40 |
| 88 | Jack Cust | .15 | .40 |
| 89 | Adam Piatt | .15 | .40 |
| 90 | Rob Ryan | .15 | .40 |
| 91 | Sean Burroughs | .15 | .40 |
| 92 | D'Angelo Jimenez | .15 | .40 |
| 93 | Chad Hermanson | .15 | .40 |
| 94 | Robert Fick | .15 | .40 |
| 95 | Ruben Mateo | .15 | .40 |
| 96 | Alex Escobar | .15 | .40 |
| 97 | Wily Pena | .15 | .40 |
| 98 | Corey Patterson | .15 | .40 |
| 99 | Eric Munson | .15 | .40 |
| 100 | Pat Burrell | .15 | .40 |
| 101 | Michael Tejera RC | 2.00 | 5.00 |
| 102 | Bobby Bradley RC | 2.00 | 5.00 |
| 103 | Larry Bigbie RC | 3.00 | 8.00 |
| 104 | B.J. Garbe RC | 2.00 | 5.00 |
| 105 | Josh Kalinowski RC | 2.00 | 5.00 |
| 106 | Brett Myers RC | 3.00 | 8.00 |
| 107 | Chris Myers RC | 2.00 | 5.00 |
| 108 | Aaron Rowand RC | 4.00 | 10.00 |
| 109 | Corey Myers RC | 2.00 | 5.00 |
| 110 | John Sneed RC | 2.00 | 5.00 |
| 111 | Ryan Christianson RC | 2.00 | 5.00 |
| 112 | Kyle Snyder RC | 2.00 | 5.00 |
| 113 | Mike Paradis RC | 2.00 | 5.00 |
| 114 | Chance Caple RC | 2.00 | 5.00 |
| 115 | Ben Christensen RC | 2.00 | 5.00 |
| 116 | Brad Baker RC | 2.00 | 5.00 |
| 117 | Rob Purvis RC | 2.00 | 5.00 |
| 118 | Rick Asadoorian RC | 2.00 | 5.00 |
| 119 | Ruben Salazar RC | 2.00 | 5.00 |
| 120 | Julio Zuleta RC | 2.00 | 5.00 |
| 121 | A.Rodriguez/K.Griffey Jr. | 1.00 | 2.50 |
| 122 | N.Garciaparra/D.Jeter | 1.25 | 3.00 |
| 123 | M.McGwire/S.Sosa | 1.50 | 4.00 |
| 124 | R.Johnson/P.Martinez | 1.00 | 2.50 |
| 125 | I.Rodriguez/M.Piazza | 1.00 | 2.50 |
| 126 | M.Ramirez/R.Alomar | .60 | 1.50 |
| 127 | C.Jones/A.Jones | 1.00 | 2.50 |
| 128 | C.Ripken/T.Gwynn | 2.00 | 5.00 |
| 129 | J.Bagwell/C.Biggio | .80 | 1.50 |
| 130 | B.Bonds/V.Guerrero | 1.50 | 2.50 |
| 131 | N.Johnson/A.Soriano | 1.50 | 2.50 |
| 132 | J.Hamilton/P.Burrell | 4.00 | 10.00 |
| 133 | C.Patterson/R.Mateo | .60 | 1.50 |
| 134 | L.Walker/T.Helton | .60 | 1.50 |
| 135 | R.Ordonez/E.Alfonzo | .60 | 1.50 |
| 136 | Derek Jeter GEM | 3.00 | 8.00 |
| 137 | Alex Rodriguez GEM | 2.00 | 5.00 |
| 138 | Chipper Jones GEM | 2.00 | 5.00 |
| 139 | Mike Piazza GEM | 2.00 | 5.00 |
| 140 | Mark McGwire GEM | 3.00 | 8.00 |
| 141 | Ivan Rodriguez GEM | 1.25 | 3.00 |
| 142 | Cal Ripken GEM | 4.00 | 10.00 |
| 143 | Vladimir Guerrero GEM | 2.00 | 5.00 |
| 144 | Randy Johnson GEM | 2.00 | 5.00 |
| 145 | Jeff Bagwell GEM | 1.25 | 3.00 |
| 146 | Ken Griffey Jr. ACTION | .60 | 1.50 |
| 146A | Ken Griffey Jr. PORT | .60 | 1.50 |
| 147 | Andruw Jones | .25 | .60 |
| 148 | Kerry Wood | .15 | .40 |
| 149 | Jim Edmonds | .15 | .40 |
| 150 | Pedro Martinez | .25 | .60 |
| 151 | Warren Morris | .15 | .40 |
| 152 | Trevor Hoffman | .15 | .40 |
| 153 | Ryan Klesko | .15 | .40 |
| 154 | Andy Pettitte | .25 | .60 |
| 155 | Frank Thomas | .40 | 1.00 |
| 156 | Damion Easley | .15 | .40 |
| 157 | Cliff Floyd | .15 | .40 |
| 158 | Ben Davis | .15 | .40 |
| 159 | John Valentin | .15 | .40 |
| 160 | Rafael Palmeiro | .25 | .60 |
| 161 | Andy Ashby | .15 | .40 |
| 162 | J.D. Drew | .15 | .40 |
| 163 | Jay Bell | .15 | .40 |
| 164 | Adam Kennedy | .15 | .40 |
| 165 | Manny Ramirez | .25 | .60 |
| 166 | John Halama | .15 | .40 |
| 167 | Octavio Dotel | .15 | .40 |
| 168 | Darin Erstad | .15 | .40 |
| 169 | Jose Lima | .15 | .40 |
| 170 | Andres Galarraga | .15 | .40 |
| 171 | Scott Rolen | .25 | .60 |
| 172 | Delino DeShields | .15 | .40 |
| 173 | J.T. Snow | .15 | .40 |
| 174 | Tony Womack | .15 | .40 |
| 175 | John Olerud | .15 | .40 |
| 176 | Jason Kendall | .15 | .40 |
| 177 | Carlos Lee | .15 | .40 |
| 178 | Eric Milton | .15 | .40 |
| 179 | Jeff Cirillo | .15 | .40 |
| 180 | Gabe Kapler | .15 | .40 |
| 181 | Greg Vaughn | .15 | .40 |
| 182 | Denny Neagle | .15 | .40 |
| 183 | Tino Martinez | .25 | .60 |
| 184 | Doug Mientkiewicz | .15 | .40 |
| 185 | Juan Gonzalez | .25 | .60 |
| 186 | Ellis Burks | .15 | .40 |
| 187 | Mike Hampton | .15 | .40 |
| 188 | Royce Clayton | .15 | .40 |
| 189 | Mike Mussina | .25 | .60 |
| 190 | Carlos Delgado | .15 | .40 |
| 191 | Ben Grieve | .15 | .40 |
| 192 | Fernando Tatis | .15 | .40 |
| 193 | Matt Williams | .25 | .60 |
| 194 | Rondell White | .15 | .40 |
| 195 | Shawn Green | .15 | .40 |
| 196 | Hideki Irabu | .15 | .40 |
| 197 | Troy Glaus | .15 | .40 |
| 198 | Roger Cedeno | .15 | .40 |
| 199 | Ray Lankford | .15 | .40 |
| 200 | Sammy Sosa | .40 | 1.00 |
| 201 | Kenny Lofton | .15 | .40 |
| 202 | Edgar Martinez | .25 | .60 |
| 203 | Mark Kotsay | .15 | .40 |
| 204 | David Wells | .15 | .40 |
| 205 | Craig Biggio | .25 | .60 |
| 206 | Ray Durham | .15 | .40 |
| 207 | Troy O'Leary | .15 | .40 |
| 208 | Rickey Henderson | .40 | 1.00 |
| 209 | Bob Abreu | .15 | .40 |
| 210 | Neifi Perez | .15 | .40 |
| 211 | Carlos Febles | .15 | .40 |
| 212 | Chuck Knoblauch | .15 | .40 |
| 213 | Moises Alou | .15 | .40 |
| 214 | Omar Vizquel | .25 | .60 |
| 215 | Vinny Castilla | .15 | .40 |
| 216 | Javy Lopez | .15 | .40 |
| 217 | Johnny Damon | .25 | .60 |
| 218 | Roger Clemens | .75 | 2.00 |
| 219 | Miguel Tejada | .15 | .40 |
| 220 | Carl Everett | .15 | .40 |
| 221 | Matt Lawton | .15 | .40 |
| 222 | Albert Belle | .15 | .40 |
| 223 | Adrian Beltre | .15 | .40 |
| 224 | Dante Bichette | .15 | .40 |
| 225 | Raul Mondesi | .15 | .40 |
| 226 | Mike Piazza | .60 | 1.50 |
| 227 | Brad Penny | .15 | .40 |
| 228 | Kip Wells | .15 | .40 |
| 229 | Adam Everett | .15 | .40 |
| 230 | Eddie Yarnall | .15 | .40 |
| 231 | Matt LeCroy | .15 | .40 |
| 232 | Jason Tyner | .15 | .40 |
| 233 | Rick Ankiel | .15 | .40 |
| 234 | Lance Berkman | .15 | .40 |
| 235 | Rafael Furcal | .15 | .40 |
| 236 | Dee Brown | .15 | .40 |
| 237 | Gookie Dawkins | .15 | .40 |
| 238 | Eric Valent | .15 | .40 |
| 239 | Peter Bergeron | .15 | .40 |
| 240 | Alfonso Soriano | .40 | 1.00 |
| 241 | Adam Dunn | .40 | 1.00 |
| 242 | Jorge Toca | .15 | .40 |
| 243 | Ryan Anderson | .15 | .40 |
| 244 | Jason Dellaero | .15 | .40 |
| 245 | Jason Grilli | .15 | .40 |
| 246 | Milton Bradley | .15 | .40 |
| 247 | Scott Downs RC | 2.00 | 5.00 |
| 248 | Keith Reed RC | 2.00 | 5.00 |
| 249 | Edgar Cruz RC | 2.00 | 5.00 |
| 250 | Wes Anderson RC | 2.00 | 5.00 |
| 251 | Lyle Overbay RC | 3.00 | 8.00 |
| 252 | Mike Lamb RC | 2.00 | 5.00 |
| 253 | Vince Faison RC | 2.00 | 5.00 |
| 254 | Chad Alexander RC | 2.00 | 5.00 |
| 255 | Chris Wakeland RC | 2.00 | 5.00 |
| 256 | Aaron McNeal RC | 2.00 | 5.00 |
| 257 | Tomo Ohka RC | 2.00 | 5.00 |
| 258 | Ty Howington RC | 2.00 | 5.00 |
| 259 | Javier Colina RC | 2.00 | 5.00 |
| 260 | Jason Jennings RC | 2.00 | 5.00 |
| 261 | Ramon Santiago RC | 2.00 | 5.00 |
| 262 | Johan Santana RC | 40.00 | 80.00 |
| 263 | Quincy Foster RC | 2.00 | 5.00 |
| 264 | Junior Brignac RC | 2.00 | 5.00 |
| 265 | Rico Washington RC | 2.00 | 5.00 |
| 266 | Scott Sobkowak RC | 2.00 | 5.00 |
| 267 | P.Martinez/R.Ankiel | .60 | 1.50 |
| 268 | M.Ramirez/V.Guerrero | 1.00 | 2.50 |
| 269 | A.Burnett/M.Mulder | .40 | 1.00 |
| 270 | M.Piazza/E.Munson | 1.00 | 2.50 |
| 271 | J.Hamilton/C.Patterson | 1.25 | 3.00 |
| 272 | K.Griffey Jr./S.Sosa | .75 | 2.00 |
| 273 | D.Jeter/A.Soriano | 1.50 | 4.00 |
| 274 | M.McGwire/P.Burrell | 1.50 | 4.00 |
| 275 | C.Jones/C.Ripken | 1.50 | 4.00 |
| 276 | N.Garciaparra/A.Rodriguez | 1.00 | 2.50 |
| 277 | Pedro Martinez GEM | 1.25 | 3.00 |
| 278 | Tony Gwynn GEM | 1.50 | 4.00 |
| 279 | Barry Bonds GEM | 3.00 | 8.00 |
| 280 | Juan Gonzalez GEM | .75 | 2.00 |
| 281 | Larry Walker GEM | .75 | 2.00 |
| 282 | Nomar Garciaparra GEM | 2.00 | 5.00 |
| 283 | Ken Griffey Jr. GEM | 2.00 | 5.00 |
| 284 | Manny Ramirez GEM | 1.25 | 3.00 |
| 285 | Shawn Green GEM | .75 | 2.00 |
| 286 | Sammy Sosa GEM | 2.00 | 5.00 |

## 2001 Finest

| | | | |
|---|------|---|---|
| | COMP. SET w/o SP's (100) | 10.00 | 25.00 |
| | COMMON CARD (1-110) | .15 | .40 |
| | COMMON SP | 4.00 | 10.00 |
| | COMMON PROSPECT (111-140) | 4.00 | 10.00 |
| 1 | Mike Piazza SP | 8.00 | 20.00 |
| 2 | Andruw Jones | .25 | .60 |
| 3 | Jason Giambi | .25 | .60 |
| 4 | Fred McGriff | .25 | .60 |
| 5 | Vladimir Guerrero SP | 4.00 | 10.00 |
| 6 | Adrian Gonzalez | .15 | .40 |
| 7 | Pedro Martinez | .25 | .60 |
| 8 | Mike Lieberthal | .15 | .40 |
| 9 | Warren Morris | .15 | .40 |
| 10 | Juan Gonzalez | .15 | .40 |
| 11 | Jose Canseco | .25 | .60 |

| # | Card | Lo | Hi |
|---|------|----|----|
| ☐ 12 | Jose Valentin | .15 | .40 |
| ☐ 13 | Jeff Cirillo | .15 | .40 |
| ☐ 14 | Pokey Reese | .15 | .40 |
| ☐ 15 | Scott Rolen | .25 | .60 |
| ☐ 16 | Greg Maddux | .60 | 1.50 |
| ☐ 17 | Carlos Delgado | .15 | .40 |
| ☐ 18 | Rick Ankiel | .15 | .40 |
| ☐ 19 | Steve Finley | .15 | .40 |
| ☐ 20 | Shawn Green | .15 | .40 |
| ☐ 21 | Orlando Cabrera | .15 | .40 |
| ☐ 22 | Roberto Alomar | .25 | .60 |
| ☐ 23 | John Olerud | .15 | .40 |
| ☐ 24 | Albert Belle | .15 | .40 |
| ☐ 25 | Edgardo Alfonzo | .15 | .40 |
| ☐ 26 | Rafael Palmeiro | .25 | .60 |
| ☐ 27 | Mike Sweeney | .15 | .40 |
| ☐ 28 | Bernie Williams | .25 | .60 |
| ☐ 29 | Larry Walker | .15 | .40 |
| ☐ 30 | Barry Bonds SP | 10.00 | 25.00 |
| ☐ 31 | Orlando Hernandez | .15 | .40 |
| ☐ 32 | Randy Johnson | .40 | 1.00 |
| ☐ 33 | Shannon Stewart | .15 | .40 |
| ☐ 34 | Mark Grace | .25 | .60 |
| ☐ 35 | Alex Rodriguez SP | 10.00 | 25.00 |
| ☐ 36 | Tino Martinez | .25 | .60 |
| ☐ 37 | Carlos Febles | .15 | .40 |
| ☐ 38 | Al Leiter | .15 | .40 |
| ☐ 39 | Omar Vizquel | .25 | .60 |
| ☐ 40 | Chuck Knoblauch | .15 | .40 |
| ☐ 41 | Tim Salmon | .25 | .60 |
| ☐ 42 | Brian Jordan | .15 | .40 |
| ☐ 43 | Edgar Renteria | .15 | .40 |
| ☐ 44 | Preston Wilson | .15 | .40 |
| ☐ 45 | Mariano Rivera | .40 | 1.00 |
| ☐ 46 | Gabe Kapler | .15 | .40 |
| ☐ 47 | Jason Kendall | .15 | .40 |
| ☐ 48 | Rickey Henderson | .40 | 1.00 |
| ☐ 49 | Luis Gonzalez | .15 | .40 |
| ☐ 50 | Tom Glavine | .25 | .60 |
| ☐ 51 | Jeromy Burnitz | .15 | .40 |
| ☐ 52 | Garret Anderson | .15 | .40 |
| ☐ 53 | Craig Biggio | .25 | .60 |
| ☐ 54 | Vinny Castilla | .15 | .40 |
| ☐ 55 | Jeff Kent | .15 | .40 |
| ☐ 56 | Gary Sheffield | .15 | .40 |
| ☐ 57 | Jorge Posada | .25 | .60 |
| ☐ 58 | Sean Casey | .15 | .40 |
| ☐ 59 | Johnny Damon | .15 | .40 |
| ☐ 60 | Dean Palmer | .15 | .40 |
| ☐ 61 | Todd Helton | .25 | .60 |
| ☐ 62 | Barry Larkin | .25 | .60 |
| ☐ 63 | Robin Ventura | .15 | .40 |
| ☐ 64 | Kenny Lofton | .15 | .40 |
| ☐ 65 | Sammy Sosa SP | 4.00 | 10.00 |
| ☐ 66 | Rafael Furcal | .15 | .40 |
| ☐ 67 | Jay Bell | .15 | .40 |
| ☐ 68 | J.T. Snow | .15 | .40 |
| ☐ 69 | Jose Vidro | .15 | .40 |
| ☐ 70 | Ivan Rodriguez | .25 | .60 |
| ☐ 71 | Jermaine Dye | .15 | .40 |
| ☐ 72 | Chipper Jones SP | 4.00 | 10.00 |
| ☐ 73 | Fernando Vina | .15 | .40 |
| ☐ 74 | Ben Grieve | .15 | .40 |
| ☐ 75 | Mark McGwire SP | 10.00 | 25.00 |
| ☐ 76 | Matt Williams | .15 | .40 |
| ☐ 77 | Mark Grudzielanek | .15 | .40 |
| ☐ 78 | Mike Hampton | .15 | .40 |
| ☐ 79 | Brian Giles | .15 | .40 |
| ☐ 80 | Tony Gwynn | .50 | 1.25 |
| ☐ 81 | Carlos Beltran | .15 | .40 |
| ☐ 82 | Ray Durham | .15 | .40 |
| ☐ 83 | Brad Radke | .15 | .40 |
| ☐ 84 | David Justice | .15 | .40 |
| ☐ 85 | Frank Thomas | .40 | 1.00 |
| ☐ 86 | Todd Zeile | .15 | .40 |
| ☐ 87 | Pat Burrell | .15 | .40 |
| ☐ 88 | Jim Thome | .25 | .60 |
| ☐ 89 | Greg Vaughn | .15 | .40 |
| ☐ 90 | Ken Griffey Jr. SP | 6.00 | 15.00 |
| ☐ 91 | Mike Mussina | .25 | .60 |
| ☐ 92 | Magglio Ordonez | .15 | .40 |
| ☐ 93 | Bob Abreu | .15 | .40 |
| ☐ 94 | Alex Gonzalez | .15 | .40 |
| ☐ 95 | Kevin Brown | .15 | .40 |
| ☐ 96 | Jay Buhner | .15 | .40 |
| ☐ 97 | Roger Clemens | .75 | 2.00 |
| ☐ 98 | Nomar Garciaparra SP | 6.00 | 15.00 |
| ☐ 99 | Derrek Lee | .25 | .60 |
| ☐ 100 | Derek Jeter SP | 10.00 | 25.00 |
| ☐ 101 | Adrian Beltre | .15 | .40 |
| ☐ 102 | Geoff Jenkins | .15 | .40 |
| ☐ 103 | Javy Lopez | .15 | .40 |
| ☐ 104 | Raul Mondesi | .15 | .40 |
| ☐ 105 | Troy Glaus | .15 | .40 |
| ☐ 106 | Jeff Bagwell | .25 | .60 |
| ☐ 107 | Eric Karros | .15 | .40 |
| ☐ 108 | Mo Vaughn | .15 | .40 |
| ☐ 109 | Cal Ripken | 1.25 | 3.00 |
| ☐ 110 | Manny Ramirez Sox | .25 | .60 |
| ☐ 111 | Scott Heard PROS | 4.00 | 10.00 |
| ☐ 112 | Luis Montanez PROS RC | 4.00 | 10.00 |
| ☐ 113 | Ben Diggins PROS | 4.00 | 10.00 |
| ☐ 114 | Shaun Boyd PROS RC | 4.00 | 10.00 |
| ☐ 115 | Sean Burnett PROS | 4.00 | 10.00 |
| ☐ 116 | Carmen Cali PROS RC | 4.00 | 10.00 |
| ☐ 117 | Derek Thompson PROS | 4.00 | 10.00 |
| ☐ 118 | David Parrish PROS RC | 4.00 | 10.00 |
| ☐ 119 | Dominic Rich PROS RC | 4.00 | 10.00 |
| ☐ 120 | Chad Petty PROS RC | 4.00 | 10.00 |
| ☐ 121 | Steve Smyth PROS RC | 4.00 | 10.00 |
| ☐ 122 | John Lackey PROS | 4.00 | 10.00 |
| ☐ 123 | Matt Galante PROS | 4.00 | 10.00 |
| ☐ 124 | Danny Borrell PROS RC | 4.00 | 10.00 |
| ☐ 125 | Bob Keppel PROS RC | 4.00 | 10.00 |
| ☐ 126 | Justin Wayne PROS RC | 4.00 | 10.00 |
| ☐ 127 | J.R. House PROS | 4.00 | 10.00 |
| ☐ 128 | Brian Sellier PROS RC | 4.00 | 10.00 |
| ☐ 129 | Dan Moylan PROS RC | 4.00 | 10.00 |
| ☐ 130 | Scott Pratt PROS RC | 4.00 | 10.00 |
| ☐ 131 | Victor Hall PROS RC | 4.00 | 10.00 |
| ☐ 132 | Joel Pineiro PROS | 4.00 | 10.00 |
| ☐ 133 | Josh Axelson PROS RC | 4.00 | 10.00 |
| ☐ 134 | Jose Reyes PROS RC | 90.00 | 150.00 |
| ☐ 135 | Greg Runser PROS RC | 4.00 | 10.00 |
| ☐ 136 | Bryan Hebson PROS RC | 4.00 | 10.00 |
| ☐ 137 | Sammy Serrano PROS RC | 4.00 | 10.00 |
| ☐ 138 | Kevin Joseph PROS RC | 4.00 | 10.00 |
| ☐ 139 | Juan Richardson PROS RC | 4.00 | 10.00 |
| ☐ 140 | Mark Fischer PROS RC | 4.00 | 10.00 |

## 2002 Finest

| # | Card | Lo | Hi |
|---|------|----|----|
| ☐ | COMP SET w/o SP's (100) | 10.00 | 25.00 |
| ☐ | COMMON CARD (1-100) | .20 | .50 |
| ☐ | COMMON CARD (101-110) | 4.00 | 10.00 |
| ☐ 1 | Mike Mussina | .30 | .75 |
| ☐ 2 | Steve Sparks | .20 | .50 |
| ☐ 3 | Randy Johnson | .50 | 1.25 |
| ☐ 4 | Orlando Cabrera | .20 | .50 |
| ☐ 5 | Jeff Kent | .20 | .50 |
| ☐ 6 | Carlos Delgado | .20 | .50 |
| ☐ 7 | Ivan Rodriguez | .30 | .75 |
| ☐ 8 | Jose Cruz | .20 | .50 |
| ☐ 9 | Jason Giambi | .20 | .50 |
| ☐ 10 | Brad Penny | .20 | .50 |
| ☐ 11 | Moises Alou | .20 | .50 |
| ☐ 12 | Mike Piazza | .75 | 2.00 |
| ☐ 13 | Ben Grieve | .20 | .50 |
| ☐ 14 | Derek Jeter | 1.25 | 3.00 |
| ☐ 15 | Roy Oswalt | .20 | .50 |
| ☐ 16 | Pat Burrell | .20 | .50 |
| ☐ 17 | Preston Wilson | .20 | .50 |
| ☐ 18 | Kevin Brown | .20 | .50 |
| ☐ 19 | Barry Bonds | 1.25 | 3.00 |
| ☐ 20 | Phil Nevin | .20 | .50 |
| ☐ 21 | Aramis Ramirez | .20 | .50 |
| ☐ 22 | Carlos Beltran | .20 | .50 |
| ☐ 23 | Chipper Jones | .50 | 1.25 |
| ☐ 24 | Curt Schilling | .20 | .50 |
| ☐ 25 | Jorge Posada | .30 | .75 |
| ☐ 26 | Alfonso Soriano | .50 | 1.25 |
| ☐ 27 | Cliff Floyd | .20 | .50 |
| ☐ 28 | Rafael Palmeiro | .30 | .75 |
| ☐ 29 | Terrence Long | .20 | .50 |
| ☐ 30 | Ken Griffey Jr. | .75 | 2.00 |
| ☐ 31 | Jason Kendall | .20 | .50 |
| ☐ 32 | Jose Vidro | .20 | .50 |
| ☐ 33 | Jermaine Dye | .20 | .50 |
| ☐ 34 | Bobby Higginson | .20 | .50 |
| ☐ 35 | Albert Pujols | 1.00 | 2.50 |
| ☐ 36 | Miguel Tejada | .20 | .50 |
| ☐ 37 | Jim Edmonds | .20 | .50 |
| ☐ 38 | Barry Zito | .20 | .50 |
| ☐ 39 | Jimmy Rollins | .20 | .50 |
| ☐ 40 | Rafael Furcal | .20 | .50 |
| ☐ 41 | Omar Vizquel | .30 | .75 |
| ☐ 42 | Kazuhiro Sasaki | .20 | .50 |
| ☐ 43 | Brian Giles | .20 | .50 |
| ☐ 44 | Darin Erstad | .20 | .50 |
| ☐ 45 | Mariano Rivera | .50 | 1.25 |
| ☐ 46 | Troy Percival | .20 | .50 |
| ☐ 47 | Mike Sweeney | .20 | .50 |
| ☐ 48 | Vladimir Guerrero | .50 | 1.25 |
| ☐ 49 | Troy Glaus | .20 | .50 |
| ☐ 50 | So Taguchi RC | 1.00 | 2.50 |
| ☐ 51 | Edgardo Alfonzo | .20 | .50 |
| ☐ 52 | Roger Clemens | 1.00 | 2.50 |
| ☐ 53 | Eric Chavez | .20 | .50 |
| ☐ 54 | Alex Rodriguez | .75 | 2.00 |
| ☐ 55 | Cristian Guzman | .20 | .50 |
| ☐ 56 | Jeff Bagwell | .30 | .75 |
| ☐ 57 | Bernie Williams | .30 | .75 |
| ☐ 58 | Kerry Wood | .20 | .50 |
| ☐ 59 | Ryan Klesko | .20 | .50 |
| ☐ 60 | Ichiro Suzuki | 1.00 | 2.50 |
| ☐ 61 | Larry Walker | .20 | .50 |
| ☐ 62 | Nomar Garciaparra | .75 | 2.00 |
| ☐ 63 | Craig Biggio | .30 | .75 |
| ☐ 64 | J.D. Drew | .20 | .50 |
| ☐ 65 | Juan Pierre | .20 | .50 |
| ☐ 66 | Roberto Alomar | .20 | .50 |
| ☐ 67 | Luis Gonzalez | .20 | .50 |
| ☐ 68 | Bud Smith | .20 | .50 |
| ☐ 69 | Magglio Ordonez | .20 | .50 |
| ☐ 70 | Scott Rolen | .20 | .50 |
| ☐ 71 | Tsuyoshi Shinjo | .20 | .50 |
| ☐ 72 | Paul Konerko | .20 | .50 |
| ☐ 73 | Garret Anderson | .20 | .50 |
| ☐ 74 | Tim Hudson | .20 | .50 |
| ☐ 75 | Adam Dunn | .20 | .50 |
| ☐ 76 | Gary Sheffield | .20 | .50 |
| ☐ 77 | Johnny Damon Sox | .30 | .75 |
| ☐ 78 | Todd Helton | .30 | .75 |
| ☐ 79 | Geoff Jenkins | .20 | .50 |
| ☐ 80 | Shawn Green | .20 | .50 |
| ☐ 81 | C.C. Sabathia | .20 | .50 |
| ☐ 82 | Kazuhisa Ishii RC | 1.00 | 2.50 |
| ☐ 83 | Rich Aurilia | .20 | .50 |
| ☐ 84 | Mike Hampton | .20 | .50 |
| ☐ 85 | Ben Sheets | .20 | .50 |
| ☐ 86 | Andruw Jones | .30 | .75 |
| ☐ 87 | Richie Sexson | .20 | .50 |
| ☐ 88 | Jim Thome | .30 | .75 |
| ☐ 89 | Sammy Sosa | .50 | 1.25 |
| ☐ 90 | Greg Maddux | .75 | 2.00 |
| ☐ 91 | Pedro Martinez | .50 | 1.25 |
| ☐ 92 | Jeromy Burnitz | .20 | .50 |
| ☐ 93 | Raul Mondesi | .20 | .50 |
| ☐ 94 | Bret Boone | .20 | .50 |
| ☐ 95 | Jerry Hairston | .20 | .50 |
| ☐ 96 | Mike Rivera | .20 | .50 |
| ☐ 97 | Juan Cruz | .20 | .50 |
| ☐ 98 | Morgan Ensberg | .20 | .50 |
| ☐ 99 | Nathan Haynes | .20 | .50 |
| ☐ 100 | Xavier Nady | .20 | .50 |
| ☐ 101 | Nic Jackson FY AU RC | 4.00 | 10.00 |
| ☐ 102 | Mauricio Lara FY AU RC | 4.00 | 10.00 |
| ☐ 103 | Freddy Sanchez FY AU RC | 6.00 | 15.00 |
| ☐ 104 | Clint Nageotte FY AU RC | 4.00 | 10.00 |
| ☐ 105 | Beltran Perez FY AU RC | 4.00 | 10.00 |
| ☐ 106 | Garrett Gentry FY AU RC | 4.00 | 10.00 |
| ☐ 107 | Chad Qualls FY AU RC | 4.00 | 10.00 |
| ☐ 108 | Jason Bay FY AU RC | 30.00 | 60.00 |
| ☐ 109 | Michael Hill FY AU RC | 4.00 | 10.00 |
| ☐ 110 | Brian Tallet FY AU RC | 4.00 | 10.00 |

## 2003 Finest

| | | |
|---|---|---|
| ☐ COMP.SET w/o SP's (100) | 10.00 | 25.00 |
| ☐ COMMON CARD (1-100) | .20 | .50 |
| ☐ COMMON CARD (101-110) | 6.00 | 15.00 |
| ☐ 1 Sammy Sosa | .50 | 1.25 |
| ☐ 2 Paul Konerko | .20 | .50 |
| ☐ 3 Todd Helton | .30 | .75 |
| ☐ 4 Mike Lowell | .20 | .50 |
| ☐ 5 Lance Berkman | .20 | .50 |
| ☐ 6 Kazuhisa Ishii | .20 | .50 |
| ☐ 7 A.J. Pierzynski | .20 | .50 |
| ☐ 8 Jose Vidro | .20 | .50 |
| ☐ 9 Roberto Alomar | .30 | .75 |
| ☐ 10 Derek Jeter | 1.25 | 3.00 |
| ☐ 11 Barry Zito | .20 | .50 |
| ☐ 12 Jimmy Rollins | .20 | .50 |
| ☐ 13 Brian Giles | .20 | .50 |
| ☐ 14 Ryan Klesko | .20 | .50 |
| ☐ 15 Rich Aurilia | .20 | .50 |
| ☐ 16 Jim Edmonds | .20 | .50 |
| ☐ 17 Aubrey Huff | .20 | .50 |
| ☐ 18 Ivan Rodriguez | .30 | .75 |
| ☐ 19 Eric Hinske | .20 | .50 |
| ☐ 20 Barry Bonds | 1.25 | 3.00 |
| ☐ 21 Darin Erstad | .20 | .50 |
| ☐ 22 Curt Schilling | .20 | .50 |
| ☐ 23 Andruw Jones | .30 | .75 |
| ☐ 24 Jay Gibbons | .20 | .50 |
| ☐ 25 Nomar Garciaparra | .75 | 2.00 |
| ☐ 26 Kerry Wood | .20 | .50 |
| ☐ 27 Magglio Ordonez | .20 | .50 |
| ☐ 28 Austin Kearns | .20 | .50 |
| ☐ 29 Jason Jennings | .20 | .50 |
| ☐ 30 Jason Giambi | .20 | .50 |
| ☐ 31 Jim Thome | .30 | .75 |
| ☐ 32 Edgar Martinez | .30 | .75 |
| ☐ 33 Carl Crawford | .20 | .50 |
| ☐ 34 Hee Seop Choi | .20 | .50 |
| ☐ 35 Vladimir Guerrero | .50 | 1.25 |
| ☐ 36 Jeff Kent | .20 | .50 |
| ☐ 37 John Smoltz | .30 | .75 |
| ☐ 38 Frank Thomas | .50 | 1.25 |
| ☐ 39 Cliff Floyd | .20 | .50 |
| ☐ 40 Mike Piazza | .75 | 2.00 |
| ☐ 41 Mark Prior | .30 | .75 |
| ☐ 42 Tim Salmon | .20 | .50 |
| ☐ 43 Shawn Green | .20 | .50 |
| ☐ 44 Bernie Williams | .30 | .75 |
| ☐ 45 Jim Thome | .30 | .75 |
| ☐ 46 John Olerud | .20 | .50 |
| ☐ 47 Orlando Hudson | .20 | .50 |
| ☐ 48 Mark Teixeira | .30 | .75 |
| ☐ 49 Gary Sheffield | .20 | .50 |
| ☐ 50 Ichiro Suzuki | 1.00 | 2.50 |
| ☐ 51 Tom Glavine | .30 | .75 |
| ☐ 52 Torii Hunter | .20 | .50 |
| ☐ 53 Craig Biggio | .20 | .50 |
| ☐ 54 Carlos Beltran | .20 | .50 |
| ☐ 55 Bartolo Colon | .20 | .50 |
| ☐ 56 Jorge Posada | .30 | .75 |
| ☐ 57 Pat Burrell | .20 | .50 |
| ☐ 58 Edgar Renteria | .20 | .50 |
| ☐ 59 Rafael Palmeiro | .30 | .75 |
| ☐ 60 Alfonso Soriano | .20 | .50 |
| ☐ 61 Brandon Phillips | .20 | .50 |
| ☐ 62 Luis Gonzalez | .20 | .50 |
| ☐ 63 Manny Ramirez | .50 | 1.25 |
| ☐ 64 Garret Anderson | .20 | .50 |
| ☐ 65 Ken Griffey Jr. | .75 | 2.00 |
| ☐ 66 A.J. Burnett | .20 | .50 |
| ☐ 67 Mike Sweeney | .20 | .50 |
| ☐ 68 Doug Mientkiewicz | .20 | .50 |
| ☐ 69 Eric Chavez | .20 | .50 |
| ☐ 70 Adam Dunn | .20 | .50 |
| ☐ 71 Shea Hillenbrand | .20 | .50 |
| ☐ 72 Troy Glaus | .20 | .50 |
| ☐ 73 Rodrigo Lopez | .20 | .50 |
| ☐ 74 Moises Alou | .20 | .50 |
| ☐ 75 Chipper Jones | .50 | 1.25 |
| ☐ 76 Bobby Abreu | .20 | .50 |
| ☐ 77 Mark Mulder | .20 | .50 |
| ☐ 78 Kevin Brown | .20 | .50 |
| ☐ 79 Josh Beckett | .20 | .50 |
| ☐ 80 Larry Walker | .20 | .50 |
| ☐ 81 Randy Johnson | .50 | 1.25 |
| ☐ 82 Greg Maddux | .75 | 2.00 |
| ☐ 83 Johnny Damon | .30 | .75 |
| ☐ 84 Omar Vizquel | .30 | .75 |
| ☐ 85 Jeff Bagwell | .30 | .75 |
| ☐ 86 Carlos Pena | .20 | .50 |
| ☐ 87 Roy Oswalt | .20 | .50 |
| ☐ 88 Richie Sexson | .20 | .50 |
| ☐ 89 Roger Clemens | 1.00 | 2.50 |
| ☐ 90 Miguel Tejada | .20 | .50 |
| ☐ 91 Vicente Padilla | .20 | .50 |
| ☐ 92 Phil Nevin | .20 | .50 |
| ☐ 93 Edgardo Alfonzo | .20 | .50 |
| ☐ 94 Bret Boone | .20 | .50 |
| ☐ 95 Albert Pujols | 1.00 | 2.50 |
| ☐ 96 Carlos Delgado | .20 | .50 |
| ☐ 97 Jose Contreras RC | .75 | 2.00 |
| ☐ 98 Scott Rolen | .30 | .75 |
| ☐ 99 Pedro Martinez | .30 | .75 |
| ☐ 100 Alex Rodriguez | .75 | 2.00 |
| ☐ 101 Adam LaRoche AU | 6.00 | 15.00 |
| ☐ 102 Andy Marte AU RC | 25.00 | 50.00 |
| ☐ 103 Daryl Clark AU RC | 4.00 | 10.00 |
| ☐ 104 J.D. Durbin AU RC | 4.00 | 10.00 |
| ☐ 105 Craig Brazell AU RC | 4.00 | 10.00 |
| ☐ 106 Brian Burgamy AU RC | 4.00 | 10.00 |
| ☐ 107 Tyler Johnson AU RC | 4.00 | 10.00 |
| ☐ 108 Joey Gomes AU RC | 4.00 | 10.00 |
| ☐ 109 Bryan Bullington AU RC | 6.00 | 15.00 |
| ☐ 110 Byron Gettis AU RC | 4.00 | 10.00 |

## 2004 Finest

| | | |
|---|---|---|
| ☐ COMP.SET w/o SP's (100) | 10.00 | 25.00 |
| ☐ COMMON CARD (1-100) | .20 | .50 |
| ☐ COMMON CARD (101-110) | 3.00 | 8.00 |
| ☐ 101-110 STATED ODDS 1:7 MINI-BOXES | | |
| ☐ COMMON CARD (111-122) | 4.00 | 10.00 |
| ☐ 111-122 STATED ODDS 1:3 MINI-BOXES | | |
| ☐ EXCHANGE DEADLINE 04/30/06 | | |
| ☐ CARD 112 EXCH UNABLE TO BE FULFILLED | | |
| ☐ 04 WS HL B.THOMSON AU SENT INSTEAD | | |
| ☐ 1 Juan Pierre | .20 | .50 |
| ☐ 2 Derek Jeter | 1.00 | 2.50 |
| ☐ 3 Garret Anderson | .20 | .50 |
| ☐ 4 Javy Lopez | .20 | .50 |
| ☐ 5 Corey Patterson | .20 | .50 |
| ☐ 6 Todd Helton | .30 | .75 |
| ☐ 7 Roy Oswalt | .20 | .50 |
| ☐ 8 Shawn Green | .20 | .50 |
| ☐ 9 Vladimir Guerrero | .50 | 1.25 |
| ☐ 10 Jorge Posada | .30 | .75 |
| ☐ 11 Jason Kendall | .20 | .50 |
| ☐ 12 Scott Rolen | .30 | .75 |
| ☐ 13 Randy Johnson | .50 | 1.25 |
| ☐ 14 Bill Mueller | .20 | .50 |
| ☐ 15 Magglio Ordonez | .20 | .50 |
| ☐ 16 Larry Walker | .20 | .50 |
| ☐ 17 Lance Berkman | .20 | .50 |
| ☐ 18 Richie Sexson | .20 | .50 |
| ☐ 19 Orlando Cabrera | .20 | .50 |
| ☐ 20 Alfonso Soriano | .20 | .50 |
| ☐ 21 Kevin Millwood | .20 | .50 |
| ☐ 22 Edgar Martinez | .30 | .75 |
| ☐ 23 Aubrey Huff | .20 | .50 |
| ☐ 24 Carlos Delgado | .20 | .50 |
| ☐ 25 Vernon Wells | .20 | .50 |
| ☐ 26 Mark Teixeira | .30 | .75 |
| ☐ 27 Troy Glaus | .20 | .50 |
| ☐ 28 Jeff Kent | .20 | .50 |
| ☐ 29 Hideo Nomo | .50 | 1.25 |
| ☐ 30 Torii Hunter | .20 | .50 |
| ☐ 31 Hank Blalock | .20 | .50 |
| ☐ 32 Brandon Webb | .20 | .50 |
| ☐ 33 Tony Batista | .20 | .50 |
| ☐ 34 Bret Boone | .20 | .50 |
| ☐ 35 Ryan Klesko | .20 | .50 |
| ☐ 36 Barry Zito | .20 | .50 |
| ☐ 37 Edgar Renteria | .20 | .50 |
| ☐ 38 Geoff Jenkins | .20 | .50 |
| ☐ 39 Jeff Bagwell | .30 | .75 |
| ☐ 40 Dontrelle Willis | .30 | .75 |
| ☐ 41 Adam Dunn | .20 | .50 |
| ☐ 42 Mark Buehrle | .20 | .50 |
| ☐ 43 Esteban Loaiza | .20 | .50 |
| ☐ 44 Angel Berroa | .20 | .50 |
| ☐ 45 Ivan Rodriguez | .30 | .75 |
| ☐ 46 Jose Vidro | .20 | .50 |
| ☐ 47 Mark Mulder | .20 | .50 |
| ☐ 48 Roger Clemens | 1.00 | 2.50 |
| ☐ 49 Jim Edmonds | .20 | .50 |
| ☐ 50 Eric Gagne | .20 | .50 |
| ☐ 51 Marcus Giles | .20 | .50 |
| ☐ 52 Curt Schilling | .30 | .75 |
| ☐ 53 Ken Griffey Jr. | .75 | 2.00 |
| ☐ 54 Jason Schmidt | .20 | .50 |
| ☐ 55 Miguel Tejada | .20 | .50 |
| ☐ 56 Dmitri Young | .20 | .50 |
| ☐ 57 Mike Lowell | .20 | .50 |
| ☐ 58 Mike Sweeney | .20 | .50 |
| ☐ 59 Scott Podsednik | .20 | .50 |
| ☐ 60 Miguel Cabrera | .30 | .75 |
| ☐ 61 Johan Santana | .50 | 1.25 |
| ☐ 62 Bernie Williams | .20 | .50 |
| ☐ 63 Eric Chavez | .20 | .50 |
| ☐ 64 Bobby Abreu | .20 | .50 |
| ☐ 65 Brian Giles | .20 | .50 |
| ☐ 66 Michael Young | .20 | .50 |
| ☐ 67 Paul Lo Duca | .20 | .50 |
| ☐ 68 Austin Kearns | .20 | .50 |
| ☐ 69 Jody Gerut | .20 | .50 |
| ☐ 70 Kerry Wood | .20 | .50 |
| ☐ 71 Luis Matos | .20 | .50 |
| ☐ 72 Greg Maddux | .75 | 2.00 |
| ☐ 73 Alex Rodriguez Yanks | .75 | 2.00 |
| ☐ 74 Mike Lieberthal | .20 | .50 |
| ☐ 75 Jim Thome | .30 | .75 |
| ☐ 76 Javier Vazquez | .20 | .50 |
| ☐ 77 Bartolo Colon | .20 | .50 |
| ☐ 78 Manny Ramirez | .50 | 1.25 |
| ☐ 79 Jacque Jones | .20 | .50 |
| ☐ 80 Johnny Damon | .30 | .75 |
| ☐ 81 Carlos Beltran | .20 | .50 |
| ☐ 82 C.C. Sabathia | .20 | .50 |
| ☐ 83 Preston Wilson | .20 | .50 |
| ☐ 84 Luis Castillo | .20 | .50 |
| ☐ 85 Kevin Brown | .20 | .50 |
| ☐ 86 Shannon Stewart | .20 | .50 |
| ☐ 87 Cliff Floyd | .20 | .50 |
| ☐ 88 Mike Mussina | .30 | .75 |
| ☐ 89 Rafael Furcal | .20 | .50 |
| ☐ 90 Roy Halladay | .20 | .50 |
| ☐ 91 Frank Thomas | .50 | 1.25 |
| ☐ 92 Melvin Mora | .20 | .50 |
| ☐ 93 Andruw Jones | .30 | .75 |
| ☐ 94 Luis Gonzalez | .20 | .50 |
| ☐ 95 David Ortiz | .50 | 1.25 |
| ☐ 96 Gary Sheffield | .20 | .50 |
| ☐ 97 Tim Hudson | .20 | .50 |
| ☐ 98 Phil Nevin | .20 | .50 |
| ☐ 99 Ichiro Suzuki | 1.00 | 2.50 |
| ☐ 100 Albert Pujols | 1.00 | 2.50 |
| ☐ 101 Nomar Garciaparra SR Jsy | 6.00 | 15.00 |
| ☐ 102 Sammy Sosa SR Jsy | 4.00 | 10.00 |
| ☐ 103 Josh Beckett SR Jsy | 3.00 | 8.00 |
| ☐ 104 Jason Giambi SR Jsy | 3.00 | 8.00 |
| ☐ 105 Rocco Baldelli SR Jsy | 3.00 | 8.00 |
| ☐ 106 Jose Reyes SR Jsy | 3.00 | 8.00 |
| ☐ 107 Chipper Jones SR Jsy | 4.00 | 10.00 |
| ☐ 108 Pedro Martinez SR Jsy | 4.00 | 10.00 |
| ☐ 109 Mike Piazza SR Jsy | 6.00 | 15.00 |
| ☐ 110 Mark Prior SR Jsy | 4.00 | 10.00 |

| | | |
|---|---|---|
| 111 Craig Ansman AU RC | 4.00 | 10.00 |
| 113 David Murphy AU RC | 4.00 | 10.00 |
| 114 Jason Hirsh AU RC | 10.00 | 25.00 |
| 115 Matt Moses AU RC | 6.00 | 15.00 |
| 116 Estee Harris AU RC | 6.00 | 15.00 |
| 117 Logan Kensing AU RC | 4.00 | 10.00 |
| 118 L.Milledge AU RC | 20.00 | 50.00 |
| 119 Merkin Valdez AU RC | 4.00 | 10.00 |
| 120 Travis Blackley AU RC | 4.00 | 10.00 |
| 121 Vito Chiaravalloti AU RC | 4.00 | 10.00 |
| 122 Dioner Navarro AU RC | 4.00 | 10.00 |

## 2005 Finest

| | | |
|---|---|---|
| COMP.SET w/o SP's (150) | 40.00 | 80.00 |
| COMMON CARD (1-140) | .20 | .50 |
| COMMON CARD (157-166) | .40 | 1.00 |
| AU p/r 970 ODDS 1:3 MINI BOXES | | |
| AU p/r 970 PRINT RUN 970 #'d SETS | | |
| AU p/r 375 ODDS 1:41 MINI BOXES | | |
| AU p/r 375 PRINT RUN 375 #'d SETS | | |
| OVERALL PLATE ODDS 1:51 MINI BOX | | |
| OVERALL AU PLATE ODDS 1:478 MINI BOX | | |
| PLATE PRINT RUN 1 SET PER COLOR | | |
| BLACK-CYAN-MAGENTA-YELLOW ISSUED | | |
| NO PLATE PRICING DUE TO SCARCITY | | |
| 1 Alexis Rios | .20 | .50 |
| 2 Hank Blalock | .20 | .50 |
| 3 Bobby Abreu | .20 | .50 |
| 4 Curt Schilling | .30 | .75 |
| 5 Albert Pujols | 1.00 | 2.50 |
| 6 Aaron Rowand | .20 | .50 |
| 7 B.J. Upton | .20 | .50 |
| 8 Andruw Jones | .30 | .75 |
| 9 Jeff Francis | .20 | .50 |
| 10 Sammy Sosa | .50 | 1.25 |
| 11 Aramis Ramirez | .20 | .50 |
| 12 Carl Pavano | .20 | .50 |
| 13 Bartolo Colon | .20 | .50 |
| 14 Greg Maddux | .75 | 2.00 |
| 15 Scott Kazmir | .20 | .50 |
| 16 Melvin Mora | .20 | .50 |
| 17 Brandon Backe | .20 | .50 |
| 18 Bobby Crosby | .20 | .50 |
| 19 Carlos Lee | .20 | .50 |
| 20 Carl Crawford | .20 | .50 |
| 21 Brian Giles | .20 | .50 |
| 22 Jeff Bagwell | .30 | .75 |
| 23 J.D. Drew | .20 | .50 |
| 24 C.C. Sabathia | .20 | .50 |
| 25 Alfonso Soriano | .20 | .50 |
| 26 Chipper Jones | .50 | 1.25 |
| 27 Austin Kearns | .20 | .50 |
| 28 Carlos Delgado | .20 | .50 |
| 29 Jack Wilson | .20 | .50 |
| 30 Dmitri Young | .20 | .50 |
| 31 Carlos Guillen | .20 | .50 |
| 32 Jim Thome | .30 | .75 |
| 33 Eric Chavez | .20 | .50 |
| 34 Jason Schmidt | .20 | .50 |
| 35 Brad Radke | .20 | .50 |
| 36 Frank Thomas | .50 | 1.25 |
| 37 Darin Erstad | .20 | .50 |
| 38 Javier Vazquez | .20 | .50 |
| 39 Garret Anderson | .20 | .50 |
| 40 David Ortiz | .50 | 1.25 |
| 41 Javy Lopez | .20 | .50 |
| 42 Geoff Jenkins | .20 | .50 |
| 43 Jose Vidro | .20 | .50 |
| 44 Aubrey Huff | .20 | .50 |
| 45 Bernie Williams | .30 | .75 |
| 46 Dontrelle Willis | .20 | .50 |
| 47 Jim Edmonds | .20 | .50 |
| 48 Ivan Rodriguez | .20 | .50 |
| 49 Gary Sheffield | .20 | .50 |
| 50 Alex Rodriguez | .75 | 2.00 |
| 51 John Buck | .20 | .50 |
| 52 Andy Pettitte | .30 | .75 |
| 53 Ichiro Suzuki | 1.00 | 2.50 |
| 54 Johnny Estrada | .20 | .50 |
| 55 Jake Peavy | .20 | .50 |
| 56 Carlos Zambrano | .20 | .50 |
| 57 Jose Reyes | .20 | .50 |
| 58 Bret Boone | .20 | .50 |
| 59 Jason Bay | .20 | .50 |
| 60 David Wright | .75 | 2.00 |
| 61 Jeromy Burnitz | .20 | .50 |
| 62 Corey Patterson | .20 | .50 |
| 63 Juan Pierre | .20 | .50 |
| 64 Zack Greinke | .20 | .50 |
| 65 Mike Lowell | .20 | .50 |
| 66 Ken Griffey Jr. | .75 | 2.00 |
| 67 Marcus Giles | .20 | .50 |
| 68 Edgar Renteria | .20 | .50 |
| 69 Ken Harvey | .20 | .50 |
| 70 Pedro Martinez | .30 | .75 |
| 71 Johnny Damon | .30 | .75 |
| 72 Lyle Overbay | .20 | .50 |
| 73 Mike Maroth | .20 | .50 |
| 74 Jorge Posada | .30 | .75 |
| 75 Carlos Beltran | .20 | .50 |
| 76 Mark Buehrle | .20 | .50 |
| 77 Khalil Greene | .20 | .50 |
| 78 Josh Beckett | .20 | .50 |
| 79 Mark Loretta | .20 | .50 |
| 80 Rafael Palmeiro | .30 | .75 |
| 81 Justin Morneau | .20 | .50 |
| 82 Rocco Baldelli | .20 | .50 |
| 83 Ben Sheets | .20 | .50 |
| 84 Kerry Wood | .20 | .50 |
| 85 Miguel Tejada | .20 | .50 |
| 86 Magglio Ordonez | .20 | .50 |
| 87 Livan Hernandez | .20 | .50 |
| 88 Kazuo Matsui | .20 | .50 |
| 89 Manny Ramirez | .30 | .75 |
| 90 Hideki Matsui | .75 | 2.00 |
| 91 Jeff Kent | .20 | .50 |
| 92 Matt Lawton | .20 | .50 |
| 93 Richie Sexson | .20 | .50 |
| 94 Mike Mussina | .30 | .75 |
| 95 Adam Dunn | .20 | .50 |
| 96 Johan Santana | .50 | 1.25 |
| 97 Nomar Garciaparra | .50 | 1.25 |
| 98 Michael Young | .20 | .50 |
| 99 Victor Martinez | .20 | .50 |
| 100 Barry Bonds | 1.25 | 3.00 |
| 101 Oliver Perez | .20 | .50 |
| 102 Randy Johnson | .50 | 1.25 |
| 103 Mark Mulder | .20 | .50 |
| 104 Pat Burrell | .20 | .50 |
| 105 Mike Sweeney | .20 | .50 |
| 106 Mark Teixeira | .30 | .75 |
| 107 Paul Lo Duca | .20 | .50 |
| 108 Jon Lieber | .20 | .50 |
| 109 Mike Piazza | .50 | 1.25 |
| 110 Roger Clemens | .75 | 2.00 |
| 111 Rafael Furcal | .20 | .50 |
| 112 Troy Glaus | .20 | .50 |
| 113 Miguel Cabrera | .30 | .75 |
| 114 Randy Wolf | .20 | .50 |
| 115 Lance Berkman | .20 | .50 |
| 116 Mark Prior | .20 | .50 |
| 117 Rich Harden | .20 | .50 |
| 118 Preston Wilson | .20 | .50 |
| 119 Roy Oswalt | .20 | .50 |
| 120 Luis Gonzalez | .20 | .50 |
| 121 Ronnie Belliard | .20 | .50 |
| 122 Sean Casey | .20 | .50 |
| 123 Barry Zito | .20 | .50 |
| 124 Larry Walker | .20 | .50 |
| 125 Derek Jeter | 1.00 | 2.50 |
| 126 Tim Hudson | .20 | .50 |
| 127 Tom Glavine | .30 | .75 |
| 128 Scott Rolen | .30 | .75 |
| 129 Torii Hunter | .20 | .50 |
| 130 Paul Konerko | .20 | .50 |
| 131 Shawn Green | .20 | .50 |
| 132 Vernon Wells | .20 | .50 |
| 133 Vernon Wells | .20 | .50 |
| 134 Sidney Ponson | .20 | .50 |
| 135 Vladimir Guerrero | .50 | 1.25 |
| 136 Mark Kotsay | .20 | .50 |
| 137 Todd Helton | .30 | .75 |
| 138 Adrian Beltre | .20 | .50 |
| 139 Wily Mo Pena | .20 | .50 |
| 140 Joe Mauer | .50 | 1.25 |
| 141 Brian Stavisky AU/970 RC | 4.00 | 10.00 |
| 142 Nate McLouth AU/970 RC | 6.00 | 15.00 |
| 143 Glen Perkins AU/375 RC | 8.00 | 20.00 |
| 144 Chip Cannon AU/970 RC | 8.00 | 20.00 |
| 145 Shane Costa AU/970 RC | 4.00 | 10.00 |
| 146 W.Swackhamer AU/970 RC | 4.00 | 10.00 |
| 147 Kevin Melillo AU/970 RC | 6.00 | 15.00 |
| 148 Billy Butler AU/970 RC | 25.00 | 50.00 |
| 149 Landon Powell AU/970 RC | 6.00 | 15.00 |
| 150 Scott Mathieson AU/970 RC | 4.00 | 10.00 |
| 151 Chris Roberston AU/970 | 4.00 | 10.00 |
| 152 Chad Orvella AU/375 RC | 6.00 | 15.00 |
| 153 Eric Nielsen AU/970 RC | 4.00 | 10.00 |
| 154 Matt Campbell AU/970 RC | 4.00 | 10.00 |
| 155 Mike Rogers AU/970 RC | 4.00 | 10.00 |
| 156 Melky Cabrera AU/970 RC | 20.00 | 40.00 |
| 157 Nolan Ryan RET | 2.00 | 5.00 |
| 158 Bo Jackson RET | .75 | 2.00 |
| 159 Wade Boggs RET | .60 | 1.50 |
| 160 Andre Dawson RET | .40 | 1.00 |
| 161 Dave Winfield RET | .40 | 1.00 |
| 162 Reggie Jackson RET | .60 | 1.50 |
| 163 David Justice RET | .75 | 2.00 |
| 164 Dale Murphy RET | .60 | 1.50 |
| 165 Paul O'Neill RET | .60 | 1.50 |
| 166 Tom Seaver RET | .60 | 1.50 |

## 2006 Finest

| | | |
|---|---|---|
| COMPLETE SET (155) | | |
| COMP.SET w/o AUs (140) | 30.00 | 60.00 |
| COMMON CARD (1-131) | .20 | .50 |
| UNLISTED STARS 1-131 | .50 | 1.25 |
| COMMON ROOKIE (132-140) | .30 | .75 |
| COMMON AUTO (141-155) | 4.00 | 10.00 |
| 141-155 AU ODDS 1:4 MINI BOX | | |
| 141-155 AU PRINT RUN 963 SETS | | |
| 141-155 AU's NOT SERIAL NUMBERED | | |
| PRINT RUN INFO PROVIDED BY TOPPS | | |
| 1-140 PLATES RANDOM INSERTS IN PACKS | | |
| AU 141-155 PLATE ODDS 1:792 MINI BOX | | |
| PLATE PRINT RUN 1 SET PER COLOR | | |
| BLACK-CYAN-MAGENTA-YELLOW ISSUED | | |
| NO PLATE PRICING DUE TO SCARCITY | | |
| 1 Vladimir Guerrero | .50 | 1.25 |
| 2 Troy Glaus | .20 | .50 |
| 3 Andruw Jones | .30 | .75 |
| 4 Miguel Tejada | .20 | .50 |
| 5 Manny Ramirez | .30 | .75 |
| 6 Curt Schilling | .30 | .75 |
| 7 Mark Prior | .20 | .50 |
| 8 Kerry Wood | .20 | .50 |
| 9 Tadahito Iguchi | .20 | .50 |
| 10 Freddy Garcia | .20 | .50 |
| 11 Ryan Howard | .75 | 2.00 |
| 12 Mark Buehrle | .20 | .50 |
| 13 Wily Mo Pena | .20 | .50 |
| 14 C.C. Sabathia | .20 | .50 |
| 15 Garret Anderson | .20 | .50 |
| 16 Shawn Green | .20 | .50 |
| 17 Rafael Furcal | .20 | .50 |
| 18 Jeff Francoeur | .50 | 1.25 |
| 19 Ken Griffey Jr. | .75 | 2.00 |
| 20 Derrek Lee | .20 | .50 |
| 21 Paul Konerko | .20 | .50 |
| 22 Rickie Weeks | .20 | .50 |
| 23 Magglio Ordonez | .20 | .50 |
| 24 Juan Pierre | .20 | .50 |
| 25 Felix Hernandez | .30 | .75 |
| 26 Roger Clemens | 1.00 | 2.50 |
| 27 Zack Greinke | .20 | .50 |
| 28 Johan Santana | .30 | .75 |

|  |  | | |
|---|---|---|---|
| 29 | Jose Reyes | .50 | 1.25 |
| 30 | Bobby Crosby | .20 | .50 |
| 31 | Jason Schmidt | .20 | .50 |
| 32 | Khalil Greene | .30 | .75 |
| 33 | Richie Sexson | .20 | .50 |
| 34 | Mark Mulder | .20 | .50 |
| 35 | Mark Teixeira | .30 | .75 |
| 36 | Nick Johnson | .20 | .50 |
| 37 | Vernon Wells | .20 | .50 |
| 38 | Scott Kazmir | .30 | .75 |
| 39 | Jim Edmonds | .30 | .75 |
| 40 | Adrian Beltre | .20 | .50 |
| 41 | Dan Johnson | .20 | .50 |
| 42 | Carlos Lee | .20 | .50 |
| 43 | Lance Berkman | .20 | .50 |
| 44 | Josh Beckett | .20 | .50 |
| 45 | Morgan Ensberg | .20 | .50 |
| 46 | Garrett Atkins | .20 | .50 |
| 47 | Chase Utley | .50 | 1.25 |
| 48 | Joe Mauer | .50 | 1.25 |
| 49 | Travis Hafner | .20 | .50 |
| 50 | Alex Rodriguez | .75 | 2.00 |
| 51 | Austin Kearns | .20 | .50 |
| 52 | Scott Podsednik | .20 | .50 |
| 53 | Jose Contreras | .20 | .50 |
| 54 | Greg Maddux | .75 | 2.00 |
| 55 | Hideki Matsui | .75 | 2.00 |
| 56 | Matt Clement | .20 | .50 |
| 57 | Javy Lopez | .20 | .50 |
| 58 | Tim Hudson | .20 | .50 |
| 59 | Luis Gonzalez | .20 | .50 |
| 60 | Bartolo Colon | .20 | .50 |
| 61 | Marcus Giles | .20 | .50 |
| 62 | Justin Morneau | .20 | .50 |
| 63 | Nomar Garciaparra | .50 | 1.25 |
| 64 | Robinson Cano | .30 | .75 |
| 65 | Ervin Santana | .20 | .50 |
| 66 | Brady Clark | .20 | .50 |
| 67 | Edgar Renteria | .20 | .50 |
| 68 | Jon Garland | .20 | .50 |
| 69 | Felipe Lopez | .20 | .50 |
| 70 | Ivan Rodriguez | .30 | .75 |
| 71 | Dontrelle Willis | .20 | .50 |
| 72 | Carlos Guillen | .20 | .50 |
| 73 | J.D. Drew | .20 | .50 |
| 74 | Rich Harden | .20 | .50 |
| 75 | Albert Pujols | 1.00 | 2.50 |
| 76 | Livan Hernandez | .20 | .50 |
| 77 | Roy Halladay | .20 | .50 |
| 78 | Hank Blalock | .20 | .50 |
| 79 | David Wright | .75 | 2.00 |
| 80 | Jimmy Rollins | .20 | .50 |
| 81 | John Smoltz | .30 | .75 |
| 82 | Miguel Cabrera | .30 | .75 |
| 83 | David DeJesus | .20 | .50 |
| 83 | Zach Duke | .20 | .50 |
| 84 | Torii Hunter | .20 | .50 |
| 85 | Adam Dunn | .20 | .50 |
| 86 | Randy Johnson | .50 | 1.25 |
| 87 | Roy Oswalt | .20 | .50 |
| 88 | Bobby Abreu | .20 | .50 |
| 89 | Rocco Baldelli | .20 | .50 |
| 90 | Ichiro Suzuki | .75 | 2.00 |
| 91 | Jorge Cantu | .20 | .50 |
| 92 | Jack Wilson | .20 | .50 |
| 93 | Jose Vidro | .20 | .50 |
| 94 | Kevin Millwood | .20 | .50 |
| 95 | David Ortiz | .30 | .75 |
| 96 | Victor Martinez | .20 | .50 |
| 97 | Jeremy Bonderman | .20 | .50 |
| 98 | Todd Helton | .30 | .75 |
| 99 | Carlos Beltran | .20 | .50 |
| 100 | Barry Bonds | 1.25 | 3.00 |
| 101 | Jeff Kent | .20 | .50 |
| 102 | Mike Sweeney | .20 | .50 |
| 103 | Ben Sheets | .20 | .50 |
| 104 | Melvin Mora | .20 | .50 |
| 105 | Gary Sheffield | .20 | .50 |
| 106 | Craig Wilson | .20 | .50 |
| 107 | Chris Carpenter | .20 | .50 |
| 108 | Michael Young | .20 | .50 |
| 109 | Gustavo Chacin | .20 | .50 |
| 110 | Chipper Jones | .50 | 1.25 |
| 111 | Mark Loretta | .20 | .50 |
| 112 | Andy Pettitte | .30 | .75 |
| 113 | Carlos Delgado | .20 | .50 |
| 114 | Pat Burrell | .20 | .50 |
| 115 | Jason Bay | .20 | .50 |

|  |  | | |
|---|---|---|---|
| 116 | Brian Roberts | .20 | .50 |
| 117 | Joe Crede | .20 | .50 |
| 118 | Jake Peavy | .20 | .50 |
| 119 | Aubrey Huff | .20 | .50 |
| 120 | Pedro Martinez | .30 | .75 |
| 121 | Jorge Posada | .30 | .75 |
| 122 | Barry Zito | .30 | .75 |
| 123 | Scott Rolen | .30 | .75 |
| 124 | Brett Myers | .20 | .50 |
| 125 | Derek Jeter | 1.25 | 3.00 |
| 126 | Eric Chavez | .20 | .50 |
| 127 | Carl Crawford | .20 | .50 |
| 128 | Jim Thome | .30 | .75 |
| 129 | Johnny Damon | .30 | .75 |
| 130 | Alfonso Soriano | .30 | .75 |
| 131 | Clint Barmes | .20 | .50 |
| 132 | Dustin Nippert (RC) | .30 | .75 |
| 133 | Hanley Ramirez (RC) | .75 | 2.00 |
| 134 | Matt Capps (RC) | .30 | .75 |
| 135 | Miguel Perez (RC) | .30 | .75 |
| 136 | Tom Gorzelanny (RC) | .30 | .75 |
| 137 | Charlton Jimerson (RC) | .30 | .75 |
| 138 | Bryan Bullington (RC) | .30 | .75 |
| 139 | Kenji Johjima RC | 1.50 | 4.00 |
| 140 | Craig Hansen RC | 1.25 | 3.00 |
| 141 | Craig Breslow AU/963 RC * | 4.00 | 10.00 |
| 142 | A.Wainwright AU/963 (RC) * | 10.00 | 25.00 |
| 143 | Joey Devine AU/963 RC * | 4.00 | 10.00 |
| 144 | H.Kuo AU/963 (RC) * | 20.00 | 50.00 |
| 145 | Jason Botts AU/963 RC * | 4.00 | 10.00 |
| 146 | J.Johnson AU/963 (RC) * | 8.00 | 20.00 |
| 147 | J.Bergmann AU/963 RC * | 4.00 | 10.00 |
| 148 | Scott Olsen AU/963 (RC) * | 6.00 | 15.00 |
| 149 | D.Rasner AU/963 (RC) * | 4.00 | 10.00 |
| 150 | Dan Ortmeier AU/963 (RC) * | 4.00 | 10.00 |
| 151 | Chuck James AU/963 (RC) * | 6.00 | 15.00 |
| 152 | Ryan Garko AU/963 (RC) * | 4.00 | 10.00 |
| 153 | Nelson Cruz AU/963 (RC) * | 6.00 | 15.00 |
| 154 | A.Lerew AU/963 (RC) * | 4.00 | 10.00 |
| 155 | F.Liriano AU/963 (RC) * | 20.00 | 50.00 |

## 2007 Finest

DEREK JETER
NEW YORK YANKEES

| | | | |
|---|---|---|---|
| COMP. SET w/o AU's (150) | | 30.00 | 60.00 |
| COMMON CARD (1-135) | | 1.25 | .40 |
| COMMON ROOKIE (136-150) | | .40 | 1.00 |
| 151-166 AU ODDS 1:3 MINI BOX | | | |
| 151-150 PLATE ODDS 1:96 MINI BOX | | | |
| AU 151-166 PLATE ODDS 1:909 MINI BOX | | | |
| PLATE PRINT RUN 1 SET PER COLOR | | | |
| BLACK-CYAN-MAGENTA-YELLOW ISSUED | | | |
| NO PLATE PRICING DUE TO SCARCITY | | | |
| EXCHANGE DEADLINE 02/28/09 | | | |
| 1 | David Wright | .60 | 1.50 |
| 2 | Jered Weaver | .25 | .60 |
| 3 | Chipper Jones | .40 | 1.00 |
| 4 | Magglio Ordonez | .15 | .40 |
| 5 | Ben Sheets | .15 | .40 |
| 6 | Nick Johnson | .15 | .40 |
| 7 | Melvin Mora | .15 | .40 |
| 8 | Chien-Ming Wang | .40 | 1.00 |
| 9 | Andre Ethier | .25 | .60 |
| 10 | Carlos Beltran | .15 | .40 |
| 11 | Ryan Zimmerman | .40 | 1.00 |
| 12 | Troy Glaus | .15 | .40 |
| 13 | Hanley Ramirez | .40 | 1.00 |
| 14 | Mark Buehrle | .15 | .40 |
| 15 | Dan Uggla | .25 | .60 |
| 16 | Richie Sexson | .15 | .40 |
| 17 | Scott Kazmir | .25 | .60 |
| 18 | Garrett Atkins | .15 | .40 |
| 19 | Matt Cain | .25 | .60 |
| 20 | Jorge Posada | .25 | .60 |
| 21 | Brett Myers | .15 | .40 |
| 22 | Jeff Francoeur | .40 | 1.00 |

|  |  | | |
|---|---|---|---|
| 23 | Scott Rolen | .25 | .60 |
| 24 | Derrek Lee | .15 | .40 |
| 25 | Manny Ramirez | .25 | .60 |
| 26 | Johnny Damon | .25 | .60 |
| 27 | Mark Teixeira | .25 | .60 |
| 28 | Mark Prior | .25 | .60 |
| 29 | Victor Martinez | .15 | .40 |
| 30 | Greg Maddux | .60 | 1.50 |
| 31 | Prince Fielder | .40 | 1.00 |
| 32 | Jeremy Bonderman | .15 | .40 |
| 33 | Paul LoDuca | .15 | .40 |
| 34 | Brandon Webb | .15 | .40 |
| 35 | Robinson Cano | .25 | .60 |
| 36 | Josh Beckett | .25 | .60 |
| 37 | David DeJesus | .15 | .40 |
| 38 | Kenny Rogers | .15 | .40 |
| 39 | Jim Thome | .25 | .60 |
| 40 | Brian McCann | .15 | .40 |
| 41 | Lance Berkman | .15 | .40 |
| 42 | Adam Dunn | .15 | .40 |
| 43 | Rocco Baldelli | .15 | .40 |
| 44 | Brian Roberts | .15 | .40 |
| 45 | Vladimir Guerrero | .40 | 1.00 |
| 46 | Dontrelle Willis | .15 | .40 |
| 47 | Eric Chavez | .15 | .40 |
| 48 | Carlos Zambrano | .15 | .40 |
| 49 | Ivan Rodriguez | .25 | .60 |
| 50 | Alex Rodriguez | .60 | 1.50 |
| 51 | Curt Schilling | .15 | .40 |
| 52 | Carlos Delgado | .15 | .40 |
| 53 | Matt Holliday | .40 | 1.00 |
| 54 | Mark Teahen | .15 | .40 |
| 55 | Frank Thomas | .40 | 1.00 |
| 56 | Grady Sizemore | .15 | .40 |
| 57 | Aramis Ramirez | .15 | .40 |
| 58 | Rafael Furcal | .15 | .40 |
| 59 | David Ortiz | .25 | .60 |
| 60 | Paul Konerko | .15 | .40 |
| 61 | Barry Zito | .15 | .40 |
| 62 | Travis Hafner | .15 | .40 |
| 63 | Nick Swisher | .15 | .40 |
| 64 | Johan Santana | .25 | .60 |
| 65 | Miguel Tejada | .15 | .40 |
| 66 | Carl Crawford | .15 | .40 |
| 67 | Kenji Johjima | .40 | 1.00 |
| 68 | Derek Jeter | 1.00 | 2.50 |
| 69 | Francisco Liriano | .75 | 2.00 |
| 70 | Ken Griffey Jr. | .60 | 1.50 |
| 71 | Pat Burrell | .15 | .40 |
| 72 | Adrian Gonzalez | .15 | .40 |
| 73 | Miguel Cabrera | .25 | .60 |
| 74 | Albert Pujols | .75 | 2.00 |
| 75 | Justin Verlander | .40 | 1.00 |
| 76 | Carlos Lee | .15 | .40 |
| 77 | John Smoltz | .25 | .60 |
| 78 | Orlando Hudson | .15 | .40 |
| 79 | Joe Mauer | .40 | 1.00 |
| 80 | Freddy Sanchez | .15 | .40 |
| 81 | Bobby Abreu | .15 | .40 |
| 82 | Pedro Martinez | .25 | .60 |
| 83 | Vernon Wells | .15 | .40 |
| 84 | Justin Morneau | .25 | .60 |
| 85 | Bill Hall | .15 | .40 |
| 86 | Jason Schmidt | .15 | .40 |
| 87 | Michael Young | .15 | .40 |
| 88 | Tadahito Iguchi | .15 | .40 |
| 89 | Kevin Millwood | .15 | .40 |
| 90 | Randy Johnson | .40 | 1.00 |
| 91 | Roy Halladay | .25 | .60 |
| 92 | Mike Lowell | .15 | .40 |
| 93 | Jake Peavy | .25 | .60 |
| 94 | Jason Varitek | .40 | 1.00 |
| 95 | Todd Helton | .25 | .60 |
| 96 | Mark Loretta | .15 | .40 |
| 97 | Gary Matthews Jr. | .15 | .40 |
| 98 | Ryan Howard | .60 | 1.50 |
| 99 | Jose Reyes | .25 | .60 |
| 100 | Chris Carpenter | .15 | .40 |
| 101 | Hideki Matsui | .40 | 1.00 |
| 102 | Brian Giles | .15 | .40 |
| 103 | Torii Hunter | .15 | .40 |
| 104 | Rich Harden | .15 | .40 |
| 105 | Ichiro Suzuki | .60 | 1.50 |
| 106 | Chase Utley | .40 | 1.00 |
| 107 | Nick Markakis | .25 | .60 |
| 108 | Marcus Giles | .15 | .40 |
| 109 | Gary Sheffield | .15 | .40 |
| 110 | Jim Edmonds | .25 | .60 |

|  |  | | |
|---|---|---|---|
| □ 111 | Brandon Phillips | .15 | .40 |
| □ 112 | Roy Oswalt | .15 | .40 |
| □ 113 | Jeff Kent | .15 | .40 |
| □ 114 | Jason Bay | .25 | .60 |
| □ 115 | Raul Ibanez | .25 | .60 |
| □ 116 | Stephen Drew | .15 | .40 |
| □ 117 | Hank Blalock | .15 | .40 |
| □ 118 | Tom Glavine | .25 | .60 |
| □ 119 | Andruw Jones | .25 | .60 |
| □ 120 | Alfonso Soriano | .15 | .40 |
| □ 121 | Mariano Rivera | .40 | 1.00 |
| □ 122 | Garret Anderson | .15 | .40 |
| □ 123 | Erik Bedard UER | .15 | .40 |
| □ 124 | Huston Street | .15 | .40 |
| □ 125 | Austin Kearns | .15 | .40 |
| □ 126 | Jermaine Dye | .15 | .40 |
| □ 127 | C.C. Sabathia | .25 | .60 |
| □ 128 | Joe Nathan | .15 | .40 |
| □ 129 | Craig Monroe | .15 | .40 |
| □ 130 | Aubrey Huff | .15 | .40 |
| □ 131 | Billy Wagner | .15 | .40 |
| □ 132 | Jorge Cantu | .15 | .40 |
| □ 133 | Trevor Hoffman | .15 | .40 |
| □ 134 | Ronnie Belliard | .15 | .40 |
| □ 135 | B.J. Ryan | .15 | .40 |
| □ 136 | Adam Lind (RC) | .40 | 1.00 |
| □ 137 | Hector Gimenez (RC) | .40 | 1.00 |
| □ 138 | Shawn Riggans UER (RC) | .40 | 1.00 |
| □ 139 | Joaquin Arias (RC) | .40 | 1.00 |
| □ 140 | Drew Anderson RC | .40 | 1.00 |
| □ 141 | Mike Rabelo RC | .40 | 1.00 |
| □ 142 | Chris Narveson (RC) | .40 | 1.00 |
| □ 143 | Ryan Feierabend (RC) | .40 | 1.00 |
| □ 144 | Vinny Rottino (RC) | .40 | 1.00 |
| □ 145 | Jon Knott (RC) | .40 | 1.00 |
| □ 146 | Oswaldo Navarro (RC) | .40 | 1.00 |
| □ 147 | Brian Stokes (RC) | .40 | 1.00 |
| □ 148 | Glen Perkins (RC) | .40 | 1.00 |
| □ 149 | Mitch Maier RC | .40 | 1.00 |
| □ 150 | Delmon Young RC | 1.00 | 2.50 |
| □ 151 | Andrew Miller AU RC | 15.00 | 40.00 |
| □ 152 | T.Tulowitzki AU (RC) | 12.50 | 30.00 |
| □ 153 | Philip Humber AU (RC) | 4.00 | 10.00 |
| □ 154 | K.Kouzmanoff AU (RC) | 6.00 | 15.00 |
| □ 155 | Michael Bourn AU (RC) | 4.00 | 10.00 |
| □ 156 | M.Montero AU (RC) EXCH | 4.00 | 10.00 |
| □ 157 | David Murphy AU (RC) | 4.00 | 10.00 |
| □ 158 | R.Sweeney AU (RC) | 4.00 | 10.00 |
| □ 159 | Jeff Baker AU (RC) | 4.00 | 10.00 |
| □ 160 | Jeff Salazar AU (RC) | 4.00 | 10.00 |
| □ 161 | J.Garcia AU RC EXCH | 4.00 | 10.00 |
| □ 162 | Josh Fields AU (RC) | 4.00 | 10.00 |
| □ 163 | Delwyn Young AU (RC) | 4.00 | 10.00 |
| □ 164 | Fred Lewis AU (RC) | 4.00 | 10.00 |
| □ 165 | Scott Moore AU (RC) | 4.00 | 10.00 |
| □ 166 | Chris Stewart AU RC | 4.00 | 10.00 |

## 2008 Finest

| | | | |
|---|---|---|---|
| □ COMP.SET w/o AUs (150) | | 40.00 | 80.00 |
| □ COMMON CARD (1-125) | | .15 | .40 |
| □ COMMON RC (126-150) | | .75 | 2.00 |
| □ COMMON AU RC (151-166) | | 4.00 | 10.00 |
| □ 151-166 AU ODDS 1:3 MINI BOX | | | |
| □ 1-150 PLATE ODDS 1:775 MINI BOX | | | |
| □ AU 151-166 PLATE ODDS 1:775 MINI BOX | | | |
| □ PLATE PRINT RUN 1 SET PER COLOR | | | |
| □ BLACK-CYAN-MAGENTA-YELLOW ISSUED | | | |
| □ NO PLATE PRICING DUE TO SCARCITY | | | |
| □ 1 | Daisuke Matsuzaka | .50 | 1.25 |
| □ 2 | Justin Upton | .25 | .60 |
| □ 3 | Andruw Jones | .15 | .40 |
| □ 4 | John Lackey | .15 | .40 |
| □ 5 | Brandon Phillips | .15 | .40 |
| □ 6 | Ryan Zimmerman | .25 | .60 |

|  |  | | |
|---|---|---|---|
| □ 7 | Tim Lincecum | .50 | 1.25 |
| □ 8 | Johnny Damon | .25 | .60 |
| □ 9 | Garrett Atkins | .15 | .40 |
| □ 10 | Magglio Ordonez | .25 | .60 |
| □ 11 | Tom Gorzelanny | .15 | .40 |
| □ 12 | Eric Chavez | .15 | .40 |
| □ 13 | Troy Tulowitzki | .25 | .60 |
| □ 14 | Mike Lowell | .15 | .40 |
| □ 15 | Brandon Webb | .25 | .60 |
| □ 16 | Chipper Jones | .50 | 1.25 |
| □ 17 | Alex Gordon | .25 | .60 |
| □ 18 | Ken Griffey Jr. | .60 | 1.50 |
| □ 19 | Roy Oswalt | .25 | .60 |
| □ 20 | Miguel Cabrera | .40 | 1.00 |
| □ 21 | Chase Utley | .25 | .60 |
| □ 22 | Scott Kazmir | .25 | .60 |
| □ 23 | Kenji Johjima | .15 | .40 |
| □ 24 | Frank Thomas | .40 | 1.00 |
| □ 25 | Ryan Braun | .50 | 1.25 |
| □ 26 | Carlos Pena | .40 | 1.00 |
| □ 27 | Robinson Cano | .25 | .60 |
| □ 28 | Ben Sheets | .25 | .60 |
| □ 29 | Russell Martin | .25 | .60 |
| □ 30 | Joe Mauer | .40 | 1.00 |
| □ 31 | Gary Sheffield | .25 | .60 |
| □ 32 | Carlos Zambrano | .15 | .40 |
| □ 33 | Jermaine Dye | .15 | .40 |
| □ 34 | Dan Uggla | .25 | .60 |
| □ 35 | Erik Bedard | .15 | .40 |
| □ 36 | Tim Hudson | .15 | .40 |
| □ 37 | David Ortiz | .25 | .60 |
| □ 38 | Tom Glavine | .25 | .60 |
| □ 39 | Adrian Gonzalez | .25 | .60 |
| □ 40 | Jorge Posada | .25 | .60 |
| □ 41 | Noah Lowry | .15 | .40 |
| □ 42 | Vernon Wells | .25 | .60 |
| □ 43 | Johan Santana | .25 | .60 |
| □ 44 | Dmitri Young | .15 | .40 |
| □ 45 | Manny Ramirez | .40 | 1.00 |
| □ 46 | Jim Edmonds | .25 | .60 |
| □ 47 | Roy Halladay | .25 | .60 |
| □ 48 | Delmon Young | .25 | .60 |
| □ 49 | Nick Swisher | .15 | .40 |
| □ 50 | David Wright | .50 | 1.25 |
| □ 51 | Paul Konerko | .15 | .40 |
| □ 52 | Curt Schilling | .25 | .60 |
| □ 53 | Torii Hunter | .15 | .40 |
| □ 54 | Gary Matthews | .15 | .40 |
| □ 55 | Derrek Lee | .25 | .60 |
| □ 56 | John Smoltz | .25 | .60 |
| □ 57 | Adam Dunn | .40 | 1.00 |
| □ 58 | C.C. Sabathia | .25 | .60 |
| □ 59 | Chris Young | .15 | .40 |
| □ 60 | Jake Peavy | .25 | .60 |
| □ 61 | Joba Chamberlain | .50 | 1.25 |
| □ 62 | Jason Bay | .25 | .60 |
| □ 63 | Chris Carpenter | .15 | .40 |
| □ 64 | Jimmy Rollins | .25 | .60 |
| □ 65 | Grady Sizemore | .25 | .60 |
| □ 66 | Joe Blanton | .15 | .40 |
| □ 67 | Justin Morneau | .25 | .60 |
| □ 68 | Lance Berkman | .25 | .60 |
| □ 69 | Jeff Francis | .15 | .40 |
| □ 70 | Nick Markakis | .25 | .60 |
| □ 71 | Orlando Cabrera | .15 | .40 |
| □ 72 | Barry Zito | .15 | .40 |
| □ 73 | Eric Byrnes | .15 | .40 |
| □ 74 | Brian McCann | .25 | .60 |
| □ 75 | Albert Pujols | .75 | 2.00 |
| □ 76 | Josh Beckett | .25 | .60 |
| □ 77 | Jim Thome | .25 | .60 |
| □ 78 | Fausto Carmona | .15 | .40 |
| □ 79 | Brad Hawpe | .15 | .40 |
| □ 80 | Prince Fielder | .40 | 1.00 |
| □ 81 | Justin Verlander | .25 | .60 |
| □ 82 | Billy Butler | .15 | .40 |
| □ 83 | J.J. Hardy | .15 | .40 |
| □ 84 | Hideki Matsui | .40 | 1.00 |
| □ 85 | Matt Holliday | .25 | .60 |
| □ 86 | Bobby Crosby | .15 | .40 |
| □ 87 | Orlando Hudson | .15 | .40 |
| □ 88 | Ichiro Suzuki | .60 | 1.50 |
| □ 89 | Troy Glaus | .25 | .60 |
| □ 90 | Hanley Ramirez | .40 | 1.00 |
| □ 91 | Carlos Beltran | .25 | .60 |
| □ 92 | Mark Buehrle | .15 | .40 |
| □ 93 | Andy Pettitte | .25 | .60 |
| □ 94 | Mark Teixeira | .25 | .60 |

|  |  | | |
|---|---|---|---|
| □ 95 | Curtis Granderson | .15 | .40 |
| □ 96 | Cole Hamels | .40 | 1.00 |
| □ 97 | Jarrod Saltalamacchia | .15 | .40 |
| □ 98 | Carl Crawford | .15 | .40 |
| □ 99 | Dontrelle Willis | .15 | .40 |
| □ 100 | Alex Rodriguez | .60 | 1.50 |
| □ 101 | Brad Penny | .15 | .40 |
| □ 102 | Michael Young | .15 | .40 |
| □ 103 | Greg Maddux | .50 | 1.25 |
| □ 104 | Brian Roberts | .25 | .60 |
| □ 105 | Hunter Pence | .40 | 1.00 |
| □ 106 | Aaron Harang | .15 | .40 |
| □ 107 | Ivan Rodriguez | .25 | .60 |
| □ 108 | Dan Haran | .15 | .40 |
| □ 109 | Freddy Sanchez | .15 | .40 |
| □ 110 | Alfonso Soriano | .25 | .60 |
| □ 111 | Hank Blalock | .15 | .40 |
| □ 112 | Chien- Ming Wang | .40 | 1.00 |
| □ 113 | Carlos Delgado | .15 | .40 |
| □ 114 | Aramis Ramirez | .15 | .40 |
| □ 115 | Jose Reyes | .25 | .60 |
| □ 116 | Victor Martinez | .25 | .60 |
| □ 117 | Carlos Lee | .15 | .40 |
| □ 118 | Jeff Kent | .15 | .40 |
| □ 119 | Miguel Tejada | .15 | .40 |
| □ 120 | Vladimir Guerrero | .40 | 1.00 |
| □ 121 | Travis Hafner | .15 | .40 |
| □ 122 | Todd Helton | .25 | .60 |
| □ 123 | Chris Young | .15 | .40 |
| □ 124 | Derek Jeter | 1.00 | 2.50 |
| □ 125 | Ryan Howard | .50 | 1.25 |
| □ 126 | Alberto Gonzalez RC | 1.25 | 3.00 |
| □ 127 | Felipe Paulino RC | 1.25 | 3.00 |
| □ 128 | Donny Lucy (RC) | .75 | 2.00 |
| □ 129 | Nick Blackburn RC | 1.25 | 3.00 |
| □ 130 | Luke Hochevar RC | 1.25 | 3.00 |
| □ 131 | Bronson Sardinha (RC) | .75 | 2.00 |
| □ 132 | Heath Phillips RC | 1.25 | 3.00 |
| □ 133 | Bryan Bullington RC | .75 | 2.00 |
| □ 134 | Jeff Clement (RC) | 1.25 | 3.00 |
| □ 135 | Josh Banks RC | .75 | 2.00 |
| □ 136 | Emilio Bonifacio RC | 2.00 | 5.00 |
| □ 137 | Ryan Hanigan RC | 1.25 | 3.00 |
| □ 138 | Erick Threets (RC) | .75 | 2.00 |
| □ 139 | Seth Smith RC | .75 | 2.00 |
| □ 140 | Billy Buckner (RC) | .75 | 2.00 |
| □ 141 | Bill Murphy (RC) | .75 | 2.00 |
| □ 142 | Radhames Liz RC | 1.25 | 3.00 |
| □ 143 | Joey Votto RC | 2.00 | 5.00 |
| □ 144 | Mel Stocker RC | .75 | 2.00 |
| □ 145 | Dan Meyer (RC) | .75 | 2.00 |
| □ 146 | Rob Johnson (RC) | .75 | 2.00 |
| □ 147 | Josh Newman RC | 1.25 | 3.00 |
| □ 148 | Gio Giese (RC) | .75 | 2.00 |
| □ 149 | Luis Mendoza (RC) | .75 | 2.00 |
| □ 150 | Wladimir Balentien (RC) | .75 | 2.00 |
| □ 151 | B.Jones AU RC | 4.00 | 10.00 |
| □ 152 | Rich Thompson AU RC | 4.00 | 10.00 |
| □ 153 | C.Hu AU (RC) | 15.00 | 40.00 |
| □ 154 | Chris Seddon AU (RC) | 4.00 | 10.00 |
| □ 155 | S.Pearce AU RC | 6.00 | 15.00 |
| □ 156 | Lance Broadway AU (RC) | 4.00 | 10.00 |
| □ 157 | Nyjer Morgan AU (RC) | 4.00 | 10.00 |
| □ 158 | Jonathan Meloan AU RC | 4.00 | 10.00 |
| □ 159 | Josh Anderson AU (RC) | 4.00 | 10.00 |
| □ 160 | C.Buchholz AU (RC) | 15.00 | 40.00 |
| □ 161 | Joe Koshansky AU (RC) | 4.00 | 10.00 |
| □ 162 | Clint Sammons AU (RC) | 4.00 | 10.00 |
| □ 163 | Daric Barton AU (RC) | 5.00 | 12.00 |
| □ 164 | Ross Detwiler AU RC | 5.00 | 12.00 |
| □ 165 | Sam Fuld AU RC | 4.00 | 10.00 |
| □ 166 | Justin Ruggiano AU RC | 4.00 | 10.00 |

## 2009 Finest

| | | | |
|---|---|---|---|
| □ COMP.SET w/o AU's (150) | | 40.00 | 80.00 |
| □ COMMON CARD (1-125) | | .15 | .40 |
| □ COMMON RC (126-150) | | .75 | 2.00 |
| □ COMMON AU RC (151-166) | | 5.00 | 12.00 |
| □ AU RC ODDS 1:2 MINI BOX | | | |
| □ LETTERS SER.#'d B/W 170-285 COPIES PER | | | |
| □ TOTAL PRINT RUNS LISTED BELOW | | | |
| □ EXCHANGE DEADLINE 4/30/2012 | | | |
| □ 1-150 PLATE ODDS 1:45 MINI BOX | | | |
| □ PLATE PRINT RUN 1 SET PER COLOR | | | |
| □ BLACK-CYAN-MAGENTA-YELLOW ISSUED | | | |
| □ NO PLATE PRICING DUE TO SCARCITY | | | |
| □ 1 | Kosuke Fukudome | .40 | 1.00 |
| □ 2 | Derek Jeter | 1.00 | 2.50 |

|  |  | | |
|---|---|---|---|
| 3 | Evan Longoria | .60 | 1.50 |
| 4 | Alex Gordon | .25 | .60 |
| 5 | David Wright | .50 | 1.25 |
| 6 | Ryan Howard | .50 | 1.25 |
| 7 | Jose Reyes | .40 | 1.00 |
| 8 | Ryan Braun | .50 | 1.25 |
| 9 | Hunter Pence | .25 | .60 |
| 10 | Chipper Jones | .40 | 1.00 |
| 11 | Jimmy Rollins | .25 | .60 |
| 12 | Alfonso Soriano | .25 | .60 |
| 13 | Alex Rodriguez | .60 | 1.50 |
| 14 | Paul Konerko | .15 | .40 |
| 15 | Dustin Pedroia | .40 | 1.00 |
| 16 | Brian McCann | .25 | .60 |
| 17 | Ken Griffey | .60 | 1.50 |
| 18 | Daisuke Matsuzaka | .60 | 1.50 |
| 19 | Josh Beckett | .25 | .60 |
| 20 | Jorge Posada | .25 | .60 |
| 21 | Nick Markakis | .25 | .60 |
| 22 | Xavier Nady | .15 | .40 |
| 23 | Carlos Pena | .25 | .60 |
| 24 | Grady Sizemore | .25 | .60 |
| 25 | Mark Teixeira | .40 | 1.00 |
| 26 | Chase Utley | .40 | 1.00 |
| 27 | Vladimir Guerrero | .40 | 1.00 |
| 28 | Prince Fielder | .40 | 1.00 |
| 29 | Brian Roberts | .15 | .40 |
| 30 | Magglio Ordonez | .25 | .60 |
| 31 | Cliff Lee | .25 | .60 |
| 32 | Josh Hamilton | .40 | 1.00 |
| 33 | Justin Morneau | .25 | .60 |
| 34 | David Ortiz | .25 | .60 |
| 35 | Cole Hamels | .40 | 1.00 |
| 36 | Edinson Volquez | .15 | .40 |
| 37 | Hanley Ramirez | .40 | 1.00 |
| 38 | Carlos Zambrano | .15 | .40 |
| 39 | Brett Myers | .15 | .40 |
| 40 | Chien-Ming Wang | .40 | 1.00 |
| 41 | John Lackey | .15 | .40 |
| 42 | B.J. Upton | .25 | .60 |
| 43 | Gary Sheffield | .15 | .40 |
| 44 | Jake Peavy | .25 | .60 |
| 45 | Carlos Lee | .15 | .40 |
| 46 | Jacoby Ellsbury | .40 | 1.00 |
| 47 | Francisco Liriano | .15 | .40 |
| 48 | Torii Hunter | .15 | .40 |
| 49 | Eric Chavez | .15 | .40 |
| 50 | Jamie Moyer | .15 | .40 |
| 51 | Ichiro Suzuki | .60 | 1.50 |
| 52 | CC Sabathia | .25 | .60 |
| 53 | Matt Holliday | .25 | .60 |
| 54 | Ervin Santana | .15 | .40 |
| 55 | Hideki Matsui | .40 | 1.00 |
| 56 | Mark Buehrle | .15 | .40 |
| 57 | Johan Santana | .40 | 1.00 |
| 58 | Francisco Rodriguez | .25 | .60 |
| 59 | Jorge Cantu | .15 | .40 |
| 60 | Joe Mauer | .40 | 1.00 |
| 61 | Ian Kinsler | .25 | .60 |
| 62 | Joba Chamberlain | .50 | 1.25 |
| 63 | Stephen Drew | .15 | .40 |
| 64 | J.D. Drew | .15 | .40 |
| 65 | Justin Upton | .25 | .60 |
| 66 | Troy Glaus | .15 | .40 |
| 67 | Chone Figgins | .15 | .40 |
| 68 | David DeJesus | .15 | .40 |
| 69 | Joey Votto | .15 | .40 |
| 70 | Alex Rios | .15 | .40 |
| 71 | Adam Jones | .25 | .60 |
| 72 | Miguel Tejada | .25 | .60 |
| 73 | Michael Young | .25 | .60 |
| 74 | Vernon Wells | .15 | .40 |
| 75 | Tim Lincecum | .50 | 1.25 |
| 76 | Ryan Zimmerman | .25 | .60 |
| 77 | Nate McLouth | .15 | .40 |
| 78 | Carl Crawford | .25 | .60 |
| 79 | Dan Haren | .15 | .40 |
| 80 | Brandon Webb | .25 | .60 |
| 81 | Tim Hudson | .15 | .40 |
| 82 | Rafael Furcal | .15 | .40 |
| 83 | Ryan Dempster | .15 | .40 |
| 84 | Carlos Beltran | .25 | .60 |
| 85 | Lance Berkman | .25 | .60 |
| 86 | Jhonny Peralta | .15 | .40 |
| 87 | Aramis Ramirez | .15 | .40 |
| 88 | Aubrey Huff | .15 | .40 |
| 89 | Johnny Damon | .25 | .60 |
| 90 | Carlos Quentin | .15 | .40 |
| 91 | Yunel Escobar | .15 | .40 |
| 92 | Scott Kazmir | .25 | .60 |
| 93 | Delmon Young | .25 | .60 |
| 94 | Jermaine Dye | .15 | .40 |
| 95 | Miguel Cabrera | .25 | .60 |
| 96 | Zack Greinke | .25 | .60 |
| 97 | Chris Young | .15 | .40 |
| 98 | Derrek Lee | .25 | .60 |
| 99 | Orlando Hudson | .15 | .40 |
| 100 | Jay Bruce | .40 | 1.00 |
| 101 | Garrett Atkins | .15 | .40 |
| 102 | Curtis Granderson | .40 | 1.00 |
| 103 | Adrian Gonzalez | .25 | .60 |
| 104 | Raul Ibanez | .25 | .60 |
| 105 | Roy Halladay | .25 | .60 |
| 106 | Jon Lester | .25 | .60 |
| 107 | Adam Dunn | .25 | .60 |
| 108 | A.J. Burnett | .25 | .60 |
| 109 | Gavin Floyd | .15 | .40 |
| 110 | Russ Martin | .25 | .60 |
| 111 | Dan Uggla | .15 | .40 |
| 112 | Andre Ethier | .25 | .60 |
| 113 | Casey Kotchman | .15 | .40 |
| 114 | Matt Garza | .15 | .40 |
| 115 | Kevin Youkilis | .25 | .60 |
| 116 | Felix Hernandez | .25 | .60 |
| 117 | Rich Harden | .15 | .40 |
| 118 | Roy Oswalt | .25 | .60 |
| 119 | Jason Bay | .25 | .60 |
| 120 | Geovany Soto | .25 | .60 |
| 121 | Ryan Ludwick | .15 | .40 |
| 122 | Joe Saunders | .15 | .40 |
| 123 | Gil Meche | .15 | .40 |
| 124 | Jim Thome | .25 | .60 |
| 125 | Albert Pujols | 1.00 | 2.50 |
| 126 | Andrew Carpenter RC | 1.25 | 3.00 |
| 127 | Aaron Cunningham RC | .75 | 2.00 |
| 128 | Phil Coke RC | 1.25 | 3.00 |
| 129 | Alcides Escobar RC | 1.25 | 3.00 |
| 130 | Dexter Fowler (RC) | 1.25 | 3.00 |
| 131 | Michael Hinckley (RC) | .75 | 2.00 |
| 132 | Brad Nelson (RC) | .75 | 2.00 |
| 133 | Scott Lewis (RC) | .75 | 2.00 |
| 134 | Juan Miranda RC | 1.25 | 3.00 |
| 135 | Jason Motte (RC) | .75 | 2.00 |
| 136 | Travis Snider RC | 2.00 | 5.00 |
| 137 | Wade LeBlanc RC | 1.25 | 3.00 |
| 138 | Matt Tuiasosopo (RC) | .75 | 2.00 |
| 139 | Humberto Sanchez (RC) | .75 | 2.00 |
| 140 | Freddy Sandoval (RC) | .75 | 2.00 |
| 141 | Chris Lambert (RC) | .75 | 2.00 |
| 142 | John Jaso RC | .75 | 2.00 |
| 143 | James McDonald RC | 1.25 | 3.00 |
| 144 | Luis Valbuena (RC) | 1.25 | 3.00 |
| 145 | Rich Rundles (RC) | .75 | 2.00 |
| 146 | Josh Whitesell RC | 1.25 | 3.00 |
| 147 | Jeff Baisley RC | .75 | 2.00 |
| 148 | Ramon Ramirez (RC) | .75 | 2.00 |
| 149 | Jason Bourgeois (RC) | .75 | 2.00 |
| 150 | Jesus Delgado RC | 1.25 | 3.00 |
| 151 | M.Gamel AU/1425 * RC | 10.00 | 25.00 |
| 152 | T.Snider AU EXCH | 10.00 | 25.00 |
| 153 | Angel Salome AU/1308 * (RC) | 5.00 | 12.00 |
| 154 | Will Venable AU/1190 * RC | 5.00 | 12.00 |
| 155 | M.Bowden AU/1308 * (RC) | 10.00 | 25.00 |
| 156 | Conor Gillaspie AU/963 * RC | 6.00 | 15.00 |
| 157 | Matt Antonelli AU/888 * RC | 5.00 | 12.00 |
| 158 | Greg Golson AU/1308 * (RC) | 5.00 | 12.00 |
| 159 | Kila Ka'aihue AU/1190 * (RC) | 5.00 | 12.00 |
| 160 | Bobby Parnell AU/1308 * RC | 5.00 | 12.00 |
| 161 | Gaby Sanchez AU/1190 * RC | 6.00 | 15.00 |
| 162 | Jonathon Niese AU/1425 * RC | 5.00 | 12.00 |
| 163 | Dexter Fowler AU EXCH | 8.00 | 20.00 |
| 164 | David Price AU/1425 * RC | 12.50 | 30.00 |

## 1960 Fleer

|  |  | | |
|---|---|---|---|
| | COMPLETE SET (79) | 300.00 | 600.00 |
| | WRAPPER (5-CENT) | 50.00 | 100.00 |
| 1 | Napoleon Lajoie DP | 12.50 | 30.00 |
| 2 | Christy Mathewson | 6.00 | 15.00 |
| 3 | Babe Ruth | 50.00 | 100.00 |
| 4 | Carl Hubbell | 3.00 | 8.00 |
| 5 | Grover C. Alexander | 4.00 | 10.00 |
| 6 | Walter Johnson DP | 4.00 | 10.00 |
| 7 | Chief Bender | 1.50 | 4.00 |
| 8 | Roger Bresnahan | 1.50 | 4.00 |
| 9 | Mordecai Brown | 1.50 | 4.00 |
| 10 | Tris Speaker | 3.00 | 8.00 |
| 11 | Arky Vaughan DP | 1.50 | 4.00 |
| 12 | Zach Wheat | 1.50 | 4.00 |
| 13 | George Sisler | 1.50 | 4.00 |
| 14 | Connie Mack | 3.00 | 8.00 |
| 15 | Clark Griffith | 1.50 | 4.00 |
| 16 | Lou Boudreau DP | 3.00 | 8.00 |
| 17 | Ernie Lombardi | 1.50 | 4.00 |
| 18 | Heinie Manush | 1.50 | 4.00 |
| 19 | Marty Marion | 2.50 | 6.00 |
| 20 | Eddie Collins DP | 1.50 | 4.00 |
| 21 | Rabbit Maranville DP | 1.50 | 4.00 |
| 22 | Joe Medwick | 1.50 | 4.00 |
| 23 | Ed Barrow | 1.50 | 4.00 |
| 24 | Mickey Cochrane | 2.50 | 6.00 |
| 25 | Jimmy Collins | 1.50 | 4.00 |
| 26 | Bob Feller DP | 6.00 | 15.00 |
| 27 | Luke Appling | 2.50 | 6.00 |
| 28 | Lou Gehrig | 40.00 | 80.00 |
| 29 | Gabby Hartnett | 1.50 | 4.00 |
| 30 | Chuck Klein | 1.50 | 4.00 |
| 31 | Tony Lazzeri DP | 2.50 | 6.00 |
| 32 | Al Simmons | 1.50 | 4.00 |
| 33 | Wilbert Robinson | 1.50 | 4.00 |
| 34 | Sam Rice | 1.50 | 4.00 |
| 35 | Herb Pennock | 1.50 | 4.00 |
| 36 | Mel Ott DP | 3.00 | 8.00 |
| 37 | Lefty O'Doul | 1.50 | 4.00 |
| 38 | Johnny Mize | 3.00 | 8.00 |
| 39 | Edmund (Bing) Miller | 1.50 | 4.00 |
| 40 | Joe Tinker | 1.50 | 4.00 |
| 41 | Frank Baker DP | 1.50 | 4.00 |
| 42 | Ty Cobb | 30.00 | 60.00 |
| 43 | Paul Derringer | 1.50 | 4.00 |
| 44 | Cap Anson | 1.50 | 4.00 |
| 45 | Jim Bottomley | 1.50 | 4.00 |
| 46 | Eddie Plank DP | 1.50 | 4.00 |
| 47 | Denton (Cy) Young | 4.00 | 10.00 |
| 48 | Hack Wilson | 2.50 | 6.00 |
| 49 | Ed Walsh UER | 1.50 | 4.00 |
| 50 | Frank Chance | 1.50 | 4.00 |
| 51 | Dazzy Vance DP | 1.50 | 4.00 |
| 52 | Bill Terry | 2.50 | 6.00 |
| 53 | Jimmie Foxx | 4.00 | 10.00 |
| 54 | Lefty Gomez | 3.00 | 8.00 |
| 55 | Branch Rickey | 1.50 | 4.00 |
| 56 | Ray Schalk DP | 1.50 | 4.00 |
| 57 | Johnny Evers | 1.50 | 4.00 |
| 58 | Charley Gehringer | 2.50 | 6.00 |
| 59 | Burleigh Grimes | 1.50 | 4.00 |
| 60 | Lefty Grove | 3.00 | 8.00 |
| 61 | Rube Waddell DP | 1.50 | 4.00 |
| 62 | Honus Wagner | 6.00 | 15.00 |
| 63 | Red Ruffing | 1.50 | 4.00 |
| 64 | Kenesaw M. Landis | 1.50 | 4.00 |
| 65 | Harry Heilmann | 1.50 | 4.00 |
| 66 | John McGraw DP | 1.50 | 4.00 |
| 67 | Hughie Jennings | 1.50 | 4.00 |
| 68 | Hal Newhouser | 2.50 | 6.00 |
| 69 | Waite Hoyt | 1.50 | 4.00 |
| 70 | Bobo Newsom | 1.50 | 4.00 |

| | | |
|---|---|---|
| ❏ 71 Earl Averill DP | 1.50 | 4.00 |
| ❏ 72 Ted Williams | 40.00 | 80.00 |
| ❏ 73 Warren Giles | 2.50 | 6.00 |
| ❏ 74 Ford Frick | 2.50 | 6.00 |
| ❏ 75 Kiki Cuyler | 1.50 | 4.00 |
| ❏ 76 Paul Waner DP | 2.50 | 6.00 |
| ❏ 77 Pie Traynor | 1.50 | 4.00 |
| ❏ 78 Lloyd Waner | 1.50 | 4.00 |
| ❏ 79 Ralph Kiner | 4.00 | 10.00 |
| ❏ 80A P.Martin SP/Eddie Collins | 1250.00 | 2500.00 |
| ❏ 80B P.Martin SP/Lefty Grove | 1000.00 | 2000.00 |
| ❏ 80C P.Martin SP/Joe Tinker | 1000.00 | 2000.00 |

## 1961 Fleer

| | | |
|---|---|---|
| ❏ COMPLETE SET (154) | 600.00 | 1200.00 |
| ❏ COMMON CARD (1-88) | 1.25 | 3.00 |
| ❏ COMMON CARD (89-154) | 3.00 | 8.00 |
| ❏ WRAPPER (5-CENT) | 50.00 | 100.00 |
| ❏ 1 Baker/Cobb/Wheat | 20.00 | 50.00 |
| ❏ 2 Grover C. Alexander | 2.50 | 6.00 |
| ❏ 3 Nick Altrock | 1.25 | 3.00 |
| ❏ 4 Cap Anson | 1.50 | 4.00 |
| ❏ 5 Earl Averill | 1.50 | 4.00 |
| ❏ 6 Frank Baker | 1.50 | 4.00 |
| ❏ 7 Dave Bancroft | 1.50 | 4.00 |
| ❏ 8 Chief Bender | 1.50 | 4.00 |
| ❏ 9 Jim Bottomley | 1.50 | 4.00 |
| ❏ 10 Roger Bresnahan | 1.50 | 4.00 |
| ❏ 11 Mordecai Brown | 1.50 | 4.00 |
| ❏ 12 Max Carey | 1.50 | 4.00 |
| ❏ 13 Jack Chesbro | 1.50 | 4.00 |
| ❏ 14 Ty Cobb | 20.00 | 50.00 |
| ❏ 15 Mickey Cochrane | 2.50 | 6.00 |
| ❏ 16 Eddie Collins | 2.50 | 6.00 |
| ❏ 17 Earle Combs | 1.50 | 4.00 |
| ❏ 18 Charles Comiskey | 1.50 | 4.00 |
| ❏ 19 Kiki Cuyler | 1.50 | 4.00 |
| ❏ 20 Paul Derringer | 1.25 | 3.00 |
| ❏ 21 Howard Ehmke | 1.25 | 3.00 |
| ❏ 22 Billy Evans UMP | 1.25 | 3.00 |
| ❏ 23 Johnny Evers | 1.50 | 4.00 |
| ❏ 24 Urban Faber | 1.50 | 4.00 |
| ❏ 25 Bob Feller | 5.00 | 12.00 |
| ❏ 26 Wes Ferrell | 1.25 | 3.00 |
| ❏ 27 Lew Fonseca | 1.25 | 3.00 |
| ❏ 28 Jimmie Foxx | 2.50 | 6.00 |
| ❏ 29 Ford Frick | 1.25 | 3.00 |
| ❏ 30 Frankie Frisch | 1.50 | 4.00 |
| ❏ 31 Lou Gehrig | 40.00 | 80.00 |
| ❏ 32 Charley Gehringer | 1.50 | 4.00 |
| ❏ 33 Warren Giles | 1.25 | 3.00 |
| ❏ 34 Lefty Gomez | 1.50 | 4.00 |
| ❏ 35 Goose Goslin | 1.50 | 4.00 |
| ❏ 36 Clark Griffith | 1.50 | 4.00 |
| ❏ 37 Burleigh Grimes | 1.50 | 4.00 |
| ❏ 38 Lefty Grove | 2.50 | 6.00 |
| ❏ 39 Chick Hafey | 1.50 | 4.00 |
| ❏ 40 Jesse Haines | 1.50 | 4.00 |
| ❏ 41 Gabby Hartnett | 1.50 | 4.00 |
| ❏ 42 Harry Heilmann | 1.50 | 4.00 |
| ❏ 43 Rogers Hornsby | 2.50 | 6.00 |
| ❏ 44 Waite Hoyt | 1.50 | 4.00 |
| ❏ 45 Carl Hubbell | 2.50 | 6.00 |
| ❏ 46 Miller Huggins | 1.50 | 4.00 |
| ❏ 47 Hughie Jennings | 1.50 | 4.00 |
| ❏ 48 Ban Johnson | 1.50 | 4.00 |
| ❏ 49 Walter Johnson | 5.00 | 12.00 |
| ❏ 50 Ralph Kiner | 2.50 | 6.00 |
| ❏ 51 Chuck Klein | 1.50 | 4.00 |
| ❏ 52 Johnny Kling | 1.25 | 3.00 |
| ❏ 53 Kenesaw M. Landis | 1.50 | 4.00 |
| ❏ 54 Tony Lazzeri | 1.50 | 4.00 |
| ❏ 55 Ernie Lombardi | 1.50 | 4.00 |
| ❏ 56 Dolf Luque | 1.25 | 3.00 |

| | | |
|---|---|---|
| ❏ 57 Heinie Manush | 1.50 | 4.00 |
| ❏ 58 Marty Marion | 1.25 | 3.00 |
| ❏ 59 Christy Mathewson | 5.00 | 12.00 |
| ❏ 60 John McGraw | 1.50 | 4.00 |
| ❏ 61 Joe Medwick | 1.50 | 4.00 |
| ❏ 62 Edmund (Bing) Miller | 1.25 | 3.00 |
| ❏ 63 Johnny Mize | 1.50 | 4.00 |
| ❏ 64 John Mostil | 1.25 | 3.00 |
| ❏ 65 Art Nehf | 1.25 | 3.00 |
| ❏ 66 Hal Newhouser | 1.50 | 4.00 |
| ❏ 67 Bobo Newsom | 1.25 | 3.00 |
| ❏ 68 Mel Ott | 2.50 | 6.00 |
| ❏ 69 Allie Reynolds | 1.25 | 3.00 |
| ❏ 70 Sam Rice | 1.50 | 4.00 |
| ❏ 71 Eppa Rixey | 1.50 | 4.00 |
| ❏ 72 Edd Roush | 1.50 | 4.00 |
| ❏ 73 Schoolboy Rowe | 1.25 | 3.00 |
| ❏ 74 Red Ruffing | 1.50 | 4.00 |
| ❏ 75 Babe Ruth | 60.00 | 120.00 |
| ❏ 76 Joe Sewell | 1.50 | 4.00 |
| ❏ 77 Al Simmons | 1.50 | 4.00 |
| ❏ 78 George Sisler | 1.50 | 4.00 |
| ❏ 79 Tris Speaker | 1.50 | 4.00 |
| ❏ 80 Fred Toney | 1.25 | 3.00 |
| ❏ 81 Dazzy Vance | 1.50 | 4.00 |
| ❏ 82 Hippo Vaughn | 1.25 | 3.00 |
| ❏ 83 Ed Walsh | 1.50 | 4.00 |
| ❏ 84 Lloyd Waner | 1.50 | 4.00 |
| ❏ 85 Paul Waner | 1.50 | 4.00 |
| ❏ 86 Zack Wheat | 1.50 | 4.00 |
| ❏ 87 Hack Wilson | 1.50 | 4.00 |
| ❏ 88 Jimmy Wilson | 1.25 | 3.00 |
| ❏ 89 G.Sisler/P.Traynor | 30.00 | 60.00 |
| ❏ 90 Babe Adams | 3.00 | 8.00 |
| ❏ 91 Dale Alexander | 3.00 | 8.00 |
| ❏ 92 Jim Bagby | 3.00 | 8.00 |
| ❏ 93 Ossie Bluege | 3.00 | 8.00 |
| ❏ 94 Lou Boudreau | 4.00 | 10.00 |
| ❏ 95 Tommy Bridges | 3.00 | 8.00 |
| ❏ 96 Donie Bush | 3.00 | 8.00 |
| ❏ 97 Dolph Camilli | 3.00 | 8.00 |
| ❏ 98 Frank Chance | 4.00 | 10.00 |
| ❏ 99 Jimmy Collins | 4.00 | 10.00 |
| ❏ 100 Stan Coveleskie | 4.00 | 10.00 |
| ❏ 101 Hugh Critz | 3.00 | 8.00 |
| ❏ 102 Alvin Crowder | 3.00 | 8.00 |
| ❏ 103 Joe Dugan | 3.00 | 8.00 |
| ❏ 104 Bibb Falk | 3.00 | 8.00 |
| ❏ 105 Rick Ferrell | 4.00 | 10.00 |
| ❏ 106 Art Fletcher | 3.00 | 8.00 |
| ❏ 107 Dennis Galehouse | 3.00 | 8.00 |
| ❏ 108 Chick Galloway | 3.00 | 8.00 |
| ❏ 109 Mule Haas | 3.00 | 8.00 |
| ❏ 110 Stan Hack | 3.00 | 8.00 |
| ❏ 111 Bump Hadley | 3.00 | 8.00 |
| ❏ 112 Billy Hamilton | 4.00 | 10.00 |
| ❏ 113 Joe Hauser | 3.00 | 8.00 |
| ❏ 114 Babe Herman | 3.00 | 8.00 |
| ❏ 115 Travis Jackson | 4.00 | 10.00 |
| ❏ 116 Eddie Joost | 3.00 | 8.00 |
| ❏ 117 Addie Joss | 4.00 | 10.00 |
| ❏ 118 Joe Judge | 3.00 | 8.00 |
| ❏ 119 Joe Kuhel | 3.00 | 8.00 |
| ❏ 120 Napoleon Lajoie | 5.00 | 12.00 |
| ❏ 121 Dutch Leonard | 3.00 | 8.00 |
| ❏ 122 Ted Lyons | 4.00 | 10.00 |
| ❏ 123 Connie Mack | 5.00 | 12.00 |
| ❏ 124 Rabbit Maranville | 4.00 | 10.00 |
| ❏ 125 Fred Marberry | 3.00 | 8.00 |
| ❏ 126 Joe McGinnity | 4.00 | 10.00 |
| ❏ 127 Oscar Melillo | 3.00 | 8.00 |
| ❏ 128 Ray Mueller | 3.00 | 8.00 |
| ❏ 129 Kid Nichols | 4.00 | 10.00 |
| ❏ 130 Lefty O'Doul | 4.00 | 10.00 |
| ❏ 131 Bob O'Farrell | 3.00 | 8.00 |
| ❏ 132 Roger Peckinpaugh | 3.00 | 8.00 |
| ❏ 133 Herb Pennock | 4.00 | 10.00 |
| ❏ 134 George Pipgras | 3.00 | 8.00 |
| ❏ 135 Eddie Plank | 4.00 | 10.00 |
| ❏ 136 Ray Schalk | 4.00 | 10.00 |
| ❏ 137 Hal Schumacher | 3.00 | 8.00 |
| ❏ 138 Luke Sewell | 3.00 | 8.00 |
| ❏ 139 Bob Shawkey | 3.00 | 8.00 |
| ❏ 140 Riggs Stephenson | 3.00 | 8.00 |
| ❏ 141 Billy Sullivan | 3.00 | 8.00 |
| ❏ 142 Bill Terry | 5.00 | 12.00 |
| ❏ 143 Joe Tinker | 4.00 | 10.00 |
| ❏ 144 Pie Traynor | 4.00 | 10.00 |

| | | |
|---|---|---|
| ❏ 145 Hal Trosky | 3.00 | 8.00 |
| ❏ 146 George Uhle | 3.00 | 8.00 |
| ❏ 147 Johnny VanderMeer | 4.00 | 10.00 |
| ❏ 148 Arky Vaughan | 4.00 | 10.00 |
| ❏ 149 Rube Waddell | 4.00 | 10.00 |
| ❏ 150 Honus Wagner | 20.00 | 50.00 |
| ❏ 151 Dixie Walker | 3.00 | 8.00 |
| ❏ 152 Ted Williams | 60.00 | 120.00 |
| ❏ 153 Cy Young | 15.00 | 40.00 |
| ❏ 154 Ross Youngs | 15.00 | 40.00 |

## 1963 Fleer

| | | |
|---|---|---|
| ❏ COMPLETE SET (67) | 1000.00 | 2000.00 |
| ❏ WRAPPER (5-CENT) | 50.00 | 100.00 |
| ❏ 1 Steve Barber | 10.00 | 25.00 |
| ❏ 2 Ron Hansen | 6.00 | 15.00 |
| ❏ 3 Milt Pappas | 8.00 | 20.00 |
| ❏ 4 Brooks Robinson | 50.00 | 100.00 |
| ❏ 5 Willie Mays | 100.00 | 200.00 |
| ❏ 6 Lou Clinton | 6.00 | 15.00 |
| ❏ 7 Bill Monbouquette | 6.00 | 15.00 |
| ❏ 8 Carl Yastrzemski | 50.00 | 100.00 |
| ❏ 9 Ray Herbert | 6.00 | 15.00 |
| ❏ 10 Jim Landis | 6.00 | 15.00 |
| ❏ 11 Dick Donovan | 6.00 | 15.00 |
| ❏ 12 Tito Francona | 6.00 | 15.00 |
| ❏ 13 Jerry Kindall | 6.00 | 15.00 |
| ❏ 14 Frank Lary | 8.00 | 20.00 |
| ❏ 15 Dick Howser | 8.00 | 20.00 |
| ❏ 16 Jerry Lumpe | 6.00 | 15.00 |
| ❏ 17 Norm Siebern | 6.00 | 15.00 |
| ❏ 18 Don Lee | 6.00 | 15.00 |
| ❏ 19 Albie Pearson | 8.00 | 20.00 |
| ❏ 20 Bob Rodgers | 8.00 | 20.00 |
| ❏ 21 Leon Wagner | 6.00 | 15.00 |
| ❏ 22 Jim Kaat | 10.00 | 25.00 |
| ❏ 23 Vic Power | 6.00 | 15.00 |
| ❏ 24 Rich Rollins | 6.00 | 15.00 |
| ❏ 25 Bobby Richardson | 10.00 | 25.00 |
| ❏ 26 Ralph Terry | 8.00 | 20.00 |
| ❏ 27 Tom Cheney | 6.00 | 15.00 |
| ❏ 28 Chuck Cottier | 6.00 | 15.00 |
| ❏ 29 Jimmy Piersall | 8.00 | 20.00 |
| ❏ 30 Dave Stenhouse | 6.00 | 15.00 |
| ❏ 31 Glen Hobbie | 6.00 | 15.00 |
| ❏ 32 Ron Santo | 10.00 | 25.00 |
| ❏ 33 Gene Freese | 6.00 | 15.00 |
| ❏ 34 Vada Pinson | 10.00 | 25.00 |
| ❏ 35 Bob Purkey | 6.00 | 15.00 |
| ❏ 36 Joe Amalfitano | 6.00 | 15.00 |
| ❏ 37 Bob Aspromonte | 6.00 | 15.00 |
| ❏ 38 Dick Farrell | 6.00 | 15.00 |
| ❏ 39 Al Spangler | 6.00 | 15.00 |
| ❏ 40 Tommy Davis | 8.00 | 20.00 |
| ❏ 41 Don Drysdale | 40.00 | 80.00 |
| ❏ 42 Sandy Koufax | 100.00 | 200.00 |
| ❏ 43 Maury Wills RC | 50.00 | 100.00 |
| ❏ 44 Frank Bolling | 6.00 | 15.00 |
| ❏ 45 Warren Spahn | 40.00 | 80.00 |
| ❏ 46 Joe Adcock SP | 75.00 | 150.00 |
| ❏ 47 Roger Craig | 8.00 | 20.00 |
| ❏ 48 Al Jackson | 8.00 | 20.00 |
| ❏ 49 Rod Kanehl | 8.00 | 20.00 |
| ❏ 50 Ruben Amaro | 6.00 | 15.00 |
| ❏ 51 Johnny Callison | 8.00 | 20.00 |
| ❏ 52 Clay Dalrymple | 6.00 | 15.00 |
| ❏ 53 Don Demeter | 6.00 | 15.00 |
| ❏ 54 Art Mahaffey | 6.00 | 15.00 |
| ❏ 55 Smoky Burgess | 6.00 | 15.00 |
| ❏ 56 Roberto Clemente | 100.00 | 200.00 |
| ❏ 57 Roy Face | 8.00 | 20.00 |
| ❏ 58 Vern Law | 8.00 | 20.00 |
| ❏ 59 Bill Mazeroski | 12.50 | 30.00 |
| ❏ 60 Ken Boyer | 10.00 | 25.00 |

| | | | |
|---|---|--:|--:|
| ☐ 61 | Bob Gibson | 40.00 | 80.00 |
| ☐ 62 | Gene Oliver | 6.00 | 15.00 |
| ☐ 63 | Bill White | 8.00 | 20.00 |
| ☐ 64 | Orlando Cepeda | 12.50 | 30.00 |
| ☐ 65 | Jim Davenport | 6.00 | 15.00 |
| ☐ 66 | Billy O'Dell | 10.00 | 25.00 |
| ☐ NNO | Checklist SP | 250.00 | 500.00 |

## 1981 Fleer

| | | | |
|---|---|--:|--:|
| ☐ | COMPLETE SET (660) | 15.00 | 40.00 |
| ☐ 1 | Pete Rose | 1.25 | 3.00 |
| ☐ 2 | Larry Bowa | .08 | .25 |
| ☐ 3 | Manny Trillo | .02 | .10 |
| ☐ 4 | Bob Boone | .08 | .25 |
| ☐ 5 | Mike Schmidt | 1.00 | 2.50 |
| ☐ 6 | Steve Carlton P1 | .20 | .50 |
| ☐ 6B | Steve Carlton P2 | .60 | 1.50 |
| ☐ 6C | Steve Carlton P3 | .75 | 2.00 |
| ☐ 7 | Tug McGraw | .08 | .25 |
| ☐ 8 | Larry Christenson | .02 | .10 |
| ☐ 9 | Bake McBride | .02 | .10 |
| ☐ 10 | Greg Luzinski | .08 | .25 |
| ☐ 11 | Ron Reed | .02 | .10 |
| ☐ 12 | Dickie Noles | .02 | .10 |
| ☐ 13 | Keith Moreland RC | .02 | .10 |
| ☐ 14 | Bob Walk RC | .20 | .50 |
| ☐ 15 | Lonnie Smith | .08 | .25 |
| ☐ 16 | Dick Ruthven | .02 | .10 |
| ☐ 17 | Sparky Lyle | .08 | .25 |
| ☐ 18 | Greg Gross | .02 | .10 |
| ☐ 19 | Garry Maddox | .02 | .10 |
| ☐ 20 | Nino Espinosa | .02 | .10 |
| ☐ 21 | George Vukovich RC | .02 | .10 |
| ☐ 22 | John Vukovich | .02 | .10 |
| ☐ 23 | Ramon Aviles | .02 | .10 |
| ☐ 24A | Kevin Saucier P1 | .02 | .10 |
| ☐ 24B | Kevin Saucier P2 | .02 | .10 |
| ☐ 24C | Kevin Saucier P3 | .20 | .50 |
| ☐ 25 | Randy Lerch | .02 | .10 |
| ☐ 26 | Del Unser | .02 | .10 |
| ☐ 27 | Tim McCarver | .08 | .25 |
| ☐ 28 | George Brett | 1.00 | 2.50 |
| ☐ 29 | Willie Wilson | .08 | .25 |
| ☐ 30 | Paul Splittorff | .02 | .10 |
| ☐ 31 | Dan Quisenberry | .08 | .25 |
| ☐ 32A | Amos Otis P1 Batting | .08 | .25 |
| ☐ 32B | Amos Otis P2 | .08 | .25 |
| ☐ 33 | Steve Busby | .02 | .10 |
| ☐ 34 | U.L. Washington | .02 | .10 |
| ☐ 35 | Dave Chalk | .02 | .10 |
| ☐ 36 | Darrell Porter | .02 | .10 |
| ☐ 37 | Marty Pattin | .02 | .10 |
| ☐ 38 | Larry Gura | .02 | .10 |
| ☐ 39 | Renie Martin | .02 | .10 |
| ☐ 40 | Rich Gale | .02 | .10 |
| ☐ 41A | Hal McRae P1 | .20 | .50 |
| ☐ 41B | Hal McRae P2 | .08 | .25 |
| ☐ 42 | Dennis Leonard | .02 | .10 |
| ☐ 43 | Willie Aikens | .02 | .10 |
| ☐ 44 | Frank White | .08 | .25 |
| ☐ 45 | Clint Hurdle | .02 | .10 |
| ☐ 46 | John Wathan | .02 | .10 |
| ☐ 47 | Pete LaCock | .02 | .10 |
| ☐ 48 | Rance Mulliniks | .02 | .10 |
| ☐ 49 | Jeff Twitty RC | .02 | .10 |
| ☐ 50 | Jamie Quirk | .02 | .10 |
| ☐ 51 | Art Howe | .02 | .10 |
| ☐ 52 | Ken Forsch | .02 | .10 |
| ☐ 53 | Vern Ruhle | .02 | .10 |
| ☐ 54 | Joe Niekro | .08 | .25 |
| ☐ 55 | Frank LaCorte | .02 | .10 |
| ☐ 56 | J.R. Richard | .08 | .25 |
| ☐ 57 | Nolan Ryan | 2.00 | 5.00 |
| ☐ 58 | Enos Cabell | .02 | .10 |

| | | | |
|---|---|--:|--:|
| ☐ 59 | Cesar Cedeno | .08 | .25 |
| ☐ 60 | Jose Cruz | .08 | .25 |
| ☐ 61 | Bill Virdon MG | .02 | .10 |
| ☐ 62 | Terry Puhl | .02 | .10 |
| ☐ 63 | Joaquin Andujar | .08 | .25 |
| ☐ 64 | Alan Ashby | .02 | .10 |
| ☐ 65 | Joe Sambito | .02 | .10 |
| ☐ 66 | Denny Walling | .02 | .10 |
| ☐ 67 | Jeff Leonard | .08 | .25 |
| ☐ 68 | Luis Pujols | .02 | .10 |
| ☐ 69 | Bruce Bochy | .02 | .10 |
| ☐ 70 | Rafael Landestoy | .02 | .10 |
| ☐ 71 | Dave Smith RC | .20 | .50 |
| ☐ 72 | Danny Heep RC | .08 | .25 |
| ☐ 73 | Julio Gonzalez | .02 | .10 |
| ☐ 74 | Craig Reynolds | .02 | .10 |
| ☐ 75 | Gary Woods | .02 | .10 |
| ☐ 76 | Dave Bergman | .02 | .10 |
| ☐ 77 | Randy Niemann | .02 | .10 |
| ☐ 78 | Joe Morgan | .20 | .50 |
| ☐ 79 | Reggie Jackson | .40 | 1.00 |
| ☐ 80 | Bucky Dent | .08 | .25 |
| ☐ 81 | Tommy John | .08 | .25 |
| ☐ 82 | Luis Tiant | .08 | .25 |
| ☐ 83 | Rick Cerone | .02 | .10 |
| ☐ 84 | Dick Howser MG | .02 | .10 |
| ☐ 85 | Lou Piniella | .08 | .25 |
| ☐ 86 | Ron Davis | .02 | .10 |
| ☐ 87A | Craig Nettles P1 | 2.00 | 5.00 |
| ☐ 87B | Graig Nettles COR | .08 | .25 |
| ☐ 88 | Ron Guidry | .08 | .25 |
| ☐ 89 | Rich Gossage | .08 | .25 |
| ☐ 90 | Rudy May | .02 | .10 |
| ☐ 91 | Gaylord Perry | .08 | .25 |
| ☐ 92 | Eric Soderholm | .02 | .10 |
| ☐ 93 | Bob Watson | .02 | .10 |
| ☐ 94 | Bobby Murcer | .08 | .25 |
| ☐ 95 | Bobby Brown | .02 | .10 |
| ☐ 96 | Jim Spencer | .02 | .10 |
| ☐ 97 | Tom Underwood | .02 | .10 |
| ☐ 98 | Oscar Gamble | .02 | .10 |
| ☐ 99 | Johnny Oates | .02 | .10 |
| ☐ 100 | Fred Stanley | .02 | .10 |
| ☐ 101 | Ruppert Jones | .02 | .10 |
| ☐ 102 | Dennis Werth RC | .02 | .10 |
| ☐ 103 | Joe Lefebvre RC | .02 | .10 |
| ☐ 104 | Brian Doyle | .02 | .10 |
| ☐ 105 | Aurelio Rodriguez | .02 | .10 |
| ☐ 106 | Doug Bird | .02 | .10 |
| ☐ 107 | Mike Griffin RC | .05 | .15 |
| ☐ 108 | Tim Lollar RC | .02 | .10 |
| ☐ 109 | Willie Randolph | .08 | .25 |
| ☐ 110 | Steve Garvey | .20 | .50 |
| ☐ 111 | Reggie Smith | .08 | .25 |
| ☐ 112 | Don Sutton | .08 | .25 |
| ☐ 113 | Burt Hooton | .02 | .10 |
| ☐ 114A | Dave Lopes P1 | .20 | .50 |
| ☐ 114B | Dave Lopes P2 | .08 | .25 |
| ☐ 115 | Dusty Baker | .08 | .25 |
| ☐ 116 | Tom Lasorda MG | .08 | .25 |
| ☐ 117 | Bill Russell | .08 | .25 |
| ☐ 118 | Jerry Reuss UER | .02 | .10 |
| ☐ 119 | Terry Forster | .08 | .25 |
| ☐ 120A | Bob Welch | .08 | .25 |
| ☐ 120B | Bob Welch (Robert) | .08 | .25 |
| ☐ 121 | Don Stanhouse | .02 | .10 |
| ☐ 122 | Rick Monday | .08 | .25 |
| ☐ 123 | Derrel Thomas | .02 | .10 |
| ☐ 124 | Joe Ferguson | .02 | .10 |
| ☐ 125 | Rick Sutcliffe | .08 | .25 |
| ☐ 126A | Ron Cey P1 | .08 | .25 |
| ☐ 126B | Ron Cey P2 | .08 | .25 |
| ☐ 127 | Dave Goltz | .02 | .10 |
| ☐ 128 | Jay Johnstone | .02 | .10 |
| ☐ 129 | Steve Yeager | .02 | .10 |
| ☐ 130 | Gary Weiss RC | .02 | .10 |
| ☐ 131 | Mike Scioscia RC | .60 | 1.50 |
| ☐ 132 | Vic Davalillo | .02 | .10 |
| ☐ 133 | Doug Rau | .02 | .10 |
| ☐ 134 | Pepe Frias | .02 | .10 |
| ☐ 135 | Mickey Hatcher | .02 | .10 |
| ☐ 136 | Steve Howe RC | .20 | .50 |
| ☐ 137 | Robert Castillo RC | .02 | .10 |
| ☐ 138 | Gary Thomasson | .02 | .10 |
| ☐ 139 | Rudy Law | .02 | .10 |
| ☐ 140 | Fernando Valenzuela RC | 2.00 | 5.00 |
| ☐ 141 | Manny Mota | .08 | .25 |
| ☐ 142 | Gary Carter | .20 | .50 |

| | | | |
|---|---|--:|--:|
| ☐ 143 | Steve Rogers | .08 | .25 |
| ☐ 144 | Warren Cromartie | .02 | .10 |
| ☐ 145 | Andre Dawson | .20 | .50 |
| ☐ 146 | Larry Parrish | .02 | .10 |
| ☐ 147 | Rowland Office | .02 | .10 |
| ☐ 148 | Ellis Valentine | .02 | .10 |
| ☐ 149 | Dick Williams MG | .02 | .10 |
| ☐ 150 | Bill Gullickson RC | .20 | .50 |
| ☐ 151 | Elias Sosa | .02 | .10 |
| ☐ 152 | John Tamargo | .02 | .10 |
| ☐ 153 | Chris Speier | .02 | .10 |
| ☐ 154 | Ron LeFlore | .08 | .25 |
| ☐ 155 | Rodney Scott | .02 | .10 |
| ☐ 156 | Stan Bahnsen | .02 | .10 |
| ☐ 157 | Bill Lee | .08 | .25 |
| ☐ 158 | Fred Norman | .02 | .10 |
| ☐ 159 | Woodie Fryman | .02 | .10 |
| ☐ 160 | David Palmer | .02 | .10 |
| ☐ 161 | Jerry White | .02 | .10 |
| ☐ 162 | Roberto Ramos RC | .02 | .10 |
| ☐ 163 | John D'Acquisto | .02 | .10 |
| ☐ 164 | Tommy Hutton | .02 | .10 |
| ☐ 165 | Charlie Lea RC | .02 | .10 |
| ☐ 166 | Scott Sanderson | .02 | .10 |
| ☐ 167 | Ken Macha | .02 | .10 |
| ☐ 168 | Tony Bernazard | .02 | .10 |
| ☐ 169 | Jim Palmer | .20 | .50 |
| ☐ 170 | Steve Stone | .02 | .10 |
| ☐ 171 | Mike Flanagan | .08 | .25 |
| ☐ 172 | Al Bumbry | .02 | .10 |
| ☐ 173 | Doug DeCinces | .08 | .25 |
| ☐ 174 | Scott McGregor | .02 | .10 |
| ☐ 175 | Mark Belanger | .02 | .10 |
| ☐ 176 | Tim Stoddard | .02 | .10 |
| ☐ 177A | Rick Dempsey P1 | .08 | .25 |
| ☐ 177B | Rick Dempsey P2 | .08 | .25 |
| ☐ 178 | Earl Weaver MG | .08 | .25 |
| ☐ 179 | Tippy Martinez | .02 | .10 |
| ☐ 180 | Dennis Martinez | .08 | .25 |
| ☐ 181 | Sammy Stewart | .02 | .10 |
| ☐ 182 | Rich Dauer | .02 | .10 |
| ☐ 183 | Lee May | .02 | .10 |
| ☐ 184 | Eddie Murray | .60 | 1.50 |
| ☐ 185 | Benny Ayala | .02 | .10 |
| ☐ 186 | John Lowenstein | .02 | .10 |
| ☐ 187 | Gary Roenicke | .02 | .10 |
| ☐ 188 | Ken Singleton | .08 | .25 |
| ☐ 189 | Dan Graham | .02 | .10 |
| ☐ 190 | Terry Crowley | .02 | .10 |
| ☐ 191 | Kiko Garcia | .02 | .10 |
| ☐ 192 | Dave Ford RC | .02 | .10 |
| ☐ 193 | Mark Corey | .02 | .10 |
| ☐ 194 | Lenn Sakata | .02 | .10 |
| ☐ 195 | Doug DeCinces | .02 | .10 |
| ☐ 196 | Johnny Bench | .40 | 1.00 |
| ☐ 197 | Dave Concepcion | .08 | .25 |
| ☐ 198 | Ray Knight | .08 | .25 |
| ☐ 199 | Ken Griffey | .08 | .25 |
| ☐ 200 | Tom Seaver | .40 | 1.00 |
| ☐ 201 | Dave Collins | .02 | .10 |
| ☐ 202A | George Foster P1 | .20 | .50 |
| ☐ 202B | George Foster P2 | .20 | .50 |
| ☐ 203 | Junior Kennedy | .02 | .10 |
| ☐ 204 | Frank Pastore | .02 | .10 |
| ☐ 205 | Dan Driessen | .02 | .10 |
| ☐ 206 | Hector Cruz | .02 | .10 |
| ☐ 207 | Paul Moskau | .02 | .10 |
| ☐ 208 | Charlie Leibrandt RC | .20 | .50 |
| ☐ 209 | Harry Spilman | .02 | .10 |
| ☐ 210 | Joe Price RC | .02 | .10 |
| ☐ 211 | Tom Hume | .02 | .10 |
| ☐ 212 | Joe Nolan RC | .02 | .10 |
| ☐ 213 | Doug Bair | .02 | .10 |
| ☐ 214 | Mario Soto | .08 | .25 |
| ☐ 215A | Bill Bonham P1 | .20 | .50 |
| ☐ 215B | Bill Bonham P2 | .08 | .25 |
| ☐ 216 | George Foster SLG | .08 | .25 |
| ☐ 217 | Paul Householder RC | .02 | .10 |
| ☐ 218 | Ron Oester | .02 | .10 |
| ☐ 219 | Sam Mejias | .02 | .10 |
| ☐ 220 | Sheldon Burnside RC | .02 | .10 |
| ☐ 221 | Carl Yastrzemski | .60 | 1.50 |
| ☐ 222 | Jim Rice | .08 | .25 |
| ☐ 223 | Fred Lynn | .08 | .25 |
| ☐ 224 | Carlton Fisk | .20 | .50 |
| ☐ 225 | Rick Burleson | .02 | .10 |
| ☐ 226 | Dennis Eckersley | .20 | .50 |
| ☐ 227 | Butch Hobson | .02 | .10 |

|  |  | | |
|---|---|---|---|
| 228 | Tom Burgmeier | .02 | .10 |
| 229 | Garry Hancock | .02 | .10 |
| 230 | Don Zimmer MG | .08 | .25 |
| 231 | Steve Renko | .02 | .10 |
| 232 | Dwight Evans | .20 | .50 |
| 233 | Mike Torrez | .02 | .10 |
| 234 | Bob Stanley | .02 | .10 |
| 235 | Jim Dwyer | .02 | .10 |
| 236 | Dave Stapleton RC | .02 | .10 |
| 237 | Glenn Hoffman RC | .02 | .10 |
| 238 | Jerry Remy | .02 | .10 |
| 239 | Dick Drago | .02 | .10 |
| 240 | Bill Campbell | .02 | .10 |
| 241 | Tony Perez | .20 | .50 |
| 242 | Phil Niekro | .08 | .25 |
| 243 | Dale Murphy | .20 | .50 |
| 244 | Bob Horner | .08 | .25 |
| 245 | Jeff Burroughs | .08 | .25 |
| 246 | Rick Camp | .02 | .10 |
| 247 | Bobby Cox MG | .08 | .25 |
| 248 | Bruce Benedict | .02 | .10 |
| 249 | Gene Garber | .02 | .10 |
| 250 | Jerry Royster | .02 | .10 |
| 251A | Gary Matthews P1 | .20 | .50 |
| 251B | Gary Matthews P2 | .08 | .25 |
| 252 | Chris Chambliss | .08 | .25 |
| 253 | Luis Gomez | .02 | .10 |
| 254 | Bill Nahorodny | .02 | .10 |
| 255 | Doyle Alexander | .02 | .10 |
| 256 | Brian Asselstine | .02 | .10 |
| 257 | Biff Pocoroba | .02 | .10 |
| 258 | Mike Lum | .02 | .10 |
| 259 | Charlie Spikes | .02 | .10 |
| 260 | Glenn Hubbard | .02 | .10 |
| 261 | Tommy Boggs | .02 | .10 |
| 262 | Al Hrabosky | .08 | .25 |
| 263 | Rick Matula | .02 | .10 |
| 264 | Preston Hanna | .02 | .10 |
| 265 | Larry Bradford | .02 | .10 |
| 266 | Rafael Ramirez RC | .02 | .10 |
| 267 | Larry McWilliams | .02 | .10 |
| 268 | Rod Carew | .20 | .50 |
| 269 | Bobby Grich | .08 | .25 |
| 270 | Carney Lansford | .08 | .25 |
| 271 | Don Baylor | .08 | .25 |
| 272 | Joe Rudi | .08 | .25 |
| 273 | Dan Ford | .02 | .10 |
| 274 | Jim Fregosi MG | .02 | .10 |
| 275 | Dave Frost | .02 | .10 |
| 276 | Frank Tanana | .08 | .25 |
| 277 | Dickie Thon | .02 | .10 |
| 278 | Jason Thompson | .02 | .10 |
| 279 | Rick Miller | .02 | .10 |
| 280 | Bert Campaneris | .08 | .25 |
| 281 | Tom Donohue | .02 | .10 |
| 282 | Brian Downing | .08 | .25 |
| 283 | Fred Patek | .02 | .10 |
| 284 | Bruce Kison | .02 | .10 |
| 285 | Dave LaRoche | .02 | .10 |
| 286 | Don Aase | .02 | .10 |
| 287 | Jim Barr | .02 | .10 |
| 288 | Alfredo Martinez RC | .02 | .10 |
| 289 | Larry Harlow | .02 | .10 |
| 290 | Andy Hassler | .02 | .10 |
| 291 | Dave Kingman | .08 | .25 |
| 292 | Bill Buckner | .08 | .25 |
| 293 | Rick Reuschel | .08 | .25 |
| 294 | Bruce Sutter | .20 | .50 |
| 295 | Jerry Martin | .02 | .10 |
| 296 | Scot Thompson | .02 | .10 |
| 297 | Ivan DeJesus | .02 | .10 |
| 298 | Steve Dillard | .02 | .10 |
| 299 | Dick Tidrow | .02 | .10 |
| 300 | Randy Martz RC | .02 | .10 |
| 301 | Lenny Randle | .02 | .10 |
| 302 | Lynn McGlothen | .02 | .10 |
| 303 | Cliff Johnson | .02 | .10 |
| 304 | Tim Blackwell | .02 | .10 |
| 305 | Dennis Lamp | .02 | .10 |
| 306 | Bill Caudill | .02 | .10 |
| 307 | Carlos Lezcano RC | .02 | .10 |
| 308 | Jim Tracy RC | .40 | 1.00 |
| 309 | Doug Capilla UER | .02 | .10 |
| 310 | Willie Hernandez | .02 | .10 |
| 311 | Mike Vail | .02 | .10 |
| 312 | Mike Krukow RC | .02 | .10 |
| 313 | Barry Foote | .02 | .10 |
| 314 | Larry Biittner | .02 | .10 |
| 315 | Mike Tyson | .02 | .10 |
| 316 | Lee Mazzilli | .06 | .25 |
| 317 | John Stearns | .02 | .10 |
| 318 | Alex Trevino | .02 | .10 |
| 319 | Craig Swan | .02 | .10 |
| 320 | Frank Taveras | .02 | .10 |
| 321 | Steve Henderson | .02 | .10 |
| 322 | Neil Allen | .02 | .10 |
| 323 | Mark Bomback RC | .02 | .10 |
| 324 | Mike Jorgensen | .02 | .10 |
| 325 | Joe Torre MG | .08 | .25 |
| 326 | Elliott Maddox | .02 | .10 |
| 327 | Pete Falcone | .02 | .10 |
| 328 | Ray Burris | .02 | .10 |
| 329 | Claudell Washington | .02 | .10 |
| 330 | Doug Flynn | .02 | .10 |
| 331 | Joel Youngblood | .02 | .10 |
| 332 | Bill Almon RC | .02 | .10 |
| 333 | Tom Hausman | .02 | .10 |
| 334 | Pat Zachry | .02 | .10 |
| 335 | Jeff Reardon RC | .40 | 1.00 |
| 336 | Wally Backman RC | .20 | .50 |
| 337 | Dan Norman | .02 | .10 |
| 338 | Jerry Morales | .02 | .10 |
| 339 | Ed Farmer | .02 | .10 |
| 340 | Bob Molinaro | .02 | .10 |
| 341 | Todd Cruz | .02 | .10 |
| 342A | Britt Burns P1 | .20 | .50 |
| 342B | Britt Burns P2 RC | .08 | .25 |
| 343 | Kevin Bell | .02 | .10 |
| 344 | Tony LaRussa MG | .08 | .25 |
| 345 | Steve Trout | .02 | .10 |
| 346 | Harold Baines RC | .75 | 2.00 |
| 347 | Richard Wortham | .02 | .10 |
| 348 | Wayne Nordhagen | .02 | .10 |
| 349 | Mike Squires | .02 | .10 |
| 350 | Lamar Johnson | .02 | .10 |
| 351 | Rickey Henderson SB | 1.25 | 3.00 |
| 352 | Francisco Barrios | .02 | .10 |
| 353 | Thad Bosley | .02 | .10 |
| 354 | Chet Lemon | .08 | .25 |
| 355 | Bruce Kimm | .02 | .10 |
| 356 | Richard Dotson RC | .02 | .10 |
| 357 | Jim Morrison | .02 | .10 |
| 358 | Mike Proly | .02 | .10 |
| 359 | Greg Pryor | .02 | .10 |
| 360 | Dave Parker | .08 | .25 |
| 361 | Omar Moreno | .02 | .10 |
| 362A | Kent Tekulve P1 | .02 | .10 |
| 362B | Kent Tekulve P2 | .02 | .10 |
| 363 | Willie Stargell | .20 | .50 |
| 364 | Phil Garner | .08 | .25 |
| 365 | Ed Ott | .02 | .10 |
| 366 | Don Robinson | .02 | .10 |
| 367 | Chuck Tanner MG | .02 | .10 |
| 368 | Jim Rooker | .02 | .10 |
| 369 | Dale Berra | .02 | .10 |
| 370 | Jim Bibby | .02 | .10 |
| 371 | Steve Nicosia | .02 | .10 |
| 372 | Mike Easler | .02 | .10 |
| 373 | Bill Robinson | .02 | .10 |
| 374 | Lee Lacy | .02 | .10 |
| 375 | John Candelaria | .08 | .25 |
| 376 | Manny Sanguillen | .08 | .25 |
| 377 | Rick Rhoden | .08 | .25 |
| 378 | Grant Jackson | .02 | .10 |
| 379 | Tim Foli | .02 | .10 |
| 380 | Rod Scurry RC | .02 | .10 |
| 381 | Bill Madlock | .08 | .25 |
| 382A | Kurt Bevacqua P1 | .08 | .25 |
| 382B | Kurt Bevacqua P2 | .02 | .10 |
| 383 | Bert Blyleven | .08 | .25 |
| 384 | Eddie Solomon | .02 | .10 |
| 385 | Enrique Romo | .02 | .10 |
| 386 | John Milner | .02 | .10 |
| 387 | Mike Hargrove | .02 | .10 |
| 388 | Jorge Orta | .02 | .10 |
| 389 | Toby Harrah | .08 | .25 |
| 390 | Tom Veryzer | .02 | .10 |
| 391 | Miguel Dilone | .02 | .10 |
| 392 | Dan Spillner | .02 | .10 |
| 393 | Jack Brohamer | .02 | .10 |
| 394 | Wayne Garland | .02 | .10 |
| 395 | Sid Monge | .02 | .10 |
| 396 | Rick Waits | .02 | .10 |
| 397 | Joe Charboneau RC | .40 | 1.00 |
| 398 | Gary Alexander | .02 | .10 |
| 399 | Jerry Dybzinski RC | .02 | .10 |
| 400 | Mike Stanton RC | .02 | .10 |
| 401 | Mike Paxton | .02 | .10 |
| 402 | Gary Gray RC | .02 | .10 |
| 403 | Rick Manning | .02 | .10 |
| 404 | Bo Diaz | .02 | .10 |
| 405 | Ron Hassey | .02 | .10 |
| 406 | Ross Grimsley | .02 | .10 |
| 407 | Victor Cruz | .02 | .10 |
| 408 | Len Barker | .08 | .25 |
| 409 | Bob Bailor | .02 | .10 |
| 410 | Otto Velez | .02 | .10 |
| 411 | Ernie Whitt | .02 | .10 |
| 412 | Jim Clancy | .02 | .10 |
| 413 | Barry Bonnell | .02 | .10 |
| 414 | Dave Stieb | .08 | .25 |
| 415 | Damaso Garcia RC | .02 | .10 |
| 416 | John Mayberry | .02 | .10 |
| 417 | Roy Howell | .02 | .10 |
| 418 | Danny Ainge RC | 1.25 | 3.00 |
| 419A | Jesse Jefferson P1 | .02 | .10 |
| 419B | Jesse Jefferson P2 | .02 | .10 |
| 419C | Jesse Jefferson P3 | .20 | .50 |
| 420 | Joey McLaughlin | .02 | .10 |
| 421 | Lloyd Moseby RC | .20 | .50 |
| 422 | Alvis Woods | .02 | .10 |
| 423 | Garth Iorg | .02 | .10 |
| 424 | Doug Ault | .02 | .10 |
| 425 | Ken Schrom RC | .02 | .10 |
| 426 | Mike Willis | .02 | .10 |
| 427 | Steve Braun | .02 | .10 |
| 428 | Bob Davis | .02 | .10 |
| 429 | Jerry Garvin | .02 | .10 |
| 430 | Alfredo Griffin | .02 | .10 |
| 431 | Bob Mattick MG RC | .02 | .10 |
| 432 | Vida Blue | .08 | .25 |
| 433 | Jack Clark | .08 | .25 |
| 434A | Darrel Evans P1 ERR | .20 | .50 |
| 434B | Darrel Evans P2 COR | .20 | .50 |
| 435 | Mike Ivie | .02 | .10 |
| 437 | Terry Whitfield | .02 | .10 |
| 438 | Rennie Stennett | .02 | .10 |
| 439 | John Montefusco | .02 | .10 |
| 440 | Jim Wohlford | .02 | .10 |
| 441 | Bill North | .02 | .10 |
| 442 | Milt May | .02 | .10 |
| 443 | Max Venable RC | .02 | .10 |
| 444 | Ed Whitson | .02 | .10 |
| 445 | Al Holland RC | .02 | .10 |
| 446 | Randy Moffitt | .02 | .10 |
| 447 | Bob Knepper | .02 | .10 |
| 448 | Gary Lavelle | .02 | .10 |
| 449 | Greg Minton | .02 | .10 |
| 450 | Johnnie LeMaster | .02 | .10 |
| 451 | Larry Herndon | .02 | .10 |
| 452 | Rich Murray RC | .02 | .10 |
| 453 | Joe Pettini RC | .02 | .10 |
| 454 | Allen Ripley | .02 | .10 |
| 455 | Dennis Littlejohn | .02 | .10 |
| 456 | Tom Griffin | .02 | .10 |
| 457 | Alan Hargesheimer RC | .02 | .10 |
| 458 | Joe Strain | .02 | .10 |
| 459 | Steve Kemp | .08 | .25 |
| 460 | Gary Anderson MG | .08 | .25 |
| 461 | Alan Trammell | .20 | .50 |
| 462 | Mark Fidrych | .08 | .25 |
| 463 | Lou Whitaker | .20 | .50 |
| 464 | Dave Rozema | .02 | .10 |
| 465 | Milt Wilcox | .02 | .10 |
| 466 | Champ Summers | .02 | .10 |
| 467 | Lance Parrish | .08 | .25 |
| 468 | Dan Petry | .02 | .10 |
| 469 | Pat Underwood | .02 | .10 |
| 470 | Rick Peters RC | .02 | .10 |
| 471 | Al Cowens | .02 | .10 |
| 472 | John Wockenfuss | .02 | .10 |
| 473 | Tom Brookens | .02 | .10 |
| 474 | Richie Hebner | .02 | .10 |
| 475 | Jack Morris | .20 | .50 |
| 476 | Jim Lentine RC | .02 | .10 |
| 477 | Bruce Robbins | .02 | .10 |
| 478 | Mark Wagner | .02 | .10 |
| 479 | Tim Corcoran | .02 | .10 |
| 480A | Stan Papi P1 | .08 | .25 |
| 480B | Stan Papi P2 | .02 | .10 |
| 481 | Kirk Gibson RC | 2.00 | 5.00 |
| 482 | Dan Schatzeder | .02 | .10 |
| 483A | Amos Otis P1 | .08 | .25 |

|  |  | | |
|---|---|---|---|
| 483B | Amos Otis P2 | .08 | .25 |
| 484 | Dave Winfield | .20 | .50 |
| 485 | Rollie Fingers | .08 | .25 |
| 486 | Gene Richards | .02 | .10 |
| 487 | Randy Jones | .02 | .10 |
| 488 | Ozzie Smith | 1.25 | 3.00 |
| 489 | Gene Tenace | .08 | .25 |
| 490 | Bill Fahey | .02 | .10 |
| 491 | John Curtis | .02 | .10 |
| 492 | Dave Cash | .02 | .10 |
| 493A | Tim Flannery P1 | .08 | .25 |
| 493B | Tim Flannery P2 | .02 | .10 |
| 494 | Jerry Mumphrey | .02 | .10 |
| 495 | Bob Shirley | .02 | .10 |
| 496 | Steve Mura | .02 | .10 |
| 497 | Eric Rasmussen | .02 | .10 |
| 498 | Broderick Perkins | .02 | .10 |
| 499 | Barry Evans RC | .02 | .10 |
| 500 | Chuck Baker | .02 | .10 |
| 501 | Luis Salazar RC | .20 | .50 |
| 502 | Gary Lucas RC | .02 | .10 |
| 503 | Mike Armstrong RC | .02 | .10 |
| 504 | Jerry Turner | .02 | .10 |
| 505 | Dennis Kinney RC | .02 | .10 |
| 506 | Willie Montanez UER | .02 | .10 |
| 507 | Gorman Thomas | .08 | .25 |
| 508 | Ben Oglivie | .08 | .25 |
| 509 | Larry Hisle | .02 | .10 |
| 510 | Sal Bando | .08 | .25 |
| 511 | Robin Yount | .60 | 1.50 |
| 512 | Mike Caldwell | .02 | .10 |
| 513 | Sixto Lezcano | .02 | .10 |
| 514A | Bill Travers P1 ERR | .08 | .25 |
| 514B | Bill Travers P2 COR | .02 | .10 |
| 515 | Paul Molitor | .40 | 1.00 |
| 516 | Moose Haas | .02 | .10 |
| 517 | Bill Castro | .02 | .10 |
| 518 | Jim Slaton | .02 | .10 |
| 519 | Larry Sorensen | .02 | .10 |
| 520 | Bob McClure | .02 | .10 |
| 521 | Charlie Moore | .02 | .10 |
| 522 | Jim Gantner | .08 | .25 |
| 523 | Reggie Cleveland | .02 | .10 |
| 524 | Don Money | .02 | .10 |
| 525 | Bill Travers | .02 | .10 |
| 526 | Buck Martinez | .02 | .10 |
| 527 | Dick Davis | .02 | .10 |
| 528 | Ted Simmons | .08 | .25 |
| 529 | Garry Templeton | .08 | .25 |
| 530 | Ken Reitz | .02 | .10 |
| 531 | Tony Scott | .02 | .10 |
| 532 | Ken Oberkfell | .02 | .10 |
| 533 | Bob Sykes | .02 | .10 |
| 534 | Keith Smith | .02 | .10 |
| 535 | John Littlefield RC | .08 | .25 |
| 536 | Jim Kaat | .08 | .25 |
| 537 | Bob Forsch | .02 | .10 |
| 538 | Mike Phillips | .02 | .10 |
| 539 | Terry Landrum RC | .02 | .10 |
| 540 | Leon Durham RC | .20 | .50 |
| 541 | Terry Kennedy | .02 | .10 |
| 542 | George Hendrick | .08 | .25 |
| 543 | Dane Iorg | .02 | .10 |
| 544 | Mark Littell | .02 | .10 |
| 545 | Keith Hernandez | .08 | .25 |
| 546 | Silvio Martinez | .02 | .10 |
| 547A | Don Hood P1 ERR | .08 | .25 |
| 547B | Don Hood P2 COR | .02 | .10 |
| 548 | Bobby Bonds | .08 | .25 |
| 549 | Mike Ramsey RC | .05 | .15 |
| 550 | Tom Herr | .02 | .10 |
| 551 | Roy Smalley | .02 | .10 |
| 552 | Jerry Koosman | .08 | .25 |
| 553 | Ken Landreaux | .02 | .10 |
| 554 | John Castino | .02 | .10 |
| 555 | Doug Corbett RC | .02 | .10 |
| 556 | Bombo Rivera | .02 | .10 |
| 557 | Ron Jackson | .02 | .10 |
| 558 | Butch Wynegar | .02 | .10 |
| 559 | Hosken Powell | .02 | .10 |
| 560 | Pete Redfern | .02 | .10 |
| 561 | Roger Erickson | .02 | .10 |
| 562 | Glenn Adams | .02 | .10 |
| 563 | Rick Sofield | .02 | .10 |
| 564 | Geoff Zahn | .02 | .10 |
| 565 | Pete Mackanin | .02 | .10 |
| 566 | Mike Cubbage | .02 | .10 |
| 567 | Darrell Jackson | .02 | .10 |
| 568 | Dave Edwards | .02 | .10 |
| 569 | Rob Wilfong | .02 | .10 |
| 570 | Sal Butera RC | .02 | .10 |
| 571 | Jose Morales | .02 | .10 |
| 572 | Rick Langford | .02 | .10 |
| 573 | Mike Norris | .02 | .10 |
| 574 | Rickey Henderson | 2.50 | 6.00 |
| 575 | Tony Armas | .08 | .25 |
| 576 | Dave Revering | .02 | .10 |
| 577 | Jeff Newman | .02 | .10 |
| 578 | Bob Lacey | .02 | .10 |
| 579 | Brian Kingman | .02 | .10 |
| 580 | Mitchell Page | .02 | .10 |
| 581 | Billy Martin MG | .20 | .50 |
| 582 | Rob Picciolo | .02 | .10 |
| 583 | Mike Heath | .02 | .10 |
| 584 | Mickey Klutts | .02 | .10 |
| 585 | Orlando Gonzalez | .02 | .10 |
| 586 | Mike Davis RC | .20 | .50 |
| 587 | Wayne Gross | .02 | .10 |
| 588 | Matt Keough | .02 | .10 |
| 589 | Steve McCatty | .02 | .10 |
| 590 | Dwayne Murphy | .02 | .10 |
| 591 | Mario Guerrero | .02 | .10 |
| 592 | Dave McKay RC | .02 | .10 |
| 593 | Jim Essian | .02 | .10 |
| 594 | Dave Heaverlo | .02 | .10 |
| 595 | Maury Wills MG | .08 | .25 |
| 596 | Juan Beniquez | .02 | .10 |
| 597 | Rodney Craig | .02 | .10 |
| 598 | Jim Anderson | .02 | .10 |
| 599 | Floyd Bannister | .02 | .10 |
| 600 | Bruce Bochte | .02 | .10 |
| 601 | Julio Cruz | .02 | .10 |
| 602 | Ted Cox | .02 | .10 |
| 603 | Dan Meyer | .02 | .10 |
| 604 | Larry Cox | .02 | .10 |
| 605 | Bill Stein | .02 | .10 |
| 606 | Steve Garvey | .20 | .50 |
| 607 | Dave Roberts | .02 | .10 |
| 608 | Leon Roberts | .02 | .10 |
| 609 | Reggie Walton RC | .02 | .10 |
| 610 | Dave Edler RC | .02 | .10 |
| 611 | Larry Milbourne | .02 | .10 |
| 612 | Kim Allen RC | .02 | .10 |
| 613 | Mario Mendoza | .02 | .10 |
| 614 | Tom Paciorek | .08 | .25 |
| 615 | Glenn Abbott | .02 | .10 |
| 616 | Joe Simpson | .02 | .10 |
| 617 | Mickey Rivers | .02 | .10 |
| 618 | Jim Kern | .02 | .10 |
| 619 | Jim Sundberg | .08 | .25 |
| 620 | Richie Zisk | .02 | .10 |
| 621 | Jon Matlack | .02 | .10 |
| 622 | Fergie Jenkins | .08 | .25 |
| 623 | Pat Corrales MG | .02 | .10 |
| 624 | Ed Figueroa | .02 | .10 |
| 625 | Buddy Bell | .08 | .25 |
| 626 | Al Oliver | .08 | .25 |
| 627 | Doc Medich | .02 | .10 |
| 628 | Bump Wills | .02 | .10 |
| 629 | Rusty Staub | .08 | .25 |
| 630 | Pat Putnam | .02 | .10 |
| 631 | John Grubb | .02 | .10 |
| 632 | Danny Darwin | .02 | .10 |
| 633 | Ken Clay | .02 | .10 |
| 634 | Jim Norris | .02 | .10 |
| 635 | John Butcher RC | .02 | .10 |
| 636 | Dave Roberts | .02 | .10 |
| 637 | Billy Sample | .02 | .10 |
| 638 | Carl Yastrzemski | .60 | 1.50 |
| 639 | Cecil Cooper | .08 | .25 |
| 640M | M.Schmidt Portrait P1 | 1.00 | 2.50 |
| 640B | M.Schmidt Portrait P2 | 1.00 | 2.50 |
| 641A | CL: Phils/Royals P1 | .08 | .25 |
| 641B | CL: Phils/Royals P2 | .08 | .25 |
| 642 | CL: Astros/Yankees | .02 | .10 |
| 643 | CL: Expos/Dodgers | .02 | .10 |
| 644A | CL: Reds/Orioles P1 | .08 | .25 |
| 644B | CL: Reds/Orioles P2 | .08 | .25 |
| 645A | Rose/Bowa/Schmidt | .60 | 1.50 |
| 645B | Rose/Bowa/Schmidt | 1.00 | 2.50 |
| 646 | CL: Braves/Red Sox | .02 | .10 |
| 647 | CL: Cubs/Angels | .02 | .10 |
| 648 | CL: Mets/White Sox | .02 | .10 |
| 649 | CL: Indians/Pirates | .02 | .10 |
| 650 | Reggie Jackson Mr. BB | .40 | 1.00 |
| 650B | R.Jackson Mr. BB P2 | .20 | .50 |
| 651 | CL: Giants/Blue Jays | .02 | .10 |
| 652A | CL: Tigers/Padres P1 | .08 | .25 |
| 652B | CL: Tigers/Padres P2 | .08 | .25 |
| 653A | Willie Wilson Most Hits | .08 | .25 |
| 653B | W.Wilson Hits P2 | .08 | .25 |
| 654A | CL:Brewers/Cards P1 | .08 | .25 |
| 654B | CL:Brewers/Cards P2 | .08 | .25 |
| 655 | George Brett .390 Avg. | 1.00 | 2.50 |
| 655B | G.Brett .390 Avg. P2 | 1.00 | 2.50 |
| 656 | CL: Twins/Oakland A's | .02 | .10 |
| 657A | Tug McGraw Saver | .08 | .25 |
| 657B | T.McGraw Saver P2 | .08 | .25 |
| 658 | CL: Rangers/Mariners | .02 | .10 |
| 659A | Checklist P1 | .02 | .10 |
| 659B | Checklist P2 | .02 | .10 |
| 660 | S.Carlton Gold Arm P1 | .20 | .50 |
| 660B | S.Carlton Golden Arm | .75 | 2.00 |

## 1982 Fleer

Tim Raines

|  |  | | |
|---|---|---|---|
| | COMPLETE SET (660) | 20.00 | 50.00 |
| 1 | Dusty Baker | .07 | .20 |
| 2 | Robert Castillo | .07 | .20 |
| 3 | Ron Cey | .07 | .20 |
| 4 | Terry Forster | .07 | .20 |
| 5 | Steve Garvey | .07 | .20 |
| 6 | Dave Goltz | .02 | .10 |
| 7 | Pedro Guerrero | .07 | .20 |
| 8 | Burt Hooton | .02 | .10 |
| 9 | Steve Howe | .02 | .10 |
| 10 | Jay Johnstone | .07 | .20 |
| 11 | Ken Landreaux | .02 | .10 |
| 12 | Dave Lopes | .07 | .20 |
| 13 | Mike A. Marshall RC | .20 | .50 |
| 14 | Bobby Mitchell | .02 | .10 |
| 15 | Rick Monday | .07 | .20 |
| 16 | Tom Niedenfuer RC | .20 | .50 |
| 17 | Ted Power RC | .05 | .15 |
| 18 | Jerry Reuss UER | .02 | .10 |
| 19 | Ron Roenicke | .02 | .10 |
| 20 | Bill Russell | .07 | .20 |
| 21 | Steve Sax RC | .40 | 1.00 |
| 22 | Mike Scioscia | .07 | .20 |
| 23 | Reggie Smith | .07 | .20 |
| 24 | Dave Stewart RC | .60 | 1.50 |
| 25 | Rick Sutcliffe | .07 | .20 |
| 26 | Derrel Thomas | .02 | .10 |
| 27 | Fernando Valenzuela | .30 | .75 |
| 28 | Bob Welch | .07 | .20 |
| 29 | Steve Yeager | .07 | .20 |
| 30 | Bobby Brown | .02 | .10 |
| 31 | Rick Cerone | .02 | .10 |
| 32 | Ron Davis | .02 | .10 |
| 33 | Bucky Dent | .07 | .20 |
| 34 | Barry Foote | .02 | .10 |
| 35 | George Frazier | .02 | .10 |
| 36 | Oscar Gamble | .07 | .20 |
| 37 | Rich Gossage | .07 | .20 |
| 38 | Ron Guidry | .07 | .20 |
| 39 | Reggie Jackson | .15 | .40 |
| 40 | Tommy John | .07 | .20 |
| 41 | Rudy May | .02 | .10 |
| 42 | Larry Milbourne | .02 | .10 |
| 43 | Jerry Mumphrey | .07 | .20 |
| 44 | Bobby Murcer | .07 | .20 |
| 45 | Gene Nelson | .02 | .10 |
| 46 | Graig Nettles | .07 | .20 |
| 47 | Johnny Oates | .07 | .20 |
| 48 | Lou Piniella | .07 | .20 |
| 49 | Willie Randolph | .07 | .20 |
| 50 | Rick Reuschel | .07 | .20 |
| 51 | Dave Revering | .02 | .10 |
| 52 | Dave Righetti RC | .60 | 1.50 |
| 53 | Aurelio Rodriguez | .02 | .10 |
| 54 | Bob Watson | .02 | .10 |

|  |  | | |
|---|---|---|---|
| ☐ 55 | Dennis Werth | .02 | .10 |
| ☐ 56 | Dave Winfield | .07 | .20 |
| ☐ 57 | Johnny Bench | .30 | .75 |
| ☐ 58 | Bruce Berenyi | .02 | .10 |
| ☐ 59 | Larry Biittner | .02 | .10 |
| ☐ 60 | Scott Brown | .02 | .10 |
| ☐ 61 | Dave Collins | .02 | .10 |
| ☐ 62 | Geoff Combe | .02 | .10 |
| ☐ 63 | Dave Concepcion | .07 | .20 |
| ☐ 64 | Dan Driessen | .02 | .10 |
| ☐ 65 | Joe Edelen | .02 | .10 |
| ☐ 66 | George Foster | .07 | .20 |
| ☐ 67 | Ken Griffey | .07 | .20 |
| ☐ 68 | Paul Householder | .02 | .10 |
| ☐ 69 | Tom Hume | .02 | .10 |
| ☐ 70 | Junior Kennedy | .02 | .10 |
| ☐ 71 | Ray Knight | .07 | .20 |
| ☐ 72 | Mike LaCoss | .02 | .10 |
| ☐ 73 | Rafael Landestoy | .02 | .10 |
| ☐ 74 | Charlie Leibrandt | .02 | .10 |
| ☐ 75 | Sam Mejias | .02 | .10 |
| ☐ 76 | Paul Moskau | .02 | .10 |
| ☐ 77 | Joe Nolan | .02 | .10 |
| ☐ 78 | Mike O'Berry | .02 | .10 |
| ☐ 79 | Ron Oester | .02 | .10 |
| ☐ 80 | Frank Pastore | .02 | .10 |
| ☐ 81 | Joe Price | .02 | .10 |
| ☐ 82 | Tom Seaver | .30 | .75 |
| ☐ 83 | Mario Soto | .07 | .20 |
| ☐ 84 | Mike Vail | .02 | .10 |
| ☐ 85 | Tony Armas | .07 | .20 |
| ☐ 86 | Shooty Babitt | .02 | .10 |
| ☐ 87 | Dave Beard | .02 | .10 |
| ☐ 88 | Rick Bosetti | .02 | .10 |
| ☐ 89 | Keith Drumwright | .02 | .10 |
| ☐ 90 | Wayne Gross | .02 | .10 |
| ☐ 91 | Mike Heath | .02 | .10 |
| ☐ 92 | Rickey Henderson | 1.00 | 2.50 |
| ☐ 93 | Cliff Johnson | .02 | .10 |
| ☐ 94 | Jeff Jones | .02 | .10 |
| ☐ 95 | Matt Keough | .02 | .10 |
| ☐ 96 | Brian Kingman | .02 | .10 |
| ☐ 97 | Mickey Klutts | .02 | .10 |
| ☐ 98 | Rick Langford | .02 | .10 |
| ☐ 99 | Steve McCatty | .02 | .10 |
| ☐ 100 | Dave McKay | .02 | .10 |
| ☐ 101 | Dwayne Murphy | .02 | .10 |
| ☐ 102 | Jeff Newman | .02 | .10 |
| ☐ 103 | Mike Norris | .02 | .10 |
| ☐ 104 | Bob Owchinko | .02 | .10 |
| ☐ 105 | Mitchell Page | .02 | .10 |
| ☐ 106 | Rob Picciolo | .02 | .10 |
| ☐ 107 | Jim Spencer | .02 | .10 |
| ☐ 108 | Fred Stanley | .02 | .10 |
| ☐ 109 | Tom Underwood | .02 | .10 |
| ☐ 110 | Joaquin Andujar | .07 | .20 |
| ☐ 111 | Steve Braun | .02 | .10 |
| ☐ 112 | Bob Forsch | .02 | .10 |
| ☐ 113 | George Hendrick | .07 | .20 |
| ☐ 114 | Keith Hernandez | .07 | .20 |
| ☐ 115 | Tom Herr | .07 | .20 |
| ☐ 116 | Dane Iorg | .02 | .10 |
| ☐ 117 | Jim Kaat | .07 | .20 |
| ☐ 118 | Tito Landrum | .02 | .10 |
| ☐ 119 | Sixto Lezcano | .02 | .10 |
| ☐ 120 | Mark Littell | .02 | .10 |
| ☐ 121 | John Martin RC | .05 | .15 |
| ☐ 122 | Silvio Martinez | .02 | .10 |
| ☐ 123 | Ken Oberkfell | .02 | .10 |
| ☐ 124 | Darrell Porter | .07 | .20 |
| ☐ 125 | Mike Ramsey | .02 | .10 |
| ☐ 126 | Orlando Sanchez | .02 | .10 |
| ☐ 127 | Bob Shirley | .02 | .10 |
| ☐ 128 | Lary Sorensen | .02 | .10 |
| ☐ 129 | Bruce Sutter | .15 | .40 |
| ☐ 130 | Bob Sykes | .02 | .10 |
| ☐ 131 | Garry Templeton | .07 | .20 |
| ☐ 132 | Gene Tenace | .07 | .20 |
| ☐ 133 | Jerry Augustine | .02 | .10 |
| ☐ 134 | Sal Bando | .07 | .20 |
| ☐ 135 | Mark Brouhard | .02 | .10 |
| ☐ 136 | Mike Caldwell | .02 | .10 |
| ☐ 137 | Reggie Cleveland | .02 | .10 |
| ☐ 138 | Cecil Cooper | .07 | .20 |
| ☐ 139 | Jamie Easterly | .02 | .10 |
| ☐ 140 | Marshall Edwards | .02 | .10 |
| ☐ 141 | Rollie Fingers | .30 | .75 |
| ☐ 142 | Jim Gantner | .02 | .10 |
| ☐ 143 | Moose Haas | .02 | .10 |
| ☐ 144 | Larry Hisle | .02 | .10 |
| ☐ 145 | Roy Howell | .02 | .10 |
| ☐ 146 | Rickey Keeton | .02 | .10 |
| ☐ 147 | Randy Lerch | .02 | .10 |
| ☐ 148 | Paul Molitor | .07 | .20 |
| ☐ 149 | Don Money | .02 | .10 |
| ☐ 150 | Charlie Moore | .02 | .10 |
| ☐ 151 | Ben Oglivie | .07 | .20 |
| ☐ 152 | Ted Simmons | .07 | .20 |
| ☐ 153 | Jim Slaton | .02 | .10 |
| ☐ 154 | Gorman Thomas | .07 | .20 |
| ☐ 155 | Robin Yount | .50 | 1.25 |
| ☐ 156 | Pete Vuckovich (Should precede Yount in the team | .02 | .10 |
| ☐ 157 | Benny Ayala | .02 | .10 |
| ☐ 158 | Mark Belanger | .02 | .10 |
| ☐ 159 | Al Bumbry | .02 | .10 |
| ☐ 160 | Terry Crowley | .02 | .10 |
| ☐ 161 | Rich Dauer | .02 | .10 |
| ☐ 162 | Doug DeCinces | .02 | .10 |
| ☐ 163 | Rick Dempsey | .02 | .10 |
| ☐ 164 | Jim Dwyer | .02 | .10 |
| ☐ 165 | Mike Flanagan | .07 | .20 |
| ☐ 166 | Dave Ford | .02 | .10 |
| ☐ 167 | Dan Graham | .02 | .10 |
| ☐ 168 | Wayne Krenchicki | .02 | .10 |
| ☐ 169 | John Lowenstein | .02 | .10 |
| ☐ 170 | Dennis Martinez | .07 | .20 |
| ☐ 171 | Tippy Martinez | .02 | .10 |
| ☐ 172 | Scott McGregor | .02 | .10 |
| ☐ 173 | Jose Morales | .02 | .10 |
| ☐ 174 | Eddie Murray | .30 | .75 |
| ☐ 175 | Jim Palmer | .07 | .20 |
| ☐ 176 | Cal Ripken RC | 10.00 | 25.00 |
| ☐ 177 | Gary Roenicke | .02 | .10 |
| ☐ 178 | Lenn Sakata | .02 | .10 |
| ☐ 179 | Ken Singleton | .07 | .20 |
| ☐ 180 | Sammy Stewart | .02 | .10 |
| ☐ 181 | Tim Stoddard | .02 | .10 |
| ☐ 182 | Steve Stone | .07 | .20 |
| ☐ 183 | Stan Bahnsen | .02 | .10 |
| ☐ 184 | Ray Burris | .02 | .10 |
| ☐ 185 | Gary Carter | .07 | .20 |
| ☐ 186 | Warren Cromartie | .02 | .10 |
| ☐ 187 | Andre Dawson | .07 | .20 |
| ☐ 188 | Terry Francona RC | 1.25 | 3.00 |
| ☐ 189 | Woodie Fryman | .02 | .10 |
| ☐ 190 | Bill Gullickson | .02 | .10 |
| ☐ 191 | Grant Jackson | .02 | .10 |
| ☐ 192 | Wallace Johnson | .02 | .10 |
| ☐ 193 | Charlie Lea | .02 | .10 |
| ☐ 194 | Bill Lee | .07 | .20 |
| ☐ 195 | Jerry Manuel | .02 | .10 |
| ☐ 196 | Brad Mills | .02 | .10 |
| ☐ 197 | John Milner | .02 | .10 |
| ☐ 198 | Rowland Office | .02 | .10 |
| ☐ 199 | David Palmer | .02 | .10 |
| ☐ 200 | Larry Parrish | .07 | .20 |
| ☐ 201 | Mike Phillips | .02 | .10 |
| ☐ 202 | Tim Raines | .15 | .40 |
| ☐ 203 | Bobby Ramos | .02 | .10 |
| ☐ 204 | Jeff Reardon | .07 | .20 |
| ☐ 205 | Steve Rogers | .02 | .10 |
| ☐ 206 | Scott Sanderson | .02 | .10 |
| ☐ 207 | Rodney Scott UER Raines | .15 | .40 |
| ☐ 208 | Elias Sosa | .02 | .10 |
| ☐ 209 | Chris Speier | .02 | .10 |
| ☐ 210 | Tim Wallach RC | .40 | 1.00 |
| ☐ 211 | Jerry White | .02 | .10 |
| ☐ 212 | Alan Ashby | .02 | .10 |
| ☐ 213 | Cesar Cedeno | .07 | .20 |
| ☐ 214 | Jose Cruz | .07 | .20 |
| ☐ 215 | Kiko Garcia | .02 | .10 |
| ☐ 216 | Phil Garner | .07 | .20 |
| ☐ 217 | Danny Heep | .02 | .10 |
| ☐ 218 | Art Howe | .02 | .10 |
| ☐ 219 | Bob Knepper | .02 | .10 |
| ☐ 220 | Frank LaCorte | .02 | .10 |
| ☐ 221 | Joe Niekro | .02 | .10 |
| ☐ 222 | Joe Pittman | .02 | .10 |
| ☐ 223 | Terry Puhl | .02 | .10 |
| ☐ 224 | Luis Pujols | .02 | .10 |
| ☐ 225 | Craig Reynolds | .02 | .10 |
| ☐ 226 | J.R. Richard | .07 | .20 |
| ☐ 227 | Dave Roberts | .02 | .10 |
| ☐ 228 | Vern Ruhle | .02 | .10 |
| ☐ 229 | Nolan Ryan | 1.50 | 4.00 |
| ☐ 230 | Joe Sambito | .02 | .10 |
| ☐ 231 | Tony Scott | .02 | .10 |
| ☐ 232 | Dave Smith | .02 | .10 |
| ☐ 233 | Harry Spilman | .02 | .10 |
| ☐ 234 | Don Sutton | .07 | .20 |
| ☐ 235 | Dickie Thon | .02 | .10 |
| ☐ 236 | Denny Walling | .02 | .10 |
| ☐ 237 | Gary Woods | .02 | .10 |
| ☐ 238 | Luis Aguayo | .02 | .10 |
| ☐ 239 | Ramon Aviles | .02 | .10 |
| ☐ 240 | Bob Boone | .07 | .20 |
| ☐ 241 | Larry Bowa | .07 | .20 |
| ☐ 242 | Warren Brusstar | .02 | .10 |
| ☐ 243 | Steve Carlton | .15 | .40 |
| ☐ 244 | Larry Christenson | .02 | .10 |
| ☐ 245 | Dick Davis | .02 | .10 |
| ☐ 246 | Greg Gross | .02 | .10 |
| ☐ 247 | Sparky Lyle | .07 | .20 |
| ☐ 248 | Garry Maddox | .02 | .10 |
| ☐ 249 | Gary Matthews | .07 | .20 |
| ☐ 250 | Bake McBride | .02 | .10 |
| ☐ 251 | Tug McGraw | .07 | .20 |
| ☐ 252 | Keith Moreland | .02 | .10 |
| ☐ 253 | Dickie Noles | .02 | .10 |
| ☐ 254 | Mike Proly | .02 | .10 |
| ☐ 255 | Ron Reed | .02 | .10 |
| ☐ 256 | Pete Rose | 1.00 | 2.50 |
| ☐ 257 | Dick Ruthven | .02 | .10 |
| ☐ 258 | Mike Schmidt | .75 | 2.00 |
| ☐ 259 | Lonnie Smith | .02 | .10 |
| ☐ 260 | Manny Trillo | .02 | .10 |
| ☐ 261 | Del Unser | .02 | .10 |
| ☐ 262 | George Vukovich | .02 | .10 |
| ☐ 263 | Tom Brookens | .02 | .10 |
| ☐ 264 | George Cappuzzello | .02 | .10 |
| ☐ 265 | Marty Castillo | .02 | .10 |
| ☐ 266 | Al Cowens | .02 | .10 |
| ☐ 267 | Kirk Gibson | .30 | .75 |
| ☐ 268 | Richie Hebner | .02 | .10 |
| ☐ 269 | Ron Jackson | .02 | .10 |
| ☐ 270 | Lynn Jones | .02 | .10 |
| ☐ 271 | Steve Kemp | .02 | .10 |
| ☐ 272 | Rick Leach | .02 | .10 |
| ☐ 273 | Aurelio Lopez | .02 | .10 |
| ☐ 274 | Jack Morris | .07 | .20 |
| ☐ 275 | Kevin Saucier | .02 | .10 |
| ☐ 276 | Lance Parrish | .07 | .20 |
| ☐ 277 | Rick Peters | .02 | .10 |
| ☐ 278 | Dan Petry | .02 | .10 |
| ☐ 279 | Dave Rozema | .02 | .10 |
| ☐ 280 | Stan Papi | .02 | .10 |
| ☐ 281 | Dan Schatzeder | .02 | .10 |
| ☐ 282 | Champ Summers | .02 | .10 |
| ☐ 283 | Alan Trammell | .07 | .20 |
| ☐ 284 | Lou Whitaker | .07 | .20 |
| ☐ 285 | Milt Wilcox | .02 | .10 |
| ☐ 286 | John Wockenfuss | .02 | .10 |
| ☐ 287 | Gary Allenson | .02 | .10 |
| ☐ 288 | Tom Burgmeier | .02 | .10 |
| ☐ 289 | Bill Campbell | .02 | .10 |
| ☐ 290 | Mark Clear | .02 | .10 |
| ☐ 291 | Steve Crawford | .02 | .10 |
| ☐ 292 | Dennis Eckersley | .15 | .40 |
| ☐ 293 | Dwight Evans | .15 | .40 |
| ☐ 294 | Rich Gedman | .20 | .50 |
| ☐ 295 | Garry Hancock | .02 | .10 |
| ☐ 296 | Glenn Hoffman | .02 | .10 |
| ☐ 297 | Bruce Hurst | .02 | .10 |
| ☐ 298 | Carney Lansford | .07 | .20 |
| ☐ 299 | Rick Miller | .02 | .10 |
| ☐ 300 | Reid Nichols | .02 | .10 |
| ☐ 301 | Bob Ojeda RC | .20 | .50 |
| ☐ 302 | Tony Perez | .15 | .40 |
| ☐ 303 | Chuck Rainey | .02 | .10 |
| ☐ 304 | Jerry Remy | .02 | .10 |
| ☐ 305 | Jim Rice | .07 | .20 |
| ☐ 306 | Joe Rudi | .07 | .20 |
| ☐ 307 | Bob Stanley | .02 | .10 |
| ☐ 308 | Dave Stapleton | .02 | .10 |
| ☐ 309 | Frank Tanana | .07 | .20 |
| ☐ 310 | Mike Torrez | .02 | .10 |
| ☐ 311 | John Tudor | .07 | .20 |
| ☐ 312 | Carl Yastrzemski | .50 | 1.25 |
| ☐ 313 | Buddy Bell | .07 | .20 |
| ☐ 314 | Steve Comer | .02 | .10 |
| ☐ 315 | Danny Darwin | .02 | .10 |
| ☐ 316 | John Ellis | .02 | .10 |

| # | Player | Price | Price |
|---|--------|-------|-------|
| 317 | John Grubb | .02 | .10 |
| 318 | Rick Honeycutt | .02 | .10 |
| 319 | Charlie Hough | .07 | .20 |
| 320 | Fergie Jenkins | .07 | .20 |
| 321 | John Henry Johnson | .02 | .10 |
| 322 | Jim Kern | .02 | .10 |
| 323 | Jon Matlack | .02 | .10 |
| 324 | Doc Medich | .02 | .10 |
| 325 | Mario Mendoza | .02 | .10 |
| 326 | Al Oliver | .07 | .20 |
| 327 | Pat Putnam | .02 | .10 |
| 328 | Mickey Rivers | .02 | .10 |
| 329 | Leon Roberts | .02 | .10 |
| 330 | Billy Sample | .02 | .10 |
| 331 | Bill Stein | .02 | .10 |
| 332 | Jim Sundberg | .07 | .20 |
| 333 | Mark Wagner | .02 | .10 |
| 334 | Bump Wills | .02 | .10 |
| 335 | Bill Almon | .02 | .10 |
| 336 | Harold Baines | .07 | .20 |
| 337 | Ross Baumgarten | .02 | .10 |
| 338 | Tony Bernazard | .02 | .10 |
| 339 | Britt Burns | .02 | .10 |
| 340 | Richard Dotson | .02 | .10 |
| 341 | Jim Essian | .02 | .10 |
| 342 | Ed Farmer | .02 | .10 |
| 343 | Carlton Fisk | .15 | .40 |
| 344 | Kevin Hickey RC | .05 | .15 |
| 345 | LaMarr Hoyt | .02 | .10 |
| 346 | Lamar Johnson | .02 | .10 |
| 347 | Jerry Koosman | .07 | .20 |
| 348 | Rusty Kuntz | .02 | .10 |
| 349 | Dennis Lamp | .02 | .10 |
| 350 | Ron LeFlore | .07 | .20 |
| 351 | Chet Lemon | .07 | .20 |
| 352 | Greg Luzinski | .07 | .20 |
| 353 | Bob Molinaro | .02 | .10 |
| 354 | Jim Morrison | .02 | .10 |
| 355 | Wayne Nordhagen | .02 | .10 |
| 356 | Greg Pryor | .02 | .10 |
| 357 | Mike Squires | .02 | .10 |
| 358 | Steve Trout | .02 | .10 |
| 359 | Alan Bannister | .02 | .10 |
| 360 | Len Barker | .02 | .10 |
| 361 | Bert Blyleven | .07 | .20 |
| 362 | Joe Charboneau | .07 | .20 |
| 363 | John Denny | .02 | .10 |
| 364 | Bo Diaz | .02 | .10 |
| 365 | Miguel Dilone | .02 | .10 |
| 366 | Jerry Dybzinski | .02 | .10 |
| 367 | Wayne Garland | .02 | .10 |
| 368 | Mike Hargrove | .02 | .10 |
| 369 | Toby Harrah | .07 | .20 |
| 370 | Ron Hassey | .02 | .10 |
| 371 | Von Hayes RC | .20 | .50 |
| 372 | Pat Kelly | .02 | .10 |
| 373 | Duane Kuiper | .02 | .10 |
| 374 | Rick Manning | .02 | .10 |
| 375 | Sid Monge | .02 | .10 |
| 376 | Jorge Orta | .02 | .10 |
| 377 | Dave Rosello | .02 | .10 |
| 378 | Dan Spillner | .02 | .10 |
| 379 | Mike Stanton | .02 | .10 |
| 380 | Andre Thornton | .07 | .20 |
| 381 | Tom Veryzer | .02 | .10 |
| 382 | Rick Waits | .02 | .10 |
| 383 | Doyle Alexander | .02 | .10 |
| 384 | Vida Blue | .07 | .20 |
| 385 | Fred Breining | .02 | .10 |
| 386 | Enos Cabell | .02 | .10 |
| 387 | Jack Clark | .07 | .20 |
| 388 | Darrell Evans | .07 | .20 |
| 389 | Tom Griffin | .02 | .10 |
| 390 | Larry Herndon | .02 | .10 |
| 391 | Al Holland | .02 | .10 |
| 392 | Gary Lavelle | .02 | .10 |
| 393 | Johnnie LeMaster | .02 | .10 |
| 394 | Jerry Martin | .02 | .10 |
| 395 | Milt May | .02 | .10 |
| 396 | Greg Minton | .02 | .10 |
| 397 | Joe Morgan | .07 | .20 |
| 398 | Joe Pettini | .02 | .10 |
| 399 | Allen Ripley | .02 | .10 |
| 400 | Billy Smith | .02 | .10 |
| 401 | Rennie Stennett | .02 | .10 |
| 402 | Ed Whitson | .02 | .10 |
| 403 | Jim Wohlford | .02 | .10 |
| 404 | Willie Aikens | .02 | .10 |
| 405 | George Brett | .75 | 2.00 |
| 406 | Ken Brett | .02 | .10 |
| 407 | Dave Chalk | .02 | .10 |
| 408 | Rich Gale | .02 | .10 |
| 409 | Cesar Geronimo | .02 | .10 |
| 410 | Larry Gura | .02 | .10 |
| 411 | Clint Hurdle | .02 | .10 |
| 412 | Mike Jones | .02 | .10 |
| 413 | Dennis Leonard | .02 | .10 |
| 414 | Renie Martin | .02 | .10 |
| 415 | Lee May | .07 | .20 |
| 416 | Hal McRae | .07 | .20 |
| 417 | Darryl Motley | .02 | .10 |
| 418 | Rance Mulliniks | .02 | .10 |
| 419 | Amos Otis | .07 | .20 |
| 420 | Ken Phelps | .02 | .10 |
| 421 | Jamie Quirk | .02 | .10 |
| 422 | Dan Quisenberry | .07 | .20 |
| 423 | Paul Splittorff | .02 | .10 |
| 424 | U.L. Washington | .02 | .10 |
| 425 | John Wathan | .02 | .10 |
| 426 | Frank White | .07 | .20 |
| 427 | Willie Wilson | .07 | .20 |
| 428 | Brian Asselstine | .02 | .10 |
| 429 | Bruce Benedict | .02 | .10 |
| 430 | Tommy Boggs | .02 | .10 |
| 431 | Larry Bradford | .02 | .10 |
| 432 | Rick Camp | .02 | .10 |
| 433 | Chris Chambliss | .07 | .20 |
| 434 | Gene Garber | .02 | .10 |
| 435 | Preston Hanna | .02 | .10 |
| 436 | Bob Horner | .07 | .20 |
| 437 | Glenn Hubbard | .02 | .10 |
| 438A | Al Hrabosky ERR | 3.00 | 8.00 |
| 438B | Al Hrabosky ERR (Height 5'1) | .15 | .40 |
| 438C | Al Hrabosky (Height 5'10) | .07 | .20 |
| 439 | Rufino Linares | .02 | .10 |
| 440 | Rick Mahler | .02 | .10 |
| 441 | Ed Miller | .02 | .10 |
| 442 | John Montefusco | .02 | .10 |
| 443 | Dale Murphy | .15 | .40 |
| 444 | Phil Niekro | .07 | .20 |
| 445 | Gaylord Perry | .07 | .20 |
| 446 | Biff Pocoroba | .02 | .10 |
| 447 | Rafael Ramirez | .02 | .10 |
| 448 | Jerry Royster | .02 | .10 |
| 449 | Claudell Washington | .02 | .10 |
| 450 | Don Aase | .02 | .10 |
| 451 | Don Baylor | .07 | .20 |
| 452 | Juan Beniquez | .02 | .10 |
| 453 | Rick Burleson | .02 | .10 |
| 454 | Bert Campaneris | .07 | .20 |
| 455 | Rod Carew | .15 | .40 |
| 456 | Bob Clark | .02 | .10 |
| 457 | Brian Downing | .07 | .20 |
| 458 | Dan Ford | .02 | .10 |
| 459 | Ken Forsch | .02 | .10 |
| 460A | Dave Frost (5 mm space before ERA) | .02 | .10 |
| 460B | Dave Frost (1 mm space) | .02 | .10 |
| 461 | Bobby Grich | .07 | .20 |
| 462 | Larry Harlow | .02 | .10 |
| 463 | John Harris | .02 | .10 |
| 464 | Andy Hassler | .02 | .10 |
| 465 | Butch Hobson | .02 | .10 |
| 466 | Jesse Jefferson | .02 | .10 |
| 467 | Bruce Kison | .02 | .10 |
| 468 | Fred Lynn | .07 | .20 |
| 469 | Angel Moreno | .02 | .10 |
| 470 | Ed Ott | .02 | .10 |
| 471 | Fred Patek | .02 | .10 |
| 472 | Steve Renko | .02 | .10 |
| 473 | Mike Witt | .20 | .50 |
| 474 | Geoff Zahn | .02 | .10 |
| 475 | Gary Alexander | .02 | .10 |
| 476 | Dale Berra | .02 | .10 |
| 477 | Kurt Bevacqua | .02 | .10 |
| 478 | Jim Bibby | .02 | .10 |
| 479 | John Candelaria | .07 | .20 |
| 480 | Victor Cruz | .02 | .10 |
| 481 | Mike Easler | .07 | .20 |
| 482 | Tim Foli | .02 | .10 |
| 483 | Lee Lacy | .02 | .10 |
| 484 | Vance Law | .02 | .10 |
| 485 | Bill Madlock | .07 | .20 |
| 486 | Willie Montanez | .02 | .10 |
| 487 | Omar Moreno | .02 | .10 |
| 488 | Steve Nicosia | .02 | * |
| 489 | Dave Parker | .07 | .20 |
| 490 | Tony Pena | .07 | .20 |
| 491 | Pascual Perez | .02 | .10 |
| 492 | Johnny Ray RC | .20 | .50 |
| 493 | Rick Rhoden | .02 | .10 |
| 494 | Bill Robinson | .02 | .10 |
| 495 | Don Robinson | .02 | .10 |
| 496 | Enrique Romo | .02 | .10 |
| 497 | Rod Scurry | .02 | .10 |
| 498 | Eddie Solomon | .02 | .10 |
| 499 | Willie Stargell | .15 | .40 |
| 500 | Kent Tekulve | .02 | .10 |
| 501 | Jason Thompson | .02 | .10 |
| 502 | Glenn Abbott | .02 | .10 |
| 503 | Jim Anderson | .02 | .10 |
| 504 | Floyd Bannister | .02 | .10 |
| 505 | Bruce Bochte | .02 | .10 |
| 506 | Jeff Burroughs | .02 | .10 |
| 507 | Bryan Clark RC | .05 | .15 |
| 508 | Ken Clay | .02 | .10 |
| 509 | Julio Cruz | .02 | .10 |
| 510 | Dick Drago | .02 | .10 |
| 511 | Gary Gray | .02 | .10 |
| 512 | Dan Meyer | .02 | .10 |
| 513 | Jerry Narron | .02 | .10 |
| 514 | Tom Paciorek | .02 | .10 |
| 515 | Casey Parsons | .02 | .10 |
| 516 | Lenny Randle | .02 | .10 |
| 517 | Shane Rawley | .02 | .10 |
| 518 | Joe Simpson | .02 | .10 |
| 519 | Richie Zisk | .02 | .10 |
| 520 | Neil Allen | .02 | .10 |
| 521 | Bob Bailor | .02 | .10 |
| 522 | Hubie Brooks | .07 | .20 |
| 523 | Mike Cubbage | .02 | .10 |
| 524 | Pete Falcone | .02 | .10 |
| 525 | Doug Flynn | .02 | .10 |
| 526 | Tom Hausman | .02 | .10 |
| 527 | Ron Hodges | .02 | .10 |
| 528 | Randy Jones | .07 | .20 |
| 529 | Mike Jorgensen | .02 | .10 |
| 530 | Dave Kingman | .07 | .20 |
| 531 | Ed Lynch | .07 | .20 |
| 532 | Mike G. Marshall | .07 | .20 |
| 533 | Lee Mazzilli | .02 | .10 |
| 534 | Dyar Miller | .02 | .10 |
| 535 | Mike Scott | .07 | .20 |
| 536 | Rusty Staub | .07 | .20 |
| 537 | John Stearns | .02 | .10 |
| 538 | Craig Swan | .02 | .10 |
| 539 | Frank Taveras | .02 | .10 |
| 540 | Alex Trevino | .02 | .10 |
| 541 | Ellis Valentine | .02 | .10 |
| 542 | Mookie Wilson | .07 | .20 |
| 543 | Joel Youngblood | .02 | .10 |
| 544 | Pat Zachry | .02 | .10 |
| 545 | Glenn Adams | .02 | .10 |
| 546 | Fernando Arroyo | .02 | .10 |
| 547 | John Verhoeven | .02 | .10 |
| 548 | Sal Butera | .02 | .10 |
| 549 | John Castino | .02 | .10 |
| 550 | Don Cooper | .02 | .10 |
| 551 | Doug Corbett | .02 | .10 |
| 552 | Dave Engle | .02 | .10 |
| 553 | Roger Erickson | .02 | .10 |
| 554 | Danny Goodwin | .02 | .10 |
| 555A | Darrell Jackson (Black cap) | .15 | .40 |
| 555B | Darrell Jackson (Red cap with ?) | .02 | .10 |
| 555C | Darrell Jackson VAR3 | 1.25 | 3.00 |
| 556 | Pete Mackanin | .02 | .10 |
| 557 | Jack O'Connor | .02 | .10 |
| 558 | Hosken Powell | .02 | .10 |
| 559 | Pete Redfern | .02 | .10 |
| 560 | Roy Smalley | .02 | .10 |
| 561 | Chuck Baker UER (Shortstop on front) | .02 | .10 |
| 562 | Gary Ward | .02 | .10 |
| 563 | Rob Wilfong | .02 | .10 |
| 564 | Al Williams | .02 | .10 |
| 565 | Butch Wynegar | .02 | .10 |
| 566 | Randy Bass | .20 | .50 |
| 567 | Juan Bonilla RC | .05 | .15 |
| 568 | Danny Boone | .02 | .10 |

| | | |
|---|---|---|
| ☐ 569 John Curtis | .02 | .10 |
| ☐ 570 Juan Eichelberger | .02 | .10 |
| ☐ 571 Barry Evans | .02 | .10 |
| ☐ 572 Tim Flannery | .02 | .10 |
| ☐ 573 Ruppert Jones | .02 | .10 |
| ☐ 574 Terry Kennedy | .02 | .10 |
| ☐ 575 Joe Lefebvre | .02 | .10 |
| ☐ 576A John Littlefield RevNg | 50.00 | 100.00 |
| ☐ 576B John Littlefield COR | | |
| (Right handed) | .07 | .20 |
| ☐ 577 Gary Lucas | .02 | .10 |
| ☐ 578 Steve Mura | .02 | .10 |
| ☐ 579 Broderick Perkins | .02 | .10 |
| ☐ 580 Gene Richards | .02 | .10 |
| ☐ 581 Luis Salazar | .02 | .10 |
| ☐ 582 Ozzie Smith | .60 | 1.50 |
| ☐ 583 John Urrea | .02 | .10 |
| ☐ 584 Chris Welsh | .02 | .10 |
| ☐ 585 Rick Wise | .02 | .10 |
| ☐ 586 Doug Bird | .02 | .10 |
| ☐ 587 Tim Blackwell | .02 | .10 |
| ☐ 588 Bobby Bonds | .07 | .20 |
| ☐ 589 Bill Buckner | .07 | .20 |
| ☐ 590 Bill Caudill | .02 | .10 |
| ☐ 591 Hector Cruz | .02 | .10 |
| ☐ 592 Jody Davis | .02 | .10 |
| ☐ 593 Ivan DeJesus | .02 | .10 |
| ☐ 594 Steve Dillard | .02 | .10 |
| ☐ 595 Leon Durham | .02 | .10 |
| ☐ 596 Rawly Eastwick | .07 | .20 |
| ☐ 597 Steve Henderson | .02 | .10 |
| ☐ 598 Mike Krukow | .02 | .10 |
| ☐ 599 Mike Lum | .02 | .10 |
| ☐ 600 Randy Martz | .02 | .10 |
| ☐ 601 Jerry Morales | .02 | .10 |
| ☐ 602 Ken Reitz | .02 | .10 |
| ☐ 603 Lee Smith RC | .75 | 2.00 |
| ☐ 603B Lee Smith RC COR | 2.50 | 6.00 |
| ☐ 604 Dick Tidrow | .02 | .10 |
| ☐ 605 Jim Tracy | .07 | .20 |
| ☐ 606 Mike Tyson | .02 | .10 |
| ☐ 607 Ty Waller | .02 | .10 |
| ☐ 608 Danny Ainge | .07 | .20 |
| ☐ 609 George Bell RC | .40 | 1.00 |
| ☐ 610 Mark Bomback | .02 | .10 |
| ☐ 611 Barry Bonnell | .02 | .10 |
| ☐ 612 Jim Clancy | .02 | .10 |
| ☐ 613 Damaso Garcia | .02 | .10 |
| ☐ 614 Jerry Garvin | .02 | .10 |
| ☐ 615 Alfredo Griffin | .02 | .10 |
| ☐ 616 Garth Iorg | .02 | .10 |
| ☐ 617 Luis Leal | .02 | .10 |
| ☐ 618 Ken Macha | .02 | .10 |
| ☐ 619 John Mayberry | .02 | .10 |
| ☐ 620 Joey McLaughlin | .02 | .10 |
| ☐ 621 Lloyd Moseby | .02 | .10 |
| ☐ 622 Dave Stieb | .07 | .20 |
| ☐ 623 Jackson Todd | .02 | .10 |
| ☐ 624 Willie Upshaw | .20 | .50 |
| ☐ 625 Otto Velez | .02 | .10 |
| ☐ 626 Ernie Whitt | .02 | .10 |
| ☐ 627 Alvis Woods | .02 | .10 |
| ☐ 628 All Star Game | | |
| Cleveland, Ohio | .07 | .20 |
| ☐ 629 All Star Infielders | | |
| Frank White | | |
| Bucky Dent | | |
| ☐ 630 Big Red Machine | .07 | .20 |
| Dan Driessen | | |
| Dave Concepcion | | |
| Ge | .07 | .20 |
| ☐ 631 Bruce Sutter | | |
| Top NL Relief Pitcher | .07 | .20 |
| ☐ 632 Steve Carlton/C.Fisk | | |
| ☐ 633 Yaz 3000th Game | .30 | .75 |
| ☐ 634 J.Bench/T.Seaver | .30 | .75 |
| ☐ 635 West Meets East | | |
| Fernando Valenzuela | | |
| and Gary Car | .02 | .10 |
| ☐ 636A Fernando Valenzuela IA | .15 | .40 |
| ☐ 636B Fernando Valenzuela: | | |
| NL SO King (%%the- NL) | .15 | .40 |
| ☐ 637 Mike Schmidt IA | .30 | .75 |
| ☐ 638 Gary Carter/D.Parker | .02 | .10 |
| ☐ 639 Perfect Game UER | | |
| Len Barker and | | |
| Bo Diaz | | |
| (Catche | .07 | .20 |

| | | |
|---|---|---|
| ☐ 640 Pete and Re-Pete | .30 | .75 |
| ☐ 641 L.Smith/Schmidt/Carlton | .30 | .75 |
| ☐ 642 Red Sox Reunion | | |
| Fred Lynn | | |
| Dwight Evans | .15 | .40 |
| ☐ 643 Rickey Henderson IA | .50 | 1.25 |
| ☐ 644 R.Fingers Most Saves | .07 | .20 |
| ☐ 645 Tom Seaver Most Wins | .07 | .20 |
| ☐ 646 R.Jackson/D.Winfield | .07 | .20 |
| ☐ 646B Reggie/D.Winfield | .07 | .20 |
| ☐ 647 CL: Yankees/Dodgers | .02 | .10 |
| ☐ 648 CL: A's/Reds | .02 | .10 |
| ☐ 649 CL: Cards/Brewers | .02 | .10 |
| ☐ 650 CL: Expos/Orioles | .02 | .10 |
| ☐ 651 CL: Astros/Phillies | .02 | .10 |
| ☐ 652 CL: Tigers/Red Sox | .02 | .10 |
| ☐ 653 CL: Rangers/White Sox | .02 | .10 |
| ☐ 654 CL: Giants/Indians | .02 | .10 |
| ☐ 655 CL: Royals/Braves | .02 | .10 |
| ☐ 656 CL: Angels/Pirates | .02 | .10 |
| ☐ 657 CL: Mariners/Mets | .02 | .10 |
| ☐ 658 CL: Padres/Twins | .02 | .10 |
| ☐ 659 CL: Blue Jays/Cubs | .02 | .10 |
| ☐ 660 CL: Specials Checklist | .02 | .10 |

## 1983 Fleer

Red Carew

| | | |
|---|---|---|
| ☐ COMPLETE SET (660) | 30.00 | 60.00 |
| ☐ 1 Joaquin Andujar | .07 | .20 |
| ☐ 2 Doug Bair | .02 | .10 |
| ☐ 3 Steve Braun | .02 | .10 |
| ☐ 4 Glenn Brummer | .02 | .10 |
| ☐ 5 Bob Forsch | .02 | .10 |
| ☐ 6 David Green RC | .20 | .50 |
| ☐ 7 George Hendrick | .07 | .20 |
| ☐ 8 Keith Hernandez | .20 | .50 |
| ☐ 9 Tom Herr | .07 | .20 |
| ☐ 10 Dane Iorg | .02 | .10 |
| ☐ 11 Jim Kaat | .07 | .20 |
| ☐ 12 Jeff Lahti | .02 | .10 |
| ☐ 13 Tito Landrum | .02 | .10 |
| ☐ 14 Dave LaPoint | .02 | .10 |
| ☐ 15 Willie McGee RC | .60 | 1.50 |
| ☐ 16 Steve Mura | .02 | .10 |
| ☐ 17 Ken Oberkfell | .02 | .10 |
| ☐ 18 Darrell Porter | .02 | .10 |
| ☐ 19 Mike Ramsey | .02 | .10 |
| ☐ 20 Gene Roof | .02 | .10 |
| ☐ 21 Lonnie Smith | .07 | .20 |
| ☐ 22 Ozzie Smith | .50 | 1.25 |
| ☐ 23 John Stuper | .02 | .10 |
| ☐ 24 Bruce Sutter | .15 | .40 |
| ☐ 25 Gene Tenace | .07 | .20 |
| ☐ 26 Jerry Augustine | .02 | .10 |
| ☐ 27 Dwight Bernard | .02 | .10 |
| ☐ 28 Mark Brouhard | .02 | .10 |
| ☐ 29 Mike Caldwell | .02 | .10 |
| ☐ 30 Cecil Cooper | .07 | .20 |
| ☐ 31 Jamie Easterly | .02 | .10 |
| ☐ 32 Marshall Edwards | .02 | .10 |
| ☐ 33 Rollie Fingers | .07 | .20 |
| ☐ 34 Jim Gantner | .07 | .20 |
| ☐ 35 Moose Haas | .02 | .10 |
| ☐ 36 Roy Howell | .02 | .10 |
| ☐ 37 Pete Ladd | .02 | .10 |
| ☐ 38 Bob McClure | .02 | .10 |
| ☐ 39 Doc Medich | .02 | .10 |
| ☐ 40 Paul Molitor | .07 | .20 |
| ☐ 41 Don Money | .02 | .10 |
| ☐ 42 Charlie Moore | .02 | .10 |
| ☐ 43 Ben Oglivie | .07 | .20 |
| ☐ 44 Ed Romero | .02 | .10 |
| ☐ 45 Ted Simmons | .07 | .20 |
| ☐ 46 Jim Slaton | .02 | .10 |
| ☐ 47 Don Sutton | .07 | .20 |

| | | |
|---|---|---|
| ☐ 48 Gorman Thomas | .07 | .20 |
| ☐ 49 Pete Vuckovich | .02 | .10 |
| ☐ 50 Ned Yost | .02 | .10 |
| ☐ 51 Robin Yount | .50 | 1.25 |
| ☐ 52 Benny Ayala | .02 | .10 |
| ☐ 53 Bob Bonner | .02 | .10 |
| ☐ 54 Al Bumbry | .02 | .10 |
| ☐ 55 Terry Crowley | .02 | .10 |
| ☐ 56 Storm Davis RC | .20 | .50 |
| ☐ 57 Rich Dauer | .02 | .10 |
| ☐ 58 Rick Dempsey UER | .02 | .10 |
| ☐ 59 Jim Dwyer | .02 | .10 |
| ☐ 60 Mike Flanagan | .02 | .10 |
| ☐ 61 Dan Ford | .02 | .10 |
| ☐ 62 Glenn Gulliver | .02 | .10 |
| ☐ 63 John Lowenstein | .02 | .10 |
| ☐ 64 Dennis Martinez | .07 | .20 |
| ☐ 65 Tippy Martinez | .02 | .10 |
| ☐ 66 Scott McGregor | .02 | .10 |
| ☐ 67 Eddie Murray | .30 | .75 |
| ☐ 68 Joe Nolan | .02 | .10 |
| ☐ 69 Jim Palmer | .30 | .75 |
| ☐ 70 Cal Ripken | 2.50 | 6.00 |
| ☐ 71 Gary Roenicke | .02 | .10 |
| ☐ 72 Lenn Sakata | .02 | .10 |
| ☐ 73 Ken Singleton | .07 | .20 |
| ☐ 74 Sammy Stewart | .02 | .10 |
| ☐ 75 Tim Stoddard | .02 | .10 |
| ☐ 76 Don Aase | .02 | .10 |
| ☐ 77 Don Baylor | .07 | .20 |
| ☐ 78 Juan Beniquez | .02 | .10 |
| ☐ 79 Bob Boone | .07 | .20 |
| ☐ 80 Rick Burleson | .02 | .10 |
| ☐ 81 Rod Carew | .15 | .40 |
| ☐ 82 Bobby Clark | .02 | .10 |
| ☐ 83 Doug Corbett | .02 | .10 |
| ☐ 84 John Curtis | .02 | .10 |
| ☐ 85 Doug DeCinces | .02 | .10 |
| ☐ 86 Brian Downing | .07 | .20 |
| ☐ 87 Joe Ferguson | .02 | .10 |
| ☐ 88 Tim Foli | .02 | .10 |
| ☐ 89 Ken Forsch | .02 | .10 |
| ☐ 90 Dave Goltz | .02 | .10 |
| ☐ 91 Bobby Grich | .07 | .20 |
| ☐ 92 Andy Hassler | .02 | .10 |
| ☐ 93 Reggie Jackson | .15 | .40 |
| ☐ 94 Ron Jackson | .02 | .10 |
| ☐ 95 Tommy John | .07 | .20 |
| ☐ 96 Bruce Kison | .02 | .10 |
| ☐ 97 Fred Lynn | .07 | .20 |
| ☐ 98 Ed Ott | .02 | .10 |
| ☐ 99 Steve Renko | .02 | .10 |
| ☐ 100 Luis Sanchez | .02 | .10 |
| ☐ 101 Rob Wilfong | .02 | .10 |
| ☐ 102 Mike Witt | .07 | .20 |
| ☐ 103 Geoff Zahn | .02 | .10 |
| ☐ 104 Willie Aikens | .02 | .10 |
| ☐ 105 Mike Armstrong | .02 | .10 |
| ☐ 106 Vida Blue | .07 | .20 |
| ☐ 107 Bud Black RC | .20 | .50 |
| ☐ 108 George Brett | .75 | 2.00 |
| ☐ 109 Bill Castro | .02 | .10 |
| ☐ 110 Onix Concepcion | .02 | .10 |
| ☐ 111 Dave Frost | .02 | .10 |
| ☐ 112 Cesar Geronimo | .02 | .10 |
| ☐ 113 Larry Gura | .02 | .10 |
| ☐ 114 Steve Hammond | .02 | .10 |
| ☐ 115 Don Hood | .02 | .10 |
| ☐ 116 Dennis Leonard | .02 | .10 |
| ☐ 117 Jerry Martin | .02 | .10 |
| ☐ 118 Lee May | .02 | .10 |
| ☐ 119 Hal McRae | .07 | .20 |
| ☐ 120 Amos Otis | .07 | .20 |
| ☐ 121 Greg Pryor | .02 | .10 |
| ☐ 122 Dan Quisenberry | .02 | .10 |
| ☐ 123 Don Slaught RC | .20 | .50 |
| ☐ 124 Paul Splittorff | .02 | .10 |
| ☐ 125 U.L. Washington | .02 | .10 |
| ☐ 126 John Wathan | .02 | .10 |
| ☐ 127 Frank White | .07 | .20 |
| ☐ 128 Willie Wilson | .07 | .20 |
| ☐ 129 Steve Bedrosian UER | | |
| (Height 6'3) | .02 | .10 |
| ☐ 130 Bruce Benedict | .02 | .10 |
| ☐ 131 Tommy Boggs | .02 | .10 |
| ☐ 132 Brett Butler | .07 | .20 |
| ☐ 133 Rick Camp | .02 | .10 |
| ☐ 134 Chris Chambliss | .07 | .20 |

|  |  | | |
|---|--------|------|------|
| ☐ 135 | Ken Dayley | .02 | .10 |
| ☐ 136 | Gene Garber | .02 | .10 |
| ☐ 137 | Terry Harper | .02 | .10 |
| ☐ 138 | Bob Horner | .07 | .20 |
| ☐ 139 | Glenn Hubbard | .02 | .10 |
| ☐ 140 | Rufino Linares | .02 | .10 |
| ☐ 141 | Rick Mahler | .02 | .10 |
| ☐ 142 | Dale Murphy | .15 | .40 |
| ☐ 143 | Phil Niekro | .07 | .20 |
| ☐ 144 | Pascual Perez | .02 | .10 |
| ☐ 145 | Biff Pocoroba | .02 | .10 |
| ☐ 146 | Rafael Ramirez | .02 | .10 |
| ☐ 147 | Jerry Royster | .02 | .10 |
| ☐ 148 | Ken Smith | .02 | .10 |
| ☐ 149 | Bob Walk | .02 | .10 |
| ☐ 150 | Claudell Washington | .02 | .10 |
| ☐ 151 | Bob Watson | .02 | .10 |
| ☐ 152 | Larry Whisenton | .02 | .10 |
| ☐ 153 | Porfirio Altamirano | .02 | .10 |
| ☐ 154 | Marty Bystrom | .02 | .10 |
| ☐ 155 | Steve Carlton | .15 | .40 |
| ☐ 156 | Larry Christenson | .02 | .10 |
| ☐ 157 | Ivan DeJesus | .02 | .10 |
| ☐ 158 | John Denny | .02 | .10 |
| ☐ 159 | Bob Dernier | .02 | .10 |
| ☐ 160 | Bo Diaz | .02 | .10 |
| ☐ 161 | Ed Farmer | .02 | .10 |
| ☐ 162 | Greg Gross | .02 | .10 |
| ☐ 163 | Mike Krukow | .02 | .10 |
| ☐ 164 | Garry Maddox | .02 | .10 |
| ☐ 165 | Gary Matthews | .07 | .20 |
| ☐ 166 | Tug McGraw | .07 | .20 |
| ☐ 167 | Bob Molinaro | .02 | .10 |
| ☐ 168 | Sid Monge | .02 | .10 |
| ☐ 169 | Ron Reed | .02 | .10 |
| ☐ 170 | Bill Robinson | .02 | .10 |
| ☐ 171 | Pete Rose | 1.00 | 2.50 |
| ☐ 172 | Dick Ruthven | .02 | .10 |
| ☐ 173 | Mike Schmidt | .75 | 2.00 |
| ☐ 174 | Manny Trillo | .02 | .10 |
| ☐ 175 | Ozzie Virgil | .02 | .10 |
| ☐ 176 | George Vukovich | .02 | .10 |
| ☐ 177 | Gary Allenson | .02 | .10 |
| ☐ 178 | Luis Aponte | .02 | .10 |
| ☐ 179 | Wade Boggs RC | 4.00 | 10.00 |
| ☐ 180 | Tom Burgmeier | .02 | .10 |
| ☐ 181 | Mark Clear | .02 | .10 |
| ☐ 182 | Dennis Eckersley | .15 | .40 |
| ☐ 183 | Dwight Evans | .15 | .40 |
| ☐ 184 | Rich Gedman | .02 | .10 |
| ☐ 185 | Glenn Hoffman | .02 | .10 |
| ☐ 186 | Bruce Hurst | .07 | .20 |
| ☐ 187 | Carney Lansford | .07 | .20 |
| ☐ 188 | Rick Miller | .02 | .10 |
| ☐ 189 | Reid Nichols | .02 | .10 |
| ☐ 190 | Bob Ojeda | .02 | .10 |
| ☐ 191 | Tony Perez | .15 | .40 |
| ☐ 192 | Chuck Rainey | .02 | .10 |
| ☐ 193 | Jerry Remy | .02 | .10 |
| ☐ 194 | Jim Rice | .07 | .20 |
| ☐ 195 | Bob Stanley | .02 | .10 |
| ☐ 196 | Dave Stapleton | .02 | .10 |
| ☐ 197 | Mike Torrez | .02 | .10 |
| ☐ 198 | John Tudor | .07 | .20 |
| ☐ 199 | Julio Valdez | .02 | .10 |
| ☐ 200 | Carl Yastrzemski | .50 | 1.25 |
| ☐ 201 | Dusty Baker | .07 | .20 |
| ☐ 202 | Joe Beckwith | .02 | .10 |
| ☐ 203 | Greg Brock | .02 | .10 |
| ☐ 204 | Ron Cey | .07 | .20 |
| ☐ 205 | Terry Forster | .02 | .10 |
| ☐ 206 | Steve Garvey | .07 | .20 |
| ☐ 207 | Pedro Guerrero | .07 | .20 |
| ☐ 208 | Burt Hooton | .02 | .10 |
| ☐ 209 | Steve Howe | .02 | .10 |
| ☐ 210 | Ken Landreaux | .02 | .10 |
| ☐ 211 | Mike Marshall | .07 | .20 |
| ☐ 212 | Candy Maldonado RC | .20 | .50 |
| ☐ 213 | Rick Monday | .02 | .10 |
| ☐ 214 | Tom Niedenfuer | .02 | .10 |
| ☐ 215 | Jorge Orta | .02 | .10 |
| ☐ 216 | Jerry Reuss UER | .02 | .10 |
| ☐ 217 | Ron Roenicke | .02 | .10 |
| ☐ 218 | Vicente Romo | .02 | .10 |
| ☐ 219 | Bill Russell | .07 | .20 |
| ☐ 220 | Steve Sax | .20 | .50 |
| ☐ 221 | Mike Scioscia | .07 | .20 |
| ☐ 222 | Dave Stewart | .07 | .20 |
| ☐ 223 | Derrel Thomas | .02 | .10 |
| ☐ 224 | Fernando Valenzuela | .07 | .20 |
| ☐ 225 | Bob Welch | .07 | .20 |
| ☐ 226 | Ricky Wright | .02 | .10 |
| ☐ 227 | Steve Yeager | .07 | .20 |
| ☐ 228 | Bill Almon | .02 | .10 |
| ☐ 229 | Harold Baines | .07 | .20 |
| ☐ 230 | Salome Barojas | .02 | .10 |
| ☐ 231 | Tony Bernazard | .02 | .10 |
| ☐ 232 | Britt Burns | .02 | .10 |
| ☐ 233 | Richard Dotson | .02 | .10 |
| ☐ 234 | Ernesto Escarrega | .02 | .10 |
| ☐ 235 | Carlton Fisk | .15 | .40 |
| ☐ 236 | Jerry Hairston | .02 | .10 |
| ☐ 237 | Kevin Hickey | .02 | .10 |
| ☐ 238 | LaMarr Hoyt | .02 | .10 |
| ☐ 239 | Steve Kemp | .02 | .10 |
| ☐ 240 | Jim Kern | .02 | .10 |
| ☐ 241 | Ron Kittle RC | .40 | 1.00 |
| ☐ 242 | Jerry Koosman | .07 | .20 |
| ☐ 243 | Dennis Lamp | .02 | .10 |
| ☐ 244 | Rudy Law | .02 | .10 |
| ☐ 245 | Vance Law | .02 | .10 |
| ☐ 246 | Ron LeFlore | .02 | .10 |
| ☐ 247 | Greg Luzinski | .07 | .20 |
| ☐ 248 | Tom Paciorek | .02 | .10 |
| ☐ 249 | Aurelio Rodriguez | .02 | .10 |
| ☐ 250 | Mike Squires | .02 | .10 |
| ☐ 251 | Steve Trout | .02 | .10 |
| ☐ 252 | Jim Barr | .02 | .10 |
| ☐ 253 | Dave Bergman | .02 | .10 |
| ☐ 254 | Fred Breining | .02 | .10 |
| ☐ 255 | Bob Brenly | .07 | .20 |
| ☐ 256 | Jack Clark | .07 | .20 |
| ☐ 257 | Chili Davis | .07 | .20 |
| ☐ 258 | Darrell Evans | .07 | .20 |
| ☐ 259 | Alan Fowlkes | .02 | .10 |
| ☐ 260 | Rich Gale | .02 | .10 |
| ☐ 261 | Atlee Hammaker | .02 | .10 |
| ☐ 262 | Al Holland | .02 | .10 |
| ☐ 263 | Duane Kuiper | .02 | .10 |
| ☐ 264 | Bill Laskey | .02 | .10 |
| ☐ 265 | Gary Lavelle | .02 | .10 |
| ☐ 266 | Johnnie LeMaster | .02 | .10 |
| ☐ 267 | Renie Martin | .02 | .10 |
| ☐ 268 | Milt May | .02 | .10 |
| ☐ 269 | Greg Minton | .02 | .10 |
| ☐ 270 | Joe Morgan | .07 | .20 |
| ☐ 271 | Tom O'Malley | .02 | .10 |
| ☐ 272 | Reggie Smith | .07 | .20 |
| ☐ 273 | Guy Sularz | .02 | .10 |
| ☐ 274 | Champ Summers | .02 | .10 |
| ☐ 275 | Max Venable | .02 | .10 |
| ☐ 276 | Jim Wohlford | .02 | .10 |
| ☐ 277 | Ray Burris | .02 | .10 |
| ☐ 278 | Gary Carter | .07 | .20 |
| ☐ 279 | Warren Cromartie | .02 | .10 |
| ☐ 280 | Andre Dawson | .07 | .20 |
| ☐ 281 | Terry Francona | .02 | .10 |
| ☐ 282 | Doug Flynn | .02 | .10 |
| ☐ 283 | Woodie Fryman | .02 | .10 |
| ☐ 284 | Bill Gullickson | .02 | .10 |
| ☐ 285 | Wallace Johnson | .02 | .10 |
| ☐ 286 | Charlie Lea | .02 | .10 |
| ☐ 287 | Randy Lerch | .02 | .10 |
| ☐ 288 | Brad Mills | .02 | .10 |
| ☐ 289 | Dan Norman | .02 | .10 |
| ☐ 290 | Al Oliver | .07 | .20 |
| ☐ 291 | David Palmer | .02 | .10 |
| ☐ 292 | Tim Raines | .07 | .20 |
| ☐ 293 | Jeff Reardon | .07 | .20 |
| ☐ 294 | Steve Rogers | .02 | .10 |
| ☐ 295 | Scott Sanderson | .02 | .10 |
| ☐ 296 | Dan Schatzeder | .02 | .10 |
| ☐ 297 | Bryn Smith | .02 | .10 |
| ☐ 298 | Chris Speier | .02 | .10 |
| ☐ 299 | Tim Wallach | .07 | .20 |
| ☐ 300 | Jerry White | .02 | .10 |
| ☐ 301 | Joel Youngblood | .02 | .10 |
| ☐ 302 | Ross Baumgarten | .02 | .10 |
| ☐ 303 | Dale Berra | .02 | .10 |
| ☐ 304 | John Candelaria | .02 | .10 |
| ☐ 305 | Dick Davis | .02 | .10 |
| ☐ 306 | Mike Easler | .02 | .10 |
| ☐ 307 | Richie Hebner | .02 | .10 |
| ☐ 308 | Lee Lacy | .02 | .10 |
| ☐ 309 | Bill Madlock | .07 | .20 |
| ☐ 310 | Larry McWilliams | .02 | .10 |
| ☐ 311 | John Milner | .02 | .10 |
| ☐ 312 | Omar Moreno | .02 | .10 |
| ☐ 313 | Jim Morrison | .02 | .10 |
| ☐ 314 | Steve Nicosia | .02 | .10 |
| ☐ 315 | Dave Parker | .07 | .20 |
| ☐ 316 | Tony Pena | .07 | .20 |
| ☐ 317 | Johnny Ray | .02 | .10 |
| ☐ 318 | Rick Rhoden | .02 | .10 |
| ☐ 319 | Don Robinson | .02 | .10 |
| ☐ 320 | Enrique Romo | .02 | .10 |
| ☐ 321 | Manny Sarmiento | .02 | .10 |
| ☐ 322 | Rod Scurry | .02 | .10 |
| ☐ 323 | Jimmy Smith | .02 | .10 |
| ☐ 324 | Willie Stargell | .15 | .40 |
| ☐ 325 | Jason Thompson | .02 | .10 |
| ☐ 326 | Kent Tekulve | .02 | .10 |
| ☐ 327A | Tom Brookens | | |
| | (Short .375~ brown box | | |
| | shaded in on | .02 | .10 |
| ☐ 327B | Tom Brookens | | |
| | (Longer 1.25~ brown box | | |
| | shaded in o | .02 | .10 |
| ☐ 328 | Enos Cabell | .02 | .10 |
| ☐ 329 | Kirk Gibson | .07 | .20 |
| ☐ 330 | Larry Herndon | .02 | .10 |
| ☐ 331 | Mike Ivie | .02 | .10 |
| ☐ 332 | Howard Johnson RC | .40 | 1.00 |
| ☐ 333 | Lynn Jones | .02 | .10 |
| ☐ 334 | Rick Leach | .02 | .10 |
| ☐ 335 | Chet Lemon | .07 | .20 |
| ☐ 336 | Jack Morris | .07 | .20 |
| ☐ 337 | Lance Parrish | .07 | .20 |
| ☐ 338 | Larry Pashnick | .02 | .10 |
| ☐ 339 | Dan Petry | .02 | .10 |
| ☐ 340 | Dave Rozema | .02 | .10 |
| ☐ 341 | Dave Rucker | .02 | .10 |
| ☐ 342 | Elias Sosa | .02 | .10 |
| ☐ 343 | Dave Tobik | .02 | .10 |
| ☐ 344 | Alan Trammell | .07 | .20 |
| ☐ 345 | Jerry Turner | .02 | .10 |
| ☐ 346 | Jerry Ujdur | .02 | .10 |
| ☐ 347 | Pat Underwood | .02 | .10 |
| ☐ 348 | Lou Whitaker | .07 | .20 |
| ☐ 349 | Milt Wilcox | .02 | .10 |
| ☐ 350 | Glenn Wilson | .20 | .50 |
| ☐ 351 | John Wockenfuss | .02 | .10 |
| ☐ 352 | Kurt Bevacqua | .02 | .10 |
| ☐ 353 | Juan Bonilla | .02 | .10 |
| ☐ 354 | Floyd Chiffer | .02 | .10 |
| ☐ 355 | Luis DeLeon | .02 | .10 |
| ☐ 356 | Dave Dravecky RC | .40 | 1.00 |
| ☐ 357 | Dave Edwards | .02 | .10 |
| ☐ 358 | Juan Eichelberger | .02 | .10 |
| ☐ 359 | Tim Flannery | .02 | .10 |
| ☐ 360 | Tony Gwynn RC | 5.00 | 12.00 |
| ☐ 361 | Ruppert Jones | .02 | .10 |
| ☐ 362 | Terry Kennedy | .02 | .10 |
| ☐ 363 | Joe Lefebvre | .02 | .10 |
| ☐ 364 | Sixto Lezcano | .02 | .10 |
| ☐ 365 | Tim Lollar | .02 | .10 |
| ☐ 366 | Gary Lucas | .02 | .10 |
| ☐ 367 | John Montefusco | .02 | .10 |
| ☐ 368 | Broderick Perkins | .02 | .10 |
| ☐ 369 | Joe Pittman | .02 | .10 |
| ☐ 370 | Gene Richards | .02 | .10 |
| ☐ 371 | Luis Salazar | .02 | .10 |
| ☐ 372 | Eric Show RC | .20 | .50 |
| ☐ 373 | Garry Templeton | .07 | .20 |
| ☐ 374 | Chris Welsh | .02 | .10 |
| ☐ 375 | Alan Wiggins | .02 | .10 |
| ☐ 376 | Rick Cerone | .02 | .10 |
| ☐ 377 | Dave Collins | .02 | .10 |
| ☐ 378 | Roger Erickson | .02 | .10 |
| ☐ 379 | George Frazier | .02 | .10 |
| ☐ 380 | Oscar Gamble | .02 | .10 |
| ☐ 381 | Rich Gossage | .07 | .20 |
| ☐ 382 | Ken Griffey | .07 | .20 |
| ☐ 383 | Ron Guidry | .07 | .20 |
| ☐ 384 | Dave LaRoche | .02 | .10 |
| ☐ 385 | Rudy May | .02 | .10 |
| ☐ 386 | John Mayberry | .02 | .10 |
| ☐ 387 | Lee Mazzilli | .02 | .10 |
| ☐ 388 | Mike Morgan | .02 | .10 |
| ☐ 389 | Jerry Mumphrey | .02 | .10 |
| ☐ 390 | Bobby Murcer | .07 | .20 |
| ☐ 391 | Graig Nettles | .07 | .20 |
| ☐ 392 | Lou Piniella | .07 | .20 |
| ☐ 393 | Willie Randolph | .07 | .20 |

|  |  | | |
|---|---|---|---|
| ☐ 394 | Shane Rawley | .02 | .10 |
| ☐ 395 | Dave Righetti | .07 | .20 |
| ☐ 396 | Andre Robertson | .02 | .10 |
| ☐ 397 | Roy Smalley | .02 | .10 |
| ☐ 398 | Dave Winfield | .07 | .20 |
| ☐ 399 | Butch Wynegar | .02 | .10 |
| ☐ 400 | Chris Bando | .02 | .10 |
| ☐ 401 | Alan Bannister | .02 | .10 |
| ☐ 402 | Len Barker | .02 | .10 |
| ☐ 403 | Tom Brennan | .02 | .10 |
| ☐ 404 | Carmelo Castillo | .02 | .10 |
| ☐ 405 | Miguel Dilone | .02 | .10 |
| ☐ 406 | Jerry Dybzinski | .02 | .10 |
| ☐ 407 | Mike Fischlin | .02 | .10 |
| ☐ 408 | Ed Glynn UER | .02 | .10 |
| ☐ 409 | Mike Hargrove | .02 | .10 |
| ☐ 410 | Toby Harrah | .07 | .20 |
| ☐ 411 | Ron Hassey | .02 | .10 |
| ☐ 412 | Von Hayes | .02 | .10 |
| ☐ 413 | Rick Manning | .02 | .10 |
| ☐ 414 | Bake McBride | .07 | .20 |
| ☐ 415 | Larry Milbourne | .02 | .10 |
| ☐ 416 | Bill Nahorodny | .02 | .10 |
| ☐ 417 | Jack Perconte | .02 | .10 |
| ☐ 418 | Lary Sorensen | .02 | .10 |
| ☐ 419 | Dan Spillner | .02 | .10 |
| ☐ 420 | Rick Sutcliffe | .07 | .20 |
| ☐ 421 | Andre Thornton | .02 | .10 |
| ☐ 422 | Rick Waits | .02 | .10 |
| ☐ 423 | Eddie Whitson | .02 | .10 |
| ☐ 424 | Jesse Barfield | .07 | .20 |
| ☐ 425 | Barry Bonnell | .02 | .10 |
| ☐ 426 | Jim Clancy | .02 | .10 |
| ☐ 427 | Damaso Garcia | .02 | .10 |
| ☐ 428 | Jerry Garvin | .02 | .10 |
| ☐ 429 | Alfredo Griffin | .02 | .10 |
| ☐ 430 | Garth Iorg | .02 | .10 |
| ☐ 431 | Roy Lee Jackson | .02 | .10 |
| ☐ 432 | Luis Leal | .02 | .10 |
| ☐ 433 | Buck Martinez | .02 | .10 |
| ☐ 434 | Joey McLaughlin | .02 | .10 |
| ☐ 435 | Lloyd Moseby | .02 | .10 |
| ☐ 436 | Rance Mulliniks | .02 | .10 |
| ☐ 437 | Dale Murray | .02 | .10 |
| ☐ 438 | Wayne Nordhagen | .02 | .10 |
| ☐ 439 | Geno Petralli | .20 | .50 |
| ☐ 440 | Hosken Powell | .02 | .10 |
| ☐ 441 | Dave Stieb | .07 | .20 |
| ☐ 442 | Willie Upshaw | .02 | .10 |
| ☐ 443 | Ernie Whitt | .02 | .10 |
| ☐ 444 | Alvis Woods | .02 | .10 |
| ☐ 445 | Alan Ashby | .02 | .10 |
| ☐ 446 | Jose Cruz | .07 | .20 |
| ☐ 447 | Kiko Garcia | .02 | .10 |
| ☐ 448 | Phil Garner | .02 | .10 |
| ☐ 449 | Danny Heep | .02 | .10 |
| ☐ 450 | Art Howe | .02 | .10 |
| ☐ 451 | Bob Knepper | .02 | .10 |
| ☐ 452 | Alan Knicely | .02 | .10 |
| ☐ 453 | Ray Knight | .07 | .20 |
| ☐ 454 | Frank LaCorte | .02 | .10 |
| ☐ 455 | Mike LaCoss | .02 | .10 |
| ☐ 456 | Randy Moffitt | .02 | .10 |
| ☐ 457 | Joe Niekro | .07 | .20 |
| ☐ 458 | Terry Puhl | .02 | .10 |
| ☐ 459 | Luis Pujols | .02 | .10 |
| ☐ 460 | Craig Reynolds | .02 | .10 |
| ☐ 461 | Bert Roberge | .02 | .10 |
| ☐ 462 | Vern Ruhle | .02 | .10 |
| ☐ 463 | Nolan Ryan | 1.50 | 4.00 |
| ☐ 464 | Joe Sambito | .02 | .10 |
| ☐ 465 | Tony Scott | .02 | .10 |
| ☐ 466 | Dave Smith | .02 | .10 |
| ☐ 467 | Harry Spilman | .02 | .10 |
| ☐ 468 | Dickie Thon | .02 | .10 |
| ☐ 469 | Denny Walling | .02 | .10 |
| ☐ 470 | Larry Andersen | .02 | .10 |
| ☐ 471 | Floyd Bannister | .02 | .10 |
| ☐ 472 | Jim Beattie | .02 | .10 |
| ☐ 473 | Bruce Bochte | .02 | .10 |
| ☐ 474 | Manny Castillo | .02 | .10 |
| ☐ 475 | Bill Caudill | .02 | .10 |
| ☐ 476 | Bryan Clark | .02 | .10 |
| ☐ 477 | Al Cowens | .02 | .10 |
| ☐ 478 | Julio Cruz | .02 | .10 |
| ☐ 479 | Todd Cruz | .02 | .10 |
| ☐ 480 | Gary Gray | .02 | .10 |
| ☐ 481 | Dave Henderson | .02 | .10 |
| ☐ 482 | Mike Moore RC | .20 | .50 |
| ☐ 483 | Gaylord Perry | .07 | .20 |
| ☐ 484 | Dave Revering | .02 | .10 |
| ☐ 485 | Joe Simpson | .02 | .10 |
| ☐ 486 | Mike Stanton | .02 | .10 |
| ☐ 487 | Rick Sweet | .02 | .10 |
| ☐ 488 | Ed VandeBerg | .02 | .10 |
| ☐ 489 | Richie Zisk | .02 | .10 |
| ☐ 490 | Doug Bird | .02 | .10 |
| ☐ 491 | Larry Bowa | .07 | .20 |
| ☐ 492 | Bill Buckner | .07 | .20 |
| ☐ 493 | Bill Campbell | .02 | .10 |
| ☐ 494 | Jody Davis | .02 | .10 |
| ☐ 495 | Leon Durham | .02 | .10 |
| ☐ 496 | Steve Henderson | .02 | .10 |
| ☐ 497 | Willie Hernandez | .07 | .20 |
| ☐ 498 | Fergie Jenkins | .07 | .20 |
| ☐ 499 | Jay Johnstone | .02 | .10 |
| ☐ 500 | Junior Kennedy | .02 | .10 |
| ☐ 501 | Randy Martz | .02 | .10 |
| ☐ 502 | Jerry Morales | .02 | .10 |
| ☐ 503 | Keith Moreland | .02 | .10 |
| ☐ 504 | Dickie Noles | .02 | .10 |
| ☐ 505 | Mike Proly | .02 | .10 |
| ☐ 506 | Allen Ripley | .02 | .10 |
| ☐ 507 | Ryne Sandberg RC | 4.00 | 10.00 |
| ☐ 508 | Lee Smith | .15 | .40 |
| ☐ 509 | Pat Tabler | .02 | .10 |
| ☐ 510 | Dick Tidrow | .02 | .10 |
| ☐ 511 | Bump Wills | .02 | .10 |
| ☐ 512 | Gary Woods | .02 | .10 |
| ☐ 513 | Tony Armas | .07 | .20 |
| ☐ 514 | Dave Beard | .02 | .10 |
| ☐ 515 | Jeff Burroughs | .02 | .10 |
| ☐ 516 | John D'Acquisto | .02 | .10 |
| ☐ 517 | Wayne Gross | .02 | .10 |
| ☐ 518 | Mike Heath | .02 | .10 |
| ☐ 519 | Rickey Henderson | .60 | 1.50 |
| ☐ 520 | Cliff Johnson | .02 | .10 |
| ☐ 521 | Matt Keough | .02 | .10 |
| ☐ 522 | Brian Kingman | .02 | .10 |
| ☐ 523 | Rick Langford | .02 | .10 |
| ☐ 524 | Dave Lopes | .07 | .20 |
| ☐ 525 | Steve McCatty | .02 | .10 |
| ☐ 526 | Dave McKay | .02 | .10 |
| ☐ 527 | Dan Meyer | .02 | .10 |
| ☐ 528 | Dwayne Murphy | .02 | .10 |
| ☐ 529 | Jeff Newman | .02 | .10 |
| ☐ 530 | Mike Norris | .02 | .10 |
| ☐ 531 | Bob Owchinko | .02 | .10 |
| ☐ 532 | Joe Rudi | .07 | .20 |
| ☐ 533 | Jimmy Sexton | .02 | .10 |
| ☐ 534 | Fred Stanley | .02 | .10 |
| ☐ 535 | Tom Underwood | .02 | .10 |
| ☐ 536 | Neil Allen | .02 | .10 |
| ☐ 537 | Wally Backman | .02 | .10 |
| ☐ 538 | Bob Bailor | .02 | .10 |
| ☐ 539 | Hubie Brooks | .02 | .10 |
| ☐ 540 | Carlos Diaz RC | .08 | .25 |
| ☐ 541 | Pete Falcone | .02 | .10 |
| ☐ 542 | George Foster | .07 | .20 |
| ☐ 543 | Ron Gardenhire | .02 | .10 |
| ☐ 544 | Brian Giles | .02 | .10 |
| ☐ 545 | Ron Hodges | .02 | .10 |
| ☐ 546 | Randy Jones | .02 | .10 |
| ☐ 547 | Mike Jorgensen | .02 | .10 |
| ☐ 548 | Dave Kingman | .07 | .20 |
| ☐ 549 | Ed Lynch | .02 | .10 |
| ☐ 550 | Jesse Orosco | .02 | .10 |
| ☐ 551 | Rick Ownbey | .02 | .10 |
| ☐ 552 | Charlie Puleo | .02 | .10 |
| ☐ 553 | Gary Rajsich | .02 | .10 |
| ☐ 554 | Mike Scott | .07 | .20 |
| ☐ 555 | Rusty Staub | .07 | .20 |
| ☐ 556 | John Stearns | .02 | .10 |
| ☐ 557 | Craig Swan | .02 | .10 |
| ☐ 558 | Ellis Valentine | .02 | .10 |
| ☐ 559 | Tom Veryzer | .02 | .10 |
| ☐ 560 | Mookie Wilson | .07 | .20 |
| ☐ 561 | Pat Zachry | .02 | .10 |
| ☐ 562 | Buddy Bell | .07 | .20 |
| ☐ 563 | John Butcher | .02 | .10 |
| ☐ 564 | Steve Comer | .02 | .10 |
| ☐ 565 | Danny Darwin | .02 | .10 |
| ☐ 566 | Bucky Dent | .07 | .20 |
| ☐ 567 | John Grubb | .02 | .10 |
| ☐ 568 | Rick Honeycutt | .02 | .10 |
| ☐ 569 | Dave Hostetler | .02 | .10 |
| ☐ 570 | Charlie Hough | .07 | .20 |
| ☐ 571 | Lamar Johnson | .02 | .10 |
| ☐ 572 | Jon Matlack | .02 | .10 |
| ☐ 573 | Paul Mirabella | .02 | .10 |
| ☐ 574 | Larry Parrish | .02 | .10 |
| ☐ 575 | Mike Richardt | .02 | .10 |
| ☐ 576 | Mickey Rivers | .02 | .10 |
| ☐ 577 | Billy Sample | .02 | .10 |
| ☐ 578 | Dave Schmidt | .02 | .10 |
| ☐ 579 | Bill Stein | .02 | .10 |
| ☐ 580 | Jim Sundberg | .07 | .20 |
| ☐ 581 | Frank Tanana | .07 | .20 |
| ☐ 582 | Mark Wagner | .02 | .10 |
| ☐ 583 | George Wright RC | .20 | .50 |
| ☐ 584 | Johnny Bench | .30 | .75 |
| ☐ 585 | Bruce Berenyi | .02 | .10 |
| ☐ 586 | Larry Biittner | .02 | .10 |
| ☐ 587 | Cesar Cedeno | .07 | .20 |
| ☐ 588 | Dave Concepcion | .07 | .20 |
| ☐ 589 | Dan Driessen | .02 | .10 |
| ☐ 590 | Greg Harris | .02 | .10 |
| ☐ 591 | Ben Hayes | .02 | .10 |
| ☐ 592 | Paul Householder | .02 | .10 |
| ☐ 593 | Tom Hume | .02 | .10 |
| ☐ 594 | Wayne Krenchicki | .02 | .10 |
| ☐ 595 | Rafael Landestoy | .02 | .10 |
| ☐ 596 | Charlie Leibrandt | .02 | .10 |
| ☐ 597 | Eddie Milner | .02 | .10 |
| ☐ 598 | Ron Oester | .02 | .10 |
| ☐ 599 | Frank Pastore | .02 | .10 |
| ☐ 600 | Joe Price | .02 | .10 |
| ☐ 601 | Tom Seaver | .30 | .75 |
| ☐ 602 | Bob Shirley | .02 | .10 |
| ☐ 603 | Mario Soto | .07 | .20 |
| ☐ 604 | Alex Trevino | .02 | .10 |
| ☐ 605 | Mike Vail | .02 | .10 |
| ☐ 606 | Duane Walker | .02 | .10 |
| ☐ 607 | Tom Brunansky | .07 | .20 |
| ☐ 608 | Bobby Castillo | .02 | .10 |
| ☐ 609 | John Castino | .02 | .10 |
| ☐ 610 | Ron Davis | .02 | .10 |
| ☐ 611 | Lenny Faedo | .02 | .10 |
| ☐ 612 | Terry Felton | .02 | .10 |
| ☐ 613 | Gary Gaetti RC | .40 | 1.00 |
| ☐ 614 | Mickey Hatcher | .02 | .10 |
| ☐ 615 | Brad Havens | .02 | .10 |
| ☐ 616 | Kent Hrbek | .07 | .20 |
| ☐ 617 | Randy Johnson | .02 | .10 |
| ☐ 618 | Tim Laudner | .02 | .10 |
| ☐ 619 | Jeff Little | .02 | .10 |
| ☐ 620 | Bobby Mitchell | .02 | .10 |
| ☐ 621 | Jack O'Connor | .02 | .10 |
| ☐ 622 | John Pacella | .02 | .10 |
| ☐ 623 | Pete Redfern | .02 | .10 |
| ☐ 624 | Jesus Vega | .02 | .10 |
| ☐ 625 | Frank Viola RC | .60 | 1.50 |
| ☐ 626 | Ron Washington | .02 | .10 |
| ☐ 627 | Gary Ward | .02 | .10 |
| ☐ 628 | Al Williams | .02 | .10 |
| ☐ 629 | Yaz/Eck/M.Clear | .30 | .75 |
| ☐ 630 | G.Perry/T.Bulling | .02 | .10 |
| ☐ 631 | D.Concepcion/M.Trillo | .07 | .20 |
| ☐ 632 | R.Yount/B.Bell | .30 | .75 |
| ☐ 633 | D.Winfield/K.Hrbek | .02 | .10 |
| ☐ 634 | P.Rose/W.Stargell | .30 | .75 |
| ☐ 635 | T.Harrah/A.Thornton | .07 | .20 |
| ☐ 636 | O.Smith/Lo.Smith | .30 | .75 |
| ☐ 637 | B.Diaz/G.Carter | .07 | .20 |
| ☐ 638 | C.Fisk/G.Carter | .07 | .20 |
| ☐ 639 | Rickey Henderson IA | .30 | .75 |
| ☐ 640 | B.Ogilvie/R.Jackson | .15 | .40 |
| ☐ 641 | Joel Youngblood | .02 | .10 |
| ☐ 642 | R.Hassey/L.Barker | .07 | .20 |
| ☐ 643 | V.Blue/Black-Blue | .02 | .10 |
| ☐ 644 | B.Black/Black-Blue | .02 | .10 |
| ☐ 645 | Reggie Jackson Power | .07 | .20 |
| ☐ 646 | Rickey Henderson Speed | .30 | .75 |
| ☐ 647 | CL: Cards/Brewers | .02 | .10 |
| ☐ 648 | CL: Orioles/Angels | .02 | .10 |
| ☐ 649 | CL: Royals/Braves | .02 | .10 |
| ☐ 650 | CL: Phillies/Red Sox | .02 | .10 |
| ☐ 651 | CL: Dodgers/White Sox | .02 | .10 |
| ☐ 652 | CL: Giants/Expos | .02 | .10 |
| ☐ 653 | CL: Pirates/Tigers | .02 | .10 |
| ☐ 654 | CL: Padres/Yankees | .02 | .10 |
| ☐ 655 | CL: Indians/Blue Jays | .02 | .10 |
| ☐ 656 | CL: Astros/Mariners | .02 | .10 |
| ☐ 657 | CL: Cubs/A's | .02 | .10 |

|  |  | | |
|---|---|---|---|
| ☐ 658 | CL: Mets/Rangers | .02 | .10 |
| ☐ 659 | CL: Reds/Twins | .02 | .10 |
| ☐ 660 | CL: Specials/Teams | .02 | .10 |

## 1984 Fleer

Tom Seaver

|  |  | | |
|---|---|---|---|
| ☐ | COMPLETE SET (660) | 25.00 | 50.00 |
| ☐ 1 | Mike Boddicker | .05 | .15 |
| ☐ 2 | Al Bumbry | .05 | .15 |
| ☐ 3 | Todd Cruz | .05 | .15 |
| ☐ 4 | Rich Dauer | .05 | .15 |
| ☐ 5 | Storm Davis | .05 | .15 |
| ☐ 6 | Rick Dempsey | .05 | .15 |
| ☐ 7 | Jim Dwyer | .05 | .15 |
| ☐ 8 | Mike Flanagan | .05 | .15 |
| ☐ 9 | Dan Ford | .05 | .15 |
| ☐ 10 | John Lowenstein | .05 | .15 |
| ☐ 11 | Dennis Martinez | .15 | .40 |
| ☐ 12 | Tippy Martinez | .05 | .15 |
| ☐ 13 | Scott McGregor | .05 | .15 |
| ☐ 14 | Eddie Murray | .60 | 1.50 |
| ☐ 15 | Joe Nolan | .05 | .15 |
| ☐ 16 | Jim Palmer | .15 | .40 |
| ☐ 17 | Cal Ripken | 4.00 | 10.00 |
| ☐ 18 | Gary Roenicke | .05 | .15 |
| ☐ 19 | Lenn Sakata | .05 | .15 |
| ☐ 20 | John Shelby | .05 | .15 |
| ☐ 21 | Ken Singleton | .15 | .40 |
| ☐ 22 | Sammy Stewart | .05 | .15 |
| ☐ 23 | Tim Stoddard | .05 | .15 |
| ☐ 24 | Marty Bystrom | .05 | .15 |
| ☐ 25 | Steve Carlton | .30 | .75 |
| ☐ 26 | Ivan DeJesus | .05 | .15 |
| ☐ 27 | John Denny | .05 | .15 |
| ☐ 28 | Bob Dernier | .05 | .15 |
| ☐ 29 | Bo Diaz | .05 | .15 |
| ☐ 30 | Kiko Garcia | .05 | .15 |
| ☐ 31 | Greg Gross | .05 | .15 |
| ☐ 32 | Kevin Gross RC | .20 | .50 |
| ☐ 33 | Von Hayes | .05 | .15 |
| ☐ 34 | Willie Hernandez | .05 | .15 |
| ☐ 35 | Al Holland | .05 | .15 |
| ☐ 36 | Charles Hudson | .05 | .15 |
| ☐ 37 | Joe Lefebvre | .05 | .15 |
| ☐ 38 | Sixto Lezcano | .05 | .15 |
| ☐ 39 | Garry Maddox | .05 | .15 |
| ☐ 40 | Gary Matthews | .15 | .40 |
| ☐ 41 | Len Matuszek | .15 | .40 |
| ☐ 42 | Tug McGraw | .15 | .40 |
| ☐ 43 | Joe Morgan | .15 | .40 |
| ☐ 44 | Tony Perez | .30 | .75 |
| ☐ 45 | Ron Reed | .05 | .15 |
| ☐ 46 | Pete Rose | 2.00 | 5.00 |
| ☐ 47 | Juan Samuel RC | .40 | 1.00 |
| ☐ 48 | Mike Schmidt | 1.50 | 4.00 |
| ☐ 49 | Ozzie Virgil | .05 | .15 |
| ☐ 50 | Juan Agosto | .05 | .15 |
| ☐ 51 | Harold Baines | .15 | .40 |
| ☐ 52 | Floyd Bannister | .05 | .15 |
| ☐ 53 | Salome Barojas | .05 | .15 |
| ☐ 54 | Britt Burns | .05 | .15 |
| ☐ 55 | Julio Cruz | .05 | .15 |
| ☐ 56 | Richard Dotson | .05 | .15 |
| ☐ 57 | Jerry Dybzinski | .05 | .15 |
| ☐ 58 | Carlton Fisk | .30 | .75 |
| ☐ 59 | Scott Fletcher | .05 | .15 |
| ☐ 60 | Jerry Hairston | .05 | .15 |
| ☐ 61 | Kevin Hickey | .05 | .15 |
| ☐ 62 | Marc Hill | .05 | .15 |
| ☐ 63 | LaMarr Hoyt | .05 | .15 |
| ☐ 64 | Ron Kittle | .15 | .40 |
| ☐ 65 | Jerry Koosman | .15 | .40 |
| ☐ 66 | Dennis Lamp | .05 | .15 |
| ☐ 67 | Rudy Law | .05 | .15 |
| ☐ 68 | Vance Law | .05 | .15 |
| ☐ 69 | Greg Luzinski | .15 | .40 |
| ☐ 70 | Tom Paciorek | .05 | .15 |
| ☐ 71 | Mike Squires | .05 | .15 |
| ☐ 72 | Dick Tidrow | .05 | .15 |
| ☐ 73 | Greg Walker | .20 | .50 |
| ☐ 74 | Glenn Abbott | .05 | .15 |
| ☐ 75 | Howard Bailey | .05 | .15 |
| ☐ 76 | Doug Bair | .05 | .15 |
| ☐ 77 | Juan Berenguer | .05 | .15 |
| ☐ 78 | Tom Brookens | .05 | .15 |
| ☐ 79 | Enos Cabell | .05 | .15 |
| ☐ 80 | Kirk Gibson | .60 | 1.50 |
| ☐ 81 | John Grubb | .05 | .15 |
| ☐ 82 | Larry Herndon | .15 | .40 |
| ☐ 83 | Wayne Krenchicki | .05 | .15 |
| ☐ 84 | Rick Leach | .05 | .15 |
| ☐ 85 | Chet Lemon | .15 | .40 |
| ☐ 86 | Aurelio Lopez | .05 | .15 |
| ☐ 87 | Jack Morris | .15 | .40 |
| ☐ 88 | Lance Parrish | .15 | .40 |
| ☐ 89 | Dan Petry | .15 | .40 |
| ☐ 90 | Dave Rozema | .05 | .15 |
| ☐ 91 | Alan Trammell | .15 | .40 |
| ☐ 92 | Lou Whitaker | .15 | .40 |
| ☐ 93 | Milt Wilcox | .05 | .15 |
| ☐ 94 | Glenn Wilson | .05 | .15 |
| ☐ 95 | John Wockenfuss | .05 | .15 |
| ☐ 96 | Dusty Baker | .15 | .40 |
| ☐ 97 | Joe Beckwith | .05 | .15 |
| ☐ 98 | Greg Brock | .05 | .15 |
| ☐ 99 | Jack Fimple | .05 | .15 |
| ☐ 100 | Pedro Guerrero | .15 | .40 |
| ☐ 101 | Rick Honeycutt | .05 | .15 |
| ☐ 102 | Burt Hooton | .05 | .15 |
| ☐ 103 | Steve Howe | .05 | .15 |
| ☐ 104 | Ken Landreaux | .05 | .15 |
| ☐ 105 | Mike Marshall | .15 | .40 |
| ☐ 106 | Rick Monday | .15 | .40 |
| ☐ 107 | Jose Morales | .05 | .15 |
| ☐ 108 | Tom Niedenfuer | .05 | .15 |
| ☐ 109 | Alejandro Pena RC* | .40 | 1.00 |
| ☐ 110 | Jerry Reuss UER (%%Home:- omitted) | .15 | .15 |
| ☐ 111 | Bill Russell | .15 | .40 |
| ☐ 112 | Steve Sax | .15 | .40 |
| ☐ 113 | Mike Scioscia | .15 | .40 |
| ☐ 114 | Derrel Thomas | .05 | .15 |
| ☐ 115 | Fernando Valenzuela | .15 | .40 |
| ☐ 116 | Bob Welch | .15 | .40 |
| ☐ 117 | Steve Yeager | .05 | .15 |
| ☐ 118 | Pat Zachry | .05 | .15 |
| ☐ 119 | Don Baylor | .15 | .40 |
| ☐ 120 | Bert Campaneris | .15 | .40 |
| ☐ 121 | Rick Cerone | .05 | .15 |
| ☐ 122 | Ray Fontenot | .05 | .15 |
| ☐ 123 | George Frazier | .05 | .15 |
| ☐ 124 | Oscar Gamble | .05 | .15 |
| ☐ 125 | Rich Gossage | .15 | .40 |
| ☐ 126 | Ken Griffey | .15 | .40 |
| ☐ 127 | Ron Guidry | .15 | .40 |
| ☐ 128 | Jay Howell | .05 | .15 |
| ☐ 129 | Steve Kemp | .05 | .15 |
| ☐ 130 | Matt Keough | .05 | .15 |
| ☐ 131 | Don Mattingly RC | 8.00 | 20.00 |
| ☐ 132 | John Montefusco | .05 | .15 |
| ☐ 133 | Omar Moreno | .05 | .15 |
| ☐ 134 | Dale Murray | .05 | .15 |
| ☐ 135 | Graig Nettles | .15 | .40 |
| ☐ 136 | Lou Piniella | .15 | .40 |
| ☐ 137 | Willie Randolph | .15 | .40 |
| ☐ 138 | Shane Rawley | .05 | .15 |
| ☐ 139 | Dave Righetti | .15 | .40 |
| ☐ 140 | Andre Robertson | .05 | .15 |
| ☐ 141 | Bob Shirley | .05 | .15 |
| ☐ 142 | Roy Smalley | .05 | .15 |
| ☐ 143 | Dave Winfield | .15 | .40 |
| ☐ 144 | Butch Wynegar | .05 | .15 |
| ☐ 145 | Jim Acker | .05 | .15 |
| ☐ 146 | Doyle Alexander | .05 | .15 |
| ☐ 147 | Jesse Barfield | .15 | .40 |
| ☐ 148 | George Bell | .15 | .40 |
| ☐ 149 | Barry Bonnell | .05 | .15 |
| ☐ 150 | Jim Clancy | .05 | .15 |
| ☐ 151 | Dave Collins | .05 | .15 |
| ☐ 152 | Tony Fernandez RC | .40 | 1.00 |
| ☐ 153 | Damaso Garcia | .05 | .15 |
| ☐ 154 | Dave Geisel | .05 | .15 |
| ☐ 155 | Jim Gott | .05 | .15 |
| ☐ 156 | Alfredo Griffin | .05 | .15 |
| ☐ 157 | Garth Iorg | .05 | .15 |
| ☐ 158 | Roy Lee Jackson | .05 | .15 |
| ☐ 159 | Cliff Johnson | .05 | .15 |
| ☐ 160 | Luis Leal | .05 | .15 |
| ☐ 161 | Buck Martinez | .05 | .15 |
| ☐ 162 | Joey McLaughlin | .05 | .15 |
| ☐ 163 | Randy Moffitt | .05 | .15 |
| ☐ 164 | Lloyd Moseby | .05 | .15 |
| ☐ 165 | Rance Mulliniks | .05 | .15 |
| ☐ 166 | Jorge Orta | .05 | .15 |
| ☐ 167 | Dave Stieb | .15 | .40 |
| ☐ 168 | Willie Upshaw | .05 | .15 |
| ☐ 169 | Ernie Whitt | .05 | .15 |
| ☐ 170 | Len Barker | .05 | .15 |
| ☐ 171 | Steve Bedrosian | .05 | .15 |
| ☐ 172 | Bruce Benedict | .05 | .15 |
| ☐ 173 | Brett Butler | .15 | .40 |
| ☐ 174 | Rick Camp | .05 | .15 |
| ☐ 175 | Chris Chambliss | .15 | .40 |
| ☐ 176 | Ken Dayley | .05 | .15 |
| ☐ 177 | Pete Falcone | .05 | .15 |
| ☐ 178 | Terry Forster | .15 | .40 |
| ☐ 179 | Gene Garber | .05 | .15 |
| ☐ 180 | Terry Harper | .05 | .15 |
| ☐ 181 | Bob Horner | .15 | .40 |
| ☐ 182 | Glenn Hubbard | .05 | .15 |
| ☐ 183 | Randy Johnson | .05 | .15 |
| ☐ 184 | Craig McMurtry | .05 | .15 |
| ☐ 185 | Donnie Moore | .05 | .15 |
| ☐ 186 | Dale Murphy | .30 | .75 |
| ☐ 187 | Phil Niekro | .15 | .40 |
| ☐ 188 | Pascual Perez | .05 | .15 |
| ☐ 189 | Biff Pocoroba | .05 | .15 |
| ☐ 190 | Rafael Ramirez | .05 | .15 |
| ☐ 191 | Jerry Royster | .05 | .15 |
| ☐ 192 | Claudell Washington | .05 | .15 |
| ☐ 193 | Bob Watson | .15 | .40 |
| ☐ 194 | Jerry Augustine | .05 | .15 |
| ☐ 195 | Mark Brouhard | .05 | .15 |
| ☐ 196 | Mike Caldwell | .05 | .15 |
| ☐ 197 | Tom Candiotti RC | .40 | 1.00 |
| ☐ 198 | Cecil Cooper | .15 | .40 |
| ☐ 199 | Rollie Fingers | .15 | .40 |
| ☐ 200 | Jim Gantner | .05 | .15 |
| ☐ 201 | Bob L. Gibson RC | .08 | .25 |
| ☐ 202 | Moose Haas | .05 | .15 |
| ☐ 203 | Roy Howell | .05 | .15 |
| ☐ 204 | Pete Ladd | .05 | .15 |
| ☐ 205 | Rick Manning | .05 | .15 |
| ☐ 206 | Bob McClure | .05 | .15 |
| ☐ 207 | Paul Molitor | .15 | .40 |
| ☐ 208 | Don Money | .05 | .15 |
| ☐ 209 | Charlie Moore | .05 | .15 |
| ☐ 210 | Ben Oglivie | .05 | .15 |
| ☐ 211 | Chuck Porter | .05 | .15 |
| ☐ 212 | Ed Romero | .05 | .15 |
| ☐ 213 | Ted Simmons | .15 | .40 |
| ☐ 214 | Jim Slaton | .05 | .15 |
| ☐ 215 | Don Sutton | .15 | .40 |
| ☐ 216 | Tom Tellmann | .05 | .15 |
| ☐ 217 | Pete Vuckovich | .05 | .15 |
| ☐ 218 | Ned Yost | .05 | .15 |
| ☐ 219 | Robin Yount | 1.00 | 2.50 |
| ☐ 220 | Alan Ashby | .05 | .15 |
| ☐ 221 | Kevin Bass | .15 | .40 |
| ☐ 222 | Jose Cruz | .15 | .40 |
| ☐ 223 | Bill Dawley | .05 | .15 |
| ☐ 224 | Frank DiPino | .05 | .15 |
| ☐ 225 | Bill Doran RC* | .20 | .50 |
| ☐ 226 | Phil Garner | .15 | .40 |
| ☐ 227 | Art Howe | .05 | .15 |
| ☐ 228 | Bob Knepper | .05 | .15 |
| ☐ 229 | Ray Knight | .15 | .40 |
| ☐ 230 | Frank LaCorte | .05 | .15 |
| ☐ 231 | Mike LaCoss | .05 | .15 |
| ☐ 232 | Mike Madden | .05 | .15 |
| ☐ 233 | Jerry Mumphrey | .05 | .15 |
| ☐ 234 | Joe Niekro | .15 | .40 |
| ☐ 235 | Terry Puhl | .05 | .15 |
| ☐ 236 | Luis Pujols | .05 | .15 |
| ☐ 237 | Craig Reynolds | .05 | .15 |
| ☐ 238 | Vern Ruhle | .05 | .15 |
| ☐ 239 | Nolan Ryan | 3.00 | 8.00 |
| ☐ 240 | Mike Scott | .15 | .40 |
| ☐ 241 | Tony Scott | .05 | .15 |
| ☐ 242 | Dave Smith | .05 | .15 |
| ☐ 243 | Dickie Thon | .05 | .15 |

|  |  | | |
|---|--------|---|---|
| 244 | Denny Walling | .05 | .15 |
| 245 | Dale Berra | .05 | .15 |
| 246 | Jim Bibby | .05 | .15 |
| 247 | John Candelaria | .05 | .15 |
| 248 | Jose DeLeon RC | .20 | .50 |
| 249 | Mike Easler | .05 | .15 |
| 250 | Cecilio Guante | .05 | .15 |
| 251 | Richie Hebner | .05 | .15 |
| 252 | Lee Lacy | .05 | .15 |
| 253 | Bill Madlock | .15 | .40 |
| 254 | Milt May | .05 | .15 |
| 255 | Lee Mazzilli | .15 | .40 |
| 256 | Larry McWilliams | .05 | .15 |
| 257 | Jim Morrison | .05 | .15 |
| 258 | Dave Parker | .15 | .40 |
| 259 | Tony Pena | .05 | .15 |
| 260 | Johnny Ray | .05 | .15 |
| 261 | Rick Rhoden | .05 | .15 |
| 262 | Don Robinson | .05 | .15 |
| 263 | Manny Sarmiento | .05 | .15 |
| 264 | Rod Scurry | .05 | .15 |
| 265 | Kent Tekulve | .05 | .15 |
| 266 | Gene Tenace | .15 | .40 |
| 267 | Jason Thompson | .05 | .15 |
| 268 | Lee Tunnell | .05 | .15 |
| 269 | Marvell Wynne | .20 | .50 |
| 270 | Ray Burris | .05 | .15 |
| 271 | Gary Carter | .15 | .40 |
| 272 | Warren Cromartie | .05 | .15 |
| 273 | Andre Dawson | .15 | .40 |
| 274 | Doug Flynn | .05 | .15 |
| 275 | Terry Francona | .15 | .40 |
| 276 | Bill Gullickson | .05 | .15 |
| 277 | Bob James | .05 | .15 |
| 278 | Charlie Lea | .05 | .15 |
| 279 | Bryan Little | .05 | .15 |
| 280 | Al Oliver | .15 | .40 |
| 281 | Tim Raines | .15 | .40 |
| 282 | Bobby Ramos | .05 | .15 |
| 283 | Jeff Reardon | .15 | .40 |
| 284 | Steve Rogers | .15 | .40 |
| 285 | Scott Sanderson | .05 | .15 |
| 286 | Dan Schatzeder | .05 | .15 |
| 287 | Bryn Smith | .05 | .15 |
| 288 | Chris Speier | .05 | .15 |
| 289 | Manny Trillo | .05 | .15 |
| 290 | Mike Vail | .05 | .15 |
| 291 | Tim Wallach | .15 | .40 |
| 292 | Chris Welsh | .05 | .15 |
| 293 | Jim Wohlford | .05 | .15 |
| 294 | Kurt Bevacqua | .05 | .15 |
| 295 | Juan Bonilla | .05 | .15 |
| 296 | Bobby Brown | .05 | .15 |
| 297 | Luis DeLeon | .05 | .15 |
| 298 | Dave Dravecky | .15 | .40 |
| 299 | Tim Flannery | .05 | .15 |
| 300 | Steve Garvey | .15 | .40 |
| 301 | Tony Gwynn | 2.50 | 6.00 |
| 302 | Andy Hawkins | .05 | .15 |
| 303 | Ruppert Jones | .05 | .15 |
| 304 | Terry Kennedy | .05 | .15 |
| 305 | Tim Lollar | .05 | .15 |
| 306 | Gary Lucas | .05 | .15 |
| 307 | Kevin McReynolds RC | .40 | 1.00 |
| 308 | Sid Monge | .05 | .15 |
| 309 | Mario Ramirez | .05 | .15 |
| 310 | Gene Richards | .05 | .15 |
| 311 | Luis Salazar | .05 | .15 |
| 312 | Eric Show | .05 | .15 |
| 313 | Elias Sosa | .05 | .15 |
| 314 | Garry Templeton | .15 | .40 |
| 315 | Mark Thurmond | .05 | .15 |
| 316 | Ed Whitson | .05 | .15 |
| 317 | Alan Wiggins | .05 | .15 |
| 318 | Neil Allen | .05 | .15 |
| 319 | Joaquin Andujar | .15 | .40 |
| 320 | Steve Braun | .05 | .15 |
| 321 | Glenn Brummer | .05 | .15 |
| 322 | Bob Forsch | .05 | .15 |
| 323 | David Green | .05 | .15 |
| 324 | George Hendrick | .15 | .40 |
| 325 | Tom Herr | .15 | .40 |
| 326 | Dane Iorg | .05 | .15 |
| 327 | Jeff Lahti | .05 | .15 |
| 328 | Dave LaPoint | .05 | .15 |
| 329 | Willie McGee | .15 | .40 |
| 330 | Ken Oberkfell | .05 | .15 |
| 331 | Darrell Porter | .05 | .15 |
| 332 | Jamie Quirk | .05 | .15 |
| 333 | Mike Ramsey | .05 | .15 |
| 334 | Floyd Rayford | .05 | .15 |
| 335 | Lonnie Smith | .05 | .15 |
| 336 | Ozzie Smith | 1.00 | 2.50 |
| 337 | John Stuper | .05 | .15 |
| 338 | Bruce Sutter | .30 | .75 |
| 339 | Andy Van Slyke RC | 1.00 | 2.50 |
| 340 | Dave Von Ohlen | .05 | .15 |
| 341 | Willie Aikens | .05 | .15 |
| 342 | Mike Armstrong | .05 | .15 |
| 343 | Bud Black | .05 | .15 |
| 344 | George Brett | 1.50 | 4.00 |
| 345 | Onix Concepcion | .05 | .15 |
| 346 | Keith Creel | .05 | .15 |
| 347 | Larry Gura | .05 | .15 |
| 348 | Don Hood | .05 | .15 |
| 349 | Dennis Leonard | .05 | .15 |
| 350 | Hal McRae | .15 | .40 |
| 351 | Amos Otis | .15 | .40 |
| 352 | Gaylord Perry | .15 | .40 |
| 353 | Greg Pryor | .05 | .15 |
| 354 | Dan Quisenberry | .15 | .40 |
| 355 | Steve Renko | .05 | .15 |
| 356 | Leon Roberts | .05 | .15 |
| 357 | Pat Sheridan | .05 | .15 |
| 358 | Joe Simpson | .05 | .15 |
| 359 | Don Slaught | .15 | .40 |
| 360 | Paul Splittorff | .05 | .15 |
| 361 | U.L. Washington | .05 | .15 |
| 362 | John Wathan | .05 | .15 |
| 363 | Frank White | .15 | .40 |
| 364 | Willie Wilson | .15 | .40 |
| 365 | Jim Barr | .05 | .15 |
| 366 | Dave Bergman | .05 | .15 |
| 367 | Fred Breining | .05 | .15 |
| 368 | Bob Brenly | .05 | .15 |
| 369 | Jack Clark | .15 | .40 |
| 370 | Chili Davis | .15 | .40 |
| 371 | Mark Davis | .15 | .40 |
| 372 | Darrell Evans | .15 | .40 |
| 373 | Atlee Hammaker | .05 | .15 |
| 374 | Mike Krukow | .05 | .15 |
| 375 | Duane Kuiper | .05 | .15 |
| 376 | Bill Laskey | .05 | .15 |
| 377 | Gary Lavelle | .05 | .15 |
| 378 | Johnnie LeMaster | .05 | .15 |
| 379 | Jeff Leonard | .05 | .15 |
| 380 | Randy Lerch | .05 | .15 |
| 381 | Renie Martin | .05 | .15 |
| 382 | Andy McGaffigan | .05 | .15 |
| 383 | Greg Minton | .05 | .15 |
| 384 | Tom O'Malley | .05 | .15 |
| 385 | Max Venable | .05 | .15 |
| 386 | Brad Wellman | .05 | .15 |
| 387 | Joel Youngblood | .05 | .15 |
| 388 | Gary Allenson | .05 | .15 |
| 389 | Luis Aponte | .05 | .15 |
| 390 | Tony Armas | .15 | .40 |
| 391 | Doug Bird | .05 | .15 |
| 392 | Wade Boggs | 1.50 | 4.00 |
| 393 | Dennis Boyd | .15 | .40 |
| 394 | Mike G. Brown UER | .08 | .25 |
| 395 | Mark Clear | .05 | .15 |
| 396 | Dennis Eckersley | .30 | .75 |
| 397 | Dwight Evans | .30 | .75 |
| 398 | Rich Gedman | .05 | .15 |
| 399 | Glenn Hoffman | .05 | .15 |
| 400 | Bruce Hurst | .15 | .40 |
| 401 | John Henry Johnson | .05 | .15 |
| 402 | Ed Jurak | .05 | .15 |
| 403 | Rick Miller | .05 | .15 |
| 404 | Jeff Newman | .05 | .15 |
| 405 | Reid Nichols | .05 | .15 |
| 406 | Bob Ojeda | .15 | .40 |
| 407 | Jerry Remy | .05 | .15 |
| 408 | Jim Rice | .15 | .40 |
| 409 | Bob Stanley | .05 | .15 |
| 410 | Dave Stapleton | .05 | .15 |
| 411 | John Tudor | .15 | .40 |
| 412 | Carl Yastrzemski | .60 | 1.50 |
| 413 | Buddy Bell | .15 | .40 |
| 414 | Larry Bittner | .05 | .15 |
| 415 | John Butcher | .05 | .15 |
| 416 | Danny Darwin | .05 | .15 |
| 417 | Bucky Dent | .15 | .40 |
| 418 | Dave Hostetler | .05 | .15 |
| 419 | Charlie Hough | .15 | .40 |
| 420 | Bobby Johnson | .05 | .15 |
| 421 | Odell Jones | .05 | .15 |
| 422 | Jon Matlack | .05 | .15 |
| 423 | Pete O'Brien RC* | .20 | .50 |
| 424 | Larry Parrish | .05 | .15 |
| 425 | Mickey Rivers | .05 | .15 |
| 426 | Billy Sample | .05 | .15 |
| 427 | Dave Schmidt | .05 | .15 |
| 428 | Mike Smithson | .05 | .15 |
| 429 | Bill Stein | .05 | .15 |
| 430 | Dave Stewart | .15 | .40 |
| 431 | Jim Sundberg | .15 | .40 |
| 432 | Frank Tanana | .15 | .40 |
| 433 | Dave Tobik | .05 | .15 |
| 434 | Wayne Tolleson | .05 | .15 |
| 435 | George Wright | .05 | .15 |
| 436 | Bill Almon | .05 | .15 |
| 437 | Keith Atherton | .05 | .15 |
| 438 | Dave Beard | .05 | .15 |
| 439 | Tom Burgmeier | .05 | .15 |
| 440 | Jeff Burroughs | .05 | .15 |
| 441 | Chris Codiroli | .05 | .15 |
| 442 | Tim Conroy | .05 | .15 |
| 443 | Mike Davis | .05 | .15 |
| 444 | Wayne Gross | .05 | .15 |
| 445 | Garry Hancock | .05 | .15 |
| 446 | Mike Heath | .05 | .15 |
| 447 | Rickey Henderson | 1.00 | 2.50 |
| 448 | Donnie Hill | .05 | .15 |
| 449 | Bob Kearney | .05 | .15 |
| 450 | Bill Krueger RC | .08 | .25 |
| 451 | Rick Langford | .05 | .15 |
| 452 | Carney Lansford | .15 | .40 |
| 453 | Dave Lopes | .15 | .40 |
| 454 | Steve McCatty | .05 | .15 |
| 455 | Dan Meyer | .05 | .15 |
| 456 | Dwayne Murphy | .05 | .15 |
| 457 | Mike Norris | .05 | .15 |
| 458 | Ricky Peters | .05 | .15 |
| 459 | Tony Phillips RC | .40 | 1.00 |
| 460 | Tom Underwood | .05 | .15 |
| 461 | Mike Warren | .05 | .15 |
| 462 | Johnny Bench | .60 | 1.50 |
| 463 | Bruce Berenyi | .05 | .15 |
| 464 | Dann Bilardello | .05 | .15 |
| 465 | Cesar Cedeno | .15 | .40 |
| 466 | Dave Concepcion | .15 | .40 |
| 467 | Dan Driessen | .05 | .15 |
| 468 | Nick Esasky | .15 | .40 |
| 469 | Rich Gale | .05 | .15 |
| 470 | Ben Hayes | .05 | .15 |
| 471 | Paul Householder | .05 | .15 |
| 472 | Tom Hume | .05 | .15 |
| 473 | Alan Knicely | .05 | .15 |
| 474 | Eddie Milner | .05 | .15 |
| 475 | Ron Oester | .05 | .15 |
| 476 | Kelly Paris | .05 | .15 |
| 477 | Frank Pastore | .05 | .15 |
| 478 | Ted Power | .05 | .15 |
| 479 | Joe Price | .05 | .15 |
| 480 | Charlie Puleo | .05 | .15 |
| 481 | Gary Redus RC* | .20 | .50 |
| 482 | Bill Scherrer | .05 | .15 |
| 483 | Mario Soto | .15 | .40 |
| 484 | Alex Trevino | .05 | .15 |
| 485 | Duane Walker | .05 | .15 |
| 486 | Larry Bowa | .15 | .40 |
| 487 | Warren Brusstar | .05 | .15 |
| 488 | Bill Buckner | .15 | .40 |
| 489 | Bill Campbell | .05 | .15 |
| 490 | Ron Cey | .15 | .40 |
| 491 | Jody Davis | .05 | .15 |
| 492 | Leon Durham | .15 | .40 |
| 493 | Mel Hall | .15 | .40 |
| 494 | Fergie Jenkins | .15 | .40 |
| 495 | Jay Johnstone | .05 | .15 |
| 496 | Craig Lefferts RC | .08 | .25 |
| 497 | Carmelo Martinez | .05 | .15 |
| 498 | Jerry Morales | .05 | .15 |
| 499 | Keith Moreland | .05 | .15 |
| 500 | Dickie Noles | .05 | .15 |
| 501 | Mike Proly | .05 | .15 |
| 502 | Chuck Rainey | .05 | .15 |
| 503 | Dick Ruthven | .05 | .15 |
| 504 | Ryne Sandberg | 2.50 | 6.00 |
| 505 | Lee Smith | .15 | .40 |
| 506 | Steve Trout | .05 | .15 |
| 507 | Gary Woods | .05 | .15 |

| | | | |
|---|---|---|---|
| ❏ 508 Juan Beniquez | .05 | .15 | |
| ❏ 509 Bob Boone | .15 | .40 | |
| ❏ 510 Rick Burleson | .05 | .15 | |
| ❏ 511 Rod Carew | .30 | .75 | |
| ❏ 512 Bobby Clark | .05 | .15 | |
| ❏ 513 John Curtis | .05 | .15 | |
| ❏ 514 Doug DeCinces | .05 | .15 | |
| ❏ 515 Brian Downing | .15 | .40 | |
| ❏ 516 Tim Foli | .05 | .15 | |
| ❏ 517 Ken Forsch | .05 | .15 | |
| ❏ 518 Bobby Grich | .15 | .40 | |
| ❏ 519 Andy Hassler | .05 | .15 | |
| ❏ 520 Reggie Jackson | .30 | .75 | |
| ❏ 521 Ron Jackson | .05 | .15 | |
| ❏ 522 Tommy John | .15 | .40 | |
| ❏ 523 Bruce Kison | .05 | .15 | |
| ❏ 524 Steve Lubratich | .05 | .15 | |
| ❏ 525 Fred Lynn | .15 | .40 | |
| ❏ 526 Gary Pettis | .05 | .15 | |
| ❏ 527 Luis Sanchez | .05 | .15 | |
| ❏ 528 Daryl Sconiers | .05 | .15 | |
| ❏ 529 Ellis Valentine | .05 | .15 | |
| ❏ 530 Rob Wilfong | .05 | .15 | |
| ❏ 531 Mike Witt | .15 | .40 | |
| ❏ 532 Geoff Zahn | .05 | .15 | |
| ❏ 533 Bud Anderson | .05 | .15 | |
| ❏ 534 Chris Bando | .05 | .15 | |
| ❏ 535 Alan Bannister | .05 | .15 | |
| ❏ 536 Bert Blyleven | .15 | .40 | |
| ❏ 537 Tom Brennan | .05 | .15 | |
| ❏ 538 Jamie Easterly | .05 | .15 | |
| ❏ 539 Juan Eichelberger | .05 | .15 | |
| ❏ 540 Jim Essian | .05 | .15 | |
| ❏ 541 Mike Fischlin | .05 | .15 | |
| ❏ 542 Julio Franco | .15 | .40 | |
| ❏ 543 Mike Hargrove | .15 | .40 | |
| ❏ 544 Toby Harrah | .15 | .40 | |
| ❏ 545 Ron Hassey | .05 | .15 | |
| ❏ 546 Neal Heaton | .05 | .15 | |
| ❏ 547 Bake McBride | .15 | .40 | |
| ❏ 548 Broderick Perkins | .05 | .15 | |
| ❏ 549 Lary Sorensen | .05 | .15 | |
| ❏ 550 Dan Spillner | .05 | .15 | |
| ❏ 551 Rick Sutcliffe | .15 | .40 | |
| ❏ 552 Pat Tabler | .15 | .40 | |
| ❏ 553 Gorman Thomas | .15 | .40 | |
| ❏ 554 Andre Thornton | .15 | .40 | |
| ❏ 555 George Vukovich | .05 | .15 | |
| ❏ 556 Darrell Brown | .05 | .15 | |
| ❏ 557 Tom Brunansky | .15 | .40 | |
| ❏ 558 Randy Bush | .05 | .15 | |
| ❏ 559 Bobby Castillo | .05 | .15 | |
| ❏ 560 John Castino | .05 | .15 | |
| ❏ 561 Ron Davis | .05 | .15 | |
| ❏ 562 Dave Engle | .05 | .15 | |
| ❏ 563 Lenny Faedo | .05 | .15 | |
| ❏ 564 Pete Filson | .05 | .15 | |
| ❏ 565 Gary Gaetti | .30 | .75 | |
| ❏ 566 Mickey Hatcher | .05 | .15 | |
| ❏ 567 Kent Hrbek | .15 | .40 | |
| ❏ 568 Rusty Kuntz | .05 | .15 | |
| ❏ 569 Tim Laudner | .05 | .15 | |
| ❏ 570 Rick Lysander | .05 | .15 | |
| ❏ 571 Bobby Mitchell | .05 | .15 | |
| ❏ 572 Ken Schrom | .05 | .15 | |
| ❏ 573 Ray Smith | .05 | .15 | |
| ❏ 574 Tim Teufel RC | .20 | .50 | |
| ❏ 575 Frank Viola | .30 | .75 | |
| ❏ 576 Gary Ward | .05 | .15 | |
| ❏ 577 Ron Washington | .05 | .15 | |
| ❏ 578 Len Whitehouse | .05 | .15 | |
| ❏ 579 Al Williams | .05 | .15 | |
| ❏ 580 Bob Bailor | .05 | .15 | |
| ❏ 581 Mark Bradley | .05 | .15 | |
| ❏ 582 Hubie Brooks | .15 | .40 | |
| ❏ 583 Carlos Diaz | .05 | .15 | |
| ❏ 584 George Foster | .15 | .40 | |
| ❏ 585 Brian Giles | .05 | .15 | |
| ❏ 586 Danny Heep | .05 | .15 | |
| ❏ 587 Keith Hernandez | .15 | .40 | |
| ❏ 588 Ron Hodges | .05 | .15 | |
| ❏ 589 Scott Holman | .05 | .15 | |
| ❏ 590 Dave Kingman | .15 | .40 | |
| ❏ 591 Ed Lynch | .05 | .15 | |
| ❏ 592 Jose Oquendo RC | .20 | .50 | |
| ❏ 593 Jesse Orosco | .05 | .15 | |
| ❏ 594 Junior Ortiz | .05 | .15 | |
| ❏ 595 Tom Seaver | .60 | 1.50 | |

| | | | |
|---|---|---|---|
| ❏ 596 Doug Sisk | .05 | .15 | |
| ❏ 597 Rusty Staub | .15 | .40 | |
| ❏ 598 John Stearns | .05 | .15 | |
| ❏ 599 Darryl Strawberry RC | 2.00 | 5.00 | |
| ❏ 600 Craig Swan | .05 | .15 | |
| ❏ 601 Walt Terrell | .05 | .15 | |
| ❏ 602 Mike Torrez | .05 | .15 | |
| ❏ 603 Mookie Wilson | .15 | .40 | |
| ❏ 604 Jamie Allen | .05 | .15 | |
| ❏ 605 Jim Beattie | .05 | .15 | |
| ❏ 606 Tony Bernazard | .05 | .15 | |
| ❏ 607 Manny Castillo | .05 | .15 | |
| ❏ 608 Bill Caudill | .05 | .15 | |
| ❏ 609 Bryan Clark | .05 | .15 | |
| ❏ 610 Al Cowens | .05 | .15 | |
| ❏ 611 Dave Henderson | .15 | .40 | |
| ❏ 612 Steve Henderson | .05 | .15 | |
| ❏ 613 Orlando Mercado | .05 | .15 | |
| ❏ 614 Mike Moore | .15 | .40 | |
| ❏ 615 Ricky Nelson UER | .05 | .15 | |
| (Jamie Nelson's | | | |
| stats on back) | | | |
| ❏ 616 Spike Owen RC | .20 | .50 | |
| ❏ 617 Pat Putnam | .05 | .15 | |
| ❏ 618 Ron Roenicke | .05 | .15 | |
| ❏ 619 Mike Stanton | .05 | .15 | |
| ❏ 620 Bob Stoddard | .05 | .15 | |
| ❏ 621 Rick Sweet | .05 | .15 | |
| ❏ 622 Roy Thomas | .05 | .15 | |
| ❏ 623 Ed VandeBerg | .05 | .15 | |
| ❏ 624 Matt Young RC | .20 | .50 | |
| ❏ 625 Richie Zisk | .05 | .15 | |
| ❏ 626 Fred Lynn | | | |
| 1982 AS Game RB | .15 | .40 | |
| ❏ 627 Manny Trillo | | | |
| 1983 AS Game RB | .05 | .15 | |
| ❏ 628 Steve Garvey Iron Man | .05 | .15 | |
| ❏ 629 Rod Carew AL RunnerUp | .15 | .40 | |
| ❏ 630 Wade Boggs AL Champ | .60 | 1.50 | |
| ❏ 631 Tim Raines IA | .15 | .40 | |
| ❏ 632 Al Oliver | | | |
| Double Trouble | .15 | .40 | |
| ❏ 633 Steve Sax | | | |
| AS Second Base | .05 | .15 | |
| ❏ 634 Dickie Thon | | | |
| AS Shortstop | .05 | .15 | |
| ❏ 635 Ace Firemen | | | |
| Dan Quisenberry | | | |
| and Tippy Martinez | .05 | .15 | |
| ❏ 636 J.Morgan/P.Rose/T.Perez | .60 | 1.50 | |
| ❏ 637 Backstop Stars | | | |
| Lance Parrish | | | |
| Bob Boone | .30 | .75 | |
| ❏ 638 G.Brett/G.Perry | .75 | 2.00 | |
| ❏ 639 1983 No Hitters | | | |
| Dave Righetti | | | |
| Mike Warren | | | |
| Bob F | .30 | .75 | |
| ❏ 640 J.Bench/C.Yastrzemski | .60 | 1.50 | |
| ❏ 641 Gaylord Perry Style | .05 | .15 | |
| ❏ 642 Steve Carlton IA | .15 | .40 | |
| ❏ 643 Joe Altobelli and | | | |
| Paul Owens | | | |
| World Series Manage | .05 | .15 | |
| ❏ 644 Rick Dempsey | | | |
| World Series MVP | .05 | .15 | |
| ❏ 645 Mike Boddicker | | | |
| WS Rookie Winner | .05 | .15 | |
| ❏ 646 Scott McGregor | | | |
| WS Clincher | .05 | .15 | |
| ❏ 647 CL: Orioles/Royals | | | |
| Joe Altobelli MG | .05 | .15 | |
| ❏ 648 CL: Phillies/Giants | | | |
| Paul Owens MG | .05 | .15 | |
| ❏ 649 CL: White Sox/Red Sox | | | |
| Tony LaRussa MG | .30 | .75 | |
| ❏ 650 CL: Tigers/Rangers | | | |
| Sparky Anderson MG | .30 | .75 | |
| ❏ 651 CL: Dodgers/A's | | | |
| Tommy Lasorda MG | .30 | .75 | |
| ❏ 652 CL: Yankees/Reds | | | |
| Billy Martin MG | .30 | .75 | |
| ❏ 653 CL: Blue Jays/Cubs | | | |
| Bobby Cox MG | .15 | .40 | |
| ❏ 654 CL: Braves/Angels | | | |
| Joe Torre MG | .30 | .75 | |
| ❏ 655 CL: Brewers/Mariners | | | |
| Rene Lachemann MG | .05 | .15 | |

| | | | |
|---|---|---|---|
| ❏ 656 CL: Astros/Twins | | | |
| Bob Lillis MG | .05 | .15 | |
| ❏ 657 CL: Pirates/Mets | | | |
| Chuck Tanner MG | .05 | .15 | |
| ❏ 658 CL: Expos/Mariners | | | |
| Bill Virdon MG | .05 | .15 | |
| ❏ 659 CL: Padres/Specials | | | |
| Dick Williams MG | .15 | .40 | |
| ❏ 660 CL: Cardinals/Teams | | | |
| Whitey Herzog MG | .30 | .75 | |

## 1985 Fleer

| | | | |
|---|---|---|---|
| ❏ COMPLETE SET (660) | | 30.00 | 60.00 |
| ❏ COMP.FACT.SET (660) | | 50.00 | 100.00 |
| ❏ 1 Doug Bair | .05 | .15 | |
| ❏ 2 Juan Berenguer | .05 | .15 | |
| ❏ 3 Dave Bergman | .05 | .15 | |
| ❏ 4 Tom Brookens | .05 | .15 | |
| ❏ 5 Marty Castillo | .05 | .15 | |
| ❏ 6 Darrell Evans | .15 | .40 | |
| ❏ 7 Barbaro Garbey | .05 | .15 | |
| ❏ 8 Kirk Gibson | .15 | .40 | |
| ❏ 9 John Grubb | .05 | .15 | |
| ❏ 10 Willie Hernandez | .15 | .40 | |
| ❏ 11 Larry Herndon | .05 | .15 | |
| ❏ 12 Howard Johnson | .15 | .40 | |
| ❏ 13 Ruppert Jones | .05 | .15 | |
| ❏ 14 Rusty Kuntz | .05 | .15 | |
| ❏ 15 Chet Lemon | .15 | .40 | |
| ❏ 16 Aurelio Lopez | .05 | .15 | |
| ❏ 17 Sid Monge | .05 | .15 | |
| ❏ 18 Jack Morris | .15 | .40 | |
| ❏ 19 Lance Parrish | .15 | .40 | |
| ❏ 20 Dan Petry | .05 | .15 | |
| ❏ 21 Dave Rozema | .05 | .15 | |
| ❏ 22 Bill Scherrer | .05 | .15 | |
| ❏ 23 Alan Trammell | .15 | .40 | |
| ❏ 24 Lou Whitaker | .15 | .40 | |
| ❏ 25 Milt Wilcox | .05 | .15 | |
| ❏ 26 Kurt Bevacqua | .05 | .15 | |
| ❏ 27 Greg Booker | .05 | .15 | |
| ❏ 28 Bobby Brown | .05 | .15 | |
| ❏ 29 Luis DeLeon | .05 | .15 | |
| ❏ 30 Dave Dravecky | .05 | .15 | |
| ❏ 31 Tim Flannery | .05 | .15 | |
| ❏ 32 Steve Garvey | .15 | .40 | |
| ❏ 33 Rich Gossage | .15 | .40 | |
| ❏ 34 Tony Gwynn | 1.00 | 2.50 | |
| ❏ 35 Greg Harris | .05 | .15 | |
| ❏ 36 Andy Hawkins | .05 | .15 | |
| ❏ 37 Terry Kennedy | .05 | .15 | |
| ❏ 38 Craig Lefferts | .05 | .15 | |
| ❏ 39 Tim Lollar | .05 | .15 | |
| ❏ 40 Carmelo Martinez | .05 | .15 | |
| ❏ 41 Kevin McReynolds | .15 | .40 | |
| ❏ 42 Graig Nettles | .15 | .40 | |
| ❏ 43 Luis Salazar | .05 | .15 | |
| ❏ 44 Eric Show | .05 | .15 | |
| ❏ 45 Garry Templeton | .15 | .40 | |
| ❏ 46 Mark Thurmond | .05 | .15 | |
| ❏ 47 Ed Whitson | .05 | .15 | |
| ❏ 48 Alan Wiggins | .05 | .15 | |
| ❏ 49 Rich Bordi | .05 | .15 | |
| ❏ 50 Larry Bowa | .15 | .40 | |
| ❏ 51 Warren Brusstar | .05 | .15 | |
| ❏ 52 Ron Cey | .15 | .40 | |
| ❏ 53 Henry Cotto RC | .08 | .25 | |
| ❏ 54 Jody Davis | .05 | .15 | |
| ❏ 55 Bob Dernier | .05 | .15 | |
| ❏ 56 Leon Durham | .05 | .15 | |
| ❏ 57 Dennis Eckersley | .30 | .75 | |
| ❏ 58 George Frazier | .05 | .15 | |
| ❏ 59 Richie Hebner | .05 | .15 | |
| ❏ 60 Dave Lopes | .15 | .40 | |

|  |  | | |
|---|--------|------|------|
| 61 | Gary Matthews | .15 | .40 |
| 62 | Keith Moreland | .05 | .15 |
| 63 | Rick Reuschel | .15 | .40 |
| 64 | Dick Ruthven | .05 | .15 |
| 65 | Ryne Sandberg | 1.00 | 2.50 |
| 66 | Scott Sanderson | .05 | .15 |
| 67 | Lee Smith | .15 | .40 |
| 68 | Tim Stoddard | .05 | .15 |
| 69 | Rick Sutcliffe | .15 | .40 |
| 70 | Steve Trout | .05 | .15 |
| 71 | Gary Woods | .05 | .15 |
| 72 | Wally Backman | .05 | .15 |
| 73 | Bruce Berenyi | .05 | .15 |
| 74 | Hubie Brooks UER (Kelvin Chapman's stats on card | .15 | .40 |
| 75 | Kelvin Chapman | .05 | .15 |
| 76 | Ron Darling | .15 | .40 |
| 77 | Sid Fernandez | .15 | .40 |
| 78 | Mike Fitzgerald | .05 | .15 |
| 79 | George Foster | .15 | .40 |
| 80 | Brent Gaff | .05 | .15 |
| 81 | Ron Gardenhire | .05 | .15 |
| 82 | Dwight Gooden RC | 1.25 | 3.00 |
| 83 | Tom Gorman | .05 | .15 |
| 84 | Danny Heep | .05 | .15 |
| 85 | Keith Hernandez | .15 | .40 |
| 86 | Ray Knight | .15 | .40 |
| 87 | Ed Lynch | .05 | .15 |
| 88 | Jose Oquendo | .15 | .40 |
| 89 | Jesse Orosco | .05 | .15 |
| 90 | Rafael Santana | .05 | .15 |
| 91 | Doug Sisk | .05 | .15 |
| 92 | Rusty Staub | .15 | .40 |
| 93 | Darryl Strawberry | .50 | 1.25 |
| 94 | Walt Terrell | .05 | .15 |
| 95 | Mookie Wilson | .15 | .40 |
| 96 | Jim Acker | .05 | .15 |
| 97 | Willie Aikens | .05 | .15 |
| 98 | Doyle Alexander | .05 | .15 |
| 99 | Jesse Barfield | .15 | .40 |
| 100 | George Bell | .15 | .40 |
| 101 | Jim Clancy | .05 | .15 |
| 102 | Dave Collins | .05 | .15 |
| 103 | Tony Fernandez | .15 | .40 |
| 104 | Damaso Garcia | .05 | .15 |
| 105 | Jim Gott | .05 | .15 |
| 106 | Alfredo Griffin | .05 | .15 |
| 107 | Garth Iorg | .05 | .15 |
| 108 | Roy Lee Jackson | .05 | .15 |
| 109 | Cliff Johnson | .05 | .15 |
| 110 | Jimmy Key RC | .40 | 1.00 |
| 111 | Dennis Lamp | .05 | .15 |
| 112 | Rick Leach | .05 | .15 |
| 113 | Luis Leal | .05 | .15 |
| 114 | Buck Martinez | .05 | .15 |
| 115 | Lloyd Moseby | .15 | .40 |
| 116 | Rance Mulliniks | .05 | .15 |
| 117 | Dave Stieb | .15 | .40 |
| 118 | Willie Upshaw | .05 | .15 |
| 119 | Ernie Whitt | .05 | .15 |
| 120 | Mike Armstrong | .05 | .15 |
| 121 | Don Baylor | .15 | .40 |
| 122 | Marty Bystrom | .05 | .15 |
| 123 | Rick Cerone | .05 | .15 |
| 124 | Joe Cowley | .05 | .15 |
| 125 | Brian Dayett | .05 | .15 |
| 126 | Tim Foli | .05 | .15 |
| 127 | Ray Fontenot | .05 | .15 |
| 128 | Ken Griffey | .15 | .40 |
| 129 | Ron Guidry | .15 | .40 |
| 130 | Toby Harrah | .05 | .15 |
| 131 | Jay Howell | .05 | .15 |
| 132 | Steve Kemp | .05 | .15 |
| 133 | Don Mattingly | 2.00 | 5.00 |
| 134 | Bobby Meacham | .05 | .15 |
| 135 | John Montefusco | .05 | .15 |
| 136 | Omar Moreno | .05 | .15 |
| 137 | Dale Murray | .05 | .15 |
| 138 | Phil Niekro | .15 | .40 |
| 139 | Mike Pagliarulo | .15 | .40 |
| 140 | Willie Randolph | .15 | .40 |
| 141 | Dennis Rasmussen | .05 | .15 |
| 142 | Dave Righetti | .15 | .40 |
| 143 | Jose Rijo RC | .40 | 1.00 |
| 144 | Andre Robertson | .05 | .15 |
| 145 | Bob Shirley | .05 | .15 |
| 146 | Dave Winfield | .15 | .40 |
| 147 | Butch Wynegar | .05 | .15 |
| 148 | Gary Allenson | .05 | .15 |
| 149 | Tony Armas | .15 | .40 |
| 150 | Marty Barrett | .05 | .15 |
| 151 | Wade Boggs | .50 | 1.25 |
| 152 | Dennis Boyd | .05 | .15 |
| 153 | Bill Buckner | .15 | .40 |
| 154 | Mark Clear | .05 | .15 |
| 155 | Roger Clemens RC | 8.00 | 20.00 |
| 156 | Steve Crawford | .05 | .15 |
| 157 | Mike Easler | .05 | .15 |
| 158 | Dwight Evans | .30 | .75 |
| 159 | Rich Gedman | .05 | .15 |
| 160 | Jackie Gutierrez w/Boggs | .15 | .40 |
| 161 | Bruce Hurst | .15 | .40 |
| 162 | John Henry Johnson | .05 | .15 |
| 163 | Rick Miller | .05 | .15 |
| 164 | Reid Nichols | .05 | .15 |
| 165 | Al Nipper | .05 | .15 |
| 166 | Bob Ojeda | .05 | .15 |
| 167 | Jerry Remy | .05 | .15 |
| 168 | Jim Rice | .15 | .40 |
| 169 | Bob Stanley | .05 | .15 |
| 170 | Mike Boddicker | .05 | .15 |
| 171 | Al Bumbry | .05 | .15 |
| 172 | Todd Cruz | .05 | .15 |
| 173 | Rich Dauer | .05 | .15 |
| 174 | Storm Davis | .05 | .15 |
| 175 | Rick Dempsey | .05 | .15 |
| 176 | Jim Dwyer | .05 | .15 |
| 177 | Mike Flanagan | .05 | .15 |
| 178 | Dan Ford | .05 | .15 |
| 179 | Wayne Gross | .05 | .15 |
| 180 | John Lowenstein | .05 | .15 |
| 181 | Dennis Martinez | .15 | .40 |
| 182 | Tippy Martinez | .05 | .15 |
| 183 | Scott McGregor | .05 | .15 |
| 184 | Eddie Murray | .50 | 1.25 |
| 185 | Joe Nolan | .05 | .15 |
| 186 | Floyd Rayford | .05 | .15 |
| 187 | Cal Ripken | 2.00 | 5.00 |
| 188 | Gary Roenicke | .05 | .15 |
| 189 | Lenn Sakata | .05 | .15 |
| 190 | John Shelby | .05 | .15 |
| 191 | Ken Singleton | .15 | .40 |
| 192 | Sammy Stewart | .05 | .15 |
| 193 | Bill Swaggerty | .05 | .15 |
| 194 | Tom Underwood | .05 | .15 |
| 195 | Mike Young | .05 | .15 |
| 196 | Steve Balboni | .05 | .15 |
| 197 | Joe Beckwith | .05 | .15 |
| 198 | Bud Black | .05 | .15 |
| 199 | George Brett | 1.25 | 3.00 |
| 200 | Onix Concepcion | .05 | .15 |
| 201 | Mark Gubicza RC* | .20 | .50 |
| 202 | Larry Gura | .05 | .15 |
| 203 | Mark Huismann | .05 | .15 |
| 204 | Dane Iorg | .05 | .15 |
| 205 | Danny Jackson | .05 | .15 |
| 206 | Charlie Leibrandt | .05 | .15 |
| 207 | Hal McRae | .15 | .40 |
| 208 | Darryl Motley | .05 | .15 |
| 209 | Jorge Orta | .05 | .15 |
| 210 | Greg Pryor | .05 | .15 |
| 211 | Dan Quisenberry | .15 | .40 |
| 212 | Bret Saberhagen RC | .60 | 1.50 |
| 213 | Pat Sheridan | .05 | .15 |
| 214 | Don Slaught | .05 | .15 |
| 215 | U.L. Washington | .05 | .15 |
| 216 | John Wathan | .05 | .15 |
| 217 | Frank White | .15 | .40 |
| 218 | Willie Wilson | .15 | .40 |
| 219 | Neil Allen | .05 | .15 |
| 220 | Joaquin Andujar | .05 | .15 |
| 221 | Steve Braun | .05 | .15 |
| 222 | Danny Cox | .05 | .15 |
| 223 | Bob Forsch | .05 | .15 |
| 224 | David Green | .05 | .15 |
| 225 | George Hendrick | .05 | .15 |
| 226 | Tom Herr | .05 | .15 |
| 227 | Ricky Horton | .05 | .15 |
| 228 | Art Howe | .05 | .15 |
| 229 | Mike Jorgensen | .05 | .15 |
| 230 | Kurt Kepshire | .05 | .15 |
| 231 | Jeff Lahti | .05 | .15 |
| 232 | Tito Landrum | .05 | .15 |
| 233 | Dave LaPoint | .05 | .15 |
| 234 | Willie McGee | .15 | .40 |
| 235 | Tom Nieto | .05 | .15 |
| 236 | Terry Pendleton RC | .40 | 1.00 |
| 237 | Darrell Porter | .05 | .15 |
| 238 | Dave Rucker | .05 | .15 |
| 239 | Lonnie Smith | .05 | .15 |
| 240 | Ozzie Smith | .75 | 2.00 |
| 241 | Bruce Sutter | .15 | .40 |
| 242 | Andy Van Slyke UER | .30 | .75 |
| 243 | Dave Von Ohlen | .05 | .15 |
| 244 | Larry Andersen | .05 | .15 |
| 245 | Bill Campbell | .05 | .15 |
| 246 | Steve Carlton | .15 | .40 |
| 247 | Tim Corcoran | .05 | .15 |
| 248 | Ivan DeJesus | .05 | .15 |
| 249 | John Denny | .05 | .15 |
| 250 | Bo Diaz | .05 | .15 |
| 251 | Greg Gross | .05 | .15 |
| 252 | Kevin Gross | .05 | .15 |
| 253 | Von Hayes | .05 | .15 |
| 254 | Al Holland | .05 | .15 |
| 255 | Charles Hudson | .05 | .15 |
| 256 | Jerry Koosman | .15 | .40 |
| 257 | Joe Lefebvre | .05 | .15 |
| 258 | Sixto Lezcano | .05 | .15 |
| 259 | Garry Maddox | .05 | .15 |
| 260 | Len Matuszek | .05 | .15 |
| 261 | Tug McGraw | .15 | .40 |
| 262 | Al Oliver | .15 | .40 |
| 263 | Shane Rawley | .05 | .15 |
| 264 | Juan Samuel | .05 | .15 |
| 265 | Mike Schmidt | 1.25 | 3.00 |
| 266 | Jeff Stone RC | .05 | .15 |
| 267 | Ozzie Virgil | .05 | .15 |
| 268 | Glenn Wilson | .05 | .15 |
| 269 | John Wockenfuss | .05 | .15 |
| 270 | Darrell Brown | .05 | .15 |
| 271 | Tom Brunansky | .15 | .40 |
| 272 | Randy Bush | .05 | .15 |
| 273 | John Butcher | .05 | .15 |
| 274 | Bobby Castillo | .05 | .15 |
| 275 | Ron Davis | .05 | .15 |
| 276 | Dave Engle | .05 | .15 |
| 277 | Pete Filson | .05 | .15 |
| 278 | Gary Gaetti | .15 | .40 |
| 279 | Mickey Hatcher | .05 | .15 |
| 280 | Ed Hodge | .05 | .15 |
| 281 | Kent Hrbek | .15 | .40 |
| 282 | Houston Jimenez | .05 | .15 |
| 283 | Tim Laudner | .05 | .15 |
| 284 | Rick Lysander | .05 | .15 |
| 285 | Dave Meier | .05 | .15 |
| 286 | Kirby Puckett RC | 6.00 | 15.00 |
| 287 | Pat Putnam | .05 | .15 |
| 288 | Ken Schrom | .05 | .15 |
| 289 | Mike Smithson | .05 | .15 |
| 290 | Tim Teufel | .05 | .15 |
| 291 | Frank Viola | .15 | .40 |
| 292 | Ron Washington | .05 | .15 |
| 293 | Don Asse | .05 | .15 |
| 294 | Juan Beniquez | .05 | .15 |
| 295 | Bob Boone | .15 | .40 |
| 296 | Mike C. Brown | .05 | .15 |
| 297 | Rod Carew | .30 | .75 |
| 298 | Doug Corbett | .05 | .15 |
| 299 | Doug DeCinces | .05 | .15 |
| 300 | Brian Downing | .15 | .40 |
| 301 | Ken Forsch | .05 | .15 |
| 302 | Bobby Grich | .15 | .40 |
| 303 | Reggie Jackson | .30 | .75 |
| 304 | Tommy John | .15 | .40 |
| 305 | Curt Kaufman | .05 | .15 |
| 306 | Bruce Kison | .05 | .15 |
| 307 | Fred Lynn | .15 | .40 |
| 308 | Gary Pettis | .05 | .15 |
| 309 | Ron Romanick | .05 | .15 |
| 310 | Luis Sanchez | .05 | .15 |
| 311 | Dick Schofield | .05 | .15 |
| 312 | Daryl Sconiers | .05 | .15 |
| 313 | Jim Slaton | .05 | .15 |
| 314 | Derrel Thomas | .05 | .15 |
| 315 | Rob Wilfong | .05 | .15 |
| 316 | Mike Witt | .05 | .15 |
| 317 | Geoff Zahn | .05 | .15 |
| 318 | Len Barker | .05 | .15 |
| 319 | Steve Bedrosian | .05 | .15 |
| 320 | Bruce Benedict | .05 | .15 |
| 321 | Rick Camp | .05 | .15 |
| 322 | Chris Chambliss | .15 | .40 |

|  |  | | |
|---|---|---|---|
| 323 | Jeff Dedmon | .05 | .15 |
| 324 | Terry Forster | .15 | .40 |
| 325 | Gene Garber | .05 | .15 |
| 326 | Albert Hall | .05 | .15 |
| 327 | Terry Harper | .05 | .15 |
| 328 | Bob Horner | .15 | .40 |
| 329 | Glenn Hubbard | .05 | .15 |
| 330 | Randy Johnson | .05 | .15 |
| 331 | Brad Komminsk | .05 | .15 |
| 332 | Rick Mahler | .05 | .15 |
| 333 | Craig McMurtry | .05 | .15 |
| 334 | Donnie Moore | .05 | .15 |
| 335 | Dale Murphy | .30 | .75 |
| 336 | Ken Oberkfell | .05 | .15 |
| 337 | Pascual Perez | .05 | .15 |
| 338 | Gerald Perry | .05 | .15 |
| 339 | Rafael Ramirez | .05 | .15 |
| 340 | Jerry Royster | .05 | .15 |
| 341 | Alex Trevino | .05 | .15 |
| 342 | Claudell Washington | .05 | .15 |
| 343 | Alan Ashby | .05 | .15 |
| 344 | Mark Bailey | .05 | .15 |
| 345 | Kevin Bass | .05 | .15 |
| 346 | Enos Cabell | .05 | .15 |
| 347 | Jose Cruz | .15 | .40 |
| 348 | Bill Dawley | .05 | .15 |
| 349 | Frank DiPino | .05 | .15 |
| 350 | Bill Doran | .05 | .15 |
| 351 | Phil Garner | .15 | .40 |
| 352 | Bob Knepper | .05 | .15 |
| 353 | Mike LaCoss | .05 | .15 |
| 354 | Jerry Mumphrey | .05 | .15 |
| 355 | Joe Niekro | .05 | .15 |
| 356 | Terry Puhl | .05 | .15 |
| 357 | Craig Reynolds | .05 | .15 |
| 358 | Vern Ruhle | .05 | .15 |
| 359 | Nolan Ryan | 2.50 | 6.00 |
| 360 | Joe Sambito | .05 | .15 |
| 361 | Mike Scott | .15 | .40 |
| 362 | Dave Smith | .05 | .15 |
| 363 | Julio Solano | .05 | .15 |
| 364 | Dickie Thon | .05 | .15 |
| 365 | Denny Walling | .05 | .15 |
| 366 | Dave Anderson | .05 | .15 |
| 367 | Bob Bailor | .05 | .15 |
| 368 | Greg Brock | .05 | .15 |
| 369 | Carlos Diaz | .05 | .15 |
| 370 | Pedro Guerrero | .15 | .40 |
| 371 | Orel Hershiser RC | 1.25 | 3.00 |
| 372 | Rick Honeycutt | .05 | .15 |
| 373 | Burt Hooton | .05 | .15 |
| 374 | Ken Howell | .05 | .15 |
| 375 | Ken Landreaux | .05 | .15 |
| 376 | Candy Maldonado | .05 | .15 |
| 377 | Mike Marshall | .15 | .40 |
| 378 | Tom Niedenfuer | .05 | .15 |
| 379 | Alejandro Pena | .05 | .15 |
| 380 | Jerry Reuss UER (%%Home:- omitted) | .05 | .15 |
| 381 | R.J. Reynolds | .05 | .15 |
| 382 | German Rivera | .05 | .40 |
| 383 | Bill Russell | .15 | .40 |
| 384 | Steve Sax | .15 | .40 |
| 385 | Mike Scioscia | .15 | .40 |
| 386 | Franklin Stubbs | .15 | .40 |
| 387 | Fernando Valenzuela | .15 | .40 |
| 388 | Bob Welch | .15 | .40 |
| 389 | Terry Whitfield | .05 | .15 |
| 390 | Steve Yeager | .15 | .40 |
| 391 | Pat Zachry | .05 | .15 |
| 392 | Fred Breining | .05 | .15 |
| 393 | Gary Carter | .15 | .40 |
| 394 | Andre Dawson | .15 | .40 |
| 395 | Miguel Dilone | .05 | .15 |
| 396 | Dan Driessen | .05 | .15 |
| 397 | Doug Flynn | .05 | .15 |
| 398 | Terry Francona | .15 | .40 |
| 399 | Bill Gullickson | .05 | .15 |
| 400 | Bob James | .05 | .15 |
| 401 | Charlie Lea | .05 | .15 |
| 402 | Bryan Little | .05 | .15 |
| 403 | Gary Lucas | .05 | .15 |
| 404 | David Palmer | .05 | .15 |
| 405 | Tim Raines | .15 | .40 |
| 406 | Mike Ramsey | .05 | .15 |
| 407 | Jeff Reardon | .15 | .40 |
| 408 | Steve Rogers | .15 | .40 |
| 409 | Dan Schatzeder | .05 | .15 |
| 410 | Bryn Smith | .05 | .15 |
| 411 | Mike Stenhouse | .05 | .15 |
| 412 | Tim Wallach | .05 | .15 |
| 413 | Jim Wohlford | .05 | .15 |
| 414 | Bill Almon | .05 | .15 |
| 415 | Keith Atherton | .05 | .15 |
| 416 | Bruce Bochte | .05 | .15 |
| 417 | Tom Burgmeier | .05 | .15 |
| 418 | Ray Burris | .05 | .15 |
| 419 | Bill Caudill | .05 | .15 |
| 420 | Chris Codiroli | .05 | .15 |
| 421 | Tim Conroy | .05 | .15 |
| 422 | Mike Davis | .05 | .15 |
| 423 | Jim Essian | .05 | .15 |
| 424 | Mike Heath | .05 | .15 |
| 425 | Rickey Henderson | .60 | 1.50 |
| 426 | Donnie Hill | .05 | .15 |
| 427 | Dave Kingman | .15 | .40 |
| 428 | Bill Krueger | .05 | .15 |
| 429 | Carney Lansford | .15 | .40 |
| 430 | Steve McCatty | .05 | .15 |
| 431 | Joe Morgan | .15 | .40 |
| 432 | Dwayne Murphy | .05 | .15 |
| 433 | Tony Phillips | .05 | .15 |
| 434 | Lary Sorensen | .05 | .15 |
| 435 | Mike Warren | .05 | .15 |
| 436 | Curt Young | .05 | .15 |
| 437 | Luis Aponte | .05 | .15 |
| 438 | Chris Bando | .05 | .15 |
| 439 | Tony Bernazard | .05 | .15 |
| 440 | Bert Blyleven | .15 | .40 |
| 441 | Brett Butler | .15 | .40 |
| 442 | Ernie Camacho | .05 | .15 |
| 443 | Joe Carter | .50 | 1.25 |
| 444 | Carmelo Castillo | .05 | .15 |
| 445 | Jamie Easterly | .05 | .15 |
| 446 | Steve Farr RC | .20 | .50 |
| 447 | Mike Fischlin | .05 | .15 |
| 448 | Julio Franco | .15 | .40 |
| 449 | Mel Hall | .05 | .15 |
| 450 | Mike Hargrove | .05 | .15 |
| 451 | Neal Heaton | .05 | .15 |
| 452 | Brook Jacoby | .05 | .15 |
| 453 | Mike Jeffcoat | .05 | .15 |
| 454 | Don Schulze | .05 | .15 |
| 455 | Roy Smith | .05 | .15 |
| 456 | Pat Tabler | .05 | .15 |
| 457 | Andre Thornton | .05 | .15 |
| 458 | George Vukovich | .05 | .15 |
| 459 | Tom Waddell | .05 | .15 |
| 460 | Jerry Willard | .05 | .15 |
| 461 | Dale Berra | .05 | .15 |
| 462 | John Candelaria | .05 | .15 |
| 463 | Jose DeLeon | .05 | .15 |
| 464 | Doug Frobel | .05 | .15 |
| 465 | Cecilio Guante | .05 | .15 |
| 466 | Brian Harper | .05 | .15 |
| 467 | Lee Lacy | .05 | .15 |
| 468 | Bill Madlock | .15 | .40 |
| 469 | Lee Mazzilli | .05 | .15 |
| 470 | Larry McWilliams | .05 | .15 |
| 471 | Jim Morrison | .05 | .15 |
| 472 | Tony Pena | .15 | .40 |
| 473 | Johnny Ray | .05 | .15 |
| 474 | Rick Rhoden | .05 | .15 |
| 475 | Don Robinson | .05 | .15 |
| 476 | Rod Scurry | .05 | .15 |
| 477 | Kent Tekulve | .05 | .15 |
| 478 | Jason Thompson | .05 | .15 |
| 479 | John Tudor | .15 | .40 |
| 480 | Lee Tunnell | .05 | .15 |
| 481 | Marvell Wynne | .05 | .15 |
| 482 | Salome Barojas | .05 | .15 |
| 483 | Dave Beard | .05 | .15 |
| 484 | Jim Beattie | .05 | .15 |
| 485 | Barry Bonnell | .05 | .15 |
| 486 | Phil Bradley | .20 | .50 |
| 487 | Al Cowens | .05 | .15 |
| 488 | Alvin Davis RC* | .20 | .50 |
| 489 | Dave Henderson | .15 | .40 |
| 490 | Steve Henderson | .05 | .15 |
| 491 | Bob Kearney | .05 | .15 |
| 492 | Mark Langston RC | .40 | 1.00 |
| 493 | Larry Milbourne | .05 | .15 |
| 494 | Paul Mirabella | .05 | .15 |
| 495 | Mike Moore | .15 | .40 |
| 496 | Edwin Nunez | .05 | .15 |
| 497 | Spike Owen | .05 | .15 |
| 498 | Jack Perconte | .05 | .15 |
| 499 | Ken Phelps | .05 | .15 |
| 500 | Jim Presley | .20 | .50 |
| 501 | Mike Stanton | .05 | .15 |
| 502 | Bob Stoddard | .05 | .15 |
| 503 | Gorman Thomas | .15 | .40 |
| 504 | Ed VandeBerg | .05 | .15 |
| 505 | Matt Young | .05 | .15 |
| 506 | Juan Agosto | .05 | .15 |
| 507 | Harold Baines | .15 | .40 |
| 508 | Floyd Bannister | .05 | .15 |
| 509 | Britt Burns | .05 | .15 |
| 510 | Julio Cruz | .05 | .15 |
| 511 | Richard Dotson | .05 | .15 |
| 512 | Jerry Dybzinski | .05 | .15 |
| 513 | Carlton Fisk | .30 | .75 |
| 514 | Scott Fletcher | .05 | .15 |
| 515 | Jerry Hairston | .05 | .15 |
| 516 | Marc Hill | .05 | .15 |
| 517 | LaMarr Hoyt | .05 | .15 |
| 518 | Ron Kittle | .05 | .15 |
| 519 | Rudy Law | .05 | .15 |
| 520 | Vance Law | .05 | .15 |
| 521 | Greg Luzinski | .15 | .40 |
| 522 | Gene Nelson | .05 | .15 |
| 523 | Tom Paciorek | .05 | .15 |
| 524 | Ron Reed | .05 | .15 |
| 525 | Bert Roberge | .05 | .15 |
| 526 | Tom Seaver | .30 | .75 |
| 527 | Roy Smalley | .05 | .15 |
| 528 | Dan Spillner | .05 | .15 |
| 529 | Mike Squires | .05 | .15 |
| 530 | Greg Walker | .05 | .15 |
| 531 | Cesar Cedeno | .15 | .40 |
| 532 | Dave Concepcion | .15 | .40 |
| 533 | Eric Davis RC | 1.25 | 3.00 |
| 534 | Nick Esasky | .05 | .15 |
| 535 | Tom Foley | .05 | .15 |
| 536 | John Franco UER RC | .40 | 1.00 |
| 537 | Brad Gulden | .05 | .15 |
| 538 | Tom Hume | .05 | .15 |
| 539 | Wayne Krenchicki | .05 | .15 |
| 540 | Andy McGaffigan | .05 | .15 |
| 541 | Eddie Milner | .05 | .15 |
| 542 | Ron Oester | .05 | .15 |
| 543 | Bob Owchinko | .05 | .15 |
| 544 | Dave Parker | .15 | .40 |
| 545 | Frank Pastore | .05 | .15 |
| 546 | Tony Perez | .30 | .75 |
| 547 | Ted Power | .05 | .15 |
| 548 | Joe Price | .05 | .15 |
| 549 | Gary Redus | .05 | .15 |
| 550 | Pete Rose | 1.50 | 4.00 |
| 551 | Jeff Russell | .15 | .40 |
| 552 | Mario Soto | .15 | .40 |
| 553 | Jay Tibbs | .05 | .15 |
| 554 | Duane Walker | .05 | .15 |
| 555 | Alan Bannister | .05 | .15 |
| 556 | Buddy Bell | .15 | .40 |
| 557 | Danny Darwin | .05 | .15 |
| 558 | Charlie Hough | .15 | .40 |
| 559 | Bobby Jones | .05 | .15 |
| 560 | Odell Jones | .05 | .15 |
| 561 | Jeff Kunkel | .05 | .15 |
| 562 | Mike Mason RC | .08 | .25 |
| 563 | Pete O'Brien | .05 | .15 |
| 564 | Larry Parrish | .05 | .15 |
| 565 | Mickey Rivers | .05 | .15 |
| 566 | Billy Sample | .05 | .15 |
| 567 | Dave Schmidt | .05 | .15 |
| 568 | Donnie Scott | .05 | .15 |
| 569 | Dave Stewart | .15 | .40 |
| 570 | Frank Tanana | .15 | .40 |
| 571 | Wayne Tolleson | .05 | .15 |
| 572 | Gary Ward | .05 | .15 |
| 573 | Curtis Wilkerson | .05 | .15 |
| 574 | George Wright | .05 | .15 |
| 575 | Ned Yost | .05 | .15 |
| 576 | Mark Brouhard | .05 | .15 |
| 577 | Mike Caldwell | .05 | .15 |
| 578 | Bobby Clark | .05 | .15 |
| 579 | Jaime Cocanower | .05 | .15 |
| 580 | Cecil Cooper | .15 | .40 |
| 581 | Rollie Fingers | .15 | .40 |
| 582 | Jim Gantner | .05 | .15 |
| 583 | Moose Haas | .05 | .15 |
| 584 | Dion James | .05 | .15 |
| 585 | Pete Ladd | .05 | .15 |

| | | |
|---|---|---|
| ☐ 586 Rick Manning | .05 | .15 |
| ☐ 587 Bob McClure | .05 | .15 |
| ☐ 588 Paul Molitor | .15 | .40 |
| ☐ 589 Charlie Moore | .05 | .15 |
| ☐ 590 Ben Oglivie | .05 | .15 |
| ☐ 591 Chuck Porter | .05 | .15 |
| ☐ 592 Randy Ready RC* | .08 | .25 |
| ☐ 593 Ed Romero | .05 | .15 |
| ☐ 594 Bill Schroeder | .05 | .15 |
| ☐ 595 Ray Searage | .05 | .15 |
| ☐ 596 Ted Simmons | .15 | .40 |
| ☐ 597 Jim Sundberg | .15 | .40 |
| ☐ 598 Don Sutton | .15 | .40 |
| ☐ 599 Tom Tellmann | .05 | .15 |
| ☐ 600 Rick Waits | .05 | .15 |
| ☐ 601 Robin Yount | .75 | 2.00 |
| ☐ 602 Dusty Baker | .15 | .40 |
| ☐ 603 Bob Brenly | .05 | .15 |
| ☐ 604 Jack Clark | .15 | .40 |
| ☐ 605 Chili Davis | .15 | .40 |
| ☐ 606 Mark Davis | .05 | .15 |
| ☐ 607 Dan Gladden RC | .20 | .50 |
| ☐ 608 Atlee Hammaker | .05 | .15 |
| ☐ 609 Mike Krukow | .05 | .15 |
| ☐ 610 Duane Kuiper | .05 | .15 |
| ☐ 611 Bob Lacey | .05 | .15 |
| ☐ 612 Bill Laskey | .05 | .15 |
| ☐ 613 Gary Lavelle | .05 | .15 |
| ☐ 614 Johnnie LeMaster | .05 | .15 |
| ☐ 615 Jeff Leonard | .05 | .15 |
| ☐ 616 Randy Lerch | .05 | .15 |
| ☐ 617 Greg Minton | .05 | .15 |
| ☐ 618 Steve Nicosia | .05 | .15 |
| ☐ 619 Gene Richards | .05 | .15 |
| ☐ 620 Jeff D. Robinson | .05 | .15 |
| ☐ 621 Scot Thompson | .05 | .15 |
| ☐ 622 Manny Trillo | .05 | .15 |
| ☐ 623 Brad Wellman | .05 | .15 |
| ☐ 624 Frank Williams | .05 | .15 |
| ☐ 625 Joel Youngblood | .05 | .15 |
| ☐ 626 Cal Ripken IA | 1.25 | 3.00 |
| ☐ 627 Mike Schmidt IA | .50 | 1.25 |
| ☐ 628 Giving The Signs | | |
| Sparky Anderson | .15 | .40 |
| ☐ 629 D.Winfield/R.Henderson | .08 | .25 |
| ☐ 630 M.Schmidt/R.Brooks | .75 | 2.00 |
| ☐ 631 Straw/Carter/Garvey/Oz | .50 | 1.25 |
| ☐ 632 A-S Winning Battery | | |
| Gary Carter | | |
| Charlie Lea | .05 | .15 |
| ☐ 633 NL Pennant Clinchers | | |
| Steve Garvey | | |
| Rich Gossage | .15 | .40 |
| ☐ 634 Dwight Gooden/J.Samuel | .50 | 1.25 |
| ☐ 635 Toronto's Big Guns | | |
| Willie Upshaw | .05 | .15 |
| ☐ 636 Toronto's Big Guns | | |
| Lloyd Moseby | .05 | .15 |
| ☐ 637 HOLLAND: Al Holland | .05 | .15 |
| ☐ 638 TUNNELL: Lee Tunnell | .05 | .15 |
| ☐ 639 Reggie Jackson IA | .15 | .40 |
| ☐ 640 Pete Rose IA | .50 | 1.25 |
| ☐ 641 Cal Ripken Jr./Sr. | 1.25 | 3.00 |
| ☐ 642 Cubs: Division Champs | .15 | .40 |
| ☐ 643 Two Perfect Games | | |
| and One No-Hitter. | | |
| Mike Witt | .15 | .40 |
| ☐ 644 M.Lozado RC/N.Mata RC | .15 | .40 |
| ☐ 645 K.Gruber RC/R.O'Neal RC | .20 | .50 |
| ☐ 646 J.Roman RC/J.Skinner | .20 | .50 |
| ☐ 647 S.Kiefer RC/D.Tartabull RC | .40 | 1.00 |
| ☐ 648 R.Deer RC/A.Sanchez RC | .20 | .50 |
| ☐ 649 B.Hatcher RC/S.Dunston RC | .40 | 1.00 |
| ☐ 650 R.Robinson RC/M.Bielecki RC | .20 | .50 |
| ☐ 651 Z.Smith RC/P.Zuvella RC | .20 | .50 |
| ☐ 652 J.Hesketh RC/G.Davis RC | .20 | .50 |
| ☐ 653 J.Russell RC/S.Jeltz RC | .05 | .15 |
| ☐ 654 CL: Tigers/Padres | | |
| and Cubs/Mets | .05 | .15 |
| ☐ 655 CL: Blue Jays/Yankees | | |
| and Red Sox/Orioles | .05 | .15 |
| ☐ 656 CL: Royals/Cardinals | | |
| and Phillies/Twins | .05 | .15 |
| ☐ 657 CL: Angels/Braves | | |
| and Astros/Dodgers | .05 | .15 |
| ☐ 658 CL: Expos/A's | | |
| and Indians/Pirates | .05 | .15 |
| ☐ 659 CL: Mariners/White Sox | | |

| | | |
|---|---|---|
| and Reds/Rangers | .05 | .15 |
| ☐ 660 CL: Brewers/Giants | | |
| and Special Cards | .05 | .15 |

## 1986 Fleer

| | | |
|---|---|---|
| ☐ COMPLETE SET (660) | 15.00 | 40.00 |
| ☐ COMP.FACT.SET (660) | 15.00 | 40.00 |
| ☐ 1 Steve Balboni | .05 | .15 |
| ☐ 2 Joe Beckwith | .05 | .15 |
| ☐ 3 Buddy Biancalana | .05 | .15 |
| ☐ 4 Bud Black | .05 | .15 |
| ☐ 5 George Brett | .75 | 2.00 |
| ☐ 6 Onix Concepcion | .05 | .15 |
| ☐ 7 Steve Farr | .05 | .15 |
| ☐ 8 Mark Gubicza | .05 | .15 |
| ☐ 9 Dane Iorg | .05 | .15 |
| ☐ 10 Danny Jackson | .05 | .15 |
| ☐ 11 Lynn Jones | .05 | .15 |
| ☐ 12 Mike Jones | .05 | .15 |
| ☐ 13 Charlie Leibrandt | .05 | .15 |
| ☐ 14 Hal McRae | .08 | .25 |
| ☐ 15 Omar Moreno | .05 | .15 |
| ☐ 16 Darryl Motley | .05 | .15 |
| ☐ 17 Jorge Orta | .05 | .15 |
| ☐ 18 Dan Quisenberry | .08 | .25 |
| ☐ 19 Bret Saberhagen | .08 | .25 |
| ☐ 20 Pat Sheridan | .05 | .15 |
| ☐ 21 Lonnie Smith | .05 | .15 |
| ☐ 22 Jim Sundberg | .08 | .25 |
| ☐ 23 John Wathan | .05 | .15 |
| ☐ 24 Frank White | .08 | .25 |
| ☐ 25 Willie Wilson | .08 | .25 |
| ☐ 26 Joaquin Andujar | .08 | .25 |
| ☐ 27 Steve Braun | .05 | .15 |
| ☐ 28 Bill Campbell | .05 | .15 |
| ☐ 29 Cesar Cedeno | .08 | .25 |
| ☐ 30 Jack Clark | .08 | .25 |
| ☐ 31 Vince Coleman RC | .40 | 1.00 |
| ☐ 32 Danny Cox | .05 | .15 |
| ☐ 33 Ken Dayley | .05 | .15 |
| ☐ 34 Ivan DeJesus | .05 | .15 |
| ☐ 35 Bob Forsch | .05 | .15 |
| ☐ 36 Brian Harper | .05 | .15 |
| ☐ 37 Tom Herr | .05 | .15 |
| ☐ 38 Ricky Horton | .05 | .15 |
| ☐ 39 Kurt Kepshire | .05 | .15 |
| ☐ 40 Jeff Lahti | .05 | .15 |
| ☐ 41 Tito Landrum | .05 | .15 |
| ☐ 42 Willie McGee | .08 | .25 |
| ☐ 43 Tom Nieto | .05 | .15 |
| ☐ 44 Terry Pendleton | .50 | 1.25 |
| ☐ 45 Darrell Porter | .05 | .15 |
| ☐ 46 Ozzie Smith | .50 | 1.25 |
| ☐ 47 John Tudor | .08 | .25 |
| ☐ 48 Andy Van Slyke | .08 | .25 |
| ☐ 49 Todd Worrell RC | .20 | .50 |
| ☐ 50 Jim Acker | .05 | .15 |
| ☐ 51 Doyle Alexander | .05 | .15 |
| ☐ 52 Jesse Barfield | .08 | .25 |
| ☐ 53 George Bell | .08 | .25 |
| ☐ 54 Jeff Burroughs | .05 | .15 |
| ☐ 55 Bill Caudill | .05 | .15 |
| ☐ 56 Jim Clancy | .05 | .15 |
| ☐ 57 Tony Fernandez | .08 | .25 |
| ☐ 58 Tom Filer | .05 | .15 |
| ☐ 59 Damaso Garcia | .05 | .15 |
| ☐ 60 Tom Henke | .08 | .25 |
| ☐ 61 Garth Iorg | .05 | .15 |
| ☐ 62 Cliff Johnson | .05 | .15 |
| ☐ 63 Jimmy Key | .08 | .25 |
| ☐ 64 Dennis Lamp | .05 | .15 |
| ☐ 65 Gary Lavelle | .05 | .15 |
| ☐ 66 Buck Martinez | .05 | .15 |
| ☐ 67 Lloyd Moseby | .05 | .15 |

| | | |
|---|---|---|
| ☐ 68 Rance Mulliniks | .05 | .15 |
| ☐ 69 Al Oliver | .08 | .25 |
| ☐ 70 Dave Stieb | .08 | .25 |
| ☐ 71 Louis Thornton | .05 | .15 |
| ☐ 72 Willie Upshaw | .05 | .15 |
| ☐ 73 Ernie Whitt | .05 | .15 |
| ☐ 74 Rick Aguilera RC | .20 | .50 |
| ☐ 75 Wally Backman | .05 | .15 |
| ☐ 76 Gary Carter | .08 | .25 |
| ☐ 77 Ron Darling | .08 | .25 |
| ☐ 78 Len Dykstra RC | .60 | 1.50 |
| ☐ 79 Sid Fernandez | .05 | .15 |
| ☐ 80 George Foster | .08 | .25 |
| ☐ 81 Dwight Gooden | .30 | .75 |
| ☐ 82 Tom Gorman | .05 | .15 |
| ☐ 83 Danny Heep | .05 | .15 |
| ☐ 84 Keith Hernandez | .08 | .25 |
| ☐ 85 Howard Johnson | .08 | .25 |
| ☐ 86 Ray Knight | .08 | .25 |
| ☐ 87 Terry Leach | .05 | .15 |
| ☐ 88 Ed Lynch | .05 | .15 |
| ☐ 89 Roger McDowell RC* | .20 | .50 |
| ☐ 90 Jesse Orosco | .05 | .15 |
| ☐ 91 Tom Paciorek | .05 | .15 |
| ☐ 92 Ronn Reynolds | .05 | .15 |
| ☐ 93 Rafael Santana | .05 | .15 |
| ☐ 94 Doug Sisk | .05 | .15 |
| ☐ 95 Rusty Staub | .08 | .25 |
| ☐ 96 Darryl Strawberry | .20 | .50 |
| ☐ 97 Mookie Wilson | .08 | .25 |
| ☐ 98 Neil Allen | .05 | .15 |
| ☐ 99 Don Baylor | .08 | .25 |
| ☐ 100 Dale Berra | .05 | .15 |
| ☐ 101 Rich Bordi | .05 | .15 |
| ☐ 102 Marty Bystrom | .05 | .15 |
| ☐ 103 Joe Cowley | .05 | .15 |
| ☐ 104 Brian Fisher RC | .05 | .15 |
| ☐ 105 Ken Griffey | .08 | .25 |
| ☐ 106 Ron Guidry | .08 | .25 |
| ☐ 107 Ron Hassey | .05 | .15 |
| ☐ 108 Rickey Henderson | .30 | .75 |
| ☐ 109 Don Mattingly | 1.00 | 2.50 |
| ☐ 110 Bobby Meacham | .05 | .15 |
| ☐ 111 John Montefusco | .05 | .15 |
| ☐ 112 Phil Niekro | .08 | .25 |
| ☐ 113 Mike Pagliarulo | .05 | .15 |
| ☐ 114 Dan Pasqua | .05 | .15 |
| ☐ 115 Willie Randolph | .08 | .25 |
| ☐ 116 Dave Righetti | .08 | .25 |
| ☐ 117 Andre Robertson | .05 | .15 |
| ☐ 118 Billy Sample | .05 | .15 |
| ☐ 119 Bob Shirley | .05 | .15 |
| ☐ 120 Ed Whitson | .05 | .15 |
| ☐ 121 Dave Winfield | .20 | .50 |
| ☐ 122 Butch Wynegar | .05 | .15 |
| ☐ 123 Dave Anderson | .05 | .15 |
| ☐ 124 Bob Bailor | .05 | .15 |
| ☐ 125 Greg Brock | .05 | .15 |
| ☐ 126 Enos Cabell | .05 | .15 |
| ☐ 127 Bobby Castillo | .05 | .15 |
| ☐ 128 Carlos Diaz | .05 | .15 |
| ☐ 129 Mariano Duncan RC | .20 | .50 |
| ☐ 130 Pedro Guerrero | .08 | .25 |
| ☐ 131 Orel Hershiser | .30 | .75 |
| ☐ 132 Rick Honeycutt | .05 | .15 |
| ☐ 133 Ken Howell | .05 | .15 |
| ☐ 134 Ken Landreaux | .05 | .15 |
| ☐ 135 Bill Madlock | .08 | .25 |
| ☐ 136 Candy Maldonado | .05 | .15 |
| ☐ 137 Mike Marshall | .08 | .25 |
| ☐ 138 Len Matuszek | .05 | .15 |
| ☐ 139 Tom Niedenfuer | .05 | .15 |
| ☐ 140 Alejandro Pena | .05 | .15 |
| ☐ 141 Jerry Reuss | .05 | .15 |
| ☐ 142 Bill Russell | .08 | .25 |
| ☐ 143 Steve Sax | .08 | .25 |
| ☐ 144 Mike Scioscia | .08 | .25 |
| ☐ 145 Fernando Valenzuela | .08 | .25 |
| ☐ 146 Bob Welch | .08 | .25 |
| ☐ 147 Terry Whitfield | .05 | .15 |
| ☐ 148 Juan Beniquez | .05 | .15 |
| ☐ 149 Bob Boone | .08 | .25 |
| ☐ 150 John Candelaria | .05 | .15 |
| ☐ 151 Rod Carew | .20 | .50 |
| ☐ 152 Stu Cliburn | .05 | .15 |
| ☐ 153 Doug DeCinces | .05 | .15 |
| ☐ 154 Brian Downing | .05 | .15 |
| ☐ 155 Ken Forsch | .05 | .15 |

|  |  | | |
|---|---|---|---|
| ☐ 156 | Craig Gerber | .05 | .15 |
| ☐ 157 | Bobby Grich | .08 | .25 |
| ☐ 158 | George Hendrick | .05 | .15 |
| ☐ 159 | Al Holland | .05 | .15 |
| ☐ 160 | Reggie Jackson | .20 | .50 |
| ☐ 161 | Ruppert Jones | .05 | .15 |
| ☐ 162 | Urbano Lugo | .05 | .15 |
| ☐ 163 | Kirk McCaskill RC | .20 | .50 |
| ☐ 164 | Donnie Moore | .05 | .15 |
| ☐ 165 | Gary Pettis | .05 | .15 |
| ☐ 166 | Ron Romanick | .05 | .15 |
| ☐ 167 | Dick Schofield | .05 | .15 |
| ☐ 168 | Daryl Sconiers | .05 | .15 |
| ☐ 169 | Jim Slaton | .05 | .15 |
| ☐ 170 | Don Sutton | .08 | .25 |
| ☐ 171 | Mike Witt | .05 | .15 |
| ☐ 172 | Buddy Bell | .08 | .25 |
| ☐ 173 | Tom Browning | .05 | .15 |
| ☐ 174 | Dave Concepcion | .08 | .25 |
| ☐ 175 | Eric Davis | .30 | .15 |
| ☐ 176 | Bo Diaz | .05 | .15 |
| ☐ 177 | Nick Esasky | .05 | .15 |
| ☐ 178 | John Franco | .08 | .25 |
| ☐ 179 | Tom Hume | .05 | .15 |
| ☐ 180 | Wayne Krenchicki | .05 | .15 |
| ☐ 181 | Andy McGaffigan | .05 | .15 |
| ☐ 182 | Eddie Milner | .05 | .15 |
| ☐ 183 | Ron Oester | .05 | .15 |
| ☐ 184 | Dave Parker | .08 | .25 |
| ☐ 185 | Frank Pastore | .05 | .15 |
| ☐ 186 | Tony Perez | .20 | .50 |
| ☐ 187 | Ted Power | .05 | .15 |
| ☐ 188 | Joe Price | .05 | .15 |
| ☐ 189 | Gary Redus | .05 | .15 |
| ☐ 190 | Ron Robinson | .05 | .15 |
| ☐ 191 | Pete Rose | 1.00 | 2.50 |
| ☐ 192 | Mario Soto | .08 | .25 |
| ☐ 193 | John Stuper | .05 | .15 |
| ☐ 194 | Jay Tibbs | .05 | .15 |
| ☐ 195 | Dave Van Gorder | .05 | .15 |
| ☐ 196 | Max Venable | .05 | .15 |
| ☐ 197 | Juan Agosto | .05 | .15 |
| ☐ 198 | Harold Baines | .08 | .25 |
| ☐ 199 | Floyd Bannister | .05 | .15 |
| ☐ 200 | Britt Burns | .05 | .15 |
| ☐ 201 | Julio Cruz | .05 | .15 |
| ☐ 202 | Joel Davis | .05 | .15 |
| ☐ 203 | Richard Dotson | .05 | .15 |
| ☐ 204 | Carlton Fisk | .20 | .50 |
| ☐ 205 | Scott Fletcher | .05 | .15 |
| ☐ 206 | Ozzie Guillen RC | .75 | 2.00 |
| ☐ 207 | Jerry Hairston | .05 | .15 |
| ☐ 208 | Tim Hulett | .05 | .15 |
| ☐ 209 | Bob James | .05 | .15 |
| ☐ 210 | Ron Kittle | .05 | .15 |
| ☐ 211 | Rudy Law | .05 | .15 |
| ☐ 212 | Bryan Little | .05 | .15 |
| ☐ 213 | Gene Nelson | .05 | .15 |
| ☐ 214 | Reid Nichols | .05 | .15 |
| ☐ 215 | Luis Salazar | .05 | .15 |
| ☐ 216 | Tom Seaver | .20 | .50 |
| ☐ 217 | Dan Spillner | .05 | .15 |
| ☐ 218 | Bruce Tanner | .05 | .15 |
| ☐ 219 | Greg Walker | .05 | .15 |
| ☐ 220 | Dave Wehrmeister | .05 | .15 |
| ☐ 221 | Juan Berenguer | .05 | .15 |
| ☐ 222 | Dave Bergman | .05 | .15 |
| ☐ 223 | Tom Brookens | .05 | .15 |
| ☐ 224 | Darrell Evans | .08 | .25 |
| ☐ 225 | Barbaro Garbey | .05 | .15 |
| ☐ 226 | Kirk Gibson | .08 | .25 |
| ☐ 227 | John Grubb | .05 | .15 |
| ☐ 228 | Willie Hernandez | .05 | .15 |
| ☐ 229 | Larry Herndon | .05 | .15 |
| ☐ 230 | Chet Lemon | .05 | .15 |
| ☐ 231 | Aurelio Lopez | .05 | .15 |
| ☐ 232 | Jack Morris | .08 | .25 |
| ☐ 233 | Randy O'Neal | .05 | .15 |
| ☐ 234 | Lance Parrish | .08 | .25 |
| ☐ 235 | Dan Petry | .05 | .15 |
| ☐ 236 | Alejandro Sanchez | .05 | .15 |
| ☐ 237 | Bill Scherrer | .05 | .15 |
| ☐ 238 | Nelson Simmons | .05 | .15 |
| ☐ 239 | Frank Tanana | .05 | .15 |
| ☐ 240 | Walt Terrell | .05 | .15 |
| ☐ 241 | Alan Trammell | .08 | .25 |
| ☐ 242 | Lou Whitaker | .08 | .25 |
| ☐ 243 | Milt Wilcox | .05 | .15 |
| ☐ 244 | Hubie Brooks | .05 | .15 |
| ☐ 245 | Tim Burke | .05 | .15 |
| ☐ 246 | Andre Dawson | .08 | .25 |
| ☐ 247 | Mike Fitzgerald | .05 | .15 |
| ☐ 248 | Terry Francona | .08 | .25 |
| ☐ 249 | Bill Gullickson | .05 | .15 |
| ☐ 250 | Joe Hesketh | .05 | .15 |
| ☐ 251 | Bill Laskey | .05 | .15 |
| ☐ 252 | Vance Law | .05 | .15 |
| ☐ 253 | Charlie Lea | .05 | .15 |
| ☐ 254 | Gary Lucas | .05 | .15 |
| ☐ 255 | David Palmer | .05 | .15 |
| ☐ 256 | Tim Raines | .08 | .25 |
| ☐ 257 | Jeff Reardon | .08 | .25 |
| ☐ 258 | Bert Roberge | .05 | .15 |
| ☐ 259 | Dan Schatzeder | .05 | .15 |
| ☐ 260 | Bryn Smith | .05 | .15 |
| ☐ 261 | Randy St.Claire | .05 | .15 |
| ☐ 262 | Scot Thompson | .05 | .15 |
| ☐ 263 | Tim Wallach | .08 | .25 |
| ☐ 264 | U.L. Washington | .05 | .15 |
| ☐ 265 | Mitch Webster | .05 | .15 |
| ☐ 266 | Herm Winningham | .05 | .15 |
| ☐ 267 | Floyd Youmans | .05 | .15 |
| ☐ 268 | Don Aase | .05 | .15 |
| ☐ 269 | Mike Boddicker | .05 | .15 |
| ☐ 270 | Rich Dauer | .05 | .15 |
| ☐ 271 | Storm Davis | .05 | .15 |
| ☐ 272 | Rick Dempsey | .05 | .15 |
| ☐ 273 | Ken Dixon | .05 | .15 |
| ☐ 274 | Jim Dwyer | .05 | .15 |
| ☐ 275 | Mike Flanagan | .08 | .25 |
| ☐ 276 | Wayne Gross | .05 | .15 |
| ☐ 277 | Lee Lacy | .05 | .15 |
| ☐ 278 | Fred Lynn | .08 | .25 |
| ☐ 279 | Tippy Martinez | .05 | .15 |
| ☐ 280 | Dennis Martinez | .08 | .25 |
| ☐ 281 | Scott McGregor | .05 | .15 |
| ☐ 282 | Eddie Murray | .30 | .75 |
| ☐ 283 | Floyd Rayford | .05 | .15 |
| ☐ 284 | Cal Ripken | 1.25 | 3.00 |
| ☐ 285 | Gary Roenicke | .05 | .15 |
| ☐ 286 | Larry Sheets | .05 | .15 |
| ☐ 287 | John Shelby | .05 | .15 |
| ☐ 288 | Nate Snell | .05 | .15 |
| ☐ 289 | Sammy Stewart | .05 | .15 |
| ☐ 290 | Alan Wiggins | .05 | .15 |
| ☐ 291 | Mike Young | .05 | .15 |
| ☐ 292 | Alan Ashby | .05 | .15 |
| ☐ 293 | Mark Bailey | .05 | .15 |
| ☐ 294 | Kevin Bass | .05 | .15 |
| ☐ 295 | Jeff Calhoun | .05 | .15 |
| ☐ 296 | Jose Cruz | .08 | .25 |
| ☐ 297 | Glenn Davis | .05 | .15 |
| ☐ 298 | Bill Dawley | .05 | .15 |
| ☐ 299 | Frank DiPino | .05 | .15 |
| ☐ 300 | Bill Doran | .08 | .25 |
| ☐ 301 | Phil Garner | .08 | .25 |
| ☐ 302 | Jeff Heathcock | .05 | .15 |
| ☐ 303 | Charlie Kerfeld | .05 | .15 |
| ☐ 304 | Bob Knepper | .05 | .15 |
| ☐ 305 | Ron Mathis | .05 | .15 |
| ☐ 306 | Jerry Mumphrey | .05 | .15 |
| ☐ 307 | Jim Pankovits | .05 | .15 |
| ☐ 308 | Terry Puhl | .05 | .15 |
| ☐ 309 | Craig Reynolds | .05 | .15 |
| ☐ 310 | Nolan Ryan | 1.50 | 4.00 |
| ☐ 311 | Mike Scott | .08 | .25 |
| ☐ 312 | Dave Smith | .05 | .15 |
| ☐ 313 | Dickie Thon | .05 | .15 |
| ☐ 314 | Denny Walling | .05 | .15 |
| ☐ 315 | Kurt Bevacqua | .05 | .15 |
| ☐ 316 | Al Bumbry | .05 | .15 |
| ☐ 317 | Jerry Davis | .05 | .15 |
| ☐ 318 | Luis DeLeon | .05 | .15 |
| ☐ 319 | Dave Dravecky | .05 | .15 |
| ☐ 320 | Tim Flannery | .05 | .15 |
| ☐ 321 | Steve Garvey | .08 | .25 |
| ☐ 322 | Rich Gossage | .08 | .25 |
| ☐ 323 | Tony Gwynn | .50 | 1.25 |
| ☐ 324 | Andy Hawkins | .05 | .15 |
| ☐ 325 | LaMarr Hoyt | .05 | .15 |
| ☐ 326 | Roy Lee Jackson | .05 | .15 |
| ☐ 327 | Terry Kennedy | .05 | .15 |
| ☐ 328 | Craig Lefferts | .05 | .15 |
| ☐ 329 | Carmelo Martinez | .05 | .15 |
| ☐ 330 | Lance McCullers | .05 | .15 |
| ☐ 331 | Kevin McReynolds | .05 | .15 |
| ☐ 332 | Graig Nettles | .08 | .25 |
| ☐ 333 | Jerry Royster | .05 | .15 |
| ☐ 334 | Eric Show | .05 | .15 |
| ☐ 335 | Tim Stoddard | .05 | .15 |
| ☐ 336 | Garry Templeton | .08 | .25 |
| ☐ 337 | Mark Thurmond | .05 | .15 |
| ☐ 338 | Ed Wojna | .05 | .15 |
| ☐ 339 | Tony Armas | .08 | .25 |
| ☐ 340 | Marty Barrett | .05 | .15 |
| ☐ 341 | Wade Boggs | .20 | .50 |
| ☐ 342 | Dennis Boyd | .05 | .15 |
| ☐ 343 | Bill Buckner | .08 | .25 |
| ☐ 344 | Mark Clear | .05 | .15 |
| ☐ 345 | Roger Clemens | 2.00 | 5.00 |
| ☐ 346 | Steve Crawford | .05 | .15 |
| ☐ 347 | Mike Easler | .05 | .15 |
| ☐ 348 | Dwight Evans | .20 | .50 |
| ☐ 349 | Rich Gedman | .05 | .15 |
| ☐ 350 | Jackie Gutierrez | .05 | .15 |
| ☐ 351 | Glenn Hoffman | .05 | .15 |
| ☐ 352 | Bruce Hurst | .05 | .15 |
| ☐ 353 | Bruce Kison | .05 | .15 |
| ☐ 354 | Tim Lollar | .05 | .15 |
| ☐ 355 | Steve Lyons | .05 | .15 |
| ☐ 356 | Al Nipper | .05 | .15 |
| ☐ 357 | Bob Ojeda | .05 | .15 |
| ☐ 358 | Jim Rice | .08 | .25 |
| ☐ 359 | Bob Stanley | .05 | .15 |
| ☐ 360 | Mike Trujillo | .05 | .15 |
| ☐ 361 | Thad Bosley | .05 | .15 |
| ☐ 362 | Warren Brusstar | .05 | .15 |
| ☐ 363 | Ron Cey | .08 | .25 |
| ☐ 364 | Jody Davis | .05 | .15 |
| ☐ 365 | Bob Dernier | .05 | .15 |
| ☐ 366 | Shawon Dunston | .08 | .25 |
| ☐ 367 | Leon Durham | .05 | .15 |
| ☐ 368 | Dennis Eckersley | .20 | .50 |
| ☐ 369 | Ray Fontenot | .05 | .15 |
| ☐ 370 | George Frazier | .05 | .15 |
| ☐ 371 | Billy Hatcher | .08 | .25 |
| ☐ 372 | Dave Lopes | .08 | .25 |
| ☐ 373 | Gary Matthews | .08 | .25 |
| ☐ 374 | Ron Meridith | .05 | .15 |
| ☐ 375 | Keith Moreland | .05 | .15 |
| ☐ 376 | Reggie Patterson | .05 | .15 |
| ☐ 377 | Dick Ruthven | .05 | .15 |
| ☐ 378 | Ryne Sandberg | .60 | 1.50 |
| ☐ 379 | Scott Sanderson | .05 | .15 |
| ☐ 380 | Lee Smith | .08 | .25 |
| ☐ 381 | Gary Sorensen | .05 | .15 |
| ☐ 382 | Chris Speier | .05 | .15 |
| ☐ 383 | Rick Sutcliffe | .08 | .25 |
| ☐ 384 | Steve Trout | .05 | .15 |
| ☐ 385 | Gary Woods | .05 | .15 |
| ☐ 386 | Bert Blyleven | .08 | .25 |
| ☐ 387 | Tom Brunansky | .05 | .15 |
| ☐ 388 | Randy Bush | .05 | .15 |
| ☐ 389 | John Butcher | .05 | .15 |
| ☐ 390 | Ron Davis | .05 | .15 |
| ☐ 391 | Dave Engle | .05 | .15 |
| ☐ 392 | Frank Eufemia | .05 | .15 |
| ☐ 393 | Pete Filson | .05 | .15 |
| ☐ 394 | Gary Gaetti | .08 | .25 |
| ☐ 395 | Greg Gagne | .05 | .15 |
| ☐ 396 | Mickey Hatcher | .05 | .15 |
| ☐ 397 | Kent Hrbek | .08 | .25 |
| ☐ 398 | Tim Laudner | .05 | .15 |
| ☐ 399 | Rick Lysander | .05 | .15 |
| ☐ 400 | Dave Meier | .05 | .15 |
| ☐ 401 | Kirby Puckett | .75 | 2.00 |
| ☐ 402 | Mark Salas | .05 | .15 |
| ☐ 403 | Ken Schrom | .05 | .15 |
| ☐ 404 | Roy Smalley | .05 | .15 |
| ☐ 405 | Mike Smithson | .05 | .15 |
| ☐ 406 | Mike Stenhouse | .05 | .15 |
| ☐ 407 | Tim Teufel | .05 | .15 |
| ☐ 408 | Frank Viola | .08 | .25 |
| ☐ 409 | Ron Washington | .05 | .15 |
| ☐ 410 | Keith Atherton | .05 | .15 |
| ☐ 411 | Dusty Baker | .08 | .25 |
| ☐ 412 | Tim Birtsas | .05 | .15 |
| ☐ 413 | Bruce Bochte | .05 | .15 |
| ☐ 414 | Chris Codiroli | .05 | .15 |
| ☐ 415 | Dave Collins | .05 | .15 |
| ☐ 416 | Mike Davis | .05 | .15 |
| ☐ 417 | Alfredo Griffin | .05 | .15 |
| ☐ 418 | Mike Heath | .05 | .15 |
| ☐ 419 | Steve Henderson | .05 | .15 |

| | | |
|---|---|---|
| ☐ 420 Donnie Hill | .05 | .15 |
| ☐ 421 Jay Howell | .05 | .15 |
| ☐ 422 Tommy John | .08 | .25 |
| ☐ 423 Dave Kingman | .08 | .25 |
| ☐ 424 Bill Krueger | .05 | .15 |
| ☐ 425 Rick Langford | .05 | .15 |
| ☐ 426 Carney Lansford | .08 | .25 |
| ☐ 427 Steve McCatty | .05 | .15 |
| ☐ 428 Dwayne Murphy | .05 | .15 |
| ☐ 429 Steve Ontiveros RC | .05 | .15 |
| ☐ 430 Tony Phillips | .05 | .15 |
| ☐ 431 Jose Rijo | .08 | .25 |
| ☐ 432 Mickey Tettleton RC | .20 | .50 |
| ☐ 433 Luis Aguayo | .05 | .15 |
| ☐ 434 Larry Andersen | .05 | .15 |
| ☐ 435 Steve Carlton | .08 | .25 |
| ☐ 436 Don Carman | .05 | .15 |
| ☐ 437 Tim Corcoran | .05 | .15 |
| ☐ 438 Darren Daulton RC | .40 | 1.00 |
| ☐ 439 John Denny | .05 | .15 |
| ☐ 440 Tom Foley | .05 | .15 |
| ☐ 441 Greg Gross | .05 | .15 |
| ☐ 442 Kevin Gross | .05 | .15 |
| ☐ 443 Von Hayes | .05 | .15 |
| ☐ 444 Charles Hudson | .05 | .15 |
| ☐ 445 Garry Maddox | .05 | .15 |
| ☐ 446 Shane Rawley | .05 | .15 |
| ☐ 447 Dave Rucker | .05 | .15 |
| ☐ 448 John Russell | .05 | .15 |
| ☐ 449 Juan Samuel | .05 | .15 |
| ☐ 450 Mike Schmidt | .75 | 2.00 |
| ☐ 451 Rick Schu | .05 | .15 |
| ☐ 452 Dave Shipanoff | .05 | .15 |
| ☐ 453 Dave Stewart | .08 | .25 |
| ☐ 454 Jeff Stone | .05 | .15 |
| ☐ 455 Kent Tekulve | .05 | .15 |
| ☐ 456 Ozzie Virgil | .05 | .15 |
| ☐ 457 Glenn Wilson | .05 | .15 |
| ☐ 458 Jim Beattie | .05 | .15 |
| ☐ 459 Karl Best | .05 | .15 |
| ☐ 460 Barry Bonnell | .05 | .15 |
| ☐ 461 Phil Bradley | .05 | .15 |
| ☐ 462 Ivan Calderon RC* | .20 | .50 |
| ☐ 463 Al Cowens | .05 | .15 |
| ☐ 464 Alvin Davis | .05 | .15 |
| ☐ 465 Dave Henderson | .05 | .15 |
| ☐ 466 Bob Kearney | .05 | .15 |
| ☐ 467 Mark Langston | .08 | .25 |
| ☐ 468 Bob Long | .05 | .15 |
| ☐ 469 Mike Moore | .05 | .15 |
| ☐ 470 Edwin Nunez | .05 | .15 |
| ☐ 471 Spike Owen | .05 | .15 |
| ☐ 472 Jack Perconte | .05 | .15 |
| ☐ 473 Jim Presley | .05 | .15 |
| ☐ 474 Donnie Scott | .05 | .15 |
| ☐ 475 Bill Swift | .05 | .15 |
| ☐ 476 Danny Tartabull | .08 | .25 |
| ☐ 477 Gorman Thomas | .08 | .25 |
| ☐ 478 Roy Thomas | .05 | .15 |
| ☐ 479 Ed VandeBerg | .05 | .15 |
| ☐ 480 Frank Wills | .05 | .15 |
| ☐ 481 Matt Young | .05 | .15 |
| ☐ 482 Ray Burris | .05 | .15 |
| ☐ 483 Jaime Cocanower | .05 | .15 |
| ☐ 484 Cecil Cooper | .08 | .25 |
| ☐ 485 Danny Darwin | .05 | .15 |
| ☐ 486 Rollie Fingers | .08 | .25 |
| ☐ 487 Jim Gantner | .05 | .15 |
| ☐ 488 Bob L. Gibson | .05 | .15 |
| ☐ 489 Moose Haas | .05 | .15 |
| ☐ 490 Teddy Higuera RC* | .20 | .50 |
| ☐ 491 Paul Householder | .05 | .15 |
| ☐ 492 Pete Ladd | .05 | .15 |
| ☐ 493 Rick Manning | .05 | .15 |
| ☐ 494 Bob McClure | .05 | .15 |
| ☐ 495 Paul Molitor | .08 | .25 |
| ☐ 496 Charlie Moore | .05 | .15 |
| ☐ 497 Ben Oglivie | .05 | .15 |
| ☐ 498 Randy Ready | .05 | .15 |
| ☐ 499 Earnie Riles | .05 | .15 |
| ☐ 500 Ed Romero | .05 | .15 |
| ☐ 501 Bill Schroeder | .05 | .15 |
| ☐ 502 Ray Searage | .05 | .15 |
| ☐ 503 Ted Simmons | .08 | .25 |
| ☐ 504 Pete Vuckovich | .05 | .15 |
| ☐ 505 Rick Waits | .05 | .15 |
| ☐ 506 Robin Yount | .50 | 1.25 |
| ☐ 507 Len Barker | .05 | .15 |
| ☐ 508 Steve Bedrosian | .05 | .15 |
| ☐ 509 Bruce Benedict | .05 | .15 |
| ☐ 510 Rick Camp | .05 | .15 |
| ☐ 511 Rick Cerone | .05 | .15 |
| ☐ 512 Chris Chambliss | .08 | .25 |
| ☐ 513 Jeff Dedmon | .05 | .15 |
| ☐ 514 Terry Forster | .08 | .25 |
| ☐ 515 Gene Garber | .05 | .15 |
| ☐ 516 Terry Harper | .05 | .15 |
| ☐ 517 Bob Horner | .08 | .25 |
| ☐ 518 Glenn Hubbard | .05 | .15 |
| ☐ 519 Joe Johnson | .05 | .15 |
| ☐ 520 Brad Komminsk | .05 | .15 |
| ☐ 521 Rick Mahler | .05 | .15 |
| ☐ 522 Dale Murphy | .20 | .50 |
| ☐ 523 Ken Oberkfell | .05 | .15 |
| ☐ 524 Pascual Perez | .05 | .15 |
| ☐ 525 Gerald Perry | .05 | .15 |
| ☐ 526 Rafael Ramirez | .05 | .15 |
| ☐ 527 Steve Shields | .05 | .15 |
| ☐ 528 Zane Smith | .05 | .15 |
| ☐ 529 Bruce Sutter | .08 | .25 |
| ☐ 530 Milt Thompson RC | .20 | .50 |
| ☐ 531 Claudell Washington | .05 | .15 |
| ☐ 532 Paul Zuvella | .05 | .15 |
| ☐ 533 Vida Blue | .08 | .25 |
| ☐ 534 Bob Brenly | .05 | .15 |
| ☐ 535 Chris Brown RC | .05 | .15 |
| ☐ 536 Chili Davis | .08 | .25 |
| ☐ 537 Mark Davis | .05 | .15 |
| ☐ 538 Rob Deer | .08 | .25 |
| ☐ 539 Dan Driessen | .05 | .15 |
| ☐ 540 Scott Garrelts | .05 | .15 |
| ☐ 541 Dan Gladden | .05 | .15 |
| ☐ 542 Jim Gott | .05 | .15 |
| ☐ 543 David Green | .05 | .15 |
| ☐ 544 Atlee Hammaker | .05 | .15 |
| ☐ 545 Mike Jeffcoat | .05 | .15 |
| ☐ 546 Mike Krukow | .05 | .15 |
| ☐ 547 Dave LaPoint | .05 | .15 |
| ☐ 548 Jeff Leonard | .05 | .15 |
| ☐ 549 Greg Minton | .05 | .15 |
| ☐ 550 Alex Trevino | .05 | .15 |
| ☐ 551 Manny Trillo | .05 | .15 |
| ☐ 552 Jose Uribe | .05 | .15 |
| ☐ 553 Brad Wellman | .05 | .15 |
| ☐ 554 Frank Williams | .05 | .15 |
| ☐ 555 Joel Youngblood | .05 | .15 |
| ☐ 556 Alan Bannister | .05 | .15 |
| ☐ 557 Glenn Brummer | .05 | .15 |
| ☐ 558 Steve Buechele RC | .20 | .50 |
| ☐ 559 Jose Guzman RC | .05 | .15 |
| ☐ 560 Toby Harrah | .08 | .25 |
| ☐ 561 Greg Harris | .05 | .15 |
| ☐ 562 Dwayne Henry | .05 | .15 |
| ☐ 563 Burt Hooton | .05 | .15 |
| ☐ 564 Charlie Hough | .08 | .25 |
| ☐ 565 Mike Mason | .05 | .15 |
| ☐ 566 Oddibe McDowell | .05 | .15 |
| ☐ 567 Dickie Noles | .05 | .15 |
| ☐ 568 Pete O'Brien | .05 | .15 |
| ☐ 569 Larry Parrish | .05 | .15 |
| ☐ 570 Dave Rozema | .05 | .15 |
| ☐ 571 Dave Schmidt | .05 | .15 |
| ☐ 572 Don Slaught | .05 | .15 |
| ☐ 573 Wayne Tolleson | .05 | .15 |
| ☐ 574 Duane Walker | .05 | .15 |
| ☐ 575 Gary Ward | .05 | .15 |
| ☐ 576 Chris Welsh | .05 | .15 |
| ☐ 577 Curtis Wilkerson | .05 | .15 |
| ☐ 578 George Wright | .05 | .15 |
| ☐ 579 Chris Bando | .05 | .15 |
| ☐ 580 Tony Bernazard | .05 | .15 |
| ☐ 581 Brett Butler | .08 | .25 |
| ☐ 582 Ernie Camacho | .05 | .15 |
| ☐ 583 Joe Carter | .05 | .15 |
| ☐ 584 Carmen Castillo | .05 | .15 |
| ☐ 585 Jamie Easterly | .05 | .15 |
| ☐ 586 Julio Franco | .05 | .15 |
| ☐ 587 Mel Hall | .05 | .15 |
| ☐ 588 Mike Hargrove | .05 | .15 |
| ☐ 589 Neal Heaton | .05 | .15 |
| ☐ 590 Brook Jacoby | .05 | .15 |
| ☐ 591 Otis Nixon RC | .40 | 1.00 |
| ☐ 592 Jerry Reed | .05 | .15 |
| ☐ 593 Vern Ruhle | .05 | .15 |
| ☐ 594 Pat Tabler | .05 | .15 |
| ☐ 595 Rich Thompson | .05 | .15 |
| ☐ 596 Andre Thornton | .05 | .15 |
| ☐ 597 Dave Von Ohlen | .05 | .15 |
| ☐ 598 George Vukovich | .05 | .15 |
| ☐ 599 Tom Waddell | .05 | .15 |
| ☐ 600 Curt Wardle | .05 | .15 |
| ☐ 601 Jerry Willard | .05 | .15 |
| ☐ 602 Bill Almon | .05 | .15 |
| ☐ 603 Mike Bielecki | .05 | .15 |
| ☐ 604 Sid Bream | .05 | .15 |
| ☐ 605 Mike C. Brown | .05 | .15 |
| ☐ 606 Pat Clements | .05 | .15 |
| ☐ 607 Jose DeLeon | .05 | .15 |
| ☐ 608 Denny Gonzalez | .05 | .15 |
| ☐ 609 Cecilio Guante | .05 | .15 |
| ☐ 610 Steve Kemp | .05 | .15 |
| ☐ 611 Sammy Khalifa | .05 | .15 |
| ☐ 612 Lee Mazzilli | .08 | .25 |
| ☐ 613 Larry McWilliams | .05 | .15 |
| ☐ 614 Jim Morrison | .05 | .15 |
| ☐ 615 Joe Orsulak RC* | .20 | .50 |
| ☐ 616 Tony Pena | .05 | .15 |
| ☐ 617 Johnny Ray | .05 | .15 |
| ☐ 618 Rick Reuschel | .08 | .25 |
| ☐ 619 R.J. Reynolds | .05 | .15 |
| ☐ 620 Rick Rhoden | .05 | .15 |
| ☐ 621 Don Robinson | .05 | .15 |
| ☐ 622 Jason Thompson | .05 | .15 |
| ☐ 623 Lee Tunnell | .05 | .15 |
| ☐ 624 Jim Winn | .05 | .15 |
| ☐ 625 Marvell Wynne | .05 | .15 |
| ☐ 626 Dwight Gooden IA | .20 | .50 |
| ☐ 627 Don Mattingly IA | .50 | 1.25 |
| ☐ 628 Pete Rose 4192 | .20 | .50 |
| ☐ 629 Rod Carew 3000 Hits | .08 | .25 |
| ☐ 630 T.Seaver/P.Niekro | .05 | .15 |
| ☐ 631 Don Baylor Ouch | .08 | .25 |
| ☐ 632 Tim Raines/Strawberry | .05 | .15 |
| ☐ 633 C.Ripken/A.Trammell | .60 | 1.50 |
| ☐ 634 Wade Boggs/G.Brett | .40 | 1.00 |
| ☐ 635 B.Horner/D.Murphy | .20 | .50 |
| ☐ 636 W.McGee/V.Coleman | .08 | .25 |
| ☐ 637 Vince Coleman IA | .08 | .25 |
| ☐ 638 Pete Rose/D.Gooden | .30 | .75 |
| ☐ 639 Wade Boggs/D.Mattingly | .50 | 1.25 |
| ☐ 640 Murphy/Garvey/Parker | .20 | .50 |
| ☐ 641 D.Gooden/F.Valenzuela | .20 | .50 |
| ☐ 642 Jimmy Key/D.Stieb | .08 | .25 |
| ☐ 643 C.Fisk/R.Gedman | .08 | .25 |
| ☐ 644 Benito Santiago AS | .75 | 2.00 |
| ☐ 645 M.Woodard/C.Ward RC | .05 | .15 |
| ☐ 646 Paul O'Neill RC | 1.50 | 4.00 |
| ☐ 647 Andres Galarraga RC | .60 | 1.50 |
| ☐ 648 B.Kipper/C.Ford RC | .05 | .15 |
| ☐ 649 Jose Canseco RC | 3.00 | 8.00 |
| ☐ 650 Mark McLemore RC | .40 | 1.00 |
| ☐ 651 R.Woodward/M.Brantley RC | .05 | .15 |
| ☐ 652 B.Robidoux/M.Funderburk RC | .05 | .15 |
| ☐ 653 Cecil Fielder RC | .75 | 2.00 |
| ☐ 654 CL: Royals/Cardinals Blue Jays/Mets | .05 | .15 |
| ☐ 655 CL: Yankees/Dodgers Angels/Reds UER (168 Darly S | .05 | .15 |
| ☐ 656 CL: White Sox/Tigers Expos/Orioles (279 Dennis&# | .05 | .15 |
| ☐ 657 CL: Astros/Padres Red Sox/Cubs | .05 | .15 |
| ☐ 658 CL: Twins/A's Phillies/Mariners | .05 | .15 |
| ☐ 659 CL: Brewers/Braves Giants/Rangers | .05 | .15 |
| ☐ 660 CL: Indians/Pirates Special Cards | .05 | .15 |

## 1987 Fleer

|  | | |
|---|---|---|
| ☐ COMPLETE SET (660) | 20.00 | 40.00 |
| ☐ COMP.FACT.SET (672) | 25.00 | 50.00 |
| ☐ 1 Rick Aguilera | .05 | .15 |
| ☐ 2 Richard Anderson | .05 | .15 |
| ☐ 3 Wally Backman | .05 | .15 |
| ☐ 4 Gary Carter | .08 | .25 |
| ☐ 5 Ron Darling | .08 | .25 |
| ☐ 6 Len Dykstra | .08 | .25 |
| ☐ 7 Kevin Elster RC | .20 | .50 |
| ☐ 8 Sid Fernandez | .05 | .15 |
| ☐ 9 Dwight Gooden | .15 | .40 |
| ☐ 10 Ed Hearn RC | .05 | .15 |
| ☐ 11 Danny Heep | .05 | .15 |
| ☐ 12 Keith Hernandez | .08 | .25 |
| ☐ 13 Howard Johnson | .08 | .25 |
| ☐ 14 Ray Knight | .08 | .25 |
| ☐ 15 Lee Mazzilli | .05 | .25 |
| ☐ 16 Roger McDowell | .05 | .15 |
| ☐ 17 Kevin Mitchell RC * | .50 | 1.25 |
| ☐ 18 Randy Niemann | .05 | .15 |
| ☐ 19 Bob Ojeda | .05 | .15 |
| ☐ 20 Jesse Orosco | .05 | .15 |
| ☐ 21 Rafael Santana | .05 | .15 |
| ☐ 22 Doug Sisk | .05 | .15 |
| ☐ 23 Darryl Strawberry | .08 | .25 |
| ☐ 24 Tim Teufel | .05 | .15 |
| ☐ 25 Mookie Wilson | .08 | .25 |
| ☐ 26 Tony Armas | .08 | .25 |
| ☐ 27 Marty Barrett | .05 | .15 |
| ☐ 28 Don Baylor | .08 | .25 |
| ☐ 29 Wade Boggs | .15 | .40 |
| ☐ 30 Oil Can Boyd | .05 | .15 |
| ☐ 31 Bill Buckner | .08 | .25 |
| ☐ 32 Roger Clemens | 1.25 | 3.00 |
| ☐ 33 Steve Crawford | .05 | .15 |
| ☐ 34 Dwight Evans | .15 | .40 |
| ☐ 35 Rich Gedman | .05 | .15 |
| ☐ 36 Dave Henderson | .05 | .15 |
| ☐ 37 Bruce Hurst | .05 | .15 |
| ☐ 38 Tim Lollar | .05 | .15 |
| ☐ 39 Al Nipper | .05 | .15 |
| ☐ 40 Spike Owen | .05 | .15 |
| ☐ 41 Jim Rice | .08 | .25 |
| ☐ 42 Ed Romero | .05 | .15 |
| ☐ 43 Joe Sambito | .05 | .15 |
| ☐ 44 Calvin Schiraldi | .05 | .15 |
| ☐ 45 Tom Seaver | .15 | .40 |
| ☐ 46 Jeff Sellers | .05 | .15 |
| ☐ 47 Bob Stanley | .05 | .15 |
| ☐ 48 Sammy Stewart | .05 | .15 |
| ☐ 49 Larry Andersen | .05 | .15 |
| ☐ 50 Alan Ashby | .05 | .15 |
| ☐ 51 Kevin Bass | .05 | .15 |
| ☐ 52 Jeff Calhoun | .05 | .15 |
| ☐ 53 Jose Cruz | .08 | .25 |
| ☐ 54 Danny Darwin | .05 | .15 |
| ☐ 55 Glenn Davis | .08 | .25 |
| ☐ 56 Jim Deshaies RC * | .08 | .25 |
| ☐ 57 Bill Doran | .05 | .15 |
| ☐ 58 Phil Garner | .05 | .15 |
| ☐ 59 Billy Hatcher | .05 | .15 |
| ☐ 60 Charlie Kerfeld | .05 | .15 |
| ☐ 61 Bob Knepper | .05 | .15 |
| ☐ 62 Dave Lopes | .08 | .25 |
| ☐ 63 Aurelio Lopez | .05 | .15 |
| ☐ 64 Jim Pankovits | .05 | .15 |
| ☐ 65 Terry Puhl | .05 | .15 |
| ☐ 66 Craig Reynolds | .05 | .15 |
| ☐ 67 Nolan Ryan | 1.25 | 3.00 |
| ☐ 68 Mike Scott | .05 | .15 |
| ☐ 69 Dave Smith | .05 | .15 |
| ☐ 70 Dickie Thon | .05 | .15 |
| ☐ 71 Tony Walker | .05 | .15 |
| ☐ 72 Denny Walling | .05 | .15 |
| ☐ 73 Bob Boone | .08 | .25 |
| ☐ 74 Rick Burleson | .05 | .15 |
| ☐ 75 John Candelaria | .05 | .15 |
| ☐ 76 Doug Corbett | .05 | .15 |
| ☐ 77 Doug DeCinces | .05 | .15 |
| ☐ 78 Brian Downing | .08 | .25 |
| ☐ 79 Chuck Finley RC | .50 | 1.25 |
| ☐ 80 Terry Forster | .08 | .25 |
| ☐ 81 Bob Grich | .08 | .25 |
| ☐ 82 George Hendrick | .08 | .25 |
| ☐ 83 Jack Howell | .05 | .15 |
| ☐ 84 Reggie Jackson | .15 | .40 |
| ☐ 85 Ruppert Jones | .05 | .15 |
| ☐ 86 Wally Joyner RC | .50 | 1.25 |
| ☐ 87 Gary Lucas | .05 | .15 |
| ☐ 88 Kirk McCaskill | .05 | .15 |
| ☐ 89 Donnie Moore | .05 | .15 |
| ☐ 90 Gary Pettis | .05 | .15 |
| ☐ 91 Vern Ruhle | .05 | .15 |
| ☐ 92 Dick Schofield | .05 | .15 |
| ☐ 93 Don Sutton | .08 | .25 |
| ☐ 94 Rob Wilfong | .05 | .15 |
| ☐ 95 Mike Witt | .05 | .15 |
| ☐ 96 Doug Drabek RC | .50 | 1.25 |
| ☐ 97 Mike Easler | .05 | .15 |
| ☐ 98 Mike Fischlin | .05 | .15 |
| ☐ 99 Brian Fisher | .05 | .15 |
| ☐ 100 Ron Guidry | .08 | .25 |
| ☐ 101 Rickey Henderson | .25 | .60 |
| ☐ 102 Tommy John | .08 | .25 |
| ☐ 103 Ron Kittle | .05 | .15 |
| ☐ 104 Don Mattingly | .75 | 2.00 |
| ☐ 105 Bobby Meacham | .05 | .15 |
| ☐ 106 Joe Niekro | .05 | .15 |
| ☐ 107 Mike Pagliarulo | .05 | .15 |
| ☐ 108 Dan Pasqua | .05 | .15 |
| ☐ 109 Willie Randolph | .08 | .25 |
| ☐ 110 Dennis Rasmussen | .05 | .15 |
| ☐ 111 Dave Righetti | .08 | .25 |
| ☐ 112 Gary Roenicke | .05 | .15 |
| ☐ 113 Rod Scurry | .05 | .15 |
| ☐ 114 Bob Shirley | .05 | .15 |
| ☐ 115 Joel Skinner | .05 | .15 |
| ☐ 116 Tim Stoddard | .05 | .15 |
| ☐ 117 Bob Tewksbury RC * | .20 | .50 |
| ☐ 118 Wayne Tolleson | .05 | .15 |
| ☐ 119 Claudell Washington | .05 | .15 |
| ☐ 120 Dave Winfield | .20 | .50 |
| ☐ 121 Steve Buechele | .05 | .15 |
| ☐ 122 Ed Correa | .05 | .15 |
| ☐ 123 Scott Fletcher | .05 | .15 |
| ☐ 124 Jose Guzman | .05 | .15 |
| ☐ 125 Toby Harrah | .08 | .25 |
| ☐ 126 Greg Harris | .05 | .15 |
| ☐ 127 Charlie Hough | .08 | .25 |
| ☐ 128 Pete Incaviglia RC * | .20 | .50 |
| ☐ 129 Mike Mason | .05 | .15 |
| ☐ 130 Oddibe McDowell | .05 | .15 |
| ☐ 131 Dale Mohorcic | .05 | .15 |
| ☐ 132 Pete O'Brien | .05 | .15 |
| ☐ 133 Tom Paciorek | .05 | .15 |
| ☐ 134 Larry Parrish | .05 | .15 |
| ☐ 135 Geno Petralli | .05 | .15 |
| ☐ 136 Darrell Porter | .05 | .15 |
| ☐ 137 Jeff Russell | .05 | .15 |
| ☐ 138 Ruben Sierra RC | .75 | 2.00 |
| ☐ 139 Don Slaught | .05 | .15 |
| ☐ 140 Gary Ward | .05 | .15 |
| ☐ 141 Curtis Wilkerson | .05 | .15 |
| ☐ 142 Mitch Williams RC * | .20 | .50 |
| ☐ 143 Bobby Witt RC | .20 | .50 |
| ☐ 144 Dave Bergman | .05 | .15 |
| ☐ 145 Tom Brookens | .05 | .15 |
| ☐ 146 Bill Campbell | .05 | .15 |
| ☐ 147 Chuck Cary | .05 | .15 |
| ☐ 148 Darnell Coles | .05 | .15 |
| ☐ 149 Dave Collins | .05 | .15 |
| ☐ 150 Darrell Evans | .08 | .25 |
| ☐ 151 Kirk Gibson | .08 | .25 |
| ☐ 152 John Grubb | .05 | .15 |
| ☐ 153 Willie Hernandez | .05 | .15 |
| ☐ 154 Larry Herndon | .05 | .15 |
| ☐ 155 Eric King | .05 | .15 |
| ☐ 156 Chet Lemon | .05 | .15 |
| ☐ 157 Dwight Lowry | .05 | .15 |
| ☐ 158 Jack Morris | .08 | .25 |
| ☐ 159 Randy O'Neal | .05 | .15 |
| ☐ 160 Lance Parrish | .08 | .25 |
| ☐ 161 Dan Petry | .05 | .15 |
| ☐ 162 Pat Sheridan | .05 | .15 |
| ☐ 163 Jim Slaton | .05 | .15 |
| ☐ 164 Frank Tanana | .08 | .25 |
| ☐ 165 Walt Terrell | .05 | .15 |
| ☐ 166 Mark Thurmond | .05 | .15 |
| ☐ 167 Alan Trammell | .08 | .25 |
| ☐ 168 Lou Whitaker | .08 | .25 |
| ☐ 169 Luis Aguayo | .05 | .15 |
| ☐ 170 Steve Bedrosian | .05 | .15 |
| ☐ 171 Don Carman | .05 | .15 |
| ☐ 172 Darren Daulton | .08 | .25 |
| ☐ 173 Greg Gross | .05 | .15 |
| ☐ 174 Kevin Gross | .05 | .15 |
| ☐ 175 Von Hayes | .05 | .15 |
| ☐ 176 Charles Hudson | .05 | .15 |
| ☐ 177 Tom Hume | .05 | .15 |
| ☐ 178 Steve Jeltz | .05 | .15 |
| ☐ 179 Mike Maddux RC | .05 | .15 |
| ☐ 180 Shane Rawley | .05 | .15 |
| ☐ 181 Gary Redus | .05 | .15 |
| ☐ 182 Ron Roenicke | .05 | .15 |
| ☐ 183 Bruce Ruffin RC | .08 | .25 |
| ☐ 184 John Russell | .05 | .15 |
| ☐ 185 Juan Samuel | .05 | .15 |
| ☐ 186 Dan Schatzeder | .05 | .15 |
| ☐ 187 Mike Schmidt | .60 | 1.50 |
| ☐ 188 Rick Schu | .05 | .15 |
| ☐ 189 Jeff Stone | .05 | .15 |
| ☐ 190 Kent Tekulve | .05 | .15 |
| ☐ 191 Milt Thompson | .05 | .15 |
| ☐ 192 Glenn Wilson | .05 | .15 |
| ☐ 193 Buddy Bell | .08 | .25 |
| ☐ 194 Tom Browning | .05 | .15 |
| ☐ 195 Sal Butera | .05 | .15 |
| ☐ 196 Dave Concepcion | .08 | .25 |
| ☐ 197 Kal Daniels | .05 | .15 |
| ☐ 198 Eric Davis | .15 | .40 |
| ☐ 199 John Denny | .05 | .15 |
| ☐ 200 Bo Diaz | .05 | .15 |
| ☐ 201 Nick Esasky | .05 | .15 |
| ☐ 202 John Franco | .08 | .25 |
| ☐ 203 Bill Gullickson | .05 | .15 |
| ☐ 204 Barry Larkin RC | 1.25 | 3.00 |
| ☐ 205 Eddie Milner | .05 | .15 |
| ☐ 206 Rob Murphy | .05 | .15 |
| ☐ 207 Ron Oester | .05 | .15 |
| ☐ 208 Dave Parker | .08 | .25 |
| ☐ 209 Tony Perez | .15 | .40 |
| ☐ 210 Ted Power | .05 | .15 |
| ☐ 211 Joe Price | .05 | .15 |
| ☐ 212 Ron Robinson | .05 | .15 |
| ☐ 213 Pete Rose | .75 | 2.00 |
| ☐ 214 Mario Soto | .08 | .25 |
| ☐ 215 Kurt Stillwell | .05 | .15 |
| ☐ 216 Max Venable | .05 | .15 |
| ☐ 217 Chris Welsh | .05 | .15 |
| ☐ 218 Carl Willis RC | .08 | .25 |
| ☐ 219 Jesse Barfield | .05 | .15 |
| ☐ 220 George Bell | .08 | .25 |
| ☐ 221 Bill Caudill | .05 | .15 |
| ☐ 222 John Cerutti | .05 | .15 |
| ☐ 223 Jim Clancy | .05 | .15 |
| ☐ 224 Mark Eichhorn | .05 | .15 |
| ☐ 225 Tony Fernandez | .05 | .15 |
| ☐ 226 Damaso Garcia | .05 | .15 |
| ☐ 227 Kelly Gruber ERR (Wrong birth year) | .05 | .15 |
| ☐ 228 Tom Henke | .05 | .15 |
| ☐ 229 Garth Iorg | .05 | .15 |
| ☐ 230 Joe Johnson | .05 | .15 |
| ☐ 231 Cliff Johnson | .05 | .15 |
| ☐ 232 Jimmy Key | .08 | .25 |
| ☐ 233 Dennis Lamp | .05 | .15 |
| ☐ 234 Rick Leach | .05 | .15 |
| ☐ 235 Buck Martinez | .05 | .15 |
| ☐ 236 Lloyd Moseby | .05 | .15 |
| ☐ 237 Rance Mulliniks | .05 | .15 |
| ☐ 238 Dave Stieb | .08 | .25 |
| ☐ 239 Willie Upshaw | .05 | .15 |
| ☐ 240 Ernie Whitt | .05 | .15 |
| ☐ 241 Andy Allanson RC | .05 | .15 |
| ☐ 242 Scott Bailes | .05 | .15 |
| ☐ 243 Chris Bando | .05 | .15 |
| ☐ 244 Tony Bernazard | .05 | .15 |
| ☐ 245 John Butcher | .05 | .15 |

|  |  | | |
|---|---|---|---|
| 246 | Brett Butler | .08 | .25 |
| 247 | Ernie Camacho | .05 | .15 |
| 248 | Tom Candiotti | .05 | .15 |
| 249 | Joe Carter | .08 | .25 |
| 250 | Carmen Castillo | .05 | .15 |
| 251 | Julio Franco | .05 | .15 |
| 252 | Mel Hall | .05 | .15 |
| 253 | Brook Jacoby | .05 | .15 |
| 254 | Phil Niekro | .08 | .25 |
| 255 | Otis Nixon | .05 | .15 |
| 256 | Dickie Noles | .05 | .15 |
| 257 | Bryan Oelkers | .05 | .15 |
| 258 | Ken Schrom | .05 | .15 |
| 259 | Don Schulze | .05 | .15 |
| 260 | Cory Snyder | .08 | .25 |
| 261 | Pat Tabler | .05 | .15 |
| 262 | Andre Thornton | .05 | .15 |
| 263 | Rich Yett | .05 | .15 |
| 264 | Mike Aldrete | .05 | .15 |
| 265 | Juan Berenguer | .05 | .15 |
| 266 | Vida Blue | .08 | .25 |
| 267 | Bob Brenly | .05 | .15 |
| 268 | Chris Brown | .05 | .15 |
| 269 | Will Clark RC | 1.25 | 3.00 |
| 270 | Chili Davis | .08 | .25 |
| 271 | Mark Davis | .05 | .15 |
| 272 | Kelly Downs RC | .08 | .25 |
| 273 | Scott Garrelts | .05 | .15 |
| 274 | Dan Gladden | .05 | .15 |
| 275 | Mike Krukow | .05 | .15 |
| 276 | Randy Kutcher | .05 | .15 |
| 277 | Mike LaCoss | .05 | .15 |
| 278 | Jeff Leonard | .05 | .15 |
| 279 | Candy Maldonado | .05 | .15 |
| 280 | Roger Mason | .05 | .15 |
| 281 | Bob Melvin | .05 | .15 |
| 282 | Greg Minton | .05 | .15 |
| 283 | Jeff D. Robinson | .05 | .15 |
| 284 | Harry Spilman | .05 | .15 |
| 285 | Robby Thompson RC * | .20 | .50 |
| 286 | Jose Uribe | .05 | .15 |
| 287 | Frank Williams | .05 | .15 |
| 288 | Joel Youngblood | .05 | .15 |
| 289 | Jack Clark | .08 | .25 |
| 290 | Vince Coleman | .05 | .15 |
| 291 | Tim Conroy | .05 | .15 |
| 292 | Danny Cox | .05 | .15 |
| 293 | Ken Dayley | .05 | .15 |
| 294 | Curt Ford | .05 | .15 |
| 295 | Bob Forsch | .05 | .15 |
| 296 | Tom Herr | .05 | .15 |
| 297 | Ricky Horton | .05 | .15 |
| 298 | Clint Hurdle | .05 | .15 |
| 299 | Jeff Lahti | .05 | .15 |
| 300 | Steve Lake | .05 | .15 |
| 301 | Tito Landrum | .05 | .15 |
| 302 | Mike LaValliere RC * | .20 | .50 |
| 303 | Greg Mathews | .05 | .15 |
| 304 | Willie McGee | .08 | .25 |
| 305 | Jose Oquendo | .05 | .15 |
| 306 | Terry Pendleton | .08 | .25 |
| 307 | Pat Perry | .05 | .15 |
| 308 | Ozzie Smith | .40 | 1.00 |
| 309 | Ray Soff | .05 | .15 |
| 310 | John Tudor | .08 | .25 |
| 311 | Andy Van Slyke UER | .15 | .40 |
| 312 | Todd Worrell | .05 | .15 |
| 313 | Dann Bilardello | .05 | .15 |
| 314 | Hubie Brooks | .05 | .15 |
| 315 | Tim Burke | .05 | .15 |
| 316 | Andre Dawson | .08 | .25 |
| 317 | Mike Fitzgerald | .05 | .15 |
| 318 | Tom Foley | .05 | .15 |
| 319 | Andres Galarraga | .08 | .25 |
| 320 | Joe Hesketh | .05 | .15 |
| 321 | Wallace Johnson | .05 | .15 |
| 322 | Wayne Krenchicki | .05 | .15 |
| 323 | Vance Law | .05 | .15 |
| 324 | Dennis Martinez | .08 | .25 |
| 325 | Bob McClure | .05 | .15 |
| 326 | Andy McGaffigan | .05 | .15 |
| 327 | Al Newman RC | .05 | .15 |
| 328 | Tim Raines | .08 | .25 |
| 329 | Jeff Reardon | .08 | .25 |
| 330 | Luis Rivera RC | .08 | .25 |
| 331 | Bob Sebra | .05 | .15 |
| 332 | Bryn Smith | .05 | .15 |
| 333 | Jay Tibbs | .05 | .15 |
| 334 | Tim Wallach | .05 | .15 |
| 335 | Mitch Webster | .05 | .15 |
| 336 | Jim Wohlford | .05 | .15 |
| 337 | Floyd Youmans | .05 | .15 |
| 338 | Chris Bosio RC | .20 | .50 |
| 339 | Glenn Braggs RC | .05 | .15 |
| 340 | Rick Cerone | .05 | .15 |
| 341 | Mark Clear | .05 | .15 |
| 342 | Bryan Clutterbuck | .05 | .15 |
| 343 | Cecil Cooper | .08 | .25 |
| 344 | Rob Deer | .05 | .15 |
| 345 | Jim Gantner | .05 | .15 |
| 346 | Ted Higuera | .05 | .15 |
| 347 | John Henry Johnson | .05 | .15 |
| 348 | Tim Leary | .05 | .15 |
| 349 | Rick Manning | .05 | .15 |
| 350 | Paul Molitor | .08 | .25 |
| 351 | Charlie Moore | .05 | .15 |
| 352 | Juan Nieves | .05 | .15 |
| 353 | Ben Oglivie | .08 | .25 |
| 354 | Dan Plesac | .08 | .25 |
| 355 | Ernest Riles | .05 | .15 |
| 356 | Billy Joe Robidoux | .05 | .15 |
| 357 | Bill Schroeder | .05 | .15 |
| 358 | Dale Sveum | .08 | .25 |
| 359 | Gorman Thomas | .08 | .25 |
| 360 | Bill Wegman | .05 | .15 |
| 361 | Robin Yount | .40 | 1.00 |
| 362 | Steve Balboni | .05 | .15 |
| 363 | Scott Bankhead | .05 | .15 |
| 364 | Buddy Biancalana | .05 | .15 |
| 365 | Bud Black | .05 | .15 |
| 366 | George Brett | .60 | 1.50 |
| 367 | Steve Farr | .05 | .15 |
| 368 | Mark Gubicza | .05 | .15 |
| 369 | Bo Jackson RC | 3.00 | 8.00 |
| 370 | Danny Jackson | .05 | .15 |
| 371 | Mike Kingery RC | .08 | .25 |
| 372 | Rudy Law | .05 | .15 |
| 373 | Charlie Leibrandt | .05 | .15 |
| 374 | Dennis Leonard | .05 | .15 |
| 375 | Hal McRae | .08 | .25 |
| 376 | Jorge Orta | .05 | .15 |
| 377 | Jamie Quirk | .05 | .15 |
| 378 | Dan Quisenberry | .08 | .25 |
| 379 | Bret Saberhagen | .08 | .25 |
| 380 | Angel Salazar | .05 | .15 |
| 381 | Lonnie Smith | .05 | .15 |
| 382 | Jim Sundberg | .05 | .15 |
| 383 | Frank White | .08 | .25 |
| 384 | Willie Wilson | .08 | .25 |
| 385 | Joaquin Andujar | .08 | .25 |
| 386 | Doug Bair | .05 | .15 |
| 387 | Dusty Baker | .08 | .25 |
| 388 | Bruce Bochte | .05 | .15 |
| 389 | Jose Canseco | .60 | 1.50 |
| 390 | Chris Codiroli | .05 | .15 |
| 391 | Mike Davis | .05 | .15 |
| 392 | Alfredo Griffin | .05 | .15 |
| 393 | Moose Haas | .05 | .15 |
| 394 | Donnie Hill | .05 | .15 |
| 395 | Jay Howell | .05 | .15 |
| 396 | Dave Kingman | .08 | .25 |
| 397 | Carney Lansford | .08 | .25 |
| 398 | Dave Leiper | .05 | .15 |
| 399 | Bill Mooneyham | .05 | .15 |
| 400 | Dwayne Murphy | .05 | .15 |
| 401 | Steve Ontiveros | .05 | .15 |
| 402 | Tony Phillips | .08 | .25 |
| 403 | Eric Plunk | .05 | .15 |
| 404 | Jose Rijo | .08 | .25 |
| 405 | Terry Steinbach RC | .50 | 1.25 |
| 406 | Dave Stewart | .08 | .25 |
| 407 | Mickey Tettleton | .08 | .25 |
| 408 | Dave Von Ohlen | .05 | .15 |
| 409 | Jerry Willard | .05 | .15 |
| 410 | Curt Young | .05 | .15 |
| 411 | Bruce Bochy | .05 | .15 |
| 412 | Dave Dravecky | .08 | .25 |
| 413 | Tim Flannery | .05 | .15 |
| 414 | Steve Garvey | .08 | .25 |
| 415 | Rich Gossage | .08 | .25 |
| 416 | Tony Gwynn | .40 | 1.00 |
| 417 | Andy Hawkins | .05 | .15 |
| 418 | LaMarr Hoyt | .05 | .15 |
| 419 | Terry Kennedy | .05 | .15 |
| 420 | John Kruk RC | .75 | 2.00 |
| 421 | Dave LaPoint | .05 | .15 |
| 422 | Craig Lefferts | .05 | .15 |
| 423 | Carmelo Martinez | .05 | .15 |
| 424 | Lance McCullers | .05 | .15 |
| 425 | Kevin McReynolds | .05 | .15 |
| 426 | Graig Nettles | .08 | .25 |
| 427 | Bip Roberts RC | .20 | .50 |
| 428 | Jerry Royster | .05 | .15 |
| 429 | Benito Santiago | .08 | .25 |
| 430 | Eric Show | .05 | .15 |
| 431 | Bob Stoddard | .05 | .15 |
| 432 | Garry Templeton | .08 | .25 |
| 433 | Gene Walter | .05 | .15 |
| 434 | Ed Whitson | .05 | .15 |
| 435 | Marvell Wynne | .05 | .15 |
| 436 | Dave Anderson | .05 | .15 |
| 437 | Greg Brock | .05 | .15 |
| 438 | Enos Cabell | .05 | .15 |
| 439 | Mariano Duncan | .05 | .15 |
| 440 | Pedro Guerrero | .08 | .25 |
| 441 | Orel Hershiser | .15 | .40 |
| 442 | Rick Honeycutt | .05 | .15 |
| 443 | Ken Howell | .05 | .15 |
| 444 | Ken Landreaux | .05 | .15 |
| 445 | Bill Madlock | .08 | .25 |
| 446 | Mike Marshall | .05 | .15 |
| 447 | Len Matuszek | .05 | .15 |
| 448 | Tom Niedenfuer | .05 | .15 |
| 449 | Alejandro Pena | .05 | .15 |
| 450 | Dennis Powell | .05 | .15 |
| 451 | Jerry Reuss | .05 | .15 |
| 452 | Bill Russell | .08 | .25 |
| 453 | Steve Sax | .08 | .25 |
| 454 | Mike Scioscia | .08 | .25 |
| 455 | Franklin Stubbs | .05 | .15 |
| 456 | Alex Trevino | .05 | .15 |
| 457 | Fernando Valenzuela | .08 | .25 |
| 458 | Ed VandeBerg | .05 | .15 |
| 459 | Bob Welch | .08 | .25 |
| 460 | Reggie Williams | .05 | .15 |
| 461 | Don Aase | .05 | .15 |
| 462 | Juan Beniquez | .05 | .15 |
| 463 | Mike Boddicker | .05 | .15 |
| 464 | Juan Bonilla | .05 | .15 |
| 465 | Rich Bordi | .05 | .15 |
| 466 | Storm Davis | .05 | .15 |
| 467 | Rick Dempsey | .05 | .15 |
| 468 | Ken Dixon | .05 | .15 |
| 469 | Jim Dwyer | .05 | .15 |
| 470 | Mike Flanagan | .08 | .25 |
| 471 | Jackie Gutierrez | .05 | .15 |
| 472 | Brad Havens | .05 | .15 |
| 473 | Lee Lacy | .05 | .15 |
| 474 | Fred Lynn | .08 | .25 |
| 475 | Scott McGregor | .05 | .15 |
| 476 | Eddie Murray | .25 | .60 |
| 477 | Tom O'Malley | .05 | .15 |
| 478 | Cal Ripken | 1.00 | 2.50 |
| 479 | Larry Sheets | .05 | .15 |
| 480 | John Shelby | .05 | .15 |
| 481 | Nate Snell | .05 | .15 |
| 482 | Jim Traber | .05 | .15 |
| 483 | Mike Young | .05 | .15 |
| 484 | Neil Allen | .05 | .15 |
| 485 | Harold Baines | .08 | .25 |
| 486 | Floyd Bannister | .05 | .15 |
| 487 | Daryl Boston | .05 | .15 |
| 488 | Ivan Calderon | .08 | .25 |
| 489 | John Cangelosi | .05 | .15 |
| 490 | Steve Carlton | .08 | .25 |
| 491 | Joe Cowley | .05 | .15 |
| 492 | Julio Cruz | .05 | .15 |
| 493 | Bill Dawley | .05 | .15 |
| 494 | Jose DeLeon | .05 | .15 |
| 495 | Richard Dotson | .05 | .15 |
| 496 | Carlton Fisk | .15 | .40 |
| 497 | Ozzie Guillen | .15 | .40 |
| 498 | Jerry Hairston | .05 | .15 |
| 499 | Ron Hassey | .05 | .15 |
| 500 | Tim Hulett | .05 | .15 |
| 501 | Bob James | .05 | .15 |
| 502 | Steve Lyons | .05 | .15 |
| 503 | Joel McKeon | .05 | .15 |
| 504 | Gene Nelson | .05 | .15 |
| 505 | Dave Schmidt | .05 | .15 |
| 506 | Ray Searage | .05 | .15 |
| 507 | Bobby Thigpen RC | .20 | .50 |
| 508 | Greg Walker | .05 | .15 |
| 509 | Jim Acker | .05 | .15 |

|  | | |
|---|---|---|
| ☐ 510 Doyle Alexander | .05 | .15 |
| ☐ 511 Paul Assenmacher | .20 | .50 |
| ☐ 512 Bruce Benedict | .05 | .15 |
| ☐ 513 Chris Chambliss | .08 | .25 |
| ☐ 514 Jeff Dedmon | .05 | .15 |
| ☐ 515 Gene Garber | .05 | .15 |
| ☐ 516 Ken Griffey | .08 | .25 |
| ☐ 517 Terry Harper | .05 | .15 |
| ☐ 518 Bob Horner | .08 | .25 |
| ☐ 519 Glenn Hubbard | .05 | .15 |
| ☐ 520 Rick Mahler | .05 | .15 |
| ☐ 521 Omar Moreno | .05 | .15 |
| ☐ 522 Dale Murphy | .15 | .40 |
| ☐ 523 Ken Oberkfell | .05 | .15 |
| ☐ 524 Ed Olwine | .05 | .15 |
| ☐ 525 David Palmer | .05 | .15 |
| ☐ 526 Rafael Ramirez | .05 | .15 |
| ☐ 527 Billy Sample | .05 | .15 |
| ☐ 528 Ted Simmons | .08 | .25 |
| ☐ 529 Zane Smith | .05 | .15 |
| ☐ 530 Bruce Sutter | .08 | .25 |
| ☐ 531 Andres Thomas | .05 | .15 |
| ☐ 532 Ozzie Virgil | .05 | .15 |
| ☐ 533 Allan Anderson RC | .05 | .15 |
| ☐ 534 Keith Atherton | .05 | .15 |
| ☐ 535 Billy Beane | .08 | .25 |
| ☐ 536 Bert Blyleven | .05 | .15 |
| ☐ 537 Tom Brunansky | .05 | .15 |
| ☐ 538 Randy Bush | .05 | .15 |
| ☐ 539 George Frazier | .05 | .15 |
| ☐ 540 Gary Gaetti | .08 | .25 |
| ☐ 541 Greg Gagne | .05 | .15 |
| ☐ 542 Mickey Hatcher | .05 | .15 |
| ☐ 543 Neal Heaton | .05 | .15 |
| ☐ 544 Kent Hrbek | .08 | .25 |
| ☐ 545 Roy Lee Jackson | .05 | .15 |
| ☐ 546 Tim Laudner | .05 | .15 |
| ☐ 547 Steve Lombardozzi | .05 | .15 |
| ☐ 548 Mark Portugal RC * | .20 | .50 |
| ☐ 549 Kirby Puckett | .40 | 1.00 |
| ☐ 550 Jeff Reed | .05 | .15 |
| ☐ 551 Mark Salas | .05 | .15 |
| ☐ 552 Roy Smalley | .05 | .15 |
| ☐ 553 Mike Smithson | .05 | .15 |
| ☐ 554 Frank Viola | .08 | .25 |
| ☐ 555 Thad Bosley | .05 | .15 |
| ☐ 556 Ron Cey | .08 | .25 |
| ☐ 557 Jody Davis | .05 | .15 |
| ☐ 558 Ron Davis | .05 | .15 |
| ☐ 559 Bob Demier | .05 | .15 |
| ☐ 560 Frank DiPino | .05 | .15 |
| ☐ 561 Shawon Dunston UER (Wrong birth year listed on c | | |
| ☐ 562 Leon Durham | .05 | .15 |
| ☐ 563 Dennis Eckersley | .15 | .40 |
| ☐ 564 Terry Francona | .08 | .25 |
| ☐ 565 Dave Gumpert | .05 | .15 |
| ☐ 566 Guy Hoffman | .05 | .15 |
| ☐ 567 Ed Lynch | .05 | .15 |
| ☐ 568 Gary Matthews | .08 | .25 |
| ☐ 569 Keith Moreland | .05 | .15 |
| ☐ 570 Jamie Moyer RC | .75 | 2.00 |
| ☐ 571 Jerry Mumphrey | .05 | .15 |
| ☐ 572 Ryne Sandberg | .50 | 1.25 |
| ☐ 573 Scott Sanderson | .05 | .15 |
| ☐ 574 Lee Smith | .08 | .25 |
| ☐ 575 Chris Speier | .05 | .15 |
| ☐ 576 Rick Sutcliffe | .08 | .25 |
| ☐ 577 Manny Trillo | .05 | .15 |
| ☐ 578 Steve Trout | .05 | .15 |
| ☐ 579 Karl Best | .05 | .15 |
| ☐ 580 Scott Bradley | .05 | .15 |
| ☐ 581 Phil Bradley | .05 | .15 |
| ☐ 582 Mickey Brantley | .05 | .15 |
| ☐ 583 Mike G. Brown P | .05 | .15 |
| ☐ 584 Alvin Davis | .05 | .15 |
| ☐ 585 Lee Guetterman | .05 | .15 |
| ☐ 586 Mark Huismann | .05 | .15 |
| ☐ 587 Bob Kearney | .05 | .15 |
| ☐ 588 Pete Ladd | .05 | .15 |
| ☐ 589 Mark Langston | .05 | .15 |
| ☐ 590 Mike Moore | .05 | .15 |
| ☐ 591 Mike Morgan | .05 | .15 |
| ☐ 592 John Moses | .05 | .15 |
| ☐ 593 Ken Phelps | .05 | .15 |
| ☐ 594 Jim Presley | .05 | .15 |
| ☐ 595 Rey Quinones UER | | |

|  | | |
|---|---|---|
| (Quinonez on front) | .05 | .15 |
| ☐ 596 Harold Reynolds | .08 | .25 |
| ☐ 597 Bill Swift | .05 | .15 |
| ☐ 598 Danny Tartabull | .05 | .15 |
| ☐ 599 Steve Yeager | .08 | .25 |
| ☐ 600 Matt Young | .05 | .15 |
| ☐ 601 Bill Almon | .05 | .15 |
| ☐ 602 Rafael Belliard RC | .20 | .50 |
| ☐ 603 Mike Bielecki | .05 | .15 |
| ☐ 604 Barry Bonds RC | 6.00 | 15.00 |
| ☐ 605 Bobby Bonilla RC | .50 | 1.25 |
| ☐ 606 Sid Bream | .05 | .15 |
| ☐ 607 Mike C. Brown | .05 | .15 |
| ☐ 608 Pat Clements | .05 | .15 |
| ☐ 609 Mike Diaz | .05 | .15 |
| ☐ 610 Cecilio Guante | .05 | .15 |
| ☐ 611 Barry Jones | .05 | .15 |
| ☐ 612 Bob Kipper | .05 | .15 |
| ☐ 613 Larry McWilliams | .05 | .15 |
| ☐ 614 Jim Morrison | .05 | .15 |
| ☐ 615 Joe Orsulak | .05 | .15 |
| ☐ 616 Junior Ortiz | .05 | .15 |
| ☐ 617 Tony Pena | .05 | .15 |
| ☐ 618 Johnny Ray | .08 | .25 |
| ☐ 619 Rick Reuschel | .05 | .15 |
| ☐ 620 R.J. Reynolds | .05 | .15 |
| ☐ 621 Rick Rhoden | .05 | .15 |
| ☐ 622 Don Robinson | .05 | .15 |
| ☐ 623 Bob Walk | .05 | .15 |
| ☐ 624 Jim Winn | .05 | .15 |
| ☐ 625 J.Canseco/P.Incaviglia | .30 | .75 |
| ☐ 626 300 Game Winners | | |
| Don Sutton | | |
| Phil Niekro | .08 | .25 |
| ☐ 627 AL Firemen | | |
| Dave Righetti | | |
| Don Aase | .05 | .15 |
| ☐ 628 J.Canseco/W.Joyner | .30 | .75 |
| ☐ 629 Magic Mets | .15 | .40 |
| ☐ 630 NL Best Righties | | |
| Mike Scott | | |
| Mike Krukow | .05 | .15 |
| ☐ 631 Sensational Southpaws | | |
| Fernando Valenzuela | | |
| John F | .05 | .15 |
| ☐ 632 Count'Em | | |
| Bob Horner | | |
| ☐ 633 J.Canseco/Rice/Puckett | .30 | .75 |
| ☐ 634 R.Clemens/G.Carter | .25 | .60 |
| ☐ 635 Steve Carlton 4000 | .08 | .25 |
| ☐ 636 Eddie Murray/G.Davis | .25 | .60 |
| ☐ 637 W.Boggs/K.Hernandez | .08 | .25 |
| ☐ 638 D.Mattingly/Strawberry | .40 | 1.00 |
| ☐ 639 R.Sandberg/D.Parker | .25 | .60 |
| ☐ 640 R.Clemens/D.Gooden | .25 | .60 |
| ☐ 641 AL West Stoppers | | |
| Mike Witt | | |
| Charlie Hough | .05 | .15 |
| ☐ 642 Doubles and Triples | | |
| Juan Samuel | | |
| Tim Raines | .08 | .25 |
| ☐ 643 Outfielders with Punch | | |
| Harold Baines | | |
| Jesse Barfi | .08 | .25 |
| ☐ 644 G.Swindell/D.Clark RC | .20 | .50 |
| ☐ 645 R.Karkovice/R.Morman RC | .20 | .50 |
| ☐ 646 D.White/W.Fraser RC | .50 | 1.25 |
| ☐ 647 M.Stanley/J.Browne RC | .20 | .50 |
| ☐ 648 D.Magadan/P.Lombardi RC | .08 | .25 |
| ☐ 649 J.Gonzalez/R.Bryant RC | .08 | .25 |
| ☐ 650 J.Jones/R.Asadoor RC | .08 | .25 |
| ☐ 651 T.Jones/M.Freeman RC | .08 | .25 |
| ☐ 652 K.Seitzer/J.Stefero RC | .20 | .50 |
| ☐ 653 R.Nelson/S.Fireovid RC | .08 | .25 |
| ☐ 654 CL: Mets/Red Sox | | |
| Astros/Angels | .05 | .15 |
| ☐ 655 CL: Yankees/Rangers | | |
| Tigers/Phillies | .05 | .15 |
| ☐ 656 CL: Reds/Blue Jays | | |
| Indians/Giants | | |
| ERR (230/231 w | .05 | .15 |
| ☐ 657 CL: Cardinals/Expos | | |
| Brewers/Royals | | |
| ☐ 658 CL: A's/Padres | | |
| Dodgers/Orioles | .05 | .15 |
| ☐ 659 CL: White Sox/Braves | | |
| Twins/Cubs | .05 | .15 |
| ☐ 660 CL: Mariners/Pirates | | |

| Special Cards | | |
|---|---|---|
| ER (580/581 w | .05 | .15 |

### 1988 Fleer

Danny Tartabull

| | | |
|---|---|---|
| ☐ COMPLETE SET (660) | 6.00 | 15.00 |
| ☐ COMP.RETAIL SET (660) | 6.00 | 15.00 |
| ☐ COMP.HOBBY SET (672) | 6.00 | 15.00 |
| ☐ 1 Keith Atherton | .02 | .10 |
| ☐ 2 Don Baylor | .05 | .15 |
| ☐ 3 Juan Berenguer | .02 | .10 |
| ☐ 4 Bert Blyleven | .05 | .15 |
| ☐ 5 Tom Brunansky | .02 | .10 |
| ☐ 6 Randy Bush | .02 | .10 |
| ☐ 7 Steve Carlton | .02 | .10 |
| ☐ 8 Mark Davidson | .02 | .10 |
| ☐ 9 George Frazier | .02 | .10 |
| ☐ 10 Gary Gaetti | .05 | .15 |
| ☐ 11 Greg Gagne | .02 | .10 |
| ☐ 12 Dan Gladden | .02 | -.10 |
| ☐ 13 Kent Hrbek | .05 | .15 |
| ☐ 14 Gene Larkin RC* | .15 | .40 |
| ☐ 15 Tim Laudner | .02 | .10 |
| ☐ 16 Steve Lombardozzi | .02 | .10 |
| ☐ 17 Al Newman | .02 | .10 |
| ☐ 18 Joe Niekro | .02 | .10 |
| ☐ 19 Kirby Puckett | .10 | .30 |
| ☐ 20 Jeff Reardon | .05 | .15 |
| ☐ 21A Dan Schatzeder ERR (Misspelled Schatzader on bac | | |
| ☐ 21B Dan Schatzeder COR | .05 | .15 |
| ☐ 22 Roy Smalley | .02 | .10 |
| ☐ 23 Mike Smithson | .02 | .10 |
| ☐ 24 Les Straker | .02 | .10 |
| ☐ 25 Frank Viola | .02 | .10 |
| ☐ 26 Jack Clark | .05 | .15 |
| ☐ 27 Vince Coleman | .02 | .10 |
| ☐ 28 Danny Cox | .02 | .10 |
| ☐ 29 Bill Dawley | .02 | .10 |
| ☐ 30 Ken Dayley | .02 | .10 |
| ☐ 31 Doug DeCinces | .02 | .10 |
| ☐ 32 Curt Ford | .02 | .10 |
| ☐ 33 Bob Forsch | .02 | .10 |
| ☐ 34 David Green | .02 | .10 |
| ☐ 35 Tom Herr | .02 | .10 |
| ☐ 36 Ricky Horton | .02 | .10 |
| ☐ 37 Lance Johnson RC | .15 | .40 |
| ☐ 38 Steve Lake | .02 | .10 |
| ☐ 39 Jim Lindeman | .02 | .10 |
| ☐ 40 Joe Magrane RC* | .15 | .40 |
| ☐ 41 Greg Mathews | .02 | .10 |
| ☐ 42 Willie McGee | .05 | .15 |
| ☐ 43 John Morris | .02 | .10 |
| ☐ 44 Jose Oquendo | .02 | .10 |
| ☐ 45 Tony Pena | .02 | .10 |
| ☐ 46 Terry Pendleton | .05 | .15 |
| ☐ 47 Ozzie Smith | .20 | .50 |
| ☐ 48 John Tudor | .02 | .10 |
| ☐ 49 Lee Tunnell | .02 | .10 |
| ☐ 50 Todd Worrell | .05 | .15 |
| ☐ 51 Doyle Alexander | .02 | .10 |
| ☐ 52 Dave Bergman | .02 | .10 |
| ☐ 53 Tom Brookens | .02 | .10 |
| ☐ 54 Darrell Evans | .05 | .15 |
| ☐ 55 Kirk Gibson | .10 | .30 |
| ☐ 56 Mike Heath | .02 | .10 |
| ☐ 57 Mike Henneman RC* | .15 | .40 |
| ☐ 58 Willie Hernandez | .02 | .10 |
| ☐ 59 Larry Herndon | .02 | .10 |
| ☐ 60 Eric King | .02 | .10 |
| ☐ 61 Chet Lemon | .02 | .10 |
| ☐ 62 Scott Lusader | .05 | .15 |
| ☐ 63 Bill Madlock | .05 | .15 |
| ☐ 64 Jack Morris | .05 | .15 |

|  |  | | |
|---|---|---|---|
| ☐ 65 | Jim Morrison | .02 | .10 |
| ☐ 66 | Matt Nokes RC* | .15 | .40 |
| ☐ 67 | Dan Petry | .02 | .10 |
| ☐ 68A | Jeff M. Robinson ERR (Stats for Jeff D. Robinson) | .07 | .20 |
| ☐ 68B | Jeff M. Robinson COR (Born 12-14-61) | .02 | .10 |
| ☐ 69 | Pat Sheridan | .02 | .10 |
| ☐ 70 | Nate Snell | .02 | .10 |
| ☐ 71 | Frank Tanana | .05 | .15 |
| ☐ 72 | Walt Terrell | .02 | .10 |
| ☐ 73 | Mark Thurmond | .02 | .10 |
| ☐ 74 | Alan Trammell | .05 | .15 |
| ☐ 75 | Lou Whitaker | .05 | .15 |
| ☐ 76 | Mike Aldrete | .02 | .10 |
| ☐ 77 | Bob Brenly | .02 | .10 |
| ☐ 78 | Will Clark | .10 | .30 |
| ☐ 79 | Chili Davis | .05 | .15 |
| ☐ 80 | Kelly Downs | .02 | .10 |
| ☐ 81 | Dave Dravecky | .02 | .10 |
| ☐ 82 | Scott Garrelts | .02 | .10 |
| ☐ 83 | Atlee Hammaker | .02 | .10 |
| ☐ 84 | Dave Henderson | .05 | .15 |
| ☐ 85 | Mike Krukow | .02 | .10 |
| ☐ 86 | Mike LaCoss | .02 | .10 |
| ☐ 87 | Craig Lefferts | .02 | .10 |
| ☐ 88 | Jeff Leonard | .02 | .10 |
| ☐ 89 | Candy Maldonado | .02 | .10 |
| ☐ 90 | Eddie Milner | .02 | .10 |
| ☐ 91 | Bob Melvin | .02 | .10 |
| ☐ 92 | Kevin Mitchell | .05 | .15 |
| ☐ 93 | Jon Perlman | .02 | .10 |
| ☐ 94 | Rick Reuschel | .05 | .15 |
| ☐ 95 | Don Robinson | .02 | .10 |
| ☐ 96 | Chris Speier | .02 | .10 |
| ☐ 97 | Harry Spilman | .02 | .10 |
| ☐ 98 | Robby Thompson | .05 | .15 |
| ☐ 99 | Jose Uribe | .02 | .10 |
| ☐ 100 | Mark Wasinger | .02 | .10 |
| ☐ 101 | Matt Williams RC | .60 | 1.50 |
| ☐ 102 | Jesse Barfield | .05 | .15 |
| ☐ 103 | George Bell | .05 | .15 |
| ☐ 104 | Juan Beniquez | .02 | .10 |
| ☐ 105 | John Cerutti | .02 | .10 |
| ☐ 106 | Jim Clancy | .02 | .10 |
| ☐ 107 | Rob Ducey | .02 | .10 |
| ☐ 108 | Mark Eichhorn | .02 | .10 |
| ☐ 109 | Tony Fernandez | .05 | .15 |
| ☐ 110 | Cecil Fielder | .05 | .15 |
| ☐ 111 | Kelly Gruber | .02 | .10 |
| ☐ 112 | Tom Henke | .02 | .10 |
| ☐ 113A | Garth Iorg ERR (Misspelled Iorq on card front) | .07 | .20 |
| ☐ 113B | Garth Iorg COR | .02 | .10 |
| ☐ 114 | Jimmy Key | .05 | .15 |
| ☐ 115 | Rick Leach | .02 | .10 |
| ☐ 116 | Manny Lee | .02 | .10 |
| ☐ 117 | Nelson Liriano | .02 | .10 |
| ☐ 118 | Fred McGriff | .10 | .30 |
| ☐ 119 | Lloyd Moseby | .02 | .10 |
| ☐ 120 | Rance Mulliniks | .02 | .10 |
| ☐ 121 | Jeff Musselman | .02 | .10 |
| ☐ 122 | Jose Nunez | .02 | .10 |
| ☐ 123 | Dave Stieb | .05 | .15 |
| ☐ 124 | Willie Upshaw | .02 | .10 |
| ☐ 125 | Duane Ward | .02 | .10 |
| ☐ 126 | Ernie Whitt | .02 | .10 |
| ☐ 127 | Rick Aguilera | .02 | .10 |
| ☐ 128 | Wally Backman | .02 | .10 |
| ☐ 129 | Mark Carreon RC | .05 | .15 |
| ☐ 130 | Gary Carter | .05 | .15 |
| ☐ 131 | David Cone | .15 | .40 |
| ☐ 132 | Ron Darling | .05 | .15 |
| ☐ 133 | Len Dykstra | .05 | .15 |
| ☐ 134 | Sid Fernandez | .02 | .10 |
| ☐ 135 | Dwight Gooden | .05 | .15 |
| ☐ 136 | Keith Hernandez | .05 | .15 |
| ☐ 137 | Gregg Jefferies RC | .15 | .40 |
| ☐ 138 | Howard Johnson | .05 | .15 |
| ☐ 139 | Terry Leach | .02 | .10 |
| ☐ 140 | Barry Lyons | .02 | .10 |
| ☐ 141 | Dave Magadan | .05 | .15 |
| ☐ 142 | Roger McDowell | .02 | .10 |
| ☐ 143 | Kevin McReynolds | .02 | .10 |
| ☐ 144 | Keith Miller RC | .15 | .40 |
| ☐ 145 | John Mitchell RC | .05 | .15 |
| ☐ 146 | Randy Myers | .05 | .15 |
| ☐ 147 | Bob Ojeda | .02 | .10 |
| ☐ 148 | Jesse Orosco | .02 | .10 |
| ☐ 149 | Rafael Santana | .02 | .10 |
| ☐ 150 | Doug Sisk | .02 | .10 |
| ☐ 151 | Darryl Strawberry | .05 | .15 |
| ☐ 152 | Tim Teufel | .02 | .10 |
| ☐ 153 | Gene Walter | .02 | .10 |
| ☐ 154 | Mookie Wilson | .05 | .15 |
| ☐ 155 | Jay Aldrich | .02 | .10 |
| ☐ 156 | Chris Bosio | .05 | .15 |
| ☐ 157 | Glenn Braggs | .02 | .10 |
| ☐ 158 | Greg Brock | .02 | .10 |
| ☐ 159 | Juan Castillo | .02 | .10 |
| ☐ 160 | Mark Clear | .02 | .10 |
| ☐ 161 | Cecil Cooper | .05 | .15 |
| ☐ 162 | Chuck Crim | .02 | .10 |
| ☐ 163 | Rob Deer | .02 | .10 |
| ☐ 164 | Mike Felder | .02 | .10 |
| ☐ 165 | Jim Gantner | .02 | .10 |
| ☐ 166 | Ted Higuera | .02 | .10 |
| ☐ 167 | Steve Kiefer | .02 | .10 |
| ☐ 168 | Rick Manning | .02 | .10 |
| ☐ 169 | Paul Molitor | .05 | .15 |
| ☐ 170 | Juan Nieves | .02 | .10 |
| ☐ 171 | Dan Plesac | .02 | .10 |
| ☐ 172 | Earnest Riles | .02 | .10 |
| ☐ 173 | Bill Schroeder | .02 | .10 |
| ☐ 174 | Steve Stanicek | .02 | .10 |
| ☐ 175 | B.J. Surhoff | .05 | .15 |
| ☐ 176 | Dale Sveum | .02 | .10 |
| ☐ 177 | Bill Wegman | .02 | .10 |
| ☐ 178 | Robin Yount | .20 | .50 |
| ☐ 179 | Hubie Brooks | .02 | .10 |
| ☐ 180 | Tim Burke | .02 | .10 |
| ☐ 181 | Casey Candaele | .02 | .10 |
| ☐ 182 | Mike Fitzgerald | .02 | .10 |
| ☐ 183 | Tom Foley | .02 | .10 |
| ☐ 184 | Andres Galarraga | .05 | .15 |
| ☐ 185 | Neal Heaton | .02 | .10 |
| ☐ 186 | Wallace Johnson | .02 | .10 |
| ☐ 187 | Vance Law | .02 | .10 |
| ☐ 188 | Dennis Martinez | .05 | .15 |
| ☐ 189 | Bob McClure | .02 | .10 |
| ☐ 190 | Andy McGaffigan | .02 | .10 |
| ☐ 191 | Reid Nichols | .02 | .10 |
| ☐ 192 | Pascual Perez | .02 | .10 |
| ☐ 193 | Tim Raines | .05 | .15 |
| ☐ 194 | Jeff Reed | .02 | .10 |
| ☐ 195 | Bob Sebra | .02 | .10 |
| ☐ 196 | Bryn Smith | .02 | .10 |
| ☐ 197 | Randy St.Claire | .02 | .10 |
| ☐ 198 | Tim Wallach | .02 | .10 |
| ☐ 199 | Mitch Webster | .02 | .10 |
| ☐ 200 | Herm Winningham | .02 | .10 |
| ☐ 201 | Floyd Youmans | .02 | .10 |
| ☐ 202 | Brad Arnsberg | .02 | .10 |
| ☐ 203 | Rick Cerone | .02 | .10 |
| ☐ 204 | Pat Clements | .02 | .10 |
| ☐ 205 | Henry Cotto | .02 | .10 |
| ☐ 206 | Mike Easler | .02 | .10 |
| ☐ 207 | Ron Guidry | .05 | .15 |
| ☐ 208 | Bill Gullickson | .02 | .10 |
| ☐ 209 | Rickey Henderson | .10 | .30 |
| ☐ 210 | Charles Hudson | .02 | .10 |
| ☐ 211 | Tommy John | .05 | .15 |
| ☐ 212 | Roberto Kelly RC | .15 | .40 |
| ☐ 213 | Ron Kittle | .02 | .10 |
| ☐ 214 | Don Mattingly | .40 | 1.00 |
| ☐ 215 | Bobby Meacham | .02 | .10 |
| ☐ 216 | Mike Pagliarulo | .02 | .10 |
| ☐ 217 | Dan Pasqua | .02 | .10 |
| ☐ 218 | Willie Randolph | .05 | .15 |
| ☐ 219 | Rick Rhoden | .02 | .10 |
| ☐ 220 | Dave Righetti | .05 | .15 |
| ☐ 221 | Jerry Royster | .02 | .10 |
| ☐ 222 | Tim Stoddard | .02 | .10 |
| ☐ 223 | Wayne Tolleson | .02 | .10 |
| ☐ 224 | Gary Ward | .02 | .10 |
| ☐ 225 | Claudell Washington | .05 | .15 |
| ☐ 226 | Dave Winfield | .05 | .15 |
| ☐ 227 | Buddy Bell | .05 | .15 |
| ☐ 228 | Tom Browning | .02 | .10 |
| ☐ 229 | Dave Concepcion | .05 | .15 |
| ☐ 230 | Kal Daniels | .02 | .10 |
| ☐ 231 | Eric Davis | .05 | .15 |
| ☐ 232 | Bo Diaz | .02 | .10 |
| ☐ 233 | Nick Esasky | .02 | .10 |
| (Has a dollar sign before '87 SB tot | | .02 | .10 |
| ☐ 234 | John Franco | .05 | .15 |
| ☐ 235 | Guy Hoffman | .02 | .10 |
| ☐ 236 | Tom Hume | .02 | .10 |
| ☐ 237 | Tracy Jones | .02 | .10 |
| ☐ 238 | Bill Landrum | .02 | .10 |
| ☐ 239 | Barry Larkin | .07 | .20 |
| ☐ 240 | Terry McGriff | .02 | .10 |
| ☐ 241 | Rob Murphy | .02 | .10 |
| ☐ 242 | Ron Oester | .02 | .10 |
| ☐ 243 | Dave Parker | .05 | .15 |
| ☐ 244 | Pat Perry | .02 | .10 |
| ☐ 245 | Ted Power | .02 | .10 |
| ☐ 246 | Dennis Rasmussen | .02 | .10 |
| ☐ 247 | Ron Robinson | .02 | .10 |
| ☐ 248 | Kurt Stillwell | .02 | .10 |
| ☐ 249 | Jeff Treadway RC | .15 | .40 |
| ☐ 250 | Frank Williams | .02 | .10 |
| ☐ 251 | Steve Balboni | .02 | .10 |
| ☐ 252 | Bud Black | .02 | .10 |
| ☐ 253 | Thad Bosley | .02 | .10 |
| ☐ 254 | George Brett | .30 | .75 |
| ☐ 255 | John Davis | .02 | .10 |
| ☐ 256 | Steve Farr | .02 | .10 |
| ☐ 257 | Gene Garber | .02 | .10 |
| ☐ 258 | Jerry Don Gleaton | .02 | .10 |
| ☐ 259 | Mark Gubicza | .02 | .10 |
| ☐ 260 | Bo Jackson | .10 | .30 |
| ☐ 261 | Danny Jackson | .02 | .10 |
| ☐ 262 | Ross Jones | .02 | .10 |
| ☐ 263 | Charlie Leibrandt | .02 | .10 |
| ☐ 264 | Bill Pecota RC* | .05 | .15 |
| ☐ 265 | Melido Perez RC | .15 | .40 |
| ☐ 266 | Jamie Quirk | .02 | .10 |
| ☐ 267 | Dan Quisenberry | .02 | .10 |
| ☐ 268 | Bret Saberhagen | .05 | .15 |
| ☐ 269 | Angel Salazar | .02 | .10 |
| ☐ 270 | Kevin Seitzer UER (Wrong birth year) | .05 | .15 |
| ☐ 271 | Danny Tartabull | .02 | .10 |
| ☐ 272 | Gary Thurman | .02 | .10 |
| ☐ 273 | Frank White | .05 | .15 |
| ☐ 274 | Willie Wilson | .05 | .15 |
| ☐ 275 | Tony Bernazard | .02 | .10 |
| ☐ 276 | Jose Canseco | .30 | .75 |
| ☐ 277 | Mike Davis | .02 | .10 |
| ☐ 278 | Storm Davis | .02 | .10 |
| ☐ 279 | Dennis Eckersley | .07 | .20 |
| ☐ 280 | Alfredo Griffin | .02 | .10 |
| ☐ 281 | Rick Honeycutt | .02 | .10 |
| ☐ 282 | Jay Howell | .02 | .10 |
| ☐ 283 | Reggie Jackson | .07 | .20 |
| ☐ 284 | Dennis Lamp | .02 | .10 |
| ☐ 285 | Carney Lansford | .05 | .15 |
| ☐ 286 | Mark McGwire | 1.00 | 2.50 |
| ☐ 287 | Dwayne Murphy | .02 | .10 |
| ☐ 288 | Gene Nelson | .02 | .10 |
| ☐ 289 | Steve Ontiveros | .02 | .10 |
| ☐ 290 | Tony Phillips | .02 | .10 |
| ☐ 291 | Eric Plunk | .02 | .10 |
| ☐ 292 | Luis Polonia RC* | .15 | .40 |
| ☐ 293 | Rick Rodriguez | .02 | .10 |
| ☐ 294 | Terry Steinbach | .05 | .15 |
| ☐ 295 | Dave Stewart | .05 | .15 |
| ☐ 296 | Curt Young | .02 | .10 |
| ☐ 297 | Luis Aguayo | .02 | .10 |
| ☐ 298 | Steve Bedrosian | .02 | .10 |
| ☐ 299 | Jeff Calhoun | .02 | .10 |
| ☐ 300 | Don Carman | .02 | .10 |
| ☐ 301 | Todd Frohwirth | .02 | .10 |
| ☐ 302 | Greg Gross | .02 | .10 |
| ☐ 303 | Kevin Gross | .02 | .10 |
| ☐ 304 | Von Hayes | .02 | .10 |
| ☐ 305 | Keith Hughes | .02 | .10 |
| ☐ 306 | Mike Jackson RC* | .15 | .40 |
| ☐ 307 | Chris James | .02 | .10 |
| ☐ 308 | Steve Jeltz | .02 | .10 |
| ☐ 309 | Mike Maddux | .02 | .10 |
| ☐ 310 | Lance Parrish | .05 | .15 |
| ☐ 311 | Shane Rawley | .02 | .10 |
| ☐ 312 | Wally Ritchie | .02 | .10 |
| ☐ 313 | Bruce Ruffin | .02 | .10 |
| ☐ 314 | Juan Samuel | .05 | .15 |
| ☐ 315 | Mike Schmidt | .30 | .75 |
| ☐ 316 | Rick Schu | .02 | .10 |
| ☐ 317 | Jeff Stone | .02 | .10 |
| ☐ 318 | Kent Tekulve | .02 | .10 |

|  |  | | |
|---|---|---|---|
| 319 | Milt Thompson | .02 | .10 |
| 320 | Glenn Wilson | .02 | .10 |
| 321 | Rafael Belliard | .02 | .10 |
| 322 | Barry Bonds | 1.00 | 2.50 |
| 323 | Bobby Bonilla | .05 | .15 |
| 324 | Sid Bream | .02 | .10 |
| 325 | John Cangelosi | .02 | .10 |
| 326 | Mike Diaz | .02 | .10 |
| 327 | Doug Drabek | .02 | .10 |
| 328 | Mike Dunne | .02 | .10 |
| 329 | Brian Fisher | .02 | .10 |
| 330 | Brett Gideon | .02 | .10 |
| 331 | Terry Harper | .02 | .10 |
| 332 | Bob Kipper | .02 | .10 |
| 333 | Mike LaValliere | .02 | .10 |
| 334 | Jose Lind RC | .15 | .40 |
| 335 | Junior Ortiz | .02 | .10 |
| 336 | Vicente Palacios | .02 | .10 |
| 337 | Bob Patterson | .02 | .10 |
| 338 | Al Pedrique | .02 | .10 |
| 339 | R.J. Reynolds | .02 | .10 |
| 340 | John Smiley RC* | .15 | .40 |
| 341 | Andy Van Slyke UER (Wrong batting and throwing ) | .07 | .20 |
| 342 | Bob Walk | .02 | .10 |
| 343 | Marty Barrett | .02 | .10 |
| 344 | Todd Benzinger RC* | .15 | .40 |
| 345 | Wade Boggs | .07 | .20 |
| 346 | Tom Bolton | .02 | .10 |
| 347 | Oil Can Boyd | .02 | .10 |
| 348 | Ellis Burks RC | .20 | .50 |
| 349 | Roger Clemens | .60 | 1.50 |
| 350 | Steve Crawford | .02 | .10 |
| 351 | Dwight Evans | .07 | .20 |
| 352 | Wes Gardner | .02 | .10 |
| 353 | Rich Gedman | .02 | .10 |
| 354 | Mike Greenwell | .05 | .15 |
| 355 | Sam Horn RC | .05 | .15 |
| 356 | Bruce Hurst | .02 | .10 |
| 357 | John Marzano | .02 | .10 |
| 358 | Al Nipper | .02 | .10 |
| 359 | Spike Owen | .02 | .10 |
| 360 | Jody Reed RC | .15 | .40 |
| 361 | Jim Rice | .05 | .15 |
| 362 | Ed Romero | .02 | .10 |
| 363 | Kevin Romine | .02 | .10 |
| 364 | Joe Sambito | .02 | .10 |
| 365 | Calvin Schiraldi | .02 | .10 |
| 366 | Jeff Sellers | .02 | .10 |
| 367 | Bob Stanley | .02 | .10 |
| 368 | Scott Bankhead | .02 | .10 |
| 369 | Phil Bradley | .02 | .10 |
| 370 | Scott Bradley | .02 | .10 |
| 371 | Mickey Brantley | .02 | .10 |
| 372 | Mike Campbell | .02 | .10 |
| 373 | Alvin Davis | .02 | .10 |
| 374 | Lee Guetterman | .02 | .10 |
| 375 | Dave Hengel | .02 | .10 |
| 376 | Mike Kingery | .02 | .10 |
| 377 | Mark Langston | .02 | .10 |
| 378 | Edgar Martinez RC* | 2.00 | 5.00 |
| 379 | Mike Moore | .02 | .10 |
| 380 | Mike Morgan | .02 | .10 |
| 381 | John Moses | .02 | .10 |
| 382 | Donell Nixon | .02 | .10 |
| 383 | Edwin Nunez | .02 | .10 |
| 384 | Ken Phelps | .02 | .10 |
| 385 | Jim Presley | .02 | .10 |
| 386 | Rey Quinones | .02 | .10 |
| 387 | Jerry Reed | .02 | .10 |
| 388 | Harold Reynolds | .05 | .15 |
| 389 | Dave Valle | .02 | .10 |
| 390 | Bill Wilkinson | .02 | .10 |
| 391 | Harold Baines | .05 | .15 |
| 392 | Floyd Bannister | .02 | .10 |
| 393 | Daryl Boston | .02 | .10 |
| 394 | Ivan Calderon | .02 | .10 |
| 395 | Jose DeLeon | .02 | .10 |
| 396 | Richard Dotson | .02 | .10 |
| 397 | Carlton Fisk | .07 | .20 |
| 398 | Ozzie Guillen | .05 | .15 |
| 399 | Ron Hassey | .02 | .10 |
| 400 | Donnie Hill | .02 | .10 |
| 401 | Bob James | .02 | .10 |
| 402 | Dave LaPoint | .02 | .10 |
| 403 | Bill Lindsey | .02 | .10 |
| 404 | Bill Long | .02 | .10 |
| 405 | Steve Lyons | .02 | .10 |
| 406 | Fred Manrique | .02 | .10 |
| 407 | Jack McDowell RC | .20 | .50 |
| 408 | Gary Redus | .02 | .10 |
| 409 | Ray Searage | .02 | .10 |
| 410 | Bobby Thigpen | .02 | .10 |
| 411 | Greg Walker | .02 | .10 |
| 412 | Ken Williams | .02 | .10 |
| 413 | Jim Winn | .02 | .10 |
| 414 | Jody Davis | .02 | .10 |
| 415 | Andre Dawson | .05 | .15 |
| 416 | Brian Dayett | .02 | .10 |
| 417 | Bob Dernier | .02 | .10 |
| 418 | Frank DiPino | .02 | .10 |
| 419 | Shawon Dunston | .05 | .15 |
| 420 | Leon Durham | .02 | .10 |
| 421 | Les Lancaster | .02 | .10 |
| 422 | Ed Lynch | .02 | .10 |
| 423 | Greg Maddux | .60 | 1.50 |
| 424 | Dave Martinez | .02 | .10 |
| 425A | Keith Moreland ERR | .60 | 1.50 |
| 425B | Keith Moreland COR (Bat on shoulder) | .05 | .15 |
| 426 | Jamie Moyer | .05 | .15 |
| 427 | Jerry Mumphrey | .02 | .10 |
| 428 | Paul Noce | .02 | .10 |
| 429 | Rafael Palmeiro | .25 | .60 |
| 430 | Wade Rowdon | .02 | .10 |
| 431 | Ryne Sandberg | .25 | .60 |
| 432 | Scott Sanderson | .02 | .10 |
| 433 | Lee Smith | .05 | .15 |
| 434 | Jim Sundberg | .02 | .10 |
| 435 | Rick Sutcliffe | .05 | .15 |
| 436 | Manny Trillo | .02 | .10 |
| 437 | Juan Agosto | .02 | .10 |
| 438 | Larry Andersen | .02 | .10 |
| 439 | Alan Ashby | .02 | .10 |
| 440 | Kevin Bass | .02 | .10 |
| 441 | Ken Caminiti RC | 1.25 | 3.00 |
| 442 | Rocky Childress | .05 | .15 |
| 443 | Jose Cruz | .05 | .15 |
| 444 | Danny Darwin | .02 | .10 |
| 445 | Glenn Davis | .05 | .15 |
| 446 | Jim Deshaies | .02 | .10 |
| 447 | Bill Doran | .02 | .10 |
| 448 | Ty Gainey | .02 | .10 |
| 449 | Billy Hatcher | .02 | .10 |
| 450 | Jeff Heathcock | .02 | .10 |
| 451 | Bob Knepper | .02 | .10 |
| 452 | Rob Mallicoat | .02 | .10 |
| 453 | Dave Meads | .02 | .10 |
| 454 | Craig Reynolds | .02 | .10 |
| 455 | Nolan Ryan | .60 | 1.50 |
| 456 | Mike Scott | .05 | .15 |
| 457 | Dave Smith | .02 | .10 |
| 458 | Denny Walling | .02 | .10 |
| 459 | Robbie Wine | .02 | .10 |
| 460 | Gerald Young | .02 | .10 |
| 461 | Bob Brower | .02 | .10 |
| 462A | Jerry Browne ERR | .60 | 1.50 |
| 462B | Jerry Browne COR (Black player) | .05 | .15 |
| 463 | Steve Buechele | .02 | .10 |
| 464 | Edwin Correa | .02 | .10 |
| 465 | Cecil Espy RC | .05 | .15 |
| 466 | Scott Fletcher | .02 | .10 |
| 467 | Jose Guzman | .02 | .10 |
| 468 | Greg Harris | .02 | .10 |
| 469 | Charlie Hough | .05 | .15 |
| 470 | Pete Incaviglia | .02 | .10 |
| 471 | Paul Kilgus | .02 | .10 |
| 472 | Mike Loynd | .02 | .10 |
| 473 | Oddibe McDowell | .02 | .10 |
| 474 | Dale Mohorcic | .02 | .10 |
| 475 | Pete O'Brien | .02 | .10 |
| 476 | Larry Parrish | .02 | .10 |
| 477 | Geno Petralli | .02 | .10 |
| 478 | Jeff Russell | .02 | .10 |
| 479 | Ruben Sierra | .15 | .40 |
| 480 | Mike Stanley | .02 | .10 |
| 481 | Curtis Wilkerson | .02 | .10 |
| 482 | Mitch Williams | .05 | .15 |
| 483 | Bobby Witt | .05 | .15 |
| 484 | Tony Armas | .05 | .15 |
| 485 | Bob Boone | .05 | .15 |
| 486 | Bill Buckner | .02 | .10 |
| 487 | DeWayne Buice | .02 | .10 |
| 488 | Brian Downing | .05 | .15 |
| 489 | Chuck Finley | .05 | .15 |
| 490 | Willie Fraser UER (Wrong bio stats& for George H) | .02 | .10 |
| 491 | Jack Howell | .02 | .10 |
| 492 | Ruppert Jones | .02 | .10 |
| 493 | Wally Joyner | .05 | .15 |
| 494 | Jack Lazorko | .02 | .10 |
| 495 | Gary Lucas | .02 | .10 |
| 496 | Kirk McCaskill | .02 | .10 |
| 497 | Mark McLemore | .02 | .10 |
| 498 | Darrell Miller | .02 | .10 |
| 499 | Greg Minton | .02 | .10 |
| 500 | Donnie Moore | .02 | .10 |
| 501 | Gus Polidor | .02 | .10 |
| 502 | Johnny Ray | .02 | .10 |
| 503 | Mark Ryal | .02 | .10 |
| 504 | Dick Schofield | .02 | .10 |
| 505 | Don Sutton | .05 | .15 |
| 506 | Devon White | .05 | .15 |
| 507 | Mike Witt | .02 | .10 |
| 508 | Dave Anderson | .02 | .10 |
| 509 | Tim Belcher | .05 | .15 |
| 510 | Ralph Bryant | .02 | .10 |
| 511 | Tim Crews RC | .15 | .40 |
| 512 | Mike Devereaux RC | .15 | .40 |
| 513 | Mariano Duncan | .02 | .10 |
| 514 | Pedro Guerrero | .05 | .15 |
| 515 | Jeff Hamilton | .02 | .10 |
| 516 | Mickey Hatcher | .02 | .10 |
| 517 | Brad Havens | .02 | .10 |
| 518 | Orel Hershiser | .05 | .15 |
| 519 | Shawn Hillegas | .02 | .10 |
| 520 | Ken Howell | .02 | .10 |
| 521 | Tim Leary | .02 | .10 |
| 522 | Mike Marshall | .02 | .10 |
| 523 | Steve Sax | .05 | .15 |
| 524 | Mike Scioscia | .05 | .15 |
| 525 | Mike Sharperson | .02 | .10 |
| 526 | John Shelby | .02 | .10 |
| 527 | Franklin Stubbs | .02 | .10 |
| 528 | Fernando Valenzuela | .05 | .15 |
| 529 | Bob Welch | .05 | .15 |
| 530 | Matt Young | .02 | .10 |
| 531 | Jim Acker | .02 | .10 |
| 532 | Paul Assenmacher | .02 | .10 |
| 533 | Jeff Blauer RC | .15 | .40 |
| 534 | Joe Boever | .02 | .10 |
| 535 | Martin Clary | .02 | .10 |
| 536 | Kevin Coffman | .02 | .10 |
| 537 | Jeff Dedmon | .02 | .10 |
| 538 | Ron Gant RC | .20 | .50 |
| 539 | Tom Glavine RC | 1.50 | 4.00 |
| 540 | Ken Griffey | .05 | .15 |
| 541 | Albert Hall | .02 | .10 |
| 542 | Glenn Hubbard | .02 | .10 |
| 543 | Dion James | .02 | .10 |
| 544 | Dale Murphy | .07 | .20 |
| 545 | Ken Oberkfell | .02 | .10 |
| 546 | David Palmer | .02 | .10 |
| 547 | Gerald Perry | .02 | .10 |
| 548 | Charlie Puleo | .02 | .10 |
| 549 | Ted Simmons | .05 | .15 |
| 550 | Zane Smith | .02 | .10 |
| 551 | Andres Thomas | .02 | .10 |
| 552 | Ozzie Virgil | .02 | .10 |
| 553 | Don Aase | .02 | .10 |
| 554 | Jeff Ballard | .02 | .10 |
| 555 | Eric Bell | .02 | .10 |
| 556 | Mike Boddicker | .02 | .10 |
| 557 | Ken Dixon | .02 | .10 |
| 558 | Jim Dwyer | .02 | .10 |
| 559 | Ken Gerhart | .02 | .10 |
| 560 | Rene Gonzales RC | .02 | .10 |
| 561 | Mike Griffin | .02 | .10 |
| 562 | John Habyan UER (Misspelled Hayban on both sides) | .02 | .10 |
| 563 | Terry Kennedy | .02 | .10 |
| 564 | Ray Knight | .05 | .15 |
| 565 | Lee Lacy | .02 | .10 |
| 566 | Fred Lynn | .05 | .15 |
| 567 | Eddie Murray | .10 | .30 |
| 568 | Tom Niedenfuer | .02 | .10 |
| 569 | Cal Ripken RC* | .15 | .40 |
| 570 | Cal Ripken | .50 | 1.25 |
| 571 | Dave Schmidt | .02 | .10 |
| 572 | Larry Sheets | .02 | .10 |

|  |  | | |
|---|---|---|---|
| 573 | Pete Stanicek | .02 | .10 |
| 574 | Mark Williamson | .02 | .10 |
| 575 | Mike Young | .02 | .10 |
| 576 | Shawn Abner | .02 | .10 |
| 577 | Greg Booker | .02 | .10 |
| 578 | Chris Brown | .02 | .10 |
| 579 | Keith Comstock | .02 | .10 |
| 580 | Joey Cora RC | .15 | .40 |
| 581 | Mark Davis | .02 | .10 |
| 582 | Tim Flannery (With surfboard) | .07 | .20 |
| 583 | Goose Gossage | .05 | .15 |
| 584 | Mark Grant | .02 | .10 |
| 585 | Tony Gwynn | .20 | .50 |
| 586 | Andy Hawkins | .02 | .10 |
| 587 | Stan Jefferson | .02 | .10 |
| 588 | Jimmy Jones | .02 | .10 |
| 589 | John Kruk | .05 | .15 |
| 590 | Shane Mack | .02 | .10 |
| 591 | Carmelo Martinez | .02 | .10 |
| 592 | Lance McCullers UER (6'11 tall) | .02 | .10 |
| 593 | Eric Nolte | .02 | .10 |
| 594 | Randy Ready | .02 | .10 |
| 595 | Luis Salazar | .02 | .10 |
| 596 | Benito Santiago | .05 | .15 |
| 597 | Eric Show | .02 | .10 |
| 598 | Garry Templeton | .05 | .15 |
| 599 | Ed Whitson | .02 | .10 |
| 600 | Scott Bailes | .02 | .10 |
| 601 | Chris Bando | .02 | .10 |
| 602 | Jay Bell RC | .20 | .50 |
| 603 | Brett Butler | .05 | .15 |
| 604 | Tom Candiotti | .02 | .10 |
| 605 | Joe Carter | .05 | .15 |
| 606 | Carmen Castillo | .02 | .10 |
| 607 | Brian Dorsett | .05 | .15 |
| 608 | John Farrell RC | .05 | .15 |
| 609 | Julio Franco | .05 | .15 |
| 610 | Mel Hall | .02 | .10 |
| 611 | Tommy Hinzo | .02 | .10 |
| 612 | Brook Jacoby | .02 | .10 |
| 613 | Doug Jones RC | .15 | .40 |
| 614 | Ken Schrom | .02 | .10 |
| 615 | Cory Snyder | .02 | .10 |
| 616 | Sammy Stewart | .02 | .10 |
| 617 | Greg Swindell | .02 | .10 |
| 618 | Pat Tabler | .02 | .10 |
| 619 | Ed VandeBerg | .02 | .10 |
| 620 | Eddie Williams RC | .05 | .15 |
| 621 | Rich Yett | .02 | .10 |
| 622 | Slugging Sophomores Wally Joyner Cory Snyder | .05 | .15 |
| 623 | Dominican Dynamite George Bell Pedro Guerrero | .02 | .10 |
| 624 | M.McGwire/J.Canseco | .60 | 1.50 |
| 625 | Classic Relief Dave Righetti Dan Plesac | .02 | .10 |
| 626 | All Star Righties Bret Saberhagen Mike Witt Jac | .05 | .15 |
| 627 | Game Closers John Franco Steve Bedrosian | .02 | .10 |
| 628 | O.Smith/R.Sandberg | .10 | .30 |
| 629 | Mark McGwire HL | .50 | 1.25 |
| 630 | Greenwell/Burks/Benz | .10 | .30 |
| 631 | Tony Gwynn/T.Raines | .07 | .20 |
| 632 | Pitching Magic Mike Scott Orel Hershiser | .05 | .15 |
| 633 | M.McGwire/P.Tabler | .50 | 1.25 |
| 634 | Tony Gwynn/V.Coleman | .07 | .20 |
| 635 | C.Ripken/Trammell/Fern | .20 | .50 |
| 636 | Mike Schmidt/G.Carter | .10 | .30 |
| 637 | D.Strawberry/E.Davis | .05 | .15 |
| 638 | M.Nokes/K.Puckett | .07 | .20 |
| 639 | NL All-Stars Keith Hernandez Dale Murphy | .05 | .15 |
| 640 | Rookie Brothers | .30 | .75 |
| 641 | Mark Grace RC | 1.25 | 3.00 |
| 642 | D.Berryhill/J.Montgomery RC | .15 | .40 |
| 643 | F.Fermin/J.Reid RC | .05 | .15 |

|  |  | | |
|---|---|---|---|
| 644 | G.Myers/G.Tabor RC | .15 | .40 |
| 645 | J.Meyer/J.Eppard RC | .05 | .15 |
| 646 | A.Peterson RC/R.Velarde RC | .15 | .40 |
| 647 | P.Smith/C.Gwynn RC | .05 | .15 |
| 648 | T.Newell/G.Jelks RC | .05 | .15 |
| 649 | M.Diaz/C.Parker RC | .05 | .15 |
| 650 | J.Savage/T.Simmons RC | .05 | .15 |
| 651 | John Burkett RC | .15 | .40 |
| 652 | Walt Weiss RC | .20 | .50 |
| 653 | Jeff King RC | .15 | .40 |
| 654 | CL: Twins/Cards Tigers/Giants UER (90 Bob Melvin) | .02 | .10 |
| 655 | CL: Blue Jays/Mets Brewers/Expos UER (Mets liste | .02 | .10 |
| 656 | CL: Yankees/Reds Royals/A's | .02 | .10 |
| 657 | CL: Phillies/Pirates Red Sox/Mariners | .02 | .10 |
| 658 | CL: White Sox/Cubs Astros/Rangers | .02 | .10 |
| 659 | CL: Angels/Dodgers Braves/Orioles | .02 | .10 |
| 660 | CL: Padres/Indians Rookies/Specials | .02 | .10 |

## 1989 Fleer

| | | | |
|---|---|---|---|
| COMPLETE SET (660) | | 6.00 | 15.00 |
| COMP.FACT.SET (672) | | 6.00 | 15.00 |
| 1 | Don Baylor | .02 | .10 |
| 2 | Lance Blankenship RC | .02 | .10 |
| 3 | Todd Burns UER | .01 | .05 |
| 4 | Greg Cadaret UER | .01 | .05 |
| 5 | Jose Canseco | .08 | .25 |
| 6 | Storm Davis | .01 | .05 |
| 7 | Dennis Eckersley | .05 | .15 |
| 8 | Mike Gallego | .01 | .05 |
| 9 | Ron Hassey | .01 | .05 |
| 10 | Dave Henderson | .01 | .05 |
| 11 | Rick Honeycutt | .01 | .05 |
| 12 | Glenn Hubbard | .01 | .05 |
| 13 | Stan Javier | .01 | .05 |
| 14 | Doug Jennings | .01 | .05 |
| 15 | Felix Jose RC | .02 | .10 |
| 16 | Carney Lansford | .01 | .05 |
| 17 | Mark McGwire | .40 | 1.00 |
| 18 | Gene Nelson | .01 | .05 |
| 19 | Dave Parker | .01 | .05 |
| 20 | Eric Plunk | .01 | .05 |
| 21 | Luis Polonia | .01 | .05 |
| 22 | Terry Steinbach | .02 | .10 |
| 23 | Dave Stewart | .01 | .05 |
| 24 | Walt Weiss | .01 | .05 |
| 25 | Bob Welch | .01 | .05 |
| 26 | Curt Young | .01 | .05 |
| 27 | Rick Aguilera | .01 | .05 |
| 28 | Wally Backman | .01 | .05 |
| 29 | Mark Carreon UER | .01 | .05 |
| 30 | Gary Carter | .02 | .10 |
| 31 | David Cone | .02 | .10 |
| 32 | Ron Darling | .02 | .10 |
| 33 | Len Dykstra | .02 | .10 |
| 34 | Kevin Elster | .01 | .05 |
| 35 | Sid Fernandez | .01 | .05 |
| 36 | Dwight Gooden | .02 | .10 |
| 37 | Keith Hernandez | .02 | .10 |
| 38 | Gregg Jefferies | .01 | .05 |
| 39 | Howard Johnson | .02 | .10 |
| 40 | Terry Leach | .01 | .05 |
| 41 | Dave Magadan UER | .01 | .05 |
| 42 | Bob McClure | .01 | .05 |
| 43 | Roger McDowell UER | .01 | .05 |
| 44 | Kevin McReynolds | .01 | .05 |

|  |  | | |
|---|---|---|---|
| 45 | Keith A. Miller | .01 | .05 |
| 46 | Randy Myers | .02 | .05 |
| 47 | Bob Ojeda | .01 | .05 |
| 48 | Mackey Sasser | .01 | .05 |
| 49 | Darryl Strawberry | .02 | .10 |
| 50 | Tim Teufel | .01 | .05 |
| 51 | Dave West RC | .02 | .10 |
| 52 | Mookie Wilson | .02 | .10 |
| 53 | Dave Anderson | .01 | .05 |
| 54 | Tim Belcher | .01 | .05 |
| 55 | Mike Davis | .01 | .05 |
| 56 | Mike Devereaux | .02 | .10 |
| 57 | Kirk Gibson | .02 | .10 |
| 58 | Alfredo Griffin | .01 | .05 |
| 59 | Chris Gwynn | .01 | .05 |
| 60 | Jeff Hamilton | .01 | .05 |
| 61A | Danny Heep ERR | .08 | .25 |
| 61B | Danny Heep COR | .02 | .10 |
| 62 | Orel Hershiser | .02 | .10 |
| 63 | Brian Holton | .01 | .05 |
| 64 | Jay Howell | .01 | .05 |
| 65 | Tim Leary | .01 | .05 |
| 66 | Mike Marshall | .01 | .05 |
| 67 | Ramon Martinez RC | .08 | .25 |
| 68 | Jesse Orosco | .01 | .05 |
| 69 | Alejandro Pena | .01 | .05 |
| 70 | Steve Sax | .01 | .05 |
| 71 | Mike Scioscia | .02 | .10 |
| 72 | Mike Sharperson | .01 | .05 |
| 73 | John Shelby | .01 | .05 |
| 74 | Franklin Stubbs | .01 | .05 |
| 75 | John Tudor | .02 | .10 |
| 76 | Fernando Valenzuela | .02 | .10 |
| 77 | Tracy Woodson | .01 | .05 |
| 78 | Marty Barrett | .01 | .05 |
| 79 | Todd Benzinger | .01 | .05 |
| 80 | Mike Boddicker UER | .01 | .05 |
| 81 | Wade Boggs | .05 | .15 |
| 82 | Oil Can Boyd | .01 | .05 |
| 83 | Ellis Burks | .02 | .10 |
| 84 | Rick Cerone | .01 | .05 |
| 85 | Roger Clemens | .40 | 1.00 |
| 86 | Steve Curry | .01 | .05 |
| 87 | Dwight Evans | .05 | .15 |
| 88 | Wes Gardner | .01 | .05 |
| 89 | Rich Gedman | .01 | .05 |
| 90 | Mike Greenwell | .01 | .05 |
| 91 | Bruce Hurst | .01 | .05 |
| 92 | Dennis Lamp | .01 | .05 |
| 93 | Spike Owen | .01 | .05 |
| 94 | Larry Parrish UER | .01 | .05 |
| 95 | Carlos Quintana RC | .02 | .10 |
| 96 | Jody Reed | .01 | .05 |
| 97 | Jim Rice | .02 | .10 |
| 98A | Kevin Romine ERR | .08 | .25 |
| 98B | Kevin Romine COR | .01 | .05 |
| 99 | Lee Smith | .02 | .10 |
| 100 | Mike Smithson | .01 | .05 |
| 101 | Bob Stanley | .01 | .05 |
| 102 | Allan Anderson | .01 | .05 |
| 103 | Keith Atherton | .01 | .05 |
| 104 | Juan Berenguer | .01 | .05 |
| 105 | Bert Blyleven | .02 | .10 |
| 106 | Eric Bullock UER | .01 | .05 |
| 107 | Randy Bush | .01 | .05 |
| 108 | John Christensen | .01 | .05 |
| 109 | Mark Davidson | .01 | .05 |
| 110 | Gary Gaetti | .01 | .05 |
| 111 | Greg Gagne | .01 | .05 |
| 112 | Dan Gladden | .01 | .05 |
| 113 | German Gonzalez | .01 | .05 |
| 114 | Brian Harper | .01 | .05 |
| 115 | Tom Herr | .01 | .05 |
| 116 | Kent Hrbek | .02 | .10 |
| 117 | Gene Larkin | .01 | .05 |
| 118 | Tim Laudner | .01 | .05 |
| 119 | Charlie Lea | .01 | .05 |
| 120 | Steve Lombardozzi | .01 | .05 |
| 121A | John Moses ERR | .08 | .25 |
| 121B | John Moses COR | .01 | .05 |
| 122 | Al Newman | .01 | .05 |
| 123 | Mark Portugal | .01 | .05 |
| 124 | Kirby Puckett | .08 | .25 |
| 125 | Jeff Reardon | .02 | .10 |
| 126 | Fred Toliver | .01 | .05 |
| 127 | Frank Viola | .02 | .10 |
| 128 | Doyle Alexander | .01 | .05 |
| 129 | Dave Bergman | .01 | .05 |

| | | | |
|---|---|---|---|
| ☐ 130A Tom Brookens ERR | .30 | .75 |
| ☐ 130B Tom Brookens COR | .01 | .05 |
| ☐ 131 Fred Gibson | .01 | .05 |
| ☐ 132A Mike Heath ERR | .30 | .75 |
| ☐ 132B Mike Heath COR | .01 | .05 |
| ☐ 133 Don Heinkel | .01 | .05 |
| ☐ 134 Mike Henneman | .01 | .05 |
| ☐ 135 Guillermo Hernandez | .01 | .05 |
| ☐ 136 Eric King | .01 | .05 |
| ☐ 137 Chet Lemon | .02 | .10 |
| ☐ 138 Fred Lynn UER | .02 | .10 |
| ☐ 139 Jack Morris | .02 | .10 |
| ☐ 140 Matt Nokes | .01 | .05 |
| ☐ 141 Gary Pettis | .01 | .05 |
| ☐ 142 Ted Power | .01 | .05 |
| ☐ 143 Jeff M. Robinson | .01 | .05 |
| ☐ 144 Luis Salazar | .01 | .05 |
| ☐ 145 Steve Searcy | .01 | .05 |
| ☐ 146 Pat Sheridan | .01 | .05 |
| ☐ 147 Frank Tanana | .02 | .10 |
| ☐ 148 Alan Trammell | .02 | .10 |
| ☐ 149 Walt Terrell | .01 | .05 |
| ☐ 150 Jim Walewander | .01 | .05 |
| ☐ 151 Lou Whitaker | .02 | .10 |
| ☐ 152 Tim Birtsas | .01 | .05 |
| ☐ 153 Tom Browning | .01 | .05 |
| ☐ 154 Keith Brown | .01 | .05 |
| ☐ 155 Norm Charlton RC | .08 | .25 |
| ☐ 156 Dave Concepcion | .02 | .10 |
| ☐ 157 Kal Daniels | .01 | .05 |
| ☐ 158 Eric Davis | .02 | .10 |
| ☐ 159 Bo Diaz | .01 | .05 |
| ☐ 160 Rob Dibble RC | .15 | .40 |
| ☐ 161 Nick Esasky | .01 | .05 |
| ☐ 162 John Franco | .02 | .10 |
| ☐ 163 Danny Jackson | .01 | .05 |
| ☐ 164 Barry Larkin | .05 | .15 |
| ☐ 165 Rob Murphy | .01 | .05 |
| ☐ 166 Paul O'Neill | .05 | .15 |
| ☐ 167 Jeff Reed | .01 | .05 |
| ☐ 168 Jose Rijo | .02 | .10 |
| ☐ 169 Ron Robinson | .01 | .05 |
| ☐ 170 Chris Sabo RC | .15 | .40 |
| ☐ 171 Candy Sierra | .01 | .05 |
| ☐ 172 Van Snider | .01 | .05 |
| ☐ 173A J.Treadway ERR Target | 10.00 | 25.00 |
| ☐ 173B Jeff Treadway No Target | .01 | .05 |
| ☐ 174 Frank Williams UER | .01 | .05 |
| ☐ 175 Herm Winningham | .01 | .05 |
| ☐ 176 Jim Adduci | .01 | .05 |
| ☐ 177 Don August | .01 | .05 |
| ☐ 178 Mike Birkbeck | .01 | .05 |
| ☐ 179 Chris Bosio | .01 | .05 |
| ☐ 180 Glenn Braggs | .01 | .05 |
| ☐ 181 Greg Brock | .01 | .05 |
| ☐ 182 Mark Clear | .01 | .05 |
| ☐ 183 Chuck Crim | .01 | .05 |
| ☐ 184 Rob Deer | .01 | .05 |
| ☐ 185 Tom Filer | .01 | .05 |
| ☐ 186 Jim Gantner | .01 | .05 |
| ☐ 187 Darryl Hamilton RC | .08 | .25 |
| ☐ 188 Ted Higuera | .01 | .05 |
| ☐ 189 Odell Jones | .01 | .05 |
| ☐ 190 Jeffrey Leonard | .01 | .05 |
| ☐ 191 Joey Meyer | .01 | .05 |
| ☐ 192 Paul Mirabella | .01 | .05 |
| ☐ 193 Paul Molitor | .02 | .10 |
| ☐ 194 Charlie O'Brien | .01 | .05 |
| ☐ 195 Dan Plesac | .01 | .05 |
| ☐ 196 Gary Sheffield RC | .60 | 1.50 |
| ☐ 197 B.J. Surhoff | .02 | .10 |
| ☐ 198 Dale Sveum | .01 | .05 |
| ☐ 199 Bill Wegman | .01 | .05 |
| ☐ 200 Robin Yount | .15 | .40 |
| ☐ 201 Rafael Bellard | .01 | .05 |
| ☐ 202 Barry Bonds | .60 | 1.50 |
| ☐ 203 Bobby Bonilla | .02 | .10 |
| ☐ 204 Sid Bream | .01 | .05 |
| ☐ 205 Benny Distefano | .01 | .05 |
| ☐ 206 Doug Drabek | .01 | .05 |
| ☐ 207 Mike Dunne | .01 | .05 |
| ☐ 208 Felix Fermin | .01 | .05 |
| ☐ 209 Brian Fisher | .01 | .05 |
| ☐ 210 Jim Gott | .01 | .05 |
| ☐ 211 Bob Kipper | .01 | .05 |
| ☐ 212 Dave LaPoint | .01 | .05 |
| ☐ 213 Mike LaValliere | .01 | .05 |
| ☐ 214 Jose Lind | .01 | .05 |

| | | |
|---|---|---|
| ☐ 215 Junior Ortiz | .01 | .05 |
| ☐ 216 Vicente Palacios | .01 | .05 |
| ☐ 217 Tom Prince | .01 | .05 |
| ☐ 218 Gary Redus | .01 | .05 |
| ☐ 219 R.J. Reynolds | .01 | .05 |
| ☐ 220 Jeff D. Robinson | .01 | .05 |
| ☐ 221 John Smiley | .01 | .05 |
| ☐ 222 Andy Van Slyke | .05 | .15 |
| ☐ 223 Bob Walk | .01 | .05 |
| ☐ 224 Glenn Wilson | .01 | .05 |
| ☐ 225 Jesse Barfield | .02 | .10 |
| ☐ 226 George Bell | .02 | .10 |
| ☐ 227 Pat Borders RC | .08 | .25 |
| ☐ 228 John Cerutti | .01 | .05 |
| ☐ 229 Jim Clancy | .01 | .05 |
| ☐ 230 Mark Eichhorn | .01 | .05 |
| ☐ 231 Tony Fernandez | .01 | .05 |
| ☐ 232 Cecil Fielder | .02 | .10 |
| ☐ 233 Mike Flanagan | .01 | .05 |
| ☐ 234 Kelly Gruber | .01 | .05 |
| ☐ 235 Tom Henke | .01 | .05 |
| ☐ 236 Jimmy Key | .02 | .10 |
| ☐ 237 Rick Leach | .01 | .05 |
| ☐ 238 Manny Lee UER | .01 | .05 |
| ☐ 239 Nelson Liriano | .01 | .05 |
| ☐ 240 Fred McGriff | .05 | .15 |
| ☐ 241 Lloyd Moseby | .01 | .05 |
| ☐ 242 Rance Mulliniks | .01 | .05 |
| ☐ 243 Jeff Musselman | .01 | .05 |
| ☐ 244 Dave Stieb | .02 | .10 |
| ☐ 245 Todd Stottlemyre | .01 | .05 |
| ☐ 246 Duane Ward | .01 | .05 |
| ☐ 247 David Wells | .02 | .10 |
| ☐ 248 Ernie Whitt UER | .01 | .05 |
| ☐ 249 Luis Aguayo | .01 | .05 |
| ☐ 250A Neil Allen ERR | .30 | .75 |
| ☐ 250B Neil Allen COR | .01 | .05 |
| ☐ 251 John Candelaria | .01 | .05 |
| ☐ 252 Jack Clark | .02 | .10 |
| ☐ 253 Richard Dotson | .01 | .05 |
| ☐ 254 Rickey Henderson | .08 | .25 |
| ☐ 255 Tommy John | .02 | .10 |
| ☐ 256 Roberto Kelly | .01 | .05 |
| ☐ 257 Al Leiter | .08 | .25 |
| ☐ 258 Don Mattingly | .25 | .60 |
| ☐ 259 Dale Mohorcic | .01 | .05 |
| ☐ 260 Hal Morris RC | .08 | .25 |
| ☐ 261 Scott Nielsen | .01 | .05 |
| ☐ 262 Mike Pagliarulo UER | .01 | .05 |
| ☐ 263 Hipolito Pena | .01 | .05 |
| ☐ 264 Ken Phelps | .01 | .05 |
| ☐ 265 Willie Randolph | .02 | .10 |
| ☐ 266 Rick Rhoden | .01 | .05 |
| ☐ 267 Dave Righetti | .02 | .10 |
| ☐ 268 Rafael Santana | .01 | .05 |
| ☐ 269 Steve Shields | .01 | .05 |
| ☐ 270 Joel Skinner | .01 | .05 |
| ☐ 271 Don Slaught | .01 | .05 |
| ☐ 272 Claudell Washington | .01 | .05 |
| ☐ 273 Gary Ward | .01 | .05 |
| ☐ 274 Dave Winfield | .02 | .10 |
| ☐ 275 Luis Aquino | .01 | .05 |
| ☐ 276 Floyd Bannister | .01 | .05 |
| ☐ 277 George Brett | .25 | .60 |
| ☐ 278 Bill Buckner | .02 | .10 |
| ☐ 279 Nick Capra | .01 | .05 |
| ☐ 280 Jose DeJesus | .01 | .05 |
| ☐ 281 Steve Farr | .01 | .05 |
| ☐ 282 Jerry Don Gleaton | .01 | .05 |
| ☐ 283 Mark Gubicza | .01 | .05 |
| ☐ 284 Tom Gordon RC | .20 | .50 |
| ☐ 285 Bo Jackson | .08 | .25 |
| ☐ 286 Charlie Leibrandt | .01 | .05 |
| ☐ 287 Mike Macfarlane RC | .08 | .25 |
| ☐ 288 Jeff Montgomery | .01 | .05 |
| ☐ 289 Bill Pecota UER | .01 | .05 |
| ☐ 290 Jamie Quirk | .01 | .05 |
| ☐ 291 Bret Saberhagen | .02 | .10 |
| ☐ 292 Kevin Seitzer | .01 | .05 |
| ☐ 293 Kurt Stillwell | .01 | .05 |
| ☐ 294 Pat Tabler | .01 | .05 |
| ☐ 295 Danny Tartabull | .02 | .10 |
| ☐ 296 Gary Thurman | .01 | .05 |
| ☐ 297 Frank White | .02 | .10 |
| ☐ 298 Willie Wilson | .02 | .10 |
| ☐ 299 Roberto Alomar | .08 | .25 |
| ☐ 300 Sandy Alomar Jr. RC | .15 | .40 |
| ☐ 301 Chris Brown | .01 | .05 |

| | | |
|---|---|---|
| ☐ 302 Mike Brumley UER | .01 | .05 |
| ☐ 303 Mark Davis | .01 | .05 |
| ☐ 304 Mark Grant | .01 | .05 |
| ☐ 305 Tony Gwynn | .10 | .30 |
| ☐ 306 Greg W.Harris RC | .02 | .10 |
| ☐ 307 Andy Hawkins | .01 | .05 |
| ☐ 308 Jimmy Jones | .01 | .05 |
| ☐ 309 John Kruk | .02 | .10 |
| ☐ 310 Dave Leiper | .01 | .05 |
| ☐ 311 Carmelo Martinez | .01 | .05 |
| ☐ 312 Lance McCullers | .01 | .05 |
| ☐ 313 Keith Moreland | .01 | .05 |
| ☐ 314 Dennis Rasmussen | .01 | .05 |
| ☐ 315 Randy Ready UER | .01 | .05 |
| ☐ 316 Benito Santiago | .02 | .10 |
| ☐ 317 Eric Show | .01 | .05 |
| ☐ 318 Todd Simmons | .01 | .05 |
| ☐ 319 Garry Templeton | .02 | .10 |
| ☐ 320 Dickie Thon | .01 | .05 |
| ☐ 321 Ed Whitson | .01 | .05 |
| ☐ 322 Marvell Wynne | .01 | .05 |
| ☐ 323 Mike Aldrete | .01 | .05 |
| ☐ 324 Brett Butler | .02 | .10 |
| ☐ 325 Will Clark | .05 | .15 |
| ☐ 326 Kelly Downs UER | .01 | .05 |
| ☐ 327 Dave Dravecky | .01 | .05 |
| ☐ 328 Scott Garrelts | .01 | .05 |
| ☐ 329 Atlee Hammaker | .01 | .05 |
| ☐ 330 Charlie Hayes RC | .08 | .25 |
| ☐ 331 Mike Krukow | .01 | .05 |
| ☐ 332 Craig Lefferts | .01 | .05 |
| ☐ 333 Candy Maldonado | .01 | .05 |
| ☐ 334 Kirt Manwaring UER | .01 | .05 |
| ☐ 335 Bob Melvin | .01 | .05 |
| ☐ 336 Kevin Mitchell | .02 | .10 |
| ☐ 337 Donell Nixon | .01 | .05 |
| ☐ 338 Tony Perezchica | .01 | .05 |
| ☐ 339 Joe Price | .01 | .05 |
| ☐ 340 Rick Reuschel | .02 | .10 |
| ☐ 341 Earnest Riles | .01 | .05 |
| ☐ 342 Don Robinson | .01 | .05 |
| ☐ 343 Chris Speier | .01 | .05 |
| ☐ 344 Robby Thompson UER | .01 | .05 |
| ☐ 345 Jose Uribe | .01 | .05 |
| ☐ 346 Matt Williams | .08 | .25 |
| ☐ 347 Trevor Wilson RC | .02 | .10 |
| ☐ 348 Juan Agosto | .01 | .05 |
| ☐ 349 Larry Andersen | .01 | .05 |
| ☐ 350A Alan Ashby ERR | .75 | 2.00 |
| ☐ 350B Alan Ashby COR | .01 | .05 |
| ☐ 351 Kevin Bass | .01 | .05 |
| ☐ 352 Buddy Bell | .02 | .10 |
| ☐ 353 Craig Biggio RC | 1.00 | 2.50 |
| ☐ 354 Danny Darwin | .01 | .05 |
| ☐ 355 Glenn Davis | .01 | .05 |
| ☐ 356 Jim Deshaies | .01 | .05 |
| ☐ 357 Bill Doran | .01 | .05 |
| ☐ 358 John Fishel | .01 | .05 |
| ☐ 359 Billy Hatcher | .01 | .05 |
| ☐ 360 Bob Knepper | .01 | .05 |
| ☐ 361 Louie Meadows UER | .01 | .05 |
| ☐ 362 Dave Meads | .01 | .05 |
| ☐ 363 Jim Pankovits | .01 | .05 |
| ☐ 364 Terry Puhl | .01 | .05 |
| ☐ 365 Rafael Ramirez | .01 | .05 |
| ☐ 366 Craig Reynolds | .01 | .05 |
| ☐ 367 Mike Scott | .02 | .10 |
| ☐ 368 Nolan Ryan | .40 | 1.00 |
| ☐ 369 Dave Smith | .01 | .05 |
| ☐ 370 Gerald Young | .01 | .05 |
| ☐ 371 Hubie Brooks | .01 | .05 |
| ☐ 372 Tim Burke | .01 | .05 |
| ☐ 373 John Dopson | .01 | .05 |
| ☐ 374 Mike R. Fitzgerald | .01 | .05 |
| ☐ 375 Tom Foley | .01 | .05 |
| ☐ 376 Andres Galarraga UER | .02 | .10 |
| ☐ 377 Neal Heaton | .01 | .05 |
| ☐ 378 Joe Hesketh | .01 | .05 |
| ☐ 379 Brian Holman RC | .02 | .10 |
| ☐ 380 Rex Hudler | .01 | .05 |
| ☐ 381 Randy Johnson RC | .75 | 2.00 |
| ☐ 381B R.Johnson Marlboro ERR | 10.00 | 25.00 |
| ☐ 382 Wallace Johnson | .01 | .05 |
| ☐ 383 Tracy Jones | .01 | .05 |
| ☐ 384 Dave Martinez | .01 | .05 |
| ☐ 385 Dennis Martinez | .02 | .10 |
| ☐ 386 Andy McGaffigan | .01 | .05 |
| ☐ 387 Otis Nixon | .01 | .05 |

|  |  | | |
|---|---|---|---|
| 388 | Johnny Paredes | .01 | .05 |
| 389 | Jeff Parrett | .01 | .05 |
| 390 | Pascual Perez | .01 | .05 |
| 391 | Tim Raines | .02 | .10 |
| 392 | Luis Rivera | .01 | .05 |
| 393 | Nelson Santovenia | .01 | .05 |
| 394 | Bryn Smith | .01 | .05 |
| 395 | Tim Wallach | .01 | .05 |
| 396 | Andy Allanson UER | .01 | .05 |
| 397 | Rod Allen | .01 | .05 |
| 398 | Scott Bailes | .01 | .05 |
| 399 | Tom Candiotti | .01 | .05 |
| 400 | Joe Carter | .02 | .10 |
| 401 | Carmen Castillo UER | .01 | .05 |
| 402 | Dave Clark UER# | .01 | .05 |
| 403 | John Farrell UER | .01 | .05 |
| 404 | Julio Franco | .02 | .10 |
| 405 | Don Gordon | .01 | .05 |
| 406 | Mel Hall | .01 | .05 |
| 407 | Brad Havens | .01 | .05 |
| 408 | Brook Jacoby | .01 | .05 |
| 409 | Doug Jones | .01 | .05 |
| 410 | Jeff Kaiser | .01 | .05 |
| 411 | Luis Medina | .01 | .05 |
| 412 | Cory Snyder | .01 | .05 |
| 413 | Greg Swindell | .01 | .05 |
| 414 | Ron Tingley UER | .01 | .05 |
| 415 | Willie Upshaw | .01 | .05 |
| 416 | Ron Washington | .01 | .05 |
| 417 | Rich Yett | .01 | .05 |
| 418 | Damon Berryhill | .01 | .05 |
| 419 | Mike Bielecki | .01 | .05 |
| 420 | Doug Dascenzo | .01 | .05 |
| 421 | Jody Davis UER | .01 | .05 |
| 422 | Andre Dawson | .02 | .10 |
| 423 | Frank DiPino | .01 | .05 |
| 424 | Shawon Dunston | .01 | .05 |
| 425 | Rich Gossage | .02 | .10 |
| 426 | Mark Grace | .08 | .25 |
| 427 | Mike Harkey RC | .02 | .10 |
| 428 | Darrin Jackson | .02 | .10 |
| 429 | Les Lancaster | .01 | .05 |
| 430 | Vance Law | .01 | .05 |
| 431 | Greg Maddux | .20 | .50 |
| 432 | Jamie Moyer | .02 | .10 |
| 433 | Al Nipper | .01 | .05 |
| 434 | Rafael Palmeiro | .08 | .25 |
| 435 | Pat Perry | .01 | .05 |
| 436 | Jeff Pico | .01 | .05 |
| 437 | Ryne Sandberg | .15 | .40 |
| 438 | Calvin Schiraldi | .01 | .05 |
| 439 | Rick Sutcliffe | .02 | .10 |
| 440A | Manny Trillo ERR | .75 | 2.00 |
| 440B | Manny Trillo COR | .01 | .05 |
| 441 | Gary Varsho UER | .01 | .05 |
| 442 | Mitch Webster | .01 | .05 |
| 443 | Luis Alicea RC | .08 | .25 |
| 444 | Tom Brunansky | .02 | .10 |
| 445 | Vince Coleman UER | .01 | .05 |
| 446 | John Costello UER | .01 | .05 |
| 447 | Danny Cox | .01 | .05 |
| 448 | Ken Dayley | .01 | .05 |
| 449 | Jose DeLeon | .01 | .05 |
| 450 | Curt Ford | .01 | .05 |
| 451 | Pedro Guerrero | .02 | .10 |
| 452 | Bob Horner | .02 | .10 |
| 453 | Tim Jones | .01 | .05 |
| 454 | Steve Lake | .01 | .05 |
| 455 | Joe Magrane UER | .01 | .05 |
| 456 | Greg Mathews | .01 | .05 |
| 457 | Willie McGee | .02 | .10 |
| 458 | Larry McWilliams | .01 | .05 |
| 459 | Jose Oquendo | .01 | .05 |
| 460 | Tony Pena | .01 | .05 |
| 461 | Terry Pendleton | .02 | .10 |
| 462 | Steve Peters UER | .01 | .05 |
| 463 | Ozzie Smith | .15 | .40 |
| 464 | Scott Terry | .01 | .05 |
| 465 | Denny Walling | .01 | .05 |
| 466 | Todd Worrell | .01 | .05 |
| 467 | Tony Armas UER | .02 | .10 |
| 468 | Dante Bichette RC | .15 | .40 |
| 469 | Bob Boone | .02 | .10 |
| 470 | Terry Clark | .01 | .05 |
| 471 | Stu Cliburn | .01 | .05 |
| 472 | Mike Cook UER | .01 | .05 |
| 473 | Sherman Corbett | .01 | .05 |
| 474 | Chili Davis | .02 | .10 |
| 475 | Brian Downing | .02 | .10 |
| 476 | Jim Eppard | .01 | .05 |
| 477 | Chuck Finley | .02 | .10 |
| 478 | Willie Fraser | .01 | .05 |
| 479 | Bryan Harvey UER RC | .08 | .25 |
| 480 | Jack Howell | .01 | .05 |
| 481 | Wally Joyner UER | .02 | .10 |
| 482 | Jack Lazorko | .01 | .05 |
| 483 | Kirk McCaskill | .01 | .05 |
| 484 | Mark McLemore | .01 | .05 |
| 485 | Greg Minton | .01 | .05 |
| 486 | Dan Petry | .01 | .05 |
| 487 | Johnny Ray | .01 | .05 |
| 488 | Dick Schofield | .01 | .05 |
| 489 | Devon White | .02 | .10 |
| 490 | Mike Witt | .01 | .05 |
| 491 | Harold Baines | .02 | .10 |
| 492 | Daryl Boston | .01 | .05 |
| 493 | Ivan Calderon UER | .01 | .05 |
| 494 | Mike Diaz | .01 | .05 |
| 495 | Carlton Fisk | .05 | .15 |
| 496 | Dave Gallagher | .01 | .05 |
| 497 | Ozzie Guillen | .02 | .10 |
| 498 | Shawn Hillegas | .01 | .05 |
| 499 | Lance Johnson | .01 | .05 |
| 500 | Barry Jones | .01 | .05 |
| 501 | Bill Long | .01 | .05 |
| 502 | Steve Lyons | .01 | .05 |
| 503 | Fred Manrique | .01 | .05 |
| 504 | Jack McDowell | .02 | .10 |
| 505 | Donn Pall | .01 | .05 |
| 506 | Kelly Paris | .01 | .05 |
| 507 | Dan Pasqua | .01 | .05 |
| 508 | Ken Patterson | .01 | .05 |
| 509 | Melido Perez | .01 | .05 |
| 510 | Jerry Reuss | .01 | .05 |
| 511 | Mark Salas | .01 | .05 |
| 512 | Bobby Thigpen UER | .01 | .05 |
| 513 | Mike Woodard | .01 | .05 |
| 514 | Bob Brower | .01 | .05 |
| 515 | Steve Buechele | .01 | .05 |
| 516 | Jose Cecena | .01 | .05 |
| 517 | Cecil Espy | .01 | .05 |
| 518 | Scott Fletcher | .01 | .05 |
| 519 | Cecilio Guante | .01 | .05 |
| 520 | Jose Guzman | .01 | .05 |
| 521 | Ray Hayward | .01 | .05 |
| 522 | Charlie Hough | .02 | .10 |
| 523 | Pete Incaviglia | .01 | .05 |
| 524 | Mike Jeffcoat | .01 | .05 |
| 525 | Paul Kilgus | .01 | .05 |
| 526 | Chad Kreuter RC | .08 | .25 |
| 527 | Jeff Kunkel | .01 | .05 |
| 528 | Oddibe McDowell | .01 | .05 |
| 529 | Pete O'Brien | .01 | .05 |
| 530 | Geno Petralli | .01 | .05 |
| 531 | Jeff Russell | .01 | .05 |
| 532 | Ruben Sierra | .02 | .10 |
| 533 | Mike Stanley | .01 | .05 |
| 534A | Ed VandeBerg ERR | .75 | 2.00 |
| 534B | Ed VandeBerg COR | .01 | .05 |
| 535 | Curtis Wilkerson ERR | .01 | .05 |
| 536 | Mitch Williams | .01 | .05 |
| 537 | Bobby Witt UER | .01 | .05 |
| 538 | Steve Balboni | .01 | .05 |
| 539 | Scott Bankhead | .01 | .05 |
| 540 | Scott Bradley | .01 | .05 |
| 541 | Mickey Brantley | .01 | .05 |
| 542 | Jay Buhner | .02 | .10 |
| 543 | Mike Campbell | .01 | .05 |
| 544 | Darnell Coles | .01 | .05 |
| 545 | Henry Cotto | .01 | .05 |
| 546 | Alvin Davis | .01 | .05 |
| 547 | Mario Diaz | .01 | .05 |
| 548 | Ken Griffey Jr. RC | 4.00 | 10.00 |
| 549 | Erik Hanson RC | .08 | .25 |
| 550 | Mike Jackson UER | .01 | .05 |
| 551 | Mark Langston | .02 | .10 |
| 552 | Edgar Martinez | .08 | .25 |
| 553 | Bill McGuire | .01 | .05 |
| 554 | Mike Moore | .01 | .05 |
| 555 | Jim Presley | .01 | .05 |
| 556 | Rey Quinones | .01 | .05 |
| 557 | Jerry Reed | .01 | .05 |
| 558 | Harold Reynolds | .02 | .10 |
| 559 | Mike Schooler | .01 | .05 |
| 560 | Bill Swift | .01 | .05 |
| 561 | Dave Valle | .01 | .05 |
| 562 | Steve Bedrosian | .01 | .05 |
| 563 | Phil Bradley | .01 | .05 |
| 564 | Don Carman | .01 | .05 |
| 565 | Bob Dernier | .01 | .05 |
| 566 | Marvin Freeman | .01 | .05 |
| 567 | Todd Frohwirth | .01 | .05 |
| 568 | Greg Gross | .01 | .05 |
| 569 | Kevin Gross | .01 | .05 |
| 570 | Greg A. Harris | .01 | .05 |
| 571 | Von Hayes | .01 | .05 |
| 572 | Chris James | .01 | .05 |
| 573 | Steve Jeltz | .01 | .05 |
| 574 | Ron Jones UER | .02 | .10 |
| 575 | Ricky Jordan RC | .08 | .25 |
| 576 | Mike Maddux | .01 | .05 |
| 577 | David Palmer | .01 | .05 |
| 578 | Lance Parrish | .02 | .10 |
| 579 | Shane Rawley | .01 | .05 |
| 580 | Bruce Ruffin | .01 | .05 |
| 581 | Juan Samuel | .01 | .05 |
| 582 | Mike Schmidt | .20 | .50 |
| 583 | Kent Tekulve | .01 | .05 |
| 584 | Milt Thompson UER | .01 | .05 |
| 585 | Jose Alvarez RC | .02 | .10 |
| 586 | Paul Assenmacher | .01 | .05 |
| 587 | Bruce Benedict | .01 | .05 |
| 588 | Jeff Blauser | .01 | .05 |
| 589 | Terry Blocker | .01 | .05 |
| 590 | Ron Gant | .02 | .10 |
| 591 | Tom Glavine | .08 | .25 |
| 592 | Tommy Gregg | .01 | .05 |
| 593 | Albert Hall | .01 | .05 |
| 594 | Dion James | .01 | .05 |
| 595 | Rick Mahler | .01 | .05 |
| 596 | Dale Murphy | .05 | .15 |
| 597 | Gerald Perry | .01 | .05 |
| 598 | Charlie Puleo | .01 | .05 |
| 599 | Ted Simmons | .02 | .10 |
| 600 | Pete Smith | .01 | .05 |
| 601 | Zane Smith | .01 | .05 |
| 602 | John Smoltz RC | .60 | 1.50 |
| 603 | Bruce Sutter | .02 | .10 |
| 604 | Andres Thomas | .01 | .05 |
| 605 | Ozzie Virgil | .01 | .05 |
| 606 | Brady Anderson RC | .15 | .40 |
| 607 | Jeff Ballard | .01 | .05 |
| 608 | Jose Bautista RC | .02 | .10 |
| 609 | Ken Gerhart | .01 | .05 |
| 610 | Terry Kennedy | .01 | .05 |
| 611 | Eddie Murray | .08 | .25 |
| 612 | Carl Nichols UER | .01 | .05 |
| 613 | Tom Niedenfuer | .01 | .05 |
| 614 | Joe Orsulak | .01 | .05 |
| 615 | Oswald Peraza UER | .01 | .05 |
| 616A | Bill Ripken Rick Face | 6.00 | 15.00 |
| 616B | Bill Ripken Whiteout | 60.00 | 120.00 |
| 616C | Bill Ripken White Scribble | 10.00 | 15.00 |
| 616D | Bill Ripken Black Scribble | 6.00 | 15.00 |
| 616E | Bill Ripken Black Box | 2.00 | 5.00 |
| 617 | Cal Ripken | .30 | .75 |
| 618 | Dave Schmidt | .01 | .05 |
| 619 | Rick Schu | .01 | .05 |
| 620 | Larry Sheets | .01 | .05 |
| 621 | Doug Sisk | .01 | .05 |
| 622 | Pete Stanicek | .01 | .05 |
| 623 | Mickey Tettleton | .01 | .05 |
| 624 | Jay Tibbs | .01 | .05 |
| 625 | Jim Traber | .01 | .05 |
| 626 | Mark Williamson | .01 | .05 |
| 627 | Craig Worthington | .01 | .05 |
| 628 | Jose Canseco 40/40 | .08 | .25 |
| 629 | Tom Browning Perfect | .01 | .05 |
| 630 | R.Alomar/S.Alomar | .08 | .25 |
| 631 | W.Clark/R.Palmeiro | .05 | .15 |
| 632 | D.Strawberry/W.Clark | .02 | .10 |
| 633 | W.Boggs/C.Lansford | .02 | .10 |
| 634 | McGwire/Cans/Stein | .30 | .75 |
| 635 | M.Davis/D.Gooden | .01 | .05 |
| 636 | D.Jackson/D.Cone UER | .01 | .05 |
| 637 | C.Sabo/B.Bonilla UER | .02 | .10 |
| 638 | A.Galarraga/G.Perry UER | .01 | .05 |
| 639 | K.Puckett/E.Davis | .05 | .15 |
| 640 | S.Wilson/C.Drew | .01 | .05 |
| 641 | K.Brown/K.Reimer | .08 | .25 |
| 642 | B.Pounders RC/J.Clark | .02 | .10 |
| 643 | M.Capel/D.Hall | .01 | .05 |
| 644 | J.Girardi RC/R.Roomes | .15 | .40 |
| 645 | L.Harris RC/M.Brown | .08 | .25 |

| | | |
|---|---|---|
| 646 L.De Los Santos/J.Campbell | .01 | .05 |
| 647 R.Kramer/M.Garcia | .01 | .05 |
| 648 T.Lovullo RC/R.Palacios | .02 | .10 |
| 649 J.Corsi/B.Milacki | .01 | .05 |
| 650 G.Hall/M.Rochford | .01 | .05 |
| 651 T.Taylor/V.Lovelace RC | .02 | .10 |
| 652 K.Hill RC/D.Cook | .08 | .25 |
| 653 S.Service/S.Turner | .01 | .05 |
| 654 CL: Oakland/Mets Dodgers/Red Sox (10 Henderson,r# | .01 | .05 |
| 655A CL: Twins/Tigers ERR Reds/Brewers (179 Bosio and | .01 | .05 |
| 655B CL: Twins/Tigers COR Reds/Brewers (179 Bosio but | | |
| 656 CL: Pirates/Blue Jays Yankees/Royals (225 Jess B | .01 | .05 |
| 657 CL: Padres/Giants Astros/Expos (367/368 wrong) | .01 | .05 |
| 658 CL: Indians/Cubs Cardinals/Angels (449 Deleon) | .01 | .05 |
| 659 CL: White Sox/Rangers Mariners/Phillies | .01 | .05 |
| 660 CL: Braves/Orioles Specials/Checklists (632 hyph | .01 | .05 |

## 1990 Fleer

| | | |
|---|---|---|
| COMPLETE SET (660) | 6.00 | 15.00 |
| COMP.RETAIL SET (660) | 6.00 | 15.00 |
| COMP.HOBBY SET (672) | 6.00 | 15.00 |
| 1 Lance Blankenship | .01 | .05 |
| 2 Todd Burns | .01 | .05 |
| 3 Jose Canseco | .05 | .15 |
| 4 Jim Corsi | .01 | .05 |
| 5 Storm Davis | .01 | .05 |
| 6 Dennis Eckersley | .02 | .10 |
| 7 Mike Gallego | .01 | .05 |
| 8 Ron Hassey | .01 | .05 |
| 9 Dave Henderson | .01 | .05 |
| 10 Rickey Henderson | .08 | .25 |
| 11 Rick Honeycutt | .01 | .05 |
| 12 Stan Javier | .01 | .05 |
| 13 Felix Jose | .05 | .15 |
| 14 Carney Lansford | .02 | .10 |
| 15 Mark McGwire | .40 | 1.00 |
| 16 Mike Moore | .01 | .05 |
| 17 Gene Nelson | .01 | .05 |
| 18 Dave Parker | .02 | .10 |
| 19 Tony Phillips | .01 | .05 |
| 20 Terry Steinbach | .02 | .10 |
| 21 Dave Stewart | .02 | .10 |
| 22 Walt Weiss | .01 | .05 |
| 23 Bob Welch | .01 | .05 |
| 24 Curt Young | .01 | .05 |
| 25 Paul Assenmacher | .01 | .05 |
| 26 Damon Berryhill | .01 | .05 |
| 27 Mike Bielecki | .01 | .05 |
| 28 Kevin Blankenship | .01 | .05 |
| 29 Andre Dawson | .02 | .10 |
| 30 Shawon Dunston | .01 | .05 |
| 31 Joe Girardi | .05 | .15 |
| 32 Mark Grace | .05 | .15 |
| 33 Mike Harkey | .01 | .05 |
| 34 Paul Kilgus | .01 | .05 |
| 35 Les Lancaster | .01 | .05 |
| 36 Vance Law | .01 | .05 |
| 37 Greg Maddux | .15 | .40 |
| 38 Lloyd McClendon | .01 | .05 |

| | | |
|---|---|---|
| 39 Jeff Pico | .01 | .05 |
| 40 Ryne Sandberg | .15 | .40 |
| 41 Scott Sanderson | .01 | .05 |
| 42 Dwight Smith | .01 | .05 |
| 43 Rick Sutcliffe | .02 | .10 |
| 44 Jerome Walton | .01 | .05 |
| 45 Mitch Webster | .01 | .05 |
| 46 Curt Wilkerson | .01 | .05 |
| 47 Dean Wilkins RC | .01 | .05 |
| 48 Mitch Williams | .01 | .05 |
| 49 Steve Wilson | .01 | .05 |
| 50 Steve Bedrosian | .01 | .05 |
| 51 Mike Benjamin | .02 | .10 |
| 52 Jeff Brantley | .01 | .05 |
| 53 Brett Butler | .02 | .10 |
| 54 Will Clark UER | .02 | .10 |
| 55 Kelly Downs | .01 | .05 |
| 56 Scott Garrelts | .01 | .05 |
| 57 Atlee Hammaker | .01 | .05 |
| 58 Terry Kennedy | .01 | .05 |
| 59 Mike LaCoss | .01 | .05 |
| 60 Craig Lefferts | .01 | .05 |
| 61 Greg Litton | .01 | .05 |
| 62 Candy Maldonado | .01 | .05 |
| 63 Kirt Manwaring UER (No '88 Phoenix stats as note | | |
| 64 Randy McCament RC | .01 | .05 |
| 65 Kevin Mitchell | .05 | .15 |
| 66 Donell Nixon | .01 | .05 |
| 67 Ken Oberkfell | .01 | .05 |
| 68 Rick Reuschel | .01 | .05 |
| 69 Ernest Riles | .01 | .05 |
| 70 Don Robinson | .01 | .05 |
| 71 Pat Sheridan | .01 | .05 |
| 72 Chris Speier | .01 | .05 |
| 73 Robby Thompson | .01 | .05 |
| 74 Jose Uribe | .01 | .05 |
| 75 Matt Williams | .02 | .10 |
| 76 George Bell | .02 | .10 |
| 77 Pat Borders | .01 | .05 |
| 78 John Cerutti | .01 | .05 |
| 79 Junior Felix | .01 | .05 |
| 80 Tony Fernandez | .01 | .05 |
| 81 Mike Flanagan | .01 | .05 |
| 82 Mauro Gozzo RC | .01 | .05 |
| 83 Kelly Gruber | .01 | .05 |
| 84 Tom Henke | .01 | .05 |
| 85 Jimmy Key | .02 | .10 |
| 86 Manny Lee | .01 | .05 |
| 87 Nelson Liriano UER | .01 | .05 |
| 88 Lee Mazzilli | .01 | .05 |
| 89 Fred McGriff | .08 | .25 |
| 90 Lloyd Moseby | .01 | .05 |
| 91 Rance Mulliniks | .01 | .05 |
| 92 Alex Sanchez | .01 | .05 |
| 93 Dave Stieb | .02 | .10 |
| 94 Todd Stottlemyre | .02 | .10 |
| 95 Duane Ward UER | .01 | .05 |
| 96 David Wells | .02 | .10 |
| 97 Ernie Whitt | .01 | .05 |
| 98 Frank Wills | .01 | .05 |
| 99 Mookie Wilson | .02 | .10 |
| 100 Kevin Appier | .05 | .15 |
| 101 Luis Aquino | .01 | .05 |
| 102 Bob Boone | .02 | .10 |
| 103 George Brett | .25 | .60 |
| 104 Jose DeJesus | .01 | .05 |
| 105 Luis De Los Santos | .01 | .05 |
| 106 Jim Eisenreich | .01 | .05 |
| 107 Steve Farr | .01 | .05 |
| 108 Tom Gordon | .02 | .10 |
| 109 Mark Gubicza | .01 | .05 |
| 110 Bo Jackson | .08 | .25 |
| 111 Terry Leach | .01 | .05 |
| 112 Charlie Leibrandt | .01 | .05 |
| 113 Rick Luecken RC | .01 | .05 |
| 114 Mike Macfarlane | .01 | .05 |
| 115 Jeff Montgomery | .02 | .10 |
| 116 Bret Saberhagen | .02 | .10 |
| 117 Kevin Seitzer | .01 | .05 |
| 118 Kurt Stillwell | .01 | .05 |
| 119 Pat Tabler | .01 | .05 |
| 120 Danny Tartabull | .02 | .10 |
| 121 Gary Thurman | .01 | .05 |
| 122 Frank White | .02 | .10 |
| 123 Willie Wilson | .01 | .05 |
| 124 Matt Winters RC | .01 | .05 |

| | | |
|---|---|---|
| 125 Jim Abbott | .05 | .15 |
| 126 Tony Armas | .01 | .05 |
| 127 Dante Bichette | .02 | .10 |
| 128 Bert Blyleven | .02 | .10 |
| 129 Chili Davis | .02 | .10 |
| 130 Brian Downing | .01 | .05 |
| 131 Mike Fetters RC | .08 | .25 |
| 132 Chuck Finley | .02 | .10 |
| 133 Willie Fraser | .01 | .05 |
| 134 Bryan Harvey | .01 | .05 |
| 135 Jack Howell | .01 | .05 |
| 136 Wally Joyner | .02 | .10 |
| 137 Jeff Manto | .01 | .05 |
| 138 Kirk McCaskill | .01 | .05 |
| 139 Bob McClure | .01 | .05 |
| 140 Greg Minton | .01 | .05 |
| 141 Lance Parrish | .01 | .05 |
| 142 Dan Petry | .01 | .05 |
| 143 Johnny Ray | .01 | .05 |
| 144 Dick Schofield | .01 | .05 |
| 145 Lee Stevens | .02 | .10 |
| 146 Claudell Washington | .01 | .05 |
| 147 Devon White | .01 | .05 |
| 148 Mike Witt | .01 | .05 |
| 149 Roberto Alomar | .05 | .15 |
| 150 Sandy Alomar Jr. | .02 | .10 |
| 151 Andy Benes | .05 | .15 |
| 152 Jack Clark | .02 | .10 |
| 153 Pat Clements | .01 | .05 |
| 154 Joey Cora | .02 | .10 |
| 155 Mark Davis | .01 | .05 |
| 156 Mark Grant | .01 | .05 |
| 157 Tony Gwynn | .10 | .30 |
| 158 Greg W. Harris | .01 | .05 |
| 159 Bruce Hurst | .01 | .05 |
| 160 Darrin Jackson | .01 | .05 |
| 161 Chris James | .01 | .05 |
| 162 Carmelo Martinez | .01 | .05 |
| 163 Mike Pagliarulo | .01 | .05 |
| 164 Mark Parent | .01 | .05 |
| 165 Dennis Rasmussen | .01 | .05 |
| 166 Bip Roberts | .01 | .05 |
| 167 Benito Santiago | .02 | .10 |
| 168 Calvin Schiraldi | .01 | .05 |
| 169 Eric Show | .01 | .05 |
| 170 Garry Templeton | .01 | .05 |
| 171 Ed Whitson | .01 | .05 |
| 172 Brady Anderson | .01 | .05 |
| 173 Jeff Ballard | .01 | .05 |
| 174 Phil Bradley | .01 | .05 |
| 175 Mike Devereaux | .01 | .05 |
| 176 Steve Finley | .02 | .10 |
| 177 Pete Harnisch | .01 | .05 |
| 178 Kevin Hickey | .01 | .05 |
| 179 Brian Holton | .01 | .05 |
| 180 Ben McDonald RC | .08 | .25 |
| 181 Bob Melvin | .01 | .05 |
| 182 Bob Milacki | .01 | .05 |
| 183 Randy Milligan UER | .01 | .05 |
| 184 Gregg Olson | .02 | .10 |
| 185 Joe Orsulak | .01 | .05 |
| 186 Bill Ripken | .01 | .05 |
| 187 Cal Ripken | .30 | .75 |
| 188 Dave Schmidt | .01 | .05 |
| 189 Larry Sheets | .01 | .05 |
| 190 Mickey Tettleton | .01 | .05 |
| 191 Mark Thurmond | .01 | .05 |
| 192 Jay Tibbs | .01 | .05 |
| 193 Jim Traber | .01 | .05 |
| 194 Mark Williamson | .01 | .05 |
| 195 Craig Worthington | .01 | .05 |
| 196 Don Aase | .01 | .05 |
| 197 Blaine Beatty RC | .02 | .10 |
| 198 Mark Carreon | .01 | .05 |
| 199 Gary Carter | .02 | .10 |
| 200 David Cone | .02 | .10 |
| 201 Ron Darling | .01 | .05 |
| 202 Kevin Elster | .01 | .05 |
| 203 Sid Fernandez | .01 | .05 |
| 204 Dwight Gooden | .02 | .10 |
| 205 Keith Hernandez | .02 | .10 |
| 206 Jeff Innis RC | .01 | .05 |
| 207 Gregg Jefferies | .02 | .10 |
| 208 Howard Johnson | .02 | .10 |
| 209 Barry Lyons UER | .01 | .05 |
| 210 Dave Magadan | .01 | .05 |
| 211 Kevin McReynolds | .01 | .05 |
| 212 Jeff Musselman | .01 | .05 |

|  |  | | |
|---|---|---|---|
| 213 | Randy Myers | .02 | .10 |
| 214 | Bob Ojeda | .01 | .05 |
| 215 | Juan Samuel | .01 | .05 |
| 216 | Mackey Sasser | .01 | .05 |
| 217 | Darryl Strawberry | .02 | .10 |
| 218 | Tim Teufel | .01 | .05 |
| 219 | Frank Viola | .01 | .05 |
| 220 | Juan Agosto | .01 | .05 |
| 221 | Larry Andersen | .01 | .05 |
| 222 | Eric Anthony RC | .02 | .10 |
| 223 | Kevin Bass | .01 | .05 |
| 224 | Craig Biggio | .08 | .25 |
| 225 | Ken Caminiti | .02 | .10 |
| 226 | Jim Clancy | .01 | .05 |
| 227 | Danny Darwin | .01 | .05 |
| 228 | Glenn Davis | .01 | .05 |
| 229 | Jim Deshaies | .01 | .05 |
| 230 | Bill Doran | .01 | .05 |
| 231 | Bob Forsch | .01 | .05 |
| 232 | Brian Meyer | .01 | .05 |
| 233 | Terry Puhl | .01 | .05 |
| 234 | Rafael Ramirez | .01 | .05 |
| 235 | Rick Rhoden | .01 | .05 |
| 236 | Dan Schatzeder | .01 | .05 |
| 237 | Mike Scott | .01 | .05 |
| 238 | Dave Smith | .01 | .05 |
| 239 | Alex Trevino | .01 | .05 |
| 240 | Glenn Wilson | .01 | .05 |
| 241 | Gerald Young | .01 | .05 |
| 242 | Tom Brunansky | .01 | .05 |
| 243 | Cris Carpenter | .01 | .05 |
| 244 | Alex Cole RC | .02 | .10 |
| 245 | Vince Coleman | .01 | .05 |
| 246 | John Costello | .01 | .05 |
| 247 | Ken Dayley | .01 | .05 |
| 248 | Jose DeLeon | .01 | .05 |
| 249 | Frank DiPino | .01 | .05 |
| 250 | Pedro Guerrero | .01 | .05 |
| 251 | Ken Hill | .02 | .10 |
| 252 | Joe Magrane | .01 | .05 |
| 253 | Willie McGee UER | .02 | .10 |
| 254 | John Morris | .01 | .05 |
| 255 | Jose Oquendo | .01 | .05 |
| 256 | Tony Pena | .01 | .05 |
| 257 | Terry Pendleton | .02 | .10 |
| 258 | Ted Power | .01 | .05 |
| 259 | Dan Quisenberry | .01 | .05 |
| 260 | Ozzie Smith | .15 | .40 |
| 261 | Scott Terry | .01 | .05 |
| 262 | Milt Thompson | .01 | .05 |
| 263 | Denny Walling | .01 | .05 |
| 264 | Todd Worrell | .01 | .05 |
| 265 | Todd Zeile | .02 | .10 |
| 266 | Marty Barrett | .01 | .05 |
| 267 | Mike Boddicker | .01 | .05 |
| 268 | Wade Boggs | .05 | .15 |
| 269 | Ellis Burks | .05 | .15 |
| 270 | Rick Cerone | .01 | .05 |
| 271 | Roger Clemens | .40 | 1.00 |
| 272 | John Dopson | .01 | .05 |
| 273 | Nick Esasky | .01 | .05 |
| 274 | Dwight Evans | .05 | .15 |
| 275 | Wes Gardner | .01 | .05 |
| 276 | Rich Gedman | .01 | .05 |
| 277 | Mike Greenwell | .01 | .05 |
| 278 | Danny Heep | .01 | .05 |
| 279 | Eric Hetzel | .01 | .05 |
| 280 | Dennis Lamp | .01 | .05 |
| 281 | Rob Murphy UER | .01 | .05 |
| 282 | Joe Price | .01 | .05 |
| 283 | Carlos Quintana | .01 | .05 |
| 284 | Jody Reed | .01 | .05 |
| 285 | Luis Rivera | .01 | .05 |
| 286 | Kevin Romine | .01 | .05 |
| 287 | Lee Smith | .02 | .10 |
| 288 | Mike Smithson | .01 | .05 |
| 289 | Bob Stanley | .01 | .05 |
| 290 | Harold Baines | .02 | .10 |
| 291 | Kevin Brown | .02 | .10 |
| 292 | Steve Buechele | .01 | .05 |
| 293 | Scott Coolbaugh RC | .01 | .05 |
| 294 | Jack Daugherty RC | .01 | .05 |
| 295 | Cecil Espy | .01 | .05 |
| 296 | Julio Franco | .02 | .10 |
| 297 | Juan Gonzalez RC | .40 | 1.00 |
| 298 | Cecilio Guante | .01 | .05 |
| 299 | Drew Hall | .01 | .05 |
| 300 | Charlie Hough | .02 | .10 |
| 301 | Pete Incaviglia | .01 | .05 |
| 302 | Mike Jeffcoat | .01 | .05 |
| 303 | Chad Kreuter | .01 | .05 |
| 304 | Jeff Kunkel | .01 | .05 |
| 305 | Rick Leach | .01 | .05 |
| 306 | Fred Manrique | .01 | .05 |
| 307 | Jamie Moyer | .02 | .10 |
| 308 | Rafael Palmeiro | .05 | .15 |
| 309 | Geno Petralli | .01 | .05 |
| 310 | Kevin Reimer | .01 | .05 |
| 311 | Kenny Rogers | .02 | .10 |
| 312 | Jeff Russell | .01 | .05 |
| 313 | Nolan Ryan | .40 | 1.00 |
| 314 | Ruben Sierra | .02 | .10 |
| 315 | Bobby Witt | .01 | .05 |
| 316 | Chris Bosio | .01 | .05 |
| 317 | Glenn Braggs UER | .01 | .05 |
| 318 | Greg Brock | .01 | .05 |
| 319 | Chuck Crim | .01 | .05 |
| 320 | Rob Deer | .01 | .05 |
| 321 | Mike Felder | .01 | .05 |
| 322 | Tom Filer | .01 | .05 |
| 323 | Tony Fossas RC | .01 | .05 |
| 324 | Jim Gantner | .01 | .05 |
| 325 | Darryl Hamilton | .01 | .05 |
| 326 | Teddy Higuera | .01 | .05 |
| 327 | Mark Knudson | .01 | .05 |
| 328 | Bill Krueger UER | .01 | .05 |
| 329 | Tim McIntosh RC | .02 | .10 |
| 330 | Paul Molitor | .02 | .10 |
| 331 | Jaime Navarro | .01 | .05 |
| 332 | Charlie O'Brien | .01 | .05 |
| 333 | Jeff Peterek RC | .01 | .05 |
| 334 | Dan Plesac | .01 | .05 |
| 335 | Jerry Reuss | .01 | .05 |
| 336 | Gary Sheffield UER | .08 | .25 |
| 337 | Bill Spiers | .01 | .05 |
| 338 | B.J. Surhoff | .02 | .10 |
| 339 | Greg Vaughn | .05 | .15 |
| 340 | Robin Yount | .15 | .40 |
| 341 | Hubie Brooks | .01 | .05 |
| 342 | Tim Burke | .01 | .05 |
| 343 | Mike Fitzgerald | .01 | .05 |
| 344 | Tom Foley | .01 | .05 |
| 345 | Andres Galarraga | .02 | .10 |
| 346 | Damaso Garcia | .01 | .05 |
| 347 | Marquis Grissom RC | .15 | .40 |
| 348 | Kevin Gross | .01 | .05 |
| 349 | Joe Hesketh | .01 | .05 |
| 350 | Jeff Huson RC | .01 | .05 |
| 351 | Wallace Johnson | .01 | .05 |
| 352 | Mark Langston | .01 | .05 |
| 353A | Dave Martinez Yellow | .75 | 2.00 |
| 353B | Dave Martinez Red | .01 | .05 |
| 354 | Dennis Martinez UER | .02 | .10 |
| 355 | Andy McGaffigan | .01 | .05 |
| 356 | Otis Nixon | .01 | .05 |
| 357 | Spike Owen | .01 | .05 |
| 358 | Pascual Perez | .01 | .05 |
| 359 | Tim Raines | .02 | .10 |
| 360 | Nelson Santovenia | .01 | .05 |
| 361 | Bryn Smith | .01 | .05 |
| 362 | Zane Smith | .01 | .05 |
| 363 | Larry Walker RC | .40 | 1.00 |
| 364 | Tim Wallach | .02 | .10 |
| 365 | Rick Aguilera | .02 | .10 |
| 366 | Allan Anderson | .01 | .05 |
| 367 | Wally Backman | .01 | .05 |
| 368 | Doug Baker | .01 | .05 |
| 369 | Juan Berenguer | .01 | .05 |
| 370 | Randy Bush | .01 | .05 |
| 371 | Carmelo Castillo | .01 | .05 |
| 372 | Mike Dyer RC | .01 | .05 |
| 373 | Gary Gaetti | .02 | .10 |
| 374 | Greg Gagne | .01 | .05 |
| 375 | Dan Gladden | .01 | .05 |
| 376 | German Gonzalez UER | .01 | .05 |
| 377 | Brian Harper | .01 | .05 |
| 378 | Kent Hrbek | .02 | .10 |
| 379 | Gene Larkin | .01 | .05 |
| 380 | Tim Laudner UER | .01 | .05 |
| 381 | John Moses | .01 | .05 |
| 382 | Al Newman | .01 | .05 |
| 383 | Kirby Puckett | .08 | .25 |
| 384 | Shane Rawley | .01 | .05 |
| 385 | Jeff Reardon | .02 | .10 |
| 386 | Roy Smith | .01 | .05 |
| 387 | Gary Wayne | .01 | .05 |
| 388 | Dave West | .01 | .05 |
| 389 | Tim Belcher | .01 | .05 |
| 390 | Tim Crews UER | .01 | .05 |
| 391 | Mike Davis | .01 | .05 |
| 392 | Rick Dempsey | .01 | .05 |
| 393 | Kirk Gibson | .02 | .10 |
| 394 | Jose Gonzalez | .01 | .05 |
| 395 | Alfredo Griffin | .01 | .05 |
| 396 | Jeff Hamilton | .01 | .05 |
| 397 | Lenny Harris | .01 | .05 |
| 398 | Mickey Hatcher | .01 | .05 |
| 399 | Orel Hershiser | .02 | .10 |
| 400 | Jay Howell | .01 | .05 |
| 401 | Mike Marshall | .01 | .05 |
| 402 | Ramon Martinez | .05 | .15 |
| 403 | Mike Morgan | .01 | .05 |
| 404 | Eddie Murray | .08 | .25 |
| 405 | Alejandro Pena | .01 | .05 |
| 406 | Willie Randolph | .02 | .10 |
| 407 | Mike Scioscia | .01 | .05 |
| 408 | Ray Searage | .01 | .05 |
| 409 | Fernando Valenzuela | .02 | .10 |
| 410 | Jose Vizcaino RC | .08 | .25 |
| 411 | John Wetteland | .08 | .25 |
| 412 | Jack Armstrong | .01 | .05 |
| 413 | Todd Benzinger UER | .01 | .05 |
| 414 | Tim Birtsas | .01 | .05 |
| 415 | Tom Browning | .01 | .05 |
| 416 | Norm Charlton | .01 | .05 |
| 417 | Eric Davis | .02 | .10 |
| 418 | Rob Dibble | .02 | .10 |
| 419 | John Franco | .02 | .10 |
| 420 | Ken Griffey Sr. | .02 | .10 |
| 421 | Chris Hammond RC | .02 | .10 |
| 422 | Danny Jackson | .01 | .05 |
| 423 | Barry Larkin | .05 | .15 |
| 424 | Tim Leary | .01 | .05 |
| 425 | Rick Mahler | .01 | .05 |
| 426 | Joe Oliver | .01 | .05 |
| 427 | Paul O'Neill | .05 | .15 |
| 428 | Luis Quinones UER | .01 | .05 |
| 429 | Jeff Reed | .01 | .05 |
| 430 | Jose Rijo | .01 | .05 |
| 431 | Ron Robinson | .01 | .05 |
| 432 | Rolando Roomes | .01 | .05 |
| 433 | Chris Sabo | .01 | .05 |
| 434 | Scott Scudder | .01 | .05 |
| 435 | Herm Winningham | .01 | .05 |
| 436 | Steve Balboni | .01 | .05 |
| 437 | Jesse Barfield | .01 | .05 |
| 438 | Mike Blowers RC | .02 | .10 |
| 439 | Tom Brookens | .01 | .05 |
| 440 | Greg Cadaret | .01 | .05 |
| 441 | Alvaro Espinoza UER | .01 | .05 |
| 442 | Bob Geren | .01 | .05 |
| 443 | Lee Guetterman | .01 | .05 |
| 444 | Mel Hall | .01 | .05 |
| 445 | Andy Hawkins | .01 | .05 |
| 446 | Roberto Kelly | .05 | .15 |
| 447 | Don Mattingly | .25 | .60 |
| 448 | Lance McCullers | .01 | .05 |
| 449 | Hensley Meulens | .01 | .05 |
| 450 | Dale Mohorcic | .01 | .05 |
| 451 | Clay Parker | .01 | .05 |
| 452 | Eric Plunk | .01 | .05 |
| 453 | Dave Righetti | .01 | .05 |
| 454 | Deion Sanders | .08 | .25 |
| 455 | Steve Sax | .01 | .05 |
| 456 | Don Slaught | .01 | .05 |
| 457 | Walt Terrell | .01 | .05 |
| 458 | Dave Winfield | .05 | .15 |
| 459 | Jay Bell | .02 | .10 |
| 460 | Rafael Belliard | .01 | .05 |
| 461 | Barry Bonds | .40 | 1.00 |
| 462 | Bobby Bonilla | .02 | .10 |
| 463 | Sid Bream | .01 | .05 |
| 464 | Benny Distefano | .01 | .05 |
| 465 | Doug Drabek | .02 | .10 |
| 466 | Jim Gott | .01 | .05 |
| 467 | Billy Hatcher UER | .01 | .05 |
| 468 | Neal Heaton | .01 | .05 |
| 469 | Jeff King | .01 | .05 |
| 470 | Bob Kipper | .01 | .05 |
| 471 | Randy Kramer | .01 | .05 |
| 472 | Bill Landrum | .01 | .05 |
| 473 | Mike LaValliere | .01 | .05 |
| 474 | Jose Lind | .01 | .05 |
| 475 | Junior Ortiz | .01 | .05 |

| | | |
|---|---|---|
| 476 Gary Redus | .01 | .05 |
| 477 Rick Reed RC | .08 | .25 |
| 478 R.J. Reynolds | .01 | .05 |
| 479 Jeff D. Robinson | .01 | .05 |
| 480 John Smiley | .01 | .05 |
| 481 Andy Van Slyke | .05 | .15 |
| 482 Bob Walk | .01 | .05 |
| 483 Andy Allanson | .01 | .05 |
| 484 Scott Bailes | .01 | .05 |
| 485 Albert Belle | .08 | .25 |
| 486 Bud Black | .01 | .05 |
| 487 Jerry Browne | .01 | .05 |
| 488 Tom Candiotti | .01 | .05 |
| 489 Joe Carter | .02 | .10 |
| 490 Dave Clark (No '84 stats) | .01 | .05 |
| 491 John Farrell | .01 | .05 |
| 492 Felix Fermin | .01 | .05 |
| 493 Brook Jacoby | .01 | .05 |
| 494 Dion James | .01 | .05 |
| 495 Doug Jones | .01 | .05 |
| 496 Brad Komminsk | .01 | .05 |
| 497 Rod Nichols | .01 | .05 |
| 498 Pete O'Brien | .01 | .05 |
| 499 Steve Olin RC | .02 | .10 |
| 500 Jesse Orosco | .01 | .05 |
| 501 Joel Skinner | .01 | .05 |
| 502 Cory Snyder | .01 | .05 |
| 503 Greg Swindell | .01 | .05 |
| 504 Rich Yett | .01 | .05 |
| 505 Scott Bankhead | .01 | .05 |
| 506 Scott Bradley | .01 | .05 |
| 507 Greg Briley UER | .01 | .05 |
| 508 Jay Buhner | .02 | .10 |
| 509 Darnell Coles | .01 | .05 |
| 510 Keith Comstock | .01 | .05 |
| 511 Henry Cotto | .01 | .05 |
| 512 Alvin Davis | .01 | .05 |
| 513 Ken Griffey Jr. | .30 | .75 |
| 514 Erik Hanson | .01 | .05 |
| 515 Gene Harris | .01 | .05 |
| 516 Brian Holman | .01 | .05 |
| 517 Mike Jackson | .01 | .05 |
| 518 Randy Johnson | .20 | .50 |
| 519 Jeffrey Leonard | .01 | .05 |
| 520 Edgar Martinez | .05 | .15 |
| 521 Dennis Powell | .01 | .05 |
| 522 Jim Presley | .01 | .05 |
| 523 Jerry Reed | .01 | .05 |
| 524 Harold Reynolds | .02 | .10 |
| 525 Mike Schooler | .01 | .05 |
| 526 Bill Swift | .01 | .05 |
| 527 Dave Valle | .01 | .05 |
| 528 Omar Vizquel | .08 | .25 |
| 529 Ivan Calderon | .01 | .05 |
| 530 Carlton Fisk UER | .05 | .15 |
| 531 Scott Fletcher | .01 | .05 |
| 532 Dave Gallagher | .01 | .05 |
| 533 Ozzie Guillen | .02 | .10 |
| 534 Greg Hibbard RC | .02 | .10 |
| 535 Shawn Hillegas | .01 | .05 |
| 536 Lance Johnson | .01 | .05 |
| 537 Eric King | .01 | .05 |
| 538 Ron Kittle | .01 | .05 |
| 539 Steve Lyons | .01 | .05 |
| 540 Carlos Martinez | .01 | .05 |
| 541 Tom McCarthy | .01 | .05 |
| 542 Matt Merullo | .01 | .05 |
| 543 Donn Pall UER | .01 | .05 |
| 544 Dan Pasqua | .01 | .05 |
| 545 Ken Patterson | .01 | .05 |
| 546 Melido Perez | .01 | .05 |
| 547 Steve Rosenberg | .01 | .05 |
| 548 Sammy Sosa RC | 1.00 | 2.50 |
| 549 Bobby Thigpen | .01 | .05 |
| 550 Robin Ventura | .08 | .25 |
| 551 Greg Walker | .01 | .05 |
| 552 Don Carman | .01 | .05 |
| 553 Pat Combs | .01 | .05 |
| 554 Dennis Cook | .01 | .05 |
| 555 Darren Daulton | .02 | .10 |
| 556 Len Dykstra | .02 | .10 |
| 557 Curt Ford | .01 | .05 |
| 558 Charlie Hayes | .01 | .05 |
| 559 Von Hayes | .01 | .05 |
| 560 Tommy Herr | .01 | .05 |
| 561 Ken Howell | .01 | .05 |
| 562 Steve Jeltz | .01 | .05 |

| | | |
|---|---|---|
| 563 Ron Jones | .01 | .05 |
| 564 Ricky Jordan UER | .01 | .05 |
| 565 John Kruk | .02 | .10 |
| 566 Steve Lake | .01 | .05 |
| 567 Roger McDowell | .01 | .05 |
| 568 Terry Mulholland UER | .01 | .05 |
| 569 Dwayne Murphy | .01 | .05 |
| 570 Jeff Parrett | .01 | .05 |
| 571 Randy Ready | .01 | .05 |
| 572 Bruce Ruffin | .01 | .05 |
| 573 Dickie Thon | .01 | .05 |
| 574 Jose Alvarez UER | .01 | .05 |
| 575 Geronimo Berroa | .01 | .05 |
| 576 Jeff Blauser | .01 | .05 |
| 577 Joe Boever | .01 | .05 |
| 578 Marty Clary UER | .01 | .05 |
| 579 Jody Davis | .01 | .05 |
| 580 Mark Eichhorn | .01 | .05 |
| 581 Darrell Evans | .02 | .10 |
| 582 Ron Gant | .02 | .10 |
| 583 Tom Glavine | .05 | .15 |
| 584 Tommy Greene RC | .02 | .10 |
| 585 Tommy Gregg | .01 | .05 |
| 586 David Justice RC | .20 | .50 |
| 587 Mark Lemke | .01 | .05 |
| 588 Derek Lilliquist | .01 | .05 |
| 589 Oddibe McDowell | .01 | .05 |
| 590 Kent Mercker RC | .01 | .05 |
| 591 Dale Murphy | .05 | .15 |
| 592 Gerald Perry | .01 | .05 |
| 593 Lonnie Smith | .01 | .05 |
| 594 Pete Smith | .01 | .05 |
| 595 John Smoltz | .08 | .25 |
| 596 Mike Stanton UER RC | .08 | .25 |
| 597 Andres Thomas | .01 | .05 |
| 598 Jeff Treadway | .01 | .05 |
| 599 Doyle Alexander | .01 | .05 |
| 600 Dave Bergman | .01 | .05 |
| 601 Brian DuBois RC | .01 | .05 |
| 602 Paul Gibson | .01 | .05 |
| 603 Mike Heath | .01 | .05 |
| 604 Mike Henneman | .01 | .05 |
| 605 Guillermo Hernandez | .01 | .05 |
| 606 Shawn Holman RC | .01 | .05 |
| 607 Tracy Jones | .01 | .05 |
| 608 Chet Lemon | .01 | .05 |
| 609 Fred Lynn | .01 | .05 |
| 610 Jack Morris | .02 | .10 |
| 611 Matt Nokes | .01 | .05 |
| 612 Gary Pettis | .01 | .05 |
| 613 Kevin Ritz RC | .01 | .05 |
| 614 Jeff M. Robinson | .01 | .05 |
| 615 Steve Searcy | .01 | .05 |
| 616 Frank Tanana | .01 | .05 |
| 617 Alan Trammell | .02 | .10 |
| 618 Gary Ward | .01 | .05 |
| 619 Lou Whitaker | .02 | .10 |
| 620 Frank Williams | .01 | .05 |
| 621A George Brett '80 ERR | .75 | 2.00 |
| 621B George Brett '80 | .10 | .30 |
| 622 Fern.Valenzuela '81 | .10 | .30 |
| 623 Dale Murphy '82 | .05 | .15 |
| 624A Cal Ripken '83 ERR | 2.00 | 5.00 |
| 624B Cal Ripken '83 COR | .15 | .40 |
| 625 Ryne Sandberg '84 | .08 | .25 |
| 626 Don Mattingly '85 | .07 | .20 |
| 627 Roger Clemens '86 | .20 | .50 |
| 628 George Bell '87 | .01 | .05 |
| 629 Jose Canseco '88 UER | .02 | .10 |
| 630A Will Clark '89 ERR 32 | .40 | 1.00 |
| 630B Will Clark '89 COR 321 | .05 | .15 |
| 631 M.Davis/M.Williams | .01 | .05 |
| 632 W.Boggs/M.Greenwell | .02 | .10 |
| 633 M.Gubicza/J.Russell | .01 | .05 |
| 634 C.Ripken/T.Fernandez | .08 | .25 |
| 635 K.Puckett/Bo Jackson | .05 | .15 |
| 636 N.Ryan/M.Scott | .15 | .40 |
| 637 W.Clark/K.Mitchell | .02 | .10 |
| 638 M.McGwire/D.Mattingly | .10 | .30 |
| 639 R.Sandberg/H.Johnson | .08 | .25 |
| 640 R.Seanez RC/C.Charland RC | .01 | .05 |
| 641 G.Canale RC/K.Maas RC | .08 | .25 |
| 642 Kelly Mann RC/D.Hansen RC | .02 | .10 |
| 643 G.Smith RC/S.Tate RC | .02 | .10 |
| 644 T.Drees RC/D.Howitt RC | .01 | .05 |
| 645 M.Roesler RC/D.May RC | .02 | .10 |
| 646 S.Hemond RC/M.Gardner RC | .01 | .05 |
| 647 John Orton RC/S.Leius RC | .02 | .10 |

| | | |
|---|---|---|
| 648 R.Monteleone RC/D.Williams RC | .02 | .10 |
| 649 M.Huff RC/S.Frey RC | .02 | .10 |
| 650 C.McElroy RC/M.Alou RC | .30 | .75 |
| 651 B.Rose RC/M.Hartley RC | .08 | .25 |
| 652 M.Kinzer RC/W.Edwards RC | .02 | .10 |
| 653 D.DeShields RC/J.Grimsley RC | .08 | .25 |
| 654 CL: A's/Cubs | | |
| Giants/Blue Jays | .01 | .05 |
| 655 CL: Royals/Angels | | |
| Padres/Orioles | .01 | .05 |
| 656 CL: Mets/Astros | | |
| Cards/Red Sox | .01 | .05 |
| 657 CL: Rangers/Brewers | | |
| Expos/Twins | .01 | .05 |
| 658 CL: Dodgers/Reds | | |
| Yankees/Pirates | .01 | .05 |
| 659 CL: Indians/Mariners | | |
| White Sox/Phillies | .01 | .05 |
| 660A CL: Braves/Tigers Specials/Checklist (Checklist | .01 | .05 |
| 660B CL: Braves/Tigers Specials/Checklists (Checklist | .01 | .05 |

## 1991 Fleer

| | | |
|---|---|---|
| COMPLETE SET (720) | 3.00 | 8.00 |
| COMP.RETAIL SET (732) | 4.00 | 10.00 |
| COMP.HOBBY SET (732) | 4.00 | 10.00 |
| 1 Troy Afenir RC | .01 | .05 |
| 2 Harold Baines | .02 | .10 |
| 3 Lance Blankenship | .01 | .05 |
| 4 Todd Burns | .01 | .05 |
| 5 Jose Canseco | .05 | .15 |
| 6 Dennis Eckersley | .02 | .10 |
| 7 Mike Gallego | .01 | .05 |
| 8 Ron Hassey | .01 | .05 |
| 9 Dave Henderson | .01 | .05 |
| 10 Rickey Henderson | .08 | .25 |
| 11 Rick Honeycutt | .01 | .05 |
| 12 Doug Jennings | .01 | .05 |
| 13 Joe Klink | .01 | .05 |
| 14 Carney Lansford | .02 | .10 |
| 15 Darren Lewis | .01 | .05 |
| 16 Willie McGee UER | .02 | .10 |
| 17 Mark McGwire UER | .30 | .75 |
| 18 Mike Moore | .01 | .05 |
| 19 Gene Nelson | .01 | .05 |
| 20 Dave Otto | .01 | .05 |
| 21 Jamie Quirk | .01 | .05 |
| 22 Willie Randolph | .02 | .10 |
| 23 Scott Sanderson | .01 | .05 |
| 24 Terry Steinbach | .02 | .10 |
| 25 Dave Stewart | .02 | .10 |
| 26 Walt Weiss | .01 | .05 |
| 27 Bob Welch | .01 | .05 |
| 28 Curt Young | .01 | .05 |
| 29 Wally Backman | .01 | .05 |
| 30 Stan Belinda UER | .01 | .05 |
| 31 Jay Bell | .02 | .10 |
| 32 Rafael Belliard | .01 | .05 |
| 33 Barry Bonds | .40 | 1.00 |
| 34 Bobby Bonilla | .02 | .10 |
| 35 Sid Bream | .01 | .05 |
| 36 Doug Drabek | .01 | .05 |
| 37 Carlos Garcia RC | .02 | .10 |
| 38 Neal Heaton | .01 | .05 |
| 39 Jeff King | .01 | .05 |
| 40 Bob Kipper | .01 | .05 |
| 41 Bill Landrum | .01 | .05 |
| 42 Mike LaValliere | .01 | .05 |
| 43 Jose Lind | .01 | .05 |
| 44 Carmelo Martinez | .01 | .05 |
| 45 Bob Patterson | .01 | .05 |

|  |  | | |
|---|--------|------|------|
| ❑ 46 | Ted Power | .01 | .05 |
| ❑ 47 | Gary Redus | .01 | .05 |
| ❑ 48 | R.J. Reynolds | .01 | .05 |
| ❑ 49 | Don Slaught | .01 | .05 |
| ❑ 50 | John Smiley | .01 | .05 |
| ❑ 51 | Zane Smith | .01 | .05 |
| ❑ 52 | Randy Tomlin RC | .02 | .10 |
| ❑ 53 | Andy Van Slyke | .05 | .15 |
| ❑ 54 | Bob Walk | .01 | .05 |
| ❑ 55 | Jack Armstrong | .01 | .05 |
| ❑ 56 | Todd Benzinger | .01 | .05 |
| ❑ 57 | Glenn Braggs | .01 | .05 |
| ❑ 58 | Keith Brown | .01 | .05 |
| ❑ 59 | Tom Browning | .01 | .05 |
| ❑ 60 | Norm Charlton | .01 | .05 |
| ❑ 61 | Eric Davis | .02 | .10 |
| ❑ 62 | Rob Dibble | .02 | .10 |
| ❑ 63 | Bill Doran | .01 | .05 |
| ❑ 64 | Mariano Duncan | .01 | .05 |
| ❑ 65 | Chris Hammond | .01 | .05 |
| ❑ 66 | Billy Hatcher | .01 | .05 |
| ❑ 67 | Danny Jackson | .01 | .05 |
| ❑ 68 | Barry Larkin | .05 | .15 |
| ❑ 69 | Tim Layana UER | .01 | .05 |
| ❑ 70 | Terry Lee RC | .01 | .05 |
| ❑ 71 | Rick Mahler | .01 | .05 |
| ❑ 72 | Hal Morris | .01 | .05 |
| ❑ 73 | Randy Myers | .01 | .05 |
| ❑ 74 | Ron Oester | .01 | .05 |
| ❑ 75 | Joe Oliver | .01 | .05 |
| ❑ 76 | Paul O'Neill | .05 | .15 |
| ❑ 77 | Luis Quinones | .01 | .05 |
| ❑ 78 | Jeff Reed | .01 | .05 |
| ❑ 79 | Jose Rijo | .01 | .05 |
| ❑ 80 | Chris Sabo | .01 | .05 |
| ❑ 81 | Scott Scudder | .01 | .05 |
| ❑ 82 | Herm Winningham | .01 | .05 |
| ❑ 83 | Larry Andersen | .01 | .05 |
| ❑ 84 | Marty Barrett | .01 | .05 |
| ❑ 85 | Mike Boddicker | .01 | .05 |
| ❑ 86 | Wade Boggs | .05 | .15 |
| ❑ 87 | Tom Bolton | .01 | .05 |
| ❑ 88 | Tom Brunansky | .01 | .05 |
| ❑ 89 | Ellis Burks | .02 | .10 |
| ❑ 90 | Roger Clemens | .30 | .75 |
| ❑ 91 | Scott Cooper | .01 | .05 |
| ❑ 92 | John Dopson | .01 | .05 |
| ❑ 93 | Dwight Evans | .05 | .15 |
| ❑ 94 | Wes Gardner | .01 | .05 |
| ❑ 95 | Jeff Gray | .01 | .05 |
| ❑ 96 | Mike Greenwell | .01 | .05 |
| ❑ 97 | Greg A. Harris | .01 | .05 |
| ❑ 98 | Daryl Irvine RC | .01 | .05 |
| ❑ 99 | Dana Kiecker | .01 | .05 |
| ❑ 100 | Randy Kutcher | .01 | .05 |
| ❑ 101 | Dennis Lamp | .01 | .05 |
| ❑ 102 | Mike Marshall | .01 | .05 |
| ❑ 103 | John Marzano | .01 | .05 |
| ❑ 104 | Rob Murphy | .01 | .05 |
| ❑ 105 | Tim Naehring | .01 | .05 |
| ❑ 106 | Tony Pena | .01 | .05 |
| ❑ 107 | Phil Plantier RC | .08 | .25 |
| ❑ 108 | Carlos Quintana | .01 | .05 |
| ❑ 109 | Jeff Reardon | .02 | .10 |
| ❑ 110 | Jerry Reed | .01 | .05 |
| ❑ 111 | Jody Reed | .01 | .05 |
| ❑ 112 | Luis Rivera UER | .01 | .05 |
| ❑ 113 | Kevin Romine | .01 | .05 |
| ❑ 114 | Phil Bradley | .01 | .05 |
| ❑ 115 | Ivan Calderon | .01 | .05 |
| ❑ 116 | Wayne Edwards | .01 | .05 |
| ❑ 117 | Alex Fernandez | .01 | .05 |
| ❑ 118 | Carlton Fisk | .05 | .15 |
| ❑ 119 | Scott Fletcher | .01 | .05 |
| ❑ 120 | Craig Grebeck | .01 | .05 |
| ❑ 121 | Ozzie Guillen | .02 | .10 |
| ❑ 122 | Greg Hibbard | .01 | .05 |
| ❑ 123 | Lance Johnson UER | .01 | .05 |
| ❑ 124 | Barry Jones | .01 | .05 |
| ❑ 125 | Ron Karkovice | .01 | .05 |
| ❑ 126 | Eric King | .01 | .05 |
| ❑ 127 | Steve Lyons | .01 | .05 |
| ❑ 128 | Carlos Martinez | .01 | .05 |
| ❑ 129 | Jack McDowell UER | .01 | .05 |
| ❑ 130 | Donn Pall | .01 | .05 |
| ❑ 131 | Dan Pasqua | .01 | .05 |
| ❑ 132 | Ken Patterson | .01 | .05 |
| ❑ 133 | Melido Perez | .01 | .05 |
| ❑ 134 | Adam Peterson | .01 | .05 |
| ❑ 135 | Scott Radinsky | .01 | .05 |
| ❑ 136 | Sammy Sosa | .08 | .25 |
| ❑ 137 | Bobby Thigpen | .01 | .05 |
| ❑ 138 | Frank Thomas | .08 | .25 |
| ❑ 139 | Robin Ventura | .02 | .10 |
| ❑ 140 | Daryl Boston | .01 | .05 |
| ❑ 141 | Chuck Carr | .01 | .05 |
| ❑ 142 | Mark Carreon | .01 | .05 |
| ❑ 143 | David Cone | .02 | .10 |
| ❑ 144 | Ron Darling | .01 | .05 |
| ❑ 145 | Kevin Elster | .01 | .05 |
| ❑ 146 | Sid Fernandez | .01 | .05 |
| ❑ 147 | John Franco | .02 | .10 |
| ❑ 148 | Dwight Gooden | .01 | .05 |
| ❑ 149 | Tom Herr | .01 | .05 |
| ❑ 150 | Todd Hundley | .01 | .05 |
| ❑ 151 | Gregg Jefferies | .01 | .05 |
| ❑ 152 | Howard Johnson | .01 | .05 |
| ❑ 153 | Dave Magadan | .01 | .05 |
| ❑ 154 | Kevin McReynolds | .01 | .05 |
| ❑ 155 | Keith Miller UER (Text says Rochester in '878 st | | |
| ❑ 156 | Bob Ojeda | .01 | .05 |
| ❑ 157 | Tom O'Malley | .01 | .05 |
| ❑ 158 | Alejandro Pena | .01 | .05 |
| ❑ 159 | Darren Reed | .01 | .05 |
| ❑ 160 | Mackey Sasser | .01 | .05 |
| ❑ 161 | Darryl Strawberry | .02 | .10 |
| ❑ 162 | Tim Teufel | .01 | .05 |
| ❑ 163 | Kelvin Torve | .01 | .05 |
| ❑ 164 | Julio Valera | .01 | .05 |
| ❑ 165 | Frank Viola | .02 | .10 |
| ❑ 166 | Wally Whitehurst | .01 | .05 |
| ❑ 167 | Jim Acker | .01 | .05 |
| ❑ 168 | Derek Bell | .02 | .10 |
| ❑ 169 | George Bell | .01 | .05 |
| ❑ 170 | Willie Blair | .01 | .05 |
| ❑ 171 | Pat Borders | .01 | .05 |
| ❑ 172 | John Cerutti | .01 | .05 |
| ❑ 173 | Junior Felix | .01 | .05 |
| ❑ 174 | Tony Fernandez | .01 | .05 |
| ❑ 175 | Kelly Gruber UER (Born in Houston& should be Bel | | |
| ❑ 176 | Tom Henke | .01 | .05 |
| ❑ 177 | Glenallen Hill | .01 | .05 |
| ❑ 178 | Jimmy Key | .02 | .10 |
| ❑ 179 | Manny Lee | .01 | .05 |
| ❑ 180 | Fred McGriff | .05 | .15 |
| ❑ 181 | Rance Mulliniks | .01 | .05 |
| ❑ 182 | Greg Myers | .01 | .05 |
| ❑ 183 | John Olerud | .02 | .10 |
| ❑ 184 | Luis Sojo | .01 | .05 |
| ❑ 185 | Dave Stieb | .01 | .05 |
| ❑ 186 | Todd Stottlemyre | .01 | .05 |
| ❑ 187 | Duane Ward | .01 | .05 |
| ❑ 188 | David Wells | .02 | .10 |
| ❑ 189 | Mark Whiten | .01 | .05 |
| ❑ 190 | Ken Williams | .01 | .05 |
| ❑ 191 | Frank Wills | .01 | .05 |
| ❑ 192 | Mookie Wilson | .02 | .10 |
| ❑ 193 | Don Aase | .01 | .05 |
| ❑ 194 | Tim Belcher UER (Born Sparta& Ohio& should say M | | |
| ❑ 195 | Hubie Brooks | .01 | .05 |
| ❑ 196 | Dennis Cook | .01 | .05 |
| ❑ 197 | Tim Crews | .01 | .05 |
| ❑ 198 | Kal Daniels | .01 | .05 |
| ❑ 199 | Kirk Gibson | .02 | .10 |
| ❑ 200 | Jim Gott | .01 | .05 |
| ❑ 201 | Alfredo Griffin | .01 | .05 |
| ❑ 202 | Chris Gwynn | .01 | .05 |
| ❑ 203 | Dave Hansen | .01 | .05 |
| ❑ 204 | Lenny Harris | .01 | .05 |
| ❑ 205 | Mike Hartley | .01 | .05 |
| ❑ 206 | Mickey Hatcher | .01 | .05 |
| ❑ 207 | Carlos Hernandez | .01 | .05 |
| ❑ 208 | Orel Hershiser | .02 | .10 |
| ❑ 209 | Jay Howell UER (No 1982 Yankee stats) | | |
| ❑ 210 | Mike Huff | .01 | .05 |
| ❑ 211 | Stan Javier | .01 | .05 |
| ❑ 212 | Ramon Martinez | .01 | .05 |
| ❑ 213 | Mike Morgan | .01 | .05 |
| ❑ 214 | Eddie Murray | .08 | .25 |
| ❑ 215 | Jim Neidlinger RC | .01 | .05 |
| ❑ 216 | Jose Offerman | .01 | .05 |
| ❑ 217 | Jim Poole | .01 | .05 |
| ❑ 218 | Juan Samuel | .01 | .05 |
| ❑ 219 | Mike Scioscia | .01 | .05 |
| ❑ 220 | Ray Searage | .01 | .05 |
| ❑ 221 | Mike Sharperson | .01 | .05 |
| ❑ 222 | Fernando Valenzuela | .02 | .10 |
| ❑ 223 | Jose Vizcaino | .01 | .05 |
| ❑ 224 | Mike Aldrete | .01 | .05 |
| ❑ 225 | Scott Anderson RC | .01 | .05 |
| ❑ 226 | Dennis Boyd | .01 | .05 |
| ❑ 227 | Tim Burke | .01 | .05 |
| ❑ 228 | Delino DeShields | .02 | .10 |
| ❑ 229 | Mike Fitzgerald | .01 | .05 |
| ❑ 230 | Tom Foley | .01 | .05 |
| ❑ 231 | Steve Frey | .01 | .05 |
| ❑ 232 | Andres Galarraga | .02 | .10 |
| ❑ 233 | Mark Gardner | .01 | .05 |
| ❑ 234 | Marquis Grissom | .02 | .10 |
| ❑ 235 | Kevin Gross (No date given for first Expos win) | .01 | .05 |
| ❑ 236 | Drew Hall | .01 | .05 |
| ❑ 237 | Dave Martinez | .01 | .05 |
| ❑ 238 | Dennis Martinez | .02 | .10 |
| ❑ 239 | Dale Mohorcic | .01 | .05 |
| ❑ 240 | Chris Nabholz | .01 | .05 |
| ❑ 241 | Otis Nixon | .01 | .05 |
| ❑ 242 | Junior Noboa | .01 | .05 |
| ❑ 243 | Spike Owen | .01 | .05 |
| ❑ 244 | Tim Raines | .02 | .10 |
| ❑ 245 | Mel Rojas UER (Stats show 3.60 ERA, bio says 3.1 | | |
| ❑ 246 | Scott Ruskin | .01 | .05 |
| ❑ 247 | Bill Sampen | .01 | .05 |
| ❑ 248 | Nelson Santovenia | .01 | .05 |
| ❑ 249 | Dave Schmidt | .01 | .05 |
| ❑ 250 | Larry Walker | .08 | .25 |
| ❑ 251 | Tim Wallach | .01 | .05 |
| ❑ 252 | Dave Anderson | .01 | .05 |
| ❑ 253 | Kevin Bass | .01 | .05 |
| ❑ 254 | Steve Bedrosian | .01 | .05 |
| ❑ 255 | Jeff Brantley | .01 | .05 |
| ❑ 256 | John Burkett | .01 | .05 |
| ❑ 257 | Brett Butler | .02 | .10 |
| ❑ 258 | Gary Carter | .01 | .05 |
| ❑ 259 | Will Clark | .05 | .15 |
| ❑ 260 | Steve Decker RC | .02 | .10 |
| ❑ 261 | Kelly Downs | .01 | .05 |
| ❑ 262 | Scott Garrelts | .01 | .05 |
| ❑ 263 | Terry Kennedy | .01 | .05 |
| ❑ 264 | Mike LaCoss | .01 | .05 |
| ❑ 265 | Mark Leonard RC | .01 | .05 |
| ❑ 266 | Greg Litton | .01 | .05 |
| ❑ 267 | Kevin Mitchell | .02 | .10 |
| ❑ 268 | Randy O'Neal | .01 | .05 |
| ❑ 269 | Rick Parker | .01 | .05 |
| ❑ 270 | Rick Reuschel | .01 | .05 |
| ❑ 271 | Ernest Riles | .01 | .05 |
| ❑ 272 | Don Robinson | .01 | .05 |
| ❑ 273 | Robby Thompson | .01 | .05 |
| ❑ 274 | Mark Thurmond | .01 | .05 |
| ❑ 275 | Jose Uribe | .01 | .05 |
| ❑ 276 | Matt Williams | .02 | .10 |
| ❑ 277 | Trevor Wilson | .01 | .05 |
| ❑ 278 | Gerald Alexander RC | .01 | .05 |
| ❑ 279 | Brad Arnsberg | .01 | .05 |
| ❑ 280 | Kevin Belcher RC | .01 | .05 |
| ❑ 281 | Joe Bitker RC | .01 | .05 |
| ❑ 282 | Kevin Brown | .02 | .10 |
| ❑ 283 | Steve Buechele | .01 | .05 |
| ❑ 284 | Jack Daugherty | .01 | .05 |
| ❑ 285 | Julio Franco | .02 | .10 |
| ❑ 286 | Juan Gonzalez | .08 | .25 |
| ❑ 287 | Bill Haselman RC | .01 | .05 |
| ❑ 288 | Charlie Hough | .01 | .05 |
| ❑ 289 | Jeff Huson | .01 | .05 |
| ❑ 290 | Pete Incaviglia | .01 | .05 |
| ❑ 291 | Mike Jeffcoat | .01 | .05 |
| ❑ 292 | Jeff Kunkel | .01 | .05 |
| ❑ 293 | Gary Mielke | .01 | .05 |
| ❑ 294 | Jamie Moyer | .01 | .05 |
| ❑ 295 | Rafael Palmeiro | .05 | .15 |
| ❑ 296 | Geno Petralli | .01 | .05 |
| ❑ 297 | Gary Pettis | .01 | .05 |
| ❑ 298 | Kevin Reimer | .01 | .05 |

|  |  | | |
|---|---|---|---|
| ❑ 299 | Kenny Rogers | .02 | .10 |
| ❑ 300 | Jeff Russell | .01 | .05 |
| ❑ 301 | John Russell | .01 | .05 |
| ❑ 302 | Nolan Ryan | .40 | 1.00 |
| ❑ 303 | Ruben Sierra | .02 | .10 |
| ❑ 304 | Bobby Witt | .01 | .05 |
| ❑ 305 | Jim Abbott | .05 | .15 |
| ❑ 306 | Kent Anderson | .01 | .05 |
| ❑ 307 | Dante Bichette | .02 | .10 |
| ❑ 308 | Bert Blyleven | .02 | .10 |
| ❑ 309 | Chili Davis | .02 | .10 |
| ❑ 310 | Brian Downing | .01 | .05 |
| ❑ 311 | Mark Eichhorn | .01 | .05 |
| ❑ 312 | Mike Fetters | .01 | .05 |
| ❑ 313 | Chuck Finley | .02 | .10 |
| ❑ 314 | Willie Fraser | .01 | .05 |
| ❑ 315 | Bryan Harvey | .01 | .05 |
| ❑ 316 | Donnie Hill | .01 | .05 |
| ❑ 317 | Wally Joyner | .02 | .10 |
| ❑ 318 | Mark Langston | .01 | .05 |
| ❑ 319 | Kirk McCaskill | .01 | .05 |
| ❑ 320 | John Orton | .01 | .05 |
| ❑ 321 | Lance Parrish | .02 | .10 |
| ❑ 322 | Luis Polonia UER | | |
| | (1984 Maddison& | | |
| | should be Madis | | |
| ❑ 323 | Johnny Ray | .01 | .05 |
| ❑ 324 | Bobby Rose | .01 | .05 |
| ❑ 325 | Dick Schofield | .01 | .05 |
| ❑ 326 | Rick Schu | .01 | .05 |
| ❑ 327 | Lee Stevens | .01 | .05 |
| ❑ 328 | Devon White | .02 | .10 |
| ❑ 329 | Dave Winfield | .05 | .15 |
| ❑ 330 | Cliff Young | .01 | .05 |
| ❑ 331 | Dave Bergman | .01 | .05 |
| ❑ 332 | Phil Clark RC | .02 | .10 |
| ❑ 333 | Darnell Coles | .01 | .05 |
| ❑ 334 | Milt Cuyler | .02 | .10 |
| ❑ 335 | Cecil Fielder | .05 | .15 |
| ❑ 336 | Travis Fryman | .02 | .10 |
| ❑ 337 | Paul Gibson | .01 | .05 |
| ❑ 338 | Jerry Don Gleaton | .01 | .05 |
| ❑ 339 | Mike Heath | .01 | .05 |
| ❑ 340 | Mike Henneman | .01 | .05 |
| ❑ 341 | Chet Lemon | .01 | .05 |
| ❑ 342 | Lance McCullers | .01 | .05 |
| ❑ 343 | Jack Morris | .02 | .10 |
| ❑ 344 | Lloyd Moseby | .01 | .05 |
| ❑ 345 | Edwin Nunez | .01 | .05 |
| ❑ 346 | Clay Parker | .01 | .05 |
| ❑ 347 | Dan Petry | .01 | .05 |
| ❑ 348 | Tony Phillips | .01 | .05 |
| ❑ 349 | Jeff M. Robinson | .01 | .05 |
| ❑ 350 | Mark Salas | .01 | .05 |
| ❑ 351 | Mike Schwabe | .01 | .05 |
| ❑ 352 | Larry Sheets | .01 | .05 |
| ❑ 353 | John Shelby | .01 | .05 |
| ❑ 354 | Frank Tanana | .01 | .05 |
| ❑ 355 | Alan Trammell | .02 | .10 |
| ❑ 356 | Gary Ward | .01 | .05 |
| ❑ 357 | Lou Whitaker | .02 | .10 |
| ❑ 358 | Beau Allred | .01 | .05 |
| ❑ 359 | Sandy Alomar Jr. | .05 | .15 |
| ❑ 360 | Carlos Baerga | .05 | .15 |
| ❑ 361 | Kevin Bearse | .01 | .05 |
| ❑ 362 | Tom Brookens | .01 | .05 |
| ❑ 363 | Jerry Browne UER | | |
| | (No dot over i in | | |
| | first text li | | |
| ❑ 364 | Tom Candiotti | .01 | .05 |
| ❑ 365 | Alex Cole | .01 | .05 |
| ❑ 366 | John Farrell UER | .01 | .05 |
| | (Born in Neptune& | | |
| | should be Mon | | |
| ❑ 367 | Felix Fermin | .01 | .05 |
| ❑ 368 | Keith Hernandez | .02 | .10 |
| ❑ 369 | Brook Jacoby | .01 | .05 |
| ❑ 370 | Chris James | .01 | .05 |
| ❑ 371 | Dion James | .01 | .05 |
| ❑ 372 | Doug Jones | .01 | .05 |
| ❑ 373 | Candy Maldonado | .01 | .05 |
| ❑ 374 | Steve Olin | .01 | .05 |
| ❑ 375 | Jesse Orosco | .01 | .05 |
| ❑ 376 | Rudy Seanez | .01 | .05 |
| ❑ 377 | Joel Skinner | .01 | .05 |
| ❑ 378 | Cory Snyder | .01 | .05 |
| ❑ 379 | Greg Swindell | .01 | .05 |
| ❑ 380 | Sergio Valdez | .01 | .05 |
| ❑ 381 | Mike Walker | .01 | .05 |
| ❑ 382 | Colby Ward RC | .01 | .05 |
| ❑ 383 | Turner Ward RC | .08 | .25 |
| ❑ 384 | Mitch Webster | .01 | .05 |
| ❑ 385 | Kevin Wickander | .01 | .05 |
| ❑ 386 | Darrel Akerfelds | .01 | .05 |
| ❑ 387 | Joe Boever | .01 | .05 |
| ❑ 388 | Rod Booker | .01 | .05 |
| ❑ 389 | Sil Campusano | .01 | .05 |
| ❑ 390 | Don Carman | .01 | .05 |
| ❑ 391 | Wes Chamberlain RC | .08 | .25 |
| ❑ 392 | Pat Combs | .01 | .05 |
| ❑ 393 | Darren Daulton | .02 | .10 |
| ❑ 394 | Jose DeJesus | .01 | .05 |
| ❑ 395A | Len Dykstra | .02 | .10 |
| ❑ 395B | Len Dykstra | .02 | .10 |
| ❑ 396 | Jason Grimsley | .01 | .05 |
| ❑ 397 | Charlie Hayes | .01 | .05 |
| ❑ 398 | Von Hayes | .01 | .05 |
| ❑ 399 | Dave Hollins UER | .01 | .05 |
| ❑ 400 | Ken Howell | .01 | .05 |
| ❑ 401 | Ricky Jordan | .01 | .05 |
| ❑ 402 | John Kruk | .02 | .10 |
| ❑ 403 | Steve Lake | .01 | .05 |
| ❑ 404 | Chuck Malone | .01 | .05 |
| ❑ 405 | Roger McDowell UER | .01 | .05 |
| | (Says Phillies is | | |
| | saves& shou | | |
| ❑ 406 | Chuck McElroy | .01 | .05 |
| ❑ 407 | Mickey Morandini | .01 | .05 |
| ❑ 408 | Terry Mulholland | .01 | .05 |
| ❑ 409 | Dale Murphy | .05 | .15 |
| ❑ 410A | Randy Ready ERR | .01 | .05 |
| | (No Brewers stats | | |
| | listed for 198 | | |
| ❑ 410B | Randy Ready COR | .01 | .05 |
| ❑ 411 | Bruce Ruffin | .01 | .05 |
| ❑ 412 | Dickie Thon | .01 | .05 |
| ❑ 413 | Paul Assenmacher | .01 | .05 |
| ❑ 414 | Damon Berryhill | .01 | .05 |
| ❑ 415 | Mike Bielecki | .01 | .05 |
| ❑ 416 | Shawn Boskie | .01 | .05 |
| ❑ 417 | Dave Clark | .01 | .05 |
| ❑ 418 | Doug Dascenzo | .01 | .05 |
| ❑ 419A | Andre Dawson ERR | .02 | .10 |
| ❑ 419B | Andre Dawson COR | .02 | .10 |
| ❑ 420 | Shawon Dunston | .01 | .05 |
| ❑ 421 | Joe Girardi | .01 | .05 |
| ❑ 422 | Mark Grace | .05 | .15 |
| ❑ 423 | Mike Harkey | .01 | .05 |
| ❑ 424 | Les Lancaster | .01 | .05 |
| ❑ 425 | Bill Long | .01 | .05 |
| ❑ 426 | Greg Maddux | .15 | .40 |
| ❑ 427 | Derrick May | .01 | .05 |
| ❑ 428 | Jeff Pico | .01 | .05 |
| ❑ 429 | Domingo Ramos | .01 | .05 |
| ❑ 430 | Luis Salazar | .01 | .05 |
| ❑ 431 | Ryne Sandberg | .15 | .40 |
| ❑ 432 | Dwight Smith | .01 | .05 |
| ❑ 433 | Greg Smith | .01 | .05 |
| ❑ 434 | Rick Sutcliffe | .02 | .10 |
| ❑ 435 | Gary Varsho | .01 | .05 |
| ❑ 436 | Hector Villanueva | .01 | .05 |
| ❑ 437 | Jerome Walton | .01 | .05 |
| ❑ 438 | Curtis Wilkerson | .01 | .05 |
| ❑ 439 | Mitch Williams | .01 | .05 |
| ❑ 440 | Steve Wilson | .01 | .05 |
| ❑ 441 | Marvell Wynne | .01 | .05 |
| ❑ 442 | Scott Bankhead | .01 | .05 |
| ❑ 443 | Scott Bradley | .01 | .05 |
| ❑ 444 | Greg Briley | .01 | .05 |
| ❑ 445 | Mike Brumley UER | .01 | .05 |
| ❑ 446 | Jay Buhner | .02 | .10 |
| ❑ 447 | Dave Burba RC | .08 | .25 |
| ❑ 448 | Henry Cotto | .01 | .05 |
| ❑ 449 | Alvin Davis | .01 | .05 |
| ❑ 450 | Ken Griffey Jr. | .20 | .50 |
| ❑ 450A | Ken Griffey Jr. ERR | .40 | 1.00 |
| ❑ 451 | Erik Hanson | .01 | .05 |
| ❑ 452 | Gene Harris UER | | |
| | (63 career runs& | | |
| | should be 73) | | |
| ❑ 453 | Brian Holman | .01 | .05 |
| ❑ 454 | Mike Jackson | .01 | .05 |
| ❑ 455 | Randy Johnson | .10 | .30 |
| ❑ 456 | Jeffrey Leonard | .01 | .05 |
| ❑ 457 | Edgar Martinez | .05 | .15 |
| ❑ 458 | Tino Martinez | .08 | .25 |
| ❑ 459 | Pete O'Brien UER | | |
| | (1987 BA .266& | | |
| | should be .286) | .01 | .05 |
| ❑ 460 | Harold Reynolds | .02 | .10 |
| ❑ 461 | Mike Schooler | .01 | .05 |
| ❑ 462 | Bill Swift | .01 | .05 |
| ❑ 463 | David Valle | .01 | .05 |
| ❑ 464 | Omar Vizquel | .05 | .15 |
| ❑ 465 | Matt Young | .01 | .05 |
| ❑ 466 | Brady Anderson | .02 | .10 |
| ❑ 467 | Jeff Ballard UER | | |
| | (Missing top of right | | |
| | parenthes | .01 | .05 |
| ❑ 468 | Juan Bell | .01 | .05 |
| ❑ 469A | Mike Devereaux | | |
| | (First line of text | | |
| | ends with six | .02 | .10 |
| ❑ 469B | Mike Devereaux | | |
| | (First line of text | | |
| | ends with nine | | |
| ❑ 470 | Steve Finley | .02 | .10 |
| ❑ 471 | Dave Gallagher | .01 | .05 |
| ❑ 472 | Leo Gomez | .01 | .05 |
| ❑ 473 | Rene Gonzales | .01 | .05 |
| ❑ 474 | Pete Harnisch | .01 | .05 |
| ❑ 475 | Kevin Hickey | .01 | .05 |
| ❑ 476 | Chris Hoiles | .01 | .05 |
| ❑ 477 | Sam Horn | .01 | .05 |
| ❑ 478 | Tim Hulett | | |
| | (Photo shows National | | |
| | Leaguer sliding | .01 | .05 |
| ❑ 479 | Dave Johnson | .01 | .05 |
| ❑ 480 | Ron Kittle UER | | |
| | (Edmonton misspelled | | |
| | as Edmundton | .01 | .05 |
| ❑ 481 | Ben McDonald | .01 | .05 |
| ❑ 482 | Bob Melvin | .01 | .05 |
| ❑ 483 | Bob Milacki | .01 | .05 |
| ❑ 484 | Randy Milligan | .01 | .05 |
| ❑ 485 | John Mitchell | .01 | .05 |
| ❑ 486 | Gregg Olson | .01 | .05 |
| ❑ 487 | Joe Orsulak | .01 | .05 |
| ❑ 488 | Joe Price | .01 | .05 |
| ❑ 489 | Bill Ripken | .01 | .05 |
| ❑ 490 | Cal Ripken | .30 | .75 |
| ❑ 491 | Curt Schilling | .08 | .25 |
| ❑ 492 | David Segui | .01 | .05 |
| ❑ 493 | Anthony Telford RC | .05 | .15 |
| ❑ 494 | Mickey Tettleton | .01 | .05 |
| ❑ 495 | Mark Williamson | .01 | .05 |
| ❑ 496 | Craig Worthington | .01 | .05 |
| ❑ 497 | Juan Agosto | .01 | .05 |
| ❑ 498 | Eric Anthony | .01 | .05 |
| ❑ 499 | Craig Biggio | .05 | .15 |
| ❑ 500 | Ken Caminiti UER | .02 | .10 |
| ❑ 501 | Casey Candaele | .01 | .05 |
| ❑ 502 | Andujar Cedeno | .01 | .05 |
| ❑ 503 | Danny Darwin | .01 | .05 |
| ❑ 504 | Mark Davidson | .01 | .05 |
| ❑ 505 | Glenn Davis | .01 | .05 |
| ❑ 506 | Jim Deshaies | .01 | .05 |
| ❑ 507 | Luis Gonzalez RC | .20 | .50 |
| ❑ 508 | Bill Gullickson | .01 | .05 |
| ❑ 509 | Xavier Hernandez | .01 | .05 |
| ❑ 510 | Brian Meyer | .01 | .05 |
| ❑ 511 | Ken Oberkfell | .01 | .05 |
| ❑ 512 | Mark Portugal | .01 | .05 |
| ❑ 513 | Rafael Ramirez | .01 | .05 |
| ❑ 514 | Karl Rhodes | .01 | .05 |
| ❑ 515 | Mike Scott | .01 | .05 |
| ❑ 516 | Mike Simms RC | .01 | .05 |
| ❑ 517 | Dave Smith | .01 | .05 |
| ❑ 518 | Franklin Stubbs | .01 | .05 |
| ❑ 519 | Glenn Wilson | .01 | .05 |
| ❑ 520 | Eric Yelding UER | | |
| | (Text has 63 steals& | | |
| | stats have | .01 | .05 |
| ❑ 521 | Gerald Young | .01 | .05 |
| ❑ 522 | Shawn Abner | .01 | .05 |
| ❑ 523 | Roberto Alomar | .05 | .15 |
| ❑ 524 | Andy Benes | .01 | .05 |
| ❑ 525 | Joe Carter | .02 | .10 |
| ❑ 526 | Jack Clark | .02 | .10 |
| ❑ 527 | Joey Cora | .01 | .05 |
| ❑ 528 | Paul Faries RC | .01 | .05 |
| ❑ 529 | Tony Gwynn | .10 | .30 |
| ❑ 530 | Atlee Hammaker | .01 | .05 |
| ❑ 531 | Greg W. Harris | .01 | .05 |

| | | |
|---|---|---|
| 532 Thomas Howard | .01 | .05 |
| 533 Bruce Hurst | .01 | .05 |
| 534 Craig Lefferts | .01 | .05 |
| 535 Derek Lilliquist | .01 | .05 |
| 536 Fred Lynn | .01 | .05 |
| 537 Mike Pagliarulo | .01 | .05 |
| 538 Mark Parent | .01 | .05 |
| 539 Dennis Rasmussen | .01 | .05 |
| 540 Bip Roberts | .01 | .05 |
| 541 Richard Rodriguez RC | .01 | .05 |
| 542 Benito Santiago | .02 | .10 |
| 543 Calvin Schiraldi | .01 | .05 |
| 544 Eric Show | .01 | .05 |
| 545 Phil Stephenson | .01 | .05 |
| 546 Garry Templeton UER (Born 3/24/57& should be 3/2 | .01 | .05 |
| 547 Ed Whitson | .01 | .05 |
| 548 Eddie Williams | .01 | .05 |
| 549 Kevin Appier | .02 | .10 |
| 550 Luis Aquino | .01 | .05 |
| 551 Bob Boone | .02 | .10 |
| 552 George Brett | .25 | .60 |
| 553 Jeff Conine RC | .15 | .40 |
| 554 Steve Crawford | .01 | .05 |
| 555 Mark Davis | .01 | .05 |
| 556 Storm Davis | .01 | .05 |
| 557 Jim Eisenreich | .01 | .05 |
| 558 Steve Farr | .01 | .05 |
| 559 Tom Gordon | .01 | .05 |
| 560 Mark Gubicza | .01 | .05 |
| 561 Bo Jackson | .08 | .25 |
| 562 Mike Macfarlane | .01 | .05 |
| 563 Brian McRae RC | .08 | .25 |
| 564 Jeff Montgomery | .01 | .05 |
| 565 Bill Pecota | .01 | .05 |
| 566 Gerald Perry | .01 | .05 |
| 567 Bret Saberhagen | .02 | .10 |
| 568 Jeff Schulz RC | .01 | .05 |
| 569 Kevin Seitzer | .01 | .05 |
| 570 Terry Shumpert | .01 | .05 |
| 571 Kurt Stillwell | .01 | .05 |
| 572 Danny Tartabull | .02 | .10 |
| 573 Gary Thurman | .01 | .05 |
| 574 Frank White | .02 | .10 |
| 575 Willie Wilson | .01 | .05 |
| 576 Chris Bosio | .01 | .05 |
| 577 Greg Brock | .01 | .05 |
| 578 George Canale | .01 | .05 |
| 579 Chuck Crim | .01 | .05 |
| 580 Rob Deer | .01 | .05 |
| 581 Edgar Diaz | .01 | .05 |
| 582 Tom Edens RC | .02 | .10 |
| 583 Mike Felder | .01 | .05 |
| 584 Jim Gantner | .01 | .05 |
| 585 Darryl Hamilton | .01 | .05 |
| 586 Ted Higuera | .01 | .05 |
| 587 Mark Knudson | .01 | .05 |
| 588 Bill Krueger | .01 | .05 |
| 589 Tim McIntosh | .01 | .05 |
| 590 Paul Mirabella | .01 | .05 |
| 591 Paul Molitor | .02 | .10 |
| 592 Jaime Navarro | .02 | .10 |
| 593 Dave Parker | .02 | .10 |
| 594 Dan Plesac | .01 | .05 |
| 595 Ron Robinson | .01 | .05 |
| 596 Gary Sheffield | .02 | .10 |
| 597 Bill Spiers | .01 | .05 |
| 598 B.J. Surhoff | .01 | .05 |
| 599 Greg Vaughn | .01 | .05 |
| 600 Randy Veres | .01 | .05 |
| 601 Robin Yount | .15 | .40 |
| 602 Rick Aguilera | .01 | .05 |
| 603 Allan Anderson | .01 | .05 |
| 604 Juan Berenguer | .01 | .05 |
| 605 Randy Bush | .01 | .05 |
| 606 Carmelo Castillo | .01 | .05 |
| 607 Tim Drummond | .01 | .05 |
| 608 Scott Erickson | .01 | .05 |
| 609 Gary Gaetti | .01 | .05 |
| 610 Greg Gagne | .01 | .05 |
| 611 Dan Gladden | .01 | .05 |
| 612 Mark Guthrie | .01 | .05 |
| 613 Brian Harper | .01 | .05 |
| 614 Kent Hrbek | .02 | .10 |
| 615 Gene Larkin | .01 | .05 |
| 616 Terry Leach | .01 | .05 |
| 617 Nelson Liriano | .01 | .05 |
| 618 Shane Mack | .01 | .05 |
| 619 John Moses | .01 | .05 |
| 620 Pedro Munoz RC | .02 | .10 |
| 621 Al Newman | .01 | .05 |
| 622 Junior Ortiz | .01 | .05 |
| 623 Kirby Puckett | .08 | .25 |
| 624 Roy Smith | .01 | .05 |
| 625 Kevin Tapani | .01 | .05 |
| 626 Gary Wayne | .01 | .05 |
| 627 David West | .01 | .05 |
| 628 Cris Carpenter | .01 | .05 |
| 629 Vince Coleman | .01 | .05 |
| 630 Ken Dayley | .01 | .05 |
| 631A Jose DeLeon ERR | .01 | .05 |
| 631B Jose DeLeon COR | .01 | .05 |
| 632 Frank DiPino | .01 | .05 |
| 633 Bernard Gilkey | .01 | .05 |
| 634A Pedro Guerrero ERR | .01 | .05 |
| 634B Pedro Guerrero COR | .02 | .10 |
| 635 Ken Hill | .01 | .05 |
| 636 Felix Jose | .01 | .05 |
| 637 Ray Lankford | .02 | .10 |
| 638 Joe Magrane | .01 | .05 |
| 639 Tom Niedenfuer | .01 | .05 |
| 640 Jose Oquendo | .01 | .05 |
| 641 Tom Pagnozzi | .01 | .05 |
| 642 Terry Pendleton | .02 | .10 |
| 643 Mike Perez RC | .02 | .10 |
| 644 Bryn Smith | .01 | .05 |
| 645 Lee Smith | .02 | .10 |
| 646 Ozzie Smith | .15 | .40 |
| 647 Scott Terry | .01 | .05 |
| 648 Bob Tewksbury | .01 | .05 |
| 649 Milt Thompson | .01 | .05 |
| 650 John Tudor | .01 | .05 |
| 651 Denny Walling | .01 | .05 |
| 652 Craig Wilson RC | .01 | .05 |
| 653 Todd Worrell | .01 | .05 |
| 654 Todd Zeile | .01 | .05 |
| 655 Oscar Azocar | .01 | .05 |
| 656 Steve Balboni UER (Born 1/5/57, should be 1/16) | .01 | .05 |
| 657 Jesse Barfield | .01 | .05 |
| 658 Greg Cadaret | .01 | .05 |
| 659 Chuck Cary | .01 | .05 |
| 660 Rick Cerone | .01 | .05 |
| 661 Dave Eiland | .01 | .05 |
| 662 Alvaro Espinoza | .01 | .05 |
| 663 Bob Geren | .01 | .05 |
| 664 Lee Guetterman | .01 | .05 |
| 665 Mel Hall | .01 | .05 |
| 666 Andy Hawkins | .01 | .05 |
| 667 Jimmy Jones | .01 | .05 |
| 668 Roberto Kelly | .01 | .05 |
| 669 Dave LaPoint UER (No '81 Brewers stats& totals a | .01 | .05 |
| 670 Tim Leary | .01 | .05 |
| 671 Jim Leyritz | .01 | .05 |
| 672 Kevin Maas | .01 | .05 |
| 673 Don Mattingly | .25 | .60 |
| 674 Matt Nokes | .01 | .05 |
| 675 Pascual Perez | .01 | .05 |
| 676 Eric Plunk | .01 | .05 |
| 677 Dave Righetti | .02 | .10 |
| 678 Jeff D. Robinson | .01 | .05 |
| 679 Steve Sax | .02 | .10 |
| 680 Mike Witt | .01 | .05 |
| 681 Steve Avery UER | .01 | .05 |
| 682 Mike Bell RC | .01 | .05 |
| 683 Jeff Blauser | .01 | .05 |
| 684 Francisco Cabrera UER (Born 10/16& should say 10 | .01 | .05 |
| 685 Tony Castillo | .01 | .05 |
| 686 Marty Clary UER (Shown pitching righty& but bio | .01 | .05 |
| 687 Nick Esasky | .01 | .05 |
| 688 Ron Gant | .02 | .10 |
| 689 Tom Glavine | .05 | .15 |
| 690 Mark Grant | .01 | .05 |
| 691 Tommy Gregg | .01 | .05 |
| 692 Dwayne Henry | .01 | .05 |
| 693 David Justice | .02 | .10 |
| 694 Jimmy Kremers | .01 | .05 |
| 695 Charlie Leibrandt | .01 | .05 |
| 696 Mark Lemke | .01 | .05 |
| 697 Oddibe McDowell | .01 | .05 |
| 698 Greg Olson | .01 | .05 |
| 699 Jeff Parrett | .01 | .05 |
| 700 Jim Presley | .01 | .05 |
| 701 Victor Rosario RC | .01 | .05 |
| 702 Lonnie Smith | .01 | .05 |
| 703 Pete Smith | .01 | .05 |
| 704 John Smoltz | .05 | .15 |
| 705 Mike Stanton | .01 | .05 |
| 706 Andres Thomas | .01 | .05 |
| 707 Jeff Treadway | .01 | .05 |
| 708 Jim Vatcher RC | .01 | .05 |
| 709 R.Sandberg/C.Fielder | .08 | .25 |
| 710 K.Griffey Jr./B.Bonds | .40 | 1.00 |
| 711 B.Bonilla/B.Larkin | .02 | .10 |
| 712 Top Game Savers Bobby Thigpen John Franco | .01 | .05 |
| 713 A.Dawson/R.Sandberg UER | .08 | .25 |
| 714 CL:A's/Pirates Reds/Red Sox | .01 | .05 |
| 715 CL:White Sox/Mets Blue Jays/Dodgers | .01 | .05 |
| 716 CL:Expos/Giants Rangers/Angels | .01 | .05 |
| 717 CL:Tigers/Indians Phillies/Cubs | .01 | .05 |
| 718 CL:Mariners/Orioles Astros/Padres | .01 | .05 |
| 719 CL:Royals/Brewers Twins/Cardinals | .01 | .05 |
| 720 CL:Yankees/Braves Superstars/Specials | .01 | .05 |

### 1992 Fleer

| | | |
|---|---|---|
| COMPLETE SET (720) | 4.00 | 10.00 |
| COMP.HOBBY SET (732) | 8.00 | 20.00 |
| COMP.RETAIL SET (732) | 8.00 | 20.00 |
| 1 Brady Anderson | .02 | .10 |
| 2 Jose Bautista | .02 | .10 |
| 3 Juan Bell | .02 | .10 |
| 4 Glenn Davis | .02 | .10 |
| 5 Mike Devereaux | .02 | .10 |
| 6 Dwight Evans | .05 | .15 |
| 7 Mike Flanagan | .02 | .10 |
| 8 Leo Gomez | .02 | .10 |
| 9 Chris Hoiles | .02 | .10 |
| 10 Sam Horn | .02 | .10 |
| 11 Tim Hulett | .02 | .10 |
| 12 Dave Johnson | .02 | .10 |
| 13 Chito Martinez | .02 | .10 |
| 14 Ben McDonald | .02 | .10 |
| 15 Bob Melvin | .02 | .10 |
| 16 Luis Mercedes | .02 | .10 |
| 17 Jose Mesa | .02 | .10 |
| 18 Bob Milacki | .02 | .10 |
| 19 Randy Milligan | .02 | .10 |
| 20 Mike Mussina | .08 | .25 |
| 21 Gregg Olson | .02 | .10 |
| 22 Joe Orsulak | .02 | .10 |
| 23 Jim Poole | .02 | .10 |
| 24 Arthur Rhodes | .02 | .10 |
| 25 Billy Ripken | .02 | .10 |
| 26 Cal Ripken | .30 | .75 |
| 27 David Segui | .02 | .10 |
| 28 Roy Smith | .02 | .10 |
| 29 Anthony Telford | .02 | .10 |
| 30 Mark Williamson | .02 | .10 |
| 31 Craig Worthington | .02 | .10 |
| 32 Mike Boddicker | .05 | .15 |
| 33 Tom Bolton | .02 | .10 |
| 34 Tom Brunansky | .02 | .10 |
| 35 Ellis Burks | .02 | .10 |

|  |  | | |
|---|--------|----|----|
| 36 | Jack Clark | .02 | .10 |
| 37 | Roger Clemens | .20 | .50 |
| 38 | Danny Darwin | .02 | .10 |
| 39 | Mike Greenwell | .02 | .10 |
| 40 | Joe Hesketh | .02 | .10 |
| 41 | Daryl Irvine | .02 | .10 |
| 42 | Dennis Lamp | .02 | .10 |
| 43 | Tony Pena | .02 | .10 |
| 44 | Phil Plantier | .02 | .10 |
| 45 | Carlos Quintana | .02 | .10 |
| 46 | Jeff Reardon | .02 | .10 |
| 47 | Jody Reed | .02 | .10 |
| 48 | Luis Rivera | .02 | .10 |
| 49 | Mo Vaughn | .02 | .10 |
| 50 | Jim Abbott | .05 | .15 |
| 51 | Kyle Abbott | .02 | .10 |
| 52 | Ruben Amaro | .02 | .10 |
| 53 | Scott Bailes | .02 | .10 |
| 54 | Chris Beasley | .02 | .10 |
| 55 | Mark Eichhorn | .02 | .10 |
| 56 | Mike Fetters | .02 | .10 |
| 57 | Chuck Finley | .02 | .10 |
| 58 | Gary Gaetti | .02 | .10 |
| 59 | Dave Gallagher | .02 | .10 |
| 60 | Donnie Hill | .02 | .10 |
| 61 | Bryan Harvey UER | | |
| | (Lee Smith led the | | |
| | Majors with | .02 | .10 |
| 62 | Wally Joyner | .02 | .10 |
| 63 | Mark Langston | .02 | .10 |
| 64 | Kirk McCaskill | .02 | .10 |
| 65 | John Orton | .02 | .10 |
| 66 | Lance Parrish | .02 | .10 |
| 67 | Luis Polonia | .02 | .10 |
| 68 | Bobby Rose | .02 | .10 |
| 69 | Dick Schofield | .02 | .10 |
| 70 | Luis Sojo | .02 | .10 |
| 71 | Lee Stevens | .02 | .10 |
| 72 | Dave Winfield | .02 | .10 |
| 73 | Cliff Young | .02 | .10 |
| 74 | Wilson Alvarez | .02 | .10 |
| 75 | Esteban Beltre | .02 | .10 |
| 76 | Joey Cora | .02 | .10 |
| 77 | Brian Drahman | .02 | .10 |
| 78 | Alex Fernandez | .02 | .10 |
| 79 | Carlton Fisk | .05 | .15 |
| 80 | Scott Fletcher | .02 | .10 |
| 81 | Craig Grebeck | .02 | .10 |
| 82 | Ozzie Guillen | .02 | .10 |
| 83 | Greg Hibbard | .02 | .10 |
| 84 | Charlie Hough | .02 | .10 |
| 85 | Mike Huff | .02 | .10 |
| 86 | Bo Jackson | .08 | .25 |
| 87 | Lance Johnson | .02 | .10 |
| 88 | Ron Karkovice | .02 | .10 |
| 89 | Jack McDowell | .02 | .10 |
| 90 | Matt Merullo | .02 | .10 |
| 91 | Warren Newson | .02 | .10 |
| 92 | Donn Pall UER | | |
| | (Called Dunn on | | |
| | card back) | .02 | .10 |
| 93 | Dan Pasqua | .02 | .10 |
| 94 | Ken Patterson | .02 | .10 |
| 95 | Melido Perez | .02 | .10 |
| 96 | Scott Radinsky | .02 | .10 |
| 97 | Tim Raines | .02 | .10 |
| 98 | Sammy Sosa | .08 | .25 |
| 99 | Bobby Thigpen | .02 | .10 |
| 100 | Frank Thomas | .08 | .25 |
| 101 | Robin Ventura | .02 | .10 |
| 102 | Mike Aldrete | .02 | .10 |
| 103 | Sandy Alomar Jr. | .02 | .10 |
| 104 | Carlos Baerga | .02 | .10 |
| 105 | Albert Belle | .02 | .10 |
| 106 | Willie Blair | .02 | .10 |
| 107 | Jerry Browne | .02 | .10 |
| 108 | Alex Cole | .02 | .10 |
| 109 | Felix Fermin | .02 | .10 |
| 110 | Glenallen Hill | .02 | .10 |
| 111 | Shawn Hillegas | .02 | .10 |
| 112 | Chris James | .02 | .10 |
| 113 | Reggie Jefferson | .02 | .10 |
| 114 | Doug Jones | .02 | .10 |
| 115 | Eric King | .02 | .10 |
| 116 | Mark Lewis | .02 | .10 |
| 117 | Carlos Martinez | .02 | .10 |
| 118 | Charles Nagy UER | | |
| | (Throws right& but | | |
| | card says le | .02 | .10 |
| 119 | Rod Nichols | .02 | .10 |
| 120 | Steve Olin | .02 | .10 |
| 121 | Jesse Orosco | .02 | .10 |
| 122 | Rudy Seanez | .02 | .10 |
| 123 | Joel Skinner | .02 | .10 |
| 124 | Greg Swindell | .02 | .10 |
| 125 | Jim Thome | .08 | .25 |
| 126 | Mark Whiten | .02 | .10 |
| 127 | Scott Aldred | .02 | .10 |
| 128 | Andy Allanson | .02 | .10 |
| 129 | John Cerutti | .02 | .10 |
| 130 | Milt Cuyler | .02 | .10 |
| 131 | Mike Dalton | .02 | .10 |
| 132 | Rob Deer | .02 | .10 |
| 133 | Cecil Fielder | .02 | .10 |
| 134 | Travis Fryman | .02 | .10 |
| 135 | Dan Gakeler | .02 | .10 |
| 136 | Paul Gibson | .02 | .10 |
| 137 | Bill Gullickson | .02 | .10 |
| 138 | Mike Henneman | .02 | .10 |
| 139 | Pete Incaviglia | .02 | .10 |
| 140 | Mark Leiter | .02 | .10 |
| 141 | Scott Livingstone | .02 | .10 |
| 142 | Lloyd Moseby | .02 | .10 |
| 143 | Tony Phillips | .02 | .10 |
| 144 | Mark Salas | .02 | .10 |
| 145 | Frank Tanana | .02 | .10 |
| 146 | Walt Terrell | .02 | .10 |
| 147 | Mickey Tettleton | .02 | .10 |
| 148 | Alan Trammell | .02 | .10 |
| 149 | Lou Whitaker | .02 | .10 |
| 150 | Kevin Appier | .02 | .10 |
| 151 | Luis Aquino | .02 | .10 |
| 152 | Todd Benzinger | .02 | .10 |
| 153 | Mike Boddicker | .02 | .10 |
| 154 | George Brett | .25 | .60 |
| 155 | Storm Davis | .02 | .10 |
| 156 | Jim Eisenreich | .02 | .10 |
| 157 | Kirk Gibson | .02 | .10 |
| 158 | Tom Gordon | .02 | .10 |
| 159 | Mark Gubicza | .02 | .10 |
| 160 | David Howard | .02 | .10 |
| 161 | Mike Macfarlane | .02 | .10 |
| 162 | Brent Mayne | .02 | .10 |
| 163 | Brian McRae | .02 | .10 |
| 164 | Jeff Montgomery | .02 | .10 |
| 165 | Bill Pecota | .02 | .10 |
| 166 | Harvey Pulliam | .02 | .10 |
| 167 | Bret Saberhagen | .02 | .10 |
| 168 | Kevin Seitzer | .02 | .10 |
| 169 | Terry Shumpert | .02 | .10 |
| 170 | Kurt Stillwell | .02 | .10 |
| 171 | Danny Tartabull | .02 | .10 |
| 172 | Gary Thurman | .02 | .10 |
| 173 | Dante Bichette | .02 | .10 |
| 174 | Kevin D. Brown | .02 | .10 |
| 175 | Chuck Crim | .02 | .10 |
| 176 | Jim Gantner | .02 | .10 |
| 177 | Darryl Hamilton | .02 | .10 |
| 178 | Ted Higuera | .02 | .10 |
| 179 | Darren Holmes | .02 | .10 |
| 180 | Mark Lee | .02 | .10 |
| 181 | Julio Machado | .02 | .10 |
| 182 | Paul Molitor | .02 | .10 |
| 183 | Jaime Navarro | .02 | .10 |
| 184 | Edwin Nunez | .02 | .10 |
| 185 | Dan Plesac | .02 | .10 |
| 186 | Willie Randolph | .02 | .10 |
| 187 | Ron Robinson | .02 | .10 |
| 188 | Gary Sheffield | .02 | .10 |
| 189 | Bill Spiers | .02 | .10 |
| 190 | B.J. Surhoff | .02 | .10 |
| 191 | Dale Sveum | .02 | .10 |
| 192 | Greg Vaughn | .02 | .10 |
| 193 | Bill Wegman | .02 | .10 |
| 194 | Robin Yount | .15 | .40 |
| 195 | Rick Aguilera | .02 | .10 |
| 196 | Allan Anderson | .02 | .10 |
| 197 | Steve Bedrosian | .02 | .10 |
| 198 | Randy Bush | .02 | .10 |
| 199 | Larry Casian | .02 | .10 |
| 200 | Chili Davis | .02 | .10 |
| 201 | Scott Erickson | .02 | .10 |
| 202 | Greg Gagne | .02 | .10 |
| 203 | Dan Gladden | .02 | .10 |
| 204 | Brian Harper | .02 | .10 |
| 205 | Kent Hrbek | .02 | .10 |
| 206 | Chuck Knoblauch UER | .02 | .10 |
| 207 | Gene Larkin | .02 | .10 |
| 208 | Terry Leach | .02 | .10 |
| 209 | Scott Leius | .02 | .10 |
| 210 | Shane Mack | .02 | .10 |
| 211 | Jack Morris | .02 | .10 |
| 212 | Pedro Munoz | .02 | .10 |
| 213 | Denny Neagle | .02 | .10 |
| 214 | Al Newman | .02 | .10 |
| 215 | Junior Ortiz | .02 | .10 |
| 216 | Mike Pagliarulo | .02 | .10 |
| 217 | Kirby Puckett | .08 | .25 |
| 218 | Paul Sorrento | .02 | .10 |
| 219 | Kevin Tapani | .02 | .10 |
| 220 | Lenny Webster | .02 | .10 |
| 221 | Jesse Barfield | .02 | .10 |
| 222 | Greg Cadaret | .02 | .10 |
| 223 | Dave Eiland | .02 | .10 |
| 224 | Alvaro Espinoza | .02 | .10 |
| 225 | Steve Farr | .02 | .10 |
| 226 | Bob Geren | .02 | .10 |
| 227 | Lee Guetterman | .02 | .10 |
| 228 | John Habyan | .02 | .10 |
| 229 | Mel Hall | .02 | .10 |
| 230 | Steve Howe | .02 | .10 |
| 231 | Mike Humphreys | .02 | .10 |
| 232 | Scott Kamieniecki | .02 | .10 |
| 233 | Pat Kelly | .02 | .10 |
| 234 | Roberto Kelly | .02 | .10 |
| 235 | Tim Leary | .02 | .10 |
| 236 | Kevin Maas | .02 | .10 |
| 237 | Don Mattingly | .25 | .60 |
| 238 | Hensley Meulens | .02 | .10 |
| 239 | Matt Nokes | .02 | .10 |
| 240 | Pascual Perez | .02 | .10 |
| 241 | Eric Plunk | .02 | .10 |
| 242 | John Ramos | .02 | .10 |
| 243 | Scott Sanderson | .02 | .10 |
| 244 | Steve Sax | .02 | .10 |
| 245 | Wade Taylor | .02 | .10 |
| 246 | Randy Velarde | .02 | .10 |
| 247 | Bernie Williams | .05 | .15 |
| 248 | Troy Afenir | .02 | .10 |
| 249 | Harold Baines | .02 | .10 |
| 250 | Lance Blankenship | .02 | .10 |
| 251 | Mike Bordick | .02 | .10 |
| 252 | Jose Canseco | .15 | .15 |
| 253 | Steve Chitren | .02 | .10 |
| 254 | Ron Darling | .02 | .10 |
| 255 | Dennis Eckersley | .02 | .10 |
| 256 | Mike Gallego | .02 | .10 |
| 257 | Dave Henderson | .02 | .10 |
| 258 | Rickey Henderson | .08 | .25 |
| 259 | Rick Honeycutt | .02 | .10 |
| 260 | Brook Jacoby | .02 | .10 |
| 261 | Carney Lansford | .02 | .10 |
| 262 | Mark McGwire | .25 | .60 |
| 263 | Mike Moore | .02 | .10 |
| 264 | Gene Nelson | .02 | .10 |
| 265 | Jamie Quirk | .02 | .10 |
| 266 | Joe Slusarski | .02 | .10 |
| 267 | Terry Steinbach | .02 | .10 |
| 268 | Dave Stewart | .02 | .10 |
| 269 | Todd Van Poppel | .02 | .10 |
| 270 | Walt Weiss | .02 | .10 |
| 271 | Bob Welch | .02 | .10 |
| 272 | Curt Young | .02 | .10 |
| 273 | Scott Bradley | .02 | .10 |
| 274 | Greg Briley | .02 | .10 |
| 275 | Jay Buhner | .02 | .10 |
| 276 | Henry Cotto | .02 | .10 |
| 277 | Alvin Davis | .02 | .10 |
| 278 | Rich DeLucia | .02 | .10 |
| 279 | Ken Griffey Jr. | .15 | .40 |
| 280 | Erik Hanson | .02 | .10 |
| 281 | Brian Holman | .02 | .10 |
| 282 | Mike Jackson | .02 | .10 |
| 283 | Randy Johnson | .06 | .25 |
| 284 | Tracy Jones | .02 | .10 |
| 285 | Bill Krueger | .02 | .10 |
| 286 | Edgar Martinez | .05 | .15 |
| 287 | Tino Martinez | .05 | .15 |
| 288 | Rob Murphy | .02 | .10 |
| 289 | Pete O'Brien | .02 | .10 |
| 290 | Alonzo Powell | .02 | .10 |
| 291 | Harold Reynolds | .02 | .10 |
| 292 | Mike Schooler | .02 | .10 |
| 293 | Russ Swan | .02 | .10 |

| | | |
|---|---|---|
| ☐ 294 Bill Swift | .02 | .10 |
| ☐ 295 Dave Valle | .02 | .10 |
| ☐ 296 Omar Vizquel | .05 | .15 |
| ☐ 297 Gerald Alexander | .02 | .10 |
| ☐ 298 Brad Arnsberg | .02 | .10 |
| ☐ 299 Kevin Brown | .02 | .10 |
| ☐ 300 Jack Daugherty | .02 | .10 |
| ☐ 301 Mario Diaz | .02 | .10 |
| ☐ 302 Brian Downing | .02 | .10 |
| ☐ 303 Julio Franco | .02 | .10 |
| ☐ 304 Juan Gonzalez | .05 | .15 |
| ☐ 305 Rich Gossage | .02 | .10 |
| ☐ 306 Jose Guzman | .02 | .10 |
| ☐ 307 Jose Hernandez RC | .08 | .25 |
| ☐ 308 Jeff Huson | .02 | .10 |
| ☐ 309 Mike Jeffcoat | .02 | .10 |
| ☐ 310 Terry Mathews | .02 | .10 |
| ☐ 311 Rafael Palmeiro | .05 | .15 |
| ☐ 312 Dean Palmer | .02 | .10 |
| ☐ 313 Geno Petralli | .02 | .10 |
| ☐ 314 Gary Pettis | .02 | .10 |
| ☐ 315 Kevin Reimer | .02 | .10 |
| ☐ 316 Ivan Rodriguez | .08 | .25 |
| ☐ 317 Kenny Rogers | .02 | .10 |
| ☐ 318 Wayne Rosenthal | .02 | .10 |
| ☐ 319 Jeff Russell | .02 | .10 |
| ☐ 320 Nolan Ryan | .40 | 1.00 |
| ☐ 321 Ruben Sierra | .02 | .10 |
| ☐ 322 Jim Acker | .02 | .10 |
| ☐ 323 Roberto Alomar | .05 | .15 |
| ☐ 324 Derek Bell | .02 | .10 |
| ☐ 325 Pat Borders | .02 | .10 |
| ☐ 326 Tom Candiotti | .02 | .10 |
| ☐ 327 Joe Carter | .02 | .10 |
| ☐ 328 Rob Ducey | .02 | .10 |
| ☐ 329 Kelly Gruber | .02 | .10 |
| ☐ 330 Juan Guzman | .02 | .10 |
| ☐ 331 Tom Henke | .02 | .10 |
| ☐ 332 Jimmy Key | .02 | .10 |
| ☐ 333 Manny Lee | .02 | .10 |
| ☐ 334 Al Leiter | .02 | .10 |
| ☐ 335 Bob MacDonald | .02 | .10 |
| ☐ 336 Candy Maldonado | .02 | .10 |
| ☐ 337 Rance Mulliniks | .02 | .10 |
| ☐ 338 Greg Myers | .02 | .10 |
| ☐ 339 John Olerud UER | .02 | .10 |
| ☐ 340 Ed Sprague | .02 | .10 |
| ☐ 341 Dave Stieb | .02 | .10 |
| ☐ 342 Todd Stottlemyre | .02 | .10 |
| ☐ 343 Mike Timlin | .02 | .10 |
| ☐ 344 Duane Ward | .02 | .10 |
| ☐ 345 David Wells | .02 | .10 |
| ☐ 346 Devon White | .02 | .10 |
| ☐ 347 Mookie Wilson | .02 | .10 |
| ☐ 348 Eddie Zosky | .02 | .10 |
| ☐ 349 Steve Avery | .02 | .10 |
| ☐ 350 Mike Bell | .02 | .10 |
| ☐ 351 Rafael Belliard | .02 | .10 |
| ☐ 352 Juan Berenguer | .02 | .10 |
| ☐ 353 Jeff Blauser | .02 | .10 |
| ☐ 354 Sid Bream | .02 | .10 |
| ☐ 355 Francisco Cabrera | .02 | .10 |
| ☐ 356 Marvin Freeman | .02 | .10 |
| ☐ 357 Ron Gant | .02 | .10 |
| ☐ 358 Tom Glavine | .05 | .15 |
| ☐ 359 Brian Hunter | .02 | .10 |
| ☐ 360 David Justice | .02 | .10 |
| ☐ 361 Charlie Leibrandt | .02 | .10 |
| ☐ 362 Mark Lemke | .02 | .10 |
| ☐ 363 Kent Mercker | .02 | .10 |
| ☐ 364 Keith Mitchell | .02 | .10 |
| ☐ 365 Greg Olson | .02 | .10 |
| ☐ 366 Terry Pendleton | .02 | .10 |
| ☐ 367 Armando Reynoso RC | .08 | .25 |
| ☐ 368 Deion Sanders | .05 | .15 |
| ☐ 369 Lonnie Smith | .02 | .10 |
| ☐ 370 Pete Smith | .02 | .10 |
| ☐ 371 John Smoltz | .05 | .15 |
| ☐ 372 Mike Stanton | .02 | .10 |
| ☐ 373 Jeff Treadway | .02 | .10 |
| ☐ 374 Mark Wohlers | .02 | .10 |
| ☐ 375 Paul Assenmacher | .02 | .10 |
| ☐ 376 George Bell | .02 | .10 |
| ☐ 377 Shawn Boskie | .02 | .10 |
| ☐ 378 Frank Castillo | .02 | .10 |
| ☐ 379 Andre Dawson | .02 | .10 |
| ☐ 380 Shawon Dunston | .02 | .10 |
| ☐ 381 Mark Grace | .05 | .15 |

| | | |
|---|---|---|
| ☐ 382 Mike Harkey | .02 | .10 |
| ☐ 383 Danny Jackson | .02 | .10 |
| ☐ 384 Les Lancaster | .02 | .10 |
| ☐ 385 Ced Landrum | .02 | .10 |
| ☐ 386 Greg Maddux | .15 | .40 |
| ☐ 387 Derrick May | .02 | .10 |
| ☐ 388 Chuck McElroy | .02 | .10 |
| ☐ 389 Ryne Sandberg | .15 | .40 |
| ☐ 390 Heathcliff Slocumb | .02 | .10 |
| ☐ 391 Dave Smith | .02 | .10 |
| ☐ 392 Dwight Smith | .02 | .10 |
| ☐ 393 Rick Sutcliffe | .02 | .10 |
| ☐ 394 Hector Villanueva | .02 | .10 |
| ☐ 395 Chico Walker | .02 | .10 |
| ☐ 396 Jerome Walton | .02 | .10 |
| ☐ 397 Rick Wilkins | .02 | .10 |
| ☐ 398 Jack Armstrong | .02 | .10 |
| ☐ 399 Freddie Benavides | .02 | .10 |
| ☐ 400 Glenn Braggs | .02 | .10 |
| ☐ 401 Tom Browning | .02 | .10 |
| ☐ 402 Norm Charlton | .02 | .10 |
| ☐ 403 Eric Davis | .02 | .10 |
| ☐ 404 Rob Dibble | .02 | .10 |
| ☐ 405 Bill Doran | .02 | .10 |
| ☐ 406 Mariano Duncan | .02 | .10 |
| ☐ 407 Kip Gross | .02 | .10 |
| ☐ 408 Chris Hammond | .02 | .10 |
| ☐ 409 Billy Hatcher | .02 | .10 |
| ☐ 410 Chris Jones | .02 | .10 |
| ☐ 411 Barry Larkin | .05 | .15 |
| ☐ 412 Hal Morris | .02 | .10 |
| ☐ 413 Randy Myers | .02 | .10 |
| ☐ 414 Joe Oliver | .02 | .10 |
| ☐ 415 Paul O'Neill | .05 | .15 |
| ☐ 416 Ted Power | .02 | .10 |
| ☐ 417 Luis Quinones | .02 | .10 |
| ☐ 418 Jeff Reed | .02 | .10 |
| ☐ 419 Jose Rijo | .02 | .10 |
| ☐ 420 Chris Sabo | .02 | .10 |
| ☐ 421 Reggie Sanders | .02 | .10 |
| ☐ 422 Scott Scudder | .02 | .10 |
| ☐ 423 Glenn Sutko | .02 | .10 |
| ☐ 424 Eric Anthony | .02 | .10 |
| ☐ 425 Jeff Bagwell | .08 | .25 |
| ☐ 426 Craig Biggio | .05 | .15 |
| ☐ 427 Ken Caminiti | .02 | .10 |
| ☐ 428 Casey Candaele | .02 | .10 |
| ☐ 429 Mike Capel | .02 | .10 |
| ☐ 430 Andujar Cedeno | .02 | .10 |
| ☐ 431 Jim Corsi | .02 | .10 |
| ☐ 432 Mark Davidson | .02 | .10 |
| ☐ 433 Steve Finley | .02 | .10 |
| ☐ 434 Luis Gonzalez | .02 | .10 |
| ☐ 435 Pete Harnisch | .02 | .10 |
| ☐ 436 Dwayne Henry | .02 | .10 |
| ☐ 437 Xavier Hernandez | .02 | .10 |
| ☐ 438 Jimmy Jones | .02 | .10 |
| ☐ 439 Darryl Kile | .02 | .10 |
| ☐ 440 Rob Mallicoat | .02 | .10 |
| ☐ 441 Andy Mota | .02 | .10 |
| ☐ 442 Al Osuna | .02 | .10 |
| ☐ 443 Mark Portugal | .02 | .10 |
| ☐ 444 Scott Servais | .02 | .10 |
| ☐ 445 Mike Simms | .02 | .10 |
| ☐ 446 Gerald Young | .02 | .10 |
| ☐ 447 Tim Belcher | .02 | .10 |
| ☐ 448 Brett Butler | .02 | .10 |
| ☐ 449 John Candelaria | .02 | .10 |
| ☐ 450 Gary Carter | .02 | .10 |
| ☐ 451 Dennis Cook | .02 | .10 |
| ☐ 452 Tim Crews | .02 | .10 |
| ☐ 453 Kal Daniels | .02 | .10 |
| ☐ 454 Jim Gott | .02 | .10 |
| ☐ 455 Alfredo Griffin | .02 | .10 |
| ☐ 456 Kevin Gross | .02 | .10 |
| ☐ 457 Chris Gwynn | .02 | .10 |
| ☐ 458 Lenny Harris | .02 | .10 |
| ☐ 459 Orel Hershiser | .02 | .10 |
| ☐ 460 Jay Howell | .02 | .10 |
| ☐ 461 Stan Javier | .02 | .10 |
| ☐ 462 Eric Karros | .02 | .10 |
| ☐ 463 Ramon Martinez UER (Card says bats right& should | .02 | .10 |
| ☐ 464 Roger McDowell UER (Wins add up to 54& totals ha | | |
| ☐ 465 Mike Morgan | .02 | .10 |

| | | |
|---|---|---|
| ☐ 466 Eddie Murray | .08 | .25 |
| ☐ 467 Jose Offerman | .02 | .10 |
| ☐ 468 Bob Ojeda | .02 | .10 |
| ☐ 469 Juan Samuel | .02 | .10 |
| ☐ 470 Mike Scioscia | .02 | .10 |
| ☐ 471 Darryl Strawberry | .02 | .10 |
| ☐ 472 Bret Barberie | .02 | .10 |
| ☐ 473 Brian Barnes | .02 | .10 |
| ☐ 474 Eric Bullock | .02 | .10 |
| ☐ 475 Ivan Calderon | .02 | .10 |
| ☐ 476 Delino DeShields | .02 | .10 |
| ☐ 477 Jeff Fassero | .02 | .10 |
| ☐ 478 Mike Fitzgerald | .02 | .10 |
| ☐ 479 Steve Frey | .02 | .10 |
| ☐ 480 Andres Galarraga | .02 | .10 |
| ☐ 481 Mark Gardner | .02 | .10 |
| ☐ 482 Marquis Grissom | .02 | .10 |
| ☐ 483 Chris Haney | .02 | .10 |
| ☐ 484 Barry Jones | .02 | .10 |
| ☐ 485 Dave Martinez | .02 | .10 |
| ☐ 486 Dennis Martinez | .02 | .10 |
| ☐ 487 Chris Nabholz | .02 | .10 |
| ☐ 488 Spike Owen | .02 | .10 |
| ☐ 489 Gilberto Reyes | .02 | .10 |
| ☐ 490 Mel Rojas | .02 | .10 |
| ☐ 491 Scott Ruskin | .02 | .10 |
| ☐ 492 Bill Sampen | .02 | .10 |
| ☐ 493 Larry Walker | .05 | .15 |
| ☐ 494 Tim Wallach | .02 | .10 |
| ☐ 495 Daryl Boston | .02 | .10 |
| ☐ 496 Hubie Brooks | .02 | .10 |
| ☐ 497 Tim Burke | .02 | .10 |
| ☐ 498 Mark Carreon | .02 | .10 |
| ☐ 499 Tony Castillo | .02 | .10 |
| ☐ 500 Vince Coleman | .02 | .10 |
| ☐ 501 David Cone | .02 | .10 |
| ☐ 502 Kevin Elster | .02 | .10 |
| ☐ 503 Sid Fernandez | .02 | .10 |
| ☐ 504 John Franco | .02 | .10 |
| ☐ 505 Dwight Gooden | .02 | .10 |
| ☐ 506 Todd Hundley | .02 | .10 |
| ☐ 507 Jeff Innis | .02 | .10 |
| ☐ 508 Gregg Jefferies | .02 | .10 |
| ☐ 509 Howard Johnson | .02 | .10 |
| ☐ 510 Dave Magadan | .02 | .10 |
| ☐ 511 Terry McDaniel | .02 | .10 |
| ☐ 512 Kevin McReynolds | .02 | .10 |
| ☐ 513 Keith Miller | .02 | .10 |
| ☐ 514 Charlie O'Brien | .02 | .10 |
| ☐ 515 Mackey Sasser | .02 | .10 |
| ☐ 516 Pete Schourek | .02 | .10 |
| ☐ 517 Julio Valera | .02 | .10 |
| ☐ 518 Frank Viola | .02 | .10 |
| ☐ 519 Wally Whitehurst | .02 | .10 |
| ☐ 520 Anthony Young | .02 | .10 |
| ☐ 521 Andy Ashby | .02 | .10 |
| ☐ 522 Kim Batiste | .02 | .10 |
| ☐ 523 Joe Boever | .02 | .10 |
| ☐ 524 Wes Chamberlain | .02 | .10 |
| ☐ 525 Pat Combs | .02 | .10 |
| ☐ 526 Danny Cox | .02 | .10 |
| ☐ 527 Darren Daulton | .02 | .10 |
| ☐ 528 Jose DeJesus | .02 | .10 |
| ☐ 529 Len Dykstra | .02 | .10 |
| ☐ 530 Darrin Fletcher | .02 | .10 |
| ☐ 531 Tommy Greene | .02 | .10 |
| ☐ 532 Jason Grimsley | .02 | .10 |
| ☐ 533 Charlie Hayes | .02 | .10 |
| ☐ 534 Von Hayes | .02 | .10 |
| ☐ 535 Dave Hollins | .02 | .10 |
| ☐ 536 Ricky Jordan | .02 | .10 |
| ☐ 537 John Kruk | .02 | .10 |
| ☐ 538 Jim Lindeman | .02 | .10 |
| ☐ 539 Mickey Morandini | .02 | .10 |
| ☐ 540 Terry Mulholland | .02 | .10 |
| ☐ 541 Dale Murphy | .05 | .15 |
| ☐ 542 Randy Ready | .02 | .10 |
| ☐ 543 Wally Ritchie UER (Letters in data are cut off o | .02 | .10 |
| ☐ 544 Bruce Ruffin | .02 | .10 |
| ☐ 545 Steve Searcy | .02 | .10 |
| ☐ 546 Dickie Thon | .02 | .10 |
| ☐ 547 Mitch Williams | .02 | .10 |
| ☐ 548 Stan Belinda | .02 | .10 |
| ☐ 549 Jay Bell | .02 | .10 |
| ☐ 550 Barry Bonds | .40 | 1.00 |
| ☐ 551 Bobby Bonilla | .02 | .10 |

| | | |
|---|---|---|
| 552 Steve Buechele | .02 | .10 |
| 553 Doug Drabek | .02 | .10 |
| 554 Neal Heaton | .02 | .10 |
| 555 Jeff King | .02 | .10 |
| 556 Bob Kipper | .02 | .10 |
| 557 Bill Landrum | .02 | .10 |
| 558 Mike LaValliere | .02 | .10 |
| 559 Jose Lind | .02 | .10 |
| 560 Lloyd McClendon | .02 | .10 |
| 561 Orlando Merced | .02 | .10 |
| 562 Bob Patterson | .02 | .10 |
| 563 Joe Redfield | .02 | .10 |
| 564 Gary Redus | .02 | .10 |
| 565 Rosario Rodriguez | .02 | .10 |
| 566 Don Slaught | .02 | .10 |
| 567 John Smiley | .02 | .10 |
| 568 Zane Smith | .02 | .10 |
| 569 Randy Tomlin | .02 | .10 |
| 570 Andy Van Slyke | .05 | .15 |
| 571 Gary Varsho | .02 | .10 |
| 572 Bob Walk | .02 | .10 |
| 573 John Wehner UER | | |
| (Actually played for | | |
| Carolina in | | |
| 574 Juan Agosto | .02 | .10 |
| 575 Cris Carpenter | .02 | .10 |
| 576 Jose DeLeon | .02 | .10 |
| 577 Rich Gedman | .02 | .10 |
| 578 Bernard Gilkey | .02 | .10 |
| 579 Pedro Guerrero | .02 | .10 |
| 580 Ken Hill | .02 | .10 |
| 581 Rex Hudler | .02 | .10 |
| 582 Felix Jose | .02 | .10 |
| 583 Ray Lankford | .02 | .10 |
| 584 Omar Olivares | .02 | .10 |
| 585 Jose Oquendo | .02 | .10 |
| 586 Tom Pagnozzi | .02 | .10 |
| 587 Geronimo Pena | .02 | .10 |
| 588 Mike Perez | .02 | .10 |
| 589 Gerald Perry | .02 | .10 |
| 590 Bryn Smith | .02 | .10 |
| 591 Lee Smith | .02 | .10 |
| 592 Ozzie Smith | .15 | .40 |
| 593 Scott Terry | .02 | .10 |
| 594 Bob Tewksbury | .02 | .10 |
| 595 Milt Thompson | .02 | .10 |
| 596 Todd Zeile | .02 | .10 |
| 597 Larry Andersen | .02 | .10 |
| 598 Oscar Azocar | .02 | .10 |
| 599 Andy Benes | .02 | .10 |
| 600 Ricky Bones | .02 | .10 |
| 601 Jerald Clark | .02 | .10 |
| 602 Pat Clements | .02 | .10 |
| 603 Paul Faries | .02 | .10 |
| 604 Tony Fernandez | .02 | .10 |
| 605 Tony Gwynn | .10 | .30 |
| 606 Greg W. Harris | .02 | .10 |
| 607 Thomas Howard | .02 | .10 |
| 608 Bruce Hurst | .02 | .10 |
| 609 Darrin Jackson | .02 | .10 |
| 610 Tom Lampkin | .02 | .10 |
| 611 Craig Lefferts | .02 | .10 |
| 612 Jim Lewis RC | .02 | .10 |
| 613 Mike Maddux | .02 | .10 |
| 614 Fred McGriff | .05 | .15 |
| 615 Jose Melendez | .02 | .10 |
| 616 Jose Mota | .02 | .10 |
| 617 Dennis Rasmussen | .02 | .10 |
| 618 Bip Roberts | .02 | .10 |
| 619 Rich Rodriguez | .02 | .10 |
| 620 Benito Santiago | .02 | .10 |
| 621 Craig Shipley | .02 | .10 |
| 622 Tim Teufel | .02 | .10 |
| 623 Kevin Ward | .02 | .10 |
| 624 Ed Whitson | .02 | .10 |
| 625 Dave Anderson | .02 | .10 |
| 626 Kevin Bass | .02 | .10 |
| 627 Rod Beck RC | .15 | .40 |
| 628 Bud Black | .02 | .10 |
| 629 Jeff Brantley | .02 | .10 |
| 630 John Burkett | .02 | .10 |
| 631 Will Clark | .05 | .15 |
| 632 Royce Clayton | .02 | .10 |
| 633 Steve Decker | .02 | .10 |
| 634 Kelly Downs | .02 | .10 |
| 635 Mike Felder | .02 | .10 |
| 636 Scott Garrelts | .02 | .10 |
| 637 Eric Gunderson | .02 | .10 |

| | | |
|---|---|---|
| 638 Bryan Hickerson RC | .02 | .10 |
| 639 Darren Lewis | .02 | .10 |
| 640 Greg Litton | .02 | .10 |
| 641 Kirt Manwaring | .02 | .10 |
| 642 Paul McClellan | .02 | .10 |
| 643 Willie McGee | .02 | .10 |
| 644 Kevin Mitchell | .02 | .10 |
| 645 Francisco Oliveras | .02 | .10 |
| 646 Mike Remlinger | .02 | .10 |
| 647 Dave Righetti | .02 | .10 |
| 648 Robby Thompson | .02 | .10 |
| 649 Jose Uribe | .02 | .10 |
| 650 Matt Williams | .02 | .10 |
| 651 Trevor Wilson | .02 | .10 |
| 652 Tom Goodwin MLP UER | .02 | .10 |
| 653 Terry Bross MLP | .02 | .10 |
| 654 Mike Christopher MLP | .02 | .10 |
| 655 Kenny Lofton | .05 | .15 |
| 656 Chris Cron MLP | .02 | .10 |
| 657 Willie Banks MLP | .02 | .10 |
| 658 Pat Rice MLP | .02 | .10 |
| 659A Rob Mauer ERR | .30 | .75 |
| 659B Rob Mauer MLP COR | .02 | .10 |
| 660 Don Harris MLP | .02 | .10 |
| 661 Henry Rodriguez MLP | .02 | .10 |
| 662 Cliff Brantley MLP | .02 | .10 |
| 663 Mike Linskey MLP UER | .02 | .10 |
| 664 Gary DiSarcina MLP | .02 | .10 |
| 665 Gil Heredia RC | .08 | .25 |
| 666 Vinny Castilla RC | .40 | 1.00 |
| 667 Paul Abbott MLP | .02 | .10 |
| 668 Monty Fariss MLP UER | | |
| (Called Paul on back) | .02 | .10 |
| 669 Jarvis Brown MLP | .02 | .10 |
| 670 Wayne Kirby RC | .02 | .10 |
| 671 Scott Brosius RC | .15 | .40 |
| 672 Bob Hamelin | .02 | .10 |
| 673 Joel Johnston MLP | .02 | .10 |
| 674 Tim Spehr MLP | .02 | .10 |
| 675A Jeff Gardner ERR P | .30 | .75 |
| 675B Jeff Gardner MLP COR | .02 | .10 |
| 676 Rico Rossy MLP | .02 | .10 |
| 677 Roberto Hernandez MLP | .02 | .10 |
| 678 Ted Wood MLP | .02 | .10 |
| 679 Cal Eldred | .02 | .10 |
| 680 Sean Berry MLP | .05 | .15 |
| 681 Rickey Henderson RS | .10 | .30 |
| 682 Nolan Ryan RS | .20 | .50 |
| 683 Dennis Martinez RS | .02 | .10 |
| 684 Wilson Alvarez RS | .02 | .10 |
| 685 Joe Carter RS | .02 | .10 |
| 686 Dave Winfield RS | .02 | .10 |
| 687 David Cone RS | .02 | .10 |
| 688 Jose Canseco LL UER | .05 | .15 |
| 689 Howard Johnson LL | .02 | .10 |
| 690 Julio Franco LL | .02 | .10 |
| 691 Terry Pendleton LL | .02 | .10 |
| 692 Cecil Fielder LL | .02 | .10 |
| 693 Scott Erickson LL | .02 | .10 |
| 694 Tom Glavine LL | .02 | .10 |
| 695 Bryan Harvey LL | .02 | .10 |
| 696 Lee Smith LL | .02 | .10 |
| 698 Roberto/Sandy Alomar | .05 | .15 |
| 699 B.Bonilla/W.Clark | .05 | .15 |
| 700 Wohlers/Mercker/Pena | .02 | .10 |
| 701 B.Jackson/F.Thomas | .05 | .15 |
| 702 P.Molitor/J.Carter | .15 | .40 |
| 703 C.Ripken/J.Carter | .15 | .40 |
| 704 B.Larkin/K.Puckett | .05 | .15 |
| 705 M.Vaughn/C.Fielder | .02 | .10 |
| 706 R.Martinez/O.Guillen | .02 | .10 |
| 707 H.Baines/W.Boggs | .02 | .10 |
| 708 Robin Yount PV | .08 | .25 |
| 709 Ken Griffey Jr. PV | .08 | .25 |
| 710 Nolan Ryan PV | .20 | .50 |
| 711 Cal Ripken PV | .15 | .40 |
| 712 Frank Thomas PV | .05 | .15 |
| 713 David Justice PV | .02 | .10 |
| 714 Checklist 1-101 | .02 | .10 |
| 715 Checklist 102-194 | .02 | .10 |
| 716 Checklist 195-296 | .02 | .10 |
| 717 Checklist 297-397 | .02 | .10 |
| 718 Checklist 398-494 | .02 | .10 |
| 719 Checklist 495-596 | .02 | .10 |
| 720A Checklist 597-720 ERR | | |
| (659 Rob Maurer) | .02 | .10 |

| | | |
|---|---|---|
| 720B Checklist 597-720 COR | | |
| (659 Rob Maurer) | .02 | .10 |

**1993 Fleer**

| | | |
|---|---|---|
| COMPLETE SET (720) | 20.00 | 40.00 |
| COMPLETE SERIES 1 (360) | 10.00 | 20.00 |
| COMPLETE SERIES 2 (360) | 10.00 | 20.00 |
| 1 Steve Avery | .02 | .10 |
| 2 Sid Bream | .02 | .10 |
| 3 Ron Gant | .07 | .20 |
| 4 Tom Glavine | .10 | .30 |
| 5 Brian Hunter | .02 | .10 |
| 6 Ryan Klesko | .07 | .20 |
| 7 Charlie Leibrandt | .02 | .10 |
| 8 Kent Mercker | .02 | .10 |
| 9 David Nied | .02 | .10 |
| 10 Otis Nixon | .02 | .10 |
| 11 Greg Olson | .02 | .10 |
| 12 Terry Pendleton | .07 | .20 |
| 13 Deion Sanders | .10 | .30 |
| 14 John Smoltz | .10 | .30 |
| 15 Mike Stanton | .02 | .10 |
| 16 Mark Wohlers | .02 | .10 |
| 17 Paul Assenmacher | .02 | .10 |
| 18 Steve Buechele | .02 | .10 |
| 19 Shawon Dunston | .02 | .10 |
| 20 Mark Grace | .10 | .30 |
| 21 Derrick May | .02 | .10 |
| 22 Chuck McElroy | .02 | .10 |
| 23 Mike Morgan | .02 | .10 |
| 24 Rey Sanchez | .02 | .10 |
| 25 Ryne Sandberg | .30 | .75 |
| 26 Bob Scanlan | .02 | .10 |
| 27 Sammy Sosa | .20 | .50 |
| 28 Rick Wilkins | .02 | .10 |
| 29 Bobby Ayala RC | .02 | .10 |
| 30 Tim Belcher | .02 | .10 |
| 31 Jeff Branson | .02 | .10 |
| 32 Norm Charlton | .02 | .10 |
| 33 Steve Foster | .02 | .10 |
| 34 Willie Greene | .02 | .10 |
| 35 Chris Hammond | .02 | .10 |
| 36 Milt Hill | .02 | .10 |
| 37 Hal Morris | .02 | .10 |
| 38 Joe Oliver | .02 | .10 |
| 39 Paul O'Neill | .10 | .30 |
| 40 Tim Pugh RC | .02 | .10 |
| 41 Jose Rijo | .02 | .10 |
| 42 Bip Roberts | .02 | .10 |
| 43 Chris Sabo | .02 | .10 |
| 44 Reggie Sanders | .07 | .20 |
| 45 Eric Anthony | .02 | .10 |
| 46 Jeff Bagwell | .10 | .30 |
| 47 Craig Biggio | .10 | .30 |
| 48 Joe Boever | .02 | .10 |
| 49 Casey Candaele | .02 | .10 |
| 50 Steve Finley | .07 | .20 |
| 51 Luis Gonzalez | .07 | .20 |
| 52 Pete Harnisch | .02 | .10 |
| 53 Xavier Hernandez | .02 | .10 |
| 54 Doug Jones | .02 | .10 |
| 55 Eddie Taubensee | .02 | .10 |
| 56 Brian Williams | .02 | .10 |
| 57 Pedro Astacio | .02 | .10 |
| 58 Todd Benzinger | .02 | .10 |
| 59 Brett Butler | .02 | .10 |
| 60 Tom Candiotti | .02 | .10 |
| 61 Lenny Harris | .02 | .10 |
| 62 Carlos Hernandez | .02 | .10 |
| 63 Orel Hershiser | .07 | .20 |
| 64 Eric Karros | .07 | .20 |
| 65 Ramon Martinez | .02 | .10 |
| 66 Jose Offerman | .02 | .10 |
| 67 Mike Scioscia | .02 | .10 |

|  |  | | |
|---|---|---|---|
| ☐ 68 | Mike Sharperson | .02 | .10 |
| ☐ 69 | Eric Young | .02 | .10 |
| ☐ 70 | Moises Alou | .07 | .20 |
| ☐ 71 | Ivan Calderon | .02 | .10 |
| ☐ 72 | Archi Cianfrocco | .02 | .10 |
| ☐ 73 | Wil Cordero | .02 | .10 |
| ☐ 74 | Delino DeShields | .02 | .10 |
| ☐ 75 | Mark Gardner | .02 | .10 |
| ☐ 76 | Ken Hill | .02 | .10 |
| ☐ 77 | Tim Laker RC | .02 | .10 |
| ☐ 78 | Chris Nabholz | .02 | .10 |
| ☐ 79 | Mel Rojas | .02 | .10 |
| ☐ 80 | John Vander Wal UER | | |
|  | (Misspelled Vander Wall in l | .02 | .10 |
| ☐ 81 | Larry Walker | .07 | .20 |
| ☐ 82 | Tim Wallach | .02 | .10 |
| ☐ 83 | John Wetteland | .07 | .20 |
| ☐ 84 | Bobby Bonilla | .07 | .20 |
| ☐ 85 | Daryl Boston | .02 | .10 |
| ☐ 86 | Sid Fernandez | .02 | .10 |
| ☐ 87 | Eric Hillman | .02 | .10 |
| ☐ 88 | Todd Hundley | .02 | .10 |
| ☐ 89 | Howard Johnson | .02 | .10 |
| ☐ 90 | Jeff Kent | .20 | .50 |
| ☐ 91 | Eddie Murray | .20 | .50 |
| ☐ 92 | Bill Pecota | .02 | .10 |
| ☐ 93 | Bret Saberhagen | .07 | .20 |
| ☐ 94 | Dick Schofield | .02 | .10 |
| ☐ 95 | Pete Schourek | .02 | .10 |
| ☐ 96 | Anthony Young | .02 | .10 |
| ☐ 97 | Ruben Amaro | .02 | .10 |
| ☐ 98 | Juan Bell | .02 | .10 |
| ☐ 99 | Wes Chamberlain | .02 | .10 |
| ☐ 100 | Darren Daulton | .07 | .20 |
| ☐ 101 | Mariano Duncan | .02 | .10 |
| ☐ 102 | Mike Hartley | .02 | .10 |
| ☐ 103 | Ricky Jordan | .02 | .10 |
| ☐ 104 | John Kruk | .07 | .20 |
| ☐ 105 | Mickey Morandini | .02 | .10 |
| ☐ 106 | Terry Mulholland | .02 | .10 |
| ☐ 107 | Ben Rivera | .02 | .10 |
| ☐ 108 | Curt Schilling | .07 | .20 |
| ☐ 109 | Keith Shepherd RC | .02 | .10 |
| ☐ 110 | Stan Belinda | .02 | .10 |
| ☐ 111 | Jay Bell | .07 | .20 |
| ☐ 112 | Barry Bonds | .60 | 1.50 |
| ☐ 113 | Jeff King | .02 | .10 |
| ☐ 114 | Mike LaValliere | .02 | .10 |
| ☐ 115 | Jose Lind | .02 | .10 |
| ☐ 116 | Roger Mason | .02 | .10 |
| ☐ 117 | Orlando Merced | .02 | .10 |
| ☐ 118 | Bob Patterson | .02 | .10 |
| ☐ 119 | Don Slaught | .02 | .10 |
| ☐ 120 | Zane Smith | .02 | .10 |
| ☐ 121 | Randy Tomlin | .02 | .10 |
| ☐ 122 | Andy Van Slyke | .10 | .30 |
| ☐ 123 | Tim Wakefield | .20 | .50 |
| ☐ 124 | Rheal Cormier | .02 | .10 |
| ☐ 125 | Bernard Gilkey | .02 | .10 |
| ☐ 126 | Felix Jose | .02 | .10 |
| ☐ 127 | Ray Lankford | .07 | .20 |
| ☐ 128 | Bob McClure | .02 | .10 |
| ☐ 129 | Donovan Osborne | .02 | .10 |
| ☐ 130 | Tom Pagnozzi | .02 | .10 |
| ☐ 131 | Geronimo Pena | .02 | .10 |
| ☐ 132 | Mike Perez | .02 | .10 |
| ☐ 133 | Lee Smith | .07 | .20 |
| ☐ 134 | Bob Tewksbury | .02 | .10 |
| ☐ 135 | Todd Worrell | .02 | .10 |
| ☐ 136 | Todd Zeile | .02 | .10 |
| ☐ 137 | Jerald Clark | .02 | .10 |
| ☐ 138 | Tony Gwynn | .25 | .60 |
| ☐ 139 | Greg W. Harris | .02 | .10 |
| ☐ 140 | Jeremy Hernandez | .02 | .10 |
| ☐ 141 | Darrin Jackson | .02 | .10 |
| ☐ 142 | Mike Maddux | .02 | .10 |
| ☐ 143 | Fred McGriff | .10 | .30 |
| ☐ 144 | Jose Melendez | .02 | .10 |
| ☐ 145 | Rich Rodriguez | .02 | .10 |
| ☐ 146 | Frank Seminara | .02 | .10 |
| ☐ 147 | Gary Sheffield | .07 | .20 |
| ☐ 148 | Kurt Stillwell | .02 | .10 |
| ☐ 149 | Dan Walters | .02 | .10 |
| ☐ 150 | Rod Beck | .02 | .10 |
| ☐ 151 | Bud Black | .02 | .10 |
| ☐ 152 | Jeff Brantley | .02 | .10 |
| ☐ 153 | John Burkett | .02 | .10 |
| ☐ 154 | Will Clark | .10 | .30 |
| ☐ 155 | Royce Clayton | .02 | .10 |
| ☐ 156 | Mike Jackson | .02 | .10 |
| ☐ 157 | Darren Lewis | .02 | .10 |
| ☐ 158 | Kirt Manwaring | .02 | .10 |
| ☐ 159 | Willie McGee | .07 | .20 |
| ☐ 160 | Cory Snyder | .02 | .10 |
| ☐ 161 | Bill Swift | .02 | .10 |
| ☐ 162 | Trevor Wilson | .02 | .10 |
| ☐ 163 | Brady Anderson | .07 | .20 |
| ☐ 164 | Glenn Davis | .02 | .10 |
| ☐ 165 | Mike Devereaux | .02 | .10 |
| ☐ 166 | Todd Frohwirth | .02 | .10 |
| ☐ 167 | Leo Gomez | .02 | .10 |
| ☐ 168 | Chris Hoiles | .02 | .10 |
| ☐ 169 | Ben McDonald | .02 | .10 |
| ☐ 170 | Randy Milligan | .02 | .10 |
| ☐ 171 | Alan Mills | .02 | .10 |
| ☐ 172 | Mike Mussina | .10 | .30 |
| ☐ 173 | Gregg Olson | .02 | .10 |
| ☐ 174 | Arthur Rhodes | .02 | .10 |
| ☐ 175 | David Segui | .02 | .10 |
| ☐ 176 | Ellis Burks | .07 | .20 |
| ☐ 177 | Roger Clemens | .40 | 1.00 |
| ☐ 178 | Scott Cooper | .02 | .10 |
| ☐ 179 | Danny Darwin | .02 | .10 |
| ☐ 180 | Tony Fossas | .02 | .10 |
| ☐ 181 | Paul Quantrill | .02 | .10 |
| ☐ 182 | Jody Reed | .02 | .10 |
| ☐ 183 | John Valentin | .02 | .10 |
| ☐ 184 | Mo Vaughn | .07 | .20 |
| ☐ 185 | Frank Viola | .07 | .20 |
| ☐ 186 | Bob Zupcic | .02 | .10 |
| ☐ 187 | Jim Abbott | .10 | .30 |
| ☐ 188 | Gary DiSarcina | .02 | .10 |
| ☐ 189 | Damion Easley | .02 | .10 |
| ☐ 190 | Junior Felix | .02 | .10 |
| ☐ 191 | Chuck Finley | .02 | .10 |
| ☐ 192 | Joe Grahe | .02 | .10 |
| ☐ 193 | Bryan Harvey | .02 | .10 |
| ☐ 194 | Mark Langston | .02 | .10 |
| ☐ 195 | John Orton | .02 | .10 |
| ☐ 196 | Luis Polonia | .02 | .10 |
| ☐ 197 | Tim Salmon | .10 | .30 |
| ☐ 198 | Luis Sojo | .02 | .10 |
| ☐ 199 | Wilson Alvarez | .02 | .10 |
| ☐ 200 | George Bell | .02 | .10 |
| ☐ 201 | Alex Fernandez | .02 | .10 |
| ☐ 202 | Craig Grebeck | .02 | .10 |
| ☐ 203 | Ozzie Guillen | .07 | .20 |
| ☐ 204 | Lance Johnson | .02 | .10 |
| ☐ 205 | Ron Karkovice | .02 | .10 |
| ☐ 206 | Kirk McCaskill | .02 | .10 |
| ☐ 207 | Jack McDowell | .07 | .20 |
| ☐ 208 | Scott Radinsky | .02 | .10 |
| ☐ 209 | Tim Raines | .07 | .20 |
| ☐ 210 | Frank Thomas | .20 | .50 |
| ☐ 211 | Robin Ventura | .07 | .20 |
| ☐ 212 | Sandy Alomar Jr. | .02 | .10 |
| ☐ 213 | Carlos Baerga | .10 | .30 |
| ☐ 214 | Dennis Cook | .02 | .10 |
| ☐ 215 | Thomas Howard | .02 | .10 |
| ☐ 216 | Mark Lewis | .02 | .10 |
| ☐ 217 | Derek Lilliquist | .02 | .10 |
| ☐ 218 | Kenny Lofton | .07 | .20 |
| ☐ 219 | Charles Nagy | .02 | .10 |
| ☐ 220 | Steve Olin | .02 | .10 |
| ☐ 221 | Paul Sorrento | .02 | .10 |
| ☐ 222 | Jim Thome | .10 | .30 |
| ☐ 223 | Mark Whiten | .02 | .10 |
| ☐ 224 | Milt Cuyler | .02 | .10 |
| ☐ 225 | Rob Deer | .02 | .10 |
| ☐ 226 | John Doherty | .02 | .10 |
| ☐ 227 | Cecil Fielder | .07 | .20 |
| ☐ 228 | Travis Fryman | .07 | .20 |
| ☐ 229 | Mike Henneman | .02 | .10 |
| ☐ 230 | John Kiely UER | | |
|  | (Card has batting stats of Pat Ke | .02 | .10 |
| ☐ 231 | Kurt Knudsen | .02 | .10 |
| ☐ 232 | Scott Livingstone | .02 | .10 |
| ☐ 233 | Tony Phillips | .02 | .10 |
| ☐ 234 | Mickey Tettleton | .02 | .10 |
| ☐ 235 | Kevin Appier | .07 | .20 |
| ☐ 236 | George Brett | .50 | 1.25 |
| ☐ 237 | Tom Gordon | .02 | .10 |
| ☐ 238 | Gregg Jefferies | .02 | .10 |
| ☐ 239 | Wally Joyner | .07 | .20 |
| ☐ 240 | Kevin Koslofski | .02 | .10 |
| ☐ 241 | Mike Macfarlane | .02 | .10 |
| ☐ 242 | Brian McRae | .02 | .10 |
| ☐ 243 | Rusty Meacham | .02 | .10 |
| ☐ 244 | Keith Miller | .02 | .10 |
| ☐ 245 | Jeff Montgomery | .02 | .10 |
| ☐ 246 | Hipolito Pichardo | .02 | .10 |
| ☐ 247 | Ricky Bones | .02 | .10 |
| ☐ 248 | Cal Eldred | .02 | .10 |
| ☐ 249 | Mike Fetters | .02 | .10 |
| ☐ 250 | Darryl Hamilton | .02 | .10 |
| ☐ 251 | Doug Henry | .02 | .10 |
| ☐ 252 | John Jaha | .02 | .10 |
| ☐ 253 | Pat Listach | .02 | .10 |
| ☐ 254 | Paul Molitor | .07 | .20 |
| ☐ 255 | Jaime Navarro | .02 | .10 |
| ☐ 256 | Kevin Seitzer | .02 | .10 |
| ☐ 257 | B.J. Surhoff | .02 | .10 |
| ☐ 258 | Greg Vaughn | .02 | .10 |
| ☐ 259 | Bill Wegman | .02 | .10 |
| ☐ 260 | Robin Yount | .30 | .75 |
| ☐ 261 | Rick Aguilera | .02 | .10 |
| ☐ 262 | Chili Davis | .07 | .20 |
| ☐ 263 | Scott Erickson | .02 | .10 |
| ☐ 264 | Greg Gagne | .02 | .10 |
| ☐ 265 | Mark Guthrie | .02 | .10 |
| ☐ 266 | Brian Harper | .02 | .10 |
| ☐ 267 | Kent Hrbek | .07 | .20 |
| ☐ 268 | Terry Jorgensen | .02 | .10 |
| ☐ 269 | Gene Larkin | .02 | .10 |
| ☐ 270 | Scott Leius | .02 | .10 |
| ☐ 271 | Pat Mahomes | .02 | .10 |
| ☐ 272 | Pedro Munoz | .02 | .10 |
| ☐ 273 | Kirby Puckett | .20 | .50 |
| ☐ 274 | Kevin Tapani | .02 | .10 |
| ☐ 275 | Carl Willis | .02 | .10 |
| ☐ 276 | Steve Farr | .02 | .10 |
| ☐ 277 | John Habyan | .02 | .10 |
| ☐ 278 | Mel Hall | .02 | .10 |
| ☐ 279 | Charlie Hayes | .02 | .10 |
| ☐ 280 | Pat Kelly | .02 | .10 |
| ☐ 281 | Don Mattingly | .50 | 1.25 |
| ☐ 282 | Sam Militello | .02 | .10 |
| ☐ 283 | Matt Nokes | .02 | .10 |
| ☐ 284 | Melido Perez | .02 | .10 |
| ☐ 285 | Andy Stankiewicz | .02 | .10 |
| ☐ 286 | Danny Tartabull | .07 | .20 |
| ☐ 287 | Randy Velarde | .02 | .10 |
| ☐ 288 | Bob Wickman | .02 | .10 |
| ☐ 289 | Bernie Williams | .10 | .30 |
| ☐ 290 | Lance Blankenship | .02 | .10 |
| ☐ 291 | Mike Bordick | .02 | .10 |
| ☐ 292 | Jerry Browne | .02 | .10 |
| ☐ 293 | Dennis Eckersley | .07 | .20 |
| ☐ 294 | Rickey Henderson | .20 | .50 |
| ☐ 295 | Vince Horsman | .02 | .10 |
| ☐ 296 | Mark McGwire | .50 | 1.25 |
| ☐ 297 | Jeff Parrett | .02 | .10 |
| ☐ 298 | Ruben Sierra | .07 | .20 |
| ☐ 299 | Terry Steinbach | .02 | .10 |
| ☐ 300 | Walt Weiss | .02 | .10 |
| ☐ 301 | Bob Welch | .02 | .10 |
| ☐ 302 | Willie Wilson | .02 | .10 |
| ☐ 303 | Bobby Witt | .02 | .10 |
| ☐ 304 | Bret Boone | .07 | .20 |
| ☐ 305 | Jay Buhner | .07 | .20 |
| ☐ 306 | Dave Fleming | .07 | .20 |
| ☐ 307 | Ken Griffey Jr. | .30 | .75 |
| ☐ 308 | Erik Hanson | .02 | .10 |
| ☐ 309 | Edgar Martinez | .10 | .30 |
| ☐ 310 | Tino Martinez | .10 | .30 |
| ☐ 311 | Jeff Nelson | .02 | .10 |
| ☐ 312 | Dennis Powell | .02 | .10 |
| ☐ 313 | Mike Schooler | .02 | .10 |
| ☐ 314 | Russ Swan | .02 | .10 |
| ☐ 315 | Dave Valle | .02 | .10 |
| ☐ 316 | Omar Vizquel | .10 | .30 |
| ☐ 317 | Kevin Brown | .07 | .20 |
| ☐ 318 | Todd Burns | .02 | .10 |
| ☐ 319 | Jose Canseco | .10 | .30 |
| ☐ 320 | Julio Franco | .07 | .20 |
| ☐ 321 | Jeff Frye | .02 | .10 |
| ☐ 322 | Juan Gonzalez | .07 | .20 |
| ☐ 323 | Jose Guzman | .02 | .10 |
| ☐ 324 | Jeff Huson | .02 | .10 |
| ☐ 325 | Dean Palmer | .07 | .20 |
| ☐ 326 | Kevin Reimer | .02 | .10 |
| ☐ 327 | Ivan Rodriguez | .10 | .30 |

|  |  | | |
|---|---|---|---|
| 328 | Kenny Rogers | .07 | .20 |
| 329 | Dan Smith | .02 | .10 |
| 330 | Roberto Alomar | .10 | .30 |
| 331 | Derek Bell | .02 | .10 |
| 332 | Pat Borders | .02 | .10 |
| 333 | Joe Carter | .07 | .20 |
| 334 | Kelly Gruber | .02 | .10 |
| 335 | Tom Henke | .02 | .10 |
| 336 | Jimmy Key | .07 | .20 |
| 337 | Manuel Lee | .02 | .10 |
| 338 | Candy Maldonado | .02 | .10 |
| 339 | John Olerud | .07 | .20 |
| 340 | Todd Stottlemyre | .02 | .10 |
| 341 | Duane Ward | .02 | .10 |
| 342 | Devon White | .07 | .20 |
| 343 | Dave Winfield | .10 | .30 |
| 344 | Edgar Martinez LL | .07 | .20 |
| 345 | Cecil Fielder LL | .02 | .10 |
| 346 | Kenny Lofton LL | .02 | .10 |
| 347 | Jack Morris LL | .02 | .10 |
| 348 | Roger Clemens LL | .20 | .50 |
| 349 | Fred McGriff RT | .02 | .10 |
| 350 | Barry Bonds | .30 | .75 |
| 351 | Gary Sheffield RT | .02 | .10 |
| 352 | Darren Daulton RT | .02 | .10 |
| 353 | Dave Hollins RT | .02 | .10 |
| 354 | P.Martinez/R.Martinez | .20 | .50 |
| 355 | K.Puckett/I.Rodriguez | .10 | .30 |
| 356 | Sandberg/Sheffield | .20 | .50 |
| 357 | R.Alomar/Knoblauch/Baerg | .07 | .20 |
| 358 | Checklist 1-120 | .02 | .10 |
| 359 | Checklist 121-240 | .02 | .10 |
| 360 | Checklist 241-360 | .02 | .10 |
| 361 | Rafael Belliard | .02 | .10 |
| 362 | Damon Berryhill | .02 | .10 |
| 363 | Mike Bielecki | .02 | .10 |
| 364 | Jeff Blauser | .02 | .10 |
| 365 | Francisco Cabrera | .02 | .10 |
| 366 | Marvin Freeman | .02 | .10 |
| 367 | David Justice | .07 | .20 |
| 368 | Mark Lemke | .02 | .10 |
| 369 | Alejandro Pena | .02 | .10 |
| 370 | Jeff Reardon | .07 | .20 |
| 371 | Lonnie Smith | .02 | .10 |
| 372 | Pete Smith | .02 | .10 |
| 373 | Shawn Boskie | .02 | .10 |
| 374 | Jim Bullinger | .02 | .10 |
| 375 | Frank Castillo | .02 | .10 |
| 376 | Doug Dascenzo | .02 | .10 |
| 377 | Andre Dawson | .07 | .20 |
| 378 | Mike Harkey | .02 | .10 |
| 379 | Greg Hibbard | .02 | .10 |
| 380 | Greg Maddux | .30 | .75 |
| 381 | Ken Patterson | .02 | .10 |
| 382 | Jeff D. Robinson | .02 | .10 |
| 383 | Luis Salazar | .02 | .10 |
| 384 | Dwight Smith | .02 | .10 |
| 385 | Jose Vizcaino | .02 | .10 |
| 386 | Scott Bankhead | .02 | .10 |
| 387 | Tom Browning | .02 | .10 |
| 388 | Darnell Coles | .02 | .10 |
| 389 | Rob Dibble | .07 | .20 |
| 390 | Bill Doran | .02 | .10 |
| 391 | Dwayne Henry | .02 | .10 |
| 392 | Cesar Hernandez | .02 | .10 |
| 393 | Roberto Kelly | .07 | .20 |
| 394 | Barry Larkin | .10 | .30 |
| 395 | Dave Martinez | .02 | .10 |
| 396 | Kevin Mitchell | .07 | .20 |
| 397 | Jeff Reed | .02 | .10 |
| 398 | Scott Ruskin | .02 | .10 |
| 399 | Greg Swindell | .02 | .10 |
| 400 | Dan Wilson | .07 | .20 |
| 401 | Andy Ashby | .02 | .10 |
| 402 | Freddie Benavides | .02 | .10 |
| 403 | Dante Bichette | .07 | .20 |
| 404 | Willie Blair | .02 | .10 |
| 405 | Dennis Boucher | .02 | .10 |
| 406 | Vinny Castilla | .02 | .10 |
| 407 | Braulio Castillo | .02 | .10 |
| 408 | Alex Cole | .02 | .10 |
| 409 | Andres Galarraga | .07 | .20 |
| 410 | Joe Girardi | .02 | .10 |
| 411 | Butch Henry | .02 | .10 |
| 412 | Darren Holmes | .02 | .10 |
| 413 | Calvin Jones | .02 | .10 |
| 414 | Steve Reed RC | .02 | .10 |
| 415 | Kevin Ritz | .02 | .10 |
| 416 | Jim Tatum RC | .02 | .10 |
| 417 | Jack Armstrong | .02 | .10 |
| 418 | Bret Barberie | .02 | .10 |
| 419 | Ryan Bowen | .02 | .10 |
| 420 | Cris Carpenter | .02 | .10 |
| 421 | Chuck Carr | .02 | .10 |
| 422 | Scott Chiamparino | .02 | .10 |
| 423 | Jeff Conine | .07 | .20 |
| 424 | Jim Corsi | .02 | .10 |
| 425 | Steve Decker | .02 | .10 |
| 426 | Chris Donnels | .02 | .10 |
| 427 | Monty Fariss | .02 | .10 |
| 428 | Bob Natal | .02 | .10 |
| 429 | Pat Rapp | .02 | .10 |
| 430 | Dave Weathers | .02 | .10 |
| 431 | Nigel Wilson | .02 | .10 |
| 432 | Ken Caminiti | .07 | .20 |
| 433 | Andujar Cedeno | .02 | .10 |
| 434 | Tom Edens | .02 | .10 |
| 435 | Juan Guerrero | .02 | .10 |
| 436 | Pete Incaviglia | .02 | .10 |
| 437 | Jimmy Jones | .02 | .10 |
| 438 | Darryl Kile | .07 | .20 |
| 439 | Rob Murphy | .02 | .10 |
| 440 | Al Osuna | .02 | .10 |
| 441 | Mark Portugal | .02 | .10 |
| 442 | Scott Servais | .02 | .10 |
| 443 | John Candelaria | .02 | .10 |
| 444 | Tim Crews | .02 | .10 |
| 445 | Eric Davis | .07 | .20 |
| 446 | Tom Goodwin | .02 | .10 |
| 447 | Jim Gott | .02 | .10 |
| 448 | Kevin Gross | .02 | .10 |
| 449 | Dave Hansen | .02 | .10 |
| 450 | Jay Howell | .02 | .10 |
| 451 | Roger McDowell | .02 | .10 |
| 452 | Bob Ojeda | .02 | .10 |
| 453 | Henry Rodriguez | .02 | .10 |
| 454 | Darryl Strawberry | .07 | .20 |
| 455 | Mitch Webster | .02 | .10 |
| 456 | Steve Wilson | .02 | .10 |
| 457 | Brian Barnes | .02 | .10 |
| 458 | Sean Berry | .02 | .10 |
| 459 | Jeff Fassero | .02 | .10 |
| 460 | Darrin Fletcher | .02 | .10 |
| 461 | Marquis Grissom | .07 | .20 |
| 462 | Dennis Martinez | .07 | .20 |
| 463 | Spike Owen | .02 | .10 |
| 464 | Matt Stairs | .02 | .10 |
| 465 | Sergio Valdez | .02 | .10 |
| 466 | Kevin Bass | .02 | .10 |
| 467 | Vince Coleman | .02 | .10 |
| 468 | Mark Dewey | .02 | .10 |
| 469 | Kevin Elster | .02 | .10 |
| 470 | Tony Fernandez | .02 | .10 |
| 471 | John Franco | .07 | .20 |
| 472 | Dave Gallagher | .02 | .10 |
| 473 | Paul Gibson | .02 | .10 |
| 474 | Dwight Gooden | .07 | .20 |
| 475 | Lee Guetterman | .02 | .10 |
| 476 | Jeff Innis | .02 | .10 |
| 477 | Dave Magadan | .02 | .10 |
| 478 | Charlie O'Brien | .02 | .10 |
| 479 | Willie Randolph | .07 | .20 |
| 480 | Mackey Sasser | .02 | .10 |
| 481 | Ryan Thompson | .02 | .10 |
| 482 | Chico Walker | .02 | .10 |
| 483 | Kyle Abbott | .02 | .10 |
| 484 | Bob Ayrault | .02 | .10 |
| 485 | Kim Batiste | .02 | .10 |
| 486 | Cliff Brantley | .02 | .10 |
| 487 | Jose DeLeon | .02 | .10 |
| 488 | Len Dykstra | .07 | .20 |
| 489 | Tommy Greene | .02 | .10 |
| 490 | Jeff Grotewold | .02 | .10 |
| 491 | Dave Hollins | .07 | .20 |
| 492 | Danny Jackson | .02 | .10 |
| 493 | Stan Javier | .02 | .10 |
| 494 | Tom Marsh | .02 | .10 |
| 495 | Greg Mathews | .02 | .10 |
| 496 | Dale Murphy | .10 | .30 |
| 497 | Todd Pratt RC | .07 | .20 |
| 498 | Mitch Williams | .02 | .10 |
| 499 | Danny Cox | .02 | .10 |
| 500 | Doug Drabek | .07 | .20 |
| 501 | Carlos Garcia | .02 | .10 |
| 502 | Lloyd McClendon | .02 | .10 |
| 503 | Denny Neagle | .07 | .20 |
| 504 | Gary Redus | .02 | .10 |
| 505 | Bob Walk | .02 | .10 |
| 506 | John Wehner | .02 | .10 |
| 507 | Luis Alicea | .02 | .10 |
| 508 | Mark Clark | .02 | .10 |
| 509 | Pedro Guerrero | .07 | .20 |
| 510 | Rex Hudler | .02 | .10 |
| 511 | Brian Jordan | .07 | .20 |
| 512 | Omar Olivares | .02 | .10 |
| 513 | Jose Oquendo | .02 | .10 |
| 514 | Gerald Perry | .02 | .10 |
| 515 | Bryn Smith | .02 | .10 |
| 516 | Craig Wilson | .02 | .10 |
| 517 | Tracy Woodson | .02 | .10 |
| 518 | Larry Andersen | .02 | .10 |
| 519 | Andy Benes | .07 | .20 |
| 520 | Jim Deshaies | .02 | .10 |
| 521 | Bruce Hurst | .02 | .10 |
| 522 | Randy Myers | .07 | .20 |
| 523 | Benito Santiago | .07 | .20 |
| 524 | Tim Scott | .02 | .10 |
| 525 | Tim Teufel | .02 | .10 |
| 526 | Mike Benjamin | .02 | .10 |
| 527 | Dave Burba | .02 | .10 |
| 528 | Craig Colbert | .02 | .10 |
| 529 | Mike Felder | .02 | .10 |
| 530 | Bryan Hickerson | .02 | .10 |
| 531 | Chris James | .02 | .10 |
| 532 | Mark Leonard | .02 | .10 |
| 533 | Greg Litton | .02 | .10 |
| 534 | Francisco Oliveras | .02 | .10 |
| 535 | John Patterson | .02 | .10 |
| 536 | Jim Pena | .02 | .10 |
| 537 | Dave Righetti | .07 | .20 |
| 538 | Robby Thompson | .02 | .10 |
| 539 | Jose Uribe | .02 | .10 |
| 540 | Matt Williams | .07 | .20 |
| 541 | Storm Davis | .02 | .10 |
| 542 | Sam Horn | .02 | .10 |
| 543 | Tim Hulett | .02 | .10 |
| 544 | Craig Lefferts | .02 | .10 |
| 545 | Chito Martinez | .02 | .10 |
| 546 | Mark McLemore | .02 | .10 |
| 547 | Luis Mercedes | .02 | .10 |
| 548 | Bob Milacki | .02 | .10 |
| 549 | Joe Orsulak | .02 | .10 |
| 550 | Billy Ripken | .02 | .10 |
| 551 | Cal Ripken | .60 | 1.50 |
| 552 | Rick Sutcliffe | .07 | .20 |
| 553 | Jeff Tackett | .02 | .10 |
| 554 | Wade Boggs | .10 | .30 |
| 555 | Tom Brunansky | .02 | .10 |
| 556 | Jack Clark | .07 | .20 |
| 557 | John Dopson | .02 | .10 |
| 558 | Mike Gardiner | .02 | .10 |
| 559 | Mike Greenwell | .07 | .20 |
| 560 | Greg A. Harris | .02 | .10 |
| 561 | Billy Hatcher | .02 | .10 |
| 562 | Joe Hesketh | .02 | .10 |
| 563 | Tony Pena | .02 | .10 |
| 564 | Phil Plantier | .07 | .20 |
| 565 | Luis Rivera | .02 | .10 |
| 566 | Herm Winningham | .02 | .10 |
| 567 | Matt Young | .02 | .10 |
| 568 | Bert Blyleven | .07 | .20 |
| 569 | Mike Butcher | .02 | .10 |
| 570 | Chuck Crim | .02 | .10 |
| 571 | Chad Curtis | .07 | .20 |
| 572 | Tim Fortugno | .02 | .10 |
| 573 | Steve Frey | .02 | .10 |
| 574 | Gary Gaetti | .07 | .20 |
| 575 | Scott Lewis | .02 | .10 |
| 576 | Lee Stevens | .02 | .10 |
| 577 | Ron Tingley | .02 | .10 |
| 578 | Julio Valera | .02 | .10 |
| 579 | Shawn Abner | .02 | .10 |
| 580 | Joey Cora | .02 | .10 |
| 581 | Chris Cron | .02 | .10 |
| 582 | Carlton Fisk | .10 | .30 |
| 583 | Roberto Hernandez | .02 | .10 |
| 584 | Charlie Hough | .07 | .20 |
| 585 | Terry Leach | .02 | .10 |
| 586 | Don Pall | .02 | .10 |
| 587 | Dan Pasqua | .02 | .10 |
| 588 | Steve Sax | .07 | .20 |
| 589 | Bobby Thigpen | .02 | .10 |
| 590 | Albert Belle | .07 | .20 |
| 591 | Felix Fermin | .02 | .10 |

|  |  | | |
|---|---|---|---|
| ❑ 592 | Glenallen Hill | .02 | .10 |
| ❑ 593 | Brook Jacoby | .02 | .10 |
| ❑ 594 | Reggie Jefferson | .02 | .10 |
| ❑ 595 | Carlos Martinez | .02 | .10 |
| ❑ 596 | Jose Mesa | .02 | .10 |
| ❑ 597 | Rod Nichols | .02 | .10 |
| ❑ 598 | Junior Ortiz | .02 | .10 |
| ❑ 599 | Eric Plunk | .02 | .10 |
| ❑ 600 | Ted Power | .02 | .10 |
| ❑ 601 | Scott Scudder | .02 | .10 |
| ❑ 602 | Kevin Wickander | .02 | .10 |
| ❑ 603 | Skeeter Barnes | .02 | .10 |
| ❑ 604 | Mark Carreon | .02 | .10 |
| ❑ 605 | Dan Gladden | .02 | .10 |
| ❑ 606 | Bill Gullickson | .02 | .10 |
| ❑ 607 | Chad Kreuter | .02 | .10 |
| ❑ 608 | Mark Leiter | .02 | .10 |
| ❑ 609 | Mike Munoz | .02 | .10 |
| ❑ 610 | Rich Rowland | .02 | .10 |
| ❑ 611 | Frank Tanana | .02 | .10 |
| ❑ 612 | Walt Terrell | .02 | .10 |
| ❑ 613 | Alan Trammell | .07 | .20 |
| ❑ 614 | Lou Whitaker | .07 | .20 |
| ❑ 615 | Luis Aquino | .02 | .10 |
| ❑ 616 | Mike Boddicker | .02 | .10 |
| ❑ 617 | Jim Eisenreich | .02 | .10 |
| ❑ 618 | Mark Gubicza | .02 | .10 |
| ❑ 619 | David Howard | .02 | .10 |
| ❑ 620 | Mike Magnante | .02 | .10 |
| ❑ 621 | Brent Mayne | .02 | .10 |
| ❑ 622 | Kevin McReynolds | .02 | .10 |
| ❑ 623 | Eddie Pierce RC | .02 | .10 |
| ❑ 624 | Bill Sampen | .02 | .10 |
| ❑ 625 | Steve Shifflett | .02 | .10 |
| ❑ 626 | Gary Thurman | .02 | .10 |
| ❑ 627 | Curt Wilkerson | .02 | .10 |
| ❑ 628 | Chris Bosio | .02 | .10 |
| ❑ 629 | Scott Fletcher | .02 | .10 |
| ❑ 630 | Jim Gantner | .02 | .10 |
| ❑ 631 | Dave Nilsson | .02 | .10 |
| ❑ 632 | Jesse Orosco | .02 | .10 |
| ❑ 633 | Dan Plesac | .02 | .10 |
| ❑ 634 | Ron Robinson | .02 | .10 |
| ❑ 635 | Bill Spiers | .02 | .10 |
| ❑ 636 | Franklin Stubbs | .02 | .10 |
| ❑ 637 | Willie Banks | .02 | .10 |
| ❑ 638 | Randy Bush | .02 | .10 |
| ❑ 639 | Chuck Knoblauch | .07 | .20 |
| ❑ 640 | Shane Mack | .02 | .10 |
| ❑ 641 | Mike Pagliarulo | .02 | .10 |
| ❑ 642 | Jeff Reboulet | .02 | .10 |
| ❑ 643 | John Smiley | .02 | .10 |
| ❑ 644 | Mike Trombley | .02 | .10 |
| ❑ 645 | Gary Wayne | .02 | .10 |
| ❑ 646 | Lenny Webster | .02 | .10 |
| ❑ 647 | Tim Burke | .02 | .10 |
| ❑ 648 | Mike Gallego | .02 | .10 |
| ❑ 649 | Dion James | .02 | .10 |
| ❑ 650 | Jeff Johnson | .02 | .10 |
| ❑ 651 | Scott Kamieniecki | .02 | .10 |
| ❑ 652 | Kevin Maas | .02 | .10 |
| ❑ 653 | Rich Monteleone | .02 | .10 |
| ❑ 654 | Jerry Nielsen | .02 | .10 |
| ❑ 655 | Scott Sanderson | .02 | .10 |
| ❑ 656 | Mike Stanley | .02 | .10 |
| ❑ 657 | Gerald Williams | .02 | .10 |
| ❑ 658 | Curt Young | .02 | .10 |
| ❑ 659 | Harold Baines | .07 | .20 |
| ❑ 660 | Kevin Campbell | .02 | .10 |
| ❑ 661 | Ron Darling | .02 | .10 |
| ❑ 662 | Kelly Downs | .02 | .10 |
| ❑ 663 | Eric Fox | .02 | .10 |
| ❑ 664 | Dave Henderson | .02 | .10 |
| ❑ 665 | Rick Honeycutt | .02 | .10 |
| ❑ 666 | Mike Moore | .02 | .10 |
| ❑ 667 | Jamie Quirk | .02 | .10 |
| ❑ 668 | Jeff Russell | .02 | .10 |
| ❑ 669 | Dave Stewart | .07 | .20 |
| ❑ 670 | Greg Briley | .02 | .10 |
| ❑ 671 | Dave Cochrane | .02 | .10 |
| ❑ 672 | Henry Cotto | .02 | .10 |
| ❑ 673 | Rich DeLucia | .02 | .10 |
| ❑ 674 | Brian Fisher | .02 | .10 |
| ❑ 675 | Mark Grant | .02 | .10 |
| ❑ 676 | Randy Johnson | .20 | .50 |
| ❑ 677 | Tim Leary | .02 | .10 |
| ❑ 678 | Pete O'Brien | .02 | .10 |
| ❑ 679 | Lance Parrish | .07 | .20 |
| ❑ 680 | Harold Reynolds | .07 | .20 |
| ❑ 681 | Shane Turner | .02 | .10 |
| ❑ 682 | Jack Daugherty | .02 | .10 |
| ❑ 683 | David Hulse RC | .02 | .10 |
| ❑ 684 | Terry Mathews | .02 | .10 |
| ❑ 685 | Al Newman | .02 | .10 |
| ❑ 686 | Edwin Nunez | .02 | .10 |
| ❑ 687 | Rafael Palmeiro | .10 | .30 |
| ❑ 688 | Roger Pavlik | .02 | .10 |
| ❑ 689 | Geno Petralli | .02 | .10 |
| ❑ 690 | Nolan Ryan | .75 | 2.00 |
| ❑ 691 | David Cone | .07 | .20 |
| ❑ 692 | Alfredo Griffin | .02 | .10 |
| ❑ 693 | Juan Guzman | .02 | .10 |
| ❑ 694 | Pat Hentgen | .02 | .10 |
| ❑ 695 | Randy Knorr | .02 | .10 |
| ❑ 696 | Bob MacDonald | .02 | .10 |
| ❑ 697 | Jack Morris | .07 | .20 |
| ❑ 698 | Ed Sprague | .02 | .10 |
| ❑ 699 | Dave Stieb | .02 | .10 |
| ❑ 700 | Pat Tabler | .02 | .10 |
| ❑ 701 | Mike Timlin | .02 | .10 |
| ❑ 702 | David Wells | .07 | .20 |
| ❑ 703 | Eddie Zosky | .02 | .10 |
| ❑ 704 | Gary Sheffield LL | .07 | .20 |
| ❑ 705 | Darren Daulton LL | .02 | .10 |
| ❑ 706 | Marquis Grissom LL | .02 | .10 |
| ❑ 707 | Greg Maddux LL | .20 | .50 |
| ❑ 708 | Bill Swift LL | .02 | .10 |
| ❑ 709 | Juan Gonzalez RT | .10 | .30 |
| ❑ 710 | Mark McGwire RT | .25 | .60 |
| ❑ 711 | Cecil Fielder RT | .07 | .20 |
| ❑ 712 | Albert Belle RT | .07 | .20 |
| ❑ 713 | Joe Carter RT | .02 | .10 |
| ❑ 714 | F.Thomas/C.Fielder | .10 | .30 |
| ❑ 715 | L.Walker/D.Justice SS | .07 | .20 |
| ❑ 716 | E.Martinez/R.Ventura SS | .07 | .20 |
| ❑ 717 | R.Clemens/D.Eckersley | .20 | .50 |
| ❑ 718 | Checklist 361-480 | .02 | .10 |
| ❑ 719 | Checklist 481-600 | .02 | .10 |
| ❑ 720 | Checklist 601-720 | .02 | .10 |

## 1994 Fleer

|  |  | | |
|---|---|---|---|
| ❑ | COMPLETE SET (720) | 25.00 | 50.00 |
| ❑ 1 | Brady Anderson | .10 | .30 |
| ❑ 2 | Harold Baines | .10 | .30 |
| ❑ 3 | Mike Devereaux | .05 | .15 |
| ❑ 4 | Todd Frohwirth | .05 | .15 |
| ❑ 5 | Jeffrey Hammonds | .05 | .15 |
| ❑ 6 | Chris Hoiles | .05 | .15 |
| ❑ 7 | Tim Hulett | .05 | .15 |
| ❑ 8 | Ben McDonald | .05 | .15 |
| ❑ 9 | Mark McLemore | .05 | .15 |
| ❑ 10 | Alan Mills | .05 | .15 |
| ❑ 11 | Jamie Moyer | .10 | .30 |
| ❑ 12 | Mike Mussina | .20 | .50 |
| ❑ 13 | Gregg Olson | .05 | .15 |
| ❑ 14 | Mike Pagliarulo | .05 | .15 |
| ❑ 15 | Brad Pennington | .05 | .15 |
| ❑ 16 | Jim Poole | .05 | .15 |
| ❑ 17 | Harold Reynolds | .10 | .30 |
| ❑ 18 | Arthur Rhodes | .05 | .15 |
| ❑ 19 | Cal Ripken | 1.00 | 2.50 |
| ❑ 20 | David Segui | .05 | .15 |
| ❑ 21 | Rick Sutcliffe | .10 | .30 |
| ❑ 22 | Fernando Valenzuela | .05 | .15 |
| ❑ 23 | Jack Voigt | .05 | .15 |
| ❑ 24 | Mark Williamson | .05 | .15 |
| ❑ 25 | Scott Bankhead | .05 | .15 |
| ❑ 26 | Roger Clemens | .60 | 1.50 |
| ❑ 27 | Scott Cooper | .05 | .15 |
| ❑ 28 | Danny Darwin | .05 | .15 |
| ❑ 29 | Andre Dawson | .10 | .30 |
| ❑ 30 | Rob Deer | .05 | .15 |
| ❑ 31 | John Dopson | .05 | .15 |
| ❑ 32 | Scott Fletcher | .05 | .15 |
| ❑ 33 | Mike Greenwell | .05 | .15 |
| ❑ 34 | Greg A. Harris | .05 | .15 |
| ❑ 35 | Billy Hatcher | .05 | .15 |
| ❑ 36 | Bob Melvin | .05 | .15 |
| ❑ 37 | Tony Pena | .05 | .15 |
| ❑ 38 | Paul Quantrill | .05 | .15 |
| ❑ 39 | Carlos Quintana | .05 | .15 |
| ❑ 40 | Ernest Riles | .05 | .15 |
| ❑ 41 | Jeff Russell | .05 | .15 |
| ❑ 42 | Ken Ryan | .05 | .15 |
| ❑ 43 | Aaron Sele | .05 | .15 |
| ❑ 44 | John Valentin | .05 | .15 |
| ❑ 45 | Mo Vaughn | .10 | .30 |
| ❑ 46 | Frank Viola | .10 | .30 |
| ❑ 47 | Bob Zupcic | .05 | .15 |
| ❑ 48 | Mike Butcher | .05 | .15 |
| ❑ 49 | Rod Correia | .05 | .15 |
| ❑ 50 | Chad Curtis | .05 | .15 |
| ❑ 51 | Chili Davis | .10 | .30 |
| ❑ 52 | Gary DiSarcina | .05 | .15 |
| ❑ 53 | Damion Easley | .05 | .15 |
| ❑ 54 | Jim Edmonds | .30 | .75 |
| ❑ 55 | Chuck Finley | .10 | .30 |
| ❑ 56 | Steve Frey | .05 | .15 |
| ❑ 57 | Rene Gonzales | .05 | .15 |
| ❑ 58 | Joe Grahe | .05 | .15 |
| ❑ 59 | Billy Hathaway | .05 | .15 |
| ❑ 60 | Stan Javier | .05 | .15 |
| ❑ 61 | Mark Langston | .05 | .15 |
| ❑ 62 | Phil Leftwich RC | .05 | .15 |
| ❑ 63 | Torey Lovullo | .05 | .15 |
| ❑ 64 | Joe Magrane | .05 | .15 |
| ❑ 65 | Greg Myers | .05 | .15 |
| ❑ 66 | Ken Patterson | .05 | .15 |
| ❑ 67 | Eduardo Perez | .05 | .15 |
| ❑ 68 | Luis Polonia | .05 | .15 |
| ❑ 69 | Tim Salmon | .20 | .50 |
| ❑ 70 | J.T.Snow | .10 | .30 |
| ❑ 71 | Ron Tingley | .05 | .15 |
| ❑ 72 | Julio Valera | .05 | .15 |
| ❑ 73 | Wilson Alvarez | .05 | .15 |
| ❑ 74 | Tim Belcher | .05 | .15 |
| ❑ 75 | George Bell | .05 | .15 |
| ❑ 76 | Jason Bere | .05 | .15 |
| ❑ 77 | Rod Bolton | .05 | .15 |
| ❑ 78 | Ellis Burks | .10 | .30 |
| ❑ 79 | Joey Cora | .05 | .15 |
| ❑ 80 | Alex Fernandez | .05 | .15 |
| ❑ 81 | Craig Grebeck | .05 | .15 |
| ❑ 82 | Ozzie Guillen | .10 | .30 |
| ❑ 83 | Roberto Hernandez | .05 | .15 |
| ❑ 84 | Bo Jackson | .30 | .75 |
| ❑ 85 | Lance Johnson | .05 | .15 |
| ❑ 86 | Ron Karkovice | .05 | .15 |
| ❑ 87 | Mike LaValliere | .05 | .15 |
| ❑ 88 | Kirk McCaskill | .05 | .15 |
| ❑ 89 | Jack McDowell | .05 | .15 |
| ❑ 90 | Warren Newson | .05 | .15 |
| ❑ 91 | Dan Pasqua | .05 | .15 |
| ❑ 92 | Scott Radinsky | .05 | .15 |
| ❑ 93 | Tim Raines | .10 | .30 |
| ❑ 94 | Steve Sax | .05 | .15 |
| ❑ 95 | Jeff Schwarz | .05 | .15 |
| ❑ 96 | Frank Thomas | .30 | .75 |
| ❑ 97 | Robin Ventura | .10 | .30 |
| ❑ 98 | Sandy Alomar Jr. | .05 | .15 |
| ❑ 99 | Carlos Baerga | .05 | .15 |
| ❑ 100 | Albert Belle | .10 | .30 |
| ❑ 101 | Mark Clark | .05 | .15 |
| ❑ 102 | Jerry DiPoto | .05 | .15 |
| ❑ 103 | Alvaro Espinoza | .05 | .15 |
| ❑ 104 | Felix Fermin | .05 | .15 |
| ❑ 105 | Jeremy Hernandez | .05 | .15 |
| ❑ 106 | Reggie Jefferson | .05 | .15 |
| ❑ 107 | Wayne Kirby | .05 | .15 |
| ❑ 108 | Tom Kramer | .05 | .15 |
| ❑ 109 | Mark Lewis | .05 | .15 |
| ❑ 110 | Derek Lilliquist | .05 | .15 |
| ❑ 111 | Kenny Lofton | .10 | .30 |
| ❑ 112 | Candy Maldonado | .05 | .15 |
| ❑ 113 | Jose Mesa | .05 | .15 |
| ❑ 114 | Jeff Mutis | .05 | .15 |
| ❑ 115 | Charles Nagy | .05 | .15 |
| ❑ 116 | Bob Ojeda | .05 | .15 |
| ❑ 117 | Junior Ortiz | .05 | .15 |
| ❑ 118 | Eric Plunk | .05 | .15 |

|  |  | | |
|---|--------|---|---|
| ☐ 119 | Manny Ramirez | .30 | .75 |
| ☐ 120 | Paul Sorrento | .05 | .15 |
| ☐ 121 | Jim Thome | .20 | .50 |
| ☐ 122 | Jeff Treadway | .05 | .15 |
| ☐ 123 | Bill Wertz | .05 | .15 |
| ☐ 124 | Skeeter Barnes | .05 | .15 |
| ☐ 125 | Milt Cuyler | .05 | .15 |
| ☐ 126 | Eric Davis | .10 | .30 |
| ☐ 127 | John Doherty | .05 | .15 |
| ☐ 128 | Cecil Fielder | .10 | .30 |
| ☐ 129 | Travis Fryman | .10 | .30 |
| ☐ 130 | Kirk Gibson | .05 | .15 |
| ☐ 131 | Dan Gladden | .05 | .15 |
| ☐ 132 | Greg Gohr | .05 | .15 |
| ☐ 133 | Chris Gomez | .05 | .15 |
| ☐ 134 | Bill Gullickson | .05 | .15 |
| ☐ 135 | Mike Henneman | .05 | .15 |
| ☐ 136 | Kurt Knudsen | .05 | .15 |
| ☐ 137 | Chad Kreuter | .05 | .15 |
| ☐ 138 | Bill Krueger | .05 | .15 |
| ☐ 139 | Scott Livingstone | .05 | .15 |
| ☐ 140 | Bob MacDonald | .05 | .15 |
| ☐ 141 | Mike Moore | .05 | .15 |
| ☐ 142 | Tony Phillips | .05 | .15 |
| ☐ 143 | Mickey Tettleton | .05 | .15 |
| ☐ 144 | Alan Trammell | .10 | .30 |
| ☐ 145 | David Wells | .10 | .30 |
| ☐ 146 | Lou Whitaker | .10 | .30 |
| ☐ 147 | Kevin Appier | .10 | .30 |
| ☐ 148 | Stan Belinda | .05 | .15 |
| ☐ 149 | George Brett | .75 | 2.00 |
| ☐ 150 | Billy Brewer | .05 | .15 |
| ☐ 151 | Hubie Brooks | .05 | .15 |
| ☐ 152 | David Cone | .10 | .30 |
| ☐ 153 | Gary Gaetti | .05 | .15 |
| ☐ 154 | Greg Gagne | .05 | .15 |
| ☐ 155 | Tom Gordon | .05 | .15 |
| ☐ 156 | Mark Gubicza | .05 | .15 |
| ☐ 157 | Chris Gwynn | .05 | .15 |
| ☐ 158 | John Habyan | .05 | .15 |
| ☐ 159 | Chris Haney | .05 | .15 |
| ☐ 160 | Phil Hiatt | .05 | .15 |
| ☐ 161 | Felix Jose | .05 | .15 |
| ☐ 162 | Wally Joyner | .10 | .30 |
| ☐ 163 | Jose Lind | .05 | .15 |
| ☐ 164 | Mike Macfarlane | .05 | .15 |
| ☐ 165 | Mike Magnante | .05 | .15 |
| ☐ 166 | Brent Mayne | .05 | .15 |
| ☐ 167 | Brian McRae | .05 | .15 |
| ☐ 168 | Kevin McReynolds | .05 | .15 |
| ☐ 169 | Keith Miller | .05 | .15 |
| ☐ 170 | Jeff Montgomery | .05 | .15 |
| ☐ 171 | Hipolito Pichardo | .05 | .15 |
| ☐ 172 | Rico Rossy | .05 | .15 |
| ☐ 173 | Juan Bell | .05 | .15 |
| ☐ 174 | Rickey Bones | .05 | .15 |
| ☐ 175 | Cal Eldred | .05 | .15 |
| ☐ 176 | Mike Fetters | .05 | .15 |
| ☐ 177 | Darryl Hamilton | .05 | .15 |
| ☐ 178 | Doug Henry | .05 | .15 |
| ☐ 179 | Mike Ignasiak | .05 | .15 |
| ☐ 180 | John Jaha | .05 | .15 |
| ☐ 181 | Pat Listach | .05 | .15 |
| ☐ 182 | Graeme Lloyd | .05 | .15 |
| ☐ 183 | Matt Mieske | .05 | .15 |
| ☐ 184 | Angel Miranda | .05 | .15 |
| ☐ 185 | Jaime Navarro | .05 | .15 |
| ☐ 186 | Dave Nilsson | .05 | .15 |
| ☐ 187 | Troy O'Leary | .05 | .15 |
| ☐ 188 | Jesse Orosco | .05 | .15 |
| ☐ 189 | Kevin Reimer | .05 | .15 |
| ☐ 190 | Kevin Seitzer | .05 | .15 |
| ☐ 191 | Bill Spiers | .05 | .15 |
| ☐ 192 | B.J. Surhoff | .10 | .30 |
| ☐ 193 | Dickie Thon | .05 | .15 |
| ☐ 194 | Jose Valentin | .05 | .15 |
| ☐ 195 | Greg Vaughn | .05 | .15 |
| ☐ 196 | Bill Wegman | .05 | .15 |
| ☐ 197 | Robin Yount | .50 | 1.25 |
| ☐ 198 | Rick Aguilera | .05 | .15 |
| ☐ 199 | Willie Banks | .05 | .15 |
| ☐ 200 | Bernardo Brito | .05 | .15 |
| ☐ 201 | Larry Casian | .05 | .15 |
| ☐ 202 | Scott Erickson | .05 | .15 |
| ☐ 203 | Eddie Guardado | .10 | .30 |
| ☐ 204 | Mark Guthrie | .05 | .15 |
| ☐ 205 | Chip Hale | .05 | .15 |
| ☐ 206 | Brian Harper | .05 | .15 |
| ☐ 207 | Mike Hartley | .05 | .15 |
| ☐ 208 | Kent Hrbek | .10 | .30 |
| ☐ 209 | Terry Jorgensen | .05 | .15 |
| ☐ 210 | Chuck Knoblauch | .10 | .30 |
| ☐ 211 | Gene Larkin | .05 | .15 |
| ☐ 212 | Shane Mack | .05 | .15 |
| ☐ 213 | David McCarty | .05 | .15 |
| ☐ 214 | Pat Meares | .05 | .15 |
| ☐ 215 | Pedro Munoz | .05 | .15 |
| ☐ 216 | Derek Parks | .05 | .15 |
| ☐ 217 | Kirby Puckett | .30 | .75 |
| ☐ 218 | Jeff Reboulet | .05 | .15 |
| ☐ 219 | Kevin Tapani | .05 | .15 |
| ☐ 220 | Mike Trombley | .05 | .15 |
| ☐ 221 | George Tsamis | .05 | .15 |
| ☐ 222 | Carl Willis | .05 | .15 |
| ☐ 223 | Dave Winfield | .10 | .30 |
| ☐ 224 | Jim Abbott | .20 | .50 |
| ☐ 225 | Paul Assenmacher | .05 | .15 |
| ☐ 226 | Wade Boggs | .20 | .50 |
| ☐ 227 | Russ Davis | .05 | .15 |
| ☐ 228 | Steve Farr | .05 | .15 |
| ☐ 229 | Mike Gallego | .05 | .15 |
| ☐ 230 | Paul Gibson | .05 | .15 |
| ☐ 231 | Steve Howe | .05 | .15 |
| ☐ 232 | Dion James | .05 | .15 |
| ☐ 233 | Domingo Jean | .05 | .15 |
| ☐ 234 | Scott Kamieniecki | .05 | .15 |
| ☐ 235 | Pat Kelly | .05 | .15 |
| ☐ 236 | Jimmy Key | .10 | .30 |
| ☐ 237 | Jim Leyritz | .05 | .15 |
| ☐ 238 | Kevin Maas | .05 | .15 |
| ☐ 239 | Don Mattingly | .75 | 2.00 |
| ☐ 240 | Rich Monteleone | .05 | .15 |
| ☐ 241 | Bobby Munoz | .05 | .15 |
| ☐ 242 | Matt Nokes | .05 | .15 |
| ☐ 243 | Paul O'Neill | .20 | .50 |
| ☐ 244 | Spike Owen | .05 | .15 |
| ☐ 245 | Melido Perez | .05 | .15 |
| ☐ 246 | Lee Smith | .10 | .30 |
| ☐ 247 | Mike Stanley | .05 | .15 |
| ☐ 248 | Danny Tartabull | .05 | .15 |
| ☐ 249 | Randy Velarde | .05 | .15 |
| ☐ 250 | Bob Wickman | .05 | .15 |
| ☐ 251 | Bernie Williams | .20 | .50 |
| ☐ 252 | Mike Aldrete | .05 | .15 |
| ☐ 253 | Marcos Armas | .05 | .15 |
| ☐ 254 | Lance Blankenship | .05 | .15 |
| ☐ 255 | Mike Bordick | .05 | .15 |
| ☐ 256 | Scott Brosius | .10 | .30 |
| ☐ 257 | Jerry Browne | .05 | .15 |
| ☐ 258 | Ron Darling | .05 | .15 |
| ☐ 259 | Kelly Downs | .05 | .15 |
| ☐ 260 | Dennis Eckersley | .10 | .30 |
| ☐ 261 | Brent Gates | .05 | .15 |
| ☐ 262 | Rich Gossage | .10 | .30 |
| ☐ 263 | Scott Hemond | .05 | .15 |
| ☐ 264 | Dave Henderson | .05 | .15 |
| ☐ 265 | Rick Honeycutt | .05 | .15 |
| ☐ 266 | Vince Horsman | .05 | .15 |
| ☐ 267 | Scott Lydy | .05 | .15 |
| ☐ 268 | Mark McGwire | .75 | 2.00 |
| ☐ 269 | Mike Mohler | .05 | .15 |
| ☐ 270 | Troy Neel | .05 | .15 |
| ☐ 271 | Edwin Nunez | .05 | .15 |
| ☐ 272 | Craig Paquette | .05 | .15 |
| ☐ 273 | Ruben Sierra | .10 | .30 |
| ☐ 274 | Terry Steinbach | .05 | .15 |
| ☐ 275 | Todd Van Poppel | .05 | .15 |
| ☐ 276 | Bob Welch | .05 | .15 |
| ☐ 277 | Bobby Witt | .05 | .15 |
| ☐ 278 | Rich Amaral | .05 | .15 |
| ☐ 279 | Mike Blowers | .05 | .15 |
| ☐ 280 | Bret Boone UER | .10 | .30 |
| ☐ 281 | Chris Bosio | .05 | .15 |
| ☐ 282 | Jay Buhner | .10 | .30 |
| ☐ 283 | Norm Charlton | .05 | .15 |
| ☐ 284 | Mike Felder | .05 | .15 |
| ☐ 285 | Dave Fleming | .05 | .15 |
| ☐ 286 | Ken Griffey Jr. | .50 | 1.25 |
| ☐ 287 | Erik Hanson | .05 | .15 |
| ☐ 288 | Bill Haselman | .05 | .15 |
| ☐ 289 | Brad Holman RC | .05 | .15 |
| ☐ 290 | Randy Johnson | .30 | .75 |
| ☐ 291 | Tim Leary | .05 | .15 |
| ☐ 292 | Greg Litton | .05 | .15 |
| ☐ 293 | Dave Magadan | .05 | .15 |
| ☐ 294 | Edgar Martinez | .20 | .50 |
| ☐ 295 | Tino Martinez | .20 | .50 |
| ☐ 296 | Jeff Nelson | .05 | .15 |
| ☐ 297 | Erik Plantenberg RC | .05 | .15 |
| ☐ 298 | Mackey Sasser | .05 | .15 |
| ☐ 299 | Brian Turang RC | .05 | .15 |
| ☐ 300 | Dave Valle | .05 | .15 |
| ☐ 301 | Omar Vizquel | .20 | .50 |
| ☐ 302 | Brian Bohanon | .05 | .15 |
| ☐ 303 | Kevin Brown | .10 | .30 |
| ☐ 304 | Jose Canseco | .20 | .50 |
| ☐ 305 | Mario Diaz | .05 | .15 |
| ☐ 306 | Julio Franco | .10 | .30 |
| ☐ 307 | Juan Gonzalez | .10 | .30 |
| ☐ 308 | Tom Henke | .05 | .15 |
| ☐ 309 | David Hulse | .05 | .15 |
| ☐ 310 | Manuel Lee | .05 | .15 |
| ☐ 311 | Craig Lefferts | .05 | .15 |
| ☐ 312 | Charlie Leibrandt | .05 | .15 |
| ☐ 313 | Rafael Palmeiro | .20 | .50 |
| ☐ 314 | Dean Palmer | .10 | .30 |
| ☐ 315 | Roger Pavlik | .05 | .15 |
| ☐ 316 | Dan Peltier | .05 | .15 |
| ☐ 317 | Gene Petralli | .05 | .15 |
| ☐ 318 | Gary Redus | .05 | .15 |
| ☐ 319 | Ivan Rodriguez | .20 | .50 |
| ☐ 320 | Kenny Rogers | .10 | .30 |
| ☐ 321 | Nolan Ryan | 1.25 | 3.00 |
| ☐ 322 | Doug Strange | .05 | .15 |
| ☐ 323 | Matt Whiteside | .05 | .15 |
| ☐ 324 | Roberto Alomar | .20 | .50 |
| ☐ 325 | Pat Borders | .05 | .15 |
| ☐ 326 | Joe Carter | .10 | .30 |
| ☐ 327 | Tony Castillo | .05 | .15 |
| ☐ 328 | Darnell Coles | .05 | .15 |
| ☐ 329 | Danny Cox | .05 | .15 |
| ☐ 330 | Mark Eichhorn | .05 | .15 |
| ☐ 331 | Tony Fernandez | .05 | .15 |
| ☐ 332 | Alfredo Griffin | .05 | .15 |
| ☐ 333 | Juan Guzman | .05 | .15 |
| ☐ 334 | Rickey Henderson | .30 | .75 |
| ☐ 335 | Pat Hentgen | .05 | .15 |
| ☐ 336 | Randy Knorr | .05 | .15 |
| ☐ 337 | Al Leiter | .10 | .30 |
| ☐ 338 | Paul Molitor | .10 | .30 |
| ☐ 339 | Jack Morris | .10 | .30 |
| ☐ 340 | John Olerud | .10 | .30 |
| ☐ 341 | Dick Schofield | .05 | .15 |
| ☐ 342 | Ed Sprague | .05 | .15 |
| ☐ 343 | Dave Stewart | .10 | .30 |
| ☐ 344 | Todd Stottlemyre | .05 | .15 |
| ☐ 345 | Mike Timlin | .05 | .15 |
| ☐ 346 | Duane Ward | .05 | .15 |
| ☐ 347 | Turner Ward | .05 | .15 |
| ☐ 348 | Devon White | .10 | .30 |
| ☐ 349 | Woody Williams | .10 | .30 |
| ☐ 350 | Steve Avery | .10 | .30 |
| ☐ 351 | Steve Bedrosian | .05 | .15 |
| ☐ 352 | Rafael Belliard | .05 | .15 |
| ☐ 353 | Damon Berryhill | .05 | .15 |
| ☐ 354 | Jeff Blauser | .05 | .15 |
| ☐ 355 | Sid Bream | .05 | .15 |
| ☐ 356 | Francisco Cabrera | .05 | .15 |
| ☐ 357 | Marvin Freeman | .05 | .15 |
| ☐ 358 | Ron Gant | .10 | .30 |
| ☐ 359 | Tom Glavine | .20 | .50 |
| ☐ 360 | Jay Howell | .05 | .15 |
| ☐ 361 | David Justice | .10 | .30 |
| ☐ 362 | Ryan Klesko | .10 | .30 |
| ☐ 363 | Mark Lemke | .05 | .15 |
| ☐ 364 | Javier Lopez | .10 | .30 |
| ☐ 365 | Greg Maddux | .50 | 1.25 |
| ☐ 366 | Fred McGriff | .20 | .50 |
| ☐ 367 | Greg McMichael | .05 | .15 |
| ☐ 368 | Kent Mercker | .05 | .15 |
| ☐ 369 | Otis Nixon | .05 | .15 |
| ☐ 370 | Greg Olson | .05 | .15 |
| ☐ 371 | Bill Pecota | .05 | .15 |
| ☐ 372 | Terry Pendleton | .10 | .30 |
| ☐ 373 | Deion Sanders | .20 | .50 |
| ☐ 374 | Pete Smith | .05 | .15 |
| ☐ 375 | John Smoltz | .20 | .50 |
| ☐ 376 | Mike Stanton | .05 | .15 |
| ☐ 377 | Tony Tarasco | .05 | .15 |
| ☐ 378 | Mark Wohlers | .05 | .15 |
| ☐ 379 | Jose Bautista | .05 | .15 |
| ☐ 380 | Shawn Boskie | .05 | .15 |
| ☐ 381 | Steve Buechele | .05 | .15 |
| ☐ 382 | Frank Castillo | .05 | .15 |

|  |  | | |
|---|--------|---|---|
| ☐ 383 | Mark Grace | .20 | .50 |
| ☐ 384 | Jose Guzman | .05 | .15 |
| ☐ 385 | Mike Harkey | .05 | .15 |
| ☐ 386 | Greg Hibbard | .05 | .15 |
| ☐ 387 | Glenallen Hill | .05 | .15 |
| ☐ 388 | Steve Lake | .05 | .15 |
| ☐ 389 | Derrick May | .05 | .15 |
| ☐ 390 | Chuck McElroy | .05 | .15 |
| ☐ 391 | Mike Morgan | .05 | .15 |
| ☐ 392 | Randy Myers | .05 | .15 |
| ☐ 393 | Dan Plesac | .05 | .15 |
| ☐ 394 | Kevin Roberson | .05 | .15 |
| ☐ 395 | Rey Sanchez | .05 | .15 |
| ☐ 396 | Ryne Sandberg | .50 | 1.25 |
| ☐ 397 | Bob Scanlan | .05 | .15 |
| ☐ 398 | Dwight Smith | .05 | .15 |
| ☐ 399 | Sammy Sosa | .30 | .75 |
| ☐ 400 | Jose Vizcaino | .05 | .15 |
| ☐ 401 | Rick Wilkins | .05 | .15 |
| ☐ 402 | Willie Wilson | .05 | .15 |
| ☐ 403 | Eric Yelding | .05 | .15 |
| ☐ 404 | Bobby Ayala | .05 | .15 |
| ☐ 405 | Jeff Branson | .05 | .15 |
| ☐ 406 | Tom Browning | .05 | .15 |
| ☐ 407 | Jacob Brumfield | .05 | .15 |
| ☐ 408 | Tim Costo | .05 | .15 |
| ☐ 409 | Rob Dibble | .10 | .30 |
| ☐ 410 | Willie Greene | .05 | .15 |
| ☐ 411 | Thomas Howard | .05 | .15 |
| ☐ 412 | Roberto Kelly | .05 | .15 |
| ☐ 413 | Bill Landrum | .05 | .15 |
| ☐ 414 | Barry Larkin | .20 | .50 |
| ☐ 415 | Larry Luebbers RC | .05 | .15 |
| ☐ 416 | Kevin Mitchell | .05 | .15 |
| ☐ 417 | Hal Morris | .05 | .15 |
| ☐ 418 | Joe Oliver | .05 | .15 |
| ☐ 419 | Tim Pugh | .05 | .15 |
| ☐ 420 | Jeff Reardon | .10 | .30 |
| ☐ 421 | Jose Rijo | .05 | .15 |
| ☐ 422 | Bip Roberts | .05 | .15 |
| ☐ 423 | John Roper | .05 | .15 |
| ☐ 424 | Johnny Ruffin | .05 | .15 |
| ☐ 425 | Chris Sabo | .05 | .15 |
| ☐ 426 | Juan Samuel | .05 | .15 |
| ☐ 427 | Reggie Sanders | .10 | .30 |
| ☐ 428 | Scott Service | .05 | .15 |
| ☐ 429 | John Smiley | .05 | .15 |
| ☐ 430 | Jerry Spradlin RC | .05 | .15 |
| ☐ 431 | Kevin Wickander | .05 | .15 |
| ☐ 432 | Freddie Benavides | .05 | .15 |
| ☐ 433 | Dante Bichette | .10 | .30 |
| ☐ 434 | Willie Blair | .05 | .15 |
| ☐ 435 | Daryl Boston | .05 | .15 |
| ☐ 436 | Kent Bottenfield | .05 | .15 |
| ☐ 437 | Vinny Castilla | .10 | .30 |
| ☐ 438 | Jerald Clark | .05 | .15 |
| ☐ 439 | Alex Cole | .05 | .15 |
| ☐ 440 | Andres Galarraga | .10 | .30 |
| ☐ 441 | Joe Girardi | .05 | .15 |
| ☐ 442 | Greg W. Harris | .05 | .15 |
| ☐ 443 | Charlie Hayes | .05 | .15 |
| ☐ 444 | Darren Holmes | .05 | .15 |
| ☐ 445 | Chris Jones | .05 | .15 |
| ☐ 446 | Roberto Mejia | .05 | .15 |
| ☐ 447 | David Nied | .05 | .15 |
| ☐ 448 | Jayhawk Owens | .05 | .15 |
| ☐ 449 | Jeff Parrett | .05 | .15 |
| ☐ 450 | Steve Reed | .05 | .15 |
| ☐ 451 | Armando Reynoso | .05 | .15 |
| ☐ 452 | Bruce Ruffin | .05 | .15 |
| ☐ 453 | Mo Sanford | .05 | .15 |
| ☐ 454 | Gary Sheaffer | .05 | .15 |
| ☐ 455 | Jim Tatum | .05 | .15 |
| ☐ 456 | Gary Wayne | .05 | .15 |
| ☐ 457 | Eric Young | .05 | .15 |
| ☐ 458 | Luis Aquino | .05 | .15 |
| ☐ 459 | Alex Arias | .05 | .15 |
| ☐ 460 | Jack Armstrong | .05 | .15 |
| ☐ 461 | Bret Barberie | .05 | .15 |
| ☐ 462 | Ryan Bowen | .05 | .15 |
| ☐ 463 | Chuck Carr | .05 | .15 |
| ☐ 464 | Jeff Conine | .10 | .30 |
| ☐ 465 | Henry Cotto | .05 | .15 |
| ☐ 466 | Orestes Destrade | .05 | .15 |
| ☐ 467 | Chris Hammond | .05 | .15 |
| ☐ 468 | Bryan Harvey | .05 | .15 |
| ☐ 469 | Charlie Hough | .10 | .30 |
| ☐ 470 | Joe Klink | .05 | .15 |
| ☐ 471 | Richie Lewis | .05 | .15 |
| ☐ 472 | Bob Natal | .05 | .15 |
| ☐ 473 | Pat Rapp | .05 | .15 |
| ☐ 474 | Rich Renteria | .05 | .15 |
| ☐ 475 | Rich Rodriguez | .05 | .15 |
| ☐ 476 | Benito Santiago | .10 | .30 |
| ☐ 477 | Gary Sheffield | .10 | .30 |
| ☐ 478 | Matt Turner | .05 | .15 |
| ☐ 479 | David Weathers | .05 | .15 |
| ☐ 480 | Walt Weiss | .05 | .15 |
| ☐ 481 | Darrell Whitmore | .05 | .15 |
| ☐ 482 | Eric Anthony | .05 | .15 |
| ☐ 483 | Jeff Bagwell | .20 | .50 |
| ☐ 484 | Kevin Bass | .05 | .15 |
| ☐ 485 | Craig Biggio | .20 | .50 |
| ☐ 486 | Ken Caminiti | .10 | .30 |
| ☐ 487 | Andujar Cedeno | .05 | .15 |
| ☐ 488 | Chris Donnels | .05 | .15 |
| ☐ 489 | Doug Drabek | .05 | .15 |
| ☐ 490 | Steve Finley | .10 | .30 |
| ☐ 491 | Luis Gonzalez | .10 | .30 |
| ☐ 492 | Pete Harnisch | .05 | .15 |
| ☐ 493 | Xavier Hernandez | .05 | .15 |
| ☐ 494 | Doug Jones | .05 | .15 |
| ☐ 495 | Todd Jones | .05 | .15 |
| ☐ 496 | Darryl Kile | .10 | .30 |
| ☐ 497 | Al Osuna | .05 | .15 |
| ☐ 498 | Mark Portugal | .05 | .15 |
| ☐ 499 | Scott Servais | .05 | .15 |
| ☐ 500 | Greg Swindell | .05 | .15 |
| ☐ 501 | Eddie Taubensee | .05 | .15 |
| ☐ 502 | Jose Uribe | .05 | .15 |
| ☐ 503 | Brian Williams | .05 | .15 |
| ☐ 504 | Billy Ashley | .05 | .15 |
| ☐ 505 | Pedro Astacio | .05 | .15 |
| ☐ 506 | Brett Butler | .10 | .30 |
| ☐ 507 | Tom Candiotti | .05 | .15 |
| ☐ 508 | Omar Daal | .05 | .15 |
| ☐ 509 | Jim Gott | .05 | .15 |
| ☐ 510 | Kevin Gross | .05 | .15 |
| ☐ 511 | Dave Hansen | .05 | .15 |
| ☐ 512 | Carlos Hernandez | .05 | .15 |
| ☐ 513 | Orel Hershiser | .10 | .30 |
| ☐ 514 | Eric Karros | .10 | .30 |
| ☐ 515 | Pedro Martinez | .30 | .75 |
| ☐ 516 | Ramon Martinez | .05 | .15 |
| ☐ 517 | Roger McDowell | .05 | .15 |
| ☐ 518 | Raul Mondesi | .05 | .15 |
| ☐ 519 | Jose Offerman | .05 | .15 |
| ☐ 520 | Mike Piazza | .60 | 1.50 |
| ☐ 521 | Jody Reed | .05 | .15 |
| ☐ 522 | Henry Rodriguez | .05 | .15 |
| ☐ 523 | Mike Sharperson | .05 | .15 |
| ☐ 524 | Cory Snyder | .05 | .15 |
| ☐ 525 | Darryl Strawberry | .10 | .30 |
| ☐ 526 | Rick Trlicek | .05 | .15 |
| ☐ 527 | Tim Wallach | .05 | .15 |
| ☐ 528 | Mitch Webster | .05 | .15 |
| ☐ 529 | Steve Wilson | .05 | .15 |
| ☐ 530 | Todd Worrell | .05 | .15 |
| ☐ 531 | Moises Alou | .10 | .30 |
| ☐ 532 | Brian Barnes | .05 | .15 |
| ☐ 533 | Sean Berry | .05 | .15 |
| ☐ 534 | Greg Colbrunn | .05 | .15 |
| ☐ 535 | Delino DeShields | .05 | .15 |
| ☐ 536 | Jeff Fassero | .05 | .15 |
| ☐ 537 | Darrin Fletcher | .05 | .15 |
| ☐ 538 | Cliff Floyd | .10 | .30 |
| ☐ 539 | Lou Frazier | .05 | .15 |
| ☐ 540 | Marquis Grissom | .10 | .30 |
| ☐ 541 | Butch Henry | .05 | .15 |
| ☐ 542 | Ken Hill | .05 | .15 |
| ☐ 543 | Mike Lansing | .05 | .15 |
| ☐ 544 | Brian Looney RC | .05 | .15 |
| ☐ 545 | Dennis Martinez | .10 | .30 |
| ☐ 546 | Chris Nabholz | .05 | .15 |
| ☐ 547 | Randy Ready | .05 | .15 |
| ☐ 548 | Mel Rojas | .05 | .15 |
| ☐ 549 | Kirk Rueter | .05 | .15 |
| ☐ 550 | Tim Scott | .05 | .15 |
| ☐ 551 | Jeff Shaw | .05 | .15 |
| ☐ 552 | Tim Spehr | .05 | .15 |
| ☐ 553 | John Vander Wal | .05 | .15 |
| ☐ 554 | Larry Walker | .10 | .30 |
| ☐ 555 | John Wetteland | .05 | .15 |
| ☐ 556 | Rondell White | .10 | .30 |
| ☐ 557 | Tim Bogar | .05 | .15 |
| ☐ 558 | Bobby Bonilla | .10 | .30 |
| ☐ 559 | Jeromy Burnitz | .10 | .30 |
| ☐ 560 | Sid Fernandez | .05 | .15 |
| ☐ 561 | John Franco | .10 | .30 |
| ☐ 562 | Dave Gallagher | .05 | .15 |
| ☐ 563 | Dwight Gooden | .10 | .30 |
| ☐ 564 | Eric Hillman | .05 | .15 |
| ☐ 565 | Todd Hundley | .05 | .15 |
| ☐ 566 | Jeff Innis | .05 | .15 |
| ☐ 567 | Darrin Jackson | .05 | .15 |
| ☐ 568 | Howard Johnson | .05 | .15 |
| ☐ 569 | Bobby Jones | .05 | .15 |
| ☐ 570 | Jeff Kent | .20 | .50 |
| ☐ 571 | Mike Maddux | .05 | .15 |
| ☐ 572 | Jeff McKnight | .05 | .15 |
| ☐ 573 | Eddie Murray | .30 | .75 |
| ☐ 574 | Charlie O'Brien | .05 | .15 |
| ☐ 575 | Joe Orsulak | .05 | .15 |
| ☐ 576 | Bret Saberhagen | .10 | .30 |
| ☐ 577 | Pete Schourek | .05 | .15 |
| ☐ 578 | Dave Telgheder | .05 | .15 |
| ☐ 579 | Ryan Thompson | .05 | .15 |
| ☐ 580 | Anthony Young | .05 | .15 |
| ☐ 581 | Ruben Amaro | .05 | .15 |
| ☐ 582 | Larry Andersen | .05 | .15 |
| ☐ 583 | Kim Batiste | .05 | .15 |
| ☐ 584 | Wes Chamberlain | .05 | .15 |
| ☐ 585 | Darren Daulton | .10 | .30 |
| ☐ 586 | Mariano Duncan | .05 | .15 |
| ☐ 587 | Lenny Dykstra | .10 | .30 |
| ☐ 588 | Jim Eisenreich | .05 | .15 |
| ☐ 589 | Tommy Greene | .05 | .15 |
| ☐ 590 | Dave Hollins | .05 | .15 |
| ☐ 591 | Pete Incaviglia | .05 | .15 |
| ☐ 592 | Danny Jackson | .05 | .15 |
| ☐ 593 | Ricky Jordan | .05 | .15 |
| ☐ 594 | John Kruk | .10 | .30 |
| ☐ 595 | Roger Mason | .05 | .15 |
| ☐ 596 | Mickey Morandini | .05 | .15 |
| ☐ 597 | Terry Mulholland | .05 | .15 |
| ☐ 598 | Todd Pratt | .05 | .15 |
| ☐ 599 | Ben Rivera | .05 | .15 |
| ☐ 600 | Curt Schilling | .10 | .30 |
| ☐ 601 | Kevin Stocker | .05 | .15 |
| ☐ 602 | Milt Thompson | .05 | .15 |
| ☐ 603 | David West | .05 | .15 |
| ☐ 604 | Mitch Williams | .05 | .15 |
| ☐ 605 | Jay Bell | .10 | .30 |
| ☐ 606 | Dave Clark | .05 | .15 |
| ☐ 607 | Steve Cooke | .05 | .15 |
| ☐ 608 | Tom Foley | .05 | .15 |
| ☐ 609 | Carlos Garcia | .05 | .15 |
| ☐ 610 | Joel Johnston | .05 | .15 |
| ☐ 611 | Jeff King | .05 | .15 |
| ☐ 612 | Al Martin | .05 | .15 |
| ☐ 613 | Lloyd McClendon | .05 | .15 |
| ☐ 614 | Orlando Merced | .05 | .15 |
| ☐ 615 | Blas Minor | .05 | .15 |
| ☐ 616 | Denny Neagle | .10 | .30 |
| ☐ 617 | Mark Petkovsek RC | .05 | .15 |
| ☐ 618 | Tom Prince | .05 | .15 |
| ☐ 619 | Don Slaught | .05 | .15 |
| ☐ 620 | Zane Smith | .05 | .15 |
| ☐ 621 | Randy Tomlin | .05 | .15 |
| ☐ 622 | Andy Van Slyke | .20 | .50 |
| ☐ 623 | Paul Wagner | .05 | .15 |
| ☐ 624 | Tim Wakefield | .20 | .50 |
| ☐ 625 | Bob Walk | .05 | .15 |
| ☐ 626 | Kevin Young | .05 | .15 |
| ☐ 627 | Luis Alicea | .05 | .15 |
| ☐ 628 | Rene Arocha | .05 | .15 |
| ☐ 629 | Rod Brewer | .05 | .15 |
| ☐ 630 | Rheal Cormier | .05 | .15 |
| ☐ 631 | Bernard Gilkey | .05 | .15 |
| ☐ 632 | Lee Guetterman | .05 | .15 |
| ☐ 633 | Gregg Jefferies | .10 | .30 |
| ☐ 634 | Brian Jordan | .10 | .30 |
| ☐ 635 | Les Lancaster | .05 | .15 |
| ☐ 636 | Ray Lankford | .10 | .30 |
| ☐ 637 | Rob Murphy | .05 | .15 |
| ☐ 638 | Omar Olivares | .05 | .15 |
| ☐ 639 | Jose Oquendo | .05 | .15 |
| ☐ 640 | Donovan Osborne | .05 | .15 |
| ☐ 641 | Tom Pagnozzi | .05 | .15 |
| ☐ 642 | Erik Pappas | .05 | .15 |
| ☐ 643 | Geronimo Pena | .05 | .15 |
| ☐ 644 | Mike Perez | .05 | .15 |
| ☐ 645 | Gerald Perry | .05 | .15 |
| ☐ 646 | Ozzie Smith | .50 | 1.25 |

| | | |
|---|---|---|
| 647 Bob Tewksbury | .05 | .15 |
| 648 Allen Watson | .05 | .15 |
| 649 Mark Whiten | .05 | .15 |
| 650 Tracy Woodson | .05 | .15 |
| 651 Todd Zeile | .05 | .15 |
| 652 Andy Ashby | .05 | .15 |
| 653 Brad Ausmus | .20 | .50 |
| 654 Billy Bean | .05 | .15 |
| 655 Derek Bell | .05 | .15 |
| 656 Andy Benes | .05 | .15 |
| 657 Doug Brocail | .05 | .15 |
| 658 Jarvis Brown | .05 | .15 |
| 659 Archi Cianfrocco | .05 | .15 |
| 660 Phil Clark | .05 | .15 |
| 661 Mark Davis | .05 | .15 |
| 662 Jeff Gardner | .05 | .15 |
| 663 Pat Gomez | .05 | .15 |
| 664 Ricky Gutierrez | .05 | .15 |
| 665 Tony Gwynn | .40 | 1.00 |
| 666 Gene Harris | .05 | .15 |
| 667 Kevin Higgins | .05 | .15 |
| 668 Trevor Hoffman | .20 | .50 |
| 669 Pedro A.Martinez RC | .05 | .15 |
| 670 Tim Mauser | .05 | .15 |
| 671 Melvin Nieves | .05 | .15 |
| 672 Phil Plantier | .05 | .15 |
| 673 Frank Seminara | .05 | .15 |
| 674 Craig Shipley | .05 | .15 |
| 675 Kerry Taylor | .05 | .15 |
| 676 Tim Teufel | .05 | .15 |
| 677 Guillermo Velasquez | .05 | .15 |
| 678 Wally Whitehurst | .05 | .15 |
| 679 Tim Worrell | .05 | .15 |
| 680 Rod Beck | .05 | .15 |
| 681 Mike Benjamin | .05 | .15 |
| 682 Todd Benzinger | .05 | .15 |
| 683 Bud Black | .05 | .15 |
| 684 Barry Bonds | .75 | 2.00 |
| 685 Jeff Brantley | .05 | .15 |
| 686 Dave Burba | .05 | .15 |
| 687 John Burkett | .05 | .15 |
| 688 Mark Carreon | .05 | .15 |
| 689 Will Clark | .20 | .50 |
| 690 Royce Clayton | .05 | .15 |
| 691 Bryan Hickerson | .05 | .15 |
| 692 Mike Jackson | .05 | .15 |
| 693 Darren Lewis | .05 | .15 |
| 694 Kirt Manwaring | .05 | .15 |
| 695 Dave Martinez | .05 | .15 |
| 696 Willie McGee | .10 | .30 |
| 697 John Patterson | .05 | .15 |
| 698 Jeff Reed | .05 | .15 |
| 699 Kevin Rogers | .05 | .15 |
| 700 Scott Sanderson | .05 | .15 |
| 701 Steve Scarsone | .05 | .15 |
| 702 Billy Swift | .05 | .15 |
| 703 Robby Thompson | .05 | .15 |
| 704 Matt Williams | .10 | .30 |
| 705 Trevor Wilson | .05 | .15 |
| 706 McGriff/Gant/Justice | .10 | .30 |
| 707 J.Olerud/P. Molitor | .10 | .30 |
| 708 M.Mussina/J.McDowell | .10 | .30 |
| 709 L.Whitaker/A.Trammell | .10 | .30 |
| 710 R.Palmeiro/J.Gonzalez | .10 | .30 |
| 711 B.Butler/T.Gwynn | .20 | .50 |
| 712 K.Puckett/C.Knoblauch | .30 | .75 |
| 713 M.Piazza/E.Karros | .30 | .75 |
| 714 Checklist 1 | .05 | .15 |
| 715 Checklist 2 | .05 | .15 |
| 716 Checklist 3 | .05 | .15 |
| 717 Checklist 4 | .05 | .15 |
| 718 Checklist 5 | .05 | .15 |
| 719 Checklist 6 | .05 | .15 |
| 720 Checklist 7 | .05 | .15 |
| P69 Tim Salmon Promo | .40 | 1.00 |

## 1995 Fleer

| | | |
|---|---|---|
| COMPLETE SET (600) | 20.00 | 50.00 |
| 1 Brady Anderson | .10 | .30 |
| 2 Harold Baines | .10 | .30 |
| 3 Damon Buford | .05 | .15 |
| 4 Mike Devereaux | .05 | .15 |
| 5 Mark Eichhorn | .05 | .15 |
| 6 Sid Fernandez | .05 | .15 |
| 7 Leo Gomez | .05 | .15 |
| 8 Jeffrey Hammonds | .05 | .15 |
| 9 Chris Hoiles | .05 | .15 |
| 10 Rick Krivda | .05 | .15 |
| 11 Ben McDonald | .05 | .15 |
| 12 Mark McLemore | .05 | .15 |
| 13 Alan Mills | .05 | .15 |
| 14 Jamie Moyer | .10 | .30 |
| 15 Mike Mussina | .20 | .50 |
| 16 Mike Oquist | .05 | .15 |
| 17 Rafael Palmeiro | .20 | .50 |
| 18 Arthur Rhodes | .05 | .15 |
| 19 Cal Ripken | 1.00 | 2.50 |
| 20 Chris Sabo | .05 | .15 |
| 21 Lee Smith | .10 | .30 |
| 22 Jack Voigt | .05 | .15 |
| 23 Damon Berryhill | .05 | .15 |
| 24 Tom Brunansky | .05 | .15 |
| 25 Wes Chamberlain | .05 | .15 |
| 26 Roger Clemens | .60 | 1.50 |
| 27 Scott Cooper | .05 | .15 |
| 28 Andre Dawson | .10 | .30 |
| 29 Gar Finnvold | .05 | .15 |
| 30 Tony Fossas | .05 | .15 |
| 31 Mike Greenwell | .05 | .15 |
| 32 Joe Hesketh | .05 | .15 |
| 33 Chris Howard | .05 | .15 |
| 34 Chris Nabholz | .05 | .15 |
| 35 Tim Naehring | .05 | .15 |
| 36 Otis Nixon | .05 | .15 |
| 37 Carlos Rodriguez | .05 | .15 |
| 38 Rich Rowland | .05 | .15 |
| 39 Ken Ryan | .05 | .15 |
| 40 Aaron Sele | .05 | .15 |
| 41 John Valentin | .05 | .15 |
| 42 Mo Vaughn | .10 | .30 |
| 43 Frank Viola | .10 | .30 |
| 44 Danny Bautista | .05 | .15 |
| 45 Joe Boever | .05 | .15 |
| 46 Milt Cuyler | .05 | .15 |
| 47 Storm Davis | .05 | .15 |
| 48 John Doherty | .05 | .15 |
| 49 Junior Felix | .05 | .15 |
| 50 Cecil Fielder | .10 | .30 |
| 51 Travis Fryman | .10 | .30 |
| 52 Mike Gardiner | .05 | .15 |
| 53 Kirk Gibson | .10 | .30 |
| 54 Chris Gomez | .05 | .15 |
| 55 Buddy Groom | .05 | .15 |
| 56 Mike Henneman | .05 | .15 |
| 57 Chad Kreuter | .05 | .15 |
| 58 Mike Moore | .05 | .15 |
| 59 Tony Phillips | .05 | .15 |
| 60 Juan Samuel | .05 | .15 |
| 61 Mickey Tettleton | .05 | .15 |
| 62 Alan Trammell | .10 | .30 |
| 63 David Wells | .10 | .30 |
| 64 Lou Whitaker | .10 | .30 |
| 65 Jim Abbott | .20 | .50 |
| 66 Joe Ausanio | .05 | .15 |
| 67 Wade Boggs | .20 | .50 |
| 68 Mike Gallego | .05 | .15 |
| 69 Xavier Hernandez | .05 | .15 |
| 70 Sterling Hitchcock | .05 | .15 |
| 71 Steve Howe | .05 | .15 |

| | | |
|---|---|---|
| 72 Scott Kamieniecki | .05 | .15 |
| 73 Pat Kelly | .05 | .15 |
| 74 Jimmy Key | .10 | .30 |
| 75 Jim Leyritz | .05 | .15 |
| 76 Don Mattingly | .75 | 2.00 |
| 77 Terry Mulholland | .05 | .15 |
| 78 Paul O'Neill | .20 | .50 |
| 79 Melido Perez | .05 | .15 |
| 80 Luis Polonia | .05 | .15 |
| 81 Mike Stanley | .05 | .15 |
| 82 Danny Tartabull | .05 | .15 |
| 83 Randy Velarde | .05 | .15 |
| 84 Bob Wickman | .05 | .15 |
| 85 Bernie Williams | .20 | .50 |
| 86 Gerald Williams | .05 | .15 |
| 87 Roberto Alomar | .20 | .50 |
| 88 Pat Borders | .05 | .15 |
| 89 Joe Carter | .10 | .30 |
| 90 Tony Castillo | .05 | .15 |
| 91 Brad Cornett RC | .05 | .15 |
| 92 Carlos Delgado | .10 | .30 |
| 93 Alex Gonzalez | .05 | .15 |
| 94 Shawn Green | .10 | .30 |
| 95 Juan Guzman | .05 | .15 |
| 96 Darren Hall | .05 | .15 |
| 97 Pat Hentgen | .05 | .15 |
| 98 Mike Huff | .05 | .15 |
| 99 Randy Knorr | .05 | .15 |
| 100 Al Leiter | .10 | .30 |
| 101 Paul Molitor | .10 | .30 |
| 102 John Olerud | .10 | .30 |
| 103 Dick Schofield | .05 | .15 |
| 104 Ed Sprague | .05 | .15 |
| 105 Dave Stewart | .10 | .30 |
| 106 Todd Stottlemyre | .05 | .15 |
| 107 Devon White | .10 | .30 |
| 108 Woody Williams | .05 | .15 |
| 109 Wilson Alvarez | .05 | .15 |
| 110 Paul Assenmacher | .05 | .15 |
| 111 Jason Bere | .05 | .15 |
| 112 Dennis Cook | .05 | .15 |
| 113 Joey Cora | .05 | .15 |
| 114 Jose DeLeon | .05 | .15 |
| 115 Alex Fernandez | .10 | .30 |
| 116 Julio Franco | .10 | .30 |
| 117 Craig Grebeck | .05 | .15 |
| 118 Ozzie Guillen | .10 | .30 |
| 119 Roberto Hernandez | .05 | .15 |
| 120 Darrin Jackson | .05 | .15 |
| 121 Lance Johnson | .05 | .15 |
| 122 Ron Karkovice | .05 | .15 |
| 123 Mike LaValliere | .05 | .15 |
| 124 Norberto Martin | .05 | .15 |
| 125 Kirk McCaskill | .05 | .15 |
| 126 Jack McDowell | .05 | .15 |
| 127 Tim Raines | .10 | .30 |
| 128 Frank Thomas | .30 | .75 |
| 129 Robin Ventura | .10 | .30 |
| 130 Sandy Alomar Jr. | .05 | .15 |
| 131 Carlos Baerga | .05 | .15 |
| 132 Albert Belle | .10 | .30 |
| 133 Mark Clark | .05 | .15 |
| 134 Alvaro Espinoza | .05 | .15 |
| 135 Jason Grimsley | .05 | .15 |
| 136 Wayne Kirby | .05 | .15 |
| 137 Kenny Lofton | .10 | .30 |
| 138 Albie Lopez | .05 | .15 |
| 139 Dennis Martinez | .10 | .30 |
| 140 Jose Mesa | .05 | .15 |
| 141 Eddie Murray | .20 | .50 |
| 142 Charles Nagy | .10 | .30 |
| 143 Tony Pena | .05 | .15 |
| 144 Eric Plunk | .05 | .15 |
| 145 Manny Ramirez | .20 | .50 |
| 146 Jeff Russell | .05 | .15 |
| 147 Paul Shuey | .05 | .15 |
| 148 Paul Sorrento | .05 | .15 |
| 149 Jim Thome | .20 | .50 |
| 150 Omar Vizquel | .20 | .50 |
| 151 Dave Winfield | .20 | .50 |
| 152 Kevin Appier | .10 | .30 |
| 153 Billy Brewer | .05 | .15 |
| 154 Vince Coleman | .05 | .15 |
| 155 David Cone | .10 | .30 |
| 156 Gary Gaetti | .10 | .30 |
| 157 Greg Gagne | .05 | .15 |
| 158 Tom Gordon | .05 | .15 |
| 159 Mark Gubicza | .05 | .15 |

|  |  | | |
|---|---|---|---|
| ☐ 160 | Bob Hamelin | .05 | .15 |
| ☐ 161 | Dave Henderson | .05 | .15 |
| ☐ 162 | Felix Jose | .05 | .15 |
| ☐ 163 | Wally Joyner | .10 | .30 |
| ☐ 164 | Jose Lind | .05 | .15 |
| ☐ 165 | Mike Macfarlane | .05 | .15 |
| ☐ 166 | Mike Magnante | .05 | .15 |
| ☐ 167 | Brent Mayne | .05 | .15 |
| ☐ 168 | Brian McRae | .05 | .15 |
| ☐ 169 | Rusty Meacham | .05 | .15 |
| ☐ 170 | Jeff Montgomery | .05 | .15 |
| ☐ 171 | Hipolito Pichardo | .05 | .15 |
| ☐ 172 | Terry Shumpert | .05 | .15 |
| ☐ 173 | Michael Tucker | .05 | .15 |
| ☐ 174 | Ricky Bones | .05 | .15 |
| ☐ 175 | Jeff Cirillo | .05 | .15 |
| ☐ 176 | Alex Diaz | .05 | .15 |
| ☐ 177 | Cal Eldred | .05 | .15 |
| ☐ 178 | Mike Fetters | .05 | .15 |
| ☐ 179 | Darryl Hamilton | .05 | .15 |
| ☐ 180 | Brian Harper | .05 | .15 |
| ☐ 181 | John Jaha | .05 | .15 |
| ☐ 182 | Pat Listach | .05 | .15 |
| ☐ 183 | Graeme Lloyd | .05 | .15 |
| ☐ 184 | Jose Mercedes | .05 | .15 |
| ☐ 185 | Matt Mieske | .05 | .15 |
| ☐ 186 | Dave Nilsson | .05 | .15 |
| ☐ 187 | Jody Reed | .05 | .15 |
| ☐ 188 | Bob Scanlan | .05 | .15 |
| ☐ 189 | Kevin Seitzer | .05 | .15 |
| ☐ 190 | Bill Spiers | .05 | .15 |
| ☐ 191 | B.J. Surhoff | .10 | .30 |
| ☐ 192 | Jose Valentin | .05 | .15 |
| ☐ 193 | Greg Vaughn | .05 | .15 |
| ☐ 194 | Turner Ward | .05 | .15 |
| ☐ 195 | Bill Wegman | .05 | .15 |
| ☐ 196 | Rick Aguilera | .05 | .15 |
| ☐ 197 | Rich Becker | .05 | .15 |
| ☐ 198 | Alex Cole | .05 | .15 |
| ☐ 199 | Marty Cordova | .05 | .15 |
| ☐ 200 | Steve Dunn | .05 | .15 |
| ☐ 201 | Scott Erickson | .05 | .15 |
| ☐ 202 | Mark Guthrie | .05 | .15 |
| ☐ 203 | Chip Hale | .05 | .15 |
| ☐ 204 | LaTroy Hawkins | .05 | .15 |
| ☐ 205 | Denny Hocking | .05 | .15 |
| ☐ 206 | Chuck Knoblauch | .10 | .30 |
| ☐ 207 | Scott Leius | .05 | .15 |
| ☐ 208 | Shane Mack | .05 | .15 |
| ☐ 209 | Pat Mahomes | .05 | .15 |
| ☐ 210 | Pat Meares | .05 | .15 |
| ☐ 211 | Pedro Munoz | .05 | .15 |
| ☐ 212 | Kirby Puckett | .30 | .75 |
| ☐ 213 | Jeff Reboulet | .05 | .15 |
| ☐ 214 | Dave Stevens | .05 | .15 |
| ☐ 215 | Kevin Tapani | .05 | .15 |
| ☐ 216 | Matt Walbeck | .05 | .15 |
| ☐ 217 | Carl Willis | .05 | .15 |
| ☐ 218 | Brian Anderson | .05 | .15 |
| ☐ 219 | Chad Curtis | .05 | .15 |
| ☐ 220 | Chili Davis | .10 | .30 |
| ☐ 221 | Gary DiSarcina | .05 | .15 |
| ☐ 222 | Damion Easley | .05 | .15 |
| ☐ 223 | Jim Edmonds | .20 | .50 |
| ☐ 224 | Chuck Finley | .10 | .30 |
| ☐ 225 | Joe Grahe | .05 | .15 |
| ☐ 226 | Rex Hudler | .05 | .15 |
| ☐ 227 | Bo Jackson | .30 | .75 |
| ☐ 228 | Mark Langston | .05 | .15 |
| ☐ 229 | Phil Leftwich | .05 | .15 |
| ☐ 230 | Mark Leiter | .05 | .15 |
| ☐ 231 | Spike Owen | .05 | .15 |
| ☐ 232 | Bob Patterson | .05 | .15 |
| ☐ 233 | Troy Percival | .10 | .30 |
| ☐ 234 | Eduardo Perez | .05 | .15 |
| ☐ 235 | Tim Salmon | .20 | .50 |
| ☐ 236 | J.T. Snow | .10 | .30 |
| ☐ 237 | Chris Turner | .05 | .15 |
| ☐ 238 | Mark Acre | .05 | .15 |
| ☐ 239 | Geronimo Berroa | .05 | .15 |
| ☐ 240 | Mike Bordick | .05 | .15 |
| ☐ 241 | John Briscoe | .05 | .15 |
| ☐ 242 | Scott Brosius | .10 | .30 |
| ☐ 243 | Ron Darling | .05 | .15 |
| ☐ 244 | Dennis Eckersley | .10 | .30 |
| ☐ 245 | Brent Gates | .05 | .15 |
| ☐ 246 | Rickey Henderson | .30 | .75 |
| ☐ 247 | Stan Javier | .05 | .15 |
| ☐ 248 | Steve Karsay | .05 | .15 |
| ☐ 249 | Mark McGwire | .75 | 2.00 |
| ☐ 250 | Troy Neel | .05 | .15 |
| ☐ 251 | Steve Ontiveros | .05 | .15 |
| ☐ 252 | Carlos Reyes | .05 | .15 |
| ☐ 253 | Ruben Sierra | .10 | .30 |
| ☐ 254 | Terry Steinbach | .05 | .15 |
| ☐ 255 | Bill Taylor | .05 | .15 |
| ☐ 256 | Todd Van Poppel | .05 | .15 |
| ☐ 257 | Bobby Witt | .05 | .15 |
| ☐ 258 | Rich Amaral | .05 | .15 |
| ☐ 259 | Eric Anthony | .05 | .15 |
| ☐ 260 | Bobby Ayala | .05 | .15 |
| ☐ 261 | Mike Blowers | .05 | .15 |
| ☐ 262 | Chris Bosio | .05 | .15 |
| ☐ 263 | Jay Buhner | .10 | .30 |
| ☐ 264 | John Cummings | .05 | .15 |
| ☐ 265 | Tim Davis | .05 | .15 |
| ☐ 266 | Felix Fermin | .05 | .15 |
| ☐ 267 | Dave Fleming | .05 | .15 |
| ☐ 268 | Goose Gossage | .10 | .30 |
| ☐ 269 | Ken Griffey Jr. | .50 | 1.25 |
| ☐ 270 | Reggie Jefferson | .05 | .15 |
| ☐ 271 | Randy Johnson | .30 | .75 |
| ☐ 272 | Edgar Martinez | .20 | .50 |
| ☐ 273 | Tino Martinez | .20 | .50 |
| ☐ 274 | Greg Pirkl | .05 | .15 |
| ☐ 275 | Bill Risley | .05 | .15 |
| ☐ 276 | Roger Salkeld | .05 | .15 |
| ☐ 277 | Luis Sojo | .05 | .15 |
| ☐ 278 | Mac Suzuki | .05 | .15 |
| ☐ 279 | Dan Wilson | .05 | .15 |
| ☐ 280 | Kevin Brown | .10 | .30 |
| ☐ 281 | Jose Canseco | .20 | .50 |
| ☐ 282 | Cris Carpenter | .05 | .15 |
| ☐ 283 | Will Clark | .20 | .50 |
| ☐ 284 | Jeff Frye | .05 | .15 |
| ☐ 285 | Juan Gonzalez | .10 | .30 |
| ☐ 286 | Rick Helling | .05 | .15 |
| ☐ 287 | Tom Henke | .05 | .15 |
| ☐ 288 | David Hulse | .05 | .15 |
| ☐ 289 | Chris James | .05 | .15 |
| ☐ 290 | Manuel Lee | .05 | .15 |
| ☐ 291 | Oddibe McDowell | .05 | .15 |
| ☐ 292 | Dean Palmer | .10 | .30 |
| ☐ 293 | Roger Pavlik | .05 | .15 |
| ☐ 294 | Bill Ripken | .05 | .15 |
| ☐ 295 | Ivan Rodriguez | .20 | .50 |
| ☐ 296 | Kenny Rogers | .10 | .30 |
| ☐ 297 | Doug Strange | .05 | .15 |
| ☐ 298 | Matt Whiteside | .05 | .15 |
| ☐ 299 | Steve Avery | .05 | .15 |
| ☐ 300 | Steve Bedrosian | .05 | .15 |
| ☐ 301 | Rafael Belliard | .05 | .15 |
| ☐ 302 | Jeff Blauser | .05 | .15 |
| ☐ 303 | Dave Gallagher | .05 | .15 |
| ☐ 304 | Tom Glavine | .20 | .50 |
| ☐ 305 | David Justice | .10 | .30 |
| ☐ 306 | Mike Kelly | .05 | .15 |
| ☐ 307 | Roberto Kelly | .05 | .15 |
| ☐ 308 | Ryan Klesko | .10 | .30 |
| ☐ 309 | Mark Lemke | .05 | .15 |
| ☐ 310 | Javier Lopez | .10 | .30 |
| ☐ 311 | Greg Maddux | .50 | 1.25 |
| ☐ 312 | Fred McGriff | .20 | .50 |
| ☐ 313 | Greg McMichael | .05 | .15 |
| ☐ 314 | Kent Mercker | .05 | .15 |
| ☐ 315 | Charlie O'Brien | .05 | .15 |
| ☐ 316 | Jose Oliva | .05 | .15 |
| ☐ 317 | Terry Pendleton | .10 | .30 |
| ☐ 318 | John Smoltz | .20 | .50 |
| ☐ 319 | Mike Stanton | .05 | .15 |
| ☐ 320 | Tony Tarasco | .05 | .15 |
| ☐ 321 | Terrell Wade | .05 | .15 |
| ☐ 322 | Mark Wohlers | .05 | .15 |
| ☐ 323 | Kurt Abbott | .05 | .15 |
| ☐ 324 | Luis Aquino | .05 | .15 |
| ☐ 325 | Bret Barberie | .05 | .15 |
| ☐ 326 | Ryan Bowen | .05 | .15 |
| ☐ 327 | Jerry Browne | .05 | .15 |
| ☐ 328 | Chuck Carr | .05 | .15 |
| ☐ 329 | Matias Carrillo | .05 | .15 |
| ☐ 330 | Greg Colbrunn | .05 | .15 |
| ☐ 331 | Jeff Conine | .10 | .30 |
| ☐ 332 | Mark Gardner | .05 | .15 |
| ☐ 333 | Chris Hammond | .05 | .15 |
| ☐ 334 | Bryan Harvey | .05 | .15 |
| ☐ 335 | Richie Lewis | .05 | .15 |
| ☐ 336 | Dave Magadan | .05 | .15 |
| ☐ 337 | Terry Mathews | .05 | .15 |
| ☐ 338 | Robb Nen | .10 | .30 |
| ☐ 339 | Yorkis Perez | .05 | .15 |
| ☐ 340 | Pat Rapp | .05 | .15 |
| ☐ 341 | Benito Santiago | .10 | .30 |
| ☐ 342 | Gary Sheffield | .10 | .30 |
| ☐ 343 | Dave Weathers | .05 | .15 |
| ☐ 344 | Moises Alou | .05 | .15 |
| ☐ 345 | Sean Berry | .05 | .15 |
| ☐ 346 | Wil Cordero | .05 | .15 |
| ☐ 347 | Joey Eischen | .05 | .15 |
| ☐ 348 | Jeff Fassero | .05 | .15 |
| ☐ 349 | Darrin Fletcher | .05 | .15 |
| ☐ 350 | Cliff Floyd | .10 | .30 |
| ☐ 351 | Marquis Grissom | .10 | .30 |
| ☐ 352 | Butch Henry | .05 | .15 |
| ☐ 353 | Gil Heredia | .05 | .15 |
| ☐ 354 | Ken Hill | .05 | .15 |
| ☐ 355 | Mike Lansing | .05 | .15 |
| ☐ 356 | Pedro Martinez | .20 | .50 |
| ☐ 357 | Mel Rojas | .05 | .15 |
| ☐ 358 | Kirk Rueter | .05 | .15 |
| ☐ 359 | Tim Scott | .05 | .15 |
| ☐ 360 | Jeff Shaw | .05 | .15 |
| ☐ 361 | Larry Walker | .10 | .30 |
| ☐ 362 | Lenny Webster | .05 | .15 |
| ☐ 363 | John Wetteland | .10 | .30 |
| ☐ 364 | Rondell White | .10 | .30 |
| ☐ 365 | Bobby Bonilla | .10 | .30 |
| ☐ 366 | Rico Brogna | .05 | .15 |
| ☐ 367 | Jeromy Burnitz | .10 | .30 |
| ☐ 368 | John Franco | .10 | .30 |
| ☐ 369 | Dwight Gooden | .10 | .30 |
| ☐ 370 | Todd Hundley | .05 | .15 |
| ☐ 371 | Jason Jacome | .05 | .15 |
| ☐ 372 | Bobby Jones | .05 | .15 |
| ☐ 373 | Jeff Kent | .10 | .30 |
| ☐ 374 | Jim Lindeman | .05 | .15 |
| ☐ 375 | Josias Manzanillo | .05 | .15 |
| ☐ 376 | Roger Mason | .05 | .15 |
| ☐ 377 | Kevin McReynolds | .05 | .15 |
| ☐ 378 | Joe Orsulak | .05 | .15 |
| ☐ 379 | Bill Pulsipher | .05 | .15 |
| ☐ 380 | Bret Saberhagen | .10 | .30 |
| ☐ 381 | David Segui | .05 | .15 |
| ☐ 382 | Pete Smith | .05 | .15 |
| ☐ 383 | Kelly Stinnett | .05 | .15 |
| ☐ 384 | Ryan Thompson | .05 | .15 |
| ☐ 385 | Jose Vizcaino | .05 | .15 |
| ☐ 386 | Toby Borland | .05 | .15 |
| ☐ 387 | Ricky Bottalico | .05 | .15 |
| ☐ 388 | Darren Daulton | .10 | .30 |
| ☐ 389 | Mariano Duncan | .05 | .15 |
| ☐ 390 | Lenny Dykstra | .10 | .30 |
| ☐ 391 | Jim Eisenreich | .05 | .15 |
| ☐ 392 | Tommy Greene | .05 | .15 |
| ☐ 393 | Dave Hollins | .05 | .15 |
| ☐ 394 | Pete Incaviglia | .05 | .15 |
| ☐ 395 | Danny Jackson | .05 | .15 |
| ☐ 396 | Doug Jones | .05 | .15 |
| ☐ 397 | Ricky Jordan | .05 | .15 |
| ☐ 398 | John Kruk | .10 | .30 |
| ☐ 399 | Mike Lieberthal | .10 | .30 |
| ☐ 400 | Tony Longmire | .05 | .15 |
| ☐ 401 | Mickey Morandini | .05 | .15 |
| ☐ 402 | Bobby Munoz | .05 | .15 |
| ☐ 403 | Curt Schilling | .10 | .30 |
| ☐ 404 | Heathcliff Slocumb | .05 | .15 |
| ☐ 405 | Kevin Stocker | .05 | .15 |
| ☐ 406 | Fernando Valenzuela | .10 | .30 |
| ☐ 407 | David West | .05 | .15 |
| ☐ 408 | Willie Banks | .05 | .15 |
| ☐ 409 | Jose Bautista | .05 | .15 |
| ☐ 410 | Steve Buechele | .05 | .15 |
| ☐ 411 | Jim Bullinger | .05 | .15 |
| ☐ 412 | Chuck Crim | .05 | .15 |
| ☐ 413 | Shawon Dunston | .05 | .15 |
| ☐ 414 | Kevin Foster | .05 | .15 |
| ☐ 415 | Mark Grace | .20 | .50 |
| ☐ 416 | Jose Hernandez | .05 | .15 |
| ☐ 417 | Glenallen Hill | .05 | .15 |
| ☐ 418 | Brooks Kieschnick | .05 | .15 |
| ☐ 419 | Derrick May | .05 | .15 |
| ☐ 420 | Randy Myers | .05 | .15 |
| ☐ 421 | Dan Plesac | .05 | .15 |
| ☐ 422 | Karl Rhodes | .05 | .15 |
| ☐ 423 | Rey Sanchez | .05 | .15 |

| | | |
|---|---|---|
| ☐ 424 Sammy Sosa | .30 | .75 |
| ☐ 425 Steve Trachsel | .05 | .15 |
| ☐ 426 Rick Wilkins | .05 | .15 |
| ☐ 427 Anthony Young | .05 | .15 |
| ☐ 428 Eddie Zambrano | .05 | .15 |
| ☐ 429 Bret Boone | .10 | .30 |
| ☐ 430 Jeff Branson | .05 | .15 |
| ☐ 431 Brian Brantley | .05 | .15 |
| ☐ 432 Hector Carrasco | .05 | .15 |
| ☐ 433 Brian Dorsett | .05 | .15 |
| ☐ 434 Tony Fernandez | .05 | .15 |
| ☐ 435 Tim Fortugno | .05 | .15 |
| ☐ 436 Erik Hanson | .05 | .15 |
| ☐ 437 Thomas Howard | .05 | .15 |
| ☐ 438 Kevin Jarvis | .05 | .15 |
| ☐ 439 Barry Larkin | .20 | .50 |
| ☐ 440 Chuck McElroy | .05 | .15 |
| ☐ 441 Kevin Mitchell | .05 | .15 |
| ☐ 442 Hal Morris | .05 | .15 |
| ☐ 443 Jose Rijo | .05 | .15 |
| ☐ 444 John Roper | .05 | .15 |
| ☐ 445 Johnny Ruffin | .05 | .15 |
| ☐ 446 Deion Sanders | .20 | .50 |
| ☐ 447 Reggie Sanders | .10 | .30 |
| ☐ 448 Pete Schourek | .05 | .15 |
| ☐ 449 John Smiley | .05 | .15 |
| ☐ 450 Eddie Taubensee | .05 | .15 |
| ☐ 451 Jeff Bagwell | .30 | .75 |
| ☐ 452 Kevin Bass | .05 | .15 |
| ☐ 453 Craig Biggio | .20 | .50 |
| ☐ 454 Ken Caminiti | .10 | .30 |
| ☐ 455 Andujar Cedeno | .05 | .15 |
| ☐ 456 Doug Drabek | .05 | .15 |
| ☐ 457 Tony Eusebio | .05 | .15 |
| ☐ 458 Mike Felder | .05 | .15 |
| ☐ 459 Steve Finley | .10 | .30 |
| ☐ 460 Luis Gonzalez | .10 | .30 |
| ☐ 461 Mike Hampton | .05 | .15 |
| ☐ 462 Pete Harnisch | .05 | .15 |
| ☐ 463 John Hudek | .05 | .15 |
| ☐ 464 Todd Jones | .05 | .15 |
| ☐ 465 Darryl Kile | .10 | .30 |
| ☐ 466 James Mouton | .05 | .15 |
| ☐ 467 Shane Reynolds | .05 | .15 |
| ☐ 468 Scott Servais | .05 | .15 |
| ☐ 469 Greg Swindell | .05 | .15 |
| ☐ 470 Dave Veres RC | .15 | .40 |
| ☐ 471 Brian Williams | .05 | .15 |
| ☐ 472 Jay Bell | .10 | .30 |
| ☐ 473 Jacob Brumfield | .05 | .15 |
| ☐ 474 Dave Clark | .05 | .15 |
| ☐ 475 Steve Cooke | .05 | .15 |
| ☐ 476 Midre Cummings | .05 | .15 |
| ☐ 477 Mark Dewey | .05 | .15 |
| ☐ 478 Tom Foley | .05 | .15 |
| ☐ 479 Carlos Garcia | .05 | .15 |
| ☐ 480 Jeff King | .05 | .15 |
| ☐ 481 Jon Lieber | .05 | .15 |
| ☐ 482 Ravelo Manzanillo | .05 | .15 |
| ☐ 483 Al Martin | .05 | .15 |
| ☐ 484 Orlando Merced | .05 | .15 |
| ☐ 485 Danny Miceli | .05 | .15 |
| ☐ 486 Denny Neagle | .10 | .30 |
| ☐ 487 Lance Parrish | .10 | .30 |
| ☐ 488 Don Slaught | .05 | .15 |
| ☐ 489 Zane Smith | .05 | .15 |
| ☐ 490 Andy Van Slyke | .20 | .50 |
| ☐ 491 Paul Wagner | .05 | .15 |
| ☐ 492 Rick White | .05 | .15 |
| ☐ 493 Luis Alicea | .05 | .15 |
| ☐ 494 Rene Arocha | .05 | .15 |
| ☐ 495 Rheal Cormier | .05 | .15 |
| ☐ 496 Bryan Eversgerd | .05 | .15 |
| ☐ 497 Bernard Gilkey | .05 | .15 |
| ☐ 498 John Habyan | .05 | .15 |
| ☐ 499 Gregg Jefferies | .05 | .15 |
| ☐ 500 Brian Jordan | .10 | .30 |
| ☐ 501 Ray Lankford | .10 | .30 |
| ☐ 502 John Mabry | .05 | .15 |
| ☐ 503 Terry McGriff | .05 | .15 |
| ☐ 504 Tom Pagnozzi | .05 | .15 |
| ☐ 505 Vicente Palacios | .05 | .15 |
| ☐ 506 Geronimo Pena | .05 | .15 |
| ☐ 507 Gerald Perry | .05 | .15 |
| ☐ 508 Rich Rodriguez | .05 | .15 |
| ☐ 509 Ozzie Smith | .50 | 1.25 |
| ☐ 510 Bob Tewksbury | .05 | .15 |
| ☐ 511 Allen Watson | .05 | .15 |
| ☐ 512 Mark Whiten | .05 | .15 |
| ☐ 513 Todd Zeile | .05 | .15 |
| ☐ 514 Dante Bichette | .10 | .30 |
| ☐ 515 Willie Blair | .05 | .15 |
| ☐ 516 Ellis Burks | .10 | .30 |
| ☐ 517 Marvin Freeman | .05 | .15 |
| ☐ 518 Andres Galarraga | .10 | .30 |
| ☐ 519 Joe Girardi | .05 | .15 |
| ☐ 520 Greg W. Harris | .05 | .15 |
| ☐ 521 Charlie Hayes | .05 | .15 |
| ☐ 522 Mike Kingery | .05 | .15 |
| ☐ 523 Nelson Liriano | .05 | .15 |
| ☐ 524 Mike Munoz | .05 | .15 |
| ☐ 525 David Nied | .05 | .15 |
| ☐ 526 Steve Reed | .05 | .15 |
| ☐ 527 Kevin Ritz | .05 | .15 |
| ☐ 528 Bruce Ruffin | .05 | .15 |
| ☐ 529 John Vander Wal | .05 | .15 |
| ☐ 530 Walt Weiss | .05 | .15 |
| ☐ 531 Eric Young | .05 | .15 |
| ☐ 532 Billy Ashley | .05 | .15 |
| ☐ 533 Pedro Astacio | .05 | .15 |
| ☐ 534 Rafael Bournigal | .05 | .15 |
| ☐ 535 Brett Butler | .10 | .30 |
| ☐ 536 Tom Candiotti | .05 | .15 |
| ☐ 537 Omar Daal | .05 | .15 |
| ☐ 538 Delino DeShields | .05 | .15 |
| ☐ 539 Darren Dreifort | .05 | .15 |
| ☐ 540 Kevin Gross | .05 | .15 |
| ☐ 541 Orel Hershiser | .10 | .30 |
| ☐ 542 Garey Ingram | .05 | .15 |
| ☐ 543 Eric Karros | .10 | .30 |
| ☐ 544 Ramon Martinez | .05 | .15 |
| ☐ 545 Raul Mondesi | .10 | .30 |
| ☐ 546 Chan Ho Park | .10 | .30 |
| ☐ 547 Mike Piazza | .50 | 1.25 |
| ☐ 548 Henry Rodriguez | .05 | .15 |
| ☐ 549 Rudy Seanez | .05 | .15 |
| ☐ 550 Ismael Valdes | .05 | .15 |
| ☐ 551 Tim Wallach | .05 | .15 |
| ☐ 552 Todd Worrell | .05 | .15 |
| ☐ 553 Andy Ashby | .05 | .15 |
| ☐ 554 Brad Ausmus | .10 | .30 |
| ☐ 555 Derek Bell | .05 | .15 |
| ☐ 556 Andy Benes | .05 | .15 |
| ☐ 557 Phil Clark | .05 | .15 |
| ☐ 558 Donnie Elliott | .05 | .15 |
| ☐ 559 Ricky Gutierrez | .05 | .15 |
| ☐ 560 Tony Gwynn | .40 | 1.00 |
| ☐ 561 Joey Hamilton | .05 | .15 |
| ☐ 562 Trevor Hoffman | .10 | .30 |
| ☐ 563 Luis Lopez | .05 | .15 |
| ☐ 564 Pedro A. Martinez | .05 | .15 |
| ☐ 565 Tim Mauser | .05 | .15 |
| ☐ 566 Phil Plantier | .05 | .15 |
| ☐ 567 Bip Roberts | .05 | .15 |
| ☐ 568 Scott Sanders | .05 | .15 |
| ☐ 569 Craig Shipley | .05 | .15 |
| ☐ 570 Jeff Tabaka | .05 | .15 |
| ☐ 571 Eddie Williams | .05 | .15 |
| ☐ 572 Rod Beck | .05 | .15 |
| ☐ 573 Mike Benjamin | .05 | .15 |
| ☐ 574 Barry Bonds | .75 | 2.00 |
| ☐ 575 Dave Burba | .05 | .15 |
| ☐ 576 John Burkett | .05 | .15 |
| ☐ 577 Mark Carreon | .05 | .15 |
| ☐ 578 Royce Clayton | .05 | .15 |
| ☐ 579 Steve Frey | .05 | .15 |
| ☐ 580 Bryan Hickerson | .05 | .15 |
| ☐ 581 Mike Jackson | .05 | .15 |
| ☐ 582 Darren Lewis | .05 | .15 |
| ☐ 583 Kirt Manwaring | .05 | .15 |
| ☐ 584 Rich Monteleone | .05 | .15 |
| ☐ 585 John Patterson | .05 | .15 |
| ☐ 586 J.R. Phillips | .05 | .15 |
| ☐ 587 Mark Portugal | .05 | .15 |
| ☐ 588 Joe Rosselli | .05 | .15 |
| ☐ 589 Darryl Strawberry | .10 | .30 |
| ☐ 590 Bill Swift | .05 | .15 |
| ☐ 591 Robby Thompson | .05 | .15 |
| ☐ 592 William VanLandingham | .05 | .15 |
| ☐ 593 Matt Williams | .10 | .30 |
| ☐ 594 Checklist | .05 | .15 |
| ☐ 595 Checklist | .05 | .15 |
| ☐ 596 Checklist | .05 | .15 |
| ☐ 597 Checklist | .05 | .15 |
| ☐ 598 Checklist | .05 | .15 |
| ☐ 599 Checklist | .05 | .15 |
| ☐ 600 Checklist | .05 | .15 |

## 1996 Fleer

| | | |
|---|---|---|
| ☐ COMPLETE SET (600) | 40.00 | 80.00 |
| ☐ 1 Manny Alexander | .10 | .30 |
| ☐ 2 Brady Anderson | .10 | .30 |
| ☐ 3 Harold Baines | .10 | .30 |
| ☐ 4 Armando Benitez | .10 | .30 |
| ☐ 5 Bobby Bonilla | .10 | .30 |
| ☐ 6 Kevin Brown | .10 | .30 |
| ☐ 7 Scott Erickson | .10 | .30 |
| ☐ 8 Curtis Goodwin | .10 | .30 |
| ☐ 9 Jeffrey Hammonds | .10 | .30 |
| ☐ 10 Jimmy Haynes | .10 | .30 |
| ☐ 11 Chris Hoiles | .10 | .30 |
| ☐ 12 Doug Jones | .10 | .30 |
| ☐ 13 Rick Krivda | .10 | .30 |
| ☐ 14 Jeff Manto | .10 | .30 |
| ☐ 15 Ben McDonald | .10 | .30 |
| ☐ 16 Jamie Moyer | .10 | .30 |
| ☐ 17 Mike Mussina | .20 | .50 |
| ☐ 18 Jesse Orosco | .10 | .30 |
| ☐ 19 Rafael Palmeiro | .20 | .50 |
| ☐ 20 Cal Ripken | 1.00 | 2.50 |
| ☐ 21 Rick Aguilera | .10 | .30 |
| ☐ 22 Luis Alicea | .10 | .30 |
| ☐ 23 Stan Belinda | .10 | .30 |
| ☐ 24 Jose Canseco | .20 | .50 |
| ☐ 25 Roger Clemens | .60 | 1.50 |
| ☐ 26 Vaughn Eshelman | .10 | .30 |
| ☐ 27 Mike Greenwell | .10 | .30 |
| ☐ 28 Erik Hanson | .10 | .30 |
| ☐ 29 Dwayne Hosey | .10 | .30 |
| ☐ 30 Mike Macfarlane UER | .10 | .30 |
| ☐ 31 Tim Naehring | .10 | .30 |
| ☐ 32 Troy O'Leary | .10 | .30 |
| ☐ 33 Aaron Sele | .10 | .30 |
| ☐ 34 Zane Smith | .10 | .30 |
| ☐ 35 Jeff Suppan | .10 | .30 |
| ☐ 36 Lee Tinsley | .10 | .30 |
| ☐ 37 John Valentin | .10 | .30 |
| ☐ 38 Mo Vaughn | .10 | .30 |
| ☐ 39 Tim Wakefield | .10 | .30 |
| ☐ 40 Jim Abbott | .20 | .50 |
| ☐ 41 Brian Anderson | .10 | .30 |
| ☐ 42 Garret Anderson | .10 | .30 |
| ☐ 43 Chili Davis | .10 | .30 |
| ☐ 44 Gary DiSarcina | .10 | .30 |
| ☐ 45 Damion Easley | .10 | .30 |
| ☐ 46 Jim Edmonds | .10 | .30 |
| ☐ 47 Chuck Finley | .10 | .30 |
| ☐ 48 Todd Greene | .10 | .30 |
| ☐ 49 Mike Harkey | .10 | .30 |
| ☐ 50 Mike James | .10 | .30 |
| ☐ 51 Mark Langston | .10 | .30 |
| ☐ 52 Greg Myers | .10 | .30 |
| ☐ 53 Orlando Palmeiro | .10 | .30 |
| ☐ 54 Bob Patterson | .10 | .30 |
| ☐ 55 Troy Percival | .10 | .30 |
| ☐ 56 Tony Phillips | .10 | .30 |
| ☐ 57 Tim Salmon | .20 | .50 |
| ☐ 58 Lee Smith | .10 | .30 |
| ☐ 59 J.T. Snow | .10 | .30 |
| ☐ 60 Randy Velarde | .10 | .30 |
| ☐ 61 Wilson Alvarez | .10 | .30 |
| ☐ 62 Luis Andujar | .10 | .30 |
| ☐ 63 Jason Bere | .10 | .30 |
| ☐ 64 Ray Durham | .10 | .30 |
| ☐ 65 Alex Fernandez | .10 | .30 |
| ☐ 66 Ozzie Guillen | .10 | .30 |
| ☐ 67 Roberto Hernandez | .10 | .30 |
| ☐ 68 Lance Johnson | .10 | .30 |
| ☐ 69 Matt Karchner | .10 | .30 |

|  |  | | |
|---|---|---|---|
| 70 | Ron Karkovice | .10 | .30 |
| 71 | Norberto Martin | .10 | .30 |
| 72 | Dave Martinez | .10 | .30 |
| 73 | Kirk McCaskill | .10 | .30 |
| 74 | Lyle Mouton | .10 | .30 |
| 75 | Tim Raines | .10 | .30 |
| 76 | Mike Sirotka RC | .10 | .30 |
| 77 | Frank Thomas | .30 | .75 |
| 78 | Larry Thomas | .10 | .30 |
| 79 | Robin Ventura | .10 | .30 |
| 80 | Sandy Alomar Jr. | .10 | .30 |
| 81 | Paul Assenmacher | .10 | .30 |
| 82 | Carlos Baerga | .10 | .30 |
| 83 | Albert Belle | .10 | .30 |
| 84 | Mark Clark | .10 | .30 |
| 85 | Alan Embree | .10 | .30 |
| 86 | Alvaro Espinoza | .10 | .30 |
| 87 | Orel Hershiser | .10 | .30 |
| 88 | Ken Hill | .10 | .30 |
| 89 | Kenny Lofton | .10 | .30 |
| 90 | Dennis Martinez | .10 | .30 |
| 91 | Jose Mesa | .10 | .30 |
| 92 | Eddie Murray | .30 | .75 |
| 93 | Charles Nagy | .10 | .30 |
| 94 | Chad Ogea | .10 | .30 |
| 95 | Tony Pena | .10 | .30 |
| 96 | Herb Perry | .10 | .30 |
| 97 | Eric Plunk | .10 | .30 |
| 98 | Jim Poole | .10 | .30 |
| 99 | Manny Ramirez | .20 | .50 |
| 100 | Paul Sorrento | .10 | .30 |
| 101 | Julian Tavarez | .10 | .30 |
| 102 | Jim Thome | .20 | .50 |
| 103 | Omar Vizquel | .20 | .50 |
| 104 | Dave Winfield | .10 | .30 |
| 105 | Danny Bautista | .10 | .30 |
| 106 | Joe Boever | .10 | .30 |
| 107 | Chad Curtis | .10 | .30 |
| 108 | John Doherty | .10 | .30 |
| 109 | Cecil Fielder | .10 | .30 |
| 110 | John Flaherty | .10 | .30 |
| 111 | Travis Fryman | .10 | .30 |
| 112 | Chris Gomez | .10 | .30 |
| 113 | Bob Higginson | .10 | .30 |
| 114 | Mark Lewis | .10 | .30 |
| 115 | Jose Lima | .10 | .30 |
| 116 | Felipe Lira | .10 | .30 |
| 117 | Brian Maxcy | .10 | .30 |
| 118 | C.J. Nitkowski | .10 | .30 |
| 119 | Phil Plantier | .10 | .30 |
| 120 | Clint Sodowsky | .10 | .30 |
| 121 | Alan Trammell | .10 | .30 |
| 122 | Lou Whitaker | .10 | .30 |
| 123 | Kevin Appier | .10 | .30 |
| 124 | Johnny Damon | .20 | .50 |
| 125 | Gary Gaetti | .10 | .30 |
| 126 | Tom Goodwin | .10 | .30 |
| 127 | Tom Gordon | .10 | .30 |
| 128 | Mark Gubicza | .10 | .30 |
| 129 | Bob Hamelin | .10 | .30 |
| 130 | David Howard | .10 | .30 |
| 131 | Jason Jacome | .10 | .30 |
| 132 | Wally Joyner | .10 | .30 |
| 133 | Keith Lockhart | .10 | .30 |
| 134 | Brent Mayne | .10 | .30 |
| 135 | Jeff Montgomery | .10 | .30 |
| 136 | Jon Nunnally | .10 | .30 |
| 137 | Juan Samuel | .10 | .30 |
| 138 | Mike Sweeney RC | .40 | 1.00 |
| 139 | Michael Tucker | .10 | .30 |
| 140 | Joe Vitiello | .10 | .30 |
| 141 | Ricky Bones | .10 | .30 |
| 142 | Chuck Carr | .10 | .30 |
| 143 | Jeff Cirillo | .10 | .30 |
| 144 | Mike Fetters | .10 | .30 |
| 145 | Darryl Hamilton | .10 | .30 |
| 146 | David Hulse | .10 | .30 |
| 147 | John Jaha | .10 | .30 |
| 148 | Scott Karl | .10 | .30 |
| 149 | Mark Kiefer | .10 | .30 |
| 150 | Pat Listach | .10 | .30 |
| 151 | Mark Loretta | .10 | .30 |
| 152 | Mike Matheny | .10 | .30 |
| 153 | Matt Mieske | .10 | .30 |
| 154 | Dave Nilsson | .10 | .30 |
| 155 | Joe Oliver | .10 | .30 |
| 156 | Al Reyes | .10 | .30 |
| 157 | Kevin Seitzer | .10 | .30 |
| 158 | Steve Sparks | .10 | .30 |
| 159 | B.J. Surhoff | .10 | .30 |
| 160 | Jose Valentin | .10 | .30 |
| 161 | Greg Vaughn | .10 | .30 |
| 162 | Fernando Vina | .10 | .30 |
| 163 | Rich Becker | .10 | .30 |
| 164 | Ron Coomer | .10 | .30 |
| 165 | Marty Cordova | .10 | .30 |
| 166 | Chuck Knoblauch | .10 | .30 |
| 167 | Matt Lawton RC | .20 | .50 |
| 168 | Pat Meares | .10 | .30 |
| 169 | Paul Molitor | .10 | .30 |
| 170 | Pedro Munoz | .10 | .30 |
| 171 | Jose Parra | .10 | .30 |
| 172 | Kirby Puckett | .30 | .75 |
| 173 | Brad Radke | .10 | .30 |
| 174 | Jeff Reboulet | .10 | .30 |
| 175 | Rich Robertson | .10 | .30 |
| 176 | Frank Rodriguez | .10 | .30 |
| 177 | Scott Stahoviak | .10 | .30 |
| 178 | Dave Stevens | .10 | .30 |
| 179 | Matt Walbeck | .10 | .30 |
| 180 | Wade Boggs | .20 | .50 |
| 181 | David Cone | .10 | .30 |
| 182 | Tony Fernandez | .10 | .30 |
| 183 | Joe Girardi | .10 | .30 |
| 184 | Derek Jeter | .75 | 2.00 |
| 185 | Scott Kamieniecki | .10 | .30 |
| 186 | Pat Kelly | .10 | .30 |
| 187 | Jim Leyritz | .10 | .30 |
| 188 | Tino Martinez | .20 | .50 |
| 189 | Don Mattingly | .75 | 2.00 |
| 190 | Jack McDowell | .10 | .30 |
| 191 | Jeff Nelson | .10 | .30 |
| 192 | Paul O'Neill | .20 | .50 |
| 193 | Melido Perez | .10 | .30 |
| 194 | Andy Pettitte | .20 | .50 |
| 195 | Mariano Rivera | .30 | .75 |
| 196 | Ruben Sierra | .10 | .30 |
| 197 | Mike Stanley | .10 | .30 |
| 198 | Darryl Strawberry | .10 | .30 |
| 199 | John Wetteland | .10 | .30 |
| 200 | Bob Wickman | .10 | .30 |
| 201 | Bernie Williams | .20 | .50 |
| 202 | Mark Acre | .10 | .30 |
| 203 | Geronimo Berroa | .10 | .30 |
| 204 | Mike Bordick | .10 | .30 |
| 205 | Scott Brosius | .10 | .30 |
| 206 | Dennis Eckersley | .10 | .30 |
| 207 | Brent Gates | .10 | .30 |
| 208 | Jason Giambi | .10 | .30 |
| 209 | Rickey Henderson | .30 | .75 |
| 210 | Jose Herrera | .10 | .30 |
| 211 | Stan Javier | .10 | .30 |
| 212 | Doug Johns | .10 | .30 |
| 213 | Mark McGwire | .75 | 2.00 |
| 214 | Steve Ontiveros | .10 | .30 |
| 215 | Craig Paquette | .10 | .30 |
| 216 | Ariel Prieto | .10 | .30 |
| 217 | Carlos Reyes | .10 | .30 |
| 218 | Terry Steinbach | .10 | .30 |
| 219 | Todd Stottlemyre | .10 | .30 |
| 220 | Danny Tartabull | .10 | .30 |
| 221 | Todd Van Poppel | .10 | .30 |
| 222 | John Wasdin | .10 | .30 |
| 223 | George Williams | .10 | .30 |
| 224 | Steve Wojciechowski | .10 | .30 |
| 225 | Rich Amaral | .10 | .30 |
| 226 | Bobby Ayala | .10 | .30 |
| 227 | Tim Belcher | .10 | .30 |
| 228 | Andy Benes | .10 | .30 |
| 229 | Chris Bosio | .10 | .30 |
| 230 | Darren Bragg | .10 | .30 |
| 231 | Jay Buhner | .10 | .30 |
| 232 | Norm Charlton | .10 | .30 |
| 233 | Vince Coleman | .10 | .30 |
| 234 | Joey Cora | .10 | .30 |
| 235 | Russ Davis | .10 | .30 |
| 236 | Alex Diaz | .10 | .30 |
| 237 | Felix Fermin | .10 | .30 |
| 238 | Ken Griffey Jr. | .50 | 1.25 |
| 239 | Sterling Hitchcock | .10 | .30 |
| 240 | Randy Johnson | .30 | .75 |
| 241 | Edgar Martinez | .20 | .50 |
| 242 | Bill Risley | .10 | .30 |
| 243 | Alex Rodriguez | .60 | 1.50 |
| 244 | Luis Sojo | .10 | .30 |
| 245 | Dan Wilson | .10 | .30 |
| 246 | Bob Wolcott | .10 | .30 |
| 247 | Will Clark | .20 | .50 |
| 248 | Jeff Frye | .10 | .30 |
| 249 | Benji Gil | .10 | .30 |
| 250 | Juan Gonzalez | .10 | .30 |
| 251 | Rusty Greer | .10 | .30 |
| 252 | Kevin Gross | .10 | .30 |
| 253 | Roger McDowell | .10 | .30 |
| 254 | Mark McLemore | .10 | .30 |
| 255 | Otis Nixon | .10 | .30 |
| 256 | Luis Ortiz | .10 | .30 |
| 257 | Mike Pagliarulo | .10 | .30 |
| 258 | Dean Palmer | .10 | .30 |
| 259 | Roger Pavlik | .10 | .30 |
| 260 | Ivan Rodriguez | .20 | .50 |
| 261 | Kenny Rogers | .10 | .30 |
| 262 | Jeff Russell | .10 | .30 |
| 263 | Mickey Tettleton | .10 | .30 |
| 264 | Bob Tewksbury | .10 | .30 |
| 265 | Dave Valle | .10 | .30 |
| 266 | Matt Whiteside | .10 | .30 |
| 267 | Roberto Alomar | .20 | .50 |
| 268 | Joe Carter | .10 | .30 |
| 269 | Tony Castillo | .10 | .30 |
| 270 | Domingo Cedeno | .10 | .30 |
| 271 | Tim Crabtree UER | .10 | .30 |
| 272 | Carlos Delgado | .10 | .30 |
| 273 | Alex Gonzalez | .10 | .30 |
| 274 | Shawn Green | .10 | .30 |
| 275 | Juan Guzman | .10 | .30 |
| 276 | Pat Hentgen | .10 | .30 |
| 277 | Al Leiter | .10 | .30 |
| 278 | Sandy Martinez | .10 | .30 |
| 279 | Paul Menhart | .10 | .30 |
| 280 | John Olerud | .10 | .30 |
| 281 | Paul Quantrill | .10 | .30 |
| 282 | Ken Robinson | .10 | .30 |
| 283 | Ed Sprague | .10 | .30 |
| 284 | Mike Timlin | .10 | .30 |
| 285 | Steve Avery | .10 | .30 |
| 286 | Rafael Belliard | .10 | .30 |
| 287 | Jeff Blauser | .10 | .30 |
| 288 | Pedro Borbon | .10 | .30 |
| 289 | Brad Clontz | .10 | .30 |
| 290 | Mike Devereaux | .10 | .30 |
| 291 | Tom Glavine | .20 | .50 |
| 292 | Marquis Grissom | .10 | .30 |
| 293 | Chipper Jones | .30 | .75 |
| 294 | David Justice | .10 | .30 |
| 295 | Mike Kelly | .10 | .30 |
| 296 | Ryan Klesko | .10 | .30 |
| 297 | Mark Lemke | .10 | .30 |
| 298 | Javier Lopez | .10 | .30 |
| 299 | Greg Maddux | .50 | 1.25 |
| 300 | Fred McGriff | .10 | .30 |
| 301 | Greg McMichael | .10 | .30 |
| 302 | Kent Mercker | .10 | .30 |
| 303 | Mike Mordecai | .10 | .30 |
| 304 | Charlie O'Brien | .10 | .30 |
| 305 | Eduardo Perez | .10 | .30 |
| 306 | Luis Polonia | .10 | .30 |
| 307 | Jason Schmidt | .20 | .50 |
| 308 | John Smoltz | .20 | .50 |
| 309 | Terrell Wade | .10 | .30 |
| 310 | Mark Wohlers | .10 | .30 |
| 311 | Scott Bullett | .10 | .30 |
| 312 | Jim Bullinger | .10 | .30 |
| 313 | Larry Casian | .10 | .30 |
| 314 | Frank Castillo | .10 | .30 |
| 315 | Shawon Dunston | .10 | .30 |
| 316 | Kevin Foster | .10 | .30 |
| 317 | Matt Franco | .10 | .30 |
| 318 | Luis Gonzalez | .10 | .30 |
| 319 | Mark Grace | .20 | .50 |
| 320 | Jose Hernandez | .10 | .30 |
| 321 | Mike Hubbard | .10 | .30 |
| 322 | Brian McRae | .10 | .30 |
| 323 | Randy Myers | .10 | .30 |
| 324 | Jaime Navarro | .10 | .30 |
| 325 | Mark Parent | .10 | .30 |
| 326 | Mike Perez | .10 | .30 |
| 327 | Rey Sanchez | .10 | .30 |
| 328 | Ryne Sandberg | .50 | 1.25 |
| 329 | Scott Servais | .10 | .30 |
| 330 | Sammy Sosa | .30 | .75 |
| 331 | Ozzie Timmons | .10 | .30 |
| 332 | Steve Trachsel | .10 | .30 |
| 333 | Todd Zeile | .10 | .30 |

|  |  | | |
|---|---|---|---|
| 334 | Bret Boone | .10 | .30 |
| 335 | Jeff Branson | .10 | .30 |
| 336 | Jeff Brantley | .10 | .30 |
| 337 | Dave Burba | .10 | .30 |
| 338 | Hector Carrasco | .10 | .30 |
| 339 | Mariano Duncan | .10 | .30 |
| 340 | Ron Gant | .10 | .30 |
| 341 | Lenny Harris | .10 | .30 |
| 342 | Xavier Hernandez | .10 | .30 |
| 343 | Thomas Howard | .10 | .30 |
| 344 | Mike Jackson | .10 | .30 |
| 345 | Barry Larkin | .20 | .50 |
| 346 | Darren Lewis | .10 | .30 |
| 347 | Hal Morris | .10 | .30 |
| 348 | Eric Owens | .10 | .30 |
| 349 | Mark Portugal | .10 | .30 |
| 350 | Jose Rijo | .10 | .30 |
| 351 | Reggie Sanders | .10 | .30 |
| 352 | Benito Santiago | .10 | .30 |
| 353 | Pete Schourek | .10 | .30 |
| 354 | John Smiley | .10 | .30 |
| 355 | Eddie Taubensee | .10 | .30 |
| 356 | Jerome Walton | .10 | .30 |
| 357 | David Wells | .10 | .30 |
| 358 | Roger Bailey | .10 | .30 |
| 359 | Jason Bates | .10 | .30 |
| 360 | Dante Bichette | .10 | .30 |
| 361 | Ellis Burks | .10 | .30 |
| 362 | Vinny Castilla | .10 | .30 |
| 363 | Andres Galarraga | .10 | .30 |
| 364 | Darren Holmes | .10 | .30 |
| 365 | Mike Kingery | .10 | .30 |
| 366 | Curt Leskanic | .10 | .30 |
| 367 | Quinton McCracken | .10 | .30 |
| 368 | Mike Munoz | .10 | .30 |
| 369 | David Nied | .10 | .30 |
| 370 | Steve Reed | .10 | .30 |
| 371 | Bryan Rekar | .10 | .30 |
| 372 | Kevin Ritz | .10 | .30 |
| 373 | Bruce Ruffin | .10 | .30 |
| 374 | Bret Saberhagen | .10 | .30 |
| 375 | Bill Swift | .10 | .30 |
| 376 | John Vander Wal | .10 | .30 |
| 377 | Larry Walker | .10 | .30 |
| 378 | Walt Weiss | .10 | .30 |
| 379 | Eric Young | .10 | .30 |
| 380 | Kurt Abbott | .10 | .30 |
| 381 | Alex Arias | .10 | .30 |
| 382 | Jerry Browne | .10 | .30 |
| 383 | John Burkett | .10 | .30 |
| 384 | Greg Colbrunn | .10 | .30 |
| 385 | Jeff Conine | .10 | .30 |
| 386 | Andre Dawson | .10 | .30 |
| 387 | Chris Hammond | .10 | .30 |
| 388 | Charles Johnson | .10 | .30 |
| 389 | Terry Mathews | .10 | .30 |
| 390 | Robb Nen | .10 | .30 |
| 391 | Joe Orsulak | .10 | .30 |
| 392 | Terry Pendleton | .10 | .30 |
| 393 | Pat Rapp | .10 | .30 |
| 394 | Gary Sheffield | .10 | .30 |
| 395 | Jesus Tavarez | .10 | .30 |
| 396 | Marc Valdes | .10 | .30 |
| 397 | Quilvio Veras | .10 | .30 |
| 398 | Randy Veres | .10 | .30 |
| 399 | Devon White | .10 | .30 |
| 400 | Jeff Bagwell | .20 | .50 |
| 401 | Derek Bell | .10 | .30 |
| 402 | Craig Biggio | .20 | .50 |
| 403 | John Cangelosi | .10 | .30 |
| 404 | Jim Dougherty | .10 | .30 |
| 405 | Doug Drabek | .10 | .30 |
| 406 | Tony Eusebio | .10 | .30 |
| 407 | Ricky Gutierrez | .10 | .30 |
| 408 | Mike Hampton | .10 | .30 |
| 409 | Dean Hartgraves | .10 | .30 |
| 410 | John Hudek | .10 | .30 |
| 411 | Brian Hunter | .10 | .30 |
| 412 | Todd Jones | .10 | .30 |
| 413 | Darryl Kile | .10 | .30 |
| 414 | Dave Magadan | .10 | .30 |
| 415 | Derrick May | .10 | .30 |
| 416 | Orlando Miller | .10 | .30 |
| 417 | James Mouton | .10 | .30 |
| 418 | Shane Reynolds | .10 | .30 |
| 419 | Greg Swindell | .10 | .30 |
| 420 | Jeff Tabaka | .10 | .30 |
| 421 | Dave Veres | .10 | .30 |
| 422 | Billy Wagner | .10 | .30 |
| 423 | Donne Wall | .10 | .30 |
| 424 | Rick Wilkins | .10 | .30 |
| 425 | Billy Ashley | .10 | .30 |
| 426 | Mike Blowers | .10 | .30 |
| 427 | Brett Butler | .10 | .30 |
| 428 | Tom Candiotti | .10 | .30 |
| 429 | Juan Castro | .10 | .30 |
| 430 | John Cummings | .10 | .30 |
| 431 | Delino DeShields | .10 | .30 |
| 432 | Joey Eischen | .10 | .30 |
| 433 | Chad Fonville | .10 | .30 |
| 434 | Greg Gagne | .10 | .30 |
| 435 | Dave Hansen | .10 | .30 |
| 436 | Carlos Hernandez | .10 | .30 |
| 437 | Todd Hollandsworth | .10 | .30 |
| 438 | Eric Karros | .10 | .30 |
| 439 | Roberto Kelly | .10 | .30 |
| 440 | Ramon Martinez | .10 | .30 |
| 441 | Raul Mondesi | .10 | .30 |
| 442 | Hideo Nomo | .30 | .75 |
| 443 | Antonio Osuna | .10 | .30 |
| 444 | Chan Ho Park | .10 | .30 |
| 445 | Mike Piazza | .50 | 1.25 |
| 446 | Felix Rodriguez | .10 | .30 |
| 447 | Kevin Tapani | .10 | .30 |
| 448 | Ismael Valdes | .10 | .30 |
| 449 | Todd Worrell | .10 | .30 |
| 450 | Moises Alou | .10 | .30 |
| 451 | Shane Andrews | .10 | .30 |
| 452 | Yamil Benitez | .10 | .30 |
| 453 | Sean Berry | .10 | .30 |
| 454 | Wil Cordero | .10 | .30 |
| 455 | Jeff Fassero | .10 | .30 |
| 456 | Darrin Fletcher | .10 | .30 |
| 457 | Cliff Floyd | .10 | .30 |
| 458 | Mark Grudzielanek | .10 | .30 |
| 459 | Gil Heredia | .10 | .30 |
| 460 | Tim Laker | .10 | .30 |
| 461 | Mike Lansing | .10 | .30 |
| 462 | Pedro Martinez | .20 | .50 |
| 463 | Carlos Perez | .10 | .30 |
| 464 | Curtis Pride | .10 | .30 |
| 465 | Mel Rojas | .10 | .30 |
| 466 | Kirk Rueter | .10 | .30 |
| 467 | F.P. Santangelo | .10 | .30 |
| 468 | Tim Scott | .10 | .30 |
| 469 | David Segui | .10 | .30 |
| 470 | Tony Tarasco | .10 | .30 |
| 471 | Rondell White | .10 | .30 |
| 472 | Edgardo Alfonzo | .10 | .30 |
| 473 | Tim Bogar | .10 | .30 |
| 474 | Rico Brogna | .10 | .30 |
| 475 | Damon Buford | .10 | .30 |
| 476 | Paul Byrd | .10 | .30 |
| 477 | Carl Everett | .10 | .30 |
| 478 | John Franco | .10 | .30 |
| 479 | Todd Hundley | .10 | .30 |
| 480 | Butch Huskey | .10 | .30 |
| 481 | Jason Isringhausen | .10 | .30 |
| 482 | Bobby Jones | .10 | .30 |
| 483 | Chris Jones | .10 | .30 |
| 484 | Jeff Kent | .10 | .30 |
| 485 | Dave Mlicki | .10 | .30 |
| 486 | Robert Person | .10 | .30 |
| 487 | Bill Pulsipher | .10 | .30 |
| 488 | Kelly Stinnett | .10 | .30 |
| 489 | Ryan Thompson | .10 | .30 |
| 490 | Jose Vizcaino | .10 | .30 |
| 491 | Howard Battle | .10 | .30 |
| 492 | Toby Borland | .10 | .30 |
| 493 | Ricky Bottalico | .10 | .30 |
| 494 | Darren Daulton | .10 | .30 |
| 495 | Lenny Dykstra | .10 | .30 |
| 496 | Jim Eisenreich | .10 | .30 |
| 497 | Sid Fernandez | .10 | .30 |
| 498 | Tyler Green | .10 | .30 |
| 499 | Charlie Hayes | .10 | .30 |
| 500 | Gregg Jefferies | .10 | .30 |
| 501 | Kevin Jordan | .10 | .30 |
| 502 | Tony Longmire | .10 | .30 |
| 503 | Tom Marsh | .10 | .30 |
| 504 | Michael Mimbs | .10 | .30 |
| 505 | Mickey Morandini | .10 | .30 |
| 506 | Gene Schall | .10 | .30 |
| 507 | Curt Schilling | .10 | .30 |
| 508 | Heathcliff Slocumb | .10 | .30 |
| 509 | Kevin Stocker | .10 | .30 |
| 510 | Andy Van Slyke | .20 | .50 |
| 511 | Lenny Webster | .10 | .30 |
| 512 | Mark Whiten | .10 | .30 |
| 513 | Mike Williams | .10 | .30 |
| 514 | Jay Bell | .10 | .30 |
| 515 | Jacob Brumfield | .10 | .30 |
| 516 | Jason Christiansen | .10 | .30 |
| 517 | Dave Clark | .10 | .30 |
| 518 | Midre Cummings | .10 | .30 |
| 519 | Angelo Encarnacion | .10 | .30 |
| 520 | John Ericks | .10 | .30 |
| 521 | Carlos Garcia | .10 | .30 |
| 522 | Mark Johnson | .10 | .30 |
| 523 | Jeff King | .10 | .30 |
| 524 | Nelson Liriano | .10 | .30 |
| 525 | Esteban Loaiza | .10 | .30 |
| 526 | Al Martin | .10 | .30 |
| 527 | Orlando Merced | .10 | .30 |
| 528 | Dan Miceli | .10 | .30 |
| 529 | Ramon Morel | .10 | .30 |
| 530 | Denny Neagle | .10 | .30 |
| 531 | Steve Parris | .10 | .30 |
| 532 | Dan Plesac | .10 | .30 |
| 533 | Don Slaught | .10 | .30 |
| 534 | Paul Wagner | .10 | .30 |
| 535 | John Wehner | .10 | .30 |
| 536 | Kevin Young | .10 | .30 |
| 537 | Allen Battle | .10 | .30 |
| 538 | David Bell | .10 | .30 |
| 539 | Alan Benes | .10 | .30 |
| 540 | Scott Cooper | .10 | .30 |
| 541 | Tripp Cromer | .10 | .30 |
| 542 | Gary Gaetti | .10 | .30 |
| 543 | Bernard Gilkey | .10 | .30 |
| 544 | Tom Henke | .10 | .30 |
| 545 | Brian Jordan | .10 | .30 |
| 546 | Ray Lankford | .10 | .30 |
| 547 | John Mabry | .10 | .30 |
| 548 | T.J. Mathews | .10 | .30 |
| 549 | Mike Morgan | .10 | .30 |
| 550 | Jose Oliva | .10 | .30 |
| 551 | Jose Oquendo | .10 | .30 |
| 552 | Donovan Osborne | .10 | .30 |
| 553 | Tom Pagnozzi | .10 | .30 |
| 554 | Mark Petkovsek | .10 | .30 |
| 555 | Danny Sheaffer | .10 | .30 |
| 556 | Ozzie Smith | .50 | 1.25 |
| 557 | Mark Sweeney | .10 | .30 |
| 558 | Allen Watson | .10 | .30 |
| 559 | Andy Ashby | .10 | .30 |
| 560 | Brad Ausmus | .10 | .30 |
| 561 | Willie Blair | .10 | .30 |
| 562 | Ken Caminiti | .10 | .30 |
| 563 | Andujar Cedeno | .10 | .30 |
| 564 | Glenn Dishman | .10 | .30 |
| 565 | Steve Finley | .10 | .30 |
| 566 | Bryce Florie | .10 | .30 |
| 567 | Tony Gwynn | .40 | 1.00 |
| 568 | Joey Hamilton | .10 | .30 |
| 569 | Dustin Hermanson UER | .10 | .30 |
| 570 | Trevor Hoffman | .10 | .30 |
| 571 | Brian Johnson | .10 | .30 |
| 572 | Marc Kroon | .10 | .30 |
| 573 | Scott Livingstone | .10 | .30 |
| 574 | Marc Newfield | .10 | .30 |
| 575 | Melvin Nieves | .10 | .30 |
| 576 | Jody Reed | .10 | .30 |
| 577 | Bip Roberts | .10 | .30 |
| 578 | Scott Sanders | .10 | .30 |
| 579 | Fernando Valenzuela | .10 | .30 |
| 580 | Eddie Williams | .10 | .30 |
| 581 | Rod Beck | .10 | .30 |
| 582 | Marvin Benard RC | .10 | .30 |
| 583 | Barry Bonds | .75 | 2.00 |
| 584 | Jamie Brewington RC | .10 | .30 |
| 585 | Mark Carreon | .10 | .30 |
| 586 | Royce Clayton | .10 | .30 |
| 587 | Shawn Estes | .10 | .30 |
| 588 | Glenallen Hill | .10 | .30 |
| 589 | Mark Leiter | .10 | .30 |
| 590 | Kirt Manwaring | .10 | .30 |
| 591 | David McCarty | .10 | .30 |
| 592 | Terry Mulholland | .10 | .30 |
| 593 | John Patterson | .10 | .30 |
| 594 | J.R. Phillips | .10 | .30 |
| 595 | Deion Sanders | .20 | .50 |
| 596 | Steve Scarsone | .10 | .30 |
| 597 | Robby Thompson | .10 | .30 |

| | | |
|---|---|---|
| ☐ 598 Sergio Valdez | .10 | .30 |
| ☐ 599 William Van Landingham | .10 | .30 |
| ☐ 600 Matt Williams | .10 | .30 |
| ☐ P20 Cal Ripken Promo | 1.25 | 3.00 |

### 1997 Fleer

| | | |
|---|---|---|
| ☐ COMPLETE SET (761) | 70.00 | 140.00 |
| ☐ COMPLETE SERIES 1 (500) | 30.00 | 60.00 |
| ☐ COMPLETE SERIES 2 (261) | 40.00 | 80.00 |
| ☐ COMMON CARD (1-750) | .10 | .30 |
| ☐ COMMON CARD (751-761) | .20 | .50 |
| ☐ 1 Roberto Alomar | .20 | .50 |
| ☐ 2 Brady Anderson | .10 | .30 |
| ☐ 3 Bobby Bonilla | .10 | .30 |
| ☐ 4 Rocky Coppinger | .10 | .30 |
| ☐ 5 Cesar Devarez | .10 | .30 |
| ☐ 6 Scott Erickson | .10 | .30 |
| ☐ 7 Jeffrey Hammonds | .10 | .30 |
| ☐ 8 Chris Hoiles | .10 | .30 |
| ☐ 9 Eddie Murray | .30 | .75 |
| ☐ 10 Mike Mussina | .20 | .50 |
| ☐ 11 Randy Myers | .10 | .30 |
| ☐ 12 Rafael Palmeiro | .20 | .50 |
| ☐ 13 Cal Ripken | 1.00 | 2.50 |
| ☐ 14 B.J. Surhoff | .10 | .30 |
| ☐ 15 David Wells | .10 | .30 |
| ☐ 16 Todd Zeile | .10 | .30 |
| ☐ 17 Darren Bragg | .10 | .30 |
| ☐ 18 Jose Canseco | .20 | .50 |
| ☐ 19 Roger Clemens | .60 | 1.50 |
| ☐ 20 Wil Cordero | .10 | .30 |
| ☐ 21 Jeff Frye | .10 | .30 |
| ☐ 22 Nomar Garciaparra | .50 | 1.25 |
| ☐ 23 Tom Gordon | .10 | .30 |
| ☐ 24 Mike Greenwell | .10 | .30 |
| ☐ 25 Reggie Jefferson | .10 | .30 |
| ☐ 26 Jose Malave | .10 | .30 |
| ☐ 27 Tim Naehring | .10 | .30 |
| ☐ 28 Troy O'Leary | .10 | .30 |
| ☐ 29 Heathcliff Slocumb | .10 | .30 |
| ☐ 30 Mike Stanley | .10 | .30 |
| ☐ 31 John Valentin | .10 | .30 |
| ☐ 32 Mo Vaughn | .10 | .30 |
| ☐ 33 Tim Wakefield | .10 | .30 |
| ☐ 34 Garret Anderson | .10 | .30 |
| ☐ 35 George Arias | .10 | .30 |
| ☐ 36 Shawn Boskie | .10 | .30 |
| ☐ 37 Chili Davis | .10 | .30 |
| ☐ 38 Jason Dickson | .10 | .30 |
| ☐ 39 Gary DiSarcina | .10 | .30 |
| ☐ 40 Jim Edmonds | .10 | .30 |
| ☐ 41 Darin Erstad | .10 | .30 |
| ☐ 42 Jorge Fabregas | .10 | .30 |
| ☐ 43 Chuck Finley | .10 | .30 |
| ☐ 44 Todd Greene | .10 | .30 |
| ☐ 45 Mike Holtz | .10 | .30 |
| ☐ 46 Rex Hudler | .10 | .30 |
| ☐ 47 Mike James | .10 | .30 |
| ☐ 48 Mark Langston | .10 | .30 |
| ☐ 49 Troy Percival | .10 | .30 |
| ☐ 50 Tim Salmon | .20 | .50 |
| ☐ 51 Jeff Schmidt | .10 | .30 |
| ☐ 52 J.T. Snow | .10 | .30 |
| ☐ 53 Randy Velarde | .10 | .30 |
| ☐ 54 Wilson Alvarez | .10 | .30 |
| ☐ 55 Harold Baines | .10 | .30 |
| ☐ 56 James Baldwin | .10 | .30 |
| ☐ 57 Jason Bere | .10 | .30 |
| ☐ 58 Mike Cameron | .10 | .30 |
| ☐ 59 Ray Durham | .10 | .30 |
| ☐ 60 Alex Fernandez | .10 | .30 |
| ☐ 61 Ozzie Guillen | .10 | .30 |
| ☐ 62 Roberto Hernandez | .10 | .30 |

| | | |
|---|---|---|
| ☐ 63 Ron Karkovice | .10 | .30 |
| ☐ 64 Darren Lewis | .10 | .30 |
| ☐ 65 Dave Martinez | .10 | .30 |
| ☐ 66 Lyle Mouton | .10 | .30 |
| ☐ 67 Greg Norton | .10 | .30 |
| ☐ 68 Tony Phillips | .10 | .30 |
| ☐ 69 Chris Snopek | .10 | .30 |
| ☐ 70 Kevin Tapani | .10 | .30 |
| ☐ 71 Danny Tartabull | .10 | .30 |
| ☐ 72 Frank Thomas | .30 | .75 |
| ☐ 73 Robin Ventura | .10 | .30 |
| ☐ 74 Sandy Alomar Jr. | .10 | .30 |
| ☐ 75 Albert Belle | .10 | .30 |
| ☐ 76 Mark Carreon | .10 | .30 |
| ☐ 77 Julio Franco | .10 | .30 |
| ☐ 78 Brian Giles RC | .60 | 1.50 |
| ☐ 79 Orel Hershiser | .10 | .30 |
| ☐ 80 Kenny Lofton | .10 | .30 |
| ☐ 81 Dennis Martinez | .10 | .30 |
| ☐ 82 Jack McDowell | .10 | .30 |
| ☐ 83 Jose Mesa | .10 | .30 |
| ☐ 84 Charles Nagy | .10 | .30 |
| ☐ 85 Chad Ogea | .10 | .30 |
| ☐ 86 Eric Plunk | .10 | .30 |
| ☐ 87 Manny Ramirez | .20 | .50 |
| ☐ 88 Kevin Seitzer | .10 | .30 |
| ☐ 89 Julian Tavarez | .10 | .30 |
| ☐ 90 Jim Thome | .20 | .50 |
| ☐ 91 Jose Vizcaino | .10 | .30 |
| ☐ 92 Omar Vizquel | .20 | .50 |
| ☐ 93 Brad Ausmus | .10 | .30 |
| ☐ 94 Kimera Bartee | .10 | .30 |
| ☐ 95 Raul Casanova | .10 | .30 |
| ☐ 96 Tony Clark | .10 | .30 |
| ☐ 97 John Cummings | .10 | .30 |
| ☐ 98 Travis Fryman | .10 | .30 |
| ☐ 99 Bob Higginson | .10 | .30 |
| ☐ 100 Mark Lewis | .10 | .30 |
| ☐ 101 Felipe Lira | .10 | .30 |
| ☐ 102 Phil Nevin | .10 | .30 |
| ☐ 103 Melvin Nieves | .10 | .30 |
| ☐ 104 Curtis Pride | .10 | .30 |
| ☐ 105 A.J. Sager | .10 | .30 |
| ☐ 106 Ruben Sierra | .10 | .30 |
| ☐ 107 Justin Thompson | .10 | .30 |
| ☐ 108 Alan Trammell | .10 | .30 |
| ☐ 109 Kevin Appier | .10 | .30 |
| ☐ 110 Tim Belcher | .10 | .30 |
| ☐ 111 Jaime Bluma | .10 | .30 |
| ☐ 112 Johnny Damon | .20 | .50 |
| ☐ 113 Tom Goodwin | .10 | .30 |
| ☐ 114 Chris Haney | .10 | .30 |
| ☐ 115 Keith Lockhart | .10 | .30 |
| ☐ 116 Mike Macfarlane | .10 | .30 |
| ☐ 117 Jeff Montgomery | .10 | .30 |
| ☐ 118 Jose Offerman | .10 | .30 |
| ☐ 119 Craig Paquette | .10 | .30 |
| ☐ 120 Joe Randa | .10 | .30 |
| ☐ 121 Bip Roberts | .10 | .30 |
| ☐ 122 Jose Rosado | .10 | .30 |
| ☐ 123 Mike Sweeney | .10 | .30 |
| ☐ 124 Michael Tucker | .10 | .30 |
| ☐ 125 Jeromy Burnitz | .10 | .30 |
| ☐ 126 Jeff Cirillo | .10 | .30 |
| ☐ 127 Jeff D'Amico | .10 | .30 |
| ☐ 128 Mike Fetters | .10 | .30 |
| ☐ 129 John Jaha | .10 | .30 |
| ☐ 130 Scott Karl | .10 | .30 |
| ☐ 131 Jesse Levis | .10 | .30 |
| ☐ 132 Mark Loretta | .10 | .30 |
| ☐ 133 Mike Matheny | .10 | .30 |
| ☐ 134 Ben McDonald | .10 | .30 |
| ☐ 135 Matt Mieske | .10 | .30 |
| ☐ 136 Marc Newfield | .10 | .30 |
| ☐ 137 Dave Nilsson | .10 | .30 |
| ☐ 138 Jose Valentin | .10 | .30 |
| ☐ 139 Fernando Vina | .10 | .30 |
| ☐ 140 Bob Wickman | .10 | .30 |
| ☐ 141 Gerald Williams | .10 | .30 |
| ☐ 142 Rick Aguilera | .10 | .30 |
| ☐ 143 Rich Becker | .10 | .30 |
| ☐ 144 Ron Coomer | .10 | .30 |
| ☐ 145 Marty Cordova | .10 | .30 |
| ☐ 146 Roberto Kelly | .10 | .30 |
| ☐ 147 Chuck Knoblauch | .10 | .30 |
| ☐ 148 Matt Lawton | .10 | .30 |
| ☐ 149 Pat Meares | .10 | .30 |
| ☐ 150 Travis Miller | .10 | .30 |

| | | |
|---|---|---|
| ☐ 151 Paul Molitor | .10 | .30 |
| ☐ 152 Greg Myers | .10 | .30 |
| ☐ 153 Dan Naulty | .10 | .30 |
| ☐ 154 Kirby Puckett | .30 | .75 |
| ☐ 155 Brad Radke | .10 | .30 |
| ☐ 156 Frank Rodriguez | .10 | .30 |
| ☐ 157 Scott Stahoviak | .10 | .30 |
| ☐ 158 Dave Stevens | .10 | .30 |
| ☐ 159 Matt Walbeck | .10 | .30 |
| ☐ 160 Todd Walker | .10 | .30 |
| ☐ 161 Wade Boggs | .20 | .50 |
| ☐ 162 David Cone | .10 | .30 |
| ☐ 163 Mariano Duncan | .10 | .30 |
| ☐ 164 Cecil Fielder | .10 | .30 |
| ☐ 165 Joe Girardi | .10 | .30 |
| ☐ 166 Dwight Gooden | .10 | .30 |
| ☐ 167 Charlie Hayes | .10 | .30 |
| ☐ 168 Derek Jeter | .75 | 2.00 |
| ☐ 169 Jimmy Key | .10 | .30 |
| ☐ 170 Jim Leyritz | .10 | .30 |
| ☐ 171 Tino Martinez | .20 | .50 |
| ☐ 172 Ramiro Mendoza RC | .10 | .30 |
| ☐ 173 Jeff Nelson | .10 | .30 |
| ☐ 174 Paul O'Neill | .20 | .50 |
| ☐ 175 Andy Pettitte | .20 | .50 |
| ☐ 176 Mariano Rivera | .30 | .75 |
| ☐ 177 Ruben Rivera | .10 | .30 |
| ☐ 178 Kenny Rogers | .10 | .30 |
| ☐ 179 Darryl Strawberry | .10 | .30 |
| ☐ 180 John Wetteland | .10 | .30 |
| ☐ 181 Bernie Williams | .20 | .50 |
| ☐ 182 Willie Adams | .10 | .30 |
| ☐ 183 Tony Batista | .10 | .30 |
| ☐ 184 Geronimo Berroa | .10 | .30 |
| ☐ 185 Mike Bordick | .10 | .30 |
| ☐ 186 Scott Brosius | .10 | .30 |
| ☐ 187 Bobby Chouinard | .10 | .30 |
| ☐ 188 Jim Corsi | .10 | .30 |
| ☐ 189 Brent Gates | .10 | .30 |
| ☐ 190 Jason Giambi | .10 | .30 |
| ☐ 191 Jose Herrera | .10 | .30 |
| ☐ 192 Damon Mashore | .10 | .30 |
| ☐ 193 Mark McGwire | .75 | 2.00 |
| ☐ 194 Mike Mohler | .10 | .30 |
| ☐ 195 Scott Spiezio | .10 | .30 |
| ☐ 196 Terry Steinbach | .10 | .30 |
| ☐ 197 Bill Taylor | .10 | .30 |
| ☐ 198 John Wasdin | .10 | .30 |
| ☐ 199 Steve Wojciechowski | .10 | .30 |
| ☐ 200 Ernie Young | .10 | .30 |
| ☐ 201 Rich Amaral | .10 | .30 |
| ☐ 202 Jay Buhner | .10 | .30 |
| ☐ 203 Norm Charlton | .10 | .30 |
| ☐ 204 Joey Cora | .10 | .30 |
| ☐ 205 Russ Davis | .10 | .30 |
| ☐ 206 Ken Griffey Jr. | .50 | 1.25 |
| ☐ 207 Sterling Hitchcock | .10 | .30 |
| ☐ 208 Brian Hunter | .10 | .30 |
| ☐ 209 Raul Ibanez | .10 | .30 |
| ☐ 210 Randy Johnson | .30 | .75 |
| ☐ 211 Edgar Martinez | .20 | .50 |
| ☐ 212 Jamie Moyer | .10 | .30 |
| ☐ 213 Alex Rodriguez | .50 | 1.25 |
| ☐ 214 Paul Sorrento | .10 | .30 |
| ☐ 215 Matt Wagner | .10 | .30 |
| ☐ 216 Bob Wells | .10 | .30 |
| ☐ 217 Dan Wilson | .10 | .30 |
| ☐ 218 Damon Buford | .10 | .30 |
| ☐ 219 Will Clark | .20 | .50 |
| ☐ 220 Kevin Elster | .10 | .30 |
| ☐ 221 Juan Gonzalez | .10 | .30 |
| ☐ 222 Rusty Greer | .10 | .30 |
| ☐ 223 Kevin Gross | .10 | .30 |
| ☐ 224 Darryl Hamilton | .10 | .30 |
| ☐ 225 Mike Henneman | .10 | .30 |
| ☐ 226 Ken Hill | .10 | .30 |
| ☐ 227 Mark McLemore | .10 | .30 |
| ☐ 228 Darren Oliver | .10 | .30 |
| ☐ 229 Dean Palmer | .10 | .30 |
| ☐ 230 Roger Pavlik | .10 | .30 |
| ☐ 231 Ivan Rodriguez | .20 | .50 |
| ☐ 232 Mickey Tettleton | .10 | .30 |
| ☐ 233 Bobby Witt | .10 | .30 |
| ☐ 234 Jacob Brumfield | .10 | .30 |
| ☐ 235 Joe Carter | .10 | .30 |
| ☐ 236 Tim Crabtree | .10 | .30 |
| ☐ 237 Carlos Delgado | .10 | .30 |
| ☐ 238 Huck Flener | .10 | .30 |

|  |  | | |
|---|---|---|---|
| 239 | Alex Gonzalez | .10 | .30 |
| 240 | Shawn Green | .10 | .30 |
| 241 | Juan Guzman | .10 | .30 |
| 242 | Pat Hentgen | .10 | .30 |
| 243 | Marty Janzen | .10 | .30 |
| 244 | Sandy Martinez | .10 | .30 |
| 245 | Otis Nixon | .10 | .30 |
| 246 | Charlie O'Brien | .10 | .30 |
| 247 | John Olerud | .10 | .30 |
| 248 | Robert Perez | .10 | .30 |
| 249 | Ed Sprague | .10 | .30 |
| 250 | Mike Timlin | .10 | .30 |
| 251 | Steve Avery | .10 | .30 |
| 252 | Jeff Blauser | .10 | .30 |
| 253 | Brad Clontz | .10 | .30 |
| 254 | Jermaine Dye | .10 | .30 |
| 255 | Tom Glavine | .20 | .50 |
| 256 | Marquis Grissom | .10 | .30 |
| 257 | Andruw Jones | .20 | .50 |
| 258 | Chipper Jones | .30 | .75 |
| 259 | David Justice | .10 | .30 |
| 260 | Ryan Klesko | .10 | .30 |
| 261 | Mark Lemke | .10 | .30 |
| 262 | Javier Lopez | .10 | .30 |
| 263 | Greg Maddux | .50 | 1.25 |
| 264 | Fred McGriff | .20 | .50 |
| 265 | Greg McMichael | .10 | .30 |
| 266 | Denny Neagle | .10 | .30 |
| 267 | Terry Pendleton | .10 | .30 |
| 268 | Eddie Perez | .10 | .30 |
| 269 | John Smoltz | .20 | .50 |
| 270 | Terrell Wade | .10 | .30 |
| 271 | Mark Wohlers | .10 | .30 |
| 272 | Terry Adams | .10 | .30 |
| 273 | Brant Brown | .10 | .30 |
| 274 | Leo Gomez | .10 | .30 |
| 275 | Luis Gonzalez | .10 | .30 |
| 276 | Mark Grace | .20 | .50 |
| 277 | Tyler Houston | .10 | .30 |
| 278 | Robin Jennings | .10 | .30 |
| 279 | Brooks Kieschnick | .10 | .30 |
| 280 | Brian McRae | .10 | .30 |
| 281 | Jaime Navarro | .10 | .30 |
| 282 | Ryne Sandberg | .50 | 1.25 |
| 283 | Scott Servais | .10 | .30 |
| 284 | Sammy Sosa | .30 | .75 |
| 285 | Dave Swartzbaugh | .10 | .30 |
| 286 | Amaury Telemaco | .10 | .30 |
| 287 | Steve Trachsel | .10 | .30 |
| 288 | Pedro Valdes | .10 | .30 |
| 289 | Turk Wendell | .10 | .30 |
| 290 | Bret Boone | .10 | .30 |
| 291 | Jeff Branson | .10 | .30 |
| 292 | Jeff Brantley | .10 | .30 |
| 293 | Eric Davis | .10 | .30 |
| 294 | Willie Greene | .10 | .30 |
| 295 | Thomas Howard | .10 | .30 |
| 296 | Barry Larkin | .20 | .50 |
| 297 | Kevin Mitchell | .10 | .30 |
| 298 | Hal Morris | .10 | .30 |
| 299 | Chad Mottola | .10 | .30 |
| 300 | Joe Oliver | .10 | .30 |
| 301 | Mark Portugal | .10 | .30 |
| 302 | Roger Salkeld | .10 | .30 |
| 303 | Reggie Sanders | .10 | .30 |
| 304 | Pete Schourek | .10 | .30 |
| 305 | John Smiley | .10 | .30 |
| 306 | Eddie Taubensee | .10 | .30 |
| 307 | Dante Bichette | .10 | .30 |
| 308 | Ellis Burks | .10 | .30 |
| 309 | Vinny Castilla | .10 | .30 |
| 310 | Andres Galarraga | .10 | .30 |
| 311 | Curt Leskanic | .10 | .30 |
| 312 | Quinton McCracken | .10 | .30 |
| 313 | Neifi Perez | .10 | .30 |
| 314 | Jeff Reed | .10 | .30 |
| 315 | Steve Reed | .10 | .30 |
| 316 | Armando Reynoso | .10 | .30 |
| 317 | Kevin Ritz | .10 | .30 |
| 318 | Bruce Ruffin | .10 | .30 |
| 319 | Larry Walker | .10 | .30 |
| 320 | Walt Weiss | .10 | .30 |
| 321 | Jamey Wright | .10 | .30 |
| 322 | Eric Young | .10 | .30 |
| 323 | Kurt Abbott | .10 | .30 |
| 324 | Alex Arias | .10 | .30 |
| 325 | Kevin Brown | .10 | .30 |
| 326 | Luis Castillo | .10 | .30 |
| 327 | Greg Colbrunn | .10 | .30 |
| 328 | Jeff Conine | .10 | .30 |
| 329 | Andre Dawson | .10 | .30 |
| 330 | Charles Johnson | .10 | .30 |
| 331 | Al Leiter | .10 | .30 |
| 332 | Ralph Milliard | .10 | .30 |
| 333 | Robb Nen | .10 | .30 |
| 334 | Pat Rapp | .10 | .30 |
| 335 | Edgar Renteria | .10 | .30 |
| 336 | Gary Sheffield | .10 | .30 |
| 337 | Devon White | .10 | .30 |
| 338 | Bob Abreu | .20 | .50 |
| 339 | Jeff Bagwell | .20 | .50 |
| 340 | Derek Bell | .10 | .30 |
| 341 | Sean Berry | .10 | .30 |
| 342 | Craig Biggio | .20 | .50 |
| 343 | Doug Drabek | .10 | .30 |
| 344 | Tony Eusebio | .10 | .30 |
| 345 | Ricky Gutierrez | .10 | .30 |
| 346 | Mike Hampton | .10 | .30 |
| 347 | Brian Hunter | .10 | .30 |
| 348 | Todd Jones | .10 | .30 |
| 349 | Darryl Kile | .10 | .30 |
| 350 | Derrick May | .10 | .30 |
| 351 | Orlando Miller | .10 | .30 |
| 352 | James Mouton | .10 | .30 |
| 353 | Shane Reynolds | .10 | .30 |
| 354 | Billy Wagner | .10 | .30 |
| 355 | Donne Wall | .10 | .30 |
| 356 | Mike Blowers | .10 | .30 |
| 357 | Brett Butler | .10 | .30 |
| 358 | Roger Cedeno | .10 | .30 |
| 359 | Chad Curtis | .10 | .30 |
| 360 | Delino DeShields | .10 | .30 |
| 361 | Greg Gagne | .10 | .30 |
| 362 | Karim Garcia | .10 | .30 |
| 363 | Wilton Guerrero | .10 | .30 |
| 364 | Todd Hollandsworth | .10 | .30 |
| 365 | Eric Karros | .10 | .30 |
| 366 | Ramon Martinez | .10 | .30 |
| 367 | Raul Mondesi | .10 | .30 |
| 368 | Hideo Nomo | .30 | .75 |
| 369 | Antonio Osuna | .10 | .30 |
| 370 | Chan Ho Park | .10 | .30 |
| 371 | Mike Piazza | .50 | 1.25 |
| 372 | Ismael Valdes | .10 | .30 |
| 373 | Todd Worrell | .10 | .30 |
| 374 | Moises Alou | .10 | .30 |
| 375 | Shane Andrews | .10 | .30 |
| 376 | Yamil Benitez | .10 | .30 |
| 377 | Jeff Fassero | .10 | .30 |
| 378 | Darrin Fletcher | .10 | .30 |
| 379 | Cliff Floyd | .10 | .30 |
| 380 | Mark Grudzielanek | .10 | .30 |
| 381 | Mike Lansing | .10 | .30 |
| 382 | Barry Manuel | .10 | .30 |
| 383 | Pedro Martinez | .20 | .50 |
| 384 | Henry Rodriguez | .10 | .30 |
| 385 | Mel Rojas | .10 | .30 |
| 386 | F.P. Santangelo | .10 | .30 |
| 387 | David Segui | .10 | .30 |
| 388 | Ugueth Urbina | .10 | .30 |
| 389 | Rondell White | .10 | .30 |
| 390 | Edgardo Alfonzo | .10 | .30 |
| 391 | Carlos Baerga | .10 | .30 |
| 392 | Mark Clark | .10 | .30 |
| 393 | Alvaro Espinoza | .10 | .30 |
| 394 | John Franco | .10 | .30 |
| 395 | Bernard Gilkey | .10 | .30 |
| 396 | Pete Harnisch | .10 | .30 |
| 397 | Todd Hundley | .10 | .30 |
| 398 | Butch Huskey | .10 | .30 |
| 399 | Jason Isringhausen | .10 | .30 |
| 400 | Lance Johnson | .10 | .30 |
| 401 | Bobby Jones | .10 | .30 |
| 402 | Alex Ochoa | .10 | .30 |
| 403 | Rey Ordonez | .10 | .30 |
| 404 | Robert Person | .10 | .30 |
| 405 | Paul Wilson | .10 | .30 |
| 406 | Matt Beech | .10 | .30 |
| 407 | Ron Blazier | .10 | .30 |
| 408 | Ricky Bottalico | .10 | .30 |
| 409 | Lenny Dykstra | .10 | .30 |
| 410 | Jim Eisenreich | .10 | .30 |
| 411 | Bobby Estalella | .10 | .30 |
| 412 | Mike Grace | .10 | .30 |
| 413 | Gregg Jefferies | .10 | .30 |
| 414 | Mike Lieberthal | .10 | .30 |
| 415 | Wendell Magee | .10 | .30 |
| 416 | Mickey Morandini | .10 | .30 |
| 417 | Ricky Otero | .10 | .30 |
| 418 | Scott Rolen | .20 | .50 |
| 419 | Ken Ryan | .10 | .30 |
| 420 | Benito Santiago | .10 | .30 |
| 421 | Curt Schilling | .10 | .30 |
| 422 | Kevin Sefcik | .10 | .30 |
| 423 | Jermaine Allensworth | .10 | .30 |
| 424 | Trey Beamon | .10 | .30 |
| 425 | Jay Bell | .10 | .30 |
| 426 | Francisco Cordova | .10 | .30 |
| 427 | Carlos Garcia | .10 | .30 |
| 428 | Mark Johnson | .10 | .30 |
| 429 | Jason Kendall | .10 | .30 |
| 430 | Jeff King | .10 | .30 |
| 431 | Jon Lieber | .10 | .30 |
| 432 | Al Martin | .10 | .30 |
| 433 | Orlando Merced | .10 | .30 |
| 434 | Ramon Morel | .10 | .30 |
| 435 | Matt Ruebel | .10 | .30 |
| 436 | Jason Schmidt | .10 | .30 |
| 437 | Marc Wilkins | .10 | .30 |
| 438 | Alan Benes | .10 | .30 |
| 439 | Andy Benes | .10 | .30 |
| 440 | Royce Clayton | .10 | .30 |
| 441 | Dennis Eckersley | .10 | .30 |
| 442 | Gary Gaetti | .10 | .30 |
| 443 | Ron Gant | .10 | .30 |
| 444 | Aaron Holbert | .10 | .30 |
| 445 | Brian Jordan | .10 | .30 |
| 446 | Ray Lankford | .10 | .30 |
| 447 | John Mabry | .10 | .30 |
| 448 | T.J. Mathews | .10 | .30 |
| 449 | Willie McGee | .10 | .30 |
| 450 | Donovan Osborne | .10 | .30 |
| 451 | Tom Pagnozzi | .10 | .30 |
| 452 | Ozzie Smith | .50 | 1.25 |
| 453 | Todd Stottlemyre | .10 | .30 |
| 454 | Mark Sweeney | .10 | .30 |
| 455 | Dmitri Young | .10 | .30 |
| 456 | Andy Ashby | .10 | .30 |
| 457 | Ken Caminiti | .10 | .30 |
| 458 | Archi Cianfrocco | .10 | .30 |
| 459 | Steve Finley | .10 | .30 |
| 460 | John Flaherty | .10 | .30 |
| 461 | Chris Gomez | .10 | .30 |
| 462 | Tony Gwynn | .40 | 1.00 |
| 463 | Joey Hamilton | .10 | .30 |
| 464 | Rickey Henderson | .30 | .75 |
| 465 | Trevor Hoffman | .10 | .30 |
| 466 | Brian Johnson | .10 | .30 |
| 467 | Wally Joyner | .10 | .30 |
| 468 | Jody Reed | .10 | .30 |
| 469 | Scott Sanders | .10 | .30 |
| 470 | Bob Tewksbury | .10 | .30 |
| 471 | Fernando Valenzuela | .10 | .30 |
| 472 | Greg Vaughn | .10 | .30 |
| 473 | Tim Worrell | .10 | .30 |
| 474 | Rich Aurilia | .10 | .30 |
| 475 | Rod Beck | .10 | .30 |
| 476 | Marvin Benard | .10 | .30 |
| 477 | Barry Bonds | .75 | 2.00 |
| 478 | Jay Canizaro | .10 | .30 |
| 479 | Shawon Dunston | .10 | .30 |
| 480 | Shawn Estes | .10 | .30 |
| 481 | Mark Gardner | .10 | .30 |
| 482 | Glenallen Hill | .10 | .30 |
| 483 | Stan Javier | .10 | .30 |
| 484 | Marcus Jensen | .10 | .30 |
| 485 | Bill Mueller RC | .50 | 1.25 |
| 486 | Wm. VanLandingham | .10 | .30 |
| 487 | Allen Watson | .10 | .30 |
| 488 | Rick Wilkins | .10 | .30 |
| 489 | Matt Williams | .10 | .30 |
| 490 | Desi Wilson | .10 | .30 |
| 491 | Albert Belle CL | .10 | .30 |
| 492 | Ken Griffey Jr. CL | .30 | .75 |
| 493 | Andruw Jones CL | .10 | .30 |
| 494 | Chipper Jones CL | .20 | .50 |
| 495 | Mark McGwire CL | .40 | 1.00 |
| 496 | Paul Molitor CL | .10 | .30 |
| 497 | Mike Piazza CL | .30 | .75 |
| 498 | Cal Ripken CL | .50 | 1.25 |
| 499 | Alex Rodriguez CL | .30 | .75 |
| 500 | Frank Thomas CL | .20 | .50 |
| 501 | Kenny Lofton | .10 | .30 |
| 502 | Carlos Perez | .10 | .30 |

|  |  | | |
|---|--------|---|---|
| ☐ 503 | Tim Raines | .10 | .30 |
| ☐ 504 | Danny Patterson | .10 | .30 |
| ☐ 505 | Derrick May | .10 | .30 |
| ☐ 506 | Dave Hollins | .10 | .30 |
| ☐ 507 | Felipe Crespo | .10 | .30 |
| ☐ 508 | Brian Banks | .10 | .30 |
| ☐ 509 | Jeff Kent | .10 | .30 |
| ☐ 510 | Bubba Trammell RC | .15 | .40 |
| ☐ 511 | Robert Person | .10 | .30 |
| ☐ 512 | David Arias-Ortiz RC | 10.00 | 25.00 |
| ☐ 513 | Ryan Jones | .10 | .30 |
| ☐ 514 | David Justice | .10 | .30 |
| ☐ 515 | Will Cunnane | .10 | .30 |
| ☐ 516 | Russ Johnson | .10 | .30 |
| ☐ 517 | John Burkett | .10 | .30 |
| ☐ 518 | Robinson Checo RC | .10 | .30 |
| ☐ 519 | Ricardo Rincon RC | .10 | .30 |
| ☐ 520 | Woody Williams | .10 | .30 |
| ☐ 521 | Rick Helling | .10 | .30 |
| ☐ 522 | Jorge Posada | .20 | .50 |
| ☐ 523 | Kevin Orie | .10 | .30 |
| ☐ 524 | Fernando Tatis RC | .10 | .30 |
| ☐ 525 | Jermaine Dye | .10 | .30 |
| ☐ 526 | Brian Hunter | .10 | .30 |
| ☐ 527 | Greg McMichael | .10 | .30 |
| ☐ 528 | Matt Wagner | .10 | .30 |
| ☐ 529 | Richie Sexson | .10 | .30 |
| ☐ 530 | Scott Ruffcorn | .10 | .30 |
| ☐ 531 | Luis Gonzalez | .10 | .30 |
| ☐ 532 | Mike Johnson RC | .10 | .30 |
| ☐ 533 | Mark Petkovsek | .10 | .30 |
| ☐ 534 | Doug Drabek | .10 | .30 |
| ☐ 535 | Jose Canseco | .20 | .50 |
| ☐ 536 | Bobby Bonilla | .10 | .30 |
| ☐ 537 | J.T. Snow | .10 | .30 |
| ☐ 538 | Shawon Dunston | .10 | .30 |
| ☐ 539 | John Ericks | .10 | .30 |
| ☐ 540 | Terry Steinbach | .10 | .30 |
| ☐ 541 | Jay Bell | .10 | .30 |
| ☐ 542 | Joe Borowski RC | .15 | .40 |
| ☐ 543 | David Wells | .10 | .30 |
| ☐ 544 | Justin Towle RC | .10 | .30 |
| ☐ 545 | Mike Blowers | .10 | .30 |
| ☐ 546 | Shannon Stewart | .10 | .30 |
| ☐ 547 | Rudy Pemberton | .10 | .30 |
| ☐ 548 | Bill Swift | .10 | .30 |
| ☐ 549 | Osvaldo Fernandez | .10 | .30 |
| ☐ 550 | Eddie Murray | .30 | .75 |
| ☐ 551 | Don Wengert | .10 | .30 |
| ☐ 552 | Brad Ausmus | .10 | .30 |
| ☐ 553 | Carlos Garcia | .10 | .30 |
| ☐ 554 | Jose Guillen | .10 | .30 |
| ☐ 555 | Rheal Cormier | .10 | .30 |
| ☐ 556 | Doug Brocail | .10 | .30 |
| ☐ 557 | Rex Hudler | .10 | .30 |
| ☐ 558 | Armando Benitez | .10 | .30 |
| ☐ 559 | Eli Marrero | .10 | .30 |
| ☐ 560 | Ricky Ledee RC | .15 | .40 |
| ☐ 561 | Bartolo Colon | .10 | .30 |
| ☐ 562 | Quilvio Veras | .10 | .30 |
| ☐ 563 | Alex Fernandez | .10 | .30 |
| ☐ 564 | Darren Dreifort | .10 | .30 |
| ☐ 565 | Benji Gil | .10 | .30 |
| ☐ 566 | Kent Mercker | .10 | .30 |
| ☐ 567 | Glendon Rusch | .10 | .30 |
| ☐ 568 | Ramon Tatis RC | .10 | .30 |
| ☐ 569 | Roger Clemens | .60 | 1.50 |
| ☐ 570 | Mark Lewis | .10 | .30 |
| ☐ 571 | Emil Brown RC | .10 | .30 |
| ☐ 572 | Jaime Navarro | .10 | .30 |
| ☐ 573 | Sherman Obando | .10 | .30 |
| ☐ 574 | John Wasdin | .10 | .30 |
| ☐ 575 | Calvin Maduro | .10 | .30 |
| ☐ 576 | Todd Jones | .10 | .30 |
| ☐ 577 | Orlando Merced | .10 | .30 |
| ☐ 578 | Cal Eldred | .10 | .30 |
| ☐ 579 | Mark Gubicza | .10 | .30 |
| ☐ 580 | Michael Tucker | .10 | .30 |
| ☐ 581 | Tony Saunders RC | .10 | .30 |
| ☐ 582 | Garvin Alston | .10 | .30 |
| ☐ 583 | Joe Roa | .10 | .30 |
| ☐ 584 | Brady Raggio RC | .10 | .30 |
| ☐ 585 | Jimmy Key | .10 | .30 |
| ☐ 586 | Marc Sagmoen RC | .10 | .30 |
| ☐ 587 | Jim Bullinger | .10 | .30 |
| ☐ 588 | Yorkis Perez | .10 | .30 |
| ☐ 589 | Jose Cruz Jr. RC | .15 | .40 |
| ☐ 590 | Mike Stanton | .10 | .30 |
| ☐ 591 | Deivi Cruz RC | .15 | .40 |
| ☐ 592 | Steve Karsay | .10 | .30 |
| ☐ 593 | Mike Trombley | .10 | .30 |
| ☐ 594 | Doug Glanville | .10 | .30 |
| ☐ 595 | Scott Sanders | .10 | .30 |
| ☐ 596 | Thomas Howard | .10 | .30 |
| ☐ 597 | T.J. Staton RC | .10 | .30 |
| ☐ 598 | Garrett Stephenson | .10 | .30 |
| ☐ 599 | Rico Brogna | .10 | .30 |
| ☐ 600 | Albert Belle | .10 | .30 |
| ☐ 601 | Jose Vizcaino | .10 | .30 |
| ☐ 602 | Chili Davis | .10 | .30 |
| ☐ 603 | Shane Mack | .10 | .30 |
| ☐ 604 | Jim Eisenreich | .10 | .30 |
| ☐ 605 | Todd Zeile | .10 | .30 |
| ☐ 606 | Brian Boehringer RC | .10 | .30 |
| ☐ 607 | Paul Shuey | .10 | .30 |
| ☐ 608 | Kevin Tapani | .10 | .30 |
| ☐ 609 | John Wetteland | .10 | .30 |
| ☐ 610 | Jim Leyritz | .10 | .30 |
| ☐ 611 | Ray Montgomery RC | .10 | .30 |
| ☐ 612 | Doug Bochtler | .10 | .30 |
| ☐ 613 | Wady Almonte RC | .10 | .30 |
| ☐ 614 | Danny Tartabull | .10 | .30 |
| ☐ 615 | Orlando Miller | .10 | .30 |
| ☐ 616 | Bobby Ayala | .10 | .30 |
| ☐ 617 | Tony Graffanino | .10 | .30 |
| ☐ 618 | Marc Valdes | .10 | .30 |
| ☐ 619 | Ron Villone | .10 | .30 |
| ☐ 620 | Derrek Lee | .20 | .50 |
| ☐ 621 | Greg Colbrunn | .10 | .30 |
| ☐ 622 | Felix Heredia RC | .15 | .40 |
| ☐ 623 | Carl Everett | .10 | .30 |
| ☐ 624 | Mark Thompson | .10 | .30 |
| ☐ 625 | Jeff Granger | .10 | .30 |
| ☐ 626 | Damian Jackson | .10 | .30 |
| ☐ 627 | Mark Leiter | .10 | .30 |
| ☐ 628 | Chris Holt | .10 | .30 |
| ☐ 629 | Dario Veras RC | .10 | .30 |
| ☐ 630 | Dave Burba | .10 | .30 |
| ☐ 631 | Darryl Hamilton | .10 | .30 |
| ☐ 632 | Mark Acre | .10 | .30 |
| ☐ 633 | Fernando Hernandez RC | .10 | .30 |
| ☐ 634 | Terry Mulholland | .10 | .30 |
| ☐ 635 | Dustin Hermanson | .10 | .30 |
| ☐ 636 | Delino DeShields | .10 | .30 |
| ☐ 637 | Steve Avery | .10 | .30 |
| ☐ 638 | Tony Womack RC | .15 | .40 |
| ☐ 639 | Mark Whiten | .10 | .30 |
| ☐ 640 | Marquis Grissom | .10 | .30 |
| ☐ 641 | Xavier Hernandez | .10 | .30 |
| ☐ 642 | Eric Davis | .10 | .30 |
| ☐ 643 | Bob Tewksbury | .10 | .30 |
| ☐ 644 | Dante Powell | .10 | .30 |
| ☐ 645 | Carlos Castillo RC | .10 | .30 |
| ☐ 646 | Chris Widger | .10 | .30 |
| ☐ 647 | Moises Alou | .10 | .30 |
| ☐ 648 | Pat Listach | .10 | .30 |
| ☐ 649 | Edgar Ramos RC | .10 | .30 |
| ☐ 650 | Deion Sanders | .20 | .50 |
| ☐ 651 | John Olerud | .10 | .30 |
| ☐ 652 | Todd Dunwoody | .10 | .30 |
| ☐ 653 | Randall Simon RC | .15 | .40 |
| ☐ 654 | Dan Carlson | .10 | .30 |
| ☐ 655 | Matt Williams | .10 | .30 |
| ☐ 656 | Jeff King | .10 | .30 |
| ☐ 657 | Luis Alicea | .10 | .30 |
| ☐ 658 | Brian Moehler RC | .15 | .40 |
| ☐ 659 | Ariel Prieto | .10 | .30 |
| ☐ 660 | Kevin Elster | .10 | .30 |
| ☐ 661 | Mark Hutton | .10 | .30 |
| ☐ 662 | Aaron Sele | .10 | .30 |
| ☐ 663 | Graeme Lloyd | .10 | .30 |
| ☐ 664 | John Burke | .10 | .30 |
| ☐ 665 | Mel Rojas | .10 | .30 |
| ☐ 666 | Sid Fernandez | .10 | .30 |
| ☐ 667 | Pedro Astacio | .10 | .30 |
| ☐ 668 | Jeff Abbott | .10 | .30 |
| ☐ 669 | Darren Daulton | .10 | .30 |
| ☐ 670 | Mike Bordick | .10 | .30 |
| ☐ 671 | Sterling Hitchcock | .10 | .30 |
| ☐ 672 | Damion Easley | .10 | .30 |
| ☐ 673 | Armando Reynoso | .10 | .30 |
| ☐ 674 | Pat Cline | .10 | .30 |
| ☐ 675 | Orlando Cabrera RC | .30 | .75 |
| ☐ 676 | Alan Embree | .10 | .30 |
| ☐ 677 | Brian Bevil | .10 | .30 |
| ☐ 678 | David Weathers | .10 | .30 |
| ☐ 679 | Cliff Floyd | .10 | .30 |
| ☐ 680 | Joe Randa | .10 | .30 |
| ☐ 681 | Bill Haselman | .10 | .30 |
| ☐ 682 | Jeff Fassero | .10 | .30 |
| ☐ 683 | Matt Morris | .10 | .30 |
| ☐ 684 | Mark Portugal | .10 | .30 |
| ☐ 685 | Lee Smith | .10 | .30 |
| ☐ 686 | Pokey Reese | .10 | .30 |
| ☐ 687 | Benito Santiago | .10 | .30 |
| ☐ 688 | Brian Johnson | .10 | .30 |
| ☐ 689 | Brent Brede RC | .10 | .30 |
| ☐ 690 | Shigetoshi Hasegawa RC | .20 | .50 |
| ☐ 691 | Julio Santana | .10 | .30 |
| ☐ 692 | Steve Kline | .10 | .30 |
| ☐ 693 | Julian Tavarez | .10 | .30 |
| ☐ 694 | John Hudek | .10 | .30 |
| ☐ 695 | Manny Alexander | .10 | .30 |
| ☐ 696 | Roberto Alomar ENC | .10 | .30 |
| ☐ 697 | Jeff Bagwell ENC | .10 | .30 |
| ☐ 698 | Barry Bonds ENC | .40 | 1.00 |
| ☐ 699 | Ken Caminiti ENC | .10 | .30 |
| ☐ 700 | Juan Gonzalez ENC | .10 | .30 |
| ☐ 701 | Ken Griffey Jr. ENC | .30 | .75 |
| ☐ 702 | Tony Gwynn ENC | .20 | .50 |
| ☐ 703 | Derek Jeter ENC | .40 | 1.00 |
| ☐ 704 | Andruw Jones ENC | .20 | .50 |
| ☐ 705 | Chipper Jones ENC | .20 | .50 |
| ☐ 706 | Barry Larkin ENC | .10 | .30 |
| ☐ 707 | Greg Maddux ENC | .30 | .75 |
| ☐ 708 | Mark McGwire ENC | .40 | 1.00 |
| ☐ 709 | Paul Molitor ENC | .10 | .30 |
| ☐ 710 | Hideo Nomo ENC | .10 | .30 |
| ☐ 711 | Andy Pettitte ENC | .10 | .30 |
| ☐ 712 | Mike Piazza ENC | .30 | .75 |
| ☐ 713 | Manny Ramirez ENC | .20 | .50 |
| ☐ 714 | Cal Ripken ENC | .50 | 1.25 |
| ☐ 715 | Alex Rodriguez ENC | .30 | .75 |
| ☐ 716 | Ryne Sandberg ENC | .30 | .75 |
| ☐ 717 | John Smoltz ENC | .10 | .30 |
| ☐ 718 | Frank Thomas ENC | .20 | .50 |
| ☐ 719 | Mo Vaughn ENC | .10 | .30 |
| ☐ 720 | Bernie Williams ENC | .10 | .30 |
| ☐ 721 | Tim Salmon CL | .10 | .30 |
| ☐ 722 | Greg Maddux CL | .30 | .75 |
| ☐ 723 | Cal Ripken CL | .50 | 1.25 |
| ☐ 724 | Mo Vaughn CL | .10 | .30 |
| ☐ 725 | Ryne Sandberg CL | .30 | .75 |
| ☐ 726 | Frank Thomas CL | .20 | .50 |
| ☐ 727 | Barry Larkin CL | .10 | .30 |
| ☐ 728 | Manny Ramirez CL | .10 | .30 |
| ☐ 729 | Andres Galarraga CL | .10 | .30 |
| ☐ 730 | Tony Clark CL | .10 | .30 |
| ☐ 731 | Gary Sheffield CL | .10 | .30 |
| ☐ 732 | Jeff Bagwell CL | .10 | .30 |
| ☐ 733 | Kevin Appier CL | .10 | .30 |
| ☐ 734 | Mike Piazza CL | .30 | .75 |
| ☐ 735 | Jeff Cirillo CL | .10 | .30 |
| ☐ 736 | Paul Molitor CL | .10 | .30 |
| ☐ 737 | Henry Rodriguez CL | .10 | .30 |
| ☐ 738 | Todd Hundley CL | .10 | .30 |
| ☐ 739 | Derek Jeter CL | .40 | 1.00 |
| ☐ 740 | Mark McGwire CL | .40 | 1.00 |
| ☐ 741 | Curt Schilling CL | .10 | .30 |
| ☐ 742 | Jason Kendall CL | .10 | .30 |
| ☐ 743 | Tony Gwynn CL | .20 | .50 |
| ☐ 744 | Barry Bonds CL | .40 | 1.00 |
| ☐ 745 | Ken Griffey Jr. CL | .30 | .75 |
| ☐ 746 | Brian Jordan CL | .10 | .30 |
| ☐ 747 | Juan Gonzalez CL | .10 | .30 |
| ☐ 748 | Joe Carter CL | .10 | .30 |
| ☐ 749 | Arizona Diamondbacks CL | .10 | .30 |
| ☐ 750 | Tampa Bay Devil Rays CL | .10 | .30 |
| ☐ 751 | Hideki Irabu RC | .30 | .75 |
| ☐ 752 | Jeremi Gonzalez RC | .20 | .50 |
| ☐ 753 | Mario Valdez RC | .10 | .30 |
| ☐ 754 | Aaron Boone | .30 | .75 |
| ☐ 755 | Brett Tomko | .10 | .30 |
| ☐ 756 | Janet Wright RC | .30 | .75 |
| ☐ 757 | Ryan McGuire | .10 | .30 |
| ☐ 758 | Jason McDonald | .20 | .50 |
| ☐ 759 | Adrian Brown RC | .20 | .50 |
| ☐ 760 | Keith Foulke RC | .75 | 2.00 |
| ☐ 761 | Bonus Checklist (751-761) | .20 | .50 |
| ☐ P489 | Matt Williams Promo | .40 | 1.00 |
| ☐ NNO | A.Jones Circa AU/200 | 10.00 | 25.00 |

## 2002 Fleer

| | | |
|---|---|---|
| ❑ COMPLETE SET (540) | 30.00 | 80.00 |
| ❑ COMMON CARD (1-540) | .08 | .25 |
| ❑ COMMON CARD (492-531) | .20 | .50 |
| ❑ 1 Darin Erstad FP | .08 | .25 |
| ❑ 2 Randy Johnson FP | .25 | .60 |
| ❑ 3 Chipper Jones FP | .25 | .60 |
| ❑ 4 Jay Gibbons FP | .08 | .25 |
| ❑ 5 Nomar Garciaparra FP | .40 | 1.00 |
| ❑ 6 Sammy Sosa FP | .25 | .60 |
| ❑ 7 Frank Thomas FP | .25 | .60 |
| ❑ 8 Ken Griffey Jr. FP | .40 | 1.00 |
| ❑ 9 Jim Thome FP | .15 | .40 |
| ❑ 10 Todd Helton FP | .15 | .40 |
| ❑ 11 Jeff Weaver FP | .08 | .25 |
| ❑ 12 Cliff Floyd FP | .08 | .25 |
| ❑ 13 Jeff Bagwell FP | .15 | .40 |
| ❑ 14 Mike Sweeney FP | .08 | .25 |
| ❑ 15 Adrian Beltre FP | .08 | .25 |
| ❑ 16 Richie Sexson FP | .08 | .25 |
| ❑ 17 Brad Radke FP | .08 | .25 |
| ❑ 18 Vladimir Guerrero FP | .25 | .60 |
| ❑ 19 Mike Piazza FP | .40 | 1.00 |
| ❑ 20 Derek Jeter FP | .50 | 1.25 |
| ❑ 21 Eric Chavez FP | .08 | .25 |
| ❑ 22 Pat Burrell FP | .08 | .25 |
| ❑ 23 Brian Giles FP | .08 | .25 |
| ❑ 24 Trevor Hoffman FP | .08 | .25 |
| ❑ 25 Barry Bonds FP | .40 | 1.00 |
| ❑ 26 Ichiro Suzuki FP | .40 | 1.00 |
| ❑ 27 Albert Pujols FP | .40 | 1.00 |
| ❑ 28 Ben Grieve FP | .08 | .25 |
| ❑ 29 Alex Rodriguez FP | .40 | 1.00 |
| ❑ 30 Carlos Delgado FP | .08 | .25 |
| ❑ 31 Miguel Tejada | .15 | .40 |
| ❑ 32 Todd Hollandsworth | .08 | .25 |
| ❑ 33 Marlon Anderson | .08 | .25 |
| ❑ 34 Kerry Robinson | .08 | .25 |
| ❑ 35 Chris Richard | .08 | .25 |
| ❑ 36 Jamey Wright | .08 | .25 |
| ❑ 37 Ray Lankford | .15 | .40 |
| ❑ 38 Mike Bordick | .15 | .40 |
| ❑ 39 Danny Graves | .15 | .40 |
| ❑ 40 A.J. Pierzynski | .15 | .40 |
| ❑ 41 Shannon Stewart | .15 | .40 |
| ❑ 42 Tony Armas Jr. | .08 | .25 |
| ❑ 43 Brad Ausmus | .15 | .40 |
| ❑ 44 Alfonso Soriano | .15 | .40 |
| ❑ 45 Junior Spivey | .08 | .25 |
| ❑ 46 Brent Mayne | .08 | .25 |
| ❑ 47 Jim Thome | .25 | .60 |
| ❑ 48 Dan Wilson | .08 | .25 |
| ❑ 49 Geoff Jenkins | .08 | .25 |
| ❑ 50 Kris Benson | .08 | .25 |
| ❑ 51 Rafael Furcal | .15 | .40 |
| ❑ 52 Wiki Gonzalez | .08 | .25 |
| ❑ 53 Jeff Kent | .15 | .40 |
| ❑ 54 Curt Schilling | .25 | .60 |
| ❑ 55 Ken Harvey | .08 | .25 |
| ❑ 56 Roosevelt Brown | .08 | .25 |
| ❑ 57 David Segui | .08 | .25 |
| ❑ 58 Mario Valdez | .08 | .25 |
| ❑ 59 Adam Dunn | .15 | .40 |
| ❑ 60 Bob Howry | .08 | .25 |
| ❑ 61 Michael Barrett | .08 | .25 |
| ❑ 62 Garret Anderson | .15 | .40 |
| ❑ 63 Kelvim Escobar | .08 | .25 |
| ❑ 64 Ben Grieve | .08 | .25 |
| ❑ 65 Randy Johnson | .40 | 1.00 |
| ❑ 66 Jose Offerman | .08 | .25 |
| ❑ 67 Jason Kendall | .15 | .40 |
| ❑ 68 Joel Pineiro | .08 | .25 |
| ❑ 69 Alex Escobar | .08 | .25 |
| ❑ 70 Chris George | .08 | .25 |
| ❑ 71 Bobby Higginson | .15 | .40 |
| ❑ 72 Nomar Garciaparra | .60 | 1.50 |
| ❑ 73 Pat Burrell | .15 | .40 |
| ❑ 74 Lee Stevens | .08 | .25 |
| ❑ 75 Felipe Lopez | .08 | .25 |
| ❑ 76 Al Leiter | .15 | .40 |
| ❑ 77 Jim Edmonds | .15 | .40 |
| ❑ 78 Al Levine | .08 | .25 |
| ❑ 79 Raul Mondesi | .15 | .40 |
| ❑ 80 Jose Valentin | .08 | .25 |
| ❑ 81 Matt Clement | .15 | .40 |
| ❑ 82 Richard Hidalgo | .08 | .25 |
| ❑ 83 Jamie Moyer | .15 | .40 |
| ❑ 84 Brian Schneider | .08 | .25 |
| ❑ 85 John Franco | .15 | .40 |
| ❑ 86 Brian Buchanan | .08 | .25 |
| ❑ 87 Roy Oswalt | .15 | .40 |
| ❑ 88 Johnny Estrada | .08 | .25 |
| ❑ 89 Marcus Giles | .15 | .40 |
| ❑ 90 Carlos Valderrama | .08 | .25 |
| ❑ 91 Mark Mulder | .15 | .40 |
| ❑ 92 Mark Grace | .25 | .60 |
| ❑ 93 Andy Ashby | .08 | .25 |
| ❑ 94 Woody Williams | .08 | .25 |
| ❑ 95 Ben Petrick | .08 | .25 |
| ❑ 96 Roy Halladay | .15 | .40 |
| ❑ 97 Fred McGriff | .25 | .60 |
| ❑ 98 Shawn Green | .15 | .40 |
| ❑ 99 Todd Hundley | .08 | .25 |
| ❑ 100 Carlos Febles | .08 | .25 |
| ❑ 101 Jason Marquis | .08 | .25 |
| ❑ 102 Mike Redmond | .08 | .25 |
| ❑ 103 Shane Halter | .08 | .25 |
| ❑ 104 Tori Nixon | .15 | .40 |
| ❑ 105 Jeremy Giambi | .08 | .25 |
| ❑ 106 Carlos Delgado | .15 | .40 |
| ❑ 107 Richie Sexson | .15 | .40 |
| ❑ 108 Russ Ortiz | .08 | .25 |
| ❑ 109 David Ortiz | .40 | 1.00 |
| ❑ 110 Curtis Leskanic | .08 | .25 |
| ❑ 111 Jay Payton | .08 | .25 |
| ❑ 112 Travis Phelps | .08 | .25 |
| ❑ 113 J.T. Snow | .15 | .40 |
| ❑ 114 Edgar Renteria | .15 | .40 |
| ❑ 115 Freddy Garcia | .15 | .40 |
| ❑ 116 Cliff Floyd | .15 | .40 |
| ❑ 117 Charles Nagy | .08 | .25 |
| ❑ 118 Tony Batista | .08 | .25 |
| ❑ 119 Rafael Palmeiro | .25 | .60 |
| ❑ 120 Darren Dreifort | .08 | .25 |
| ❑ 121 Warren Morris | .08 | .25 |
| ❑ 122 Augie Ojeda | .08 | .25 |
| ❑ 123 Rusty Greer | .15 | .40 |
| ❑ 124 Esteban Yan | .08 | .25 |
| ❑ 125 Corey Patterson | .15 | .40 |
| ❑ 126 Matt Ginter | .08 | .25 |
| ❑ 127 Matt Lawton | .08 | .25 |
| ❑ 128 Miguel Batista | .08 | .25 |
| ❑ 129 Randy Winn | .08 | .25 |
| ❑ 130 Eric Milton | .08 | .25 |
| ❑ 131 Jack Wilson | .08 | .25 |
| ❑ 132 Sean Casey | .15 | .40 |
| ❑ 133 Mike Sweeney | .15 | .40 |
| ❑ 134 Jason Tyner | .08 | .25 |
| ❑ 135 Carlos Hernandez | .08 | .25 |
| ❑ 136 Shea Hillenbrand | .15 | .40 |
| ❑ 137 Shawn Wooten | .08 | .25 |
| ❑ 138 Peter Bergeron | .08 | .25 |
| ❑ 139 Travis Lee | .08 | .25 |
| ❑ 140 Craig Wilson | .08 | .25 |
| ❑ 141 Carlos Guillen | .15 | .40 |
| ❑ 142 Chipper Jones | .40 | 1.00 |
| ❑ 143 Gabe Kapler | .15 | .40 |
| ❑ 144 Raul Ibanez | .08 | .25 |
| ❑ 145 Eric Chavez | .15 | .40 |
| ❑ 146 D'Angelo Jimenez | .08 | .25 |
| ❑ 147 Chad Hermansen | .08 | .25 |
| ❑ 148 Joe Kennedy | .08 | .25 |
| ❑ 149 Mariano Rivera | .40 | 1.00 |
| ❑ 150 Jeff Bagwell | .25 | .60 |
| ❑ 151 Joe McEwing | .08 | .25 |
| ❑ 152 Ronnie Belliard | .08 | .25 |
| ❑ 153 Desi Relaford | .08 | .25 |
| ❑ 154 Vinny Castilla | .15 | .40 |
| ❑ 155 Tim Hudson | .15 | .40 |
| ❑ 156 Wilton Guerrero | .08 | .25 |
| ❑ 157 Raul Casanova | .08 | .25 |
| ❑ 158 Edgardo Alfonzo | .08 | .25 |
| ❑ 159 Derrek Lee | .25 | .60 |
| ❑ 160 Phil Nevin | .15 | .40 |
| ❑ 161 Roger Clemens | .75 | 2.00 |
| ❑ 162 Jason LaRue | .08 | .25 |
| ❑ 163 Brian Lawrence | .08 | .25 |
| ❑ 164 Adrian Beltre | .15 | .40 |
| ❑ 165 Troy Glaus | .15 | .40 |
| ❑ 166 Jeff Weaver | .08 | .25 |
| ❑ 167 B.J. Surhoff | .08 | .25 |
| ❑ 168 Eric Byrnes | .08 | .25 |
| ❑ 169 Mike Sirotka | .08 | .25 |
| ❑ 170 Bill Haselman | .08 | .25 |
| ❑ 171 Javier Vazquez | .15 | .40 |
| ❑ 172 Sidney Ponson | .08 | .25 |
| ❑ 173 Adam Everett | .08 | .25 |
| ❑ 174 Bubba Trammell | .08 | .25 |
| ❑ 175 Robb Nen | .15 | .40 |
| ❑ 176 Barry Larkin | .25 | .60 |
| ❑ 177 Tony Graffanino | .08 | .25 |
| ❑ 178 Rich Garces | .08 | .25 |
| ❑ 179 Juan Uribe | .08 | .25 |
| ❑ 180 Tom Glavine | .25 | .60 |
| ❑ 181 Eric Karros | .15 | .40 |
| ❑ 182 Michael Cuddyer | .08 | .25 |
| ❑ 183 Wade Miller | .08 | .25 |
| ❑ 184 Matt Williams | .15 | .40 |
| ❑ 185 Matt Morris | .15 | .40 |
| ❑ 186 Rickey Henderson | .40 | 1.00 |
| ❑ 187 Trevor Hoffman | .15 | .40 |
| ❑ 188 Wilson Betemit | .08 | .25 |
| ❑ 189 Steve Karsay | .08 | .25 |
| ❑ 190 Frank Catalanotto | .08 | .25 |
| ❑ 191 Jason Schmidt | .15 | .40 |
| ❑ 192 Roger Cedeno | .08 | .25 |
| ❑ 193 Magglio Ordonez | .15 | .40 |
| ❑ 194 Pat Hentgen | .08 | .25 |
| ❑ 195 Mike Lieberthal | .15 | .40 |
| ❑ 196 Andy Pettitte | .25 | .60 |
| ❑ 197 Jay Gibbons | .25 | .60 |
| ❑ 198 Rolando Arrojo | .08 | .25 |
| ❑ 199 Joe Mays | .08 | .25 |
| ❑ 200 Aubrey Huff | .15 | .40 |
| ❑ 201 Nelson Figueroa | .08 | .25 |
| ❑ 202 Paul Konerko | .15 | .40 |
| ❑ 203 Ken Griffey Jr. | .60 | 1.50 |
| ❑ 204 Brandon Duckworth | .08 | .25 |
| ❑ 205 Sammy Sosa | .40 | 1.00 |
| ❑ 206 Carl Everett | .15 | .40 |
| ❑ 207 Scott Rolen | .25 | .60 |
| ❑ 208 Orlando Hernandez | .15 | .40 |
| ❑ 209 Todd Helton | .25 | .60 |
| ❑ 210 Preston Wilson | .15 | .40 |
| ❑ 211 Gil Meche | .08 | .25 |
| ❑ 212 Bill Mueller | .15 | .40 |
| ❑ 213 Craig Biggio | .25 | .60 |
| ❑ 214 Dean Palmer | .15 | .40 |
| ❑ 215 Randy Wolf | .08 | .25 |
| ❑ 216 Jeff Suppan | .08 | .25 |
| ❑ 217 Jimmy Rollins | .15 | .40 |
| ❑ 218 Alexis Gomez | .08 | .25 |
| ❑ 219 Ellis Burks | .15 | .40 |
| ❑ 220 Ramon E. Martinez | .08 | .25 |
| ❑ 221 Ramiro Mendoza | .08 | .25 |
| ❑ 222 Einar Diaz | .08 | .25 |
| ❑ 223 Brent Abernathy | .08 | .25 |
| ❑ 224 Darin Erstad | .15 | .40 |
| ❑ 225 Reggie Taylor | .08 | .25 |
| ❑ 226 Jason Jennings | .08 | .25 |
| ❑ 227 Ray Durham | .15 | .40 |
| ❑ 228 John Parrish | .08 | .25 |
| ❑ 229 Kevin Young | .08 | .25 |
| ❑ 230 Xavier Nady | .08 | .25 |
| ❑ 231 Juan Cruz | .08 | .25 |
| ❑ 232 Greg Norton | .08 | .25 |
| ❑ 233 Barry Bonds | 1.00 | 2.50 |
| ❑ 234 Kip Wells | .08 | .25 |
| ❑ 235 Paul LoDuca | .15 | .40 |
| ❑ 236 Javy Lopez | .15 | .40 |
| ❑ 237 Luis Castillo | .08 | .25 |
| ❑ 238 Tom Gordon | .08 | .25 |
| ❑ 239 Mike Mordecai | .08 | .25 |
| ❑ 240 Damian Rolls | .08 | .25 |
| ❑ 241 Julio Lugo | .08 | .25 |
| ❑ 242 Ichiro Suzuki | .75 | 2.00 |
| ❑ 243 Tony Womack | .08 | .25 |
| ❑ 244 Marlon Anderson | .08 | .25 |
| ❑ 245 Carlos Lee | .15 | .40 |

|  |  | | |
|---|--------|------|------|
| 246 | Alex Rodriguez | .60 | 1.50 |
| 247 | Bernie Williams | .25 | .60 |
| 248 | Scott Sullivan | .08 | .25 |
| 249 | Mike Hampton | .15 | .40 |
| 250 | Orlando Cabrera | .15 | .40 |
| 251 | Benito Santiago | .15 | .40 |
| 252 | Steve Finley | .15 | .40 |
| 253 | Dave Williams | .08 | .25 |
| 254 | Adam Kennedy | .08 | .25 |
| 255 | Omar Vizquel | .25 | .60 |
| 256 | Garrett Stephenson | .08 | .25 |
| 257 | Fernando Tatis | .08 | .25 |
| 258 | Mike Piazza | .60 | 1.50 |
| 259 | Scott Spiezio | .08 | .25 |
| 260 | Jacque Jones | .15 | .40 |
| 261 | Russell Branyan | .08 | .25 |
| 262 | Mark McLemore | .08 | .25 |
| 263 | Mitch Meluskey | .08 | .25 |
| 264 | Marlon Byrd | .08 | .25 |
| 265 | Kyle Farnsworth | .08 | .25 |
| 266 | Billy Sylvester | .08 | .25 |
| 267 | C.C. Sabathia | .15 | .40 |
| 268 | Mark Buehrle | .08 | .25 |
| 269 | Geoff Blum | .08 | .25 |
| 270 | Bret Prinz | .08 | .25 |
| 271 | Placido Polanco | .08 | .25 |
| 272 | John Olerud | .25 | .40 |
| 273 | Pedro Martinez | .25 | .60 |
| 274 | Doug Mientkiewicz | .15 | .40 |
| 275 | Jason Bere | .08 | .25 |
| 276 | Bud Smith | .08 | .25 |
| 277 | Terrence Long | .08 | .25 |
| 278 | Troy Percival | .15 | .40 |
| 279 | Derek Jeter | 1.00 | 2.50 |
| 280 | Eric Owens | .08 | .25 |
| 281 | Jay Bell | .15 | .40 |
| 282 | Mike Cameron | .08 | .25 |
| 283 | Joe Randa | .08 | .25 |
| 284 | Brian Roberts | .15 | .40 |
| 285 | Ryan Klesko | .15 | .40 |
| 286 | Ryan Dempster | .08 | .25 |
| 287 | Cristian Guzman | .08 | .25 |
| 288 | Tim Salmon | .25 | .60 |
| 289 | Mark Johnson | .08 | .25 |
| 290 | Brian Giles | .15 | .40 |
| 291 | Jon Lieber | .08 | .25 |
| 292 | Fernando Vina | .08 | .25 |
| 293 | Mike Mussina | .25 | .60 |
| 294 | Juan Pierre | .15 | .40 |
| 295 | Carlos Beltran | .25 | .60 |
| 296 | Vladimir Guerrero | .40 | 1.00 |
| 297 | Orlando Merced | .08 | .25 |
| 298 | Jose Hernandez | .08 | .25 |
| 299 | Mike Lamb | .08 | .25 |
| 300 | David Eckstein | .15 | .40 |
| 301 | Mark Loretta | .08 | .25 |
| 302 | Greg Vaughn | .08 | .25 |
| 303 | Jose Vidro | .15 | .40 |
| 304 | Jose Ortiz | .08 | .25 |
| 305 | Mark Grudzielanek | .08 | .25 |
| 306 | Rob Bell | .08 | .25 |
| 307 | Elmer Dessens | .08 | .25 |
| 308 | Tomas Perez | .08 | .25 |
| 309 | Jerry Hairston Jr. | .08 | .25 |
| 310 | Mike Stanton | .08 | .25 |
| 311 | Todd Walker | .08 | .25 |
| 312 | Jason Varitek | .40 | 1.00 |
| 313 | Masato Yoshii | .08 | .25 |
| 314 | Ben Sheets | .15 | .40 |
| 315 | Roberto Hernandez | .08 | .25 |
| 316 | Eli Marrero | .08 | .25 |
| 317 | Josh Beckett | .15 | .40 |
| 318 | Robert Fick | .08 | .25 |
| 319 | Aramis Ramirez | .15 | .40 |
| 320 | Bartolo Colon | .15 | .40 |
| 321 | Kenny Kelly | .08 | .25 |
| 322 | Luis Gonzalez | .15 | .40 |
| 323 | John Smoltz | .25 | .60 |
| 324 | Homer Bush | .08 | .25 |
| 325 | Kevin Millwood | .15 | .40 |
| 326 | Manny Ramirez | .25 | .60 |
| 327 | Armando Benitez | .08 | .25 |
| 328 | Luis Alicea | .08 | .25 |
| 329 | Mark Kotsay | .15 | .40 |
| 330 | Felix Rodriguez | .08 | .25 |
| 331 | Eddie Taubensee | .08 | .25 |
| 332 | John Burkett | .08 | .25 |
| 333 | Ramon Ortiz | .08 | .25 |
| 334 | Daryle Ward | .08 | .25 |
| 335 | Jarrod Washburn | .08 | .25 |
| 336 | Benji Gil | .08 | .25 |
| 337 | Mike Lowell | .15 | .40 |
| 338 | Larry Walker | .15 | .40 |
| 339 | Andruw Jones | .25 | .60 |
| 340 | Scott Elarton | .08 | .25 |
| 341 | Tony McKnight | .08 | .25 |
| 342 | Frank Thomas | .40 | 1.00 |
| 343 | Kevin Brown | .15 | .40 |
| 344 | Jermaine Dye | .15 | .40 |
| 345 | Luis Rivas | .08 | .25 |
| 346 | Jeff Conine | .15 | .40 |
| 347 | Bobby Kielty | .08 | .25 |
| 348 | Jeffrey Hammonds | .08 | .25 |
| 349 | Keith Foulke | .15 | .40 |
| 350 | Dave Martinez | .08 | .25 |
| 351 | Adam Eaton | .08 | .25 |
| 352 | Brandon Inge | .08 | .25 |
| 353 | Tyler Houston | .08 | .25 |
| 354 | Bobby Abreu | .15 | .40 |
| 355 | Ivan Rodriguez | .25 | .60 |
| 356 | Doug Glanville | .08 | .25 |
| 357 | Jorge Julio | .08 | .25 |
| 358 | Kerry Wood | .15 | .40 |
| 359 | Eric Munson | .08 | .25 |
| 360 | Joe Crede | .15 | .40 |
| 361 | Denny Neagle | .08 | .25 |
| 362 | Vance Wilson | .08 | .25 |
| 363 | Neifi Perez | .08 | .25 |
| 364 | Darryl Kile | .15 | .40 |
| 365 | Jose Macias | .08 | .25 |
| 366 | Michael Coleman | .08 | .25 |
| 367 | Erubiel Durazo | .08 | .25 |
| 368 | Darrin Fletcher | .08 | .25 |
| 369 | Matt White | .08 | .25 |
| 370 | Marvin Benard | .08 | .25 |
| 371 | Brad Penny | .08 | .25 |
| 372 | Chuck Finley | .15 | .40 |
| 373 | Delino DeShields | .08 | .25 |
| 374 | Adrian Brown | .08 | .25 |
| 375 | Corey Koskie | .08 | .25 |
| 376 | Kazuhiro Sasaki | .15 | .40 |
| 377 | Brent Butler | .08 | .25 |
| 378 | Paul Wilson | .08 | .25 |
| 379 | Scott Williamson | .08 | .25 |
| 380 | Mike Young | .40 | 1.00 |
| 381 | Toby Hall | .08 | .25 |
| 382 | Shane Reynolds | .08 | .25 |
| 383 | Tom Goodwin | .08 | .25 |
| 384 | Seth Etherton | .08 | .25 |
| 385 | Billy Wagner | .15 | .40 |
| 386 | Josh Phelps | .08 | .25 |
| 387 | Kyle Lohse | .08 | .25 |
| 388 | Jeremy Fikac | .08 | .25 |
| 389 | Jorge Posada | .25 | .60 |
| 390 | Bret Boone | .15 | .40 |
| 391 | Angel Berroa | .08 | .25 |
| 392 | Matt Mantei | .08 | .25 |
| 393 | Alex Gonzalez | .08 | .25 |
| 394 | Scott Strickland | .08 | .25 |
| 395 | Charles Johnson | .15 | .40 |
| 396 | Ramon Hernandez | .08 | .25 |
| 397 | Damian Jackson | .08 | .25 |
| 398 | Albert Pujols | .75 | 2.00 |
| 399 | Gary Bennett | .08 | .25 |
| 400 | Edgar Martinez | .25 | .60 |
| 401 | Carl Pavano | .08 | .25 |
| 402 | Chris Gomez | .08 | .25 |
| 403 | Jaret Wright | .08 | .25 |
| 404 | Lance Berkman | .15 | .40 |
| 405 | Robert Person | .08 | .25 |
| 406 | Brook Fordyce | .08 | .25 |
| 407 | Adam Pettyjohn | .08 | .25 |
| 408 | Chris Carpenter | .08 | .25 |
| 409 | Rey Ordonez | .08 | .25 |
| 410 | Eric Gagne | .15 | .40 |
| 411 | Damion Easley | .08 | .25 |
| 412 | A.J. Burnett | .15 | .40 |
| 413 | Aaron Boone | .15 | .40 |
| 414 | J.D. Drew | .25 | .60 |
| 415 | Kelly Stinnett | .08 | .25 |
| 416 | Mark Quinn | .08 | .25 |
| 417 | Brad Radke | .15 | .40 |
| 418 | Jose Cruz Jr. | .15 | .40 |
| 419 | Greg Maddux | .60 | 1.50 |
| 420 | Steve Cox | .08 | .25 |
| 421 | Torii Hunter | .15 | .40 |
| 422 | Sandy Alomar Jr. | .08 | .25 |
| 423 | Barry Zito | .15 | .40 |
| 424 | Bill Hall | .15 | .40 |
| 425 | Marquis Grissom | .15 | .40 |
| 426 | Rich Aurilia | .08 | .25 |
| 427 | Royce Clayton | .08 | .25 |
| 428 | Travis Fryman | .15 | .40 |
| 429 | Pablo Ozuna | .08 | .25 |
| 430 | David Dellucci | .08 | .25 |
| 431 | Vernon Wells | .15 | .40 |
| 432 | Gregg Zaun CP | .08 | .25 |
| 433 | Alex Gonzalez CP | .08 | .25 |
| 434 | Hideo Nomo CP | .40 | 1.00 |
| 435 | Jeromy Burnitz CP | .15 | .40 |
| 436 | Gary Sheffield CP | .15 | .40 |
| 437 | Tino Martinez CP | .25 | .60 |
| 438 | Tsuyoshi Shinjo CP | .15 | .40 |
| 439 | Chan Ho Park CP | .15 | .40 |
| 440 | Tony Clark CP | .08 | .25 |
| 441 | Brad Fullmer CP | .08 | .25 |
| 442 | Jason Giambi CP | .25 | .60 |
| 443 | Billy Koch CP | .08 | .25 |
| 444 | Mo Vaughn CP | .15 | .40 |
| 445 | Alex Ochoa CP | .08 | .25 |
| 446 | Darren Lewis CP | .08 | .25 |
| 447 | John Rocker CP | .15 | .40 |
| 448 | Scott Hatteberg CP | .08 | .25 |
| 449 | Brady Anderson CP | .15 | .40 |
| 450 | Chuck Knoblauch CP | .15 | .40 |
| 451 | Pokey Reese CP | .08 | .25 |
| 452 | Brian Jordan CP | .15 | .40 |
| 453 | Albie Lopez CP | .08 | .25 |
| 454 | David Bell CP | .08 | .25 |
| 455 | Juan Gonzalez CP | .15 | .40 |
| 456 | Terry Adams CP | .08 | .25 |
| 457 | Kenny Lofton CP | .15 | .40 |
| 458 | Shawn Estes CP | .08 | .25 |
| 459 | Josh Fogg CP | .08 | .25 |
| 460 | Dmitri Young CP | .08 | .25 |
| 461 | Johnny Damon Sox CP | .25 | .60 |
| 462 | Chris Singleton CP | .08 | .25 |
| 463 | Ricky Ledee CP | .08 | .25 |
| 464 | Dustin Hermanson CP | .08 | .25 |
| 465 | Aaron Sele CP | .08 | .25 |
| 466 | Chris Stynes CP | .08 | .25 |
| 467 | Matt Stairs CP | .08 | .25 |
| 468 | Kevin Appier CP | .15 | .40 |
| 469 | Omar Daal CP | .08 | .25 |
| 470 | Moises Alou CP | .15 | .40 |
| 471 | Juan Encarnacion CP | .08 | .25 |
| 472 | Robin Ventura CP | .15 | .40 |
| 473 | Eric Hinske CP | .25 | .60 |
| 474 | Rondell White CP | .15 | .40 |
| 475 | Carlos Pena CP | .08 | .25 |
| 476 | Craig Paquette CP | .08 | .25 |
| 477 | Marty Cordova CP | .08 | .25 |
| 478 | Brett Tomko CP | .08 | .25 |
| 479 | Reggie Sanders CP | .08 | .25 |
| 480 | Roberto Alomar CP | .25 | .60 |
| 481 | Jeff Cirillo CP | .08 | .25 |
| 482 | Todd Zeile CP | .15 | .40 |
| 483 | John Vander Wal CP | .08 | .25 |
| 484 | Rick Helling CP | .08 | .25 |
| 485 | Jeff D'Amico CP | .08 | .25 |
| 486 | David Justice CP | .15 | .40 |
| 487 | Jason Isringhausen CP | .15 | .40 |
| 488 | Shigetoshi Hasegawa CP | .15 | .40 |
| 489 | Eric Young CP | .08 | .25 |
| 490 | David Wells CP | .15 | .40 |
| 491 | Ruben Sierra CP | .08 | .25 |
| 492 | Aaron Cook FF RC | .30 | .75 |
| 493 | Takahito Nomura FF RC | .30 | .75 |
| 494 | Austin Kearns FF RC | .50 | 1.25 |
| 495 | Kazuhisa Ishii FF RC | .50 | 1.25 |
| 496 | Mark Teixeira FF RC | .75 | 2.00 |
| 497 | Rene Reyes FF RC | .30 | .75 |
| 498 | Tim Spooneybarger FF RC | .20 | .50 |
| 499 | Ben Broussard FF RC | .20 | .50 |
| 500 | Eric Cyr FF RC | .20 | .50 |
| 501 | Anastacio Martinez FF RC | .30 | .75 |
| 502 | Morgan Ensberg FF RC | .30 | .75 |
| 503 | Steve Kent FF RC | .20 | .50 |
| 504 | Franklin Nunez FF RC | .30 | .75 |
| 505 | Adam Walker FF RC | .20 | .50 |
| 506 | Anderson Machado FF RC | .30 | .75 |
| 507 | Ryan Drese FF RC | .20 | .50 |
| 508 | Luis Ugueto FF RC | .20 | .50 |
| 509 | Jorge Nunez FF RC | .30 | .75 |

| | | |
|---|---|---|
| ☐ 510 Colby Lewis | .20 | .50 |
| ☐ 511 Ron Calloway FF RC | .30 | .75 |
| ☐ 512 Hansel Izquierdo FF RC | .30 | .75 |
| ☐ 513 Jason Lane FF | .30 | .75 |
| ☐ 514 Rafael Soriano FF | .20 | .50 |
| ☐ 515 Jackson Melian FF | .20 | .50 |
| ☐ 516 Edwin Almonte FF RC | .30 | .75 |
| ☐ 517 Satoru Komiyama FF RC | .30 | .75 |
| ☐ 518 Corey Thurman FF RC | .30 | .75 |
| ☐ 519 Jorge De La Rosa FF RC | .30 | .75 |
| ☐ 520 Victor Martinez FF | .75 | 2.00 |
| ☐ 521 Dewon Brazelton FF | .20 | .50 |
| ☐ 522 Marlon Byrd FF | .20 | .50 |
| ☐ 523 Jae Seo FF | .20 | .50 |
| ☐ 524 Orlando Hudson FF | .20 | .50 |
| ☐ 525 Sean Burroughs FF | .20 | .50 |
| ☐ 526 Ryan Langerhans FF | .30 | .75 |
| ☐ 527 David Kelton FF | .20 | .50 |
| ☐ 528 So Taguchi FF RC | .50 | 1.25 |
| ☐ 529 Tyler Walker FF | .20 | .50 |
| ☐ 530 Hank Blalock FF | .50 | 1.25 |
| ☐ 531 Mark Prior FF | .50 | 1.25 |
| ☐ 532 Yankee Stadium CL | .15 | .40 |
| ☐ 533 Fenway Park CL | .15 | .40 |
| ☐ 534 Wrigley Field CL | .15 | .40 |
| ☐ 535 Dodger Stadium CL | .15 | .40 |
| ☐ 536 Camden Yards CL | .15 | .40 |
| ☐ 537 PacBell Park CL | .08 | .25 |
| ☐ 538 Jacobs Field CL | .08 | .25 |
| ☐ 539 SAFECO Field CL | .08 | .25 |
| ☐ 540 Miller Field CL | .08 | .25 |
| ☐ P279 Derek Jeter Promo | | |

## 2006 Fleer

| | | |
|---|---|---|
| ☐ Alay Soler RC | | |
| ☐ COMP.FACT.SET (430) | 20.00 | 50.00 |
| ☐ COMPLETE SET (400) | 15.00 | 40.00 |
| ☐ COMMON CARD (1-400) | .15 | .40 |
| ☐ COMMON ROOKIE | .20 | .50 |
| ☐ COMMON ROOKIE (401-430) | .25 | .60 |
| ☐ 401-430 AVAIL. IN FLEER FACT.SET | | |
| ☐ 1 Adam Kennedy | .15 | .40 |
| ☐ 2 Bartolo Colon | .15 | .40 |
| ☐ 3 Bengie Molina | .15 | .40 |
| ☐ 4 Chone Figgins | .15 | .40 |
| ☐ 5 Dallas McPherson | .15 | .40 |
| ☐ 6 Darin Erstad | .15 | .40 |
| ☐ 7 Francisco Rodriguez | .15 | .40 |
| ☐ 8 Garret Anderson | .15 | .40 |
| ☐ 9 Jarrod Washburn | .15 | .40 |
| ☐ 10 John Lackey | .15 | .40 |
| ☐ 11 Orlando Cabrera | .15 | .40 |
| ☐ 12 Ryan Theriot RC | .20 | .50 |
| ☐ 13 Steve Finley | .15 | .40 |
| ☐ 14 Vladimir Guerrero | .40 | 1.00 |
| ☐ 15 Adam Everett | .15 | .40 |
| ☐ 16 Andy Pettitte | .25 | .60 |
| ☐ 17 Charlton Jimerson (RC) | .20 | .50 |
| ☐ 18 Brad Lidge | .15 | .40 |
| ☐ 19 Chris Burke | .15 | .40 |
| ☐ 20 Craig Biggio | .25 | .60 |
| ☐ 21 Jason Lane | .15 | .40 |
| ☐ 22 Jeff Bagwell | .25 | .60 |
| ☐ 23 Lance Berkman | .15 | .40 |
| ☐ 24 Morgan Ensberg | .15 | .40 |
| ☐ 25 Roger Clemens | .75 | 2.00 |
| ☐ 26 Roy Oswalt | .15 | .40 |
| ☐ 27 Willy Taveras | .15 | .40 |
| ☐ 28 Barry Zito | .15 | .40 |
| ☐ 29 Bobby Crosby | .15 | .40 |
| ☐ 30 Bobby Kielty | .15 | .40 |
| ☐ 31 Dan Johnson | .15 | .40 |
| ☐ 32 Danny Haren | .15 | .40 |
| ☐ 33 Eric Chavez | .15 | .40 |

| | | |
|---|---|---|
| ☐ 34 Huston Street | .15 | .40 |
| ☐ 35 Jason Kendall | .15 | .40 |
| ☐ 36 Jay Payton | .15 | .40 |
| ☐ 37 Joe Blanton | .15 | .40 |
| ☐ 38 Mark Kotsay | .15 | .40 |
| ☐ 39 Nick Swisher | .15 | .40 |
| ☐ 40 Rich Harden | .15 | .40 |
| ☐ 41 Ron Flores RC | .20 | .50 |
| ☐ 42 Alex Rios | .15 | .40 |
| ☐ 43 John-Ford Griffin (RC) | .20 | .50 |
| ☐ 44 Dave Bush | .15 | .40 |
| ☐ 45 Eric Hinske | .15 | .40 |
| ☐ 46 Frank Catalanotto | .15 | .40 |
| ☐ 47 Gustavo Chacin | .15 | .40 |
| ☐ 48 Josh Towers | .15 | .40 |
| ☐ 49 Miguel Batista | .15 | .40 |
| ☐ 50 Orlando Hudson | .15 | .40 |
| ☐ 51 Roy Halladay | .15 | .40 |
| ☐ 52 Shea Hillenbrand | .15 | .40 |
| ☐ 53 Shaun Marcum (RC) | .20 | .50 |
| ☐ 54 Vernon Wells | .15 | .40 |
| ☐ 55 Adam LaRoche | .15 | .40 |
| ☐ 56 Andruw Jones | .25 | .60 |
| ☐ 57 Chipper Jones | .40 | 1.00 |
| ☐ 58 Anthony Lerew (RC) | .20 | .50 |
| ☐ 59 Jeff Francoeur | .40 | 1.00 |
| ☐ 60 John Smoltz | .25 | .60 |
| ☐ 61 Johnny Estrada | .15 | .40 |
| ☐ 62 Julio Franco | .15 | .40 |
| ☐ 63 Joey Devine RC | .20 | .50 |
| ☐ 64 Marcus Giles | .15 | .40 |
| ☐ 65 Mike Hampton | .15 | .40 |
| ☐ 66 Rafael Furcal | .15 | .40 |
| ☐ 67 Chuck James (RC) | .30 | .75 |
| ☐ 68 Tim Hudson | .15 | .40 |
| ☐ 69 Ben Sheets | .15 | .40 |
| ☐ 70 Bill Hall | .15 | .40 |
| ☐ 71 Brady Clark | .15 | .40 |
| ☐ 72 Carlos Lee | .15 | .40 |
| ☐ 73 Chris Capuano | .15 | .40 |
| ☐ 74 Nelson Cruz (RC) | .30 | .75 |
| ☐ 75 Derrick Turnbow | .15 | .40 |
| ☐ 76 Doug Davis | .15 | .40 |
| ☐ 77 Geoff Jenkins | .15 | .40 |
| ☐ 78 J.J. Hardy | .15 | .40 |
| ☐ 79 Lyle Overbay | .15 | .40 |
| ☐ 80 Prince Fielder | .60 | 1.50 |
| ☐ 81 Rickie Weeks | .15 | .40 |
| ☐ 82 Albert Pujols | .75 | 2.00 |
| ☐ 83 Chris Carpenter | .15 | .40 |
| ☐ 84 David Eckstein | .15 | .40 |
| ☐ 85 Jason Isringhausen | .15 | .40 |
| ☐ 86 Tyler Johnson (RC) | .20 | .50 |
| ☐ 87 Adam Wainwright (RC) | .30 | .75 |
| ☐ 88 Jim Edmonds | .25 | .60 |
| ☐ 89 Chris Duncan (RC) | .20 | .50 |
| ☐ 90 Mark Grudzielanek | .15 | .40 |
| ☐ 91 Mark Mulder | .15 | .40 |
| ☐ 92 Matt Morris | .15 | .40 |
| ☐ 93 Reggie Sanders | .15 | .40 |
| ☐ 94 Scott Rolen | .25 | .60 |
| ☐ 95 Yadier Molina | .15 | .40 |
| ☐ 96 Aramis Ramirez | .15 | .40 |
| ☐ 97 Carlos Zambrano | .15 | .40 |
| ☐ 98 Corey Patterson | .15 | .40 |
| ☐ 99 Derrek Lee | .15 | .40 |
| ☐ 100 Glendon Rusch | .15 | .40 |
| ☐ 101 Greg Maddux | .60 | 1.50 |
| ☐ 102 Jeromy Burnitz | .15 | .40 |
| ☐ 103 Kerry Wood | .15 | .40 |
| ☐ 104 Mark Prior | .25 | .60 |
| ☐ 105 Michael Barrett | .15 | .40 |
| ☐ 106 Geovany Soto (RC) | .50 | 1.25 |
| ☐ 107 Nomar Garciaparra | .40 | 1.00 |
| ☐ 108 Ryan Dempster | .15 | .40 |
| ☐ 109 Todd Walker | .15 | .40 |
| ☐ 110 Alex S. Gonzalez | .15 | .40 |
| ☐ 111 Aubrey Huff | .15 | .40 |
| ☐ 112 Victor Diaz | .15 | .40 |
| ☐ 113 Carl Crawford | .15 | .40 |
| ☐ 114 Danys Baez | .15 | .40 |
| ☐ 115 Joey Gathright | .15 | .40 |
| ☐ 116 Jonny Gomes | .15 | .40 |
| ☐ 117 Jorge Cantu | .15 | .40 |
| ☐ 118 Julio Lugo | .15 | .40 |
| ☐ 119 Rocco Baldelli | .15 | .40 |
| ☐ 120 Scott Kazmir | .25 | .60 |
| ☐ 121 Toby Hall | .15 | .40 |

| | | |
|---|---|---|
| ☐ 122 Tim Corcoran RC | .20 | .50 |
| ☐ 123 Alex Cintron | .15 | .40 |
| ☐ 124 Brandon Webb | .15 | .40 |
| ☐ 125 Chad Tracy | .15 | .40 |
| ☐ 126 Dustin Nippert (RC) | .20 | .50 |
| ☐ 127 Claudio Vargas | .15 | .40 |
| ☐ 128 Craig Counsell | .15 | .40 |
| ☐ 129 Javier Vazquez | .15 | .40 |
| ☐ 130 Jose Valverde | .15 | .40 |
| ☐ 131 Luis Gonzalez | .15 | .40 |
| ☐ 132 Royce Clayton | .15 | .40 |
| ☐ 133 Russ Ortiz | .15 | .40 |
| ☐ 134 Shawn Green | .15 | .40 |
| ☐ 135 Tony Clark | .15 | .40 |
| ☐ 136 Troy Glaus | .15 | .40 |
| ☐ 137 Brad Penny | .15 | .40 |
| ☐ 138 Cesar Izturis | .15 | .40 |
| ☐ 139 Derek Lowe | .15 | .40 |
| ☐ 140 Eric Gagne | .15 | .40 |
| ☐ 141 Hee Seop Choi | .15 | .40 |
| ☐ 142 J.D. Drew | .15 | .40 |
| ☐ 143 Jason Phillips | .15 | .40 |
| ☐ 144 Jayson Werth | .15 | .40 |
| ☐ 145 Jeff Kent | .15 | .40 |
| ☐ 146 Jeff Weaver | .15 | .40 |
| ☐ 147 Milton Bradley | .15 | .40 |
| ☐ 148 Odalis Perez | .15 | .40 |
| ☐ 149 Hong-Chih Kuo (RC) | .50 | 1.25 |
| ☐ 150 Brian Myrow RC | .20 | .50 |
| ☐ 151 Armando Benitez | .15 | .40 |
| ☐ 152 Edgardo Alfonzo | .15 | .40 |
| ☐ 153 J.T. Snow | .15 | .40 |
| ☐ 154 Jason Schmidt | .15 | .40 |
| ☐ 155 Lance Niekro | .15 | .40 |
| ☐ 156 Doug Clark (RC) | .20 | .50 |
| ☐ 157 Dan Ortmeier (RC) | .20 | .50 |
| ☐ 158 Moises Alou | .15 | .40 |
| ☐ 159 Noah Lowry | .15 | .40 |
| ☐ 160 Omar Vizquel | .25 | .60 |
| ☐ 161 Pedro Feliz | .15 | .40 |
| ☐ 162 Randy Winn | .15 | .40 |
| ☐ 163 Jeremy Accardo RC | .20 | .50 |
| ☐ 164 Aaron Boone | .15 | .40 |
| ☐ 165 Ryan Garko (RC) | .20 | .50 |
| ☐ 166 C.C. Sabathia | .15 | .40 |
| ☐ 167 Casey Blake | .15 | .40 |
| ☐ 168 Cliff Lee | .15 | .40 |
| ☐ 169 Coco Crisp | .15 | .40 |
| ☐ 170 Grady Sizemore | .25 | .60 |
| ☐ 171 Jake Westbrook | .15 | .40 |
| ☐ 172 Jhonny Peralta | .15 | .40 |
| ☐ 173 Kevin Millwood | .15 | .40 |
| ☐ 174 Scott Elarton | .15 | .40 |
| ☐ 175 Travis Hafner | .15 | .40 |
| ☐ 176 Victor Martinez | .15 | .40 |
| ☐ 177 Adrian Beltre | .15 | .40 |
| ☐ 178 Eddie Guardado | .15 | .40 |
| ☐ 179 Felix Hernandez | .25 | .60 |
| ☐ 180 Gil Meche | .15 | .40 |
| ☐ 181 Ichiro Suzuki | .60 | 1.50 |
| ☐ 182 Jamie Moyer | .15 | .40 |
| ☐ 183 Jeremy Reed | .15 | .40 |
| ☐ 184 Jaime Bubela (RC) | .25 | .60 |
| ☐ 185 Raul Ibanez | .25 | .60 |
| ☐ 186 Richie Sexson | .15 | .40 |
| ☐ 187 Ryan Franklin | .15 | .40 |
| ☐ 188 Jeff Harris RC | .15 | .40 |
| ☐ 189 A.J. Burnett | .15 | .40 |
| ☐ 190 Josh Wilson (RC) | .20 | .50 |
| ☐ 191 Josh Johnson (RC) | .30 | .75 |
| ☐ 192 Carlos Delgado | .15 | .40 |
| ☐ 193 Dontrelle Willis | .15 | .40 |
| ☐ 194 Bernie Castro (RC) | .20 | .50 |
| ☐ 195 Josh Beckett | .15 | .40 |
| ☐ 196 Juan Encarnacion | .15 | .40 |
| ☐ 197 Juan Pierre | .15 | .40 |
| ☐ 198 Robert Andino RC | .20 | .50 |
| ☐ 199 Miguel Cabrera | .25 | .60 |
| ☐ 200 Ryan Jorgensen RC | .20 | .50 |
| ☐ 201 Paul Lo Duca | .15 | .40 |
| ☐ 202 Todd Jones | .15 | .40 |
| ☐ 203 Braden Looper | .15 | .40 |
| ☐ 204 Carlos Beltran | .15 | .40 |
| ☐ 205 Cliff Floyd | .15 | .40 |
| ☐ 206 David Wright | .60 | 1.50 |
| ☐ 207 Doug Mientkiewicz | .15 | .40 |
| ☐ 208 Jae Seo | .15 | .40 |
| ☐ 209 Jose Reyes | .40 | 1.00 |

|  |  | | |
|---|---|---|---|
| 210 | Anderson Hernandez (RC) | .20 | .50 |
| 211 | Miguel Cairo | .15 | .40 |
| 212 | Mike Cameron | .15 | .40 |
| 213 | Mike Piazza | .40 | 1.00 |
| 214 | Pedro Martinez | .25 | .60 |
| 215 | Tom Glavine | .25 | .60 |
| 216 | Tim Hamulack (RC) | .15 | .40 |
| 217 | Brad Wilkerson | .15 | .40 |
| 218 | Darrell Rasner (RC) | .15 | .40 |
| 219 | Chad Cordero | .15 | .40 |
| 220 | Cristian Guzman | .15 | .40 |
| 221 | Jason Bergmann RC | .20 | .50 |
| 222 | John Patterson | .15 | .40 |
| 223 | Jose Guillen | .15 | .40 |
| 224 | Jose Vidro | .15 | .40 |
| 225 | Livan Hernandez | .15 | .40 |
| 226 | Nick Johnson | .15 | .40 |
| 227 | Preston Wilson | .15 | .40 |
| 228 | Ryan Zimmerman (RC) | 1.00 | 2.50 |
| 229 | Vinny Castilla | .15 | .40 |
| 230 | B.J. Ryan | .15 | .40 |
| 231 | B.J. Surhoff | .15 | .40 |
| 232 | Brian Roberts | .15 | .40 |
| 233 | Walter Young (RC) | .20 | .50 |
| 234 | Daniel Cabrera | .15 | .40 |
| 235 | Erik Bedard | .15 | .40 |
| 236 | Javy Lopez | .15 | .40 |
| 237 | Jay Gibbons | .15 | .40 |
| 238 | Luis Matos | .15 | .40 |
| 239 | Melvin Mora | .15 | .40 |
| 240 | Miguel Tejada | .15 | .40 |
| 241 | Rafael Palmeiro | .25 | .60 |
| 242 | Alejandro Freire RC | .15 | .40 |
| 243 | Sammy Sosa | .40 | 1.00 |
| 244 | Adam Eaton | .15 | .40 |
| 245 | Brian Giles | .15 | .40 |
| 246 | Brian Lawrence | .15 | .40 |
| 247 | Dave Roberts | .15 | .40 |
| 248 | Jake Peavy | .15 | .40 |
| 249 | Khalil Greene | .25 | .60 |
| 250 | Mark Loretta | .15 | .40 |
| 251 | Ramon Hernandez | .15 | .40 |
| 252 | Ryan Klesko | .15 | .40 |
| 253 | Trevor Hoffman | .15 | .40 |
| 254 | Woody Williams | .15 | .40 |
| 255 | Craig Breslow RC | .20 | .50 |
| 256 | Billy Wagner | .15 | .40 |
| 257 | Bobby Abreu | .15 | .40 |
| 258 | Brett Myers | .15 | .40 |
| 259 | Chase Utley | .40 | 1.00 |
| 260 | David Bell | .15 | .40 |
| 261 | Jim Thome | .25 | .60 |
| 262 | Jimmy Rollins | .15 | .40 |
| 263 | Jon Lieber | .15 | .40 |
| 264 | Danny Sandoval RC | .20 | .50 |
| 265 | Mike Lieberthal | .15 | .40 |
| 266 | Pat Burrell | .15 | .40 |
| 267 | Randy Wolf | .15 | .40 |
| 268 | Ryan Howard | .60 | 1.50 |
| 269 | J.J. Furmaniak (RC) | .20 | .50 |
| 270 | Ronny Paulino (RC) | .20 | .50 |
| 271 | Craig Wilson | .15 | .40 |
| 272 | Bryan Bullington (RC) | .20 | .50 |
| 273 | Jack Wilson | .15 | .40 |
| 274 | Jason Bay | .15 | .40 |
| 275 | Matt Capps (RC) | .20 | .50 |
| 276 | Oliver Perez | .15 | .40 |
| 277 | Rob Mackowiak | .15 | .40 |
| 278 | Tom Gorzelanny (RC) | .15 | .40 |
| 279 | Zach Duke | .15 | .40 |
| 280 | Alfonso Soriano | .15 | .40 |
| 281 | Chris R. Young | .15 | .40 |
| 282 | David Dellucci | .15 | .40 |
| 283 | Francisco Cordero | .15 | .40 |
| 284 | Jason Botts (RC) UER | .20 | .50 |
| 285 | Hank Blalock | .15 | .40 |
| 286 | Josh Rupe (RC) | .20 | .50 |
| 287 | Kevin Mench | .15 | .40 |
| 288 | Laynce Nix | .15 | .40 |
| 289 | Mark Teixeira | .25 | .60 |
| 290 | Michael Young | .15 | .40 |
| 291 | Richard Hidalgo | .15 | .40 |
| 292 | Scott Feldman RC | .30 | .75 |
| 293 | Bill Mueller | .15 | .40 |
| 294 | Hanley Ramirez (RC) | .50 | 1.25 |
| 295 | Curt Schilling | .15 | .40 |
| 296 | David Ortiz | .25 | .60 |
| 297 | Alejandro Machado (RC) | .20 | .50 |
| 298 | Edgar Renteria | .15 | .40 |
| 299 | Jason Varitek | .40 | 1.00 |
| 300 | Johnny Damon | .25 | .60 |
| 301 | Keith Foulke | .15 | .40 |
| 302 | Manny Ramirez | .25 | .60 |
| 303 | Matt Clement | .15 | .40 |
| 304 | Craig Hansen RC | .75 | 2.00 |
| 305 | Tim Wakefield | .15 | .40 |
| 306 | Trot Nixon | .15 | .40 |
| 307 | Aaron Harang | .15 | .40 |
| 308 | Adam Dunn | .15 | .40 |
| 309 | Austin Kearns | .15 | .40 |
| 310 | Brandon Claussen | .15 | .40 |
| 311 | Chris Booker | .15 | .40 |
| 312 | Edwin Encarnacion | .15 | .40 |
| 313 | Chris Denorfia (RC) | .20 | .50 |
| 314 | Felipe Lopez | .15 | .40 |
| 315 | Miguel Perez (RC) | .20 | .50 |
| 316 | Ken Griffey Jr. | .60 | 1.50 |
| 317 | Ryan Freel | .15 | .40 |
| 318 | Sean Casey | .15 | .40 |
| 319 | Wily Mo Pena | .15 | .40 |
| 320 | Mike Esposito (RC) | .20 | .50 |
| 321 | Aaron Miles | .15 | .40 |
| 322 | Brad Hawpe | .15 | .40 |
| 323 | Brian Fuentes | .15 | .40 |
| 324 | Clint Barmes | .15 | .40 |
| 325 | Cory Sullivan | .15 | .40 |
| 326 | Garrett Atkins | .15 | .40 |
| 327 | J.D. Closser | .15 | .40 |
| 328 | Jeff Francis | .15 | .40 |
| 329 | Luis Gonzalez | .15 | .40 |
| 330 | Matt Holliday | .40 | 1.00 |
| 331 | Todd Helton | .25 | .60 |
| 332 | Angel Berroa | .15 | .40 |
| 333 | David DeJesus | .15 | .40 |
| 334 | Emil Brown | .15 | .40 |
| 335 | Jeremy Affeldt | .15 | .40 |
| 336 | Chris Demaria RC | .20 | .50 |
| 337 | Mark Teahen | .15 | .40 |
| 338 | Matt Stairs | .15 | .40 |
| 339 | Steve Stemle RC | .20 | .50 |
| 340 | Mike Sweeney | .15 | .40 |
| 341 | Runelvys Hernandez | .15 | .40 |
| 342 | Jonah Bayliss RC | .20 | .50 |
| 343 | Zack Greinke | .15 | .40 |
| 344 | Brandon Inge | .15 | .40 |
| 345 | Carlos Guillen | .15 | .40 |
| 346 | Carlos Pena | .15 | .40 |
| 347 | Chris Shelton | .15 | .40 |
| 348 | Craig Monroe | .15 | .40 |
| 349 | Dmitri Young | .15 | .40 |
| 350 | Ivan Rodriguez | .25 | .60 |
| 351 | Jeremy Bonderman | .15 | .40 |
| 352 | Magglio Ordonez | .15 | .40 |
| 353 | Mark Woodyard (RC) | .20 | .50 |
| 354 | Omar Infante | .15 | .40 |
| 355 | Placido Polanco | .15 | .40 |
| 356 | Rondell White | .15 | .40 |
| 357 | Brad Radke | .15 | .40 |
| 358 | Carlos Silva | .15 | .40 |
| 359 | Jacque Jones | .15 | .40 |
| 360 | Joe Mauer | .40 | 1.00 |
| 361 | Chris Heintz RC | .20 | .50 |
| 362 | Joe Nathan | .15 | .40 |
| 363 | Johan Santana | .25 | .60 |
| 364 | Justin Morneau | .15 | .40 |
| 365 | Francisco Liriano (RC) | 1.00 | 2.50 |
| 366 | Travis Bowyer (RC) | .20 | .50 |
| 367 | Michael Cuddyer | .15 | .40 |
| 368 | Scott Baker | .15 | .40 |
| 369 | Shannon Stewart | .15 | .40 |
| 370 | Torii Hunter | .15 | .40 |
| 371 | A.J. Pierzynski | .15 | .40 |
| 372 | Aaron Rowand | .15 | .40 |
| 373 | Carl Everett | .15 | .40 |
| 374 | Dustin Hermanson | .15 | .40 |
| 375 | Frank Thomas | .40 | 1.00 |
| 376 | Freddy Garcia | .15 | .40 |
| 377 | Jermaine Dye | .15 | .40 |
| 378 | Joe Crede | .15 | .40 |
| 379 | Jon Garland | .15 | .40 |
| 380 | Jose Contreras | .15 | .40 |
| 381 | Juan Uribe | .15 | .40 |
| 382 | Mark Buehrle | .15 | .40 |
| 383 | Orlando Hernandez | .15 | .40 |
| 384 | Paul Konerko | .15 | .40 |
| 385 | Scott Podsednik | .15 | .40 |
| 386 | Tadahito Iguchi | .15 | .40 |
| 387 | Alex Rodriguez | .60 | 1.50 |
| 388 | Bernie Williams | .25 | .60 |
| 389 | Chien-Ming Wang | .40 | 1.00 |
| 390 | Derek Jeter | 1.00 | 2.50 |
| 391 | Gary Sheffield | .15 | .40 |
| 392 | Hideki Matsui | .60 | 1.50 |
| 393 | Jason Giambi | .15 | .40 |
| 394 | Jorge Posada | .25 | .60 |
| 395 | Mike Vento (RC) | .20 | .50 |
| 396 | Mariano Rivera | .40 | 1.00 |
| 397 | Mike Mussina | .25 | .60 |
| 398 | Randy Johnson | .40 | 1.00 |
| 399 | Robinson Cano | .25 | .60 |
| 400 | Tino Martinez | .15 | .40 |
| 401 | Alay Soler RC | .25 | .60 |
| 402 | Boof Bonser RC | .40 | 1.00 |
| 403 | Cole Hamels (RC) | 1.00 | 2.50 |
| 404 | Ian Kinsler (RC) | .75 | 2.00 |
| 405 | Jason Kubel (RC) | .25 | .60 |
| 406 | Joel Zumaya (RC) | .60 | 1.50 |
| 407 | Jonathan Papelbon (RC) | 1.25 | 3.00 |
| 408 | Jered Weaver (RC) | 1.25 | 3.00 |
| 409 | Kendry Morales (RC) | .60 | 1.50 |
| 410 | Lastings Milledge (RC) | .60 | 1.50 |
| 411 | Matt Kemp (RC) | .60 | 1.50 |
| 412 | Taylor Buchholz (RC) | .60 | 1.50 |
| 413 | Andre Ethier (RC) | .60 | 1.50 |
| 414 | Dan Uggla (RC) | .60 | 1.50 |
| 415 | Jeremy Sowers (RC) | .25 | .60 |
| 416 | Chad Billingsley (RC) | .40 | 1.00 |
| 417 | Josh Barfield (RC) | .25 | .60 |
| 418 | Matt Cain (RC) | .40 | 1.00 |
| 419 | Fausto Carmona (RC) | .40 | 1.00 |
| 420 | Josh Willingham (RC) | .40 | 1.00 |
| 421 | Jeremy Hermida (RC) | .40 | 1.00 |
| 422 | Conor Jackson (RC) | .40 | 1.00 |
| 423 | Dave Gasner (RC) | .25 | .60 |
| 424 | Brian Bannister (RC) | .25 | .60 |
| 425 | Fernando Nieve (RC) | .25 | .60 |
| 426 | Justin Verlander (RC) | 1.00 | 2.50 |
| 427 | Scott Olsen (RC) | .25 | .60 |
| 428 | Takashi Saito RC | .25 | .60 |
| 429 | Willie Eyre (RC) | .25 | .60 |
| 430 | Travis Ishikawa (RC) | .25 | .60 |

## 2007 Fleer

| | | | |
|---|---|---|---|
| COMPLETE SET (400) | | 30.00 | 60.00 |
| COMP.FACT.SET (430) | | 30.00 | 60.00 |
| COMMON CARD (1-430) | | .12 | .30 |
| COMMON RC | | .25 | .60 |
| 401-430 ISSUED IN FACT.SET | | | |
| OVERALL PRINTING PLATE ODDS 1:720 | | | |
| PLATE PRINT RUN 1 SET PER COLOR | | | |
| BLACK-CYAN-MAGENTA-YELLOW ISSUED | | | |
| NO PLATE PRICING DUE TO SCARCITY | | | |
| 1 | Chad Cordero | .12 | .30 |
| 2 | Alfonso Soriano | .12 | .30 |
| 3 | Nick Johnson | .12 | .30 |
| 4 | Austin Kearns | .12 | .30 |
| 5 | Ramon Ortiz | .12 | .30 |
| 6 | Brian Schneider | .12 | .30 |
| 7 | Ryan Zimmerman | .30 | .75 |
| 8 | Jose Vidro | .12 | .30 |
| 9 | Felipe Lopez | .12 | .30 |
| 10 | Cristian Guzman | .12 | .30 |
| 11 | B.J. Ryan | .12 | .30 |
| 12 | Alex Rios | .12 | .30 |
| 13 | Vernon Wells | .12 | .30 |
| 14 | Roy Halladay | .12 | .30 |
| 15 | A.J. Burnett | .12 | .30 |
| 16 | Lyle Overbay | .12 | .30 |
| 17 | Troy Glaus | .12 | .30 |
| 18 | Bengie Molina | .12 | .30 |

|  |  | | |  |  | | |  |  | | |
|---|--------|---|---|---|--------|---|---|---|--------|---|---|
| 19 | Gustavo Chacin | .12 | .30 | 107 | Brett Myers | .12 | .30 | 195 | Craig Biggio | .20 | .50 |
| 20 | Aaron Hill | .12 | .30 | 108 | Nick Swisher | .12 | .30 | 196 | Andy Pettitte | .20 | .50 |
| 21 | Vicente Padilla | .12 | .30 | 109 | Barry Zito | .12 | .30 | 197 | Roy Oswalt | .12 | .30 |
| 22 | Kevin Millwood | .12 | .30 | 110 | Jason Kendall | .12 | .30 | 198 | Lance Berkman | .12 | .30 |
| 23 | Akinori Otsuka | .12 | .30 | 111 | Milton Bradley | .12 | .30 | 199 | Morgan Ensberg | .12 | .30 |
| 24 | Adam Eaton | .12 | .30 | 112 | Bobby Crosby | .12 | .30 | 200 | Brad Lidge | .12 | .30 |
| 25 | Hank Blalock | .12 | .30 | 113 | Huston Street | .12 | .30 | 201 | Chris Burke | .12 | .30 |
| 26 | Mark Teixeira | .20 | .50 | 114 | Eric Chavez | .12 | .30 | 202 | Miguel Cabrera | .20 | .50 |
| 27 | Michael Young | .12 | .30 | 115 | Frank Thomas | .30 | .75 | 203 | Dontrelle Willis | .12 | .30 |
| 28 | Mark DeRosa | .12 | .30 | 116 | Dan Haren | .12 | .30 | 204 | Josh Johnson | .12 | .30 |
| 29 | Gary Matthews | .12 | .30 | 117 | Jay Payton | .12 | .30 | 205 | Ricky Nolasco | .12 | .30 |
| 30 | Ian Kinsler | .12 | .30 | 118 | Randy Johnson | .30 | .75 | 206 | Dan Uggla | .20 | .50 |
| 31 | Carlos Lee | .12 | .30 | 119 | Mike Mussina | .20 | .50 | 207 | Jeremy Hermida | .12 | .30 |
| 32 | James Shields | .12 | .30 | 120 | Bobby Abreu | .12 | .30 | 208 | Scott Olsen | .12 | .30 |
| 33 | Scott Kazmir | .20 | .50 | 121 | Jason Giambi | .12 | .30 | 209 | Josh Willingham | .12 | .30 |
| 34 | Carl Crawford | .12 | .30 | 122 | Derek Jeter | .75 | 2.00 | 210 | Joe Borowski | .12 | .30 |
| 35 | Jonny Gomes | .12 | .30 | 123 | Alex Rodriguez | .50 | 1.25 | 211 | Hanley Ramirez | .20 | .50 |
| 36 | Tim Corcoran | .12 | .30 | 124 | Jorge Posada | .20 | .50 | 212 | Mike Jacobs | .12 | .30 |
| 37 | B.J. Upton | .12 | .30 | 125 | Robinson Cano | .20 | .50 | 213 | Kenny Rogers | .12 | .30 |
| 38 | Rocco Baldelli | .12 | .30 | 126 | Mariano Rivera | .30 | .75 | 214 | Justin Verlander | .30 | .75 |
| 39 | Jae Seo | .12 | .30 | 127 | Chien-Ming Wang | .30 | .75 | 215 | Ivan Rodriguez | .20 | .50 |
| 40 | Jorge Cantu | .12 | .30 | 128 | Hideki Matsui | .30 | .75 | 216 | Magglio Ordonez | .12 | .30 |
| 41 | Ty Wigginton | .12 | .30 | 129 | Gary Sheffield | .12 | .30 | 217 | Todd Jones | .12 | .30 |
| 42 | Chris Carpenter | .12 | .30 | 130 | Lastings Milledge | .20 | .50 | 218 | Joel Zumaya | .20 | .50 |
| 43 | Albert Pujols | .60 | 1.50 | 131 | Tom Glavine | .20 | .50 | 219 | Jeremy Bonderman | .12 | .30 |
| 44 | Scott Rolen | .20 | .50 | 132 | Billy Wagner | .12 | .30 | 220 | Nate Robertson | .12 | .30 |
| 45 | Jim Edmonds | .20 | .50 | 133 | Pedro Martinez | .20 | .50 | 221 | Brandon Inge | .12 | .30 |
| 46 | Jason Isringhausen | .12 | .30 | 134 | Paul LoDuca | .12 | .30 | 222 | Craig Monroe | .12 | .30 |
| 47 | Yadier Molina | .12 | .30 | 135 | Carlos Delgado | .12 | .30 | 223 | Carlos Guillen | .12 | .30 |
| 48 | Adam Wainwright | .20 | .50 | 136 | Carlos Beltran | .12 | .30 | 224 | Jeff Francis | .12 | .30 |
| 49 | Mark Mulder | .12 | .30 | 137 | David Wright | .50 | 1.25 | 225 | Brian Fuentes | .12 | .30 |
| 50 | Jason Marquis | .12 | .30 | 138 | Jose Reyes | .12 | .30 | 226 | Todd Helton | .20 | .50 |
| 51 | Juan Encarnacion | .12 | .30 | 139 | Julio Franco | .12 | .30 | 227 | Matt Holliday | .30 | .75 |
| 52 | Aaron Miles | .12 | .30 | 140 | Michael Cuddyer | .12 | .30 | 228 | Garrett Atkins | .12 | .30 |
| 53 | Ichiro Suzuki | .50 | 1.25 | 141 | Justin Morneau | .12 | .30 | 229 | Clint Barmes | .12 | .30 |
| 54 | Felix Hernandez | .20 | .50 | 142 | Johan Santana | .20 | .50 | 230 | Jason Jennings | .12 | .30 |
| 55 | Kenji Johjima | .30 | .75 | 143 | Francisco Liriano | .30 | .75 | 231 | Aaron Cook | .12 | .30 |
| 56 | Richie Sexson | .12 | .30 | 144 | Joe Mauer | .30 | .75 | 232 | Brad Hawpe | .12 | .30 |
| 57 | Yuniesky Betancourt | .12 | .30 | 145 | Torii Hunter | .12 | .30 | 233 | Cory Sullivan | .12 | .30 |
| 58 | J.J. Putz | .12 | .30 | 146 | Luis Castillo | .12 | .30 | 234 | Aaron Boone | .12 | .30 |
| 59 | Jarrod Washburn | .12 | .30 | 147 | Joe Nathan | .12 | .30 | 235 | C.C. Sabathia | .12 | .30 |
| 60 | Ben Broussard | .12 | .30 | 148 | Carlos Silva | .12 | .30 | 236 | Grady Sizemore | .20 | .50 |
| 61 | Adrian Beltre | .12 | .30 | 149 | Boof Bonser | .12 | .30 | 237 | Travis Hafner | .12 | .30 |
| 62 | Raul Ibanez | .20 | .50 | 150 | Ben Sheets | .12 | .30 | 238 | Jhonny Peralta | .12 | .30 |
| 63 | Jose Lopez | .12 | .30 | 151 | Prince Fielder | .30 | .75 | 239 | Jake Westbrook | .12 | .30 |
| 64 | Matt Cain | .20 | .50 | 152 | Bill Hall | .12 | .30 | 240 | Jeremy Sowers | .12 | .30 |
| 65 | Noah Lowry | .12 | .30 | 153 | Rickie Weeks | .12 | .30 | 241 | Andy Marte | .12 | .30 |
| 66 | Jason Schmidt | .12 | .30 | 154 | Geoff Jenkins | .12 | .30 | 242 | Victor Martinez | .20 | .50 |
| 67 | Pedro Feliz | .12 | .30 | 155 | Kevin Mench | .12 | .30 | 243 | Jason Michaels | .12 | .30 |
| 68 | Matt Morris | .12 | .30 | 156 | Francisco Cordero | .12 | .30 | 244 | Cliff Lee | .12 | .30 |
| 69 | Ray Durham | .12 | .30 | 157 | Chris Capuano | .12 | .30 | 245 | Bronson Arroyo | .12 | .30 |
| 70 | Steve Finley | .12 | .30 | 158 | Brady Clark | .12 | .30 | 246 | Aaron Harang | .12 | .30 |
| 71 | Randy Winn | .12 | .30 | 159 | Tony Gwynn Jr. | .12 | .30 | 247 | Ken Griffey Jr. | .50 | 1.25 |
| 72 | Moises Alou | .12 | .30 | 160 | Chad Billingsley | .12 | .30 | 248 | Adam Dunn | .12 | .30 |
| 73 | Eliezer Alfonzo | .12 | .30 | 161 | Russell Martin | .12 | .30 | 249 | Rich Aurilia | .12 | .30 |
| 74 | Armando Benitez | .12 | .30 | 162 | Wilson Betemit | .12 | .30 | 250 | Eric Milton | .12 | .30 |
| 75 | Omar Vizquel | .20 | .50 | 163 | Nomar Garciaparra | .30 | .75 | 251 | David Ross | .12 | .30 |
| 76 | Chris R. Young | .12 | .30 | 164 | Kenny Lofton | .12 | .30 | 252 | Brandon Phillips | .12 | .30 |
| 77 | Adrian Gonzalez | .12 | .30 | 165 | Rafael Furcal | .12 | .30 | 253 | Ryan Freel | .12 | .30 |
| 78 | Khalil Greene | .20 | .50 | 166 | Julio Lugo | .12 | .30 | 254 | Eddie Guardado | .12 | .30 |
| 79 | Mike Piazza | .30 | .75 | 167 | Brad Penny | .12 | .30 | 255 | Jose Contreras | .12 | .30 |
| 80 | Josh Barfield | .12 | .30 | 168 | Jeff Kent | .12 | .30 | 256 | Freddy Garcia | .12 | .30 |
| 81 | Brian Giles | .12 | .30 | 169 | Greg Maddux | .50 | 1.25 | 257 | Jon Garland | .12 | .30 |
| 82 | Jake Peavy | .12 | .30 | 170 | Derek Lowe | .12 | .30 | 258 | Mark Buehrle | .12 | .30 |
| 83 | Trevor Hoffman | .12 | .30 | 171 | Andre Ethier | .20 | .50 | 259 | Bobby Jenks | .12 | .30 |
| 84 | Mike Cameron | .12 | .30 | 172 | Chone Figgins | .12 | .30 | 260 | Paul Konerko | .20 | .50 |
| 85 | Dave Roberts | .12 | .30 | 173 | Francisco Rodriguez | .12 | .30 | 261 | Jermaine Dye | .12 | .30 |
| 86 | David Wells | .12 | .30 | 174 | Garret Anderson | .12 | .30 | 262 | Joe Crede | .12 | .30 |
| 87 | Zach Duke | .12 | .30 | 175 | Orlando Cabrera | .12 | .30 | 263 | Jim Thome | .30 | .75 |
| 88 | Ian Snell | .12 | .30 | 176 | Adam Kennedy | .12 | .30 | 264 | Javier Vazquez | .12 | .30 |
| 89 | Jason Bay | .20 | .50 | 177 | John Lackey | .12 | .30 | 265 | A.J. Pierzynski | .12 | .30 |
| 90 | Freddy Sanchez | .12 | .30 | 178 | Vladimir Guerrero | .30 | .75 | 266 | Tadahito Iguchi | .12 | .30 |
| 91 | Jack Wilson | .12 | .30 | 179 | Bartolo Colon | .12 | .30 | 267 | Carlos Zambrano | .20 | .50 |
| 92 | Tom Gorzelanny | .12 | .30 | 180 | Jered Weaver | .20 | .50 | 268 | Derrek Lee | .12 | .30 |
| 93 | Chris Duffy | .12 | .30 | 181 | Juan Rivera | .12 | .30 | 269 | Aramis Ramirez | .12 | .30 |
| 94 | Jose Castillo | .12 | .30 | 182 | Howie Kendrick | .12 | .30 | 270 | Ryan Theriot | .12 | .30 |
| 95 | Matt Capps | .12 | .30 | 183 | Ervin Santana | .12 | .30 | 271 | Juan Pierre | .12 | .30 |
| 96 | Mike Gonzalez | .12 | .30 | 184 | Mark Redman | .12 | .30 | 272 | Rich Hill | .12 | .30 |
| 97 | Chase Utley | .30 | .75 | 185 | David DeJesus | .12 | .30 | 273 | Ryan Dempster | .12 | .30 |
| 98 | Jimmy Rollins | .30 | .75 | 186 | Joey Gathright | .12 | .30 | 274 | Jacque Jones | .12 | .30 |
| 99 | Aaron Rowand | .12 | .30 | 187 | Mike Sweeney | .12 | .30 | 275 | Mark Prior | .20 | .50 |
| 100 | Ryan Howard | .50 | 1.25 | 188 | Mark Teahen | .12 | .30 | 276 | Kerry Wood | .20 | .50 |
| 101 | Cole Hamels | .30 | .75 | 189 | Angel Berroa | .12 | .30 | 277 | Josh Beckett | .20 | .50 |
| 102 | Pat Burrell | .12 | .30 | 190 | Ambiorix Burgos | .12 | .30 | 278 | David Ortiz | .30 | .75 |
| 103 | Shane Victorino | .12 | .30 | 191 | Luke Hudson | .12 | .30 | 279 | Kevin Youkilis | .20 | .50 |
| 104 | Jamie Moyer | .12 | .30 | 192 | Mark Grudzielanek | .12 | .30 | 280 | Jason Varitek | .30 | .75 |
| 105 | Mike Lieberthal | .12 | .30 | 193 | Roger Clemens | .50 | 1.25 | 281 | Manny Ramirez | .30 | .75 |
| 106 | Tom Gordon | .12 | .30 | 194 | Willy Taveras | .12 | .30 | 282 | Curt Schilling | .20 | .50 |

|  | | |
|---|---|---|
| 283 Jon Lester | .20 | .50 |
| 284 Jonathan Papelbon | .30 | .75 |
| 285 Alex Gonzalez | .12 | .30 |
| 286 Mike Lowell | .12 | .30 |
| 287 Kyle Snyder | .12 | .30 |
| 288 Miguel Tejada | .12 | .30 |
| 289 Erik Bedard | .12 | .30 |
| 290 Ramon Hernandez | .12 | .30 |
| 291 Melvin Mora | .12 | .30 |
| 292 Nick Markakis | .20 | .50 |
| 293 Brian Roberts | .12 | .30 |
| 294 Corey Patterson | .12 | .30 |
| 295 Kris Benson | .12 | .30 |
| 296 Jay Gibbons | .12 | .30 |
| 297 Rodrigo Lopez | .12 | .30 |
| 298 Chris Ray | .12 | .30 |
| 299 Andruw Jones | .20 | .50 |
| 300 Brian McCann | .12 | .30 |
| 301 Jeff Francoeur | .30 | .75 |
| 302 Chuck James | .12 | .30 |
| 303 John Smoltz | .20 | .50 |
| 304 Bob Wickman | .12 | .30 |
| 305 Edgar Renteria | .12 | .30 |
| 306 Adam LaRoche | .12 | .30 |
| 307 Marcus Giles | .12 | .30 |
| 308 Tim Hudson | .12 | .30 |
| 309 Chipper Jones | .30 | .75 |
| 310 Miguel Batista | .12 | .30 |
| 311 Claudio Vargas | .12 | .30 |
| 312 Brandon Webb | .12 | .30 |
| 313 Luis Gonzalez | .12 | .30 |
| 314 Livan Hernandez | .12 | .30 |
| 315 Stephen Drew | .20 | .50 |
| 316 Johnny Estrada | .12 | .30 |
| 317 Orlando Hudson | .12 | .30 |
| 318 Conor Jackson | .12 | .30 |
| 319 Chad Tracy | .12 | .30 |
| 320 Carlos Quentin | .12 | .30 |
| 321 Alvin Colina RC | .60 | 1.50 |
| 322 Miguel Montero (RC) | .25 | .60 |
| 323 Jeff Fiorentino (RC) | .25 | .60 |
| 324 Jeff Baker (RC) | .25 | .60 |
| 325 Brian Burres (RC) | .25 | .60 |
| 326 David Murphy (RC) | .25 | .60 |
| 327 Francisco Cruceta (RC) | .25 | .60 |
| 328 Beltran Perez (RC) | .25 | .60 |
| 329 Scott Moore (RC) | .25 | .60 |
| 330 Sean Henn (RC) | .25 | .60 |
| 331 Ryan Sweeney (RC) | .25 | .60 |
| 332 Josh Fields (RC) | .25 | .60 |
| 333 Jerry Owens (RC) | .25 | .60 |
| 334 Vinny Rottino (RC) | .25 | .60 |
| 335 Kevin Kouzmanoff (RC) | .25 | .60 |
| 336 Alexi Casilla RC | .40 | 1.00 |
| 337 Justin Hampson (RC) | .25 | .60 |
| 338 Troy Tulowitzki (RC) | .60 | 1.50 |
| 339 Jose Garcia RC | .25 | .60 |
| 340 Andrew Miller RC | 1.50 | 4.00 |
| 341 Glen Perkins (RC) | .25 | .60 |
| 342 Ubaldo Jimenez (RC) | .25 | .60 |
| 343 Doug Slaten RC | .25 | .60 |
| 344 Angel Sanchez RC | .25 | .60 |
| 345 Mitch Maier RC | .25 | .60 |
| 346 Ryan Braun RC | .25 | .60 |
| 347 Joselo Diaz (RC) | .25 | .60 |
| 348 Delwyn Young (RC) | .25 | .60 |
| 349 Kevin Hooper (RC) | .25 | .60 |
| 350 Dennis Sarfate (RC) | .25 | .60 |
| 351 Andy Cannizaro (RC) | .25 | .60 |
| 352 Devern Hansack RC | .25 | .60 |
| 353 Michael Bourn (RC) | .25 | .60 |
| 354 Carlos Maldonado (RC) | .25 | .60 |
| 355 Shane Youman RC | .25 | .60 |
| 356 Phillip Humber (RC) | .40 | 1.00 |
| 357 Hector Gimenez (RC) | .25 | .60 |
| 358 Fred Lewis (RC) | .25 | .60 |
| 359 Ryan Feierabend (RC) | .25 | .60 |
| 360 Juan Morillo (RC) | .25 | .60 |
| 361 Travis Chick (RC) | .25 | .60 |
| 362 Oswaldo Navarro RC | .25 | .60 |
| 363 Cesar Jimenez RC | .25 | .60 |
| 364 Brian Stokes (RC) | .25 | .60 |
| 365 Delmon Young (RC) | .60 | 1.50 |
| 366 Juan Salas (RC) | .25 | .60 |
| 367 Shawn Riggans (RC) | .25 | .60 |
| 368 Adam Lind (RC) | .25 | .60 |
| 369 Joaquin Arias (RC) | .25 | .60 |
| 370 Eric Stults RC | .25 | .60 |

|  | | |
|---|---|---|
| 371 Brandon Webb CL | .12 | .30 |
| 372 John Smoltz CL | .20 | .50 |
| 373 Miguel Tejada CL | .12 | .30 |
| 374 David Ortiz CL | .20 | .50 |
| 375 Carlos Zambrano CL | .12 | .30 |
| 376 Jermaine Dye CL | .12 | .30 |
| 377 Ken Griffey Jr. CL | .50 | 1.25 |
| 378 Victor Martinez CL | .12 | .30 |
| 379 Todd Helton CL | .20 | .50 |
| 380 Ivan Rodriguez CL | .20 | .50 |
| 381 Miguel Cabrera CL | .20 | .50 |
| 382 Lance Berkman CL | .12 | .30 |
| 383 Mike Sweeney CL | .12 | .30 |
| 384 Vladimir Guerrero CL | .30 | .75 |
| 385 Derek Lowe CL | .12 | .30 |
| 386 Bill Hall CL | .12 | .30 |
| 387 Johan Santana CL | .20 | .50 |
| 388 Carlos Beltran CL | .12 | .30 |
| 389 Derek Jeter CL | .75 | 2.00 |
| 390 Nick Swisher CL | .12 | .30 |
| 391 Ryan Howard CL | .50 | 1.25 |
| 392 Jason Bay CL | .20 | .50 |
| 393 Trevor Hoffman CL | .12 | .30 |
| 394 Omar Vizquel CL | .20 | .50 |
| 395 Ichiro Suzuki CL | .50 | 1.25 |
| 396 Albert Pujols CL | .60 | 1.50 |
| 397 Carl Crawford CL | .12 | .30 |
| 398 Mark Teixeira CL | .20 | .50 |
| 399 Roy Halladay CL | .12 | .30 |
| 400 Ryan Zimmerman CL | .30 | .75 |
| 401 Mark Reynolds RC | 1.50 | 4.00 |
| 402 Micah Owings (RC) | .25 | .60 |
| 403 Jarrod Saltalamacchia (RC) | .40 | 1.00 |
| 406 Felix Pie (RC) | .25 | .60 |
| 407 Mike Fontenot (RC) | .25 | .60 |
| 408 John Danks RC | .25 | .60 |
| 409 Josh Hamilton RC | .60 | 1.50 |
| 410 Homey Bailey (RC) | .40 | 1.00 |
| 411 Alejandro De Aza RC | .40 | 1.00 |
| 412 Matt Lindstrom (RC) | .25 | .60 |
| 415 Billy Butler (RC) | .40 | 1.00 |
| 416 Brandon Wood (RC) | .25 | .60 |
| 417 Andy LaRoche (RC) | .25 | .60 |
| 419 Joe Smith RC | .25 | .60 |
| 420 Carlos Gomez RC | .40 | 1.00 |
| 421 Tyler Clippard (RC) | .25 | .60 |
| 422 Matt DeSalvo (RC) | .25 | .60 |
| 424 Kei Igawa RC | .60 | 1.50 |
| 425 Chase Wright RC | .60 | 1.50 |
| 426 Travis Buck (RC) | .25 | .60 |
| 427 Zack Segovia (RC) | .25 | .60 |
| 429 Elijah Dukes (RC) | .40 | 1.00 |
| 430 Akinori Iwamura RC | .60 | 1.50 |

## 2002 Fleer Tradition

| | | |
|---|---|---|
| COMPLETE SET (500) | 125.00 | 200.00 |
| COMP.SET w/o SP's (400) | 20.00 | 50.00 |
| COMMON SP (1-100) | .10 | .30 |
| COMMON SP (1-100) | 1.25 | 3.00 |
| COMMON CARD (436-470) | .20 | .50 |
| 1 Barry Bonds SP | 5.00 | 12.00 |
| 2 Cal Ripken SP | 6.00 | 15.00 |
| 3 Tony Gwynn SP | 2.50 | 6.00 |
| 4 Brad Radke SP | 1.25 | 3.00 |
| 5 Jose Ortiz SP | 1.25 | 3.00 |
| 6 Mark Mulder SP | 1.25 | 3.00 |
| 7 Jon Lieber SP | 1.25 | 3.00 |
| 8 John Olerud SP | 1.25 | 3.00 |
| 9 Phil Nevin SP | 1.25 | 3.00 |
| 10 Craig Biggio SP | 1.25 | 3.00 |
| 11 Pedro Martinez SP | 1.25 | 3.00 |
| 12 Fred McGriff SP | 1.25 | 3.00 |
| 13 Vladimir Guerrero SP | 2.00 | 5.00 |
| 14 Jason Giambi SP | 1.25 | 3.00 |

|  | | |
|---|---|---|
| 15 Mark Kotsay SP | 1.25 | 3.00 |
| 16 Bud Smith SP | 1.25 | 3.00 |
| 17 Kevin Brown SP | 1.25 | 3.00 |
| 18 Darin Erstad SP | 1.25 | 3.00 |
| 19 Julio Franco SP | 1.25 | 3.00 |
| 20 C.C. Sabathia SP | 1.25 | 3.00 |
| 21 Larry Walker SP | 1.25 | 3.00 |
| 22 Doug Mientkiewicz SP | 1.25 | 3.00 |
| 23 Luis Gonzalez SP | 1.25 | 3.00 |
| 24 Albert Pujols SP | 4.00 | 10.00 |
| 25 Brian Lawrence SP | 1.25 | 3.00 |
| 26 Al Leiter SP | 1.25 | 3.00 |
| 27 Mike Sweeney SP | 1.25 | 3.00 |
| 28 Jeff Weaver SP | 1.25 | 3.00 |
| 29 Matt Morris SP | 1.25 | 3.00 |
| 30 Hideo Nomo SP | 2.00 | 5.00 |
| 31 Tom Glavine SP | 1.25 | 3.00 |
| 32 Magglio Ordonez SP | 1.25 | 3.00 |
| 33 Roberto Alomar SP | 1.25 | 3.00 |
| 34 Roger Cedeno SP | 1.25 | 3.00 |
| 35 Greg Vaughn SP | 1.25 | 3.00 |
| 36 Chan Ho Park SP | 1.25 | 3.00 |
| 37 Rich Aurilia SP | 1.25 | 3.00 |
| 38 Tsuyoshi Shinjo SP | 1.25 | 3.00 |
| 39 Eric Young SP | 1.25 | 3.00 |
| 40 Bobby Higginson SP | 1.25 | 3.00 |
| 41 Marlon Anderson SP | 1.25 | 3.00 |
| 42 Mark Grace SP | 1.25 | 3.00 |
| 43 Steve Cox SP | 1.25 | 3.00 |
| 44 Cliff Floyd SP | 1.25 | 3.00 |
| 45 Brian Roberts SP | 1.25 | 3.00 |
| 46 Paul Konerko SP | 1.25 | 3.00 |
| 47 Brandon Duckworth SP | 1.25 | 3.00 |
| 48 Josh Beckett SP | 1.25 | 3.00 |
| 49 David Ortiz SP | 2.00 | 5.00 |
| 50 Geoff Jenkins SP | 1.25 | 3.00 |
| 51 Ruben Sierra SP | 1.25 | 3.00 |
| 52 John Franco SP | 1.25 | 3.00 |
| 53 Einar Diaz SP | 1.25 | 3.00 |
| 54 Luis Castillo SP | 1.25 | 3.00 |
| 55 Mark Quinn SP | 1.25 | 3.00 |
| 56 Shea Hillenbrand SP | 1.25 | 3.00 |
| 57 Rafael Palmeiro SP | 1.25 | 3.00 |
| 58 Paul O'Neill SP | 1.25 | 3.00 |
| 59 Andruw Jones SP | 1.25 | 3.00 |
| 60 Lance Berkman SP | 1.25 | 3.00 |
| 61 Jimmy Rollins SP | 1.25 | 3.00 |
| 62 Jose Hernandez SP | 1.25 | 3.00 |
| 63 Rusty Greer SP | 1.25 | 3.00 |
| 64 Wade Miller SP | 1.25 | 3.00 |
| 65 David Eckstein SP | 1.25 | 3.00 |
| 66 Jose Valentin SP | 1.25 | 3.00 |
| 67 Javier Vazquez SP | 1.25 | 3.00 |
| 68 Roger Clemens SP | 4.00 | 10.00 |
| 69 Omar Vizquel SP | 1.25 | 3.00 |
| 70 Roy Oswalt SP | 1.25 | 3.00 |
| 71 Shannon Stewart SP | 1.25 | 3.00 |
| 72 Byung-Hyun Kim SP | 1.25 | 3.00 |
| 73 Jay Gibbons SP | 1.25 | 3.00 |
| 74 Barry Larkin SP | 1.25 | 3.00 |
| 75 Brian Giles SP | 1.25 | 3.00 |
| 76 Andres Galarraga SP | 1.25 | 3.00 |
| 77 Sammy Sosa SP | 2.00 | 5.00 |
| 78 Manny Ramirez SP | 1.25 | 3.00 |
| 79 Carlos Delgado SP | 1.25 | 3.00 |
| 80 Jorge Posada SP | 1.25 | 3.00 |
| 81 Todd Ritchie SP | 1.25 | 3.00 |
| 82 Russ Ortiz SP | 1.25 | 3.00 |
| 83 Brent Mayne SP | 1.25 | 3.00 |
| 84 Mike Mussina SP | 1.25 | 3.00 |
| 85 Raul Mondesi SP | 1.25 | 3.00 |
| 86 Mark Loretta SP | 1.25 | 3.00 |
| 87 Tim Raines SP | 1.25 | 3.00 |
| 88 Ichiro Suzuki SP | 4.00 | 10.00 |
| 89 Juan Pierre SP | 1.25 | 3.00 |
| 90 Adam Dunn SP | 1.25 | 3.00 |
| 91 Jason Tyner SP | 1.25 | 3.00 |
| 92 Miguel Tejada SP | 1.25 | 3.00 |
| 93 Epidio Guzman SP | 1.25 | 3.00 |
| 94 Freddy Garcia SP | 1.25 | 3.00 |
| 95 Marcus Giles SP | 1.25 | 3.00 |
| 96 Junior Spivey SP | 1.25 | 3.00 |
| 97 Aramis Ramirez SP | 1.25 | 3.00 |
| 98 Jose Rijo SP | 1.25 | 3.00 |
| 99 Paul LoDuca SP | 1.25 | 3.00 |
| 100 Mike Cameron SP | 1.25 | 3.00 |
| 101 Alex Hernandez | .10 | .30 |
| 102 Benji Gil | .10 | .30 |

|  |  | | |
|---|---|---|---|
| ☐ 103 | Benito Santiago | .10 | .30 |
| ☐ 104 | Bobby Abreu | .10 | .30 |
| ☐ 105 | Brad Penny | .10 | .30 |
| ☐ 106 | Calvin Murray | .10 | .30 |
| ☐ 107 | Chad Durbin | .10 | .30 |
| ☐ 108 | Chris Singleton | .10 | .30 |
| ☐ 109 | Chris Carpenter | .10 | .30 |
| ☐ 110 | David Justice | .10 | .30 |
| ☐ 111 | Eric Chavez | .10 | .30 |
| ☐ 112 | Fernando Tatis | .10 | .30 |
| ☐ 113 | Frank Castillo | .10 | .30 |
| ☐ 114 | Jason LaRue | .10 | .30 |
| ☐ 115 | Jim Edmonds | .10 | .30 |
| ☐ 116 | Joe Kennedy | .10 | .30 |
| ☐ 117 | Jose Jimenez | .10 | .30 |
| ☐ 118 | Josh Towers | .10 | .30 |
| ☐ 119 | Junior Herndon | .10 | .30 |
| ☐ 120 | Luke Prokopec | .10 | .30 |
| ☐ 121 | Mac Suzuki | .10 | .30 |
| ☐ 122 | Mark DeRosa | .10 | .30 |
| ☐ 123 | Marty Cordova | .10 | .30 |
| ☐ 124 | Michael Tucker | .10 | .30 |
| ☐ 125 | Michael Young | .30 | .75 |
| ☐ 126 | Robin Ventura | .10 | .30 |
| ☐ 127 | Shane Halter | .10 | .30 |
| ☐ 128 | Shane Reynolds | .10 | .30 |
| ☐ 129 | Tony Womack | .10 | .30 |
| ☐ 130 | A.J. Pierzynski | .10 | .30 |
| ☐ 131 | Aaron Rowand | .10 | .30 |
| ☐ 132 | Antonio Alfonseca | .10 | .30 |
| ☐ 133 | Arthur Rhodes | .10 | .30 |
| ☐ 134 | Bob Wickman | .10 | .30 |
| ☐ 135 | Brady Clark | .10 | .30 |
| ☐ 136 | Chad Hermansen | .10 | .30 |
| ☐ 137 | Marlon Byrd | .10 | .30 |
| ☐ 138 | Dan Wilson | .10 | .30 |
| ☐ 139 | David Cone | .10 | .30 |
| ☐ 140 | Dean Palmer | .10 | .30 |
| ☐ 141 | Denny Neagle | .10 | .30 |
| ☐ 142 | Derek Jeter | .75 | 2.00 |
| ☐ 143 | Erubiel Durazo | .10 | .30 |
| ☐ 144 | Felix Rodriguez | .10 | .30 |
| ☐ 145 | Jason Hart | .10 | .30 |
| ☐ 146 | Jay Bell | .10 | .30 |
| ☐ 147 | Jeff Suppan | .10 | .30 |
| ☐ 148 | Jeff Zimmerman | .10 | .30 |
| ☐ 149 | Kerry Wood | .10 | .30 |
| ☐ 150 | Kerry Robinson | .10 | .30 |
| ☐ 151 | Kevin Appier | .10 | .30 |
| ☐ 152 | Michael Barrett | .10 | .30 |
| ☐ 153 | Mo Vaughn | .10 | .30 |
| ☐ 154 | Rafael Furcal | .10 | .30 |
| ☐ 155 | Sidney Ponson | .10 | .30 |
| ☐ 156 | Terry Adams | .10 | .30 |
| ☐ 157 | Tim Redding | .10 | .30 |
| ☐ 158 | Toby Hall | .10 | .30 |
| ☐ 159 | Aaron Sele | .10 | .30 |
| ☐ 160 | Bartolo Colon | .10 | .30 |
| ☐ 161 | Brad Ausmus | .10 | .30 |
| ☐ 162 | Carlos Pena | .10 | .30 |
| ☐ 163 | Jace Brewer | .10 | .30 |
| ☐ 164 | David Wells | .10 | .30 |
| ☐ 165 | David Segui | .10 | .30 |
| ☐ 166 | Derek Lowe | .10 | .30 |
| ☐ 167 | Derek Bell | .10 | .30 |
| ☐ 168 | Jason Grabowski | .10 | .30 |
| ☐ 169 | Johnny Damon | .20 | .50 |
| ☐ 170 | Jose Mesa | .10 | .30 |
| ☐ 171 | Juan Encarnacion | .10 | .30 |
| ☐ 172 | Ken Caminiti | .10 | .30 |
| ☐ 173 | Ken Griffey Jr. | .50 | 1.25 |
| ☐ 174 | Luis Rivas | .10 | .30 |
| ☐ 175 | Mariano Rivera | .30 | .75 |
| ☐ 176 | Mark Grudzielanek | .10 | .30 |
| ☐ 177 | Mark McGwire | .75 | 2.00 |
| ☐ 178 | Mike Bordick | .10 | .30 |
| ☐ 179 | Mike Hampton | .10 | .30 |
| ☐ 180 | Nick Bierbrodt | .10 | .30 |
| ☐ 181 | Paul Byrd | .10 | .30 |
| ☐ 182 | Robb Nen | .10 | .30 |
| ☐ 183 | Ryan Dempster | .10 | .30 |
| ☐ 184 | Ryan Klesko | .10 | .30 |
| ☐ 185 | Scott Spiezio | .10 | .30 |
| ☐ 186 | Scott Strickland | .10 | .30 |
| ☐ 187 | Todd Zeile | .10 | .30 |
| ☐ 188 | Tom Gordon | .10 | .30 |
| ☐ 189 | Troy Glaus | .10 | .30 |
| ☐ 190 | Matt Williams | .10 | .30 |
| ☐ 191 | Wes Helms | .10 | .30 |
| ☐ 192 | Jerry Hairston Jr. | .10 | .30 |
| ☐ 193 | Brook Fordyce | .10 | .30 |
| ☐ 194 | Nomar Garciaparra | .50 | 1.25 |
| ☐ 195 | Kevin Tapani | .10 | .30 |
| ☐ 196 | Mark Buehrle | .10 | .30 |
| ☐ 197 | Dmitri Young | .10 | .30 |
| ☐ 198 | John Rocker | .10 | .30 |
| ☐ 199 | Juan Uribe | .10 | .30 |
| ☐ 200 | Matt Anderson | .10 | .30 |
| ☐ 201 | Alex Gonzalez | .10 | .30 |
| ☐ 202 | Julio Lugo | .10 | .30 |
| ☐ 203 | Roberto Hernandez | .10 | .30 |
| ☐ 204 | Richie Sexson | .10 | .30 |
| ☐ 205 | Corey Koskie | .10 | .30 |
| ☐ 206 | Tony Armas Jr. | .10 | .30 |
| ☐ 207 | Rey Ordonez | .10 | .30 |
| ☐ 208 | Orlando Hernandez | .10 | .30 |
| ☐ 209 | Pokey Reese | .10 | .30 |
| ☐ 210 | Mike Lieberthal | .10 | .30 |
| ☐ 211 | Kris Benson | .10 | .30 |
| ☐ 212 | Jermaine Dye | .10 | .30 |
| ☐ 213 | Livan Hernandez | .10 | .30 |
| ☐ 214 | Bret Boone | .10 | .30 |
| ☐ 215 | Dustin Hermanson | .10 | .30 |
| ☐ 216 | Placido Polanco | .10 | .30 |
| ☐ 217 | Jesus Colome | .10 | .30 |
| ☐ 218 | Alex Gonzalez | .10 | .30 |
| ☐ 219 | Adam Everett | .10 | .30 |
| ☐ 220 | Adam Piatt | .10 | .30 |
| ☐ 221 | Brad Fullmer | .10 | .30 |
| ☐ 222 | Brian Buchanan | .10 | .30 |
| ☐ 223 | Chipper Jones | .30 | .75 |
| ☐ 224 | Chuck Finley | .10 | .30 |
| ☐ 225 | David Bell | .10 | .30 |
| ☐ 226 | Jack Wilson | .10 | .30 |
| ☐ 227 | Jason Bere | .10 | .30 |
| ☐ 228 | Jeff Conine | .10 | .30 |
| ☐ 229 | Jeff Bagwell | .20 | .50 |
| ☐ 230 | Joe McEwing | .10 | .30 |
| ☐ 231 | Kip Wells | .10 | .30 |
| ☐ 232 | Mike Lansing | .10 | .30 |
| ☐ 233 | Neifi Perez | .10 | .30 |
| ☐ 234 | Omar Daal | .10 | .30 |
| ☐ 235 | Reggie Sanders | .10 | .30 |
| ☐ 236 | Shawn Wooten | .10 | .30 |
| ☐ 237 | Shawn Chacon | .10 | .30 |
| ☐ 238 | Shawn Estes | .10 | .30 |
| ☐ 239 | Steve Sparks | .10 | .30 |
| ☐ 240 | Steve Kline | .10 | .30 |
| ☐ 241 | Tino Martinez | .20 | .50 |
| ☐ 242 | Tyler Houston | .10 | .30 |
| ☐ 243 | Xavier Nady | .10 | .30 |
| ☐ 244 | Bengie Molina | .10 | .30 |
| ☐ 245 | Ben Davis | .10 | .30 |
| ☐ 246 | Casey Fossum | .10 | .30 |
| ☐ 247 | Chris Stynes | .10 | .30 |
| ☐ 248 | Danny Graves | .10 | .30 |
| ☐ 249 | Pedro Feliz | .10 | .30 |
| ☐ 250 | Darren Oliver | .10 | .30 |
| ☐ 251 | Dave Veres | .10 | .30 |
| ☐ 252 | Deivi Cruz | .10 | .30 |
| ☐ 253 | Desi Relaford | .10 | .30 |
| ☐ 254 | Devon White | .10 | .30 |
| ☐ 255 | Edgar Martinez | .20 | .50 |
| ☐ 256 | Eric Munson | .10 | .30 |
| ☐ 257 | Eric Karros | .10 | .30 |
| ☐ 258 | Homer Bush | .10 | .30 |
| ☐ 259 | Jason Kendall | .10 | .30 |
| ☐ 260 | Javy Lopez | .10 | .30 |
| ☐ 261 | Keith Foulke | .10 | .30 |
| ☐ 262 | Keith Ginter | .10 | .30 |
| ☐ 263 | Nick Johnson | .10 | .30 |
| ☐ 264 | Pat Burrell | .10 | .30 |
| ☐ 265 | Ricky Gutierrez | .10 | .30 |
| ☐ 266 | Russ Johnson | .10 | .30 |
| ☐ 267 | Steve Finley | .10 | .30 |
| ☐ 268 | Terrence Long | .10 | .30 |
| ☐ 269 | Tony Batista | .10 | .30 |
| ☐ 270 | Torii Hunter | .10 | .30 |
| ☐ 271 | Vinny Castilla | .10 | .30 |
| ☐ 272 | A.J. Burnett | .10 | .30 |
| ☐ 273 | Adrian Beltre | .10 | .30 |
| ☐ 274 | Alex Rodriguez | .50 | 1.25 |
| ☐ 275 | Armando Benitez | .10 | .30 |
| ☐ 276 | Billy Koch | .10 | .30 |
| ☐ 277 | Brady Anderson | .10 | .30 |
| ☐ 278 | Brian Jordan | .10 | .30 |
| ☐ 279 | Carlos Febles | .10 | .30 |
| ☐ 280 | Daryle Ward | .10 | .30 |
| ☐ 281 | Eli Marrero | .10 | .30 |
| ☐ 282 | Garret Anderson | .10 | .30 |
| ☐ 283 | Jack Cust | .10 | .30 |
| ☐ 284 | Jacque Jones | .10 | .30 |
| ☐ 285 | Jamie Moyer | .10 | .30 |
| ☐ 286 | Jeffrey Hammonds | .10 | .30 |
| ☐ 287 | Jim Thome | .20 | .50 |
| ☐ 288 | Jon Garland | .10 | .30 |
| ☐ 289 | Jose Offerman | .10 | .30 |
| ☐ 290 | Matt Stairs | .10 | .30 |
| ☐ 291 | Orlando Cabrera | .10 | .30 |
| ☐ 292 | Ramiro Mendoza | .10 | .30 |
| ☐ 293 | Ray Durham | .10 | .30 |
| ☐ 294 | Rickey Henderson | .30 | .75 |
| ☐ 295 | Rob Mackowiak | .10 | .30 |
| ☐ 296 | Scott Rolen | .20 | .50 |
| ☐ 297 | Tim Hudson | .10 | .30 |
| ☐ 298 | Todd Helton | .20 | .50 |
| ☐ 299 | Tony Clark | .10 | .30 |
| ☐ 300 | B.J. Surhoff | .10 | .30 |
| ☐ 301 | Bernie Williams | .20 | .50 |
| ☐ 302 | Bill Mueller | .10 | .30 |
| ☐ 303 | Chris Richard | .10 | .30 |
| ☐ 304 | Craig Paquette | .10 | .30 |
| ☐ 305 | Curt Schilling | .10 | .30 |
| ☐ 306 | Damian Jackson | .10 | .30 |
| ☐ 307 | Derrek Lee | .20 | .50 |
| ☐ 308 | Eric Milton | .10 | .30 |
| ☐ 309 | Frank Catalanotto | .10 | .30 |
| ☐ 310 | J.T. Snow | .10 | .30 |
| ☐ 311 | Jared Sandberg | .10 | .30 |
| ☐ 312 | Jason Varitek | .30 | .75 |
| ☐ 313 | Jeff Cirillo | .10 | .30 |
| ☐ 314 | Jeromy Burnitz | .10 | .30 |
| ☐ 315 | Joe Crede | .10 | .30 |
| ☐ 316 | Joel Pineiro | .10 | .30 |
| ☐ 317 | Jose Cruz Jr. | .10 | .30 |
| ☐ 318 | Kevin Young | .10 | .30 |
| ☐ 319 | Marquis Grissom | .10 | .30 |
| ☐ 320 | Moises Alou | .10 | .30 |
| ☐ 321 | Randall Simon | .10 | .30 |
| ☐ 322 | Royce Clayton | .10 | .30 |
| ☐ 323 | Tim Salmon | .20 | .50 |
| ☐ 324 | Travis Fryman | .10 | .30 |
| ☐ 325 | Travis Lee | .10 | .30 |
| ☐ 326 | Vance Wilson | .10 | .30 |
| ☐ 327 | Jarrod Washburn | .10 | .30 |
| ☐ 328 | Ben Petrick | .10 | .30 |
| ☐ 329 | Ben Grieve | .10 | .30 |
| ☐ 330 | Carl Everett | .10 | .30 |
| ☐ 331 | Eric Byrnes | .10 | .30 |
| ☐ 332 | Doug Glanville | .10 | .30 |
| ☐ 333 | Edgardo Alfonzo | .10 | .30 |
| ☐ 334 | Ellis Burks | .10 | .30 |
| ☐ 335 | Gabe Kapler | .10 | .30 |
| ☐ 336 | Gary Sheffield | .10 | .30 |
| ☐ 337 | Greg Maddux | .50 | 1.25 |
| ☐ 338 | J.D. Drew | .10 | .30 |
| ☐ 339 | Jamey Wright | .10 | .30 |
| ☐ 340 | Jeff Kent | .10 | .30 |
| ☐ 341 | Jeremy Giambi | .10 | .30 |
| ☐ 342 | Joe Randa | .10 | .30 |
| ☐ 343 | Joe Mays | .10 | .30 |
| ☐ 344 | Jose Macias | .10 | .30 |
| ☐ 345 | Kazuhiro Sasaki | .10 | .30 |
| ☐ 346 | Mike Kinkade | .10 | .30 |
| ☐ 347 | Mike Lowell | .10 | .30 |
| ☐ 348 | Randy Johnson | .30 | .75 |
| ☐ 349 | Randy Wolf | .10 | .30 |
| ☐ 350 | Richard Hidalgo | .10 | .30 |
| ☐ 351 | Ron Coomer | .10 | .30 |
| ☐ 352 | Sandy Alomar Jr. | .10 | .30 |
| ☐ 353 | Sean Casey | .10 | .30 |
| ☐ 354 | Trevor Hoffman | .10 | .30 |
| ☐ 355 | Adam Eaton | .10 | .30 |
| ☐ 356 | Alfonso Soriano | .10 | .30 |
| ☐ 357 | Barry Zito | .10 | .30 |
| ☐ 358 | Billy Wagner | .10 | .30 |
| ☐ 359 | Brent Abernathy | .10 | .30 |
| ☐ 360 | Bret Prinz | .10 | .30 |
| ☐ 361 | Carlos Beltran | .10 | .30 |
| ☐ 362 | Carlos Guillen | .10 | .30 |
| ☐ 363 | Charles Johnson | .10 | .30 |
| ☐ 364 | Cristian Guzman | .10 | .30 |
| ☐ 365 | Damion Easley | .10 | .30 |
| ☐ 366 | Darryl Kile | .10 | .30 |

| | | |
|---|---|---|
| 367 Delino DeShields | .10 | .30 |
| 368 Eric Davis | .10 | .30 |
| 369 Frank Thomas | .30 | .75 |
| 370 Ivan Rodriguez | .20 | .50 |
| 371 Jay Payton | .10 | .30 |
| 372 Jeff D'Amico | .10 | .30 |
| 373 John Burkett | .10 | .30 |
| 374 Melvin Mora | .10 | .30 |
| 375 Ramon Ortiz | .10 | .30 |
| 376 Robert Person | .10 | .30 |
| 377 Russell Branyan | .10 | .30 |
| 378 Shawn Green | .10 | .30 |
| 379 Todd Hollandsworth | .10 | .30 |
| 380 Tony McKnight | .10 | .30 |
| 381 Trot Nixon | .10 | .30 |
| 382 Vernon Wells | .10 | .30 |
| 383 Troy Percival | .10 | .30 |
| 384 Albie Lopez | .10 | .30 |
| 385 Alex Ochoa | .10 | .30 |
| 386 Andy Pettitte | .20 | .50 |
| 387 Brandon Inge | .10 | .30 |
| 388 Bubba Trammell | .10 | .30 |
| 389 Corey Patterson | .10 | .30 |
| 390 Damian Rolls | .10 | .30 |
| 391 Dee Brown | .10 | .30 |
| 392 Edgar Renteria | .10 | .30 |
| 393 Eric Gagne | .10 | .30 |
| 394 Jason Johnson | .10 | .30 |
| 395 Jeff Nelson | .10 | .30 |
| 396 John Vander Wal | .10 | .30 |
| 397 Johnny Estrada | .10 | .30 |
| 398 Jose Canseco | .20 | .50 |
| 399 Juan Gonzalez | .10 | .30 |
| 400 Kevin Millwood | .10 | .30 |
| 401 Lee Stevens | .10 | .30 |
| 402 Matt Lawton | .10 | .30 |
| 403 Mike Lamb | .10 | .30 |
| 404 Octavio Dotel | .10 | .30 |
| 405 Ramon Hernandez | .10 | .30 |
| 406 Ruben Quevedo | .10 | .30 |
| 407 Todd Walker | .10 | .30 |
| 408 Troy O'Leary | .10 | .30 |
| 409 Wascar Serrano | .10 | .30 |
| 410 Aaron Boone | .10 | .30 |
| 411 Aubrey Huff | .10 | .30 |
| 412 Ben Sheets | .10 | .30 |
| 413 Carlos Lee | .10 | .30 |
| 414 Chuck Knoblauch | .10 | .30 |
| 415 Steve Karsay | .10 | .30 |
| 416 Dante Bichette | .10 | .30 |
| 417 David Dellucci | .10 | .30 |
| 418 Esteban Loaiza | .10 | .30 |
| 419 Fernando Vina | .10 | .30 |
| 420 Ismael Valdes | .10 | .30 |
| 421 Jason Isringhausen | .10 | .30 |
| 422 Jeff Shaw | .10 | .30 |
| 423 John Smoltz | .20 | .50 |
| 424 Jose Vidro | .10 | .30 |
| 425 Kenny Lofton | .10 | .30 |
| 426 Mark Little | .10 | .30 |
| 427 Mark McLemore | .10 | .30 |
| 428 Marvin Benard | .10 | .30 |
| 429 Mike Piazza | .50 | 1.25 |
| 430 Pat Hentgen | .10 | .30 |
| 431 Preston Wilson | .10 | .30 |
| 432 Rick Helling | .10 | .30 |
| 433 Robert Fick | .10 | .30 |
| 434 Rondell White | .10 | .30 |
| 435 Adam Kennedy | .10 | .30 |
| 436 David Espinosa PROS | .20 | .50 |
| 437 Dewon Brazelton PROS | .20 | .50 |
| 438 Drew Henson PROS | .20 | .50 |
| 439 Juan Cruz PROS | .20 | .50 |
| 440 Jason Jennings PROS | .20 | .50 |
| 441 Carlos Garcia PROS | .20 | .50 |
| 442 Carlos Hernandez PROS | .20 | .50 |
| 443 Wilkin Ruan PROS | .20 | .50 |
| 444 Wilson Betemit PROS | .20 | .50 |
| 445 Horacio Ramirez PROS | .20 | .50 |
| 446 Danys Baez PROS | .20 | .50 |
| 447 Abraham Nunez PROS | .20 | .50 |
| 448 Josh Hamilton PROS | .40 | 1.00 |
| 449 Chris George PROS | .20 | .50 |
| 450 Rick Bauer PROS | .20 | .50 |
| 451 Donnie Bridges PROS | .20 | .50 |
| 452 Erick Almonte PROS | .20 | .50 |
| 453 Cory Aldridge PROS | .20 | .50 |
| 454 Ryan Drese PROS | .20 | .50 |
| 455 Jason Romano PROS | .20 | .50 |
| 456 Corky Miller PROS | .20 | .50 |
| 457 Rafael Soriano PROS | .20 | .50 |
| 458 Mark Prior PROS | .50 | 1.25 |
| 459 Mark Teixeira PROS | .50 | 1.25 |
| 460 Adrian Hernandez PROS | .20 | .50 |
| 461 Tim Spooneybarger PROS | .20 | .50 |
| 462 Bill Ortega PROS | .20 | .50 |
| 463 D'Angelo Jimenez PROS | .20 | .50 |
| 464 Andres Torres PROS | .20 | .50 |
| 465 Alexis Gomez PROS | .20 | .50 |
| 466 Angel Berroa PROS | .20 | .50 |
| 467 Henry Mateo PROS | .20 | .50 |
| 468 Endy Chavez PROS | .20 | .50 |
| 469 Billy Sylvester PROS | .20 | .50 |
| 470 Nate Frese PROS | .20 | .50 |
| 471 Luis Gonzalez BNR | .10 | .30 |
| 472 Barry Bonds BNR | .75 | 2.00 |
| 473 Rich Aurilia BNR | .10 | .30 |
| 474 Albert Pujols BNR | .60 | 1.50 |
| 475 Todd Helton BNR | .30 | .75 |
| 476 Moises Alou BNR | .10 | .30 |
| 477 Lance Berkman BNR | .10 | .30 |
| 478 Brian Giles BNR | .10 | .30 |
| 479 Cliff Floyd BNR | .10 | .30 |
| 480 Sammy Sosa BNR | .30 | .75 |
| 481 Shawn Green BNR | .10 | .30 |
| 482 Jon Lieber BNR | .10 | .30 |
| 483 Matt Morris BNR | .10 | .30 |
| 484 Curt Schilling BNR | .10 | .30 |
| 485 Randy Johnson BNR | .20 | .50 |
| 486 Manny Ramirez BNR | .20 | .50 |
| 487 Ichiro Suzuki BNR | .60 | 1.50 |
| 488 Juan Gonzalez BNR | .10 | .30 |
| 489 Derek Jeter BNR | .75 | 2.00 |
| 490 Alex Rodriguez BNR | .50 | 1.25 |
| 491 Bret Boone BNR | .10 | .30 |
| 492 Roberto Alomar BNR | .10 | .30 |
| 493 Jason Giambi BNR | .10 | .30 |
| 494 Rafael Palmeiro BNR | .10 | .30 |
| 495 Doug Mientkiewicz BNR | .10 | .30 |
| 496 Jim Thome BNR | .20 | .50 |
| 497 Freddy Garcia BNR | .10 | .30 |
| 498 Mark Buehrle BNR | .10 | .30 |
| 499 Mark Mulder BNR | .10 | .30 |
| 500 Roger Clemens BNR | .60 | 1.50 |

## 2003 Fleer Tradition

| | | |
|---|---|---|
| COMPLETE SET (485) | 75.00 | 150.00 |
| COMP.SET w/o SP (385) | 15.00 | 40.00 |
| COMMON CARD (1-30) | .40 | 1.00 |
| COMMON SP (31-66/86-100) | .40 | 1.00 |
| COMMON ML (67-85) | .60 | 1.50 |
| COMMON CARD (101-485) | .10 | .30 |
| COMMON PR (426-460) | .10 | .30 |
| 1 Wash/Giaus/And/Ortiz TL | .40 | 1.00 |
| 2 L.Gonzalez/R.Johnson TL | .60 | 1.50 |
| 3 Andruw/Chip/Glav/Millt TL | .60 | 1.50 |
| 4 T.Batista/R.Lopez TL | .40 | 1.00 |
| 5 Ram/Nomar/Low/Pedro TL | .60 | 1.50 |
| 6 Sosa/Clement/Wood TL | 1.00 | 2.50 |
| 7 Buehrle/Magglio/Wright TL | .40 | 1.00 |
| 8 Dunn/Boone/Haynes TL | .40 | 1.00 |
| 9 C.Sabathia/J.Thome TL | .40 | 1.00 |
| 10 T.Helton/J.Jennings TL | .60 | 1.50 |
| 11 Simon/Sparks/Redman TL | .40 | 1.00 |
| 12 Lee/Lowell/Burnett TL | .60 | 1.50 |
| 13 L.Berkman/R.Oswalt TL | .60 | 1.50 |
| 14 P.Byrd/C.Beltran TL | .40 | 1.00 |
| 15 S.Green/H.Nomo TL | .60 | 1.50 |
| 16 R.Sexson/B.Sheets TL | .40 | 1.00 |
| 17 Hunter/Lohse/Santana TL | .40 | 1.00 |
| 18 Vladdie/Ohka/Vazquez TL | .60 | 1.50 |
| 19 M.Piazza/A.Leiter TL | 1.00 | 2.50 |
| 20 Giambi/Wells/Clemens TL | 1.00 | 2.50 |
| 21 Chavez/Tejada/Zito TL | .40 | 1.00 |
| 22 Burrell/Padilla/Wolf TL | .40 | 1.00 |
| 23 Giles/Fogg/Wells TL | .40 | 1.00 |
| 24 R.Klesko/S.Lawrence TL | .40 | 1.00 |
| 25 Bonds/Ortiz/Schmidt TL | 1.00 | 2.50 |
| 26 Cameron/Boone/Garcia TL | .40 | 1.00 |
| 27 A.Pujols/M.Morris TL | 1.00 | 2.50 |
| 28 Huff/Winn/Kenn/Sturtze TL | .40 | 1.00 |
| 29 A-Rod/Rogers/Park TL | 1.00 | 2.50 |
| 30 C.Delgado/R.Halladay TL | .40 | 1.00 |
| 31 Greg Maddux SP | 1.50 | 4.00 |
| 32 Nick Neugebauer SP | .40 | 1.00 |
| 33 Larry Walker SP | .40 | 1.00 |
| 34 Freddy Garcia SP | .40 | 1.00 |
| 35 Rich Aurilia SP | .40 | 1.00 |
| 36 Craig Wilson SP | .40 | 1.00 |
| 37 Jeff Suppan SP | .40 | 1.00 |
| 38 Joel Pineiro SP | .40 | 1.00 |
| 39 Pedro Feliz SP | .40 | 1.00 |
| 40 Bartolo Colon SP | .40 | 1.00 |
| 41 Pete Walker SP | .40 | 1.00 |
| 42 Mo Vaughn SP | .40 | 1.00 |
| 43 Sidney Ponson SP | .40 | 1.00 |
| 44 Jason Isringhausen SP | .40 | 1.00 |
| 45 Hideki Irabu SP | .40 | 1.00 |
| 46 Pedro Martinez SP | .60 | 1.50 |
| 47 Tom Glavine SP | .60 | 1.50 |
| 48 Matt Lawton SP | .40 | 1.00 |
| 49 Kyle Lohse SP | .40 | 1.00 |
| 50 Corey Patterson SP | .40 | 1.00 |
| 51 Ichiro Suzuki SP | 2.00 | 5.00 |
| 52 Wade Miller SP | .40 | 1.00 |
| 53 Ben Diggins SP | .40 | 1.00 |
| 54 Jayson Werth SP | .40 | 1.00 |
| 55 Masato Yoshii SP | .40 | 1.00 |
| 56 Mark Buehrle SP | .40 | 1.00 |
| 57 Drew Henson SP | .40 | 1.00 |
| 58 Dave Williams SP | .40 | 1.00 |
| 59 Juan Rivera SP | .40 | 1.00 |
| 60 Scott Schoeneweis SP | .40 | 1.00 |
| 61 Josh Beckett SP | .40 | 1.00 |
| 62 Vinny Castilla SP | .40 | 1.00 |
| 63 Barry Zito SP | .40 | 1.00 |
| 64 Jose Valentin SP | .40 | 1.00 |
| 65 Jon Lieber SP | .40 | 1.00 |
| 66 Jorge Padilla SP | .40 | 1.00 |
| 67 Luis Aparicio ML SP | .60 | 1.50 |
| 68 Boog Powell ML SP | 1.00 | 2.50 |
| 69 Dick Radatz ML SP | .60 | 1.50 |
| 70 Frank Malzone ML SP | .60 | 1.50 |
| 71 Lou Brock ML SP | 1.00 | 2.50 |
| 72 Billy Williams ML SP | .60 | 1.50 |
| 73 Early Wynn ML SP | .60 | 1.50 |
| 74 Jim Bunning ML SP | 1.00 | 2.50 |
| 75 Al Kaline ML SP | 1.50 | 4.00 |
| 76 Eddie Mathews ML SP | 1.50 | 4.00 |
| 77 Harmon Killebrew ML SP | 1.00 | 2.50 |
| 78 Gil Hodges ML SP | 1.00 | 2.50 |
| 79 Duke Snider ML SP | 1.00 | 2.50 |
| 80 Yogi Berra ML SP | 1.50 | 4.00 |
| 81 Whitey Ford ML SP | 1.00 | 2.50 |
| 82 Willie Stargell ML SP | 1.00 | 2.50 |
| 83 Willie McCovey ML SP | .60 | 1.50 |
| 84 Gaylord Perry ML SP | .60 | 1.50 |
| 85 Red Schoendienst ML SP | .60 | 1.50 |
| 86 Luis Castillo SP | .40 | 1.00 |
| 87 Derek Jeter SP | 2.50 | 6.00 |
| 88 Orlando Hudson SP | .40 | 1.00 |
| 89 Bobby Higginson SP | .40 | 1.00 |
| 90 Brent Butler SP | .40 | 1.00 |
| 91 Brad Wilkerson SP | .40 | 1.00 |
| 92 Craig Biggio SP | .60 | 1.50 |
| 93 Marlon Anderson SP | .40 | 1.00 |
| 94 Ty Wigginton SP | .40 | 1.00 |
| 95 Hideo Nomo SP | 1.00 | 2.50 |
| 96 Barry Larkin SP | .60 | 1.50 |
| 97 Roberto Alomar SP | .60 | 1.50 |
| 98 Omar Vizquel SP | .60 | 1.50 |
| 99 Andres Galarraga SP | .60 | 1.50 |
| 100 Shawn Green SP | .40 | 1.00 |
| 101 Rafael Furcal | .10 | .30 |
| 102 Bill Selby | .10 | .30 |
| 103 Brent Abernathy | .10 | .30 |
| 104 Nomar Garciaparra | .50 | 1.25 |
| 105 Michael Barrett | .10 | .30 |
| 106 Travis Hafner | .10 | .30 |
| 107 Carl Crawford | .10 | .30 |

|  |  | | |  |  | | |  |  | | |
|---|---|---|---|---|---|---|---|---|---|---|---|
| 108 | Jeff Cirillo | .10 | .30 | 196 | Kenny Lofton | .10 | .30 | 284 | Ray Durham | .10 | .30 |
| 109 | Mike Hampton | .10 | .30 | 197 | A.J. Pierzynski | .10 | .30 | 285 | Trot Nixon | .10 | .30 |
| 110 | Kip Wells | .10 | .30 | 198 | Larry Bigbie | .10 | .30 | 286 | Rondell White | .10 | .30 |
| 111 | Luis Alicea | .10 | .30 | 199 | Juan Uribe | .10 | .30 | 287 | Alex Gonzalez | .10 | .30 |
| 112 | Ellis Burks | .10 | .30 | 200 | Jeff Bagwell | .20 | .50 | 288 | Tomas Perez | .10 | .30 |
| 113 | Matt Anderson | .10 | .30 | 201 | Timo Perez | .10 | .30 | 289 | Jared Sandberg | .10 | .30 |
| 114 | Carlos Beltran | .10 | .30 | 202 | Jeremy Giambi | .10 | .30 | 290 | Jacque Jones | .10 | .30 |
| 115 | Paul Lo Duca | .10 | .30 | 203 | Deivi Cruz | .10 | .30 | 291 | Cliff Floyd | .10 | .30 |
| 116 | Lance Berkman | .10 | .30 | 204 | Marquis Grissom | .10 | .30 | 292 | Ryan Klesko | .10 | .30 |
| 117 | Moises Alou | .10 | .30 | 205 | Chipper Jones | .30 | .75 | 293 | Morgan Ensberg | .10 | .30 |
| 118 | Roger Cedeno | .10 | .30 | 206 | Alex Gonzalez | .10 | .30 | 294 | Jerry Hairston | .10 | .30 |
| 119 | Brad Fullmer | .10 | .30 | 207 | Steve Finley | .10 | .30 | 295 | Doug Mientkiewicz | .10 | .30 |
| 120 | Sean Burroughs | .10 | .30 | 208 | Ben Davis | .10 | .30 | 296 | Darin Erstad | .10 | .30 |
| 121 | Eric Byrnes | .10 | .30 | 209 | Mike Bordick | .10 | .30 | 297 | Jeff Conine | .10 | .30 |
| 122 | Milton Bradley | .10 | .30 | 210 | Casey Fossum | .10 | .30 | 298 | Johnny Estrada | .10 | .30 |
| 123 | Jason Giambi | .10 | .30 | 211 | Aramis Ramirez | .10 | .30 | 299 | Mark Mulder | .10 | .30 |
| 124 | Brook Fordyce | .10 | .30 | 212 | Aaron Boone | .10 | .30 | 300 | Jeff Kent | .10 | .30 |
| 125 | Kevin Appier | .10 | .30 | 213 | Orlando Cabrera | .10 | .30 | 301 | Roger Clemens | .60 | 1.50 |
| 126 | Steve Cox | .10 | .30 | 214 | Hee Seop Choi | .10 | .30 | 302 | Endy Chavez | .10 | .30 |
| 127 | Danny Bautista | .10 | .30 | 215 | Jeromy Burnitz | .10 | .30 | 303 | Joe Crede | .10 | .30 |
| 128 | Edgardo Alfonzo | .10 | .30 | 216 | Todd Hollandsworth | .10 | .30 | 304 | J.D. Drew | .10 | .30 |
| 129 | Matt Clement | .10 | .30 | 217 | Rey Sanchez | .10 | .30 | 305 | David Dellucci | .10 | .30 |
| 130 | Robb Nen | .10 | .30 | 218 | Jose Cruz | .10 | .30 | 306 | Eli Marrero | .10 | .30 |
| 131 | Roy Halladay | .10 | .30 | 219 | Roosevelt Brown | .10 | .30 | 307 | Josh Fogg | .10 | .30 |
| 132 | Brian Jordan | .10 | .30 | 220 | Odalis Perez | .10 | .30 | 308 | Mike Crudale | .10 | .30 |
| 133 | A.J. Burnett | .10 | .30 | 221 | Carlos Delgado | .10 | .30 | 309 | Bret Boone | .10 | .30 |
| 134 | Aaron Cook | .10 | .30 | 222 | Orlando Hernandez | .10 | .30 | 310 | Mariano Rivera | .30 | .75 |
| 135 | Paul Byrd | .10 | .30 | 223 | Adam Everett | .10 | .30 | 311 | Mike Piazza | .50 | 1.25 |
| 136 | Ramon Ortiz | .10 | .30 | 224 | Adrian Beltre | .10 | .30 | 312 | Jason Jennings | .10 | .30 |
| 137 | Adam Hyzdu | .10 | .30 | 225 | Ken Griffey Jr. | .50 | 1.25 | 313 | Jason Varitek | .30 | .75 |
| 138 | Rafael Soriano | .10 | .30 | 226 | Brad Penny | .10 | .30 | 314 | Vicente Padilla | .10 | .30 |
| 139 | Marty Cordova | .10 | .30 | 227 | Carlos Lee | .10 | .30 | 315 | Kevin Millwood | .10 | .30 |
| 140 | Nelson Cruz | .10 | .30 | 228 | J.C. Romero | .10 | .30 | 316 | Nick Johnson | .10 | .30 |
| 141 | Jamie Moyer | .10 | .30 | 229 | Ramon Martinez | .10 | .30 | 317 | Shane Reynolds | .10 | .30 |
| 142 | Raul Mondesi | .10 | .30 | 230 | Matt Morris | .10 | .30 | 318 | Joe Thurston | .10 | .30 |
| 143 | Josh Bard | .10 | .30 | 231 | Ben Howard | .10 | .30 | 319 | Mike Lamb | .10 | .30 |
| 144 | Elmer Dessens | .10 | .30 | 232 | Damon Minor | .10 | .30 | 320 | Aaron Sele | .10 | .30 |
| 145 | Rickey Henderson | .30 | .75 | 233 | Jason Marquis | .10 | .30 | 321 | Fernando Tatis | .10 | .30 |
| 146 | Joe McEwing | .10 | .30 | 234 | Paul Wilson | .10 | .30 | 322 | Randy Wolf | .10 | .30 |
| 147 | Luis Rivas | .10 | .30 | 235 | Ryan Dempster | .10 | .30 | 323 | David Justice | .10 | .30 |
| 148 | Armando Benitez | .10 | .30 | 236 | Jeffrey Hammonds | .10 | .30 | 324 | Andy Pettitte | .20 | .50 |
| 149 | Keith Foulke | .10 | .30 | 237 | Jaret Wright | .10 | .30 | 325 | Freddy Sanchez | .10 | .30 |
| 150 | Zach Day | .10 | .30 | 238 | Carlos Pena | .10 | .30 | 326 | Scott Spiezio | .10 | .30 |
| 151 | Trey Lunsford | .10 | .30 | 239 | Toby Hall | .10 | .30 | 327 | Randy Johnson | .30 | .75 |
| 152 | Bobby Abreu | .10 | .30 | 240 | Rick Helling | .10 | .30 | 328 | Karim Garcia | .10 | .30 |
| 153 | Juan Cruz | .10 | .30 | 241 | Alex Escobar | .10 | .30 | 329 | Eric Milton | .10 | .30 |
| 154 | Ramon Hernandez | .10 | .30 | 242 | Trevor Hoffman | .10 | .30 | 330 | Jermaine Dye | .10 | .30 |
| 155 | Brandon Duckworth | .10 | .30 | 243 | Bernie Williams | .20 | .50 | 331 | Kevin Brown | .10 | .30 |
| 156 | Matt Ginter | .10 | .30 | 244 | Jorge Julio | .10 | .30 | 332 | Adam Pettyjohn | .10 | .30 |
| 157 | Rob Mackowiak | .10 | .30 | 245 | Byung-Hyun Kim | .10 | .30 | 333 | Jason Lane | .10 | .30 |
| 158 | Josh Pearce | .10 | .30 | 246 | Mike Redmond | .10 | .30 | 334 | Mark Prior | .20 | .50 |
| 159 | Marlon Byrd | .10 | .30 | 247 | Tony Armas | .10 | .30 | 335 | Mike Lieberthal | .10 | .30 |
| 160 | Todd Walker | .10 | .30 | 248 | Aaron Rowand | .10 | .30 | 336 | Matt White | .10 | .30 |
| 161 | Chad Hermansen | .10 | .30 | 249 | Rusty Greer | .10 | .30 | 337 | John Patterson | .10 | .30 |
| 162 | Felix Escalona | .10 | .30 | 250 | Aaron Harang | .10 | .30 | 338 | Marcus Giles | .10 | .30 |
| 163 | Ruben Mateo | .10 | .30 | 251 | Jeremy Fikac | .10 | .30 | 339 | Kazuhisa Ishii | .10 | .30 |
| 164 | Mark Johnson | .10 | .30 | 252 | Jay Gibbons | .10 | .30 | 340 | Willie Harris | .10 | .30 |
| 165 | Juan Pierre | .10 | .30 | 253 | Brandon Puffer | .10 | .30 | 341 | Travis Phelps | .10 | .30 |
| 166 | Gary Sheffield | .10 | .30 | 254 | Dewayne Wise | .10 | .30 | 342 | Randall Simon | .10 | .30 |
| 167 | Edgar Martinez | .20 | .50 | 255 | Chan Ho Park | .10 | .30 | 343 | Manny Ramirez | .20 | .50 |
| 168 | Randy Winn | .10 | .30 | 256 | David Bell | .10 | .30 | 344 | Kerry Wood | .10 | .30 |
| 169 | Pokey Reese | .10 | .30 | 257 | Kenny Rogers | .10 | .30 | 345 | Shannon Stewart | .10 | .30 |
| 170 | Kevin Mench | .10 | .30 | 258 | Mark Quinn | .10 | .30 | 346 | Mike Mussina | .20 | .50 |
| 171 | Albert Pujols | .60 | 1.50 | 259 | Greg LaRocca | .10 | .30 | 347 | Joe Borchard | .10 | .30 |
| 172 | J.T. Snow | .10 | .30 | 260 | Reggie Taylor | .10 | .30 | 348 | Tyler Walker | .10 | .30 |
| 173 | Dean Palmer | .10 | .30 | 261 | Brett Tomko | .10 | .30 | 349 | Preston Wilson | .10 | .30 |
| 174 | Jay Payton | .10 | .30 | 262 | Jack Wilson | .10 | .30 | 350 | Damian Moss | .10 | .30 |
| 175 | Abraham Nunez | .10 | .30 | 263 | Billy Wagner | .10 | .30 | 351 | Eric Karros | .10 | .30 |
| 176 | Richie Sexson | .10 | .30 | 264 | Greg Norton | .10 | .30 | 352 | Bobby Kielty | .10 | .30 |
| 177 | Jose Vidro | .10 | .30 | 265 | Tim Salmon | .20 | .50 | 353 | Jason LaRue | .10 | .30 |
| 178 | Geoff Jenkins | .10 | .30 | 266 | Joe Randa | .10 | .30 | 354 | Phil Nevin | .10 | .30 |
| 179 | Dan Wilson | .10 | .30 | 267 | Geronimo Gil | .10 | .30 | 355 | Tony Graffanino | .10 | .30 |
| 180 | John Olerud | .10 | .30 | 268 | Johnny Damon | 1.00 | 2.50 | 356 | Antonio Alfonseca | .10 | .30 |
| 181 | Javy Lopez | .10 | .30 | 269 | Robin Ventura | .10 | .30 | 357 | Eddie Taubensee | .10 | .30 |
| 182 | Carl Everett | .10 | .30 | 270 | Frank Thomas | .30 | .75 | 358 | Luis Ugueto | .10 | .30 |
| 183 | Vernon Wells | .30 | .75 | 271 | Terrence Long | .10 | .30 | 359 | Greg Vaughn | .10 | .30 |
| 184 | Juan Gonzalez | .10 | .30 | 272 | Mark Redman | .10 | .30 | 360 | Corey Thurman | .10 | .30 |
| 185 | Jorge Posada | .20 | .50 | 273 | Mark Kotsay | .10 | .30 | 361 | Omar Infante | .10 | .30 |
| 186 | Mike Sweeney | .10 | .30 | 274 | Ben Sheets | .10 | .30 | 362 | Alex Cintron | .10 | .30 |
| 187 | Cesar Izturis | .10 | .30 | 275 | Reggie Sanders | .10 | .30 | 363 | Esteban Loaiza | .10 | .30 |
| 188 | Jason Schmidt | .10 | .30 | 276 | Mark Grace | .20 | .50 | 364 | Tino Martinez | .20 | .50 |
| 189 | Chris Richard | .10 | .30 | 277 | Eddie Guardado | .10 | .30 | 365 | David Eckstein | .10 | .30 |
| 190 | Jason Phillips | .10 | .30 | 278 | Julio Mateo | .10 | .30 | 366 | Dave Pember RC | .10 | .30 |
| 191 | Fred McGriff | .20 | .50 | 279 | Bengie Molina | .10 | .30 | 367 | Damian Rolls | .10 | .30 |
| 192 | Shea Hillenbrand | .10 | .30 | 280 | Bill Hall | .10 | .30 | 368 | Richard Hidalgo | .10 | .30 |
| 193 | Ivan Rodriguez | .20 | .50 | 281 | Eric Chavez | .10 | .30 | 369 | Brad Radke | .10 | .30 |
| 194 | Mike Lowell | .10 | .30 | 282 | Joe Kennedy | .10 | .30 | 370 | Alex Sanchez | .10 | .30 |
| 195 | Nerli Perez | .10 | .30 | 283 | John Valentin | .10 | .30 | 371 | Ben Grieve | .10 | .30 |

| | | |
|---|---|---|
| 372 Brandon Inge | .10 | .30 |
| 373 Adam Piatt | .10 | .30 |
| 374 Charles Johnson | .10 | .30 |
| 375 Rafael Palmeiro | .20 | .50 |
| 376 Joe Mays | .10 | .30 |
| 377 Derrek Lee | .20 | .50 |
| 378 Fernando Vina | .10 | .30 |
| 379 Andruw Jones | .20 | .50 |
| 380 Troy Glaus | .10 | .30 |
| 381 Bobby Hill | .10 | .30 |
| 382 C.C. Sabathia | .10 | .30 |
| 383 Jose Hernandez | .10 | .30 |
| 384 Al Leiter | .10 | .30 |
| 385 Jarrod Washburn | .10 | .30 |
| 386 Cody Ransom | .10 | .30 |
| 387 Matt Stairs | .10 | .30 |
| 388 Edgar Renteria | .10 | .30 |
| 389 Tsuyoshi Shinjo | .10 | .30 |
| 390 Matt Williams | .10 | .30 |
| 391 Bubba Trammell | .10 | .30 |
| 392 Jason Kendall | .10 | .30 |
| 393 Scott Rolen | .20 | .50 |
| 394 Chuck Knoblauch | .10 | .30 |
| 395 Jimmy Rollins | .10 | .30 |
| 396 Gary Bennett | .10 | .30 |
| 397 David Wells | .10 | .30 |
| 398 Ronnie Belliard | .10 | .30 |
| 399 Austin Kearns | .10 | .30 |
| 400 Tim Hudson | .10 | .30 |
| 401 Andy Van Hekken | .10 | .30 |
| 402 Ray Lankford | .10 | .30 |
| 403 Todd Helton | .20 | .50 |
| 404 Jeff Weaver | .10 | .30 |
| 405 Gabe Kapler | .10 | .30 |
| 406 Luis Gonzalez | .10 | .30 |
| 407 Sean Casey | .10 | .30 |
| 408 Kazuhiro Sasaki | .10 | .30 |
| 409 Mark Teixeira | .20 | .50 |
| 410 Brian Giles | .10 | .30 |
| 411 Robert Fick | .10 | .30 |
| 412 Wilkin Ruan | .10 | .30 |
| 413 Jose Rijo | .10 | .30 |
| 414 Ben Broussard | .10 | .30 |
| 415 Aubrey Huff | .10 | .30 |
| 416 Magglio Ordonez | .10 | .30 |
| 417 Barry Bonds AW | .40 | 1.00 |
| 418 Miguel Tejada AW | .10 | .30 |
| 419 Randy Johnson AW | .20 | .50 |
| 420 Barry Zito AW | .10 | .30 |
| 421 Jason Jennings AW | .10 | .30 |
| 422 Eric Hinske AW | .10 | .30 |
| 423 Benito Santiago AW | .10 | .30 |
| 424 Adam Kennedy AW | .10 | .30 |
| 425 Troy Glaus AW | .10 | .30 |
| 426 Brandon Phillips PR | .10 | .30 |
| 427 Jake Peavy PR | .10 | .30 |
| 428 Jason Romano PR | .10 | .30 |
| 429 Jerome Robertson PR | .10 | .30 |
| 430 Aaron Guiel PR | .10 | .30 |
| 431 Hank Blalock PR | .10 | .30 |
| 432 Brad Lidge PR | .10 | .30 |
| 433 Francisco Rodriguez PR | .10 | .30 |
| 434 Jaime Cerda PR | .10 | .30 |
| 435 Jung Bong PR | .10 | .30 |
| 436 Reed Johnson PR | .10 | .30 |
| 437 Rene Reyes PR | .10 | .30 |
| 438 Chris Snelling PR | .10 | .30 |
| 439 Miguel Olivo PR | .10 | .30 |
| 440 Brian Banks PR | .10 | .30 |
| 441 Eric Junge PR | .10 | .30 |
| 442 Kirk Saarloos PR | .10 | .30 |
| 443 Jamey Carroll PR | .10 | .30 |
| 444 Josh Hancock PR | .10 | .30 |
| 445 Michael Restovich PR | .10 | .30 |
| 446 Willie Bloomquist PR | .10 | .30 |
| 447 John Lackey PR | .10 | .30 |
| 448 Marcus Thames PR | .10 | .30 |
| 449 Victor Martinez PR | .20 | .50 |
| 450 Brett Myers PR | .10 | .30 |
| 451 Wes Obermueller PR | .10 | .30 |
| 452 Hansel Izquierdo PR | .10 | .30 |
| 453 Brian Tallet PR | .10 | .30 |
| 454 Craig Monroe PR | .10 | .30 |
| 455 Doug Devore PR | .10 | .30 |
| 456 John Buck PR | .10 | .30 |
| 457 Tony Alvarez PR | .10 | .30 |
| 458 Willy Mo Pena PR | .10 | .30 |
| 459 John Stephens PR | .10 | .30 |

| | | |
|---|---|---|
| 460 Tony Torcato PR | .10 | .30 |
| 461 Adam Kennedy BNR | .10 | .30 |
| 462 Alex Rodriguez BNR | .30 | .75 |
| 463 Derek Lowe BNR | .10 | .30 |
| 464 Garret Anderson BNR | .10 | .30 |
| 465 Pat Burrell BNR | .10 | .30 |
| 466 Eric Gagne BNR | .10 | .30 |
| 467 Tomo Ohka BNR | .10 | .30 |
| 468 Josh Phelps BNR | .10 | .30 |
| 469 Sammy Sosa BNR | .30 | .75 |
| 470 Jim Thome BNR | .30 | .75 |
| 471 Vladimir Guerrero BNR | .20 | .50 |
| 472 Jason Simontacchi BNR | .10 | .30 |
| 473 Adam Dunn BNR | .10 | .30 |
| 474 Jim Edmonds BNR | .10 | .30 |
| 475 Barry Bonds BNR | .40 | 1.00 |
| 476 Paul Konerko BNR | .10 | .30 |
| 477 Alfonso Soriano BNR | .10 | .30 |
| 478 Curt Schilling BNR | .10 | .30 |
| 479 John Smoltz BNR | .10 | .30 |
| 480 Torii Hunter BNR | .10 | .30 |
| 481 Rodrigo Lopez BNR | .10 | .30 |
| 482 Miguel Tejada BNR | .10 | .30 |
| 483 Eric Hinske BNR | .10 | .30 |
| 484 Roy Oswalt BNR | .10 | .30 |
| 485 Junior Spivey BNR | .10 | .30 |
| P1 Barry Bonds Pin | 3.00 | 8.00 |
| P87 Derek Jeter Promo | .75 | 2.00 |

## 2004 Fleer Tradition

| | | |
|---|---|---|
| COMPLETE SET (500) | 75.00 | 150.00 |
| COMP.SET w/o SP's (400) | 15.00 | 40.00 |
| COMMON CARD (1-400) | .10 | .30 |
| COMMON CARD (401-470) | .40 | 1.00 |
| COMMON CARD (471-500) | .40 | 1.00 |
| 401-445 STATED ODDS 1:2 | | |
| 446-461 STATED ODDS 1:6 | | |
| 462-470 STATED ODDS 1:9 | | |
| 471-500 STATED ODDS 1:3 | | |
| 1 Juan Pierre WS | .10 | .30 |
| 2 Josh Beckett WS | .10 | .30 |
| 3 Ivan Rodriguez WS | .20 | .50 |
| 4 Miguel Cabrera WS | .20 | .50 |
| 5 Dontrelle Willis WS | .20 | .50 |
| 6 Derek Jeter WS | .60 | 1.50 |
| 7 Jason Giambi WS | .10 | .30 |
| 8 Bernie Williams WS | .10 | .30 |
| 9 Alfonso Soriano WS | .10 | .30 |
| 10 Hideki Matsui WS | .50 | 1.25 |
| 11 Anderson/Ortiz/Lackey TL | .10 | .30 |
| 12 Gonzalez/Webb/Schilling TL | .10 | .30 |
| 13 Lopez/Sheffield/Ortiz TL | .10 | .30 |
| 14 Batista/Gibb/Ponson/John TL | .10 | .30 |
| 15 Manny/Nomar/Lowe/Pedro TL | .20 | .50 |
| 16 Sosa/Prior/Wood TL | .20 | .50 |
| 17 Thomas/Lee/Loaiza TL | .20 | .50 |
| 18 Dunn/Casey/Reit/Wilson TL | .10 | .30 |
| 19 Gerut/Sabathia TL | .10 | .30 |
| 20 Wilson/Oliver/Jennings TL | .10 | .30 |
| 21 Young/Maroth/Bonderman TL | .10 | .30 |
| 22 Lowell/Willis/Beckett TL | .20 | .50 |
| 23 Bagwell/Robertson/Miller TL | .20 | .50 |
| 24 Beltran/May TL | .10 | .30 |
| 25 Beltre/Green/Nomo/Brown TL | .10 | .30 |
| 26 Sexson/Sheets TL | .10 | .30 |
| 27 Hunter/Radke/Santana TL | .20 | .50 |
| 28 Vlad/Cabrera/Leiyh/Vazq TL | .20 | .50 |
| 29 Floyd/Wigg/Trach/Leiter TL | .10 | .30 |
| 30 Giambi/Pettitte/Mussina TL | .20 | .50 |
| 31 Chavez/Tejada/Hudson TL | .10 | .30 |
| 32 Thome/Wolf TL | .10 | .30 |
| 33 Sanders/Fogg/Wells TL | .10 | .30 |
| 34 Klesko/Loretta/Peavy TL | .10 | .30 |
| 35 Cruz Jr./Alfonzo/Schmidt TL | .10 | .30 |

| | | |
|---|---|---|
| 36 Boone/Moyer/Pineiro TL | .30 | .75 |
| 37 Pujols/Williams TL | .30 | .75 |
| 38 Huff/Zambrano TL | .10 | .30 |
| 39 A.Rodriguez/Thomson TL | .30 | .75 |
| 40 Delgado/Halladay TL | .10 | .30 |
| 41 Greg Maddux | .50 | 1.25 |
| 42 Ben Grieve | .10 | .30 |
| 43 Darin Erstad | .10 | .30 |
| 44 Ruben Sierra | .10 | .30 |
| 45 Byung-Hyung Kim | .10 | .30 |
| 46 Freddy Garcia | .10 | .30 |
| 47 Richard Hidalgo | .10 | .30 |
| 48 Tike Redman | .10 | .30 |
| 49 Kevin Millwood | .10 | .30 |
| 50 Marquis Grissom | .10 | .30 |
| 51 Jae Weong Seo | .10 | .30 |
| 52 Wil Cordero | .10 | .30 |
| 53 LaTroy Hawkins | .10 | .30 |
| 54 Jolbert Cabrera | .10 | .30 |
| 55 Kevin Appier | .10 | .30 |
| 56 John Lackey | .10 | .30 |
| 57 Garret Anderson | .10 | .30 |
| 58 R.A. Dickey | .10 | .30 |
| 59 David Segui | .10 | .30 |
| 60 Erubiel Durazo | .10 | .30 |
| 61 Bobby Abreu | .10 | .30 |
| 62 Travis Hafner | .10 | .30 |
| 63 Victor Zambrano | .10 | .30 |
| 64 Randy Johnson | .30 | .75 |
| 65 Bernie Williams | .20 | .50 |
| 66 J.T. Snow | .10 | .30 |
| 67 Sammy Sosa | .30 | .75 |
| 68 Al Leiter | .10 | .30 |
| 69 Jason Jennings | .10 | .30 |
| 70 Matt Morris | .10 | .30 |
| 71 Mike Hampton | .10 | .30 |
| 72 Juan Encarnacion | .10 | .30 |
| 73 Alex Gonzalez | .10 | .30 |
| 74 Bartolo Colon | .10 | .30 |
| 75 Brett Myers | .10 | .30 |
| 76 Michael Young | .10 | .30 |
| 77 Ichiro Suzuki | .60 | 1.50 |
| 78 Jason Johnson | .10 | .30 |
| 79 Brad Ausmus | .10 | .30 |
| 80 Ted Lilly | .10 | .30 |
| 81 Ken Griffey Jr. | .50 | 1.25 |
| 82 Chone Figgins | .10 | .30 |
| 83 Edgar Martinez | .20 | .50 |
| 84 Adam Eaton | .10 | .30 |
| 85 Ken Harvey | .10 | .30 |
| 86 Francisco Rodriguez | .10 | .30 |
| 87 Bill Mueller | .10 | .30 |
| 88 Mike Maroth | .10 | .30 |
| 89 Charles Johnson | .10 | .30 |
| 90 Jhonny Peralta | .10 | .30 |
| 91 Kip Wells | .10 | .30 |
| 92 Cesar Izturis | .10 | .30 |
| 93 Matt Clement | .10 | .30 |
| 94 Lyle Overbay | .10 | .30 |
| 95 Kirk Rueter | .10 | .30 |
| 96 Cristian Guzman | .10 | .30 |
| 97 Garrett Stephenson | .10 | .30 |
| 98 Lance Berkman | .10 | .30 |
| 99 Brett Tomko | .10 | .30 |
| 100 Chris Stynes | .10 | .30 |
| 101 Nate Cornejo | .10 | .30 |
| 102 Aaron Rowand | .10 | .30 |
| 103 Javier Vazquez | .10 | .30 |
| 104 Jason Kendall | .10 | .30 |
| 105 Mark Redman | .10 | .30 |
| 106 Benito Santiago | .10 | .30 |
| 107 C.C. Sabathia | .10 | .30 |
| 108 David Wells | .10 | .30 |
| 109 Mark Ellis | .10 | .30 |
| 110 Casey Blake | .10 | .30 |
| 111 Sean Burroughs | .10 | .30 |
| 112 Carlos Beltran | .10 | .30 |
| 113 Ramon Hernandez | .10 | .30 |
| 114 Eric Hinske | .10 | .30 |
| 115 Luis Gonzalez | .10 | .30 |
| 116 Jarrod Washburn | .10 | .30 |
| 117 Ronnie Belliard | .10 | .30 |
| 118 Troy Percival | .10 | .30 |
| 119 Jose Valentin | .10 | .30 |
| 120 Chase Utley | .20 | .50 |
| 121 Odalis Perez | .10 | .30 |
| 122 Steve Finley | .10 | .30 |
| 123 Bret Boone | .10 | .30 |

|  |  | | |
|---|--------|------|------|
| 124 | Jeff Conine | .10 | .30 |
| 125 | Josh Fogg | .10 | .30 |
| 126 | Neifi Perez | .10 | .30 |
| 127 | Ben Sheets | .10 | .30 |
| 128 | Randy Winn | .10 | .30 |
| 129 | Matt Stairs | .10 | .30 |
| 130 | Carlos Delgado | .10 | .30 |
| 131 | Morgan Ensberg | .10 | .30 |
| 132 | Vinny Castilla | .10 | .30 |
| 133 | Matt Mantei | .10 | .30 |
| 134 | Alex Rodriguez | .50 | 1.25 |
| 135 | Matthew LeCroy | .10 | .30 |
| 136 | Woody Williams | .10 | .30 |
| 137 | Frank Catalanotto | .10 | .30 |
| 138 | Rondell White | .10 | .30 |
| 139 | Scott Rolen | .20 | .50 |
| 140 | Cliff Floyd | .10 | .30 |
| 141 | Chipper Jones | .30 | .75 |
| 142 | Robin Ventura | .10 | .30 |
| 143 | Mariano Rivera | .30 | .75 |
| 144 | Brady Clark | .10 | .30 |
| 145 | Ramon Ortiz | .10 | .30 |
| 146 | Omar Infante | .10 | .30 |
| 147 | Mike Matheny | .10 | .30 |
| 148 | Pedro Martinez | .20 | .50 |
| 149 | Carlos Baerga | .10 | .30 |
| 150 | Shannon Stewart | .10 | .30 |
| 151 | Travis Lee | .10 | .30 |
| 152 | Eric Byrnes | .10 | .30 |
| 153 | Rafael Furcal | .10 | .30 |
| 154 | B.J. Surhoff | .10 | .30 |
| 155 | Zach Day | .10 | .30 |
| 156 | Marlon Anderson | .10 | .30 |
| 157 | Mark Hendrickson | .10 | .30 |
| 158 | Mike Mussina | .20 | .50 |
| 159 | Randall Simon | .10 | .30 |
| 160 | Jeff DaVanon | .10 | .30 |
| 161 | Joel Pineiro | .10 | .30 |
| 162 | Vernon Wells | .10 | .30 |
| 163 | Adam Kennedy | .10 | .30 |
| 164 | Trot Nixon | .10 | .30 |
| 165 | Rodrigo Lopez | .10 | .30 |
| 166 | Curt Schilling | .10 | .30 |
| 167 | Horacio Ramirez | .10 | .30 |
| 168 | Jason Marquis | .10 | .30 |
| 169 | Magglio Ordonez | .10 | .30 |
| 170 | Scott Schoeneweis | .10 | .30 |
| 171 | Andruw Jones | .20 | .50 |
| 172 | Tino Martinez | .10 | .50 |
| 173 | Moises Alou | .10 | .30 |
| 174 | Kelvim Escobar | .10 | .30 |
| 175 | Xavier Nady | .10 | .30 |
| 176 | Ramon Martinez | .10 | .30 |
| 177 | Pat Hentgen | .10 | .30 |
| 178 | Austin Kearns | .10 | .30 |
| 179 | D'Angelo Jimenez | .10 | .30 |
| 180 | Deivi Cruz | .10 | .30 |
| 181 | John Smoltz | .20 | .50 |
| 182 | Toby Hall | .10 | .30 |
| 183 | Mark Buehrle | .10 | .30 |
| 184 | Howie Clark | .10 | .30 |
| 185 | David Ortiz | .30 | .75 |
| 186 | Raul Mondesi | .10 | .30 |
| 187 | Milton Bradley | .10 | .30 |
| 188 | Jorge Julio | .10 | .30 |
| 189 | Victor Martinez | .10 | .30 |
| 190 | Gabe Kapler | .10 | .30 |
| 191 | Julio Franco | .10 | .30 |
| 192 | Ryan Freel | .10 | .30 |
| 193 | Brad Fullmer | .10 | .30 |
| 194 | Joe Borowski | .10 | .30 |
| 195 | Darren Oliver | .10 | .30 |
| 196 | Jason Varitek | .30 | .75 |
| 197 | Greg Myers | .10 | .30 |
| 198 | Eric Munson | .10 | .30 |
| 199 | Tim Wakefield | .10 | .30 |
| 200 | Kyle Farnsworth | .10 | .30 |
| 201 | Johnny Vander Wal | .10 | .30 |
| 202 | Alex Escobar | .10 | .30 |
| 203 | Sean Casey | .10 | .30 |
| 204 | John Thomson | .10 | .30 |
| 205 | Carlos Zambrano | .10 | .30 |
| 206 | Kenny Lofton | .10 | .30 |
| 207 | Marcus Giles | .10 | .30 |
| 208 | Wade Miller | .10 | .30 |
| 209 | Geoff Blum | .10 | .30 |
| 210 | Jason LaRue | .10 | .30 |
| 211 | Omar Vizquel | .20 | .50 |
| 212 | Carlos Pena | .10 | .30 |
| 213 | Adam Dunn | .10 | .30 |
| 214 | Oscar Villarreal | .10 | .30 |
| 215 | Paul Konerko | .10 | .30 |
| 216 | Hideo Nomo | .30 | .75 |
| 217 | Mike Sweeney | .10 | .30 |
| 218 | Coco Crisp | .10 | .30 |
| 219 | Shawn Chacon | .10 | .30 |
| 220 | Brook Fordyce | .10 | .30 |
| 221 | Josh Beckett | .10 | .30 |
| 222 | Paul Wilson | .10 | .30 |
| 223 | Josh Towers | .10 | .30 |
| 224 | Geoff Jenkins | .10 | .30 |
| 225 | Shawn Green | .10 | .30 |
| 226 | Derek Lee | .20 | .50 |
| 227 | Karim Garcia | .10 | .30 |
| 228 | Preston Wilson | .10 | .30 |
| 229 | Dane Sardinha | .10 | .30 |
| 230 | Aramis Ramirez | .10 | .30 |
| 231 | Doug Mientkiewicz | .10 | .30 |
| 232 | Jay Gibbons | .10 | .30 |
| 233 | Adam Everett | .10 | .30 |
| 234 | Brooks Kieschnick | .10 | .30 |
| 235 | Dmitri Young | .10 | .30 |
| 236 | Brad Penny | .10 | .30 |
| 237 | Todd Zeile | .10 | .30 |
| 238 | Eric Gagne | .10 | .30 |
| 239 | Esteban Loaiza | .10 | .30 |
| 240 | Billy Wagner | .10 | .30 |
| 241 | Nomar Garciaparra | .50 | 1.25 |
| 242 | Desi Relaford | .10 | .30 |
| 243 | Luis Rivas | .10 | .30 |
| 244 | Andy Pettitte | .20 | .50 |
| 245 | Ty Wigginton | .10 | .30 |
| 246 | Edgar Gonzalez | .10 | .30 |
| 247 | Brian Anderson | .10 | .30 |
| 248 | Richie Sexson | .10 | .30 |
| 249 | Russell Branyan | .10 | .30 |
| 250 | Jose Guillen | .10 | .30 |
| 251 | Chin-Hui Tsao | .10 | .30 |
| 252 | Jose Hernandez | .10 | .30 |
| 253 | Kevin Brown | .10 | .30 |
| 254 | Pete LaForest | .10 | .30 |
| 255 | Adrian Beltre | .10 | .30 |
| 256 | Jacque Jones | .10 | .30 |
| 257 | Jimmy Rollins | .10 | .30 |
| 258 | Brandon Phillips | .10 | .30 |
| 259 | Derek Jeter | .60 | 1.50 |
| 260 | Carl Everett | .10 | .30 |
| 261 | Wes Helms | .10 | .30 |
| 262 | Kyle Lohse | .10 | .30 |
| 263 | Jason Phillips | .10 | .30 |
| 264 | Jake Peavy | .10 | .30 |
| 265 | Orlando Hernandez | .10 | .30 |
| 266 | Keith Foulke | .10 | .30 |
| 267 | Brad Wilkerson | .10 | .30 |
| 268 | Corey Koskie | .10 | .30 |
| 269 | Josh Hall | .10 | .30 |
| 270 | Bobby Higginson | .10 | .30 |
| 271 | Andres Galarraga | .10 | .30 |
| 272 | Alfonso Soriano | .10 | .30 |
| 273 | Carlos Rivera | .10 | .30 |
| 274 | Steve Trachsel | .10 | .30 |
| 275 | David Bell | .10 | .30 |
| 276 | Endy Chavez | .10 | .30 |
| 277 | Jay Payton | .10 | .30 |
| 278 | Mark Mulder | .10 | .30 |
| 279 | Terrence Long | .10 | .30 |
| 280 | A.J. Burnett | .10 | .30 |
| 281 | Pokey Reese | .10 | .30 |
| 282 | Phil Nevin | .10 | .30 |
| 283 | Jose Contreras | .10 | .30 |
| 284 | Jim Thome | .20 | .50 |
| 285 | Pat Burrell | .10 | .30 |
| 286 | Luis Castillo | .10 | .30 |
| 287 | Juan Uribe | .10 | .30 |
| 288 | Raul Ibanez | .10 | .30 |
| 289 | Sidney Ponson | .10 | .30 |
| 290 | Scott Hatteberg | .10 | .30 |
| 291 | Jack Wilson | .10 | .30 |
| 292 | Reggie Sanders | .10 | .30 |
| 293 | Brian Giles | .10 | .30 |
| 294 | Craig Biggio | .20 | .50 |
| 295 | Kazuhisa Ishii | .10 | .30 |
| 296 | Jim Edmonds | .10 | .30 |
| 297 | Trevor Hoffman | .10 | .30 |
| 298 | Ray Durham | .10 | .30 |
| 299 | Mike Lieberthal | .10 | .30 |
| 300 | Tim Worrell | .10 | .30 |
| 301 | Chris George | .10 | .30 |
| 302 | Jamie Moyer | .10 | .30 |
| 303 | Mike Cameron | .10 | .30 |
| 304 | Matt Kinney | .10 | .30 |
| 305 | Aubrey Huff | .10 | .30 |
| 306 | Brian Lawrence | .10 | .30 |
| 307 | Carlos Guillen | .10 | .30 |
| 308 | J.D. Drew | .10 | .30 |
| 309 | Paul Lo Duca | .10 | .30 |
| 310 | Tim Salmon | .20 | .50 |
| 311 | Jason Schmidt | .10 | .30 |
| 312 | A.J. Pierzynski | .10 | .30 |
| 313 | Lance Carter | .10 | .30 |
| 314 | Julio Lugo | .10 | .30 |
| 315 | Johan Santana | .30 | .75 |
| 316 | Laynce Nix | .10 | .30 |
| 317 | John Olerud | .10 | .30 |
| 318 | Robb Quinlan | .10 | .30 |
| 319 | Scott Spiezio | .10 | .30 |
| 320 | Tony Clark | .10 | .30 |
| 321 | Jose Vidro | .10 | .30 |
| 322 | Shea Hillenbrand | .10 | .30 |
| 323 | Doug Glanville | .10 | .30 |
| 324 | Orlando Palmeiro | .10 | .30 |
| 325 | Juan Gonzalez | .10 | .30 |
| 326 | Jason Giambi | .10 | .30 |
| 327 | Junior Spivey | .10 | .30 |
| 328 | Tom Glavine | .20 | .50 |
| 329 | Reed Johnson | .10 | .30 |
| 330 | David Eckstein | .10 | .30 |
| 331 | Damian Jackson | .10 | .30 |
| 332 | Orlando Hudson | .10 | .30 |
| 333 | Barry Zito | .10 | .30 |
| 334 | Robert Fick | .10 | .30 |
| 335 | Aaron Boone | .10 | .30 |
| 336 | Rafael Palmeiro | .20 | .50 |
| 337 | Bobby Kielty | .10 | .30 |
| 338 | Tony Batista | .10 | .30 |
| 339 | Ryan Dempster | .10 | .30 |
| 340 | Derek Lowe | .10 | .30 |
| 341 | Alex Cintron | .10 | .30 |
| 342 | Jermaine Dye | .10 | .30 |
| 343 | John Burkett | .10 | .30 |
| 344 | Javy Lopez | .10 | .30 |
| 345 | Eric Karros | .10 | .30 |
| 346 | Corey Patterson | .10 | .30 |
| 347 | Josh Phelps | .10 | .30 |
| 348 | Ryan Klesko | .10 | .30 |
| 349 | Craig Wilson | .10 | .30 |
| 350 | Brian Roberts | .10 | .30 |
| 351 | Roberto Alomar | .20 | .50 |
| 352 | Frank Thomas | .30 | .75 |
| 353 | Gary Sheffield | .20 | .50 |
| 354 | Alex Gonzalez | .10 | .30 |
| 355 | Jose Cruz Jr. | .10 | .30 |
| 356 | Jerome Williams | .10 | .30 |
| 357 | Mark Kotsay | .10 | .30 |
| 358 | Chris Reitsma | .10 | .30 |
| 359 | Carlos Lee | .10 | .30 |
| 360 | Todd Helton | .20 | .50 |
| 361 | Gil Meche | .10 | .30 |
| 362 | Ryan Franklin | .10 | .30 |
| 363 | Josh Bard | .10 | .30 |
| 364 | Juan Pierre | .10 | .30 |
| 365 | Barry Larkin | .20 | .50 |
| 366 | Edgar Renteria | .10 | .30 |
| 367 | Alex Sanchez | .10 | .30 |
| 368 | Jeff Bagwell | .20 | .50 |
| 369 | Ben Broussard | .10 | .30 |
| 370 | Chan-Ho Park | .10 | .30 |
| 371 | Darrell May | .10 | .30 |
| 372 | Roy Oswalt | .10 | .30 |
| 373 | Craig Monroe | .10 | .30 |
| 374 | Fred McGriff | .20 | .50 |
| 375 | Bengie Molina | .10 | .30 |
| 376 | Aaron Guiel | .10 | .30 |
| 377 | Jerome Robertson | .10 | .30 |
| 378 | Kenny Rogers | .10 | .30 |
| 379 | Colby Lewis | .10 | .30 |
| 380 | Jeromy Burnitz | .10 | .30 |
| 381 | Orlando Cabrera | .10 | .30 |
| 382 | Joe Randa | .10 | .30 |
| 383 | Miguel Batista | .10 | .30 |
| 384 | Brad Radke | .10 | .30 |
| 385 | Jeremy Giambi | .10 | .30 |
| 386 | Vladimir Guerrero | .30 | .75 |
| 387 | Melvin Mora | .10 | .30 |

|  | | |
|---|---|---|
| 388 Royce Clayton | .10 | .30 |
| 389 Danny Garcia | .10 | .30 |
| 390 Manny Ramirez | .20 | .50 |
| 391 Dave McCarty | .10 | .30 |
| 392 Mark Grudzielanek | .10 | .30 |
| 393 Mike Piazza | .50 | 1.25 |
| 394 Jorge Posada | .20 | .50 |
| 395 Tim Hudson | .10 | .30 |
| 396 Placido Polanco | .10 | .30 |
| 397 Mark Loretta | .10 | .30 |
| 398 Jesse Foppert | .10 | .30 |
| 399 Albert Pujols | .60 | 1.50 |
| 400 Jeremi Gonzalez | .10 | .30 |
| 401 Paul Bako SP | .40 | 1.00 |
| 402 Luis Matos SP | .40 | 1.00 |
| 403 Johnny Damon SP | .60 | 1.50 |
| 404 Kerry Wood SP | .40 | 1.00 |
| 405 Joe Crede SP | .40 | 1.00 |
| 406 Jason Davis SP | .40 | 1.00 |
| 407 Larry Walker SP | .40 | 1.00 |
| 408 Ivan Rodriguez SP | .60 | 1.50 |
| 409 Nick Johnson SP | .40 | 1.00 |
| 410 Jose Lima SP | .40 | 1.00 |
| 411 Brian Jordan SP | .40 | 1.00 |
| 412 Eddie Guardado SP • | .40 | 1.00 |
| 413 Ron Calloway SP | .40 | 1.00 |
| 414 Aaron Heilman SP | .40 | 1.00 |
| 415 Eric Chavez SP | .40 | 1.00 |
| 416 Randy Wolf SP | .40 | 1.00 |
| 417 Jason Bay SP | .40 | 1.00 |
| 418 Edgardo Alfonzo SP | .40 | 1.00 |
| 419 Kazuhiro Sasaki SP | .40 | 1.00 |
| 420 Eduardo Perez SP | .40 | 1.00 |
| 421 Carl Crawford SP | .40 | 1.00 |
| 422 Troy Glaus SP | .40 | 1.00 |
| 423 Joaquin Benoit SP | .40 | 1.00 |
| 424 Russ Ortiz SP | .40 | 1.00 |
| 425 Larry Bigbie SP | .40 | 1.00 |
| 426 Todd Walker SP | .40 | 1.00 |
| 427 Kris Benson SP | .40 | 1.00 |
| 428 Sandy Alomar Jr. SP | .40 | 1.00 |
| 429 Jody Gerut SP | .40 | 1.00 |
| 430 Rene Reyes SP | .40 | 1.00 |
| 431 Mike Lowell SP | .40 | 1.00 |
| 432 Jeff Kent SP | .40 | 1.00 |
| 433 Mike MacDougal SP | .40 | 1.00 |
| 434 Dave Roberts SP | .40 | 1.00 |
| 435 Torii Hunter SP | .40 | 1.00 |
| 436 Tomo Ohka SP | .40 | 1.00 |
| 437 Jeremy Griffiths SP | .40 | 1.00 |
| 438 Miguel Tejada SP | .40 | 1.00 |
| 439 Vicente Padilla SP | .40 | 1.00 |
| 440 Bobby Hill SP | .40 | 1.00 |
| 441 Rich Aurilia SP | .40 | 1.00 |
| 442 Shigetoshi Hasegawa SP | .40 | 1.00 |
| 443 So Taguchi SP | .40 | 1.00 |
| 444 Damian Rolls SP | .40 | 1.00 |
| 445 Roy Halladay SP | .40 | 1.00 |
| 446 Rocco Baldelli SO SP | .40 | 1.00 |
| 447 Dontrelle Willis SO SP | .60 | 1.50 |
| 448 Mark Prior SO SP | .60 | 1.50 |
| 449 Jason Lane SO SP | .40 | 1.00 |
| 450 Angel Berroa SO SP | .40 | 1.00 |
| 451 Jose Reyes SO SP | .40 | 1.00 |
| 452 Ryan Wagner SO SP | .40 | 1.00 |
| 453 Marlon Byrd SO SP | .40 | 1.00 |
| 454 Hee Seop Choi SO SP | .40 | 1.00 |
| 455 Brandon Webb SO SP | .40 | 1.00 |
| 456 Bo Hart SO SP | .40 | 1.00 |
| 457 Hank Blalock SO SP | .40 | 1.00 |
| 458 Mark Teixeira SO SP | .60 | 1.50 |
| 459 Hideki Matsui SO SP | 1.50 | 4.00 |
| 460 Scott Podsednik SO SP | .40 | 1.00 |
| 461 Miguel Cabrera SO SP | .50 | 1.50 |
| 462 Josh Beckett AW SP | .40 | 1.00 |
| 463 Mariano Rivera AW SP | 1.00 | 2.50 |
| 464 Ivan Rodriguez AW SP | .60 | 1.50 |
| 465 Alex Rodriguez AW SP | 1.50 | 4.00 |
| 466 Albert Pujols AW SP | 2.00 | 5.00 |
| 467 Roy Halladay AW SP | .40 | 1.00 |
| 468 Eric Gagne AW SP | .40 | 1.00 |
| 469 Angel Berroa AW SP | .40 | 1.00 |
| 470 Dontrelle Willis AW SP | .60 | 1.50 |
| 471 Boof/Gregorio/Fischer SP | .40 | 1.00 |
| 472 Kata/Olson/Hammock SP | .40 | 1.00 |
| 473 Hessman/Waters/Aquino SP | .40 | 1.00 |
| 474 Mendez/Cabrera/Guthrie SP | .40 | 1.00 |
| 475 Almonte/Seibel/Sanchez SP | .40 | 1.00 |
| 476 Wellemeyer/Leicester/Mitre SP | .40 | 1.00 |
| 477 Stewart/Cotts/Miles SP | .40 | 1.00 |
| 478 Sledge/Hall/Clausen SP | .40 | 1.00 |
| 479 Cruceta/Stanford/Betan SP | .40 | 1.00 |
| 480 Lopez/Atkins/Barnes SP | .60 | 1.50 |
| 481 Ledez/Logan/Bonderman SP | .60 | 1.50 |
| 482 Willingham/Hoop/Roberts SP | .40 | 1.00 |
| 483 Porter/Gallo/Matranga SP | .40 | 1.00 |
| 484 DeJesus/Gilliam/Gobble SP | .40 | 1.00 |
| 485 Hill/Gonzalez/Brown SP | .40 | 1.00 |
| 486 Weeks/Liriano/Oberm SP | .60 | 1.50 |
| 487 Prieto/Ryan/Ford SP | .40 | 1.00 |
| 488 Manon/Ayala/Song SP | .40 | 1.00 |
| 489 Duncan/Hedman/Brazell SP | .40 | 1.00 |
| 490 Wang/M.Hern/M.Gonz SP | 2.00 | 5.00 |
| 491 Harden/Neu/Geary SP | .60 | 1.50 |
| 492 Markwell/Gaudin/Sanders SP | .40 | 1.00 |
| 493 Kemp/Nakamura/Carrasco SP | .40 | 1.00 |
| 494 Greene/Ojeda/Castro SP | 1.00 | 2.50 |
| 495 Lowry/Linden/Correia SP | .60 | 1.50 |
| 496 Looper/Sweeney/R.John SP | .40 | 1.00 |
| 497 J.Gall RC/Haren/Ohme SP | 1.00 | 2.50 |
| 498 Young/Waechter/Diaz SP | 1.00 | 2.50 |
| 499 Laird/Garcia/Nivar SP | .40 | 1.00 |
| 500 Rios/Quiroz/Rosario SP | .60 | 1.50 |

## 2005 Fleer Tradition

|  | | |
|---|---|---|
| COMPLETE SET (350) | 75.00 | 150.00 |
| COMP.SET w/o SP's (300) | 15.00 | 40.00 |
| COMMON CARD (1-300) | .10 | .30 |
| COMMON CARD (301-330) | 2.00 | 5.00 |
| COMMON CARD (331-350) | .40 | 1.00 |
| 301-350 STATED ODDS 1:2 H, 1:4 R | | |

|  | | |
|---|---|---|
| 1 Johan/Schil/Westbrook SL | .20 | .50 |
| 2 Sheets/Peavy/Randy SL | .20 | .50 |
| 3 Johan/Colon/Schilling SL | .10 | .30 |
| 4 Pavano/Oswalt/Clemens SL | .30 | .75 |
| 5 Johan/Pedro/Schilling SL | .10 | .30 |
| 6 Schmidt/Randy/Sheets SL | .20 | .50 |
| 7 Mora/Guerrero/Ichiro SL | .30 | .75 |
| 8 Beltra/Helton/Loretta SL | .10 | .30 |
| 9 Manny/Konerko/Ortiz SL | .20 | .50 |
| 10 Pujols/Beltre/Dunn SL | .30 | .75 |
| 11 Ortiz/Manny/Tejada SL | .20 | .50 |
| 12 Pujols/Castilla/Rolen SL | .20 | .50 |
| 13 Jason Bay | .10 | .30 |
| 14 Greg Maddux | .50 | 1.25 |
| 15 Melvin Mora | .10 | .30 |
| 16 Matt Stairs | .10 | .30 |
| 17 Scott Podsednik | .10 | .30 |
| 18 Bartolo Colon | .10 | .30 |
| 19 Roger Clemens | .50 | 1.25 |
| 20 Eric Hinske | .10 | .30 |
| 21 Johnny Estrada | .10 | .30 |
| 22 Brett Tomko | .10 | .30 |
| 23 John Buck | .10 | .30 |
| 24 Nomar Garciaparra | .30 | .75 |
| 25 Milton Bradley | .10 | .30 |
| 26 Craig Biggio | .20 | .50 |
| 27 Kyle Denney | .10 | .30 |
| 28 Brad Penny | .10 | .30 |
| 29 Todd Helton | .20 | .50 |
| 30 Luis Gonzalez | .10 | .30 |
| 31 Bill Hall | .10 | .30 |
| 32 Ruben Sierra | .10 | .30 |
| 33 Zack Greinke | .30 | .75 |
| 34 Sandy Alomar Jr. | .10 | .30 |
| 35 Jason Giambi | .10 | .30 |
| 36 Ben Sheets | .10 | .30 |
| 37 Edgardo Alfonzo | .10 | .30 |
| 38 Kenny Rogers | .10 | .30 |
| 39 Coco Crisp | .10 | .30 |
| 40 Randy Choate | .10 | .30 |
| 41 Braden Looper | .10 | .30 |
| 42 Adam Dunn | .10 | .30 |
| 43 Adam Eaton | .10 | .30 |
| 44 Luis Castillo | .10 | .30 |
| 45 Casey Fossum | .10 | .30 |
| 46 Mike Piazza | .30 | .75 |
| 47 Juan Pierre | .10 | .30 |
| 48 Doug Davis | .10 | .30 |
| 49 Manny Ramirez | .20 | .50 |
| 50 Travis Hafner | .10 | .30 |
| 51 Jack Wilson | .10 | .30 |
| 52 Mike Maroth | .10 | .30 |
| 53 Ken Harvey | .10 | .30 |
| 54 Brooks Kieschnick | .10 | .30 |
| 55 Brad Fullmer | .10 | .30 |
| 56 Octavio Dotel | .10 | .30 |
| 57 Mike Matheny | .10 | .30 |
| 58 Andruw Jones | .20 | .50 |
| 59 Alfonso Soriano | .10 | .30 |
| 60 Royce Clayton | .10 | .30 |
| 61 Jon Garland | .10 | .30 |
| 62 John Mabry | .10 | .30 |
| 63 Rafael Palmeiro | .20 | .50 |
| 64 Garett Atkins | .10 | .30 |
| 65 Brian Meadows | .10 | .30 |
| 66 Tony Armas Jr. | .10 | .30 |
| 67 Toby Hall | .10 | .30 |
| 68 Carlos Baerga | .10 | .30 |
| 69 Barry Larkin | .20 | .50 |
| 70 Jody Gerut | .10 | .30 |
| 71 Brent Mayne | .10 | .30 |
| 72 Shigetoshi Hasegawa | .10 | .30 |
| 73 Jose Cruz Jr. | .10 | .30 |
| 74 Dan Wilson | .10 | .30 |
| 75 Sidney Ponson | .10 | .30 |
| 76 Jason Jennings | .10 | .30 |
| 77 A.J. Burnett | .10 | .30 |
| 78 Tony Batista | .10 | .30 |
| 79 Kris Benson | .10 | .30 |
| 80 Sean Burroughs | .10 | .30 |
| 81 Eric Young | .10 | .30 |
| 82 Casey Kotchman | .10 | .30 |
| 83 Derrek Lee | .20 | .50 |
| 84 Mariano Rivera | .30 | .75 |
| 85 Julio Franco | .10 | .30 |
| 86 Corey Patterson | .10 | .30 |
| 87 Carlos Beltran | .30 | .75 |
| 88 Trevor Hoffman | .10 | .30 |
| 89 Danny Garcia | .10 | .30 |
| 90 Marcos Scutaro | .10 | .30 |
| 91 Marquis Grissom | .10 | .30 |
| 92 Aubrey Huff | .10 | .30 |
| 93 Tony Womack | .10 | .30 |
| 94 Placido Polanco | .10 | .30 |
| 95 Bengie Molina | .10 | .30 |
| 96 Roger Cedeno | .10 | .30 |
| 97 Geoff Jenkins | .10 | .30 |
| 98 Kip Wells | .10 | .30 |
| 99 Derek Jeter | .60 | 1.50 |
| 100 Omar Infante | .10 | .30 |
| 101 Phil Nevin | .10 | .30 |
| 102 Edgar Renteria | .10 | .30 |
| 103 B.J. Surhoff | .10 | .30 |
| 104 David DeJesus | .10 | .30 |
| 105 Raul Ibanez | .10 | .30 |
| 106 Hank Blalock | .10 | .30 |
| 107 Shawn Estes | .10 | .30 |
| 108 Willy Mo Pena | .10 | .30 |
| 109 Shawn Green | .10 | .30 |
| 110 David Wright | .75 | 2.00 |
| 111 Kenny Lofton | .10 | .30 |
| 112 Matt Clement | .10 | .30 |
| 113 Cesar Izturis | .10 | .30 |
| 114 John Lackey | .10 | .30 |
| 115 Torii Hunter | .10 | .30 |
| 116 Charles Johnson | .10 | .30 |
| 117 Ray Durham | .10 | .30 |
| 118 Luke Hudson | .10 | .30 |
| 119 Jeremy Bonderman | .10 | .30 |
| 120 Sean Casey | .10 | .30 |
| 121 Johnny Damon | .20 | .50 |
| 122 Eric Milton | .10 | .30 |
| 123 Shea Hillenbrand | .10 | .30 |
| 124 Johan Santana | .30 | .75 |
| 125 Jim Edmonds | .10 | .30 |
| 126 Javier Vazquez | .10 | .30 |
| 127 Jon Adkins | .10 | .30 |
| 128 Mike Lowell | .10 | .30 |
| 129 Khalil Greene | .20 | .50 |

## 2006 Fleer Tradition

ICHIRO

| | | |
|---|---|---|
| 19 Casey Kotchman | .12 | .30 |
| 20 Lance Berkman | .12 | .30 |
| 21 Craig Biggio | .20 | .50 |
| 22 Andy Pettitte | .20 | .50 |
| 23 Morgan Ensberg | .12 | .30 |
| 24 Brad Lidge | .12 | .30 |
| 25 Jered Weaver (RC) | 1.00 | 2.50 |
| 26 Roy Oswalt | .12 | .30 |
| 27 Eric Chavez | .12 | .30 |
| 28 Rich Harden | .12 | .30 |
| 29 Cole Hamels (RC) | .75 | 2.00 |
| 30 Huston Street | .12 | .30 |
| 31 Bobby Crosby | .12 | .30 |
| 32 Nick Swisher | .12 | .30 |
| 33 Vernon Wells | .12 | .30 |
| 34 Roy Halladay | .12 | .30 |
| 35 A.J. Burnett | .12 | .30 |
| 36 Troy Glaus | .12 | .30 |
| 37 B.J. Ryan | .12 | .30 |
| 38 Bengie Molina | .12 | .30 |
| 39 Alex Rios | .12 | .30 |
| 40 Prince Fielder | .75 | 2.00 |
| 41 Jose Capellan (RC) | .20 | .50 |
| 42 Rickie Weeks | .12 | .30 |
| 43 Ben Sheets | .12 | .30 |
| 44 Carlos Lee | .12 | .30 |
| 45 J.J. Hardy | .12 | .30 |
| 46 Albert Pujols | .60 | 1.50 |
| 47 Skip Schumaker (RC) | .20 | .50 |
| 48 Adam Wainwright (RC) | .30 | .75 |
| 49 Jim Edmonds | .20 | .50 |
| 50 Scott Rolen | .20 | .50 |
| 51 Chris Carpenter | .12 | .30 |
| 52 David Eckstein | .12 | .30 |
| 53 Derrek Lee | .12 | .30 |
| 54 Jon Lester RC | 1.25 | 3.00 |
| 55 Mark Prior | .20 | .50 |
| 56 Aramis Ramirez | .12 | .30 |
| 57 Juan Pierre | .12 | .30 |
| 58 Greg Maddux | .50 | 1.25 |
| 59 Michael Barrett | .12 | .30 |
| 60 Carl Crawford | .12 | .30 |
| 61 Scott Kazmir | .20 | .50 |
| 62 Jorge Cantu | .12 | .30 |
| 63 Jonny Gomes | .12 | .30 |
| 64 Julio Lugo | .12 | .30 |
| 65 Aubrey Huff | .12 | .30 |
| 66 Jeff Kent | .12 | .30 |
| 67 Nomar Garciaparra | .30 | .75 |
| 68 Rafael Furcal | .12 | .30 |
| 69 Tim Hamulack (RC) | .20 | .50 |
| 70 Chad Billingsley (RC) | .30 | .75 |
| 71 Hong-Chih Kuo (RC) | .50 | 1.25 |
| 72 J.D. Drew | .12 | .30 |
| 73 Moises Alou | .12 | .30 |
| 74 Randy Winn | .12 | .30 |
| 75 Jason Schmidt | .12 | .30 |
| 76 Jeremy Accardo (RC) | .12 | .30 |
| 77 Matt Cain (RC) | .30 | .75 |
| 78 Joel Zumaya (RC) | .50 | 1.25 |
| 79 Travis Hafner | .12 | .30 |
| 80 Victor Martinez | .12 | .30 |
| 81 Grady Sizemore | .20 | .50 |
| 82 C.C. Sabathia | .12 | .30 |
| 83 Jhonny Peralta | .12 | .30 |
| 84 Jason Michaels | .12 | .30 |
| 85 Jeremy Sowers (RC) | .20 | .50 |
| 86 Ichiro Suzuki | .50 | 1.25 |
| 87 Richie Sexson | .12 | .30 |
| 88 Adrian Beltre | .12 | .30 |
| 89 Felix Hernandez | .20 | .50 |
| 90 Kenji Johjima RC | 1.00 | 2.50 |
| 91 Jeff Harris RC | .20 | .50 |
| 92 Taylor Buchholz (RC) | .30 | .75 |
| 93 Miguel Cabrera | .30 | .75 |
| 94 Dontrelle Willis | .20 | .50 |
| 95 Jeremy Hermida (RC) | .20 | .50 |
| 96 Mike Jacobs (RC) | .12 | .30 |
| 97 Josh Johnson (RC) | .30 | .75 |
| 98 Hanley Ramirez (RC) | .50 | 1.25 |
| 99 Josh Willingham (RC) | .20 | .50 |
| 100 Dan Uggla (RC) | .50 | 1.25 |
| 101 David Wright | .50 | 1.25 |
| 102 Jose Reyes | .30 | .75 |
| 103 Pedro Martinez | .20 | .50 |
| 104 Carlos Beltran | .12 | .30 |
| 105 Carlos Delgado | .12 | .30 |
| 106 Billy Wagner | .12 | .30 |
| 107 Lastings Milledge (RC) | .30 | .75 |
| 108 Alfonso Soriano | .12 | .30 |
| 109 Jose Vidro | .12 | .30 |
| 110 Livan Hernandez | .12 | .30 |
| 111 Matt Kemp (RC) | .50 | 1.25 |
| 112 Brandon Watson (RC) | .20 | .50 |
| 113 Ryan Zimmerman (RC) | 1.00 | 2.50 |
| 114 Miguel Tejada | .12 | .30 |
| 115 Ramon Hernandez | .12 | .30 |
| 116 Brian Roberts | .12 | .30 |
| 117 Melvin Mora | .12 | .30 |
| 118 Erik Bedard | .12 | .30 |
| 119 Jay Gibbons | .12 | .30 |
| 120 Aaron Rakers (RC) | .20 | .50 |
| 121 Jake Peavy | .12 | .30 |
| 122 Brian Giles | .12 | .30 |
| 123 Khalil Greene | .12 | .30 |
| 124 Trevor Hoffman | .12 | .30 |
| 125 Josh Barfield (RC) | .20 | .50 |
| 126 Ben Johnson (RC) | .20 | .50 |
| 127 Ryan Howard | .50 | 1.25 |
| 128 Bobby Abreu | .12 | .30 |
| 129 Chase Utley | .30 | .75 |
| 130 Pat Burrell | .12 | .30 |
| 131 Jimmy Rollins | .12 | .30 |
| 132 Brett Myers | .12 | .30 |
| 133 Mike Thompson RC | .12 | .30 |
| 134 Jason Bay | .12 | .30 |
| 135 Oliver Perez | .12 | .30 |
| 136 Matt Capps (RC) | .20 | .50 |
| 137 Paul Maholm (RC) | .20 | .50 |
| 138 Nate McLouth (RC) | .20 | .50 |
| 139 John Van Benschoten (RC) | .20 | .50 |
| 140 Mark Teixeira | .20 | .50 |
| 141 Michael Young | .12 | .30 |
| 142 Hank Blalock | .12 | .30 |
| 143 Kevin Millwood | .12 | .30 |
| 144 Laynce Nix | .12 | .30 |
| 145 Francisco Cordero | .12 | .30 |
| 146 Ian Kinsler (RC) | .60 | 1.50 |
| 147 David Ortiz | .20 | .50 |
| 148 Manny Ramirez | .30 | .75 |
| 149 Jason Varitek | .20 | .50 |
| 150 Curt Schilling | .20 | .50 |
| 151 Josh Beckett | .12 | .30 |
| 152 Coco Crisp | .12 | .30 |
| 153 Jonathan Papelbon (RC) | 1.00 | 2.50 |
| 154 Ken Griffey Jr. | .50 | 1.25 |
| 155 Adam Dunn | .12 | .30 |
| 156 Felipe Lopez | .12 | .30 |
| 157 Bronson Arroyo | .12 | .30 |
| 158 Ryan Freel | .12 | .30 |
| 159 Chris Denorfia (RC) | .20 | .50 |
| 160 Todd Helton | .20 | .50 |
| 161 Garrett Atkins | .12 | .30 |
| 162 Matt Holliday | .30 | .75 |
| 163 Clint Barmes | .12 | .30 |
| 164 Kendry Morales (RC) | .50 | 1.25 |
| 165 Ryan Shealy (RC) | .20 | .50 |
| 166 Josh Wilson (RC) | .20 | .50 |
| 167 Reggie Sanders | .12 | .30 |
| 168 Angel Berroa | .12 | .30 |
| 169 Mike Sweeney | .12 | .30 |
| 170 Mark Grudzielanek | .12 | .30 |
| 171 Jeremy Affeldt | .12 | .30 |
| 172 Steve Stemle RC | .20 | .50 |
| 173 Justin Verlander (RC) | .75 | 2.00 |
| 174 Ivan Rodriguez | .20 | .50 |
| 175 Chris Shelton | .12 | .30 |
| 176 Jeremy Bonderman | .12 | .30 |
| 177 Magglio Ordonez | .12 | .30 |
| 178 Carlos Guillen | .12 | .30 |
| 179 Placido Polanco | .12 | .30 |
| 180 Johan Santana | .20 | .50 |
| 181 Torii Hunter | .12 | .30 |
| 182 Joe Nathan | .12 | .30 |
| 183 Joe Mauer | .30 | .75 |
| 184 Dave Gassner (RC) | .20 | .50 |
| 185 Jason Kubel (RC) | .20 | .50 |
| 186 Francisco Liriano (RC) | 1.00 | 2.50 |
| 187 Jim Thome | .20 | .50 |
| 188 Paul Konerko | .12 | .30 |
| 189 Scott Podsednik | .12 | .30 |
| 190 Tadahito Iguchi | .12 | .30 |
| 191 A.J. Pierzynski | .12 | .30 |
| 192 Jose Contreras | .12 | .30 |
| 193 Brian Anderson (RC) | .20 | .50 |
| 194 Hideki Matsui | .30 | .75 |
| 195 Wil Nieves | .20 | .50 |
| 196 Alex Rodriguez | .50 | 1.25 |
| 197 Gary Sheffield | .12 | .30 |
| 198 Randy Johnson | .30 | .75 |
| 199 Johnny Damon | .20 | .50 |
| 200 Derek Jeter | .75 | 2.00 |
| NNO Exquisite Redemption | | |

## 1933 Goudey

| | | |
|---|---|---|
| COMPLETE SET (239) | 25000.00 | 40000.00 |
| COMMON CARD (1-52) | 45.00 | 75.00 |
| COMMON (41/43/53-240) | 35.00 | 60.00 |
| WRAPPER (1-CENT, BAT.) | 75.00 | 100.00 |
| WRAPPER (1-CENT, AD) | 150.00 | 175.00 |
| 1 Benny Bengough RC | 900.00 | 1500.00 |
| 2 Dazzy Vance RC | 125.00 | 200.00 |
| 3 Hugh Critz BAT RC | 40.00 | 75.00 |
| 4 Heinie Schuble RC | 45.00 | 75.00 |
| 5 Babe Herman RC | 40.00 | 75.00 |
| 6 Jimmy Dykes RC | 40.00 | 75.00 |
| 7 Ted Lyons RC | 90.00 | 150.00 |
| 8 Roy Johnson RC | 45.00 | 75.00 |
| 9 Dave Harris RC | 45.00 | 75.00 |
| 10 Glenn Myatt RC | 45.00 | 75.00 |
| 11 Billy Rogell RC | 45.00 | 75.00 |
| 12 George Pipgras RC | 45.00 | 75.00 |
| 13 Fresco Thompson RC | 45.00 | 75.00 |
| 14 Henry Johnson RC | 45.00 | 75.00 |
| 15 Victor Sorrell RC | 45.00 | 75.00 |
| 16 George Blaeholder RC | 45.00 | 75.00 |
| 17 Watson Clark RC | 45.00 | 75.00 |
| 18 Muddy Ruel RC | 45.00 | 75.00 |
| 19 Bill Dickey RC | 200.00 | 350.00 |
| 20 Bill Terry THROW RC | 150.00 | 250.00 |
| 21 Phil Collins RC | 45.00 | 75.00 |
| 22 Pie Traynor RC | 150.00 | 250.00 |
| 23 Kiki Cuyler RC | 125.00 | 200.00 |
| 24 Horace Ford RC | 45.00 | 75.00 |
| 25 Paul Waner RC | 125.00 | 200.00 |
| 26 Bill Cissell RC | 45.00 | 75.00 |
| 27 George Connally RC | 45.00 | 75.00 |
| 28 Dick Bartell RC | 40.00 | 75.00 |
| 29 Jimmie Foxx RC | 350.00 | 600.00 |
| 30 Frank Hogan RC | 45.00 | 75.00 |
| 31 Tony Lazzeri RC | 250.00 | 400.00 |
| 32 Bud Clancy RC | 40.00 | 75.00 |
| 33 Ralph Kress RC | 45.00 | 75.00 |
| 34 Bob O'Farrell RC | 45.00 | 75.00 |
| 35 Al Simmons RC | 200.00 | 350.00 |
| 36 Tommy Thevenow RC | 45.00 | 75.00 |
| 37 Jimmy Wilson RC | 45.00 | 75.00 |
| 38 Fred Brickell RC | 45.00 | 75.00 |
| 39 Mark Koenig RC | 40.00 | 75.00 |
| 40 Taylor Douthit RC | 45.00 | 75.00 |
| 41 Gus Mancuso CATCH | 35.00 | 60.00 |
| 42 Eddie Collins RC | 90.00 | 150.00 |
| 43 Lew Fonseca RC | 35.00 | 60.00 |
| 44 Jim Bottomley RC | 90.00 | 150.00 |
| 45 Larry Benton RC | 45.00 | 75.00 |
| 46 Ethan Allen RC | 40.00 | 75.00 |
| 47 Heinie Manush BAT RC | 100.00 | 175.00 |
| 48 Marty McManus RC | 45.00 | 75.00 |
| 49 Frankie Frisch RC | 175.00 | 300.00 |
| 50 Ed Brandt RC | 45.00 | 75.00 |
| 51 Charlie Grimm RC | 40.00 | 75.00 |
| 52 Andy Cohen RC | 45.00 | 75.00 |
| 53 Babe Ruth RC | 5000.00 | 8000.00 |
| 54 Ray Kremer RC | 35.00 | 60.00 |
| 55 Pat Malone RC | 35.00 | 60.00 |
| 56 Red Ruffing RC | 100.00 | 175.00 |
| 57 Earl Clark RC | 35.00 | 60.00 |
| 58 Lefty O'Doul RC | 75.00 | 125.00 |
| 59 Bing Miller RC | 35.00 | 60.00 |
| 60 Waite Hoyt RC | 75.00 | 125.00 |
| 61 Max Bishop RC | 35.00 | 60.00 |

| | | | | | | | | | |
|---|---|---|---|---|---|---|---|---|---|
| ❑ 62 Pepper Martin RC | 75.00 | 125.00 | ❑ 150 Ray Kolp RC | 35.00 | 60.00 | ❑ 238 Hugh Critz FIELD RC | 35.00 | 60.00 |
| ❑ 63 Joe Cronin BAT RC | 90.00 | 150.00 | ❑ 151 Jake Flowers RC | 35.00 | 60.00 | ❑ 239 Leroy Parmelee RC | 35.00 | 60.00 |
| ❑ 64 Burleigh Grimes RC | 150.00 | 250.00 | ❑ 152 Zack Taylor RC | 35.00 | 60.00 | ❑ 240 Hal Schumacher RC | 75.00 | 125.00 |
| ❑ 65 Milt Gaston RC | 35.00 | 60.00 | ❑ 153 Buddy Myer RC | 35.00 | 60.00 | | | |
| ❑ 66 George Grantham RC | 35.00 | 60.00 | ❑ 154 Jimmie Foxx RC | 350.00 | 600.00 | **1934 Goudey** | | |
| ❑ 67 Guy Bush RC | 35.00 | 60.00 | ❑ 155 Joe Judge RC | 35.00 | 60.00 | | | |
| ❑ 68 Horace Lisenbee RC | 35.00 | 60.00 | ❑ 156 Danny MacFayden RC | 35.00 | 60.00 | | | |
| ❑ 69 Randy Moore RC | 35.00 | 60.00 | ❑ 157 Sam Byrd RC | 35.00 | 60.00 | | | |
| ❑ 70 Floyd (Pete) Scott RC | 35.00 | 60.00 | ❑ 158 Moe Berg RC | 250.00 | 400.00 | | | |
| ❑ 71 Robert J. Burke RC | 35.00 | 60.00 | ❑ 159 Oswald Bluege FIELD RC | 35.00 | 60.00 | | | |
| ❑ 72 Owen Carroll RC | 35.00 | 60.00 | ❑ 160 Lou Gehrig RC | 1800.00 | 3000.00 | | | |
| ❑ 73 Jesse Haines RC | 75.00 | 125.00 | ❑ 161 Al Spohrer RC | 35.00 | 60.00 | | | |
| ❑ 74 Eppa Rixey RC | 90.00 | 150.00 | ❑ 162 Leo Mangum RC | 35.00 | 60.00 | | | |
| ❑ 75 Willie Kamm RC | 35.00 | 60.00 | ❑ 163 Luke Sewell POR RC | 45.00 | 75.00 | | | |
| ❑ 76 Mickey Cochrane RC | 300.00 | 500.00 | ❑ 164 Lloyd Waner RC | 150.00 | 250.00 | | | |
| ❑ 77 Adam Comorosky RC | 35.00 | 60.00 | ❑ 165 Joe Sewell RC | 75.00 | 125.00 | | | |
| ❑ 78 Jack Quinn RC | 35.00 | 60.00 | ❑ 166 Sam West RC | 35.00 | 60.00 | | | |
| ❑ 79 Red Faber RC | 75.00 | 125.00 | ❑ 167 Jack Russell RC | 35.00 | 60.00 | | | |
| ❑ 80 Clyde Manion RC | 35.00 | 60.00 | ❑ 168 Goose Goslin RC | 125.00 | 200.00 | ❑ COMPLETE SET (96) | 9000.00 | 16000.00 |
| ❑ 81 Sam Jones RC | 35.00 | 60.00 | ❑ 169 Al Thomas RC | 35.00 | 60.00 | ❑ COMMON CARD (1-48) | 30.00 | 50.00 |
| ❑ 82 Dib Williams RC | 35.00 | 60.00 | ❑ 170 Harry McCurdy RC | 35.00 | 60.00 | ❑ COMMON CARD (49-72) | 40.00 | 75.00 |
| ❑ 83 Pete Jablonowski RC | 35.00 | 60.00 | ❑ 171 Charlie Jamieson RC | 35.00 | 60.00 | ❑ COMMON CARD (73-96) | 100.00 | 175.00 |
| ❑ 84 Glenn Spencer RC | 35.00 | 60.00 | ❑ 172 Billy Hargrave RC | 35.00 | 60.00 | ❑ WRAPPER (1-CENT, WHT.) | 75.00 | 100.00 |
| ❑ 85 Heinie Sand RC | 35.00 | 60.00 | ❑ 173 Roscoe Holm RC | 35.00 | 60.00 | ❑ WRAPPER (1-CENT, CLR.) | 75.00 | 100.00 |
| ❑ 86 Phil Todt RC | 35.00 | 60.00 | ❑ 174 Warren (Curly) Ogden RC | 35.00 | 60.00 | ❑ 1 Jimmie Foxx | 450.00 | 750.00 |
| ❑ 87 Frank O'Rourke RC | 35.00 | 60.00 | ❑ 175 Dan Howley MG RC | 35.00 | 60.00 | ❑ 2 Mickey Cochrane | 100.00 | 175.00 |
| ❑ 88 Russell Rollings RC | 35.00 | 60.00 | ❑ 176 John Ogden RC | 35.00 | 60.00 | ❑ 3 Charlie Grimm | 35.00 | 60.00 |
| ❑ 89 Tris Speaker RET | 175.00 | 300.00 | ❑ 177 Walter French RC | 35.00 | 60.00 | ❑ 4 Woody English | 30.00 | 50.00 |
| ❑ 90 Jess Petty RC | 35.00 | 60.00 | ❑ 178 Jackie Warner RC | 35.00 | 60.00 | ❑ 5 Ed Brandt | 30.00 | 50.00 |
| ❑ 91 Tom Zachary RC | 35.00 | 60.00 | ❑ 179 Fred Leach RC | 35.00 | 60.00 | ❑ 6 Dizzy Dean | 400.00 | 700.00 |
| ❑ 92 Lou Gehrig RC | 1500.00 | 2500.00 | ❑ 180 Eddie Moore RC | 35.00 | 60.00 | ❑ 7 Leo Durocher | 100.00 | 175.00 |
| ❑ 93 John Welch RC | 35.00 | 60.00 | ❑ 181 Babe Ruth RC | 3500.00 | 5000.00 | ❑ 8 Tony Piet | 30.00 | 50.00 |
| ❑ 94 Bill Walker RC | 35.00 | 60.00 | ❑ 182 Andy High RC | 35.00 | 60.00 | ❑ 9 Ben Chapman | 35.00 | 60.00 |
| ❑ 95 Alvin Crowder RC | 35.00 | 60.00 | ❑ 183 Rube Walberg RC | 35.00 | 60.00 | ❑ 10 Chuck Klein | 90.00 | 150.00 |
| ❑ 96 Willis Hudlin RC | 35.00 | 60.00 | ❑ 184 Charley Berry RC | 35.00 | 60.00 | ❑ 11 Paul Waner | 90.00 | 150.00 |
| ❑ 97 Joe Morrissey RC | 35.00 | 60.00 | ❑ 185 Bob Smith RC | 35.00 | 60.00 | ❑ 12 Carl Hubbell | 100.00 | 175.00 |
| ❑ 98 Wally Berger RC | 45.00 | 75.00 | ❑ 186 John Schulte RC | 35.00 | 60.00 | ❑ 13 Frankie Frisch | 100.00 | 175.00 |
| ❑ 99 Tony Cuccinello RC | 45.00 | 75.00 | ❑ 187 Heinie Manush RC | 90.00 | 150.00 | ❑ 14 Willie Kamm | 30.00 | 50.00 |
| ❑ 100 George Uhle RC | 35.00 | 60.00 | ❑ 188 Rogers Hornsby RC | 350.00 | 600.00 | ❑ 15 Alvin Crowder | 30.00 | 50.00 |
| ❑ 101 Richard Coffman RC | 35.00 | 60.00 | ❑ 189 Joe Cronin RC | 125.00 | 200.00 | ❑ 16 Joe Kuhel | 30.00 | 50.00 |
| ❑ 102 Travis Jackson RC | 90.00 | 150.00 | ❑ 190 Fred Schulte RC | 35.00 | 60.00 | ❑ 17 Hugh Critz | 30.00 | 50.00 |
| ❑ 103 Earle Combs RC | 75.00 | 125.00 | ❑ 191 Ben Chapman RC | 45.00 | 75.00 | ❑ 18 Heinie Manush | 75.00 | 125.00 |
| ❑ 104 Fred Marberry RC | 35.00 | 60.00 | ❑ 192 Walter Brown RC | 35.00 | 60.00 | ❑ 19 Lefty Grove | 175.00 | 300.00 |
| ❑ 105 Bernie Friberg RC | 35.00 | 60.00 | ❑ 193 Lynford Lary RC | 35.00 | 60.00 | ❑ 20 Frank Hogan | 30.00 | 50.00 |
| ❑ 106 Napoleon Lajoie SP | 15000.00 | 25000.00 | ❑ 194 Earl Averill RC | 125.00 | 200.00 | ❑ 21 Bill Terry | 125.00 | 200.00 |
| ❑ 107 Heinie Manush RC | 75.00 | 125.00 | ❑ 195 Evar Swanson RC | 35.00 | 60.00 | ❑ 22 Arky Vaughan | 75.00 | 125.00 |
| ❑ 108 Joe Kuhel RC | 35.00 | 60.00 | ❑ 196 Leroy Mahaffey RC | 35.00 | 60.00 | ❑ 23 Charley Gehringer | 125.00 | 200.00 |
| ❑ 109 Joe Cronin RC | 175.00 | 300.00 | ❑ 197 Rick Ferrell RC | 75.00 | 125.00 | ❑ 24 Ray Benge | 30.00 | 50.00 |
| ❑ 110 Goose Goslin RC | 150.00 | 250.00 | ❑ 198 Jack Burns RC | 35.00 | 60.00 | ❑ 25 Roger Cramer RC | 35.00 | 60.00 |
| ❑ 111 Monte Weaver RC | 35.00 | 60.00 | ❑ 199 Tom Bridges RC | 35.00 | 60.00 | ❑ 26 Gerald Walker RC | 30.00 | 50.00 |
| ❑ 112 Fred Schulte RC | 35.00 | 60.00 | ❑ 200 Bill Hallahan RC | 35.00 | 60.00 | ❑ 27 Luke Appling RC | 90.00 | 150.00 |
| ❑ 113 Oswald Bluege POR RC | 45.00 | 75.00 | ❑ 201 Ernie Orsatti RC | 35.00 | 60.00 | ❑ 28 Ed Coleman RC | 30.00 | 50.00 |
| ❑ 114 Luke Sewell FIELD RC | 45.00 | 75.00 | ❑ 202 Gabby Hartnett RC | 150.00 | 250.00 | ❑ 29 Larry French RC | 30.00 | 50.00 |
| ❑ 115 Cliff Heathcote RC | 35.00 | 60.00 | ❑ 203 Lon Warneke RC | 35.00 | 60.00 | ❑ 30 Julius Solters RC | 30.00 | 50.00 |
| ❑ 116 Eddie Morgan RC | 35.00 | 60.00 | ❑ 204 Riggs Stephenson RC | 35.00 | 60.00 | ❑ 31 Buck Jordan RC | 30.00 | 50.00 |
| ❑ 117 Rabbit Maranville RC | 75.00 | 125.00 | ❑ 205 Heinie Meine RC | 35.00 | 60.00 | ❑ 32 Blondy Ryan RC | 30.00 | 50.00 |
| ❑ 118 Val Picinich RC | 35.00 | 60.00 | ❑ 206 Gus Suhr RC | 35.00 | 60.00 | ❑ 33 Don Hurst RC | 30.00 | 50.00 |
| ❑ 119 Rogers Hornsby Field RC | 350.00 | 600.00 | ❑ 207 Mel Ott Bat RC | 250.00 | 400.00 | ❑ 34 Chick Hafey RC | 75.00 | 125.00 |
| ❑ 120 Carl Reynolds RC | 35.00 | 60.00 | ❑ 208 Bernie James RC | 35.00 | 60.00 | ❑ 35 Ernie Lombardi RC | 90.00 | 150.00 |
| ❑ 121 Walter Stewart RC | 35.00 | 60.00 | ❑ 209 Adolfo Luque RC | 45.00 | 75.00 | ❑ 36 Walter Betts RC | 30.00 | 50.00 |
| ❑ 122 Alvin Crowder RC | 35.00 | 60.00 | ❑ 210 Spud Davis RC | 35.00 | 60.00 | ❑ 37 Lou Gehrig | 2000.00 | 3000.00 |
| ❑ 123 Jack Russell RC | 35.00 | 60.00 | ❑ 211 Hack Wilson RC | 250.00 | 400.00 | ❑ 38 Oral Hildebrand RC | 30.00 | 50.00 |
| ❑ 124 Earl Whitehill RC | 35.00 | 60.00 | ❑ 212 Billy Urbanski RC | 35.00 | 60.00 | ❑ 39 Fred Walker RC | 30.00 | 50.00 |
| ❑ 125 Bill Terry RC | 150.00 | 250.00 | ❑ 213 Earl Adams RC | 35.00 | 60.00 | ❑ 40 John Stone | 30.00 | 50.00 |
| ❑ 126 Joe Moore BAT RC | 35.00 | 60.00 | ❑ 214 John Kerr RC | 35.00 | 60.00 | ❑ 41 George Earnshaw RC | 30.00 | 50.00 |
| ❑ 127 Mel Ott RC | 250.00 | 400.00 | ❑ 215 Russ Van Atta RC | 35.00 | 60.00 | ❑ 42 John Allen RC | 30.00 | 50.00 |
| ❑ 128 Chuck Klein RC | 100.00 | 175.00 | ❑ 216 Lefty Gomez RC | 175.00 | 300.00 | ❑ 43 Dick Porter RC | 30.00 | 50.00 |
| ❑ 129 Hal Schumacher PIT RC | 35.00 | 60.00 | ❑ 217 Frank Crosetti RC | 90.00 | 150.00 | ❑ 44 Tom Bridges | 35.00 | 60.00 |
| ❑ 130 Fred Fitzsimmons POR RC | 35.00 | 60.00 | ❑ 218 Wes Ferrell RC | 45.00 | 75.00 | ❑ 45 Oscar Melillo RC | 30.00 | 50.00 |
| ❑ 131 Fred Frankhouse RC | 35.00 | 60.00 | ❑ 219 Mule Haas UER RC | 35.00 | 60.00 | ❑ 46 Joe Stripp RC | 30.00 | 50.00 |
| ❑ 132 Jim Elliott RC | 35.00 | 60.00 | ❑ 220 Lefty Grove RC | 300.00 | 500.00 | ❑ 47 John Frederick RC | 30.00 | 50.00 |
| ❑ 133 Fred Lindstrom RC | 75.00 | 125.00 | ❑ 221 Dale Alexander RC | 35.00 | 60.00 | ❑ 48 Tex Carleton RC | 30.00 | 50.00 |
| ❑ 134 Sam Rice RC | 125.00 | 200.00 | ❑ 222 Charley Gehringer RC | 250.00 | 400.00 | ❑ 49 Sam Leslie RC | 40.00 | 75.00 |
| ❑ 135 Woody English RC | 35.00 | 60.00 | ❑ 223 Dizzy Dean RC | 500.00 | 800.00 | ❑ 50 Walter Beck RC | 40.00 | 75.00 |
| ❑ 136 Flint Rhem RC | 35.00 | 60.00 | ❑ 224 Frank Demaree RC | 35.00 | 60.00 | ❑ 51 Rip Collins RC | 40.00 | 75.00 |
| ❑ 137 Red Lucas RC | 35.00 | 60.00 | ❑ 225 Bill Jurges RC | 35.00 | 60.00 | ❑ 52 Herman Bell RC | 40.00 | 75.00 |
| ❑ 138 Herb Pennock RC | 100.00 | 175.00 | ❑ 226 Charley Root RC | 35.00 | 60.00 | ❑ 53 George Watkins RC | 40.00 | 75.00 |
| ❑ 139 Ben Cantwell RC | 35.00 | 60.00 | ❑ 227 Billy Herman RC | 90.00 | 150.00 | ❑ 54 Wesley Schulmerich RC | 40.00 | 75.00 |
| ❑ 140 Bump Hadley RC | 35.00 | 60.00 | ❑ 228 Tony Piet RC | 35.00 | 60.00 | ❑ 55 Ed Holley RC | 40.00 | 75.00 |
| ❑ 141 Ray Benge RC | 35.00 | 60.00 | ❑ 229 Arky Vaughan RC | 90.00 | 150.00 | ❑ 56 Mark Koenig | 60.00 | 100.00 |
| ❑ 142 Paul Richards RC | 45.00 | 75.00 | ❑ 230 Carl Hubbell PIT RC | 250.00 | 400.00 | ❑ 57 Bill Swift RC | 40.00 | 75.00 |
| ❑ 143 Glenn Wright RC | 35.00 | 60.00 | ❑ 231 Joe Moore FIELD RC | 35.00 | 60.00 | ❑ 58 Earl Grace RC | 40.00 | 75.00 |
| ❑ 144 Babe Ruth Bat DP RC | 2500.00 | 4000.00 | ❑ 232 Lefty O'Doul RC | 75.00 | 125.00 | ❑ 59 Joe Mowry RC | 40.00 | 75.00 |
| ❑ 145 Rube Walberg RC | 35.00 | 60.00 | ❑ 233 Johnny Vergez RC | 35.00 | 60.00 | ❑ 60 Lynn Nelson RC | 40.00 | 75.00 |
| ❑ 146 Walter Stewart PIT RC | 35.00 | 60.00 | ❑ 234 Carl Hubbell RC | 250.00 | 400.00 | ❑ 61 Lou Gehrig | 2000.00 | 3000.00 |
| ❑ 147 Leo Durocher RC | 125.00 | 200.00 | ❑ 235 Fred Fitzsimmons PIT RC | 35.00 | 60.00 | ❑ 62 Hank Greenberg RC | 400.00 | 700.00 |
| ❑ 148 Eddie Farrell RC | 35.00 | 60.00 | ❑ 236 George Davis RC | 35.00 | 60.00 | ❑ 63 Minter Hayes RC | 40.00 | 75.00 |
| ❑ 149 Babe Ruth RC | 3000.00 | 5000.00 | ❑ 237 Gus Mancuso FIELD RC | 35.00 | 60.00 | | | |

| | | |
|---|---|---|
| 64 Frank Grube RC | 40.00 | 75.00 |
| 65 Cliff Bolton RC | 40.00 | 75.00 |
| 66 Mel Harder RC | 60.00 | 100.00 |
| 67 Bob Weiland RC | 40.00 | 75.00 |
| 68 Bob Johnson RC | 60.00 | 100.00 |
| 69 John Marcum RC | 40.00 | 75.00 |
| 70 Pete Fox RC | 40.00 | 75.00 |
| 71 Lyle Tinning RC | 40.00 | 75.00 |
| 72 Arndt Jorgens RC | 40.00 | 75.00 |
| 73 Ed Wells RC | 100.00 | 175.00 |
| 74 Bob Boken RC | 100.00 | 175.00 |
| 75 Bill Werber RC | 100.00 | 175.00 |
| 76 Hal Trosky RC | 125.00 | 200.00 |
| 77 Joe Vosmik RC | 100.00 | 175.00 |
| 78 Pinky Higgins RC | 125.00 | 200.00 |
| 79 Eddie Durham RC | 100.00 | 175.00 |
| 80 Marty McManus CK | 100.00 | 175.00 |
| 81 Bob Brown CK RC | 100.00 | 175.00 |
| 82 Bill Hallahan CK | 100.00 | 175.00 |
| 83 Jim Mooney CK RC | 100.00 | 175.00 |
| 84 Paul Derringer CK RC | 125.00 | 225.00 |
| 85 Adam Comorosky CK | 100.00 | 175.00 |
| 86 Lloyd Johnson CK RC | 100.00 | 175.00 |
| 87 George Darrow CK RC | 100.00 | 175.00 |
| 88 Homer Peel CK RC | 100.00 | 175.00 |
| 89 Linus Frey CK RC | 100.00 | 175.00 |
| 90 KiKi Cuyler CK | 200.00 | 350.00 |
| 91 Dolph Camilli CK RC | 125.00 | 200.00 |
| 92 Steve Larkin RC | 100.00 | 175.00 |
| 93 Fred Ostermueller RC | 100.00 | 175.00 |
| 94 Red Rolfe RC | 125.00 | 200.00 |
| 95 Myril Hoag RC | 100.00 | 175.00 |
| 96 James DeShong RC | 300.00 | 500.00 |

## 1949 Leaf

TED WILLIAMS

| | | |
|---|---|---|
| COMPLETE SET (98) | 25000.00 | 40000.00 |
| COMMON CARD (1-168) | 15.00 | 25.00 |
| COMMON SP's | 200.00 | 350.00 |
| WRAPPER (1-CENT) | 120.00 | 160.00 |
| 1 Joe DiMaggio | 1800.00 | 3000.00 |
| 3 Babe Ruth | 1500.00 | 2500.00 |
| 4 Stan Musial | 600.00 | 1000.00 |
| 5 Virgil Trucks SP RC | 250.00 | 400.00 |
| 8 S.Paige SP RC | 9000.00 | 15000.00 |
| 10 Dizzy Trout | 25.00 | 40.00 |
| 11 Phil Rizzuto | 200.00 | 350.00 |
| 13 Cass Michaels SP RC | 200.00 | 300.00 |
| 14 Billy Johnson | 15.00 | 25.00 |
| 17 Frank Overmire RC | 15.00 | 25.00 |
| 19 Johnny Wyrostek SP | 200.00 | 300.00 |
| 20 Hank Sauer SP RC | 250.00 | 400.00 |
| 22 Al Evans RC | 15.00 | 25.00 |
| 26 Sam Chapman | 25.00 | 40.00 |
| 27 Mickey Harris RC | 15.00 | 25.00 |
| 28 Jim Hegan RC | 25.00 | 40.00 |
| 29 Elmer Valo RC | 25.00 | 40.00 |
| 30 Billy Goodman SP RC | 250.00 | 400.00 |
| 31 Lou Brissie RC | 15.00 | 25.00 |
| 32 Warren Spahn | 200.00 | 350.00 |
| 33 Peanuts Lowrey SP RC | 200.00 | 300.00 |
| 36 Al Zarilla SP | 200.00 | 300.00 |
| 38 Ted Kluszewski RC | 125.00 | 200.00 |
| 39 Ewell Blackwell | 35.00 | 60.00 |
| 43 Ed Stevens SP RC | 200.00 | 300.00 |
| 45 Ken Keltner SP RC | 200.00 | 300.00 |
| 46 Johnny Mize | 60.00 | 100.00 |
| 47 George Vico RC | 15.00 | 25.00 |
| 48 Johnny Schmitz SP RC | 200.00 | 300.00 |
| 49 Del Ennis RC | 35.00 | 60.00 |
| 50 Dick Wakefield RC | 15.00 | 25.00 |
| 51 Alvin Dark SP RC | 300.00 | 500.00 |
| 53 Johnny VanderMeer RC | 60.00 | 100.00 |
| 54 Bobby Adams SP RC | 200.00 | 300.00 |
| 55 Tommy Henrich SP | 300.00 | 500.00 |
| 56 Larry Jansen RC | 25.00 | 40.00 |
| 57 Bob McCall RC | 15.00 | 25.00 |
| 59 Luke Appling | 60.00 | 100.00 |
| 61 Jake Early RC | 15.00 | 25.00 |
| 62 Eddie Joost SP | 200.00 | 300.00 |
| 63 Barney McCosky SP | 200.00 | 300.00 |
| 65 Bob Elliott UER | 60.00 | 100.00 |
| 66 Orval Grove SP RC | 200.00 | 300.00 |
| 68 Eddie Miller SP | 200.00 | 300.00 |
| 70 Honus Wagner | 200.00 | 350.00 |
| 72 Hank Edwards RC | 15.00 | 25.00 |
| 73 Pat Seerey RC | 15.00 | 25.00 |
| 75 Dom DiMaggio SP | 350.00 | 600.00 |
| 76 Ted Williams | 700.00 | 1200.00 |
| 77 Roy Smalley RC | 15.00 | 25.00 |
| 78 Hoot Evers SP RC | 200.00 | 300.00 |
| 79 Jackie Robinson SP | 1200.00 | 2000.00 |
| 81 Whitey Kurowski SP RC | 200.00 | 300.00 |
| 82 Johnny Lindell | 25.00 | 40.00 |
| 83 Bobby Doerr | 60.00 | 100.00 |
| 84 Sid Hudson | 15.00 | 25.00 |
| 85 Dave Philley SP RC | 250.00 | 400.00 |
| 86 Ralph Weigel RC | 15.00 | 25.00 |
| 88 Frank Gustine SP RC | 200.00 | 300.00 |
| 91 Ralph Kiner | 125.00 | 200.00 |
| 93 Bob Feller SP | 1400.00 | 2000.00 |
| 95 Snuffy Stirnweiss | 25.00 | 40.00 |
| 97 Marty Marion | 35.00 | 60.00 |
| 98 Hal Newhouser SP RC | 350.00 | 600.00 |
| 104 Eddie Stewart SP RC | 200.00 | 300.00 |
| 106 Lou Boudreau MG RC | 60.00 | 100.00 |
| 108 Matt Batts SP RC | 200.00 | 300.00 |
| 111 Jerry Priddy RC | 15.00 | 25.00 |
| 113 Dutch Leonard SP | 200.00 | 300.00 |
| 117 Joe Gordon RC | 25.00 | 40.00 |
| 122 George Kell SP RC | 350.00 | 600.00 |
| 121 Johnny Pesky SP RC | 250.00 | 400.00 |
| 123 Cliff Fannin SP RC | 200.00 | 300.00 |
| 125 Andy Pafko RC | 15.00 | 25.00 |
| 127 Enos Slaughter SP | 500.00 | 800.00 |
| 128 Buddy Rosar | 15.00 | 25.00 |
| 129 Kirby Higbe SP | 200.00 | 300.00 |
| 131 Sid Gordon SP | 200.00 | 300.00 |
| 133 Tommy Holmes SP RC | 300.00 | 500.00 |
| 137 Harry Walker SP RC | 250.00 | 400.00 |
| 138 Larry Doby SP RC | 400.00 | 700.00 |
| 139 Johnny Hopp RC | 15.00 | 25.00 |
| 142 D.Murtaugh SP RC | 250.00 | 400.00 |
| 143 Dick Sisler SP RC | 200.00 | 300.00 |
| 144 Bob Dillinger SP RC | 200.00 | 300.00 |
| 146 Pete Reiser SP | 300.00 | 500.00 |
| 149 Hank Majeski SP RC | 200.00 | 300.00 |
| 153 Floyd Baker SP RC | 200.00 | 300.00 |
| 156 H.Brecheen SP RC | 250.00 | 400.00 |
| 159 Mizell Platt RC | 15.00 | 25.00 |
| 160 Bob Scheffing SP RC | 200.00 | 300.00 |
| 161 V.Stephens SP RC | 250.00 | 400.00 |
| 163 F.Hutchinson SP RC | 250.00 | 400.00 |
| 165 Dale Mitchell SP RC | 250.00 | 400.00 |
| 168 Phil Cavarretta SP | 300.00 | 500.00 |
| 42A Kent Peterson RC | 15.00 | 25.00 |
| 42B Kent Peterson Red Cap | | |
| NNO Album | | |
| 102A G.Hermanski ERR | 150.00 | 250.00 |
| 102B Gene Hermanski COR RC | 25.00 | 40.00 |
| 136A C.Aberson Full Slv RC | 15.00 | 25.00 |
| 136B C.Aberson Short Slv | 150.00 | 250.00 |

## 2009 O-Pee-Chee

| | | |
|---|---|---|
| COMPLETE SET (600) | 60.00 | 120.00 |
| COMMON CARD (1-600) | .15 | .40 |
| COMMON OLSEN (561-600) | .40 | 1.00 |
| RC ODDS 1:3 HOBBY/RETAIL | | |
| CL ODDS 1:3 HOBBY/RETAIL | | |
| MOMENT ODDS 1:6 HOBBY/RETAIL | | |
| LL ODDS 1:8 HOBBY/RETAIL | | |
| 1 Melvin Mora | .15 | .40 |
| 2 Jim Thome | .25 | .60 |
| 3 Jonathan Sanchez | .15 | .40 |
| 4 Cesar Izturis | .15 | .40 |
| 5 A.J. Pierzynski | .15 | .40 |
| 6 Brian Schneider | .15 | .40 |
| 7 J.D. Drew | .15 | .40 |
| 8 Brian Schneider | .15 | .40 |
| 9 John Grabow | .15 | .40 |
| 10 Jimmy Rollins | .25 | .60 |
| 11 Jeff Baker | .15 | .40 |
| 12 Daniel Cabrera | .15 | .40 |
| 13 Kyle Lohse | .15 | .40 |
| 14 Jason Giambi | .15 | .40 |
| 15 Nate McLouth | .15 | .40 |
| 16 Gary Matthews | .15 | .40 |
| 17 Cody Ross | .15 | .40 |
| 18 Justin Masterson | .25 | .60 |
| 19 Jose Lopez | .15 | .40 |
| 20 Brian Roberts | .15 | .40 |
| 21 Cla Meredith | .15 | .40 |
| 22 Ben Francisco | .15 | .40 |
| 23 Brian McCann | .25 | .60 |
| 24 Carlos Guillen | .15 | .40 |
| 25 Chien-Ming Wang | .40 | 1.00 |
| 26 Brandon Phillips | .25 | .60 |
| 27 Saul Rivera | .15 | .40 |
| 28 Torii Hunter | .15 | .40 |
| 29 Jamie Moyer | .15 | .40 |
| 30 Kevin Youkilis | .25 | .60 |
| 31 Martin Prado | .15 | .40 |
| 32 Magglio Ordonez | .25 | .60 |
| 33 Nomar Garciaparra | .25 | .60 |
| 34 Takashi Saito | .15 | .40 |
| 35 Chase Headley | .15 | .40 |
| 36 Mike Pelfrey | .15 | .40 |
| 37 Ronny Cedeno | .15 | .40 |
| 38 Dallas McPherson | .15 | .40 |
| 39 Zack Greinke | .25 | .60 |
| 40 Matt Cain | .15 | .40 |
| 41 Xavier Nady | .15 | .40 |
| 42 Willie Aybar | .15 | .40 |
| 43 Edgar Gonzalez | .15 | .40 |
| 44 Gabe Gross | .15 | .40 |
| 45 Joey Votto | .25 | .60 |
| 46 Jason Michaels | .15 | .40 |
| 47 Eric Chavez | .15 | .40 |
| 48 Jason Bartlett | .15 | .40 |
| 49 Jeremy Guthrie | .15 | .40 |
| 50 Matt Holliday | .25 | .60 |
| 51 Ross Ohlendorf | .15 | .40 |
| 52 Gil Meche | .15 | .40 |
| 53 B.J. Upton | .25 | .60 |
| 54 Ryan Doumit | .15 | .40 |
| 55 Jay Bruce | .40 | 1.00 |
| 56 Huston Street | .15 | .40 |
| 57 Bobby Crosby | .15 | .40 |
| 58 Jose Valverde | .15 | .40 |
| 59 Brian Tallet | .15 | .40 |
| 60 Adam Dunn | .25 | .60 |
| 61 Victor Martinez | .25 | .60 |
| 62 Jeff Francoeur | .25 | .60 |
| 63 Emilio Bonifacio | .15 | .40 |
| 64 Chone Figgins | .15 | .40 |
| 65 Alexei Ramirez | .25 | .60 |
| 66 Brian Giles | .15 | .40 |
| 67 Khalil Greene | .15 | .40 |
| 68 Phil Hughes | .25 | .60 |
| 69 Mike Aviles | .15 | .40 |
| 70 Ryan Braun | .50 | 1.25 |
| 71 Braden Looper | .15 | .40 |
| 72 Jhonny Peralta | .15 | .40 |
| 73 Ian Stewart | .15 | .40 |
| 74 James Loney | .25 | .60 |
| 75 Chase Utley | .40 | 1.00 |
| 76 Reed Johnson | .15 | .40 |
| 77 Jorge Cantu | .15 | .40 |
| 78 Julio Lugo | .15 | .40 |
| 79 Raul Ibanez | .25 | .60 |
| 80 Lance Berkman | .25 | .60 |
| 81 Joel Peralta | .15 | .40 |
| 82 Mark Hendrickson | .15 | .40 |
| 83 Jeff Suppan | .15 | .40 |
| 84 Scott Olsen | .15 | .40 |
| 85 Joba Chamberlain | .50 | 1.25 |
| 86 Fausto Carmona | .15 | .40 |
| 87 Andy Pettitte | .25 | .60 |
| 88 Jim Johnson | .15 | .40 |
| 89 Chris Snyder | .15 | .40 |
| 90 Nick Swisher | .25 | .60 |
| 91 Edgar Renteria | .15 | .40 |
| 92 Brandon Inge | .15 | .40 |
| 93 Aubrey Huff | .15 | .40 |
| 94 Stephen Drew | .25 | .60 |
| 95 Denard Span | .25 | .60 |
| 96 Carl Crawford | .25 | .60 |
| 97 Felix Pie | .15 | .40 |
| 98 Jeremy Sowers | .15 | .40 |
| 99 Trevor Hoffman | .15 | .40 |
| 100 Albert Pujols | 1.00 | 2.50 |
| 101 Radhames Liz | .15 | .40 |
| 102 Doug Davis | .15 | .40 |

|  |  | | |
|---|------|---|---|
| 103 | Joel Hanrahan | .15 | .40 |
| 104 | Seth Smith | .15 | .40 |
| 105 | Francisco Liriano | .15 | .40 |
| 106 | Bobby Abreu | .15 | .40 |
| 107 | Willie Harris | .15 | .40 |
| 108 | Travis Ishikawa | .15 | .40 |
| 109 | Travis Hafner | .15 | .40 |
| 110 | Adrian Gonzalez | .25 | .60 |
| 111 | Shin-Soo Choo | .15 | .40 |
| 112 | Robinson Cano | .25 | .60 |
| 113 | Matt Capps | .15 | .40 |
| 114 | Gerald Laird | .15 | .40 |
| 115 | Max Scherzer | .25 | .60 |
| 116 | Mike Jacobs | .15 | .40 |
| 117 | Asdrubal Cabrera | .15 | .40 |
| 118 | J.J. Hardy | .15 | .40 |
| 119 | Justin Upton | .25 | .60 |
| 120 | Mariano Rivera | .25 | .60 |
| 121 | Jack Cust | .15 | .40 |
| 122 | Orlando Hudson | .15 | .40 |
| 123 | Brian Wilson | .15 | .40 |
| 124 | Heath Bell | .15 | .40 |
| 125 | Chipper Jones | .40 | 1.00 |
| 126 | Jason Marquis | .15 | .40 |
| 127 | Rocco Baldelli | .15 | .40 |
| 128 | Rafael Perez | .15 | .40 |
| 129 | Carlos Gomez | .15 | .40 |
| 130 | Kerry Wood | .15 | .40 |
| 131 | Adam Wainwright | .25 | .60 |
| 132 | Michael Bourn | .15 | .40 |
| 133 | Cristian Guzman | .15 | .40 |
| 134 | Dustin McGowan | .15 | .40 |
| 135 | James Shields | .15 | .40 |
| 136 | Matt Lindstrom | .15 | .40 |
| 137 | Rick Ankiel | .25 | .60 |
| 138 | J.P. Howell | .15 | .40 |
| 139 | Ben Zobrist | .15 | .40 |
| 140 | Tim Hudson | .15 | .40 |
| 141 | Clayton Kershaw | .40 | 1.00 |
| 142 | Edwin Encarnacion | .15 | .40 |
| 143 | Kevin Millwood | .15 | .40 |
| 144 | Jack Hannahan | .15 | .40 |
| 145 | Alex Gordon | .25 | .60 |
| 146 | Chad Durbin | .15 | .40 |
| 147 | Derrek Lee | .25 | .60 |
| 148 | Kevin Gregg | .15 | .40 |
| 149 | Clint Barmes | .15 | .40 |
| 150 | Dustin Pedroia | .50 | 1.25 |
| 151 | Brad Hawpe | .15 | .40 |
| 152 | Steven Shell | .15 | .40 |
| 153 | Jesse Crain | .15 | .40 |
| 154 | Edwar Ramirez | .15 | .40 |
| 155 | Jair Jurrjens | .25 | .60 |
| 156 | Matt Albers | .15 | .40 |
| 157 | Endy Chavez | .15 | .40 |
| 158 | Steve Pearce | .15 | .40 |
| 159 | John Maine | .15 | .40 |
| 160 | Ryan Theriot | .15 | .40 |
| 161 | Eric Stults | .15 | .40 |
| 162 | Cha-Seung Baek | .15 | .40 |
| 163 | Alex Gonzalez | .15 | .40 |
| 164 | Dan Haren | .15 | .40 |
| 165 | Edwin Jackson | .15 | .40 |
| 166 | Felipe Lopez | .15 | .40 |
| 167 | David DeJesus | .15 | .40 |
| 168 | Todd Wellemeyer | .15 | .40 |
| 169 | Joey Gathright | .15 | .40 |
| 170 | Roy Oswalt | .25 | .60 |
| 171 | Carlos Pena | .25 | .60 |
| 172 | Nick Hundley | .15 | .40 |
| 173 | Adrian Beltre | .15 | .40 |
| 174 | Omar Vizquel | .15 | .40 |
| 175 | Cole Hamels | .40 | 1.00 |
| 176 | Jarrod Saltalamacchia | .15 | .40 |
| 177 | Yuniesky Betancourt | .15 | .40 |
| 178 | Placido Polanco | .15 | .40 |
| 179 | Ryan Spilborghs | .15 | .40 |
| 180 | Josh Beckett | .25 | .60 |
| 181 | Cory Wade | .15 | .40 |
| 182 | Aaron Laffey | .15 | .40 |
| 183 | Kosuke Fukudome | .40 | 1.00 |
| 184 | Miguel Montero | .15 | .40 |
| 185 | Edinson Volquez | .15 | .40 |
| 186 | Jon Garland | .15 | .40 |
| 187 | Andruw Jones | .15 | .40 |
| 188 | Vernon Wells | .15 | .40 |
| 189 | Zach Duke | .15 | .40 |
| 190 | David Wright | .50 | 1.25 |
| 191 | Ryan Madson | .15 | .40 |
| 192 | Hideki Okajima | .15 | .40 |
| 193 | Ryan Church | .15 | .40 |
| 194 | Adam Jones | .25 | .60 |
| 195 | Geovany Soto | .25 | .60 |
| 196 | Jeremy Hermida | .15 | .40 |
| 197 | Juan Rivera | .15 | .40 |
| 198 | David Weathers | .15 | .40 |
| 199 | Jorge Campillo | .15 | .40 |
| 200 | Derek Jeter | 1.00 | 2.50 |
| 201 | Brett Myers | .15 | .40 |
| 202 | Brett Gardner | .15 | .40 |
| 203 | Rafael Furcal | .15 | .40 |
| 204 | Wandy Rodriguez | .15 | .40 |
| 205 | Ricky Nolasco | .15 | .40 |
| 206 | Ryan Freel | .15 | .40 |
| 207 | Jeremy Bonderman | .15 | .40 |
| 208 | Michael Wuertz | .15 | .40 |
| 209 | Hank Blalock | .15 | .40 |
| 210 | Alfonso Soriano | .25 | .60 |
| 211 | Jeff Clement | .15 | .40 |
| 212 | Garrett Atkins | .15 | .40 |
| 213 | Luis Vizcaino | .15 | .40 |
| 214 | Tim Redding | .15 | .40 |
| 215 | Ryan Ludwick | .25 | .60 |
| 216 | Mark Teahen | .15 | .40 |
| 217 | Chris Young | .15 | .40 |
| 218 | David Aardsma | .15 | .40 |
| 219 | Ubaldo Jimenez | .15 | .40 |
| 220 | Ryan Howard | .50 | 1.25 |
| 221 | Skip Schumaker | .15 | .40 |
| 222 | Craig Counsell | .15 | .40 |
| 223 | Chris Iannetta | .15 | .40 |
| 224 | Jason Kubel | .15 | .40 |
| 225 | Johan Santana | .40 | 1.00 |
| 226 | Luke Hochevar | .15 | .40 |
| 227 | Jason Bay | .25 | .60 |
| 228 | Alex Hinshaw | .15 | .40 |
| 229 | Jon Rauch | .15 | .40 |
| 230 | Carlos Quentin | .15 | .40 |
| 231 | Coco Crisp | .15 | .40 |
| 232 | Casey Blake | .15 | .40 |
| 233 | Carlos Marmol | .15 | .40 |
| 234 | Fernando Rodney | .15 | .40 |
| 235 | Jed Lowrie | .25 | .60 |
| 236 | Brad Penny | .15 | .40 |
| 237 | Reggie Willits | .15 | .40 |
| 238 | Mike Hampton | .15 | .40 |
| 239 | Mike Lowell | .15 | .40 |
| 240 | Randy Johnson | .40 | 1.00 |
| 241 | Jarrod Washburn | .15 | .40 |
| 242 | B.J. Ryan | .15 | .40 |
| 243 | Javier Vazquez | .15 | .40 |
| 244 | Todd Helton | .25 | .60 |
| 245 | Matt Garza | .15 | .40 |
| 246 | Ramon Hernandez | .15 | .40 |
| 247 | Johnny Cueto | .15 | .40 |
| 248 | Willy Taveras | .15 | .40 |
| 249 | Carlos Silva | .15 | .40 |
| 250 | Manny Ramirez | .40 | 1.00 |
| 251 | A.J. Burnett | .25 | .60 |
| 252 | Aaron Cook | .15 | .40 |
| 253 | Josh Bard | .15 | .40 |
| 254 | Aaron Harang | .15 | .40 |
| 255 | Jeff Samardzija | .25 | .60 |
| 256 | Brad Lidge | .15 | .40 |
| 257 | Pedro Feliz | .15 | .40 |
| 258 | Kazuo Matsui | .15 | .40 |
| 259 | Joe Blanton | .15 | .40 |
| 260 | Ian Kinsler | .25 | .60 |
| 261 | Rich Harden | .15 | .40 |
| 262 | Kelly Johnson | .15 | .40 |
| 263 | Anibal Sanchez | .15 | .40 |
| 264 | Mike Adams | .15 | .40 |
| 265 | Chad Billingsley | .25 | .60 |
| 266 | Chris Davis | .15 | .40 |
| 267 | Brandon Moss | .15 | .40 |
| 268 | Matt Kemp | .40 | 1.00 |
| 269 | Jose Arredondo | .15 | .40 |
| 270 | Mark Teixeira | .40 | 1.00 |
| 271 | Glen Perkins | .15 | .40 |
| 272 | Pat Burrell | .25 | .60 |
| 273 | Luke Scott | .15 | .40 |
| 274 | Scott Feldman | .15 | .40 |
| 275 | Ichiro Suzuki | .60 | 1.50 |
| 276 | Cliff Floyd | .15 | .40 |
| 277 | Bill Hall | .15 | .40 |
| 278 | Bronson Arroyo | .15 | .40 |
| 279 | Lyle Overbay | .15 | .40 |
| 280 | Aramis Ramirez | .15 | .40 |
| 281 | Jeff Keppinger | .15 | .40 |
| 282 | Brandon Morrow | .15 | .40 |
| 283 | Ryan Shealy | .15 | .40 |
| 284 | Andy Sonnanstine | .15 | .40 |
| 285 | Josh Johnson | .15 | .40 |
| 286 | Carlos Ruiz | .15 | .40 |
| 287 | Gregg Zaun | .15 | .40 |
| 288 | Kenji Johjima | .25 | .60 |
| 289 | Mike Gonzalez | .15 | .40 |
| 290 | Carlos Delgado | .25 | .60 |
| 291 | Gary Sheffield | .25 | .60 |
| 292 | Brian Anderson | .15 | .40 |
| 293 | Josh Hamilton | .40 | 1.00 |
| 294 | Tom Gorzelanny | .15 | .40 |
| 295 | Yunel Escobar | .15 | .40 |
| 296 | Scott Hairston | .15 | .40 |
| 297 | Luis Castillo | .15 | .40 |
| 298 | Gabe Kapler | .15 | .40 |
| 299 | Nelson Cruz | .15 | .40 |
| 300 | Tim Lincecum | .50 | 1.25 |
| 301 | Brian Bannister | .15 | .40 |
| 302 | Frank Francisco | .15 | .40 |
| 303 | Jose Guillen | .15 | .40 |
| 304 | Erick Aybar | .15 | .40 |
| 305 | Brad Ziegler | .15 | .40 |
| 306 | John Baker | .15 | .40 |
| 307 | Hong-Chih Kuo | .15 | .40 |
| 308 | Jo Jo Reyes | .15 | .40 |
| 309 | Josh Willingham | .15 | .40 |
| 310 | Billy Wagner | .15 | .40 |
| 311 | Nick Blackburn | .15 | .40 |
| 312 | David Purcey | .15 | .40 |
| 313 | Rafael Soriano | .15 | .40 |
| 314 | Zach Miner | .15 | .40 |
| 315 | Andre Ethier | .25 | .60 |
| 316 | Rickie Weeks | .15 | .40 |
| 317 | Akinori Iwamura | .25 | .60 |
| 318 | Hideki Matsui | .40 | 1.00 |
| 319 | Ryan Rowland-Smith | .15 | .40 |
| 320 | Miguel Cabrera | .25 | .60 |
| 321 | Manny Parra | .15 | .40 |
| 322 | Jack Wilson | .15 | .40 |
| 323 | Jeremy Reed | .15 | .40 |
| 324 | Chris Coste | .15 | .40 |
| 325 | Grady Sizemore | .25 | .60 |
| 326 | Andy LaRoche | .15 | .40 |
| 327 | Joel Pineiro | .15 | .40 |
| 328 | Brian Buscher | .15 | .40 |
| 329 | Randy Wolf | .15 | .40 |
| 330 | Jake Peavy | .25 | .60 |
| 331 | Curtis Granderson | .40 | 1.00 |
| 332 | Kyle Kendrick | .15 | .40 |
| 333 | Joe Saunders | .15 | .40 |
| 334 | Russell Martin | .25 | .60 |
| 335 | Conor Jackson | .15 | .40 |
| 336 | Paul Konerko | .15 | .40 |
| 337 | Kevin Slowey | .15 | .40 |
| 338 | Mark DeRosa | .15 | .40 |
| 339 | Garret Anderson | .15 | .40 |
| 340 | Michael Young | .25 | .60 |
| 341 | Greg Dobbs | .15 | .40 |
| 342 | Brian Moehler | .15 | .40 |
| 343 | Alex Rios | .15 | .40 |
| 344 | Mike Napoli | .15 | .40 |
| 345 | Bobby Jenks | .15 | .40 |
| 346 | Daric Barton | .15 | .40 |
| 347 | Jason Kendall | .15 | .40 |
| 348 | Chad Qualls | .15 | .40 |
| 349 | Milton Bradley | .15 | .40 |
| 350 | Joe Mauer | .40 | 1.00 |
| 351 | Livan Hernandez | .15 | .40 |
| 352 | Chris Ray | .15 | .40 |
| 353 | Bob Howry | .15 | .40 |
| 354 | Manny Corpas | .15 | .40 |
| 355 | Ervin Santana | .15 | .40 |
| 356 | Billy Butler | .15 | .40 |
| 357 | Russ Springer | .15 | .40 |
| 358 | Micah Owings | .15 | .40 |
| 359 | Corey Hart | .15 | .40 |
| 360 | Francisco Rodriguez | .25 | .60 |
| 361 | Ted Lilly | .15 | .40 |
| 362 | Adam Everett | .15 | .40 |
| 363 | Scott Rolen | .40 | 1.00 |
| 364 | Troy Tulowitzki | .25 | .60 |
| 365 | Jacoby Ellsbury | .40 | 1.00 |
| 366 | Jayson Werth | .15 | .40 |

|  |  | | |
|---|---|---|---|
| ☐ 367 | Gio Gonzalez | .15 | .40 |
| ☐ 368 | Mark Ellis | .15 | .40 |
| ☐ 369 | Brendan Harris | .15 | .40 |
| ☐ 370 | David Ortiz | .25 | .60 |
| ☐ 371 | Carlos Lee | .15 | .40 |
| ☐ 372 | Jonathan Broxton | .15 | .40 |
| ☐ 373 | Jesse Litsch | .15 | .40 |
| ☐ 374 | Barry Zito | .15 | .40 |
| ☐ 375 | Daisuke Matsuzaka | .60 | 1.50 |
| ☐ 376 | Kevin Kouzmanoff | .15 | .40 |
| ☐ 377 | Jesse Carlson | .15 | .40 |
| ☐ 378 | Brian Fuentes | .15 | .40 |
| ☐ 379 | Mark Reynolds | .15 | .40 |
| ☐ 380 | Brandon Webb | .25 | .60 |
| ☐ 381 | Scott Kazmir | .25 | .60 |
| ☐ 382 | Blake DeWitt | .15 | .40 |
| ☐ 383 | Kurt Suzuki | .15 | .40 |
| ☐ 384 | Chris Volstad | .15 | .40 |
| ☐ 385 | Gavin Floyd | .15 | .40 |
| ☐ 386 | Paul Maholm | .15 | .40 |
| ☐ 387 | Freddy Sanchez | .15 | .40 |
| ☐ 388 | Scott Baker | .15 | .40 |
| ☐ 389 | John Danks | .15 | .40 |
| ☐ 390 | CC Sabathia | .25 | .60 |
| ☐ 391 | Ryan Dempster | .15 | .40 |
| ☐ 392 | Tim Wakefield | .15 | .40 |
| ☐ 393 | Mike Cameron | .15 | .40 |
| ☐ 394 | Aaron Rowand | .15 | .40 |
| ☐ 395 | Howie Kendrick | .15 | .40 |
| ☐ 396 | Marlon Byrd | .15 | .40 |
| ☐ 397 | Dave Bush | .15 | .40 |
| ☐ 398 | George Sherrill | .15 | .40 |
| ☐ 399 | Francisco Cordero | .15 | .40 |
| ☐ 400 | Evan Longoria | .60 | 1.50 |
| ☐ 401 | Hiroki Kuroda | .15 | .40 |
| ☐ 402 | Sean Gallagher | .15 | .40 |
| ☐ 403 | Yovani Gallardo | .15 | .40 |
| ☐ 404 | Ryan Sweeney | .15 | .40 |
| ☐ 405 | Chris Dickerson | .15 | .40 |
| ☐ 406 | Jason Varitek | .25 | .60 |
| ☐ 407 | Erik Bedard | .15 | .40 |
| ☐ 408 | J.J. Putz | .15 | .40 |
| ☐ 409 | Wily Mo Pena | .15 | .40 |
| ☐ 410 | Rich Hill | .15 | .40 |
| ☐ 411 | Delmon Young | .25 | .60 |
| ☐ 412 | David Eckstein | .15 | .40 |
| ☐ 413 | Marcus Thames | .15 | .40 |
| ☐ 414 | Dontrelle Willis | .15 | .40 |
| ☐ 415 | Joakim Soria | .15 | .40 |
| ☐ 416 | Chan Ho Park | .15 | .40 |
| ☐ 417 | Jered Weaver | .25 | .60 |
| ☐ 418 | Justin Duchscherer | .15 | .40 |
| ☐ 419 | Casey Kotchman | .15 | .40 |
| ☐ 420 | John Lackey | .15 | .40 |
| ☐ 421 | Peter Moylan | .15 | .40 |
| ☐ 422 | Bengie Molina | .15 | .40 |
| ☐ 423 | Mark Loretta | .15 | .40 |
| ☐ 424 | Dan Wheeler | .15 | .40 |
| ☐ 425 | Ken Griffey Jr. | .60 | 1.50 |
| ☐ 426 | Justin Verlander | .25 | .60 |
| ☐ 427 | Troy Glaus | .15 | .40 |
| ☐ 428 | Daniel Murphy RC | 1.00 | 2.50 |
| ☐ 429 | Brandon Backe | .15 | .40 |
| ☐ 430 | Nick Markakis | .25 | .60 |
| ☐ 431 | Travis Metcalf | .15 | .40 |
| ☐ 432 | Austin Kearns | .15 | .40 |
| ☐ 433 | Adam Lind | .15 | .40 |
| ☐ 434 | Jody Gerut | .15 | .40 |
| ☐ 435 | Jonathan Papelbon | .25 | .60 |
| ☐ 436 | Duaner Sanchez | .15 | .40 |
| ☐ 437 | David Murphy | .15 | .40 |
| ☐ 438 | Eddie Guardado | .15 | .40 |
| ☐ 439 | Johnny Damon | .25 | .60 |
| ☐ 440 | Derek Lowe | .15 | .40 |
| ☐ 441 | Miguel Olivo | .15 | .40 |
| ☐ 442 | Shaun Marcum | .15 | .40 |
| ☐ 443 | Ty Wigginton | .15 | .40 |
| ☐ 444 | Elijah Dukes | .15 | .40 |
| ☐ 445 | Felix Hernandez | .25 | .60 |
| ☐ 446 | Joe Inglett | .15 | .40 |
| ☐ 447 | Kelly Shoppach | .15 | .40 |
| ☐ 448 | Eric Hinske | .15 | .40 |
| ☐ 449 | Fred Lewis | .15 | .40 |
| ☐ 450 | Cliff Lee | .25 | .60 |
| ☐ 451 | Miguel Tejada | .25 | .60 |
| ☐ 452 | Jensen Lewis | .15 | .40 |
| ☐ 453 | Ryan Zimmerman | .25 | .60 |
| ☐ 454 | Jon Lester | .25 | .60 |
| ☐ 455 | Justin Morneau | .25 | .60 |
| ☐ 456 | John Smoltz | .40 | 1.00 |
| ☐ 457 | Emmanuel Burriss | .15 | .40 |
| ☐ 458 | Joe Nathan | .15 | .40 |
| ☐ 459 | Jeff Niemann | .15 | .40 |
| ☐ 460 | Roy Halladay | .25 | .60 |
| ☐ 461 | Matt Diaz | .15 | .40 |
| ☐ 462 | Oscar Salazar | .15 | .40 |
| ☐ 463 | Chris Perez | .15 | .40 |
| ☐ 464 | Matt Joyce | .15 | .40 |
| ☐ 465 | Dan Uggla | .15 | .40 |
| ☐ 466 | Jermaine Dye | .15 | .40 |
| ☐ 467 | Shane Victorino | .15 | .40 |
| ☐ 468 | Chris Getz | .15 | .40 |
| ☐ 469 | Chris B. Young | .15 | .40 |
| ☐ 470 | Prince Fielder | .40 | 1.00 |
| ☐ 471 | Juan Pierre | .15 | .40 |
| ☐ 472 | Travis Buck | .15 | .40 |
| ☐ 473 | Dioner Navarro | .15 | .40 |
| ☐ 474 | Mark Buehrle | .15 | .40 |
| ☐ 475 | Hanley Ramirez | .40 | 1.00 |
| ☐ 476 | John Lannan | .15 | .40 |
| ☐ 477 | Lastings Milledge | .15 | .40 |
| ☐ 478 | Dallas Braden | .15 | .40 |
| ☐ 479 | Orlando Cabrera | .15 | .40 |
| ☐ 480 | Jose Reyes | .40 | 1.00 |
| ☐ 481 | Jorge Posada | .25 | .60 |
| ☐ 482 | Jason Isringhausen | .15 | .40 |
| ☐ 483 | Rich Aurilia | .15 | .40 |
| ☐ 484 | Hunter Pence | .25 | .60 |
| ☐ 485 | Carlos Zambrano | .15 | .40 |
| ☐ 486 | Randy Winn | .15 | .40 |
| ☐ 487 | Carlos Beltran | .15 | .40 |
| ☐ 488 | Armando Galarraga | .15 | .40 |
| ☐ 489 | Wilson Betemit | .15 | .40 |
| ☐ 490 | Vladimir Guerrero | .40 | 1.00 |
| ☐ 491 | Ryan Garko | .15 | .40 |
| ☐ 492 | Ian Snell | .15 | .40 |
| ☐ 493 | Yadier Molina | .25 | .60 |
| ☐ 494 | Tom Glavine | .25 | .60 |
| ☐ 495 | Cameron Maybin | .25 | .60 |
| ☐ 496 | Vicente Padilla | .15 | .40 |
| ☐ 497 | Keiichi Yabu | .15 | .40 |
| ☐ 498 | Oliver Perez | .15 | .40 |
| ☐ 499 | Carlos Villanueva | .15 | .40 |
| ☐ 500 | Alex Rodriguez | .60 | 1.50 |
| ☐ 501 | Baltimore Orioles CL | .15 | .40 |
| ☐ 502 | Boston Red Sox CL | .25 | .60 |
| ☐ 503 | Chicago White Sox CL | .15 | .40 |
| ☐ 504 | Houston Astros CL | .15 | .40 |
| ☐ 505 | Oakland Athletics CL | .15 | .40 |
| ☐ 506 | Toronto Blue Jays CL | .15 | .40 |
| ☐ 507 | Atlanta Braves CL | .15 | .40 |
| ☐ 508 | Milwaukee Brewers CL | .15 | .40 |
| ☐ 509 | St. Louis Cardinals CL | .25 | .60 |
| ☐ 510 | Chicago Cubs CL | .25 | .60 |
| ☐ 511 | Arizona Diamondbacks CL | .15 | .40 |
| ☐ 512 | Los Angeles Dodgers CL | .25 | .60 |
| ☐ 513 | San Francisco Giants CL | .15 | .40 |
| ☐ 514 | Cleveland Indians CL | .15 | .40 |
| ☐ 515 | Seattle Mariners CL | .25 | .60 |
| ☐ 516 | Florida Marlins CL | .15 | .40 |
| ☐ 517 | New York Mets CL | .25 | .60 |
| ☐ 518 | Washington Nationals CL | .15 | .40 |
| ☐ 519 | San Diego Padres CL | .15 | .40 |
| ☐ 520 | Pittsburgh Pirates CL | .15 | .40 |
| ☐ 521 | Tampa Bay Rays CL | .25 | .60 |
| ☐ 522 | Cincinnati Reds CL | .15 | .40 |
| ☐ 523 | Colorado Rockies CL | .15 | .40 |
| ☐ 524 | Kansas City Royals CL | .15 | .40 |
| ☐ 525 | Detroit Tigers CL | .15 | .40 |
| ☐ 526 | Minnesota Twins CL | .15 | .40 |
| ☐ 527 | New York Yankees CL | .25 | .60 |
| ☐ 528 | Philadelphia Phillies CL | .25 | .60 |
| ☐ 529 | Los Angeles Angels CL | .15 | .40 |
| ☐ 530 | Texas Rangers CL | .15 | .40 |
| ☐ 531 | Bradley/Mauer/Pedroia | .50 | 1.25 |
| ☐ 532 | Chipper/Holliday/Pujols | 1.00 | 2.50 |
| ☐ 533 | M.Cabrera/ARod/Quentin | .50 | 1.25 |
| ☐ 534 | Delgado/Dunn/Howard | .50 | 1.25 |
| ☐ 535 | Justin Morneau/Josh Hamilton /Miguel Cabrera | .40 | 1.00 |
| ☐ 536 | Howard/Wright/A.Gon | .50 | 1.25 |
| ☐ 537 | C.Lee/D.Matsu/Halladay | .25 | .60 |
| ☐ 538 | Santana/Peavy/Lince | .50 | 1.25 |
| ☐ 539 | C.Lee/D.Matsu/Halladay | .25 | .60 |
| ☐ 540 | Lince/Dempster/Webb | .50 | 1.25 |
| ☐ 541 | Ervin Santana/Roy Halladay/A.J. Burnett | .25 | .60 |
| ☐ 542 | Santana/Lince/Haren | .50 | 1.25 |
| ☐ 543 | Grady Sizemore | .25 | .60 |
| ☐ 544 | Ichiro Suzuki | .60 | 1.50 |
| ☐ 545 | Hanley Ramirez | .40 | 1.00 |
| ☐ 546 | Jose Reyes | .40 | 1.00 |
| ☐ 547 | Johan Santana | .40 | 1.00 |
| ☐ 548 | Adrian Gonzalez | .25 | .60 |
| ☐ 549 | Carlos Zambrano | .15 | .40 |
| ☐ 550 | Jonathan Papelbon | .25 | .60 |
| ☐ 551 | Josh Hamilton | .40 | 1.00 |
| ☐ 552 | Derek Jeter | 1.00 | 1.50 |
| ☐ 553 | Kevin Youkilis | .25 | .60 |
| ☐ 554 | Joe Mauer | .40 | 1.00 |
| ☐ 555 | Kosuke Fukudome | .40 | 1.00 |
| ☐ 556 | Chipper Jones | .40 | 1.00 |
| ☐ 557 | Lance Berkman | .25 | .60 |
| ☐ 558 | Michael Young | .25 | .60 |
| ☐ 559 | Evan Longoria | .60 | 1.50 |
| ☐ 560 | Alex Rodriguez | .60 | 1.50 |
| ☐ 561 | Travis Snider RC | 1.00 | 1.50 |
| ☐ 562 | James McDonald RC | .60 | 1.50 |
| ☐ 563 | Brian Duensing RC | .60 | 1.50 |
| ☐ 564 | Josh Outman RC | .60 | 1.50 |
| ☐ 565 | Josh Geer (RC) | .60 | 1.50 |
| ☐ 566 | Kevin Jepsen (RC) | .40 | 1.00 |
| ☐ 567 | Scott Lewis (RC) | .40 | 1.00 |
| ☐ 568 | Jason Motte (RC) | .40 | 1.00 |
| ☐ 569 | Ricky Romero (RC) | .40 | 1.00 |
| ☐ 570 | Landon Powell (RC) | .40 | 1.00 |
| ☐ 571 | Scott Elbert (RC) | .40 | 1.00 |
| ☐ 572 | Bobby Parnell RC | .60 | 1.50 |
| ☐ 573 | Ryan Perry RC | 1.00 | 2.50 |
| ☐ 574 | Phil Coke RC | .60 | 1.50 |
| ☐ 575 | Trevor Cahill RC | .60 | 1.50 |
| ☐ 576 | Jesse Chavez RC | .40 | 1.00 |
| ☐ 577 | George Kottaras (RC) | .40 | 1.00 |
| ☐ 578 | Trevor Crowe RC | .60 | 1.50 |
| ☐ 579 | David Freese RC | 1.00 | 2.50 |
| ☐ 580 | Matt Tuiasosopo (RC) | .40 | 1.00 |
| ☐ 581 | Brett Anderson RC | .60 | 1.50 |
| ☐ 582 | Casey McGehee (RC) | .60 | 1.50 |
| ☐ 583 | Elvis Andrus RC | 1.00 | 2.50 |
| ☐ 584 | Shawn Kelley RC | .40 | 1.00 |
| ☐ 585 | Mike Hinckley (RC) | .40 | 1.00 |
| ☐ 586 | Donald Veal RC | .60 | 1.50 |
| ☐ 587 | Colby Rasmus (RC) | .60 | 1.50 |
| ☐ 588 | Shairon Martis RC | .60 | 1.50 |
| ☐ 589 | Walter Silva RC | .60 | 1.50 |
| ☐ 590 | Chris Jakubauskas RC | .60 | 1.50 |
| ☐ 591 | Brad Nelson (RC) | .40 | 1.00 |
| ☐ 592 | Alfredo Simon (RC) | .40 | 1.00 |
| ☐ 593 | Koji Uehara RC | 1.00 | 2.50 |
| ☐ 594 | Rick Porcello RC | 1.50 | 4.00 |
| ☐ 595 | Kenshin Kawakami RC | .60 | 1.50 |
| ☐ 596 | Dexter Fowler (RC) | .60 | 1.50 |
| ☐ 597 | Jordan Schafer (RC) | .60 | 1.50 |
| ☐ 598 | David Patton RC | .60 | 1.50 |
| ☐ 599 | Luis Cruz RC | .40 | 1.00 |
| ☐ 600 | Joe Martinez RC | .60 | 1.50 |

## 1939 Play Ball

| | | | |
|---|---|---|---|
| ☐ | COMPLETE SET (161) | 6000.00 | 10000.00 |
| ☐ | COMMON CARD (1-115) | 12.00 | 20.00 |
| ☐ | COMMON CARD (116-162) | 40.00 | 75.00 |
| ☐ | WRAPPER (1-CENT) | 150.00 | 200.00 |
| ☐ 1 | Jake Powell RC | 30.00 | 60.00 |
| ☐ 2 | Lee Grissom RC | 12.00 | 20.00 |
| ☐ 3 | Red Ruffing | 40.00 | 75.00 |
| ☐ 4 | Eldon Auker RC | 12.00 | 20.00 |
| ☐ 5 | Luke Sewell | 15.00 | 25.00 |
| ☐ 6 | Leo Durocher | 60.00 | 100.00 |
| ☐ 7 | Bobby Doerr RC | 40.00 | 75.00 |
| ☐ 8 | Henry Pippen RC | 12.00 | 20.00 |
| ☐ 9 | James Tobin RC | 12.00 | 20.00 |

| | | |
|---|---|---|
| ❏ 10 James DeShong | 12.00 | 20.00 |
| ❏ 11 Johnny Rizzo RC | 12.00 | 20.00 |
| ❏ 12 Hershel Martin RC | 12.00 | 20.00 |
| ❏ 13 Luke Hamlin RC | 12.00 | 20.00 |
| ❏ 14 Jim Tabor RC | 12.00 | 20.00 |
| ❏ 15 Paul Derringer | 18.00 | 30.00 |
| ❏ 16 John Peacock RC | 12.00 | 20.00 |
| ❏ 17 Emerson Dickman RC | 12.00 | 20.00 |
| ❏ 18 Harry Danning RC | 12.00 | 20.00 |
| ❏ 19 Paul Dean RC | 25.00 | 40.00 |
| ❏ 20 Joe Heving RC | 12.00 | 20.00 |
| ❏ 21 Dutch Leonard | 18.00 | 30.00 |
| ❏ 22 Bucky Walters RC | 18.00 | 30.00 |
| ❏ 23 Burgess Whitehead RC | 12.00 | 20.00 |
| ❏ 24 Richard Coffman | 12.00 | 20.00 |
| ❏ 25 George Selkirk RC | 25.00 | 40.00 |
| ❏ 26 Joe DiMaggio | 900.00 | 1400.00 |
| ❏ 27 Fred Ostermueller | 12.00 | 20.00 |
| ❏ 28 Sylvester Johnson RC | 12.00 | 20.00 |
| ❏ 29 John(Jack) Wilson RC | 12.00 | 20.00 |
| ❏ 30 Bill Dickey | 75.00 | 125.00 |
| ❏ 31 Sam West | 12.00 | 20.00 |
| ❏ 32 Bob Seeds RC | 12.00 | 20.00 |
| ❏ 33 Del Young RC | 12.00 | 20.00 |
| ❏ 34 Frank Demaree | 12.00 | 20.00 |
| ❏ 35 Bill Jurges | 12.00 | 20.00 |
| ❏ 36 Frank McCormick RC | 12.00 | 20.00 |
| ❏ 37 Virgil Davis | 12.00 | 20.00 |
| ❏ 38 Billy Myers RC | 12.00 | 20.00 |
| ❏ 39 Rick Ferrell | 40.00 | 75.00 |
| ❏ 40 James Bagby Jr. RC | 12.00 | 20.00 |
| ❏ 41 Lon Warneke | 15.00 | 25.00 |
| ❏ 42 Arndt Jorgens | 12.00 | 20.00 |
| ❏ 43 Melo Almada RC | 15.00 | 25.00 |
| ❏ 44 Don Heffner RC | 12.00 | 20.00 |
| ❏ 45 Merrill May RC | 12.00 | 20.00 |
| ❏ 46 Morris Arnovich RC | 12.00 | 20.00 |
| ❏ 47 Buddy Lewis RC | 12.00 | 20.00 |
| ❏ 48 Lefty Gomez | 75.00 | 125.00 |
| ❏ 49 Eddie Miller RC | 12.00 | 20.00 |
| ❏ 50 Charley Gehringer | 75.00 | 125.00 |
| ❏ 51 Mel Ott | 75.00 | 125.00 |
| ❏ 52 Tommy Henrich RC | 25.00 | 40.00 |
| ❏ 53 Carl Hubbell | 75.00 | 125.00 |
| ❏ 54 Harry Gumpert RC | 12.00 | 20.00 |
| ❏ 55 Arky Vaughan | 40.00 | 75.00 |
| ❏ 56 Hank Greenberg | 125.00 | 200.00 |
| ❏ 57 Buddy Hassett RC | 12.00 | 20.00 |
| ❏ 58 Lou Chiozza RC | 12.00 | 20.00 |
| ❏ 59 Ken Chase RC | 12.00 | 20.00 |
| ❏ 60 Schoolboy Rowe RC | 25.00 | 40.00 |
| ❏ 61 Tony Cuccinello | 15.00 | 25.00 |
| ❏ 62 Tom Carey RC | 12.00 | 20.00 |
| ❏ 63 Emmett Mueller RC | 12.00 | 20.00 |
| ❏ 64 Wally Moses RC | 15.00 | 25.00 |
| ❏ 65 Harry Craft RC | 15.00 | 25.00 |
| ❏ 66 Jimmy Ripple RC | 12.00 | 20.00 |
| ❏ 67 Ed Joost RC | 15.00 | 25.00 |
| ❏ 68 Fred Sington RC | 12.00 | 20.00 |
| ❏ 69 Elbie Fletcher RC | 12.00 | 20.00 |
| ❏ 70 Fred Frankhouse | 12.00 | 20.00 |
| ❏ 71 Monte Pearson RC | 18.00 | 30.00 |
| ❏ 72 Debs Garms RC | 12.00 | 20.00 |
| ❏ 73 Hal Schumacher | 15.00 | 25.00 |
| ❏ 74 Cookie Lavagetto RC | 12.00 | 20.00 |
| ❏ 75 Stan Bordagaray RC | 12.00 | 20.00 |
| ❏ 76 Goody Rosen RC | 12.00 | 20.00 |
| ❏ 77 Lew Riggs RC | 12.00 | 20.00 |
| ❏ 78 Julius Solters | 12.00 | 20.00 |
| ❏ 79 Jo Jo Moore | 12.00 | 20.00 |
| ❏ 80 Pete Fox | 12.00 | 20.00 |
| ❏ 81 Babe Dahlgren RC | 18.00 | 30.00 |
| ❏ 82 Chuck Klein | 60.00 | 100.00 |
| ❏ 83 Gus Suhr | 12.00 | 20.00 |
| ❏ 84 Skeeter Newsom RC | 12.00 | 20.00 |
| ❏ 85 Johnny Cooney RC | 12.00 | 20.00 |
| ❏ 86 Dolph Camilli | 15.00 | 25.00 |
| ❏ 87 Milburn Shoffner RC | 12.00 | 20.00 |
| ❏ 88 Charlie Keller RC | 25.00 | 40.00 |
| ❏ 89 Lloyd Waner | 40.00 | 75.00 |
| ❏ 90 Robert Klinger RC | 12.00 | 20.00 |
| ❏ 91 John Knott RC | 12.00 | 20.00 |
| ❏ 92 Ted Williams RC | 1000.00 | 1800.00 |
| ❏ 93 Charles Gelbert RC | 12.00 | 20.00 |
| ❏ 94 Heinie Manush | 40.00 | 75.00 |
| ❏ 95 Whit Wyatt RC | 12.00 | 20.00 |
| ❏ 96 Babe Phelps RC | 12.00 | 20.00 |
| ❏ 97 Bob Johnson | 18.00 | 30.00 |

| | | |
|---|---|---|
| ❏ 98 Pinky Whitney RC | 12.00 | 20.00 |
| ❏ 99 Wally Berger | 18.00 | 30.00 |
| ❏ 100 Buddy Myer | 15.00 | 25.00 |
| ❏ 101 Roger Cramer | 15.00 | 25.00 |
| ❏ 102 Lem (Pep) Young RC | 12.00 | 20.00 |
| ❏ 103 Moe Berg | 75.00 | 125.00 |
| ❏ 104 Tom Bridges | 15.00 | 25.00 |
| ❏ 105 Rabbit McNair RC | 12.00 | 20.00 |
| ❏ 106 Dolly Stark UMP | 18.00 | 30.00 |
| ❏ 107 Joe Vosmik | 12.00 | 20.00 |
| ❏ 108 Frank Hayes | 12.00 | 20.00 |
| ❏ 109 Myril Hoag | 12.00 | 20.00 |
| ❏ 110 Fred Fitzsimmons | 15.00 | 25.00 |
| ❏ 111 Van Lingle Mungo RC | 18.00 | 30.00 |
| ❏ 112 Paul Waner | 60.00 | 100.00 |
| ❏ 113 Al Schacht | 18.00 | 30.00 |
| ❏ 114 Cecil Travis | 15.00 | 25.00 |
| ❏ 115 Ralph Kress | 12.00 | 20.00 |
| ❏ 116 Gene Desautels RC | 40.00 | 75.00 |
| ❏ 117 Wayne Ambler RC | 40.00 | 75.00 |
| ❏ 118 Lynn Nelson | 40.00 | 75.00 |
| ❏ 119 Will Hershberger RC | 50.00 | 100.00 |
| ❏ 120 Rabbit Warstler RC | 40.00 | 75.00 |
| ❏ 121 Bill Posedel RC | 40.00 | 75.00 |
| ❏ 122 George McQuinn RC | 40.00 | 75.00 |
| ❏ 123 Ray T. Davis RC | 40.00 | 75.00 |
| ❏ 124 Walter Brown | 40.00 | 75.00 |
| ❏ 125 Cliff Melton RC | 40.00 | 75.00 |
| ❏ 126 Not issued | | |
| ❏ 127 Gil Brack RC | 40.00 | 75.00 |
| ❏ 128 Joe Bowman RC | 40.00 | 75.00 |
| ❏ 129 Bill Swift | 40.00 | 75.00 |
| ❏ 130 Bill Brubaker RC | 40.00 | 75.00 |
| ❏ 131 Mort Cooper RC | 50.00 | 100.00 |
| ❏ 132 Jim Brown RC | 40.00 | 75.00 |
| ❏ 133 Lynn Myers RC | 40.00 | 75.00 |
| ❏ 134 Tot Presnell RC | 40.00 | 75.00 |
| ❏ 135 Mickey Owen RC | 50.00 | 100.00 |
| ❏ 136 Roy Bell RC | 40.00 | 75.00 |
| ❏ 137 Pete Appleton | 40.00 | 75.00 |
| ❏ 138 George Case RC | 50.00 | 100.00 |
| ❏ 139 Vito Tamulis RC | 40.00 | 75.00 |
| ❏ 140 Ray Hayworth RC | 40.00 | 75.00 |
| ❏ 141 Pete Coscarart RC | 40.00 | 75.00 |
| ❏ 142 Ira Hutchinson RC | 40.00 | 75.00 |
| ❏ 143 Earl Averill | 100.00 | 175.00 |
| ❏ 144 Zeke Bonura RC | 50.00 | 100.00 |
| ❏ 145 Hugh Mulcahy RC | 40.00 | 75.00 |
| ❏ 146 Tom Sunkel RC | 40.00 | 75.00 |
| ❏ 147 George Coffman RC | 40.00 | 75.00 |
| ❏ 148 Bill Trotter RC | 40.00 | 75.00 |
| ❏ 149 Max West RC | 40.00 | 75.00 |
| ❏ 150 James Walkup RC | 40.00 | 75.00 |
| ❏ 151 Hugh Casey RC | 50.00 | 100.00 |
| ❏ 152 Roy Weatherly RC | 40.00 | 75.00 |
| ❏ 153 Dizzy Trout RC | 50.00 | 100.00 |
| ❏ 154 Johnny Hudson RC | 40.00 | 75.00 |
| ❏ 155 Jimmy Outlaw RC | 40.00 | 75.00 |
| ❏ 156 Ray Berres RC | 40.00 | 75.00 |
| ❏ 157 Don Padgett RC | 40.00 | 75.00 |
| ❏ 158 Bud Thomas RC | 40.00 | 75.00 |
| ❏ 159 Red Evans RC | 40.00 | 75.00 |
| ❏ 160 Gene Moore RC | 40.00 | 75.00 |
| ❏ 161 Lonnie Frey | 40.00 | 75.00 |
| ❏ 162 Whitey Moore RC | 50.00 | 100.00 |

## 1940 Play Ball

| | | |
|---|---|---|
| ❏ COMPLETE SET (240) | 10000.00 | 15000.00 |
| ❏ COMMON CARD (1-120) | 12.00 | 20.00 |
| ❏ COMMON CARD (121-180) | 12.00 | 20.00 |
| ❏ COMMON CARD (181-240) | 35.00 | 70.00 |
| ❏ WRAP.(1-CENT, DIFF. COL.) | 700.00 | 800.00 |
| ❏ 1 Joe DiMaggio | 1500.00 | 2500.00 |
| ❏ 2 Art Jorgens | 15.00 | 25.00 |
| ❏ 3 Babe Dahlgren | 15.00 | 25.00 |

| | | |
|---|---|---|
| ❏ 4 Tommy Henrich | 25.00 | 50.00 |
| ❏ 5 Monte Pearson | 15.00 | 25.00 |
| ❏ 6 Lefty Gomez | 90.00 | 150.00 |
| ❏ 7 Bill Dickey | 100.00 | 175.00 |
| ❏ 8 George Selkirk | 15.00 | 25.00 |
| ❏ 9 Charlie Keller | 25.00 | 50.00 |
| ❏ 10 Red Ruffing | 50.00 | 90.00 |
| ❏ 11 Jake Powell | 12.00 | 20.00 |
| ❏ 12 Johnny Schulte | 12.00 | 20.00 |
| ❏ 13 Jack Knott | 12.00 | 20.00 |
| ❏ 14 Rabbit McNair | 12.00 | 20.00 |
| ❏ 15 George Case | 15.00 | 25.00 |
| ❏ 16 Cecil Travis | 15.00 | 25.00 |
| ❏ 17 Buddy Myer | 15.00 | 25.00 |
| ❏ 18 Charlie Gelbert | 12.00 | 20.00 |
| ❏ 19 Ken Chase | 12.00 | 20.00 |
| ❏ 20 Buddy Lewis | 12.00 | 20.00 |
| ❏ 21 Rick Ferrell | 45.00 | 80.00 |
| ❏ 22 Sammy West | 15.00 | 25.00 |
| ❏ 23 Dutch Leonard | 15.00 | 25.00 |
| ❏ 24 Frank Hayes | 15.00 | 25.00 |
| ❏ 25 Bob Johnson | 15.00 | 25.00 |
| ❏ 26 Wally Moses | 15.00 | 25.00 |
| ❏ 27 Ted Williams | 800.00 | 1200.00 |
| ❏ 28 Gene Desautels | 15.00 | 25.00 |
| ❏ 29 Doc Cramer | 15.00 | 25.00 |
| ❏ 30 Moe Berg | 90.00 | 150.00 |
| ❏ 31 Jack Wilson | 12.00 | 20.00 |
| ❏ 32 Jim Bagby | 12.00 | 20.00 |
| ❏ 33 Fritz Ostermueller | 12.00 | 20.00 |
| ❏ 34 John Peacock | 12.00 | 20.00 |
| ❏ 35 Joe Heving | 12.00 | 20.00 |
| ❏ 36 Jim Tabor | 12.00 | 20.00 |
| ❏ 37 Emerson Dickman | 12.00 | 20.00 |
| ❏ 38 Bobby Doerr | 50.00 | 90.00 |
| ❏ 39 Tom Carey | 12.00 | 20.00 |
| ❏ 40 Hank Greenberg | 100.00 | 200.00 |
| ❏ 41 Charley Gehringer | 90.00 | 150.00 |
| ❏ 42 Bud Thomas | 12.00 | 20.00 |
| ❏ 43 Pete Fox | 12.00 | 20.00 |
| ❏ 44 Dizzy Trout | 15.00 | 25.00 |
| ❏ 45 Red Kress | 15.00 | 25.00 |
| ❏ 46 Earl Averill | 50.00 | 90.00 |
| ❏ 47 Oscar Vitt RC | 15.00 | 25.00 |
| ❏ 48 Luke Sewell | 15.00 | 25.00 |
| ❏ 49 Stormy Weatherly | 15.00 | 25.00 |
| ❏ 50 Hal Trosky | 15.00 | 25.00 |
| ❏ 51 Don Heffner | 12.00 | 20.00 |
| ❏ 52 Myril Hoag | 12.00 | 20.00 |
| ❏ 53 George McQuinn | 15.00 | 25.00 |
| ❏ 54 Bill Trotter | 12.00 | 20.00 |
| ❏ 55 Slick Coffman | 15.00 | 25.00 |
| ❏ 56 Eddie Miller RC | 15.00 | 25.00 |
| ❏ 57 Max West | 12.00 | 20.00 |
| ❏ 58 Bill Posedel | 12.00 | 20.00 |
| ❏ 59 Rabbit Warstler | 12.00 | 20.00 |
| ❏ 60 John Cooney | 12.00 | 20.00 |
| ❏ 61 Tony Cuccinello | 15.00 | 25.00 |
| ❏ 62 Buddy Hassett | 12.00 | 20.00 |
| ❏ 63 Pete Coscarart | 12.00 | 20.00 |
| ❏ 64 Van Lingle Mungo | 15.00 | 25.00 |
| ❏ 65 Fred Fitzsimmons | 15.00 | 25.00 |
| ❏ 66 Babe Phelps | 15.00 | 25.00 |
| ❏ 67 Whit Wyatt | 15.00 | 25.00 |
| ❏ 68 Dolph Camilli | 15.00 | 25.00 |
| ❏ 69 Cookie Lavagetto | 15.00 | 25.00 |
| ❏ 70 Luke Hamlin (Hot Potato) | 12.00 | 20.00 |
| ❏ 71 Mel Almada | 12.00 | 20.00 |
| ❏ 72 Chuck Dressen RC | 15.00 | 25.00 |
| ❏ 73 Bucky Walters | 15.00 | 25.00 |
| ❏ 74 Paul (Duke) Derringer | 15.00 | 25.00 |
| ❏ 75 Frank (Buck) McCormick | 15.00 | 25.00 |
| ❏ 76 Lonny Frey | 12.00 | 20.00 |
| ❏ 77 Willard Hershberger | 12.00 | 20.00 |
| ❏ 78 Lew Riggs | 12.00 | 20.00 |
| ❏ 79 Harry Craft | 15.00 | 25.00 |
| ❏ 80 Billy Myers | 12.00 | 20.00 |
| ❏ 81 Wally Berger | 15.00 | 25.00 |
| ❏ 82 Hank Gowdy CO | 15.00 | 25.00 |
| ❏ 83 Cliff Melton | 12.00 | 20.00 |
| ❏ 84 Jo Jo Moore | 12.00 | 20.00 |
| ❏ 85 Hal Schumacher | 15.00 | 25.00 |
| ❏ 86 Harry Gumbert | 12.00 | 20.00 |
| ❏ 87 Carl Hubbell | 75.00 | 125.00 |
| ❏ 98 Mel Ott | 100.00 | 175.00 |
| ❏ 89 Bill Jurges | 12.00 | 20.00 |
| ❏ 90 Frank Demaree | 12.00 | 20.00 |

|  |  | | |
|---|---|---|---|
| 91 | Bob Seeds | 12.00 | 20.00 |
| 92 | Whitey Whitehead | 12.00 | 20.00 |
| 93 | Harry Danning | 12.00 | 20.00 |
| 94 | Gus Suhr | 12.00 | 20.00 |
| 95 | Hugh Mulcahy | 12.00 | 20.00 |
| 96 | Heinie Mueller | 12.00 | 20.00 |
| 97 | Morry Arnovich | 12.00 | 20.00 |
| 98 | Pinky May | 12.00 | 20.00 |
| 99 | Syl Johnson | 12.00 | 20.00 |
| 100 | Hersh Martin | 12.00 | 20.00 |
| 101 | Del Young | 12.00 | 20.00 |
| 102 | Chuck Klein | 60.00 | 100.00 |
| 103 | Elbie Fletcher | 12.00 | 20.00 |
| 104 | Paul Waner | 50.00 | 90.00 |
| 105 | Lloyd Waner | 45.00 | 80.00 |
| 106 | Pep Young | 12.00 | 20.00 |
| 107 | Arky Vaughan | 45.00 | 80.00 |
| 108 | Johnny Rizzo | 12.00 | 20.00 |
| 109 | Don Padgett | 12.00 | 20.00 |
| 110 | Tom Sunkel | 12.00 | 20.00 |
| 111 | Mickey Owen | 15.00 | 25.00 |
| 112 | Jimmy Brown | 12.00 | 20.00 |
| 113 | Mort Cooper | 15.00 | 25.00 |
| 114 | Lon Warneke | 15.00 | 25.00 |
| 115 | Mike Gonzalez CO | 15.00 | 25.00 |
| 116 | Al Schacht | 15.00 | 25.00 |
| 117 | Dolly Stark UMP | 15.00 | 25.00 |
| 118 | Waite Hoyt | 50.00 | 90.00 |
| 119 | Grover C. Alexander | 100.00 | 175.00 |
| 120 | Walter Johnson | 100.00 | 200.00 |
| 121 | Atley Donald RC | 15.00 | 25.00 |
| 122 | Sandy Sundra RC | 15.00 | 25.00 |
| 123 | Hildy Hildebrand | 15.00 | 25.00 |
| 124 | Earle Combs | 60.00 | 100.00 |
| 125 | Art Fletcher RC | 15.00 | 25.00 |
| 126 | Jake Solters | 12.00 | 20.00 |
| 127 | Muddy Ruel | 12.00 | 20.00 |
| 128 | Pete Appleton | 12.00 | 20.00 |
| 129 | Bucky Harris MG RC | 45.00 | 80.00 |
| 130 | Clyde Milan RC | 15.00 | 25.00 |
| 131 | Zeke Bonura | 15.00 | 25.00 |
| 132 | Connie Mack MG RC | 75.00 | 150.00 |
| 133 | Jimmie Foxx | 100.00 | 200.00 |
| 134 | Joe Cronin | 60.00 | 100.00 |
| 135 | Line Drive Nelson | 12.00 | 20.00 |
| 136 | Cotton Pippen | 12.00 | 20.00 |
| 137 | Bing Miller | 12.00 | 20.00 |
| 138 | Beau Bell | 12.00 | 20.00 |
| 139 | Elden Auker | 12.00 | 20.00 |
| 140 | Dick Coffman | 12.00 | 20.00 |
| 141 | Casey Stengel MG RC | 100.00 | 175.00 |
| 142 | George Kelly RC | 50.00 | 90.00 |
| 143 | Gene Moore | 12.00 | 20.00 |
| 144 | Joe Vosmik | 12.00 | 20.00 |
| 145 | Vito Tamulis | 12.00 | 20.00 |
| 146 | Tot Pressnell | 12.00 | 20.00 |
| 147 | Johnny Hudson | 12.00 | 20.00 |
| 148 | Hugh Casey | 15.00 | 25.00 |
| 149 | Pinky Shoffner | 12.00 | 20.00 |
| 150 | Whitey Moore | 12.00 | 20.00 |
| 151 | Edwin Joost | 15.00 | 25.00 |
| 152 | Jimmy Wilson | 12.00 | 20.00 |
| 153 | Bill McKechnie MG RC | 45.00 | 80.00 |
| 154 | Jumbo Brown | 12.00 | 20.00 |
| 155 | Ray Hayworth | 12.00 | 20.00 |
| 156 | Daffy Dean | 25.00 | 50.00 |
| 157 | Lou Chiozza | 12.00 | 20.00 |
| 158 | Travis Jackson | 50.00 | 90.00 |
| 159 | Pancho Snyder RC | 12.00 | 20.00 |
| 160 | Hans Lobert CO | 12.00 | 20.00 |
| 161 | Debs Garms | 12.00 | 20.00 |
| 162 | Joe Bowman | 12.00 | 20.00 |
| 163 | Spud Davis | 12.00 | 20.00 |
| 164 | Ray Berres | 12.00 | 20.00 |
| 165 | Bob Klinger | 12.00 | 20.00 |
| 166 | Bill Brubaker | 12.00 | 20.00 |
| 167 | Frankie Frisch MG | 50.00 | 90.00 |
| 168 | Honus Wagner CO | 100.00 | 200.00 |
| 169 | Gabby Street | 12.00 | 20.00 |
| 170 | Tris Speaker | 100.00 | 175.00 |
| 171 | Harry Heilmann | 45.00 | 80.00 |
| 172 | Chief Bender | 45.00 | 80.00 |
| 173 | Napoleon Lajoie | 100.00 | 175.00 |
| 174 | Johnny Evers | 50.00 | 90.00 |
| 175 | Christy Mathewson | 150.00 | 250.00 |
| 176 | Heinie Manush | 50.00 | 90.00 |
| 177 | Frank Baker | 60.00 | 100.00 |
| 178 | Max Carey | 50.00 | 90.00 |
| 179 | George Sisler | 75.00 | 125.00 |
| 180 | Mickey Cochrane | 90.00 | 150.00 |
| 181 | Spud Chandler RC | 45.00 | 80.00 |
| 182 | Knick Knickerbocker RC | 35.00 | 70.00 |
| 183 | Marvin Breuer RC | 35.00 | 70.00 |
| 184 | Mule Haas | 35.00 | 70.00 |
| 185 | Joe Kuhel | 35.00 | 70.00 |
| 186 | Taft Wright RC | 35.00 | 70.00 |
| 187 | Jimmy Dykes MG | 45.00 | 80.00 |
| 188 | Joe Krakauskas RC | 35.00 | 70.00 |
| 189 | Jim Bloodworth RC | 35.00 | 70.00 |
| 190 | Charley Berry | 35.00 | 70.00 |
| 191 | John Babich RC | 35.00 | 70.00 |
| 192 | Dick Siebert RC | 35.00 | 70.00 |
| 193 | Chubby Dean RC | 35.00 | 70.00 |
| 194 | Sam Chapman RC | 35.00 | 70.00 |
| 195 | Dee Miles RC | 35.00 | 70.00 |
| 196 | Red (Nonny) Nonnenkamp RC | 35.00 | 70.00 |
| 197 | Lou Finney RC | 35.00 | 70.00 |
| 198 | Denny Galehouse RC | 35.00 | 70.00 |
| 199 | Pinky Higgins | 35.00 | 70.00 |
| 200 | Soup Campbell RC | 35.00 | 70.00 |
| 201 | Barney McCosky RC | 35.00 | 70.00 |
| 202 | Al Milnar RC | 35.00 | 70.00 |
| 203 | Bad News Hale RC | 35.00 | 70.00 |
| 204 | Harry Eisenstat RC | 35.00 | 70.00 |
| 205 | Rollie Hemsley RC | 35.00 | 70.00 |
| 206 | Chet Laabs RC | 35.00 | 70.00 |
| 207 | Gus Mancuso | 35.00 | 70.00 |
| 208 | Lee Gamble RC | 35.00 | 70.00 |
| 209 | Hy Vandenberg RC | 35.00 | 70.00 |
| 210 | Bill Lohrman RC | 35.00 | 70.00 |
| 211 | Pop Joiner RC | 35.00 | 70.00 |
| 212 | Babe Young RC | 35.00 | 70.00 |
| 213 | John Rucker RC | 35.00 | 70.00 |
| 214 | Ken O'Dea RC | 35.00 | 70.00 |
| 215 | Johnnie McCarthy RC | 35.00 | 70.00 |
| 216 | Joe Marty RC | 35.00 | 70.00 |
| 217 | Walter Beck | 35.00 | 70.00 |
| 218 | Wally Millies RC | 35.00 | 70.00 |
| 219 | Russ Bauers RC | 35.00 | 70.00 |
| 220 | Mace Brown RC | 35.00 | 70.00 |
| 221 | Lee Handley RC | 35.00 | 70.00 |
| 222 | Max Butcher RC | 35.00 | 70.00 |
| 223 | Hughie Jennings | 90.00 | 150.00 |
| 224 | Pie Traynor | 100.00 | 175.00 |
| 225 | Joe Jackson | 1500.00 | 2500.00 |
| 226 | Harry Hooper | 90.00 | 150.00 |
| 227 | Jesse Haines | 90.00 | 150.00 |
| 228 | Charlie Grimm | 45.00 | 80.00 |
| 229 | Buck Herzog | 35.00 | 70.00 |
| 230 | Red Faber | 100.00 | 175.00 |
| 231 | Doll Luque | 60.00 | 100.00 |
| 232 | Goose Goslin | 90.00 | 150.00 |
| 233 | George Earnshaw | 45.00 | 80.00 |
| 234 | Frank Chance | 90.00 | 150.00 |
| 235 | John McGraw | 90.00 | 150.00 |
| 236 | Jim Bottomley | 90.00 | 150.00 |
| 237 | Willie Keeler | 100.00 | 175.00 |
| 238 | Tony Lazzeri | 100.00 | 175.00 |
| 239 | George Uhle | 35.00 | 70.00 |
| 240 | Bill Atwood RC | 60.00 | 100.00 |

## 1941 Play Ball

HARRY "DUNDOAT" GUMBERT

| | | | |
|---|---|---|---|
| | COMPLETE SET (72) | 6000.00 | 10000.00 |
| | COMMON CARD (1-48) | 20.00 | 40.00 |
| | COMMON CARD (49-72) | 35.00 | 70.00 |
| | WRAPPER (1-CENT) | 700.00 | 800.00 |
| 1 | Eddie Miller | 75.00 | 125.00 |
| 2 | Max West | 20.00 | 40.00 |
| 3 | Bucky Walters | 25.00 | 45.00 |
| 4 | Paul Derringer | 30.00 | 50.00 |
| 5 | Frank (Buck) McCormick | 25.00 | 45.00 |
| 6 | Carl Hubbell | 100.00 | 175.00 |
| 7 | Harry Danning | 20.00 | 40.00 |
| 8 | Mel Ott | 125.00 | 225.00 |
| 9 | Pinky May | 20.00 | 40.00 |
| 10 | Arky Vaughan | 60.00 | 100.00 |
| 11 | Debs Garms | 20.00 | 40.00 |
| 12 | Jimmy Brown | 20.00 | 40.00 |
| 13 | Jimmie Foxx | 175.00 | 300.00 |
| 14 | Ted Williams | 900.00 | 1500.00 |
| 15 | Joe Cronin | 75.00 | 125.00 |
| 16 | Hal Trosky | 25.00 | 45.00 |
| 17 | Roy Weatherly | 20.00 | 40.00 |
| 18 | Hank Greenberg | 175.00 | 300.00 |
| 19 | Charley Gehringer | 125.00 | 200.00 |
| 20 | Red Ruffing | 75.00 | 125.00 |
| 21 | Charlie Keller | 35.00 | 60.00 |
| 22 | Bob Johnson | 30.00 | 50.00 |
| 23 | George McQuinn | 25.00 | 45.00 |
| 24 | Dutch Leonard | 25.00 | 45.00 |
| 25 | Gene Moore | 20.00 | 40.00 |
| 26 | Harry Gumpert | 20.00 | 40.00 |
| 27 | Babe Young | 20.00 | 40.00 |
| 28 | Joe Marty | 20.00 | 40.00 |
| 29 | Jack Wilson | 20.00 | 40.00 |
| 30 | Lou Finney | 20.00 | 40.00 |
| 31 | Joe Kuhel | 20.00 | 40.00 |
| 32 | Taft Wright | 20.00 | 40.00 |
| 33 | Al Milnar | 20.00 | 40.00 |
| 34 | Rollie Hemsley | 20.00 | 40.00 |
| 35 | Pinky Higgins | 25.00 | 45.00 |
| 36 | Barney McCosky | 20.00 | 40.00 |
| 37 | Bruce Campbell RC | 20.00 | 40.00 |
| 38 | Atley Donald | 30.00 | 50.00 |
| 39 | Tommy Henrich | 35.00 | 60.00 |
| 40 | John Babich | 20.00 | 40.00 |
| 41 | Frank (Blimp) Hayes | 20.00 | 40.00 |
| 42 | Wally Moses | 25.00 | 45.00 |
| 43 | Al Brancato RC | 20.00 | 40.00 |
| 44 | Sam Chapman | 20.00 | 40.00 |
| 45 | Eldon Auker | 20.00 | 40.00 |
| 46 | Sid Hudson RC | 20.00 | 40.00 |
| 47 | Buddy Lewis | 20.00 | 40.00 |
| 48 | Cecil Travis | 25.00 | 45.00 |
| 49 | Babe Dahlgren | 35.00 | 65.00 |
| 50 | Johnny Cooney | 30.00 | 60.00 |
| 51 | Dolph Camilli | 35.00 | 65.00 |
| 52 | Kirby Higbe RC | 30.00 | 60.00 |
| 53 | Luke Hamlin | 30.00 | 60.00 |
| 54 | Pee Wee Reese RC | 350.00 | 600.00 |
| 55 | Whit Wyatt | 35.00 | 65.00 |
| 56 | Johnny VanderMeer RC | 60.00 | 100.00 |
| 57 | Moe Arnovich | 30.00 | 60.00 |
| 58 | Frank Demaree | 30.00 | 60.00 |
| 59 | Bill Jurges | 30.00 | 60.00 |
| 60 | Chuck Klein | 90.00 | 150.00 |
| 61 | Vince DiMaggio RC | 125.00 | 225.00 |
| 62 | Elbie Fletcher | 30.00 | 60.00 |
| 63 | Dom DiMaggio RC | 150.00 | 250.00 |
| 64 | Bobby Doerr | 100.00 | 175.00 |
| 65 | Tommy Bridges | 35.00 | 65.00 |
| 66 | Harland Clift RC | 30.00 | 60.00 |
| 67 | Walt Judnich RC | 30.00 | 60.00 |
| 68 | John Knott | 30.00 | 60.00 |
| 69 | George Case | 35.00 | 65.00 |
| 70 | Bill Dickey | 250.00 | 400.00 |
| 71 | Joe DiMaggio | 1500.00 | 2500.00 |
| 72 | Lefty Gomez | 275.00 | 475.00 |

## 2008 Playoff Contenders

| | | | |
|---|---|---|---|
| | COMP.SET w/o AU's (50) | 8.00 | 20.00 |
| | COMMON CARD (1-50) | .25 | .60 |
| | COMMON AU (51-130) | 3.00 | 8.00 |
| | OVERALL AUTO ODDS 5 PER BOX | | |
| | EXCHANGE DEADLINE 8/4/2010 | | |
| 1 | Aaron Shafer | .25 | .60 |

| | | |
|---|---|---|
| ❏ 2 Adrian Nieto | .25 | .60 |
| ❏ 3 Andrew Liebel | .25 | .60 |
| ❏ 4 Blake Tekotte | .40 | 1.00 |
| ❏ 5 Brad Mills | .25 | .60 |
| ❏ 6 Brandon Waring | .75 | 2.00 |
| ❏ 7 Brett Hunter | .25 | .60 |
| ❏ 8 Byron Wiley | .25 | .60 |
| ❏ 9 Caleb Gindl | .25 | .60 |
| ❏ 10 Carlos Peguero | .40 | 1.00 |
| ❏ 11 Carson Blair | .25 | .60 |
| ❏ 12 Charlie Blackmon | .25 | .60 |
| ❏ 13 Chris Johnson | .25 | .60 |
| ❏ 14 Cody Adams | .40 | 1.00 |
| ❏ 15 Cody Satterwhite | .40 | 1.00 |
| ❏ 16 Cole Rohrbough | .25 | .60 |
| ❏ 17 Cole St. Clair | .25 | .60 |
| ❏ 18 Daniel Thomas | .25 | .60 |
| ❏ 19 Dennis Raben | .40 | 1.00 |
| ❏ 20 Derek Norris | .60 | 1.50 |
| ❏ 21 Dominic Brown | .75 | 2.00 |
| ❏ 22 Dusty Coleman | .25 | .60 |
| ❏ 23 Gerardo Parra | .25 | .60 |
| ❏ 24 Greg Halman | .60 | 1.50 |
| ❏ 25 J.P. Ramirez | .25 | .60 |
| ❏ 26 James Darnell | .25 | .60 |
| ❏ 27 Jason Knapp | .25 | .60 |
| ❏ 28 Jay Austin | .25 | .60 |
| ❏ 29 Jesus Montero | 1.25 | 3.00 |
| ❏ 30 Jharmidy De Jesus | .25 | .60 |
| ❏ 31 Jose Duran | .40 | 1.00 |
| ❏ 32 Josh Vitters | .25 | .60 |
| ❏ 33 Kenn Kasparek | .60 | 1.50 |
| ❏ 34 L. J. Hoes | .60 | 1.50 |
| ❏ 35 Logan Schafer | .25 | .60 |
| ❏ 36 Matt Harrison | .25 | .60 |
| ❏ 37 Matt Mitchell | .25 | .60 |
| ❏ 38 Max Ramirez | .25 | .60 |
| ❏ 39 Mike Cisco | .25 | .60 |
| ❏ 40 Niko Vasquez | .60 | 1.50 |
| ❏ 41 Rolando Gomez | .40 | 1.00 |
| ❏ 42 Ryan Kalish | .25 | .60 |
| ❏ 43 Stolmy Pimentel | .25 | .60 |
| ❏ 44 T.J. Steele | .40 | 1.00 |
| ❏ 45 Tim Murphy | .25 | .60 |
| ❏ 46 Tony Delmonico | .40 | 1.00 |
| ❏ 47 Tyler Ladendorf | .40 | 1.00 |
| ❏ 48 Tyler Sample | .25 | .60 |
| ❏ 49 Vance Worley | .25 | .60 |
| ❏ 50 Xavier Avery | .60 | 1.50 |
| ❏ 51 A.Cunningham AU/283 * | 5.00 | 12.00 |
| ❏ 52 Alex Buchholz AU | 3.00 | 8.00 |
| ❏ 53 Allan Dykstra AU | 3.00 | 8.00 |
| ❏ 54 A.Cashner AU/216 * | 6.00 | 15.00 |
| ❏ 55 A.Walker AU/288 * | 3.00 | 8.00 |
| ❏ 56 Angel Morales AU | 3.00 | 8.00 |
| ❏ 57 Angel Villalona AU | 10.00 | 25.00 |
| ❏ 58 Anthony Hewitt AU | 4.00 | 10.00 |
| ❏ 59 B.Hand AU/274 * | 3.00 | 8.00 |
| ❏ 60 B.Holt AU/236 * | 6.00 | 15.00 |
| ❏ 61 B.Crawford AU/339 * | 4.00 | 10.00 |
| ❏ 62 B.Price AU/165 * | 10.00 | 25.00 |
| ❏ 63 Buster Posey AU | 15.00 | 40.00 |
| ❏ 64 C.Gutierrez AU/87 * | 15.00 | 40.00 |
| ❏ 65 C.D'Arnaud AU/304 * | 6.00 | 15.00 |
| ❏ 66 Chris Davis AU | 6.00 | 15.00 |
| ❏ 67 C.Hicks AU/230 * | 3.00 | 8.00 |
| ❏ 68 Christian Friedrich AU | 6.00 | 15.00 |
| ❏ 69 Clark Murphy AU | 3.00 | 8.00 |
| ❏ 70 C.Phelps AU/244 * | 3.00 | 8.00 |
| ❏ 71 Curtis Petersen AU/244 * | 3.00 | 8.00 |
| ❏ 72 D.Cortes AU/292 * | 4.00 | 10.00 |
| ❏ 73 D.Schlereth AU/317 * | 4.00 | 10.00 |
| ❏ 74 Danny Carroll AU | 3.00 | 8.00 |
| ❏ 75 Danny Espinosa AU/395 * | 3.00 | 8.00 |
| ❏ 76 D.Viciedo AU/395 * | 30.00 | 80.00 |
| ❏ 77 Derek Holland AU | 8.00 | 20.00 |
| ❏ 78 D.Rose AU/88 * | 75.00 | 150.00 |
| ❏ 79 Devaris Gordon AU | 4.00 | 10.00 |
| ❏ 80 Engel Beltre AU | 5.00 | 12.00 |
| ❏ 81 E.Frederickson AU/177 * | 5.00 | 12.00 |
| ❏ 82 Gordon Beckham AU | 20.00 | 50.00 |
| ❏ 83 G.Veloz AU/339 * | 3.00 | 8.00 |
| ❏ 84 Ike Davis AU | 3.00 | 8.00 |
| ❏ 85 Isaac Galloway AU | 3.00 | 8.00 |
| ❏ 86 Jared Bolden AU | 3.00 | 8.00 |
| ❏ 87 J.Cunningham AU/229 * | 8.00 | 20.00 |
| ❏ 88 Jhoulys Chacin AU | 3.00 | 8.00 |
| ❏ 89 Jon Jay AU | 3.00 | 8.00 |

| | | |
|---|---|---|
| ❏ 90 J.Danks AU/354 * | 10.00 | 25.00 |
| ❏ 91 J.Lindblom AU/288 * | 4.00 | 10.00 |
| ❏ 92 Juan Carlos Subaran AU | 3.00 | 8.00 |
| ❏ 93 J.Ramirez AU/267 * | 4.00 | 10.00 |
| ❏ 94 J.Parker AU/229 * | 6.00 | 15.00 |
| ❏ 95 Kirk Nieuwenhuis AU | 4.00 | 10.00 |
| ❏ 96 Pat Venditte AU | 10.00 | 25.00 |
| ❏ 97 Lance Lynn AU | 3.00 | 8.00 |
| ❏ 98 L.Forsythe AU/262 * | 3.00 | 8.00 |
| ❏ 99 L.Morrison AU/314 * | 12.50 | 30.00 |
| ❏ 100 Marcus Lemon AU | 3.00 | 8.00 |
| ❏ 101 M.Sobolewski AU/277? * | 3.00 | 8.00 |
| ❏ 102 Mat Gamel AU | 10.00 | 25.00 |
| ❏ 103 M.Beasley AU/88 * | 30.00 | 60.00 |
| ❏ 104 Michael Kohn AU | 3.00 | 8.00 |
| ❏ 105 Mt Taylor AU/382 * | 20.00 | 50.00 |
| ❏ 106 Michel Inoa AU | 5.00 | 12.00 |
| ❏ 107 Mike Jones AU | 3.00 | 8.00 |
| ❏ 108 Mike Montgomery AU | 3.00 | 8.00 |
| ❏ 109 M.Stanton AU/149 * | 90.00 | 150.00 |
| ❏ 110 N.Feliz AU/246 * | 20.00 | 50.00 |
| ❏ 111 N.Soto AU/249 * | 8.00 | 20.00 |
| ❏ 112 O.Mayo AU/88 * | 40.00 | 80.00 |
| ❏ 113 Pedro Baez AU EXCH | 3.00 | 8.00 |
| ❏ 114 Petey Paramore AU | 3.00 | 8.00 |
| ❏ 115 Rafael Rodriguez AU | 6.00 | 20.00 |
| ❏ 116 Rashun Dixon AU | 6.00 | 15.00 |
| ❏ 117 Rick Porcello AU | 15.00 | 40.00 |
| ❏ 118 R.Grossman AU/227 * | 3.00 | 8.00 |
| ❏ 119 R.Kieschnick AU/289 * | 5.00 | 12.00 |
| ❏ 120 Ryan Perry AU | 3.00 | 8.00 |
| ❏ 121 S.Peterson AU/399 * | 3.00 | 8.00 |
| ❏ 122 Shooter Hunt AU/52 * | 90.00 | 150.00 |
| ❏ 123 T.Haley AU/309 * | 4.00 | 10.00 |
| ❏ 124 Tyler Chatwood AU | 3.00 | 8.00 |
| ❏ 125 Tyson Ross AU | 3.00 | 8.00 |
| ❏ 126 Wilin Rosario AU | 4.00 | 10.00 |
| ❏ 127 W.Flores AU/75 * EXCH | 150.00 | 250.00 |
| ❏ 128 Yamaico Navarro AU | 4.00 | 10.00 |
| ❏ 129 Z.Collier AU/200 * | 5.00 | 12.00 |
| ❏ 130 Zach Putnam AU | 3.00 | 8.00 |

### 1988 Score

OZZIE SMITH

| | | |
|---|---|---|
| ❏ COMPLETE SET (660) | 5.00 | 10.00 |
| ❏ COMP.FACT.SET (660) | 7.50 | 15.00 |
| ❏ 1 Don Mattingly | .25 | .60 |
| ❏ 2 Wade Boggs | .05 | .15 |
| ❏ 3 Tim Raines | .02 | .10 |
| ❏ 4 Andre Dawson | .02 | .10 |
| ❏ 5 Mark McGwire | .60 | 1.50 |
| ❏ 6 Kevin Seitzer | .01 | .05 |
| ❏ 7 Wally Joyner | .02 | .10 |
| ❏ 8 Jesse Barfield | .02 | .10 |
| ❏ 9 Pedro Guerrero | .02 | .10 |
| ❏ 10 Eric Davis | .02 | .10 |
| ❏ 11 George Brett | .10 | .25 |
| ❏ 12 Ozzie Smith | .07 | .20 |
| ❏ 13 Rickey Henderson | .07 | .20 |
| ❏ 14 Jim Rice | .02 | .10 |
| ❏ 15 Matt Nokes RC* | .08 | .25 |
| ❏ 16 Mike Schmidt | .20 | .50 |
| ❏ 17 Dave Parker | .02 | .10 |
| ❏ 18 Eddie Murray | .07 | .20 |
| ❏ 19 Andres Galarraga | .02 | .10 |
| ❏ 20 Tony Fernandez | .01 | .05 |
| ❏ 21 Kevin McReynolds | .01 | .05 |
| ❏ 22 B.J. Surhoff | .02 | .10 |
| ❏ 23 Pat Tabler | .01 | .05 |
| ❏ 24 Kirby Puckett | .07 | .20 |
| ❏ 25 Benito Santiago | .02 | .10 |
| ❏ 26 Ryne Sandberg | .15 | .40 |
| ❏ 27 Kelly Downs | .01 | .05 |
| ❏ 28 Jose Cruz | .02 | .10 |
| ❏ 29 Pete O'Brien | .01 | .05 |

| | | |
|---|---|---|
| ❏ 30 Mark Langston | .01 | .05 |
| ❏ 31 Lee Smith | .02 | .10 |
| ❏ 32 Juan Samuel | .01 | .05 |
| ❏ 33 Kevin Bass | .01 | .05 |
| ❏ 34 R.J. Reynolds | .01 | .05 |
| ❏ 35 Steve Sax | .01 | .05 |
| ❏ 36 John Kruk | .02 | .10 |
| ❏ 37 Alan Trammell | .02 | .10 |
| ❏ 38 Chris Bosio | .01 | .05 |
| ❏ 39 Brook Jacoby | .01 | .05 |
| ❏ 40 Willie McGee UER | | |
| (Excited misspelled | | |
| as excitd) | .02 | .10 |
| ❏ 41 Dave Magadan | .01 | .05 |
| ❏ 42 Fred Lynn | .02 | .10 |
| ❏ 43 Kent Hrbek | .02 | .10 |
| ❏ 44 Brian Downing | .01 | .05 |
| ❏ 45 Jose Canseco | .20 | .50 |
| ❏ 46 Jim Presley | .01 | .05 |
| ❏ 47 Mike Stanley | .01 | .05 |
| ❏ 48 Tony Pena | .01 | .05 |
| ❏ 49 David Cone | .02 | .10 |
| ❏ 50 Rick Sutcliffe | .02 | .10 |
| ❏ 51 Doug Drabek | .01 | .05 |
| ❏ 52 Bill Doran | .01 | .05 |
| ❏ 53 Mike Scioscia | .01 | .05 |
| ❏ 54 Candy Maldonado | .01 | .05 |
| ❏ 55 Dave Winfield | .02 | .10 |
| ❏ 56 Lou Whitaker | .02 | .10 |
| ❏ 57 Tom Henke | .01 | .05 |
| ❏ 58 Ken Gerhart | .01 | .05 |
| ❏ 59 Glenn Braggs | .01 | .05 |
| ❏ 60 Julio Franco | .02 | .10 |
| ❏ 61 Charlie Leibrandt | .01 | .05 |
| ❏ 62 Gary Gaetti | .01 | .05 |
| ❏ 63 Bob Boone | .02 | .10 |
| ❏ 64 Luis Polonia RC* | .08 | .25 |
| ❏ 65 Dwight Evans | .05 | .15 |
| ❏ 66 Phil Bradley | .01 | .05 |
| ❏ 67 Mike Boddicker | .01 | .05 |
| ❏ 68 Vince Coleman | .02 | .10 |
| ❏ 69 Howard Johnson | .02 | .10 |
| ❏ 70 Tim Wallach | .02 | .10 |
| ❏ 71 Keith Moreland | .01 | .05 |
| ❏ 72 Barry Larkin | .05 | .15 |
| ❏ 73 Alan Ashby | .01 | .05 |
| ❏ 74 Rick Rhoden | .01 | .05 |
| ❏ 75 Darrell Evans | .02 | .10 |
| ❏ 76 Dave Slieb | .02 | .10 |
| ❏ 77 Dan Plesac | .01 | .05 |
| ❏ 78 Will Clark | .07 | .20 |
| ❏ 79 Frank White | .02 | .10 |
| ❏ 80 Joe Carter | .05 | .15 |
| ❏ 81 Mike Witt | .01 | .05 |
| ❏ 82 Terry Steinbach | .02 | .10 |
| ❏ 83 Alvin Davis | .01 | .05 |
| ❏ 84 Tommy Herr | .01 | .05 |
| ❏ 85 Vance Law | .01 | .05 |
| ❏ 86 Kal Daniels | .01 | .05 |
| ❏ 87 Rick Honeycutt UER | | |
| (Wrong years for | | |
| stats on bac | | |
| ❏ 88 Alfredo Griffin | .01 | .05 |
| ❏ 89 Bret Saberhagen | .02 | .10 |
| ❏ 90 Bert Blyleven | .02 | .10 |
| ❏ 91 Jeff Reardon | .02 | .10 |
| ❏ 92 Cory Snyder | .01 | .05 |
| ❏ 93A Greg Walker ERR | .75 | 2.00 |
| ❏ 93B Greg Walker COR | | |
| (93 of 660) | .01 | .05 |
| ❏ 94 Joe Magrane RC* | .08 | .25 |
| ❏ 95 Rob Deer | .02 | .10 |
| ❏ 96 Ray Knight | .02 | .10 |
| ❏ 97 Casey Candaele | .01 | .05 |
| ❏ 98 John Cerutti | .01 | .05 |
| ❏ 99 Buddy Bell | .02 | .10 |
| ❏ 100 Jack Clark | .02 | .10 |
| ❏ 101 Eric Bell | .01 | .05 |
| ❏ 102 Willie Wilson | .02 | .10 |
| ❏ 103 Dave Schmidt | .01 | .05 |
| ❏ 104 Dennis Eckersley UER | .05 | .15 |
| ❏ 105 Don Sutton | .02 | .10 |
| ❏ 106 Danny Tartabull | .02 | .10 |
| ❏ 107 Fred McGriff | .07 | .20 |
| ❏ 108 Les Straker | .01 | .05 |
| ❏ 109 Lloyd Moseby | .01 | .05 |
| ❏ 110 Roger Clemens | .40 | 1.00 |
| ❏ 111 Glenn Hubbard | .01 | .05 |

|  |  | | |
|---|---|---|---|
| 112 | Ken Williams | .01 | .05 |
| 113 | Ruben Sierra | .02 | .10 |
| 114 | Stan Jefferson | .01 | .05 |
| 115 | Milt Thompson | .01 | .05 |
| 116 | Bobby Bonilla | .02 | .10 |
| 117 | Wayne Tolleson | .01 | .05 |
| 118 | Matt Williams RC | .30 | .75 |
| 119 | Chet Lemon | .02 | .10 |
| 120 | Dale Sveum | .01 | .05 |
| 121 | Dennis Boyd | .01 | .05 |
| 122 | Brett Butler | .02 | .10 |
| 123 | Terry Kennedy | .01 | .05 |
| 124 | Jack Howell | .01 | .05 |
| 125 | Curt Young | .01 | .05 |
| 126A | Dave Valle ERR (Misspelled Dale on card front) | .02 | .10 |
| 126B | Dave Valle COR | .02 | .10 |
| 127 | Curt Wilkerson | .01 | .05 |
| 128 | Tim Teufel | .01 | .05 |
| 129 | Ozzie Virgil | .01 | .05 |
| 130 | Brian Fisher | .01 | .05 |
| 131 | Lance Parrish | .02 | .10 |
| 132 | Tom Browning | .01 | .05 |
| 133A | Larry Andersen ERR (Misspelled Anderson on card) | .02 | .10 |
| 133B | Larry Andersen COR | .01 | .05 |
| 134A | Bob Brenly ERR (Misspelled Brenley on card front) | .02 | .10 |
| 134B | Bob Brenly COR | .01 | .05 |
| 135 | Mike Marshall | .01 | .05 |
| 136 | Gerald Perry | .01 | .05 |
| 137 | Bobby Meacham | .01 | .05 |
| 138 | Larry Herndon | .01 | .05 |
| 139 | Fred Manrique | .01 | .05 |
| 140 | Charlie Hough | .02 | .10 |
| 141 | Ron Darling | .02 | .10 |
| 142 | Herm Winningham | .01 | .05 |
| 143 | Mike Diaz | .01 | .05 |
| 144 | Mike Jackson RC* | .08 | .25 |
| 145 | Denny Walling | .01 | .05 |
| 146 | Robby Thompson | .01 | .05 |
| 147 | Franklin Stubbs | .01 | .05 |
| 148 | Albert Hall | .01 | .05 |
| 149 | Bobby Witt | .01 | .05 |
| 150 | Lance McCullers | .01 | .05 |
| 151 | Scott Bradley | .01 | .05 |
| 152 | Mark McLemore | .01 | .05 |
| 153 | Tim Laudner | .01 | .05 |
| 154 | Greg Swindell | .01 | .05 |
| 155 | Marty Barrett | .01 | .05 |
| 156 | Mike Heath | .01 | .05 |
| 157 | Gary Ward | .01 | .05 |
| 158A | Lee Mazzilli ERR (Misspelled Mazzilli on card fro) | .02 | .10 |
| 158B | Lee Mazzilli COR | .02 | .10 |
| 159 | Tom Foley | .01 | .05 |
| 160 | Robin Yount | .10 | .30 |
| 161 | Steve Bedrosian | .01 | .05 |
| 162 | Bob Walk | .01 | .05 |
| 163 | Nick Esasky | .01 | .05 |
| 164 | Ken Caminiti RC | .75 | 2.00 |
| 165 | Jose Uribe | .01 | .05 |
| 166 | Dave Anderson | .01 | .05 |
| 167 | Ed Whitson | .01 | .05 |
| 168 | Ernie Whitt | .01 | .05 |
| 169 | Cecil Cooper | .02 | .10 |
| 170 | Mike Pagliarulo | .01 | .05 |
| 171 | Pat Sheridan | .01 | .05 |
| 172 | Chris Bando | .01 | .05 |
| 173 | Lee Lacy | .01 | .05 |
| 174 | Steve Lombardozzi | .01 | .05 |
| 175 | Mike Greenwell | .01 | .05 |
| 176 | Greg Minton | .01 | .05 |
| 177 | Moose Haas | .01 | .05 |
| 178 | Mike Kingery | .01 | .05 |
| 179 | Greg A. Harris | .01 | .05 |
| 180 | Bo Jackson | .07 | .20 |
| 181 | Carmelo Martinez | .01 | .05 |
| 182 | Alex Trevino | .01 | .05 |
| 183 | Ron Oester | .01 | .05 |
| 184 | Danny Darwin | .01 | .05 |
| 185 | Mike Krukow | .01 | .05 |
| 186 | Rafael Palmeiro | .15 | .40 |
| 187 | Tim Burke | .01 | .05 |
| 188 | Roger McDowell | .01 | .05 |
| 189 | Garry Templeton | .02 | .10 |
| 190 | Terry Pendleton | .02 | .10 |
| 191 | Larry Parrish | .01 | .05 |
| 192 | Rey Quinones | .01 | .05 |
| 193 | Joaquin Andujar | .02 | .10 |
| 194 | Tom Brunansky | .02 | .10 |
| 195 | Donnie Moore | .01 | .05 |
| 196 | Dan Pasqua | .01 | .05 |
| 197 | Jim Gantner | .01 | .05 |
| 198 | Mark Eichhorn | .01 | .05 |
| 199 | John Grubb | .01 | .05 |
| 200 | Bill Ripken RC* | .08 | .25 |
| 201 | Sam Horn RC | .02 | .10 |
| 202 | Todd Worrell | .01 | .05 |
| 203 | Terry Leach | .01 | .05 |
| 204 | Garth Iorg | .01 | .05 |
| 205 | Brian Dayett | .01 | .05 |
| 206 | Bo Diaz | .01 | .05 |
| 207 | Craig Reynolds | .01 | .05 |
| 208 | Brian Holton | .01 | .05 |
| 209 | Marvell Wynne UER (Misspelled Marvelle on card f | .01 | .05 |
| 210 | Dave Concepcion | .01 | .05 |
| 211 | Mike Davis | .01 | .05 |
| 212 | Devon White | .02 | .10 |
| 213 | Mickey Brantley | .01 | .05 |
| 214 | Greg Gagne | .01 | .05 |
| 215 | Oddibe McDowell | .01 | .05 |
| 216 | Jimmy Key | .02 | .10 |
| 217 | Dave Bergman | .01 | .05 |
| 218 | Calvin Schiraldi | .01 | .05 |
| 219 | Larry Sheets | .01 | .05 |
| 220 | Mike Easler | .01 | .05 |
| 221 | Kurt Stillwell | .01 | .05 |
| 222 | Chuck Jackson | .01 | .05 |
| 223 | Dave Martinez | .01 | .05 |
| 224 | Tim Leary | .01 | .05 |
| 225 | Steve Garvey | .02 | .10 |
| 226 | Greg Mathews | .01 | .05 |
| 227 | Doug Sisk | .01 | .05 |
| 228 | Dave Henderson (Wearing Red Sox uniform; Red Sox | .01 | .05 |
| 229 | Jimmy Dwyer | .01 | .05 |
| 230 | Larry Owen | .01 | .05 |
| 231 | Andre Thornton | .01 | .05 |
| 232 | Mark Salas | .01 | .05 |
| 233 | Tom Brookens | .01 | .05 |
| 234 | Greg Brock | .01 | .05 |
| 235 | Rance Mulliniks | .01 | .05 |
| 236 | Bob Brower | .01 | .05 |
| 237 | Joe Niekro | .01 | .05 |
| 238 | Scott Bankhead | .01 | .05 |
| 239 | Doug DeCinces | .01 | .05 |
| 240 | Tommy John | .02 | .10 |
| 241 | Rich Gedman | .01 | .05 |
| 242 | Ted Power | .01 | .05 |
| 243 | Dave Meads | .01 | .05 |
| 244 | Jim Sundberg | .02 | .10 |
| 245 | Ken Oberkfell | .01 | .05 |
| 246 | Jimmy Jones | .01 | .05 |
| 247 | Ken Landreaux | .01 | .05 |
| 248 | Jose Oquendo | .01 | .05 |
| 249 | John Mitchell RC | .02 | .10 |
| 250 | Don Baylor | .02 | .10 |
| 251 | Scott Fletcher | .01 | .05 |
| 252 | Al Newman | .01 | .05 |
| 253 | Carney Lansford | .02 | .10 |
| 254 | Johnny Ray | .01 | .05 |
| 255 | Gary Pettis | .01 | .05 |
| 256 | Ken Phelps | .01 | .05 |
| 257 | Rick Leach | .01 | .05 |
| 258 | Tim Stoddard | .01 | .05 |
| 259 | Ed Romero | .01 | .05 |
| 260 | Sid Bream | .01 | .05 |
| 261A | Tom Niedenfuer ERR (Misspelled Neidenfuer on | .02 | .10 |
| 261B | Tom Niedenfuer COR | .01 | .05 |
| 262 | Rick Dempsey | .01 | .05 |
| 263 | Lonnie Smith | .01 | .05 |
| 264 | Bob Forsch | .01 | .05 |
| 265 | Barry Bonds | .75 | 2.00 |
| 266 | Willie Randolph | .01 | .05 |
| 267 | Don Ramsey | .01 | .05 |
| 268 | Don Slaught | .01 | .05 |
| 269 | Mickey Tettleton | .01 | .05 |
| 270 | Jerry Reuss | .01 | .05 |
| 271 | Marc Sullivan | .01 | .05 |
| 272 | Jim Morrison | .01 | .05 |
| 273 | Steve Balboni | .01 | .05 |
| 274 | Dick Schofield | .01 | .05 |
| 275 | John Tudor | .02 | .10 |
| 276 | Gene Larkin RC* | .08 | .25 |
| 277 | Harold Reynolds | .02 | .10 |
| 278 | Jerry Browne | .01 | .05 |
| 279 | Willie Upshaw | .01 | .05 |
| 280 | Ted Higuera | .01 | .05 |
| 281 | Terry McGriff | .01 | .05 |
| 282 | Terry Puhl | .01 | .05 |
| 283 | Mark Wasinger | .01 | .05 |
| 284 | Luis Salazar | .01 | .05 |
| 285 | Ted Simmons | .02 | .10 |
| 286 | John Shelby | .01 | .05 |
| 287 | John Smiley RC* | .08 | .25 |
| 288 | Curt Ford | .01 | .05 |
| 289 | Steve Crawford | .01 | .05 |
| 290 | Dan Quisenberry | .01 | .05 |
| 291 | Alan Wiggins | .01 | .05 |
| 292 | Randy Bush | .01 | .05 |
| 293 | John Candelaria | .01 | .05 |
| 294 | Tony Phillips | .01 | .05 |
| 295 | Mike Morgan | .01 | .05 |
| 296 | Bill Wegman | .01 | .05 |
| 297A | Terry Francona ERR (Misspelled Franconia on card) | .02 | .10 |
| 297B | Terry Francona COR | .01 | .05 |
| 298 | Mickey Hatcher | .01 | .05 |
| 299 | Andres Thomas | .01 | .05 |
| 300 | Bob Stanley | .01 | .05 |
| 301 | Al Pedrique | .01 | .05 |
| 302 | Jim Lindeman | .01 | .05 |
| 303 | Wally Backman | .01 | .05 |
| 304 | Paul O'Neill | .05 | .15 |
| 305 | Hubie Brooks | .01 | .05 |
| 306 | Steve Buechele | .01 | .05 |
| 307 | Bobby Thigpen | .01 | .05 |
| 308 | George Hendrick | .02 | .10 |
| 309 | John Moses | .01 | .05 |
| 310 | Ron Guidry | .02 | .10 |
| 311 | Bill Schroeder | .01 | .05 |
| 312 | Jose Nunez | .01 | .05 |
| 313 | Bud Black | .01 | .05 |
| 314 | Joe Sambito | .01 | .05 |
| 315 | Scott McGregor | .01 | .05 |
| 316 | Rafael Santana | .01 | .05 |
| 317 | Frank Williams | .01 | .05 |
| 318 | Mike Fitzgerald | .01 | .05 |
| 319 | Rick Mahler | .01 | .05 |
| 320 | Jim Gott | .01 | .05 |
| 321 | Mariano Duncan | .01 | .05 |
| 322 | Jose Guzman | .02 | .10 |
| 323 | Lee Guetterman | .01 | .05 |
| 324 | Dan Gladden | .01 | .05 |
| 325 | Gary Carter | .02 | .10 |
| 326 | Tracy Jones | .01 | .05 |
| 327 | Floyd Youmans | .01 | .05 |
| 328 | Bill Dawley | .01 | .05 |
| 329 | Paul Noce | .01 | .05 |
| 330 | Angel Salazar | .01 | .05 |
| 331 | Goose Gossage | .02 | .10 |
| 332 | George Frazier | .01 | .05 |
| 333 | Ruppert Jones | .01 | .05 |
| 334 | Billy Joe Robidoux | .01 | .05 |
| 335 | Mike Scott | .02 | .10 |
| 336 | Randy Myers | .02 | .10 |
| 337 | Bob Sebra | .01 | .05 |
| 338 | Eric Show | .01 | .05 |
| 339 | Mitch Williams | .02 | .10 |
| 340 | Paul Molitor | .02 | .10 |
| 341 | Gus Polidor | .01 | .05 |
| 342 | Steve Trout | .01 | .05 |
| 343 | Jerry Don Gleaton | .01 | .05 |
| 344 | Bob Knepper | .01 | .05 |
| 345 | Mitch Webster | .01 | .05 |
| 346 | John Morris | .01 | .05 |
| 347 | Andy Hawkins | .01 | .05 |
| 348 | Dave Leiper | .01 | .05 |
| 349 | Ernest Riles | .01 | .05 |
| 350 | Dwight Gooden | .10 | .30 |
| 351 | Dave Righetti | .02 | .10 |
| 352 | Pat Dodson | .01 | .05 |
| 353 | John Habyan | .01 | .05 |

|  |  | | |
|---|---|---|---|
| ☐ 354 | Jim Deshaies | .01 | .05 |
| ☐ 355 | Butch Wynegar | .01 | .05 |
| ☐ 356 | Bryn Smith | .01 | .05 |
| ☐ 357 | Matt Young | .01 | .05 |
| ☐ 358 | Tom Pagnozzi RC | .02 | .10 |
| ☐ 359 | Floyd Rayford | .01 | .05 |
| ☐ 360 | Darryl Strawberry | .02 | .10 |
| ☐ 361 | Sal Butera | .01 | .05 |
| ☐ 362 | Domingo Ramos | .01 | .05 |
| ☐ 363 | Chris Brown | .01 | .05 |
| ☐ 364 | Jose Gonzalez | .01 | .05 |
| ☐ 365 | Dave Smith | .01 | .05 |
| ☐ 366 | Andy McGaffigan | .01 | .05 |
| ☐ 367 | Stan Javier | .01 | .05 |
| ☐ 368 | Henry Cotto | .01 | .05 |
| ☐ 369 | Mike Birkbeck | .01 | .05 |
| ☐ 370 | Len Dykstra | .02 | .10 |
| ☐ 371 | Dave Collins | .01 | .05 |
| ☐ 372 | Spike Owen | .01 | .05 |
| ☐ 373 | Geno Petralli | .01 | .05 |
| ☐ 374 | Ron Karkovice | .01 | .05 |
| ☐ 375 | Shane Rawley | .01 | .05 |
| ☐ 376 | DeWayne Buice | .01 | .05 |
| ☐ 377 | Bill Pecota RC* | .01 | .05 |
| ☐ 378 | Leon Durham | .01 | .05 |
| ☐ 379 | Ed Olwine | .01 | .05 |
| ☐ 380 | Bruce Hurst | .01 | .05 |
| ☐ 381 | Bob McClure | .01 | .05 |
| ☐ 382 | Mark Thurmond | .01 | .05 |
| ☐ 383 | Buddy Biancalana | .01 | .05 |
| ☐ 384 | Tim Conroy | .01 | .05 |
| ☐ 385 | Tony Gwynn | .10 | .30 |
| ☐ 386 | Greg Gross | .01 | .05 |
| ☐ 387 | Barry Lyons | .01 | .05 |
| ☐ 388 | Mike Felder | .01 | .05 |
| ☐ 389 | Pat Clements | .01 | .05 |
| ☐ 390 | Ken Griffey | .02 | .10 |
| ☐ 391 | Mark Davis | .01 | .05 |
| ☐ 392 | Jose Rijo | .02 | .10 |
| ☐ 393 | Mike Young | .01 | .05 |
| ☐ 394 | Willie Fraser | .01 | .05 |
| ☐ 395 | Dion James | .01 | .05 |
| ☐ 396 | Steve Shields | .01 | .05 |
| ☐ 397 | Randy St.Claire | .01 | .05 |
| ☐ 398 | Danny Jackson | .01 | .05 |
| ☐ 399 | Cecil Fielder | .02 | .10 |
| ☐ 400 | Keith Hernandez | .02 | .10 |
| ☐ 401 | Don Carman | .01 | .05 |
| ☐ 402 | Chuck Crim | .01 | .05 |
| ☐ 403 | Rob Woodward | .01 | .05 |
| ☐ 404 | Junior Ortiz | .01 | .05 |
| ☐ 405 | Glenn Wilson | .01 | .05 |
| ☐ 406 | Ken Howell | .01 | .05 |
| ☐ 407 | Jeff Kunkel | .01 | .05 |
| ☐ 408 | Jeff Reed | .01 | .05 |
| ☐ 409 | Chris James | .01 | .05 |
| ☐ 410 | Zane Smith | .01 | .05 |
| ☐ 411 | Ken Dixon | .01 | .05 |
| ☐ 412 | Ricky Horton | .01 | .05 |
| ☐ 413 | Frank DiPino | .01 | .05 |
| ☐ 414 | Shane Mack | .01 | .05 |
| ☐ 415 | Danny Cox | .01 | .05 |
| ☐ 416 | Andy Van Slyke | .05 | .15 |
| ☐ 417 | Danny Heep | .01 | .05 |
| ☐ 418 | John Cangelosi | .01 | .05 |
| ☐ 419A | John Christensen ERR (Christiansen on card front) | .02 | .10 |
| ☐ 419B | John Christensen COR | .01 | .05 |
| ☐ 420 | Joey Cora RC | .08 | .25 |
| ☐ 421 | Mike LaValliere | .01 | .05 |
| ☐ 422 | Kelly Gruber | .01 | .05 |
| ☐ 423 | Bruce Benedict | .01 | .05 |
| ☐ 424 | Len Matuszek | .01 | .05 |
| ☐ 425 | Kent Tekulve | .01 | .05 |
| ☐ 426 | Rafael Ramirez | .01 | .05 |
| ☐ 427 | Mike Flanagan | .01 | .05 |
| ☐ 428 | Mike Gallego | .01 | .05 |
| ☐ 429 | Juan Castillo | .01 | .05 |
| ☐ 430 | Neal Heaton | .01 | .05 |
| ☐ 431 | Phil Garner | .02 | .10 |
| ☐ 432 | Mike Dunne | .01 | .05 |
| ☐ 433 | Wallace Johnson | .01 | .05 |
| ☐ 434 | Jack O'Connor | .01 | .05 |
| ☐ 435 | Steve Jeltz | .01 | .05 |
| ☐ 436 | Donell Nixon | .01 | .05 |
| ☐ 437 | Jack Lazorko | .01 | .05 |
| ☐ 438 | Keith Comstock | .01 | .05 |
| ☐ 439 | Jeff D. Robinson | .01 | .05 |
| ☐ 440 | Graig Nettles | .02 | .10 |
| ☐ 441 | Mel Hall | .01 | .05 |
| ☐ 442 | Gerald Young | .01 | .05 |
| ☐ 443 | Gary Redus | .01 | .05 |
| ☐ 444 | Charlie Moore | .01 | .05 |
| ☐ 445 | Bill Madlock | .02 | .10 |
| ☐ 446 | Mark Clear | .01 | .05 |
| ☐ 447 | Greg Booker | .01 | .05 |
| ☐ 448 | Rick Schu | .01 | .05 |
| ☐ 449 | Ron Kittle | .01 | .05 |
| ☐ 450 | Dale Murphy | .05 | .15 |
| ☐ 451 | Bob Dernier | .01 | .05 |
| ☐ 452 | Dale Mohorcic | .01 | .05 |
| ☐ 453 | Rafael Belliard | .01 | .05 |
| ☐ 454 | Charlie Puleo | .01 | .05 |
| ☐ 455 | Dwayne Murphy | .01 | .05 |
| ☐ 456 | Jim Eisenreich | .01 | .05 |
| ☐ 457 | David Palmer | .01 | .05 |
| ☐ 458 | Dave Stewart | .02 | .10 |
| ☐ 459 | Pascual Perez | .01 | .05 |
| ☐ 460 | Glenn Davis | .01 | .05 |
| ☐ 461 | Dan Petry | .01 | .05 |
| ☐ 462 | Jim Winn | .01 | .05 |
| ☐ 463 | Darrell Miller | .01 | .05 |
| ☐ 464 | Mike Moore | .01 | .05 |
| ☐ 465 | Mike LaCoss | .01 | .05 |
| ☐ 466 | Steve Farr | .01 | .05 |
| ☐ 467 | Jerry Mumphrey | .01 | .05 |
| ☐ 468 | Kevin Gross | .01 | .05 |
| ☐ 469 | Bruce Bochy | .01 | .05 |
| ☐ 470 | Orel Hershiser | .02 | .10 |
| ☐ 471 | Eric King | .01 | .05 |
| ☐ 472 | Ellis Burks RC | .15 | .40 |
| ☐ 473 | Darren Daulton | .02 | .10 |
| ☐ 474 | Mookie Wilson | .02 | .10 |
| ☐ 475 | Frank Viola | .02 | .10 |
| ☐ 476 | Ron Robinson | .01 | .05 |
| ☐ 477 | Bob Melvin | .01 | .05 |
| ☐ 478 | Jeff Musselman | .01 | .05 |
| ☐ 479 | Charlie Kerfeld | .01 | .05 |
| ☐ 480 | Richard Dotson | .01 | .05 |
| ☐ 481 | Kevin Mitchell | .02 | .10 |
| ☐ 482 | Gary Roenicke | .01 | .05 |
| ☐ 483 | Tim Flannery | .01 | .05 |
| ☐ 484 | Rich Yett | .01 | .05 |
| ☐ 485 | Pete Incaviglia | .02 | .10 |
| ☐ 486 | Rick Cerone | .01 | .05 |
| ☐ 487 | Tony Armas | .02 | .10 |
| ☐ 488 | Jerry Reed | .01 | .05 |
| ☐ 489 | Dave Lopes | .02 | .10 |
| ☐ 490 | Frank Tanana | .02 | .10 |
| ☐ 491 | Mike Loynd | .01 | .05 |
| ☐ 492 | Bruce Ruffin | .01 | .05 |
| ☐ 493 | Chris Speier | .01 | .05 |
| ☐ 494 | Tom Hume | .01 | .05 |
| ☐ 495 | Jesse Orosco | .01 | .05 |
| ☐ 496 | Robbie Wine UER (Misspelled Robby on card front) | .01 | .05 |
| ☐ 497 | Jeff Montgomery RC | .08 | .25 |
| ☐ 498 | Jeff Dedmon | .01 | .05 |
| ☐ 499 | Luis Aguayo | .01 | .05 |
| ☐ 500 | Reggie Jackson A's | .05 | .15 |
| ☐ 501 | Reggie Jackson O's | .05 | .15 |
| ☐ 502 | Reggie Jackson Yankees | .05 | .15 |
| ☐ 503 | Reggie Jackson Angels | .05 | .15 |
| ☐ 504 | Reggie Jackson A's | .05 | .15 |
| ☐ 505 | Billy Hatcher | .01 | .05 |
| ☐ 506 | Ed Lynch | .01 | .05 |
| ☐ 507 | Willie Hernandez | .01 | .05 |
| ☐ 508 | Jose DeLeon | .01 | .05 |
| ☐ 509 | Joel Youngblood | .01 | .05 |
| ☐ 510 | Bob Welch | .02 | .10 |
| ☐ 511 | Steve Ontiveros | .01 | .05 |
| ☐ 512 | Randy Ready | .01 | .05 |
| ☐ 513 | Juan Nieves | .01 | .05 |
| ☐ 514 | Jeff Russell | .01 | .05 |
| ☐ 515 | Von Hayes | .02 | .10 |
| ☐ 516 | Mark Gubicza | .02 | .10 |
| ☐ 517 | Ken Dayley | .01 | .05 |
| ☐ 518 | Don Aase | .01 | .05 |
| ☐ 519 | Rick Reuschel | .02 | .10 |
| ☐ 520 | Mike Henneman RC* | .08 | .25 |
| ☐ 521 | Rick Aguilera | .02 | .10 |
| ☐ 522 | Jay Howell | .01 | .05 |
| ☐ 523 | Ed Correa | .01 | .05 |
| ☐ 524 | Manny Trillo | .01 | .05 |
| ☐ 525 | Kirk Gibson | .07 | .20 |
| ☐ 526 | Wally Ritchie | .01 | .05 |
| ☐ 527 | Al Nipper | .01 | .05 |
| ☐ 528 | Atlee Hammaker | .01 | .05 |
| ☐ 529 | Shawon Dunston | .01 | .05 |
| ☐ 530 | Jim Clancy | .01 | .05 |
| ☐ 531 | Tom Paciorek | .01 | .05 |
| ☐ 532 | Joel Skinner | .01 | .05 |
| ☐ 533 | Scott Garrelts | .01 | .05 |
| ☐ 534 | Tom O'Malley | .01 | .05 |
| ☐ 535 | John Franco | .02 | .10 |
| ☐ 536 | Paul Kilgus | .01 | .05 |
| ☐ 537 | Darnell Porter | .01 | .05 |
| ☐ 538 | Walt Terrell | .01 | .05 |
| ☐ 539 | Bill Long | .01 | .05 |
| ☐ 540 | George Bell | .02 | .10 |
| ☐ 541 | Jeff Sellers | .01 | .05 |
| ☐ 542 | Joe Boever | .01 | .05 |
| ☐ 543 | Steve Howe | .01 | .05 |
| ☐ 544 | Scott Sanderson | .01 | .05 |
| ☐ 545 | Jack Morris | .02 | .10 |
| ☐ 546 | Todd Benzinger RC* | .08 | .25 |
| ☐ 547 | Steve Henderson | .01 | .05 |
| ☐ 548 | Eddie Milner | .01 | .05 |
| ☐ 549 | Jeff M. Robinson | .01 | .05 |
| ☐ 550 | Cal Ripken | .30 | .75 |
| ☐ 551 | Jody Davis | .01 | .05 |
| ☐ 552 | Kirk McCaskill | .01 | .05 |
| ☐ 553 | Craig Lefferts | .01 | .05 |
| ☐ 554 | Darnell Coles | .01 | .05 |
| ☐ 555 | Phil Niekro | .02 | .10 |
| ☐ 556 | Mike Aldrete | .01 | .05 |
| ☐ 557 | Pat Perry | .01 | .05 |
| ☐ 558 | Juan Agosto | .01 | .05 |
| ☐ 559 | Rob Murphy | .01 | .05 |
| ☐ 560 | Dennis Rasmussen | .01 | .05 |
| ☐ 561 | Manny Lee | .01 | .05 |
| ☐ 562 | Jeff Blauser RC | .08 | .25 |
| ☐ 563 | Bob Ojeda | .01 | .05 |
| ☐ 564 | Dave Dravecky | .01 | .05 |
| ☐ 565 | Gene Garber | .01 | .05 |
| ☐ 566 | Ron Roenicke | .01 | .05 |
| ☐ 567 | Tommy Hinzo | .01 | .05 |
| ☐ 568 | Eric Nolte | .01 | .05 |
| ☐ 569 | Ed Hearn | .01 | .05 |
| ☐ 570 | Mark Davidson | .01 | .05 |
| ☐ 571 | Jim Walewander | .01 | .05 |
| ☐ 572 | Donnie Hill UER (84 Stolen Base total listed as | .01 | .05 |
| ☐ 573 | Jamie Moyer | .02 | .10 |
| ☐ 574 | Ken Schrom | .01 | .05 |
| ☐ 575 | Nolan Ryan | .40 | 1.00 |
| ☐ 576 | Jim Acker | .01 | .05 |
| ☐ 577 | Jamie Quirk | .01 | .05 |
| ☐ 578 | Jay Aldrich | .01 | .05 |
| ☐ 579 | Claudell Washington | .01 | .05 |
| ☐ 580 | Jeff Leonard | .01 | .05 |
| ☐ 581 | Carmen Castillo | .01 | .05 |
| ☐ 582 | Daryl Boston | .01 | .05 |
| ☐ 583 | Jeff DeWillis | .01 | .05 |
| ☐ 584 | John Marzano | .01 | .05 |
| ☐ 585 | Bill Gullickson | .01 | .05 |
| ☐ 586 | Andy Allanson | .01 | .05 |
| ☐ 587 | Lee Tunnell UER (1987 stat line reads 4.84 ERA) | .01 | .05 |
| ☐ 588 | Gene Nelson | .01 | .05 |
| ☐ 589 | Dave LaPoint | .01 | .05 |
| ☐ 590 | Harold Baines | .02 | .10 |
| ☐ 591 | Bill Buckner | .02 | .10 |
| ☐ 592 | Carlton Fisk | .05 | .15 |
| ☐ 593 | Rick Manning | .01 | .05 |
| ☐ 594 | Doug Jones RC | .08 | .25 |
| ☐ 595 | Tom Candiotti | .01 | .05 |
| ☐ 596 | Steve Lake | .01 | .05 |
| ☐ 597 | Jose Lind RC | .08 | .25 |
| ☐ 598 | Ross Jones | .01 | .05 |
| ☐ 599 | Gary Matthews | .02 | .10 |
| ☐ 600 | Fernando Valenzuela | .02 | .10 |
| ☐ 601 | Dennis Martinez | .02 | .10 |
| ☐ 602 | Les Lancaster | .01 | .05 |
| ☐ 603 | Ozzie Guillen | .02 | .10 |
| ☐ 604 | Tony Bernazard | .01 | .05 |
| ☐ 605 | Chili Davis | .02 | .10 |
| ☐ 606 | Roy Smalley | .01 | .05 |
| ☐ 607 | Ivan Calderon | .01 | .05 |
| ☐ 608 | Jay Tibbs | .01 | .05 |

|  | | |
|---|---|---|
| 609 Guy Hoffman | .01 | .05 |
| 610 Doyle Alexander | .01 | .05 |
| 611 Mike Bielecki | .01 | .05 |
| 612 Shawn Hillegas | .01 | .05 |
| 613 Keith Atherton | .01 | .05 |
| 614 Eric Plunk | .01 | .05 |
| 615 Sid Fernandez | .01 | .05 |
| 616 Dennis Lamp | .01 | .05 |
| 617 Dave Engle | .01 | .05 |
| 618 Harry Spilman | .01 | .05 |
| 619 Don Robinson | .01 | .05 |
| 620 John Farrell RC | .02 | .10 |
| 621 Nelson Liriano | .01 | .05 |
| 622 Floyd Bannister | .01 | .05 |
| 623 Randy Milligan RC | .02 | .10 |
| 624 Kevin Elster | .01 | .05 |
| 625 Jody Reed RC | .08 | .25 |
| 626 Shawn Abner | .01 | .05 |
| 627 Kirt Manwaring RC | .08 | .25 |
| 628 Pete Stanicek | .01 | .05 |
| 629 Rob Ducey | .01 | .05 |
| 630 Steve Kiefer | .01 | .05 |
| 631 Gary Thurman | .01 | .05 |
| 632 Darrel Akerfelds | .01 | .05 |
| 633 Dave Clark | .01 | .05 |
| 634 Roberto Kelly RC | .08 | .25 |
| 635 Keith Hughes | .01 | .05 |
| 636 John Davis | .01 | .05 |
| 637 Mike Devereaux RC | .08 | .25 |
| 638 Tom Glavine RC | 1.00 | 2.50 |
| 639 Keith Miller RC | .08 | .25 |
| 640 Chris Gwynn UER RC | .08 | .25 |
| 641 Tim Crews RC | .08 | .25 |
| 642 Mackey Sasser RC | .08 | .25 |
| 643 Vicente Palacios | .01 | .05 |
| 644 Kevin Romine | .01 | .05 |
| 645 Gregg Jefferies RC | .08 | .25 |
| 646 Jeff Treadway RC | .08 | .25 |
| 647 Ron Gant RC | .15 | .40 |
| 648 M.McGwire/M.Nokes | .30 | .75 |
| 649 Eric Davis and Tim Raines (Speed and Power) | .02 | .10 |
| 650 Don Mattingly/J.Clark | .10 | .30 |
| 651 C.Ripken/Trammell/Fem | .08 | .25 |
| 652 Vince Coleman HL 100 Stolen Bases | .01 | .05 |
| 653 Kirby Puckett HL | .05 | .15 |
| 654 Benito Santiago HL | .01 | .05 |
| 655 Juan Nieves HL No Hitter | .01 | .05 |
| 656 Steve Bedrosian HL Saves Record | .07 | .20 |
| 657 Mike Schmidt HL | .10 | .30 |
| 658 Don Mattingly HL | .10 | .30 |
| 659 Mark McGwire HL | .30 | .75 |
| 660 Paul Molitor HL | .01 | .05 |

## 1989 Score

| | | |
|---|---|---|
| COMPLETE SET (660) | 6.00 | 15.00 |
| COMP.FACT.SET (660) | 6.00 | 15.00 |
| 1 Jose Canseco | .08 | .25 |
| 2 Andre Dawson | .02 | .10 |
| 3 Mark McGwire | .40 | 1.00 |
| 4 Benito Santiago | .02 | .10 |
| 5 Rick Reuschel | .01 | .05 |
| 6 Fred McGriff | .05 | .15 |
| 7 Kal Daniels | .01 | .05 |
| 8 Gary Gaetti | .02 | .10 |
| 9 Ellis Burks | .02 | .10 |
| 10 Darryl Strawberry | .02 | .10 |
| 11 Julio Franco | .02 | .10 |
| 12 Lloyd Moseby | .01 | .05 |
| 13 Jeff Pico | .01 | .05 |
| 14 Johnny Ray | .01 | .05 |
| 15 Cal Ripken | .30 | .75 |
| 16 Dick Schofield | .01 | .05 |
| 17 Mel Hall | .01 | .05 |
| 18 Bill Ripken | .01 | .05 |
| 19 Brook Jacoby | .01 | .05 |
| 20 Kirby Puckett | .08 | .25 |
| 21 Bill Doran | .01 | .05 |
| 22 Pete O'Brien | .01 | .05 |
| 23 Matt Nokes | .01 | .05 |
| 24 Brian Fisher | .01 | .05 |
| 25 Jack Clark | .02 | .10 |
| 26 Gary Pettis | .01 | .05 |
| 27 Dave Valle | .01 | .05 |
| 28 Willie Wilson | .02 | .10 |
| 29 Curt Young | .01 | .05 |
| 30 Dale Murphy | .05 | .15 |
| 31 Barry Larkin | .05 | .15 |
| 32 Dave Stewart | .02 | .10 |
| 33 Mike LaValliere | .01 | .05 |
| 34 Glenn Hubbard | .01 | .05 |
| 35 Ryne Sandberg | .15 | .40 |
| 36 Tony Pena | .01 | .05 |
| 37 Greg Walker | .01 | .05 |
| 38 Von Hayes | .01 | .05 |
| 39 Kevin Mitchell | .02 | .10 |
| 40 Tim Raines | .02 | .10 |
| 41 Keith Hernandez | .02 | .10 |
| 42 Keith Moreland | .01 | .05 |
| 43 Ruben Sierra | .02 | .10 |
| 44 Chet Lemon | .01 | .05 |
| 45 Willie Randolph | .02 | .10 |
| 46 Andy Allanson | .01 | .05 |
| 47 Candy Maldonado | .01 | .05 |
| 48 Sid Bream | .01 | .05 |
| 49 Denny Walling | .01 | .05 |
| 50 Dave Winfield | .02 | .10 |
| 51 Alvin Davis | .01 | .05 |
| 52 Cory Snyder | .01 | .05 |
| 53 Hubie Brooks | .01 | .05 |
| 54 Chili Davis | .02 | .10 |
| 55 Kevin Seitzer | .01 | .05 |
| 56 Jose Uribe | .01 | .05 |
| 57 Tony Fernandez | .01 | .05 |
| 58 Tim Teufel | .01 | .05 |
| 59 Oddibe McDowell | .01 | .05 |
| 60 Les Lancaster | .01 | .05 |
| 61 Billy Hatcher | .01 | .05 |
| 62 Dan Gladden | .01 | .05 |
| 63 Marty Barrett | .01 | .05 |
| 64 Nick Esasky | .01 | .05 |
| 65 Wally Joyner | .02 | .10 |
| 66 Mike Greenwell | .01 | .05 |
| 67 Ken Williams | .01 | .05 |
| 68 Bob Horner | .02 | .10 |
| 69 Steve Sax | .01 | .05 |
| 70 Rickey Henderson | .08 | .25 |
| 71 Mitch Webster | .01 | .05 |
| 72 Rob Deer | .01 | .05 |
| 73 Jim Presley | .01 | .05 |
| 74 Albert Hall | .01 | .05 |
| 75 George Brett | .25 | .60 |
| 75A George Brett 33 ERR | .40 | 1.00 |
| 76 Brian Downing | .02 | .10 |
| 77 Dave Martinez | .01 | .05 |
| 78 Scott Fletcher | .01 | .05 |
| 79 Phil Bradley | .01 | .05 |
| 80 Ozzie Smith | .15 | .40 |
| 81 Larry Sheets | .01 | .05 |
| 82 Mike Aldrete | .01 | .05 |
| 83 Darnell Coles | .01 | .05 |
| 84 Len Dykstra | .02 | .10 |
| 85 Jim Rice | .02 | .10 |
| 86 Jeff Treadway | .01 | .05 |
| 87 Jose Lind | .01 | .05 |
| 88 Willie McGee | .02 | .10 |
| 89 Mickey Brantley | .01 | .05 |
| 90 Tony Gwynn | .10 | .30 |
| 91 R.J. Reynolds | .01 | .05 |
| 92 Milt Thompson | .01 | .05 |
| 93 Kevin McReynolds | .01 | .05 |
| 94 Eddie Murray | .08 | .25 |
| 95 Ron Kittle | .01 | .05 |
| 96 Ron Kittle | .01 | .05 |
| 97 Gerald Young | .01 | .05 |
| 98 Ernie Whit | .01 | .05 |
| 99 Jeff Reed | .01 | .05 |
| 100 Don Mattingly | .25 | .60 |
| 101 Gerald Perry | .01 | .05 |
| 102 Vance Law | .01 | .05 |
| 103 John Shelby | .01 | .05 |
| 104 Chris Sabo RC * | .15 | .40 |
| 105 Danny Tartabull | .01 | .05 |
| 106 Glenn Wilson | .01 | .05 |
| 107 Mark Davidson | .01 | .05 |
| 108 Dave Parker | .02 | .10 |
| 109 Eric Davis | .02 | .10 |
| 110 Alan Trammell | .02 | .10 |
| 111 Ozzie Virgil | .01 | .05 |
| 112 Frank Tanana | .02 | .10 |
| 113 Rafael Ramirez | .01 | .05 |
| 114 Dennis Martinez | .02 | .10 |
| 115 Jose DeLeon | .01 | .05 |
| 116 Bob Ojeda | .01 | .05 |
| 117 Doug Drabek | .02 | .10 |
| 118 Andy Hawkins | .01 | .05 |
| 119 Greg Maddux | .20 | .50 |
| 120 Cecil Fielder RevNeg UER | | |
| 121 Mike Scioscia | .02 | .10 |
| 122 Dan Petry | .01 | .05 |
| 123 Terry Kennedy | .01 | .05 |
| 124 Kelly Downs | .01 | .05 |
| 125 Greg Gross UER (Gregg on back) | .01 | .05 |
| 126 Fred Lynn | .02 | .10 |
| 127 Barry Bonds | .60 | 1.50 |
| 128 Harold Baines | .02 | .10 |
| 129 Doyle Alexander | .01 | .05 |
| 130 Kevin Elster | .01 | .05 |
| 131 Mike Heath | .01 | .05 |
| 132 Teddy Higuera | .01 | .05 |
| 133 Charlie Leibrandt | .01 | .05 |
| 134 Tim Laudner | .01 | .05 |
| 135A Ray Knight ERR (Reverse negative) | .02 | .10 |
| 135B Ray Knight COR | .02 | .10 |
| 136 Howard Johnson | .02 | .10 |
| 137 Terry Pendleton | .02 | .10 |
| 138 Andy McGaffigan | .01 | .05 |
| 139 Ken Oberkfell | .01 | .05 |
| 140 Butch Wynegar | .01 | .05 |
| 141 Rob Murphy | .01 | .05 |
| 142 Rich Renteria | .01 | .05 |
| 143 Jose Guzman | .01 | .05 |
| 144 Andres Galarraga | .02 | .10 |
| 145 Ricky Horton | .01 | .05 |
| 146 Frank DiPino | .01 | .05 |
| 147 Glenn Braggs | .01 | .05 |
| 148 John Kruk | .02 | .10 |
| 149 Mike Schmidt | .20 | .50 |
| 150 Lee Smith | .02 | .10 |
| 151 Robin Yount * | .15 | .40 |
| 152 Mark Eichhorn | .01 | .05 |
| 153 DeWayne Buice | .01 | .05 |
| 154 B.J. Surhoff | .02 | .10 |
| 155 Vince Coleman | .01 | .05 |
| 156 Tony Phillips | .01 | .05 |
| 157 Willie Fraser | .01 | .05 |
| 158 Lance McCullers | .01 | .05 |
| 159 Greg Gagne | .01 | .05 |
| 160 Jesse Barfield | .02 | .10 |
| 161 Mark Langston | .02 | .10 |
| 162 Kurt Stillwell | .01 | .05 |
| 163 Dion James | .01 | .05 |
| 164 Glenn Davis | .01 | .05 |
| 165 Walt Weiss | .01 | .05 |
| 166 Dave Concepcion | .02 | .10 |
| 167 Alfredo Griffin | .01 | .05 |
| 168 Don Heinkel | .01 | .05 |
| 169 Luis Rivera | .01 | .05 |
| 170 Shane Rawley | .01 | .05 |
| 171 Darrell Evans | .02 | .10 |
| 172 Robby Thompson | .01 | .05 |
| 173 Jody Davis | .01 | .05 |
| 174 Andy Van Slyke | .05 | .15 |
| 175 Wade Boggs ERR | .05 | .15 |
| 176 Garry Templeton ('85 stats off-centered) | .02 | .10 |
| 177 Gary Redus | .01 | .05 |
| 178 Craig Lefferts | .01 | .05 |
| 179 Carney Lansford | .02 | .10 |
| 180 Ron Darling | .01 | .05 |
| 181 Kirk McCaskill | .01 | .05 |
| 182 Tony Armas | .01 | .05 |
| 183 Steve Farr | .01 | .05 |

|  |  | | |
|---|---|---|---|
| ☐ 184 | Tom Brunansky | .01 | .05 |
| ☐ 185 | Bryan Harvey UER RC * | .08 | .25 |
| ☐ 186 | Mike Marshall | .01 | .05 |
| ☐ 187 | Bo Diaz | .01 | .05 |
| ☐ 188 | Willie Upshaw | .01 | .05 |
| ☐ 189 | Mike Pagliarulo | .01 | .05 |
| ☐ 190 | Mike Krukow | .01 | .05 |
| ☐ 191 | Tommy Herr | .01 | .05 |
| ☐ 192 | Jim Pankovits | .01 | .05 |
| ☐ 193 | Dwight Evans | .05 | .15 |
| ☐ 194 | Kelly Gruber | .01 | .05 |
| ☐ 195 | Bobby Bonilla | .02 | .10 |
| ☐ 196 | Wallace Johnson | .01 | .05 |
| ☐ 197 | Dave Stieb | .02 | .10 |
| ☐ 198 | Pat Borders RC * | .08 | .25 |
| ☐ 199 | Rafael Palmeiro | .08 | .25 |
| ☐ 200 | Dwight Gooden | .05 | .15 |
| ☐ 201 | Pete Incaviglia | .01 | .05 |
| ☐ 202 | Chris James | .01 | .05 |
| ☐ 203 | Marvell Wynne | .01 | .05 |
| ☐ 204 | Pat Sheridan | .01 | .05 |
| ☐ 205 | Don Baylor | .02 | .10 |
| ☐ 206 | Paul O'Neill | .05 | .15 |
| ☐ 207 | Pete Smith | .01 | .05 |
| ☐ 208 | Mark McLemore | .01 | .05 |
| ☐ 209 | Henry Cotto | .01 | .05 |
| ☐ 210 | Kirk Gibson | .02 | .10 |
| ☐ 211 | Claudell Washington | .01 | .05 |
| ☐ 212 | Randy Bush | .01 | .05 |
| ☐ 213 | Joe Carter | .02 | .10 |
| ☐ 214 | Bill Buckner | .02 | .10 |
| ☐ 215 | Bert Blyleven UER | .02 | .10 |
| ☐ 216 | Brett Butler | .02 | .10 |
| ☐ 217 | Lee Mazzilli | .01 | .05 |
| ☐ 218 | Spike Owen | .01 | .05 |
| ☐ 219 | Bill Swift | .01 | .05 |
| ☐ 220 | Tim Wallach | .01 | .05 |
| ☐ 221 | David Cone | .02 | .10 |
| ☐ 222 | Don Carman | .01 | .05 |
| ☐ 223 | Rich Gossage | .02 | .10 |
| ☐ 224 | Bob Walk | .01 | .05 |
| ☐ 225 | Dave Righetti | .02 | .10 |
| ☐ 226 | Kevin Bass | .01 | .05 |
| ☐ 227 | Kevin Gross | .01 | .05 |
| ☐ 228 | Tim Burke | .01 | .05 |
| ☐ 229 | Rick Mahler | .01 | .05 |
| ☐ 230 | Lou Whitaker UER (252 games in '85& should be 15 | .02 | .10 |
| ☐ 231 | Luis Alicea RC * | .08 | .25 |
| ☐ 232 | Roberto Alomar | .08 | .25 |
| ☐ 233 | Bob Boone | .02 | .10 |
| ☐ 234 | Dickie Thon | .01 | .05 |
| ☐ 235 | Shawon Dunston | .01 | .05 |
| ☐ 236 | Pete Stanicek | .01 | .05 |
| ☐ 237 | Craig Biggio RC | 1.50 | 4.00 |
| ☐ 238 | Dennis Boyd | .01 | .05 |
| ☐ 239 | Tom Candiotti | .01 | .05 |
| ☐ 240 | Gary Carter | .02 | .10 |
| ☐ 241 | Mike Stanley | .01 | .05 |
| ☐ 242 | Ken Phelps | .01 | .05 |
| ☐ 243 | Chris Bosio | .01 | .05 |
| ☐ 244 | Les Straker | .01 | .05 |
| ☐ 245 | Dave Smith | .01 | .05 |
| ☐ 246 | John Candelaria | .01 | .05 |
| ☐ 247 | Joe Orsulak | .01 | .05 |
| ☐ 248 | Storm Davis | .01 | .05 |
| ☐ 249 | Floyd Bannister UER (ML Batting Record) | .01 | .05 |
| ☐ 250 | Jack Morris | .02 | .10 |
| ☐ 251 | Bret Saberhagen | .01 | .05 |
| ☐ 252 | Tom Niedenfuer | .01 | .05 |
| ☐ 253 | Neal Heaton | .01 | .05 |
| ☐ 254 | Eric Show | .01 | .05 |
| ☐ 255 | Juan Samuel | .01 | .05 |
| ☐ 256 | Dale Sveum | .01 | .05 |
| ☐ 257 | Jim Gott | .01 | .05 |
| ☐ 258 | Scott Garrelts | .01 | .05 |
| ☐ 259 | Larry McWilliams | .01 | .05 |
| ☐ 260 | Steve Bedrosian | .01 | .05 |
| ☐ 261 | Jack Howell | .01 | .05 |
| ☐ 262 | Jay Tibbs | .01 | .05 |
| ☐ 263 | Jamie Moyer | .01 | .05 |
| ☐ 264 | Doug Sisk | .01 | .05 |
| ☐ 265 | Todd Worrell | .01 | .05 |
| ☐ 266 | John Farrell | .01 | .05 |
| ☐ 267 | Dave Collins | .01 | .05 |
| ☐ 268 | Sid Fernandez | .01 | .05 |

|  |  | | |
|---|---|---|---|
| ☐ 269 | Tom Brookens | .01 | .05 |
| ☐ 270 | Shane Mack | .01 | .05 |
| ☐ 271 | Paul Kilgus | .01 | .05 |
| ☐ 272 | Chuck Crim | .01 | .05 |
| ☐ 273 | Bob Knepper | .01 | .05 |
| ☐ 274 | Mike Moore | .01 | .05 |
| ☐ 275 | Guillermo Hernandez | .01 | .05 |
| ☐ 276 | Dennis Eckersley | .05 | .15 |
| ☐ 277 | Graig Nettles | .02 | .10 |
| ☐ 278 | Rich Dotson | .01 | .05 |
| ☐ 279 | Larry Herndon | .01 | .05 |
| ☐ 280 | Gene Larkin | .01 | .05 |
| ☐ 281 | Roger McDowell | .01 | .05 |
| ☐ 282 | Greg Swindell | .01 | .05 |
| ☐ 283 | Juan Agosto | .01 | .05 |
| ☐ 284 | Jeff M. Robinson | .01 | .05 |
| ☐ 285 | Mike Dunne | .01 | .05 |
| ☐ 286 | Greg Mathews | .01 | .05 |
| ☐ 287 | Kent Tekulve | .01 | .05 |
| ☐ 288 | Jerry Mumphrey | .01 | .05 |
| ☐ 289 | Jack McDowell | .02 | .10 |
| ☐ 290 | Frank Viola | .02 | .10 |
| ☐ 291 | Mark Gubicza | .01 | .05 |
| ☐ 292 | Dave Schmidt | .01 | .05 |
| ☐ 293 | Mike Henneman | .01 | .05 |
| ☐ 294 | Jimmy Jones | .01 | .05 |
| ☐ 295 | Charlie Hough | .02 | .10 |
| ☐ 296 | Rafael Santana | .01 | .05 |
| ☐ 297 | Chris Speier | .01 | .05 |
| ☐ 298 | Mike Witt | .01 | .05 |
| ☐ 299 | Pascual Perez | .01 | .05 |
| ☐ 300 | Nolan Ryan | .40 | 1.00 |
| ☐ 301 | Mitch Williams | .01 | .05 |
| ☐ 302 | Mookie Wilson | .02 | .10 |
| ☐ 303 | Mackey Sasser | .01 | .05 |
| ☐ 304 | John Cerutti | .01 | .05 |
| ☐ 305 | Jeff Reardon | .02 | .10 |
| ☐ 306 | Randy Myers UER (6 hits in '87 should be 61) | .02 | .10 |
| ☐ 307 | Greg Brock | .01 | .05 |
| ☐ 308 | Bob Welch | .01 | .05 |
| ☐ 309 | Jeff D. Robinson | .01 | .05 |
| ☐ 310 | Harold Reynolds | .02 | .10 |
| ☐ 311 | Jim Walewander | .01 | .05 |
| ☐ 312 | Dave Magadan | .01 | .05 |
| ☐ 313 | Jim Gantner | .01 | .05 |
| ☐ 314 | Walt Terrell | .01 | .05 |
| ☐ 315 | Wally Backman | .01 | .05 |
| ☐ 316 | Luis Salazar | .01 | .05 |
| ☐ 317 | Rick Rhoden | .01 | .05 |
| ☐ 318 | Tom Henke | .01 | .05 |
| ☐ 319 | Mike Macfarlane RC * | .08 | .25 |
| ☐ 320 | Dan Plesac | .01 | .05 |
| ☐ 321 | Calvin Schiraldi | .01 | .05 |
| ☐ 322 | Stan Javier | .01 | .05 |
| ☐ 323 | Devon White | .02 | .10 |
| ☐ 324 | Scott Bradley | .01 | .05 |
| ☐ 325 | Bruce Hurst | .01 | .05 |
| ☐ 326 | Manny Lee | .01 | .05 |
| ☐ 327 | Rick Aguilera | .01 | .05 |
| ☐ 328 | Bruce Ruffin | .01 | .05 |
| ☐ 329 | Ed Whitson | .01 | .05 |
| ☐ 330 | Bo Jackson | .08 | .25 |
| ☐ 331 | Ivan Calderon | .01 | .05 |
| ☐ 332 | Mickey Hatcher | .01 | .05 |
| ☐ 333 | Barry Jones | .01 | .05 |
| ☐ 334 | Ron Hassey | .01 | .05 |
| ☐ 335 | Bill Wegman | .01 | .05 |
| ☐ 336 | Damon Berryhill | .01 | .05 |
| ☐ 337 | Steve Ontiveros | .01 | .05 |
| ☐ 338 | Dan Pasqua | .01 | .05 |
| ☐ 339 | Bill Pecota | .01 | .05 |
| ☐ 340 | Greg Cadaret | .01 | .05 |
| ☐ 341 | Scott Bankhead | .01 | .05 |
| ☐ 342 | Ron Guidry | .02 | .10 |
| ☐ 343 | Danny Heep | .01 | .05 |
| ☐ 344 | Bob Brower | .01 | .05 |
| ☐ 345 | Rich Gedman | .01 | .05 |
| ☐ 346 | Nelson Santovenia | .01 | .05 |
| ☐ 347 | George Bell | .02 | .10 |
| ☐ 348 | Ted Power | .01 | .05 |
| ☐ 349 | Mark Grant | .01 | .05 |
| ☐ 350 | Roger Clemens | .40 | 1.00 |
| ☐ 350A | Roger Clemens 778 ERR | .75 | 2.00 |
| ☐ 351 | Bill Long | .01 | .05 |
| ☐ 352 | Jay Bell | .02 | .10 |
| ☐ 353 | Steve Balboni | .01 | .05 |

|  |  | | |
|---|---|---|---|
| ☐ 354 | Bob Kipper | .01 | .05 |
| ☐ 355 | Steve Jeltz | .01 | .05 |
| ☐ 356 | Jesse Orosco | .01 | .05 |
| ☐ 357 | Bob Dernier | .01 | .05 |
| ☐ 358 | Mickey Tettleton | .01 | .05 |
| ☐ 359 | Duane Ward | .01 | .05 |
| ☐ 360 | Darrin Jackson | .02 | .10 |
| ☐ 361 | Rey Quinones | .01 | .05 |
| ☐ 362 | Mark Grace | .08 | .25 |
| ☐ 363 | Steve Lyons | .01 | .05 |
| ☐ 364 | Pat Perry | .01 | .05 |
| ☐ 365 | Terry Steinbach | .02 | .10 |
| ☐ 366 | Alan Ashby | .01 | .05 |
| ☐ 367 | Jeff Montgomery | .01 | .05 |
| ☐ 368 | Steve Buechele | .01 | .05 |
| ☐ 369 | Chris Brown | .01 | .05 |
| ☐ 370 | Orel Hershiser | .02 | .10 |
| ☐ 371 | Todd Benzinger | .01 | .05 |
| ☐ 372 | Ron Gant | .02 | .10 |
| ☐ 373 | Paul Assenmacher | .01 | .05 |
| ☐ 374 | Joey Meyer | .01 | .05 |
| ☐ 375 | Neil Allen | .01 | .05 |
| ☐ 376 | Mike Davis | .01 | .05 |
| ☐ 377 | Jeff Parrett | .01 | .05 |
| ☐ 378 | Jay Howell | .01 | .05 |
| ☐ 379 | Rafael Belliard | .01 | .05 |
| ☐ 380 | Luis Polonia UER (2 triples in '87& should be 10 | .01 | .05 |
| ☐ 381 | Keith Atherton | .01 | .05 |
| ☐ 382 | Kent Hrbek | .02 | .10 |
| ☐ 383 | Bob Stanley | .01 | .05 |
| ☐ 384 | Dave LaPoint | .01 | .05 |
| ☐ 385 | Rance Mulliniks | .01 | .05 |
| ☐ 386 | Melido Perez | .01 | .05 |
| ☐ 387 | Doug Jones | .01 | .05 |
| ☐ 388 | Steve Lyons | .01 | .05 |
| ☐ 389 | Alejandro Pena | .01 | .05 |
| ☐ 390 | Frank White | .02 | .10 |
| ☐ 391 | Pat Tabler | .01 | .05 |
| ☐ 392 | Eric Plunk | .01 | .05 |
| ☐ 393 | Mike Maddux | .01 | .05 |
| ☐ 394 | Allan Anderson | .01 | .05 |
| ☐ 395 | Bob Brenly | .01 | .05 |
| ☐ 396 | Rick Cerone | .01 | .05 |
| ☐ 397 | Scott Terry | .01 | .05 |
| ☐ 398 | Mike Jackson | .01 | .05 |
| ☐ 399 | Bobby Thigpen UER (Bio says 37 saves in '88& sho | .01 | .05 |
| ☐ 400 | Don Sutton | .02 | .10 |
| ☐ 401 | Cecil Espy | .01 | .05 |
| ☐ 402 | Junior Ortiz | .01 | .05 |
| ☐ 403 | Mike Smithson | .01 | .05 |
| ☐ 404 | Bud Black | .01 | .05 |
| ☐ 405 | Tom Foley | .01 | .05 |
| ☐ 406 | Andres Thomas | .01 | .05 |
| ☐ 407 | Rick Sutcliffe | .02 | .10 |
| ☐ 408 | Brian Harper | .01 | .05 |
| ☐ 409 | John Smiley | .01 | .05 |
| ☐ 410 | Juan Nieves | .01 | .05 |
| ☐ 411 | Shawn Abner | .01 | .05 |
| ☐ 412 | Wes Gardner | .01 | .05 |
| ☐ 413 | Darren Daulton | .02 | .10 |
| ☐ 414 | Juan Berenguer | .01 | .05 |
| ☐ 415 | Charles Hudson | .01 | .05 |
| ☐ 416 | Rick Honeycutt | .01 | .05 |
| ☐ 417 | Greg Booker | .01 | .05 |
| ☐ 418 | Tim Belcher | .01 | .05 |
| ☐ 419 | Don August | .01 | .05 |
| ☐ 420 | Dale Mohorcic | .01 | .05 |
| ☐ 421 | Steve Lombardozzi | .01 | .05 |
| ☐ 422 | Atlee Hammaker | .01 | .05 |
| ☐ 423 | Jerry Don Gleaton | .01 | .05 |
| ☐ 424 | Scott Bailes | .01 | .05 |
| ☐ 425 | Bruce Sutter | .02 | .10 |
| ☐ 426 | Randy Ready | .01 | .05 |
| ☐ 427 | Jerry Reed | .01 | .05 |
| ☐ 428 | Bryn Smith | .01 | .05 |
| ☐ 429 | Tim Leary | .01 | .05 |
| ☐ 430 | Mark Clear | .01 | .05 |
| ☐ 431 | Terry Leach | .01 | .05 |
| ☐ 432 | John Moses | .01 | .05 |
| ☐ 433 | Ozzie Guillen | .02 | .10 |
| ☐ 434 | Gene Nelson | .01 | .05 |
| ☐ 435 | Gary Ward | .01 | .05 |
| ☐ 436 | Luis Aguayo | .01 | .05 |
| ☐ 437 | Fernando Valenzuela | .02 | .10 |

| | | |
|---|---|---|
| ☐ 438 Jeff Russell UER | | |
| (Saves total does | | |
| not add up co | .01 | .05 |
| ☐ 439 Cecilio Guante | .01 | .05 |
| ☐ 440 Don Robinson | .01 | .05 |
| ☐ 441 Rick Anderson | .01 | .05 |
| ☐ 442 Tom Glavine | .08 | .25 |
| ☐ 443 Daryl Boston | .01 | .05 |
| ☐ 444 Joe Price | .01 | .05 |
| ☐ 445 Stu Cliburn | .01 | .05 |
| ☐ 446 Manny Trillo | .01 | .05 |
| ☐ 447 Joel Skinner | .01 | .05 |
| ☐ 448 Charlie Puleo | .01 | .05 |
| ☐ 449 Carlton Fisk | .05 | .15 |
| ☐ 450 Will Clark | .05 | .15 |
| ☐ 451 Otis Nixon | .01 | .05 |
| ☐ 452 Rick Schu | .01 | .05 |
| ☐ 453 Todd Stottlemyre UER | | |
| (ML Batting Record) | | |
| ☐ 454 Tim Birtsas | .01 | .05 |
| ☐ 455 Dave Gallagher | .01 | .05 |
| ☐ 456 Barry Lyons | .01 | .05 |
| ☐ 457 Fred Manrique | .01 | .05 |
| ☐ 458 Ernest Riles | .01 | .05 |
| ☐ 459 Doug Jennings | .01 | .05 |
| ☐ 460 Joe Magrane | .01 | .05 |
| ☐ 461 Jamie Quirk | .01 | .05 |
| ☐ 462 Jack Armstrong RC * | .08 | .25 |
| ☐ 463 Bobby Witt | .01 | .05 |
| ☐ 464 Keith A. Miller | .01 | .05 |
| ☐ 465 Todd Burns | .01 | .05 |
| ☐ 466 John Dopson | .01 | .05 |
| ☐ 467 Rich Yett | .01 | .05 |
| ☐ 468 Craig Reynolds | .01 | .05 |
| ☐ 469 Dave Bergman | .01 | .05 |
| ☐ 470 Rex Hudler | .01 | .05 |
| ☐ 471 Eric King | .01 | .05 |
| ☐ 472 Joaquin Andujar | .02 | .10 |
| ☐ 473 Sil Campusano | .01 | .05 |
| ☐ 474 Terry Mulholland | .01 | .05 |
| ☐ 475 Mike Flanagan | .01 | .05 |
| ☐ 476 Greg A. Harris | .01 | .05 |
| ☐ 477 Tommy John | .02 | .10 |
| ☐ 478 Dave Anderson | .01 | .05 |
| ☐ 479 Fred Toliver | .01 | .05 |
| ☐ 480 Jimmy Key | .02 | .10 |
| ☐ 481 Donell Nixon | .01 | .05 |
| ☐ 482 Mark Portugal | .01 | .05 |
| ☐ 483 Tom Pagnozzi | .01 | .05 |
| ☐ 484 Jeff Kunkel | .01 | .05 |
| ☐ 485 Frank Williams | .01 | .05 |
| ☐ 486 Jody Reed | .01 | .05 |
| ☐ 487 Roberto Kelly | .01 | .05 |
| ☐ 488 Shawn Hillegas UER | | |
| (165 innings in '87& | | |
| should b | .01 | .05 |
| ☐ 489 Jerry Reuss | .01 | .05 |
| ☐ 490 Mark Davis | .01 | .05 |
| ☐ 491 Jeff Sellers | .01 | .05 |
| ☐ 492 Zane Smith | .01 | .05 |
| ☐ 493 Al Newman | .01 | .05 |
| ☐ 494 Mike Young | .01 | .05 |
| ☐ 495 Larry Parrish | .01 | .05 |
| ☐ 496 Herm Winningham | .01 | .05 |
| ☐ 497 Carmen Castillo | .01 | .05 |
| ☐ 498 Joe Hesketh | .01 | .05 |
| ☐ 499 Darrell Miller | .01 | .05 |
| ☐ 500 Mike LaCoss | .01 | .05 |
| ☐ 501 Charlie Lea | .01 | .05 |
| ☐ 502 Bruce Benedict | .01 | .05 |
| ☐ 503 Chuck Finley | .02 | .10 |
| ☐ 504 Brad Wellman | .01 | .05 |
| ☐ 505 Tim Crews | .01 | .05 |
| ☐ 506 Ken Gerhart | .01 | .05 |
| ☐ 507A Brian Holton ERR | | |
| (Born 1/25/65 Denver& | | |
| should be | .01 | .05 |
| ☐ 507B Brian Holton COR | .75 | 2.00 |
| ☐ 508 Dennis Lamp | .01 | .05 |
| ☐ 509 Bobby Meacham UER | | |
| ('84 games 099) | | |
| ☐ 510 Tracy Jones | .01 | .05 |
| ☐ 511 Mike R. Fitzgerald | .01 | .05 |
| ☐ 512 Jeff Bittiger | .01 | .05 |
| ☐ 513 Tim Flannery | .01 | .05 |
| ☐ 514 Ray Hayward | .01 | .05 |
| ☐ 515 Dave Leiper | .01 | .05 |
| ☐ 516 Rod Scurry | .01 | .05 |

| | | |
|---|---|---|
| ☐ 517 Carmelo Martinez | .01 | .05 |
| ☐ 518 Curtis Wilkerson | .01 | .05 |
| ☐ 519 Stan Jefferson | .01 | .05 |
| ☐ 520 Dan Quisenberry | .01 | .05 |
| ☐ 521 Lloyd McClendon | .01 | .05 |
| ☐ 522 Steve Trout | .01 | .05 |
| ☐ 523 Larry Andersen | .01 | .05 |
| ☐ 524 Don Aase | .01 | .05 |
| ☐ 525 Bob Forsch | .01 | .05 |
| ☐ 526 Geno Petralli | .01 | .05 |
| ☐ 527 Angel Salazar | .01 | .05 |
| ☐ 528 Mike Schooler | .01 | .05 |
| ☐ 529 Jose Oquendo | .01 | .05 |
| ☐ 530 Jay Buhner | .02 | .10 |
| ☐ 531 Tom Bolton | .01 | .05 |
| ☐ 532 Al Nipper | .01 | .05 |
| ☐ 533 Dave Henderson | .01 | .05 |
| ☐ 534 John Costello | .01 | .05 |
| ☐ 535 Donnie Moore | .01 | .05 |
| ☐ 536 Mike Laga | .01 | .05 |
| ☐ 537 Mike Gallego | .01 | .05 |
| ☐ 538 Jim Clancy | .01 | .05 |
| ☐ 539 Joel Youngblood | .01 | .05 |
| ☐ 540 Rick Leach | .01 | .05 |
| ☐ 541 Kevin Romine | .01 | .05 |
| ☐ 542 Mark Salas | .01 | .05 |
| ☐ 543 Greg Minton | .01 | .05 |
| ☐ 544 Dave Palmer | .01 | .05 |
| ☐ 545 Dwayne Murphy UER | | |
| (Game-sinning) | .01 | .05 |
| ☐ 546 Jim Deshaies | .01 | .05 |
| ☐ 547 Don Gordon | .01 | .05 |
| ☐ 548 Ricky Jordan RC * | .08 | .25 |
| ☐ 549 Mike Boddicker | .01 | .05 |
| ☐ 550 Mike Scott | .02 | .10 |
| ☐ 551 Jeff Ballard | .01 | .05 |
| ☐ 552A Jose Rijo ERR | | |
| (Uniform listed as | | |
| 27 on back) | .02 | .10 |
| ☐ 552B Jose Rijo COR | | |
| (Uniform listed as | | |
| 24 on back) | .02 | .10 |
| ☐ 553 Danny Darwin | .01 | .05 |
| ☐ 554 Tom Browning | .01 | .05 |
| ☐ 555 Danny Jackson | .01 | .05 |
| ☐ 556 Rick Dempsey | .01 | .05 |
| ☐ 557 Jeffrey Leonard | .01 | .05 |
| ☐ 558 Jeff Musselman | .01 | .05 |
| ☐ 559 Ron Robinson | .01 | .05 |
| ☐ 560 John Tudor | .02 | .10 |
| ☐ 561 Don Slaught UER | | |
| (237 games in 1987) | | |
| ☐ 562 Dennis Rasmussen | .01 | .05 |
| ☐ 563 Brady Anderson RC | .15 | .40 |
| ☐ 564 Pedro Guerrero | .02 | .10 |
| ☐ 565 Paul Molitor | .02 | .10 |
| ☐ 566 Terry Clark | .01 | .05 |
| ☐ 567 Terry Puhl | .01 | .05 |
| ☐ 568 Mike Campbell | .01 | .05 |
| ☐ 569 Paul Mirabella | .01 | .05 |
| ☐ 570 Jeff Hamilton | .01 | .05 |
| ☐ 571 Oswald Peraza | .01 | .05 |
| ☐ 572 Bob McClure | .01 | .05 |
| ☐ 573 Jose Bautista RC | .02 | .10 |
| ☐ 574 Alex Trevino | .01 | .05 |
| ☐ 575 John Franco | .02 | .10 |
| ☐ 576 Mark Parent | .01 | .05 |
| ☐ 577 Nelson Liriano | .01 | .05 |
| ☐ 578 Steve Shields | .01 | .05 |
| ☐ 579 Odell Jones | .01 | .05 |
| ☐ 580 Al Leiter | .08 | .25 |
| ☐ 581 Dave Stapleton | .01 | .05 |
| ☐ 582 Hersh/Cans/Gibs/Stew WS | .08 | .25 |
| ☐ 583 Donnie Hill | .01 | .05 |
| ☐ 584 Chuck Jackson | .01 | .05 |
| ☐ 585 Rene Gonzales | .01 | .05 |
| ☐ 586 Tracy Woodson | .01 | .05 |
| ☐ 587 Jim Adduci | .01 | .05 |
| ☐ 588 Mario Soto | .02 | .10 |
| ☐ 589 Jeff Blauser | .01 | .05 |
| ☐ 590 Jim Traber | .01 | .05 |
| ☐ 591 Jon Perlman | .01 | .05 |
| ☐ 592 Mark Williamson | .01 | .05 |
| ☐ 593 Dave Meads | .01 | .05 |
| ☐ 594 Jim Eisenreich | .01 | .05 |
| ☐ 595A Paul Gibson P1 | .40 | 1.00 |
| ☐ 595B Paul Gibson P2 | | |
| (Airbrushed leg on | | |

| | | |
|---|---|---|
| player in back | .01 | .05 |
| ☐ 596 Mike Birkbeck | .01 | .05 |
| ☐ 597 Terry Francona | .02 | .10 |
| ☐ 598 Paul Zuvella | .01 | .05 |
| ☐ 599 Franklin Stubbs | .01 | .05 |
| ☐ 600 Gregg Jefferies | .01 | .05 |
| ☐ 601 John Cangelosi | .01 | .05 |
| ☐ 602 Mike Sharperson | .01 | .05 |
| ☐ 603 Mike Diaz | .01 | .05 |
| ☐ 604 Gary Varsho | .01 | .05 |
| ☐ 605 Terry Blocker | .01 | .05 |
| ☐ 606 Charlie O'Brien | .01 | .05 |
| ☐ 607 Jim Eppard | .01 | .05 |
| ☐ 608 John Davis | .01 | .05 |
| ☐ 609 Ken Griffey Sr. | .02 | .10 |
| ☐ 610 Buddy Bell | .02 | .10 |
| ☐ 611 Ted Simmons UER | | |
| ('78 stats Cardinal) | | |
| ☐ 612 Matt Williams | .08 | .25 |
| ☐ 613 Danny Cox | .01 | .05 |
| ☐ 614 Al Pedrique | .01 | .05 |
| ☐ 615 Ron Oester | .01 | .05 |
| ☐ 616 John Smoltz RC | .60 | 1.50 |
| ☐ 617 Bob Melvin | .01 | .05 |
| ☐ 618 Rob Dibble RC * | .15 | .40 |
| ☐ 619 Kirt Manwaring | .01 | .05 |
| ☐ 620 Felix Fermin | .01 | .05 |
| ☐ 621 Doug Dascenzo | .01 | .05 |
| ☐ 622 Bill Brennan | .01 | .05 |
| ☐ 623 Carlos Quintana RC | .02 | .10 |
| ☐ 624 Mike Harkey UER RC | .02 | .10 |
| ☐ 625 Gary Sheffield RC | .60 | 1.50 |
| ☐ 626 Tom Prince | .01 | .05 |
| ☐ 627 Steve Searcy | .01 | .05 |
| ☐ 628 Charlie Hayes RC | .08 | .25 |
| ☐ 629 Felix Jose UER RC | .02 | .10 |
| ☐ 630 Sandy Alomar Jr. RC | .15 | .40 |
| ☐ 631 Derek Lilliquist RC | .02 | .10 |
| ☐ 632 Geronimo Berroa | .01 | .05 |
| ☐ 633 Luis Medina | .01 | .05 |
| ☐ 634 Tom Gordon RC | .20 | .50 |
| ☐ 635 Ramon Martinez RC | .08 | .25 |
| ☐ 636 Craig Worthington | .01 | .05 |
| ☐ 637 Edgar Martinez | .08 | .25 |
| ☐ 638 Chad Kreuter RC | .08 | .25 |
| ☐ 639 Ron Jones | .02 | .10 |
| ☐ 640 Van Snider RC | .02 | .10 |
| ☐ 641 Lance Blankenship RC | .02 | .10 |
| ☐ 642 Dwight Smith UER RC | .08 | .25 |
| ☐ 643 Cameron Drew | .01 | .05 |
| ☐ 644 Jerald Clark RC | .02 | .10 |
| ☐ 645 Randy Johnson RC | 1.00 | 2.50 |
| ☐ 646 Norm Charlton RC | .08 | .25 |
| ☐ 647 Todd Frohwirth UER | | |
| (Southpaw on back) | | |
| ☐ 648 Luis De Los Santos | .01 | .05 |
| ☐ 649 Tim Jones | .01 | .05 |
| ☐ 65u Dave West UER RC | .02 | .10 |
| ☐ 651 Bob Milacki | .01 | .05 |
| ☐ 652 Wrigley Field HL | .01 | .05 |
| ☐ 653 Orel Hershiser HL | .01 | .05 |
| ☐ 654A W.Boggs HL seeason ERR | .05 | .15 |
| ☐ 654B Wade Boggs HL COR | .02 | .10 |
| ☐ 655 Jose Canseco HL | .08 | .25 |
| ☐ 656 Nolan Ryan HL | .01 | .05 |
| ☐ 657 Rickey Henderson HL | .05 | .15 |
| ☐ 658 Tom Browning HL | .01 | .05 |
| ☐ 659 Mike Greenwell HL | .01 | .05 |
| ☐ 660 Boston Red Sox HL | | |
| (Joe Morgan MG& | | |
| Sox Sock 'Em) | .01 | .05 |

**1990 Score**

| | | |
|---|---|---|
| ☐ COMPLETE SET (704) | 6.00 | 15.00 |

| Card | Low | High |
|---|---|---|
| COMP.RETAIL SET (704) | 6.00 | 15.00 |
| COMP.HOBBY SET (714) | 6.00 | 15.00 |
| 1 Don Mattingly | .25 | .60 |
| 2 Cal Ripken | .30 | .75 |
| 3 Dwight Evans | .05 | .15 |
| 4 Barry Bonds | .40 | 1.00 |
| 5 Kevin McReynolds | .01 | .05 |
| 6 Ozzie Guillen | .02 | .10 |
| 7 Terry Kennedy | .01 | .05 |
| 8 Bryan Harvey | .01 | .05 |
| 9 Alan Trammell | .02 | .10 |
| 10 Cory Snyder | .01 | .05 |
| 11 Jody Reed | .01 | .05 |
| 12 Roberto Alomar | .05 | .15 |
| 13 Pedro Guerrero | .01 | .05 |
| 14 Gary Redus | .01 | .05 |
| 15 Marty Barrett | .01 | .05 |
| 16 Ricky Jordan | .01 | .05 |
| 17 Joe Magrane | .01 | .05 |
| 18 Sid Fernandez | .01 | .05 |
| 19 Richard Dotson | .01 | .05 |
| 20 Jack Clark | .02 | .10 |
| 21 Bob Walk | .01 | .05 |
| 22 Ron Karkovice | .01 | .05 |
| 23 Lenny Harris | .01 | .05 |
| 24 Phil Bradley | .01 | .05 |
| 25 Andres Galarraga | .02 | .10 |
| 26 Brian Downing | .01 | .05 |
| 27 Dave Martinez | .01 | .05 |
| 28 Eric King | .01 | .05 |
| 29 Barry Lyons | .01 | .05 |
| 30 Dave Schmidt | .01 | .05 |
| 31 Mike Boddicker | .01 | .05 |
| 32 Tom Foley | .01 | .05 |
| 33 Brady Anderson | .02 | .10 |
| 34 Jim Presley | .01 | .05 |
| 35 Lance Parrish | .01 | .05 |
| 36 Von Hayes | .01 | .05 |
| 37 Lee Smith | .02 | .10 |
| 38 Herm Winningham | .01 | .05 |
| 39 Alejandro Pena | .01 | .05 |
| 40 Mike Scott | .01 | .05 |
| 41 Joe Orsulak | .01 | .05 |
| 42 Rafael Ramirez | .01 | .05 |
| 43 Gerald Young | .01 | .05 |
| 44 Dick Schofield | .01 | .05 |
| 45 Dave Smith | .01 | .05 |
| 46 Dave Magadan | .02 | .10 |
| 47 Dennis Martinez | .02 | .10 |
| 48 Greg Minton | .01 | .05 |
| 49 Milt Thompson | .01 | .05 |
| 50 Orel Hershiser | .02 | .10 |
| 51 Bip Roberts | .01 | .05 |
| 52 Jerry Browne | .01 | .05 |
| 53 Bob Ojeda | .01 | .05 |
| 54 Fernando Valenzuela | .02 | .10 |
| 55 Matt Nokes | .01 | .05 |
| 56 Brook Jacoby | .01 | .05 |
| 57 Frank Tanana | .01 | .05 |
| 58 Scott Fletcher | .01 | .05 |
| 59 Ron Oester | .01 | .05 |
| 60 Bob Boone | .02 | .10 |
| 61 Dan Gladden | .01 | .05 |
| 62 Darnell Coles | .01 | .05 |
| 63 Gregg Olson | .02 | .10 |
| 64 Todd Burns | .01 | .05 |
| 65 Todd Benzinger | .01 | .05 |
| 66 Dale Murphy | .05 | .15 |
| 67 Mike Flanagan | .01 | .05 |
| 68 Jose Oquendo | .01 | .05 |
| 69 Cecil Espy | .01 | .05 |
| 70 Chris Sabo | .02 | .10 |
| 71 Shane Rawley | .01 | .05 |
| 72 Tom Brunansky | .01 | .05 |
| 73 Vance Law | .01 | .05 |
| 74 B.J. Surhoff | .02 | .10 |
| 75 Lou Whitaker | .02 | .10 |
| 76 Ken Caminiti UER | .02 | .10 |
| 77 Nelson Liriano | .01 | .05 |
| 78 Tommy Gregg | .01 | .05 |
| 79 Don Slaught | .01 | .05 |
| 80 Eddie Murray | .08 | .25 |
| 81 Joe Boever | .01 | .05 |
| 82 Charlie Leibrandt | .01 | .05 |
| 83 Jose Lind | .01 | .05 |
| 84 Tony Phillips | .01 | .05 |
| 85 Mitch Webster | .01 | .05 |
| 86 Dan Plesac | .01 | .05 |
| 87 Rick Mahler | .01 | .05 |
| 88 Steve Lyons | .01 | .05 |
| 89 Tony Fernandez | .01 | .05 |
| 90 Ryne Sandberg | .15 | .40 |
| 91 Nick Esasky | .01 | .05 |
| 92 Luis Salazar | .01 | .05 |
| 93 Pete Incaviglia | .01 | .05 |
| 94 Ivan Calderon | .01 | .05 |
| 95 Jeff Treadway | .01 | .05 |
| 96 Kurt Stillwell | .01 | .05 |
| 97 Gary Sheffield | .08 | .25 |
| 98 Jeffrey Leonard | .01 | .05 |
| 99 Andres Thomas | .01 | .05 |
| 100 Roberto Kelly | .01 | .05 |
| 101 Alvaro Espinoza | .01 | .05 |
| 102 Greg Gagne | .01 | .05 |
| 103 John Farrell | .01 | .05 |
| 104 Willie Wilson | .01 | .05 |
| 105 Glenn Braggs | .01 | .05 |
| 106 Chet Lemon | .01 | .05 |
| 107A Jamie Moyer ERR | .02 | .10 |
| 107B Jamie Moyer COR | .20 | .50 |
| 108 Chuck Crim | .01 | .05 |
| 109 Dave Valle | .01 | .05 |
| 110 Walt Weiss | .01 | .05 |
| 111 Larry Sheets | .01 | .05 |
| 112 Don Robinson | .01 | .05 |
| 113 Danny Heep | .01 | .05 |
| 114 Carmelo Martinez | .01 | .05 |
| 115 Dave Gallagher | .01 | .05 |
| 116 Mike LaValliere | .01 | .05 |
| 117 Bob McClure | .01 | .05 |
| 118 Rene Gonzales | .01 | .05 |
| 119 Mark Parent | .01 | .05 |
| 120 Wally Joyner | .02 | .10 |
| 121 Mark Gubicza | .01 | .05 |
| 122 Tony Pena | .01 | .05 |
| 123 Carmelo Castillo | .01 | .05 |
| 124 Howard Johnson | .02 | .10 |
| 125 Steve Sax | .02 | .10 |
| 126 Tim Belcher | .01 | .05 |
| 127 Tim Burke | .01 | .05 |
| 128 Al Newman | .01 | .05 |
| 129 Dennis Rasmussen | .01 | .05 |
| 130 Doug Jones | .01 | .05 |
| 131 Fred Lynn | .01 | .05 |
| 132 Jeff Hamilton | .01 | .05 |
| 133 German Gonzalez | .01 | .05 |
| 134 John Morris | .01 | .05 |
| 135 Dave Parker | .02 | .10 |
| 136 Gary Pettis | .01 | .05 |
| 137 Dennis Boyd | .01 | .05 |
| 138 Candy Maldonado | .01 | .05 |
| 139 Rick Cerone | .01 | .05 |
| 140 George Brett | .25 | .60 |
| 141 Dave Clark | .01 | .05 |
| 142 Dickie Thon | .01 | .05 |
| 143 Junior Ortiz | .01 | .05 |
| 144 Don August | .01 | .05 |
| 145 Gary Gaetti | .02 | .10 |
| 146 Kirt Manwaring | .01 | .05 |
| 147 Jeff Reed | .01 | .05 |
| 148 Jose Alvarez | .01 | .05 |
| 149 Mike Schooler | .01 | .05 |
| 150 Mark Grace | .05 | .15 |
| 151 Geronimo Berroa | .01 | .05 |
| 152 Barry Jones | .01 | .05 |
| 153 Geno Petralli | .01 | .05 |
| 154 Jim Deshaies | .01 | .05 |
| 155 Barry Larkin | .05 | .15 |
| 156 Alfredo Griffin | .01 | .05 |
| 157 Tom Henke | .01 | .05 |
| 158 Mike Jeffcoat | .01 | .05 |
| 159 Bob Welch | .01 | .05 |
| 160 Julio Franco | .02 | .10 |
| 161 Henry Cotto | .01 | .05 |
| 162 Terry Steinbach | .01 | .05 |
| 163 Damon Berryhill | .01 | .05 |
| 164 Tim Crews | .01 | .05 |
| 165 Tom Browning | .01 | .05 |
| 166 Fred Manrique | .01 | .05 |
| 167 Harold Reynolds | .02 | .10 |
| 168B Ron Hassey ERR (27 on back) | .01 | .05 |
| 168B Ron Hassey COR | .20 | .50 |
| 169 Shawon Dunston | .01 | .05 |
| 170 Bobby Bonilla | .02 | .10 |
| 171 Tommy Herr | .01 | .05 |
| 172 Mike Heath | .01 | .05 |
| 173 Rich Gedman | .01 | .05 |
| 174 Bill Ripken | .01 | .05 |
| 175 Pete O'Brien | .01 | .05 |
| 176A Lloyd McClendon ERR (Uniform number on back list) | .01 | .05 |
| 176B Lloyd McClendon COR (Uniform number on back list) | .20 | .50 |
| 177 Brian Holton | .01 | .05 |
| 178 Jeff Blauser | .01 | .05 |
| 179 Jim Eisenreich | .01 | .05 |
| 180 Bert Blyleven | .02 | .10 |
| 181 Rob Murphy | .01 | .05 |
| 182 Bill Doran | .01 | .05 |
| 183 Curt Ford | .01 | .05 |
| 184 Mike Henneman | .01 | .05 |
| 185 Eric Davis | .02 | .10 |
| 186 Lance McCullers | .01 | .05 |
| 187 Steve Davis RC | .01 | .05 |
| 188 Bill Wegman | .01 | .05 |
| 189 Brian Harper | .01 | .05 |
| 190 Mike Moore | .01 | .05 |
| 191 Dale Mohorcic | .01 | .05 |
| 192 Tim Wallach | .01 | .05 |
| 193 Keith Hernandez | .01 | .05 |
| 194 Dave Righetti | .01 | .05 |
| 195A Bret Saberhagen ERR (Joke) | .02 | .10 |
| 195B Bret Saberhagen COR (Joker) | .20 | .50 |
| 196 Paul Kilgus | .01 | .05 |
| 197 Bud Black | .01 | .05 |
| 198 Juan Samuel | .01 | .05 |
| 199 Kevin Seitzer | .01 | .05 |
| 200 Darryl Strawberry | .02 | .10 |
| 201 Dave Stieb | .02 | .10 |
| 202 Charlie Hough | .01 | .05 |
| 203 Jack Morris | .02 | .10 |
| 204 Rance Mulliniks | .01 | .05 |
| 205 Alvin Davis | .01 | .05 |
| 206 Jack Howell | .01 | .05 |
| 207 Ken Patterson | .01 | .05 |
| 208 Terry Pendleton | .02 | .10 |
| 209 Craig Lefferts | .01 | .05 |
| 210 Kevin Brown UER (First mention of '89 Rangers sh) | .02 | .10 |
| 211 Dan Petry | .01 | .05 |
| 212 Dave Leiper | .01 | .05 |
| 213 Daryl Boston | .01 | .05 |
| 214 Kevin Hickey | .01 | .05 |
| 215 Mike Krukow | .01 | .05 |
| 216 Terry Francona | .02 | .10 |
| 217 Kirk McCaskill | .01 | .05 |
| 218 Scott Bailes | .01 | .05 |
| 219 Bob Forsch | .01 | .05 |
| 220A Mike Aldrete ERR (25 on back) | .01 | .05 |
| 220B Mike Aldrete COR (24 on back) | .20 | .50 |
| 221 Steve Buechele | .01 | .05 |
| 222 Jesse Barfield | .01 | .05 |
| 223 Juan Berenguer | .01 | .05 |
| 224 Andy McGaffigan | .01 | .05 |
| 225 Pete Smith | .01 | .05 |
| 226 Mike Witt | .01 | .05 |
| 227 Jay Howell | .01 | .05 |
| 228 Scott Bradley | .01 | .05 |
| 229 Jerome Walton | .01 | .05 |
| 230 Greg Swindell | .01 | .05 |
| 231 Atlee Hammaker | .01 | .05 |
| 232A Mike Devereaux ERR (RF on front) | .01 | .05 |
| 232B Mike Devereaux COR | .20 | .50 |
| 233 Ken Hill | .02 | .10 |
| 234 Craig Worthington | .01 | .05 |
| 235 Scott Terry | .01 | .05 |
| 236 Brett Butler | .02 | .10 |
| 237 Doyle Alexander | .01 | .05 |
| 238 Dave Anderson | .01 | .05 |
| 239 Bob Milacki | .01 | .05 |
| 240 Dwight Smith | .01 | .05 |
| 241 Otis Nixon | .01 | .05 |
| 242 Pat Tabler | .01 | .05 |
| 243 Derek Lilliquist | .01 | .05 |
| 244 Danny Tartabull | .01 | .05 |

|  |  | | |
|---|---|---|---|
| 245 | Wade Boggs | .05 | .15 |
| 246 | Scott Garrelts (Should say Relief Pitcher on fro | .01 | .05 |
| 247 | Spike Owen | .01 | .05 |
| 248 | Norm Charlton | .01 | .05 |
| 249 | Gerald Perry | .01 | .05 |
| 250 | Nolan Ryan | .40 | 1.00 |
| 251 | Kevin Gross | .01 | .05 |
| 252 | Randy Milligan | .01 | .05 |
| 253 | Mike LaCoss | .01 | .05 |
| 254 | Dave Bergman | .01 | .05 |
| 255 | Tony Gwynn | .10 | .30 |
| 256 | Felix Fermin | .01 | .05 |
| 257 | Greg W. Harris | .01 | .05 |
| 258 | Junior Felix | .01 | .05 |
| 259 | Mark Davis | .01 | .05 |
| 260 | Vince Coleman | .01 | .05 |
| 261 | Paul Gibson | .01 | .05 |
| 262 | Mitch Williams | .01 | .05 |
| 263 | Jeff Russell | .01 | .05 |
| 264 | Omar Vizquel | .08 | .25 |
| 265 | Andre Dawson | .02 | .10 |
| 266 | Storm Davis | .01 | .05 |
| 267 | Guillermo Hernandez | .01 | .05 |
| 268 | Mike Felder | .01 | .05 |
| 269 | Tom Candiotti | .01 | .05 |
| 270 | Bruce Hurst | .01 | .05 |
| 271 | Fred McGriff | .08 | .25 |
| 272 | Glenn Davis | .01 | .05 |
| 273 | John Franco | .02 | .10 |
| 274 | Rich Yett | .01 | .05 |
| 275 | Craig Biggio | .08 | .25 |
| 276 | Gene Larkin | .01 | .05 |
| 277 | Rob Dibble | .02 | .10 |
| 278 | Randy Bush | .01 | .05 |
| 279 | Kevin Bass | .01 | .05 |
| 280A | Bo Jackson ERR Watham | .08 | .25 |
| 280B | Bo Jackson COR Watham | .30 | .75 |
| 281 | Wally Backman | .01 | .05 |
| 282 | Larry Andersen | .01 | .05 |
| 283 | Chris Bosio | .01 | .05 |
| 284 | Juan Agosto | .01 | .05 |
| 285 | Ozzie Smith | .15 | .40 |
| 286 | George Bell | .05 | .15 |
| 287 | Rex Hudler | .01 | .05 |
| 288 | Pat Borders | .01 | .05 |
| 289 | Danny Jackson | .01 | .05 |
| 290 | Carlton Fisk | .05 | .15 |
| 291 | Tracy Jones | .01 | .05 |
| 292 | Allan Anderson | .01 | .05 |
| 293 | Johnny Ray | .01 | .05 |
| 294 | Lee Guetterman | .01 | .05 |
| 295 | Paul O'Neill | .05 | .15 |
| 296 | Carney Lansford | .02 | .10 |
| 297 | Tom Brookens | .01 | .05 |
| 298 | Claudell Washington | .01 | .05 |
| 299 | Hubie Brooks | .01 | .05 |
| 300 | Will Clark | .05 | .15 |
| 301 | Kenny Rogers | .02 | .10 |
| 302 | Darrell Evans | .02 | .10 |
| 303 | Greg Briley | .01 | .05 |
| 304 | Donn Pall | .01 | .05 |
| 305 | Teddy Higuera | .01 | .05 |
| 306 | Dan Pasqua | .01 | .05 |
| 307 | Dave Winfield | .02 | .10 |
| 308 | Dennis Powell | .01 | .05 |
| 309 | Jose DeLeon | .01 | .05 |
| 310 | Roger Clemens | .40 | 1.00 |
| 311 | Melido Perez | .01 | .05 |
| 312 | Devon White | .02 | .10 |
| 313 | Dwight Gooden | .02 | .10 |
| 314 | Carlos Martinez | .01 | .05 |
| 315 | Dennis Eckersley | .02 | .10 |
| 316 | Clay Parker UER (Height 6'11-inch) | .01 | .05 |
| 317 | Rick Honeycutt | .01 | .05 |
| 318 | Tim Laudner | .01 | .05 |
| 319 | Joe Carter | .02 | .10 |
| 320 | Robin Yount | .15 | .40 |
| 321 | Felix Jose | .01 | .05 |
| 322 | Mickey Tettleton | .01 | .05 |
| 323 | Mike Gallego | .01 | .05 |
| 324 | Edgar Martinez | .05 | .15 |
| 325 | Dave Henderson | .01 | .05 |
| 326 | Chili Davis | .02 | .10 |
| 327 | Steve Balboni | .01 | .05 |
| 328 | Jody Davis | .01 | .05 |
| 329 | Shawn Hillegas | .01 | .05 |
| 330 | Jim Abbott | .05 | .15 |
| 331 | John Dopson | .01 | .05 |
| 332 | Mark Williamson | .01 | .05 |
| 333 | Jeff D. Robinson | .01 | .05 |
| 334 | John Smiley | .01 | .05 |
| 335 | Bobby Thigpen | .01 | .05 |
| 336 | Garry Templeton | .01 | .05 |
| 337 | Marvell Wynne | .01 | .05 |
| 338A | Ken Griffey Sr. ERR (Uniform number on back list | .02 | .10 |
| 338B | Ken Griffey Sr. COR | .20 | .50 |
| 339 | Steve Finley | .02 | .10 |
| 340 | Ellis Burks | .05 | .15 |
| 341 | Frank Williams | .01 | .05 |
| 342 | Mike Morgan | .01 | .05 |
| 343 | Kevin Mitchell | .05 | .15 |
| 344 | Joel Youngblood | .01 | .05 |
| 345 | Mike Greenwell | .01 | .05 |
| 346 | Glenn Wilson | .01 | .05 |
| 347 | John Costello | .01 | .05 |
| 348 | Wes Gardner | .01 | .05 |
| 349 | Jeff Ballard | .01 | .05 |
| 350 | Mark Thurmond UER (ERA is 192, should be 1.92) | .01 | .05 |
| 351 | Randy Myers | .02 | .10 |
| 352 | Shawn Abner | .01 | .05 |
| 353 | Jesse Orosco | .01 | .05 |
| 354 | Greg Walker | .01 | .05 |
| 355 | Pete Harnisch | .02 | .10 |
| 356 | Steve Farr | .01 | .05 |
| 357 | Dave LaPoint | .01 | .05 |
| 358 | Willie Fraser | .01 | .05 |
| 359 | Mickey Hatcher | .01 | .05 |
| 360 | Rickey Henderson | .08 | .25 |
| 361 | Mike Fitzgerald | .01 | .05 |
| 362 | Bill Schroeder | .01 | .05 |
| 363 | Mark Carreon | .01 | .05 |
| 364 | Ron Jones | .01 | .05 |
| 365 | Jeff Montgomery | .02 | .10 |
| 366 | Bill Krueger | .01 | .05 |
| 367 | John Cangelosi | .01 | .05 |
| 368 | Jose Gonzalez | .01 | .05 |
| 369 | Greg Hibbard RC | .02 | .10 |
| 370 | John Smoltz | .08 | .25 |
| 371 | Jeff Brantley | .01 | .05 |
| 372 | Frank White | .02 | .10 |
| 373 | Ed Whitson | .01 | .05 |
| 374 | Willie McGee | .02 | .10 |
| 375 | Jose Canseco | .05 | .15 |
| 376 | Randy Ready | .01 | .05 |
| 377 | Don Aase | .01 | .05 |
| 378 | Tony Armas | .01 | .05 |
| 379 | Steve Bedrosian | .01 | .05 |
| 380 | Chuck Finley | .02 | .10 |
| 381 | Kent Hrbek | .02 | .10 |
| 382 | Jim Gantner | .01 | .05 |
| 383 | Mel Hall | .01 | .05 |
| 384 | Mike Marshall | .01 | .05 |
| 385 | Mark McGwire | .40 | 1.00 |
| 386 | Wayne Tolleson | .01 | .05 |
| 387 | Brian Holman | .01 | .05 |
| 388 | John Wetteland | .08 | .25 |
| 389 | Darren Daulton | .02 | .10 |
| 390 | Rob Deer | .01 | .05 |
| 391 | John Moses | .01 | .05 |
| 392 | Todd Worrell | .01 | .05 |
| 393 | Chuck Cary | .01 | .05 |
| 394 | Stan Javier | .01 | .05 |
| 395 | Willie Randolph | .02 | .10 |
| 396 | Bill Buckner | .01 | .05 |
| 397 | Robby Thompson | .01 | .05 |
| 398 | Mike Scioscia | .01 | .05 |
| 399 | Lonnie Smith | .01 | .05 |
| 400 | Kirby Puckett | .08 | .25 |
| 401 | Mark Langston | .01 | .05 |
| 402 | Danny Darwin | .01 | .05 |
| 403 | Greg Maddux | .15 | .40 |
| 404 | Lloyd Moseby | .01 | .05 |
| 405 | Rafael Palmeiro | .05 | .15 |
| 406 | Chad Kreuter | .01 | .05 |
| 407 | Jimmy Key | .02 | .10 |
| 408 | Tim Birtsas | .01 | .05 |
| 409 | Tim Raines | .02 | .10 |
| 410 | Dave Stewart | .02 | .10 |
| 411 | Eric Yelding RC | .01 | .05 |
| 412 | Kent Anderson | .01 | .05 |
| 413 | Les Lancaster | .01 | .05 |
| 414 | Rick Dempsey | .01 | .05 |
| 415 | Randy Johnson | .20 | .50 |
| 416 | Gary Carter | .02 | .10 |
| 417 | Rolando Roomes | .01 | .05 |
| 418 | Dan Schatzeder | .01 | .05 |
| 419 | Bryn Smith | .01 | .05 |
| 420 | Ruben Sierra | .02 | .10 |
| 421 | Steve Jeltz | .01 | .05 |
| 422 | Ken Oberkfell | .01 | .05 |
| 423 | Sid Bream | .01 | .05 |
| 424 | Jim Clancy | .01 | .05 |
| 425 | Kelly Gruber | .01 | .05 |
| 426 | Rick Leach | .01 | .05 |
| 427 | Len Dykstra | .02 | .10 |
| 428 | Jeff Pico | .01 | .05 |
| 429 | John Cerutti | .01 | .05 |
| 430 | David Cone | .02 | .10 |
| 431 | Jeff Kunkel | .01 | .05 |
| 432 | Luis Aquino | .01 | .05 |
| 433 | Ernie Whitt | .01 | .05 |
| 434 | Bo Diaz | .01 | .05 |
| 435 | Steve Lake | .01 | .05 |
| 436 | Pat Perry | .01 | .05 |
| 437 | Mike Davis | .01 | .05 |
| 438 | Cecilio Guante | .01 | .05 |
| 439 | Duane Ward | .01 | .05 |
| 440 | Andy Van Slyke | .05 | .15 |
| 441 | Gene Nelson | .01 | .05 |
| 442 | Luis Polonia | .01 | .05 |
| 443 | Kevin Elster | .01 | .05 |
| 444 | Keith Moreland | .01 | .05 |
| 445 | Roger McDowell | .01 | .05 |
| 446 | Ron Darling | .01 | .05 |
| 447 | Ernest Riles | .01 | .05 |
| 448 | Mookie Wilson | .02 | .10 |
| 449A | Billy Spiers ERR (No birth year) | .01 | .05 |
| 449B | Billy Spiers COR (Born in 1966) | .20 | .50 |
| 450 | Rick Sutcliffe | .02 | .10 |
| 451 | Nelson Santovenia | .01 | .05 |
| 452 | Andy Allanson | .01 | .05 |
| 453 | Bob Melvin | .01 | .05 |
| 454 | Benito Santiago | .02 | .10 |
| 455 | Jose Uribe | .01 | .05 |
| 456 | Bill Landrum | .01 | .05 |
| 457 | Bobby Witt | .01 | .05 |
| 458 | Kevin Romine | .01 | .05 |
| 459 | Lee Mazzilli | .01 | .05 |
| 460 | Paul Molitor | .02 | .10 |
| 461 | Ramon Martinez | .01 | .05 |
| 462 | Frank DiPino | .01 | .05 |
| 463 | Walt Terrell | .01 | .05 |
| 464 | Bob Geren | .01 | .05 |
| 465 | Rick Reuschel | .01 | .05 |
| 466 | Mark Grant | .01 | .05 |
| 467 | John Kruk | .02 | .10 |
| 468 | Gregg Jefferies | .02 | .10 |
| 469 | R.J. Reynolds | .01 | .05 |
| 470 | Harold Baines | .02 | .10 |
| 471 | Dennis Lamp | .01 | .05 |
| 472 | Tom Gordon | .02 | .10 |
| 473 | Terry Puhl | .01 | .05 |
| 474 | Curt Wilkerson | .01 | .05 |
| 475 | Dan Quisenberry | .01 | .05 |
| 476 | Oddibe McDowell | .01 | .05 |
| 477A | Zane Smith ERR | .01 | .05 |
| 477B | Zane Smith COR | .20 | .50 |
| 478 | Franklin Stubbs | .01 | .05 |
| 479 | Wallace Johnson | .01 | .05 |
| 480 | Jay Tibbs | .01 | .05 |
| 481 | Tom Glavine | .05 | .15 |
| 482 | Manny Lee | .01 | .05 |
| 483 | Joe Hesketh UER (Says Rookies on back& should s | .01 | .05 |
| 484 | Mike Bielecki | .01 | .05 |
| 485 | Greg Brock | .01 | .05 |
| 486 | Pascual Perez | .01 | .05 |
| 487 | Kirk Gibson | .02 | .10 |
| 488 | Scott Sanderson | .01 | .05 |
| 489 | Domingo Ramos | .01 | .05 |
| 490 | Kal Daniels | .01 | .05 |
| 491A | David Wells ERR | .02 | .10 |
| 491B | David Wells COR | .20 | .50 |
| 492 | Jerry Reed | .01 | .05 |

|  |  | | |
|---|---|---|---|
| 493 | Eric Show | .01 | .05 |
| 494 | Mike Pagliarulo | .01 | .05 |
| 495 | Ron Robinson | .01 | .05 |
| 496 | Brad Komminsk | .01 | .05 |
| 497 | Greg Litton | .01 | .05 |
| 498 | Chris James | .01 | .05 |
| 499 | Luis Quinones | .01 | .05 |
| 500 | Frank Viola | .01 | .05 |
| 501 | Tim Teufel UER (Twins '85& the s is lower case& | .01 | .05 |
| 502 | Terry Leach | .01 | .05 |
| 503 | Matt Williams | .02 | .10 |
| 504 | Tim Leary | .01 | .05 |
| 505 | Doug Drabek | .01 | .05 |
| 506 | Mariano Duncan | .01 | .05 |
| 507 | Charlie Hayes | .01 | .05 |
| 508 | Albert Belle | .08 | .25 |
| 509 | Pat Sheridan | .01 | .05 |
| 510 | Mackey Sasser | .01 | .05 |
| 511 | Jose Rijo | .01 | .05 |
| 512 | Mike Smithson | .01 | .05 |
| 513 | Gary Ward | .01 | .05 |
| 514 | Dion James | .01 | .05 |
| 515 | Jim Gott | .01 | .05 |
| 516 | Drew Hall | .01 | .05 |
| 517 | Doug Bair | .01 | .05 |
| 518 | Scott Scudder | .01 | .05 |
| 519 | Rick Aguilera | .02 | .10 |
| 520 | Rafael Belliard | .01 | .05 |
| 521 | Jay Buhner | .02 | .10 |
| 522 | Jeff Reardon | .02 | .10 |
| 523 | Steve Rosenberg | .01 | .05 |
| 524 | Randy Velarde | .01 | .05 |
| 525 | Jeff Musselman | .01 | .05 |
| 526 | Bill Long | .01 | .05 |
| 527 | Gary Wayne | .01 | .05 |
| 528 | Dave Wayne Johnson RC | .01 | .05 |
| 529 | Ron Kittle | .01 | .05 |
| 530 | Erik Hanson UER (5th line on back says season& sh | .01 | .05 |
| 531 | Steve Wilson | .01 | .05 |
| 532 | Joey Meyer | .01 | .05 |
| 533 | Curt Young | .01 | .05 |
| 534 | Kelly Downs | .01 | .05 |
| 535 | Joe Girardi | .05 | .15 |
| 536 | Lance Blankenship | .01 | .05 |
| 537 | Greg Mathews | .01 | .05 |
| 538 | Donell Nixon | .01 | .05 |
| 539 | Mark Knudson | .01 | .05 |
| 540 | Jeff Wetherby RC | .01 | .05 |
| 541 | Darrin Jackson | .01 | .05 |
| 542 | Terry Mulholland | .01 | .05 |
| 543 | Eric Hetzel | .01 | .05 |
| 544 | Rick Reed RC | .08 | .25 |
| 545 | Dennis Cook | .01 | .05 |
| 546 | Mike Jackson | .01 | .05 |
| 547 | Brian Fisher | .01 | .05 |
| 548 | Gene Harris | .01 | .05 |
| 549 | Jeff King | .01 | .05 |
| 550 | Dave Dravecky | .08 | .25 |
| 551 | Randy Kutcher | .01 | .05 |
| 552 | Mark Portugal | .01 | .05 |
| 553 | Jim Corsi | .01 | .05 |
| 554 | Todd Stottlemyre | .02 | .10 |
| 555 | Scott Bankhead | .01 | .05 |
| 556 | Ken Dayley | .01 | .05 |
| 557 | Rick Wrona | .01 | .05 |
| 558 | Sammy Sosa RC | 1.00 | 2.50 |
| 559 | Keith Miller | .01 | .05 |
| 560 | Ken Griffey Jr. | .30 | .75 |
| 561A | R.Sandberg HL ERR 3B | 3.00 | 8.00 |
| 561B | R.Sandberg HL COR | .08 | .25 |
| 562 | Billy Hatcher | .01 | .05 |
| 563 | Jay Bell | .02 | .10 |
| 564 | Jack Daugherty RC | .01 | .05 |
| 565 | Rich Monteleone | .01 | .05 |
| 566 | Bo Jackson AS-MVP | .02 | .10 |
| 567 | Tony Fossas RC | .01 | .05 |
| 568 | Roy Smith | .01 | .05 |
| 569 | Jaime Navarro | .01 | .05 |
| 570 | Lance Johnson | .01 | .05 |
| 571 | Mike Dyer RC | .01 | .05 |
| 572 | Kevin Ritz RC | .01 | .05 |
| 573 | Dave West | .01 | .05 |
| 574 | Gary Mielke RC | .01 | .05 |
| 575 | Scott Lusader | .01 | .05 |
| 576 | Joe Oliver | .01 | .05 |
| 577 | Sandy Alomar Jr. | .02 | .10 |
| 578 | Andy Benes UER | .02 | .10 |
| 579 | Tim Jones | .01 | .05 |
| 580 | Randy McCament RC | .01 | .05 |
| 581 | Curt Schilling | .40 | 1.00 |
| 582 | John Orton RC | .02 | .10 |
| 583A | Milt Cuyler ERR RC | .02 | .10 |
| 583B | Milt Cuyler COR | .20 | .50 |
| 584 | Eric Anthony RC | .02 | .10 |
| 585 | Greg Vaughn | .02 | .10 |
| 586 | Deion Sanders | .08 | .25 |
| 587 | Jose DeJesus | .01 | .05 |
| 588 | Chip Hale RC | .01 | .05 |
| 589 | John Olerud RC | .20 | .50 |
| 590 | Steve Olin RC | .08 | .25 |
| 591 | Marquis Grissom RC | .15 | .40 |
| 592 | Moises Alou RC | .30 | .75 |
| 593 | Mark Lemke | .01 | .05 |
| 594 | Dean Palmer RC | .08 | .25 |
| 595 | Robin Ventura | .20 | .50 |
| 596 | Tino Martinez | .20 | .50 |
| 597 | Mike Huff RC | .01 | .05 |
| 598 | Scott Hemond RC | .02 | .10 |
| 599 | Wally Whitehurst | .01 | .05 |
| 600 | Todd Zeile | .02 | .10 |
| 601 | Glenallen Hill | .01 | .05 |
| 602 | Hal Morris | .05 | .15 |
| 603 | Juan Bell | .01 | .05 |
| 604 | Bobby Rose | .01 | .05 |
| 605 | Matt Merullo | .01 | .05 |
| 606 | Kevin Maas RC | .08 | .25 |
| 607 | Randy Nosek RC | .01 | .05 |
| 608A | Billy Bates RC | .01 | .05 |
| 608B | Billy Bates (Text has no mention of triples) | .01 | .05 |
| 609 | Mike Stanton RC | .08 | .25 |
| 610 | Mauro Gozzo RC | .01 | .05 |
| 611 | Charles Nagy RC | .08 | .25 |
| 612 | Scott Coolbaugh RC | .01 | .05 |
| 613 | Jose Vizcaino RC | .08 | .25 |
| 614 | Greg Smith RC | .01 | .05 |
| 615 | Jeff Huson RC | .02 | .10 |
| 616 | Mickey Weston RC | .01 | .05 |
| 617 | John Pawlowski | .01 | .05 |
| 618A | Joe Skalski ERR (27 on back) | .01 | .05 |
| 618B | Joe Skalski COR | .01 | .05 |
| 619 | Bernie Williams RC | .60 | 1.50 |
| 620 | Shawn Holman RC | .01 | .05 |
| 621 | Gary Eave RC | .01 | .05 |
| 622 | Darren Fletcher UER RC | .02 | .10 |
| 623 | Pat Combs | .01 | .05 |
| 624 | Mike Blowers RC | .02 | .10 |
| 625 | Kevin Appier | .02 | .10 |
| 626 | Pat Austin | .01 | .05 |
| 627 | Kelly Mann RC | .01 | .05 |
| 628 | Matt Kinzer RC | .01 | .05 |
| 629 | Chris Hammond RC | .02 | .10 |
| 630 | Dean Wilkins RC | .01 | .05 |
| 631 | Larry Walker RC | .40 | 1.00 |
| 632 | Blaine Beatty RC | .01 | .05 |
| 633A | Tommy Barrett ERR | .01 | .05 |
| 633B | Tommy Barrett COR | .20 | .50 |
| 634 | Stan Belinda RC | .02 | .10 |
| 635 | Mike (Texas) Smith RC | .01 | .05 |
| 636 | Hensley Meulens | .02 | .10 |
| 637 | Juan Gonzalez RC | .40 | 1.00 |
| 638 | Lenny Webster RC | .02 | .10 |
| 639 | Mark Gardner RC | .02 | .10 |
| 640 | Tommy Greene RC | .02 | .10 |
| 641 | Mike Hartley RC | .01 | .05 |
| 642 | Phil Stephenson | .01 | .05 |
| 643 | Kevin Mmahat RC | .01 | .05 |
| 644 | Ed Whited RC | .01 | .05 |
| 645 | Delino DeShields RC | .08 | .25 |
| 646 | Kevin Blankenship | .01 | .05 |
| 647 | Paul Sorrento RC | .08 | .25 |
| 648 | Mike Roesler RC | .01 | .05 |
| 649 | Jason Grimsley RC | .02 | .10 |
| 650 | David Justice RC | .20 | .50 |
| 651 | Scott Cooper RC | .02 | .10 |
| 652 | Dave Eiland | .01 | .05 |
| 653 | Mike Munoz RC | .01 | .05 |
| 654 | Jeff Fischer RC | .01 | .05 |
| 655 | Terry Jorgensen RC | .01 | .05 |
| 656 | George Canale RC | .01 | .05 |
| 657 | Brian DuBois UER RC | .01 | .05 |
| 658 | Carlos Quintana | .01 | .05 |
| 659 | Luis de los Santos | .01 | .05 |
| 660 | Jerald Clark | .01 | .05 |
| 661 | Donald Harris RC | .01 | .05 |
| 662 | Paul Coleman RC | .02 | .10 |
| 663 | Frank Thomas RC | .75 | 2.00 |
| 664 | Brent Mayne RC | .08 | .25 |
| 665 | Eddie Zosky RC | .02 | .10 |
| 666 | Steve Hosey RC | .08 | .25 |
| 667 | Scott Bryant RC | .02 | .10 |
| 668 | Tom Goodwin RC | .08 | .25 |
| 669 | Cal Eldred RC | .08 | .25 |
| 670 | Earl Cunningham RC | .02 | .10 |
| 671 | Alan Zinter RC | .02 | .10 |
| 672 | Chuck Knoblauch RC | .15 | .40 |
| 673 | Kyle Abbott RC | .01 | .05 |
| 674 | Roger Salkeld RC | .01 | .05 |
| 675 | Mo Vaughn RC | .20 | .50 |
| 676 | Keith (Kiki) Jones RC | .01 | .05 |
| 677 | Tyler Houston RC | .08 | .25 |
| 678 | Jeff Jackson RC | .02 | .10 |
| 679 | Greg Gohr RC | .02 | .10 |
| 680 | Ben McDonald RC | .08 | .25 |
| 681 | Greg Blosser RC | .02 | .10 |
| 682 | Willie Greene RC | .08 | .25 |
| 683A | Wade Boggs DT ERR | .02 | .10 |
| 683B | Wade Boggs DT COR | .20 | .50 |
| 684 | Will Clark DT | .02 | .10 |
| 685 | Tony Gwynn DT | .05 | .15 |
| 686 | Rickey Henderson DT | .02 | .10 |
| 687 | Bo Jackson DT | .02 | .10 |
| 688 | Mark Langston DT | .01 | .05 |
| 689 | Barry Larkin DT | .02 | .10 |
| 690 | Kirby Puckett DT | .05 | .15 |
| 691 | Ryne Sandberg DT | .08 | .25 |
| 692 | Mike Scott DT | .01 | .05 |
| 693A | Terry Steinbach DT ERR (cathers) | .01 | .05 |
| 693B | Terry Steinbach DT COR (catchers) | .01 | .05 |
| 694 | Bobby Thigpen DT | .01 | .05 |
| 695 | Mitch Williams DT | .01 | .05 |
| 696 | Nolan Ryan HL | .15 | .40 |
| 697 | Bo Jackson FB/BB | .20 | .50 |
| 698 | Rickey Henderson ALCS | .05 | .15 |
| 699 | Will Clark NLCS | .02 | .10 |
| 700 | WS Games 1/2 (Dave Stewart Mike Moore) | .02 | .10 |
| 701 | Candlestick/Earthquake | .08 | .25 |
| 702 | WS Game 3 | .05 | .15 |
| 703 | WS Game 4/Wrap-up A's Sweep Battle of the Bay | .01 | .05 |
| 704 | Wade Boggs HL | .02 | .10 |

## 1991 Score

|  |  | | |
|---|---|---|---|
| | COMPLETE SET (893) | 8.00 | 20.00 |
| | COMP.FACT.SET (900) | 10.00 | 25.00 |
| 1 | Jose Canseco | .05 | .15 |
| 2 | Ken Griffey Jr. | .20 | .50 |
| 3 | Ryne Sandberg | .15 | .40 |
| 4 | Nolan Ryan | .40 | 1.00 |
| 5 | Bo Jackson | .08 | .25 |
| 6 | Bret Saberhagen UER (In bio& missed misspelled a | .01 | .05 |
| 7 | Will Clark | .05 | .15 |
| 8 | Ellis Burks | .01 | .05 |
| 9 | Joe Carter | .02 | .10 |
| 10 | Rickey Henderson | .08 | .25 |
| 11 | Ozzie Guillen | .01 | .05 |
| 12 | Wade Boggs | .05 | .15 |
| 13 | Jerome Walton | .01 | .05 |
| 14 | John Franco | .02 | .10 |
| 15 | Ricky Jordan UER (League misspelled as leaue) | .01 | .05 |
| 16 | Wally Backman | .01 | .05 |
| 17 | Rob Dibble | .02 | .10 |
| 18 | Glenn Braggs | .01 | .05 |
| 19 | Cory Snyder | .01 | .05 |
| 20 | Kal Daniels | .01 | .05 |
| 21 | Mark Langston | .01 | .05 |
| 22 | Kevin Gross | .01 | .05 |
| 23 | Don Mattingly | .25 | .60 |
| 24 | Dave Righetti | .02 | .10 |

|  | | |
|------|------|------|
| ☐ 25 Roberto Alomar | .05 | .15 |
| ☐ 26 Bobby Thompson | .01 | .05 |
| ☐ 27 Jack McDowell | .01 | .05 |
| ☐ 28 Bip Roberts UER | .01 | .05 |
| (Bio reads playd) | | |
| ☐ 29 Jay Howell | .01 | .05 |
| ☐ 30 Dave Stieb UER | .01 | .05 |
| (17 wins in bio& | | |
| 18 in stats) | | |
| ☐ 31 Johnny Ray | .01 | .05 |
| ☐ 32 Steve Sax | .01 | .05 |
| ☐ 33 Terry Mulholland | .01 | .05 |
| ☐ 34 Lee Guetterman | .01 | .05 |
| ☐ 35 Tim Raines | .02 | .10 |
| ☐ 36 Scott Fletcher | .01 | .05 |
| ☐ 37 Lance Parrish | .02 | .10 |
| ☐ 38 Tony Phillips UER | | |
| (Born 4/15& | | |
| should be 4/25) | .01 | .05 |
| ☐ 39 Todd Stottlemyre | .01 | .05 |
| ☐ 40 Alan Trammell | .02 | .10 |
| ☐ 41 Todd Burns | .01 | .05 |
| ☐ 42 Mookie Wilson | .02 | .10 |
| ☐ 43 Chris Bosio | .01 | .05 |
| ☐ 44 Jeffrey Leonard | .01 | .05 |
| ☐ 45 Doug Jones | .01 | .05 |
| ☐ 46 Mike Scott UER | .01 | .05 |
| ☐ 47 Andy Hawkins | .01 | .05 |
| ☐ 48 Harold Reynolds | .02 | .10 |
| ☐ 49 Paul Molitor | .02 | .10 |
| ☐ 50 John Farrell | .01 | .05 |
| ☐ 51 Danny Darwin | .01 | .05 |
| ☐ 52 Jeff Blauser | .01 | .05 |
| ☐ 53 John Tudor UER | | |
| (41 wins in '81) | .01 | .05 |
| ☐ 54 Milt Thompson | .01 | .05 |
| ☐ 55 David Justice | .02 | .10 |
| ☐ 56 Greg Olson | .01 | .05 |
| ☐ 57 Willie Blair | .01 | .05 |
| ☐ 58 Rick Parker | .01 | .05 |
| ☐ 59 Shawn Boskie | .01 | .05 |
| ☐ 60 Kevin Tapani | .01 | .05 |
| ☐ 61 Dave Hollins | .01 | .05 |
| ☐ 62 Scott Radinsky | .01 | .05 |
| ☐ 63 Francisco Cabrera | .01 | .05 |
| ☐ 64 Tim Layana | .01 | .05 |
| ☐ 65 Jim Leyritz | .01 | .05 |
| ☐ 66 Wayne Edwards | .01 | .05 |
| ☐ 67 Lee Stevens | .01 | .05 |
| ☐ 68 Bill Sampen UER | | |
| (Fourth line& long | | |
| is spelled al | .01 | .05 |
| ☐ 69 Craig Grebeck UER | | |
| (Born in Cerritos& | | |
| not Johnsto | .01 | .05 |
| ☐ 70 John Burkett | .01 | .05 |
| ☐ 71 Hector Villanueva | .01 | .05 |
| ☐ 72 Oscar Azocar | .01 | .05 |
| ☐ 73 Alan Mills | .01 | .05 |
| ☐ 74 Carlos Baerga | .01 | .05 |
| ☐ 75 Charles Nagy | .01 | .05 |
| ☐ 76 Tim Drummond | .01 | .05 |
| ☐ 77 Dana Kiecker | .01 | .05 |
| ☐ 78 Tom Edens RC | .01 | .05 |
| ☐ 79 Kent Mercker | .01 | .05 |
| ☐ 80 Steve Avery | .01 | .05 |
| ☐ 81 Lee Smith | .02 | .10 |
| ☐ 82 Dave Martinez | .01 | .05 |
| ☐ 83 Dave Winfield | .02 | .10 |
| ☐ 84 Bill Spiers | .01 | .05 |
| ☐ 85 Dan Pasqua | .01 | .05 |
| ☐ 86 Randy Milligan | .01 | .05 |
| ☐ 87 Tracy Jones | .01 | .05 |
| ☐ 88 Greg Myers | .01 | .05 |
| ☐ 89 Keith Hernandez | .02 | .10 |
| ☐ 90 Todd Benzinger | .01 | .05 |
| ☐ 91 Mike Jackson | .01 | .05 |
| ☐ 92 Mike Stanley | .01 | .05 |
| ☐ 93 Candy Maldonado | .01 | .05 |
| ☐ 94 John Kruk UER | .02 | .10 |
| ☐ 95 Cal Ripken | .30 | .75 |
| ☐ 96 Willie Fraser | .01 | .05 |
| ☐ 97 Mike Felder | .01 | .05 |
| ☐ 98 Bill Landrum | .01 | .05 |
| ☐ 99 Chuck Crim | .01 | .05 |
| ☐ 100 Chuck Finley | .01 | .05 |
| ☐ 101 Kirt Manwaring | .01 | .05 |
| ☐ 102 Jaime Navarro | .01 | .05 |
| ☐ 103 Dickie Thon | .01 | .05 |
| ☐ 104 Brian Downing | .01 | .05 |
| ☐ 105 Jim Abbott | .05 | .15 |
| ☐ 106 Tom Brookens | .01 | .05 |
| ☐ 107 Darryl Hamilton UER | .01 | .05 |
| (Bio info is for | | |
| Jeff Hamilt | | |
| ☐ 108 Bryan Harvey | .01 | .05 |
| ☐ 109 Greg A. Harris UER | .01 | .05 |
| (Shown pitching lefty& | | |
| bio sa | | |
| ☐ 110 Greg Swindell | .01 | .05 |
| ☐ 111 Juan Berenguer | .01 | .05 |
| ☐ 112 Mike Heath | .01 | .05 |
| ☐ 113 Scott Bradley | .01 | .05 |
| ☐ 114 Jack Morris | .02 | .10 |
| ☐ 115 Barry Jones | .01 | .05 |
| ☐ 116 Kevin Romine | .01 | .05 |
| ☐ 117 Garry Templeton | .01 | .05 |
| ☐ 118 Scott Sanderson | .01 | .05 |
| ☐ 119 Roberto Kelly | .01 | .05 |
| ☐ 120 George Brett | .25 | .60 |
| ☐ 121 Oddibe McDowell | .01 | .05 |
| ☐ 122 Jim Acker | .01 | .05 |
| ☐ 123 Bill Swift UER | .01 | .05 |
| (Born 12/27/61, | | |
| should be 10/27) | | |
| ☐ 124 Eric King | .01 | .05 |
| ☐ 125 Jay Buhner | .02 | .10 |
| ☐ 126 Matt Young | .01 | .05 |
| ☐ 127 Alvaro Espinoza | .01 | .05 |
| ☐ 128 Greg Hibbard | .01 | .05 |
| ☐ 129 Jeff M. Robinson | .01 | .05 |
| ☐ 130 Mike Greenwell | .01 | .05 |
| ☐ 131 Dion James | .01 | .05 |
| ☐ 132 Donn Pall UER | | |
| (1988 ERA in stats 0.00) | .01 | .05 |
| ☐ 133 Lloyd Moseby | .01 | .05 |
| ☐ 134 Randy Velarde | .01 | .05 |
| ☐ 135 Allan Anderson | .01 | .05 |
| ☐ 136 Mark Davis | .01 | .05 |
| ☐ 137 Eric Davis | .02 | .10 |
| ☐ 138 Phil Stephenson | .01 | .05 |
| ☐ 139 Felix Fermin | .01 | .05 |
| ☐ 140 Pedro Guerrero | .02 | .10 |
| ☐ 141 Charlie Hough | .02 | .10 |
| ☐ 142 Mike Henneman | .01 | .05 |
| ☐ 143 Jeff Montgomery | .01 | .05 |
| ☐ 144 Lenny Harris | .01 | .05 |
| ☐ 145 Bruce Hurst | .01 | .05 |
| ☐ 146 Eric Anthony | .01 | .05 |
| ☐ 147 Paul Assenmacher | .01 | .05 |
| ☐ 148 Jesse Barfield | .01 | .05 |
| ☐ 149 Carlos Quintana | .01 | .05 |
| ☐ 150 Dave Stewart | .02 | .10 |
| ☐ 151 Roy Smith | .01 | .05 |
| ☐ 152 Paul Gibson | .01 | .05 |
| ☐ 153 Mickey Hatcher | .01 | .05 |
| ☐ 154 Jim Eisenreich | .01 | .05 |
| ☐ 155 Kenny Rogers | .02 | .10 |
| ☐ 156 Dave Schmidt | .01 | .05 |
| ☐ 157 Lance Johnson | .01 | .05 |
| ☐ 158 Dave West | .01 | .05 |
| ☐ 159 Steve Balboni | .01 | .05 |
| ☐ 160 Jeff Brantley | .01 | .05 |
| ☐ 161 Craig Biggio | .05 | .15 |
| ☐ 162 Brook Jacoby | .01 | .05 |
| ☐ 163 Dan Gladden | .01 | .05 |
| ☐ 164 Jeff Reardon UER | .02 | .10 |
| ☐ 165 Mark Carreon | .01 | .05 |
| ☐ 166 Mel Hall | .01 | .05 |
| ☐ 167 Gary Mielke | .01 | .05 |
| ☐ 168 Cecil Fielder | .02 | .10 |
| ☐ 169 Darrin Jackson | .01 | .05 |
| ☐ 170 Rick Aguilera | .02 | .10 |
| ☐ 171 Walt Weiss | .01 | .05 |
| ☐ 172 Steve Farr | .01 | .05 |
| ☐ 173 Jody Reed | .01 | .05 |
| ☐ 174 Mike Jeffcoat | .01 | .05 |
| ☐ 175 Mark Grace | .05 | .15 |
| ☐ 176 Larry Sheets | .01 | .05 |
| ☐ 177 Bill Gullickson | .01 | .05 |
| ☐ 178 Chris Gwynn | .01 | .05 |
| ☐ 179 Melido Perez | .01 | .05 |
| ☐ 180 Sid Fernandez UER | .01 | .05 |
| (778 runs in 1990) | | |
| ☐ 181 Tim Burke | .01 | .05 |
| ☐ 182 Gary Pettis | .01 | .05 |
| ☐ 183 Rob Murphy | .01 | .05 |
| ☐ 184 Craig Lefferts | .01 | .05 |
| ☐ 185 Howard Johnson | .01 | .05 |
| ☐ 186 Ken Caminiti | .02 | .10 |
| ☐ 187 Tim Belcher | .01 | .05 |
| ☐ 188 Greg Cadaret | .01 | .05 |
| ☐ 189 Matt Williams | .02 | .10 |
| ☐ 190 Dave Magadan | .01 | .05 |
| ☐ 191 Geno Petralli | .01 | .05 |
| ☐ 192 Jeff D. Robinson | .01 | .05 |
| ☐ 193 Jim Deshaies | .01 | .05 |
| ☐ 194 Willie Randolph | .02 | .10 |
| ☐ 195 George Bell | .01 | .05 |
| ☐ 196 Huble Brooks | .01 | .05 |
| ☐ 197 Tom Gordon | .01 | .05 |
| ☐ 198 Mike Fitzgerald | .01 | .05 |
| ☐ 199 Mike Pagliarulo | .01 | .05 |
| ☐ 200 Kirby Puckett | .08 | .25 |
| ☐ 201 Shawon Dunston | .01 | .05 |
| ☐ 202 Dennis Boyd | .01 | .05 |
| ☐ 203 Junior Felix UER | | |
| (Text has him in NL) | | |
| ☐ 204 Alejandro Pena | .01 | .05 |
| ☐ 205 Pete Smith | .01 | .05 |
| ☐ 206 Tom Glavine | .05 | .15 |
| ☐ 207 Luis Salazar | .01 | .05 |
| ☐ 208 John Smoltz | .05 | .15 |
| ☐ 209 Doug Dascenzo | .01 | .05 |
| ☐ 210 Tim Wallach | .01 | .05 |
| ☐ 211 Greg Gagne | .01 | .05 |
| ☐ 212 Mark Gubicza | .01 | .05 |
| ☐ 213 Mark Parent | .01 | .05 |
| ☐ 214 Ken Oberkfell | .01 | .05 |
| ☐ 215 Gary Carter | .02 | .10 |
| ☐ 216 Rafael Palmeiro | .05 | .15 |
| ☐ 217 Tom Niedenfuer | .01 | .05 |
| ☐ 218 Dave LaPoint | .01 | .05 |
| ☐ 219 Jeff Treadway | .01 | .05 |
| ☐ 220 Mitch Williams UER | | |
| ('89 ERA shown as 2.76& | | |
| shoul | .01 | .05 |
| ☐ 221 Jose DeLeon | .01 | .05 |
| ☐ 222 Mike LaValliere | .01 | .05 |
| ☐ 223 Darrel Akerfelds | .01 | .05 |
| ☐ 224A Kent Anderson ERR | | |
| (First line& flachy | | |
| should rea | .02 | .10 |
| ☐ 224B Kent Anderson COR | | |
| (Corrected in | | |
| factory sets) | .02 | .10 |
| ☐ 225 Dwight Evans | .05 | .15 |
| ☐ 226 Gary Redus | .01 | .05 |
| ☐ 227 Paul O'Neill | .05 | .15 |
| ☐ 228 Marty Barrett | .01 | .05 |
| ☐ 229 Tom Browning | .01 | .05 |
| ☐ 230 Terry Pendleton | .05 | .15 |
| ☐ 231 Jack Armstrong | .01 | .05 |
| ☐ 232 Mike Boddicker | .01 | .05 |
| ☐ 233 Neal Heaton | .01 | .05 |
| ☐ 234 Marquis Grissom | .02 | .10 |
| ☐ 235 Bert Blyleven | .02 | .10 |
| ☐ 236 Curt Young | .01 | .05 |
| ☐ 237 Don Carman | .01 | .05 |
| ☐ 238 Charlie Hayes | .01 | .05 |
| ☐ 239 Mark Knudson | .01 | .05 |
| ☐ 240 Todd Zeile | .01 | .05 |
| ☐ 241 Larry Walker | .08 | .25 |
| ☐ 242 Jerald Clark | .01 | .05 |
| ☐ 243 Jeff Ballard | .01 | .05 |
| ☐ 244 Jeff King | .01 | .05 |
| ☐ 245 Tom Brunansky | .01 | .05 |
| ☐ 246 Darren Daulton | .02 | .10 |
| ☐ 247 Scott Terry | .01 | .05 |
| ☐ 248 Rob Deer | .01 | .05 |
| ☐ 249 Brady Anderson UER | .02 | .10 |
| ☐ 250 Len Dykstra | .02 | .10 |
| ☐ 251 Greg W. Harris | .01 | .05 |
| ☐ 252 Mike Hartley | .01 | .05 |
| ☐ 253 Joey Cora | .01 | .05 |
| ☐ 254 Ivan Calderon | .01 | .05 |
| ☐ 255 Ted Power | .01 | .05 |
| ☐ 256 Sammy Sosa | .08 | .25 |
| ☐ 257 Steve Buechele | .01 | .05 |
| ☐ 258 Mike Devereaux UER | | |
| (No comma between | | |
| city and st | .01 | .05 |
| ☐ 259 Brad Komminsk UER | | |
| (Last text line& | | |

Ba should be
- 260 Ted Higuera .01 .05
- 261 Shawn Abner .01 .05
- 262 Dave Valle .01 .05
- 263 Jeff Huson .01 .05
- 264 Edgar Martinez .05 .15
- 265 Carlton Fisk .05 .15
- 266 Steve Finley .01 .05
- 267 John Wetteland .02 .10
- 268 Kevin Appier .05 .15
- 269 Steve Lyons .01 .05
- 270 Mickey Tettleton .01 .05
- 271 Luis Rivera .01 .05
- 272 Steve Jeltz .01 .05
- 273 R.J. Reynolds .01 .05
- 274 Carlos Martinez .01 .05
- 275 Dan Plesac .01 .05
- 276 Mike Morgan UER .01 .05
  (Total IP shown as
  1149.1& shoul
- 277 Jeff Russell .01 .05
- 278 Pete Incaviglia .01 .05
- 279 Kevin Seitzer UER
  (Bio has 200 hits twice
  and .3
- 280 Bobby Thigpen .01 .05
- 281 Stan Javier UER
  (Born 1/9,
  should say 9/11)
- 282 Henry Cotto .01 .05
- 283 Gary Wayne .01 .05
- 284 Shane Mack .01 .05
- 285 Brian Holman .01 .05
- 286 Gerald Perry .01 .05
- 287 Steve Crawford .01 .05
- 288 Nelson Liriano .01 .05
- 289 Don Aase .01 .05
- 290 Randy Johnson .10 .30
- 291 Harold Baines .02 .10
- 292 Kent Hrbek .02 .10
- 293A Les Lancaster ERR
  (No comma between
  Dallas and T .01 .05
- 293B Les Lancaster COR
  (Corrected in
  factory sets) .01 .05
- 294 Jeff Musselman .01 .05
- 295 Kurt Stillwell .01 .05
- 296 Stan Belinda .01 .05
- 297 Lou Whitaker .02 .10
- 298 Glenn Wilson .01 .05
- 299 Omar Vizquel UER .05 .15
- 300 Ramon Martinez .05 .15
- 301 Dwight Smith .01 .05
- 302 Tim Crews .01 .05
- 303 Lance Blankenship .01 .05
- 304 Sid Bream .01 .05
- 305 Rafael Ramirez .01 .05
- 306 Steve Wilson .01 .05
- 307 Mackey Sasser .01 .05
- 308 Franklin Stubbs .01 .05
- 309 Jack Daugherty UER
  (Born 6/3/60,
  should say July .01 .05
- 310 Eddie Murray .08 .25
- 311 Bob Welch .01 .05
- 312 Brian Harper .01 .05
- 313 Lance McCullers .01 .05
- 314 Dave Smith .01 .05
- 315 Bobby Bonilla .02 .10
- 316 Jerry Don Gleaton .01 .05
- 317 Greg Maddux .15 .40
- 318 Keith Miller .01 .05
- 319 Mark Portugal .01 .05
- 320 Robin Ventura .02 .10
- 321 Bob Ojeda .01 .05
- 322 Mike Harkey .01 .05
- 323 Jay Bell .02 .10
- 324 Mark McGwire .30 .75
- 325 Gary Gaetti .02 .10
- 326 Jeff Pico .01 .05
- 327 Kevin McReynolds .01 .05
- 328 Frank Tanana .01 .05
- 329 Eric Yelding UER
  (Listed as 6'3
  should be 5'11 .01 .05
- 330 Barry Bonds .40 1.00
- 331 Brian McRae RC .08 .25
- 332 Pedro Munoz RC .02 .10
- 333 Daryl Irvine RC .01 .05
- 334 Chris Hoiles .01 .05
- 335 Thomas Howard .01 .05
- 336 Jeff Schulz RC .01 .05
- 337 Jeff Manto .01 .05
- 338 Beau Allred .01 .05
- 339 Mike Bordick RC .15 .40
- 340 Todd Hundley .01 .05
- 341 Jim Vatcher UER RC .01 .05
- 342 Luis Sojo .01 .05
- 343 Jose Offerman UER .05 .15
- 344 Pete Coachman RC .01 .05
- 345 Mike Benjamin .01 .05
- 346 Ozzie Canseco .01 .05
- 347 Tim McIntosh .01 .05
- 348 Phil Plantier RC .02 .10
- 349 Terry Shumpert .01 .05
- 350 Darren Lewis FSC .01 .05
- 351 David Walsh RC .01 .05
- 352A Scott Chiamparino
  ERR (Bats left&
  should be righ .02 .10
- 352B Scott Chiamparino
  COR (corrected in
  factory sets .02 .10
- 353 Julio Valera
  UER (Progressed mis-
  spelled as pro .01 .05
- 354 Anthony Telford RC .01 .05
- 355 Kevin Wickander .01 .05
- 356 Tim Naehring .01 .05
- 357 Jim Poole .01 .05
- 358 Mark Whiten FSC UER .01 .05
- 359 Terry Wells RC .01 .05
- 360 Rafael Valdez .01 .05
- 361 Mel Stottlemyre Jr. .01 .05
- 362 David Segui .01 .05
- 363 Paul Abbott RC .01 .05
- 364 Steve Howard .01 .05
- 365 Karl Rhodes .01 .05
- 366 Rafael Novoa RC .01 .05
- 367 Joe Grahe RC .02 .10
- 368 Darren Reed .01 .05
- 369 Jeff McKnight .01 .05
- 370 Scott Leius .01 .05
- 371 Mark Dewey RC .01 .05
- 372 Mark Lee UER RC .02 .10
- 373 Rosario Rodriguez UER RC .01 .05
- 374 Chuck McElroy .01 .05
- 375 Mike Bell RC .01 .05
- 376 Mickey Morandini .01 .05
- 377 Bill Haselman RC .01 .05
- 378 Dave Pavlas RC .01 .05
- 379 Derrick May .01 .05
- 380 Jeromy Burnitz RC .15 .40
- 381 Donald Peters RC .01 .05
- 382 Alex Fernandez .05 .15
- 383 Mike Mussina RC .75 2.00
- 384 Dan Smith RC .02 .10
- 385 Lance Dickson RC .02 .10
- 386 Carl Everett RC .20 .50
- 387 Tom Nevers RC .02 .10
- 388 Adam Hyzdu RC .08 .25
- 389 Todd Van Poppel RC .08 .25
- 390 Rondell White RC .15 .40
- 391 Marc Newfield RC .02 .10
- 392 Julio Franco AS .01 .05
- 393 Wade Boggs AS .02 .10
- 394 Ozzie Guillen AS .01 .05
- 395 Cecil Fielder AS .05 .15
- 396 Ken Griffey Jr. AS .08 .25
- 397 Rickey Henderson AS .05 .15
- 398 Jose Canseco AS .05 .15
- 399 Roger Clemens AS .05 .15
- 400 Sandy Alomar Jr. AS .01 .05
- 401 Bobby Thigpen AS .01 .05
- 402 Bobby Bonilla MB .01 .05
- 403 Eric Davis MB .01 .05
- 404 Fred McGriff MB .02 .10
- 405 Glenn Davis MB .01 .05
- 406 Kevin Mitchell MB .01 .05
- 407 Rob Dibble KM .01 .05
- 408 Ramon Martinez KM .01 .05
- 409 David Cone KM .01 .05
- 410 Bobby Witt KM .01 .05
- 411 Mark Langston KM .01 .05
- 412 Bo Jackson RIF .02 .10
- 413 Shawon Dunston RIF
  UER (In the baseball&
  should .01 .05
- 414 Jesse Barfield RIF .01 .05
- 415 Ken Caminiti RIF .01 .05
- 416 Benito Santiago RIF .01 .05
- 417 Nolan Ryan HL .20 .50
- 418 Bobby Thigpen HL UER
  (Back refers to Hal
  McRea J
- 419 Ramon Martinez HL .01 .05
- 420 Bo Jackson HL .02 .10
- 421 Carlton Fisk HL .02 .10
- 422 Jimmy Key .01 .05
- 423 Junior Noboa .01 .05
- 424 Al Newman .01 .05
- 425 Pat Borders .01 .05
- 426 Von Hayes .01 .05
- 427 Tim Teufel .01 .05
- 428 Eric Plunk UER
  (Text says Eric's had&
  no apostro
- 429 John Moses .01 .05
- 430 Mike Witt .01 .05
- 431 Otis Nixon .01 .05
- 432 Tony Fernandez .01 .05
- 433 Rance Mulliniks .01 .05
- 434 Dan Petry .01 .05
- 435 Bob Geren .01 .05
- 436 Steve Frey .01 .05
- 437 Jamie Moyer .02 .10
- 438 Junior Ortiz .01 .05
- 439 Tom O'Malley .01 .05
- 440 Pat Combs .01 .05
- 441 Jose Canseco DT .05 .15
- 442 Alfredo Griffin .01 .05
- 443 Andres Galarraga .02 .10
- 444 Bryn Smith .01 .05
- 445 Andre Dawson .02 .10
- 446 Juan Samuel .01 .05
- 447 Mike Aldrete .01 .05
- 448 Ron Gant .02 .10
- 449 Fernando Valenzuela .02 .10
- 450 Vince Coleman UER
  (Should say topped
  majors in s .01 .05
- 451 Kevin Mitchell .01 .05
- 452 Spike Owen .01 .05
- 453 Mike Bielecki .01 .05
- 454 Dennis Martinez .02 .10
- 455 Brett Butler .02 .10
- 456 Ron Darling .01 .05
- 457 Dennis Rasmussen .01 .05
- 458 Ken Howell .01 .05
- 459 Steve Bedrosian .01 .05
- 460 Frank Viola .02 .10
- 461 Jose Lind .01 .05
- 462 Chris Sabo .01 .05
- 463 Dante Bichette .02 .10
- 464 Rick Mahler .01 .05
- 465 John Smiley .02 .10
- 466 Devon White .02 .10
- 467 John Orton .02 .10
- 468 Mike Stanton .01 .05
- 469 Billy Hatcher .01 .05
- 470 Wally Joyner .02 .10
- 471 Gene Larkin .01 .05
- 472 Doug Drabek .01 .05
- 473 Gary Sheffield .02 .10
- 474 David Wells .02 .10
- 475 Andy Van Slyke .05 .15
- 476 Mike Gallego .01 .05
- 477 B.J. Surhoff .01 .05
- 478 Gene Nelson .01 .05
- 479 Mariano Duncan .01 .05
- 480 Fred McGriff .05 .15
- 481 Jerry Browne .01 .05
- 482 Alvin Davis .01 .05
- 483 Bill Wegman .01 .05
- 484 Dave Parker .02 .10
- 485 Dennis Eckersley .02 .10
- 486 Erik Hanson UER
  (Basketball misspelled
  as baseke .01 .05
- 487 Bill Ripken .01 .05
- 488 Tom Candiotti .01 .05
- 489 Mike Schooler .01 .05
- 490 Gregg Olson .01 .05

|  |  | | |
|---|------|---|---|
| ❑ 491 | Chris James | .01 | .05 |
| ❑ 492 | Pete Harnisch | .01 | .05 |
| ❑ 493 | Julio Franco | .02 | .10 |
| ❑ 494 | Greg Briley | .01 | .05 |
| ❑ 495 | Ruben Sierra | .02 | .10 |
| ❑ 496 | Steve Olin | .01 | .05 |
| ❑ 497 | Mike Fetters | .01 | .05 |
| ❑ 498 | Mark Williamson | .01 | .05 |
| ❑ 499 | Bob Tewksbury | .01 | .05 |
| ❑ 500 | Tony Gwynn | .10 | .30 |
| ❑ 501 | Randy Myers | .01 | .05 |
| ❑ 502 | Keith Comstock | .01 | .05 |
| ❑ 503 | Craig Worthington UER (DeCinces misspelled DiCin | .01 | .05 |
| ❑ 504 | Mark Eichhorn UER (Stats incomplete& doesn't hav | .01 | .05 |
| ❑ 505 | Barry Larkin | .05 | .15 |
| ❑ 506 | Dave Johnson | .01 | .05 |
| ❑ 507 | Bobby Witt | .01 | .05 |
| ❑ 508 | Joe Orsulak | .01 | .05 |
| ❑ 509 | Pete O'Brien | .01 | .05 |
| ❑ 510 | Brad Arnsberg | .01 | .05 |
| ❑ 511 | Storm Davis | .01 | .05 |
| ❑ 512 | Bob Milacki | .01 | .05 |
| ❑ 513 | Bill Pecota | .01 | .05 |
| ❑ 514 | Glenallen Hill | .01 | .05 |
| ❑ 515 | Danny Tartabull | .01 | .05 |
| ❑ 516 | Mike Moore | .01 | .05 |
| ❑ 517 | Ron Robinson UER (577 K's in 1990) | .01 | .05 |
| ❑ 518 | Mark Gardner | .01 | .05 |
| ❑ 519 | Rick Wrona | .01 | .05 |
| ❑ 520 | Mike Scioscia | .01 | .05 |
| ❑ 521 | Frank Wills | .01 | .05 |
| ❑ 522 | Greg Brock | .01 | .05 |
| ❑ 523 | Jack Clark | .02 | .10 |
| ❑ 524 | Bruce Ruffin | .01 | .05 |
| ❑ 525 | Robin Yount | .15 | .40 |
| ❑ 526 | Tom Foley | .01 | .05 |
| ❑ 527 | Pat Perry | .01 | .05 |
| ❑ 528 | Greg Vaughn | .01 | .05 |
| ❑ 529 | Wally Whitehurst | .01 | .05 |
| ❑ 530 | Norm Charlton | .01 | .05 |
| ❑ 531 | Marvell Wynne | .01 | .05 |
| ❑ 532 | Jim Gantner | .01 | .05 |
| ❑ 533 | Greg Litton | .01 | .05 |
| ❑ 534 | Manny Lee | .01 | .05 |
| ❑ 535 | Scott Bailes | .01 | .05 |
| ❑ 536 | Charlie Leibrandt | .01 | .05 |
| ❑ 537 | Roger McDowell | .01 | .05 |
| ❑ 538 | Andy Benes | .01 | .05 |
| ❑ 539 | Rick Honeycutt | .01 | .05 |
| ❑ 540 | Dwight Gooden | .02 | .10 |
| ❑ 541 | Scott Garrelts | .01 | .05 |
| ❑ 542 | Dave Clark | .01 | .05 |
| ❑ 543 | Lonnie Smith | .01 | .05 |
| ❑ 544 | Rick Reuschel | .01 | .05 |
| ❑ 545 | Delino DeShields | .02 | .10 |
| ❑ 546 | Mike Sharperson | .01 | .05 |
| ❑ 547 | Mike Kingery | .01 | .05 |
| ❑ 548 | Terry Kennedy | .01 | .05 |
| ❑ 549 | David Cone | .02 | .10 |
| ❑ 550 | Orel Hershiser | .02 | .10 |
| ❑ 551 | Matt Nokes | .01 | .05 |
| ❑ 552 | Eddie Williams | .01 | .05 |
| ❑ 553 | Frank DiPino | .01 | .05 |
| ❑ 554 | Fred Lynn | .01 | .05 |
| ❑ 555 | Alex Cole | .01 | .05 |
| ❑ 556 | Terry Leach | .01 | .05 |
| ❑ 557 | Chet Lemon | .01 | .05 |
| ❑ 558 | Paul Mirabella | .01 | .05 |
| ❑ 559 | Bill Long | .01 | .05 |
| ❑ 560 | Phil Bradley | .01 | .05 |
| ❑ 561 | Duane Ward | .01 | .05 |
| ❑ 562 | Dave Bergman | .01 | .05 |
| ❑ 563 | Eric Show | .01 | .05 |
| ❑ 564 | Xavier Hernandez | .01 | .05 |
| ❑ 565 | Jeff Parrett | .01 | .05 |
| ❑ 566 | Chuck Cary | .01 | .05 |
| ❑ 567 | Ken Hill | .01 | .05 |
| ❑ 568 | Bob Welch Hand (Complement should be compliment) | .01 | .05 |
| ❑ 569 | John Mitchell | .01 | .05 |
| ❑ 570 | Travis Fryman | .02 | .10 |
| ❑ 571 | Derek Lilliquist | .01 | .05 |
| ❑ 572 | Steve Lake | .01 | .05 |
| ❑ 573 | John Barfield | .01 | .05 |
| ❑ 574 | Randy Bush | .01 | .05 |
| ❑ 575 | Joe Magrane | .01 | .05 |
| ❑ 576 | Eddie Diaz | .01 | .05 |
| ❑ 577 | Casey Candaele | .01 | .05 |
| ❑ 578 | Jesse Orosco | .01 | .05 |
| ❑ 579 | Tom Henke | .01 | .05 |
| ❑ 580 | Rick Cerone UER (Actually has third go-toard wt | .01 | .05 |
| ❑ 581 | Drew Hall | .01 | .05 |
| ❑ 582 | Tony Castillo | .01 | .05 |
| ❑ 583 | Jimmy Jones | .01 | .05 |
| ❑ 584 | Rick Reed | .01 | .05 |
| ❑ 585 | Joe Girardi | .01 | .05 |
| ❑ 586 | Jeff Gray RC | .01 | .05 |
| ❑ 587 | Luis Polonia | .01 | .05 |
| ❑ 588 | Joe Klink | .01 | .05 |
| ❑ 589 | Rex Hudler | .01 | .05 |
| ❑ 590 | Kirk McCaskill | .01 | .05 |
| ❑ 591 | Juan Agosto | .01 | .05 |
| ❑ 592 | Wes Gardner | .01 | .05 |
| ❑ 593 | Rich Rodriguez RC | .01 | .05 |
| ❑ 594 | Mitch Webster | .01 | .05 |
| ❑ 595 | Kelly Gruber | .01 | .05 |
| ❑ 596 | Dale Mohorcic | .01 | .05 |
| ❑ 597 | Willie McGee | .02 | .10 |
| ❑ 598 | Bill Krueger | .01 | .05 |
| ❑ 599 | Bob Walk UER (Cards says he's 33& but actually | .01 | .05 |
| ❑ 600 | Kevin Maas | .01 | .05 |
| ❑ 601 | Danny Jackson | .01 | .05 |
| ❑ 602 | Craig McMurtry UER (Anonymously misspelled anoni | .01 | .05 |
| ❑ 603 | Curtis Wilkerson | .01 | .05 |
| ❑ 604 | Adam Peterson | .01 | .05 |
| ❑ 605 | Sam Horn | .01 | .05 |
| ❑ 606 | Tommy Gregg | .01 | .05 |
| ❑ 607 | Ken Dayley | .01 | .05 |
| ❑ 608 | Carmelo Castillo | .01 | .05 |
| ❑ 609 | John Shelby | .01 | .05 |
| ❑ 610 | Don Slaught | .01 | .05 |
| ❑ 611 | Calvin Schiraldi | .01 | .05 |
| ❑ 612 | Dennis Lamp | .01 | .05 |
| ❑ 613 | Andres Thomas | .01 | .05 |
| ❑ 614 | Jose Gonzalez | .01 | .05 |
| ❑ 615 | Randy Ready | .01 | .05 |
| ❑ 616 | Kevin Bass | .01 | .05 |
| ❑ 617 | Mike Marshall | .01 | .05 |
| ❑ 618 | Daryl Boston | .01 | .05 |
| ❑ 619 | Andy McGaffigan | .01 | .05 |
| ❑ 620 | Joe Oliver | .01 | .05 |
| ❑ 621 | Jim Gott | .01 | .05 |
| ❑ 622 | Jose Oquendo | .01 | .05 |
| ❑ 623 | Jose DeJesus | .01 | .05 |
| ❑ 624 | Mike Brumley | .01 | .05 |
| ❑ 625 | John Olerud | .02 | .10 |
| ❑ 626 | Ernest Riles | .01 | .05 |
| ❑ 627 | Gene Harris | .01 | .05 |
| ❑ 628 | Jose Uribe | .01 | .05 |
| ❑ 629 | Darnell Coles | .01 | .05 |
| ❑ 630 | Carney Lansford | .02 | .10 |
| ❑ 631 | Tim Leary | .01 | .05 |
| ❑ 632 | Tim Hulett | .01 | .05 |
| ❑ 633 | Kevin Elster | .01 | .05 |
| ❑ 634 | Tony Fossas | .01 | .05 |
| ❑ 635 | Francisco Oliveras | .01 | .05 |
| ❑ 636 | Bob Patterson | .01 | .05 |
| ❑ 637 | Gary Ward | .01 | .05 |
| ❑ 638 | Rene Gonzales | .01 | .05 |
| ❑ 639 | Don Robinson | .01 | .05 |
| ❑ 640 | Darryl Strawberry | .02 | .10 |
| ❑ 641 | Dave Anderson | .01 | .05 |
| ❑ 642 | Scott Scudder | .01 | .05 |
| ❑ 643 | Reggie Harris UER (Hepatitis misspelled as hepit | .01 | .05 |
| ❑ 644 | Dave Henderson | .01 | .05 |
| ❑ 645 | Ben McDonald | .01 | .05 |
| ❑ 646 | Bob Kipper | .01 | .05 |
| ❑ 647 | Hal Morris UER (It's should be its) | .01 | .05 |
| ❑ 648 | Tim Birtsas | .01 | .05 |
| ❑ 649 | Steve Searcy | .01 | .05 |
| ❑ 650 | Dale Murphy | .05 | .15 |
| ❑ 651 | Ron Oester | .01 | .05 |
| ❑ 652 | Mike LaCoss | .01 | .05 |
| ❑ 653 | Ron Jones | .01 | .05 |
| ❑ 654 | Kelly Downs | .01 | .05 |
| ❑ 655 | Roger Clemens | .30 | .75 |
| ❑ 656 | Herm Winningham | .01 | .05 |
| ❑ 657 | Trevor Wilson | .01 | .05 |
| ❑ 658 | Jose Rijo | .01 | .05 |
| ❑ 659 | Dann Bilardello UER (Bio has 13 games& 1 hit& an | .01 | .05 |
| ❑ 660 | Gregg Jefferies | .01 | .05 |
| ❑ 661 | Doug Drabek AS UER (Through is misspelled thou | .01 | .05 |
| ❑ 662 | Randy Myers AS | .01 | .05 |
| ❑ 663 | Benny Santiago AS | .01 | .05 |
| ❑ 664 | Will Clark AS | .02 | .10 |
| ❑ 665 | Ryne Sandberg AS | .08 | .25 |
| ❑ 666 | Barry Larkin AS UER (Line 13& coolly misspelled | .02 | .10 |
| ❑ 667 | Matt Williams AS | .01 | .05 |
| ❑ 668 | Barry Bonds AS | .20 | .50 |
| ❑ 669 | Eric Davis AS | .01 | .05 |
| ❑ 670 | Bobby Bonilla AS | .02 | .10 |
| ❑ 671 | Chipper Jones RC | 1.50 | 4.00 |
| ❑ 672 | Eric Christopherson RC | .02 | .10 |
| ❑ 673 | Robbie Beckett RC | .08 | .25 |
| ❑ 674 | Shane Andrews RC | .08 | .25 |
| ❑ 675 | Steve Karsay RC | .08 | .25 |
| ❑ 676 | Aaron Holbert RC | .02 | .10 |
| ❑ 677 | Donovan Osborne RC | .08 | .25 |
| ❑ 678 | Todd Ritchie RC | .08 | .25 |
| ❑ 679 | Ronnie Walden RC | .02 | .10 |
| ❑ 680 | Tim Costo RC | .02 | .10 |
| ❑ 681 | Dan Wilson RC | .08 | .25 |
| ❑ 682 | Kurt Miller RC | | |
| ❑ 683 | Mike Lieberthal RC | .15 | .40 |
| ❑ 684 | Roger Clemens KM | .15 | .40 |
| ❑ 685 | Dwight Gooden KM | .01 | .05 |
| ❑ 686 | Nolan Ryan KM | .20 | .50 |
| ❑ 687 | Frank Viola KM | .01 | .05 |
| ❑ 688 | Matt Williams MB | .01 | .05 |
| ❑ 689 | Jose Canseco MB | .02 | .10 |
| ❑ 690 | Darryl Strawberry MB | .01 | .05 |
| ❑ 691 | Bo Jackson MB | .02 | .10 |
| ❑ 692 | Cecil Fielder MB | .01 | .05 |
| ❑ 693 | Sandy Alomar Jr. RF | .01 | .05 |
| ❑ 694 | Ken Griffey Jr. RF | .08 | .25 |
| ❑ 695 | Coy Snyder RF | .01 | .05 |
| ❑ 696 | Eric Davis RF | .01 | .05 |
| ❑ 697 | Ken Griffey Jr. RF | .08 | .25 |
| ❑ 698 | Andy Van Slyke RF UER | .02 | .10 |
| ❑ 699 | Langston/Witt NH Mark Langston Mike Witt | .01 | .05 |
| ❑ 700 | Randy Johnson NH | .05 | .15 |
| ❑ 701 | Nolan Ryan NH | .20 | .50 |
| ❑ 702 | Dave Stewart NH | .01 | .05 |
| ❑ 703 | Fernando Valenzuela NH | .01 | .05 |
| ❑ 704 | Andy Hawkins NH | .01 | .05 |
| ❑ 705 | Melido Perez NH | .01 | .05 |
| ❑ 706 | Terry Mulholland NH | .01 | .05 |
| ❑ 707 | Dave Stieb NH | .01 | .05 |
| ❑ 708 | Brian Barnes RC | .01 | .05 |
| ❑ 709 | Bernard Gilkey RC | .01 | .05 |
| ❑ 710 | Steve Decker RC | .01 | .05 |
| ❑ 711 | Paul Faries RC | .01 | .05 |
| ❑ 712 | Paul Marak RC | .01 | .05 |
| ❑ 713 | Wes Chamberlain RC | .02 | .10 |
| ❑ 714 | Kevin Belcher RC | .01 | .05 |
| ❑ 715 | Dan Boone UER (IP adds up to 101, but card has 1 | .01 | .05 |
| ❑ 716 | Steve Adkins RC | .01 | .05 |
| ❑ 717 | Geronimo Pena | .01 | .05 |
| ❑ 718 | Howard Farmer | .01 | .05 |
| ❑ 719 | Mark Leonard RC | .01 | .05 |
| ❑ 720 | Tom Lampkin | .01 | .05 |
| ❑ 721 | Mike Gardiner RC | .01 | .05 |
| ❑ 722 | Jeff Conine RC | .15 | .40 |
| ❑ 723 | Efrain Valdez RC | .01 | .05 |
| ❑ 724 | Chuck Malone | .01 | .05 |
| ❑ 725 | Leo Gomez | | |
| ❑ 726 | Paul McClellan RC | .01 | .05 |
| ❑ 727 | Mark Leiter RC | .02 | .10 |
| ❑ 728 | Rich DeLucia RC | .01 | .05 |

|  | | |
|---|---|---|
| ☐ 729 Mel Rojas | .01 | .05 |
| ☐ 730 Hector Wagner RC | .01 | .05 |
| ☐ 731 Ray Lankford | .02 | .10 |
| ☐ 732 Turner Ward RC | .02 | .10 |
| ☐ 733 Gerald Alexander RC | .01 | .05 |
| ☐ 734 Scott Anderson RC | .01 | .05 |
| ☐ 735 Tony Perezchica | .01 | .05 |
| ☐ 736 Jimmy Kremers | .01 | .05 |
| ☐ 737 American Flag/Peace | .08 | .25 |
| ☐ 738 Mike York RC | .01 | .05 |
| ☐ 739 Mike Rochford | .01 | .05 |
| ☐ 740 Scott Aldred | .01 | .05 |
| ☐ 741 Rico Brogna | .01 | .05 |
| ☐ 742 Dave Burba RC | .08 | .25 |
| ☐ 743 Ray Stephens RC | .01 | .05 |
| ☐ 744 Eric Gunderson | .01 | .05 |
| ☐ 745 Troy Afenir RC | .01 | .05 |
| ☐ 746 Jeff Shaw | .01 | .05 |
| ☐ 747 Orlando Merced RC | .02 | .10 |
| ☐ 748 Omar Olivares UER RC | .02 | .10 |
| ☐ 749 Jerry Kutzler | .01 | .05 |
| ☐ 750 Mo Vaughn | .02 | .10 |
| ☐ 751 Matt Stark RC | .01 | .05 |
| ☐ 752 Randy Hennis RC | .01 | .05 |
| ☐ 753 Andujar Cedeno | .01 | .05 |
| ☐ 754 Kelvin Torve | .01 | .05 |
| ☐ 755 Joe Kraemer | .01 | .05 |
| ☐ 756 Phil Clark RC | .02 | .10 |
| ☐ 757 Ed Vosberg RC | .01 | .05 |
| ☐ 758 Mike Perez RC | .02 | .10 |
| ☐ 759 Scott Lewis RC | .01 | .05 |
| ☐ 760 Steve Chitren RC | .01 | .05 |
| ☐ 761 Ray Young RC | .01 | .05 |
| ☐ 762 Andres Santana | .01 | .05 |
| ☐ 763 Rodney McCray RC | .01 | .05 |
| ☐ 764 Sean Berry UER RC | .02 | .10 |
| ☐ 765 Brent Mayne | .01 | .05 |
| ☐ 766 Mike Simms RC | .02 | .10 |
| ☐ 767 Glenn Sutko RC | .01 | .05 |
| ☐ 768 Gary DiSarcina | .01 | .05 |
| ☐ 769 George Brett HL | .08 | .25 |
| ☐ 770 Cecil Fielder HL | .05 | .15 |
| ☐ 771 Jim Presley | .01 | .05 |
| ☐ 772 John Dopson | .01 | .05 |
| ☐ 773 Bo Jackson Breaker | .02 | .10 |
| ☐ 774 Brent Knackert UER | | |
| (Born in 1954& shown | | |
| throwing | .01 | .05 |
| ☐ 775 Bill Doran UER | | |
| (Reds in NL East) | .01 | .05 |
| ☐ 776 Dick Schofield | .01 | .05 |
| ☐ 777 Nelson Santovenia | .01 | .05 |
| ☐ 778 Mark Guthrie | .01 | .05 |
| ☐ 779 Mark Lemke | .01 | .05 |
| ☐ 780 Terry Steinbach | .01 | .05 |
| ☐ 781 Tom Bolton | .01 | .05 |
| ☐ 782 Randy Tomlin RC | .02 | .10 |
| ☐ 783 Jeff Kunkel | .01 | .05 |
| ☐ 784 Felix Jose | .01 | .05 |
| ☐ 785 Rick Sutcliffe | .02 | .10 |
| ☐ 786 John Cerutti | .01 | .05 |
| ☐ 787 Jose Vizcaino UER | .01 | .05 |
| ☐ 788 Curt Schilling | .08 | .25 |
| ☐ 789 Ed Whitson | .01 | .05 |
| ☐ 790 Tony Pena | .01 | .05 |
| ☐ 791 John Candelaria | .01 | .05 |
| ☐ 792 Carmelo Martinez | .01 | .05 |
| ☐ 793 Sandy Alomar Jr. UER | .01 | .05 |
| ☐ 794 Jim Neidlinger RC | .01 | .05 |
| ☐ 795 Barry Larkin WS | | |
| and Chris Sabo | .02 | .10 |
| ☐ 796 Paul Sorrento | .02 | .10 |
| ☐ 797 Tom Pagnozzi | .01 | .05 |
| ☐ 798 Tino Martinez | .08 | .25 |
| ☐ 799 Scott Ruskin UER | | |
| (Text says first three | | |
| seasons | .01 | .05 |
| ☐ 800 Kirk Gibson | .01 | .05 |
| ☐ 801 Walt Terrell | .02 | .10 |
| ☐ 802 John Russell | .01 | .05 |
| ☐ 803 Chili Davis | .02 | .10 |
| ☐ 804 Chris Nabholz | .02 | .10 |
| ☐ 805 Juan Gonzalez | .08 | .25 |
| ☐ 806 Ron Hassey | .01 | .05 |
| ☐ 807 Todd Worrell | .01 | .05 |
| ☐ 808 Tommy Greene | .01 | .05 |
| ☐ 809 Joel Skinner UER | | |
| (Joel& not Bob& was | | |

|  | | |
|---|---|---|
| drafted in | .01 | .05 |
| ☐ 810 Benito Santiago | .02 | .10 |
| ☐ 811 Pat Tabler UER | | |
| (Line 3& always | | |
| misspelled annual) | .01 | .05 |
| ☐ 812 Scott Erickson UER RC | .01 | .05 |
| ☐ 813 Moises Alou | .02 | .10 |
| ☐ 814 Dale Sveum | .01 | .05 |
| ☐ 815 Rayne Sandberg MANYR | .08 | .25 |
| ☐ 816 Rick Dempsey | .01 | .05 |
| ☐ 817 Scott Bankhead | .01 | .05 |
| ☐ 818 Jason Grimsley | .01 | .05 |
| ☐ 819 Doug Jennings | .01 | .05 |
| ☐ 820 Tom Herr | .01 | .05 |
| ☐ 821 Rob Ducey | .01 | .05 |
| ☐ 822 Luis Quinones | .01 | .05 |
| ☐ 823 Greg Minton | .01 | .05 |
| ☐ 824 Mark Grant | .01 | .05 |
| ☐ 825 Ozzie Smith | .15 | .40 |
| ☐ 826 Dave Eiland | .01 | .05 |
| ☐ 827 Danny Heep | .01 | .05 |
| ☐ 828 Hensley Meulens | .02 | .10 |
| ☐ 829 Charlie O'Brien | .01 | .05 |
| ☐ 830 Glenn Davis | .01 | .05 |
| ☐ 831 John Marzano UER | | |
| (International mis- | | |
| spelled Int | .01 | .05 |
| ☐ 832 Steve Ontiveros | .01 | .05 |
| ☐ 833 Ron Karkovice | .01 | .05 |
| ☐ 834 Jerry Goff | .01 | .05 |
| ☐ 835 Ken Griffey Sr. | .02 | .10 |
| ☐ 836 Kevin Reimer | .01 | .05 |
| ☐ 837 Randy Kutcher UER | | |
| (Infectous mis- | | |
| spelled infec | .01 | .05 |
| ☐ 838 Mike Blowers | .01 | .05 |
| ☐ 839 Mike Macfarlane | .01 | .05 |
| ☐ 840 Frank Thomas | .08 | .25 |
| ☐ 841 K.Griffey Jr./K.Griffey Sr. | .15 | .40 |
| ☐ 842 Jack Howell | .01 | .05 |
| ☐ 843 Goose Gozzo | .01 | .05 |
| ☐ 844 Gerald Young | .01 | .05 |
| ☐ 845 Zane Smith | .01 | .05 |
| ☐ 846 Kevin Brown | .02 | .10 |
| ☐ 847 Sil Campusano | .01 | .05 |
| ☐ 848 Larry Andersen | .01 | .05 |
| ☐ 849 Cal Ripken FRAN | .15 | .40 |
| ☐ 850 Roger Clemens FRAN | .15 | .40 |
| ☐ 851 Sandy Alomar Jr. FRAN | .01 | .05 |
| ☐ 852 Alan Trammell FRAN | .02 | .10 |
| ☐ 853 George Brett FRAN | .08 | .25 |
| ☐ 854 Robin Yount FRAN | .08 | .25 |
| ☐ 855 Kirby Puckett FRAN | .05 | .15 |
| ☐ 856 Don Mattingly FRAN | .10 | .30 |
| ☐ 857 Rickey Henderson FRAN | .05 | .15 |
| ☐ 858 Ken Griffey Jr. FRAN | .08 | .25 |
| ☐ 859 Ruben Sierra FRAN | .01 | .05 |
| ☐ 860 John Olerud FRAN | .01 | .05 |
| ☐ 861 Chris Sabo FRAN | .01 | .05 |
| ☐ 862 Ryne Sandberg FRAN | .05 | .15 |
| ☐ 863 Eric Davis FRAN | .01 | .05 |
| ☐ 864 Darryl Strawberry FRAN | .02 | .10 |
| ☐ 865 Tim Wallach FRAN | .01 | .05 |
| ☐ 866 Dwight Gooden FRAN | .01 | .05 |
| ☐ 867 Len Dykstra FRAN | .01 | .05 |
| ☐ 868 Barry Bonds FRAN | .20 | .50 |
| ☐ 869 Todd Zeile FRAN | .01 | .05 |
| ☐ 870 Benito Santiago FRAN | .01 | .05 |
| ☐ 871 Will Clark FRAN | .02 | .10 |
| ☐ 872 Craig Biggio FRAN | .02 | .10 |
| ☐ 873 Wally Joyner FRAN | .01 | .05 |
| ☐ 874 Frank Thomas FRAN | .05 | .15 |
| ☐ 875 Rickey Henderson MVP | .05 | .15 |
| ☐ 876 Barry Bonds MVP | .20 | .50 |
| ☐ 877 Bob Welch CY | .01 | .05 |
| ☐ 878 Doug Drabek CY | .01 | .05 |
| ☐ 879 Sandy Alomar Jr. ROY | .01 | .05 |
| ☐ 880 David Justice ROY | .05 | .15 |
| ☐ 881 Damon Berryhill | .01 | .05 |
| ☐ 882 Frank Viola DT | .01 | .05 |
| ☐ 883 Dave Stewart DT | .01 | .05 |
| ☐ 884 Doug Jones DT | .01 | .05 |
| ☐ 885 Randy Myers DT | .01 | .05 |
| ☐ 886 Will Clark DT | .02 | .10 |
| ☐ 887 Roberto Alomar DT | .02 | .10 |
| ☐ 888 Barry Larkin DT | .02 | .10 |
| ☐ 889 Wade Boggs DT | .05 | .15 |
| ☐ 890 Rickey Henderson DT | .08 | .25 |

|  | | |
|---|---|---|
| ☐ 891 Kirby Puckett DT | .05 | .15 |
| ☐ 892 Ken Griffey Jr. DT | .20 | .50 |
| ☐ 893 Benny Santiago DT | .02 | .10 |

### 1992 Score

| | | |
|---|---|---|
| ☐ COMPLETE SET (893) | 6.00 | 15.00 |
| ☐ COMP.FACT.SET (910) | 8.00 | 20.00 |
| ☐ COMPLETE SERIES 1 (442) | 3.00 | 8.00 |
| ☐ COMPLETE SERIES 2 (451) | 3.00 | 8.00 |
| ☐ 1 Ken Griffey Jr. | .15 | .40 |
| ☐ 2 Nolan Ryan | .40 | 1.00 |
| ☐ 3 Will Clark | .05 | .15 |
| ☐ 4 David Justice | .02 | .10 |
| ☐ 5 Dave Henderson | .01 | .05 |
| ☐ 6 Bret Saberhagen | .01 | .05 |
| ☐ 7 Fred McGriff | .05 | .15 |
| ☐ 8 Erik Hanson | .01 | .05 |
| ☐ 9 Darryl Strawberry | .02 | .10 |
| ☐ 10 Dwight Gooden | .02 | .10 |
| ☐ 11 Juan Gonzalez | .05 | .15 |
| ☐ 12 Mark Langston | .01 | .05 |
| ☐ 13 Lonnie Smith | .01 | .05 |
| ☐ 14 Jeff Montgomery | .01 | .05 |
| ☐ 15 Roberto Alomar | .05 | .15 |
| ☐ 16 Delino DeShields | .01 | .05 |
| ☐ 17 Steve Bedrosian | .01 | .05 |
| ☐ 18 Terry Pendleton | .02 | .10 |
| ☐ 19 Mark Carreon | .01 | .05 |
| ☐ 20 Mark McGwire | .25 | .60 |
| ☐ 21 Roger Clemens | .20 | .50 |
| ☐ 22 Chuck Crim | .01 | .05 |
| ☐ 23 Don Mattingly | .25 | .60 |
| ☐ 24 Dickie Thon | .01 | .05 |
| ☐ 25 Ron Gant | .02 | .10 |
| ☐ 26 Milt Cuyler | .01 | .05 |
| ☐ 27 Mike Macfarlane | .01 | .05 |
| ☐ 28 Dan Gladden | .01 | .05 |
| ☐ 29 Melido Perez | .01 | .05 |
| ☐ 30 Willie Randolph | .02 | .10 |
| ☐ 31 Albert Belle | .05 | .15 |
| ☐ 32 Dave Winfield | .05 | .15 |
| ☐ 33 Jimmy Jones | .01 | .05 |
| ☐ 34 Kevin Gross | .01 | .05 |
| ☐ 35 Andres Galarraga | .02 | .10 |
| ☐ 36 Mike Devereaux | .01 | .05 |
| ☐ 37 Chris Bosio | .01 | .05 |
| ☐ 38 Mike LaValliere | .01 | .05 |
| ☐ 39 Gary Gaetti | .02 | .10 |
| ☐ 40 Felix Jose | .01 | .05 |
| ☐ 41 Alvaro Espinoza | .01 | .05 |
| ☐ 42 Rick Aguilera | .01 | .05 |
| ☐ 43 Mike Gallego | .01 | .05 |
| ☐ 44 Eric Davis | .01 | .05 |
| ☐ 45 George Bell | .05 | .15 |
| ☐ 46 Tom Brunansky | .02 | .10 |
| ☐ 47 Steve Farr | .01 | .05 |
| ☐ 48 Duane Ward | .01 | .05 |
| ☐ 49 David Wells | .02 | .10 |
| ☐ 50 Cecil Fielder | .08 | .25 |
| ☐ 51 Walt Weiss | .01 | .05 |
| ☐ 52 Todd Zeile | .02 | .10 |
| ☐ 53 Doug Jones | .01 | .05 |
| ☐ 54 Bob Walk | .01 | .05 |
| ☐ 55 Rafael Palmeiro | .05 | .15 |
| ☐ 56 Rob Deer | .01 | .05 |
| ☐ 57 Paul O'Neill | .02 | .10 |
| ☐ 58 Jeff Reardon | .02 | .10 |
| ☐ 59 Randy Ready | .01 | .05 |
| ☐ 60 Scott Erickson | .02 | .10 |
| ☐ 61 Paul Molitor | .02 | .10 |
| ☐ 62 Jack McDowell | .05 | .15 |
| ☐ 63 Jim Acker | .01 | .05 |
| ☐ 64 Jay Buhner | .02 | .10 |
| ☐ 65 Travis Fryman | .05 | .15 |

|  |  | | |
|---|---|---|---|
| ☐ 66 Marquis Grissom | .02 | .10 |
| ☐ 67 Mike Harkey | .01 | .05 |
| ☐ 68 Luis Polonia | .01 | .05 |
| ☐ 69 Ken Caminiti | .02 | .10 |
| ☐ 70 Chris Sabo | .01 | .05 |
| ☐ 71 Gregg Olson | .01 | .05 |
| ☐ 72 Carlton Fisk | .05 | .15 |
| ☐ 73 Juan Samuel | .01 | .05 |
| ☐ 74 Todd Stottlemyre | .01 | .05 |
| ☐ 75 Andre Dawson | .02 | .10 |
| ☐ 76 Alvin Davis | .01 | .05 |
| ☐ 77 Bill Doran | .01 | .05 |
| ☐ 78 B.J. Surhoff | .01 | .05 |
| ☐ 79 Kirk McCaskill | .01 | .05 |
| ☐ 80 Dale Murphy | .05 | .15 |
| ☐ 81 Jose DeLeon | .01 | .05 |
| ☐ 82 Alex Fernandez | .01 | .05 |
| ☐ 83 Ivan Calderon | .01 | .05 |
| ☐ 84 Brent Mayne | .01 | .05 |
| ☐ 85 Jody Reed | .01 | .05 |
| ☐ 86 Randy Tomlin | .01 | .05 |
| ☐ 87 Randy Milligan | .01 | .05 |
| ☐ 88 Pascual Perez | .01 | .05 |
| ☐ 89 Hensley Meulens | .01 | .05 |
| ☐ 90 Joe Carter | .02 | .10 |
| ☐ 91 Mike Moore | .01 | .05 |
| ☐ 92 Ozzie Guillen | .02 | .10 |
| ☐ 93 Shawn Hillegas | .01 | .05 |
| ☐ 94 Chili Davis | .02 | .10 |
| ☐ 95 Vince Coleman | .01 | .05 |
| ☐ 96 Jimmy Key | .02 | .10 |
| ☐ 97 Billy Ripken | .01 | .05 |
| ☐ 98 Dave Smith | .01 | .05 |
| ☐ 99 Tom Bolton | .01 | .05 |
| ☐ 100 Barry Larkin | .05 | .15 |
| ☐ 101 Kenny Rogers | .02 | .10 |
| ☐ 102 Mike Boddicker | .01 | .05 |
| ☐ 103 Kevin Elster | .01 | .05 |
| ☐ 104 Ken Hill | .01 | .05 |
| ☐ 105 Charlie Leibrandt | .01 | .05 |
| ☐ 106 Pat Combs | .01 | .05 |
| ☐ 107 Hubie Brooks | .01 | .05 |
| ☐ 108 Julio Franco | .02 | .10 |
| ☐ 109 Vicente Palacios | .01 | .05 |
| ☐ 110 Kal Daniels | .01 | .05 |
| ☐ 111 Bruce Hurst | .01 | .05 |
| ☐ 112 Willie McGee | .02 | .10 |
| ☐ 113 Ted Power | .01 | .05 |
| ☐ 114 Milt Thompson | .01 | .05 |
| ☐ 115 Doug Drabek | .01 | .05 |
| ☐ 116 Rafael Belliard | .01 | .05 |
| ☐ 117 Scott Garrelts | .01 | .05 |
| ☐ 118 Terry Mulholland | .01 | .05 |
| ☐ 119 Jay Howell | .01 | .05 |
| ☐ 120 Danny Jackson | .01 | .05 |
| ☐ 121 Scott Ruskin | .01 | .05 |
| ☐ 122 Robin Ventura | .02 | .10 |
| ☐ 123 Bip Roberts | .01 | .05 |
| ☐ 124 Jeff Russell | .01 | .05 |
| ☐ 125 Hal Morris | .01 | .05 |
| ☐ 126 Teddy Higuera | .01 | .05 |
| ☐ 127 Luis Sojo | .01 | .05 |
| ☐ 128 Carlos Baerga | .01 | .05 |
| ☐ 129 Jeff Ballard | .01 | .05 |
| ☐ 130 Tom Gordon | .01 | .05 |
| ☐ 131 Sid Bream | .01 | .05 |
| ☐ 132 Rance Mulliniks | .01 | .05 |
| ☐ 133 Andy Benes | .01 | .05 |
| ☐ 134 Mickey Tettleton | .01 | .05 |
| ☐ 135 Rich DeLucia | .01 | .05 |
| ☐ 136 Tom Pagnozzi | .01 | .05 |
| ☐ 137 Harold Baines | .02 | .10 |
| ☐ 138 Danny Darwin | .01 | .05 |
| ☐ 139 Kevin Bass | .01 | .05 |
| ☐ 140 Chris Nabholz | .01 | .05 |
| ☐ 141 Pete O'Brien | .01 | .05 |
| ☐ 142 Jeff Treadway | .01 | .05 |
| ☐ 143 Mickey Morandini | .01 | .05 |
| ☐ 144 Eric King | .01 | .05 |
| ☐ 145 Danny Tartabull | .05 | .15 |
| ☐ 146 Lance Johnson | .01 | .05 |
| ☐ 147 Casey Candaele | .01 | .05 |
| ☐ 148 Felix Fermin | .01 | .05 |
| ☐ 149 Rich Rodriguez | .01 | .05 |
| ☐ 150 Dwight Evans | .05 | .15 |
| ☐ 151 Joe Klink | .01 | .05 |
| ☐ 152 Kevin Reimer | .01 | .05 |
| ☐ 153 Orlando Merced | .01 | .05 |
| ☐ 154 Mel Hall | .01 | .05 |
| ☐ 155 Randy Myers | .01 | .05 |
| ☐ 156 Greg A. Harris | .01 | .05 |
| ☐ 157 Jeff Brantley | .01 | .05 |
| ☐ 158 Jim Eisenreich | .01 | .05 |
| ☐ 159 Luis Rivera | .01 | .05 |
| ☐ 160 Cris Carpenter | .01 | .05 |
| ☐ 161 Bruce Ruffin | .01 | .05 |
| ☐ 162 Omar Vizquel | .05 | .15 |
| ☐ 163 Gerald Alexander | .01 | .05 |
| ☐ 164 Mark Guthrie | .01 | .05 |
| ☐ 165 Scott Lewis | .01 | .05 |
| ☐ 166 Bill Sampen | .01 | .05 |
| ☐ 167 Dave Anderson | .01 | .05 |
| ☐ 168 Kevin McReynolds | .01 | .05 |
| ☐ 169 Jose Vizcaino | .01 | .05 |
| ☐ 170 Bob Geren | .01 | .05 |
| ☐ 171 Mike Morgan | .01 | .05 |
| ☐ 172 Jim Gott | .01 | .05 |
| ☐ 173 Mike Pagliarulo | .01 | .05 |
| ☐ 174 Mike Jeffcoat | .01 | .05 |
| ☐ 175 Craig Lefferts | .01 | .05 |
| ☐ 176 Steve Finley | .02 | .10 |
| ☐ 177 Wally Backman | .01 | .05 |
| ☐ 178 Kent Mercker | .01 | .05 |
| ☐ 179 John Cerutti | .01 | .05 |
| ☐ 180 Jay Bell | .02 | .10 |
| ☐ 181 Dale Sveum | .01 | .05 |
| ☐ 182 Greg Gagne | .01 | .05 |
| ☐ 183 Donnie Hill | .01 | .05 |
| ☐ 184 Rex Hudler | .01 | .05 |
| ☐ 185 Pat Kelly | .01 | .05 |
| ☐ 186 Jeff D. Robinson | .01 | .05 |
| ☐ 187 Jeff Gray | .01 | .05 |
| ☐ 188 Jerry Willard | .01 | .05 |
| ☐ 189 Carlos Quintana | .01 | .05 |
| ☐ 190 Dennis Eckersley | .02 | .10 |
| ☐ 191 Kelly Downs | .01 | .05 |
| ☐ 192 Gregg Jefferies | .01 | .05 |
| ☐ 193 Darrin Fletcher | .01 | .05 |
| ☐ 194 Mike Jackson | .01 | .05 |
| ☐ 195 Eddie Murray | .08 | .25 |
| ☐ 196 Bill Landrum | .01 | .05 |
| ☐ 197 Eric Yelding | .01 | .05 |
| ☐ 198 Devon White | .02 | .10 |
| ☐ 199 Larry Walker | .01 | .05 |
| ☐ 200 Ryne Sandberg | .15 | .40 |
| ☐ 201 Dave Magadan | .01 | .05 |
| ☐ 202 Steve Chitren | .01 | .05 |
| ☐ 203 Scott Fletcher | .01 | .05 |
| ☐ 204 Dwayne Henry | .01 | .05 |
| ☐ 205 Scott Coolbaugh | .01 | .05 |
| ☐ 206 Tracy Jones | .01 | .05 |
| ☐ 207 Von Hayes | .01 | .05 |
| ☐ 208 Bob Melvin | .01 | .05 |
| ☐ 209 Scott Scudder | .01 | .05 |
| ☐ 210 Luis Gonzalez | .02 | .10 |
| ☐ 211 Scott Sanderson | .01 | .05 |
| ☐ 212 Chris Donnels | .01 | .05 |
| ☐ 213 Heathcliff Slocumb | .01 | .05 |
| ☐ 214 Mike Timlin | .01 | .05 |
| ☐ 215 Brian Harper | .01 | .05 |
| ☐ 216 Juan Berenguer UER (Decimal point missing in IP) | .01 | .05 |
| ☐ 217 Mike Henneman | .01 | .05 |
| ☐ 218 Bill Spiers | .01 | .05 |
| ☐ 219 Scott Terry | .01 | .05 |
| ☐ 220 Frank Viola | .02 | .10 |
| ☐ 221 Mark Eichhorn | .01 | .05 |
| ☐ 222 Ernest Riles | .01 | .05 |
| ☐ 223 Ray Lankford | .02 | .10 |
| ☐ 224 Pete Harnisch | .01 | .05 |
| ☐ 225 Bobby Bonilla | .01 | .05 |
| ☐ 226 Mike Scioscia | .01 | .05 |
| ☐ 227 Joel Skinner | .01 | .05 |
| ☐ 228 Brian Holman | .01 | .05 |
| ☐ 229 Gilberto Reyes | .01 | .05 |
| ☐ 230 Matt Williams | .02 | .10 |
| ☐ 231 Jaime Navarro | .01 | .05 |
| ☐ 232 Jose Rijo | .01 | .05 |
| ☐ 233 Atlee Hammaker | .01 | .05 |
| ☐ 234 Tim Teufel | .01 | .05 |
| ☐ 235 John Kruk | .02 | .10 |
| ☐ 236 Kurt Stillwell | .01 | .05 |
| ☐ 237 Dan Pasqua | .01 | .05 |
| ☐ 238 Tim Crews | .01 | .05 |
| ☐ 239 Dave Gallagher | .01 | .05 |
| ☐ 240 Leo Gomez | .01 | .05 |
| ☐ 241 Steve Avery | .01 | .05 |
| ☐ 242 Bill Gullickson | .01 | .05 |
| ☐ 243 Mark Portugal | .01 | .05 |
| ☐ 244 Lee Guetterman | .01 | .05 |
| ☐ 245 Benito Santiago | .02 | .10 |
| ☐ 246 Jim Gantner | .01 | .05 |
| ☐ 247 Robby Thompson | .01 | .05 |
| ☐ 248 Terry Shumpert | .01 | .05 |
| ☐ 249 Mike Bell | .01 | .05 |
| ☐ 250 Harold Reynolds | .02 | .10 |
| ☐ 251 Mike Felder | .01 | .05 |
| ☐ 252 Bill Pecota | .01 | .05 |
| ☐ 253 Bill Krueger | .01 | .05 |
| ☐ 254 Alfredo Griffin | .01 | .05 |
| ☐ 255 Lou Whitaker | .02 | .10 |
| ☐ 256 Roy Smith | .01 | .05 |
| ☐ 257 Jerald Clark | .01 | .05 |
| ☐ 258 Sammy Sosa | .06 | .25 |
| ☐ 259 Tim Naehring | .01 | .05 |
| ☐ 260 Dave Righetti | .02 | .10 |
| ☐ 261 Paul Gibson | .01 | .05 |
| ☐ 262 Chris James | .01 | .05 |
| ☐ 263 Larry Andersen | .01 | .05 |
| ☐ 264 Storm Davis | .01 | .05 |
| ☐ 265 Jose Lind | .01 | .05 |
| ☐ 266 Greg Hibbard | .01 | .05 |
| ☐ 267 Norm Charlton | .01 | .05 |
| ☐ 268 Paul Kilgus | .01 | .05 |
| ☐ 269 Greg Maddux | .15 | .40 |
| ☐ 270 Ellis Burks | .02 | .10 |
| ☐ 271 Frank Tanana | .01 | .05 |
| ☐ 272 Gene Larkin | .01 | .05 |
| ☐ 273 Ron Hassey | .01 | .05 |
| ☐ 274 Jeff M. Robinson | .01 | .05 |
| ☐ 275 Steve Howe | .01 | .05 |
| ☐ 276 Daryl Boston | .01 | .05 |
| ☐ 277 Mark Lee | .01 | .05 |
| ☐ 278 Jose Segura | .01 | .05 |
| ☐ 279 Lance Blankenship | .01 | .05 |
| ☐ 280 Don Slaught | .01 | .05 |
| ☐ 281 Russ Swan | .01 | .05 |
| ☐ 282 Bob Tewksbury | .01 | .05 |
| ☐ 283 Geno Petralli | .01 | .05 |
| ☐ 284 Shane Mack | .01 | .05 |
| ☐ 285 Bob Scanlan | .01 | .05 |
| ☐ 286 Tim Leary | .01 | .05 |
| ☐ 287 John Smoltz | .05 | .15 |
| ☐ 288 Pat Borders | .01 | .05 |
| ☐ 289 Mark Davidson | .01 | .05 |
| ☐ 290 Sam Horn | .01 | .05 |
| ☐ 291 Lenny Harris | .01 | .05 |
| ☐ 292 Franklin Stubbs | .01 | .05 |
| ☐ 293 Thomas Howard | .01 | .05 |
| ☐ 294 Steve Lyons | .01 | .05 |
| ☐ 295 Francisco Oliveras | .01 | .05 |
| ☐ 296 Terry Leach | .01 | .05 |
| ☐ 297 Barry Jones | .01 | .05 |
| ☐ 298 Lance Parrish | .02 | .10 |
| ☐ 299 Wally Whitehurst | .01 | .05 |
| ☐ 300 Bob Welch | .01 | .05 |
| ☐ 301 Charlie Hayes | .01 | .05 |
| ☐ 302 Charlie Hough | .02 | .10 |
| ☐ 303 Gary Redus | .01 | .05 |
| ☐ 304 Scott Bradley | .01 | .05 |
| ☐ 305 Jose Oquendo | .01 | .05 |
| ☐ 306 Pete Incaviglia | .01 | .05 |
| ☐ 307 Marvin Freeman | .01 | .05 |
| ☐ 308 Gary Pettis | .01 | .05 |
| ☐ 309 Joe Slusarski | .01 | .05 |
| ☐ 310 Kevin Seitzer | .01 | .05 |
| ☐ 311 Jeff Reed | .01 | .05 |
| ☐ 312 Pat Tabler | .01 | .05 |
| ☐ 313 Mike Maddux | .01 | .05 |
| ☐ 314 Bob Milacki | .01 | .05 |
| ☐ 315 Eric Anthony | .01 | .05 |
| ☐ 316 Dante Bichette | .02 | .10 |
| ☐ 317 Steve Decker | .01 | .05 |
| ☐ 318 Jack Clark | .02 | .10 |
| ☐ 319 Doug Dascenzo | .01 | .05 |
| ☐ 320 Scott Leius | .01 | .05 |
| ☐ 321 Jim Leyritz | .01 | .05 |
| ☐ 322 Bryan Harvey | .01 | .05 |
| ☐ 323 Spike Owen | .01 | .05 |
| ☐ 324 Roberto Kelly | .01 | .05 |
| ☐ 325 Stan Belinda | .01 | .05 |
| ☐ 326 Joey Cora | .01 | .05 |
| ☐ 327 Jeff Innis | .01 | .05 |

|  |  | | |
|---|---|---|---|
| ❑ 328 | Willie Wilson | .01 | .05 |
| ❑ 329 | Juan Agosto | .01 | .05 |
| ❑ 330 | Charles Nagy | .01 | .05 |
| ❑ 331 | Scott Bailes | .01 | .05 |
| ❑ 332 | Pete Schourek | .01 | .05 |
| ❑ 333 | Mike Flanagan | .01 | .05 |
| ❑ 334 | Omar Olivares | .01 | .05 |
| ❑ 335 | Dennis Lamp | .01 | .05 |
| ❑ 336 | Tommy Greene | .01 | .05 |
| ❑ 337 | Randy Velarde | .01 | .05 |
| ❑ 338 | Tom Lampkin | .01 | .05 |
| ❑ 339 | John Russell | .01 | .05 |
| ❑ 340 | Bob Kipper | .01 | .05 |
| ❑ 341 | Todd Burns | .01 | .05 |
| ❑ 342 | Ron Jones | .01 | .05 |
| ❑ 343 | Dave Valle | .01 | .05 |
| ❑ 344 | Mike Heath | .01 | .05 |
| ❑ 345 | John Olerud | .02 | .10 |
| ❑ 346 | Gerald Young | .01 | .05 |
| ❑ 347 | Ken Patterson | .01 | .05 |
| ❑ 348 | Les Lancaster | .01 | .05 |
| ❑ 349 | Steve Crawford | .01 | .05 |
| ❑ 350 | John Candelaria | .01 | .05 |
| ❑ 351 | Mike Aldrete | .01 | .05 |
| ❑ 352 | Mariano Duncan | .01 | .05 |
| ❑ 353 | Julio Machado | .01 | .05 |
| ❑ 354 | Ken Williams | .01 | .05 |
| ❑ 355 | Walt Terrell | .01 | .05 |
| ❑ 356 | Mitch Williams | .01 | .05 |
| ❑ 357 | Al Newman | .01 | .05 |
| ❑ 358 | Bud Black | .01 | .05 |
| ❑ 359 | Joe Hesketh | .01 | .05 |
| ❑ 360 | Paul Assenmacher | .01 | .05 |
| ❑ 361 | Bo Jackson | .08 | .25 |
| ❑ 362 | Jeff Blauser | .01 | .05 |
| ❑ 363 | Mike Brumley | .01 | .05 |
| ❑ 364 | Jim Deshaies | .01 | .05 |
| ❑ 365 | Brady Anderson | .02 | .10 |
| ❑ 366 | Chuck McElroy | .01 | .05 |
| ❑ 367 | Matt Merullo | .01 | .05 |
| ❑ 368 | Tim Belcher | .01 | .05 |
| ❑ 369 | Luis Aquino | .01 | .05 |
| ❑ 370 | Joe Oliver | .01 | .05 |
| ❑ 371 | Greg Swindell | .01 | .05 |
| ❑ 372 | Lee Stevens | .01 | .05 |
| ❑ 373 | Mark Knudson | .01 | .05 |
| ❑ 374 | Bill Wegman | .01 | .05 |
| ❑ 375 | Jerry Don Gleaton | .01 | .05 |
| ❑ 376 | Pedro Guerrero | .02 | .10 |
| ❑ 377 | Randy Bush | .01 | .05 |
| ❑ 378 | Greg W. Harris | .01 | .05 |
| ❑ 379 | Eric Plunk | .01 | .05 |
| ❑ 380 | Jose DeJesus | .01 | .05 |
| ❑ 381 | Bobby Witt | .01 | .05 |
| ❑ 382 | Curtis Wilkerson | .01 | .05 |
| ❑ 383 | Gene Nelson | .01 | .05 |
| ❑ 384 | Wes Chamberlain | .01 | .05 |
| ❑ 385 | Tom Henke | .01 | .05 |
| ❑ 386 | Mark Lemke | .01 | .05 |
| ❑ 387 | Greg Briley | .01 | .05 |
| ❑ 388 | Rafael Ramirez | .01 | .05 |
| ❑ 389 | Tony Fossas | .01 | .05 |
| ❑ 390 | Henry Cotto | .01 | .05 |
| ❑ 391 | Tim Hulett | .01 | .05 |
| ❑ 392 | Dean Palmer | .02 | .10 |
| ❑ 393 | Glenn Braggs | .01 | .05 |
| ❑ 394 | Mark Salas | .01 | .05 |
| ❑ 395 | Rusty Meacham | .01 | .05 |
| ❑ 396 | Andy Ashby | .01 | .05 |
| ❑ 397 | Jose Melendez | .01 | .05 |
| ❑ 398 | Warren Newson | .01 | .05 |
| ❑ 399 | Frank Castillo | .01 | .05 |
| ❑ 400 | Chito Martinez | .01 | .05 |
| ❑ 401 | Bernie Williams | .05 | .15 |
| ❑ 402 | Derek Bell | .02 | .10 |
| ❑ 403 | Javier Ortiz | .01 | .05 |
| ❑ 404 | Tim Sherrill | .01 | .05 |
| ❑ 405 | Rob MacDonald | .01 | .05 |
| ❑ 406 | Phil Plantier | .05 | .15 |
| ❑ 407 | Troy Afenir | .01 | .05 |
| ❑ 408 | Gino Minutelli | .01 | .05 |
| ❑ 409 | Reggie Jefferson | .05 | .15 |
| ❑ 410 | Mike Remlinger | .01 | .05 |
| ❑ 411 | Carlos Rodriguez | .01 | .05 |
| ❑ 412 | Joe Redfield | .01 | .05 |
| ❑ 413 | Alonzo Powell | .01 | .05 |
| ❑ 414 | Scott Livingstone UER (Travis Fryman) | | |
| ❑ 415 | Scott Kamieniecki | .01 | .05 |
| ❑ 416 | Tim Spehr | .01 | .05 |
| ❑ 417 | Brian Hunter | .01 | .05 |
| ❑ 418 | Ced Landrum | .01 | .05 |
| ❑ 419 | Bret Barberie | .01 | .05 |
| ❑ 420 | Kevin Morton | .01 | .05 |
| ❑ 421 | Doug Henry RC | .02 | .10 |
| ❑ 422 | Doug Piatt | .01 | .05 |
| ❑ 423 | Pat Rice | .01 | .05 |
| ❑ 424 | Juan Guzman | .05 | .15 |
| ❑ 425 | Nolan Ryan SPEC | .20 | .50 |
| ❑ 426 | Tommy Greene NH | .01 | .05 |
| ❑ 427 | Bob Milacki and Mike Flanagan NH (Mark Williamson) | .01 | .05 |
| ❑ 428 | Wilson Alvarez NH | .01 | .05 |
| ❑ 429 | Otis Nixon HL | .01 | .05 |
| ❑ 430 | Rickey Henderson HL | .05 | .15 |
| ❑ 431 | Cecil Fielder AS | .01 | .05 |
| ❑ 432 | Julio Franco AS | .15 | .40 |
| ❑ 433 | Cal Ripken AS | .15 | .40 |
| ❑ 434 | Wade Boggs AS | .02 | .10 |
| ❑ 435 | Joe Carter AS | .01 | .05 |
| ❑ 436 | Ken Griffey Jr. AS | .08 | .25 |
| ❑ 437 | Ruben Sierra AS | .01 | .05 |
| ❑ 438 | Scott Erickson AS | .01 | .05 |
| ❑ 439 | Tom Henke AS | .01 | .05 |
| ❑ 440 | Terry Steinbach AS | .01 | .05 |
| ❑ 441 | Rickey Henderson DT | .08 | .25 |
| ❑ 442 | Ryne Sandberg DT | .15 | .40 |
| ❑ 443 | Otis Nixon | .01 | .05 |
| ❑ 444 | Scott Radinsky | .01 | .05 |
| ❑ 445 | Mark Grace | .05 | .15 |
| ❑ 446 | Tony Pena | .01 | .05 |
| ❑ 447 | Billy Hatcher | .01 | .05 |
| ❑ 448 | Glenallen Hill | .01 | .05 |
| ❑ 449 | Chris Gwynn | .01 | .05 |
| ❑ 450 | Tom Glavine | .05 | .15 |
| ❑ 451 | John Habyan | .01 | .05 |
| ❑ 452 | Al Osuna | .01 | .05 |
| ❑ 453 | Tony Phillips | .01 | .05 |
| ❑ 454 | Greg Cadaret | .01 | .05 |
| ❑ 455 | Rob Dibble | .02 | .10 |
| ❑ 456 | Rick Honeycutt | .01 | .05 |
| ❑ 457 | Jerome Walton | .01 | .05 |
| ❑ 458 | Mookie Wilson | .02 | .10 |
| ❑ 459 | Mark Gubicza | .01 | .05 |
| ❑ 460 | Craig Biggio | .05 | .15 |
| ❑ 461 | Dave Cochrane | .01 | .05 |
| ❑ 462 | Keith Miller | .01 | .05 |
| ❑ 463 | Alex Cole | .01 | .05 |
| ❑ 464 | Pete Smith | .01 | .05 |
| ❑ 465 | Brett Butler | .02 | .10 |
| ❑ 466 | Jeff Huson | .01 | .05 |
| ❑ 467 | Steve Lake | .01 | .05 |
| ❑ 468 | Lloyd Moseby | .01 | .05 |
| ❑ 469 | Tim McIntosh | .01 | .05 |
| ❑ 470 | Dennis Martinez | .02 | .10 |
| ❑ 471 | Greg Myers | .01 | .05 |
| ❑ 472 | Mackey Sasser | .01 | .05 |
| ❑ 473 | Junior Ortiz | .01 | .05 |
| ❑ 474 | Greg Olson | .01 | .05 |
| ❑ 475 | Steve Sax | .02 | .10 |
| ❑ 476 | Ricky Jordan | .01 | .05 |
| ❑ 477 | Max Venable | .01 | .05 |
| ❑ 478 | Brian McRae | .05 | .15 |
| ❑ 479 | Doug Simons | .01 | .05 |
| ❑ 480 | Rickey Henderson | .08 | .25 |
| ❑ 481 | Gary Varsho | .01 | .05 |
| ❑ 482 | Carl Willis | .01 | .05 |
| ❑ 483 | Rick Wilkins | .01 | .05 |
| ❑ 484 | Donn Pall | .01 | .05 |
| ❑ 485 | Edgar Martinez | .05 | .15 |
| ❑ 486 | Tom Foley | .01 | .05 |
| ❑ 487 | Mark Williamson | .01 | .05 |
| ❑ 488 | Jack Armstrong | .01 | .05 |
| ❑ 489 | Gary Carter | .02 | .10 |
| ❑ 490 | Ruben Sierra | .10 | .25 |
| ❑ 491 | Gerald Perry | .01 | .05 |
| ❑ 492 | Rob Murphy | .01 | .05 |
| ❑ 493 | Zane Smith | .01 | .05 |
| ❑ 494 | Darryl Kile | .02 | .10 |
| ❑ 495 | Kelly Gruber | .01 | .05 |
| ❑ 496 | Jerry Browne | .01 | .05 |
| ❑ 497 | Darryl Hamilton | .01 | .05 |
| ❑ 498 | Mike Stanton | .01 | .05 |
| ❑ 499 | Mark Leonard | .01 | .05 |
| ❑ 500 | Jose Canseco | .05 | .15 |
| ❑ 501 | Dave Martinez | .01 | .05 |
| ❑ 502 | Jose Guzman | .01 | .05 |
| ❑ 503 | Terry Kennedy | .01 | .05 |
| ❑ 504 | Ed Sprague | .01 | .05 |
| ❑ 505 | Frank Thomas | .08 | .25 |
| ❑ 506 | Darren Daulton | .02 | .10 |
| ❑ 507 | Kevin Tapani | .01 | .05 |
| ❑ 508 | Luis Salazar | .01 | .05 |
| ❑ 509 | Paul Faries | .01 | .05 |
| ❑ 510 | Sandy Alomar Jr. | .01 | .05 |
| ❑ 511 | Jeff King | .01 | .05 |
| ❑ 512 | Gary Thurman | .01 | .05 |
| ❑ 513 | Chris Hammond | .01 | .05 |
| ❑ 514 | Pedro Munoz | .01 | .05 |
| ❑ 515 | Alan Trammell | .02 | .10 |
| ❑ 516 | Geronimo Pena | .01 | .05 |
| ❑ 517 | Rodney McCray UER (Stole 6 bases in 1990& not 5; | | |
| ❑ 518 | Manny Lee | .01 | .05 |
| ❑ 519 | Junior Felix | .01 | .05 |
| ❑ 520 | Kirk Gibson | .02 | .10 |
| ❑ 521 | Darrin Jackson | .01 | .05 |
| ❑ 522 | John Burkett | .01 | .05 |
| ❑ 523 | Jeff Johnson | .01 | .05 |
| ❑ 524 | Jim Corsi | .01 | .05 |
| ❑ 525 | Robin Yount | .15 | .40 |
| ❑ 526 | Jamie Quirk | .01 | .05 |
| ❑ 527 | Bob Ojeda | .01 | .05 |
| ❑ 528 | Mark Lewis | .01 | .05 |
| ❑ 529 | Bryn Smith | .01 | .05 |
| ❑ 530 | Kent Hrbek | .02 | .10 |
| ❑ 531 | Dennis Boyd | .01 | .05 |
| ❑ 532 | Ron Karkovice | .01 | .05 |
| ❑ 533 | Don August | .01 | .05 |
| ❑ 534 | Todd Frohwirth | .01 | .05 |
| ❑ 535 | Wally Joyner | .02 | .10 |
| ❑ 536 | Dennis Rasmussen | .01 | .05 |
| ❑ 537 | Andy Allanson | .01 | .05 |
| ❑ 538 | Rich Gossage | .02 | .10 |
| ❑ 539 | John Marzano | .01 | .05 |
| ❑ 540 | Cal Ripken | .30 | .75 |
| ❑ 541 | Bill Swift UER (Brewers logo on front) | .01 | .05 |
| ❑ 542 | Kevin Appier | .02 | .10 |
| ❑ 543 | Dave Bergman | .01 | .05 |
| ❑ 544 | Bernard Gilkey | .01 | .05 |
| ❑ 545 | Mike Greenwell | .01 | .05 |
| ❑ 546 | Jose Uribe | .01 | .05 |
| ❑ 547 | Jesse Orosco | .01 | .05 |
| ❑ 548 | Bob Patterson | .01 | .05 |
| ❑ 549 | Mike Stanley | .01 | .05 |
| ❑ 550 | Howard Johnson | .01 | .05 |
| ❑ 551 | Joe Orsulak | .01 | .05 |
| ❑ 552 | Dick Schofield | .01 | .05 |
| ❑ 553 | Dave Hollins | .02 | .10 |
| ❑ 554 | David Segui | .01 | .05 |
| ❑ 555 | Barry Bonds | .40 | 1.00 |
| ❑ 556 | Mo Vaughn | .02 | .10 |
| ❑ 557 | Craig Wilson | .01 | .05 |
| ❑ 558 | Bobby Rose | .01 | .05 |
| ❑ 559 | Rod Nichols | .01 | .05 |
| ❑ 560 | Len Dykstra | .02 | .10 |
| ❑ 561 | Craig Grebeck | .01 | .05 |
| ❑ 562 | Darren Lewis | .01 | .05 |
| ❑ 563 | Todd Benzinger | .01 | .05 |
| ❑ 564 | Ed Whitson | .01 | .05 |
| ❑ 565 | Jesse Barfield | .01 | .05 |
| ❑ 566 | Lloyd McClendon | .01 | .05 |
| ❑ 567 | Dan Plesac | .01 | .05 |
| ❑ 568 | Danny Cox | .01 | .05 |
| ❑ 569 | Skeeter Barnes | .01 | .05 |
| ❑ 570 | Bobby Thigpen | .01 | .05 |
| ❑ 571 | Deion Sanders | .05 | .15 |
| ❑ 572 | Chuck Knoblauch | .02 | .10 |
| ❑ 573 | Matt Nokes | .01 | .05 |
| ❑ 574 | Herm Winningham | .01 | .05 |
| ❑ 575 | Tom Candiotti | .01 | .05 |
| ❑ 576 | Jeff Bagwell | .08 | .25 |
| ❑ 577 | Brook Jacoby | .01 | .05 |
| ❑ 578 | Chico Walker | .01 | .05 |
| ❑ 579 | Brian Downing | .01 | .05 |
| ❑ 580 | Dave Stewart | .02 | .10 |
| ❑ 581 | Francisco Cabrera | .01 | .05 |
| ❑ 582 | Rene Gonzales | .01 | .05 |
| ❑ 583 | Stan Javier | .01 | .05 |
| ❑ 584 | Randy Johnson | .08 | .25 |

not Woody&

|  |  | | |
|---|---|---|---|
| 585 | Chuck Finley | .02 | .10 |
| 586 | Mark Gardner | .01 | .05 |
| 587 | Mark Whiten | .01 | .05 |
| 588 | Garry Templeton | .01 | .05 |
| 589 | Gary Sheffield | .02 | .10 |
| 590 | Ozzie Smith | .15 | .40 |
| 591 | Candy Maldonado | .01 | .05 |
| 592 | Mike Sharperson | .01 | .05 |
| 593 | Carlos Martinez | .01 | .05 |
| 594 | Scott Bankhead | .01 | .05 |
| 595 | Tim Wallach | .01 | .05 |
| 596 | Tino Martinez | .05 | .15 |
| 597 | Roger McDowell | .01 | .05 |
| 598 | Cory Snyder | .01 | .05 |
| 599 | Andujar Cedeno | .01 | .05 |
| 600 | Kirby Puckett | .08 | .25 |
| 601 | Rick Parker | .01 | .05 |
| 602 | Todd Hundley | .01 | .05 |
| 603 | Greg Litton | .01 | .05 |
| 604 | Dave Johnson | .01 | .05 |
| 605 | John Franco | .02 | .10 |
| 606 | Mike Fetters | .01 | .05 |
| 607 | Luis Alicea | .01 | .05 |
| 608 | Trevor Wilson | .01 | .05 |
| 609 | Rob Ducey | .01 | .05 |
| 610 | Ramon Martinez | .01 | .05 |
| 611 | Dave Burba | .01 | .05 |
| 612 | Dwight Smith | .01 | .05 |
| 613 | Kevin Maas | .01 | .05 |
| 614 | John Costello | .01 | .05 |
| 615 | Glenn Davis | .01 | .05 |
| 616 | Shawn Abner | .01 | .05 |
| 617 | Scott Hemond | .01 | .05 |
| 618 | Tom Prince | .01 | .05 |
| 619 | Wally Ritchie | .01 | .05 |
| 620 | Jim Abbott | .05 | .15 |
| 621 | Charlie O'Brien | .01 | .05 |
| 622 | Jack Daugherty | .01 | .05 |
| 623 | Tommy Gregg | .01 | .05 |
| 624 | Jeff Shaw | .01 | .05 |
| 625 | Tony Gwynn | .10 | .30 |
| 626 | Mark Leiter | .01 | .05 |
| 627 | Jim Clancy | .01 | .05 |
| 628 | Tim Layana | .01 | .05 |
| 629 | Jeff Schaefer | .01 | .05 |
| 630 | Lee Smith | .02 | .10 |
| 631 | Wade Taylor | .01 | .05 |
| 632 | Mike Simms | .01 | .05 |
| 633 | Terry Steinbach | .01 | .05 |
| 634 | Shawon Dunston | .01 | .05 |
| 635 | Tim Raines | .02 | .10 |
| 636 | Kirt Manwaring | .01 | .05 |
| 637 | Warren Cromartie | .01 | .05 |
| 638 | Luis Quinones | .01 | .05 |
| 639 | Greg Vaughn | .01 | .05 |
| 640 | Kevin Mitchell | .05 | .15 |
| 641 | Chris Hoiles | .01 | .05 |
| 642 | Tom Browning | .01 | .05 |
| 643 | Mitch Webster | .01 | .05 |
| 644 | Steve Olin | .01 | .05 |
| 645 | Tony Fernandez | .01 | .05 |
| 646 | Juan Bell | .01 | .05 |
| 647 | Joe Boever | .01 | .05 |
| 648 | Carney Lansford | .02 | .10 |
| 649 | Mike Benjamin | .01 | .05 |
| 650 | George Brett | .25 | .60 |
| 651 | Tim Burke | .01 | .05 |
| 652 | Jack Morris | .02 | .10 |
| 653 | Orel Hershiser | .02 | .10 |
| 654 | Mike Schooler | .01 | .05 |
| 655 | Andy Van Slyke | .05 | .15 |
| 656 | Dave Stieb | .01 | .05 |
| 657 | Dave Clark | .01 | .05 |
| 658 | Ben McDonald | .05 | .15 |
| 659 | John Smiley | .01 | .05 |
| 660 | Wade Boggs | .05 | .15 |
| 661 | Eric Bullock | .01 | .05 |
| 662 | Eric Show | .01 | .05 |
| 663 | Lenny Webster | .01 | .05 |
| 664 | Mike Huff | .01 | .05 |
| 665 | Rick Sutcliffe | .01 | .05 |
| 666 | Jeff Manto | .01 | .05 |
| 667 | Mike Fitzgerald | .01 | .05 |
| 668 | Matt Young | .01 | .05 |
| 669 | Dave West | .01 | .05 |
| 670 | Mike Hartley | .01 | .05 |
| 671 | Curt Schilling | .05 | .15 |
| 672 | Brian Bohanon | .01 | .05 |
| 673 | Cecil Espy | .01 | .05 |
| 674 | Joe Grahe | .01 | .05 |
| 675 | Sid Fernandez | .01 | .05 |
| 676 | Edwin Nunez | .01 | .05 |
| 677 | Hector Villanueva | .01 | .05 |
| 678 | Sean Berry | .01 | .05 |
| 679 | Dave Eiland | .01 | .05 |
| 680 | David Cone | .02 | .10 |
| 681 | Mike Bordick | .01 | .05 |
| 682 | Tony Castillo | .01 | .05 |
| 683 | John Barfield | .01 | .05 |
| 684 | Jeff Hamilton | .01 | .05 |
| 685 | Ken Dayley | .01 | .05 |
| 686 | Carmelo Martinez | .01 | .05 |
| 687 | Mike Capel | .01 | .05 |
| 688 | Scott Chiamparino | .01 | .05 |
| 689 | Rich Gedman | .01 | .05 |
| 690 | Rich Monteleone | .01 | .05 |
| 691 | Alejandro Pena | .01 | .05 |
| 692 | Oscar Azocar | .01 | .05 |
| 693 | Jim Poole | .01 | .05 |
| 694 | Mike Gardner | .01 | .05 |
| 695 | Steve Buechele | .01 | .05 |
| 696 | Rudy Seanez | .01 | .05 |
| 697 | Paul Abbott | .01 | .05 |
| 698 | Steve Searcy | .01 | .05 |
| 699 | Jose Offerman | .01 | .05 |
| 700 | Ivan Rodriguez | .08 | .25 |
| 701 | Joe Girardi | .01 | .05 |
| 702 | Tony Perezchica | .01 | .05 |
| 703 | Paul McClellan | .01 | .05 |
| 704 | David Howard | .01 | .05 |
| 705 | Dan Petry | .01 | .05 |
| 706 | Jack Howell | .01 | .05 |
| 707 | Jose Mesa | .01 | .05 |
| 708 | Randy St. Claire | .01 | .05 |
| 709 | Kevin Brown | .02 | .10 |
| 710 | Ron Darling | .01 | .05 |
| 711 | Jason Grimsley | .01 | .05 |
| 712 | John Orton | .01 | .05 |
| 713 | Shawn Boskie | .01 | .05 |
| 714 | Pat Clements | .01 | .05 |
| 715 | Brian Barnes | .01 | .05 |
| 716 | Luis Lopez | .01 | .05 |
| 717 | Bob McClure | .01 | .05 |
| 718 | Mark Davis | .01 | .05 |
| 719 | Dann Bilardello | .01 | .05 |
| 720 | Tom Edens | .01 | .05 |
| 721 | Willie Fraser | .01 | .05 |
| 722 | Curt Young | .01 | .05 |
| 723 | Neal Heaton | .01 | .05 |
| 724 | Craig Worthington | .01 | .05 |
| 725 | Mel Rojas | .01 | .05 |
| 726 | Daryl Irvine | .01 | .05 |
| 727 | Roger Mason | .01 | .05 |
| 728 | Kirk Dressendorfer | .01 | .05 |
| 729 | Scott Aldred | .01 | .05 |
| 730 | Willie Blair | .01 | .05 |
| 731 | Allan Anderson | .01 | .05 |
| 732 | Dana Kiecker | .01 | .05 |
| 733 | Jose Gonzalez | .01 | .05 |
| 734 | Brian Drahman | .01 | .05 |
| 735 | Brad Komminsk | .01 | .05 |
| 736 | Arthur Rhodes | .01 | .05 |
| 737 | Terry Mathews | .01 | .05 |
| 738 | Jeff Fassero | .01 | .05 |
| 739 | Mike Magnante RC | .02 | .10 |
| 740 | Kip Gross | .01 | .05 |
| 741 | Jim Hunter | .01 | .05 |
| 742 | Jose Mota | .01 | .05 |
| 743 | Joe Bitker | .01 | .05 |
| 744 | Tim Mauser | .01 | .05 |
| 745 | Ramon Garcia | .01 | .05 |
| 746 | Rod Beck RC | .08 | .25 |
| 747 | Jim Austin RC | .01 | .05 |
| 748 | Keith Mitchell | .01 | .05 |
| 749 | Wayne Rosenthal | .01 | .05 |
| 750 | Bryan Hickerson RC | .02 | .10 |
| 751 | Bruce Egloff | .01 | .05 |
| 752 | John Wehner | .01 | .05 |
| 753 | Darren Holmes | .01 | .05 |
| 754 | Dave Hansen | .01 | .05 |
| 755 | Mike Mussina | .08 | .25 |
| 756 | Anthony Young | .01 | .05 |
| 757 | Ron Tingley | .01 | .05 |
| 758 | Ricky Bones | .01 | .05 |
| 759 | Mark Wohlers | .01 | .05 |
| 760 | Wilson Alvarez | .01 | .05 |
| 761 | Harvey Pulliam | .01 | .05 |
| 762 | Ryan Bowen | .01 | .05 |
| 763 | Terry Bross | .01 | .05 |
| 764 | Joel Johnston | .01 | .05 |
| 765 | Terry McDaniel | .01 | .05 |
| 766 | Esteban Beltre | .01 | .05 |
| 767 | Rob Maurer | .01 | .05 |
| 768 | Ted Wood | .01 | .05 |
| 769 | Mo Sanford | .01 | .05 |
| 770 | Jeff Carter | .01 | .05 |
| 771 | Gil Heredia RC | .08 | .25 |
| 772 | Monty Farias | .01 | .05 |
| 773 | Will Clark AS | .02 | .10 |
| 774 | Ryne Sandberg AS | .08 | .25 |
| 775 | Barry Larkin AS | .02 | .10 |
| 776 | Howard Johnson AS | .01 | .05 |
| 777 | Barry Bonds AS | .20 | .50 |
| 778 | Brett Butler AS | .01 | .05 |
| 779 | Tony Gwynn AS | .05 | .15 |
| 780 | Ramon Martinez AS | .01 | .05 |
| 781 | Lee Smith AS | .01 | .05 |
| 782 | Mike Scioscia AS | .01 | .05 |
| 783 | Dennis Martinez HL UER | .01 | .05 |
| 784 | Dennis Martinez NH | .01 | .05 |
| 785 | Mark Gardner NH | .01 | .05 |
| 786 | Bret Saberhagen NH | .01 | .05 |
| 787 | Kent Mercker NH | | |
| | Mark Wohlers | | |
| | Alejandro Pena | .01 | .05 |
| 788 | Cal Ripken MVP | .15 | .40 |
| 789 | Terry Pendleton MVP | .01 | .05 |
| 790 | Roger Clemens CY | .08 | .25 |
| 791 | Tom Glavine CY | .02 | .10 |
| 792 | Chuck Knoblauch ROY | .01 | .05 |
| 793 | Jeff Bagwell ROY | .05 | .15 |
| 794 | Cal Ripken MOY | .15 | .40 |
| 795 | David Cone HL | .01 | .05 |
| 796 | Kirby Puckett HL | .05 | .15 |
| 797 | Steve Avery HL | .01 | .05 |
| 798 | Jack Morris HL | .01 | .05 |
| 799 | Allen Watson RC | .02 | .10 |
| 800 | Manny Ramirez RC | 1.50 | 4.00 |
| 801 | Cliff Floyd RC | .30 | .75 |
| 802 | Al Shirley RC | .02 | .10 |
| 803 | Brian Barber RC | .02 | .10 |
| 804 | Jon Farrell RC | .02 | .10 |
| 805 | Brent Gates RC | .02 | .10 |
| 806 | Scott Ruffcorn RC | .02 | .10 |
| 807 | Tyrone Hill RC | .02 | .10 |
| 808 | Benji Gil RC | .08 | .25 |
| 809 | Aaron Sele RC | .08 | .25 |
| 810 | Tyler Green RC | .02 | .10 |
| 811 | Chris Jones | .01 | .05 |
| 812 | Steve Wilson | .01 | .05 |
| 813 | Freddie Benavides | .01 | .05 |
| 814 | Don Wakamatsu | .01 | .05 |
| 815 | Mike Humphreys | .01 | .05 |
| 816 | Scott Servais | .01 | .05 |
| 817 | Rico Rossy | .01 | .05 |
| 818 | John Ramos | .01 | .05 |
| 819 | Rob Mallicoat | .01 | .05 |
| 820 | Milt Hill | .01 | .05 |
| 821 | Carlos Garcia | .01 | .05 |
| 822 | Stan Royer | .01 | .05 |
| 823 | Jeff Plympton | .01 | .05 |
| 824 | Braulio Castillo | .01 | .05 |
| 825 | David Haas | .01 | .05 |
| 826 | Luis Mercedes | .01 | .05 |
| 827 | Eric Karros | .02 | .10 |
| 828 | Shawn Hare RC | .02 | .10 |
| 829 | Reggie Sanders | .02 | .10 |
| 830 | Tom Goodwin | .01 | .05 |
| 831 | Dan Gakeler | .01 | .05 |
| 832 | Stacy Jones | .01 | .05 |
| 833 | Kim Batiste | .01 | .05 |
| 834 | Cal Eldred | .01 | .05 |
| 835 | Chris George | .01 | .05 |
| 836 | Wayne Housie | .01 | .05 |
| 837 | Mike Ignasiak | .01 | .05 |
| 838 | Josias Manzanillo RC | .02 | .10 |
| 839 | Jim Olander | .01 | .05 |
| 840 | Gary Cooper | .01 | .05 |
| 841 | Royce Clayton | .02 | .10 |
| 842 | Hector Fajardo RC | .02 | .10 |
| 843 | Blaine Beatty | .01 | .05 |
| 844 | Jorge Pedre | .01 | .05 |
| 845 | Kenny Lofton | .05 | .15 |
| 846 | Scott Brosius RC | .20 | .50 |

|  |  | | |
|---|---|---|---|
| ☐ 847 | Chris Cron | .01 | .05 |
| ☐ 848 | Dennis Boucher | .01 | .05 |
| ☐ 849 | Kyle Abbott | .01 | .05 |
| ☐ 850 | Bob Zupcic RC | .02 | .10 |
| ☐ 851 | Rheal Cormier | .01 | .05 |
| ☐ 852 | Jimmy Lewis RC | .01 | .05 |
| ☐ 853 | Anthony Telford | .01 | .05 |
| ☐ 854 | Cliff Brantley | .01 | .05 |
| ☐ 855 | Kevin Campbell | .01 | .05 |
| ☐ 856 | Craig Shipley | .01 | .05 |
| ☐ 857 | Chuck Carr | .01 | .05 |
| ☐ 858 | Tony Eusebio | .02 | .10 |
| ☐ 859 | Jim Thome | .40 | 1.00 |
| ☐ 860 | Vinny Castilla RC | .40 | 1.00 |
| ☐ 861 | Darin Howitt | .01 | .05 |
| ☐ 862 | Kevin Ward | .01 | .05 |
| ☐ 863 | Steve Wapnick | .01 | .05 |
| ☐ 864 | Rod Brewer RC | .02 | .10 |
| ☐ 865 | Todd Van Poppel | .08 | .25 |
| ☐ 866 | Jose Hernandez RC | .08 | .25 |
| ☐ 867 | Amalio Carreno | .01 | .05 |
| ☐ 868 | Calvin Jones | .01 | .05 |
| ☐ 869 | Jeff Gardner | .01 | .05 |
| ☐ 870 | Jarvis Brown | .01 | .05 |
| ☐ 871 | Eddie Taubensee RC | .08 | .25 |
| ☐ 872 | Andy Mota | .01 | .05 |
| ☐ 873 | Chris Haney | .01 | .05 |
| ☐ 874 | Roberto Hernandez | .01 | .05 |
| ☐ 875 | Laddie Renfroe | .01 | .05 |
| ☐ 876 | Scott Cooper | .08 | .25 |
| ☐ 877 | Armando Reynoso RC | .08 | .25 |
| ☐ 878 | Ty Cobb MEMO | .08 | .25 |
| ☐ 879 | Babe Ruth MEMO | .20 | .50 |
| ☐ 880 | Honus Wagner MEMO | .08 | .25 |
| ☐ 881 | Lou Gehrig MEMO | .15 | .40 |
| ☐ 882 | Satchel Paige MEMO | .08 | .25 |
| ☐ 883 | Will Clark DT | .02 | .10 |
| ☐ 884 | Cal Ripken DT | .75 | 2.00 |
| ☐ 885 | Wade Boggs DT | .05 | .15 |
| ☐ 886 | Kirby Puckett DT | .05 | .15 |
| ☐ 887 | Tony Gwynn DT | .05 | .15 |
| ☐ 888 | Craig Biggio DT | .01 | .05 |
| ☐ 889 | Scott Erickson DT | .01 | .05 |
| ☐ 890 | Tom Glavine DT | .05 | .15 |
| ☐ 891 | Rob Dibble DT | .02 | .10 |
| ☐ 892 | Mitch Williams DT | .01 | .05 |
| ☐ 893 | Frank Thomas DT | .05 | .15 |
| ☐ X672 | C.Knob 90S AU/3000 | 10.00 | 25.00 |

## 1993 Score

|  |  | | |
|---|---|---|---|
| ☐ | COMPLETE SET (660) | 15.00 | 40.00 |
| ☐ 1 | Ken Griffey Jr. | .30 | .75 |
| ☐ 2 | Gary Sheffield | .30 | .75 |
| ☐ 3 | Frank Thomas | .20 | .50 |
| ☐ 4 | Ryne Sandberg | .30 | .75 |
| ☐ 5 | Larry Walker | .10 | .30 |
| ☐ 6 | Cal Ripken | .60 | 1.50 |
| ☐ 7 | Roger Clemens | .40 | 1.00 |
| ☐ 8 | Bobby Bonilla | .07 | .20 |
| ☐ 9 | Carlos Baerga | .02 | .10 |
| ☐ 10 | Darren Daulton | .07 | .20 |
| ☐ 11 | Travis Fryman | .07 | .20 |
| ☐ 12 | Andy Van Slyke | .10 | .30 |
| ☐ 13 | Jose Canseco | .10 | .30 |
| ☐ 14 | Roberto Alomar | .10 | .30 |
| ☐ 15 | Tom Glavine | .10 | .30 |
| ☐ 16 | Barry Larkin | .10 | .30 |
| ☐ 17 | Gregg Jefferies | .07 | .20 |
| ☐ 18 | Craig Biggio | .02 | .10 |
| ☐ 19 | Shane Mack | .02 | .10 |
| ☐ 20 | Brett Butler | .07 | .20 |
| ☐ 21 | Dennis Eckersley | .10 | .30 |
| ☐ 22 | Will Clark | .10 | .30 |
| ☐ 23 | Don Mattingly | .50 | 1.25 |

|  |  | | |
|---|---|---|---|
| ☐ 24 | Tony Gwynn | .25 | .60 |
| ☐ 25 | Ivan Rodriguez | .10 | .30 |
| ☐ 26 | Shawon Dunston | .02 | .10 |
| ☐ 27 | Mike Mussina | .10 | .30 |
| ☐ 28 | Marquis Grissom | .07 | .20 |
| ☐ 29 | Charles Nagy | .02 | .10 |
| ☐ 30 | Len Dykstra | .07 | .20 |
| ☐ 31 | Cecil Fielder | .07 | .20 |
| ☐ 32 | Jay Bell | .02 | .10 |
| ☐ 33 | B.J. Surhoff | .07 | .20 |
| ☐ 34 | Bob Tewksbury | .02 | .10 |
| ☐ 35 | Danny Tartabull | .07 | .20 |
| ☐ 36 | Terry Pendleton | .07 | .20 |
| ☐ 37 | Jack Morris | .07 | .20 |
| ☐ 38 | Hal Morris | .02 | .10 |
| ☐ 39 | Luis Polonia | .02 | .10 |
| ☐ 40 | Ken Caminiti | .07 | .20 |
| ☐ 41 | Robin Ventura | .07 | .20 |
| ☐ 42 | Darryl Strawberry | .07 | .20 |
| ☐ 43 | Wally Joyner | .07 | .20 |
| ☐ 44 | Fred McGriff | .10 | .30 |
| ☐ 45 | Kevin Tapani | .02 | .10 |
| ☐ 46 | Matt Williams | .07 | .20 |
| ☐ 47 | Robin Yount | .30 | .75 |
| ☐ 48 | Ken Hill | .02 | .10 |
| ☐ 49 | Edgar Martinez | .10 | .30 |
| ☐ 50 | Mark Grace | .10 | .30 |
| ☐ 51 | Juan Gonzalez | .07 | .20 |
| ☐ 52 | Curt Schilling | .07 | .20 |
| ☐ 53 | Dwight Gooden | .07 | .20 |
| ☐ 54 | Chris Hoiles | .02 | .10 |
| ☐ 55 | Frank Viola | .07 | .20 |
| ☐ 56 | Ray Lankford | .07 | .20 |
| ☐ 57 | George Brett | .50 | 1.25 |
| ☐ 58 | Kenny Lofton | .07 | .20 |
| ☐ 59 | Nolan Ryan | .75 | 2.00 |
| ☐ 60 | Mickey Tettleton | .07 | .20 |
| ☐ 61 | John Smoltz | .10 | .30 |
| ☐ 62 | Howard Johnson | .02 | .10 |
| ☐ 63 | Eric Karros | .07 | .20 |
| ☐ 64 | Rick Aguilera | .02 | .10 |
| ☐ 65 | Steve Finley | .07 | .20 |
| ☐ 66 | Mark Langston | .02 | .10 |
| ☐ 67 | Bill Swift | .02 | .10 |
| ☐ 68 | John Olerud | .07 | .20 |
| ☐ 69 | Kevin McReynolds | .02 | .10 |
| ☐ 70 | Jack McDowell | .02 | .10 |
| ☐ 71 | Rickey Henderson | .20 | .50 |
| ☐ 72 | Brian Harper | .02 | .10 |
| ☐ 73 | Mike Morgan | .02 | .10 |
| ☐ 74 | Rafael Palmeiro | .10 | .30 |
| ☐ 75 | Dennis Martinez | .07 | .20 |
| ☐ 76 | Tino Martinez | .10 | .30 |
| ☐ 77 | Eddie Murray | .20 | .50 |
| ☐ 78 | Ellis Burks | .07 | .20 |
| ☐ 79 | John Kruk | .07 | .20 |
| ☐ 80 | Gregg Olson | .02 | .10 |
| ☐ 81 | Bernard Gilkey | .02 | .10 |
| ☐ 82 | Milt Cuyler | .02 | .10 |
| ☐ 83 | Mike LaValliere | .02 | .10 |
| ☐ 84 | Albert Belle | .07 | .20 |
| ☐ 85 | Bip Roberts | .02 | .10 |
| ☐ 86 | Melido Perez | .02 | .10 |
| ☐ 87 | Otis Nixon | .02 | .10 |
| ☐ 88 | Bill Spiers | .02 | .10 |
| ☐ 89 | Jeff Bagwell | .20 | .50 |
| ☐ 90 | Orel Hershiser | .07 | .20 |
| ☐ 91 | Andy Benes | .07 | .20 |
| ☐ 92 | Devon White | .07 | .20 |
| ☐ 93 | Willie McGee | .07 | .20 |
| ☐ 94 | Ozzie Guillen | .02 | .10 |
| ☐ 95 | Ivan Calderon | .02 | .10 |
| ☐ 96 | Keith Miller | .02 | .10 |
| ☐ 97 | Steve Buechele | .02 | .10 |
| ☐ 98 | Kent Hrbek | .07 | .20 |
| ☐ 99 | Dave Hollins | .07 | .20 |
| ☐ 100 | Mike Bordick | .07 | .20 |
| ☐ 101 | Randy Tomlin | .02 | .10 |
| ☐ 102 | Omar Vizquel | .10 | .30 |
| ☐ 103 | Lee Smith | .07 | .20 |
| ☐ 104 | Leo Gomez | .07 | .20 |
| ☐ 105 | Jose Rijo | .02 | .10 |
| ☐ 106 | Mark Whiten | .02 | .10 |
| ☐ 107 | David Justice | .07 | .20 |
| ☐ 108 | Eddie Taubensee | .02 | .10 |
| ☐ 109 | Lance Johnson | .02 | .10 |
| ☐ 110 | Felix Jose | .07 | .20 |
| ☐ 111 | Mike Harkey | .02 | .10 |

|  |  | | |
|---|---|---|---|
| ☐ 112 | Randy Milligan | .02 | .10 |
| ☐ 113 | Anthony Young | .02 | .10 |
| ☐ 114 | Rico Brogna | .02 | .10 |
| ☐ 115 | Bret Saberhagen | .07 | .20 |
| ☐ 116 | Sandy Alomar Jr. | .02 | .10 |
| ☐ 117 | Terry Mulholland | .02 | .10 |
| ☐ 118 | Darryl Hamilton | .02 | .10 |
| ☐ 119 | Todd Zeile | .02 | .10 |
| ☐ 120 | Bernie Williams | .10 | .30 |
| ☐ 121 | Zane Smith | .02 | .10 |
| ☐ 122 | Derek Bell | .02 | .10 |
| ☐ 123 | Deion Sanders | .07 | .20 |
| ☐ 124 | Luis Sojo | .02 | .10 |
| ☐ 125 | Joe Oliver | .02 | .10 |
| ☐ 126 | Craig Grebeck | .02 | .10 |
| ☐ 127 | Andujar Cedeno | .02 | .10 |
| ☐ 128 | Brian McRae | .02 | .10 |
| ☐ 129 | Jose Offerman | .02 | .10 |
| ☐ 130 | Pedro Munoz | .02 | .10 |
| ☐ 131 | Bud Black | .02 | .10 |
| ☐ 132 | Mo Vaughn | .07 | .20 |
| ☐ 133 | Bruce Hurst | .02 | .10 |
| ☐ 134 | Dave Henderson | .02 | .10 |
| ☐ 135 | Tom Pagnozzi | .02 | .10 |
| ☐ 136 | Erik Hanson | .02 | .10 |
| ☐ 137 | Orlando Merced | .02 | .10 |
| ☐ 138 | Dean Palmer | .07 | .20 |
| ☐ 139 | John Franco | .02 | .10 |
| ☐ 140 | Brady Anderson | .07 | .20 |
| ☐ 141 | Ricky Jordan | .02 | .10 |
| ☐ 142 | Jeff Blauser | .02 | .10 |
| ☐ 143 | Sammy Sosa | .20 | .50 |
| ☐ 144 | Bob Walk | .02 | .10 |
| ☐ 145 | Delino DeShields | .07 | .20 |
| ☐ 146 | Kevin Brown | .07 | .20 |
| ☐ 147 | Mark Lemke | .02 | .10 |
| ☐ 148 | Chuck Knoblauch | .07 | .20 |
| ☐ 149 | Chris Sabo | .02 | .10 |
| ☐ 150 | Bobby Witt | .02 | .10 |
| ☐ 151 | Luis Gonzalez | .07 | .20 |
| ☐ 152 | Ron Karkovice | .02 | .10 |
| ☐ 153 | Jeff Brantley | .02 | .10 |
| ☐ 154 | Kevin Appier | .07 | .20 |
| ☐ 155 | Darrin Jackson | .02 | .10 |
| ☐ 156 | Kelly Gruber | .02 | .10 |
| ☐ 157 | Royce Clayton | .07 | .20 |
| ☐ 158 | Chuck Finley | .07 | .20 |
| ☐ 159 | Jeff King | .02 | .10 |
| ☐ 160 | Greg Vaughn | .02 | .10 |
| ☐ 161 | Geronimo Pena | .02 | .10 |
| ☐ 162 | Steve Farr | .02 | .10 |
| ☐ 163 | Jose Oquendo | .02 | .10 |
| ☐ 164 | Mark Lewis | .02 | .10 |
| ☐ 165 | John Wetteland | .07 | .20 |
| ☐ 166 | Mike Henneman | .02 | .10 |
| ☐ 167 | Todd Hundley | .02 | .10 |
| ☐ 168 | Wes Chamberlain | .02 | .10 |
| ☐ 169 | Steve Avery | .07 | .20 |
| ☐ 170 | Mike Devereaux | .07 | .20 |
| ☐ 171 | Reggie Sanders | .07 | .20 |
| ☐ 172 | Jay Buhner | .07 | .20 |
| ☐ 173 | Eric Anthony | .02 | .10 |
| ☐ 174 | John Burkett | .02 | .10 |
| ☐ 175 | Tom Candiotti | .02 | .10 |
| ☐ 176 | Phil Plantier | .07 | .20 |
| ☐ 177 | Doug Henry | .02 | .10 |
| ☐ 178 | Scott Leius | .02 | .10 |
| ☐ 179 | Kirt Manwaring | .02 | .10 |
| ☐ 180 | Jeff Parrett | .02 | .10 |
| ☐ 181 | Don Slaught | .02 | .10 |
| ☐ 182 | Scott Radinsky | .02 | .10 |
| ☐ 183 | Luis Alicea | .02 | .10 |
| ☐ 184 | Tom Gordon | .02 | .10 |
| ☐ 185 | Rick Wilkins | .02 | .10 |
| ☐ 186 | Todd Stottlemyre | .02 | .10 |
| ☐ 187 | Moises Alou | .07 | .20 |
| ☐ 188 | Joe Grahe | .02 | .10 |
| ☐ 189 | Jeff Kent | .20 | .50 |
| ☐ 190 | Bill Wegman | .02 | .10 |
| ☐ 191 | Kim Batiste | .02 | .10 |
| ☐ 192 | Matt Nokes | .02 | .10 |
| ☐ 193 | Mark Wohlers | .07 | .20 |
| ☐ 194 | Paul Sorrento | .02 | .10 |
| ☐ 195 | Chris Hammond | .02 | .10 |
| ☐ 196 | Scott Livingstone | .02 | .10 |
| ☐ 197 | Doug Jones | .02 | .10 |
| ☐ 198 | Scott Cooper | .02 | .10 |
| ☐ 199 | Ramon Martinez | .07 | .20 |

|  |  | | |
|---|---|---|---|
| 200 | Dave Valle | .02 | .10 |
| 201 | Mariano Duncan | .02 | .10 |
| 202 | Ben McDonald | .02 | .10 |
| 203 | Darren Lewis | .02 | .10 |
| 204 | Kenny Rogers | .07 | .20 |
| 205 | Manuel Lee | .02 | .10 |
| 206 | Scott Erickson | .02 | .10 |
| 207 | Dan Gladden | .02 | .10 |
| 208 | Bob Welch | .02 | .10 |
| 209 | Greg Olson | .02 | .10 |
| 210 | Dan Pasqua | .02 | .10 |
| 211 | Tim Wallach | .02 | .10 |
| 212 | Jeff Montgomery | .02 | .10 |
| 213 | Derrick May | .02 | .10 |
| 214 | Ed Sprague | .02 | .10 |
| 215 | David Haas | .02 | .10 |
| 216 | Darrin Fletcher | .02 | .10 |
| 217 | Brian Jordan | .07 | .20 |
| 218 | Jaime Navarro | .02 | .10 |
| 219 | Randy Velarde | .02 | .10 |
| 220 | Ron Gant | .07 | .20 |
| 221 | Paul Quantrill | .02 | .10 |
| 222 | Damion Easley | .02 | .10 |
| 223 | Charlie Hough | .07 | .20 |
| 224 | Brad Brink | .02 | .10 |
| 225 | Gary Manuel | .02 | .10 |
| 226 | Kevin Koslofski | .02 | .10 |
| 227 | Ryan Thompson | .02 | .10 |
| 228 | Mike Munoz | .02 | .10 |
| 229 | Dan Wilson | .07 | .20 |
| 230 | Peter Hoy | .02 | .10 |
| 231 | Pedro Astacio | .02 | .10 |
| 232 | Matt Stairs | .02 | .10 |
| 233 | Jeff Reboulet | .02 | .10 |
| 234 | Manny Alexander | .02 | .10 |
| 235 | Willie Banks | .02 | .10 |
| 236 | John Jaha | .02 | .10 |
| 237 | Scooter Tucker | .02 | .10 |
| 238 | Russ Springer | .02 | .10 |
| 239 | Paul Miller | .02 | .10 |
| 240 | Dan Peltier | .02 | .10 |
| 241 | Ozzie Canseco | .02 | .10 |
| 242 | Ben Rivera | .02 | .10 |
| 243 | John Valentin | .02 | .10 |
| 244 | Henry Rodriguez | .02 | .10 |
| 245 | Derek Parks | .02 | .10 |
| 246 | Carlos Garcia | .02 | .10 |
| 247 | Tim Pugh RC | .02 | .10 |
| 248 | Melvin Nieves | .02 | .10 |
| 249 | Rich Amaral | .02 | .10 |
| 250 | Willie Greene | .02 | .10 |
| 251 | Tim Scott | .02 | .10 |
| 252 | Dave Silvestri | .02 | .10 |
| 253 | Rob Mallicoat | .02 | .10 |
| 254 | Donald Harris | .02 | .10 |
| 255 | Craig Colbert | .02 | .10 |
| 256 | Jose Guzman | .02 | .10 |
| 257 | Domingo Martinez RC | .02 | .10 |
| 258 | William Suero | .02 | .10 |
| 259 | Juan Guerrero | .02 | .10 |
| 260 | J.T. Snow RC | .20 | .50 |
| 261 | Tony Pena | .02 | .10 |
| 262 | Tim Fortugno | .02 | .10 |
| 263 | Tom Marsh | .02 | .10 |
| 264 | Kurt Knudsen | .02 | .10 |
| 265 | Tim Costo | .02 | .10 |
| 266 | Steve Shifflett | .02 | .10 |
| 267 | Billy Ashley | .02 | .10 |
| 268 | Jerry Nielsen | .02 | .10 |
| 269 | Pete Young | .02 | .10 |
| 270 | Johnny Guzman | .02 | .10 |
| 271 | Greg Colbrunn | .02 | .10 |
| 272 | Jeff Nelson | .02 | .10 |
| 273 | Kevin Young | .07 | .20 |
| 274 | Jeff Frye | .02 | .10 |
| 275 | J.T. Bruett | .02 | .10 |
| 276 | Todd Pratt RC | .08 | .25 |
| 277 | Mike Butcher | .02 | .10 |
| 278 | John Flaherty | .02 | .10 |
| 279 | John Patterson | .02 | .10 |
| 280 | Eric Hillman | .02 | .10 |
| 281 | Bien Figueroa | .02 | .10 |
| 282 | Shane Reynolds | .02 | .10 |
| 283 | Rich Rowland | .02 | .10 |
| 284 | Steve Foster | .02 | .10 |
| 285 | Dave Mlicki | .02 | .10 |
| 286 | Mike Piazza | 1.25 | 3.00 |
| 287 | Mike Trombley | .02 | .10 |
| 288 | Jim Pena | .02 | .10 |
| 289 | Bob Ayrault | .02 | .10 |
| 290 | Henry Mercedes | .02 | .10 |
| 291 | Bob Wickman | .02 | .10 |
| 292 | Jacob Brumfield | .02 | .10 |
| 293 | David Hulse RC | .02 | .10 |
| 294 | Ryan Klesko | .07 | .20 |
| 295 | Doug Linton | .02 | .10 |
| 296 | Steve Cooke | .02 | .10 |
| 297 | Eddie Zosky | .02 | .10 |
| 298 | Gerald Williams | .02 | .10 |
| 299 | Jonathan Hurst | .02 | .10 |
| 300 | Larry Carter RC | .02 | .10 |
| 301 | William Pennyfeather | .02 | .10 |
| 302 | Cesar Hernandez | .02 | .10 |
| 303 | Steve Hosey | .02 | .10 |
| 304 | Blas Minor | .02 | .10 |
| 305 | Jeff Grotewald | .02 | .10 |
| 306 | Bernardo Brito | .02 | .10 |
| 307 | Rafael Bournigal | .02 | .10 |
| 308 | Jeff Branson | .02 | .10 |
| 309 | Tom Quinlan RC | .02 | .10 |
| 310 | Pat Gomez RC | .02 | .10 |
| 311 | Sterling Hitchcock RC | .08 | .25 |
| 312 | Kent Bottenfield | .02 | .10 |
| 313 | Alan Trammell | .07 | .20 |
| 314 | Cris Colon | .02 | .10 |
| 315 | Paul Wagner | .02 | .10 |
| 316 | Matt Maysey | .02 | .10 |
| 317 | Mike Stanton | .02 | .10 |
| 318 | Rick Trlicek | .02 | .10 |
| 319 | Kevin Rogers | .02 | .10 |
| 320 | Mark Clark | .02 | .10 |
| 321 | Pedro Martinez | .40 | 1.00 |
| 322 | Al Martin | .02 | .10 |
| 323 | Mike Macfarlane | .02 | .10 |
| 324 | Rey Sanchez | .02 | .10 |
| 325 | Roger Pavlik | .02 | .10 |
| 326 | Troy Neel | .02 | .10 |
| 327 | Kerry Woodson | .02 | .10 |
| 328 | Wayne Kirby | .02 | .10 |
| 329 | Ken Ryan RC | .08 | .25 |
| 330 | Jesse Levis | .02 | .10 |
| 331 | Jim Austin | .02 | .10 |
| 332 | Dan Walters | .02 | .10 |
| 333 | Brian Williams | .02 | .10 |
| 334 | Wil Cordero | .07 | .20 |
| 335 | Bret Boone | .07 | .20 |
| 336 | Hipolito Pichardo | .02 | .10 |
| 337 | Pat Mahomes | .02 | .10 |
| 338 | Andy Stankiewicz | .02 | .10 |
| 339 | Jim Bullinger | .02 | .10 |
| 340 | Archi Cianfrocco | .02 | .10 |
| 341 | Ruben Amaro | .02 | .10 |
| 342 | Frank Seminara | .02 | .10 |
| 343 | Pat Hentgen | .02 | .10 |
| 344 | Dave Nilsson | .02 | .10 |
| 345 | Mike Perez | .02 | .10 |
| 346 | Tim Salmon | .10 | .30 |
| 347 | Tim Wakefield | .20 | .50 |
| 348 | Carlos Hernandez | .02 | .10 |
| 349 | Donovan Osborne | .07 | .20 |
| 350 | Denny Neagle | .07 | .20 |
| 351 | Sam Militello | .02 | .10 |
| 352 | Eric Fox | .02 | .10 |
| 353 | John Doherty | .02 | .10 |
| 354 | Chad Curtis | .02 | .10 |
| 355 | Jeff Tackett | .02 | .10 |
| 356 | Dave Fleming | .02 | .10 |
| 357 | Pat Listach | .02 | .10 |
| 358 | Kevin Wickander | .02 | .10 |
| 359 | John Vander Wal | .02 | .10 |
| 360 | Arthur Rhodes | .02 | .10 |
| 361 | Bob Scanlan | .02 | .10 |
| 362 | Bob Zupcic | .02 | .10 |
| 363 | Mel Rojas | .02 | .10 |
| 364 | Jim Thome | .10 | .30 |
| 365 | Bill Pecota | .02 | .10 |
| 366 | Mark Carreon | .02 | .10 |
| 367 | Mitch Williams | .02 | .10 |
| 368 | Cal Eldred | .02 | .10 |
| 369 | Stan Belinda | .02 | .10 |
| 370 | Pat Kelly | .02 | .10 |
| 371 | Rheal Cormier | .02 | .10 |
| 372 | Juan Guzman | .02 | .10 |
| 373 | Damon Berryhill | .02 | .10 |
| 374 | Gary DiSarcina | .02 | .10 |
| 375 | Norm Charlton | .02 | .10 |
| 376 | Roberto Hernandez | .02 | .10 |
| 377 | Scott Kamieniecki | .02 | .10 |
| 378 | Rusty Meacham | .02 | .10 |
| 379 | Kurt Stillwell | .02 | .10 |
| 380 | Lloyd McClendon | .02 | .10 |
| 381 | Mark Leonard | .02 | .10 |
| 382 | Jerry Browne | .02 | .10 |
| 383 | Glenn Davis | .02 | .10 |
| 384 | Randy Johnson | .20 | .50 |
| 385 | Mike Greenwell | .02 | .10 |
| 386 | Scott Chiamparino | .02 | .10 |
| 387 | George Bell | .02 | .10 |
| 388 | Steve Olin | .02 | .10 |
| 389 | Chuck McElroy | .02 | .10 |
| 390 | Mark Gardner | .02 | .10 |
| 391 | Rod Beck | .02 | .10 |
| 392 | Dennis Rasmussen | .02 | .10 |
| 393 | Charlie Leibrandt | .02 | .10 |
| 394 | Julio Franco | .07 | .20 |
| 395 | Pete Harnisch | .02 | .10 |
| 396 | Sid Bream | .02 | .10 |
| 397 | Milt Thompson | .02 | .10 |
| 398 | Glenallen Hill | .02 | .10 |
| 399 | Chico Walker | .02 | .10 |
| 400 | Alex Cole | .02 | .10 |
| 401 | Trevor Wilson | .02 | .10 |
| 402 | Jeff Conine | .07 | .20 |
| 403 | Kyle Abbott | .02 | .10 |
| 404 | Tom Browning | .02 | .10 |
| 405 | Jerald Clark | .02 | .10 |
| 406 | Vince Horsman | .02 | .10 |
| 407 | Kevin Mitchell | .02 | .10 |
| 408 | Pete Smith | .02 | .10 |
| 409 | Jeff Innis | .02 | .10 |
| 410 | Mike Timlin | .02 | .10 |
| 411 | Charlie Hayes | .02 | .10 |
| 412 | Alex Fernandez | .02 | .10 |
| 413 | Jeff Russell | .02 | .10 |
| 414 | Jody Reed | .02 | .10 |
| 415 | Mickey Morandini | .02 | .10 |
| 416 | Darnell Coles | .02 | .10 |
| 417 | Xavier Hernandez | .02 | .10 |
| 418 | Steve Sax | .02 | .10 |
| 419 | Joe Girardi | .02 | .10 |
| 420 | Mike Fetters | .02 | .10 |
| 421 | Danny Jackson | .02 | .10 |
| 422 | Jim Gott | .02 | .10 |
| 423 | Tim Belcher | .02 | .10 |
| 424 | Jose Mesa | .02 | .10 |
| 425 | Junior Felix | .02 | .10 |
| 426 | Thomas Howard | .02 | .10 |
| 427 | Julio Valera | .02 | .10 |
| 428 | Dante Bichette | .07 | .20 |
| 429 | Mike Sharperson | .02 | .10 |
| 430 | Darryl Kile | .07 | .20 |
| 431 | Lonnie Smith | .02 | .10 |
| 432 | Monty Fariss | .02 | .10 |
| 433 | Reggie Jefferson | .02 | .10 |
| 434 | Bob McClure | .02 | .10 |
| 435 | Craig Lefferts | .02 | .10 |
| 436 | Duane Ward | .02 | .10 |
| 437 | Shawn Abner | .02 | .10 |
| 438 | Roberto Kelly | .02 | .10 |
| 439 | Paul O'Neill | .10 | .30 |
| 440 | Alan Mills | .02 | .10 |
| 441 | Roger Mason | .02 | .10 |
| 442 | Gary Pettis | .02 | .10 |
| 443 | Steve Lake | .02 | .10 |
| 444 | Gene Larkin | .02 | .10 |
| 445 | Larry Andersen | .02 | .10 |
| 446 | Doug Dascenzo | .02 | .10 |
| 447 | Daryl Boston | .02 | .10 |
| 448 | John Candelaria | .02 | .10 |
| 449 | Storm Davis | .02 | .10 |
| 450 | Tom Edens | .02 | .10 |
| 451 | Mike Maddux | .02 | .10 |
| 452 | Tim Naehring | .02 | .10 |
| 453 | John Orton | .02 | .10 |
| 454 | Joey Cora | .02 | .10 |
| 455 | Chuck Crim | .02 | .10 |
| 456 | Dan Plesac | .02 | .10 |
| 457 | Mike Bielecki | .02 | .10 |
| 458 | Terry Jorgensen | .02 | .10 |
| 459 | John Habyan | .02 | .10 |
| 460 | Pete O'Brien | .02 | .10 |
| 461 | Jeff Treadway | .02 | .10 |
| 462 | Frank Castillo | .02 | .10 |
| 463 | Jimmy Jones | .02 | .10 |

|  | | |
|---|---|---|
| 464 Tommy Greene | .02 | .10 |
| 465 Tracy Woodson | .02 | .10 |
| 466 Rich Rodriguez | .02 | .10 |
| 467 Joe Hesketh | .02 | .10 |
| 468 Greg Myers | .02 | .10 |
| 469 Kirk McCaskill | .02 | .10 |
| 470 Ricky Bones | .02 | .10 |
| 471 Lenny Webster | .02 | .10 |
| 472 Francisco Cabrera | .02 | .10 |
| 473 Turner Ward | .02 | .10 |
| 474 Dwayne Henry | .02 | .10 |
| 475 Al Osuna | .02 | .10 |
| 476 Craig Wilson | .02 | .10 |
| 477 Chris Nabholz | .02 | .10 |
| 478 Rafael Belliard | .02 | .10 |
| 479 Terry Leach | .02 | .10 |
| 480 Tim Teufel | .02 | .10 |
| 481 Dennis Eckersley AW | .07 | .20 |
| 482 Barry Bonds MVP | .30 | .75 |
| 483 Dennis Eckersley AW | .07 | .20 |
| 484 Greg Maddux CY | .20 | .50 |
| 485 Pat Listach AW | .02 | .10 |
| 486 Eric Karros AW | .07 | .10 |
| 487 Jamie Arnold RC | .02 | .10 |
| 488 B.J. Wallace | .02 | .10 |
| 489 Derek Jeter RC | 5.00 | 12.00 |
| 490 Jason Kendall RC | .40 | 1.00 |
| 491 Rick Helling | .02 | .10 |
| 492 Derek Wallace RC | .02 | .10 |
| 493 Sean Lowe RC | .02 | .10 |
| 494 Shannon Stewart RC | .30 | .75 |
| 495 Benji Grigsby RC | .02 | .10 |
| 496 Todd Steverson RC | .02 | .10 |
| 497 Dan Serafini RC | .02 | .10 |
| 498 Michael Tucker | .02 | .10 |
| 499 Chris Roberts | .02 | .10 |
| 500 Pete Janicki RC | .02 | .10 |
| 501 Jeff Schmidt RC | .02 | .10 |
| 502 Edgar Martinez AS | .07 | .20 |
| 503 Omar Vizquel AS | .07 | .20 |
| 504 Ken Griffey Jr. AS | .20 | .50 |
| 505 Kirby Puckett AS | .07 | .20 |
| 506 Joe Carter AS | .02 | .10 |
| 507 Ivan Rodriguez AS | .07 | .20 |
| 508 Jack Morris AS | .02 | .10 |
| 509 Dennis Eckersley AS | .07 | .20 |
| 510 Frank Thomas AS | .10 | .30 |
| 511 Roberto Alomar AS | .07 | .20 |
| 512 Mickey Morandini AS | .02 | .10 |
| 513 Dennis Eckersley HL | .07 | .20 |
| 514 Jeff Reardon HL | .02 | .10 |
| 515 Danny Tartabull AS | .02 | .10 |
| 516 Bip Roberts HL | .02 | .10 |
| 517 George Brett HL | .25 | .60 |
| 518 Robin Yount HL | .20 | .50 |
| 519 Kevin Gross HL | .02 | .10 |
| 520 Ed Sprague WS | .02 | .10 |
| 521 Dave Winfield WS | .20 | .50 |
| 522 Ozzie Smith AS | .20 | .50 |
| 523 Barry Bonds AS | .30 | .75 |
| 524 Andy Van Slyke AS | .07 | .20 |
| 525 Tony Gwynn AS | .10 | .30 |
| 526 Darren Daulton AS | .02 | .10 |
| 527 Greg Maddux AS | .20 | .50 |
| 528 Fred McGriff AS | .10 | .30 |
| 529 Lee Smith AS | .02 | .10 |
| 530 Ryne Sandberg AS | .20 | .50 |
| 531 Gary Sheffield AS | .10 | .30 |
| 532 Ozzie Smith DT | .20 | .50 |
| 533 Kirby Puckett DT | .10 | .30 |
| 534 Gary Sheffield DT | .10 | .30 |
| 535 Andy Van Slyke DT | .07 | .20 |
| 536 Ken Griffey Jr. DT | .20 | .50 |
| 537 Ivan Rodriguez DT | .07 | .20 |
| 538 Charles Nagy DT | .02 | .10 |
| 539 Tom Glavine DT | .07 | .20 |
| 540 Dennis Eckersley DT | .07 | .20 |
| 541 Frank Thomas DT | .10 | .30 |
| 542 Roberto Alomar DT | .07 | .20 |
| 543 Sean Berry | .02 | .10 |
| 544 Mike Schooler | .02 | .10 |
| 545 Chuck Carr | .02 | .10 |
| 546 Lenny Harris | .02 | .10 |
| 547 Gary Scott | .02 | .10 |
| 548 Derek Lilliquist | .02 | .10 |
| 549 Brian Hunter | .02 | .10 |
| 550 Kirby Puckett MOY | .10 | .30 |
| 551 Jim Eisenreich | .02 | .10 |

|  | | |
|---|---|---|
| 552 Andre Dawson | .07 | .20 |
| 553 David Nied | .02 | .10 |
| 554 Spike Owen | .02 | .10 |
| 555 Greg Gagne | .02 | .10 |
| 556 Sid Fernandez | .02 | .10 |
| 557 Mark McGwire | .50 | 1.25 |
| 558 Bryan Harvey | .02 | .10 |
| 559 Harold Reynolds | .07 | .20 |
| 560 Barry Bonds | .60 | 1.50 |
| 561 Eric Wedge RC | .08 | .25 |
| 562 Ozzie Smith | .30 | .75 |
| 563 Rick Sutcliffe | .07 | .20 |
| 564 Jeff Reardon | .07 | .20 |
| 565 Alex Arias | .02 | .10 |
| 566 Greg Swindell | .02 | .10 |
| 567 Brook Jacoby | .02 | .10 |
| 568 Pete Incaviglia | .02 | .10 |
| 569 Butch Henry | .02 | .10 |
| 570 Eric Davis | .07 | .20 |
| 571 Kevin Seitzer | .02 | .10 |
| 572 Tony Fernandez | .02 | .10 |
| 573 Steve Reed RC | .02 | .10 |
| 574 Cory Snyder | .02 | .10 |
| 575 Joe Carter | .07 | .20 |
| 576 Greg Maddux | .30 | .75 |
| 577 Bert Blyleven UER | .07 | .20 |
| 578 Kevin Bass | .02 | .10 |
| 579 Carlton Fisk | .10 | .30 |
| 580 Doug Drabek | .02 | .10 |
| 581 Mark Gubicza | .02 | .10 |
| 582 Bobby Thigpen | .02 | .10 |
| 583 Chili Davis | .07 | .20 |
| 584 Scott Bankhead | .02 | .10 |
| 585 Harold Baines | .07 | .20 |
| 586 Eric Young | .07 | .20 |
| 587 Lance Parrish | .07 | .20 |
| 588 Juan Bell | .02 | .10 |
| 589 Bob Ojeda | .02 | .10 |
| 590 Joe Orsulak | .02 | .10 |
| 591 Benito Santiago | .07 | .20 |
| 592 Wade Boggs | .10 | .30 |
| 593 Robby Thompson | .02 | .10 |
| 594 Eric Plunk | .02 | .10 |
| 595 Hensley Meulens | .02 | .10 |
| 596 Lou Whitaker | .07 | .20 |
| 597 Dale Murphy | .10 | .30 |
| 598 Paul Molitor | .10 | .30 |
| 599 Greg W. Harris | .02 | .10 |
| 600 Darren Holmes | .02 | .10 |
| 601 Dave Martinez | .02 | .10 |
| 602 Tom Henke | .02 | .10 |
| 603 Mike Benjamin | .02 | .10 |
| 604 Rene Gonzales | .02 | .10 |
| 605 Roger McDowell | .02 | .10 |
| 606 Kirby Puckett | .20 | .50 |
| 607 Randy Myers | .02 | .10 |
| 608 Ruben Sierra | .07 | .20 |
| 609 Wilson Alvarez | .02 | .10 |
| 610 David Segui | .02 | .10 |
| 611 Juan Samuel | .02 | .10 |
| 612 Tom Brunansky | .07 | .20 |
| 613 Willie Randolph | .07 | .20 |
| 614 Tony Phillips | .02 | .10 |
| 615 Candy Maldonado | .02 | .10 |
| 616 Chris Bosio | .02 | .10 |
| 617 Bret Barberie | .02 | .10 |
| 618 Scott Sanderson | .02 | .10 |
| 619 Ron Darling | .02 | .10 |
| 620 Dave Winfield | .07 | .20 |
| 621 Mike Felder | .02 | .10 |
| 622 Greg Hibbard | .02 | .10 |
| 623 Mike Scioscia | .02 | .10 |
| 624 John Smiley | .07 | .20 |
| 625 Alejandro Pena | .02 | .10 |
| 626 Terry Steinbach | .02 | .10 |
| 627 Freddie Benavides | .02 | .10 |
| 628 Kevin Reimer | .02 | .10 |
| 629 Braulio Castillo | .02 | .10 |
| 630 Dave Shieb | .02 | .10 |
| 631 Dave Magadan | .02 | .10 |
| 632 Scott Fletcher | .02 | .10 |
| 633 Cris Carpenter | .02 | .10 |
| 634 Kevin Maas | .02 | .10 |
| 635 Todd Worrell | .02 | .10 |
| 636 Rob Deer | .07 | .20 |
| 637 Dwight Smith | .02 | .10 |
| 638 Chito Martinez | .02 | .10 |
| 639 Jimmy Key | .07 | .20 |

|  | | |
|---|---|---|
| 640 Greg A. Harris | .02 | .10 |
| 641 Mike Moore | .02 | .10 |
| 642 Pat Borders | .02 | .10 |
| 643 Bill Gullickson | .02 | .10 |
| 644 Gary Gaetti | .07 | .20 |
| 645 David Howard | .02 | .10 |
| 646 Jim Abbott | .10 | .30 |
| 647 Willie Wilson | .02 | .10 |
| 648 David Wells | .07 | .20 |
| 649 Andres Galarraga | .07 | .20 |
| 650 Vince Coleman | .02 | .10 |
| 651 Rob Dibble | .07 | .20 |
| 652 Frank Tanana | .02 | .10 |
| 653 Steve Decker | .02 | .10 |
| 654 David Cone | .07 | .20 |
| 655 Jack Armstrong | .02 | .10 |
| 656 Dave Stewart | .07 | .20 |
| 657 Billy Hatcher | .02 | .10 |
| 658 Tim Raines | .07 | .20 |
| 659 Walt Weiss | .02 | .10 |
| 660 Jose Lind | .02 | .10 |

## 1994 Score

| | | |
|---|---|---|
| COMPLETE SET (660) | 10.00 | 24.00 |
| COMPLETE SERIES 1 (330) | 5.00 | 12.00 |
| COMPLETE SERIES 2 (330) | 5.00 | 12.00 |
| 1 Barry Bonds | .60 | 1.50 |
| 2 John Olerud | .07 | .20 |
| 3 Ken Griffey Jr. | .30 | .75 |
| 4 Jeff Bagwell | .10 | .30 |
| 5 John Burkett | .02 | .10 |
| 6 Jack McDowell | .02 | .10 |
| 7 Albert Belle | .07 | .20 |
| 8 Andres Galarraga | .07 | .20 |
| 9 Mike Mussina | .10 | .30 |
| 10 Will Clark | .10 | .30 |
| 11 Travis Fryman | .07 | .20 |
| 12 Tony Gwynn | .25 | .60 |
| 13 Robin Yount | .30 | .75 |
| 14 Dave Magadan | .02 | .10 |
| 15 Paul O'Neill | .10 | .30 |
| 16 Ray Lankford | .07 | .20 |
| 17 Damion Easley | .02 | .10 |
| 18 Andy Van Slyke | .10 | .30 |
| 19 Brian McRae | .02 | .10 |
| 20 Ryne Sandberg | .30 | .75 |
| 21 Kirby Puckett | .20 | .50 |
| 22 Dwight Gooden | .07 | .20 |
| 23 Don Mattingly | .50 | 1.25 |
| 24 Kevin Mitchell | .02 | .10 |
| 25 Roger Clemens | .40 | 1.00 |
| 26 Eric Karros | .07 | .20 |
| 27 Juan Gonzalez | .20 | .50 |
| 28 John Kruk | .07 | .20 |
| 29 Gregg Jefferies | .02 | .10 |
| 30 Tom Glavine | .10 | .30 |
| 31 Ivan Rodriguez | .10 | .30 |
| 32 Jay Bell | .07 | .20 |
| 33 Randy Johnson | .20 | .50 |
| 34 Darren Daulton | .07 | .20 |
| 35 Rickey Henderson | .20 | .50 |
| 36 Eddie Murray | .20 | .50 |
| 37 Brian Harper | .02 | .10 |
| 38 Delino DeShields | .02 | .10 |
| 39 Jose Lind | .02 | .10 |
| 40 Benito Santiago | .07 | .20 |
| 41 Frank Thomas | .20 | .50 |
| 42 Mark Grace | .10 | .30 |
| 43 Roberto Alomar | .10 | .30 |
| 44 Andy Benes | .02 | .10 |
| 45 Luis Polonia | .02 | .10 |
| 46 Brett Butler | .07 | .20 |
| 47 Terry Steinbach | .02 | .10 |
| 48 Craig Biggio | .10 | .30 |

|  |  | | |
|---|---|---|---|
| 49 | Greg Vaughn | .02 | .10 |
| 50 | Charlie Hayes | .02 | .10 |
| 51 | Mickey Tettleton | .02 | .10 |
| 52 | Jose Rijo | .02 | .10 |
| 53 | Carlos Baerga | .02 | .10 |
| 54 | Jeff Blauser | .02 | .10 |
| 55 | Leo Gomez | .02 | .10 |
| 56 | Bob Tewksbury | .02 | .10 |
| 57 | Mo Vaughn | .07 | .20 |
| 58 | Orlando Merced | .02 | .10 |
| 59 | Tino Martinez | .10 | .30 |
| 60 | Lenny Dykstra | .07 | .20 |
| 61 | Jose Canseco | .10 | .30 |
| 62 | Tony Fernandez | .02 | .10 |
| 63 | Donovan Osborne | .02 | .10 |
| 64 | Ken Hill | .02 | .10 |
| 65 | Kent Hrbek | .07 | .20 |
| 66 | Bryan Harvey | .07 | .20 |
| 67 | Wally Joyner | .07 | .20 |
| 68 | Derrick May | .07 | .20 |
| 69 | Lance Johnson | .02 | .10 |
| 70 | Willie McGee | .07 | .20 |
| 71 | Mark Langston | .07 | .20 |
| 72 | Terry Pendleton | .07 | .20 |
| 73 | Joe Carter | .07 | .20 |
| 74 | Barry Larkin | .10 | .30 |
| 75 | Jimmy Key | .07 | .20 |
| 76 | Joe Girardi | .02 | .10 |
| 77 | B.J. Surhoff | .07 | .20 |
| 78 | Pete Harnisch | .02 | .10 |
| 79 | Lou Whitaker UER | .07 | .20 |
| 80 | Cory Snyder | .02 | .10 |
| 81 | Kenny Lofton | .07 | .20 |
| 82 | Fred McGriff | .10 | .30 |
| 83 | Mike Greenwell | .02 | .10 |
| 84 | Mike Perez | .02 | .10 |
| 85 | Cal Ripken | .60 | 1.50 |
| 86 | Don Slaught | .02 | .10 |
| 87 | Omar Vizquel | .10 | .30 |
| 88 | Curt Schilling | .07 | .20 |
| 89 | Chuck Knoblauch | .07 | .20 |
| 90 | Moises Alou | .07 | .20 |
| 91 | Greg Gagne | .02 | .10 |
| 92 | Bret Saberhagen | .07 | .20 |
| 93 | Ozzie Guillen | .02 | .10 |
| 94 | Matt Williams | .07 | .20 |
| 95 | Chad Curtis | .02 | .10 |
| 96 | Mike Harkey | .02 | .10 |
| 97 | Devon White | .07 | .20 |
| 98 | Walt Weiss | .02 | .10 |
| 99 | Kevin Brown | .07 | .20 |
| 100 | Gary Sheffield | .07 | .20 |
| 101 | Wade Boggs | .10 | .30 |
| 102 | Orel Hershiser | .07 | .20 |
| 103 | Tony Phillips | .02 | .10 |
| 104 | Andujar Cedeno | .02 | .10 |
| 105 | Bill Spiers | .02 | .10 |
| 106 | Otis Nixon | .02 | .10 |
| 107 | Felix Fermin | .02 | .10 |
| 108 | Bip Roberts | .02 | .10 |
| 109 | Dennis Eckersley | .07 | .20 |
| 110 | Dante Bichette | .02 | .10 |
| 111 | Ben McDonald | .02 | .10 |
| 112 | Jim Poole | .02 | .10 |
| 113 | John Dopson | .02 | .10 |
| 114 | Rob Dibble | .07 | .20 |
| 115 | Jeff Treadway | .02 | .10 |
| 116 | Ricky Jordan | .02 | .10 |
| 117 | Mike Henneman | .02 | .10 |
| 118 | Willie Blair | .02 | .10 |
| 119 | Doug Henry | .02 | .10 |
| 120 | Gerald Perry | .02 | .10 |
| 121 | Greg Myers | .02 | .10 |
| 122 | John Franco | .07 | .20 |
| 123 | Roger Mason | .02 | .10 |
| 124 | Chris Hammond | .02 | .10 |
| 125 | Hubie Brooks | .02 | .10 |
| 126 | Kent Mercker | .02 | .10 |
| 127 | Jim Abbott | .10 | .30 |
| 128 | Kevin Bass | .02 | .10 |
| 129 | Rick Aguilera | .02 | .10 |
| 130 | Mitch Webster | .02 | .10 |
| 131 | Eric Plunk | .02 | .10 |
| 132 | Mark Carreon | .02 | .10 |
| 133 | Dave Stewart | .07 | .20 |
| 134 | Willie Wilson | .02 | .10 |
| 135 | Dave Fleming | .02 | .10 |
| 136 | Jeff Tackett | .02 | .10 |
| 137 | Geno Petralli | .02 | .10 |
| 138 | Gene Harris | .02 | .10 |
| 139 | Scott Bankhead | .02 | .10 |
| 140 | Trevor Wilson | .02 | .10 |
| 141 | Alvaro Espinoza | .02 | .10 |
| 142 | Ryan Bowen | .02 | .10 |
| 143 | Mike Moore | .02 | .10 |
| 144 | Bill Pecota | .02 | .10 |
| 145 | Jaime Navarro | .02 | .10 |
| 146 | Jack Daugherty | .02 | .10 |
| 147 | Bob Wickman | .07 | .20 |
| 148 | Chris Jones | .02 | .10 |
| 149 | Todd Stottlemyre | .02 | .10 |
| 150 | Brian Williams | .02 | .10 |
| 151 | Chuck Finley | .07 | .20 |
| 152 | Lenny Harris | .02 | .10 |
| 153 | Alex Fernandez | .02 | .10 |
| 154 | Candy Maldonado | .02 | .10 |
| 155 | Jeff Montgomery | .02 | .10 |
| 156 | David West | .02 | .10 |
| 157 | Mark Williamson | .02 | .10 |
| 158 | Milt Thompson | .02 | .10 |
| 159 | Ron Darling | .02 | .10 |
| 160 | Stan Belinda | .02 | .10 |
| 161 | Henry Cotto | .02 | .10 |
| 162 | Mel Rojas | .02 | .10 |
| 163 | Doug Strange | .02 | .10 |
| 164 | Rene Arocha | .02 | .10 |
| 165 | Tim Hulett | .02 | .10 |
| 166 | Steve Avery | .07 | .20 |
| 167 | Jim Thome | .10 | .30 |
| 168 | Tom Browning | .02 | .10 |
| 169 | Mario Diaz | .02 | .10 |
| 170 | Steve Reed | .02 | .10 |
| 171 | Scott Livingstone | .02 | .10 |
| 172 | Chris Donnels | .02 | .10 |
| 173 | John Jaha | .07 | .20 |
| 174 | Carlos Hernandez | .02 | .10 |
| 175 | Dion James | .02 | .10 |
| 176 | Bud Black | .02 | .10 |
| 177 | Tony Castillo | .02 | .10 |
| 178 | Jose Guzman | .02 | .10 |
| 179 | Torey Lovullo | .02 | .10 |
| 180 | John Vander Wal | .02 | .10 |
| 181 | Mike LaValliere | .02 | .10 |
| 182 | Sid Fernandez | .07 | .20 |
| 183 | Brent Mayne | .02 | .10 |
| 184 | Terry Mulholland | .02 | .10 |
| 185 | Willie Banks | .02 | .10 |
| 186 | Steve Cooke | .02 | .10 |
| 187 | Brent Gates | .07 | .20 |
| 188 | Erik Pappas | .02 | .10 |
| 189 | Bill Haselman | .02 | .10 |
| 190 | Fernando Valenzuela | .07 | .20 |
| 191 | Gary Redus | .02 | .10 |
| 192 | Danny Darwin | .02 | .10 |
| 193 | Mark Portugal | .02 | .10 |
| 194 | Derek Lilliquist | .02 | .10 |
| 195 | Charlie O'Brien | .02 | .10 |
| 196 | Matt Nokes | .02 | .10 |
| 197 | Danny Sheaffer | .02 | .10 |
| 198 | Bill Gullickson | .02 | .10 |
| 199 | Alex Arias | .02 | .10 |
| 200 | Mike Fetters | .02 | .10 |
| 201 | Brian Jordan | .07 | .20 |
| 202 | Joe Grahe | .02 | .10 |
| 203 | Tom Candiotti | .02 | .10 |
| 204 | Jeremy Hernandez | .02 | .10 |
| 205 | Mike Stanton | .02 | .10 |
| 206 | David Howard | .02 | .10 |
| 207 | Darren Holmes | .02 | .10 |
| 208 | Rick Honeycutt | .02 | .10 |
| 209 | Danny Jackson | .02 | .10 |
| 210 | Rich Amaral | .02 | .10 |
| 211 | Blas Minor | .02 | .10 |
| 212 | Kenny Rogers | .07 | .20 |
| 213 | Jim Leyritz | .02 | .10 |
| 214 | Mike Morgan | .02 | .10 |
| 215 | Dan Gladden | .02 | .10 |
| 216 | Randy Velarde | .02 | .10 |
| 217 | Hipolito Pichardo | .02 | .10 |
| 218 | Dave Burba | .02 | .10 |
| 220 | Wilson Alvarez | .02 | .10 |
| 221 | Bob Zupcic | .02 | .10 |
| 222 | Francisco Cabrera | .02 | .10 |
| 223 | Julio Valera | .02 | .10 |
| 224 | Paul Assenmacher | .02 | .10 |
| 225 | Jeff Branson | .02 | .10 |
| 226 | Todd Frohwirth | .02 | .10 |
| 227 | Armando Reynoso | .02 | .10 |
| 228 | Rich Rowland | .02 | .10 |
| 229 | Freddie Benavides | .02 | .10 |
| 230 | Wayne Kirby | .02 | .10 |
| 231 | Darryl Kile | .07 | .20 |
| 232 | Skeeter Barnes | .02 | .10 |
| 233 | Ramon Martinez | .07 | .20 |
| 234 | Tom Gordon | .02 | .10 |
| 235 | Dave Gallagher | .02 | .10 |
| 236 | Ricky Bones | .02 | .10 |
| 237 | Larry Andersen | .02 | .10 |
| 238 | Pat Meares | .02 | .10 |
| 239 | Zane Smith | .02 | .10 |
| 240 | Tim Leary | .02 | .10 |
| 241 | Phil Clark | .02 | .10 |
| 242 | Danny Cox | .02 | .10 |
| 243 | Mike Jackson | .02 | .10 |
| 244 | Mike Gallego | .02 | .10 |
| 245 | Lee Smith | .07 | .20 |
| 246 | Todd Jones | .02 | .10 |
| 247 | Steve Bedrosian | .02 | .10 |
| 248 | Troy Neel | .02 | .10 |
| 249 | Jose Bautista | .02 | .10 |
| 250 | Steve Frey | .02 | .10 |
| 251 | Jeff Reardon | .07 | .20 |
| 252 | Stan Javier | .02 | .10 |
| 253 | Mo Sanford | .02 | .10 |
| 254 | Luis Aquino | .02 | .10 |
| 255 | Domingo Jean | .02 | .10 |
| 256 | Scott Servais | .02 | .10 |
| 257 | Brad Pennington | .02 | .10 |
| 258 | Dave Hansen | .02 | .10 |
| 259 | Rich Gossage | .07 | .20 |
| 260 | Jeff Fassero | .02 | .10 |
| 261 | Junior Ortiz | .02 | .10 |
| 262 | Anthony Young | .02 | .10 |
| 263 | Chris Bosio | .02 | .10 |
| 264 | Ruben Amaro | .02 | .10 |
| 265 | Mark Eichhorn | .02 | .10 |
| 266 | Dave Clark | .02 | .10 |
| 267 | Gary Thurman | .02 | .10 |
| 268 | Les Lancaster | .02 | .10 |
| 269 | Jamie Moyer | .07 | .20 |
| 270 | Ricky Gutierrez | .02 | .10 |
| 271 | Greg A. Harris | .02 | .10 |
| 272 | Mike Benjamin | .02 | .10 |
| 273 | Gene Nelson | .02 | .10 |
| 274 | Damon Berryhill | .02 | .10 |
| 275 | Scott Radinsky | .02 | .10 |
| 276 | Mike Aldrete | .02 | .10 |
| 277 | Jerry DiPoto | .02 | .10 |
| 278 | Chris Haney | .02 | .10 |
| 279 | Richie Lewis | .02 | .10 |
| 280 | Jarvis Brown | .02 | .10 |
| 281 | Juan Bell | .02 | .10 |
| 282 | Joe Klink | .02 | .10 |
| 283 | Graeme Lloyd | .02 | .10 |
| 284 | Casey Candaele | .02 | .10 |
| 285 | Bob MacDonald | .02 | .10 |
| 286 | Mike Sharperson | .02 | .10 |
| 287 | Gene Larkin | .02 | .10 |
| 288 | Brian Barnes | .02 | .10 |
| 289 | David McCarty | .07 | .20 |
| 290 | Jeff Innis | .02 | .10 |
| 291 | Bob Patterson | .02 | .10 |
| 292 | Ben Rivera | .02 | .10 |
| 293 | John Habyan | .02 | .10 |
| 294 | Rich Rodriguez | .02 | .10 |
| 295 | Edwin Nunez | .02 | .10 |
| 296 | Rod Brewer | .02 | .10 |
| 297 | Mike Timlin | .02 | .10 |
| 298 | Jesse Orosco | .02 | .10 |
| 299 | Gary Gaetti | .07 | .20 |
| 300 | Todd Benzinger | .02 | .10 |
| 301 | Jeff Nelson | .02 | .10 |
| 302 | Rafael Belliard | .02 | .10 |
| 303 | Matt Whiteside | .02 | .10 |
| 304 | Vinny Castilla | .07 | .20 |
| 305 | Matt Turner | .02 | .10 |
| 306 | Eduardo Perez | .02 | .10 |
| 307 | Joel Johnston | .02 | .10 |
| 308 | Chris Gomez | .02 | .10 |
| 309 | Pat Rapp | .02 | .10 |
| 310 | Jim Tatum | .02 | .10 |
| 311 | Kirk Rueter | .02 | .10 |

|  |  | | |
|---|---|---|---|
| ❑ 313 | John Flaherty | .02 | .10 |
| ❑ 314 | Tom Kramer | .02 | .10 |
| ❑ 315 | Mark Whiten | .02 | .10 |
| ❑ 316 | Chris Bosio | .02 | .10 |
| ❑ 317 | Baltimore Orioles CL | .02 | .10 |
| ❑ 318 | Boston Red Sox CL UER | | |
| | (Viola listed as 316; shoul | | |
| ❑ 319 | California Angels CL | .02 | .10 |
| ❑ 320 | Chicago White Sox CL | .02 | .10 |
| ❑ 321 | Cleveland Indians CL | .02 | .10 |
| ❑ 322 | Detroit Tigers CL | .02 | .10 |
| ❑ 323 | Kansas City Royals CL | .02 | .10 |
| ❑ 324 | Milwaukee Brewers CL | .02 | .10 |
| ❑ 325 | Minnesota Twins CL | .02 | .10 |
| ❑ 326 | New York Yankees CL | .02 | .10 |
| ❑ 327 | Oakland Athletics CL | .02 | .10 |
| ❑ 328 | Seattle Mariners CL | .02 | .10 |
| ❑ 329 | Texas Rangers CL | .02 | .10 |
| ❑ 330 | Toronto Blue Jays CL | .02 | .10 |
| ❑ 331 | Frank Viola | .07 | .20 |
| ❑ 332 | Ron Gant | .07 | .20 |
| ❑ 333 | Charles Nagy | .02 | .10 |
| ❑ 334 | Roberto Kelly | .02 | .10 |
| ❑ 335 | Brady Anderson | .07 | .20 |
| ❑ 336 | Alex Cole | .02 | .10 |
| ❑ 337 | Alan Trammell | .07 | .20 |
| ❑ 338 | Derek Bell | .07 | .20 |
| ❑ 339 | Bernie Williams | .10 | .30 |
| ❑ 340 | Jose Offerman | .02 | .10 |
| ❑ 341 | Bill Wegman | .02 | .10 |
| ❑ 342 | Ken Caminiti | .07 | .20 |
| ❑ 343 | Pat Borders | .02 | .10 |
| ❑ 344 | Kirt Manwaring | .02 | .10 |
| ❑ 345 | Chili Davis | .07 | .20 |
| ❑ 346 | Steve Buechele | .02 | .10 |
| ❑ 347 | Robin Ventura | .07 | .20 |
| ❑ 348 | Teddy Higuera | .02 | .10 |
| ❑ 349 | Jerry Browne | .02 | .10 |
| ❑ 350 | Scott Kamieniecki | .02 | .10 |
| ❑ 351 | Kevin Tapani | .02 | .10 |
| ❑ 352 | Marquis Grissom | .07 | .20 |
| ❑ 353 | Jay Buhner | .07 | .20 |
| ❑ 354 | Dave Hollins | .02 | .10 |
| ❑ 355 | Dan Wilson | .02 | .10 |
| ❑ 356 | Bob Walk | .02 | .10 |
| ❑ 357 | Chris Hoiles | .02 | .10 |
| ❑ 358 | Todd Zeile | .02 | .10 |
| ❑ 359 | Kevin Appier | .07 | .20 |
| ❑ 360 | Chris Sabo | .02 | .10 |
| ❑ 361 | David Segui | .02 | .10 |
| ❑ 362 | Jerald Clark | .02 | .10 |
| ❑ 363 | Tony Pena | .02 | .10 |
| ❑ 364 | Steve Finley | .07 | .20 |
| ❑ 365 | Roger Pavlik | .02 | .10 |
| ❑ 366 | John Smoltz | .10 | .30 |
| ❑ 367 | Scott Fletcher | .02 | .10 |
| ❑ 368 | Jody Reed | .02 | .10 |
| ❑ 369 | David Wells | .07 | .20 |
| ❑ 370 | Jose Vizcaino | .02 | .10 |
| ❑ 371 | Pat Listach | .02 | .10 |
| ❑ 372 | Orestes Destrade | .02 | .10 |
| ❑ 373 | Danny Tartabull | .07 | .20 |
| ❑ 374 | Greg W. Harris | .02 | .10 |
| ❑ 375 | Juan Guzman | .07 | .20 |
| ❑ 376 | Larry Walker | .07 | .20 |
| ❑ 377 | Gary DiSarcina | .02 | .10 |
| ❑ 378 | Bobby Bonilla | .07 | .20 |
| ❑ 379 | Tim Raines | .07 | .20 |
| ❑ 380 | Tommy Greene | .02 | .10 |
| ❑ 381 | Tony Gwynn | .07 | .20 |
| ❑ 382 | Jeff King | .02 | .10 |
| ❑ 383 | Shane Mack | .02 | .10 |
| ❑ 384 | Ozzie Smith | .30 | .75 |
| ❑ 385 | Eddie Zambrano RC | .02 | .10 |
| ❑ 386 | Mike Devereaux | .02 | .10 |
| ❑ 387 | Erik Hanson | .02 | .10 |
| ❑ 388 | Scott Cooper | .07 | .20 |
| ❑ 389 | Dean Palmer | .07 | .20 |
| ❑ 390 | John Wetteland | .07 | .20 |
| ❑ 391 | Reggie Jefferson | .02 | .10 |
| ❑ 392 | Mark Lemke | .02 | .10 |
| ❑ 393 | Cecil Fielder | .07 | .20 |
| ❑ 394 | Reggie Sanders | .07 | .20 |
| ❑ 395 | Darryl Hamilton | .02 | .10 |
| ❑ 396 | Daryl Boston | .02 | .10 |
| ❑ 397 | Pat Kelly | .02 | .10 |
| ❑ 398 | Joe Orsulak | .02 | .10 |
| ❑ 399 | Ed Sprague | .02 | .10 |
| ❑ 400 | Eric Anthony | .02 | .10 |
| ❑ 401 | Scott Sanderson | .02 | .10 |
| ❑ 402 | Jim Gott | .02 | .10 |
| ❑ 403 | Ron Karkovice | .02 | .10 |
| ❑ 404 | Phil Plantier | .07 | .20 |
| ❑ 405 | David Cone | .07 | .20 |
| ❑ 406 | Robby Thompson | .02 | .10 |
| ❑ 407 | Dave Winfield | .20 | .50 |
| ❑ 408 | Dwight Smith | .02 | .10 |
| ❑ 409 | Ruben Sierra | .07 | .20 |
| ❑ 410 | Jack Armstrong | .02 | .10 |
| ❑ 411 | Mike Felder | .02 | .10 |
| ❑ 412 | Wil Cordero | .07 | .20 |
| ❑ 413 | Julio Franco | .07 | .20 |
| ❑ 414 | Howard Johnson | .07 | .20 |
| ❑ 415 | Mark McLemore | .02 | .10 |
| ❑ 416 | Pete Incaviglia | .02 | .10 |
| ❑ 417 | John Valentin | .02 | .10 |
| ❑ 418 | Tim Wakefield | .10 | .30 |
| ❑ 419 | Jose Mesa | .02 | .10 |
| ❑ 420 | Bernard Gilkey | .02 | .10 |
| ❑ 421 | Kirk Gibson | .07 | .20 |
| ❑ 422 | David Justice | .07 | .20 |
| ❑ 423 | Tom Brunansky | .02 | .10 |
| ❑ 424 | John Smiley | .02 | .10 |
| ❑ 425 | Kevin Maas | .02 | .10 |
| ❑ 426 | Doug Drabek | .02 | .10 |
| ❑ 427 | Paul Molitor | .07 | .20 |
| ❑ 428 | Darryl Strawberry | .07 | .20 |
| ❑ 429 | Tim Naehring | .02 | .10 |
| ❑ 430 | Bill Swift | .02 | .10 |
| ❑ 431 | Ellis Burks | .07 | .20 |
| ❑ 432 | Greg Hibbard | .02 | .10 |
| ❑ 433 | Felix Jose | .02 | .10 |
| ❑ 434 | Bret Barberie | .02 | .10 |
| ❑ 435 | Pedro Munoz | .02 | .10 |
| ❑ 436 | Darrin Fletcher | .02 | .10 |
| ❑ 437 | Bobby Witt | .02 | .10 |
| ❑ 438 | Wes Chamberlain | .02 | .10 |
| ❑ 439 | Mackey Sasser | .02 | .10 |
| ❑ 440 | Mark Whiten | .02 | .10 |
| ❑ 441 | Harold Reynolds | .02 | .10 |
| ❑ 442 | Greg Olson | .02 | .10 |
| ❑ 443 | Billy Hatcher | .02 | .10 |
| ❑ 444 | Joe Oliver | .02 | .10 |
| ❑ 445 | Sandy Alomar Jr. | .02 | .10 |
| ❑ 446 | Tim Wallach | .02 | .10 |
| ❑ 447 | Karl Rhodes | .02 | .10 |
| ❑ 448 | Royce Clayton | .02 | .10 |
| ❑ 449 | Cal Eldred | .07 | .20 |
| ❑ 450 | Rick Wilkins | .02 | .10 |
| ❑ 451 | Mike Stanley | .02 | .10 |
| ❑ 452 | Charlie Hough | .07 | .20 |
| ❑ 453 | Jack Morris | .07 | .20 |
| ❑ 454 | Jon Ratliff RC | .02 | .10 |
| ❑ 455 | Rene Gonzales | .02 | .10 |
| ❑ 456 | Eddie Taubensee | .02 | .10 |
| ❑ 457 | Roberto Hernandez | .02 | .10 |
| ❑ 458 | Todd Hundley | .02 | .10 |
| ❑ 459 | Mike Macfarlane | .02 | .10 |
| ❑ 460 | Mickey Morandini | .02 | .10 |
| ❑ 461 | Scott Erickson | .02 | .10 |
| ❑ 462 | Lonnie Smith | .02 | .10 |
| ❑ 463 | Dave Henderson | .02 | .10 |
| ❑ 464 | Ryan Klesko | .07 | .20 |
| ❑ 465 | Edgar Martinez | .10 | .30 |
| ❑ 466 | Tom Pagnozzi | .02 | .10 |
| ❑ 467 | Charlie Leibrandt | .02 | .10 |
| ❑ 468 | Brian Anderson RC | .08 | .25 |
| ❑ 469 | Harold Baines | .07 | .20 |
| ❑ 470 | Tim Belcher | .02 | .10 |
| ❑ 471 | Andre Dawson | .07 | .20 |
| ❑ 472 | Eric Young | .02 | .10 |
| ❑ 473 | Paul Sorrento | .02 | .10 |
| ❑ 474 | Luis Gonzalez | .07 | .20 |
| ❑ 475 | Rob Deer | .02 | .10 |
| ❑ 476 | Mike Piazza | .40 | 1.00 |
| ❑ 477 | Kevin Reimer | .02 | .10 |
| ❑ 478 | Jeff Gardner | .02 | .10 |
| ❑ 479 | Melido Perez | .02 | .10 |
| ❑ 480 | Darren Lewis | .02 | .10 |
| ❑ 481 | Duane Ward | .02 | .10 |
| ❑ 482 | Rey Sanchez | .02 | .10 |
| ❑ 483 | Mark Lewis | .02 | .10 |
| ❑ 484 | Jeff Conine | .07 | .20 |
| ❑ 485 | Joey Cora | .02 | .10 |
| ❑ 486 | Trot Nixon RC | .40 | 1.00 |
| ❑ 487 | Kevin McReynolds | .02 | .10 |
| ❑ 488 | Mike Lansing | .02 | .10 |
| ❑ 489 | Mike Pagliarulo | .02 | .10 |
| ❑ 490 | Mariano Duncan | .02 | .10 |
| ❑ 491 | Mike Bordick | .02 | .10 |
| ❑ 492 | Kevin Young | .02 | .10 |
| ❑ 493 | Dave Valle | .02 | .10 |
| ❑ 494 | Wayne Gomes RC | .02 | .10 |
| ❑ 495 | Rafael Palmeiro | .10 | .30 |
| ❑ 496 | Deion Sanders | .10 | .30 |
| ❑ 497 | Rick Sutcliffe | .07 | .20 |
| ❑ 498 | Randy Milligan | .02 | .10 |
| ❑ 499 | Carlos Quintana | .02 | .10 |
| ❑ 500 | Chris Turner | .02 | .10 |
| ❑ 501 | Thomas Howard | .02 | .10 |
| ❑ 502 | Greg Swindell | .02 | .10 |
| ❑ 503 | Chad Kreuter | .02 | .10 |
| ❑ 504 | Eric Davis | .07 | .20 |
| ❑ 505 | Dickie Thon | .02 | .10 |
| ❑ 506 | Matt Drews RC | .10 | .30 |
| ❑ 507 | Spike Owen | .02 | .10 |
| ❑ 508 | Rod Beck | .02 | .10 |
| ❑ 509 | Pat Hentgen | .02 | .10 |
| ❑ 510 | Sammy Sosa | .20 | .50 |
| ❑ 511 | J.T. Snow | .07 | .20 |
| ❑ 512 | Chuck Carr | .02 | .10 |
| ❑ 513 | Bo Jackson | .20 | .50 |
| ❑ 514 | Dennis Martinez | .07 | .20 |
| ❑ 515 | Phil Hiatt | .02 | .10 |
| ❑ 516 | Jeff Kent | .10 | .30 |
| ❑ 517 | Brooks Kieschnick RC | .07 | .20 |
| ❑ 518 | Kirk Presley RC | .10 | .30 |
| ❑ 519 | Kevin Seitzer | .02 | .10 |
| ❑ 520 | Carlos Garcia | .02 | .10 |
| ❑ 521 | Mike Blowers | .02 | .10 |
| ❑ 522 | Luis Alicea | .02 | .10 |
| ❑ 523 | David Hulse | .02 | .10 |
| ❑ 524 | Greg Maddux | .30 | .75 |
| ❑ 525 | Gregg Olson | .02 | .10 |
| ❑ 526 | Hal Morris | .02 | .10 |
| ❑ 527 | Daron Kirkreit | .02 | .10 |
| ❑ 528 | David Nied | .07 | .20 |
| ❑ 529 | Jeff Russell | .02 | .10 |
| ❑ 530 | Kevin Gross | .02 | .10 |
| ❑ 531 | John Doherty | .02 | .10 |
| ❑ 532 | Matt Brunson RC | .02 | .10 |
| ❑ 533 | Dave Nilsson | .02 | .10 |
| ❑ 534 | Randy Myers | .02 | .10 |
| ❑ 535 | Steve Farr | .02 | .10 |
| ❑ 536 | Billy Wagner RC | .50 | 1.25 |
| ❑ 537 | Darnell Coles | .02 | .10 |
| ❑ 538 | Frank Tanana | .02 | .10 |
| ❑ 539 | Tim Salmon | .10 | .30 |
| ❑ 540 | Kim Batiste | .02 | .10 |
| ❑ 541 | George Bell | .07 | .20 |
| ❑ 542 | Tom Henke | .02 | .10 |
| ❑ 543 | Sam Horn | .02 | .10 |
| ❑ 544 | Doug Jones | .02 | .10 |
| ❑ 545 | Scott Leius | .02 | .10 |
| ❑ 546 | Al Martin | .02 | .10 |
| ❑ 547 | Bob Welch | .02 | .10 |
| ❑ 548 | Scott Christman RC | .02 | .10 |
| ❑ 549 | Norm Charlton | .02 | .10 |
| ❑ 550 | Mark McGwire | .50 | 1.25 |
| ❑ 551 | Greg McMichael | .02 | .10 |
| ❑ 552 | Tim Costo | .02 | .10 |
| ❑ 553 | Rodney Bolton | .02 | .10 |
| ❑ 554 | Pedro Martinez | .20 | .50 |
| ❑ 555 | Marc Valdes | .02 | .10 |
| ❑ 556 | Darrell Whitmore | .02 | .10 |
| ❑ 557 | Tim Bogar | .02 | .10 |
| ❑ 558 | Steve Karsay | .02 | .10 |
| ❑ 559 | Danny Bautista | .02 | .10 |
| ❑ 560 | Jeffrey Hammonds | .07 | .20 |
| ❑ 561 | Aaron Sele | .07 | .20 |
| ❑ 562 | Russ Springer | .02 | .10 |
| ❑ 563 | Jason Bere | .07 | .20 |
| ❑ 564 | Billy Brewer | .02 | .10 |
| ❑ 565 | Sterling Hitchcock | .02 | .10 |
| ❑ 566 | Bobby Munoz | .02 | .10 |
| ❑ 567 | Craig Paquette | .07 | .20 |
| ❑ 568 | Bret Boone | .07 | .20 |
| ❑ 569 | Dan Peltier | .02 | .10 |
| ❑ 570 | Jeromy Burnitz | .07 | .20 |
| ❑ 571 | John Wasdin RC | .02 | .10 |
| ❑ 572 | Chipper Jones | .20 | .50 |
| ❑ 573 | Jamey Wright RC | .02 | .10 |
| ❑ 574 | Jeff Granger | .02 | .10 |
| ❑ 575 | Jay Powell RC | .02 | .10 |

| | | |
|---|---|---|
| ❑ 576 Ryan Thompson | .02 | .10 |
| ❑ 577 Lou Frazier | .02 | .10 |
| ❑ 578 Paul Wagner | .02 | .10 |
| ❑ 579 Brad Ausmus | .10 | .30 |
| ❑ 580 Jack Voigt | .02 | .10 |
| ❑ 581 Kevin Rogers | .02 | .10 |
| ❑ 582 Damon Buford | .02 | .10 |
| ❑ 583 Paul Quantrill | .02 | .10 |
| ❑ 584 Marc Newfield | .02 | .10 |
| ❑ 585 Derrek Lee RC | .60 | 1.50 |
| ❑ 586 Shane Reynolds | .02 | .10 |
| ❑ 587 Cliff Floyd | .07 | .20 |
| ❑ 588 Jeff Schwarz | .02 | .10 |
| ❑ 589 Ross Powell RC | .02 | .10 |
| ❑ 590 Gerald Williams | .02 | .10 |
| ❑ 591 Mike Trombley | .02 | .10 |
| ❑ 592 Ken Ryan | .02 | .10 |
| ❑ 593 John O'Donoghue | .02 | .10 |
| ❑ 594 Rod Correia | .02 | .10 |
| ❑ 595 Darrell Sherman | .02 | .10 |
| ❑ 596 Steve Scarsone | .02 | .10 |
| ❑ 597 Sherman Obando | .02 | .10 |
| ❑ 598 Kurt Abbott RC | .02 | .10 |
| ❑ 599 Dave Telgheder | .02 | .10 |
| ❑ 600 Rick Trlicek | .02 | .10 |
| ❑ 601 Carl Everett | .07 | .20 |
| ❑ 602 Luis Ortiz | .02 | .10 |
| ❑ 603 Larry Luebbers | .02 | .10 |
| ❑ 604 Kevin Roberson | .02 | .10 |
| ❑ 605 Butch Huskey | .02 | .10 |
| ❑ 606 Benji Gil | .02 | .10 |
| ❑ 607 Todd Van Poppel | .02 | .10 |
| ❑ 608 Mark Hutton | .02 | .10 |
| ❑ 609 Chip Hale | .02 | .10 |
| ❑ 610 Matt Maysey | .02 | .10 |
| ❑ 611 Scott Ruffcorn | .02 | .10 |
| ❑ 612 Hilly Hathaway | .02 | .10 |
| ❑ 613 Allen Watson | .02 | .10 |
| ❑ 614 Carlos Delgado | .10 | .30 |
| ❑ 615 Roberto Mejia | .02 | .10 |
| ❑ 616 Turk Wendell | .02 | .10 |
| ❑ 617 Tony Tarasco | .02 | .10 |
| ❑ 618 Raul Mondesi | .07 | .20 |
| ❑ 619 Kevin Stocker | .02 | .10 |
| ❑ 620 Javier Lopez | .07 | .20 |
| ❑ 621 Keith Kessinger | .02 | .10 |
| ❑ 622 Bob Hamelin | .02 | .10 |
| ❑ 623 John Roper | .02 | .10 |
| ❑ 624 Lenny Dykstra WS | .02 | .10 |
| ❑ 625 Joe Carter WS | .02 | .10 |
| ❑ 626 Jim Abbott HL | .07 | .20 |
| ❑ 627 Lee Smith HL | .02 | .10 |
| ❑ 628 Ken Griffey Jr. HL | .20 | .50 |
| ❑ 629 Dave Winfield HL | .02 | .10 |
| ❑ 630 Darryl Kile HL | .02 | .10 |
| ❑ 631 Frank Thomas MVP | .10 | .30 |
| ❑ 632 Barry Bonds MVP | .30 | .75 |
| ❑ 633 Jack McDowell AL CY | .02 | .10 |
| ❑ 634 Greg Maddux CY | .20 | .50 |
| ❑ 635 Tim Salmon ROY | .07 | .20 |
| ❑ 636 Mike Piazza ROY | .20 | .50 |
| ❑ 637 Brian Turang RC | .02 | .10 |
| ❑ 638 Rondell White | .07 | .20 |
| ❑ 639 Nigel Wilson | .02 | .10 |
| ❑ 640 Torii Hunter RC | .40 | 1.00 |
| ❑ 641 Salomon Torres | .02 | .10 |
| ❑ 642 Kevin Higgins | .02 | .10 |
| ❑ 643 Eric Wedge | .02 | .10 |
| ❑ 644 Roger Salkeld | .02 | .10 |
| ❑ 645 Manny Ramirez | .20 | .50 |
| ❑ 646 Jeff McNeely | .02 | .10 |
| ❑ 647 Checklist | | |
| Atlanta Braves | .02 | .10 |
| ❑ 648 Checklist | | |
| Chicago Cubs | .02 | .10 |
| ❑ 649 Checklist | | |
| Cincinnati Reds | .02 | .10 |
| ❑ 650 Checklist | | |
| Colorado Rockies | .02 | .10 |
| ❑ 651 Checklist | | |
| Florida Marlins | .02 | .10 |
| ❑ 652 Checklist | | |
| Houston Astros | .02 | .10 |
| ❑ 653 Checklist | | |
| Los Angeles Dodgers | .02 | .10 |
| ❑ 654 Checklist | | |
| Montreal Expos | .02 | .10 |
| ❑ 655 Checklist | | |

| | | |
|---|---|---|
| New York Mets | .02 | .10 |
| ❑ 656 Checklist | | |
| Philadelphia Phillies | .02 | .10 |
| ❑ 657 Checklist | | |
| Pittsburgh Pirates | .02 | .10 |
| ❑ 658 Checklist | | |
| St. Louis Cardinals | .02 | .10 |
| ❑ 659 Checklist | | |
| San Diego Padres | | .10 |
| ❑ 660 Checklist | | |
| San Francisco Giants | .02 | .10 |

## 1995 Score

| | | |
|---|---|---|
| ❑ COMPLETE SET (605) | 10.00 | 24.00 |
| ❑ COMPLETE SERIES 1 (330) | 5.00 | 12.00 |
| ❑ COMPLETE SERIES 2 (275) | 5.00 | 12.00 |
| ❑ 1 Frank Thomas | .20 | .50 |
| ❑ 2 Roberto Alomar | .10 | .30 |
| ❑ 3 Cal Ripken | .60 | 1.50 |
| ❑ 4 Jose Canseco | .10 | .30 |
| ❑ 5 Matt Williams | .07 | .20 |
| ❑ 6 Esteban Beltre | .02 | .10 |
| ❑ 7 Domingo Cedeno | .02 | .10 |
| ❑ 8 John Valentin | .02 | .10 |
| ❑ 9 Glenallen Hill | .02 | .10 |
| ❑ 10 Rafael Belliard | .02 | .10 |
| ❑ 11 Randy Myers | .02 | .10 |
| ❑ 12 Mo Vaughn | .07 | .20 |
| ❑ 13 Hector Carrasco | .02 | .10 |
| ❑ 14 Chili Davis | .07 | .20 |
| ❑ 15 Dante Bichette | .07 | .20 |
| ❑ 16 Darrin Jackson | .02 | .10 |
| ❑ 17 Mike Piazza | .30 | .75 |
| ❑ 18 Junior Felix | .02 | .10 |
| ❑ 19 Moises Alou | .07 | .20 |
| ❑ 20 Mark Gubicza | .02 | .10 |
| ❑ 21 Bret Saberhagen | .07 | .20 |
| ❑ 22 Lenny Dykstra | .07 | .20 |
| ❑ 23 Steve Howe | .02 | .10 |
| ❑ 24 Mark Dewey | .02 | .10 |
| ❑ 25 Brian Harper | .02 | .10 |
| ❑ 26 Ozzie Smith | .30 | .75 |
| ❑ 27 Scott Erickson | .02 | .10 |
| ❑ 28 Tony Gwynn | .25 | .60 |
| ❑ 29 Bob Welch | .02 | .10 |
| ❑ 30 Barry Bonds | .60 | 1.50 |
| ❑ 31 Leo Gomez | .02 | .10 |
| ❑ 32 Greg Maddux | .30 | .75 |
| ❑ 33 Mike Greenwell | .02 | .10 |
| ❑ 34 Sammy Sosa | .20 | .50 |
| ❑ 35 Darnell Coles | .02 | .10 |
| ❑ 36 Henry Mercker | .02 | .10 |
| ❑ 37 Will Clark | .10 | .30 |
| ❑ 38 Steve Ontiveros | .02 | .10 |
| ❑ 39 Stan Javier | .02 | .10 |
| ❑ 40 Bip Roberts | .02 | .10 |
| ❑ 41 Paul O'Neill | .10 | .30 |
| ❑ 42 Bill Haselman | .02 | .10 |
| ❑ 43 Shane Mack | .02 | .10 |
| ❑ 44 Orlando Merced | .02 | .10 |
| ❑ 45 Kevin Seitzer | .02 | .10 |
| ❑ 46 Trevor Hoffman | .07 | .20 |
| ❑ 47 Greg Gagne | .02 | .10 |
| ❑ 48 Jeff Kent | .07 | .20 |
| ❑ 49 Tony Phillips | .02 | .10 |
| ❑ 50 Ken Hill | .02 | .10 |
| ❑ 51 Carlos Baerga | .07 | .20 |
| ❑ 52 Henry Rodriguez | .02 | .10 |
| ❑ 53 Scott Sanderson | .02 | .10 |
| ❑ 54 Jeff Conine | .07 | .20 |
| ❑ 55 Chris Turner | .02 | .10 |
| ❑ 56 Ken Caminiti | .07 | .20 |
| ❑ 57 Harold Baines | .07 | .20 |
| ❑ 58 Charlie Hayes | .02 | .10 |

| | | |
|---|---|---|
| ❑ 59 Roberto Kelly | .02 | .10 |
| ❑ 60 John Olerud | .07 | .20 |
| ❑ 61 Tim Davis | .02 | .10 |
| ❑ 62 Rich Rowland | .02 | .10 |
| ❑ 63 Rey Sanchez | .02 | .10 |
| ❑ 64 Junior Ortiz | .02 | .10 |
| ❑ 65 Ricky Gutierrez | .02 | .10 |
| ❑ 66 Rex Hudler | .02 | .10 |
| ❑ 67 Johnny Ruffin | .02 | .10 |
| ❑ 68 Jay Buhner | .07 | .20 |
| ❑ 69 Tom Pagnozzi | .02 | .10 |
| ❑ 70 Julio Franco | .07 | .20 |
| ❑ 71 Eric Young | .02 | .10 |
| ❑ 72 Mike Bordick | .02 | .10 |
| ❑ 73 Don Slaught | .02 | .10 |
| ❑ 74 Goose Gossage | .07 | .20 |
| ❑ 75 Lonnie Smith | .02 | .10 |
| ❑ 76 Jimmy Key | .07 | .20 |
| ❑ 77 Dave Hollins | .02 | .10 |
| ❑ 78 Mickey Tettleton | .02 | .10 |
| ❑ 79 Luis Gonzalez | .07 | .20 |
| ❑ 80 Dave Winfield | .07 | .20 |
| ❑ 81 Ryan Thompson | .02 | .10 |
| ❑ 82 Felix Jose | .02 | .10 |
| ❑ 83 Rusty Meacham | .02 | .10 |
| ❑ 84 Darryl Hamilton | .02 | .10 |
| ❑ 85 John Wetteland | .07 | .20 |
| ❑ 86 Tom Brunansky | .02 | .10 |
| ❑ 87 Mark Lemke | .02 | .10 |
| ❑ 88 Spike Owen | .02 | .10 |
| ❑ 89 Shawon Dunston | .02 | .10 |
| ❑ 90 Wilson Alvarez | .02 | .10 |
| ❑ 91 Lee Smith | .07 | .20 |
| ❑ 92 Scott Kamieniecki | .02 | .10 |
| ❑ 93 Jacob Brumfield | .02 | .10 |
| ❑ 94 Kirk Gibson | .07 | .20 |
| ❑ 95 Joe Girardi | .02 | .10 |
| ❑ 96 Mike Macfarlane | .02 | .10 |
| ❑ 97 Greg Colbrunn | .02 | .10 |
| ❑ 98 Ricky Bones | .02 | .10 |
| ❑ 99 Delino DeShields | .02 | .10 |
| ❑ 100 Pat Meares | .02 | .10 |
| ❑ 101 Jeff Fassero | .02 | .10 |
| ❑ 102 Jim Leyritz | .02 | .10 |
| ❑ 103 Gary Redus | .02 | .10 |
| ❑ 104 Terry Steinbach | .02 | .10 |
| ❑ 105 Kevin McReynolds | .02 | .10 |
| ❑ 106 Felix Fermin | .02 | .10 |
| ❑ 107 Danny Jackson | .02 | .10 |
| ❑ 108 Chris James | .02 | .10 |
| ❑ 109 Jeff King | .02 | .10 |
| ❑ 110 Pat Hentgen | .02 | .10 |
| ❑ 111 Gerald Perry | .02 | .10 |
| ❑ 112 Tim Raines | .07 | .20 |
| ❑ 113 Eddie Williams | .02 | .10 |
| ❑ 114 Jamie Moyer | .07 | .20 |
| ❑ 115 Bud Black | .02 | .10 |
| ❑ 116 Chris Gomez | .02 | .10 |
| ❑ 117 Luis Lopez | .02 | .10 |
| ❑ 118 Roger Clemens | .40 | 1.00 |
| ❑ 119 Javier Lopez | .02 | .10 |
| ❑ 120 Dave Nilsson | .02 | .10 |
| ❑ 121 Karl Rhodes | .02 | .10 |
| ❑ 122 Rick Aguilera | .02 | .10 |
| ❑ 123 Tony Fernandez | .02 | .10 |
| ❑ 124 Bernie Williams | .10 | .30 |
| ❑ 125 James Mouton | .02 | .10 |
| ❑ 126 Mark Langston | .07 | .20 |
| ❑ 127 Mike Lansing | .02 | .10 |
| ❑ 128 Tino Martinez | .10 | .30 |
| ❑ 129 Joe Orsulak | .02 | .10 |
| ❑ 130 David Hulse | .02 | .10 |
| ❑ 131 Pete Incaviglia | .02 | .10 |
| ❑ 132 Mark Clark | .02 | .10 |
| ❑ 133 Tony Eusebio | .02 | .10 |
| ❑ 134 Chuck Finley | .07 | .20 |
| ❑ 135 Lou Frazier | .02 | .10 |
| ❑ 136 Craig Grebeck | .02 | .10 |
| ❑ 137 Kelly Stinnett | .02 | .10 |
| ❑ 138 Paul Shuey | .02 | .10 |
| ❑ 139 David Nied | .02 | .10 |
| ❑ 140 Billy Brewer | .02 | .10 |
| ❑ 141 Dave Weathers | .02 | .10 |
| ❑ 142 Scott Leius | .02 | .10 |
| ❑ 143 Brian Jordan | .07 | .20 |
| ❑ 144 Melido Perez | .02 | .10 |
| ❑ 145 Tony Tarasco | .02 | .10 |
| ❑ 146 Dan Wilson | .02 | .10 |

|  |  | | |
|---|---|---|---|
| 147 | Rondell White | .07 | .20 |
| 148 | Mike Henneman | .02 | .10 |
| 149 | Brian Johnson | .02 | .10 |
| 150 | Tom Henke | .02 | .10 |
| 151 | John Patterson | .02 | .10 |
| 152 | Bobby Witt | .02 | .10 |
| 153 | Eddie Taubensee | .02 | .10 |
| 154 | Pat Borders | .02 | .10 |
| 155 | Ramon Martinez | .02 | .10 |
| 156 | Mike Kingery | .02 | .10 |
| 157 | Zane Smith | .02 | .10 |
| 158 | Benito Santiago | .07 | .20 |
| 159 | Matias Carrillo | .02 | .10 |
| 160 | Scott Brosius | .02 | .10 |
| 161 | Dave Clark | .02 | .10 |
| 162 | Mark McLemore | .02 | .10 |
| 163 | Curt Schilling | .07 | .20 |
| 164 | J.T. Snow | .07 | .20 |
| 165 | Rod Beck | .02 | .10 |
| 166 | Scott Fletcher | .02 | .10 |
| 167 | Bob Tewksbury | .02 | .10 |
| 168 | Mike LaValliere | .02 | .10 |
| 169 | Dave Hansen | .02 | .10 |
| 170 | Pedro Martinez | .10 | .30 |
| 171 | Kirk Rueter | .02 | .10 |
| 172 | Jose Lind | .02 | .10 |
| 173 | Luis Alicea | .02 | .10 |
| 174 | Mike Moore | .02 | .10 |
| 175 | Andy Ashby | .02 | .10 |
| 176 | Jody Reed | .02 | .10 |
| 177 | Darryl Kile | .07 | .20 |
| 178 | Carl Willis | .02 | .10 |
| 179 | Jeromy Burnitz | .07 | .20 |
| 180 | Mike Gallego | .02 | .10 |
| 181 | Bill VanLandingham | .02 | .10 |
| 182 | Sid Fernandez | .02 | .10 |
| 183 | Kim Batiste | .02 | .10 |
| 184 | Greg Myers | .02 | .10 |
| 185 | Steve Avery | .07 | .20 |
| 186 | Steve Farr | .02 | .10 |
| 187 | Robb Nen | .07 | .20 |
| 188 | Dan Pasqua | .02 | .10 |
| 189 | Bruce Ruffin | .02 | .10 |
| 190 | Jose Valentin | .02 | .10 |
| 191 | Willie Banks | .02 | .10 |
| 192 | Mike Aldrete | .02 | .10 |
| 193 | Randy Milligan | .02 | .10 |
| 194 | Steve Karsay | .02 | .10 |
| 195 | Mike Stanley | .02 | .10 |
| 196 | Jose Mesa | .02 | .10 |
| 197 | Tom Browning | .02 | .10 |
| 198 | John Vander Wal | .02 | .10 |
| 199 | Kevin Brown | .07 | .20 |
| 200 | Mike Oquist | .02 | .10 |
| 201 | Greg Swindell | .02 | .10 |
| 202 | Eddie Zambrano | .02 | .10 |
| 203 | Joe Boever | .02 | .10 |
| 204 | Gary Varsho | .02 | .10 |
| 205 | Greg Gwynn | .02 | .10 |
| 206 | David Howard | .02 | .10 |
| 207 | Jerome Walton | .02 | .10 |
| 208 | Danny Darwin | .02 | .10 |
| 209 | Darryl Strawberry | .07 | .20 |
| 210 | Todd Van Poppel | .02 | .10 |
| 211 | Scott Livingstone | .02 | .10 |
| 212 | Dave Fleming | .02 | .10 |
| 213 | Todd Worrell | .02 | .10 |
| 214 | Carlos Delgado | .07 | .20 |
| 215 | Bill Pecota | .02 | .10 |
| 216 | Jim Lindeman | .02 | .10 |
| 217 | Rick White | .02 | .10 |
| 218 | Jose Oquendo | .02 | .10 |
| 219 | Tony Castillo | .02 | .10 |
| 220 | Fernando Vina | .02 | .10 |
| 221 | Jeff Bagwell | .10 | .30 |
| 222 | Randy Johnson | .20 | .50 |
| 223 | Albert Belle | .07 | .20 |
| 224 | Chuck Carr | .02 | .10 |
| 225 | Mark Leiter | .02 | .10 |
| 226 | Hal Morris | .02 | .10 |
| 227 | Robin Ventura | .07 | .20 |
| 228 | Mike Munoz | .02 | .10 |
| 229 | Jim Thome | .10 | .30 |
| 230 | Mario Diaz | .02 | .10 |
| 231 | John Doherty | .02 | .10 |
| 232 | Bobby Jones | .07 | .20 |
| 233 | Raul Mondesi | .07 | .20 |
| 234 | Ricky Jordan | .02 | .10 |
| 235 | John Jaha | .02 | .10 |
| 236 | Carlos Garcia | .02 | .10 |
| 237 | Kirby Puckett | .20 | .50 |
| 238 | Orel Hershiser | .07 | .20 |
| 239 | Don Mattingly | .50 | 1.25 |
| 240 | Sid Bream | .02 | .10 |
| 241 | Brent Gates | .02 | .10 |
| 242 | Tony Longmire | .02 | .10 |
| 243 | Robby Thompson | .02 | .10 |
| 244 | Rick Sutcliffe | .07 | .20 |
| 245 | Dean Palmer | .07 | .20 |
| 246 | Marquis Grissom | .07 | .20 |
| 247 | Paul Molitor | .07 | .20 |
| 248 | Mark Carreon | .02 | .10 |
| 249 | Jack Voigt | .02 | .10 |
| 250 | Greg McMichael UER | .02 | .10 |
| 251 | Damon Berryhill | .02 | .10 |
| 252 | Brian Dorsett | .02 | .10 |
| 253 | Jim Edmonds | .10 | .30 |
| 254 | Barry Larkin | .10 | .30 |
| 255 | Jack McDowell | .02 | .10 |
| 256 | Wally Joyner | .07 | .20 |
| 257 | Eddie Murray | .20 | .50 |
| 258 | Lenny Webster | .02 | .10 |
| 259 | Milt Cuyler | .02 | .10 |
| 260 | Todd Benzinger | .02 | .10 |
| 261 | Vince Coleman | .02 | .10 |
| 262 | Todd Stottlemyre | .02 | .10 |
| 263 | Turner Ward | .02 | .10 |
| 264 | Ray Lankford | .07 | .20 |
| 265 | Matt Walbeck | .02 | .10 |
| 266 | Deion Sanders | .10 | .30 |
| 267 | Gerald Williams | .02 | .10 |
| 268 | Jim Gott | .02 | .10 |
| 269 | Jeff Frye | .02 | .10 |
| 270 | Jose Rijo | .02 | .10 |
| 271 | David Justice | .07 | .20 |
| 272 | Ismael Valdes | .02 | .10 |
| 273 | Ben McDonald | .02 | .10 |
| 274 | Darren Lewis | .02 | .10 |
| 275 | Graeme Lloyd | .02 | .10 |
| 276 | Luis Ortiz | .02 | .10 |
| 277 | Julian Tavarez | .02 | .10 |
| 278 | Mark Dalesandro | .02 | .10 |
| 279 | Brett Merriman | .02 | .10 |
| 280 | Ricky Bottalico | .02 | .10 |
| 281 | Robert Eenhoorn | .02 | .10 |
| 282 | Rikkert Faneyte | .02 | .10 |
| 283 | Mike Kelly | .02 | .10 |
| 284 | Mark Smith | .02 | .10 |
| 285 | Turk Wendell | .02 | .10 |
| 286 | Greg Blosser | .02 | .10 |
| 287 | Garey Ingram | .02 | .10 |
| 288 | Jorge Fabregas | .02 | .10 |
| 289 | Blaise Ilsley | .02 | .10 |
| 290 | Joe Hall | .02 | .10 |
| 291 | Orlando Miller | .02 | .10 |
| 292 | Jose Lima | .02 | .10 |
| 293 | Greg O'Halloran RC | .02 | .10 |
| 294 | Mark Kiefer | .02 | .10 |
| 295 | Jose Oliva | .02 | .10 |
| 296 | Rich Becker | .02 | .10 |
| 297 | Brian L. Hunter | .02 | .10 |
| 298 | Dave Silvestri | .02 | .10 |
| 299 | Armando Benitez | .07 | .20 |
| 300 | Darren Dreifort | .02 | .10 |
| 301 | John Mabry | .07 | .20 |
| 302 | Greg Pirkl | .02 | .10 |
| 303 | J.R. Phillips | .02 | .10 |
| 304 | Shawn Green | .07 | .20 |
| 305 | Roberto Petagine | .02 | .10 |
| 306 | Keith Lockhart | .02 | .10 |
| 307 | Jonathan Hurst | .02 | .10 |
| 308 | Paul Spoljaric | .02 | .10 |
| 309 | Mike Lieberthal | .07 | .20 |
| 310 | Garret Anderson | .07 | .20 |
| 311 | John Johnstone | .02 | .10 |
| 312 | Alex Rodriguez | .50 | 1.25 |
| 313 | Kent Mercker | .02 | .10 |
| 314 | John Valentin | .02 | .10 |
| 315 | Kenny Rogers | .07 | .20 |
| 316 | Fred McGriff AS MVP | .07 | .20 |
| 317 | Team Checklists | .02 | .10 |
| 318 | Team Checklists | .02 | .10 |
| 319 | Team Checklists | .02 | .10 |
| 320 | Team Checklists | .02 | .10 |
| 321 | Team Checklists | .02 | .10 |
| 322 | Team Checklists | .02 | .10 |
| 323 | Team Checklists | .02 | .10 |
| 324 | Team Checklists | .02 | .10 |
| 325 | Team Checklists | .02 | .10 |
| 326 | Team Checklists | .02 | .10 |
| 327 | Team Checklists | .02 | .10 |
| 328 | Team Checklists | .02 | .10 |
| 329 | Team Checklists | .02 | .10 |
| 330 | Team Checklists | .02 | .10 |
| 331 | Pedro Munoz | .02 | .10 |
| 332 | Ryan Klesko | .07 | .20 |
| 333 | Andre Dawson | .07 | .20 |
| 334 | Derrick May | .02 | .10 |
| 335 | Aaron Sele | .07 | .20 |
| 336 | Kevin Mitchell | .02 | .10 |
| 337 | Steve Trachsel | .02 | .10 |
| 338 | Andres Galarraga | .07 | .20 |
| 339 | Terry Pendleton | .07 | .20 |
| 340 | Gary Sheffield | .07 | .20 |
| 341 | Travis Fryman | .07 | .20 |
| 342 | Bo Jackson | .20 | .50 |
| 343 | Gary Gaetti | .02 | .10 |
| 344 | Brett Butler | .07 | .20 |
| 345 | B.J. Surhoff | .02 | .10 |
| 346 | Larry Walker | .07 | .20 |
| 347 | Kevin Tapani | .02 | .10 |
| 348 | Rick Wilkins | .02 | .10 |
| 349 | Wade Boggs | .10 | .30 |
| 350 | Mariano Duncan | .02 | .10 |
| 351 | Ruben Sierra | .07 | .20 |
| 352 | Andy Van Slyke | .10 | .30 |
| 353 | Reggie Jefferson | .02 | .10 |
| 354 | Gregg Jefferies | .02 | .10 |
| 355 | Tim Naehring | .02 | .10 |
| 356 | John Roper | .02 | .10 |
| 357 | Joe Carter | .07 | .20 |
| 358 | Kurt Abbott | .02 | .10 |
| 359 | Lenny Harris | .02 | .10 |
| 360 | Lance Johnson | .02 | .10 |
| 361 | Brian Anderson | .02 | .10 |
| 362 | Jim Eisenreich | .02 | .10 |
| 363 | Jerry Browne | .02 | .10 |
| 364 | Mark Grace | .10 | .30 |
| 365 | Devon White | .07 | .20 |
| 366 | Reggie Sanders | .07 | .20 |
| 367 | Ivan Rodriguez | .10 | .30 |
| 368 | Kirt Manwaring | .02 | .10 |
| 369 | Pat Kelly | .02 | .10 |
| 370 | Ellis Burks | .02 | .10 |
| 371 | Charles Nagy | .02 | .10 |
| 372 | Kevin Bass | .02 | .10 |
| 373 | Lou Whitaker | .07 | .20 |
| 374 | Rene Arocha | .02 | .10 |
| 375 | Derek Parks | .02 | .10 |
| 376 | Mark Whiten | .02 | .10 |
| 377 | Mark McGwire | .50 | 1.25 |
| 378 | Doug Drabek | .02 | .10 |
| 379 | Greg Vaughn | .02 | .10 |
| 380 | Al Martin | .02 | .10 |
| 381 | Ron Darling | .02 | .10 |
| 382 | Tim Wallach | .02 | .10 |
| 383 | Alan Trammell | .07 | .20 |
| 384 | Randy Velarde | .02 | .10 |
| 385 | Chris Sabo | .02 | .10 |
| 386 | Wil Cordero | .02 | .10 |
| 387 | Darrin Fletcher | .02 | .10 |
| 388 | David Segui | .02 | .10 |
| 389 | Steve Buechele | .02 | .10 |
| 390 | Dave Gallagher | .02 | .10 |
| 391 | Thomas Howard | .02 | .10 |
| 392 | Chad Curtis | .02 | .10 |
| 393 | Cal Eldred | .07 | .20 |
| 394 | Jason Bere | .02 | .10 |
| 395 | Bret Barberie | .02 | .10 |
| 396 | Paul Sorrento | .02 | .10 |
| 397 | Steve Finley | .07 | .20 |
| 398 | Cecil Fielder | .07 | .20 |
| 399 | Eric Karros | .07 | .20 |
| 400 | Jeff Montgomery | .02 | .10 |
| 401 | Cliff Floyd | .07 | .20 |
| 402 | Matt Mieske | .02 | .10 |
| 403 | Brian Hunter | .02 | .10 |
| 404 | Alex Cole | .02 | .10 |
| 405 | Kevin Stocker | .02 | .10 |
| 406 | Eric Davis | .07 | .20 |
| 407 | Marvin Freeman | .02 | .10 |
| 408 | Dennis Eckersley | .07 | .20 |
| 409 | Todd Zeile | .02 | .10 |
| 410 | Keith Mitchell | .02 | .10 |

|  |  | | |
|---|---|---|---|
| ❑ 411 | Andy Benes | .02 | .10 |
| ❑ 412 | Juan Bell | .02 | .10 |
| ❑ 413 | Royce Clayton | .02 | .10 |
| ❑ 414 | Ed Sprague | .02 | .10 |
| ❑ 415 | Mike Mussina | .10 | .30 |
| ❑ 416 | Todd Hundley | .02 | .10 |
| ❑ 417 | Pat Listach | .02 | .10 |
| ❑ 418 | Joe Oliver | .02 | .10 |
| ❑ 419 | Rafael Palmeiro | .10 | .30 |
| ❑ 420 | Tim Salmon | .10 | .30 |
| ❑ 421 | Brady Anderson | .07 | .20 |
| ❑ 422 | Kenny Lofton | .07 | .20 |
| ❑ 423 | Craig Biggio | .07 | .20 |
| ❑ 424 | Bobby Bonilla | .07 | .20 |
| ❑ 425 | Kenny Rogers | .02 | .10 |
| ❑ 426 | Derek Bell | .02 | .10 |
| ❑ 427 | Scott Cooper | .02 | .10 |
| ❑ 428 | Ozzie Guillen | .07 | .20 |
| ❑ 429 | Omar Vizquel | .10 | .30 |
| ❑ 430 | Phil Plantier | .02 | .10 |
| ❑ 431 | Chuck Knoblauch | .07 | .20 |
| ❑ 432 | Darren Daulton | .07 | .20 |
| ❑ 433 | Bob Hamelin | .02 | .10 |
| ❑ 434 | Tom Glavine | .10 | .30 |
| ❑ 435 | Walt Weiss | .02 | .10 |
| ❑ 436 | Jose Vizcaino | .02 | .10 |
| ❑ 437 | Ken Griffey Jr. | .30 | .75 |
| ❑ 438 | Jay Bell | .07 | .20 |
| ❑ 439 | Juan Gonzalez | .20 | .50 |
| ❑ 440 | Jeff Blauser | .02 | .10 |
| ❑ 441 | Rickey Henderson | .20 | .50 |
| ❑ 442 | Bobby Ayala | .02 | .10 |
| ❑ 443 | David Cone | .07 | .20 |
| ❑ 444 | Pedro Martinez | .10 | .30 |
| ❑ 445 | Manny Ramirez | .10 | .30 |
| ❑ 446 | Mark Portugal | .02 | .10 |
| ❑ 447 | Damion Easley | .02 | .10 |
| ❑ 448 | Gary DiSarcina | .02 | .10 |
| ❑ 449 | Roberto Hernandez | .02 | .10 |
| ❑ 450 | Jeffrey Hammonds | .02 | .10 |
| ❑ 451 | Jeff Treadway | .02 | .10 |
| ❑ 452 | Jim Abbott | .10 | .30 |
| ❑ 453 | Carlos Rodriguez | .02 | .10 |
| ❑ 454 | Joey Cora | .02 | .10 |
| ❑ 455 | Bret Boone | .07 | .20 |
| ❑ 456 | Danny Tartabull | .07 | .20 |
| ❑ 457 | John Franco | .02 | .10 |
| ❑ 458 | Roger Salkeld | .02 | .10 |
| ❑ 459 | Fred McGriff | .10 | .30 |
| ❑ 460 | Pedro Astacio | .02 | .10 |
| ❑ 461 | Jon Lieber | .02 | .10 |
| ❑ 462 | Luis Polonia | .02 | .10 |
| ❑ 463 | Geronimo Pena | .02 | .10 |
| ❑ 464 | Tom Gordon | .02 | .10 |
| ❑ 465 | Brad Ausmus | .07 | .20 |
| ❑ 466 | Willie McGee | .07 | .20 |
| ❑ 467 | Doug Jones | .02 | .10 |
| ❑ 468 | John Smoltz | .10 | .30 |
| ❑ 469 | Troy Neel | .02 | .10 |
| ❑ 470 | Luis Sojo | .02 | .10 |
| ❑ 471 | John Smiley | .02 | .10 |
| ❑ 472 | Rafael Bournigal | .02 | .10 |
| ❑ 473 | Bill Taylor | .02 | .10 |
| ❑ 474 | Juan Guzman | .07 | .20 |
| ❑ 475 | Dave Magadan | .02 | .10 |
| ❑ 476 | Mike Devereaux | .02 | .10 |
| ❑ 477 | Andujar Cedeno | .02 | .10 |
| ❑ 478 | Edgar Martinez | .10 | .30 |
| ❑ 479 | Milt Thompson | .02 | .10 |
| ❑ 480 | Allen Watson | .02 | .10 |
| ❑ 481 | Ron Karkovice | .02 | .10 |
| ❑ 482 | Joey Hamilton | .07 | .20 |
| ❑ 483 | Vinny Castilla | .07 | .20 |
| ❑ 484 | Tim Belcher | .02 | .10 |
| ❑ 485 | Bernard Gilkey | .02 | .10 |
| ❑ 486 | Scott Servais | .02 | .10 |
| ❑ 487 | Cory Snyder | .02 | .10 |
| ❑ 488 | Mel Rojas | .02 | .10 |
| ❑ 489 | Carlos Reyes | .02 | .10 |
| ❑ 490 | Chip Hale | .02 | .10 |
| ❑ 491 | Bill Swift | .07 | .20 |
| ❑ 492 | Pat Rapp | .02 | .10 |
| ❑ 493 | Brian McRae | .02 | .10 |
| ❑ 494 | Mickey Morandini | .02 | .10 |
| ❑ 495 | Tony Pena | .02 | .10 |
| ❑ 496 | Danny Bautista | .02 | .10 |
| ❑ 497 | Armando Reynoso | .02 | .10 |
| ❑ 498 | Ken Ryan | .02 | .10 |
| ❑ 499 | Billy Ripken | .02 | .10 |
| ❑ 500 | Pat Mahomes | .02 | .10 |
| ❑ 501 | Mark Acre | .02 | .10 |
| ❑ 502 | Geronimo Berroa | .02 | .10 |
| ❑ 503 | Norberto Martin | .02 | .10 |
| ❑ 504 | Chad Kreuter | .02 | .10 |
| ❑ 505 | Howard Johnson | .02 | .10 |
| ❑ 506 | Eric Anthony | .02 | .10 |
| ❑ 507 | Mark Wohlers | .02 | .10 |
| ❑ 508 | Scott Sanders | .02 | .10 |
| ❑ 509 | Pete Harnisch | .02 | .10 |
| ❑ 510 | Wes Chamberlain | .02 | .10 |
| ❑ 511 | Tom Candiotti | .02 | .10 |
| ❑ 512 | Albie Lopez | .02 | .10 |
| ❑ 513 | Denny Neagle | .07 | .20 |
| ❑ 514 | Sean Berry | .02 | .10 |
| ❑ 515 | Billy Hatcher | .02 | .10 |
| ❑ 516 | Todd Jones | .02 | .10 |
| ❑ 517 | Wayne Kirby | .02 | .10 |
| ❑ 518 | Butch Henry | .02 | .10 |
| ❑ 519 | Sandy Alomar Jr. | .02 | .10 |
| ❑ 520 | Kevin Appier | .07 | .20 |
| ❑ 521 | Roberto Mejia | .02 | .10 |
| ❑ 522 | Steve Cooke | .02 | .10 |
| ❑ 523 | Terry Shumpert | .02 | .10 |
| ❑ 524 | Mike Jackson | .02 | .10 |
| ❑ 525 | Kent Mercker | .02 | .10 |
| ❑ 526 | David Wells | .02 | .10 |
| ❑ 527 | Juan Samuel | .02 | .10 |
| ❑ 528 | Salomon Torres | .02 | .10 |
| ❑ 529 | Duane Ward | .02 | .10 |
| ❑ 530 | Rob Dibble | .07 | .20 |
| ❑ 531 | Mike Blowers | .02 | .10 |
| ❑ 532 | Mark Eichhorn | .02 | .10 |
| ❑ 533 | Alex Diaz | .02 | .10 |
| ❑ 534 | Dan Miceli | .02 | .10 |
| ❑ 535 | Jeff Branson | .02 | .10 |
| ❑ 536 | Dave Stevens | .02 | .10 |
| ❑ 537 | Charlie O'Brien | .02 | .10 |
| ❑ 538 | Shane Reynolds | .02 | .10 |
| ❑ 539 | Rich Amaral | .02 | .10 |
| ❑ 540 | Rusty Greer | .07 | .20 |
| ❑ 541 | Alex Arias | .02 | .10 |
| ❑ 542 | Eric Plunk | .02 | .10 |
| ❑ 543 | John Hudek | .02 | .10 |
| ❑ 544 | Kirk McCaskill | .02 | .10 |
| ❑ 545 | Jeff Reboulet | .02 | .10 |
| ❑ 546 | Sterling Hitchcock | .02 | .10 |
| ❑ 547 | Warren Newson | .02 | .10 * |
| ❑ 548 | Bryan Harvey | .02 | .10 |
| ❑ 549 | Mike Huff | .02 | .10 |
| ❑ 550 | Lance Parrish | .07 | .20 |
| ❑ 551 | Ken Griffey Jr. HIT | .20 | .50 |
| ❑ 552 | Matt Williams HIT | .07 | .20 |
| ❑ 553 | Roberto Alomar HIT | .07 | .20 |
| ❑ 554 | Jeff Bagwell HIT | .07 | .20 |
| ❑ 555 | David Justice HIT | .07 | .20 |
| ❑ 556 | Cal Ripken HIT | .30 | .75 |
| ❑ 557 | Albert Belle HIT | .02 | .10 |
| ❑ 558 | Mike Piazza HIT | .15 | .40 |
| ❑ 559 | Kirby Puckett HIT | .10 | .30 |
| ❑ 560 | Wade Boggs HIT | .07 | .20 |
| ❑ 561 | Tony Gwynn HIT | .10 | .30 |
| ❑ 562 | Barry Bonds HIT | .30 | .75 |
| ❑ 563 | Mo Vaughn HIT | .02 | .10 |
| ❑ 564 | Don Mattingly HIT | .25 | .60 |
| ❑ 565 | Carlos Baerga HIT | .02 | .10 |
| ❑ 566 | Paul Molitor HIT | .07 | .20 |
| ❑ 567 | Raul Mondesi HIT | .02 | .10 |
| ❑ 568 | Manny Ramirez HIT | .07 | .20 |
| ❑ 569 | Alex Rodriguez HIT | .20 | .50 |
| ❑ 570 | Will Clark HIT | .07 | .20 |
| ❑ 571 | Frank Thomas HIT | .10 | .30 |
| ❑ 572 | Moises Alou HIT | .02 | .10 |
| ❑ 573 | Jeff Conine HIT | .02 | .10 |
| ❑ 574 | Joe Ausanio | .02 | .10 |
| ❑ 575 | Charles Johnson | .07 | .20 |
| ❑ 576 | Ernie Young | .02 | .10 |
| ❑ 577 | Jeff Granger | .02 | .10 |
| ❑ 578 | Robert Perez | .02 | .10 |
| ❑ 579 | Melvin Nieves | .02 | .10 |
| ❑ 580 | Gar Finnvold | .02 | .10 |
| ❑ 581 | Duane Singleton | .02 | .10 |
| ❑ 582 | Chan Ho Park | .07 | .20 |
| ❑ 583 | Fausto Cruz | .02 | .10 |
| ❑ 584 | Dave Staton | .02 | .10 |
| ❑ 585 | Denny Hocking | .02 | .10 |
| ❑ 586 | Nate Minchey | .02 | .10 |
| ❑ 587 | Marc Newfield | .02 | .10 |
| ❑ 588 | Jayhawk Owens | .02 | .10 |
| ❑ 589 | Darren Bragg | .02 | .10 |
| ❑ 590 | Kevin King | .02 | .10 |
| ❑ 591 | Kurt Miller | .02 | .10 |
| ❑ 592 | Aaron Small | .02 | .10 |
| ❑ 593 | Troy O'Leary | .02 | .10 |
| ❑ 594 | Phil Stidham | .02 | .10 |
| ❑ 595 | Steve Dunn | .02 | .10 |
| ❑ 596 | Cory Bailey | .02 | .10 |
| ❑ 597 | Alex Gonzalez | .07 | .20 |
| ❑ 598 | Jim Bowie RC | .02 | .10 |
| ❑ 599 | Jeff Cirillo | .02 | .10 |
| ❑ 600 | Mark Hutton | .02 | .10 |
| ❑ 601 | Russ Davis | .02 | .10 |
| ❑ 602 | Checklist | .02 | .10 |
| ❑ 603 | Checklist | .02 | .10 |
| ❑ 604 | Checklist | .02 | .10 |
| ❑ 605 | Checklist | .02 | .10 |
| ❑ RG1 | R.Klesko Rook.Great. | .40 | 1.00 |
| ❑ SG1 | Ryan Klesko AU/6100 | 4.00 | 10.00 |

## 1996 Score

| | | | |
|---|---|---|---|
| ❑ | COMPLETE SET (517) | 10.00 | 24.00 |
| ❑ | COMPLETE SERIES 1 (275) | 5.00 | 12.00 |
| ❑ | COMPLETE SERIES 2 (242) | 5.00 | 12.00 |
| ❑ 1 | Will Clark | .10 | .30 |
| ❑ 2 | Rich Becker | .07 | .20 |
| ❑ 3 | Ryan Klesko | .07 | .20 |
| ❑ 4 | Jim Edmonds | .07 | .20 |
| ❑ 5 | Barry Larkin | .10 | .30 |
| ❑ 6 | Jim Thome | .10 | .30 |
| ❑ 7 | Raul Mondesi | .07 | .20 |
| ❑ 8 | Don Mattingly | .50 | 1.25 |
| ❑ 9 | Jeff Conine | .07 | .20 |
| ❑ 10 | Rickey Henderson | .20 | .50 |
| ❑ 11 | Chad Curtis | .07 | .20 |
| ❑ 12 | Darren Daulton | .07 | .20 |
| ❑ 13 | Larry Walker | .07 | .20 |
| ❑ 14 | Carlos Garcia | .07 | .20 |
| ❑ 15 | Carlos Baerga | .07 | .20 |
| ❑ 16 | Tony Gwynn | .25 | .60 |
| ❑ 17 | Jon Nunnally | .07 | .20 |
| ❑ 18 | Deion Sanders | .10 | .30 |
| ❑ 19 | Mark Grace | .10 | .30 |
| ❑ 20 | Alex Rodriguez | .40 | 1.00 |
| ❑ 21 | Frank Thomas | .20 | .50 |
| ❑ 22 | Brian Jordan | .07 | .20 |
| ❑ 23 | J.T. Snow | .07 | .20 |
| ❑ 24 | Shawn Green | .07 | .20 |
| ❑ 25 | Tim Wakefield | .07 | .20 |
| ❑ 26 | Curtis Goodwin | .07 | .20 |
| ❑ 27 | John Smoltz | .07 | .20 |
| ❑ 28 | Devon White | .07 | .20 |
| ❑ 29 | Brian L. Hunter | .10 | .30 |
| ❑ 30 | Tim Salmon | .10 | .30 |
| ❑ 31 | Rafael Palmeiro | .07 | .20 |
| ❑ 32 | Bernard Gilkey | .07 | .20 |
| ❑ 33 | John Valentin | .07 | .20 |
| ❑ 34 | Randy Johnson | .20 | .50 |
| ❑ 35 | Garret Anderson | .07 | .20 |
| ❑ 36 | Rikkert Faneyte | .07 | .20 |
| ❑ 37 | Ray Durham | .07 | .20 |
| ❑ 38 | Bip Roberts | .07 | .20 |
| ❑ 39 | Jaime Navarro | .07 | .20 |
| ❑ 40 | Mark Johnson | .07 | .20 |
| ❑ 41 | Darren Lewis | .07 | .20 |
| ❑ 42 | Tyler Green | .07 | .20 |
| ❑ 43 | Bill Pulsipher | .07 | .20 |
| ❑ 44 | Jason Giambi | .20 | .50 |
| ❑ 45 | Kevin Ritz | .07 | .20 |
| ❑ 46 | Jack McDowell | .07 | .20 |
| ❑ 47 | Felipe Lira | .07 | .20 |
| ❑ 48 | Rico Brogna | .07 | .20 |

|  |  | | |
|---|---|---|---|
| 49 | Terry Pendleton | .07 | .20 |
| 50 | Rondell White | .07 | .20 |
| 51 | Andre Dawson | .07 | .20 |
| 52 | Kirby Puckett | .20 | .50 |
| 53 | Wally Joyner | .07 | .20 |
| 54 | B.J. Surhoff | .07 | .20 |
| 55 | Randy Velarde | .07 | .20 |
| 56 | Greg Vaughn | .07 | .20 |
| 57 | Roberto Alomar | .10 | .30 |
| 58 | David Justice | .07 | .20 |
| 59 | Kevin Seitzer | .07 | .20 |
| 60 | Cal Ripken | .60 | 1.50 |
| 61 | Ozzie Smith | .30 | .75 |
| 62 | Mo Vaughn | .07 | .20 |
| 63 | Ricky Bones | .07 | .20 |
| 64 | Gary DiSarcina | .07 | .20 |
| 65 | Matt Williams | .07 | .20 |
| 66 | Wilson Alvarez | .07 | .20 |
| 67 | Lenny Dykstra | .07 | .20 |
| 68 | Brian McRae | .07 | .20 |
| 69 | Todd Stottlemyre | .07 | .20 |
| 70 | Bret Boone | .07 | .20 |
| 71 | Sterling Hitchcock | .07 | .20 |
| 72 | Albert Belle | .07 | .20 |
| 73 | Todd Hundley | .07 | .20 |
| 74 | Vinny Castilla | .07 | .20 |
| 75 | Moises Alou | .07 | .20 |
| 76 | Cecil Fielder | .07 | .20 |
| 77 | Brad Radke | .07 | .20 |
| 78 | Quilvio Veras | .07 | .20 |
| 79 | Eddie Murray | .20 | .50 |
| 80 | James Mouton | .07 | .20 |
| 81 | Pat Listach | .07 | .20 |
| 82 | Mark Gubicza | .07 | .20 |
| 83 | Dave Winfield | .07 | .20 |
| 84 | Fred McGriff | .10 | .30 |
| 85 | Darryl Hamilton | .07 | .20 |
| 86 | Jeffrey Hammonds | .07 | .20 |
| 87 | Pedro Munoz | .07 | .20 |
| 88 | Craig Biggio | .10 | .30 |
| 89 | Cliff Floyd | .07 | .20 |
| 90 | Tim Naehring | .07 | .20 |
| 91 | Brett Butler | .07 | .20 |
| 92 | Kevin Foster | .07 | .20 |
| 93 | Pat Kelly | .07 | .20 |
| 94 | John Smiley | .07 | .20 |
| 95 | Terry Steinbach | .07 | .20 |
| 96 | Orel Hershiser | .07 | .20 |
| 97 | Darrin Fletcher | .07 | .20 |
| 98 | Walt Weiss | .07 | .20 |
| 99 | John Wetteland | .07 | .20 |
| 100 | Alan Trammell | .07 | .20 |
| 101 | Steve Avery | .07 | .20 |
| 102 | Tony Eusebio | .07 | .20 |
| 103 | Sandy Alomar Jr. | .07 | .20 |
| 104 | Joe Girardi | .07 | .20 |
| 105 | Rick Aguilera | .07 | .20 |
| 106 | Tony Tarasco | .07 | .20 |
| 107 | Chris Hammond | .07 | .20 |
| 108 | Mike MacFarlane | .07 | .20 |
| 109 | Doug Drabek | .07 | .20 |
| 110 | Derek Bell | .07 | .20 |
| 111 | Ed Sprague | .07 | .20 |
| 112 | Todd Hollandsworth | .07 | .20 |
| 113 | Otis Nixon | .07 | .20 |
| 114 | Keith Lockhart | .07 | .20 |
| 115 | Donovan Osborne | .07 | .20 |
| 116 | Dave Magadan | .07 | .20 |
| 117 | Edgar Martinez | .10 | .30 |
| 118 | Chuck Carr | .07 | .20 |
| 119 | J.R. Phillips | .07 | .20 |
| 120 | Sean Bergman | .07 | .20 |
| 121 | Andujar Cedeno | .07 | .20 |
| 122 | Eric Young | .07 | .20 |
| 123 | Al Martin | .07 | .20 |
| 124 | Mark Lemke | .07 | .20 |
| 125 | Jim Eisenreich | .07 | .20 |
| 126 | Benito Santiago | .07 | .20 |
| 127 | Ariel Prieto | .07 | .20 |
| 128 | Jim Bullinger | .07 | .20 |
| 129 | Russ Davis | .07 | .20 |
| 130 | Jim Abbott | .10 | .30 |
| 131 | Jason Isringhausen | .07 | .20 |
| 132 | Carlos Perez | .07 | .20 |
| 133 | David Segui | .07 | .20 |
| 134 | Troy O'Leary | .07 | .20 |
| 135 | Pat Meares | .07 | .20 |
| 136 | Chris Hoiles | .07 | .20 |
| 137 | Ismael Valdes | .07 | .20 |
| 138 | Jose Oliva | .07 | .20 |
| 139 | Carlos Delgado | .07 | .20 |
| 140 | Tom Goodwin | .07 | .20 |
| 141 | Bob Tewksbury | .07 | .20 |
| 142 | Chris Gomez | .07 | .20 |
| 143 | Jose Oquendo | .07 | .20 |
| 144 | Mark Lewis | .07 | .20 |
| 145 | Salomon Torres | .07 | .20 |
| 146 | Luis Gonzalez | .07 | .20 |
| 147 | Mark Carreon | .07 | .20 |
| 148 | Lance Johnson | .07 | .20 |
| 149 | Melvin Nieves | .07 | .20 |
| 150 | Lee Smith | .07 | .20 |
| 151 | Jacob Brumfield | .07 | .20 |
| 152 | Armando Benitez | .07 | .20 |
| 153 | Curt Schilling | .07 | .20 |
| 154 | Javier Lopez | .07 | .20 |
| 155 | Frank Rodriguez | .07 | .20 |
| 156 | Alex Gonzalez | .07 | .20 |
| 157 | Todd Worrell | .07 | .20 |
| 158 | Benji Gil | .07 | .20 |
| 159 | Greg Gagne | .07 | .20 |
| 160 | Tom Henke | .07 | .20 |
| 161 | Randy Myers | .07 | .20 |
| 162 | Joey Cora | .07 | .20 |
| 163 | Scott Ruffcorn | .07 | .20 |
| 164 | W. VanLandingham | .07 | .20 |
| 165 | Tony Phillips | .07 | .20 |
| 166 | Eddie Williams | .07 | .20 |
| 167 | Bobby Bonilla | .07 | .20 |
| 168 | Denny Neagle | .07 | .20 |
| 169 | Troy Percival | .07 | .20 |
| 170 | Billy Ashley | .07 | .20 |
| 171 | Andy Van Slyke | .10 | .30 |
| 172 | Jose Offerman | .07 | .20 |
| 173 | Mark Parent | .07 | .20 |
| 174 | Edgardo Alfonzo | .07 | .20 |
| 175 | Trevor Hoffman | .07 | .20 |
| 176 | David Cone | .07 | .20 |
| 177 | Dan Wilson | .07 | .20 |
| 178 | Steve Ontiveros | .07 | .20 |
| 179 | Dean Palmer | .07 | .20 |
| 180 | Mike Kelly | .07 | .20 |
| 181 | Jim Leyritz | .07 | .20 |
| 182 | Ron Karkovice | .07 | .20 |
| 183 | Kevin Brown | .07 | .20 |
| 184 | Jose Valentin | .07 | .20 |
| 185 | Jorge Fabregas | .07 | .20 |
| 186 | Jose Mesa | .07 | .20 |
| 187 | Brent Mayne | .07 | .20 |
| 188 | Carl Everett | .07 | .20 |
| 189 | Paul Sorrento | .07 | .20 |
| 190 | Pete Schourek | .07 | .20 |
| 191 | Scott Kamieniecki | .07 | .20 |
| 192 | Roberto Hernandez | .07 | .20 |
| 193 | Randy Johnson RR | .10 | .30 |
| 194 | Greg Maddux RR | .20 | .50 |
| 195 | Hideo Nomo RR | .10 | .30 |
| 196 | David Cone RR | .07 | .20 |
| 197 | Mike Mussina RR | .07 | .20 |
| 198 | Andy Benes RR | .07 | .20 |
| 199 | Kevin Appier RR | .07 | .20 |
| 200 | John Smoltz RR | .07 | .20 |
| 201 | John Wetteland RR | .07 | .20 |
| 202 | Mark Wohlers RR | .07 | .20 |
| 203 | Stan Belinda | .07 | .20 |
| 204 | Brian Anderson | .07 | .20 |
| 205 | Mike Devereaux | .07 | .20 |
| 206 | Mark Wohlers | .07 | .20 |
| 207 | Omar Vizquel | .10 | .30 |
| 208 | Jose Rijo | .07 | .20 |
| 209 | Willie Blair | .07 | .20 |
| 210 | Jamie Moyer | .07 | .20 |
| 211 | Craig Shipley | .07 | .20 |
| 212 | Shane Reynolds | .07 | .20 |
| 213 | Chad Fonville | .07 | .20 |
| 214 | Jose Vizcaino | .07 | .20 |
| 215 | Sid Fernandez | .07 | .20 |
| 216 | Andy Ashby | .07 | .20 |
| 217 | Frank Castillo | .07 | .20 |
| 218 | Kevin Tapani | .07 | .20 |
| 219 | Kent Mercker | .07 | .20 |
| 220 | Karim Garcia | .07 | .20 |
| 221 | Antonio Osuna | .07 | .20 |
| 222 | Tim Unroe | .07 | .20 |
| 223 | Johnny Damon | .07 | .30 |
| 224 | LaTroy Hawkins | .07 | .20 |
| 225 | Mariano Rivera | .20 | .50 |
| 226 | Jose Alberro | .07 | .20 |
| 227 | Angel Martinez | .07 | .20 |
| 228 | Jason Schmidt | .10 | .30 |
| 229 | Tony Clark | .07 | .20 |
| 230 | Kevin Jordan | .07 | .20 |
| 231 | Mark Thompson | .07 | .20 |
| 232 | Jim Dougherty | .07 | .20 |
| 233 | Roger Cedeno | .07 | .20 |
| 234 | Ugueth Urbina | .07 | .20 |
| 235 | Ricky Otero | .07 | .20 |
| 236 | Mark Smith | .07 | .20 |
| 237 | Brian Barber | .07 | .20 |
| 238 | Kevin Flora | .07 | .20 |
| 239 | Joe Rosselli | .07 | .20 |
| 240 | Derek Jeter | .50 | 1.25 |
| 241 | Michael Tucker | .07 | .20 |
| 242 | Ben Blomdahl | .07 | .20 |
| 243 | Joe Vitiello | .07 | .20 |
| 244 | Todd Steverson | .07 | .20 |
| 245 | James Baldwin | .07 | .20 |
| 246 | Alan Embree | .07 | .20 |
| 247 | Shannon Penn | .07 | .20 |
| 248 | Chris Stynes | .07 | .20 |
| 249 | Oscar Munoz | .07 | .20 |
| 250 | Jose Herrera | .07 | .20 |
| 251 | Scott Sullivan | .07 | .20 |
| 252 | Reggie Williams | .07 | .20 |
| 253 | Mark Grudzielanek | .07 | .20 |
| 254 | Steve Rodriguez | .07 | .20 |
| 255 | Terry Bradshaw | .07 | .20 |
| 256 | F.P. Santangelo | .07 | .20 |
| 257 | Lyle Mouton | .07 | .20 |
| 258 | George Williams | .07 | .20 |
| 259 | Larry Thomas | .07 | .20 |
| 260 | Rudy Pemberton | .07 | .20 |
| 261 | Jim Pittsley | .07 | .20 |
| 262 | Les Norman | .07 | .20 |
| 263 | Ruben Rivera | .07 | .20 |
| 264 | Cesar Devarez | .07 | .20 |
| 265 | Greg Zaun | .07 | .20 |
| 266 | Dustin Hermanson | .07 | .20 |
| 267 | John Frascatore | .07 | .20 |
| 268 | Joe Randa | .07 | .20 |
| 269 | Jeff Bagwell CL | .07 | .20 |
| 270 | Mike Piazza CL | .20 | .50 |
| 271 | Dante Bichette CL | .07 | .20 |
| 272 | Frank Thomas CL | .10 | .30 |
| 273 | Ken Griffey Jr. CL | .20 | .50 |
| 274 | Cal Ripken CL | .30 | .75 |
| 275 | G.Maddux/A.Belle CL | .07 | .20 |
| 276 | Greg Maddux | .30 | .75 |
| 277 | Pedro Martinez | .10 | .30 |
| 278 | Bobby Higginson | .07 | .20 |
| 279 | Ray Lankford | .07 | .20 |
| 280 | Shawon Dunston | .07 | .20 |
| 281 | Gary Sheffield | .07 | .20 |
| 282 | Ken Griffey Jr. | .30 | .75 |
| 283 | Paul Molitor | .07 | .20 |
| 284 | Kevin Appier | .07 | .20 |
| 285 | Chuck Knoblauch | .07 | .20 |
| 286 | Alex Fernandez | .07 | .20 |
| 287 | Steve Finley | .07 | .20 |
| 288 | Jeff Blauser | .07 | .20 |
| 289 | Charles Johnson | .07 | .20 |
| 290 | John Franco | .07 | .20 |
| 291 | Mark Langston | .07 | .20 |
| 292 | Bret Saberhagen | .07 | .20 |
| 293 | John Mabry | .07 | .20 |
| 294 | Ramon Martinez | .07 | .20 |
| 295 | Mike Blowers | .07 | .20 |
| 296 | Paul O'Neill | .10 | .30 |
| 297 | Dave Nilsson | .07 | .20 |
| 298 | Dante Bichette | .07 | .20 |
| 299 | Marty Cordova | .07 | .20 |
| 300 | Jay Bell | .07 | .20 |
| 301 | Mike Mussina | .10 | .30 |
| 302 | Ivan Rodriguez | .10 | .30 |
| 303 | Jose Canseco | .10 | .30 |
| 304 | Jeff Bagwell | .10 | .30 |
| 305 | Manny Ramirez | .10 | .30 |
| 306 | Dennis Martinez | .07 | .20 |
| 307 | Charlie Hayes | .07 | .20 |
| 308 | Joe Carter | .07 | .20 |
| 309 | Travis Fryman | .07 | .20 |
| 310 | Mark McGwire | .50 | 1.25 |
| 311 | Reggie Sanders | .07 | .20 |
| 312 | Julian Tavarez | .07 | .20 |

| | | |
|---|---|---|
| ☐ 313 Jeff Montgomery | .07 | .20 |
| ☐ 314 Andy Benes | .07 | .20 |
| ☐ 315 John Jaha | .07 | .20 |
| ☐ 316 Jeff Kent | .07 | .20 |
| ☐ 317 Mike Piazza | .30 | .75 |
| ☐ 318 Erik Hanson | .07 | .20 |
| ☐ 319 Kenny Rogers | .07 | .20 |
| ☐ 320 Hideo Nomo | .20 | .50 |
| ☐ 321 Gregg Jefferies | .07 | .20 |
| ☐ 322 Chipper Jones | .20 | .50 |
| ☐ 323 Jay Buhner | .07 | .20 |
| ☐ 324 Dennis Eckersley | .07 | .20 |
| ☐ 325 Kenny Lofton | .07 | .20 |
| ☐ 326 Robin Ventura | .07 | .20 |
| ☐ 327 Tom Glavine | .10 | .30 |
| ☐ 328 Tim Salmon | .10 | .30 |
| ☐ 329 Andres Galarraga | .07 | .20 |
| ☐ 330 Hal Morris | .07 | .20 |
| ☐ 331 Brady Anderson | .07 | .20 |
| ☐ 332 Chili Davis | .07 | .20 |
| ☐ 333 Roger Clemens | .40 | 1.00 |
| ☐ 334 Marquis Grissom | .07 | .20 |
| ☐ 335 Mike Greenwell UER front reads Jeff Greenwell | .07 | .20 |
| ☐ 336 Sammy Sosa | .20 | .50 |
| ☐ 337 Ron Gant | .07 | .20 |
| ☐ 338 Ken Caminiti | .07 | .20 |
| ☐ 339 Danny Tartabull | .07 | .20 |
| ☐ 340 Barry Bonds | .60 | 1.50 |
| ☐ 341 Ben McDonald | .07 | .20 |
| ☐ 342 Ruben Sierra | .07 | .20 |
| ☐ 343 Bernie Williams | .10 | .30 |
| ☐ 344 Wil Cordero | .07 | .20 |
| ☐ 345 Wade Boggs | .10 | .30 |
| ☐ 346 Gary Gaetti | .07 | .20 |
| ☐ 347 Greg Colbrunn | .07 | .20 |
| ☐ 348 Juan Gonzalez | .20 | .50 |
| ☐ 349 Marc Newfield | .07 | .20 |
| ☐ 350 Charles Nagy | .07 | .20 |
| ☐ 351 Robby Thompson | .07 | .20 |
| ☐ 352 Roberto Petagine | .07 | .20 |
| ☐ 353 Darryl Strawberry | .07 | .20 |
| ☐ 354 Tino Martinez | .10 | .30 |
| ☐ 355 Eric Karros | .07 | .20 |
| ☐ 356 Cal Ripken SS | .30 | .75 |
| ☐ 357 Cecil Fielder SS | .07 | .20 |
| ☐ 358 Kirby Puckett SS | .10 | .30 |
| ☐ 359 Jim Edmonds SS | .07 | .20 |
| ☐ 360 Matt Williams SS | .07 | .20 |
| ☐ 361 Alex Rodriguez SS | .20 | .50 |
| ☐ 362 Barry Larkin SS | .07 | .20 |
| ☐ 363 Rafael Palmeiro SS | .07 | .20 |
| ☐ 364 David Cone SS | .07 | .20 |
| ☐ 365 Roberto Alomar SS | .10 | .30 |
| ☐ 366 Eddie Murray SS | .10 | .30 |
| ☐ 367 Randy Johnson SS | .10 | .30 |
| ☐ 368 Ryan Klesko SS | .07 | .20 |
| ☐ 369 Raul Mondesi SS | .07 | .20 |
| ☐ 370 Mo Vaughn SS | .07 | .20 |
| ☐ 371 Will Clark SS | .07 | .20 |
| ☐ 372 Carlos Baerga SS | .07 | .20 |
| ☐ 373 Frank Thomas SS | .10 | .30 |
| ☐ 374 Larry Walker SS | .07 | .20 |
| ☐ 375 Garret Anderson SS | .07 | .20 |
| ☐ 376 Edgar Martinez SS | .07 | .20 |
| ☐ 377 Don Mattingly SS | .25 | .60 |
| ☐ 378 Tony Gwynn SS | .10 | .30 |
| ☐ 379 Albert Belle SS | .07 | .20 |
| ☐ 380 Jason Isringhausen SS | .07 | .20 |
| ☐ 381 Ruben Rivera SS | .07 | .20 |
| ☐ 382 Johnny Damon SS | .07 | .20 |
| ☐ 383 Karim Garcia SS | .07 | .20 |
| ☐ 384 Derek Jeter SS | .25 | .60 |
| ☐ 385 David Justice SS | .07 | .20 |
| ☐ 386 Royce Clayton | .07 | .20 |
| ☐ 387 Mark Whiten | .07 | .20 |
| ☐ 388 Mickey Tettleton | .07 | .20 |
| ☐ 389 Steve Trachsel | .07 | .20 |
| ☐ 390 Danny Bautista | .07 | .20 |
| ☐ 391 Midre Cummings | .07 | .20 |
| ☐ 392 Scott Leius | .07 | .20 |
| ☐ 393 Manny Alexander | .07 | .20 |
| ☐ 394 Brent Gates | .07 | .20 |
| ☐ 395 Rey Sanchez | .07 | .20 |
| ☐ 396 Andy Pettitte | .10 | .30 |
| ☐ 397 Jeff Cirillo | .07 | .20 |
| ☐ 398 Kurt Abbott | .07 | .20 |
| ☐ 399 Lee Tinsley | .07 | .20 |

| | | |
|---|---|---|
| ☐ 400 Paul Assenmacher | .07 | .20 |
| ☐ 401 Scott Erickson | .07 | .20 |
| ☐ 402 Todd Zeile | .07 | .20 |
| ☐ 403 Tom Pagnozzi | .07 | .20 |
| ☐ 404 Ozzie Guillen | .07 | .20 |
| ☐ 405 Jeff Frye | .07 | .20 |
| ☐ 406 Kirt Manwaring | .07 | .20 |
| ☐ 407 Chad Ogea | .07 | .20 |
| ☐ 408 Harold Baines | .07 | .20 |
| ☐ 409 Jason Bere | .07 | .20 |
| ☐ 410 Chuck Finley | .07 | .20 |
| ☐ 411 Jeff Fassero | .07 | .20 |
| ☐ 412 Joey Hamilton | .07 | .20 |
| ☐ 413 John Olerud | .07 | .20 |
| ☐ 414 Kevin Stocker | .07 | .20 |
| ☐ 415 Eric Anthony | .07 | .20 |
| ☐ 416 Aaron Sele | .07 | .20 |
| ☐ 417 Chris Bosio | .07 | .20 |
| ☐ 418 Michael Mimbs | .07 | .20 |
| ☐ 419 Orlando Miller | .07 | .20 |
| ☐ 420 Stan Javier | .07 | .20 |
| ☐ 421 Matt Mieske | .07 | .20 |
| ☐ 422 Jason Bates | .07 | .20 |
| ☐ 423 Orlando Merced | .07 | .20 |
| ☐ 424 John Flaherty | .07 | .20 |
| ☐ 425 Reggie Jefferson | .07 | .20 |
| ☐ 426 Scott Stahoviak | .07 | .20 |
| ☐ 427 John Burkett | .07 | .20 |
| ☐ 428 Rod Beck | .07 | .20 |
| ☐ 429 Bill Swift | .07 | .20 |
| ☐ 430 Scott Cooper | .07 | .20 |
| ☐ 431 Mel Rojas | .07 | .20 |
| ☐ 432 Todd Van Poppel | .07 | .20 |
| ☐ 433 Bobby Jones | .07 | .20 |
| ☐ 434 Mike Harkey | .07 | .20 |
| ☐ 435 Sean Berry | .07 | .20 |
| ☐ 436 Glenallen Hill | .07 | .20 |
| ☐ 437 Ryan Thompson | .07 | .20 |
| ☐ 438 Luis Alicea | .07 | .20 |
| ☐ 439 Esteban Loaiza | .07 | .20 |
| ☐ 440 Jeff Reboulet | .07 | .20 |
| ☐ 441 Vince Coleman | .07 | .20 |
| ☐ 442 Ellis Burks | .07 | .20 |
| ☐ 443 Allen Battle | .07 | .20 |
| ☐ 444 Jimmy Key | .07 | .20 |
| ☐ 445 Ricky Bottalico | .07 | .20 |
| ☐ 446 Delino DeShields | .07 | .20 |
| ☐ 447 Albie Lopez | .07 | .20 |
| ☐ 448 Mark Petkovsek | .07 | .20 |
| ☐ 449 Tim Raines | .07 | .20 |
| ☐ 450 Bryan Harvey | .07 | .20 |
| ☐ 451 Pat Hentgen | .07 | .20 |
| ☐ 452 Tim Laker | .07 | .20 |
| ☐ 453 Tom Gordon | .07 | .20 |
| ☐ 454 Phil Plantier | .07 | .20 |
| ☐ 455 Ernie Young | .07 | .20 |
| ☐ 456 Pete Harnisch | .07 | .20 |
| ☐ 457 Roberto Kelly | .07 | .20 |
| ☐ 458 Mark Portugal | .07 | .20 |
| ☐ 459 Mark Leiter | .07 | .20 |
| ☐ 460 Tony Pena | .07 | .20 |
| ☐ 461 Roger Pavlik | .07 | .20 |
| ☐ 462 Jeff King | .07 | .20 |
| ☐ 463 Bryan Rekar | .07 | .20 |
| ☐ 464 Al Leiter | .07 | .20 |
| ☐ 465 Phil Nevin | .07 | .20 |
| ☐ 466 Jose Lima | .07 | .20 |
| ☐ 467 Mike Stanley | .07 | .20 |
| ☐ 468 David McCarty | .07 | .20 |
| ☐ 469 Herb Perry | .07 | .20 |
| ☐ 470 Geronimo Berroa | .07 | .20 |
| ☐ 471 David Wells | .07 | .20 |
| ☐ 472 Vaughn Eshelman | .07 | .20 |
| ☐ 473 Greg Swindell | .07 | .20 |
| ☐ 474 Steve Sparks | .07 | .20 |
| ☐ 475 Luis Sojo | .07 | .20 |
| ☐ 476 Derrick May | .07 | .20 |
| ☐ 477 Joe Oliver | .07 | .20 |
| ☐ 478 Alex Arias | .07 | .20 |
| ☐ 479 Brad Ausmus | .07 | .20 |
| ☐ 480 Gabe White | .07 | .20 |
| ☐ 481 Pat Rapp | .07 | .20 |
| ☐ 482 Damon Buford | .07 | .20 |
| ☐ 483 Turk Wendell | .07 | .20 |
| ☐ 484 Jeff Brantley | .07 | .20 |
| ☐ 485 Curtis Leskanic | .07 | .20 |
| ☐ 486 Robb Nen | .07 | .20 |
| ☐ 487 Lou Whitaker | .07 | .20 |

| | | |
|---|---|---|
| ☐ 488 Melido Perez | .07 | .20 |
| ☐ 489 Luis Polonia | .07 | .20 |
| ☐ 490 Scott Brosius | .07 | .20 |
| ☐ 491 Robert Perez | .07 | .20 |
| ☐ 492 Mike Sweeney RC | .30 | .75 |
| ☐ 493 Mark Loretta | .07 | .20 |
| ☐ 494 Alex Ochoa | .07 | .20 |
| ☐ 495 Matt Lawton RC | .07 | .20 |
| ☐ 496 Shawn Estes | .07 | .20 |
| ☐ 497 John Wasdin | .07 | .20 |
| ☐ 498 Marc Kroon | .07 | .20 |
| ☐ 499 Chris Snopek | .07 | .20 |
| ☐ 500 Jeff Suppan | .07 | .20 |
| ☐ 501 Terrell Wade | .07 | .20 |
| ☐ 502 Marvin Benard RC | .07 | .20 |
| ☐ 503 Chris Widger | .07 | .20 |
| ☐ 504 Quinton McCracken | .07 | .20 |
| ☐ 505 Bob Wolcott | .07 | .20 |
| ☐ 506 C.J. Nitkowski | .07 | .20 |
| ☐ 507 Aaron Ledesma | .07 | .20 |
| ☐ 508 Scott Hatteberg | .07 | .20 |
| ☐ 509 Jimmy Haynes | .07 | .20 |
| ☐ 510 Howard Battle | .07 | .20 |
| ☐ 511 Marty Cordova CL | .07 | .20 |
| ☐ 512 Randy Johnson CL | .10 | .30 |
| ☐ 513 Mo Vaughn CL | .07 | .20 |
| ☐ 514 Hideo Nomo CL | .07 | .20 |
| ☐ 515 Greg Maddux CL | .20 | .50 |
| ☐ 516 Barry Larkin CL | .07 | .20 |
| ☐ 517 Tom Glavine CL | .07 | .20 |
| ☐ NNO Cal Ripken 2131 | 8.00 | 20.00 |

## 1997 Score

| | | |
|---|---|---|
| ☐ COMPLETE SET (551) | 15.00 | 40.00 |
| ☐ COMP.FACT.SET (551) | 15.00 | 40.00 |
| ☐ COMPLETE SERIES 1 (330) | 6.00 | 15.00 |
| ☐ COMPLETE SERIES 2 (221) | 10.00 | 25.00 |
| ☐ 1 Jeff Bagwell | .10 | .30 |
| ☐ 2 Mickey Tettleton | .07 | .20 |
| ☐ 3 Johnny Damon | .07 | .20 |
| ☐ 4 Jeff Conine | .07 | .20 |
| ☐ 5 Bernie Williams | .10 | .30 |
| ☐ 6 Will Clark | .10 | .30 |
| ☐ 7 Ryan Klesko | .07 | .20 |
| ☐ 8 Cecil Fielder | .07 | .20 |
| ☐ 9 Paul Wilson | .07 | .20 |
| ☐ 10 Gregg Jefferies | .07 | .20 |
| ☐ 11 Chili Davis | .07 | .20 |
| ☐ 12 Albert Belle | .20 | .50 |
| ☐ 13 Ken Hill | .07 | .20 |
| ☐ 14 Cliff Floyd | .07 | .20 |
| ☐ 15 Jaime Navarro | .07 | .20 |
| ☐ 16 Ismael Valdes | .07 | .20 |
| ☐ 17 Jeff King | .07 | .20 |
| ☐ 18 Chris Bosio | .07 | .20 |
| ☐ 19 Reggie Sanders | .07 | .20 |
| ☐ 20 Darren Daulton | .07 | .20 |
| ☐ 21 Ken Caminiti | .07 | .20 |
| ☐ 22 Mike Piazza | .30 | .75 |
| ☐ 23 Chad Mottola | .07 | .20 |
| ☐ 24 Darin Erstad | .07 | .20 |
| ☐ 25 Dante Bichette | .07 | .20 |
| ☐ 26 Frank Thomas | .20 | .50 |
| ☐ 27 Ben McDonald | .07 | .20 |
| ☐ 28 Raul Casanova | .07 | .20 |
| ☐ 29 Kevin Ritz | .07 | .20 |
| ☐ 30 Garret Anderson | .07 | .20 |
| ☐ 31 Jason Kendall | .07 | .20 |
| ☐ 32 Billy Wagner | .07 | .20 |
| ☐ 33 Dave Justice | .07 | .20 |
| ☐ 34 Marty Cordova | .07 | .20 |
| ☐ 35 Derek Jeter | .50 | 1.25 |
| ☐ 36 Trevor Hoffman | .07 | .20 |
| ☐ 37 Geronimo Berroa | .07 | .20 |

|  |  | | |
|---|---|---|---|
| 38 | Walt Weiss | .07 | .20 |
| 39 | Kirt Manwaring | .07 | .20 |
| 40 | Alex Gonzalez | .07 | .20 |
| 41 | Sean Berry | .07 | .20 |
| 42 | Kevin Appier | .07 | .20 |
| 43 | Rusty Greer | .07 | .20 |
| 44 | Pete Incaviglia | .07 | .20 |
| 45 | Rafael Palmeiro | .10 | .30 |
| 46 | Eddie Murray | .20 | .50 |
| 47 | Moises Alou | .07 | .20 |
| 48 | Mark Lewis | .07 | .20 |
| 49 | Hal Morris | .07 | .20 |
| 50 | Edgar Renteria | .07 | .20 |
| 51 | Rickey Henderson | .20 | .50 |
| 52 | Pat Listach | .07 | .20 |
| 53 | John Wasdin | .07 | .20 |
| 54 | James Baldwin | .07 | .20 |
| 55 | Brian Jordan | .07 | .20 |
| 56 | Edgar Martinez | .10 | .30 |
| 57 | Wil Cordero | .07 | .20 |
| 58 | Danny Tartabull | .07 | .20 |
| 59 | Keith Lockhart | .07 | .20 |
| 60 | Rico Brogna | .07 | .20 |
| 61 | Ricky Bottalico | .07 | .20 |
| 62 | Terry Pendleton | .07 | .20 |
| 63 | Bret Boone | .07 | .20 |
| 64 | Charlie Hayes | .07 | .20 |
| 65 | Marc Newfield | .07 | .20 |
| 66 | Sterling Hitchcock | .07 | .20 |
| 67 | Roberto Alomar | .10 | .30 |
| 68 | John Jaha | .07 | .20 |
| 69 | Greg Colbrunn | .07 | .20 |
| 70 | Sal Fasano | .07 | .20 |
| 71 | Brooks Kieschnick | .07 | .20 |
| 72 | Pedro Martinez | .10 | .30 |
| 73 | Kevin Elster | .07 | .20 |
| 74 | Ellis Burks | .07 | .20 |
| 75 | Chuck Finley | .07 | .20 |
| 76 | John Olerud | .07 | .20 |
| 77 | Jay Bell | .07 | .20 |
| 78 | Allen Watson | .07 | .20 |
| 79 | Darryl Strawberry | .10 | .30 |
| 80 | Orlando Miller | .07 | .20 |
| 81 | Jose Herrera | .07 | .20 |
| 82 | Andy Pettitte | .10 | .30 |
| 83 | Juan Guzman | .07 | .20 |
| 84 | Alan Benes | .07 | .20 |
| 85 | Jack McDowell | .07 | .20 |
| 86 | Ugueth Urbina | .07 | .20 |
| 87 | Rocky Coppinger | .07 | .20 |
| 88 | Jeff Cirillo | .07 | .20 |
| 89 | Tom Glavine | .10 | .30 |
| 90 | Robby Thompson | .07 | .20 |
| 91 | Barry Bonds | .60 | 1.50 |
| 92 | Carlos Delgado | .07 | .20 |
| 93 | Mo Vaughn | .20 | .50 |
| 94 | Ryne Sandberg | .30 | .75 |
| 95 | Alex Rodriguez | .30 | .75 |
| 96 | Brady Anderson | .07 | .20 |
| 97 | Scott Brosius | .07 | .20 |
| 98 | Dennis Eckersley | .07 | .20 |
| 99 | Brian McRae | .07 | .20 |
| 100 | Rey Ordonez | .07 | .20 |
| 101 | John Valentin | .07 | .20 |
| 102 | Brett Butler | .07 | .20 |
| 103 | Eric Karros | .07 | .20 |
| 104 | Harold Baines | .07 | .20 |
| 105 | Javier Lopez | .07 | .20 |
| 106 | Alan Trammell | .07 | .20 |
| 107 | Jim Thome | .10 | .30 |
| 108 | Frank Rodriguez | .07 | .20 |
| 109 | Bernard Gilkey | .07 | .20 |
| 110 | Reggie Jefferson | .07 | .20 |
| 111 | Scott Stahoviak | .07 | .20 |
| 112 | Steve Gibralter | .07 | .20 |
| 113 | Todd Hollandsworth | .07 | .20 |
| 114 | Ruben Rivera | .07 | .20 |
| 115 | Dennis Martinez | .07 | .20 |
| 116 | Mariano Rivera | .20 | .50 |
| 117 | John Smoltz | .10 | .30 |
| 118 | John Mabry | .07 | .20 |
| 119 | Tom Gordon | .07 | .20 |
| 120 | Alex Ochoa | .07 | .20 |
| 121 | Jamey Wright | .07 | .20 |
| 122 | Dave Nilsson | .07 | .20 |
| 123 | Bobby Bonilla | .07 | .20 |
| 124 | Al Leiter | .07 | .20 |
| 125 | Rick Aguilera | .07 | .20 |
| 126 | Jeff Brantley | .07 | .20 |
| 127 | Kevin Brown | .07 | .20 |
| 128 | George Arias | .07 | .20 |
| 129 | Darren Oliver | .07 | .20 |
| 130 | Bill Pulsipher | .07 | .20 |
| 131 | Roberto Hernandez | .07 | .20 |
| 132 | Delino DeShields | .07 | .20 |
| 133 | Mark Grudzielanek | .07 | .20 |
| 134 | John Wetteland | .07 | .20 |
| 135 | Carlos Baerga | .07 | .20 |
| 136 | Paul Sorrento | .07 | .20 |
| 137 | Leo Gomez | .07 | .20 |
| 138 | Andy Ashby | .07 | .20 |
| 139 | Julio Franco | .07 | .20 |
| 140 | Brian Hunter | .07 | .20 |
| 141 | Jermaine Dye | .07 | .20 |
| 142 | Tony Clark | .07 | .20 |
| 143 | Ruben Sierra | .07 | .20 |
| 144 | Donovan Osborne | .07 | .20 |
| 145 | Mark McLemore | .07 | .20 |
| 146 | Terry Steinbach | .07 | .20 |
| 147 | Bob Wells | .07 | .20 |
| 148 | Chan Ho Park | .20 | .50 |
| 149 | Tim Salmon | .10 | .30 |
| 150 | Paul O'Neill | .10 | .30 |
| 151 | Cal Ripken | .60 | 1.50 |
| 152 | Wally Joyner | .07 | .20 |
| 153 | Omar Vizquel | .10 | .30 |
| 154 | Mike Mussina | .10 | .30 |
| 155 | Andres Galarraga | .07 | .20 |
| 156 | Ken Griffey Jr. | .30 | .75 |
| 157 | Kenny Lofton | .20 | .50 |
| 158 | Ray Durham | .07 | .20 |
| 159 | Hideo Nomo | .20 | .50 |
| 160 | Ozzie Guillen | .07 | .20 |
| 161 | Roger Pavlik | .07 | .20 |
| 162 | Manny Ramirez | .10 | .30 |
| 163 | Mark Lemke | .07 | .20 |
| 164 | Mike Stanley | .07 | .20 |
| 165 | Chuck Knoblauch | .10 | .30 |
| 166 | Kimera Bartee | .07 | .20 |
| 167 | Wade Boggs | .10 | .30 |
| 168 | Jay Buhner | .07 | .20 |
| 169 | Eric Young | .07 | .20 |
| 170 | Jose Canseco | .10 | .30 |
| 171 | Dwight Gooden | .07 | .20 |
| 172 | Fred McGriff | .10 | .30 |
| 173 | Sandy Alomar Jr. | .07 | .20 |
| 174 | Andy Benes | .07 | .20 |
| 175 | Dean Palmer | .07 | .20 |
| 176 | Larry Walker | .07 | .20 |
| 177 | Charles Nagy | .07 | .20 |
| 178 | David Cone | .07 | .20 |
| 179 | Mark Grace | .10 | .30 |
| 180 | Robin Ventura | .07 | .20 |
| 181 | Roger Clemens | .40 | 1.00 |
| 182 | Bobby Witt | .07 | .20 |
| 183 | Vinny Castilla | .07 | .20 |
| 184 | Gary Sheffield | .07 | .20 |
| 185 | Dan Wilson | .07 | .20 |
| 186 | Roger Cedeno | .07 | .20 |
| 187 | Mark McGwire | .50 | 1.25 |
| 188 | Darren Bragg | .07 | .20 |
| 189 | Quinton McCracken | .07 | .20 |
| 190 | Randy Myers | .07 | .20 |
| 191 | Jeromy Burnitz | .07 | .20 |
| 192 | Randy Johnson | .20 | .50 |
| 193 | Chipper Jones | .20 | .50 |
| 194 | Greg Vaughn | .07 | .20 |
| 195 | Travis Fryman | .07 | .20 |
| 196 | Tim Naehring | .07 | .20 |
| 197 | B.J. Surhoff | .07 | .20 |
| 198 | Juan Gonzalez | .20 | .50 |
| 199 | Terrell Wade | .07 | .20 |
| 200 | Jeff Frye | .07 | .20 |
| 201 | Joey Cora | .07 | .20 |
| 202 | Raul Mondesi | .07 | .20 |
| 203 | Ivan Rodriguez | .10 | .30 |
| 204 | Armando Reynoso | .07 | .20 |
| 205 | Jeffrey Hammonds | .07 | .20 |
| 206 | Darren Dreifort | .07 | .20 |
| 207 | Kevin Seitzer | .07 | .20 |
| 208 | Tino Martinez | .10 | .30 |
| 209 | Jim Bruske SP | .07 | .20 |
| 210 | Jeff Suppan | .07 | .20 |
| 211 | Mark Carreon | .07 | .20 |
| 212 | Wilson Alvarez | .07 | .20 |
| 213 | John Burkett | .07 | .20 |
| 214 | Tony Phillips | .07 | .20 |
| 215 | Greg Maddux | .30 | .75 |
| 216 | Mark Whiten | .07 | .20 |
| 217 | Curtis Pride | .07 | .20 |
| 218 | Lyle Mouton | .07 | .20 |
| 219 | Todd Hundley | .07 | .20 |
| 220 | Greg Gagne | .07 | .20 |
| 221 | Rich Amaral | .07 | .20 |
| 222 | Tom Goodwin | .07 | .20 |
| 223 | Chris Hoiles | .07 | .20 |
| 224 | Jayhawk Owens | .07 | .20 |
| 225 | Kenny Rogers | .07 | .20 |
| 226 | Mike Greenwell | .07 | .20 |
| 227 | Mark Wohlers | .07 | .20 |
| 228 | Henry Rodriguez | .07 | .20 |
| 229 | Robert Perez | .07 | .20 |
| 230 | Jeff Kent | .07 | .20 |
| 231 | Darryl Hamilton | .07 | .20 |
| 232 | Alex Fernandez | .07 | .20 |
| 233 | Ron Karkovice | .07 | .20 |
| 234 | Jimmy Haynes | .07 | .20 |
| 235 | Craig Biggio | .10 | .30 |
| 236 | Ray Lankford | .07 | .20 |
| 237 | Lance Johnson | .07 | .20 |
| 238 | Matt Williams | .07 | .20 |
| 239 | Chad Curtis | .07 | .20 |
| 240 | Mark Thompson | .07 | .20 |
| 241 | Jason Giambi | .07 | .20 |
| 242 | Barry Larkin | .10 | .30 |
| 243 | Paul Molitor | .10 | .30 |
| 244 | Sammy Sosa | .20 | .50 |
| 245 | Kevin Tapani | .07 | .20 |
| 246 | Marquis Grissom | .07 | .20 |
| 247 | Joe Carter | .07 | .20 |
| 248 | Ramon Martinez | .07 | .20 |
| 249 | Tony Gwynn | .25 | .60 |
| 250 | Andy Fox | .07 | .20 |
| 251 | Troy O'Leary | .07 | .20 |
| 252 | Warren Newson | .07 | .20 |
| 253 | Troy Percival | .07 | .20 |
| 254 | Jamie Moyer | .07 | .20 |
| 255 | Danny Graves | .07 | .20 |
| 256 | David Wells | .07 | .20 |
| 257 | Todd Zeile | .07 | .20 |
| 258 | Raul Ibanez | .07 | .20 |
| 259 | Tyler Houston | .07 | .20 |
| 260 | LaTroy Hawkins | .07 | .20 |
| 261 | Joey Hamilton | .07 | .20 |
| 262 | Mike Sweeney | .07 | .20 |
| 263 | Brant Brown | .07 | .20 |
| 264 | Pat Hentgen | .07 | .20 |
| 265 | Mark Johnson | .07 | .20 |
| 266 | Robb Nen | .07 | .20 |
| 267 | Justin Thompson | .07 | .20 |
| 268 | Ron Gant | .07 | .20 |
| 269 | Jeff D'Amico | .07 | .20 |
| 270 | Shawn Estes | .07 | .20 |
| 271 | Derek Bell | .07 | .20 |
| 272 | Fernando Valenzuela | .07 | .20 |
| 273 | Tom Pagnozzi | .07 | .20 |
| 274 | John Burke | .07 | .20 |
| 275 | Ed Sprague | .07 | .20 |
| 276 | F.P. Santangelo | .07 | .20 |
| 277 | Todd Greene | .07 | .20 |
| 278 | Butch Huskey | .07 | .20 |
| 279 | Steve Finley | .07 | .20 |
| 280 | Eric Davis | .07 | .20 |
| 281 | Shawn Green | .07 | .20 |
| 282 | Al Martin | .07 | .20 |
| 283 | Michael Tucker | .07 | .20 |
| 284 | Shane Reynolds | .07 | .20 |
| 285 | Matt Mieske | .07 | .20 |
| 286 | Jose Rosado | .07 | .20 |
| 287 | Mark Langston | .07 | .20 |
| 288 | Ralph Milliard | .07 | .20 |
| 289 | Mike Lansing | .07 | .20 |
| 290 | Scott Servais | .07 | .20 |
| 291 | Royce Clayton | .07 | .20 |
| 292 | Mike Grace | .07 | .20 |
| 293 | James Mouton | .07 | .20 |
| 294 | Charles Johnson | .07 | .20 |
| 295 | Gary Gaetti | .07 | .20 |
| 296 | Kevin Mitchell | .07 | .20 |
| 297 | Carlos Garcia | .07 | .20 |
| 298 | Desi Relaford | .07 | .20 |
| 299 | Jason Thompson | .07 | .20 |
| 300 | Osvaldo Fernandez | .07 | .20 |
| 301 | Fernando Vina | .07 | .20 |

|  |  | | |
|---|---|---|---|
| ☐ 302 | Jose Offerman | .07 | .20 |
| ☐ 303 | Yamil Benitez | .07 | .20 |
| ☐ 304 | J.T. Snow | .07 | .20 |
| ☐ 305 | Rafael Bournigal | .07 | .20 |
| ☐ 306 | Jason Isringhausen | .07 | .20 |
| ☐ 307 | Bobby Higginson | .07 | .20 |
| ☐ 308 | Nerio Rodriguez RC | .07 | .20 |
| ☐ 309 | Brian Giles RC | .40 | 1.00 |
| ☐ 310 | Andruw Jones | .10 | .30 |
| ☐ 311 | Tony Graffanino | .07 | .20 |
| ☐ 312 | Arquimedez Pozo | .07 | .20 |
| ☐ 313 | Jermaine Allensworth | .07 | .20 |
| ☐ 314 | Jeff Darwin | .07 | .20 |
| ☐ 315 | George Williams | .07 | .20 |
| ☐ 316 | Karim Garcia | .07 | .20 |
| ☐ 317 | Trey Beamon | .07 | .20 |
| ☐ 318 | Mac Suzuki | .07 | .20 |
| ☐ 319 | Robin Jennings | .07 | .20 |
| ☐ 320 | Danny Patterson | .07 | .20 |
| ☐ 321 | Damon Mashore | .07 | .20 |
| ☐ 322 | Wendell Magee | .07 | .20 |
| ☐ 323 | Dax Jones | .07 | .20 |
| ☐ 324 | Todd Walker | .07 | .20 |
| ☐ 325 | Marvin Benard | .07 | .20 |
| ☐ 326 | Mike Cameron | .07 | .20 |
| ☐ 327 | Marcus Jensen | .07 | .20 |
| ☐ 328 | Eddie Murray CL | .10 | .30 |
| ☐ 329 | Paul Molitor CL | .07 | .20 |
| ☐ 330 | Todd Hundley CL | .07 | .20 |
| ☐ 331 | Norm Charlton | .07 | .20 |
| ☐ 332 | Bruce Ruffin | .07 | .20 |
| ☐ 333 | John Wetteland | .07 | .20 |
| ☐ 334 | Marquis Grissom | .07 | .20 |
| ☐ 335 | Sterling Hitchcock | .07 | .20 |
| ☐ 336 | John Olerud | .07 | .20 |
| ☐ 337 | David Wells | .07 | .20 |
| ☐ 338 | Chili Davis | .07 | .20 |
| ☐ 339 | Mark Lewis | .07 | .20 |
| ☐ 340 | Kenny Lofton | .07 | .20 |
| ☐ 341 | Alex Fernandez | .07 | .20 |
| ☐ 342 | Ruben Sierra | .07 | .20 |
| ☐ 343 | Delino DeShields | .07 | .20 |
| ☐ 344 | John Wasdin | .07 | .20 |
| ☐ 345 | Dennis Martinez | .07 | .20 |
| ☐ 346 | Kevin Elster | .07 | .20 |
| ☐ 347 | Bobby Bonilla | .07 | .20 |
| ☐ 348 | Jaime Navarro | .07 | .20 |
| ☐ 349 | Chad Curtis | .07 | .20 |
| ☐ 350 | Terry Steinbach | .07 | .20 |
| ☐ 351 | Ariel Prieto | .07 | .20 |
| ☐ 352 | Jeff Kent | .07 | .20 |
| ☐ 353 | Carlos Garcia | .07 | .20 |
| ☐ 354 | Mark Whiten | .07 | .20 |
| ☐ 355 | Todd Zeile | .07 | .20 |
| ☐ 356 | Eric Davis | .07 | .20 |
| ☐ 357 | Greg Colbrunn | .07 | .20 |
| ☐ 358 | Moises Alou | .07 | .20 |
| ☐ 359 | Allen Watson | .07 | .20 |
| ☐ 360 | Jose Canseco | .10 | .30 |
| ☐ 361 | Matt Williams | .07 | .20 |
| ☐ 362 | Jeff King | .07 | .20 |
| ☐ 363 | Darryl Hamilton | .07 | .20 |
| ☐ 364 | Mark Clark | .07 | .20 |
| ☐ 365 | J.T. Snow | .07 | .20 |
| ☐ 366 | Kevin Mitchell | .07 | .20 |
| ☐ 367 | Orlando Miller | .07 | .20 |
| ☐ 368 | Rico Brogna | .07 | .20 |
| ☐ 369 | Mike James | .07 | .20 |
| ☐ 370 | Brad Ausmus | .07 | .20 |
| ☐ 371 | Darryl Kile | .07 | .20 |
| ☐ 372 | Edgardo Alfonzo | .07 | .20 |
| ☐ 373 | Julian Tavarez | .07 | .20 |
| ☐ 374 | Darren Lewis | .07 | .20 |
| ☐ 375 | Steve Karsay | .07 | .20 |
| ☐ 376 | Lee Stevens | .07 | .20 |
| ☐ 377 | Albie Lopez | .07 | .20 |
| ☐ 378 | Orel Hershiser | .07 | .20 |
| ☐ 379 | Lee Smith | .07 | .20 |
| ☐ 380 | Rick Helling | .07 | .20 |
| ☐ 381 | Carlos Perez | .07 | .20 |
| ☐ 382 | Tony Tarasco | .07 | .20 |
| ☐ 383 | Melvin Nieves | .07 | .20 |
| ☐ 384 | Benji Gil | .07 | .20 |
| ☐ 385 | Devon White | .07 | .20 |
| ☐ 386 | Armando Benitez | .07 | .20 |
| ☐ 387 | Bill Swift | .07 | .20 |
| ☐ 388 | John Smiley | .07 | .20 |
| ☐ 389 | Midre Cummings | .07 | .20 |
| ☐ 390 | Tim Belcher | .07 | .20 |
| ☐ 391 | Tim Raines | .07 | .20 |
| ☐ 392 | Todd Worrell | .07 | .20 |
| ☐ 393 | Quilvio Veras | .07 | .20 |
| ☐ 394 | Matt Lawton | .07 | .20 |
| ☐ 395 | Aaron Sele | .07 | .20 |
| ☐ 396 | Bip Roberts | .07 | .20 |
| ☐ 397 | Denny Neagle | .07 | .20 |
| ☐ 398 | Tyler Green | .07 | .20 |
| ☐ 399 | Hipolito Pichardo | .07 | .20 |
| ☐ 400 | Scott Erickson | .07 | .20 |
| ☐ 401 | Bobby Jones | .07 | .20 |
| ☐ 402 | Jim Edmonds | .07 | .20 |
| ☐ 403 | Chad Ogea | .07 | .20 |
| ☐ 404 | Cal Eldred | .07 | .20 |
| ☐ 405 | Pat Listach | .07 | .20 |
| ☐ 406 | Todd Stottlemyre | .07 | .20 |
| ☐ 407 | Phil Nevin | .07 | .20 |
| ☐ 408 | Otis Nixon | .07 | .20 |
| ☐ 409 | Billy Ashley | .07 | .20 |
| ☐ 410 | Jimmy Key | .07 | .20 |
| ☐ 411 | Mike Timlin | .07 | .20 |
| ☐ 412 | Joe Vitiello | .07 | .20 |
| ☐ 413 | Rondell White | .07 | .20 |
| ☐ 414 | Jeff Fassero | .07 | .20 |
| ☐ 415 | Rex Hudler | .07 | .20 |
| ☐ 416 | Curt Schilling | .07 | .20 |
| ☐ 417 | Rich Becker | .07 | .20 |
| ☐ 418 | William Van Landingham | .07 | .20 |
| ☐ 419 | Chris Snopek | .07 | .20 |
| ☐ 420 | David Segui | .07 | .20 |
| ☐ 421 | Eddie Murray | .20 | .50 |
| ☐ 422 | Shane Andrews | .07 | .20 |
| ☐ 423 | Gary DiSarcina | .07 | .20 |
| ☐ 424 | Brian Hunter | .07 | .20 |
| ☐ 425 | Willie Greene | .07 | .20 |
| ☐ 426 | Felipe Crespo | .07 | .20 |
| ☐ 427 | Jason Bates | .07 | .20 |
| ☐ 428 | Albert Belle | .20 | .50 |
| ☐ 429 | Rey Sanchez | .07 | .20 |
| ☐ 430 | Roger Clemens | .40 | 1.00 |
| ☐ 431 | Deion Sanders | .10 | .30 |
| ☐ 432 | Ernie Young | .07 | .20 |
| ☐ 433 | Jay Bell | .07 | .20 |
| ☐ 434 | Jeff Blauser | .07 | .20 |
| ☐ 435 | Lenny Dykstra | .07 | .20 |
| ☐ 436 | Chuck Carr | .07 | .20 |
| ☐ 437 | Russ Davis | .07 | .20 |
| ☐ 438 | Carl Everett | .07 | .20 |
| ☐ 439 | Damion Easley | .07 | .20 |
| ☐ 440 | Pat Kelly | .07 | .20 |
| ☐ 441 | Pat Rapp | .07 | .20 |
| ☐ 442 | Dave Justice | .07 | .20 |
| ☐ 443 | Graeme Lloyd | .07 | .20 |
| ☐ 444 | Damon Buford | .07 | .20 |
| ☐ 445 | Jose Valentin | .07 | .20 |
| ☐ 446 | Jason Schmidt | .07 | .20 |
| ☐ 447 | Dave Martinez | .07 | .20 |
| ☐ 448 | Danny Tartabull | .07 | .20 |
| ☐ 449 | Jose Vizcaino | .07 | .20 |
| ☐ 450 | Steve Avery | .07 | .20 |
| ☐ 451 | Mike Devereaux | .07 | .20 |
| ☐ 452 | Jim Eisenreich | .07 | .20 |
| ☐ 453 | Mark Leiter | .07 | .20 |
| ☐ 454 | Roberto Kelly | .07 | .20 |
| ☐ 455 | Benito Santiago | .07 | .20 |
| ☐ 456 | Steve Trachsel | .07 | .20 |
| ☐ 457 | Gerald Williams | .07 | .20 |
| ☐ 458 | Pete Schourek | .07 | .20 |
| ☐ 459 | Esteban Loaiza | .07 | .20 |
| ☐ 460 | Mel Rojas | .07 | .20 |
| ☐ 461 | Tim Wakefield | .07 | .20 |
| ☐ 462 | Tony Fernandez | .07 | .20 |
| ☐ 463 | Doug Drabek | .07 | .20 |
| ☐ 464 | Joe Girardi | .07 | .20 |
| ☐ 465 | Mike Bordick | .07 | .20 |
| ☐ 466 | Jim Leyritz | .07 | .20 |
| ☐ 467 | Erik Hanson | .07 | .20 |
| ☐ 468 | Michael Tucker | .07 | .20 |
| ☐ 469 | Tony Womack RC | .07 | .20 |
| ☐ 470 | Doug Glanville | .07 | .20 |
| ☐ 471 | Rudy Pemberton | .07 | .20 |
| ☐ 472 | Keith Lockhart | .07 | .20 |
| ☐ 473 | Nomar Garciaparra | .30 | .75 |
| ☐ 474 | Scott Rolen | .10 | .30 |
| ☐ 475 | Jason Dickson | .07 | .20 |
| ☐ 476 | Glendon Rusch | .07 | .20 |
| ☐ 477 | Todd Walker | .07 | .20 |
| ☐ 478 | Dmitri Young | .07 | .20 |
| ☐ 479 | Roy Myers | .07 | .20 |
| ☐ 480 | Wilton Guerrero | .07 | .20 |
| ☐ 481 | Jorge Posada | .10 | .30 |
| ☐ 482 | Brant Brown | .07 | .20 |
| ☐ 483 | Bubba Trammell RC | .07 | .20 |
| ☐ 484 | Jose Guillen | .07 | .20 |
| ☐ 485 | Scott Spiezio | .07 | .20 |
| ☐ 486 | Bob Abreu | .10 | .30 |
| ☐ 487 | Chris Holt | .07 | .20 |
| ☐ 488 | Deivi Cruz RC | .07 | .20 |
| ☐ 489 | Vladimir Guerrero | .20 | .50 |
| ☐ 490 | Julio Santana | .07 | .20 |
| ☐ 491 | Ray Montgomery RC | .07 | .20 |
| ☐ 492 | Kevin Orie | .07 | .20 |
| ☐ 493 | Todd Hundley GY | .07 | .20 |
| ☐ 494 | Tim Salmon GY | .07 | .20 |
| ☐ 495 | Albert Belle GY | .07 | .20 |
| ☐ 496 | Manny Ramirez GY | .07 | .20 |
| ☐ 497 | Rafael Palmeiro GY | .07 | .20 |
| ☐ 498 | Juan Gonzalez GY | .07 | .20 |
| ☐ 499 | Ken Griffey Jr. GY | .20 | .50 |
| ☐ 500 | Andruw Jones GY | .10 | .30 |
| ☐ 501 | Mike Piazza GY | .20 | .50 |
| ☐ 502 | Jeff Bagwell GY | .20 | .50 |
| ☐ 503 | Bernie Williams GY | .07 | .20 |
| ☐ 504 | Barry Bonds GY | .30 | .75 |
| ☐ 505 | Ken Caminiti GY | .07 | .20 |
| ☐ 506 | Darin Erstad GY | .07 | .20 |
| ☐ 507 | Alex Rodriguez GY | .20 | .50 |
| ☐ 508 | Frank Thomas GY | .10 | .30 |
| ☐ 509 | Chipper Jones GY | .10 | .30 |
| ☐ 510 | Mo Vaughn GY | .07 | .20 |
| ☐ 511 | Mark McGwire GY | .25 | .60 |
| ☐ 512 | Fred McGriff GY | .07 | .20 |
| ☐ 513 | Jay Buhner RF | .07 | .20 |
| ☐ 514 | Jim Thome RF | .07 | .20 |
| ☐ 515 | Gary Sheffield RF | .07 | .20 |
| ☐ 516 | Dean Palmer RF | .07 | .20 |
| ☐ 517 | Henry Rodriguez RF | .07 | .20 |
| ☐ 518 | Andy Pettitte RF | .07 | .20 |
| ☐ 519 | Mike Mussina RF | .07 | .20 |
| ☐ 520 | Greg Maddux RF | .20 | .50 |
| ☐ 521 | John Smoltz RF | .07 | .20 |
| ☐ 522 | Hideo Nomo RF | .07 | .20 |
| ☐ 523 | Troy Percival RF | .07 | .20 |
| ☐ 524 | John Wetteland RF | .07 | .20 |
| ☐ 525 | Roger Clemens RF | .20 | .50 |
| ☐ 526 | Charles Nagy RF | .07 | .20 |
| ☐ 527 | Mariano Rivera RF | .10 | .30 |
| ☐ 528 | Tom Glavine RF | .07 | .20 |
| ☐ 529 | Randy Johnson RF | .10 | .30 |
| ☐ 530 | Jason Isringhausen RF | .07 | .20 |
| ☐ 531 | Alex Fernandez RF | .07 | .20 |
| ☐ 532 | Kevin Brown RF | .07 | .20 |
| ☐ 533 | Chuck Knoblauch TG | .07 | .20 |
| ☐ 534 | Rusty Greer TG | .07 | .20 |
| ☐ 535 | Tony Gwynn TG | .10 | .30 |
| ☐ 536 | Ryan Klesko TG | .07 | .20 |
| ☐ 537 | Ryne Sandberg TG | .20 | .50 |
| ☐ 538 | Barry Larkin TG | .07 | .20 |
| ☐ 539 | Will Clark TG | .07 | .20 |
| ☐ 540 | Kenny Lofton TG | .07 | .20 |
| ☐ 541 | Paul Molitor TG | .07 | .20 |
| ☐ 542 | Roberto Alomar TG | .07 | .20 |
| ☐ 543 | Rey Ordonez TG | .07 | .20 |
| ☐ 544 | Jason Giambi TG | .07 | .20 |
| ☐ 545 | Derek Jeter TG | .25 | .60 |
| ☐ 546 | Cal Ripken TG | .30 | .75 |
| ☐ 547 | Ivan Rodriguez TG | .07 | .20 |
| ☐ 548 | Ken Griffey Jr. CL | .20 | .50 |
| ☐ 549 | Frank Thomas CL | .10 | .30 |
| ☐ 550 | Mike Piazza CL | .20 | .50 |
| ☐ 551A | Hideki Irabu English SP | 1.00 | 2.50 |
| ☐ 551B | Hideki Irabu Japanese SP | 1.00 | 2.50 |

# 1998 Score

| | | |
|---|---|---|
| ❑ COMPLETE SET (270) | 15.00 | 40.00 |
| ❑ 1 Andruw Jones | .10 | .30 |
| ❑ 2 Dan Wilson | .07 | .20 |
| ❑ 3 Hideo Nomo | .20 | .50 |
| ❑ 4 Chuck Carr | .07 | .20 |
| ❑ 5 Barry Bonds | .60 | 1.50 |
| ❑ 6 Jack McDowell | .07 | .20 |
| ❑ 7 Albert Belle | .07 | .20 |
| ❑ 8 Francisco Cordova | .07 | .20 |
| ❑ 9 Greg Maddux | .30 | .75 |
| ❑ 10 Alex Rodriguez | .30 | .75 |
| ❑ 11 Steve Avery | .07 | .20 |
| ❑ 12 Chuck McElroy | .07 | .20 |
| ❑ 13 Larry Walker | .07 | .20 |
| ❑ 14 Hideki Irabu | .07 | .20 |
| ❑ 15 Roberto Alomar | .10 | .30 |
| ❑ 16 Neifi Perez | .07 | .20 |
| ❑ 17 Jim Thome | .10 | .30 |
| ❑ 18 Rickey Henderson | .20 | .50 |
| ❑ 19 Andres Galarraga | .20 | .50 |
| ❑ 20 Jeff Fassero | .07 | .20 |
| ❑ 21 Kevin Young | .07 | .20 |
| ❑ 22 Derek Jeter | .50 | 1.25 |
| ❑ 23 Andy Benes | .07 | .20 |
| ❑ 24 Mike Piazza | .30 | .75 |
| ❑ 25 Todd Stottlemyre | .07 | .20 |
| ❑ 26 Michael Tucker | .07 | .20 |
| ❑ 27 Denny Neagle | .07 | .20 |
| ❑ 28 Javier Lopez | .07 | .20 |
| ❑ 29 Aaron Sele | .07 | .20 |
| ❑ 30 Ryan Klesko | .07 | .20 |
| ❑ 31 Dennis Eckersley | .07 | .20 |
| ❑ 32 Quinton McCracken | .07 | .20 |
| ❑ 33 Brian Anderson | .07 | .20 |
| ❑ 34 Ken Griffey Jr. | .30 | .75 |
| ❑ 35 Shawn Estes | .07 | .20 |
| ❑ 36 Tim Wakefield | .07 | .20 |
| ❑ 37 Jimmy Key | .07 | .20 |
| ❑ 38 Jeff Bagwell | .10 | .30 |
| ❑ 39 Edgardo Alfonzo | .07 | .20 |
| ❑ 40 Mike Cameron | .07 | .20 |
| ❑ 41 Mark McGwire | .50 | 1.25 |
| ❑ 42 Tino Martinez | .10 | .30 |
| ❑ 43 Cal Ripken | .60 | 1.50 |
| ❑ 44 Curtis Goodwin | .07 | .20 |
| ❑ 45 Bobby Ayala | .07 | .20 |
| ❑ 46 Sandy Alomar Jr. | .07 | .20 |
| ❑ 47 Bobby Jones | .07 | .20 |
| ❑ 48 Omar Vizquel | .10 | .30 |
| ❑ 49 Roger Clemens | .40 | 1.00 |
| ❑ 50 Tony Gwynn | .25 | .60 |
| ❑ 51 Chipper Jones | .20 | .50 |
| ❑ 52 Ron Coomer | .07 | .20 |
| ❑ 53 Dmitri Young | .07 | .20 |
| ❑ 54 Brian Giles | .07 | .20 |
| ❑ 55 Steve Finley | .07 | .20 |
| ❑ 56 David Cone | .07 | .20 |
| ❑ 57 Andy Pettitte | .10 | .30 |
| ❑ 58 Wilton Guerrero | .07 | .20 |
| ❑ 59 Deion Sanders | .10 | .30 |
| ❑ 60 Carlos Delgado | .07 | .20 |
| ❑ 61 Jason Giambi | .07 | .20 |
| ❑ 62 Ozzie Guillen | .07 | .20 |
| ❑ 63 Jay Bell | .07 | .20 |
| ❑ 64 Barry Larkin | .10 | .30 |
| ❑ 65 Sammy Sosa | .20 | .50 |
| ❑ 66 Bernie Williams | .10 | .30 |
| ❑ 67 Terry Steinbach | .07 | .20 |
| ❑ 68 Scott Rolen | .20 | .50 |
| ❑ 69 Melvin Nieves | .07 | .20 |
| ❑ 70 Craig Biggio | .10 | .30 |
| ❑ 71 Todd Greene | .07 | .20 |

| | | |
|---|---|---|
| ❑ 72 Greg Gagne | .07 | .20 |
| ❑ 73 Shigetoshi Hasegawa | .07 | .20 |
| ❑ 74 Mark McLemore | .07 | .20 |
| ❑ 75 Darren Bragg | .07 | .20 |
| ❑ 76 Brett Butler | .07 | .20 |
| ❑ 77 Ron Gant | .07 | .20 |
| ❑ 78 Mike Difelice RC | .07 | .20 |
| ❑ 79 Charles Nagy | .07 | .20 |
| ❑ 80 Scott Hatteberg | .07 | .20 |
| ❑ 81 Brady Anderson | .07 | .20 |
| ❑ 82 Jay Buhner | .07 | .20 |
| ❑ 83 Todd Hollandsworth | .07 | .20 |
| ❑ 84 Geronimo Berroa | .07 | .20 |
| ❑ 85 Jeff Suppan | .07 | .20 |
| ❑ 86 Pedro Martinez | .10 | .30 |
| ❑ 87 Roger Cedeno | .07 | .20 |
| ❑ 88 Ivan Rodriguez | .10 | .30 |
| ❑ 89 Jaime Navarro | .07 | .20 |
| ❑ 90 Chris Hoiles | .07 | .20 |
| ❑ 91 Nomar Garciaparra | .30 | .75 |
| ❑ 92 Rafael Palmeiro | .10 | .30 |
| ❑ 93 Darin Erstad | .07 | .20 |
| ❑ 94 Kenny Lofton | .07 | .20 |
| ❑ 95 Mike Timlin | .07 | .20 |
| ❑ 96 Chris Clemons | .07 | .20 |
| ❑ 97 Vinny Castilla | .07 | .20 |
| ❑ 98 Charlie Hayes | .07 | .20 |
| ❑ 99 Lyle Mouton | .07 | .20 |
| ❑ 100 Jason Dickson | .07 | .20 |
| ❑ 101 Justin Thompson | .07 | .20 |
| ❑ 102 Pat Kelly | .07 | .20 |
| ❑ 103 Chan Ho Park | .07 | .20 |
| ❑ 104 Ray Lankford | .07 | .20 |
| ❑ 105 Frank Thomas | .20 | .50 |
| ❑ 106 Jermaine Allensworth | .07 | .20 |
| ❑ 107 Doug Drabek | .07 | .20 |
| ❑ 108 Todd Hundley | .07 | .20 |
| ❑ 109 Carl Everett | .07 | .20 |
| ❑ 110 Edgar Martinez | .10 | .30 |
| ❑ 111 Robin Ventura | .07 | .20 |
| ❑ 112 John Wetteland | .07 | .20 |
| ❑ 113 Mariano Rivera | .20 | .50 |
| ❑ 114 Jose Rosado | .07 | .20 |
| ❑ 115 Ken Caminiti | .07 | .20 |
| ❑ 116 Paul O'Neill | .10 | .30 |
| ❑ 117 Tim Salmon | .10 | .30 |
| ❑ 118 Eduardo Perez | .07 | .20 |
| ❑ 119 Mike Jackson | .07 | .20 |
| ❑ 120 John Smoltz | .10 | .30 |
| ❑ 121 Brant Brown | .07 | .20 |
| ❑ 122 John Mabry | .07 | .20 |
| ❑ 123 Chuck Knoblauch | .10 | .30 |
| ❑ 124 Reggie Sanders | .07 | .20 |
| ❑ 125 Ken Hill | .07 | .20 |
| ❑ 126 Mike Mussina | .10 | .30 |
| ❑ 127 Chad Curtis | .07 | .20 |
| ❑ 128 Todd Worrell | .07 | .20 |
| ❑ 129 Chris Widger | .07 | .20 |
| ❑ 130 Damon Mashore | .07 | .20 |
| ❑ 131 Kevin Brown | .10 | .30 |
| ❑ 132 Bip Roberts | .07 | .20 |
| ❑ 133 Tim Naehring | .07 | .20 |
| ❑ 134 Dave Martinez | .07 | .20 |
| ❑ 135 Jeff Blauser | .07 | .20 |
| ❑ 136 David Justice | .07 | .20 |
| ❑ 137 Dave Hollins | .07 | .20 |
| ❑ 138 Pat Hentgen | .07 | .20 |
| ❑ 139 Darren Daulton | .07 | .20 |
| ❑ 140 Ramon Martinez | .07 | .20 |
| ❑ 141 Raul Casanova | .07 | .20 |
| ❑ 142 Tom Glavine | .10 | .30 |
| ❑ 143 J.T. Snow | .07 | .20 |
| ❑ 144 Tony Graffanino | .07 | .20 |
| ❑ 145 Randy Johnson | .20 | .50 |
| ❑ 146 Orlando Merced | .07 | .20 |
| ❑ 147 Jeff Juden | .07 | .20 |
| ❑ 148 Darryl Kile | .07 | .20 |
| ❑ 149 Ray Durham | .07 | .20 |
| ❑ 150 Alex Fernandez | .07 | .20 |
| ❑ 151 Joey Cora | .07 | .20 |
| ❑ 152 Royce Clayton | .07 | .20 |
| ❑ 153 Randy Myers | .07 | .20 |
| ❑ 154 Charles Johnson | .07 | .20 |
| ❑ 155 Alan Benes | .07 | .20 |
| ❑ 156 Mike Bordick | .07 | .20 |
| ❑ 157 Heathcliff Slocumb | .07 | .20 |
| ❑ 158 Roger Bailey | .07 | .20 |
| ❑ 159 Reggie Jefferson | .07 | .20 |

| | | |
|---|---|---|
| ❑ 160 Ricky Bottalico | .07 | .20 |
| ❑ 161 Scott Erickson | .07 | .20 |
| ❑ 162 Matt Williams | .07 | .20 |
| ❑ 163 Robb Nen | .07 | .20 |
| ❑ 164 Matt Stairs | .07 | .20 |
| ❑ 165 Ismael Valdes | .07 | .20 |
| ❑ 166 Lee Stevens | .07 | .20 |
| ❑ 167 Gary DiSarcina | .07 | .20 |
| ❑ 168 Brad Radke | .07 | .20 |
| ❑ 169 Mike Lansing | .07 | .20 |
| ❑ 170 Armando Benitez | .07 | .20 |
| ❑ 171 Mike James | .07 | .20 |
| ❑ 172 Russ Davis | .07 | .20 |
| ❑ 173 Lance Johnson | .07 | .20 |
| ❑ 174 Joey Hamilton | .07 | .20 |
| ❑ 175 John Valentin | .07 | .20 |
| ❑ 176 David Segui | .07 | .20 |
| ❑ 177 David Wells | .07 | .20 |
| ❑ 178 Delino DeShields | .07 | .20 |
| ❑ 179 Eric Karros | .07 | .20 |
| ❑ 180 Jim Leyritz | .07 | .20 |
| ❑ 181 Raul Mondesi | .07 | .20 |
| ❑ 182 Travis Fryman | .07 | .20 |
| ❑ 183 Todd Zeile | .07 | .20 |
| ❑ 184 Brian Jordan | .07 | .20 |
| ❑ 185 Rey Ordonez | .07 | .20 |
| ❑ 186 Jim Edmonds | .07 | .20 |
| ❑ 187 Terrell Wade | .07 | .20 |
| ❑ 188 Marquis Grissom | .07 | .20 |
| ❑ 189 Chris Snopek | .07 | .20 |
| ❑ 190 Shane Reynolds | .07 | .20 |
| ❑ 191 Jeff Frye | .07 | .20 |
| ❑ 192 Paul Sorrento | .07 | .20 |
| ❑ 193 James Baldwin | .07 | .20 |
| ❑ 194 Brian McRae | .07 | .20 |
| ❑ 195 Fred McGriff | .10 | .30 |
| ❑ 196 Troy Percival | .07 | .20 |
| ❑ 197 Rich Amaral | .07 | .20 |
| ❑ 198 Juan Guzman | .07 | .20 |
| ❑ 199 Cecil Fielder | .07 | .20 |
| ❑ 200 Willie Blair | .07 | .20 |
| ❑ 201 Chili Davis | .07 | .20 |
| ❑ 202 Gary Gaetti | .07 | .20 |
| ❑ 203 B.J. Surhoff | .07 | .20 |
| ❑ 204 Steve Cooke | .07 | .20 |
| ❑ 205 Chuck Finley | .07 | .20 |
| ❑ 206 Jeff Kent | .07 | .20 |
| ❑ 207 Ben McDonald | .07 | .20 |
| ❑ 208 Jeffrey Hammonds | .07 | .20 |
| ❑ 209 Tom Goodwin | .07 | .20 |
| ❑ 210 Billy Ashley | .07 | .20 |
| ❑ 211 Wil Cordero | .07 | .20 |
| ❑ 212 Shawon Dunston | .07 | .20 |
| ❑ 213 Tony Phillips | .07 | .20 |
| ❑ 214 Jamie Moyer | .07 | .20 |
| ❑ 215 John Jaha | .07 | .20 |
| ❑ 216 Troy O'Leary | .07 | .20 |
| ❑ 217 Brad Ausmus | .07 | .20 |
| ❑ 218 Garret Anderson | .07 | .20 |
| ❑ 219 Wilson Alvarez | .07 | .20 |
| ❑ 220 Kent Mercker | .07 | .20 |
| ❑ 221 Wade Boggs | .10 | .30 |
| ❑ 222 Mark Wohlers | .07 | .20 |
| ❑ 223 Kevin Appier | .07 | .20 |
| ❑ 224 Tony Fernandez | .07 | .20 |
| ❑ 225 Ugueth Urbina | .07 | .20 |
| ❑ 226 Gregg Jefferies | .07 | .20 |
| ❑ 227 Mo Vaughn | .07 | .20 |
| ❑ 228 Arthur Rhodes | .07 | .20 |
| ❑ 229 Jorge Fabregas | .07 | .20 |
| ❑ 230 Mark Gardner | .07 | .20 |
| ❑ 231 Shane Mack | .07 | .20 |
| ❑ 232 Jorge Posada | .10 | .30 |
| ❑ 233 Jose Cruz Jr. | .10 | .30 |
| ❑ 234 Paul Konerko | .07 | .20 |
| ❑ 235 Derek Lee | .10 | .30 |
| ❑ 236 Steve Woodard | .07 | .20 |
| ❑ 237 Todd Dunwoody | .07 | .20 |
| ❑ 238 Fernando Tatis | .07 | .20 |
| ❑ 239 Jacob Cruz | .07 | .20 |
| ❑ 240 Pokey Reese | .07 | .20 |
| ❑ 241 Mark Kotsay | .07 | .20 |
| ❑ 242 Matt Morris | .07 | .20 |
| ❑ 243 Antone Williamson | .07 | .20 |
| ❑ 244 Ben Grieve | .07 | .20 |
| ❑ 245 Ryan McGuire | .07 | .20 |
| ❑ 246 Lou Collier | .07 | .20 |
| ❑ 247 Shannon Stewart | .07 | .20 |

| | | |
|---|---|---|
| □ 248 Brett Tomko | .07 | .20 |
| □ 249 Bobby Estalella | .07 | .20 |
| □ 250 Livan Hernandez | .07 | .20 |
| □ 251 Todd Helton | .10 | .30 |
| □ 252 Jaret Wright | .07 | .20 |
| □ 253 Darryl Hamilton IM | .07 | .20 |
| □ 254 Stan Javier IM | .07 | .20 |
| □ 255 Glenallen Hill IM | .07 | .20 |
| □ 256 Mark Gardner IM | .07 | .20 |
| □ 257 Cal Ripken IM | .30 | .75 |
| □ 258 Mike Mussina IM | .07 | .20 |
| □ 259 Mike Piazza IM | .20 | .50 |
| □ 260 Sammy Sosa IM | .10 | .30 |
| □ 261 Todd Hundley IM | .07 | .20 |
| □ 262 Eric Karros IM | .07 | .20 |
| □ 263 Denny Neagle IM | .07 | .20 |
| □ 264 Jeromy Burnitz IM | .07 | .20 |
| □ 265 Greg Maddux IM | .20 | .50 |
| □ 266 Tony Clark IM | .07 | .20 |
| □ 267 Vladimir Guerrero IM | .10 | .30 |
| □ 268 Cal Ripken CL UER | .30 | .75 |
| □ 269 Ken Griffey Jr. CL | .20 | .50 |
| □ 270 Mark McGwire CL | .25 | .60 |
| □ NNO Checklist Regular Issue | .07 | .20 |
| □ NNO Checklist All-Star Edition | .10 | .30 |

## 1993 SP

| | | |
|---|---|---|
| □ COMPLETE SET (290) | 40.00 | 80.00 |
| □ COMMON CARD (1-270) | .20 | .50 |
| □ FOIL PROSPECTS (271-290) | .40 | 1.00 |
| □ 1 Roberto Alomar AS | .50 | 1.25 |
| □ 2 Wade Boggs AS | .50 | 1.25 |
| □ 3 Joe Carter AS | .20 | .50 |
| □ 4 Ken Griffey Jr. AS | 1.25 | 3.00 |
| □ 5 Mark Langston AS | .20 | .50 |
| □ 6 John Olerud AS | .30 | .75 |
| □ 7 Kirby Puckett AS | .75 | 2.00 |
| □ 8 Cal Ripken AS | 2.50 | 6.00 |
| □ 9 Ivan Rodriguez AS | .50 | 1.25 |
| □ 10 Barry Bonds AS | 2.00 | 5.00 |
| □ 11 Darren Daulton AS | .30 | .75 |
| □ 12 Marquis Grissom AS | .30 | .75 |
| □ 13 David Justice AS | .30 | .75 |
| □ 14 John Kruk AS | .30 | .75 |
| □ 15 Barry Larkin AS | .50 | 1.25 |
| □ 16 Terry Mulholland AS | .20 | .50 |
| □ 17 Ryne Sandberg AS | 1.25 | 3.00 |
| □ 18 Gary Sheffield AS | .30 | .75 |
| □ 19 Chad Curtis | .20 | .50 |
| □ 20 Chili Davis | .30 | .75 |
| □ 21 Gary DiSarcina | .20 | .50 |
| □ 22 Damion Easley | .20 | .50 |
| □ 23 Chuck Finley | .20 | .50 |
| □ 24 Luis Polonia | .20 | .50 |
| □ 25 Tim Salmon | .50 | 1.25 |
| □ 26 J.T.Snow RC | .50 | 1.25 |
| □ 27 Russ Springer | .20 | .50 |
| □ 28 Jeff Bagwell | .50 | 1.25 |
| □ 29 Craig Biggio | .50 | 1.25 |
| □ 30 Ken Caminiti | .30 | .75 |
| □ 31 Andujar Cedeno | .20 | .50 |
| □ 32 Doug Drabek | .20 | .50 |
| □ 33 Steve Finley | .30 | .75 |
| □ 34 Luis Gonzalez | .30 | .75 |
| □ 35 Pete Harnisch | .20 | .50 |
| □ 36 Darryl Kile | .20 | .50 |
| □ 37 Mike Bordick | .20 | .50 |
| □ 38 Dennis Eckersley | .30 | .75 |
| □ 39 Brent Gates | .20 | .50 |
| □ 40 Rickey Henderson | .75 | 2.00 |
| □ 41 Mark McGwire | 2.00 | 5.00 |
| □ 42 Craig Paquette | .20 | .50 |
| □ 43 Ruben Sierra | .30 | .75 |
| □ 44 Terry Steinbach | .20 | .50 |

| | | |
|---|---|---|
| □ 45 Todd Van Poppel | .20 | .50 |
| □ 46 Pat Borders | .20 | .50 |
| □ 47 Tony Fernandez | .20 | .50 |
| □ 48 Juan Guzman | .20 | .50 |
| □ 49 Pat Hentgen | .20 | .50 |
| □ 50 Paul Molitor | .30 | .75 |
| □ 51 Jack Morris | .30 | .75 |
| □ 52 Ed Sprague | .20 | .50 |
| □ 53 Duane Ward | .20 | .50 |
| □ 54 Devon White | .20 | .50 |
| □ 55 Steve Avery | .20 | .50 |
| □ 56 Jeff Blauser | .20 | .50 |
| □ 57 Ron Gant | .30 | .75 |
| □ 58 Tom Glavine | .50 | 1.25 |
| □ 59 Greg Maddux | 1.25 | 3.00 |
| □ 60 Fred McGriff | .50 | 1.25 |
| □ 61 Terry Pendleton | .30 | .75 |
| □ 62 Deion Sanders | .50 | 1.25 |
| □ 63 John Smoltz | .50 | 1.25 |
| □ 64 Cal Eldred | .20 | .50 |
| □ 65 Darryl Hamilton | .20 | .50 |
| □ 66 John Jaha | .20 | .50 |
| □ 67 Pat Listach | .20 | .50 |
| □ 68 Jaime Navarro | .20 | .50 |
| □ 69 Kevin Reimer | .20 | .50 |
| □ 70 B.J. Surhoff | .30 | .75 |
| □ 71 Greg Vaughn | .20 | .50 |
| □ 72 Robin Yount | 1.25 | 3.00 |
| □ 73 Rene Arocha RC | .20 | .50 |
| □ 74 Bernard Gilkey | .20 | .50 |
| □ 75 Gregg Jefferies | .20 | .50 |
| □ 76 Ray Lankford | .30 | .75 |
| □ 77 Tom Pagnozzi | .20 | .50 |
| □ 78 Lee Smith | .30 | .75 |
| □ 79 Ozzie Smith | 1.25 | 3.00 |
| □ 80 Bob Tewksbury | .20 | .50 |
| □ 81 Mark Whiten | .20 | .50 |
| □ 82 Steve Buechele | .20 | .50 |
| □ 83 Mark Grace | .50 | 1.25 |
| □ 84 Jose Guzman | .20 | .50 |
| □ 85 Derrick May | .20 | .50 |
| □ 86 Mike Morgan | .20 | .50 |
| □ 87 Randy Myers | .20 | .50 |
| □ 88 Kevin Roberson RC | .20 | .50 |
| □ 89 Sammy Sosa | .75 | 2.00 |
| □ 90 Rick Wilkins | .20 | .50 |
| □ 91 Brett Butler | .30 | .75 |
| □ 92 Eric Davis | .30 | .75 |
| □ 93 Orel Hershiser | .30 | .75 |
| □ 94 Eric Karros | .30 | .75 |
| □ 95 Ramon Martinez | .30 | .75 |
| □ 96 Raul Mondesi | .30 | .75 |
| □ 97 Jose Offerman | .20 | .50 |
| □ 98 Mike Piazza | 2.00 | 5.00 |
| □ 99 Darryl Strawberry | .30 | .75 |
| □ 100 Moises Alou | .30 | .75 |
| □ 101 Wil Cordero | .20 | .50 |
| □ 102 Delino DeShields | .20 | .50 |
| □ 103 Darrin Fletcher | .20 | .50 |
| □ 104 Ken Hill | .20 | .50 |
| □ 105 Mike Lansing RC | .30 | .75 |
| □ 106 Dennis Martinez | .30 | .75 |
| □ 107 Larry Walker | .30 | .75 |
| □ 108 John Wetteland | .20 | .50 |
| □ 109 Rod Beck | .20 | .50 |
| □ 110 John Burkett | .20 | .50 |
| □ 111 Will Clark | .50 | 1.25 |
| □ 112 Royce Clayton | .20 | .50 |
| □ 113 Darren Lewis | .20 | .50 |
| □ 114 Willie McGee | .30 | .75 |
| □ 115 Bill Swift | .20 | .50 |
| □ 116 Robby Thompson | .20 | .50 |
| □ 117 Matt Williams | .30 | .75 |
| □ 118 Sandy Alomar Jr. | .20 | .50 |
| □ 119 Carlos Baerga | .30 | .75 |
| □ 120 Albert Belle | .30 | .75 |
| □ 121 Reggie Jefferson | .20 | .50 |
| □ 122 Wayne Kirby | .20 | .50 |
| □ 123 Kenny Lofton | .30 | .75 |
| □ 124 Carlos Martinez | .20 | .50 |
| □ 125 Charles Nagy | .20 | .50 |
| □ 126 Paul Sorrento | .20 | .50 |
| □ 127 Rich Amaral | .20 | .50 |
| □ 128 Jay Buhner | .30 | .75 |
| □ 129 Norm Charlton | .20 | .50 |
| □ 130 Dave Fleming | .20 | .50 |
| □ 131 Erik Hanson | .20 | .50 |
| □ 132 Randy Johnson | .75 | 2.00 |

| | | |
|---|---|---|
| □ 133 Edgar Martinez | .50 | 1.25 |
| □ 134 Tino Martinez | .50 | 1.25 |
| □ 135 Omar Vizquel | .50 | 1.25 |
| □ 136 Bret Barberie | .20 | .50 |
| □ 137 Chuck Carr | .20 | .50 |
| □ 138 Jeff Conine | .30 | .75 |
| □ 139 Orestes Destrade | .20 | .50 |
| □ 140 Chris Hammond | .20 | .50 |
| □ 141 Bryan Harvey | .20 | .50 |
| □ 142 Benito Santiago | .30 | .75 |
| □ 143 Walt Weiss | .20 | .50 |
| □ 144 Darrell Whitmore RC | .20 | .50 |
| □ 145 Tim Bogar RC | .20 | .50 |
| □ 146 Bobby Bonilla | .30 | .75 |
| □ 147 Jeromy Burnitz | .30 | .75 |
| □ 148 Vince Coleman | .20 | .50 |
| □ 149 Dwight Gooden | .30 | .75 |
| □ 150 Todd Hundley | .20 | .50 |
| □ 151 Howard Johnson | .20 | .50 |
| □ 152 Eddie Murray | .75 | 2.00 |
| □ 153 Bret Saberhagen | .20 | .50 |
| □ 154 Brady Anderson | .30 | .75 |
| □ 155 Mike Devereaux | .20 | .50 |
| □ 156 Jeffrey Hammonds | .20 | .50 |
| □ 157 Chris Hoiles | .20 | .50 |
| □ 158 Ben McDonald | .20 | .50 |
| □ 159 Mark McLemore | .20 | .50 |
| □ 160 Mike Mussina | .50 | 1.25 |
| □ 161 Gregg Olson | .20 | .50 |
| □ 162 David Segui | .20 | .50 |
| □ 163 Derek Bell | .20 | .50 |
| □ 164 Andy Benes | .20 | .50 |
| □ 165 Archi Cianfrocco | .20 | .50 |
| □ 166 Ricky Gutierrez | .20 | .50 |
| □ 167 Tony Gwynn | 1.00 | 2.50 |
| □ 168 Gene Harris | .20 | .50 |
| □ 169 Trevor Hoffman | .75 | 2.00 |
| □ 170 Ray McDavid RC | .20 | .50 |
| □ 171 Phil Plantier | .20 | .50 |
| □ 172 Mariano Duncan | .20 | .50 |
| □ 173 Len Dykstra | .30 | .75 |
| □ 174 Tommy Greene | .20 | .50 |
| □ 175 Dave Hollins | .20 | .50 |
| □ 176 Pete Incaviglia | .20 | .50 |
| □ 177 Mickey Morandini | .20 | .50 |
| □ 178 Curt Schilling | .30 | .75 |
| □ 179 Kevin Stocker | .20 | .50 |
| □ 180 Mitch Williams | .20 | .50 |
| □ 181 Stan Belinda | .20 | .50 |
| □ 182 Jay Bell | .30 | .75 |
| □ 183 Steve Cooke | .20 | .50 |
| □ 184 Carlos Garcia | .20 | .50 |
| □ 185 Jeff King | .20 | .50 |
| □ 186 Orlando Merced | .20 | .50 |
| □ 187 Don Slaught | .20 | .50 |
| □ 188 Andy Van Slyke | .50 | 1.25 |
| □ 189 Kevin Young | .20 | .50 |
| □ 190 Kevin Brown | .20 | .50 |
| □ 191 Jose Canseco | .50 | 1.25 |
| □ 192 Julio Franco | .30 | .75 |
| □ 193 Benji Gil | .20 | .50 |
| □ 194 Juan Gonzalez | .30 | .75 |
| □ 195 Tom Henke | .20 | .50 |
| □ 196 Rafael Palmeiro | .50 | 1.25 |
| □ 197 Dean Palmer | .30 | .75 |
| □ 198 Nolan Ryan | 3.00 | 8.00 |
| □ 199 Roger Clemens | 1.50 | 4.00 |
| □ 200 Scott Cooper | .20 | .50 |
| □ 201 Andre Dawson | .30 | .75 |
| □ 202 Mike Greenwell | .20 | .50 |
| □ 203 Carlos Quintana | .20 | .50 |
| □ 204 Jeff Russell | .20 | .50 |
| □ 205 Aaron Sele | .20 | .50 |
| □ 206 Mo Vaughn | .30 | .75 |
| □ 207 Frank Viola | .20 | .50 |
| □ 208 Rob Dibble | .20 | .50 |
| □ 209 Roberto Kelly | .20 | .50 |
| □ 210 Kevin Mitchell | .20 | .50 |
| □ 211 Hal Morris | .20 | .50 |
| □ 212 Joe Oliver | .20 | .50 |
| □ 213 Jose Rijo | .20 | .50 |
| □ 214 Bip Roberts | .20 | .50 |
| □ 215 Chris Sabo | .20 | .50 |
| □ 216 Reggie Sanders | .30 | .75 |
| □ 217 Dante Bichette | .30 | .75 |
| □ 218 Jerald Clark | .20 | .50 |
| □ 219 Alex Cole | .20 | .50 |
| □ 220 Andres Galarraga | .30 | .75 |

| | | |
|---|---|---|
| 221 Joe Girardi | .20 | .50 |
| 222 Charlie Hayes | .20 | .50 |
| 223 Roberto Mejia RC | .20 | .50 |
| 224 Armando Reynoso | .20 | .50 |
| 225 Eric Young | .20 | .50 |
| 226 Kevin Appier | .30 | .75 |
| 227 George Brett | 2.00 | 5.00 |
| 228 David Cone | .30 | .75 |
| 229 Phil Hiatt | .20 | .50 |
| 230 Felix Jose | .20 | .50 |
| 231 Wally Joyner | .30 | .75 |
| 232 Mike Macfarlane | .20 | .50 |
| 233 Brian McRae | .20 | .50 |
| 234 Jeff Montgomery | .20 | .50 |
| 235 Rob Deer | .20 | .50 |
| 236 Cecil Fielder | .30 | .75 |
| 237 Travis Fryman | .30 | .75 |
| 238 Mike Henneman | .20 | .50 |
| 239 Tony Phillips | .20 | .50 |
| 240 Mickey Tettleton | .20 | .50 |
| 241 Alan Trammell | .30 | .75 |
| 242 David Wells | .30 | .75 |
| 243 Lou Whitaker | .30 | .75 |
| 244 Rick Aguilera | .20 | .50 |
| 245 Scott Erickson | .20 | .50 |
| 246 Brian Harper | .20 | .50 |
| 247 Kent Hrbek | .30 | .75 |
| 248 Chuck Knoblauch | .30 | .75 |
| 249 Shane Mack | .20 | .50 |
| 250 David McCarty | .20 | .50 |
| 251 Pedro Munoz | .20 | .50 |
| 252 Dave Winfield | .20 | .50 |
| 253 Alex Fernandez | .20 | .50 |
| 254 Ozzie Guillen | .30 | .75 |
| 255 Bo Jackson | .75 | 2.00 |
| 256 Lance Johnson | .20 | .50 |
| 257 Ron Karkovice | .20 | .50 |
| 258 Jack McDowell | .20 | .50 |
| 259 Tim Raines | .30 | .75 |
| 260 Frank Thomas | .75 | 2.00 |
| 261 Robin Ventura | .50 | 1.25 |
| 262 Jim Abbott | .50 | 1.25 |
| 263 Steve Farr | .20 | .50 |
| 264 Jimmy Key | .30 | .75 |
| 265 Don Mattingly | 2.00 | 5.00 |
| 266 Paul O'Neill | .50 | 1.25 |
| 267 Mike Stanley | .20 | .50 |
| 268 Danny Tartabull | .20 | .50 |
| 269 Bob Wickman | .20 | .50 |
| 270 Bernie Williams | .50 | 1.25 |
| 271 Jason Bere FOIL | .40 | 1.00 |
| 272 Roger Cedeno FOIL RC | .60 | 1.50 |
| 273 Johnny Damon FOIL RC | 6.00 | 15.00 |
| 274 Russ Davis FOIL RC | .60 | 1.50 |
| 275 Carlos Delgado FOIL | 1.50 | 4.00 |
| 276 Carl Everett FOIL | .60 | 1.50 |
| 277 Cliff Floyd FOIL | .30 | .75 |
| 278 Alex Gonzalez FOIL | .40 | 1.00 |
| 279 Derek Jeter FOIL RC ! | 50.00 | 100.00 |
| 280 Chipper Jones FOIL | 1.50 | 4.00 |
| 281 Javier Lopez FOIL | .50 | 1.25 |
| 282 Chad Mottola FOIL RC | .60 | 1.50 |
| 283 Marc Newfield FOIL | .40 | 1.00 |
| 284 Eduardo Perez FOIL | .40 | 1.00 |
| 285 Manny Ramirez FOIL | 2.00 | 5.00 |
| 286 Todd Steverson FOIL RC | .40 | 1.00 |
| 287 Michael Tucker FOIL | .40 | 1.00 |
| 288 Allen Watson FOIL | .40 | 1.00 |
| 289 Rondell White FOIL | .60 | 1.50 |
| 290 Dmitri Young FOIL | .60 | 1.50 |

**1994 SP**

| | | |
|---|---|---|
| COMPLETE SET (200) | 125.00 | 250.00 |
| COMMON CARD (21-200) | .07 | .20 |

| | | |
|---|---|---|
| COMMON FOIL (1-20) | .20 | .50 |
| 1 Mike Bell FOIL RC | .20 | .50 |
| 2 D.J. Boston FOIL RC | .20 | .50 |
| 3 Johnny Damon FOIL | .75 | 2.00 |
| 4 Brad Fullmer FOIL RC | .40 | 1.00 |
| 5 Joey Hamilton FOIL | .20 | .50 |
| 6 Todd Hollandsworth FOIL | .20 | .50 |
| 7 Brian L.Hunter FOIL | .20 | .50 |
| 8 LaTroy Hawkins FOIL RC | .40 | 1.00 |
| 9 Brooks Kieschnick FOIL RC | .20 | .50 |
| 10 Derrek Lee FOIL RC | 5.00 | 12.00 |
| 11 Trot Nixon FOIL RC | 1.50 | 4.00 |
| 12 Alex Ochoa FOIL | .20 | .50 |
| 13 Chan Ho Park FOIL RC | .75 | 2.00 |
| 14 Kirk Presley FOIL RC | .20 | .50 |
| 15 Alex Rodriguez FOIL RC | 40.00 | 80.00 |
| 16 Jose Silva FOIL RC | .20 | .50 |
| 17 Terrell Wade FOIL RC | .20 | .50 |
| 18 Billy Wagner FOIL RC | 1.50 | 4.00 |
| 19 Glenn Williams FOIL RC | .20 | .50 |
| 20 Preston Wilson FOIL | .40 | 1.00 |
| 21 Brian Anderson RC | .15 | .40 |
| 22 Chad Curtis | .07 | .20 |
| 23 Chili Davis | .15 | .40 |
| 24 Bo Jackson | .40 | 1.00 |
| 25 Mark Langston | .07 | .20 |
| 26 Tim Salmon | .25 | .60 |
| 27 Jeff Bagwell | .25 | .60 |
| 28 Craig Biggio | .25 | .60 |
| 29 Ken Caminiti | .15 | .40 |
| 30 Doug Drabek | .07 | .20 |
| 31 John Hudek RC | .07 | .20 |
| 32 Greg Swindell | .07 | .20 |
| 33 Brent Gates | .07 | .20 |
| 34 Rickey Henderson | .40 | 1.00 |
| 35 Steve Karsay | .07 | .20 |
| 36 Mark McGwire | 1.00 | 2.50 |
| 37 Ruben Sierra | .15 | .40 |
| 38 Terry Steinbach | .07 | .20 |
| 39 Roberto Alomar | .25 | .60 |
| 40 Joe Carter | .15 | .40 |
| 41 Carlos Delgado | .25 | .60 |
| 42 Alex Gonzalez | .07 | .20 |
| 43 Juan Guzman | .07 | .20 |
| 44 Paul Molitor | .15 | .40 |
| 45 John Olerud | .15 | .40 |
| 46 Devon White | .07 | .20 |
| 47 Steve Avery | .07 | .20 |
| 48 Jeff Blauser | .07 | .20 |
| 49 Tom Glavine | .25 | .60 |
| 50 David Justice | .15 | .40 |
| 51 Roberto Kelly | .15 | .40 |
| 52 Ryan Klesko | .15 | .40 |
| 53 Javier Lopez | .15 | .40 |
| 54 Greg Maddux | .60 | 1.50 |
| 55 Fred McGriff | .25 | .60 |
| 56 Ricky Bones | .07 | .20 |
| 57 Cal Eldred | .07 | .20 |
| 58 Brian Harper | .07 | .20 |
| 59 Pat Listach | .07 | .20 |
| 60 B.J. Surhoff | .15 | .40 |
| 61 Greg Vaughn | .07 | .20 |
| 62 Bernard Gilkey | .07 | .20 |
| 63 Gregg Jefferies | .15 | .40 |
| 64 Ray Lankford | .15 | .40 |
| 65 Ozzie Smith | .60 | 1.50 |
| 66 Bob Tewksbury | .07 | .20 |
| 67 Mark Whiten | .07 | .20 |
| 68 Todd Zeile | .07 | .20 |
| 69 Mark Grace | .25 | .60 |
| 70 Randy Myers | .07 | .20 |
| 71 Ryne Sandberg | .60 | 1.50 |
| 72 Sammy Sosa | .40 | 1.00 |
| 73 Steve Trachsel | .07 | .20 |
| 74 Rick Wilkins | .07 | .20 |
| 75 Brett Butler | .15 | .40 |
| 76 Delino DeShields | .15 | .40 |
| 77 Orel Hershiser | .15 | .40 |
| 78 Eric Karros | .15 | .40 |
| 79 Raul Mondesi | .15 | .40 |
| 80 Mike Piazza | .75 | 2.00 |
| 81 Tim Wallach | .07 | .20 |
| 82 Moises Alou | .15 | .40 |
| 83 Cliff Floyd | .15 | .40 |
| 84 Marquis Grissom | .15 | .40 |
| 85 Pedro Martinez | .40 | 1.00 |
| 86 Larry Walker | .25 | .60 |
| 87 John Wetteland | .15 | .40 |

| | | |
|---|---|---|
| 88 Rondell White | .15 | .40 |
| 89 Rod Beck | .07 | .20 |
| 90 Barry Bonds | 1.00 | 2.50 |
| 91 John Burkett | .07 | .20 |
| 92 Royce Clayton | .07 | .20 |
| 93 Billy Swift | .07 | .20 |
| 94 Robby Thompson | .07 | .20 |
| 95 Matt Williams | .15 | .40 |
| 96 Carlos Baerga | .07 | .20 |
| 97 Albert Belle | .15 | .40 |
| 98 Kenny Lofton | .15 | .40 |
| 99 Dennis Martinez | .15 | .40 |
| 100 Eddie Murray | .40 | 1.00 |
| 101 Manny Ramirez | .40 | 1.00 |
| 102 Eric Anthony | .07 | .20 |
| 103 Chris Bosio | .07 | .20 |
| 104 Jay Buhner | .15 | .40 |
| 105 Ken Griffey Jr. | .60 | 1.50 |
| 106 Randy Johnson | .40 | 1.00 |
| 107 Edgar Martinez | .25 | .60 |
| 108 Chuck Carr | .07 | .20 |
| 109 Jeff Conine | .15 | .40 |
| 110 Carl Everett | .15 | .40 |
| 111 Chris Hammond | .07 | .20 |
| 112 Bryan Harvey | .07 | .20 |
| 113 Charles Johnson | .15 | .40 |
| 114 Gary Sheffield | .15 | .40 |
| 115 Bobby Bonilla | .15 | .40 |
| 116 Dwight Gooden | .15 | .40 |
| 117 Todd Hundley | .07 | .20 |
| 118 Bobby Jones | .07 | .20 |
| 119 Jeff Kent | .25 | .60 |
| 120 Bret Saberhagen | .15 | .40 |
| 121 Jeffrey Hammonds | .07 | .20 |
| 122 Chris Hoiles | .07 | .20 |
| 123 Ben McDonald | .07 | .20 |
| 124 Mike Mussina | .25 | .60 |
| 125 Rafael Palmeiro | .15 | .40 |
| 126 Cal Ripken | 1.25 | 3.00 |
| 127 Lee Smith | .07 | .20 |
| 128 Derek Bell | .07 | .20 |
| 129 Andy Benes | .07 | .20 |
| 130 Tony Gwynn | .50 | 1.25 |
| 131 Trevor Hoffman | .25 | .60 |
| 132 Phil Plantier | .07 | .20 |
| 133 Bip Roberts | .07 | .20 |
| 134 Darren Daulton | .15 | .40 |
| 135 Lenny Dykstra | .15 | .40 |
| 136 Dave Hollins | .07 | .20 |
| 137 Danny Jackson | .07 | .20 |
| 138 John Kruk | .15 | .40 |
| 139 Kevin Stocker | .07 | .20 |
| 140 Jay Bell | .15 | .40 |
| 141 Carlos Garcia | .07 | .20 |
| 142 Jeff King | .07 | .20 |
| 143 Orlando Merced | .07 | .20 |
| 144 Andy Van Slyke | .25 | .60 |
| 145 Rick White | .07 | .20 |
| 146 Jose Canseco | .25 | .60 |
| 147 Will Clark | .25 | .60 |
| 148 Juan Gonzalez | .15 | .40 |
| 149 Rick Helling | .07 | .20 |
| 150 Dean Palmer | .15 | .40 |
| 151 Ivan Rodriguez | .25 | .60 |
| 152 Roger Clemens | .75 | 2.00 |
| 153 Scott Cooper | .07 | .20 |
| 154 Andre Dawson | .15 | .40 |
| 155 Mike Greenwell | .07 | .20 |
| 156 Aaron Sele | .15 | .40 |
| 157 Mo Vaughn | .15 | .40 |
| 158 Bret Boone | .15 | .40 |
| 159 Barry Larkin | .25 | .60 |
| 160 Kevin Mitchell | .07 | .20 |
| 161 Jose Rijo | .07 | .20 |
| 162 Deion Sanders | .25 | .60 |
| 163 Reggie Sanders | .15 | .40 |
| 164 Dante Bichette | .15 | .40 |
| 165 Ellis Burks | .15 | .40 |
| 166 Andres Galarraga | .15 | .40 |
| 167 Charlie Hayes | .07 | .20 |
| 168 David Nied | .07 | .20 |
| 169 Walt Weiss | .07 | .20 |
| 170 Kevin Appier | .07 | .20 |
| 171 David Cone | .15 | .40 |
| 172 Jeff Granger | .07 | .20 |
| 173 Felix Jose | .07 | .20 |
| 174 Wally Joyner | .07 | .20 |
| 175 Brian McRae | .07 | .20 |

| | | |
|---|---|---|
| 176 Cecil Fielder | .15 | .40 |
| 177 Travis Fryman | .15 | .40 |
| 178 Mike Henneman | .07 | .20 |
| 179 Tony Phillips | .07 | .20 |
| 180 Mickey Tettleton | .07 | .20 |
| 181 Alan Trammell | .15 | .40 |
| 182 Rick Aguilera | .07 | .20 |
| 183 Rich Becker | .07 | .20 |
| 184 Scott Erickson | .07 | .20 |
| 185 Chuck Knoblauch | .15 | .40 |
| 186 Kirby Puckett | .40 | 1.00 |
| 187 Dave Winfield | .15 | .40 |
| 188 Wilson Alvarez | .07 | .20 |
| 189 Jason Bere | .07 | .20 |
| 190 Alex Fernandez | .07 | .20 |
| 191 Julio Franco | .15 | .40 |
| 192 Jack McDowell | .07 | .20 |
| 193 Frank Thomas | .40 | 1.00 |
| 194 Robin Ventura | .15 | .40 |
| 195 Jim Abbott | .25 | .60 |
| 196 Wade Boggs | .25 | .60 |
| 197 Jimmy Key | .15 | .40 |
| 198 Don Mattingly | 1.00 | 2.50 |
| 199 Paul O'Neill | .25 | .60 |
| 200 Danny Tartabull | .07 | .20 |
| P24 Ken Griffey Jr. Promo | .75 | 2.00 |

## 1998 SP Authentic

| | | |
|---|---|---|
| COMPLETE SET (198) | 15.00 | 40.00 |
| 1 Travis Lee FOIL | .15 | .40 |
| 2 Mike Caruso FOIL | .15 | .40 |
| 3 Kerry Wood FOIL | .20 | .50 |
| 4 Mark Kotsay FOIL | .15 | .40 |
| 5 Magglio Ordonez FOIL RC | 5.00 | 12.00 |
| 6 Scott Elarton FOIL | .15 | .40 |
| 7 Carl Pavano FOIL | .15 | .40 |
| 8 A.J. Hinch FOIL | .15 | .40 |
| 9 Rolando Arrojo FOIL RC | .15 | .40 |
| 10 Ben Grieve FOIL | .15 | .40 |
| 11 Gabe Alvarez FOIL | .15 | .40 |
| 12 Mike Kinkade FOIL RC | .15 | .40 |
| 13 Bruce Chen FOIL | .15 | .40 |
| 14 Juan Encarnacion FOIL | .15 | .40 |
| 15 Todd Helton FOIL | .25 | .60 |
| 16 Aaron Boone FOIL | .15 | .40 |
| 17 Sean Casey FOIL | .15 | .40 |
| 18 Ramon Hernandez FOIL | .15 | .40 |
| 19 Daryle Ward FOIL | .15 | .40 |
| 20 Paul Konerko FOIL | .15 | .40 |
| 21 David Ortiz FOIL | .50 | 1.25 |
| 22 Derrek Lee FOIL | .25 | .60 |
| 23 Brad Fullmer FOIL | .15 | .40 |
| 24 Javier Vazquez FOIL | .15 | .40 |
| 25 Miguel Tejada FOIL | .40 | 1.00 |
| 26 Dave Dellucci FOIL RC | .25 | .60 |
| 27 Alex Gonzalez FOIL | .15 | .40 |
| 28 Matt Clement FOIL | .15 | .40 |
| 29 Masato Yoshii FOIL RC | .15 | .40 |
| 30 Russell Branyan FOIL | .15 | .40 |
| 31 Chuck Finley | .15 | .40 |
| 32 Jim Edmonds | .15 | .40 |
| 33 Darin Erstad | .15 | .40 |
| 34 Jason Dickson | .15 | .40 |
| 35 Tim Salmon | .25 | .60 |
| 36 Cecil Fielder | .15 | .40 |
| 37 Todd Greene | .15 | .40 |
| 38 Andy Benes | .15 | .40 |
| 39 Jay Bell | .15 | .40 |
| 40 Matt Williams | .15 | .40 |
| 41 Brian Anderson | .15 | .40 |
| 42 Karim Garcia | .15 | .40 |
| 43 Javy Lopez | .15 | .40 |
| 44 Tom Glavine | .25 | .60 |
| 45 Greg Maddux | .60 | 1.50 |

| | | |
|---|---|---|
| 46 Andruw Jones | .25 | .60 |
| 47 Chipper Jones | .40 | 1.00 |
| 48 Ryan Klesko | .15 | .40 |
| 49 John Smoltz | .25 | .60 |
| 50 Andres Galarraga | .25 | .60 |
| 51 Rafael Palmeiro | .25 | .60 |
| 52 Mike Mussina | .25 | .60 |
| 53 Roberto Alomar | .25 | .60 |
| 54 Joe Carter | .15 | .40 |
| 55 Cal Ripken | 1.25 | 3.00 |
| 56 Brady Anderson | .15 | .40 |
| 57 Mo Vaughn | .15 | .40 |
| 58 John Valentin | .15 | .40 |
| 59 Dennis Eckersley | .15 | .40 |
| 60 Nomar Garciaparra | .60 | 1.50 |
| 61 Pedro Martinez | .25 | .60 |
| 62 Jeff Blauser | .15 | .40 |
| 63 Kevin Orie | .15 | .40 |
| 64 Henry Rodriguez | .15 | .40 |
| 65 Mark Grace | .25 | .60 |
| 66 Albert Belle | .15 | .40 |
| 67 Mike Cameron | .15 | .40 |
| 68 Robin Ventura | .15 | .40 |
| 69 Frank Thomas | .40 | 1.00 |
| 70 Barry Larkin | .25 | .60 |
| 71 Brett Tomko | .15 | .40 |
| 72 Willie Greene | .15 | .40 |
| 73 Reggie Sanders | .15 | .40 |
| 74 Sandy Alomar Jr. | .15 | .40 |
| 75 Kenny Lofton | .15 | .40 |
| 76 Jaret Wright | .15 | .40 |
| 77 David Justice | .15 | .40 |
| 78 Omar Vizquel | .25 | .60 |
| 79 Manny Ramirez | .25 | .60 |
| 80 Jim Thome | .25 | .60 |
| 81 Travis Fryman | .15 | .40 |
| 82 Neifi Perez | .15 | .40 |
| 83 Mike Lansing | .15 | .40 |
| 84 Vinny Castilla | .15 | .40 |
| 85 Larry Walker | .15 | .40 |
| 86 Dante Bichette | .15 | .40 |
| 87 Darryl Kile | .15 | .40 |
| 88 Justin Thompson | .15 | .40 |
| 89 Damion Easley | .15 | .40 |
| 90 Tony Clark | .15 | .40 |
| 91 Bobby Higginson | .15 | .40 |
| 92 Brian Hunter | .15 | .40 |
| 93 Edgar Renteria | .15 | .40 |
| 94 Craig Counsell | .15 | .40 |
| 95 Mike Piazza | .60 | 1.50 |
| 96 Livan Hernandez | .15 | .40 |
| 97 Todd Zeile | .15 | .40 |
| 98 Richard Hidalgo | .15 | .40 |
| 99 Moises Alou | .15 | .40 |
| 100 Jeff Bagwell | .25 | .60 |
| 101 Mike Hampton | .15 | .40 |
| 102 Craig Biggio | .25 | .60 |
| 103 Dean Palmer | .15 | .40 |
| 104 Tim Belcher | .15 | .40 |
| 105 Jeff King | .15 | .40 |
| 106 Jeff Conine | .15 | .40 |
| 107 Johnny Damon | .15 | .40 |
| 108 Hideo Nomo | .40 | 1.00 |
| 109 Raul Mondesi | .15 | .40 |
| 110 Gary Sheffield | .15 | .40 |
| 111 Ramon Martinez | .15 | .40 |
| 112 Chan Ho Park | .15 | .40 |
| 113 Eric Young | .15 | .40 |
| 114 Charles Johnson | .15 | .40 |
| 115 Eric Karros | .15 | .40 |
| 116 Bobby Bonilla | .15 | .40 |
| 117 Jeromy Burnitz | .15 | .40 |
| 118 Cal Eldred | .15 | .40 |
| 119 Jeff D'Amico | .15 | .40 |
| 120 Marquis Grissom | .15 | .40 |
| 121 Dave Nilsson | .15 | .40 |
| 122 Brad Radke | .15 | .40 |
| 123 Marty Cordova | .15 | .40 |
| 124 Ron Coomer | .15 | .40 |
| 125 Paul Molitor | .15 | .40 |
| 126 Todd Walker | .15 | .40 |
| 127 Rondell White | .15 | .40 |
| 128 Mark Grudzielanek | .15 | .40 |
| 129 Carlos Perez | .15 | .40 |
| 130 Vladimir Guerrero | .40 | 1.00 |
| 131 Dustin Hermanson | .15 | .40 |
| 132 Butch Huskey | .15 | .40 |
| 133 John Franco | .15 | .40 |

| | | |
|---|---|---|
| 134 Rey Ordonez | .15 | .40 |
| 135 Todd Hundley | .15 | .40 |
| 136 Edgardo Alfonzo | .15 | .40 |
| 137 Bobby Jones | .15 | .40 |
| 138 John Olerud | .15 | .40 |
| 139 Chili Davis | .15 | .40 |
| 140 Tino Martinez | .25 | .60 |
| 141 Andy Pettitte | .25 | .60 |
| 142 Chuck Knoblauch | .15 | .40 |
| 143 Bernie Williams | .25 | .60 |
| 144 David Cone | .15 | .40 |
| 145 Derek Jeter | 1.00 | 2.50 |
| 146 Paul O'Neill | .25 | .60 |
| 147 Rickey Henderson | .40 | 1.00 |
| 148 Jason Giambi | .15 | .40 |
| 149 Kenny Rogers | .15 | .40 |
| 150 Scott Rolen | .25 | .60 |
| 151 Curt Schilling | .15 | .40 |
| 152 Ricky Bottalico | .15 | .40 |
| 153 Mike Lieberthal | .15 | .40 |
| 154 Francisco Cordova | .15 | .40 |
| 155 Jose Guillen | .15 | .40 |
| 156 Jason Schmidt | .15 | .40 |
| 157 Jason Kendall | .15 | .40 |
| 158 Kevin Young | .15 | .40 |
| 159 Delino DeShields | .15 | .40 |
| 160 Mark McGwire | 1.00 | 2.50 |
| 161 Ray Lankford | .15 | .40 |
| 162 Brian Jordan | .15 | .40 |
| 163 Ron Gant | .15 | .40 |
| 164 Todd Stottlemyre | .15 | .40 |
| 165 Ken Caminiti | .15 | .40 |
| 166 Kevin Brown | .25 | .60 |
| 167 Trevor Hoffman | .15 | .40 |
| 168 Steve Finley | .15 | .40 |
| 169 Wally Joyner | .15 | .40 |
| 170 Tony Gwynn | .50 | 1.25 |
| 171 Shawn Estes | .15 | .40 |
| 172 J.T. Snow | .15 | .40 |
| 173 Jeff Kent | .15 | .40 |
| 174 Robb Nen | .15 | .40 |
| 175 Barry Bonds | 1.00 | 2.50 |
| 176 Randy Johnson | .40 | 1.00 |
| 177 Edgar Martinez | .25 | .60 |
| 178 Jay Buhner | .15 | .40 |
| 179 Alex Rodriguez | .60 | 1.50 |
| 180 Ken Griffey Jr. | .60 | 1.50 |
| 181 Ken Cloude | .15 | .40 |
| 182 Wade Boggs | .25 | .60 |
| 183 Tony Saunders | .15 | .40 |
| 184 Wilson Alvarez | .15 | .40 |
| 185 Fred McGriff | .25 | .60 |
| 186 Roberto Hernandez | .15 | .40 |
| 187 Kevin Stocker | .15 | .40 |
| 188 Fernando Tatis | .15 | .40 |
| 189 Will Clark | .25 | .60 |
| 190 Juan Gonzalez | .25 | .60 |
| 191 Rusty Greer | .15 | .40 |
| 192 Ivan Rodriguez | .25 | .60 |
| 193 Jose Canseco | .15 | .40 |
| 194 Carlos Delgado | .15 | .40 |
| 195 Roger Clemens | .75 | 2.00 |
| 196 Pat Hentgen | .15 | .40 |
| 197 Randy Myers | .15 | .40 |
| 198 Ken Griffey Jr. CL | .40 | 1.00 |
| S123 Ken Griffey Jr. Sample | .75 | 2.00 |

## 1999 SP Authentic

| | | |
|---|---|---|
| COMP.SET w/o SP's (90) | 10.00 | 25.00 |
| COMMON CARD (1-90) | .15 | .40 |
| COMMON TR (91-120) | 4.00 | 10.00 |
| COMMON STR (121-135) | 1.25 | 3.00 |
| 1 Mo Vaughn | .15 | .40 |
| 2 Jim Edmonds | .15 | .40 |

|  |  | | |
|---|---|--:|--:|
| 3 | Darin Erstad | .15 | .40 |
| 4 | Travis Lee | .15 | .40 |
| 5 | Matt Williams | .15 | .40 |
| 6 | Randy Johnson | .40 | 1.00 |
| 7 | Chipper Jones | .40 | 1.00 |
| 8 | Greg Maddux | .60 | 1.50 |
| 9 | Andruw Jones | .25 | .60 |
| 10 | Andres Galarraga | .15 | .40 |
| 11 | Tom Glavine | .25 | .60 |
| 12 | Cal Ripken | 1.25 | 3.00 |
| 13 | Brady Anderson | .15 | .40 |
| 14 | Albert Belle | .15 | .40 |
| 15 | Nomar Garciaparra | .60 | 1.50 |
| 16 | Donnie Sadler | .15 | .40 |
| 17 | Pedro Martinez | .25 | .60 |
| 18 | Sammy Sosa | .40 | .40 |
| 19 | Kerry Wood | .15 | .40 |
| 20 | Mark Grace | .25 | .60 |
| 21 | Mike Caruso | .15 | .40 |
| 22 | Frank Thomas | .40 | 1.00 |
| 23 | Paul Konerko | .15 | .40 |
| 24 | Sean Casey | .15 | .40 |
| 25 | Barry Larkin | .25 | .60 |
| 26 | Kenny Lofton | .15 | .40 |
| 27 | Manny Ramirez | .25 | .60 |
| 28 | Jim Thome | .25 | .60 |
| 29 | Bartolo Colon | .15 | .40 |
| 30 | Jaret Wright | .15 | .40 |
| 31 | Larry Walker | .15 | .40 |
| 32 | Todd Helton | .25 | .60 |
| 33 | Tony Clark | .15 | .40 |
| 34 | Dean Palmer | .15 | .40 |
| 35 | Mark Kotsay | .15 | .40 |
| 36 | Cliff Floyd | .15 | .40 |
| 37 | Ken Caminiti | .15 | .40 |
| 38 | Craig Biggio | .25 | .60 |
| 39 | Jeff Bagwell | .25 | .60 |
| 40 | Moises Alou | .15 | .40 |
| 41 | Johnny Damon | .25 | .60 |
| 42 | Larry Sutton | .15 | .40 |
| 43 | Kevin Brown | .25 | .60 |
| 44 | Gary Sheffield | .15 | .40 |
| 45 | Raul Mondesi | .15 | .40 |
| 46 | Jeromy Burnitz | .15 | .40 |
| 47 | Jeff Cirillo | .15 | .40 |
| 48 | Todd Walker | .15 | .40 |
| 49 | David Ortiz | .40 | 1.00 |
| 50 | Brad Radke | .15 | .40 |
| 51 | Vladimir Guerrero | .40 | 1.00 |
| 52 | Rondell White | .15 | .40 |
| 53 | Brad Fullmer | .15 | .40 |
| 54 | Mike Piazza | .60 | 1.50 |
| 55 | Robin Ventura | .15 | .40 |
| 56 | John Olerud | .15 | .40 |
| 57 | Derek Jeter | 1.00 | 2.50 |
| 58 | Tino Martinez | .25 | .60 |
| 59 | Bernie Williams | .25 | .60 |
| 60 | Roger Clemens | .75 | 2.00 |
| 61 | Ben Grieve | .15 | .40 |
| 62 | Miguel Tejada | .15 | .40 |
| 63 | A.J. Hinch | .15 | .40 |
| 64 | Scott Rolen | .25 | .60 |
| 65 | Curt Schilling | .15 | .40 |
| 66 | Doug Glanville | .15 | .40 |
| 67 | Aramis Ramirez | .15 | .40 |
| 68 | Tony Womack | .15 | .40 |
| 69 | Jason Kendall | .15 | .40 |
| 70 | Tony Gwynn | .50 | 1.25 |
| 71 | Wally Joyner | .15 | .40 |
| 72 | Greg Vaughn | .15 | .40 |
| 73 | Barry Bonds | 1.00 | 2.50 |
| 74 | Ellis Burks | .15 | .40 |
| 75 | Jeff Kent | .15 | .40 |
| 76 | Ken Griffey Jr. | .60 | 1.50 |
| 77 | Alex Rodriguez | .60 | 1.50 |
| 78 | Edgar Martinez | .25 | .60 |
| 79 | Mark McGwire | 1.00 | 2.50 |
| 80 | Eli Marrero | .15 | .40 |
| 81 | Matt Morris | .15 | .40 |
| 82 | Rolando Arrojo | .15 | .40 |
| 83 | Quinton McCracken | .15 | .40 |
| 84 | Jose Canseco | .25 | .60 |
| 85 | Ivan Rodriguez | .25 | .60 |
| 86 | Juan Gonzalez | .40 | 1.00 |
| 87 | Royce Clayton | .15 | .40 |
| 88 | Shawn Green | .15 | .40 |
| 89 | Jose Cruz Jr. | .15 | .40 |
| 90 | Carlos Delgado | .15 | .40 |
| 91 | Troy Glaus FW | 5.00 | 12.00 |
| 92 | George Lombard FW | 4.00 | 10.00 |
| 93 | Ryan Minor FW | 4.00 | 10.00 |
| 94 | Calvin Pickering FW | 4.00 | 10.00 |
| 95 | Jin Ho Cho FW | 4.00 | 10.00 |
| 96 | Russ Branyan FW | 4.00 | 10.00 |
| 97 | Derrick Gibson FW | 4.00 | 10.00 |
| 98 | Gabe Kapler FW | 4.00 | 10.00 |
| 99 | Matt Anderson FW | 4.00 | 10.00 |
| 100 | Preston Wilson FW | 4.00 | 10.00 |
| 101 | Alex Gonzalez FW | 4.00 | 10.00 |
| 102 | Carlos Beltran FW | 4.00 | 10.00 |
| 103 | Dee Brown FW | 4.00 | 10.00 |
| 104 | Jeremy Giambi FW | 4.00 | 10.00 |
| 105 | Angel Pena FW | 4.00 | 10.00 |
| 106 | Geoff Jenkins FW | 4.00 | 10.00 |
| 107 | Corey Koskie FW | 4.00 | 10.00 |
| 108 | A.J. Pierzynski FW | 4.00 | 10.00 |
| 109 | Michael Barrett FW | 4.00 | 10.00 |
| 110 | Fernando Seguignol FW | 4.00 | 10.00 |
| 111 | Mike Kinkade FW | 4.00 | 10.00 |
| 112 | Ricky Ledee FW | 4.00 | 10.00 |
| 113 | Mike Lowell FW | 4.00 | 10.00 |
| 114 | Eric Chavez FW | 4.00 | 10.00 |
| 115 | Matt Clement FW | 4.00 | 10.00 |
| 116 | Shane Monahan FW | 4.00 | 10.00 |
| 117 | J.D. Drew FW | 4.00 | 10.00 |
| 118 | Bubba Trammell FW | 4.00 | 10.00 |
| 119 | Kevin Witt FW | 4.00 | 10.00 |
| 120 | Roy Halladay FW | 4.00 | 10.00 |
| 121 | Mark McGwire STR | 5.00 | 12.00 |
| 122 | McGwire/S.Sosa STR | 4.00 | 10.00 |
| 123 | Sammy Sosa STR | 2.00 | 5.00 |
| 124 | Ken Griffey Jr. STR | 3.00 | 8.00 |
| 125 | Cal Ripken STR | 6.00 | 15.00 |
| 126 | Juan Gonzalez STR | 1.25 | 3.00 |
| 127 | Kerry Wood STR | 1.25 | 3.00 |
| 128 | Trevor Hoffman STR | 1.25 | 3.00 |
| 129 | Barry Bonds STR | 5.00 | 12.00 |
| 130 | Alex Rodriguez STR | 3.00 | 8.00 |
| 131 | Ben Grieve STR | 1.25 | 3.00 |
| 132 | Tom Glavine STR | 1.25 | 3.00 |
| 133 | David Wells STR | 1.25 | 3.00 |
| 134 | Mike Piazza STR | 3.00 | 8.00 |
| 135 | Scott Brosius STR | 1.25 | 3.00 |

## 2000 SP Authentic

|  |  | | |
|---|---|--:|--:|
| | COMP.BASIC w/o SP's (90) | 10.00 | 25.00 |
| | COMP.UPDATE w/o SP'S (30) | 4.00 | 10.00 |
| | COMMON CARD | .15 | .40 |
| | COMMON SUP (91-105) | 1.25 | 3.00 |
| | COMMON FW (106-135) | 2.00 | 5.00 |
| | COMMON FW (136-164) | 2.00 | 5.00 |
| | COMMON SUP (166-195) | .25 | .60 |
| 1 | Mo Vaughn | .15 | .40 |
| 2 | Troy Glaus | .15 | .40 |
| 3 | Jason Giambi | .15 | .40 |
| 4 | Tim Hudson | .15 | .40 |
| 5 | Eric Chavez | .15 | .40 |
| 6 | Shannon Stewart | .15 | .40 |
| 7 | Raul Mondesi | .15 | .40 |
| 8 | Carlos Delgado | .15 | .40 |
| 9 | Jose Canseco | .25 | .60 |
| 10 | Vinny Castilla | .15 | .40 |
| 11 | Greg Vaughn | .15 | .40 |
| 12 | Manny Ramirez | .25 | .60 |
| 13 | Roberto Alomar | .25 | .60 |
| 14 | Jim Thome | .25 | .60 |
| 15 | Richie Sexson | .15 | .40 |
| 16 | Alex Rodriguez | .60 | 1.50 |
| 17 | Freddy Garcia | .15 | .40 |
| 18 | John Olerud | .15 | .40 |
| 19 | Albert Belle | .15 | .40 |
| 20 | Cal Ripken | 1.25 | 3.00 |
| 21 | Mike Mussina | .25 | .60 |
| 22 | Ivan Rodriguez | .25 | .60 |
| 23 | Gabe Kapler | .15 | .40 |
| 24 | Rafael Palmeiro | .25 | .60 |
| 25 | Nomar Garciaparra | .60 | 1.50 |
| 26 | Pedro Martinez | .25 | .60 |
| 27 | Carl Everett | .15 | .40 |
| 28 | Carlos Beltran | .15 | .40 |
| 29 | Jermaine Dye | .15 | .40 |
| 30 | Juan Gonzalez | .15 | .40 |
| 31 | Dean Palmer | .15 | .40 |
| 32 | Corey Koskie | .15 | .40 |
| 33 | Jacque Jones | .15 | .40 |
| 34 | Frank Thomas | .40 | 1.00 |
| 35 | Paul Konerko | .15 | .40 |
| 36 | Magglio Ordonez | .15 | .40 |
| 37 | Bernie Williams | .25 | .60 |
| 38 | Derek Jeter | 1.00 | 3.00 |
| 39 | Roger Clemens | .75 | 2.00 |
| 40 | Mariano Rivera | .40 | 1.00 |
| 41 | Jeff Bagwell | .25 | .60 |
| 42 | Craig Biggio | .25 | .60 |
| 43 | Jose Lima | .15 | .40 |
| 44 | Moises Alou | .15 | .40 |
| 45 | Chipper Jones | .40 | 1.00 |
| 46 | Greg Maddux | .60 | 1.50 |
| 47 | Andruw Jones | .25 | .60 |
| 48 | Andres Galarraga | .15 | .40 |
| 49 | Jeromy Burnitz | .15 | .40 |
| 50 | Geoff Jenkins | .15 | .40 |
| 51 | Mark McGwire | 1.00 | 2.50 |
| 52 | Fernando Tatis | .15 | .40 |
| 53 | J.D. Drew | .15 | .40 |
| 54 | Sammy Sosa | .40 | 1.00 |
| 55 | Kerry Wood | .15 | .40 |
| 56 | Mark Grace | .25 | .60 |
| 57 | Matt Williams | .15 | .40 |
| 58 | Randy Johnson | .40 | 1.00 |
| 59 | Erubiel Durazo | .15 | .40 |
| 60 | Gary Sheffield | .15 | .40 |
| 61 | Kevin Brown | .25 | .60 |
| 62 | Shawn Green | .15 | .40 |
| 63 | Vladimir Guerrero | .40 | 1.00 |
| 64 | Michael Barrett | .15 | .40 |
| 65 | Barry Bonds | 1.00 | 2.50 |
| 66 | Jeff Kent | .15 | .40 |
| 67 | Russ Ortiz | .15 | .40 |
| 68 | Preston Wilson | .15 | .40 |
| 69 | Mike Lowell | .15 | .40 |
| 70 | Mike Piazza | .60 | 1.50 |
| 71 | Mike Hampton | .15 | .40 |
| 72 | Robin Ventura | .15 | .40 |
| 73 | Edgardo Alfonzo | .15 | .40 |
| 74 | Tony Gwynn | .50 | 1.25 |
| 75 | Ryan Klesko | .15 | .40 |
| 76 | Trevor Hoffman | .15 | .40 |
| 77 | Scott Rolen | .25 | .60 |
| 78 | Bob Abreu | .15 | .40 |
| 79 | Mike Lieberthal | .15 | .40 |
| 80 | Curt Schilling | .15 | .40 |
| 81 | Jason Kendall | .15 | .40 |
| 82 | Brian Giles | .15 | .40 |
| 83 | Kris Benson | .15 | .40 |
| 84 | Ken Griffey Jr. | .60 | 1.50 |
| 85 | Sean Casey | .15 | .40 |
| 86 | Pokey Reese | .15 | .40 |
| 87 | Barry Larkin | .25 | .60 |
| 88 | Larry Walker | .15 | .40 |
| 89 | Todd Helton | .25 | .60 |
| 90 | Jeff Cirillo | .15 | .40 |
| 91 | Ken Griffey Jr. SUP | 3.00 | 8.00 |
| 92 | Mark McGwire SUP | 5.00 | 12.00 |
| 93 | Chipper Jones SUP | 2.00 | 5.00 |
| 94 | Derek Jeter SUP | 5.00 | 12.00 |
| 95 | Shawn Green SUP | 1.25 | 3.00 |
| 96 | Pedro Martinez SUP | 1.25 | 3.00 |
| 97 | Mike Piazza SUP | 3.00 | 8.00 |
| 98 | Alex Rodriguez SUP | 3.00 | 8.00 |
| 99 | Jeff Bagwell SUP | 1.25 | 3.00 |
| 100 | Cal Ripken SUP | 6.00 | 15.00 |
| 101 | Sammy Sosa SUP | 2.00 | 5.00 |
| 102 | Barry Bonds SUP | 5.00 | 12.00 |
| 103 | Jose Canseco SUP | 1.25 | 3.00 |
| 104 | Nomar Garciaparra SUP | 3.00 | 8.00 |
| 105 | Ivan Rodriguez SUP | 1.25 | 3.00 |
| 106 | Rick Ankiel FW | 3.00 | 8.00 |
| 107 | Pat Burrell FW | 1.25 | 3.00 |
| 108 | Vernon Wells FW | 2.00 | 5.00 |

| | | |
|---|---|---|
| ☐ 109 Nick Johnson FW | 2.00 | 5.00 |
| ☐ 110 Kip Wells FW | 2.00 | 5.00 |
| ☐ 111 Matt Riley FW | 2.00 | 5.00 |
| ☐ 112 Alfonso Soriano FW | 3.00 | 8.00 |
| ☐ 113 Josh Beckett FW | 3.00 | 8.00 |
| ☐ 114 Danys Baez FW RC | 2.00 | 5.00 |
| ☐ 115 Travis Dawkins FW | 2.00 | 5.00 |
| ☐ 116 Eric Gagne FW | 3.00 | 8.00 |
| ☐ 117 Mike Lamb FW RC | 3.00 | 8.00 |
| ☐ 118 Eric Munson FW | 2.00 | 5.00 |
| ☐ 119 Wilfredo Rodriguez FW RC | 2.00 | 5.00 |
| ☐ 120 Kazuhiro Sasaki FW | 3.00 | 8.00 |
| ☐ 121 Chad Hutchinson FW | 2.00 | 5.00 |
| ☐ 122 Peter Bergeron FW | 2.00 | 5.00 |
| ☐ 123 Wascar Serrano FW RC | 2.00 | 5.00 |
| ☐ 124 Tony Armas Jr. FW | 2.00 | 5.00 |
| ☐ 125 Ramon Ortiz FW | 2.00 | 5.00 |
| ☐ 126 Adam Kennedy FW | 2.00 | 5.00 |
| ☐ 127 Joe Crede FW | 4.00 | 10.00 |
| ☐ 128 Roosevelt Brown FW | 2.00 | 5.00 |
| ☐ 129 Mark Mulder FW | 2.00 | 5.00 |
| ☐ 130 Brad Penny FW | 2.00 | 5.00 |
| ☐ 131 Terrence Long FW | 2.00 | 5.00 |
| ☐ 132 Ruben Mateo FW | 2.00 | 5.00 |
| ☐ 133 Willy Mo Pena FW | 2.00 | 5.00 |
| ☐ 134 Rafael Furcal FW | 2.00 | 5.00 |
| ☐ 135 Mario Encarnacion FW | 2.00 | 5.00 |
| ☐ 136 Barry Zito FW RC | 8.00 | 20.00 |
| ☐ 137 Aaron McNeal FW RC | 2.00 | 5.00 |
| ☐ 138 Timo Perez FW RC | 2.00 | 5.00 |
| ☐ 139 Sun Woo Kim FW RC | 2.00 | 5.00 |
| ☐ 140 Xavier Nady FW RC | 4.00 | 10.00 |
| ☐ 141 Matt Wheatland FW RC | 2.00 | 5.00 |
| ☐ 142 Brent Abernathy FW RC | 2.00 | 5.00 |
| ☐ 143 Cory Vance FW RC | 2.00 | 5.00 |
| ☐ 144 Scott Heard FW RC | 2.00 | 5.00 |
| ☐ 145 Mike Meyers FW RC | 2.00 | 5.00 |
| ☐ 146 Ben Diggins FW RC | 2.00 | 5.00 |
| ☐ 147 Luis Matos FW RC | 2.00 | 5.00 |
| ☐ 148 Ben Sheets FW RC | 5.00 | 12.00 |
| ☐ 149 Kurt Ainsworth FW RC | 2.00 | 5.00 |
| ☐ 150 Dave Krynzel FW RC | 2.00 | 5.00 |
| ☐ 151 Alex Cabrera FW RC | 2.00 | 5.00 |
| ☐ 152 Mike Tonis FW RC | 2.00 | 5.00 |
| ☐ 153 Dane Sardinha FW RC | 2.00 | 5.00 |
| ☐ 154 Keith Ginter FW RC | 2.00 | 5.00 |
| ☐ 155 David Espinosa FW RC | 2.00 | 5.00 |
| ☐ 156 Joe Torres FW RC | 2.00 | 5.00 |
| ☐ 157 Daylan Holt FW RC | 2.00 | 5.00 |
| ☐ 158 Koyie Hill FW RC | 2.00 | 5.00 |
| ☐ 159 Brad Wilkerson FW RC | 3.00 | 8.00 |
| ☐ 160 Juan Pierre FW RC | 3.00 | 8.00 |
| ☐ 161 Matt Ginter FW RC | 2.00 | 5.00 |
| ☐ 162 Dane Artman FW RC | 2.00 | 5.00 |
| ☐ 163 Jon Rauch FW RC | 2.00 | 5.00 |
| ☐ 164 Sean Burnett FW RC | 2.00 | 5.00 |
| ☐ 165 Does Not Exist | | |
| ☐ 166 Darin Erstad | .25 | .60 |
| ☐ 167 Ben Grieve | .25 | .60 |
| ☐ 168 David Wells | .25 | .60 |
| ☐ 169 Fred McGriff | .40 | 1.00 |
| ☐ 170 Bob Wickman | .25 | .60 |
| ☐ 171 Al Martin | .25 | .60 |
| ☐ 172 Melvin Mora | .25 | .60 |
| ☐ 173 Ricky Ledee | .15 | .40 |
| ☐ 174 Dante Bichette | .25 | .60 |
| ☐ 175 Mike Sweeney | .25 | .60 |
| ☐ 176 Bobby Higginson | .25 | .60 |
| ☐ 177 Matt Lawton | .25 | .60 |
| ☐ 178 Charles Johnson | .25 | .60 |
| ☐ 179 David Justice | .25 | .60 |
| ☐ 180 Richard Hidalgo | .25 | .60 |
| ☐ 181 B.J. Surhoff | .15 | .40 |
| ☐ 182 Richie Sexson | .25 | .60 |
| ☐ 183 Jim Edmonds | .25 | .60 |
| ☐ 184 Rondell White | .25 | .60 |
| ☐ 185 Curt Schilling | .25 | .60 |
| ☐ 186 Tom Goodwin | .15 | .40 |
| ☐ 187 Jose Vidro | .25 | .60 |
| ☐ 188 Ellis Burks | .25 | .60 |
| ☐ 189 Henry Rodriguez | .25 | .60 |
| ☐ 190 Mike Bordick | .25 | .60 |
| ☐ 191 Eric Owens | .25 | .60 |
| ☐ 192 Travis Lee | .25 | .60 |
| ☐ 193 Kevin Young | .25 | .60 |
| ☐ 194 Aaron Boone | .25 | .60 |
| ☐ 195 Todd Hollandsworth | .25 | .60 |
| ☐ SPA Ken Griffey Jr. Sample | .75 | 2.00 |

## 2001 SP Authentic

| | | |
|---|---|---|
| ☐ COMP.BASIC w/o SP's (90) | 10.00 | 25.00 |
| ☐ COMP.UPDATE w/o SP's (30) | 4.00 | 10.00 |
| ☐ COMMON CARD (1-90) | .15 | .40 |
| ☐ COMMON FW (91-135) | 3.00 | 8.00 |
| ☐ COMMON SS (136-180) | 2.00 | 5.00 |
| ☐ COMMON CARD (181-210) | .25 | .60 |
| ☐ COMMON CARD (211-240) | 2.50 | 6.00 |
| ☐ 1 Troy Glaus | .15 | .40 |
| ☐ 2 Darin Erstad | .15 | .40 |
| ☐ 3 Jason Giambi | .15 | .40 |
| ☐ 4 Tim Hudson | .15 | .40 |
| ☐ 5 Eric Chavez | .15 | .40 |
| ☐ 6 Miguel Tejada | .15 | .40 |
| ☐ 7 Jose Ortiz | .15 | .40 |
| ☐ 8 Carlos Delgado | .15 | .40 |
| ☐ 9 Tony Batista | .15 | .40 |
| ☐ 10 Raul Mondesi | .15 | .40 |
| ☐ 11 Aubrey Huff | .15 | .40 |
| ☐ 12 Greg Vaughn | .15 | .40 |
| ☐ 13 Roberto Alomar | .25 | .60 |
| ☐ 14 Juan Gonzalez | .25 | .60 |
| ☐ 15 Jim Thome | .25 | .60 |
| ☐ 16 Omar Vizquel | .15 | .40 |
| ☐ 17 Edgar Martinez | .25 | .60 |
| ☐ 18 Freddy Garcia | .15 | .40 |
| ☐ 19 Cal Ripken | 1.25 | 3.00 |
| ☐ 20 Ivan Rodriguez | .25 | .60 |
| ☐ 21 Rafael Palmeiro | .25 | .60 |
| ☐ 22 Alex Rodriguez | .60 | 1.50 |
| ☐ 23 Manny Ramirez Sox | .25 | .60 |
| ☐ 24 Pedro Martinez | .25 | .60 |
| ☐ 25 Nomar Garciaparra | .60 | 1.50 |
| ☐ 26 Mike Sweeney | .15 | .40 |
| ☐ 27 Jermaine Dye | .15 | .40 |
| ☐ 28 Bobby Higginson | .15 | .40 |
| ☐ 29 Dean Palmer | .15 | .40 |
| ☐ 30 Matt Lawton | .15 | .40 |
| ☐ 31 Eric Milton | .15 | .40 |
| ☐ 32 Frank Thomas | .40 | 1.00 |
| ☐ 33 Magglio Ordonez | .15 | .40 |
| ☐ 34 David Wells | .15 | .40 |
| ☐ 35 Paul Konerko | .15 | .40 |
| ☐ 36 Derek Jeter | 1.00 | 2.50 |
| ☐ 37 Bernie Williams | .25 | .60 |
| ☐ 38 Roger Clemens | .75 | 2.00 |
| ☐ 39 Mike Mussina | .25 | .60 |
| ☐ 40 Jorge Posada | .25 | .60 |
| ☐ 41 Jeff Bagwell | .25 | .60 |
| ☐ 42 Richard Hidalgo | .15 | .40 |
| ☐ 43 Craig Biggio | .25 | .60 |
| ☐ 44 Greg Maddux | .60 | 1.50 |
| ☐ 45 Chipper Jones | .40 | 1.00 |
| ☐ 46 Andruw Jones | .25 | .60 |
| ☐ 47 Rafael Furcal | .15 | .40 |
| ☐ 48 Tom Glavine | .25 | .60 |
| ☐ 49 Jeromy Burnitz | .15 | .40 |
| ☐ 50 Jeffrey Hammonds | .15 | .40 |
| ☐ 51 Mark McGwire | 1.00 | 2.50 |
| ☐ 52 Jim Edmonds | .25 | .60 |
| ☐ 53 Rick Ankiel | .15 | .40 |
| ☐ 54 J.D. Drew | .25 | .60 |
| ☐ 55 Sammy Sosa | .40 | 1.00 |
| ☐ 56 Corey Patterson | .25 | .60 |
| ☐ 57 Kerry Wood | .15 | .40 |
| ☐ 58 Randy Johnson | .40 | 1.00 |
| ☐ 59 Luis Gonzalez | .15 | .40 |
| ☐ 60 Curt Schilling | .15 | .40 |
| ☐ 61 Gary Sheffield | .15 | .40 |
| ☐ 62 Shawn Green | .15 | .40 |
| ☐ 63 Kevin Brown | .15 | .40 |
| ☐ 64 Vladimir Guerrero | .40 | 1.00 |
| ☐ 65 Jose Vidro | .15 | .40 |

| | | |
|---|---|---|
| ☐ 66 Barry Bonds | 1.00 | 2.50 |
| ☐ 67 Jeff Kent | .15 | .40 |
| ☐ 68 Livan Hernandez | .15 | .40 |
| ☐ 69 Preston Wilson | .15 | .40 |
| ☐ 70 Charles Johnson | .15 | .40 |
| ☐ 71 Ryan Dempster | .15 | .40 |
| ☐ 72 Mike Piazza | .60 | 1.50 |
| ☐ 73 Al Leiter | .15 | .40 |
| ☐ 74 Edgardo Alfonzo | .15 | .40 |
| ☐ 75 Robin Ventura | .15 | .40 |
| ☐ 76 Tony Gwynn | .50 | 1.25 |
| ☐ 77 Phil Nevin | .15 | .40 |
| ☐ 78 Trevor Hoffman | .15 | .40 |
| ☐ 79 Scott Rolen | .25 | .60 |
| ☐ 80 Pat Burrell | .15 | .40 |
| ☐ 81 Bob Abreu | .15 | .40 |
| ☐ 82 Jason Kendall | .15 | .40 |
| ☐ 83 Brian Giles | .15 | .40 |
| ☐ 84 Kris Benson | .15 | .40 |
| ☐ 85 Ken Griffey Jr. | .60 | 1.50 |
| ☐ 86 Barry Larkin | .25 | .60 |
| ☐ 87 Sean Casey | .15 | .40 |
| ☐ 88 Todd Helton | .25 | .60 |
| ☐ 89 Mike Hampton | .15 | .40 |
| ☐ 90 Larry Walker | .15 | .40 |
| ☐ 91 Ichiro Suzuki FW RC | 60.00 | 120.00 |
| ☐ 92 Wilson Betemit FW RC | 6.00 | 15.00 |
| ☐ 93 Adrian Hernandez FW RC | 3.00 | 8.00 |
| ☐ 94 Juan Uribe FW RC | 4.00 | 10.00 |
| ☐ 95 Travis Hafner FW RC | 20.00 | 50.00 |
| ☐ 96 Morgan Ensberg FW RC | 6.00 | 15.00 |
| ☐ 97 Sean Douglass FW RC | 3.00 | 8.00 |
| ☐ 98 Juan Diaz FW RC | 3.00 | 8.00 |
| ☐ 99 Erick Almonte FW RC | 3.00 | 8.00 |
| ☐ 100 Ryan Freel FW RC | 3.00 | 8.00 |
| ☐ 101 Elpidio Guzman FW RC | 3.00 | 8.00 |
| ☐ 102 Christian Parker FW RC | 3.00 | 8.00 |
| ☐ 103 Josh Fogg FW RC | 3.00 | 8.00 |
| ☐ 104 Bert Snow FW RC | 3.00 | 8.00 |
| ☐ 105 Horacio Ramirez FW RC | 4.00 | 10.00 |
| ☐ 106 Ricardo Rodriguez FW RC | 3.00 | 8.00 |
| ☐ 107 Tyler Walker FW RC | 3.00 | 8.00 |
| ☐ 108 Jose Mieses FW RC | 3.00 | 8.00 |
| ☐ 109 Billy Sylvester FW RC | 3.00 | 8.00 |
| ☐ 110 Martin Vargas FW RC | 3.00 | 8.00 |
| ☐ 111 Andres Torres FW RC | 3.00 | 8.00 |
| ☐ 112 Greg Miller FW RC | 3.00 | 8.00 |
| ☐ 113 Alexis Gomez FW RC | 3.00 | 8.00 |
| ☐ 114 Grant Balfour FW RC | 3.00 | 8.00 |
| ☐ 115 Henry Mateo FW RC | -3.00 | 8.00 |
| ☐ 116 Esix Snead FW RC | 3.00 | 8.00 |
| ☐ 117 Jackson Melian FW RC | 3.00 | 8.00 |
| ☐ 118 Nate Teut FW RC | 3.00 | 8.00 |
| ☐ 119 Tsuyoshi Shinjo FW RC | 4.00 | 10.00 |
| ☐ 120 Carlos Valderrama FW RC | 3.00 | 8.00 |
| ☐ 121 Johnny Estrada FW RC | 4.00 | 10.00 |
| ☐ 122 Jason Michaels FW RC | 3.00 | 8.00 |
| ☐ 123 William Ortega FW RC | 3.00 | 8.00 |
| ☐ 124 Jason Smith FW RC | 3.00 | 8.00 |
| ☐ 125 Brian Lawrence FW RC | 3.00 | 8.00 |
| ☐ 126 Albert Pujols FW RC | 200.00 | 300.00 |
| ☐ 127 Wilkin Ruan FW RC | 3.00 | 8.00 |
| ☐ 128 Josh Towers FW RC | 4.00 | 10.00 |
| ☐ 129 Kris Keller FW RC | 3.00 | 8.00 |
| ☐ 130 Nick Maness FW RC | 3.00 | 8.00 |
| ☐ 131 Jack Wilson FW RC | 4.00 | 10.00 |
| ☐ 132 Brandon Duckworth FW RC | 3.00 | 8.00 |
| ☐ 133 Mike Penney FW RC | 3.00 | 8.00 |
| ☐ 134 Jay Gibbons FW RC | 4.00 | 10.00 |
| ☐ 135 Cesar Crespo FW RC | 3.00 | 8.00 |
| ☐ 136 Ken Griffey Jr. SS | 4.00 | 10.00 |
| ☐ 137 Mark McGwire SS | 6.00 | 15.00 |
| ☐ 138 Derek Jeter SS | 6.00 | 15.00 |
| ☐ 139 Alex Rodriguez SS | 4.00 | 10.00 |
| ☐ 140 Sammy Sosa SS | 2.50 | 6.00 |
| ☐ 141 Carlos Delgado SS | 2.00 | 5.00 |
| ☐ 142 Cal Ripken SS | 8.00 | 20.00 |
| ☐ 143 Pedro Martinez SS | 2.50 | 6.00 |
| ☐ 144 Frank Thomas SS | 2.50 | 6.00 |
| ☐ 145 Juan Gonzalez SS | 2.00 | 5.00 |
| ☐ 146 Troy Glaus SS | 2.00 | 5.00 |
| ☐ 147 Jason Giambi SS | 2.00 | 5.00 |
| ☐ 148 Ivan Rodriguez SS | 2.00 | 5.00 |
| ☐ 149 Chipper Jones SS | 2.50 | 6.00 |
| ☐ 150 Vladimir Guerrero SS | 2.50 | 6.00 |
| ☐ 151 Mike Piazza SS | 4.00 | 10.00 |
| ☐ 152 Jeff Bagwell SS | 2.00 | 5.00 |
| ☐ 153 Randy Johnson SS | 2.50 | 6.00 |

### 2002 SP Authentic

| # | Card | Lo | Hi |
|---|------|----|----|
| 154 | Todd Helton SS | 2.00 | 5.00 |
| 155 | Gary Sheffield SS | 2.00 | 5.00 |
| 156 | Tony Gwynn SS | 3.00 | 8.00 |
| 157 | Barry Bonds SS | 6.00 | 15.00 |
| 158 | Nomar Garciaparra SS | 4.00 | 10.00 |
| 159 | Bernie Williams SS | 2.00 | 5.00 |
| 160 | Greg Vaughn SS | 2.00 | 5.00 |
| 161 | David Wells SS | 2.00 | 5.00 |
| 162 | Roberto Alomar SS | 2.00 | 5.00 |
| 163 | Jermaine Dye SS | 2.00 | 5.00 |
| 164 | Rafael Palmeiro SS | 2.00 | 5.00 |
| 165 | Andruw Jones SS | 2.00 | 5.00 |
| 166 | Preston Wilson SS | 2.00 | 5.00 |
| 167 | Edgardo Alfonzo SS | 2.00 | 5.00 |
| 168 | Pat Burrell SS | 2.00 | 5.00 |
| 169 | Jim Edmonds SS | 2.00 | 5.00 |
| 170 | Mike Hampton SS | 2.00 | 5.00 |
| 171 | Jeff Kent SS | 2.00 | 5.00 |
| 172 | Kevin Brown SS | 2.00 | 5.00 |
| 173 | Manny Ramirez Sox SS | 2.00 | 5.00 |
| 174 | Maggio Ordonez SS | 2.00 | 5.00 |
| 175 | Roger Clemens SS | 5.00 | 12.00 |
| 176 | Jim Thome SS | 2.00 | 5.00 |
| 177 | Barry Zito SS | 2.00 | 5.00 |
| 178 | Brian Giles SS | 2.00 | 5.00 |
| 179 | Rick Ankiel SS | 2.00 | 5.00 |
| 180 | Corey Patterson SS | 2.00 | 5.00 |
| 181 | Garret Anderson | .25 | .60 |
| 182 | Jermaine Dye | .25 | .60 |
| 183 | Shannon Stewart | .25 | .60 |
| 184 | Ben Grieve | .25 | .60 |
| 185 | Ellis Burks | .25 | .60 |
| 186 | John Olerud | .25 | .60 |
| 187 | Tony Batista | .25 | .60 |
| 188 | Ruben Sierra | .25 | .60 |
| 189 | Carl Everett | .25 | .60 |
| 190 | Neifi Perez | .25 | .60 |
| 191 | Tony Clark | .25 | .60 |
| 192 | Doug Mientkiewicz | .25 | .60 |
| 193 | Carlos Lee | .25 | .60 |
| 194 | Jorge Posada | .40 | 1.00 |
| 195 | Lance Berkman | .40 | 1.00 |
| 196 | Ken Caminiti | .25 | .60 |
| 197 | Ben Sheets | .40 | 1.00 |
| 198 | Matt Morris | .25 | .60 |
| 199 | Fred McGriff | .40 | 1.00 |
| 200 | Mark Grace | .40 | 1.00 |
| 201 | Paul LoDuca | .25 | .60 |
| 202 | Tony Armas Jr. | .25 | .60 |
| 203 | Andres Galarraga | .25 | .60 |
| 204 | Cliff Floyd | .25 | .60 |
| 205 | Matt Lawton | .25 | .60 |
| 206 | Ryan Klesko | .25 | .60 |
| 207 | Jimmy Rollins | .25 | .60 |
| 208 | Aramis Ramirez | .25 | .60 |
| 209 | Aaron Boone | .25 | .60 |
| 210 | Jose Ortiz | .25 | .60 |
| 211 | Mark Prior FW RC | 6.00 | 15.00 |
| 212 | Mark Teixeira FW RC | 50.00 | 100.00 |
| 213 | Bud Smith FW RC | 2.50 | 6.00 |
| 214 | Wilmy Caceres FW RC | 2.50 | 6.00 |
| 215 | Dave Williams FW RC | 2.50 | 6.00 |
| 216 | Delvin James FW RC | 2.50 | 6.00 |
| 217 | Endy Chavez FW RC | 2.50 | 6.00 |
| 218 | Doug Nickle FW RC | 2.50 | 6.00 |
| 219 | Bret Prinz FW RC | 2.50 | 6.00 |
| 220 | Troy Mattes FW RC | 2.50 | 6.00 |
| 221 | Duaner Sanchez FW RC | 2.50 | 6.00 |
| 222 | Dewon Brazelton FW RC | 2.50 | 6.00 |
| 223 | Brian Bowles FW RC | 2.50 | 6.00 |
| 224 | Donaldo Mendez FW RC | 2.50 | 6.00 |
| 225 | Jorge Julio FW RC | 2.50 | 6.00 |
| 226 | Matt White FW RC | 2.50 | 6.00 |
| 227 | Casey Fossum FW RC | 2.50 | 6.00 |
| 228 | Mike Rivera FW RC | 2.50 | 6.00 |
| 229 | Joe Kennedy FW RC | 3.00 | 8.00 |
| 230 | Kyle Lohse FW RC | 3.00 | 8.00 |
| 231 | Juan Cruz FW RC | 3.00 | 8.00 |
| 232 | Jeremy Affeldt FW RC | 2.50 | 6.00 |
| 233 | Brandon Lyon FW RC | 2.50 | 6.00 |
| 234 | Brian Roberts FW RC | 8.00 | 20.00 |
| 235 | Willie Harris FW RC | 2.50 | 6.00 |
| 236 | Pedro Santana FW RC | 2.50 | 6.00 |
| 237 | Rafael Soriano FW RC | 2.50 | 6.00 |
| 238 | Steve Green FW RC | 2.50 | 6.00 |
| 239 | Junior Spivey FW RC | 3.00 | 8.00 |
| 240 | Rob Mackowiak FW RC | 3.00 | 8.00 |
| NNO | Ken Griffey Jr. Promo | .75 | 2.00 |

| # | Card | Lo | Hi |
|---|------|----|----|
|  | COMP.LOW w/o SP's (90) | 6.00 | 15.00 |
|  | COMP.UPDATE w/o SP's (30) | 4.00 | 10.00 |
|  | COMMON CARD (1-90) | .15 | .40 |
|  | COMMON (91-135/201-230) | 2.00 | 5.00 |
|  | COMMON CARD (136-170) | 4.00 | 10.00 |
|  | COMMON CARD (171-200) | .25 | .60 |
| 1 | Troy Glaus | .15 | .40 |
| 2 | Darin Erstad | .15 | .40 |
| 3 | Barry Zito | .15 | .40 |
| 4 | Eric Chavez | .15 | .40 |
| 5 | Tim Hudson | .15 | .40 |
| 6 | Miguel Tejada | .15 | .40 |
| 7 | Carlos Delgado | .15 | .40 |
| 8 | Shannon Stewart | .15 | .40 |
| 9 | Ben Grieve | .15 | .40 |
| 10 | Jim Thome | .25 | .60 |
| 11 | C.C. Sabathia | .25 | .60 |
| 12 | Ichiro Suzuki | .75 | 2.00 |
| 13 | Freddy Garcia | .15 | .40 |
| 14 | Edgar Martinez | .25 | .60 |
| 15 | Bret Boone | .15 | .40 |
| 16 | Jeff Conine | .15 | .40 |
| 17 | Alex Rodriguez | .60 | 1.50 |
| 18 | Juan Gonzalez | .15 | .40 |
| 19 | Ivan Rodriguez | .25 | .60 |
| 20 | Rafael Palmeiro | .25 | .60 |
| 21 | Hank Blalock | .25 | .60 |
| 22 | Pedro Martinez | .25 | .60 |
| 23 | Manny Ramirez | .25 | .60 |
| 24 | Nomar Garciaparra | .60 | 1.50 |
| 25 | Carlos Beltran | .15 | .40 |
| 26 | Mike Sweeney | .15 | .40 |
| 27 | Randall Simon | .15 | .40 |
| 28 | Dmitri Young | .15 | .40 |
| 29 | Bobby Higginson | .15 | .40 |
| 30 | Corey Koskie | .15 | .40 |
| 31 | Eric Milton | .15 | .40 |
| 32 | Torii Hunter | .15 | .40 |
| 33 | Joe Mays | .15 | .40 |
| 34 | Frank Thomas | .40 | 1.00 |
| 35 | Mark Buehrle | .15 | .40 |
| 36 | Magglio Ordonez | .15 | .40 |
| 37 | Kenny Lofton | .15 | .40 |
| 38 | Roger Clemens | .75 | 2.00 |
| 39 | Derek Jeter | 1.00 | 2.50 |
| 40 | Jason Giambi | .15 | .40 |
| 41 | Bernie Williams | .25 | .60 |
| 42 | Alfonso Soriano | .15 | .40 |
| 43 | Lance Berkman | .15 | .40 |
| 44 | Roy Oswalt | .15 | .40 |
| 45 | Jeff Bagwell | .25 | .60 |
| 46 | Craig Biggio | .15 | .40 |
| 47 | Chipper Jones | .40 | 1.00 |
| 48 | Greg Maddux | .60 | 1.50 |
| 49 | Gary Sheffield | .15 | .40 |
| 50 | Andruw Jones | .15 | .40 |
| 51 | Ben Sheets | .15 | .40 |
| 52 | Richie Sexson | .15 | .40 |
| 53 | Albert Pujols | .75 | 2.00 |
| 54 | Matt Morris | .15 | .40 |
| 55 | J.D. Drew | .15 | .40 |
| 56 | Sammy Sosa | .40 | 1.00 |
| 57 | Kerry Wood | .15 | .40 |
| 58 | Corey Patterson | .15 | .40 |
| 59 | Mark Prior | .75 | 2.00 |
| 60 | Randy Johnson | .40 | 1.00 |
| 61 | Luis Gonzalez | .15 | .40 |
| 62 | Curt Schilling | .15 | .40 |
| 63 | Shawn Green | .15 | .40 |
| 64 | Kevin Brown | .15 | .40 |
| 65 | Hideo Nomo | .40 | 1.00 |
| 66 | Vladimir Guerrero | .40 | 1.00 |

| # | Card | Lo | Hi |
|---|------|----|----|
| 67 | Jose Vidro | .15 | .40 |
| 68 | Barry Bonds | 1.00 | 2.50 |
| 69 | Jeff Kent | .15 | .40 |
| 70 | Rich Aurilia | .15 | .40 |
| 71 | Preston Wilson | .15 | .40 |
| 72 | Josh Beckett | .15 | .40 |
| 73 | Mike Lowell | .15 | .40 |
| 74 | Roberto Alomar | .25 | .60 |
| 75 | Mo Vaughn | .15 | .40 |
| 76 | Jeromy Burnitz | .15 | .40 |
| 77 | Mike Piazza | .60 | 1.50 |
| 78 | Sean Burroughs | .15 | .40 |
| 79 | Phil Nevin | .15 | .40 |
| 80 | Bobby Abreu | .15 | .40 |
| 81 | Pat Burrell | .15 | .40 |
| 82 | Scott Rolen | .25 | .60 |
| 83 | Jason Kendall | .15 | .40 |
| 84 | Brian Giles | .15 | .40 |
| 85 | Ken Griffey Jr. | .60 | 1.50 |
| 86 | Adam Dunn | .15 | .40 |
| 87 | Sean Casey | .15 | .40 |
| 88 | Todd Helton | .25 | .60 |
| 89 | Larry Walker | .15 | .40 |
| 90 | Mike Hampton | .15 | .40 |
| 91 | Brandon Puffer FW RC | 2.00 | 5.00 |
| 92 | Tom Sheam FW RC | 2.00 | 5.00 |
| 93 | Chris Baker FW RC | 2.00 | 5.00 |
| 94 | Gustavo Chacin FW RC | 3.00 | 8.00 |
| 95 | Joe Orloski FW RC | 2.00 | 5.00 |
| 96 | Mike Smith FW RC | 2.00 | 5.00 |
| 97 | John Ennis FW RC | 2.00 | 5.00 |
| 98 | John Fosler FW RC | 2.00 | 5.00 |
| 99 | Kevin Gryboski FW RC | 2.00 | 5.00 |
| 100 | Brian Mallette FW RC | 2.00 | 5.00 |
| 101 | Takahito Nomura FW RC | 2.00 | 5.00 |
| 102 | So Taguchi FW RC | 3.00 | 8.00 |
| 103 | Jeremy Lambert FW RC | 2.00 | 5.00 |
| 104 | Jason Simontacchi FW RC | 2.00 | 5.00 |
| 105 | Jorge Sosa FW RC | 3.00 | 8.00 |
| 106 | Brandon Backe FW RC | 3.00 | 8.00 |
| 107 | P.J. Bevis FW RC | 2.00 | 5.00 |
| 108 | Jeremy Ward FW RC | 2.00 | 5.00 |
| 109 | Doug Devore FW RC | 2.00 | 5.00 |
| 110 | Ron Chiavacci FW RC | 2.00 | 5.00 |
| 111 | Ron Calloway FW RC | 2.00 | 5.00 |
| 112 | Nelson Castro FW RC | 2.00 | 5.00 |
| 113 | Deivis Santos FW RC | 2.00 | 5.00 |
| 114 | Earl Snyder FW RC | 2.00 | 5.00 |
| 115 | Julio Mateo FW RC | 2.00 | 5.00 |
| 116 | J.J. Putz FW RC | 2.00 | 5.00 |
| 117 | Allan Simpson FW RC | 2.00 | 5.00 |
| 118 | Satoru Komiyama FW RC | 2.00 | 5.00 |
| 119 | Adam Walker FW RC | 2.00 | 5.00 |
| 120 | Oliver Perez FW RC | 3.00 | 8.00 |
| 121 | Cliff Bartosh FW RC | 2.00 | 5.00 |
| 122 | Todd Donovan FW RC | 2.00 | 5.00 |
| 123 | Elio Serrano FW RC | 2.00 | 5.00 |
| 124 | Pete Zamora FW RC | 2.00 | 5.00 |
| 125 | Mike Gonzalez FW RC | 2.00 | 5.00 |
| 126 | Travis Hughes FW RC | 2.00 | 5.00 |
| 127 | Jorge De La Rosa FW RC | 2.00 | 5.00 |
| 128 | Anastacio Martinez FW RC | 2.00 | 5.00 |
| 129 | Colin Young FW RC | 2.00 | 5.00 |
| 130 | Nate Field FW RC | 2.00 | 5.00 |
| 131 | Tim Kalita FW RC | 2.00 | 5.00 |
| 132 | Julius Matos FW RC | 2.00 | 5.00 |
| 133 | Terry Pearson FW RC | 2.00 | 5.00 |
| 134 | Kyle Kane FW RC | 2.00 | 5.00 |
| 135 | Mitch Wylie FW RC | 2.00 | 5.00 |
| 136 | Rodrigo Rosario AU RC | 4.00 | 10.00 |
| 137 | Franklyn German AU RC | 4.00 | 10.00 |
| 138 | Reed Johnson AU RC | 8.00 | 20.00 |
| 139 | Luis Martinez AU RC | 4.00 | 10.00 |
| 140 | Michael Crudale AU RC | 4.00 | 10.00 |
| 141 | Francis Beltran AU RC | 4.00 | 10.00 |
| 142 | Steve Kent AU RC | 4.00 | 10.00 |
| 143 | Felix Escalona AU RC | 4.00 | 10.00 |
| 144 | Jose Valverde AU RC | 4.00 | 10.00 |
| 145 | Victor Alvarez AU RC | 4.00 | 10.00 |
| 146 | Kazuhisa Ishii AU/249 RC | 15.00 | 40.00 |
| 147 | Jorge Nunez AU RC | 4.00 | 10.00 |
| 148 | Eric Good AU RC | 4.00 | 10.00 |
| 149 | Luis Ugueto AU RC | 4.00 | 10.00 |
| 150 | Matt Thornton AU RC | 4.00 | 10.00 |
| 151 | Wilson Valdez AU RC | 4.00 | 10.00 |
| 152 | Han Izquierdo AU/249 RC | 15.00 | 40.00 |
| 153 | Jaime Cerda AU RC | 4.00 | 10.00 |
| 154 | Mark Corey AU RC | 4.00 | 10.00 |

| # | | Lo | Hi |
|---|---|----|----|
| 155 | Tyler Yates AU RC | 4.00 | 10.00 |
| 156 | Steve Bechler AU RC | 4.00 | 10.00 |
| 157 | Ben Howard AU/249 RC | 15.00 | 40.00 |
| 158 | Anderson Machado AU RC | 4.00 | 10.00 |
| 159 | Jorge Padilla AU RC | 4.00 | 10.00 |
| 160 | Eric Junge AU RC | 4.00 | 10.00 |
| 161 | Adrian Burnside AU RC | 4.00 | 10.00 |
| 162 | Josh Hancock AU RC | 8.00 | 20.00 |
| 163 | Chris Booker AU RC | 4.00 | 10.00 |
| 164 | Cam Esslinger AU RC | 4.00 | 10.00 |
| 165 | Rene Reyes AU RC | 4.00 | 10.00 |
| 166 | Aaron Cook AU RC | 6.00 | 15.00 |
| 167 | Juan Brito AU RC | 4.00 | 10.00 |
| 168 | Miguel Ascencio AU RC | 4.00 | 10.00 |
| 169 | Kevin Frederick AU RC | 4.00 | 10.00 |
| 170 | Edwin Almonte AU RC | 4.00 | 10.00 |
| 171 | Enubiel Durazo | .25 | .60 |
| 172 | Junior Spivey | .25 | .60 |
| 173 | Geronimo Gil | .25 | .60 |
| 174 | Cliff Floyd | .25 | .60 |
| 175 | Brandon Larson | .25 | .60 |
| 176 | Aaron Boone | .25 | .60 |
| 177 | Shawn Estes | .25 | .60 |
| 178 | Austin Kearns | .25 | .60 |
| 179 | Joe Borchard | .25 | .60 |
| 180 | Russell Branyan | .25 | .60 |
| 181 | Jay Payton | .25 | .60 |
| 182 | Andres Torres | .25 | .60 |
| 183 | Andy Van Hekken | .25 | .60 |
| 184 | Alex Sanchez | .25 | .60 |
| 185 | Endy Chavez | .25 | .60 |
| 186 | Bartolo Colon | .25 | .60 |
| 187 | Raul Mondesi | .25 | .60 |
| 188 | Robin Ventura | .25 | .60 |
| 189 | Mike Mussina | .40 | 1.00 |
| 190 | Jorge Posada | .40 | 1.00 |
| 191 | Ted Lilly | .25 | .60 |
| 192 | Ray Durham | .25 | .60 |
| 193 | Brett Myers | .25 | .60 |
| 194 | Marlon Byrd | .25 | .60 |
| 195 | Vicente Padilla | .25 | .60 |
| 196 | Josh Fogg | .25 | .60 |
| 197 | Kenny Lofton | .25 | .60 |
| 198 | Scott Rolen | .40 | 1.00 |
| 199 | Jason Lane | .25 | .60 |
| 200 | Josh Phelps | .25 | .60 |
| 201 | Travis Driskill FW RC | 2.00 | 5.00 |
| 202 | Howie Clark FW RC | 2.00 | 5.00 |
| 203 | Mike Mahoney FW | 2.00 | 5.00 |
| 204 | Brian Tallet FW RC | 2.00 | 5.00 |
| 205 | Kirk Saarloos FW RC | 2.00 | 5.00 |
| 206 | Barry Wesson FW RC | 2.00 | 5.00 |
| 207 | Aaron Guiel FW RC | 2.00 | 5.00 |
| 208 | Shawn Sedlacek FW RC | 2.00 | 5.00 |
| 209 | Jose Diaz FW | 2.00 | 5.00 |
| 210 | Jorge Nunez FW | 2.00 | 5.00 |
| 211 | Danny Mota FW RC | 2.00 | 5.00 |
| 212 | David Ross FW RC | 3.00 | 8.00 |
| 213 | Jayson Durocher FW RC | 2.00 | 5.00 |
| 214 | Shane Nance FW RC | 2.00 | 5.00 |
| 215 | Wil Nieves FW RC | 2.00 | 5.00 |
| 216 | Freddy Sarithez FW RC | 4.00 | 10.00 |
| 217 | Alex Pelaez FW RC | 2.00 | 5.00 |
| 218 | Jamey Carroll FW RC | 3.00 | 8.00 |
| 219 | J.J. Trujillo FW RC | 2.00 | 5.00 |
| 220 | Kevin Pickford FW RC | 2.00 | 5.00 |
| 221 | Clay Condrey FW RC | 2.00 | 5.00 |
| 222 | Chris Snelling FW RC | 2.50 | 6.00 |
| 223 | Cliff Lee FW RC | 5.00 | 12.00 |
| 224 | Jeremy Hill FW RC | 2.00 | 5.00 |
| 225 | Jose Rodriguez FW RC | 2.00 | 5.00 |
| 226 | Lance Carter FW RC | 2.00 | 5.00 |
| 227 | Ken Huckaby FW RC | 2.00 | 5.00 |
| 228 | Scott Wiggins FW RC | 2.00 | 5.00 |
| 229 | Corey Thurman FW RC | 2.50 | 6.00 |
| 230 | Kevin Cash FW RC | 2.00 | 5.00 |
| RJD | Joe DiMaggio AU Poster | 125.00 | 200.00 |

# 2003 SP Authentic

| | Lo | Hi |
|---|----|----|
| COMP.LO SET w/o SP's (90) | 6.00 | 15.00 |
| COMMON CARD (1-90) | .15 | |
| COMMON CARD (91-123) | 1.25 | 3.00 |
| COMMON CARD (124-150) | 1.25 | 3.00 |
| COMMON CARD (151-180) | 2.00 | 5.00 |
| COMMON CARD (181-189) | 6.00 | 15.00 |
| 91-189 RANDOM INSERTS IN PACKS | | |
| COMMON CARD (190-239) | 2.00 | 5.00 |
| 190-239 RANDOM IN 03 UD FINITE PACKS | | |
| 190-239 PRINT RUN 699 SERIAL #'d SETS | | |

| # | | Lo | Hi |
|---|---|----|----|
| 1 | Darin Erstad | .15 | .40 |
| 2 | Garret Anderson | .15 | .40 |
| 3 | Troy Glaus | .15 | .40 |
| 4 | Eric Chavez | .15 | .40 |
| 5 | Barry Zito | .15 | .40 |
| 6 | Miguel Tejada | .15 | .40 |
| 7 | Eric Hinske | .15 | .40 |
| 8 | Carlos Delgado | .15 | .40 |
| 9 | Josh Phelps | .15 | .40 |
| 10 | Ben Grieve | .15 | .40 |
| 11 | Carl Crawford | .15 | .40 |
| 12 | Omar Vizquel | .25 | .60 |
| 13 | Matt Lawton | .15 | .40 |
| 14 | C.C. Sabathia | .15 | .40 |
| 15 | Ichiro Suzuki | .75 | 2.00 |
| 16 | John Olerud | .15 | .40 |
| 17 | Freddy Garcia | .15 | .40 |
| 18 | Jay Gibbons | .15 | .40 |
| 19 | Tony Batista | .15 | .40 |
| 20 | Melvin Mora | .15 | .40 |
| 21 | Alex Rodriguez | .60 | 1.50 |
| 22 | Rafael Palmeiro | .25 | .60 |
| 23 | Hank Blalock | .15 | .40 |
| 24 | Nomar Garciaparra | .60 | 1.50 |
| 25 | Pedro Martinez | .25 | .60 |
| 26 | Johnny Damon | .25 | .60 |
| 27 | Mike Sweeney | .15 | .40 |
| 28 | Carlos Febles | .15 | .40 |
| 29 | Carlos Beltran | .15 | .40 |
| 30 | Carlos Pena | .15 | .40 |
| 31 | Eric Munson | .15 | .40 |
| 32 | Bobby Higginson | .15 | .40 |
| 33 | Torii Hunter | .15 | .40 |
| 34 | Doug Mientkiewicz | .15 | .40 |
| 35 | Jacque Jones | .15 | .40 |
| 36 | Paul Konerko | .15 | .40 |
| 37 | Bartolo Colon | .15 | .40 |
| 38 | Magglio Ordonez | .15 | .40 |
| 39 | Derek Jeter | 1.00 | 2.50 |
| 40 | Bernie Williams | .25 | .60 |
| 41 | Jason Giambi | .40 | 1.00 |
| 42 | Alfonso Soriano | .40 | 1.00 |
| 43 | Roger Clemens | .75 | 2.00 |
| 44 | Jeff Bagwell | .25 | .60 |
| 45 | Jeff Kent | .15 | .40 |
| 46 | Lance Berkman | .15 | .40 |
| 47 | Chipper Jones | .40 | 1.00 |
| 48 | Andruw Jones | .25 | .60 |
| 49 | Gary Sheffield | .15 | .40 |
| 50 | Ben Sheets | .15 | .40 |
| 51 | Richie Sexson | .15 | .40 |
| 52 | Geoff Jenkins | .15 | .40 |
| 53 | Jim Edmonds | .15 | .40 |
| 54 | Albert Pujols | .75 | 2.00 |
| 55 | Scott Rolen | .25 | .60 |
| 56 | Sammy Sosa | .40 | 1.00 |
| 57 | Kerry Wood | .15 | .40 |
| 58 | Eric Karros | .15 | .40 |
| 59 | Luis Gonzalez | .15 | .40 |
| 60 | Randy Johnson | .40 | 1.00 |
| 61 | Curt Schilling | .15 | .40 |
| 62 | Fred McGriff | .25 | .60 |
| 63 | Shawn Green | .15 | .40 |
| 64 | Paul Lo Duca | .15 | .40 |
| 65 | Vladimir Guerrero | .40 | 1.00 |
| 66 | Jose Vidro | .15 | .40 |
| 67 | Barry Bonds | 1.00 | 2.50 |
| 68 | Rich Aurilia | .15 | .40 |
| 69 | Edgardo Alfonzo | .15 | .40 |
| 70 | Ivan Rodriguez | .25 | .60 |
| 71 | Mike Lowell | .15 | .40 |
| 72 | Derek Lee | .25 | .60 |
| 73 | Tom Glavine | .25 | .60 |
| 74 | Mike Piazza | .60 | 1.50 |
| 75 | Roberto Alomar | .15 | .40 |
| 76 | Ryan Klesko | .15 | .40 |
| 77 | Phil Nevin | .15 | .40 |
| 78 | Mark Kotsay | .15 | .40 |
| 79 | Jim Thome | .25 | .60 |
| 80 | Pat Burrell | .15 | .40 |
| 81 | Bobby Abreu | .15 | .40 |
| 82 | Jason Kendall | .15 | .40 |
| 83 | Brian Giles | .15 | .40 |
| 84 | Aramis Ramirez | .15 | .40 |
| 85 | Austin Kearns | .15 | .40 |
| 86 | Ken Griffey Jr. | .60 | 1.50 |
| 87 | Adam Dunn | .15 | .40 |
| 88 | Larry Walker | .15 | .40 |
| 89 | Todd Helton | .25 | .60 |
| 90 | Preston Wilson | .15 | .40 |
| 91 | Derek Jeter RA | 3.00 | 8.00 |
| 92 | Johnny Damon RA | 1.25 | 3.00 |
| 93 | Chipper Jones RA | 1.25 | 3.00 |
| 94 | Manny Ramirez RA | 1.25 | 3.00 |
| 95 | Trot Nixon RA | 1.25 | 3.00 |
| 96 | Alex Rodriguez RA | 2.00 | 5.00 |
| 97 | Chan Ho Park RA | 1.25 | 3.00 |
| 98 | Brad Fullmer RA | 1.25 | 3.00 |
| 99 | Billy Wagner RA | 1.25 | 3.00 |
| 100 | Hideo Nomo RA | 1.25 | 3.00 |
| 101 | Freddy Garcia RA | 1.25 | 3.00 |
| 102 | Darin Erstad RA | 1.25 | 3.00 |
| 103 | Jose Cruz Jr. RA | 1.25 | 3.00 |
| 104 | Nomar Garciaparra RA | 2.00 | 5.00 |
| 105 | Magglio Ordonez RA | 1.25 | 3.00 |
| 106 | Kerry Wood RA | 1.25 | 3.00 |
| 107 | Troy Glaus RA | 1.25 | 3.00 |
| 108 | J.D. Drew RA | 1.25 | 3.00 |
| 109 | Alfonso Soriano RA | 1.25 | 3.00 |
| 110 | Danys Baez RA | 1.25 | 3.00 |
| 111 | Kazuhiro Sasaki RA | 1.25 | 3.00 |
| 112 | Barry Zito RA | 1.25 | 3.00 |
| 113 | Brent Abernathy RA | 1.25 | 3.00 |
| 114 | Ben Diggins RA | 1.25 | 3.00 |
| 115 | Ben Sheets RA | 1.25 | 3.00 |
| 116 | Brad Wilkerson RA | 1.25 | 3.00 |
| 117 | Juan Pierre RA | 1.25 | 3.00 |
| 118 | Jon Rauch RA | 1.25 | 3.00 |
| 119 | Ichiro Suzuki RA | 2.50 | 6.00 |
| 120 | Albert Pujols RA | 2.50 | 6.00 |
| 121 | Mark Prior RA | 1.25 | 3.00 |
| 122 | Mark Teixeira RA | 1.25 | 3.00 |
| 123 | Kazuhisa Ishii RA | 1.25 | 3.00 |
| 124 | Troy Glaus B93 | 1.25 | 3.00 |
| 125 | Randy Johnson B93 | 1.25 | 3.00 |
| 126 | Curt Schilling B93 | 1.25 | 3.00 |
| 127 | Chipper Jones B93 | 2.00 | 5.00 |
| 128 | Greg Maddux B93 | 2.00 | 5.00 |
| 129 | Nomar Garciaparra B93 | 2.00 | 5.00 |
| 130 | Pedro Martinez B93 | 1.25 | 3.00 |
| 131 | Sammy Sosa B93 | 1.25 | 3.00 |
| 132 | Mark Prior B93 | 1.25 | 3.00 |
| 133 | Ken Griffey Jr. B93 | 2.00 | 5.00 |
| 134 | Adam Dunn B93 | 1.25 | 3.00 |
| 135 | Jeff Bagwell B93 | 1.25 | 3.00 |
| 136 | Vladimir Guerrero B93 | 1.25 | 3.00 |
| 137 | Mike Piazza B93 | 2.00 | 5.00 |
| 138 | Tom Glavine B93 | 1.25 | 3.00 |
| 139 | Derek Jeter B93 | 3.00 | 8.00 |
| 140 | Roger Clemens B93 | 2.50 | 6.00 |
| 141 | Jason Giambi B93 | 1.25 | 3.00 |
| 142 | Alfonso Soriano B93 | 1.25 | 3.00 |
| 143 | Miguel Tejada B93 | 1.25 | 3.00 |
| 144 | Barry Zito B93 | 1.25 | 3.00 |
| 145 | Jim Thome B93 | 1.25 | 3.00 |
| 146 | Barry Bonds B93 | 3.00 | 8.00 |
| 147 | Ichiro Suzuki B93 | 2.50 | 6.00 |
| 148 | Albert Pujols B93 | 2.50 | 6.00 |
| 149 | Alex Rodriguez B93 | 2.00 | 5.00 |
| 150 | Carlos Delgado B93 | 1.25 | 3.00 |

| | | |
|---|---|---|
| 151 Rich Fischar FW RC | 2.00 | 5.00 |
| 152 Brandon Webb FW RC | 10.00 | 25.00 |
| 153 Rob Hammock FW RC | 2.00 | 5.00 |
| 154 Matt Kata FW RC | 2.00 | 5.00 |
| 155 Tim Olson FW RC | 2.00 | 5.00 |
| 156 Oscar Villarreal FW RC | 2.00 | 5.00 |
| 157 Michael Hessman FW RC | 2.00 | 5.00 |
| 158 Daniel Cabrera FW RC | 3.00 | 8.00 |
| 159 Jon Leicester FW RC | 2.00 | 5.00 |
| 160 Todd Wellemeyer FW RC | 2.00 | 5.00 |
| 161 Felix Sanchez FW RC | 2.00 | 5.00 |
| 162 David Sanders FW RC | 2.00 | 5.00 |
| 163 Josh Stewart FW RC | 2.00 | 5.00 |
| 164 Arnie Munoz FW RC | 2.00 | 5.00 |
| 165 Ryan Cameron FW RC | 2.00 | 5.00 |
| 166 Clint Barmes FW RC | 10.00 | 25.00 |
| 167 Josh Willingham FW RC | 4.00 | 10.00 |
| 169 Willie Eyre FW RC | 2.00 | 5.00 |
| 170 Brent Hoard FW RC | 2.00 | 5.00 |
| 171 Termel Sledge FW RC | 2.00 | 5.00 |
| 172 Phil Seibel FW RC | 2.00 | 5.00 |
| 173 Craig Brazell FW RC | 2.00 | 5.00 |
| 174 Jeff Duncan FW RC | 2.00 | 5.00 |
| 176 Bernie Castro FW RC | 2.00 | 5.00 |
| 177 Mike Nicolas FW RC | 2.00 | 5.00 |
| 178 Rett Johnson FW RC | 2.00 | 5.00 |
| 179 Bobby Madritsch FW RC | 2.00 | 5.00 |
| 180 Chris Capuano FW RC | 10.00 | 25.00 |
| 181 Hid Matsui FW AU RC | 175.00 | 300.00 |
| 182 Jose Contreras FW AU RC | 12.50 | 30.00 |
| 183 Lew Ford FW AU RC | 10.00 | 25.00 |
| 184 Jeremy Griffiths FW AU RC | 6.00 | 15.00 |
| 185 G.Quinz FW AU RC | 6.00 | 15.00 |
| 186 Alej Machado FW AU RC | 6.00 | 15.00 |
| 187 Fran Cruceta FW AU RC | 6.00 | 15.00 |
| 188 Prentice Redman FW AU RC | 6.00 | 15.00 |
| 189 Shane Bazzell FW AU RC | 6.00 | 15.00 |
| 190 Aaron Looper FW RC | 2.00 | 5.00 |
| 191 Alex Prieto FW RC | 2.00 | 5.00 |
| 192 Alfredo Gonzalez FW RC | 2.00 | 5.00 |
| 193 Andrew Brown FW RC | 3.00 | 8.00 |
| 194 Anthony Ferrari FW RC | 2.00 | 5.00 |
| 195 Aquilino Lopez FW RC | 2.00 | 5.00 |
| 196 Beau Kemp FW RC | 2.00 | 5.00 |
| 197 Bo Hart FW RC | 2.00 | 5.00 |
| 198 Chad Gaudin FW RC | 2.00 | 5.00 |
| 199 Colin Porter FW RC | 2.00 | 5.00 |
| 200 D.J. Carrasco FW RC | 2.00 | 5.00 |
| 201 Dan Haren FW RC | 3.00 | 8.00 |
| 202 Danny Garcia FW RC | 2.00 | 5.00 |
| 203 Jon Switzer FW RC | 2.00 | 5.00 |
| 204 Edwin Jackson FW RC | 3.00 | 8.00 |
| 205 Fernando Cabrera FW RC | 2.00 | 5.00 |
| 206 Garrett Atkins FW RC | 2.00 | 5.00 |
| 207 Gerald Laird FW RC | 2.00 | 5.00 |
| 208 Greg Jones FW RC | 2.00 | 5.00 |
| 209 Ian Ferguson FW RC | 2.00 | 5.00 |
| 210 Jason Roach FW RC | 2.00 | 5.00 |
| 211 Jason Shiell FW RC | 2.00 | 5.00 |
| 212 Jeremy Bonderman FW RC | 10.00 | 25.00 |
| 213 Jeremy Wedel FW RC | 2.00 | 5.00 |
| 214 Jhonny Peralta FW RC | 3.00 | 8.00 |
| 215 Delmon Young FW RC | 25.00 | 50.00 |
| 216 Jorge DePaula FW RC | 2.00 | 5.00 |
| 217 Josh Hall FW RC | 2.00 | 5.00 |
| 218 Julio Manon FW RC | 2.00 | 5.00 |
| 219 Kevin Correia FW RC | 2.00 | 5.00 |
| 220 Kevin Ohme FW RC | 2.00 | 5.00 |
| 221 Kevin Tolar FW RC | 2.00 | 5.00 |
| 222 Luis Ayala FW RC | 2.00 | 5.00 |
| 223 Luis De Los Santos FW | 2.00 | 5.00 |
| 224 Chad Cordero FW RC | 4.00 | 10.00 |
| 225 Mark Malaska FW RC | 2.00 | 5.00 |
| 226 Khalil Greene FW | 3.00 | 8.00 |
| 227 Michael Nakamura FW RC | 2.00 | 5.00 |
| 228 Michel Hernandez FW RC | 2.00 | 5.00 |
| 229 Miguel Ojeda FW RC | 2.00 | 5.00 |
| 230 Mike Neu FW RC | 2.00 | 5.00 |
| 231 Nate Bland FW RC | 2.00 | 5.00 |
| 232 Pete LaForest FW RC | 2.00 | 5.00 |
| 233 Rickie Weeks FW RC | 8.00 | 20.00 |
| 234 Rosman Garcia FW RC | 2.00 | 5.00 |
| 235 Ryan Wagner FW RC | 2.00 | 5.00 |
| 236 Lance Niekro FW | 2.00 | 5.00 |
| 237 Tom Gregorio FW RC | 2.00 | 5.00 |
| 238 Tommy Phelps FW RC | 2.00 | 5.00 |
| 239 Wilfredo Ledezma FW RC | 2.00 | 5.00 |

**2004 SP Authentic**

| | | |
|---|---|---|
| COMP SET w/o SP's (90) | 6.00 | 15.00 |
| COMMON CARD (1-90) | .15 | .40 |
| COMMON (91-132/178-191) | 2.00 | 5.00 |
| 91-132/178-191 OVERALL ODDS 1:24 | | |
| 91-132/178-179/181-191 PRINT 704 #'d SETS | | |
| 91-132/178-191/181-191 #'d FROM 296-999 | | |
| CARD 180 PRINT RUN 999 #'d COPIES | | |
| CARD 180 #'d FROM 1-999 | | |
| COMMON CARD (133-177) | 1.25 | 3.00 |
| 133-177 STATED ODDS 1:24 | | |
| 133-177 PRINT RUN 999 SERIAL #'d SETS | | |
| 1 Bret Boone | .15 | .40 |
| 2 Gary Sheffield | .15 | .40 |
| 3 Rafael Palmeiro | .25 | .60 |
| 4 Jorge Posada | .25 | .60 |
| 5 Derek Jeter | .75 | 2.00 |
| 6 Garret Anderson | .15 | .40 |
| 7 Bartolo Colon | .15 | .40 |
| 8 Kevin Brown | .15 | .40 |
| 9 Shea Hillenbrand | .15 | .40 |
| 10 Ryan Klesko | .15 | .40 |
| 11 Bobby Abreu | .15 | .40 |
| 12 Scott Rolen | .25 | .60 |
| 13 Alfonso Soriano | .25 | .60 |
| 14 Jason Giambi | .15 | .40 |
| 15 Tom Glavine | .25 | .60 |
| 16 Hideo Nomo | .40 | 1.00 |
| 17 Johan Santana | .40 | 1.00 |
| 18 Sammy Sosa | .40 | 1.00 |
| 19 Rickie Weeks | .15 | .40 |
| 20 Barry Zito | .15 | .40 |
| 21 Kerry Wood | .15 | .40 |
| 22 Austin Kearns | .15 | .40 |
| 23 Shawn Green | .15 | .40 |
| 24 Miguel Cabrera | .25 | .60 |
| 25 Richard Hidalgo | .15 | .40 |
| 26 Andruw Jones | .25 | .60 |
| 27 Randy Wolf | .15 | .40 |
| 28 David Ortiz | .40 | 1.00 |
| 29 Roy Oswalt | .15 | .40 |
| 30 Vernon Wells | .15 | .40 |
| 31 Ben Sheets | .15 | .40 |
| 32 Mike Lowell | .15 | .40 |
| 33 Todd Helton | .25 | .60 |
| 34 Jacque Jones | .15 | .40 |
| 35 Mike Sweeney | .15 | .40 |
| 36 Hank Blalock | .15 | .40 |
| 37 Jason Schmidt | .15 | .40 |
| 38 Jeff Kent | .15 | .40 |
| 39 Josh Beckett | .25 | .60 |
| 40 Manny Ramirez | .25 | .60 |
| 41 Torii Hunter | .15 | .40 |
| 42 Brian Giles | .15 | .40 |
| 43 Javier Vazquez | .15 | .40 |
| 44 Jim Edmonds | .15 | .40 |
| 45 Dmitri Young | .15 | .40 |
| 46 Preston Wilson | .15 | .40 |
| 47 Jeff Bagwell | .25 | .60 |
| 48 Pedro Martinez | .25 | .60 |
| 49 Eric Chavez | .15 | .40 |
| 50 Ken Griffey Jr. | .60 | 1.50 |
| 51 Shannon Stewart | .15 | .40 |
| 52 Rafael Furcal | .15 | .40 |
| 53 Brandon Webb | .15 | .40 |
| 54 Juan Pierre | .15 | .40 |
| 55 Roger Clemens | .75 | 2.00 |
| 56 Geoff Jenkins | .15 | .40 |
| 57 Lance Berkman | .15 | .40 |
| 58 Albert Pujols | .75 | 2.00 |
| 59 Frank Thomas | .40 | 1.00 |
| 60 Edgar Martinez | .15 | .40 |
| 61 Tim Hudson | .15 | .40 |

| | | |
|---|---|---|
| 62 Eric Gagne | .15 | .40 |
| 63 Richie Sexson | .15 | .40 |
| 64 Corey Patterson | .15 | .40 |
| 65 Nomar Garciaparra | .60 | 1.50 |
| 66 Hideki Matsui | .60 | 1.50 |
| 67 Mark Teixeira | .25 | .60 |
| 68 Troy Glaus | .15 | .40 |
| 69 Carlos Lee | .15 | .40 |
| 70 Mike Mussina | .25 | .60 |
| 71 Magglio Ordonez | .15 | .40 |
| 72 Roy Halladay | .15 | .40 |
| 73 Ichiro Suzuki | .75 | 2.00 |
| 74 Randy Johnson | .40 | 1.00 |
| 75 Luis Gonzalez | .15 | .40 |
| 76 Mark Prior | .25 | .60 |
| 77 Carlos Beltran | .25 | .60 |
| 78 Ivan Rodriguez | .25 | .60 |
| 79 Alex Rodriguez | .60 | 1.50 |
| 80 Dontrelle Willis | .25 | .60 |
| 81 Mike Piazza | .60 | 1.50 |
| 82 Curt Schilling | .25 | .60 |
| 83 Vladimir Guerrero | .40 | 1.00 |
| 84 Greg Maddux | .60 | 1.50 |
| 85 Jim Thome | .25 | .60 |
| 86 Miguel Tejada | .15 | .40 |
| 87 Carlos Delgado | .15 | .40 |
| 88 Jose Reyes | .15 | .40 |
| 89 Matt Morris | .15 | .40 |
| 90 Mark Mulder | .15 | .40 |
| 91 Angel Chavez FW RC | 2.00 | 5.00 |
| 92 Brandon Medders FW RC | 2.00 | 5.00 |
| 93 Carlos Vasquez FW RC | 2.00 | 5.00 |
| 94 Chris Aguila FW RC | 2.00 | 5.00 |
| 95 Colby Miller FW RC | 2.00 | 5.00 |
| 96 Dave Crouthers FW RC | 2.00 | 5.00 |
| 97 Dennis Sarfate FW RC | 2.00 | 5.00 |
| 98 Donnie Kelly FW RC | 2.00 | 5.00 |
| 99 Merkin Valdez FW RC | 2.00 | 5.00 |
| 100 Eddy Rodriguez FW RC | 2.00 | 5.00 |
| 101 Edwin Moreno FW RC | 2.00 | 5.00 |
| 102 Enemencio Pacheco FW RC | 2.00 | 5.00 |
| 103 Roberto Novoa FW RC | 2.00 | 5.00 |
| 104 Greg Dobbs FW RC | 2.00 | 5.00 |
| 105 Hector Gimenez FW RC | 2.00 | 5.00 |
| 106 Ian Snell FW RC | 3.00 | 8.00 |
| 107 Jake Woods FW RC | 2.00 | 5.00 |
| 108 Jamie Brown FW RC | 2.00 | 5.00 |
| 109 Jason Frasor FW RC | 2.00 | 5.00 |
| 110 Jerome Gamble FW RC | 2.00 | 5.00 |
| 111 Jerry Gil FW RC | 2.00 | 5.00 |
| 112 Jesse Harper FW RC | 2.00 | 5.00 |
| 113 Jorge Vasquez FW RC | 2.00 | 5.00 |
| 114 Jose Capellan FW RC | 2.00 | 5.00 |
| 115 Josh Labandeira FW RC | 2.00 | 5.00 |
| 116 Justin Hampson FW RC | 2.00 | 5.00 |
| 117 Justin Huisman FW RC | 2.00 | 5.00 |
| 118 Justin Leone FW RC | 2.00 | 5.00 |
| 119 Lincoln Holdzkom FW RC | 2.00 | 5.00 |
| 120 Lino Urdaneta FW RC | 2.00 | 5.00 |
| 121 Mike Gosling FW RC | 2.00 | 5.00 |
| 122 Mike Johnston FW RC | 2.00 | 5.00 |
| 123 Mike Rouse FW RC | 2.00 | 5.00 |
| 124 Scott Proctor FW RC | 2.00 | 5.00 |
| 125 Roman Colon FW RC | 2.00 | 5.00 |
| 126 Ronny Cedeno FW RC | 3.00 | 8.00 |
| 127 Ryan Meaux FW RC | 2.00 | 5.00 |
| 128 Scott Dohmann FW RC | 2.00 | 5.00 |
| 129 Sean Henn FW RC | 2.00 | 5.00 |
| 130 Tim Bausher FW RC | 2.00 | 5.00 |
| 131 Tim Bittner FW RC | 2.00 | 5.00 |
| 132 William Bergolla FW RC | 2.00 | 5.00 |
| 133 Rick Ferrell ASM | 1.25 | 3.00 |
| 134 Joe DiMaggio ASM | 2.00 | 5.00 |
| 135 Bob Feller ASM | 1.25 | 3.00 |
| 136 Ted Williams ASM | 3.00 | 8.00 |
| 137 Stan Musial ASM | 2.00 | 5.00 |
| 138 Larry Doby ASM | 1.25 | 3.00 |
| 139 Red Schoendienst ASM | 1.25 | 3.00 |
| 140 Enos Slaughter ASM | 1.25 | 3.00 |
| 141 Stan Musial ASM | 2.00 | 5.00 |
| 142 Mickey Mantle ASM | 4.00 | 10.00 |
| 143 Ted Williams ASM | 3.00 | 8.00 |
| 144 Mickey Mantle ASM | 4.00 | 10.00 |
| 145 Stan Musial ASM | 2.00 | 5.00 |
| 146 Tom Seaver ASM | 1.50 | 4.00 |
| 147 Willie McCovey ASM | 1.50 | 4.00 |
| 148 Bob Gibson ASM | 1.25 | 3.00 |
| 149 Frank Robinson ASM | 1.25 | 3.00 |

| | | | | | | |
|---|---|---|---|---|---|---|
| □ 150 Joe Morgan ASM | 1.25 | 3.00 | | □ 22 Chone Figgins | .15 | .40 |
| □ 151 Billy Williams ASM | 1.25 | 3.00 | | □ 23 Corey Patterson | .15 | .40 |
| □ 152 Catfish Hunter ASM | 1.50 | 4.00 | | □ 24 Craig Biggio | .25 | .60 |
| □ 153 Joe Morgan ASM | 1.25 | 3.00 | | □ 25 Dale Murphy | .25 | .60 |
| □ 154 Joe Morgan ASM | 1.25 | 3.00 | | □ 26 Dallas McPherson | .15 | .40 |
| □ 155 Mike Schmidt ASM | 3.00 | 8.00 | | □ 27 Danny Haren | .15 | .40 |
| □ 156 Tommy Lasorda ASM | 1.25 | 3.00 | | □ 28 Darryl Strawberry | .15 | .40 |
| □ 157 Robin Yount ASM | 1.50 | 4.00 | | □ 29 David Ortiz | .25 | .60 |
| □ 158 Nolan Ryan ASM | 4.00 | 10.00 | | □ 30 David Wright | .60 | 1.50 |
| □ 159 John Franco ASM | 1.25 | 3.00 | | □ 31 Derek Jeter | .75 | 2.00 |
| □ 160 Nolan Ryan ASM | 4.00 | 10.00 | | □ 32 Derrek Lee | .25 | .60 |
| □ 161 Ken Griffey Jr. ASM | 2.00 | 5.00 | | □ 33 Don Mattingly | .75 | 2.00 |
| □ 162 Cal Ripken ASM | 4.00 | 10.00 | | □ 34 Dwight Gooden | .15 | .40 |
| □ 163 Ken Griffey Jr. ASM | 2.00 | 5.00 | | □ 35 Edgar Renteria | .15 | .40 |
| □ 164 Gary Sheffield ASM | 1.25 | 3.00 | | □ 36 Eric Chavez | .15 | .40 |
| □ 165 Fred McGriff ASM | 1.50 | 4.00 | | □ 37 Eric Gagne | .15 | .40 |
| □ 166 Hideo Nomo ASM | 1.50 | 4.00 | | □ 38 Gary Sheffield | .15 | .40 |
| □ 167 Mike Piazza ASM | 2.00 | 5.00 | | □ 39 Gavin Floyd | .15 | .40 |
| □ 168 Sandy Alomar Jr. ASM | 1.25 | 3.00 | | □ 40 Pedro Martinez | .25 | .60 |
| □ 169 Roberto Alomar ASM | 1.50 | 4.00 | | □ 41 Greg Maddux | .60 | 1.50 |
| □ 170 Ted Williams ASM | 3.00 | 8.00 | | □ 42 Hank Blalock | .15 | .40 |
| □ 171 Pedro Martinez ASM | 1.50 | 4.00 | | □ 43 Huston Street | .25 | .60 |
| □ 172 Derek Jeter ASM | 2.50 | 6.00 | | □ 44 J.D. Drew | .15 | .40 |
| □ 173 Cal Ripken ASM | 4.00 | 10.00 | | □ 45 Jake Peavy | .15 | .40 |
| □ 174 Torii Hunter ASM | 1.25 | 3.00 | | □ 46 Jake Westbrook | .15 | .40 |
| □ 175 Alfonso Soriano ASM | 1.25 | 3.00 | | □ 47 Jason Bay | .15 | .40 |
| □ 176 Hank Blalock ASM | 1.25 | 3.00 | | □ 48 Austin Kearns | .15 | .40 |
| □ 177 Ichiro Suzuki ASM | 2.50 | 6.00 | | □ 49 Jeremy Reed | .15 | .40 |
| □ 178 Orlando Rodriguez FW RC | 2.00 | 5.00 | | □ 50 Jim Rice | .15 | .40 |
| □ 179 Ramon Ramirez FW RC | 2.00 | 5.00 | | □ 51 Jimmy Rollins | .15 | .40 |
| □ 180 Kazuo Matsui FW RC | 2.00 | 5.00 | | □ 52 Joe Blanton | .15 | .40 |
| □ 181 Kevin Cave FW RC | 2.00 | 5.00 | | □ 53 Joe Mauer | .40 | 1.00 |
| □ 182 John Gall FW RC | 2.00 | 5.00 | | □ 54 Johan Santana | .40 | 1.00 |
| □ 183 Freddy Guzman FW RC | 2.00 | 5.00 | | □ 55 John Smoltz | .25 | .60 |
| □ 184 Chris Oxspring FW RC | 2.00 | 5.00 | | □ 56 Johnny Estrada | .15 | .40 |
| □ 185 Rusty Tucker FW RC | 2.00 | 5.00 | | □ 57 Jose Reyes | .15 | .40 |
| □ 186 Jorge Sequea FW RC | 2.00 | 5.00 | | □ 58 Ken Griffey Jr. | .60 | 1.50 |
| □ 187 Carlos Hines FW RC | 2.00 | 5.00 | | □ 59 Kerry Wood | .15 | .40 |
| □ 188 Michael Vento FW RC | 2.00 | 5.00 | | □ 60 Khalil Greene | .15 | .40 |
| □ 189 Ryan Wing FW RC | 2.00 | 5.00 | | □ 61 Marcus Giles | .15 | .40 |
| □ 190 Jeff Bennett FW RC | 2.00 | 5.00 | | □ 62 Melvin Mora | .15 | .40 |
| □ 191 Luis A. Gonzalez FW RC | 2.00 | 5.00 | | □ 63 Mark Grace | .25 | .60 |

### 2005 SP Authentic

| | | |
|---|---|---|
| □ COMP. BASIC SET (100) | 10.00 | 25.00 |
| □ COMMON CARD (1-100) | .15 | .40 |
| □ COMMON RETIRED 1-100 | .15 | .40 |
| □ 1-100 ISSUED IN 05 SP COLLECTION PACKS | | |
| □ COMMON AUTO (101-186) | 4.00 | 10.00 |
| □ 101-186 ODDS APPX 1:8 '05 UD UPDATE | | |
| □ 101-186 PRINT RUN 185 SERIAL #'d SETS | | |
| □ 105, 115, 118-119, 142, 154 DO NOT EXIST | | |
| □ 161, 180, 183, 186 DO NOT EXIST | | |
| □ 1 A.J. Burnett | .15 | .40 |
| □ 2 Aaron Rowand | .15 | .40 |
| □ 3 Adam Dunn | .15 | .40 |
| □ 4 Adrian Beltre | .15 | .40 |
| □ 5 Adrian Gonzalez | .15 | .40 |
| □ 6 Akinori Otsuka | .15 | .40 |
| □ 7 Albert Crawford | .75 | 2.00 |
| □ 8 Andre Dawson | .15 | .40 |
| □ 9 Andruw Jones | .25 | .60 |
| □ 10 Aramis Ramirez | .15 | .40 |
| □ 11 Barry Larkin | .25 | .60 |
| □ 12 Ben Sheets | .15 | .40 |
| □ 13 Bo Jackson | .40 | 1.00 |
| □ 14 Bobby Abreu | .15 | .40 |
| □ 15 Bobby Crosby | .15 | .40 |
| □ 16 Bronson Arroyo | .15 | .40 |
| □ 17 Cal Ripken | 1.25 | 3.00 |
| □ 18 Carl Crawford | .15 | .40 |
| □ 19 Carlos Zambrano | .15 | .40 |
| □ 20 Casey Kotchman | .15 | .40 |
| □ 21 Cesar Izturis | .15 | .40 |

| | | | | | | |
|---|---|---|---|---|---|---|
| □ 64 Mark Mulder | .15 | .40 | | □ 111 Chris Resop AU RC | 6.00 | 15.00 |
| □ 65 Mark Prior | .25 | .60 | | □ 112 Chris Roberson AU RC | 4.00 | 10.00 |
| □ 66 Mark Teixeira | .25 | .60 | | □ 113 Chris Seddon AU RC | 4.00 | 10.00 |
| □ 67 Matt Clement | .15 | .40 | | □ 114 Colter Bean AU RC | 6.00 | 15.00 |
| □ 68 Michael Young | .15 | .40 | | □ 116 Dave Gassner AU RC | 4.00 | 10.00 |
| □ 69 Miguel Cabrera | .25 | .60 | | □ 117 Brian Anderson AU RC | 15.00 | 40.00 |
| □ 70 Miguel Tejada | .15 | .40 | | □ 120 Devon Lowery AU RC | 4.00 | 10.00 |
| □ 71 Mike Piazza | .40 | 1.00 | | □ 121 Enrique Gonzalez AU RC | 6.00 | 15.00 |
| □ 72 Mike Schmidt | .75 | 2.00 | | □ 122 Eude Brito AU RC | 4.00 | 10.00 |
| □ 73 Nolan Ryan | 1.00 | 2.50 | | □ 123 Francisco Butto AU RC | 4.00 | 10.00 |
| □ 74 Oliver Perez | .15 | .40 | | □ 124 Franquelis Osoria AU RC | 4.00 | 10.00 |
| □ 75 Nick Johnson | .15 | .40 | | □ 125 Garrett Jones AU RC | 30.00 | 60.00 |
| □ 76 Paul Molitor | .25 | .60 | | □ 126 Geovany Soto AU RC | 75.00 | 150.00 |
| □ 77 Rafael Palmeiro | .15 | .40 | | □ 127 Hayden Penn AU RC | 10.00 | 25.00 |
| □ 78 Randy Johnson | .40 | 1.00 | | □ 128 Ismael Ramirez AU RC | 4.00 | 10.00 |
| □ 79 Reggie Jackson | .25 | .60 | | □ 129 Jared Gothreaux AU RC | 4.00 | 10.00 |
| □ 80 Rich Harden | .15 | .40 | | □ 130 Jason Hammel AU RC | 4.00 | 10.00 |
| □ 81 Rickie Weeks | .15 | .40 | | □ 131 Jeff Miller AU RC | 4.00 | 10.00 |
| □ 82 Robin Yount | .40 | 1.00 | | □ 132 Jeff Niemann AU RC | 12.50 | 30.00 |
| □ 83 Roger Clemens | .60 | 1.50 | | □ 133 Joel Peralta AU RC | 4.00 | 10.00 |
| □ 84 Roy Oswalt | .15 | .40 | | □ 134 John Hattig AU RC | 4.00 | 10.00 |
| □ 85 Ryan Howard | 1.00 | 2.50 | | □ 135 Jorge Campillo AU RC | 4.00 | 10.00 |
| □ 86 Ryne Sandberg | .75 | 2.00 | | □ 136 Juan Morillo AU RC | 4.00 | 10.00 |
| □ 87 Scott Kazmir | .15 | .40 | | □ 137 Justin Verlander AU RC | 90.00 | 150.00 |
| □ 88 Scott Rolen | .25 | .60 | | □ 138 Ryan Garko AU RC | 25.00 | 50.00 |
| □ 89 Sean Burroughs | .15 | .40 | | □ 139 Keiichi Yabu AU RC | 6.00 | 15.00 |
| □ 90 Sean Casey | .15 | .40 | | □ 140 Kendry Morales AU RC | 40.00 | 80.00 |
| □ 91 Shingo Takatsu | .15 | .40 | | □ 141 Luis Hernandez AU RC | 4.00 | 10.00 |
| □ 92 Tim Hudson | .15 | .40 | | □ 143 Luis O.Rodriguez AU RC | 4.00 | 10.00 |
| □ 93 Tony Gwynn | .50 | 1.25 | | □ 144 Luke Scott AU RC | 30.00 | 60.00 |
| □ 94 Torii Hunter | .15 | .40 | | □ 145 Marcos Carvajal AU RC | 4.00 | 10.00 |
| □ 95 Travis Hafner | .15 | .40 | | □ 146 Mark Woodyard AU RC | 4.00 | 10.00 |
| □ 96 Victor Martinez | .15 | .40 | | □ 147 Matt A.Smith AU RC | 4.00 | 10.00 |
| □ 97 Vladimir Guerrero | .40 | 1.00 | | □ 148 Matthew Lindstrom AU RC | 4.00 | 10.00 |
| □ 98 Wade Boggs | .25 | .60 | | □ 149 Miguel Negron AU RC | 6.00 | 15.00 |
| □ 99 Will Clark | .25 | .60 | | □ 150 Mike Morse AU RC | 8.00 | 20.00 |
| □ 100 Yadier Molina | .15 | .40 | | □ 151 Nate McLouth AU RC | 50.00 | 100.00 |
| □ 101 Adam Shabala AU RC | 4.00 | 10.00 | | □ 152 Nelson Cruz AU RC | 50.00 | 100.00 |
| □ 102 Ambiorix Burgos AU RC | 4.00 | 10.00 | | □ 153 Nick Masset AU RC | 4.00 | 10.00 |
| □ 103 Ambiorix Concepcion AU RC | 4.00 | 10.00 | | □ 155 Paulino Reynoso AU RC | 4.00 | 10.00 |
| □ 104 Anibal Sanchez AU RC | 15.00 | 40.00 | | □ 156 Pedro Lopez AU RC | 4.00 | 10.00 |
| □ 106 Brandon McCarthy AU RC | 15.00 | 40.00 | | □ 157 Pete Orr AU RC | 4.00 | 10.00 |
| □ 107 Brian Burres AU RC | 4.00 | 10.00 | | □ 159 Philip Humber AU RC | 12.50 | 30.00 |
| □ 108 Carlos Ruiz AU RC | 10.00 | 25.00 | | □ 160 Prince Fielder AU RC | 225.00 | 300.00 |
| □ 109 Casey Rogowski AU RC | 6.00 | 15.00 | | □ 161 Randy Messenger AU RC | 4.00 | 10.00 |
| □ 110 Chad Orvella AU RC | 4.00 | 10.00 | | □ 162 Raul Tablado AU RC | 4.00 | 10.00 |
| | | | | □ 163 Ronny Paulino AU RC | 10.00 | 25.00 |
| | | | | □ 164 Russ Rohlicek AU RC | 4.00 | 10.00 |
| | | | | □ 165 Russell Martin AU RC | 60.00 | 120.00 |
| | | | | □ 166 Scott Baker AU RC | 6.00 | 15.00 |
| | | | | □ 167 Scott Munter AU RC | 4.00 | 10.00 |
| | | | | □ 168 Sean Thompson AU RC | 4.00 | 10.00 |
| | | | | □ 169 Sean Tracey AU RC | 4.00 | 10.00 |
| | | | | □ 170 Shane Costa AU RC | 4.00 | 10.00 |
| | | | | □ 171 Stephen Drew AU RC | 30.00 | 60.00 |
| | | | | □ 172 Steve Schmoll AU RC | 4.00 | 10.00 |
| | | | | □ 173 Tadahito Iguchi AU RC | 20.00 | 50.00 |
| | | | | □ 174 Tony Giarratano AU RC | 4.00 | 10.00 |
| | | | | □ 175 Tony Pena AU RC | 4.00 | 10.00 |
| | | | | □ 176 Travis Bowyer AU RC | 4.00 | 10.00 |
| | | | | □ 177 Ubaldo Jimenez AU RC | 20.00 | 50.00 |
| | | | | □ 178 Wladimir Balentien AU RC | 50.00 | 100.00 |
| | | | | □ 179 Yorman Bazardo AU RC | 4.00 | 10.00 |
| | | | | □ 181 Ryan Zimmerman AU RC | 150.00 | 225.00 |
| | | | | □ 182 Chris Denorfia AU RC | 10.00 | 25.00 |
| | | | | □ 184 Jermaine Van Buren AU | 4.00 | 10.00 |
| | | | | □ 185 Mark McLemore AU RC | 4.00 | 10.00 |

### 2006 SP Authentic

| | | |
|---|---|---|
| □ COMP.SET w/o SP's (100) | 6.00 | 15.00 |
| □ 1 Erik Bedard | .15 | .40 |
| □ 2 Corey Patterson | .15 | .40 |
| □ 3 Ramon Hernandez | .15 | .40 |
| □ 4 Kris Benson | .15 | .40 |

|  |  | | |
|---|---|---|---|
| ❑ 5 | Miguel Batista | .15 | .40 |
| ❑ 6 | Orlando Hudson | .15 | .40 |
| ❑ 7 | Shawn Green | .15 | .40 |
| ❑ 8 | Jeff Francoeur | .15 | 1.00 |
| ❑ 9 | Marcus Giles | .15 | .40 |
| ❑ 10 | Edgar Renteria | .15 | .40 |
| ❑ 11 | Tim Hudson | .15 | .40 |
| ❑ 12 | Tim Wakefield | .15 | .40 |
| ❑ 13 | Mark Loretta | .15 | .40 |
| ❑ 14 | Kevin Youkilis | .15 | .40 |
| ❑ 15 | Mike Lowell | .15 | .40 |
| ❑ 16 | Coco Crisp | .15 | .40 |
| ❑ 17 | Tadahito Iguchi | .15 | .40 |
| ❑ 18 | Scott Podsednik | .15 | .40 |
| ❑ 19 | Jermaine Dye | .15 | .40 |
| ❑ 20 | Jose Contreras | .15 | .40 |
| ❑ 21 | Carlos Zambrano | .15 | .40 |
| ❑ 22 | Aramis Ramirez | .15 | .40 |
| ❑ 23 | Jacque Jones | .15 | .40 |
| ❑ 24 | Austin Kearns | .15 | .40 |
| ❑ 25 | Felipe Lopez | .15 | .40 |
| ❑ 26 | Brandon Phillips | .15 | .40 |
| ❑ 27 | Aaron Harang | .15 | .40 |
| ❑ 28 | Cliff Lee | .15 | .40 |
| ❑ 29 | Jhonny Peralta | .15 | .40 |
| ❑ 30 | Jason Michaels | .15 | .40 |
| ❑ 31 | Clint Barmes | .15 | .40 |
| ❑ 32 | Brad Hawpe | .15 | .40 |
| ❑ 33 | Aaron Cook | .15 | .40 |
| ❑ 34 | Kenny Rogers | .15 | .40 |
| ❑ 35 | Carlos Guillen | .15 | .40 |
| ❑ 36 | Brian Moehler | .15 | .40 |
| ❑ 37 | Andy Pettitte | .25 | .60 |
| ❑ 38 | Wandy Rodriguez | .15 | .40 |
| ❑ 39 | Morgan Ensberg | .15 | .40 |
| ❑ 40 | Preston Wilson | .15 | .40 |
| ❑ 41 | Mark Grudzielanek | .15 | .40 |
| ❑ 42 | Angel Berroa | .15 | .40 |
| ❑ 43 | Jeremy Affeldt | .15 | .40 |
| ❑ 44 | Zack Greinke | .15 | .40 |
| ❑ 45 | Orlando Cabrera | .15 | .40 |
| ❑ 46 | Garret Anderson | .15 | .40 |
| ❑ 47 | Ervin Santana | .15 | .40 |
| ❑ 48 | Derek Lowe | .15 | .40 |
| ❑ 49 | Nomar Garciaparra | .40 | 1.00 |
| ❑ 50 | J.D. Drew | .15 | .40 |
| ❑ 51 | Rafael Furcal | .15 | .40 |
| ❑ 52 | Rickie Weeks | .15 | .40 |
| ❑ 53 | Geoff Jenkins | .15 | .40 |
| ❑ 54 | Bill Hall | .15 | .40 |
| ❑ 55 | Chris Capuano | .15 | .40 |
| ❑ 56 | Derrick Turnbow | .15 | .40 |
| ❑ 57 | Justin Morneau | .15 | .40 |
| ❑ 58 | Michael Cuddyer | .15 | .40 |
| ❑ 59 | Luis Castillo | .15 | .40 |
| ❑ 60 | Hideki Matsui | .40 | 1.00 |
| ❑ 61 | Jason Giambi | .15 | .40 |
| ❑ 62 | Jorge Posada | .25 | .60 |
| ❑ 63 | Mariano Rivera | .40 | 1.00 |
| ❑ 64 | Billy Wagner | .15 | .40 |
| ❑ 65 | Carlos Delgado | .15 | .40 |
| ❑ 66 | Jose Reyes | .40 | 1.00 |
| ❑ 67 | Nick Swisher | .15 | .40 |
| ❑ 68 | Bobby Crosby | .15 | .40 |
| ❑ 69 | Frank Thomas | .40 | 1.00 |
| ❑ 70 | Ryan Howard | .60 | 1.50 |
| ❑ 71 | Pat Burrell | .15 | .40 |
| ❑ 72 | Jimmy Rollins | .15 | .40 |
| ❑ 73 | Craig Wilson | .15 | .40 |
| ❑ 74 | Freddy Sanchez | .15 | .40 |
| ❑ 75 | Sean Casey | .15 | .40 |
| ❑ 76 | Mike Piazza | .40 | 1.00 |
| ❑ 77 | Dave Roberts | .15 | .40 |
| ❑ 78 | Chris Young | .15 | .40 |
| ❑ 79 | Noah Lowry | .15 | .40 |
| ❑ 80 | Armando Benitez | .15 | .40 |
| ❑ 81 | Pedro Feliz | .15 | .40 |
| ❑ 82 | Jose Lopez | .15 | .40 |
| ❑ 83 | Adrian Beltre | .15 | .40 |
| ❑ 84 | Jamie Moyer | .15 | .40 |
| ❑ 85 | Jason Isringhausen | .15 | .40 |
| ❑ 86 | Jason Marquis | .15 | .40 |
| ❑ 87 | David Eckstein | .15 | .40 |
| ❑ 88 | Juan Encarnacion | .15 | .40 |
| ❑ 89 | Julio Lugo | .15 | .40 |
| ❑ 90 | Ty Wigginton | .15 | .40 |
| ❑ 91 | Jorge Cantu | .15 | .40 |
| ❑ 92 | Akinori Otsuka | .15 | .40 |
| ❑ 93 | Hank Blalock | .15 | .40 |
| ❑ 94 | Kevin Mench | .15 | .40 |
| ❑ 95 | Lyle Overbay | .15 | .40 |
| ❑ 96 | Shea Hillenbrand | .15 | .40 |
| ❑ 97 | B.J. Ryan | .15 | .40 |
| ❑ 98 | Tony Armas | .15 | .40 |
| ❑ 99 | Chad Cordero | .15 | .40 |
| ❑ 100 | Jose Guillen | .15 | .40 |
| ❑ 101 | Miguel Tejada | 1.50 | 4.00 |
| ❑ 102 | Brian Roberts | 1.50 | 4.00 |
| ❑ 103 | Melvin Mora | 1.50 | 4.00 |
| ❑ 104 | Brandon Webb | 1.50 | 4.00 |
| ❑ 105 | Chad Tracy | 1.50 | 4.00 |
| ❑ 106 | Luis Gonzalez | 1.50 | 4.00 |
| ❑ 107 | Andruw Jones | 2.00 | 5.00 |
| ❑ 108 | Chipper Jones | 2.00 | 5.00 |
| ❑ 109 | John Smoltz | 2.00 | 5.00 |
| ❑ 110 | Curt Schilling | 2.00 | 5.00 |
| ❑ 111 | Josh Beckett | 1.50 | 4.00 |
| ❑ 112 | David Ortiz | 2.00 | 5.00 |
| ❑ 113 | Manny Ramirez | 2.00 | 5.00 |
| ❑ 114 | Jason Varitek | 1.50 | 4.00 |
| ❑ 115 | Jim Thome | 2.00 | 5.00 |
| ❑ 116 | Paul Konerko | 1.50 | 4.00 |
| ❑ 117 | Javier Vazquez | 1.50 | 4.00 |
| ❑ 118 | Mark Prior | 1.50 | 4.00 |
| ❑ 119 | Derrek Lee | 1.50 | 4.00 |
| ❑ 120 | Greg Maddux | 3.00 | 8.00 |
| ❑ 121 | Ken Griffey Jr. | 3.00 | 8.00 |
| ❑ 122 | Adam Dunn | 1.50 | 4.00 |
| ❑ 123 | Bronson Arroyo | 2.00 | 5.00 |
| ❑ 124 | Travis Hafner | 1.50 | 4.00 |
| ❑ 125 | Victor Martinez | 1.50 | 4.00 |
| ❑ 126 | Grady Sizemore | 2.00 | 5.00 |
| ❑ 127 | C.C. Sabathia | 1.50 | 4.00 |
| ❑ 128 | Todd Helton | 2.00 | 5.00 |
| ❑ 129 | Matt Holliday | 1.50 | 4.00 |
| ❑ 130 | Garrett Atkins | 1.50 | 4.00 |
| ❑ 131 | Jeff Francis | 1.50 | 4.00 |
| ❑ 132 | Jeremy Bonderman | 1.50 | 4.00 |
| ❑ 133 | Ivan Rodriguez | 2.00 | 5.00 |
| ❑ 134 | Chris Shelton | 1.50 | 4.00 |
| ❑ 135 | Magglio Ordonez | 1.50 | 4.00 |
| ❑ 136 | Dontrelle Willis | 1.50 | 4.00 |
| ❑ 137 | Miguel Cabrera | 2.00 | 5.00 |
| ❑ 138 | Roger Clemens | 3.00 | 8.00 |
| ❑ 139 | Roy Oswalt | 1.50 | 4.00 |
| ❑ 140 | Lance Berkman | 1.50 | 4.00 |
| ❑ 141 | Reggie Sanders | 1.50 | 4.00 |
| ❑ 142 | Vladimir Guerrero | 2.00 | 5.00 |
| ❑ 143 | Bartolo Colon | 1.50 | 4.00 |
| ❑ 144 | Chone Figgins | 1.50 | 4.00 |
| ❑ 145 | Francisco Rodriguez | 1.50 | 4.00 |
| ❑ 146 | Brad Penny | 1.50 | 4.00 |
| ❑ 147 | Jeff Kent | 1.50 | 4.00 |
| ❑ 148 | Eric Gagne | 1.50 | 4.00 |
| ❑ 149 | Carlos Lee | 1.50 | 4.00 |
| ❑ 150 | Ben Sheets | 1.50 | 4.00 |
| ❑ 151 | Johan Santana | 2.00 | 5.00 |
| ❑ 152 | Torii Hunter | 1.50 | 4.00 |
| ❑ 153 | Joe Nathan | 1.50 | 4.00 |
| ❑ 154 | Alex Rodriguez | 3.00 | 8.00 |
| ❑ 155 | Derek Jeter | 4.00 | 10.00 |
| ❑ 156 | Randy Johnson | 2.00 | 5.00 |
| ❑ 157 | Johnny Damon | 2.00 | 5.00 |
| ❑ 158 | Mike Mussina | 2.00 | 5.00 |
| ❑ 159 | Pedro Martinez | 2.00 | 5.00 |
| ❑ 160 | Tom Glavine | 2.00 | 5.00 |
| ❑ 161 | David Wright | 3.00 | 8.00 |
| ❑ 162 | Carlos Beltran | 1.50 | 4.00 |
| ❑ 163 | Rich Harden | 1.50 | 4.00 |
| ❑ 164 | Barry Zito | 1.50 | 4.00 |
| ❑ 165 | Eric Chavez | 1.50 | 4.00 |
| ❑ 166 | Huston Street | 1.50 | 4.00 |
| ❑ 167 | Bobby Abreu | 1.50 | 4.00 |
| ❑ 168 | Chase Utley | 2.00 | 5.00 |
| ❑ 169 | Brett Myers | 1.50 | 4.00 |
| ❑ 170 | Jason Bay | 1.50 | 4.00 |
| ❑ 171 | Zach Duke | 1.50 | 4.00 |
| ❑ 172 | Jake Peavy | 1.50 | 4.00 |
| ❑ 173 | Brian Giles | 1.50 | 4.00 |
| ❑ 174 | Khalil Greene | 2.00 | 5.00 |
| ❑ 175 | Trevor Hoffman | 1.50 | 4.00 |
| ❑ 176 | Jason Schmidt | 1.50 | 4.00 |
| ❑ 177 | Randy Winn | 1.50 | 4.00 |
| ❑ 178 | Omar Vizquel | 2.00 | 5.00 |
| ❑ 179 | Kenji Johjima | 3.00 | 8.00 |
| ❑ 180 | Ichiro Suzuki | 3.00 | 8.00 |
| ❑ 181 | Richie Sexson | 1.50 | 4.00 |
| ❑ 182 | Felix Hernandez | 2.00 | 5.00 |
| ❑ 183 | Albert Pujols | 4.00 | 10.00 |
| ❑ 184 | Chris Carpenter | 2.00 | 5.00 |
| ❑ 185 | Jim Edmonds | 2.00 | 5.00 |
| ❑ 186 | Scott Rolen | 2.00 | 5.00 |
| ❑ 187 | Carl Crawford | 1.50 | 4.00 |
| ❑ 188 | Scott Kazmir | 1.50 | 4.00 |
| ❑ 189 | Jonny Gomes | 1.50 | 4.00 |
| ❑ 190 | Mark Teixeira | 2.00 | 5.00 |
| ❑ 191 | Michael Young | 1.50 | 4.00 |
| ❑ 192 | Kevin Millwood | 1.50 | 4.00 |
| ❑ 193 | Vernon Wells | 1.50 | 4.00 |
| ❑ 194 | Troy Glaus | 1.50 | 4.00 |
| ❑ 195 | Roy Halladay | 1.50 | 4.00 |
| ❑ 196 | Alex Rios | 1.50 | 4.00 |
| ❑ 197 | Nick Johnson | 1.50 | 4.00 |
| ❑ 198 | Livan Hernandez | 1.50 | 4.00 |
| ❑ 199 | Alfonso Soriano | 2.00 | 5.00 |
| ❑ 200 | Jose Vidro | 1.50 | 4.00 |
| ❑ 201 | A.Rakers AU/399 (RC) | 3.00 | 8.00 |
| ❑ 202 | A.Pagan AU/399 (RC) | 6.00 | 15.00 |
| ❑ 203 | B.Hendrick AU/399 (RC) | 3.00 | 8.00 |
| ❑ 204 | B.Livingston AU/399 (RC) | 3.00 | 8.00 |
| ❑ 205 | D.Rasner AU/399 (RC) | 3.00 | 8.00 |
| ❑ 206 | B.Bannister AU/399 (RC) | 12.50 | 30.00 |
| ❑ 207 | B.Wilson AU/899 RC | 3.00 | 8.00 |
| ❑ 208 | B.Keppel AU/199 (RC) | 6.00 | 15.00 |
| ❑ 209 | C.Freeman AU/399 (RC) | 3.00 | 8.00 |
| ❑ 210 | C.Booker AU/399 (RC) | 3.00 | 8.00 |
| ❑ 211 | C.Britton AU/399 (RC) | 4.00 | 10.00 |
| ❑ 212 | C.Demaria AU/329 RC | 4.00 | 10.00 |
| ❑ 213 | C.Resop AU/399 (RC) | 3.00 | 8.00 |
| ❑ 214 | T.Gwynn Jr. AU/299 | 30.00 | 60.00 |
| ❑ 215 | E.Reed AU/399 (RC) | 3.00 | 8.00 |
| ❑ 216 | F.Castro AU/399 RC | 3.00 | 8.00 |
| ❑ 217 | F.Nieve AU/299 (RC) | 4.00 | 10.00 |
| ❑ 218 | F.Bynum AU/899 (RC) | 3.00 | 8.00 |
| ❑ 219 | G.Quiroz AU/399 (RC) | 3.00 | 8.00 |
| ❑ 220 | H.Kuo AU/899 (RC) | 30.00 | 60.00 |
| ❑ 221 | R.Theriot AU/399 (RC) | 30.00 | 60.00 |
| ❑ 222 | J.Taschner AU/899 (RC) | 3.00 | 8.00 |
| ❑ 223 | J.Bergmann AU/899 (RC) | 3.00 | 8.00 |
| ❑ 224 | J.Hammel AU/399 (RC) | 3.00 | 8.00 |
| ❑ 225 | J.Harris AU/399 RC | 3.00 | 8.00 |
| ❑ 226 | J.Accardo AU/399 RC | 4.00 | 10.00 |
| ❑ 227 | J.Taubenheim AU/399 RC | 12.50 | 30.00 |
| ❑ 228 | J.Zumaya AU/399 (RC) | 15.00 | 40.00 |
| ❑ 229 | J.Koronka AU/399 (RC) | 3.00 | 8.00 |
| ❑ 230 | E.Aybar AU/399 (RC) | 3.00 | 8.00 |
| ❑ 231 | J.Tata AU/399 RC | 6.00 | 15.00 |
| ❑ 232 | R.Martin AU/399 (RC) | 15.00 | 40.00 |
| ❑ 233 | J.Rupe AU/199 (RC) | 3.00 | 8.00 |
| ❑ 234 | K.Frandsen AU/399 (RC) | 6.00 | 15.00 |
| ❑ 235 | M.Prado AU/399 RC | 6.00 | 15.00 |
| ❑ 236 | M.Capps AU/399 RC | 3.00 | 8.00 |
| ❑ 237 | A.Montero AU/199 RC | 4.00 | 10.00 |
| ❑ 238 | M.Thompson AU/399 RC | 3.00 | 8.00 |
| ❑ 239 | M.McLouth AU/399 (RC) | 8.00 | 20.00 |
| ❑ 240 | P.Moylan AU/399 RC | 3.00 | 8.00 |
| ❑ 241 | R.Abercrom AU/399 RC | 3.00 | 8.00 |
| ❑ 242 | C.Quentin AU/399 (RC) | 8.00 | 20.00 |
| ❑ 243 | R.Flores AU/399 RC | 3.00 | 8.00 |
| ❑ 244 | R.Shealy AU/399 (RC) | 8.00 | 20.00 |
| ❑ 245 | M.Rouse AU/399 (RC) | 3.00 | 8.00 |
| ❑ 246 | S.Ramirez AU/399 (RC) | 3.00 | 8.00 |
| ❑ 247 | C.Hensley AU/399 (RC) | 3.00 | 8.00 |
| ❑ 248 | S.Schumaker AU/399 (RC) | 4.00 | 10.00 |
| ❑ 249 | E.Alfonzo AU/899 RC | 3.00 | 8.00 |
| ❑ 250 | S.Stemle AU/399 RC | 3.00 | 8.00 |
| ❑ 251 | T.Hamulack AU/399 (RC) | 3.00 | 8.00 |
| ❑ 252 | T.Pena Jr. AU/299 RC | 4.00 | 10.00 |
| ❑ 253 | E.Fruto AU/899 RC | 3.00 | 8.00 |
| ❑ 254 | W.Nieves AU/399 RC | 4.00 | 10.00 |
| ❑ 255 | J.Devine AU/399 RC | 4.00 | 10.00 |
| ❑ 256 | A.Wainwright AU/399 (RC) | 12.50 | 30.00 |
| ❑ 257 | A.Ethier AU/399 (RC) | 10.00 | 25.00 |
| ❑ 258 | B.Johnson AU/399 (RC) | 3.00 | 8.00 |
| ❑ 259 | B.Logan AU/399 (RC) | 6.00 | 15.00 |
| ❑ 260 | C.Denorfia AU/899 (RC) | 4.00 | 10.00 |
| ❑ 261 | A.Soler AU/299 RC | 6.00 | 15.00 |
| ❑ 262 | C.Ross AU/899 (RC) | 3.00 | 8.00 |
| ❑ 263 | D.Gassner AU/399 (RC) | 3.00 | 8.00 |
| ❑ 264 | F.Carmona AU/399 (RC) | 10.00 | 25.00 |
| ❑ 265 | J.Sowers AU/299 RC | 10.00 | 25.00 |
| ❑ 266 | J.Kubel AU/399 (RC) | 4.00 | 10.00 |
| ❑ 267 | J.VanBenSch AU/399 (RC) | 3.00 | 8.00 |
| ❑ 268 | J.Capellan AU/399 (RC) | 3.00 | 8.00 |

|  |  | | |
|---|---|---|---|
| 269 | J.Wilson AU/399 (RC) | 3.00 | 8.00 |
| 270 | K.Shoppach AU/399 (RC) | 3.00 | 8.00 |
| 271 | M.McBride AU/399 (RC) | 4.00 | 10.00 |
| 272 | M.Cain AU/399 (RC) | 10.00 | 25.00 |
| 273 | M.Jacobs AU/399 (RC) | 6.00 | 15.00 |
| 274 | P.Maholm AU/399 (RC) | 4.00 | 10.00 |
| 275 | C.Billingsley AU/399 (RC) | 12.50 | 30.00 |
| 276 | R.Lugo AU/399 (RC) | 3.00 | 8.00 |
| 277 | J.Lester AU/399 RC * | 30.00 | 60.00 |
| 278 | S.Marshall AU/383 (RC) | 10.00 | 25.00 |
| 279 | Me.Cabrera AU/399 (RC) | 15.00 | 40.00 |
| 280 | Y.Petit AU/399 (RC) | 4.00 | 10.00 |
| 281 | A.Hernandez AU/299 (RC) | 4.00 | 10.00 |
| 282 | B.Anderson AU/499 (RC) | 4.00 | 10.00 |
| 283 | C.Hamels AU/299 (RC) | 60.00 | 120.00 |
| 284 | B.Bonser AU/299 (RC) | 6.00 | 15.00 |
| 285 | D.Uggla AU/199 (RC) | 20.00 | 50.00 |
| 286 | F.Liriano AU/299 (RC) | 15.00 | 40.00 |
| 287 | H.Ramirez AU/199 (RC) | 30.00 | 60.00 |
| 288 | I.Kinsler AU/299 (RC) | 40.00 | 80.00 |
| 289 | J.Hermida AU/299 (RC) | 6.00 | 15.00 |
| 290 | J.Papelbon AU/199 (RC) | 30.00 | 60.00 |
| 291 | J.Weaver AU/199 (RC) | 15.00 | 40.00 |
| 292 | J.Johnson AU/299 (RC) | 6.00 | 15.00 |
| 293 | J.Willingham AU/199 (RC) | 6.00 | 15.00 |
| 294 | J.Verlander AU/199 (RC) | 40.00 | 80.00 |
| 295 | S.Drew AU/299 (RC) | 12.50 | 30.00 |
| 296 | P.Fielder AU/125 (RC) | 60.00 | 120.00 |
| 297 | Ry.Zimmer AU/199 (RC) | 40.00 | 70.00 |
| 298 | T.Sato AU/283 RC | 15.00 | 40.00 |
| 299 | T.Buchholz AU/299 (RC) | 40.00 | 100.00 |
| 300 | Co.Jackson AU/299 (RC) | 6.00 | 15.00 |

## 2007 SP Authentic

| | | | |
|---|---|---|---|
| COMP.SET w/o RCs (100) | | 6.00 | 15.00 |
| COMMON CARD (1-100) | | .15 | .40 |
| COMMON AU (101-158) | | 5.00 | 12.00 |
| OVERALL BY THE LETTER AUTOS 1:12 | | | |
| AU RC PRINT RUN BETWEEN 20-120 COPIES PER | | | |
| EXCHANGE DEADLINE 11/08/2008 | | | |
| 1 | Chipper Jones | .40 | 1.00 |
| 2 | Andruw Jones | .25 | .60 |
| 3 | John Smoltz | .25 | .60 |
| 4 | Carlos Quentin | .15 | .40 |
| 5 | Randy Johnson | .40 | 1.00 |
| 6 | Brandon Webb | .15 | .40 |
| 7 | Alfonso Soriano | .15 | .40 |
| 8 | Derrek Lee | .15 | .40 |
| 9 | Aramis Ramirez | .15 | .40 |
| 10 | Carlos Zambrano | .15 | .40 |
| 11 | Ken Griffey Jr. | .60 | 1.50 |
| 12 | Adam Dunn | .15 | .40 |
| 13 | Josh Hamilton | .40 | 1.00 |
| 14 | Todd Helton | .25 | .60 |
| 15 | Jeff Francis | .15 | .40 |
| 16 | Matt Holliday | .40 | 1.00 |
| 17 | Hanley Ramirez | .25 | .60 |
| 18 | Dontrelle Willis | .15 | .40 |
| 19 | Miguel Cabrera | .25 | .60 |
| 20 | Lance Berkman | .15 | .40 |
| 21 | Roy Oswalt | .15 | .40 |
| 22 | Carlos Lee | .15 | .40 |
| 23 | Nomar Garciaparra | .40 | 1.00 |
| 24 | Derek Lowe | .15 | .40 |
| 25 | Juan Pierre | .15 | .40 |
| 26 | Rafael Furcal | .15 | .40 |
| 27 | Rickie Weeks | .15 | .40 |
| 28 | Prince Fielder | .40 | 1.00 |
| 29 | Ben Sheets | .15 | .40 |
| 30 | David Wright | .60 | 1.50 |
| 31 | Jose Reyes | .40 | 1.00 |
| 32 | Tom Glavine | .25 | .60 |

|  |  | | |
|---|---|---|---|
| 33 | Carlos Beltran | .15 | .40 |
| 34 | Cole Hamels | .40 | 1.00 |
| 35 | Jimmy Rollins | .15 | .40 |
| 36 | Ryan Howard | .60 | 1.50 |
| 37 | Jason Bay | .25 | .60 |
| 38 | Freddy Sanchez | .15 | .40 |
| 39 | Ian Snell | .15 | .40 |
| 40 | Jake Peavy | .15 | .40 |
| 41 | Greg Maddux | .60 | 1.50 |
| 42 | Trevor Hoffman | .15 | .40 |
| 43 | Matt Cain | .25 | .60 |
| 44 | Barry Zito | .15 | .40 |
| 45 | Ray Durham | .15 | .40 |
| 46 | Albert Pujols | .75 | 2.00 |
| 47 | Chris Carpenter | .15 | .40 |
| 48 | Jim Edmonds | .25 | .60 |
| 49 | Scott Rolen | .25 | .60 |
| 50 | Ryan Zimmerman | .40 | 1.00 |
| 51 | Felipe Lopez | .15 | .40 |
| 52 | Austin Kearns | .15 | .40 |
| 53 | Miguel Tejada | .15 | .40 |
| 54 | Erik Bedard | .15 | .40 |
| 55 | Daniel Cabrera | .15 | .40 |
| 56 | David Ortiz | .25 | .60 |
| 57 | Curt Schilling | .25 | .60 |
| 58 | Manny Ramirez | .25 | .60 |
| 59 | Jonathan Papelbon | .40 | 1.00 |
| 60 | Jim Thome | .25 | .60 |
| 61 | Paul Konerko | .15 | .40 |
| 62 | Bobby Jenks | .15 | .40 |
| 63 | Grady Sizemore | .25 | .60 |
| 64 | Victor Martinez | .15 | .40 |
| 65 | Travis Hafner | .15 | .40 |
| 66 | Ivan Rodriguez | .25 | .60 |
| 67 | Justin Verlander | .40 | 1.00 |
| 68 | Joel Zumaya | .15 | .40 |
| 69 | Jeremy Bonderman | .15 | .40 |
| 70 | Gil Meche | .15 | .40 |
| 71 | Mike Sweeney | .15 | .40 |
| 72 | Mark Teahen | .15 | .40 |
| 73 | Vladimir Guerrero | .40 | 1.00 |
| 74 | Howie Kendrick | .25 | .60 |
| 75 | Francisco Rodriguez | .15 | .40 |
| 76 | Johan Santana | .25 | .60 |
| 77 | Justin Morneau | .15 | .40 |
| 78 | Joe Mauer | .40 | 1.00 |
| 79 | Joe Nathan | .15 | .40 |
| 80a | Alex Rodriguez | .60 | 1.50 |
| 80b | A.Rodriguez Angels | | |
| 80c | A.Rodriguez Cubs | | |
| 80d | A.Rodriguez Dodgers | | |
| 80e | A.Rodriguez Mariners | | |
| 80f | A.Rodriguez Red Sox | | |
| 81 | Derek Jeter | 1.00 | 2.50 |
| 82 | Johnny Damon | .25 | .60 |
| 83 | Chien-Ming Wang | .40 | 1.00 |
| 84 | Rich Harden | .15 | .40 |
| 85 | Mike Piazza | .40 | 1.00 |
| 86 | Dan Haren | .15 | .40 |
| 87 | Ichiro Suzuki | .60 | 1.50 |
| 88 | Felix Hernandez | .25 | .60 |
| 89 | Kenji Johjima | .40 | 1.00 |
| 90 | Adrian Beltre | .15 | .40 |
| 91 | Carl Crawford | .25 | .60 |
| 92 | Scott Kazmir | .25 | .60 |
| 93 | Delmon Young | .25 | .60 |
| 94 | Michael Young | .15 | .40 |
| 95 | Mark Teixeira | .25 | .60 |
| 96 | Eric Gagne | .15 | .40 |
| 97 | Hank Blalock | .15 | .40 |
| 98 | Vernon Wells | .15 | .40 |
| 99 | Roy Halladay | .15 | .40 |
| 100 | Frank Thomas | .40 | 1.00 |
| 101 | Joaquin Arias AU/75 (RC) | 5.00 | 12.00 |
| 102 | Jeff Baker AU (75) EXCH | 5.00 | 12.00 |
| 103 | M.Bourn AU/75 (RC) | 6.00 | 15.00 |
| 104 | Brian Burres AU/75 (RC) | 6.00 | 15.00 |
| 105 | Jared Burton AU/75 RC | 6.00 | 15.00 |
| 106 | Ryan Braun AU/50 (RC) | 60.00 | 150.00 |
| 109 | Alex Gordon AU/50 RC | 20.00 | 50.00 |
| 112 | Sean Henn AU/75 (RC) | 10.00 | 25.00 |
| 113 | P.Hughes AU (RC) EXCH | 40.00 | 80.00 |
| 114 | Kei Igawa AU/25 RC | 30.00 | 60.00 |

|  |  | | |
|---|---|---|---|
| 115 | A.Iwamura AU/20 RC | 40.00 | 80.00 |
| 119 | Adam Lind AU/75 (RC) | 10.00 | 25.00 |
| 123 | Brad Salmon AU/75 RC | 5.00 | 12.00 |
| 127 | Cesar Jimenez AU RC EXCH | 5.00 | 12.00 |
| 129 | T.Tulowit AU (RC) EXCH | 30.00 | 60.00 |
| 130 | Chase Wright AU/75 RC | 12.50 | 30.00 |
| 131 | Delmon Young AU/20 (RC) | 20.00 | 50.00 |
| 132 | Brian Barden AU/75 RC | 5.00 | 12.00 |
| 137 | Billy Butler AU/75 (RC) | 20.00 | 50.00 |
| 139 | Kory Casto AU/75 (RC) | 6.00 | 15.00 |
| 140 | Matt Chico AU/75 (RC) | 6.00 | 15.00 |
| 141 | John Danks AU/75 (RC) | 10.00 | 25.00 |
| 142 | Andrew Miller AU/50 RC | 20.00 | 50.00 |
| 145 | D.Hansack AU RC EXCH | 6.00 | 15.00 |
| 146 | Mike Rabelo AU/75 RC | 6.00 | 15.00 |
| 150a | D.Matsuzaka AU/20 RC | 175.00 | 300.00 |
| 152 | Micah Owings AU/75 (RC) | 20.00 | 50.00 |
| 153 | Hunter Pence AU/75 (RC) | 10.00 | 25.00 |
| 156 | Danny Putnam AU/75 (RC) | 6.00 | 15.00 |
| 159 | Doug Slaten AU/75 RC | 6.00 | 15.00 |
| 160 | Joe Smith AU/75 RC | 8.00 | 20.00 |
| 161 | Justin Upton AU/120 RC | 30.00 | 60.00 |
| 162 | J.Chamberlain AU/60 RC | 50.00 | 100.00 |
| 107a | Y.Gallardo AU/75 (RC) | 20.00 | 50.00 |
| 107b | Y.Gallardo AU/35 (RC) | 30.00 | 60.00 |
| 108a | H.Gimenez AU/75 (RC) | 6.00 | 15.00 |
| 108b | H.Gimenez AU/50 (RC) | 6.00 | 15.00 |
| 110a | J.Hamilton AU/50 (RC) | 30.00 | 60.00 |
| 110b | J.Hamilton AU/35 (RC) | 40.00 | 80.00 |
| 111a | Justin Hampson AU/75 (RC) | 5.00 | 12.00 |
| 111b | Justin Hampson AU/50 (RC) | 5.00 | 12.00 |
| 116a | M.Reynolds AU/75 RC | 20.00 | 50.00 |
| 116b | M.Reynolds AU/35 RC | 30.00 | 60.00 |
| 117a | Homer Bailey AU/75 (RC) | 10.00 | 25.00 |
| 117b | Homer Bailey AU/50 (RC) | 10.00 | 25.00 |
| 118a | K.Kouzmanoff AU/75 (RC) | 8.00 | 20.00 |
| 118b | K.Kouzmanoff AU/40 (RC) | 8.00 | 20.00 |
| 120a | Carlos Gomez AU/75 RC | 20.00 | 50.00 |
| 120b | Carlos Gomez AU/50 (RC) | 20.00 | 50.00 |
| 121a | Glen Perkins AU/75 (RC) | 6.00 | 15.00 |
| 121b | Glen Perkins AU/50 (RC) | 6.00 | 15.00 |
| 122a | R.Vanden Hurk AU/75 RC | 10.00 | 25.00 |
| 122b | R.Vanden Hurk AU/35 (RC) | 12.50 | 30.00 |
| 124a | Zack Segovia AU/75 (RC) | 5.00 | 12.00 |
| 124b | Zack Segovia AU/50 (RC) | 5.00 | 12.00 |
| 125a | Kurt Suzuki AU/75 (RC) | 12.50 | 30.00 |
| 125b | Kurt Suzuki AU/50 (RC) | 12.50 | 30.00 |
| 126a | Chris Stewart AU/75 (RC) | 5.00 | 12.00 |
| 126b | Chris Stewart AU/50 (RC) | 5.00 | 12.00 |
| 128a | Ryan Sweeney AU/75 (RC) | 6.00 | 15.00 |
| 128b | Ryan Sweeney AU/40 (RC) | 6.00 | 15.00 |
| 133a | Tony Abreu AU/75 RC | 10.00 | 25.00 |
| 133b | Tony Abreu AU/57 (RC) | 10.00 | 25.00 |
| 133c | Tony Abreu AU/50 (RC) | 10.00 | 25.00 |
| 134a | C.Thigpen AU/75 (RC) | 10.00 | 25.00 |
| 134b | C.Thigpen AU/40 (RC) | 10.00 | 25.00 |
| 135a | Jon Coutlangus AU/75 (RC) | 5.00 | 12.00 |
| 135b | Jon Coutlangus AU/50 (RC) | 5.00 | 12.00 |
| 136a | Kevin Cameron AU/75 RC | 5.00 | 12.00 |
| 136b | Kevin Cameron AU/50 (RC) | 5.00 | 12.00 |
| 138a | A.Casilla AU/75 RC | 6.00 | 15.00 |
| 138b | A.Casilla AU/50 (RC) | 6.00 | 15.00 |
| 143a | B.Francisco AU/75 (RC) | 6.00 | 15.00 |
| 143b | B.Francisco AU/40 (RC) | 6.00 | 15.00 |
| 144a | Andy Gonzalez AU/75 RC | 5.00 | 12.00 |
| 144b | Andy Gonzalez AU/50 (RC) | 5.00 | 12.00 |
| 147a | Tim Lincecum AU/50 RC | 75.00 | 150.00 |
| 147b | Tim Lincecum AU/25 (RC) | 125.00 | 250.00 |
| 148a | M.Lindstrom AU/75 (RC) | 6.00 | 15.00 |
| 148b | M.Lindstrom AU/40 (RC) | 6.00 | 15.00 |
| 149a | Jay Marshall AU/75 (RC) | 5.00 | 12.00 |
| 149b | Jay Marshall AU/50 (RC) | 5.00 | 12.00 |
| 150b | D.Matsuzaka AU/10 RC | | |
| 151a | M.Montero AU/75 (RC) | 6.00 | 15.00 |
| 151b | M.Montero AU/60 (RC) | 6.00 | 15.00 |
| 154a | Brandon Wood AU/75 (RC) | 6.00 | 15.00 |
| 155a | Felix Pie AU/75 (RC) | 12.50 | 30.00 |
| 155b | Felix Pie AU/70 (RC) | 12.50 | 30.00 |
| 157a | Andy LaRoche AU/50 (RC) | 6.00 | 15.00 |
| 157b | Andy LaRoche AU/40 (RC) | 6.00 | 15.00 |
| 158a | J.Saltalamac AU/75 (RC) | 10.00 | 25.00 |
| 158b | J.Saltalamac AU/25 (RC) | 12.50 | 30.00 |

## 2008 SP Authentic

| | | |
|---|---|---|
| COMP. SET w/o RCs (100) | 8.00 | 20.00 |
| COMMON CARD | .15 | .40 |
| COMMON AU RC (101-191) | 3.00 | 8.00 |
| AU PRINT RUNS 149-999 PER | | |
| OVERALL AU ODDS 1:8 HOBBY | | |
| COMMON JSY AU RC (101-191) | 4.00 | 10.00 |
| JSY AU PRINT RUNS 299-999 PER | | |
| OVERALL AU ODDS 1:8 HOBBY | | |
| EXCH DEADLINE 9/18/2010 | | |
| 1 Ken Griffey Jr. | .60 | 1.50 |
| 2 Derek Jeter | 1.00 | 2.50 |
| 3 Albert Pujols | .75 | 2.00 |
| 4 Ichiro Suzuki | .60 | 1.50 |
| 5 Daisuke Matsuzaka | .50 | 1.25 |
| 6 Vladimir Guerrero | .40 | 1.00 |
| 7 Magglio Ordonez | .25 | .60 |
| 8 Eric Chavez | .15 | .40 |
| 9 Randy Johnson | .40 | 1.00 |
| 10 Ryan Braun | .50 | 1.25 |
| 11 Phil Hughes | .40 | 1.00 |
| 12 Joba Chamberlain | .50 | 1.25 |
| 13 B.J. Upton | .25 | .60 |
| 14 Frank Thomas | .40 | 1.00 |
| 15 Greg Maddux | .50 | 1.25 |
| 16 Delmon Young | .25 | .60 |
| 17 Carlos Beltran | .15 | .40 |
| 18 Derrek Lee | .25 | .60 |
| 19 Aramis Ramirez | .15 | .40 |
| 20 Miguel Tejada | .15 | .40 |
| 21 Manny Ramirez | .40 | 1.00 |
| 22 Justin Upton | .40 | 1.00 |
| 23 Miguel Cabrera | .25 | .60 |
| 24 Prince Fielder | .40 | 1.00 |
| 25 Adam Dunn | .15 | .40 |
| 26 Jose Reyes | .25 | .60 |
| 27 Chase Utley | .40 | 1.00 |
| 28 Jimmy Rollins | .25 | .60 |
| 29 Joe Blanton | .15 | .40 |
| 30 Mark Teixeira | .25 | .60 |
| 31 Brian McCann | .25 | .60 |
| 32 Russell Martin | .15 | .40 |
| 33 Ian Kinsler | .25 | .60 |
| 34 Travis Hafner | .15 | .40 |
| 35 Victor Martinez | .15 | .40 |
| 36 Grady Sizemore | .25 | .60 |
| 37 Alex Rodriguez | .60 | 1.50 |
| 38 David Wright | .50 | 1.25 |
| 39 Ryan Howard | .50 | 1.25 |
| 40 Carlos Lee | .15 | .40 |
| 41 Lance Berkman | .25 | .60 |
| 42 Hunter Pence | .40 | 1.00 |
| 43 John Lackey | .15 | .40 |
| 44 C.C. Sabathia | .15 | .40 |
| 45 Michael Young | .25 | .60 |
| 46 Carl Crawford | .15 | .40 |
| 47 Carlos Pena | .40 | 1.00 |
| 48 Justin Verlander | .25 | .60 |
| 49 Cole Hamels | .40 | 1.00 |
| 50 Carlos Zambrano | .15 | .40 |
| 51 Jake Peavy | .25 | .60 |
| 52 Khalil Greene | .25 | .60 |
| 53 Chris Young | .15 | .40 |
| 54 Vernon Wells | .25 | .60 |
| 55 Alex Rios | .15 | .40 |
| 56 Roy Halladay | .25 | .60 |
| 57 Roy Oswalt | .15 | .40 |
| 58 Ben Sheets | .25 | .60 |
| 59 J.J. Hardy | .25 | .60 |
| 60 Pedro Martinez | .25 | .60 |
| 61 Nick Swisher | .15 | .40 |
| 62 Curtis Granderson | .15 | .40 |
| 63 Johnny Damon | .25 | .60 |
| 64 Mariano Rivera | .40 | 1.00 |
| 65 Josh Beckett | .25 | .60 |
| 66 Erik Bedard | .15 | .40 |
| 67 Johan Santana | .25 | .60 |
| 68 Joe Mauer | .40 | 1.00 |
| 69 Justin Morneau | .25 | .60 |
| 70 Torii Hunter | .15 | .40 |
| 71 Alex Gordon | .25 | .60 |
| 72 Jose Guillen | .15 | .40 |
| 73 Jim Thome | .25 | .60 |
| 74 Paul Konerko | .25 | .60 |
| 75 Josh Hamilton | .50 | 1.25 |
| 76 Hanley Ramirez | .40 | 1.00 |
| 77 Dontrelle Willis | .15 | .40 |
| 78 Dan Uggla | .25 | .60 |
| 79 Brandon Phillips | .15 | .40 |
| 80 Rick Ankiel | .15 | .40 |
| 81 Nick Markakis | .25 | .60 |
| 82 Ryan Zimmerman | .25 | .60 |
| 83 Brian Roberts | .15 | .40 |
| 84 Lastings Milledge | .15 | .40 |
| 85 Freddy Sanchez | .15 | .40 |
| 86 Barry Zito | .15 | .40 |
| 87 Matt Cain | .15 | .40 |
| 88 Andruw Jones | .15 | .40 |
| 89 Dan Haren | .15 | .40 |
| 90 Chien-Ming Wang | .40 | 1.00 |
| 91 Jonathan Papelbon | .25 | .60 |
| 92 Felix Hernandez | .25 | .60 |
| 93 David Ortiz | .25 | .60 |
| 94 Jason Bay | .25 | .60 |
| 95 Matt Holliday | .25 | .60 |
| 96 Troy Tulowitzki | .40 | 1.00 |
| 97 Hideki Matsui | .40 | 1.00 |
| 98 Jeff Francoeur | .25 | .60 |
| 99 Alfonso Soriano | .25 | .60 |
| 100 Curt Schilling | .25 | .60 |
| 101 Alex Romero Jsy AU/799 (RC) | 4.00 | 10.00 |
| 102 Matt Tolbert Jsy/699 RC | 5.00 | 12.00 |
| 103 Bobby Wilson AU/699 RC | 6.00 | 15.00 |
| 104 B.Lillibridge AU/599 (RC) | 5.00 | 12.00 |
| 105 Brian Barton AU/698 RC | 6.00 | 15.00 |
| 106 B.Bass Jsy AU/799 (RC) | 8.00 | 20.00 |
| 107 Brian Bixler AU/698 (RC) | 3.00 | 8.00 |
| 108 Brian Bocock Jsy AU/599 RC | 4.00 | 10.00 |
| 109 B.Badenhop AU/797 RC | 3.00 | 8.00 |
| 110 C.Hu Jsy AU/999 (RC) | 10.00 | 25.00 |
| 111 Chris Perez AU/699 RC | 5.00 | 12.00 |
| 112 Buchholz Jsy AU/699 (RC) | 8.00 | 20.00 |
| 113 Kershaw Jsy AU/999 RC EXCH | 12.50 | 30.00 |
| 114 Colt Morton Jsy AU/574 RC | 4.00 | 10.00 |
| 115 Daric Barton Jsy AU/799 (RC) | 4.00 | 10.00 |
| 116 Darren O'Day AU/798 RC | 3.00 | 8.00 |
| 117 David Purcey AU/599 (RC) | 4.00 | 10.00 |
| 118 D.Span Jsy AU/299 (RC) EXCH | 8.00 | 20.00 |
| 119 E.Johnson AU/798 (RC) | 3.00 | 8.00 |
| 120 E.Burriss AU/299 RC EXCH | 4.00 | 10.00 |
| 121 E.Longoria Jsy AU/499 RC | 60.00 | 120.00 |
| 122 Evan Meek Jsy AU/648 RC | 5.00 | 12.00 |
| 123 Felipe Paulino Jsy AU/799 RC | 4.00 | 10.00 |
| 124 C.Gonzalez Jsy AU/599 (RC) EXCH | 10.00 | 25.00 |
| 125 German Duran AU/699 RC | 4.00 | 10.00 |
| 126 Greg Reynolds AU/149 RC | 3.00 | 8.00 |
| 127 Greg Smith Jsy AU/799 RC | 5.00 | 12.00 |
| 128 Harvey Garcia Jsy AU/999 RC | 4.00 | 10.00 |
| 129 Heman Iribarren Jsy AU/799 (RC) | 4.00 | 10.00 |
| 130 I.Kennedy Jsy AU/999 RC | 10.00 | 25.00 |
| 131 J.R. Towles Jsy AU/499 RC | 4.00 | 10.00 |
| 132 Jay Bruce Jsy AU/549 (RC) | 20.00 | 50.00 |
| 133 Jayson Nix Jsy AU/299 (RC) EXCH | 4.00 | 10.00 |
| 134 Jed Lowrie AU/499 (RC) | 10.00 | 25.00 |
| 135 Jeff Clement AU/399 (RC) | 6.00 | 15.00 |
| 136 Jonathan Herrera AU/699 RC | 3.00 | 8.00 |
| 137 Joey Votto Jsy AU/999 (RC) | 10.00 | 25.00 |
| 138 J.Cueto Jsy AU/999 RC | 8.00 | 20.00 |
| 139 Jonathan Albaladejo Jsy AU/799 RC | 4.00 | 10.00 |
| 140 J.Masterson AU/699 RC | 20.00 | 50.00 |
| 141 J.Ruggiano AU/149 RC | 3.00 | 8.00 |
| 142 Kevin Hart Jsy AU/749 (RC) | 4.00 | 10.00 |
| 143 K.Fukudome Jsy/799 RC | 12.50 | 30.00 |
| 144 Luis Mendoza Jsy AU/299 (RC) | 4.00 | 10.00 |
| 145 Luke Carlin AU/699 RC | 6.00 | 15.00 |
| 146 L.Hochevar AU/798 RC | 4.00 | 10.00 |
| 147 Scherzer Jsy AU/999 RC EXCH | 12.50 | 30.00 |
| 148 M.Hoffpauir AU/699 RC | 15.00 | 40.00 |
| 149 Mike Parisi AU/999 RC | 8.00 | 20.00 |
| 150 N.Adenhart AU/599 (RC) | 10.00 | 25.00 |
| 151 Blackburn Jsy AU/799 RC | 8.00 | 20.00 |
| 152 Nyjer Morgan Jsy AU/999 (RC) | 4.00 | 10.00 |
| 153 Troncoso Jsy AU/399 RC | 5.00 | 12.00 |
| 154 Randor Bierd AU/799 RC | 4.00 | 10.00 |
| 155 R.Thompson AU/398 RC | 5.00 | 12.00 |
| 156 Washington Jsy AU/799 RC | 4.00 | 10.00 |
| 157 Ross Ohlendorf Jsy AU/999 RC | 4.00 | 10.00 |
| 158 Steve Holm Jsy AU/999 RC | 4.00 | 10.00 |
| 159 Wesley Wright Jsy AU/849 RC | 4.00 | 10.00 |
| 160 Wladimir Balentien AU/599 (RC) | 3.00 | 8.00 |
| 161 Alex Hinshaw AU/699 RC EXCH | 3.00 | 8.00 |
| 162 Bobby Korecky AU/999 RC | 5.00 | 12.00 |
| 163 Brad Harman AU/999 RC | 5.00 | 12.00 |
| 164 Brandon Boggs AU/999 (RC) | 3.00 | 8.00 |
| 165 Callix Crabbe AU/325 (RC) | 3.00 | 8.00 |
| 166 Clay Timpner AU/849 (RC) | 3.00 | 8.00 |
| 167 Clete Thomas AU/850 RC | 6.00 | 15.00 |
| 168 Cory Wade AU/999 (RC) | 3.00 | 8.00 |
| 169 Doug Mathis AU/999 RC | 3.00 | 8.00 |
| 170 Elder Torres AU/999 RC | 5.00 | 12.00 |
| 171 Gregorio Petit AU/999 RC | 4.00 | 10.00 |
| 172 M.Aubrey AU/499 RC EXCH | 4.00 | 10.00 |
| 173 Jesse Carlson AU/599 RC | 8.00 | 20.00 |
| 174 Billy Buckner AU/999 RC | 3.00 | 8.00 |
| 175 Josh Newman AU/699 RC | 3.00 | 8.00 |
| 176 Matt Tupman AU/999 RC | 3.00 | 8.00 |
| 177 Matt Joyce AU/999 RC | 8.00 | 20.00 |
| 178 Paul Janish AU/999 (RC) | 5.00 | 12.00 |
| 179 Robinzon Diaz AU/999 (RC) | 3.00 | 8.00 |
| 180 Fernando Hernandez AU/999 RC | 3.00 | 8.00 |
| 181 Brandon Jones AU/999 RC | 3.00 | 8.00 |
| 182 Eddie Bonine AU/899 RC | 3.00 | 8.00 |
| 183 Chris Smith AU/384 (RC) | 6.00 | 15.00 |
| 184 J.Van Every AU/999 RC | 4.00 | 10.00 |
| 185 Marino Salas AU/999 RC | 6.00 | 15.00 |
| 186 Mike Aviles AU/899 RC | 6.00 | 15.00 |
| 187 M.Boggs AU/699 (RC) EXCH | 4.00 | 10.00 |
| 188 C.Carter AU/699 (RC) EXCH | 5.00 | 12.00 |
| 189 Travis Denker AU/699 RC EXCH | 3.00 | 8.00 |
| 190 Carlos Rosa AU/699 RC | 5.00 | 12.00 |
| 191 E.Longoria AU/360 (RC) | 50.00 | 100.00 |

## 2001 SP Legendary Cuts

| | | |
|---|---|---|
| COMPLETE SET (90) | 10.00 | 25.00 |
| 1 Al Simmons | .10 | .30 |
| 2 Jimmie Foxx | .30 | .75 |
| 3 Mickey Cochrane | .20 | .50 |
| 4 Phil Niekro | .10 | .30 |
| 5 Eddie Mathews | .30 | .75 |
| 6 Gary Matthews | .10 | .30 |
| 7 Hank Aaron | .60 | 1.50 |
| 8 Joe Adcock | .10 | .30 |
| 9 Warren Spahn | .20 | .50 |
| 10 George Sisler | .10 | .30 |
| 11 Stan Musial | .50 | 1.25 |
| 12 Dizzy Dean | .30 | .75 |
| 13 Frankie Frisch | .10 | .30 |
| 14 Harvey Haddix | .10 | .30 |
| 15 Johnny Mize | .20 | .50 |
| 16 Ken Boyer | .10 | .30 |
| 17 Rogers Hornsby | .30 | .75 |
| 18 Cap Anson | .30 | .75 |
| 19 Andre Dawson | .10 | .30 |
| 20 Billy Williams | .10 | .30 |
| 21 Billy Herman | .10 | .30 |
| 22 Hack Wilson | .20 | .50 |
| 23 Ron Santo | .20 | .50 |
| 24 Ryne Sandberg | .50 | 1.25 |
| 25 Ernie Banks | .30 | .75 |
| 26 Burleigh Grimes | .10 | .30 |
| 27 Don Drysdale | .20 | .50 |
| 28 Gil Hodges | .30 | .75 |
| 29 Jackie Robinson | .30 | .75 |
| 30 Tommy Lasorda | .10 | .30 |
| 31 Pee Wee Reese | .30 | .75 |
| 32 Roy Campanella | .30 | .75 |

| | | |
|---|---|---|
| ❑ 33 Tommy Davis | .10 | .30 |
| ❑ 34 Branch Rickey | .10 | .30 |
| ❑ 35 Leo Durocher | .20 | .50 |
| ❑ 36 Walt Alston | .10 | .30 |
| ❑ 37 Bill Terry | .10 | .30 |
| ❑ 38 Carl Hubbell | .20 | .50 |
| ❑ 39 Eddie Stanky | .10 | .30 |
| ❑ 40 George Kelly | .10 | .30 |
| ❑ 41 Mel Ott | .30 | .75 |
| ❑ 42 Juan Marichal | .10 | .30 |
| ❑ 43 Rube Marquard | .10 | .30 |
| ❑ 44 Travis Jackson | .10 | .30 |
| ❑ 45 Bob Feller | .10 | .30 |
| ❑ 46 Earl Averill | .10 | .30 |
| ❑ 47 Elmer Flick | .10 | .30 |
| ❑ 48 Ken Keltner | .10 | .30 |
| ❑ 49 Lou Boudreau | .20 | .50 |
| ❑ 50 Early Wynn | .20 | .50 |
| ❑ 51 Satchel Paige | .30 | .75 |
| ❑ 52 Ron Hunt | .10 | .30 |
| ❑ 53 Tom Seaver | .20 | .50 |
| ❑ 54 Richie Ashburn | .20 | .50 |
| ❑ 55 Mike Schmidt | .60 | 1.50 |
| ❑ 56 Honus Wagner | .40 | 1.00 |
| ❑ 57 Lloyd Waner | .20 | .50 |
| ❑ 58 Max Carey | .10 | .30 |
| ❑ 59 Paul Waner | .20 | .50 |
| ❑ 60 Roberto Clemente | .75 | 2.00 |
| ❑ 61 Nolan Ryan | .75 | 2.00 |
| ❑ 62 Bobby Doerr | .20 | .50 |
| ❑ 63 Carlton Fisk | .20 | .50 |
| ❑ 64 Joe Cronin | .20 | .50 |
| ❑ 65 Joe Wood | .20 | .50 |
| ❑ 66 Tony Conigliaro | .20 | .50 |
| ❑ 67 Edd Roush | .10 | .30 |
| ❑ 68 Johnny VanderMeer | .10 | .30 |
| ❑ 69 Walter Johnson | .30 | .75 |
| ❑ 70 Charlie Gehringer | .10 | .30 |
| ❑ 71 Al Kaline | .30 | .75 |
| ❑ 72 Ty Cobb | .50 | 1.25 |
| ❑ 73 Tony Oliva | .10 | .30 |
| ❑ 74 Luke Appling | .10 | .30 |
| ❑ 75 Minnie Minoso | .10 | .30 |
| ❑ 76 Nellie Fox | .20 | .50 |
| ❑ 77 Joe Jackson | .60 | 1.50 |
| ❑ 78 Babe Ruth | 1.00 | 2.50 |
| ❑ 79 Bill Dickey | .20 | .50 |
| ❑ 80 Elston Howard | .20 | .50 |
| ❑ 81 Joe DiMaggio | .60 | 1.50 |
| ❑ 82 Lefty Gomez | .30 | .75 |
| ❑ 83 Lou Gehrig | .60 | 1.50 |
| ❑ 84 Mickey Mantle | 1.25 | 3.00 |
| ❑ 85 Reggie Jackson | .20 | .50 |
| ❑ 86 Roger Maris | .30 | .75 |
| ❑ 87 Whitey Ford | .20 | .50 |
| ❑ 88 Waite Hoyt | .10 | .30 |
| ❑ 89 Yogi Berra | .30 | .75 |
| ❑ 90 Casey Stengel | .30 | .75 |

## 2002 SP Legendary Cuts

| | | |
|---|---|---|
| ❑ COMPLETE SET (90) | 10.00 | 25.00 |
| ❑ 1 Al Kaline | .60 | 1.50 |
| ❑ 2 Alvin Dark | .25 | .60 |
| ❑ 3 Andre Dawson | .25 | .60 |
| ❑ 4 Babe Ruth | 2.00 | 5.00 |
| ❑ 5 Ernie Banks | .60 | 1.50 |
| ❑ 6 Bob Lemon | .40 | 1.00 |
| ❑ 7 Bobby Bonds | .25 | .60 |
| ❑ 8 Carl Erskine | .25 | .60 |
| ❑ 9 Carl Hubbell | .40 | 1.00 |
| ❑ 10 Casey Stengel | .60 | 1.50 |
| ❑ 11 Charlie Gehringer | .40 | 1.00 |
| ❑ 12 Christy Mathewson | .60 | 1.50 |
| ❑ 13 Dale Murphy | .40 | 1.00 |

| | | |
|---|---|---|
| ❑ 14 Dave Concepcion | .25 | .60 |
| ❑ 15 Dave Parker | .25 | .60 |
| ❑ 16 Dazzy Vance | .25 | .60 |
| ❑ 17 Dizzy Dean | .40 | 1.00 |
| ❑ 18 Don Baylor | .25 | .60 |
| ❑ 19 Don Drysdale | .40 | 1.00 |
| ❑ 20 Duke Snider | .40 | 1.00 |
| ❑ 21 Earl Averill | .25 | .60 |
| ❑ 22 Early Wynn | .25 | .60 |
| ❑ 23 Edd Roush | .25 | .60 |
| ❑ 24 Elston Howard | .25 | .60 |
| ❑ 25 Ferguson Jenkins | .25 | .60 |
| ❑ 26 Frank Crosetti | .25 | .60 |
| ❑ 27 Frankie Frisch | .25 | .60 |
| ❑ 28 Gaylord Perry | .25 | .60 |
| ❑ 29 George Foster | .25 | .60 |
| ❑ 30 George Kell | .25 | .60 |
| ❑ 31 Gil Hodges | .40 | 1.00 |
| ❑ 32 Hank Greenberg | .60 | 1.50 |
| ❑ 33 Phil Niekro | .25 | .60 |
| ❑ 34 Harvey Haddix | .25 | .60 |
| ❑ 35 Harvey Kuenn | .25 | .60 |
| ❑ 36 Honus Wagner | 1.00 | 2.50 |
| ❑ 37 Jackie Robinson | .60 | 1.50 |
| ❑ 38 Orlando Cepeda | .25 | .60 |
| ❑ 39 Joe Adcock | .25 | .60 |
| ❑ 40 Joe Cronin | .25 | .60 |
| ❑ 41 Joe DiMaggio | 1.00 | 2.50 |
| ❑ 42 Joe Morgan | .25 | .60 |
| ❑ 43 Johnny Mize | .25 | .60 |
| ❑ 44 Lefty Gomez | .40 | 1.00 |
| ❑ 45 Lefty Grove | .40 | 1.00 |
| ❑ 46 Jim Palmer | .25 | .60 |
| ❑ 47 Lou Boudreau | .25 | .60 |
| ❑ 48 Lou Gehrig | 1.00 | 2.50 |
| ❑ 49 Luke Appling | .25 | .60 |
| ❑ 50 Mark McGwire | 2.00 | 5.00 |
| ❑ 51 Mel Ott | .60 | 1.50 |
| ❑ 52 Mickey Cochrane | .40 | 1.00 |
| ❑ 53 Mickey Mantle | 2.00 | 5.00 |
| ❑ 54 Minnie Minoso | .25 | .60 |
| ❑ 55 Brooks Robinson | .40 | 1.00 |
| ❑ 56 Nellie Fox | .40 | 1.00 |
| ❑ 57 Nolan Ryan | 1.50 | 4.00 |
| ❑ 58 Rollie Fingers | .25 | .60 |
| ❑ 59 Pee Wee Reese | .40 | 1.00 |
| ❑ 60 Phil Rizzuto | .40 | 1.00 |
| ❑ 61 Ralph Kiner | .25 | .60 |
| ❑ 62 Ray Dandridge | .25 | .60 |
| ❑ 63 Richie Ashburn | .40 | 1.00 |
| ❑ 64 Robin Yount | .60 | 1.50 |
| ❑ 65 Rocky Colavito | .40 | 1.00 |
| ❑ 66 Roger Maris | .60 | 1.50 |
| ❑ 67 Rogers Hornsby | .60 | 1.50 |
| ❑ 68 Ron Santo | .25 | .60 |
| ❑ 69 Ryne Sandberg | 1.25 | 3.00 |
| ❑ 70 Stan Musial | 1.00 | 2.50 |
| ❑ 71 Sam McDowell | .25 | .60 |
| ❑ 72 Satchel Paige | .60 | 1.50 |
| ❑ 73 Willie McCovey | .40 | 1.00 |
| ❑ 74 Steve Garvey | .25 | .60 |
| ❑ 75 Ted Kluszewski | .40 | 1.00 |
| ❑ 76 Catfish Hunter | .40 | 1.00 |
| ❑ 77 Terry Moore | .15 | .40 |
| ❑ 78 Thurman Munson | .60 | 1.50 |
| ❑ 79 Tom Seaver | .40 | 1.00 |
| ❑ 80 Tommy John | .25 | .60 |
| ❑ 81 Tony Gwynn | .75 | 2.00 |
| ❑ 82 Tony Kubek | .40 | 1.00 |
| ❑ 83 Tony Lazzeri | .25 | .60 |
| ❑ 84 Ty Cobb | 1.00 | 2.50 |
| ❑ 85 Wade Boggs | .40 | 1.00 |
| ❑ 86 Waite Hoyt | .25 | .60 |
| ❑ 87 Walter Johnson | .60 | 1.50 |
| ❑ 88 Willie Stargell | .40 | 1.00 |
| ❑ 89 Yogi Berra | .60 | 1.50 |
| ❑ 90 Zack Wheat | .25 | .60 |
| ❑ MM M.McGwire AU/100 EX | | |

## 2003 SP Legendary Cuts

WARREN SPAHN

| | | |
|---|---|---|
| ❑ COMP.SET w/o SP's (100) | 15.00 | 40.00 |
| ❑ COMMON CARD | .15 | .40 |
| ❑ COMMON SP | 3.00 | 8.00 |
| ❑ 1 Luis Aparicio | .25 | .60 |
| ❑ 2 Al Barlick | .15 | .40 |
| ❑ 3 Al Lopez | .25 | .60 |
| ❑ 4 Ernie Banks | .60 | 1.50 |
| ❑ 5 Alexander Cartwright | .25 | .60 |
| ❑ 6 Lou Brock | .25 | .60 |
| ❑ 7 Babe Ruth/1299 | 6.00 | 15.00 |
| ❑ 8 Bill Dickey | .40 | 1.00 |
| ❑ 9 Bill Mazeroski | .40 | 1.00 |
| ❑ 10 Bob Feller | .25 | .60 |
| ❑ 11 Billy Herman | .25 | .60 |
| ❑ 12 Billy Williams | .25 | .60 |
| ❑ 13 Bob Gibson/1299 | 4.00 | 10.00 |
| ❑ 14 Bob Lemon | .25 | .60 |
| ❑ 15 Bobby Doerr | .25 | .60 |
| ❑ 16 Branch Rickey | .25 | .60 |
| ❑ 17 Gary Carter | .25 | .60 |
| ❑ 18 Burleigh Grimes | .25 | .60 |
| ❑ 19 Cap Anson | .40 | 1.00 |
| ❑ 20 Carl Hubbell | .40 | 1.00 |
| ❑ 21 Carlton Fisk | .40 | 1.00 |
| ❑ 22 Casey Stengel | .25 | .60 |
| ❑ 23 Charlie Gehringer | .25 | .60 |
| ❑ 24 Chief Bender | .25 | .60 |
| ❑ 25 Christy Mathewson/1299 | 4.00 | 10.00 |
| ❑ 26 Cy Young | .60 | 1.50 |
| ❑ 27 Dave Winfield | .25 | .60 |
| ❑ 28 Dazzy Vance | .25 | .60 |
| ❑ 29 Dizzy Dean/1299 | 4.00 | 10.00 |
| ❑ 30 Don Drysdale/1299 | 4.00 | 10.00 |
| ❑ 31 Duke Snider/1299 | 4.00 | 10.00 |
| ❑ 32 Earl Averill | .25 | .60 |
| ❑ 33 Earle Combs | .25 | .60 |
| ❑ 34 Edd Roush | .25 | .60 |
| ❑ 35 Earl Weaver | .25 | .60 |
| ❑ 36 Eddie Collins | .25 | .60 |
| ❑ 37 Eddie Plank | .25 | .60 |
| ❑ 38 Elmer Flick | .25 | .60 |
| ❑ 39 Enos Slaughter | .25 | .60 |
| ❑ 40 Ernie Lombardi | .25 | .60 |
| ❑ 41 Ford Frick | .15 | .40 |
| ❑ 42 Jim Hunter | .40 | 1.00 |
| ❑ 43 Frankie Frisch | .25 | .60 |
| ❑ 44 Gabby Hartnett | .25 | .60 |
| ❑ 45 George Kell | .25 | .60 |
| ❑ 46 Early Wynn | .25 | .60 |
| ❑ 47 Ferguson Jenkins | .25 | .60 |
| ❑ 48 Al Kaline | .60 | 1.50 |
| ❑ 49 Harmon Killebrew | .60 | 1.50 |
| ❑ 50 Hal Newhouser | .25 | .60 |
| ❑ 51 Hank Greenberg/1299 | 4.00 | 10.00 |
| ❑ 52 Harry Caray | .40 | 1.00 |
| ❑ 53 Tommy Lasorda | .25 | .60 |
| ❑ 54 Honus Wagner/1299 | 4.00 | 10.00 |
| ❑ 55 Hoyt Wilhelm/1299 | 3.00 | 8.00 |
| ❑ 56 Jackie Robinson/1299 | 4.00 | 10.00 |
| ❑ 57 Jim Bottomley | .25 | .60 |
| ❑ 58 Jim Bunning/1299 | 4.00 | 10.00 |
| ❑ 59 Jimmie Foxx/1299 | 4.00 | 10.00 |
| ❑ 60 Eddie Mathews | .60 | 1.50 |
| ❑ 61 Joe Cronin | .25 | .60 |
| ❑ 62 Joe DiMaggio/1299 | 4.00 | 10.00 |
| ❑ 63 Joe McCarthy/1299 | 3.00 | 8.00 |
| ❑ 64 Joe Morgan/1299 | 3.00 | 8.00 |
| ❑ 65 Willie McCovey | .25 | .60 |
| ❑ 66 Joe Tinker | .25 | .60 |
| ❑ 67 Johnny Bench/1299 | 4.00 | 10.00 |
| ❑ 68 Johnny Evers/1299 | 3.00 | 8.00 |
| ❑ 69 Johnny Mize/1299 | 3.00 | 8.00 |

| | | |
|---|---|---|
| ❑ 70 Josh Gibson/1299 | 4.00 | 10.00 |
| ❑ 71 Juan Marichal | .25 | .60 |
| ❑ 72 Judy Johnson | .25 | .60 |
| ❑ 73 Stan Musial | 1.00 | 2.50 |
| ❑ 74 Kiki Cuyler | .25 | .60 |
| ❑ 75 Larry Doby | .25 | .60 |
| ❑ 76 Nap Lajoie | .40 | 1.00 |
| ❑ 77 Larry MacPhail | .15 | .40 |
| ❑ 78 Phil Niekro | .25 | .60 |
| ❑ 79 Lefty Gomez/1299 | 4.00 | 10.00 |
| ❑ 80 Lefty Grove/1299 | 4.00 | 10.00 |
| ❑ 81 Leo Durocher/1299 | 3.00 | 8.00 |
| ❑ 82 Leon Day | .25 | .60 |
| ❑ 83 Gaylord Perry/1299 | 3.00 | 8.00 |
| ❑ 84 Lou Boudreau | .25 | .60 |
| ❑ 85 Lou Gehrig | 1.00 | 2.50 |
| ❑ 86 Luke Appling | .25 | .60 |
| ❑ 87 Max Carey | .25 | .60 |
| ❑ 88 Mel Allen/1299 | 3.00 | 8.00 |
| ❑ 89 Mel Ott/1299 | 4.00 | 10.00 |
| ❑ 90 Mickey Cochrane | .25 | .60 |
| ❑ 91 Mickey Mantle | 2.00 | 5.00 |
| ❑ 92 Brooks Robinson | .40 | 1.00 |
| ❑ 93 Monte Irvin | .25 | .60 |
| ❑ 94 Nellie Fox | .40 | 1.00 |
| ❑ 95 Nolan Ryan/1299 | 5.00 | 12.00 |
| ❑ 96 Ozzie Smith/1299 | 4.00 | 10.00 |
| ❑ 97 Mike Schmidt | 1.25 | 3.00 |
| ❑ 98 Pee Wee Reese/1299 | 4.00 | 10.00 |
| ❑ 99 Phil Rizzuto | .40 | 1.00 |
| ❑ 100 Ralph Kiner | .25 | .60 |
| ❑ 101 Ray Dandridge | .25 | .60 |
| ❑ 102 Richie Ashburn | .40 | 1.00 |
| ❑ 103 Rick Ferrell | .25 | .60 |
| ❑ 104 Roberto Clemente | 1.50 | 4.00 |
| ❑ 105 Robin Roberts | .25 | .60 |
| ❑ 106 Robin Yount | .60 | 1.50 |
| ❑ 107 Rogers Hornsby | .25 | .60 |
| ❑ 108 Rollie Fingers | .25 | .60 |
| ❑ 109 Roy Campanella | .60 | 1.50 |
| ❑ 110 Rube Marquard | .25 | .60 |
| ❑ 111 Sam Crawford | .25 | .60 |
| ❑ 112 Steve Carlton | .25 | .60 |
| ❑ 113 Satchel Paige/1299 | 4.00 | 10.00 |
| ❑ 114 Sparky Anderson | .25 | .60 |
| ❑ 115 Stan Coveleski | .25 | .60 |
| ❑ 116 Red Schoendienst | .40 | 1.00 |
| ❑ 117 Ted Williams | 1.25 | 3.00 |
| ❑ 118 Tom Seaver | .40 | 1.00 |
| ❑ 119 Tom Yawkey | .15 | .40 |
| ❑ 120 Tony Lazzeri | .25 | .60 |
| ❑ 121 Tony Perez | .25 | .60 |
| ❑ 122 Tris Speaker | .60 | 1.50 |
| ❑ 123 Ty Cobb | 1.00 | 2.50 |
| ❑ 124 Waite Hoyt/1299 | 3.00 | 8.00 |
| ❑ 125 Walter Alston | .25 | .60 |
| ❑ 126 Walter Johnson | .60 | 1.50 |
| ❑ 127 Warren Spahn | .40 | 1.00 |
| ❑ 128 Whitey Ford | .40 | 1.00 |
| ❑ 129 Willie Stargell | .25 | .60 |
| ❑ 130 Yogi Berra | .60 | 1.50 |

## 2004 SP Legendary Cuts

| | | |
|---|---|---|
| ❑ COMPLETE SET (126) | 15.00 | 40.00 |
| ❑ 1 Al Kaline | .60 | 1.50 |
| ❑ 2 Al Lopez | .25 | .60 |
| ❑ 3 Alan Trammell | .25 | .60 |
| ❑ 4 Andre Dawson | .25 | .60 |
| ❑ 5 Babe Ruth | 2.00 | 5.00 |
| ❑ 6 Bert Campaneris | .15 | .40 |
| ❑ 7 Bill Mazeroski | .25 | .60 |
| ❑ 8 Bill Russell | .15 | .40 |
| ❑ 9 Billy Williams | .25 | .60 |
| ❑ 10 Bob Feller | .40 | 1.00 |

| | | |
|---|---|---|
| ❑ 11 Bob Gibson | .40 | 1.00 |
| ❑ 12 Bob Lemon | .25 | .60 |
| ❑ 13 Bobby Doerr | .25 | .60 |
| ❑ 14 Brooks Robinson | .40 | 1.00 |
| ❑ 15 Cal Ripken | 2.00 | 5.00 |
| ❑ 16 Carl Yastrzemski | 1.00 | 2.50 |
| ❑ 17 Carlton Fisk | .40 | 1.00 |
| ❑ 18 Catfish Hunter | .25 | .60 |
| ❑ 19 Dale Murphy | .40 | 1.00 |
| ❑ 20 Darryl Strawberry | .25 | .60 |
| ❑ 21 Dave Concepcion | .25 | .60 |
| ❑ 22 Dave Winfield | .25 | .60 |
| ❑ 23 Dennis Eckersley | .25 | .60 |
| ❑ 24 Denny McLain | .25 | .60 |
| ❑ 25 Don Drysdale | .40 | 1.00 |
| ❑ 26 Don Larsen | .25 | .60 |
| ❑ 27 Don Mattingly | 1.25 | 3.00 |
| ❑ 28 Don Sutton | .25 | .60 |
| ❑ 29 Duke Snider | .40 | 1.00 |
| ❑ 30 Dusty Baker | .25 | .60 |
| ❑ 31 Dwight Gooden | .25 | .60 |
| ❑ 32 Earl Weaver | .15 | .40 |
| ❑ 33 Early Wynn | .25 | .60 |
| ❑ 34 Eddie Mathews | .60 | 1.50 |
| ❑ 35 Eddie Murray | .60 | 1.50 |
| ❑ 36 Enos Slaughter | .60 | 1.50 |
| ❑ 37 Ernie Banks | .60 | 1.50 |
| ❑ 38 Fergie Jenkins | .25 | .60 |
| ❑ 39 Frank Robinson | .60 | 1.50 |
| ❑ 40 Fred Lynn | .15 | .40 |
| ❑ 41 Gary Carter | .25 | .60 |
| ❑ 42 Gaylord Perry | .25 | .60 |
| ❑ 43 George Brett | 1.25 | 3.00 |
| ❑ 44 George Foster | .15 | .40 |
| ❑ 45 George Kell | .25 | .60 |
| ❑ 46 Greg Luzinski | .25 | .60 |
| ❑ 47 Hal Newhouser | .25 | .60 |
| ❑ 48 Hank Greenberg | .60 | 1.50 |
| ❑ 49 Harmon Killebrew | .60 | 1.50 |
| ❑ 50 Honus Wagner | .60 | 1.50 |
| ❑ 51 Hoyt Wilhelm | .25 | .60 |
| ❑ 52 Jackie Robinson | .60 | 1.50 |
| ❑ 53 Jim Bunning | .40 | 1.00 |
| ❑ 54 Jim Palmer | .25 | .60 |
| ❑ 55 Jimmie Foxx | .60 | 1.50 |
| ❑ 56 Joe Carter | .25 | .60 |
| ❑ 57 Joe DiMaggio | 1.00 | 2.50 |
| ❑ 58 Joe Morgan | .25 | .60 |
| ❑ 59 Joe Torre | .40 | 1.00 |
| ❑ 60 Johnny Bench | .60 | 1.50 |
| ❑ 61 Johnny Podres | .25 | .60 |
| ❑ 62 Johnny Roseboro | .15 | .40 |
| ❑ 63 Johnny Sain | .25 | .60 |
| ❑ 64 Juan Marichal | .25 | .60 |
| ❑ 65 Keith Hernandez | .25 | .60 |
| ❑ 66 Kirby Puckett | .60 | 1.50 |
| ❑ 67 Kirk Gibson | .25 | .60 |
| ❑ 68 Will Clark | .40 | 1.00 |
| ❑ 69 Jim Rice | .25 | .60 |
| ❑ 70 Larry Doby | .25 | .60 |
| ❑ 71 Lou Boudreau | .25 | .60 |
| ❑ 72 Lou Brock | .40 | 1.00 |
| ❑ 73 Lou Gehrig | 1.00 | 2.50 |
| ❑ 74 Lou Piniella | .25 | .60 |
| ❑ 75 Luis Aparicio | .25 | .60 |
| ❑ 76 Mark Grace | .40 | 1.00 |
| ❑ 77 Mel Ott | .60 | 1.50 |
| ❑ 78 Mickey Lolich | .25 | .60 |
| ❑ 79 Mickey Mantle | 3.00 | 8.00 |
| ❑ 80 Mike Greenwell | .15 | .40 |
| ❑ 81 Mike Schmidt | 1.25 | 3.00 |
| ❑ 82 Monte Irvin | .25 | .60 |
| ❑ 83 Nellie Fox | .40 | 1.00 |
| ❑ 84 Nolan Ryan | 1.50 | 4.00 |
| ❑ 85 Orlando Cepeda | .25 | .60 |
| ❑ 86 Ozzie Smith | 1.00 | 2.50 |
| ❑ 87 Paul Molitor | .25 | .60 |
| ❑ 88 Pee Wee Reese | .40 | 1.00 |
| ❑ 89 Phil Niekro | .25 | .60 |
| ❑ 90 Phil Rizzuto | .40 | 1.00 |
| ❑ 91 Ralph Kiner | .40 | 1.00 |
| ❑ 92 Red Rolfe | .15 | .40 |
| ❑ 93 Red Schoendienst | .25 | .60 |
| ❑ 94 Reggie Smith | .15 | .40 |
| ❑ 95 Rich Gossage | .25 | .60 |
| ❑ 96 Richie Ashburn | .40 | 1.00 |
| ❑ 97 Rick Ferrell | .25 | .60 |
| ❑ 98 Elston Howard | .25 | .60 |

| | | |
|---|---|---|
| ❑ 99 Roberto Clemente | 1.50 | 4.00 |
| ❑ 100 Robin Roberts | .25 | .60 |
| ❑ 101 Robin Yount | .60 | 1.50 |
| ❑ 102 Roger Maris | .60 | 1.50 |
| ❑ 103 Rollie Fingers | .25 | .60 |
| ❑ 104 Ron Santo | .40 | 1.00 |
| ❑ 105 Roy Campanella | .60 | 1.50 |
| ❑ 106 Ryne Sandberg | 1.25 | 3.00 |
| ❑ 107 Sparky Anderson | .25 | .60 |
| ❑ 108 Sparky Lyle | .15 | .40 |
| ❑ 109 Stan Musial | 1.00 | 2.50 |
| ❑ 110 Steve Carlton | .25 | .60 |
| ❑ 111 Steve Garvey | .25 | .60 |
| ❑ 112 Ted Williams | 1.25 | 3.00 |
| ❑ 113 Thurman Munson | .60 | 1.50 |
| ❑ 114 Tom Seaver | .40 | 1.00 |
| ❑ 115 Tommy Henrich | .25 | .60 |
| ❑ 116 Tommy Lasorda | .25 | .60 |
| ❑ 117 Tony Gwynn | .75 | 2.00 |
| ❑ 118 Tony Perez | .25 | .60 |
| ❑ 119 Ty Cobb | .75 | 2.00 |
| ❑ 120 Wade Boggs | .40 | 1.00 |
| ❑ 121 Warren Spahn | .40 | 1.00 |
| ❑ 122 Whitey Ford | .40 | 1.00 |
| ❑ 123 Willie McCovey | .40 | 1.00 |
| ❑ 124 Willie Randolph | .25 | .60 |
| ❑ 125 Willie Stargell | .40 | 1.00 |
| ❑ 126 Yogi Berra | .60 | 1.50 |

## 2005 SP Legendary Cuts

| | | |
|---|---|---|
| ❑ COMPLETE SET (90) | 10.00 | 25.00 |
| ❑ COMMON CARD (1-90) | .15 | .40 |
| ❑ 1 Al Kaline | .60 | 1.50 |
| ❑ 2 Babe Ruth | 2.00 | 5.00 |
| ❑ 3 Bill Mazeroski | .40 | 1.00 |
| ❑ 4 Billy Williams | .25 | .60 |
| ❑ 5 Bob Feller | .40 | 1.00 |
| ❑ 6 Bob Gibson | .40 | 1.00 |
| ❑ 7 Bob Lemon | .25 | .60 |
| ❑ 8 Bobby Doerr | .25 | .60 |
| ❑ 9 Brooks Robinson | .40 | 1.00 |
| ❑ 10 Carl Yastrzemski | 1.00 | 2.50 |
| ❑ 11 Carlton Fisk | .40 | 1.00 |
| ❑ 12 Casey Stengel | .40 | 1.00 |
| ❑ 13 Catfish Hunter | .25 | .60 |
| ❑ 14 Christy Mathewson | .60 | 1.50 |
| ❑ 15 Cy Young | .60 | 1.50 |
| ❑ 16 Dennis Eckersley | .25 | .60 |
| ❑ 17 Dizzy Dean | .40 | 1.00 |
| ❑ 18 Don Drysdale | .40 | 1.00 |
| ❑ 19 Don Sutton | .25 | .60 |
| ❑ 20 Duke Snider | .40 | 1.00 |
| ❑ 21 Early Wynn | .25 | .60 |
| ❑ 22 Eddie Mathews | .60 | 1.50 |
| ❑ 23 Eddie Murray | .60 | 1.50 |
| ❑ 24 Enos Slaughter | .60 | 1.50 |
| ❑ 25 Ernie Banks | .60 | 1.50 |
| ❑ 26 Fergie Jenkins | .25 | .60 |
| ❑ 27 Frank Robinson | .60 | 1.50 |
| ❑ 28 Gary Carter | .25 | .60 |
| ❑ 29 Gaylord Perry | .25 | .60 |
| ❑ 30 Reggie Jackson | .40 | 1.00 |
| ❑ 31 George Kell | .25 | .60 |
| ❑ 32 George Sisler | .25 | .60 |
| ❑ 33 Hal Newhouser | .25 | .60 |
| ❑ 34 Harmon Killebrew | .60 | 1.50 |
| ❑ 35 Honus Wagner | .60 | 1.50 |
| ❑ 36 Jackie Robinson | .60 | 1.50 |
| ❑ 37 Jim Bunning | .40 | 1.00 |
| ❑ 38 Jim Palmer | .25 | .60 |
| ❑ 39 Jimmie Foxx | .60 | 1.50 |
| ❑ 40 Joe DiMaggio | 1.00 | 2.50 |
| ❑ 41 Joe Morgan | .25 | .60 |
| ❑ 42 Johnny Bench | .60 | 1.50 |

|  |  | | |
|---|------|------|------|
| 43 | Johnny Mize | .25 | .60 |
| 44 | Juan Marichal | .25 | .60 |
| 45 | Kirby Puckett | .60 | 1.50 |
| 46 | Larry Doby | .25 | .60 |
| 47 | Lefty Grove | .40 | 1.00 |
| 48 | Lou Boudreau | .25 | .60 |
| 49 | Lou Brock | .40 | 1.00 |
| 50 | Lou Gehrig | 1.00 | 2.50 |
| 51 | Luis Aparicio | .25 | .60 |
| 52 | Mel Ott | .60 | 1.50 |
| 53 | Mickey Cochrane | .25 | .60 |
| 54 | Mickey Mantle | 3.00 | 8.00 |
| 55 | Mike Schmidt | 1.25 | 3.00 |
| 56 | Monte Irvin | .25 | .60 |
| 57 | Nolan Ryan | 1.50 | 4.00 |
| 58 | Orlando Cepeda | .25 | .60 |
| 59 | Ozzie Smith | 1.00 | 2.50 |
| 60 | Paul Molitor | .25 | .60 |
| 61 | Pee Wee Reese | .40 | 1.00 |
| 62 | Phil Niekro | .25 | .60 |
| 63 | Phil Rizzuto | .25 | .60 |
| 64 | Ralph Kiner | .40 | 1.00 |
| 65 | Red Schoendienst | .25 | .60 |
| 66 | Richie Ashburn | .40 | 1.00 |
| 67 | Rick Ferrell | .25 | .60 |
| 68 | Robin Roberts | .25 | .60 |
| 69 | Robin Yount | .60 | 1.50 |
| 70 | Rod Carew | .40 | 1.00 |
| 71 | Rogers Hornsby | .40 | 1.00 |
| 72 | Rollie Fingers | .25 | .60 |
| 73 | Roy Campanella | 1.25 | 3.00 |
| 74 | Ryne Sandberg | .60 | 1.50 |
| 75 | Satchel Paige | 1.00 | 2.50 |
| 77 | Steve Carlton | .25 | .60 |
| 78 | Ted Williams | 1.25 | 3.00 |
| 79 | Thurman Munson | .60 | 1.50 |
| 80 | Tom Seaver | .40 | 1.00 |
| 81 | Tony Gwynn | .75 | 2.00 |
| 82 | Tony Perez | .25 | .60 |
| 83 | Ty Cobb | .75 | 2.00 |
| 84 | Wade Boggs | .40 | 1.00 |
| 85 | Walter Johnson | .60 | 1.50 |
| 86 | Warren Spahn | .40 | 1.00 |
| 87 | Whitey Ford | .40 | 1.00 |
| 88 | Willie McCovey | .25 | .60 |
| 89 | Willie Stargell | .40 | 1.00 |
| 90 | Yogi Berra | .60 | 1.50 |

## 2006 SP Legendary Cuts

| | | | |
|---|------|------|------|
| COMP.SET w/o SP's (100) | | 10.00 | 25.00 |
| COMMON CARD (1-100) | | .25 | .60 |
| COMMON CARD (101-200) | | 2.00 | 5.00 |
| 101-200: ONE BASIC OR BRONZE PER BOX | | | |
| 101-200 PRINT RUN 550 SERIAL #'d SETS | | | |
| EXQUISITE EXCH ODDS 1:60 | | | |
| EXQUISITE EXCH DEADLINE 07/27/07 | | | |
| 1 | Juan Marichal | .25 | .60 |
| 2 | Monte Irvin | .25 | .60 |
| 3 | Will Clark | .40 | 1.00 |
| 4 | Willie McCovey | .40 | 1.00 |
| 5 | Eddie Gaedel | .25 | .60 |
| 6 | Ken Williams | .25 | .60 |
| 7 | Earl Battey | .25 | .60 |
| 8 | Rick Ferrell | .25 | .60 |
| 9 | Bob Gibson | .40 | 1.00 |
| 10 | Elmer Flick | .25 | .60 |
| 11 | Joe Medwick | .25 | .60 |
| 12 | Lou Brock | .40 | 1.00 |
| 13 | Ozzie Smith | 1.00 | 2.50 |
| 14 | Red Schoendienst | .25 | .60 |
| 15 | Stan Musial | 1.00 | 2.50 |
| 16 | Tony Oliva | .25 | .60 |
| 17 | Phil Niekro | .25 | .60 |

|  |  | | |
|---|------|------|------|
| 18 | Boog Powell | .25 | .60 |
| 19 | Brooks Robinson | .40 | 1.00 |
| 20 | Cal Ripken | 2.50 | 6.00 |
| 21 | Eddie Murray | .60 | 1.50 |
| 22 | Frank Robinson | .25 | .60 |
| 23 | Jim Palmer | .25 | .60 |
| 24 | Jocko Conlon | .25 | .60 |
| 25 | Carlton Fisk | .40 | 1.00 |
| 26 | Dwight Evans | .25 | .60 |
| 27 | Fred Lynn | .25 | .60 |
| 28 | Jim Rice | .25 | .60 |
| 29 | Ted Williams | 1.50 | 4.00 |
| 30 | Wade Boggs | .40 | 1.00 |
| 31 | Hugh Duffy | .25 | .60 |
| 32 | Kid Nichols | .25 | .60 |
| 33 | Johnny Vander Meer | .25 | .60 |
| 34 | Dolph Camilli | .25 | .60 |
| 35 | Carl Yastrzemski | 1.00 | 2.50 |
| 36 | Chick Hafey | .25 | .60 |
| 37 | Kirby Higbe | .25 | .60 |
| 38 | Pee Wee Reese | .40 | 1.00 |
| 39 | Pete Reiser | .25 | .60 |
| 40 | Don Sutton | .25 | .60 |
| 41 | Rod Carew | .40 | 1.00 |
| 42 | Andre Dawson | .25 | .60 |
| 43 | Billy Herman | .25 | .60 |
| 44 | Billy Williams | .25 | .60 |
| 45 | Charley Root | .25 | .60 |
| 46 | Hack Wilson | .40 | 1.00 |
| 47 | Ernie Banks | .60 | 1.50 |
| 48 | Fergie Jenkins | .25 | .60 |
| 49 | Gabby Hartnett | .25 | .60 |
| 50 | Ken Hubbs | .25 | .60 |
| 51 | Kiki Cuyler | .25 | .60 |
| 52 | Mark Grace | .40 | 1.00 |
| 53 | Ryne Sandberg | 1.25 | 3.00 |
| 54 | Harold Newhouser | .25 | .60 |
| 55 | Charlie Robertson | .25 | .60 |
| 56 | Harold Baines | .25 | .60 |
| 57 | Luis Aparicio | .25 | .60 |
| 58 | Luke Appling | .25 | .60 |
| 59 | Nellie Fox | .40 | 1.00 |
| 60 | Ray Schalk | .25 | .60 |
| 61 | Red Faber | .25 | .60 |
| 62 | Sloppy Thurston | .25 | .60 |
| 63 | Freddie Lindstrom | .25 | .60 |
| 64 | Vern Kennedy | .25 | .60 |
| 65 | Barry Larkin | .40 | 1.00 |
| 66 | Bucky Walters | .25 | .60 |
| 67 | Dolf Luque | .25 | .60 |
| 68 | Al Campanis | .25 | .60 |
| 69 | Ernie Lombardi | .25 | .60 |
| 70 | George Foster | .25 | .60 |
| 71 | Joe Morgan | .25 | .60 |
| 72 | Johnny Bench | .60 | 1.50 |
| 73 | Ken Griffey Sr. | .25 | .60 |
| 74 | Ted Kluszewski | .40 | 1.00 |
| 75 | Tony Perez | .25 | .60 |
| 76 | Wally Post | .25 | .60 |
| 77 | Bob Feller | .25 | .60 |
| 78 | Bob Lemon | .25 | .60 |
| 79 | Earl Averill | .25 | .60 |
| 80 | Joe Sewell | .25 | .60 |
| 81 | Johnny Hodapp | .25 | .60 |
| 82 | Larry Doby | .25 | .60 |
| 83 | Lou Boudreau | .25 | .60 |
| 84 | Rocky Colavito | .40 | 1.00 |
| 85 | Stan Coveleski | .25 | .60 |
| 86 | Nap Lajoie | .40 | 1.00 |
| 87 | Al Kaline | .60 | 1.50 |
| 88 | Alan Trammell | .25 | .60 |
| 89 | Charlie Gehringer | .25 | .60 |
| 90 | Denny McLain | .25 | .60 |
| 91 | Hank Greenberg | .60 | 1.50 |
| 92 | Jack Morris | .25 | .60 |
| 93 | Mark Fidrych | .25 | .60 |
| 94 | Ray Boone | .25 | .60 |
| 95 | Rudy York | .25 | .60 |
| 96 | Buck Leonard | .25 | .60 |
| 97 | Bo Jackson | .60 | 1.50 |
| 98 | Zoilo Versalles | .25 | .60 |
| 99 | John Kruk | .25 | .60 |
| 100 | Don Drysdale | .40 | 1.00 |
| 101 | Cecil Cooper | 2.00 | 5.00 |
| 102 | Vic Wertz | 2.00 | 5.00 |
| 103 | Kirk Gibson | 2.00 | 5.00 |
| 104 | Maury Wills | 2.00 | 5.00 |
| 105 | Steve Garvey | 2.00 | 5.00 |

|  |  | | |
|---|------|------|------|
| 106 | Warren Spahn | 3.00 | 8.00 |
| 107 | Paul Molitor | 2.00 | 5.00 |
| 108 | Robin Yount | 3.00 | 8.00 |
| 109 | Rollie Fingers | 2.00 | 5.00 |
| 110 | Bob Allison | 2.00 | 5.00 |
| 111 | Kirby Puckett | 3.00 | 8.00 |
| 112 | Tim Raines | 2.00 | 5.00 |
| 113 | George Pipgras | 2.00 | 5.00 |
| 114 | Eddie Grant | 2.00 | 5.00 |
| 115 | Hoyt Wilhelm | 2.00 | 5.00 |
| 116 | Sal Maglie | 2.00 | 5.00 |
| 117 | Ron Santo | 3.00 | 8.00 |
| 118 | Wally Joyner | 2.00 | 5.00 |
| 119 | Tom Seaver | 3.00 | 8.00 |
| 120 | Tommie Agee | 2.00 | 5.00 |
| 121 | Harmon Killebrew | 3.00 | 8.00 |
| 122 | Bill Dickey | 2.00 | 5.00 |
| 123 | Early Wynn | 2.00 | 5.00 |
| 124 | Bobby Murcer | 3.00 | 8.00 |
| 125 | Bucky Dent | 2.00 | 5.00 |
| 126 | Dave Winfield | 3.00 | 8.00 |
| 127 | Don Larsen | 2.00 | 5.00 |
| 128 | Don Mattingly | 4.00 | 10.00 |
| 129 | Earle Combs | 2.00 | 5.00 |
| 130 | Ed Lopat | 2.00 | 5.00 |
| 131 | Elston Howard | 2.00 | 5.00 |
| 132 | Everett Scott | 2.00 | 5.00 |
| 133 | Goose Gossage | 2.00 | 5.00 |
| 134 | Graig Nettles | 2.00 | 5.00 |
| 135 | Joe DiMaggio | 4.00 | 10.00 |
| 136 | Lou Piniella | 2.00 | 5.00 |
| 137 | Bill Skowron | 2.00 | 5.00 |
| 138 | Phil Rizzuto | 3.00 | 8.00 |
| 139 | Red Ruffing | 2.00 | 5.00 |
| 140 | Reggie Jackson | 3.00 | 8.00 |
| 141 | Roger Maris | 3.00 | 8.00 |
| 142 | Ron Guidry | 2.00 | 5.00 |
| 143 | Tiny Bonham | 2.00 | 5.00 |
| 144 | Bruce Sutter | 2.00 | 5.00 |
| 145 | Tony Lazzeri | 2.00 | 5.00 |
| 146 | Waite Hoyt | 2.00 | 5.00 |
| 147 | Whitey Ford | 3.00 | 8.00 |
| 148 | Steve Sax | 2.00 | 5.00 |
| 149 | Yogi Berra | 3.00 | 8.00 |
| 150 | Enos Slaughter | 2.00 | 5.00 |
| 151 | Catfish Hunter | 2.00 | 5.00 |
| 152 | Dennis Eckersley | 2.00 | 5.00 |
| 153 | Jose Canseco | 2.00 | 5.00 |
| 154 | Al Rosen | 2.00 | 5.00 |
| 155 | Al Simmons | 2.00 | 5.00 |
| 156 | Chief Bender | 2.00 | 5.00 |
| 157 | Cy Williams | 2.00 | 5.00 |
| 158 | Mike Schmidt | 4.00 | 10.00 |
| 159 | Richie Ashburn | 3.00 | 8.00 |
| 160 | Robin Roberts | 2.00 | 5.00 |
| 161 | Steve Carlton | 2.00 | 5.00 |
| 162 | Judy Johnson | 2.00 | 5.00 |
| 163 | Al Oliver | 2.00 | 5.00 |
| 164 | Bill Mazeroski | 3.00 | 8.00 |
| 165 | Dave Parker | 2.00 | 5.00 |
| 166 | Max Carey | 2.00 | 5.00 |
| 167 | Pie Traynor | 2.00 | 5.00 |
| 168 | Ralph Kiner | 2.00 | 5.00 |
| 169 | Roberto Clemente | 6.00 | 15.00 |
| 170 | Willie Stargell | 2.00 | 5.00 |
| 171 | Gaylord Perry | 2.00 | 5.00 |
| 172 | Tony Gwynn | 3.00 | 8.00 |
| 173 | Nolan Ryan | 4.00 | 10.00 |
| 174 | Joe Carter | 2.00 | 5.00 |
| 175 | Frank Howard | 2.00 | 5.00 |
| 176 | George Kell | 2.00 | 5.00 |
| 177 | Heinie Manush | 2.00 | 5.00 |
| 178 | Sam Rice | 2.00 | 5.00 |
| 179 | Babe Ruth | 6.00 | 15.00 |
| 180 | Casey Stengel | 3.00 | 8.00 |
| 181 | Christy Mathewson | 3.00 | 8.00 |
| 182 | Cy Young | 3.00 | 8.00 |
| 183 | Dizzy Dean | 3.00 | 8.00 |
| 184 | Eddie Mathews | 3.00 | 8.00 |
| 185 | George Sisler | 2.00 | 5.00 |
| 186 | Honus Wagner | 3.00 | 8.00 |
| 187 | Jackie Robinson | 3.00 | 8.00 |
| 188 | Jimmie Foxx | 3.00 | 8.00 |
| 189 | Johnny Mize | 2.00 | 5.00 |
| 190 | Lefty Grove | 2.00 | 5.00 |
| 191 | Lou Gehrig | 4.00 | 10.00 |
| 192 | Mel Ott | 3.00 | 8.00 |
| 193 | Mickey Cochrane | 2.00 | 5.00 |

| | | |
|---|---|---|
| ☐ 194 Rogers Hornsby | 3.00 | 8.00 |
| ☐ 195 Roy Campanella | 3.00 | 8.00 |
| ☐ 196 Satchel Paige | 3.00 | 8.00 |
| ☐ 197 Thurman Munson | 3.00 | 8.00 |
| ☐ 198 Ty Cobb | 4.00 | 10.00 |
| ☐ 199 Walter Johnson | 3.00 | 8.00 |
| ☐ 200 Lefty Grove | 2.00 | 5.00 |
| ☐ NNO Exquisite Redemption | | |

## 2007 SP Legendary Cuts

| | | |
|---|---|---|
| ☐ COMP.SET w/o SP's (100) | 10.00 | 25.00 |
| ☐ COMMON CARD (1-100) | .25 | .60 |
| ☐ COMMON CARD (101-200) | 2.00 | 5.00 |
| ☐ 101-200 RANDOMLY INSERTED | | |
| ☐ 101-200 PRINT RUN 550 SERIAL #'d SETS | | |
| ☐ 1 Phil Niekro | .25 | .60 |
| ☐ 2 Brooks Robinson | .40 | 1.00 |
| ☐ 3 Frank Robinson | .40 | 1.00 |
| ☐ 4 Jim Palmer | .25 | .60 |
| ☐ 5 Cal Ripken Jr. | 2.50 | 6.00 |
| ☐ 6 Warren Spahn | .40 | 1.00 |
| ☐ 7 Cy Young | .60 | 1.50 |
| ☐ 8 Carl Yastrzemski | 1.00 | 2.50 |
| ☐ 9 Wade Boggs | .40 | 1.00 |
| ☐ 10 Carlton Fisk | .40 | 1.00 |
| ☐ 11 Joe Cronin | .25 | .60 |
| ☐ 12 Bobby Doerr | .25 | .60 |
| ☐ 13 Roy Campanella | .60 | 1.50 |
| ☐ 14 Pee Wee Reese | .40 | 1.00 |
| ☐ 15 Rod Carew | .40 | 1.00 |
| ☐ 16 Ernie Banks | .60 | 1.50 |
| ☐ 17 Fergie Jenkins | .25 | .60 |
| ☐ 18 Billy Williams | .25 | .60 |
| ☐ 19 Gabby Hartnett | .25 | .60 |
| ☐ 20 Luis Aparicio | .25 | .60 |
| ☐ 21 Nellie Fox | .40 | 1.00 |
| ☐ 22 Luke Appling | .25 | .60 |
| ☐ 23 Joe Morgan | .25 | .60 |
| ☐ 24 Johnny Bench | .60 | 1.50 |
| ☐ 25 Tony Perez | .25 | .60 |
| ☐ 26 George Foster | .25 | .60 |
| ☐ 27 Johnny Vander Meer | .25 | .60 |
| ☐ 28 Bob Feller | .25 | .60 |
| ☐ 29 Bob Lemon | .25 | .60 |
| ☐ 30 Lou Boudreau | .25 | .60 |
| ☐ 31 Early Wynn | .25 | .60 |
| ☐ 32 Charlie Gehringer | .25 | .60 |
| ☐ 33 George Kell | .25 | .60 |
| ☐ 34 Hal Newhouser | .25 | .60 |
| ☐ 35 Al Kaline | .60 | 1.50 |
| ☐ 36 Ted Kluszewski | .40 | 1.00 |
| ☐ 37 Harvey Kuenn | .25 | .60 |
| ☐ 38 Maury Wills | .25 | .60 |
| ☐ 39 Don Drysdale | .40 | 1.00 |
| ☐ 40 Don Sutton | .25 | .60 |
| ☐ 41 Eddie Mathews | .60 | 1.50 |
| ☐ 42 Joe Adcock | .25 | .60 |
| ☐ 43 Paul Molitor | .40 | 1.00 |
| ☐ 44 Kirby Puckett | .60 | 1.50 |
| ☐ 45 Harmon Killebrew | .60 | 1.50 |
| ☐ 46 Monte Irvin | .40 | 1.00 |
| ☐ 47 Ralph Kiner | .40 | 1.00 |
| ☐ 48 Christy Mathewson | .60 | 1.50 |
| ☐ 49 Hoyt Wilhelm | .25 | .60 |
| ☐ 50 Tom Seaver | .40 | 1.00 |
| ☐ 51 Allie Reynolds | .25 | .60 |
| ☐ 52 Joe DiMaggio | 1.25 | 3.00 |
| ☐ 53 Lou Gehrig | 1.25 | 3.00 |
| ☐ 54 Babe Ruth | 1.50 | 4.00 |
| ☐ 55 Casey Stengel | .25 | .60 |
| ☐ 56 Phil Rizzuto | .40 | 1.00 |
| ☐ 57 Thurman Munson | .60 | 1.50 |
| ☐ 58 Johnny Mize | .25 | .60 |
| ☐ 59 Yogi Berra | .60 | 1.50 |
| ☐ 60 Rube Marquard | .25 | .60 |
| ☐ 61 Don Mattingly | 1.25 | 3.00 |
| ☐ 62 Ray Dandridge | .25 | .60 |
| ☐ 63 Rollie Fingers | .25 | .60 |
| ☐ 64 Roberto Clemente | 2.00 | 5.00 |
| ☐ 65 Reggie Jackson | .40 | 1.00 |
| ☐ 66 Dennis Eckersley | .25 | .60 |
| ☐ 67 Robin Yount | .60 | 1.50 |
| ☐ 68 Jimmie Foxx | .60 | 1.50 |
| ☐ 69 Lefty Grove | .25 | .60 |
| ☐ 70 Richie Ashburn | .40 | 1.00 |
| ☐ 71 Jim Bunning | .25 | .60 |
| ☐ 72 Steve Carlton | .25 | .60 |
| ☐ 73 Robin Roberts | .25 | .60 |
| ☐ 74 Mike Schmidt | 1.00 | 2.50 |
| ☐ 75 Willie Stargell | .40 | 1.00 |
| ☐ 76 Ozzie Smith | 1.00 | 2.50 |
| ☐ 77 Bill Mazeroski | .40 | 1.00 |
| ☐ 78 Honus Wagner | .60 | 1.50 |
| ☐ 79 Pie Traynor | .25 | .60 |
| ☐ 80 Tony Gwynn | .60 | 1.50 |
| ☐ 81 Willie McCovey | .40 | 1.00 |
| ☐ 82 Gaylord Perry | .25 | .60 |
| ☐ 83 Juan Marichal | .25 | .60 |
| ☐ 84 Orlando Cepeda | .25 | .60 |
| ☐ 85 Satchel Paige | .60 | 1.50 |
| ☐ 86 George Sisler | .25 | .60 |
| ☐ 87 Ken Boyer | .25 | .60 |
| ☐ 88 Joe Medwick | .25 | .60 |
| ☐ 89 Travis Jackson | .25 | .60 |
| ☐ 90 Stan Musial | 1.00 | 2.50 |
| ☐ 91 Dizzy Dean | .40 | 1.00 |
| ☐ 92 Bob Gibson | .40 | 1.00 |
| ☐ 93 Red Schoendienst | .25 | .60 |
| ☐ 94 Lou Brock | .40 | 1.00 |
| ☐ 95 Enos Slaughter | .25 | .60 |
| ☐ 96 Nolan Ryan | 1.50 | 4.00 |
| ☐ 97 Smokey Burgess | .25 | .60 |
| ☐ 98 Mickey Vernon | .25 | .60 |
| ☐ 99 Vern Stephens | .25 | .60 |
| ☐ 100 Rick Ferrell | .25 | .60 |
| ☐ 101 Phil Niekro LL | 2.00 | 5.00 |
| ☐ 102 Brooks Robinson LL | 3.00 | 8.00 |
| ☐ 103 Frank Robinson LL | 3.00 | 8.00 |
| ☐ 104 Jim Palmer LL | 2.00 | 5.00 |
| ☐ 105 Cal Ripken Jr. LL | 5.00 | 12.00 |
| ☐ 106 Warren Spahn LL | 3.00 | 8.00 |
| ☐ 107 Cy Young LL | 3.00 | 8.00 |
| ☐ 108 Nellie Fox LL | 2.00 | 5.00 |
| ☐ 109 Carl Yastrzemski LL | 3.00 | 8.00 |
| ☐ 110 Joe Sewell LL | 2.00 | 5.00 |
| ☐ 111 Wade Boggs LL | 3.00 | 8.00 |
| ☐ 112 Carlton Fisk LL | 3.00 | 8.00 |
| ☐ 113 Jackie Robinson LL | 4.00 | 10.00 |
| ☐ 114 Roy Campanella LL | 3.00 | 8.00 |
| ☐ 115 Pee Wee Reese LL | 3.00 | 8.00 |
| ☐ 116 Earl Averill LL | 2.00 | 5.00 |
| ☐ 117 Rod Carew LL | 2.00 | 5.00 |
| ☐ 118 Ernie Banks LL | 3.00 | 8.00 |
| ☐ 119 Fergie Jenkins LL | 2.00 | 5.00 |
| ☐ 120 Billy Williams LL | 2.00 | 5.00 |
| ☐ 121 Al Lopez LL | 2.00 | 5.00 |
| ☐ 122 Luis Aparicio LL | 2.00 | 5.00 |
| ☐ 123 Luke Appling LL | 2.00 | 5.00 |
| ☐ 124 Joe Morgan LL | 2.00 | 5.00 |
| ☐ 125 Johnny Bench LL | 3.00 | 8.00 |
| ☐ 126 Tony Perez LL | 2.00 | 5.00 |
| ☐ 127 George Foster LL | 2.00 | 5.00 |
| ☐ 128 Bob Feller LL | 2.00 | 5.00 |
| ☐ 129 Bob Lemon LL | 2.00 | 5.00 |
| ☐ 130 Larry Doby LL | 2.00 | 5.00 |
| ☐ 131 Lou Boudreau LL | 2.00 | 5.00 |
| ☐ 132 George Kell LL | 2.00 | 5.00 |
| ☐ 133 Hal Newhouser LL | 2.00 | 5.00 |
| ☐ 134 Al Kaline LL | 3.00 | 8.00 |
| ☐ 135 Ty Cobb LL | 4.00 | 10.00 |
| ☐ 136 Charlie Keller LL | 2.00 | 5.00 |
| ☐ 137 Buck Leonard LL | 2.00 | 5.00 |
| ☐ 138 Maury Wills LL | 2.00 | 5.00 |
| ☐ 139 Don Drysdale LL | 3.00 | 8.00 |
| ☐ 140 Don Sutton LL | 2.00 | 5.00 |
| ☐ 141 Eddie Mathews LL | 3.00 | 8.00 |
| ☐ 142 Paul Molitor LL | 2.00 | 5.00 |
| ☐ 143 Kirby Puckett LL | 4.00 | 10.00 |
| ☐ 144 Harmon Killebrew LL | 3.00 | 8.00 |
| ☐ 145 Monte Irvin LL | 2.00 | 5.00 |
| ☐ 146 Mel Ott LL | 2.00 | 5.00 |
| ☐ 147 Charlie Gehringer LL | 2.00 | 5.00 |
| ☐ 148 Hoyt Wilhelm LL | 2.00 | 5.00 |
| ☐ 149 Tom Seaver LL | 3.00 | 8.00 |
| ☐ 150 Ted Kluszewski LL | 3.00 | 8.00 |
| ☐ 151 Joe DiMaggio LL | 4.00 | 10.00 |
| ☐ 152 Lou Gehrig LL | 4.00 | 10.00 |
| ☐ 153 Babe Ruth LL | 5.00 | 12.00 |
| ☐ 154 Casey Stengel LL | 2.00 | 5.00 |
| ☐ 155 Phil Rizzuto LL | 3.00 | 8.00 |
| ☐ 156 Thurman Munson LL | 3.00 | 8.00 |
| ☐ 157 Johnny Mize LL | 2.00 | 5.00 |
| ☐ 158 Yogi Berra LL | 3.00 | 8.00 |
| ☐ 159 Roger Maris LL | 3.00 | 8.00 |
| ☐ 160 Early Wynn LL | 2.00 | 5.00 |
| ☐ 161 Bobby Doerr LL | 2.00 | 5.00 |
| ☐ 162 Joe Cronin LL | 2.00 | 5.00 |
| ☐ 163 Don Mattingly LL | 4.00 | 10.00 |
| ☐ 164 Ray Dandridge LL | 2.00 | 5.00 |
| ☐ 165 Rollie Fingers LL | 2.00 | 5.00 |
| ☐ 166 Christy Mathewson LL | 3.00 | 8.00 |
| ☐ 167 Reggie Jackson LL | 3.00 | 8.00 |
| ☐ 168 Dennis Eckersley LL | 2.00 | 5.00 |
| ☐ 169 Mickey Cochrane LL | 2.00 | 5.00 |
| ☐ 170 Jimmie Foxx LL | 3.00 | 8.00 |
| ☐ 171 Lefty Gomez LL | 2.00 | 5.00 |
| ☐ 172 Jim Bunning LL | 2.00 | 5.00 |
| ☐ 173 Steve Carlton LL | 2.00 | 5.00 |
| ☐ 174 Robin Roberts LL | 2.00 | 5.00 |
| ☐ 175 Richie Ashburn LL | 2.00 | 5.00 |
| ☐ 176 Mike Schmidt LL | 3.00 | 8.00 |
| ☐ 177 Ralph Kiner LL | 2.00 | 5.00 |
| ☐ 178 Willie Stargell LL | 3.00 | 8.00 |
| ☐ 179 Roberto Clemente LL | 6.00 | 15.00 |
| ☐ 180 Bill Mazeroski LL | 3.00 | 8.00 |
| ☐ 181 Honus Wagner LL | 3.00 | 8.00 |
| ☐ 182 Pie Traynor LL | 2.00 | 5.00 |
| ☐ 183 Tony Gwynn LL | 3.00 | 8.00 |
| ☐ 184 Willie McCovey LL | 3.00 | 8.00 |
| ☐ 185 Gaylord Perry LL | 2.00 | 5.00 |
| ☐ 186 Juan Marichal LL | 2.00 | 5.00 |
| ☐ 187 Orlando Cepeda LL | 2.00 | 5.00 |
| ☐ 188 Satchel Paige LL | 3.00 | 8.00 |
| ☐ 189 George Sisler LL | 3.00 | 8.00 |
| ☐ 190 Rogers Hornsby LL | 3.00 | 8.00 |
| ☐ 191 Stan Musial LL | 3.00 | 8.00 |
| ☐ 192 Dizzy Dean LL | 2.00 | 5.00 |
| ☐ 193 Bob Gibson LL | 3.00 | 8.00 |
| ☐ 194 Red Schoendienst LL | 2.00 | 5.00 |
| ☐ 195 Lou Brock LL | 3.00 | 8.00 |
| ☐ 196 Enos Slaughter LL | 2.00 | 5.00 |
| ☐ 197 Nolan Ryan LL | 5.00 | 12.00 |
| ☐ 198 Mickey Vernon LL | 2.00 | 5.00 |
| ☐ 199 Walter Johnson LL | 3.00 | 8.00 |
| ☐ 200 Rick Ferrell LL | 2.00 | 5.00 |

## 2008 SP Legendary Cuts

| | | |
|---|---|---|
| ☐ COMP.SET w/o SP's (100) | 8.00 | 20.00 |
| ☐ COMMON CARD (1-100) | .20 | .50 |
| ☐ COMMON CARD (101-146) | 2.00 | 5.00 |
| ☐ COMMON CARD (147-200) | 2.00 | 5.00 |
| ☐ 101-200 RANDOMLY INSERTED | | |
| ☐ 101-200 PRINT RUN 550 SERIAL #'d SETS | | |
| ☐ 1 Ken Griffey Jr. | .75 | 2.00 |
| ☐ 2 Derek Jeter | 1.25 | 3.00 |
| ☐ 3 Albert Pujols | 1.00 | 2.50 |
| ☐ 4 Ichiro Suzuki | .75 | 2.00 |
| ☐ 5 Ryan Braun | .60 | 1.50 |
| ☐ 6 Manny Ramirez | .50 | 1.25 |
| ☐ 7 David Ortiz | .30 | .75 |
| ☐ 8 Greg Maddux | .60 | 1.50 |
| ☐ 9 Roger Clemens | .50 | 1.25 |
| ☐ 10 Chase Utley | .50 | 1.25 |
| ☐ 11 Vladimir Guerrero | .50 | 1.25 |
| ☐ 12 Johan Santana | .30 | .75 |
| ☐ 13 Chipper Jones | .50 | 1.25 |

|  |  | | |
|---|---|---|---|
| 14 | Tom Glavine | .30 | .75 |
| 15 | Ryan Howard | .60 | 1.50 |
| 16 | Hunter Pence | .50 | 1.25 |
| 17 | Prince Fielder | .30 | .75 |
| 18 | Jeff Francoeur | .30 | .75 |
| 19 | David Wright | .60 | 1.50 |
| 20 | Carlos Beltran | .20 | .50 |
| 21 | Carlos Lee | .20 | .50 |
| 22 | Cole Hamels | .50 | 1.25 |
| 23 | Jered Weaver | .20 | .50 |
| 24 | B.J. Upton | .30 | .75 |
| 25 | Akinori Iwamura | .20 | .50 |
| 26 | Daisuke Matsuzaka | .60 | 1.50 |
| 27 | Curt Schilling | .30 | .75 |
| 28 | Adam Dunn | .20 | .50 |
| 29 | Jose Reyes | .30 | .75 |
| 30 | Nomar Garciaparra | .20 | 1.25 |
| 31 | Hideki Matsui | .50 | 1.25 |
| 32 | Matt Holliday | .30 | .75 |
| 33 | Jason Bay | .30 | .75 |
| 34 | Grady Sizemore | .20 | .75 |
| 35 | Travis Hafner | .20 | .50 |
| 36 | Victor Martinez | .20 | .50 |
| 37 | C.C. Sabathia | .20 | .50 |
| 38 | Justin Morneau | .30 | .75 |
| 39 | Torii Hunter | .20 | .50 |
| 40 | Joe Mauer | .50 | 1.25 |
| 41 | Russell Martin | .20 | .50 |
| 42 | Frank Thomas | .40 | 1.00 |
| 43 | Miguel Tejada | .20 | .50 |
| 44 | Brian Roberts | .30 | .75 |
| 45 | Justin Verlander | .30 | .75 |
| 46 | Gary Sheffield | .20 | .50 |
| 47 | Magglio Ordonez | .30 | .75 |
| 48 | Alex Rodriguez | .75 | 2.00 |
| 49 | Bobby Abreu | .20 | .50 |
| 50 | Mark Teixeira | .30 | .75 |
| 51 | Andruw Jones | .20 | .50 |
| 52 | Derrek Lee | .30 | .75 |
| 53 | Aramis Ramirez | .20 | .50 |
| 54 | Carlos Zambrano | .30 | .75 |
| 55 | Alfonso Soriano | .30 | .75 |
| 56 | Omar Vizquel | .20 | .50 |
| 57 | Lance Berkman | .20 | .50 |
| 58 | Roy Oswalt | .20 | .50 |
| 59 | Jake Peavy | .30 | .75 |
| 60 | Chris R. Young | .20 | .50 |
| 61 | Khalil Greene | .30 | .75 |
| 62 | Troy Tulowitzki | .30 | .75 |
| 63 | Todd Helton | .30 | .75 |
| 64 | Josh Beckett | .30 | .75 |
| 65 | Miguel Cabrera | .30 | .75 |
| 66 | Hanley Ramirez | .50 | 1.25 |
| 67 | Dan Uggla | .30 | .75 |
| 68 | Scott Kazmir | .30 | .75 |
| 69 | Delmon Young | .30 | .75 |
| 70 | Erik Bedard | .20 | .50 |
| 71 | Alex Gordon | .30 | .75 |
| 72 | Felix Hernandez | .30 | .75 |
| 73 | Kenji Johjima | .20 | .50 |
| 74 | John Lackey | .20 | .50 |
| 75 | Ryan Zimmerman | .30 | .75 |
| 76 | Jeremy Bonderman | .20 | .50 |
| 77 | Chien-Ming Wang | .50 | 1.25 |
| 78 | Jim Thome | .30 | .75 |
| 79 | Jimmy Rollins | .30 | .75 |
| 80 | Mariano Rivera | .50 | 1.25 |
| 81 | Curtis Granderson | .20 | .50 |
| 82 | Nick Markakis | .30 | .75 |
| 83 | Trevor Hoffman | .20 | .50 |
| 84 | Barry Zito | .20 | .50 |
| 85 | Yovani Gallardo | .20 | .50 |
| 86 | Dan Haren | .20 | .50 |
| 87 | Vernon Wells | .20 | .50 |
| 88 | Ian Kennedy RC | .50 | 1.25 |
| 89 | Phil Hughes | .50 | 1.25 |
| 90 | Brian McCann | .30 | .75 |
| 91 | J.J. Hardy | .20 | .50 |
| 92 | Roy Halladay | .20 | .50 |
| 93 | Mike Piazza | .50 | 1.25 |
| 94 | Ivan Rodriguez | .30 | .75 |
| 95 | Dontrelle Willis | .30 | .75 |
| 96 | Brandon Webb | .30 | .75 |
| 97 | Carl Crawford | .30 | .75 |
| 98 | Tim Lincecum | .60 | 1.50 |
| 99 | Jason Varitek | .50 | 1.25 |
| 100 | Freddy Sanchez | .20 | .50 |
| 101 | Abraham Lincoln | 4.00 | 10.00 |
| 102 | Ulysses S. Grant | 3.00 | 8.00 |
| 103 | Andrew Johnson | 2.00 | 5.00 |
| 104 | George Washington | 3.00 | 8.00 |
| 105 | Thomas Jefferson | 2.00 | 5.00 |
| 106 | Andrew Jackson | 2.00 | 5.00 |
| 107 | James Madison | 2.00 | 5.00 |
| 108 | James Monroe | 2.00 | 5.00 |
| 109 | Benjamin Franklin | 2.50 | 6.00 |
| 110 | Alexander Graham Bell | 2.00 | 5.00 |
| 111 | Thomas Edison | 2.00 | 5.00 |
| 112 | Red Baron | 2.00 | 5.00 |
| 113 | Robert E. Lee | 3.00 | 8.00 |
| 114 | Mark Twain | 2.00 | 5.00 |
| 115 | Arthur Conan Doyle | 2.00 | 5.00 |
| 116 | Bram Stoker | 2.00 | 5.00 |
| 117 | Jules Verne | 2.00 | 5.00 |
| 118 | Billy the Kid | 2.50 | 6.00 |
| 119 | Harriet Beecher Stowe | 2.00 | 5.00 |
| 120 | Andrew Carnegie | 2.00 | 5.00 |
| 121 | Lewis Carroll | 2.00 | 5.00 |
| 122 | Cornelius Vanderbilt | 2.00 | 5.00 |
| 123 | Brigham Young | 2.00 | 5.00 |
| 124 | Charles Dickens | 2.00 | 5.00 |
| 125 | Vincent Van Gogh | 2.00 | 5.00 |
| 126 | Claude Monet | 2.00 | 5.00 |
| 127 | Jesse James | 2.50 | 6.00 |
| 128 | John D. Rockefeller | 2.00 | 5.00 |
| 129 | Harry Longabaugh | 2.00 | 5.00 |
| 130 | John F. Kennedy | 4.00 | 10.00 |
| 131 | Richard Nixon | 2.50 | 6.00 |
| 132 | Lyndon B. Johnson | 2.50 | 6.00 |
| 133 | Dwight D. Eisenhower | 2.00 | 5.00 |
| 134 | Franklin D. Roosevelt | 2.00 | 5.00 |
| 135 | Harry Truman | 2.00 | 5.00 |
| 136 | Ronald Reagan | 4.00 | 10.00 |
| 137 | Bill Clinton | 2.50 | 6.00 |
| 138 | George H.W. Bush | 2.50 | 6.00 |
| 139 | Jimmy Carter | 2.50 | 6.00 |
| 140 | Gerald Ford | 2.00 | 5.00 |
| 141 | Herbert Hoover | 2.00 | 5.00 |
| 142 | Calvin Coolidge | 2.00 | 5.00 |
| 143 | Warren G. Harding | 2.00 | 5.00 |
| 144 | Woodrow Wilson | 2.00 | 5.00 |
| 145 | William Taft | 2.00 | 5.00 |
| 146 | Theodore Roosevelt | 2.50 | 6.00 |
| 147 | Phil Niekro | 2.00 | 5.00 |
| 148 | Brooks Robinson | 3.00 | 8.00 |
| 149 | Cal Ripken Jr. | 6.00 | 15.00 |
| 150 | Eddie Murray | 3.00 | 8.00 |
| 151 | Jim Palmer | 2.00 | 5.00 |
| 152 | Abner Doubleday | 2.00 | 5.00 |
| 153 | Wade Boggs | 2.00 | 5.00 |
| 154 | Carl Yastrzemski | 5.00 | 12.00 |
| 155 | Bobby Doerr | 2.00 | 5.00 |
| 156 | Carlton Fisk | 3.00 | 8.00 |
| 157 | Pee Wee Reese | 3.00 | 8.00 |
| 158 | Ernie Banks | 2.00 | 5.00 |
| 159 | Fergie Jenkins | 2.00 | 5.00 |
| 160 | Billy Williams | 2.00 | 5.00 |
| 161 | Ryne Sandberg | 4.00 | 10.00 |
| 162 | Luis Aparicio | 2.00 | 5.00 |
| 163 | Joe Morgan | 2.00 | 5.00 |
| 164 | Johnny Bench | 4.00 | 10.00 |
| 165 | Tony Perez | 2.00 | 5.00 |
| 166 | Bob Feller | 2.00 | 5.00 |
| 167 | Larry Doby | 2.00 | 5.00 |
| 168 | Bob Lemon | 2.00 | 5.00 |
| 169 | Al Kaline | 3.00 | 8.00 |
| 170 | Warren Spahn | 3.00 | 8.00 |
| 171 | Robin Yount | 3.00 | 8.00 |
| 172 | Rollie Fingers | 2.00 | 5.00 |
| 173 | Harmon Killebrew | 2.00 | 5.00 |
| 174 | Rod Carew | 2.00 | 5.00 |
| 175 | Babe Ruth | 5.00 | 12.00 |
| 176 | Monte Irvin | 2.00 | 5.00 |
| 177 | Tom Seaver | 2.00 | 5.00 |
| 178 | Phil Rizzuto | 2.00 | 5.00 |
| 179 | Jack Chesbro | 2.00 | 5.00 |
| 180 | Catfish Hunter | 2.00 | 5.00 |
| 181 | Babe Ruth | 5.00 | 12.00 |
| 182 | Reggie Jackson | 2.00 | 5.00 |
| 183 | Dennis Eckersley | 2.00 | 5.00 |
| 184 | Steve Carlton | 2.00 | 5.00 |
| 185 | Ed Delahanty | 2.00 | 5.00 |
| 186 | Mike Schmidt | 4.00 | 10.00 |
| 187 | Jim Bunning | 2.00 | 5.00 |
| 188 | Robin Roberts | 2.00 | 5.00 |
| 189 | Willie Stargell | 3.00 | 8.00 |
| 190 | Bill Mazeroski | 3.00 | 8.00 |
| 191 | Ralph Kiner | 3.00 | 8.00 |
| 192 | Tony Gwynn | 6.00 | 15.00 |
| 193 | Juan Marichal | 2.00 | 5.00 |
| 194 | Willie McCovey | 3.00 | 8.00 |
| 195 | Orlando Cepeda | 2.00 | 5.00 |
| 196 | Stan Musial | 4.00 | 10.00 |
| 197 | Ozzie Smith | 4.00 | 10.00 |
| 198 | Bob Gibson | 3.00 | 8.00 |
| 199 | Bruce Sutter | 2.00 | 5.00 |
| 200 | Nolan Ryan | 5.00 | 12.00 |

## 2009 SP Legendary Cuts

|  |  | | |
|---|---|---|---|
| | COMP.SET w/o SP's (100) | 10.00 | 25.00 |
| | COMMON CARD (1-100) | .15 | .40 |
| | COMMON CARD (101-147) | 2.00 | 5.00 |
| | COMMON CARD (148-200) | 2.00 | 5.00 |
| | 101-200 APPX.ODDS ONE PER BOX | | |
| | 101-200 PRINT RUN 550 SERIAL #'d SETS | | |
| 1 | Brian Roberts | .15 | .40 |
| 2 | Derek Jeter | 1.00 | 2.50 |
| 3 | Evan Longoria | .60 | 1.50 |
| 4 | Brandon Phillips | .15 | .40 |
| 5 | David Wright | .50 | 1.25 |
| 6 | Ryan Howard | .50 | 1.25 |
| 7 | Jose Reyes | .40 | 1.00 |
| 8 | Ryan Braun | .50 | 1.25 |
| 9 | Jim Thome | .25 | .60 |
| 10 | Chipper Jones | .40 | 1.00 |
| 11 | Jimmy Rollins | .25 | .60 |
| 12 | Alfonso Soriano | .25 | .60 |
| 13 | Alex Rodriguez | .60 | 1.50 |
| 14 | David Price RC | 1.00 | 2.50 |
| 15 | Carlos Beltran | .15 | .40 |
| 16 | Aramis Ramirez | .15 | .40 |
| 17 | Ken Griffey Jr. | .60 | 1.50 |
| 18 | Daisuke Matsuzaka | .60 | 1.50 |
| 19 | Josh Beckett | .25 | .60 |
| 20 | Kevin Youkilis | .25 | .60 |
| 21 | Carlos Delgado | .15 | .40 |
| 22 | Clayton Kershaw | .40 | 1.00 |
| 23 | Adrian Gonzalez | .25 | .60 |
| 24 | Grady Sizemore | .25 | .60 |
| 25 | Mark Teixeira | .40 | 1.00 |
| 26 | Chase Utley | .40 | 1.00 |
| 27 | Vladimir Guerrero | .40 | 1.00 |
| 28 | Prince Fielder | .40 | 1.00 |
| 29 | Jeff Samardzija | .25 | .60 |
| 30 | Magglio Ordonez | .25 | .60 |
| 31 | Cliff Lee | .40 | 1.00 |
| 32 | Josh Hamilton | .40 | 1.00 |
| 33 | Justin Morneau | .25 | .60 |
| 34 | David Ortiz | .25 | .60 |
| 35 | Cole Hamels | .40 | 1.00 |
| 36 | Edinson Volquez | .15 | .40 |
| 37 | Nick Markakis | .15 | .40 |
| 38 | Carlos Zambrano | .15 | .40 |
| 39 | Max Scherzer | .25 | .60 |
| 40 | Rich Harden | .15 | .40 |
| 41 | Ryan Doumit | .15 | .40 |
| 42 | Mariano Rivera | .25 | .60 |
| 43 | Alexei Ramirez | .25 | .60 |
| 44 | Jake Peavy | .25 | .60 |
| 45 | Trevor Hoffman | .15 | .40 |
| 46 | Ryan Dempster | .15 | .40 |
| 47 | Francisco Liriano | .15 | .40 |
| 48 | Travis Hafner | .15 | .40 |
| 49 | Joakim Soria | .15 | .40 |
| 50 | Albert Pujols | 1.00 | 2.50 |
| 51 | Ichiro Suzuki | .60 | 1.50 |
| 52 | CC Sabathia | .25 | .60 |
| 53 | Ryan Ludwick | .25 | .60 |
| 54 | Mike Lowell | .15 | .40 |
| 55 | Tim Lincecum | .50 | 1.25 |
| 56 | Francisco Rodriguez | .25 | .60 |
| 57 | Johan Santana | .40 | 1.00 |
| 58 | Jonathan Papelbon | .25 | .60 |
| 59 | Geovany Soto | .25 | .60 |
| 60 | Jacoby Ellsbury | .40 | 1.00 |
| 61 | Jon Lester | .25 | .60 |
| 62 | Joba Chamberlain | .50 | 1.25 |
| 63 | Rick Ankiel | .15 | .40 |
| 64 | Chad Billingsley | .25 | .60 |
| 65 | Chien-Ming Wang | .40 | 1.00 |
| 66 | Stephen Drew | .15 | .40 |
| 67 | Roy Halladay | .25 | .60 |
| 68 | Ian Kinsler | .25 | .60 |
| 69 | Scott Kazmir | .25 | .60 |

| | | |
|---|---|---|
| 70 Miguel Tejada | .25 | .60 |
| 71 Carlos Lee | .15 | .40 |
| 72 Hanley Ramirez | .40 | 1.00 |
| 73 Carlos Pena | .25 | .60 |
| 74 Alex Gordon | .25 | .60 |
| 75 Pat Burrell | .25 | .60 |
| 76 Dan Uggla | .15 | .40 |
| 77 Joe Mauer | .40 | 1.00 |
| 78 Felix Hernandez | .25 | .60 |
| 79 Jermaine Dye | .15 | .40 |
| 80 Carlos Quentin | .15 | .40 |
| 81 Lance Berkman | .25 | .60 |
| 82 Randy Johnson | .40 | 1.00 |
| 83 Matt Holliday | .25 | .60 |
| 84 Curtis Granderson | .40 | 1.00 |
| 85 Miguel Cabrera | .25 | .60 |
| 86 Matt Cain | .15 | .40 |
| 87 Troy Tulowitzki | .25 | .60 |
| 88 Brian McCann | .25 | .60 |
| 89 Adam Dunn | .25 | .60 |
| 90 Matt Kemp | .40 | 1.00 |
| 91 B.J. Upton | .25 | .60 |
| 92 A.J. Burnett | .25 | .60 |
| 93 Carl Crawford | .25 | .60 |
| 94 Nate McLouth | .15 | .40 |
| 95 Derrek Lee | .25 | .60 |
| 96 Dustin Pedroia | .50 | 1.25 |
| 97 Russell Martin | .25 | .60 |
| 98 John Lackey | .15 | .40 |
| 99 Manny Ramirez | .40 | 1.00 |
| 100 Jay Bruce | .40 | 1.00 |
| 101 Ozzie Smith | 4.00 | 10.00 |
| 102 Luis Aparicio | 2.00 | 5.00 |
| 103 Johnny Bench | 3.00 | 8.00 |
| 104 Yogi Berra | 3.00 | 8.00 |
| 105 Lou Brock | 2.50 | 6.00 |
| 106 Rod Carew | 2.50 | 6.00 |
| 107 Whitey Ford | 2.50 | 6.00 |
| 108 Dennis Eckersley | 2.00 | 5.00 |
| 109 Bob Feller | 2.00 | 5.00 |
| 110 Rollie Fingers | 2.00 | 5.00 |
| 111 Carlton Fisk | 2.50 | 6.00 |
| 112 Bob Gibson | 2.50 | 6.00 |
| 113 Catfish Hunter | 2.00 | 5.00 |
| 114 Reggie Jackson | 2.50 | 6.00 |
| 115 Fergie Jenkins | 2.00 | 5.00 |
| 116 Al Kaline | 3.00 | 8.00 |
| 117 Harmon Killebrew | 3.00 | 8.00 |
| 118 Ralph Kiner | 2.50 | 6.00 |
| 119 Juan Marichal | 2.00 | 5.00 |
| 120 Vince Coleman | 2.00 | 5.00 |
| 121 Bill Mazeroski | 2.50 | 6.00 |
| 122 Don Newcombe | 2.00 | 5.00 |
| 123 Joe Morgan | 2.00 | 5.00 |
| 124 Eddie Murray | 2.50 | 5.00 |
| 125 Phil Niekro | 3.00 | 5.00 |
| 126 Mike Schmidt | 4.00 | 10.00 |
| 127 John Kruk | 2.00 | 5.00 |
| 128 Steve Carlton | 2.00 | 5.00 |
| 129 Brooks Robinson | 2.50 | 6.00 |
| 130 Nolan Ryan | 6.00 | 15.00 |
| 131 Dave Winfield | 2.00 | 5.00 |
| 132 Bo Jackson | 3.00 | 8.00 |
| 133 Paul Molitor | 3.00 | 8.00 |
| 134 Billy Williams | 2.00 | 5.00 |
| 135 Robin Yount | 3.00 | 8.00 |
| 136 Don Mattingly | 5.00 | 12.00 |
| 137 Cal Ripken Jr. | 6.00 | 15.00 |
| 138 Bobby Doerr | 2.00 | 5.00 |
| 139 Goose Gossage | 2.00 | 5.00 |
| 140 Wade Boggs | 2.50 | 6.00 |
| 141 Jim Palmer | 2.00 | 5.00 |
| 142 Carl Yastrzemski | 4.00 | 10.00 |
| 143 Frank Robinson | 2.50 | 6.00 |
| 144 Joe Carter | 2.00 | 5.00 |
| 145 Oil Can Boyd | 2.00 | 5.00 |
| 146 Tony Perez | 2.00 | 5.00 |
| 147 Gaylord Perry | 2.00 | 5.00 |
| 148 Jules Verne | 2.00 | 5.00 |
| 149 James K. Polk | 2.00 | 5.00 |
| 150 William Henry Harrison | 2.00 | 5.00 |
| 151 Manfred von Richthofen | 2.00 | 5.00 |
| 152 William Jennings Bryan | 2.00 | 5.00 |
| 153 Susan B. Anthony | 2.00 | 5.00 |
| 154 Gentleman Jim Corbett | 3.00 | 8.00 |
| 155 Cornelius Vanderbilt | 2.00 | 5.00 |
| 156 John L. Sullivan | 3.00 | 8.00 |
| 157 Daniel Boone | 2.00 | 5.00 |
| 158 Davy Crockett | 3.00 | 8.00 |
| 159 Edgar Allen Poe | 2.00 | 5.00 |
| 160 George Custer | 2.00 | 5.00 |
| 161 Harriet Tubman | 2.00 | 5.00 |
| 162 Adolphus Busch | 2.00 | 5.00 |
| 163 Bonnie Parker | 2.00 | 5.00 |
| 164 Clyde Barrow | 2.00 | 5.00 |
| 165 Winston Churchill | 2.00 | 5.00 |
| 166 Sir Isaac Newton | 2.00 | 5.00 |
| 167 Christopher Columbus | 2.00 | 5.00 |
| 168 Doc Holliday | 2.00 | 5.00 |
| 169 Wyatt Earp | 2.00 | 5.00 |
| 170 Sam Houston | 2.00 | 5.00 |
| 171 Francis Scott Key | 2.00 | 5.00 |
| 172 Betsy Ross | 2.00 | 5.00 |
| 173 John Hancock | 2.00 | 5.00 |
| 174 Vincent Van Gogh | 2.00 | 5.00 |
| 175 Charles Dickens | 2.00 | 5.00 |
| 176 Pope John Paul II | 3.00 | 8.00 |
| 177 Woodrow Wilson | 2.00 | 5.00 |
| 178 James A. Garfield | 2.00 | 5.00 |
| 179 Robert E. Lee | 3.00 | 8.00 |
| 180 Julius Caesar | 2.00 | 5.00 |
| 181 Napoleon Bonaparte | 2.00 | 5.00 |
| 182 Alexander Hamilton | 2.00 | 5.00 |
| 183 Frederick Douglass | 2.00 | 5.00 |
| 184 Booker T. Washington | 2.00 | 5.00 |
| 185 Paul Revere | 2.00 | 5.00 |
| 186 Grover Cleveland | 2.00 | 5.00 |
| 187 Andrew Johnson | 2.00 | 5.00 |
| 188 Billy the Kid | 2.00 | 5.00 |
| 189 Samuel Adams | 2.00 | 5.00 |
| 190 Dwight D. Eisenhower | 2.00 | 5.00 |
| 191 Theodore Roosevelt | 2.00 | 5.00 |
| 192 Ulysses S. Grant | 2.00 | 5.00 |
| 193 George Washington | 4.00 | 10.00 |
| 194 John D. Rockefeller | 2.00 | 5.00 |
| 195 Martin Van Buren | 2.00 | 5.00 |
| 196 John Adams | 2.00 | 5.00 |
| 197 Andrew Jackson | 2.00 | 5.00 |
| 198 Jesse James | 3.00 | 8.00 |
| 199 Thomas Jefferson | 2.00 | 5.00 |
| 200 Abraham Lincoln | 4.00 | 10.00 |

## 1996 SPx

| | | |
|---|---|---|
| COMPLETE SET (60) | 20.00 | 50.00 |
| 1 Greg Maddux | 1.25 | 3.00 |
| 2 Chipper Jones | .75 | 2.00 |
| 3 Fred McGriff | .50 | 1.25 |
| 4 Tom Glavine | .50 | 1.25 |
| 5 Cal Ripken | 2.50 | 6.00 |
| 6 Roberto Alomar | .50 | 1.25 |
| 7 Rafael Palmeiro | .50 | 1.25 |
| 8 Jose Canseco | .50 | 1.25 |
| 9 Roger Clemens | 1.50 | 4.00 |
| 10 Mo Vaughn | .30 | .75 |
| 11 Jim Edmonds | .30 | .75 |
| 12 Tim Salmon | .50 | 1.25 |
| 13 Sammy Sosa | .75 | 2.00 |
| 14 Ryne Sandberg | 1.25 | 3.00 |
| 15 Mark Grace | .50 | 1.25 |
| 16 Frank Thomas | .75 | 2.00 |
| 17 Barry Larkin | .50 | 1.25 |
| 18 Kenny Lofton | .30 | .75 |
| 19 Albert Belle | .30 | .75 |
| 20 Eddie Murray | .75 | 2.00 |
| 21 Manny Ramirez | .50 | 1.25 |
| 22 Dante Bichette | .30 | .75 |
| 23 Larry Walker | .30 | .75 |
| 24 Vinny Castilla | .30 | .75 |
| 25 Andres Galarraga | .30 | .75 |
| 26 Cecil Fielder | .30 | .75 |
| 27 Gary Sheffield | .30 | .75 |
| 28 Craig Biggio | .50 | 1.25 |
| 29 Jeff Bagwell | .50 | 1.25 |
| 30 Derek Bell | .30 | .75 |
| 31 Johnny Damon | .50 | 1.25 |
| 32 Eric Karros | .30 | .75 |
| 33 Mike Piazza | 1.25 | 3.00 |
| 34 Raul Mondesi | .30 | .75 |
| 35 Hideo Nomo | .75 | 2.00 |
| 36 Kirby Puckett | .75 | 2.00 |
| 37 Paul Molitor | .30 | .75 |
| 38 Marty Cordova | .30 | .75 |
| 39 Rondell White | .30 | .75 |
| 40 Jason Isringhausen | .30 | .75 |
| 41 Paul Wilson | .30 | .75 |
| 42 Rey Ordonez | .30 | .75 |
| 43 Derek Jeter | 2.00 | 5.00 |
| 44 Wade Boggs | .50 | 1.25 |
| 45 Mark McGwire | 1.25 | 3.00 |
| 46 Jason Kendall | .30 | .75 |
| 47 Ron Gant | .30 | .75 |
| 48 Ozzie Smith | 1.25 | 3.00 |
| 49 Tony Gwynn | 1.00 | 2.50 |
| 50 Ken Caminiti | .30 | .75 |
| 51 Barry Bonds | 2.00 | 5.00 |
| 52 Matt Williams | .30 | .75 |
| 53 Osvaldo Fernandez | .30 | .75 |
| 54 Jay Buhner | .30 | .75 |
| 55 Ken Griffey Jr. | 1.25 | 3.00 |
| 56 Randy Johnson | .75 | 2.00 |
| 57 Alex Rodriguez | 1.50 | 4.00 |
| 58 Juan Gonzalez | .30 | .75 |
| 59 Joe Carter | .30 | .75 |
| 60 Carlos Delgado | .30 | .75 |
| KG1 Ken Griffey Jr. Comm. | 2.00 | 5.00 |
| MP1 Mike Piazza Trib. | 2.00 | 5.00 |
| KGA1 Ken Griffey Jr. Auto. | 150.00 | 250.00 |
| MPA1 Mike Piazza Auto. | 125.00 | 200.00 |

## 1997 SPx

| | | |
|---|---|---|
| COMPLETE SET (50) | 25.00 | 60.00 |
| 1 Eddie Murray | .60 | 1.50 |
| 2 Darin Erstad | .60 | 1.50 |
| 3 Tim Salmon | .40 | 1.00 |
| 4 Andruw Jones | .40 | 1.00 |
| 5 Chipper Jones | .60 | 1.50 |
| 6 John Smoltz | .40 | 1.00 |
| 7 Greg Maddux | 1.00 | 2.50 |
| 8 Kenny Lofton | .25 | .60 |
| 9 Roberto Alomar | .40 | 1.00 |
| 10 Rafael Palmeiro | .40 | 1.00 |
| 11 Brady Anderson | .25 | .60 |
| 12 Cal Ripken | 2.00 | 5.00 |
| 13 Nomar Garciaparra | 1.00 | 2.50 |
| 14 Mo Vaughn | .25 | .60 |
| 15 Ryne Sandberg | 1.00 | 2.50 |
| 16 Sammy Sosa | .60 | 1.50 |
| 17 Frank Thomas | .60 | 1.50 |
| 18 Albert Belle | .25 | .60 |
| 19 Barry Larkin | .25 | .60 |
| 20 Deion Sanders | .40 | 1.00 |
| 21 Manny Ramirez | .40 | 1.00 |
| 22 Jim Thome | .40 | 1.00 |
| 23 Dante Bichette | .25 | .60 |
| 24 Andres Galarraga | .25 | .60 |
| 25 Larry Walker | .25 | .60 |
| 26 Gary Sheffield | .25 | .60 |
| 27 Jeff Bagwell | .40 | 1.00 |
| 28 Raul Mondesi | .25 | .60 |
| 29 Hideo Nomo | .60 | 1.50 |
| 30 Mike Piazza | - 1.00 | 2.50 |
| 31 Paul Molitor | .25 | .60 |
| 32 Todd Walker | .25 | .60 |
| 33 Vladimir Guerrero | .60 | 1.50 |
| 34 Todd Hundley | .25 | .60 |
| 35 Andy Pettitte | .40 | 1.00 |

| | | |
|---|---|---|
| ☐ 36 Derek Jeter | 1.50 | 4.00 |
| ☐ 37 Jose Canseco | .40 | 1.00 |
| ☐ 38 Mark McGwire | 1.50 | 4.00 |
| ☐ 39 Scott Rolen | .40 | 1.00 |
| ☐ 40 Ron Gant | .25 | .60 |
| ☐ 41 Ken Caminiti | .25 | .60 |
| ☐ 42 Tony Gwynn | .75 | 2.00 |
| ☐ 43 Barry Bonds | 1.50 | 4.00 |
| ☐ 44 Jay Buhner | .25 | .60 |
| ☐ 45 Ken Griffey Jr. | 1.00 | 2.50 |
| ☐ 46 Alex Rodriguez | 1.00 | 2.50 |
| ☐ 47 Jose Cruz Jr. RC | .40 | 1.00 |
| ☐ 48 Juan Gonzalez | .25 | .60 |
| ☐ 49 Ivan Rodriguez | .40 | 1.00 |
| ☐ 50 Roger Clemens | 1.25 | 3.00 |
| ☐ S45 Ken Griffey Jr. Sample | .75 | 2.00 |

## 1998 SPx Finite

| | | |
|---|---|---|
| ☐ COMP.YM SER.1 (30) | 15.00 | 40.00 |
| ☐ COMMON YM (1-30) | .60 | 1.50 |
| ☐ COMP.PE SER.1 (20) | 50.00 | 120.00 |
| ☐ COMMON PE (31-50) | 1.00 | 2.50 |
| ☐ COMP.BASIC SER.1 (90) | 30.00 | 80.00 |
| ☐ COMMON CARD (51-140) | .40 | 1.00 |
| ☐ COMP.SF SER.1 (30) | 40.00 | 100.00 |
| ☐ COMMON SF (141-170) | .50 | 1.25 |
| ☐ COMP.HG SER.1 (10) | 60.00 | 150.00 |
| ☐ COMMON HG (171-180) | 1.50 | 4.00 |
| ☐ COMP.YM SER.2 (30) | 25.00 | 60.00 |
| ☐ COMMON YM (181-210) | .60 | 1.50 |
| ☐ COMP.PP SER.2 (30) | 30.00 | 80.00 |
| ☐ COMMON PP (211-240) | .50 | 1.25 |
| ☐ COMP.BASIC SER.2 (90) | 20.00 | 50.00 |
| ☐ COMMON CARD (241-330) | .40 | 1.00 |
| ☐ COMP.TW SER.2 (20) | 12.50 | 30.00 |
| ☐ COMMON TW (331-350) | 1.00 | 2.50 |
| ☐ COMP.CG SER.2 (10) | 60.00 | 150.00 |
| ☐ COMMON CG (351-360) | 1.50 | 4.00 |
| ☐ 1 Nomar Garciaparra YM | 2.50 | 6.00 |
| ☐ 2 Miguel Tejada YM | .60 | 1.50 |
| ☐ 3 Mike Cameron YM | .60 | 1.50 |
| ☐ 4 Ken Cloude YM | .60 | 1.50 |
| ☐ 5 Jaret Wright YM | .60 | 1.50 |
| ☐ 6 Mark Kotsay YM | .60 | 1.50 |
| ☐ 7 Craig Counsell YM | .60 | 1.50 |
| ☐ 8 Jose Guillen YM | .60 | 1.50 |
| ☐ 9 Neifi Perez YM | .60 | 1.50 |
| ☐ 10 Jose Cruz Jr. YM | .60 | 1.50 |
| ☐ 11 Brett Tomko YM | .60 | 1.50 |
| ☐ 12 Matt Morris YM | .60 | 1.50 |
| ☐ 13 Justin Thompson YM | .60 | 1.50 |
| ☐ 14 Jeremi Gonzalez YM | .60 | 1.50 |
| ☐ 15 Scott Rolen YM | 1.00 | 2.50 |
| ☐ 16 Vladimir Guerrero YM | 1.50 | 4.00 |
| ☐ 17 Brad Fullmer YM | .60 | 1.50 |
| ☐ 18 Brian Giles YM | .60 | 1.50 |
| ☐ 19 Todd Dunwoody YM | .60 | 1.50 |
| ☐ 20 Ben Grieve YM | .60 | 1.50 |
| ☐ 21 Juan Encarnacion YM | .60 | 1.50 |
| ☐ 22 Aaron Boone YM | .60 | 1.50 |
| ☐ 23 Richie Sexson YM | .60 | 1.50 |
| ☐ 24 Richard Hidalgo YM | .60 | 1.50 |
| ☐ 25 Andruw Jones YM | 1.00 | 2.50 |
| ☐ 26 Todd Helton YM | 1.00 | 2.50 |
| ☐ 27 Paul Konerko YM | .60 | 1.50 |
| ☐ 28 Dante Powell YM | .60 | 1.50 |
| ☐ 29 Eli Marrero YM | .60 | 1.50 |
| ☐ 30 Derek Jeter YM | 4.00 | 10.00 |
| ☐ 31 Mike Piazza YM | 4.00 | 10.00 |
| ☐ 32 Tony Clark PE | 1.00 | 2.50 |
| ☐ 33 Larry Walker PE | 1.00 | 2.50 |
| ☐ 34 Jim Thome PE | 1.50 | 4.00 |
| ☐ 35 Juan Gonzalez PE | 2.00 | 5.00 |
| ☐ 36 Jeff Bagwell PE | 1.50 | 4.00 |
| ☐ 37 Jay Buhner PE | 1.00 | 2.50 |
| ☐ 38 Tim Salmon PE | 1.50 | 4.00 |
| ☐ 39 Albert Belle PE | 1.00 | 2.50 |
| ☐ 40 Mark McGwire PE | 6.00 | 15.00 |
| ☐ 41 Sammy Sosa PE | 2.50 | 6.00 |
| ☐ 42 Mo Vaughn PE | 1.00 | 2.50 |
| ☐ 43 Manny Ramirez PE | 1.50 | 4.00 |
| ☐ 44 Tino Martinez PE | 1.50 | 4.00 |
| ☐ 45 Frank Thomas PE | 2.50 | 6.00 |
| ☐ 46 Nomar Garciaparra PE | 4.00 | 10.00 |
| ☐ 47 Alex Rodriguez PE | 4.00 | 10.00 |
| ☐ 48 Chipper Jones PE | 2.50 | 6.00 |
| ☐ 49 Barry Bonds PE | 6.00 | 15.00 |
| ☐ 50 Ken Griffey Jr. PE | 4.00 | 10.00 |
| ☐ 51 Jason Dickson | .40 | 1.00 |
| ☐ 52 Jim Edmonds | .40 | 1.00 |
| ☐ 53 Darin Erstad | .40 | 1.00 |
| ☐ 54 Tim Salmon | .60 | 1.50 |
| ☐ 55 Chipper Jones | 1.00 | 2.50 |
| ☐ 56 Ryan Klesko | .40 | 1.00 |
| ☐ 57 Tom Glavine | .60 | 1.50 |
| ☐ 58 Denny Neagle | .40 | 1.00 |
| ☐ 59 John Smoltz | .60 | 1.50 |
| ☐ 60 Javy Lopez | .60 | 1.50 |
| ☐ 61 Roberto Alomar | .60 | 1.50 |
| ☐ 62 Rafael Palmeiro | .60 | 1.50 |
| ☐ 63 Mike Mussina | .60 | 1.50 |
| ☐ 64 Cal Ripken | 3.00 | 8.00 |
| ☐ 65 Mo Vaughn | .40 | 1.00 |
| ☐ 66 Tim Naehring | .40 | 1.00 |
| ☐ 67 John Valentin | .40 | 1.00 |
| ☐ 68 Mark Grace | .60 | 1.50 |
| ☐ 69 Kevin Orie | .40 | 1.00 |
| ☐ 70 Sammy Sosa | 1.00 | 2.50 |
| ☐ 71 Albert Belle | .60 | 1.50 |
| ☐ 72 Frank Thomas | 1.00 | 2.50 |
| ☐ 73 Robin Ventura | .40 | 1.00 |
| ☐ 74 David Justice | .40 | 1.00 |
| ☐ 75 Kenny Lofton | .40 | 1.00 |
| ☐ 76 Omar Vizquel | .60 | 1.50 |
| ☐ 77 Manny Ramirez | .60 | 1.50 |
| ☐ 78 Jim Thome | .60 | 1.50 |
| ☐ 79 Dante Bichette | .40 | 1.00 |
| ☐ 80 Larry Walker | .60 | 1.50 |
| ☐ 81 Vinny Castilla | .40 | 1.00 |
| ☐ 82 Ellis Burks | .40 | 1.00 |
| ☐ 83 Bobby Higginson | .40 | 1.00 |
| ☐ 84 Brian Hunter | .40 | 1.00 |
| ☐ 85 Tony Clark | .60 | 1.50 |
| ☐ 86 Mike Hampton | .40 | 1.00 |
| ☐ 87 Jeff Bagwell | .60 | 1.50 |
| ☐ 88 Craig Biggio | .60 | 1.50 |
| ☐ 89 Derek Bell | .40 | 1.00 |
| ☐ 90 Mike Piazza | 1.50 | 4.00 |
| ☐ 91 Ramon Martinez | .40 | 1.00 |
| ☐ 92 Raul Mondesi | .40 | 1.00 |
| ☐ 93 Hideo Nomo | 1.00 | 2.50 |
| ☐ 94 Eric Karros | .40 | 1.00 |
| ☐ 95 Paul Molitor | .40 | 1.00 |
| ☐ 96 Marty Cordova | .40 | 1.00 |
| ☐ 97 Brad Radke | .40 | 1.00 |
| ☐ 98 Mark Grudzielanek | .40 | 1.00 |
| ☐ 99 Carlos Perez | .40 | 1.00 |
| ☐ 100 Rondell White | .40 | 1.00 |
| ☐ 101 Todd Hundley | .40 | 1.00 |
| ☐ 102 Edgardo Alfonzo | .40 | 1.00 |
| ☐ 103 John Franco | .40 | 1.00 |
| ☐ 104 John Olerud | .40 | 1.00 |
| ☐ 105 Tino Martinez | .60 | 1.50 |
| ☐ 106 David Cone | .40 | 1.00 |
| ☐ 107 Paul O'Neill | .60 | 1.50 |
| ☐ 108 Andy Pettitte | .60 | 1.50 |
| ☐ 109 Bernie Williams | .60 | 1.50 |
| ☐ 110 Rickey Henderson | 1.50 | 4.00 |
| ☐ 111 Jason Giambi | .40 | 1.00 |
| ☐ 112 Matt Stairs | .40 | 1.00 |
| ☐ 113 Gregg Jefferies | .40 | 1.00 |
| ☐ 114 Rico Brogna | .40 | 1.00 |
| ☐ 115 Curt Schilling | .40 | 1.00 |
| ☐ 116 Jason Schmidt | .40 | 1.00 |
| ☐ 117 Jose Guillen | .40 | 1.00 |
| ☐ 118 Kevin Young | .40 | 1.00 |
| ☐ 119 Ray Lankford | .40 | 1.00 |
| ☐ 120 Mark McGwire | 2.50 | 6.00 |
| ☐ 121 Delino DeShields | .40 | 1.00 |
| ☐ 122 Ken Caminiti | .40 | 1.00 |
| ☐ 123 Tony Gwynn | 1.25 | 3.00 |
| ☐ 124 Trevor Hoffman | .40 | 1.00 |
| ☐ 125 Barry Bonds | 2.50 | 6.00 |
| ☐ 126 Jeff Kent | .40 | 1.00 |
| ☐ 127 Shawn Estes | .40 | 1.00 |
| ☐ 128 J.T. Snow | .40 | 1.00 |
| ☐ 129 Jay Johnson | .40 | 1.00 |
| ☐ 130 Ken Griffey Jr. | 1.50 | 4.00 |
| ☐ 131 Dan Wilson | .40 | 1.00 |
| ☐ 132 Edgar Martinez | .60 | 1.50 |
| ☐ 133 Alex Rodriguez | 1.50 | 4.00 |
| ☐ 134 Rusty Greer | .40 | 1.00 |
| ☐ 135 Juan Gonzalez | .40 | 1.00 |
| ☐ 136 Fernando Tatis | .40 | 1.00 |
| ☐ 137 Ivan Rodriguez | .60 | 1.50 |
| ☐ 138 Carlos Delgado | .40 | 1.00 |
| ☐ 139 Pat Hentgen | .40 | 1.00 |
| ☐ 140 Roger Clemens | 2.00 | 5.00 |
| ☐ 141 Chipper Jones SF | 1.25 | 3.00 |
| ☐ 142 Greg Maddux SF | 2.00 | 5.00 |
| ☐ 143 Rafael Palmeiro SF | .75 | 2.00 |
| ☐ 144 Mike Mussina SF | .75 | 2.00 |
| ☐ 145 Cal Ripken SF | 4.00 | 10.00 |
| ☐ 146 Nomar Garciaparra SF | 2.00 | 5.00 |
| ☐ 147 Mo Vaughn SF | .50 | 1.25 |
| ☐ 148 Sammy Sosa SF | 1.25 | 3.00 |
| ☐ 149 Albert Belle SF | .50 | 1.25 |
| ☐ 150 Frank Thomas SF | 1.25 | 3.00 |
| ☐ 151 Jim Thome SF | .75 | 2.00 |
| ☐ 152 Kenny Lofton SF | .50 | 1.25 |
| ☐ 153 Manny Ramirez SF | .75 | 2.00 |
| ☐ 154 Larry Walker SF | .50 | 1.25 |
| ☐ 155 Jeff Bagwell SF | .75 | 2.00 |
| ☐ 156 Craig Biggio SF | .75 | 2.00 |
| ☐ 157 Mike Piazza SF | 2.00 | 5.00 |
| ☐ 158 Paul Molitor SF | .50 | 1.25 |
| ☐ 159 Derek Jeter SF | 3.00 | 8.00 |
| ☐ 160 Tino Martinez SF | .75 | 2.00 |
| ☐ 161 Curt Schilling SF | .50 | 1.25 |
| ☐ 162 Mark McGwire SF | 3.00 | 8.00 |
| ☐ 163 Tony Gwynn SF | 1.50 | 4.00 |
| ☐ 164 Barry Bonds SF | 3.00 | 8.00 |
| ☐ 165 Ken Griffey Jr. SF | 2.00 | 5.00 |
| ☐ 166 Randy Johnson SF | 1.25 | 3.00 |
| ☐ 167 Alex Rodriguez SF | 2.00 | 5.00 |
| ☐ 168 Juan Gonzalez SF | .50 | 1.25 |
| ☐ 169 Ivan Rodriguez SF | .75 | 2.00 |
| ☐ 170 Roger Clemens SF | 2.50 | 6.00 |
| ☐ 171 Greg Maddux HG | 6.00 | 15.00 |
| ☐ 172 Cal Ripken HG | 12.50 | 30.00 |
| ☐ 173 Frank Thomas HG | 4.00 | 10.00 |
| ☐ 174 Jeff Bagwell HG | 2.50 | 6.00 |
| ☐ 175 Mike Piazza HG | 6.00 | 15.00 |
| ☐ 176 Mark McGwire HG | 10.00 | 25.00 |
| ☐ 177 Barry Bonds HG | 10.00 | 25.00 |
| ☐ 178 Ken Griffey Jr. HG | 6.00 | 15.00 |
| ☐ 179 Alex Rodriguez HG | 6.00 | 15.00 |
| ☐ 180 Roger Clemens HG | 8.00 | 20.00 |
| ☐ 181 Mike Caruso | .60 | 1.50 |
| ☐ 182 David Ortiz YM | 2.00 | 5.00 |
| ☐ 183 Gabe Alvarez YM | .60 | 1.50 |
| ☐ 184 Gary Matthews Jr. YM RC | 1.00 | 2.50 |
| ☐ 185 Kerry Wood YM | .75 | 2.00 |
| ☐ 186 Carl Pavano YM | .60 | 1.50 |
| ☐ 187 Alex Gonzalez YM | .60 | 1.50 |
| ☐ 188 Masato Yoshii YM RC | .60 | 1.50 |
| ☐ 189 Larry Sutton YM | .60 | 1.50 |
| ☐ 190 Russell Branyan YM | .60 | 1.50 |
| ☐ 191 Bruce Chen YM | .60 | 1.50 |
| ☐ 192 Rolando Arrojo YM RC | .60 | 1.50 |
| ☐ 193 Ryan Christenson YM RC | .60 | 1.50 |
| ☐ 194 Cliff Politte YM | .60 | 1.50 |
| ☐ 195 A.J. Hinch YM | .60 | 1.50 |
| ☐ 196 Kevin Witt YM | .60 | 1.50 |
| ☐ 197 Daryle Ward YM | .60 | 1.50 |
| ☐ 198 Corey Koskie YM RC | 1.00 | 2.50 |
| ☐ 199 Mike Lowell YM RC | 4.00 | 10.00 |
| ☐ 200 Travis Lee YM | .60 | 1.50 |
| ☐ 201 Kevin Millwood YM RC | 2.00 | 5.00 |
| ☐ 202 Robert Smith YM | .60 | 1.50 |
| ☐ 203 Magglio Ordonez YM RC | 6.00 | 15.00 |
| ☐ 204 Eric Milton YM | .60 | 1.50 |
| ☐ 205 Geoff Jenkins YM | .60 | 1.50 |
| ☐ 206 Rich Butler YM RC | .60 | 1.50 |
| ☐ 207 Mike Kinkade YM RC | .60 | 1.50 |
| ☐ 208 Braden Looper YM | .60 | 1.50 |
| ☐ 209 Matt Clement YM | .60 | 1.50 |
| ☐ 210 Derrek Lee YM | 1.00 | 2.50 |
| ☐ 211 Randy Johnson PP | 1.25 | 3.00 |
| ☐ 212 John Smoltz PP | .75 | 2.00 |

|  |  | | |
|---|---|---|---|
| ❏ 213 | Roger Clemens PP | 2.50 | 6.00 |
| ❏ 214 | Curt Schilling PP | .50 | 1.25 |
| ❏ 215 | Pedro Martinez PP | .75 | 2.00 |
| ❏ 216 | Vinny Castilla PP | .50 | 1.25 |
| ❏ 217 | Jose Cruz Jr. PP | .50 | 1.25 |
| ❏ 218 | Jim Thome PP | .75 | 2.00 |
| ❏ 219 | Alex Rodriguez PP | 2.00 | 5.00 |
| ❏ 220 | Frank Thomas PP | 1.25 | 3.00 |
| ❏ 221 | Tim Salmon PP | .50 | 1.25 |
| ❏ 222 | Larry Walker PP | .50 | 1.25 |
| ❏ 223 | Albert Belle PP | .50 | 1.25 |
| ❏ 224 | Manny Ramirez PP | .75 | 2.00 |
| ❏ 225 | Mark McGwire PP | 3.00 | 8.00 |
| ❏ 226 | Mo Vaughn PP | .50 | 1.25 |
| ❏ 227 | Andres Galarraga PP | .50 | 1.25 |
| ❏ 228 | Scott Rolen PP | .75 | 2.00 |
| ❏ 229 | Travis Lee PP | .50 | 1.25 |
| ❏ 230 | Mike Piazza PP | 2.00 | 5.00 |
| ❏ 231 | Nomar Garciaparra PP | 2.00 | 5.00 |
| ❏ 232 | Andruw Jones PP | .75 | 2.00 |
| ❏ 233 | Barry Bonds PP | 3.00 | 8.00 |
| ❏ 234 | Jeff Bagwell PP | .75 | 2.00 |
| ❏ 235 | Juan Gonzalez PP | .50 | 1.25 |
| ❏ 236 | Tino Martinez PP | .75 | 2.00 |
| ❏ 237 | Vladimir Guerrero PP | 1.25 | 3.00 |
| ❏ 238 | Rafael Palmeiro PP | .75 | 2.00 |
| ❏ 239 | Russell Branyan PP | .50 | 1.25 |
| ❏ 240 | Ken Griffey Jr. PP | 2.00 | 5.00 |
| ❏ 241 | Cecil Fielder | .40 | 1.00 |
| ❏ 242 | Chuck Finley | .40 | 1.00 |
| ❏ 243 | Jay Bell | .40 | 1.00 |
| ❏ 244 | Andy Benes | .40 | 1.00 |
| ❏ 245 | Matt Williams | .40 | 1.00 |
| ❏ 246 | Brian Anderson | .40 | 1.00 |
| ❏ 247 | Dave Dellucci RC | .60 | 1.50 |
| ❏ 248 | Andres Galarraga | .40 | 1.00 |
| ❏ 249 | Andruw Jones | .40 | 1.00 |
| ❏ 250 | Greg Maddux | 1.50 | 4.00 |
| ❏ 251 | Brady Anderson | .40 | 1.00 |
| ❏ 252 | Joe Carter | .40 | 1.00 |
| ❏ 253 | Eric Davis | .40 | 1.00 |
| ❏ 254 | Pedro Martinez | .60 | 1.50 |
| ❏ 255 | Nomar Garciaparra | 1.50 | 4.00 |
| ❏ 256 | Dennis Eckersley | .40 | 1.00 |
| ❏ 257 | Henry Rodriguez | .40 | 1.00 |
| ❏ 258 | Jeff Blauser | .40 | 1.00 |
| ❏ 259 | Jaime Navarro | .40 | 1.00 |
| ❏ 260 | Ray Durham | .40 | 1.00 |
| ❏ 261 | Chris Stynes | .40 | 1.00 |
| ❏ 262 | Willie Greene | .40 | 1.00 |
| ❏ 263 | Reggie Sanders | .40 | 1.00 |
| ❏ 264 | Bret Boone | .40 | 1.00 |
| ❏ 265 | Barry Larkin | .60 | 1.50 |
| ❏ 266 | Travis Fryman | .40 | 1.00 |
| ❏ 267 | Charles Nagy | .40 | 1.00 |
| ❏ 268 | Sandy Alomar Jr. | .40 | 1.00 |
| ❏ 269 | Darryl Kile | .40 | 1.00 |
| ❏ 270 | Mike Lansing | .40 | 1.00 |
| ❏ 271 | Pedro Astacio | .40 | 1.00 |
| ❏ 272 | Damion Easley | .40 | 1.00 |
| ❏ 273 | Joe Randa | .40 | 1.00 |
| ❏ 274 | Luis Gonzalez | .40 | 1.00 |
| ❏ 275 | Mike Piazza | 1.50 | 4.00 |
| ❏ 276 | Todd Zeile | .40 | 1.00 |
| ❏ 277 | Edgar Renteria | .40 | 1.00 |
| ❏ 278 | Livan Hernandez | .40 | 1.00 |
| ❏ 279 | Cliff Floyd | .40 | 1.00 |
| ❏ 280 | Moises Alou | .40 | 1.00 |
| ❏ 281 | Billy Wagner | .40 | 1.00 |
| ❏ 282 | Jeff King | .40 | 1.00 |
| ❏ 283 | Hal Morris | .40 | 1.00 |
| ❏ 284 | Johnny Damon | .60 | 1.50 |
| ❏ 285 | Dean Palmer | .40 | 1.00 |
| ❏ 286 | Tim Belcher | .40 | 1.00 |
| ❏ 287 | Eric Young | .40 | 1.00 |
| ❏ 288 | Bobby Bonilla | .40 | 1.00 |
| ❏ 289 | Gary Sheffield | .40 | 1.00 |
| ❏ 290 | Chan Ho Park | .40 | 1.00 |
| ❏ 291 | Charles Johnson | .40 | 1.00 |
| ❏ 292 | Jeff Cirillo | .40 | 1.00 |
| ❏ 293 | Jeromy Burnitz | .40 | 1.00 |
| ❏ 294 | Jose Valentin | .40 | 1.00 |
| ❏ 295 | Marquis Grissom | .40 | 1.00 |
| ❏ 296 | Todd Walker | .40 | 1.00 |
| ❏ 297 | Terry Steinbach | .40 | 1.00 |
| ❏ 298 | Rick Aguilera | .40 | 1.00 |
| ❏ 299 | Vladimir Guerrero | 1.00 | 2.50 |
| ❏ 300 | Rey Ordonez | .40 | 1.00 |
| ❏ 301 | Butch Huskey | .40 | 1.00 |
| ❏ 302 | Bernard Gilkey | .40 | 1.00 |
| ❏ 303 | Mariano Rivera | 1.00 | 2.50 |
| ❏ 304 | Chuck Knoblauch | .40 | 1.00 |
| ❏ 305 | Derek Jeter | 2.50 | 6.00 |
| ❏ 306 | Ricky Bottalico | .40 | 1.00 |
| ❏ 307 | Bob Abreu | .40 | 1.00 |
| ❏ 308 | Scott Rolen | .60 | 1.50 |
| ❏ 309 | Al Martin | .40 | 1.00 |
| ❏ 310 | Jason Kendall | .40 | 1.00 |
| ❏ 311 | Brian Jordan | .40 | 1.00 |
| ❏ 312 | Ron Gant | .40 | 1.00 |
| ❏ 313 | Todd Stottlemyre | .40 | 1.00 |
| ❏ 314 | Greg Vaughn | .40 | 1.00 |
| ❏ 315 | Kevin Brown | .60 | 1.50 |
| ❏ 316 | Wally Joyner | .40 | 1.00 |
| ❏ 317 | Robb Nen | .40 | 1.00 |
| ❏ 318 | Orel Hershiser | .40 | 1.00 |
| ❏ 319 | Russ Davis | .40 | 1.00 |
| ❏ 320 | Randy Johnson | 1.00 | 2.50 |
| ❏ 321 | Quinton McCracken | .40 | 1.00 |
| ❏ 322 | Tony Saunders | .40 | 1.00 |
| ❏ 323 | Wilson Alvarez | .40 | 1.00 |
| ❏ 324 | Wade Boggs | .60 | 1.50 |
| ❏ 325 | Fred McGriff | .60 | 1.50 |
| ❏ 326 | Lee Stevens | .40 | 1.00 |
| ❏ 327 | John Wetteland | .40 | 1.00 |
| ❏ 328 | Jose Canseco | .60 | 1.50 |
| ❏ 329 | Randy Myers | .40 | 1.00 |
| ❏ 330 | Jose Cruz Jr. | .40 | 1.00 |
| ❏ 331 | Matt Williams TW | 1.00 | 2.50 |
| ❏ 332 | Andres Galarraga TW | 1.00 | 2.50 |
| ❏ 333 | Walt Weiss TW | 1.00 | 2.50 |
| ❏ 334 | Joe Carter TW | 1.00 | 2.50 |
| ❏ 335 | Pedro Martinez TW | 1.50 | 4.00 |
| ❏ 336 | Henry Rodriguez TW | 1.00 | 2.50 |
| ❏ 337 | Travis Fryman TW | 1.00 | 2.50 |
| ❏ 338 | Darryl Kile TW | 1.00 | 2.50 |
| ❏ 339 | Mike Lansing TW | 1.00 | 2.50 |
| ❏ 340 | Mike Piazza TW | 4.00 | 10.00 |
| ❏ 341 | Moises Alou TW | 1.00 | 2.50 |
| ❏ 342 | Charles Johnson TW | 1.00 | 2.50 |
| ❏ 343 | Chuck Knoblauch TW | 1.00 | 2.50 |
| ❏ 344 | Rickey Henderson TW | 2.50 | 6.00 |
| ❏ 345 | Kevin Brown TW | 1.50 | 4.00 |
| ❏ 346 | Orel Hershiser TW | 1.00 | 2.50 |
| ❏ 347 | Wade Boggs TW | 1.50 | 4.00 |
| ❏ 348 | Fred McGriff TW | 1.50 | 4.00 |
| ❏ 349 | Jose Canseco TW | 1.50 | 4.00 |
| ❏ 350 | Gary Sheffield TW | 1.00 | 2.50 |
| ❏ 351 | Travis Lee CG | 1.50 | 4.00 |
| ❏ 352 | Nomar Garciaparra CG | 6.00 | 15.00 |
| ❏ 353 | Frank Thomas CG | 4.00 | 10.00 |
| ❏ 354 | Cal Ripken CG | 12.50 | 30.00 |
| ❏ 355 | Mark McGwire CG | 10.00 | 25.00 |
| ❏ 356 | Mike Piazza CG | 6.00 | 15.00 |
| ❏ 357 | Alex Rodriguez CG | 6.00 | 15.00 |
| ❏ 358 | Barry Bonds CG | 10.00 | 25.00 |
| ❏ 359 | Tony Gwynn CG | 5.00 | 12.00 |
| ❏ 360 | Ken Griffey Jr. CG | 6.00 | 15.00 |

## 1999 SPx

| | | |
|---|---|---|
| ❏ COMP.SET w/o SP's (80) | 10.00 | 25.00 |
| ❏ COMMON MCGWIRE (1-10) | .60 | 1.50 |
| ❏ COMMON CARD (11-80) | .20 | .50 |
| ❏ COMMON SP (81-120) | 4.00 | 10.00 |
| ❏ 1 Mark McGwire 61 | 1.25 | 3.00 |
| ❏ 2 Mark McGwire 62 | 1.25 | 3.00 |
| ❏ 3 Mark McGwire 63 | .60 | 1.50 |
| ❏ 4 Mark McGwire 64 | .60 | 1.50 |
| ❏ 5 Mark McGwire 65 | .60 | 1.50 |
| ❏ 6 Mark McGwire 66 | .60 | 1.50 |
| ❏ 7 Mark McGwire 67 | .60 | 1.50 |
| ❏ 8 Mark McGwire 68 | .60 | 1.50 |
| ❏ 9 Mark McGwire 69 | .60 | 1.50 |
| ❏ 10 Mark McGwire 70 | 1.50 | 4.00 |
| ❏ 11 Mo Vaughn | .20 | .50 |
| ❏ 12 Darin Erstad | .20 | .50 |
| ❏ 13 Travis Lee | .20 | .50 |
| ❏ 14 Randy Johnson | .50 | 1.25 |
| ❏ 15 Matt Williams | .20 | .50 |
| ❏ 16 Chipper Jones | .50 | 1.25 |
| ❏ 17 Greg Maddux | .75 | 2.00 |
| ❏ 18 Andruw Jones | .30 | .75 |
| ❏ 19 Andres Galarraga | .30 | .75 |
| ❏ 20 Cal Ripken | 1.50 | 4.00 |
| ❏ 21 Albert Belle | .20 | .50 |
| ❏ 22 Mike Mussina | .30 | .75 |
| ❏ 23 Nomar Garciaparra | .75 | 2.00 |
| ❏ 24 Pedro Martinez | .30 | .75 |
| ❏ 25 John Valentin | .20 | .50 |
| ❏ 26 Kerry Wood | .20 | .50 |
| ❏ 27 Sammy Sosa | .50 | 1.25 |
| ❏ 28 Mark Grace | .30 | .75 |
| ❏ 29 Frank Thomas | .50 | 1.25 |
| ❏ 30 Mike Caruso | .20 | .50 |
| ❏ 31 Barry Larkin | .30 | .75 |
| ❏ 32 Sean Casey | .20 | .50 |
| ❏ 33 Jim Thome | .30 | .75 |
| ❏ 34 Kenny Lofton | .30 | .75 |
| ❏ 35 Manny Ramirez | .30 | .75 |
| ❏ 36 Larry Walker | .20 | .50 |
| ❏ 37 Todd Helton | .30 | .75 |
| ❏ 38 Vinny Castilla | .20 | .50 |
| ❏ 39 Tony Clark | .20 | .50 |
| ❏ 40 Derrek Lee | .30 | .75 |
| ❏ 41 Mark Kotsay | .20 | .50 |
| ❏ 42 Jeff Bagwell | .50 | 1.25 |
| ❏ 43 Craig Biggio | .30 | .75 |
| ❏ 44 Moises Alou | .20 | .50 |
| ❏ 45 Larry Sutton | .20 | .50 |
| ❏ 46 Johnny Damon | .30 | .75 |
| ❏ 47 Gary Sheffield | .20 | .50 |
| ❏ 48 Raul Mondesi | .20 | .50 |
| ❏ 49 Jeromy Burnitz | .20 | .50 |
| ❏ 50 Todd Walker | .20 | .50 |
| ❏ 51 David Ortiz | .50 | 1.25 |
| ❏ 52 Vladimir Guerrero | .50 | 1.25 |
| ❏ 53 Rondell White | .20 | .50 |
| ❏ 54 Mike Piazza | .75 | 2.00 |
| ❏ 55 Derek Jeter | 1.25 | 3.00 |
| ❏ 56 Tino Martinez | .30 | .75 |
| ❏ 57 Roger Clemens | 1.00 | 2.50 |
| ❏ 58 Ben Grieve | .20 | .50 |
| ❏ 59 A.J. Hinch | .20 | .50 |
| ❏ 60 Scott Rolen | .30 | .75 |
| ❏ 61 Doug Glanville | .20 | .50 |
| ❏ 62 Aramis Ramirez | .20 | .50 |
| ❏ 63 Jose Guillen | .20 | .50 |
| ❏ 64 Tony Gwynn | .60 | 1.50 |
| ❏ 65 Greg Vaughn | .20 | .50 |
| ❏ 66 Ruben Rivera | .20 | .50 |
| ❏ 67 Barry Bonds | 1.25 | 3.00 |
| ❏ 68 J.T. Snow | .20 | .50 |
| ❏ 69 Alex Rodriguez | .75 | 2.00 |
| ❏ 70 Ken Griffey Jr. | .75 | 2.00 |
| ❏ 71 Jay Buhner | .20 | .50 |
| ❏ 72 Mark McGwire | 1.25 | 3.00 |
| ❏ 73 Fernando Tatis | .20 | .50 |
| ❏ 74 Quinton McCracken | .20 | .50 |
| ❏ 75 Wade Boggs | .30 | .75 |
| ❏ 76 Ivan Rodriguez | .30 | .75 |
| ❏ 77 Juan Gonzalez | .50 | 1.25 |
| ❏ 78 Rafael Palmeiro | .30 | .75 |
| ❏ 79 Jose Cruz Jr. | .20 | .50 |
| ❏ 80 Carlos Delgado | .20 | .50 |
| ❏ 81 Troy Glaus SP | 6.00 | 15.00 |
| ❏ 82 Vladimir Nunez SP | 4.00 | 10.00 |
| ❏ 83 George Lombard SP | 4.00 | 10.00 |
| ❏ 84 Bruce Chen SP | 4.00 | 10.00 |
| ❏ 85 Ryan Minor SP | 4.00 | 10.00 |
| ❏ 86 Calvin Pickering SP | 4.00 | 10.00 |
| ❏ 87 Jin Ho Cho SP | 4.00 | 10.00 |
| ❏ 88 Russ Branyan SP | 4.00 | 10.00 |
| ❏ 89 Derrick Gibson SP | 4.00 | 10.00 |
| ❏ 90 Gabe Kapler SP AU | 6.00 | 15.00 |
| ❏ 91 Matt Anderson SP | 4.00 | 10.00 |
| ❏ 92 Robert Fick SP | 4.00 | 10.00 |
| ❏ 93 Juan Encarnacion SP | 4.00 | 10.00 |
| ❏ 94 Preston Wilson SP | 4.00 | 10.00 |
| ❏ 95 Alex Gonzalez SP | 4.00 | 10.00 |
| ❏ 96 Carlos Beltran SP | 6.00 | 15.00 |

| | | |
|---|---|---|
| 97 Jeremy Giambi SP | 4.00 | 10.00 |
| 98 Dee Brown SP | 4.00 | 10.00 |
| 99 Adrian Beltre SP | 4.00 | 10.00 |
| 100 Alex Cora SP | 4.00 | 10.00 |
| 101 Angel Pena SP | 4.00 | 10.00 |
| 102 Geoff Jenkins SP | 4.00 | 10.00 |
| 103 Ronnie Belliard SP | 4.00 | 10.00 |
| 104 Corey Koskie SP | 4.00 | 10.00 |
| 105 A.J. Pierzynski SP | 4.00 | 10.00 |
| 106 Michael Barrett SP | 4.00 | 10.00 |
| 107 Fernando Seguignol SP | 4.00 | 10.00 |
| 108 Mike Kinkade SP | 4.00 | 10.00 |
| 109 Mike Lowell SP | 4.00 | 10.00 |
| 110 Ricky Ledee SP | 4.00 | 10.00 |
| 111 Eric Chavez SP | 4.00 | 10.00 |
| 112 Abraham Nunez SP | 4.00 | 10.00 |
| 113 Matt Clement SP | 4.00 | 10.00 |
| 114 Ben Davis SP | 4.00 | 10.00 |
| 115 Mike Darr SP | 4.00 | 10.00 |
| 116 Ramon E.Martinez SP RC | 4.00 | 10.00 |
| 117 Carlos Guillen SP | 4.00 | 10.00 |
| 118 Shane Monahan SP | 4.00 | 10.00 |
| 119 J.D. Drew AU | 6.00 | 15.00 |
| 120 Kevin Witt SP | 4.00 | 10.00 |
| 24EAST Ken Griffey Jr. Sample | .75 | 2.00 |

## 2000 SPx

| | | |
|---|---|---|
| COMP.BASIC w/o SP's (90) | 10.00 | 25.00 |
| COMP.UPDATE w/o SP's (30) | 4.00 | 10.00 |
| COMMON CARD (1-90) | .20 | .50 |
| COMMON AU/1500 (91-120) | 4.00 | 10.00 |
| COMMON (121-135/182-196) | 3.00 | 8.00 |
| COMMON (136-151) | 4.00 | 10.00 |
| COMMON CARD (152-181) | .30 | .75 |
| 1 Troy Glaus | .20 | .50 |
| 2 Mo Vaughn | .20 | .50 |
| 3 Ramon Ortiz | .20 | .50 |
| 4 Jeff Bagwell | .30 | .75 |
| 5 Moises Alou | .20 | .50 |
| 6 Craig Biggio | .30 | .75 |
| 7 Jose Lima | .20 | .50 |
| 8 Jason Giambi | .20 | .50 |
| 9 John Jaha | .20 | .50 |
| 10 Matt Stairs | .20 | .50 |
| 11 Chipper Jones | .50 | 1.25 |
| 12 Greg Maddux | .75 | 2.00 |
| 13 Andres Galarraga | .30 | .75 |
| 14 Andruw Jones | .30 | .75 |
| 15 Jeromy Burnitz | .20 | .50 |
| 16 Ron Belliard | .20 | .50 |
| 17 Carlos Delgado | .20 | .50 |
| 18 David Wells | .20 | .50 |
| 19 Tony Batista | .20 | .50 |
| 20 Shannon Stewart | .20 | .50 |
| 21 Sammy Sosa | .50 | 1.25 |
| 22 Mark Grace | .30 | .75 |
| 23 Henry Rodriguez | .20 | .50 |
| 24 Mark McGwire | 1.25 | 3.00 |
| 25 J.D. Drew | .20 | .50 |
| 26 Luis Gonzalez | .20 | .50 |
| 27 Randy Johnson | .50 | 1.25 |
| 28 Matt Williams | .20 | .50 |
| 29 Steve Finley | .20 | .50 |
| 30 Shawn Green | .20 | .50 |
| 31 Kevin Brown | .30 | .75 |
| 32 Gary Sheffield | .30 | .75 |
| 33 Jose Canseco | .30 | .75 |
| 34 Greg Vaughn | .20 | .50 |
| 35 Vladimir Guerrero | .50 | 1.25 |
| 36 Michael Barrett | .20 | .50 |
| 37 Russ Ortiz | .20 | .50 |
| 38 Barry Bonds | 1.25 | 3.00 |
| 39 Jeff Kent | .20 | .50 |
| 40 Richie Sexson | .20 | .50 |
| 41 Manny Ramirez | .30 | .75 |
| 42 Jim Thome | .30 | .75 |
| 43 Roberto Alomar | .30 | .75 |
| 44 Edgar Martinez | .30 | .75 |
| 45 Alex Rodriguez | .75 | 2.00 |
| 46 John Olerud | .20 | .50 |
| 47 Alex Gonzalez | .20 | .50 |
| 48 Cliff Floyd | .20 | .50 |
| 49 Mike Piazza | .75 | 2.00 |
| 50 Al Leiter | .20 | .50 |
| 51 Robin Ventura | .30 | .75 |
| 52 Edgardo Alfonzo | .20 | .50 |
| 53 Albert Belle | .20 | .50 |
| 54 Cal Ripken | 1.50 | 4.00 |
| 55 B.J. Surhoff | .20 | .50 |
| 56 Tony Gwynn | .60 | 1.50 |
| 57 Trevor Hoffman | .20 | .50 |
| 58 Brian Giles | .20 | .50 |
| 59 Jason Kendall | .20 | .50 |
| 60 Kris Benson | .20 | .50 |
| 61 Bob Abreu | .20 | .50 |
| 62 Scott Rolen | .20 | .50 |
| 63 Curt Schilling | .20 | .50 |
| 64 Mike Lieberthal | .20 | .50 |
| 65 Sean Casey | .20 | .50 |
| 66 Dante Bichette | .20 | .50 |
| 67 Ken Griffey Jr. | .75 | 2.00 |
| 68 Pokey Reese | .20 | .50 |
| 69 Mike Sweeney | .20 | .50 |
| 70 Carlos Febles | .20 | .50 |
| 71 Ivan Rodriguez | .30 | .75 |
| 72 Ruben Mateo | .20 | .50 |
| 73 Rafael Palmeiro | .30 | .75 |
| 74 Larry Walker | .30 | .75 |
| 75 Todd Helton | .30 | .75 |
| 76 Nomar Garciaparra | .75 | 2.00 |
| 77 Pedro Martinez | .30 | .75 |
| 78 Troy O'Leary | .20 | .50 |
| 79 Jacque Jones | .20 | .50 |
| 80 Corey Koskie | .20 | .50 |
| 81 Juan Gonzalez | .20 | .50 |
| 82 Dean Palmer | .20 | .50 |
| 83 Juan Encarnacion | .20 | .50 |
| 84 Frank Thomas | .50 | 1.25 |
| 85 Magglio Ordonez | .20 | .50 |
| 86 Paul Konerko | .20 | .50 |
| 87 Bernie Williams | .30 | .75 |
| 88 Derek Jeter | 1.25 | 3.00 |
| 89 Roger Clemens | 1.00 | 2.50 |
| 90 Orlando Hernandez | .20 | .50 |
| 91 Vernon Wells AU/1500 | 10.00 | 25.00 |
| 92 Rick Ankiel AU/1500 | 40.00 | 80.00 |
| 93 Eric Chavez AU/1500 | 10.00 | 25.00 |
| 94 Alfonso Soriano AU/1500 | 30.00 | 60.00 |
| 95 Eric Gagne AU/1500 | 30.00 | 60.00 |
| 96 Rob Bell AU/1500 | 4.00 | 10.00 |
| 97 Matt Riley AU/1500 | 4.00 | 10.00 |
| 98 Josh Beckett AU/1500 | 40.00 | 80.00 |
| 99 Ben Petrick AU/1500 | 4.00 | 10.00 |
| 100 Rob Ramsay AU/1500 | 4.00 | 10.00 |
| 101 Scott Williamson AU/1500 | 4.00 | 10.00 |
| 102 Doug Davis AU/1500 | 6.00 | 15.00 |
| 103 Eric Munson AU/1500 | 4.00 | 10.00 |
| 104 Pat Burrell AU/1500 | 30.00 | 60.00 |
| 105 Jim Morris AU/1500 | 10.00 | 25.00 |
| 106 Gabe Kapler AU/1500 | 15.00 | 40.00 |
| 107 Lance Berkman/1000 | 3.00 | 8.00 |
| 108 Erubiel Durazo AU/1500 | 4.00 | 10.00 |
| 109 Tim Hudson AU/1500 | 15.00 | 40.00 |
| 110 Ben Davis AU/1500 | 4.00 | 10.00 |
| 111 Nick Johnson AU/1500 | 6.00 | 15.00 |
| 112 Octavio Dotel AU/1500 | 4.00 | 10.00 |
| 113 Jerry Hairston/1000 | 3.00 | 8.00 |
| 114 Ruben Mateo/1000 | 3.00 | 8.00 |
| 115 Chris Singleton/1000 | 3.00 | 8.00 |
| 116 Bruce Chen AU/1500 | 4.00 | 10.00 |
| 117 Derrick Gibson/1000 | 3.00 | 8.00 |
| 118 Carlos Beltran AU/500 | 75.00 | 125.00 |
| 119 Freddy Garcia AU/1500 | 6.00 | 15.00 |
| 120 Preston Wilson AU/1500 | 6.00 | 15.00 |
| 121 Brad Wilkerson/1600 RC | 4.00 | 10.00 |
| 122 Roy Oswalt/1600 RC | 60.00 | 120.00 |
| 123 Wascar Serrano/1600 RC | 3.00 | 8.00 |
| 124 Sean Burnett/1600 RC | 3.00 | 8.00 |
| 125 Alex Cabrera/1600 RC | 3.00 | 8.00 |
| 126 Timo Perez/1600 RC | 3.00 | 8.00 |
| 127 Juan Pierre/1600 RC | 4.00 | 10.00 |
| 128 Daylan Holt/1600 RC | 3.00 | 8.00 |
| 129 Tomokazu Ohka/1600 RC | 3.00 | 8.00 |
| 130 Kazuhiro Sasaki/1600 RC | 4.00 | 10.00 |
| 131 Kurt Ainsworth/1600 RC | 3.00 | 8.00 |
| 132 Brent Abernathy/1600 RC | 3.00 | 8.00 |
| 133 Danys Baez/1600 RC | 3.00 | 8.00 |
| 134 Brad Cresse/1600 RC | 3.00 | 8.00 |
| 135 Ryan Franklin/1600 RC | 3.00 | 8.00 |
| 136 Mike Lamb AU/1500 | 6.00 | 15.00 |
| 137 David Espinosa AU/1500 RC | 4.00 | 10.00 |
| 138 Matt Wheatland AU/1500 RC | 4.00 | 10.00 |
| 139 Xavier Nady AU/1500 RC | 15.00 | 40.00 |
| 140 Scott Heard AU/1500 RC | 4.00 | 10.00 |
| 141 P.Coco AU/1500 UER54 RC | 4.00 | 10.00 |
| 142 Justin Miller AU/1500 RC | 4.00 | 10.00 |
| 143 Dave Krynzel AU/1500 RC | 4.00 | 10.00 |
| 144 Dane Sardinha AU/1500 RC | 4.00 | 10.00 |
| 145 Ben Sheets AU/1500 RC | 30.00 | 60.00 |
| 146 Leo Estrella AU/1500 RC | 4.00 | 10.00 |
| 147 Ben Diggins AU/1500 RC | 4.00 | 10.00 |
| 148 Barry Zito AU/1500 RC | 20.00 | 50.00 |
| 149 Joe Torres AU/1500 RC | 4.00 | 10.00 |
| 150 Mike Meyers AU/1500 RC | 4.00 | 10.00 |
| 151 Kris Wilson AU/1500 RC | 4.00 | 10.00 |
| 152 Darin Erstad | .30 | .75 |
| 153 Richard Hidalgo | .30 | .75 |
| 154 Eric Chavez | .30 | .75 |
| 155 B.J. Surhoff | .30 | .75 |
| 156 Richie Sexson | .30 | .75 |
| 157 Raul Mondesi | .30 | .75 |
| 158 Rondell White | .30 | .75 |
| 159 Jim Edmonds | .30 | .75 |
| 160 Curt Schilling | .30 | .75 |
| 161 Tom Goodwin | .30 | .75 |
| 162 Fred McGriff | .50 | 1.25 |
| 163 Jose Vidro | .30 | .75 |
| 164 Ellis Burks | .30 | .75 |
| 165 David Segui | .30 | .75 |
| 166 Aaron Sele | .30 | .75 |
| 167 Henry Rodriguez | .30 | .75 |
| 168 Mike Bordick | .30 | .75 |
| 169 Mike Mussina | .50 | 1.25 |
| 170 Ryan Klesko | .30 | .75 |
| 171 Kevin Young | .30 | .75 |
| 172 Travis Lee | .30 | .75 |
| 173 Aaron Boone | .30 | .75 |
| 174 Jermaine Dye | .30 | .75 |
| 175 Ricky Ledee | .30 | .75 |
| 176 Jeffrey Hammonds | .30 | .75 |
| 177 Carl Everett | .30 | .75 |
| 178 Matt Lawton | .30 | .75 |
| 179 Bobby Higginson | .30 | .75 |
| 180 Charles Johnson | .30 | .75 |
| 181 David Justice | .50 | 1.25 |
| 182 Joey Nation/1600 RC | 3.00 | 8.00 |
| 183 Rico Washington/1600 RC | 3.00 | 8.00 |
| 184 Luis Matos/1600 RC | 3.00 | 8.00 |
| 185 Chris Wakeland/1600 RC | 3.00 | 8.00 |
| 186 Sun Woo Kim/1600 RC | 3.00 | 8.00 |
| 187 Keith Ginter/1600 RC | 3.00 | 8.00 |
| 188 Geraldo Guzman/1600 RC | 3.00 | 8.00 |
| 189 Jay Spurgeon/1600 RC | 3.00 | 8.00 |
| 190 Jace Brewer/1600 RC | 3.00 | 8.00 |
| 191 Juan Guzman/1600 RC | 3.00 | 8.00 |
| 192 Ross Gload/1600 RC | 3.00 | 8.00 |
| 193 Paxton Crawford/1600 RC | 3.00 | 8.00 |
| 194 Ryan Kohlmeier/1600 RC | 3.00 | 8.00 |
| 195 Julio Zuleta/1600 RC | 3.00 | 8.00 |
| 196 Matt Ginter/1600 RC | 3.00 | 8.00 |

## 2001 SPx

| | | |
|---|---|---|
| COMP.BASIC w/o SP's (90) | 10.00 | 25.00 |
| COMP.UPDATE w/o SP's (30) | 4.00 | 10.00 |
| COMMON CARD (1-90) | .20 | .50 |
| COMMON YS (91-120) | 2.00 | 5.00 |

| | | |
|---|---|---|
| COMMON JSY (121-135) | 3.00 | 8.00 |
| COMMON JSY AU (136-150) | 6.00 | 15.00 |
| COMMON CARD (151-180) | .30 | .75 |
| COMMON CARD (181-205) | 2.00 | 5.00 |
| 1 Darin Erstad | .20 | .50 |
| 2 Troy Glaus | .20 | .50 |
| 3 Mo Vaughn | .20 | .50 |
| 4 Johnny Damon | .30 | .75 |
| 5 Jason Giambi | .20 | .50 |
| 6 Tim Hudson | .20 | .50 |
| 7 Miguel Tejada | .20 | .50 |
| 8 Carlos Delgado | .20 | .50 |
| 9 Raul Mondesi | .20 | .50 |
| 10 Tony Batista | .20 | .50 |
| 11 Ben Grieve | .20 | .50 |
| 12 Greg Vaughn | .20 | .50 |
| 13 Juan Gonzalez | .20 | .50 |
| 14 Jim Thome | .30 | .75 |
| 15 Roberto Alomar | .30 | .75 |
| 16 John Olerud | .20 | .50 |
| 17 Edgar Martinez | .20 | .50 |
| 18 Albert Belle | .20 | .50 |
| 19 Cal Ripken | 1.50 | 4.00 |
| 20 Ivan Rodriguez | .30 | .75 |
| 21 Rafael Palmeiro | .20 | .50 |
| 22 Alex Rodriguez | .75 | 2.00 |
| 23 Nomar Garciaparra | .75 | 2.00 |
| 24 Pedro Martinez | .30 | .75 |
| 25 Manny Ramirez Sox | .30 | .75 |
| 26 Jermaine Dye | .20 | .50 |
| 27 Mark Quinn | .20 | .50 |
| 28 Carlos Beltran | .20 | .50 |
| 29 Tony Clark | .20 | .50 |
| 30 Bobby Higginson | .20 | .50 |
| 31 Eric Milton | .20 | .50 |
| 32 Matt Lawton | .20 | .50 |
| 33 Frank Thomas | .50 | 1.25 |
| 34 Magglio Ordonez | .20 | .50 |
| 35 Ray Durham | .20 | .50 |
| 36 David Wells | .20 | .50 |
| 37 Derek Jeter | 1.25 | 3.00 |
| 38 Bernie Williams | .30 | .75 |
| 39 Roger Clemens | 1.00 | 2.50 |
| 40 David Justice | .20 | .50 |
| 41 Jeff Bagwell | .30 | .75 |
| 42 Richard Hidalgo | .20 | .50 |
| 43 Moises Alou | .20 | .50 |
| 44 Chipper Jones | .50 | 1.25 |
| 45 Andruw Jones | .30 | .75 |
| 46 Greg Maddux | .75 | 2.00 |
| 47 Rafael Furcal | .20 | .50 |
| 48 Jeromy Burnitz | .20 | .50 |
| 49 Geoff Jenkins | .20 | .50 |
| 50 Mark McGwire | 1.25 | 3.00 |
| 51 Jim Edmonds | .20 | .50 |
| 52 Rick Ankiel | .20 | .50 |
| 53 Edgar Renteria | .20 | .50 |
| 54 Sammy Sosa | .50 | 1.25 |
| 55 Kerry Wood | .20 | .50 |
| 56 Rondell White | .20 | .50 |
| 57 Randy Johnson | .50 | 1.25 |
| 58 Steve Finley | .20 | .50 |
| 59 Matt Williams | .20 | .50 |
| 60 Luis Gonzalez | .20 | .50 |
| 61 Kevin Brown | .20 | .50 |
| 62 Gary Sheffield | .20 | .50 |
| 63 Shawn Green | .20 | .50 |
| 64 Vladimir Guerrero | .50 | 1.25 |
| 65 Jose Vidro | .20 | .50 |
| 66 Barry Bonds | 1.25 | 3.00 |
| 67 Jeff Kent | .20 | .50 |
| 68 Livan Hernandez | .20 | .50 |
| 69 Preston Wilson | .20 | .50 |
| 70 Charles Johnson | .20 | .50 |
| 71 Cliff Floyd | .20 | .50 |
| 72 Mike Piazza | .75 | 2.00 |
| 73 Edgardo Alfonzo | .20 | .50 |
| 74 Jay Payton | .20 | .50 |
| 75 Robin Ventura | .20 | .50 |
| 76 Tony Gwynn | .60 | 1.50 |
| 77 Phil Nevin | .20 | .50 |
| 78 Ryan Klesko | .20 | .50 |
| 79 Scott Rolen | .30 | .75 |
| 80 Pat Burrell | .20 | .50 |
| 81 Bob Abreu | .20 | .50 |
| 82 Brian Giles | .20 | .50 |
| 83 Kris Benson | .20 | .50 |
| 84 Jason Kendall | .20 | .50 |
| 85 Ken Griffey Jr. | .75 | 2.00 |
| 86 Barry Larkin | .30 | .75 |
| 87 Sean Casey | .20 | .50 |
| 88 Todd Helton | .30 | .75 |
| 89 Larry Walker | .20 | .50 |
| 90 Mike Hampton | .20 | .50 |
| 91 Billy Sylvester YS RC | 2.00 | 5.00 |
| 92 Josh Towers YS RC | 3.00 | 8.00 |
| 93 Zach Day YS RC | 2.00 | 5.00 |
| 94 Martin Vargas YS RC | 2.00 | 5.00 |
| 95 Adam Pettyjohn YS RC | 2.00 | 5.00 |
| 96 Andres Torres YS RC | 2.00 | 5.00 |
| 97 Kris Keller YS RC | 2.00 | 5.00 |
| 98 Blaine Neal YS RC | 2.00 | 5.00 |
| 99 Kyle Kessel YS RC | 2.00 | 5.00 |
| 100 Greg Miller YS RC | 2.00 | 5.00 |
| 101 Shawn Sonnier YS | 2.00 | 5.00 |
| 102 Alexis Gomez YS RC | 2.00 | 5.00 |
| 103 Grant Balfour YS RC | 2.00 | 5.00 |
| 104 Henry Mateo YS RC | 2.00 | 5.00 |
| 105 Wilken Ruan YS RC | 2.00 | 5.00 |
| 106 Nick Maness YS RC | 2.00 | 5.00 |
| 107 Jason Michaels YS RC | 2.00 | 5.00 |
| 108 Esix Snead YS RC | 2.00 | 5.00 |
| 109 William Ortega YS RC | 2.00 | 5.00 |
| 110 David Elder YS RC | 2.00 | 5.00 |
| 111 Jackson Melian YS RC | 2.00 | 5.00 |
| 112 Nate Teut YS RC | 2.00 | 5.00 |
| 113 Jason Smith YS RC | 2.00 | 5.00 |
| 114 Mike Penney YS RC | 2.00 | 5.00 |
| 115 Jose Mieses YS RC | 2.00 | 5.00 |
| 116 Juan Pena YS | 2.00 | 5.00 |
| 117 Brian Lawrence YS RC | 2.00 | 5.00 |
| 118 Jeremy Owens YS RC | 2.00 | 5.00 |
| 119 Carlos Valderrama YS RC | 2.00 | 5.00 |
| 120 Rafael Soriano YS RC | 2.00 | 5.00 |
| 121 Horacio Ramirez JSY RC | 4.00 | 10.00 |
| 122 Ricardo Rodriguez JSY RC | 3.00 | 8.00 |
| 123 Juan Diaz JSY RC | 3.00 | 8.00 |
| 124 Donnie Bridges JSY | 3.00 | 8.00 |
| 125 Tyler Walker JSY RC | 3.00 | 8.00 |
| 126 Erick Almonte JSY RC | 3.00 | 8.00 |
| 127 Jesus Colome JSY | 3.00 | 8.00 |
| 128 Ryan Freel JSY RC | 4.00 | 10.00 |
| 129 Elpidio Guzman JSY RC | 3.00 | 8.00 |
| 130 Jack Cust JSY | 3.00 | 8.00 |
| 131 Eric Hinske JSY RC | 4.00 | 10.00 |
| 132 Josh Fogg JSY RC | 4.00 | 10.00 |
| 133 Juan Uribe JSY RC | 4.00 | 10.00 |
| 134 Bert Snow JSY RC | 3.00 | 8.00 |
| 135 Pedro Feliz JSY | 3.00 | 8.00 |
| 136 Wilson Betemit JSY AU RC | 15.00 | 40.00 |
| 137 Sean Douglass JSY AU | 6.00 | 15.00 |
| 138 Demell Stenson JSY AU | 6.00 | 15.00 |
| 139 Brandon Inge JSY AU | 10.00 | 25.00 |
| 140 Mor.Ensberg JSY AU RC | 15.00 | 40.00 |
| 141 Brian Cole JSY AU | 6.00 | 15.00 |
| 142 A.Hernandez JSY AU RC | 6.00 | 15.00 |
| 143 B.Duckworth JSY AU RC | 6.00 | 15.00 |
| 144 Jack Wilson JSY AU RC | 10.00 | 25.00 |
| 145 Travis Hafner JSY AU | 40.00 | 80.00 |
| 146 Carlos Pena JSY AU | 10.00 | 25.00 |
| 147 Corey Patterson JSY AU | 6.00 | 15.00 |
| 148 Xavier Nady JSY AU | 6.00 | 15.00 |
| 149 Jason Hart JSY AU | 6.00 | 15.00 |
| 150 I.Suzuki JSY AU RC | 700.00 | 900.00 |
| 151 Garret Anderson | .30 | .75 |
| 152 Jermaine Dye | .30 | .75 |
| 153 Shannon Stewart | .30 | .75 |
| 154 Toby Hall | .30 | .75 |
| 155 C.C. Sabathia | .30 | .75 |
| 156 Bret Boone | .30 | .75 |
| 157 Tony Batista | .30 | .75 |
| 158 Gabe Kapler | .30 | .75 |
| 159 Carl Everett | .30 | .75 |
| 160 Mike Sweeney | .30 | .75 |
| 161 Dean Palmer | .30 | .75 |
| 162 Doug Mientkiewicz | .30 | .75 |
| 163 Carlos Lee | .30 | .75 |
| 164 Mike Mussina | .50 | 1.25 |
| 165 Lance Berkman | .30 | .75 |
| 166 Ken Caminiti | .30 | .75 |
| 167 Ben Sheets | .50 | 1.25 |
| 168 Matt Morris | .30 | .75 |
| 169 Fred McGriff | .50 | 1.25 |
| 170 Curt Schilling | .50 | 1.25 |
| 171 Paul LoDuca | .30 | .75 |
| 172 Javier Vazquez | .30 | .75 |
| 173 Rich Aurilia | .30 | .75 |
| 174 A.J. Burnett | .30 | .75 |
| 175 Al Leiter | .30 | .75 |
| 176 Mark Kotsay | .30 | .75 |
| 177 Jimmy Rollins | .30 | .75 |
| 178 Aramis Ramirez | .30 | .75 |
| 179 Aaron Boone | .30 | .75 |
| 180 Jeff Cirillo | .30 | .75 |
| 181 Johnny Estrada YS RC | 3.00 | 8.00 |
| 182 Dave Williams YS RC | 2.00 | 5.00 |
| 183 Donaldo Mendez YS RC | 2.00 | 5.00 |
| 184 Junior Spivey YS RC | 3.00 | 8.00 |
| 185 Jay Gibbons YS RC | 3.00 | 8.00 |
| 186 Kyle Lohse YS RC | 3.00 | 8.00 |
| 187 Willie Harris YS RC | 2.00 | 5.00 |
| 188 Juan Cruz YS RC | 2.00 | 5.00 |
| 189 Joe Kennedy YS RC | 3.00 | 8.00 |
| 190 Duaner Sanchez YS RC | 2.00 | 5.00 |
| 191 Jorge Julio YS RC | 2.00 | 5.00 |
| 192 Cesar Crespo YS RC | 2.00 | 5.00 |
| 193 Casey Fossum YS RC | 2.00 | 5.00 |
| 194 Brian Roberts YS RC | 6.00 | 15.00 |
| 195 Troy Mattes YS RC | 2.00 | 5.00 |
| 196 Rob Mackowiak YS RC | 3.00 | 8.00 |
| 197 Tsuyoshi Shinjo YS RC | 3.00 | 8.00 |
| 198 Nick Punto YS RC | 2.00 | 5.00 |
| 199 Wilmy Caceres YS RC | 2.00 | 5.00 |
| 200 Jeremy Affeldt YS RC | 3.00 | 8.00 |
| 201 Bret Prinz YS RC | 2.00 | 5.00 |
| 202 Delvin James YS RC | 2.00 | 5.00 |
| 203 Luis Pineda YS RC | 2.00 | 5.00 |
| 204 Matt White YS RC | 2.00 | 5.00 |
| 205 Brandon Knight YS RC | 2.00 | 5.00 |
| 206 Albert Pujols YS AU RC | 350.00 | 600.00 |
| 207 Mark Teixeira YS AU RC | 75.00 | 150.00 |
| 208 Mark Prior YS AU RC | 15.00 | 40.00 |
| 209 Dewon Brazelton YS AU RC | 6.00 | 15.00 |
| 210 Bud Smith YS AU RC | 6.00 | 15.00 |

## 2002 SPx

| | | |
|---|---|---|
| COMP LOW w/o SP's (90) | 10.00 | 25.00 |
| COMP UPDATE w/o SP's (90) | 4.00 | 10.00 |
| COMMON CARD (1-90) | .20 | .50 |
| COMMON CARD (91-120) | 3.00 | 8.00 |
| COMMON CARD (121-150) | 6.00 | 15.00 |
| COMMON CARD (151-190) | 3.00 | 8.00 |
| COMMON CARD (191-220) | .30 | .75 |
| COMMON CARD (221-250) | 4.00 | 10.00 |
| 1 Troy Glaus | .20 | .50 |
| 2 Darin Erstad | .20 | .50 |
| 3 David Justice | .20 | .50 |
| 4 Tim Hudson | .20 | .50 |
| 5 Miguel Tejada | .20 | .50 |
| 6 Barry Zito | .20 | .50 |
| 7 Carlos Delgado | .20 | .50 |
| 8 Shannon Stewart | .20 | .50 |
| 9 Greg Vaughn | .20 | .50 |
| 10 Toby Hall | .20 | .50 |
| 11 Jim Thome | .30 | .75 |
| 12 C.C. Sabathia | .20 | .50 |
| 13 Ichiro Suzuki | 1.00 | 2.50 |
| 14 Edgar Martinez | .20 | .50 |
| 15 Freddy Garcia | .20 | .50 |
| 16 Mike Cameron | .20 | .50 |
| 17 Jeff Conine | .20 | .50 |
| 18 Tony Batista | .20 | .50 |
| 19 Alex Rodriguez | .75 | 2.00 |
| 20 Rafael Palmeiro | .30 | .75 |
| 21 Ivan Rodriguez | .30 | .75 |
| 22 Carl Everett | .20 | .50 |
| 23 Pedro Martinez | .30 | .75 |
| 24 Manny Ramirez | .30 | .75 |
| 25 Nomar Garciaparra | .75 | 2.00 |
| 26 Johnny Damon Sox | .20 | .50 |

|  |  | | |
|---|---|---|---|
| 27 | Mike Sweeney | .20 | .50 |
| 28 | Carlos Beltran | .20 | .50 |
| 29 | Dmitri Young | .20 | .50 |
| 30 | Joe Mays | .20 | .50 |
| 31 | Doug Mientkiewicz | .20 | .50 |
| 32 | Cristian Guzman | .20 | .50 |
| 33 | Corey Koskie | .20 | .50 |
| 34 | Frank Thomas | .50 | 1.25 |
| 35 | Magglio Ordonez | .20 | .50 |
| 36 | Mark Buehrle | .20 | .50 |
| 37 | Bernie Williams | .30 | .75 |
| 38 | Roger Clemens | 1.00 | 2.50 |
| 39 | Derek Jeter | 1.25 | 3.00 |
| 40 | Jason Giambi | .20 | .50 |
| 41 | Mike Mussina | .30 | .75 |
| 42 | Lance Berkman | .20 | .50 |
| 43 | Jeff Bagwell | .30 | .75 |
| 44 | Roy Oswalt | .20 | .50 |
| 45 | Greg Maddux | .75 | 2.00 |
| 46 | Chipper Jones | .50 | 1.25 |
| 47 | Andruw Jones | .30 | .75 |
| 48 | Gary Sheffield | .20 | .50 |
| 49 | Geoff Jenkins | .20 | .50 |
| 50 | Richie Sexson | .20 | .50 |
| 51 | Ben Sheets | .20 | .50 |
| 52 | Albert Pujols | 1.00 | 2.50 |
| 53 | J.D. Drew | .20 | .50 |
| 54 | Jim Edmonds | .20 | .50 |
| 55 | Sammy Sosa | .50 | 1.25 |
| 56 | Moises Alou | .20 | .50 |
| 57 | Kerry Wood | .20 | .50 |
| 58 | Jon Lieber | .20 | .50 |
| 59 | Fred McGriff | .30 | .75 |
| 60 | Randy Johnson | .50 | 1.25 |
| 61 | Luis Gonzalez | .20 | .50 |
| 62 | Curt Schilling | .30 | .75 |
| 63 | Kevin Brown | .20 | .50 |
| 64 | Hideo Nomo | .50 | 1.25 |
| 65 | Shawn Green | .50 | 1.25 |
| 66 | Vladimir Guerrero | .50 | 1.25 |
| 67 | Jose Vidro | .20 | .50 |
| 68 | Barry Bonds | 1.25 | 3.00 |
| 69 | Jeff Kent | .20 | .50 |
| 70 | Rich Aurilia | .20 | .50 |
| 71 | Cliff Floyd | .20 | .50 |
| 72 | Josh Beckett | .20 | .50 |
| 73 | Preston Wilson | .20 | .50 |
| 74 | Mike Piazza | .75 | 2.00 |
| 75 | Mo Vaughn | .20 | .50 |
| 76 | Jeromy Burnitz | .20 | .50 |
| 77 | Roberto Alomar | .30 | .75 |
| 78 | Phil Nevin | .20 | .50 |
| 79 | Ryan Klesko | .20 | .50 |
| 80 | Scott Rolen | .30 | .75 |
| 81 | Bobby Abreu | .20 | .50 |
| 82 | Jimmy Rollins | .20 | .50 |
| 83 | Brian Giles | .20 | .50 |
| 84 | Aramis Ramirez | .20 | .50 |
| 85 | Ken Griffey Jr. | .75 | 2.00 |
| 86 | Sean Casey | .20 | .50 |
| 87 | Barry Larkin | .30 | .75 |
| 88 | Mike Hampton | .20 | .50 |
| 89 | Larry Walker | .20 | .50 |
| 90 | Todd Helton | .30 | .75 |
| 91A | Ron Calloway YS RC | 3.00 | 8.00 |
| 91P | Ron Calloway YS RC | 3.00 | 8.00 |
| 92A | Joe Orloski YS RC | 3.00 | 8.00 |
| 92P | Joe Orloski YS RC | 3.00 | 8.00 |
| 93A | Anderson Machado YS RC | 3.00 | 8.00 |
| 93P | Anderson Machado YS RC | 3.00 | 8.00 |
| 94A | Eric Good YS RC | 3.00 | 8.00 |
| 94P | Eric Good YS RC | 3.00 | 8.00 |
| 95A | Reed Johnson YS RC | 4.00 | 10.00 |
| 95P | Reed Johnson YS RC | 4.00 | 10.00 |
| 96A | Brendan Donnelly YS RC | 3.00 | 8.00 |
| 96P | Brendan Donnelly YS RC | 3.00 | 8.00 |
| 97A | Chris Baker YS RC | 3.00 | 8.00 |
| 97P | Chris Baker YS RC | 3.00 | 8.00 |
| 98A | Wilson Valdez YS RC | 3.00 | 8.00 |
| 98P | Wilson Valdez YS RC | 3.00 | 8.00 |
| 99A | Scotty Layfield YS RC | 3.00 | 8.00 |
| 99P | Scotty Layfield YS RC | 3.00 | 8.00 |
| 100A | P.J. Bevis YS RC | 3.00 | 8.00 |
| 100P | P.J. Bevis YS RC | 3.00 | 8.00 |
| 101A | Edwin Almonte YS RC | 3.00 | 8.00 |
| 101P | Edwin Almonte YS RC | 3.00 | 8.00 |
| 102A | Francis Beltran YS RC | 3.00 | 8.00 |
| 102P | Francis Beltran YS RC | 3.00 | 8.00 |
| 103A | Val Pascucci YS | 3.00 | 8.00 |
| 103P | Val Pascucci YS | 3.00 | 8.00 |
| 104A | Nelson Castro YS RC | 3.00 | 8.00 |
| 104P | Nelson Castro YS RC | 3.00 | 8.00 |
| 105A | Michael Crudale YS RC | 3.00 | 8.00 |
| 105P | Michael Crudale YS RC | 3.00 | 8.00 |
| 106A | Colin Young YS RC | 3.00 | 8.00 |
| 106P | Colin Young YS RC | 3.00 | 8.00 |
| 107A | Todd Donovan YS RC | 3.00 | 8.00 |
| 107P | Todd Donovan YS RC | 3.00 | 8.00 |
| 108A | Felix Escalona YS RC | 3.00 | 8.00 |
| 108P | Felix Escalona YS RC | 3.00 | 8.00 |
| 109A | Brandon Backe YS RC | 4.00 | 10.00 |
| 109P | Brandon Backe YS RC | 4.00 | 10.00 |
| 110A | Corey Thurman YS RC | 3.00 | 8.00 |
| 110P | Corey Thurman YS RC | 3.00 | 8.00 |
| 111A | Kyle Kane YS RC | 3.00 | 8.00 |
| 111P | Kyle Kane YS RC | 3.00 | 8.00 |
| 112A | Allan Simpson YS RC | 3.00 | 8.00 |
| 112P | Allan Simpson YS RC | 3.00 | 8.00 |
| 113A | Jose Valverde YS RC | 3.00 | 8.00 |
| 113P | Jose Valverde YS RC | 3.00 | 8.00 |
| 114A | Chris Booker YS RC | 3.00 | 8.00 |
| 114P | Chris Booker YS RC | 3.00 | 8.00 |
| 115A | Brandon Puffer YS RC | 3.00 | 8.00 |
| 115P | Brandon Puffer YS RC | 3.00 | 8.00 |
| 116A | John Foster YS RC | 3.00 | 8.00 |
| 116P | John Foster YS RC | 3.00 | 8.00 |
| 117A | Cliff Bartosh YS RC | 3.00 | 8.00 |
| 117P | Cliff Bartosh YS RC | 3.00 | 8.00 |
| 118A | Gustavo Chacin YS RC | 4.00 | 10.00 |
| 118P | Gustavo Chacin YS RC | 4.00 | 10.00 |
| 119A | Steve Kent YS RC | 3.00 | 8.00 |
| 119P | Steve Kent YS RC | 3.00 | 8.00 |
| 120A | Nate Field YS RC | 3.00 | 8.00 |
| 120P | Nate Field YS RC | 3.00 | 8.00 |
| 121 | Victor Alvarez AU RC | 4.00 | 10.00 |
| 122 | Steve Bechler AU RC | 4.00 | 10.00 |
| 123 | Adrian Burnside AU RC | 4.00 | 10.00 |
| 124 | Marlon Byrd AU | 6.00 | 15.00 |
| 125 | Jaime Cerda AU RC | 4.00 | 10.00 |
| 126 | Brandon Claussen AU | 6.00 | 15.00 |
| 127 | Mark Corey AU RC | 4.00 | 10.00 |
| 128 | Doug Devore AU RC | 4.00 | 10.00 |
| 129 | Kazuhisa Ishii AU SP RC | 30.00 | 60.00 |
| 130 | John Ennis AU RC | 4.00 | 10.00 |
| 131 | Kevin Frederick AU RC | 4.00 | 10.00 |
| 132 | Josh Hancock AU RC | 8.00 | 20.00 |
| 133 | Ben Howard AU RC | 4.00 | 10.00 |
| 134 | Orlando Hudson AU | 6.00 | 15.00 |
| 135 | Hansel Izquierdo AU RC | 4.00 | 10.00 |
| 136 | Eric Junge AU RC | 4.00 | 10.00 |
| 137 | Austin Kearns AU | 6.00 | 15.00 |
| 138 | Victor Martinez AU | 10.00 | 25.00 |
| 139 | Luis Martinez AU RC | 4.00 | 10.00 |
| 140 | Danny Mota AU RC | 4.00 | 10.00 |
| 141 | Jorge Padilla AU RC | 4.00 | 10.00 |
| 142 | Andy Pratt AU RC | 4.00 | 10.00 |
| 143 | Rene Reyes AU RC | 4.00 | 10.00 |
| 144 | Rodrigo Rosario AU RC | 4.00 | 10.00 |
| 145 | Tom Sheam AU RC | 4.00 | 10.00 |
| 146 | So Taguchi AU SP RC | 10.00 | 25.00 |
| 147 | Dennis Tankersley AU | 6.00 | 15.00 |
| 148 | Matt Thornton AU RC | 4.00 | 10.00 |
| 149 | Jeremy Ward AU RC | 4.00 | 10.00 |
| 150 | Mitch Wylie AU RC | 4.00 | 10.00 |
| 151 | Pedro Martinez JSY/800 | 4.00 | 10.00 |
| 152 | Cal Ripken JSY/800 | 10.00 | 25.00 |
| 153 | Roger Clemens JSY/800 | 6.00 | 15.00 |
| 154 | Bernie Williams JSY/800 | 4.00 | 10.00 |
| 155 | Jason Giambi JSY/700 | 3.00 | 8.00 |
| 156 | Robin Ventura JSY/800 | 3.00 | 8.00 |
| 157 | Carlos Delgado JSY/800 | 3.00 | 8.00 |
| 158 | Frank Thomas JSY/800 | 6.00 | 15.00 |
| 159 | Magglio Ordonez JSY/800 | 3.00 | 8.00 |
| 160 | Jim Thome JSY/800 | 4.00 | 10.00 |
| 161 | Darin Erstad JSY/800 | 3.00 | 8.00 |
| 162 | Tim Salmon JSY/800 | 3.00 | 8.00 |
| 163 | Tim Hudson JSY/800 | 3.00 | 8.00 |
| 164 | Barry Zito JSY/800 | 3.00 | 8.00 |
| 165 | Ichiro Suzuki JSY/800 | 10.00 | 25.00 |
| 166 | Edgar Martinez JSY/800 | 4.00 | 10.00 |
| 167 | Alex Rodriguez JSY/800 | 6.00 | 15.00 |
| 168 | Ivan Rodriguez JSY/800 | 4.00 | 10.00 |
| 169 | Juan Gonzalez JSY/800 | 4.00 | 10.00 |
| 170 | Greg Maddux JSY/800 | 6.00 | 15.00 |
| 171 | Chipper Jones JSY/800 | 4.00 | 10.00 |
| 172 | Andruw Jones JSY/800 | 4.00 | 10.00 |
| 173 | Tom Glavine JSY/800 | 4.00 | 10.00 |
| 174 | Mike Piazza JSY/800 | 6.00 | 15.00 |
| 175 | Roberto Alomar JSY/800 | 4.00 | 10.00 |
| 176 | Scott Rolen JSY/800 | 4.00 | 10.00 |
| 177 | Sammy Sosa JSY/800 | 4.00 | 10.00 |
| 178 | Moises Alou JSY/800 | 3.00 | 8.00 |
| 179 | Ken Griffey Jr. JSY/700 | 8.00 | 20.00 |
| 180 | Jeff Bagwell JSY/800 | 4.00 | 10.00 |
| 181 | Jim Edmonds JSY/800 | 3.00 | 8.00 |
| 182 | J.D. Drew JSY/800 | 3.00 | 8.00 |
| 183 | Brian Giles JSY/800 | 3.00 | 8.00 |
| 184 | Randy Johnson JSY/800 | 4.00 | 10.00 |
| 185 | Curt Schilling JSY/800 | 3.00 | 8.00 |
| 186 | Luis Gonzalez JSY/800 | 3.00 | 8.00 |
| 187 | Todd Helton JSY/800 | 4.00 | 10.00 |
| 188 | Shawn Green JSY/800 | 3.00 | 8.00 |
| 189 | David Wells JSY/800 | 3.00 | 8.00 |
| 190 | Jeff Kent JSY/800 | 3.00 | 8.00 |
| 191 | Tom Glavine | .50 | 1.25 |
| 192 | Cliff Floyd | .30 | .75 |
| 193 | Mark Prior | .50 | 1.25 |
| 194 | Corey Patterson | .30 | .75 |
| 195 | Paul Konerko | .30 | .75 |
| 196 | Adam Dunn | .30 | .75 |
| 197 | Joe Borchard | .30 | .75 |
| 198 | Carlos Pena | .30 | .75 |
| 199 | Juan Encarnacion | .30 | .75 |
| 200 | Luis Castillo | .30 | .75 |
| 201 | Torii Hunter | .30 | .75 |
| 202 | Hee Seop Choi | .30 | .75 |
| 203 | Bartolo Colon | .30 | .75 |
| 204 | Raul Mondesi | .30 | .75 |
| 205 | Jeff Weaver | .30 | .75 |
| 206 | Eric Munson | .30 | .75 |
| 207 | Alfonso Soriano | .30 | .75 |
| 208 | Ray Durham | .30 | .75 |
| 209 | Eric Chavez | .30 | .75 |
| 210 | Brett Myers | .30 | .75 |
| 211 | Jeremy Giambi | .30 | .75 |
| 212 | Vicente Padilla | .30 | .75 |
| 213 | Felipe Lopez | .30 | .75 |
| 214 | Sean Burroughs | .30 | .75 |
| 215 | Kenny Lofton | .30 | .75 |
| 216 | Scott Rolen | .50 | 1.25 |
| 217 | Carl Crawford | .30 | .75 |
| 218 | Juan Gonzalez | .30 | .75 |
| 219 | Orlando Hudson | .30 | .75 |
| 220 | Eric Hinske | .30 | .75 |
| 221 | Adam Walker AU RC | 4.00 | 10.00 |
| 222 | Aaron Cook AU RC | 6.00 | 15.00 |
| 223 | Cam Esslinger AU RC | 4.00 | 10.00 |
| 224 | Kirk Saarloos AU RC | 4.00 | 10.00 |
| 225 | Jose Diaz AU RC | 4.00 | 10.00 |
| 226 | David Ross AU RC | 10.00 | 25.00 |
| 227 | Jorge Durocher AU RC | 4.00 | 10.00 |
| 228 | Brian Mallette AU RC | 4.00 | 10.00 |
| 229 | Aaron Guiel AU RC | 4.00 | 10.00 |
| 230 | Jorge Nunez AU RC | 4.00 | 10.00 |
| 231 | Satoru Komiyama AU RC | 10.00 | 25.00 |
| 232 | Tyler Yates AU RC | 4.00 | 10.00 |
| 233 | Pete Zamora AU RC | 4.00 | 10.00 |
| 234 | Mike Gonzalez AU RC | 4.00 | 10.00 |
| 235 | Oliver Perez AU RC | 12.50 | 30.00 |
| 236 | Julius Matos AU RC | 4.00 | 10.00 |
| 237 | Andy Shibilo AU RC | 4.00 | 10.00 |
| 238 | Jason Simontacchi AU RC | 4.00 | 10.00 |
| 239 | Ron Chiavacci AU RC | 4.00 | 10.00 |
| 240 | Deivis Santos AU RC | 4.00 | 10.00 |
| 241 | Travis Driskill AU RC | 4.00 | 10.00 |
| 242 | Jorge De La Rosa AU RC | 4.00 | 10.00 |
| 243 | Anastacio Martinez AU RC | 4.00 | 10.00 |
| 244 | Earl Snyder AU RC | 4.00 | 10.00 |
| 245 | Freddy Sanchez AU RC | 12.50 | 30.00 |
| 246 | Miguel Asencio AU RC | 4.00 | 10.00 |
| 247 | Juan Brito AU RC | 4.00 | 10.00 |
| 248 | Franklyn German AU RC | 4.00 | 10.00 |
| 249 | Chris Snelling AU RC | 6.00 | 15.00 |
| 250 | Ken Huckaby AU RC | 4.00 | 10.00 |

## 2003 SPx

| | | |
|---|---|---|
| COMP.LO SET w/o SP's (100) | 10.00 | 25.00 |
| COMP.LO SET w/ SP's (125) | 50.00 | 100.00 |
| COMMON CARD (1-125) | .20 | .50 |
| COMMON SP (1-125) | 1.50 | 4.00 |
| COMMON CARD (126-160) | 3.00 | 8.00 |
| COMMON CARD (161-178) | 6.00 | 15.00 |
| 163-178 PRINT RUN 1224 SERIAL #'d SETS | | |

| | | |
|---|---|---|
| ❑ 126-178 RANDOM INSERTS IN SPx PACKS | | |
| ❑ COMMON CARD (179-193) | 6.00 | 15.00 |
| ❑ COMMON CARD (381-387) | 6.00 | 15.00 |
| ❑ 1 Darin Erstad | .20 | .50 |
| ❑ 2 Garret Anderson | .20 | .50 |
| ❑ 3 Tim Salmon | .30 | .75 |
| ❑ 4 Troy Glaus SP | 1.50 | 4.00 |
| ❑ 5 Luis Gonzalez | .20 | .50 |
| ❑ 6 Randy Johnson | .50 | 1.25 |
| ❑ 7 Curt Schilling | .50 | 1.25 |
| ❑ 8 Lyle Overbay | .20 | .50 |
| ❑ 9 Andruw Jones SP | 1.50 | 4.00 |
| ❑ 10 Gary Sheffield | .20 | .50 |
| ❑ 11 Rafael Furcal | .20 | .50 |
| ❑ 12 Greg Maddux | .75 | 2.00 |
| ❑ 13 Chipper Jones SP | 2.00 | 5.00 |
| ❑ 14 Tony Batista | .20 | .50 |
| ❑ 15 Rodrigo Lopez | .20 | .50 |
| ❑ 16 Jay Gibbons | .20 | .50 |
| ❑ 17 Byung-Hyun Kim | .20 | .50 |
| ❑ 18 Johnny Damon | .30 | .75 |
| ❑ 19 Derek Lowe | .20 | .50 |
| ❑ 20 Nomar Garciaparra SP | 3.00 | 8.00 |
| ❑ 21 Pedro Martinez | .30 | .75 |
| ❑ 22 Manny Ramirez SP | 1.50 | 4.00 |
| ❑ 23 Mark Prior | .50 | 1.25 |
| ❑ 24 Kerry Wood | .20 | .50 |
| ❑ 25 Corey Patterson | .20 | .50 |
| ❑ 26 Sammy Sosa SP | 2.00 | 5.00 |
| ❑ 27 Moises Alou | .20 | .50 |
| ❑ 28 Magglio Ordonez | .20 | .50 |
| ❑ 29 Frank Thomas | .50 | 1.25 |
| ❑ 30 Paul Konerko | .20 | .50 |
| ❑ 31 Bartolo Colon | .20 | .50 |
| ❑ 32 Adam Dunn | .20 | .50 |
| ❑ 33 Austin Kearns | .20 | .50 |
| ❑ 34 Aaron Boone | .20 | .50 |
| ❑ 35 Ken Griffey Jr. SP | 3.00 | 8.00 |
| ❑ 36 Omar Vizquel | .20 | .50 |
| ❑ 37 C.C. Sabathia | .20 | .50 |
| ❑ 38 Jason Davis | .20 | .50 |
| ❑ 39 Travis Hafner | .20 | .50 |
| ❑ 40 Brandon Phillips | .20 | .50 |
| ❑ 41 Larry Walker | .20 | .50 |
| ❑ 42 Preston Wilson | .20 | .50 |
| ❑ 43 Jay Payton | .20 | .50 |
| ❑ 44 Todd Helton | .30 | .75 |
| ❑ 45 Carlos Pena | .20 | .50 |
| ❑ 46 Eric Munson | .20 | .50 |
| ❑ 47 Ivan Rodriguez | .30 | .75 |
| ❑ 48 Josh Beckett | .20 | .50 |
| ❑ 49 Alex Gonzalez | .20 | .50 |
| ❑ 50 Roy Oswalt | .20 | .50 |
| ❑ 51 Craig Biggio | .30 | .75 |
| ❑ 52 Jeff Bagwell | .50 | 1.25 |
| ❑ 53 Dontrelle Willis SP | 2.00 | 5.00 |
| ❑ 54 Mike Sweeney | .20 | .50 |
| ❑ 55 Carlos Beltran | .20 | .50 |
| ❑ 56 Brent Mayne | .20 | .50 |
| ❑ 57 Hideo Nomo | .50 | 1.25 |
| ❑ 58 Rickey Henderson | .50 | 1.25 |
| ❑ 59 Adrian Beltre | .20 | .50 |
| ❑ 60 Miguel Cabrera SP | 2.00 | 5.00 |
| ❑ 61 Kazuhisa Ishii | .20 | .50 |
| ❑ 62 Ben Sheets | .20 | .50 |
| ❑ 63 Richie Sexson | .20 | .50 |
| ❑ 64 Torii Hunter SP | 1.50 | 4.00 |
| ❑ 65 Jacque Jones | .20 | .50 |
| ❑ 66 Joe Mays | .20 | .50 |
| ❑ 67 Corey Koskie | .20 | .50 |
| ❑ 68 A.J. Pierzynski | .20 | .50 |
| ❑ 69 Jose Vidro | .20 | .50 |
| ❑ 70 Vladimir Guerrero SP | 2.00 | 5.00 |
| ❑ 71 Tom Glavine | .30 | .75 |

| | | |
|---|---|---|
| ❑ 72 Jose Reyes SP | 1.50 | 4.00 |
| ❑ 73 Aaron Heilman | .20 | .50 |
| ❑ 74 Mike Piazza | .75 | 2.00 |
| ❑ 75 Jorge Posada | .30 | .75 |
| ❑ 76 Mike Mussina | .30 | .75 |
| ❑ 77 Robin Ventura | .20 | .50 |
| ❑ 78 Mariano Rivera | .50 | 1.25 |
| ❑ 79 Roger Clemens SP | 4.00 | 10.00 |
| ❑ 80 Jason Giambi | .20 | .50 |
| ❑ 81 Bernie Williams | .30 | .75 |
| ❑ 82 Alfonso Soriano SP | 1.50 | 4.00 |
| ❑ 83 Derek Jeter SP | 5.00 | 12.00 |
| ❑ 84 Miguel Tejada SP | 1.50 | 4.00 |
| ❑ 85 Eric Chavez | .20 | .50 |
| ❑ 86 Tim Hudson | .20 | .50 |
| ❑ 87 Barry Zito | .20 | .50 |
| ❑ 88 Mark Mulder | .20 | .50 |
| ❑ 89 Erubiel Durazo | .20 | .50 |
| ❑ 90 Pat Burrell | .20 | .50 |
| ❑ 91 Jim Thome SP | 1.50 | 4.00 |
| ❑ 92 Bobby Abreu | .20 | .50 |
| ❑ 93 Brian Giles | .20 | .50 |
| ❑ 94 Reggie Sanders SP | 1.50 | 4.00 |
| ❑ 95 Kenny Lofton | .20 | .50 |
| ❑ 96 Ryan Klesko | .20 | .50 |
| ❑ 97 Sean Burroughs | .20 | .50 |
| ❑ 98 Edgardo Alfonzo | .20 | .50 |
| ❑ 99 Rich Aurilia | .20 | .50 |
| ❑ 100 Jose Cruz Jr. | .20 | .50 |
| ❑ 101 Barry Bonds SP | 5.00 | 12.00 |
| ❑ 102 Mike Cameron | .20 | .50 |
| ❑ 103 Kazuhiro Sasaki | .20 | .50 |
| ❑ 104 Bret Boone | .20 | .50 |
| ❑ 105 Ichiro Suzuki SP | 4.00 | 10.00 |
| ❑ 106 J.D. Drew | .20 | .50 |
| ❑ 107 Jim Edmonds | .20 | .50 |
| ❑ 108 Scott Rolen SP | 1.50 | 4.00 |
| ❑ 109 Matt Morris | .20 | .50 |
| ❑ 110 Tino Martinez | .30 | .75 |
| ❑ 111 Albert Pujols SP | 4.00 | 10.00 |
| ❑ 112 Damian Rolls | .20 | .50 |
| ❑ 113 Carl Crawford | .20 | .50 |
| ❑ 114 Rocco Baldelli SP | 1.50 | 4.00 |
| ❑ 115 Hank Blalock | .20 | .50 |
| ❑ 116 Alex Rodriguez SP | 3.00 | 8.00 |
| ❑ 117 Kevin Mench | .20 | .50 |
| ❑ 118 Rafael Palmeiro | .30 | .75 |
| ❑ 119 Mark Teixeira | .20 | .50 |
| ❑ 120 Shannon Stewart | .20 | .50 |
| ❑ 121 Vernon Wells | .20 | .50 |
| ❑ 122 Josh Phelps | .20 | .50 |
| ❑ 123 Eric Hinske | .20 | .50 |
| ❑ 124 Orlando Hudson | .20 | .50 |
| ❑ 125 Carlos Delgado SP | 1.50 | 4.00 |
| ❑ 126 Jason Roach ROO RC | 3.00 | 8.00 |
| ❑ 127 Dan Haren ROO RC | 4.00 | 10.00 |
| ❑ 128 Luis Ayala ROO RC | 3.00 | 8.00 |
| ❑ 129 Bo Hart ROO RC | 3.00 | 8.00 |
| ❑ 130 Wilfredo Ledezma ROO RC | 3.00 | 8.00 |
| ❑ 131 Rick Roberts ROO RC | 3.00 | 8.00 |
| ❑ 132 Miguel Ojeda ROO RC | 3.00 | 8.00 |
| ❑ 133 Aquilino Lopez ROO RC | 3.00 | 8.00 |
| ❑ 134 Roger Deago ROO RC | 3.00 | 8.00 |
| ❑ 135 Arnie Munoz ROO RC | 3.00 | 8.00 |
| ❑ 136 Brent Hoard ROO RC | 3.00 | 8.00 |
| ❑ 137 Termel Sledge ROO RC | 3.00 | 8.00 |
| ❑ 138 Ryan Cameron ROO RC | 3.00 | 8.00 |
| ❑ 139 Prentice Redman ROO RC | 3.00 | 8.00 |
| ❑ 140 Clint Barmes ROO RC | 2.50 | 8.00 |
| ❑ 141 Jeremy Griffiths ROO RC | 3.00 | 8.00 |
| ❑ 142 Jon Leicester ROO RC | 3.00 | 8.00 |
| ❑ 143 Brandon Webb ROO RC | 5.00 | 12.00 |
| ❑ 144 Todd Wellemeyer ROO RC | 3.00 | 8.00 |
| ❑ 145 Felix Sanchez ROO RC | 3.00 | 8.00 |
| ❑ 146 Anthony Ferrari ROO RC | 3.00 | 8.00 |
| ❑ 147 Ian Ferguson ROO RC | 3.00 | 8.00 |
| ❑ 148 Michael Nakamura ROO RC | 3.00 | 8.00 |
| ❑ 149 Lew Ford ROO RC | 4.00 | 10.00 |
| ❑ 150 Nate Bland ROO RC | 3.00 | 8.00 |
| ❑ 151 David Matranga ROO RC | 3.00 | 8.00 |
| ❑ 152 Edgar Gonzalez ROO RC | 3.00 | 8.00 |
| ❑ 153 Carlos Mendez ROO RC | 3.00 | 8.00 |
| ❑ 154 Jason Gilfillan ROO RC | 3.00 | 8.00 |
| ❑ 155 Mike Neu ROO RC | 3.00 | 8.00 |
| ❑ 156 Jason Shiell ROO RC | 3.00 | 8.00 |
| ❑ 157 Jeff Duncan ROO RC | 3.00 | 8.00 |
| ❑ 158 Oscar Villarreal ROO RC | 3.00 | 8.00 |
| ❑ 159 Diegomar Markwell ROO RC | 3.00 | 8.00 |

| | | |
|---|---|---|
| ❑ 160 Joe Valentine ROO RC | 3.00 | 8.00 |
| ❑ 161 Hideki Matsui AU JSY RC | 150.00 | 250.00 |
| ❑ 162 Jose Contreras AU RC | 20.00 | 40.00 |
| ❑ 163 Willie Eyre AU JSY RC | 6.00 | 15.00 |
| ❑ 164 Matt Bruback AU JSY RC | 6.00 | 15.00 |
| ❑ 165 Rett Johnson AU JSY RC | 6.00 | 15.00 |
| ❑ 166 Jeremy Griffiths AU JSY | 6.00 | 15.00 |
| ❑ 167 Fran Cruceta AU JSY RC | 6.00 | 15.00 |
| ❑ 168 Fern Cabrera AU JSY RC | 6.00 | 15.00 |
| ❑ 169 Jhonny Peralta AU JSY | 6.00 | 15.00 |
| ❑ 170 Shane Bazzell AU JSY RC | 6.00 | 15.00 |
| ❑ 171 Bob Madritsch AU JSY RC | 10.00 | 25.00 |
| ❑ 172 Phil Seibel AU JSY RC | 6.00 | 15.00 |
| ❑ 173 J.Willingham AU JSY RC | 10.00 | 25.00 |
| ❑ 174 Rob Hammock AU JSY RC | 6.00 | 15.00 |
| ❑ 175 A.Machado AU JSY RC | 6.00 | 15.00 |
| ❑ 176 David Sanders AU JSY RC | 6.00 | 15.00 |
| ❑ 177 Matt Kata AU JSY RC | 6.00 | 15.00 |
| ❑ 178 Heath Bell AU JSY RC | 6.00 | 15.00 |
| ❑ 179 Chad Gaudin ROO RC | 6.00 | 15.00 |
| ❑ 180 Chris Capuano ROO RC | 10.00 | 25.00 |
| ❑ 181 Danny Garcia ROO RC | 6.00 | 15.00 |
| ❑ 182 Delmon Young ROO RC | 50.00 | 80.00 |
| ❑ 183 Edwin Jackson ROO RC | 8.00 | 20.00 |
| ❑ 184 Greg Jones ROO RC | 6.00 | 15.00 |
| ❑ 185 Jeremy Bonderman ROO RC | 20.00 | 50.00 |
| ❑ 186 Jorge DePaula ROO RC | 6.00 | 15.00 |
| ❑ 187 Khalil Greene ROO RC | 8.00 | 20.00 |
| ❑ 188 Chad Cordero ROO RC | 10.00 | 25.00 |
| ❑ 189 Miguel Cabrera ROO RC | 8.00 | 20.00 |
| ❑ 190 Rich Harden ROO RC | 8.00 | 20.00 |
| ❑ 191 Rickie Weeks ROO RC | 15.00 | 40.00 |
| ❑ 192 Rosman Garcia ROO RC | 6.00 | 15.00 |
| ❑ 193 Tom Gregorio ROO RC | 6.00 | 15.00 |
| ❑ 381 Andrew Brown AU JSY RC | 6.00 | 15.00 |
| ❑ 382 Delmon Young AU JSY RC | 350.00 | 450.00 |
| ❑ 383 Colin Porter AU JSY RC | 6.00 | 15.00 |
| ❑ 385 Rick. Weeks AU JSY RC | 40.00 | 80.00 |
| ❑ 386 Bob Madritsch AU JSY RC | 6.00 | 15.00 |
| ❑ 387 Bo Hart AU JSY | 6.00 | 15.00 |

## 2004 SPx

| | | |
|---|---|---|
| ❑ COMP.SET w/o SP's (100) | 10.00 | 25.00 |
| ❑ COMMON CARD (1-100) | .20 | .50 |
| ❑ COMMON CARD (101-110) | 3.00 | 8.00 |
| ❑ 101-110 STATED ODDS 1:18 | | |
| ❑ COMMON CARD (111-145) | 2.00 | 5.00 |
| ❑ 111-145 PRINT RUN 1599 SERIAL #'d SETS | | |
| ❑ COMMON CARD (146-154) | 3.00 | 8.00 |
| ❑ 146-154 PRINT RUN 499 SERIAL #'d SETS | | |
| ❑ COMMON CARD (155-160) | 3.00 | 8.00 |
| ❑ 155-160 PRINT RUN 299 SERIAL #'d SETS | | |
| ❑ 111-160 ODDS W/SPECTRUM 1:9 | | |
| ❑ 161-202 ODDS W/SPECTRUM 1:18 | | |
| ❑ 161-202 PRINT RUN 799 SERIAL #'d SETS | | |
| ❑ EXCHANGE DEADLINE 12/03/07 | | |
| ❑ MASTER PLATE ODDS 1:2500 | | |
| ❑ MASTER PLATE PRINT RUN 1 #'d SET | | |
| ❑ NO PLATE PRICING DUE TO SCARCITY | | |
| ❑ 1 Alfonso Soriano | .20 | .50 |
| ❑ 2 Todd Helton | .30 | .75 |
| ❑ 3 Andruw Jones | .20 | .50 |
| ❑ 4 Eric Gagne | .20 | .50 |
| ❑ 5 Craig Wilson | .20 | .50 |
| ❑ 6 Brian Giles | .20 | .50 |
| ❑ 7 Miguel Tejada | .20 | .50 |
| ❑ 8 Kevin Brown | .20 | .50 |
| ❑ 9 Shawn Green | .20 | .50 |
| ❑ 10 Ben Sheets | .20 | .50 |
| ❑ 11 John Smoltz | .30 | .75 |
| ❑ 12 Tim Hudson | .20 | .50 |
| ❑ 13 Jason Schmidt | .20 | .50 |
| ❑ 14 Paul Konerko | .20 | .50 |
| ❑ 15 Randy Johnson | .50 | 1.25 |

|  |  | | |
|---|---|---|---|
| ☐ 16 | Roy Oswalt | .20 | .50 |
| ☐ 17 | Mike Lowell | .20 | .50 |
| ☐ 18 | Carlos Lee | .20 | .50 |
| ☐ 19 | Sean Burroughs | .20 | .50 |
| ☐ 20 | Edgar Renteria | .20 | .50 |
| ☐ 21 | Michael Young | .20 | .50 |
| ☐ 22 | Jose Vidro | .20 | .50 |
| ☐ 23 | Scott Rolen | .30 | .75 |
| ☐ 24 | Rafael Furcal | .20 | .50 |
| ☐ 25 | Tom Glavine | .30 | .75 |
| ☐ 26 | Scott Podsednik | .20 | .50 |
| ☐ 27 | Gary Sheffield | .20 | .50 |
| ☐ 28 | Eric Chavez | .20 | .50 |
| ☐ 29 | Mark Prior | .30 | .75 |
| ☐ 30 | Chipper Jones | .50 | 1.25 |
| ☐ 31 | Frank Thomas | .50 | 1.25 |
| ☐ 32 | Victor Martinez | .20 | .50 |
| ☐ 33 | Jake Peavy | .20 | .50 |
| ☐ 34 | Carlos Beltran | .20 | .50 |
| ☐ 35 | Roy Halladay | .20 | .50 |
| ☐ 36 | Mark Teixeira | .20 | .50 |
| ☐ 37 | Jacque Jones | .20 | .50 |
| ☐ 38 | Mike Sweeney | .20 | .50 |
| ☐ 39 | Troy Glaus | .20 | .50 |
| ☐ 40 | Pat Burrell | .20 | .50 |
| ☐ 41 | Ichiro Suzuki | 1.00 | 2.50 |
| ☐ 42 | Vladimir Guerrero | .50 | 1.25 |
| ☐ 43 | Bobby Abreu | .20 | .50 |
| ☐ 44 | Jim Edmonds | .20 | .50 |
| ☐ 45 | Garret Anderson | .20 | .50 |
| ☐ 46 | J.D. Drew | .20 | .50 |
| ☐ 47 | C.C. Sabathia | .20 | .50 |
| ☐ 48 | Joe Mauer | .50 | 1.25 |
| ☐ 49 | Phil Nevin | .20 | .50 |
| ☐ 50 | Hank Blalock | .20 | .50 |
| ☐ 51 | Carlos Zambrano | .20 | .50 |
| ☐ 52 | Mike Piazza | .75 | 2.00 |
| ☐ 53 | Manny Ramirez | .30 | .75 |
| ☐ 54 | Lance Berkman | .20 | .50 |
| ☐ 55 | Delmon Young | .30 | .75 |
| ☐ 56 | Nomar Garciaparra | .75 | 2.00 |
| ☐ 57 | Alex Rodriguez | .75 | 2.00 |
| ☐ 58 | Rickie Weeks | .20 | .50 |
| ☐ 59 | Adrian Beltre | .20 | .50 |
| ☐ 60 | Albert Pujols | 1.00 | 2.50 |
| ☐ 61 | Richie Sexson | .20 | .50 |
| ☐ 62 | Magglio Ordonez | .20 | .50 |
| ☐ 63 | Derrek Lee | .30 | .75 |
| ☐ 64 | Sammy Sosa | .50 | 1.25 |
| ☐ 65 | Jason Giambi | .20 | .50 |
| ☐ 66 | Curt Schilling | .30 | .75 |
| ☐ 67 | Jorge Posada | .30 | .75 |
| ☐ 68 | Rafael Palmeiro | .30 | .75 |
| ☐ 69 | Jeff Kent | .20 | .50 |
| ☐ 70 | Jose Reyes | .20 | .50 |
| ☐ 71 | David Ortiz | .50 | 1.25 |
| ☐ 72 | Aubrey Huff | .20 | .50 |
| ☐ 73 | Jim Thome | .30 | .75 |
| ☐ 74 | Andy Pettitte | .30 | .75 |
| ☐ 75 | Barry Zito | .20 | .50 |
| ☐ 76 | Carlos Delgado | .20 | .50 |
| ☐ 77 | Hideki Matsui | .75 | 2.00 |
| ☐ 78 | Sean Casey | .20 | .50 |
| ☐ 79 | Luis Gonzalez | .20 | .50 |
| ☐ 80 | Marcus Giles | .20 | .50 |
| ☐ 81 | Preston Wilson | .20 | .50 |
| ☐ 82 | Javy Lopez | .20 | .50 |
| ☐ 83 | Mark Mulder | .20 | .50 |
| ☐ 84 | Derek Jeter | 1.00 | 2.50 |
| ☐ 85 | Miguel Cabrera | .30 | .75 |
| ☐ 86 | Vernon Wells | .20 | .50 |
| ☐ 87 | Roger Clemens | 1.00 | 2.50 |
| ☐ 88 | Lyle Overbay | .20 | .50 |
| ☐ 89 | Bret Boone | .20 | .50 |
| ☐ 90 | Melvin Mora | .20 | .50 |
| ☐ 91 | Greg Maddux | .75 | 2.00 |
| ☐ 92 | Kerry Wood | .20 | .50 |
| ☐ 93 | Ivan Rodriguez | .30 | .75 |
| ☐ 94 | Pedro Martinez | .30 | .75 |
| ☐ 95 | Jeff Bagwell | .30 | .75 |
| ☐ 96 | Torii Hunter | .20 | .50 |
| ☐ 97 | Ken Griffey Jr. | .75 | 2.00 |
| ☐ 98 | Mike Mussina | .30 | .75 |
| ☐ 99 | Oliver Perez | .20 | .50 |
| ☐ 100 | Josh Beckett | .20 | .50 |
| ☐ 101 | Bob Gibson LGD | 3.00 | 8.00 |
| ☐ 102 | Cal Ripken LGD | 6.00 | 15.00 |
| ☐ 103 | Ted Williams LGD | 3.00 | 8.00 |
| ☐ 104 | Nolan Ryan LGD | 4.00 | 10.00 |
| ☐ 105 | Mickey Mantle LGD | 6.00 | 15.00 |
| ☐ 106 | Ernie Banks LGD | 3.00 | 8.00 |
| ☐ 107 | Joe DiMaggio LGD | 3.00 | 8.00 |
| ☐ 108 | Stan Musial LGD | 3.00 | 8.00 |
| ☐ 109 | Tom Seaver LGD | 3.00 | 8.00 |
| ☐ 110 | Mike Schmidt LGD | 4.00 | 10.00 |
| ☐ 111 | Jerry Gil T1 RC | 2.00 | 5.00 |
| ☐ 112 | Dioner Navarro T1 RC | 3.00 | 8.00 |
| ☐ 113 | Bartolome Fortunato T1 RC | 2.00 | 5.00 |
| ☐ 114 | Carlos Hines T1 RC | 2.00 | 5.00 |
| ☐ 115 | Franklyn Gracesqui T1 RC | 2.00 | 5.00 |
| ☐ 116 | Aarom Baldiris T1 RC | 3.00 | 8.00 |
| ☐ 117 | Casey Daigle T1 RC | 2.00 | 5.00 |
| ☐ 118 | Joey Gathright T1 RC | 3.00 | 8.00 |
| ☐ 119 | William Bergolla T1 RC | 2.00 | 5.00 |
| ☐ 120 | Jeff Bennett T1 RC | 2.00 | 5.00 |
| ☐ 121 | Lincoln Holdzkom T1 RC | 2.00 | 5.00 |
| ☐ 122 | Jorge Vasquez T1 RC | 2.00 | 5.00 |
| ☐ 123 | Donnie Kelly T1 RC | 2.00 | 5.00 |
| ☐ 124 | Yadier Molina T1 RC | 3.00 | 8.00 |
| ☐ 125 | Ryan Wing T1 RC | 2.00 | 5.00 |
| ☐ 126 | Justin Germano T1 RC | 2.00 | 5.00 |
| ☐ 127 | Freddy Guzman T1 RC | 2.00 | 5.00 |
| ☐ 128 | Onil Joseph T1 RC | 2.00 | 5.00 |
| ☐ 129 | Roman Colon T1 RC | 2.00 | 5.00 |
| ☐ 130 | Roberto Novoa T1 RC | 3.00 | 8.00 |
| ☐ 131 | Renyel Pinto T1 RC | 3.00 | 8.00 |
| ☐ 132 | Evan Rust T1 RC | 2.00 | 5.00 |
| ☐ 133 | Orlando Rodriguez T1 RC | 2.00 | 5.00 |
| ☐ 134 | Edwardo Sierra T1 RC | 3.00 | 8.00 |
| ☐ 135 | Mike Rose T1 RC | 2.00 | 5.00 |
| ☐ 136 | Phil Stockman T1 RC | 2.00 | 5.00 |
| ☐ 137 | Greg Dobbs T1 RC | 2.00 | 5.00 |
| ☐ 138 | Brad Halsey T1 RC | 3.00 | 8.00 |
| ☐ 139 | David Aardsma T1 RC | 3.00 | 8.00 |
| ☐ 140 | Joe Hietpas T1 RC | 2.00 | 5.00 |
| ☐ 141 | Josh Labandeira T1 RC | 2.00 | 5.00 |
| ☐ 142 | Mariano Gomez T1 RC | 2.00 | 5.00 |
| ☐ 143 | Jeff Bajenaru T1 RC | 2.00 | 5.00 |
| ☐ 144 | Travis Blackley T1 RC | 2.00 | 5.00 |
| ☐ 145 | Abe Alvarez T1 RC | 3.00 | 8.00 |
| ☐ 146 | Ramon Ramirez T2 RC | 3.00 | 8.00 |
| ☐ 147 | Edwin Moreno T2 RC | 4.00 | 10.00 |
| ☐ 148 | Ronny Cedeno T2 RC | 4.00 | 10.00 |
| ☐ 149 | Hector Gimenez T2 RC | 3.00 | 8.00 |
| ☐ 150 | Carlos Vasquez T2 RC | 4.00 | 10.00 |
| ☐ 151 | Jesse Crain T2 RC | 6.00 | 15.00 |
| ☐ 152 | Logan Kensing T2 RC | 3.00 | 8.00 |
| ☐ 153 | Sean Henn T2 RC | 3.00 | 8.00 |
| ☐ 154 | Rusty Tucker T2 RC | 4.00 | 10.00 |
| ☐ 155 | Justin Lehr T3 RC | 3.00 | 8.00 |
| ☐ 156 | Ian Snell T3 RC | 4.00 | 10.00 |
| ☐ 157 | Merkin Valdez T3 RC | 3.00 | 8.00 |
| ☐ 158 | Scott Proctor T3 RC | 4.00 | 10.00 |
| ☐ 159 | Jose Capellan T3 RC | 4.00 | 10.00 |
| ☐ 160 | Kazuo Matsui T3 RC | 3.00 | 8.00 |
| ☐ 161 | Chris Oxspring AU JSY RC | 6.00 | 15.00 |
| ☐ 162 | Jimmy Serrano AU JSY RC | 6.00 | 15.00 |
| ☐ 163 | Jeff Keppinger AU JSY RC | 8.00 | 20.00 |
| ☐ 164 | B.Medders AU JSY RC | 6.00 | 15.00 |
| ☐ 165 | Brian Dallimore AU JSY RC | 6.00 | 15.00 |
| ☐ 166 | Chad Bentz AU JSY RC | 6.00 | 15.00 |
| ☐ 167 | Chris Aguila AU JSY RC | 6.00 | 15.00 |
| ☐ 168 | Chris Saenz AU JSY RC | 6.00 | 15.00 |
| ☐ 169 | Frank Francisco AU JSY RC | 6.00 | 15.00 |
| ☐ 170 | Colby Miller AU JSY RC | 6.00 | 15.00 |
| ☐ 171 | D.Crouth AU JSY RC EXCH | 6.00 | 15.00 |
| ☐ 172 | Charles Thomas AU JSY RC | 6.00 | 15.00 |
| ☐ 173 | Dennis Sarfate AU JSY RC | 6.00 | 15.00 |
| ☐ 174 | Lance Cormier AU JSY RC | 6.00 | 15.00 |
| ☐ 175 | Joe Horgan AU JSY RC | 6.00 | 15.00 |
| ☐ 176 | Fernando Nieve AU JSY RC | 6.00 | 15.00 |
| ☐ 177 | Jake Woods AU JSY RC | 6.00 | 15.00 |
| ☐ 178 | Matt Treanor AU JSY RC | 6.00 | 15.00 |
| ☐ 179 | Jerome Gamble AU JSY RC | 6.00 | 15.00 |
| ☐ 180 | John Gall AU JSY RC | 10.00 | 25.00 |
| ☐ 181 | Jorge Sequea AU JSY RC | 6.00 | 15.00 |
| ☐ 182 | Justin Hampson AU JSY RC | 6.00 | 15.00 |
| ☐ 183 | Justin Huisman AU JSY RC | 6.00 | 15.00 |
| ☐ 184 | Justin Knoedler AU JSY RC | 6.00 | 15.00 |
| ☐ 185 | Justin Leone AU JSY RC | 10.00 | 25.00 |
| ☐ 186 | Scott Atchison AU JSY RC | 6.00 | 15.00 |
| ☐ 187 | Jon Knott AU JSY RC | 6.00 | 15.00 |
| ☐ 188 | Kevin Cave AU JSY RC | 6.00 | 15.00 |
| ☐ 189 | Jason Frasor AU JSY RC | 6.00 | 15.00 |
| ☐ 190 | George Sherrill AU JSY RC | 6.00 | 15.00 |
| ☐ 191 | Mike Gosling AU JSY RC | 6.00 | 15.00 |
| ☐ 192 | Mike Johnston AU JSY RC | 6.00 | 15.00 |
| ☐ 193 | Mike Rouse AU JSY RC | 6.00 | 15.00 |
| ☐ 194 | Nick Regilio AU JSY RC | 6.00 | 15.00 |
| ☐ 195 | Ryan Meaux AU JSY RC | 6.00 | 15.00 |
| ☐ 196 | Scott Dohmann AU JSY RC | 6.00 | 15.00 |
| ☐ 197 | Shawn Camp AU JSY RC | 6.00 | 15.00 |
| ☐ 198 | Shawn Hill AU JSY RC | 6.00 | 15.00 |
| ☐ 199 | Shingo Takatsu AU JSY RC | 6.00 | 15.00 |
| ☐ 200 | Tim Bausher AU JSY RC | 6.00 | 15.00 |
| ☐ 201 | Tim Bittner AU JSY RC | 6.00 | 15.00 |
| ☐ 202 | Scott Kazmir AU JSY RC | 12.50 | 30.00 |

## 2005 SPx

| | | | |
|---|---|---|---|
| ☐ COMP.BASIC SET (100) | | 10.00 | 25.00 |
| ☐ COMMON CARD (1-100) | | .15 | .40 |
| ☐ COMMON RC (1-100) | | .15 | .40 |
| ☐ 1-100 ISSUED IN 05 SP COLLECTION PACKS | | | |
| ☐ COMMON AUTO (101-180) | | 4.00 | 10.00 |
| ☐ 101-180 ODDS APPX 1:8 '05 UD UPDATE | | | |
| ☐ 101-180 PRINT RUN 185 SERIAL #'d SETS | | | |
| ☐ 105, 117, 139, 149, 155, 172 DO NOT EXIST | | | |
| ☐ 175, 178, 180 DO NOT EXIST | | | |
| ☐ 1 | Aaron Harang | .15 | .40 |
| ☐ 2 | Aaron Rowand | .15 | .40 |
| ☐ 3 | Aaron Miles | .15 | .40 |
| ☐ 4 | Adrian Gonzalez | .15 | .40 |
| ☐ 5 | Alex Rios | .15 | .40 |
| ☐ 6 | Angel Berroa | .15 | .40 |
| ☐ 7 | B.J. Upton | .15 | .40 |
| ☐ 8 | Brandon Claussen | .15 | .40 |
| ☐ 9 | Andy Marte | .15 | .40 |
| ☐ 10 | Brandon Webb | .15 | .40 |
| ☐ 11 | Bronson Arroyo | .15 | .40 |
| ☐ 12 | Casey Kotchman | .15 | .40 |
| ☐ 13 | Cesar Izturis | .15 | .40 |
| ☐ 14 | Chad Cordero | .15 | .40 |
| ☐ 15 | Chad Tracy | .15 | .40 |
| ☐ 16 | Charles Thomas | .15 | .40 |
| ☐ 17 | Chase Utley | .25 | .60 |
| ☐ 18 | Chone Figgins | .15 | .40 |
| ☐ 19 | Chris Burke | .15 | .40 |
| ☐ 20 | Cliff Lee | .15 | .40 |
| ☐ 21 | Clint Barmes | .15 | .40 |
| ☐ 22 | Coco Crisp | .15 | .40 |
| ☐ 23 | Bill Hall | .15 | .40 |
| ☐ 24 | Dallas McPherson | .15 | .40 |
| ☐ 25 | Brad Halsey | .15 | .40 |
| ☐ 26 | Daniel Cabrera | .15 | .40 |
| ☐ 27 | Danny Haren | .15 | .40 |
| ☐ 28 | Dave Bush | .15 | .40 |
| ☐ 29 | David DeJesus | .15 | .40 |
| ☐ 30 | D.J. Houlton RC | .25 | .60 |
| ☐ 31 | Derek Jeter | .75 | 2.00 |
| ☐ 32 | Dewon Brazelton | .15 | .40 |
| ☐ 33 | Edwin Jackson | .15 | .40 |
| ☐ 34 | Brad Hawpe | .15 | .40 |
| ☐ 35 | Brandon Inge | .15 | .40 |
| ☐ 36 | Brett Myers | .15 | .40 |
| ☐ 37 | Garrett Atkins | .15 | .40 |
| ☐ 38 | Gavin Floyd | .15 | .40 |
| ☐ 39 | Grady Sizemore | .25 | .60 |
| ☐ 40 | Guillermo Mota | .15 | .40 |
| ☐ 41 | Carlos Guillen | .15 | .40 |
| ☐ 42 | Gustavo Chacin | .15 | .40 |
| ☐ 43 | Huston Street | .15 | .40 |
| ☐ 44 | Chris Duffy | .15 | .40 |
| ☐ 45 | J.D. Closser | .15 | .40 |
| ☐ 46 | J.J. Hardy | .15 | .40 |
| ☐ 47 | Jason Bartlett | .15 | .40 |
| ☐ 48 | Jason DuBois | .15 | .40 |
| ☐ 49 | Chris Shelton | .25 | .60 |
| ☐ 50 | Jason Lane | .15 | .40 |
| ☐ 51 | Jayson Werth | .15 | .40 |
| ☐ 52 | Jeff Baker | .15 | .40 |

| Card | .15 | .40 |
|---|---|---|
| 53 Jeff Francis | .15 | .40 |
| 54 Jeremy Bonderman | .15 | .40 |
| 55 Jeremy Reed | .15 | .40 |
| 56 Jerome Williams | .15 | .40 |
| 57 Jesse Crain | .15 | .40 |
| 58 Chris Young | .15 | .40 |
| 59 Jhonny Peralta | .15 | .40 |
| 60 Joe Blanton | .15 | .40 |
| 61 Joe Crede | .15 | .40 |
| 62 Joel Pineiro | .15 | .40 |
| 63 Joey Gathright | .15 | .40 |
| 64 John Buck | .15 | .40 |
| 65 Jonny Gomes | .15 | .40 |
| 66 Jorge Cantu | .15 | .40 |
| 67 Dan Johnson | .15 | .40 |
| 68 Jose Valverde | .15 | .40 |
| 69 Ervin Santana | .15 | .40 |
| 70 Justin Morneau | .15 | .40 |
| 71 Keiichi Yabu RC | .25 | .60 |
| 72 Ken Griffey Jr. | .60 | 1.50 |
| 73 Jason Repko | .15 | .40 |
| 74 Kevin Youkilis | .15 | .40 |
| 75 Koyie Hill | .15 | .40 |
| 76 Laynce Nix | .15 | .40 |
| 77 Luke Scott RC | .75 | 2.00 |
| 78 Juan Rivera | .15 | .40 |
| 79 Justin Duchscherer | .15 | .40 |
| 80 Mark Teahen | .15 | .40 |
| 81 Lance Niekro | .15 | .40 |
| 82 Michael Cuddyer | .15 | .40 |
| 83 Nick Swisher | .15 | .40 |
| 84 Noah Lowry | .15 | .40 |
| 85 Matt Holliday | .20 | .50 |
| 86 Reed Johnson | .15 | .40 |
| 87 Rich Harden | .15 | .40 |
| 88 Robb Quinlan | .15 | .40 |
| 89 Nick Johnson | .15 | .40 |
| 90 Ryan Howard | 1.00 | 2.50 |
| 91 Nook Logan | .15 | .40 |
| 92 Steve Schmoll RC | .25 | .60 |
| 93 Tadahito Iguchi RC | 1.50 | 4.00 |
| 94 Willy Taveras | .15 | .40 |
| 95 Wily Mo Pena | .15 | .40 |
| 96 Xavier Nady | .15 | .40 |
| 97 Yadier Molina | .15 | .40 |
| 98 Yhency Brazoban | .15 | .40 |
| 99 Ryan Freel | .15 | .40 |
| 100 Zack Greinke | .15 | .40 |
| 101 Adam Shabala AU RC | 4.00 | 10.00 |
| 102 Ambiorix Burgos AU RC | 4.00 | 10.00 |
| 103 Ambiorix Concepcion AU RC | 4.00 | 10.00 |
| 104 Anibal Sanchez AU RC | 15.00 | 40.00 |
| 106 Brandon McCarthy AU RC | 12.50 | 30.00 |
| 107 Brian Burres AU RC | 4.00 | 10.00 |
| 108 Carlos Ruiz AU RC | 6.00 | 15.00 |
| 109 Casey Rogowski AU RC | 6.00 | 15.00 |
| 110 Chad Orvella AU RC | 4.00 | 10.00 |
| 111 Chris Resop AU RC | 6.00 | 15.00 |
| 112 Chris Roberson AU RC | 4.00 | 10.00 |
| 113 Chris Seddon AU RC | 4.00 | 10.00 |
| 114 Colter Bean AU RC | 6.00 | 15.00 |
| 115 Dave Gassner AU RC | 4.00 | 10.00 |
| 116 Brian Anderson AU RC | 15.00 | 40.00 |
| 118 Devon Lowery AU RC | 4.00 | 10.00 |
| 119 Enrique Gonzalez AU RC | 6.00 | 15.00 |
| 120 Eude Brito AU RC | 4.00 | 10.00 |
| 121 Francisco Butto AU RC | 4.00 | 10.00 |
| 122 Franquelis Osoria AU RC | 4.00 | 10.00 |
| 123 Garrett Jones AU RC | 15.00 | 40.00 |
| 124 Geovany Soto AU RC | 60.00 | 120.00 |
| 125 Hayden Penn AU RC | 8.00 | 20.00 |
| 126 Ismael Ramirez AU RC | 4.00 | 10.00 |
| 127 Jared Gothreaux AU RC | 4.00 | 10.00 |
| 128 Jason Hammel AU RC | 4.00 | 10.00 |
| 129 Jeff Miller AU RC | 4.00 | 10.00 |
| 130 Jeff Niemann AU RC | 12.50 | 30.00 |
| 131 Joel Peralta AU RC | 4.00 | 10.00 |
| 132 John Hattig AU RC | 4.00 | 10.00 |
| 133 Jorge Campillo AU RC | 4.00 | 10.00 |
| 134 Juan Morillo AU RC | 4.00 | 10.00 |
| 135 Justin Verlander AU RC | 125.00 | 200.00 |
| 136 Ryan Garko AU RC | 15.00 | 40.00 |
| 137 Kendry Morales AU RC | 30.00 | 60.00 |
| 138 Luis Hernandez AU RC | 4.00 | 10.00 |
| 140 Luis O.Rodriguez AU RC | 4.00 | 10.00 |
| 141 Mark Woodyard AU RC | 4.00 | 10.00 |
| 142 Matt A.Smith AU RC | 4.00 | 10.00 |
| 143 Matthew Lindstrom AU RC | 4.00 | 10.00 |
| 144 Miguel Negron AU RC | 6.00 | 15.00 |
| 145 Mike Morse AU RC | 8.00 | 20.00 |
| 146 Nate McLouth AU RC | 20.00 | 50.00 |
| 147 Nelson Cruz AU RC | 20.00 | 50.00 |
| 148 Nick Masset AU RC | 4.00 | 10.00 |
| 150 Paulino Reynoso AU RC | 4.00 | 10.00 |
| 151 Pedro Lopez AU RC | 4.00 | 10.00 |
| 152 Philip Humber AU RC | 12.50 | 30.00 |
| 153 Prince Fielder AU RC | 75.00 | 150.00 |
| 154 Randy Messenger AU RC | 4.00 | 10.00 |
| 156 Raul Tablado AU RC | 4.00 | 10.00 |
| 157 Ronny Paulino AU RC | 6.00 | 15.00 |
| 158 Russ Rohlicek AU RC | 4.00 | 10.00 |
| 159 Russell Martin AU RC | 30.00 | 60.00 |
| 160 Scott Baker AU RC | 6.00 | 15.00 |
| 161 Scott Munter AU RC | 4.00 | 10.00 |
| 162 Sean Thompson AU RC | 4.00 | 10.00 |
| 163 Sean Tracey AU RC | 4.00 | 10.00 |
| 164 Shane Costa AU RC | 4.00 | 10.00 |
| 165 Stephen Drew AU RC | 30.00 | 60.00 |
| 166 Tony Giarratano AU RC | 4.00 | 10.00 |
| 167 Tony Pena AU RC | 4.00 | 10.00 |
| 168 Travis Bowyer AU RC | 4.00 | 10.00 |
| 169 Ubaldo Jimenez AU RC | 20.00 | 50.00 |
| 170 Wladimir Balentien AU RC | 40.00 | 80.00 |
| 171 Yorman Bazardo AU RC | 4.00 | 10.00 |
| 173 Ryan Zimmerman AU RC | 60.00 | 120.00 |
| 174 Chris Denorfia AU RC | 6.00 | 15.00 |
| 176 Jermaine Van Buren AU | 4.00 | 10.00 |
| 177 Mark McLemore AU | 4.00 | 10.00 |
| 179 Ryan Speier AU RC | 4.00 | 10.00 |

## 2006 SPx

GARCIAPARRA

| | | |
|---|---|---|
| COMP.BASIC SET (100) | 10.00 | 25.00 |
| COMMON CARD (1-100) | .15 | .40 |
| COMMON AU p/r 659-999 | 4.00 | 10.00 |
| COMMON AU p/r 350-500 | 4.00 | 10.00 |
| OVERALL 101-161 AU ODDS 1:9 | | |
| 101-161 AU EXCH DEADLINE 09/07/08 | | |
| 101-161 AU PRINT RUN B/WN 190-999 PER | | |
| 101-161 PRINTING PLATE ODDS 1:224 | | |
| 101-161 PLATES PRINT RUN 1 SET PER CLR | | |
| 101-161 PLATES FEATURE AUTOS | | |
| BLACK-CYAN-MAGENTA-YELLOW ISSUED | | |
| NO PLATE PRICING DUE TO SCARCITY | | |
| EXQUISITE EXCH ODDS 1:36 | | |
| EXQUISITE EXCH DEADLINE 07/27/07 | | |
| 1 Luis Gonzalez | .15 | .40 |
| 2 Chad Tracy | .15 | .40 |
| 3 Brandon Webb | .15 | .40 |
| 4 Andruw Jones | .25 | .60 |
| 5 Chipper Jones | .40 | 1.00 |
| 6 John Smoltz | .25 | .60 |
| 7 Tim Hudson | .15 | .40 |
| 8 Miguel Tejada | .15 | .40 |
| 9 Brian Roberts | .15 | .40 |
| 10 Ramon Hernandez | .15 | .40 |
| 11 Curt Schilling | .25 | .60 |
| 12 David Ortiz | .25 | .60 |
| 13 Manny Ramirez | .25 | .60 |
| 14 Jason Varitek | .40 | 1.00 |
| 15 Josh Beckett | .15 | .40 |
| 16 Greg Maddux | .60 | 1.50 |
| 17 Derrek Lee | .15 | .40 |
| 18 Mark Prior | .25 | .60 |
| 19 Aramis Ramirez | .15 | .40 |
| 20 Jim Thome | .25 | .60 |
| 21 Paul Konerko | .15 | .40 |
| 22 Scott Podsednik | .15 | .40 |
| 23 Jose Contreras | .15 | .40 |
| 24 Ken Griffey Jr. | .60 | 1.50 |
| 25 Adam Dunn | .15 | .40 |
| 26 Felipe Lopez | .15 | .40 |
| 27 Travis Hafner | .15 | .40 |
| 28 Victor Martinez | .15 | .40 |
| 29 Grady Sizemore | .25 | .60 |
| 30 Jhonny Peralta | .15 | .40 |
| 31 Todd Helton | .25 | .60 |
| 32 Garrett Atkins | .15 | .40 |
| 33 Clint Barmes | .15 | .40 |
| 34 Ivan Rodriguez | .15 | .40 |
| 35 Chris Shelton | .15 | .40 |
| 36 Jeremy Bonderman | .15 | .40 |
| 37 Miguel Cabrera | .25 | .60 |
| 38 Dontrelle Willis | .15 | .40 |
| 39 Lance Berkman | .15 | .40 |
| 40 Morgan Ensberg | .15 | .40 |
| 41 Roy Oswalt | .15 | .40 |
| 42 Reggie Sanders | .15 | .40 |
| 43 Mike Sweeney | .15 | .40 |
| 44 Vladimir Guerrero | .40 | 1.00 |
| 45 Bartolo Colon | .15 | .40 |
| 46 Chone Figgins | .15 | .40 |
| 47 Nomar Garciaparra | .40 | 1.00 |
| 48 Jeff Kent | .15 | .40 |
| 49 J.D. Drew | .15 | .40 |
| 50 Carlos Lee | .15 | .40 |
| 51 Ben Sheets | .15 | .40 |
| 52 Rickie Weeks | .15 | .40 |
| 53 Johan Santana | .25 | .60 |
| 54 Torii Hunter | .15 | .40 |
| 55 Joe Mauer | .40 | 1.00 |
| 56 Pedro Martinez | .25 | .60 |
| 57 David Wright | .60 | 1.50 |
| 58 Carlos Beltran | .15 | .40 |
| 59 Carlos Delgado | .15 | .40 |
| 60 Jose Reyes | .40 | 1.00 |
| 61 Derek Jeter | 1.00 | 2.50 |
| 62 Alex Rodriguez | .60 | 1.50 |
| 63 Randy Johnson | .40 | 1.00 |
| 64 Hideki Matsui | .40 | 1.00 |
| 65 Gary Sheffield | .15 | .40 |
| 66 Rich Harden | .15 | .40 |
| 67 Eric Chavez | .15 | .40 |
| 68 Huston Street | .15 | .40 |
| 69 Bobby Crosby | .15 | .40 |
| 70 Bobby Abreu | .15 | .40 |
| 71 Ryan Howard | .60 | 1.50 |
| 72 Chase Utley | .40 | 1.00 |
| 73 Pat Burrell | .15 | .40 |
| 74 Jason Bay | .15 | .40 |
| 75 Sean Casey | .15 | .40 |
| 76 Mike Piazza | .40 | 1.00 |
| 77 Jake Peavy | .15 | .40 |
| 78 Brian Giles | .15 | .40 |
| 79 Milton Bradley | .15 | .40 |
| 80 Omar Vizquel | .15 | .40 |
| 81 Jason Schmidt | .15 | .40 |
| 82 Ichiro Suzuki | .60 | 1.50 |
| 83 Felix Hernandez | .25 | .60 |
| 84 Richie Sexson | .15 | .40 |
| 85 Albert Pujols | .75 | 2.00 |
| 86 Chris Carpenter | .25 | .60 |
| 87 Scott Rolen | .25 | .60 |
| 88 Jim Edmonds | .25 | .60 |
| 89 Carl Crawford | .15 | .40 |
| 90 Jonny Gomes | .15 | .40 |
| 91 Scott Kazmir | .25 | .60 |
| 92 Mark Teixeira | .25 | .60 |
| 93 Michael Young | .15 | .40 |
| 94 Phil Nevin | .15 | .40 |
| 95 Vernon Wells | .15 | .40 |
| 96 Roy Halladay | .15 | .40 |
| 97 Troy Glaus | .15 | .40 |
| 98 Alfonso Soriano | .15 | .40 |
| 99 Nick Johnson | .15 | .40 |
| 100 Jose Vidro | .15 | .40 |
| 101 Conor Jackson AU/999 (RC) | 6.00 | 15.00 |
| 102 J.Weaver AU/299 (RC) RC | 15.00 | 40.00 |
| 103 Macay McBride AU/999 (RC) | 4.00 | 10.00 |
| 104 Aaron Rakers AU/499 (RC) | 4.00 | 10.00 |
| 105 J.Papelbon AU/499 (RC) | 12.50 | 30.00 |
| 106 J.Bergmann AU/999 (RC) | 4.00 | 10.00 |
| 107 S.Drew AU/350 (RC) | 12.50 | 30.00 |
| 108 Chris Denorfia AU/999 (RC) | 4.00 | 10.00 |
| 109 Kelly Shoppach AU/999 (RC) | 4.00 | 10.00 |
| 110 Ryan Shealy AU/999 (RC) | 4.00 | 10.00 |
| 111 Josh Wilson AU/999 (RC) | 4.00 | 10.00 |
| 112 Brian Anderson AU/999 (RC) | 4.00 | 10.00 |
| 113 J.Verlander AU/749 (RC) | 20.00 | 50.00 |
| 114 J.Hermida AU/999 (RC) | 6.00 | 15.00 |
| 115 M.Jacobs AU/999 (RC) | 6.00 | 15.00 |

| | | |
|---|---|---|
| 116 Josh Johnson AU/999 (RC) | 8.00 | 20.00 |
| 117 Hanley Ramirez AU/659 (RC) | 20.00 | 50.00 |
| 118 Chris Resop AU/999 (RC) | 4.00 | 10.00 |
| 119 J.Willingham AU/999 (RC) | 4.00 | 10.00 |
| 120 Cole Hamels AU/499 (RC) | 20.00 | 50.00 |
| 121 Matt Cain AU/999 (RC) | 8.00 | 20.00 |
| 122 Steve Stemle AU/999 RC | 4.00 | 10.00 |
| 123 Tim Hamulack AU/999 (RC) | 4.00 | 10.00 |
| 124 Choo Freeman AU/999 (RC) | 4.00 | 10.00 |
| 125 H.Kuo AU/999 (RC) | 20.00 | 50.00 |
| 126 Cody Ross AU/999 (RC) | 4.00 | 10.00 |
| 127 Jose Capellan AU/999 (RC) | 4.00 | 10.00 |
| 128 Prince Fielder AU/999 (RC) | 60.00 | 120.00 |
| 129 David Gassner AU/999 (RC) | 4.00 | 10.00 |
| 130 Jason Kubel AU/999 (RC) | 4.00 | 10.00 |
| 131 F.Liriano AU/299 (RC) | 20.00 | 50.00 |
| 132 A.Hernandez AU/999 (RC) | 6.00 | 15.00 |
| 133 Joey Devine AU/999 (RC) | 4.00 | 10.00 |
| 134 Chris Booker AU/999 (RC) | 4.00 | 10.00 |
| 135 Matt Capps AU/999 (RC) | 4.00 | 10.00 |
| 136 Paul Maholm AU/999 (RC) | 4.00 | 10.00 |
| 137 N.McLouth AU/999 (RC) | 8.00 | 20.00 |
| 138 J.Van Benschoten AU/999 (RC) | 4.00 | 10.00 |
| 139 Jeff Harris AU/999 (RC) | 4.00 | 10.00 |
| 140 Ben Johnson AU/999 (RC) | 4.00 | 10.00 |
| 141 Wil Nieves AU/999 (RC) | 4.00 | 10.00 |
| 142 G.Quiroz AU/999 (RC) | 4.00 | 10.00 |
| 143 Josh Rupe AU/500 (RC) | 4.00 | 10.00 |
| 144 Skip Schumaker AU/999 (RC) | 4.00 | 10.00 |
| 145 Jack Taschner AU/999 (RC) | 4.00 | 10.00 |
| 146 A.Wainwright AU/999 (RC) | 10.00 | 25.00 |
| 147 Alay Soler AU/499 RC | 10.00 | 25.00 |
| 148 Kendry Morales AU/999 (RC) | 6.00 | 15.00 |
| 149 Ian Kinsler AU/999 (RC) | 10.00 | 25.00 |
| 150 Jason Hammel AU/999 (RC) | 4.00 | 10.00 |
| 151 C.Billingsley AU/499 (RC) | 15.00 | 40.00 |
| 152 Boof Bonser AU/999 (RC) | 6.00 | 15.00 |
| 153 Peter Moylan AU/999 RC | 4.00 | 10.00 |
| 154 Chris Britton AU/999 RC | 4.00 | 10.00 |
| 155 Takashi Saito AU/999 (RC) | 12.50 | 30.00 |
| 156 Scott Dunn AU/999 (RC) | 4.00 | 10.00 |
| 157 J.Zumaya AU/299 (RC) EXCH | 12.50 | 30.00 |
| 158 Dan Uggla AU/999 (RC) | 10.00 | 25.00 |
| 159 Taylor Buchholz AU/999 (RC) | 4.00 | 10.00 |
| 160 M.Cabrera AU/999 (RC) EXCH | 15.00 | 40.00 |
| NNO Exquisite Redemption | | |

## 2007 SPx

| | | |
|---|---|---|
| COMMON CARD (1-100) | .30 | .75 |
| COMMON AU RC (101-150) | 3.00 | 8.00 |
| OVERALL 101-150 AU RC ODDS 1:3 | | |
| 101-150 AU RC EXCH DEADLINE 05/10/2010 | | |
| ASTERISK EQUALS PARTIAL EXCH | | |
| APPX.PRINTING PLATE ODDS 2 PER CASE | | |
| PLATES PRINT RUN 1 SET PER COLOR | | |
| BLACK-CYAN-MAGENTA-YELLOW ISSUED | | |
| NO PLATE PRICING DUE TO SCARCITY | | |
| 1 Miguel Tejada | .30 | .75 |
| 2 Brian Roberts | .30 | .75 |
| 3 Melvin Mora | .30 | .75 |
| 4 David Ortiz | .75 | 2.00 |
| 5 Manny Ramirez | .50 | 1.25 |
| 6 Jason Varitek | .75 | 2.00 |
| 7 Curt Schilling | .50 | 1.25 |
| 8 Jim Thome | .50 | 1.25 |
| 9 Paul Konerko | .30 | .75 |
| 10 Jermaine Dye | .30 | .75 |
| 11 Travis Hafner | .30 | .75 |
| 12 Victor Martinez | .30 | .75 |
| 13 Grady Sizemore | .50 | 1.25 |
| 14 C.C. Sabathia | .50 | 1.25 |
| 15 Ivan Rodriguez | .50 | 1.25 |
| 16 Magglio Ordonez | .30 | .75 |
| 17 Carlos Guillen | .30 | .75 |
| 18 Justin Verlander | .75 | 2.00 |
| 19 Shane Costa | .30 | .75 |
| 20 Emil Brown | .30 | .75 |
| 21 Mark Teahen | .30 | .75 |
| 22 Vladimir Guerrero | .75 | 2.00 |
| 23 Jered Weaver | .50 | 1.25 |
| 24 Juan Rivera | .30 | .75 |
| 25 Justin Morneau | .50 | 1.25 |
| 26 Joe Mauer | .50 | 1.25 |
| 27 Torii Hunter | .30 | .75 |
| 28 Johan Santana | .50 | 1.25 |
| 29 Derek Jeter | 2.00 | 5.00 |
| 30 Alex Rodriguez | 1.25 | 3.00 |
| 31 Johnny Damon | .50 | 1.25 |
| 32 Jason Giambi | .30 | .75 |
| 33 Bobby Crosby | .30 | .75 |
| 34 Nick Swisher | .30 | .75 |
| 35 Eric Chavez | .30 | .75 |
| 36 Ichiro Suzuki | 1.25 | 3.00 |
| 37 Raul Ibanez | .30 | .75 |
| 38 Richie Sexson | .30 | .75 |
| 39 Carl Crawford | .30 | .75 |
| 40 Rocco Baldelli | .30 | .75 |
| 41 Scott Kazmir | .50 | 1.25 |
| 42 Michael Young | .50 | 1.25 |
| 43 Mark Teixeira | .50 | 1.25 |
| 44 Ian Kinsler | .30 | .75 |
| 45 Troy Glaus | .30 | .75 |
| 46 Vernon Wells | .30 | .75 |
| 47 Roy Halladay | .30 | .75 |
| 48 Lyle Overbay | .30 | .75 |
| 49 Brandon Webb | .30 | .75 |
| 50 Conor Jackson | .30 | .75 |
| 51 Stephen Drew | .50 | 1.25 |
| 52 Chipper Jones | .75 | 2.00 |
| 53 Andruw Jones | .50 | 1.25 |
| 54 Adam LaRoche | .30 | .75 |
| 55 John Smoltz | .50 | 1.25 |
| 56 Derrek Lee | .30 | .75 |
| 57 Aramis Ramirez | .30 | .75 |
| 58 Carlos Zambrano | .30 | .75 |
| 59 Ken Griffey Jr. | 1.25 | 3.00 |
| 60 Adam Dunn | .30 | .75 |
| 61 Aaron Harang | .30 | .75 |
| 62 Todd Helton | .50 | 1.25 |
| 63 Matt Holliday | .40 | 1.00 |
| 64 Garrett Atkins | .30 | .75 |
| 65 Miguel Cabrera | .50 | 1.25 |
| 66 Hanley Ramirez | .50 | 1.25 |
| 67 Dontrelle Willis | .30 | .75 |
| 68 Lance Berkman | .30 | .75 |
| 69 Roy Oswalt | .30 | .75 |
| 70 Craig Biggio | .50 | 1.25 |
| 71 J.D. Drew | .30 | .75 |
| 72 Nomar Garciaparra | .75 | 2.00 |
| 73 Rafael Furcal | .30 | .75 |
| 74 Jeff Kent | .30 | .75 |
| 75 Prince Fielder | .75 | 2.00 |
| 76 Bill Hall | .30 | .75 |
| 77 Rickie Weeks | .30 | .75 |
| 78 Jose Reyes | .50 | 1.25 |
| 79 David Wright | 1.25 | 3.00 |
| 80 Carlos Delgado | .30 | .75 |
| 81 Carlos Beltran | .30 | .75 |
| 82 Ryan Howard | .75 | 2.00 |
| 83 Chase Utley | .75 | 2.00 |
| 84 Jimmy Rollins | .50 | 1.25 |
| 85 Jason Bay | .50 | 1.25 |
| 86 Freddy Sanchez | .30 | .75 |
| 87 Zach Duke | .30 | .75 |
| 88 Trevor Hoffman | .30 | .75 |
| 89 Adrian Gonzalez | .30 | .75 |
| 90 Chris Young | .30 | .75 |
| 91 Ray Durham | .30 | .75 |
| 92 Omar Vizquel | .50 | 1.25 |
| 93 Jason Schmidt | .30 | .75 |
| 94 Albert Pujols | 1.50 | 4.00 |
| 95 Scott Rolen | .50 | 1.25 |
| 96 Jim Edmonds | .50 | 1.25 |
| 97 Chris Carpenter | .30 | .75 |
| 98 Alfonso Soriano | .30 | .75 |
| 99 Ryan Zimmerman | .75 | 2.00 |
| 100 Nick Johnson | .30 | .75 |
| 101 Delmon Young AU (RC) | 10.00 | 25.00 |
| 102 A.Miller AU RC EXCH * | 10.00 | 25.00 |
| 103 Troy Tulowitzki AU (RC) | 12.50 | 30.00 |
| 104 Jeff Fiorentino AU (RC) | 3.00 | 8.00 |
| 105 David Murphy AU (RC) | 3.00 | 8.00 |
| 106 T.Lincecum AU RC | 75.00 | 150.00 |
| 107 P.Hughes AU (RC) EXCH | 15.00 | 40.00 |
| 108 K.Kouzmanoff AU (RC) EXCH | 6.00 | 15.00 |
| 109 A.Lind AU (RC) EXCH * | 3.00 | 8.00 |
| 110 M.Reynolds AU RC EXCH | 20.00 | 50.00 |
| 111 Kevin Hooper AU (RC) | 3.00 | 8.00 |
| 112 Mitch Maier AU RC | 3.00 | 8.00 |
| 113 Homey Bailey AU (RC) EXCH | 10.00 | 25.00 |
| 114 Dennis Sarfate AU (RC) | 3.00 | 8.00 |
| 115 Drew Anderson AU RC | 3.00 | 8.00 |
| 116 Miguel Montero AU (RC) | 3.00 | 8.00 |
| 117 G.Perkins AU (RC) EXCH | 3.00 | 8.00 |
| 118 Kevin Slowey AU (RC) EXCH | 10.00 | 25.00 |
| 119 Tim Gradoville AU RC | 3.00 | 8.00 |
| 120 Ryan Braun AU (RC) | 30.00 | 60.00 |
| 121 Chris Narveson AU (RC) | 3.00 | 8.00 |
| 122 P.Misch AU (RC) EXCH * | 3.00 | 8.00 |
| 123 Juan Salas AU (RC) | 3.00 | 8.00 |
| 124 Beltran Perez AU (RC) | 3.00 | 8.00 |
| 125 Joaquin Arias AU (RC) | 3.00 | 8.00 |
| 126 Philip Humber AU (RC) | 6.00 | 15.00 |
| 127 Kei Igawa AU RC | 6.00 | 15.00 |
| 128 Daisuke Matsuzaka AU (RC) | 90.00 | 150.00 |
| 129 Andy Cannizaro AU RC | 6.00 | 15.00 |
| 130 Ubaldo Jimenez AU (RC) | 6.00 | 15.00 |
| 131 Fred Lewis AU (RC) | 6.00 | 15.00 |
| 132 Ryan Sweeney AU (RC) | 3.00 | 8.00 |
| 133 Jeff Baker AU (RC) | 3.00 | 8.00 |
| 134 Michael Bourn AU (RC) | 6.00 | 15.00 |
| 135 Akinori Iwamura AU RC | 6.00 | 15.00 |
| 136 Oswaldo Navarro AU RC | 3.00 | 8.00 |
| 137 Hunter Pence AU (RC) | 12.50 | 30.00 |
| 138 Jon Knott AU (RC) | 3.00 | 8.00 |
| 139 J.Hampson AU (RC) EXCH | 3.00 | 8.00 |
| 140 J.Salazar AU (RC) EXCH | 3.00 | 8.00 |
| 141 Juan Morillo AU (RC) | 3.00 | 8.00 |
| 142 Delwyn Young AU (RC) | 3.00 | 8.00 |
| 143 Brian Burres AU (RC) | 5.00 | 12.00 |
| 144 Chris Stewart AU RC | 3.00 | 8.00 |
| 145 Eric Stults AU RC | 3.00 | 8.00 |
| 146 Carlos Maldonado AU (RC) | 3.00 | 8.00 |
| 147 Angel Sanchez AU RC | 3.00 | 8.00 |
| 148 Cesar Jimenez AU RC | 3.00 | 8.00 |
| 149 Shawn Riggans AU (RC) | 3.00 | 8.00 |
| 150 John Nelson AU (RC) | 3.00 | 8.00 |

## 2008 SPx

| | | |
|---|---|---|
| COMMON CARD (1-100) | .25 | .60 |
| COMMON AU RC (101-150) | .25 | .60 |
| OVERALL AU ODDS FOUR PER BOX | | |
| 1 Brandon Webb | .40 | 1.00 |
| 2 Chris B. Young | .25 | .60 |
| 3 Eric Byrnes | .25 | .60 |
| 4 Dan Haren | .25 | .60 |
| 5 Mark Teixeira | .40 | 1.00 |
| 6 Chipper Jones | .75 | 2.00 |
| 7 John Smoltz | .60 | 1.50 |
| 8 Erik Bedard | .25 | .60 |
| 9 Nick Markakis | .40 | 1.00 |
| 10 Brian Roberts | .40 | 1.00 |
| 11 David Ortiz | .40 | 1.00 |
| 12 Curt Schilling | .60 | 1.50 |
| 13 Manny Ramirez | .60 | 1.50 |
| 14 Daisuke Matsuzaka | .75 | 2.00 |
| 15 Josh Beckett | .40 | 1.00 |
| 16 Derrek Lee | .40 | 1.00 |
| 17 Alfonso Soriano | .40 | 1.00 |
| 18 Carlos Zambrano | .25 | .60 |
| 19 Aramis Ramirez | .25 | .60 |
| 20 Jermaine Dye | .25 | .60 |
| 21 Jim Thome | .40 | 1.00 |
| 22 Nick Swisher | .25 | .60 |
| 23 Ken Griffey Jr. | 1.00 | 2.50 |
| 24 Adam Dunn | .25 | .60 |
| 25 Brandon Phillips | .25 | .60 |
| 26 Grady Sizemore | .40 | 1.00 |
| 27 Victor Martinez | .25 | .60 |
| 28 C.C. Sabathia | .25 | .60 |
| 29 Travis Hafner | .25 | .60 |
| 30 Matt Holliday | .40 | 1.00 |
| 31 Todd Helton | .40 | 1.00 |
| 32 Troy Tulowitzki | .40 | 1.00 |
| 33 Magglio Ordonez | .40 | 1.00 |
| 34 Gary Sheffield | .25 | .60 |
| 35 Justin Verlander | .40 | 1.00 |
| 36 Curtis Granderson | .25 | .60 |
| 37 Miguel Cabrera | .60 | 1.50 |
| 38 Hanley Ramirez | .60 | 1.50 |

|  |  | | |
|---|---|---|---|
| ❑ 39 | Dan Uggla | .40 | 1.00 |
| ❑ 40 | Miguel Tejada | .25 | .60 |
| ❑ 41 | Lance Berkman | .40 | 1.00 |
| ❑ 42 | Hunter Pence | .60 | 1.50 |
| ❑ 43 | Carlos Lee | .25 | .60 |
| ❑ 44 | Alex Gordon | .40 | 1.00 |
| ❑ 45 | David DeJesus | .25 | .60 |
| ❑ 46 | Vladimir Guerrero | .60 | 1.50 |
| ❑ 47 | Jered Weaver | .25 | .60 |
| ❑ 48 | Torii Hunter | .25 | .60 |
| ❑ 49 | Andruw Jones | .25 | .60 |
| ❑ 50 | Rafael Furcal | .25 | .60 |
| ❑ 51 | Russell Martin | .25 | .60 |
| ❑ 52 | Brad Penny | .25 | .60 |
| ❑ 53 | Ryan Braun | .75 | 2.00 |
| ❑ 54 | Prince Fielder | .60 | 1.50 |
| ❑ 55 | J.J. Hardy | .25 | .60 |
| ❑ 56 | Justin Morneau | .25 | .60 |
| ❑ 57 | Johan Santana | .40 | 1.00 |
| ❑ 58 | Joe Mauer | .60 | 1.50 |
| ❑ 59 | Delmon Young | .40 | 1.00 |
| ❑ 60 | Jose Reyes | .40 | 1.00 |
| ❑ 61 | David Wright | .75 | 2.00 |
| ❑ 62 | Carlos Beltran | .25 | .60 |
| ❑ 63 | Pedro Martinez | .40 | 1.00 |
| ❑ 64 | Chien-Ming Wang | .60 | 1.50 |
| ❑ 65 | Alex Rodriguez | 1.00 | 2.50 |
| ❑ 66 | Derek Jeter | 1.50 | 4.00 |
| ❑ 67 | Robinson Cano | .40 | 1.00 |
| ❑ 68 | Hideki Matsui | .60 | 1.50 |
| ❑ 69 | Joe Blanton | .25 | .60 |
| ❑ 70 | Jack Cust | .25 | .60 |
| ❑ 71 | Cole Hamels | .60 | 1.50 |
| ❑ 72 | Jimmy Rollins | .40 | 1.00 |
| ❑ 73 | Ryan Howard | .75 | 2.00 |
| ❑ 74 | Chase Utley | .60 | 1.50 |
| ❑ 75 | Jason Bay | .40 | 1.00 |
| ❑ 76 | Freddy Sanchez | .25 | .60 |
| ❑ 77 | Jake Peavy | .40 | 1.00 |
| ❑ 78 | Greg Maddux | .75 | 2.00 |
| ❑ 79 | Adrian Gonzalez | .40 | 1.00 |
| ❑ 80 | Barry Zito | .25 | .60 |
| ❑ 81 | Omar Vizquel | .25 | .60 |
| ❑ 82 | Tim Lincecum | .75 | 2.00 |
| ❑ 83 | Ichiro Suzuki | 1.00 | 2.50 |
| ❑ 84 | Felix Hernandez | .40 | 1.00 |
| ❑ 85 | Kenji Johjima | .25 | .60 |
| ❑ 86 | Albert Pujols | 1.25 | 3.00 |
| ❑ 87 | Scott Rolen | .40 | 1.00 |
| ❑ 88 | Chris Carpenter | .25 | .60 |
| ❑ 89 | Rick Ankiel | .25 | .60 |
| ❑ 90 | Scott Kazmir | .40 | 1.00 |
| ❑ 91 | Carl Crawford | .40 | 1.00 |
| ❑ 92 | B.J. Upton | .40 | 1.00 |
| ❑ 93 | Michael Young | .25 | .60 |
| ❑ 94 | Josh Hamilton | .75 | 2.00 |
| ❑ 95 | Hank Blalock | .25 | .60 |
| ❑ 96 | Roy Halladay | .25 | .60 |
| ❑ 97 | Vernon Wells | .25 | .60 |
| ❑ 98 | Alex Rios | .25 | .60 |
| ❑ 99 | Ryan Zimmerman | .40 | 1.00 |
| ❑ 100 | Dmitri Young | .25 | .60 |
| ❑ 101 | Bill Murphy AU (RC) | 3.00 | 8.00 |
| ❑ 102 | Emilio Bonifacio AU RC | 5.00 | 12.00 |
| ❑ 103 | Brandon Jones AU RC | 3.00 | 8.00 |
| ❑ 104 | Clint Sammons AU (RC) | 3.00 | 8.00 |
| ❑ 105 | Clay Buchholz AU (RC) | 10.00 | 25.00 |
| ❑ 106 | Kevin Hart AU (RC) | 3.00 | 8.00 |
| ❑ 107 | Donny Lucy AU (RC) | 3.00 | 8.00 |
| ❑ 108 | Lance Broadway AU (RC) | 3.00 | 8.00 |
| ❑ 109 | Joey Votto AU (RC) | 10.00 | 25.00 |
| ❑ 110 | Ryan Hanigan AU RC | 3.00 | 8.00 |
| ❑ 111 | Joe Koshansky AU (RC) | 3.00 | 8.00 |
| ❑ 112 | Josh Newman AU RC | 3.00 | 8.00 |
| ❑ 113 | Seth Smith AU (RC) | 3.00 | 8.00 |
| ❑ 114 | Chris Seddon AU (RC) | 3.00 | 8.00 |
| ❑ 115 | Harvey Garcia AU (RC) | 3.00 | 8.00 |
| ❑ 116 | Felipe Paulino AU RC | 4.00 | 10.00 |
| ❑ 117 | J.R. Towles AU RC | 4.00 | 10.00 |
| ❑ 118 | Josh Anderson AU (RC) | 3.00 | 8.00 |
| ❑ 119 | Troy Patton AU (RC) | 3.00 | 8.00 |
| ❑ 120 | Billy Buckner AU (RC) | 3.00 | 8.00 |
| ❑ 121 | Luke Hochevar AU RC | 3.00 | 8.00 |
| ❑ 122 | Chin-Lung Hu AU (RC) | 6.00 | 15.00 |
| ❑ 123 | Jonathan Meloan AU RC | | |
| ❑ 124 | Jose Morales (RC) | 6.00 | 15.00 |
| ❑ 125 | Carlos Muniz AU RC | | |
| ❑ 126 | Alberto Gonzalez AU RC | 3.00 | 8.00 |

|  |  | | |
|---|---|---|---|
| ❑ 127 | Bronson Sardinha AU (RC) | 3.00 | 8.00 |
| ❑ 128 | Ian Kennedy AU (RC) | 10.00 | 25.00 |
| ❑ 129 | Ross Ohlendorf AU RC | 3.00 | 8.00 |
| ❑ 130 | Daric Barton AU (RC) | 6.00 | 15.00 |
| ❑ 131 | Jerry Blevins AU RC | 3.00 | 8.00 |
| ❑ 132 | Dave Davidson AU RC | 3.00 | 8.00 |
| ❑ 133 | Nyjer Morgan AU (RC) | 3.00 | 8.00 |
| ❑ 134 | Steve Pearce AU RC | 3.00 | 8.00 |
| ❑ 135 | Colt Morton AU RC | 3.00 | 8.00 |
| ❑ 136 | Eugenio Velez AU RC | 3.00 | 8.00 |
| ❑ 137 | Jeff Clement AU (RC) | | |
| ❑ 138 | Rob Johnson AU (RC) | 3.00 | 8.00 |
| ❑ 139 | Wladimir Balentien AU (RC) | 3.00 | 8.00 |
| ❑ 140 | Justin Ruggiano AU RC | 3.00 | 8.00 |
| ❑ 141 | Bill White AU RC | 3.00 | 8.00 |
| ❑ 142 | Luis Mendoza AU (RC) | 3.00 | 8.00 |
| ❑ 143 | Jonathan Albaladejo AU RC | 3.00 | 8.00 |
| ❑ 144 | Justin Maxwell AU RC | | |
| ❑ 145 | Ross Detwiler AU RC | 6.00 | 15.00 |
| ❑ 146 | J.Bruce AU (RC) UER | | |
| ❑ 147 | C.Gonzalez AU (RC) EXCH | | |
| ❑ 148 | E.Longoria AU RC EXCH | 50.00 | 100.00 |
| ❑ 149 | C.Balester AU (RC) EXCH | | |
| ❑ 150 | M.Scherzer AU RC EXCH | | |
| ❑ 151 | C.Kershaw AU RC EXCH | 8.00 | 20.00 |
| ❑ 152 | A.Ramirez AU RC EXCH | | |

## 2009 SPx

| | | | |
|---|---|---|---|
| ❑ COMP.SET w/o AU's (100) | | 12.50 | 30.00 |
| ❑ COMMON CARD (1-100) | | .20 | .50 |
| ❑ COMMON AU RC (101-123) | | 4.00 | 10.00 |
| ❑ OVERALL AUTO ODDS 1:18 | | | |
| ❑ AU RC PRINT RUN 99 SER.#'d SETS | | | |
| ❑ 1 | Ichiro Suzuki | .75 | 2.00 |
| ❑ 2 | Rick Ankiel | .30 | .75 |
| ❑ 3 | Garrett Atkins | .20 | .50 |
| ❑ 4 | Jason Bay | .30 | .75 |
| ❑ 5 | Josh Beckett | .30 | .75 |
| ❑ 6 | Erik Bedard | .20 | .50 |
| ❑ 7 | Carlos Beltran | .20 | .50 |
| ❑ 8 | Lance Berkman | .30 | .75 |
| ❑ 9 | Ryan Braun | .60 | 1.50 |
| ❑ 10 | Jay Bruce | .50 | 1.25 |
| ❑ 11 | Miguel Cabrera | .30 | .75 |
| ❑ 12 | Matt Cain | .20 | .50 |
| ❑ 13 | Joba Chamberlain | .60 | 1.50 |
| ❑ 14 | Carl Crawford | .30 | .75 |
| ❑ 15 | Jack Cust | .20 | .50 |
| ❑ 16 | Joe DiMaggio | 1.25 | 3.00 |
| ❑ 17 | Ryan Doumit | .20 | .50 |
| ❑ 18 | Justin Duchscherer | .20 | .50 |
| ❑ 19 | Adam Dunn | .30 | .75 |
| ❑ 20 | Prince Fielder | .50 | 1.25 |
| ❑ 21 | Kosuke Fukudome | .50 | 1.25 |
| ❑ 22 | Troy Glaus | .20 | .50 |
| ❑ 23 | Tom Glavine | .30 | .75 |
| ❑ 24 | Adrian Gonzalez | .30 | .75 |
| ❑ 25 | Alex Gordon | .30 | .75 |
| ❑ 26 | Zack Greinke | .30 | .75 |
| ❑ 27 | Ken Griffey Jr. | .75 | 2.00 |
| ❑ 28 | Vladimir Guerrero | .50 | 1.25 |
| ❑ 29 | Travis Hafner | .20 | .50 |
| ❑ 30 | Roy Halladay | .30 | .75 |
| ❑ 31 | Cole Hamels | .50 | 1.25 |
| ❑ 32 | Josh Hamilton | .50 | 1.25 |
| ❑ 33 | Rich Harden | .20 | .50 |
| ❑ 34 | Dan Haren | .20 | .50 |
| ❑ 35 | Felix Hernandez | .30 | .75 |
| ❑ 36 | Trevor Hoffman | .20 | .50 |
| ❑ 37 | Matt Holliday | .30 | .75 |
| ❑ 38 | Ryan Howard | .60 | 1.50 |
| ❑ 39 | Torii Hunter | .20 | .50 |
| ❑ 40 | Derek Jeter | 1.25 | 3.00 |
| ❑ 41 | Randy Johnson | .50 | 1.25 |
| ❑ 42 | Chipper Jones | .50 | 1.25 |
| ❑ 43 | Scott Kazmir | .30 | .75 |
| ❑ 44 | Matt Kemp | .50 | 1.25 |
| ❑ 45 | Clayton Kershaw | .50 | 1.25 |
| ❑ 46 | Ian Kinsler | .30 | .75 |
| ❑ 47 | John Lackey | .20 | .50 |
| ❑ 48 | Carlos Lee | .20 | .50 |
| ❑ 49 | Derrek Lee | .30 | .75 |
| ❑ 50 | Tim Lincecum | .60 | 1.50 |
| ❑ 51 | Evan Longoria | .75 | 2.00 |
| ❑ 52 | Nick Markakis | .30 | .75 |
| ❑ 53 | Russell Martin | .30 | .75 |
| ❑ 54 | Victor Martinez | .30 | .75 |
| ❑ 55 | Hideki Matsui | .50 | 1.25 |

|  |  | | |
|---|---|---|---|
| ❑ 56 | Daisuke Matsuzaka | .75 | 2.00 |
| ❑ 57 | Joe Mauer | .50 | 1.25 |
| ❑ 58 | Brian McCann | .30 | .75 |
| ❑ 59 | Nate McLouth | .20 | .50 |
| ❑ 60 | Lastings Milledge | .20 | .50 |
| ❑ 61 | Justin Morneau | .30 | .75 |
| ❑ 62 | Magglio Ordonez | .30 | .75 |
| ❑ 63 | David Ortiz | .30 | .75 |
| ❑ 64 | Roy Oswalt | .30 | .75 |
| ❑ 65 | Jonathan Papelbon | .30 | .75 |
| ❑ 66 | Jake Peavy | .30 | .75 |
| ❑ 67 | Dustin Pedroia | .60 | 1.50 |
| ❑ 68 | Brandon Phillips | .20 | .50 |
| ❑ 69 | Albert Pujols | 1.25 | 3.00 |
| ❑ 70 | Carlos Quentin | .20 | .50 |
| ❑ 71 | Aramis Ramirez | .20 | .50 |
| ❑ 72 | Hanley Ramirez | .50 | 1.25 |
| ❑ 73 | Manny Ramirez | .50 | 1.25 |
| ❑ 74 | Jose Reyes | .50 | 1.25 |
| ❑ 75 | Alex Rios | .20 | .50 |
| ❑ 76 | Mariano Rivera | .30 | .75 |
| ❑ 77 | Brian Roberts | .20 | .50 |
| ❑ 78 | Alex Rodriguez | .75 | 2.00 |
| ❑ 79 | Ivan Rodriguez | .30 | .75 |
| ❑ 80 | Jimmy Rollins | .30 | .75 |
| ❑ 81 | CC Sabathia | .30 | .75 |
| ❑ 82 | Johan Santana | .50 | 1.25 |
| ❑ 83 | Grady Sizemore | .50 | 1.25 |
| ❑ 84 | John Smoltz | .50 | 1.25 |
| ❑ 85 | Alfonso Soriano | .30 | .75 |
| ❑ 86 | Mark Teixeira | .50 | 1.25 |
| ❑ 87 | Miguel Tejada | .30 | .75 |
| ❑ 88 | Jim Thome | .30 | .75 |
| ❑ 89 | Troy Tulowitzki | .30 | .75 |
| ❑ 90 | Dan Uggla | .20 | .50 |
| ❑ 91 | B.J. Upton | .30 | .75 |
| ❑ 92 | Chase Utley | .50 | 1.25 |
| ❑ 93 | Edinson Volquez | .20 | .50 |
| ❑ 94 | Chien-Ming Wang | .50 | 1.25 |
| ❑ 95 | Brandon Webb | .30 | .75 |
| ❑ 96 | Vernon Wells | .20 | .50 |
| ❑ 97 | David Wright | .60 | 1.50 |
| ❑ 98 | Michael Young | .30 | .75 |
| ❑ 99 | Carlos Zambrano | .20 | .50 |
| ❑ 100 | Ryan Zimmerman | .30 | .75 |
| ❑ 101 | David Price AU RC | 50.00 | 100.00 |
| ❑ 102 | A.Cunningham AU RC | 12.50 | 30.00 |
| ❑ 103 | A.Salome AU (RC) | 10.00 | 25.00 |
| ❑ 104 | C.Gillaspie AU RC | 12.50 | 30.00 |
| ❑ 105 | C.Lambert AU (RC) | 8.00 | 20.00 |
| ❑ 106 | D.Fowler AU (RC) | 6.00 | 15.00 |
| ❑ 107 | F.Cervelli AU RC EXCH | 10.00 | 25.00 |
| ❑ 108 | G.Golson AU (RC) | 8.00 | 20.00 |
| ❑ 109 | Josh Geer AU (RC) | 4.00 | 10.00 |
| ❑ 110 | J.Outman AU RC | 4.00 | 10.00 |
| ❑ 111 | James Parr AU (RC) | 8.00 | 20.00 |
| ❑ 112 | K.Ka'aihue AU (RC) | 4.00 | 10.00 |
| ❑ 113 | Luis Cruz AU RC | 10.00 | 25.00 |
| ❑ 114 | L.Marson AU (RC) | 15.00 | 40.00 |
| ❑ 115 | M.Antonelli AU RC | 15.00 | 40.00 |
| ❑ 116 | M.Bowden AU (RC) | 15.00 | 40.00 |
| ❑ 117 | Mat Gamel AU RC | 20.00 | 50.00 |
| ❑ 118 | Tuiasosopo AU (RC) | 15.00 | 40.00 |
| ❑ 119 | Phil Coke AU RC | 20.00 | 50.00 |
| ❑ 120 | J.McDonald AU RC | 30.00 | 60.00 |
| ❑ 121 | S.Martis AU RC EXCH | 10.00 | 25.00 |
| ❑ 122 | Travis Snider AU RC | 75.00 | 150.00 |
| ❑ 123 | Wade LeBlanc AU RC | 4.00 | 10.00 |
| ❑ 124 | Matt Wieters AU RC | 90.00 | 150.00 |
| ❑ 125 | Colby Rasmus AU (RC) | 20.00 | 50.00 |
| ❑ 126 | A.McCutchen AU (RC) | 20.00 | 50.00 |
| ❑ 130 | Koji Uehara AU RC | 50.00 | 100.00 |

## 1991 Stadium Club

| | | |
|---|---|---|
| ❑ COMPLETE SET (600) | 25.00 | 60.00 |
| ❑ COMPLETE SERIES 1 (300) | 15.00 | 40.00 |
| ❑ COMPLETE SERIES 2 (300) | 8.00 | 20.00 |
| ❑ 1 Dave Stewart Tuxedo | .20 | .50 |
| ❑ 2 Wally Joyner | .20 | .50 |
| ❑ 3 Shawon Dunston | .08 | .25 |
| ❑ 4 Darren Daulton | .20 | .50 |
| ❑ 5 Will Clark | .30 | .75 |
| ❑ 6 Sammy Sosa | .50 | 1.25 |
| ❑ 7 Dan Plesac | .08 | .25 |
| ❑ 8 Marquis Grissom | .20 | .50 |
| ❑ 9 Erik Hanson | .08 | .25 |
| ❑ 10 Geno Petralli | .08 | .25 |
| ❑ 11 Jose Rijo | .08 | .25 |
| ❑ 12 Carlos Quintana | .08 | .25 |
| ❑ 13 Junior Ortiz | .08 | .25 |
| ❑ 14 Bob Walk | .08 | .25 |
| ❑ 15 Mike Macfarlane | .08 | .25 |
| ❑ 16 Eric Yelding | .08 | .25 |
| ❑ 17 Bryn Smith | .08 | .25 |
| ❑ 18 Bip Roberts | .08 | .25 |
| ❑ 19 Mike Scioscia | .08 | .25 |
| ❑ 20 Mark Williamson | .08 | .25 |
| ❑ 21 Don Mattingly | 1.25 | 3.00 |
| ❑ 22 John Franco | .20 | .50 |
| ❑ 23 Chet Lemon | .08 | .25 |
| ❑ 24 Tom Henke | .08 | .25 |
| ❑ 25 Jerry Browne | .08 | .25 |
| ❑ 26 David Justice | .20 | .50 |
| ❑ 27 Mark Langston | .08 | .25 |
| ❑ 28 Damon Berryhill | .08 | .25 |
| ❑ 29 Kevin Bass | .08 | .25 |
| ❑ 30 Scott Fletcher | .08 | .25 |
| ❑ 31 Moises Alou | .20 | .50 |
| ❑ 32 Dave Valle | .08 | .25 |
| ❑ 33 Jody Reed | .08 | .25 |
| ❑ 34 Dave West | .08 | .25 |
| ❑ 35 Kevin McReynolds | .08 | .25 |
| ❑ 36 Pat Combs | .08 | .25 |
| ❑ 37 Eric Davis | .20 | .50 |
| ❑ 38 Bret Saberhagen | .20 | .50 |
| ❑ 39 Stan Javier | .08 | .25 |
| ❑ 40 Chuck Cary | .08 | .25 |
| ❑ 41 Tony Phillips | .08 | .25 |
| ❑ 42 Lee Smith | .20 | .50 |
| ❑ 43 Tim Teufel | .08 | .25 |
| ❑ 44 Lance Dickson RC | .15 | .40 |
| ❑ 45 Greg Litton | .08 | .25 |
| ❑ 46 Ted Higuera | .08 | .25 |
| ❑ 47 Edgar Martinez | .30 | .75 |
| ❑ 48 Steve Avery | .20 | .50 |
| ❑ 49 Walt Weiss | .08 | .25 |
| ❑ 50 David Segui | .08 | .25 |
| ❑ 51 Andy Benes | .08 | .25 |
| ❑ 52 Karl Rhodes | .08 | .25 |
| ❑ 53 Neal Heaton | .08 | .25 |
| ❑ 54 Danny Gladden | .08 | .25 |
| ❑ 55 Luis Rivera | .08 | .25 |
| ❑ 56 Kevin Brown | .20 | .50 |
| ❑ 57 Frank Thomas | .50 | 1.25 |
| ❑ 58 Terry Mulholland | .08 | .25 |
| ❑ 59 Dick Schofield | .08 | .25 |
| ❑ 60 Ron Darling | .08 | .25 |
| ❑ 61 Sandy Alomar Jr. | .08 | .25 |
| ❑ 62 Dave Stieb | .08 | .25 |
| ❑ 63 Alan Trammell | .20 | .50 |
| ❑ 64 Matt Nokes | .08 | .25 |
| ❑ 65 Lenny Harris | .08 | .25 |
| ❑ 66 Milt Thompson | .08 | .25 |
| ❑ 67 Storm Davis | .08 | .25 |
| ❑ 68 Joe Oliver | .08 | .25 |
| ❑ 69 Andres Galarraga | .20 | .50 |
| ❑ 70 Ozzie Guillen | .20 | .50 |
| ❑ 71 Ken Howell | .08 | .25 |
| ❑ 72 Garry Templeton | .08 | .25 |
| ❑ 73 Derrick May | .08 | .25 |
| ❑ 74 Xavier Hernandez | .08 | .25 |
| ❑ 75 Dave Parker | .20 | .50 |
| ❑ 76 Rick Aguilera | .20 | .50 |
| ❑ 77 Robby Thompson | .08 | .25 |
| ❑ 78 Pete Incaviglia | .08 | .25 |
| ❑ 79 Bob Welch | .08 | .25 |
| ❑ 80 Randy Milligan | .08 | .25 |
| ❑ 81 Chuck Finley | .20 | .50 |
| ❑ 82 Alvin Davis | .08 | .25 |
| ❑ 83 Tim Naehring | .08 | .25 |
| ❑ 84 Jay Bell | .20 | .50 |
| ❑ 85 Joe Magrane | .08 | .25 |
| ❑ 86 Howard Johnson | .08 | .25 |
| ❑ 87 Jack McDowell | .08 | .25 |
| ❑ 88 Kevin Seitzer | .08 | .25 |
| ❑ 89 Bruce Ruffin | .08 | .25 |
| ❑ 90 Fernando Valenzuela | .20 | .50 |
| ❑ 91 Terry Kennedy | .08 | .25 |
| ❑ 92 Barry Larkin | .30 | .75 |
| ❑ 93 Larry Walker | .50 | 1.25 |
| ❑ 94 Luis Salazar | .08 | .25 |
| ❑ 95 Gary Sheffield | .20 | .50 |
| ❑ 96 Bobby Witt | .08 | .25 |
| ❑ 97 Lonnie Smith | .08 | .25 |
| ❑ 98 Bryan Harvey | .08 | .25 |
| ❑ 99 Mookie Wilson | .20 | .50 |
| ❑ 100 Dwight Gooden | .20 | .50 |
| ❑ 101 Lou Whitaker | .20 | .50 |
| ❑ 102 Ron Karkovice | .08 | .25 |
| ❑ 103 Jesse Barfield | .08 | .25 |
| ❑ 104 Jose DeJesus | .08 | .25 |
| ❑ 105 Benito Santiago | .20 | .50 |
| ❑ 106 Brian Holman | .08 | .25 |
| ❑ 107 Rafael Ramirez | .08 | .25 |
| ❑ 108 Ellis Burks | .08 | .25 |
| ❑ 109 Mike Bielecki | .08 | .25 |
| ❑ 110 Kirby Puckett | .50 | 1.25 |
| ❑ 111 Terry Shumpert | .08 | .25 |
| ❑ 112 Chuck Crim | .08 | .25 |
| ❑ 113 Todd Benzinger | .08 | .25 |
| ❑ 114 Brian Barnes RC | .15 | .40 |
| ❑ 115 Carlos Baerga | .20 | .50 |
| ❑ 116 Kal Daniels | .08 | .25 |
| ❑ 117 Dave Johnson | .08 | .25 |
| ❑ 118 Andy Van Slyke | .30 | .75 |
| ❑ 119 John Burkett | .08 | .25 |
| ❑ 120 Rickey Henderson | .50 | 1.25 |
| ❑ 121 Tim Jones | .08 | .25 |
| ❑ 122 Daryl Irvine RC | .08 | .25 |
| ❑ 123 Ruben Sierra | .20 | .50 |
| ❑ 124 Jim Abbott | .30 | .75 |
| ❑ 125 Daryl Boston | .08 | .25 |
| ❑ 126 Greg Maddux | .75 | 2.00 |
| ❑ 127 Von Hayes | .08 | .25 |
| ❑ 128 Mike Fitzgerald | .08 | .25 |
| ❑ 129 Wayne Edwards | .08 | .25 |
| ❑ 130 Greg Briley | .08 | .25 |
| ❑ 131 Rob Dibble | .20 | .50 |
| ❑ 132 Gene Larkin | .08 | .25 |
| ❑ 133 David Wells | .08 | .25 |
| ❑ 134 Steve Balboni | .08 | .25 |
| ❑ 135 Greg Vaughn | .08 | .25 |
| ❑ 136 Mark Davis | .08 | .25 |
| ❑ 137 Dave Rhode | .08 | .25 |
| ❑ 138 Eric Show | .08 | .25 |
| ❑ 139 Bobby Bonilla | .20 | .50 |
| ❑ 140 Dana Kiecker | .08 | .25 |
| ❑ 141 Gary Pettis | .08 | .25 |
| ❑ 142 Dennis Boyd | .08 | .25 |
| ❑ 143 Mike Benjamin | .08 | .25 |
| ❑ 144 Luis Polonia | .08 | .25 |
| ❑ 145 Doug Jones | .08 | .25 |
| ❑ 146 Al Newman | .08 | .25 |
| ❑ 147 Alex Fernandez | .20 | .50 |
| ❑ 148 Bill Doran | .08 | .25 |
| ❑ 149 Kevin Elster | .08 | .25 |
| ❑ 150 Len Dykstra | .20 | .50 |
| ❑ 151 Mike Gallego | .08 | .25 |
| ❑ 152 Tim Belcher | .08 | .25 |
| ❑ 153 Jay Buhner | .20 | .50 |
| ❑ 154 Ozzie Smith | .75 | 2.00 |
| ❑ 155 Jose Canseco | .30 | .75 |
| ❑ 156 Gregg Olson | .08 | .25 |
| ❑ 157 Charlie O'Brien | .08 | .25 |
| ❑ 158 Frank Tanana | .08 | .25 |
| ❑ 159 George Brett | 1.25 | 3.00 |
| ❑ 160 Jeff Huson | .08 | .25 |
| ❑ 161 Kevin Tapani | .08 | .25 |
| ❑ 162 Jerome Walton | .08 | .25 |
| ❑ 163 Charlie Hayes | .08 | .25 |
| ❑ 164 Chris Bosio | .08 | .25 |
| ❑ 165 Chris Sabo | .08 | .25 |
| ❑ 166 Lance Parrish | .20 | .50 |
| ❑ 167 Don Robinson | .08 | .25 |
| ❑ 168 Manny Lee | .08 | .25 |
| ❑ 169 Dennis Rasmussen | .08 | .25 |
| ❑ 170 Wade Boggs | .30 | .75 |
| ❑ 171 Bob Geren | .08 | .25 |
| ❑ 172 Mackey Sasser | .08 | .25 |
| ❑ 173 Julio Franco | .20 | .50 |
| ❑ 174 Otis Nixon | .08 | .25 |
| ❑ 175 Bert Blyleven | .20 | .50 |
| ❑ 176 Craig Biggio | .30 | .75 |
| ❑ 177 Eddie Murray | .50 | 1.25 |
| ❑ 178 Randy Tomlin RC | .15 | .40 |
| ❑ 179 Tino Martinez | .50 | 1.25 |
| ❑ 180 Carlton Fisk | .30 | .75 |
| ❑ 181 Dwight Smith | .08 | .25 |
| ❑ 182 Scott Garrelts | .08 | .25 |
| ❑ 183 Jim Gantner | .08 | .25 |
| ❑ 184 Dickie Thon | .08 | .25 |
| ❑ 185 John Farrell | .08 | .25 |
| ❑ 186 Cecil Fielder | .20 | .50 |
| ❑ 187 Glenn Braggs | .08 | .25 |
| ❑ 188 Allan Anderson | .08 | .25 |
| ❑ 189 Kurt Stillwell | .08 | .25 |
| ❑ 190 Jose Oquendo | .08 | .25 |
| ❑ 191 Joe Orsulak | .08 | .25 |
| ❑ 192 Ricky Jordan | .08 | .25 |
| ❑ 193 Kelly Downs | .08 | .25 |
| ❑ 194 Delino DeShields | .08 | .25 |
| ❑ 195 Omar Vizquel | .30 | .75 |
| ❑ 196 Mark Carreon | .08 | .25 |
| ❑ 197 Mike Harkey | .08 | .25 |
| ❑ 198 Jack Howell | .08 | .25 |
| ❑ 199 Lance Johnson | .08 | .25 |
| ❑ 200 Nolan Ryan Tuxedo | 2.00 | 5.00 |
| ❑ 201 John Marzano | .08 | .25 |
| ❑ 202 Doug Drabek | .08 | .25 |
| ❑ 203 Mark Lemke | .08 | .25 |
| ❑ 204 Steve Sax | .08 | .25 |
| ❑ 205 Greg Harris | .08 | .25 |
| ❑ 206 B.J. Surhoff | .20 | .50 |
| ❑ 207 Todd Burns | .08 | .25 |
| ❑ 208 Jose Gonzalez | .08 | .25 |
| ❑ 209 Mike Scott | .08 | .25 |
| ❑ 210 Dave Magadan | .08 | .25 |
| ❑ 211 Dante Bichette | .08 | .25 |
| ❑ 212 Trevor Wilson | .08 | .25 |
| ❑ 213 Hector Villanueva | .08 | .25 |
| ❑ 214 Dan Pasqua | .08 | .25 |
| ❑ 215 Greg Colbrunn RC | .25 | .60 |
| ❑ 216 Mike Jeffcoat | .08 | .25 |
| ❑ 217 Harold Reynolds | .20 | .50 |
| ❑ 218 Paul O'Neill | .30 | .75 |
| ❑ 219 Mark Guthrie | .08 | .25 |
| ❑ 220 Barry Bonds | 1.50 | 4.00 |
| ❑ 221 Jimmy Key | .20 | .50 |
| ❑ 222 Billy Ripken | .08 | .25 |
| ❑ 223 Tom Pagnozzi | .08 | .25 |
| ❑ 224 Bo Jackson | .50 | 1.25 |
| ❑ 225 Sid Fernandez | .08 | .25 |
| ❑ 226 Mike Marshall | .08 | .25 |
| ❑ 227 John Kruk | .20 | .50 |
| ❑ 228 Mike Fetters | .08 | .25 |
| ❑ 229 Eric Anthony | .08 | .25 |
| ❑ 230 Ryne Sandberg | .75 | 2.00 |
| ❑ 231 Carney Lansford | .20 | .50 |
| ❑ 232 Melido Perez | .08 | .25 |
| ❑ 233 Jose Lind | .08 | .25 |
| ❑ 234 Darryl Hamilton | .08 | .25 |
| ❑ 235 Tom Browning | .08 | .25 |
| ❑ 236 Spike Owen | .08 | .25 |
| ❑ 237 Juan Gonzalez | .50 | 1.25 |
| ❑ 238 Felix Fermin | .08 | .25 |
| ❑ 239 Keith Miller | .08 | .25 |
| ❑ 240 Mark Gubicza | .08 | .25 |
| ❑ 241 Kent Anderson | .08 | .25 |
| ❑ 242 Alvaro Espinoza | .08 | .25 |
| ❑ 243 Dale Murphy | .30 | .75 |
| ❑ 244 Orel Hershiser | .20 | .50 |
| ❑ 245 Paul Molitor | .20 | .50 |

|  |  | | |
|---|------|-----|-----|
| 246 | Eddie Whitson | .08 | .25 |
| 247 | Joe Girardi | .08 | .25 |
| 248 | Kent Hrbek | .20 | .50 |
| 249 | Bill Sampen | .08 | .25 |
| 250 | Kevin Mitchell | .08 | .25 |
| 251 | Mariano Duncan | .08 | .25 |
| 252 | Scott Bradley | .08 | .25 |
| 253 | Mike Greenwell | .08 | .25 |
| 254 | Tom Gordon | .08 | .25 |
| 255 | Todd Zeile | .08 | .25 |
| 256 | Bobby Thigpen | .08 | .25 |
| 257 | Gregg Jefferies | .08 | .25 |
| 258 | Kenny Rogers | .20 | .50 |
| 259 | Shane Mack | .08 | .25 |
| 260 | Zane Smith | .08 | .25 |
| 261 | Mitch Williams | .08 | .25 |
| 262 | Jim Deshaies | .08 | .25 |
| 263 | Dave Winfield | .20 | .50 |
| 264 | Ben McDonald | .08 | .25 |
| 265 | Randy Ready | .08 | .25 |
| 266 | Pat Borders | .08 | .25 |
| 267 | Jose Uribe | .08 | .25 |
| 268 | Derek Lilliquist | .08 | .25 |
| 269 | Greg Brock | .08 | .25 |
| 270 | Ken Griffey Jr. | 1.00 | 2.50 |
| 271 | Jeff Gray RC | .08 | .25 |
| 272 | Danny Tartabull | .08 | .25 |
| 273 | Dennis Martinez | .20 | .50 |
| 274 | Robin Ventura | .20 | .50 |
| 275 | Randy Myers | .08 | .25 |
| 276 | Jack Daugherty | .08 | .25 |
| 277 | Greg Gagne | .08 | .25 |
| 278 | Jay Howell | .08 | .25 |
| 279 | Mike LaValliere | .08 | .25 |
| 280 | Rex Hudler | .08 | .25 |
| 281 | Mike Simms RC | .08 | .25 |
| 282 | Kevin Maas | .08 | .25 |
| 283 | Jeff Ballard | .08 | .25 |
| 284 | Dave Henderson | .08 | .25 |
| 285 | Pete O'Brien | .08 | .25 |
| 286 | Brook Jacoby | .08 | .25 |
| 287 | Mike Henneman | .08 | .25 |
| 288 | Greg Olson | .08 | .25 |
| 289 | Greg Myers | .08 | .25 |
| 290 | Mark Grace | .30 | .75 |
| 291 | Shawn Abner | .08 | .25 |
| 292 | Frank Viola | .20 | .50 |
| 293 | Lee Stevens | .08 | .25 |
| 294 | Jason Grimsley | .08 | .25 |
| 295 | Matt Williams | .20 | .50 |
| 296 | Ron Robinson | .08 | .25 |
| 297 | Tom Brunansky | .08 | .25 |
| 298 | Checklist 1-100 | .08 | .25 |
| 299 | Checklist 101-200 | .08 | .25 |
| 300 | Checklist 201-300 | .08 | .25 |
| 301 | Darryl Strawberry | .20 | .50 |
| 302 | Bud Black | .08 | .25 |
| 303 | Harold Baines | .20 | .50 |
| 304 | Roberto Alomar | .30 | .75 |
| 305 | Norm Charlton | .08 | .25 |
| 306 | Gary Thurman | .08 | .25 |
| 307 | Mike Felder | .08 | .25 |
| 308 | Tony Gwynn | .60 | 1.50 |
| 309 | Roger Clemens | 1.50 | 4.00 |
| 310 | Andre Dawson | .20 | .50 |
| 311 | Scott Radinsky | .08 | .25 |
| 312 | Bob Melvin | .08 | .25 |
| 313 | Kirk McCaskill | .08 | .25 |
| 314 | Pedro Guerrero | .20 | .50 |
| 315 | Walt Terrell | .08 | .25 |
| 316 | Sam Horn | .08 | .25 |
| 317 | Wes Chamberlain UER RC | .25 | .60 |
| 318 | Pedro Munoz RC | .15 | .40 |
| 319 | Roberto Kelly | .08 | .25 |
| 320 | Mark Portugal | .08 | .25 |
| 321 | Tim McIntosh | .08 | .25 |
| 322 | Jesse Orosco | .08 | .25 |
| 323 | Gary Green | .08 | .25 |
| 324 | Greg Harris | .08 | .25 |
| 325 | Hubie Brooks | .08 | .25 |
| 326 | Chris Nabholz | .08 | .25 |
| 327 | Terry Pendleton | .20 | .50 |
| 328 | Eric King | .08 | .25 |
| 329 | Chili Davis | .20 | .50 |
| 330 | Anthony Telford RC | .08 | .25 |
| 331 | Kelly Gruber | .08 | .25 |
| 332 | Dennis Eckersley | .20 | .50 |
| 333 | Mel Hall | .08 | .25 |
| 334 | Bob Kipper | .08 | .25 |
| 335 | Willie McGee | .20 | .50 |
| 336 | Steve Olin | .08 | .25 |
| 337 | Steve Buechele | .08 | .25 |
| 338 | Scott Leius | .08 | .25 |
| 339 | Hal Morris | .08 | .25 |
| 340 | Jose Offerman | .08 | .25 |
| 341 | Kent Mercker | .08 | .25 |
| 342 | Ken Griffey Sr. | .20 | .50 |
| 343 | Pete Harnisch | .08 | .25 |
| 344 | Kirk Gibson | .20 | .50 |
| 345 | Dave Smith | .08 | .25 |
| 346 | Dave Martinez | .08 | .25 |
| 347 | Atlee Hammaker | .08 | .25 |
| 348 | Brian Downing | .08 | .25 |
| 349 | Todd Hundley | .08 | .25 |
| 350 | Candy Maldonado | .08 | .25 |
| 351 | Dwight Evans | .30 | .75 |
| 352 | Steve Searcy | .08 | .25 |
| 353 | Gary Gaetti | .20 | .50 |
| 354 | Jeff Reardon | .20 | .50 |
| 355 | Travis Fryman | .20 | .50 |
| 356 | Dave Righetti | .08 | .25 |
| 357 | Fred McGriff | .30 | .75 |
| 358 | Don Slaught | .08 | .25 |
| 359 | Gene Nelson | .08 | .25 |
| 360 | Billy Spiers | .08 | .25 |
| 361 | Lee Guetterman | .08 | .25 |
| 362 | Darren Lewis | .08 | .25 |
| 363 | Duane Ward | .08 | .25 |
| 364 | Lloyd Moseby | .08 | .25 |
| 365 | John Smoltz | .30 | .75 |
| 366 | Felix Jose | .08 | .25 |
| 367 | David Cone | .20 | .50 |
| 368 | Wally Backman | .08 | .25 |
| 369 | Jeff Montgomery | .08 | .25 |
| 370 | Rich Garces RC | .15 | .40 |
| 371 | Billy Hatcher | .08 | .25 |
| 372 | Bill Swift | .08 | .25 |
| 373 | Jim Eisenreich | .08 | .25 |
| 374 | Rob Ducey | .08 | .25 |
| 375 | Tim Crews | .08 | .25 |
| 376 | Steve Finley | .20 | .50 |
| 377 | Jeff Blauser | .08 | .25 |
| 378 | Willie Wilson | .08 | .25 |
| 379 | Gerald Perry | .08 | .25 |
| 380 | Jose Mesa | .08 | .25 |
| 381 | Pat Kelly RC | .25 | .60 |
| 382 | Matt Merullo | .08 | .25 |
| 383 | Ivan Calderon | .08 | .25 |
| 384 | Scott Chiamparino | .08 | .25 |
| 385 | Lloyd McClendon | .08 | .25 |
| 386 | Dave Bergman | .08 | .25 |
| 387 | Ed Sprague | .08 | .25 |
| 388 | Jeff Bagwell RC | 1.25 | 3.00 |
| 389 | Brett Butler | .20 | .50 |
| 390 | Larry Andersen | .08 | .25 |
| 391 | Glenn Davis | .08 | .25 |
| 392 | Alex Cole UER | | |
|  | (Front photo actually | | |
|  | Otis Nixon) | .08 | .25 |
| 393 | Mike Heath | .08 | .25 |
| 394 | Danny Darwin | .08 | .25 |
| 395 | Steve Lake | .08 | .25 |
| 396 | Tim Layana | .08 | .25 |
| 397 | Terry Leach | .08 | .25 |
| 398 | Bill Wegman | .08 | .25 |
| 399 | Mark McGwire | 1.50 | 4.00 |
| 400 | Mike Boddicker | .08 | .25 |
| 401 | Steve Howe | .08 | .25 |
| 402 | Bernard Gilkey | .08 | .25 |
| 403 | Thomas Howard | .08 | .25 |
| 404 | Rafael Belliard | .08 | .25 |
| 405 | Tom Candiotti | .08 | .25 |
| 406 | Rene Gonzales | .08 | .25 |
| 407 | Chuck McElroy | .08 | .25 |
| 408 | Paul Sorrento | .08 | .25 |
| 409 | Randy Johnson | .60 | 1.50 |
| 410 | Brady Anderson | .20 | .50 |
| 411 | Dennis Cook | .08 | .25 |
| 412 | Mickey Tettleton | .08 | .25 |
| 413 | Mike Stanton | .08 | .25 |
| 414 | Ken Oberkfell | .08 | .25 |
| 415 | Rick Honeycutt | .08 | .25 |
| 416 | Nelson Santovenia | .08 | .25 |
| 417 | Bob Tewksbury | .08 | .25 |
| 418 | Brent Mayne | .08 | .25 |
| 419 | Steve Farr | .08 | .25 |
| 420 | Phil Stephenson | .08 | .25 |
| 421 | Jeff Russell | .08 | .25 |
| 422 | Chris James | .08 | .25 |
| 423 | Tim Leary | .08 | .25 |
| 424 | Gary Carter | .20 | .50 |
| 425 | Glenallen Hill | .08 | .25 |
| 426 | Matt Young UER | .08 | .25 |
| 427 | Sid Bream | .08 | .25 |
| 428 | Greg Swindell | .08 | .25 |
| 429 | Scott Aldred | .08 | .25 |
| 430 | Cal Ripken | 1.50 | 4.00 |
| 431 | Bill Landrum | .08 | .25 |
| 432 | Earnest Riles | .08 | .25 |
| 433 | Danny Jackson | .08 | .25 |
| 434 | Casey Candaele | .08 | .25 |
| 435 | Ken Hill | .08 | .25 |
| 436 | Jaime Navarro | .08 | .25 |
| 437 | Lance Blankenship | .08 | .25 |
| 438 | Randy Velarde | .08 | .25 |
| 439 | Frank DiPino | .08 | .25 |
| 440 | Carl Nichols | .08 | .25 |
| 441 | Jeff M. Robinson | .08 | .25 |
| 442 | Deion Sanders | .30 | .75 |
| 443 | Vicente Palacios | .08 | .25 |
| 444 | Devon White | .20 | .50 |
| 445 | John Cerutti | .08 | .25 |
| 446 | Tracy Jones | .08 | .25 |
| 447 | Jack Morris | .20 | .50 |
| 448 | Mitch Webster | .08 | .25 |
| 449 | Bob Ojeda | .08 | .25 |
| 450 | Oscar Azocar | .08 | .25 |
| 451 | Luis Aquino | .08 | .25 |
| 452 | Mark Whiten | .08 | .25 |
| 453 | Stan Belinda | .08 | .25 |
| 454 | Ron Gant | .20 | .50 |
| 455 | Jose DeLeon | .08 | .25 |
| 456 | Mark Salas UER | | |
|  | (Back has 85T photo& | | |
|  | but calls it | .08 | .25 |
| 457 | Junior Felix | .08 | .25 |
| 458 | Wally Whitehurst | .08 | .25 |
| 459 | Phil Plantier RC | .25 | .60 |
| 460 | Juan Berenguer | .08 | .25 |
| 461 | Franklin Stubbs | .08 | .25 |
| 462 | Joe Boever | .08 | .25 |
| 463 | Tim Wallach | .08 | .25 |
| 464 | Mike Moore | .08 | .25 |
| 465 | Albert Belle | .20 | .50 |
| 466 | Mike Witt | .08 | .25 |
| 467 | Craig Worthington | .08 | .25 |
| 468 | Jerald Clark | .08 | .25 |
| 469 | Scott Terry | .08 | .25 |
| 470 | Milt Cuyler | .08 | .25 |
| 471 | John Smiley | .08 | .25 |
| 472 | Charles Nagy | .25 | .60 |
| 473 | Alan Mills | .08 | .25 |
| 474 | John Russell | .08 | .25 |
| 475 | Bruce Hurst | .08 | .25 |
| 476 | Andujar Cedeno | .08 | .25 |
| 477 | Dave Eiland | .08 | .25 |
| 478 | Brian McRae RC | .25 | .60 |
| 479 | Mike LaCoss | .08 | .25 |
| 480 | Chris Gwynn | .08 | .25 |
| 481 | Jamie Moyer | .20 | .50 |
| 482 | John Olerud | .20 | .50 |
| 483 | Efrain Valdez RC | .08 | .25 |
| 484 | Sil Campusano | .08 | .25 |
| 485 | Pascual Perez | .08 | .25 |
| 486 | Gary Redus | .08 | .25 |
| 487 | Andy Hawkins | .08 | .25 |
| 488 | Cory Snyder | .08 | .25 |
| 489 | Chris Hoiles | .08 | .25 |
| 490 | Ron Hassey | .08 | .25 |
| 491 | Gary Wayne | .08 | .25 |
| 492 | Mark Lewis | .08 | .25 |
| 493 | Scott Coolbaugh | .08 | .25 |
| 494 | Gerald Young | .08 | .25 |
| 495 | Juan Samuel | .08 | .25 |
| 496 | Willie Fraser | .08 | .25 |
| 497 | Jeff Treadway | .08 | .25 |
| 498 | Vince Coleman | .08 | .25 |
| 499 | Cris Carpenter | .08 | .25 |
| 500 | Jack Clark | .20 | .50 |
| 501 | Kevin Appier | .20 | .50 |
| 502 | Rafael Palmeiro | .30 | .75 |
| 503 | Hensley Meulens | .08 | .25 |
| 504 | George Bell | .08 | .25 |
| 505 | Tony Pena | .08 | .25 |

| | | |
|---|---|---|
| 506 Roger McDowell | .08 | .25 |
| 507 Luis Sojo | .08 | .25 |
| 508 Mike Schooler | .08 | .25 |
| 509 Robin Yount | .75 | 2.00 |
| 510 Jack Armstrong | .08 | .25 |
| 511 Rick Cerone | .08 | .25 |
| 512 Curt Wilkerson | .08 | .25 |
| 513 Joe Carter | .20 | .50 |
| 514 Tim Burke | .08 | .25 |
| 515 Tony Fernandez | .08 | .25 |
| 516 Ramon Martinez | .08 | .25 |
| 517 Tim Hulett | .08 | .25 |
| 518 Terry Steinbach | .08 | .25 |
| 519 Pete Smith | .08 | .25 |
| 520 Ken Caminiti | .20 | .50 |
| 521 Shawn Boskie | .08 | .25 |
| 522 Mike Pagliarulo | .08 | .25 |
| 523 Tim Raines | .20 | .50 |
| 524 Alfredo Griffin | .08 | .25 |
| 525 Henry Cotto | .08 | .25 |
| 526 Mike Stanley | .08 | .25 |
| 527 Charlie Leibrandt | .08 | .25 |
| 528 Jeff King | .08 | .25 |
| 529 Eric Plunk | .08 | .25 |
| 530 Tom Lampkin | .08 | .25 |
| 531 Steve Bedrosian | .08 | .25 |
| 532 Tom Herr | .08 | .25 |
| 533 Craig Lefferts | .08 | .25 |
| 534 Jeff Reed | .08 | .25 |
| 535 Mickey Morandini | .08 | .25 |
| 536 Greg Cadaret | .08 | .25 |
| 537 Ray Lankford | .20 | .50 |
| 538 John Candelaria | .08 | .25 |
| 539 Rob Deer | .08 | .25 |
| 540 Brad Arnsberg | .08 | .25 |
| 541 Mike Sharperson | .08 | .25 |
| 542 Jeff D. Robinson | .08 | .25 |
| 543 Mo Vaughn | .20 | .50 |
| 544 Jeff Parrett | .08 | .25 |
| 545 Willie Randolph | .20 | .50 |
| 546 Herm Winningham | .08 | .25 |
| 547 Jeff Innis | .08 | .25 |
| 548 Chuck Knoblauch | .20 | .50 |
| 549 Tommy Greene UER | .08 | .25 |
| 550 Jeff Hamilton | .08 | .25 |
| 551 Barry Jones | .08 | .25 |
| 552 Ken Dayley | .08 | .25 |
| 553 Rick Dempsey | .08 | .25 |
| 554 Greg Smith | .08 | .25 |
| 555 Mike Devereaux | .08 | .25 |
| 556 Keith Comstock | .08 | .25 |
| 557 Paul Faries RC | .08 | .25 |
| 558 Tom Glavine | .30 | .75 |
| 559 Craig Grebeck | .08 | .25 |
| 560 Scott Erickson | .08 | .25 |
| 561 Joel Skinner | .08 | .25 |
| 562 Mike Morgan | .08 | .25 |
| 563 Dave Gallagher | .08 | .25 |
| 564 Todd Stottlemyre | .08 | .25 |
| 565 Rich Rodriguez RC | .08 | .25 |
| 566 Craig Wilson RC | .08 | .25 |
| 567 Jeff Brantley | .08 | .25 |
| 568 Scott Kamieniecki RC | .25 | .60 |
| 569 Steve Decker RC | .15 | .40 |
| 570 Juan Agosto | .08 | .25 |
| 571 Tommy Gregg | .08 | .25 |
| 572 Kevin Wickander | .08 | .25 |
| 573 Jamie Quirk UER (Rookie card is 1976& but card b | .08 | .25 |
| 574 Jerry Don Gleaton | .08 | .25 |
| 575 Chris Hammond | .08 | .25 |
| 576 Luis Gonzalez RC | .60 | 1.50 |
| 577 Russ Swan | .08 | .25 |
| 578 Jeff Conine RC | .40 | 1.00 |
| 579 Charlie Hough | .20 | .50 |
| 580 Jeff Kunkel | .08 | .25 |
| 581 Darrel Akerfelds | .08 | .25 |
| 582 Jeff Manto | .08 | .25 |
| 583 Alejandro Pena | .08 | .25 |
| 584 Mark Davidson | .08 | .25 |
| 585 Bob MacDonald RC | .15 | .40 |
| 586 Paul Assenmacher | .08 | .25 |
| 587 Dan Wilson RC | .25 | .60 |
| 588 Tom Bolton | .08 | .25 |
| 589 Brian Harper | .08 | .25 |
| 590 John Habyan | .08 | .25 |
| 591 John Orton | .08 | .25 |

| | | |
|---|---|---|
| 592 Mark Gardner | .08 | .25 |
| 593 Turner Ward RC | .25 | .60 |
| 594 Bob Patterson | .08 | .25 |
| 595 Ed Nunez | .08 | .25 |
| 596 Gary Scott UER RC | .15 | .40 |
| 597 Scott Bankhead | .08 | .25 |
| 598 Checklist 301-400 | .08 | .25 |
| 599 Checklist 401-500 | .08 | .25 |
| 600 Checklist 501-600 | .08 | .25 |

## 1993 Stadium Club Murphy

| | | |
|---|---|---|
| COMP.FACT.SET (212) | 15.00 | 40.00 |
| COMPLETE SET (200) | 12.00 | 30.00 |
| COMMON CARD (1-200) | .05 | .15 |
| COMMON RC | .05 | .15 |
| STATED PRINT RUN 128,000 SETS | | |
| 1 Dave Winfield WS | .05 | .15 |
| 2 Juan Guzman AS | .05 | .15 |
| 3 Tony Gwynn AS | .40 | 1.00 |
| 4 Chris Roberts USA | .05 | .15 |
| 5 Benny Santiago | .10 | .30 |
| 6 Sherard Clinkscales RC | .05 | .15 |
| 7 Jon Nunnally RC | .20 | .50 |
| 8 Chuck Knoblauch | .10 | .30 |
| 9 Bob Wolcott RC | .05 | .15 |
| 10 Steve Rodriguez USA | .05 | .15 |
| 11 Mark Williams RC | .05 | .15 |
| 12 Danny Clyburn RC | .05 | .15 |
| 13 Darren Dreifort USA | .05 | .15 |
| 14 Andy Van Slyke | .20 | .50 |
| 15 Wade Boggs AS | .20 | .50 |
| 16 Scott Patton RC | .05 | .15 |
| 17 Gary Sheffield AS | .10 | .30 |
| 18 Ron Villone USA | .05 | .15 |
| 19 Roberto Alomar ALCS | .20 | .50 |
| 20 Marc Valdes USA | .05 | .15 |
| 21 Darron Kirkreit USA | .05 | .15 |
| 22 Jeff Granger USA | .05 | .15 |
| 23 Levon Largusa RC | .05 | .15 |
| 24 Jimmy Key | .10 | .30 |
| 25 Kevin Pearson RC | .05 | .15 |
| 26 Michael Moore RC | .05 | .15 |
| 27 Preston Wilson RC | .60 | 1.50 |
| 28 Kirby Puckett AS | .30 | .75 |
| 29 Tim Crabtree RC | .05 | .15 |
| 30 Bip Roberts | .05 | .15 |
| 31 Kelly Gruber | .05 | .15 |
| 32 Tony Fernandez | .05 | .15 |
| 33 Jason Angel RC | .05 | .15 |
| 34 Calvin Murray USA | .05 | .15 |
| 35 Chad McConnell | .05 | .15 |
| 36 Jason Moler USA | .05 | .15 |
| 37 Mark Lemke | .05 | .15 |
| 38 Tom Knauss RC | .05 | .15 |
| 39 Larry Mitchell RC | .05 | .15 |
| 40 Doug Mirabelli RC | .20 | .50 |
| 41 Everett Stull RC | .05 | .15 |
| 42 Chris Wimmer USA | .05 | .15 |
| 43 Dan Serafini RC | .10 | .30 |
| 44 Ryne Sandberg AS | .50 | 1.25 |
| 45 Steve Lyons RC | .05 | .15 |
| 46 Ryan Freeburg RC | .05 | .15 |
| 47 Ruben Sierra | .10 | .30 |
| 48 David Mysel RC | .05 | .15 |
| 49 Joe Hamilton RC | .05 | .15 |
| 50 Steve Rodriguez | .05 | .15 |
| 51 Tim Wakefield | .30 | .75 |
| 52 Scott Gentile RC | .05 | .15 |
| 53 Doug Jones | .05 | .15 |
| 54 Willie Brown RC | .05 | .15 |
| 55 Chad Mottola RC | .20 | .50 |
| 56 Ken Griffey Jr. AS | .50 | 1.25 |
| 57 Jon Lieber RC | 1.00 | 2.50 |

| | | |
|---|---|---|
| 58 Dennis Martinez | .10 | .30 |
| 59 Joe Petzka RC | .05 | .15 |
| 60 Benji Simonton RC | .05 | .15 |
| 61 Brett Backlund RC | .05 | .15 |
| 62 Damon Berryhill | .05 | .15 |
| 63 Juan Guzman ALCS | .05 | .15 |
| 64 Doug Hecker RC | .05 | .15 |
| 65 Jamie Arnold RC | .05 | .15 |
| 66 Bob Tewksbury | .05 | .15 |
| 67 Tim Leger RC | .05 | .15 |
| 68 Todd Etler RC | .05 | .15 |
| 69 Lloyd McClendon | .05 | .15 |
| 70 Kurt Ehmann RC | .05 | .15 |
| 71 Rick Magdaleno RC | .05 | .15 |
| 72 Tom Pagnozzi | .05 | .15 |
| 73 Jeffrey Hammonds USA | .05 | .15 |
| 74 Joe Carter AS | .10 | .30 |
| 75 Chris Holt RC | .10 | .30 |
| 76 Charles Johnson USA | .10 | .30 |
| 77 Bob Walk | .05 | .15 |
| 78 Fred McGriff AS | .20 | .50 |
| 79 Tom Evans RC | .05 | .15 |
| 80 Scott Klingenbeck RC | .05 | .15 |
| 81 Chad McConnell USA | .05 | .15 |
| 82 Chris Eddy RC | .05 | .15 |
| 83 Phil Nevin USA | .10 | .30 |
| 84 John Kruk | .10 | .30 |
| 85 Tony Sheffield RC | .05 | .15 |
| 86 John Smoltz | .20 | .50 |
| 87 Trevor Humphry RC | .05 | .15 |
| 88 Charles Nagy | .05 | .15 |
| 89 Sean Runyan RC | .05 | .15 |
| 90 Mike Gulan RC | .05 | .15 |
| 91 Darren Daulton | .10 | .30 |
| 92 Otis Nixon | .05 | .15 |
| 93 Nomar Garciaparra USA | 2.00 | 5.00 |
| 94 Larry Walker AS | .10 | .30 |
| 95 Hut Smith RC | .05 | .15 |
| 96 Rick Helling USA | .05 | .15 |
| 97 Roger Clemens AS | .60 | 1.50 |
| 98 Ron Gant | .10 | .30 |
| 99 Kenny Felder RC | .05 | .15 |
| 100 Steve Murphy RC | .05 | .15 |
| 101 Mike Smith RC | .05 | .15 |
| 102 Terry Pendleton | .10 | .30 |
| 103 Tim Davis USA | .05 | .15 |
| 104 Jeff Patzke RC | .05 | .15 |
| 105 Craig Wilson USA | .05 | .15 |
| 106 Tom Glavine AS | .20 | .50 |
| 107 Mark Langston | .05 | .15 |
| 108 Mark Thompson RC | .05 | .15 |
| 109 Eric Owens RC | .05 | .15 |
| 110 Keith Johnson RC | .05 | .15 |
| 111 Robin Ventura AS | .10 | .30 |
| 112 Ed Sprague | .05 | .15 |
| 113 Jeff Schmidt RC | .05 | .15 |
| 114 Don Wengert RC | .05 | .15 |
| 115 Craig Biggio | .20 | .50 |
| 116 Kenny Carlyle RC | .05 | .15 |
| 117 Derek Jeter RC | 20.00 | 50.00 |
| 118 Manuel Lee | .05 | .15 |
| 119 Jeff Haas RC | .05 | .15 |
| 120 Roger Bailey RC | .05 | .15 |
| 121 Sean Lowe RC | .05 | .15 |
| 122 Rick Aguilera | .05 | .15 |
| 123 Sandy Alomar Jr. | .05 | .15 |
| 124 Derek Wallace RC | .05 | .15 |
| 125 B.J. Wallace USA | .05 | .15 |
| 126 Greg Maddux AS | .50 | 1.25 |
| 127 Tim Moore RC | .05 | .15 |
| 128 Lee Smith | .10 | .30 |
| 129 Todd Steverson RC | .05 | .15 |
| 130 Chris Widger RC | .05 | .15 |
| 131 Paul Molitor | .10 | .30 |
| 132 Chris Smith RC | .05 | .15 |
| 133 Chris Gomez RC | .20 | .50 |
| 134 Jimmy Baron RC | .05 | .15 |
| 135 John Smoltz | .20 | .50 |
| 136 Pat Borders | .05 | .15 |
| 137 Donnie Leshnock | .05 | .15 |
| 138 Gus Gandarillas RC | .05 | .15 |
| 139 Will Clark | .20 | .50 |
| 140 Ryan Luzinski RC | .05 | .15 |
| 141 Cal Ripken AS | 1.00 | 2.50 |
| 142 B.J. Wallace | .05 | .15 |
| 143 Trey Beamon RC | .20 | .50 |
| 144 Norm Charlton | .05 | .15 |
| 145 Mike Mussina | .20 | .50 |

|  |  | | |
|---|---|---|---|
| 146 | Billy Owens RC | .05 | .15 |
| 147 | Ozzie Smith AS | .50 | 1.25 |
| 148 | Jason Kendall RC | .60 | 1.50 |
| 149 | Mike Matthews RC | .05 | .15 |
| 150 | David Spykstra RC | .05 | .15 |
| 151 | Benji Grigsby RC | .05 | .15 |
| 152 | Sean Smith RC | .05 | .15 |
| 153 | Mark McGwire AS | .75 | 2.00 |
| 154 | David Cone | .10 | .30 |
| 155 | Shon Walker RC | .05 | .15 |
| 156 | Jason Giambi USA | .40 | 1.00 |
| 157 | Jack McDowell AS | .05 | .15 |
| 158 | Paxton Briley RC | .05 | .15 |
| 159 | Edgar Martinez | .20 | .50 |
| 160 | Brian Sackinsky RC | .05 | .15 |
| 161 | Barry Bonds AS | .75 | 2.00 |
| 162 | Roberto Kelly | .05 | .15 |
| 163 | Jeff Alkire | .05 | .15 |
| 164 | Mike Sharperson | .05 | .15 |
| 165 | Jamie Taylor RC | .05 | .15 |
| 166 | John Saffer UER RC | .05 | .15 |
| 167 | Jerry Browne | .05 | .15 |
| 168 | Travis Fryman AS | .10 | .30 |
| 169 | Brady Anderson | .10 | .30 |
| 170 | Chris Roberts | .05 | .15 |
| 171 | Lloyd Peever RC | .05 | .15 |
| 172 | Francisco Cabrera | .05 | .15 |
| 173 | Ramiro Martinez RC | .05 | .15 |
| 174 | Jeff Alkire USA | .05 | .15 |
| 175 | Ivan Rodriguez AS | .20 | .50 |
| 176 | Kevin Brown | .10 | .30 |
| 177 | Chad Roper RC | .05 | .15 |
| 178 | Rod Henderson RC | .05 | .15 |
| 179 | Dennis Eckersley | .10 | .30 |
| 180 | Shannon Stewart RC | .60 | 1.50 |
| 181 | DeShawn Warren RC | .05 | .15 |
| 182 | Lonnie Smith | .05 | .15 |
| 183 | Willie Adams USA | .05 | .15 |
| 184 | Jeff Montgomery | .05 | .15 |
| 185 | Damon Hollins RC | .20 | .50 |
| 186 | Byron Mathews RC | .05 | .15 |
| 187 | Harold Baines | .10 | .30 |
| 188 | Rick Greene USA | .05 | .15 |
| 189 | Carlos Baerga AS | .05 | .15 |
| 190 | Brandon Cromer RC | .05 | .15 |
| 191 | Roberto Alomar AS | .20 | .50 |
| 192 | Rich Ireland RC | .05 | .15 |
| 193 | Steve Montgomery RC | .05 | .15 |
| 194 | Brant Brown RC | .05 | .15 |
| 195 | Ritchie Moody RC | .05 | .15 |
| 196 | Michael Tucker USA | .05 | .15 |
| 197 | Jason Varitek USA | 2.00 | 5.00 |
| 198 | David Manning RC | .05 | .15 |
| 199 | Marquis Riley RC | .05 | .15 |
| 200 | Jason Giambi | .40 | 1.00 |

## 2001 Stadium Club

| | | | |
|---|---|---|---|
| COMPLETE SET (200) | | 50.00 | 120.00 |
| COMP.SET w/o SP's (175) | | 10.00 | 25.00 |
| COMMON CARD (1-150) | | .10 | .30 |
| COMMON SP (151-200) | | 1.25 | 3.00 |
| 1 | Nomar Garciaparra | .50 | 1.25 |
| 2 | Chipper Jones | .30 | .75 |
| 3 | Jeff Bagwell | .20 | .50 |
| 4 | Chad Kreuter | .10 | .30 |
| 5 | Randy Johnson | .30 | .75 |
| 6 | Mike Hampton | .10 | .30 |
| 7 | Barry Larkin | .20 | .50 |
| 8 | Bernie Williams | .20 | .50 |
| 9 | Chris Singleton | .10 | .30 |
| 10 | Larry Walker | .20 | .50 |
| 11 | Brad Ausmus | .10 | .30 |
| 12 | Ron Coomer | .10 | .30 |
| 13 | Edgardo Alfonzo | .10 | .30 |
| 14 | Delino DeShields | .10 | .30 |
| 15 | Tony Gwynn | .40 | 1.00 |
| 16 | Andruw Jones | .20 | .50 |
| 17 | Raul Mondesi | .10 | .30 |
| 18 | Troy Glaus | .10 | .30 |
| 19 | Ben Grieve | .10 | .30 |
| 20 | Sammy Sosa | .30 | .75 |
| 21 | Fernando Vina | .10 | .30 |
| 22 | Jeromy Burnitz | .10 | .30 |
| 23 | Jay Bell | .10 | .30 |
| 24 | Pete Harnisch | .10 | .30 |
| 25 | Barry Bonds | .75 | 2.00 |
| 26 | Eric Karros | .10 | .30 |
| 27 | Alex Gonzalez | .10 | .30 |
| 28 | Mike Lieberthal | .10 | .30 |
| 29 | Juan Encarnacion | .10 | .30 |
| 30 | Derek Jeter | .75 | 2.00 |
| 31 | Luis Sojo | .10 | .30 |
| 32 | Eric Milton | .10 | .30 |
| 33 | Aaron Boone | .10 | .30 |
| 34 | Roberto Alomar | .20 | .50 |
| 35 | John Olerud | .10 | .30 |
| 36 | Orlando Cabrera | .10 | .30 |
| 37 | Shawn Green | .10 | .30 |
| 38 | Roger Cedeno | .10 | .30 |
| 39 | Garret Anderson | .10 | .30 |
| 40 | Jim Thome | .20 | .50 |
| 41 | Gabe Kapler | .10 | .30 |
| 42 | Mo Vaughn | .10 | .30 |
| 43 | Sean Casey | .10 | .30 |
| 44 | Preston Wilson | .10 | .30 |
| 45 | Juvy Lopez | .10 | .30 |
| 46 | Ryan Klesko | .10 | .30 |
| 47 | Ray Durham | .10 | .30 |
| 48 | Dean Palmer | .10 | .30 |
| 49 | Jorge Posada | .20 | .50 |
| 50 | Alex Rodriguez | .50 | 1.25 |
| 51 | Tom Glavine | .20 | .50 |
| 52 | Ray Lankford | .10 | .30 |
| 53 | Jose Canseco | .20 | .50 |
| 54 | Tim Salmon | .10 | .30 |
| 55 | Cal Ripken | 1.00 | 2.50 |
| 56 | Bob Abreu | .10 | .30 |
| 57 | Robin Ventura | .10 | .30 |
| 58 | Damion Easley | .10 | .30 |
| 59 | Paul O'Neill | .20 | .50 |
| 60 | Ivan Rodriguez | .20 | .50 |
| 61 | Carl Everett | .10 | .30 |
| 62 | Doug Glanville | .10 | .30 |
| 63 | Jeff Kent | .20 | .50 |
| 64 | Jay Buhner | .10 | .30 |
| 65 | Cliff Floyd | .10 | .30 |
| 66 | Rick Ankiel | .10 | .30 |
| 67 | Mark Grace | .20 | .50 |
| 68 | Brian Jordan | .10 | .30 |
| 69 | Craig Biggio | .20 | .50 |
| 70 | Carlos Delgado | .10 | .30 |
| 71 | Brad Radke | .10 | .30 |
| 72 | Greg Maddux | .50 | 1.25 |
| 73 | Al Leiter | .10 | .30 |
| 74 | Pokey Reese | .10 | .30 |
| 75 | Todd Helton | .20 | .50 |
| 76 | Mariano Rivera | .30 | .75 |
| 77 | Shane Spencer | .10 | .30 |
| 78 | Jason Kendall | .10 | .30 |
| 79 | Chuck Knoblauch | .10 | .30 |
| 80 | Scott Rolen | .20 | .50 |
| 81 | Jose Offerman | .10 | .30 |
| 82 | J.T. Snow | .10 | .30 |
| 83 | Pat Meares | .10 | .30 |
| 84 | Quilvio Veras | .10 | .30 |
| 85 | Edgar Renteria | .10 | .30 |
| 86 | Luis Matos | .10 | .30 |
| 87 | Adrian Beltre | .10 | .30 |
| 88 | Luis Gonzalez | .10 | .30 |
| 89 | Rickey Henderson | .30 | .75 |
| 90 | Brian Giles | .10 | .30 |
| 91 | Carlos Febles | .10 | .30 |
| 92 | Tino Martinez | .20 | .50 |
| 93 | Magglio Ordonez | .10 | .30 |
| 94 | Rafael Furcal | .10 | .30 |
| 95 | Mike Mussina | .20 | .50 |
| 96 | Gary Sheffield | .10 | .30 |
| 97 | Kenny Lofton | .10 | .30 |
| 98 | Fred McGriff | .20 | .50 |
| 99 | Ken Caminiti | .10 | .30 |
| 100 | Mark McGwire | .75 | 2.00 |
| 101 | Tom Goodwin | .10 | .30 |
| 102 | Mark Grudzielanek | .10 | .30 |
| 103 | Derek Bell | .10 | .30 |
| 104 | Mike Lowell | .10 | .30 |
| 105 | Jeff Cirillo | .10 | .30 |
| 106 | Orlando Hernandez | .10 | .30 |
| 107 | Jose Valentin | .10 | .30 |
| 108 | Warren Morris | .10 | .30 |
| 109 | Mike Williams | .10 | .30 |
| 110 | Greg Zaun | .10 | .30 |
| 111 | Jose Vidro | .10 | .30 |
| 112 | Omar Vizquel | .20 | .50 |
| 113 | Vinny Castilla | .10 | .30 |
| 114 | Gregg Jefferies | .10 | .30 |
| 115 | Kevin Brown | .10 | .30 |
| 116 | Shannon Stewart | .10 | .30 |
| 117 | Marquis Grissom | .10 | .30 |
| 118 | Manny Ramirez | .20 | .50 |
| 119 | Albert Belle | .10 | .30 |
| 120 | Bret Boone | .10 | .30 |
| 121 | Johnny Damon | .20 | .50 |
| 122 | Juan Gonzalez | .20 | .50 |
| 123 | David Justice | .10 | .30 |
| 124 | Jeffrey Hammonds | .10 | .30 |
| 125 | Ken Griffey Jr. | .50 | 1.25 |
| 126 | Mike Sweeney | .10 | .30 |
| 127 | Tony Clark | .10 | .30 |
| 128 | Todd Zeile | .10 | .30 |
| 129 | Mark Johnson | .10 | .30 |
| 130 | Matt Williams | .10 | .30 |
| 131 | Geoff Jenkins | .10 | .30 |
| 132 | Jason Giambi | .20 | .50 |
| 133 | Steve Finley | .10 | .30 |
| 134 | Derrek Lee | .20 | .50 |
| 135 | Royce Clayton | .10 | .30 |
| 136 | Joe Randa | .10 | .30 |
| 137 | Rafael Palmeiro | .20 | .50 |
| 138 | Kevin Young | .10 | .30 |
| 139 | Mike Redmond | .10 | .30 |
| 140 | Vladimir Guerrero | .30 | .75 |
| 141 | Greg Vaughn | .10 | .30 |
| 142 | Jermaine Dye | .20 | .50 |
| 143 | Roger Clemens | .60 | 1.50 |
| 144 | Denny Hocking | .10 | .30 |
| 145 | Frank Thomas | .30 | .75 |
| 146 | Carlos Beltran | .10 | .30 |
| 147 | Eric Young | .10 | .30 |
| 148 | Pat Burrell | .10 | .30 |
| 149 | Pedro Martinez | .20 | .50 |
| 150 | Mike Piazza | .50 | 1.25 |
| 151 | Adrian Gonzalez | .20 | .50 |
| 152 | Adam Johnson | .20 | .50 |
| 153 | Luis Montanez SP RC | 1.25 | 3.00 |
| 154 | Mike Stodolka | .20 | .50 |
| 155 | Phil Dumatrait | .20 | .50 |
| 156 | Sean Burnett SP | 1.25 | 3.00 |
| 157 | Dominic Rich SP RC | 1.25 | 3.00 |
| 158 | Adam Wainwright | .40 | 1.00 |
| 159 | Scott Thorman | .20 | .50 |
| 160 | Scott Heard SP | 1.25 | 3.00 |
| 161 | Chad Petty SP RC | 1.25 | 3.00 |
| 162 | Matt Wheatland | .20 | .50 |
| 163 | Bryan Digby | .20 | .50 |
| 164 | Rocco Baldelli | .20 | .50 |
| 165 | Grady Sizemore | .75 | 2.00 |
| 166 | Brian Sellier SP RC | 1.25 | 3.00 |
| 167 | Rick Brosseau SP RC | 1.25 | 3.00 |
| 168 | Shawn Fagan SP RC | 1.25 | 3.00 |
| 169 | Sean Smith SP | 1.25 | 3.00 |
| 170 | Chris Bass SP RC | 1.25 | 3.00 |
| 171 | Corey Patterson | .20 | .50 |
| 172 | Sean Burroughs | .20 | .50 |
| 173 | Ben Petrick | .20 | .50 |
| 174 | Mike Glendenning | .20 | .50 |
| 175 | Barry Zito | .30 | .75 |
| 176 | Milton Bradley | .20 | .50 |
| 177 | Bobby Bradley | .20 | .50 |
| 178 | Jason Hart | .20 | .50 |
| 179 | Ryan Anderson | .20 | .50 |
| 180 | Ben Sheets | .30 | .75 |
| 181 | Adam Everett | .20 | .50 |
| 182 | Alfonso Soriano | .40 | 1.00 |
| 183 | Josh Hamilton | .40 | 1.00 |
| 184 | Eric Munson | .20 | .50 |
| 185 | Chin-Feng Chen | .20 | .50 |
| 186 | Tim Christman SP RC | 1.25 | 3.00 |
| 187 | J.R. House SP | 1.25 | 3.00 |
| 188 | Brandon Parker SP RC | 1.25 | 3.00 |
| 189 | Sean Fesh SP RC | 1.25 | 3.00 |

|  |  | | |
|---|---|---|---|
| 190 | Joel Pineiro SP | 1.25 | 3.00 |
| 191 | Oscar Ramirez SP RC | 1.25 | 3.00 |
| 192 | Alex Santos SP RC | 1.25 | 3.00 |
| 193 | Eddy Reyes SP RC | 1.25 | 3.00 |
| 194 | Mike Jacobs SP RC | 6.00 | 15.00 |
| 195 | Erick Almonte SP RC | 1.25 | 3.00 |
| 196 | Brandon Claussen SP RC | 1.25 | 3.00 |
| 197 | Kris Koller SP RC | 1.25 | 3.00 |
| 198 | Wilson Betemit SP RC | 3.00 | 8.00 |
| 199 | Andy Phillips SP RC | 6.00 | 15.00 |
| 200 | Adam Pettyjohn SP RC | 1.25 | 3.00 |

## 2008 Stadium Club

| | | | |
|---|---|---|---|
| COMMON CARD(1-100) | | .40 | 1.00 |
| COMMON 999 (1-100) | | .75 | 2.00 |
| COMMON RC (1-150) | | 1.00 | |
| COMMON RC 999 (1-150) | | .60 | 1.50 |
| COMMON RC (151-185) | | 4.00 | 10.00 |
| AU RC A ODDS 1:3 | | | |
| AU RC B ODDS 1:8 | | | |
| EXCHANGE DEADLINE 10/31/2010 | | | |
| PRINTING PLATE ODDS 1:85 HOBBY | | | |
| PRINT.PLATE AUTO ODDS 1:198 HOBBY | | | |
| PLATE PRINT RUN 1 SET PER COLOR | | | |
| BLACK-CYAN-MAGENTA-YELLOW ISSUED | | | |
| NO PLATE PRICING DUE TO SCARCITY | | | |
| 1 | Chase Utley | 1.00 | 2.50 |
| 2 | Tim Lincecum | 1.25 | 3.00 |
| 3 | Ryan Zimmerman/999 | 1.00 | 2.50 |
| 4 | Todd Helton | .60 | 1.50 |
| 5 | Russell Martin | .40 | 1.00 |
| 6 | Curtis Granderson/999 | .60 | 1.50 |
| 7 | Torii Hunter | .40 | 1.00 |
| 8 | Mark Teixeira | .60 | 1.50 |
| 9 | Alfonso Soriano/999 | 1.00 | 2.50 |
| 10 | C.C. Sabathia | .40 | 1.00 |
| 11 | David Ortiz | .60 | 1.50 |
| 12 | Miguel Tejada/999 | .60 | 1.50 |
| 13 | Alex Rodriguez | 1.50 | 4.00 |
| 14 | Prince Fielder | 1.00 | 2.50 |
| 15 | Alex Gordon/999 | 1.00 | 2.50 |
| 16 | Jake Peavy | .60 | 1.50 |
| 17 | B.J. Upton | .60 | 1.50 |
| 18 | Michael Young/999 | .60 | 1.50 |
| 19 | Jason Bay | .60 | 1.50 |
| 20 | Jorge Posada | .60 | 1.50 |
| 21 | Jacoby Ellsbury/999 | 2.50 | 6.00 |
| 22 | Nick Markakis | .60 | 1.50 |
| 23 | Tom Glavine | .60 | 1.50 |
| 24 | Justin Upton/999 | 1.50 | 4.00 |
| 25 | Edinson Volquez | .40 | 1.00 |
| 26 | Miguel Cabrera | .60 | 1.50 |
| 27 | Carlos Lee/999 | .60 | 1.50 |
| 28 | Ryan Church | .40 | 1.00 |
| 29 | Delmon Young | .60 | 1.50 |
| 30 | Carlos Quentin/999 | .40 | 1.00 |
| 31 | Carl Crawford | .40 | 1.00 |
| 32 | Roy Halladay | .40 | 1.00 |
| 33 | Brandon Webb/999 | 1.00 | 2.50 |
| 34 | Brian Roberts | .40 | 1.00 |
| 35 | Ken Griffey Jr. | 1.50 | 4.00 |
| 36 | Troy Tulowitzki/999 | 1.00 | 2.50 |
| 37 | Hanley Ramirez | 1.00 | 2.50 |
| 38 | Hunter Pence | 1.00 | 2.50 |
| 39 | Johnny Damon/999 | 1.00 | 2.50 |
| 40 | Eric Chavez | .40 | 1.00 |
| 41 | Adrian Gonzalez | .60 | 1.50 |
| 42 | Carlos Pena/999 | 1.50 | 4.00 |
| 43 | Felix Hernandez | .60 | 1.50 |
| 44 | Magglio Ordonez | .60 | 1.50 |
| 45 | Josh Beckett/999 | 1.00 | 2.50 |
| 46 | Fausto Carmona | .40 | 1.00 |
| 47 | Chris Young | .40 | 1.00 |
| 48 | John Lackey/999 | .60 | 1.50 |
| 49 | John Smoltz | 1.00 | 2.50 |
| 50 | David Wright | 1.25 | 3.00 |
| 51 | Ichiro Suzuki/999 | 2.50 | 6.00 |
| 52 | Vernon Wells | .40 | 1.00 |
| 53 | Josh Hamilton | 1.25 | 3.00 |
| 54 | Albert Pujols/999 | 3.00 | 8.00 |
| 55 | Dustin Pedroia | 1.25 | 3.00 |
| 56 | Garrett Atkins | .40 | 1.00 |
| 57 | Roy Oswalt/999 | .60 | 1.50 |
| 58 | Jose Reyes | .60 | 1.50 |
| 59 | Derek Jeter | 2.50 | 6.00 |
| 60 | Scott Kazmir/999 | 1.00 | 2.50 |
| 61 | Vladimir Guerrero | 1.00 | 2.50 |
| 62 | Joba Chamberlain | 1.25 | 3.00 |
| 63 | Kevin Youkilis/999 | 1.00 | 2.50 |
| 64 | Victor Martinez | .40 | 1.00 |
| 65 | Nick Swisher | .40 | 1.00 |
| 66 | Carlos Beltran/999 | .60 | 1.50 |
| 67 | Joe Mauer | 1.00 | 2.50 |
| 68 | Gary Sheffield | .40 | 1.00 |
| 69 | Cole Hamels/999 | 1.50 | 4.00 |
| 70 | Brian McCann | .60 | 1.50 |
| 71 | Grady Sizemore | .60 | 1.50 |
| 72 | Robinson Cano/999 | 1.00 | 2.50 |
| 73 | Greg Maddux | 1.25 | 3.00 |
| 74 | Rich Harden | .40 | 1.00 |
| 75 | Ryan Howard/999 | 2.00 | 5.00 |
| 76 | Johan Santana | .60 | 1.50 |
| 77 | Dan Uggla | .60 | 1.50 |
| 78 | Justin Verlander/999 | 1.00 | 2.50 |
| 79 | Derrek Lee | .60 | 1.50 |
| 80 | Ryan Braun | 1.25 | 3.00 |
| 81 | Lance Berkman/999 | 1.00 | 2.50 |
| 82 | Manny Ramirez | 1.00 | 2.50 |
| 83 | Chipper Jones | 1.25 | 3.00 |
| 84 | Daisuke Matsuzaka/999 | 2.00 | 5.00 |
| 85 | Matt Holliday | .60 | 1.50 |
| 86 | Justin Morneau | .60 | 1.50 |
| 87 | Jimmy Rollins/999 | 1.00 | 2.50 |
| 88 | Hideki Matsui | 1.00 | 2.50 |
| 89 | Pedro Martinez | .60 | 1.50 |
| 90 | Carlos Zambrano/999 | .60 | 1.50 |
| 91 | Jackie Robinson | 1.00 | 2.50 |
| 92 | Mickey Mantle | 4.00 | 10.00 |
| 93 | Ty Cobb/999 | 2.50 | 6.00 |
| 94 | J.DiMaggio Cut Out | | |
| 95 | Honus Wagner | 1.00 | 2.50 |
| 96 | Babe Ruth/999 | 4.00 | 10.00 |
| 97 | Nolan Ryan | 3.00 | 8.00 |
| 98 | Roberto Clemente | 2.00 | 5.00 |
| 99 | Ted Williams/999 | 4.00 | 10.00 |
| 100 | Tom Seaver | .60 | 1.50 |
| 101a | Luke Hochevar RC | .60 | 1.50 |
| 101b | Luke Hochevar VAR/999 (RC) | .60 | 1.50 |
| 102a | Daric Barton/999 (RC) | .60 | 1.50 |
| 102b | Daric Barton VAR/999 (RC) | .60 | 1.50 |
| 103a | Nick Adenhart RC | .40 | 1.00 |
| 103b | Nick Adenhart VAR/999 (RC) | .60 | 1.50 |
| 104a | Gregor Blanco RC | .40 | 1.00 |
| 104b | Gregor Blanco VAR/999 (RC) | .60 | 1.50 |
| 105a | Chris Carter/999 (RC) | 1.00 | 2.50 |
| 105b | Chris Carter VAR/999 (RC) | .60 | 1.50 |
| 106a | Eric Hurley RC | .40 | 1.00 |
| 106b | Eric Hurley VAR/999 (RC) | .40 | 1.00 |
| 107a | Clayton Kershaw RC | 2.00 | 5.00 |
| 107b | Clayton Kershaw VAR/999 (RC) | 3.00 | 8.00 |
| 108a | Evan Longoria RC | 5.00 | 12.00 |
| 108b | Evan Longoria VAR/999 (RC) | 5.00 | 12.00 |
| 109a | Garrett Mock RC | .40 | 1.00 |
| 109b | Garrett Mock VAR/999 (RC) | .60 | 1.50 |
| 110a | David Purcey RC | .40 | 1.00 |
| 110b | David Purcey VAR/999 (RC) | .60 | 1.50 |
| 111a | Ryan Tucker/999 (RC) | .60 | 1.50 |
| 111b | Ryan Tucker VAR/999 (RC) | .60 | 1.50 |
| 112a | Joey Votto RC | 1.00 | 2.50 |
| 112b | Joey Votto VAR/999 (RC) | 1.50 | 4.00 |
| 113a | Jeff Clement (RC) | .60 | 1.50 |
| 113b | Jeff Clement VAR/999 (RC) | 1.00 | 2.50 |
| 114a | Michael Aubrey RC | 1.00 | 2.50 |
| 114b | Michael Aubrey VAR/999 (RC) | 1.00 | 2.50 |
| 115a | Brandon Boggs (RC) | .60 | 1.50 |
| 115b | Brandon Boggs VAR/999 (RC) | 1.00 | 2.50 |
| 116a | Johnny Cueto RC | .60 | 1.50 |
| 116b | Johnny Cueto VAR/999 (RC) | 1.00 | 2.50 |
| 117a | Heman Iribarren/999 (RC) | .60 | 1.50 |
| 117b | Heman Iribarren VAR/999 (RC) | .60 | 1.50 |
| 118a | Masahide Kobayashi/999 (RC) | .60 | 1.50 |
| 118b | Masahide Kobayashi VAR/999 (RC) | 1.00 | 2.50 |
| 119a | Jed Lowrie (RC) | 1.00 | 2.50 |
| 119b | Jed Lowrie VAR/999 (RC) | 1.50 | 4.00 |
| 120a | Greg Reynolds/999 RC | 1.00 | 2.50 |
| 120b | Greg Reynolds VAR/999 (RC) | 1.00 | 2.50 |
| 121a | Matt Tolbert RC | .60 | 1.50 |
| 121b | Matt Tolbert VAR/999 (RC) | .60 | 1.50 |
| 122a | Jonathan Herrera RC | .60 | 1.50 |
| 122b | Jonathan Herrera VAR/999 (RC) | 1.00 | 2.50 |
| 123a | J.R. Towles/999 RC | 1.00 | 2.50 |
| 123b | J.R. Towles VAR/999 (RC) | 1.00 | 2.50 |
| 124a | Armando Galarraga RC | .60 | 1.50 |
| 124b | Armando Galarraga VAR/999 (RC) | 1.00 | 2.50 |
| 125a | Josh Banks (RC) | .60 | 1.50 |
| 125b | Josh Banks VAR/999 (RC) | .60 | 1.50 |
| 126a | Mitch Boggs/999 (RC) | .60 | 1.50 |
| 126b | Mitch Boggs VAR/999 (RC) | .60 | 1.50 |
| 127a | Blake DeWitt RC | 1.00 | 2.50 |
| 127b | Blake DeWitt VAR/999 (RC) | 1.50 | 4.00 |
| 128a | Carlos Gonzalez RC | .40 | 1.00 |
| 128b | Carlos Gonzalez VAR/999 (RC) | 1.00 | 2.50 |
| 129a | Elliot Johnson/999 (RC) | .60 | 1.50 |
| 129b | Elliot Johnson VAR/999 (RC) | .60 | 1.50 |
| 130a | Brian Barton RC | .60 | 1.50 |
| 130b | Brian Barton VAR/999 (RC) | 1.00 | 2.50 |
| 131a | Sean Rodriguez RC | .60 | 1.50 |
| 131b | Sean Rodriguez VAR/999 (RC) | .60 | 1.50 |
| 132a | Kosuke Fukudome/999 RC | 2.00 | 5.00 |
| 132b | Kosuke Fukudome VAR/999 RC | 2.00 | 5.00 |
| 133a | Chin-Lung Hu (RC) | 1.00 | 2.50 |
| 133b | Chin-Lung Hu VAR/999 (RC) | 1.00 | 2.50 |
| 134a | Wladimir Balentien RC | .40 | 1.00 |
| 134b | Wladimir Balentien VAR/999 (RC) | .60 | 1.50 |
| 135a | Jeff Niemann/999 (RC) | .60 | 1.50 |
| 135b | Jeff Niemann VAR/999 (RC) | .60 | 1.50 |
| 136a | Jay Bruce RC | 1.50 | 4.00 |
| 136b | Jay Bruce VAR/999 (RC) | 2.00 | 5.00 |
| 137a | Brandon Jones RC | 1.00 | 2.50 |
| 137b | Brandon Jones VAR/999 (RC) | 1.50 | 4.00 |
| 138a | Justin Masterson/999 RC | 3.00 | 8.00 |
| 138b | Justin Masterson VAR/999 RC | 3.00 | 8.00 |
| 139a | Jayson Nix (RC) | .40 | 1.00 |
| 139b | Jayson Nix VAR/999 (RC) | .60 | 1.50 |
| 140a | Max Scherzer RC | 1.00 | 2.50 |
| 140b | Max Scherzer VAR/999 (RC) | 1.50 | 4.00 |
| 141a | Mike Aviles RC | 1.00 | 2.50 |
| 141b | Mike Aviles VAR/999 RC | 1.00 | 2.50 |
| 142a | Greg Smith RC | .40 | 1.00 |
| 142b | Greg Smith VAR/999 (RC) | .60 | 1.50 |
| 143a | Nick Blackburn RC | .60 | 1.50 |
| 143b | Nick Blackburn VAR/999 (RC) | 1.00 | 2.50 |
| 144a | Justin Ruggiano/999 RC | 1.00 | 2.50 |
| 144b | Justin Ruggiano VAR/999 (RC) | 1.00 | 2.50 |
| 145a | Clay Buchholz RC | 1.00 | 2.50 |
| 145b | Clay Buchholz VAR/999 (RC) | 1.50 | 4.00 |
| 146a | German Duran RC | 1.00 | 2.50 |
| 146b | German Duran VAR/999 (RC) | 1.00 | 2.50 |
| 147a | Radhames Liz/999 RC | 1.00 | 2.50 |
| 147b | Radhames Liz VAR/999 RC | 1.00 | 2.50 |
| 148a | Chris Perez RC | .60 | 1.50 |
| 148b | Chris Perez VAR/999 (RC) | 1.00 | 2.50 |
| 149a | Hiroki Kuroda RC | .60 | 1.50 |
| 149b | Hiroki Kuroda VAR/999 (RC) | 1.00 | 2.50 |
| 150a | Gregorio Petit RC | 1.00 | 2.50 |
| 150b | Gregorio Petit VAR/999 (RC) | 1.00 | 2.50 |
| 151 | Emmanuel Burriss AU RC EXCH A | 4.00 | 10.00 |
| 152 | Elliot Johnson AU (RC) A | 4.00 | 10.00 |
| 153 | Jonathan Van Every AU RC A | 4.00 | 10.00 |
| 154 | Darren O'Day AU RC A | 4.00 | 10.00 |
| 155 | Matt Joyce AU RC A | 6.00 | 15.00 |
| 156 | Burke Badenhop AU RC A | 4.00 | 10.00 |
| 157 | Brent Lillibridge AU (RC) A | 4.00 | 10.00 |
| 158 | J.Cueto AU (RC) EXCH A | 5.00 | 12.00 |
| 159 | Jeff Niemann AU (RC) A | 4.00 | 10.00 |
| 160 | John Bowker AU (RC) A | 4.00 | 10.00 |
| 161 | Brandon Boggs AU (RC) A | 4.00 | 10.00 |
| 162 | J.Masterson AU (RC) A | 12.50 | 30.00 |
| 163 | M.Kobayashi AU (RC) A | 5.00 | 12.00 |
| 164 | Nick Adenhart AU (RC) A | 12.50 | 30.00 |
| 165 | Chris Perez AU (RC) EXCH A | 4.00 | 10.00 |
| 166 | Gregor Blanco AU (RC) A | 4.00 | 10.00 |
| 167 | Travis Denker AU RC A | 4.00 | 10.00 |
| 168 | Jeff Clement AU (RC) EXCH A | 4.00 | 10.00 |
| 169 | E.Longoria AU (RC) A | 30.00 | 60.00 |
| 170 | Greg Smith AU (RC) A | 4.00 | 10.00 |
| 171 | Jay Bruce AU (RC) B | 12.50 | 30.00 |
| 172 | Brian Barton AU (RC) B | 6.00 | 15.00 |
| 173 | Max Scherzer AU (RC) B | 6.00 | 15.00 |
| 174 | Blake DeWitt AU (RC) B | 6.00 | 15.00 |

| | | |
|---|---|---|
| ☐ 175 J.Lowrie AU (RC) EXCH B | 6.00 | 15.00 |
| ☐ 176 C.Kershaw AU (RC) B | 10.00 | 25.00 |
| ☐ 177 Jonathan Albaladejo AU RC B | 4.00 | 10.00 |
| ☐ 178 Josh Banks AU (RC) B | 4.00 | 10.00 |
| ☐ 179 Brian Horwitz AU RC B | 4.00 | 10.00 |
| ☐ 180 Micah Hoffpauir AU RC B | 8.00 | 20.00 |
| ☐ 181 Robinzon Diaz AU (RC) B | 4.00 | 10.00 |
| ☐ 182 Nick Evans AU RC B | 6.00 | 15.00 |
| ☐ 183 J.Mather AU EXCH B | 5.00 | 12.00 |
| ☐ 184 Danny Herrera AU RC B | 4.00 | 10.00 |
| ☐ 185 Eugenio Velez AU RC B | 4.00 | 10.00 |

## 2001 Sweet Spot

| | | |
|---|---|---|
| ☐ COMP.BASIC w/o SP's (60) | 8.00 | 20.00 |
| ☐ COMP.UPDATE w/o SP's (30) | 4.00 | 10.00 |
| ☐ COMMON CARD (1-60) | .15 | .40 |
| ☐ COMMON CARD (61-90) | 4.00 | 10.00 |
| ☐ COMMON CARD (91-120) | .25 | .60 |
| ☐ COMMON CARD (121-150) | 2.00 | 5.00 |
| ☐ 1 Troy Glaus | .15 | .40 |
| ☐ 2 Darin Erstad | .15 | .40 |
| ☐ 3 Jason Giambi | .15 | .40 |
| ☐ 4 Tim Hudson | .15 | .40 |
| ☐ 5 Ben Grieve | .15 | .40 |
| ☐ 6 Carlos Delgado | .15 | .40 |
| ☐ 7 David Wells | .15 | .40 |
| ☐ 8 Greg Vaughn | .15 | .40 |
| ☐ 9 Roberto Alomar | .25 | .60 |
| ☐ 10 Jim Thome | .25 | .60 |
| ☐ 11 John Olerud | .15 | .40 |
| ☐ 12 Edgar Martinez | .15 | .40 |
| ☐ 13 Cal Ripken | 1.25 | 3.00 |
| ☐ 14 Albert Belle | .15 | .40 |
| ☐ 15 Ivan Rodriguez | .25 | .60 |
| ☐ 16 Alex Rodriguez Rangers | 1.25 | 3.00 |
| ☐ 17 Pedro Martinez | .25 | .60 |
| ☐ 18 Nomar Garciaparra | .60 | 1.50 |
| ☐ 19 Manny Ramirez | .25 | .60 |
| ☐ 20 Jermaine Dye | .15 | .40 |
| ☐ 21 Juan Gonzalez | .25 | .60 |
| ☐ 22 Dean Palmer | .15 | .40 |
| ☐ 23 Matt Lawton | .15 | .40 |
| ☐ 24 Eric Milton | .15 | .40 |
| ☐ 25 Frank Thomas | .40 | 1.00 |
| ☐ 26 Magglio Ordonez | .15 | .40 |
| ☐ 27 Derek Jeter | 1.00 | 2.50 |
| ☐ 28 Bernie Williams | .25 | .60 |
| ☐ 29 Roger Clemens | .75 | 2.00 |
| ☐ 30 Jeff Bagwell | .25 | .60 |
| ☐ 31 Richard Hidalgo | .15 | .40 |
| ☐ 32 Chipper Jones | .40 | 1.00 |
| ☐ 33 Greg Maddux | .60 | 1.50 |
| ☐ 34 Richie Sexson | .15 | .40 |
| ☐ 35 Jeromy Burnitz | .15 | .40 |
| ☐ 36 Mark McGwire | 1.00 | 2.50 |
| ☐ 37 Jim Edmonds | .15 | .40 |
| ☐ 38 Sammy Sosa | .40 | 1.00 |
| ☐ 39 Randy Johnson | .40 | 1.00 |
| ☐ 40 Steve Finley | .15 | .40 |
| ☐ 41 Gary Sheffield | .15 | .40 |
| ☐ 42 Shawn Green | .15 | .40 |
| ☐ 43 Vladimir Guerrero | .40 | 1.00 |
| ☐ 44 Jose Vidro | .15 | .40 |
| ☐ 45 Barry Bonds | 1.00 | 2.50 |
| ☐ 46 Jeff Kent | .15 | .40 |
| ☐ 47 Preston Wilson | .15 | .40 |
| ☐ 48 Luis Castillo | .15 | .40 |
| ☐ 49 Mike Piazza | .60 | 1.50 |
| ☐ 50 Edgardo Alfonzo | .15 | .40 |
| ☐ 51 Tony Gwynn | .50 | 1.25 |
| ☐ 52 Ryan Klesko | .15 | .40 |
| ☐ 53 Scott Rolen | .25 | .60 |
| ☐ 54 Bob Abreu | .15 | .40 |
| ☐ 55 Jason Kendall | .15 | .40 |

| | | |
|---|---|---|
| ☐ 56 Brian Giles | .15 | .40 |
| ☐ 57 Ken Griffey Jr. | .60 | 1.50 |
| ☐ 58 Barry Larkin | .25 | .60 |
| ☐ 59 Todd Helton | .25 | .60 |
| ☐ 60 Mike Hampton UER | .15 | .40 |
| ☐ 61 Corey Patterson SB | 4.00 | 10.00 |
| ☐ 62 Ichiro Suzuki SB RC | 125.00 | 200.00 |
| ☐ 63 Jason Grilli SB | 4.00 | 10.00 |
| ☐ 64 Brian Cole SB | 4.00 | 10.00 |
| ☐ 65 Juan Pierre SB | 4.00 | 10.00 |
| ☐ 66 Matt Ginter SB | 4.00 | 10.00 |
| ☐ 67 Jimmy Rollins SB | 4.00 | 10.00 |
| ☐ 68 Jason Smith SB RC | 4.00 | 10.00 |
| ☐ 69 Israel Alcantara SB | 4.00 | 10.00 |
| ☐ 70 Adam Piatlyjohn SB RC | 4.00 | 10.00 |
| ☐ 71 Luke Hudson SB | 4.00 | 10.00 |
| ☐ 72 Barry Zito SB | 5.00 | 12.00 |
| ☐ 73 Keith Ginter SB | 4.00 | 10.00 |
| ☐ 74 Sun Woo Kim SB | 4.00 | 10.00 |
| ☐ 75 Ross Gload SB | 4.00 | 10.00 |
| ☐ 76 Matt Wise SB | 4.00 | 10.00 |
| ☐ 77 Aubrey Huff SB | 4.00 | 10.00 |
| ☐ 78 Ryan Franklin SB | 4.00 | 10.00 |
| ☐ 79 Brandon Inge SB | 4.00 | 10.00 |
| ☐ 80 Wes Helms SB | 4.00 | 10.00 |
| ☐ 81 Junior Spivey SB RC | 5.00 | 12.00 |
| ☐ 82 Ryan Vogelsong SB | 4.00 | 10.00 |
| ☐ 83 John Parrish SB | 4.00 | 10.00 |
| ☐ 84 Joe Crede SB | 5.00 | 12.00 |
| ☐ 85 Damian Rolls SB | 4.00 | 10.00 |
| ☐ 86 Esix Snead SB RC | 4.00 | 10.00 |
| ☐ 87 Rocky Biddle SB | 4.00 | 10.00 |
| ☐ 88 Brady Clark SB | 4.00 | 10.00 |
| ☐ 89 Timo Perez SB | 4.00 | 10.00 |
| ☐ 90 Jay Spurgeon SB | 4.00 | 10.00 |
| ☐ 91 Garret Anderson | .25 | .60 |
| ☐ 92 Jermaine Dye | .25 | .60 |
| ☐ 93 Shannon Stewart | .25 | .60 |
| ☐ 94 Ben Grieve | .25 | .60 |
| ☐ 95 Juan Gonzalez | .25 | .60 |
| ☐ 96 Brett Boone | .25 | .60 |
| ☐ 97 Tony Batista | .25 | .60 |
| ☐ 98 Rafael Palmeiro | .40 | 1.00 |
| ☐ 99 Carl Everett | .25 | .60 |
| ☐ 100 Mike Sweeney | .25 | .60 |
| ☐ 101 Tony Clark | .25 | .60 |
| ☐ 102 Doug Mientkiewicz | .25 | .60 |
| ☐ 103 Jose Canseco | .40 | 1.00 |
| ☐ 104 Mike Mussina | .40 | 1.00 |
| ☐ 105 Lance Berkman | .25 | .60 |
| ☐ 106 Andruw Jones | .25 | .60 |
| ☐ 107 Geoff Jenkins | .25 | .60 |
| ☐ 108 Matt Morris | .25 | .60 |
| ☐ 109 Fred McGriff | .40 | 1.00 |
| ☐ 110 Luis Gonzalez | .25 | .60 |
| ☐ 111 Kevin Brown | .25 | .60 |
| ☐ 112 Tony Armas Jr. | .25 | .60 |
| ☐ 113 John Vander Wal | .25 | .60 |
| ☐ 114 Cliff Floyd | .25 | .60 |
| ☐ 115 Matt Lawton | .25 | .60 |
| ☐ 116 Phil Nevin | .25 | .60 |
| ☐ 117 Pat Burrell | .25 | .60 |
| ☐ 118 Aramis Ramirez | .25 | .60 |
| ☐ 119 Sean Casey | .25 | .60 |
| ☐ 120 Larry Walker | .25 | .60 |
| ☐ 121 Albert Pujols SB RC | 60.00 | 120.00 |
| ☐ 122 Johnny Estrada SB RC | 2.00 | 5.00 |
| ☐ 123 Wilson Betemit SB RC | 3.00 | 8.00 |
| ☐ 124 Adrian Hernandez SB RC | 2.00 | 5.00 |
| ☐ 125 Morgan Ensberg SB RC | 3.00 | 8.00 |
| ☐ 126 Horacio Ramirez SB RC | 2.00 | 5.00 |
| ☐ 127 Josh Towers SB RC | 2.00 | 5.00 |
| ☐ 128 Juan Uribe SB RC | 2.00 | 5.00 |
| ☐ 129 Wilken Ruan SB RC | 2.00 | 5.00 |
| ☐ 130 Andres Torres SB RC | 2.00 | 5.00 |
| ☐ 131 Brian Lawrence SB RC | 2.00 | 5.00 |
| ☐ 132 Ryan Freel SB RC | 2.00 | 5.00 |
| ☐ 133 Brandon Duckworth SB RC | 2.00 | 5.00 |
| ☐ 134 Juan Diaz SB RC | 2.00 | 5.00 |
| ☐ 135 Rafael Soriano SB RC | 2.00 | 5.00 |
| ☐ 136 Ricardo Rodriguez SB RC | 2.00 | 5.00 |
| ☐ 137 Bud Smith SB RC | 2.00 | 5.00 |
| ☐ 138 Mark Teixeira SB RC | 15.00 | 40.00 |
| ☐ 139 Mark Prior SB RC | 6.00 | 15.00 |
| ☐ 140 Jackson Melian SB RC | 2.00 | 5.00 |
| ☐ 141 Dewon Brazelton SB RC | 2.00 | 5.00 |
| ☐ 142 Greg Miller SB RC | 2.00 | 5.00 |
| ☐ 143 Billy Sylvester SB RC | 2.00 | 5.00 |

| | | |
|---|---|---|
| ☐ 144 Elpidio Guzman SB RC | 2.00 | 5.00 |
| ☐ 145 Jack Wilson SB RC | 2.00 | 5.00 |
| ☐ 146 Jose Mieses SB RC | 2.00 | 5.00 |
| ☐ 147 Brandon Lyon SB RC | 2.00 | 5.00 |
| ☐ 148 Tsuyoshi Shinjo SB RC | 2.00 | 5.00 |
| ☐ 149 Juan Cruz SB RC | 2.00 | 5.00 |
| ☐ 150 Jay Gibbons SB RC | 2.00 | 5.00 |

## 2002 Sweet Spot

| | | |
|---|---|---|
| ☐ COMP.SET w/o SP's (90) | 8.00 | 20.00 |
| ☐ COMMON CARD (1-90) | .15 | .40 |
| ☐ COMMON CARD (91-130) | 1.50 | 4.00 |
| ☐ COMMON TIER 1 AU (131-145) | 6.00 | 15.00 |
| ☐ COMMON TIER 2 AU (131-145) | 10.00 | 25.00 |
| ☐ COMMON CARD (146-175) | 4.00 | 10.00 |
| MCGWIRE AU EXCH.RANDOM IN PACKS | | |
| ☐ 1 Troy Glaus | .15 | .40 |
| ☐ 2 Darin Erstad | .15 | .40 |
| ☐ 3 Tim Hudson | .15 | .40 |
| ☐ 4 Eric Chavez | .15 | .40 |
| ☐ 5 Barry Zito | .15 | .40 |
| ☐ 6 Miguel Tejada | .15 | .40 |
| ☐ 7 Carlos Delgado | .15 | .40 |
| ☐ 8 Eric Hinske | .15 | .40 |
| ☐ 9 Ben Grieve | .15 | .40 |
| ☐ 10 Jim Thome | .25 | .60 |
| ☐ 11 C.C. Sabathia | .15 | .40 |
| ☐ 12 Omar Vizquel | .25 | .60 |
| ☐ 13 Ichiro Suzuki | .75 | 2.00 |
| ☐ 14 Edgar Martinez | .25 | .60 |
| ☐ 15 Bret Boone | .15 | .40 |
| ☐ 16 Freddy Garcia | .15 | .40 |
| ☐ 17 Tony Batista | .15 | .40 |
| ☐ 18 Geronimo Gil | .15 | .40 |
| ☐ 19 Alex Rodriguez | .60 | 1.50 |
| ☐ 20 Rafael Palmeiro | .25 | .60 |
| ☐ 21 Ivan Rodriguez | .25 | .60 |
| ☐ 22 Hank Blalock | .25 | .60 |
| ☐ 23 Juan Gonzalez | .15 | .40 |
| ☐ 24 Nomar Garciaparra | .60 | 1.50 |
| ☐ 25 Pedro Martinez | .25 | .60 |
| ☐ 26 Manny Ramirez | .25 | .60 |
| ☐ 27 Mike Sweeney | .15 | .40 |
| ☐ 28 Carlos Beltran | .15 | .40 |
| ☐ 29 Dmitri Young | .15 | .40 |
| ☐ 30 Toril Hunter | .15 | .40 |
| ☐ 31 Eric Milton | .15 | .40 |
| ☐ 32 Corey Koskie | .15 | .40 |
| ☐ 33 Frank Thomas | .40 | 1.00 |
| ☐ 34 Mark Buehrle | .15 | .40 |
| ☐ 35 Magglio Ordonez | .15 | .40 |
| ☐ 36 Roger Clemens | .75 | 2.00 |
| ☐ 37 Derek Jeter | 1.00 | 2.50 |
| ☐ 38 Jason Giambi | .15 | .40 |
| ☐ 39 Alfonso Soriano | .25 | .60 |
| ☐ 40 Bernie Williams | .25 | .60 |
| ☐ 41 Jeff Bagwell | .25 | .60 |
| ☐ 42 Roy Oswalt | .15 | .40 |
| ☐ 43 Lance Berkman | .15 | .40 |
| ☐ 44 Greg Maddux | .60 | 1.50 |
| ☐ 45 Chipper Jones | .40 | 1.00 |
| ☐ 46 Gary Sheffield | .15 | .40 |
| ☐ 47 Andruw Jones | .25 | .60 |
| ☐ 48 Richie Sexson | .15 | .40 |
| ☐ 49 Ben Sheets | .15 | .40 |
| ☐ 50 Albert Pujols | .75 | 2.00 |
| ☐ 51 Matt Morris | .15 | .40 |
| ☐ 52 J.D. Drew | .15 | .40 |
| ☐ 53 Sammy Sosa | .40 | 1.00 |
| ☐ 54 Kerry Wood | .15 | .40 |
| ☐ 55 Mark Prior | .25 | .60 |
| ☐ 56 Moises Alou | .15 | .40 |
| ☐ 57 Corey Patterson | .15 | .40 |
| ☐ 58 Randy Johnson | .40 | 1.00 |

|  |  | | |
|---|--------|------|------|
| 59 | Luis Gonzalez | .15 | .40 |
| 60 | Curt Schilling | .15 | .40 |
| 61 | Shawn Green | .15 | .40 |
| 62 | Kevin Brown | .15 | .40 |
| 63 | Paul Lo Duca | .15 | .40 |
| 64 | Adrian Beltre | .15 | .40 |
| 65 | Vladimir Guerrero | .40 | 1.00 |
| 66 | Jose Vidro | .15 | .40 |
| 67 | Javier Vazquez | .15 | .40 |
| 68 | Barry Bonds | 1.00 | 2.50 |
| 69 | Jeff Kent | .15 | .40 |
| 70 | Rich Aurilia | .15 | .40 |
| 71 | Mike Lowell | .15 | .40 |
| 72 | Josh Beckett | .15 | .40 |
| 73 | Brad Penny | .15 | .40 |
| 74 | Roberto Alomar | .25 | .60 |
| 75 | Mike Piazza | .60 | 1.50 |
| 76 | Jeromy Burnitz | .15 | .40 |
| 77 | Mo Vaughn | .15 | .40 |
| 78 | Phil Nevin | .15 | .40 |
| 79 | Sean Burroughs | .15 | .40 |
| 80 | Jeremy Giambi | .15 | .40 |
| 81 | Bobby Abreu | .15 | .40 |
| 82 | Jimmy Rollins | .15 | .40 |
| 83 | Pat Burrell | .15 | .40 |
| 84 | Brian Giles | .15 | .40 |
| 85 | Aramis Ramirez | .15 | .40 |
| 86 | Ken Griffey Jr. | .60 | 1.50 |
| 87 | Adam Dunn | .15 | .40 |
| 88 | Austin Kearns | .15 | .40 |
| 89 | Todd Helton | .25 | .60 |
| 90 | Larry Walker | .15 | .40 |
| 91 | Earl Snyder SB RC | 1.50 | 4.00 |
| 92 | Jorge Padilla SB RC | 1.50 | 4.00 |
| 93 | Felix Escalona SB RC | 1.50 | 4.00 |
| 94 | John Foster SB RC | 1.50 | 4.00 |
| 95 | Brandon Puffer SB RC | 1.50 | 4.00 |
| 96 | Steve Bechler SB RC | 1.50 | 4.00 |
| 97 | Hansel Izquierdo SB RC | 1.50 | 4.00 |
| 98 | Chris Baker SB RC | 1.50 | 4.00 |
| 99 | Jeremy Ward SB RC | 1.50 | 4.00 |
| 100 | Kevin Frederick SB RC | 1.50 | 4.00 |
| 101 | Josh Hancock SB RC | 2.00 | 5.00 |
| 102 | Allan Simpson SB RC | 1.50 | 4.00 |
| 103 | Mitch Wylie SB RC | 1.50 | 4.00 |
| 104 | Mark Corey SB RC | 1.50 | 4.00 |
| 105 | Victor Alvarez SB RC | 1.50 | 4.00 |
| 106 | Todd Donovan SB RC | 1.50 | 4.00 |
| 107 | Nelson Castro SB RC | 1.50 | 4.00 |
| 108 | Chris Booker SB RC | 1.50 | 4.00 |
| 109 | Corey Thurman SB RC | 1.50 | 4.00 |
| 110 | Kirk Saarloos SB RC | 1.50 | 4.00 |
| 111 | Michael Crudale SB RC | 1.50 | 4.00 |
| 112 | Jason Simontacchi SB RC | 1.50 | 4.00 |
| 113 | Ron Calloway SB RC | 1.50 | 4.00 |
| 114 | Brandon Backe SB RC | 2.00 | 5.00 |
| 115 | Tom Sheam SB RC | 1.50 | 4.00 |
| 116 | Oliver Perez SB RC | 2.00 | 5.00 |
| 117 | Kyle Kane SB RC | 1.50 | 4.00 |
| 118 | Francis Beltran SB RC | 1.50 | 4.00 |
| 119 | So Taguchi SB RC | 2.00 | 5.00 |
| 120 | Doug Devore SB RC | 1.50 | 4.00 |
| 121 | Juan Brito SB RC | 1.50 | 4.00 |
| 122 | Cliff Bartosh SB RC | 1.50 | 4.00 |
| 123 | Eric Junge SB RC | 1.50 | 4.00 |
| 124 | Joe Orloski SB RC | 1.50 | 4.00 |
| 125 | Scotty Layfield SB RC | 1.50 | 4.00 |
| 126 | Jorge Sosa SB RC | 2.00 | 5.00 |
| 127 | Satoru Komiyama SB RC | 1.50 | 4.00 |
| 128 | Edwin Almonte SB RC | 1.50 | 4.00 |
| 129 | Takahito Nomura SB RC | 1.50 | 4.00 |
| 130 | John Ennis SB RC | 1.50 | 4.00 |
| 131 | Kazuhisa Ishii T2 AU RC | 40.00 | 80.00 |
| 132 | Ben Howard T2 AU RC | 10.00 | 25.00 |
| 133 | Aaron Cook T1 AU RC | 8.00 | 20.00 |
| 134 | Andy Machado T1 AU RC | 6.00 | 15.00 |
| 135 | Luis Ugueto T1 AU RC | 6.00 | 15.00 |
| 136 | Tyler Yates T1 AU RC | 6.00 | 15.00 |
| 137 | Rodrigo Rosario T1 AU RC | 6.00 | 15.00 |
| 138 | Jaime Cerda T1 AU RC | 6.00 | 15.00 |
| 139 | Luis Martinez T1 AU RC | 6.00 | 15.00 |
| 140 | Rene Reyes T1 AU RC | 6.00 | 15.00 |
| 141 | Eric Good T1 AU RC | 6.00 | 15.00 |
| 142 | Matt Thornton T2 AU RC | 10.00 | 25.00 |
| 143 | Steve Kent T1 AU RC | 6.00 | 15.00 |
| 144 | Jose Valverde T1 AU RC | 6.00 | 15.00 |
| 145 | Adrian Burnside T1 AU RC | 6.00 | 15.00 |
| 146 | Barry Bonds GF | 10.00 | 25.00 |

|  |  | | |
|---|--------|------|------|
| 147 | Ken Griffey Jr. GF | 6.00 | 15.00 |
| 148 | Alex Rodriguez GF | 6.00 | 15.00 |
| 149 | Jason Giambi GF | 1.50 | 4.00 |
| 150 | Chipper Jones GF | 4.00 | 10.00 |
| 151 | Nomar Garciaparra GF | 6.00 | 15.00 |
| 152 | Mike Piazza GF | 4.00 | 10.00 |
| 153 | Sammy Sosa GF | 4.00 | 10.00 |
| 154 | Derek Jeter GF | 10.00 | 25.00 |
| 155 | Jeff Bagwell GF | 4.00 | 10.00 |
| 156 | Albert Pujols GF | 6.00 | 15.00 |
| 157 | Ichiro Suzuki GF | 6.00 | 15.00 |
| 158 | Randy Johnson GF | 4.00 | 10.00 |
| 159 | Frank Thomas GF | 4.00 | 10.00 |
| 160 | Greg Maddux GF | 6.00 | 15.00 |
| 161 | Jim Thome GF | 4.00 | 10.00 |
| 162 | Scott Rolen GF | 4.00 | 10.00 |
| 163 | Shawn Green GF | 4.00 | 10.00 |
| 164 | Vladimir Guerrero GF | 4.00 | 10.00 |
| 165 | Troy Glaus GF | 4.00 | 10.00 |
| 166 | Carlos Delgado GF | 4.00 | 10.00 |
| 167 | Luis Gonzalez GF | 4.00 | 10.00 |
| 168 | Roger Clemens GF | 8.00 | 20.00 |
| 169 | Todd Helton GF | 4.00 | 10.00 |
| 170 | Eric Chavez GF | 4.00 | 10.00 |
| 171 | Rafael Palmeiro GF | 4.00 | 10.00 |
| 172 | Pedro Martinez GF | 4.00 | 10.00 |
| 173 | Lance Berkman GF | 4.00 | 10.00 |
| 174 | Josh Beckett GF | 4.00 | 10.00 |
| 175 | Sean Burroughs GF | 4.00 | 10.00 |
| MM | Mark McGwire AU EXCH/100 | | |

## 2003 Sweet Spot

|  | | |
|------|------|------|
| COMP.SET w/o SP's (100) | 8.00 | 20.00 |
| COMP.SET w/SP's (130) | 60.00 | 120.00 |
| COMMON CARD (1-130) | .20 | .50 |
| COMMON SP (1-130) | 1.25 | 3.00 |
| COMMON CARD (131-190) | 1.25 | 3.00 |
| 131-190 PRINT RUN 2000 SERIAL #'d SETS | | |
| COMMON P1 (191-232) | 1.50 | 4.00 |
| P1 191-232 PRINT RUN 500 SERIAL #'d SETS | | |
| COMMON P2-P3 (191-232) | 1.25 | 3.00 |
| P2 191-232 PRINT RUN 1200 SERIAL #'d SETS | | |
| P3 191-232 PRINT RUN 1430 #'d SETS | | |
| 1 Darin Erstad | .20 | .50 |
| 2 Garret Anderson | .20 | .50 |
| 3 Tim Salmon | .30 | .75 |
| 4 Troy Glaus | .20 | .50 |
| 5 Luis Gonzalez | .20 | .50 |
| 6 Randy Johnson | .50 | 1.25 |
| 7 Curt Schilling | .20 | .50 |
| 8 Lyle Overbay | .20 | .50 |
| 9 Andruw Jones SP | 1.50 | 4.00 |
| 10 Gary Sheffield SP | 1.25 | 3.00 |
| 11 Rafael Furcal SP | 1.25 | 3.00 |
| 12 Greg Maddux SP | 2.50 | 6.00 |
| 13 Chipper Jones SP | 1.50 | 4.00 |
| 14 Tony Batista | .20 | .50 |
| 15 Rodrigo Lopez | .20 | .50 |
| 16 Jay Gibbons | .20 | .50 |
| 17 Jason Johnson | .20 | .50 |
| 18 Byung-Hyun Kim SP | 1.25 | 3.00 |
| 19 Johnny Damon SP | 1.50 | 4.00 |
| 20 Derek Lowe SP | 1.25 | 3.00 |
| 21 Nomar Garciaparra SP | 2.50 | 6.00 |
| 22 Pedro Martinez SP | 1.50 | 4.00 |
| 23 Manny Ramirez SP | 1.50 | 4.00 |
| 24 Mark Prior | .30 | .75 |
| 25 Kerry Wood | .30 | .75 |
| 26 Corey Patterson | .20 | .50 |
| 27 Sammy Sosa | .50 | 1.25 |
| 28 Moises Alou | .20 | .50 |
| 29 Magglio Ordonez | .20 | .50 |
| 30 Frank Thomas | .50 | 1.25 |
| 31 Paul Konerko | .20 | .50 |

|  |  | | |
|---|--------|------|------|
| 32 | Roberto Alomar | .30 | .75 |
| 33 | Adam Dunn | .20 | .50 |
| 34 | Austin Kearns | .20 | .50 |
| 35 | Ryan Wagner RC | .20 | .50 |
| 36 | Ken Griffey Jr. | .75 | 2.00 |
| 37 | Sean Casey | .20 | .50 |
| 38 | Omar Vizquel | .30 | .75 |
| 39 | C.C. Sabathia | .20 | .50 |
| 40 | Jason Davis | .20 | .50 |
| 41 | Travis Hafner | .20 | .50 |
| 42 | Brandon Phillips | .20 | .50 |
| 43 | Larry Walker | .20 | .50 |
| 44 | Preston Wilson | .20 | .50 |
| 45 | Jay Payton | .20 | .50 |
| 46 | Todd Helton | .30 | .75 |
| 47 | Carlos Pena | .20 | .50 |
| 48 | Eric Munson | .20 | .50 |
| 49 | Ivan Rodriguez | .30 | .75 |
| 50 | Josh Beckett | .20 | .50 |
| 51 | Alex Gonzalez | .20 | .50 |
| 52 | Roy Oswalt | .20 | .50 |
| 53 | Craig Biggio | .30 | .75 |
| 54 | Jeff Bagwell | .30 | .75 |
| 55 | Lance Berkman | .20 | .50 |
| 56 | Mike Sweeney | .20 | .50 |
| 57 | Carlos Beltran | .20 | .50 |
| 58 | Brent Mayne | .20 | .50 |
| 59 | Mike MacDougal | .20 | .50 |
| 60 | Hideo Nomo | .50 | 1.25 |
| 61 | Dave Roberts | .20 | .50 |
| 62 | Adrian Beltre | .20 | .50 |
| 63 | Shawn Green | .20 | .50 |
| 64 | Kazuhisa Ishii | .20 | .50 |
| 65 | Rickey Henderson | .50 | 1.25 |
| 66 | Richie Sexson | .20 | .50 |
| 67 | Torii Hunter | .20 | .50 |
| 68 | Jacque Jones | .20 | .50 |
| 69 | Joe Mays | .20 | .50 |
| 70 | Corey Koskie | .20 | .50 |
| 71 | A.J. Pierzynski | .20 | .50 |
| 72 | Jose Vidro | .20 | .50 |
| 73 | Vladimir Guerrero | .50 | 1.25 |
| 74 | Tom Glavine | .30 | .75 |
| 75 | Mike Piazza | .75 | 2.00 |
| 76 | Jose Reyes | .20 | .50 |
| 77 | Jae Weong Seo | .20 | .50 |
| 78 | Jorge Posada | .50 | 1.25 |
| 79 | Mike Mussina | .50 | 1.25 |
| 80 | Robin Ventura SP | 1.25 | 3.00 |
| 81 | Mariano Rivera SP | 1.50 | 4.00 |
| 82 | Roger Clemens SP | 3.00 | 8.00 |
| 83 | Jason Giambi SP | 1.25 | 3.00 |
| 84 | Bernie Williams SP | 1.50 | 4.00 |
| 85 | Alfonso Soriano SP | 1.25 | 3.00 |
| 86 | Derek Jeter SP | 3.00 | 8.00 |
| 87 | Miguel Tejada | .20 | .50 |
| 88 | Eric Chavez | .20 | .50 |
| 89 | Tim Hudson | .20 | .50 |
| 90 | Barry Zito | .20 | .50 |
| 91 | Mark Mulder | .20 | .50 |
| 92 | Erubiel Durazo | .20 | .50 |
| 93 | Pat Burrell | .20 | .50 |
| 94 | Jim Thome | .30 | .75 |
| 95 | Bobby Abreu | .20 | .50 |
| 96 | Brian Giles | .20 | .50 |
| 97 | Reggie Sanders | .20 | .50 |
| 98 | Jose Hernandez | .20 | .50 |
| 99 | Ryan Klesko | .20 | .50 |
| 100 | Sean Burroughs | .20 | .50 |
| 101 | Edgardo Alfonzo SP | 1.25 | 3.00 |
| 102 | Rich Aurilia SP | 1.25 | 3.00 |
| 103 | Jose Cruz Jr. SP | 1.25 | 3.00 |
| 104 | Barry Bonds SP | 4.00 | 10.00 |
| 105 | Andres Galarraga SP | 1.25 | 3.00 |
| 106 | Mike Cameron | .20 | .50 |
| 107 | Kazuhiro Sasaki | .20 | .50 |
| 108 | Bret Boone | .20 | .50 |
| 109 | Ichiro Suzuki | 1.00 | 2.50 |
| 110 | John Olerud | .20 | .50 |
| 111 | J.D. Drew SP | 1.25 | 3.00 |
| 112 | Jim Edmonds SP | 1.25 | 3.00 |
| 113 | Scott Rolen SP | 1.50 | 4.00 |
| 114 | Matt Morris SP | 1.25 | 3.00 |
| 115 | Tino Martinez SP | 1.50 | 4.00 |
| 116 | Albert Pujols SP | 3.00 | 8.00 |
| 117 | Jared Sandberg | .20 | .50 |
| 118 | Carl Crawford | .20 | .50 |
| 119 | Rafael Palmeiro | .30 | .75 |

| | | |
|---|---|---|
| ☐ 120 Hank Blalock | .20 | .50 |
| ☐ 121 Alex Rodriguez SP | 2.50 | 6.00 |
| ☐ 122 Kevin Mench | .20 | .50 |
| ☐ 123 Juan Gonzalez | .20 | .50 |
| ☐ 124 Mark Teixeira | .30 | .75 |
| ☐ 125 Shannon Stewart | .20 | .50 |
| ☐ 126 Vernon Wells | .20 | .50 |
| ☐ 127 Josh Phelps | .20 | .50 |
| ☐ 128 Eric Hinske | .20 | .50 |
| ☐ 129 Orlando Hudson | .20 | .50 |
| ☐ 130 Carlos Delgado | .20 | .50 |
| ☐ 131 Jason Shiell SB RC | 1.25 | 3.00 |
| ☐ 132 Kevin Tolar SB RC | 1.25 | 3.00 |
| ☐ 133 Nathan Bland SB RC | 1.25 | 3.00 |
| ☐ 134 Brent Hoard SB RC | 1.25 | 3.00 |
| ☐ 135 Jon Pridie SB RC | 1.25 | 3.00 |
| ☐ 136 Mike Ryan SB RC | 1.25 | 3.00 |
| ☐ 137 Francisco Rosario SB RC | 1.25 | 3.00 |
| ☐ 138 Runelvys Hernandez SB | 1.25 | 3.00 |
| ☐ 139 Guillermo Quiroz SB RC | 1.25 | 3.00 |
| ☐ 140 Chin-Hui Tsao SB | 1.25 | 3.00 |
| ☐ 141 Rett Johnson SB RC | 1.25 | 3.00 |
| ☐ 142 Colin Porter SB RC | 1.25 | 3.00 |
| ☐ 143 Jose Castillo SB | 1.25 | 3.00 |
| ☐ 144 Chris Waters SB RC | 1.25 | 3.00 |
| ☐ 145 Jeremy Guthrie SB | 1.25 | 3.00 |
| ☐ 146 Pedro Liriano SB | 1.25 | 3.00 |
| ☐ 147 Joe Borowski SB | 1.25 | 3.00 |
| ☐ 148 Felix Sanchez SB RC | 1.25 | 3.00 |
| ☐ 149 Todd Wellemeyer SB RC | 1.25 | 3.00 |
| ☐ 150 Gerald Laird SB | 1.25 | 3.00 |
| ☐ 151 Brandon Webb SB | 3.00 | 8.00 |
| ☐ 152 Tommy Whiteman SB | 1.25 | 3.00 |
| ☐ 153 Carlos Rivera SB | 1.25 | 3.00 |
| ☐ 154 Rick Roberts SB RC | 1.25 | 3.00 |
| ☐ 155 Termel Sledge SB RC | 1.25 | 3.00 |
| ☐ 156 Jeff Duncan SB RC | 1.25 | 3.00 |
| ☐ 157 Craig Brazell SB RC | 1.25 | 3.00 |
| ☐ 158 Bernie Castro SB RC | 1.25 | 3.00 |
| ☐ 159 Cory Stewart SB RC | 1.25 | 3.00 |
| ☐ 160 Brandon Villafuerte SB | 1.25 | 3.00 |
| ☐ 161 Tommy Phelps SB | 1.25 | 3.00 |
| ☐ 162 Josh Hall SB RC | 1.25 | 3.00 |
| ☐ 163 Ryan Cameron SB RC | 1.25 | 3.00 |
| ☐ 164 Garret Atkins SB | 1.25 | 3.00 |
| ☐ 165 Brian Stokes SB RC | 1.25 | 3.00 |
| ☐ 166 Rafael Betancourt SB RC | 1.50 | 4.00 |
| ☐ 167 Jaime Cerda SB | 1.25 | 3.00 |
| ☐ 168 D.J. Carrasco SB RC | 1.25 | 3.00 |
| ☐ 169 Ian Ferguson SB RC | 1.25 | 3.00 |
| ☐ 170 Jorge Cordova SB RC | 1.25 | 3.00 |
| ☐ 171 Eric Munson SB | 1.25 | 3.00 |
| ☐ 172 Nook Logan SB RC | 1.50 | 4.00 |
| ☐ 173 Jeremy Bonderman SB RC | 5.00 | 12.00 |
| ☐ 174 Kyle Snyder SB | 1.25 | 3.00 |
| ☐ 175 Rich Harden SB | 1.50 | 4.00 |
| ☐ 176 Kevin Ohme SB RC | 1.25 | 3.00 |
| ☐ 177 Roger Deago SB RC | 1.25 | 3.00 |
| ☐ 178 Marlon Byrd SB | 1.25 | 3.00 |
| ☐ 179 Dontrelle Willis SB | 1.50 | 4.00 |
| ☐ 180 Bobby Hill SB | 1.25 | 3.00 |
| ☐ 181 Jesse Foppert SB | 1.25 | 3.00 |
| ☐ 182 Andrew Good SB | 1.25 | 3.00 |
| ☐ 183 Chase Utley SB | 1.50 | 4.00 |
| ☐ 184 Bo Hart SB RC | 1.25 | 3.00 |
| ☐ 185 Dan Haren SB RC | 1.50 | 4.00 |
| ☐ 186 Tim Olson SB RC | 1.25 | 3.00 |
| ☐ 187 Joe Thurston SB | 1.25 | 3.00 |
| ☐ 188 Jason Anderson SB | 1.25 | 3.00 |
| ☐ 189 Jason Gilfillan SB RC | 1.25 | 3.00 |
| ☐ 190 Rickie Weeks SB RC | 1.50 | 4.00 |
| ☐ 191 Hideki Matsui SB P1 RC | 10.00 | 25.00 |
| ☐ 192 Jose Contreras SB P3 RC | 1.50 | 4.00 |
| ☐ 193 Willie Eyre SB P3 RC | 1.25 | 3.00 |
| ☐ 194 Matt Bruback SB P3 RC | 1.25 | 3.00 |
| ☐ 195 Heath Bell SB P3 RC | 1.25 | 3.00 |
| ☐ 196 Lew Ford SB P3 RC | 1.50 | 4.00 |
| ☐ 197 Jeremy Griffiths SB P3 RC | 1.50 | 4.00 |
| ☐ 198 Oscar Villarreal SB P1 RC | 1.50 | 4.00 |
| ☐ 199 Francisco Cruceta SB P3 RC | 1.25 | 3.00 |
| ☐ 200 Fern Cabrera SB P3 RC | 1.25 | 3.00 |
| ☐ 201 Jhonny Peralta SB P3 | 1.50 | 4.00 |
| ☐ 202 Shane Bazzell SB P3 RC | 1.50 | 4.00 |
| ☐ 203 Bobby Madritsch SB P1 RC | 1.50 | 4.00 |
| ☐ 204 Phil Seibel SB P3 RC | 1.25 | 3.00 |
| ☐ 205 Josh Willingham SB P3 RC | 2.00 | 5.00 |
| ☐ 206 Rob Hammock SB P1 RC | 1.50 | 4.00 |
| ☐ 207 Alejandro Machado SB P3 RC | 1.25 | 3.00 |

| | | |
|---|---|---|
| ☐ 208 David Sanders SB P3 RC | 1.25 | 3.00 |
| ☐ 209 Mike Neu SB P1 RC | 1.50 | 4.00 |
| ☐ 210 Andrew Brown SB P3 RC | 1.50 | 4.00 |
| ☐ 211 Nate Robertson SB P3 RC | 2.00 | 5.00 |
| ☐ 212 Miguel Ojeda SB P3 RC | 1.25 | 3.00 |
| ☐ 213 Beau Kemp SB P3 RC | 1.25 | 3.00 |
| ☐ 214 Aaron Looper SB P3 RC | 1.25 | 3.00 |
| ☐ 215 Alfredo Gonzalez SB P3 RC | 1.25 | 3.00 |
| ☐ 216 Rich Fischer SB P1 RC | 1.50 | 4.00 |
| ☐ 218 Jeremy Wedel SB P1 RC | 1.25 | 3.00 |
| ☐ 219 Prentice Redman SB P3 RC | 1.25 | 3.00 |
| ☐ 220 Michel Hernandez SB P3 RC | 1.25 | 3.00 |
| ☐ 221 Rocco Baldelli SB P1 | 1.50 | 4.00 |
| ☐ 222 Luis Ayala SB P3 RC | 1.25 | 3.00 |
| ☐ 223 Arnaldo Munoz SB P3 RC | 1.25 | 3.00 |
| ☐ 224 Wilfredo Ledezma SB P3 RC | 1.25 | 3.00 |
| ☐ 225 Chris Capuano SB P3 RC | 1.50 | 4.00 |
| ☐ 226 Aquilino Lopez SB P3 RC | 1.25 | 3.00 |
| ☐ 227 Joe Valentine SB P1 RC | 1.50 | 4.00 |
| ☐ 228 Matt Kata SB P2 RC | 1.25 | 3.00 |
| ☐ 229 Diegomar Markwell SB P2 RC | 1.25 | 3.00 |
| ☐ 230 Clint Barmes SB P2 RC | 1.25 | 3.00 |
| ☐ 231 Mike Nicolas SB P1 RC | 1.50 | 4.00 |
| ☐ 232 Jon Leicester SB P2 RC | 1.25 | 3.00 |

## 2004 Sweet Spot

| | | |
|---|---|---|
| ☐ COMP.SET w/o SP's (90) | 8.00 | 20.00 |
| ☐ COMMON CARD (1-90) | .20 | .50 |
| ☐ COMMON (91-170/261-262) | 1.50 | 4.00 |
| ☐ 91-170/261-262 STATED ODDS 1:12 | | |
| ☐ 171/170/261-262 PRINT RUN 799 #'d SETS | | |
| ☐ COMMON CARD (171-230) | 1.50 | 4.00 |
| ☐ 171-230 PRINT RUN 399 SERIAL #'d SETS | | |
| ☐ COMMON CARD (231-250) | 1.50 | 4.00 |
| ☐ 231-250 PRINT RUN 299 SERIAL #'d SETS | | |
| ☐ COMMON CARD (251-260) | 2.50 | 6.00 |
| ☐ 251-260 PRINT RUN 199 SERIAL #'d SETS | | |
| ☐ 171-260/Lid 10/W99 OVERALL ODDS 1:12 | | |
| ☐ OVERALL PLATES ODDS 1:360 HOBBY | | |
| ☐ PLATES PRINT RUN 1 SET PER COLOR | | |
| ☐ BLACK-CYAN-MAGENTA-YELLOW ISSUED | | |
| ☐ NO PLATES PRICING DUE TO SACRCITY | | |
| ☐ 1 Albert Pujols | 1.00 | 2.50 |
| ☐ 2 Alex Rodriguez | .75 | 2.00 |
| ☐ 3 Alfonso Soriano | .20 | .50 |
| ☐ 4 Andruw Jones | .30 | .75 |
| ☐ 5 Andy Pettitte | .30 | .75 |
| ☐ 6 Aubrey Huff | .20 | .50 |
| ☐ 7 Austin Kearns | .20 | .50 |
| ☐ 8 Barry Zito | .20 | .50 |
| ☐ 9 Bobby Abreu | .20 | .50 |
| ☐ 10 Brandon Webb | .20 | .50 |
| ☐ 11 Bret Boone | .20 | .50 |
| ☐ 12 Brian Giles | .20 | .50 |
| ☐ 13 C.C. Sabathia | .20 | .50 |
| ☐ 14 Carlos Beltran | .20 | .50 |
| ☐ 15 Carlos Delgado | .20 | .50 |
| ☐ 16 Chipper Jones | .50 | 1.25 |
| ☐ 17 Cliff Floyd | .20 | .50 |
| ☐ 18 Curt Schilling | .30 | .75 |
| ☐ 19 Delmon Young | .30 | .75 |
| ☐ 20 Derek Jeter | 1.00 | 2.50 |
| ☐ 21 Dontrelle Willis | .30 | .75 |
| ☐ 22 Edgar Martinez | .30 | .75 |
| ☐ 23 Edgar Renteria | .20 | .50 |
| ☐ 24 Eric Chavez | .20 | .50 |
| ☐ 25 Eric Gagne | .20 | .50 |
| ☐ 26 Frank Thomas | .50 | 1.25 |
| ☐ 27 Garret Anderson | .20 | .50 |
| ☐ 28 Gary Sheffield | .30 | .75 |
| ☐ 29 Geoff Jenkins | .20 | .50 |
| ☐ 30 Greg Maddux | .75 | 2.00 |
| ☐ 31 Hank Blalock | .20 | .50 |
| ☐ 32 Hideo Nomo | .50 | 1.25 |

| | | |
|---|---|---|
| ☐ 33 Ichiro Suzuki | 1.00 | 2.50 |
| ☐ 34 Ivan Rodriguez | .30 | .75 |
| ☐ 35 Jacque Jones | .20 | .50 |
| ☐ 36 Jason Gambi | .20 | .50 |
| ☐ 37 Jason Schmidt | .20 | .50 |
| ☐ 38 Javier Vazquez | .20 | .50 |
| ☐ 39 Javy Lopez | .20 | .50 |
| ☐ 40 Jeff Bagwell | .30 | .75 |
| ☐ 41 Jim Edmonds | .20 | .50 |
| ☐ 42 Jim Thome | .30 | .75 |
| ☐ 43 Joe Mauer | .50 | 1.25 |
| ☐ 44 John Smoltz | .20 | .50 |
| ☐ 45 Jose Cruz Jr. | .20 | .50 |
| ☐ 46 Jose Reyes | .20 | .50 |
| ☐ 47 Jose Vidro | .20 | .50 |
| ☐ 48 Josh Beckett | .20 | .50 |
| ☐ 49 Ken Griffey Jr. | .75 | 2.00 |
| ☐ 50 Kerry Wood | .20 | .50 |
| ☐ 51 Kevin Brown | .20 | .50 |
| ☐ 52 Larry Walker | .20 | .50 |
| ☐ 53 Magglio Ordonez | .20 | .50 |
| ☐ 54 Manny Ramirez | .30 | .75 |
| ☐ 55 Mark Mulder | .20 | .50 |
| ☐ 56 Mark Prior | .30 | .75 |
| ☐ 57 Mark Teixeira | .30 | .75 |
| ☐ 58 Miguel Cabrera | .30 | .75 |
| ☐ 59 Miguel Tejada | .20 | .50 |
| ☐ 60 Mike Lowell | .20 | .50 |
| ☐ 61 Mike Mussina | .30 | .75 |
| ☐ 62 Mike Piazza | .75 | 2.00 |
| ☐ 63 Nomar Garciaparra | .75 | 2.00 |
| ☐ 64 Orlando Cabrera | .20 | .50 |
| ☐ 65 Pat Burrell | .20 | .50 |
| ☐ 66 Pedro Martinez | .30 | .75 |
| ☐ 67 Phil Nevin | .20 | .50 |
| ☐ 68 Preston Wilson | .20 | .50 |
| ☐ 69 Rafael Furcal | .20 | .50 |
| ☐ 70 Rafael Palmeiro | .30 | .75 |
| ☐ 71 Randy Johnson | .50 | 1.25 |
| ☐ 72 Craig Wilson | .20 | .50 |
| ☐ 73 Rich Harden | .20 | .50 |
| ☐ 74 Richie Sexson | .20 | .50 |
| ☐ 75 Rickie Weeks | .20 | .50 |
| ☐ 76 Rocco Baldelli | .20 | .50 |
| ☐ 77 Roger Clemens | 1.00 | 2.50 |
| ☐ 78 Roy Halladay | .20 | .50 |
| ☐ 79 Roy Oswalt | .20 | .50 |
| ☐ 80 Ryan Klesko | .20 | .50 |
| ☐ 81 Sammy Sosa | .50 | 1.25 |
| ☐ 82 Scott Podsednik | .20 | .50 |
| ☐ 83 Scott Rolen | .30 | .75 |
| ☐ 84 Shawn Green | .20 | .50 |
| ☐ 85 Tim Hudson | .20 | .50 |
| ☐ 86 Todd Helton | .30 | .75 |
| ☐ 87 Torii Hunter | .20 | .50 |
| ☐ 88 Troy Glaus | .20 | .50 |
| ☐ 89 Vernon Wells | .20 | .50 |
| ☐ 90 Vladimir Guerrero | .50 | 1.25 |
| ☐ 91 Aarom Baldiris SB RC | 2.00 | 5.00 |
| ☐ 92 Akinori Otsuka SB RC | 1.50 | 4.00 |
| ☐ 93 Andres Blanco SB RC | 1.50 | 4.00 |
| ☐ 94 Angel Chavez SB RC | 1.50 | 4.00 |
| ☐ 95 Brian Dallimore SB RC | 1.50 | 4.00 |
| ☐ 96 Carlos Hines SB RC | 1.50 | 4.00 |
| ☐ 97 Carlos Vasquez SB RC | 2.00 | 5.00 |
| ☐ 98 Casey Daigle SB RC | 1.50 | 4.00 |
| ☐ 99 Chad Bentz SB RC | 1.50 | 4.00 |
| ☐ 100 Chris Aguila SB RC | 1.50 | 4.00 |
| ☐ 101 Chris Oxspring SB RC | 1.50 | 4.00 |
| ☐ 102 Chris Saenz SB RC | 1.50 | 4.00 |
| ☐ 103 Chris Shelton SB RC | 2.00 | 5.00 |
| ☐ 104 Colby Miller SB RC | 1.50 | 4.00 |
| ☐ 105 Dave Crouthers SB RC | 1.50 | 4.00 |
| ☐ 106 David Aardsma SB RC | 1.50 | 4.00 |
| ☐ 107 Dennis Sarfate SB RC | 1.50 | 4.00 |
| ☐ 108 Donnie Kelly SB RC | 1.50 | 4.00 |
| ☐ 109 Eddy Rodriguez SB RC | 2.00 | 5.00 |
| ☐ 110 Eduardo Villacis SB RC | 1.50 | 4.00 |
| ☐ 111 Edwin Moreno SB RC | 2.00 | 5.00 |
| ☐ 112 Enemencio Pacheco SB RC | 1.50 | 4.00 |
| ☐ 113 Fernando Nieve SB RC | 2.00 | 5.00 |
| ☐ 114 Franklyn Gracesqui SB RC | 1.50 | 4.00 |
| ☐ 115 Freddy Guzman SB RC | 1.50 | 4.00 |
| ☐ 116 Greg Dobbs SB RC | 1.50 | 4.00 |
| ☐ 117 Hector Gimenez SB RC | 1.50 | 4.00 |
| ☐ 118 Ian Snell SB RC | 2.00 | 5.00 |
| ☐ 119 Ivan Ochoa SB RC | 1.50 | 4.00 |
| ☐ 120 Jake Woods SB RC | 1.50 | 4.00 |

| | | |
|---|---|---|
| ❑ 121 Jamie Brown SB RC | 1.50 | 4.00 |
| ❑ 122 Jason Bartlett SB RC | 2.00 | 5.00 |
| ❑ 123 Jason Frasor SB RC | 1.50 | 4.00 |
| ❑ 124 Jeff Bennett SB RC | 1.50 | 4.00 |
| ❑ 125 Jerome Gamble SB RC | 1.50 | 4.00 |
| ❑ 126 Jerry Gil SB RC | 1.50 | 4.00 |
| ❑ 127 Brandon Medders SB RC | 1.50 | 4.00 |
| ❑ 128 Ryan Meaux SB RC | 1.50 | 4.00 |
| ❑ 129 John Gall SB RC | 2.00 | 5.00 |
| ❑ 130 Jorge Sequea SB RC | 1.50 | 4.00 |
| ❑ 131 Jorge Vasquez SB RC | 1.50 | 4.00 |
| ❑ 132 Jose Capellan SB RC | 2.00 | 5.00 |
| ❑ 133 Josh Labandeira SB RC | 1.50 | 4.00 |
| ❑ 134 Justin Germano SB RC | 1.50 | 4.00 |
| ❑ 135 Justin Hampson SB RC | 1.50 | 4.00 |
| ❑ 136 Justin Huisman SB RC | 1.50 | 4.00 |
| ❑ 137 Justin Knoedler SB RC | 1.50 | 4.00 |
| ❑ 138 Justin Leone SB RC | 2.00 | 5.00 |
| ❑ 139 Kazuhito Tadano SB RC | 2.00 | 5.00 |
| ❑ 140 Kazuo Matsui SB RC | 2.00 | 5.00 |
| ❑ 141 Kevin Cave SB RC | 1.50 | 4.00 |
| ❑ 142 Lincoln Holdzkom SB RC | 1.50 | 4.00 |
| ❑ 143 Lino Urdaneta SB RC | 1.50 | 4.00 |
| ❑ 144 Luis A. Gonzalez SB RC | 1.50 | 4.00 |
| ❑ 145 Mariano Gomez SB RC | 1.50 | 4.00 |
| ❑ 146 Merkin Valdez SB RC | 2.00 | 5.00 |
| ❑ 147 Michael Vento SB RC | 2.00 | 5.00 |
| ❑ 148 Michael Wuertz SB RC | 2.00 | 5.00 |
| ❑ 149 Mike Gosling SB RC | 1.50 | 4.00 |
| ❑ 150 Mike Johnston SB RC | 1.50 | 4.00 |
| ❑ 151 Mike Rouse SB RC | 1.50 | 4.00 |
| ❑ 152 Nick Regilio SB RC | 1.50 | 4.00 |
| ❑ 153 Onil Joseph SB RC | 1.50 | 4.00 |
| ❑ 154 Orlando Rodriguez SB RC | 1.50 | 4.00 |
| ❑ 155 Ramon Ramirez SB RC | 1.50 | 4.00 |
| ❑ 156 Renyel Pinto SB RC | 1.50 | 4.00 |
| ❑ 157 Roberto Novoa SB RC | 2.00 | 5.00 |
| ❑ 158 Roman Colon SB RC | 1.50 | 4.00 |
| ❑ 159 Ronald Belisario SB RC | 1.50 | 4.00 |
| ❑ 160 Ronny Cedeno SB RC | 2.00 | 5.00 |
| ❑ 161 Rusty Tucker SB RC | 2.00 | 5.00 |
| ❑ 162 Ryan Wing SB RC | 1.50 | 4.00 |
| ❑ 163 Scott Dohmann SB RC | 1.50 | 4.00 |
| ❑ 164 Scott Proctor SB RC | 1.50 | 4.00 |
| ❑ 165 Sean Henn SB RC | 1.50 | 4.00 |
| ❑ 166 Shawn Camp SB RC | 1.50 | 4.00 |
| ❑ 167 Shawn Hill SB RC | 1.50 | 4.00 |
| ❑ 168 Shingo Takatsu SB RC | 2.00 | 5.00 |
| ❑ 169 Tim Hamulack SB RC | 1.50 | 4.00 |
| ❑ 170 William Bergolla SB RC | 1.50 | 4.00 |
| ❑ 171 Adam Dunn SF | 1.50 | 4.00 |
| ❑ 172 Albert Pujols SF | 4.00 | 10.00 |
| ❑ 173 Alex Rodriguez SF | 3.00 | 8.00 |
| ❑ 174 Alfonso Soriano SF | 1.50 | 4.00 |
| ❑ 175 Andruw Jones SF | 1.50 | 4.00 |
| ❑ 176 Bret Boone SF | 1.50 | 4.00 |
| ❑ 177 Brian Giles SF | 1.50 | 4.00 |
| ❑ 178 Carlos Delgado SF | 1.50 | 4.00 |
| ❑ 179 Derrek Lee SF | 1.50 | 4.00 |
| ❑ 180 Eric Chavez SF | 1.50 | 4.00 |
| ❑ 181 Frank Thomas SF | 2.00 | 5.00 |
| ❑ 182 Garret Anderson SF | 1.50 | 4.00 |
| ❑ 183 Gary Sheffield SF | 1.50 | 4.00 |
| ❑ 184 Hank Blalock SF | 1.50 | 4.00 |
| ❑ 185 Jason Giambi SF | 1.50 | 4.00 |
| ❑ 186 Javy Lopez SF | 1.50 | 4.00 |
| ❑ 187 Jeff Bagwell SF | 2.00 | 5.00 |
| ❑ 188 Jim Edmonds SF | 1.50 | 4.00 |
| ❑ 189 Jim Thome SF | 2.00 | 5.00 |
| ❑ 190 Ken Griffey Jr. SF | 3.00 | 8.00 |
| ❑ 191 Lance Berkman SF | 1.50 | 4.00 |
| ❑ 192 Magglio Ordonez SF | 1.50 | 4.00 |
| ❑ 193 Manny Ramirez SF | 2.00 | 5.00 |
| ❑ 194 Mike Lowell SF | 1.50 | 4.00 |
| ❑ 195 Mike Piazza SF | 3.00 | 8.00 |
| ❑ 196 Preston Wilson SF | 1.50 | 4.00 |
| ❑ 197 Rafael Palmeiro SF | 2.00 | 5.00 |
| ❑ 198 Richie Sexson SF | 1.50 | 4.00 |
| ❑ 199 Sammy Sosa SF | 2.00 | 5.00 |
| ❑ 200 Scott Rolen SF | 1.50 | 4.00 |
| ❑ 201 Shawn Green SF | 1.50 | 4.00 |
| ❑ 202 Todd Helton SF | 2.00 | 5.00 |
| ❑ 203 Troy Glaus SF | 1.50 | 4.00 |
| ❑ 204 Vernon Wells SF | 1.50 | 4.00 |
| ❑ 205 Vladimir Guerrero SF | 2.00 | 5.00 |
| ❑ 206 G.Anderson/V.Guerrero SL | 1.50 | 4.00 |
| ❑ 207 L.Gonzalez/R.Sexson SL | 1.50 | 4.00 |
| ❑ 208 A.Jones/C.Jones SL | 2.00 | 5.00 |
| ❑ 209 J.Lopez/M.Tejada SL | 1.50 | 4.00 |
| ❑ 210 M.Ramirez/D.Ortiz SL | 2.00 | 5.00 |
| ❑ 211 D.Lee/S.Sosa SL | 2.00 | 5.00 |
| ❑ 212 F.Thomas/M.Ordonez SL | 2.00 | 5.00 |
| ❑ 213 A.Kearns/K.Griffey Jr. SL | 3.00 | 8.00 |
| ❑ 214 P.Wilson/T.Helton SL | 2.00 | 5.00 |
| ❑ 215 D.Young/I.Rodriguez SL | 2.00 | 5.00 |
| ❑ 216 M.Cabrera/M.Lowell SL | 2.00 | 5.00 |
| ❑ 217 J.Bagwell/L.Berkman SL | 2.00 | 5.00 |
| ❑ 218 L.Overbay/G.Jenkins SL | 1.50 | 4.00 |
| ❑ 219 A.Beltre/S.Green SL | 1.50 | 4.00 |
| ❑ 220 J.Jones/T.Hunter SL | 1.50 | 4.00 |
| ❑ 221 J.Vidro/N.Johnson SL | 1.50 | 4.00 |
| ❑ 222 K.Matsui/M.Piazza SL | 3.00 | 8.00 |
| ❑ 223 A.Rodriguez/J.Giambi SL | 3.00 | 8.00 |
| ❑ 224 E.Chavez/J.Dye SL | 1.50 | 4.00 |
| ❑ 225 J.Thome/P.Burrell SL | 2.00 | 5.00 |
| ❑ 226 B.Giles/P.Nevin SL | 1.50 | 4.00 |
| ❑ 227 B.Boone/I.Suzuki SL | 4.00 | 10.00 |
| ❑ 228 A.Pujols/S.Rolen SL | 4.00 | 10.00 |
| ❑ 229 H.Blalock/M.Teixeira SL | 1.50 | 4.00 |
| ❑ 230 C.Delgado/V.Wells SL | 1.50 | 4.00 |
| ❑ 231 Albert Pujols PD | 4.00 | 10.00 |
| ❑ 232 Alex Rodriguez PD | 3.00 | 8.00 |
| ❑ 233 Chipper Jones PD | 2.00 | 5.00 |
| ❑ 234 Craig Biggio PD | 2.00 | 5.00 |
| ❑ 235 Curt Schilling PD | 2.00 | 5.00 |
| ❑ 236 Derek Jeter PD | 4.00 | 10.00 |
| ❑ 237 Ivan Rodriguez PD | 2.00 | 5.00 |
| ❑ 238 Jeff Bagwell PD | 2.00 | 5.00 |
| ❑ 239 Jim Edmonds PD | 1.50 | 4.00 |
| ❑ 240 Jim Thome PD | 2.00 | 5.00 |
| ❑ 241 Josh Beckett PD | 1.50 | 4.00 |
| ❑ 242 Kerry Wood PD | 1.50 | 4.00 |
| ❑ 243 Kevin Brown PD | 1.50 | 4.00 |
| ❑ 244 Mark Prior PD | 2.00 | 5.00 |
| ❑ 245 Miguel Tejada PD | 1.50 | 4.00 |
| ❑ 246 Mike Mussina PD | 2.00 | 5.00 |
| ❑ 247 Nomar Garciaparra PD | 3.00 | 8.00 |
| ❑ 248 Pedro Martinez PD | 3.00 | 8.00 |
| ❑ 249 Randy Johnson PD | 2.00 | 5.00 |
| ❑ 250 Roger Clemens PD | 4.00 | 10.00 |
| ❑ 251 A.Rodriguez/D.Jeter DD | 6.00 | 15.00 |
| ❑ 252 A.Soriano/H.Blalock DD | 2.50 | 6.00 |
| ❑ 253 B.Abreu/P.Burrell DD | 2.50 | 6.00 |
| ❑ 254 E.Renteria/S.Rolen DD | 3.00 | 8.00 |
| ❑ 255 G.Anderson/V.Guerrero DD | 3.00 | 8.00 |
| ❑ 256 J.Bagwell/J.Kent DD | 3.00 | 8.00 |
| ❑ 257 J.Reyes/K.Matsui DD | 3.00 | 8.00 |
| ❑ 258 K.Greene/S.Burroughs DD | 3.00 | 8.00 |
| ❑ 259 M.Giles/R.Furcal DD | 2.50 | 6.00 |
| ❑ 260 M.Ramirez/J.Damon DD | 3.00 | 8.00 |
| ❑ 261 Tim Bausher SB RC | 1.50 | 4.00 |
| ❑ 262 Tim Bittner SB RC | 1.50 | 4.00 |

## 2005 Sweet Spot

| | | |
|---|---|---|
| ❑ COMP.BASIC SET (90) | 8.00 | 20.00 |
| ❑ COMP.UPDATE SET (84) | 10.00 | 25.00 |
| ❑ COMMON CARD (1-90) | .20 | .50 |
| ❑ COMMON CARD (91-174) | .40 | 1.00 |
| ❑ 91-174 ONE PER '05 UD UPDATE PACK | | |
| ❑ 1 Magglio Ordonez | .20 | .50 |
| ❑ 2 Craig Biggio | .30 | .75 |
| ❑ 3 Hank Blalock | .20 | .50 |
| ❑ 4 Nomar Garciaparra | .50 | 1.25 |
| ❑ 5 Ken Griffey Jr. | .75 | 2.00 |
| ❑ 6 Khalil Greene | .30 | .75 |
| ❑ 7 Andruw Jones | .30 | .75 |
| ❑ 8 Ichiro Suzuki | 1.00 | 2.50 |
| ❑ 9 Philip Humber RC | .50 | 1.25 |
| ❑ 10 Vladimir Guerrero | .50 | 1.25 |
| ❑ 11 Carlos Delgado | .20 | .50 |
| ❑ 12 Jeff Niemann RC | .50 | 1.25 |
| ❑ 13 Chipper Jones | .50 | 1.25 |
| ❑ 14 Jose Vidro | .20 | .50 |
| ❑ 15 Miguel Cabrera | .30 | .75 |
| ❑ 16 Albert Pujols | 1.00 | 2.50 |
| ❑ 17 Tadahito Iguchi RC | .75 | 2.00 |
| ❑ 18 Norihiro Nakamura RC | .60 | 1.50 |
| ❑ 19 Jeff Bagwell | .30 | .75 |
| ❑ 20 Troy Glaus | .20 | .50 |
| ❑ 21 Scott Rolen | .20 | .50 |
| ❑ 22 Derek Lowe | .20 | .50 |
| ❑ 23 Mark Prior | .30 | .75 |
| ❑ 24 Bobby Abreu | .20 | .50 |
| ❑ 25 David Wright | .75 | 2.00 |
| ❑ 26 Barry Zito | .20 | .50 |
| ❑ 27 Livan Hernandez | .20 | .50 |
| ❑ 28 Mark Teixeira | .30 | .75 |
| ❑ 29 Manny Ramirez | .30 | .75 |
| ❑ 30 Paul Konerko | .20 | .50 |
| ❑ 31 Victor Martinez | .20 | .50 |
| ❑ 32 Greg Maddux | .75 | 2.00 |
| ❑ 33 Jim Thome | .30 | .75 |
| ❑ 34 Miguel Tejada | .20 | .50 |
| ❑ 35 Ivan Rodriguez | .30 | .75 |
| ❑ 36 Carlos Beltran | .20 | .50 |
| ❑ 37 Steve Finley | .20 | .50 |
| ❑ 38 Torii Hunter | .20 | .50 |
| ❑ 39 Bobby Crosby | .20 | .50 |
| ❑ 40 Jorge Posada | .30 | .75 |
| ❑ 41 Ben Sheets | .20 | .50 |
| ❑ 42 Mike Piazza | .50 | 1.25 |
| ❑ 43 Luis Gonzalez | .20 | .50 |
| ❑ 44 Joe Mauer | .50 | 1.25 |
| ❑ 45 Shawn Green | .20 | .50 |
| ❑ 46 Eric Gagne | .20 | .50 |
| ❑ 47 Kerry Wood | .20 | .50 |
| ❑ 48 Derek Jeter | 1.25 | 3.00 |
| ❑ 49 Josh Beckett | .20 | .50 |
| ❑ 50 Alex Rodriguez | .75 | 2.00 |
| ❑ 51 Aubrey Huff | .20 | .50 |
| ❑ 52 Eric Chavez | .20 | .50 |
| ❑ 53 Sammy Sosa | .50 | 1.25 |
| ❑ 54 Roger Clemens | .75 | 2.00 |
| ❑ 55 Mike Mussina | .30 | .75 |
| ❑ 56 Mike Sweeney | .20 | .50 |
| ❑ 57 Oliver Perez | .20 | .50 |
| ❑ 58 Tim Hudson | .20 | .50 |
| ❑ 59 Justin Verlander RC | 1.50 | 4.00 |
| ❑ 60 Johan Santana | .50 | 1.25 |
| ❑ 61 Hideki Matsui | .75 | 2.00 |
| ❑ 62 Mark Mulder | .20 | .50 |
| ❑ 63 Jake Peavy | .20 | .50 |
| ❑ 64 Adam Dunn | .20 | .50 |
| ❑ 65 Dallas McPherson | .20 | .50 |
| ❑ 66 Jeff Kent | .30 | .75 |
| ❑ 67 Pedro Martinez | .50 | 1.25 |
| ❑ 68 J.D. Drew | .20 | .50 |
| ❑ 69 Frank Thomas | .50 | 1.25 |
| ❑ 70 Kazuo Matsui | .20 | .50 |
| ❑ 71 Travis Hafner | .20 | .50 |
| ❑ 72 John Smoltz | .30 | .75 |
| ❑ 73 Jason Schmidt | .20 | .50 |
| ❑ 74 Carlos Lee | .20 | .50 |
| ❑ 75 Todd Helton | .30 | .75 |
| ❑ 76 David Ortiz | .50 | 1.25 |
| ❑ 77 Roy Oswalt | .20 | .50 |
| ❑ 78 Brian Giles | .20 | .50 |
| ❑ 79 Gary Sheffield | .20 | .50 |
| ❑ 80 Jason Bay | .20 | .50 |
| ❑ 81 Alfonso Soriano | .20 | .50 |
| ❑ 82 Randy Johnson | .30 | .75 |
| ❑ 83 Tom Glavine | .30 | .75 |
| ❑ 84 Richie Sexson | .20 | .50 |
| ❑ 85 Curt Schilling | .30 | .75 |
| ❑ 86 Adrian Beltre | .20 | .50 |
| ❑ 87 Jim Edmonds | .20 | .50 |
| ❑ 88 Roy Halladay | .30 | .75 |
| ❑ 89 Johnny Damon | .30 | .75 |
| ❑ 90 Lance Berkman | .20 | .50 |
| ❑ 91 Adam Shabala SB RC | .40 | 1.00 |
| ❑ 92 Ambiorix Burgos SB RC | .40 | 1.00 |
| ❑ 93 Ambiorix Concepcion SB RC | .40 | 1.00 |
| ❑ 94 Anibal Sanchez SB RC | 1.25 | 3.00 |
| ❑ 95 Bill McCarthy SB RC | .40 | 1.00 |
| ❑ 96 Brandon McCarthy SB RC | .60 | 1.50 |
| ❑ 97 Brian Burres SB RC | .40 | 1.00 |
| ❑ 98 Carlos Ruiz SB RC | .40 | 1.00 |
| ❑ 99 Casey Rogowski SB RC | .50 | 1.25 |
| ❑ 100 Chad Orvella SB RC | .40 | 1.00 |
| ❑ 101 Chris Resop SB RC | .40 | 1.00 |

|  | | |
|---|---|---|
| ☐ 102 Chris Roberson SB RC | .40 | 1.00 |
| ☐ 103 Chris Seddon SB RC | .40 | 1.00 |
| ☐ 104 Colter Bean SB RC | .40 | 1.00 |
| ☐ 105 Dae-Sung Koo SB RC | .40 | 1.00 |
| ☐ 106 Ryan Zimmerman SB RC | 3.00 | 8.00 |
| ☐ 107 Dave Gassner SB RC | .40 | 1.00 |
| ☐ 108 Brian Anderson SB RC | .60 | 1.50 |
| ☐ 109 D.J. Houlton SB RC | .40 | 1.00 |
| ☐ 110 Derek Wathan SB RC | .40 | 1.00 |
| ☐ 111 Devon Lowery SB RC | .40 | 1.00 |
| ☐ 112 Enrique Gonzalez SB RC | .40 | 1.00 |
| ☐ 113 Chris Denorfia SB RC | .50 | 1.25 |
| ☐ 114 Eude Brito SB RC | .40 | 1.00 |
| ☐ 115 Francisco Butto SB RC | .40 | 1.00 |
| ☐ 116 Franquelis Osoria SB RC | .40 | 1.00 |
| ☐ 117 Garrett Jones SB RC | .40 | 1.00 |
| ☐ 118 Geovany Soto SB RC | 1.50 | 4.00 |
| ☐ 119 Hayden Penn SB RC | .50 | 1.25 |
| ☐ 120 Ismael Ramirez SB RC | .40 | 1.00 |
| ☐ 121 Jared Gothreaux SB RC | .40 | 1.00 |
| ☐ 122 Jason Hammel SB RC | .40 | 1.00 |
| ☐ 123 Dana Eveland SB RC | .40 | 1.00 |
| ☐ 124 Jeff Miller SB RC | .40 | 1.00 |
| ☐ 125 Jermaine Van Buren SB | .40 | 1.00 |
| ☐ 126 Joel Peralta SB RC | .40 | 1.00 |
| ☐ 127 John Hattig SB RC | .40 | 1.00 |
| ☐ 128 Jorge Campillo SB RC | .40 | 1.00 |
| ☐ 129 Juan Morillo SB RC | .40 | 1.00 |
| ☐ 130 Ryan Garko SB RC | .75 | 2.00 |
| ☐ 131 Keiichi Yabu SB RC | .40 | 1.00 |
| ☐ 132 Kendry Morales SB RC | 1.00 | 2.50 |
| ☐ 133 Luis Hernandez SB RC | .40 | 1.00 |
| ☐ 134 Mark McLemore SB RC | .40 | 1.00 |
| ☐ 135 Luis Pena SB RC | .40 | 1.00 |
| ☐ 136 Luis O.Rodriguez SB RC | .40 | 1.00 |
| ☐ 137 Luke Scott SB RC | .75 | 2.00 |
| ☐ 138 Marcos Carvajal SB RC | .40 | 1.00 |
| ☐ 139 Mark Woodyard SB RC | .40 | 1.00 |
| ☐ 140 Matt A.Smith SB RC | .40 | 1.00 |
| ☐ 141 Matthew Lindstrom SB RC | .40 | 1.00 |
| ☐ 142 Miguel Negron SB RC | .50 | 1.25 |
| ☐ 143 Mike Morse SB RC | .40 | 1.00 |
| ☐ 144 Nate McLouth SB RC | .50 | 1.25 |
| ☐ 145 Nelson Cruz SB RC | 1.25 | 3.00 |
| ☐ 146 Nick Masset SB RC | .40 | 1.00 |
| ☐ 147 Ryan Spilborghs SB RC | .50 | 1.25 |
| ☐ 148 Oscar Robles SB RC | .40 | 1.00 |
| ☐ 149 Paulino Reynoso SB RC | .40 | 1.00 |
| ☐ 150 Pedro Lopez SB RC | .40 | 1.00 |
| ☐ 151 Pete Orr SB RC | .40 | 1.00 |
| ☐ 152 Prince Fielder SB RC | 1.50 | 4.00 |
| ☐ 153 Randy Messenger SB RC | .40 | 1.00 |
| ☐ 154 Randy Williams SB RC | .40 | 1.00 |
| ☐ 155 Raul Tablado SB RC | .40 | 1.00 |
| ☐ 156 Ronny Paulino SB RC | .50 | 1.25 |
| ☐ 157 Russ Rohlicek SB RC | .40 | 1.00 |
| ☐ 158 Russell Martin SB RC | .75 | 2.00 |
| ☐ 159 Scott Baker SB RC | .50 | 1.25 |
| ☐ 160 Scott Munter SB RC | .40 | 1.00 |
| ☐ 161 Sean Thompson SB RC | .40 | 1.00 |
| ☐ 162 Sean Tracey SB RC | .40 | 1.00 |
| ☐ 163 Shane Costa SB RC | .40 | 1.00 |
| ☐ 164 Stephen Drew SB RC | 2.00 | 5.00 |
| ☐ 165 Steve Schmoll SB RC | .40 | 1.00 |
| ☐ 166 Ryan Speier SB RC | .40 | 1.00 |
| ☐ 167 Tadahito Iguchi SB | .75 | 2.00 |
| ☐ 168 Tony Giarratano SB RC | .40 | 1.00 |
| ☐ 169 Tony Pena SB RC | .40 | 1.00 |
| ☐ 170 Travis Bowyer SB RC | .40 | 1.00 |
| ☐ 171 Ubaldo Jimenez SB RC | .75 | 2.00 |
| ☐ 172 Wladimir Balentien SB RC | .50 | 1.25 |
| ☐ 173 Yorman Bazardo SB RC | .40 | 1.00 |
| ☐ 174 Yuniesky Betancourt SB RC | .75 | 2.00 |

**2006 Sweet Spot**

|  | | |
|---|---|---|
| ☐ COMP.SET w/o AU's (100) | 10.00 | 25.00 |
| ☐ COMMON CARD (1-100) | .20 | .50 |
| ☐ OVERALL AU ODDS 1:12 | | |
| ☐ AU PRINT RUNS B/WN 45-275 PER | | |
| ☐ EXCHANGE DEADLINE 05/25/08 | | |
| ☐ ASTERISK = PARTIAL EXCHANGE | | |
| ☐ 1 Bartolo Colon | .20 | .50 |
| ☐ 2 Garret Anderson | .20 | .50 |
| ☐ 3 Francisco Rodriguez | .20 | .50 |
| ☐ 4 Dallas McPherson | .20 | .50 |
| ☐ 5 Andy Pettitte | .30 | .75 |
| ☐ 6 Lance Berkman | .20 | .50 |
| ☐ 7 Willy Taveras | .20 | .50 |
| ☐ 8 Bobby Crosby | .20 | .50 |
| ☐ 9 Dan Haren | .20 | .50 |
| ☐ 10 Nick Swisher | .20 | .50 |
| ☐ 11 Vernon Wells | .20 | .50 |
| ☐ 12 Orlando Hudson | .20 | .50 |
| ☐ 13 Roy Halladay | .20 | .50 |
| ☐ 14 Andruw Jones | .30 | .75 |
| ☐ 15 Chipper Jones | .50 | 1.25 |
| ☐ 16 Jeff Francoeur | .50 | 1.25 |
| ☐ 17 John Smoltz | .30 | .75 |
| ☐ 18 Carlos Lee | .20 | .50 |
| ☐ 19 Rickie Weeks | .20 | .50 |
| ☐ 20 Bill Hall | .20 | .50 |
| ☐ 21 Jim Edmonds | .30 | .75 |
| ☐ 22 David Eckstein | .20 | .50 |
| ☐ 23 Mark Mulder | .20 | .50 |
| ☐ 24 Aramis Ramirez | .20 | .50 |
| ☐ 25 Greg Maddux | .75 | 2.00 |
| ☐ 26 Nomar Garciaparra | .50 | 1.25 |
| ☐ 27 Carlos Zambrano | .20 | .50 |
| ☐ 28 Scott Kazmir | .30 | .75 |
| ☐ 29 Jorge Cantu | .20 | .50 |
| ☐ 30 Carl Crawford | .20 | .50 |
| ☐ 31 Luis Gonzalez | .20 | .50 |
| ☐ 32 Troy Glaus | .20 | .50 |
| ☐ 33 Shawn Green | .20 | .50 |
| ☐ 34 Jeff Kent | .20 | .50 |
| ☐ 35 Milton Bradley | .20 | .50 |
| ☐ 36 Cesar Izturis | .20 | .50 |
| ☐ 37 Omar Vizquel | .30 | .75 |
| ☐ 38 Moises Alou | .20 | .50 |
| ☐ 39 Randy Winn | .20 | .50 |
| ☐ 40 Jason Schmidt | .20 | .50 |
| ☐ 41 Coco Crisp | .20 | .50 |
| ☐ 42 C.C. Sabathia | .20 | .50 |
| ☐ 43 Cliff Lee | .20 | .50 |
| ☐ 44 Ichiro Suzuki | .75 | 2.00 |
| ☐ 45 Richie Sexson | .20 | .50 |
| ☐ 46 Jeremy Reed | .20 | .50 |
| ☐ 47 Carlos Delgado | .20 | .50 |
| ☐ 48 Miguel Cabrera | .30 | .75 |
| ☐ 49 Luis Castillo | .20 | .50 |
| ☐ 50 Carlos Beltran | .20 | .50 |
| ☐ 51 Tom Glavine | .30 | .75 |
| ☐ 52 David Wright | .75 | 2.00 |
| ☐ 53 Cliff Floyd | .20 | .50 |
| ☐ 54 Chad Cordero | .20 | .50 |
| ☐ 55 Jose Vidro | .20 | .50 |
| ☐ 56 Jose Guillen | .20 | .50 |
| ☐ 57 Nick Johnson | .20 | .50 |
| ☐ 58 Miguel Tejada | .20 | .50 |
| ☐ 59 Melvin Mora | .20 | .50 |
| ☐ 60 Javy Lopez | .20 | .50 |
| ☐ 61 Khalil Greene | .30 | .75 |
| ☐ 62 Brian Giles | .20 | .50 |
| ☐ 63 Trevor Hoffman | .20 | .50 |
| ☐ 64 Bobby Abreu | .20 | .50 |
| ☐ 65 Jimmy Rollins | .20 | .50 |
| ☐ 66 Pat Burrell | .20 | .50 |
| ☐ 67 Billy Wagner | .20 | .50 |
| ☐ 68 Jack Wilson | .20 | .50 |
| ☐ 69 Zach Duke | .20 | .50 |
| ☐ 70 Craig Wilson | .20 | .50 |
| ☐ 71 Mark Teixeira | .30 | .75 |
| ☐ 72 Hank Blalock | .20 | .50 |
| ☐ 73 David Dellucci | .20 | .50 |
| ☐ 74 Manny Ramirez | .30 | .75 |
| ☐ 75 Johnny Damon | .30 | .75 |
| ☐ 76 Jason Varitek | .50 | 1.25 |
| ☐ 77 Trot Nixon | .20 | .50 |
| ☐ 78 Adam Dunn | .20 | .50 |
| ☐ 79 Felipe Lopez | .20 | .50 |
| ☐ 80 Brandon Claussen | .20 | .50 |
| ☐ 81 Sean Casey | .20 | .50 |
| ☐ 82 Todd Helton | .30 | .75 |

|  | | |
|---|---|---|
| ☐ 83 Clint Barmes | .20 | .50 |
| ☐ 84 Matt Holliday | .50 | 1.25 |
| ☐ 85 Mike Sweeney | .20 | .50 |
| ☐ 86 Zack Greinke | .20 | .50 |
| ☐ 87 David DeJesus | .20 | .50 |
| ☐ 88 Ivan Rodriguez | .30 | .75 |
| ☐ 89 Jeremy Bonderman | .20 | .50 |
| ☐ 90 Magglio Ordonez | .20 | .50 |
| ☐ 91 Torii Hunter | .20 | .50 |
| ☐ 92 Joe Nathan | .20 | .50 |
| ☐ 93 Michael Cuddyer | .20 | .50 |
| ☐ 94 Paul Konerko | .20 | .50 |
| ☐ 95 Jermaine Dye | .20 | .50 |
| ☐ 96 Jon Garland | .20 | .50 |
| ☐ 97 Alex Rodriguez | .75 | 2.00 |
| ☐ 98 Hideki Matsui | .50 | 1.25 |
| ☐ 99 Jason Giambi | .20 | .50 |
| ☐ 100 Mariano Rivera | .50 | 1.25 |
| ☐ 101 Adrian Beltre AU/99 | 15.00 | 40.00 |
| ☐ 102 Matt Cain AU/275 | 15.00 | 40.00 |
| ☐ 103 Craig Biggio AU/99 | 30.00 | 60.00 |
| ☐ 104 Eric Chavez AU/99 | 12.50 | 30.00 |
| ☐ 105 J.D. Drew AU/99 | 12.50 | 30.00 |
| ☐ 106 Eric Gagne AU/99 | 20.00 | 50.00 |
| ☐ 107 Tim Hudson AU/99 | 15.00 | 40.00 |
| ☐ 108 Tom Glavine AU/275 | 20.00 | 50.00 |
| ☐ 109 David Ortiz AU/99 | 40.00 | 80.00 |
| ☐ 110 Scott Rolen AU/275 | 15.00 | 40.00 |
| ☐ 111 Johan Santana AU/99 | 20.00 | 50.00 |
| ☐ 112 Curt Schilling AU/99 | 40.00 | 80.00 |
| ☐ 113 John Smoltz AU/99 | 30.00 | 60.00 |
| ☐ 114 Alfonso Soriano AU/99 | 30.00 | 60.00 |
| ☐ 115 Kerry Wood AU/99 | 12.50 | 30.00 |
| ☐ 116 Edwin Jackson AU/99 | 8.00 | 20.00 |
| ☐ 117 Felix Hernandez AU/275 | 20.00 | 50.00 |
| ☐ 118 Prince Fielder AU/99 (RC) | 60.00 | 120.00 |
| ☐ 119 Vladimir Guerrero AU/86 | 30.00 | 60.00 |
| ☐ 120 Roger Clemens AU/99 | 30.00 | 60.00 |
| ☐ 121 Albert Pujols AU/45 | 175.00 | 300.00 |
| ☐ 122 Chris Carpenter AU/99 | 20.00 | 50.00 |
| ☐ 123 Derrek Lee AU/99 | 15.00 | 40.00 |
| ☐ 124 Dontrelle Willis AU/99 | 12.50 | 30.00 |
| ☐ 125 Roy Oswalt AU/99 | 15.00 | 40.00 |
| ☐ 126 Ryan Garko AU/275 (RC) | 10.00 | 25.00 |
| ☐ 127 Tadahito Iguchi AU/275 | 20.00 | 50.00 |
| ☐ 128 Mark Loretta AU/275 | 10.00 | 25.00 |
| ☐ 129 Joe Mauer AU/275 | 20.00 | 50.00 |
| ☐ 130 Victor Martinez AU/275 | 8.00 | 20.00 |
| ☐ 131 Willy Mo Pena AU/275 | 10.00 | 25.00 |
| ☐ 132 Oliver Perez AU/274 | 6.00 | 15.00 |
| ☐ 133 C.Patterson AU/275 EXCH | 10.00 | 25.00 |
| ☐ 134 Ben Sheets AU/275 | 10.00 | 25.00 |
| ☐ 135 Michael Young AU/275 | 10.00 | 25.00 |
| ☐ 136 Jonny Gomes AU/275 | 6.00 | 15.00 |
| ☐ 137 Derek Jeter AU/275 | 125.00 | 200.00 |
| ☐ 138 K.Griffey Jr. AU/275 EXCH * | 30.00 | 60.00 |
| ☐ 139 R.Zimmerman AU/275 (RC) | 30.00 | 60.00 |
| ☐ 140 Scott Baker AU/275 (RC) | 6.00 | 15.00 |
| ☐ 141 Huston Street AU/275 | 10.00 | 25.00 |
| ☐ 142 Jason Bay AU/275 EXCH | 10.00 | 25.00 |
| ☐ 143 Ryan Howard AU/275 | 40.00 | 80.00 |
| ☐ 144 Travis Hafner AU/275 | 6.00 | 15.00 |
| ☐ 145 Brian Myrow AU/275 RC | 6.00 | 15.00 |
| ☐ 146 Scott Podsednik AU/275 | 10.00 | 25.00 |
| ☐ 147 Brian Roberts AU/275 | 10.00 | 25.00 |
| ☐ 148 Grady Sizemore AU/135 | 15.00 | 40.00 |
| ☐ 149 Chris Demaria AU/275 | 6.00 | 15.00 |
| ☐ 150 Jonah Bayliss AU/275 RC | 6.00 | 15.00 |
| ☐ 151 Geovany Soto AU/275 (RC) | 15.00 | 40.00 |
| ☐ 152 Lyle Overbay AU/275 | 6.00 | 15.00 |
| ☐ 153 Joey Devine AU/275 RC | 6.00 | 15.00 |
| ☐ 154 A.Freire AU/275 RC | 6.00 | 15.00 |
| ☐ 155 Conor Jackson AU/275 (RC) | 10.00 | 25.00 |
| ☐ 156 Danny Sandoval AU/275 RC | 6.00 | 15.00 |
| ☐ 157 Chase Utley AU/275 | 20.00 | 50.00 |
| ☐ 158 Jeff Harris AU/275 RC | 6.00 | 15.00 |
| ☐ 159 Ron Flores AU/275 RC | 6.00 | 15.00 |
| ☐ 160 Scott Feldman AU/275 RC | 6.00 | 15.00 |
| ☐ 161 Yadier Molina AU/275 | 10.00 | 25.00 |
| ☐ 162 Tim Corcoran AU/275 RC | 6.00 | 15.00 |
| ☐ 163 Craig Hansen AU/275 RC | 15.00 | 40.00 |
| ☐ 164 Jason Bergmann AU/275 RC | 6.00 | 15.00 |
| ☐ 165 Craig Breslow AU/275 RC | 6.00 | 15.00 |
| ☐ 166 Jhonny Peralta AU/275 | 6.00 | 15.00 |
| ☐ 167 J.Hermida AU/275 (RC) | 10.00 | 25.00 |
| ☐ 168 Scott Kazmir AU/275 | 15.00 | 40.00 |
| ☐ 169 Bobby Crosby AU/99 | 12.50 | 30.00 |
| ☐ 170 Rich Harden AU/275 | 6.00 | 15.00 |

| | | |
|---|---|---|
| ❑ 172 Casey Kotchman AU/275 | 6.00 | 15.00 |
| ❑ 173 Tim Hamulack AU/275 (RC) | 6.00 | 15.00 |
| ❑ 174 Justin Morneau AU/275 | 10.00 | 25.00 |
| ❑ 175 Jake Peavy AU/275 | 10.00 | 25.00 |
| ❑ 176 Y.Betancourt AU/275 | 10.00 | 25.00 |
| ❑ 177 Jeremy Accardo AU/275 RC | 6.00 | 15.00 |
| ❑ 178 Jorge Cantu AU/200 | 10.00 | 25.00 |
| ❑ 179 Marlon Byrd AU/275 | 6.00 | 15.00 |
| ❑ 180 R.Jorgensen AU/275 RC | 6.00 | 15.00 |
| ❑ 181 C.Denorfia AU/275 RC | 6.00 | 15.00 |
| ❑ 182 Steve Stemle AU/275 RC | 6.00 | 15.00 |
| ❑ 183 Robert Andino AU/275 RC | 6.00 | 15.00 |
| ❑ 184 Chris Heintz AU/275 RC | 6.00 | 15.00 |

## 2007 Sweet Spot

| | | |
|---|---|---|
| ❑ COMMON CARD (1-100) | .75 | 2.00 |
| ❑ STATED PRINT RUN 850 SER.#'d SETS | | |
| ❑ TWO BASE CARDS PER TIN | | |
| ❑ COMMON AU RC (101-142) | 3.00 | 8.00 |
| ❑ OVERALL AU ODDS ONE PER TIN | | |
| ❑ EXCHANGE DEADLINE 11/9/2009 | | |
| ❑ 1 Adam Dunn | .75 | 2.00 |
| ❑ 2 Adrian Beltre | .75 | 2.00 |
| ❑ 3 Albert Pujols | 4.00 | 10.00 |
| ❑ 4 Alex Rios | .75 | 2.00 |
| ❑ 5 Alex Rodriguez | 3.00 | 8.00 |
| ❑ 6 Alfonso Soriano | .75 | 2.00 |
| ❑ 7 Andruw Jones | 1.25 | 3.00 |
| ❑ 8 Aramis Ramirez | .75 | 2.00 |
| ❑ 9 B.J. Upton | .75 | 2.00 |
| ❑ 10 Barry Zito | .75 | 2.00 |
| ❑ 11 Bartolo Colon | .75 | 2.00 |
| ❑ 12 Ben Sheets | .75 | 2.00 |
| ❑ 13 Bill Hall | .75 | 2.00 |
| ❑ 14 Brad Penny | .75 | 2.00 |
| ❑ 15 Brandon Webb | .75 | 2.00 |
| ❑ 16 C.C. Sabathia | .75 | 2.00 |
| ❑ 17 Carl Crawford | .75 | 2.00 |
| ❑ 18 Carlos Beltran | .75 | 2.00 |
| ❑ 19 Carlos Guillen | .75 | 2.00 |
| ❑ 20 Carlos Lee | .75 | 2.00 |
| ❑ 21 Chase Utley | 2.00 | 5.00 |
| ❑ 22 Chien-Ming Wang | 2.00 | 5.00 |
| ❑ 23 Chipper Jones | 2.00 | 5.00 |
| ❑ 24 Chris Carpenter | .75 | 2.00 |
| ❑ 25 Cole Hamels | 2.00 | 5.00 |
| ❑ 26 Craig Biggio | 1.25 | 3.00 |
| ❑ 27 Curt Schilling | 1.25 | 3.00 |
| ❑ 28 Dan Haren | .75 | 2.00 |
| ❑ 29 David Ortiz | 1.25 | 3.00 |
| ❑ 30 David Wright | 3.00 | 8.00 |
| ❑ 31 Delmon Young | 1.25 | 3.00 |
| ❑ 32 Derek Jeter | 5.00 | 12.00 |
| ❑ 33 Derek Lee | .75 | 2.00 |
| ❑ 34 Dontrelle Willis | .75 | 2.00 |
| ❑ 35 Felix Hernandez | 1.25 | 3.00 |
| ❑ 36 Frank Thomas | 2.00 | 5.00 |
| ❑ 37 Gil Meche | .75 | 2.00 |
| ❑ 38 Grady Sizemore | 1.25 | 3.00 |
| ❑ 39 Greg Maddux | 3.00 | 8.00 |
| ❑ 40 Ian Kinsler | .75 | 2.00 |
| ❑ 41 Ichiro Suzuki | 3.00 | 8.00 |
| ❑ 42 Ivan Rodriguez | 1.25 | 3.00 |
| ❑ 43 Jake Peavy | .75 | 2.00 |
| ❑ 44 Jason Bay | 1.25 | 3.00 |
| ❑ 45 Jason Varitek | 2.00 | 5.00 |
| ❑ 46 Jeff Kent | .75 | 2.00 |
| ❑ 47 Jermaine Dye | .75 | 2.00 |
| ❑ 48 Jim Edmonds | 1.25 | 3.00 |
| ❑ 49 Jim Thome | 1.25 | 3.00 |
| ❑ 50 Jimmy Rollins | .75 | 2.00 |
| ❑ 51 Joe Mauer | 2.00 | 5.00 |
| ❑ 52 John Santana | 1.25 | 3.00 |
| ❑ 53 John Smoltz | 1.25 | 3.00 |
| ❑ 54 Jonathan Papelbon | 2.00 | 5.00 |
| ❑ 55 Jorge Posada | 1.25 | 3.00 |
| ❑ 56 Jose Reyes | 2.00 | 5.00 |
| ❑ 57 Josh Beckett | 1.25 | 3.00 |
| ❑ 58 Justin Morneau | .75 | 2.00 |
| ❑ 59 Justin Verlander | 2.00 | 5.00 |
| ❑ 60 Ken Griffey Jr. | 3.00 | 8.00 |
| ❑ 61 Kenji Johjima | 2.00 | 5.00 |
| ❑ 62 Lance Berkman | .75 | 2.00 |
| ❑ 63 Magglio Ordonez | .75 | 2.00 |
| ❑ 64 Manny Ramirez | 1.25 | 3.00 |
| ❑ 65 Mariano Rivera | 2.00 | 5.00 |
| ❑ 66 Mark Buehrle | .75 | 2.00 |
| ❑ 67 Mark Teixeira | 1.25 | 3.00 |
| ❑ 68 Matt Holliday | 2.00 | 5.00 |
| ❑ 69 Matt Morris | .75 | 2.00 |
| ❑ 70 Melvin Mora | .75 | 2.00 |
| ❑ 71 Michael Young | 1.25 | 3.00 |
| ❑ 72 Miguel Cabrera | 1.25 | 3.00 |
| ❑ 73 Miguel Tejada | .75 | 2.00 |
| ❑ 74 Mike Lowell | .75 | 2.00 |
| ❑ 75 Mike Mussina | 1.25 | 3.00 |
| ❑ 76 Mike Piazza | 2.00 | 5.00 |
| ❑ 77 Nick Swisher | .75 | 2.00 |
| ❑ 78 Orlando Hudson | .75 | 2.00 |
| ❑ 79 Paul Konerko | .75 | 2.00 |
| ❑ 80 Paul Lo Duca | .75 | 2.00 |
| ❑ 81 Pedro Martinez | 1.25 | 3.00 |
| ❑ 82 Prince Fielder | 2.00 | 5.00 |
| ❑ 83 Randy Johnson | 2.00 | 5.00 |
| ❑ 84 Rickie Weeks | .75 | 2.00 |
| ❑ 85 Roger Clemens | 3.00 | 8.00 |
| ❑ 86 Roy Halladay | 2.00 | 5.00 |
| ❑ 87 Roy Oswalt | .75 | 2.00 |
| ❑ 88 Russell Martin | .75 | 2.00 |
| ❑ 89 Ryan Howard | 3.00 | 8.00 |
| ❑ 90 Ryan Zimmerman | 2.00 | 5.00 |
| ❑ 91 Sammy Sosa | 2.00 | 5.00 |
| ❑ 92 Scott Rolen | 1.25 | 3.00 |
| ❑ 93 Shawn Green | .75 | 2.00 |
| ❑ 94 Todd Helton | 1.25 | 3.00 |
| ❑ 95 Tom Glavine | 1.25 | 3.00 |
| ❑ 96 Torii Hunter | .75 | 2.00 |
| ❑ 97 Travis Hafner | .75 | 2.00 |
| ❑ 98 Vernon Wells | .75 | 2.00 |
| ❑ 99 Victor Martinez | .75 | 2.00 |
| ❑ 100 Vladimir Guerrero | 2.00 | 5.00 |
| ❑ 101 Adam Lind AU (RC) | 2.00 | 5.00 |
| ❑ 102 Akinori Iwamura AU SP RC | 10.00 | 25.00 |
| ❑ 103 Alex Gordon AU RC | 12.50 | 30.00 |
| ❑ 104 Alexi Casilla AU (RC) | 6.00 | 15.00 |
| ❑ 105 Andy LaRoche AU (RC) | 6.00 | 15.00 |
| ❑ 106 Billy Butler AU (RC) | 6.00 | 15.00 |
| ❑ 107 Ryan Rowland-Smith AU RC | 6.00 | 15.00 |
| ❑ 108 Brandon Wood AU (RC) | 6.00 | 15.00 |
| ❑ 109 Brian Burres AU (RC) | 3.00 | 8.00 |
| ❑ 110 Chase Wright AU RC | 4.00 | 10.00 |
| ❑ 111 Chris Stewart AU RC | 3.00 | 8.00 |
| ❑ 112 Daisuke Matsuzaka AU SP RC | 150.00 | 250.00 |
| ❑ 113 Delmon Young AU SP (RC) | 6.00 | 15.00 |
| ❑ 114 Andy Sonnanstine AU RC | 6.00 | 15.00 |
| ❑ 115 Andrew Miller AU RC | | |
| ❑ 116 Fred Lewis AU (RC) | 4.00 | 10.00 |
| ❑ 117 Glen Perkins AU SP (RC) | 10.00 | 25.00 |
| ❑ 118 David Murphy AU (RC) | 3.00 | 8.00 |
| ❑ 119 Hunter Pence AU (RC) | 12.50 | 30.00 |
| ❑ 120 Jarrod Saltalamacchia AU (RC) | 6.00 | 15.00 |
| ❑ 121 Jeff Baker AU SP (RC) | 3.00 | 8.00 |
| ❑ 122 Jesus Flores AU SP RC | 10.00 | 25.00 |
| ❑ 123 Joakim Soria AU SP RC | 10.00 | 25.00 |
| ❑ 124 Joe Smith AU RC | 4.00 | 10.00 |
| ❑ 125 Jon Knott AU (RC) | 3.00 | 8.00 |
| ❑ 126 Josh Hamilton AU (RC) | 15.00 | 40.00 |
| ❑ 127 Justin Hampson AU (RC) | 3.00 | 8.00 |
| ❑ 128 Kei Igawa AU SP RC | 10.00 | 25.00 |
| ❑ 129 Kevin Cameron AU RC | 3.00 | 8.00 |
| ❑ 130 Matt Chico AU (RC) | 4.00 | 10.00 |
| ❑ 131 Matt DeSalvo AU (RC) | 4.00 | 10.00 |
| ❑ 132 Micah Owings AU SP (RC) | 10.00 | 25.00 |
| ❑ 133 Michael Bourn AU (RC) | 4.00 | 10.00 |
| ❑ 134 Miguel Montero AU (RC) | 3.00 | 8.00 |
| ❑ 135 Phil Hughes AU SP RC | 20.00 | 50.00 |
| ❑ 136 Rick Vanden Hurk AU RC | 3.00 | 8.00 |
| ❑ 137 Ryan Sweeney AU SP (RC) | | |
| ❑ 138 Tim Lincecum AU RC | | |
| ❑ 139 Travis Buck AU (RC) | 4.00 | 10.00 |
| ❑ 140 Troy Tulowitzki AU SP (RC) | 20.00 | 50.00 |
| ❑ 141 Sean Henn AU (RC) | 4.00 | 10.00 |
| ❑ 142 Zack Segovia AU (RC) | 4.00 | 10.00 |
| ❑ NNO Michael Buysner | 15.00 | 40.00 |

## 2008 Sweet Spot

| | | |
|---|---|---|
| ❑ COMMON CARD (1-100) | .40 | 1.00 |
| ❑ COMMON AUTO (101-150) | 3.00 | 8.00 |
| ❑ AU PRINT RUNS B/WN 199-699 COPIES PER | | |
| ❑ OVERALL AUTO ODDS 1:3 PACKS | | |
| ❑ EXCH DEADLINE 11/10/2010 | | |
| ❑ 1 Aaron Harang | .40 | 1.00 |
| ❑ 2 Aaron Rowland | .40 | 1.00 |
| ❑ 3 Adam Dunn | .40 | 1.00 |
| ❑ 4 Albert Pujols | 2.00 | 5.00 |
| ❑ 5 Alex Gordon | .60 | 1.50 |
| ❑ 6 Alex Rios | .40 | 1.00 |
| ❑ 7 Alex Rodriguez | 1.50 | 4.00 |
| ❑ 8 Alfonso Soriano | .60 | 1.50 |
| ❑ 9 Andruw Jones | .60 | 1.50 |
| ❑ 10 Aramis Ramirez | .40 | 1.00 |
| ❑ 11 B.J. Upton | .60 | 1.50 |
| ❑ 12 Barry Zito | .40 | 1.00 |
| ❑ 13 Billy Butler | .40 | 1.00 |
| ❑ 14 Brandon Phillips | .40 | 1.00 |
| ❑ 15 Brandon Webb | .60 | 1.50 |
| ❑ 16 Brian McCann | .60 | 1.50 |
| ❑ 17 Brian Roberts | .60 | 1.50 |
| ❑ 18 CC Sabathia | .40 | 1.00 |
| ❑ 19 Carl Crawford | .40 | 1.00 |
| ❑ 20 Carlos Beltran | .40 | 1.00 |
| ❑ 21 Carlos Lee | .40 | 1.00 |
| ❑ 22 Carlos Pena | 1.00 | 2.50 |
| ❑ 23 Carlos Zambrano | .40 | 1.00 |
| ❑ 24 Chase Utley | 1.00 | 2.50 |
| ❑ 25 Chipper Jones | 1.25 | 3.00 |
| ❑ 26 Chris B. Young | .40 | 1.00 |
| ❑ 27 Chris Carpenter | .40 | 1.00 |
| ❑ 28 Cole Hamels | 1.00 | 2.50 |
| ❑ 29 Daisuke Matsuzaka | 1.25 | 3.00 |
| ❑ 30 Dan Haren | .40 | 1.00 |
| ❑ 31 Dan Uggla | .60 | 1.50 |
| ❑ 32 David Ortiz | .60 | 1.50 |
| ❑ 33 David Wright | 1.25 | 3.00 |
| ❑ 34 Derek Jeter | 2.50 | 6.00 |
| ❑ 35 Dontrelle Willis | .40 | 1.00 |
| ❑ 36 Dustin Pedroia | 1.25 | 3.00 |
| ❑ 37 Erik Bedard | .40 | 1.00 |
| ❑ 38 Felix Hernandez | .60 | 1.50 |
| ❑ 39 Frank Thomas | 1.00 | 2.50 |
| ❑ 40 Froddy Sanchez | .40 | 1.00 |
| ❑ 41 Gary Sheffield | .60 | 1.50 |
| ❑ 42 Grady Sizemore | .60 | 1.50 |
| ❑ 43 Greg Maddux | 1.25 | 3.00 |
| ❑ 44 Hanley Ramirez | 1.00 | 2.50 |
| ❑ 45 Hideki Matsui | 1.00 | 2.50 |
| ❑ 46 Hunter Pence | 1.00 | 2.50 |
| ❑ 47 Ichiro Suzuki | 1.50 | 4.00 |
| ❑ 48 Ivan Rodriguez | .60 | 1.50 |
| ❑ 49 Jake Peavy | .60 | 1.50 |
| ❑ 50 Jason Bay | .60 | 1.50 |
| ❑ 51 Jeff Francoeur | .60 | 1.50 |
| ❑ 52 Jeff Kent | .40 | 1.00 |
| ❑ 53 Jim Thome | .60 | 1.50 |
| ❑ 54 Jimmy Rollins | .60 | 1.50 |
| ❑ 55 Joba Chamberlain | 1.25 | 3.00 |
| ❑ 56 Joe Blanton | .40 | 1.00 |
| ❑ 57 Joe Mauer | 1.00 | 2.50 |
| ❑ 58 Johan Santana | 1.00 | 2.50 |
| ❑ 59 John Smoltz | 1.00 | 2.50 |
| ❑ 60 Jonathan Papelbon | .60 | 1.50 |
| ❑ 61 Jose Reyes | .60 | 1.50 |
| ❑ 62 Josh Beckett | .60 | 1.50 |
| ❑ 63 Josh Hamilton | 1.25 | 3.00 |
| ❑ 64 Justin Morneau | .60 | 1.50 |
| ❑ 65 Justin Verlander | .60 | 1.50 |

| | | |
|---|---:|---:|
| ☐ 66 Ken Griffey Jr. | 1.50 | 4.00 |
| ☐ 67 Lance Berkman | .60 | 1.50 |
| ☐ 68 Lastings Milledge | .40 | 1.00 |
| ☐ 69 Magglio Ordonez | .60 | 1.50 |
| ☐ 70 Manny Ramirez | 1.00 | 2.50 |
| ☐ 71 Mariano Rivera | 1.00 | 2.50 |
| ☐ 72 Mark Teixeira | .60 | 1.50 |
| ☐ 73 Matt Holliday | .60 | 1.50 |
| ☐ 74 Michael Young | .40 | 1.00 |
| ☐ 75 Miguel Cabrera | .60 | 1.50 |
| ☐ 76 Miguel Tejada | .60 | 1.50 |
| ☐ 77 Mike Lowell | .40 | 1.00 |
| ☐ 78 Nick Markakis | .60 | 1.50 |
| ☐ 79 Nick Swisher | .40 | 1.00 |
| ☐ 80 Paul Konerko | .40 | 1.00 |
| ☐ 81 Pedro Martinez | .60 | 1.50 |
| ☐ 82 Phil Hughes | 1.00 | 2.50 |
| ☐ 83 Prince Fielder | 1.00 | 2.50 |
| ☐ 84 Randy Johnson | 1.00 | 2.50 |
| ☐ 85 Rich Harden | .40 | 1.00 |
| ☐ 86 Robinson Cano | .60 | 1.50 |
| ☐ 87 Roy Oswalt | .40 | 1.00 |
| ☐ 88 Russell Martin | .40 | 1.00 |
| ☐ 89 Ryan Braun | 1.25 | 3.00 |
| ☐ 90 Ryan Howard | 1.25 | 3.00 |
| ☐ 91 Ryan Zimmerman | .60 | 1.50 |
| ☐ 92 Scott Rolen | .60 | 1.50 |
| ☐ 93 Tom Glavine | .60 | 1.50 |
| ☐ 94 Torii Hunter | .40 | 1.00 |
| ☐ 95 Travis Hafner | .40 | 1.00 |
| ☐ 96 Trevor Hoffman | .40 | 1.00 |
| ☐ 97 Troy Tulowitzki | .60 | 1.50 |
| ☐ 98 Vernon Wells | .40 | 1.00 |
| ☐ 99 Victor Martinez | .40 | 1.00 |
| ☐ 100 Vladimir Guerrero | 1.00 | 2.50 |
| ☐ 101 Alex Romero AU/499 (RC) | .40 | 1.00 |
| ☐ 102 Alexei Ramirez AU/399 RC | 60.00 | 120.00 |
| ☐ 103 Bobby Korecky AU/399 RC | 3.00 | 8.00 |
| ☐ 104 Bobby Wilson AU/699 RC | 3.00 | 8.00 |
| ☐ 105 Brad Harman AU/699 RC | 3.00 | 8.00 |
| ☐ 106 Brandon Boggs AU/699 (RC) | 3.00 | 8.00 |
| ☐ 107 Brent Lillibridge AU/399 (RC) | 4.00 | 10.00 |
| ☐ 108 Brian Barton AU/699 RC | 3.00 | 8.00 |
| ☐ 109 Brian Bass AU/699 (RC) | 3.00 | 8.00 |
| ☐ 110 Brian Bixler AU/699 (RC) | 3.00 | 8.00 |
| ☐ 111 Brian Bocock AU/399 RC | 3.00 | 8.00 |
| ☐ 112 Burke Badenhop AU/699 RC | 3.00 | 8.00 |
| ☐ 113 Chin-Lung Hu AU/199 | 12.50 | 30.00 |
| ☐ 114 Clay Buchholz AU/199 (RC) | 12.50 | 30.00 |
| ☐ 115 Clay Timpner AU/699 (RC) | 3.00 | 8.00 |
| ☐ 116 Cory Wade AU/699 (RC) | 3.00 | 8.00 |
| ☐ 117 Daric Barton AU/399 RC | 3.00 | 8.00 |
| ☐ 118 Eider Torres AU/699 (RC) | 3.00 | 8.00 |
| ☐ 119 Jonathan Van Every AU/399 RC | 3.00 | 8.00 |
| ☐ 120 Emmanuel Burriss AU/399 RC | 3.00 | 8.00 |
| ☐ 121 Evan Longoria AU/249 RC | 60.00 | 120.00 |
| ☐ 122 Felipe Paulino AU/499 RC | 3.00 | 8.00 |
| ☐ 123 Fernando Hernandez AU/499 RC | 3.00 | 8.00 |
| ☐ 124 German Duran AU/499 RC | 3.00 | 8.00 |
| ☐ 125 Greg Smith AU/399 RC | 3.00 | 8.00 |
| ☐ 126 Hernan Iribarren AU/699 (RC) EXCH | 3.00 | 8.00 |
| ☐ 127 Kennedy AU/249 RC EXCH | 8.00 | 20.00 |
| ☐ 128 Jed Lowrie AU/349 (RC) | 10.00 | 25.00 |
| ☐ 129 Jeff Clement AU/199 (RC) | 15.00 | 40.00 |
| ☐ 130 Jesse Carlson AU/649 RC | 3.00 | 8.00 |
| ☐ 131 Johnny Cueto AU/249 RC | 6.00 | 15.00 |
| ☐ 132 J.Albaladejo AU/399 RC | | |
| ☐ 133 C.Kershaw AU/199 RC | 15.00 | 40.00 |
| ☐ 134 Josh Newman AU/699 RC | 3.00 | 8.00 |
| ☐ 135 J.Masterson AU/399 RC | 12.50 | 30.00 |
| ☐ 136 Kevin Hart AU/399 (RC) | 3.00 | 8.00 |
| ☐ 137 Luke Hochevar AU/199 RC | 6.00 | 15.00 |
| ☐ 138 Jay Bruce AU/349 (RC) | 15.00 | 40.00 |
| ☐ 139 Max Scherzer AU/299 RC | 10.00 | 25.00 |
| ☐ 140 Nick Adenhart AU/399 (RC) | 15.00 | 40.00 |
| ☐ 141 Nick Blackburn AU/399 RC | 4.00 | 10.00 |
| ☐ 142 Nyjer Morgan AU/399 (RC) | 4.00 | 10.00 |
| ☐ 143 Ramon Troncoso AU/699 RC | 3.00 | 8.00 |
| ☐ 144 Randor Bierd AU/499 RC | 3.00 | 8.00 |
| ☐ 145 Rich Thompson AU/399 RC | 3.00 | 8.00 |
| ☐ 146 Robinzon Diaz AU/699 (RC) | 3.00 | 8.00 |
| ☐ 147 Ross Ohlendorf AU/399 RC | 3.00 | 8.00 |
| ☐ 148 Steve Holm AU/699 RC | 3.00 | 8.00 |
| ☐ 149 Wesley Wright AU/499 RC | 3.00 | 8.00 |
| ☐ 150 W.Balentien AU/399 (RC) | 3.00 | 8.00 |

## 2002 Sweet Spot Classics

| | | |
|---|---:|---:|
| ☐ COMPLETE SET (90) | 15.00 | 40.00 |
| ☐ 1 Mickey Mantle | 2.50 | 6.00 |
| ☐ 2 Joe DiMaggio | 1.25 | 3.00 |
| ☐ 3 Babe Ruth | 2.00 | 5.00 |
| ☐ 4 Ty Cobb | 1.00 | 2.50 |
| ☐ 5 Nolan Ryan | 1.50 | 4.00 |
| ☐ 6 Sandy Koufax | 1.25 | 3.00 |
| ☐ 7 Cy Young | .60 | 1.50 |
| ☐ 8 Roberto Clemente | 1.50 | 4.00 |
| ☐ 9 Lefty Grove | .40 | 1.00 |
| ☐ 10 Lou Gehrig | 1.25 | 3.00 |
| ☐ 11 Walter Johnson | .60 | 1.50 |
| ☐ 12 Honus Wagner | .75 | 2.00 |
| ☐ 13 Christy Mathewson | .60 | 1.50 |
| ☐ 14 Jackie Robinson | .60 | 1.50 |
| ☐ 15 Joe Morgan | .40 | 1.00 |
| ☐ 16 Reggie Jackson | .40 | 1.00 |
| ☐ 17 Eddie Collins | .40 | 1.00 |
| ☐ 18 Cal Ripken | 2.00 | 5.00 |
| ☐ 19 Hank Greenberg | .60 | 1.50 |
| ☐ 20 Harmon Killebrew | .60 | 1.50 |
| ☐ 21 Johnny Bench | .60 | 1.50 |
| ☐ 22 Ernie Banks | .60 | 1.50 |
| ☐ 23 Willie McCovey | .40 | 1.00 |
| ☐ 24 Mel Ott | .60 | 1.50 |
| ☐ 25 Tom Seaver | .40 | 1.00 |
| ☐ 26 Tony Gwynn | .75 | 2.00 |
| ☐ 27 Dave Winfield | .40 | 1.00 |
| ☐ 28 Willie Stargell | .40 | 1.00 |
| ☐ 29 Mark McGwire | 1.50 | 4.00 |
| ☐ 30 Al Kaline | .60 | 1.50 |
| ☐ 31 Jimmie Foxx | .60 | 1.50 |
| ☐ 32 Satchel Paige | .60 | 1.50 |
| ☐ 33 Eddie Murray | .60 | 1.50 |
| ☐ 34 Lou Boudreau | .40 | 1.00 |
| ☐ 35 Joe Jackson | 1.25 | 3.00 |
| ☐ 36 Luke Appling | .40 | 1.00 |
| ☐ 37 Ralph Kiner | .40 | 1.00 |
| ☐ 38 Robin Yount | .60 | 1.50 |
| ☐ 39 Paul Molitor | .40 | 1.00 |
| ☐ 40 Juan Marichal | .40 | 1.00 |
| ☐ 41 Brooks Robinson | .40 | 1.00 |
| ☐ 42 Wade Boggs | .60 | 1.50 |
| ☐ 43 Kirby Puckett | .60 | 1.50 |
| ☐ 44 Yogi Berra | .60 | 1.50 |
| ☐ 45 George Sisler | .40 | 1.00 |
| ☐ 46 Buck Leonard | .40 | 1.00 |
| ☐ 47 Billy Williams | .40 | 1.00 |
| ☐ 48 Duke Snider | .40 | 1.00 |
| ☐ 49 Don Drysdale | .40 | 1.00 |
| ☐ 50 Bill Mazeroski | .40 | 1.00 |
| ☐ 51 Tony Oliva | .40 | 1.00 |
| ☐ 52 Luis Aparicio | .40 | 1.00 |
| ☐ 53 Carlton Fisk | .40 | 1.00 |
| ☐ 54 Kirk Gibson | .40 | 1.00 |
| ☐ 55 Catfish Hunter | .40 | 1.00 |
| ☐ 56 Joe Carter | .40 | 1.00 |
| ☐ 57 Gaylord Perry | .40 | 1.00 |
| ☐ 58 Don Mattingly | 1.25 | 3.00 |
| ☐ 59 Eddie Mathews | .60 | 1.50 |
| ☐ 60 Fergie Jenkins | .40 | 1.00 |
| ☐ 61 Roy Campanella | .60 | 1.50 |
| ☐ 62 Orlando Cepeda | .40 | 1.00 |
| ☐ 63 Tony Perez | .40 | 1.00 |
| ☐ 64 Dave Parker | .40 | 1.00 |
| ☐ 65 Richie Ashburn | .40 | 1.00 |
| ☐ 66 Andre Dawson | .40 | 1.00 |
| ☐ 67 Dwight Evans | .40 | 1.00 |
| ☐ 68 Rollie Fingers | .40 | 1.00 |
| ☐ 69 Dale Murphy | .40 | 1.00 |
| ☐ 70 Ron Santo | .40 | 1.00 |

| | | |
|---|---:|---:|
| ☐ 71 Steve Garvey | .40 | 1.00 |
| ☐ 72 Monte Irvin | .40 | 1.00 |
| ☐ 73 Alan Trammell | .40 | 1.00 |
| ☐ 74 Ryne Sandberg | 1.00 | 2.50 |
| ☐ 75 Gary Carter | .40 | 1.00 |
| ☐ 76 Fred Lynn | .40 | 1.00 |
| ☐ 77 Maury Wills | .40 | 1.00 |
| ☐ 78 Ozzie Smith | 1.00 | 2.50 |
| ☐ 79 Bobby Bonds | .40 | 1.00 |
| ☐ 80 Mickey Cochrane | .40 | 1.00 |
| ☐ 81 Dizzy Dean | .60 | 1.50 |
| ☐ 82 Graig Nettles | .40 | 1.00 |
| ☐ 83 Keith Hernandez | .40 | 1.00 |
| ☐ 84 Boog Powell | .40 | 1.00 |
| ☐ 85 Jack Clark | .40 | 1.00 |
| ☐ 86 Dave Stewart | .40 | 1.00 |
| ☐ 87 Tommy Lasorda | .40 | 1.00 |
| ☐ 88 Dennis Eckersley | .40 | 1.00 |
| ☐ 89 Ken Griffey Sr. | .40 | 1.00 |
| ☐ 90 Bucky Dent | .40 | 1.00 |

## 2003 Sweet Spot Classics

| | | |
|---|---:|---:|
| ☐ COMP.SET w/o SP's (89) | 15.00 | 40.00 |
| ☐ COMMON (1-74/76-90) | .30 | .75 |
| ☐ COMMON CARD (91-120) | 3.00 | 8.00 |
| ☐ COMMON CARD (121-150) | 2.00 | 5.00 |
| ☐ 1 Al Hrabosky | .30 | .75 |
| ☐ 2 Al Lopez | .30 | .75 |
| ☐ 3 Andre Dawson | .30 | .75 |
| ☐ 4 Bill Buckner | .30 | .75 |
| ☐ 5 Billy Williams | .30 | .75 |
| ☐ 6 Bob Feller | .30 | .75 |
| ☐ 7 Bob Lemon | .30 | .75 |
| ☐ 8 Bobby Doerr | .30 | .75 |
| ☐ 9 Cecil Cooper | .30 | .75 |
| ☐ 10 Cal Ripken | 2.50 | 6.00 |
| ☐ 11 Carlton Fisk | .50 | 1.25 |
| ☐ 12 Catfish Hunter | .50 | 1.25 |
| ☐ 13 Chris Chambliss | .30 | .75 |
| ☐ 14 Dale Murphy | .50 | 1.25 |
| ☐ 15 Gaylord Perry | .30 | .75 |
| ☐ 16 Dave Kingman | .30 | .75 |
| ☐ 17 Dave Parker | .30 | .75 |
| ☐ 18 Dave Stewart | .30 | .75 |
| ☐ 19 David Cone | .30 | .75 |
| ☐ 20 Dennis Eckersley | .30 | .75 |
| ☐ 21 Don Baylor | .30 | .75 |
| ☐ 22 Don Sutton | .30 | .75 |
| ☐ 23 Duke Snider | .50 | 1.25 |
| ☐ 24 Dwight Evans | .50 | 1.25 |
| ☐ 25 Dwight Gooden | .30 | .75 |
| ☐ 26 Earl Weaver MG | .30 | .75 |
| ☐ 27 Early Wynn | .30 | .75 |
| ☐ 28 Eddie Mathews | .75 | 2.00 |
| ☐ 29 Enos Slaughter | .30 | .75 |
| ☐ 30 Ernie Banks | .75 | 2.00 |
| ☐ 31 Fred Lynn | .30 | .75 |
| ☐ 32 Fred Stanley | .30 | .75 |
| ☐ 33 Gary Carter | .30 | .75 |
| ☐ 34 George Foster | .30 | .75 |
| ☐ 35 Hal Newhouser | .30 | .75 |
| ☐ 36 George Kell | .30 | .75 |
| ☐ 37 Harmon Killebrew | .75 | 2.00 |
| ☐ 38 Hoyt Wilhelm | .30 | .75 |
| ☐ 39 Jack Morris | .30 | .75 |
| ☐ 40 Jim Bunning | .30 | .75 |
| ☐ 41 Jim Gilliam | .30 | .75 |
| ☐ 42 Jim Leyritz | .30 | .75 |
| ☐ 43 Jimmy Key | .30 | .75 |
| ☐ 44 Joe Carter | .30 | .75 |
| ☐ 45 Joe Morgan | .30 | .75 |
| ☐ 46 John Montefusco | .30 | .75 |
| ☐ 47 Johnny Bench | .75 | 2.00 |

| | | |
|---|---|---|
| ❑ 48 Johnny Podres | .30 | .75 |
| ❑ 49 Jose Canseco | .50 | 1.25 |
| ❑ 50 Juan Marichal | .30 | .75 |
| ❑ 51 Keith Hernandez | .30 | .75 |
| ❑ 52 Ken Griffey Sr. | .30 | .75 |
| ❑ 53 Kirby Puckett | .75 | 2.00 |
| ❑ 54 Kirk Gibson | .30 | .75 |
| ❑ 55 Larry Doby | .30 | .75 |
| ❑ 56 Lee May | .30 | .75 |
| ❑ 57 Lee Mazzilli | .30 | .75 |
| ❑ 58 Lou Boudreau | .30 | .75 |
| ❑ 59 Mark McGwire | 2.00 | 5.00 |
| ❑ 60 Maury Wills | .30 | .75 |
| ❑ 61 Mike Pagliarulo | .30 | .75 |
| ❑ 62 Monte Irvin | .30 | .75 |
| ❑ 63 Nolan Ryan | 2.00 | 5.00 |
| ❑ 64 Orlando Cepeda | .30 | .75 |
| ❑ 65 Ozzie Smith | 1.25 | 3.00 |
| ❑ 66 Paul O'Neill | .50 | 1.25 |
| ❑ 67 Pee Wee Reese | .50 | 1.25 |
| ❑ 68 Phil Niekro | .30 | .75 |
| ❑ 69 Ralph Kiner | .30 | .75 |
| ❑ 70 Red Schoendienst | .30 | .75 |
| ❑ 71 Richie Ashburn | .50 | 1.25 |
| ❑ 72 Rick Ferrell | .30 | .75 |
| ❑ 73 Robin Roberts | .30 | .75 |
| ❑ 74 Robin Yount | .75 | 2.00 |
| ❑ 75 Hideki Matsui/1999 XRC | 6.00 | 15.00 |
| ❑ 75B Rod Carew ERR | | |
| ❑ 76 Rollie Fingers | .30 | .75 |
| ❑ 77 Ron Cey | .30 | .75 |
| ❑ 78 Tom Seaver | .50 | 1.25 |
| ❑ 79 Sparky Anderson MG | .30 | .75 |
| ❑ 80 Stan Musial | 1.25 | 3.00 |
| ❑ 81 Steve Garvey | .30 | .75 |
| ❑ 82 Ted Williams | 1.50 | 4.00 |
| ❑ 83 Tommy Lasorda | .30 | .75 |
| ❑ 84 Tony Gwynn | 1.00 | 2.50 |
| ❑ 85 Tony Perez | .30 | .75 |
| ❑ 86 Vida Blue | .30 | .75 |
| ❑ 87 Warren Spahn | .50 | 1.25 |
| ❑ 88 Bob Gibson | .50 | 1.25 |
| ❑ 89 Willie McCovey | .30 | .75 |
| ❑ 90 Willie Stargell | .50 | 1.25 |
| ❑ 91 Ted Williams TB | 3.00 | 8.00 |
| ❑ 92 Ted Williams TB | 3.00 | 8.00 |
| ❑ 93 Ted Williams TB | 3.00 | 8.00 |
| ❑ 94 Ted Williams TB | 3.00 | 8.00 |
| ❑ 95 Ted Williams TB | 3.00 | 8.00 |
| ❑ 96 Ted Williams TB | 3.00 | 8.00 |
| ❑ 97 Ted Williams TB | 3.00 | 8.00 |
| ❑ 98 Ted Williams TB | 3.00 | 8.00 |
| ❑ 99 Ted Williams TB | 3.00 | 8.00 |
| ❑ 100 Ted Williams TB | 3.00 | 8.00 |
| ❑ 101 Ted Williams TB | 3.00 | 8.00 |
| ❑ 102 Ted Williams TB | 3.00 | 8.00 |
| ❑ 103 Ted Williams TB | 3.00 | 8.00 |
| ❑ 104 Ted Williams TB | 3.00 | 8.00 |
| ❑ 105 Ted Williams TB | 3.00 | 8.00 |
| ❑ 106B Ted Williams TB | 3.00 | 8.00 |
| ❑ 107 Ted Williams TB | 3.00 | 8.00 |
| ❑ 108 Ted Williams TB | 3.00 | 8.00 |
| ❑ 109 Ted Williams TB | 3.00 | 8.00 |
| ❑ 110 Ted Williams TB | 3.00 | 8.00 |
| ❑ 111 Ted Williams TB | 3.00 | 8.00 |
| ❑ 112 Ted Williams TB | 3.00 | 8.00 |
| ❑ 113 Ted Williams TB | 3.00 | 8.00 |
| ❑ 114 Ted Williams TB | 3.00 | 8.00 |
| ❑ 115 Ted Williams TB | 3.00 | 8.00 |
| ❑ 116 Ted Williams TB | 3.00 | 8.00 |
| ❑ 117 Ted Williams TB | 3.00 | 8.00 |
| ❑ 118 Ted Williams TB | 3.00 | 8.00 |
| ❑ 119 Ted Williams TB | 3.00 | 8.00 |
| ❑ 120 Ted Williams TB | 3.00 | 8.00 |
| ❑ 121 Babe Ruth YH | 6.00 | 15.00 |
| ❑ 122 Bucky Dent YH | 2.00 | 5.00 |
| ❑ 123 Casey Stengel YH | 2.00 | 5.00 |
| ❑ 124 Dave Righetti YH | 2.00 | 5.00 |
| ❑ 125 Dave Winfield YH | 2.00 | 5.00 |
| ❑ 126 Dick Tidrow YH | 2.00 | 5.00 |
| ❑ 127 Dock Ellis YH | 2.00 | 5.00 |
| ❑ 128 Don Mattingly YH | 5.00 | 12.00 |
| ❑ 129 Hank Bauer YH | 2.00 | 5.00 |
| ❑ 130 Jim Bouton YH | 2.00 | 5.00 |
| ❑ 131 Jim Kaat YH | 2.00 | 5.00 |
| ❑ 132 Joe DiMaggio YH | 4.00 | 10.00 |
| ❑ 133 Joe Torre YH | 2.00 | 5.00 |
| ❑ 134 Lou Piniella YH | 2.00 | 5.00 |

| | | |
|---|---|---|
| ❑ 135 Mel Stottlemyre YH | 2.00 | 5.00 |
| ❑ 136 Mickey Mantle YH | 8.00 | 20.00 |
| ❑ 137 Mickey Rivers YH | 2.00 | 5.00 |
| ❑ 138 Phil Rizzuto YH | 2.00 | 5.00 |
| ❑ 139 Ralph Branca YH | 2.00 | 5.00 |
| ❑ 140 Ralph Houk YH | 2.00 | 5.00 |
| ❑ 141 Roger Maris YH | 3.00 | 8.00 |
| ❑ 142 Ron Guidry YH | 2.00 | 5.00 |
| ❑ 143 Ruben Amaro Sr. YH | 2.00 | 5.00 |
| ❑ 144 Sparky Lyle YH | 2.00 | 5.00 |
| ❑ 145 Thurman Munson YH | 3.00 | 8.00 |
| ❑ 146 Tommy Henrich YH | 2.00 | 5.00 |
| ❑ 147 Tommy John YH | 2.00 | 5.00 |
| ❑ 148 Tony Kubek YH | 2.00 | 5.00 |
| ❑ 149 Whitey Ford YH | 2.00 | 5.00 |
| ❑ 150 Yogi Berra YH | 3.00 | 8.00 |

## 2004 Sweet Spot Classic

| | | |
|---|---|---|
| ❑ COMP.SET w/o SP'S (90) | 15.00 | 40.00 |
| ❑ COMMON CARD (1-90) | .30 | .75 |
| ❑ COMMON CARD (91-161) | 2.00 | 5.00 |
| ❑ 91-161 STATED ODDS 1:3 | | |
| ❑ 1 Al Kaline | .75 | 2.00 |
| ❑ 2 Andre Dawson | .30 | .75 |
| ❑ 3 Bert Blyleven | .30 | .75 |
| ❑ 4 Bill Dickey | .50 | 1.25 |
| ❑ 5 Bill Mazeroski | .50 | 1.25 |
| ❑ 6 Billy Martin | .50 | 1.25 |
| ❑ 7 Bob Feller | .30 | .75 |
| ❑ 8 Bob Gibson | .50 | 1.25 |
| ❑ 9 Bob Lemon | .30 | .75 |
| ❑ 10 George Kell | .30 | .75 |
| ❑ 11 Bobby Doerr | .30 | .75 |
| ❑ 12 Brooks Robinson | .50 | 1.25 |
| ❑ 13 Cal Ripken | 2.50 | 6.00 |
| ❑ 14 Carl Hubbell | .50 | 1.25 |
| ❑ 15 Carl Yastrzemski | 1.25 | 3.00 |
| ❑ 16 Charlie Keller | .30 | .75 |
| ❑ 17 Chuck Dressen | .30 | .75 |
| ❑ 18 Cy Young | .75 | 2.00 |
| ❑ 19 Dave Winfield | .75 | 2.00 |
| ❑ 20 Dizzy Dean | .50 | 1.25 |
| ❑ 21 Don Drysdale | .50 | 1.25 |
| ❑ 22 Don Larsen | .30 | .75 |
| ❑ 23 Don Mattingly | 1.50 | 4.00 |
| ❑ 24 Don Newcombe | .30 | .75 |
| ❑ 25 Duke Snider | .50 | 1.25 |
| ❑ 26 Early Wynn | .30 | .75 |
| ❑ 27 Eddie Mathews | .75 | 2.00 |
| ❑ 28 Elston Howard | .30 | .75 |
| ❑ 29 Frank Robinson | .30 | .75 |
| ❑ 30 Gary Carter | .30 | .75 |
| ❑ 31 Gil Hodges | .50 | 1.25 |
| ❑ 32 Gil McDougald | .50 | 1.25 |
| ❑ 33 Hank Greenberg | .75 | 2.00 |
| ❑ 34 Harmon Killebrew | .75 | 2.00 |
| ❑ 35 Harry Caray | .75 | 2.00 |
| ❑ 36 Honus Wagner | .75 | 2.00 |
| ❑ 37 Hoyt Wilhelm | .30 | .75 |
| ❑ 38 Jackie Robinson | .75 | 2.00 |
| ❑ 39 Jim Bunning | .30 | .75 |
| ❑ 40 Jim Palmer | .30 | .75 |
| ❑ 41 Jimmie Foxx | .75 | 2.00 |
| ❑ 42 Jimmy Wynn | .30 | .75 |
| ❑ 43 Joe DiMaggio | 1.50 | 4.00 |
| ❑ 44 Joe Torre | .50 | 1.25 |
| ❑ 45 Johnny Mize | .30 | .75 |
| ❑ 46 Juan Marichal | .30 | .75 |
| ❑ 47 Larry Doby | .30 | .75 |
| ❑ 48 Lefty Gomez | .30 | .75 |
| ❑ 49 Lefty Grove | .50 | 1.25 |
| ❑ 50 Leo Durocher | .30 | .75 |
| ❑ 51 Lou Boudreau | .30 | .75 |

| | | |
|---|---|---|
| ❑ 52 Lou Brock | .50 | 1.25 |
| ❑ 53 Lou Gehrig | 1.50 | 4.00 |
| ❑ 54 Luis Aparicio | .30 | .75 |
| ❑ 55 Maury Wills | .30 | .75 |
| ❑ 56 Mel Allen | .30 | .75 |
| ❑ 57 Mel Ott | .75 | 2.00 |
| ❑ 58 Mickey Cochrane | .30 | .75 |
| ❑ 59 Mickey Mantle | 3.00 | 8.00 |
| ❑ 60 Mike Schmidt | 1.50 | 4.00 |
| ❑ 61 Monte Irvin | .30 | .75 |
| ❑ 62 Nolan Ryan | 2.00 | 5.00 |
| ❑ 63 Pee Wee Reese | .50 | 1.25 |
| ❑ 64 Phil Rizzuto | .50 | 1.25 |
| ❑ 65 Ralph Kiner | .30 | .75 |
| ❑ 66 Richie Ashburn | .50 | 1.25 |
| ❑ 67 Rick Ferrell | .30 | .75 |
| ❑ 68 Roberto Clemente | 2.00 | 5.00 |
| ❑ 69 Robin Roberts | .30 | .75 |
| ❑ 70 Robin Yount | .75 | 2.00 |
| ❑ 71 Rogers Hornsby | .75 | 2.00 |
| ❑ 72 Rollie Fingers | .30 | .75 |
| ❑ 73 Roy Campanella | .75 | 2.00 |
| ❑ 74 Ryne Sandberg | 1.50 | 4.00 |
| ❑ 75 Tony Gwynn | 1.00 | 2.50 |
| ❑ 76 Satchel Paige | .75 | 2.00 |
| ❑ 77 Shoeless Joe Jackson | 1.25 | 3.00 |
| ❑ 78 Stan Musial | 1.25 | 3.00 |
| ❑ 79 Ted Williams | 1.50 | 4.00 |
| ❑ 80 Thurman Munson | .75 | 2.00 |
| ❑ 81 Tom Seaver | .50 | 1.25 |
| ❑ 82 Tommy Henrich | .30 | .75 |
| ❑ 83 Tony Perez | .30 | .75 |
| ❑ 84 Tris Speaker | .50 | 1.25 |
| ❑ 85 Vida Blue | .30 | .75 |
| ❑ 86 Wade Boggs | .50 | 1.25 |
| ❑ 87 Walter Johnson | .75 | 2.00 |
| ❑ 88 Warren Spahn | .50 | 1.25 |
| ❑ 89 Whitey Ford | .50 | 1.25 |
| ❑ 90 Willie McCovey | .30 | .75 |
| ❑ 91 Andre Dawson FF/1987 | 2.00 | 5.00 |
| ❑ 92 Andre Dawson FF/1990 | 2.00 | 5.00 |
| ❑ 93 Ernie Banks FF/1958 | 3.00 | 8.00 |
| ❑ 94 Bob Lemon FF/1948 | 2.00 | 5.00 |
| ❑ 95 Cal Ripken FF/1982 | 6.00 | 15.00 |
| ❑ 96 Cal Ripken FF/1995 | 6.00 | 15.00 |
| ❑ 97 Carl Yastrzemski FF/1979 | 3.00 | 8.00 |
| ❑ 98 Carlton Fisk FF/1972 | 3.00 | 8.00 |
| ❑ 99 Cy Young FF/1910 | 3.00 | 8.00 |
| ❑ 100 Don Larsen FF/1956 | 2.00 | 5.00 |
| ❑ 101 Don Newcombe FF/1949 | 2.00 | 5.00 |
| ❑ 102 Don Newcombe FF/1956 | 2.00 | 5.00 |
| ❑ 103 Dwight Evans FF/1986 | 3.00 | 8.00 |
| ❑ 104 Elston Howard FF/1955 | 2.00 | 5.00 |
| ❑ 105 Frank Robinson FF/1956 | 2.00 | 5.00 |
| ❑ 106 Frank Robinson FF/1966 | 2.00 | 5.00 |
| ❑ 107 Frank Robinson FF/1973 | 2.00 | 5.00 |
| ❑ 108 Gil McDougald FF/1951 | 3.00 | 8.00 |
| ❑ 109 Hank Greenberg FF/1941 | 3.00 | 8.00 |
| ❑ 110 Harmon Killebrew FF/1964 | 3.00 | 8.00 |
| ❑ 111 Hoyt Wilhelm FF/1952 | 2.00 | 5.00 |
| ❑ 112 Hoyt Wilhelm FF/1958 | 2.00 | 5.00 |
| ❑ 113 Jackie Robinson FF/1946 | 3.00 | 8.00 |
| ❑ 114 J.Robinson FF Black/1947 | 3.00 | 8.00 |
| ❑ 115 J.Robinson FF ROY/1947 | 3.00 | 8.00 |
| ❑ 116 Jackie Robinson FF/1997 | 3.00 | 8.00 |
| ❑ 117 Jim Bunning FF/1964 | 2.00 | 5.00 |
| ❑ 118 J.DiMaggio FF Bench/1936 | 4.00 | 10.00 |
| ❑ 119 Joe Morgan FF/1976 | 2.00 | 5.00 |
| ❑ 120 Johnny Mize FF/1939 | 2.00 | 5.00 |
| ❑ 121 Johnny Mize FF/1947 | 2.00 | 5.00 |
| ❑ 122 Juan Marichal FF/1968 | 2.00 | 5.00 |
| ❑ 123 Ken Griffey Sr. FF/1990 | 2.00 | 5.00 |
| ❑ 124 Larry Doby FF/1947 | 2.00 | 5.00 |
| ❑ 125 Lefty Gomez FF/1933 | 3.00 | 8.00 |
| ❑ 126 Lou Boudreau FF/1946 | 2.00 | 5.00 |
| ❑ 127 Lou Gehrig FF Lineup/1939 | 5.00 | 12.00 |
| ❑ 128 Lou Gehrig FF Number/1939 | 4.00 | 10.00 |
| ❑ 129 Mark McGwire FF/1989 | 5.00 | 12.00 |
| ❑ 130 Mark McGwire FF/1998 | 5.00 | 12.00 |
| ❑ 131 Maury Wills FF/1962 | 2.00 | 5.00 |
| ❑ 132 Mel Ott FF/1946 | 3.00 | 8.00 |
| ❑ 133 Mike Schmidt FF/1980 | 4.00 | 10.00 |
| ❑ 134 Nolan Ryan FF/1973 | 5.00 | 12.00 |
| ❑ 135 Nolan Ryan FF/1989 | 5.00 | 12.00 |
| ❑ 136 Pee Wee Reese FF/1955 | 3.00 | 8.00 |
| ❑ 137 Nolan Ryan FF/1979 | 5.00 | 12.00 |
| ❑ 138 Richie Ashburn FF/1962 | 3.00 | 8.00 |
| ❑ 139 Roberto Clemente FF/1971 | 5.00 | 12.00 |

|  |  | | |
|---|---|---|---|
| 140 | Roberto Clemente FF/1973 | 5.00 | 12.00 |
| 141 | Robin Roberts FF/1956 | 2.00 | 5.00 |
| 142 | Robin Yount FF/1982 | 3.00 | 8.00 |
| 144 | Rollie Fingers FF/1975 | 2.00 | 5.00 |
| 145 | Rollie Fingers FF/1981 | 2.00 | 5.00 |
| 146 | Roy Campanella FF/1953 | 3.00 | 8.00 |
| 147 | Ryne Sandberg FF/1990 | 4.00 | 10.00 |
| 149 | Satchel Paige FF/1948 | 3.00 | 8.00 |
| 150 | Stan Musial FF/1952 | 3.00 | 8.00 |
| 151 | Stan Musial FF/1954 | 3.00 | 8.00 |
| 152 | Stan Musial FF/1963 | 3.00 | 8.00 |
| 153 | Ted Williams FF/1947 | 4.00 | 10.00 |
| 154 | Ted Williams FF/1957 | 4.00 | 10.00 |
| 155 | Tom Seaver FF/1970 | 3.00 | 8.00 |
| 156 | Tom Seaver FF/1975 | 3.00 | 8.00 |
| 157 | Wade Boggs FF/1999 | 3.00 | 8.00 |
| 158 | Warren Spahn FF/1957 | 3.00 | 8.00 |
| 159 | Warren Spahn FF/1958 | 3.00 | 8.00 |
| 160 | Joe DiMaggio FF AS/1950 | 4.00 | 10.00 |
| 161 | Yogi Berra FF/1947 | 3.00 | 8.00 |

## 2005 Sweet Spot Classic

|  |  | | |
|---|---|---|---|
| | COMPLETE SET (100) | 15.00 | 40.00 |
| 1 | Al Kaline | .75 | 2.00 |
| 2 | Al Rosen | .30 | .75 |
| 3 | Babe Ruth | 2.50 | 6.00 |
| 4 | Bill Mazeroski | .50 | 1.25 |
| 5 | Billy Williams | .30 | .75 |
| 6 | Bob Feller | .50 | 1.25 |
| 7 | Bob Gibson | .50 | 1.25 |
| 8 | Bobby Doerr | .30 | .75 |
| 9 | Brooks Robinson | .50 | 1.25 |
| 10 | Cal Ripken | 2.50 | 6.00 |
| 11 | Carl Yastrzemski | 1.25 | 3.00 |
| 12 | Carlton Fisk | .50 | 1.25 |
| 13 | Casey Stengel | .50 | 1.25 |
| 14 | Christy Mathewson | .75 | 2.00 |
| 15 | Cy Young | .75 | 2.00 |
| 16 | Dale Murphy | .50 | 1.25 |
| 17 | Dave Winfield | .30 | .75 |
| 18 | Dennis Eckersley | .50 | .75 |
| 19 | Dizzy Dean | .50 | 1.25 |
| 20 | Don Drysdale | .50 | 1.25 |
| 21 | Don Mattingly | 1.50 | 4.00 |
| 22 | Don Newcombe | .30 | .75 |
| 23 | Don Sutton | .30 | .75 |
| 24 | Duke Snider | .50 | 1.25 |
| 25 | Dwight Evans | .50 | 1.25 |
| 26 | Eddie Mathews | .75 | 2.00 |
| 27 | Eddie Murray | .75 | 2.00 |
| 28 | Enos Slaughter | .30 | .75 |
| 29 | Ernie Banks | .75 | 2.00 |
| 30 | Frank Howard | .30 | .75 |
| 31 | Frank Robinson | .30 | .75 |
| 32 | Gary Carter | .30 | .75 |
| 33 | Gaylord Perry | .30 | .75 |
| 34 | George Brett | 1.50 | 4.00 |
| 35 | George Kell | .30 | .75 |
| 36 | George Sisler | .30 | .75 |
| 37 | Larry Doby | .30 | .75 |
| 38 | Harmon Killebrew | .75 | 2.00 |
| 39 | Honus Wagner | .75 | 2.00 |
| 40 | Jackie Robinson | .75 | 2.00 |
| 41 | Jim Bunning | .30 | .75 |
| 42 | Jim Palmer | .30 | .75 |
| 43 | Jim Rice | .30 | .75 |
| 44 | Jimmie Foxx | .75 | 2.00 |
| 45 | Joe DiMaggio | 1.50 | 4.00 |
| 46 | Joe Morgan | .30 | .75 |
| 47 | Johnny Bench | .75 | 2.00 |
| 48 | Johnny Mize | .30 | .75 |
| 49 | Johnny Podres | .30 | .75 |
| 50 | Juan Marichal | .30 | .75 |
| 51 | Keith Hernandez | .30 | .75 |
| 52 | Kirby Puckett | .75 | 2.00 |
| 53 | Lefty Grove | .30 | .75 |
| 54 | Lou Brock | .50 | 1.25 |
| 55 | Lou Gehrig | 1.50 | 4.00 |
| 56 | Luis Aparicio | .30 | .75 |
| 57 | Fergie Jenkins | .30 | .75 |
| 58 | Maury Wills | .30 | .75 |
| 59 | Mel Ott | .75 | 2.00 |
| 60 | Mickey Cochrane | .30 | .75 |
| 61 | Mickey Mantle | 3.00 | 8.00 |
| 62 | Mike Schmidt | 1.50 | 4.00 |
| 63 | Monte Irvin | .30 | .75 |
| 64 | Nolan Ryan | 2.00 | 5.00 |
| 65 | Orlando Cepeda | .30 | .75 |
| 66 | Ozzie Smith | 1.25 | 3.00 |
| 67 | Paul Molitor | .30 | .75 |
| 68 | Pee Wee Reese | .50 | 1.25 |
| 69 | Phil Niekro | .30 | .75 |
| 70 | Phil Rizzuto | .50 | 1.25 |
| 71 | Ralph Kiner | .50 | 1.25 |
| 72 | Richie Ashburn | .50 | 1.25 |
| 73 | Roberto Clemente | 2.00 | 5.00 |
| 74 | Robin Roberts | .30 | .75 |
| 75 | Robin Yount | .75 | 2.00 |
| 76 | Rocky Colavito | .50 | 1.25 |
| 77 | Rod Carew | .50 | 1.25 |
| 78 | Rogers Hornsby | .75 | 2.00 |
| 79 | Rollie Fingers | .30 | .75 |
| 80 | Roy Campanella | .75 | 2.00 |
| 81 | Bob Lemon | .30 | .75 |
| 82 | Red Schoendienst | .30 | .75 |
| 83 | Satchel Paige | .75 | 2.00 |
| 84 | Stan Musial | 1.25 | 3.00 |
| 85 | Steve Carlton | .30 | .75 |
| 86 | Ted Williams | 1.50 | 4.00 |
| 87 | Thurman Munson | .75 | 2.00 |
| 88 | Tom Seaver | .50 | 1.25 |
| 89 | Tony Gwynn | 1.00 | 2.50 |
| 90 | Tony Perez | .50 | 1.25 |
| 91 | Ty Cobb | 1.25 | 3.00 |
| 92 | Wade Boggs | .50 | 1.25 |
| 93 | Walter Johnson | .75 | 2.00 |
| 94 | Warren Spahn | .50 | 1.25 |
| 95 | Whitey Ford | .50 | 1.25 |
| 96 | Will Clark | .50 | 1.25 |
| 97 | Catfish Hunter | .50 | 1.25 |
| 98 | Willie McCovey | .50 | 1.25 |
| 99 | Willie Stargell | .50 | 1.25 |
| 100 | Yogi Berra | .75 | 2.00 |

## 2007 Sweet Spot Classic

|  |  | | |
|---|---|---|---|
| | COMMON CARD | .60 | 1.50 |
| | STATED PRINT RUN 575 SER.#'d SETS | | |
| 1 | Phil Niekro | .60 | 1.50 |
| 2 | Fred McGriff | 1.00 | 2.50 |
| 3 | Bob Horner | .60 | 1.50 |
| 4 | Earl Weaver | .60 | 1.50 |
| 5 | Boog Powell | .60 | 1.50 |
| 6 | Eddie Murray | 1.50 | 4.00 |
| 7 | Fred Lynn | .60 | 1.50 |
| 8 | Dwight Evans | .60 | 1.50 |
| 9 | Jim Rice | .60 | 1.50 |
| 10 | Carlton Fisk | 1.00 | 2.50 |
| 11 | Luis Tiant | .60 | 1.50 |
| 12 | Robin Yount | 1.50 | 4.00 |
| 13 | Bobby Doerr | .60 | 1.50 |
| 14 | Ryne Sandberg | 3.00 | 8.00 |
| 15 | Billy Williams | .60 | 1.50 |
| 16 | Andre Dawson | .60 | 1.50 |
| 17 | Mark Grace | 1.00 | 2.50 |
| 18 | Ron Santo | 1.00 | 2.50 |
| 19 | Shawon Dunston | .60 | 1.50 |
| 20 | Harold Baines | .60 | 1.50 |
| 21 | Carlton Fisk | 1.00 | 2.50 |
| 22 | Sparky Anderson | .60 | 1.50 |
| 23 | George Foster | .60 | 1.50 |
| 24 | Dave Parker | .60 | 1.50 |
| 25 | Ken Griffey Sr. | .60 | 1.50 |
| 26 | Dave Concepcion | .60 | 1.50 |
| 27 | Rafael Palmeiro | 1.00 | 2.50 |
| 28 | Al Rosen | .60 | 1.50 |
| 29 | Kirk Gibson | .60 | 1.50 |
| 30 | Alan Trammell | .60 | 1.50 |
| 31 | Jack Morris | .60 | 1.50 |
| 32 | Willie Horton | .60 | 1.50 |
| 33 | JR Richard | .60 | 1.50 |
| 34 | Jose Cruz | .60 | 1.50 |
| 36 | Willie Wilson | .60 | 1.50 |
| 37 | Bo Jackson | 1.50 | 4.00 |
| 38 | Nolan Ryan | 4.00 | 10.00 |
| 39 | Don Baylor | .60 | 1.50 |
| 40 | Maury Wills | .60 | 1.50 |
| 41 | Tommy John | .60 | 1.50 |
| 42 | Ron Cey | .60 | 1.50 |
| 43 | Davey Lopes | .60 | 1.50 |
| 44 | Tommy Lasorda | .60 | 1.50 |
| 45 | Burt Hooton | .60 | 1.50 |
| 46 | Reggie Smith | .60 | 1.50 |
| 47 | Rollie Fingers | .60 | 1.50 |
| 48 | Cecil Cooper | .60 | 1.50 |
| 49 | Paul Molitor | .60 | 1.50 |
| 50 | Vern Stephens | .60 | 1.50 |
| 51 | Tony Oliva | .60 | 1.50 |
| 52 | Andres Galarraga | .60 | 1.50 |
| 53 | Tim Raines | .60 | 1.50 |
| 54 | Dennis Martinez | .60 | 1.50 |
| 55 | Lee Mazzilli | .60 | 1.50 |
| 56 | Rusty Staub | .60 | 1.50 |
| 57 | David Cone | .60 | 1.50 |
| 58 | Reggie Jackson | 1.00 | 2.50 |
| 59 | Ron Guidry | .60 | 1.50 |
| 60 | Tino Martinez | .60 | 1.50 |
| 61 | Don Mattingly | 3.00 | 8.00 |
| 62 | Chris Chambliss | .60 | 1.50 |
| 63 | Sparky Lyle | .60 | 1.50 |
| 64 | Goose Gossage | .60 | 1.50 |
| 65 | Dave Righetti | .60 | 1.50 |
| 66 | Phil Garner | .60 | 1.50 |
| 67 | Bill Madlock | .60 | 1.50 |
| 68 | Kent Hrbek | .60 | 1.50 |
| 69 | Al Oliver | .60 | 1.50 |
| 70 | John Kruk | .60 | 1.50 |
| 71 | Greg Luzinski | .60 | 1.50 |
| 72 | Dick Allen | .60 | 1.50 |
| 73 | Richie Ashburn | 1.00 | 2.50 |
| 74 | Gary Matthews | .60 | 1.50 |
| 75 | Mike Schmidt | 2.50 | 6.00 |
| 76 | Waite Hoyt | .60 | 1.50 |
| 77 | Bruce Sutter | .60 | 1.50 |
| 78 | Roger Maris | 1.50 | 4.00 |
| 79 | Joe Torre | 1.00 | 2.50 |
| 80 | Kevin Mitchell | .60 | 1.50 |
| 81 | John Montefusco | .60 | 1.50 |
| 82 | Rick Reuschel | .60 | 1.50 |
| 83 | Will Clark | 1.00 | 2.50 |
| 84 | Jack Clark | .60 | 1.50 |
| 85 | Matt Williams | .60 | 1.50 |
| 86 | Steve Garvey | .60 | 1.50 |
| 87 | Dave Winfield | .60 | 1.50 |
| 88 | Jay Buhner | .60 | 1.50 |
| 89 | Edgar Martinez | 1.00 | 2.50 |
| 90 | Carney Lansford | .60 | 1.50 |
| 91 | Sal Bando | .60 | 1.50 |
| 92 | Dave Stewart | .60 | 1.50 |
| 93 | Dennis Eckersley | .60 | 1.50 |
| 94 | Jose Canseco | 1.00 | 2.50 |
| 95 | Dennis Eckersley | .60 | 1.50 |
| 96 | Roberto Alomar | 1.00 | 2.50 |
| 97 | George Bell | .60 | 1.50 |
| 98 | Joe Carter | .60 | 1.50 |
| 99 | Frank Howard | .60 | 1.50 |
| 100 | Brooks Robinson | 1.00 | 2.50 |
| 101 | Frank Robinson | .60 | 1.50 |
| 102 | Jim Palmer | .60 | 1.50 |
| 103 | Cal Ripken Jr. | 6.00 | 15.00 |
| 104 | Warren Spahn | 1.00 | 2.50 |
| 105 | Cy Young | 1.50 | 4.00 |
| 106 | Waite Hoyt | .60 | 1.50 |
| 107 | Carl Yastrzemski | 2.50 | 6.00 |
| 108 | Johnny Pesky | .60 | 1.50 |

|  |  | | |
|---|---|---|---|
| 110 | Wade Boggs | 1.00 | 2.50 |
| 111 | Jackie Robinson | 1.50 | 4.00 |
| 112 | Roy Campanella | 1.50 | 4.00 |
| 113 | Pee Wee Reese | 1.00 | 2.50 |
| 114 | Don Newcombe | .60 | 1.50 |
| 115 | Rod Carew | 1.00 | 2.50 |
| 116 | Ernie Banks | 1.50 | 4.00 |
| 117 | Fergie Jenkins | .60 | 1.50 |
| 118 | Al Lopez | .60 | 1.50 |
| 119 | Luis Aparicio | .60 | 1.50 |
| 120 | Toby Harrah | .60 | 1.50 |
| 121 | Joe Morgan | .60 | 1.50 |
| 122 | Johnny Bench | 1.50 | 4.00 |
| 123 | Tony Perez | .50 | 1.50 |
| 124 | Ted Kluszewski | 1.00 | 2.50 |
| 125 | Bob Feller | .60 | 1.50 |
| 126 | Bob Lemon | .60 | 1.50 |
| 127 | Larry Doby | .60 | 1.50 |
| 128 | Lou Boudreau | .60 | 1.50 |
| 129 | George Kell | .60 | 1.50 |
| 130 | Hal Newhouser | .60 | 1.50 |
| 131 | Al Kaline | 1.50 | 4.00 |
| 132 | Ty Cobb | 2.50 | 6.00 |
| 133 | Denny McLain | .60 | 1.50 |
| 134 | Buck Leonard | .60 | 1.50 |
| 135 | Dean Chance | .60 | 1.50 |
| 136 | Don Drysdale | 1.00 | 2.50 |
| 137 | Don Sutton | .60 | 1.50 |
| 138 | Eddie Mathews | 1.50 | 4.00 |
| 139 | Paul Molitor | .60 | 1.50 |
| 140 | Kirby Puckett | 1.50 | 4.00 |
| 141 | Rod Carew | 1.00 | 2.50 |
| 142 | Harmon Killebrew | 1.50 | 4.00 |
| 143 | Monte Irvin | .60 | 1.50 |
| 144 | Mel Ott | .60 | 1.50 |
| 145 | Christy Mathewson | 1.50 | 4.00 |
| 146 | Hoyt Wilhelm | .60 | 1.50 |
| 147 | Tom Seaver | 1.00 | 2.50 |
| 148 | Joe McCarthy | .60 | 1.50 |
| 149 | Joe DiMaggio | 3.00 | 8.00 |
| 150 | Lou Gehrig | 3.00 | 8.00 |
| 151 | Babe Ruth | 4.00 | 10.00 |
| 152 | Casey Stengel | .60 | 1.50 |
| 153 | Phil Rizzuto | 1.00 | 2.50 |
| 154 | Thurman Munson | 1.50 | 4.00 |
| 155 | Johnny Mize | .60 | 1.50 |
| 156 | Yogi Berra | 1.50 | 4.00 |
| 157 | Roger Maris | 1.50 | 4.00 |
| 158 | Don Larsen | .60 | 1.50 |
| 159 | Bill Skowron | .60 | 1.50 |
| 160 | Lou Piniella | .60 | 1.50 |
| 161 | Joe Pepitone | .60 | 1.50 |
| 162 | Ray Dandridge | .60 | 1.50 |
| 163 | Rollie Fingers | .60 | 1.50 |
| 165 | Reggie Jackson | 1.00 | 2.50 |
| 166 | Mickey Cochrane | .60 | 1.50 |
| 167 | Jimmie Foxx | 1.50 | 4.00 |
| 168 | Lefty Grove | .60 | 1.50 |
| 169 | Gus Zernial | .60 | 1.50 |
| 170 | Jim Bunning | .60 | 1.50 |
| 171 | Steve Carlton | .60 | 1.50 |
| 172 | Robin Roberts | .60 | 1.50 |
| 173 | Ralph Kiner | 1.00 | 2.50 |
| 174 | Willie Stargell | 1.00 | 2.50 |
| 175 | Roberto Clemente | 5.00 | 12.00 |
| 176 | Bill Mazeroski | 1.00 | 2.50 |
| 177 | Honus Wagner | 1.50 | 4.00 |
| 178 | Pie Traynor | .60 | 1.50 |
| 179 | Elroy Face | .60 | 1.50 |
| 180 | Dick Groat | .60 | 1.50 |
| 181 | Tony Gwynn | 1.50 | 4.00 |
| 182 | Willie McCovey | 1.00 | 2.50 |
| 183 | Gaylord Perry | .60 | 1.50 |
| 184 | Juan Marichal | .60 | 1.50 |
| 185 | Orlando Cepeda | .60 | 1.50 |
| 186 | Satchel Paige | 1.50 | 4.00 |
| 187 | George Sisler | .60 | 1.50 |
| 188 | Rogers Hornsby | 1.00 | 2.50 |
| 189 | Stan Musial | 2.50 | 6.00 |
| 190 | Dizzy Dean | 1.00 | 2.50 |
| 191 | Bob Gibson | 1.00 | 2.50 |
| 192 | Red Schoendienst | .60 | 1.50 |
| 193 | Lou Brock | 1.00 | 2.50 |
| 194 | Enos Slaughter | .60 | 1.50 |
| 195 | Nolan Ryan | 4.00 | 10.00 |
| 196 | Mickey Vernon | .60 | 1.50 |
| 197 | Walter Johnson | 1.50 | 4.00 |
| 198 | Rick Ferrell | .60 | 1.50 |
| 199 | Roy Sievers | .60 | 1.50 |
| 200 | Judy Johnson | .60 | 1.50 |

## 2006 Sweet Spot Update

|  | | |
|---|---|---|
| COMP.SET w/o AU's (100) | 10.00 | 25.00 |
| COMMON CARD (1-100) | .20 | .50 |
| COMMON AU pr 399-499 | 3.00 | 8.00 |
| COMMON AU pr 150-240 | 4.00 | 10.00 |
| COMMON AU pr 98-125 | 4.00 | 10.00 |
| OVERALL AU ODDS 1:6 | | |
| AU PRINT RUNS B/WN 98-499 PER | | |
| EXCHANGE DEADLINE 12/19/09 | | |

|  |  | | |
|---|---|---|---|
| 1 | Luis Gonzalez | .20 | .50 |
| 2 | Chad Tracy | .20 | .50 |
| 3 | Brandon Webb | .20 | .50 |
| 4 | Andruw Jones | .30 | .75 |
| 5 | Chipper Jones | .50 | 1.25 |
| 6 | John Smoltz | .30 | .75 |
| 7 | Tim Hudson | .20 | .50 |
| 8 | Miguel Tejada | .20 | .50 |
| 9 | Brian Roberts | .20 | .50 |
| 10 | Ramon Hernandez | .20 | .50 |
| 11 | Curt Schilling | .30 | .75 |
| 12 | David Ortiz | .50 | 1.25 |
| 13 | Manny Ramirez | .30 | .75 |
| 14 | Jason Varitek | .50 | 1.25 |
| 15 | Josh Beckett | .30 | .75 |
| 16 | Greg Maddux | .75 | 2.00 |
| 17 | Derrek Lee | .20 | .50 |
| 18 | Mark Prior | .30 | .75 |
| 19 | Aramis Ramirez | .20 | .50 |
| 20 | Jim Thome | .30 | .75 |
| 21 | Paul Konerko | .20 | .50 |
| 22 | Scott Podsednik | .20 | .50 |
| 23 | Jose Contreras | .20 | .50 |
| 24 | Ken Griffey Jr. | .75 | 2.00 |
| 25 | Adam Dunn | .20 | .50 |
| 26 | Felipe Lopez | .20 | .50 |
| 27 | Travis Hafner | .20 | .50 |
| 28 | Victor Martinez | .20 | .50 |
| 29 | Grady Sizemore | .30 | .75 |
| 30 | Jhonny Peralta | .20 | .50 |
| 31 | Todd Helton | .30 | .75 |
| 32 | Garrett Atkins | .20 | .50 |
| 33 | Clint Barmes | .20 | .50 |
| 34 | Ivan Rodriguez | .30 | .75 |
| 35 | Chris Shelton | .20 | .50 |
| 36 | Jeremy Bonderman | .20 | .50 |
| 37 | Miguel Cabrera | .50 | 1.25 |
| 38 | Dontrelle Willis | .20 | .50 |
| 39 | Lance Berkman | .20 | .50 |
| 40 | Morgan Ensberg | .20 | .50 |
| 41 | Roy Oswalt | .20 | .50 |
| 42 | Reggie Sanders | .20 | .50 |
| 43 | Mike Sweeney | .20 | .50 |
| 44 | Vladimir Guerrero | .50 | 1.25 |
| 45 | Bartolo Colon | .20 | .50 |
| 46 | Chone Figgins | .20 | .50 |
| 47 | Nomar Garciaparra | .50 | 1.25 |
| 48 | Jeff Kent | .20 | .50 |
| 49 | J.D. Drew | .20 | .50 |
| 50 | Carlos Lee | .20 | .50 |
| 51 | Ben Sheets | .20 | .50 |
| 52 | Rickie Weeks | .20 | .50 |
| 53 | Johan Santana | .30 | .75 |
| 54 | Torii Hunter | .20 | .50 |
| 55 | Joe Mauer | .50 | 1.25 |
| 56 | Pedro Martinez | .30 | .75 |
| 57 | David Wright | .75 | 2.00 |
| 58 | Carlos Beltran | .20 | .50 |
| 59 | Carlos Delgado | .20 | .50 |
| 60 | Jose Reyes | .50 | 1.25 |
| 61 | Derek Jeter | 1.25 | 3.00 |
| 62 | Alex Rodriguez | .75 | 2.00 |
| 63 | Randy Johnson | .50 | 1.25 |
| 64 | Hideki Matsui | .50 | 1.25 |
| 65 | Gary Sheffield | .20 | .50 |
| 66 | Rich Harden | .20 | .50 |
| 67 | Eric Chavez | .20 | .50 |
| 68 | Huston Street | .20 | .50 |
| 69 | Bobby Crosby | .20 | .50 |
| 70 | Bobby Abreu | .20 | .50 |
| 71 | Ryan Howard | .75 | 2.00 |
| 72 | Chase Utley | .50 | 1.25 |
| 73 | Pat Burrell | .20 | .50 |
| 74 | Jason Bay | .20 | .50 |
| 75 | Sean Casey | .20 | .50 |
| 76 | Mike Piazza | .50 | 1.25 |
| 77 | Jake Peavy | .20 | .50 |
| 78 | Brian Giles | .20 | .50 |
| 79 | Milton Bradley | .20 | .50 |
| 80 | Omar Vizquel | .30 | .75 |
| 81 | Jason Schmidt | .20 | .50 |
| 82 | Ichiro Suzuki | .75 | 2.00 |
| 83 | Felix Hernandez | .30 | .75 |
| 84 | Kenji Johjima RC | 1.00 | 2.50 |
| 85 | Albert Pujols | 1.00 | 2.50 |
| 86 | Chris Carpenter | .20 | .50 |
| 87 | Scott Rolen | .30 | .75 |
| 88 | Jim Edmonds | .20 | .50 |
| 89 | Carl Crawford | .20 | .50 |
| 90 | Jonny Gomes | .20 | .50 |
| 91 | Scott Kazmir | .30 | .75 |
| 92 | Mark Teixeira | .30 | .75 |
| 93 | Michael Young | .20 | .50 |
| 94 | Phil Nevin | .20 | .50 |
| 95 | Vernon Wells | .20 | .50 |
| 96 | Roy Halladay | .20 | .50 |
| 97 | Troy Glaus | .20 | .50 |
| 98 | Alfonso Soriano | .20 | .50 |
| 99 | Nick Johnson | .20 | .50 |
| 100 | Jose Vidro | .20 | .50 |
| 101 | A.Wainwright AU/100 (RC) | 15.00 | 40.00 |
| 102 | A.Hernandez AU/100 (RC) EXCH | 6.00 | 15.00 |
| 103 | A.Ethier AU/150 (RC) | 12.50 | 30.00 |
| 104 | J.Botts AU/100 (RC) EXCH | 6.00 | 15.00 |
| 105 | B.Johnson AU/400 (RC) | 3.00 | 8.00 |
| 106 | B.Bonser AU/100 (RC) | 6.00 | 15.00 |
| 107 | B.Logan AU/200 RC | 4.00 | 10.00 |
| 108 | B.Anderson AU/200 (RC) | 4.00 | 10.00 |
| 109 | B.Bannister AU/100 (RC) | 8.00 | 20.00 |
| 110 | C.Demorfia AU/100 (RC) | 4.00 | 10.00 |
| 111 | A.Montero AU/100 (RC) | 6.00 | 15.00 |
| 112 | C.Ross AU/100 (RC) | 4.00 | 10.00 |
| 113 | C.Hamels AU/399 (RC) | 20.00 | 50.00 |
| 114 | J.Jackson AU/400 (RC) | 4.00 | 10.00 |
| 115 | D.Uggla AU/125 (RC) | 12.50 | 30.00 |
| 116 | D.Gassner AU/100 (RC) | 4.00 | 10.00 |
| 117 | C.Wilson AU/150 (RC) | 4.00 | 10.00 |
| 118 | E.Reed AU/150 (RC) | 4.00 | 10.00 |
| 119 | F.Carmona AU/99 (RC) | 10.00 | 25.00 |
| 120 | F.Nieve AU/100 (RC) | 4.00 | 10.00 |
| 121 | F.Liriano AU/499 (RC) | 10.00 | 25.00 |
| 122 | F.Bynum AU/100 (RC) | • 4.00 | 10.00 |
| 123 | H.Ramirez AU/100 (RC) | 15.00 | 40.00 |
| 124 | H.Kuo AU/100 (RC) | 75.00 | 150.00 |
| 125 | I.Kinsler AU/100 (RC) | 12.50 | 30.00 |
| 126 | C.Marmol AU/100 RC | 6.00 | 15.00 |
| 127 | B.Keppel AU/200 (RC) | 4.00 | 10.00 |
| 128 | J.Kubel AU/100 (RC) | 6.00 | 15.00 |
| 129 | J.Harris AU/100 RC | 4.00 | 10.00 |
| 130 | A.Soler AU/100 RC | 6.00 | 15.00 |
| 131 | J.Weaver AU/100 (RC) EXCH | 10.00 | 25.00 |
| 132 | C.Quentin AU/100 (RC) | 12.50 | 30.00 |
| 133 | J.Hermida AU/100 (RC) | 6.00 | 15.00 |
| 134 | J.Zumaya AU/100 (RC) | 20.00 | 50.00 |
| 135 | J.Devine AU/100 RC | 4.00 | 10.00 |
| 136 | J.Koronka AU/98 (RC) | 4.00 | 10.00 |
| 137 | J.Papelbon AU/399 (RC) | 15.00 | 40.00 |
| 138 | J.Capellan AU/240 (RC) | 4.00 | 10.00 |
| 139 | J.Johnson AU/100 (RC) | 6.00 | 15.00 |
| 140 | J.Rupe AU/100 (RC) EXCH | 4.00 | 10.00 |
| 141 | J.Willingham AU/100 (RC) | 4.00 | 10.00 |
| 142 | J.Verlander AU/100 (RC) | 15.00 | 40.00 |
| 143 | K.Shoppach AU/100 (RC) | 6.00 | 15.00 |
| 144 | K.Thompson AU/100 (RC) | 4.00 | 10.00 |
| 145 | K.Morales AU/100 (RC) EXCH | 4.00 | 10.00 |
| 146 | K.Thompson AU/100 (RC) | 4.00 | 10.00 |
| 147 | M.McBride AU/100 (RC) | 4.00 | 10.00 |
| 148 | M.Prado AU/100 (RC) EXCH | 4.00 | 10.00 |
| 149 | M.Cain AU/150 (RC) EXCH | 6.00 | 15.00 |

|  | | |
|---|---|---|
| 150 C.Hensley AU/100 (RC) | 4.00 | 10.00 |
| 151 T.Taubenheim AU/100 RC | 10.00 | 25.00 |
| 152 M.Jacobs AU/200 RC | 4.00 | 10.00 |
| 153 S.Rivera AU/100 (RC) | 4.00 | 10.00 |
| 154 M.Thompson AU/100 RC | 4.00 | 10.00 |
| 155 N.McLouth AU/100 (RC) | 10.00 | 25.00 |
| 156 M.Vento AU/100 (RC) | 4.00 | 10.00 |
| 157 P.Maholm AU/200 (RC) | 4.00 | 10.00 |
| 159 R.Abercrombie AU/100 (RC) | 4.00 | 10.00 |
| 160 M.Rouse AU/100 (RC) | 4.00 | 10.00 |
| 161 K.Ray AU/100 (RC) | 4.00 | 10.00 |
| 162 R.Flores AU/100 (RC) | 4.00 | 10.00 |
| 163 R.Zimmerman AU/100 (RC) | 30.00 | 60.00 |
| 164 E.Aybar AU/100 (RC) | 6.00 | 15.00 |
| 165 S.Marshall AU/150 (RC) | 8.00 | 20.00 |
| 166 T.Saito AU/100 RC EXCH | | |
| 167 T.Buchholz AU/100 (RC) | 4.00 | 10.00 |
| 168 M.Murton AU/100 (RC) | 12.50 | 30.00 |
| 169 L.Figueroa AU/100 RC EXCH | | |
| 170 W.Nieves AU/100 (RC) | 6.00 | 15.00 |
| 171 J.Shields AU/100 RC | 6.00 | 15.00 |
| 172 J.Lester AU/399 RC | 20.00 | 50.00 |
| 173 C.Hansen AU/100 RC EXCH | 12.50 | 30.00 |
| 174 A.Rakers AU/100 (RC) | 6.00 | 15.00 |
| 175 B.Livingston AU/100 (RC) | 4.00 | 10.00 |
| 176 B.Harris AU/100 (RC) | 4.00 | 10.00 |
| 177 Z.Jackson AU/100 (RC) | 6.00 | 15.00 |
| 178 C.Britton AU/100 RC | 6.00 | 15.00 |
| 179 H.Kendrick AU/399 (RC) | 10.00 | 25.00 |
| 180 Z.Miner AU/100 (RC) | 4.00 | 10.00 |
| 181 K.Frandsen AU/100 (RC) | 4.00 | 10.00 |
| 182 M.Capps AU/100 (RC) | 4.00 | 10.00 |
| 183 P.Moylan AU/100 RC | 4.00 | 10.00 |
| 184 M.Cabrera AU/100 (RC) EXCH | 20.00 | 50.00 |

## 1911 T205 Gold Border

|  | | |
|---|---|---|
| COMPLETE SET (218) | 25000.00 | 50000.00 |
| COMMON MAJOR (1-186) | 90.00 | 150.00 |
| COM. MINOR (187-198) | 150.00 | 300.00 |
| 1 Ed Abbaticchio | 60.00 | 100.00 |
| 2 Merle (Doc) Adkins | 125.00 | 200.00 |
| 3 Red Ames | 60.00 | 100.00 |
| 4 Jimmy Archer | 60.00 | 100.00 |
| 5 Jimmy Austin | 60.00 | 100.00 |
| 6 Bill Bailey | 60.00 | 100.00 |
| 7 Frank Baker | 175.00 | 300.00 |
| 8 Neal Ball | 60.00 | 100.00 |
| 9 Cy Barger Full B | 60.00 | 100.00 |
| 10 Cy Barger Part B | 250.00 | 400.00 |
| 11 Jack Barry | 60.00 | 100.00 |
| 12 Emil Batch | 125.00 | 200.00 |
| 13 Johnny Bates | 60.00 | 100.00 |
| 14 Fred Beck | 60.00 | 100.00 |
| 15 Beals Becker | 60.00 | 100.00 |
| 16 George Bell | 60.00 | 100.00 |
| 17 Chief Bender | 175.00 | 300.00 |
| 18 Bill Bergen | 60.00 | 100.00 |
| 19 Bob Bescher | 60.00 | 100.00 |
| 20 Joe Birmingham | 60.00 | 100.00 |
| 21 Russ Blackburne | 60.00 | 100.00 |
| 22 Kitty Bransfield | 60.00 | 100.00 |
| 23 R.Bresnahan Closed | 175.00 | 300.00 |
| 24 R.Bresnahan Open | 300.00 | 500.00 |
| 25 Al Bridwell | 60.00 | 100.00 |
| 26 Mordecai Brown | 175.00 | 300.00 |
| 27 Bobby Byrne | 60.00 | 100.00 |
| 28 Hick Cady | 150.00 | 250.00 |
| 29 Howie Camnitz | 60.00 | 100.00 |
| 30 Bill Carrigan | 60.00 | 100.00 |
| 31 Frank Chance | 175.00 | 300.00 |
| 32A Hal Chase Both - Ends | 125.00 | 200.00 |
| 32B Hal Chase Both - Extends | 125.00 | 200.00 |
| 33 Hal Chase Left Ear | 300.00 | 500.00 |
| 34 Eddie Cicotte | 250.00 | 400.00 |
| 35 Fred Clarke | 150.00 | 250.00 |
| 36 Ty Cobb | 2500.00 | 4000.00 |
| 37 E.Collins Mouth Closed | 175.00 | 300.00 |
| 38 E.Collins Mouth Open | 350.00 | 600.00 |
| 39 Jimmy Collins | 250.00 | 400.00 |
| 40 Frank Corridon | 60.00 | 100.00 |
| 41A Otis Crandall (Olis) | 150.00 | 250.00 |
| 41B Otis Crandall (Olis) | 90.00 | 150.00 |
| 42 Lou Criger | 60.00 | 100.00 |
| 43 Bill Dahlen | 250.00 | 400.00 |
| 44 Jake Daubert | 60.00 | 100.00 |
| 45 Jim Delahanty | 60.00 | 100.00 |
| 46 Art Devlin | 60.00 | 100.00 |
| 47 Josh Devore | 60.00 | 100.00 |
| 48 Walt Dickson | 60.00 | 100.00 |
| 49 Jiggs Donohue | 250.00 | 400.00 |
| 50 Red Dooin | 60.00 | 100.00 |
| 51 Mickey Doolan | 60.00 | 100.00 |
| 52A Patsy Dougherty Red | 150.00 | 250.00 |
| 52B Patsy Dougherty White | 150.00 | 250.00 |
| 53 Tom Downey | 60.00 | 100.00 |
| 54 Larry Doyle | 60.00 | 100.00 |
| 55 Hugh Duffy | 175.00 | 300.00 |
| 56 Jack Dunn | 175.00 | 300.00 |
| 57 Jimmy Dygert | 60.00 | 100.00 |
| 58 Dick Egan | 60.00 | 100.00 |
| 59 Kid Elberfeld | 60.00 | 100.00 |
| 60 Clyde Engle | 60.00 | 100.00 |
| 61 Steve Evans | 60.00 | 100.00 |
| 62 Johnny Evers | 300.00 | 500.00 |
| 63 Bob Ewing | 60.00 | 100.00 |
| 64 George Ferguson | 60.00 | 100.00 |
| 65 Ray Fisher | 175.00 | 300.00 |
| 66 Art Fletcher | 60.00 | 100.00 |
| 67 John Flynn | 60.00 | 100.00 |
| 68 Russ Ford Dark Cap | 60.00 | 100.00 |
| 69 Russ Ford Light Cap | 250.00 | 400.00 |
| 70 Bill Foxen | 60.00 | 100.00 |
| 71 James Frick | 150.00 | 250.00 |
| 72 Art Fromme | 60.00 | 100.00 |
| 73 Earl Gardner | 60.00 | 100.00 |
| 74 Harry Gaspar | 60.00 | 100.00 |
| 75 George Gibson | 60.00 | 100.00 |
| 76 Wilbur Good | 60.00 | 100.00 |
| 77 P.Graham Cubs | 250.00 | 400.00 |
| 78 P.Graham Rustlers | 250.00 | 400.00 |
| 79 Eddie Grant | 250.00 | 400.00 |
| 80A Dolly Gray w/o Stats | 150.00 | 250.00 |
| 80B Dolly Gray w/Stats | 600.00 | 1000.00 |
| 81 Clark Griffith | 175.00 | 300.00 |
| 82 Bob Groom | 60.00 | 100.00 |
| 83 Charles Hanford | 150.00 | 250.00 |
| 84 Bob Harmon Both Ears | 60.00 | 100.00 |
| 85 Bob Harmon Left Ear | 250.00 | 400.00 |
| 86 Topsy Hartsel | 60.00 | 100.00 |
| 87 Arnold Hauser | 60.00 | 100.00 |
| 88 Charlie Hemphill | 60.00 | 100.00 |
| 89 Buck Herzog | 60.00 | 100.00 |
| 90A D.Hoblitzell No Stats | 7000.00 | 12000.00 |
| 90B D.Hoblitzell w/CIN | 90.00 | 150.00 |
| 90C D.Hoblitzell (Hoblitzel) | 350.00 | 600.00 |
| 90D D.Hoblitzell w/o CIN | 350.00 | 600.00 |
| 91 Danny Hoffman | 60.00 | 100.00 |
| 92 Miller Huggins | 175.00 | 300.00 |
| 93 John Hummell | 60.00 | 100.00 |
| 94 Fred Jacklitsch | 60.00 | 100.00 |
| 95 Hughie Jennings | 175.00 | 300.00 |
| 96 Walter Johnson | 1000.00 | 1800.00 |
| 97 Davy Jones | 60.00 | 100.00 |
| 98 Tom Jones | 60.00 | 100.00 |
| 99 Addie Joss | 900.00 | 1500.00 |
| 100 Ed Karger | 250.00 | 400.00 |
| 101 Ed Killian | 60.00 | 100.00 |
| 102 Red Kleinow | 250.00 | 400.00 |
| 103 John King | 60.00 | 100.00 |
| 104 John Knight | 60.00 | 100.00 |
| 105 Ed Konetchy | 60.00 | 100.00 |
| 106 Harry Krause | 60.00 | 100.00 |
| 107 Rube Kroh | 60.00 | 100.00 |
| 108 Frank Lang | 60.00 | 100.00 |
| 109 Frank LaPorte | 60.00 | 100.00 |
| 110A Arlie Latham (A.) | 125.00 | 200.00 |
| 110B Arlie Latham (A.P.) | 250.00 | 400.00 |
| 111 Tommy Leach | 60.00 | 100.00 |
| 112 Wyatt Lee | 90.00 | 150.00 |
| 113 Sam Leever | 60.00 | 100.00 |
| 114A Lefty Leifield (A.) | 150.00 | 250.00 |
| 114B Lefty Leifield (A.P.) | 250.00 | 400.00 |
| 115 Ed Lennox | 60.00 | 100.00 |
| 116 Paddy Livingston | 60.00 | 100.00 |
| 117 Hans Lobert | 60.00 | 100.00 |
| 118 Bris Lord | 60.00 | 100.00 |
| 119 Harry Lord | 60.00 | 100.00 |
| 120 John Lush | 60.00 | 100.00 |
| 121 Nick Maddox | 60.00 | 100.00 |
| 122 Sherry Magee | 60.00 | 100.00 |
| 123 Rube Marquard | 175.00 | 300.00 |
| 124 Christy Mathewson | 1000.00 | 1800.00 |
| 125 Al Mattern | 60.00 | 100.00 |
| 126 Lewis McAllister | 90.00 | 150.00 |
| 127 George McBride | 60.00 | 100.00 |
| 128 Amby McConnell | 60.00 | 100.00 |
| 129 Pryor McElveen | 60.00 | 100.00 |
| 130 John McGraw MG | 175.00 | 300.00 |
| 131 Harry McIntire | 60.00 | 100.00 |
| 132 Matty McIntyre | 60.00 | 100.00 |
| 133 Larry McLean | 60.00 | 100.00 |
| 134 Fred Merkle | 60.00 | 100.00 |
| 135 George Merritt | 150.00 | 250.00 |
| 136 Chief Meyers | 60.00 | 100.00 |
| 137 Clyde Milan | 60.00 | 100.00 |
| 138 Dots Miller | 60.00 | 100.00 |
| 139 Mike Mitchell | 60.00 | 100.00 |
| 140A Pat Moran Extra Stat | 900.00 | 1500.00 |
| 140B Pat Moran | 60.00 | 100.00 |
| 141 George Moriarty | 60.00 | 100.00 |
| 142 George Mullin | 60.00 | 100.00 |
| 143 Danny Murphy | 60.00 | 100.00 |
| 144 Red Murray | 60.00 | 100.00 |
| 145 John Nee | 150.00 | 250.00 |
| 146 Tom Needham | 60.00 | 100.00 |
| 147 Rebel Oakes | 60.00 | 100.00 |
| 148 Rube Oldring | 60.00 | 100.00 |
| 149 Charley O'Leary | 60.00 | 100.00 |
| 150 Fred Olmstead | 60.00 | 100.00 |
| 151 Orval Overall | 60.00 | 100.00 |
| 152 Freddy Parent | 60.00 | 100.00 |
| 153 Dode Paskert | 60.00 | 100.00 |
| 154 Fred Payne | 60.00 | 100.00 |
| 155 Barney Pelty | 60.00 | 100.00 |
| 156 Jack Pfiester | 60.00 | 100.00 |
| 157 James Phelan | 150.00 | 250.00 |
| 158 Ed Phelps | 60.00 | 100.00 |
| 159 Decon Phillippe | 60.00 | 100.00 |
| 160 Jack Quinn | 60.00 | 100.00 |
| 161 Bugs Raymond | 250.00 | 400.00 |
| 162 Ed Reulbach | 60.00 | 100.00 |
| 163 Lewis Richie | 60.00 | 100.00 |
| 164 Jack Rowan | 175.00 | 300.00 |
| 165 Nap Rucker | 60.00 | 100.00 |
| 166 Doc Scanlan | 250.00 | 400.00 |
| 167 Germany Schaefer | 60.00 | 100.00 |
| 168 Admiral Schlei | 60.00 | 100.00 |
| 169 Boss Schmidt | 60.00 | 100.00 |
| 170 Wildfire Schulte | 60.00 | 100.00 |
| 171 Jim Scott | 60.00 | 100.00 |
| 172 Bayard Sharpe | 60.00 | 100.00 |
| 173 David Shean Cubs | 175.00 | 300.00 |
| 174 David Shean Rustlers | 60.00 | 100.00 |
| 175 Jimmy Sheckard | 60.00 | 100.00 |
| 176 Hack Simmons | 60.00 | 100.00 |
| 177 Tony Smith | 60.00 | 100.00 |
| 178 Fred Snodgrass | 60.00 | 100.00 |
| 179 Tris Speaker | 500.00 | 800.00 |
| 180 Jake Stahl | 60.00 | 100.00 |
| 181 Oscar Strange | 60.00 | 100.00 |
| 182 Harry Steinfeldt | 60.00 | 100.00 |
| 183 George Stone | 60.00 | 100.00 |
| 184 George Stovall | 60.00 | 100.00 |
| 185 Gabby Street | 60.00 | 100.00 |
| 186 George Suggs | 250.00 | 400.00 |
| 187 Ed Summers | 60.00 | 100.00 |
| 188 Jeff Sweeney | 250.00 | 400.00 |
| 189 Lee Tannehill | 60.00 | 100.00 |
| 190 Ira Thomas | 60.00 | 100.00 |
| 191 Joe Tinker | 175.00 | 300.00 |
| 192 John Titus | 60.00 | 100.00 |
| 193 Terry Turner | 250.00 | 400.00 |
| 194 Hippo Vaughn | 300.00 | 500.00 |
| 195 Heinie Wagner | 175.00 | 300.00 |
| 196 B.Wallace w/cap | 150.00 | 250.00 |
| 197A B.Wallace w/Cap 1 Line | 1200.00 | 2000.00 |
| 197B B.Wallace w/Cap 2 Lines | 700.00 | 1200.00 |
| 198 Ed Walsh | 500.00 | 800.00 |
| 199 Zach Wheat | 175.00 | 300.00 |
| 200 Doc White | 60.00 | 100.00 |

☐ 201 Kirby White 250.00 400.00
☐ 202A Irvin K. Wilhelm 350.00 600.00
☐ 202B Irvin K. Wilhelm Missing Letter 175.00 300.00
☐ 203 Ed Willett 60.00 100.00
☐ 204 Owen Wilson 60.00 100.00
☐ 205 H.Wiltse Both Ears 60.00 100.00
☐ 206 H.Wiltse Right Ear 250.00 400.00
☐ 207 Harry Wolter 60.00 100.00
☐ 208 Cy Young 1000.00 1800.00

**1909-11 T206**

☐ COMPLETE SET (520) 30000.00 55000.00
☐ COMMON MAJOR (1-389) 50.00 100.00
☐ COMMON MINOR (390-475) 50.00 100.00
☐ COM. SO. LEA. (476-523) 125.00 250.00
☐ CARDS PRICED IN EXMT CONDITION
☐ HONUS WAGNER PRICED IN GOOD CONDITION
☐ 1 Ed Abbaticchio Blue 85.00 135.00
☐ 2 Ed Abbaticchio Brown 85.00 135.00
☐ 3 Fred Abbott 60.00 100.00
☐ 4 Bill Abstein 60.00 100.00
☐ 5 Doc Adkins 125.00 200.00
☐ 6 Whitey Alperman 60.00 100.00
☐ 7 Red Ames Hands at 150.00 250.00
☐ 8 Red Ames Hands over 60.00 100.00
☐ 9 Red Ames Portrait 60.00 100.00
☐ 10 John Anderson 60.00 100.00
☐ 11 Frank Arellanes 60.00 100.00
☐ 12 Herman Armbruster 60.00 100.00
☐ 13 Harry Arndt 70.00 120.00
☐ 14 Jake Atz 60.00 100.00
☐ 15 Home Run Baker 250.00 400.00
☐ 16 Neal Ball Cleveland 60.00 100.00
☐ 17 Neal Ball New York 60.00 100.00
☐ 18 Jap Barbeau 60.00 100.00
☐ 19 Cy Barger 60.00 100.00
☐ 20 Jack Barry 60.00 100.00
☐ 21 Shad Barry 60.00 100.00
☐ 22 Jack Bastian 175.00 300.00
☐ 23 Emil Batch 60.00 100.00
☐ 24 Johnny Bates 60.00 100.00
☐ 25 Harry Bay 175.00 300.00
☐ 26 Ginger Beaumont 60.00 100.00
☐ 27 Fred Beck 60.00 100.00
☐ 28 Beals Becker 60.00 100.00
☐ 29 Jake Beckley 175.00 300.00
☐ 30 George Bell Follow 60.00 100.00
☐ 31 George Bell Hands above 60.00 100.00
☐ 32 Chief Bender Pitching 250.00 400.00
☐ 33 Chief Bender Pitching Trees 250.00 400.00
☐ 34 Chief Bender Portrait 300.00 500.00
☐ 35 Bill Bergen Batting 60.00 100.00
☐ 36 Bill Bergen Catching 60.00 100.00
☐ 37 Heinie Berger 60.00 100.00
☐ 38 Bob Bescher Hands 175.00 300.00
☐ 39 Bob Bescher Hands above 60.00 100.00
☐ 40 Bob Bescher Portrait 60.00 100.00
☐ 41 Joe Birmingham 90.00 150.00
☐ 42 Lena Blackburne 60.00 100.00
☐ 43 Jack Bliss 60.00 100.00
☐ 44 Frank Bowerman 60.00 100.00
☐ 45 Bill Bradley with Bat 60.00 100.00
☐ 46 Bill Bradley Portrait 60.00 100.00
☐ 47 David Brain 60.00 100.00
☐ 48 Kitty Bransfield 60.00 100.00
☐ 49 Roy Brashear 60.00 100.00
☐ 50 Ted Breitenstein 175.00 300.00
☐ 51 Roger Bresnahan Portrait 175.00 300.00
☐ 52 Roger Bresnahan with Bat 175.00 300.00
☐ 53 Al Bridwell No Cap 60.00 100.00
☐ 54 Al Bridwell with Cap 60.00 100.00
☐ 55 George Brown Chicago 125.00 200.00
☐ 56 George Brown Washington 300.00 500.00
☐ 57 Mordecai Brown Chicago 200.00 350.00

☐ 58 Mordecai Brown Cubs 350.00 600.00
☐ 59 Mordecai Brown Portrait 300.00 500.00
☐ 60 Al Burch Batting 125.00 200.00
☐ 61 Al Burch Fielding 60.00 100.00
☐ 62 Fred Burchell 60.00 100.00
☐ 63 Jimmy Burke 60.00 100.00
☐ 64 Bill Burns 60.00 100.00
☐ 65 Donie Bush 60.00 100.00
☐ 66 John Butler 60.00 100.00
☐ 67 Bobby Byrne 60.00 100.00
☐ 68 Howie Camnitz Arm at Side 60.00 100.00
☐ 69 Howie Camnitz Folded 60.00 100.00
☐ 70 Howie Camnitz Hands 60.00 100.00
☐ 71 Billy Campbell 60.00 100.00
☐ 72 Scoops Carey 175.00 300.00
☐ 73 Charley Carr 60.00 100.00
☐ 74 Bill Carrigan 60.00 100.00
☐ 75 Doc Casey 60.00 100.00
☐ 76 Peter Cassidy 60.00 100.00
☐ 77 Frank Chance Batting 250.00 400.00
☐ 78 F.Chance Portrait Red 300.00 500.00
☐ 79 F.Chance Portrait Yel 250.00 400.00
☐ 80 Bill Chappelle 60.00 100.00
☐ 81 Chappie Charles 60.00 100.00
☐ 82 Hal Chase Dark Cap 90.00 150.00
☐ 83 Hal Chase Holding Trophy 150.00 250.00
☐ 84 Hal Chase Holding Bat 90.00 150.00
☐ 85 Hal Chase Portrait Pink 250.00 400.00
☐ 86 Hal Chase White Cap 125.00 200.00
☐ 87 Jack Chesbro 250.00 400.00
☐ 88 Ed Cicotte 175.00 300.00
☐ 89 Bill Clancy (Clancey) 60.00 100.00
☐ 90 Fred Clarke Holding Bat 250.00 400.00
☐ 91 Fred Clarke Portrait 250.00 400.00
☐ 92 Josh Clark (Clarke) ML 60.00 100.00
☐ 93 J.J. (Nig) Clarke 60.00 100.00
☐ 94 Bill Clymer 60.00 100.00
☐ 95 Ty Cobb Bat off Shoulder 1500.00 2500.00
☐ 96 Ty Cobb Bat on Shoulder 1500.00 2500.00
☐ 97 Ty Cobb Portrait Green 3500.00 5000.00
☐ 98 Ty Cobb Portrait Red 1200.00 2000.00
☐ 99 Cad Coles 175.00 300.00
☐ 100 Eddie Collins 200.00 350.00
☐ 101 Jimmy Collins 175.00 300.00
☐ 102 Bunk Congalton 60.00 100.00
☐ 103 Wid Conroy Fielding 60.00 100.00
☐ 104 Wid Conroy with Bat 60.00 100.00
☐ 105 Harry Covaleski (Coveleski) 60.00 100.00
☐ 106 Doc Crandall No Cap 60.00 100.00
☐ 107 Doc Crandall with Cap 60.00 100.00
☐ 108 Bill Cranston 175.00 300.00
☐ 109 Gavvy Cravath 60.00 100.00
☐ 110 Sam Crawford Throwing 250.00 400.00
☐ 111 Sam Crawford with Bat 250.00 400.00
☐ 112 Birdie Cree 60.00 100.00
☐ 113 Lou Criger 60.00 100.00
☐ 114 Dode Criss 60.00 100.00
☐ 115 Monte Cross 60.00 100.00
☐ 116 Bill Dahlen Boston 90.00 150.00
☐ 117 Bill Dahlen Brooklyn 300.00 500.00
☐ 118 Paul Davidson 60.00 100.00
☐ 119 George Davis 175.00 300.00
☐ 120 Harry Davis (Davis on Front) 60.00 100.00
☐ 121 Harry Davis (H.Davis on Front) 60.00 100.00
☐ 122 Frank Delehanty 60.00 100.00
☐ 123 Jim Delehanty 60.00 100.00
☐ 124 Ray Demmitt New York 70.00 120.00
☐ 125 Ray Demmitt St. Louis 6000.00 10000.00
☐ 126 Rube Dessau 85.00 135.00
☐ 127 Art Devlin 60.00 100.00
☐ 128 Josh Devore 60.00 100.00
☐ 129 Bill Dineen 60.00 100.00
☐ 130 Mike Donlin Fielding 125.00 200.00
☐ 131 Mike Donlin Sitting 60.00 100.00
☐ 132 Mike Donlin with Bat 60.00 100.00
☐ 133 Jiggs Donahue (Donohue) 60.00 100.00
☐ 134 Wild Bill Donovan Portrait 60.00 100.00
☐ 135 Wild Bill Donovan Throwing 60.00 100.00
☐ 136 Red Dooin 60.00 100.00
☐ 137 Mickey Doolan Batting 60.00 100.00
☐ 138 Mickey Doolan Fielding 60.00 100.00
☐ 139 Mickey Doolin Portrait (Doolan) 60.00 100.00
☐ 140 Gus Dorner ML 60.00 100.00
☐ 141 Gus Dorner Dopner 60.00 100.00
☐ 142 Patsy Dougherty Arm in Air 60.00 100.00
☐ 143 Patsy Dougherty Arm at Side 60.00 100.00
☐ 144 Tom Downey Batting 60.00 100.00
☐ 145 Tom Downey Fielding 60.00 100.00

☐ 146 Jerry Downs 60.00 100.00
☐ 147 Joe Doyle 350.00 600.00
☐ 148 Joe Doyle Nat'l 60.00 100.00
☐ 149 Larry Doyle Portrait 60.00 100.00
☐ 150 Larry Doyle Throwing 60.00 100.00
☐ 151 Larry Doyle with Bat 60.00 100.00
☐ 152 Jean Dubuc 60.00 100.00
☐ 153 Hugh Duffy 175.00 300.00
☐ 154 Jack Dunn Baltimore 60.00 100.00
☐ 155 Joe Dunn Brooklyn 60.00 100.00
☐ 156 Bull Durham 60.00 100.00
☐ 157 Jimmy Dygert 60.00 100.00
☐ 158 Ted Easterly 60.00 100.00
☐ 159 Dick Egan 90.00 150.00
☐ 160 Kid Elberfeld Fielding 60.00 100.00
☐ 161 Kid Elberfeld Port NY 60.00 100.00
☐ 162 Kid Elberfeld Port Wash 1800.00 3000.00
☐ 163 Roy Ellam 175.00 300.00
☐ 164 Clyde Engle 60.00 100.00
☐ 165 Steve Evans 60.00 100.00
☐ 166 J.Evers Portrait 350.00 600.00
☐ 167 J.Evers Chi Shirt 250.00 400.00
☐ 168 J.Evers Cubs Shirt 500.00 800.00
☐ 169 Bob Ewing 60.00 100.00
☐ 170 Cecil Ferguson 60.00 100.00
☐ 171 Hobe Ferris 60.00 100.00
☐ 172 Lou Fiene Portrait 60.00 100.00
☐ 173 Lou Fiene Throwing 60.00 100.00
☐ 174 Steamer Flanagan 60.00 100.00
☐ 175 Art Fletcher 60.00 100.00
☐ 176 Elmer Flick 175.00 300.00
☐ 177 Russ Ford 60.00 100.00
☐ 178 Ed Foster 175.00 300.00
☐ 179 Jerry Freeman 60.00 100.00
☐ 180 John Frill 60.00 100.00
☐ 181 Charlie Fritz 175.00 300.00
☐ 182 Art Fromme 60.00 100.00
☐ 183 Chick Gandil 175.00 300.00
☐ 184 Bob Ganley 60.00 100.00
☐ 185 John Ganzel 60.00 100.00
☐ 186 Harry Gasper (Gaspar) 60.00 100.00
☐ 187 Rube Geyer 60.00 100.00
☐ 188 George Gibson 60.00 100.00
☐ 189 Billy Gilbert 60.00 100.00
☐ 190 Wilbur Goode (Good) 60.00 100.00
☐ 191 Bill Graham St. Louis 60.00 100.00
☐ 192 Peaches Graham 70.00 120.00
☐ 193 Dolly Gray 60.00 100.00
☐ 194 Ed Greminger 175.00 300.00
☐ 195 Clark Griffith Batting 175.00 300.00
☐ 196 Clark Griffith Portrait 175.00 300.00
☐ 197 Moose Grimshaw 60.00 100.00
☐ 198 Bob Groom 60.00 100.00
☐ 199 Tom Guiheen 175.00 300.00
☐ 200 Ed Hahn 60.00 100.00
☐ 201 Bob Hall 60.00 100.00
☐ 202 Bill Hallman 60.00 100.00
☐ 203 Jack Hannifan (Hannifin) 60.00 100.00
☐ 204 Bill Hart Little Rock 175.00 300.00
☐ 205 Jimmy Hart Montgomery 175.00 300.00
☐ 206 Topsy Hartsel 60.00 100.00
☐ 207 Jack Hayden 60.00 100.00
☐ 208 J.Ross Helm 175.00 300.00
☐ 209 Charlie Hemphill 60.00 100.00
☐ 210 Buck Herzog Boston 60.00 100.00
☐ 211 Buck Herzog New York 60.00 100.00
☐ 212 Gordon Hickman 175.00 300.00
☐ 213 Bill Hinchman 60.00 100.00
☐ 214 Harry Hinchman 60.00 100.00
☐ 215 Doc Hoblitzell 60.00 100.00
☐ 216 Danny Hoffman St. Louis 60.00 100.00
☐ 217 Izzy Hoffman Providence 60.00 100.00
☐ 218 Solly Hofman 60.00 100.00
☐ 219 Buck Hooker 175.00 300.00
☐ 220 Del Howard Chicago 60.00 100.00
☐ 221 Ernie Howard Savannah 175.00 300.00
☐ 222 Harry Howell Hand at Waist 60.00 100.00
☐ 223 Harry Howell Portrait 60.00 100.00
☐ 224 M.Huggins Mouth 175.00 300.00
☐ 225 M.Huggins Portrait 175.00 300.00
☐ 226 Rudy Hulswitt 60.00 100.00
☐ 227 John Hummel 60.00 100.00
☐ 228 George Hunter 60.00 100.00
☐ 229 Frank Isbell 60.00 100.00
☐ 230 Fred Jacklitsch 60.00 100.00
☐ 231 Jimmy Jackson 60.00 100.00
☐ 232 H.Jennings Both 175.00 300.00
☐ 233 H.Jennings One 175.00 300.00

| | | |
|---|---|---|
| ❑ 234 H.Jennings Portrait | 175.00 | 300.00 |
| ❑ 235 Walter Johnson Hands | 700.00 | 1200.00 |
| ❑ 236 Walter Johnson Port | 1000.00 | 1800.00 |
| ❑ 237 Davy Jones Detroit | 60.00 | 100.00 |
| ❑ 238 Fielder Jones Hands at Hips | 60.00 | 100.00 |
| ❑ 239 Fielder Jones Portrait | 60.00 | 100.00 |
| ❑ 240 Tom Jones St. Louis | 60.00 | 100.00 |
| ❑ 241 Dutch Jordan Atlanta | 175.00 | 300.00 |
| ❑ 242 Tim Jordan Batting | 60.00 | 100.00 |
| ❑ 243 Tim Jordan Portrait | 60.00 | 100.00 |
| ❑ 244 Addie Joss Pitching | 175.00 | 300.00 |
| ❑ 245 Addie Joss Portrait | 250.00 | 400.00 |
| ❑ 246 Ed Karger | 60.00 | 100.00 |
| ❑ 247 Willie Keeler Portrait | 350.00 | 600.00 |
| ❑ 248 Willie Keeler Batting | 350.00 | 600.00 |
| ❑ 249 Joe Kelley | 150.00 | 250.00 |
| ❑ 250 J.F. Kiernan | 300.00 | 500.00 |
| ❑ 251 Ed Killian Pitching | 60.00 | 100.00 |
| ❑ 252 Ed Killian Portrait | 60.00 | 100.00 |
| ❑ 253 Frank King | 175.00 | 300.00 |
| ❑ 254 Rube Kisinger (Kissinger) | 60.00 | 100.00 |
| ❑ 255 Red Kleinow Boston | 300.00 | 500.00 |
| ❑ 256 Red Kleinow NY Catch | 60.00 | 100.00 |
| ❑ 257 Red Kleinow NY Bat | 60.00 | 100.00 |
| ❑ 258 Johnny Kling | 60.00 | 100.00 |
| ❑ 259 Otto Knabe | 60.00 | 100.00 |
| ❑ 260 Jack Knight Portrait | 60.00 | 100.00 |
| ❑ 261 Jack Knight with Bat | 60.00 | 100.00 |
| ❑ 262 Ed Konetchy Glove Lo | 60.00 | 100.00 |
| ❑ 263 Ed Konetchy Glove Hi | 60.00 | 100.00 |
| ❑ 264 Harry Krause Pitching | 60.00 | 100.00 |
| ❑ 265 Harry Krause Portrait | 60.00 | 100.00 |
| ❑ 266 Rube Kroh | 60.00 | 100.00 |
| ❑ 267 Otto Kruger (Krueger) | 60.00 | 100.00 |
| ❑ 268 James LaFitte | 175.00 | 300.00 |
| ❑ 269 Nap Lajoie Portrait | 500.00 | 800.00 |
| ❑ 270 Nap Lajoie Throwing | 400.00 | 700.00 |
| ❑ 271 Nap Lajoie with Bat | 400.00 | 700.00 |
| ❑ 272 Joe Lake NY | 60.00 | 100.00 |
| ❑ 273 Joe Lake Stl No Ball | 60.00 | 100.00 |
| ❑ 274 Joe Lake Stl with Ball | 60.00 | 100.00 |
| ❑ 275 Frank LaPorte | 60.00 | 100.00 |
| ❑ 276 Arlie Latham | 60.00 | 100.00 |
| ❑ 277 Bill Lattimore | 60.00 | 100.00 |
| ❑ 278 Jimmy Lavender | 60.00 | 100.00 |
| ❑ 279 Tommy Leach Bending Over | 60.00 | 100.00 |
| ❑ 280 Tommy Leach Portrait | 60.00 | 100.00 |
| ❑ 281 Lefty Leifield Batting | 60.00 | 100.00 |
| ❑ 282 Lefty Leifield Pitching | 60.00 | 100.00 |
| ❑ 283 Ed Lennox | 60.00 | 100.00 |
| ❑ 284 Harry Lentz (Sentz) SL | 250.00 | 400.00 |
| ❑ 285 Glenn Liebhardt | 60.00 | 100.00 |
| ❑ 286 Vive Lindaman | 60.00 | 100.00 |
| ❑ 287 Perry Lipe | 175.00 | 300.00 |
| ❑ 288 Paddy Livingstone (Livingston) | 60.00 | 100.00 |
| ❑ 289 Hans Lobert | 60.00 | 100.00 |
| ❑ 290 Harry Lord | 60.00 | 100.00 |
| ❑ 291 Harry Lumley | 60.00 | 100.00 |
| ❑ 292 Carl Lundgren Chicago | 500.00 | 800.00 |
| ❑ 293 Carl Lundgren Kansas City | 125.00 | 200.00 |
| ❑ 294 Nick Maddox | 60.00 | 100.00 |
| ❑ 294 Sherry Magie Portrait ERR | 15000.00 | 25000.00 |
| ❑ 295 Sherry Magee with Bat | 60.00 | 100.00 |
| ❑ 296 Sherry Magee Portrait | 150.00 | 250.00 |
| ❑ 298 Bill Malarkey | 60.00 | 100.00 |
| ❑ 299 Bill Maloney | 60.00 | 100.00 |
| ❑ 300 George Manion | 175.00 | 300.00 |
| ❑ 301 Rube Manning Batting | 60.00 | 100.00 |
| ❑ 302 Rube Manning Pitching | 60.00 | 100.00 |
| ❑ 303 R.Marquard Follow | 175.00 | 300.00 |
| ❑ 304 R.Marquard Hands | 175.00 | 300.00 |
| ❑ 305 R.Marquard Portrait | 200.00 | 350.00 |
| ❑ 306 Doc Marshall | 60.00 | 100.00 |
| ❑ 307 C.Mathewson Drk Cap | 700.00 | 1200.00 |
| ❑ 308 C.Mathewson Portrait | 900.00 | 1500.00 |
| ❑ 309 C.Mathewson Wht Cap | 900.00 | 1500.00 |
| ❑ 310 Al Mattern | 60.00 | 100.00 |
| ❑ 311 John McAleese | 60.00 | 100.00 |
| ❑ 312 George McBride | 60.00 | 100.00 |
| ❑ 313 Pat McCauley | 175.00 | 300.00 |
| ❑ 314 Moose McCormick | 60.00 | 100.00 |
| ❑ 315 Pryor McElveen | 60.00 | 100.00 |
| ❑ 316 Dennis McGann | 60.00 | 100.00 |
| ❑ 317 Jim McGinley | 60.00 | 100.00 |
| ❑ 318 Iron Man McGinnity | 175.00 | 300.00 |
| ❑ 319 Stoney McGlynn | 60.00 | 100.00 |
| ❑ 320 J.McGraw Finger | 250.00 | 400.00 |
| ❑ 321 J.McGraw Glove-Hip | 250.00 | 400.00 |
| ❑ 322 J.McGraw w/o Cap | 250.00 | 400.00 |
| ❑ 323 J.McGraw w/Cap | 250.00 | 400.00 |
| ❑ 324 Harry McIntyre Brooklyn | 60.00 | 100.00 |
| ❑ 325 Harry McIntyre Brooklyn-Chicago | 60.00 | 100.00 |
| ❑ 326 Matty McIntyre Detroit | 60.00 | 100.00 |
| ❑ 327 Larry McLean | 60.00 | 100.00 |
| ❑ 328 George McQuillan Ball in Hand | 60.00 | 100.00 |
| ❑ 329 George McQuillan with Bat | 60.00 | 100.00 |
| ❑ 330 Fred Merkle Portrait | 70.00 | 120.00 |
| ❑ 331 Fred Merkle Throwing | 90.00 | 150.00 |
| ❑ 332 George Merritt | 60.00 | 100.00 |
| ❑ 333 Chief Meyers | 60.00 | 100.00 |
| ❑ 334 Chief Myers Batting (Meyers) | 70.00 | 120.00 |
| ❑ 335 Chief Myers Fielding (Meyers) | 60.00 | 100.00 |
| ❑ 336 Clyde Milan | 60.00 | 100.00 |
| ❑ 337 Molly Miller Dallas | 175.00 | 300.00 |
| ❑ 338 Dots Miller Pittsburgh | 60.00 | 100.00 |
| ❑ 339 Bill Milligan | 60.00 | 100.00 |
| ❑ 340 Fred Mitchell Toronto | 60.00 | 100.00 |
| ❑ 341 Mike Mitchell Cincinnati | 60.00 | 100.00 |
| ❑ 342 Dan Moeller | 60.00 | 100.00 |
| ❑ 343 Carleton Molesworth | 175.00 | 300.00 |
| ❑ 344 Herbie Moran Providence | 60.00 | 100.00 |
| ❑ 345 Pat Moran Chicago | 60.00 | 100.00 |
| ❑ 346 George Moriarty | 60.00 | 100.00 |
| ❑ 347 Mike Mowrey | 60.00 | 100.00 |
| ❑ 348 Dom Mullaney | 175.00 | 300.00 |
| ❑ 349 George Mullen (Mullin) | 60.00 | 100.00 |
| ❑ 350 George Mullin with Bat | 60.00 | 100.00 |
| ❑ 351 George Mullin Throwing | 60.00 | 100.00 |
| ❑ 352 Danny Murphy Batting | 60.00 | 100.00 |
| ❑ 353 Danny Murphy Throwing | 60.00 | 100.00 |
| ❑ 354 Red Murray Batting | 60.00 | 100.00 |
| ❑ 355 Red Murray Portrait | 60.00 | 100.00 |
| ❑ 356 Billy Nattress | 60.00 | 100.00 |
| ❑ 357 Tom Needham | 60.00 | 100.00 |
| ❑ 358 Simon Nicholls Hands on Knees | 60.00 | 100.00 |
| ❑ 359 Simon Nichols Batting (Nicholls) | 60.00 | 100.00 |
| ❑ 360 Harry Niles | 60.00 | 100.00 |
| ❑ 361 Rebel Oakes | 60.00 | 100.00 |
| ❑ 362 Frank Oberlin | 60.00 | 100.00 |
| ❑ 363 Peter O'Brien | 60.00 | 100.00 |
| ❑ 364 Bill O'Hara NY | 60.00 | 100.00 |
| ❑ 365 Bill O'Hara Stl | 6000.00 | 10000.00 |
| ❑ 366 Rube Oldring Batting | 60.00 | 100.00 |
| ❑ 367 Rube Oldring Fielding | 60.00 | 100.00 |
| ❑ 368 Charley O'Leary Hands on Knees | 60.00 | 100.00 |
| ❑ 369 Charley O'Leary Portrait | 60.00 | 100.00 |
| ❑ 370 William O'Neil | 150.00 | 250.00 |
| ❑ 371 Albert Orth | 175.00 | 300.00 |
| ❑ 372 William Otey | 175.00 | 300.00 |
| ❑ 373 Orval Overall Hand at Face | 60.00 | 100.00 |
| ❑ 374 Orval Overall Hands at Waist | 60.00 | 100.00 |
| ❑ 375 Orval Overall Portrait | 60.00 | 100.00 |
| ❑ 376 Frank Owen (Owens) | 60.00 | 100.00 |
| ❑ 377 George Paige | 175.00 | 300.00 |
| ❑ 378 Fred Parent | 60.00 | 100.00 |
| ❑ 379 Dode Paskert | 60.00 | 100.00 |
| ❑ 380 Jim Pastorius | 60.00 | 100.00 |
| ❑ 381 Harry Pattee | 60.00 | 100.00 |
| ❑ 382 Fred Payne | 60.00 | 100.00 |
| ❑ 383 Barney Pelty Horizontal | 60.00 | 100.00 |
| ❑ 384 Barney Pelty Vertical | 60.00 | 100.00 |
| ❑ 385 Hub Perdue | 175.00 | 300.00 |
| ❑ 386 George Perring | 60.00 | 100.00 |
| ❑ 387 Arch Persons | 175.00 | 300.00 |
| ❑ 388 Francis Pfeffer | 60.00 | 100.00 |
| ❑ 389 Jake Pfeister Seated (Pfiester) | 60.00 | 100.00 |
| ❑ 390 Jake Pfeister Throwing (Pfiester) | 60.00 | 100.00 |
| ❑ 391 Jimmy Phelan | 60.00 | 100.00 |
| ❑ 392 Eddie Phelps | 60.00 | 100.00 |
| ❑ 393 Deacon Phillippe | 60.00 | 100.00 |
| ❑ 394 Ollie Pickering | 60.00 | 100.00 |
| ❑ 395 Eddie Plank | 45000.00 | 60000.00 |
| ❑ 396 Phil Poland | 60.00 | 100.00 |
| ❑ 397 Jack Powell | 60.00 | 100.00 |
| ❑ 398 Mike Powers | 60.00 | 100.00 |
| ❑ 399 Billy Purtell | 60.00 | 100.00 |
| ❑ 400 Ambrose Puttman (Puttmann) | 85.00 | 135.00 |
| ❑ 401 Lee Quillen (Quillin) | 60.00 | 100.00 |
| ❑ 402 Jack Quinn | 60.00 | 100.00 |
| ❑ 403 Newt Randall | 60.00 | 100.00 |
| ❑ 404 Bugs Raymond | 60.00 | 100.00 |
| ❑ 405 Ed Reagan | 175.00 | 300.00 |
| ❑ 406 Ed Reulbach Glove | 60.00 | 100.00 |
| ❑ 407 Ed Reulbach No Glove | 70.00 | 120.00 |
| ❑ 408 Dutch Revelle | 175.00 | 300.00 |
| ❑ 409 Bob Rhoades Hands | 60.00 | 100.00 |
| ❑ 410 Bob Rhoades Right | 60.00 | 100.00 |
| ❑ 411 Charlie Rhodes | 60.00 | 100.00 |
| ❑ 412 Claude Ritchey | 60.00 | 100.00 |
| ❑ 413 Lou Ritter | 60.00 | 100.00 |
| ❑ 414 Ike Rockenfeld | 175.00 | 300.00 |
| ❑ 415 Claude Rossman | 60.00 | 100.00 |
| ❑ 416 Nap Rucker Portrait | 60.00 | 100.00 |
| ❑ 417 Nap Rucker Throwing | 60.00 | 100.00 |
| ❑ 418 Dick Rudolph | 60.00 | 100.00 |
| ❑ 419 Ray Ryan | 175.00 | 300.00 |
| ❑ 420 Germany Schaefer Det | 60.00 | 100.00 |
| ❑ 421 Germany Schaefer Wash | 60.00 | 100.00 |
| ❑ 422 George Schirm | 85.00 | 135.00 |
| ❑ 423 Larry Schlafly | 60.00 | 100.00 |
| ❑ 424 Admiral Schlei Batting | 60.00 | 100.00 |
| ❑ 425 Admiral Schlei Catching | 60.00 | 100.00 |
| ❑ 426 Admiral Schlei Portrait | 60.00 | 100.00 |
| ❑ 427 Boss Schmidt Portrait | 60.00 | 100.00 |
| ❑ 428 Boss Schmidt Throwing | 60.00 | 100.00 |
| ❑ 429 Ossee Schreck (Schreckengost) | 70.00 | 120.00 |
| ❑ 430 Wildfire Schulte Back View | 60.00 | 100.00 |
| ❑ 431 Wildfire Schulte Front View | 175.00 | 300.00 |
| ❑ 432 Jim Scott | 60.00 | 100.00 |
| ❑ 433 Charles Seitz | 175.00 | 300.00 |
| ❑ 434 Cy Seymour Batting | 60.00 | 100.00 |
| ❑ 435 Cy Seymour Portrait | 60.00 | 100.00 |
| ❑ 436 Cy Seymour Throwing | 60.00 | 100.00 |
| ❑ 437 Spike Shannon | 60.00 | 100.00 |
| ❑ 438 Bud Sharpe | 60.00 | 100.00 |
| ❑ 439 Bud Shappe ERR (Sharpe) ML | | |
| ❑ 440 Frank Shaughnessy SL | 175.00 | 300.00 |
| ❑ 441 Al Shaw St. Louis | 60.00 | 100.00 |
| ❑ 442 Hunky Shaw Providence | 60.00 | 100.00 |
| ❑ 443 Jimmy Sheckard Glove | 60.00 | 100.00 |
| ❑ 444 Jimmy Sheckard No Glove | 60.00 | 100.00 |
| ❑ 445 Bill Shipke | 60.00 | 100.00 |
| ❑ 446 Jimmy Slagle | 60.00 | 100.00 |
| ❑ 447 Carlos Smith Shreveport | 175.00 | 300.00 |
| ❑ 448 Frank Smith Chi-Bos | 350.00 | 600.00 |
| ❑ 449 Frank Smith Chi F.Smith | 60.00 | 100.00 |
| ❑ 450 Frank Smith Chi Whit Cap | 60.00 | 100.00 |
| ❑ 451 Heinie Smith Buffalo | 60.00 | 100.00 |
| ❑ 452 Happy Smith Brooklyn | 60.00 | 100.00 |
| ❑ 453 Sid Smith Atlanta | 175.00 | 300.00 |
| ❑ 454 F.Snodgrass Batting | 60.00 | 100.00 |
| ❑ 455 F.nodgrass Batting ERR | | |
| ❑ 456 F.Snodgrass Catching | 60.00 | 100.00 |
| ❑ 457 Bob Spade | 60.00 | 100.00 |
| ❑ 458 Tris Speaker | 600.00 | 1000.00 |
| ❑ 459 Tubby Spencer | 60.00 | 100.00 |
| ❑ 460 Jake Stahl Glove | 85.00 | 135.00 |
| ❑ 461 Jake Stahl No Glove | 60.00 | 100.00 |
| ❑ 462 Oscar Stanage | 60.00 | 100.00 |
| ❑ 463 Dolly Stark | 175.00 | 300.00 |
| ❑ 464 Charlie Starr | 60.00 | 100.00 |
| ❑ 465 Harry Steinfeldt with Bat | 60.00 | 100.00 |
| ❑ 466 Harry Steinfeldt Portrait | 60.00 | 100.00 |
| ❑ 467 Jim Stephens | 60.00 | 100.00 |
| ❑ 468 George Stone | 60.00 | 100.00 |
| ❑ 469 George Stovall Batting | 60.00 | 100.00 |
| ❑ 470 George Stovall Portrait | 60.00 | 100.00 |
| ❑ 471 Sam Strang | 60.00 | 100.00 |
| ❑ 472 Gabby Street Catching | 60.00 | 100.00 |
| ❑ 473 Gabby Street Portrait | 60.00 | 100.00 |
| ❑ 474 Billy Sullivan | 60.00 | 100.00 |
| ❑ 475 Ed Summers | 60.00 | 100.00 |
| ❑ 476 Bill Sweeney Boston | 60.00 | 100.00 |
| ❑ 477 Jeff Sweeney New York | 60.00 | 100.00 |
| ❑ 478 Jesse Tannehill Washington | 60.00 | 100.00 |
| ❑ 479 Lee Tannehill Chi L.Tannehill | 60.00 | 100.00 |
| ❑ 480 Lee Tannehill Chi Tannehill | 60.00 | 100.00 |
| ❑ 481 Dummy Taylor | 60.00 | 100.00 |
| ❑ 482 Fred Tenney | 60.00 | 100.00 |
| ❑ 483 Tony Thebo | 175.00 | 300.00 |
| ❑ 484 Jake Thielman | 90.00 | 150.00 |
| ❑ 485 Ira Thomas | 60.00 | 100.00 |
| ❑ 486 Woodie Thornton | 175.00 | 300.00 |
| ❑ 487 J.Tinker Bat off Shldr | 250.00 | 400.00 |
| ❑ 488 J.Tinker Bat on Shldr | 400.00 | 400.00 |
| ❑ 489 J.Tinker Hand-Knee | 350.00 | 600.00 |
| ❑ 490 J.Tinker Portrait | 350.00 | 600.00 |
| ❑ 491 John Titus | 60.00 | 100.00 |
| ❑ 492 Terry Turner | 60.00 | 100.00 |
| ❑ 493 Bob Unglaub | 60.00 | 100.00 |
| ❑ 494 Juan Violat (Viola) | 175.00 | 300.00 |
| ❑ 495 R.Waddell Portrait | 250.00 | 400.00 |
| ❑ 496 R.Waddell Throwing | 250.00 | 400.00 |
| ❑ 497 Heinie Wagner on Left | 60.00 | 100.00 |

| | | |
|---|---|---|
| 498 Heinie Wagner on Right | 60.00 | 100.00 |
| 499 Honus Wagner | 250000.00 | 350000.00 |
| 500 Bobby Wallace | 175.00 | 300.00 |
| 501 Ed Walsh | 250.00 | 400.00 |
| 502 Jack Warhop | 60.00 | 100.00 |
| 503 Jake Weimer | 60.00 | 100.00 |
| 504 James Westlake | 175.00 | 300.00 |
| 505 Zack Wheat | 200.00 | 350.00 |
| 506 Doc White Pitching | 60.00 | 100.00 |
| 507 Doc White Portrait | 60.00 | 100.00 |
| 508 Foley White Houston | 175.00 | 300.00 |
| 509 Jack White Buffalo | 60.00 | 100.00 |
| 510 Kaiser Wilhelm Hands | 60.00 | 100.00 |
| 511 Kaiser Wilhelm with Bat | 60.00 | 100.00 |
| 512 Ed Willett with Bat | 60.00 | 100.00 |
| 513 Ed Willetts Throwing (Willett) | 60.00 | 100.00 |
| 514 Jimmy Williams | 60.00 | 100.00 |
| 515 Vic Willis Pitt | 200.00 | 350.00 |
| 516 Vic Willis Stl Throw | 175.00 | 300.00 |
| 517 Vic Willis Stl Bat | 175.00 | 300.00 |
| 518 Owen Wilson | 60.00 | 100.00 |
| 519 Hooks Wiltse Pitching | 60.00 | 100.00 |
| 520 Hooks Wiltse Portrait | 60.00 | 100.00 |
| 521 Hooks Wiltse Sweater | 60.00 | 100.00 |
| 522 Lucky Wright | 60.00 | 100.00 |
| 523 Cy Young Bare Hand | 700.00 | 1200.00 |
| 524 Cy Young w/Glove | 700.00 | 1200.00 |
| 525 Cy Young Portrait | 1000.00 | 1800.00 |
| 526 Irv Young Minneapolis | 70.00 | 120.00 |
| 527 Heinie Zimmerman | 60.00 | 100.00 |

## 1952 Topps

| | | |
|---|---|---|
| COMP.MASTER SET (487) | 40000.00 | 80000.00 |
| COMPLETE SET (407) | 40000.00 | 65000.00 |
| COMMON CARD (1-80) | 35.00 | 60.00 |
| COMMON CARD (81-250) | 20.00 | 40.00 |
| COMMON CARD (251-310) | 30.00 | 50.00 |
| COMMON CARD (311-407) | 150.00 | 250.00 |
| WRAPPER (1-CENT) | 200.00 | 250.00 |
| WRAPPER (5-CENT) | 75.00 | 100.00 |
| 1 Andy Pafko | 3000.00 | 5000.00 |
| 1A Andy Pafko Black | 1800.00 | 3000.00 |
| 2 Pete Runnels RC | 150.00 | 250.00 |
| 2A Pete Runnels Black | 150.00 | 250.00 |
| 3 Hank Thompson | 40.00 | 70.00 |
| 3A Hank Thompson Black | 40.00 | 70.00 |
| 4 Don Lenhardt | 35.00 | 60.00 |
| 4A Don Lenhardt Black | 35.00 | 60.00 |
| 5 Larry Jansen | 40.00 | 70.00 |
| 5A Larry Jansen Black | 40.00 | 70.00 |
| 6 Grady Hatton | 35.00 | 60.00 |
| 6A Grady Hatton Black | 35.00 | 60.00 |
| 7 Wayne Terwilliger | 35.00 | 60.00 |
| 7A Wayne Terwilliger Black | 35.00 | 60.00 |
| 8 Fred Marsh RC | 35.00 | 60.00 |
| 8A Fred Marsh Black | 35.00 | 60.00 |
| 9 Robert Hogue RC | 35.00 | 60.00 |
| 9A Robert Hogue Black | 35.00 | 60.00 |
| 10 Al Rosen | 40.00 | 70.00 |
| 10A Al Rosen Black | 40.00 | 70.00 |
| 11 Phil Rizzuto | 250.00 | 400.00 |
| 11A Phil Rizzuto Black | 200.00 | 350.00 |
| 12 Monty Basgall RC | 35.00 | 60.00 |
| 12A Monty Basgall Black | 35.00 | 60.00 |
| 13 Johnny Wyrostek | 35.00 | 60.00 |
| 13A Johnny Wyrostek Black | 35.00 | 60.00 |
| 14 Bob Elliott | 40.00 | 70.00 |
| 14A Bob Elliott Black | 40.00 | 70.00 |
| 15 Johnny Pesky | 40.00 | 70.00 |
| 15A Johnny Pesky Black | 40.00 | 70.00 |
| 16 Gene Hermanski | 35.00 | 60.00 |
| 16A Gene Hermanski Black | 35.00 | 60.00 |
| 17 Jim Hegan | 40.00 | 70.00 |
| 17A Jim Hegan Black | 40.00 | 70.00 |

| | | |
|---|---|---|
| 18 Merrill Combs RC | 35.00 | 60.00 |
| 18A Merrill Combs Black | 35.00 | 60.00 |
| 19 Johnny Bucha RC | 35.00 | 60.00 |
| 19A Johnny Bucha Black | 35.00 | 60.00 |
| 20 Billy Loes SP RC | 90.00 | 150.00 |
| 20A Billy Loes Black | 90.00 | 150.00 |
| 21 Ferris Fain | 40.00 | 70.00 |
| 21A Ferris Fain Black | 40.00 | 70.00 |
| 22 Dom DiMaggio | 75.00 | 125.00 |
| 22A Dom DiMaggio Black | 60.00 | 100.00 |
| 23 Billy Goodman | 40.00 | 70.00 |
| 23A Billy Goodman Black | 40.00 | 70.00 |
| 24 Luke Easter | 50.00 | 80.00 |
| 24A Luke Easter Black | 50.00 | 80.00 |
| 25 Johnny Groth | 35.00 | 60.00 |
| 25A Johnny Groth Black | 35.00 | 60.00 |
| 26 Monte Irvin | 90.00 | 150.00 |
| 26A Monte Irvin Black | 90.00 | 150.00 |
| 27 Sam Jethroe | 40.00 | 70.00 |
| 27A Sam Jethroe Black | 40.00 | 70.00 |
| 28 Jerry Priddy | 35.00 | 60.00 |
| 28A Jerry Priddy Black | 35.00 | 60.00 |
| 29 Ted Kluszewski | 75.00 | 125.00 |
| 29A Ted Kluszewski Black | 75.00 | 125.00 |
| 30 Mel Parnell | 40.00 | 70.00 |
| 30A Mel Parnell Black | 40.00 | 70.00 |
| 31 Gus Zernial Baseballs | 50.00 | 80.00 |
| 31A Gus Zernial Black | 50.00 | 80.00 |
| 32 Eddie Robinson | 35.00 | 60.00 |
| 32A Eddie Robinson Black | 35.00 | 60.00 |
| 33 Warren Spahn | 175.00 | 300.00 |
| 33A Warren Spahn Black | 175.00 | 300.00 |
| 34 Elmer Valo | 35.00 | 60.00 |
| 34A Elmer Valo Black | 35.00 | 60.00 |
| 35 Hank Sauer | 40.00 | 70.00 |
| 35A Hank Sauer Black | 40.00 | 70.00 |
| 36 Gil Hodges | 175.00 | 300.00 |
| 36A Gil Hodges Black | 175.00 | 300.00 |
| 37 Duke Snider | 300.00 | 500.00 |
| 37A Duke Snider Black | 300.00 | 500.00 |
| 38 Wally Westlake | 35.00 | 60.00 |
| 38A Wally Westlake Black | 35.00 | 60.00 |
| 39 Dizzy Trout | 40.00 | 70.00 |
| 39A Dizzy Trout Black | 40.00 | 70.00 |
| 40 Irv Noren | 40.00 | 70.00 |
| 40A Irv Noren Black | 40.00 | 70.00 |
| 41 Bob Wellman RC | 35.00 | 60.00 |
| 41A Bob Wellman Black | 35.00 | 60.00 |
| 42 Lou Kretlow RC | 35.00 | 60.00 |
| 42A Lou Kretlow Black | 35.00 | 60.00 |
| 43 Ray Scarborough | 35.00 | 60.00 |
| 43A Ray Scarborough Black | 35.00 | 60.00 |
| 44 Con Dempsey RC | 35.00 | 60.00 |
| 44A Con Dempsey Black | 35.00 | 60.00 |
| 45 Eddie Joost | 35.00 | 60.00 |
| 45A Eddie Joost Black | 35.00 | 60.00 |
| 46 Gordon Goldsberry RC | 35.00 | 60.00 |
| 46A Gordon Goldsberry Black | 35.00 | 60.00 |
| 47 Willie Jones | 40.00 | 70.00 |
| 47A Willie Jones Black | 40.00 | 70.00 |
| 48A Joe Page ERR BLA | 250.00 | 400.00 |
| 48B Joe Page COR Black | 75.00 | 125.00 |
| 48C Joe Page COR Red | 75.00 | 125.00 |
| 49A John Sain ERR BLA | 250.00 | 400.00 |
| 49B John Sain COR BLA | 75.00 | 125.00 |
| 49C Joe Page COR Red | 75.00 | 125.00 |
| 50 Marv Rickert RC | 35.00 | 60.00 |
| 50A Marv Rickert Black | 35.00 | 60.00 |
| 51 Jim Russell | 35.00 | 60.00 |
| 51A Jim Russell Black | 35.00 | 60.00 |
| 52 Don Mueller | 40.00 | 70.00 |
| 52A Don Mueller Black | 40.00 | 70.00 |
| 53 Chris Van Cuyk RC | 35.00 | 60.00 |
| 53A Chris Van Cuyk Black | 35.00 | 60.00 |
| 54 Leo Kiely RC | 35.00 | 60.00 |
| 54A Leo Kiely Black | 35.00 | 60.00 |
| 55 Ray Boone | 50.00 | 80.00 |
| 55A Ray Boone Black | 50.00 | 80.00 |
| 56 Tommy Glaviano | 35.00 | 60.00 |
| 56A Tommy Glaviano Black | 35.00 | 60.00 |
| 57 Ed Lopat | 60.00 | 100.00 |
| 57A Ed Lopat Black | 60.00 | 100.00 |
| 58 Bob Mahoney RC | 35.00 | 60.00 |
| 58A Bob Mahoney Black | 35.00 | 60.00 |
| 59 Robin Roberts | 100.00 | 175.00 |
| 59A Robin Roberts Black | 100.00 | 175.00 |
| 60 Sid Hudson | 35.00 | 60.00 |
| 60A Sid Hudson Black | 35.00 | 60.00 |

| | | |
|---|---|---|
| 61 Tookie Gilbert | 35.00 | 60.00 |
| 61A Tookie Gilbert Black | 35.00 | 60.00 |
| 62 Chuck Stobbs RC | 35.00 | 60.00 |
| 62A Chuck Stobbs Black | 35.00 | 60.00 |
| 63 Howie Pollet | 35.00 | 60.00 |
| 63A Howie Pollet Black | 35.00 | 60.00 |
| 64 Roy Sievers | 40.00 | 70.00 |
| 64A Roy Sievers Black | 40.00 | 70.00 |
| 65 Enos Slaughter | 100.00 | 175.00 |
| 65A Enos Slaughter Black | 100.00 | 175.00 |
| 66 Preacher Roe | 60.00 | 100.00 |
| 66A Preacher Roe Black | 60.00 | 100.00 |
| 67 Allie Reynolds | 75.00 | 125.00 |
| 67A Allie Reynolds Black | 75.00 | 125.00 |
| 68 Cliff Chambers | 35.00 | 60.00 |
| 68A Cliff Chambers Black | 35.00 | 60.00 |
| 69 Virgil Stallcup | 35.00 | 60.00 |
| 69A Virgil Stallcup Black | 35.00 | 60.00 |
| 70 Al Zarilla | 35.00 | 60.00 |
| 70A Al Zarilla Black | 35.00 | 60.00 |
| 71 Tom Upton RC | 35.00 | 60.00 |
| 71A Tom Upton Black | 35.00 | 60.00 |
| 72 Karl Olson RC | 35.00 | 60.00 |
| 72A Karl Olson Black | 35.00 | 60.00 |
| 73 Bill Werle | 35.00 | 60.00 |
| 73A Bill Werle Black | 35.00 | 60.00 |
| 74 Andy Hansen RC | 35.00 | 60.00 |
| 74A Andy Hansen Black | 35.00 | 60.00 |
| 75 Wes Westrum | 40.00 | 70.00 |
| 75A Wes Westrum Black | 40.00 | 70.00 |
| 76 Eddie Stanky | 40.00 | 70.00 |
| 76A Eddie Stanky Black | 40.00 | 70.00 |
| 77 Bob Kennedy | 40.00 | 70.00 |
| 77A Bob Kennedy Black | 40.00 | 70.00 |
| 78 Ellis Kinder | 35.00 | 60.00 |
| 78A Ellis Kinder Black | 35.00 | 60.00 |
| 79 Gerry Staley | 35.00 | 60.00 |
| 79A Gerry Staley Black | 35.00 | 60.00 |
| 80 Herman Wehmeier | 50.00 | 80.00 |
| 80A Herman Wehmeier Black | 50.00 | 80.00 |
| 81 Vern Law | 50.00 | 80.00 |
| 82 Duane Pillette | 20.00 | 40.00 |
| 83 Billy Johnson | 20.00 | 40.00 |
| 84 Vern Stephens | 30.00 | 50.00 |
| 85 Bob Kuzava | 30.00 | 50.00 |
| 86 Ted Gray | 20.00 | 40.00 |
| 87 Dale Coogan | 20.00 | 40.00 |
| 88 Bob Feller | 150.00 | 250.00 |
| 89 Johnny Lipon | 20.00 | 40.00 |
| 90 Mickey Grasso | 20.00 | 40.00 |
| 91 Red Schoendienst | 90.00 | 150.00 |
| 92 Dale Mitchell | 30.00 | 50.00 |
| 93 Al Sima RC | 20.00 | 40.00 |
| 94 Sam Mele | 20.00 | 40.00 |
| 95 Ken Holcombe | 20.00 | 40.00 |
| 96 Willard Marshall | 20.00 | 40.00 |
| 97 Earl Torgeson | 20.00 | 40.00 |
| 98 Billy Pierce | 30.00 | 50.00 |
| 99 Gene Woodling | 35.00 | 60.00 |
| 100 Del Rice | 20.00 | 40.00 |
| 101 Max Lanier | 20.00 | 40.00 |
| 102 Bill Kennedy | 20.00 | 40.00 |
| 103 Cliff Mapes | 20.00 | 40.00 |
| 104 Don Kolloway | 20.00 | 40.00 |
| 105 Johnny Pramesa | 20.00 | 40.00 |
| 106 Mickey Vernon | 35.00 | 60.00 |
| 107 Connie Ryan | 20.00 | 40.00 |
| 108 Jim Konstanty | 35.00 | 60.00 |
| 109 Ted Wilks | 20.00 | 40.00 |
| 110 Dutch Leonard | 20.00 | 40.00 |
| 111 Peanuts Lowrey | 20.00 | 40.00 |
| 112 Hank Majeski | 20.00 | 40.00 |
| 113 Dick Sisler | 30.00 | 50.00 |
| 114 Willard Ramsdell | 20.00 | 40.00 |
| 115 George Munger | 20.00 | 40.00 |
| 116 Carl Scheib | 20.00 | 40.00 |
| 117 Sherm Lollar | 30.00 | 50.00 |
| 118 Ken Raffensberger | 20.00 | 40.00 |
| 119 Mickey McDermott | 20.00 | 40.00 |
| 120 Bob Chakales RC | 20.00 | 40.00 |
| 121 Gus Niarhos | 20.00 | 40.00 |
| 122 Jackie Jensen | 50.00 | 80.00 |
| 123 Eddie Yost | 30.00 | 50.00 |
| 124 Monte Kennedy | 20.00 | 40.00 |
| 125 Bill Rigney | 20.00 | 40.00 |
| 126 Fred Hutchinson | 30.00 | 50.00 |
| 127 Paul Minner RC | 20.00 | 40.00 |
| 128 Don Bollweg RC | 20.00 | 40.00 |

|  |  | | |
|---|---|---|---|
| 129 | Johnny Mize | 90.00 | 150.00 |
| 130 | Sheldon Jones | 20.00 | 40.00 |
| 131 | Morrie Martin RC | 20.00 | 40.00 |
| 132 | Clyde Klutz RC | 20.00 | 40.00 |
| 133 | Al Widmar | 20.00 | 40.00 |
| 134 | Joe Tipton | 20.00 | 40.00 |
| 135 | Dixie Howell | 20.00 | 40.00 |
| 136 | Johnny Schmitz | 20.00 | 40.00 |
| 137 | Roy McMillan RC | 30.00 | 50.00 |
| 138 | Bill MacDonald | 20.00 | 40.00 |
| 139 | Ken Wood | 20.00 | 40.00 |
| 140 | Johnny Antonelli | 35.00 | 60.00 |
| 141 | Clint Hartung | 20.00 | 40.00 |
| 142 | Harry Perkowski RC | 20.00 | 40.00 |
| 143 | Les Moss | 20.00 | 40.00 |
| 144 | Ed Blake RC | 20.00 | 40.00 |
| 145 | Joe Haynes | 20.00 | 40.00 |
| 146 | Frank House RC | 20.00 | 40.00 |
| 147 | Bob Young RC | 20.00 | 40.00 |
| 148 | Johnny Klippstein | 20.00 | 40.00 |
| 149 | Dick Kryhoski | 20.00 | 40.00 |
| 150 | Ted Beard | 20.00 | 40.00 |
| 151 | Wally Post RC | 30.00 | 50.00 |
| 152 | Al Evans | 20.00 | 40.00 |
| 153 | Bob Rush | 20.00 | 40.00 |
| 154 | Joe Muir RC | 20.00 | 40.00 |
| 155 | Frank Overmire | 20.00 | 40.00 |
| 156 | Frank Hiller RC | 20.00 | 40.00 |
| 157 | Bob Usher | 20.00 | 40.00 |
| 158 | Eddie Waitkus | 20.00 | 40.00 |
| 159 | Saul Rogovin RC | 20.00 | 40.00 |
| 160 | Owen Friend | 20.00 | 40.00 |
| 161 | Bud Byerly RC | 20.00 | 40.00 |
| 162 | Del Crandall | 30.00 | 50.00 |
| 163 | Stan Rojek | 20.00 | 40.00 |
| 164 | Walt Dubiel | 20.00 | 40.00 |
| 165 | Eddie Kazak | 20.00 | 40.00 |
| 166 | Paul LaPalme RC | 20.00 | 40.00 |
| 167 | Bill Howerton | 20.00 | 40.00 |
| 168 | Charlie Silvera RC | 35.00 | 60.00 |
| 169 | Howie Judson | 20.00 | 40.00 |
| 170 | Gus Bell | 30.00 | 50.00 |
| 171 | Ed Erautt RC | 20.00 | 40.00 |
| 172 | Eddie Miksis | 20.00 | 40.00 |
| 173 | Roy Smalley | 20.00 | 40.00 |
| 174 | Clarence Marshall RC | 35.00 | 60.00 |
| 175 | Billy Martin RC | 300.00 | 500.00 |
| 176 | Hank Edwards | 20.00 | 40.00 |
| 177 | Bill Wight | 20.00 | 40.00 |
| 178 | Cass Michaels | 20.00 | 40.00 |
| 179 | Frank Smith RC | 20.00 | 40.00 |
| 180 | Charlie Maxwell RC | 30.00 | 50.00 |
| 181 | Bob Swift | 20.00 | 40.00 |
| 182 | Billy Hitchcock | 20.00 | 40.00 |
| 183 | Erv Dusak | 20.00 | 40.00 |
| 184 | Bob Ramazzotti | 20.00 | 40.00 |
| 185 | Bill Nicholson | 30.00 | 50.00 |
| 186 | Walt Masterson | 20.00 | 40.00 |
| 187 | Bob Miller | 20.00 | 40.00 |
| 188 | Clarence Podbielan RC | 20.00 | 40.00 |
| 189 | Pete Reiser | 35.00 | 60.00 |
| 190 | Don Johnson RC | 20.00 | 40.00 |
| 191 | Yogi Berra | 500.00 | 800.00 |
| 192 | Myron Ginsberg RC | 20.00 | 40.00 |
| 193 | Harry Simpson RC | 30.00 | 50.00 |
| 194 | Joe Hatton | 20.00 | 40.00 |
| 195 | Minnie Minoso RC | 90.00 | 150.00 |
| 196 | Solly Hemus RC | 35.00 | 60.00 |
| 197 | George Strickland RC | 20.00 | 40.00 |
| 198 | Phil Haugstad RC | 20.00 | 40.00 |
| 199 | George Zuverink RC | 20.00 | 40.00 |
| 200 | Ralph Houk RC | 50.00 | 80.00 |
| 201 | Alex Kellner | 20.00 | 40.00 |
| 202 | Joe Collins RC | 35.00 | 60.00 |
| 203 | Curt Simmons | 35.00 | 60.00 |
| 204 | Ron Northey | 20.00 | 40.00 |
| 205 | Clyde King | 35.00 | 60.00 |
| 206 | Joe Ostrowski RC | 20.00 | 40.00 |
| 207 | Mickey Harris | 20.00 | 40.00 |
| 208 | Marlin Stuart RC | 20.00 | 40.00 |
| 209 | Howie Fox | 20.00 | 40.00 |
| 210 | Dick Fowler | 20.00 | 40.00 |
| 211 | Ray Coleman | 20.00 | 40.00 |
| 212 | Ned Garver | 20.00 | 40.00 |
| 213 | Nippy Jones | 20.00 | 40.00 |
| 214 | Johnny Hopp | 30.00 | 50.00 |
| 215 | Hank Bauer | 60.00 | 100.00 |
| 216 | Richie Ashburn | 150.00 | 250.00 |
| 217 | Snuffy Stirnweiss | 30.00 | 50.00 |
| 218 | Clyde McCullough | 20.00 | 40.00 |
| 219 | Bobby Shantz | 35.00 | 60.00 |
| 220 | Joe Presko RC | 20.00 | 40.00 |
| 221 | Granny Hamner | 20.00 | 40.00 |
| 222 | Hoot Evers | 20.00 | 40.00 |
| 223 | Del Ennis | 30.00 | 50.00 |
| 224 | Bruce Edwards | 20.00 | 40.00 |
| 225 | Frank Baumholtz | 20.00 | 40.00 |
| 226 | Dave Philley | 20.00 | 40.00 |
| 227 | Joe Garagiola | 50.00 | 80.00 |
| 228 | Al Brazle | 20.00 | 40.00 |
| 229 | Gene Bearden UER | 20.00 | 40.00 |
| 230 | Matt Batts | 20.00 | 40.00 |
| 231 | Sam Zoldak | 20.00 | 40.00 |
| 232 | Billy Cox | 30.00 | 50.00 |
| 233 | Bob Friend RC | 50.00 | 80.00 |
| 234 | Steve Souchock RC | 20.00 | 40.00 |
| 235 | Walt Dropo | 20.00 | 40.00 |
| 236 | Ed Fitzgerald | 20.00 | 40.00 |
| 237 | Jerry Coleman | 35.00 | 60.00 |
| 238 | Art Houtteman | 20.00 | 40.00 |
| 239 | Rocky Bridges RC | 30.00 | 50.00 |
| 240 | Jack Phillips RC | 20.00 | 40.00 |
| 241 | Tommy Byrne | 20.00 | 40.00 |
| 242 | Tom Poholsky RC | 20.00 | 40.00 |
| 243 | Larry Doby | 50.00 | 80.00 |
| 244 | Vic Wertz | 20.00 | 40.00 |
| 245 | Sherry Robertson | 20.00 | 40.00 |
| 246 | George Kell | 50.00 | 80.00 |
| 247 | Randy Gumpert | 20.00 | 40.00 |
| 248 | Frank Shea | 20.00 | 40.00 |
| 249 | Bobby Adams | 20.00 | 40.00 |
| 250 | Carl Erskine | 60.00 | 100.00 |
| 251 | Chico Carrasquel | 30.00 | 50.00 |
| 252 | Vern Bickford | 20.00 | 40.00 |
| 253 | John Berardino | 60.00 | 100.00 |
| 254 | Joe Dobson | 30.00 | 50.00 |
| 255 | Clyde Vollmer | 20.00 | 40.00 |
| 256 | Pete Suder | 20.00 | 40.00 |
| 257 | Bobby Avila | 35.00 | 60.00 |
| 258 | Steve Gromek | 35.00 | 60.00 |
| 259 | Bob Addis RC | 20.00 | 40.00 |
| 260 | Pete Castiglione | 30.00 | 50.00 |
| 261 | Willie Mays | 2000.00 | 3000.00 |
| 262 | Virgil Trucks | 35.00 | 60.00 |
| 263 | Harry Brecheen | 35.00 | 60.00 |
| 264 | Roy Hartsfield | 30.00 | 50.00 |
| 265 | Chuck Diering | 30.00 | 50.00 |
| 266 | Murry Dickson | 30.00 | 50.00 |
| 267 | Sid Gordon | 35.00 | 60.00 |
| 268 | Bob Lemon | 90.00 | 150.00 |
| 269 | Willard Nixon | 30.00 | 50.00 |
| 270 | Lou Brissie | 30.00 | 50.00 |
| 271 | Jim Delsing | 30.00 | 50.00 |
| 272 | Mike Garcia | 50.00 | 80.00 |
| 273 | Erv Palica | 30.00 | 50.00 |
| 274 | Ralph Branca | 75.00 | 125.00 |
| 275 | Pat Mullin | 30.00 | 50.00 |
| 276 | Jim Wilson RC | 30.00 | 50.00 |
| 277 | Early Wynn | 100.00 | 175.00 |
| 278 | Allie Clark | 30.00 | 50.00 |
| 279 | Eddie Stewart | 30.00 | 50.00 |
| 280 | Cloyd Boyer | 30.00 | 50.00 |
| 281 | Tommy Brown SP | 50.00 | 80.00 |
| 282 | Birdie Tebbetts SP | 50.00 | 80.00 |
| 283 | Phil Masi SP | 35.00 | 60.00 |
| 284 | Hank Arft SP | 35.00 | 60.00 |
| 285 | Cliff Fannin SP | 35.00 | 60.00 |
| 286 | Joe DeMaestri SP RC | 50.00 | 80.00 |
| 287 | Steve Bilko SP | 35.00 | 60.00 |
| 288 | Chet Nichols SP RC | 35.00 | 60.00 |
| 289 | Tommy Holmes MG | 60.00 | 100.00 |
| 290 | Joe Astroth SP | 35.00 | 60.00 |
| 291 | Gil Coan SP | 35.00 | 60.00 |
| 292 | Floyd Baker SP | 35.00 | 60.00 |
| 293 | Sibby Sisti SP | 35.00 | 60.00 |
| 294 | Walker Cooper SP | 35.00 | 60.00 |
| 295 | Phil Cavarretta | 50.00 | 80.00 |
| 296 | Red Rolfe MG | 35.00 | 60.00 |
| 297 | Andy Seminick SP | 35.00 | 60.00 |
| 298 | Bob Ross SP RC | 35.00 | 60.00 |
| 299 | Ray Murray SP RC | 35.00 | 60.00 |
| 300 | Barney McCosky SP | 50.00 | 80.00 |
| 301 | Bob Porterfield | 30.00 | 50.00 |
| 302 | Max Surkont RC | 30.00 | 50.00 |
| 303 | Harry Dorish | 30.00 | 50.00 |
| 304 | Sam Dente | 30.00 | 50.00 |
| 305 | Paul Richards MG | 35.00 | 60.00 |
| 306 | Lou Sleater RC | 30.00 | 50.00 |
| 307 | Frank Campos RC | 30.00 | 50.00 |
| 307A | Frank Campos Star | | |
| 308 | Luis Aloma | 30.00 | 50.00 |
| 309 | Jim Busby | 35.00 | 60.00 |
| 310 | George Metkovich | 60.00 | 100.00 |
| 311 | Mickey Mantle DP | 18000.00 | 30000.00 |
| 311B | Mickey Mantle DP | 18000.00 | 30000.00 |
| 312 | Jackie Robinson DP | 1500.00 | 2500.00 |
| 312B | Jackie Robinson Stitch | 1500.00 | 2500.00 |
| 313 | Bobby Thomson DP | 200.00 | 350.00 |
| 313B | Bobby Thomson Stitch | 200.00 | 350.00 |
| 314 | Roy Campanella | 1500.00 | 2500.00 |
| 315 | Leo Durocher MG | 350.00 | 600.00 |
| 316 | Dave Williams RC | 175.00 | 300.00 |
| 317 | Conrado Marrero | 175.00 | 300.00 |
| 318 | Harold Gregg RC | 175.00 | 300.00 |
| 319 | Rube Walker RC | 150.00 | 250.00 |
| 320 | John Rutherford RC | 175.00 | 300.00 |
| 321 | Joe Black RC | 350.00 | 500.00 |
| 322 | Randy Jackson RC | 175.00 | 300.00 |
| 323 | Bubba Church | 150.00 | 250.00 |
| 324 | Warren Hacker | 150.00 | 250.00 |
| 325 | Bill Serena | 175.00 | 300.00 |
| 326 | George Shuba RC | 350.00 | 500.00 |
| 327 | Al Wilson RC | 150.00 | 250.00 |
| 328 | Bob Borkowski RC | 175.00 | 300.00 |
| 329 | Ike Delock RC | 175.00 | 300.00 |
| 330 | Turk Lown RC | 175.00 | 300.00 |
| 331 | Tom Morgan RC | 175.00 | 300.00 |
| 332 | Tony Bartirome RC | 175.00 | 300.00 |
| 333 | Pee Wee Reese | 1000.00 | 1800.00 |
| 334 | Wilmer Mizell RC | 175.00 | 300.00 |
| 335 | Ted Lepcio RC | 150.00 | 250.00 |
| 336 | Dave Koslo | 150.00 | 250.00 |
| 337 | Jim Hearn | 175.00 | 300.00 |
| 338 | Sal Yvars RC | 175.00 | 300.00 |
| 339 | Russ Meyer | 175.00 | 300.00 |
| 340 | Bob Hooper | 175.00 | 300.00 |
| 341 | Hal Jeffcoat | 175.00 | 300.00 |
| 342 | Clem Labine RC | 350.00 | 500.00 |
| 343 | Dick Gernert RC | 150.00 | 250.00 |
| 344 | Ewell Blackwell | 175.00 | 300.00 |
| 345 | Sammy White RC | 150.00 | 250.00 |
| 346 | George Spencer RC | 175.00 | 300.00 |
| 347 | Joe Adcock | 250.00 | 400.00 |
| 348 | Robert Kelly RC | 150.00 | 250.00 |
| 349 | Bob Cain | 175.00 | 300.00 |
| 350 | Cal Abrams | 175.00 | 300.00 |
| 351 | Alvin Dark | 175.00 | 300.00 |
| 352 | Karl Drews | 175.00 | 300.00 |
| 353 | Bobby Del Greco RC | 175.00 | 300.00 |
| 354 | Fred Hatfield RC | 175.00 | 300.00 |
| 355 | Bobby Morgan | 175.00 | 300.00 |
| 356 | Toby Atwell RC | 175.00 | 300.00 |
| 357 | Smoky Burgess | 175.00 | 300.00 |
| 358 | John Kucab RC | 175.00 | 300.00 |
| 359 | Dee Fondy RC | 150.00 | 250.00 |
| 360 | George Crowe RC | 175.00 | 300.00 |
| 361 | Bill Posedel CO | 150.00 | 250.00 |
| 362 | Ken Heintzelman | 175.00 | 300.00 |
| 363 | Dick Rozek RC | 175.00 | 300.00 |
| 364 | Clyde Sukeforth CO RC | 175.00 | 300.00 |
| 365 | Cookie Lavagetto CO | 250.00 | 400.00 |
| 366 | Dave Madison RC | 150.00 | 250.00 |
| 367 | Ben Thorpe RC | 175.00 | 300.00 |
| 368 | Ed Wright RC | 175.00 | 300.00 |
| 369 | Dick Groat RC | 350.00 | 500.00 |
| 370 | Billy Hoeft RC | 175.00 | 300.00 |
| 371 | Bobby Hofman | 150.00 | 250.00 |
| 372 | Gil McDougald RC | 300.00 | 500.00 |
| 373 | Jim Turner CO RC | 250.00 | 400.00 |
| 374 | Al Benton RC | 150.00 | 250.00 |
| 375 | John Merson RC | 150.00 | 250.00 |
| 376 | Faye Throneberry RC | 150.00 | 250.00 |
| 377 | Chuck Dressen MG | 250.00 | 400.00 |
| 378 | Leroy Fusselman RC | 175.00 | 300.00 |
| 379 | Joe Rossi RC | 150.00 | 250.00 |
| 380 | Clem Koshorek RC | 150.00 | 250.00 |
| 381 | Milton Stock CO RC | 175.00 | 300.00 |
| 382 | Sam Jones RC | 200.00 | 350.00 |
| 383 | Del Wilber RC | 150.00 | 250.00 |
| 384 | Frank Crosetti CO | 300.00 | 500.00 |
| 385 | Herman Franks CO RC | 150.00 | 250.00 |
| 386 | Ed Yuhas RC | 175.00 | 300.00 |
| 387 | Billy Meyer RC | 150.00 | 250.00 |
| 388 | Bob Chipman | 150.00 | 250.00 |

| # | Card | Price 1 | Price 2 |
|---|------|---------|---------|
| ☐ 389 | Ben Wade RC | 175.00 | 300.00 |
| ☐ 390 | Rocky Nelson RC | 175.00 | 300.00 |
| ☐ 391 | Ben Chapman CO UER | 150.00 | 250.00 |
| ☐ 392 | Hoyt Wilhelm RC | 600.00 | 1000.00 |
| ☐ 393 | Ebba St.Claire RC | 175.00 | 300.00 |
| ☐ 394 | Billy Herman CO | 350.00 | 600.00 |
| ☐ 395 | Jake Pitler CO | 175.00 | 300.00 |
| ☐ 396 | Dick Williams RC | 300.00 | 500.00 |
| ☐ 397 | Forrest Main RC | 150.00 | 250.00 |
| ☐ 398 | Hal Rice | 150.00 | 250.00 |
| ☐ 399 | Jim Fridley RC | 150.00 | 250.00 |
| ☐ 400 | Bill Dickey CO | 1000.00 | 1800.00 |
| ☐ 401 | Bob Schultz RC | 175.00 | 300.00 |
| ☐ 402 | Earl Harrist RC | 175.00 | 300.00 |
| ☐ 403 | Bill Miller RC | 175.00 | 300.00 |
| ☐ 404 | Dick Brodowski RC | 175.00 | 300.00 |
| ☐ 405 | Eddie Pellagrini | 175.00 | 300.00 |
| ☐ 406 | Joe Nuxhall RC | 250.00 | 400.00 |
| ☐ 407 | Eddie Mathews RC | 6000.00 | 10000.00 |

### 1953 Topps

WILLIE MAYS
NEW YORK GIANTS

| | | Price 1 | Price 2 |
|---|------|---------|---------|
| ☐ | COMPLETE SET (274) | 9000.00 | 15000.00 |
| ☐ | COMMON CARD (1-165) | 15.00 | 30.00 |
| ☐ | COMMON DP (1-165) | 7.50 | 15.00 |
| ☐ | COMMON CARD (166-220) | 12.50 | 25.00 |
| ☐ | COMMON CARD (221-280) | 50.00 | 100.00 |
| ☐ | NOT ISSUED (253/261/267) | | |
| ☐ | NOT ISSUED (268/271/275) | | |
| ☐ | WRAP.(1-CENT, DATED) | 150.00 | 200.00 |
| ☐ | WRAP.(1-CENT,NO DATE) | 250.00 | 300.00 |
| ☐ | WRAP.(5-CENT, DATED) | 300.00 | 400.00 |
| ☐ | WRAP.(5-CENT,NO DATE) | 275.00 | 350.00 |
| ☐ 1 | Jackie Robinson DP | 500.00 | 800.00 |
| ☐ 2 | Luke Easter DP | 10.00 | 20.00 |
| ☐ 3 | George Crowe | 25.00 | 40.00 |
| ☐ 4 | Ben Wade | 15.00 | 30.00 |
| ☐ 5 | Joe Dobson | 15.00 | 30.00 |
| ☐ 6 | Sam Jones | 25.00 | 40.00 |
| ☐ 7 | Bob Borkowski DP | 7.50 | 15.00 |
| ☐ 8 | Clem Koshorek DP | 7.50 | 15.00 |
| ☐ 9 | Joe Collins | 35.00 | 60.00 |
| ☐ 10 | Smoky Burgess SP | 50.00 | 80.00 |
| ☐ 11 | Sal Yvars | 15.00 | 30.00 |
| ☐ 12 | Howie Judson DP | 7.50 | 15.00 |
| ☐ 13 | Conrado Marrero DP | 7.50 | 15.00 |
| ☐ 14 | Clem Labine DP | 10.00 | 20.00 |
| ☐ 15 | Bobo Newsom DP RC | 10.00 | 20.00 |
| ☐ 16 | Peanuts Lowrey DP | 7.50 | 15.00 |
| ☐ 17 | Billy Hitchcock | 15.00 | 30.00 |
| ☐ 18 | Ted Lepcio DP | 7.50 | 15.00 |
| ☐ 19 | Mel Parnell DP | 10.00 | 20.00 |
| ☐ 20 | Hank Thompson | 25.00 | 40.00 |
| ☐ 21 | Billy Johnson | 15.00 | 30.00 |
| ☐ 22 | Howie Fox | 15.00 | 30.00 |
| ☐ 23 | Toby Atwell DP | 7.50 | 15.00 |
| ☐ 24 | Ferris Fain | 25.00 | 40.00 |
| ☐ 25 | Ray Boone | 25.00 | 40.00 |
| ☐ 26 | Dale Mitchell DP | 10.00 | 20.00 |
| ☐ 27 | Roy Campanella DP | 175.00 | 300.00 |
| ☐ 28 | Eddie Pellagrini | 15.00 | 30.00 |
| ☐ 29 | Hal Jeffcoat | 15.00 | 30.00 |
| ☐ 30 | Willard Nixon | 15.00 | 30.00 |
| ☐ 31 | Ewell Blackwell | 35.00 | 60.00 |
| ☐ 32 | Clyde Vollmer | 15.00 | 30.00 |
| ☐ 33 | Bob Kennedy DP | 7.50 | 15.00 |
| ☐ 34 | George Shuba | 25.00 | 40.00 |
| ☐ 35 | Irv Noren DP | 7.50 | 15.00 |
| ☐ 36 | Johnny Groth DP | 7.50 | 15.00 |
| ☐ 37 | Eddie Mathews DP | 150.00 | 250.00 |
| ☐ 38 | Jim Hearn DP | 7.50 | 15.00 |
| ☐ 39 | Eddie Miksis | 15.00 | 30.00 |
| ☐ 40 | John Lipon | 15.00 | 30.00 |
| ☐ 41 | Enos Slaughter | 50.00 | 80.00 |
| ☐ 42 | Gus Zernial DP | 10.00 | 20.00 |
| ☐ 43 | Gil McDougald | 35.00 | 60.00 |
| ☐ 44 | Ellis Kinder SP | 35.00 | 60.00 |
| ☐ 45 | Grady Hatton DP | 7.50 | 15.00 |
| ☐ 46 | Johnny Klippstein DP | 7.50 | 15.00 |
| ☐ 47 | Bubba Church DP | 7.50 | 15.00 |
| ☐ 48 | Bob Del Greco DP | 7.50 | 15.00 |
| ☐ 49 | Faye Throneberry DP | 7.50 | 15.00 |
| ☐ 50 | Chuck Dressen DP | 10.00 | 20.00 |
| ☐ 51 | Frank Campos DP | 7.50 | 15.00 |
| ☐ 52 | Ted Gray DP | 7.50 | 15.00 |
| ☐ 53 | Sherm Lollar DP | 10.00 | 20.00 |
| ☐ 54 | Bob Feller DP | 90.00 | 150.00 |
| ☐ 55 | Maurice McDermott DP | 7.50 | 15.00 |
| ☐ 56 | Gerry Staley DP | 7.50 | 15.00 |
| ☐ 57 | Carl Scheib | 15.00 | 30.00 |
| ☐ 58 | George Metkovich | 15.00 | 30.00 |
| ☐ 59 | Karl Drews DP | 7.50 | 15.00 |
| ☐ 60 | Cloyd Boyer DP | 7.50 | 15.00 |
| ☐ 61 | Early Wynn SP | 75.00 | 125.00 |
| ☐ 62 | Monte Irvin DP | 25.00 | 40.00 |
| ☐ 63 | Gus Niarhos DP | 7.50 | 15.00 |
| ☐ 64 | Dave Philley | 15.00 | 30.00 |
| ☐ 65 | Earl Harrist | 15.00 | 30.00 |
| ☐ 66 | Minnie Minoso | 35.00 | 60.00 |
| ☐ 67 | Roy Sievers DP | 10.00 | 20.00 |
| ☐ 68 | Del Rice | 15.00 | 30.00 |
| ☐ 69 | Dick Brodowski | 15.00 | 30.00 |
| ☐ 70 | Ed Yuhas | 15.00 | 30.00 |
| ☐ 71 | Tony Bartirome | 15.00 | 30.00 |
| ☐ 72 | Fred Hutchinson SP | 35.00 | 60.00 |
| ☐ 73 | Eddie Robinson | 15.00 | 30.00 |
| ☐ 74 | Joe Rossi | 15.00 | 30.00 |
| ☐ 75 | Mike Garcia | 25.00 | 40.00 |
| ☐ 76 | Pee Wee Reese | 100.00 | 175.00 |
| ☐ 77 | Johnny Mize DP | 50.00 | 80.00 |
| ☐ 78 | Red Schoendienst | 50.00 | 80.00 |
| ☐ 79 | Johnny Wyrostek | 15.00 | 30.00 |
| ☐ 80 | Jim Hegan | 25.00 | 40.00 |
| ☐ 81 | Joe Black SP | 50.00 | 80.00 |
| ☐ 82 | Mickey Mantle | 2000.00 | 3000.00 |
| ☐ 83 | Howie Pollet | 15.00 | 30.00 |
| ☐ 84 | Bob Hooper DP | 7.50 | 15.00 |
| ☐ 85 | Bobby Morgan DP | 7.50 | 15.00 |
| ☐ 86 | Billy Martin | 75.00 | 125.00 |
| ☐ 87 | Ed Lopat | 35.00 | 60.00 |
| ☐ 88 | Willie Jones DP | 7.50 | 15.00 |
| ☐ 89 | Chuck Stobbs DP | 7.50 | 15.00 |
| ☐ 90 | Hank Edwards DP | 7.50 | 15.00 |
| ☐ 91 | Ebba St.Claire DP | 7.50 | 15.00 |
| ☐ 92 | Paul Minner DP | 7.50 | 15.00 |
| ☐ 93 | Hal Rice DP | 7.50 | 15.00 |
| ☐ 94 | Bill Kennedy DP | 7.50 | 15.00 |
| ☐ 95 | Willard Marshall DP | 7.50 | 15.00 |
| ☐ 96 | Virgil Trucks | 25.00 | 40.00 |
| ☐ 97 | Don Kolloway DP | 7.50 | 15.00 |
| ☐ 98 | Cal Abrams DP | 7.50 | 15.00 |
| ☐ 99 | Dave Madison | 15.00 | 30.00 |
| ☐ 100 | Bill Miller | 15.00 | 30.00 |
| ☐ 101 | Ted Wilks | 15.00 | 30.00 |
| ☐ 102 | Connie Ryan DP | 7.50 | 15.00 |
| ☐ 103 | Joe Astroth DP | 7.50 | 15.00 |
| ☐ 104 | Yogi Berra | 250.00 | 400.00 |
| ☐ 105 | Joe Nuxhall DP | 10.00 | 20.00 |
| ☐ 106 | Johnny Antonelli | 25.00 | 40.00 |
| ☐ 107 | Danny O'Connell DP | 7.50 | 15.00 |
| ☐ 108 | Bob Porterfield DP | 7.50 | 15.00 |
| ☐ 109 | Alvin Dark | 35.00 | 60.00 |
| ☐ 110 | Herman Wehmeier DP | 7.50 | 15.00 |
| ☐ 111 | Hank Sauer DP | 7.50 | 15.00 |
| ☐ 112 | Ned Garver DP | 7.50 | 15.00 |
| ☐ 113 | Jerry Priddy | 15.00 | 30.00 |
| ☐ 114 | Phil Rizzuto | 150.00 | 250.00 |
| ☐ 115 | George Spencer | 15.00 | 30.00 |
| ☐ 116 | Frank Smith DP | 7.50 | 15.00 |
| ☐ 117 | Sid Gordon DP | 7.50 | 15.00 |
| ☐ 118 | Gus Bell DP | 10.00 | 20.00 |
| ☐ 119 | Johnny Sain SP | 45.00 | 80.00 |
| ☐ 120 | Davey Williams | 25.00 | 40.00 |
| ☐ 121 | Walt Dropo | 25.00 | 40.00 |
| ☐ 122 | Elmer Valo | 15.00 | 30.00 |
| ☐ 123 | Tommy Byrne DP | 7.50 | 15.00 |
| ☐ 124 | Sibby Sisti DP | 7.50 | 15.00 |
| ☐ 125 | Dick Williams DP | 10.00 | 20.00 |
| ☐ 126 | Bill Connelly DP RC | 7.50 | 15.00 |
| ☐ 127 | Clint Courtney DP RC | 7.50 | 15.00 |
| ☐ 128 | Wilmer Mizell DP | 10.00 | 20.00 |
| ☐ 129 | Keith Thomas RC | 15.00 | 30.00 |
| ☐ 130 | Turk Lown DP | 7.50 | 15.00 |
| ☐ 131 | Harry Byrd DP RC | 7.50 | 15.00 |
| ☐ 132 | Tom Morgan | 15.00 | 30.00 |
| ☐ 133 | Gil Coan | 15.00 | 30.00 |
| ☐ 134 | Rube Walker | 25.00 | 40.00 |
| ☐ 135 | Al Rosen DP | 10.00 | 20.00 |
| ☐ 136 | Ken Heintzelman DP | 7.50 | 15.00 |
| ☐ 137 | John Rutherford DP | 7.50 | 15.00 |
| ☐ 138 | George Kell | 50.00 | 80.00 |
| ☐ 139 | Sammy White | 15.00 | 30.00 |
| ☐ 140 | Tommy Glaviano | 15.00 | 30.00 |
| ☐ 141 | Allie Reynolds DP | 7.50 | 15.00 |
| ☐ 142 | Vic Wertz | 25.00 | 40.00 |
| ☐ 143 | Billy Pierce | 35.00 | 60.00 |
| ☐ 144 | Bob Schultz DP | 7.50 | 15.00 |
| ☐ 145 | Harry Dorish DP | 7.50 | 15.00 |
| ☐ 146 | Granny Hamner | 15.00 | 30.00 |
| ☐ 147 | Warren Spahn | 100.00 | 175.00 |
| ☐ 148 | Mickey Grasso | 15.00 | 30.00 |
| ☐ 149 | Dom DiMaggio DP | 7.50 | 15.00 |
| ☐ 150 | Harry Simpson DP | 7.50 | 15.00 |
| ☐ 151 | Hoyt Wilhelm | 60.00 | 100.00 |
| ☐ 152 | Bob Adams DP | 7.50 | 15.00 |
| ☐ 153 | Andy Seminick DP | 7.50 | 15.00 |
| ☐ 154 | Dick Groat | 25.00 | 40.00 |
| ☐ 155 | Dutch Leonard | 15.00 | 30.00 |
| ☐ 156 | Jim Rivera DP RC | 10.00 | 20.00 |
| ☐ 157 | Bob Addis DP | 7.50 | 15.00 |
| ☐ 158 | Johnny Logan RC | 25.00 | 40.00 |
| ☐ 159 | Wayne Terwilliger DP | 7.50 | 15.00 |
| ☐ 160 | Bob Young | 15.00 | 30.00 |
| ☐ 161 | Vern Bickford DP | 7.50 | 15.00 |
| ☐ 162 | Ted Kluszewski | 35.00 | 60.00 |
| ☐ 163 | Fred Hatfield DP | 7.50 | 15.00 |
| ☐ 164 | Frank Shea DP | 7.50 | 15.00 |
| ☐ 165 | Billy Hoeft | 15.00 | 30.00 |
| ☐ 166 | Billy Hunter RC | 12.50 | 25.00 |
| ☐ 167 | Art Schult RC | 12.50 | 25.00 |
| ☐ 168 | Willard Schmidt RC | 12.50 | 25.00 |
| ☐ 169 | Dizzy Trout | 15.00 | 30.00 |
| ☐ 170 | Bill Werle | 12.50 | 25.00 |
| ☐ 171 | Bill Glynn RC | 12.50 | 25.00 |
| ☐ 172 | Rip Repulski RC | 12.50 | 25.00 |
| ☐ 173 | Preston Ward | 12.50 | 25.00 |
| ☐ 174 | Billy Loes | 15.00 | 30.00 |
| ☐ 175 | Ron Kline RC | 12.50 | 25.00 |
| ☐ 176 | Don Hoak RC | 25.00 | 40.00 |
| ☐ 177 | Jim Dyck RC | 12.50 | 25.00 |
| ☐ 178 | Jim Waugh RC | 12.50 | 25.00 |
| ☐ 179 | Gene Hermanski | 12.50 | 25.00 |
| ☐ 180 | Virgil Stallcup | 12.50 | 25.00 |
| ☐ 181 | Al Zarilla | 12.50 | 25.00 |
| ☐ 182 | Bobby Hofman | 12.50 | 25.00 |
| ☐ 183 | Stu Miller RC | 25.00 | 40.00 |
| ☐ 184 | Hal Brown RC | 12.50 | 25.00 |
| ☐ 185 | Jim Pendleton RC | 12.50 | 25.00 |
| ☐ 186 | Charlie Bishop RC | 12.50 | 25.00 |
| ☐ 187 | Jim Fridley | 12.50 | 25.00 |
| ☐ 188 | Andy Carey RC | 25.00 | 40.00 |
| ☐ 189 | Ray Jablonski RC | 12.50 | 25.00 |
| ☐ 190 | Dixie Walker CO | 15.00 | 30.00 |
| ☐ 191 | Ralph Kiner | 50.00 | 80.00 |
| ☐ 192 | Wally Westlake | 12.50 | 25.00 |
| ☐ 193 | Mike Clark RC | 12.50 | 25.00 |
| ☐ 194 | Eddie Kazak | 12.50 | 25.00 |
| ☐ 195 | Ed McGhee RC | 12.50 | 25.00 |
| ☐ 196 | Bob Keegan RC | 12.50 | 25.00 |
| ☐ 197 | Del Crandall | 25.00 | 40.00 |
| ☐ 198 | Forrest Main | 12.50 | 25.00 |
| ☐ 199 | Marion Fricano RC | 12.50 | 25.00 |
| ☐ 200 | Gordon Goldsberry | 12.50 | 25.00 |
| ☐ 201 | Paul LaPalme | 12.50 | 25.00 |
| ☐ 202 | Carl Sawatski RC | 12.50 | 25.00 |
| ☐ 203 | Cliff Fannin | 12.50 | 25.00 |
| ☐ 204 | Dick Bokelman RC | 12.50 | 25.00 |
| ☐ 205 | Vern Benson RC | 12.50 | 25.00 |
| ☐ 206 | Ed Bailey RC | 15.00 | 30.00 |
| ☐ 207 | Whitey Ford | 175.00 | 300.00 |
| ☐ 208 | Jim Wilson | 12.50 | 25.00 |
| ☐ 209 | Jim Greengrass RC | 12.50 | 25.00 |
| ☐ 210 | Bob Cerv RC | 25.00 | 40.00 |
| ☐ 211 | J.W. Porter RC | 12.50 | 25.00 |
| ☐ 212 | Jack Dittmer RC | 12.50 | 25.00 |
| ☐ 213 | Ray Scarborough | 12.50 | 25.00 |
| ☐ 214 | Bill Bruton RC | 25.00 | 40.00 |
| ☐ 215 | Gene Conley RC | 15.00 | 30.00 |
| ☐ 216 | Jim Hughes RC | 12.50 | 25.00 |
| ☐ 217 | Murray Wall RC | 12.50 | 25.00 |
| ☐ 218 | Les Fusselman | 12.50 | 25.00 |

# 348 / 1954 Topps

|  | | |
|---|---|---|
| 219 Pete Runnels UER (Photo actually Don Johnson) | 15.00 | 30.00 |
| 220 Satchel Paige UER | 350.00 | 600.00 |
| 221 Bob Milliken RC | 50.00 | 100.00 |
| 222 Vic Janowicz DP RC | 25.00 | 50.00 |
| 223 Johnny O'Brien DP RC | 25.00 | 50.00 |
| 224 Lou Sleater DP | 25.00 | 50.00 |
| 225 Bobby Shantz | 75.00 | 125.00 |
| 226 Ed Erautt | 50.00 | 100.00 |
| 227 Morrie Martin | 50.00 | 100.00 |
| 228 Hal Newhouser | 90.00 | 150.00 |
| 229 Rocky Krsnich DP | 50.00 | 100.00 |
| 230 Johnny Lindell DP | 25.00 | 50.00 |
| 231 Solly Hemus DP | 25.00 | 50.00 |
| 232 Dick Kokos | 50.00 | 100.00 |
| 233 Al Aber RC | 50.00 | 100.00 |
| 234 Ray Murray DP | 25.00 | 50.00 |
| 235 John Hetki DP RC | 25.00 | 50.00 |
| 236 Harry Perkowski DP | 25.00 | 50.00 |
| 237 Bud Podbielan DP | 25.00 | 50.00 |
| 238 Cal Hogue DP RC | 25.00 | 50.00 |
| 239 Jim Delsing | 50.00 | 100.00 |
| 240 Fred Marsh | 50.00 | 100.00 |
| 241 Al Sima DP | 25.00 | 50.00 |
| 242 Charlie Silvera | 75.00 | 125.00 |
| 243 Carlos Bernier DP RC | 25.00 | 50.00 |
| 244 Willie Mays | 1500.00 | 2500.00 |
| 245 Bill Norman CO | 50.00 | 100.00 |
| 246 Roy Face RC DP RC | 50.00 | 80.00 |
| 247 Mike Sandlock DP RC | 25.00 | 50.00 |
| 248 Gene Stephens DP RC | 25.00 | 50.00 |
| 249 Eddie O'Brien RC | 50.00 | 100.00 |
| 250 Bob Wilson RC | 50.00 | 100.00 |
| 251 Sid Hudson | 50.00 | 100.00 |
| 252 Hank Foiles RC | 50.00 | 100.00 |
| 253 Does not exist | | |
| 254 Preacher Roe DP | 50.00 | 80.00 |
| 255 Dixie Howell | 50.00 | 100.00 |
| 256 Les Peden RC | 50.00 | 100.00 |
| 257 Bob Boyd RC | 50.00 | 100.00 |
| 258 Jim Gilliam RC | 250.00 | 400.00 |
| 259 Roy McMillan DP | 25.00 | 50.00 |
| 260 Sam Calderone RC | 50.00 | 100.00 |
| 261 Does not exist | | |
| 262 Bob Oldis RC | 50.00 | 100.00 |
| 263 Johnny Podres RC | 175.00 | 300.00 |
| 264 Gene Woodling DP | 30.00 | 60.00 |
| 265 Jackie Jensen | 75.00 | 125.00 |
| 266 Bob Cain | 50.00 | 100.00 |
| 267 Does not exist | | |
| 268 Does not exist | | |
| 269 Duane Pillette | 50.00 | 100.00 |
| 270 Vern Stephens | 75.00 | 125.00 |
| 271 Does not exist | | |
| 272 Bill Antonello RC | 50.00 | 100.00 |
| 273 Harvey Haddix RC | 90.00 | 150.00 |
| 274 John Riddle CO | 50.00 | 100.00 |
| 275 Does not exist | | |
| 276 Ken Raffensberger | 50.00 | 100.00 |
| 277 Don Lund RC | 50.00 | 100.00 |
| 278 Willie Miranda RC | 50.00 | 100.00 |
| 279 Joe Coleman DP | 25.00 | 50.00 |
| 280 Milt Bolling RC | 200.00 | 350.00 |

## 1954 Topps

| | | |
|---|---|---|
| COMPLETE SET (250) | 5000.00 | 8000.00 |
| COMMON (1-50/76-250) | 7.50 | 15.00 |
| COMMON CARD (51-75) | 12.50 | 25.00 |
| WRAP (1-CENT, DATED) | 150.00 | 200.00 |
| WRAP (1-CENT, UNDAT) | 100.00 | 150.00 |
| WRAP (5-CENT, DATED) | 250.00 | 300.00 |
| WRAP (5-CENT, UNDAT) | 200.00 | 250.00 |
| 1 Ted Williams | 500.00 | 800.00 |
| 2 Gus Zernial | 12.50 | 25.00 |
| 3 Monte Irvin | 25.00 | 50.00 |
| 4 Hank Sauer | 12.50 | 25.00 |
| 5 Ed Lopat | 12.50 | 25.00 |
| 6 Pete Runnels | 12.50 | 25.00 |
| 7 Ted Kluszewski | 25.00 | 50.00 |
| 8 Bob Young | 7.50 | 15.00 |
| 9 Harvey Haddix | 12.50 | 25.00 |
| 10 Jackie Robinson | 250.00 | 450.00 |
| 11 Paul Leslie Smith RC | 7.50 | 15.00 |
| 12 Del Crandall | 12.50 | 25.00 |
| 13 Billy Martin | 60.00 | 100.00 |
| 14 Preacher Roe DP | 12.50 | 25.00 |
| 15 Al Rosen | 12.50 | 25.00 |
| 16 Vic Janowicz | 12.50 | 25.00 |
| 17 Phil Rizzuto | 75.00 | 125.00 |
| 18 Walt Dropo | 7.50 | 15.00 |
| 19 Johnny Lipon | 7.50 | 15.00 |
| 20 Warren Spahn | 75.00 | 125.00 |
| 21 Bobby Shantz | 7.50 | 15.00 |
| 22 Jim Greengrass | 7.50 | 15.00 |
| 23 Luke Easter | 12.50 | 25.00 |
| 24 Granny Hamner | 7.50 | 15.00 |
| 25 Harvey Kuenn RC | 20.00 | 40.00 |
| 26 Ray Jablonski | 7.50 | 15.00 |
| 27 Ferris Fain | 12.50 | 25.00 |
| 28 Paul Minner | 7.50 | 15.00 |
| 29 Jim Hegan | 12.50 | 25.00 |
| 30 Eddie Mathews | 60.00 | 100.00 |
| 31 Johnny Klippstein | 7.50 | 15.00 |
| 32 Duke Snider | 125.00 | 200.00 |
| 33 Johnny Schmitz | 7.50 | 15.00 |
| 34 Jim Rivera | 7.50 | 15.00 |
| 35 Junior Gilliam | 25.00 | 50.00 |
| 36 Hoyt Wilhelm | 25.00 | 50.00 |
| 37 Whitey Ford | 125.00 | 200.00 |
| 38 Eddie Stanky MG | 12.50 | 25.00 |
| 39 Sherm Lollar | 12.50 | 25.00 |
| 40 Mel Parnell | 12.50 | 25.00 |
| 41 Willie Jones | 7.50 | 15.00 |
| 42 Don Mueller | 7.50 | 15.00 |
| 43 Dick Groat | 12.50 | 25.00 |
| 44 Ned Garver | 7.50 | 15.00 |
| 45 Richie Ashburn | 50.00 | 80.00 |
| 46 Ken Raffensberger | 7.50 | 15.00 |
| 47 Ellis Kinder | 7.50 | 15.00 |
| 48 Billy Hunter | 12.50 | 25.00 |
| 49 Ray Murray | 7.50 | 15.00 |
| 50 Yogi Berra | 175.00 | 300.00 |
| 51 Johnny Lindell | 12.50 | 25.00 |
| 52 Vic Power RC | 15.00 | 30.00 |
| 53 Jack Dittmer | 12.50 | 25.00 |
| 54 Vern Stephens | 15.00 | 30.00 |
| 55 Phil Cavarretta MG | 15.00 | 30.00 |
| 56 Willie Miranda | 12.50 | 25.00 |
| 57 Luis Aloma | 12.50 | 25.00 |
| 58 Bob Wilson | 12.50 | 25.00 |
| 59 Gene Conley | 15.00 | 30.00 |
| 60 Frank Baumholtz | 12.50 | 25.00 |
| 61 Bob Cain | 12.50 | 25.00 |
| 62 Eddie Robinson | 12.50 | 25.00 |
| 63 Johnny Pesky | 15.00 | 30.00 |
| 64 Hank Thompson | 12.50 | 25.00 |
| 65 Bob Swift CO | 12.50 | 25.00 |
| 66 Ted Lepcio | 12.50 | 25.00 |
| 67 Jim Willis RC | 12.50 | 25.00 |
| 68 Sam Calderone | 12.50 | 25.00 |
| 69 Bud Podbielan | 12.50 | 25.00 |
| 70 Larry Doby | 30.00 | 60.00 |
| 71 Frank Smith | 12.50 | 25.00 |
| 72 Preston Ward | 12.50 | 25.00 |
| 73 Wayne Terwilliger | 12.50 | 25.00 |
| 74 Bill Taylor RC | 12.50 | 25.00 |
| 75 Fred Haney MG RC | 12.50 | 25.00 |
| 76 Bob Scheffing CO | 7.50 | 15.00 |
| 77 Ray Boone | 12.50 | 25.00 |
| 78 Ted Kazanski RC | 7.50 | 15.00 |
| 79 Andy Pafko | 12.50 | 25.00 |
| 80 Jackie Jensen | 12.50 | 25.00 |
| 81 Dave Hoskins RC | 7.50 | 15.00 |
| 82 Milt Bolling | 7.50 | 15.00 |
| 83 Joe Collins | 12.50 | 25.00 |
| 84 Dick Cole RC | 7.50 | 15.00 |
| 85 Bob Turley RC | 20.00 | 40.00 |
| 86 Billy Herman CO | 12.50 | 25.00 |
| 87 Roy Face | 12.50 | 25.00 |
| 88 Matt Batts | 7.50 | 15.00 |
| 89 Howie Pollet | 7.50 | 15.00 |
| 90 Willie Mays | 500.00 | 800.00 |
| 91 Bob Oldis | 7.50 | 15.00 |
| 92 Wally Westlake | 7.50 | 15.00 |
| 93 Sid Hudson | 7.50 | 15.00 |
| 94 Ernie Banks RC | 900.00 | 1500.00 |
| 95 Hal Rice | 7.50 | 15.00 |
| 96 Charlie Silvera | 12.50 | 25.00 |
| 97 Jerald Hal Lane RC | 7.50 | 15.00 |
| 98 Joe Black | 20.00 | 40.00 |
| 99 Bobby Hofman | 7.50 | 15.00 |
| 100 Bob Keegan | 7.50 | 15.00 |
| 101 Gene Woodling | 12.50 | 25.00 |
| 102 Gil Hodges | 50.00 | 80.00 |
| 103 Jim Lemon RC | 7.50 | 15.00 |
| 104 Mike Sandlock | 7.50 | 15.00 |
| 105 Andy Carey | 12.50 | 25.00 |
| 106 Dick Kokos | 7.50 | 15.00 |
| 107 Duane Pillette | 7.50 | 15.00 |
| 108 Thornton Kipper RC | 7.50 | 15.00 |
| 109 Bill Bruton | 12.50 | 25.00 |
| 110 Harry Dorish | 7.50 | 15.00 |
| 111 Jim Delsing | 7.50 | 15.00 |
| 112 Bill Renna RC | 7.50 | 15.00 |
| 113 Bob Boyd | 7.50 | 15.00 |
| 114 Dean Stone RC | 7.50 | 15.00 |
| 115 Rip Repulski | 7.50 | 15.00 |
| 116 Steve Bilko | 7.50 | 15.00 |
| 117 Solly Hemus | 7.50 | 15.00 |
| 118 Carl Scheib | 7.50 | 15.00 |
| 119 Johnny Antonelli | 12.50 | 25.00 |
| 120 Roy McMillan | 12.50 | 25.00 |
| 121 Clem Labine | 12.50 | 25.00 |
| 122 Johnny Logan | 12.50 | 25.00 |
| 123 Bobby Adams | 7.50 | 15.00 |
| 124 Marion Fricano | 7.50 | 15.00 |
| 125 Harry Perkowski | 7.50 | 15.00 |
| 126 Ben Wade | 7.50 | 15.00 |
| 127 Steve O'Neill MG | 7.50 | 15.00 |
| 128 Hank Aaron RC | 1000.00 | 1800.00 |
| 129 Forrest Jacobs RC | 7.50 | 15.00 |
| 130 Hank Bauer | 12.50 | 25.00 |
| 131 Reno Bertoia RC | 7.50 | 15.00 |
| 132 Tommy Lasorda RC | 150.00 | 250.00 |
| 133 Del Baker CO | 7.50 | 15.00 |
| 134 Cal Hogue | 7.50 | 15.00 |
| 135 Joe Presko | 7.50 | 15.00 |
| 136 Connie Ryan | 7.50 | 15.00 |
| 137 Wally Moon RC | 20.00 | 40.00 |
| 138 Bob Borkowski | 7.50 | 15.00 |
| 139 J.O'Brien/E.O'Brien | 25.00 | 50.00 |
| 140 Tom Wright | 7.50 | 15.00 |
| 141 Joey Jay RC | 12.50 | 25.00 |
| 142 Tom Poholsky | 7.50 | 15.00 |
| 143 Rollie Hemsley CO | 7.50 | 15.00 |
| 144 Bill Werle | 7.50 | 15.00 |
| 145 Elmer Valo | 7.50 | 15.00 |
| 146 Don Johnson | 7.50 | 15.00 |
| 147 Johnny Riddle CO | 7.50 | 15.00 |
| 148 Bob Trice RC | 7.50 | 15.00 |
| 149 Al Robertson | 7.50 | 15.00 |
| 150 Dick Kryhoski | 7.50 | 15.00 |
| 151 Alex Grammas RC | 12.50 | 25.00 |
| 152 Michael Blyzka RC | 7.50 | 15.00 |
| 153 Al Walker | 12.50 | 25.00 |
| 154 Mike Fornieles RC | 7.50 | 15.00 |
| 155 Bob Kennedy | 12.50 | 25.00 |
| 156 Joe Coleman | 12.50 | 25.00 |
| 157 Don Lenhardt | 12.50 | 25.00 |
| 158 Peanuts Lowrey | 7.50 | 15.00 |
| 159 Dave Philley | 7.50 | 15.00 |
| 160 Ralph Kress CO | 7.50 | 15.00 |
| 161 John Hetki | 7.50 | 15.00 |
| 162 Herman Wehmeier | 7.50 | 15.00 |
| 163 Frank House | 7.50 | 15.00 |
| 164 Stu Miller | 12.50 | 25.00 |
| 165 Jim Pendleton | 7.50 | 15.00 |
| 166 Johnny Podres | 20.00 | 40.00 |
| 167 Don Lund | 7.50 | 15.00 |
| 168 Morrie Martin | 12.50 | 25.00 |
| 169 Jim Hughes | 20.00 | 40.00 |
| 170 Dusty Rhodes RC | 12.50 | 25.00 |
| 171 Leo Kiely | 7.50 | 15.00 |
| 172 Harold Brown RC | 7.50 | 15.00 |
| 173 Jack Harshman RC | 7.50 | 15.00 |
| 174 Tom Qualters RC | 7.50 | 15.00 |
| 175 Frank Leja RC | 12.50 | 25.00 |
| 176 Robert Keely CO | 7.50 | 15.00 |
| 177 Bob Milliken | 7.50 | 15.00 |

| | | |
|---|---|---|
| ❑ 178 Bill Glynn UER | 7.50 | 15.00 |
| ❑ 179 Gair Allie RC | 7.50 | 15.00 |
| ❑ 180 Wes Westrum | 12.50 | 25.00 |
| ❑ 181 Mel Roach RC | 7.50 | 15.00 |
| ❑ 182 Chuck Harmon RC | 7.50 | 15.00 |
| ❑ 183 Earle Combs RC | 12.50 | 25.00 |
| ❑ 184 Ed Bailey | 7.50 | 15.00 |
| ❑ 185 Chuck Stobbs | 7.50 | 15.00 |
| ❑ 186 Karl Olson | 7.50 | 15.00 |
| ❑ 187 Heinie Manush CO | 12.50 | 25.00 |
| ❑ 188 Dave Jolly RC | 7.50 | 15.00 |
| ❑ 189 Bob Ross | 7.50 | 15.00 |
| ❑ 190 Ray Herbert RC | 7.50 | 15.00 |
| ❑ 191 Dick Schofield RC | 12.50 | 25.00 |
| ❑ 192 Ellis Deal CO | 7.50 | 15.00 |
| ❑ 193 Johnny Hopp CO | 12.50 | 25.00 |
| ❑ 194 Bill Sarni RC | 7.50 | 15.00 |
| ❑ 195 Billy Consolo RC | 7.50 | 15.00 |
| ❑ 196 Stan Jok RC | 7.50 | 15.00 |
| ❑ 197 Lynwood Rowe CO | 12.50 | 25.00 |
| ❑ 198 Carl Sawatski | 7.50 | 15.00 |
| ❑ 199 Glenn (Rocky) Nelson | 7.50 | 15.00 |
| ❑ 200 Larry Jansen | 12.50 | 25.00 |
| ❑ 201 Al Kaline RC | 400.00 | 700.00 |
| ❑ 202 Bob Purkey RC | 12.50 | 25.00 |
| ❑ 203 Harry Brecheen CO | 12.50 | 25.00 |
| ❑ 204 Angel Scull RC | 7.50 | 15.00 |
| ❑ 205 Johnny Sain | 20.00 | 40.00 |
| ❑ 206 Ray Crone RC | 7.50 | 15.00 |
| ❑ 207 Tom Oliver CO RC | 7.50 | 15.00 |
| ❑ 208 Grady Hatton | 7.50 | 15.00 |
| ❑ 209 Chuck Thompson RC | 7.50 | 15.00 |
| ❑ 210 Bob Buhl RC | 12.50 | 25.00 |
| ❑ 211 Don Hoak | 12.50 | 25.00 |
| ❑ 212 Bob Micelotta RC | 7.50 | 15.00 |
| ❑ 213 Johnny Fitzpatrick CO RC | 7.50 | 15.00 |
| ❑ 214 Amie Portocarrero RC | 7.50 | 15.00 |
| ❑ 215 Ed McGhee | 12.50 | 25.00 |
| ❑ 216 Al Sima | 7.50 | 15.00 |
| ❑ 217 Paul Schreiber CO RC | 7.50 | 15.00 |
| ❑ 218 Fred Marsh | 7.50 | 15.00 |
| ❑ 219 Chuck Kress RC | 7.50 | 15.00 |
| ❑ 220 Ruben Gomez RC | 12.50 | 25.00 |
| ❑ 221 Dick Brodowski | 7.50 | 15.00 |
| ❑ 222 Bill Wilson RC | 7.50 | 15.00 |
| ❑ 223 Joe Haynes CO RC | 7.50 | 15.00 |
| ❑ 224 Dick Weik RC | 7.50 | 15.00 |
| ❑ 225 Don Liddle RC | 7.50 | 15.00 |
| ❑ 226 Jehosie Heard RC | 12.50 | 25.00 |
| ❑ 227 Buster Mills CO RC | 7.50 | 15.00 |
| ❑ 228 Gene Hermanski RC | 7.50 | 15.00 |
| ❑ 229 Bob Talbot RC | 7.50 | 15.00 |
| ❑ 230 Bob Kuzava | 12.50 | 25.00 |
| ❑ 231 Roy Smalley | 7.50 | 15.00 |
| ❑ 232 Lou Limmer RC | 7.50 | 15.00 |
| ❑ 233 Augie Galan CO | 7.50 | 15.00 |
| ❑ 234 Jerry Lynch RC | 7.50 | 15.00 |
| ❑ 235 Vern Law | 12.50 | 25.00 |
| ❑ 236 Paul Penson RC | 7.50 | 15.00 |
| ❑ 237 Mike Ryba CO RC | 7.50 | 15.00 |
| ❑ 238 Al Aber | 7.50 | 15.00 |
| ❑ 239 Bill Skowron RC | 60.00 | 100.00 |
| ❑ 240 Sam Mele | 12.50 | 25.00 |
| ❑ 241 Robert Miller RC | 7.50 | 15.00 |
| ❑ 242 Curt Roberts RC | 7.50 | 15.00 |
| ❑ 243 Ray Blades CO RC | 7.50 | 15.00 |
| ❑ 244 Leroy Wheat RC | 7.50 | 15.00 |
| ❑ 245 Roy Sievers | 12.50 | 25.00 |
| ❑ 246 Howie Fox | 7.50 | 15.00 |
| ❑ 247 Ed Mayo CO | 7.50 | 15.00 |
| ❑ 248 Al Smith RC | 12.50 | 25.00 |
| ❑ 249 Wilmer Mizell | 12.50 | 25.00 |
| ❑ 250 Ted Williams | 500.00 | 1000.00 |

**1955 Topps**

HANK SAUER

| | | |
|---|---|---|
| ❑ COMPLETE SET (206) | 5000.00 | 8000.00 |
| ❑ COMMON CARD (1-150) | 6.00 | 12.00 |
| ❑ COMMON CARD (151-160) | 10.00 | 20.00 |
| ❑ COMMON CARD (161-210) | 15.00 | 30.00 |
| ❑ NOT ISSUED (175/186/203/209) | | |
| ❑ WRAP (1-CENT, DATED) | 100.00 | 150.00 |
| ❑ WRAP (1-CENT, UNDAT) | 40.00 | 50.00 |
| ❑ WRAP (5-CENT, DATED) | 100.00 | 150.00 |
| ❑ WRAP (5-CENT, UNDAT) | 75.00 | 100.00 |
| ❑ 1 Dusty Rhodes | 75.00 | 125.00 |
| ❑ 2 Ted Williams | 400.00 | 700.00 |
| ❑ 3 Art Fowler RC | 7.50 | 15.00 |
| ❑ 4 Al Kaline | 90.00 | 150.00 |
| ❑ 5 Jim Gilliam | 20.00 | 40.00 |
| ❑ 6 Stan Hack MG RC | 12.50 | 25.00 |
| ❑ 7 Jim Hegan | 7.50 | 15.00 |
| ❑ 8 Harold Smith RC | 6.00 | 12.00 |
| ❑ 9 Robert Miller | 6.00 | 12.00 |
| ❑ 10 Bob Keegan | 6.00 | 12.00 |
| ❑ 11 Ferris Fain | 7.50 | 15.00 |
| ❑ 12 Vernon (Jake) Thies RC | 6.00 | 12.00 |
| ❑ 13 Fred Marsh | 6.00 | 12.00 |
| ❑ 14 Jim Finigan RC | 6.00 | 12.00 |
| ❑ 15 Jim Pendleton | 6.00 | 12.00 |
| ❑ 16 Roy Sievers | 7.50 | 15.00 |
| ❑ 17 Bobby Hofman | 6.00 | 12.00 |
| ❑ 18 Russ Kemmerer RC | 6.00 | 12.00 |
| ❑ 19 Billy Herman CO | 7.50 | 15.00 |
| ❑ 20 Andy Carey | 6.00 | 12.00 |
| ❑ 21 Alex Grammas RC | 6.00 | 12.00 |
| ❑ 22 Bill Skowron | 20.00 | 40.00 |
| ❑ 23 Jack Parks RC | 6.00 | 12.00 |
| ❑ 24 Hal Newhouser | 20.00 | 40.00 |
| ❑ 25 Johnny Podres | 12.50 | 25.00 |
| ❑ 26 Dick Groat | 7.50 | 15.00 |
| ❑ 27 Billy Gardner RC | 7.50 | 15.00 |
| ❑ 28 Ernie Banks | 125.00 | 200.00 |
| ❑ 29 Herman Wehmeier | 6.00 | 12.00 |
| ❑ 30 Vic Power | 7.50 | 15.00 |
| ❑ 31 Warren Spahn | 60.00 | 100.00 |
| ❑ 32 Warren McGhee RC | 6.00 | 12.00 |
| ❑ 33 Tom Qualters | 6.00 | 12.00 |
| ❑ 34 Wayne Terwilliger | 6.00 | 12.00 |
| ❑ 35 Dave Jolly | 6.00 | 12.00 |
| ❑ 36 Leo Kiely | 6.00 | 12.00 |
| ❑ 37 Joe Cunningham RC | 7.50 | 15.00 |
| ❑ 38 Bob Turley | 7.50 | 15.00 |
| ❑ 39 Bill Glynn | 6.00 | 12.00 |
| ❑ 40 Don Hoak | 7.50 | 15.00 |
| ❑ 41 Chuck Stobbs | 6.00 | 12.00 |
| ❑ 42 John (Windy) McCall RC | 6.00 | 12.00 |
| ❑ 43 Harvey Haddix | 7.50 | 15.00 |
| ❑ 44 Harold Valentine RC | 6.00 | 12.00 |
| ❑ 45 Hank Sauer | 7.50 | 15.00 |
| ❑ 46 Ted Kazanski | 6.00 | 12.00 |
| ❑ 47 Hank Aaron | 250.00 | 400.00 |
| ❑ 48 Bob Kennedy | 7.50 | 15.00 |
| ❑ 49 J.W. Porter | 6.00 | 12.00 |
| ❑ 50 Jackie Robinson | 300.00 | 500.00 |
| ❑ 51 Jim Hughes | 7.50 | 15.00 |
| ❑ 52 Bill Tremel RC | 6.00 | 12.00 |
| ❑ 53 Bill Taylor | 6.00 | 12.00 |
| ❑ 54 Lou Limmer | 6.00 | 12.00 |
| ❑ 55 Rip Repulski | 6.00 | 12.00 |
| ❑ 56 Ray Jablonski | 6.00 | 12.00 |
| ❑ 57 Billy O'Dell RC | 6.00 | 12.00 |
| ❑ 58 Jim Rivera | 6.00 | 12.00 |
| ❑ 59 Gair Allie | 6.00 | 12.00 |
| ❑ 60 Dean Stone | 6.00 | 12.00 |
| ❑ 61 Forrest Jacobs | 6.00 | 12.00 |
| ❑ 62 Thornton Kipper | 6.00 | 12.00 |
| ❑ 63 Joe Collins | 7.50 | 15.00 |
| ❑ 64 Gus Triandos RC | 7.50 | 15.00 |
| ❑ 65 Ray Boone | 7.50 | 15.00 |
| ❑ 66 Ron Jackson RC | 6.00 | 12.00 |
| ❑ 67 Wally Moon | 7.50 | 15.00 |
| ❑ 68 Jim Davis RC | 6.00 | 12.00 |
| ❑ 69 Ed Bailey | 7.50 | 15.00 |
| ❑ 70 Al Rosen | 7.50 | 15.00 |
| ❑ 71 Ruben Gomez | 6.00 | 12.00 |
| ❑ 72 Karl Olson | 6.00 | 12.00 |
| ❑ 73 Jack Shepard RC | 6.00 | 12.00 |
| ❑ 74 Bob Borkowski | 6.00 | 12.00 |
| ❑ 75 Sandy Amoros RC | 20.00 | 40.00 |
| ❑ 76 Howie Pollet | 6.00 | 12.00 |
| ❑ 77 Amie Portocarrero | 6.00 | 12.00 |
| ❑ 78 Gordon Jones RC | 6.00 | 12.00 |
| ❑ 79 Clyde (Danny) Schell RC | 6.00 | 12.00 |

| | | |
|---|---|---|
| ❑ 80 Bob Grim RC | 7.50 | 15.00 |
| ❑ 81 Gene Conley | 7.50 | 15.00 |
| ❑ 82 Chuck Harmon | 6.00 | 12.00 |
| ❑ 83 Tom Brewer RC | 6.00 | 12.00 |
| ❑ 84 Camilo Pascual RC | 7.50 | 15.00 |
| ❑ 85 Don Mossi RC | 12.50 | 25.00 |
| ❑ 86 Bill Wilson | 6.00 | 12.00 |
| ❑ 87 Frank House | 6.00 | 12.00 |
| ❑ 88 Bob Skinner RC | 7.50 | 15.00 |
| ❑ 89 Joe Frazier RC | 7.50 | 15.00 |
| ❑ 90 Karl Spooner RC | 7.50 | 15.00 |
| ❑ 91 Milt Bolling | 6.00 | 12.00 |
| ❑ 92 Don Zimmer RC | 12.50 | 25.00 |
| ❑ 93 Steve Bilko | 6.00 | 12.00 |
| ❑ 94 Reno Bertoia | 6.00 | 12.00 |
| ❑ 95 Preston Ward | 6.00 | 12.00 |
| ❑ 96 Chuck Bishop | 6.00 | 12.00 |
| ❑ 97 Carlos Paula RC | 6.00 | 12.00 |
| ❑ 98 John Riddle CO | 6.00 | 12.00 |
| ❑ 99 Frank Leja | 6.00 | 12.00 |
| ❑ 100 Monte Irvin | 20.00 | 40.00 |
| ❑ 101 Johnny Gray RC | 6.00 | 12.00 |
| ❑ 102 Wally Westlake | 6.00 | 12.00 |
| ❑ 103 Chuck White RC | 6.00 | 12.00 |
| ❑ 104 Jack Harshman | 6.00 | 12.00 |
| ❑ 105 Chuck Diering | 6.00 | 12.00 |
| ❑ 106 Frank Sullivan RC | 6.00 | 12.00 |
| ❑ 107 Curt Roberts | 6.00 | 12.00 |
| ❑ 108 Rube Walker | 7.50 | 15.00 |
| ❑ 109 Ed Lopat | 7.50 | 15.00 |
| ❑ 110 Gus Zernial | 7.50 | 15.00 |
| ❑ 111 Bob Milliken | 6.00 | 12.00 |
| ❑ 112 Nelson King RC | 6.00 | 12.00 |
| ❑ 113 Harry Brecheen CO | 7.50 | 15.00 |
| ❑ 114 Louis Ortiz RC | 6.00 | 12.00 |
| ❑ 115 Ellis Kinder | 6.00 | 12.00 |
| ❑ 116 Tom Hurd RC | 6.00 | 12.00 |
| ❑ 117 Mel Roach | 6.00 | 12.00 |
| ❑ 118 Bob Purkey | 6.00 | 12.00 |
| ❑ 119 Bob Lennon RC | 6.00 | 12.00 |
| ❑ 120 Ted Kluszewski | 50.00 | 80.00 |
| ❑ 121 Bill Renna | 6.00 | 12.00 |
| ❑ 122 Carl Sawatski | 6.00 | 12.00 |
| ❑ 123 Sandy Koufax RC | 700.00 | 1200.00 |
| ❑ 124 Harmon Killebrew RC | 150.00 | 250.00 |
| ❑ 125 Ken Boyer RC | 50.00 | 80.00 |
| ❑ 126 Dick Hall RC | 6.00 | 12.00 |
| ❑ 127 Dale Long RC | 7.50 | 15.00 |
| ❑ 128 Ted Lepcio | 6.00 | 12.00 |
| ❑ 129 Elvin Tappe | 7.50 | 15.00 |
| ❑ 130 Mayo Smith MG RC | 6.00 | 12.00 |
| ❑ 131 Grady Hatton | 6.00 | 12.00 |
| ❑ 132 Bob Trice | 6.00 | 12.00 |
| ❑ 133 Dave Hoskins | 6.00 | 12.00 |
| ❑ 134 Joey Jay | 7.50 | 15.00 |
| ❑ 135 Johnny O'Brien | 6.00 | 12.00 |
| ❑ 136 Veston (Bunky) Stewart RC | 6.00 | 12.00 |
| ❑ 137 Harry Elliott RC | 6.00 | 12.00 |
| ❑ 138 Ray Herbert | 6.00 | 12.00 |
| ❑ 139 Steve Kraly RC | 6.00 | 12.00 |
| ❑ 140 Mel Parnell | 7.50 | 15.00 |
| ❑ 141 Tom Wright | 6.00 | 12.00 |
| ❑ 142 Jerry Lynch | 7.50 | 15.00 |
| ❑ 143 John Schofield | 6.00 | 12.00 |
| ❑ 144 Joe Amalfitano RC | 6.00 | 12.00 |
| ❑ 145 Elmer Valo | 6.00 | 12.00 |
| ❑ 146 Dick Donovan RC | 7.50 | 15.00 |
| ❑ 147 Hugh Pepper RC | 6.00 | 12.00 |
| ❑ 148 Hector Brown | 6.00 | 12.00 |
| ❑ 149 Ray Crone | 6.00 | 12.00 |
| ❑ 150 Mike Higgins MG | 6.00 | 12.00 |
| ❑ 151 Ralph Kress CO | 10.00 | 20.00 |
| ❑ 152 Harry Agganis RC | 60.00 | 100.00 |
| ❑ 153 Bud Podbielan | 12.50 | 25.00 |
| ❑ 154 Willie Miranda | 10.00 | 20.00 |
| ❑ 155 Eddie Mathews | 125.00 | 200.00 |
| ❑ 156 Joe Black | 30.00 | 50.00 |
| ❑ 157 Robert Miller | 10.00 | 20.00 |
| ❑ 158 Tommy Carroll RC | 12.50 | 25.00 |
| ❑ 159 Johnny Schmitz | 10.00 | 20.00 |
| ❑ 160 Ray Narleski RC | 15.00 | 30.00 |
| ❑ 161 Chuck Tanner RC | 20.00 | 40.00 |
| ❑ 162 Joe Coleman | 15.00 | 30.00 |
| ❑ 163 Faye Throneberry | 15.00 | 30.00 |
| ❑ 164 Roberto Clemente RC | 1400.00 | 2200.00 |
| ❑ 165 Don Johnson | 15.00 | 30.00 |
| ❑ 166 Hank Bauer | 50.00 | 80.00 |
| ❑ 167 Tom Casagrande RC | 15.00 | 30.00 |

| Card | Low | High |
|---|---|---|
| 168 Duane Pillette | 15.00 | 30.00 |
| 169 Bob Oldis | 20.00 | 40.00 |
| 170 Jim Pearce DP RC | 7.50 | 15.00 |
| 171 Dick Brodowski | 15.00 | 30.00 |
| 172 Frank Baumholtz RC | 7.50 | 15.00 |
| 173 Bob Kline RC | 15.00 | 30.00 |
| 174 Rudy Minarcin RC | 15.00 | 30.00 |
| 175 Does not exist | | |
| 176 Norm Zauchin RC | 15.00 | 30.00 |
| 177 Al Robertson | | |
| 178 Bobby Adams | 15.00 | 30.00 |
| 179 Jim Bolger RC | 15.00 | 30.00 |
| 180 Clem Labine | 30.00 | 60.00 |
| 181 Roy McMillan | 20.00 | 40.00 |
| 182 Humberto Robinson RC | 15.00 | 30.00 |
| 183 Anthony Jacobs RC | 15.00 | 30.00 |
| 184 Harry Perkowski DP | 7.50 | 15.00 |
| 185 Don Ferrarese RC | 15.00 | 30.00 |
| 186 Does not exist | | |
| 187 Gil Hodges | 100.00 | 175.00 |
| 188 Charlie Silvera DP | 7.50 | 15.00 |
| 189 Phil Rizzuto | 100.00 | 175.00 |
| 190 Gene Woodling | 20.00 | 40.00 |
| 191 Eddie Stanky MG | 20.00 | 40.00 |
| 192 Jim Delsing | 20.00 | 40.00 |
| 193 Johnny Sain | 30.00 | 60.00 |
| 194 Willie Mays | 350.00 | 600.00 |
| 195 Ed Roebuck RC | 30.00 | 60.00 |
| 196 Gale Wade RC | 15.00 | 30.00 |
| 197 Al Smith | 30.00 | 60.00 |
| 198 Yogi Berra | 175.00 | 300.00 |
| 199 Bert Hamric RC | 20.00 | 40.00 |
| 200 Jackie Jensen | 30.00 | 60.00 |
| 201 Sherman Lollar | 20.00 | 40.00 |
| 202 Jim Owens RC | 15.00 | 30.00 |
| 203 Does not exist | | |
| 204 Frank Smith | 15.00 | 30.00 |
| 205 Gene Freese RC | 20.00 | 40.00 |
| 206 Pete Daley RC | 15.00 | 30.00 |
| 207 Billy Consolo | 15.00 | 30.00 |
| 208 Ray Moore RC | 20.00 | 40.00 |
| 209 Does not exist | | |
| 210 Duke Snider | 350.00 | 600.00 |

## 1956 Topps

| Card | Low | High |
|---|---|---|
| COMPLETE SET (340) | 5000.00 | 8000.00 |
| COMMON CARD (1-100) | 5.00 | 10.00 |
| COMMON CARD (101-180) | 6.00 | 12.00 |
| COMMON CARD (261-340) | 6.00 | 12.00 |
| COMMON CARD (181-260) | 7.50 | 15.00 |
| WRAP (1-CENT) | 200.00 | 250.00 |
| WRAP (1-CENT, REPEAT) | 75.00 | 100.00 |
| WRAPPER (5-CENT) | 150.00 | 200.00 |
| 1 Will Harridge PRES | 75.00 | 125.00 |
| 2 Warren Giles PRES DP | 30.00 | 50.00 |
| 3 Elmer Valo | 7.50 | 15.00 |
| 4 Carlos Paula | 7.50 | 15.00 |
| 5 Ted Williams | 300.00 | 500.00 |
| 6 Ray Boone | 15.00 | 25.00 |
| 7 Ron Negray RC | 5.00 | 10.00 |
| 8 Walter Alston MG RC | 25.00 | 40.00 |
| 9 Ruben Gomez DP | 5.00 | 10.00 |
| 10 Warren Spahn | 70.00 | 120.00 |
| 11A Chicago Cubs TC Center | 15.00 | 30.00 |
| 11B Chicago Cubs TC D'55 | 50.00 | 80.00 |
| 11C Chicago Cubs TC Left | 15.00 | 30.00 |
| 12 Andy Carey | 7.50 | 15.00 |
| 13 Roy Face | 7.50 | 15.00 |
| 14 Ken Boyer DP | 7.50 | 15.00 |
| 15 Ernie Banks DP | 60.00 | 100.00 |
| 16 Hector Lopez RC | 7.50 | 15.00 |
| 17 Gene Conley | 7.50 | 15.00 |
| 18 Dick Donovan | 5.00 | 10.00 |
| 19 Chuck Diering DP | 5.00 | 10.00 |
| 20 Al Kaline | 75.00 | 125.00 |
| 21 Joe Collins DP | 7.50 | 15.00 |
| 22 Jim Finigan | 5.00 | 10.00 |
| 23 Fred Marsh | 5.00 | 10.00 |
| 24 Dick Groat | 7.50 | 15.00 |
| 25 Ted Kluszewski | 50.00 | 80.00 |
| 25A Ted Kluszewski GB | | |
| 26 Grady Hatton | 5.00 | 10.00 |
| 27 Nelson Burbrink DP RC | 5.00 | 10.00 |
| 28 Bobby Hofman | 5.00 | 10.00 |
| 29 Jack Harshman | 5.00 | 10.00 |
| 30 Jackie Robinson DP | 150.00 | 250.00 |
| 31 Hank Aaron UER RC | 200.00 | 350.00 |
| 32 Frank House | 5.00 | 10.00 |
| 33 Roberto Clemente | 250.00 | 400.00 |
| 34 Tom Brewer DP | 5.00 | 10.00 |
| 35 Al Rosen | 7.50 | 15.00 |
| 36 Rudy Minarcin | 7.50 | 15.00 |
| 37 Alex Grammas | 5.00 | 10.00 |
| 38 Bob Kennedy | 7.50 | 15.00 |
| 39 Don Mossi | 7.50 | 15.00 |
| 40 Bob Turley | 7.50 | 15.00 |
| 41 Hank Sauer | 7.50 | 15.00 |
| 42 Sandy Amoros | 15.00 | 25.00 |
| 43 Ray Moore | 5.00 | 10.00 |
| 44 Windy McCall | 5.00 | 10.00 |
| 45 Gus Zernial | 7.50 | 15.00 |
| 46 Gene Freese DP | 5.00 | 10.00 |
| 47 Art Fowler | 5.00 | 10.00 |
| 48 Jim Hegan | 7.50 | 15.00 |
| 49 Pedro Ramos RC | 5.00 | 10.00 |
| 50 Dusty Rhodes DP | 7.50 | 15.00 |
| 51 Ernie Oravetz RC | 5.00 | 10.00 |
| 52 Bob Grim DP | 7.50 | 15.00 |
| 53 Arnie Portocarrero | 5.00 | 10.00 |
| 54 Bob Keegan | 5.00 | 10.00 |
| 55 Wally Moon | 7.50 | 15.00 |
| 56 Dale Long | 7.50 | 15.00 |
| 57 Duke Maas RC | 5.00 | 10.00 |
| 58 Ed Roebuck | 15.00 | 25.00 |
| 59 Jose Santiago RC | 5.00 | 10.00 |
| 60 Mayo Smith MG DP | 5.00 | 10.00 |
| 61 Bill Skowron | 15.00 | 25.00 |
| 62 Hal Smith | 7.50 | 15.00 |
| 63 Roger Craig RC | 25.00 | 40.00 |
| 64 Luis Arroyo RC | 7.50 | 15.00 |
| 65 Johnny O'Brien | 7.50 | 15.00 |
| 66 Bob Speake DP RC | 5.00 | 10.00 |
| 67 Vic Power | 7.50 | 15.00 |
| 68 Chuck Stobbs | 5.00 | 10.00 |
| 69 Chuck Tanner | 7.50 | 15.00 |
| 70 Jim Rivera | 5.00 | 10.00 |
| 71 Frank Sullivan | 5.00 | 10.00 |
| 72A Philadelphia Phillies TC Center | 15.00 | 30.00 |
| 72B Philadelphia Phillies TC D'55 | 50.00 | 80.00 |
| 72C Philadelphia Phillies TC Left DP | 15.00 | 30.00 |
| 73 Wayne Terwilliger | 5.00 | 10.00 |
| 74 Jim King RC | 5.00 | 10.00 |
| 75 Roy Sievers DP | 7.50 | 15.00 |
| 76 Ray Crone | 5.00 | 10.00 |
| 77 Harvey Haddix | 7.50 | 15.00 |
| 78 Herman Wehmeier | 5.00 | 10.00 |
| 79 Sandy Koufax | 200.00 | 350.00 |
| 80 Gus Triandos DP | 5.00 | 10.00 |
| 81 Wally Westlake | 5.00 | 10.00 |
| 82 Bill Renna DP | 5.00 | 10.00 |
| 83 Karl Spooner | 7.50 | 15.00 |
| 84 Babe Birrer RC | 5.00 | 10.00 |
| 85A Cleveland Indians TC Center | 15.00 | 30.00 |
| 85B Cleveland Indians TC D'55 | 50.00 | 80.00 |
| 85C Cleveland Indians TC Left | 15.00 | 30.00 |
| 86 Ray Jablonski DP | 5.00 | 10.00 |
| 87 Dean Stone | 5.00 | 10.00 |
| 88 Johnny Kucks RC | 7.50 | 15.00 |
| 89 Norm Zauchin | 5.00 | 10.00 |
| 90A Cincinnati Redlegs TC Center | 15.00 | 30.00 |
| 90B Cincinnati Reds TC D'55 | 50.00 | 80.00 |
| 90C Cincinnati Reds TC Left | 15.00 | 30.00 |
| 91 Gail Harris RC | 5.00 | 10.00 |
| 92 Bob (Red) Wilson | 5.00 | 10.00 |
| 93 George Susce | 5.00 | 10.00 |
| 94 Ron Kline | 5.00 | 10.00 |
| 95A Milwaukee Braves TC Center | 20.00 | 40.00 |
| 95B Milwaukee Braves TC D'55 | 50.00 | 80.00 |
| 95C Milwaukee Braves TC Left | 20.00 | 40.00 |
| 96 Bill Tremel | 5.00 | 10.00 |
| 97 Jerry Lynch | 7.50 | 15.00 |
| 98 Camilo Pascual | 7.50 | 15.00 |
| 99 Don Zimmer | 15.00 | 25.00 |
| 100A Baltimore Orioles TC Center | 20.00 | 40.00 |
| 100B Baltimore Orioles TC D'55 | 50.00 | 80.00 |
| 100C Baltimore Orioles TC Left | 20.00 | 40.00 |
| 101 Roy Campanella | 90.00 | 150.00 |
| 102 Jim Davis | 6.00 | 12.00 |
| 103 Willie Miranda | 6.00 | 12.00 |
| 104 Bob Lennon | 6.00 | 12.00 |
| 105 Al Smith | 6.00 | 12.00 |
| 106 Joe Astroth | 6.00 | 12.00 |
| 107 Eddie Mathews | 60.00 | 100.00 |
| 108 Laurin Pepper | 6.00 | 12.00 |
| 109 Enos Slaughter | 25.00 | 40.00 |
| 110 Yogi Berra | 100.00 | 175.00 |
| 111 Boston Red Sox TC | 20.00 | 40.00 |
| 112 Dee Fondy | 6.00 | 12.00 |
| 113 Phil Rizzuto | 90.00 | 150.00 |
| 114 Jim Owens | 7.50 | 15.00 |
| 115 Jackie Jensen | 7.50 | 15.00 |
| 116 Eddie O'Brien | 7.50 | 15.00 |
| 117 Virgil Trucks | 7.50 | 15.00 |
| 118 Nellie Fox | 50.00 | 80.00 |
| 119 Larry Jackson RC | 7.50 | 15.00 |
| 120 Richie Ashburn | 35.00 | 60.00 |
| 121 Pittsburgh Pirates TC | 20.00 | 40.00 |
| 122 Willard Nixon | 6.00 | 12.00 |
| 123 Roy McMillan | 7.50 | 15.00 |
| 124 Don Kaiser | 6.00 | 12.00 |
| 125 Minnie Minoso | 25.00 | 40.00 |
| 126 Jim Brady RC | 6.00 | 12.00 |
| 127 Willie Jones | 7.50 | 15.00 |
| 128 Eddie Yost | 7.50 | 15.00 |
| 129 Jake Martin RC | 6.00 | 12.00 |
| 130 Willie Mays | 175.00 | 300.00 |
| 131 Bob Roselli RC | 6.00 | 12.00 |
| 132 Bobby Avila | 6.00 | 12.00 |
| 133 Ray Narleski | 6.00 | 12.00 |
| 134 St. Louis Cardinals TC | 20.00 | 40.00 |
| 135 Mickey Mantle | 900.00 | 1500.00 |
| 136 Johnny Logan | 7.50 | 15.00 |
| 137 Al Silvera RC | 6.00 | 12.00 |
| 138 Johnny Antonelli | 7.50 | 15.00 |
| 139 Tommy Carroll | 7.50 | 15.00 |
| 140 Herb Score RC | 35.00 | 60.00 |
| 141 Joe Frazier | 6.00 | 12.00 |
| 142 Gene Baker | 6.00 | 12.00 |
| 143 Jim Piersall | 7.50 | 15.00 |
| 144 Leroy Powell RC | 6.00 | 12.00 |
| 145 Gil Hodges | 35.00 | 60.00 |
| 146 Washington Nationals TC | 20.00 | 40.00 |
| 147 Earl Torgeson | 6.00 | 12.00 |
| 148 Alvin Dark | 7.50 | 15.00 |
| 149 Dixie Howell | 6.00 | 12.00 |
| 150 Duke Snider | 75.00 | 125.00 |
| 151 Spook Jacobs | 7.50 | 15.00 |
| 152 Billy Hoeft | 7.50 | 15.00 |
| 153 Frank Thomas | 7.50 | 15.00 |
| 154 Dave Pope | 6.00 | 12.00 |
| 155 Harvey Kuenn | 7.50 | 15.00 |
| 156 Wes Westrum | 7.50 | 15.00 |
| 157 Dick Brodowski | 6.00 | 12.00 |
| 158 Wally Post | 6.00 | 12.00 |
| 159 Clint Courtney | 6.00 | 12.00 |
| 160 Billy Pierce | 7.50 | 15.00 |
| 161 Joe DeMaestri | 6.00 | 12.00 |
| 162 Dave (Gus) Bell | 7.50 | 15.00 |
| 163 Gene Woodling | 7.50 | 15.00 |
| 164 Harmon Killebrew | 60.00 | 100.00 |
| 165 Red Schoendienst | 25.00 | 40.00 |
| 166 Brooklyn Dodgers TC | 125.00 | 200.00 |
| 167 Harry Dorish | 6.00 | 12.00 |
| 168 Sammy White | 6.00 | 12.00 |
| 169 Bob Nelson RC | 6.00 | 12.00 |
| 170 Bill Virdon | 7.50 | 15.00 |
| 171 Jim Wilson | 6.00 | 12.00 |
| 172 Frank Torre DP | 7.50 | 15.00 |
| 173 Johnny Podres | 15.00 | 25.00 |
| 174 Glen Gorbous RC | 6.00 | 12.00 |
| 175 Del Crandall | 7.50 | 15.00 |
| 176 Alex Kellner | 6.00 | 12.00 |
| 177 Hank Bauer | 15.00 | 25.00 |
| 178 Joe Black | 7.50 | 15.00 |
| 179 Harry Chiti | 6.00 | 12.00 |
| 180 Robin Roberts | 30.00 | 50.00 |
| 181 Billy Martin | 75.00 | 125.00 |
| 182 Paul Minner | 7.50 | 15.00 |
| 183 Stan Lopata | 10.00 | 20.00 |
| 184 Don Bessent RC | 10.00 | 20.00 |

| | | | | | | | | | |
|---|---|---|---|---|---|---|---|---|---|
| ❑ 185 Bill Bruton | 10.00 | 20.00 | | ❑ 273 Walker Cooper | 6.00 | 12.00 | | ❑ COMMON CARD (89-176) | 4.00 | 8.00 |
| ❑ 186 Ron Jackson | 7.50 | 15.00 | | ❑ 274 Frank Baumholtz | 6.00 | 12.00 | | ❑ COMMON CARD (177-264) | 4.00 | 8.00 |
| ❑ 187 Early Wynn | 30.00 | 50.00 | | ❑ 275 Jim Greengrass | 6.00 | 12.00 | | ❑ COMMON CARD (265-352) | 10.00 | 20.00 |
| ❑ 188 Chicago White Sox TC | 30.00 | 50.00 | | ❑ 276 George Zuverink | 6.00 | 12.00 | | ❑ COMMON CARD (353-407) | 4.00 | 8.00 |
| ❑ 189 Ned Garver | 7.50 | 15.00 | | ❑ 277 Daryl Spencer | 6.00 | 12.00 | | ❑ COMMON DP (265-352) | 6.00 | 12.00 |
| ❑ 190 Carl Furillo | 18.00 | 30.00 | | ❑ 278 Chet Nichols | 6.00 | 12.00 | | ❑ WRAPPER (1-CENT) | 250.00 | 300.00 |
| ❑ 191 Frank Lary | 10.00 | 20.00 | | ❑ 279 Johnny Groth | 6.00 | 12.00 | | ❑ WRAPPER (5-CENT) | 150.00 | 200.00 |
| ❑ 192 Smoky Burgess | 10.00 | 20.00 | | ❑ 280 Jim Gilliam | 25.00 | 40.00 | | ❑ 1 Ted Williams | 350.00 | 600.00 |
| ❑ 193 Wilmer Mizell | 10.00 | 20.00 | | ❑ 281 Art Houtteman | 6.00 | 12.00 | | ❑ 2 Yogi Berra | 125.00 | 200.00 |
| ❑ 194 Monte Irvin | 18.00 | 30.00 | | ❑ 282 Warren Hacker | 6.00 | 12.00 | | ❑ 3 Dale Long | 10.00 | 20.00 |
| ❑ 195 George Kell | 18.00 | 30.00 | | ❑ 283 Hal R.Smith RC | 7.50 | 15.00 | | ❑ 4 Johnny Logan | 10.00 | 20.00 |
| ❑ 196 Tom Poholsky | 7.50 | 15.00 | | ❑ 284 Ike Delock | 6.00 | 12.00 | | ❑ 5 Sal Maglie | 10.00 | 20.00 |
| ❑ 197 Granny Hamner | 7.50 | 15.00 | | ❑ 285 Eddie Miksis | 6.00 | 12.00 | | ❑ 6 Hector Lopez | 7.50 | 15.00 |
| ❑ 198 Ed Fitzgerald | 7.50 | 15.00 | | ❑ 286 Bill Wight | 6.00 | 12.00 | | ❑ 7 Luis Aparicio | 15.00 | 30.00 |
| ❑ 199 Hank Thompson | 10.00 | 20.00 | | ❑ 287 Bobby Adams | 6.00 | 12.00 | | ❑ 8 Don Mossi | 7.50 | 15.00 |
| ❑ 200 Bob Feller | 75.00 | 125.00 | | ❑ 288 Bob Cerv | 25.00 | 40.00 | | ❑ 9 Johnny Temple | 7.50 | 15.00 |
| ❑ 201 Rip Repulski | 7.50 | 15.00 | | ❑ 289 Hal Jeffcoat | 6.00 | 12.00 | | ❑ 10 Willie Mays | 250.00 | 400.00 |
| ❑ 202 Jim Hearn | 7.50 | 15.00 | | ❑ 290 Curt Simmons | 7.50 | 15.00 | | ❑ 11 George Zuverink | 5.00 | 10.00 |
| ❑ 203 Bill Tuttle | 7.50 | 15.00 | | ❑ 291 Frank Kellert RC | 6.00 | 12.00 | | ❑ 12 Dick Groat | 10.00 | 20.00 |
| ❑ 204 Art Swanson RC | 7.50 | 15.00 | | ❑ 292 Luis Aparicio RC | 90.00 | 150.00 | | ❑ 13 Wally Burnette RC | 5.00 | 10.00 |
| ❑ 205 Whitey Lockman | 10.00 | 20.00 | | ❑ 293 Stu Miller | 15.00 | 25.00 | | ❑ 14 Bob Nieman | 5.00 | 10.00 |
| ❑ 206 Erv Palica | 7.50 | 15.00 | | ❑ 294 Ernie Johnson | 7.50 | 15.00 | | ❑ 15 Robin Roberts | 15.00 | 30.00 |
| ❑ 207 Jim Small RC | 7.50 | 15.00 | | ❑ 295 Clem Labine | 7.50 | 15.00 | | ❑ 16 Walt Moryn | 5.00 | 10.00 |
| ❑ 208 Elston Howard | 35.00 | 60.00 | | ❑ 296 Andy Seminick | 6.00 | 12.00 | | ❑ 17 Billy Gardner | 5.00 | 10.00 |
| ❑ 209 Max Surkont | 7.50 | 15.00 | | ❑ 297 Bob Skinner | 7.50 | 15.00 | | ❑ 18 Don Drysdale RC | 150.00 | 250.00 |
| ❑ 210 Mike Garcia | 10.00 | 20.00 | | ❑ 298 Johnny Schmitz | 6.00 | 12.00 | | ❑ 19 Bob Wilson | 5.00 | 10.00 |
| ❑ 211 Murry Dickson | 7.50 | 15.00 | | ❑ 299 Charlie Neal | 25.00 | 40.00 | | ❑ 20 Hank Aaron UER | 175.00 | 300.00 |
| ❑ 212 Johnny Temple | 7.50 | 15.00 | | ❑ 300 Vic Wertz | 7.50 | 15.00 | | ❑ 21 Frank Sullivan | 5.00 | 10.00 |
| ❑ 213 Detroit Tigers TC | 35.00 | 60.00 | | ❑ 301 Marv Grissom | 6.00 | 12.00 | | ❑ 22 Jerry Snyder UER | 5.00 | 10.00 |
| ❑ 214 Bob Rush | 7.50 | 15.00 | | ❑ 302 Eddie Robinson | 6.00 | 12.00 | | ❑ 23 Sherm Lollar | 7.50 | 15.00 |
| ❑ 215 Tommy Byrne | 10.00 | 20.00 | | ❑ 303 Jim Dyck | 6.00 | 12.00 | | ❑ 24 Bill Mazeroski RC | 50.00 | 80.00 |
| ❑ 216 Jerry Schoonmaker RC | 7.50 | 15.00 | | ❑ 304 Frank Malzone | 7.50 | 15.00 | | ❑ 25 Whitey Ford | 100.00 | 175.00 |
| ❑ 217 Billy Klaus | 7.50 | 15.00 | | ❑ 305 Brooks Lawrence | 6.00 | 12.00 | | ❑ 26 Bob Boyd | 5.00 | 10.00 |
| ❑ 218 Joe Nuxhall UER | 10.00 | 20.00 | | ❑ 306 Curt Roberts | 6.00 | 12.00 | | ❑ 27 Ted Kazanski | 5.00 | 10.00 |
| ❑ 219 Lew Burdette | 10.00 | 20.00 | | ❑ 307 Hoyt Wilhelm | 25.00 | 40.00 | | ❑ 28 Gene Conley | 7.50 | 15.00 |
| ❑ 220 Del Ennis | 10.00 | 20.00 | | ❑ 308 Chuck Harmon | 6.00 | 12.00 | | ❑ 29 Whitey Herzog RC | 15.00 | 30.00 |
| ❑ 221 Bob Friend | 10.00 | 20.00 | | ❑ 309 Don Blasingame RC | 7.50 | 15.00 | | ❑ 30 Pee Wee Reese | 50.00 | 80.00 |
| ❑ 222 Dave Philley | 7.50 | 15.00 | | ❑ 310 Steve Gromek | 6.00 | 12.00 | | ❑ 31 Ron Northey | 5.00 | 10.00 |
| ❑ 223 Randy Jackson | 7.50 | 15.00 | | ❑ 311 Hal Naragon | 6.00 | 12.00 | | ❑ 32 Hershell Freeman | 5.00 | 10.00 |
| ❑ 224 Bud Podbielan | 7.50 | 15.00 | | ❑ 312 Andy Pafko | 7.50 | 15.00 | | ❑ 33 Jim Small | 5.00 | 10.00 |
| ❑ 225 Gil McDougald | 30.00 | 50.00 | | ❑ 313 Gene Stephens | 6.00 | 12.00 | | ❑ 34 Tom Sturdivant RC | 7.50 | 15.00 |
| ❑ 226 New York Giants TC | 50.00 | 80.00 | | ❑ 314 Hobie Landrith | 6.00 | 12.00 | | ❑ 35 Frank Robinson RC | 175.00 | 300.00 |
| ❑ 227 Russ Meyer | 7.50 | 15.00 | | ❑ 315 Milt Bolling | 6.00 | 12.00 | | ❑ 36 Bob Grim | 5.00 | 10.00 |
| ❑ 228 Mickey Vernon | 10.50 | 20.00 | | ❑ 316 Jerry Coleman | 7.50 | 15.00 | | ❑ 37 Frank Torre | 7.50 | 15.00 |
| ❑ 229 Harry Brecheen CO | 10.00 | 20.00 | | ❑ 317 Al Aber | 6.00 | 12.00 | | ❑ 38 Nellie Fox | 30.00 | 50.00 |
| ❑ 230 Chico Carrasquel | 7.50 | 15.00 | | ❑ 318 Fred Hatfield | 6.00 | 12.00 | | ❑ 39 Al Worthington RC | 5.00 | 10.00 |
| ❑ 231 Bob Hale RC | 7.50 | 15.00 | | ❑ 319 Jack Crimian RC | 6.00 | 12.00 | | ❑ 40 Early Wynn | 15.00 | 30.00 |
| ❑ 232 Toby Atwell | 7.50 | 15.00 | | ❑ 320 Joe Adcock | 7.50 | 15.00 | | ❑ 41 Hal W. Smith | 5.00 | 10.00 |
| ❑ 233 Carl Erskine | 18.00 | 30.00 | | ❑ 321 Jim Konstanty | 7.50 | 15.00 | | ❑ 42 Dee Fondy | 5.00 | 10.00 |
| ❑ 234 Pete Runnels | 7.50 | 15.00 | | ❑ 322 Karl Olson | 6.00 | 12.00 | | ❑ 43 Connie Johnson | 5.00 | 10.00 |
| ❑ 235 Don Newcombe | 30.00 | 50.00 | | ❑ 323 Willard Schmidt | 6.00 | 12.00 | | ❑ 44 Joe DeMaestri | 5.00 | 10.00 |
| ❑ 236 Kansas City Athletics TC | 20.00 | 40.00 | | ❑ 324 Rocky Bridges | 7.50 | 15.00 | | ❑ 45 Carl Furillo | 15.00 | 30.00 |
| ❑ 237 Jose Valdivielso RC | 7.50 | 15.00 | | ❑ 325 Don Liddle | 6.00 | 12.00 | | ❑ 46 Robert J. Miller | 5.00 | 10.00 |
| ❑ 238 Walt Dropo | 10.00 | 20.00 | | ❑ 326 Connie Johnson RC | 6.00 | 12.00 | | ❑ 47 Don Blasingame | 5.00 | 10.00 |
| ❑ 239 Harry Simpson | 7.50 | 15.00 | | ❑ 327 Bob Wiesler RC | 6.00 | 12.00 | | ❑ 48 Bill Bruton | 7.50 | 15.00 |
| ❑ 240 Whitey Ford | 75.00 | 125.00 | | ❑ 328 Preston Ward | 6.00 | 12.00 | | ❑ 49 Daryl Spencer | 5.00 | 10.00 |
| ❑ 241 Don Mueller UER | 10.00 | 20.00 | | ❑ 329 Lou Berberet RC | 6.00 | 12.00 | | ❑ 50 Herb Score | 15.00 | 30.00 |
| ❑ 242 Hershell Freeman | 7.50 | 15.00 | | ❑ 330 Jim Busby | 7.50 | 15.00 | | ❑ 51 Clint Courtney | 5.00 | 10.00 |
| ❑ 243 Sherm Lollar | 10.00 | 20.00 | | ❑ 331 Dick Hall | 6.00 | 12.00 | | ❑ 52 Lee Walls | 5.00 | 10.00 |
| ❑ 244 Bob Buhl | 18.00 | 30.00 | | ❑ 332 Don Larsen | 35.00 | 60.00 | | ❑ 53 Clem Labine | 10.00 | 20.00 |
| ❑ 245 Billy Goodman | 10.00 | 20.00 | | ❑ 333 Rube Walker | 6.00 | 12.00 | | ❑ 54 Elmer Valo | 5.00 | 10.00 |
| ❑ 246 Tom Gorman | 7.50 | 15.00 | | ❑ 334 Bob Miller | 7.50 | 15.00 | | ❑ 55 Ernie Banks | 75.00 | 125.00 |
| ❑ 247 Bill Sarni | 7.50 | 15.00 | | ❑ 335 Don Hoak | 7.50 | 15.00 | | ❑ 56 Dave Sisler RC | 5.00 | 10.00 |
| ❑ 248 Bob Porterfield | 7.50 | 15.00 | | ❑ 336 Ellis Kinder | 6.00 | 12.00 | | ❑ 57 Jim Lemon | 7.50 | 15.00 |
| ❑ 249 Johnny Klippstein | 7.50 | 15.00 | | ❑ 337 Bobby Morgan | 6.00 | 12.00 | | ❑ 58 Ruben Gomez | 5.00 | 10.00 |
| ❑ 250 Larry Doby | 18.00 | 30.00 | | ❑ 338 Jim Delsing | 6.00 | 12.00 | | ❑ 59 Dick Williams | 7.50 | 15.00 |
| ❑ 251 New York Yankees TC UER | 150.00 | 250.00 | | ❑ 339 Rance Pless RC | 6.00 | 12.00 | | ❑ 60 Billy Hoeft | 5.00 | 10.00 |
| ❑ 252 Vern Law | 10.00 | 20.00 | | ❑ 340 Mickey McDermott | 35.00 | 60.00 | | ❑ 61 Dusty Rhodes | 7.50 | 15.00 |
| ❑ 253 Irv Noren | 18.00 | 30.00 | | ❑ CL1 Checklist 1/3 | 175.00 | 300.00 | | ❑ 62 Billy Martin | 35.00 | 60.00 |
| ❑ 254 George Crowe | 7.50 | 15.00 | | ❑ CL2 Checklist 2/4 | 175.00 | 300.00 | | ❑ 63 Ike Delock | 5.00 | 10.00 |
| ❑ 255 Bob Lemon | 30.00 | 50.00 | | | | | | ❑ 64 Pete Runnels | 5.00 | 10.00 |
| ❑ 256 Tom Hurd | 7.50 | 15.00 | | **1957 Topps** | | | | ❑ 65 Wally Moon | 7.50 | 15.00 |
| ❑ 257 Bobby Thomson | 18.00 | 30.00 | | | | | | ❑ 66 Brooks Lawrence | 5.00 | 10.00 |
| ❑ 258 Art Ditmar | 7.50 | 15.00 | | | | | | ❑ 67 Chico Carrasquel | 5.00 | 10.00 |
| ❑ 259 Sam Jones | 10.00 | 20.00 | | | | | | ❑ 68 Ray Crone | 5.00 | 10.00 |
| ❑ 260 Pee Wee Reese | 90.00 | 150.00 | | | | | | ❑ 69 Roy McMillan | 7.50 | 15.00 |
| ❑ 261 Bobby Shantz | 7.50 | 15.00 | | | | | | ❑ 70 Richie Ashburn | 30.00 | 50.00 |
| ❑ 262 Howie Pollet | 6.00 | 12.00 | | | | | | ❑ 71 Murry Dickson | 5.00 | 10.00 |
| ❑ 263 Bob Miller | 6.00 | 12.00 | | | | | | ❑ 72 Bill Tuttle | 5.00 | 10.00 |
| ❑ 264 Ray Monzant RC | 6.00 | 12.00 | | | | | | ❑ 73 George Crowe | 5.00 | 10.00 |
| ❑ 265 Sandy Consuegra | 6.00 | 12.00 | | | | | | ❑ 74 Vito Valentinetti RC | 5.00 | 10.00 |
| ❑ 266 Don Ferrarese | 6.00 | 12.00 | | | | | | ❑ 75 Jimmy Piersall | 7.50 | 15.00 |
| ❑ 267 Bob Nieman | 6.00 | 12.00 | | | | | | ❑ 76 Roberto Clemente | 175.00 | 300.00 |
| ❑ 268 Dale Mitchell | 7.50 | 15.00 | | | | | | ❑ 77 Paul Foytack RC | 5.00 | 10.00 |
| ❑ 269 Jack Meyer RC | 6.00 | 12.00 | | | | | | ❑ 78 Vic Wertz | 7.50 | 15.00 |
| ❑ 270 Billy Loes | 7.50 | 15.00 | | | | | | ❑ 79 Lindy McDaniel RC | 7.50 | 15.00 |
| ❑ 271 Foster Castleman RC | 6.00 | 12.00 | | ❑ COMPLETE SET (407) | 7000.00 | 10000.00 | | ❑ 80 Gil Hodges | 30.00 | 50.00 |
| ❑ 272 Danny O'Connell | 6.00 | 12.00 | | ❑ COMMON CARD (1-88) | 5.00 | 10.00 | | ❑ 81 Herman Wehmeier | 5.00 | 10.00 |

| | | |
|---|---|---|
| ❑ 82 Elston Howard | 15.00 | 30.00 |
| ❑ 83 Lou Skizas RC | 5.00 | 10.00 |
| ❑ 84 Moe Drabowsky RC | 7.50 | 15.00 |
| ❑ 85 Larry Doby | 15.00 | 30.00 |
| ❑ 86 Bill Sarni | 5.00 | 10.00 |
| ❑ 87 Tom Gorman | 5.00 | 10.00 |
| ❑ 88 Harvey Kuenn | 7.50 | 15.00 |
| ❑ 89 Roy Sievers | 7.50 | 15.00 |
| ❑ 90 Warren Spahn | 50.00 | 80.00 |
| ❑ 91 Mack Burk RC | 4.00 | 8.00 |
| ❑ 92 Mickey Vernon | 7.50 | 15.00 |
| ❑ 93 Hal Jeffcoat | 4.00 | 8.00 |
| ❑ 94 Bobby Del Greco | 4.00 | 8.00 |
| ❑ 95 Mickey Mantle | 700.00 | 1200.00 |
| ❑ 96 Hank Aguirre RC | 4.00 | 8.00 |
| ❑ 97 New York Yankees TC | 60.00 | 100.00 |
| ❑ 98 Alvin Dark | 7.50 | 15.00 |
| ❑ 99 Bob Keegan | 4.00 | 8.00 |
| ❑ 100 W.Giles/W.Harridge | 7.50 | 15.00 |
| ❑ 101 Chuck Stobbs | 4.00 | 8.00 |
| ❑ 102 Ray Boone | 7.50 | 15.00 |
| ❑ 103 Joe Nuxhall | 7.50 | 15.00 |
| ❑ 104 Hank Foiles | 4.00 | 8.00 |
| ❑ 105 Johnny Antonelli | 7.50 | 15.00 |
| ❑ 106 Ray Moore | 4.00 | 8.00 |
| ❑ 107 Jim Rivera | 4.00 | 8.00 |
| ❑ 108 Tommy Byrne | 7.50 | 15.00 |
| ❑ 109 Hank Thompson | 4.00 | 8.00 |
| ❑ 110 Bill Virdon | 7.50 | 15.00 |
| ❑ 111 Hal R. Smith | 4.00 | 8.00 |
| ❑ 112 Tom Brewer | 4.00 | 8.00 |
| ❑ 113 Wilmer Mizell | 7.50 | 15.00 |
| ❑ 114 Milwaukee Braves TC | 10.00 | 20.00 |
| ❑ 115 Jim Gilliam | 7.50 | 15.00 |
| ❑ 116 Mike Fornieles | 4.00 | 8.00 |
| ❑ 117 Joe Adcock | 10.00 | 20.00 |
| ❑ 118 Bob Porterfield | 4.00 | 8.00 |
| ❑ 119 Stan Lopata | 4.00 | 8.00 |
| ❑ 120 Bob Lemon | 15.00 | 30.00 |
| ❑ 121 Clete Boyer RC | 15.00 | 30.00 |
| ❑ 122 Ken Boyer | 10.00 | 20.00 |
| ❑ 123 Steve Ridzik | 4.00 | 8.00 |
| ❑ 124 Dave Philley | 4.00 | 8.00 |
| ❑ 125 Al Kaline | 60.00 | 100.00 |
| ❑ 126 Bob Wiesler | 4.00 | 8.00 |
| ❑ 127 Bob Buhl | 7.50 | 15.00 |
| ❑ 128 Ed Bailey | 7.50 | 15.00 |
| ❑ 129 Saul Rogovin | 4.00 | 8.00 |
| ❑ 130 Don Newcombe | 10.00 | 20.00 |
| ❑ 131 Milt Bolling | 4.00 | 8.00 |
| ❑ 132 Art Ditmar | 7.50 | 15.00 |
| ❑ 133 Del Crandall | 7.50 | 15.00 |
| ❑ 134 Don Kaiser | 4.00 | 8.00 |
| ❑ 135 Bill Skowron | 10.00 | 20.00 |
| ❑ 136 Jim Hegan | 7.50 | 15.00 |
| ❑ 137 Bob Rush | 4.00 | 8.00 |
| ❑ 138 Minnie Minoso | 10.00 | 20.00 |
| ❑ 139 Lou Kretlow | 4.00 | 8.00 |
| ❑ 140 Frank Thomas | 7.50 | 15.00 |
| ❑ 141 Al Aber | 4.00 | 8.00 |
| ❑ 142 Charley Thompson | 4.00 | 8.00 |
| ❑ 143 Andy Pafko | 7.50 | 15.00 |
| ❑ 144 Ray Narleski | 4.00 | 8.00 |
| ❑ 145 Al Smith | 4.00 | 8.00 |
| ❑ 146 Don Ferrarese | 4.00 | 8.00 |
| ❑ 147 Al Walker | 4.00 | 8.00 |
| ❑ 148 Don Mueller | 7.50 | 15.00 |
| ❑ 149 Bob Kennedy | 7.50 | 15.00 |
| ❑ 150 Bob Friend | 7.50 | 15.00 |
| ❑ 151 Willie Miranda | 4.00 | 8.00 |
| ❑ 152 Jack Harshman | 4.00 | 8.00 |
| ❑ 153 Karl Olson | 4.00 | 8.00 |
| ❑ 154 Red Schoendienst | 15.00 | 30.00 |
| ❑ 155 Jim Brosnan | 7.50 | 15.00 |
| ❑ 156 Gus Triandos | 7.50 | 15.00 |
| ❑ 157 Wally Post | 7.50 | 15.00 |
| ❑ 158 Curt Simmons | 7.50 | 15.00 |
| ❑ 159 Solly Drake RC | 4.00 | 8.00 |
| ❑ 160 Billy Pierce | 7.50 | 15.00 |
| ❑ 161 Pittsburgh Pirates TC | 7.50 | 15.00 |
| ❑ 162 Jack Meyer | 4.00 | 8.00 |
| ❑ 163 Sammy White | 4.00 | 8.00 |
| ❑ 164 Tommy Carroll | 4.00 | 8.00 |
| ❑ 165 Ted Kluszewski | 60.00 | 100.00 |
| ❑ 166 Roy Face | 7.50 | 15.00 |
| ❑ 167 Vic Power | 7.50 | 15.00 |
| ❑ 168 Frank Lary | 7.50 | 15.00 |
| ❑ 169 Herb Plews RC | 4.00 | 8.00 |
| ❑ 170 Duke Snider | 75.00 | 125.00 |
| ❑ 171 Boston Red Sox TC | 7.50 | 15.00 |
| ❑ 172 Gene Woodling | 7.50 | 15.00 |
| ❑ 173 Roger Craig | 7.50 | 15.00 |
| ❑ 174 Willie Jones | 4.00 | 8.00 |
| ❑ 175 Don Larsen | 15.00 | 30.00 |
| ❑ 176A Gene Bakep ERR | 200.00 | 350.00 |
| ❑ 176B Gene Baker COR | 7.50 | 15.00 |
| ❑ 177 Eddie Yost | 4.00 | 8.00 |
| ❑ 178 Don Bessent | 4.00 | 8.00 |
| ❑ 179 Ernie Oravetz | 4.00 | 8.00 |
| ❑ 180 Gus Bell | 7.50 | 15.00 |
| ❑ 181 Dick Donovan | 4.00 | 8.00 |
| ❑ 182 Hobie Landrith | 4.00 | 8.00 |
| ❑ 183 Chicago Cubs TC | 7.50 | 15.00 |
| ❑ 184 Tito Francona RC | 4.00 | 8.00 |
| ❑ 185 Johnny Kucks | 7.50 | 15.00 |
| ❑ 186 Jim King | 7.50 | 15.00 |
| ❑ 187 Virgil Trucks | 7.50 | 15.00 |
| ❑ 188 Felix Mantilla RC | 7.50 | 15.00 |
| ❑ 189 Willard Nixon | 4.00 | 8.00 |
| ❑ 190 Randy Jackson | 4.00 | 8.00 |
| ❑ 191 Joe Margoneri RC | 4.00 | 8.00 |
| ❑ 192 Jerry Coleman | 7.50 | 15.00 |
| ❑ 193 Del Rice | 4.00 | 8.00 |
| ❑ 194 Hal Brown | 4.00 | 8.00 |
| ❑ 195 Bobby Avila | 4.00 | 8.00 |
| ❑ 196 Larry Jackson | 7.50 | 15.00 |
| ❑ 197 Hank Sauer | 7.50 | 15.00 |
| ❑ 198 Detroit Tigers TC | 7.50 | 15.00 |
| ❑ 199 Vern Law | 7.50 | 15.00 |
| ❑ 200 Gil McDougald | 10.00 | 20.00 |
| ❑ 201 Sandy Amoros | 7.50 | 15.00 |
| ❑ 202 Dick Gernert | 4.00 | 8.00 |
| ❑ 203 Hoyt Wilhelm | 15.00 | 30.00 |
| ❑ 204 Kansas City Athletics TC | 7.50 | 15.00 |
| ❑ 205 Charlie Maxwell | 4.00 | 8.00 |
| ❑ 206 Willard Schmidt | 4.00 | 8.00 |
| ❑ 207 Gordon (Billy) Hunter | 4.00 | 8.00 |
| ❑ 208 Lew Burdette | 7.50 | 15.00 |
| ❑ 209 Bob Skinner | 7.50 | 15.00 |
| ❑ 210 Roy Campanella | 90.00 | 150.00 |
| ❑ 211 Camilo Pascual | 7.50 | 15.00 |
| ❑ 212 Rocky Colavito RC | 75.00 | 125.00 |
| ❑ 213 Les Moss | 4.00 | 8.00 |
| ❑ 214 Philadelphia Phillies TC | 7.50 | 15.00 |
| ❑ 215 Enos Slaughter | 15.00 | 30.00 |
| ❑ 216 Marv Grissom | 4.00 | 8.00 |
| ❑ 217 Gene Stephens | 4.00 | 8.00 |
| ❑ 218 Ray Jablonski | 4.00 | 8.00 |
| ❑ 219 Tom Acker RC | 4.00 | 8.00 |
| ❑ 220 Jackie Jensen | 10.00 | 20.00 |
| ❑ 221 Dixie Howell | 4.00 | 8.00 |
| ❑ 222 Alex Grammas | 4.00 | 8.00 |
| ❑ 223 Frank House | 4.00 | 8.00 |
| ❑ 224 Marv Blaylock | 4.00 | 8.00 |
| ❑ 225 Harry Simpson | 4.00 | 8.00 |
| ❑ 226 Preston Ward | 4.00 | 8.00 |
| ❑ 227 Gerry Staley | 4.00 | 8.00 |
| ❑ 228 Smoky Burgess UER | 7.50 | 15.00 |
| ❑ 229 George Susce | 4.00 | 8.00 |
| ❑ 230 George Kell | 15.00 | 30.00 |
| ❑ 231 Solly Hemus | 4.00 | 8.00 |
| ❑ 232 Whitey Lockman | 7.50 | 15.00 |
| ❑ 233 Art Fowler | 4.00 | 8.00 |
| ❑ 234 Dick Cole | 4.00 | 8.00 |
| ❑ 235 Tom Poholsky | 7.50 | 15.00 |
| ❑ 236 Joe Ginsberg | 4.00 | 8.00 |
| ❑ 237 Foster Castleman | 4.00 | 8.00 |
| ❑ 238 Eddie Robinson | 4.00 | 8.00 |
| ❑ 239 Tom Morgan | 4.00 | 8.00 |
| ❑ 240 Hank Bauer | 7.50 | 15.00 |
| ❑ 241 Joe Lonnett RC | 4.00 | 8.00 |
| ❑ 242 Charlie Neal | 7.50 | 15.00 |
| ❑ 243 St. Louis Cardinals TC | 7.50 | 15.00 |
| ❑ 244 Billy Loes | 4.00 | 8.00 |
| ❑ 245 Rip Repulski | 4.00 | 8.00 |
| ❑ 246 Jose Valdivielso | 4.00 | 8.00 |
| ❑ 247 Turk Lown | 4.00 | 8.00 |
| ❑ 248 Jim Finigan | 4.00 | 8.00 |
| ❑ 249 Dave Pope | 4.00 | 8.00 |
| ❑ 250 Eddie Mathews | 30.00 | 50.00 |
| ❑ 251 Baltimore Orioles TC | 7.50 | 15.00 |
| ❑ 252 Carl Erskine | 7.50 | 15.00 |
| ❑ 253 Gus Zernial | 7.50 | 15.00 |
| ❑ 254 Ron Negray | 4.00 | 8.00 |
| ❑ 255 Charlie Silvera | 7.50 | 15.00 |
| ❑ 256 Ron Kline | 4.00 | 8.00 |
| ❑ 257 Walt Dropo | 4.00 | 8.00 |
| ❑ 258 Steve Gromek | 4.00 | 8.00 |
| ❑ 259 Eddie O'Brien | 4.00 | 8.00 |
| ❑ 260 Del Ennis | 7.50 | 15.00 |
| ❑ 261 Bob Chakales | 4.00 | 8.00 |
| ❑ 262 Bobby Thomson | 7.50 | 15.00 |
| ❑ 263 George Strickland | 4.00 | 8.00 |
| ❑ 264 Bob Turley | 7.50 | 15.00 |
| ❑ 265 Harvey Haddix DP | 6.00 | 12.00 |
| ❑ 266 Ken Kuhn DP RC | 6.00 | 12.00 |
| ❑ 267 Danny Kravitz RC | 10.00 | 20.00 |
| ❑ 268 Jack Collum | 10.00 | 20.00 |
| ❑ 269 Bob Cerv | 15.00 | 30.00 |
| ❑ 270 Washington Senators TC | 35.00 | 60.00 |
| ❑ 271 Danny O'Connell DP | 6.00 | 12.00 |
| ❑ 272 Bobby Shantz | 15.00 | 30.00 |
| ❑ 273 Jim Davis | 10.00 | 20.00 |
| ❑ 274 Don Hoak | 7.50 | 15.00 |
| ❑ 275 Cleveland Indians TC UER | 35.00 | 60.00 |
| ❑ 276 Jim Pyburn RC | 10.00 | 20.00 |
| ❑ 277 Johnny Podres | 20.00 | 40.00 |
| ❑ 278 Fred Hatfield DP | 6.00 | 12.00 |
| ❑ 279 Bob Thurman RC | 10.00 | 20.00 |
| ❑ 280 Alex Kellner | 10.00 | 20.00 |
| ❑ 281 Gail Harris | 10.00 | 20.00 |
| ❑ 282 Jack Dittmer DP | 6.00 | 12.00 |
| ❑ 283 Wes Covington DP RC | 6.00 | 12.00 |
| ❑ 284 Don Zimmer | 20.00 | 40.00 |
| ❑ 285 Ned Garver | 10.00 | 20.00 |
| ❑ 286 Bobby Richardson RC | 75.00 | 125.00 |
| ❑ 287 Sam Jones | 10.00 | 20.00 |
| ❑ 288 Ted Lepcio | 10.00 | 20.00 |
| ❑ 289 Jim Bolger DP | 6.00 | 12.00 |
| ❑ 290 Andy Carey DP | 20.00 | 40.00 |
| ❑ 291 Windy McCall | 10.00 | 20.00 |
| ❑ 292 Billy Klaus | 10.00 | 20.00 |
| ❑ 293 Ted Abernathy RC | 10.00 | 20.00 |
| ❑ 294 Rocky Bridges DP | 6.00 | 12.00 |
| ❑ 295 Joe Collins DP | 20.00 | 40.00 |
| ❑ 296 Johnny Klippstein | 10.00 | 20.00 |
| ❑ 297 Jack Crimian | 10.00 | 20.00 |
| ❑ 298 Irv Noren DP | 6.00 | 12.00 |
| ❑ 299 Chuck Harmon | 10.00 | 20.00 |
| ❑ 300 Mike Garcia | 15.00 | 30.00 |
| ❑ 301 Sammy Esposito DP RC | 10.00 | 20.00 |
| ❑ 302 Sandy Koufax DP | 200.00 | 350.00 |
| ❑ 303 Billy Goodman | 15.00 | 30.00 |
| ❑ 304 Joe Cunningham | 15.00 | 30.00 |
| ❑ 305 Chico Fernandez | 10.00 | 20.00 |
| ❑ 306 Darrell Johnson DP RC | 6.00 | 12.00 |
| ❑ 307 Jack D. Phillips DP | 6.00 | 12.00 |
| ❑ 308 Dick Hall | 10.00 | 20.00 |
| ❑ 309 Jim Busby DP | 6.00 | 12.00 |
| ❑ 310 Max Surkont DP | 6.00 | 12.00 |
| ❑ 311 Al Pilarcik DP RC | 6.00 | 12.00 |
| ❑ 312 Tony Kubek DP RC | 60.00 | 100.00 |
| ❑ 313 Mel Parnell | 7.50 | 15.00 |
| ❑ 314 Ed Bouchee DP RC | 6.00 | 12.00 |
| ❑ 315 Lou Berberet DP | 6.00 | 12.00 |
| ❑ 316 Billy O'Dell | 10.00 | 20.00 |
| ❑ 317 New York Giants TC | 50.00 | 80.00 |
| ❑ 318 Mickey McDermott | 10.00 | 20.00 |
| ❑ 319 Gino Cimoli RC | 10.00 | 20.00 |
| ❑ 320 Neil Chrisley RC | 10.00 | 20.00 |
| ❑ 321 John (Red) Murff RC | 10.00 | 20.00 |
| ❑ 322 Cincinnati Reds TC | 50.00 | 80.00 |
| ❑ 323 Wes Westrum | 15.00 | 30.00 |
| ❑ 324 Brooklyn Dodgers TC | 90.00 | 150.00 |
| ❑ 325 Frank Bolling | 10.00 | 20.00 |
| ❑ 326 Pedro Ramos | 10.00 | 20.00 |
| ❑ 327 Jim Pendleton | 10.00 | 20.00 |
| ❑ 328 Brooks Robinson RC | 250.00 | 400.00 |
| ❑ 329 Chicago White Sox TC | 35.00 | 60.00 |
| ❑ 330 Jim Wilson | 10.00 | 20.00 |
| ❑ 331 Ray Katt | 10.00 | 20.00 |
| ❑ 332 Bob Bowman RC | 10.00 | 20.00 |
| ❑ 333 Ernie Johnson | 10.00 | 20.00 |
| ❑ 334 Jerry Schoonmaker | 10.00 | 20.00 |
| ❑ 335 Granny Hamner | 10.00 | 20.00 |
| ❑ 336 Haywood Sullivan RC | 20.00 | 40.00 |
| ❑ 337 Rene Valdes RC | 10.00 | 20.00 |
| ❑ 338 Jim Bunning RC | 90.00 | 150.00 |
| ❑ 339 Bob Speake | 10.00 | 20.00 |
| ❑ 340 Bill Wight | 10.00 | 20.00 |
| ❑ 341 Don Gross DP | 10.00 | 20.00 |
| ❑ 342 Gene Mauch | 15.00 | 30.00 |
| ❑ 343 Taylor Phillips RC | 7.50 | 15.00 |
| ❑ 344 Paul LaPalme | 10.00 | 20.00 |

|  |  | | |
|---|---|---|---|
| 345 | Paul Smith | 10.00 | 20.00 |
| 346 | Dick Littlefield | 10.00 | 20.00 |
| 347 | Hal Naragon | 10.00 | 20.00 |
| 348 | Jim Hearn | 10.00 | 20.00 |
| 349 | Nellie King | 10.00 | 20.00 |
| 350 | Eddie Miksis | 10.00 | 20.00 |
| 351 | Dave Hillman RC | 10.00 | 20.00 |
| 352 | Elvis Kinder | 10.00 | 20.00 |
| 353 | Cal Neeman RC | 4.00 | 8.00 |
| 354 | Rip Coleman RC | 4.00 | 8.00 |
| 355 | Frank Malzone | 7.50 | 15.00 |
| 356 | Faye Throneberry | 4.00 | 8.00 |
| 357 | Earl Torgeson | 4.00 | 8.00 |
| 358 | Jerry Lynch | 7.50 | 15.00 |
| 359 | Tom Cheney RC | 4.00 | 8.00 |
| 360 | Johnny Groth | 4.00 | 8.00 |
| 361 | Curt Barclay RC | 4.00 | 8.00 |
| 362 | Roman Mejias RC | 7.50 | 15.00 |
| 363 | Eddie Kasko RC | 4.00 | 8.00 |
| 364 | Cal McLish RC | 7.50 | 15.00 |
| 365 | Ozzie Virgil RC | 4.00 | 8.00 |
| 366 | Ken Lehman | 4.00 | 8.00 |
| 367 | Ed Fitzgerald | 4.00 | 8.00 |
| 368 | Bob Purkey | 4.00 | 8.00 |
| 369 | Milt Graff RC | 4.00 | 8.00 |
| 370 | Warren Hacker | 4.00 | 8.00 |
| 371 | Bob Lennon | 4.00 | 8.00 |
| 372 | Norm Zauchin | 4.00 | 8.00 |
| 373 | Pete Whisenant RC | 4.00 | 8.00 |
| 374 | Don Cardwell RC | 4.00 | 8.00 |
| 375 | Jim Landis RC | 7.50 | 15.00 |
| 376 | Don Elston RC | 4.00 | 8.00 |
| 377 | Andre Rodgers RC | 4.00 | 8.00 |
| 378 | Elmer Singleton RC | 4.00 | 8.00 |
| 379 | Don Lee RC | 4.00 | 8.00 |
| 380 | Walker Cooper | 4.00 | 8.00 |
| 381 | Dean Stone | 4.00 | 8.00 |
| 382 | Jim Brideweaser | 4.00 | 8.00 |
| 383 | Juan Pizarro RC | 4.00 | 8.00 |
| 384 | Bobby G. Smith RC | 4.00 | 8.00 |
| 385 | Art Houtteman | 4.00 | 8.00 |
| 386 | Lyle Luttrell RC | 4.00 | 8.00 |
| 387 | Jack Sanford RC | 7.50 | 15.00 |
| 388 | Pete Daley | 4.00 | 8.00 |
| 389 | Dave Jolly | 4.00 | 8.00 |
| 390 | Reno Bertoia | 4.00 | 8.00 |
| 391 | Ralph Terry RC | 7.50 | 15.00 |
| 392 | Chuck Tanner | 7.50 | 15.00 |
| 393 | Raul Sanchez RC | 4.00 | 8.00 |
| 394 | Luis Arroyo | 7.50 | 15.00 |
| 395 | Bubba Phillips | 4.00 | 8.00 |
| 396 | Casey Wise RC | 4.00 | 8.00 |
| 397 | Roy Smalley | 4.00 | 8.00 |
| 398 | Al Cicotte RC | 7.50 | 15.00 |
| 399 | Billy Consolo | 4.00 | 8.00 |
| 400 | Fur/Hodges/Campy/Snider | 150.00 | 250.00 |
| 401 | Earl Battey RC | 7.50 | 15.00 |
| 402 | Jim Pisoni RC | 4.00 | 8.00 |
| 403 | Dick Hyde RC | 4.00 | 8.00 |
| 404 | Harry Anderson RC | 4.00 | 8.00 |
| 405 | Duke Maas | 4.00 | 8.00 |
| 406 | Bob Hale | 4.00 | 8.00 |
| 407 | Y.Berra/M.Mantle | 350.00 | 600.00 |
| CC1 | Contest May 4 | 60.00 | 100.00 |
| CC2 | Contest May 25 | 60.00 | 100.00 |
| CC3 | Contest June 22 | 75.00 | 125.00 |
| CC4 | Contest July 19 | 75.00 | 125.00 |
| NNO | Checklist 1/2 Bazooka | 150.00 | 250.00 |
| NNO | Checklist 1/2 Blony | 150.00 | 250.00 |
| NNO | Checklist 2/3 Bazooka | 250.00 | 400.00 |
| NNO | Checklist 2/3 Blony | 250.00 | 400.00 |
| NNO | Checklist 3/4 Bazooka | 500.00 | 800.00 |
| NNO | Checklist 3/4 Blony | 350.00 | 600.00 |
| NNO | Checklist 4/5 Bazooka | 600.00 | 1000.00 |
| NNO | Checklist 4/5 Blony | 500.00 | 800.00 |
| NNO | Lucky Penny Card | 60.00 | 100.00 |

## 1958 Topps

| | | |
|---|---|---|
| COMP. MASTER SET (534) | 8000.00 | 12000.00 |
| COMPLETE SET (494) | 4000.00 | 6000.00 |
| COMMON CARD (1-110) | 6.00 | 12.00 |
| COMMON CARD (111-495) | 4.00 | 8.00 |
| WRAPPER (1-CENT) | 75.00 | 100.00 |
| WRAPPER (5-CENT) | 100.00 | 125.00 |
| 1 Ted Williams | 350.00 | 600.00 |
| 2A Bob Lemon | 15.00 | 30.00 |
| 2B Bob Lemon YT | 35.00 | 60.00 |
| 3 Alex Kellner | 6.00 | 12.00 |

|  |  | | |
|---|---|---|---|
| 4 | Hank Foiles | 6.00 | 12.00 |
| 5 | Willie Mays | 175.00 | 300.00 |
| 6 | George Zuverink | 6.00 | 12.00 |
| 7 | Dale Long | 7.50 | 15.00 |
| 8A | Eddie Kasko | 6.00 | 12.00 |
| 8B | Eddie Kasko YN | 20.00 | 40.00 |
| 9 | Hank Bauer | 10.00 | 20.00 |
| 10 | Lew Burdette | 10.00 | 20.00 |
| 11A | Jim Rivera | 6.00 | 12.00 |
| 11B | Jim Rivera YT | 20.00 | 40.00 |
| 12 | George Crowe | 6.00 | 12.00 |
| 13A | Billy Hoeft | 6.00 | 12.00 |
| 13B | Billy Hoeft YN | 20.00 | 40.00 |
| 14 | Rip Repulski | 6.00 | 12.00 |
| 15 | Jim Lemon | 7.50 | 15.00 |
| 16 | Charlie Neal | 7.50 | 15.00 |
| 17 | Felix Mantilla | 6.00 | 12.00 |
| 18 | Frank Sullivan | 6.00 | 12.00 |
| 19 | San Francisco Giants TC | 20.00 | 40.00 |
| 20A | Gil McDougald | 20.00 | 40.00 |
| 20B | Gil McDougald YN | 35.00 | 60.00 |
| 21 | Curt Barclay | 6.00 | 12.00 |
| 22 | Hal Naragon | 6.00 | 12.00 |
| 23A | Bill Tuttle | 6.00 | 12.00 |
| 23B | Bill Tuttle YN | 20.00 | 40.00 |
| 24A | Hobie Landrith | 6.00 | 12.00 |
| 24B | Hobie Landrith YN | 20.00 | 40.00 |
| 25 | Don Drysdale | 60.00 | 120.00 |
| 26 | Ron Jackson | 6.00 | 12.00 |
| 27 | Bud Freeman | 6.00 | 12.00 |
| 28 | Jim Busby | 6.00 | 12.00 |
| 29 | Ted Lepcio | 6.00 | 12.00 |
| 30A | Hank Aaron | 125.00 | 200.00 |
| 30B | Hank Aaron YN | 350.00 | 600.00 |
| 31 | Tex Clevenger RC | 6.00 | 12.00 |
| 32A | J.W. Porter | 6.00 | 12.00 |
| 32B | J.W. Porter YN | 20.00 | 40.00 |
| 33A | Cal Neeman | 6.00 | 12.00 |
| 33B | Cal Neeman YT | 20.00 | 40.00 |
| 34 | Bob Thurman | 6.00 | 12.00 |
| 35A | Don Mossi | 7.50 | 15.00 |
| 35B | Don Mossi YT | 20.00 | 40.00 |
| 36 | Ted Kazanski | 6.00 | 12.00 |
| 37 | Mike McCormick UER RC | 7.50 | 15.00 |
| 38 | Dick Gernert | 6.00 | 12.00 |
| 39 | Bob Martyn RC | 6.00 | 12.00 |
| 40 | George Kell | 15.00 | 30.00 |
| 41 | Dave Hillman | 6.00 | 12.00 |
| 42 | John Roseboro RC | 15.00 | 30.00 |
| 43 | Sal Maglie | 7.50 | 15.00 |
| 44 | Washington Senators TC | 10.00 | 20.00 |
| 45 | Dick Groat | 7.50 | 15.00 |
| 46A | Lou Sleater | 6.00 | 12.00 |
| 46B | Lou Sleater YN | 20.00 | 40.00 |
| 47 | Roger Maris RC | 300.00 | 500.00 |
| 48 | Chuck Harmon | 6.00 | 12.00 |
| 49 | Smoky Burgess | 7.50 | 15.00 |
| 50A | Billy Pierce | 7.50 | 15.00 |
| 50B | Billy Pierce YT | 20.00 | 40.00 |
| 51 | Del Rice | 6.00 | 12.00 |
| 52A | Roberto Clemente | 175.00 | 300.00 |
| 52B | Roberto Clemente YT | 300.00 | 500.00 |
| 53A | Morrie Martin | 6.00 | 12.00 |
| 53B | Morrie Martin YN | 20.00 | 40.00 |
| 54 | Norm Siebern RC | 10.00 | 20.00 |
| 55 | Chico Carrasquel | 6.00 | 12.00 |
| 56 | Bill Fischer RC | 6.00 | 12.00 |
| 57A | Tim Thompson | 6.00 | 12.00 |
| 57B | Tim Thompson YN | 20.00 | 40.00 |
| 58A | Art Schult | 6.00 | 12.00 |
| 58B | Art Schult YT | 20.00 | 40.00 |
| 59 | Dave Sisler | 6.00 | 12.00 |
| 60A | Del Ennis | 7.50 | 15.00 |
| 60B | Del Ennis YN | 20.00 | 40.00 |
| 61A | Darrell Johnson | 6.00 | 12.00 |
| 61B | Darrell Johnson YN | 20.00 | 40.00 |
| 62 | Joe DeMaestri | 6.00 | 12.00 |
| 63 | Joe Nuxhall | 7.50 | 15.00 |
| 64 | Joe Lonnett | 6.00 | 12.00 |
| 65A | Von McDaniel RC | 6.00 | 12.00 |
| 65B | Von McDaniel YN | 20.00 | 40.00 |
| 66 | Lee Walls | 6.00 | 12.00 |
| 67 | Joe Ginsberg | 6.00 | 12.00 |
| 68 | Daryl Spencer | 6.00 | 12.00 |
| 69 | Wally Moon | 7.50 | 15.00 |
| 70A | Al Kaline | 60.00 | 100.00 |
| 70B | Al Kaline YN | 150.00 | 250.00 |
| 71 | Los Angeles Dodgers TC | 35.00 | 60.00 |

|  |  | | |
|---|---|---|---|
| 72 | Bud Byerly UER | 6.00 | 12.00 |
| 73 | Pete Daley | 6.00 | 12.00 |
| 74 | Roy Face | 7.50 | 15.00 |
| 75 | Gus Bell | 7.50 | 15.00 |
| 76A | Dick Farrell RC | 6.00 | 12.00 |
| 76B | Dick Farrell YT | 20.00 | 40.00 |
| 77A | Don Zimmer | 7.50 | 15.00 |
| 77B | Don Zimmer YT | 20.00 | 40.00 |
| 78A | Ernie Johnson | 7.50 | 15.00 |
| 78B | Ernie Johnson YN | 20.00 | 40.00 |
| 79A | Dick Williams | 7.50 | 15.00 |
| 79B | Dick Williams YT | 20.00 | 40.00 |
| 80 | Dick Drott RC | 6.00 | 12.00 |
| 81A | Steve Boros RC | 6.00 | 12.00 |
| 81B | Steve Boros YT | 20.00 | 40.00 |
| 82 | Ron Kline | 6.00 | 12.00 |
| 83 | Bob Hazle RC | 6.00 | 12.00 |
| 84 | Billy O'Dell | 6.00 | 12.00 |
| 85A | Luis Aparicio | 15.00 | 30.00 |
| 85B | Luis Aparicio YT | 50.00 | 80.00 |
| 86 | Valmy Thomas RC | 6.00 | 12.00 |
| 87 | Johnny Kucks | 6.00 | 12.00 |
| 88 | Duke Snider | 50.00 | 80.00 |
| 89 | Billy Klaus | 6.00 | 12.00 |
| 90 | Robin Roberts | 15.00 | 30.00 |
| 91 | Chuck Tanner | 7.50 | 15.00 |
| 92A | Clint Courtney | 6.00 | 12.00 |
| 92B | Clint Courtney YN | 20.00 | 40.00 |
| 93 | Sandy Amoros | 7.50 | 15.00 |
| 94 | Bob Skinner | 7.50 | 15.00 |
| 95 | Frank Bolling | 6.00 | 12.00 |
| 96 | Joe Durham RC | 6.00 | 12.00 |
| 97A | Larry Jackson | 6.00 | 12.00 |
| 97B | Larry Jackson YN | 20.00 | 40.00 |
| 98A | Billy Hunter | 6.00 | 12.00 |
| 98B | Billy Hunter YN | 20.00 | 40.00 |
| 99 | Bobby Adams | 6.00 | 12.00 |
| 100A | Early Wynn | 15.00 | 30.00 |
| 100B | Early Wynn YT | 50.00 | 80.00 |
| 101A | Bobby Richardson | 15.00 | 30.00 |
| 101B | B.Richardson YN | 35.00 | 60.00 |
| 102 | George Strickland | 6.00 | 12.00 |
| 103 | Jerry Lynch | 7.50 | 15.00 |
| 104 | Jim Pendleton | 6.00 | 12.00 |
| 105 | Billy Gardner | 6.00 | 12.00 |
| 106 | Dick Schofield | 7.50 | 15.00 |
| 107 | Ossie Virgil | 6.00 | 12.00 |
| 108A | Jim Landis | 6.00 | 12.00 |
| 108B | Jim Landis YT | 20.00 | 40.00 |
| 109 | Herb Plews | 6.00 | 12.00 |
| 110 | Johnny Logan | 7.50 | 15.00 |
| 111 | Stu Miller | 5.00 | 10.00 |
| 112 | Gus Zernial | 5.00 | 10.00 |
| 113 | Jerry Walker RC | 4.00 | 8.00 |
| 114 | Irv Noren | 4.00 | 8.00 |
| 115 | Jim Bunning | 15.00 | 30.00 |
| 116 | Dave Philley | 4.00 | 8.00 |
| 117 | Frank Torre | 5.00 | 10.00 |
| 118 | Harvey Haddix | 5.00 | 10.00 |
| 119 | Harry Chiti | 4.00 | 8.00 |
| 120 | Johnny Podres | 5.00 | 10.00 |
| 121 | Eddie Miksis | 4.00 | 8.00 |
| 122 | Walt Moryn | 4.00 | 8.00 |
| 123 | Dick Tomanek RC | 4.00 | 8.00 |
| 124 | Bobby Usher | 4.00 | 8.00 |
| 125 | Alvin Dark | 5.00 | 10.00 |
| 126 | Stan Palys RC | 4.00 | 8.00 |
| 127 | Tom Sturdivant | 5.00 | 10.00 |
| 128 | Willie Kirkland RC | 5.00 | 10.00 |
| 129 | Jim Derrington RC | 4.00 | 8.00 |
| 130 | Jackie Jensen | 5.00 | 10.00 |
| 131 | Bob Henrich RC | 4.00 | 8.00 |
| 132 | Vern Law | 5.00 | 10.00 |
| 133 | Russ Nixon RC | 4.00 | 8.00 |
| 134 | Philadelphia Phillies TC | 7.50 | 15.00 |
| 135 | Mike (Moe)Drabowsky | 5.00 | 10.00 |
| 136 | Jim Finigan | 4.00 | 8.00 |
| 137 | Russ Kemmerer | 4.00 | 8.00 |
| 138 | Earl Torgeson | 4.00 | 8.00 |
| 139 | George Brunet RC | 4.00 | 8.00 |
| 140 | Wes Covington | 5.00 | 10.00 |
| 141 | Ken Lehman | 4.00 | 8.00 |
| 142 | Enos Slaughter | 12.50 | 25.00 |
| 143 | Billy Muffett RC | 4.00 | 8.00 |
| 144 | Bobby Morgan | 4.00 | 8.00 |
| 145 | Never issued | | |
| 146 | Dick Gray RC | 4.00 | 8.00 |
| 147 | Don McMahon RC | 4.00 | 8.00 |

| # | Card | Low | High |
|---|---|---|---|
| 148 | Billy Consolo | 4.00 | 8.00 |
| 149 | Tom Acker | 4.00 | 8.00 |
| 150 | Mickey Mantle | 600.00 | 1000.00 |
| 151 | Buddy Pritchard RC | 4.00 | 8.00 |
| 152 | Johnny Antonelli | 5.00 | 10.00 |
| 153 | Les Moss | 4.00 | 8.00 |
| 154 | Harry Byrd | 4.00 | 8.00 |
| 155 | Hector Lopez | 5.00 | 10.00 |
| 156 | Dick Hyde | 4.00 | 8.00 |
| 157 | Dee Fondy | 4.00 | 8.00 |
| 158 | Cleveland Indians TC | 7.50 | 15.00 |
| 159 | Taylor Phillips | 4.00 | 8.00 |
| 160 | Don Hoak | 5.00 | 10.00 |
| 161 | Don Larsen | 7.50 | 15.00 |
| 162 | Gil Hodges | 20.00 | 40.00 |
| 163 | Jim Wilson | 4.00 | 8.00 |
| 164 | Bob Taylor RC | 4.00 | 8.00 |
| 165 | Bob Nieman | 4.00 | 8.00 |
| 166 | Danny O'Connell | 4.00 | 8.00 |
| 167 | Frank Baumann RC | 4.00 | 8.00 |
| 168 | Joe Cunningham | 4.00 | 8.00 |
| 169 | Ralph Terry | 5.00 | 10.00 |
| 170 | Vic Wertz | 5.00 | 10.00 |
| 171 | Harry Anderson | 4.00 | 8.00 |
| 172 | Don Gross | 4.00 | 8.00 |
| 173 | Eddie Yost | 4.00 | 8.00 |
| 174 | Kansas City Athletics TC | 7.50 | 15.00 |
| 175 | Marv Throneberry RC | 7.50 | 15.00 |
| 176 | Bob Buhl | 5.00 | 10.00 |
| 177 | Al Smith | 4.00 | 8.00 |
| 178 | Ted Kluszewski | 12.50 | 25.00 |
| 179 | Willie Miranda | 4.00 | 8.00 |
| 180 | Lindy McDaniel | 5.00 | 10.00 |
| 181 | Willie Jones | 4.00 | 8.00 |
| 182 | Joe Caffie RC | 4.00 | 8.00 |
| 183 | Dave Jolly | 4.00 | 8.00 |
| 184 | Elvin Tappe | 4.00 | 8.00 |
| 185 | Ray Boone | 5.00 | 10.00 |
| 186 | Jack Meyer | 4.00 | 8.00 |
| 187 | Sandy Koufax | 150.00 | 250.00 |
| 188 | Milt Bolling UER | 4.00 | 8.00 |
| 189 | George Susce | 4.00 | 8.00 |
| 190 | Red Schoendienst | 12.50 | 25.00 |
| 191 | Art Ceccarelli RC | 4.00 | 8.00 |
| 192 | Milt Graff | 4.00 | 8.00 |
| 193 | Jerry Lumpe RC | 5.00 | 10.00 |
| 194 | Roger Craig | 5.00 | 10.00 |
| 195 | Whitey Lockman | 5.00 | 10.00 |
| 196 | Mike Garcia | 5.00 | 10.00 |
| 197 | Haywood Sullivan | 4.00 | 8.00 |
| 198 | Bill Virdon | 5.00 | 10.00 |
| 199 | Don Blasingame | 4.00 | 8.00 |
| 200 | Bob Keegan | 4.00 | 8.00 |
| 201 | Jim Bolger | 4.00 | 8.00 |
| 202 | Woody Held RC | 4.00 | 8.00 |
| 203 | Al Walker | 4.00 | 8.00 |
| 204 | Leo Kiely | 4.00 | 8.00 |
| 205 | Johnny Temple | 5.00 | 10.00 |
| 206 | Bob Shaw RC | 4.00 | 8.00 |
| 207 | Solly Hemus | 4.00 | 8.00 |
| 208 | Cal McLish | 4.00 | 8.00 |
| 209 | Bob Anderson RC | 4.00 | 8.00 |
| 210 | Wally Moon | 5.00 | 10.00 |
| 211 | Pete Burnside RC | 4.00 | 8.00 |
| 212 | Bubba Phillips | 4.00 | 8.00 |
| 213 | Red Wilson | 4.00 | 8.00 |
| 214 | Willard Schmidt | 4.00 | 8.00 |
| 215 | Jim Gilliam | 7.50 | 15.00 |
| 216 | St. Louis Cardinals TC | 7.50 | 15.00 |
| 217 | Jack Harshman | 4.00 | 8.00 |
| 218 | Dick Rand RC | 4.00 | 8.00 |
| 219 | Camilo Pascual | 5.00 | 10.00 |
| 220 | Tom Brewer | 4.00 | 8.00 |
| 221 | Jerry Kindall RC | 4.00 | 8.00 |
| 222 | Bud Daley RC | 4.00 | 8.00 |
| 223 | Andy Pafko | 5.00 | 10.00 |
| 224 | Bob Grim | 5.00 | 10.00 |
| 225 | Billy Goodman | 5.00 | 10.00 |
| 226 | Bob Smith RC | 4.00 | 8.00 |
| 227 | Gene Stephens | 4.00 | 8.00 |
| 228 | Duke Maas | 4.00 | 8.00 |
| 229 | Frank Zupo RC | 4.00 | 8.00 |
| 230 | Richie Ashburn | 20.00 | 40.00 |
| 231 | Lloyd Merritt RC | 4.00 | 8.00 |
| 232 | Reno Bertoia | 4.00 | 8.00 |
| 233 | Mickey Vernon | 5.00 | 10.00 |
| 234 | Carl Sawatski | 4.00 | 8.00 |
| 235 | Tom Gorman | 4.00 | 8.00 |
| 236 | Ed Fitzgerald | 4.00 | 8.00 |
| 237 | Bill Wight | 4.00 | 8.00 |
| 238 | Bill Mazeroski | 15.00 | 30.00 |
| 239 | Chuck Stobbs | 4.00 | 8.00 |
| 240 | Bill Skowron | 12.50 | 25.00 |
| 241 | Dick Littlefield | 4.00 | 8.00 |
| 242 | Johnny Klippstein | 4.00 | 8.00 |
| 243 | Larry Raines RC | 4.00 | 8.00 |
| 244 | Don Demeter RC | 4.00 | 8.00 |
| 245 | Frank Lary | 5.00 | 10.00 |
| 246 | New York Yankees TC | 60.00 | 100.00 |
| 247 | Casey Wise | 4.00 | 8.00 |
| 248 | Herman Wehmeier | 4.00 | 8.00 |
| 249 | Ray Moore | 4.00 | 8.00 |
| 250 | Roy Sievers | 5.00 | 10.00 |
| 251 | Warren Hacker | 4.00 | 8.00 |
| 252 | Bob Trowbridge RC | 4.00 | 8.00 |
| 253 | Don Mueller | 5.00 | 10.00 |
| 254 | Alex Grammas | 4.00 | 8.00 |
| 255 | Bob Turley | 5.00 | 10.00 |
| 256 | Chicago White Sox TC | 7.50 | 15.00 |
| 257 | Hal Smith | 4.00 | 8.00 |
| 258 | Carl Erskine | 7.50 | 15.00 |
| 259 | Al Pilarcik | 4.00 | 8.00 |
| 260 | Frank Malzone | 5.00 | 10.00 |
| 261 | Turk Lown | 4.00 | 8.00 |
| 262 | Johnny Groth | 4.00 | 8.00 |
| 263 | Eddie Bressoud RC | 5.00 | 10.00 |
| 264 | Jack Sanford | 5.00 | 10.00 |
| 265 | Pete Runnels | 4.00 | 8.00 |
| 266 | Connie Johnson | 4.00 | 8.00 |
| 267 | Sherm Lollar | 5.00 | 10.00 |
| 268 | Granny Hamner | 4.00 | 8.00 |
| 269 | Paul Smith | 4.00 | 8.00 |
| 270 | Warren Spahn | 35.00 | 60.00 |
| 271 | Billy Martin | 20.00 | 40.00 |
| 272 | Ray Crone | 4.00 | 8.00 |
| 273 | Hal Smith | 4.00 | 8.00 |
| 274 | Rocky Bridges | 4.00 | 8.00 |
| 275 | Elston Howard | 7.50 | 15.00 |
| 276 | Bobby Avila | 4.00 | 8.00 |
| 277 | Virgil Trucks | 5.00 | 10.00 |
| 278 | Mack Burk | 4.00 | 8.00 |
| 279 | Bob Boyd | 4.00 | 8.00 |
| 280 | Jim Piersall | 5.00 | 10.00 |
| 281 | Sammy Taylor RC | 4.00 | 8.00 |
| 282 | Paul Foytack | 4.00 | 8.00 |
| 283 | Ray Shearer RC | 4.00 | 8.00 |
| 284 | Ray Katt | 4.00 | 8.00 |
| 285 | Frank Robinson | 60.00 | 100.00 |
| 286 | Gino Cimoli | 4.00 | 8.00 |
| 287 | Sam Jones | 5.00 | 10.00 |
| 288 | Harmon Killebrew | 60.00 | 100.00 |
| 289 | B.Shantz/L.Burdette | 5.00 | 10.00 |
| 290 | Dick Donovan | 4.00 | 8.00 |
| 291 | Don Landrum RC | 4.00 | 8.00 |
| 292 | Ned Garver | 4.00 | 8.00 |
| 293 | Gene Freese | 4.00 | 8.00 |
| 294 | Hal Jeffcoat | 4.00 | 8.00 |
| 295 | Minnie Minoso | 12.50 | 25.00 |
| 296 | Ryne Duren RC | 7.50 | 15.00 |
| 297 | Don Buddin RC | 4.00 | 8.00 |
| 298 | Jim Hearn | 4.00 | 8.00 |
| 299 | Harry Simpson | 4.00 | 8.00 |
| 300 | W.Harridge/W.Giles | 7.50 | 15.00 |
| 301 | Randy Jackson | 4.00 | 8.00 |
| 302 | Mike Baxes RC | 4.00 | 8.00 |
| 303 | Neil Chrisley | 4.00 | 8.00 |
| 304 | H.Kuenn/A.Kaline | 12.50 | 25.00 |
| 305 | Clem Labine | 5.00 | 10.00 |
| 306 | Whammy Douglas RC | 4.00 | 8.00 |
| 307 | Brooks Robinson | 60.00 | 100.00 |
| 308 | Paul Giel | 5.00 | 10.00 |
| 309 | Gail Harris | 4.00 | 8.00 |
| 310 | Ernie Banks | 60.00 | 100.00 |
| 311 | Bob Purkey | 4.00 | 8.00 |
| 312 | Boston Red Sox TC | 7.50 | 15.00 |
| 313 | Bob Rush | 4.00 | 8.00 |
| 314 | D.Snider/W.Alston | 30.00 | 50.00 |
| 315 | Bob Friend | 5.00 | 10.00 |
| 316 | Tito Francona | 4.00 | 8.00 |
| 317 | Albie Pearson RC | 5.00 | 10.00 |
| 318 | Frank House | 4.00 | 8.00 |
| 319 | Lou Skizas | 4.00 | 8.00 |
| 320 | Whitey Ford | 35.00 | 50.00 |
| 321 | T.Kluszewski/T.Williams | 60.00 | 100.00 |
| 322 | Harding Peterson RC | 5.00 | 10.00 |
| 323 | Elmer Valo | 4.00 | 8.00 |
| 324 | Hoyt Wilhelm | 12.50 | 25.00 |
| 325 | Joe Adcock | 5.00 | 10.00 |
| 326 | Bob Miller | 4.00 | 8.00 |
| 327 | Chicago Cubs TC | 7.50 | 15.00 |
| 328 | Ike Delock | 4.00 | 8.00 |
| 329 | Bob Cerv | 5.00 | 10.00 |
| 330 | Ed Bailey | 5.00 | 10.00 |
| 331 | Pedro Ramos | 4.00 | 8.00 |
| 332 | Jim King | 4.00 | 8.00 |
| 333 | Andy Carey | 5.00 | 10.00 |
| 334 | B.Friend/B.Pierce | 5.00 | 10.00 |
| 335 | Ruben Gomez | 4.00 | 8.00 |
| 336 | Bert Hamric | 4.00 | 8.00 |
| 337 | Hank Aguirre | 4.00 | 8.00 |
| 338 | Walt Dropo | 5.00 | 10.00 |
| 339 | Fred Hatfield | 4.00 | 8.00 |
| 340 | Don Newcombe | 7.50 | 15.00 |
| 341 | Pittsburgh Pirates TC | 7.50 | 15.00 |
| 342 | Jim Brosnan | 5.00 | 10.00 |
| 343 | Orlando Cepeda RC | 60.00 | 100.00 |
| 344 | Bob Porterfield | 4.00 | 8.00 |
| 345 | Jim Hegan | 5.00 | 10.00 |
| 346 | Steve Bilko | 4.00 | 8.00 |
| 347 | Don Rudolph RC | 4.00 | 8.00 |
| 348 | Chico Fernandez | 4.00 | 8.00 |
| 349 | Murry Dickson | 4.00 | 8.00 |
| 350 | Ken Boyer | 12.50 | 25.00 |
| 351 | Cran/Math/Aaron/Adcock | 20.00 | 40.00 |
| 352 | Herb Score | 7.50 | 15.00 |
| 353 | Stan Lopata | 4.00 | 8.00 |
| 354 | Art Ditmar | 5.00 | 10.00 |
| 355 | Bill Bruton | 5.00 | 10.00 |
| 356 | Bob Malkmus RC | 4.00 | 8.00 |
| 357 | Danny McDevitt RC | 4.00 | 8.00 |
| 358 | Gene Baker | 4.00 | 8.00 |
| 359 | Billy Loes | 5.00 | 10.00 |
| 360 | Roy McMillan | 5.00 | 10.00 |
| 361 | Mike Fornieles | 4.00 | 8.00 |
| 362 | Ray Jablonski | 4.00 | 8.00 |
| 363 | Don Elston | 4.00 | 8.00 |
| 364 | Earl Battey | 4.00 | 8.00 |
| 365 | Tom Morgan | 4.00 | 8.00 |
| 366 | Gene Green RC | 4.00 | 8.00 |
| 367 | Jack Urban RC | 4.00 | 8.00 |
| 368 | Rocky Colavito | 30.00 | 50.00 |
| 369 | Ralph Lumenti RC | 4.00 | 8.00 |
| 370 | Yogi Berra | 60.00 | 100.00 |
| 371 | Marty Keough RC | 4.00 | 8.00 |
| 372 | Don Cardwell | 4.00 | 8.00 |
| 373 | Joe Pignatano RC | 4.00 | 8.00 |
| 374 | Brooks Lawrence | 4.00 | 8.00 |
| 375 | Pee Wee Reese | 50.00 | 80.00 |
| 376 | Charley Rabe RC | 4.00 | 8.00 |
| 377A | Milwaukee Braves TC Alpha | 7.50 | 15.00 |
| 377B | Milwaukee Braves TC Num | 60.00 | 100.00 |
| 378 | Hank Sauer | 5.00 | 10.00 |
| 379 | Ray Herbert | 4.00 | 8.00 |
| 380 | Charlie Maxwell | 5.00 | 10.00 |
| 381 | Hal Brown | 4.00 | 8.00 |
| 382 | Al Cicotte | 4.00 | 8.00 |
| 383 | Lou Berberet | 4.00 | 8.00 |
| 384 | John Goryl RC | 4.00 | 8.00 |
| 385 | Wilmer Mizell | 5.00 | 10.00 |
| 386 | Bailey/Tebbets/F.Rob | 7.50 | 15.00 |
| 387 | Wally Post | 5.00 | 10.00 |
| 388 | Billy Moran RC | 4.00 | 8.00 |
| 389 | Bill Taylor | 4.00 | 8.00 |
| 390 | Del Crandall | 5.00 | 10.00 |
| 391 | Dave Melton RC | 4.00 | 8.00 |
| 392 | Bennie Daniels RC | 4.00 | 8.00 |
| 393 | Tony Kubek | 15.00 | 30.00 |
| 394 | Jim Grant RC | 4.00 | 8.00 |
| 395 | Willard Nixon | 4.00 | 8.00 |
| 396 | Dutch Dotterer RC | 4.00 | 8.00 |
| 397A | Detroit Tigers TC Alpha | 7.50 | 15.00 |
| 397B | Detroit Tigers TC Num | 60.00 | 100.00 |
| 398 | Gene Woodling | 5.00 | 10.00 |
| 399 | Marv Grissom | 4.00 | 8.00 |
| 400 | Nellie Fox | 20.00 | 40.00 |
| 401 | Don Bessent | 4.00 | 8.00 |
| 402 | Bobby Gene Smith | 4.00 | 8.00 |
| 403 | Steve Korcheck RC | 4.00 | 8.00 |
| 404 | Curt Simmons | 5.00 | 10.00 |
| 405 | Ken Aspromonte RC | 4.00 | 8.00 |
| 406 | Vic Power | 5.00 | 10.00 |
| 407 | Carlton Willey RC | 5.00 | 10.00 |
| 408A | Baltimore Orioles TC Alpha | 7.50 | 15.00 |
| 408B | Baltimore Orioles TC Num | 60.00 | 100.00 |

| | | |
|---|---|---|
| ❏ 409 Frank Thomas | 5.00 | 10.00 |
| ❏ 410 Murray Wall | 4.00 | 8.00 |
| ❏ 411 Tony Taylor RC | 5.00 | 10.00 |
| ❏ 412 Gerry Staley | 4.00 | 8.00 |
| ❏ 413 Jim Davenport RC | 4.00 | 8.00 |
| ❏ 414 Sammy White | 4.00 | 8.00 |
| ❏ 415 Bob Bowman | 4.00 | 8.00 |
| ❏ 416 Foster Castleman | 4.00 | 8.00 |
| ❏ 417 Carl Furillo | 7.50 | 15.00 |
| ❏ 418 M.Mantle/H.Aaron | 250.00 | 400.00 |
| ❏ 419 Bobby Shantz | 5.00 | 10.00 |
| ❏ 420 Vada Pinson RC | 20.00 | 40.00 |
| ❏ 421 Dixie Howell | 4.00 | 8.00 |
| ❏ 422 Norm Zauchin | 4.00 | 8.00 |
| ❏ 423 Phil Clark RC | 4.00 | 8.00 |
| ❏ 424 Larry Doby | 12.50 | 25.00 |
| ❏ 425 Sammy Esposito | 4.00 | 8.00 |
| ❏ 426 Johnny O'Brien | 5.00 | 10.00 |
| ❏ 427 Al Worthington | 4.00 | 8.00 |
| ❏ 428A Cincinnati Reds TC Alpha | 7.50 | 15.00 |
| ❏ 428B Cincinnati Reds TC Num | 60.00 | 100.00 |
| ❏ 429 Gus Triandos | 5.00 | 10.00 |
| ❏ 430 Bobby Thomson | 5.00 | 10.00 |
| ❏ 431 Gene Conley | 5.00 | 10.00 |
| ❏ 432 John Powers RC | 4.00 | 8.00 |
| ❏ 433A Pancho Herrera COR RC | 5.00 | 10.00 |
| ❏ 433B Pancho Herrera ERR (No a) | 350.00 | 600.00 |
| ❏ 434 Harvey Kuenn | 5.00 | 10.00 |
| ❏ 435 Ed Roebuck | 5.00 | 10.00 |
| ❏ 436 W.Mays/D.Snider | 60.00 | 100.00 |
| ❏ 437 Bob Speake | 4.00 | 8.00 |
| ❏ 438 Whitey Herzog | 5.00 | 10.00 |
| ❏ 439 Ray Narleski | 4.00 | 8.00 |
| ❏ 440 Eddie Mathews | 50.00 | 80.00 |
| ❏ 441 Jim Marshall RC | 5.00 | 10.00 |
| ❏ 442 Phil Paine RC | 4.00 | 8.00 |
| ❏ 443 Billy Harrell SP RC | 10.00 | 20.00 |
| ❏ 444 Danny Kravitz | 4.00 | 8.00 |
| ❏ 445 Bob Smith RC | 4.00 | 8.00 |
| ❏ 446 Carroll Hardy SP RC | 10.00 | 20.00 |
| ❏ 447 Ray Monzant | 4.00 | 8.00 |
| ❏ 448 Charley Lau RC | 5.00 | 10.00 |
| ❏ 449 Gene Fodge RC | 4.00 | 8.00 |
| ❏ 450 Preston Ward SP | 10.00 | 20.00 |
| ❏ 451 Joe Taylor RC | 4.00 | 8.00 |
| ❏ 452 Roman Mejias | 4.00 | 8.00 |
| ❏ 453 Tom Qualters | 4.00 | 8.00 |
| ❏ 454 Harry Hanebrink RC | 4.00 | 8.00 |
| ❏ 455 Hal Griggs RC | 4.00 | 8.00 |
| ❏ 456 Dick Brown RC | 4.00 | 8.00 |
| ❏ 457 Milt Pappas RC | 5.00 | 10.00 |
| ❏ 458 Julio Becquer RC | 4.00 | 8.00 |
| ❏ 459 Ron Blackburn RC | 4.00 | 8.00 |
| ❏ 460 Chuck Essegian RC | 4.00 | 8.00 |
| ❏ 461 Ed Mayer RC | 4.00 | 8.00 |
| ❏ 462 Gary Geiger SP RC | 10.00 | 20.00 |
| ❏ 463 Vito Valentinetti | 4.00 | 8.00 |
| ❏ 464 Curt Flood RC | 15.00 | 30.00 |
| ❏ 465 Arnie Portocarrero | 4.00 | 8.00 |
| ❏ 466 Pete Whisenant | 4.00 | 8.00 |
| ❏ 467 Glen Hobbie RC | 4.00 | 8.00 |
| ❏ 468 Bob Schmidt RC | 4.00 | 8.00 |
| ❏ 469 Don Ferrarese | 4.00 | 8.00 |
| ❏ 470 R.C. Stevens RC | 4.00 | 8.00 |
| ❏ 471 Lenny Green RC | 4.00 | 8.00 |
| ❏ 472 Joey Jay | 5.00 | 10.00 |
| ❏ 473 Bill Renna | 4.00 | 8.00 |
| ❏ 474 Roman Semproch RC | 4.00 | 8.00 |
| ❏ 475 F.Haney/C.Stengel AS | 12.50 | 25.00 |
| ❏ 476 Stan Musial AS TP | 30.00 | 50.00 |
| ❏ 477 Bill Skowron AS | 5.00 | 10.00 |
| ❏ 478 Johnny Temple AS UER | 4.00 | 8.00 |
| ❏ 479 Nellie Fox AS | 7.50 | 15.00 |
| ❏ 480 Eddie Mathews AS | 15.00 | 30.00 |
| ❏ 481 Frank Malzone AS | 4.00 | 8.00 |
| ❏ 482 Ernie Banks AS | 20.00 | 40.00 |
| ❏ 483 Luis Aparicio AS | 7.50 | 15.00 |
| ❏ 484 Frank Robinson AS | 20.00 | 40.00 |
| ❏ 485 Ted Williams AS | 90.00 | 150.00 |
| ❏ 486 Willie Mays AS | 35.00 | 60.00 |
| ❏ 487 Mickey Mantle AS TP | 125.00 | 200.00 |
| ❏ 488 Hank Aaron AS | 35.00 | 60.00 |
| ❏ 489 Jackie Jensen AS | 5.00 | 10.00 |
| ❏ 490 Ed Bailey AS | 4.00 | 8.00 |
| ❏ 491 Sherm Lollar AS | 4.00 | 8.00 |
| ❏ 492 Bob Friend AS | 4.00 | 8.00 |
| ❏ 493 Bob Turley AS | 5.00 | 10.00 |
| ❏ 494 Warren Spahn AS | 12.50 | 25.00 |

| | | |
|---|---|---|
| ❏ 495 Herb Score AS | 7.50 | 15.00 |
| ❏ NNO Contest Cards | 20.00 | 40.00 |
| ❏ NNO Felt Emblem Insert | | |

## 1959 Topps

| | | |
|---|---|---|
| ❏ COMPLETE SET (572) | 5000.00 | 8000.00 |
| ❏ COMMON CARD (1-110) | 3.00 | 6.00 |
| ❏ COMMON CARD (111-506) | 3.00 | 6.00 |
| ❏ COMMON CARD (507-572) | 7.50 | 15.00 |
| ❏ WRAPPER (1-CENT) | 100.00 | 125.00 |
| ❏ WRAPPER (5-CENT) | 75.00 | 100.00 |
| ❏ 1 Ford Frick COMM | 35.00 | 60.00 |
| ❏ 2 Eddie Yost | 4.00 | 8.00 |
| ❏ 3 Don McMahon | 4.00 | 8.00 |
| ❏ 4 Albie Pearson | 4.00 | 8.00 |
| ❏ 5 Dick Donovan | 3.00 | 6.00 |
| ❏ 6 Alex Grammas | 3.00 | 6.00 |
| ❏ 7 Al Pilarcik | 3.00 | 6.00 |
| ❏ 8 Philadelphia Phillies CL | 50.00 | 80.00 |
| ❏ 9 Paul Giel | 4.00 | 8.00 |
| ❏ 10 Mickey Mantle | 600.00 | 1000.00 |
| ❏ 11 Billy Hunter | 4.00 | 8.00 |
| ❏ 12 Vern Law | 4.00 | 8.00 |
| ❏ 13 Dick Gernert | 3.00 | 6.00 |
| ❏ 14 Pete Whisenant | 3.00 | 6.00 |
| ❏ 15 Dick Drott | 3.00 | 6.00 |
| ❏ 16 Joe Pignatano | 3.00 | 6.00 |
| ❏ 17 Thomas/Murtaugh/Klusz | 3.00 | 6.00 |
| ❏ 18 Jack Urban | 3.00 | 6.00 |
| ❏ 19 Eddie Bressoud | 3.00 | 6.00 |
| ❏ 20 Duke Snider | 35.00 | 60.00 |
| ❏ 21 Connie Johnson | 3.00 | 6.00 |
| ❏ 22 Al Smith | 4.00 | 8.00 |
| ❏ 23 Murry Dickson | 4.00 | 8.00 |
| ❏ 24 Red Wilson | 3.00 | 6.00 |
| ❏ 25 Don Hoak | 4.00 | 8.00 |
| ❏ 26 Chuck Stobbs | 3.00 | 6.00 |
| ❏ 27 Andy Pafko | 4.00 | 8.00 |
| ❏ 28 Al Worthington | 3.00 | 6.00 |
| ❏ 29 Jim Bolger | 3.00 | 6.00 |
| ❏ 30 Nellie Fox | 15.00 | 30.00 |
| ❏ 31 Ken Lehman | 3.00 | 6.00 |
| ❏ 32 Don Buddin | 3.00 | 6.00 |
| ❏ 33 Ed Fitzgerald | 3.00 | 6.00 |
| ❏ 34 Al Kaline/C.Maxwell | 10.00 | 20.00 |
| ❏ 35 Ted Kluszewski | 6.00 | 12.00 |
| ❏ 36 Hank Aguirre | 3.00 | 6.00 |
| ❏ 37 Gene Green | 3.00 | 6.00 |
| ❏ 38 Morrie Martin | 3.00 | 6.00 |
| ❏ 39 Ed Bouchee | 3.00 | 6.00 |
| ❏ 40A Warren Spahn ERR | 50.00 | 80.00 |
| ❏ 40B Warren Spahn ERR | 60.00 | 100.00 |
| ❏ 40C Warren Spahn COR | 35.00 | 60.00 |
| ❏ 41 Bob Martyn | 3.00 | 6.00 |
| ❏ 42 Murray Wall | 3.00 | 6.00 |
| ❏ 43 Steve Bilko | 3.00 | 6.00 |
| ❏ 44 Vito Valentinetti | 3.00 | 6.00 |
| ❏ 45 Andy Carey | 3.00 | 6.00 |
| ❏ 46 Bill R. Henry | 3.00 | 6.00 |
| ❏ 47 Jim Finigan | 3.00 | 6.00 |
| ❏ 48 Baltimore Orioles CL | 12.50 | 25.00 |
| ❏ 49 Bill Hall RC | 3.00 | 6.00 |
| ❏ 50 Willie Mays | 100.00 | 175.00 |
| ❏ 51 Rip Coleman | 3.00 | 6.00 |
| ❏ 52 Coot Veal RC | 3.00 | 6.00 |
| ❏ 53 Stan Williams RC | 4.00 | 8.00 |
| ❏ 54 Mel Roach | 3.00 | 6.00 |
| ❏ 55 Tom Brewer | 3.00 | 6.00 |
| ❏ 56 Carl Sawatski | 3.00 | 6.00 |
| ❏ 57 Al Cicotte | 3.00 | 6.00 |
| ❏ 58 Eddie Miksis | 3.00 | 6.00 |
| ❏ 59 Irv Noren | 3.00 | 6.00 |
| ❏ 60 Bob Turley | 4.00 | 8.00 |
| ❏ 61 Dick Brown | 3.00 | 6.00 |

| | | |
|---|---|---|
| ❏ 62 Tony Taylor | 4.00 | 8.00 |
| ❏ 63 Jim Hearn | 3.00 | 6.00 |
| ❏ 64 Joe DeMaestri | 3.00 | 6.00 |
| ❏ 65 Frank Torre | 4.00 | 8.00 |
| ❏ 66 Joe Ginsberg | 3.00 | 6.00 |
| ❏ 67 Brooks Lawrence | 3.00 | 6.00 |
| ❏ 68 Dick Schofield | 3.00 | 6.00 |
| ❏ 69 San Francisco Giants CL | 12.50 | 25.00 |
| ❏ 70 Harvey Kuenn | 4.00 | 8.00 |
| ❏ 71 Don Bessent | 3.00 | 6.00 |
| ❏ 72 Bill Renna | 3.00 | 6.00 |
| ❏ 73 Ron Jackson | 3.00 | 6.00 |
| ❏ 74 Lemon/Lavagetto/Sievers | 4.00 | 8.00 |
| ❏ 75 Sam Jones | 4.00 | 8.00 |
| ❏ 76 Bobby Richardson | 10.00 | 20.00 |
| ❏ 77 John Goryl | 3.00 | 6.00 |
| ❏ 78 Pedro Ramos | 3.00 | 6.00 |
| ❏ 79 Harry Chiti | 3.00 | 6.00 |
| ❏ 80 Minnie Minoso | 6.00 | 12.00 |
| ❏ 81 Hal Jeffcoat | 3.00 | 6.00 |
| ❏ 82 Bob Boyd | 3.00 | 6.00 |
| ❏ 83 Bob Smith | 3.00 | 6.00 |
| ❏ 84 Reno Bertoia | 3.00 | 6.00 |
| ❏ 85 Harry Anderson | 3.00 | 6.00 |
| ❏ 86 Bob Keegan | 4.00 | 8.00 |
| ❏ 87 Danny O'Connell | 3.00 | 6.00 |
| ❏ 88 Herb Score | 6.00 | 12.00 |
| ❏ 89 Billy Gardner | 3.00 | 6.00 |
| ❏ 90 Bill Skowron | 6.00 | 12.00 |
| ❏ 91 Herb Moford RC | 3.00 | 6.00 |
| ❏ 92 Dave Philley | 3.00 | 6.00 |
| ❏ 93 Julio Becquer | 3.00 | 6.00 |
| ❏ 94 Chicago White Sox CL | 20.00 | 40.00 |
| ❏ 95 Carl Willey | 3.00 | 6.00 |
| ❏ 96 Lou Berberet | 3.00 | 6.00 |
| ❏ 97 Jerry Lynch | 3.00 | 6.00 |
| ❏ 98 Arnie Portocarrero | 3.00 | 6.00 |
| ❏ 99 Ted Kazanski | 3.00 | 6.00 |
| ❏ 100 Bob Cerv | 4.00 | 8.00 |
| ❏ 101 Alex Kellner | 3.00 | 6.00 |
| ❏ 102 Felipe Alou RC | 15.00 | 30.00 |
| ❏ 103 Billy Goodman | 4.00 | 8.00 |
| ❏ 104 Del Rice | 3.00 | 6.00 |
| ❏ 105 Lee Walls | 3.00 | 6.00 |
| ❏ 106 Hal Woodeshick RC | 3.00 | 6.00 |
| ❏ 107 Norm Larker RC | 4.00 | 8.00 |
| ❏ 108 Zack Monroe RC | 4.00 | 8.00 |
| ❏ 109 Bob Schmidt | 3.00 | 6.00 |
| ❏ 110 George Witt RC | 4.00 | 8.00 |
| ❏ 111 Cincinnati Redlegs CL | 7.50 | 15.00 |
| ❏ 112 Billy Consolo | 3.00 | 6.00 |
| ❏ 113 Taylor Phillips | 2.00 | 4.00 |
| ❏ 114 Earl Battey | 4.00 | 8.00 |
| ❏ 115 Mickey Vernon | 4.00 | 8.00 |
| ❏ 116 Bob Allison RS RC | 6.00 | 12.00 |
| ❏ 117 John Blanchard RS RC | 6.00 | 12.00 |
| ❏ 118 John Buzhardt RS RC | 2.50 | 5.00 |
| ❏ 119 Johnny Callison RS RC | 6.00 | 12.00 |
| ❏ 120 Chuck Coles RS RC | 2.50 | 5.00 |
| ❏ 121 Bob Conley RS RC | 2.50 | 5.00 |
| ❏ 122 Bennie Daniels RS | 2.50 | 5.00 |
| ❏ 123 Don Dillard RS RC | 2.50 | 5.00 |
| ❏ 124 Dan Dobbek RS RC | 2.50 | 5.00 |
| ❏ 125 Ron Fairly RS RC | 6.00 | 12.00 |
| ❏ 126 Eddie Haas RS RC | 2.50 | 5.00 |
| ❏ 127 Kent Hadley RS RC | 2.50 | 5.00 |
| ❏ 128 Bob Hartman RS RC | 2.50 | 5.00 |
| ❏ 129 Frank Herrera RS | 2.50 | 5.00 |
| ❏ 130 Lou Jackson RS RC | 2.50 | 5.00 |
| ❏ 131 Deron Johnson RS RC | 6.00 | 12.00 |
| ❏ 132 Don Lee RS | 2.50 | 5.00 |
| ❏ 133 Bob Lillis RS RC | 2.50 | 5.00 |
| ❏ 134 Jim McDaniel RS RC | 2.50 | 5.00 |
| ❏ 135 Gene Oliver RS RC | 2.50 | 5.00 |
| ❏ 136 Jim O'Toole RS RC | 2.50 | 5.00 |
| ❏ 137 Dick Ricketts RS RC | 2.50 | 5.00 |
| ❏ 138 John Romano RS RC | 2.50 | 5.00 |
| ❏ 139 Ed Sadowski RS RC | 2.50 | 5.00 |
| ❏ 140 Charlie Secrest RS RC | 2.50 | 5.00 |
| ❏ 141 Joe Shipley RS RC | 2.50 | 5.00 |
| ❏ 142 Dick Stigman RS RC | 2.50 | 5.00 |
| ❏ 143 Willie Tasby RS RC | 2.50 | 5.00 |
| ❏ 144 Jerry Walker RS | 2.50 | 5.00 |
| ❏ 145 Dom Zanni RS RC | 2.50 | 5.00 |
| ❏ 146 Jerry Zimmerman RS RC | 2.50 | 5.00 |
| ❏ 147 Long/Banks/Moryn | 15.00 | 30.00 |
| ❏ 148 Mike McCormick | 4.00 | 8.00 |
| ❏ 149 Jim Bunning | 10.00 | 20.00 |

|  |  | | |
|---|---|---:|---:|
| 150 | Stan Musial | 60.00 | 120.00 |
| 151 | Bob Malkmus | 2.00 | 4.00 |
| 152 | Johnny Klippstein | 2.00 | 4.00 |
| 153 | Jim Marshall | 2.00 | 4.00 |
| 154 | Ray Herbert | 2.00 | 4.00 |
| 155 | Enos Slaughter | 10.00 | 20.00 |
| 156 | B.Pierce/R.Roberts | 6.00 | 12.00 |
| 157 | Felix Mantilla | 2.00 | 4.00 |
| 158 | Walt Dropo | 2.00 | 4.00 |
| 159 | Bob Shaw | 4.00 | 8.00 |
| 160 | Dick Groat | 4.00 | 8.00 |
| 161 | Frank Baumann | 2.00 | 4.00 |
| 162 | Bobby G. Smith | 2.00 | 4.00 |
| 163 | Sandy Koufax | 90.00 | 150.00 |
| 164 | Johnny Groth | 2.00 | 4.00 |
| 165 | Bill Bruton | 2.00 | 4.00 |
| 166 | Minoso/Colavito/Doby | 15.00 | 30.00 |
| 167 | Duke Maas | 2.00 | 4.00 |
| 168 | Carroll Hardy | 2.00 | 4.00 |
| 169 | Ted Abernathy | 2.00 | 4.00 |
| 170 | Gene Woodling | 4.00 | 8.00 |
| 171 | Willard Schmidt | 2.00 | 4.00 |
| 172 | Kansas City Athletics CL | 7.50 | 15.00 |
| 173 | Bill Monbouquette RC | 4.00 | 8.00 |
| 174 | Jim Pendleton | 2.00 | 4.00 |
| 175 | Dick Farrell | 2.00 | 4.00 |
| 176 | Preston Ward | 2.00 | 4.00 |
| 177 | John Briggs RC | 2.00 | 4.00 |
| 178 | Ruben Amaro RC | 6.00 | 12.00 |
| 179 | Don Rudolph | 2.00 | 4.00 |
| 180 | Yogi Berra | 50.00 | 80.00 |
| 181 | Bob Porterfield | 2.00 | 4.00 |
| 182 | Milt Graff | 2.00 | 4.00 |
| 183 | Stu Miller | 4.00 | 8.00 |
| 184 | Harvey Haddix | 4.00 | 8.00 |
| 185 | Jim Busby | 2.00 | 4.00 |
| 186 | Mudcat Grant | 4.00 | 8.00 |
| 187 | Bubba Phillips | 4.00 | 8.00 |
| 188 | Juan Pizarro | 2.00 | 4.00 |
| 189 | Neil Chrisley | 2.00 | 4.00 |
| 190 | Bill Virdon | 4.00 | 8.00 |
| 191 | Russ Kemmerer | 2.00 | 4.00 |
| 192 | Charlie Beamon RC | 2.00 | 4.00 |
| 193 | Sammy Taylor | 2.00 | 4.00 |
| 194 | Jim Brosnan | 4.00 | 8.00 |
| 195 | Rip Repulski | 2.00 | 4.00 |
| 196 | Billy Moran | 2.00 | 4.00 |
| 197 | Ray Semproch | 2.00 | 4.00 |
| 198 | Jim Davenport | 4.00 | 8.00 |
| 199 | Leo Kiely | 2.00 | 4.00 |
| 200 | W.Giles NL PRES | 4.00 | 8.00 |
| 201 | Tom Acker | 2.00 | 4.00 |
| 202 | Roger Maris | 75.00 | 125.00 |
| 203 | Ossie Virgil | 2.00 | 4.00 |
| 204 | Casey Wise | 2.00 | 4.00 |
| 205 | Don Larsen | 4.00 | 8.00 |
| 206 | Carl Furillo | 6.00 | 12.00 |
| 207 | George Strickland | 2.00 | 4.00 |
| 208 | Willie Jones | 2.00 | 4.00 |
| 209 | Lenny Green | 2.00 | 4.00 |
| 210 | Ed Bailey | 2.00 | 4.00 |
| 211 | Bob Blaylock RC | 2.00 | 4.00 |
| 212 | H.Aaron/E.Mathews | 50.00 | 80.00 |
| 213 | Jim Rivera | 4.00 | 8.00 |
| 214 | Marcelino Solis RC | 4.00 | 8.00 |
| 215 | Jim Lemon | 4.00 | 8.00 |
| 216 | Andre Rodgers | 2.00 | 4.00 |
| 217 | Carl Erskine | 6.00 | 12.00 |
| 218 | Roman Mejias | 2.00 | 4.00 |
| 219 | George Zuverink | 2.00 | 4.00 |
| 220 | Frank Malzone | 4.00 | 8.00 |
| 221 | Bob Bowman | 2.00 | 4.00 |
| 222 | Bobby Shantz | 4.00 | 8.00 |
| 223 | St. Louis Cardinals CL | 7.50 | 15.00 |
| 224 | Claude Osteen RC | 4.00 | 8.00 |
| 225 | Johnny Logan | 4.00 | 8.00 |
| 226 | Art Ceccarelli | 2.00 | 4.00 |
| 227 | Hal W. Smith | 2.00 | 4.00 |
| 228 | Don Gross | 2.00 | 4.00 |
| 229 | Vic Power | 4.00 | 8.00 |
| 230 | Bill Fischer | 2.00 | 4.00 |
| 231 | Ellis Burton RC | 2.00 | 4.00 |
| 232 | Eddie Kasko | 4.00 | 8.00 |
| 233 | Paul Foytack | 2.00 | 4.00 |
| 234 | Chuck Tanner | 4.00 | 8.00 |
| 235 | Valmy Thomas | 2.00 | 4.00 |
| 236 | Ted Bowsfield RC | 2.00 | 4.00 |
| 237 | McDougald/Turley/B.Rich | 6.00 | 12.00 |
| 238 | Gene Baker | 2.00 | 4.00 |
| 239 | Bob Trowbridge | 2.00 | 4.00 |
| 240 | Hank Bauer | 6.00 | 12.00 |
| 241 | Billy Muffett | 2.00 | 4.00 |
| 242 | Ron Samford RC | 2.00 | 4.00 |
| 243 | Marv Grissom | 2.00 | 4.00 |
| 244 | Ted Gray | 2.00 | 4.00 |
| 245 | Ned Garver | 2.00 | 4.00 |
| 246 | J.W. Porter | 2.00 | 4.00 |
| 247 | Don Ferrarese | 2.00 | 4.00 |
| 248 | Boston Red Sox CL | 7.50 | 15.00 |
| 249 | Bobby Adams | 2.00 | 4.00 |
| 250 | Billy O'Dell | 4.00 | 8.00 |
| 251 | Clete Boyer | 6.00 | 12.00 |
| 252 | Ray Boone | 4.00 | 8.00 |
| 253 | Seth Morehead RC | 2.00 | 4.00 |
| 254 | Zeke Bella RC | 2.00 | 4.00 |
| 255 | Del Ennis | 4.00 | 8.00 |
| 256 | Jerry Davie RC | 2.00 | 4.00 |
| 257 | Leon Wagner RC | 4.00 | 8.00 |
| 258 | Fred Kipp RC | 2.00 | 4.00 |
| 259 | Jim Pisoni | 2.00 | 4.00 |
| 260 | Early Wynn UER | 10.00 | 20.00 |
| 261 | Gene Stephens | 2.00 | 4.00 |
| 262 | Podres/Labine/Drysdale | 6.00 | 12.00 |
| 263 | Bud Daley | 2.00 | 4.00 |
| 264 | Chico Carrasquel | 2.00 | 4.00 |
| 265 | Ron Kline | 2.00 | 4.00 |
| 266 | Woody Held | 4.00 | 8.00 |
| 267 | John Romonosky RC | 2.00 | 4.00 |
| 268 | Tito Francona | 4.00 | 8.00 |
| 269 | Jack Meyer | 2.00 | 4.00 |
| 270 | Gil Hodges | 15.00 | 30.00 |
| 271 | Orlando Pena RC | 2.00 | 4.00 |
| 272 | Jerry Lumpe | 4.00 | 8.00 |
| 273 | Joey Jay | 4.00 | 8.00 |
| 274 | Jerry Kindall | 4.00 | 8.00 |
| 275 | Jack Sanford | 4.00 | 8.00 |
| 276 | Pete Daley | 2.00 | 4.00 |
| 277 | Turk Lown | 2.00 | 4.00 |
| 278 | Chuck Essegian | 2.00 | 4.00 |
| 279 | Ernie Johnson | 2.00 | 4.00 |
| 280 | Frank Bolling | 2.00 | 4.00 |
| 281 | Walt Craddock RC | 2.00 | 4.00 |
| 282 | R.C. Stevens | 2.00 | 4.00 |
| 283 | Russ Heman RC | 2.00 | 4.00 |
| 284 | Steve Korcheck | 2.00 | 4.00 |
| 285 | Joe Cunningham | 2.00 | 4.00 |
| 286 | Dean Stone | 2.00 | 4.00 |
| 287 | Don Zimmer | 6.00 | 12.00 |
| 288 | Dutch Dotterer | 2.00 | 4.00 |
| 289 | Johnny Kucks | 4.00 | 8.00 |
| 290 | Wes Covington | 2.00 | 4.00 |
| 291 | P.Ramos/C.Pascual | 2.00 | 4.00 |
| 292 | Dick Williams | 4.00 | 8.00 |
| 293 | Ray Moore | 2.00 | 4.00 |
| 294 | Hank Foiles | 2.00 | 4.00 |
| 295 | Billy Martin | 15.00 | 30.00 |
| 296 | Ernie Broglio RC | 4.00 | 8.00 |
| 297 | Jackie Brandt RC | 2.00 | 4.00 |
| 298 | Tex Clevenger | 2.00 | 4.00 |
| 299 | Billy Klaus | 2.00 | 4.00 |
| 300 | Richie Ashburn | 15.00 | 30.00 |
| 301 | Earl Averill Jr. RC | 2.00 | 4.00 |
| 302 | Don Mossi | 4.00 | 8.00 |
| 303 | Marty Keough | 2.00 | 4.00 |
| 304 | Chicago Cubs CL | 7.50 | 15.00 |
| 305 | Curt Raydon RC | 2.00 | 4.00 |
| 306 | Jim Gilliam | 4.00 | 8.00 |
| 307 | Curt Barclay | 2.00 | 4.00 |
| 308 | Norm Siebern | 4.00 | 8.00 |
| 309 | Sal Maglie | 4.00 | 8.00 |
| 310 | Luis Aparicio | 10.00 | 20.00 |
| 311 | Norm Zauchin | 2.00 | 4.00 |
| 312 | Don Newcombe | 4.00 | 8.00 |
| 313 | Frank House | 2.00 | 4.00 |
| 314 | Don Cardwell | 2.00 | 4.00 |
| 315 | Joe Adcock | 4.00 | 8.00 |
| 316A | Ralph Lumenti UER | 2.00 | 4.00 |
| 316B | Ralph Lumenti UER | 50.00 | 80.00 |
| 317 | R.Ashburn/W.Mays | 50.00 | 80.00 |
| 318 | Rocky Bridges | 2.00 | 4.00 |
| 319 | Dave Hillman | 2.00 | 4.00 |
| 320 | Bob Skinner | 4.00 | 8.00 |
| 321A | Bob Giallombardo RC | 4.00 | 8.00 |
| 321B | Bob Giallombardo ERR | 50.00 | 80.00 |
| 322A | Harry Hanebrink TR | 4.00 | 8.00 |
| 322B | H.Hanebrink ERR | 50.00 | 80.00 |
| 323 | Frank Sullivan | 2.00 | 4.00 |
| 324 | Don Demeter | 2.00 | 4.00 |
| 325 | Ken Boyer | 6.00 | 12.00 |
| 326 | Marv Throneberry | 4.00 | 8.00 |
| 327 | Gary Bell RC | 2.00 | 4.00 |
| 328 | Lou Skizas | 2.00 | 4.00 |
| 329 | Detroit Tigers CL | 7.50 | 15.00 |
| 330 | Gus Triandos | 4.00 | 8.00 |
| 331 | Steve Boros | 2.00 | 4.00 |
| 332 | Ray Monzant | 2.00 | 4.00 |
| 333 | Harry Simpson | 4.00 | 8.00 |
| 334 | Glen Hobbie | 2.00 | 4.00 |
| 335 | Johnny Temple | 4.00 | 8.00 |
| 336A | Billy Loes TR | 4.00 | 8.00 |
| 336B | Billy Loes ERR | 50.00 | 80.00 |
| 337 | George Crowe | 2.00 | 4.00 |
| 338 | Sparky Anderson RC | 35.00 | 60.00 |
| 339 | Roy Face | 4.00 | 8.00 |
| 340 | Roy Sievers | 4.00 | 8.00 |
| 341 | Tom Qualters | 2.00 | 4.00 |
| 342 | Ray Jablonski | 2.00 | 4.00 |
| 343 | Billy Hoeft | 2.00 | 4.00 |
| 344 | Russ Nixon | 2.00 | 4.00 |
| 345 | Gil McDougald | 6.00 | 12.00 |
| 346 | D.Sisler/T.Brewer | 2.00 | 4.00 |
| 347 | Bob Buhl | 2.00 | 4.00 |
| 348 | Ted Lepcio | 2.00 | 4.00 |
| 349 | Hoyt Wilhelm | 10.00 | 20.00 |
| 350 | Ernie Banks | 50.00 | 80.00 |
| 351 | Earl Torgeson | 2.00 | 4.00 |
| 352 | Robin Roberts | 10.00 | 20.00 |
| 353 | Curt Flood | 4.00 | 8.00 |
| 354 | Pete Burnside | 2.00 | 4.00 |
| 355 | Jimmy Piersall | 4.00 | 8.00 |
| 356 | Bob Mabe RC | 2.00 | 4.00 |
| 357 | Dick Stuart RC | 4.00 | 8.00 |
| 358 | Ralph Terry | 4.00 | 8.00 |
| 359 | Bill White RC | 10.00 | 20.00 |
| 360 | Al Kaline | 35.00 | 60.00 |
| 361 | Willard Nixon | 2.00 | 4.00 |
| 362A | Dolan Nichols RC | 4.00 | 8.00 |
| 362B | Dolan Nichols ERR | 50.00 | 80.00 |
| 363 | Bobby Avila | 2.00 | 4.00 |
| 364 | Danny McDevitt | 2.00 | 4.00 |
| 365 | Gus Bell | 4.00 | 8.00 |
| 366 | Humberto Robinson | 2.00 | 4.00 |
| 367 | Cal Neeman | 2.00 | 4.00 |
| 368 | Don Mueller | 4.00 | 8.00 |
| 369 | Dick Tomanek | 2.00 | 4.00 |
| 370 | Pete Runnels | 4.00 | 8.00 |
| 371 | Dick Brodowski | 2.00 | 4.00 |
| 372 | Jim Hegan | 4.00 | 8.00 |
| 373 | Herb Plews | 2.00 | 4.00 |
| 374 | Art Ditmar | 4.00 | 8.00 |
| 375 | Bob Nieman | 2.00 | 4.00 |
| 376 | Hal Naragon | 2.00 | 4.00 |
| 377 | John Antonelli | 4.00 | 8.00 |
| 378 | Gail Harris | 2.00 | 4.00 |
| 379 | Bob Miller | 2.00 | 4.00 |
| 380 | Hank Aaron | 90.00 | 150.00 |
| 381 | Mike Baxes | 2.00 | 4.00 |
| 382 | Curt Simmons | 4.00 | 8.00 |
| 383 | D.Larsen/C.Stengel | 6.00 | 12.00 |
| 384 | Dave Sisler | 2.00 | 4.00 |
| 385 | Sherm Lollar | 4.00 | 8.00 |
| 386 | Jim Delsing | 2.00 | 4.00 |
| 387 | Don Drysdale | 30.00 | 50.00 |
| 388 | Bob Will RC | 2.00 | 4.00 |
| 389 | Joe Nuxhall | 4.00 | 8.00 |
| 390 | Orlando Cepeda | 10.00 | 20.00 |
| 391 | Milt Pappas | 4.00 | 8.00 |
| 392 | Whitey Herzog | 4.00 | 8.00 |
| 393 | Frank Lary | 4.00 | 8.00 |
| 394 | Randy Jackson | 2.00 | 4.00 |
| 395 | Elston Howard | 6.00 | 12.00 |
| 396 | Bob Rush | 2.00 | 4.00 |
| 397 | Washington Senators CL | 7.50 | 15.00 |
| 398 | Wally Post | 2.00 | 4.00 |
| 399 | Larry Jackson | 2.00 | 4.00 |
| 400 | Jackie Jensen | 4.00 | 8.00 |
| 401 | Ron Blackburn | 2.00 | 4.00 |
| 402 | Hector Lopez | 2.00 | 4.00 |
| 403 | Clem Labine | 4.00 | 8.00 |
| 404 | Hank Sauer | 4.00 | 8.00 |
| 405 | Roy McMillan | 4.00 | 8.00 |
| 406 | Solly Drake | 2.00 | 4.00 |
| 407 | Moe Drabowsky | 4.00 | 8.00 |
| 408 | N.Fox/L.Aparicio | 20.00 | 40.00 |

| | | |
|---|---|---|
| ☐ 409 Gus Zernial | 4.00 | 8.00 |
| ☐ 410 Billy Pierce | 4.00 | 8.00 |
| ☐ 411 Whitey Lockman | 4.00 | 8.00 |
| ☐ 412 Stan Lopata | 2.00 | 4.00 |
| ☐ 413 Camilo Pascual UER | 4.00 | 8.00 |
| ☐ 414 Dale Long | 4.00 | 8.00 |
| ☐ 415 Bill Mazeroski | 6.00 | 12.00 |
| ☐ 416 Haywood Sullivan | 4.00 | 8.00 |
| ☐ 417 Virgil Trucks | 4.00 | 8.00 |
| ☐ 418 Gino Cimoli | 2.00 | 4.00 |
| ☐ 419 Milwaukee Braves CL | 7.50 | 15.00 |
| ☐ 420 Rocky Colavito | 15.00 | 30.00 |
| ☐ 421 Herman Wehmeier | 2.00 | 4.00 |
| ☐ 422 Hobie Landrith | 2.00 | 4.00 |
| ☐ 423 Bob Grim | 4.00 | 8.00 |
| ☐ 424 Ken Aspromonte | 2.00 | 4.00 |
| ☐ 425 Del Crandall | 4.00 | 8.00 |
| ☐ 426 Gerry Staley | 4.00 | 8.00 |
| ☐ 427 Charlie Neal | 4.00 | 8.00 |
| ☐ 428 Kline/French/Law/Face | 2.00 | 4.00 |
| ☐ 429 Bobby Thomson | 4.00 | 8.00 |
| ☐ 430 Whitey Ford | 35.00 | 60.00 |
| ☐ 431 Whammy Douglas | 2.00 | 4.00 |
| ☐ 432 Smoky Burgess | 4.00 | 8.00 |
| ☐ 433 Billy Harrell | 2.00 | 4.00 |
| ☐ 434 Hal Griggs | 2.00 | 4.00 |
| ☐ 435 Frank Robinson | 30.00 | 50.00 |
| ☐ 436 Granny Hamner | 2.00 | 4.00 |
| ☐ 437 Ike Delock | 2.00 | 4.00 |
| ☐ 438 Sammy Esposito | 2.00 | 4.00 |
| ☐ 439 Brooks Robinson | 30.00 | 50.00 |
| ☐ 440 Lew Burdette UER | 4.00 | 8.00 |
| ☐ 441 John Roseboro | 4.00 | 8.00 |
| ☐ 442 Ray Narleski | 2.00 | 4.00 |
| ☐ 443 Daryl Spencer | 2.00 | 4.00 |
| ☐ 444 Ron Hansen RC | 4.00 | 8.00 |
| ☐ 445 Cal McLish | 2.00 | 4.00 |
| ☐ 446 Rocky Nelson | 2.00 | 4.00 |
| ☐ 447 Bob Anderson | 2.00 | 4.00 |
| ☐ 448 Vada Pinson UER | 6.00 | 12.00 |
| ☐ 449 Tom Gorman | 2.00 | 4.00 |
| ☐ 450 Eddie Mathews | 20.00 | 40.00 |
| ☐ 451 Jimmy Constable RC | 2.00 | 4.00 |
| ☐ 452 Chico Fernandez | 2.00 | 4.00 |
| ☐ 453 Les Moss | 2.00 | 4.00 |
| ☐ 454 Phil Clark | 2.00 | 4.00 |
| ☐ 455 Larry Doby | 6.00 | 12.00 |
| ☐ 456 Jerry Casale RC | 2.00 | 4.00 |
| ☐ 457 Los Angeles Dodgers CL | 15.00 | 30.00 |
| ☐ 458 Gordon Jones | 2.00 | 4.00 |
| ☐ 459 Bill Tuttle | 2.00 | 4.00 |
| ☐ 460 Bob Friend | 4.00 | 8.00 |
| ☐ 461 Mickey Mantle BT | 75.00 | 125.00 |
| ☐ 462 Rocky Colavito BT | 6.00 | 12.00 |
| ☐ 463 Al Kaline BT | 15.00 | 30.00 |
| ☐ 464 Willie Mays BT | 20.00 | 40.00 |
| ☐ 465 Roy Sievers BT | 4.00 | 8.00 |
| ☐ 466 Billy Pierce BT | 4.00 | 8.00 |
| ☐ 467 Hank Aaron BT | 20.00 | 40.00 |
| ☐ 468 Duke Snider BT | 10.00 | 20.00 |
| ☐ 469 Ernie Banks BT | 10.00 | 20.00 |
| ☐ 470 Stan Musial BT | 15.00 | 30.00 |
| ☐ 471 Tom Sturdivant | 2.00 | 4.00 |
| ☐ 472 Gene Freese | 2.00 | 4.00 |
| ☐ 473 Mike Fornieles | 2.00 | 4.00 |
| ☐ 474 Moe Thacker RC | 2.00 | 4.00 |
| ☐ 475 Jack Harshman | 2.00 | 4.00 |
| ☐ 476 Cleveland Indians CL | 7.50 | 15.00 |
| ☐ 477 Barry Latman RC | 2.00 | 4.00 |
| ☐ 478 Roberto Clemente | 100.00 | 175.00 |
| ☐ 479 Lindy McDaniel | 4.00 | 8.00 |
| ☐ 480 Red Schoendienst | 6.00 | 12.00 |
| ☐ 481 Charlie Maxwell | 4.00 | 8.00 |
| ☐ 482 Russ Meyer | 2.00 | 4.00 |
| ☐ 483 Clint Courtney | 2.00 | 4.00 |
| ☐ 484 Willie Kirkland | 2.00 | 4.00 |
| ☐ 485 Ryne Duren | 4.00 | 8.00 |
| ☐ 486 Sammy White | 2.00 | 4.00 |
| ☐ 487 Hal Brown | 2.00 | 4.00 |
| ☐ 488 Walt Moryn | 2.00 | 4.00 |
| ☐ 489 John Powers | 2.00 | 4.00 |
| ☐ 490 Frank Thomas | 4.00 | 8.00 |
| ☐ 491 Don Blasingame | 2.00 | 4.00 |
| ☐ 492 Gene Conley | 4.00 | 8.00 |
| ☐ 493 Jim Landis | 4.00 | 8.00 |
| ☐ 494 Don Pavletich RC | 2.00 | 4.00 |
| ☐ 495 Johnny Podres | 6.00 | 12.00 |
| ☐ 496 Wayne Terwilliger UER | 2.00 | 4.00 |

| | | |
|---|---|---|
| ☐ 497 Hal R. Smith | 2.00 | 4.00 |
| ☐ 498 Dick Hyde | 2.00 | 4.00 |
| ☐ 499 Johnny O'Brien | 4.00 | 8.00 |
| ☐ 500 Vic Wertz | 4.00 | 8.00 |
| ☐ 501 Bob Tiefenauer RC | 2.00 | 4.00 |
| ☐ 502 Alvin Dark | 4.00 | 8.00 |
| ☐ 503 Jim Owens | 2.00 | 4.00 |
| ☐ 504 Ossie Alvarez RC | 2.00 | 4.00 |
| ☐ 505 Tony Kubek | 6.00 | 12.00 |
| ☐ 506 Bob Purkey | 4.00 | 8.00 |
| ☐ 507 Bob Hale | 7.50 | 15.00 |
| ☐ 508 Art Fowler | 7.50 | 15.00 |
| ☐ 509 Norm Cash RC | 50.00 | 80.00 |
| ☐ 510 New York Yankees CL | 75.00 | 125.00 |
| ☐ 511 George Susce | 7.50 | 15.00 |
| ☐ 512 George Altman RC | 7.50 | 15.00 |
| ☐ 513 Tommy Carroll | 7.50 | 15.00 |
| ☐ 514 Bob Gibson RC | 175.00 | 300.00 |
| ☐ 515 Harmon Killebrew | 75.00 | 125.00 |
| ☐ 516 Mike Garcia | 10.00 | 20.00 |
| ☐ 517 Joe Koppe RC | 7.50 | 15.00 |
| ☐ 518 Mike Cuellar UER RC | 18.00 | 30.00 |
| ☐ 519 Runnels/Gernert/Malzone | 10.00 | 20.00 |
| ☐ 520 Don Elston | 7.50 | 15.00 |
| ☐ 521 Gary Geiger | 7.50 | 15.00 |
| ☐ 522 Gene Snyder RC | 7.50 | 15.00 |
| ☐ 523 Harry Bright RC | 7.50 | 15.00 |
| ☐ 524 Larry Osborne RC | 7.50 | 15.00 |
| ☐ 525 Jim Coates RC | 10.00 | 20.00 |
| ☐ 526 Bob Speake | 7.50 | 15.00 |
| ☐ 527 Solly Hemus | 7.50 | 15.00 |
| ☐ 528 Pittsburgh Pirates CL | 50.00 | 80.00 |
| ☐ 529 George Bamberger RC | 10.00 | 20.00 |
| ☐ 530 Wally Moon | 10.00 | 20.00 |
| ☐ 531 Ray Webster RC | 7.50 | 15.00 |
| ☐ 532 Mark Freeman RC | 7.50 | 15.00 |
| ☐ 533 Darrell Johnson | 10.00 | 20.00 |
| ☐ 534 Faye Throneberry | 7.50 | 15.00 |
| ☐ 535 Ruben Gomez | 7.50 | 15.00 |
| ☐ 536 Danny Kravitz | 7.50 | 15.00 |
| ☐ 537 Rudolph Arias RC | 7.50 | 15.00 |
| ☐ 538 Chick King | 7.50 | 15.00 |
| ☐ 539 Gary Blaylock RC | 7.50 | 15.00 |
| ☐ 540 Willie Miranda | 7.50 | 15.00 |
| ☐ 541 Bob Thurman | 7.50 | 15.00 |
| ☐ 542 Jim Perry RC | 18.00 | 30.00 |
| ☐ 543 Skinner/Virdon/Clemente | 75.00 | 125.00 |
| ☐ 544 Lee Tate RC | 7.50 | 15.00 |
| ☐ 545 Tom Morgan | 7.50 | 15.00 |
| ☐ 546 Al Schroll | 7.50 | 15.00 |
| ☐ 547 Jim Baxes RC | 7.50 | 15.00 |
| ☐ 548 Elmer Singleton | 7.50 | 15.00 |
| ☐ 549 Howie Nunn RC | 7.50 | 15.00 |
| ☐ 550 H.Campanella Courage | 90.00 | 150.00 |
| ☐ 551 Fred Haney AS MG | 7.50 | 15.00 |
| ☐ 552 Casey Stengel AS | 18.00 | 30.00 |
| ☐ 553 Orlando Cepeda AS | 18.00 | 30.00 |
| ☐ 554 Bill Skowron AS | 10.00 | 20.00 |
| ☐ 555 Bill Mazeroski AS | 18.00 | 30.00 |
| ☐ 556 Nellie Fox AS | 20.00 | 40.00 |
| ☐ 557 Ken Boyer AS | 18.00 | 30.00 |
| ☐ 558 Frank Malzone AS | 7.50 | 15.00 |
| ☐ 559 Ernie Banks AS | 35.00 | 60.00 |
| ☐ 560 Luis Aparicio AS | 25.00 | 40.00 |
| ☐ 561 Hank Aaron AS | 75.00 | 125.00 |
| ☐ 562 Al Kaline AS | 35.00 | 60.00 |
| ☐ 563 Willie Mays AS | 75.00 | 125.00 |
| ☐ 564 Mickey Mantle AS | 175.00 | 300.00 |
| ☐ 565 Wes Covington AS | 10.00 | 20.00 |
| ☐ 566 Roy Sievers AS | 7.50 | 15.00 |
| ☐ 567 Del Crandall AS | 7.50 | 15.00 |
| ☐ 568 Gus Triandos AS | 7.50 | 15.00 |
| ☐ 569 Bob Friend AS | 7.50 | 15.00 |
| ☐ 570 Bob Turley AS | 7.50 | 15.00 |
| ☐ 571 Warren Spahn AS | 30.00 | 50.00 |
| ☐ 572 Billy Pierce AS | 25.00 | 40.00 |

## 1960 Topps

| | | |
|---|---|---|
| ☐ COMPLETE SET (572) | 2500.00 | 5000.00 |
| ☐ COMMON CARD (1-440) | 1.50 | 4.00 |
| ☐ COMMON CARD (441-506) | 3.00 | 8.00 |
| ☐ COMMON CARD (507-572) | 6.00 | 15.00 |
| ☐ WRAPPER (1-CENT) | 500.00 | 1000.00 |
| ☐ WRAP. (1-CENT REPEAT) | 250.00 | 500.00 |
| ☐ WRAPPER (5-CENT) | 15.00 | 40.00 |
| ☐ 1 Early Wynn | 15.00 | 10.00 |
| ☐ 2 Roman Mejias | 1.50 | 4.00 |
| ☐ 3 Joe Adcock | 2.50 | 6.00 |

| | | |
|---|---|---|
| ☐ 4 Bob Purkey | 1.50 | 4.00 |
| ☐ 5 Wally Moon | 2.50 | 6.00 |
| ☐ 6 Lou Berberet | 1.50 | 4.00 |
| ☐ 7 W.Mays/B.Rigney | 10.00 | 25.00 |
| ☐ 8 Bud Daley | 1.50 | 4.00 |
| ☐ 9 Faye Throneberry | 1.50 | 4.00 |
| ☐ 10 Ernie Banks | 20.00 | 50.00 |
| ☐ 11 Norm Siebern | 1.50 | 4.00 |
| ☐ 12 Milt Pappas | 2.50 | 6.00 |
| ☐ 13 Wally Post | 2.50 | 6.00 |
| ☐ 14 Jim Grant | 2.50 | 6.00 |
| ☐ 15 Pete Runnels | 2.50 | 6.00 |
| ☐ 16 Ernie Broglio | 2.50 | 6.00 |
| ☐ 17 Johnny Callison | 2.50 | 6.00 |
| ☐ 18 Los Angeles Dodgers CL | 20.00 | 50.00 |
| ☐ 19 Felix Mantilla | 1.50 | 4.00 |
| ☐ 20 Roy Face | 2.50 | 6.00 |
| ☐ 21 Dutch Dotterer | 1.50 | 4.00 |
| ☐ 22 Rocky Bridges | 1.50 | 4.00 |
| ☐ 23 Eddie Fisher RC | 1.50 | 4.00 |
| ☐ 24 Dick Gray | 1.50 | 4.00 |
| ☐ 25 Roy Sievers | 2.50 | 6.00 |
| ☐ 26 Wayne Terwilliger | 1.50 | 4.00 |
| ☐ 27 Dick Drott | 1.50 | 4.00 |
| ☐ 28 Brooks Robinson | 20.00 | 50.00 |
| ☐ 29 Clem Labine | 2.50 | 6.00 |
| ☐ 30 Tito Francona | 1.50 | 4.00 |
| ☐ 31 Sammy Esposito | 1.50 | 4.00 |
| ☐ 32 J.O'Toole/V.Pinson | 1.50 | 4.00 |
| ☐ 33 Tom Morgan | 1.50 | 4.00 |
| ☐ 34 Sparky Anderson | 6.00 | 15.00 |
| ☐ 35 Whitey Ford | 20.00 | 50.00 |
| ☐ 36 Russ Nixon | 1.50 | 4.00 |
| ☐ 37 Bill Bruton | 1.50 | 4.00 |
| ☐ 38 Jerry Casale | 1.50 | 4.00 |
| ☐ 39 Earl Averill Jr. | 1.50 | 4.00 |
| ☐ 40 Joe Cunningham | 1.50 | 4.00 |
| ☐ 41 Barry Latman | 1.50 | 4.00 |
| ☐ 42 Hobie Landrith | 1.50 | 4.00 |
| ☐ 43 Washington Senators CL | 4.00 | 10.00 |
| ☐ 44 Bobby Locke RC | 1.50 | 4.00 |
| ☐ 45 Roy McMillan | 2.50 | 6.00 |
| ☐ 46 Jack Fisher RC | 1.50 | 4.00 |
| ☐ 47 Don Zimmer | 2.50 | 6.00 |
| ☐ 48 Hal W. Smith | 1.50 | 4.00 |
| ☐ 49 Curt Raydon | 1.50 | 4.00 |
| ☐ 50 Al Kaline | 20.00 | 50.00 |
| ☐ 51 Jim Coates | 2.50 | 6.00 |
| ☐ 52 Dave Philley | 1.50 | 4.00 |
| ☐ 53 Jackie Brandt | 1.50 | 4.00 |
| ☐ 54 Mike Fornieles | 1.50 | 4.00 |
| ☐ 55 Bill Mazeroski | 6.00 | 15.00 |
| ☐ 56 Steve Korcheck | 1.50 | 4.00 |
| ☐ 57 T.Lown/G.Staley | 1.50 | 4.00 |
| ☐ 58 Gino Cimoli | 1.50 | 4.00 |
| ☐ 58A Gino Cimoli Cards | | |
| ☐ 59 Juan Pizarro | 1.50 | 4.00 |
| ☐ 60 Gus Triandos | 2.50 | 6.00 |
| ☐ 61 Eddie Kasko | 1.50 | 4.00 |
| ☐ 62 Roger Craig | 2.50 | 6.00 |
| ☐ 63 George Strickland | 1.50 | 4.00 |
| ☐ 64 Jack Meyer | 1.50 | 4.00 |
| ☐ 65 Elston Howard | 2.50 | 6.00 |
| ☐ 66 Bob Trowbridge | 1.50 | 4.00 |
| ☐ 67 Jose Pagan RC | 1.50 | 4.00 |
| ☐ 68 Dave Hillman | 1.50 | 4.00 |
| ☐ 69 Billy Goodman | 2.50 | 6.00 |
| ☐ 70 Lew Burdette UER | 2.50 | 6.00 |
| ☐ 71 Marty Keough | 1.50 | 4.00 |
| ☐ 72 Detroit Tigers CL | 10.00 | 25.00 |
| ☐ 73 Bob Gibson | 20.00 | 50.00 |
| ☐ 74 Walt Moryn | 1.50 | 4.00 |
| ☐ 75 Vic Power | 2.50 | 6.00 |
| ☐ 76 Bill Fischer | 1.50 | 4.00 |

|  |  | | |
|---|---|---|---|
| 77 | Hank Foiles | 1.50 | 4.00 |
| 78 | Bob Grim | 1.50 | 4.00 |
| 79 | Walt Dropo | 1.50 | 4.00 |
| 80 | Johnny Antonelli | 2.50 | 6.00 |
| 81 | Russ Snyder RC | 1.50 | 4.00 |
| 82 | Ruben Gomez | 1.50 | 4.00 |
| 83 | Tony Kubek | 6.00 | 15.00 |
| 84 | Hal R. Smith | 1.50 | 4.00 |
| 85 | Frank Lary | 2.50 | 6.00 |
| 86 | Dick Gernert | 1.50 | 4.00 |
| 87 | John Romonosky | 1.50 | 4.00 |
| 88 | John Roseboro | 2.50 | 6.00 |
| 89 | Hal Brown | 1.50 | 4.00 |
| 90 | Bobby Avila | 1.50 | 4.00 |
| 91 | Bennie Daniels | 1.50 | 4.00 |
| 92 | Whitey Herzog | 2.50 | 6.00 |
| 93 | Art Schult | 1.50 | 4.00 |
| 94 | Leo Kiely | 1.50 | 4.00 |
| 95 | Frank Thomas | 2.50 | 6.00 |
| 96 | Ralph Terry | 2.50 | 6.00 |
| 97 | Ted Lepcio | 1.50 | 4.00 |
| 98 | Gordon Jones | 1.50 | 4.00 |
| 99 | Lenny Green | 1.50 | 4.00 |
| 100 | Nellie Fox | 8.00 | 20.00 |
| 101 | Bob Miller RC | 1.50 | 4.00 |
| 102 | Kent Hadley | 1.50 | 4.00 |
| 102A | Kent Hadley A's | | |
| 103 | Dick Farrell | 2.50 | 6.00 |
| 104 | Dick Schofield | 2.50 | 6.00 |
| 105 | Larry Sherry RC | 2.50 | 6.00 |
| 106 | Billy Gardner | 1.50 | 4.00 |
| 107 | Carlton Willey | 1.50 | 4.00 |
| 108 | Pete Daley | 1.50 | 4.00 |
| 109 | Clete Boyer | 6.00 | 15.00 |
| 110 | Cal McLish | 1.50 | 4.00 |
| 111 | Vic Wertz | 2.50 | 6.00 |
| 112 | Jack Harshman | 1.50 | 4.00 |
| 113 | Bob Skinner | 1.50 | 4.00 |
| 114 | Ken Aspromonte | 1.50 | 4.00 |
| 115 | R.Face/H.Wilhelm | 2.50 | 6.00 |
| 116 | Jim Rivera | 1.50 | 4.00 |
| 117 | Tom Borland RS | 1.50 | 4.00 |
| 118 | Bob Bruce RS RC | 1.50 | 4.00 |
| 119 | Chico Cardenas RS RC | 2.50 | 6.00 |
| 120 | Duke Carmel RS RC | 1.50 | 4.00 |
| 121 | Camilo Carreon RS RC | 1.50 | 4.00 |
| 122 | Don Dillard RS | 1.50 | 4.00 |
| 123 | Dan Dobbek RS | 1.50 | 4.00 |
| 124 | Jim Donohue RS RC | 1.50 | 4.00 |
| 125 | Dick Ellsworth RS RC | 2.50 | 6.00 |
| 126 | Chuck Estrada RS RC | 1.50 | 4.00 |
| 127 | Ron Hansen RS | 2.50 | 6.00 |
| 128 | Bill Harris RS RC | 1.50 | 4.00 |
| 129 | Bob Hartman RS | 1.50 | 4.00 |
| 130 | Frank Herrera RS | 1.50 | 4.00 |
| 131 | Ed Hobaugh RS RC | 1.50 | 4.00 |
| 132 | Frank Howard RS RC | 10.00 | 25.00 |
| 133 | Julian Javier RS RC | 2.50 | 6.00 |
| 134 | Deron Johnson RS | 2.50 | 6.00 |
| 135 | Ken Johnson RS RC | 1.50 | 4.00 |
| 136 | Jim Kaat RS RC | 15.00 | 40.00 |
| 137 | Lou Klimchock RS RC | 1.50 | 4.00 |
| 138 | Art Mahaffey RS RC | 2.50 | 6.00 |
| 139 | Carl Mathias RS RC | 1.50 | 4.00 |
| 140 | Julio Navarro RS RC | 1.50 | 4.00 |
| 141 | Jim Proctor RS RC | 1.50 | 4.00 |
| 142 | Bill Short RS RC | 1.50 | 4.00 |
| 143 | Al Spangler RS RC | 1.50 | 4.00 |
| 144 | Al Stieglitz RS RC | 1.50 | 4.00 |
| 145 | Jim Umbricht RS RC | 1.50 | 4.00 |
| 146 | Ted Wieand RS RC | 1.50 | 4.00 |
| 147 | Bob Will RS | 1.50 | 4.00 |
| 148 | C.Yastrzemski RS RC | 100.00 | 200.00 |
| 149 | Bob Nieman | 1.50 | 4.00 |
| 150 | Billy Pierce | 2.50 | 6.00 |
| 151 | San Francisco Giants CL | 4.00 | 10.00 |
| 152 | Gail Harris | 1.50 | 4.00 |
| 153 | Bobby Thomson | 2.50 | 6.00 |
| 154 | Jim Davenport | 2.50 | 6.00 |
| 155 | Charlie Neal | 2.50 | 6.00 |
| 156 | Art Ceccarelli | 1.50 | 4.00 |
| 157 | Rocky Nelson | 2.50 | 6.00 |
| 158 | Wes Covington | 1.50 | 4.00 |
| 159 | Jim Piersall | 2.50 | 6.00 |
| 160 | N.Mantle/K.Boyer | 60.00 | 120.00 |
| 161 | Ray Narleski | 1.50 | 4.00 |
| 162 | Sammy Taylor | 1.50 | 4.00 |
| 163 | Hector Lopez | 2.50 | 6.00 |
| 164 | Cincinnati Reds CL | 4.00 | 10.00 |
| 165 | Jack Sanford | 2.50 | 6.00 |
| 166 | Chuck Essegian | 1.50 | 4.00 |
| 167 | Valmy Thomas | 1.50 | 4.00 |
| 168 | Alex Grammas | 1.50 | 4.00 |
| 169 | Jake Striker RC | 1.50 | 4.00 |
| 170 | Del Crandall | 2.50 | 6.00 |
| 171 | Johnny Groth | 1.50 | 4.00 |
| 172 | Willie Kirkland | 1.50 | 4.00 |
| 173 | Billy Martin | 8.00 | 20.00 |
| 174 | Cleveland Indians CL | 4.00 | 10.00 |
| 175 | Pedro Ramos | 1.50 | 4.00 |
| 176 | Vada Pinson | 2.50 | 6.00 |
| 177 | Johnny Kucks | 1.50 | 4.00 |
| 178 | Woody Held | 1.50 | 4.00 |
| 179 | Rip Coleman | 1.50 | 4.00 |
| 180 | Harry Simpson | 1.50 | 4.00 |
| 181 | Billy Loes | 2.50 | 6.00 |
| 182 | Glen Hobbie | 1.50 | 4.00 |
| 183 | Eli Grba RC | 1.50 | 4.00 |
| 184 | Gary Geiger | 1.50 | 4.00 |
| 185 | Jim Owens | 1.50 | 4.00 |
| 186 | Dave Sisler | 1.50 | 4.00 |
| 187 | Jay Hook RC | 1.50 | 4.00 |
| 188 | Dick Williams | 2.50 | 6.00 |
| 189 | Don McMahon | 1.50 | 4.00 |
| 190 | Gene Woodling | 2.50 | 6.00 |
| 191 | Johnny Klippstein | 1.50 | 4.00 |
| 192 | Danny O'Connell | 1.50 | 4.00 |
| 193 | Dick Hyde | 1.50 | 4.00 |
| 194 | Bobby Gene Smith | 1.50 | 4.00 |
| 195 | Lindy McDaniel | 2.50 | 6.00 |
| 196 | Andy Carey | 2.50 | 6.00 |
| 197 | Ron Kline | 1.50 | 4.00 |
| 198 | Jerry Lynch | 2.50 | 6.00 |
| 199 | Dick Donovan | 2.50 | 6.00 |
| 200 | Willie Mays | 60.00 | 120.00 |
| 201 | Larry Osborne | 1.50 | 4.00 |
| 202 | Fred Kipp | 1.50 | 4.00 |
| 203 | Sammy White | 1.50 | 4.00 |
| 204 | Ryne Duren | 2.50 | 6.00 |
| 205 | Johnny Logan | 2.50 | 6.00 |
| 206 | Claude Osteen | 2.50 | 6.00 |
| 207 | Bob Boyd | 1.50 | 4.00 |
| 208 | Chicago White Sox CL | 4.00 | 10.00 |
| 209 | Ron Blackburn | 1.50 | 4.00 |
| 210 | Harmon Killebrew | 15.00 | 40.00 |
| 211 | Taylor Phillips | 1.50 | 4.00 |
| 212 | Walter Alston MG | 4.00 | 10.00 |
| 213 | Chuck Dressen MG | 2.50 | 6.00 |
| 214 | Jimmy Dykes MG | 2.50 | 6.00 |
| 215 | Bob Elliott MG | 2.50 | 6.00 |
| 216 | Joe Gordon MG | 2.50 | 6.00 |
| 217 | Charlie Grimm MG | 2.50 | 6.00 |
| 218 | Solly Hemus MG | 1.50 | 4.00 |
| 219 | Fred Hutchinson MG | 2.50 | 6.00 |
| 220 | Billy Jurges MG | 1.50 | 4.00 |
| 221 | Cookie Lavagetto MG | 1.50 | 4.00 |
| 222 | Al Lopez MG | 4.00 | 10.00 |
| 223 | Danny Murtaugh MG | 2.50 | 6.00 |
| 224 | Paul Richards MG | 2.50 | 6.00 |
| 225 | Bill Rigney MG | 1.50 | 4.00 |
| 226 | Eddie Sawyer MG | 1.50 | 4.00 |
| 227 | Casey Stengel MG | 6.00 | 15.00 |
| 228 | Ernie Johnson | 2.50 | 6.00 |
| 229 | Joe M. Morgan RC | 1.50 | 4.00 |
| 230 | Burdette/Spahn/Buhl | 4.00 | 10.00 |
| 231 | Hal Naragon | 1.50 | 4.00 |
| 232 | Jim Busby | 1.50 | 4.00 |
| 233 | Don Elston | 1.50 | 4.00 |
| 234 | Don Demeter | 1.50 | 4.00 |
| 235 | Gus Bell | 2.50 | 6.00 |
| 236 | Dick Ricketts | 1.50 | 4.00 |
| 237 | Elmer Valo | 1.50 | 4.00 |
| 238 | Danny Kravitz | 1.50 | 4.00 |
| 239 | Joe Shipley | 1.50 | 4.00 |
| 240 | Luis Aparicio | 6.00 | 15.00 |
| 241 | Albie Pearson | 2.50 | 6.00 |
| 242 | St. Louis Cardinals CL | 4.00 | 10.00 |
| 243 | Bubba Phillips | 1.50 | 4.00 |
| 244 | Hal Griggs | 1.50 | 4.00 |
| 245 | Eddie Yost | 2.50 | 6.00 |
| 246 | Lee Maye RC | 2.50 | 6.00 |
| 247 | Gil McDougald | 4.00 | 10.00 |
| 248 | Del Rice | 1.50 | 4.00 |
| 249 | Earl Wilson RC | 2.50 | 6.00 |
| 250 | Stan Musial | 50.00 | 100.00 |
| 251 | Bob Malkmus | 1.50 | 4.00 |
| 252 | Ray Herbert | 1.50 | 4.00 |
| 253 | Eddie Bressoud | 1.50 | 4.00 |
| 254 | Arnie Portocarrero | 1.50 | 4.00 |
| 255 | Jim Gilliam | 2.50 | 6.00 |
| 256 | Dick Brown | 1.50 | 4.00 |
| 257 | Gordy Coleman RC | 1.50 | 4.00 |
| 258 | Dick Groat | 2.50 | 6.00 |
| 259 | George Altman | 1.50 | 4.00 |
| 260 | R.Colavito/T.Francona | 6.00 | 15.00 |
| 261 | Pete Burnside | 1.50 | 4.00 |
| 262 | Hank Bauer | 2.50 | 6.00 |
| 263 | Darrell Johnson | 1.50 | 4.00 |
| 264 | Robin Roberts | 6.00 | 15.00 |
| 265 | Rip Repulski | 1.50 | 4.00 |
| 266 | Joey Jay | 2.50 | 6.00 |
| 267 | Jim Marshall | 1.50 | 4.00 |
| 268 | Al Worthington | 1.50 | 4.00 |
| 269 | Gene Green | 1.50 | 4.00 |
| 270 | Bob Turley | 2.50 | 6.00 |
| 271 | Julio Becquer | 1.50 | 4.00 |
| 272 | Fred Green RC | 2.50 | 6.00 |
| 273 | Neil Chrisley | 1.50 | 4.00 |
| 274 | Tom Acker | 1.50 | 4.00 |
| 275 | Curt Flood | 2.50 | 6.00 |
| 276 | Ken McBride RC | 1.50 | 4.00 |
| 277 | Harry Bright | 1.50 | 4.00 |
| 278 | Stan Williams | 2.50 | 6.00 |
| 279 | Chuck Tanner | 1.50 | 4.00 |
| 280 | Frank Sullivan | 1.50 | 4.00 |
| 281 | Ray Boone | 2.50 | 6.00 |
| 282 | Joe Nuxhall | 2.50 | 6.00 |
| 283 | Johnny Blanchard | 2.50 | 6.00 |
| 284 | Don Gross | 1.50 | 4.00 |
| 285 | Harry Anderson | 1.50 | 4.00 |
| 286 | Ray Semproch | 1.50 | 4.00 |
| 287 | Felipe Alou | 2.50 | 6.00 |
| 288 | Bob Mabe | 1.50 | 4.00 |
| 289 | Willie Jones | 1.50 | 4.00 |
| 290 | Jerry Lumpe | 1.50 | 4.00 |
| 291 | Bob Keegan | 1.50 | 4.00 |
| 292 | J.Pignatano/J.Roseboro | 2.50 | 6.00 |
| 293 | Gene Conley | 2.50 | 6.00 |
| 294 | Tony Taylor | 2.50 | 6.00 |
| 295 | Gil Hodges | 10.00 | 25.00 |
| 296 | Nelson Chittum RC | 1.50 | 4.00 |
| 297 | Reno Bertoia | 1.50 | 4.00 |
| 298 | George Witt | 1.50 | 4.00 |
| 299 | Earl Torgeson | 1.50 | 4.00 |
| 300 | Hank Aaron | 60.00 | 120.00 |
| 301 | Jerry Davie | 1.50 | 4.00 |
| 302 | Philadelphia Phillies CL | 4.00 | 10.00 |
| 303 | Billy O'Dell | 1.50 | 4.00 |
| 304 | Joe Ginsberg | 1.50 | 4.00 |
| 305 | Richie Ashburn | 8.00 | 20.00 |
| 306 | Frank Baumann | 1.50 | 4.00 |
| 307 | Gene Oliver | 1.50 | 4.00 |
| 308 | Dick Hall | 1.50 | 4.00 |
| 309 | Bob Hale | 1.50 | 4.00 |
| 310 | Frank Malzone | 2.50 | 6.00 |
| 311 | Raul Sanchez | 1.50 | 4.00 |
| 312 | Charley Lau | 2.50 | 6.00 |
| 313 | Turk Lown | 1.50 | 4.00 |
| 314 | Chico Fernandez | 1.50 | 4.00 |
| 315 | Bobby Shantz | 4.00 | 10.00 |
| 316 | W.McCovey ASR RC | 60.00 | 120.00 |
| 317 | Pumpsie Green ASR | 2.50 | 6.00 |
| 318 | Jim Baxes ASR | 2.50 | 6.00 |
| 319 | Joe Koppe ASR | 2.50 | 6.00 |
| 320 | Bob Allison ASR | 2.50 | 6.00 |
| 321 | Ron Fairly ASR | 2.50 | 6.00 |
| 322 | Willie Tasby ASR | 2.50 | 6.00 |
| 323 | John Romano ASR | 2.50 | 6.00 |
| 324 | Jim Perry ASR | 2.50 | 6.00 |
| 325 | Jim O'Toole ASR | 2.50 | 6.00 |
| 326 | Roberto Clemente | 100.00 | 200.00 |
| 327 | Ray Sadecki RC | 1.50 | 4.00 |
| 328 | Earl Battey | 2.50 | 6.00 |
| 329 | Zack Monroe | 1.50 | 4.00 |
| 330 | Harvey Kuenn | 2.50 | 6.00 |
| 331 | Henry Mason RC | 1.50 | 4.00 |
| 332 | New York Yankees CL | 40.00 | 80.00 |
| 333 | Danny McDevitt | 1.50 | 4.00 |
| 334 | Ted Abernathy | 1.50 | 4.00 |
| 335 | Red Schoendienst | 6.00 | 15.00 |
| 336 | Ike Delock | 1.50 | 4.00 |
| 337 | Cal Neeman | 1.50 | 4.00 |
| 338 | Ray Monzant | 1.50 | 4.00 |
| 339 | Harry Chiti | 1.50 | 4.00 |

| | | |
|---|---|---|
| ❑ 340 Harvey Haddix | 2.50 | 6.00 |
| ❑ 341 Carroll Hardy | 1.50 | 4.00 |
| ❑ 342 Casey Wise | 1.50 | 4.00 |
| ❑ 343 Sandy Koufax | 60.00 | 120.00 |
| ❑ 344 Clint Courtney | 1.50 | 4.00 |
| ❑ 345 Don Newcombe | 2.50 | 6.00 |
| ❑ 346 J.C. Martin UER RC | 2.50 | 6.00 |
| ❑ 347 Ed Bouchee | 1.50 | 4.00 |
| ❑ 348 Barry Shetrone RC | 1.50 | 4.00 |
| ❑ 349 Moe Drabowsky | 2.50 | 6.00 |
| ❑ 350 Mickey Mantle | 300.00 | 600.00 |
| ❑ 351 Don Nottebart RC | 1.50 | 4.00 |
| ❑ 352 Bell/F. Robinson/Lynch | 4.00 | 10.00 |
| ❑ 353 Don Larsen | 2.50 | 6.00 |
| ❑ 354 Bob Lillis | 1.50 | 4.00 |
| ❑ 355 Bill White | 2.50 | 6.00 |
| ❑ 356 Joe Amalfitano | 1.50 | 4.00 |
| ❑ 357 Al Schroll | 1.50 | 4.00 |
| ❑ 358 Joe DeMaestri | 1.50 | 4.00 |
| ❑ 359 Buddy Gilbert RC | 1.50 | 4.00 |
| ❑ 360 Herb Score | 6.00 | 6.00 |
| ❑ 361 Bob Oldis | 2.50 | 6.00 |
| ❑ 362 Russ Kemmerer | 1.50 | 4.00 |
| ❑ 363 Gene Stephens | 1.50 | 4.00 |
| ❑ 364 Paul Foytack | 1.50 | 4.00 |
| ❑ 365 Minnie Minoso | 4.00 | 10.00 |
| ❑ 366 Dallas Green RC | 4.00 | 10.00 |
| ❑ 367 Bill Tuttle | 1.50 | 4.00 |
| ❑ 368 Daryl Spencer | 1.50 | 4.00 |
| ❑ 369 Billy Hoeft | 1.50 | 4.00 |
| ❑ 370 Bill Skowron | 4.00 | 10.00 |
| ❑ 371 Bud Byerly | 1.50 | 4.00 |
| ❑ 372 Frank House | 1.50 | 4.00 |
| ❑ 373 Don Hoak | 2.50 | 6.00 |
| ❑ 374 Bob Buhl | 2.50 | 6.00 |
| ❑ 375 Dale Long | 4.00 | 10.00 |
| ❑ 376 John Briggs | 1.50 | 4.00 |
| ❑ 377 Roger Maris | 50.00 | 100.00 |
| ❑ 378 Stu Miller | 2.50 | 6.00 |
| ❑ 379 Red Wilson | 1.50 | 4.00 |
| ❑ 380 Bob Shaw | 1.50 | 4.00 |
| ❑ 381 Milwaukee Braves CL | 4.00 | 10.00 |
| ❑ 382 Ted Bowsfield | 1.50 | 4.00 |
| ❑ 383 Leon Wagner | 1.50 | 4.00 |
| ❑ 384 Don Cardwell | 1.50 | 4.00 |
| ❑ 385 Charlie Neal WS1 | 3.00 | 8.00 |
| ❑ 386 Charlie Neal WS2 | 3.00 | 8.00 |
| ❑ 387 Carl Furillo WS3 | 3.00 | 8.00 |
| ❑ 388 Gil Hodges WS4 | 4.00 | 10.00 |
| ❑ 389 L.Aparicio WS5 w/M.Wills | 3.00 | 8.00 |
| ❑ 390 Scrambling After Ball WS6 | 3.00 | 8.00 |
| ❑ 391 Champs Celebrate WS | 3.00 | 8.00 |
| ❑ 392 Tex Clevenger | 1.50 | 4.00 |
| ❑ 393 Smoky Burgess | 2.50 | 6.00 |
| ❑ 394 Norm Larker | 2.50 | 6.00 |
| ❑ 395 Hoyt Wilhelm | 6.00 | 15.00 |
| ❑ 396 Steve Bilko | 1.50 | 4.00 |
| ❑ 397 Don Blasingame | 1.50 | 4.00 |
| ❑ 398 Mike Cuellar | 2.50 | 6.00 |
| ❑ 399 Pappas/Fisher/Walker | 2.50 | 6.00 |
| ❑ 400 Rocky Colavito | 8.00 | 20.00 |
| ❑ 401 Bob Duliba RC | 1.50 | 4.00 |
| ❑ 402 Dick Stuart | 6.00 | 15.00 |
| ❑ 403 Ed Sadowski | 1.50 | 4.00 |
| ❑ 404 Bob Rush | 1.50 | 4.00 |
| ❑ 405 Bobby Richardson | 6.00 | 15.00 |
| ❑ 406 Billy Klaus | 1.50 | 4.00 |
| ❑ 407 Gary Peters UER RC | 2.50 | 6.00 |
| ❑ 408 Carl Furillo | 4.00 | 10.00 |
| ❑ 409 Ron Samford | 1.50 | 4.00 |
| ❑ 410 Sam Jones | 2.50 | 6.00 |
| ❑ 411 Ed Bailey | 1.50 | 4.00 |
| ❑ 412 Bob Anderson | 1.50 | 4.00 |
| ❑ 413 Kansas City Athletics CL | 4.00 | 10.00 |
| ❑ 414 Don Williams RC | 1.50 | 4.00 |
| ❑ 415 Bob Cerv | 1.50 | 4.00 |
| ❑ 416 Humberto Robinson | 1.50 | 4.00 |
| ❑ 417 Chuck Cottier RC | 1.50 | 4.00 |
| ❑ 418 Don Mossi | 2.50 | 6.00 |
| ❑ 419 George Crowe | 1.50 | 4.00 |
| ❑ 420 Eddie Mathews | 15.00 | 40.00 |
| ❑ 421 Duke Maas | 1.50 | 4.00 |
| ❑ 422 John Powers | 1.50 | 4.00 |
| ❑ 423 Ed Fitzgerald | 1.50 | 4.00 |
| ❑ 424 Pete Whisenant | 1.50 | 4.00 |
| ❑ 425 Johnny Podres | 2.50 | 6.00 |
| ❑ 426 Ron Jackson | 1.50 | 4.00 |
| ❑ 427 Al Grunwald RC | 1.50 | 4.00 |

| | | |
|---|---|---|
| ❑ 428 Al Smith | 1.50 | 4.00 |
| ❑ 429 Nellie Fox/H.Kuenn | 4.00 | 10.00 |
| ❑ 430 Art Ditmar | 1.50 | 4.00 |
| ❑ 431 Andre Rodgers | 1.50 | 4.00 |
| ❑ 432 Chuck Stobbs | 1.50 | 4.00 |
| ❑ 433 Irv Noren | 1.50 | 4.00 |
| ❑ 434 Brooks Lawrence | 2.50 | 6.00 |
| ❑ 435 Gene Freese | 1.50 | 4.00 |
| ❑ 436 Marv Throneberry | 2.50 | 6.00 |
| ❑ 437 Bob Friend | 2.50 | 6.00 |
| ❑ 438 Jim Coker RC | 1.50 | 4.00 |
| ❑ 439 Tom Brewer | 1.50 | 4.00 |
| ❑ 440 Jim Lemon | 2.50 | 6.00 |
| ❑ 441 Gary Bell | 4.00 | 10.00 |
| ❑ 442 Joe Pignatano | 3.00 | 8.00 |
| ❑ 443 Charlie Maxwell | 3.00 | 8.00 |
| ❑ 444 Jerry Kindall | 3.00 | 8.00 |
| ❑ 445 Warren Spahn | 20.00 | 50.00 |
| ❑ 446 Ellis Burton | 3.00 | 8.00 |
| ❑ 447 Ray Moore | 3.00 | 8.00 |
| ❑ 448 Jim Gentile RC | 6.00 | 15.00 |
| ❑ 449 Jim Brosnan | 3.00 | 8.00 |
| ❑ 450 Orlando Cepeda | 10.00 | 25.00 |
| ❑ 451 Curt Simmons | 3.00 | 8.00 |
| ❑ 452 Ray Webster | 3.00 | 8.00 |
| ❑ 453 Vern Law | 10.00 | 25.00 |
| ❑ 454 Hal Woodeshick | 3.00 | 8.00 |
| ❑ 455 Baltimore Coaches | 3.00 | 8.00 |
| ❑ 456 Red Sox Coaches | 4.00 | 10.00 |
| ❑ 457 Cubs Coaches | 3.00 | 8.00 |
| ❑ 458 White Sox Coaches | 3.00 | 8.00 |
| ❑ 459 Reds Coaches | 3.00 | 8.00 |
| ❑ 460 Indians Coaches | 6.00 | 15.00 |
| ❑ 461 Tigers Coaches | 3.00 | 8.00 |
| ❑ 462 Athletics Coaches | 3.00 | 8.00 |
| ❑ 463 Dodgers Coaches | 3.00 | 8.00 |
| ❑ 464 Braves Coaches | 3.00 | 8.00 |
| ❑ 465 Yankees Coaches | 10.00 | 25.00 |
| ❑ 466 Phillies Coaches | 3.00 | 8.00 |
| ❑ 467 Pirates Coaches | 3.00 | 8.00 |
| ❑ 468 Cardinals Coaches | 3.00 | 8.00 |
| ❑ 469 Giants Coaches | 3.00 | 8.00 |
| ❑ 470 Senators Coaches | 3.00 | 8.00 |
| ❑ 471 Ned Garver | 3.00 | 8.00 |
| ❑ 472 Alvin Dark | 3.00 | 8.00 |
| ❑ 473 Al Cicotte | 3.00 | 8.00 |
| ❑ 474 Haywood Sullivan | 4.00 | 10.00 |
| ❑ 475 Don Drysdale | 15.00 | 40.00 |
| ❑ 476 Lou Johnson RC | 3.00 | 8.00 |
| ❑ 477 Don Ferrarese | 3.00 | 8.00 |
| ❑ 478 Frank Torre | 3.00 | 8.00 |
| ❑ 479 Georges Maranda RC | 3.00 | 8.00 |
| ❑ 480 Yogi Berra | 40.00 | 80.00 |
| ❑ 481 Wes Stock RC | 3.00 | 8.00 |
| ❑ 482 Frank Bolling | 3.00 | 8.00 |
| ❑ 483 Camilo Pascual | 3.00 | 8.00 |
| ❑ 484 Pittsburgh Pirates CL | 15.00 | 40.00 |
| ❑ 485 Ken Boyer | 6.00 | 15.00 |
| ❑ 486 Bobby Del Greco | 3.00 | 8.00 |
| ❑ 487 Tom Sturdivant | 3.00 | 8.00 |
| ❑ 488 Norm Cash | 10.00 | 25.00 |
| ❑ 489 Steve Ridzik | 3.00 | 8.00 |
| ❑ 490 Frank Robinson | 20.00 | 50.00 |
| ❑ 491 Mel Roach | 3.00 | 8.00 |
| ❑ 492 Larry Jackson | 3.00 | 8.00 |
| ❑ 493 Duke Snider | 20.00 | 50.00 |
| ❑ 494 Baltimore Orioles CL | 10.00 | 25.00 |
| ❑ 495 Sherm Lollar | 3.00 | 8.00 |
| ❑ 496 Bill Virdon | 4.00 | 10.00 |
| ❑ 497 John Tsitouris | 3.00 | 8.00 |
| ❑ 498 Al Pilarcik | 3.00 | 8.00 |
| ❑ 499 Johnny James RC | 4.00 | 10.00 |
| ❑ 500 Johnny Temple | 3.00 | 8.00 |
| ❑ 501 Bob Schmidt | 3.00 | 8.00 |
| ❑ 502 Jim Bunning | 10.00 | 25.00 |
| ❑ 503 Don Lee | 3.00 | 8.00 |
| ❑ 504 Seth Morehead | 3.00 | 8.00 |
| ❑ 505 Ted Kluszewski | 10.00 | 25.00 |
| ❑ 506 Lee Walls | 3.00 | 8.00 |
| ❑ 507 Dick Stigman | 6.00 | 15.00 |
| ❑ 508 Billy Consolo | 6.00 | 15.00 |
| ❑ 509 Tommy Davis RC | 10.00 | 25.00 |
| ❑ 510 Gerry Staley | 6.00 | 15.00 |
| ❑ 511 Ken Walters RC | 6.00 | 15.00 |
| ❑ 512 Joe Gibbon RC | 6.00 | 15.00 |
| ❑ 513 Chicago Cubs CL | 12.50 | 30.00 |
| ❑ 514 Steve Barber RC | 6.00 | 15.00 |
| ❑ 515 Stan Lopata | 6.00 | 15.00 |

| | | |
|---|---|---|
| ❑ 516 Marty Kutyna RC | 6.00 | 15.00 |
| ❑ 517 Charlie James RC | 10.00 | 25.00 |
| ❑ 518 Tony Gonzalez RC | 6.00 | 15.00 |
| ❑ 519 Ed Roebuck | 6.00 | 15.00 |
| ❑ 520 Don Buddin | 6.00 | 15.00 |
| ❑ 521 Mike Lee RC | 6.00 | 15.00 |
| ❑ 522 Ken Hunt RC | 12.50 | 30.00 |
| ❑ 523 Clay Dalrymple RC | 6.00 | 15.00 |
| ❑ 524 Bill Henry | 6.00 | 15.00 |
| ❑ 525 Marv Breeding RC | 6.00 | 15.00 |
| ❑ 526 Paul Giel | 10.00 | 25.00 |
| ❑ 527 Jose Valdivielso | 10.00 | 25.00 |
| ❑ 528 Ben Johnson RC | 6.00 | 15.00 |
| ❑ 529 Norm Sherry RC | 8.00 | 20.00 |
| ❑ 530 Mike McCormick | 6.00 | 15.00 |
| ❑ 531 Sandy Amoros | 8.00 | 20.00 |
| ❑ 532 Mike Garcia | 8.00 | 20.00 |
| ❑ 533 Lu Clinton RC | 6.00 | 15.00 |
| ❑ 534 Ken MacKenzie RC | 6.00 | 15.00 |
| ❑ 535 Whitey Lockman | 6.00 | 15.00 |
| ❑ 536 Wynn Hawkins RC | 6.00 | 15.00 |
| ❑ 537 Boston Red Sox CL | 12.50 | 30.00 |
| ❑ 538 Frank Barnes RC | 6.00 | 15.00 |
| ❑ 539 Gene Baker | 6.00 | 15.00 |
| ❑ 540 Jerry Walker | 6.00 | 15.00 |
| ❑ 541 Tony Curry RC | 6.00 | 15.00 |
| ❑ 542 Ken Hamlin RC | 6.00 | 15.00 |
| ❑ 543 Elio Chacon RC | 6.00 | 15.00 |
| ❑ 544 Bill Monbouquette | 8.00 | 20.00 |
| ❑ 545 Carl Sawatski | 6.00 | 15.00 |
| ❑ 546 Hank Aguirre | 6.00 | 15.00 |
| ❑ 547 Bob Aspromonte RC | 8.00 | 20.00 |
| ❑ 548 Don Mincher RC | 6.00 | 15.00 |
| ❑ 549 John Buzhardt | 6.00 | 15.00 |
| ❑ 550 Jim Landis | 6.00 | 15.00 |
| ❑ 551 Ed Rakow RC | 6.00 | 15.00 |
| ❑ 552 Walt Bond RC | 6.00 | 15.00 |
| ❑ 553 Bill Skowron AS | 8.00 | 20.00 |
| ❑ 554 Willie McCovey AS | 15.00 | 40.00 |
| ❑ 555 Nellie Fox AS | 12.50 | 30.00 |
| ❑ 556 Charlie Neal AS | 6.00 | 15.00 |
| ❑ 557 Frank Malzone AS | 6.00 | 15.00 |
| ❑ 558 Eddie Mathews AS | 15.00 | 40.00 |
| ❑ 559 Luis Aparicio AS | 12.50 | 30.00 |
| ❑ 560 Ernie Banks AS | 30.00 | 60.00 |
| ❑ 561 Al Kaline AS | 30.00 | 60.00 |
| ❑ 562 Joe Cunningham AS | 6.00 | 15.00 |
| ❑ 563 Mickey Mantle AS | 125.00 | 250.00 |
| ❑ 564 Willie Mays AS | 50.00 | 100.00 |
| ❑ 565 Roger Maris AS | 50.00 | 100.00 |
| ❑ 566 Hank Aaron AS | 50.00 | 100.00 |
| ❑ 567 Sherm Lollar AS | 6.00 | 15.00 |
| ❑ 568 Del Crandall AS | 6.00 | 15.00 |
| ❑ 569 Camilo Pascual AS | 6.00 | 15.00 |
| ❑ 570 Don Drysdale AS | 15.00 | 40.00 |
| ❑ 571 Billy Pierce AS | 6.00 | 15.00 |
| ❑ 572 Johnny Antonelli AS | 12.50 | 30.00 |

## 1961 Topps

| | | |
|---|---|---|
| ❑ COMPLETE SET (587) | 3500.00 | 7000.00 |
| ❑ COMMON CARD (1-370) | 1.25 | 3.00 |
| ❑ COMMON CARD (371-446) | 1.50 | 4.00 |
| ❑ COMMON CARD (447-522) | 3.00 | 8.00 |
| ❑ COMMON CARD (523-589) | 12.50 | 30.00 |
| ❑ NOT ISSUED (587/588) | | |
| ❑ WRAPPER (1-CENT) | 100.00 | 200.00 |
| ❑ WRAP.(1-CENT, REPEAT) | 50.00 | 100.00 |
| ❑ WRAPPER (5-CENT) | 15.00 | 40.00 |
| ❑ 1 Dick Groat | 12.50 | 30.00 |
| ❑ 2 Roger Maris | 125.00 | 250.00 |
| ❑ 3 John Buzhardt | 1.25 | 3.00 |
| ❑ 4 Lenny Green | 1.25 | 3.00 |
| ❑ 5 John Romano | 1.25 | 3.00 |
| ❑ 6 Ed Roebuck | 1.25 | 3.00 |

| No. | Card | Price | Price |
|---|---|---|---|
| 7 | Chicago White Sox TC | 3.00 | 8.00 |
| 8 | Dick Williams | 2.50 | 6.00 |
| 9 | Bob Purkey | 1.25 | 3.00 |
| 10 | Brooks Robinson | 20.00 | 50.00 |
| 11 | Curt Simmons | 2.50 | 6.00 |
| 12 | Moe Thacker | 1.25 | 3.00 |
| 13 | Chuck Cottier | 1.25 | 3.00 |
| 14 | Don Mossi | 2.50 | 6.00 |
| 15 | Willie Kirkland | 1.25 | 3.00 |
| 16 | Billy Muffett | 1.25 | 3.00 |
| 17 | Checklist 1 | 4.00 | 10.00 |
| 18 | Jim Grant | 2.50 | 6.00 |
| 19 | Clete Boyer | 3.00 | 8.00 |
| 20 | Robin Roberts | 6.00 | 15.00 |
| 21 | Zoilo Versalles UER RC | 3.00 | 8.00 |
| 22 | Clem Labine | 2.50 | 6.00 |
| 23 | Don Demeter | 1.25 | 3.00 |
| 24 | Ken Johnson | 2.50 | 6.00 |
| 25 | Pinson/Bell/F. Robinson | 3.00 | 8.00 |
| 26 | Wes Stock | 1.25 | 3.00 |
| 27 | Jerry Kindall | 1.25 | 3.00 |
| 28 | Hector Lopez | 2.50 | 6.00 |
| 29 | Don Nottebart | 1.25 | 3.00 |
| 30 | Nellie Fox | 6.00 | 15.00 |
| 31 | Bob Schmidt | 1.25 | 3.00 |
| 32 | Ray Sadecki | 1.25 | 3.00 |
| 33 | Gary Geiger | 1.25 | 3.00 |
| 34 | Wynn Hawkins | 1.25 | 3.00 |
| 35 | Ron Santo RC | 15.00 | 40.00 |
| 36 | Jack Kralick RC | 1.25 | 3.00 |
| 37 | Charley Maxwell | 2.50 | 6.00 |
| 38 | Bob Lillis | 1.25 | 3.00 |
| 39 | Leo Posada RC | 1.25 | 3.00 |
| 40 | Bob Turley | 2.50 | 6.00 |
| 41 | Groat/Mays/Clemente LL | 15.00 | 40.00 |
| 42 | Runnels/Minoso/Skow LL | 3.00 | 8.00 |
| 43 | Banks/Aaron/Mathews LL | 12.50 | 30.00 |
| 44 | Manta/Maris/Colavito LL | 40.00 | 80.00 |
| 45 | McCormick/Drysdale LL | 3.00 | 8.00 |
| 46 | Baumann/Bunning/Dit LL | 3.00 | 8.00 |
| 47 | Broglio/Spahn/Burdette LL | 3.00 | 8.00 |
| 48 | Estrada/Perry/Daley LL | 3.00 | 8.00 |
| 49 | Drysdale/Koufax LL | 8.00 | 20.00 |
| 50 | Bunning/Ramos/Wynn LL | 3.00 | 8.00 |
| 51 | Detroit Tigers TC | 3.00 | 8.00 |
| 52 | George Crowe | 1.25 | 3.00 |
| 53 | Russ Nixon | 1.50 | 3.00 |
| 54 | Earl Francis RC | 1.25 | 3.00 |
| 55 | Jim Davenport | 2.50 | 6.00 |
| 56 | Russ Kemmerer | 1.25 | 3.00 |
| 57 | Marv Throneberry | 2.50 | 6.00 |
| 58 | Joe Schaffernoth RC | 1.25 | 3.00 |
| 59 | Jim Woods | 1.25 | 3.00 |
| 60 | Woody Held | 1.25 | 3.00 |
| 61 | Ron Piche RC | 1.25 | 3.00 |
| 62 | Al Pilarcik | 1.25 | 3.00 |
| 63 | Jim Kaat | 3.00 | 8.00 |
| 64 | Alex Grammas | 1.25 | 3.00 |
| 65 | Ted Kluszewski | 3.00 | 8.00 |
| 66 | Bill Henry | 1.25 | 3.00 |
| 67 | Ossie Virgil | 1.25 | 3.00 |
| 68 | Deron Johnson | 2.50 | 6.00 |
| 69 | Earl Wilson | 2.50 | 6.00 |
| 70 | Bill Virdon | 2.50 | 6.00 |
| 71 | Jerry Adair | 1.25 | 3.00 |
| 72 | Stu Miller | 2.50 | 6.00 |
| 73 | Al Spangler | 1.25 | 3.00 |
| 74 | Joe Pignatano | 1.25 | 3.00 |
| 75 | L. McDaniel/L. Jackson | 2.50 | 6.00 |
| 76 | Harry Anderson | 1.25 | 3.00 |
| 77 | Dick Stigman | 1.25 | 3.00 |
| 78 | Lee Walls | 2.50 | 6.00 |
| 79 | Joe Ginsberg | 1.25 | 3.00 |
| 80 | Harmon Killebrew | 8.00 | 20.00 |
| 81 | Tracy Stallard RC | 1.25 | 3.00 |
| 82 | Joe Christopher RC | 1.25 | 3.00 |
| 83 | Bob Bruce | 1.25 | 3.00 |
| 84 | Lee Maye | 1.25 | 3.00 |
| 85 | Jerry Walker | 1.25 | 3.00 |
| 86 | Los Angeles Dodgers TC | 3.00 | 8.00 |
| 87 | Joe Amalfitano | 1.25 | 3.00 |
| 88 | Richie Ashburn | 6.00 | 15.00 |
| 89 | Billy Martin | 6.00 | 15.00 |
| 90 | Gerry Staley | 1.25 | 3.00 |
| 91 | Walt Moryn | 1.25 | 3.00 |
| 92 | Hal Naragon | 1.25 | 3.00 |
| 93 | Tony Gonzalez | 1.25 | 3.00 |
| 94 | Johnny Kucks | 1.25 | 3.00 |
| 95 | Norm Cash | 3.00 | 8.00 |
| 96 | Billy O'Dell | 1.25 | 3.00 |
| 97 | Jerry Lynch | 2.50 | 6.00 |
| 98A | Checklist 2 Red | 4.00 | 10.00 |
| 98B | Checklist 2 Yellow B/W | 4.00 | 10.00 |
| 98C | Checklist 2 Yellow W/B | 4.00 | 10.00 |
| 99 | Don Buddin UER | 1.25 | 3.00 |
| 100 | Harvey Haddix | 2.50 | 6.00 |
| 101 | Bubba Phillips | 1.25 | 3.00 |
| 102 | Gene Stephens | 1.25 | 3.00 |
| 103 | Ruben Amaro | 1.25 | 3.00 |
| 104 | John Blanchard | 3.00 | 8.00 |
| 105 | Carl Willey | 1.25 | 3.00 |
| 106 | Whitey Herzog | 1.25 | 3.00 |
| 107 | Seth Morehead | 1.25 | 3.00 |
| 108 | Dan Dobbek | 1.25 | 3.00 |
| 109 | Johnny Podres | 3.00 | 8.00 |
| 110 | Vada Pinson | 3.00 | 8.00 |
| 111 | Jack Meyer | 1.25 | 3.00 |
| 112 | Chico Fernandez | 1.25 | 3.00 |
| 113 | Mike Fornieles | 1.25 | 3.00 |
| 114 | Hobie Landrith | 1.25 | 3.00 |
| 115 | Johnny Antonelli | 2.50 | 6.00 |
| 116 | Joe DeMaestri | 1.25 | 3.00 |
| 117 | Dale Long | 2.50 | 6.00 |
| 118 | Chris Cannizzaro RC | 1.25 | 3.00 |
| 119 | Sieben/Bauer/Lumpe | 2.50 | 6.00 |
| 120 | Eddie Mathews | 12.50 | 30.00 |
| 121 | Eli Grba | 2.50 | 6.00 |
| 122 | Chicago Cubs TC | 3.00 | 8.00 |
| 123 | Billy Gardner | 1.25 | 3.00 |
| 124 | J.C. Martin | 1.25 | 3.00 |
| 125 | Steve Barber | 1.25 | 3.00 |
| 126 | Dick Stuart | 2.50 | 6.00 |
| 127 | Ron Kline | 1.25 | 3.00 |
| 128 | Rip Repulski | 1.25 | 3.00 |
| 129 | Ed Hobaugh | 1.25 | 3.00 |
| 130 | Norm Larker | 2.50 | 6.00 |
| 131 | Paul Richards MG | 2.50 | 6.00 |
| 132 | Al Lopez MG | 3.00 | 8.00 |
| 133 | Ralph Houk MG | 2.50 | 6.00 |
| 134 | Mickey Vernon MG | 2.50 | 6.00 |
| 135 | Fred Hutchinson MG | 2.50 | 6.00 |
| 136 | Walter Alston MG | 2.50 | 6.00 |
| 137 | Chuck Dressen MG | 2.50 | 6.00 |
| 138 | Danny Murtaugh MG | 2.50 | 6.00 |
| 139 | Solly Hemus MG | 2.50 | 6.00 |
| 140 | Gus Triandos | 2.50 | 6.00 |
| 141 | Billy Williams RC | 30.00 | 60.00 |
| 142 | Luis Arroyo | 2.50 | 6.00 |
| 143 | Russ Snyder | 1.25 | 3.00 |
| 144 | Jim Coker | 1.25 | 3.00 |
| 145 | Bob Buhl | 2.50 | 6.00 |
| 146 | Marty Keough | 1.25 | 3.00 |
| 147 | Ed Rakow | 1.25 | 3.00 |
| 148 | Julian Javier | 2.50 | 6.00 |
| 149 | Bob Oldis | 1.25 | 3.00 |
| 150 | Willie Mays | 50.00 | 100.00 |
| 151 | Jim Donohue | 1.25 | 3.00 |
| 152 | Earl Torgeson | 1.25 | 3.00 |
| 153 | Don Lee | 1.25 | 3.00 |
| 154 | Bobby Del Greco | 1.25 | 3.00 |
| 155 | Johnny Temple | 1.25 | 3.00 |
| 156 | Ken Hunt | 1.25 | 3.00 |
| 157 | Cal McLish | 1.25 | 3.00 |
| 158 | Pete Daley | 1.25 | 3.90 |
| 159 | Baltimore Orioles TC | 3.00 | 8.00 |
| 160 | Whitey Ford UER | 20.00 | 50.00 |
| 161 | Sherman Jones UER RC | 1.25 | 3.00 |
| 162 | Jay Hook | 1.25 | 3.00 |
| 163 | Ed Sadowski | 1.25 | 3.00 |
| 164 | Felix Mantilla | 1.25 | 3.00 |
| 165 | Gino Cimoli | 1.25 | 3.00 |
| 166 | Danny Kravitz | 1.25 | 3.00 |
| 167 | San Francisco Giants TC | 3.00 | 8.00 |
| 168 | Tommy Davis | 3.00 | 8.00 |
| 169 | Don Elston | 1.25 | 3.00 |
| 170 | Al Smith | 1.25 | 3.00 |
| 171 | Paul Foytack | 1.25 | 3.00 |
| 172 | Don Dillard | 1.25 | 3.00 |
| 173 | Malzone/Wertz/Jensen | 2.50 | 6.00 |
| 174 | Ray Semproch | 1.25 | 3.00 |
| 175 | Gene Freese | 1.25 | 3.00 |
| 176 | Ken Aspromonte | 1.25 | 3.00 |
| 177 | Don Larsen | 2.50 | 6.00 |
| 178 | Bob Nieman | 1.25 | 3.00 |
| 179 | Joe Koppe | 1.25 | 3.00 |
| 180 | Bobby Richardson | 5.00 | 12.00 |
| 181 | Fred Green | 1.25 | 3.00 |
| 182 | Dave Nicholson RC | 1.25 | 3.00 |
| 183 | Andre Rodgers | 1.25 | 3.00 |
| 184 | Steve Bilko | 2.50 | 6.00 |
| 185 | Herb Score | 2.50 | 6.00 |
| 186 | Elmer Valo | 2.50 | 6.00 |
| 187 | Billy Klaus | 1.25 | 3.00 |
| 188 | Jim Marshall | 1.25 | 3.00 |
| 189A | Checklist 3 Copyright 263 | 4.00 | 10.00 |
| 189B | Checklist 3 Copyright 264 | 4.00 | 10.00 |
| 190 | Stan Williams | 2.50 | 6.00 |
| 191 | Mike de la Hoz RC | 1.25 | 3.00 |
| 192 | Dick Brown | 1.25 | 3.00 |
| 193 | Gene Conley | 2.50 | 6.00 |
| 194 | Gordy Coleman | 2.50 | 6.00 |
| 195 | Jerry Casale | 1.25 | 3.00 |
| 196 | Ed Bouchee | 1.25 | 3.00 |
| 197 | Dick Hall | 1.25 | 3.00 |
| 198 | Carl Sawatski | 1.25 | 3.00 |
| 199 | Bob Boyd | 1.25 | 3.00 |
| 200 | Warren Spahn | 15.00 | 40.00 |
| 201 | Pete Whisenant | 1.25 | 3.00 |
| 202 | Al Neiger RC | 1.25 | 3.00 |
| 203 | Eddie Bressoud | 1.25 | 3.00 |
| 204 | Bob Skinner | 2.50 | 6.00 |
| 205 | Billy Pierce | 2.50 | 6.00 |
| 206 | Gene Green | 1.25 | 3.00 |
| 207 | S. Koufax/J. Podres | 12.50 | 30.00 |
| 208 | Larry Osborne | 1.25 | 3.00 |
| 209 | Ken McBride | 1.25 | 3.00 |
| 210 | Pete Runnels | 2.50 | 6.00 |
| 211 | Bob Gibson | 15.00 | 40.00 |
| 212 | Haywood Sullivan | 1.25 | 3.00 |
| 213 | Bill Stafford RC | 1.25 | 3.00 |
| 214 | Danny Murphy RC | 1.25 | 3.00 |
| 215 | Gus Bell | 2.50 | 6.00 |
| 216 | Ted Bowsfield | 1.25 | 3.00 |
| 217 | Mel Roach | 1.25 | 3.00 |
| 218 | Hal Brown | 1.25 | 3.00 |
| 219 | Gene Mauch MG | 2.50 | 6.00 |
| 220 | Alvin Dark MG | 2.50 | 6.00 |
| 221 | Mike Higgins MG | 1.25 | 3.00 |
| 222 | Jimmy Dykes MG | 2.50 | 6.00 |
| 223 | Bob Scheffing MG | 1.25 | 3.00 |
| 224 | Joe Gordon MG | 2.50 | 6.00 |
| 225 | Bill Rigney MG | 2.50 | 6.00 |
| 226 | Cookie Lavagetto MG | 2.50 | 6.00 |
| 227 | Juan Pizarro | 1.25 | 3.00 |
| 228 | New York Yankees TC | 30.00 | 60.00 |
| 229 | Rudy Hernandez RC | 1.25 | 3.00 |
| 230 | Don Hoak | 2.50 | 6.00 |
| 231 | Dick Drott | 1.25 | 3.00 |
| 232 | Bill White | 2.50 | 6.00 |
| 233 | Joey Jay | 1.25 | 3.00 |
| 234 | Ted Lepcio | 1.25 | 3.00 |
| 235 | Camilo Pascual | 2.50 | 6.00 |
| 236 | Don Gile RC | 1.25 | 3.00 |
| 237 | Billy Loes | 2.50 | 6.00 |
| 238 | Jim Gilliam | 2.50 | 6.00 |
| 239 | Dave Sisler | 1.25 | 3.00 |
| 240 | Ron Hansen | 1.25 | 3.00 |
| 241 | Al Cicotte | 1.25 | 3.00 |
| 242 | Hal Smith | 1.25 | 3.00 |
| 243 | Frank Lary | 2.50 | 6.00 |
| 244 | Chico Cardenas | 2.50 | 6.00 |
| 245 | Joe Adcock | 2.50 | 6.00 |
| 246 | Bob Davis RC | 1.25 | 3.00 |
| 247 | Billy Goodman | 2.50 | 6.00 |
| 248 | Ed Keegan RC | 1.25 | 3.00 |
| 249 | Cincinnati Reds TC | 3.00 | 8.00 |
| 250 | V. Law/R. Face | 2.50 | 6.00 |
| 251 | Bill Bruton | 2.50 | 6.00 |
| 252 | Bill Short | 1.25 | 3.00 |
| 253 | Sammy Taylor | 1.25 | 3.00 |
| 254 | Ted Sadowski RC | 1.25 | 3.00 |
| 255 | Vic Power | 2.50 | 6.00 |
| 256 | Billy Hoeft | 1.25 | 3.00 |
| 257 | Carroll Hardy | 1.25 | 3.00 |
| 258 | Jack Sanford | 2.50 | 6.00 |
| 259 | John Schaive RC | 1.25 | 3.00 |
| 260 | Don Drysdale | 12.50 | 30.00 |
| 261 | Charlie Lau | 2.50 | 6.00 |
| 262 | Tony Curry | 1.25 | 3.00 |
| 263 | Ken Hamlin | 1.25 | 3.00 |
| 264 | Glen Hobbie | 1.25 | 3.00 |
| 265 | Tony Kubek | 5.00 | 12.00 |
| 266 | Lindy McDaniel | 2.50 | 6.00 |
| 267 | Norm Siebern | 1.25 | 3.00 |

|  |  | | |
|---|---|---|---|
| 268 | Ike Delock | 1.25 | 3.00 |
| 269 | Harry Chiti | 1.25 | 3.00 |
| 270 | Bob Friend | 2.50 | 3.00 |
| 271 | Jim Landis | 1.25 | 3.00 |
| 272 | Tom Morgan | 1.25 | 3.00 |
| 273A | Checklist 4 Copyright 336 | 6.00 | 15.00 |
| 273B | Checklist 4 Copyright 339 | 4.00 | 10.00 |
| 274 | Gary Bell | 1.25 | 3.00 |
| 275 | Gene Woodling | 2.50 | 3.00 |
| 276 | Ray Rippelmeyer RC | 1.25 | 3.00 |
| 277 | Hank Foiles | 1.25 | 3.00 |
| 278 | Don McMahon | 1.25 | 3.00 |
| 279 | Jose Pagan | 1.25 | 3.00 |
| 280 | Frank Howard | 3.00 | 8.00 |
| 281 | Frank Sullivan | 1.25 | 3.00 |
| 282 | Faye Throneberry | 1.25 | 3.00 |
| 283 | Bob Anderson | 1.25 | 3.00 |
| 284 | Dick Gernert | 1.25 | 3.00 |
| 285 | Sherm Lollar | 2.50 | 6.00 |
| 286 | George Witt | 1.25 | 3.00 |
| 287 | Carl Yastrzemski | 20.00 | 50.00 |
| 288 | Albie Pearson | 2.50 | 6.00 |
| 289 | Ray Moore | 1.25 | 3.00 |
| 290 | Stan Musial | 50.00 | 100.00 |
| 291 | Tex Clevenger | 1.25 | 3.00 |
| 292 | Jim Baumer RC | 1.25 | 3.00 |
| 293 | Tom Sturdivant | 1.25 | 3.00 |
| 294 | Don Blasingame | 1.25 | 3.00 |
| 295 | Milt Pappas | 2.50 | 6.00 |
| 296 | Wes Covington | 2.50 | 6.00 |
| 297 | Kansas City Athletics TC | 3.00 | 8.00 |
| 298 | Jim Golden RC | 1.25 | 3.00 |
| 299 | Clay Dalrymple | 1.25 | 3.00 |
| 300 | Mickey Mantle | 300.00 | 600.00 |
| 301 | Chet Nichols | 1.25 | 3.00 |
| 302 | Al Heist RC | 1.25 | 3.00 |
| 303 | Gary Peters | 2.50 | 6.00 |
| 304 | Rocky Nelson | 1.25 | 3.00 |
| 305 | Mike McCormick | 2.50 | 6.00 |
| 306 | Bill Virdon WS | 4.00 | 10.00 |
| 307 | Mickey Mantle WS2 | 40.00 | 80.00 |
| 308 | Bobby Richardson WS3 | 5.00 | 12.00 |
| 309 | Gino Cimoli WS4 | 4.00 | 10.00 |
| 310 | Roy Face WS5 | 4.00 | 10.00 |
| 311 | Whitey Ford WS6 | 6.00 | 15.00 |
| 312 | Bill Mazeroski WS7 | 6.00 | 15.00 |
| 313 | Pirates Celebrate WS | 6.00 | 15.00 |
| 314 | Bob Miller | 1.25 | 3.00 |
| 315 | Earl Battey | 2.50 | 6.00 |
| 316 | Bobby Gene Smith | 1.25 | 3.00 |
| 317 | Jim Brewer RC | 1.25 | 3.00 |
| 318 | Danny O'Connell | 1.25 | 3.00 |
| 319 | Valmy Thomas | 1.25 | 3.00 |
| 320 | Lou Burdette | 2.50 | 6.00 |
| 321 | Marv Breeding | 1.25 | 3.00 |
| 322 | Bill Kunkel RC | 2.50 | 6.00 |
| 323 | Sammy Esposito | 1.25 | 3.00 |
| 324 | Hank Aguirre | 1.25 | 3.00 |
| 325 | Wally Moon | 2.50 | 6.00 |
| 326 | Dave Hillman | 1.25 | 3.00 |
| 327 | Matty Alou RC | 5.00 | 12.00 |
| 328 | Jim O'Toole | 2.50 | 6.00 |
| 329 | Julio Becquer | 1.25 | 3.00 |
| 330 | Rocky Colavito | 8.00 | 20.00 |
| 331 | Ned Garver | 1.25 | 3.00 |
| 332 | Dutch Dotterer UER | 1.25 | 3.00 |
| 333 | Fritz Brickell RC | 1.25 | 3.00 |
| 334 | Walt Bond | 1.25 | 3.00 |
| 335 | Frank Bolling | 1.25 | 3.00 |
| 336 | Don Mincher | 2.50 | 6.00 |
| 337 | Wynn/Lopez/Score | 3.00 | 8.00 |
| 338 | Don Landrum | 1.25 | 3.00 |
| 339 | Gene Baker | 1.25 | 3.00 |
| 340 | Vic Wertz | 2.50 | 6.00 |
| 341 | Jim Owens | 1.25 | 3.00 |
| 342 | Clint Courtney | 1.25 | 3.00 |
| 343 | Earl Robinson RC | 1.25 | 3.00 |
| 344 | Sandy Koufax | 50.00 | 100.00 |
| 345 | Jimmy Piersall | 3.00 | 8.00 |
| 346 | Howie Nunn | 1.25 | 3.00 |
| 347 | St. Louis Cardinals TC | 3.00 | 8.00 |
| 348 | Steve Boros | 1.25 | 3.00 |
| 349 | Danny McDevitt | 1.25 | 3.00 |
| 350 | Ernie Banks | 15.00 | 40.00 |
| 351 | Jim King | 1.25 | 3.00 |
| 352 | Bob Shaw | 1.25 | 3.00 |
| 353 | Howie Bedell RC | 1.25 | 3.00 |
| 354 | Billy Harrell | 2.50 | 6.00 |
| 355 | Bob Allison | 3.00 | 8.00 |
| 356 | Ryne Duren | 1.25 | 3.00 |
| 357 | Daryl Spencer | 1.25 | 3.00 |
| 358 | Earl Averill Jr. | 2.50 | 6.00 |
| 359 | Dallas Green | 1.25 | 3.00 |
| 360 | Frank Robinson | 15.00 | 40.00 |
| 361A | Checklist 5 No Ad on Back | 6.00 | 15.00 |
| 361B | Checklist 5 Ad on Back | 6.00 | 15.00 |
| 362 | Frank Funk RC | 1.25 | 3.00 |
| 363 | John Roseboro | 2.50 | 6.00 |
| 364 | Moe Drabowsky | 2.50 | 6.00 |
| 365 | Jerry Lumpe | 1.25 | 3.00 |
| 366 | Eddie Fisher | 1.25 | 3.00 |
| 367 | Jim Rivera | 1.25 | 3.00 |
| 368 | Bennie Daniels | 1.25 | 3.00 |
| 369 | Dave Philley | 1.25 | 3.00 |
| 370 | Roy Face | 2.50 | 6.00 |
| 371 | Bill Skowron SP | 20.00 | 50.00 |
| 372 | Bob Hendley RC | 1.50 | 4.00 |
| 373 | Boston Red Sox TC | 3.00 | 8.00 |
| 374 | Paul Giel | 1.50 | 4.00 |
| 375 | Ken Boyer | 5.00 | 12.00 |
| 376 | Mike Roarke RC | 2.50 | 6.00 |
| 377 | Ruben Gomez | 1.50 | 4.00 |
| 378 | Wally Post | 2.50 | 6.00 |
| 379 | Bobby Shantz | 1.50 | 4.00 |
| 380 | Minnie Minoso | 3.00 | 8.00 |
| 381 | Dave Wickersham RC | 1.50 | 4.00 |
| 382 | Frank Thomas | 2.50 | 6.00 |
| 383 | McCormick/Sanford/O'Dell | 2.50 | 6.00 |
| 384 | Chuck Essegian | 1.50 | 4.00 |
| 385 | Jim Perry | 2.50 | 6.00 |
| 386 | Joe Hicks | 1.50 | 4.00 |
| 387 | Duke Maas | 1.50 | 4.00 |
| 388 | Roberto Clemente | 60.00 | 120.00 |
| 389 | Ralph Terry | 2.50 | 6.00 |
| 390 | Del Crandall | 3.00 | 8.00 |
| 391 | Winston Brown RC | 1.50 | 4.00 |
| 392 | Reno Bertoia | 1.50 | 4.00 |
| 393 | D.Cardwell/G.Hobbie | 1.50 | 4.00 |
| 394 | Ken Walters | 1.50 | 4.00 |
| 395 | Chuck Estrada | 2.50 | 6.00 |
| 396 | Bob Aspromonte | 1.50 | 4.00 |
| 397 | Hal Woodeshick | 1.50 | 4.00 |
| 398 | Hank Bauer | 2.50 | 6.00 |
| 399 | Cliff Cook RC | 1.50 | 4.00 |
| 400 | Vern Law | 2.50 | 6.00 |
| 401 | Babe Ruth 60th HR | 30.00 | 60.00 |
| 402 | Don Larsen Perfect SP | 10.00 | 25.00 |
| 403 | 26 Inning Tie/Oeschger/Cadore | 3.00 | 8.00 |
| 404 | Rogers Hornsby .424 | 5.00 | 12.00 |
| 405 | Lou Gehrig Streak | 40.00 | 80.00 |
| 406 | Mickey Mantle 565 HR | 50.00 | 100.00 |
| 407 | Jack Chesbro Wins 41 | 8.00 | 20.00 |
| 408 | Christy Mathewson K's SP | 8.00 | 20.00 |
| 409 | Walter Johnson Shutout | 5.00 | 12.00 |
| 410 | Harvey Haddix 12 Innings | 3.00 | 8.00 |
| 411 | Tony Taylor | 2.50 | 6.00 |
| 412 | Larry Sherry | 2.50 | 6.00 |
| 413 | Eddie Yost | 2.50 | 6.00 |
| 414 | Dick Donovan | 2.50 | 6.00 |
| 415 | Hank Aaron | 60.00 | 120.00 |
| 416 | Dick Howser RC | 3.00 | 8.00 |
| 417 | Juan Marichal SP RC | 50.00 | 100.00 |
| 418 | Ed Bailey | 2.50 | 6.00 |
| 419 | Tom Borland | 1.50 | 4.00 |
| 420 | Ernie Broglio | 2.50 | 6.00 |
| 421 | Ty Cline RC | 2.50 | 6.00 |
| 422 | Bud Daley | 1.50 | 4.00 |
| 423 | Charlie Neal SP | 8.00 | 20.00 |
| 424 | Turk Lown | 1.50 | 4.00 |
| 425 | Yogi Berra | 40.00 | 80.00 |
| 426 | Milwaukee Braves TC UER | 5.00 | 12.00 |
| 427 | Dick Ellsworth | 2.50 | 6.00 |
| 428 | Ray Barker SP RC | 8.00 | 20.00 |
| 429 | Al Kaline | 20.00 | 50.00 |
| 430 | Bill Mazeroski SP | 20.00 | 50.00 |
| 431 | Chuck Stobbs | 1.50 | 4.00 |
| 432 | Coot Veal | 2.50 | 6.00 |
| 433 | Art Mahaffey | 1.50 | 4.00 |
| 434 | Tom Brewer | 1.50 | 4.00 |
| 435 | Orlando Cepeda UER | 5.00 | 12.00 |
| 436 | Jim Maloney SP RC | -8.00 | 20.00 |
| 437A | Checklist 6 440 Louis | 6.00 | 15.00 |
| 437B | Checklist 6 440 Luis | 6.00 | 15.00 |
| 438 | Curt Flood | 3.00 | 8.00 |
| 439 | Phil Regan RC | 2.50 | 6.00 |
| 440 | Luis Aparicio | 5.00 | 12.00 |
| 441 | Dick Bertell RC | 1.50 | 4.00 |
| 442 | Gordon Jones | 1.50 | 4.00 |
| 443 | Duke Snider | 20.00 | 50.00 |
| 444 | Joe Nuxhall | 2.50 | 6.00 |
| 445 | Frank Malzone | 2.50 | 6.00 |
| 446 | Bob Taylor | 1.50 | 4.00 |
| 447 | Harry Bright | 1.50 | 4.00 |
| 448 | Del Rice | 6.00 | 15.00 |
| 449 | Bob Bolin RC | 1.50 | 4.00 |
| 450 | Jim Lemon | 3.00 | 8.00 |
| 451 | Spencer/White/Broglio | 3.00 | 8.00 |
| 452 | Bob Allen RC | 3.00 | 8.00 |
| 453 | Dick Schofield | 3.00 | 8.00 |
| 454 | Pumpsie Green | 3.00 | 8.00 |
| 455 | Early Wynn | 6.00 | 15.00 |
| 456 | Hal Bevan | 3.00 | 8.00 |
| 457 | Johnny James | 3.00 | 8.00 |
| 458 | Willie Tasby | 3.00 | 8.00 |
| 459 | Terry Fox RC | 4.00 | 10.00 |
| 460 | Gil Hodges | 10.00 | 25.00 |
| 461 | Smoky Burgess | 6.00 | 15.00 |
| 462 | Lou Klimchock | 3.00 | 8.00 |
| 463 | Jack Fisher See 426 | 3.00 | 8.00 |
| 464 | Lee Thomas RC | 4.00 | 10.00 |
| 465 | Roy McMillan | 6.00 | 15.00 |
| 466 | Ron Moeller RC | 3.00 | 8.00 |
| 467 | Cleveland Indians TC | 5.00 | 12.00 |
| 468 | John Callison | 4.00 | 10.00 |
| 469 | Ralph Lumenti | 3.00 | 8.00 |
| 470 | Roy Sievers | 4.00 | 10.00 |
| 471 | Phil Rizzuto MVP | 10.00 | 25.00 |
| 472 | Yogi Berra MVP | 20.00 | 50.00 |
| 473 | Bob Shantz MVP | 3.00 | 8.00 |
| 474 | Al Rosen MVP | 4.00 | 10.00 |
| 475 | Mickey Mantle MVP | 100.00 | 200.00 |
| 476 | Jackie Jensen MVP | 6.00 | 15.00 |
| 477 | Nellie Fox MVP | 4.00 | 10.00 |
| 478 | Roger Maris MVP | 30.00 | 60.00 |
| 479 | Jim Konstanty MVP | 3.00 | 8.00 |
| 480 | Roy Campanella MVP | 15.00 | 40.00 |
| 481 | Hank Sauer MVP | 3.00 | 8.00 |
| 482 | Willie Mays MVP | 20.00 | 50.00 |
| 483 | Don Newcombe MVP | 4.00 | 10.00 |
| 484 | Hank Aaron MVP | 20.00 | 50.00 |
| 485 | Ernie Banks MVP | 15.00 | 40.00 |
| 486 | Dick Groat MVP | 4.00 | 10.00 |
| 487 | Gene Oliver | 3.00 | 8.00 |
| 488 | Joe McClain RC | 4.00 | 10.00 |
| 489 | Walt Dropo | 3.00 | 8.00 |
| 490 | Jim Bunning | 10.00 | 25.00 |
| 491 | Philadelphia Phillies TC | 5.00 | 12.00 |
| 492A | R.Fairly White | 4.00 | 10.00 |
| 492B | R.Fairly Green | 8.00 | 20.00 |
| 493 | Don Zimmer UER | 4.00 | 10.00 |
| 494 | Tom Cheney | 6.00 | 15.00 |
| 495 | Elston Howard | 6.00 | 15.00 |
| 496 | Ken MacKenzie | 3.00 | 8.00 |
| 497 | Willie Jones | 3.00 | 8.00 |
| 498 | Ray Herbert | 3.00 | 8.00 |
| 499 | Chuck Schilling RC | 3.00 | 8.00 |
| 500 | Harvey Kuenn | 4.00 | 10.00 |
| 501 | John DeMerit RC | 3.00 | 8.00 |
| 502 | Choo Choo Coleman RC | 4.00 | 10.00 |
| 503 | Tito Francona | 3.00 | 8.00 |
| 504 | Billy Consolo | 3.00 | 8.00 |
| 505 | Red Schoendienst | 6.00 | 15.00 |
| 506 | Willie Davis RC | 6.00 | 15.00 |
| 507 | Pete Burnside | 3.00 | 8.00 |
| 508 | Rocky Bridges | 3.00 | 8.00 |
| 509 | Camilo Carreon | 3.00 | 8.00 |
| 510 | Art Ditmar | 3.00 | 8.00 |
| 511 | Joe M. Morgan | 3.00 | 8.00 |
| 512 | Bob Will | 3.00 | 8.00 |
| 513 | Jim Brosnan | 3.00 | 8.00 |
| 514 | Jake Wood RC | 3.00 | 8.00 |
| 515 | Jackie Brandt | 3.00 | 8.00 |
| 516 | Checklist 7 | 6.00 | 15.00 |
| 517 | Willie McCovey | 15.00 | 40.00 |
| 518 | Andy Carey | 3.00 | 8.00 |
| 519 | Jim Pagliaroni RC | 3.00 | 8.00 |
| 520 | Joe Cunningham | 3.00 | 8.00 |
| 521 | N.Sherry/L.Sherry | 3.00 | 8.00 |
| 522 | Dick Farrell UER | 6.00 | 15.00 |
| 523 | Joe Gibbon | 12.50 | 30.00 |
| 524 | Johnny Logan | 12.50 | 30.00 |
| 525 | Ron Perranoski RC | 30.00 | 60.00 |
| 526 | R.C. Stevens | 12.50 | 30.00 |
| 527 | Gene Leek RC | 12.50 | 30.00 |

|  | | |
|---|---|---|
| 528 Pedro Ramos | 12.50 | 30.00 |
| 529 Bob Roselli | 12.50 | 30.00 |
| 530 Bob Malkmus | 12.50 | 30.00 |
| 531 Jim Coates | 20.00 | 50.00 |
| 532 Bob Hale | 12.50 | 30.00 |
| 533 Jack Curtis RC | 12.50 | 30.00 |
| 534 Eddie Kasko | 15.00 | 40.00 |
| 535 Larry Jackson | 12.50 | 30.00 |
| 536 Bill Tuttle | 12.50 | 30.00 |
| 537 Bobby Locke | 12.50 | 30.00 |
| 538 Chuck Hiller RC | 12.50 | 30.00 |
| 539 Johnny Klippstein | 12.50 | 30.00 |
| 540 Jackie Jensen | 15.00 | 40.00 |
| 541 Rollie Sheldon RC | 20.00 | 50.00 |
| 542 Minnesota Twins TC | 30.00 | 60.00 |
| 543 Roger Craig | 15.00 | 40.00 |
| 544 George Thomas RC | 20.00 | 50.00 |
| 545 Hoyt Wilhelm | 30.00 | 60.00 |
| 546 Marty Kutyna | 12.50 | 30.00 |
| 547 Leon Wagner | 12.50 | 30.00 |
| 548 Ted Wills | 12.50 | 30.00 |
| 549 Hal R. Smith | 12.50 | 30.00 |
| 550 Frank Baumann | 12.50 | 30.00 |
| 551 George Altman | 15.00 | 40.00 |
| 552 Jim Archer RC | 12.50 | 30.00 |
| 553 Bill Fischer | 12.50 | 30.00 |
| 554 Pittsburgh Pirates TC | 40.00 | 80.00 |
| 555 Sam Jones | 12.50 | 30.00 |
| 556 Ken R. Hunt RC | 12.50 | 30.00 |
| 557 Jose Valdivielso | 12.50 | 30.00 |
| 558 Don Ferrarese | 12.50 | 30.00 |
| 559 Jim Gentile | 30.00 | 60.00 |
| 560 Barry Latman | 15.00 | 40.00 |
| 561 Charley James | 12.50 | 30.00 |
| 562 Bill Monbouquette | 12.50 | 30.00 |
| 563 Bob Cerv | 30.00 | 60.00 |
| 564 Don Cardwell | 12.50 | 30.00 |
| 565 Felipe Alou | 30.00 | 60.00 |
| 566 Paul Richards AS MG | 12.50 | 30.00 |
| 567 Danny Murtaugh AS MG | 12.50 | 30.00 |
| 568 Bill Skowron AS | 20.00 | 50.00 |
| 569 Frank Herrera AS | 15.00 | 40.00 |
| 570 Nellie Fox AS | 30.00 | 60.00 |
| 571 Bill Mazeroski AS | 30.00 | 60.00 |
| 572 Brooks Robinson AS | 40.00 | 80.00 |
| 573 Ken Boyer AS | 20.00 | 50.00 |
| 574 Luis Aparicio AS | 30.00 | 60.00 |
| 575 Ernie Banks AS | 40.00 | 80.00 |
| 576 Roger Maris AS | 100.00 | 200.00 |
| 577 Hank Aaron AS | 75.00 | 150.00 |
| 578 Mickey Mantle AS | 250.00 | 500.00 |
| 579 Willie Mays AS | 75.00 | 150.00 |
| 580 Al Kaline AS | 40.00 | 80.00 |
| 581 Frank Robinson AS | 40.00 | 80.00 |
| 582 Earl Battey AS | 12.50 | 30.00 |
| 583 Del Crandall AS | 12.50 | 30.00 |
| 584 Jim Perry AS | 12.50 | 30.00 |
| 585 Bob Friend AS | 12.50 | 30.00 |
| 586 Whitey Ford AS | 50.00 | 100.00 |
| 589 Warren Spahn AS | 50.00 | 100.00 |

## 1962 Topps

| | | |
|---|---|---|
| COMP. MASTER SET (689) | 5000.00 | 10000.00 |
| COMPLETE SET (598) | 4000.00 | 8000.00 |
| COMMON CARD (1-370) | 2.00 | 5.00 |
| COMMON CARD (371-446) | 2.50 | 6.00 |
| COMMON CARD (447-522) | 5.00 | 12.00 |
| COMMON CARD (523-598) | 8.00 | 20.00 |
| WRAPPER (1-CENT) | 50.00 | 100.00 |
| WRAPPER (5-CENT) | 12.50 | 30.00 |
| 1 Roger Maris | 250.00 | 500.00 |
| 2 Jim Brosnan | 2.00 | 5.00 |
| 3 Pete Runnels | 2.00 | 5.00 |
| 4 John DeMerit | 3.00 | 8.00 |

|  | | |
|---|---|---|
| 5 Sandy Koufax UER | 75.00 | 150.00 |
| 6 Marv Breeding | 2.00 | 5.00 |
| 7 Frank Thomas | 4.00 | 10.00 |
| 8 Ray Herbert | 2.00 | 5.00 |
| 9 Jim Davenport | 3.00 | 8.00 |
| 10 Roberto Clemente | 100.00 | 200.00 |
| 11 Tom Morgan | 2.00 | 5.00 |
| 12 Harry Craft MG | 3.00 | 8.00 |
| 13 Dick Howser | 3.00 | 8.00 |
| 14 Bill White | 3.00 | 8.00 |
| 15 Dick Donovan | 2.00 | 5.00 |
| 16 Darrell Johnson | 2.00 | 5.00 |
| 17 Johnny Callison | 3.00 | 8.00 |
| 18 M.Mantle/W.Mays | 100.00 | 200.00 |
| 19 Ray Washburn RC | 2.00 | 5.00 |
| 20 Rocky Colavito | 6.00 | 15.00 |
| 21 Jim Kaat | 3.00 | 8.00 |
| 22A Checklist 1 ERR | 5.00 | 12.00 |
| 22B Checklist 1 COR | 5.00 | 12.00 |
| 23 Norm Larker | 2.00 | 5.00 |
| 24 Detroit Tigers TC | 4.00 | 10.00 |
| 25 Ernie Banks | 20.00 | 50.00 |
| 26 Chris Cannizzaro | 3.00 | 8.00 |
| 27 Chuck Cottier | 2.00 | 5.00 |
| 28 Minnie Minoso | 4.00 | 10.00 |
| 29 Casey Stengel MG | 8.00 | 20.00 |
| 30 Eddie Mathews | 6.00 | 15.00 |
| 31 Tom Tresh RC | 6.00 | 15.00 |
| 32 John Roseboro | 3.00 | 8.00 |
| 33 Don Larsen | 3.00 | 8.00 |
| 34 Johnny Temple | 2.00 | 5.00 |
| 35 Don Schwall RC | 4.00 | 10.00 |
| 36 Don Leppert RC | 2.00 | 5.00 |
| 37 Latman/Stigman/Perry | 2.00 | 5.00 |
| 38 Gene Stephens | 2.00 | 5.00 |
| 39 Joe Koppe | 2.00 | 5.00 |
| 40 Orlando Cepeda | 6.00 | 15.00 |
| 41 Cliff Cook | 2.00 | 5.00 |
| 42 Jim King | 2.00 | 5.00 |
| 43 Los Angeles Dodgers TC | 4.00 | 10.00 |
| 44 Don Taussig RC | 2.00 | 5.00 |
| 45 Brooks Robinson | 20.00 | 50.00 |
| 46 Jack Baldschun RC | 2.00 | 5.00 |
| 47 Bob Will | 2.00 | 5.00 |
| 48 Ralph Terry | 3.00 | 8.00 |
| 49 Hal Jones RC | 2.00 | 5.00 |
| 50 Stan Musial | 50.00 | 100.00 |
| 51 Cash/Kaline/Howard LL | 3.00 | 8.00 |
| 52 Clemente/Pins/Boyer LL | 8.00 | 20.00 |
| 53 Maris/Mantle/Kill LL | 50.00 | 100.00 |
| 54 Cepeda/Mays/F.Rob LL | 3.00 | 8.00 |
| 55 Donovan/Stafl/Mossi LL | 3.00 | 8.00 |
| 56 Spahn/O'Toole/Simm LL | 3.00 | 8.00 |
| 57 Ford/Lary/Bunning LL | 3.00 | 8.00 |
| 58 Spahn/Jay/O'Toole LL | 3.00 | 8.00 |
| 59 Pascual/Ford/Bunning LL | 3.00 | 8.00 |
| 60 Koufax/Will/Drysdale LL | 8.00 | 20.00 |
| 61 St. Louis Cardinals TC | 4.00 | 10.00 |
| 62 Steve Boros | 2.00 | 5.00 |
| 63 Tony Cloninger RC | 3.00 | 8.00 |
| 64 Russ Snyder | 2.00 | 5.00 |
| 65 Bobby Richardson | 4.00 | 10.00 |
| 66 Cuno Barragan RC | 3.00 | 8.00 |
| 67 Harvey Haddix | 3.00 | 8.00 |
| 68 Ken Hunt | 2.00 | 5.00 |
| 69 Phil Ortega RC | 2.00 | 5.00 |
| 70 Harmon Killebrew | 10.00 | 25.00 |
| 71 Dick LeMay RC | 2.00 | 5.00 |
| 72 Boros/Scheffing/Wood | 2.00 | 5.00 |
| 73 Nellie Fox | 6.00 | 15.00 |
| 74 Bob Lillis | 3.00 | 8.00 |
| 75 Milt Pappas | 3.00 | 8.00 |
| 76 Howie Bedell | 2.00 | 5.00 |
| 77 Tony Taylor | 3.00 | 8.00 |
| 78 Gene Green | 2.00 | 5.00 |
| 79 Ed Hobaugh | 2.00 | 5.00 |
| 80 Vada Pinson | 3.00 | 8.00 |
| 81 Jim Pagliaroni | 2.00 | 5.00 |
| 82 Deron Johnson | 3.00 | 8.00 |
| 83 Larry Jackson | 2.00 | 5.00 |
| 84 Lenny Green | 2.00 | 5.00 |
| 85 Gil Hodges | 8.00 | 20.00 |
| 86 Donn Clendenon RC | 3.00 | 8.00 |
| 87 Mike Roarke | 2.00 | 5.00 |
| 88 Ralph Houk MG | 3.00 | 8.00 |
| 89 Barney Schultz RC | 2.00 | 5.00 |
| 90 Jimmy Piersall | 3.00 | 8.00 |
| 91 J.C. Martin | 2.00 | 5.00 |

|  | | |
|---|---|---|
| 92 Sam Jones | 2.00 | 5.00 |
| 93 John Blanchard | 3.00 | 8.00 |
| 94 Jay Hook | 3.00 | 8.00 |
| 95 Don Hoak | 3.00 | 8.00 |
| 96 Eli Grba | 2.00 | 5.00 |
| 97 Tito Francona | 2.00 | 5.00 |
| 98 Checklist 2 | 5.00 | 12.00 |
| 99 Boog Powell RC | 12.50 | 30.00 |
| 100 Warren Spahn | 15.00 | 40.00 |
| 101 Carroll Hardy | 2.00 | 5.00 |
| 102 Al Schroll | 2.00 | 5.00 |
| 103 Don Blasingame | 2.00 | 5.00 |
| 104 Ted Savage RC | 2.00 | 5.00 |
| 105 Don Mossi | 3.00 | 8.00 |
| 106 Carl Sawatski | 2.00 | 5.00 |
| 107 Mike McCormick | 3.00 | 8.00 |
| 108 Willie Davis | 3.00 | 8.00 |
| 109 Bob Shaw | 2.00 | 5.00 |
| 110 Bill Skowron | 3.00 | 8.00 |
| 110A Bill Skowron Green Tint | 3.00 | 8.00 |
| 111 Dallas Green | 3.00 | 8.00 |
| 111A Dallas Green Green Tint | 3.00 | 8.00 |
| 112 Hank Foiles | 2.00 | 5.00 |
| 112A Hank Foiles Green Tint | 2.00 | 5.00 |
| 113 Chicago White Sox TC | 4.00 | 10.00 |
| 113A Chicago White Sox TC Green Tint | 4.00 | 10.00 |
| 114 Howie Koplitz RC | 3.00 | 8.00 |
| 114A Howie Koplitz Green Tint | 2.00 | 5.00 |
| 115 Bob Skinner | 3.00 | 8.00 |
| 115A Bob Skinner Green Tint | 2.00 | 5.00 |
| 116 Herb Score | 3.00 | 8.00 |
| 116A Herb Score Green Tint | 2.00 | 5.00 |
| 117 Gary Geiger | 2.00 | 5.00 |
| 117A Gary Geiger Green Tint | 2.00 | 5.00 |
| 118 Julian Javier | 3.00 | 8.00 |
| 118A Julian Javier Green Tint | 2.00 | 5.00 |
| 119 Danny Murphy | 2.00 | 5.00 |
| 119A Danny Murphy Green Tint | 2.00 | 5.00 |
| 120 Bob Purkey | 2.00 | 5.00 |
| 120A Bob Purkey Green Tint | 2.00 | 5.00 |
| 121 Billy Hitchcock MG | 2.00 | 5.00 |
| 121A Billy Hitchcock Green Tint | 2.00 | 5.00 |
| 122 Norm Bass RC | 2.00 | 5.00 |
| 122A Norm Bass Green Tint | 2.00 | 5.00 |
| 123 Mike de la Hoz | 2.00 | 5.00 |
| 123A Mike de la Hoz Green Tint | 2.00 | 5.00 |
| 124 Bill Pleis RC | 2.00 | 5.00 |
| 124A Bill Pleis Green Tint | 2.00 | 5.00 |
| 125 Gene Woodling | 3.00 | 8.00 |
| 125A Gene Woodling Green Tint | 3.00 | 8.00 |
| 126 Al Cicotte | 2.00 | 5.00 |
| 126A Al Cicotte Green Tint | 2.00 | 5.00 |
| 127 Siebern/Bauer/Lumpe | 2.00 | 5.00 |
| 127A Siebern/Bauer/Lumpe Green Tint | 2.00 | 5.00 |
| 128 Art Fowler | 2.00 | 5.00 |
| 128A Art Fowler Green Tint | 2.00 | 5.00 |
| 129A Lee Walls Facing Right | 2.00 | 5.00 |
| 129B Lee Walls Facing Left | 12.50 | 30.00 |
| 130 Frank Bolling | 2.00 | 5.00 |
| 130A Frank Bolling Green Tint | 2.00 | 5.00 |
| 131 Pete Richert RC | 2.00 | 5.00 |
| 131A Pete Richert Green Tint | 2.00 | 5.00 |
| 131A Los Angeles Angels TC w/o Photo | 4.00 | 10.00 |
| 132B Los Angeles Angels TC w/Photo | 12.50 | 30.00 |
| 133 Felipe Alou | 3.00 | 8.00 |
| 133A Felipe Alou Green Tint | 3.00 | 8.00 |
| 134A Billy Hoeft Blue Sky | 3.00 | 8.00 |
| 134B Billy Hoeft Green Sky | 12.50 | 30.00 |
| 135 Babe as a Boy | 8.00 | 20.00 |
| 135A Babe as a Boy Green | 8.00 | 20.00 |
| 136 Babe Joins Yanks | 8.00 | 20.00 |
| 136A Babe Joins Yanks Green | 8.00 | 20.00 |
| 137 Babe with Mgr. Huggins | 8.00 | 20.00 |
| 137A Babe w/ Mgr. Huggins Green | 8.00 | 20.00 |
| 138 The Famous Slugger | 8.00 | 20.00 |
| 138A The Famous Slugger Green | 8.00 | 20.00 |
| 139A1 Babe Hits 60 (Pole) | 12.50 | 30.00 |
| 139B Hal Reniff Portrait | 6.00 | 15.00 |
| 139C Hal Reniff Pitching | 30.00 | 60.00 |
| 140 Gehrig and Ruth | 30.00 | 60.00 |
| 140A Gehrig and Ruth Green | 30.00 | 60.00 |
| 141 Twilight Years | 8.00 | 20.00 |
| 141A Twilight Years Green | 8.00 | 20.00 |
| 142 Coaching the Dodgers | 8.00 | 20.00 |
| 142A Coaching the Dodgers Green | 8.00 | 20.00 |
| 143 Greatest Sports Hero | 8.00 | 20.00 |
| 143A Greatest Sports Hero Green | 8.00 | 20.00 |
| 144 Farewell Speech | 8.00 | 20.00 |

| Card | Price 1 | Price 2 |
|---|---|---|
| ☐ 144A Farewell Speech Green | 8.00 | 20.00 |
| ☐ 145 Barry Latman | 2.00 | 5.00 |
| ☐ 145A Barry Latman Green Tint | 2.00 | 5.00 |
| ☐ 146 Don Demeter | 2.00 | 5.00 |
| ☐ 146A Don Demeter Green Tint | 2.00 | 5.00 |
| ☐ 147A Bill Kunkel Portrait | 2.00 | 5.00 |
| ☐ 147B Bill Kunkel Pitching | 12.50 | 30.00 |
| ☐ 148 Wally Post | 2.00 | 5.00 |
| ☐ 148A Wally Post Green Tint | 2.00 | 5.00 |
| ☐ 149 Bob Duliba | 2.00 | 5.00 |
| ☐ 149A Bob Duliba Green Tint | 2.00 | 5.00 |
| ☐ 150 Al Kaline | 20.00 | 50.00 |
| ☐ 150A Al Kaline Green Tint | 20.00 | 50.00 |
| ☐ 151 Johnny Klippstein | 2.00 | 5.00 |
| ☐ 151A Johnny Klippstein Green Tint | 2.00 | 5.00 |
| ☐ 152 Mickey Vernon MG | 3.00 | 8.00 |
| ☐ 152A Mickey Vernon MG Green Tint | 3.00 | 8.00 |
| ☐ 153 Pumpsie Green | 2.50 | 6.00 |
| ☐ 153A Pumpsie Green Green Tint | 2.50 | 6.00 |
| ☐ 154 Lee Thomas | 2.50 | 6.00 |
| ☐ 154A Lee Thomas Green Tint | 2.50 | 6.00 |
| ☐ 155 Stu Miller | 2.50 | 5.00 |
| ☐ 155A Stu Miller Green Tint | 2.50 | 5.00 |
| ☐ 156 Merritt Ranew RC | 2.00 | 5.00 |
| ☐ 156A Merritt Ranew Green Tint | 2.00 | 5.00 |
| ☐ 157 Wes Covington | 3.00 | 8.00 |
| ☐ 157A Wes Covington Green Tint | 3.00 | 8.00 |
| ☐ 158 Milwaukee Braves TC | 4.00 | 10.00 |
| ☐ 158A Milwaukee Braves TC Green Tint | 6.00 | 15.00 |
| ☐ 159 Hal Reniff RC | 3.00 | 8.00 |
| ☐ 160 Dick Stuart | 3.00 | 8.00 |
| ☐ 160A Dick Stuart Green Tint | 3.00 | 8.00 |
| ☐ 161 Frank Baumann | 2.00 | 5.00 |
| ☐ 161A Frank Baumann Green Tint | 2.00 | 5.00 |
| ☐ 162 Sammy Drake RC | 2.00 | 5.00 |
| ☐ 162A Sammy Drake Green Tint | 2.00 | 5.00 |
| ☐ 163 B.Gardner/C.Boyer | 3.00 | 8.00 |
| ☐ 163A B.Gardner/C.Boyer Green Tint | 3.00 | 8.00 |
| ☐ 164 Hal Naragon | 2.00 | 5.00 |
| ☐ 164A Hal Naragon Green Tint | 2.00 | 5.00 |
| ☐ 165 Jackie Brandt | 2.00 | 5.00 |
| ☐ 165A Jackie Brandt Green Tint | 2.00 | 5.00 |
| ☐ 166 Don Lee | 2.00 | 5.00 |
| ☐ 166A Don Lee Green Tint | 2.00 | 5.00 |
| ☐ 167 Tim McCarver RC | 12.50 | 30.00 |
| ☐ 167A Tim McCarver Green Tint | 12.50 | 30.00 |
| ☐ 168 Leo Posada | 2.00 | 5.00 |
| ☐ 168A Leo Posada Green Tint | 2.00 | 5.00 |
| ☐ 169 Bob Cerv | 4.00 | 10.00 |
| ☐ 169A Bob Cerv Green Tint | 4.00 | 10.00 |
| ☐ 170 Ron Santo | 6.00 | 15.00 |
| ☐ 170A Ron Santo Green Tint | 6.00 | 15.00 |
| ☐ 171 Dave Sisler | 2.00 | 5.00 |
| ☐ 171A Dave Sisler Green Tint | 2.00 | 5.00 |
| ☐ 172 Fred Hutchinson MG | 3.00 | 8.00 |
| ☐ 172A Fred Hutchinson MG Green Tint | 3.00 | 8.00 |
| ☐ 173 Chico Fernandez | 2.00 | 5.00 |
| ☐ 173A Chico Fernandez Green Tint | 2.00 | 5.00 |
| ☐ 174A Carl Willey w/o Cap | 4.00 | 10.00 |
| ☐ 174B Carl Willey w/Cap | 12.50 | 30.00 |
| ☐ 175 Frank Howard | 4.00 | 10.00 |
| ☐ 175A Frank Howard Green Tint | 4.00 | 10.00 |
| ☐ 176A Eddie Yost Portrait | 2.00 | 5.00 |
| ☐ 176B Eddie Yost Batting | 12.50 | 30.00 |
| ☐ 177 Bobby Shantz | 3.00 | 8.00 |
| ☐ 177A Bobby Shantz Green Tint | 3.00 | 8.00 |
| ☐ 178 Camilo Carreon | 2.00 | 5.00 |
| ☐ 178A Camilo Carreon Green Tint | 2.00 | 5.00 |
| ☐ 179 Tom Sturdivant | 2.00 | 5.00 |
| ☐ 179A Tom Sturdivant Green Tint | 2.00 | 5.00 |
| ☐ 180 Bob Allison | 4.00 | 10.00 |
| ☐ 180A Bob Allison Green Tint | 4.00 | 10.00 |
| ☐ 181 Paul Brown RC | 2.00 | 5.00 |
| ☐ 181A Paul Brown Green Tint | 2.00 | 5.00 |
| ☐ 182 Bob Nieman | 2.00 | 5.00 |
| ☐ 182A Bob Nieman Green Tint | 2.00 | 5.00 |
| ☐ 183 Roger Craig | 3.00 | 8.00 |
| ☐ 183A Roger Craig Green Tint | 3.00 | 8.00 |
| ☐ 184 Haywood Sullivan | 3.00 | 8.00 |
| ☐ 184A Haywood Sullivan Green Tint | 3.00 | 8.00 |
| ☐ 185 Roland Sheldon | 3.00 | 8.00 |
| ☐ 185A Roland Sheldon Green Tint | 4.00 | 10.00 |
| ☐ 186 Mack Jones RC | 2.00 | 5.00 |
| ☐ 186A Mack Jones Green Tint | 2.00 | 5.00 |
| ☐ 187 Gene Conley | 2.00 | 5.00 |
| ☐ 187A Gene Conley Green Tint | 2.00 | 5.00 |
| ☐ 188 Chuck Hiller | 2.00 | 5.00 |
| ☐ 188A Chuck Hiller Green Tint | 2.00 | 5.00 |
| ☐ 189 Dick Hall | 2.00 | 5.00 |
| ☐ 189A Dick Hall Green Tint | 2.00 | 5.00 |
| ☐ 190A Wally Moon Portrait | 3.00 | 8.00 |
| ☐ 190B Wally Moon Batting | 12.50 | 30.00 |
| ☐ 191 Jim Brewer | 2.00 | 5.00 |
| ☐ 191A Jim Brewer Green Tint | 2.00 | 5.00 |
| ☐ 192A Checklist 3 w/o Comma | 5.00 | 12.00 |
| ☐ 192B Checklist 3 w/Comma | 6.00 | 15.00 |
| ☐ 193 Eddie Kasko | 2.00 | 5.00 |
| ☐ 193A Eddie Kasko Green Tint | 2.00 | 5.00 |
| ☐ 194 Dean Chance RC | 3.00 | 8.00 |
| ☐ 194A Dean Chance Green Tint | 3.00 | 8.00 |
| ☐ 195 Joe Cunningham | 2.00 | 5.00 |
| ☐ 195A Joe Cunningham Green Tint | 2.00 | 5.00 |
| ☐ 196 Terry Fox | 2.00 | 5.00 |
| ☐ 196A Terry Fox Green Tint | 2.00 | 5.00 |
| ☐ 197 Daryl Spencer | 2.00 | 5.00 |
| ☐ 198 Johnny Keane MG | 2.00 | 5.00 |
| ☐ 199 Gaylord Perry RC | 40.00 | 80.00 |
| ☐ 200 Mickey Mantle | 300.00 | 600.00 |
| ☐ 201 Ike Delock | 2.00 | 5.00 |
| ☐ 202 Carl Warwick RC | 2.00 | 5.00 |
| ☐ 203 Jack Fisher | 2.00 | 5.00 |
| ☐ 204 Johnny Weekly RC | 2.00 | 5.00 |
| ☐ 205 Gene Freese | 2.00 | 5.00 |
| ☐ 206 Washington Senators TC | 4.00 | 10.00 |
| ☐ 207 Pete Burnside | 2.00 | 5.00 |
| ☐ 208 Billy Martin | 8.00 | 20.00 |
| ☐ 209 Jim Fregosi RC | 6.00 | 15.00 |
| ☐ 210 Roy Face | 3.00 | 8.00 |
| ☐ 211 F.Bolling/R.McMillan | 2.00 | 5.00 |
| ☐ 212 Jim Owens | 2.00 | 5.00 |
| ☐ 213 Richie Ashburn | 8.00 | 20.00 |
| ☐ 214 Dom Zanni | 2.00 | 5.00 |
| ☐ 215 Woody Held | 2.00 | 5.00 |
| ☐ 216 Ron Kline | 2.00 | 5.00 |
| ☐ 217 Walter Alston MG * | 4.00 | 10.00 |
| ☐ 218 Joe Torre RC | 15.00 | 40.00 |
| ☐ 219 Al Downing RC | 3.00 | 8.00 |
| ☐ 220 Roy Sievers | 3.00 | 8.00 |
| ☐ 221 Bill Short | 2.00 | 5.00 |
| ☐ 222 Jerry Zimmerman | 2.00 | 5.00 |
| ☐ 223 Alex Grammas | 2.00 | 5.00 |
| ☐ 224 Don Rudolph | 2.00 | 5.00 |
| ☐ 225 Frank Malzone | 3.00 | 8.00 |
| ☐ 226 San Francisco Giants TC | 4.00 | 10.00 |
| ☐ 227 Bob Tiefenauer | 2.00 | 5.00 |
| ☐ 228 Dale Long | 2.00 | 5.00 |
| ☐ 229 Jesus McFarlane RC | 2.00 | 5.00 |
| ☐ 230 Camilo Pascual | 3.00 | 8.00 |
| ☐ 231 Ernie Bowman RC | 2.00 | 5.00 |
| ☐ 232 Ellie Howard WS1 | 4.00 | 10.00 |
| ☐ 233 Joey Jay WS2 | 4.00 | 10.00 |
| ☐ 234 Roger Maris WS3 | 10.00 | 25.00 |
| ☐ 235 Whitey Ford WS4 | 5.00 | 12.00 |
| ☐ 236 Yanks Crush Reds WS5 | 4.00 | 10.00 |
| ☐ 237 Yanks Celebrate WS | 4.00 | 10.00 |
| ☐ 238 Norm Sherry | 2.00 | 5.00 |
| ☐ 239 Cecil Butler RC | 2.00 | 5.00 |
| ☐ 240 George Altman | 2.00 | 5.00 |
| ☐ 241 Johnny Kucks | 2.00 | 5.00 |
| ☐ 242 Mel McGaha MG RC | 2.00 | 5.00 |
| ☐ 243 Robin Roberts | 6.00 | 15.00 |
| ☐ 244 Don Gile | 2.00 | 5.00 |
| ☐ 245 Ron Hansen | 2.00 | 5.00 |
| ☐ 246 Art Ditmar | 2.00 | 5.00 |
| ☐ 247 Joe Pignatano | 2.00 | 5.00 |
| ☐ 248 Bob Aspromonte | 3.00 | 8.00 |
| ☐ 249 Ed Keegan | 2.00 | 5.00 |
| ☐ 250 Norm Cash | 4.00 | 10.00 |
| ☐ 251 New York Yankees TC | 20.00 | 50.00 |
| ☐ 252 Earl Francis | 2.00 | 5.00 |
| ☐ 253 Harry Chiti CO | 2.00 | 5.00 |
| ☐ 254 Gordon Windhorn RC | 2.00 | 5.00 |
| ☐ 255 Juan Pizarro | 2.00 | 5.00 |
| ☐ 256 Elio Chacon | 3.00 | 8.00 |
| ☐ 257 Jack Spring RC | 2.00 | 5.00 |
| ☐ 258 Marty Keough | 2.00 | 5.00 |
| ☐ 259 Lou Klimchock | 2.00 | 5.00 |
| ☐ 260 Billy Pierce | 3.00 | 8.00 |
| ☐ 261 George Alusik RC | 2.00 | 5.00 |
| ☐ 262 Bob Schmidt | 2.00 | 5.00 |
| ☐ 263 Purkey/Turner/Jay | 2.00 | 5.00 |
| ☐ 264 Dick Ellsworth | 3.00 | 8.00 |
| ☐ 265 Joe Adcock | 3.00 | 8.00 |
| ☐ 266 John Anderson RC | 2.00 | 5.00 |
| ☐ 267 Dan Dobbek | 2.00 | 5.00 |
| ☐ 268 Ken McBride | 2.00 | 5.00 |
| ☐ 269 Bob Oldis | 2.00 | 5.00 |
| ☐ 270 Dick Groat | 3.00 | 8.00 |
| ☐ 271 Ray Rippelmeyer | 2.00 | 5.00 |
| ☐ 272 Earl Robinson | 2.00 | 5.00 |
| ☐ 273 Gary Bell | 2.00 | 5.00 |
| ☐ 274 Sammy Taylor | 2.00 | 5.00 |
| ☐ 275 Norm Siebern | 2.00 | 5.00 |
| ☐ 276 Hal Kolstad RC | 2.00 | 5.00 |
| ☐ 277 Checklist 4 | 6.00 | 15.00 |
| ☐ 278 Ken Johnson | 3.00 | 8.00 |
| ☐ 279 Hobie Landrith UER | 3.00 | 8.00 |
| ☐ 280 Johnny Podres | 3.00 | 8.00 |
| ☐ 281 Jake Gibbs RC | 4.00 | 10.00 |
| ☐ 282 Dave Hillman | 2.00 | 5.00 |
| ☐ 283 Charlie Smith RC | 2.00 | 5.00 |
| ☐ 284 Ruben Amaro | 2.00 | 5.00 |
| ☐ 285 Curt Simmons | 3.00 | 8.00 |
| ☐ 286 Al Lopez MG | 4.00 | 10.00 |
| ☐ 287 George Witt | 2.00 | 5.00 |
| ☐ 288 Billy Williams | 12.50 | 30.00 |
| ☐ 289 Mike Krsnich RC | 2.00 | 5.00 |
| ☐ 290 Jim Gentile | 3.00 | 8.00 |
| ☐ 291 Hal Stowe RC | 2.00 | 5.00 |
| ☐ 292 Jerry Kindall | 2.00 | 5.00 |
| ☐ 293 Bob Miller | 3.00 | 8.00 |
| ☐ 294 Philadelphia Phillies TC | 4.00 | 10.00 |
| ☐ 295 Vern Law | 3.00 | 8.00 |
| ☐ 296 Ken Hamlin | 2.00 | 5.00 |
| ☐ 297 Ron Perranoski | 3.00 | 8.00 |
| ☐ 298 Bill Tuttle | 2.00 | 5.00 |
| ☐ 299 Don Wert RC | 2.00 | 5.00 |
| ☐ 300 Willie Mays | 125.00 | 250.00 |
| ☐ 301 Galen Cisco RC | 2.00 | 5.00 |
| ☐ 302 Johnny Edwards RC | 2.00 | 5.00 |
| ☐ 303 Frank Torre | 3.00 | 8.00 |
| ☐ 304 Dick Farrell | 2.00 | 5.00 |
| ☐ 305 Jerry Lumpe | 2.00 | 5.00 |
| ☐ 306 L.McDaniel/L.Jackson | 2.00 | 5.00 |
| ☐ 307 Jim Grant | 3.00 | 8.00 |
| ☐ 308 Neil Chrisley | 2.00 | 5.00 |
| ☐ 309 Moe Morhardt RC | 2.00 | 5.00 |
| ☐ 310 Whitey Ford | 20.00 | 50.00 |
| ☐ 311 Tony Kubek IA | 4.00 | 10.00 |
| ☐ 312 Warren Spahn IA | 6.00 | 15.00 |
| ☐ 313 Roger Maris IA | 40.00 | 80.00 |
| ☐ 314 Rocky Colavito IA | 3.00 | 8.00 |
| ☐ 315 Whitey Ford IA | 6.00 | 15.00 |
| ☐ 316 Harmon Killebrew IA | 6.00 | 15.00 |
| ☐ 317 Stan Musial IA | 8.00 | 20.00 |
| ☐ 318 Mickey Mantle IA | 75.00 | 150.00 |
| ☐ 319 Mike McCormick IA | 2.00 | 5.00 |
| ☐ 320 Hank Aaron | 75.00 | 150.00 |
| ☐ 321 Lee Stange RC | 2.00 | 5.00 |
| ☐ 322 Alvin Dark MG | 3.00 | 8.00 |
| ☐ 323 Don Landrum | 2.00 | 5.00 |
| ☐ 324 Joe McClain | 2.00 | 5.00 |
| ☐ 325 Luis Aparicio | 6.00 | 15.00 |
| ☐ 326 Tom Parsons RC | 2.00 | 5.00 |
| ☐ 327 Ozzie Virgil | 2.00 | 5.00 |
| ☐ 328 Ken Walters | 2.00 | 5.00 |
| ☐ 329 Bob Bolin | 2.00 | 5.00 |
| ☐ 330 John Romano | 2.00 | 5.00 |
| ☐ 331 Moe Drabowsky | 3.00 | 8.00 |
| ☐ 332 Don Buddin | 2.00 | 5.00 |
| ☐ 333 Frank Cipriani RC | 2.00 | 5.00 |
| ☐ 334 Boston Red Sox TC | 4.00 | 10.00 |
| ☐ 335 Bill Bruton | 2.00 | 5.00 |
| ☐ 336 Billy Muffett | 2.00 | 5.00 |
| ☐ 337 Jim Marshall | 3.00 | 8.00 |
| ☐ 338 Billy Gardner | 2.00 | 5.00 |
| ☐ 339 Jose Valdivielso | 2.00 | 5.00 |
| ☐ 340 Don Drysdale | 20.00 | 50.00 |
| ☐ 341 Mike Hershberger RC | 2.00 | 5.00 |
| ☐ 342 Ed Rakow | 2.00 | 5.00 |
| ☐ 343 Albie Pearson | 3.00 | 8.00 |
| ☐ 344 Ed Bauta RC | 2.00 | 5.00 |
| ☐ 345 Chuck Schilling | 2.00 | 5.00 |
| ☐ 346 Jack Kralick | 2.00 | 5.00 |
| ☐ 347 Chuck Hinton RC | 2.00 | 5.00 |
| ☐ 348 Larry Burright RC | 3.00 | 8.00 |
| ☐ 349 Paul Foytack | 2.00 | 5.00 |
| ☐ 350 Frank Robinson | 20.00 | 50.00 |
| ☐ 351 J.Torre/D.Crandall | 3.00 | 8.00 |
| ☐ 352 Frank Sullivan | 2.00 | 5.00 |
| ☐ 353 Bill Mazeroski | 6.00 | 15.00 |
| ☐ 354 Roman Mejias | 3.00 | 8.00 |
| ☐ 355 Steve Barber | 2.00 | 5.00 |
| ☐ 356 Tom Haller RC | 2.00 | 5.00 |

| No. | Player | | | No. | Player | | | No. | Player | | |
|---|---|---|---|---|---|---|---|---|---|---|---|
| 357 | Jerry Walker | 2.00 | 5.00 | 445 | Vic Power | 3.00 | 8.00 | 530 | Bob Gibson SP | 60.00 | 120.00 |
| 358 | Tommy Davis | 3.00 | 8.00 | 446 | Don Elston | 2.50 | 6.00 | 531 | Bobby G. Smith | 8.00 | 20.00 |
| 359 | Bobby Locke | 2.00 | 5.00 | 447 | Willie Kirkland | 5.00 | 12.00 | 532 | Dick Stigman | 8.00 | 20.00 |
| 360 | Yogi Berra | 40.00 | 80.00 | 448 | Joe Gibbon | 5.00 | 12.00 | 533 | Charley Lau SP | 12.50 | 30.00 |
| 361 | Bob Hendley | 2.00 | 5.00 | 449 | Jerry Adair | 5.00 | 12.00 | 534 | Tony Gonzalez SP | 12.50 | 30.00 |
| 362 | Ty Cline | 2.00 | 5.00 | 450 | Jim O'Toole | 6.00 | 15.00 | 535 | Ed Roebuck | 8.00 | 20.00 |
| 363 | Bob Roselli | 2.00 | 5.00 | 451 | Jose Tartabull RC | 6.00 | 15.00 | 536 | Dick Gernert | 8.00 | 20.00 |
| 364 | Ken Hunt | 2.00 | 5.00 | 452 | Earl Averill Jr. | 5.00 | 12.00 | 537 | Cleveland Indians TC | 20.00 | 50.00 |
| 365 | Charlie Neal | 3.00 | 8.00 | 453 | Cal McLish | 5.00 | 12.00 | 538 | Jack Sanford | 8.00 | 20.00 |
| 366 | Phil Regan | 3.00 | 8.00 | 454 | Floyd Robinson RC | 5.00 | 12.00 | 539 | Billy Moran | 8.00 | 20.00 |
| 367 | Checklist 5 | 6.00 | 15.00 | 455 | Luis Arroyo | 6.00 | 15.00 | 540 | Jim Landis SP | 12.50 | 30.00 |
| 368 | Bob Tillman RC | 2.00 | 5.00 | 456 | Joe Amalfitano | 6.00 | 15.00 | 541 | Don Nottebart SP | 12.50 | 30.00 |
| 369 | Ted Bowsfield | 2.00 | 5.00 | 457 | Lou Clinton | 5.00 | 12.00 | 542 | Dave Philley | 8.00 | 20.00 |
| 370 | Ken Boyer | 4.00 | 10.00 | 458A | Bob Buhl Emblem | | | 543 | Bob Allen SP | 12.50 | 30.00 |
| 371 | Earl Battey | 2.50 | 6.00 | 458B | Bob Buhl No Emblem | 20.00 | 50.00 | 544 | Willie McCovey SP | 60.00 | 120.00 |
| 372 | Jack Curtis | 2.50 | 6.00 | 459 | Ed Bailey | 5.00 | 12.00 | 545 | Hoyt Wilhelm SP | 20.00 | 50.00 |
| 373 | Al Heist | 2.50 | 6.00 | 460 | Jim Bunning | 8.00 | 20.00 | 546 | Moe Thacker SP | 12.50 | 30.00 |
| 374 | Gene Mauch MG | 4.00 | 10.00 | 461 | Ken Hubbs AS | 12.50 | 30.00 | 547 | Don Ferrarese | 8.00 | 20.00 |
| 375 | Ron Fairly | 4.00 | 10.00 | 462A | Willie Tasby Emblem | 5.00 | 12.00 | 548 | Bobby Del Greco | 8.00 | 20.00 |
| 376 | Bud Daley | 3.00 | 8.00 | 462B | Willie Tasby No Emblem | 20.00 | 50.00 | 549 | Bill Rigney MG SP | 12.50 | 30.00 |
| 377 | John Orsino RC | 2.50 | 6.00 | 463 | Hank Bauer MG | 6.00 | 15.00 | 550 | Art Mahaffey SP | 12.50 | 30.00 |
| 378 | Bennie Daniels | 2.50 | 6.00 | 464 | Al Jackson RC | 5.00 | 12.00 | 551 | Harry Bright | 8.00 | 20.00 |
| 379 | Chuck Essegian | 2.50 | 6.00 | 465 | Cincinnati Reds TC | 8.00 | 20.00 | 552 | Chicago Cubs TC SP | 20.00 | 50.00 |
| 380 | Lew Burdette | 4.00 | 10.00 | 466 | Norm Cash AS | 6.00 | 15.00 | 553 | Jim Coates | 12.50 | 30.00 |
| 381 | Chico Cardenas | 4.00 | 10.00 | 467 | Chuck Schilling AS | 5.00 | 12.00 | 554 | Bubba Morton SP RC | 12.50 | 30.00 |
| 382 | Dick Williams | 3.00 | 8.00 | 468 | Brooks Robinson AS | 10.00 | 25.00 | 555 | John Buzhardt SP | 12.50 | 30.00 |
| 383 | Ray Sadecki | 2.50 | 6.00 | 469 | Luis Aparicio AS | 6.00 | 15.00 | 556 | Al Spangler | 8.00 | 20.00 |
| 384 | Kansas City Athletics TC | 4.00 | 10.00 | 470 | Al Kaline AS | 10.00 | 25.00 | 557 | Bob Anderson SP | 12.50 | 30.00 |
| 385 | Early Wynn | 6.00 | 15.00 | 471 | Mickey Mantle AS | 100.00 | 200.00 | 558 | John Goryl | 8.00 | 20.00 |
| 386 | Don Mincher | 3.00 | 8.00 | 472 | Rocky Colavito AS | 6.00 | 15.00 | 559 | Mike Higgins MG | 8.00 | 20.00 |
| 387 | Lou Brock RC | 60.00 | 120.00 | 473 | Elston Howard AS | 6.00 | 15.00 | 560 | Chuck Estrada SP | 12.50 | 30.00 |
| 388 | Ryne Duren | 3.00 | 8.00 | 474 | Frank Lary AS | 5.00 | 12.00 | 561 | Gene Oliver SP | 12.50 | 30.00 |
| 389 | Smoky Burgess | 4.00 | 10.00 | 475 | Whitey Ford AS | 8.00 | 20.00 | 562 | Bill Henry | 8.00 | 20.00 |
| 390 | Orlando Cepeda AS | 4.00 | 10.00 | 476 | Baltimore Orioles TC | 8.00 | 20.00 | 563 | Ken Aspromonte | 8.00 | 20.00 |
| 391 | Bill Mazeroski AS | 4.00 | 10.00 | 477 | Andre Rodgers | 5.00 | 12.00 | 564 | Bob Grim | 8.00 | 20.00 |
| 392 | Ken Boyer AS UER | 3.00 | 8.00 | 478 | Don Zimmer | 6.00 | 15.00 | 565 | Jose Pagan | 8.00 | 20.00 |
| 393 | Roy McMillan AS | 2.50 | 6.00 | 479 | Joel Horlen RC | 5.00 | 12.00 | 566 | Marty Kutyna SP | 12.50 | 30.00 |
| 394 | Hank Aaron AS | 20.00 | 50.00 | 480 | Harvey Kuenn | 6.00 | 15.00 | 567 | Tracy Stallard SP | 12.50 | 30.00 |
| 395 | Willie Mays AS | 20.00 | 50.00 | 481 | Vic Wertz | 6.00 | 15.00 | 568 | Jim Golden | 8.00 | 20.00 |
| 396 | Frank Robinson AS | 6.00 | 15.00 | 482 | Sam Mele MG | 5.00 | 12.00 | 569 | Ed Sadowski SP | 12.50 | 30.00 |
| 397 | John Roseboro AS | 2.50 | 6.00 | 483 | Don McMahon | 5.00 | 12.00 | 570 | Bill Stafford SP | 12.50 | 30.00 |
| 398 | Don Drysdale AS | 6.00 | 15.00 | 484 | Dick Schofield | 5.00 | 12.00 | 571 | Billy Klaus SP | 12.50 | 30.00 |
| 399 | Warren Spahn AS | 6.00 | 15.00 | 485 | Pedro Ramos | 5.00 | 12.00 | 572 | Bob G. Miller SP | 12.50 | 30.00 |
| 400 | Elston Howard | 4.00 | 10.00 | 486 | Jim Gilliam | 6.00 | 15.00 | 573 | Johnny Logan | 8.00 | 20.00 |
| 401 | O.Cepeda/R.Maris | 30.00 | 60.00 | 487 | Jerry Lynch | 5.00 | 12.00 | 574 | Dean Stone | 8.00 | 20.00 |
| 402 | Gino Cimoli | 2.50 | 6.00 | 488 | Hal Brown | 5.00 | 12.00 | 575 | Red Schoendienst SP | 20.00 | 50.00 |
| 403 | Chet Nichols | 2.50 | 6.00 | 489 | Julio Gotay RC | 5.00 | 12.00 | 576 | Russ Kemmerer SP | 12.50 | 30.00 |
| 404 | Tim Harkness RC | 3.00 | 8.00 | 490 | Clete Boyer UER | 6.00 | 15.00 | 577 | Dave Nicholson SP | 12.50 | 30.00 |
| 405 | Jim Perry | 3.00 | 8.00 | 491 | Leon Wagner | 5.00 | 12.00 | 578 | Jim Duffalo RC | 8.00 | 20.00 |
| 406 | Bob Taylor | 2.50 | 6.00 | 492 | Hal W. Smith | 5.00 | 12.00 | 579 | Jim Schaffer SP RC | 12.50 | 30.00 |
| 407 | Hank Aguirre | 2.50 | 6.00 | 493 | Danny McDevitt | 5.00 | 12.00 | 580 | Bill Monbouquette | 8.00 | 20.00 |
| 408 | Gus Bell | 3.00 | 8.00 | 494 | Sammy White | 5.00 | 12.00 | 581 | Mel Roach | 8.00 | 20.00 |
| 409 | Pittsburgh Pirates TC | 4.00 | 10.00 | 495 | Don Cardwell | 5.00 | 12.00 | 582 | Ron Piche | 8.00 | 20.00 |
| 410 | Al Smith | 2.50 | 6.00 | 496 | Wayne Causey RC | 5.00 | 12.00 | 583 | Larry Osborne | 8.00 | 20.00 |
| 411 | Danny O'Connell | 2.50 | 6.00 | 497 | Ed Bouchee | 6.00 | 15.00 | 584 | Minnesota Twins SP | 30.00 | 60.00 |
| 412 | Charlie James | 2.50 | 6.00 | 498 | Jim Donohue | 5.00 | 12.00 | 585 | Glen Hobbie SP | 12.50 | 30.00 |
| 413 | Matty Alou | 4.00 | 10.00 | 499 | Zoilo Versalles | 6.00 | 15.00 | 586 | Sammy Esposito SP | 12.50 | 30.00 |
| 414 | Joe Gaines RC | 2.50 | 6.00 | 500 | Duke Snider | 30.00 | 60.00 | 587 | Frank Funk SP | 12.50 | 30.00 |
| 415 | Bill Virdon | 4.00 | 10.00 | 501 | Claude Osteen | 6.00 | 15.00 | 588 | Birdie Tebbetts MG | 8.00 | 20.00 |
| 416 | Bob Scheffing MG | 2.50 | 6.00 | 502 | Hector Lopez | 6.00 | 15.00 | 589 | Bob Turley | 12.50 | 30.00 |
| 417 | Joe Azcue RC | 2.50 | 6.00 | 503 | Danny Murtaugh MG | 6.00 | 15.00 | 590 | Curt Flood | 12.50 | 30.00 |
| 418 | Andy Carey | 2.50 | 6.00 | 504 | Eddie Bressoud | 5.00 | 12.00 | 591 | Sam McDowell SP RC | 40.00 | 80.00 |
| 419 | Bob Bruce | 3.00 | 8.00 | 505 | Juan Marichal | 15.00 | 40.00 | 592 | Jim Bouton SP RC | 40.00 | 80.00 |
| 420 | Gus Triandos | 3.00 | 8.00 | 506 | Charlie Maxwell | 6.00 | 15.00 | 593 | Rookie Pitchers SP | 20.00 | 50.00 |
| 421 | Ken MacKenzie | 3.00 | 8.00 | 507 | Ernie Broglio | 6.00 | 15.00 | 594 | Bob Uecker SP RC | 40.00 | 80.00 |
| 422 | Steve Bilko | 2.50 | 6.00 | 508 | Gordy Coleman | 6.00 | 15.00 | 595 | Rookie Infielders SP | 20.00 | 50.00 |
| 423 | R.Face/H.Wilhelm | 4.00 | 10.00 | 509 | Dave Giusti RC | 6.00 | 15.00 | 596 | Joe Pepitone SP RC | 40.00 | 80.00 |
| 424 | Al McBean RC | 2.50 | 6.00 | 510 | Jim Lemon | 5.00 | 12.00 | 597 | Rookie Infield SP | 20.00 | 50.00 |
| 425 | Carl Yastrzemski | 60.00 | 120.00 | 511 | Bubba Phillips | 5.00 | 12.00 | 598 | Rookie Outfielders SP | 40.00 | 80.00 |
| 426 | Bob Farley RC | 2.50 | 6.00 | 512 | Mike Fornieles | 5.00 | 12.00 | | | | |
| 427 | Jake Wood | 2.50 | 6.00 | 513 | Whitey Herzog | 6.00 | 15.00 | | | | |
| 428 | Joe Hicks | 2.50 | 6.00 | 514 | Sherm Lollar | 6.00 | 15.00 | | | | |
| 429 | Billy O'Dell | 2.50 | 6.00 | 515 | Stan Williams | 6.00 | 15.00 | | | | |
| 430 | Tony Kubek | 6.00 | 15.00 | 516A | Checklist 7 White | 6.00 | 15.00 | | | | |
| 431 | Bob (Buck) Rodgers RC | 3.00 | 8.00 | 516B | Checklist 7 Yellow | 6.00 | 15.00 | | | | |
| 432 | Jim Pendleton | 2.50 | 6.00 | 517 | Dave Wickersham | 5.00 | 12.00 | | | | |
| 433 | Jim Archer | 2.50 | 6.00 | 518 | Lee Maye | 5.00 | 12.00 | | | | |
| 434 | Clay Dalrymple | 2.50 | 6.00 | 519 | Bob Johnson RC | 5.00 | 12.00 | | | | |
| 435 | Larry Sherry | 3.00 | 8.00 | 520 | Bob Friend | 6.00 | 15.00 | | | | |
| 436 | Felix Mantilla | 3.00 | 8.00 | 521 | Jackie Davis UER RC | 5.00 | 12.00 | | | | |
| 437 | Ray Moore | 2.50 | 6.00 | 522 | Lindy McDaniel | 5.00 | 12.00 | | | | |
| 438 | Dick Brown | 2.50 | 6.00 | 523 | Russ Nixon SP | 12.50 | 30.00 | | | | |
| 439 | Jerry Buchek RC | 2.50 | 6.00 | 524 | Howie Nunn SP | 12.50 | 30.00 | | | | |
| 440 | Joey Jay | 2.50 | 6.00 | 525 | George Thomas | 8.00 | 20.00 | | | | |
| 441 | Checklist 6 | 6.00 | 15.00 | 526 | Hal Woodeshick SP | 12.50 | 30.00 | | | | |
| 442 | Wes Stock | 2.50 | 6.00 | 527 | Dick McAuliffe RC | 12.50 | 30.00 | | | | |
| 443 | Del Crandall | 3.00 | 8.00 | 528 | Turk Lown | 8.00 | 20.00 | | | | |
| 444 | Ted Wills | 2.50 | 6.00 | 529 | John Schaive SP | 12.50 | 30.00 | | | | |

**1963 Topps**

ALLISON

| | | | |
|---|---|---|---|
| COMPLETE SET (576) | | 3000.00 | 6000.00 |
| COMMON CARD (1-196) | | 1.50 | 4.00 |
| COMMON CARD (197-283) | | 2.00 | 5.00 |

|  | | |
|---|---:|---:|
| COMMON CARD (284-370) | 2.00 | 5.00 |
| COMMON CARD (371-446) | 2.00 | 5.00 |
| COMMON CARD (447-522) | 10.00 | 25.00 |
| COMMON CARD (523-576) | 6.00 | 15.00 |
| WRAPPER (1-CENT) | 15.00 | 40.00 |
| WRAPPER (5-CENT) | 12.50 | 30.00 |
| 1 F.Rob/Musial/Aaron LL | 15.00 | 40.00 |
| 2 Runnels/Mantle/Rob LL | 20.00 | 50.00 |
| 3 Mays/Aaron/Rob/Cep/Banks LL | 15.00 | 40.00 |
| 4 Kill/Cash/Colav/Maris LL | 8.00 | 20.00 |
| 5 Koufax/Gibson/Drysdale LL | 10.00 | 25.00 |
| 6 Aguirre/Roberts/Ford LL | 4.00 | 10.00 |
| 7 Drysdale/Sanf/Purk LL | 4.00 | 10.00 |
| 8 Terry/Donovan/Bunning LL | 3.00 | 8.00 |
| 9 Drysdale/Koufax/Gibson LL | 12.50 | 30.00 |
| 10 Pascual/Bunning/Kaat LL | 3.00 | 8.00 |
| 11 Lee Walls | 1.50 | 4.00 |
| 12 Steve Barber | 1.50 | 4.00 |
| 13 Philadelphia Phillies TC | 3.00 | 8.00 |
| 14 Pedro Ramos | 1.50 | 4.00 |
| 15 Ken Hubbs UER NPO | 4.00 | 10.00 |
| 16 Al Smith | 1.50 | 4.00 |
| 17 Ryne Duren | 3.00 | 8.00 |
| 18 Buhg/Stu/Clemente/Skin | 40.00 | 80.00 |
| 19 Pete Burnside | 1.50 | 4.00 |
| 20 Tony Kubek | 4.00 | 10.00 |
| 21 Marty Keough | 1.50 | 4.00 |
| 22 Curt Simmons | 3.00 | 8.00 |
| 23 Ed Lopat MG | 3.00 | 8.00 |
| 24 Bob Bruce | 1.50 | 4.00 |
| 25 Al Kaline | 20.00 | 50.00 |
| 26 Ray Moore | 1.50 | 4.00 |
| 27 Choo Choo Coleman | 3.00 | 8.00 |
| 28 Mike Fornieles | 1.50 | 4.00 |
| 29A Rookie Stars 1962 | 4.00 | 10.00 |
| 29B Rookie Stars 1963 | 1.50 | 4.00 |
| 30 Harvey Kuenn | 3.00 | 8.00 |
| 31 Cal Koonce RC | 1.50 | 4.00 |
| 32 Tony Gonzalez | 1.50 | 4.00 |
| 33 Bo Belinsky | 3.00 | 8.00 |
| 34 Dick Schofield | 1.50 | 4.00 |
| 35 John Buzhardt | 1.50 | 4.00 |
| 36 Jerry Kindall | 1.50 | 4.00 |
| 37 Jerry Lynch | 1.50 | 4.00 |
| 38 Bud Daley | 3.00 | 8.00 |
| 39 Los Angeles Angels TC | 3.00 | 8.00 |
| 40 Vic Power | 3.00 | 8.00 |
| 41 Charley Lau | 3.00 | 8.00 |
| 42 Stan Williams | 3.00 | 8.00 |
| 43 C.Stengel/G.Woodling | 8.00 | 20.00 |
| 44 Terry Fox | 1.50 | 4.00 |
| 45 Bob Aspromonte | 1.50 | 4.00 |
| 46 Tommie Aaron RC | 3.00 | 8.00 |
| 47 Don Lock RC | 1.50 | 4.00 |
| 48 Birdie Tebbetts MG | 3.00 | 8.00 |
| 49 Dal Maxvill RC | 3.00 | 8.00 |
| 50 Billy Pierce | 3.00 | 8.00 |
| 51 George Alusik | 1.50 | 4.00 |
| 52 Chuck Schilling | 1.50 | 4.00 |
| 53 Joe Moeller RC | 3.00 | 8.00 |
| 54A Dave DeBusschere 62 | 6.00 | 15.00 |
| 54B Dave DeBusschere 63 RC | 3.00 | 8.00 |
| 55 Bill Virdon | 3.00 | 8.00 |
| 56 Dennis Bennett RC | 1.50 | 4.00 |
| 57 Billy Moran | 1.50 | 4.00 |
| 58 Bob Will | 1.50 | 4.00 |
| 59 Craig Anderson | 1.50 | 4.00 |
| 60 Elston Howard | 3.00 | 8.00 |
| 61 Ernie Bowman | 1.50 | 4.00 |
| 62 Bob Hendley | 1.50 | 4.00 |
| 63 Cincinnati Reds TC | 3.00 | 8.00 |
| 64 Dick McAuliffe | 3.00 | 8.00 |
| 65 Jackie Brandt | 1.50 | 4.00 |
| 66 Mike Joyce RC | 1.50 | 4.00 |
| 67 Ed Charles | 1.50 | 4.00 |
| 68 G.Hodges/D.Snider | 10.00 | 25.00 |
| 69 Bud Zipfel RC | 1.50 | 4.00 |
| 70 Jim O'Toole | 3.00 | 8.00 |
| 71 Bobby Wine RC | 3.00 | 8.00 |
| 72 Johnny Romano | 1.50 | 4.00 |
| 73 Bobby Bragan MG RC | 3.00 | 8.00 |
| 74 Denny Lemaster RC | 1.50 | 4.00 |
| 75 Bob Allison | 3.00 | 8.00 |
| 76 Earl Wilson | 3.00 | 8.00 |
| 77 Al Spangler | 1.50 | 4.00 |
| 78 Marv Throneberry | 3.00 | 8.00 |
| 79 Checklist 1 | 5.00 | 12.00 |
| 80 Jim Gilliam | 3.00 | 8.00 |
| 81 Jim Schaffer | 1.50 | 4.00 |
| 82 Ed Rakow | 1.50 | 4.00 |
| 83 Charley James | 1.50 | 4.00 |
| 84 Ron Kline | 1.50 | 4.00 |
| 85 Tom Haller | 3.00 | 8.00 |
| 86 Charley Maxwell | 3.00 | 8.00 |
| 87 Bob Veale | 3.00 | 8.00 |
| 88 Ron Hansen | 1.50 | 4.00 |
| 89 Dick Stigman | 1.50 | 4.00 |
| 90 Gordy Coleman | 3.00 | 8.00 |
| 91 Dallas Green | 3.00 | 8.00 |
| 92 Hector Lopez | 3.00 | 8.00 |
| 93 Galen Cisco | 1.50 | 4.00 |
| 94 Bob Schmidt | 1.50 | 4.00 |
| 95 Larry Jackson | 1.50 | 4.00 |
| 96 Lou Clinton | 1.50 | 4.00 |
| 97 Bob Duliba | 1.50 | 4.00 |
| 98 George Thomas | 1.50 | 4.00 |
| 99 Jim Umbricht | 1.50 | 4.00 |
| 100 Joe Cunningham | 1.50 | 4.00 |
| 101 Joe Gibbon | 1.50 | 4.00 |
| 102A Checklist 2 Red/Yellow | 5.00 | 12.00 |
| 102B Checklist 2 White/Red | 12.00 | 12.00 |
| 103 Chuck Essegian | 1.50 | 4.00 |
| 104 Lew Krausse RC | 1.50 | 4.00 |
| 105 Ron Fairly | 3.00 | 8.00 |
| 106 Bobby Bolin | 1.50 | 4.00 |
| 107 Jim Hickman | 3.00 | 8.00 |
| 108 Hoyt Wilhelm | 4.00 | 10.00 |
| 109 Lee Maye | 1.50 | 4.00 |
| 110 Rich Rollins | 3.00 | 8.00 |
| 111 Al Jackson | 1.50 | 4.00 |
| 112 Dick Brown | 1.50 | 4.00 |
| 113 Don Landrum UER | 1.50 | 4.00 |
| 114 Dan Osinski RC | 1.50 | 4.00 |
| 115 Carl Yastrzemski | 15.00 | 40.00 |
| 116 Jim Brosnan | 3.00 | 8.00 |
| 117 Jacke Davis | 1.50 | 4.00 |
| 118 Sherm Lollar | 1.50 | 4.00 |
| 119 Bob Lillis | 1.50 | 4.00 |
| 120 Roger Maris | 40.00 | 80.00 |
| 121 Jim Hannan RC | 1.50 | 4.00 |
| 122 Julio Gotay | 1.50 | 4.00 |
| 123 Frank Howard | 3.00 | 8.00 |
| 124 Dick Howser | 3.00 | 8.00 |
| 125 Robin Roberts | 6.00 | 15.00 |
| 126 Bob Uecker | 6.00 | 15.00 |
| 127 Bill Tuttle | 1.50 | 4.00 |
| 128 Matty Alou | 3.00 | 8.00 |
| 129 Gary Bell | 1.50 | 4.00 |
| 130 Dick Groat | 3.00 | 8.00 |
| 131 Washington Senators TC | 3.00 | 8.00 |
| 132 Jack Hamilton | 1.50 | 4.00 |
| 133 Gene Freese | 1.50 | 4.00 |
| 134 Bob Scheffing MG | 1.50 | 4.00 |
| 135 Richie Ashburn | 8.00 | 20.00 |
| 136 Ike Delock | 1.50 | 4.00 |
| 137 Mack Jones | 1.50 | 4.00 |
| 138 W.Mays/S.Musial | 40.00 | 80.00 |
| 139 Earl Averill Jr. | 1.50 | 4.00 |
| 140 Frank Lary | 3.00 | 8.00 |
| 141 Manny Mota RC | 3.00 | 8.00 |
| 142 Whitey Ford WS1 | 4.00 | 10.00 |
| 143 Jack Sanford WS2 | 3.00 | 8.00 |
| 144 Roger Maris WS3 | 6.00 | 15.00 |
| 145 Chuck Hiller WS4 | 3.00 | 8.00 |
| 146 Tom Tresh WS5 | 3.00 | 8.00 |
| 147 Billy Pierce WS6 | 3.00 | 8.00 |
| 148 Ralph Terry WS7 | 3.00 | 8.00 |
| 149 Marv Breeding | 1.50 | 4.00 |
| 150 Johnny Podres | 3.00 | 8.00 |
| 151 Pittsburgh Pirates TC | 3.00 | 8.00 |
| 152 Ron Nischwitz | 1.50 | 4.00 |
| 153 Hal Smith | 1.50 | 4.00 |
| 154 Walter Alston MG | 3.00 | 8.00 |
| 155 Bill Stafford | 1.50 | 4.00 |
| 156 Roy McMillan | 3.00 | 8.00 |
| 157 Diego Segui RC | 3.00 | 8.00 |
| 158 Tommy Harper RC | 3.00 | 8.00 |
| 159 Jim Pagliaroni | 1.50 | 4.00 |
| 160 Juan Pizarro | 1.50 | 4.00 |
| 161 Frank Torre | 3.00 | 8.00 |
| 162 Minnesota Twins TC | 3.00 | 8.00 |
| 163 Don Larsen | 3.00 | 8.00 |
| 164 Bubba Morton | 1.50 | 4.00 |
| 165 Jim Kaat | 3.00 | 8.00 |
| 166 Johnny Keane MG | 1.50 | 4.00 |
| 167 Jim Fregosi | 3.00 | 8.00 |
| 168 Russ Nixon | 1.50 | 4.00 |
| 169 Gaylord Perry | 10.00 | 25.00 |
| 170 Joe Adcock | 3.00 | 8.00 |
| 171 Steve Hamilton RC | 1.50 | 4.00 |
| 172 Gene Oliver | 1.50 | 4.00 |
| 173 Tresh/Mantle/Richardson | 75.00 | 150.00 |
| 174 Larry Burright | 1.50 | 4.00 |
| 175 Bob Buhl | 3.00 | 8.00 |
| 176 Jim King | 1.50 | 4.00 |
| 177 Bubba Phillips | 1.50 | 4.00 |
| 178 Johnny Edwards | 1.50 | 4.00 |
| 179 Ron Piche | 1.50 | 4.00 |
| 180 Bill Skowron | 3.00 | 8.00 |
| 181 Sammy Esposito | 1.50 | 4.00 |
| 182 Albie Pearson | 3.00 | 8.00 |
| 183 Joe Pepitone | 3.00 | 8.00 |
| 184 Vern Law | 3.00 | 8.00 |
| 185 Chuck Hiller | 1.50 | 4.00 |
| 186 Jerry Zimmerman | 1.50 | 4.00 |
| 187 Willie Kirkland | 1.50 | 4.00 |
| 188 Eddie Bressoud | 1.50 | 4.00 |
| 189 Dave Giusti | 3.00 | 8.00 |
| 190 Minnie Minoso | 5.00 | 12.00 |
| 191 Checklist 3 | 5.00 | 12.00 |
| 192 Clay Dalrymple | 1.50 | 4.00 |
| 193 Andre Rodgers | 1.50 | 4.00 |
| 194 Joe Nuxhall | 3.00 | 8.00 |
| 195 Manny Jimenez | 1.50 | 4.00 |
| 196 Doug Camilli | 1.50 | 4.00 |
| 197 Roger Craig | 3.00 | 8.00 |
| 198 Lenny Green | 2.00 | 5.00 |
| 199 Joe Amalfitano | 2.00 | 5.00 |
| 200 Mickey Mantle | 300.00 | 600.00 |
| 201 Cecil Butler | 2.00 | 5.00 |
| 202 Boston Red Sox TC | 3.00 | 8.00 |
| 203 Chico Cardenas | 2.00 | 5.00 |
| 204 Don Nottebart | 2.00 | 5.00 |
| 205 Luis Aparicio | 6.00 | 15.00 |
| 206 Ray Washburn | 2.00 | 5.00 |
| 207 Ken Hunt | 2.00 | 5.00 |
| 208 Rookie Stars | 2.00 | 5.00 |
| 209 Hobie Landrith | 2.00 | 5.00 |
| 210 Sandy Koufax | 75.00 | 150.00 |
| 211 Fred Whitfield RC | 2.00 | 5.00 |
| 212 Glen Hobbie | 2.00 | 5.00 |
| 213 Billy Hitchcock MG | 2.00 | 5.00 |
| 214 Orlando Pena | 2.00 | 5.00 |
| 215 Bob Skinner | 3.00 | 8.00 |
| 216 Gene Conley | 2.00 | 5.00 |
| 217 Joe Christopher | 2.00 | 5.00 |
| 218 Lary/Mossi/Bunning | 2.00 | 5.00 |
| 219 Chuck Cottier | 2.00 | 5.00 |
| 220 Camilo Pascual | 3.00 | 8.00 |
| 221 Cookie Rojas RC | 3.00 | 8.00 |
| 222 Chicago Cubs TC | 3.00 | 8.00 |
| 223 Eddie Fisher | 2.00 | 5.00 |
| 224 Mike Roarke | 2.00 | 5.00 |
| 225 Joey Jay | 3.00 | 8.00 |
| 226 Julian Javier | 3.00 | 8.00 |
| 227 Jim Grant | 3.00 | 8.00 |
| 228 Tony Oliva LL | 20.00 | 50.00 |
| 229 Willie Davis | 3.00 | 8.00 |
| 230 Pete Runnels | 2.00 | 5.00 |
| 231 Eli Grba UER | 2.00 | 5.00 |
| 232 Frank Malzone | 2.00 | 5.00 |
| 233 Casey Stengel MG | 8.00 | 20.00 |
| 234 Dave Nicholson | 2.00 | 5.00 |
| 235 Billy O'Dell | 2.00 | 5.00 |
| 236 Bill Bryan RC | 2.00 | 5.00 |
| 237 Jim Coates | 3.00 | 8.00 |
| 238 Lou Johnson | 2.00 | 5.00 |
| 239 Harvey Haddix | 3.00 | 8.00 |
| 240 Rocky Colavito | 6.00 | 15.00 |
| 241 Billy Smith RC | 2.00 | 5.00 |
| 242 E.Banks/H.Aaron | 30.00 | 60.00 |
| 243 Don Leppert | 2.00 | 5.00 |
| 244 John Tsitouris | 2.00 | 5.00 |
| 245 Gil Hodges | 8.00 | 20.00 |
| 246 Lee Stange | 2.00 | 5.00 |
| 247 New York Yankees TC | 20.00 | 50.00 |
| 248 Tito Francona | 2.00 | 5.00 |
| 249 Leo Burke RC | 2.00 | 5.00 |
| 250 Stan Musial | 50.00 | 100.00 |
| 251 Jack Lamabe | 2.00 | 5.00 |
| 252 Ron Santo | 4.00 | 10.00 |
| 253 Rookie Stars | 2.00 | 5.00 |
| 254 Mike Hershberger | 2.00 | 5.00 |
| 255 Bob Shaw | 2.00 | 5.00 |

| # | Card | Low | High |
|---|---|---|---|
| 256 | Jerry Lumpe | 2.00 | 5.00 |
| 257 | Hank Aguirre | 2.00 | 5.00 |
| 258 | Alvin Dark MG | 3.00 | 8.00 |
| 259 | Johnny Logan | 2.00 | 8.00 |
| 260 | Jim Gentile | 3.00 | 8.00 |
| 261 | Bob Miller | 2.00 | 5.00 |
| 262 | Ellis Burton | 2.00 | 5.00 |
| 263 | Dave Stenhouse | 2.00 | 5.00 |
| 264 | Phil Linz | 2.00 | 5.00 |
| 265 | Vada Pinson | 3.00 | 8.00 |
| 266 | Bob Allen | 2.00 | 5.00 |
| 267 | Carl Sawatski | 2.00 | 5.00 |
| 268 | Don Demeter | 2.00 | 5.00 |
| 269 | Don Mincher | 2.00 | 5.00 |
| 270 | Felipe Alou | 3.00 | 8.00 |
| 271 | Dean Stone | 2.00 | 5.00 |
| 272 | Danny Murphy | 2.00 | 5.00 |
| 273 | Sammy Taylor | 2.00 | 5.00 |
| 274 | Checklist 4 | 5.00 | 12.00 |
| 275 | Eddie Mathews | 12.50 | 30.00 |
| 276 | Barry Shetrone | 2.00 | 5.00 |
| 277 | Dick Farrell | 2.00 | 5.00 |
| 278 | Chico Fernandez | 2.00 | 5.00 |
| 279 | Wally Moon | 3.00 | 8.00 |
| 280 | Bob (Buck) Rodgers | 2.00 | 5.00 |
| 281 | Tom Sturdivant | 2.00 | 5.00 |
| 282 | Bobby Del Greco | 2.00 | 5.00 |
| 283 | Roy Sievers | 3.00 | 8.00 |
| 284 | Dave Sisler | 2.00 | 5.00 |
| 285 | Dick Stuart | 3.00 | 8.00 |
| 286 | Stu Miller | 3.00 | 8.00 |
| 287 | Dick Bertell | 2.00 | 5.00 |
| 288 | Chicago White Sox TC | 4.00 | 10.00 |
| 289 | Hal Brown | 2.00 | 5.00 |
| 290 | Bill White | 3.00 | 8.00 |
| 291 | Don Rudolph | 2.00 | 5.00 |
| 292 | Pumpsie Green | 3.00 | 8.00 |
| 293 | Bill Pleis | 2.00 | 5.00 |
| 294 | Bill Rigney MG | 2.00 | 5.00 |
| 295 | Ed Roebuck | 2.00 | 5.00 |
| 296 | Doc Edwards | 2.00 | 5.00 |
| 297 | Jim Golden | 2.00 | 5.00 |
| 298 | Don Dillard | 2.00 | 5.00 |
| 299 | Rookie Stars | 3.00 | 8.00 |
| 300 | Willie Mays | 75.00 | 150.00 |
| 301 | Bill Fischer | 2.00 | 5.00 |
| 302 | Whitey Herzog | 2.00 | 5.00 |
| 303 | Earl Francis | 2.00 | 5.00 |
| 304 | Harry Bright | 2.00 | 5.00 |
| 305 | Don Hoak | 2.00 | 5.00 |
| 306 | E. Battey/E. Howard | 4.00 | 10.00 |
| 307 | Chet Nichols | 2.00 | 5.00 |
| 308 | Camilo Carreon | 2.00 | 5.00 |
| 309 | Jim Brewer | 2.00 | 5.00 |
| 310 | Tommy Davis | 3.00 | 8.00 |
| 311 | Joe McClain | 2.00 | 5.00 |
| 312 | Houston Colts TC | 10.00 | 25.00 |
| 313 | Ernie Broglio | 2.00 | 5.00 |
| 314 | John Goryl | 2.00 | 5.00 |
| 315 | Ralph Terry | 3.00 | 8.00 |
| 316 | Norm Sherry | 2.00 | 5.00 |
| 317 | Sam McDowell | 3.00 | 8.00 |
| 318 | Gene Mauch MG | 3.00 | 8.00 |
| 319 | Joe Gaines | 2.00 | 5.00 |
| 320 | Warren Spahn | 30.00 | 60.00 |
| 321 | Gino Cimoli | 2.00 | 5.00 |
| 322 | Bob Turley | 6.00 | 15.00 |
| 323 | Bill Mazeroski | 6.00 | 15.00 |
| 324 | Vic Davalillo RC | 3.00 | 8.00 |
| 325 | Jack Sanford | 2.00 | 5.00 |
| 326 | Hank Foiles | 2.00 | 5.00 |
| 327 | Paul Foytack | 2.00 | 5.00 |
| 328 | Dick Williams | 3.00 | 8.00 |
| 329 | Lindy McDaniel | 3.00 | 8.00 |
| 330 | Chuck Hinton | 3.00 | 8.00 |
| 331 | Stafford/Pierce | 3.00 | 8.00 |
| 332 | Joel Horlen | 3.00 | 8.00 |
| 333 | Carl Warwick | 2.00 | 5.00 |
| 334 | Wynn Hawkins | 2.00 | 5.00 |
| 335 | Leon Wagner | 2.00 | 5.00 |
| 336 | Ed Bauta | 2.00 | 5.00 |
| 337 | Los Angeles Dodgers TC | 10.00 | 25.00 |
| 338 | Russ Kemmerer | 2.00 | 5.00 |
| 339 | Ted Bowsfield | 2.00 | 5.00 |
| 340 | Yogi Berra P/CO | 50.00 | 100.00 |
| 341 | Jack Baldschun | 2.00 | 5.00 |
| 342 | Gene Woodling | 3.00 | 8.00 |
| 343 | Johnny Pesky MG | 3.00 | 8.00 |
| 344 | Don Schwall | 2.00 | 5.00 |
| 345 | Brooks Robinson | 30.00 | 60.00 |
| 346 | Billy Hoeft | 2.00 | 5.00 |
| 347 | Joe Torre | 6.00 | 15.00 |
| 348 | Vic Wertz | 3.00 | 8.00 |
| 349 | Zoilo Versalles | 3.00 | 8.00 |
| 350 | Bob Purkey | 2.00 | 5.00 |
| 351 | Al Luplow | 2.00 | 5.00 |
| 352 | Ken Johnson | 2.00 | 5.00 |
| 353 | Billy Williams | 12.50 | 30.00 |
| 354 | Dom Zanni | 2.00 | 5.00 |
| 355 | Dean Chance | 2.00 | 5.00 |
| 356 | John Schaive | 2.00 | 5.00 |
| 357 | George Altman | 2.00 | 5.00 |
| 358 | Milt Pappas | 3.00 | 8.00 |
| 359 | Haywood Sullivan | 3.00 | 8.00 |
| 360 | Don Drysdale | 30.00 | 60.00 |
| 361 | Clete Boyer | 3.00 | 8.00 |
| 362 | Checklist 5 | 5.00 | 12.00 |
| 363 | Dick Radatz | 3.00 | 8.00 |
| 364 | Howie Goss | 2.00 | 5.00 |
| 365 | Jim Bunning | 8.00 | 20.00 |
| 366 | Tony Taylor | 3.00 | 8.00 |
| 367 | Tony Cloninger | 2.00 | 5.00 |
| 368 | Ed Bailey | 2.00 | 5.00 |
| 369 | Jim Lemon | 2.00 | 5.00 |
| 370 | Dick Donovan | 2.00 | 5.00 |
| 371 | Rod Kanehl | 3.00 | 8.00 |
| 372 | Don Lee | 2.00 | 5.00 |
| 373 | Jim Campbell RC | 2.00 | 5.00 |
| 374 | Claude Osteen | 3.00 | 8.00 |
| 375 | Ken Boyer | 6.00 | 15.00 |
| 376 | John Wyatt RC | 2.00 | 5.00 |
| 377 | Baltimore Orioles TC | 4.00 | 10.00 |
| 378 | Bill Henry | 2.00 | 5.00 |
| 379 | Bob Anderson | 2.00 | 5.00 |
| 380 | Ernie Banks UER | 50.00 | 100.00 |
| 381 | Frank Baumann | 2.00 | 5.00 |
| 382 | Ralph Houk MG | 4.00 | 10.00 |
| 383 | Pete Richert | 2.00 | 5.00 |
| 384 | Bob Tillman | 2.00 | 5.00 |
| 385 | Art Mahaffey | 2.00 | 5.00 |
| 386 | Rookie Stars | 2.00 | 5.00 |
| 387 | Al McBean | 2.00 | 5.00 |
| 388 | Jim Davenport | 3.00 | 8.00 |
| 389 | Frank Sullivan | 2.00 | 5.00 |
| 390 | Hank Aaron | 100.00 | 200.00 |
| 391 | Bill Dailey RC | 2.00 | 5.00 |
| 392 | Romano/Francona | 2.00 | 5.00 |
| 393 | Ken MacKenzie | 3.00 | 8.00 |
| 394 | Tim McCarver | 6.00 | 15.00 |
| 395 | Don McMahon | 2.00 | 5.00 |
| 396 | Joe Koppe | 2.00 | 5.00 |
| 397 | Kansas City Athletics TC | 4.00 | 10.00 |
| 398 | Boog Powell | 10.00 | 25.00 |
| 399 | Dick Ellsworth | 2.00 | 5.00 |
| 400 | Frank Robinson | 30.00 | 60.00 |
| 401 | Jim Bouton | 6.00 | 15.00 |
| 402 | Mickey Vernon MG | 3.00 | 8.00 |
| 403 | Ron Perranoski | 3.00 | 8.00 |
| 404 | Bob Oldis | 2.00 | 5.00 |
| 405 | Floyd Robinson | 2.00 | 5.00 |
| 406 | Howie Koplitz | 2.00 | 5.00 |
| 407 | Rookie Stars | 3.00 | 8.00 |
| 408 | Billy Gardner | 2.00 | 5.00 |
| 409 | Roy Face | 3.00 | 8.00 |
| 410 | Earl Battey | 2.00 | 5.00 |
| 411 | Jim Constable | 2.00 | 5.00 |
| 412 | Pospho/Drysdale/Koufax | 20.00 | 50.00 |
| 413 | Jerry Walker | 2.00 | 5.00 |
| 414 | Ty Cline | 2.00 | 5.00 |
| 415 | Bob Gibson | 30.00 | 60.00 |
| 416 | Alex Grammas | 2.00 | 5.00 |
| 417 | San Francisco Giants TC | 4.00 | 10.00 |
| 418 | John Orsino | 2.00 | 5.00 |
| 419 | Tracy Stallard | 2.00 | 5.00 |
| 420 | Bobby Richardson | 6.00 | 15.00 |
| 421 | Tom Morgan | 2.00 | 5.00 |
| 422 | Fred Hutchinson MG | 3.00 | 8.00 |
| 423 | Ed Hobaugh | 2.00 | 5.00 |
| 424 | Charlie Smith | 2.00 | 5.00 |
| 425 | Smoky Burgess | 3.00 | 8.00 |
| 426 | Barry Latman | 2.00 | 5.00 |
| 427 | Bernie Allen | 2.00 | 5.00 |
| 428 | Carl Boles RC | 2.00 | 5.00 |
| 429 | Lew Burdette | 3.00 | 8.00 |
| 430 | Norm Siebern | 2.00 | 5.00 |
| 431A | Checklist 6 White/Red | 5.00 | 12.00 |
| 431B | Checklist 6 Black/Orange | 12.50 | 30.00 |
| 432 | Roman Mejias | 2.00 | 5.00 |
| 433 | Denis Menke | 2.00 | 5.00 |
| 434 | John Callison | 3.00 | 8.00 |
| 435 | Woody Held | 2.00 | 5.00 |
| 436 | Tim Harkness | 3.00 | 8.00 |
| 437 | Bill Bruton | 2.00 | 5.00 |
| 438 | Wes Stock | 2.00 | 5.00 |
| 439 | Don Zimmer | 3.00 | 8.00 |
| 440 | Juan Marichal | 12.50 | 30.00 |
| 441 | Lee Thomas | 3.00 | 8.00 |
| 442 | J.C. Hartman RC | 2.00 | 5.00 |
| 443 | Jimmy Piersall | 3.00 | 8.00 |
| 444 | Jim Maloney | 3.00 | 8.00 |
| 445 | Norm Cash | 4.00 | 10.00 |
| 446 | Whitey Ford | 30.00 | 60.00 |
| 447 | Felix Mantilla | 10.00 | 25.00 |
| 448 | Jack Kralick | 10.00 | 25.00 |
| 449 | Jose Tartabull | 10.00 | 25.00 |
| 450 | Bob Friend | 12.50 | 30.00 |
| 451 | Cleveland Indians TC | 15.00 | 40.00 |
| 452 | Barney Schultz | 10.00 | 25.00 |
| 453 | Jake Wood | 10.00 | 25.00 |
| 454A | Art Fowler White | 10.00 | 25.00 |
| 454B | Art Fowler Orange | 12.50 | 30.00 |
| 455 | Ruben Amaro | 10.00 | 25.00 |
| 456 | Jim Coker | 10.00 | 25.00 |
| 457 | Tex Clevenger | 10.00 | 25.00 |
| 458 | Al Lopez MG | 12.50 | 30.00 |
| 459 | Dick LeMay | 10.00 | 25.00 |
| 460 | Del Crandall | 12.50 | 30.00 |
| 461 | Norm Bass | 10.00 | 25.00 |
| 462 | Wally Post | 10.00 | 25.00 |
| 463 | Joe Schaffernoth | 10.00 | 25.00 |
| 464 | Ken Aspromonte | 10.00 | 25.00 |
| 465 | Chuck Estrada | 10.00 | 25.00 |
| 466 | Bill Freehan SP RC | 30.00 | 60.00 |
| 467 | Phil Ortega | 10.00 | 25.00 |
| 468 | Carroll Hardy | 12.50 | 30.00 |
| 469 | Jay Hook | 12.50 | 30.00 |
| 470 | Tom Tresh SP | 30.00 | 60.00 |
| 471 | Ken Retzer | 10.00 | 25.00 |
| 472 | Lou Brock | 40.00 | 80.00 |
| 473 | New York Mets TC | 50.00 | 100.00 |
| 474 | Jack Fisher | 10.00 | 25.00 |
| 475 | Gus Triandos | 12.50 | 30.00 |
| 476 | Frank Funk | 10.00 | 25.00 |
| 477 | Donn Clendenon | 12.50 | 30.00 |
| 478 | Paul Brown | 10.00 | 25.00 |
| 479 | Ed Brinkman RC | 10.00 | 25.00 |
| 480 | Bill Monbouquette | 10.00 | 25.00 |
| 481 | Bob Taylor | 10.00 | 25.00 |
| 482 | Felix Torres | 10.00 | 25.00 |
| 483 | Jim Owens UER | 10.00 | 25.00 |
| 484 | Dale Long SP | 12.50 | 30.00 |
| 485 | Jim Landis | 10.00 | 25.00 |
| 486 | Ray Sadecki | 10.00 | 25.00 |
| 487 | John Roseboro | 12.50 | 30.00 |
| 488 | Jerry Adair | 10.00 | 25.00 |
| 489 | Paul Toth RC | 10.00 | 25.00 |
| 490 | Willie McCovey | 50.00 | 100.00 |
| 491 | Harry Craft MG | 10.00 | 25.00 |
| 492 | Dave Wickersham | 10.00 | 25.00 |
| 493 | Walt Bond | 10.00 | 25.00 |
| 494 | Phil Regan | 10.00 | 25.00 |
| 495 | Frank Thomas SP | 12.50 | 30.00 |
| 496 | Rookie Stars | 12.50 | 30.00 |
| 497 | Bennie Daniels | 10.00 | 25.00 |
| 498 | Eddie Kasko | 10.00 | 25.00 |
| 499 | J.C. Martin | 10.00 | 25.00 |
| 500 | Harmon Killebrew SP | 75.00 | 150.00 |
| 501 | Joe Azcue | 10.00 | 25.00 |
| 502 | Daryl Spencer | 10.00 | 25.00 |
| 503 | Milwaukee Braves TC | 15.00 | 40.00 |
| 504 | Bob Johnson | 10.00 | 25.00 |
| 505 | Curt Flood | 15.00 | 40.00 |
| 506 | Gene Green | 10.00 | 25.00 |
| 507 | Roland Sheldon | 12.50 | 30.00 |
| 508 | Ted Savage | 10.00 | 25.00 |
| 509A | Checklist 7 Centered | 10.00 | 25.00 |
| 509B | Checklist 7 Right | 12.50 | 30.00 |
| 510 | Ken McBride | 10.00 | 25.00 |
| 511 | Charlie Neal | 12.50 | 30.00 |
| 512 | Cal McLish | 10.00 | 25.00 |
| 513 | Gary Geiger | 10.00 | 25.00 |
| 514 | Larry Osborne | 10.00 | 25.00 |
| 515 | Don Elston | 10.00 | 25.00 |
| 516 | Purnell Goldy RC | 10.00 | 25.00 |

| Card | Low | High |
|---|---|---|
| ❑ 517 Hal Woodeshick | 10.00 | 25.00 |
| ❑ 518 Don Blasingame | 10.00 | 25.00 |
| ❑ 519 Claude Raymond RC | 10.00 | 25.00 |
| ❑ 520 Orlando Cepeda | 15.00 | 40.00 |
| ❑ 521 Dan Pfister | 10.00 | 25.00 |
| ❑ 522 Rookie Stars | 12.50 | 30.00 |
| ❑ 523 Bill Kunkel | 6.00 | 15.00 |
| ❑ 524 St. Louis Cardinals TC | 12.50 | 30.00 |
| ❑ 525 Nellie Fox | 20.00 | 50.00 |
| ❑ 526 Dick Hall | 6.00 | 15.00 |
| ❑ 527 Ed Sadowski | 6.00 | 15.00 |
| ❑ 528 Carl Willey | 6.00 | 15.00 |
| ❑ 529 Wes Covington | 6.00 | 15.00 |
| ❑ 530 Don Mossi | 8.00 | 20.00 |
| ❑ 531 Sam Mele MG | 6.00 | 15.00 |
| ❑ 532 Steve Boros | 6.00 | 15.00 |
| ❑ 533 Bobby Shantz | 8.00 | 20.00 |
| ❑ 534 Ken Walters | 6.00 | 15.00 |
| ❑ 535 Jim Perry | 8.00 | 20.00 |
| ❑ 536 Norm Larker | 6.00 | 15.00 |
| ❑ 537 Pete Rose RC | 500.00 | 1000.00 |
| ❑ 538 George Brunet | 6.00 | 15.00 |
| ❑ 539 Wayne Causey | 6.00 | 15.00 |
| ❑ 540 Roberto Clemente | 125.00 | 250.00 |
| ❑ 541 Ron Moeller | 6.00 | 15.00 |
| ❑ 542 Lou Klimchock | 6.00 | 15.00 |
| ❑ 543 Russ Snyder | 6.00 | 15.00 |
| ❑ 544 Rusty Staub RC | 20.00 | 50.00 |
| ❑ 545 Jose Pagan | 6.00 | 15.00 |
| ❑ 546 Hal Reniff | 8.00 | 20.00 |
| ❑ 547 Gus Bell | 6.00 | 15.00 |
| ❑ 548 Tom Satriano RC | 6.00 | 15.00 |
| ❑ 549 Rookie Stars | 6.00 | 15.00 |
| ❑ 550 Duke Snider | 40.00 | 80.00 |
| ❑ 551 Billy Klaus | 6.00 | 15.00 |
| ❑ 552 Detroit Tigers TC | 20.00 | 50.00 |
| ❑ 553 Willie Stargell RC | 60.00 | 120.00 |
| ❑ 554 Hank Fischer RC | 6.00 | 15.00 |
| ❑ 555 John Blanchard | 8.00 | 20.00 |
| ❑ 556 Al Worthington | 6.00 | 15.00 |
| ❑ 557 Cuno Barragan | 6.00 | 15.00 |
| ❑ 558 Ron Hunt RC | 8.00 | 20.00 |
| ❑ 559 Danny Murtaugh MG | 6.00 | 15.00 |
| ❑ 560 Ray Herbert | 6.00 | 15.00 |
| ❑ 561 Mike De La Hoz | 6.00 | 15.00 |
| ❑ 562 Dave McNally RC | 12.50 | 30.00 |
| ❑ 563 Mike McCormick | 6.00 | 15.00 |
| ❑ 564 George Banks RC | 6.00 | 15.00 |
| ❑ 565 Larry Sherry | 6.00 | 15.00 |
| ❑ 566 Cliff Cook | 6.00 | 15.00 |
| ❑ 567 Jim Duffalo | 6.00 | 15.00 |
| ❑ 568 Bob Sadowski | 6.00 | 15.00 |
| ❑ 569 Luis Arroyo | 8.00 | 20.00 |
| ❑ 570 Frank Bolling | 6.00 | 15.00 |
| ❑ 571 Johnny Klippstein | 6.00 | 15.00 |
| ❑ 572 Jack Spring | 6.00 | 15.00 |
| ❑ 573 Coot Veal | 6.00 | 15.00 |
| ❑ 574 Hal Kolstad | 6.00 | 15.00 |
| ❑ 575 Don Cardwell | 6.00 | 15.00 |
| ❑ 576 Johnny Temple | 12.50 | 30.00 |

## 1964 Topps

BRAVES

ED MATHEWS

| | | |
|---|---|---|
| ❑ COMPLETE SET (587) | 2750.00 | 3500.00 |
| ❑ COMMON CARD (1-196) | 1.25 | 3.00 |
| ❑ COMMON CARD (197-370) | 1.50 | 4.00 |
| ❑ COMMON CARD (371-522) | 3.00 | 8.00 |
| ❑ COMMON CARD (523-587) | 6.00 | 15.00 |
| ❑ WRAPPER (1-CENT) | 50.00 | 100.00 |
| ❑ WRAP.(1-CENT, REPEAT) | 60.00 | 120.00 |
| ❑ WRAPPER (5-CENT) | 12.50 | 30.00 |
| ❑ WRAPPER (5-CENT, COIN) | 15.00 | 40.00 |
| ❑ 1 Koufax/Ellis/Friend LL | 12.50 | 30.00 |
| ❑ 2 Peters/Pizarro/Pascual LL | 3.00 | 8.00 |
| ❑ 3 Koufax/Marichal/Spahn LL | 8.00 | 20.00 |

| Card | Low | High |
|---|---|---|
| ❑ 4 Ford/Pascual/Bouton LL | 3.00 | 8.00 |
| ❑ 5 Koufax/Malon/Drysdale LL | 6.00 | 15.00 |
| ❑ 6 Pascual/Bunning/Stigman LL | 3.00 | 8.00 |
| ❑ 7 Clemente/Groat/Aaron LL | 8.00 | 20.00 |
| ❑ 8 Yaz/Kaline/Rollins LL | 6.00 | 15.00 |
| ❑ 9 Aaron/McCov/Mays/Cep LL | 12.50 | 30.00 |
| ❑ 10 Killebrew/Stuart/Allison LL | 3.00 | 8.00 |
| ❑ 11 Aaron/Boyer/White LL | 6.00 | 15.00 |
| ❑ 12 Stuart/Kaline/Killebrew LL | 3.00 | 8.00 |
| ❑ 13 Hoyt Wilhelm | 5.00 | 12.00 |
| ❑ 14 D.Nen RC/N.Willhite RC | 1.25 | 3.00 |
| ❑ 15 Zoilo Versalles | 2.50 | 6.00 |
| ❑ 16 John Boozer | 1.25 | 3.00 |
| ❑ 17 Willie Kirkland | 1.25 | 3.00 |
| ❑ 18 Billy O'Dell | 1.25 | 3.00 |
| ❑ 19 Don Wert | 1.25 | 3.00 |
| ❑ 20 Bob Friend | 2.50 | 6.00 |
| ❑ 21 Yogi Berra MG | 15.00 | 40.00 |
| ❑ 22 Jerry Adair | 1.25 | 3.00 |
| ❑ 23 Chris Zachary RC | 1.25 | 3.00 |
| ❑ 24 Carl Sawatski | 1.25 | 3.00 |
| ❑ 25 Bill Monbouquette | 1.25 | 3.00 |
| ❑ 26 Gino Cimoli | 1.25 | 3.00 |
| ❑ 27 New York Mets TC | 3.00 | 8.00 |
| ❑ 28 Claude Osteen | 2.50 | 6.00 |
| ❑ 29 Lou Brock | 15.00 | 40.00 |
| ❑ 30 Ron Perranoski | 2.50 | 6.00 |
| ❑ 31 Dave Nicholson | 1.25 | 3.00 |
| ❑ 32 Dean Chance | 2.50 | 6.00 |
| ❑ 33 S.Ellis/M.Queen | 2.50 | 6.00 |
| ❑ 34 Jim Perry | 2.50 | 6.00 |
| ❑ 35 Eddie Mathews | 8.00 | 20.00 |
| ❑ 36 Hal Reniff | 1.25 | 3.00 |
| ❑ 37 Smoky Burgess | 2.50 | 6.00 |
| ❑ 38 Jim Wynn RC | 3.00 | 8.00 |
| ❑ 39 Hank Aguirre | 1.25 | 3.00 |
| ❑ 40 Dick Groat | 2.50 | 6.00 |
| ❑ 41 W.McCovey/L.Wagner | 3.00 | 8.00 |
| ❑ 42 Moe Drabowsky | 2.50 | 6.00 |
| ❑ 43 Roy Sievers | 2.50 | 6.00 |
| ❑ 44 Duke Carmel | 1.25 | 3.00 |
| ❑ 45 Milt Pappas | 2.50 | 6.00 |
| ❑ 46 Ed Brinkman | 1.25 | 3.00 |
| ❑ 47 J.Alou RC/R.Herbel | 2.50 | 6.00 |
| ❑ 48 Bob Perry RC | 1.25 | 3.00 |
| ❑ 49 Bill Henry | 1.25 | 3.00 |
| ❑ 50 Mickey Mantle | 250.00 | 500.00 |
| ❑ 51 Pete Richert | 1.25 | 3.00 |
| ❑ 52 Chuck Hinton | 1.25 | 3.00 |
| ❑ 53 Denis Menke | 1.25 | 3.00 |
| ❑ 54 Sam Mele MG | 1.25 | 3.00 |
| ❑ 55 Ernie Banks | 15.00 | 40.00 |
| ❑ 56 Hal Brown | 1.25 | 3.00 |
| ❑ 57 Tim Harkness | 2.50 | 6.00 |
| ❑ 58 Don Demeter | 2.50 | 6.00 |
| ❑ 59 Ernie Broglio | 1.25 | 3.00 |
| ❑ 60 Frank Malzone | 2.50 | 6.00 |
| ❑ 61 B.Rodgers/E.Sadowski | 2.50 | 6.00 |
| ❑ 62 Ted Savage | 1.25 | 3.00 |
| ❑ 63 John Orsino | 1.25 | 3.00 |
| ❑ 64 Ted Abernathy | 1.25 | 3.00 |
| ❑ 65 Felipe Alou | 2.50 | 6.00 |
| ❑ 66 Eddie Fisher | 1.25 | 3.00 |
| ❑ 67 Detroit Tigers TC | 2.50 | 6.00 |
| ❑ 68 Willie Davis | 2.50 | 6.00 |
| ❑ 69 Clete Boyer | 2.50 | 6.00 |
| ❑ 70 Joe Torre | 3.00 | 8.00 |
| ❑ 71 Jack Spring | 1.25 | 3.00 |
| ❑ 72 Chico Cardenas | 2.50 | 6.00 |
| ❑ 73 Jimmie Hall RC | 3.00 | 8.00 |
| ❑ 74 B.Priddy RC/T.Butters | 1.25 | 3.00 |
| ❑ 75 Wayne Causey | 1.25 | 3.00 |
| ❑ 76 Checklist 1 | 4.00 | 10.00 |
| ❑ 77 Jerry Walker | 1.25 | 3.00 |
| ❑ 78 Merritt Ranew | 1.25 | 3.00 |
| ❑ 79 Bob Heffner RC | 1.25 | 3.00 |
| ❑ 80 Vada Pinson | 3.00 | 8.00 |
| ❑ 81 N.Fox/H.Killebrew | 5.00 | 12.00 |
| ❑ 82 Jim Davenport | 2.50 | 6.00 |
| ❑ 83 Gus Triandos | 2.50 | 6.00 |
| ❑ 84 Carl Willey | 1.25 | 3.00 |
| ❑ 85 Pete Ward | 1.25 | 3.00 |
| ❑ 86 Al Downing | 2.50 | 6.00 |
| ❑ 87 St. Louis Cardinals TC | 2.50 | 6.00 |
| ❑ 88 John Roseboro | 2.50 | 6.00 |
| ❑ 89 Boog Powell | 5.00 | 12.00 |
| ❑ 90 Earl Battey | 1.25 | 3.00 |
| ❑ 91 Bob Bailey | 2.50 | 6.00 |

| Card | Low | High |
|---|---|---|
| ❑ 92 Steve Ridzik | 1.25 | 3.00 |
| ❑ 93 Gary Geiger | 1.25 | 3.00 |
| ❑ 94 J.Britton RC/L.Maxie RC | 1.25 | 3.00 |
| ❑ 95 George Altman | 1.25 | 3.00 |
| ❑ 96 Bob Buhl | 2.50 | 6.00 |
| ❑ 97 Jim Fregosi | 2.50 | 6.00 |
| ❑ 98 Bill Bruton | 1.25 | 3.00 |
| ❑ 99 Al Stanek RC | 1.25 | 3.00 |
| ❑ 100 Elston Howard | 2.50 | 6.00 |
| ❑ 101 Walt Alston MG | 3.00 | 8.00 |
| ❑ 102 Checklist 2 | 4.00 | 10.00 |
| ❑ 103 Curt Flood | 2.50 | 6.00 |
| ❑ 104 Art Mahaffey | 2.50 | 6.00 |
| ❑ 105 Woody Held | 1.25 | 3.00 |
| ❑ 106 Joe Nuxhall | 2.50 | 6.00 |
| ❑ 107 B.Howard RC/F.Kruetzer RC | 1.25 | 3.00 |
| ❑ 108 John Wyatt | 1.25 | 3.00 |
| ❑ 109 Rusty Staub | 2.50 | 6.00 |
| ❑ 110 Albie Pearson | 2.50 | 6.00 |
| ❑ 111 Don Elston | 1.25 | 3.00 |
| ❑ 112 Bob Tillman | 1.25 | 3.00 |
| ❑ 113 Grover Powell RC | 2.50 | 6.00 |
| ❑ 114 Don Lock | 1.25 | 3.00 |
| ❑ 115 Frank Bolling | 1.25 | 3.00 |
| ❑ 116 J.Ward RC/T.Oliva | 5.00 | 12.00 |
| ❑ 117 Earl Francis | 1.25 | 3.00 |
| ❑ 118 John Blanchard | 2.50 | 6.00 |
| ❑ 119 Gary Kolb RC | 1.25 | 3.00 |
| ❑ 120 Don Drysdale | 8.00 | 20.00 |
| ❑ 121 Pete Runnels | 2.50 | 6.00 |
| ❑ 122 Don McMahon | 1.25 | 3.00 |
| ❑ 123 Jose Pagan | 1.25 | 3.00 |
| ❑ 124 Orlando Pena | 1.25 | 3.00 |
| ❑ 125 Pete Rose UER | 125.00 | 250.00 |
| ❑ 126 Russ Snyder | 1.25 | 3.00 |
| ❑ 127 A.Gatewood RC/D.Simpson | 1.25 | 3.00 |
| ❑ 128 Mickey Lolich RC | 8.00 | 20.00 |
| ❑ 129 Amado Samuel | 1.25 | 3.00 |
| ❑ 130 Gary Peters | 2.50 | 6.00 |
| ❑ 131 Steve Boros | 1.25 | 3.00 |
| ❑ 132 Milwaukee Braves TC | 2.50 | 6.00 |
| ❑ 133 Jim Grant | 2.50 | 6.00 |
| ❑ 134 Don Zimmer | 2.50 | 6.00 |
| ❑ 135 Johnny Callison | 2.50 | 6.00 |
| ❑ 136 Sandy Koufax WS1 | 8.00 | 20.00 |
| ❑ 137 Willie Davis WS2 | 3.00 | 8.00 |
| ❑ 138 Ron Fairly WS3 | 3.00 | 8.00 |
| ❑ 139 Frank Howard WS4 | 3.00 | 8.00 |
| ❑ 140 Dodgers Celebrate WS | 3.00 | 8.00 |
| ❑ 141 Danny Murtaugh MG | 2.50 | 6.00 |
| ❑ 142 John Bateman | 1.25 | 3.00 |
| ❑ 143 Bubba Phillips | 1.25 | 3.00 |
| ❑ 144 Al Worthington | 1.25 | 3.00 |
| ❑ 145 Norm Siebern | 1.25 | 3.00 |
| ❑ 146 T.John RC/B.Chance RC | 12.50 | 30.00 |
| ❑ 147 Ray Sadecki | 1.25 | 3.00 |
| ❑ 148 J.C. Martin | 1.25 | 3.00 |
| ❑ 149 Paul Foytack | 1.25 | 3.00 |
| ❑ 150 Willie Mays | 60.00 | 120.00 |
| ❑ 151 Kansas City Athletics TC | 2.50 | 6.00 |
| ❑ 152 Denny Lemaster | 1.25 | 3.00 |
| ❑ 153 Dick Williams | 2.50 | 6.00 |
| ❑ 154 Dick Tracewski RC | 2.50 | 6.00 |
| ❑ 155 Duke Snider | 12.50 | 30.00 |
| ❑ 156 Bill Dailey | 1.25 | 3.00 |
| ❑ 157 Gene Mauch MG | 2.50 | 6.00 |
| ❑ 158 Ken Johnson | 1.25 | 3.00 |
| ❑ 159 Charlie Dees RC | 1.25 | 3.00 |
| ❑ 160 Ken Boyer | 2.50 | 6.00 |
| ❑ 161 Dave McNally | 2.50 | 6.00 |
| ❑ 162 D.Sisler/V.Pinson | 2.50 | 6.00 |
| ❑ 163 Donn Clendenon | 2.50 | 6.00 |
| ❑ 164 Bud Daley | 1.25 | 3.00 |
| ❑ 165 Jerry Lumpe | 1.25 | 3.00 |
| ❑ 166 Marty Keough | 1.25 | 3.00 |
| ❑ 167 M.Brumley RC/L.Piniella RC | 12.50 | 30.00 |
| ❑ 168 Al Weis | 1.25 | 3.00 |
| ❑ 169 Del Crandall | 2.50 | 6.00 |
| ❑ 170 Dick Radatz | 2.50 | 6.00 |
| ❑ 171 Ty Cline | 1.25 | 3.00 |
| ❑ 172 Cleveland Indians TC | 2.50 | 6.00 |
| ❑ 173 Ryne Duren | 2.50 | 6.00 |
| ❑ 174 Doc Edwards | 1.25 | 3.00 |
| ❑ 175 Billy Williams | 5.00 | 12.00 |
| ❑ 176 Tracy Stallard | 1.25 | 3.00 |
| ❑ 177 Harmon Killebrew | 8.00 | 20.00 |
| ❑ 178 Hank Bauer MG | 2.50 | 6.00 |
| ❑ 179 Carl Warwick | 1.25 | 3.00 |

|  |  | | |
|---|------|---|---|
| 180 | Tommy Davis | 2.50 | 6.00 |
| 181 | Dave Wickersham | 1.25 | 3.00 |
| 182 | C.Yastrzemski/C.Schilling | 6.00 | 15.00 |
| 183 | Ron Taylor | 1.25 | 3.00 |
| 184 | Al Luplow | 1.25 | 3.00 |
| 185 | Jim O'Toole | 2.50 | 6.00 |
| 186 | Roman Mejias | 1.25 | 3.00 |
| 187 | Ed Roebuck | 1.25 | 3.00 |
| 188 | Checklist 3 | 4.00 | 10.00 |
| 189 | Bob Hendley | 1.25 | 3.00 |
| 190 | Bobby Richardson | 3.00 | 8.00 |
| 191 | Clay Dalrymple | 2.50 | 6.00 |
| 192 | J.Boccabella RC/B.Cowan RC | 1.25 | 3.00 |
| 193 | Jerry Lynch | 1.25 | 3.00 |
| 194 | John Goryl | 1.25 | 3.00 |
| 195 | Floyd Robinson | 1.25 | 3.00 |
| 196 | Jim Gentile | 1.25 | 3.00 |
| 197 | Frank Lary | 2.50 | 6.00 |
| 198 | Len Gabrielson | 1.50 | 4.00 |
| 199 | Joe Azcue | 1.50 | 4.00 |
| 200 | Sandy Koufax | 60.00 | 120.00 |
| 201 | S.Bowens RC/W.Bunker RC | 2.50 | 6.00 |
| 202 | Galen Cisco | 2.50 | 6.00 |
| 203 | John Kennedy RC | 2.50 | 6.00 |
| 204 | Matty Alou | 2.50 | 6.00 |
| 205 | Nellie Fox | 5.00 | 12.00 |
| 206 | Steve Hamilton | 2.50 | 6.00 |
| 207 | Fred Hutchinson MG | 2.50 | 6.00 |
| 208 | Wes Covington | 2.50 | 6.00 |
| 209 | Bob Allen | 1.50 | 4.00 |
| 210 | Carl Yastrzemski | 15.00 | 40.00 |
| 211 | Jim Coker | 1.50 | 4.00 |
| 212 | Pete Lovrich | 1.50 | 4.00 |
| 213 | Los Angeles Angels TC | 2.50 | 6.00 |
| 214 | Ken McMullen | 2.50 | 6.00 |
| 215 | Ray Herbert | 1.50 | 4.00 |
| 216 | Mike de la Hoz | 1.50 | 4.00 |
| 217 | Jim King | 1.50 | 4.00 |
| 218 | Hank Fischer | 1.50 | 4.00 |
| 219 | A.Downing/J.Bouton | 2.50 | 6.00 |
| 220 | Dick Ellsworth | 2.50 | 6.00 |
| 221 | Bob Saverine | 1.50 | 4.00 |
| 222 | Billy Pierce | 2.50 | 6.00 |
| 223 | George Banks | 1.50 | 4.00 |
| 224 | Tommie Sisk | 1.50 | 4.00 |
| 225 | Roger Maris | 30.00 | 60.00 |
| 226 | J.Grote RC/L.Yellen RC | 2.50 | 6.00 |
| 227 | Barry Latman | 1.50 | 4.00 |
| 228 | Felix Mantilla | 1.50 | 4.00 |
| 229 | Charley Lau | 2.50 | 6.00 |
| 230 | Brooks Robinson | 15.00 | 40.00 |
| 231 | Dick Calmus RC | 1.50 | 4.00 |
| 232 | Al Lopez MG | 3.00 | 8.00 |
| 233 | Hal Smith | 1.50 | 4.00 |
| 234 | Gary Bell | 1.50 | 4.00 |
| 235 | Ron Hunt | 1.50 | 4.00 |
| 236 | Bill Faul | 1.50 | 4.00 |
| 237 | Chicago Cubs TC | 2.50 | 6.00 |
| 238 | Roy McMillan | 2.50 | 6.00 |
| 239 | Herm Starrette RC | 1.50 | 4.00 |
| 240 | Bill White | 2.50 | 6.00 |
| 241 | Jim Owens | 1.50 | 4.00 |
| 242 | Harvey Kuenn | 2.50 | 6.00 |
| 243 | R.Allen RC/J.Hernstein | 12.50 | 30.00 |
| 244 | Tony LaRussa RC | 12.50 | 30.00 |
| 245 | Dick Stigman | 1.50 | 4.00 |
| 246 | Manny Mota | 2.50 | 6.00 |
| 247 | Dave DeBusschere | 2.50 | 6.00 |
| 248 | Johnny Pesky MG | 2.50 | 6.00 |
| 249 | Doug Camilli | 1.50 | 4.00 |
| 250 | Al Kaline | 15.00 | 40.00 |
| 251 | Choo Choo Coleman | 2.50 | 6.00 |
| 252 | Ken Aspromonte | 1.50 | 4.00 |
| 253 | Wally Post | 2.50 | 6.00 |
| 254 | Don Hoak | 2.50 | 6.00 |
| 255 | Lee Thomas | 2.50 | 6.00 |
| 256 | Johnny Weekly | 1.50 | 4.00 |
| 257 | San Francisco Giants TC | 2.50 | 6.00 |
| 258 | Garry Roggenburk | 1.50 | 4.00 |
| 259 | Harry Bright | 1.50 | 4.00 |
| 260 | Frank Robinson | 15.00 | 40.00 |
| 261 | Jim Hannan | 1.50 | 4.00 |
| 262 | M.Shannon RC/H.Fanok | 3.00 | 8.00 |
| 263 | Chuck Estrada | 1.50 | 4.00 |
| 264 | Jim Landis | 1.50 | 4.00 |
| 265 | Jim Bunning | 5.00 | 12.00 |
| 266 | Gene Freese | 1.50 | 4.00 |
| 267 | Wilbur Wood RC | 2.50 | 6.00 |
| 268 | D.Murtaugh/B.Virdon | 2.50 | 6.00 |
| 269 | Ellis Burton | 1.50 | 4.00 |
| 270 | Rich Rollins | 2.50 | 6.00 |
| 271 | Bob Sadowski | 1.50 | 4.00 |
| 272 | Jake Wood | 1.50 | 4.00 |
| 273 | Mel Nelson | 1.50 | 4.00 |
| 274 | Checklist 4 | 4.00 | 10.00 |
| 275 | John Tsitouris | 1.50 | 4.00 |
| 276 | Jose Tartabull | 2.50 | 6.00 |
| 277 | Ken Retzer | 1.50 | 4.00 |
| 278 | Bobby Shantz | 2.50 | 6.00 |
| 279 | Joe Koppe | 1.50 | 4.00 |
| 280 | Juan Marichal | 6.00 | 15.00 |
| 281 | J.Gibbs/T.Metclaf RC | 2.50 | 6.00 |
| 282 | Bob Bruce | 1.50 | 4.00 |
| 283 | Tom McCraw RC | 1.50 | 4.00 |
| 284 | Dick Schofield | 1.50 | 4.00 |
| 285 | Robin Roberts | 6.00 | 15.00 |
| 286 | Don Landrum | 1.50 | 4.00 |
| 287 | T.Conig.RC/B.Spans.RC | 20.00 | 50.00 |
| 288 | Al Moran | 1.50 | 4.00 |
| 289 | Frank Funk | 1.50 | 4.00 |
| 290 | Bob Allison | 2.50 | 6.00 |
| 291 | Phil Ortega | 1.50 | 4.00 |
| 292 | Mike Roarke | 1.50 | 4.00 |
| 293 | Philadelphia Phillies TC | 2.50 | 6.00 |
| 294 | Ken L. Hunt | 1.50 | 4.00 |
| 295 | Roger Craig | 2.50 | 6.00 |
| 296 | Ed Kirkpatrick | 1.50 | 4.00 |
| 297 | Ken MacKenzie | 1.50 | 4.00 |
| 298 | Harry Craft MG | 1.50 | 4.00 |
| 299 | Bill Stafford | 1.50 | 4.00 |
| 300 | Hank Aaron | 50.00 | 100.00 |
| 301 | Larry Brown RC | 1.50 | 4.00 |
| 302 | Dan Pfister | 1.50 | 4.00 |
| 303 | Jim Campbell | 1.50 | 4.00 |
| 304 | Bob Johnson | 1.50 | 4.00 |
| 305 | Jack Lamabe | 1.50 | 4.00 |
| 306 | Willie Mays/O.Cepeda | 15.00 | 40.00 |
| 307 | Joe Gibbon | 1.50 | 4.00 |
| 308 | Gene Stephens | 1.50 | 4.00 |
| 309 | Paul Toth | 1.50 | 4.00 |
| 310 | Jim Gilliam | 2.50 | 6.00 |
| 311 | Tom W. Brown RC | 2.50 | 6.00 |
| 312 | F.Fisher RC/F.Gladding RC | 1.50 | 4.00 |
| 313 | Chuck Hiller | 1.50 | 4.00 |
| 314 | Jerry Buchek | 1.50 | 4.00 |
| 315 | Bo Belinsky | 2.50 | 6.00 |
| 316 | Gene Oliver | 1.50 | 4.00 |
| 317 | Al Smith | 1.50 | 4.00 |
| 318 | Minnesota Twins TC | 2.50 | 6.00 |
| 319 | Paul Brown | 1.50 | 4.00 |
| 320 | Rocky Colavito | 5.00 | 12.00 |
| 321 | Bob Lillis | 1.50 | 4.00 |
| 322 | George Brunet | 1.50 | 4.00 |
| 323 | John Buzhardt | 1.50 | 4.00 |
| 324 | Casey Stengel MG | 6.00 | 15.00 |
| 325 | Hector Lopez | 2.50 | 6.00 |
| 326 | Ron Brand RC | 1.50 | 4.00 |
| 327 | Don Blasingame | 1.50 | 4.00 |
| 328 | Bob Shaw | 1.50 | 4.00 |
| 329 | Russ Nixon | 1.50 | 4.00 |
| 330 | Tommy Harper | 2.50 | 6.00 |
| 331 | Maris/Cash/Mantle/Kaline | 75.00 | 150.00 |
| 332 | Ray Washburn | 1.50 | 4.00 |
| 333 | Billy Moran | 1.50 | 4.00 |
| 334 | Lew Krausse | 1.50 | 4.00 |
| 335 | Don Mossi | 2.50 | 6.00 |
| 336 | Andre Rodgers | 1.50 | 4.00 |
| 337 | A.Ferrara RC/J.Torborg RC | 2.50 | 6.00 |
| 338 | Jack Kralick | 1.50 | 4.00 |
| 339 | Walt Bond | 1.50 | 4.00 |
| 340 | Joe Cunningham | 1.50 | 4.00 |
| 341 | Jim Roland | 1.50 | 4.00 |
| 342 | Willie Stargell | 12.50 | 30.00 |
| 343 | Washington Senators TC | 2.50 | 6.00 |
| 344 | Phil Linz | 2.50 | 6.00 |
| 345 | Frank Thomas | 3.00 | 8.00 |
| 346 | Joey Jay | 1.50 | 4.00 |
| 347 | Bobby Wine | 2.50 | 6.00 |
| 348 | Ed Lopat MG | 2.50 | 6.00 |
| 349 | Art Fowler | 1.50 | 4.00 |
| 350 | Willie McCovey | 10.00 | 25.00 |
| 351 | Dan Schneider | 1.50 | 4.00 |
| 352 | Eddie Bressoud | 1.50 | 4.00 |
| 353 | Wally Moon | 2.50 | 6.00 |
| 354 | Dave Giusti | 1.50 | 4.00 |
| 355 | Vic Power | 2.50 | 6.00 |
| 356 | B.McCool RC/C.Ruiz | 2.50 | 6.00 |
| 357 | Charley James | 1.50 | 4.00 |
| 358 | Ron Kline | 1.50 | 4.00 |
| 359 | Jim Schaffer | 1.50 | 4.00 |
| 360 | Joe Pepitone | 5.00 | 12.00 |
| 361 | Jay Hook | 1.50 | 4.00 |
| 362 | Checklist 5 | 4.00 | 10.00 |
| 363 | Dick McAuliffe | 2.50 | 6.00 |
| 364 | Joe Gaines | 1.50 | 4.00 |
| 365 | Cal McLish | 2.50 | 6.00 |
| 366 | Nelson Mathews | 1.50 | 4.00 |
| 367 | Fred Whitfield | 1.50 | 4.00 |
| 368 | F.Ackley RC/D.Buford RC | 2.50 | 6.00 |
| 369 | Jerry Zimmerman | 1.50 | 4.00 |
| 370 | Hal Woodeshick | 1.50 | 4.00 |
| 371 | Frank Howard | 3.00 | 8.00 |
| 372 | Howie Koplitz | 3.00 | 8.00 |
| 373 | Pittsburgh Pirates TC | 5.00 | 12.00 |
| 374 | Bobby Bolin | 3.00 | 8.00 |
| 375 | Ron Santo | 4.00 | 10.00 |
| 376 | Dave Morehead | 3.00 | 8.00 |
| 377 | Bob Skinner | 3.00 | 8.00 |
| 378 | W.Woodward RC/J.Smith | 4.00 | 10.00 |
| 379 | Tony Gonzalez | 3.00 | 8.00 |
| 380 | Whitey Ford | 15.00 | 40.00 |
| 381 | Bob Taylor | 3.00 | 8.00 |
| 382 | Wes Stock | 3.00 | 8.00 |
| 383 | Bill Rigney MG | 3.00 | 8.00 |
| 384 | Ron Hansen | 3.00 | 8.00 |
| 385 | Curt Simmons | 4.00 | 10.00 |
| 386 | Lenny Green | 3.00 | 8.00 |
| 387 | Terry Fox | 3.00 | 8.00 |
| 388 | J.O'Donoghue RC/G.Williams | 4.00 | 10.00 |
| 389 | Jim Umbricht | 4.00 | 10.00 |
| 390 | Orlando Cepeda | 10.00 | 25.00 |
| 391 | Sam McDowell | 4.00 | 10.00 |
| 392 | Jim Pagliaroni | 3.00 | 8.00 |
| 393 | C.Stengel/E.Kranepool | 6.00 | 15.00 |
| 394 | Bob Miller | 3.00 | 8.00 |
| 395 | Tom Tresh | 4.00 | 10.00 |
| 396 | Dennis Bennett | 3.00 | 8.00 |
| 397 | Chuck Cottier | 3.00 | 8.00 |
| 398 | B.Haas/D.Smith | 4.00 | 10.00 |
| 399 | Jackie Brandt | 3.00 | 8.00 |
| 400 | Warren Spahn | 15.00 | 40.00 |
| 401 | Charlie Maxwell | 3.00 | 8.00 |
| 402 | Tom Sturdivant | 3.00 | 8.00 |
| 403 | Cincinnati Reds TC | 5.00 | 12.00 |
| 404 | Tony Martinez | 3.00 | 8.00 |
| 405 | Ken McBride | 3.00 | 8.00 |
| 406 | Al Spangler | 3.00 | 8.00 |
| 407 | Bill Freehan | 4.00 | 10.00 |
| 408 | J.Stewart RC/F.Burdette RC | 4.00 | 10.00 |
| 409 | Bill Fischer | 4.00 | 10.00 |
| 410 | Dick Stuart | 4.00 | 10.00 |
| 411 | Lee Walls | 3.00 | 8.00 |
| 412 | Ray Culp | 3.00 | 8.00 |
| 413 | Johnny Keane MG | 3.00 | 8.00 |
| 414 | Jack Sanford | 3.00 | 8.00 |
| 415 | Tony Kubek | 6.00 | 15.00 |
| 416 | Lee Maye | 3.00 | 8.00 |
| 417 | Don Cardwell | 3.00 | 8.00 |
| 418 | D.Knowles RC/B.Narum RC | 4.00 | 10.00 |
| 419 | Ken Harrelson RC | 6.00 | 15.00 |
| 420 | Jim Maloney | 4.00 | 10.00 |
| 421 | Camilo Carreon | 3.00 | 8.00 |
| 422 | Jack Fisher | 3.00 | 8.00 |
| 423 | H.Aaron/W.Mays | 60.00 | 120.00 |
| 424 | Dick Bertell | 3.00 | 8.00 |
| 425 | Norm Cash | 4.00 | 10.00 |
| 426 | Bob Rodgers | 3.00 | 8.00 |
| 427 | Don Rudolph | 3.00 | 8.00 |
| 428 | A.Skeen RC/P.Smith RC | 3.00 | 8.00 |
| 429 | Tim McCarver | 4.00 | 10.00 |
| 430 | Juan Pizarro | 3.00 | 8.00 |
| 431 | George Alusik | 3.00 | 8.00 |
| 432 | Ruben Amaro | 4.00 | 10.00 |
| 433 | New York Yankees TC | 15.00 | 40.00 |
| 434 | Don Nottebart | 3.00 | 8.00 |
| 435 | Vic Davalillo | 3.00 | 8.00 |
| 436 | Charlie Neal | 4.00 | 10.00 |
| 437 | Ed Bailey | 3.00 | 8.00 |
| 438 | Checklist 6 | 6.00 | 15.00 |
| 439 | Harvey Haddix | 4.00 | 10.00 |
| 440 | Roberto Clemente UER | 100.00 | 200.00 |
| 441 | Bob Duliba | 3.00 | 8.00 |
| 442 | Pumpsie Green | 4.00 | 10.00 |
| 443 | Chuck Dressen MG | 4.00 | 10.00 |

|  |  | | |
|---|---|---|---|
| 444 | Larry Jackson | 3.00 | 8.00 |
| 445 | Bill Skowron | 4.00 | 10.00 |
| 446 | Julian Javier | 6.00 | 15.00 |
| 447 | Ted Bowsfield | 3.00 | 8.00 |
| 448 | Cookie Rojas | 4.00 | 10.00 |
| 449 | Deron Johnson | 4.00 | 10.00 |
| 450 | Steve Barber | 3.00 | 8.00 |
| 451 | Joe Amalfitano | 3.00 | 8.00 |
| 452 | G.Garrido RC/J.Hart RC | 4.00 | 10.00 |
| 453 | Frank Baumann | 3.00 | 8.00 |
| 454 | Tommie Aaron | 4.00 | 10.00 |
| 455 | Bernie Allen | 3.00 | 8.00 |
| 456 | W.Parker RC/J.Werhas RC | 4.00 | 10.00 |
| 457 | Jesse Gonder | 3.00 | 8.00 |
| 458 | Ralph Terry | 4.00 | 10.00 |
| 459 | P.Charton RC/D.Jones RC | 3.00 | 8.00 |
| 460 | Bob Gibson | 15.00 | 40.00 |
| 461 | George Thomas | 3.00 | 8.00 |
| 462 | Birdie Tebbetts MG | 3.00 | 8.00 |
| 463 | Don Leppert | 3.00 | 8.00 |
| 464 | Dallas Green | 6.00 | 15.00 |
| 465 | Mike Hershberger | 3.00 | 8.00 |
| 466 | D.Green RC/A.Monteagudo RC | 4.00 | 10.00 |
| 467 | Bob Aspromonte | 3.00 | 8.00 |
| 468 | Gaylord Perry | 15.00 | 40.00 |
| 469 | F.Norman RC/S.Slaughter RC | 4.00 | 10.00 |
| 470 | Jim Bouton | 4.00 | 10.00 |
| 471 | Gates Brown RC | 4.00 | 10.00 |
| 472 | Vern Law | 4.00 | 10.00 |
| 473 | Baltimore Orioles TC | 5.00 | 12.00 |
| 474 | Larry Sherry | 4.00 | 10.00 |
| 475 | Ed Charles | 3.00 | 8.00 |
| 476 | R.Carty RC/D.Kelley RC | 6.00 | 15.00 |
| 477 | Mike Joyce | 3.00 | 8.00 |
| 478 | Dick Howser | 4.00 | 10.00 |
| 479 | D.Bakenhaster RC/J.Lewis RC | 3.00 | 8.00 |
| 480 | Bob Purkey | 3.00 | 8.00 |
| 481 | Chuck Schilling | 3.00 | 8.00 |
| 482 | J.Briggs RC/D.Cater RC | 4.00 | 10.00 |
| 483 | Fred Valentine RC | 3.00 | 8.00 |
| 484 | Bill Pleis | 3.00 | 8.00 |
| 485 | Tom Haller | 3.00 | 8.00 |
| 486 | Bob Kennedy MG | 3.00 | 8.00 |
| 487 | Mike McCormick | 4.00 | 10.00 |
| 488 | P.Mikkelsen RC/B.Meyer RC | 6.00 | 15.00 |
| 489 | Julio Navarro | 3.00 | 8.00 |
| 490 | Ron Fairly | 4.00 | 10.00 |
| 491 | Ed Rakow | 3.00 | 8.00 |
| 492 | J.Beauchamp RC/M.White RC | 3.00 | 8.00 |
| 493 | Don Lee | 3.00 | 8.00 |
| 494 | Al Jackson | 3.00 | 8.00 |
| 495 | Bill Virdon | 4.00 | 10.00 |
| 496 | Chicago White Sox TC | 5.00 | 12.00 |
| 497 | Jeoff Long RC | 3.00 | 8.00 |
| 498 | Dave Stenhouse | 3.00 | 8.00 |
| 499 | C.Slamon RC/G.Seyfried RC | 3.00 | 8.00 |
| 500 | Camilo Pascual | 4.00 | 10.00 |
| 501 | Bob Veale | 4.00 | 10.00 |
| 502 | B.Knoop RC/B.Lee RC | 4.00 | 10.00 |
| 503 | Earl Wilson | 3.00 | 8.00 |
| 504 | Claude Raymond | 3.00 | 8.00 |
| 505 | Stan Williams | 3.00 | 8.00 |
| 506 | Bobby Bragan MG | 3.00 | 8.00 |
| 507 | Johnny Edwards | 3.00 | 8.00 |
| 508 | Diego Segui | 3.00 | 8.00 |
| 509 | G.Alley RC/O.McFarlane RC | 4.00 | 10.00 |
| 510 | Lindy McDaniel | 4.00 | 10.00 |
| 511 | Lou Jackson | 4.00 | 10.00 |
| 512 | W.Horton RC/J.Sparma RC | 6.00 | 15.00 |
| 513 | Don Larsen | 4.00 | 10.00 |
| 514 | Jim Hickman | 4.00 | 10.00 |
| 515 | Johnny Romano | 3.00 | 8.00 |
| 516 | J.Arrigo RC/D.Siebler RC | 3.00 | 8.00 |
| 517A | Checklist 7 ERR | 10.00 | 25.00 |
| 517B | Checklist 7 COR | 6.00 | 15.00 |
| 518 | Carl Bouldin | 3.00 | 8.00 |
| 519 | Charlie Smith | 3.00 | 8.00 |
| 520 | Jack Baldschun | 4.00 | 10.00 |
| 521 | Tom Satriano | 3.00 | 8.00 |
| 522 | Bob Tiefenauer | 3.00 | 8.00 |
| 523 | Lou Burdette UER | 8.00 | 20.00 |
| 524 | J.Dickson RC/B.Klaus RC | 6.00 | 15.00 |
| 525 | Al McBean | 6.00 | 15.00 |
| 526 | Lou Clinton | 3.00 | 8.00 |
| 527 | Larry Bearnarth | 6.00 | 15.00 |
| 528 | D.Duncan RC/T.Reynolds RC | 8.00 | 20.00 |
| 529 | Alvin Dark MG | 8.00 | 20.00 |
| 530 | Leon Wagner | 6.00 | 15.00 |
| 531 | Los Angeles Dodgers TC | 10.00 | 25.00 |
| 532 | B.Bloomfield RC/J.Nossek RC | 6.00 | 15.00 |
| 533 | Johnny Klippstein | 6.00 | 15.00 |
| 534 | Gus Bell | 6.00 | 15.00 |
| 535 | Phil Regan | 6.00 | 15.00 |
| 536 | L.Elliot/J.Stephenson RC | 6.00 | 15.00 |
| 537 | Dan Osinski | 6.00 | 15.00 |
| 538 | Minnie Minoso | 8.00 | 20.00 |
| 539 | Roy Face | 8.00 | 20.00 |
| 540 | Luis Aparicio | 15.00 | 40.00 |
| 541 | P.Roof/P.Niekro RC | 40.00 | 80.00 |
| 542 | Don Mincher | 6.00 | 15.00 |
| 543 | Bob Uecker | 15.00 | 40.00 |
| 544 | S.Hertz RC/J.Hoerner RC | 6.00 | 15.00 |
| 545 | Max Alvis | 6.00 | 15.00 |
| 546 | Joe Christopher | 6.00 | 15.00 |
| 547 | Gil Hodges MG | 12.50 | 30.00 |
| 548 | W.Schurr RC/P.Speckenbach RC | 8.00 | 20.00 |
| 549 | Joe Moeller | 6.00 | 15.00 |
| 550 | Ken Hubbs MEM | 15.00 | 40.00 |
| 551 | Billy Hoeft | 6.00 | 15.00 |
| 552 | T.Kelley RC/S.Siebert RC | 6.00 | 15.00 |
| 553 | Jim Brewer | 6.00 | 15.00 |
| 554 | Hank Foiles | 6.00 | 15.00 |
| 555 | Lee Stange | 6.00 | 15.00 |
| 556 | S.Dillon RC/R.Locke RC | 6.00 | 15.00 |
| 557 | Leo Burke | 6.00 | 15.00 |
| 558 | Don Schwall | 6.00 | 15.00 |
| 559 | Dick Phillips | 6.00 | 15.00 |
| 560 | Dick Farrell | 6.00 | 15.00 |
| 561 | D.Bennett RC/R.Wise RC | 8.00 | 20.00 |
| 562 | Pedro Ramos | 6.00 | 15.00 |
| 563 | Dal Maxvill | 8.00 | 20.00 |
| 564 | J.McCabe RC/J.McNertney RC | 6.00 | 15.00 |
| 565 | Stu Miller | 6.00 | 15.00 |
| 566 | Ed Kranepool | 8.00 | 20.00 |
| 567 | Jim Kaat | 8.00 | 20.00 |
| 568 | P.Gagliano RC/C.Peterson RC | 6.00 | 15.00 |
| 569 | Fred Newman | 6.00 | 15.00 |
| 570 | Bill Mazeroski | 15.00 | 40.00 |
| 571 | Gene Conley | 6.00 | 15.00 |
| 572 | D.Grey RC/D.Egan RC | 6.00 | 15.00 |
| 573 | Jim Duffalo | 6.00 | 15.00 |
| 574 | Manny Jimenez | 6.00 | 15.00 |
| 575 | Tony Cloninger | 6.00 | 15.00 |
| 576 | J.Hinsley RC/B.Wakefield RC | 6.00 | 15.00 |
| 577 | Glen Hobbie | 6.00 | 15.00 |
| 578 | Boston Red Sox TC | 10.00 | 25.00 |
| 579 | Johnny Podres | 8.00 | 20.00 |
| 580 | P.Gonzalez/A.Moore RC | 8.00 | 20.00 |
| 581 | Rod Kanehl | 8.00 | 20.00 |
| 582 | Tito Francona | 6.00 | 15.00 |
| 583 | Joel Horlen | 6.00 | 15.00 |
| 584 | Tony Taylor | 8.00 | 20.00 |
| 585 | Jimmy Piersall | 8.00 | 20.00 |
| 586 | Bennie Daniels | 8.00 | 20.00 |
| 587 | Bennie Daniels | 8.00 | 20.00 |

## 1965 Topps

JUAN MARICHAL

| | | |
|---|---|---|
| COMPLETE SET (598) | 2500.00 | 5000.00 |
| COMMON CARD (1-196) | .75 | 2.00 |
| COMMON CARD (197-283) | 1.00 | 2.50 |
| COMMON CARD (284-370) | 1.50 | 4.00 |
| COMMON CARD (371-598) | 3.00 | 8.00 |
| WRAPPER (1-CENT) | 60.00 | 120.00 |
| WRAPPER (5-CENT) | 50.00 | 100.00 |

|  |  | | |
|---|---|---|---|
| 1 | Oliva/Howard/Brooks LL | 8.00 | 20.00 |
| 2 | Clemente/Aaron/Carty LL | 10.00 | 25.00 |
| 3 | Killebrew/Mantle/Powell LL | 20.00 | 50.00 |
| 4 | Mays/B.Will/Cepeda LL | 6.00 | 15.00 |
| 5 | Brooks/Kill/Mantle LL | 15.00 | 40.00 |
| 6 | Boyer/Mays Santo LL | 5.00 | 12.00 |
| 7 | D.Chance/J.Horlen LL | 2.00 | 5.00 |
| 8 | S.Koufax/D.Drysdale LL | 8.00 | 20.00 |
| 9 | Chance/Peters/Wick LL | 2.00 | 5.00 |
| 10 | Jackson/Sad/Marichal LL | 2.00 | 5.00 |
| 11 | Downing/Chance/Pascual LL | 2.00 | 5.00 |
| 12 | Veale/Drysdale/Gibson LL | 4.00 | 10.00 |
| 13 | Pedro Ramos | 1.50 | 4.00 |
| 14 | Len Gabrielson | .75 | 2.00 |
| 15 | Robin Roberts | 4.00 | 10.00 |
| 16 | Joe Morgan RC DP | 30.00 | 60.00 |
| 17 | Johnny Romano | .75 | 2.00 |
| 18 | Bill McCool | .75 | 2.00 |
| 19 | Gates Brown | 1.50 | 4.00 |
| 20 | Jim Bunning | 4.00 | 10.00 |
| 21 | Don Blasingame | .75 | 2.00 |
| 22 | Charlie Smith | .75 | 2.00 |
| 23 | Bob Tiefenauer | .75 | 2.00 |
| 24 | Minnesota Twins TC | 2.50 | 6.00 |
| 25 | Al McBean | .75 | 2.00 |
| 26 | Bobby Knoop | .75 | 2.00 |
| 27 | Dick Bertell | .75 | 2.00 |
| 28 | Barney Schultz | .75 | 2.00 |
| 29 | Felix Mantilla | .75 | 2.00 |
| 30 | Jim Bouton | 2.50 | 6.00 |
| 31 | Mike White | .75 | 2.00 |
| 32 | Herman Franks MG | .75 | 2.00 |
| 33 | Jackie Brandt | .75 | 2.00 |
| 34 | Cal Koonce | .75 | 2.00 |
| 35 | Ed Charles | .75 | 2.00 |
| 36 | Bobby Wine | .75 | 2.00 |
| 37 | Fred Gladding | .75 | 2.00 |
| 38 | Jim King | .75 | 2.00 |
| 39 | Gerry Arrigo | .75 | 2.00 |
| 40 | Frank Howard | 2.50 | 6.00 |
| 41 | B.Howard/M.Staehle RC | .75 | 2.00 |
| 42 | Earl Wilson | 1.50 | 4.00 |
| 43 | Mike Shannon | 1.50 | 4.00 |
| 44 | Wade Blasingame RC | .75 | 2.00 |
| 45 | Roy McMillan | 1.50 | 4.00 |
| 46 | Bob Lee | .75 | 2.00 |
| 47 | Tommy Harper | 1.50 | 4.00 |
| 48 | Claude Raymond | 1.50 | 4.00 |
| 49 | C.Blefary RC/J.Miller | 1.50 | 4.00 |
| 50 | Juan Marichal | 4.00 | 10.00 |
| 51 | Bill Bryan | .75 | 2.00 |
| 52 | Ed Roebuck | .75 | 2.00 |
| 53 | Dick McAuliffe | 1.50 | 4.00 |
| 54 | Joe Gibbon | .75 | 2.00 |
| 55 | Tony Conigliaro | 6.00 | 15.00 |
| 56 | Ron Kline | .75 | 2.00 |
| 57 | St. Louis Cardinals TC | 2.50 | 6.00 |
| 58 | Fred Talbot RC | .75 | 2.00 |
| 59 | Nate Oliver | .75 | 2.00 |
| 60 | Jim O'Toole | 1.50 | 4.00 |
| 61 | Chris Cannizzaro | .75 | 2.00 |
| 62 | Jim Kaat UER DP | 2.50 | 6.00 |
| 63 | Ty Cline | .75 | 2.00 |
| 64 | Lou Burdette | 1.50 | 4.00 |
| 65 | Tony Kubek | 4.00 | 10.00 |
| 66 | Bill Rigney MG | .75 | 2.00 |
| 67 | Harvey Haddix | 1.50 | 4.00 |
| 68 | Del Crandall | 1.50 | 4.00 |
| 69 | Bill Virdon | 1.50 | 4.00 |
| 70 | Bill Skowron | 2.50 | 6.00 |
| 71 | John O'Donoghue | .75 | 2.00 |
| 72 | Tony Gonzalez | .75 | 2.00 |
| 73 | Dennis Ribant RC | .75 | 2.00 |
| 74 | R.Petrocelli RC/J.Steph RC | 4.00 | 10.00 |
| 75 | Deron Johnson | 1.50 | 4.00 |
| 76 | Sam McDowell | 2.50 | 6.00 |
| 77 | Doug Camilli | .75 | 2.00 |
| 78 | Dal Maxvill | .75 | 2.00 |
| 79A | Checklist 1 Cannizzaro | 4.00 | 10.00 |
| 79B | Checklist 1 C.Cannizzaro | 4.00 | 10.00 |
| 80 | Turk Farrell | .75 | 2.00 |
| 81 | Don Buford | 1.50 | 4.00 |
| 82 | S.Alomar RC/J.Braun RC | 2.50 | 6.00 |
| 83 | George Thomas | .75 | 2.00 |
| 84 | Ron Herbel | .75 | 2.00 |
| 85 | Willie Smith RC | .75 | 2.00 |
| 86 | Buster Narum | .75 | 2.00 |
| 87 | Nelson Mathews | .75 | 2.00 |
| 88 | Jack Lamabe | .75 | 2.00 |
| 89 | Mike Hershberger | .75 | 2.00 |
| 90 | Rich Rollins | 1.50 | 4.00 |
| 91 | Chicago Cubs TC | 2.50 | 6.00 |
| 92 | Dick Howser | 1.50 | 4.00 |
| 93 | Jack Fisher | .75 | 2.00 |
| 94 | Charlie Lau | 1.50 | 4.00 |
| 95 | Bill Mazeroski DP | 2.50 | 6.00 |

|  |  | | |
|---|---|---|---|
| 96 | Sonny Siebert | 1.50 | 4.00 |
| 97 | Pedro Gonzalez | .75 | 2.00 |
| 98 | Bob Miller | .75 | 2.00 |
| 99 | Gil Hodges MG | 2.50 | 6.00 |
| 100 | Ken Boyer | 4.00 | 10.00 |
| 101 | Fred Newman | .75 | 2.00 |
| 102 | Steve Boros | .75 | 2.00 |
| 103 | Harvey Kuenn | 1.50 | 4.00 |
| 104 | Checklist 2 | 4.00 | 10.00 |
| 105 | Chico Salmon | .75 | 2.00 |
| 106 | Gene Oliver | .75 | 2.00 |
| 107 | P.Corrales RC/C.Shockley RC | 1.50 | 4.00 |
| 108 | Don Mincher | .75 | 2.00 |
| 109 | Walt Bond | .75 | 2.00 |
| 110 | Ron Santo | 2.50 | 6.00 |
| 111 | Lee Thomas | 1.50 | 4.00 |
| 112 | Derrell Griffith RC | .75 | 2.00 |
| 113 | Steve Barber | .75 | 2.00 |
| 114 | Jim Hickman | 1.50 | 4.00 |
| 115 | Bobby Richardson | 4.00 | 10.00 |
| 116 | D.Dowling RC/B.Tolan RC | 1.50 | 4.00 |
| 117 | Wes Stock | .75 | 2.00 |
| 118 | Hal Lanier RC | 1.50 | 4.00 |
| 119 | John Kennedy | .75 | 2.00 |
| 120 | Frank Robinson | 15.00 | 40.00 |
| 121 | Gene Alley | 1.50 | 4.00 |
| 122 | Bill Pleis | .75 | 2.00 |
| 123 | Frank Thomas | 1.50 | 4.00 |
| 124 | Tom Satriano | .75 | 2.00 |
| 125 | Juan Pizarro | .75 | 2.00 |
| 126 | Los Angeles Dodgers TC | 2.50 | 6.00 |
| 127 | Frank Lary | .75 | 2.00 |
| 128 | Vic Davalillo | .75 | 2.00 |
| 129 | Bennie Daniels | .75 | 2.00 |
| 130 | Al Kaline | 15.00 | 40.00 |
| 131 | Johnny Keane MG | .75 | 2.00 |
| 132 | Cards Take Opener WS1 | 4.00 | 10.00 |
| 133 | Mel Stottlemyre WS2 | 2.50 | 6.00 |
| 134 | Mickey Mantle WS3 | 40.00 | 80.00 |
| 135 | Ken Boyer WS4 | 4.00 | 10.00 |
| 136 | Tim McCarver WS5 | 2.50 | 6.00 |
| 137 | Jim Bouton WS6 | 2.50 | 6.00 |
| 138 | Bob Gibson WS7 | 5.00 | 12.00 |
| 139 | Cards Celebrate WS | 2.50 | 6.00 |
| 140 | Dean Chance | 1.50 | 4.00 |
| 141 | Charlie James | .75 | 2.00 |
| 142 | Bill Monbouquette | .75 | 2.00 |
| 143 | J.Gelnar RC/J.May RC | .75 | 2.00 |
| 144 | Ed Kranepool | 1.50 | 4.00 |
| 145 | Luis Tiant RC | 4.00 | 10.00 |
| 146 | Ron Hansen | .75 | 2.00 |
| 147 | Dennis Bennett | .75 | 2.00 |
| 148 | Willie Kirkland | .75 | 2.00 |
| 149 | Wayne Schurr | .75 | 2.00 |
| 150 | Brooks Robinson | 15.00 | 40.00 |
| 151 | Kansas City Athletics TC | 2.50 | 6.00 |
| 152 | Phil Ortega | .75 | 2.00 |
| 153 | Norm Cash | 2.50 | 6.00 |
| 154 | Bob Humphreys RC | .75 | 2.00 |
| 155 | Roger Maris | 30.00 | 60.00 |
| 156 | Bob Sadowski | .75 | 2.00 |
| 157 | Zoilo Versalles | 1.50 | 4.00 |
| 158 | Dick Sisler | .75 | 2.00 |
| 159 | Jim Duffalo | .75 | 2.00 |
| 160 | Roberto Clemente UER | 100.00 | 200.00 |
| 161 | Frank Baumann | .75 | 2.00 |
| 162 | Russ Nixon | .75 | 2.00 |
| 163 | Johnny Briggs | .75 | 2.00 |
| 164 | Al Spangler | .75 | 2.00 |
| 165 | Dick Ellsworth | .75 | 2.00 |
| 166 | G.Culver RC/T.Agee RC | 1.50 | 4.00 |
| 167 | Bill Wakefield | .75 | 2.00 |
| 168 | Dick Green | .75 | 2.00 |
| 169 | Dave Vineyard RC | .75 | 2.00 |
| 170 | Hank Aaron | 75.00 | 150.00 |
| 171 | Jim Roland | .75 | 2.00 |
| 172 | Jimmy Piersall | 2.50 | 6.00 |
| 173 | Detroit Tigers TC | 2.50 | 6.00 |
| 174 | Joey Jay | .75 | 2.00 |
| 175 | Bob Aspromonte | .75 | 2.00 |
| 176 | Willie McCovey | 8.00 | 20.00 |
| 177 | Pete Mikkelsen | .75 | 2.00 |
| 178 | Dalton Jones | .75 | 2.00 |
| 179 | Hal Woodeshick | .75 | 2.00 |
| 180 | Bob Allison | 1.50 | 4.00 |
| 181 | D.Loun RC/J.McCabe RC | .75 | 2.00 |
| 182 | Mike de la Hoz | .75 | 2.00 |
| 183 | Dave Nicholson | .75 | 2.00 |
| 184 | John Boozer | .75 | 2.00 |
| 185 | Max Alvis | .75 | 2.00 |
| 186 | Billy Cowan | .75 | 2.00 |
| 187 | Casey Stengel MG | 6.00 | 15.00 |
| 188 | Sam Bowens | .75 | 2.00 |
| 189 | Checklist 3 | 4.00 | 10.00 |
| 190 | Bill White | 2.50 | 6.00 |
| 191 | Phil Regan | 1.50 | 4.00 |
| 192 | Jim Coker | .75 | 2.00 |
| 193 | Gaylord Perry | 6.00 | 15.00 |
| 194 | B.Kelso RC/R.Reichardt RC | .75 | 2.00 |
| 195 | Bob Veale | 1.50 | 4.00 |
| 196 | Ron Fairly | 1.50 | 4.00 |
| 197 | Diego Segui | 1.00 | 2.50 |
| 198 | Smoky Burgess | 1.50 | 4.00 |
| 199 | Bob Heffner | 1.00 | 2.50 |
| 200 | Joe Torre | 2.50 | 6.00 |
| 201 | S.Valdespino RC/C.Tovar RC | 1.50 | 4.00 |
| 202 | Leo Burke | 1.00 | 2.50 |
| 203 | Dallas Green | 1.50 | 4.00 |
| 204 | Russ Snyder | 1.00 | 2.50 |
| 205 | Warren Spahn | 12.50 | 30.00 |
| 206 | Willie Horton | 1.50 | 4.00 |
| 207 | Pete Rose | 100.00 | 200.00 |
| 208 | Tommy John | 2.50 | 6.00 |
| 209 | Pittsburgh Pirates TC | 2.50 | 6.00 |
| 210 | Jim Fregosi | 1.50 | 4.00 |
| 211 | Steve Ridzik | 1.00 | 2.50 |
| 212 | Ron Brand | 1.00 | 2.50 |
| 213 | Jim Davenport | 1.00 | 2.50 |
| 214 | Bob Purkey | 1.00 | 2.50 |
| 215 | Pete Ward | 1.50 | 4.00 |
| 216 | Al Worthington | 1.00 | 2.50 |
| 217 | Walter Alston MG | 2.50 | 6.00 |
| 218 | Dick Schofield | 1.00 | 2.50 |
| 219 | Bob Meyer | 1.00 | 2.50 |
| 220 | Billy Williams | 4.00 | 10.00 |
| 221 | John Tsitouris | 1.00 | 2.50 |
| 222 | Bob Tillman | 1.00 | 2.50 |
| 223 | Dan Osinski | 1.00 | 2.50 |
| 224 | Bob Chance | 1.00 | 2.50 |
| 225 | Bo Belinsky | 1.50 | 4.00 |
| 226 | E.Jimenez RC/J.Gibbs RC | 1.00 | 2.50 |
| 227 | Bobby Klaus | 1.00 | 2.50 |
| 228 | Jack Sanford | 1.00 | 2.50 |
| 229 | Lou Clinton | 1.00 | 2.50 |
| 230 | Ray Sadecki | 1.00 | 2.50 |
| 231 | Jerry Adair | 1.00 | 2.50 |
| 232 | Steve Blass RC | 1.50 | 4.00 |
| 233 | Don Zimmer | 1.50 | 4.00 |
| 234 | Chicago White Sox TC | 2.50 | 6.00 |
| 235 | Chuck Hinton | 1.00 | 2.50 |
| 236 | Denny McLain RC | 10.00 | 25.00 |
| 237 | Bernie Allen | 1.00 | 2.50 |
| 238 | Joe Moeller | 1.00 | 2.50 |
| 239 | Doc Edwards | 1.00 | 2.50 |
| 240 | Bob Bruce | 1.00 | 2.50 |
| 241 | Mack Jones | 1.00 | 2.50 |
| 242 | George Brunet | 1.00 | 2.50 |
| 243 | T.Davidson RC/T.Helms RC | 1.50 | 4.00 |
| 244 | Lindy McDaniel | 1.50 | 4.00 |
| 245 | Joe Pepitone | 2.50 | 6.00 |
| 246 | Tom Butters | 1.50 | 4.00 |
| 247 | Wally Moon | 1.50 | 4.00 |
| 248 | Gus Triandos | 1.50 | 4.00 |
| 249 | Dave McNally | 1.50 | 4.00 |
| 250 | Willie Mays | 75.00 | 150.00 |
| 251 | Billy Herman MG | 1.50 | 4.00 |
| 252 | Pete Richert | 1.00 | 2.50 |
| 253 | Danny Cater | 1.00 | 2.50 |
| 254 | Roland Sheldon | 1.00 | 2.50 |
| 255 | Camilo Pascual | 1.50 | 4.00 |
| 256 | Tito Francona | 1.00 | 2.50 |
| 257 | Jim Wynn | 1.50 | 4.00 |
| 258 | Larry Bearnarth | 1.00 | 2.50 |
| 259 | J.Northrup RC/R.Oyler RC | 2.50 | 6.00 |
| 260 | Don Drysdale | 8.00 | 20.00 |
| 261 | Duke Carmel | 1.00 | 2.50 |
| 262 | Bud Daley | 1.00 | 2.50 |
| 263 | Marty Keough | 1.00 | 2.50 |
| 264 | Bob Buhl | 1.00 | 2.50 |
| 265 | Jim Pagliaroni | 1.00 | 2.50 |
| 266 | Bert Campaneris RC | 4.00 | 10.00 |
| 267 | Washington Senators TC | 2.50 | 6.00 |
| 268 | Ken McBride | 1.00 | 2.50 |
| 269 | Frank Bolling | 1.00 | 2.50 |
| 270 | Milt Pappas | 1.50 | 4.00 |
| 271 | Don Wert | 1.50 | 4.00 |
| 272 | Chuck Schilling | 1.00 | 2.50 |
| 273 | Checklist 4 | 4.00 | 10.00 |
| 274 | Lum Harris MG RC | 1.00 | 2.50 |
| 275 | Dick Groat | 2.50 | 6.00 |
| 276 | Hoyt Wilhelm | 4.00 | 10.00 |
| 277 | Johnny Lewis | 1.00 | 2.50 |
| 278 | Ken Retzer | 1.00 | 2.50 |
| 279 | Dick Tracewski | 1.00 | 2.50 |
| 280 | Dick Stuart | 1.50 | 4.00 |
| 281 | Bill Stafford | 1.00 | 2.50 |
| 282 | D.Est RC/M.Murakami RC | 15.00 | 40.00 |
| 283 | Fred Whitfield | 1.00 | 2.50 |
| 284 | Nick Willhite | 1.50 | 4.00 |
| 285 | Ron Hunt | 1.50 | 4.00 |
| 286 | J.Dickson/A.Monteagudo | 1.50 | 4.00 |
| 287 | Gary Kolb | 1.50 | 4.00 |
| 288 | Jack Hamilton | 1.50 | 4.00 |
| 289 | Gordy Coleman | 2.50 | 6.00 |
| 290 | Wally Bunker | 1.50 | 4.00 |
| 291 | Jerry Lynch | 1.50 | 4.00 |
| 292 | Larry Yellen | 1.50 | 4.00 |
| 293 | Los Angeles Angels TC | 2.50 | 6.00 |
| 294 | Tim McCarver | 4.00 | 10.00 |
| 295 | Dick Radatz | 2.50 | 6.00 |
| 296 | Tony Taylor | 1.50 | 4.00 |
| 297 | Dave DeBusschere | 4.00 | 10.00 |
| 298 | Jim Stewart | 1.50 | 4.00 |
| 299 | Jerry Zimmerman | 1.50 | 4.00 |
| 300 | Sandy Koufax | 50.00 | 100.00 |
| 301 | Birdie Tebbetts MG | 2.50 | 6.00 |
| 302 | Al Stanek | 1.50 | 4.00 |
| 303 | John Orsino | 1.50 | 4.00 |
| 304 | Dave Stenhouse | 1.50 | 4.00 |
| 305 | Rico Carty | 2.50 | 6.00 |
| 306 | Bubba Phillips | 1.50 | 4.00 |
| 307 | Barry Latman | 1.50 | 4.00 |
| 308 | C.Jones RC/T.Parsons | 2.50 | 6.00 |
| 309 | Steve Hamilton | 2.50 | 6.00 |
| 310 | Johnny Callison | 2.50 | 6.00 |
| 311 | Orlando Pena | 1.50 | 4.00 |
| 312 | Joe Nuxhall | 1.50 | 4.00 |
| 313 | Jim Schaffer | 1.50 | 4.00 |
| 314 | Sterling Slaughter | 1.50 | 4.00 |
| 315 | Frank Malzone | 2.50 | 6.00 |
| 316 | Cincinnati Reds TC | 2.50 | 6.00 |
| 317 | Don McMahon | 1.50 | 4.00 |
| 318 | Matty Alou | 2.50 | 6.00 |
| 319 | Ken McMullen | 1.50 | 4.00 |
| 320 | Bob Gibson | 20.00 | 50.00 |
| 321 | Rusty Staub | 4.00 | 10.00 |
| 322 | Rick Wise | 2.50 | 6.00 |
| 323 | Hank Bauer MG | 2.50 | 6.00 |
| 324 | Bobby Locke | 1.50 | 4.00 |
| 325 | Donn Clendenon | 2.50 | 6.00 |
| 326 | Dwight Siebler | 1.50 | 4.00 |
| 327 | Denis Menke | 1.50 | 4.00 |
| 328 | Eddie Fisher | 1.50 | 4.00 |
| 329 | Hawk Taylor RC | 1.50 | 4.00 |
| 330 | Whitey Ford | 15.00 | 40.00 |
| 331 | A.Ferrara/J.Purdin RC | 2.50 | 6.00 |
| 332 | Ted Abernathy | 1.50 | 4.00 |
| 333 | Tom Reynolds | 1.50 | 4.00 |
| 334 | Vic Roznovsky RC | 1.50 | 4.00 |
| 335 | Mickey Lolich | 2.50 | 6.00 |
| 336 | Woody Held | 1.50 | 4.00 |
| 337 | Mike Cuellar | 2.50 | 6.00 |
| 338 | Philadelphia Phillies TC | 2.50 | 6.00 |
| 339 | Ryne Duren | 2.50 | 6.00 |
| 340 | Tony Oliva | 8.00 | 20.00 |
| 341 | Bob Bolin | 1.50 | 4.00 |
| 342 | Bob Rodgers | 2.50 | 6.00 |
| 343 | Mike McCormick | 2.50 | 6.00 |
| 344 | Wes Parker | 2.50 | 6.00 |
| 345 | Floyd Robinson | 1.50 | 4.00 |
| 346 | Bobby Bragan MG | 1.50 | 4.00 |
| 347 | Roy Face | 2.50 | 6.00 |
| 348 | George Banks | 1.50 | 4.00 |
| 349 | Larry Miller RC | 1.50 | 4.00 |
| 350 | Mickey Mantle | 300.00 | 600.00 |
| 351 | Jim Perry | 2.50 | 6.00 |
| 352 | Alex Johnson RC | 2.50 | 6.00 |
| 353 | Jerry Lumpe | 1.50 | 4.00 |
| 354 | B.Ott RC/D.Warner RC | 1.50 | 4.00 |
| 355 | Vada Pinson | 4.00 | 10.00 |
| 356 | Bill Spanswick | 1.50 | 4.00 |
| 357 | Carl Warwick | 1.50 | 4.00 |
| 358 | Albie Pearson | 2.50 | 6.00 |
| 359 | Ken Johnson | 1.50 | 4.00 |

| Card | Price | Price |
|---|---|---|
| ☐ 360 Orlando Cepeda | 6.00 | 15.00 |
| ☐ 361 Checklist 5 | 5.00 | 12.00 |
| ☐ 362 Don Schwall | 1.50 | 4.00 |
| ☐ 363 Bob Johnson | 1.50 | 4.00 |
| ☐ 364 Galen Cisco | 1.50 | 4.00 |
| ☐ 365 Jim Gentile | 2.50 | 6.00 |
| ☐ 366 Dan Schneider | 1.50 | 4.00 |
| ☐ 367 Leon Wagner | 1.50 | 4.00 |
| ☐ 368 K.Berry RC/J.Gibson RC | 2.50 | 6.00 |
| ☐ 369 Phil Linz | 2.50 | 6.00 |
| ☐ 370 Tommy Davis | 2.50 | 6.00 |
| ☐ 371 Frank Kreutzer | 3.00 | 8.00 |
| ☐ 372 Clay Dalrymple | 3.00 | 8.00 |
| ☐ 373 Curt Simmons | 3.00 | 8.00 |
| ☐ 374 J.Cardenal RC/D.Simpson | 3.00 | 8.00 |
| ☐ 375 Dave Wickersham | 3.00 | 8.00 |
| ☐ 376 Jim Landis | 3.00 | 8.00 |
| ☐ 377 Willie Stargell | 10.00 | 25.00 |
| ☐ 378 Chuck Estrada | 3.00 | 8.00 |
| ☐ 379 San Francisco Giants TC | 5.00 | 12.00 |
| ☐ 380 Rocky Colavito | 10.00 | 25.00 |
| ☐ 381 Al Jackson | 3.00 | 8.00 |
| ☐ 382 J.C. Martin | 3.00 | 8.00 |
| ☐ 383 Felipe Alou | 6.00 | 15.00 |
| ☐ 384 Johnny Klippstein | 3.00 | 8.00 |
| ☐ 385 Carl Yastrzemski | 30.00 | 60.00 |
| ☐ 386 P.Jaeckel RC/F.Norman | 3.00 | 8.00 |
| ☐ 387 Johnny Podres | 6.00 | 15.00 |
| ☐ 388 John Blanchard | 6.00 | 15.00 |
| ☐ 389 Don Larsen | 6.00 | 15.00 |
| ☐ 390 Bill Freehan | 6.00 | 15.00 |
| ☐ 391 Mel McGaha MG | 6.00 | 15.00 |
| ☐ 392 Bob Friend | 6.00 | 15.00 |
| ☐ 393 Ed Kirkpatrick | 3.00 | 8.00 |
| ☐ 394 Jim Hannan | 3.00 | 8.00 |
| ☐ 395 Jim Ray Hart | 3.00 | 8.00 |
| ☐ 396 Frank Bertaina RC | 3.00 | 8.00 |
| ☐ 397 Jerry Buchek | 3.00 | 8.00 |
| ☐ 398 D.Neville RC/A.Shamsky RC | 6.00 | 15.00 |
| ☐ 399 Ray Herbert | 3.00 | 8.00 |
| ☐ 400 Harmon Killebrew | 20.00 | 50.00 |
| ☐ 401 Carl Willey | 3.00 | 8.00 |
| ☐ 402 Joe Amalfitano | 3.00 | 8.00 |
| ☐ 403 Boston Red Sox TC | 5.00 | 12.00 |
| ☐ 404 Stan Williams | 3.00 | 8.00 |
| ☐ 405 John Roseboro | 8.00 | 20.00 |
| ☐ 406 Ralph Terry | 6.00 | 15.00 |
| ☐ 407 Lee Maye | 3.00 | 8.00 |
| ☐ 408 Larry Sherry | 3.00 | 8.00 |
| ☐ 409 J.Beauchamp RC/L.Dierker RC | 6.00 | 15.00 |
| ☐ 410 Luis Aparicio | 10.00 | 25.00 |
| ☐ 411 Roger Craig | 6.00 | 15.00 |
| ☐ 412 Bob Bailey | 3.00 | 8.00 |
| ☐ 413 Hal Reniff | 3.00 | 8.00 |
| ☐ 414 Al Lopez MG | 6.00 | 15.00 |
| ☐ 415 Curt Flood | 6.00 | 15.00 |
| ☐ 416 Jim Brewer | 3.00 | 8.00 |
| ☐ 417 Ed Brinkman | 3.00 | 8.00 |
| ☐ 418 Johnny Edwards | 3.00 | 8.00 |
| ☐ 419 Ruben Amaro | 3.00 | 8.00 |
| ☐ 420 Larry Jackson | 3.00 | 8.00 |
| ☐ 421 G.Dotter RC/J.Ward | 3.00 | 8.00 |
| ☐ 422 Aubrey Gatewood | 3.00 | 8.00 |
| ☐ 423 Jesse Gonder | 3.00 | 8.00 |
| ☐ 424 Gary Bell | 3.00 | 8.00 |
| ☐ 425 Wayne Causey | 3.00 | 8.00 |
| ☐ 426 Milwaukee Braves TC | 3.00 | 8.00 |
| ☐ 427 Bob Saverine | 3.00 | 8.00 |
| ☐ 428 Bob Shaw | 3.00 | 8.00 |
| ☐ 429 Don Demeter | 3.00 | 8.00 |
| ☐ 430 Gary Peters | 3.00 | 8.00 |
| ☐ 431 N.Briles RC/W.Spiezio RC | 6.00 | 15.00 |
| ☐ 432 Jim Grant | 6.00 | 15.00 |
| ☐ 433 John Bateman | 3.00 | 8.00 |
| ☐ 434 Dave Morehead | 3.00 | 8.00 |
| ☐ 435 Willie Davis | 3.00 | 8.00 |
| ☐ 436 Don Elston | 3.00 | 8.00 |
| ☐ 437 Chico Cardenas | 6.00 | 15.00 |
| ☐ 438 Harry Walker MG | 3.00 | 8.00 |
| ☐ 439 Moe Drabowsky | 6.00 | 15.00 |
| ☐ 440 Tom Tresh | 6.00 | 15.00 |
| ☐ 441 Denny Lemaster | 3.00 | 8.00 |
| ☐ 442 Vic Power | 3.00 | 8.00 |
| ☐ 443 Checklist 6 | 5.00 | 12.00 |
| ☐ 444 Bob Hendley | 3.00 | 8.00 |
| ☐ 445 Don Lock | 3.00 | 8.00 |
| ☐ 446 Art Mahaffey | 6.00 | 15.00 |
| ☐ 447 Julian Javier | 6.00 | 15.00 |
| ☐ 448 Lee Stange | 3.00 | 8.00 |
| ☐ 449 J.Hinsley/G.Kroll RC | 6.00 | 15.00 |
| ☐ 450 Elston Howard | 6.00 | 15.00 |
| ☐ 451 Jim Owens | 3.00 | 8.00 |
| ☐ 452 Gary Geiger | 3.00 | 8.00 |
| ☐ 453 W.Crawford RC/J.Werhas | 6.00 | 15.00 |
| ☐ 454 Ed Rakow | 3.00 | 8.00 |
| ☐ 455 Norm Siebern | 3.00 | 8.00 |
| ☐ 456 Bill Henry | 3.00 | 8.00 |
| ☐ 457 Bob Kennedy MG | 6.00 | 15.00 |
| ☐ 458 John Buzhardt | 3.00 | 8.00 |
| ☐ 459 Frank Kostro | 3.00 | 8.00 |
| ☐ 460 Richie Allen | 15.00 | 40.00 |
| ☐ 461 C.Carroll RC/P.Niekro | 20.00 | 50.00 |
| ☐ 462 Lew Krausse UER | 3.00 | 8.00 |
| ☐ 463 Manny Mota | 6.00 | 15.00 |
| ☐ 464 Ron Piche | 3.00 | 8.00 |
| ☐ 465 Tom Haller | 6.00 | 15.00 |
| ☐ 466 P.Craig RC/D.Nen | 3.00 | 8.00 |
| ☐ 467 Ray Washburn | 3.00 | 8.00 |
| ☐ 468 Larry Brown | 3.00 | 8.00 |
| ☐ 469 Don Nottebart | 3.00 | 8.00 |
| ☐ 470 Yogi Berra RTC | 20.00 | 50.00 |
| ☐ 471 Billy Hoeft | 3.00 | 8.00 |
| ☐ 472 Don Pavletich | 3.00 | 8.00 |
| ☐ 473 P.Blair RC/D.Johnson RC | 6.00 | 15.00 |
| ☐ 474 Cookie Rojas | 6.00 | 15.00 |
| ☐ 475 Clete Boyer | 6.00 | 15.00 |
| ☐ 476 Billy O'Dell | 3.00 | 8.00 |
| ☐ 477 Steve Carlton RC | 100.00 | 200.00 |
| ☐ 478 Wilbur Wood | 6.00 | 15.00 |
| ☐ 479 Ken Harrelson | 6.00 | 15.00 |
| ☐ 480 Joel Horlen | 3.00 | 8.00 |
| ☐ 481 Cleveland Indians TC | 4.00 | 10.00 |
| ☐ 482 Bob Priddy | 3.00 | 8.00 |
| ☐ 483 George Smith RC | 3.00 | 8.00 |
| ☐ 484 Ron Perranoski | 8.00 | 20.00 |
| ☐ 485 Nellie Fox | 10.00 | 25.00 |
| ☐ 486 T.Egan/P.Rogan RC | 3.00 | 8.00 |
| ☐ 487 Woody Woodward | 6.00 | 15.00 |
| ☐ 488 Ted Wills | 3.00 | 8.00 |
| ☐ 489 Gene Mauch MG | 6.00 | 15.00 |
| ☐ 490 Earl Battey | 3.00 | 8.00 |
| ☐ 491 Tracy Stallard | 3.00 | 8.00 |
| ☐ 492 Gene Freese | 3.00 | 8.00 |
| ☐ 493 B.Roman RC/B.Brubaker RC | 3.00 | 8.00 |
| ☐ 494 Jay Ritchie RC | 3.00 | 8.00 |
| ☐ 495 Joe Christopher | 3.00 | 8.00 |
| ☐ 496 Joe Cunningham | 3.00 | 8.00 |
| ☐ 497 K.Henderson RC/J.Hiatt RC | 6.00 | 15.00 |
| ☐ 498 Gene Stephens | 3.00 | 8.00 |
| ☐ 499 Stu Miller | 3.00 | 8.00 |
| ☐ 500 Eddie Mathews | 15.00 | 40.00 |
| ☐ 501 R.Gagliano RC/J.Rittwage RC | 3.00 | 8.00 |
| ☐ 502 Don Cardwell | 3.00 | 8.00 |
| ☐ 503 Phil Gagliano | 3.00 | 8.00 |
| ☐ 504 Jerry Grote | 6.00 | 15.00 |
| ☐ 505 Ray Culp | 3.00 | 8.00 |
| ☐ 506 Sam Mele MG | 3.00 | 8.00 |
| ☐ 507 Sammy Ellis | 3.00 | 8.00 |
| ☐ 508 Checklist 7 | 5.00 | 12.00 |
| ☐ 509 B.Guindon RC/G.Vezendy RC | 3.00 | 8.00 |
| ☐ 510 Ernie Banks | 40.00 | 80.00 |
| ☐ 511 Ron Locke | 3.00 | 8.00 |
| ☐ 512 Cap Peterson | 3.00 | 8.00 |
| ☐ 513 New York Yankees TC | 15.00 | 40.00 |
| ☐ 514 Joe Azcue | 3.00 | 8.00 |
| ☐ 515 Vern Law | 6.00 | 15.00 |
| ☐ 516 Al Weis | 3.00 | 8.00 |
| ☐ 517 P.Schaal RC/J.Warner | 6.00 | 15.00 |
| ☐ 518 Ken Rowe | 3.00 | 8.00 |
| ☐ 519 Bob Uecker UER | 12.50 | 30.00 |
| ☐ 520 Tony Cloninger | 3.00 | 8.00 |
| ☐ 521 D.Bennett/M.Stevens RC | 3.00 | 8.00 |
| ☐ 522 Hank Aguirre | 3.00 | 8.00 |
| ☐ 523 Mike Brumley SP | 5.00 | 12.00 |
| ☐ 524 Dave Giusti SP | 5.00 | 12.00 |
| ☐ 525 Eddie Bressoud | 5.00 | 12.00 |
| ☐ 526 J.Odom/J.Hunter SP RC | 40.00 | 80.00 |
| ☐ 527 Jeff Torborg SP | 5.00 | 12.00 |
| ☐ 528 George Altman | 3.00 | 8.00 |
| ☐ 529 Jerry Fosnow SP RC | 5.00 | 12.00 |
| ☐ 530 Jim Maloney | 6.00 | 15.00 |
| ☐ 531 Chuck Hiller | 3.00 | 8.00 |
| ☐ 532 Hector Lopez | 6.00 | 15.00 |
| ☐ 533 R.Swob/T.McGraw SP RC | 10.00 | 25.00 |
| ☐ 534 John Hermstein | 3.00 | 8.00 |
| ☐ 535 Jack Kralick SP | 5.00 | 12.00 |
| ☐ 536 Andre Rodgers SP | 5.00 | 12.00 |
| ☐ 537 Lopez/Roof/May RC | 3.00 | 8.00 |
| ☐ 538 Chuck Dressen MG SP | 5.00 | 12.00 |
| ☐ 539 Herm Starrette | 3.00 | 8.00 |
| ☐ 540 Lou Brock SP | 20.00 | 50.00 |
| ☐ 541 G.Bollo RC/B.Locker RC | 3.00 | 8.00 |
| ☐ 542 Lou Klimchock | 3.00 | 8.00 |
| ☐ 543 Ed Connolly SP RC | 5.00 | 12.00 |
| ☐ 544 Howie Reed SP | 3.00 | 8.00 |
| ☐ 545 Jesus Alou SP | 6.00 | 15.00 |
| ☐ 546 Davis/Hed/Bark/Weav RC | 3.00 | 8.00 |
| ☐ 547 Jake Wood SP | 5.00 | 12.00 |
| ☐ 548 Dick Stigman | 3.00 | 8.00 |
| ☐ 549 R.Pena RC/G.Beckert RC | 8.00 | 20.00 |
| ☐ 550 Mel Stottlemyre SP RC | 12.50 | 30.00 |
| ☐ 551 New York Mets TC SP | 12.50 | 30.00 |
| ☐ 552 Julio Gotay | 3.00 | 8.00 |
| ☐ 553 Coombs/Ratlif/McClure RC | 3.00 | 8.00 |
| ☐ 554 Chico Ruiz SP | 5.00 | 12.00 |
| ☐ 555 Jack Baldschun SP | 5.00 | 12.00 |
| ☐ 556 R.Schoendienst SP | 10.00 | 25.00 |
| ☐ 557 Jose Santiago RC | 3.00 | 8.00 |
| ☐ 558 Tommie Sisk | 3.00 | 8.00 |
| ☐ 559 Ed Bailey SP | 5.00 | 12.00 |
| ☐ 560 Boog Powell SP | 10.00 | 25.00 |
| ☐ 561 Dab/Kek/Valle/Lefebvre RC | 6.00 | 15.00 |
| ☐ 562 Billy Moran | 3.00 | 8.00 |
| ☐ 563 Julio Navarro | 3.00 | 8.00 |
| ☐ 564 Mel Nelson | 3.00 | 8.00 |
| ☐ 565 Ernie Broglio SP | 5.00 | 12.00 |
| ☐ 566 Blanco/Moschitto/Lopez SP | 5.00 | 12.00 |
| ☐ 567 Tommie Aaron | 3.00 | 8.00 |
| ☐ 568 Ron Taylor SP | 5.00 | 12.00 |
| ☐ 569 Gino Cimoli SP | 5.00 | 12.00 |
| ☐ 570 Claude Osteen SP | 6.00 | 15.00 |
| ☐ 571 Ossie Virgil SP | 5.00 | 12.00 |
| ☐ 572 Baltimore Orioles TC SP | 10.00 | 25.00 |
| ☐ 573 Jim Lonborg SP RC | 10.00 | 25.00 |
| ☐ 574 Roy Sievers | 6.00 | 15.00 |
| ☐ 575 Jose Pagan | 3.00 | 8.00 |
| ☐ 576 Terry Fox SP | 5.00 | 12.00 |
| ☐ 577 Knowles/Busch/Schein RC | 5.00 | 12.00 |
| ☐ 578 Camilo Carreon SP | 5.00 | 12.00 |
| ☐ 579 Dick Smith SP | 5.00 | 12.00 |
| ☐ 580 Jimmie Hall SP | 5.00 | 12.00 |
| ☐ 581 Tony Perez SP RC | 40.00 | 80.00 |
| ☐ 582 Bob Schmidt SP | 5.00 | 12.00 |
| ☐ 583 Wes Covington SP | 5.00 | 12.00 |
| ☐ 584 Harry Bright | 6.00 | 15.00 |
| ☐ 585 Hank Fischer | 3.00 | 8.00 |
| ☐ 586 Tom McCraw SP | 5.00 | 12.00 |
| ☐ 587 Joe Sparma | 3.00 | 8.00 |
| ☐ 588 Lenny Green | 3.00 | 8.00 |
| ☐ 589 F.Linzy RC/B.Schroder RC | 5.00 | 12.00 |
| ☐ 590 John Wyatt | 5.00 | 12.00 |
| ☐ 591 Bob Skinner SP | 5.00 | 12.00 |
| ☐ 592 Frank Bork SP RC | 5.00 | 12.00 |
| ☐ 593 J.Sullivan RC/J.Moore RC SP | 5.00 | 12.00 |
| ☐ 594 Joe Gaines | 3.00 | 8.00 |
| ☐ 595 Don Lee | 3.00 | 8.00 |
| ☐ 596 Don Landrum SP | 5.00 | 12.00 |
| ☐ 597 Nossek/Sevcik/Reese SP | 3.00 | 8.00 |
| ☐ 598 Al Downing SP | 10.00 | 25.00 |

### 1966 Topps

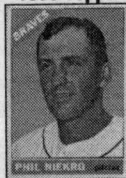

| | | |
|---|---|---|
| ☐ COMPLETE SET (598) | 2500.00 | 4000.00 |
| ☐ COMMON CARD (1-109) | .60 | 1.50 |
| ☐ COMMON CARD (110-283) | .75 | 2.00 |
| ☐ COMMON CARD (284-370) | 1.25 | 3.00 |
| ☐ COMMON CARD (371-446) | 2.00 | 5.00 |
| ☐ COMMON CARD (447-522) | 4.00 | 10.00 |
| ☐ COMMON SP (523-598) | 6.00 | 15.00 |
| ☐ COMMON SP (523-598) | 12.50 | 30.00 |
| ☐ WRAPPER (5-CENT) | 10.00 | 25.00 |

| # | Card | Low | High |
|---|---|---|---|
| 1 | Willie Mays | 125.00 | 250.00 |
| 2 | Ted Abernathy | .60 | 1.50 |
| 3 | Sam Mele MG | .60 | 1.50 |
| 4 | Ray Culp | .60 | 1.50 |
| 5 | Jim Fregosi | .75 | 2.00 |
| 6 | Chuck Schilling | .60 | 1.50 |
| 7 | Tracy Stallard | .60 | 1.50 |
| 8 | Floyd Robinson | .60 | 1.50 |
| 9 | Clete Boyer | .75 | 2.00 |
| 10 | Tony Cloninger | .60 | 1.50 |
| 11 | B.Alyea RC/P.Craig | .60 | 1.50 |
| 12 | John Tsitouris | .60 | 1.50 |
| 13 | Lou Johnson | .75 | 2.00 |
| 14 | Norm Siebern | .60 | 1.50 |
| 15 | Vern Law | .75 | 2.00 |
| 16 | Larry Brown | .60 | 1.50 |
| 17 | John Stephenson | .60 | 1.50 |
| 18 | Roland Sheldon | .60 | 1.50 |
| 19 | San Francisco Giants TC | 2.00 | 5.00 |
| 20 | Willie Horton | .75 | 2.00 |
| 21 | Don Nottebart | .60 | 1.50 |
| 22 | Joe Nossek | .60 | 1.50 |
| 23 | Jack Sanford | .60 | 1.50 |
| 24 | Don Kessinger RC | 1.50 | 4.00 |
| 25 | Pete Ward | .60 | 1.50 |
| 26 | Ray Sadecki | .60 | 1.50 |
| 27 | D.Knowles/A.Etchebarren RC | .60 | 1.50 |
| 28 | Phil Niekro | 8.00 | 20.00 |
| 29 | Mike Brumley | .60 | 1.50 |
| 30 | Pete Rose UER DP | 50.00 | 100.00 |
| 31 | Jack Cullen | .75 | 2.00 |
| 32 | Adolfo Phillips RC | .60 | 1.50 |
| 33 | Jim Pagliaroni | .60 | 1.50 |
| 34 | Checklist 1 | 3.00 | 8.00 |
| 35 | Ron Swoboda | 1.50 | 4.00 |
| 36 | Jim Hunter UER DP | 8.00 | 20.00 |
| 37 | Billy Herman MG | .75 | 2.00 |
| 38 | Ron Nischwitz | .60 | 1.50 |
| 39 | Ken Henderson | .60 | 1.50 |
| 40 | Jim Grant | .60 | 1.50 |
| 41 | Don LeJohn RC | .60 | 1.50 |
| 42 | Aubrey Gatewood | .60 | 1.50 |
| 43A | D.Landrum Dark Button | .75 | 2.00 |
| 43B | D.Landrum Airbrush Button | 8.00 | 20.00 |
| 43C | D.Landrum No Button | .75 | 2.00 |
| 44 | B.Davis/T.Kelley | .60 | 1.50 |
| 45 | Jim Gentile | .60 | 1.50 |
| 46 | Howie Koplitz | .60 | 1.50 |
| 47 | J.C. Martin | .60 | 1.50 |
| 48 | Paul Blair | .75 | 2.00 |
| 49 | Woody Woodward | .75 | 2.00 |
| 50 | Mickey Mantle DP | 175.00 | 350.00 |
| 51 | Gordon Richardson RC | .60 | 1.50 |
| 52 | W.Covington/J.Callison | 1.50 | 4.00 |
| 53 | Bob Duliba | .60 | 1.50 |
| 54 | Jose Pagan | .60 | 1.50 |
| 55 | Ken Harrelson | .75 | 2.00 |
| 56 | Sandy Valdespino | .60 | 1.50 |
| 57 | Jim Lefebvre | .75 | 2.00 |
| 58 | Dave Wickersham | .60 | 1.50 |
| 59 | Cincinnati Reds TC | 2.00 | 5.00 |
| 60 | Curt Flood | 1.50 | 4.00 |
| 61 | Bob Bolin | .60 | 1.50 |
| 62A | Merritt Ranew Sold Line | .75 | 2.00 |
| 62B | Merritt Ranew NTR | 12.50 | 30.00 |
| 63 | Jim Stewart | .60 | 1.50 |
| 64 | Bob Bruce | .60 | 1.50 |
| 65 | Leon Wagner | .60 | 1.50 |
| 66 | Al Weis | .60 | 1.50 |
| 67 | C.Jones/D.Selma RC | 1.50 | 4.00 |
| 68 | Hal Reniff | .60 | 1.50 |
| 69 | Ken Hamlin | .60 | 1.50 |
| 70 | Carl Yastrzemski | 12.50 | 30.00 |
| 71 | Frank Carpin RC | .60 | 1.50 |
| 72 | Tony Perez | 10.00 | 25.00 |
| 73 | Jerry Zimmerman | .60 | 1.50 |
| 74 | Don Mossi | .75 | 2.00 |
| 75 | Tommy Davis | .75 | 2.00 |
| 76 | Red Schoendienst MG | 1.50 | 4.00 |
| 77 | John Orsino | .60 | 1.50 |
| 78 | Frank Linzy | .60 | 1.50 |
| 79 | Joe Pepitone | 1.50 | 4.00 |
| 80 | Richie Allen | 2.50 | 6.00 |
| 81 | Ray Oyler | .60 | 1.50 |
| 82 | Bob Hendley | .60 | 1.50 |
| 83 | Albie Pearson | .75 | 2.00 |
| 84 | J.Beauchamp/D.Kelley | .60 | 1.50 |
| 85 | Eddie Fisher | .60 | 1.50 |
| 86 | John Bateman | .60 | 1.50 |
| 87 | Dan Napoleon | .60 | 1.50 |
| 88 | Fred Whitfield | .60 | 1.50 |
| 89 | Ted Davidson | .60 | 1.50 |
| 90 | Luis Aparicio DP | 3.00 | 8.00 |
| 91A | Bob Uecker TR | 4.00 | 10.00 |
| 91B | Bob Uecker NTR | 15.00 | 40.00 |
| 92 | New York Yankees TC | 6.00 | 15.00 |
| 93 | Jim Lonborg DP | .75 | 2.00 |
| 94 | Matty Alou | .75 | 2.00 |
| 95 | Pete Richert | .60 | 1.50 |
| 96 | Felipe Alou | 1.50 | 4.00 |
| 97 | Jim Merritt RC | .60 | 1.50 |
| 98 | Don Demeter | .60 | 1.50 |
| 99 | W.Stargell/D.Clendenon | 2.50 | 6.00 |
| 100 | Sandy Koufax DP | 50.00 | 100.00 |
| 101A | Checklist 2 Spahn ERR | 6.00 | 15.00 |
| 101B | Checklist 2 Henry COR | 4.00 | 10.00 |
| 102 | Ed Kirkpatrick | .60 | 1.50 |
| 103A | Dick Groat TR | .75 | 2.00 |
| 103B | Dick Groat NTR | 15.00 | 40.00 |
| 104A | Alex Johnson TR | .75 | 2.00 |
| 104B | Alex Johnson NTR | 12.50 | 30.00 |
| 105 | Milt Pappas | .75 | 2.00 |
| 106 | Rusty Staub | 1.50 | 4.00 |
| 107 | L.Stahl RC/R.Tompkins RC | .60 | 1.50 |
| 108 | Bobby Klaus | .60 | 1.50 |
| 109 | Ralph Terry | .75 | 2.00 |
| 110 | Ernie Banks | 12.50 | 30.00 |
| 111 | Gary Peters | .75 | 2.00 |
| 112 | Manny Mota | 1.50 | 4.00 |
| 113 | Hank Aguirre | .75 | 2.00 |
| 114 | Jim Gosger | .75 | 2.00 |
| 115 | Bill Henry | .75 | 2.00 |
| 116 | Walter Alston MG | 2.50 | 6.00 |
| 117 | Jake Gibbs | .75 | 2.00 |
| 118 | Mike McCormick | .75 | 2.00 |
| 119 | Art Shamsky | .75 | 2.00 |
| 120 | Harmon Killebrew | 6.00 | 15.00 |
| 121 | Ray Herbert | .75 | 2.00 |
| 122 | Joe Gaines | .75 | 2.00 |
| 123 | F.Bork/J.May | .75 | 2.00 |
| 124 | Tug McGraw | 1.50 | 4.00 |
| 125 | Lou Brock | 8.00 | 20.00 |
| 126 | Jim Palmer UER RC | 50.00 | 100.00 |
| 127 | Ken Berry | .75 | 2.00 |
| 128 | Jim Landis | .75 | 2.00 |
| 129 | Jack Kralick | .75 | 2.00 |
| 130 | Joe Torre | 2.50 | 6.00 |
| 131 | California Angels TC | 2.00 | 5.00 |
| 132 | Orlando Cepeda | 3.00 | 8.00 |
| 133 | Don McMahon | .75 | 2.00 |
| 134 | Wes Parker | 1.50 | 4.00 |
| 135 | Dave Morehead | .75 | 2.00 |
| 136 | Woody Held | .75 | 2.00 |
| 137 | Pat Corrales | .75 | 2.00 |
| 138 | Roger Repoz RC | .75 | 2.00 |
| 139 | B.Browne RC/D.Young RC | .75 | 2.00 |
| 140 | Jim Maloney | 1.50 | 4.00 |
| 141 | Tom McCraw | .75 | 2.00 |
| 142 | Don Dennis RC | .75 | 2.00 |
| 143 | Jose Tartabull | 1.50 | 4.00 |
| 144 | Don Schwall | .75 | 2.00 |
| 145 | Bill Freehan | 1.50 | 4.00 |
| 146 | George Altman | .75 | 2.00 |
| 147 | Lum Harris MG | .75 | 2.00 |
| 148 | Bob Johnson | .75 | 2.00 |
| 149 | Dick Nen | .75 | 2.00 |
| 150 | Rocky Colavito | 3.00 | 8.00 |
| 151 | Gary Wagner RC | .75 | 2.00 |
| 152 | Frank Malzone | 1.50 | 4.00 |
| 153 | Rico Carty | 1.50 | 4.00 |
| 154 | Chuck Hiller | .75 | 2.00 |
| 155 | Marcelino Lopez | .75 | 2.00 |
| 156 | D.Schofield/H.Lanier | .75 | 2.00 |
| 157 | Rene Lachemann | .75 | 2.00 |
| 158 | Jim Brewer | .75 | 2.00 |
| 159 | Chico Ruiz | .75 | 2.00 |
| 160 | Whitey Ford | 12.50 | 30.00 |
| 161 | Jerry Lumpe | .75 | 2.00 |
| 162 | Lee Maye | .75 | 2.00 |
| 163 | Tito Francona | .75 | 2.00 |
| 164 | T.Agee/M.Stahle | 1.50 | 4.00 |
| 165 | Don Lock | .75 | 2.00 |
| 166 | Chris Krug RC | .75 | 2.00 |
| 167 | Boog Powell | 2.50 | 6.00 |
| 168 | Dan Osinski | .75 | 2.00 |
| 169 | Duke Sims RC | .75 | 2.00 |
| 170 | Cookie Rojas | 1.50 | 4.00 |
| 171 | Nick Willhite | .75 | 2.00 |
| 172 | New York Mets TC | 2.00 | 5.00 |
| 173 | Al Spangler | .75 | 2.00 |
| 174 | Ron Taylor | .75 | 2.00 |
| 175 | Bert Campaneris | 1.50 | 4.00 |
| 176 | Jim Davenport | .75 | 2.00 |
| 177 | Hector Lopez | .75 | 2.00 |
| 178 | Bob Tillman | .75 | 2.00 |
| 179 | D.Aust RC/B.Tolan | 1.50 | 4.00 |
| 180 | Vada Pinson | 1.50 | 4.00 |
| 181 | Al Worthington | .75 | 2.00 |
| 182 | Jerry Lynch | .75 | 2.00 |
| 183A | Checklist 3 Large Print | 3.00 | 8.00 |
| 183B | Checklist 3 Small Print | 3.00 | 8.00 |
| 184 | Denis Menke | .75 | 2.00 |
| 185 | Bob Buhl | 1.50 | 4.00 |
| 186 | Ruben Amaro | .75 | 2.00 |
| 187 | Chuck Dressen MG | 1.50 | 4.00 |
| 188 | Al Luplow | .75 | 2.00 |
| 189 | John Roseboro | 1.50 | 4.00 |
| 190 | Jimmie Hall | .75 | 2.00 |
| 191 | Darrell Sutherland RC | .75 | 2.00 |
| 192 | Vic Power | 1.50 | 4.00 |
| 193 | Dave McNally | 1.50 | 4.00 |
| 194 | Washington Senators TC | 2.00 | 5.00 |
| 195 | Joe Morgan | 6.00 | 15.00 |
| 196 | Don Pavletich | .75 | 2.00 |
| 197 | Sonny Siebert | .75 | 2.00 |
| 198 | Mickey Stanley RC | 2.50 | 6.00 |
| 199 | Skowron/Romano/Robinson | 1.50 | 4.00 |
| 200 | Eddie Mathews | 6.00 | 15.00 |
| 201 | Jim Dickson | .75 | 2.00 |
| 202 | Clay Dalrymple | .75 | 2.00 |
| 203 | Jose Santiago | .75 | 2.00 |
| 204 | Chicago Cubs TC | 2.00 | 5.00 |
| 205 | Tom Tresh | 1.50 | 4.00 |
| 206 | Al Jackson | .75 | 2.00 |
| 207 | Frank Quilici RC | .75 | 2.00 |
| 208 | Bob Miller | .75 | 2.00 |
| 209 | F.Fisher/J.Hiller RC | 1.50 | 4.00 |
| 210 | Bill Mazeroski | 3.00 | 8.00 |
| 211 | Frank Kreutzer | .75 | 2.00 |
| 212 | Ed Kranepool | 1.50 | 4.00 |
| 213 | Fred Newman | .75 | 2.00 |
| 214 | Tommy Harper | 1.50 | 4.00 |
| 215 | Clemente/Aaron/Mays LL | 20.00 | 50.00 |
| 216 | Oliva/Yaz/Davalillo LL | 2.00 | 5.00 |
| 217 | Mays/McCovey/B.Will LL | 8.00 | 20.00 |
| 218 | Conigliaro/Cash/Horton LL | 2.00 | 5.00 |
| 219 | Johnson/F.Rob/Mays LL | 5.00 | 12.00 |
| 220 | Colavito/Horton/Oliva LL | 2.00 | 5.00 |
| 221 | Koufax/Marichal/Law LL | 5.00 | 12.00 |
| 222 | McDowell/Fisher/Siebert LL | 2.00 | 5.00 |
| 223 | Koufax/Clon/Drysdale LL | 5.00 | 12.00 |
| 224 | Grant/Stottlemyre/Kaat LL | 2.00 | 5.00 |
| 225 | Koufax/Veale/Gibson LL | 5.00 | 12.00 |
| 226 | McDowell/Lolich/McLain LL | 2.00 | 5.00 |
| 227 | Russ Nixon | .75 | 2.00 |
| 228 | Larry Dierker | 1.50 | 4.00 |
| 229 | Hank Bauer MG | 1.50 | 4.00 |
| 230 | Johnny Callison | 1.50 | 4.00 |
| 231 | Floyd Weaver | .75 | 2.00 |
| 232 | Glenn Beckert | 1.50 | 4.00 |
| 233 | Dom Zanni | .75 | 2.00 |
| 234 | R.Beck RC/R.White RC | 3.00 | 8.00 |
| 235 | Don Cardwell | .75 | 2.00 |
| 236 | Mike Hershberger | .75 | 2.00 |
| 237 | Billy O'Dell | .75 | 2.00 |
| 238 | Los Angeles Dodgers TC | 2.00 | 5.00 |
| 239 | Orlando Pena | .75 | 2.00 |
| 240 | Earl Battey | .75 | 2.00 |
| 241 | Dennis Ribant | .75 | 2.00 |
| 242 | Jesus Alou | .75 | 2.00 |
| 243 | Nelson Briles | 1.50 | 4.00 |
| 244 | C.Harrison RC/S.Jackson | .75 | 2.00 |
| 245 | John Buzhardt | .75 | 2.00 |
| 246 | Ed Bailey | .75 | 2.00 |
| 247 | Carl Warwick | .75 | 2.00 |
| 248 | Pete Mikkelsen | .75 | 2.00 |
| 249 | Bill Rigney MG | .75 | 2.00 |
| 250 | Sammy Ellis | .75 | 2.00 |
| 251 | Ed Brinkman | .75 | 2.00 |
| 252 | Denny Lemaster | .75 | 2.00 |
| 253 | Don Wert | .75 | 2.00 |
| 254 | Fergie Jenkins RC | 30.00 | 60.00 |
| 255 | Willie Stargell | 8.00 | 20.00 |
| 256 | Lew Krausse | .75 | 2.00 |

| # | Player | Low | High |
|---|--------|-----|------|
| 257 | Jeff Torborg | 1.50 | 4.00 |
| 258 | Dave Giusti | .75 | 2.00 |
| 259 | Boston Red Sox TC | 2.00 | 5.00 |
| 260 | Bob Shaw | .75 | 2.00 |
| 261 | Ron Hansen | .75 | 2.00 |
| 262 | Jack Hamilton | .75 | 2.00 |
| 263 | Tom Egan | .75 | 2.00 |
| 264 | A.Kosco RC/T.Uhlaender RC | .75 | 2.00 |
| 265 | Stu Miller | 1.50 | 4.00 |
| 266 | Pedro Gonzalez UER | .75 | 2.00 |
| 267 | Joe Sparma | .75 | 2.00 |
| 268 | John Blanchard | .75 | 2.00 |
| 269 | Don Heffner MG | .75 | 2.00 |
| 270 | Claude Osteen | 1.50 | 4.00 |
| 271 | Hal Lanier | .75 | 2.00 |
| 272 | Jack Baldschun | .75 | 2.00 |
| 273 | B.Aspromonte/R.Staub | 1.50 | 4.00 |
| 274 | Buster Narum | .75 | 2.00 |
| 275 | Tim McCarver | 1.50 | 4.00 |
| 276 | Jim Bouton | 1.50 | 4.00 |
| 277 | George Thomas | .75 | 2.00 |
| 278 | Cal Koonce | .75 | 2.00 |
| 279A | Checklist 4 Black Cap | 3.00 | 8.00 |
| 279B | Checklist 4 Red Cap | 3.00 | 8.00 |
| 280 | Bobby Knoop | .75 | 2.00 |
| 281 | Bruce Howard | .75 | 2.00 |
| 282 | Johnny Lewis | .75 | 2.00 |
| 283 | Jim Perry | 1.50 | 4.00 |
| 284 | Bobby Wine | 1.25 | 3.00 |
| 285 | Luis Tiant | 2.00 | 5.00 |
| 286 | Gary Geiger | 1.25 | 3.00 |
| 287 | Jack Aker RC | 1.25 | 3.00 |
| 288 | D.Sutton RC/B.Singer RC | 30.00 | 60.00 |
| 289 | Larry Sherry | 1.25 | 3.00 |
| 290 | Ron Santo | 2.00 | 5.00 |
| 291 | Moe Drabowsky | 1.25 | 3.00 |
| 292 | Jim Coker | 1.25 | 3.00 |
| 293 | Mike Shannon | 2.00 | 5.00 |
| 294 | Steve Ridzik | 1.25 | 3.00 |
| 295 | Jim Ray Hart | 2.00 | 5.00 |
| 296 | Johnny Keane MG | 2.00 | 5.00 |
| 297 | Jim Owens | 1.25 | 3.00 |
| 298 | Rico Petrocelli | 2.00 | 5.00 |
| 299 | Lou Burdette | 2.00 | 5.00 |
| 300 | Roberto Clemente | 75.00 | 150.00 |
| 301 | Greg Bollo | 1.25 | 3.00 |
| 302 | Ernie Bowman | 1.25 | 3.00 |
| 303 | Cleveland Indians TC | 2.00 | 5.00 |
| 304 | John Hermstein | 1.25 | 3.00 |
| 305 | Camilo Pascual | 2.00 | 5.00 |
| 306 | Ty Cline | 1.25 | 3.00 |
| 307 | Clay Carroll | 2.00 | 5.00 |
| 308 | Tom Haller | 1.25 | 3.00 |
| 309 | Diego Segui | 1.25 | 3.00 |
| 310 | Frank Robinson | 15.00 | 40.00 |
| 311 | T.Helms/D.Simpson | 2.00 | 5.00 |
| 312 | Bob Saverine | 1.25 | 3.00 |
| 313 | Chris Zachary | 1.25 | 3.00 |
| 314 | Hector Valle | 1.25 | 3.00 |
| 315 | Norm Cash | 2.00 | 5.00 |
| 316 | Jack Fisher | 1.25 | 3.00 |
| 317 | Dalton Jones | 1.25 | 3.00 |
| 318 | Harry Walker MG | 1.25 | 3.00 |
| 319 | Gene Freese | 1.25 | 3.00 |
| 320 | Bob Gibson | 10.00 | 25.00 |
| 321 | Rick Reichardt | 1.25 | 3.00 |
| 322 | Bill Faul | 1.25 | 3.00 |
| 323 | Ray Barker | 1.25 | 3.00 |
| 324 | John Boozer | 1.25 | 3.00 |
| 325 | Vic Davalillo | 1.25 | 3.00 |
| 326 | Atlanta Braves TC | 2.00 | 5.00 |
| 327 | Bernie Allen | 1.25 | 3.00 |
| 328 | Jerry Grote | 2.00 | 5.00 |
| 329 | Pete Charton | 1.25 | 3.00 |
| 330 | Ron Fairly | 2.00 | 5.00 |
| 331 | Ron Herbel | 1.25 | 3.00 |
| 332 | Bill Bryan | 1.25 | 3.00 |
| 333 | J.Coleman RC/J.French RC | 1.25 | 3.00 |
| 334 | Marty Keough | 1.25 | 3.00 |
| 335 | Juan Pizarro | 1.25 | 3.00 |
| 336 | Gene Alley | 2.00 | 5.00 |
| 337 | Fred Gladding | 1.25 | 3.00 |
| 338 | Dal Maxvill | 1.25 | 3.00 |
| 339 | Del Crandall | 2.00 | 5.00 |
| 340 | Dean Chance | 2.00 | 5.00 |
| 341 | Wes Westrum MG | 2.00 | 5.00 |
| 342 | Bob Humphreys | 1.25 | 3.00 |
| 343 | Joe Christopher | 1.25 | 3.00 |
| 344 | Steve Blass | 2.00 | 5.00 |
| 345 | Bob Allison | 2.00 | 5.00 |
| 346 | Mike de la Hoz | 1.25 | 3.00 |
| 347 | Phil Regan | 1.25 | 3.00 |
| 348 | Baltimore Orioles TC | 3.00 | 8.00 |
| 349 | Cap Peterson | 1.25 | 3.00 |
| 350 | Mel Stottlemyre | 3.00 | 8.00 |
| 351 | Fred Valentine | 1.25 | 3.00 |
| 352 | Bob Aspromonte | 1.25 | 3.00 |
| 353 | Al McBean | 1.25 | 3.00 |
| 354 | Smoky Burgess | 2.00 | 5.00 |
| 355 | Wade Blasingame | 1.25 | 3.00 |
| 356 | O.Johnson RC/K.Sanders RC | 1.25 | 3.00 |
| 357 | Gerry Arrigo | 1.25 | 3.00 |
| 358 | Charlie Smith | 1.25 | 3.00 |
| 359 | Johnny Briggs | 1.25 | 3.00 |
| 360 | Ron Hunt | 1.25 | 3.00 |
| 361 | Tom Satriano | 1.25 | 3.00 |
| 362 | Gates Brown | 2.00 | 5.00 |
| 363 | Checklist 5 | 4.00 | 10.00 |
| 364 | Nate Oliver | 1.25 | 3.00 |
| 365 | Roger Maris UER | 20.00 | 50.00 |
| 366 | Wayne Causey | 1.25 | 3.00 |
| 367 | Mel Nelson | 1.25 | 3.00 |
| 368 | Charlie Lau | 2.00 | 5.00 |
| 369 | Jim King | 1.25 | 3.00 |
| 370 | Chico Cardenas | 1.25 | 3.00 |
| 371 | Lee Stange | 1.25 | 3.00 |
| 372 | Harvey Kuenn | 3.00 | 8.00 |
| 373 | J.Hiatt/D.Estelle | 1.25 | 3.00 |
| 374 | Bob Locker | 2.00 | 5.00 |
| 375 | Donn Clendenon | 3.00 | 8.00 |
| 376 | Paul Schaal | 2.00 | 5.00 |
| 377 | Turk Farrell | 2.00 | 5.00 |
| 378 | Dick Tracewski | 2.00 | 5.00 |
| 379 | St. Louis Cardinals TC | 4.00 | 10.00 |
| 380 | Jim Coniglaro | 4.00 | 10.00 |
| 381 | Hank Fischer | 1.25 | 3.00 |
| 382 | Phil Roof | 2.00 | 5.00 |
| 383 | Jackie Brandt | 2.00 | 5.00 |
| 384 | Al Downing | 3.00 | 8.00 |
| 385 | Ken Boyer | 4.00 | 10.00 |
| 386 | Gil Hodges MG | 3.00 | 8.00 |
| 387 | Howie Reed | 2.00 | 5.00 |
| 388 | Don Mincher | 2.00 | 5.00 |
| 389 | Jim O'Toole | 2.00 | 5.00 |
| 390 | Brooks Robinson | 20.00 | 50.00 |
| 391 | Chuck Hinton | 2.00 | 5.00 |
| 392 | B.Hands RC/R.Hundley RC | 3.00 | 8.00 |
| 393 | George Brunet | 2.00 | 5.00 |
| 394 | Ron Brand | 2.00 | 5.00 |
| 395 | Len Gabrielson | 2.00 | 5.00 |
| 396 | Jerry Stephenson | 2.00 | 5.00 |
| 397 | Bill White | 3.00 | 8.00 |
| 398 | Danny Cater | 2.00 | 5.00 |
| 399 | Ray Washburn | 2.00 | 5.00 |
| 400 | Zoilo Versalles | 3.00 | 8.00 |
| 401 | Ken McMullen | 2.00 | 5.00 |
| 402 | Jim Hickman | 2.00 | 5.00 |
| 403 | Fred Talbot | 2.00 | 5.00 |
| 404 | Pittsburgh Pirates TC | 4.00 | 10.00 |
| 405 | Elston Howard | 3.00 | 8.00 |
| 406 | Joey Jay | 2.00 | 5.00 |
| 407 | John Kennedy | 2.00 | 5.00 |
| 408 | Lee Thomas | 2.00 | 5.00 |
| 409 | Billy Hoeft | 2.00 | 5.00 |
| 410 | Al Kaline | 15.00 | 40.00 |
| 411 | Gene Mauch MG | 2.00 | 5.00 |
| 412 | Sam Bowens | 2.00 | 5.00 |
| 413 | Johnny Romano | 2.00 | 5.00 |
| 414 | Dan Coombs | 2.00 | 5.00 |
| 415 | Max Alvis | 2.00 | 5.00 |
| 416 | Phil Ortega | 2.00 | 5.00 |
| 417 | J.McGlothlin RC/E.Sukla RC | 2.00 | 5.00 |
| 418 | Phil Gagliano | 2.00 | 5.00 |
| 419 | Mike Ryan | 2.00 | 5.00 |
| 420 | Juan Marichal | 6.00 | 15.00 |
| 421 | Roy McMillan | 2.00 | 5.00 |
| 422 | Ed Charles | 2.00 | 5.00 |
| 423 | Ernie Broglio | 2.00 | 5.00 |
| 424 | L.May RC/D.Osteen RC | 4.00 | 10.00 |
| 425 | Bob Veale | 3.00 | 8.00 |
| 426 | Chicago White Sox TC | 4.00 | 10.00 |
| 427 | John Miller | 2.00 | 5.00 |
| 428 | Sandy Alomar | 2.00 | 5.00 |
| 429 | Bill Monbouquette | 2.00 | 5.00 |
| 430 | Don Drysdale | 8.00 | 20.00 |
| 431 | Walt Bond | 2.00 | 5.00 |
| 432 | Bob Heffner | 2.00 | 5.00 |
| 433 | Alvin Dark MG | 3.00 | 8.00 |
| 434 | Willie Kirkland | 2.00 | 5.00 |
| 435 | Jim Bunning | 6.00 | 15.00 |
| 436 | Julian Javier | 3.00 | 8.00 |
| 437 | Al Stanek | 2.00 | 5.00 |
| 438 | Willie Smith | 2.00 | 5.00 |
| 439 | Pedro Ramos | 2.00 | 5.00 |
| 440 | Deron Johnson | 3.00 | 8.00 |
| 441 | Tommie Sisk | 2.00 | 5.00 |
| 442 | E.Bamowski RC/E.Watt RC | 2.00 | 5.00 |
| 443 | Bill Wakefield | 1.25 | 3.00 |
| 444 | Checklist 6 | 4.00 | 10.00 |
| 445 | Jim Kaat | 4.00 | 10.00 |
| 446 | Mack Jones | 2.00 | 5.00 |
| 447 | D.Elston UER Hubbs | 6.00 | 15.00 |
| 448 | Eddie Stanky MG | 3.00 | 8.00 |
| 449 | Joe Moeller | 4.00 | 10.00 |
| 450 | Tony Oliva | 6.00 | 15.00 |
| 451 | Barry Latman | 4.00 | 10.00 |
| 452 | Joe Azcue | 4.00 | 10.00 |
| 453 | Ron Kline | 4.00 | 10.00 |
| 454 | Jerry Buchek | 4.00 | 10.00 |
| 455 | Mickey Lolich | 6.00 | 15.00 |
| 456 | D.Brandon RC/J.Foy RC | 4.00 | 10.00 |
| 457 | Joe Gibbon | 4.00 | 10.00 |
| 458 | Manny Jiminez | 4.00 | 10.00 |
| 459 | Bill McCool | 4.00 | 10.00 |
| 460 | Curt Blefary | 4.00 | 10.00 |
| 461 | Roy Face | 6.00 | 15.00 |
| 462 | Bob Rodgers | 4.00 | 10.00 |
| 463 | Philadelphia Phillies TC | 6.00 | 15.00 |
| 464 | Larry Beamarth | 4.00 | 10.00 |
| 465 | Don Buford | 4.00 | 10.00 |
| 466 | Ken Johnson | 4.00 | 10.00 |
| 467 | Vic Roznovsky | 4.00 | 10.00 |
| 468 | Johnny Podres | 6.00 | 15.00 |
| 469 | B.Murcer RC/D.Womack RC | 12.50 | 30.00 |
| 470 | Sam McDowell | 6.00 | 15.00 |
| 471 | Bob Skinner | 4.00 | 10.00 |
| 472 | Terry Fox | 4.00 | 10.00 |
| 473 | Rich Rollins | 4.00 | 10.00 |
| 474 | Dick Schofield | 4.00 | 10.00 |
| 475 | Dick Radatz | 4.00 | 10.00 |
| 476 | Bobby Bragan MG | 4.00 | 10.00 |
| 477 | Steve Barber | 4.00 | 10.00 |
| 478 | Tony Gonzalez | 4.00 | 10.00 |
| 479 | Jim Hannan | 4.00 | 10.00 |
| 480 | Dick Stuart | 4.00 | 10.00 |
| 481 | Bob Lee | 4.00 | 10.00 |
| 482 | J.Boccabella/D.Dowling | 4.00 | 10.00 |
| 483 | Joe Nuxhall | 4.00 | 10.00 |
| 484 | Wes Covington | 4.00 | 10.00 |
| 485 | Bob Bailey | 4.00 | 10.00 |
| 486 | Tommy John | 6.00 | 15.00 |
| 487 | Al Ferrara | 4.00 | 10.00 |
| 488 | George Banks | 4.00 | 10.00 |
| 489 | Curt Simmons | 4.00 | 10.00 |
| 490 | Bobby Richardson | 10.00 | 25.00 |
| 491 | Dennis Bennett | 4.00 | 10.00 |
| 492 | Kansas City Athletics TC | 6.00 | 15.00 |
| 493 | Johnny Klippstein | 4.00 | 10.00 |
| 494 | Gordy Coleman | 4.00 | 10.00 |
| 495 | Dick McAuliffe | 6.00 | 15.00 |
| 496 | Lindy McDaniel | 4.00 | 10.00 |
| 497 | Chris Cannizzaro | 4.00 | 10.00 |
| 498 | L.Walker RC/W.Fryman RC | 4.00 | 10.00 |
| 499 | Wally Bunker | 4.00 | 10.00 |
| 500 | Hank Aaron | 60.00 | 120.00 |
| 501 | John O'Donoghue | 4.00 | 10.00 |
| 502 | Lenny Green UER | 4.00 | 10.00 |
| 503 | Steve Hamilton | 6.00 | 15.00 |
| 504 | Grady Hatton MG | 4.00 | 10.00 |
| 505 | Jose Cardenal | 6.00 | 15.00 |
| 506 | Bo Belinsky | 4.00 | 10.00 |
| 507 | Johnny Edwards | 4.00 | 10.00 |
| 508 | Steve Hargan RC | 6.00 | 15.00 |
| 509 | Jake Wood | 4.00 | 10.00 |
| 510 | Hoyt Wilhelm | 10.00 | 25.00 |
| 511 | B.Barton RC/T.Fuentes RC | 6.00 | 15.00 |
| 512 | Dick Stigman | 4.00 | 10.00 |
| 513 | Camilo Carreon | 4.00 | 10.00 |
| 514 | Hal Woodeshick | 4.00 | 10.00 |
| 515 | Frank Howard | 6.00 | 15.00 |
| 516 | Eddie Bressoud | 4.00 | 10.00 |
| 517A | Checklist 7 White Sox | 6.00 | 15.00 |
| 517B | Checklist 7 W.Sox | 6.00 | 15.00 |
| 518 | H.Hippauf RC/A.Umbach RC | 4.00 | 10.00 |

| | | |
|---|---|---|
| ❏ 519 Bob Friend | 6.00 | 15.00 |
| ❏ 520 Jim Wynn | 6.00 | 15.00 |
| ❏ 521 John Wyatt | 4.00 | 10.00 |
| ❏ 522 Phil Linz | 4.00 | 10.00 |
| ❏ 523 Bob Sadowski | 4.00 | 10.00 |
| ❏ 524 O.Brown RC/D.Mason RC SP | 12.50 | 30.00 |
| ❏ 525 Gary Bell SP | 12.50 | 30.00 |
| ❏ 526 Minnesota Twins TC SP | 50.00 | 100.00 |
| ❏ 527 Julio Navarro | 6.00 | 15.00 |
| ❏ 528 Jesse Gonder SP | 12.50 | 30.00 |
| ❏ 529 Elia/Higgins/Voss RC | 6.00 | 15.00 |
| ❏ 530 Robin Roberts | 20.00 | 50.00 |
| ❏ 531 Joe Cunningham | 6.00 | 15.00 |
| ❏ 532 A.Monteagudo SP | 12.50 | 30.00 |
| ❏ 533 Jerry Adair SP | 12.50 | 30.00 |
| ❏ 534 D.Eilers RC/R.Gardner RC | 6.00 | 15.00 |
| ❏ 535 Willie Davis SP | 15.00 | 40.00 |
| ❏ 536 Dick Egan | 6.00 | 15.00 |
| ❏ 537 Herman Franks MG | 6.00 | 15.00 |
| ❏ 538 Bob Allen SP | 12.50 | 30.00 |
| ❏ 539 B.Heath RC/C.Sembera RC | 10.00 | 25.00 |
| ❏ 540 Denny McLain SP | 30.00 | 60.00 |
| ❏ 541 Gene Oliver SP | 12.50 | 30.00 |
| ❏ 542 George Smith | 6.00 | 15.00 |
| ❏ 543 Roger Craig SP | 12.50 | 30.00 |
| ❏ 544 Hoerner/Kernek/Williams RC SP | 12.50 | 30.00 |
| ❏ 545 Dick Green SP | 12.50 | 30.00 |
| ❏ 546 Dwight Siebler | 12.50 | 30.00 |
| ❏ 547 Horace Clarke SR RC | 15.00 | 40.00 |
| ❏ 548 Gary Kroll SP | 12.50 | 30.00 |
| ❏ 549 A.Closter RC/C.Cox RC | 6.00 | 15.00 |
| ❏ 550 Willie McCovey SP | 50.00 | 100.00 |
| ❏ 551 Bob Purkey SP | 12.50 | 30.00 |
| ❏ 552 B.Tebbetts MG SP | 12.50 | 30.00 |
| ❏ 553 P.Garrett RC/J.Warner | 6.00 | 15.00 |
| ❏ 554 Jim Northrup SP | 12.50 | 30.00 |
| ❏ 555 Ron Perranoski SP | 12.50 | 30.00 |
| ❏ 556 Mel Queen SP | 12.50 | 30.00 |
| ❏ 557 Felix Mantilla SP | 12.50 | 30.00 |
| ❏ 558 Grilli/Magrini/Scott RC | 8.00 | 20.00 |
| ❏ 559 Roberto Pena SP | 12.50 | 30.00 |
| ❏ 560 Joel Horlen | 6.00 | 15.00 |
| ❏ 561 Choo Choo Coleman SP | 12.50 | 30.00 |
| ❏ 562 Russ Snyder | 10.00 | 25.00 |
| ❏ 563 P.Cimino RC/C.Tovar RC | 6.00 | 15.00 |
| ❏ 564 Bob Chance SP | 12.50 | 30.00 |
| ❏ 565 Jimmy Piersall SP | 15.00 | 40.00 |
| ❏ 566 Mike Cuellar SP | 12.50 | 30.00 |
| ❏ 567 Dick Howser SP | 15.00 | 40.00 |
| ❏ 568 P.Lindblad RC/R.Stone RC | 6.00 | 15.00 |
| ❏ 569 Orlando McFarlane SP | 12.50 | 30.00 |
| ❏ 570 Art Mahaffey SP | 12.50 | 30.00 |
| ❏ 571 Dave Roberts SP | 12.50 | 30.00 |
| ❏ 572 Bob Priddy | 6.00 | 15.00 |
| ❏ 573 Derrell Griffith | 6.00 | 15.00 |
| ❏ 574 B.Hepler RC/B.Murphy RC | 6.00 | 15.00 |
| ❏ 575 Earl Wilson | 6.00 | 15.00 |
| ❏ 576 Dave Nicholson SP | 12.50 | 30.00 |
| ❏ 577 Jack Lamabe SP | 12.50 | 30.00 |
| ❏ 578 Chi Chi Olivo SP RC | 12.50 | 30.00 |
| ❏ 579 Bertaina/Brabender/Johnson RC | 8.00 | 20.00 |
| ❏ 580 Billy Williams SP | 30.00 | 60.00 |
| ❏ 581 Tony Martinez | 6.00 | 15.00 |
| ❏ 582 Garry Roggenburk | 6.00 | 15.00 |
| ❏ 583 Detroit Tigers TC SP | 60.00 | 120.00 |
| ❏ 584 F.Fernandez RC/F.Peterson RC | 6.00 | 15.00 |
| ❏ 585 Tony Taylor SP | 10.00 | 25.00 |
| ❏ 586 Claude Raymond SP | 12.50 | 30.00 |
| ❏ 587 Dick Bertell | 6.00 | 15.00 |
| ❏ 588 C.Dobson RC/R.Suarez RC | 6.00 | 15.00 |
| ❏ 589 Lou Klimchock SP | 12.50 | 30.00 |
| ❏ 590 Bill Skowron SP | 15.00 | 40.00 |
| ❏ 591 B.Shirley RC/J.Jackson RC SP | 15.00 | 40.00 |
| ❏ 592 Andre Rodgers | 6.00 | 15.00 |
| ❏ 593 Doug Camilli SP | 12.50 | 30.00 |
| ❏ 594 Chico Salmon | 6.00 | 15.00 |
| ❏ 595 Larry Jackson SP | 12.50 | 30.00 |
| ❏ 596 N.Colbert RC/G.Sims RC SP | 12.50 | 30.00 |
| ❏ 597 John Sullivan | 6.00 | 15.00 |
| ❏ 598 Gaylord Perry SP | 100.00 | 200.00 |

### 1967 Topps

| | | |
|---|---|---|
| ❏ COMPLETE SET (609) | 2500.00 | 5000.00 |
| ❏ COMMON CARD (1-109) | .60 | 1.50 |
| ❏ COMMON CARD (110-283) | .75 | 2.00 |
| ❏ COMMON CARD (284-370) | 1.00 | 2.50 |
| ❏ COMMON CARD (371-457) | 1.50 | 4.00 |
| ❏ COMMON CARD (458-533) | 2.50 | 6.00 |
| ❏ COMMON CARD (534-609) | 6.00 | 15.00 |
| ❏ COMMON DP (534-609) | 3.00 | 8.00 |
| ❏ WRAPPER (5-CENT) | 10.00 | 25.00 |
| ❏ 1 Robinson/Bauer/Robinson DP | 10.00 | 25.00 |
| ❏ 2 Jack Hamilton | .60 | 1.50 |
| ❏ 3 Duke Sims | .60 | 1.50 |
| ❏ 4 Hal Lanier | .60 | 1.50 |
| ❏ 5 Whitey Ford UER | 8.00 | 20.00 |
| ❏ 6 Dick Simpson | .60 | 1.50 |
| ❏ 7 Don McMahon | .60 | 1.50 |
| ❏ 8 Chuck Harrison | .60 | 1.50 |
| ❏ 9 Ron Hansen | .60 | 1.50 |
| ❏ 10 Matty Alou | 1.50 | 4.00 |
| ❏ 11 Barry Moore RC | .60 | 1.50 |
| ❏ 12 J.Campanis RC/B.Singer | 1.50 | 4.00 |
| ❏ 13 Joe Sparma | .60 | 1.50 |
| ❏ 14 Phil Linz | 1.50 | 4.00 |
| ❏ 15 Earl Battey | .60 | 1.50 |
| ❏ 16 Bill Hands | .60 | 1.50 |
| ❏ 17 Jim Gosger | .60 | 1.50 |
| ❏ 18 Gene Oliver | .60 | 1.50 |
| ❏ 19 Jim McGlothlin | .60 | 1.50 |
| ❏ 20 Orlando Cepeda | 3.00 | 8.00 |
| ❏ 21 Dave Bristol MG RC | .60 | 1.50 |
| ❏ 22 Gene Brabender | .60 | 1.50 |
| ❏ 23 Larry Elliot | .60 | 1.50 |
| ❏ 24 Bob Allen | .60 | 1.50 |
| ❏ 25 Elston Howard | 1.50 | 4.00 |
| ❏ 26A Bob Priddy NTR | 12.50 | 30.00 |
| ❏ 26B Bob Priddy TR | 1.50 | 4.00 |
| ❏ 27 Bob Saverine | .60 | 1.50 |
| ❏ 28 Barry Latman | .60 | 1.50 |
| ❏ 29 Tom McCraw | .60 | 1.50 |
| ❏ 30 Al Kaline DP | 8.00 | 20.00 |
| ❏ 31 Jim Brewer | .60 | 1.50 |
| ❏ 32 Bob Bailey | 1.50 | 4.00 |
| ❏ 33 S.Bando RC/R.Schwartz RC | 2.50 | 6.00 |
| ❏ 34 Pete Cimino | .60 | 1.50 |
| ❏ 35 Rico Carty | 1.50 | 4.00 |
| ❏ 36 Bob Tillman | .60 | 1.50 |
| ❏ 37 Rick Wise | 1.50 | 4.00 |
| ❏ 38 Bob Johnson | .60 | 1.50 |
| ❏ 39 Curt Simmons | 1.50 | 4.00 |
| ❏ 40 Rick Reichardt | .60 | 1.50 |
| ❏ 41 Joe Hoerner | .60 | 1.50 |
| ❏ 42 New York Mets TC | 4.00 | 10.00 |
| ❏ 43 Chico Salmon | .60 | 1.50 |
| ❏ 44 Joe Nuxhall | 1.50 | 4.00 |
| ❏ 45 Roger Maris | 20.00 | 50.00 |
| ❏ 45A R.Maris Yanks/Blank Back | 900.00 | 1500.00 |
| ❏ 46 Lindy McDaniel | .60 | 1.50 |
| ❏ 47 Ken McMullen | .60 | 1.50 |
| ❏ 48 Bill Freehan | 1.50 | 4.00 |
| ❏ 49 Roy Face | 1.50 | 4.00 |
| ❏ 50 Tony Oliva | 2.50 | 6.00 |
| ❏ 51 D.Adlesh RC/W.Bales RC | .60 | 1.50 |
| ❏ 52 Dennis Higgins | .60 | 1.50 |
| ❏ 53 Clay Dalrymple | .60 | 1.50 |
| ❏ 54 Dick Green | .60 | 1.50 |
| ❏ 55 Don Drysdale | 6.00 | 15.00 |
| ❏ 56 Jose Tartabull | .60 | 1.50 |
| ❏ 57 Pat Jarvis RC | 1.50 | 4.00 |
| ❏ 58A P.Schaal Green Bat | 8.00 | 20.00 |
| ❏ 58B P.Schaal Normal Bat | .60 | 1.50 |
| ❏ 59 Ralph Terry | 1.50 | 4.00 |
| ❏ 60 Luis Aparicio | 3.00 | 8.00 |
| ❏ 61 Gordy Coleman | .60 | 1.50 |
| ❏ 62 Frank Robinson CL1 | 3.00 | 8.00 |
| ❏ 63 L.Brock/C.Flood | 3.00 | 8.00 |
| ❏ 64 Fred Valentine | .60 | 1.50 |
| ❏ 65 Tom Haller | 1.50 | 4.00 |
| ❏ 66 Manny Mota | 1.50 | 4.00 |
| ❏ 67 Ken Berry | .60 | 1.50 |
| ❏ 68 Bob Buhl | 1.50 | 4.00 |
| ❏ 69 Vic Davalillo | .60 | 1.50 |
| ❏ 70 Ron Santo | 2.50 | 6.00 |
| ❏ 71 Camilo Pascual | 1.50 | 4.00 |
| ❏ 72 G.Korince ERR RC/T.Matchick RC | .60 | 1.50 |
| ❏ 73 Rusty Staub | 2.50 | 6.00 |
| ❏ 74 Wes Stock | .60 | 1.50 |
| ❏ 75 George Scott | 1.50 | 4.00 |
| ❏ 76 Jim Barbieri RC | .60 | 1.50 |
| ❏ 77 Dooley Womack | 1.50 | 4.00 |
| ❏ 78 Pat Corrales | 1.50 | 4.00 |
| ❏ 79 Bubba Morton | .60 | 1.50 |
| ❏ 80 Jim Maloney | 1.50 | 4.00 |
| ❏ 81 Eddie Stanky MG | 1.50 | 4.00 |
| ❏ 82 Steve Barber | .60 | 1.50 |
| ❏ 83 Ollie Brown | .60 | 1.50 |
| ❏ 84 Tommie Sisk | .60 | 1.50 |
| ❏ 85 Johnny Callison | 1.50 | 4.00 |
| ❏ 86A Mike McCormick NTR | 12.50 | 30.00 |
| ❏ 86B Mike McCormick TR | 1.50 | 4.00 |
| ❏ 87 George Altman | .60 | 1.50 |
| ❏ 88 Mickey Lolich | 1.50 | 4.00 |
| ❏ 89 Felix Millan RC | 1.50 | 4.00 |
| ❏ 90 Jim Nash RC | .60 | 1.50 |
| ❏ 91 Johnny Lewis | .60 | 1.50 |
| ❏ 92 Ray Washburn | .60 | 1.50 |
| ❏ 93 S.Bahnsen RC/B.Murcer | 6.00 | 15.00 |
| ❏ 94 Ron Fairly | 1.50 | 4.00 |
| ❏ 95 Sonny Siebert | .60 | 1.50 |
| ❏ 96 Art Shamsky | .60 | 1.50 |
| ❏ 97 Mike Cuellar | 1.50 | 4.00 |
| ❏ 98 Rich Rollins | .60 | 1.50 |
| ❏ 99 Lee Stange | .60 | 1.50 |
| ❏ 100 Frank Robinson DP | 6.00 | 15.00 |
| ❏ 101 Ken Johnson | .60 | 1.50 |
| ❏ 102 Philadelphia Phillies TC | 1.50 | 4.00 |
| ❏ 103A Mickey Mantle CL2 DP D.Mc | 8.00 | 20.00 |
| ❏ 104 Minnie Rojas RC | .60 | 1.50 |
| ❏ 105 Ken Boyer | 2.50 | 6.00 |
| ❏ 106 Randy Hundley | 1.50 | 4.00 |
| ❏ 107 Joel Horlen | .60 | 1.50 |
| ❏ 108 Alex Johnson | 1.50 | 4.00 |
| ❏ 109 R.Colavito/L.Wagner | 2.50 | 6.00 |
| ❏ 110 Jack Aker | .75 | 2.00 |
| ❏ 111 John Kennedy | .75 | 2.00 |
| ❏ 112 Dave Wickersham | .75 | 2.00 |
| ❏ 113 Dave Nicholson | .75 | 2.00 |
| ❏ 114 Jack Baldschun | .75 | 2.00 |
| ❏ 115 Paul Casanova RC | .75 | 2.00 |
| ❏ 116 Herman Franks MG | .75 | 2.00 |
| ❏ 117 Darrell Brandon | .75 | 2.00 |
| ❏ 118 Bernie Allen | .75 | 2.00 |
| ❏ 119 Wade Blasingame | .75 | 2.00 |
| ❏ 120 Floyd Robinson | .75 | 2.00 |
| ❏ 121 Eddie Bressoud | .75 | 2.00 |
| ❏ 122 George Brunet | .75 | 2.00 |
| ❏ 123 J.Price RC/L.Walker | 1.50 | 4.00 |
| ❏ 124 Jim Stewart | .75 | 2.00 |
| ❏ 125 Moe Drabowsky | 1.50 | 4.00 |
| ❏ 126 Tony Taylor | .75 | 2.00 |
| ❏ 127 John O'Donoghue | .75 | 2.00 |
| ❏ 128 Ed Spiezio RC | .75 | 2.00 |
| ❏ 129 Phil Roof | .75 | 2.00 |
| ❏ 130 Phil Regan | 1.50 | 4.00 |
| ❏ 131 New York Yankees TC | 4.00 | 10.00 |
| ❏ 132 Ozzie Virgil | .75 | 2.00 |
| ❏ 133 Ron Kline | .75 | 2.00 |
| ❏ 134 Gates Brown | 2.50 | 6.00 |
| ❏ 135 Deron Johnson | 1.50 | 4.00 |
| ❏ 136 Carroll Sembera | .75 | 2.00 |
| ❏ 137 R.Clark RC/J.Ollum | .75 | 2.00 |
| ❏ 138 Dick Kelley | .75 | 2.00 |
| ❏ 139 Dalton Jones | 1.50 | 4.00 |
| ❏ 140 Willie Stargell | 8.00 | 20.00 |
| ❏ 141 John Miller | .75 | 2.00 |
| ❏ 142 Jackie Brandt | .75 | 2.00 |
| ❏ 143 P.Ward/D.Buford | .75 | 2.00 |
| ❏ 144 Bill Hepler | .75 | 2.00 |
| ❏ 145 Larry Brown | .75 | 2.00 |
| ❏ 146 Steve Carlton | 20.00 | 50.00 |
| ❏ 147 Tom Egan | .75 | 2.00 |
| ❏ 148 Adolfo Phillips | .75 | 2.00 |
| ❏ 149 Joe Moeller | .75 | 2.00 |
| ❏ 150 Mickey Mantle | 175.00 | 350.00 |
| ❏ 151 Moe Drabowsky WS1 | 2.00 | 5.00 |
| ❏ 152 Jim Palmer WS2 | 3.00 | 8.00 |
| ❏ 153 Paul Blair WS3 | 2.00 | 5.00 |
| ❏ 154 Robinson/McNally WS4 | 2.00 | 5.00 |
| ❏ 155 Orioles Celebrate WS | 2.00 | 5.00 |

|  |  | | |
|---|---|---|---|
| 156 | Ron Herbel | .75 | 2.00 |
| 157 | Danny Cater | .75 | 2.00 |
| 158 | Jimmie Coker | .75 | 2.00 |
| 159 | Bruce Howard | .75 | 2.00 |
| 160 | Willie Davis | 1.50 | 4.00 |
| 161 | Dick Williams MG | 1.50 | 4.00 |
| 162 | Billy O'Dell | .75 | 2.00 |
| 163 | Vic Roznovsky | .75 | 2.00 |
| 164 | Dwight Siebler UER | .75 | 2.00 |
| 165 | Cleon Jones | 1.50 | 4.00 |
| 166 | Eddie Mathews | 6.00 | 15.00 |
| 167 | J.Coleman RC/T.Cullen RC | .75 | 2.00 |
| 168 | Ray Culp | .75 | 2.00 |
| 169 | Horace Clarke | 1.50 | 4.00 |
| 170 | Dick McAuliffe | 1.50 | 4.00 |
| 171 | Cal Koonce | .75 | 2.00 |
| 172 | Bill Heath | .75 | 2.00 |
| 173 | St. Louis Cardinals TC | 1.50 | 4.00 |
| 174 | Dick Radatz | 1.50 | 4.00 |
| 175 | Bobby Knoop | .75 | 2.00 |
| 176 | Sammy Ellis | .75 | 2.00 |
| 177 | Tito Fuentes | .60 | 1.50 |
| 178 | John Buzhardt | .75 | 2.00 |
| 179 | C.Vaughan RC/C.Epshaw RC | 1.50 | 4.00 |
| 180 | Curt Blefary | .75 | 2.00 |
| 181 | Terry Fox | .75 | 2.00 |
| 182 | Ed Charles | .75 | 2.00 |
| 183 | Jim Pagliaroni | .75 | 2.00 |
| 184 | George Thomas | .75 | 2.00 |
| 185 | Ken Holtzman RC | 1.50 | 4.00 |
| 186 | E.Kranepool/R.Swoboda | 1.50 | 4.00 |
| 187 | Pedro Ramos | .75 | 2.00 |
| 188 | Ken Harrelson | 1.50 | 4.00 |
| 189 | Chuck Hinton | .75 | 2.00 |
| 190 | Turk Farrell | .75 | 2.00 |
| 191A | W.Mays CL3 214 Tom | 4.00 | 10.00 |
| 191B | W.Mays CL3 214 Dick | 5.00 | 12.00 |
| 192 | Fred Gladding | .75 | 2.00 |
| 193 | Jose Cardenal | 1.50 | 4.00 |
| 194 | Bob Allison | 1.50 | 4.00 |
| 195 | Al Jackson | .75 | 2.00 |
| 196 | Johnny Romano | .75 | 2.00 |
| 197 | Ron Perranoski | 1.50 | 4.00 |
| 198 | Chuck Hiller | .75 | 2.00 |
| 199 | Billy Hitchcock MG | .75 | 2.00 |
| 200 | Willie Mays UER | 50.00 | 100.00 |
| 201 | Hal Reniff | 1.50 | 4.00 |
| 202 | Johnny Edwards | .75 | 2.00 |
| 203 | Al McBean | .75 | 2.00 |
| 204 | M.Epstein RC/T.Phoebus RC | 2.50 | 6.00 |
| 205 | Dick Groat | 1.50 | 4.00 |
| 206 | Dennis Bennett | .75 | 2.00 |
| 207 | John Orsino | .75 | 2.00 |
| 208 | Jack Lamabe | .75 | 2.00 |
| 209 | Joe Nossek | .75 | 2.00 |
| 210 | Bob Gibson | 8.00 | 20.00 |
| 211 | Minnesota Twins TC | 1.50 | 4.00 |
| 212 | Chris Zachary | .75 | 2.00 |
| 213 | Jay Johnstone RC | 1.50 | 4.00 |
| 214 | Dick Kelley | .75 | 2.00 |
| 215 | Ernie Banks | 8.00 | 20.00 |
| 216 | A.Kaline/N.Cash | 3.00 | 8.00 |
| 217 | Rob Gardner | .75 | 2.00 |
| 218 | Wes Parker | 1.50 | 4.00 |
| 219 | Clay Carroll | 1.50 | 4.00 |
| 220 | Jim Ray Hart | 1.50 | 4.00 |
| 221 | Woody Fryman | 1.50 | 4.00 |
| 222 | O.Osteen/L.May | 1.50 | 4.00 |
| 223 | Mike Ryan | 1.50 | 4.00 |
| 224 | Walt Bond | .75 | 2.00 |
| 225 | Mel Stottlemyre | 2.50 | 6.00 |
| 226 | Julian Javier | 1.50 | 4.00 |
| 227 | Paul Lindblad | .75 | 2.00 |
| 228 | Gil Hodges MG | 2.50 | 6.00 |
| 229 | Larry Jackson | .75 | 2.00 |
| 230 | Boog Powell | 2.50 | 6.00 |
| 231 | John Bateman | .75 | 2.00 |
| 232 | Don Buford | .75 | 2.00 |
| 233 | Peters/Horlen/Hargan LL | 1.50 | 4.00 |
| 234 | Koufax/Cuellar/Marichal LL | 6.00 | 15.00 |
| 235 | Kaat/McLain/Wilson LL | 2.50 | 6.00 |
| 236 | Koufax/Mari/Gibs/Perry LL | 10.00 | 25.00 |
| 237 | McDowell/Kaat/Wilson LL | 2.50 | 6.00 |
| 238 | Koufax/Bunning/Veale LL | 5.00 | 12.00 |
| 239 | F.Rob/Oliva/Kaline LL | 2.50 | 6.00 |
| 240 | Alou/Alcar/Carty LL | 2.50 | 6.00 |
| 241 | F.Rob/Killebrew/Powell LL | 4.00 | 10.00 |
| 242 | Aaron/Clemente/Allen LL | 10.00 | 25.00 |
| 243 | F.Rob/Killebrew/Powell LL | 4.00 | 10.00 |
| 244 | Aaron/Allen/Mays LL | 8.00 | 20.00 |
| 245 | Curt Flood | 2.50 | 6.00 |
| 246 | Jim Perry | 1.50 | 4.00 |
| 247 | Jerry Lumpe | .75 | 2.00 |
| 248 | Gene Mauch MG | 1.50 | 4.00 |
| 249 | Nick Willhite | .75 | 2.00 |
| 250 | Hank Aaron RR | 40.00 | 80.00 |
| 251 | Woody Held | .75 | 2.00 |
| 252 | Bob Bolin | .75 | 2.00 |
| 253 | B.Davis/G.Gil RC | .75 | 2.00 |
| 254 | Milt Pappas | 1.50 | 4.00 |
| 255 | Frank Howard | 1.50 | 4.00 |
| 256 | Bob Hendley | .75 | 2.00 |
| 257 | Charlie Smith | .75 | 2.00 |
| 258 | Lee Maye | .75 | 2.00 |
| 259 | Don Dennis | .75 | 2.00 |
| 260 | Jim Lefebvre | 1.50 | 4.00 |
| 261 | John Wyatt | .75 | 2.00 |
| 262 | Kansas City Athletics TC | 1.50 | 4.00 |
| 263 | Hank Aguirre | .75 | 2.00 |
| 264 | Ron Swoboda | 1.50 | 4.00 |
| 265 | Lou Burdette | 1.50 | 4.00 |
| 266 | W.Stargell/D.Clendenon | 1.50 | 4.00 |
| 267 | Don Schwall | .75 | 2.00 |
| 268 | Johnny Briggs | .75 | 2.00 |
| 269 | Don Nottebart | .75 | 2.00 |
| 270 | Zoilo Versalles | .75 | 2.00 |
| 271 | Eddie Watt | .75 | 2.00 |
| 272 | B.Connors RC/D.Dowling | 1.50 | 4.00 |
| 273 | Dick Lines RC | .75 | 2.00 |
| 274 | Bob Aspromonte | .75 | 2.00 |
| 275 | Fred Whitfield | .75 | 2.00 |
| 276 | Bruce Brubaker | .75 | 2.00 |
| 277 | Steve Whitaker RC | 2.50 | 6.00 |
| 278 | Jim Kaat CL4 | 3.00 | 8.00 |
| 279 | Frank Linzy | .75 | 2.00 |
| 280 | Tony Conigliaro | 3.00 | 8.00 |
| 281 | Bob Rodgers | .75 | 2.00 |
| 282 | John Odom | .75 | 2.00 |
| 283 | Gene Alley | 1.50 | 4.00 |
| 284 | Johnny Podres | 1.50 | 4.00 |
| 285 | Lou Brock | 8.00 | 20.00 |
| 286 | Wayne Causey | 1.00 | 2.50 |
| 287 | G.Goosen RC/B.Shirley | 1.00 | 2.50 |
| 288 | Denny Lemaster | 1.00 | 2.50 |
| 289 | Tom Tresh | 2.00 | 5.00 |
| 290 | Bill White | 2.00 | 5.00 |
| 291 | Jim Hannan | 1.00 | 2.50 |
| 292 | Jim Pavletich | 1.00 | 2.50 |
| 293 | Ed Kirkpatrick | 1.00 | 2.50 |
| 294 | Walter Alston MG | 3.00 | 8.00 |
| 295 | Sam McDowell | 2.00 | 5.00 |
| 296 | Glenn Beckert | 2.00 | 5.00 |
| 297 | Dave Morehead | 1.00 | 2.50 |
| 298 | Ron Davis RC | 1.00 | 2.50 |
| 299 | Norm Siebern | 1.00 | 2.50 |
| 300 | Jim Kaat | 5.00 | 12.00 |
| 301 | Jesse Gonder | 1.00 | 2.50 |
| 302 | Baltimore Orioles TC | 2.00 | 5.00 |
| 303 | Gil Blanco | 1.00 | 2.50 |
| 304 | Phil Gagliano | 1.00 | 2.50 |
| 305 | Earl Wilson | 1.00 | 2.50 |
| 306 | Bud Harrelson RC | 2.00 | 5.00 |
| 307 | Jim Beauchamp | 1.00 | 2.50 |
| 308 | Al Downing | 2.00 | 5.00 |
| 309 | J.Callison/R.Allen | 2.00 | 5.00 |
| 310 | Gary Peters | 1.00 | 2.50 |
| 311 | Ed Brinkman | 1.00 | 2.50 |
| 312 | Don Mincher | 1.00 | 2.50 |
| 313 | Bob Lee | 1.00 | 2.50 |
| 314 | M.Andrews RC/R.Smith RC | 3.00 | 8.00 |
| 315 | Billy Williams | 6.00 | 15.00 |
| 316 | Jack Kralick | 1.00 | 2.50 |
| 317 | Cesar Tovar | 1.00 | 2.50 |
| 318 | Dave Giusti | 1.00 | 2.50 |
| 319 | Paul Blair | 2.00 | 5.00 |
| 320 | Gaylord Perry | 6.00 | 15.00 |
| 321 | Mayo Smith MG | 1.00 | 2.50 |
| 322 | Jose Pagan | 1.00 | 2.50 |
| 323 | Mike Hershberger | 1.00 | 2.50 |
| 324 | Hal Woodeshick | 1.00 | 2.50 |
| 325 | Chico Cardenas | 1.00 | 2.50 |
| 326 | Bob Uecker | 4.00 | 10.00 |
| 327 | California Angels TC | 2.00 | 5.00 |
| 328 | Clete Boyer UER | 2.00 | 5.00 |
| 329 | Charlie Lau | 2.00 | 5.00 |
| 330 | Claude Osteen | 2.00 | 5.00 |
| 331 | Joe Foy | 2.00 | 5.00 |
| 332 | Jesus Alou | 1.00 | 2.50 |
| 333 | Fergie Jenkins | 8.00 | 20.00 |
| 334 | H.Killebrew/B.Allison | 4.00 | 10.00 |
| 335 | Bob Veale | 2.00 | 5.00 |
| 336 | Joe Azcue | 1.00 | 2.50 |
| 337 | Joe Morgan | 6.00 | 15.00 |
| 338 | Bob Locker | 1.00 | 2.50 |
| 339 | Chico Ruiz | 1.00 | 2.50 |
| 340 | Joe Pepitone | 3.00 | 8.00 |
| 341 | D.Dietz RC/B.Sorrell | 1.00 | 2.50 |
| 342 | Hank Fischer | 1.00 | 2.50 |
| 343 | Tom Satriano | 1.00 | 2.50 |
| 344 | Ossie Chavarria RC | 1.00 | 2.50 |
| 345 | Stu Miller | 2.00 | 5.00 |
| 346 | Jim Hickman | 1.00 | 2.50 |
| 347 | Grady Hatton MG | 1.00 | 2.50 |
| 348 | Tug McGraw | 3.00 | 8.00 |
| 349 | Bob Chance | 1.00 | 2.50 |
| 350 | Joe Torre | 3.00 | 8.00 |
| 351 | Vern Law | 2.00 | 5.00 |
| 352 | Ray Oyler | 1.00 | 2.50 |
| 353 | Bill McCool | 1.00 | 2.50 |
| 354 | Chicago Cubs TC | 3.00 | 8.00 |
| 355 | Carl Yastrzemski | 30.00 | 60.00 |
| 356 | Larry Jaster RC | 1.00 | 2.50 |
| 357 | Bill Skowron | 2.00 | 5.00 |
| 358 | Ruben Amaro | 1.00 | 2.50 |
| 359 | Dick Ellsworth | 1.00 | 2.50 |
| 360 | Leon Wagner | 1.00 | 2.50 |
| 361 | Roberto Clemente CL5 | 6.00 | 15.00 |
| 362 | Darold Knowles | 1.00 | 2.50 |
| 363 | Davey Johnson | 2.00 | 5.00 |
| 364 | Claude Raymond | 1.00 | 2.50 |
| 365 | John Roseboro | 2.00 | 5.00 |
| 366 | Andy Kosco | 1.00 | 2.50 |
| 367 | B.Kelso/D.Wallace RC | 1.00 | 2.50 |
| 368 | Jack Hiatt | 1.00 | 2.50 |
| 369 | Jim Hunter | 6.00 | 15.00 |
| 370 | Tommy Davis | 2.00 | 5.00 |
| 371 | Jim Lonborg | 3.00 | 8.00 |
| 372 | Mike de la Hoz | 1.00 | 4.00 |
| 373 | D.Josephson RC/F.Klages RC DP | 1.50 | 4.00 |
| 374A | Mel Queen ERR | 8.00 | 20.00 |
| 374B | Mel Queen COR DP | 1.50 | 4.00 |
| 375 | Jake Gibbs | 1.00 | 2.50 |
| 376 | Don Lock DP | 1.00 | 2.50 |
| 377 | Luis Tiant | 3.00 | 8.00 |
| 378 | Detroit Tigers TC UER | 3.00 | 8.00 |
| 379 | Jerry May DP | 1.00 | 2.50 |
| 380 | Dean Chance DP | 1.50 | 4.00 |
| 381 | Dick Schofield DP | 1.00 | 2.50 |
| 382 | Dave McNally | 3.00 | 8.00 |
| 383 | Ken Henderson DP | 1.50 | 4.00 |
| 384 | J.Cosman RC/D.Hughes RC | 1.50 | 4.00 |
| 385 | Jim Fregosi | 3.00 | 8.00 |
| 386 | Dick Selma DP | 1.50 | 4.00 |
| 387 | Cap Peterson DP | 1.50 | 4.00 |
| 388 | Arnold Earley DP | 1.50 | 4.00 |
| 389 | Alvin Dark MG DP | 3.00 | 8.00 |
| 390 | Jim Wynn DP | 3.00 | 8.00 |
| 391 | Wilbur Wood DP | 1.50 | 4.00 |
| 392 | Tommy Harper DP | 3.00 | 8.00 |
| 393 | Jim Bouton DP | 3.00 | 8.00 |
| 394 | Jake Wood DP | 1.50 | 4.00 |
| 395 | Chris Short DP | 3.00 | 8.00 |
| 396 | D.Menke/T.Cloninger | 1.50 | 4.00 |
| 397 | Willie Smith DP | 1.50 | 4.00 |
| 398 | Jeff Torborg | 3.00 | 8.00 |
| 399 | Al Worthington DP | 1.50 | 4.00 |
| 400 | Roberto Clemente DP | 60.00 | 120.00 |
| 401 | Jim Coates DP | 1.50 | 4.00 |
| 402A | G.Jackson/B.Wilson Stat Line | 8.00 | 20.00 |
| 402B | G.Jackson/B.Wilson RC DP | 3.00 | 8.00 |
| 403 | Dick Nen DP | 1.50 | 4.00 |
| 404 | Nelson Briles | 3.00 | 8.00 |
| 405 | Russ Snyder DP | 1.50 | 4.00 |
| 406 | Lee Elia DP | 1.50 | 4.00 |
| 407 | Cincinnati Reds TC | 3.00 | 8.00 |
| 408 | Jim Northrup DP | 3.00 | 8.00 |
| 409 | Ray Sadecki DP | 1.50 | 4.00 |
| 410 | Lou Johnson DP | 1.50 | 4.00 |
| 411 | Dick Howser DP | 1.50 | 4.00 |
| 412 | N.Miller RC/D.Rader RC | 1.50 | 4.00 |
| 413 | Jerry Grote | 3.00 | 8.00 |
| 414 | Casey Cox | 1.50 | 4.00 |
| 415 | Sonny Jackson | 1.50 | 4.00 |
| 416 | Roger Repoz | 1.50 | 4.00 |

| | | |
|---|---|---|
| 417A Bob Bruce ERR | 12.50 | 30.00 |
| 417B Bob Bruce COR DP | 1.50 | 4.00 |
| 418 Sam Mele MG | 1.50 | 4.00 |
| 419 Don Kessinger DP | 4.00 | 8.00 |
| 420 Denny McLain | 5.00 | 12.00 |
| 421 Dal Maxvill DP | 1.50 | 4.00 |
| 422 Hoyt Wilhelm | 6.00 | 15.00 |
| 423 W.Mays/W.McCovey DP | 10.00 | 25.00 |
| 424 Pedro Gonzalez | 1.50 | 4.00 |
| 425 Pete Mikkelsen | 1.50 | 4.00 |
| 426 Lou Clinton | 1.50 | 4.00 |
| 427A Ruben Gomez ERR | 8.00 | 20.00 |
| 427B Ruben Gomez COR DP | 1.50 | 4.00 |
| 428 T.Hutton RC/G.Michael RC DP | 3.00 | 8.00 |
| 429 Garry Roggenburk DP | 1.50 | 4.00 |
| 430 Pete Rose | 50.00 | 100.00 |
| 431 Ted Uhlaender | 1.50 | 4.00 |
| 432 Jimmie Hall DP | 1.50 | 4.00 |
| 433 Al Luplow DP | 1.50 | 4.00 |
| 434 Eddie Fisher DP | 1.50 | 4.00 |
| 435 Mack Jones DP | 1.50 | 4.00 |
| 436 Pete Ward | 1.50 | 4.00 |
| 437 Washington Senators TC | 3.00 | 6.00 |
| 438 Chuck Dobson | 1.50 | 4.00 |
| 439 Byron Browne | 1.50 | 4.00 |
| 440 Steve Hargan | 1.50 | 4.00 |
| 441 Jim Davenport | 1.50 | 4.00 |
| 442 B.Robinson RC/J.Verbanic RC DP | 3.00 | 8.00 |
| 443 Tito Francona DP | 1.50 | 4.00 |
| 444 George Smith | 1.50 | 4.00 |
| 445 Don Sutton | 10.00 | 25.00 |
| 446 Russ Nixon DP | 1.50 | 4.00 |
| 447A Bo Belinsky ERR DP | 1.50 | 4.00 |
| 447B Bo Belinsky COR | 3.00 | 6.00 |
| 448 Harry Walker MG DP | 1.50 | 4.00 |
| 449 Orlando Pena | 1.50 | 4.00 |
| 450 Richie Allen | 3.00 | 8.00 |
| 451 Fred Newman DP | 1.50 | 4.00 |
| 452 Ed Kranepool | 3.00 | 8.00 |
| 453 Aurelio Monteagudo DP | 1.50 | 4.00 |
| 454A J.Marichal CL6 No Ear DP | 5.00 | 12.00 |
| 454B Juan Marichal CL6 w/Ear DP | 5.00 | 12.00 |
| 455 Tommie Agee | 2.50 | 6.00 |
| 456 Phil Niekro UER | 6.00 | 15.00 |
| 457 Andy Etchebarren DP | 3.00 | 8.00 |
| 458 Lee Thomas | 2.50 | 6.00 |
| 459 D.Bosman RC/P.Craig | 2.50 | 6.00 |
| 460 Harmon Killebrew | 30.00 | 60.00 |
| 461 Bob Miller | 5.00 | 12.00 |
| 462 Bob Barton | 2.50 | 6.00 |
| 463 S.McDowell/S.Siebert | 5.00 | 12.00 |
| 464 Dan Coombs | 2.50 | 6.00 |
| 465 Willie Horton | 5.00 | 12.00 |
| 466 Bobby Wine | 2.50 | 6.00 |
| 467 Jim O'Toole | 2.50 | 6.00 |
| 468 Ralph Houk MG | 2.50 | 6.00 |
| 469 Len Gabrielson | 2.50 | 6.00 |
| 470 Bob Shaw | 2.50 | 6.00 |
| 471 Rene Lachemann | 2.50 | 6.00 |
| 472 J.Gelnar/G.Spriggs RC | 2.50 | 6.00 |
| 473 Jose Santiago | 2.50 | 6.00 |
| 474 Bob Tolan | 2.50 | 6.00 |
| 475 Jim Palmer | 40.00 | 80.00 |
| 476 Tony Perez SP | 30.00 | 60.00 |
| 477 Atlanta Braves TC | 6.00 | 15.00 |
| 478 Bob Humphreys | 2.50 | 6.00 |
| 479 Gary Bell | 2.50 | 6.00 |
| 480 Willie McCovey | 15.00 | 40.00 |
| 481 Leo Durocher MG | 8.00 | 20.00 |
| 482 Bill Monbouquette | 2.50 | 6.00 |
| 483 Jim Landis | 2.50 | 6.00 |
| 484 Jerry Adair | 2.50 | 6.00 |
| 485 Tim McCarver | 10.00 | 25.00 |
| 486 R.Reese RC/E.Whitby RC | 2.50 | 6.00 |
| 487 Tommie Reynolds | 2.50 | 6.00 |
| 488 Gerry Arrigo | 2.50 | 6.00 |
| 489 Doug Clemens RC | 2.50 | 6.00 |
| 490 Tony Cloninger | 2.50 | 6.00 |
| 491 Sam Bowens | 2.50 | 6.00 |
| 492 Pittsburgh Pirates TC | 6.00 | 15.00 |
| 493 Phil Ortega | 2.50 | 6.00 |
| 494 Bill Rigney MG | 2.50 | 6.00 |
| 495 Fritz Peterson | 2.50 | 6.00 |
| 496 Orlando McFarlane | 2.50 | 6.00 |
| 497 Ron Campbell RC | 2.50 | 6.00 |
| 498 Larry Dierker | 5.00 | 12.00 |
| 499 G.Culver/J.Vidal RC | 2.50 | 6.00 |
| 500 Juan Marichal | 10.00 | 25.00 |

| | | |
|---|---|---|
| 501 Jerry Zimmerman | 2.50 | 6.00 |
| 502 Derrell Griffith | 2.50 | 6.00 |
| 503 Los Angeles Dodgers TC | 8.00 | 20.00 |
| 504 Orlando Martinez RC | 2.50 | 6.00 |
| 505 Tommy Helms | 5.00 | 12.00 |
| 506 Smoky Burgess | 2.50 | 6.00 |
| 507 E.Barnowski/L.Haney RC | 2.50 | 6.00 |
| 508 Dick Hall | 2.50 | 6.00 |
| 509 Jim King | 2.50 | 6.00 |
| 510 Bill Mazeroski | 10.00 | 25.00 |
| 511 Don Wert | 2.50 | 6.00 |
| 512 Red Schoendienst MG | 10.00 | 25.00 |
| 513 Marcelino Lopez | 2.50 | 6.00 |
| 514 John Werhas | 2.50 | 6.00 |
| 515 Bert Campaneris | 5.00 | 12.00 |
| 516 San Francisco Giants TC | 6.00 | 15.00 |
| 517 Fred Talbot | 2.50 | 6.00 |
| 518 Denis Menke | 2.50 | 6.00 |
| 519 Ted Davidson | 2.50 | 6.00 |
| 520 Max Alvis | 2.50 | 6.00 |
| 521 B.Powell/C.Blefary | 5.00 | 12.00 |
| 522 John Stephenson | 2.50 | 6.00 |
| 523 Jim Merritt | 2.50 | 6.00 |
| 524 Felix Mantilla | 2.50 | 6.00 |
| 525 Ron Hunt | 2.50 | 6.00 |
| 526 P.Dobson RC/G.Korince RC | 2.50 | 6.00 |
| 527 Dennis Ribant | 2.50 | 6.00 |
| 528 Rico Petrocelli | 8.00 | 20.00 |
| 529 Gary Wagner | 2.50 | 6.00 |
| 530 Felipe Alou | 5.00 | 12.00 |
| 531 B.Robinson CL7 DP | 6.00 | 15.00 |
| 532 Jim Hicks RC | 2.50 | 6.00 |
| 533 Jack Fisher | 2.50 | 6.00 |
| 534 Hank Bauer MG DP | 3.00 | 8.00 |
| 535 Donn Clendenon | 10.00 | 25.00 |
| 536 J.Niekro RC/P.Popovich RC | 20.00 | 50.00 |
| 537 Chuck Estrada DP | 3.00 | 8.00 |
| 538 J.C. Martin | 6.00 | 15.00 |
| 539 Dick Egan DP | 3.00 | 8.00 |
| 540 Norm Cash | 20.00 | 50.00 |
| 541 Joe Gibbon | 6.00 | 15.00 |
| 542 R.Monday RC/T.Pierce RC DP | 6.00 | 15.00 |
| 543 Dan Schneider | 6.00 | 15.00 |
| 544 Cleveland Indians TC | 12.50 | 30.00 |
| 545 Jim Grant | 10.00 | 25.00 |
| 546 Woody Woodward | 10.00 | 25.00 |
| 547 R.Gibson RC/B.Rohr RC DP | 3.00 | 8.00 |
| 548 Tony Gonzalez DP | 3.00 | 8.00 |
| 549 Jack Sanford | 6.00 | 15.00 |
| 550 Vada Pinson DP | 4.00 | 10.00 |
| 551 Doug Camilli DP | 3.00 | 8.00 |
| 552 Ted Savage | 10.00 | 25.00 |
| 553 M.Hegan RC/T.Tillotson | 15.00 | 40.00 |
| 554 Andre Rodgers DP | 3.00 | 8.00 |
| 555 Don Cardwell | 10.00 | 25.00 |
| 556 Al Weis DP | 3.00 | 8.00 |
| 557 Al Ferrara | 10.00 | 25.00 |
| 558 M.Belanger RC/B.Dillman RC | 20.00 | 50.00 |
| 559 Dick Tracewski DP | 3.00 | 8.00 |
| 560 Jim Bunning | 30.00 | 60.00 |
| 561 Sandy Alomar | 15.00 | 40.00 |
| 562 Steve Blass DP | 3.00 | 8.00 |
| 563 Joe Adcock MG | 15.00 | 40.00 |
| 564 A.Harris RC/A.Pointer RC DP | 3.00 | 8.00 |
| 565 Lew Krausse | 10.00 | 25.00 |
| 566 Gary Geiger DP | 3.00 | 8.00 |
| 567 Steve Hamilton | 15.00 | 40.00 |
| 568 John Sullivan | 15.00 | 40.00 |
| 569 Rod Carew RC DP | 150.00 | 300.00 |
| 570 Maury Wills | 40.00 | 80.00 |
| 571 Larry Sherry | 10.00 | 25.00 |
| 572 Don Demeter | 10.00 | 25.00 |
| 573 Chicago White Sox TC | 12.50 | 30.00 |
| 574 Jerry Buchek | 10.00 | 25.00 |
| 575 Dave Boswell RC | 6.00 | 15.00 |
| 576 R.Hernandez RC/N.Gigon RC | 15.00 | 40.00 |
| 577 Bill Short | 6.00 | 15.00 |
| 578 John Boccabella | 6.00 | 15.00 |
| 579 Bill Henry | 6.00 | 15.00 |
| 580 Rocky Colavito | 75.00 | 150.00 |
| 581 Tom Seaver RC | 300.00 | 600.00 |
| 582 Jim Owens DP | 3.00 | 8.00 |
| 583 Ray Barker | 15.00 | 40.00 |
| 584 Jimmy Piersall | 15.00 | 40.00 |
| 585 Wally Bunker | 10.00 | 25.00 |
| 586 Manny Jimenez | 6.00 | 15.00 |
| 587 D.Shaw RC/G.Sutherland RC | 15.00 | 40.00 |
| 588 Johnny Klippstein DP | 3.00 | 8.00 |

| | | |
|---|---|---|
| 589 Dave Ricketts DP | 3.00 | 8.00 |
| 590 Pete Richert | 6.00 | 15.00 |
| 591 Ty Cline | 10.00 | 25.00 |
| 592 J.Shellenback RC/R.Willis RC | 10.00 | 25.00 |
| 593 Wes Westrum MG | 20.00 | 50.00 |
| 594 Dan Osinski | 15.00 | 40.00 |
| 595 Cookie Rojas | 15.00 | 40.00 |
| 596 Galen Cisco DP | 3.00 | 8.00 |
| 597 Ted Abernathy | 6.00 | 15.00 |
| 598 W.Williams RC/E.Stroud RC | 10.00 | 25.00 |
| 599 Bob Duliba DP | 3.00 | 8.00 |
| 600 Brooks Robinson | 125.00 | 250.00 |
| 601 Bill Bryan DP | 3.00 | 8.00 |
| 602 Juan Pizarro | 15.00 | 40.00 |
| 603 T.Talton RC/R.Webster RC | 10.00 | 25.00 |
| 604 Boston Red Sox TC | 60.00 | 120.00 |
| 605 Mike Shannon | 20.00 | 50.00 |
| 606 Ron Taylor | 10.00 | 25.00 |
| 607 Mickey Stanley | 20.00 | 50.00 |
| 608 R.Nye RC/J.Upham RC DP | 3.00 | 8.00 |
| 609 Tommy John | 40.00 | 100.00 |

## 1968 Topps

| | | |
|---|---|---|
| COMPLETE SET (598) | 1500.00 | 3000.00 |
| COMMON CARD (1-457) | .75 | 2.00 |
| COMMON CARD (458-598) | 1.50 | 4.00 |
| WRAPPER DP | 10.00 | 25.00 |
| 1 Clemente/Gonz/Alou LL | 12.50 | 30.00 |
| 2 Yaz/F.Rob/Kaline LL | 6.00 | 15.00 |
| 3 Cep/Clemente/Aaron LL | 8.00 | 20.00 |
| 4 Yaz/Killebrew/F.Rob LL | 6.00 | 15.00 |
| 5 Aaron/Santo/McCovey LL | 3.00 | 8.00 |
| 6 Yaz/Killebrew/Howard LL | 3.00 | 8.00 |
| 7 Niekro/Bunning/Short LL | 1.50 | 4.00 |
| 8 Horlen/Peters/Siebert LL | 1.50 | 4.00 |
| 9 McCor/Jenkins/Bunning LL | 1.50 | 4.00 |
| 10A Lonb/Wiis/Chance LL ERR | 1.50 | 4.00 |
| 10B Lonb/Wiis/Chance LL COR | 1.50 | 4.00 |
| 11 Bunning/Jenkins/Perry LL | 2.50 | 6.00 |
| 12 Lonborg/McDowl/Chance LL | 1.50 | 4.00 |
| 13 Chuck Hartenstein RC | .75 | 2.00 |
| 14 Jerry McNertney | .75 | 2.00 |
| 15 Ron Hunt | .75 | 2.00 |
| 16 L.Piniella/R.Scheinblum | 2.50 | 6.00 |
| 17 Dick Hall | .75 | 2.00 |
| 18 Mike Hershberger | .75 | 2.00 |
| 19 Juan Pizarro | .75 | 2.00 |
| 20 Brooks Robinson | 10.00 | 25.00 |
| 21 Ron Davis | .75 | 2.00 |
| 22 Pat Dobson | 1.50 | 4.00 |
| 23 Chico Cardenas | 1.50 | 4.00 |
| 24 Bobby Locke | .75 | 2.00 |
| 25 Julian Javier | 1.50 | 4.00 |
| 26 Darrell Brandon | .75 | 2.00 |
| 27 Gil Hodges MG | 3.00 | 8.00 |
| 28 Ted Uhlaender | .75 | 2.00 |
| 29 Joe Verbanic | .75 | 2.00 |
| 30 Joe Torre | 2.50 | 6.00 |
| 31 Ed Stroud | .75 | 2.00 |
| 32 Joe Gibbon | .75 | 2.00 |
| 33 Pete Ward | .75 | 2.00 |
| 34 Al Ferrara | .75 | 2.00 |
| 35 Steve Hargan | .75 | 2.00 |
| 36 B.Moose RC/B.Robertson RC | 1.50 | 4.00 |
| 37 Billy Williams | 3.00 | 8.00 |
| 38 Tony Pierce | .75 | 2.00 |
| 39 Cookie Rojas | .75 | 2.00 |
| 40 Denny McLain | 3.00 | 8.00 |
| 41 Julio Gotay | .75 | 2.00 |
| 42 Larry Haney | .75 | 2.00 |
| 43 Gary Bell | .75 | 2.00 |
| 44 Frank Kostro | .75 | 2.00 |
| 45 Tom Seaver DP | 20.00 | 50.00 |
| 46 Dave Ricketts | .75 | 2.00 |

| Card | Name | Price 1 | Price 2 |
|---|---|---|---|
| 47 | Ralph Houk MG | 1.50 | 4.00 |
| 48 | Ted Davidson | .75 | 2.00 |
| 49A | E.Brinkman White | .75 | 2.00 |
| 49B | E.Brinkman Yellow Tm | 20.00 | 50.00 |
| 50 | Willie Mays | 30.00 | 60.00 |
| 51 | Bob Locker | .75 | 2.00 |
| 52 | Hawk Taylor | .75 | 2.00 |
| 53 | Gene Alley | 1.50 | 4.00 |
| 54 | Stan Williams | .75 | 2.00 |
| 55 | Felipe Alou | 1.50 | 4.00 |
| 56 | D.Leonhard RC/D.May RC | .75 | 2.00 |
| 57 | Dan Schneider | .75 | 2.00 |
| 58 | Eddie Mathews | 6.00 | 15.00 |
| 59 | Don Lock | .75 | 2.00 |
| 60 | Ken Holtzman | 1.50 | 4.00 |
| 61 | Reggie Smith | 1.50 | 4.00 |
| 62 | Chuck Dobson | .75 | 2.00 |
| 63 | Dick Kenworthy RC | .75 | 2.00 |
| 64 | Jim Merritt | .75 | 2.00 |
| 65 | John Roseboro | 1.50 | 4.00 |
| 66A | Casey Cox White | .75 | 2.00 |
| 66B | C.Cox Yellow Tm | 50.00 | 100.00 |
| 67 | Checklist 1/Kaat | 2.50 | 6.00 |
| 68 | Ron Willis | .75 | 2.00 |
| 69 | Tom Tresh | 1.50 | 4.00 |
| 70 | Bob Veale | 1.50 | 4.00 |
| 71 | Vern Fuller RC | .75 | 2.00 |
| 72 | Tommy John | 2.50 | 6.00 |
| 73 | Jim Ray Hart | 1.50 | 4.00 |
| 74 | Milt Pappas | 1.50 | 4.00 |
| 75 | Don Mincher | .75 | 2.00 |
| 76 | J.Britton/R.Reed RC | 1.50 | 4.00 |
| 77 | Don Wilson RC | 1.50 | 4.00 |
| 78 | Jim Northrup | 2.50 | 6.00 |
| 79 | Ted Kubiak RC | .75 | 2.00 |
| 80 | Rod Carew | 20.00 | 50.00 |
| 81 | Larry Jackson | .75 | 2.00 |
| 82 | Sam Bowens | .75 | 2.00 |
| 83 | John Stephenson | .75 | 2.00 |
| 84 | Bob Tolan | .75 | 2.00 |
| 85 | Gaylord Perry | 3.00 | 8.00 |
| 86 | Willie Stargell | 3.00 | 8.00 |
| 87 | Dick Williams MG | 1.50 | 4.00 |
| 88 | Phil Regan | 1.50 | 4.00 |
| 89 | Jake Gibbs | 1.50 | 4.00 |
| 90 | Vada Pinson | 1.50 | 4.00 |
| 91 | Jim Ollom RC | .75 | 2.00 |
| 92 | Ed Kranepool | 1.50 | 4.00 |
| 93 | Tony Cloninger | .75 | 2.00 |
| 94 | Lee Maye | .75 | 2.00 |
| 95 | Bob Aspromonte | .75 | 2.00 |
| 96 | F.Coggins RC/D.Nold | .75 | 2.00 |
| 97 | Tom Phoebus | .75 | 2.00 |
| 98 | Gary Sutherland | .75 | 2.00 |
| 99 | Rocky Colavito | 3.00 | 8.00 |
| 100 | Bob Gibson | 10.00 | 25.00 |
| 101 | Glenn Beckert | 1.50 | 4.00 |
| 102 | Jose Cardenal | 1.50 | 4.00 |
| 103 | Don Sutton | 3.00 | 8.00 |
| 104 | Dick Dietz | .75 | 2.00 |
| 105 | Al Downing | 1.50 | 4.00 |
| 106 | Dalton Jones | .75 | 2.00 |
| 107A | Checklist 2/Marichal Wide | 2.50 | 6.00 |
| 107B | Checklist 2/J.Marichal Fine | 2.50 | 6.00 |
| 108 | Don Pavletich | .75 | 2.00 |
| 109 | Bert Campaneris | 1.50 | 4.00 |
| 110 | Hank Aaron | 30.00 | 60.00 |
| 111 | Rich Reese | .75 | 2.00 |
| 112 | Woody Fryman | .75 | 2.00 |
| 113 | T.Matchick/D.Patterson RC | 1.50 | 4.00 |
| 114 | Ron Swoboda | 1.50 | 4.00 |
| 115 | Sam McDowell | 1.50 | 4.00 |
| 116 | Ken McMullen | .75 | 2.00 |
| 117 | Larry Jaster | .75 | 2.00 |
| 118 | Mark Belanger | 1.50 | 4.00 |
| 119 | Ted Savage | .75 | 2.00 |
| 120 | Mel Stottlemyre | 1.50 | 4.00 |
| 121 | Jimmie Hall | .75 | 2.00 |
| 122 | Gene Mauch MG | 1.50 | 4.00 |
| 123 | Jose Santiago | .75 | 2.00 |
| 124 | Nate Oliver | .75 | 2.00 |
| 125 | Joel Horlen | .75 | 2.00 |
| 126 | Bobby Etheridge RC | .75 | 2.00 |
| 127 | Paul Lindblad | .75 | 2.00 |
| 128 | T.Dukes RC/A.Harris | .75 | 2.00 |
| 129 | Mickey Stanley | 2.50 | 6.00 |
| 130 | Tony Perez | 3.00 | 8.00 |
| 131 | Frank Bertaina | .75 | 2.00 |
| 132 | Bud Harrelson | 1.50 | 4.00 |
| 133 | Fred Whitfield | .75 | 2.00 |
| 134 | Pat Jarvis | .75 | 2.00 |
| 135 | Paul Blair | 1.50 | 4.00 |
| 136 | Randy Hundley | 1.50 | 4.00 |
| 137 | Minnesota Twins TC | 1.50 | 4.00 |
| 138 | Ruben Amaro | .75 | 2.00 |
| 139 | Chris Short | .75 | 2.00 |
| 140 | Tony Conigliaro | 3.00 | 8.00 |
| 141 | Dal Maxvill | .75 | 2.00 |
| 142 | B.Bradford RC/B.Voss | .75 | 2.00 |
| 143 | Pete Cimino | .75 | 2.00 |
| 144 | Joe Morgan | 5.00 | 12.00 |
| 145 | Don Drysdale | 5.00 | 12.00 |
| 146 | Sal Bando | 1.50 | 4.00 |
| 147 | Frank Linzy | .75 | 2.00 |
| 148 | Dave Bristol MG | .75 | 2.00 |
| 149 | Bob Saverine | .75 | 2.00 |
| 150 | Roberto Clemente | 40.00 | 80.00 |
| 151 | Lou Brock WS1 | 4.00 | 10.00 |
| 152 | Carl Yastrzemski WS2 | 4.00 | 10.00 |
| 153 | Nelson Briles WS3 | 2.00 | 5.00 |
| 154 | Bob Gibson WS4 | 4.00 | 10.00 |
| 155 | Jim Lonborg WS5 | 2.00 | 5.00 |
| 156 | Rico Petrocelli WS6 | 2.00 | 5.00 |
| 157 | St. Louis Wins It WS7 | 2.00 | 5.00 |
| 158 | Cardinals Celebrate WS | 2.00 | 5.00 |
| 159 | Don Kessinger | 1.50 | 4.00 |
| 160 | Earl Wilson | .75 | 2.00 |
| 161 | Norm Miller | .75 | 2.00 |
| 162 | H.Gilson RC/M.Torrez RC | 1.50 | 4.00 |
| 163 | Gene Brabender | .75 | 2.00 |
| 164 | Ramon Webster | .75 | 2.00 |
| 165 | Tony Oliva | 2.50 | 6.00 |
| 166 | Claude Raymond | .75 | 2.00 |
| 167 | Elston Howard | 2.50 | 6.00 |
| 168 | Los Angeles Dodgers TC | 1.50 | 4.00 |
| 169 | Bob Bolin | .75 | 2.00 |
| 170 | Jim Fregosi | .75 | 2.00 |
| 171 | Don Nottebart | .75 | 2.00 |
| 172 | Walt Williams | .75 | 2.00 |
| 173 | John Boozer | .75 | 2.00 |
| 174 | Bob Tillman | .75 | 2.00 |
| 175 | Maury Wills | 2.50 | 6.00 |
| 176 | Bob Allen | .75 | 2.00 |
| 177 | N.Ryan RC/J.Koosman RC | 250.00 | 500.00 |
| 178 | Don Wert | 1.50 | 4.00 |
| 179 | Bill Stoneman RC | .75 | 2.00 |
| 180 | Curt Flood | 2.50 | 6.00 |
| 181 | Jerry Zimmerman | .75 | 2.00 |
| 182 | Dave Giusti | .75 | 2.00 |
| 183 | Bob Kennedy MG | 1.50 | 4.00 |
| 184 | Lou Johnson | .75 | 2.00 |
| 185 | Tom Haller | .75 | 2.00 |
| 186 | Eddie Watt | .75 | 2.00 |
| 187 | Sonny Jackson | .75 | 2.00 |
| 188 | Cap Peterson | .75 | 2.00 |
| 189 | Bill Landis RC | .75 | 2.00 |
| 190 | Bill White | 1.50 | 4.00 |
| 191 | Dan Frisella RC | .75 | 2.00 |
| 192A | Checklist 3/Yaz Ball | 3.00 | 8.00 |
| 192B | Checklist 3/Yaz Game | 3.00 | 8.00 |
| 193 | Jack Hamilton | .75 | 2.00 |
| 194 | Don Buford | .75 | 2.00 |
| 195 | Joe Pepitone | 1.50 | 4.00 |
| 196 | Gary Nolan RC | 1.50 | 4.00 |
| 197 | Larry Brown | .75 | 2.00 |
| 198 | Roy Face | 1.50 | 4.00 |
| 199 | F.Rodriguez RC/D.Rosen | .75 | 2.00 |
| 200 | Orlando Cepeda | 3.00 | 8.00 |
| 201 | Mike Marshall RC | 1.50 | 4.00 |
| 202 | Adolfo Phillips | .75 | 2.00 |
| 203 | Dick Kelley | .75 | 2.00 |
| 204 | Andy Etchebarren | .75 | 2.00 |
| 205 | Juan Marichal | 3.00 | 8.00 |
| 206 | Cal Ermer MG RC | .75 | 2.00 |
| 207 | Carroll Sembera | .75 | 2.00 |
| 208 | Willie Davis | 1.50 | 4.00 |
| 209 | Tim Cullen | .75 | 2.00 |
| 210 | Gary Peters | .75 | 2.00 |
| 211 | J.C. Martin | .75 | 2.00 |
| 212 | Dave Morehead | .75 | 2.00 |
| 213 | Chico Ruiz | .75 | 2.00 |
| 214 | S.Bahnsen/F.Fernandez | 1.50 | 4.00 |
| 215 | Jim Bunning | 3.00 | 8.00 |
| 216 | Bubba Morton | .75 | 2.00 |
| 217 | Dick Farrell | .75 | 2.00 |
| 218 | Ken Suarez | .75 | 2.00 |
| 219 | Rob Gardner | .75 | 2.00 |
| 220 | Harmon Killebrew | 6.00 | 15.00 |
| 221 | Atlanta Braves TC | 1.50 | 4.00 |
| 222 | Jim Hardin RC | .75 | 2.00 |
| 223 | Ollie Brown | .75 | 2.00 |
| 224 | Jack Aker | .75 | 2.00 |
| 225 | Richie Allen | 2.50 | 6.00 |
| 226 | Jimmie Price | .75 | 2.00 |
| 227 | Joe Hoerner | .75 | 2.00 |
| 228 | J.Billingham RC/J.Fairey RC | 1.50 | 4.00 |
| 229 | Fred Klages | .75 | 2.00 |
| 230 | Pete Rose | 30.00 | 60.00 |
| 231 | Dave Baldwin RC | .75 | 2.00 |
| 232 | Denis Menke | .75 | 2.00 |
| 233 | George Scott | 1.50 | 4.00 |
| 234 | Bill Monbouquette | .75 | 2.00 |
| 235 | Ron Santo | 3.00 | 8.00 |
| 236 | Tug McGraw | 2.50 | 6.00 |
| 237 | Alvin Dark MG | 1.50 | 4.00 |
| 238 | Tom Satriano | .75 | 2.00 |
| 239 | Bill Henry | .75 | 2.00 |
| 240 | Al Kaline | 15.00 | 40.00 |
| 241 | Felix Millan | .75 | 2.00 |
| 242 | Moe Drabowsky | 1.50 | 4.00 |
| 243 | Rich Rollins | .75 | 2.00 |
| 244 | John Donaldson RC | .75 | 2.00 |
| 245 | Tony Gonzalez | .75 | 2.00 |
| 246 | Fritz Peterson | 1.50 | 4.00 |
| 247 | Johnny Bench RC | 60.00 | 120.00 |
| 248 | Fred Valentine | .75 | 2.00 |
| 249 | Bill Singer | .75 | 2.00 |
| 250 | Carl Yastrzemski | 12.50 | 30.00 |
| 251 | Manny Sanguillen RC | 2.50 | 6.00 |
| 252 | California Angels TC | 1.50 | 4.00 |
| 253 | Dick Hughes | .75 | 2.00 |
| 254 | Cleon Jones | 1.50 | 4.00 |
| 255 | Dean Chance | 1.50 | 4.00 |
| 256 | Norm Cash | 2.50 | 6.00 |
| 257 | Phil Niekro | 3.00 | 8.00 |
| 258 | J.Arcia RC/B.Schlesinger | .75 | 2.00 |
| 259 | Ken Boyer | 2.50 | 6.00 |
| 260 | Jim Wynn | 1.50 | 4.00 |
| 261 | Dave Duncan | 1.50 | 4.00 |
| 262 | Rick Wise | 1.50 | 4.00 |
| 263 | Horace Clarke | 1.50 | 4.00 |
| 264 | Ted Abernathy | .75 | 2.00 |
| 265 | Tommy Davis | 1.50 | 4.00 |
| 266 | Paul Popovich | .75 | 2.00 |
| 267 | Herman Franks MG | .75 | 2.00 |
| 268 | Bob Humphreys | .75 | 2.00 |
| 269 | Bob Tiefenauer | .75 | 2.00 |
| 270 | Matty Alou | 1.50 | 4.00 |
| 271 | Bobby Knoop | .75 | 2.00 |
| 272 | Ray Culp | .75 | 2.00 |
| 273 | Dave Johnson | 1.50 | 4.00 |
| 274 | Mike Cuellar | 1.50 | 4.00 |
| 275 | Tim McCarver | 2.50 | 6.00 |
| 276 | Jim Roland | .75 | 2.00 |
| 277 | Jerry Buchek | .75 | 2.00 |
| 278 | Checklist 4/Cepeda | 2.50 | 6.00 |
| 279 | Bill Hands | .75 | 2.00 |
| 280 | Mickey Mantle | 175.00 | 350.00 |
| 281 | Jim Campanis | .75 | 2.00 |
| 282 | Rick Monday | 1.50 | 4.00 |
| 283 | Mel Queen | .75 | 2.00 |
| 284 | Johnny Briggs | .75 | 2.00 |
| 285 | Dick McAuliffe | 2.50 | 6.00 |
| 286 | Cecil Upshaw | .75 | 2.00 |
| 287 | M.Abarbanel RC/C.Carlos RC | .75 | 2.00 |
| 288 | Dave Wickersham | .75 | 2.00 |
| 289 | Woody Held | .75 | 2.00 |
| 290 | Willie McCovey | 5.00 | 12.00 |
| 291 | Dick Lines | .75 | 2.00 |
| 292 | Art Shamsky | .75 | 2.00 |
| 293 | Bruce Howard | .75 | 2.00 |
| 294 | Red Schoendienst MG | 2.50 | 6.00 |
| 295 | Sonny Siebert | .75 | 2.00 |
| 296 | Byron Browne | .75 | 2.00 |
| 297 | Russ Gibson | .75 | 2.00 |
| 298 | Jim Brewer | .75 | 2.00 |
| 299 | Gene Michael | 1.50 | 4.00 |
| 300 | Rusty Staub | 1.50 | 4.00 |
| 301 | G.Mitterwald RC/R.Renick RC | .75 | 2.00 |
| 302 | Gerry Arrigo | .75 | 2.00 |
| 303 | Dick Green | 1.50 | 4.00 |
| 304 | Sandy Valdespino | .75 | 2.00 |
| 305 | Minnie Rojas | .75 | 2.00 |
| 306 | Mike Ryan | .75 | 2.00 |

|  |  | | |
|---|---|---|---|
| 307 | John Hiller | 1.50 | 4.00 |
| 308 | Pittsburgh Pirates TC | 1.50 | 4.00 |
| 309 | Ken Henderson | .75 | 2.00 |
| 310 | Luis Aparicio | 3.00 | 8.00 |
| 311 | Jack Lamabe | .75 | 2.00 |
| 312 | Curt Blefary | .75 | 2.00 |
| 313 | Al Weis | .75 | 2.00 |
| 314 | B.Rohr/G.Spriggs | .75 | 2.00 |
| 315 | Zoilo Versalles | .75 | 2.00 |
| 316 | Steve Barber | .75 | 2.00 |
| 317 | Ron Brand | .75 | 2.00 |
| 318 | Chico Salmon | .75 | 2.00 |
| 319 | George Culver | .75 | 2.00 |
| 320 | Frank Howard | 1.50 | 4.00 |
| 321 | Leo Durocher MG | 2.50 | 6.00 |
| 322 | Dave Boswell | .75 | 2.00 |
| 323 | Deron Johnson | 1.50 | 4.00 |
| 324 | Jim Nash | .75 | 2.00 |
| 325 | Manny Mota | 1.50 | 4.00 |
| 326 | Dennis Ribant | .75 | 2.00 |
| 327 | Tony Taylor | 1.50 | 4.00 |
| 328 | C.Vinson RC/J.Weaver RC | .75 | 2.00 |
| 329 | Duane Josephson | .75 | 2.00 |
| 330 | Roger Maris | 20.00 | 50.00 |
| 331 | Dan Osinski | .75 | 2.00 |
| 332 | Doug Rader | 1.50 | 4.00 |
| 333 | Ron Herbel | .75 | 2.00 |
| 334 | Baltimore Orioles TC | 1.50 | 4.00 |
| 335 | Bob Allison | .75 | 4.00 |
| 336 | John Purdin | .75 | 2.00 |
| 337 | Bill Robinson | 1.50 | 4.00 |
| 338 | Bob Johnson | .75 | 2.00 |
| 339 | Rich Nye | .75 | 2.00 |
| 340 | Max Alvis | .75 | 2.00 |
| 341 | Jim Lemon MG | .75 | 2.00 |
| 342 | Ken Johnson | .75 | 2.00 |
| 343 | Jim Gosger | .75 | 2.00 |
| 344 | Donn Clendenon | 1.50 | 4.00 |
| 345 | Bob Hendley | .75 | 2.00 |
| 346 | Jerry Adair | .75 | 2.00 |
| 347 | George Brunet | .75 | 2.00 |
| 348 | L.Colton RC/D.Thoenen RC | .75 | 2.00 |
| 349 | Ed Spiezio | 1.50 | 4.00 |
| 350 | Hoyt Wilhelm | 3.00 | 8.00 |
| 351 | Bob Barton | .75 | 2.00 |
| 352 | Jackie Hernandez RC | .75 | 2.00 |
| 353 | Mack Jones | .75 | 2.00 |
| 354 | Pete Richert | .75 | 2.00 |
| 355 | Ernie Banks | 10.00 | 25.00 |
| 356A | Checklist 5/Holtzman Center | 2.50 | 6.00 |
| 356B | Checklist 5/Holtzman Right | 2.50 | 6.00 |
| 357 | Len Gabrielson | .75 | 2.00 |
| 358 | Mike Epstein | .75 | 2.00 |
| 359 | Joe Moeller | .75 | 2.00 |
| 360 | Willie Horton | 2.50 | 6.00 |
| 361 | Harmon Killebrew AS | 3.00 | 8.00 |
| 362 | Orlando Cepeda AS | 2.50 | 6.00 |
| 363 | Rod Carew AS | 3.00 | 8.00 |
| 364 | Joe Morgan AS | 3.00 | 8.00 |
| 365 | Brooks Robinson AS | 3.00 | 8.00 |
| 366 | Ron Santo AS | 2.50 | 6.00 |
| 367 | Jim Fregosi AS | .75 | 4.00 |
| 368 | Gene Alley AS | 1.50 | 4.00 |
| 369 | Carl Yastrzemski AS | 4.00 | 10.00 |
| 370 | Hank Aaron AS | 8.00 | 20.00 |
| 371 | Tony Oliva AS | 2.50 | 6.00 |
| 372 | Lou Brock AS | 3.00 | 8.00 |
| 373 | Frank Robinson AS | 3.00 | 8.00 |
| 374 | Roberto Clemente AS | 12.50 | 30.00 |
| 375 | Bill Freehan AS | 1.50 | 4.00 |
| 376 | Tim McCarver AS | 1.50 | 4.00 |
| 377 | Joel Horlen AS | 1.50 | 4.00 |
| 378 | Bob Gibson AS | 3.00 | 8.00 |
| 379 | Gary Peters AS | 1.50 | 4.00 |
| 380 | Ken Holtzman AS | 1.50 | 4.00 |
| 381 | Boog Powell | 1.50 | 4.00 |
| 382 | Ramon Hernandez | .75 | 2.00 |
| 383 | Steve Whitaker | .75 | 2.00 |
| 384 | B.Henry/H.McRae RC | 2.50 | 6.00 |
| 385 | Jim Hunter | 4.00 | 10.00 |
| 386 | Greg Goossen | .75 | 2.00 |
| 387 | Joe Foy | .75 | 2.00 |
| 388 | Ray Washburn | .75 | 2.00 |
| 389 | Jay Johnstone | 1.50 | 4.00 |
| 390 | Bill Mazeroski | 3.00 | 8.00 |
| 391 | Bob Priddy | .75 | 2.00 |
| 392 | Grady Hatton MG | .75 | 2.00 |
| 393 | Jim Perry | 1.50 | 4.00 |
| 394 | Tommie Aaron | 2.50 | 6.00 |
| 395 | Camilo Pascual | 1.50 | 4.00 |
| 396 | Bobby Wine | .75 | 2.00 |
| 397 | Vic Davalillo | .75 | 2.00 |
| 398 | Jim Grant | .75 | 2.00 |
| 399 | Ray Oyler | 1.50 | 4.00 |
| 400A | Mike McCormick YT | 1.50 | 4.00 |
| 400B | M.McCormick White Tm | 75.00 | 150.00 |
| 401 | Mets Team | 1.50 | 4.00 |
| 402 | Mike Hegan | 1.50 | 4.00 |
| 403 | John Buzhardt | .75 | 2.00 |
| 404 | Floyd Robinson | .75 | 2.00 |
| 405 | Tommy Helms | 1.50 | 4.00 |
| 406 | Dick Ellsworth | .75 | 2.00 |
| 407 | Gary Kolb | .75 | 2.00 |
| 408 | Steve Carlton | 12.50 | 30.00 |
| 409 | F.Peters RC/F.Stone | .75 | 2.00 |
| 410 | Ferguson Jenkins | 4.00 | 10.00 |
| 411 | Ron Hansen | .75 | 2.00 |
| 412 | Clay Carroll | 1.50 | 4.00 |
| 413 | Tom McCraw | .75 | 2.00 |
| 414 | Mickey Lolich | 3.00 | 8.00 |
| 415 | Johnny Callison | 1.50 | 4.00 |
| 416 | Bill Rigney MG | .75 | 2.00 |
| 417 | Willie Crawford | .75 | 2.00 |
| 418 | Eddie Fisher | .75 | 2.00 |
| 419 | Jack Hiatt | .75 | 2.00 |
| 420 | Cesar Tovar | .75 | 2.00 |
| 421 | Ron Taylor | .75 | 2.00 |
| 422 | Rene Lachemann | .75 | 2.00 |
| 423 | Fred Gladding | .75 | 2.00 |
| 424 | Chicago White Sox TC | 1.50 | 4.00 |
| 425 | Jim Maloney | .75 | 4.00 |
| 426 | Hank Allen | .75 | 2.00 |
| 427 | Dick Calmus | .75 | 2.00 |
| 428 | Vic Roznovsky | .75 | 2.00 |
| 429 | Tommie Sisk | .75 | 2.00 |
| 430 | Rico Petrocelli | 1.50 | 4.00 |
| 431 | Dooley Womack | .75 | 2.00 |
| 432 | B.Davis/J.Vidal | .75 | 2.00 |
| 433 | Bob Rodgers | .75 | 2.00 |
| 434 | Ricardo Joseph RC | .75 | 2.00 |
| 435 | Ron Perranoski | 1.50 | 4.00 |
| 436 | Hal Lanier | .75 | 2.00 |
| 437 | Don Cardwell | .75 | 2.00 |
| 438 | Lee Thomas | 1.50 | 4.00 |
| 439 | Lum Harris MG | .75 | 2.00 |
| 440 | Claude Osteen | 1.50 | 4.00 |
| 441 | Alex Johnson | 1.50 | 4.00 |
| 442 | Dick Bosman | .75 | 4.00 |
| 443 | Joe Azcue | .75 | 2.00 |
| 444 | Jack Fisher | .75 | 2.00 |
| 445 | Mike Shannon | 1.50 | 4.00 |
| 446 | Ron Kline | .75 | 2.00 |
| 447 | G.Korince/F.Lasher RC | 1.50 | 4.00 |
| 448 | Gary Wagner | .75 | 2.00 |
| 449 | Gene Oliver | .75 | 2.00 |
| 450 | Jim Kaat | 2.50 | 6.00 |
| 451 | Al Spangler | .75 | 2.00 |
| 452 | Jesus Alou | .75 | 2.00 |
| 453 | Sammy Ellis | .75 | 2.00 |
| 454A | Checklist 6/F.Rob Complete | 3.00 | 8.00 |
| 454B | Checklist 6/F.Rob Partial | 3.00 | 8.00 |
| 455 | Rico Carty | 1.50 | 4.00 |
| 456 | John O'Donoghue | .75 | 2.00 |
| 457 | Jim Lefebvre | 1.50 | 4.00 |
| 458 | Lew Krausse | 2.50 | 6.00 |
| 459 | Dick Simpson | 1.50 | 4.00 |
| 460 | Jim Lonborg | 2.50 | 6.00 |
| 461 | Chuck Hiller | 1.50 | 4.00 |
| 462 | Barry Moore | 1.50 | 4.00 |
| 463 | Jim Schaffer | 1.50 | 4.00 |
| 464 | Don McMahon | 1.50 | 4.00 |
| 465 | Tommie Agee | 4.00 | 10.00 |
| 466 | Bill Dillman | 1.50 | 4.00 |
| 467 | Dick Howser | 4.00 | 10.00 |
| 468 | Larry Sherry | 1.50 | 4.00 |
| 469 | Ty Cline | 1.50 | 4.00 |
| 470 | Bill Freehan | 4.00 | 10.00 |
| 471 | Orlando Pena | 1.50 | 4.00 |
| 472 | Walter Alston MG | 2.50 | 6.00 |
| 473 | Al Worthington | 1.50 | 4.00 |
| 474 | Paul Schaal | 1.50 | 4.00 |
| 475 | Joe Niekro | 2.50 | 6.00 |
| 476 | Woody Woodward | 1.50 | 4.00 |
| 477 | Philadelphia Phillies TC | 3.00 | 8.00 |
| 478 | Dave McNally | 2.50 | 6.00 |
| 479 | Phil Gagliano | 2.50 | 6.00 |
| 480 | Ofira/Chico/Clemente | 40.00 | 80.00 |
| 481 | John Wyatt | 1.50 | 4.00 |
| 482 | Jose Pagan | 1.50 | 4.00 |
| 483 | Darold Knowles | 1.50 | 4.00 |
| 484 | Phil Roof | 1.50 | 4.00 |
| 485 | Ken Berry | 2.50 | 6.00 |
| 486 | Cal Koonce | 1.50 | 4.00 |
| 487 | Lee May | 4.00 | 10.00 |
| 488 | Dick Tracewski | 2.50 | 6.00 |
| 489 | Wally Bunker | 1.50 | 4.00 |
| 490 | Kill/Mays/Mantle | 75.00 | 150.00 |
| 491 | Denny Lemaster | 1.50 | 4.00 |
| 492 | Jeff Torborg | 2.50 | 6.00 |
| 493 | Jim McGlothlin | 1.50 | 4.00 |
| 494 | Ray Sadecki | 1.50 | 4.00 |
| 495 | Leon Wagner | 1.50 | 4.00 |
| 496 | Steve Hamilton | 2.50 | 6.00 |
| 497 | St. Louis Cardinals TC | 3.00 | 8.00 |
| 498 | Bill Bryan | 2.50 | 6.00 |
| 499 | Steve Blass | 2.50 | 6.00 |
| 500 | Frank Robinson | 12.50 | 30.00 |
| 501 | John Odom | 2.50 | 6.00 |
| 502 | Mike Andrews | 1.50 | 4.00 |
| 503 | Al Jackson | 2.50 | 6.00 |
| 504 | Russ Snyder | 1.50 | 4.00 |
| 505 | Joe Sparma | 4.00 | 10.00 |
| 506 | Clarence Jones RC | 1.50 | 4.00 |
| 507 | Wade Blasingame | 1.50 | 4.00 |
| 508 | Duke Sims | 1.50 | 4.00 |
| 509 | Dennis Higgins | 1.50 | 4.00 |
| 510 | Ron Fairly | 4.00 | 10.00 |
| 511 | Bill Kelso | 1.50 | 4.00 |
| 512 | Grant Jackson | 1.50 | 4.00 |
| 513 | Hank Bauer MG | 2.50 | 6.00 |
| 514 | Al McBean | 1.50 | 4.00 |
| 515 | Russ Nixon | 1.50 | 4.00 |
| 516 | Pete Mikkelsen | 1.50 | 4.00 |
| 517 | Diego Segui | 2.50 | 6.00 |
| 518A | Checklist 7/Boyer ERR | 5.00 | 12.00 |
| 518B | Checklist 7/Boyer COR | 5.00 | 12.00 |
| 519 | Jerry Stephenson | 1.50 | 4.00 |
| 520 | Lou Brock | 10.00 | 25.00 |
| 521 | Don Shaw | 1.50 | 4.00 |
| 522 | Wayne Causey | 1.50 | 4.00 |
| 523 | John Tsitouris | 1.50 | 4.00 |
| 524 | Andy Kosco | 2.50 | 6.00 |
| 525 | Jim Davenport | 1.50 | 4.00 |
| 526 | Bill Denehy | 1.50 | 4.00 |
| 527 | Tito Francona | 1.50 | 4.00 |
| 528 | Detroit Tigers TC | 30.00 | 60.00 |
| 529 | Bruce Von Hoff RC | 1.50 | 4.00 |
| 530 | B.Robinson/F.Robinson | 15.00 | 40.00 |
| 531 | Chuck Hinton | 1.50 | 4.00 |
| 532 | Luis Tiant | 2.50 | 6.00 |
| 533 | Wes Parker | 2.50 | 6.00 |
| 534 | Bob Miller | 2.50 | 6.00 |
| 535 | Danny Cater | 2.50 | 6.00 |
| 536 | Bill Short | 1.50 | 4.00 |
| 537 | Norm Siebern | 2.50 | 6.00 |
| 538 | Manny Jimenez | 2.50 | 6.00 |
| 539 | J.Ray RC/M.Ferraro RC | 1.50 | 4.00 |
| 540 | Nelson Briles | 2.50 | 6.00 |
| 541 | Sandy Alomar | 2.50 | 6.00 |
| 542 | John Boccabella | 1.50 | 4.00 |
| 543 | Bob Lee | 1.50 | 4.00 |
| 544 | Mayo Smith MG | 5.00 | 12.00 |
| 545 | Lindy McDaniel | 2.50 | 6.00 |
| 546 | Roy White | 2.50 | 6.00 |
| 547 | Dan Coombs | 1.50 | 4.00 |
| 548 | Bernie Allen | 1.50 | 4.00 |
| 549 | C.Motton RC/R.Nelson RC | 1.50 | 4.00 |
| 550 | Cleto Boyer | 2.50 | 6.00 |
| 551 | Darrell Sutherland | 1.50 | 4.00 |
| 552 | Ed Kirkpatrick | 1.50 | 4.00 |
| 553 | Hank Aguirre | 1.50 | 4.00 |
| 554 | Oakland Athletics TC | 4.00 | 10.00 |
| 555 | Jose Tartabull | 2.50 | 6.00 |
| 556 | Dick Selma | 1.50 | 4.00 |
| 557 | Frank Quilici | 2.50 | 6.00 |
| 558 | Johnny Edwards | 1.50 | 4.00 |
| 559 | C.Taylor RC/L.Walker | 1.50 | 4.00 |
| 560 | Paul Casanova | 1.50 | 4.00 |
| 561 | Lee Elia | | |
| 562 | Jim Bouton | 2.50 | 6.00 |
| 563 | Ed Charles | 1.50 | 4.00 |
| 564 | Eddie Stanky MG | 1.50 | 4.00 |
| 565 | Larry Dierker | 2.50 | 6.00 |
| 566 | Ken Harrelson | 2.50 | 6.00 |

| | | |
|---|---|---|
| □ 567 Clay Dalrymple | 1.50 | 4.00 |
| □ 568 Willie Smith | 1.50 | 4.00 |
| □ 569 J.Murrell RC/L.Rohr RC | 1.50 | 4.00 |
| □ 570 Rick Reichardt | 1.50 | 4.00 |
| □ 571 Tony LaRussa | 5.00 | 12.00 |
| □ 572 Don Bosch RC | 1.50 | 4.00 |
| □ 573 Joe Coleman | 1.50 | 4.00 |
| □ 574 Cincinnati Reds TC | 4.00 | 10.00 |
| □ 575 Jim Palmer | 15.00 | 40.00 |
| □ 576 Dave Adlesh | 1.50 | 4.00 |
| □ 577 Fred Talbot | 1.50 | 4.00 |
| □ 578 Orlando Martinez | 1.50 | 4.00 |
| □ 579 L.Hisle RC/M.Lum RC | 4.00 | 10.00 |
| □ 580 Bob Bailey | 1.50 | 4.00 |
| □ 581 Garry Roggenburk | 1.50 | 4.00 |
| □ 582 Jerry Grote | 4.00 | 10.00 |
| □ 583 Gates Brown | 4.00 | 10.00 |
| □ 584 Larry Shepard MG RC | 1.50 | 4.00 |
| □ 585 Wilbur Wood | 2.50 | 6.00 |
| □ 586 Jim Pagliaroni | 2.50 | 6.00 |
| □ 587 Roger Repoz | 1.50 | 4.00 |
| □ 588 Dick Schofield | 1.50 | 4.00 |
| □ 589 R.Clark/M.Ogier RC | 1.50 | 4.00 |
| □ 590 Tommy Harper | 2.50 | 6.00 |
| □ 591 Dick Nen | 1.50 | 4.00 |
| □ 592 John Bateman | 1.50 | 4.00 |
| □ 593 Lee Stange | 1.50 | 4.00 |
| □ 594 Phil Linz | 2.50 | 6.00 |
| □ 595 Phil Ortega | 1.50 | 4.00 |
| □ 596 Charlie Smith | 1.50 | 4.00 |
| □ 597 Bill McCool | 1.50 | 4.00 |
| □ 598 Jerry May | 2.50 | 6.00 |

## 1969 Topps

| | | |
|---|---|---|
| □ COMP. MASTER SET (695) | 2500.00 | 5000.00 |
| □ COMPLETE SET (664) | 1500.00 | 3000.00 |
| □ COMMON CARD (1-218/328-512) | .60 | 1.50 |
| □ COMMON CARD (219-327) | 1.00 | 2.50 |
| □ COMMON CARD (513-588) | .75 | 2.00 |
| □ COMMON CARD (589-664) | 1.25 | 3.00 |
| □ WRAPPER (5-CENT) | 8.00 | 20.00 |
| □ 1 Yaz/Cater/Oliva LL | 6.00 | 15.00 |
| □ 2 Rose/Alou/Alou LL | 3.00 | 8.00 |
| □ 3 Harrelson/Howard/North LL | 1.50 | 4.00 |
| □ 4 McCovey/Santo/B.Will LL | 2.50 | 6.00 |
| □ 5 Howard/Horton/Harrelson LL | 1.50 | 4.00 |
| □ 6 McCovey/Allen/Banks LL | 2.50 | 6.00 |
| □ 7 Tiant/McDow/McNally LL | 1.50 | 4.00 |
| □ 8 Gibson/Bolin/Veale LL | 2.50 | 6.00 |
| □ 9 McLain/McNal/Tiant/Stott LL | 1.50 | 4.00 |
| □ 10 Marichal/Gibson/Jenkins LL | 3.00 | 8.00 |
| □ 11 McDowell/McLain/Tiant LL | 1.50 | 4.00 |
| □ 12 Gibson/Jenkins/Singer LL | 1.50 | 4.00 |
| □ 13 Mickey Stanley | 1.00 | 2.50 |
| □ 14 Al McBean | .60 | 1.50 |
| □ 15 Boog Powell | 1.50 | 4.00 |
| □ 16 C.Gutierrez RC/R.Robertson RC | .60 | 1.50 |
| □ 17 Mike Marshall | 1.00 | 2.50 |
| □ 18 Dick Schofield | .60 | 1.50 |
| □ 19 Ken Suarez | .60 | 1.50 |
| □ 20 Ernie Banks | 8.00 | 20.00 |
| □ 21 Jose Santiago | 1.00 | 2.50 |
| □ 22 Jesus Alou | 1.00 | 2.50 |
| □ 23 Lew Krausse | 1.00 | 2.50 |
| □ 24 Walt Alston MG | 1.50 | 4.00 |
| □ 25 Roy White | 1.00 | 2.50 |
| □ 26 Clay Carroll | 1.00 | 2.50 |
| □ 27 Bernie Allen | .60 | 1.50 |
| □ 28 Mike Ryan | .60 | 1.50 |
| □ 29 Dave Morehead | .60 | 1.50 |
| □ 30 Bob Allison | 1.00 | 2.50 |
| □ 31 G.Gentry RC/A.Otis RC | 1.00 | 2.50 |
| □ 32 Sammy Ellis | .60 | 1.50 |
| □ 33 Wayne Causey | .60 | 1.50 |

| | | |
|---|---|---|
| □ 34 Gary Peters | .60 | 1.50 |
| □ 35 Joe Morgan | 4.00 | 10.00 |
| □ 36 Luke Walker | .60 | 1.50 |
| □ 37 Curt Motton | .60 | 1.50 |
| □ 38 Zoilo Versalles | 1.00 | 2.50 |
| □ 39 Dick Hughes | .60 | 1.50 |
| □ 40 Mayo Smith MG | .60 | 1.50 |
| □ 41 Bob Barton | .60 | 1.50 |
| □ 42 Tommy Harper | 1.00 | 2.50 |
| □ 43 Joe Niekro | 1.00 | 2.50 |
| □ 44 Danny Cater | .60 | 1.50 |
| □ 45 Maury Wills | 1.50 | 4.00 |
| □ 46 Fritz Peterson | 1.00 | 2.50 |
| □ 47A P.Popovich Thick Airbrush | 1.00 | 2.50 |
| □ 47B P.Popovich Light Airbrush | 1.00 | 2.50 |
| □ 47C P.Popovich C on Helmet | 10.00 | 25.00 |
| □ 48 Brant Alyea | .60 | 1.50 |
| □ 49A S.Jones/E.Rodriguez ERR | 10.00 | 25.00 |
| □ 49B S.Jones RC/E.Rodriguez RC | 1.00 | 2.50 |
| □ 50 Roberto Clemente UER | 30.00 | 60.00 |
| □ 51 Woody Fryman | 1.00 | 2.50 |
| □ 52 Mike Andrews | .60 | 1.50 |
| □ 53 Sonny Jackson | .60 | 1.50 |
| □ 54 Cisco Carlos | .60 | 1.50 |
| □ 55 Jerry Grote | 1.00 | 2.50 |
| □ 56 Rich Reese | .60 | 1.50 |
| □ 57 Checklist 1/McLain | 2.50 | 6.00 |
| □ 58 Fred Gladding | .60 | 1.50 |
| □ 59 Jay Johnstone | 1.00 | 2.50 |
| □ 60 Nelson Briles | 1.00 | 2.50 |
| □ 61 Jimmie Hall | .60 | 1.50 |
| □ 62 Chico Salmon | 1.00 | 2.50 |
| □ 63 Jim Hickman | 1.00 | 2.50 |
| □ 64 Bill Monbouquette | .60 | 1.50 |
| □ 65 Willie Davis | 1.00 | 2.50 |
| □ 66 M.Adamson RC/M.Rettenmund RC | 1.00 | 2.50 |
| □ 67 Bill Stoneman | 1.00 | 2.50 |
| □ 68 Dave Duncan | 1.00 | 2.50 |
| □ 69 Steve Hamilton | 1.00 | 2.50 |
| □ 70 Tommy Helms | 1.00 | 2.50 |
| □ 71 Steve Whitaker | 1.00 | 2.50 |
| □ 72 Ron Taylor | .60 | 1.50 |
| □ 73 Johnny Briggs | 1.00 | 2.50 |
| □ 74 Preston Gomez MG | 1.00 | 2.50 |
| □ 75 Luis Aparicio | 2.50 | 6.00 |
| □ 76 Norm Miller | .60 | 1.50 |
| □ 77A R.Perranoski No LA | 1.00 | 2.50 |
| □ 77B R.Perranoski LA Cap | 10.00 | 25.00 |
| □ 78 Tom Satriano | .60 | 1.50 |
| □ 79 Milt Pappas | 1.00 | 2.50 |
| □ 80 Norm Cash | 1.00 | 2.50 |
| □ 81 Mel Queen | .60 | 1.50 |
| □ 82 R.Hebner RC/A.Oliver RC | 3.00 | 8.00 |
| □ 83 Mike Ferraro | .60 | 1.50 |
| □ 84 Bob Humphreys | .60 | 1.50 |
| □ 85 Lou Brock | 8.00 | 20.00 |
| □ 86 Pete Richert | .60 | 1.50 |
| □ 87 Horace Clarke | 1.00 | 2.50 |
| □ 88 Rich Nye | .60 | 1.50 |
| □ 89 Russ Gibson | .60 | 1.50 |
| □ 90 Jerry Koosman | 1.00 | 2.50 |
| □ 91 Alvin Dark MG | 1.00 | 2.50 |
| □ 92 Jack Billingham | .60 | 1.50 |
| □ 93 Joe Foy | 1.00 | 2.50 |
| □ 94 Hank Aguirre | .60 | 1.50 |
| □ 95 Johnny Bench | 20.00 | 50.00 |
| □ 96 Denny Lemaster | .60 | 1.50 |
| □ 97 Buddy Bradford | .60 | 1.50 |
| □ 98 Dave Giusti | .60 | 1.50 |
| □ 99A D.Morris RC/G.Nettles RC | 6.00 | 15.00 |
| □ 99B D.Morris/G.Nettles ERR | 6.00 | 15.00 |
| □ 100 Hank Aaron | 20.00 | 50.00 |
| □ 101 Daryl Patterson | .60 | 1.50 |
| □ 102 Jim Davenport | .60 | 1.50 |
| □ 103 Roger Repoz | .60 | 1.50 |
| □ 104 Steve Blass | 1.00 | 2.50 |
| □ 105 Rick Monday | .60 | 1.50 |
| □ 106 Jim Hannan | .60 | 1.50 |
| □ 107A Checklist 2/Gibson ERR | .60 | 1.50 |
| □ 107B Checklist 2/Gibson COR | 3.00 | 8.00 |
| □ 108 Tony Taylor | 1.00 | 2.50 |
| □ 109 Jim Lonborg | 1.00 | 2.50 |
| □ 110 Mike Shannon | 1.00 | 2.50 |
| □ 111 John Morris RC | .60 | 1.50 |
| □ 112 J.C. Martin | .60 | 1.50 |
| □ 113 Dave May | .60 | 1.50 |
| □ 114 A.Closter/J.Cumberland RC | .60 | 1.50 |
| □ 115 Bill Hands | .60 | 1.50 |

| | | |
|---|---|---|
| □ 116 Chuck Harrison | .60 | 1.50 |
| □ 117 Jim Fairey | 1.00 | 2.50 |
| □ 118 Stan Williams | .60 | 1.50 |
| □ 119 Doug Rader | 1.00 | 2.50 |
| □ 120 Pete Rose | 20.00 | 50.00 |
| □ 121 Joe Grzenda RC | .60 | 1.50 |
| □ 122 Ron Fairly | 1.00 | 2.50 |
| □ 123 Wilbur Wood | 1.00 | 2.50 |
| □ 124 Hank Bauer MG | 1.00 | 2.50 |
| □ 125 Ray Sadecki | .60 | 1.50 |
| □ 126 Dick Tracewski | .60 | 1.50 |
| □ 127 Kevin Collins | .60 | 1.50 |
| □ 128 Tommie Aaron | 1.00 | 2.50 |
| □ 129 Bill McCool | .60 | 1.50 |
| □ 130 Carl Yastrzemski | 8.00 | 20.00 |
| □ 131 Chris Cannizzaro | .60 | 1.50 |
| □ 132 Dave Baldwin | .60 | 1.50 |
| □ 133 Johnny Callison | 1.00 | 2.50 |
| □ 134 Jim Weaver | .60 | 1.50 |
| □ 135 Tommy Davis | 1.00 | 2.50 |
| □ 136 S.Huntz RC/M.Torrez | 1.00 | 2.50 |
| □ 137 Wally Bunker | .60 | 1.50 |
| □ 138 John Bateman | .60 | 1.50 |
| □ 139 Andy Kosco | 1.00 | 2.50 |
| □ 140 Jim Lefebvre | 1.00 | 2.50 |
| □ 141 Bill Dillman | .60 | 1.50 |
| □ 142 Woody Woodward | .60 | 1.50 |
| □ 143 Joe Nossek | .60 | 1.50 |
| □ 144 Bob Hendley | 1.00 | 2.50 |
| □ 145 Max Alvis | .60 | 1.50 |
| □ 146 Jim Perry | 1.00 | 2.50 |
| □ 147 Leo Durocher MG | 1.50 | 4.00 |
| □ 148 Lee Stange | .60 | 1.50 |
| □ 149 Ollie Brown | .60 | 1.50 |
| □ 150 Denny McLain | 1.50 | 4.00 |
| □ 151A C.Dalrymple Portrait | .60 | 1.50 |
| □ 151B C.Dalrymple Catch | 6.00 | 15.00 |
| □ 152 Tommie Sisk | .60 | 1.50 |
| □ 153 Ed Brinkman | .60 | 1.50 |
| □ 154 Jim Britton | .60 | 1.50 |
| □ 155 Pete Ward | .60 | 1.50 |
| □ 156 H.Gilson/L.McFadden RC | .60 | 1.50 |
| □ 157 Bob Rodgers | 1.00 | 2.50 |
| □ 158 Joe Gibbon | .60 | 1.50 |
| □ 159 Jerry Adair | .60 | 1.50 |
| □ 160 Vada Pinson | 1.00 | 2.50 |
| □ 161 John Purdin | .60 | 1.50 |
| □ 162 Bob Gibson WS1 | 3.00 | 8.00 |
| □ 163 Willie Horton WS2 | 2.50 | 6.00 |
| □ 164 T.McCarv w/Maris WS3 | 5.00 | 12.00 |
| □ 165 Lou Brock WS4 | 3.00 | 8.00 |
| □ 166 Al Kaline WS5 | 3.00 | 8.00 |
| □ 167 Jim Northrup WS6 | 2.50 | 6.00 |
| □ 168 M.Lolich/B.Gibson WS7 | 3.00 | 8.00 |
| □ 169 Tigers Celebrate WS | 2.50 | 6.00 |
| □ 170 Frank Howard | 1.00 | 2.50 |
| □ 171 Glenn Beckert | 1.00 | 2.50 |
| □ 172 Jerry Stephenson | .60 | 1.50 |
| □ 173 B.Christian RC/G.Nyman RC | .60 | 1.50 |
| □ 174 Grant Jackson | .60 | 1.50 |
| □ 175 Jim Bunning | 2.50 | 6.00 |
| □ 176 Joe Azcue | .60 | 1.50 |
| □ 177 Ron Reed | .60 | 1.50 |
| □ 178 Ray Oyler | 1.00 | 2.50 |
| □ 179 Don Pavletich | .60 | 1.50 |
| □ 180 Willie Horton | 1.00 | 2.50 |
| □ 181 Mel Nelson | .60 | 1.50 |
| □ 182 Bill Rigney MG | .60 | 1.50 |
| □ 183 Don Shaw | 1.00 | 2.50 |
| □ 184 Roberto Pena | .60 | 1.50 |
| □ 185 Tom Phoebus | .60 | 1.50 |
| □ 186 Johnny Edwards | .60 | 1.50 |
| □ 187 Leon Wagner | .60 | 1.50 |
| □ 188 Rick Wise | 1.00 | 2.50 |
| □ 189 J.Lahoud RC/J.Thibodeau RC | .60 | 1.50 |
| □ 190 Willie Mays | 40.00 | 80.00 |
| □ 191 Lindy McDaniel | 1.00 | 2.50 |
| □ 192 Jose Pagan | 1.00 | 2.50 |
| □ 193 Don Cardwell | 1.00 | 2.50 |
| □ 194 Ted Uhlaender | .60 | 1.50 |
| □ 195 John Odom | .60 | 1.50 |
| □ 196 Lum Harris MG | .60 | 1.50 |
| □ 197 Dick Selma | .60 | 1.50 |
| □ 198 Willie Smith | .60 | 1.50 |
| □ 199 Jim French | .60 | 1.50 |
| □ 200 Bob Gibson | 5.00 | 12.00 |
| □ 201 Russ Snyder | .60 | 1.50 |
| □ 202 Don Wilson | 1.00 | 2.50 |

|  | | |
|---|---|---|
| ❏ 203 Dave Johnson | 1.00 | 2.50 |
| ❏ 204 Jack Hiatt | .60 | 1.50 |
| ❏ 205 Rick Reichardt | .60 | 1.50 |
| ❏ 206 L.Hisle/B.Lersch RC | 1.00 | 2.50 |
| ❏ 207 Roy Face | 1.00 | 2.50 |
| ❏ 208A D.Clendenon Houston | 1.00 | 2.50 |
| ❏ 208B D.Clendenon Expos | 6.00 | 15.00 |
| ❏ 209 Larry Haney UER | .60 | 1.50 |
| ❏ 210 Felix Millan | .60 | 1.50 |
| ❏ 211 Galen Cisco | .60 | 1.50 |
| ❏ 212 Tom Tresh | 1.00 | 2.50 |
| ❏ 213 Gerry Arrigo | .60 | 1.50 |
| ❏ 214 Checklist 3 | 2.50 | 6.00 |
| ❏ 215 Rico Petrocelli | 1.00 | 2.50 |
| ❏ 216 Don Sutton DP | 2.50 | 6.00 |
| ❏ 217 John Donaldson | .60 | 1.50 |
| ❏ 218 John Roseboro | 1.00 | 2.50 |
| ❏ 219 Fred Patek RC | 1.50 | 4.00 |
| ❏ 220 Sam McDowell | 1.50 | 4.00 |
| ❏ 221 Art Shamsky | 1.50 | 4.00 |
| ❏ 222 Duane Josephson | 1.00 | 2.50 |
| ❏ 223 Tom Dukes | 1.00 | 2.50 |
| ❏ 224 B.Harrelson RC/S.Kealey RC | 1.00 | 2.50 |
| ❏ 225 Don Kessinger | 1.50 | 4.00 |
| ❏ 226 Bruce Howard | 1.00 | 2.50 |
| ❏ 227 Frank Johnson RC | 1.00 | 2.50 |
| ❏ 228 Dave Leonhard | 1.00 | 2.50 |
| ❏ 229 Don Lock | 1.00 | 2.50 |
| ❏ 230 Rusty Staub UER | 1.50 | 4.00 |
| ❏ 231 Pat Dobson | 1.50 | 4.00 |
| ❏ 232 Dave Ricketts | 1.00 | 2.50 |
| ❏ 233 Steve Barber | 1.50 | 4.00 |
| ❏ 234 Dave Bristol MG | 1.00 | 2.50 |
| ❏ 235 Jim Hunter | 4.00 | 10.00 |
| ❏ 236 Manny Mota | 1.50 | 4.00 |
| ❏ 237 Bobby Cox RC | 8.00 | 20.00 |
| ❏ 238 Ken Johnson | 1.00 | 2.50 |
| ❏ 239 Bob Taylor | 1.50 | 4.00 |
| ❏ 240 Ken Harrelson | 1.50 | 4.00 |
| ❏ 241 Jim Brewer | 1.00 | 2.50 |
| ❏ 242 Frank Kostro | 1.00 | 2.50 |
| ❏ 243 Ron Kline | 1.00 | 2.50 |
| ❏ 244 R.Fosse RC/G.Woodson RC | 1.50 | 4.00 |
| ❏ 245 Ed Charles | 1.50 | 4.00 |
| ❏ 246 Joe Coleman | 1.00 | 2.50 |
| ❏ 247 Gene Oliver | 1.00 | 2.50 |
| ❏ 248 Bob Priddy | 1.00 | 2.50 |
| ❏ 249 Ed Spiezio | 1.00 | 2.50 |
| ❏ 250 Frank Robinson | 8.00 | 20.00 |
| ❏ 251 Ron Herbel | 1.00 | 2.50 |
| ❏ 252 Chuck Cottier | 1.00 | 2.50 |
| ❏ 253 Jerry Johnson RC | 1.00 | 2.50 |
| ❏ 254 Joe Schultz MG RC | 1.50 | 4.00 |
| ❏ 255 Steve Carlton | 12.50 | 30.00 |
| ❏ 256 Gates Brown | 1.00 | 2.50 |
| ❏ 257 Jim Ray | 1.00 | 2.50 |
| ❏ 258 Jackie Hernandez | 1.00 | 2.50 |
| ❏ 259 Bill Short | 1.00 | 2.50 |
| ❏ 260 Reggie Jackson RC | 150.00 | 300.00 |
| ❏ 261 Bob Johnson | 1.00 | 2.50 |
| ❏ 262 Mike Kekich | 1.00 | 2.50 |
| ❏ 263 Jerry May | 1.00 | 2.50 |
| ❏ 264 Bill Landis | 1.00 | 2.50 |
| ❏ 265 Chico Cardenas | 1.50 | 4.00 |
| ❏ 266 T.Hutton/A.Foster RC | 1.50 | 4.00 |
| ❏ 267 Vicente Romo RC | 1.00 | 2.50 |
| ❏ 268 Al Spangler | .60 | 1.50 |
| ❏ 269 Al Weis | 1.50 | 4.00 |
| ❏ 270 Mickey Lolich | 1.50 | 4.00 |
| ❏ 271 Larry Stahl | 1.00 | 2.50 |
| ❏ 272 Ed Stroud | 1.00 | 2.50 |
| ❏ 273 Ron Willis | 1.00 | 2.50 |
| ❏ 274 Clyde King MG | 1.50 | 4.00 |
| ❏ 275 Vic Davalillo | 1.00 | 2.50 |
| ❏ 276 Gary Wagner | 1.00 | 2.50 |
| ❏ 277 Elrod Hendricks RC | 1.00 | 2.50 |
| ❏ 278 Gary Geiger UER | 1.50 | 4.00 |
| ❏ 279 Roger Nelson | 1.00 | 2.50 |
| ❏ 280 Alex Johnson | 1.50 | 4.00 |
| ❏ 281 Ted Kubiak | 1.00 | 2.50 |
| ❏ 282 Pat Jarvis | 1.00 | 2.50 |
| ❏ 283 Sandy Alomar | 1.50 | 4.00 |
| ❏ 284 J.Robertson RC/M.Wegener RC | 1.50 | 4.00 |
| ❏ 285 Don Mincher | 1.00 | 2.50 |
| ❏ 286 Dock Ellis RC | 1.50 | 4.00 |
| ❏ 287 Jose Tartabull | 1.50 | 4.00 |
| ❏ 288 Ken Holtzman | 1.50 | 4.00 |
| ❏ 289 Bart Shirley | 1.00 | 2.50 |
| ❏ 290 Jim Kaat | 1.50 | 4.00 |
| ❏ 291 Vern Fuller | 1.00 | 2.50 |
| ❏ 292 Al Downing | 1.50 | 4.00 |
| ❏ 293 Dick Dietz | 1.50 | 4.00 |
| ❏ 294 Jim Lemon MG | 1.00 | 2.50 |
| ❏ 295 Tony Perez | 5.00 | 12.00 |
| ❏ 296 Andy Messersmith RC | 1.50 | 4.00 |
| ❏ 297 Deron Johnson | 1.00 | 2.50 |
| ❏ 298 Dave Nicholson | 1.50 | 4.00 |
| ❏ 299 Mark Belanger | 1.50 | 4.00 |
| ❏ 300 Felipe Alou | 1.50 | 4.00 |
| ❏ 301 Darrell Brandon | 1.00 | 2.50 |
| ❏ 302 Jim Pagliaroni | 1.00 | 2.50 |
| ❏ 303 Cal Koonce | 1.50 | 4.00 |
| ❏ 304 B.Davis/C.Gaston RC | 2.50 | 6.00 |
| ❏ 305 Dick McAuliffe | 1.50 | 4.00 |
| ❏ 306 Jim Grant | 1.50 | 4.00 |
| ❏ 307 Gary Kolb | 1.00 | 2.50 |
| ❏ 308 Wade Blasingame | 1.00 | 2.50 |
| ❏ 309 Walt Williams | 1.00 | 2.50 |
| ❏ 310 Tom Haller | 1.00 | 2.50 |
| ❏ 311 Sparky Lyle RC | 4.00 | 10.00 |
| ❏ 312 Lee Elia | 1.50 | 4.00 |
| ❏ 313 Bill Robinson | 1.50 | 4.00 |
| ❏ 314 Checklist 4/Drysdale | 2.50 | 6.00 |
| ❏ 315 Eddie Fisher | 1.00 | 2.50 |
| ❏ 316 Hal Lanier | 1.50 | 4.00 |
| ❏ 317 Bruce Look RC | 1.00 | 2.50 |
| ❏ 318 Jack Fisher | 1.00 | 2.50 |
| ❏ 319 Ken McMullen UER | 1.00 | 2.50 |
| ❏ 320 Dal Maxvill | 1.00 | 2.50 |
| ❏ 321 Jim McAndrew RC | 1.50 | 4.00 |
| ❏ 322 Jose Vidal | 1.00 | 2.50 |
| ❏ 323 Larry Miller | 1.00 | 2.50 |
| ❏ 324 L.Cain RC/D.Campbell RC | 1.50 | 4.00 |
| ❏ 325 Jose Cardenal | 1.50 | 4.00 |
| ❏ 326 Gary Sutherland | 1.50 | 4.00 |
| ❏ 327 Willie Crawford | 1.00 | 2.50 |
| ❏ 328 Joel Horlen | .60 | 1.50 |
| ❏ 329 Rick Joseph | .60 | 1.50 |
| ❏ 330 Tony Conigliaro | 1.50 | 4.00 |
| ❏ 331 G.Garrido/T.House RC | 1.00 | 2.50 |
| ❏ 332 Fred Talbot | .60 | 1.50 |
| ❏ 333 Ivan Murrell | .60 | 1.50 |
| ❏ 334 Phil Roof | .60 | 1.50 |
| ❏ 335 Bill Mazeroski | 2.50 | 6.00 |
| ❏ 336 Jim Roland | .60 | 1.50 |
| ❏ 337 Marty Martinez RC | .60 | 1.50 |
| ❏ 338 Del Unser RC | .60 | 1.50 |
| ❏ 339 S.Mingori RC/J.Pena RC | .60 | 1.50 |
| ❏ 340 Dave McNally | 1.00 | 2.50 |
| ❏ 341 Dave Adlesh | .60 | 1.50 |
| ❏ 342 Bubba Morton | .60 | 1.50 |
| ❏ 343 Dan Frisella | .60 | 1.50 |
| ❏ 344 Tom Matchick | .60 | 1.50 |
| ❏ 345 Frank Linzy | .60 | 1.50 |
| ❏ 346 Wayne Comer RC | .60 | 1.50 |
| ❏ 347 Randy Hundley | 1.00 | 2.50 |
| ❏ 348 Steve Hargan | .60 | 1.50 |
| ❏ 349 Dick Williams MG | 1.50 | 4.00 |
| ❏ 350 Richie Allen | 1.50 | 4.00 |
| ❏ 351 Carroll Sembera | .60 | 1.50 |
| ❏ 352 Paul Schaal | 1.00 | 2.50 |
| ❏ 353 Jeff Torborg | 1.00 | 2.50 |
| ❏ 354 Nate Oliver | .60 | 1.50 |
| ❏ 355 Phil Niekro | 2.50 | 6.00 |
| ❏ 356 Frank Quilici | .60 | 1.50 |
| ❏ 357 Carl Taylor | .60 | 1.50 |
| ❏ 358 G.Lauzerique RC/R.Rodriguez | .60 | 1.50 |
| ❏ 359 Dick Kelley | .60 | 1.50 |
| ❏ 360 Jim Wynn | 1.00 | 2.50 |
| ❏ 361 Gary Holman RC | .60 | 1.50 |
| ❏ 362 Jim Maloney | 1.00 | 2.50 |
| ❏ 363 Russ Nixon | .60 | 1.50 |
| ❏ 364 Tommie Agee | 1.50 | 4.00 |
| ❏ 365 Jim Fregosi | 1.00 | 2.50 |
| ❏ 366 Bo Belinsky | 1.00 | 2.50 |
| ❏ 367 Lou Johnson | 1.00 | 2.50 |
| ❏ 368 Vic Roznovsky | .60 | 1.50 |
| ❏ 369 Bob Skinner MG | 1.00 | 2.50 |
| ❏ 370 Juan Marichal | 3.00 | 8.00 |
| ❏ 371 Sal Bando | 1.00 | 2.50 |
| ❏ 372 Adolfo Phillips | .60 | 1.50 |
| ❏ 373 Fred Lasher | .60 | 1.50 |
| ❏ 374 Bob Tillman | .60 | 1.50 |
| ❏ 375 Harmon Killebrew | 6.00 | 15.00 |
| ❏ 376 M.Fiore RC/J.Rooker RC | .60 | 1.50 |
| ❏ 377 Gary Bell | 1.00 | 2.50 |
| ❏ 378 Jose Herrera RC | .60 | 1.50 |
| ❏ 379 Ken Boyer | 1.00 | 2.50 |
| ❏ 380 Stan Bahnsen | 1.00 | 2.50 |
| ❏ 381 Ed Kranepool | 1.00 | 2.50 |
| ❏ 382 Pat Corrales | 1.00 | 2.50 |
| ❏ 383 Casey Cox | .60 | 1.50 |
| ❏ 384 Larry Shepard MG | .60 | 1.50 |
| ❏ 385 Orlando Cepeda | 2.50 | 6.00 |
| ❏ 386 Jim McGlothlin | .60 | 1.50 |
| ❏ 387 Bobby Klaus | .60 | 1.50 |
| ❏ 388 Tom McCraw | .60 | 1.50 |
| ❏ 389 Dan Coombs | .60 | 1.50 |
| ❏ 390 Bill Freehan | 1.00 | 2.50 |
| ❏ 391 Ray Culp | .60 | 1.50 |
| ❏ 392 Bob Burda RC | .60 | 1.50 |
| ❏ 393 Gene Brabender | 1.00 | 2.50 |
| ❏ 394 L.Piniella/M.Staehle | 2.50 | 6.00 |
| ❏ 395 Chris Short | .60 | 1.50 |
| ❏ 396 Jim Campanis | .60 | 1.50 |
| ❏ 397 Chuck Dobson | .60 | 1.50 |
| ❏ 398 Tito Francona | .60 | 1.50 |
| ❏ 399 Bob Bailey | 1.00 | 2.50 |
| ❏ 400 Don Drysdale | 6.00 | 15.00 |
| ❏ 401 Jake Gibbs | 1.00 | 2.50 |
| ❏ 402 Ken Boswell RC | 1.00 | 2.50 |
| ❏ 403 Bob Miller | .60 | 1.50 |
| ❏ 404 V.LaRose RC/G.Ross RC | 1.00 | 2.50 |
| ❏ 405 Lee May | 1.00 | 2.50 |
| ❏ 406 Phil Ortega | .60 | 1.50 |
| ❏ 407 Tom Egan | .60 | 1.50 |
| ❏ 408 Nate Colbert | .60 | 1.50 |
| ❏ 409 Bob Moose | .60 | 1.50 |
| ❏ 410 Al Kaline | 10.00 | 25.00 |
| ❏ 411 Larry Dierker | 1.00 | 2.50 |
| ❏ 412 Checklist 5/Mantle DP | 6.00 | 15.00 |
| ❏ 413 Roland Sheldon | 1.00 | 2.50 |
| ❏ 414 Duke Sims | .60 | 1.50 |
| ❏ 415 Ray Washburn | .60 | 1.50 |
| ❏ 416 Willie McCovey AS | 3.00 | 8.00 |
| ❏ 417 Ken Harrelson AS | 1.25 | 3.00 |
| ❏ 418 Tommy Helms AS | 1.25 | 3.00 |
| ❏ 419 Rod Carew AS | 4.00 | 10.00 |
| ❏ 420 Ron Santo AS | 1.50 | 4.00 |
| ❏ 421 Brooks Robinson AS | 3.00 | 8.00 |
| ❏ 422 Don Kessinger AS | 1.25 | 3.00 |
| ❏ 423 Bert Campaneris AS | 1.50 | 4.00 |
| ❏ 424 Pete Rose AS | 6.00 | 15.00 |
| ❏ 425 Carl Yastrzemski AS | 4.00 | 10.00 |
| ❏ 426 Curt Flood AS | 1.50 | 4.00 |
| ❏ 427 Tony Oliva AS | 1.50 | 4.00 |
| ❏ 428 Lou Brock AS | 2.50 | 6.00 |
| ❏ 429 Willie Horton AS | 1.25 | 3.00 |
| ❏ 430 Johnny Bench AS | 4.00 | 10.00 |
| ❏ 431 Bill Freehan AS | 1.50 | 4.00 |
| ❏ 432 Bob Gibson AS | 2.50 | 6.00 |
| ❏ 433 Denny McLain AS | 1.25 | 3.00 |
| ❏ 434 Jerry Koosman AS | 1.25 | 3.00 |
| ❏ 435 Sam McDowell AS | 1.00 | 2.50 |
| ❏ 436 Gene Alley | 1.00 | 2.50 |
| ❏ 437 Luis Alcaraz RC | .60 | 1.50 |
| ❏ 438 Gary Waslewski RC | .60 | 1.50 |
| ❏ 439 E.Hermann RC/D.Lazar RC | .60 | 1.50 |
| ❏ 440A Willie McCovey | 6.00 | 15.00 |
| ❏ 440B Willie McCovey WL | 50.00 | 100.00 |
| ❏ 441A Dennis Higgins | .60 | 1.50 |
| ❏ 441B Dennis Higgins WL | 10.00 | 25.00 |
| ❏ 442 Ty Cline | .60 | 1.50 |
| ❏ 443 Don Wert | .60 | 1.50 |
| ❏ 444A Joe Moeller | .60 | 1.50 |
| ❏ 444B Joe Moeller WL | 10.00 | 25.00 |
| ❏ 445 Bobby Knoop | .60 | 1.50 |
| ❏ 446 Claude Raymond | .60 | 1.50 |
| ❏ 447A Ralph Houk MG | 1.00 | 2.50 |
| ❏ 447B Ralph Houk MG WL | 10.00 | 25.00 |
| ❏ 448 Bob Tolan | 1.00 | 2.50 |
| ❏ 449 Paul Lindblad | .60 | 1.50 |
| ❏ 450 Billy Williams | 3.00 | 8.00 |
| ❏ 451A Rich Rollins | 1.00 | 2.50 |
| ❏ 451B Rich Rollins WL | 10.00 | 25.00 |
| ❏ 452A Al Ferrara | .60 | 1.50 |
| ❏ 452B Al Ferrara WL | 10.00 | 25.00 |
| ❏ 453 Mike Cuellar | 1.00 | 2.50 |
| ❏ 454A L.Colton/D.Money RC | 1.00 | 2.50 |
| ❏ 454B L.Colton/D.Money WL | 10.00 | 25.00 |
| ❏ 455 Sonny Siebert | .60 | 1.50 |
| ❏ 456 Bud Harrelson | 1.00 | 2.50 |
| ❏ 457 Dalton Jones | .60 | 1.50 |
| ❏ 458 Curt Blefary | .60 | 1.50 |

|  | | |
|---|---|---|
| 459 Dave Boswell | .60 | 1.50 |
| 460 Joe Torre | 1.50 | 4.00 |
| 461A Mike Epstein | .60 | 1.50 |
| 461B Mike Epstein WL | 10.00 | 25.00 |
| 462 R.Schoendienst MG | 1.00 | 2.50 |
| 463 Dennis Ribant | .60 | 1.50 |
| 464A Dave Marshall RC | .60 | 1.50 |
| 464B Dave Marshall WL | 10.00 | 25.00 |
| 465 Tommy John | 1.50 | 4.00 |
| 466 John Boccabella | 1.00 | 2.50 |
| 467 Tommie Reynolds | .60 | 1.50 |
| 468A B.Dal Canton RC/B.Robertson | .60 | 1.50 |
| 468B B.Dal Canton RC/B.Robertson WL | 10.00 | 25.00 |
| 469 Chico Ruiz | .60 | 1.50 |
| 470A Mel Stottlemyre | 1.00 | 2.50 |
| 470B Mel Stottlemyre WL | 12.50 | 30.00 |
| 471A Ted Savage | .60 | 1.50 |
| 471B Ted Savage WL | 10.00 | 25.00 |
| 472 Jim Price | .60 | 1.50 |
| 473A Jose Arcia | .60 | 1.50 |
| 473B Jose Arcia WL | 10.00 | 25.00 |
| 474 Tom Murphy RC | .60 | 1.50 |
| 475 Tim McCarver | 1.50 | 4.00 |
| 476A K.Brett RC/G.Moses | 1.00 | 2.50 |
| 476B K.Brett/G.Moses WL | 12.50 | 30.00 |
| 477 Jeff James RC | .60 | 1.50 |
| 478 Don Buford | .60 | 1.50 |
| 479 Richie Scheinblum | .60 | 1.50 |
| 480 Tom Seaver | 40.00 | 80.00 |
| 481 Bill Melton RC | 1.00 | 2.50 |
| 482A Jim Gosger | .60 | 1.50 |
| 482B Jim Gosger WL | 10.00 | 25.00 |
| 483 Ted Abernathy | .60 | 1.50 |
| 484 Joe Gordon MG | 1.00 | 2.50 |
| 485A Gaylord Perry | 4.00 | 10.00 |
| 485B Gaylord Perry WL | 40.00 | 80.00 |
| 486A Paul Casanova | .60 | 1.50 |
| 486B Paul Casanova WL | 10.00 | 25.00 |
| 487 Denis Menke | .60 | 1.50 |
| 488 Joe Sparma | .60 | 1.50 |
| 489 Clete Boyer | 1.00 | 2.50 |
| 490 Matty Alou | 1.00 | 2.50 |
| 491A J.Crider RC/G.Mitterwald | .60 | 1.50 |
| 491B J.Crider/G.Mitterwald WL | 10.00 | 25.00 |
| 492 Tony Cloninger | .60 | 1.50 |
| 493A Wes Parker | 1.00 | 2.50 |
| 493B Wes Parker WL | 10.00 | 25.00 |
| 494 Ken Berry | .60 | 1.50 |
| 495 Bert Campaneris | 1.00 | 2.50 |
| 496 Larry Jaster | .60 | 1.50 |
| 497 Julian Javier | 1.00 | 2.50 |
| 498 Juan Pizarro | 1.00 | 2.50 |
| 499 D.Bryant RC/S.Shea RC | .60 | 1.50 |
| 500A Mickey Mantle UER | 175.00 | 350.00 |
| 500B Mickey Mantle UER WL | 1000.00 | 2000.00 |
| 501A Tony Gonzalez | 1.00 | 2.50 |
| 501B Tony Gonzalez WL | 10.00 | 25.00 |
| 502 Minnie Rojas | .60 | 1.50 |
| 503 Larry Brown | .60 | 1.50 |
| 504 Checklist 6/B.Robinson | 3.00 | 8.00 |
| 505A Bobby Bolin | .60 | 1.50 |
| 505B Bobby Bolin WL | 10.00 | 25.00 |
| 506 Paul Blair | 1.00 | 2.50 |
| 507 Cookie Rojas | 1.00 | 2.50 |
| 508 Moe Drabowsky | 1.00 | 2.50 |
| 509 Manny Sanguillen | 1.00 | 2.50 |
| 510 Rod Carew | 15.00 | 40.00 |
| 511A Diego Segui | 1.00 | 2.50 |
| 511B Diego Segui WL | 10.00 | 25.00 |
| 512 Cleon Jones | -1.00 | 2.50 |
| 513 Camilo Pascual | 1.25 | 3.00 |
| 514 Mike Lum | .75 | 2.00 |
| 515 Dick Green | .75 | 2.00 |
| 516 Earl Weaver MG RC | 8.00 | 20.00 |
| 517 Mike McCormick | 1.25 | 3.00 |
| 518 Fred Whitfield | .75 | 2.00 |
| 519 J.Kenney RC/L.Boehmer RC | .75 | 2.00 |
| 520 Bob Veale | 1.25 | 3.00 |
| 521 George Thomas | .75 | 2.00 |
| 522 Joe Hoerner | .75 | 2.00 |
| 523 Bob Chance | .75 | 2.00 |
| 524 J.Laboy RC/F.Wicker RC | 1.25 | 3.00 |
| 525 Earl Wilson | 1.25 | 3.00 |
| 526 Hector Torres RC | .75 | 2.00 |
| 527 Al Lopez MG | 2.00 | 5.00 |
| 528 Claude Osteen | 1.25 | 3.00 |
| 529 Ed Kirkpatrick | 1.25 | 3.00 |
| 530 Cesar Tovar | .75 | 2.00 |

|  | | |
|---|---|---|
| 531 Dick Farrell | .75 | 2.00 |
| 532 Phoeb/Hard/McNally/Cuellar | 1.25 | 3.00 |
| 533 Nolan Ryan | 100.00 | 200.00 |
| 534 Jerry McNertney | 1.25 | 3.00 |
| 535 Phil Regan | 1.25 | 3.00 |
| 536 D.Breeden RC/D.Roberts RC | .75 | 2.00 |
| 537 Mike Paul RC | .75 | 2.00 |
| 538 Charlie Smith | .75 | 2.00 |
| 539 T.Williams/M.Epstein | 5.00 | 12.00 |
| 540 Curt Flood | 1.25 | 3.00 |
| 541 Joe Verbanic | .75 | 2.00 |
| 542 Bob Aspromonte | .75 | 2.00 |
| 543 Fred Newman | .75 | 2.00 |
| 544 M.Kilkenny RC/R.Woods RC | .75 | 2.00 |
| 545 Willie Stargell | 5.00 | 12.00 |
| 546 Jim Nash | .75 | 2.00 |
| 547 Billy Martin MG | 2.00 | 5.00 |
| 548 Bob Locker | .75 | 2.00 |
| 549 Ron Brand | .75 | 2.00 |
| 550 Brooks Robinson | 12.50 | 30.00 |
| 551 Wayne Granger RC | .75 | 2.00 |
| 552 T.Sizemore RC/B.Sudakis RC | 1.25 | 3.00 |
| 553 Ron Davis | .75 | 2.00 |
| 554 Frank Bertaina | .75 | 2.00 |
| 555 Jim Ray Hart | 1.25 | 3.00 |
| 556 Bando/Campaneris/Cater | 1.25 | 3.00 |
| 557 Frank Fernandez | .75 | 2.00 |
| 558 Tom Burgmeier RC | 1.25 | 3.00 |
| 559 J.Hague RC/J.Hicks | .75 | 2.00 |
| 560 Luis Tiant | 1.25 | 3.00 |
| 561 Ron Clark | .75 | 2.00 |
| 562 Bob Watson RC | 3.00 | 8.00 |
| 563 Marty Pattin RC | 1.25 | 3.00 |
| 564 Gil Hodges MG | 4.00 | 10.00 |
| 565 Hoyt Wilhelm | 3.00 | 8.00 |
| 566 Ron Hansen | .75 | 2.00 |
| 567 E.Jimenez/J.Shellenback | .75 | 2.00 |
| 568 Cecil Upshaw | .75 | 2.00 |
| 569 Billy Harris | .60 | 1.50 |
| 570 Ron Santo | 3.00 | 8.00 |
| 571 Cap Peterson | .75 | 2.00 |
| 572 W.McCovey/J.Marichal | 6.00 | 15.00 |
| 573 Jim Palmer | 12.50 | 30.00 |
| 574 George Scott | 1.25 | 3.00 |
| 575 Bill Singer | 1.25 | 3.00 |
| 576 R.Stone/B.Wilson | .75 | 2.00 |
| 577 Mike Hegan | 1.25 | 3.00 |
| 578 Don Bosch | .75 | 2.00 |
| 579 Dave Nelson RC | .75 | 2.00 |
| 580 Jim Northrup | 1.25 | 3.00 |
| 581 Gary Nolan | 1.25 | 3.00 |
| 582A Checklist 7/Oliva White | 2.50 | 6.00 |
| 582B Checklist 7/Oliva Red | 3.00 | 8.00 |
| 583 Clyde Wright RC | .75 | 2.00 |
| 584 Don Mason | .75 | 2.00 |
| 585 Ron Swoboda | 1.25 | 3.00 |
| 586 Tim Cullen | .75 | 2.00 |
| 587 Joe Rudi RC | 3.00 | 8.00 |
| 588 Bill White | 1.25 | 3.00 |
| 589 Joe Pepitone | 2.00 | 5.00 |
| 590 Rico Carty | 2.00 | 5.00 |
| 591 Mike Hedlund | 1.25 | 3.00 |
| 592 R.Robles RC/A.Santorini RC | 1.25 | 3.00 |
| 593 Don Nottebart | 1.25 | 3.00 |
| 594 Dooley Womack | 1.25 | 3.00 |
| 595 Lee Maye | 1.25 | 3.00 |
| 596 Chuck Hartenstein | 1.25 | 3.00 |
| 597 Rollie Fingers RC | 15.00 | 40.00 |
| 598 Ruben Amaro | 1.25 | 3.00 |
| 599 John Boozer | 1.25 | 3.00 |
| 600 Tony Oliva | 3.00 | 8.00 |
| 601 Tug McGraw SP | 3.00 | 8.00 |
| 602 Distaso/Young/Qualls RC | 2.00 | 5.00 |
| 603 Joe Keough RC | 1.25 | 3.00 |
| 604 Bobby Etheridge | 1.25 | 3.00 |
| 605 Dick Ellsworth | 1.25 | 3.00 |
| 606 Gene Mauch MG | 2.00 | 5.00 |
| 607 Dick Bosman | 1.25 | 3.00 |
| 608 Dick Simpson | 1.25 | 3.00 |
| 609 Phil Gagliano | 1.25 | 3.00 |
| 610 Jim Hardin | 1.25 | 3.00 |
| 611 Didier/Hriniak/Niebauer RC | 2.00 | 5.00 |
| 612 Jack Aker | 1.25 | 3.00 |
| 613 Jim Beauchamp | 1.25 | 3.00 |
| 614 T.Griffin RC/S.Guinn RC | 1.25 | 3.00 |
| 615 Len Gabrielson | 1.25 | 3.00 |
| 616 Don McMahon | 1.25 | 3.00 |
| 617 Jesse Gonder | 1.25 | 3.00 |

|  | | |
|---|---|---|
| 618 Ramon Webster | 1.25 | 3.00 |
| 619 Butler/Kelly/Rios RC | 2.00 | 5.00 |
| 620 Dean Chance | 2.00 | 5.00 |
| 621 Bill Voss | 1.25 | 3.00 |
| 622 Dan Osinski | 1.25 | 3.00 |
| 623 Hank Allen | 1.25 | 3.00 |
| 624 Chaney/Dyer/Harmon RC | 2.00 | 5.00 |
| 625 Mack Jones UER | 2.00 | 5.00 |
| 626 Gene Michael | 2.00 | 5.00 |
| 627 George Stone RC | 1.25 | 3.00 |
| 628 Conigliaro/O'Brien/Wenz RC | 2.00 | 5.00 |
| 629 Jack Hamilton | 1.25 | 3.00 |
| 630 Bobby Bonds RC | 12.50 | 30.00 |
| 631 John Kennedy | 2.00 | 5.00 |
| 632 Jon Warden RC | 1.25 | 3.00 |
| 633 Harry Walker MG | 1.25 | 3.00 |
| 634 Andy Etchebarren | 1.25 | 3.00 |
| 635 George Culver | 1.25 | 3.00 |
| 636 Woody Held | 1.25 | 3.00 |
| 637 DaVanon/Rieberger/Kirby RC | 2.00 | 5.00 |
| 638 Ed Sprague RC | 1.25 | 3.00 |
| 639 Barry Moore | 1.25 | 3.00 |
| 640 Ferguson Jenkins | 8.00 | 20.00 |
| 641 Darwin/Miller/Dean RC | 2.00 | 5.00 |
| 642 John Hiller | 1.25 | 3.00 |
| 643 Billy Cowan | 1.25 | 3.00 |
| 644 Chuck Hinton | 1.25 | 3.00 |
| 645 George Brunet | 1.25 | 3.00 |
| 646 D.McGinn RC/C.Morton RC | 2.00 | 5.00 |
| 647 Dave Wickersham | 1.25 | 3.00 |
| 648 Bobby Wine | 2.00 | 5.00 |
| 649 Al Jackson | 1.25 | 3.00 |
| 650 Ted Williams MG | 8.00 | 20.00 |
| 651 Gus Gil | 1.25 | 3.00 |
| 652 Eddie Watt | 1.25 | 3.00 |
| 653 Aurelio Rodriguez UER RC | 1.25 | 3.00 |
| 654 May/Secrist/Morales RC | 2.00 | 5.00 |
| 655 Mike Hershberger | 1.25 | 3.00 |
| 656 Dan Schneider | 1.25 | 3.00 |
| 657 Bobby Murcer | 3.00 | 8.00 |
| 658 Hall/Burbach/Miles RC | 2.00 | 5.00 |
| 659 Johnny Podres | 2.00 | 5.00 |
| 660 Reggie Smith | 2.00 | 5.00 |
| 661 Jim Merritt | 1.25 | 3.00 |
| 662 Drago/Spriggs/Oliver RC | 2.00 | 5.00 |
| 663 Dick Radatz | 2.00 | 5.00 |
| 664 Ron Hunt | 2.00 | 5.00 |

## 1970 Topps

Billy Williams OUTFIELD

| | | |
|---|---|---|
| COMPLETE SET (720) | 1000.00 | 2000.00 |
| COMMON CARD (1-132) | .30 | .75 |
| COMMON CARD (133-372) | .40 | 1.00 |
| COMMON CARD (373-459) | .60 | 1.50 |
| COMMON CARD (460-546) | .75 | 2.00 |
| COMMON CARD (547-633) | 1.50 | 4.00 |
| COMMON CARD (634-720) | 4.00 | 10.00 |
| WRAPPER (10-CENT) | 8.00 | 20.00 |
| 1 New York Mets TC | 12.50 | 30.00 |
| 2 Diego Segui | .40 | 1.00 |
| 3 Darrel Chaney | .30 | .75 |
| 4 Tom Egan | .30 | .75 |
| 5 Wes Parker | .40 | 1.00 |
| 6 Grant Jackson | .30 | .75 |
| 7 G.Boyd RC/R.Nagelson RC | .30 | .75 |
| 8 Jose Martinez RC | .30 | .75 |
| 9 Checklist 1 | 5.00 | 12.00 |
| 10 Carl Yastrzemski | 8.00 | 20.00 |
| 11 Nate Colbert | .30 | .75 |
| 12 John Hiller | .30 | .75 |
| 13 Jack Hiatt | .30 | .75 |
| 14 Hank Allen | .30 | .75 |
| 15 Larry Dierker | .30 | .75 |
| 16 Charlie Metro MG RC | .30 | .75 |
| 17 Hoyt Wilhelm | 1.50 | 4.00 |

|  |  | | |
|---|---|---|---|
| 18 | Carlos May | .40 | 1.00 |
| 19 | John Boccabella | .40 | 1.00 |
| 20 | Dave McNally | .40 | 1.00 |
| 21 | V.Blue RC/G.Tenace RC | 1.50 | 4.00 |
| 22 | Ray Washburn | .30 | .75 |
| 23 | Bill Robinson | .40 | 1.00 |
| 24 | Dick Selma | .30 | .75 |
| 25 | Cesar Tovar | .30 | .75 |
| 26 | Tug McGraw | .75 | 2.00 |
| 27 | Chuck Hinton | .30 | .75 |
| 28 | Billy Wilson | .30 | .75 |
| 29 | Sandy Alomar | .40 | 1.00 |
| 30 | Matty Alou | .40 | 1.00 |
| 31 | Marty Pattin | .40 | 1.00 |
| 32 | Harry Walker MG | .30 | .75 |
| 33 | Don Wert | .30 | .75 |
| 34 | Willie Crawford | .30 | .75 |
| 35 | Joel Horlen | .30 | .75 |
| 36 | D.Breeden/B.Carbo RC | .40 | 1.00 |
| 37 | Dick Drago | .30 | .75 |
| 38 | Mack Jones | .30 | .75 |
| 39 | Mike Nagy RC | .40 | 1.00 |
| 40 | Richie Allen | .75 | 2.00 |
| 41 | George Lauzerique | .30 | .75 |
| 42 | Tito Fuentes | .30 | .75 |
| 43 | Jack Aker | .30 | .75 |
| 44 | Roberto Pena | .30 | .75 |
| 45 | Dave Johnson | .40 | 1.00 |
| 46 | Ken Rudolph RC | .40 | 1.00 |
| 47 | Bob Miller | .30 | .75 |
| 48 | Gil Garrido | .30 | .75 |
| 49 | Tim Cullen | .30 | .75 |
| 50 | Tommie Agee | .40 | 1.00 |
| 51 | Bob Christian | .30 | .75 |
| 52 | Bruce Dal Canton | .30 | .75 |
| 53 | John Kennedy | .30 | .75 |
| 54 | Jeff Torborg | .40 | 1.00 |
| 55 | John Odom | .30 | .75 |
| 56 | L.Lis RC/S.Reid RC | .30 | .75 |
| 57 | Pat Kelly | .30 | .75 |
| 58 | Dave Marshall | .30 | .75 |
| 59 | Dick Ellsworth | .30 | .75 |
| 60 | Jim Wynn | .40 | 1.00 |
| 61 | Rose/Clemente/Jones LL | 5.00 | 12.00 |
| 62 | Carew/Smith/Oliva LL | .75 | 2.00 |
| 63 | McCovey/Santo/Perez LL | .75 | 2.00 |
| 64 | Kill/Powell/Jackson LL | 1.50 | 4.00 |
| 65 | McCovey/Aaron/May LL | 1.50 | 4.00 |
| 66 | Kill/Howard/Jackson LL | 1.50 | 4.00 |
| 67 | Marichal/Carlton/Gibson LL | 1.50 | 4.00 |
| 68 | Bosman/Palmer/Cuellar LL | .40 | 1.00 |
| 69 | Seav/Niek/Jenk/Mari LL | 1.50 | 4.00 |
| 70 | McLain/Cuellar/Boswell LL | .40 | 1.00 |
| 71 | Jenkins/Gibson/Singer LL | .75 | 2.00 |
| 72 | McDowell/Lolich/Mess LL | .40 | 1.00 |
| 73 | Wayne Granger | .30 | .75 |
| 74 | G.Washburn RC/W.Wolf | .30 | .75 |
| 75 | Jim Kaat | .40 | 1.00 |
| 76 | Carl Taylor | .30 | .75 |
| 77 | Frank Linzy | .30 | .75 |
| 78 | Joe Lahoud | .30 | .75 |
| 79 | Clay Kirby | .30 | .75 |
| 80 | Don Kessinger | .40 | 1.00 |
| 81 | Dave May | .30 | .75 |
| 82 | Frank Fernandez | .30 | .75 |
| 83 | Don Cardwell | .30 | .75 |
| 84 | Paul Casanova | .30 | .75 |
| 85 | Max Alvis | .30 | .75 |
| 86 | Lum Harris MG | .30 | .75 |
| 87 | Steve Renko RC | .30 | .75 |
| 88 | M.Fuentes RC/D.Baney RC | .40 | 1.00 |
| 89 | Juan Rios | .30 | .75 |
| 90 | Tim McCarver | .40 | 1.00 |
| 91 | Rich Morales | .30 | .75 |
| 92 | George Culver | .30 | .75 |
| 93 | Rick Renick | .30 | .75 |
| 94 | Freddie Patek | .40 | 1.00 |
| 95 | Earl Wilson | .40 | 1.00 |
| 96 | L.Lee RC/J.Reuss RC | .40 | 1.00 |
| 97 | Joe Moeller | .30 | .75 |
| 98 | Gates Brown | .40 | 1.00 |
| 99 | Bobby Pfeil RC | .30 | .75 |
| 100 | Mel Stottlemyre | .40 | 1.00 |
| 101 | Bobby Floyd | .30 | .75 |
| 102 | Joe Rudi | .40 | 1.00 |
| 103 | Frank Reberger | .30 | .75 |
| 104 | Gerry Moses | .30 | .75 |
| 105 | Tony Gonzalez | .30 | .75 |
| 106 | Darold Knowles | .30 | .75 |
| 107 | Bobby Etheridge | .30 | .75 |
| 108 | Tom Burgmeier | .30 | .75 |
| 109 | G.Jestadt RC/C.Morton | .30 | .75 |
| 110 | Bob Moose | .30 | .75 |
| 111 | Mike Hegan | .40 | 1.00 |
| 112 | Dave Nelson | .40 | 1.00 |
| 113 | Jim Ray | .30 | .75 |
| 114 | Gene Michael | .40 | 1.00 |
| 115 | Alex Johnson | .40 | 1.00 |
| 116 | Sparky Lyle | .40 | 1.00 |
| 117 | Don Young | .30 | .75 |
| 118 | George Mitterwald | .30 | .75 |
| 119 | Chuck Taylor RC | .30 | .75 |
| 120 | Sal Bando | .40 | 1.00 |
| 121 | F.Beene RC/T.Crowley RC | .30 | .75 |
| 122 | George Stone | .30 | .75 |
| 123 | Don Gutteridge MG RC | .30 | .75 |
| 124 | Larry Jaster | .30 | .75 |
| 125 | Deron Johnson | .30 | .75 |
| 126 | Marty Martinez | .30 | .75 |
| 127 | Joe Coleman | .30 | .75 |
| 128A | Checklist 2 R.Perranoski | 2.50 | 6.00 |
| 128B | Checklist 2 R.Perranoski | 2.50 | 6.00 |
| 129 | Jimmie Price | .30 | .75 |
| 130 | Ollie Brown | .30 | .75 |
| 131 | R.Lamb RC/B.Stinson RC | .30 | .75 |
| 132 | Jim McGlothlin | .30 | .75 |
| 133 | Clay Carroll | .40 | 1.00 |
| 134 | Danny Walton RC | .40 | 1.00 |
| 135 | Dick Dietz | .40 | 1.00 |
| 136 | Steve Hargan | .40 | 1.00 |
| 137 | Art Shamsky | .40 | 1.00 |
| 138 | Joe Foy | .40 | 1.00 |
| 139 | Rich Nye | .40 | 1.00 |
| 140 | Reggie Jackson | 20.00 | 50.00 |
| 141 | D.Cash RC/J.Jeter RC | .60 | 1.50 |
| 142 | Fritz Peterson | .40 | 1.00 |
| 143 | Phil Gagliano | .40 | 1.00 |
| 144 | Ray Culp | .40 | 1.00 |
| 145 | Rico Carty | .60 | 1.50 |
| 146 | Danny Murphy | .40 | 1.00 |
| 147 | Angel Hermoso RC | .40 | 1.00 |
| 148 | Earl Weaver MG | 1.25 | 3.00 |
| 149 | Billy Champion RC | .40 | 1.00 |
| 150 | Harmon Killebrew | 3.00 | 8.00 |
| 151 | Dave Roberts | .40 | 1.00 |
| 152 | Ike Brown RC | .40 | 1.00 |
| 153 | Gary Gentry | .40 | 1.00 |
| 154 | J.Miles/J.Dukes RC | .40 | 1.00 |
| 155 | Denis Menke | .40 | 1.00 |
| 156 | Eddie Fisher | .40 | 1.00 |
| 157 | Manny Mota | .60 | 1.50 |
| 158 | Jerry McNertney | .60 | 1.50 |
| 159 | Tommy Helms | .60 | 1.50 |
| 160 | Phil Niekro | 2.00 | 5.00 |
| 161 | Richie Scheinblum | .40 | 1.00 |
| 162 | Jerry Johnson | .40 | 1.00 |
| 163 | Syd O'Brien | .40 | 1.00 |
| 164 | Ty Cline | .40 | 1.00 |
| 165 | Ed Kirkpatrick | .40 | 1.00 |
| 166 | Al Oliver | 1.25 | 3.00 |
| 167 | Bill Burbach | .40 | 1.00 |
| 168 | Dave Watkins RC | .40 | 1.00 |
| 169 | Tom Hall | .40 | 1.00 |
| 170 | Billy Williams | 2.00 | 5.00 |
| 171 | Jim Nash | .40 | 1.00 |
| 172 | G.Hill RC/R.Garr RC | .60 | 1.50 |
| 173 | Jim Hicks | .40 | 1.00 |
| 174 | Ted Sizemore | .60 | 1.50 |
| 175 | Dick Bosman | .40 | 1.00 |
| 176 | Jim Ray Hart | .60 | 1.50 |
| 177 | Jim Northrup | .60 | 1.50 |
| 178 | Denny Lemaster | .40 | 1.00 |
| 179 | Ivan Murrell | .40 | 1.00 |
| 180 | Tommy John | .60 | 1.50 |
| 181 | Sparky Anderson MG | 2.00 | 5.00 |
| 182 | Dick Hall | .40 | 1.00 |
| 183 | Jerry Grote | .60 | 1.50 |
| 184 | Ray Fosse | .60 | 1.50 |
| 185 | Don Mincher | .60 | 1.50 |
| 186 | Rick Joseph | .40 | 1.00 |
| 187 | Mike Hedlund | .40 | 1.00 |
| 188 | Manny Sanguillen | .60 | 1.50 |
| 189 | Thurman Munson RC | 50.00 | 100.00 |
| 190 | Joe Torre | 1.25 | 3.00 |
| 191 | Vicente Romo | .40 | 1.00 |
| 192 | Jim Qualls | .40 | 1.00 |
| 193 | Mike Wegener | .40 | 1.00 |
| 194 | Chuck Manuel RC | .40 | 1.00 |
| 195 | Tom Seaver NLCS1 | 6.00 | 15.00 |
| 196 | Ken Boswell NLCS2 | .75 | 2.00 |
| 197 | Nolan Ryan NLCS3 | 12.50 | 30.00 |
| 198 | Mets Celebrate/w/Ryan | 6.00 | 15.00 |
| 199 | Mike Cuellar ALCS1 | .75 | 2.00 |
| 200 | Boog Powell ALCS2 | 1.25 | 3.00 |
| 201 | B.Powell/A.Etch ALCS3 | .75 | 2.00 |
| 202 | Orioles Celebrate ALCS | .75 | 2.00 |
| 203 | Rudy May | .40 | 1.00 |
| 204 | Len Gabrielson | .40 | 1.00 |
| 205 | Bert Campaneris | .60 | 1.50 |
| 206 | Clete Boyer | .60 | 1.50 |
| 207 | N.McRae RC/B.Reed RC | .40 | 1.00 |
| 208 | Fred Gladding | .40 | 1.00 |
| 209 | Ken Suarez | .40 | 1.00 |
| 210 | Juan Marichal | 6.00 | 15.00 |
| 211 | Ted Williams MG UER | 6.00 | 15.00 |
| 212 | Al Santorini | .40 | 1.00 |
| 213 | Andy Etchebarren | .40 | 1.00 |
| 214 | Ken Boswell | .40 | 1.00 |
| 215 | Reggie Smith | .60 | 1.50 |
| 216 | Chuck Hartenstein | .40 | 1.00 |
| 217 | Ron Hansen | .40 | 1.00 |
| 218 | Ron Stone | .40 | 1.00 |
| 219 | Jerry Kenney | .40 | 1.00 |
| 220 | Steve Carlton | 6.00 | 15.00 |
| 221 | Ron Brand | .40 | 1.00 |
| 222 | Jim Rooker | .40 | 1.00 |
| 223 | Nate Oliver | .40 | 1.00 |
| 224 | Steve Barber | .60 | 1.50 |
| 225 | Lee May | .60 | 1.50 |
| 226 | Ron Perranoski | .40 | 1.00 |
| 227 | J.Mayberry RC/B.Watkins RC | .60 | 1.50 |
| 228 | Aurelio Rodriguez | .40 | 1.00 |
| 229 | Rich Robertson | .40 | 1.00 |
| 230 | Brooks Robinson | 6.00 | 15.00 |
| 231 | Luis Tiant | .60 | 1.50 |
| 232 | Bob Didier | .40 | 1.00 |
| 233 | Lew Krausse | .40 | 1.00 |
| 234 | Tommy Dean | .40 | 1.00 |
| 235 | Mike Epstein | .40 | 1.00 |
| 236 | Bob Veale | .40 | 1.00 |
| 237 | Russ Gibson | .40 | 1.00 |
| 238 | Jose Laboy | .40 | 1.00 |
| 239 | Ken Berry | .40 | 1.00 |
| 240 | Ferguson Jenkins | 2.00 | 5.00 |
| 241 | A.Fitzmorris RC/S.Northey RC | .40 | 1.00 |
| 242 | Walt Alston MG | 1.25 | 3.00 |
| 243 | Joe Sparma | .40 | 1.00 |
| 244A | Checklist 3 Red Bat | 2.50 | 6.00 |
| 244B | Checklist 3 Brown Bat | 2.50 | 6.00 |
| 245 | Leo Cardenas | .40 | 1.00 |
| 246 | Jim McAndrew | .40 | 1.00 |
| 247 | Lou Klimchock | .40 | 1.00 |
| 248 | Jesus Alou | .40 | 1.00 |
| 249 | Bob Locker | .40 | 1.00 |
| 250 | Willie McCovey UER | 4.00 | 10.00 |
| 251 | Dick Schofield | .40 | 1.00 |
| 252 | Lowell Palmer RC | .40 | 1.00 |
| 253 | Ron Woods | .40 | 1.00 |
| 254 | Camilo Pascual | .40 | 1.00 |
| 255 | Jim Spencer RC | .40 | 1.00 |
| 256 | Vic Davalillo | .40 | 1.00 |
| 257 | Dennis Higgins | .40 | 1.00 |
| 258 | Paul Popovich | .40 | 1.00 |
| 259 | Tommie Reynolds | .40 | 1.00 |
| 260 | Claude Osteen | .40 | 1.00 |
| 261 | Curt Motton | .40 | 1.00 |
| 262 | J.Morales RC/J.Williams RC | .40 | 1.00 |
| 263 | Duane Josephson | .40 | 1.00 |
| 264 | Rich Hebner | .40 | 1.00 |
| 265 | Randy Hundley | .40 | 1.00 |
| 266 | Wally Bunker | .40 | 1.00 |
| 267 | H.Hill RC/P.Ratliff | .40 | 1.00 |
| 268 | Claude Raymond | .40 | 1.00 |
| 269 | Cesar Gutierrez | .40 | 1.00 |
| 270 | Chris Short | .40 | 1.00 |
| 271 | Greg Goossen | .60 | 1.50 |
| 272 | Hector Torres | .40 | 1.00 |
| 273 | Ralph Houk MG | .60 | 1.50 |
| 274 | Gerry Arrigo | .40 | 1.00 |
| 275 | Duke Sims | .40 | 1.00 |
| 276 | Ron Hunt | .40 | 1.00 |
| 277 | Paul Doyle RC | .40 | 1.00 |
| 278 | Tommie Aaron | .40 | 1.00 |
| 279 | Bill Lee RC | .60 | 1.50 |

|  |  | | |
|---|---|---|---|
| 280 Donn Clendenon | | .60 | 1.50 |
| 281 Casey Cox | | .40 | 1.00 |
| 282 Steve Huntz | | .40 | 1.00 |
| 283 Angel Bravo RC | | .40 | 1.00 |
| 284 Jack Baldschun | | .40 | 1.00 |
| 285 Paul Blair | | .60 | 1.50 |
| 286 J.Jenkins RC/B.Buckner RC | | 2.00 | 5.00 |
| 287 Fred Talbot | | .40 | 1.00 |
| 288 Larry Hisle | | .60 | 1.50 |
| 289 Gene Brabender | | .40 | 1.00 |
| 290 Rod Carew | | 6.00 | 15.00 |
| 291 Leo Durocher MG | | 1.25 | 3.00 |
| 292 Eddie Leon RC | | .40 | 1.00 |
| 293 Bob Bailey | | .40 | 1.00 |
| 294 Jose Azcue | | .40 | 1.00 |
| 295 Cecil Upshaw | | .40 | 1.00 |
| 296 Woody Woodward | | .40 | 1.00 |
| 297 Curt Blefary | | .40 | 1.00 |
| 298 Ken Henderson | | .40 | 1.00 |
| 299 Buddy Bradford | | .40 | 1.00 |
| 300 Tom Seaver | | 12.50 | 30.00 |
| 301 Chico Salmon | | .40 | 1.00 |
| 302 Jeff James | | .40 | 1.00 |
| 303 Brant Alyea | | .40 | 1.00 |
| 304 Bill Russell RC | | 2.00 | 5.00 |
| 305 Don Buford WS1 | | 1.50 | 4.00 |
| 306 Donn Clendenon WS2 | | 1.50 | 4.00 |
| 307 Tommie Agee WS3 | | 1.50 | 4.00 |
| 308 J.C. Martin WS4 | | 1.50 | 4.00 |
| 309 Jerry Koosman WS5 | | 1.50 | 4.00 |
| 310 Mets Celebrate WS | | 2.00 | 5.00 |
| 311 Dick Green | | .40 | 1.00 |
| 312 Mike Torrez | | .40 | 1.00 |
| 313 Mayo Smith MG | | .40 | 1.00 |
| 314 Bill McCool | | .40 | 1.00 |
| 315 Luis Aparicio | | 2.00 | 5.00 |
| 316 Skip Guinn | | .40 | 1.00 |
| 317 B.Conigliaro/L.Alvarado RC | | .60 | 1.50 |
| 318 Willie Smith | | .40 | 1.00 |
| 319 Clay Dalrymple | | .40 | 1.00 |
| 320 Jim Maloney | | .60 | 1.50 |
| 321 Lou Piniella | | .60 | 1.50 |
| 322 Luke Walker | | .40 | 1.00 |
| 323 Wayne Comer | | .40 | 1.00 |
| 324 Tony Taylor | | .60 | 1.50 |
| 325 Dave Boswell | | .40 | 1.00 |
| 326 Bill Voss | | .40 | 1.00 |
| 327 Hal King RC | | .40 | 1.00 |
| 328 George Brunet | | .40 | 1.00 |
| 329 Chris Cannizzaro | | .40 | 1.00 |
| 330 Lou Brock | | 4.00 | 10.00 |
| 331 Chuck Dobson | | .40 | 1.00 |
| 332 Bobby Wine | | .40 | 1.00 |
| 333 Bobby Murcer | | .60 | 1.50 |
| 334 Phil Regan | | .40 | 1.00 |
| 335 Bill Freehan | | .60 | 1.50 |
| 336 Del Unser | | .40 | 1.00 |
| 337 Mike McCormick | | .40 | 1.00 |
| 338 Paul Schaal | | .40 | 1.00 |
| 339 Johnny Edwards | | .40 | 1.00 |
| 340 Tony Conigliaro | | 1.25 | 3.00 |
| 341 Bill Sudakis | | .40 | 1.00 |
| 342 Wilbur Wood | | .60 | 1.50 |
| 343A Checklist 4 Red Bat | | 2.50 | 6.00 |
| 343B Checklist 4 Brown Bat | | 2.50 | 6.00 |
| 344 Marcelino Lopez | | .40 | 1.00 |
| 345 Al Ferrara | | .40 | 1.00 |
| 346 Red Schoendienst MG | | .60 | 1.50 |
| 347 Russ Snyder | | .40 | 1.00 |
| 348 W.Jorgensen RC/J.Hudson RC | | .60 | 1.50 |
| 349 Steve Hamilton | | .40 | 1.00 |
| 350 Roberto Clemente | | 30.00 | 60.00 |
| 351 Tom Murphy | | .40 | 1.00 |
| 352 Bob Barton | | .40 | 1.00 |
| 353 Stan Williams | | .40 | 1.00 |
| 354 Amos Otis | | .60 | 1.50 |
| 355 Doug Rader | | .40 | 1.00 |
| 356 Fred Lasher | | .40 | 1.00 |
| 357 Bob Burda | | .40 | 1.00 |
| 358 Pedro Borbon RC | | .60 | 1.50 |
| 359 Phil Roof | | .40 | 1.00 |
| 360 Curt Flood | | .60 | 1.50 |
| 361 Ray Jarvis | | .40 | 1.00 |
| 362 Joe Hague | | .40 | 1.00 |
| 363 Tom Shopay RC | | .40 | 1.00 |
| 364 Dan McGinn | | .40 | 1.00 |
| 365 Zoilo Versalles | | .40 | 1.00 |
| 366 Barry Moore | | .40 | 1.00 |
| 367 Mike Lum | | .40 | 1.00 |
| 368 Ed Herrmann | | .40 | 1.00 |
| 369 Alan Foster | | .40 | 1.00 |
| 370 Tommy Harper | | .40 | 1.00 |
| 371 Rod Gaspar RC | | .40 | 1.00 |
| 372 Dave Giusti | | .40 | 1.00 |
| 373 Roy White | | .75 | 2.00 |
| 374 Tommie Sisk | | .60 | 1.50 |
| 375 Johnny Callison | | .75 | 2.00 |
| 376 Lefty Phillips MG RC | | .60 | 1.50 |
| 377 Bill Butler | | .60 | 1.50 |
| 378 Jim Davenport | | .60 | 1.50 |
| 379 Tom Tischinski RC | | .60 | 1.50 |
| 380 Tony Perez | | 2.50 | 6.00 |
| 381 B.Brooks RC/M.Olivo RC | | .60 | 1.50 |
| 382 Jack DiLauro RC | | .60 | 1.50 |
| 383 Mickey Stanley | | .75 | 2.00 |
| 384 Gary Neibauer | | .60 | 1.50 |
| 385 George Scott | | .75 | 2.00 |
| 386 Bill Dillman | | .60 | 1.50 |
| 387 Baltimore Orioles TC | | 1.25 | 3.00 |
| 388 Byron Browne | | .60 | 1.50 |
| 389 Jim Shellenback | | .60 | 1.50 |
| 390 Willie Davis | | .75 | 2.00 |
| 391 Larry Brown | | .60 | 1.50 |
| 392 Walt Hriniak | | .75 | 2.00 |
| 393 John Gelnar | | .60 | 1.50 |
| 394 Gil Hodges MG | | 1.50 | 4.00 |
| 395 Walt Williams | | .60 | 1.50 |
| 396 Steve Blass | | .75 | 2.00 |
| 397 Roger Repoz | | .60 | 1.50 |
| 398 Bill Stoneman | | .60 | 1.50 |
| 399 New York Yankees TC | | 1.25 | 3.00 |
| 400 Denny McLain | | 1.50 | 4.00 |
| 401 J.Harrell RC/B.Williams RC | | .60 | 1.50 |
| 402 Ellie Rodriguez | | .60 | 1.50 |
| 403 Jim Bunning | | 2.50 | 6.00 |
| 404 Rich Reese | | .60 | 1.50 |
| 405 Bill Hands | | .60 | 1.50 |
| 406 Mike Andrews | | .60 | 1.50 |
| 407 Bob Watson | | .75 | 2.00 |
| 408 Paul Lindblad | | .60 | 1.50 |
| 409 Bob Tolan | | .60 | 1.50 |
| 410 Boog Powell | | 1.50 | 4.00 |
| 411 Los Angeles Dodgers TC | | 1.25 | 3.00 |
| 412 Larry Burchart | | .60 | 1.50 |
| 413 Sonny Jackson | | .60 | 1.50 |
| 414 Paul Edmondson RC | | .60 | 1.50 |
| 415 Julian Javier | | .75 | 2.00 |
| 416 Joe Verbanic | | .60 | 1.50 |
| 417 John Bateman | | .60 | 1.50 |
| 418 John Donaldson | | .60 | 1.50 |
| 419 Ron Taylor | | .60 | 1.50 |
| 420 Ken McMullen | | .75 | 2.00 |
| 421 Pat Dobson | | .75 | 2.00 |
| 422 Kansas City Royals TC | | 1.25 | 3.00 |
| 423 Jerry May | | .60 | 1.50 |
| 424 Mike Kilkenny | | .60 | 1.50 |
| 425 Bobby Bonds | | 2.50 | 6.00 |
| 426 Bill Rigney MG | | .60 | 1.50 |
| 427 Fred Norman | | .60 | 1.50 |
| 428 Don Buford | | .60 | 1.50 |
| 429 R.Robb RC/J.Cosman | | .60 | 1.50 |
| 430 Andy Messersmith | | .75 | 2.00 |
| 431 Ron Swoboda | | .75 | 2.00 |
| 432A Checklist 5 Yellow Ltr | | 2.50 | 6.00 |
| 432B Checklist 5 White Ltr | | 2.50 | 6.00 |
| 433 Ron Bryant RC | | .60 | 1.50 |
| 434 Felipe Alou | | .75 | 2.00 |
| 435 Nelson Briles | | .75 | 2.00 |
| 436 Philadelphia Phillies TC | | 1.25 | 3.00 |
| 437 Danny Cater | | .60 | 1.50 |
| 438 Pat Jarvis | | .60 | 1.50 |
| 439 Lee Maye | | .60 | 1.50 |
| 440 Bill Mazeroski | | 2.50 | 6.00 |
| 441 John O'Donoghue | | .60 | 1.50 |
| 442 Gene Mauch MG | | .75 | 2.00 |
| 443 Al Jackson | | .60 | 1.50 |
| 444 B.Farmer RC/J.Matias RC | | .60 | 1.50 |
| 445 Vada Pinson | | .75 | 2.00 |
| 446 Billy Grabarkewitz RC | | .60 | 1.50 |
| 447 Lee Stange | | .60 | 1.50 |
| 448 Houston Astros TC | | 1.25 | 3.00 |
| 449 Jim Palmer | | 5.00 | 12.00 |
| 450 Willie McCovey AS | | 2.50 | 6.00 |
| 451 Boog Powell AS | | 1.50 | 4.00 |
| 452 Felix Millan AS | | .75 | 2.00 |
| 453 Rod Carew AS | | 2.50 | 6.00 |
| 454 Ron Santo AS | | 1.50 | 4.00 |
| 455 Brooks Robinson AS | | 2.50 | 6.00 |
| 456 Don Kessinger AS | | .75 | 2.00 |
| 457 Rico Petrocelli AS | | 1.50 | 4.00 |
| 458 Pete Rose AS | | 6.00 | 15.00 |
| 459 Reggie Jackson AS | | 5.00 | 12.00 |
| 460 Matty Alou AS | | 1.25 | 3.00 |
| 461 Carl Yastrzemski AS | | 4.00 | 10.00 |
| 462 Hank Aaron AS | | 6.00 | 15.00 |
| 463 Frank Robinson AS | | 3.00 | 8.00 |
| 464 Johnny Bench AS | | 6.00 | 15.00 |
| 465 Bill Freehan AS | | 1.25 | 3.00 |
| 466 Juan Marichal AS | | 2.00 | 5.00 |
| 467 Denny McLain AS | | 1.25 | 3.00 |
| 468 Jerry Koosman AS | | 1.25 | 3.00 |
| 469 Sam McDowell AS | | 1.25 | 3.00 |
| 470 Willie Stargell AS | | 4.00 | 10.00 |
| 471 Chris Zachary | | .75 | 2.00 |
| 472 Atlanta Braves TC | | 1.50 | 4.00 |
| 473 Don Bryant | | .75 | 2.00 |
| 474 Dick Kelley | | .75 | 2.00 |
| 475 Dick McAuliffe | | 1.25 | 3.00 |
| 476 Don Shaw | | .75 | 2.00 |
| 477 A.Severinsen RC/R.Freed RC | | .75 | 2.00 |
| 478 Bobby Heise RC | | .75 | 2.00 |
| 479 Dick Woodson RC | | .75 | 2.00 |
| 480 Glenn Beckert | | 1.25 | 3.00 |
| 481 Jose Tartabull | | .75 | 2.00 |
| 482 Tom Hilgendorf RC | | .75 | 2.00 |
| 483 Gail Hopkins RC | | .75 | 2.00 |
| 484 Gary Nolan | | 1.25 | 3.00 |
| 485 Jay Johnstone | | 1.25 | 3.00 |
| 486 Terry Harmon | | .75 | 2.00 |
| 487 Cisco Carlos | | .75 | 2.00 |
| 488 J.C. Martin | | .75 | 2.00 |
| 489 Eddie Kasko RC | | .75 | 2.00 |
| 490 Bill Singer | | 1.25 | 3.00 |
| 491 Graig Nettles | | 2.00 | 5.00 |
| 492 K.Lampard RC/S.Spinks RC | | .75 | 2.00 |
| 493 Lindy McDaniel | | 1.25 | 3.00 |
| 494 Larry Stahl | | .75 | 2.00 |
| 495 Dave Morehead | | .75 | 2.00 |
| 496 Steve Whitaker | | .75 | 2.00 |
| 497 Eddie Watt | | .75 | 2.00 |
| 498 Al Weis | | .75 | 2.00 |
| 499 Skip Lockwood | | 1.25 | 3.00 |
| 500 Hank Aaron | | 20.00 | 50.00 |
| 501 Chicago White Sox TC | | 1.50 | 4.00 |
| 502 Rollie Fingers | | 4.00 | 10.00 |
| 503 Dal Maxvill | | .75 | 2.00 |
| 504 Don Pavletich | | .75 | 2.00 |
| 505 Ken Holtzman | | 1.25 | 3.00 |
| 506 Ed Stroud | | .75 | 2.00 |
| 507 Pat Corrales | | .75 | 2.00 |
| 508 Joe Niekro | | 1.25 | 3.00 |
| 509 Montreal Expos TC | | 1.50 | 4.00 |
| 510 Tony Oliva | | 2.00 | 5.00 |
| 511 Joe Hoerner | | .75 | 2.00 |
| 512 Billy Harris | | .75 | 2.00 |
| 513 Preston Gomez MG | | .75 | 2.00 |
| 514 Steve Hovley RC | | .75 | 2.00 |
| 515 Don Wilson | | 1.25 | 3.00 |
| 516 J.Ellis RC/J.Lyttle RC | | .75 | 2.00 |
| 517 Joe Gibbon | | .75 | 2.00 |
| 518 Bill Melton | | .75 | 2.00 |
| 519 Don McMahon | | .75 | 2.00 |
| 520 Willie Horton | | 1.25 | 3.00 |
| 521 Cal Koonce | | .75 | 2.00 |
| 522 California Angels TC | | 1.50 | 4.00 |
| 523 Jose Pena | | .75 | 2.00 |
| 524 Alvin Dark MG | | 1.25 | 3.00 |
| 525 Jerry Adair | | .75 | 2.00 |
| 526 Ron Herbel | | .75 | 2.00 |
| 527 Don Bosch | | .75 | 2.00 |
| 528 Elrod Hendricks | | .75 | 2.00 |
| 529 Bob Aspromonte | | .75 | 2.00 |
| 530 Bob Gibson | | 6.00 | 15.00 |
| 531 Ron Clark | | .75 | 2.00 |
| 532 Danny Murtaugh MG | | 1.25 | 3.00 |
| 533 Buzz Stephen RC | | .75 | 2.00 |
| 534 Minnesota Twins TC | | 1.50 | 4.00 |
| 535 Andy Kosco | | .75 | 2.00 |
| 536 Mike Kekich | | .75 | 2.00 |
| 537 Joe Morgan | | 4.00 | 10.00 |
| 538 Bob Humphreys | | .75 | 2.00 |
| 539 D.Doyle RC/L.Bowa RC | | 3.00 | 8.00 |
| 540 Gary Peters | | .75 | 2.00 |
| 541 Bill Heath | | .75 | 2.00 |

|  |  | | |
|---|---|---|---|
| 542A | Checklist 6 Brown Bat | 2.50 | 6.00 |
| 543 | Clyde Wright | .75 | 2.00 |
| 544 | Cincinnati Reds TC | 1.50 | 4.00 |
| 545 | Ken Harrelson | 1.25 | 3.00 |
| 546 | Ron Reed | .75 | 2.00 |
| 547 | Rick Monday | 2.50 | 6.00 |
| 548 | Howie Reed | 1.50 | 4.00 |
| 549 | St. Louis Cardinals TC | 2.50 | 6.00 |
| 550 | Frank Howard | 2.50 | 6.00 |
| 551 | Dock Ellis | 2.50 | 6.00 |
| 552 | O'Riley/Paepke/Rico RC | 1.50 | 4.00 |
| 553 | Jim Lefebvre | 2.50 | 6.00 |
| 554 | Tom Timmermann RC | 1.50 | 4.00 |
| 555 | Orlando Cepeda | 5.00 | 12.00 |
| 556 | Dave Bristol MG | 2.50 | 6.00 |
| 557 | Ed Kranepool | 2.50 | 6.00 |
| 558 | Vern Fuller | 1.50 | 4.00 |
| 559 | Tommy Davis | 2.50 | 6.00 |
| 560 | Gaylord Perry | 5.00 | 12.00 |
| 561 | Tom McCraw | 1.50 | 4.00 |
| 562 | Ted Abernathy | 1.50 | 4.00 |
| 563 | Boston Red Sox TC | 2.50 | 6.00 |
| 564 | Johnny Briggs | 1.50 | 4.00 |
| 565 | Jim Hunter | 5.00 | 12.00 |
| 566 | Gene Alley | 1.50 | 4.00 |
| 567 | Bob Oliver | 1.50 | 4.00 |
| 568 | Stan Bahnsen | 2.50 | 6.00 |
| 569 | Cookie Rojas | 2.50 | 6.00 |
| 570 | Jim Fregosi | 2.50 | 6.00 |
| 571 | Jim Brewer | 1.50 | 4.00 |
| 572 | Frank Quilici | 1.50 | 4.00 |
| 573 | Corkins/Robles/Slocum RC | 1.50 | 4.00 |
| 574 | Bobby Bolin | 2.50 | 6.00 |
| 575 | Cleon Jones | 2.50 | 6.00 |
| 576 | Milt Pappas | 2.50 | 6.00 |
| 577 | Bernie Allen | 1.50 | 4.00 |
| 578 | Tom Griffin | 1.50 | 4.00 |
| 579 | Detroit Tigers TC | 2.50 | 6.00 |
| 580 | Pete Rose | 30.00 | 60.00 |
| 581 | Tom Satriano | 1.50 | 4.00 |
| 582 | Mike Paul | 1.50 | 4.00 |
| 583 | Hal Lanier | 1.50 | 4.00 |
| 584 | Al Downing | 2.50 | 6.00 |
| 585 | Rusty Staub | 3.00 | 8.00 |
| 586 | Rickey Clark RC | 1.50 | 4.00 |
| 587 | Jose Arcia | 1.50 | 4.00 |
| 588A | Checklist 7 Adolfo | 3.00 | 8.00 |
| 588B | Checklist 7 Adolpho | 2.50 | 6.00 |
| 589 | Joe Keough | 1.50 | 4.00 |
| 590 | Mike Cuellar | 2.50 | 6.00 |
| 591 | Mike Ryan UER | 1.50 | 4.00 |
| 592 | Daryl Patterson | 1.50 | 4.00 |
| 593 | Chicago Cubs TC | 3.00 | 8.00 |
| 594 | Jake Gibbs | 1.50 | 4.00 |
| 595 | Maury Wills | 3.00 | 8.00 |
| 596 | Mike Hershberger | 2.50 | 6.00 |
| 597 | Sonny Siebert | 1.50 | 4.00 |
| 598 | Joe Pepitone | 2.50 | 6.00 |
| 599 | Stelmaszek/Martin/Such RC | 1.50 | 4.00 |
| 600 | Willie Mays | 40.00 | 80.00 |
| 601 | Pete Richert | 1.50 | 4.00 |
| 602 | Ted Savage | 1.50 | 4.00 |
| 603 | Ray Oyler | 1.50 | 4.00 |
| 604 | Cito Gaston | 2.50 | 6.00 |
| 605 | Rick Wise | 1.50 | 4.00 |
| 606 | Chico Ruiz | 1.50 | 4.00 |
| 607 | Gary Waslewski | 1.50 | 4.00 |
| 608 | Pittsburgh Pirates TC | 2.50 | 6.00 |
| 609 | Buck Martinez RC | 2.50 | 6.00 |
| 610 | Jerry Koosman | 3.00 | 8.00 |
| 611 | Norm Cash | 2.50 | 6.00 |
| 612 | Jim Hickman | 2.50 | 6.00 |
| 613 | Dave Baldwin | 2.50 | 6.00 |
| 614 | Mike Shannon | 2.50 | 6.00 |
| 615 | Mark Belanger | 2.50 | 6.00 |
| 616 | Jim Merritt | 1.50 | 4.00 |
| 617 | Jim French | 1.50 | 4.00 |
| 618 | Billy Wynne RC | 1.50 | 4.00 |
| 619 | Norm Miller. | 1.50 | 4.00 |
| 620 | Jim Perry | 2.50 | 6.00 |
| 621 | McQueen/Evans/Kester RC | 5.00 | 12.00 |
| 622 | Don Sutton | 5.00 | 12.00 |
| 623 | Horace Clarke | 2.50 | 6.00 |
| 624 | Clyde King MG | 1.50 | 4.00 |
| 625 | Dean Chance | 1.50 | 4.00 |
| 626 | Dave Ricketts | 1.50 | 4.00 |
| 627 | Gary Wagner | 1.50 | 4.00 |
| 628 | Wayne Garrett RC | 1.50 | 4.00 |
| 629 | Merv Rettenmund | 1.50 | 4.00 |
| 630 | Ernie Banks | 20.00 | 50.00 |
| 631 | Oakland Athletics TC | 2.50 | 6.00 |
| 632 | Gary Sutherland | 1.50 | 4.00 |
| 633 | Roger Nelson | 4.00 | 10.00 |
| 634 | Bud Harrelson | 6.00 | 15.00 |
| 635 | Bob Allison | 6.00 | 15.00 |
| 636 | Jim Stewart | 4.00 | 10.00 |
| 637 | Cleveland Indians TC | 5.00 | 12.00 |
| 638 | Frank Bertaina | 4.00 | 10.00 |
| 639 | Dave Campbell | 6.00 | 15.00 |
| 640 | Al Kaline | 20.00 | 50.00 |
| 641 | Al McBean | 4.00 | 10.00 |
| 642 | Garrett/Lum/Tatum RC | 4.00 | 10.00 |
| 643 | Jose Pagan | 4.00 | 10.00 |
| 644 | Gerry Nyman | 4.00 | 10.00 |
| 645 | Don Money | 6.00 | 15.00 |
| 646 | Jim Britton | 4.00 | 10.00 |
| 647 | Tom Matchick | 4.00 | 10.00 |
| 648 | Larry Haney | 4.00 | 10.00 |
| 649 | Jimmie Hall | 4.00 | 10.00 |
| 650 | Sam McDowell | 6.00 | 15.00 |
| 651 | Jim Gosger | 4.00 | 10.00 |
| 652 | Rich Rollins | 6.00 | 15.00 |
| 653 | Moe Drabowsky | 6.00 | 15.00 |
| 654 | Gamble/Day/Mangual RC | 6.00 | 15.00 |
| 655 | John Roseboro | 6.00 | 15.00 |
| 656 | Jim Hardin | 4.00 | 10.00 |
| 657 | San Diego Padres TC | 5.00 | 12.00 |
| 658 | Ken Tatum RC | 4.00 | 10.00 |
| 659 | Pete Ward | 4.00 | 10.00 |
| 660 | Johnny Bench | 40.00 | 80.00 |
| 661 | Jerry Robertson | 4.00 | 10.00 |
| 662 | Frank Lucchesi MG RC | 4.00 | 10.00 |
| 663 | Tito Francona | 4.00 | 10.00 |
| 664 | Bob Robertson | 4.00 | 10.00 |
| 665 | Jim Lonborg | 6.00 | 15.00 |
| 666 | Adolpho Phillips | 4.00 | 10.00 |
| 667 | Bob Meyer | 6.00 | 15.00 |
| 668 | Bob Tillman | 4.00 | 10.00 |
| 669 | Johnson/Lazar/Scott RC | 4.00 | 10.00 |
| 670 | Ron Santo | 6.00 | 15.00 |
| 671 | Jim Campanis | 4.00 | 10.00 |
| 672 | Leon McFadden | 4.00 | 10.00 |
| 673 | Ted Uhlaender | 4.00 | 10.00 |
| 674 | Dave Leonhard | 4.00 | 10.00 |
| 675 | Jose Cardenal | 6.00 | 15.00 |
| 676 | Washington Senators TC | 5.00 | 12.00 |
| 677 | Woodie Fryman | 4.00 | 10.00 |
| 678 | Dave Duncan | 6.00 | 15.00 |
| 679 | Ray Sadecki | 4.00 | 10.00 |
| 680 | Rico Petrocelli | 6.00 | 15.00 |
| 681 | Bob Garibaldi RC | 4.00 | 10.00 |
| 682 | Dalton Jones | 4.00 | 10.00 |
| 683 | Geishart/McRae/Simpson RC | 6.00 | 15.00 |
| 684 | Jack Fisher | 4.00 | 10.00 |
| 685 | Tom Haller | 4.00 | 10.00 |
| 686 | Jackie Hernandez | 4.00 | 10.00 |
| 687 | Bob Priddy | 4.00 | 10.00 |
| 688 | Ted Kubiak | 4.00 | 10.00 |
| 689 | Frank Tepedino | 6.00 | 15.00 |
| 690 | Ron Fairly | 6.00 | 15.00 |
| 691 | Joe Grzenda | 4.00 | 10.00 |
| 692 | Duffy Dyer | 4.00 | 10.00 |
| 693 | Bob Johnson | 4.00 | 10.00 |
| 694 | Gary Ross | 4.00 | 10.00 |
| 695 | Bobby Knoop | 4.00 | 10.00 |
| 696 | San Francisco Giants TC | 5.00 | 12.00 |
| 697 | Jim Hannan | 4.00 | 10.00 |
| 698 | Tom Tresh | 6.00 | 15.00 |
| 699 | Hank Aguirre | 4.00 | 10.00 |
| 700 | Frank Robinson | 20.00 | 50.00 |
| 701 | Jack Billingham | 4.00 | 10.00 |
| 702 | Johnson/Klimkowski/Zepp RC | 4.00 | 10.00 |
| 703 | Lou Marone RC | 4.00 | 10.00 |
| 704 | Frank Baker RC | 4.00 | 10.00 |
| 705 | Tony Cloninger UER | 4.00 | 10.00 |
| 706 | John McNamara MG RC | 4.00 | 10.00 |
| 707 | Kevin Collins | 4.00 | 10.00 |
| 708 | Jose Santiago | 4.00 | 10.00 |
| 709 | Mike Fiore | 4.00 | 10.00 |
| 710 | Felix Millan | 4.00 | 10.00 |
| 711 | Ed Brinkman | 4.00 | 10.00 |
| 712 | Nolan Ryan | 100.00 | 200.00 |
| 713 | Seattle Pilots TC | 10.00 | 25.00 |
| 714 | Al Spangler | 4.00 | 10.00 |
| 715 | Mickey Lolich | 6.00 | 15.00 |
| 716 | Campisi/Cleveland/Guzman RC | 6.00 | 15.00 |
| 717 | Tom Phoebus | 4.00 | 10.00 |
| 718 | Ed Spiezio | 4.00 | 10.00 |
| 719 | Jim Roland | 4.00 | 10.00 |
| 720 | Rick Reichardt | 6.00 | 15.00 |

## 1971 Topps

PIRATES — roberto clemente of

| | | | |
|---|---|---|---|
| COMPLETE SET (752) | | 1250.00 | 2500.00 |
| COMMON CARD (1-393) | | .60 | 1.50 |
| COMMON CARD (394-523) | | 1.00 | 2.50 |
| COMMON CARD (524-643) | | 1.50 | 4.00 |
| COMMON CARD (644-752) | | 3.00 | 8.00 |
| COMMON SP (644-752) | | 5.00 | 12.00 |
| WRAPPER (10-CENT) | | 5.00 | 12.00 |
| 1 | Baltimore Orioles TC | 8.00 | 20.00 |
| 2 | Dock Ellis | .60 | 1.50 |
| 3 | Dick McAuliffe | .75 | 2.00 |
| 4 | Vic Davalillo | .60 | 1.50 |
| 5 | Thurman Munson | 60.00 | 120.00 |
| 6 | Ed Spiezio | .60 | 1.50 |
| 7 | Jim Holt RC | .60 | 1.50 |
| 8 | Mike McQueen | .60 | 1.50 |
| 9 | George Scott | .75 | 2.00 |
| 10 | Claude Osteen | .75 | 2.00 |
| 11 | Elliott Maddox RC | .60 | 1.50 |
| 12 | Johnny Callison | .60 | 1.50 |
| 13 | C.Brinkman RC/D.Moloney RC | .60 | 1.50 |
| 14 | Dave Concepcion RC | 6.00 | 15.00 |
| 15 | Andy Messersmith | .75 | 2.00 |
| 16 | Ken Singleton RC | 1.50 | 4.00 |
| 17 | Billy Sorrell | .60 | 1.50 |
| 18 | Norm Miller | .60 | 1.50 |
| 19 | Skip Pitlock RC | .60 | 1.50 |
| 20 | Reggie Jackson | 20.00 | 50.00 |
| 21 | Dan McGinn | .60 | 1.50 |
| 22 | Phil Roof | .60 | 1.50 |
| 23 | Oscar Gamble | .60 | 1.50 |
| 24 | Rich Hand RC | .60 | 1.50 |
| 25 | Clito Gaston | .75 | 2.00 |
| 26 | Bert Blyleven RC | 8.00 | 20.00 |
| 27 | F.Cambria RC/G.Clines RC | .60 | 1.50 |
| 28 | Ron Klimkowski | .60 | 1.50 |
| 29 | Don Buford | .60 | 1.50 |
| 30 | Phil Niekro | 2.50 | 6.00 |
| 31 | Eddie Kasko MG | .60 | 1.50 |
| 32 | Jerry DaVanon | .60 | 1.50 |
| 33 | Del Unser | .60 | 1.50 |
| 34 | Sandy Vance RC | .60 | 1.50 |
| 35 | Lou Piniella | .75 | 2.00 |
| 36 | Dean Chance | .75 | 2.00 |
| 37 | Rich McKinney RC | .60 | 1.50 |
| 38 | Jim Colborn RC | .60 | 1.50 |
| 39 | L.LaGrow RC/G.Lamont RC | .75 | 2.00 |
| 40 | Lee May | .75 | 2.00 |
| 41 | Rick Austin RC | .60 | 1.50 |
| 42 | Boots Day | .60 | 1.50 |
| 43 | Steve Kealey | .60 | 1.50 |
| 44 | Johnny Edwards | .60 | 1.50 |
| 45 | Jim Hunter | 2.50 | 6.00 |
| 46 | Dave Campbell | .75 | 2.00 |
| 47 | Johnny Jeter | .60 | 1.50 |
| 48 | Dave Baldwin | .60 | 1.50 |
| 49 | Don Money | .60 | 1.50 |
| 50 | Willie McCovey | 4.00 | 10.00 |
| 51 | Steve Kline | .60 | 1.50 |
| 52 | O.Brown RC/E.Williams RC | .60 | 1.50 |
| 53 | Paul Blair | .75 | 2.00 |
| 54 | Checklist 1 | 4.00 | 10.00 |
| 55 | Steve Carlton | 8.00 | 20.00 |
| 56 | Duane Josephson | .60 | 1.50 |
| 57 | Von Joshua RC | .60 | 1.50 |
| 58 | Bill Lee | .75 | 2.00 |
| 59 | Gene Mauch MG | .75 | 2.00 |
| 60 | Dick Bosman | .60 | 1.50 |
| 61 | Johnson/Yaz/Oliva LL | 1.50 | 4.00 |

| # | Card | Lo | Hi |
|---|------|----|----|
| 62 | Carty/Torre/Sang LL | .75 | 2.00 |
| 63 | Howard/Conig/Powell LL | 1.50 | 4.00 |
| 64 | Bench/Perez/B.Will LL | 2.50 | 6.00 |
| 65 | Howard/Killebrew/Yaz LL | 1.50 | 4.00 |
| 66 | Bench/B.Will/Perez LL | 2.50 | 6.00 |
| 67 | Segui/Palmer/Wright LL | 1.50 | 4.00 |
| 68 | Seaver/Simp/Walk LL | 1.50 | 4.00 |
| 69 | Cuellar/McNally/Perry LL | .75 | 2.00 |
| 70 | Gibson/Perry/Jenkins LL | 2.50 | 6.00 |
| 71 | McDowell/Lolich/John LL | .75 | 2.00 |
| 72 | Seaver/Gibson/Jenkins LL | 2.50 | 6.00 |
| 73 | George Brunet | .60 | 1.50 |
| 74 | P.Hamm RC/J.Nettles RC | .75 | 2.00 |
| 75 | Gary Nolan | .75 | 2.00 |
| 76 | Ted Savage | .60 | 1.50 |
| 77 | Mike Compton RC | .60 | 1.50 |
| 78 | Jim Spencer | .60 | 1.50 |
| 79 | Wade Blasingame | .60 | 1.50 |
| 80 | Bill Melton | .60 | 1.50 |
| 81 | Felix Millan | .60 | 1.50 |
| 82 | Casey Cox | .60 | 1.50 |
| 83 | T.Foli RC/R.Bobb | .75 | 2.00 |
| 84 | Marcel Lachemann RC | .60 | 1.50 |
| 85 | Billy Grabarkewitz | .60 | 1.50 |
| 86 | Mike Kilkenny | .60 | 1.50 |
| 87 | Jack Heidemann RC | .60 | 1.50 |
| 88 | Hal King | .60 | 1.50 |
| 89 | Ken Brett | .60 | 1.50 |
| 90 | Joe Pepitone | .75 | 2.00 |
| 91 | Bob Lemon MG | .75 | 2.00 |
| 92 | Fred Wenz | .60 | 1.50 |
| 93 | N.McRae/D.Riddleberger | .60 | 1.50 |
| 94 | Don Hahn RC | .60 | 1.50 |
| 95 | Luis Tiant | .75 | 2.00 |
| 96 | Joe Hague | .60 | 1.50 |
| 97 | Floyd Wicker | .60 | 1.50 |
| 98 | Joe Decker RC | .60 | 1.50 |
| 99 | Mark Belanger | .75 | 2.00 |
| 100 | Pete Rose | 40.00 | 80.00 |
| 101 | Les Cain | .60 | 1.50 |
| 102 | K.Forsch RC/L.Howard RC | .75 | 2.00 |
| 103 | Rich Severson RC | .60 | 1.50 |
| 104 | Dan Frisella | .60 | 1.50 |
| 105 | Tony Conigliaro | .75 | 2.00 |
| 106 | Tom Dukes | .60 | 1.50 |
| 107 | Roy Foster RC | .60 | 1.50 |
| 108 | John Cumberland | .60 | 1.50 |
| 109 | Steve Hovley | .60 | 1.50 |
| 110 | Bill Mazeroski | 2.50 | 6.00 |
| 111 | L.Colson RC/B.Mitchell RC | .60 | 1.50 |
| 112 | Manny Mota | .75 | 2.00 |
| 113 | Jerry Crider | .60 | 1.50 |
| 114 | Billy Conigliaro | .75 | 2.00 |
| 115 | Donn Clendenon | .75 | 2.00 |
| 116 | Ken Sanders | .60 | 1.50 |
| 117 | Ted Simmons RC | 3.00 | 8.00 |
| 118 | Cookie Rojas | .60 | 1.50 |
| 119 | Frank Lucchesi MG | .60 | 1.50 |
| 120 | Willie Horton | .75 | 2.00 |
| 121 | J.Dunegan/R.Skidmore RC | .60 | 1.50 |
| 122 | Eddie Watt | .60 | 1.50 |
| 123A | Checklist 2 Right | 4.00 | 10.00 |
| 123B | Checklist 2 Centered | 4.00 | 10.00 |
| 124 | Don Gullett RC | .75 | 2.00 |
| 125 | Ray Fosse | .60 | 1.50 |
| 126 | Danny Coombs | .60 | 1.50 |
| 127 | Danny Thompson RC | .60 | 1.50 |
| 128 | Frank Johnson | .60 | 1.50 |
| 129 | Aurelio Monteagudo | .60 | 1.50 |
| 130 | Denis Menke | .60 | 1.50 |
| 131 | Curt Blefary | .60 | 1.50 |
| 132 | Jose Laboy | .60 | 1.50 |
| 133 | Mickey Lolich | .75 | 2.00 |
| 134 | Jose Arcia | .60 | 1.50 |
| 135 | Rick Monday | .75 | 2.00 |
| 136 | Duffy Dyer | .60 | 1.50 |
| 137 | Marcelino Lopez | .60 | 1.50 |
| 138 | J.Liis/W.Montanez RC | .75 | 2.00 |
| 139 | Paul Casanova | .60 | 1.50 |
| 140 | Gaylord Perry | 2.50 | 6.00 |
| 141 | Frank Quilici | .60 | 1.50 |
| 142 | Mack Jones | .60 | 1.50 |
| 143 | Steve Blass | .75 | 2.00 |
| 144 | Jackie Hernandez | .60 | 1.50 |
| 145 | Bill Singer | .75 | 2.00 |
| 146 | Ralph Houk MG | .60 | 1.50 |
| 147 | Bob Priddy | .60 | 1.50 |
| 148 | John Mayberry | .75 | 2.00 |
| 149 | Mike Hershberger | .60 | 1.50 |
| 150 | Sam McDowell | .75 | 2.00 |
| 151 | Tommy Davis | .75 | 2.00 |
| 152 | L.Allen RC/M.Llenas RC | .60 | 1.50 |
| 153 | Gary Ross | .60 | 1.50 |
| 154 | Cesar Gutierrez | .60 | 1.50 |
| 155 | Ken Henderson | .60 | 1.50 |
| 156 | Bart Johnson | .60 | 1.50 |
| 157 | Bob Bailey | .75 | 2.00 |
| 158 | Jerry Reuss | .75 | 2.00 |
| 159 | Jarvis Tatum | .60 | 1.50 |
| 160 | Tom Seaver | 12.50 | 30.00 |
| 161 | Coin Checklist | 4.00 | 10.00 |
| 162 | Jack Billingham | .60 | 1.50 |
| 163 | Buck Martinez | .75 | 2.00 |
| 164 | F.Duffy RC/M.Wilcox RC | .75 | 2.00 |
| 165 | Cesar Tovar | .60 | 1.50 |
| 166 | Joe Hoerner | .60 | 1.50 |
| 167 | Tom Grieve RC | .75 | 2.00 |
| 168 | Bruce Dal Canton | .60 | 1.50 |
| 169 | Ed Herrmann | .60 | 1.50 |
| 170 | Mike Cuellar | .75 | 2.00 |
| 171 | Bobby Wine | .60 | 1.50 |
| 172 | Duke Sims | .60 | 1.50 |
| 173 | Gil Garrido | .60 | 1.50 |
| 174 | Dave LaRoche RC | .60 | 1.50 |
| 175 | Jim Hickman | .60 | 1.50 |
| 176 | B.Montgomery RC/D.Griffin RC | .75 | 2.00 |
| 177 | Hal McRae | .75 | 2.00 |
| 178 | Dave Duncan | .75 | 2.00 |
| 179 | Mike Corkins | .60 | 1.50 |
| 180 | Al Kaline UER | 8.00 | 20.00 |
| 181 | Hal Lanier | .60 | 1.50 |
| 182 | Al Downing | .75 | 2.00 |
| 183 | Gil Hodges MG | 1.50 | 4.00 |
| 184 | Stan Bahnsen | .60 | 1.50 |
| 185 | Julian Javier | .60 | 1.50 |
| 186 | Bob Spence RC | .60 | 1.50 |
| 187 | Ted Abernathy | .60 | 1.50 |
| 188 | B.Valentine RC/M.Strahler RC | 2.50 | 6.00 |
| 189 | George Mitterwald | .60 | 1.50 |
| 190 | Bob Tolan | .60 | 1.50 |
| 191 | Mike Andrews | .60 | 1.50 |
| 192 | Billy Wilson | .60 | 1.50 |
| 193 | Bob Grich RC | 1.50 | 4.00 |
| 194 | Mike Lum | .60 | 1.50 |
| 195 | Boog Powell ALCS | .75 | 2.00 |
| 196 | Dave McNally ALCS | .75 | 2.00 |
| 197 | Jim Palmer ALCS | 1.50 | 4.00 |
| 198 | Orioles Celebrate ALCS | .75 | 2.00 |
| 199 | Ty Cline NLCS | .75 | 2.00 |
| 200 | Bobby Tolan NLCS | .75 | 2.00 |
| 201 | Ty Cline NLCS | .75 | 2.00 |
| 202 | Reds Celebrate NLCS | .75 | 2.00 |
| 203 | Larry Gura RC | .75 | 2.00 |
| 204 | B.Smith RC/G.Kopacz RC | .60 | 1.50 |
| 205 | Gerry Moses | .60 | 1.50 |
| 206 | Checklist 3 | 4.00 | 10.00 |
| 207 | Alan Foster | .60 | 1.50 |
| 208 | Billy Martin MG | 1.50 | 4.00 |
| 209 | Steve Renko | .60 | 1.50 |
| 210 | Rod Carew | 6.00 | 15.00 |
| 211 | Phil Hennigan RC | .60 | 1.50 |
| 212 | Rich Hebner | .75 | 2.00 |
| 213 | Frank Baker RC | .60 | 1.50 |
| 214 | Al Ferrara | .60 | 1.50 |
| 215 | Diego Segui | .60 | 1.50 |
| 216 | R.Cleveland/L.Melendez RC | .60 | 1.50 |
| 217 | Ed Stroud | .60 | 1.50 |
| 218 | Tony Cloninger | .60 | 1.50 |
| 219 | Elrod Hendricks | .60 | 1.50 |
| 220 | Ron Santo | 1.50 | 4.00 |
| 221 | Dave Morehead | .60 | 1.50 |
| 222 | Bob Watson | .75 | 2.00 |
| 223 | Cecil Upshaw | .60 | 1.50 |
| 224 | Alan Gallagher | .60 | 1.50 |
| 225 | Gary Peters | .60 | 1.50 |
| 226 | Bill Russell | .75 | 2.00 |
| 227 | Floyd Weaver | .60 | 1.50 |
| 228 | Wayne Garrett | .60 | 1.50 |
| 229 | Jim Hannan | .60 | 1.50 |
| 230 | Willie Stargell | 6.00 | 15.00 |
| 231 | V.Colbert RC/J.Lowenstein RC | .75 | 2.00 |
| 232 | John Strohmayer RC | .60 | 1.50 |
| 233 | Larry Bowa | .75 | 2.00 |
| 234 | Jim Lyttle | .60 | 1.50 |
| 235 | Nate Colbert | .60 | 1.50 |
| 236 | Bob Humphreys | .60 | 1.50 |
| 237 | Cesar Cedeno RC | .75 | 2.00 |
| 238 | Chuck Dobson | .60 | 1.50 |
| 239 | Red Schoendienst MG | .75 | 2.00 |
| 240 | Clyde Wright | .60 | 1.50 |
| 241 | Dave Nelson | .60 | 1.50 |
| 242 | Jim Ray | .60 | 1.50 |
| 243 | Carlos May | .60 | 1.50 |
| 244 | Bob Tillman | .60 | 1.50 |
| 245 | Jim Kaat | .75 | 2.00 |
| 246 | Tony Taylor | .60 | 1.50 |
| 247 | J.Cram RC/P.Splittorff RC | .75 | 2.00 |
| 248 | Hoyt Wilhelm | 2.50 | 6.00 |
| 249 | Chico Salmon | .60 | 1.50 |
| 250 | Johnny Bench | 20.00 | 50.00 |
| 251 | Frank Reberger | .60 | 1.50 |
| 252 | Eddie Leon | .60 | 1.50 |
| 253 | Bill Sudakis | .60 | 1.50 |
| 254 | Cal Koonce | .60 | 1.50 |
| 255 | Bob Robertson | .75 | 2.00 |
| 256 | Tony Gonzalez | .60 | 1.50 |
| 257 | Nelson Briles | .75 | 2.00 |
| 258 | Dick Green | .60 | 1.50 |
| 259 | Dave Marshall | .60 | 1.50 |
| 260 | Tommy Harper | .75 | 2.00 |
| 261 | Darold Knowles | .60 | 1.50 |
| 262 | J.Williams/D.Robinson RC | .60 | 1.50 |
| 263 | John Ellis | .60 | 1.50 |
| 264 | Joe Morgan | 3.00 | 8.00 |
| 265 | Jim Northrup | .75 | 2.00 |
| 266 | Bill Stoneman | .60 | 1.50 |
| 267 | Rich Morales | .60 | 1.50 |
| 268 | Philadelphia Phillies TC | 1.50 | 4.00 |
| 269 | Gail Hopkins | .60 | 1.50 |
| 270 | Rico Carty | .75 | 2.00 |
| 271 | Bill Zepp | .60 | 1.50 |
| 272 | Tommy Helms | .75 | 2.00 |
| 273 | Pete Richert | .60 | 1.50 |
| 274 | Ron Slocum | .60 | 1.50 |
| 275 | Vada Pinson | .75 | 2.00 |
| 276 | M.Davison RC/G.Foster RC | 3.00 | 8.00 |
| 277 | Gary Waslewski | .60 | 1.50 |
| 278 | Jerry Grote | .75 | 2.00 |
| 279 | Lefty Phillips MG | .60 | 1.50 |
| 280 | Ferguson Jenkins | 2.50 | 6.00 |
| 281 | Danny Walton | .60 | 1.50 |
| 282 | Jose Pagan | .60 | 1.50 |
| 283 | Dick Such | .60 | 1.50 |
| 284 | Jim Gosger | .60 | 1.50 |
| 285 | Sal Bando | .75 | 2.00 |
| 286 | Jerry McNertney | .60 | 1.50 |
| 287 | Mike Fiore | .60 | 1.50 |
| 288 | Joe Moeller | .60 | 1.50 |
| 289 | Chicago White Sox TC | 1.50 | 4.00 |
| 290 | Tony Oliva | 1.50 | 4.00 |
| 291 | George Culver | .60 | 1.50 |
| 292 | Jay Johnstone | .75 | 2.00 |
| 293 | Pat Corrales | .75 | 2.00 |
| 294 | Steve Dunning RC | .60 | 1.50 |
| 295 | Bobby Bonds | 1.50 | 4.00 |
| 296 | Tom Timmermann | .60 | 1.50 |
| 297 | Johnny Briggs | .60 | 1.50 |
| 298 | Jim Nelson RC | .60 | 1.50 |
| 299 | Ed Kirkpatrick | .60 | 1.50 |
| 300 | Brooks Robinson | 8.00 | 20.00 |
| 301 | Earl Wilson | .60 | 1.50 |
| 302 | Phil Gagliano | .60 | 1.50 |
| 303 | Lindy McDaniel | .75 | 2.00 |
| 304 | Ron Brand | .60 | 1.50 |
| 305 | Reggie Smith | .75 | 2.00 |
| 306 | Jim Nash | .60 | 1.50 |
| 307 | Don Wert | .60 | 1.50 |
| 308 | St. Louis Cardinals TC | 1.50 | 4.00 |
| 309 | Dick Ellsworth | .60 | 1.50 |
| 310 | Tommie Agee | .75 | 2.00 |
| 311 | Lee Stange | .60 | 1.50 |
| 312 | Harry Walker MG | .60 | 1.50 |
| 313 | Tom Hall | .60 | 1.50 |
| 314 | Jeff Torborg | .75 | 2.00 |
| 315 | Ron Fairly | .75 | 2.00 |
| 316 | Fred Scherman RC | .60 | 1.50 |
| 317 | J.Driscoll RC/A.Mangual | .60 | 1.50 |
| 318 | Rudy May | .60 | 1.50 |
| 319 | Ty Cline | .60 | 1.50 |
| 320 | Dave McNally | .75 | 2.00 |
| 321 | Tom Matchick | .60 | 1.50 |
| 322 | Jim Beauchamp | .60 | 1.50 |
| 323 | Billy Champion | .60 | 1.50 |
| 324 | Graig Nettles | .75 | 2.00 |

|  | | |
|---|---|---|
| ☐ 325 Juan Marichal | 3.00 | 8.00 |
| ☐ 326 Richie Scheinblum | .60 | 1.50 |
| ☐ 327 Boog Powell WS | .75 | 2.00 |
| ☐ 328 Don Buford WS | .75 | 2.00 |
| ☐ 329 Frank Robinson WS | 1.50 | 4.00 |
| ☐ 330 Reds Stay Alive WS | .75 | 2.00 |
| ☐ 331 Brooks Robinson WS | 2.50 | 6.00 |
| ☐ 332 Orioles Celebrate WS | .75 | 2.00 |
| ☐ 333 Clay Kirby | .60 | 1.50 |
| ☐ 334 Roberto Pena | .60 | 1.50 |
| ☐ 335 Jerry Koosman | .75 | 2.00 |
| ☐ 336 Detroit Tigers TC | 1.50 | 4.00 |
| ☐ 337 Jesus Alou | .60 | 1.50 |
| ☐ 338 Gene Tenace | .75 | 2.00 |
| ☐ 339 Wayne Simpson | .60 | 1.50 |
| ☐ 340 Rico Petrocelli | .75 | 2.00 |
| ☐ 341 Steve Garvey RC | 12.50 | 40.00 |
| ☐ 342 Frank Tepedino | .75 | 2.00 |
| ☐ 343 E.Acosta RC/M.May RC | .75 | 2.00 |
| ☐ 344 Ellie Rodriguez | .60 | 1.50 |
| ☐ 345 Joel Horlen | .60 | 1.50 |
| ☐ 346 Lum Harris MG | .60 | 1.50 |
| ☐ 347 Ted Uhlaender | .60 | 1.50 |
| ☐ 348 Fred Norman | .60 | 1.50 |
| ☐ 349 Rich Reese | .60 | 1.50 |
| ☐ 350 Billy Williams | 2.50 | 6.00 |
| ☐ 351 Jim Shellenback | .60 | 1.50 |
| ☐ 352 Denny Doyle | .60 | 1.50 |
| ☐ 353 Carl Taylor | .60 | 1.50 |
| ☐ 354 Don McMahon | .60 | 1.50 |
| ☐ 355 Bud Harrelson w/Ryan | 1.50 | 4.00 |
| ☐ 356 Bob Locker | .60 | 1.50 |
| ☐ 357 Cincinnati Reds TC | 1.50 | 4.00 |
| ☐ 358 Danny Cater | .60 | 1.50 |
| ☐ 359 Ron Reed | .60 | 1.50 |
| ☐ 360 Jim Fregosi | .75 | 2.00 |
| ☐ 361 Don Sutton | 2.50 | 6.00 |
| ☐ 362 M.Adamson/R.Freed | .60 | 1.50 |
| ☐ 363 Mike Nagy | .60 | 1.50 |
| ☐ 364 Tommy Dean | .60 | 1.50 |
| ☐ 365 Bob Johnson | .60 | 1.50 |
| ☐ 366 Ron Stone | .60 | 1.50 |
| ☐ 367 Dalton Jones | .60 | 1.50 |
| ☐ 368 Bob Veale | .75 | 2.00 |
| ☐ 369 Checklist 4 | 4.00 | 10.00 |
| ☐ 370 Joe Torre | 1.50 | 4.00 |
| ☐ 371 Jack Hiatt | .60 | 1.50 |
| ☐ 372 Lew Krausse | .60 | 1.50 |
| ☐ 373 Tom McCraw | .60 | 1.50 |
| ☐ 374 Clete Boyer | .75 | 2.00 |
| ☐ 375 Steve Hargan | .60 | 1.50 |
| ☐ 376 C.Mashore RC/E.McAnally RC | .60 | 1.50 |
| ☐ 377 Greg Garrett | .60 | 1.50 |
| ☐ 378 Tito Fuentes | .60 | 1.50 |
| ☐ 379 Wayne Granger | .60 | 1.50 |
| ☐ 380 Ted Williams MG | 5.00 | 12.00 |
| ☐ 381 Fred Gladding | .60 | 1.50 |
| ☐ 382 Jake Gibbs | .60 | 1.50 |
| ☐ 383 Rod Gaspar | .60 | 1.50 |
| ☐ 384 Rollie Fingers | 2.50 | 6.00 |
| ☐ 385 Maury Wills | 1.50 | 4.00 |
| ☐ 386 Boston Red Sox TC | 1.50 | 4.00 |
| ☐ 387 Ron Herbel | .60 | 1.50 |
| ☐ 388 Al Oliver | 1.50 | 4.00 |
| ☐ 389 Ed Brinkman | .60 | 1.50 |
| ☐ 390 Glenn Beckert | .75 | 2.00 |
| ☐ 391 S.Brye RC/C.Nash RC | .75 | 2.00 |
| ☐ 392 Grant Jackson | .60 | 1.50 |
| ☐ 393 Merv Rettenmund | .75 | 2.00 |
| ☐ 394 Clay Carroll . | 1.00 | 2.50 |
| ☐ 395 Roy White | 1.50 | 4.00 |
| ☐ 396 Dick Schofield | 1.00 | 2.50 |
| ☐ 397 Alvin Dark MG | 1.50 | 4.00 |
| ☐ 398 Howie Reed | 1.00 | 2.50 |
| ☐ 399 Jim French | 1.00 | 2.50 |
| ☐ 400 Hank Aaron | 30.00 | 60.00 |
| ☐ 401 Tom Murphy | 1.00 | 2.50 |
| ☐ 402 Los Angeles Dodgers TC | 2.50 | 6.00 |
| ☐ 403 Joe Coleman | 1.00 | 2.50 |
| ☐ 404 B.Harris RC/R.Metzger RC | 1.00 | 2.50 |
| ☐ 405 Leo Cardenas | 1.00 | 2.50 |
| ☐ 406 Ray Sadecki | 1.00 | 2.50 |
| ☐ 407 Joe Rudi | 1.50 | 4.00 |
| ☐ 408 Rafael Robles | 1.00 | 2.50 |
| ☐ 409 Don Pavletich | 1.00 | 2.50 |
| ☐ 410 Ken Holtzman | 1.50* | 4.00 |
| ☐ 411 George Spriggs | 1.00 | 2.50 |
| ☐ 412 Jerry Johnson | 1.00 | 2.50 |
| ☐ 413 Pat Kelly | 1.00 | 2.50 |
| ☐ 414 Woodie Fryman | 1.00 | 2.50 |
| ☐ 415 Mike Hegan | 1.00 | 2.50 |
| ☐ 416 Gene Alley | 1.00 | 2.50 |
| ☐ 417 Dick Hall | 1.00 | 2.50 |
| ☐ 418 Adolfo Phillips | 1.00 | 2.50 |
| ☐ 419 Ron Hansen | 1.00 | 2.50 |
| ☐ 420 Jim Merritt | 1.00 | 2.50 |
| ☐ 421 John Stephenson | 1.00 | 2.50 |
| ☐ 422 Frank Bertaina | 1.00 | 2.50 |
| ☐ 423 D.Saunders/T.Marting RC | 1.00 | 2.50 |
| ☐ 424 Roberto Rodriguez | 1.00 | 2.50 |
| ☐ 425 Doug Rader | 1.50 | 4.00 |
| ☐ 426 Chris Cannizzaro | 1.00 | 2.50 |
| ☐ 427 Bernie Allen | 1.00 | 2.50 |
| ☐ 428 Jim McAndrew | 1.00 | 2.50 |
| ☐ 429 Chuck Hinton | 1.00 | 2.50 |
| ☐ 430 Wes Parker | 1.50 | 4.00 |
| ☐ 431 Tom Burgmeier | 1.00 | 2.50 |
| ☐ 432 Bob Didier | 1.00 | 2.50 |
| ☐ 433 Skip Lockwood | 1.00 | 2.50 |
| ☐ 434 Gary Sutherland | 1.00 | 2.50 |
| ☐ 435 Jose Cardenal | 1.50 | 4.00 |
| ☐ 436 Wilbur Wood | 1.50 | 4.00 |
| ☐ 437 Danny Murtaugh MG | 1.50 | 4.00 |
| ☐ 438 Mike McCormick | 1.50 | 4.00 |
| ☐ 439 G.Luzinski RC/S.Reid | 2.50 | 6.00 |
| ☐ 440 Bert Campaneris | 1.50 | 4.00 |
| ☐ 441 Milt Pappas | 1.50 | 4.00 |
| ☐ 442 California Angels TC | 1.50 | 4.00 |
| ☐ 443 Rich Robertson | 1.00 | 2.50 |
| ☐ 444 Jimmie Price | 1.00 | 2.50 |
| ☐ 445 Art Shamsky | 1.00 | 2.50 |
| ☐ 446 Bobby Bolin | 1.00 | 2.50 |
| ☐ 447 Cesar Geronimo RC | 1.50 | 4.00 |
| ☐ 448 Dave Roberts | 1.00 | 2.50 |
| ☐ 449 Brant Alyea | 1.00 | 2.50 |
| ☐ 450 Bob Gibson | 6.00 | 15.00 |
| ☐ 451 Joe Keough | 1.00 | 2.50 |
| ☐ 452 John Boccabella | 1.00 | 2.50 |
| ☐ 453 Terry Crowley | 1.00 | 2.50 |
| ☐ 454 Mike Paul | 1.00 | 2.50 |
| ☐ 455 Don Kessinger | 1.50 | 4.00 |
| ☐ 456 Bob Meyer | 1.00 | 2.50 |
| ☐ 457 Willie Smith | 1.00 | 2.50 |
| ☐ 458 R.Lolich RC/D.Lemonds RC | 1.00 | 2.50 |
| ☐ 459 Jim Lefebvre | 1.00 | 2.50 |
| ☐ 460 Fritz Peterson | 1.00 | 2.50 |
| ☐ 461 Jim Ray Hart | 1.50 | 4.00 |
| ☐ 462 Washington Senators TC | 2.50 | 6.00 |
| ☐ 463 Tom Kelley | 1.00 | 2.50 |
| ☐ 464 Aurelio Rodriguez | 1.00 | 2.50 |
| ☐ 465 Tim McCarver | 2.50 | 6.00 |
| ☐ 466 Ken Berry | 1.00 | 2.50 |
| ☐ 467 Al Santorini | 1.00 | 2.50 |
| ☐ 468 Frank Fernandez | 1.00 | 2.50 |
| ☐ 469 Bob Aspromonte | 1.00 | 2.50 |
| ☐ 470 Bob Oliver | 1.00 | 2.50 |
| ☐ 471 Tom Griffin | 1.00 | 2.50 |
| ☐ 472 Ken Rudolph | 1.00 | 2.50 |
| ☐ 473 Gary Wagner | 1.00 | 2.50 |
| ☐ 474 Jim Fairey | 1.00 | 2.50 |
| ☐ 475 Ron Perranoski | 1.50 | 4.00 |
| ☐ 476 Dal Maxvill | 1.00 | 2.50 |
| ☐ 477 Earl Weaver MG | 2.50 | 6.00 |
| ☐ 478 Bernie Carbo | 1.00 | 2.50 |
| ☐ 479 Dennis Higgins | 1.00 | 2.50 |
| ☐ 480 Manny Sanguillen | 1.50 | 4.00 |
| ☐ 481 Daryl Patterson | 1.00 | 2.50 |
| ☐ 482 San Diego Padres TC | 2.50 | 6.00 |
| ☐ 483 Gene Michael | 1.50 | 4.00 |
| ☐ 484 Don Wilson | 1.00 | 2.50 |
| ☐ 485 Ken McMullen | 1.00 | 2.50 |
| ☐ 486 Steve Huntz | 1.00 | 2.50 |
| ☐ 487 Paul Schaal | 1.00 | 2.50 |
| ☐ 488 Jerry Stephenson | 1.00 | 2.50 |
| ☐ 489 Luis Alvarado | 1.00 | 2.50 |
| ☐ 490 Deron Johnson | 1.00 | 2.50 |
| ☐ 491 Jim Hardin | 1.00 | 2.50 |
| ☐ 492 Ken Boswell | 1.00 | 2.50 |
| ☐ 493 Dave Way | 1.00 | 2.50 |
| ☐ 494 R.Garr/R.Kester | 1.50 | 4.00 |
| ☐ 495 Felipe Alou | 1.50 | 4.00 |
| ☐ 496 Woody Woodward | 1.00 | 2.50 |
| ☐ 497 Horacio Pina RC | 1.00 | 2.50 |
| ☐ 498 John Kennedy | 1.00 | 2.50 |
| ☐ 499 Checklist 5 | 4.00 | 10.00 |
| ☐ 500 Jim Perry | 1.50 | 4.00 |
| ☐ 501 Andy Etchebarren | 1.00 | 2.50 |
| ☐ 502 Chicago Cubs TC | 2.50 | 6.00 |
| ☐ 503 Gates Brown | 1.50 | 4.00 |
| ☐ 504 Ken Wright RC | 1.00 | 2.50 |
| ☐ 505 Ollie Brown | 1.00 | 2.50 |
| ☐ 506 Bobby Knoop | 1.00 | 2.50 |
| ☐ 507 George Stone | 1.00 | 2.50 |
| ☐ 508 Roger Repoz | 1.00 | 2.50 |
| ☐ 509 Jim Grant | 1.00 | 2.50 |
| ☐ 510 Ken Harrelson | 1.50 | 4.00 |
| ☐ 511 Chris Short w/Rose | 2.50 | 6.00 |
| ☐ 512 D.Mills RC/M.Garman RC | 1.00 | 2.50 |
| ☐ 513 Nolan Ryan | 75.00 | 150.00 |
| ☐ 514 Ron Woods | 1.00 | 2.50 |
| ☐ 515 Carl Morton | 1.00 | 2.50 |
| ☐ 516 Ted Kubiak | 1.00 | 2.50 |
| ☐ 517 Charlie Fox MG RC | 1.00 | 2.50 |
| ☐ 518 Joe Grzenda | 1.00 | 2.50 |
| ☐ 519 Willie Crawford | 1.00 | 2.50 |
| ☐ 520 Tommy John | 2.50 | 6.00 |
| ☐ 521 Leron Lee | 1.00 | 2.50 |
| ☐ 522 Minnesota Twins TC | 2.50 | 6.00 |
| ☐ 523 John Odom | 1.00 | 2.50 |
| ☐ 524 Mickey Stanley | 2.50 | 6.00 |
| ☐ 525 Ernie Banks | 20.00 | 50.00 |
| ☐ 526 Ray Jarvis | 1.50 | 4.00 |
| ☐ 527 Cleon Jones | 2.50 | 6.00 |
| ☐ 528 Wally Bunker | 1.50 | 4.00 |
| ☐ 529 Hernandez/Bucker/Perez RC | 2.50 | 6.00 |
| ☐ 530 Carl Yastrzemski | 12.50 | 30.00 |
| ☐ 531 Mike Torrez | 1.50 | 4.00 |
| ☐ 532 Bill Rigney MG | 1.50 | 4.00 |
| ☐ 533 Mike Ryan | 1.50 | 4.00 |
| ☐ 534 Luke Walker | 1.50 | 4.00 |
| ☐ 535 Curt Flood | 2.50 | 6.00 |
| ☐ 536 Claude Raymond | 1.50 | 4.00 |
| ☐ 537 Tom Egan | 1.50 | 4.00 |
| ☐ 538 Angel Bravo | 1.50 | 4.00 |
| ☐ 539 Larry Brown | 1.50 | 4.00 |
| ☐ 540 Larry Dierker | 2.50 | 6.00 |
| ☐ 541 Bob Burda | 1.50 | 4.00 |
| ☐ 542 Bob Miller | 1.50 | 4.00 |
| ☐ 543 New York Yankees TC | 4.00 | 10.00 |
| ☐ 544 Vida Blue | 2.50 | 6.00 |
| ☐ 545 Dick Dietz | 1.50 | 4.00 |
| ☐ 546 John Matias | 1.50 | 4.00 |
| ☐ 547 Pat Dobson | 2.50 | 6.00 |
| ☐ 548 Don Mason | 1.50 | 4.00 |
| ☐ 549 Jim Brewer | 2.50 | 6.00 |
| ☐ 550 Harmon Killebrew | 10.00 | 25.00 |
| ☐ 551 Frank Linzy | 1.50 | 4.00 |
| ☐ 552 Buddy Bradford | 1.50 | 4.00 |
| ☐ 553 Kevin Collins | 1.50 | 4.00 |
| ☐ 554 Lowell Palmer | 1.50 | 4.00 |
| ☐ 555 Walt Williams | 1.50 | 4.00 |
| ☐ 556 Jim McGlothlin | 1.50 | 4.00 |
| ☐ 557 Tom Satriano | 1.50 | 4.00 |
| ☐ 558 Hector Torres | 1.50 | 4.00 |
| ☐ 559 Cox/Gogolewski/Jones RC | 1.50 | 4.00 |
| ☐ 560 Rusty Staub | 2.50 | 6.00 |
| ☐ 561 Syd O'Brien | 1.50 | 4.00 |
| ☐ 562 Dave Giusti | 1.50 | 4.00 |
| ☐ 563 San Francisco Giants TC | 3.00 | 8.00 |
| ☐ 564 Al Fitzmorris | 1.50 | 4.00 |
| ☐ 565 Jim Wynn | 2.50 | 6.00 |
| ☐ 566 Tim Cullen | 1.50 | 4.00 |
| ☐ 567 Walt Alston MG | 3.00 | 8.00 |
| ☐ 568 Sal Campisi | 1.50 | 4.00 |
| ☐ 569 Ivan Murrell | 1.50 | 4.00 |
| ☐ 570 Jim Palmer | 12.50 | 30.00 |
| ☐ 571 Ted Sizemore | 1.50 | 4.00 |
| ☐ 572 Jerry Kenney | 1.50 | 4.00 |
| ☐ 573 Ed Kranepool | 2.50 | 6.00 |
| ☐ 574 Jim Bunning | 3.00 | 8.00 |
| ☐ 575 Bill Freehan | 2.50 | 6.00 |
| ☐ 576 Garrett/Davis/Jestadt RC | 1.50 | 4.00 |
| ☐ 577 Jim Lonborg | 2.50 | 6.00 |
| ☐ 578 Ron Hunt | 1.50 | 4.00 |
| ☐ 579 Marty Pattin | 1.50 | 4.00 |
| ☐ 580 Tony Perez | 8.00 | 20.00 |
| ☐ 581 Roger Nelson | 1.50 | 4.00 |
| ☐ 582 Dave Cash | 2.50 | 6.00 |
| ☐ 583 Ron Cook RC | 1.50 | 4.00 |
| ☐ 584 Cleveland Indians TC | 3.00 | 8.00 |
| ☐ 585 Willie Davis | 2.50 | 6.00 |
| ☐ 586 Dick Woodson | 1.50 | 4.00 |
| ☐ 587 Sonny Jackson | 1.50 | 4.00 |
| ☐ 588 Tom Bradley RC | 1.50 | 4.00 |

| | | |
|---|---|---|
| ☐ 589 Bob Barton | 1.50 | 4.00 |
| ☐ 590 Alex Johnson | 2.50 | 6.00 |
| ☐ 591 Jackie Brown RC | 1.50 | 4.00 |
| ☐ 592 Randy Hundley | 2.50 | 6.00 |
| ☐ 593 Jack Aker | 1.50 | 4.00 |
| ☐ 594 Chlupsa/Stinson/Hrabosky RC | 2.50 | 6.00 |
| ☐ 595 Dave Johnson | 2.50 | 6.00 |
| ☐ 596 Mike Jorgensen | 1.50 | 4.00 |
| ☐ 597 Ken Suarez | 1.50 | 4.00 |
| ☐ 598 Rick Wise | 2.50 | 6.00 |
| ☐ 599 Norm Cash | 2.50 | 6.00 |
| ☐ 600 Willie Mays | 50.00 | 100.00 |
| ☐ 601 Ken Tatum | 1.50 | 4.00 |
| ☐ 602 Marty Gelhaar | 1.50 | 4.00 |
| ☐ 603 Pittsburgh Pirates TC | 3.00 | 8.00 |
| ☐ 604 John Gelnar | 1.50 | 4.00 |
| ☐ 605 Orlando Cepeda | 3.00 | 8.00 |
| ☐ 606 Chuck Taylor | 1.50 | 4.00 |
| ☐ 607 Paul Ratliff | 1.50 | 4.00 |
| ☐ 608 Mike Wegener | 1.50 | 4.00 |
| ☐ 609 Leo Durocher MG | 3.00 | 8.00 |
| ☐ 610 Amos Otis | 2.50 | 6.00 |
| ☐ 611 Tom Phoebus | 1.50 | 4.00 |
| ☐ 612 Camilli/Ford/Mingori RC | 1.50 | 4.00 |
| ☐ 613 Pedro Borbon | 1.50 | 4.00 |
| ☐ 614 Billy Cowan | 1.50 | 4.00 |
| ☐ 615 Mel Stottlemyre | 2.50 | 6.00 |
| ☐ 616 Larry Hisle | 2.50 | 6.00 |
| ☐ 617 Clay Dalrymple | 1.50 | 4.00 |
| ☐ 618 Tug McGraw | 2.50 | 6.00 |
| ☐ 619A Checklist 6 ERR w/o Copy | 4.00 | 10.00 |
| ☐ 619B Checklist 6 COR w/Copy | 4.00 | 10.00 |
| ☐ 620 Frank Howard | 2.50 | 6.00 |
| ☐ 621 Ron Bryant | 1.50 | 4.00 |
| ☐ 622 Joe Lahoud | 1.50 | 4.00 |
| ☐ 623 Pat Jarvis | 1.50 | 4.00 |
| ☐ 624 Oakland Athletics TC | 3.00 | 8.00 |
| ☐ 625 Lou Brock | 12.50 | 30.00 |
| ☐ 626 Freddie Patek | 2.50 | 6.00 |
| ☐ 627 Steve Hamilton | 1.50 | 4.00 |
| ☐ 628 John Bateman | 1.50 | 4.00 |
| ☐ 629 John Hiller | 2.50 | 6.00 |
| ☐ 630 Roberto Clemente | 75.00 | 150.00 |
| ☐ 631 Eddie Fisher | 1.50 | 4.00 |
| ☐ 632 Darrel Chaney | 1.50 | 4.00 |
| ☐ 633 Brooks/Koegel/Northey RC | 1.50 | 4.00 |
| ☐ 634 Phil Regan | 1.50 | 4.00 |
| ☐ 635 Bobby Murcer | 2.50 | 6.00 |
| ☐ 636 Denny Lemaster | 1.50 | 4.00 |
| ☐ 637 Dave Bristol MG | 1.50 | 4.00 |
| ☐ 638 Stan Williams | 1.50 | 4.00 |
| ☐ 639 Tom Haller | 1.50 | 4.00 |
| ☐ 640 Frank Robinson | 12.50 | 40.00 |
| ☐ 641 New York Mets TC | 6.00 | 15.00 |
| ☐ 642 Jim Roland | 1.50 | 4.00 |
| ☐ 643 Rick Reichardt | 1.50 | 4.00 |
| ☐ 644 Jim Stewart SP | 5.00 | 12.00 |
| ☐ 645 Jim Maloney SP | 6.00 | 15.00 |
| ☐ 646 Bobby Floyd SP | 5.00 | 12.00 |
| ☐ 647 Juan Pizarro | 3.00 | 8.00 |
| ☐ 648 Folkers/Martinez/Matlack SP RC | 10.00 | 25.00 |
| ☐ 649 Sparky Lyle SP | 6.00 | 15.00 |
| ☐ 650 Richie Allen SP | 12.50 | 30.00 |
| ☐ 651 Jerry Robertson SP | 5.00 | 12.00 |
| ☐ 652 Atlanta Braves TC | 5.00 | 12.00 |
| ☐ 653 Russ Snyder SP | 5.00 | 12.00 |
| ☐ 654 Don Shaw SP | 5.00 | 12.00 |
| ☐ 655 Mike Epstein SP | 5.00 | 12.00 |
| ☐ 656 Gerry Nyman SP | 5.00 | 12.00 |
| ☐ 657 Jose Azcue | 3.00 | 8.00 |
| ☐ 658 Paul Lindblad SP | 5.00 | 12.00 |
| ☐ 659 Byron Browne SP | 5.00 | 12.00 |
| ☐ 660 Ray Culp | 3.00 | 8.00 |
| ☐ 661 Chuck Tanner MG SP | 6.00 | 15.00 |
| ☐ 662 Mike Hedlund SP | 5.00 | 12.00 |
| ☐ 663 Marv Staehle | 5.00 | 12.00 |
| ☐ 664 Reyes/Reynolds/Reynolds SP RC | 5.00 | 12.00 |
| ☐ 665 Ron Swoboda SP | 6.00 | 15.00 |
| ☐ 666 Gene Brabender SP | 5.00 | 12.00 |
| ☐ 667 Pete Ward | 3.00 | 8.00 |
| ☐ 668 Gary Neibauer | 3.00 | 8.00 |
| ☐ 669 Ike Brown SP | 5.00 | 12.00 |
| ☐ 670 Bill Hands | 3.00 | 8.00 |
| ☐ 671 Bill Voss SP | 5.00 | 12.00 |
| ☐ 672 Ed Crosby SP RC | 5.00 | 12.00 |
| ☐ 673 Gerry Janeski SP RC | 5.00 | 12.00 |
| ☐ 674 Montreal Expos TC | 5.00 | 12.00 |
| ☐ 675 Dave Boswell | 3.00 | 8.00 |

| | | |
|---|---|---|
| ☐ 676 Tommie Reynolds | 3.00 | 8.00 |
| ☐ 677 Jack DiLauro SP | 5.00 | 12.00 |
| ☐ 678 George Thomas | 3.00 | 8.00 |
| ☐ 679 Don O'Riley | 3.00 | 8.00 |
| ☐ 680 Don Mincher SP | 5.00 | 12.00 |
| ☐ 681 Bill Butler | 3.00 | 8.00 |
| ☐ 682 Terry Harmon | 3.00 | 8.00 |
| ☐ 683 Bill Burbach SP | 5.00 | 12.00 |
| ☐ 684 Curt Motton | 3.00 | 8.00 |
| ☐ 685 Moe Drabowsky | 3.00 | 8.00 |
| ☐ 686 Chico Ruiz SP | 5.00 | 12.00 |
| ☐ 687 Ron Taylor SP | 5.00 | 12.00 |
| ☐ 688 S.Anderson MG SP | 12.50 | 30.00 |
| ☐ 689 Frank Baker | 3.00 | 8.00 |
| ☐ 690 Bob Moose | 3.00 | 8.00 |
| ☐ 691 Bobby Heise | 3.00 | 8.00 |
| ☐ 692 Haydel/Moret/Twitchell SP RC | 5.00 | 12.00 |
| ☐ 693 Jose Pena SP | 5.00 | 12.00 |
| ☐ 694 Rick Renick SP | 5.00 | 12.00 |
| ☐ 695 Joe Niekro | 5.00 | 12.00 |
| ☐ 696 Jerry Morales | 3.00 | 8.00 |
| ☐ 697 Rickey Clark SP | 5.00 | 12.00 |
| ☐ 698 Milwaukee Brewers TC SP | 8.00 | 20.00 |
| ☐ 699 Jim Britton | 3.00 | 8.00 |
| ☐ 700 Boog Powell SP | 10.00 | 25.00 |
| ☐ 701 Bob Garibaldi | 3.00 | 8.00 |
| ☐ 702 Milt Ramirez RC | 3.00 | 8.00 |
| ☐ 703 Mike Kekich | 3.00 | 8.00 |
| ☐ 704 J.C. Martin SP | 5.00 | 12.00 |
| ☐ 705 Dick Selma SP | 5.00 | 12.00 |
| ☐ 706 Joe Foy SP | 5.00 | 12.00 |
| ☐ 707 Fred Lasher | 3.00 | 8.00 |
| ☐ 708 Russ Nagelson SP | 5.00 | 12.00 |
| ☐ 709 Baker/Baylor/Pac SP RC | 40.00 | 80.00 |
| ☐ 710 Sonny Siebert | 3.00 | 8.00 |
| ☐ 711 Larry Stahl SP | 5.00 | 12.00 |
| ☐ 712 Jose Martinez | 3.00 | 8.00 |
| ☐ 713 Mike Marshall SP | 6.00 | 15.00 |
| ☐ 714 Dick Williams MG SP | 6.00 | 15.00 |
| ☐ 715 Horace Clarke SP | 6.00 | 15.00 |
| ☐ 716 Dave Leonhard | 3.00 | 8.00 |
| ☐ 717 Tommie Aaron SP | 5.00 | 12.00 |
| ☐ 718 Billy Wynne | 3.00 | 8.00 |
| ☐ 719 Jerry May SP | 5.00 | 12.00 |
| ☐ 720 Matty Alou | 5.00 | 12.00 |
| ☐ 721 John Morris | 3.00 | 8.00 |
| ☐ 722 Houston Astros TC SP | 8.00 | 20.00 |
| ☐ 723 Vicente Romo SP | 5.00 | 12.00 |
| ☐ 724 Tom Tischinski SP | 5.00 | 12.00 |
| ☐ 725 Gary Gentry SP | 5.00 | 12.00 |
| ☐ 726 Paul Popovich | 3.00 | 8.00 |
| ☐ 727 Ray Lamb SP | 5.00 | 12.00 |
| ☐ 728 Redmond/Lampard/Williams SP | 3.00 | 8.00 |
| ☐ 729 Dick Billings SP | 3.00 | 8.00 |
| ☐ 730 Jim Rooker | 3.00 | 8.00 |
| ☐ 731 Jim Qualls SP | 5.00 | 12.00 |
| ☐ 732 Bob Reed | 3.00 | 8.00 |
| ☐ 733 Lee Maye SP | 5.00 | 12.00 |
| ☐ 734 Rob Gardner SP | 5.00 | 12.00 |
| ☐ 735 Mike Shannon SP | 6.00 | 15.00 |
| ☐ 736 Mel Queen SP | 5.00 | 12.00 |
| ☐ 737 Preston Gomez MG SP | 5.00 | 12.00 |
| ☐ 738 Russ Gibson SP | 5.00 | 12.00 |
| ☐ 739 Barry Lersch SP | 5.00 | 12.00 |
| ☐ 740 Luis Aparicio SP | 12.50 | 30.00 |
| ☐ 741 Skip Guinn | 3.00 | 8.00 |
| ☐ 742 Kansas City Royals TC | 5.00 | 12.00 |
| ☐ 743 John O'Donoghue SP | 5.00 | 12.00 |
| ☐ 744 Chuck Manuel SP | 5.00 | 12.00 |
| ☐ 745 Sandy Alomar SP | 5.00 | 12.00 |
| ☐ 746 Andy Kosco | 3.00 | 8.00 |
| ☐ 747 Severinsen/Spinks/Moore RC | 5.00 | 12.00 |
| ☐ 748 John Purdin SP | 5.00 | 12.00 |
| ☐ 749 Ken Szotkiewicz RC | 3.00 | 8.00 |
| ☐ 750 Denny McLain SP | 10.00 | 25.00 |
| ☐ 751 Al Weis SP | 5.00 | 12.00 |
| ☐ 752 Dick Drago | 5.00 | 12.00 |

## 1972 Topps

| | | |
|---|---|---|
| ☐ COMPLETE SET (787) | 750.00 | 1500.00 |
| ☐ COMMON CARD (1-132) | .25 | .60 |
| ☐ COMMON CARD (133-263) | .40 | 1.00 |
| ☐ COMMON CARD (264-394) | .50 | 1.25 |
| ☐ COMMON CARD (395-525) | .60 | 1.50 |
| ☐ COMMON CARD (526-656) | 1.50 | 4.00 |
| ☐ COMMON CARD (657-787) | 5.00 | 8.00 |
| ☐ WRAPPER (10-CENT) | 6.00 | 15.00 |
| ☐ 1 Pittsburgh Pirates TC | 3.00 | 8.00 |

CARDINALS — BOB GIBSON

| | | |
|---|---|---|
| ☐ 2 Ray Culp | .25 | .60 |
| ☐ 3 Bob Tolan | .25 | .60 |
| ☐ 4 Checklist 1-132 | 2.50 | 6.00 |
| ☐ 5 John Bateman | .25 | .60 |
| ☐ 6 Fred Scherman | .25 | .60 |
| ☐ 7 Enzo Hernandez | .25 | .60 |
| ☐ 8 Ron Swoboda | .50 | 1.25 |
| ☐ 9 Stan Williams | .25 | .60 |
| ☐ 10 Amos Otis | .50 | 1.25 |
| ☐ 11 Bobby Valentine | .50 | 1.25 |
| ☐ 12 Jose Cardenal | .25 | .60 |
| ☐ 13 Joe Grzenda | .25 | .60 |
| ☐ 14 Koegel/Anderson/Twitchell RC | .25 | .60 |
| ☐ 15 Walt Williams | .25 | .60 |
| ☐ 16 Mike Jorgensen | .25 | .60 |
| ☐ 17 Dave Duncan | .50 | 1.25 |
| ☐ 18A Juan Pizarro Yellow | .25 | .60 |
| ☐ 18B Juan Pizarro Green | 2.00 | 5.00 |
| ☐ 19 Billy Cowan | .25 | .60 |
| ☐ 20 Don Wilson | .25 | .60 |
| ☐ 21 Atlanta Braves TC | .60 | 1.50 |
| ☐ 22 Rob Gardner | .25 | .60 |
| ☐ 23 Ted Kubiak | .25 | .60 |
| ☐ 24 Ted Ford | .25 | .60 |
| ☐ 25 Bill Singer | .25 | .60 |
| ☐ 26 Andy Etchebarren | .25 | .60 |
| ☐ 27 Bob Johnson | .25 | .60 |
| ☐ 28 Gebhard/Brye Haydel RC | .25 | .60 |
| ☐ 29A Bill Bonham Yellow RC | .25 | .60 |
| ☐ 29B Bill Bonham Green | 2.00 | 5.00 |
| ☐ 30 Rico Petrocelli | .50 | 1.25 |
| ☐ 31 Cleon Jones | .25 | .60 |
| ☐ 32 Cleon Jones IA | .25 | .60 |
| ☐ 33 Billy Martin MG | 1.50 | 4.00 |
| ☐ 34 Billy Martin IA | 1.00 | 2.50 |
| ☐ 35 Jerry Johnson | .25 | .60 |
| ☐ 36 Jerry Johnson IA | .25 | .60 |
| ☐ 37 Carl Yastrzemski | 4.00 | 10.00 |
| ☐ 38 Carl Yastrzemski IA | 3.00 | 8.00 |
| ☐ 39 Bob Barton | .25 | .60 |
| ☐ 40 Bob Barton IA | .25 | .60 |
| ☐ 41 Tommy Davis | .50 | 1.25 |
| ☐ 42 Tommy Davis IA | .25 | .60 |
| ☐ 43 Rick Wise | .50 | 1.25 |
| ☐ 44 Rick Wise IA | .25 | .60 |
| ☐ 45A Glenn Beckert Yellow | .50 | 1.25 |
| ☐ 45B Glenn Beckert Green | 2.00 | 5.00 |
| ☐ 46 Glenn Beckert IA | .25 | .60 |
| ☐ 47 John Ellis | .25 | .60 |
| ☐ 48 John Ellis IA | .25 | .60 |
| ☐ 49 Willie Mays | 12.50 | 40.00 |
| ☐ 50 Willie Mays IA | 8.00 | 20.00 |
| ☐ 51 Harmon Killebrew | 3.00 | 8.00 |
| ☐ 52 Harmon Killebrew IA | 1.50 | 4.00 |
| ☐ 53 Bud Harrelson | .50 | 1.25 |
| ☐ 54 Bud Harrelson IA | .25 | .60 |
| ☐ 55 Clyde Wright | .25 | .60 |
| ☐ 56 Rich Chiles RC | .25 | .60 |
| ☐ 57 Bob Oliver | .25 | .60 |
| ☐ 58 Ernie McAnally | .25 | .60 |
| ☐ 59 Fred Stanley RC | .25 | .60 |
| ☐ 60 Manny Sanguillen | .50 | 1.25 |
| ☐ 61 Hooten/Hisler/Stephenson RC | .50 | 1.25 |
| ☐ 62 Angel Mangual | .25 | .60 |
| ☐ 63 Duke Sims | .25 | .60 |
| ☐ 64 Pete Broberg RC | .25 | .60 |
| ☐ 65 Cesar Cedeno | .50 | 1.25 |
| ☐ 66 Ray Corbin RC | .25 | .60 |
| ☐ 67 Red Schoendienst MG | 1.00 | 2.50 |
| ☐ 68 Jim York RC | .25 | .60 |
| ☐ 69 Roger Freed | .25 | .60 |
| ☐ 70 Mike Cuellar | .50 | 1.25 |
| ☐ 71 California Angels TC | .60 | 1.50 |
| ☐ 72 Bruce Kison RC | .25 | .60 |

# 388 / 1972 Topps

|  |  | | |
|---|---|---|---|
| 73 | Steve Huntz | .25 | .60 |
| 74 | Cecil Upshaw | .25 | .60 |
| 75 | Bert Campaneris | .50 | 1.25 |
| 76 | Don Carrithers RC | .25 | .60 |
| 77 | Ron Theobald RC | .25 | .60 |
| 78 | Steve Arlin RC | .25 | .60 |
| 79 | C.Fisk RC/C.Cooper RC | 20.00 | 50.00 |
| 80 | Tony Perez | 1.50 | 4.00 |
| 81 | Mike Hedlund | .25 | .60 |
| 82 | Ron Woods | .25 | .60 |
| 83 | Dalton Jones | .25 | .60 |
| 84 | Vince Colbert | .25 | .60 |
| 85 | Torre/Garr/Beckert LL | 1.00 | 2.50 |
| 86 | Oliva/Murcer/Rett LL | 1.00 | 2.50 |
| 87 | Torre/Stargell/Aaron LL | 1.50 | 4.00 |
| 88 | Kill/F.Rob/Smith LL | 1.50 | 4.00 |
| 89 | Stargell/Aaron/May LL | 1.00 | 2.50 |
| 90 | Melton/Cash/Jackson LL | 1.00 | 2.50 |
| 91 | Seaver/Roberts/Wilson LL | 1.00 | 2.50 |
| 92 | Blue/Wood/Palmer LL | 1.00 | 2.50 |
| 93 | Jenkins/Carlton/Seaver LL | 1.50 | 4.00 |
| 94 | Lolich/Blue/Wood LL | 1.00 | 2.50 |
| 95 | Seaver/Jenkins/Stone LL | 1.00 | 2.50 |
| 96 | Lolich/Blue/Coleman LL | 1.00 | 2.50 |
| 97 | Tom Kelley | .25 | .60 |
| 98 | Chuck Tanner MG | .50 | 1.25 |
| 99 | Ross Grimsley RC | .25 | .60 |
| 100 | Frank Robinson | 3.00 | 8.00 |
| 101 | Grief/Richardt/Busse RC | 1.00 | 2.50 |
| 102 | Lloyd Allen | .25 | .60 |
| 103 | Checklist 133-263 | 2.50 | 6.00 |
| 104 | Toby Harrah RC | .50 | 1.25 |
| 105 | Gary Gentry | .25 | .60 |
| 106 | Milwaukee Brewers TC | .60 | 1.50 |
| 107 | Jose Cruz RC | .50 | 1.25 |
| 108 | Gary Wasilewski | .25 | .60 |
| 109 | Jerry May | .25 | .60 |
| 110 | Ron Hunt | .25 | .60 |
| 111 | Jim Grant | .25 | .60 |
| 112 | Greg Luzinski | .50 | 1.25 |
| 113 | Rogelio Moret | .25 | .60 |
| 114 | Bill Buckner | .50 | 1.25 |
| 115 | Jim Fregosi | .50 | 1.25 |
| 116 | Ed Farmer RC | .25 | .60 |
| 117A | Cleo James Yellow RC | .25 | .60 |
| 117B | Cleo James Green | 2.00 | 5.00 |
| 118 | Skip Lockwood | .25 | .60 |
| 119 | Marty Perez | .25 | .60 |
| 120 | Bill Freehan | .50 | 1.25 |
| 121 | Ed Sprague | .25 | .60 |
| 122 | Larry Bittner RC | .25 | .60 |
| 123 | Ed Acosta | .25 | .60 |
| 124 | Closter/Torres/Hambright RC | .25 | .60 |
| 125 | Dave Cash | .50 | 1.25 |
| 126 | Bart Johnson | .25 | .60 |
| 127 | Duffy Dyer | .25 | .60 |
| 128 | Eddie Watt | .25 | .60 |
| 129 | Charlie Fox MG | .25 | .60 |
| 130 | Bob Gibson | 3.00 | 8.00 |
| 131 | Jim Nettles | .25 | .60 |
| 132 | Joe Morgan | 2.50 | 6.00 |
| 133 | Joe Keough | .40 | 1.00 |
| 134 | Carl Morton | .40 | 1.00 |
| 135 | Vada Pinson | .75 | 2.00 |
| 136 | Darral Chaney | .40 | 1.00 |
| 137 | Dick Williams MG | .75 | 2.00 |
| 138 | Mike Kekich | .40 | 1.00 |
| 139 | Tim McCarver | .75 | 2.00 |
| 140 | Pat Dobson | .75 | 2.00 |
| 141 | Capra/Stanton/Matlack RC | .75 | 2.00 |
| 142 | Chris Chambliss RC | 1.50 | 4.00 |
| 143 | Garry Jestadt | .40 | 1.00 |
| 144 | Marty Pattin | .40 | 1.00 |
| 145 | Don Kessinger | .75 | 2.00 |
| 146 | Steve Kealey | .40 | 1.00 |
| 147 | Dave Kingman RC | 2.50 | 6.00 |
| 148 | Dick Billings | .40 | 1.00 |
| 149 | Gary Neibauer | .40 | 1.00 |
| 150 | Norm Cash | .75 | 2.00 |
| 151 | Jim Brewer | .40 | 1.00 |
| 152 | Gene Clines | .40 | 1.00 |
| 153 | Rick Auerbach RC | .40 | 1.00 |
| 154 | Ted Simmons | 1.50 | 4.00 |
| 155 | Larry Dierker | .40 | 1.00 |
| 156 | Minnesota Twins TC | .75 | 2.00 |
| 157 | Don Gullett | .40 | 1.00 |
| 158 | Jerry Kenney | .40 | 1.00 |
| 159 | John Boccabella | .40 | 1.00 |
| 160 | Andy Messersmith | .75 | 2.00 |
| 161 | Brock Davis | .40 | 1.00 |
| 162 | Bell/Porter/Reynolds RC | .75 | 2.00 |
| 163 | Tug McGraw | 1.50 | 4.00 |
| 164 | Tug McGraw IA | .75 | 2.00 |
| 165 | Chris Speier RC | .75 | 2.00 |
| 166 | Chris Speier IA | .40 | 1.00 |
| 167 | Deron Johnson | .40 | 1.00 |
| 168 | Deron Johnson IA | .40 | 1.00 |
| 169 | Vida Blue | 1.50 | 4.00 |
| 170 | Vida Blue IA | .75 | 2.00 |
| 171 | Darrell Evans | .75 | 2.00 |
| 172 | Darrell Evans IA | .75 | 2.00 |
| 173 | Clay Kirby | .40 | 1.00 |
| 174 | Clay Kirby IA | .40 | 1.00 |
| 175 | Tom Haller | .40 | 1.00 |
| 176 | Tom Haller IA | .40 | 1.00 |
| 177 | Paul Schaal | .40 | 1.00 |
| 178 | Paul Schaal IA | .40 | 1.00 |
| 179 | Dock Ellis | .40 | 1.00 |
| 180 | Dock Ellis IA | .40 | 1.00 |
| 181 | Ed Kranepool | .75 | 2.00 |
| 182 | Ed Kranepool IA | .40 | 1.00 |
| 183 | Bill Melton | .40 | 1.00 |
| 184 | Bill Melton IA | .40 | 1.00 |
| 185 | Ron Bryant | .40 | 1.00 |
| 186 | Ron Bryant IA | .40 | 1.00 |
| 187 | Gates Brown | .40 | 1.00 |
| 188 | Frank Lucchesi MG | .40 | 1.00 |
| 189 | Gene Tenace | .75 | 2.00 |
| 190 | Dave Giusti | .40 | 1.00 |
| 191 | Jeff Burroughs RC | 1.50 | 4.00 |
| 192 | Chicago Cubs TC | .75 | 2.00 |
| 193 | Kurt Bevacqua RC | .40 | 1.00 |
| 194 | Fred Norman | .40 | 1.00 |
| 195 | Orlando Cepeda | 2.50 | 6.00 |
| 196 | Mel Queen | .40 | 1.00 |
| 197 | Johnny Briggs | .40 | 1.00 |
| 198 | Hough/O'Brien/Strahler RC | 2.50 | 6.00 |
| 199 | Mike Fiore | .40 | 1.00 |
| 200 | Lou Brock | 3.00 | 8.00 |
| 201 | Phil Roof | .40 | 1.00 |
| 202 | Scipio Spinks | .40 | 1.00 |
| 203 | Ron Blomberg RC | .40 | 1.00 |
| 204 | Tommy Helms | .40 | 1.00 |
| 205 | Dick Drago | .40 | 1.00 |
| 206 | Dal Maxvill | .40 | 1.00 |
| 207 | Tom Egan | .40 | 1.00 |
| 208 | Milt Pappas | .75 | 2.00 |
| 209 | Joe Rudi | .75 | 2.00 |
| 210 | Denny McLain | .75 | 2.00 |
| 211 | Gary Sutherland | .40 | 1.00 |
| 212 | Grant Jackson | .40 | 1.00 |
| 213 | Parker/Kusnyer/Silverio RC | .40 | 1.00 |
| 214 | Mike McQueen | .40 | 1.00 |
| 215 | Alex Johnson | .75 | 2.00 |
| 216 | Joe Niekro | .75 | 2.00 |
| 217 | Roger Metzger | .40 | 1.00 |
| 218 | Eddie Kasko MG | .40 | 1.00 |
| 219 | Rennie Stennett RC | .75 | 2.00 |
| 220 | Jim Perry | .75 | 2.00 |
| 221 | NL Playoffs Bucs | .75 | 2.00 |
| 222 | AL Playoffs B.Robinson | 1.50 | 4.00 |
| 223 | Dave McNally WS | .75 | 2.00 |
| 224 | D.Johnson/M.Belanger WS | .75 | 2.00 |
| 225 | Manny Sanguillen WS | .75 | 2.00 |
| 226 | Roberto Clemente WS | 3.00 | 8.00 |
| 227 | Nellie Briles WS | .75 | 2.00 |
| 228 | F.Robinson/M.Sanguillen WS | .75 | 2.00 |
| 229 | Steve Blass WS | .75 | 2.00 |
| 230 | Pirates Celebrate WS | .75 | 2.00 |
| 231 | Casey Cox | .40 | 1.00 |
| 232 | Arnold/Barr/Rader RC | .40 | 1.00 |
| 233 | Jay Johnstone | .75 | 2.00 |
| 234 | Ron Taylor | .40 | 1.00 |
| 235 | Merv Rettenmund | .40 | 1.00 |
| 236 | Jim McGlothlin | .40 | 1.00 |
| 237 | New York Yankees TC | .75 | 2.00 |
| 238 | Leron Lee | .40 | 1.00 |
| 239 | Tom Timmermann | .40 | 1.00 |
| 240 | Richie Allen | .75 | 2.00 |
| 241 | Rollie Fingers | 2.50 | 6.00 |
| 242 | Don Mincher | .40 | 1.00 |
| 243 | Frank Linzy | .40 | 1.00 |
| 244 | Steve Braun RC | .40 | 1.00 |
| 245 | Tommie Agee | .75 | 2.00 |
| 246 | Tom Burgmeier | .40 | 1.00 |
| 247 | Milt May | .40 | 1.00 |
| 248 | Tom Bradley | .40 | 1.00 |
| 249 | Harry Walker MG | .40 | 1.00 |
| 250 | Boog Powell | .75 | 2.00 |
| 251 | Checklist 264-394 | 2.50 | 6.00 |
| 252 | Ken Reynolds | .40 | 1.00 |
| 253 | Sandy Alomar | .75 | 2.00 |
| 254 | Boots Day | .40 | 1.00 |
| 255 | Jim Lonborg | .75 | 2.00 |
| 256 | George Foster | .75 | 2.00 |
| 257 | Foor/Hosley/Jata RC | .40 | 1.00 |
| 258 | Randy Hundley | .40 | 1.00 |
| 259 | Sparky Lyle | .75 | 2.00 |
| 260 | Ralph Garr | .75 | 2.00 |
| 261 | Steve Mingori | .40 | 1.00 |
| 262 | San Diego Padres TC | .75 | 2.00 |
| 263 | Felipe Alou | .75 | 2.00 |
| 264 | Tommy John | .75 | 2.00 |
| 265 | Wes Parker | .75 | 2.00 |
| 266 | Bobby Bolin | .50 | 1.25 |
| 267 | Dave Concepcion | 1.50 | 4.00 |
| 268 | D.Anderson RC/C.Floethe RC | .50 | 1.25 |
| 269 | Don Hahn | .50 | 1.25 |
| 270 | Jim Palmer | 3.00 | 8.00 |
| 271 | Ken Rudolph | .50 | 1.25 |
| 272 | Mickey Rivers RC | .75 | 2.00 |
| 273 | Bobby Floyd | .50 | 1.25 |
| 274 | Al Severinsen | .50 | 1.25 |
| 275 | Cesar Tovar | .50 | 1.25 |
| 276 | Gene Mauch MG | .75 | 2.00 |
| 277 | Elliott Maddox | .50 | 1.25 |
| 278 | Dennis Higgins | .50 | 1.25 |
| 279 | Larry Brown | .50 | 1.25 |
| 280 | Willie McCovey | 2.50 | 6.00 |
| 281 | Bill Parsons RC | .50 | 1.25 |
| 282 | Houston Astros TC | .75 | 2.00 |
| 283 | Darrell Brandon | .50 | 1.25 |
| 284 | Ike Brown | .50 | 1.25 |
| 285 | Gaylord Perry | 2.50 | 6.00 |
| 286 | Gene Alley | .50 | 1.25 |
| 287 | Jim Hardin | .50 | 1.25 |
| 288 | Johnny Jeter | .50 | 1.25 |
| 289 | Syd O'Brien | .50 | 1.25 |
| 290 | Sonny Siebert | .50 | 1.25 |
| 291 | Hal McRae | .75 | 2.00 |
| 292 | Hal McRae IA | .50 | 1.25 |
| 293 | Dan Frisella | .50 | 1.25 |
| 294 | Dan Frisella IA | .50 | 1.25 |
| 295 | Dick Dietz | .50 | 1.25 |
| 296 | Dick Dietz IA | .50 | 1.25 |
| 297 | Claude Osteen | .75 | 2.00 |
| 298 | Claude Osteen IA | .50 | 1.25 |
| 299 | Hank Aaron | 12.50 | 40.00 |
| 300 | Hank Aaron IA | 8.00 | 20.00 |
| 301 | George Mitterwald | .50 | 1.25 |
| 302 | George Mitterwald IA | .50 | 1.25 |
| 303 | Joe Pepitone | .75 | 2.00 |
| 304 | Joe Pepitone IA | .50 | 1.25 |
| 305 | Ken Boswell | .50 | 1.25 |
| 306 | Ken Boswell IA | .50 | 1.25 |
| 307 | Steve Renko | .50 | 1.25 |
| 308 | Steve Renko IA | .50 | 1.25 |
| 309 | Roberto Clemente | 20.00 | 50.00 |
| 310 | Roberto Clemente IA | 10.00 | 25.00 |
| 311 | Clay Carroll | .50 | 1.25 |
| 312 | Clay Carroll IA | .50 | 1.25 |
| 313 | Luis Aparicio | 2.50 | 6.00 |
| 314 | Luis Aparicio IA | .75 | 2.00 |
| 315 | Paul Splittorff | .50 | 1.25 |
| 316 | Bibby/Roque/Guzman RC | .75 | 2.00 |
| 317 | Rich Hand | .50 | 1.25 |
| 318 | Sonny Jackson | .50 | 1.25 |
| 319 | Aurelio Rodriguez | .50 | 1.25 |
| 320 | Steve Blass | .75 | 2.00 |
| 321 | Joe Lahoud | .50 | 1.25 |
| 322 | Jose Pena | .50 | 1.25 |
| 323 | Earl Weaver MG | 1.50 | 4.00 |
| 324 | Mike Ryan | .50 | 1.25 |
| 325 | Mel Stottlemyre | .75 | 2.00 |
| 326 | Pat Kelly | .50 | 1.25 |
| 327 | Steve Stone RC | .75 | 2.00 |
| 328 | Boston Red Sox TC | .75 | 2.00 |
| 329 | Roy Foster | .50 | 1.25 |
| 330 | Jim Hunter | 2.50 | 6.00 |
| 331 | Stan Swanson IA | .50 | 1.25 |
| 332 | Buck Martinez | .50 | 1.25 |
| 333 | Steve Barber | .50 | 1.25 |
| 334 | Fahey/Mason Ragland RC | .50 | 1.25 |
| 335 | Bill Hands | .50 | 1.25 |

|  |  | | |
|---|---|---|---|
| 336 | Marty Martinez | .50 | 1.25 |
| 337 | Mike Kilkenny | .50 | 1.25 |
| 338 | Bob Grich | .75 | 2.00 |
| 339 | Ron Cook | .50 | 1.25 |
| 340 | Roy White | .75 | 2.00 |
| 341 | Joe Torre KP | .50 | 1.25 |
| 342 | Wilbur Wood KP | .50 | 1.25 |
| 343 | Willie Stargell KP | .75 | 2.00 |
| 344 | Dave McNally KP | .50 | 1.25 |
| 345 | Rick Wise KP | .50 | 1.25 |
| 346 | Jim Fregosi KP | .50 | 1.25 |
| 347 | Tom Seaver KP | 1.50 | 4.00 |
| 348 | Sal Bando KP | .50 | 1.25 |
| 349 | Al Fitzmorris | .50 | 1.25 |
| 350 | Frank Howard | .75 | 2.00 |
| 351 | House/Kester/Britton | .75 | 2.00 |
| 352 | Dave LaRoche | .50 | 1.25 |
| 353 | Art Shamsky | .50 | 1.25 |
| 354 | Tom Murphy | .50 | 1.25 |
| 355 | Bob Watson | .75 | 2.00 |
| 356 | Gerry Moses | .50 | 1.25 |
| 357 | Woody Fryman | .50 | 1.25 |
| 358 | Sparky Anderson MG | 1.50 | 4.00 |
| 359 | Don Pavletich | .50 | 1.25 |
| 360 | Dave Roberts | .50 | 1.25 |
| 361 | Mike Andrews | .50 | 1.25 |
| 362 | New York Mets TC | .75 | 2.00 |
| 363 | Ron Klimkowski | .50 | 1.25 |
| 364 | Johnny Callison | .75 | 2.00 |
| 365 | Dick Bosman | .50 | 1.25 |
| 366 | Jimmy Rosario RC | .50 | 1.25 |
| 367 | Ron Perranoski | .50 | 1.25 |
| 368 | Danny Thompson | .50 | 1.25 |
| 369 | Jim Lefebvre | .75 | 2.00 |
| 370 | Don Buford | .50 | 1.25 |
| 371 | Denny Lemaster | .50 | 1.25 |
| 372 | L.Clemons RC/M.Montgomery RC | .50 | 1.25 |
| 373 | John Mayberry | .75 | 2.00 |
| 374 | Jack Heidemann | .50 | 1.25 |
| 375 | Reggie Cleveland | .50 | 1.25 |
| 376 | Andy Kosco | .50 | 1.25 |
| 377 | Terry Harmon | .50 | 1.25 |
| 378 | Checklist 395-525 | 2.50 | 6.00 |
| 379 | Ken Berry | .50 | 1.25 |
| 380 | Earl Williams | .50 | 1.25 |
| 381 | Chicago White Sox TC | .75 | 2.00 |
| 382 | Joe Gibbon | .50 | 1.25 |
| 383 | Brant Alyea | .50 | 1.25 |
| 384 | Dave Campbell | .75 | 2.00 |
| 385 | Mickey Stanley | .75 | 2.00 |
| 386 | Jim Colborn | .50 | 1.25 |
| 387 | Horace Clarke | .75 | 2.00 |
| 388 | Charlie Williams RC | .50 | 1.25 |
| 389 | Bill Rigney MG | .50 | 1.25 |
| 390 | Willie Davis | .75 | 2.00 |
| 391 | Ken Sanders | .50 | 1.25 |
| 392 | F.Cambria/R.Zisk RC | .75 | 2.00 |
| 393 | Curt Motton | .50 | 1.25 |
| 394 | Ken Forsch | .75 | 2.00 |
| 395 | Matty Alou | .75 | 2.00 |
| 396 | Paul Lindblad | .60 | 1.50 |
| 397 | Philadelphia Phillies TC | .75 | 2.00 |
| 398 | Larry Hisle | .75 | 2.00 |
| 399 | Milt Wilcox | .75 | 2.00 |
| 400 | Tony Oliva | 1.50 | 4.00 |
| 401 | Jim Nash | .60 | 1.50 |
| 402 | Bobby Heise | .60 | 1.50 |
| 403 | John Cumberland | .60 | 1.50 |
| 404 | Jeff Torborg | .75 | 2.00 |
| 405 | Ron Fairly | .75 | 2.00 |
| 406 | George Hendrick RC | .75 | 2.00 |
| 407 | Chuck Taylor | .60 | 1.50 |
| 408 | Jim Northrup | .75 | 2.00 |
| 409 | Frank Baker | .60 | 1.50 |
| 410 | Ferguson Jenkins | 2.50 | 6.00 |
| 411 | Bob Montgomery | .60 | 1.50 |
| 412 | Dick Kelley | .60 | 1.50 |
| 413 | D.Eddy RC/D.Lemonds | .60 | 1.50 |
| 414 | Bob Miller | .60 | 1.50 |
| 415 | Cookie Rojas | .75 | 2.00 |
| 416 | Johnny Edwards | .60 | 1.50 |
| 417 | Tom Hall | .60 | 1.50 |
| 418 | Tom Shopay | .60 | 1.50 |
| 419 | Jim Spencer | .60 | 1.50 |
| 420 | Steve Carlton | 8.00 | 20.00 |
| 421 | Ellie Rodriguez | .60 | 1.50 |
| 422 | Ray Lamb | .60 | 1.50 |
| 423 | Oscar Gamble | .75 | 2.00 |
| 424 | Bill Gogolewski | .60 | 1.50 |
| 425 | Ken Singleton | .75 | 2.00 |
| 426 | Ken Singleton IA | .60 | 1.50 |
| 427 | Tito Fuentes | .60 | 1.50 |
| 428 | Tito Fuentes IA | .60 | 1.50 |
| 429 | Bob Robertson | .60 | 1.50 |
| 430 | Bob Robertson IA | .60 | 1.50 |
| 431 | Cito Gaston | .75 | 2.00 |
| 432 | Cito Gaston IA | .75 | 2.00 |
| 433 | Johnny Bench | 10.00 | 25.00 |
| 434 | Johnny Bench IA | 6.00 | 15.00 |
| 435 | Reggie Jackson | 12.50 | 30.00 |
| 436 | Reggie Jackson IA | 5.00 | 12.00 |
| 437 | Maury Wills | .75 | 2.00 |
| 438 | Maury Wills IA | .75 | 2.00 |
| 439 | Billy Williams | 2.50 | 6.00 |
| 440 | Billy Williams IA | 1.50 | 4.00 |
| 441 | Thurman Munson | 6.00 | 15.00 |
| 442 | Thurman Munson IA | 3.00 | 8.00 |
| 443 | Ken Henderson | .60 | 1.50 |
| 444 | Ken Henderson IA | .60 | 1.50 |
| 445 | Tom Seaver | 12.50 | 30.00 |
| 446 | Tom Seaver IA | 6.00 | 15.00 |
| 447 | Willie Stargell | 3.00 | 8.00 |
| 448 | Willie Stargell IA | 1.50 | 4.00 |
| 449 | Bob Lemon MG | .75 | 2.00 |
| 450 | Mickey Lolich | .75 | 2.00 |
| 451 | Tony LaRussa | 1.50 | 4.00 |
| 452 | Ed Herrmann | .60 | 1.50 |
| 453 | Barry Lersch | .60 | 1.50 |
| 454 | Oakland Athletics TC | .75 | 2.00 |
| 455 | Tommy Harper | .75 | 2.00 |
| 456 | Mark Belanger | .75 | 2.00 |
| 457 | Fast/Thomas/Ivie RC | .60 | 1.50 |
| 458 | Aurelio Monteagudo | .60 | 1.50 |
| 459 | Rick Renick | .60 | 1.50 |
| 460 | Al Downing | .60 | 1.50 |
| 461 | Tim Cullen | .60 | 1.50 |
| 462 | Rickey Clark | .60 | 1.50 |
| 463 | Bernie Carbo | .60 | 1.50 |
| 464 | Jim Roland | .60 | 1.50 |
| 465 | Gil Hodges MG | 1.50 | 4.00 |
| 466 | Norm Miller | .60 | 1.50 |
| 467 | Steve Kline | .60 | 1.50 |
| 468 | Richie Scheinblum | .60 | 1.50 |
| 469 | Ron Herbel | .60 | 1.50 |
| 470 | Ray Fosse | .60 | 1.50 |
| 471 | Luke Walker | .60 | 1.50 |
| 472 | Phil Gagliano | .60 | 1.50 |
| 473 | Dan McGinn | .60 | 1.50 |
| 474 | Baylor/Harrison/Oates RC | 6.00 | 15.00 |
| 475 | Gary Nolan | .75 | 2.00 |
| 476 | Lee Richard RC | .60 | 1.50 |
| 477 | Tom Phoebus | .60 | 1.50 |
| 478 | Checklist 526-656 | 2.50 | 6.00 |
| 479 | Don Shaw | .60 | 1.50 |
| 480 | Lee May | .75 | 2.00 |
| 481 | Billy Conigliaro | .75 | 2.00 |
| 482 | Joe Hoerner | .60 | 1.50 |
| 483 | Ken Suarez | .60 | 1.50 |
| 484 | Lum Harris MG | .60 | 1.50 |
| 485 | Phil Regan | .75 | 2.00 |
| 486 | John Lowenstein | .60 | 1.50 |
| 487 | Detroit Tigers TC | .75 | 2.00 |
| 488 | Mike Nagy | .60 | 1.50 |
| 489 | T.Humphrey RC/K.Lampard | .60 | 1.50 |
| 490 | Dave McNally | .75 | 2.00 |
| 491 | Lou Piniella KP | .75 | 2.00 |
| 492 | Mel Stottlemyre KP | .75 | 2.00 |
| 493 | Bob Bailey KP | .75 | 2.00 |
| 494 | Willie Horton KP | .75 | 2.00 |
| 495 | Bill Melton KP | .75 | 2.00 |
| 496 | Bud Harrelson KP | .75 | 2.00 |
| 497 | Jim Perry KP | .75 | 2.00 |
| 498 | Brooks Robinson KP | 1.50 | 4.00 |
| 499 | Vicente Romo | .60 | 1.50 |
| 500 | Joe Torre | 1.50 | 4.00 |
| 501 | Pete Hamm | .60 | 1.50 |
| 502 | Jackie Hernandez | .60 | 1.50 |
| 503 | Gary Peters | .60 | 1.50 |
| 504 | Ed Spiezio | .60 | 1.50 |
| 505 | Mike Marshall | .75 | 2.00 |
| 506 | Ley/Moyer/Tidrow RC | .60 | 1.50 |
| 507 | Fred Gladding | .60 | 1.50 |
| 508 | Elrod Hendricks | .60 | 1.50 |
| 509 | Don McMahon | .60 | 1.50 |
| 510 | Ted Williams MG | 5.00 | 12.00 |
| 511 | Tony Taylor | .75 | 2.00 |
| 512 | Paul Popovich | .60 | 1.50 |
| 513 | Lindy McDaniel | .75 | 2.00 |
| 514 | Ted Sizemore | .60 | 1.50 |
| 515 | Bert Blyleven | 1.50 | 4.00 |
| 516 | Oscar Brown | .60 | 1.50 |
| 517 | Ken Brett | .60 | 1.50 |
| 518 | Wayne Garrett | .60 | 1.50 |
| 519 | Ted Abernathy | .60 | 1.50 |
| 520 | Larry Bowa | .75 | 2.00 |
| 521 | Alan Foster | .60 | 1.50 |
| 522 | Los Angeles Dodgers TC | .75 | 2.00 |
| 523 | Chuck Dobson | .60 | 1.50 |
| 524 | E.Armbrister RC/M.Behney RC | .60 | 1.50 |
| 525 | Carlos May | .75 | 2.00 |
| 526 | Bob Bailey | 2.50 | 6.00 |
| 527 | Dave Leonhard | 1.50 | 4.00 |
| 528 | Ron Stone | 1.50 | 4.00 |
| 529 | Dave Nelson | 2.50 | 6.00 |
| 530 | Don Sutton | 5.00 | 12.00 |
| 531 | Freddie Patek | 2.50 | 6.00 |
| 532 | Fred Kendall RC | 1.50 | 4.00 |
| 533 | Ralph Houk MG | 2.50 | 6.00 |
| 534 | Jim Hickman | 1.50 | 4.00 |
| 535 | Ed Brinkman | 1.50 | 4.00 |
| 536 | Doug Rader | 2.50 | 6.00 |
| 537 | Bob Locker | 1.50 | 4.00 |
| 538 | Charlie Sands RC | 1.50 | 4.00 |
| 539 | Terry Forster RC | 2.50 | 6.00 |
| 540 | Felix Millan | 1.50 | 4.00 |
| 541 | Roger Repoz | 1.50 | 4.00 |
| 542 | Jack Billingham | 1.50 | 4.00 |
| 543 | Duane Josephson | 1.50 | 4.00 |
| 544 | Ted Martinez | 1.50 | 4.00 |
| 545 | Wayne Granger | 1.50 | 4.00 |
| 546 | Joe Hague | 1.50 | 4.00 |
| 547 | Cleveland Indians TC | 3.00 | 6.00 |
| 548 | Frank Reberger | 1.50 | 4.00 |
| 549 | Dave May | 1.50 | 4.00 |
| 550 | Brooks Robinson | 10.00 | 25.00 |
| 551 | Ollie Brown | 1.50 | 4.00 |
| 552 | Ollie Brown IA | 1.50 | 4.00 |
| 553 | Wilbur Wood | 2.50 | 6.00 |
| 554 | Wilbur Wood IA | 1.50 | 4.00 |
| 555 | Ron Santo | 3.00 | 8.00 |
| 556 | Ron Santo IA | 1.50 | 6.00 |
| 557 | John Odom | 1.50 | 4.00 |
| 558 | John Odom IA | 1.50 | 4.00 |
| 559 | Pete Rose | 20.00 | 50.00 |
| 560 | Pete Rose IA | 10.00 | 25.00 |
| 561 | Leo Cardenas | 1.50 | 4.00 |
| 562 | Leo Cardenas IA | 1.50 | 4.00 |
| 563 | Ray Sadecki | 1.50 | 4.00 |
| 564 | Ray Sadecki IA | 1.50 | 4.00 |
| 565 | Reggie Smith | 2.50 | 6.00 |
| 566 | Reggie Smith IA | 1.50 | 4.00 |
| 567 | Juan Marichal | 5.00 | 12.00 |
| 568 | Juan Marichal IA | 2.50 | 6.00 |
| 569 | Ed Kirkpatrick | 1.50 | 4.00 |
| 570 | Ed Kirkpatrick IA | 1.50 | 4.00 |
| 571 | Nate Colbert | 1.50 | 4.00 |
| 572 | Nate Colbert IA | 1.50 | 4.00 |
| 573 | Fritz Peterson | 1.50 | 4.00 |
| 574 | Fritz Peterson IA | 1.50 | 4.00 |
| 575 | Al Oliver | 3.00 | 8.00 |
| 576 | Leo Durocher MG | 2.50 | 6.00 |
| 577 | Mike Paul | 2.50 | 6.00 |
| 578 | Billy Grabarkewitz | 1.50 | 4.00 |
| 579 | Doyle Alexander RC | 2.50 | 6.00 |
| 580 | Lou Piniella | 2.50 | 6.00 |
| 581 | Wade Blasingame | 1.50 | 4.00 |
| 582 | Montreal Expos TC | 3.00 | 8.00 |
| 583 | Darold Knowles | 1.50 | 4.00 |
| 584 | Jerry McNertney | 1.50 | 4.00 |
| 585 | George Scott | 2.50 | 6.00 |
| 586 | Denis Menke | 1.50 | 4.00 |
| 587 | Billy Wilson | 1.50 | 4.00 |
| 588 | Jim Holt | 1.50 | 4.00 |
| 589 | Hal Lanier | 1.50 | 4.00 |
| 590 | Graig Nettles | 3.00 | 8.00 |
| 591 | Paul Casanova | 1.50 | 4.00 |
| 592 | Lew Krausse | 1.50 | 4.00 |
| 593 | Rich Morales | 1.50 | 4.00 |
| 594 | Jim Beauchamp | 1.50 | 4.00 |
| 595 | Nolan Ryan | 50.00 | 100.00 |
| 596 | Manny Mota | 2.50 | 6.00 |
| 597 | Jim Magnuson RC | 1.50 | 4.00 |
| 598 | Hal King | 2.50 | 6.00 |
| 599 | Billy Champion | 1.50 | 4.00 |

|  |  | | |
|---|------|------|------|
| 600 | Al Kaline | 10.00 | 25.00 |
| 601 | George Stone | 1.50 | 4.00 |
| 602 | Dave Bristol MG | 1.50 | 4.00 |
| 603 | Jim Ray | 1.50 | 4.00 |
| 604A | Checklist 657-787 Right Copy | 2.50 | 12.00 |
| 604B | Checklist 657-787 Left Copy | 5.00 | 12.00 |
| 605 | Nelson Briles | 2.50 | 6.00 |
| 606 | Luis Melendez | 1.50 | 4.00 |
| 607 | Frank Duffy | 1.50 | 4.00 |
| 608 | Mike Corkins | 1.50 | 4.00 |
| 609 | Tom Grieve | 2.50 | 6.00 |
| 610 | Bill Stoneman | 2.50 | 6.00 |
| 611 | Rich Reese | 1.50 | 4.00 |
| 612 | Joe Decker | 1.50 | 4.00 |
| 613 | Mike Ferraro | 1.50 | 4.00 |
| 614 | Ted Uhlaender | 1.50 | 4.00 |
| 615 | Steve Hargan | 1.50 | 4.00 |
| 616 | Joe Ferguson RC | 2.50 | 6.00 |
| 617 | Kansas City Royals TC | 3.00 | 8.00 |
| 618 | Rich Robertson | 1.50 | 4.00 |
| 619 | Rich McKinney | 1.50 | 4.00 |
| 620 | Phil Niekro | 5.00 | 12.00 |
| 621 | Commish Award | 3.00 | 8.00 |
| 622 | MVP Award | 3.00 | 8.00 |
| 623 | Cy Young Award | 3.00 | 8.00 |
| 624 | Minor Lg POY Award | 3.00 | 8.00 |
| 625 | Rookie of the Year | 3.00 | 8.00 |
| 626 | Babe Ruth Award | 3.00 | 8.00 |
| 627 | Moe Drabowsky | 1.50 | 4.00 |
| 628 | Terry Crowley | 1.50 | 4.00 |
| 629 | Paul Doyle | 1.50 | 4.00 |
| 630 | Rich Hebner | 2.50 | 6.00 |
| 631 | John Strohmayer | 1.50 | 4.00 |
| 632 | Mike Hegan | 1.50 | 4.00 |
| 633 | Jack Hiatt | 1.50 | 4.00 |
| 634 | Dick Woodson | 1.50 | 4.00 |
| 635 | Don Money | 2.50 | 6.00 |
| 636 | Bill Lee | 2.50 | 6.00 |
| 637 | Preston Gomez MG | 1.50 | 4.00 |
| 638 | Ken Wright | 1.50 | 4.00 |
| 639 | J.C. Martin | 1.50 | 4.00 |
| 640 | Joe Coleman | 1.50 | 4.00 |
| 641 | Mike Lum | 1.50 | 4.00 |
| 642 | Dennis Riddleberger RC | 1.50 | 4.00 |
| 643 | Russ Gibson | 1.50 | 4.00 |
| 644 | Bernie Allen | 1.50 | 4.00 |
| 645 | Jim Maloney | 2.50 | 6.00 |
| 646 | Chico Salmon | 1.50 | 4.00 |
| 647 | Bob Moose | 1.50 | 4.00 |
| 648 | Jim Lyttle | 1.50 | 4.00 |
| 649 | Pete Richert | 1.50 | 4.00 |
| 650 | Sal Bando | 2.50 | 6.00 |
| 651 | Cincinnati Reds TC | 3.00 | 8.00 |
| 652 | Marcelino Lopez | 1.50 | 4.00 |
| 653 | Jim Fairey | 1.50 | 4.00 |
| 654 | Horacio Pina | 2.50 | 6.00 |
| 655 | Jerry Grote | 1.50 | 4.00 |
| 656 | Rudy May | 1.50 | 4.00 |
| 657 | Bobby Wine | 5.00 | 12.00 |
| 658 | Steve Dunning | 5.00 | 12.00 |
| 659 | Bob Aspromonte | 5.00 | 12.00 |
| 660 | Paul Blair | 6.00 | 15.00 |
| 661 | Bill Virdon MG | 5.00 | 12.00 |
| 662 | Stan Bahnsen | 5.00 | 12.00 |
| 663 | Fran Healy RC | 6.00 | 15.00 |
| 664 | Bobby Knoop | 5.00 | 12.00 |
| 665 | Chris Short | 5.00 | 12.00 |
| 666 | Hector Torres | 5.00 | 12.00 |
| 667 | Ray Newman RC | 5.00 | 12.00 |
| 668 | Texas Rangers TC | 12.50 | 30.00 |
| 669 | Willie Crawford | 5.00 | 12.00 |
| 670 | Ken Holtzman | 6.00 | 15.00 |
| 671 | Don Clendenon | 6.00 | 15.00 |
| 672 | Archie Reynolds | 5.00 | 12.00 |
| 673 | Dave Marshall | 5.00 | 12.00 |
| 674 | John Kennedy | 5.00 | 12.00 |
| 675 | Pat Jarvis | 5.00 | 12.00 |
| 676 | Danny Cater | 5.00 | 12.00 |
| 677 | Ivan Murrell | 5.00 | 12.00 |
| 678 | Steve Luebber RC | 5.00 | 12.00 |
| 679 | B.Fenwick RC/B.Stinson | 5.00 | 12.00 |
| 680 | Dave Johnson | 6.00 | 15.00 |
| 681 | Bobby Pfeil | 5.00 | 12.00 |
| 682 | Mike McCormick | 6.00 | 15.00 |
| 683 | Steve Hovley | 5.00 | 12.00 |
| 684 | Hal Breeden RC | 5.00 | 12.00 |
| 685 | Joel Horlen | 5.00 | 12.00 |
| 686 | Steve Garvey | 12.50 | 40.00 |
| 687 | Del Unser | 5.00 | 12.00 |
| 688 | St. Louis Cardinals TC | 8.00 | 20.00 |
| 689 | Eddie Fisher | 5.00 | 12.00 |
| 690 | Willie Montanez | 6.00 | 15.00 |
| 691 | Curt Blefary | 5.00 | 12.00 |
| 692 | Curt Blefary IA | 5.00 | 12.00 |
| 693 | Alan Gallagher | 5.00 | 12.00 |
| 694 | Alan Gallagher IA | 5.00 | 12.00 |
| 695 | Rod Carew | 20.00 | 50.00 |
| 696 | Rod Carew IA | 12.50 | 30.00 |
| 697 | Jerry Koosman | 6.00 | 15.00 |
| 698 | Jerry Koosman IA | 6.00 | 15.00 |
| 699 | Bobby Murcer | 6.00 | 15.00 |
| 700 | Bobby Murcer IA | 6.00 | 15.00 |
| 701 | Jose Pagan | 5.00 | 12.00 |
| 702 | Jose Pagan IA | 5.00 | 12.00 |
| 703 | Doug Griffin | 5.00 | 12.00 |
| 704 | Doug Griffin IA | 5.00 | 12.00 |
| 705 | Pat Corrales | 6.00 | 15.00 |
| 706 | Pat Corrales IA | 5.00 | 12.00 |
| 707 | Tim Foli | 5.00 | 12.00 |
| 708 | Tim Foli IA | 5.00 | 12.00 |
| 709 | Jim Kaat | 6.00 | 15.00 |
| 710 | Jim Kaat IA | 5.00 | 12.00 |
| 711 | Bobby Bonds | 8.00 | 20.00 |
| 712 | Bobby Bonds IA | 6.00 | 15.00 |
| 713 | Gene Michael | 8.00 | 20.00 |
| 714 | Gene Michael IA | 5.00 | 12.00 |
| 715 | Mike Epstein | 5.00 | 12.00 |
| 716 | Jesus Alou | 5.00 | 12.00 |
| 717 | Bruce Dal Canton | 5.00 | 12.00 |
| 718 | Del Rice MG | 5.00 | 12.00 |
| 719 | Cesar Geronimo | 5.00 | 12.00 |
| 720 | Sam McDowell | 6.00 | 15.00 |
| 721 | Eddie Leon | 5.00 | 12.00 |
| 722 | Bill Sudakis | 5.00 | 12.00 |
| 723 | Al Santorini | 5.00 | 12.00 |
| 724 | Curtis/Hinton/Scott RC | 5.00 | 12.00 |
| 725 | Dick McAuliffe | 6.00 | 15.00 |
| 726 | Dick Selma | 5.00 | 12.00 |
| 727 | Jose Laboy | 5.00 | 12.00 |
| 728 | Gail Hopkins | 5.00 | 12.00 |
| 729 | Bob Veale | 6.00 | 15.00 |
| 730 | Rick Monday | 6.00 | 15.00 |
| 731 | Baltimore Orioles TC | 8.00 | 20.00 |
| 732 | George Culver | 5.00 | 12.00 |
| 733 | Jim Ray Hart | 6.00 | 15.00 |
| 734 | Bob Burda | 5.00 | 12.00 |
| 735 | Diego Segui | 5.00 | 12.00 |
| 736 | Bill Russell | 6.00 | 15.00 |
| 737 | Len Randle RC | 6.00 | 15.00 |
| 738 | Jim Merritt | 5.00 | 12.00 |
| 739 | Don Mason | 5.00 | 12.00 |
| 740 | Rico Carty | 6.00 | 15.00 |
| 741 | Hutton/Milner/Miller RC | 6.00 | 15.00 |
| 742 | Jim Rooker | 5.00 | 12.00 |
| 743 | Cesar Gutierrez | 5.00 | 12.00 |
| 744 | Jim Slaton RC | 6.00 | 15.00 |
| 745 | Julian Javier | 6.00 | 15.00 |
| 746 | Lowell Palmer | 5.00 | 12.00 |
| 747 | Jim Stewart | 5.00 | 12.00 |
| 748 | Phil Hennigan | 5.00 | 12.00 |
| 749 | Walt Alston MG | 8.00 | 20.00 |
| 750 | Willie Horton | 6.00 | 15.00 |
| 751 | Steve Carlton TR | 12.50 | 40.00 |
| 752 | Joe Morgan TR | 12.50 | 40.00 |
| 753 | Denny McLain TR | 8.00 | 20.00 |
| 754 | Frank Robinson TR | 12.50 | 40.00 |
| 755 | Jim Fregosi TR | 6.00 | 15.00 |
| 756 | Rick Wise TR | 6.00 | 15.00 |
| 757 | Jose Cardenal TR | 5.00 | 12.00 |
| 758 | Gil Garrido | 5.00 | 12.00 |
| 759 | Chris Cannizzaro | 5.00 | 12.00 |
| 760 | Bill Mazeroski | 10.00 | 25.00 |
| 761 | Oglivie/Cey/Williams RC | 10.00 | 25.00 |
| 762 | Wayne Simpson | 5.00 | 12.00 |
| 763 | Ron Hansen | 5.00 | 12.00 |
| 764 | Dusty Baker | 8.00 | 20.00 |
| 765 | Ken McMullen | 5.00 | 12.00 |
| 766 | Steve Hamilton | 5.00 | 12.00 |
| 767 | Tom McCraw | 6.00 | 15.00 |
| 768 | Denny Doyle | 5.00 | 12.00 |
| 769 | Jack Aker | 5.00 | 12.00 |
| 770 | Jim Wynn | 6.00 | 15.00 |
| 771 | San Francisco Giants TC | 8.00 | 20.00 |
| 772 | Ken Tatum | 5.00 | 12.00 |
| 773 | Ron Brand | 5.00 | 12.00 |
| 774 | Luis Alvarado | 5.00 | 12.00 |
| 775 | Jerry Reuss | 6.00 | 15.00 |
| 776 | Bill Voss | 5.00 | 12.00 |
| 777 | Hoyt Wilhelm | 10.00 | 25.00 |
| 778 | Albury/Dempsey/Strickland RC | 8.00 | 20.00 |
| 779 | Tony Cloninger | 5.00 | 12.00 |
| 780 | Dick Green | 5.00 | 12.00 |
| 781 | Jim McAndrew | 5.00 | 12.00 |
| 782 | Larry Stahl | 5.00 | 12.00 |
| 783 | Les Cain | 5.00 | 12.00 |
| 784 | Ken Aspromonte | 5.00 | 12.00 |
| 785 | Vic Davalillo | 5.00 | 12.00 |
| 786 | Chuck Brinkman | 5.00 | 12.00 |
| 787 | Ron Reed | 6.00 | 15.00 |

## 1973 Topps

AL KALINE
DETROIT TIGERS OUTFIELD

|  |  | | |
|---|------|------|------|
| | COMPLETE SET (660) | 350.00 | 700.00 |
| | COMMON CARD (1-264) | .20 | .50 |
| | COMMON CARD (265-396) | .30 | .75 |
| | COMMON CARD (397-528) | .50 | 1.25 |
| | COMMON CARD (529-660) | 1.25 | 3.00 |
| | WRAPPER (10-CENT, BAT) | 6.00 | 15.00 |
| | WRAPPER (10-CENT) | 6.00 | 15.00 |
| 1 | Ruth/Aaron/Mays HR | 12.50 | 40.00 |
| 2 | Rich Hebner | .60 | 1.50 |
| 3 | Jim Lonborg | .60 | 1.50 |
| 4 | John Milner | .20 | .50 |
| 5 | Ed Brinkman | .20 | .50 |
| 6 | Mac Scarce RC | .20 | .50 |
| 7 | Texas Rangers TC | .75 | 2.00 |
| 8 | Tom Hall | .20 | .50 |
| 9 | Johnny Oates | .60 | 1.50 |
| 10 | Don Sutton | 1.50 | 4.00 |
| 11 | Chris Chambliss UER | .60 | 1.50 |
| 12A | Don Zimmer MG wo Ear | 1.25 | 3.00 |
| 12B | Don Zimmer MG w/Ear | .30 | .75 |
| 13 | George Hendrick | .60 | 1.50 |
| 14 | Sonny Siebert | .20 | .50 |
| 15 | Ralph Garr | .60 | 1.50 |
| 16 | Steve Braun | .20 | .50 |
| 17 | Fred Gladding | .20 | .50 |
| 18 | Leroy Stanton | .20 | .50 |
| 19 | Tim Foli | .20 | .50 |
| 20 | Stan Bahnsen | .20 | .50 |
| 21 | Randy Hundley | .60 | 1.50 |
| 22 | Ted Abernathy | .20 | .50 |
| 23 | Dave Kingman | .60 | 1.50 |
| 24 | Al Santorini | .20 | .50 |
| 25 | Roy White | .60 | 1.50 |
| 26 | Pittsburgh Pirates TC | .75 | 2.00 |
| 27 | Bill Gogolewski | .20 | .50 |
| 28 | Hal McRae | .60 | 1.50 |
| 29 | Tony Taylor | .60 | 1.50 |
| 30 | Tug McGraw | .60 | 1.50 |
| 31 | Buddy Bell RC | 1.00 | 2.50 |
| 32 | Fred Norman | .20 | .50 |
| 33 | Jim Breazeale RC | .20 | .50 |
| 34 | Pat Dobson | .20 | .50 |
| 35 | Willie Davis | .60 | 1.50 |
| 36 | Steve Barber | .20 | .50 |
| 37 | Bill Robinson | .60 | 1.50 |
| 38 | Mike Epstein | .20 | .50 |
| 39 | Dave Roberts | .20 | .50 |
| 40 | Reggie Smith | .60 | 1.50 |
| 41 | Tom Walker RC | .20 | .50 |
| 42 | Mike Andrews | .20 | .50 |
| 43 | Randy Moffitt RC | .20 | .50 |
| 44 | Rick Monday | .60 | 1.50 |
| 45 | Ellie Rodriguez UER | .20 | .50 |
| 46 | Lindy McDaniel | .60 | 1.50 |
| 47 | Luis Melendez | .20 | .50 |
| 48 | Paul Splittorff | .20 | .50 |
| 49A | Frank Quilici MG Solid | 1.25 | 3.00 |
| 49B | Frank Quilici MG Natural | .30 | .75 |
| 50 | Roberto Clemente | 12.50 | 40.00 |

| # | Card | Lo | Hi |
|---|------|-----|------|
| 51 | Chuck Seelbach RC | .20 | .50 |
| 52 | Denis Menke | .20 | .50 |
| 53 | Steve Dunning | .20 | .50 |
| 54 | Checklist 1-132 | 1.25 | 3.00 |
| 55 | Jon Matlack | .60 | 1.50 |
| 56 | Merv Rettenmund | .20 | .50 |
| 57 | Derrel Thomas | .20 | .50 |
| 58 | Mike Paul | .20 | .50 |
| 59 | Steve Yeager RC | .60 | 1.50 |
| 60 | Ken Holtzman | .60 | 1.50 |
| 61 | B.Williams/R.Carew LL | 1.00 | 2.50 |
| 62 | J.Bench/D.Allen LL | 1.00 | 2.50 |
| 63 | J.Bench/D.Allen LL | 1.00 | 2.50 |
| 64 | L.Brock/Campaneris LL | .60 | 1.50 |
| 65 | S.Carlton/L.Tiant LL | .60 | 1.50 |
| 66 | Carlton/Perry/Wood LL | .60 | 1.50 |
| 67 | S.Carlton/N.Ryan LL | 10.00 | 25.00 |
| 68 | C.Carroll/S.Lyle LL | .60 | 1.50 |
| 69 | Phil Gagliano | .20 | .50 |
| 70 | Milt Pappas | .20 | .50 |
| 71 | Johnny Briggs | .20 | .50 |
| 72 | Ron Reed | .20 | .50 |
| 73 | Ed Herrmann | .20 | .50 |
| 74 | Billy Champion | .20 | .50 |
| 75 | Vada Pinson | .60 | 1.50 |
| 76 | Doug Rader | .20 | .50 |
| 77 | Mike Torrez | .60 | 1.50 |
| 78 | Richie Scheinblum | .20 | .50 |
| 79 | Jim Willoughby RC | .20 | .50 |
| 80 | Tony Oliva UER | 1.00 | 2.50 |
| 81A | W.Lockman MG w/Banks Solid | .60 | 1.50 |
| 81B | W.Lockman MG w/Banks Natural | .20 | .50 |
| 82 | Fritz Peterson | .20 | .50 |
| 83 | Leron Lee | .20 | .50 |
| 84 | Rollie Fingers | 1.50 | 4.00 |
| 85 | Ted Simmons | .60 | 1.50 |
| 86 | Tom McCraw | .20 | .50 |
| 87 | Ken Boswell | .20 | .50 |
| 88 | Mickey Stanley | .60 | 1.50 |
| 89 | Jack Billingham | .20 | .50 |
| 90 | Brooks Robinson | 3.00 | 8.00 |
| 91 | Los Angeles Dodgers TC | .75 | 2.00 |
| 92 | Jerry Bell | .20 | .50 |
| 93 | Jesus Alou | .20 | .50 |
| 94 | Dick Billings | .20 | .50 |
| 95 | Steve Blass | .60 | 1.50 |
| 96 | Doug Griffin | .20 | .50 |
| 97 | Willie Montanez | .20 | .50 |
| 98 | Dick Woodson | .20 | .50 |
| 99 | Carl Taylor | .20 | .50 |
| 100 | Hank Aaron | 12.50 | 40.00 |
| 101 | Ken Henderson | .20 | .50 |
| 102 | Rudy May | .20 | .50 |
| 103 | Celerino Sanchez RC | .20 | .50 |
| 104 | Reggie Cleveland | .20 | .50 |
| 105 | Carlos May | .20 | .50 |
| 106 | Terry Humphrey | .20 | .50 |
| 107 | Phil Hennigan | .20 | .50 |
| 108 | Bill Russell | .60 | 1.50 |
| 109 | Doyle Alexander | .60 | 1.50 |
| 110 | Bob Watson | .60 | 1.50 |
| 111 | Dave Nelson | .20 | .50 |
| 112 | Gary Ross | .20 | .50 |
| 113 | Jerry Grote | .20 | .50 |
| 114 | Lynn McGlothen RC | .20 | .50 |
| 115 | Ron Santo | .60 | 1.50 |
| 116A | Ralph Houk MG Solid | 1.25 | 3.00 |
| 116B | Ralph Houk MG Natural | .30 | .75 |
| 117 | Ramon Hernandez | .20 | .50 |
| 118 | John Mayberry | .60 | 1.50 |
| 119 | Larry Bowa | .60 | 1.50 |
| 120 | Joe Coleman | .20 | .50 |
| 121 | Dave Rader | .20 | .50 |
| 122 | Jim Strickland | .20 | .50 |
| 123 | Sandy Alomar | .60 | 1.50 |
| 124 | Jim Hardin | .20 | .50 |
| 125 | Ron Fairly | .60 | 1.50 |
| 126 | Jim Brewer | .20 | .50 |
| 127 | Milwaukee Brewers TC | .75 | 2.00 |
| 128 | Ted Sizemore | .20 | .50 |
| 129 | Terry Forster | .60 | 1.50 |
| 130 | Pete Rose | 12.50 | 30.00 |
| 131A | Eddie Kasko MG w/oEar | 1.25 | 3.00 |
| 131B | Eddie Kasko MG w/Ear | .30 | .75 |
| 132 | Matty Alou | .60 | 1.50 |
| 133 | Dave Roberts RC | .20 | .50 |
| 134 | Milt Wilcox RC | .60 | 1.50 |
| 135 | Lee May UER | .60 | 1.50 |
| 136A | Earl Weaver MG Orange | .60 | 1.50 |
| 136B | Earl Weaver MG Pale | 1.25 | 3.00 |
| 137 | Jim Beauchamp | .20 | .50 |
| 138 | Horacio Pina | .20 | .50 |
| 139 | Carmen Fanzone RC | .20 | .50 |
| 140 | Lou Piniella | 1.00 | 2.50 |
| 141 | Bruce Kison | .20 | .50 |
| 142 | Thurman Munson | 3.00 | 8.00 |
| 143 | John Curtis | .20 | .50 |
| 144 | Marty Perez | .20 | .50 |
| 145 | Bobby Bonds | 1.00 | 2.50 |
| 146 | Woodie Fryman | .20 | .50 |
| 147 | Mike Anderson | .20 | .50 |
| 148 | Dave Goltz RC | .20 | .50 |
| 149 | Ron Hunt | .20 | .50 |
| 150 | Wilbur Wood | .60 | 1.50 |
| 151 | Wes Parker | .60 | 1.50 |
| 152 | Dave May | .20 | .50 |
| 153 | Al Hrabosky | .60 | 1.50 |
| 154 | Jeff Torborg | .60 | 1.50 |
| 155 | Sal Bando | .60 | 1.50 |
| 156 | Cesar Geronimo | .20 | .50 |
| 157 | Denny Riddleberger | .20 | .50 |
| 158 | Houston Astros TC | .75 | 2.00 |
| 159 | Clito Gaston | .60 | 1.50 |
| 160 | Jim Palmer | 2.50 | 6.00 |
| 161 | Ted Martinez | .20 | .50 |
| 162 | Pete Broberg | .20 | .50 |
| 163 | Vic Davalillo | .20 | .50 |
| 164 | Monty Montgomery | .20 | .50 |
| 165 | Luis Aparicio | 1.50 | 4.00 |
| 166 | Terry Harmon | .20 | .50 |
| 167 | Steve Stone | .60 | 1.50 |
| 168 | Jim Northrup | .60 | 1.50 |
| 169 | Ron Schueler RC | .60 | 1.50 |
| 170 | Harmon Killebrew | 2.00 | 5.00 |
| 171 | Bernie Carbo | .20 | .50 |
| 172 | Steve Kline | .20 | .50 |
| 173 | Hal Breeden | .20 | .50 |
| 174 | Goose Gossage RC | 2.50 | 6.00 |
| 175 | Frank Robinson | 2.50 | 6.00 |
| 176 | Chuck Taylor | .20 | .50 |
| 177 | Bill Plummer RC | .20 | .50 |
| 178 | Don Rose RC | .20 | .50 |
| 179A | Dick Williams w/Ear | 1.50 | 4.00 |
| 179B | Dick Williams w/o Ear | .60 | 1.50 |
| 180 | Ferguson Jenkins | 1.50 | 4.00 |
| 181 | Jack Brohamer RC | .20 | .50 |
| 182 | Mike Caldwell RC | .60 | 1.50 |
| 183 | Don Buford | .20 | .50 |
| 184 | Jerry Koosman | .60 | 1.50 |
| 185 | Jim Wynn | .60 | 1.50 |
| 186 | Bill Fahey | .20 | .50 |
| 187 | Luke Walker | .20 | .50 |
| 188 | Cookie Rojas | .60 | 1.50 |
| 189 | Greg Luzinski | 1.00 | 2.50 |
| 190 | Bob Gibson | 3.00 | 8.00 |
| 191 | Detroit Tigers TC | 1.00 | 2.50 |
| 192 | Pat Jarvis | .20 | .50 |
| 193 | Carlton Fisk | 4.00 | 10.00 |
| 194 | Jorge Orta RC | .20 | .50 |
| 195 | Clay Carroll | .20 | .50 |
| 196 | Ken McMullen | .20 | .50 |
| 197 | Ed Goodson RC | .20 | .50 |
| 198 | Horace Clarke | .20 | .50 |
| 199 | Bert Blyleven | 1.00 | 2.50 |
| 200 | Billy Williams | 1.50 | 4.00 |
| 201 | George Hendrick ALCS | .60 | 1.50 |
| 202 | George Foster NLCS | .60 | 1.50 |
| 203 | Gene Tenace WS | .60 | 1.50 |
| 204 | A's Two Straight WS | .60 | 1.50 |
| 205 | Tony Perez WS | 1.00 | 2.50 |
| 206 | Gene Tenace WS | .60 | 1.50 |
| 207 | Blue Moon Odom WS | .60 | 1.50 |
| 208 | Johnny Bench WS | 2.00 | 5.00 |
| 209 | Bert Campaneris WS | .60 | 1.50 |
| 210 | A's Win WS | .60 | 1.50 |
| 211 | Balor Moore | .20 | .50 |
| 212 | Joe Lahoud | .20 | .50 |
| 213 | Steve Garvey | 2.00 | 5.00 |
| 214 | Dave Hamilton RC | .20 | .50 |
| 215 | Dusty Baker | 1.00 | 2.50 |
| 216 | Toby Harrah | .60 | 1.50 |
| 217 | Don Wilson | .20 | .50 |
| 218 | Aurelio Rodriguez | .20 | .50 |
| 219 | St. Louis Cardinals TC | 1.00 | 2.50 |
| 220 | Nolan Ryan | 20.00 | 50.00 |
| 221 | Fred Kendall | .20 | .50 |
| 222 | Rob Gardner | .20 | .50 |
| 223 | Bud Harrelson | .60 | 1.50 |
| 224 | Bill Lee | .60 | 1.50 |
| 225 | Al Oliver | .60 | 1.50 |
| 226 | Ray Fosse | .20 | .50 |
| 227 | Wayne Twitchell | .20 | .50 |
| 228 | Bobby Darwin | .20 | .50 |
| 229 | Roric Harrison | .20 | .50 |
| 230 | Joe Morgan | 2.50 | 6.00 |
| 231 | Bill Parsons | .20 | .50 |
| 232 | Ken Singleton | .60 | 1.50 |
| 233 | Ed Kirkpatrick | .20 | .50 |
| 234 | Bill North RC | .20 | .50 |
| 235 | Jim Hunter | 1.50 | 4.00 |
| 236 | Tito Fuentes | .20 | .50 |
| 237A | Eddie Mathews MG w/Ear | .60 | 1.50 |
| 237B | Eddie Mathews MG w/o Ear | 1.25 | 3.00 |
| 238 | Tony Muser RC | .20 | .50 |
| 239 | Pete Richert | .20 | .50 |
| 240 | Bobby Murcer | .60 | 1.50 |
| 241 | Dwain Anderson | .20 | .50 |
| 242 | George Culver | .20 | .50 |
| 243 | California Angels TC | 1.00 | 2.50 |
| 244 | Ed Acosta | .20 | .50 |
| 245 | Carl Yastrzemski | 4.00 | 10.00 |
| 246 | Ken Sanders | .20 | .50 |
| 247 | Del Unser | .20 | .50 |
| 248 | Jerry Johnson | .20 | .50 |
| 249 | Larry Biittner | .20 | .50 |
| 250 | Manny Sanguillen | .60 | 1.50 |
| 251 | Roger Nelson | .20 | .50 |
| 252A | Charlie Fox MG Orange | 1.50 | 4.00 |
| 252B | Charlie Fox MG Pale | .60 | 1.50 |
| 253 | Mark Belanger | .60 | 1.50 |
| 254 | Bill Stoneman | .20 | .50 |
| 255 | Reggie Jackson | 6.00 | 15.00 |
| 256 | Chris Zachary | .20 | .50 |
| 257A | Yogi Berra MG Orange | 1.25 | 3.00 |
| 257B | Yogi Berra MG Pale | 2.00 | 5.00 |
| 258 | Tommy John | .60 | 1.50 |
| 259 | Jim Holt | .20 | .50 |
| 260 | Gary Nolan | .60 | 1.50 |
| 261 | Pat Kelly | .20 | .50 |
| 262 | Jack Aker | .20 | .50 |
| 263 | George Scott | .60 | 1.50 |
| 264 | Checklist 133-264 | 1.25 | 3.00 |
| 265 | Gene Michael | .60 | 1.50 |
| 266 | Mike Lum | .30 | .75 |
| 267 | Lloyd Allen | .30 | .75 |
| 268 | Jerry Morales | .30 | .75 |
| 269 | Tim McCarver | .60 | 1.50 |
| 270 | Luis Tiant | .60 | 1.50 |
| 271 | Tom Hutton | .30 | .75 |
| 272 | Ed Farmer | .30 | .75 |
| 273 | Chris Speier | .30 | .75 |
| 274 | Darold Knowles | .30 | .75 |
| 275 | Tony Perez | 1.50 | 4.00 |
| 276 | Joe Lovitto RC | .30 | .75 |
| 277 | Bob Miller | .30 | .75 |
| 278 | Baltimore Orioles TC | .60 | 1.50 |
| 279 | Mike Strahler | .30 | .75 |
| 280 | Al Kaline | 3.00 | 8.00 |
| 281 | Mike Jorgensen | .30 | .75 |
| 282 | Steve Hovley | .30 | .75 |
| 283 | Ray Sadecki | .30 | .75 |
| 284 | Glenn Borgmann RC | .30 | .75 |
| 285 | Don Kessinger | .60 | 1.50 |
| 286 | Frank Linzy | .30 | .75 |
| 287 | Eddie Leon | .30 | .75 |
| 288 | Gary Gentry | .30 | .75 |
| 289 | Bob Oliver | .30 | .75 |
| 290 | Cesar Cedeno | .60 | 1.50 |
| 291 | Rogelio Moret | .30 | .75 |
| 292 | Jose Cruz | .60 | 1.50 |
| 293 | Bernie Allen | .30 | .75 |
| 294 | Steve Arlin | .30 | .75 |
| 295 | Bert Campaneris | .60 | 1.50 |
| 296 | Sparky Anderson MG | 1.00 | 2.50 |
| 297 | Walt Williams | .30 | .75 |
| 298 | Ron Bryant | .30 | .75 |
| 299 | Ted Ford | .30 | .75 |
| 300 | Steve Carlton | 4.00 | 10.00 |
| 301 | Billy Grabarkewitz | .30 | .75 |
| 302 | Terry Crowley | .30 | .75 |
| 303 | Nelson Briles | .30 | .75 |
| 304 | Duke Sims | .30 | .75 |
| 305 | Willie Mays | 12.50 | 40.00 |
| 306 | Tom Burgmeier | .30 | .75 |

|  |  | | |
|---|---|---|---|
| 307 | Boots Day | .30 | .75 |
| 308 | Skip Lockwood | .30 | .75 |
| 309 | Paul Popovich | .30 | .75 |
| 310 | Dick Allen | .60 | 1.50 |
| 311 | Joe Decker | .30 | .75 |
| 312 | Oscar Brown | .30 | .75 |
| 313 | Jim Ray | .30 | .75 |
| 314 | Ron Swoboda | .60 | 1.50 |
| 315 | John Odom | .30 | .75 |
| 316 | San Diego Padres TC | .60 | 1.50 |
| 317 | Danny Cater | .30 | .75 |
| 318 | Jim McGlothlin | .30 | .75 |
| 319 | Jim Spencer | .30 | .75 |
| 320 | Lou Brock | 3.00 | 8.00 |
| 321 | Rich Hinton | .30 | .75 |
| 322 | Garry Maddox RC | .60 | 1.50 |
| 323 | Billy Martin MG | .60 | 1.50 |
| 324 | Al Downing | .30 | .75 |
| 325 | Boog Powell | .60 | 1.50 |
| 326 | Darrell Brandon | .30 | .75 |
| 327 | John Lowenstein | .30 | .75 |
| 328 | Bill Bonham | .30 | .75 |
| 329 | Ed Kranepool | .60 | 1.50 |
| 330 | Rod Carew | 3.00 | 8.00 |
| 331 | Carl Morton | .30 | .75 |
| 332 | John Felske RC | .30 | .75 |
| 333 | Gene Clines | .30 | .75 |
| 334 | Freddie Patek | .30 | .75 |
| 335 | Bob Tolan | .30 | .75 |
| 336 | Tom Bradley | .30 | .75 |
| 337 | Dave Duncan | .60 | 1.50 |
| 338 | Checklist 265-396 | 1.25 | 3.00 |
| 339 | Dick Tidrow | .30 | .75 |
| 340 | Nate Colbert | .30 | .75 |
| 341 | Jim Palmer KP | 1.00 | 2.50 |
| 342 | Sam McDowell KP | .30 | .75 |
| 343 | Bobby Murcer KP | .30 | .75 |
| 344 | Jim Hunter KP | 1.00 | 2.50 |
| 345 | Chris Speier KP | .30 | .75 |
| 346 | Gaylord Perry KP | .60 | 1.50 |
| 347 | Kansas City Royals TC | .60 | 1.50 |
| 348 | Rennie Stennett | .30 | .75 |
| 349 | Dick McAuliffe | .30 | .75 |
| 350 | Tom Seaver | 5.00 | 12.00 |
| 351 | Jimmy Stewart | .30 | .75 |
| 352 | Don Stanhouse RC | .30 | .75 |
| 353 | Steve Brye | .30 | .75 |
| 354 | Billy Parker | .30 | .75 |
| 355 | Mike Marshall | .60 | 1.50 |
| 356 | Chuck Tanner MG | 1.50 | 4.00 |
| 357 | Ross Grimsley | .30 | .75 |
| 358 | Jim Nettles | .30 | .75 |
| 359 | Cecil Upshaw | .30 | .75 |
| 360 | Joe Rudi UER | .60 | 1.50 |
| 361 | Fran Healy | .30 | .75 |
| 362 | Eddie Watt | .30 | .75 |
| 363 | Jackie Hernandez | .30 | .75 |
| 364 | Rick Wise | .30 | .75 |
| 365 | Rico Petrocelli | .60 | 1.50 |
| 366 | Brock Davis | .30 | .75 |
| 367 | Burt Hooton | .60 | 1.50 |
| 368 | Bill Buckner | .60 | 1.50 |
| 369 | Lerrin LaGrow | .30 | .75 |
| 370 | Willie Stargell | 2.00 | 5.00 |
| 371 | Mike Kekich | .30 | .75 |
| 372 | Oscar Gamble | .30 | .75 |
| 373 | Clyde Wright | .30 | .75 |
| 374 | Darrell Evans | .60 | 1.50 |
| 375 | Larry Dierker | .60 | 1.50 |
| 376 | Frank Duffy | .30 | .75 |
| 377 | Gene Mauch MG | 1.50 | 4.00 |
| 378 | Len Randle | .30 | .75 |
| 379 | Cy Acosta RC | .30 | .75 |
| 380 | Johnny Bench | 5.00 | 12.00 |
| 381 | Vicente Romo | .30 | .75 |
| 382 | Mike Hegan | .30 | .75 |
| 383 | Diego Segui | .30 | .75 |
| 384 | Don Baylor | 1.50 | 4.00 |
| 385 | Jim Perry | .60 | 1.50 |
| 386 | Don Money | .30 | .75 |
| 387 | Jim Barr | .30 | .75 |
| 388 | Ben Oglivie | .60 | 1.50 |
| 389 | New York Mets TC | 1.50 | 4.00 |
| 390 | Mickey Lolich | .60 | 1.50 |
| 391 | Lee Lacy RC | .60 | 1.50 |
| 392 | Dick Drago | .30 | .75 |
| 393 | Jose Cardenal | .30 | .75 |
| 394 | Sparky Lyle | .60 | 1.50 |
| 395 | Roger Metzger | .30 | .75 |
| 396 | Grant Jackson | .30 | .75 |
| 397 | Dave Cash | .50 | 1.25 |
| 398 | Rich Hand | .50 | 1.25 |
| 399 | George Foster | .75 | 2.00 |
| 400 | Gaylord Perry | 2.00 | 5.00 |
| 401 | Clyde Mashore | .50 | 1.25 |
| 402 | Jack Hiatt | .50 | 1.25 |
| 403 | Sonny Jackson | .50 | 1.25 |
| 404 | Chuck Brinkman | .50 | 1.25 |
| 405 | Cesar Tovar | .50 | 1.25 |
| 406 | Paul Lindblad | .50 | 1.25 |
| 407 | Felix Millan | .50 | 1.25 |
| 408 | Jim Colborn | .50 | 1.25 |
| 409 | Ivan Murrell | .50 | 1.25 |
| 410 | Willie McCovey | 2.50 | 6.00 |
| 411 | Ray Corbin | .50 | 1.25 |
| 412 | Manny Mota | .75 | 2.00 |
| 413 | Tom Timmermann | .50 | 1.25 |
| 414 | Ken Rudolph | .50 | 1.25 |
| 415 | Marty Pattin | .50 | 1.25 |
| 416 | Paul Schaal | .50 | 1.25 |
| 417 | Scipio Spinks | .50 | 1.25 |
| 418 | Bob Grich | .75 | 2.00 |
| 419 | Casey Cox | .50 | 1.25 |
| 420 | Tommie Agee | .75 | 2.00 |
| 421A | B.Winkles MG RC Orange | .60 | 1.50 |
| 421B | Bobby Winkles MG Pale | 1.25 | 3.00 |
| 422 | Bob Robertson | .50 | 1.25 |
| 423 | Johnny Jeter | .50 | 1.25 |
| 424 | Denny Doyle | .50 | 1.25 |
| 425 | Alex Johnson | .50 | 1.25 |
| 426 | Dave LaRoche | .50 | 1.25 |
| 427 | Rick Auerbach | .50 | 1.25 |
| 428 | Wayne Simpson | .50 | 1.25 |
| 429 | Jim Fairey | .50 | 1.25 |
| 430 | Vida Blue | .75 | 2.00 |
| 431 | Gerry Moses | .50 | 1.25 |
| 432 | Dan Frisella | .50 | 1.25 |
| 433 | Willie Horton | .75 | 2.00 |
| 434 | San Francisco Giants TC | 1.25 | 3.00 |
| 435 | Rico Carty | .75 | 2.00 |
| 436 | Jim McAndrew | .50 | 1.25 |
| 437 | John Kennedy | .50 | 1.25 |
| 438 | Enzo Hernandez | .50 | 1.25 |
| 439 | Eddie Fisher | .50 | 1.25 |
| 440 | Glenn Beckert | .50 | 1.25 |
| 441 | Gail Hopkins | .50 | 1.25 |
| 442 | Dick Dietz | .50 | 1.25 |
| 443 | Danny Thompson | .50 | 1.25 |
| 444 | Ken Brett | .75 | 2.00 |
| 445 | Ken Berry | .50 | 1.25 |
| 446 | Jerry Reuss | .75 | 2.00 |
| 447 | Joe Hague | .50 | 1.25 |
| 448 | John Hiller | .50 | 1.25 |
| 449A | K.Aspro MG w/Spahn Point | 1.50 | 4.00 |
| 449B | K.Aspro MG w/Spahn Round | 1.50 | 4.00 |
| 450 | Joe Torre | 1.25 | 3.00 |
| 451 | John Vukovich RC | .50 | 1.25 |
| 452 | Paul Casanova | .50 | 1.25 |
| 453 | Checklist 397-528 | 1.25 | 3.00 |
| 454 | Tom Haller | .50 | 1.25 |
| 455 | Bill Melton | .50 | 1.25 |
| 456 | Dick Green | .50 | 1.25 |
| 457 | John Strohmayer | .50 | 1.25 |
| 458 | Jim Mason | .50 | 1.25 |
| 459 | Jimmy Howarth RC | .50 | 1.25 |
| 460 | Bill Freehan | .75 | 2.00 |
| 461 | Mike Corkins | .50 | 1.25 |
| 462 | Ron Blomberg | .50 | 1.25 |
| 463 | Ken Tatum | .50 | 1.25 |
| 464 | Chicago Cubs TC | 1.25 | 3.00 |
| 465 | Dave Giusti | .50 | 1.25 |
| 466 | Jose Arcia | .50 | 1.25 |
| 467 | Mike Ryan | .50 | 1.25 |
| 468 | Tom Griffin | .50 | 1.25 |
| 469 | Dan Monzon RC | .50 | 1.25 |
| 470 | Mike Cuellar | .75 | 2.00 |
| 471 | Ty Cobb LDR | 4.00 | 10.00 |
| 472 | Lou Gehrig LDR | 6.00 | 15.00 |
| 473 | Hank Aaron LDR | 4.00 | 10.00 |
| 474 | Babe Ruth LDR | 8.00 | 20.00 |
| 475 | Ty Cobb LDR | 3.00 | 8.00 |
| 476 | Walter Johnson LDR | 1.25 | 3.00 |
| 477 | Cy Young LDR | 1.25 | 3.00 |
| 478 | Walter Johnson LDR | 1.25 | 3.00 |
| 479 | Hal Lanier | .50 | 1.25 |
| 480 | Juan Marichal | 2.00 | 5.00 |
| 481 | Chicago White Sox TC | 1.25 | 3.00 |
| 482 | Rick Reuschel RC | 1.25 | 3.00 |
| 483 | Dal Maxvill | .50 | 1.25 |
| 484 | Ernie McAnally | .50 | 1.25 |
| 485 | Norm Cash | .75 | 2.00 |
| 486A | D.Ozark MG RC Orange | .60 | 1.50 |
| 486B | Danny Ozark MG Pale | 1.25 | 3.00 |
| 487 | Bruce Dal Canton | .50 | 1.25 |
| 488 | Dave Campbell | .75 | 2.00 |
| 489 | Jeff Burroughs | .75 | 2.00 |
| 490 | Claude Osteen | .75 | 2.00 |
| 491 | Bob Montgomery | .50 | 1.25 |
| 492 | Pedro Borbon | .50 | 1.25 |
| 493 | Duffy Dyer | .50 | 1.25 |
| 494 | Rich Morales | .50 | 1.25 |
| 495 | Tommy Helms | .50 | 1.25 |
| 496 | Ray Lamb | .50 | 1.25 |
| 497A | R.Schoen MG Orange | .75 | 2.00 |
| 497B | R.Schoen MG Pale | 1.25 | 3.00 |
| 498 | Graig Nettles | 1.25 | 3.00 |
| 499 | Bob Moose | .50 | 1.25 |
| 500 | Oakland Athletics TC | 1.25 | 3.00 |
| 501 | Larry Gura | .50 | 1.25 |
| 502 | Bobby Valentine | 1.25 | 3.00 |
| 503 | Phil Niekro | 2.00 | 5.00 |
| 504 | Earl Williams | .50 | 1.25 |
| 505 | Bob Bailey | .50 | 1.25 |
| 506 | Bart Johnson | .50 | 1.25 |
| 507 | Darrel Chaney | .50 | 1.25 |
| 508 | Gates Brown | .50 | 1.25 |
| 509 | Jim Nash | .50 | 1.25 |
| 510 | Amos Otis | .75 | 2.00 |
| 511 | Sam McDowell | .75 | 2.00 |
| 512 | Dalton Jones | .50 | 1.25 |
| 513 | Dave Marshall | .50 | 1.25 |
| 514 | Jerry Kenney | .50 | 1.25 |
| 515 | Andy Messersmith | .75 | 2.00 |
| 516 | Danny Walton | .50 | 1.25 |
| 517A | Bill Virdon MG w/o Ear | .50 | 1.25 |
| 517B | Bill Virdon MG w/Ear | 1.25 | 3.00 |
| 518 | Bob Veale | .50 | 1.25 |
| 519 | Johnny Edwards | .50 | 1.25 |
| 520 | Mel Stottlemyre | .75 | 2.00 |
| 521 | Atlanta Braves TC | 1.25 | 3.00 |
| 522 | Leo Cardenas | .50 | 1.25 |
| 523 | Wayne Granger | .50 | 1.25 |
| 524 | Gene Tenace | .75 | 2.00 |
| 525 | Jim Fregosi | .75 | 2.00 |
| 526 | Ollie Brown | .50 | 1.25 |
| 527 | Dan McGinn | .50 | 1.25 |
| 528 | Paul Blair | .50 | 1.25 |
| 529 | Milt May | 1.25 | 3.00 |
| 530 | Jim Kaat | 2.00 | 5.00 |
| 531 | Ron Woods | 1.25 | 3.00 |
| 532 | Steve Mingori | 1.25 | 3.00 |
| 533 | Larry Stahl | 1.25 | 3.00 |
| 534 | Dave Lemonds | 1.25 | 3.00 |
| 535 | Johnny Callison | 2.00 | 5.00 |
| 536 | Philadelphia Phillies TC | 2.50 | 6.00 |
| 537 | Bill Slayback RC | 1.25 | 3.00 |
| 538 | Jim Ray Hart | 2.00 | 5.00 |
| 539 | Tom Murphy | 1.25 | 3.00 |
| 540 | Cleon Jones | 2.00 | 5.00 |
| 541 | Bob Bolin | 1.25 | 3.00 |
| 542 | Pat Corrales | 2.00 | 5.00 |
| 543 | Alan Foster | 1.25 | 3.00 |
| 544 | Von Joshua | 1.25 | 3.00 |
| 545 | Orlando Cepeda | 3.00 | 8.00 |
| 546 | Jim York | 1.25 | 3.00 |
| 547 | Bobby Heise | 1.25 | 3.00 |
| 548 | Don Durham RC | 1.25 | 3.00 |
| 549 | Whitey Herzog MG | 2.00 | 5.00 |
| 550 | Dave Johnson | 2.00 | 5.00 |
| 551 | Mike Kilkenny | 1.25 | 3.00 |
| 552 | J.C. Martin | 1.25 | 3.00 |
| 553 | Mickey Scott | 1.25 | 3.00 |
| 554 | Dave Concepcion | 2.00 | 5.00 |
| 555 | Bill Hands | 1.25 | 3.00 |
| 556 | New York Yankees TC | 3.00 | 8.00 |
| 557 | Bernie Williams | 1.25 | 3.00 |
| 558 | Jerry May | 1.25 | 3.00 |
| 559 | Barry Lersch | 1.25 | 3.00 |
| 560 | Frank Howard | 2.00 | 5.00 |
| 561 | Jim Geddes RC | 1.25 | 3.00 |
| 562 | Wayne Garrett | 1.25 | 3.00 |
| 563 | Larry Haney | 1.25 | 3.00 |
| 564 | Mike Thompson RC | 1.25 | 3.00 |
| 565 | Jim Hickman | 1.25 | 3.00 |

| | | |
|---|---|---|
| 566 Lew Krausse | 1.25 | 3.00 |
| 567 Bob Fenwick | 1.25 | 3.00 |
| 568 Ray Newman | 1.25 | 3.00 |
| 569 Walt Alston MG | 3.00 | 8.00 |
| 570 Bill Singer | 2.00 | 5.00 |
| 571 Rusty Torres | 1.25 | 3.00 |
| 572 Gary Sutherland | 1.25 | 3.00 |
| 573 Fred Beene | 1.25 | 3.00 |
| 574 Bob Didier | 1.25 | 3.00 |
| 575 Dock Ellis | 1.25 | 3.00 |
| 576 Montreal Expos TC | 2.50 | 6.00 |
| 577 Eric Soderholm RC | 1.25 | 3.00 |
| 578 Ken Wright | 1.25 | 3.00 |
| 579 Tom Grieve | 2.00 | 5.00 |
| 580 Joe Pepitone | 2.00 | 5.00 |
| 581 Steve Kealey | 1.25 | 3.00 |
| 582 Darrell Porter | 2.00 | 5.00 |
| 583 Bill Greif | 1.25 | 3.00 |
| 584 Chris Arnold | 1.25 | 3.00 |
| 585 Joe Niekro | 2.00 | 5.00 |
| 586 Bill Sudakis | 1.25 | 3.00 |
| 587 Rich McKinney | 1.25 | 3.00 |
| 588 Checklist 529-660 | 6.00 | 20.00 |
| 589 Ken Forsch | 1.25 | 3.00 |
| 590 Deron Johnson | 1.25 | 3.00 |
| 591 Mike Hedlund | 1.25 | 3.00 |
| 592 John Boccabella | 1.25 | 3.00 |
| 593 Jack McKeon MG RC | 1.50 | 4.00 |
| 594 Vic Harris RC | 1.25 | 3.00 |
| 595 Don Gullett | 2.00 | 5.00 |
| 596 Boston Red Sox TC | 2.50 | 6.00 |
| 597 Mickey Rivers | 2.00 | 5.00 |
| 598 Phil Roof | 1.25 | 3.00 |
| 599 Ed Crosby | 1.25 | 3.00 |
| 600 Dave McNally | 2.00 | 5.00 |
| 601 Robles/Pena/Stalmaszek RC | 2.00 | 5.00 |
| 602 Behney/Garcia/Rau RC | 2.00 | 5.00 |
| 603 Hughes/McNulty/Reitz RC | 2.00 | 5.00 |
| 604 Jefferson/O'Toole/Stampe RC | 2.00 | 5.00 |
| 605 Cabell/Bourque/Marquez RC | 2.00 | 5.00 |
| 606 Matthews/Pac/Roque RC | 2.00 | 5.00 |
| 607 Frias/Busse/Guerrero RC | 2.00 | 5.00 |
| 608 Busby/Colpaert/Medich RC | 2.00 | 5.00 |
| 609 Blanks/Garcia/Lopes RC | 2.00 | 5.00 |
| 610 Freeman/Hough/Webb RC | 2.00 | 5.00 |
| 611 Coggins/Wohlford/Zisk RC | 2.00 | 5.00 |
| 612 Lawson/Reynolds/Strom RC | 2.00 | 5.00 |
| 613 Boone/Jutze/Ivie RC | 6.00 | 15.00 |
| 614 Bumbry/Evans/Spikes RC | 8.00 | 20.00 |
| 615 Mike Schmidt RC | 75.00 | 150.00 |
| 616 Angelini/Biateric/Garman RC | 2.00 | 5.00 |
| 617 Rich Chiles | 1.25 | 3.00 |
| 618 Andy Etchebarren | 1.25 | 3.00 |
| 619 Billy Wilson | 1.25 | 3.00 |
| 620 Tommy Harper | 2.00 | 5.00 |
| 621 Joe Ferguson | 2.00 | 5.00 |
| 622 Larry Hisle | 1.25 | 3.00 |
| 623 Steve Renko | 1.25 | 3.00 |
| 624 Leo Durocher MG | 2.00 | 5.00 |
| 625 Angel Mangual | 1.25 | 3.00 |
| 626 Bob Barton | 1.25 | 3.00 |
| 627 Luis Alvarado | 1.25 | 3.00 |
| 628 Jim Slaton | 1.25 | 3.00 |
| 629 Cleveland Indians TC | 2.50 | 6.00 |
| 630 Denny McLain | 3.00 | 8.00 |
| 631 Tom Matchick | 1.25 | 3.00 |
| 632 Dick Selma | 1.25 | 3.00 |
| 633 Ike Brown | 1.25 | 3.00 |
| 634 Alan Closter | 1.25 | 3.00 |
| 635 Gene Alley | 2.00 | 5.00 |
| 636 Rickey Clark | 1.25 | 3.00 |
| 637 Norm Miller | 1.25 | 3.00 |
| 638 Ken Reynolds | 1.25 | 3.00 |
| 639 Willie Crawford | 1.25 | 3.00 |
| 640 Dick Bosman | 1.25 | 3.00 |
| 641 Cincinnati Reds TC | 2.50 | 6.00 |
| 642 Jose Laboy | 1.25 | 3.00 |
| 643 Al Fitzmorris | 1.25 | 3.00 |
| 644 Jack Heidemann | 1.25 | 3.00 |
| 645 Bob Locker | 1.25 | 3.00 |
| 646 Del Crandall MG | 1.50 | 4.00 |
| 647 George Stone | 1.25 | 3.00 |
| 648 Tom Egan | 1.25 | 3.00 |
| 649 Rich Folkers | 1.25 | 3.00 |
| 650 Felipe Alou | 2.00 | 5.00 |
| 651 Don Carrithers | 1.25 | 3.00 |
| 652 Ted Kubiak | 1.25 | 3.00 |
| 653 Joe Hoerner | 1.25 | 3.00 |

| | | |
|---|---|---|
| 654 Minnesota Twins TC | 2.50 | 6.00 |
| 655 Clay Kirby | 1.25 | 3.00 |
| 656 John Ellis | 1.25 | 3.00 |
| 657 Bob Johnson | 1.25 | 3.00 |
| 658 Elliott Maddox | 1.25 | 3.00 |
| 659 Jose Pagan | 1.25 | 3.00 |
| 660 Fred Scherman | 2.00 | 5.00 |

## 1974 Topps

| | | |
|---|---|---|
| COMPLETE SET (660) | 200.00 | 400.00 |
| COMP.FACT.SET (660) | 300.00 | 600.00 |
| WRAPPERS (10-CENTS) | 4.00 | 10.00 |
| 1 Hank Aaron 715 | 20.00 | 50.00 |
| 2 Aaron Special 54-57 | 3.00 | 8.00 |
| 3 Aaron Special 58-61 | 3.00 | 8.00 |
| 4 Aaron Special 62-65 | 3.00 | 8.00 |
| 5 Aaron Special 66-69 | 3.00 | 8.00 |
| 6 Aaron Special 70-73 | 3.00 | 8.00 |
| 7 Jim Hunter | 1.50 | 4.00 |
| 8 George Theodore RC | .20 | .50 |
| 9 Mickey Lolich | 1.00 | 3.00 |
| 10 Johnny Bench | 6.00 | 15.00 |
| 11 Jim Bibby | .20 | .50 |
| 12 Dave May | .20 | .50 |
| 13 Tom Hilgendorf | .20 | .50 |
| 14 Paul Popovich | .20 | .50 |
| 15 Joe Torre | .75 | 2.00 |
| 16 Baltimore Orioles TC | .40 | 1.00 |
| 17 Doug Bird RC | .20 | .50 |
| 18 Gary Thomasson RC | .20 | .50 |
| 19 Gerry Moses | .20 | .50 |
| 20 Nolan Ryan | 12.50 | 40.00 |
| 21 Bob Gallagher RC | .20 | .50 |
| 22 Cy Acosta | .20 | .50 |
| 23 Craig Robinson RC | .20 | .50 |
| 24 John Hiller | .40 | 1.00 |
| 25 Ken Singleton | .40 | 1.00 |
| 26 Bill Campbell RC | .20 | .50 |
| 27 George Scott | .40 | 1.00 |
| 28 Manny Sanguillen | .40 | 1.00 |
| 29 Phil Niekro | 1.25 | 3.00 |
| 30 Bobby Bonds | .75 | 2.00 |
| 31 Preston Gomez MG | .40 | 1.00 |
| 32A Johnny Grubb SD RC | .40 | 1.00 |
| 32B Johnny Grubb WASH | 1.50 | 4.00 |
| 33 Don Newhauser RC | .20 | .50 |
| 34 Andy Kosco | .20 | .50 |
| 35 Gaylord Perry | 1.25 | 3.00 |
| 36 St. Louis Cardinals TC | .40 | 1.00 |
| 37 Dave Sells RC | .20 | .50 |
| 38 Don Kessinger | .40 | 1.00 |
| 39 Ken Suarez | .20 | .50 |
| 40 Jim Palmer | 3.00 | 8.00 |
| 41 Bobby Floyd | .20 | .50 |
| 42 Claude Osteen | .40 | 1.00 |
| 43 Jim Wynn | .40 | 1.00 |
| 44 Mel Stottlemyre | .40 | 1.00 |
| 45 Dave Johnson | .40 | 1.00 |
| 46 Pat Kelly | .20 | .50 |
| 47 Dick Ruthven RC | .20 | .50 |
| 48 Dick Sharon RC | .20 | .50 |
| 49 Steve Renko | .20 | .50 |
| 50 Rod Carew | 3.00 | 8.00 |
| 51 Bobby Heise | .20 | .50 |
| 52 Al Oliver | .40 | 1.00 |
| 53A Fred Kendall SD | .40 | 1.00 |
| 53B Fred Kendall WASH | 1.50 | 4.00 |
| 54 Elias Sosa RC | .20 | .50 |
| 55 Frank Robinson | 3.00 | 8.00 |
| 56 New York Mets TC | .40 | 1.00 |
| 57 Darold Knowles | .20 | .50 |
| 58 Charlie Spikes | .20 | .50 |
| 59 Ross Grimsley | .20 | .50 |
| 60 Lou Brock | 2.50 | 5.00 |

| | | |
|---|---|---|
| 61 Luis Aparicio | 1.25 | 3.00 |
| 62 Bob Locker | .20 | .50 |
| 63 Bill Sudakis | .20 | .50 |
| 64 Doug Rau | .20 | .50 |
| 65 Amos Otis | .40 | 1.00 |
| 66 Sparky Lyle | .40 | 1.00 |
| 67 Tommy Helms | .20 | .50 |
| 68 Grant Jackson | .20 | .50 |
| 69 Del Unser | .20 | .50 |
| 70 Dick Allen | .75 | 2.00 |
| 71 Dan Frisella | .20 | .50 |
| 72 Aurelio Rodriguez | .20 | .50 |
| 73 Mike Marshall | .75 | 2.00 |
| 74 Minnesota Twins TC | .40 | 1.00 |
| 75 Jim Colborn | .20 | .50 |
| 76 Mickey Rivers | .40 | 1.00 |
| 77A Rich Troedson SD | .40 | 1.00 |
| 77B Rich Troedson WASH | 1.50 | 4.00 |
| 78 Charlie Fox MG | .20 | .50 |
| 79 Gene Tenace | .40 | 1.00 |
| 80 Tom Seaver | 5.00 | 12.00 |
| 81 Frank Duffy | .20 | .50 |
| 82 Dave Giusti | .20 | .50 |
| 83 Orlando Cepeda | 1.25 | 3.00 |
| 84 Rick Wise | .20 | .50 |
| 85 Joe Morgan | 3.00 | 8.00 |
| 86 Joe Ferguson | .40 | 1.00 |
| 87 Fergie Jenkins | 1.25 | 3.00 |
| 88 Freddie Patek | .40 | 1.00 |
| 89 Jackie Brown | .20 | .50 |
| 90 Bobby Murcer | .40 | 1.00 |
| 91 Ken Forsch | .20 | .50 |
| 92 Paul Blair | .40 | 1.00 |
| 93 Rod Gilbreath RC | .20 | .50 |
| 94 Detroit Tigers TC | .40 | 1.00 |
| 95 Steve Carlton | 3.00 | 8.00 |
| 96 Jerry Hairston RC | .20 | .50 |
| 97 Bob Bailey | .20 | .50 |
| 98 Bert Blyleven | .75 | 2.00 |
| 99 Del Crandall MG | .40 | 1.00 |
| 100 Willie Stargell | 2.50 | 6.00 |
| 101 Bobby Valentine | .40 | 1.00 |
| 102A Bill Greif SD | .40 | 1.00 |
| 102B Bill Greif WASH | 1.50 | 4.00 |
| 103 Sal Bando | .40 | 1.00 |
| 104 Ron Bryant | .20 | .50 |
| 105 Carlton Fisk | 5.00 | 12.00 |
| 106 Harry Parker RC | .20 | .50 |
| 107 Alex Johnson | .20 | .50 |
| 108 Al Hrabosky | .40 | 1.00 |
| 109 Bob Grich | .40 | 1.00 |
| 110 Billy Williams | 1.25 | 3.00 |
| 111 Clay Carroll | .20 | .50 |
| 112 Davey Lopes | .75 | 2.00 |
| 113 Dick Drago | .20 | .50 |
| 114 California Angels TC | .40 | 1.00 |
| 115 Willie Horton | .40 | 1.00 |
| 116 Jerry Reuss | .40 | 1.00 |
| 117 Ron Blomberg | .20 | .50 |
| 118 Bill Lee | .40 | 1.00 |
| 119 Danny Ozark MG | .40 | 1.00 |
| 120 Wilbur Wood | .20 | .50 |
| 121 Larry Lintz RC | .20 | .50 |
| 122 Jim Holt | .20 | .50 |
| 123 Nelson Briles | .40 | 1.00 |
| 124 Bobby Coluccio RC | .20 | .50 |
| 125A Nate Colbert SD | .40 | 1.00 |
| 125B Nate Colbert WASH | 1.50 | 4.00 |
| 126 Checklist 1-132 | 1.25 | 3.00 |
| 127 Tom Paciorek | .40 | 1.00 |
| 128 John Ellis | .20 | .50 |
| 129 Chris Speier | .20 | .50 |
| 130 Reggie Jackson | 6.00 | 15.00 |
| 131 Bob Boone | .75 | 2.00 |
| 132 Felix Millan | .20 | .50 |
| 133 David Clyde RC | .40 | 1.00 |
| 134 Denis Menke | .20 | .50 |
| 135 Roy White | .40 | 1.00 |
| 136 Rick Reuschel | .40 | 1.00 |
| 137 Al Bumbry | .40 | 1.00 |
| 138 Eddie Brinkman | .20 | .50 |
| 139 Aurelio Monteagudo | .20 | .50 |
| 140 Darrell Evans | .75 | 2.00 |
| 141 Pat Bourque | .20 | .50 |
| 142 Pedro Garcia | .20 | .50 |
| 143 Dick Woodson | .20 | .50 |
| 144 Walter Alston MG | 1.25 | 3.00 |
| 145 Dock Ellis | .20 | .50 |

| # | Card | Price 1 | Price 2 |
|---|------|---------|---------|
| 146 | Ron Fairly | .40 | 1.00 |
| 147 | Bart Johnson | .20 | .50 |
| 148A | Dave Hilton SD | .40 | 1.00 |
| 148B | Dave Hilton WASH | 1.50 | 4.00 |
| 149 | Mac Scarce | .20 | .50 |
| 150 | John Mayberry | .40 | 1.00 |
| 151 | Diego Segui | .20 | .50 |
| 152 | Oscar Gamble | .40 | 1.00 |
| 153 | Jon Matlack | .40 | 1.00 |
| 154 | Houston Astros TC | .40 | 1.00 |
| 155 | Bert Campaneris | .40 | 1.00 |
| 156 | Randy Moffitt | .20 | .50 |
| 157 | Vic Harris | .20 | .50 |
| 158 | Jack Billingham | .20 | .50 |
| 159 | Jim Ray Hart | .20 | .50 |
| 160 | Brooks Robinson | 3.00 | 8.00 |
| 161 | Ray Burris UER RC | .40 | 1.00 |
| 162 | Bill Freehan | .40 | 1.00 |
| 163 | Ken Berry | .20 | .50 |
| 164 | Tom House | .20 | .50 |
| 165 | Willie Davis | .40 | 1.00 |
| 166 | Jack McKeon MG | .40 | 1.00 |
| 167 | Luis Tiant | .75 | 2.00 |
| 168 | Danny Thompson | .20 | .50 |
| 169 | Steve Rogers RC | .75 | 2.00 |
| 170 | Bill Melton | .20 | .50 |
| 171 | Eduardo Rodriguez RC | .20 | .50 |
| 172 | Gene Clines | .20 | .50 |
| 173A | Randy Jones SD | .75 | 2.00 |
| 173B | Randy Jones WASH | 2.00 | 5.00 |
| 174 | Bill Robinson | .40 | 1.00 |
| 175 | Reggie Cleveland | .20 | .50 |
| 176 | John Lowenstein | .20 | .50 |
| 177 | Dave Roberts | .20 | .50 |
| 178 | Garry Maddox | .40 | 1.00 |
| 179 | Yogi Berra MG | 2.00 | 5.00 |
| 180 | Ken Holtzman | .40 | 1.00 |
| 181 | Cesar Geronimo | .20 | .50 |
| 182 | Lindy McDaniel | .20 | .50 |
| 183 | Johnny Oates | .40 | 1.00 |
| 184 | Texas Rangers TC | .40 | 1.00 |
| 185 | Jose Cardenal | .20 | .50 |
| 186 | Fred Scherman | .20 | .50 |
| 187 | Don Baylor | .75 | 2.00 |
| 188 | Rudy Meoli RC | .20 | .50 |
| 189 | Jim Brewer | .20 | .50 |
| 190 | Tony Oliva | .75 | 2.00 |
| 191 | Al Fitzmorris | .20 | .50 |
| 192 | Mario Guerrero | .20 | .50 |
| 193 | Tom Walker | .20 | .50 |
| 194 | Darrell Porter | .40 | 1.00 |
| 195 | Carlos May | .20 | .50 |
| 196 | Jim Fregosi | .40 | 1.00 |
| 197A | Vicente Romo SD | .40 | 1.00 |
| 197B | Vicente Romo WASH | 1.50 | 4.00 |
| 198 | Dave Cash | .20 | .50 |
| 199 | Mike Kekich | .20 | .50 |
| 200 | Cesar Cedeno | .40 | 1.00 |
| 201 | R.Carew/P.Rose LL | 2.50 | 6.00 |
| 202 | R.Jackson/W.Stargell LL | 2.00 | 5.00 |
| 203 | R.Jackson/W.Stargell LL | 2.00 | 5.00 |
| 204 | T.Harper/L.Brock LL | .75 | 2.00 |
| 205 | W.Wood/R.Bryant LL | .40 | 1.00 |
| 206 | J.Palmer/T.Seaver LL | 2.00 | 5.00 |
| 207 | N.Ryan/T.Seaver LL | 5.00 | 12.00 |
| 208 | J.Hiller/M.Marshall LL | .40 | 1.00 |
| 209 | Ted Sizemore | .20 | .50 |
| 210 | Bill Singer | .20 | .50 |
| 211 | Chicago Cubs TC | .40 | 1.00 |
| 212 | Rollie Fingers | 1.25 | 3.00 |
| 213 | Dave Rader | .20 | .50 |
| 214 | Billy Grabarkewitz | .20 | .50 |
| 215 | A.Kaline UER | 4.00 | 10.00 |
| 216 | Ray Sadecki | .20 | .50 |
| 217 | Tim Foli | .20 | .50 |
| 218 | Johnny Briggs | .20 | .50 |
| 219 | Doug Griffin | .20 | .50 |
| 220 | Don Sutton | 1.25 | 3.00 |
| 221 | Chuck Tanner MG | .40 | 1.00 |
| 222 | Ramon Hernandez | .20 | .50 |
| 223 | Jeff Burroughs | .75 | 2.00 |
| 224 | Roger Metzger | .20 | .50 |
| 225 | Paul Splittorff | .20 | .50 |
| 226A | San Diego Padres TC SD | .75 | 2.00 |
| 226B | San Diego Padres TC WASH | 3.00 | 8.00 |
| 227 | Mike Lum | .20 | .50 |
| 228 | Ted Kubiak | .20 | .50 |
| 229 | Fritz Peterson | .20 | .50 |
| 230 | Tony Perez | 1.50 | 4.00 |
| 231 | Dick Tidrow | .20 | .50 |
| 232 | Steve Brye | .20 | .50 |
| 233 | Jim Barr | .20 | .50 |
| 234 | John Milner | .20 | .50 |
| 235 | Dave McNally | .40 | 1.00 |
| 236 | Red Schoendienst MG | 1.25 | 3.00 |
| 237 | Ken Brett | .20 | .50 |
| 238 | F.Healy w/Munson | .40 | 1.00 |
| 239 | Bill Russell | .40 | 1.00 |
| 240 | Joe Coleman | .20 | .50 |
| 241A | Glenn Beckert SD | .40 | 1.00 |
| 241B | Glenn Beckert WASH | 1.50 | 4.00 |
| 242 | Bill Gogolewski | .20 | .50 |
| 243 | Bob Oliver | .20 | .50 |
| 244 | Carl Morton | .20 | .50 |
| 245 | Cleon Jones | .20 | .50 |
| 246 | Oakland Athletics TC | .75 | 2.00 |
| 247 | Rick Miller | .20 | .50 |
| 248 | Tom Hall | .20 | .50 |
| 249 | George Mitterwald | .20 | .50 |
| 250A | Willie McCovey SD | 3.00 | 8.00 |
| 250B | Willie McCovey WASH | 10.00 | 25.00 |
| 251 | Graig Nettles | .75 | 2.00 |
| 252 | Dave Parker RC | 4.00 | 10.00 |
| 253 | John Boccabella | .20 | .50 |
| 254 | Stan Bahnsen | .20 | .50 |
| 255 | Larry Bowa | .40 | 1.00 |
| 256 | Tom Griffin | .20 | .50 |
| 257 | Buddy Bell | .75 | 2.00 |
| 258 | Jerry Morales | .20 | .50 |
| 259 | Bob Reynolds | .20 | .50 |
| 260 | Ted Simmons | .75 | 2.00 |
| 261 | Jerry Bell | .20 | .50 |
| 262 | Ed Kirkpatrick | .20 | .50 |
| 263 | Checklist 133-264 | 1.25 | 3.00 |
| 264 | Joe Rudi | .40 | 1.00 |
| 265 | Tug McGraw | .75 | 2.00 |
| 266 | Jim Northrup | .40 | 1.00 |
| 267 | Andy Messersmith | .40 | 1.00 |
| 268 | Tom Grieve | .40 | 1.00 |
| 269 | Bob Johnson | .20 | .50 |
| 270 | Ron Santo | .75 | 2.00 |
| 271 | Bill Hands | .20 | .50 |
| 272 | Paul Casanova | .20 | .50 |
| 273 | Checklist 265-396 | 1.25 | 3.00 |
| 274 | Fred Beene | .20 | .50 |
| 275 | Ron Hunt | .20 | .50 |
| 276 | Bobby Winkles MG | .40 | 1.00 |
| 277 | Gary Nolan | .40 | 1.00 |
| 278 | Cookie Rojas | .40 | 1.00 |
| 279 | Jim Crawford RC | .20 | .50 |
| 280 | Carl Yastrzemski | 5.00 | 12.00 |
| 281 | San Francisco Giants TC | .40 | 1.00 |
| 282 | Doyle Alexander | .40 | 1.00 |
| 283 | Mike Schmidt | 8.00 | 20.00 |
| 284 | Dave Duncan | .20 | .50 |
| 285 | Reggie Smith | .40 | 1.00 |
| 286 | Tony Muser | .20 | .50 |
| 287 | Clay Kirby | .20 | .50 |
| 288 | Gorman Thomas RC | .75 | 2.00 |
| 289 | Rick Auerbach | .20 | .50 |
| 290 | Vida Blue | .40 | 1.00 |
| 291 | Don Hahn | .20 | .50 |
| 292 | Chuck Seelbach | .20 | .50 |
| 293 | Milt May | .20 | .50 |
| 294 | Steve Foucault RC | .20 | .50 |
| 295 | Rick Monday | .40 | 1.00 |
| 296 | Ray Corbin | .20 | .50 |
| 297 | Hal Breeden | .20 | .50 |
| 298 | Roric Harrison | .20 | .50 |
| 299 | Gene Michael | .20 | .50 |
| 300 | Pete Rose | 10.00 | 25.00 |
| 301 | Bob Montgomery | .20 | .50 |
| 302 | Rudy May | .20 | .50 |
| 303 | George Hendrick | .40 | 1.00 |
| 304 | Don Wilson | .20 | .50 |
| 305 | Tito Fuentes | .20 | .50 |
| 306 | Earl Weaver MG | 1.25 | 3.00 |
| 307 | Luis Melendez | .20 | .50 |
| 308 | Bruce Dal Canton | .20 | .50 |
| 309A | Dave Roberts SD | .40 | 1.00 |
| 309B | Dave Roberts WASH | 2.50 | 6.00 |
| 310 | Terry Forster | .40 | 1.00 |
| 311 | Jerry Grote | .40 | 1.00 |
| 312 | Deron Johnson | .20 | .50 |
| 313 | Barry Lersch | .20 | .50 |
| 314 | Milwaukee Brewers TC | .40 | 1.00 |
| 315 | Ron Cey | .75 | 2.00 |
| 316 | Jim Perry | .40 | 1.00 |
| 317 | Richie Zisk | .40 | 1.00 |
| 318 | Jim Merritt | .20 | .50 |
| 319 | Randy Hundley | .20 | .50 |
| 320 | Dusty Baker | .75 | 2.00 |
| 321 | Steve Braun | .20 | .50 |
| 322 | Ernie McAnally | .20 | .50 |
| 323 | Richie Scheinblum | .20 | .50 |
| 324 | Steve Kline | .20 | .50 |
| 325 | Tommy Harper | .40 | 1.00 |
| 326 | Sparky Anderson MG | 1.25 | 3.00 |
| 327 | Tom Timmermann | .20 | .50 |
| 328 | Skip Jutze | .20 | .50 |
| 329 | Mark Belanger | .40 | 1.00 |
| 330 | Juan Marichal | 2.00 | 5.00 |
| 331 | C.Fisk/J.Bench AS | 2.00 | 5.00 |
| 332 | D.Allen/H.Aaron AS | 3.00 | 8.00 |
| 333 | R.Carew/J.Morgan AS | 1.50 | 4.00 |
| 334 | B.Robinson/R.Santo AS | .75 | 2.00 |
| 335 | B.Campaneris/C.Speier AS | .40 | 1.00 |
| 336 | B.Murcer/P.Rose AS | 2.00 | 5.00 |
| 337 | A.Otis/C.Cedeno AS | .40 | 1.00 |
| 338 | R.Jackson/B.Williams AS | 2.00 | 5.00 |
| 339 | J.Hunter/R.Wise AS | 1.25 | 3.00 |
| 340 | Thurman Munson | 3.00 | 8.00 |
| 341 | Dan Driessen RC | .40 | 1.00 |
| 342 | Jim Lonborg | .40 | 1.00 |
| 343 | Kansas City Royals TC | .40 | 1.00 |
| 344 | Mike Caldwell | .20 | .50 |
| 345 | Bill North | .20 | .50 |
| 346 | Ron Reed | .20 | .50 |
| 347 | Sandy Alomar | .40 | 1.00 |
| 348 | Pete Richert | .20 | .50 |
| 349 | John Vukovich | .20 | .50 |
| 350 | Bob Gibson | 3.00 | 8.00 |
| 351 | Dwight Evans | 1.25 | 3.00 |
| 352 | Bill Stoneman | .20 | .50 |
| 353 | Rich Coggins | .20 | .50 |
| 354 | Whitey Lockman MG | .40 | 1.00 |
| 355 | Dave Nelson | .20 | .50 |
| 356 | Jerry Koosman | .40 | 1.00 |
| 357 | Buddy Bradford | .20 | .50 |
| 358 | Dal Maxvill | .20 | .50 |
| 359 | Brent Strom | .20 | .50 |
| 360 | Greg Luzinski | .75 | 2.00 |
| 361 | Don Carrithers | .20 | .50 |
| 362 | Hal King | .20 | .50 |
| 363 | New York Yankees TC | .75 | 2.00 |
| 364A | Cito Gaston SD | .75 | 2.00 |
| 364B | Cito Gaston WASH | 3.00 | 8.00 |
| 365 | Steve Busby | .40 | 1.00 |
| 366 | Larry Hisle | .40 | 1.00 |
| 367 | Norm Cash | .75 | 2.00 |
| 368 | Manny Mota | .40 | 1.00 |
| 369 | Paul Lindblad | .20 | .50 |
| 370 | Bob Watson | .40 | 1.00 |
| 371 | Jim Slaton | .20 | .50 |
| 372 | Ken Reitz | .20 | .50 |
| 373 | John Curtis | .20 | .50 |
| 374 | Marty Perez | .20 | .50 |
| 375 | Earl Williams | .20 | .50 |
| 376 | Jorge Orta | .20 | .50 |
| 377 | Ron Woods | .20 | .50 |
| 378 | Burt Hooton | .40 | 1.00 |
| 379 | Billy Martin MG | .75 | 2.00 |
| 380 | Bud Harrelson | .40 | 1.00 |
| 381 | Charlie Sands | .20 | .50 |
| 382 | Bob Moose | .20 | .50 |
| 383 | Philadelphia Phillies TC | .40 | 1.00 |
| 384 | Chris Chambliss | .40 | 1.00 |
| 385 | Don Gullett | .40 | 1.00 |
| 386 | Gary Matthews | .75 | 2.00 |
| 387A | Rich Morales SD | .40 | 1.00 |
| 387B | Rich Morales WASH | 2.50 | 6.00 |
| 388 | Phil Roof | .20 | .50 |
| 389 | Gates Brown | .20 | .50 |
| 390 | Lou Piniella | .75 | 2.00 |
| 391 | Billy Champion | .20 | .50 |
| 392 | Dick Green | .20 | .50 |
| 393 | Orlando Pena | .20 | .50 |
| 394 | Ken Henderson | .20 | .50 |
| 395 | Doug Rader | .20 | .50 |
| 396 | Tommy Davis | .40 | 1.00 |
| 397 | George Stone | .20 | .50 |
| 398 | Duke Sims | .20 | .50 |
| 399 | Mike Paul | .20 | .50 |
| 400 | Harmon Killebrew | 2.50 | 6.00 |

|  |  | | |
|---|---|---|---|
| ☐ 401 | Elliott Maddox | .20 | .50 |
| ☐ 402 | Jim Rooker | .20 | .50 |
| ☐ 403 | Darrell Johnson MG | .40 | 1.00 |
| ☐ 404 | Jim Howarth | .20 | .50 |
| ☐ 405 | Ellie Rodriguez | .20 | .50 |
| ☐ 406 | Steve Arlin | .20 | .50 |
| ☐ 407 | Jim Wohlford | .20 | .50 |
| ☐ 408 | Charlie Hough | .40 | 1.00 |
| ☐ 409 | Ike Brown | .20 | .50 |
| ☐ 410 | Pedro Borbon | .20 | .50 |
| ☐ 411 | Frank Baker | .20 | .50 |
| ☐ 412 | Chuck Taylor | .20 | .50 |
| ☐ 413 | Don Money | .40 | 1.00 |
| ☐ 414 | Checklist 397-528 | 1.25 | 3.00 |
| ☐ 415 | Gary Gentry | .20 | .50 |
| ☐ 416 | Chicago White Sox TC | .40 | 1.00 |
| ☐ 417 | Rich Folkers | .20 | .50 |
| ☐ 418 | Walt Williams | .20 | .50 |
| ☐ 419 | Wayne Twitchell | .20 | .50 |
| ☐ 420 | Ray Fosse | .20 | .50 |
| ☐ 421 | Dan Fife RC | .20 | .50 |
| ☐ 422 | Gonzalo Marquez | .20 | .50 |
| ☐ 423 | Fred Stanley | .20 | .50 |
| ☐ 424 | Jim Beauchamp | .20 | .50 |
| ☐ 425 | Pete Broberg | .20 | .50 |
| ☐ 426 | Rennie Stennett | .20 | .50 |
| ☐ 427 | Bobby Bolin | .20 | .50 |
| ☐ 428 | Gary Sutherland | .20 | .50 |
| ☐ 429 | Dick Lange RC | .20 | .50 |
| ☐ 430 | Matty Alou | .40 | 1.00 |
| ☐ 431 | Gene Garber RC | .40 | 1.00 |
| ☐ 432 | Chris Arnold | .20 | .50 |
| ☐ 433 | Lerrin LaGrow | .20 | .50 |
| ☐ 434 | Ken McMullen | .20 | .50 |
| ☐ 435 | Dave Concepcion | .75 | 2.00 |
| ☐ 436 | Don Hood RC | .20 | .50 |
| ☐ 437 | Jim Lyttle | .20 | .50 |
| ☐ 438 | Ed Herrmann | .20 | .50 |
| ☐ 439 | Norm Miller | .20 | .50 |
| ☐ 440 | Jim Kaat | .75 | 2.00 |
| ☐ 441 | Tom Ragland | .20 | .50 |
| ☐ 442 | Alan Foster | .20 | .50 |
| ☐ 443 | Tom Hutton | .20 | .50 |
| ☐ 444 | Vic Davalillo | .20 | .50 |
| ☐ 445 | George Medich | .20 | .50 |
| ☐ 446 | Len Randle | .20 | .50 |
| ☐ 447 | Frank Quilici MG | .40 | 1.00 |
| ☐ 448 | Ron Hodges RC | .20 | .50 |
| ☐ 449 | Tom McCraw | .20 | .50 |
| ☐ 450 | Rich Hebner | .40 | 1.00 |
| ☐ 451 | Tommy John | .75 | 2.00 |
| ☐ 452 | Gene Hiser | .20 | .50 |
| ☐ 453 | Balor Moore | .20 | .50 |
| ☐ 454 | Kurt Bevacqua | .20 | .50 |
| ☐ 455 | Tom Bradley | .20 | .50 |
| ☐ 456 | Dave Winfield RC | 20.00 | 50.00 |
| ☐ 457 | Chuck Goggin RC | .20 | .50 |
| ☐ 458 | Jim Ray | .20 | .50 |
| ☐ 459 | Cincinnati Reds TC | .75 | 2.00 |
| ☐ 460 | Boog Powell | .75 | 2.00 |
| ☐ 461 | John Odom | .20 | .50 |
| ☐ 462 | Luis Alvarado | .20 | .50 |
| ☐ 463 | Pat Dobson | .20 | .50 |
| ☐ 464 | Jose Cruz | .75 | 2.00 |
| ☐ 465 | Dick Bosman | .20 | .50 |
| ☐ 466 | Dick Billings | .20 | .50 |
| ☐ 467 | Winston Llenas | .20 | .50 |
| ☐ 468 | Pepe Frias | .20 | .50 |
| ☐ 469 | Joe Decker | .20 | .50 |
| ☐ 470 | Reggie Jackson ALCS | 2.00 | 5.00 |
| ☐ 471 | Jon Matlack NLCS | .40 | 1.00 |
| ☐ 472 | Darold Knowles WS1 | .40 | 1.00 |
| ☐ 473 | Willie Mays WS | 3.00 | 8.00 |
| ☐ 474 | Bert Campaneris WS3 | .40 | 1.00 |
| ☐ 475 | Rusty Staub WS4 | .40 | 1.00 |
| ☐ 476 | Cleon Jones WS5 | .40 | 1.00 |
| ☐ 477 | Reggie Jackson WS6 | 2.00 | 5.00 |
| ☐ 478 | Bert Campaneris WS7 | .40 | 1.00 |
| ☐ 479 | A's Celebrate WS | .40 | 1.00 |
| ☐ 480 | Willie Crawford | .20 | .50 |
| ☐ 481 | Jerry Terrell RC | .20 | .50 |
| ☐ 482 | Bob Didier | .20 | .50 |
| ☐ 483 | Atlanta Braves TC | .40 | 1.00 |
| ☐ 484 | Carmen Fanzone | .20 | .50 |
| ☐ 485 | Felipe Alou | .75 | 2.00 |
| ☐ 486 | Steve Stone | .40 | 1.00 |
| ☐ 487 | Ted Martinez | .20 | .50 |
| ☐ 488 | Andy Etchebarren | .20 | .50 |
| ☐ 489 | Danny Murtaugh MG | .40 | 1.00 |
| ☐ 490 | Vada Pinson | .75 | 2.00 |
| ☐ 491 | Roger Nelson | .20 | .50 |
| ☐ 492 | Mike Rogodzinski RC | .20 | .50 |
| ☐ 493 | Joe Hoerner | .20 | .50 |
| ☐ 494 | Ed Goodson | .20 | .50 |
| ☐ 495 | Dick McAuliffe | .40 | 1.00 |
| ☐ 496 | Tom Murphy | .20 | .50 |
| ☐ 497 | Bobby Mitchell | .20 | .50 |
| ☐ 498 | Pat Corrales | .20 | .50 |
| ☐ 499 | Rusty Torres | .20 | .50 |
| ☐ 500 | Lee May | .40 | 1.00 |
| ☐ 501 | Eddie Leon | .20 | .50 |
| ☐ 502 | Dave LaRoche | .20 | .50 |
| ☐ 503 | Eric Soderholm | .20 | .50 |
| ☐ 504 | Joe Niekro | .40 | 1.00 |
| ☐ 505 | Bill Buckner | .40 | 1.00 |
| ☐ 506 | Ed Farmer | .20 | .50 |
| ☐ 507 | Larry Stahl | .20 | .50 |
| ☐ 508 | Montreal Expos TC | .40 | 1.00 |
| ☐ 509 | Jesse Jefferson | .20 | .50 |
| ☐ 510 | Wayne Garrett | .20 | .50 |
| ☐ 511 | Toby Harrah | .40 | 1.00 |
| ☐ 512 | Joe Lahoud | .20 | .50 |
| ☐ 513 | Jim Campanis | .20 | .50 |
| ☐ 514 | Paul Schaal | .20 | .50 |
| ☐ 515 | Willie Montanez | .20 | .50 |
| ☐ 516 | Horacio Pina | .20 | .50 |
| ☐ 517 | Mike Hegan | .20 | .50 |
| ☐ 518 | Derrel Thomas | .20 | .50 |
| ☐ 519 | Bill Sharp RC | .20 | .50 |
| ☐ 520 | Tim McCarver | .75 | 2.00 |
| ☐ 521 | Ken Aspromonte MG | .40 | 1.00 |
| ☐ 522 | J.R. Richard | .75 | 2.00 |
| ☐ 523 | Cecil Cooper | .75 | 2.00 |
| ☐ 524 | Bill Plummer | .20 | .50 |
| ☐ 525 | Clyde Wright | .20 | .50 |
| ☐ 526 | Frank Tepedino | .40 | 1.00 |
| ☐ 527 | Bobby Darwin | .20 | .50 |
| ☐ 528 | Bill Bonham | .20 | .50 |
| ☐ 529 | Horace Clarke | .40 | 1.00 |
| ☐ 530 | Mickey Stanley | .40 | 1.00 |
| ☐ 531 | Gene Mauch MG | .40 | 1.00 |
| ☐ 532 | Skip Lockwood | .20 | .50 |
| ☐ 533 | Mike Phillips RC | .20 | .50 |
| ☐ 534 | Eddie Watt | .20 | .50 |
| ☐ 535 | Bob Tolan | .20 | .50 |
| ☐ 536 | Duffy Dyer | .20 | .50 |
| ☐ 537 | Steve Mingori | .20 | .50 |
| ☐ 538 | Cesar Tovar | .20 | .50 |
| ☐ 539 | Lloyd Allen | .20 | .50 |
| ☐ 540 | Bob Robertson | .20 | .50 |
| ☐ 541 | Cleveland Indians TC | .40 | 1.00 |
| ☐ 542 | Goose Gossage | .75 | 2.00 |
| ☐ 543 | Danny Cater | .20 | .50 |
| ☐ 544 | Ron Schueler | .20 | .50 |
| ☐ 545 | Billy Conigliaro | .40 | 1.00 |
| ☐ 546 | Mike Corkins | .20 | .50 |
| ☐ 547 | Glenn Borgmann | .20 | .50 |
| ☐ 548 | Sonny Siebert | .20 | .50 |
| ☐ 549 | Mike Jorgensen | .20 | .50 |
| ☐ 550 | Sam McDowell | .40 | 1.00 |
| ☐ 551 | Von Joshua | .20 | .50 |
| ☐ 552 | Denny Doyle | .20 | .50 |
| ☐ 553 | Jim Willoughby | .20 | .50 |
| ☐ 554 | Tim Johnson RC | .20 | .50 |
| ☐ 555 | Woodie Fryman | .20 | .50 |
| ☐ 556 | Dave Campbell | .40 | 1.00 |
| ☐ 557 | Jim McGlothlin | .20 | .50 |
| ☐ 558 | Bill Fahey | .20 | .50 |
| ☐ 559 | Darrel Chaney | .20 | .50 |
| ☐ 560 | Mike Cuellar | .40 | 1.00 |
| ☐ 561 | Ed Kranepool | .40 | 1.00 |
| ☐ 562 | Jack Aker | .20 | .50 |
| ☐ 563 | Hal McRae | .40 | 1.00 |
| ☐ 564 | Mike Ryan | .20 | .50 |
| ☐ 565 | Milt Wilcox | .20 | .50 |
| ☐ 566 | Jackie Hernandez | .20 | .50 |
| ☐ 567 | Boston Red Sox TC | .40 | 1.00 |
| ☐ 568 | Mike Torrez | .40 | 1.00 |
| ☐ 569 | Rick Dempsey | .40 | 1.00 |
| ☐ 570 | Ralph Garr | .40 | 1.00 |
| ☐ 571 | Rich Hand | .20 | .50 |
| ☐ 572 | Enzo Hernandez | .20 | .50 |
| ☐ 573 | Mike Adams RC | .20 | .50 |
| ☐ 574 | Bill Parsons | .20 | .50 |
| ☐ 575 | Steve Garvey | 1.25 | 3.00 |
| ☐ 576 | Scipio Spinks | .20 | .50 |
| ☐ 577 | Mike Sadek RC | .20 | .50 |
| ☐ 578 | Ralph Houk MG | .40 | 1.00 |
| ☐ 579 | Cecil Upshaw | .20 | .50 |
| ☐ 580 | Jim Spencer | .20 | .50 |
| ☐ 581 | Fred Norman | .20 | .50 |
| ☐ 582 | Bucky Dent RC | 2.00 | 5.00 |
| ☐ 583 | Marty Pattin | .20 | .50 |
| ☐ 584 | Ken Rudolph | .20 | .50 |
| ☐ 585 | Merv Rettenmund | .20 | .50 |
| ☐ 586 | Jack Brohamer | .20 | .50 |
| ☐ 587 | Larry Christenson RC | .20 | .50 |
| ☐ 588 | Hal Lanier | .20 | .50 |
| ☐ 589 | Boots Day | .20 | .50 |
| ☐ 590 | Roger Moret | .20 | .50 |
| ☐ 591 | Sonny Jackson | .20 | .50 |
| ☐ 592 | Ed Bane RC | .20 | .50 |
| ☐ 593 | Steve Yeager | .40 | 1.00 |
| ☐ 594 | Leroy Stanton | .20 | .50 |
| ☐ 595 | Steve Blass | .40 | 1.00 |
| ☐ 596 | Garr/Hold/Lit/Pole RC | .20 | .50 |
| ☐ 597 | Chalk/Gam/Mac/Trillo RC | .40 | 1.00 |
| ☐ 598 | Ken Griffey RC | 5.00 | 12.00 |
| ☐ 599A | Dior/Freis/Ric/Shan Wash | .75 | 2.00 |
| ☐ 599B | Dior/Freis/Ric/Shan San | 6.00 | 15.00 |
| ☐ 599C | Dior/Freis/Ric/Shan Snt | 2.50 | 6.00 |
| ☐ 600 | Cash/Cox/Madlock/Sand RC | 2.00 | 5.00 |
| ☐ 601 | Arm/Bladt/Downing/McBride RC | 1.25 | 3.00 |
| ☐ 602 | Ado/Henn/Swan/Voss RC | .40 | 1.00 |
| ☐ 603 | Foote/Lund/Moore/Robles RC | .40 | 1.00 |
| ☐ 604 | Hugh/Knox/Thornton/White RC | 2.00 | 5.00 |
| ☐ 605 | Alb/Palt/Kob/Tanana RC | 1.50 | 4.00 |
| ☐ 606 | Fuller/Howard/Smith/Velez RC | .40 | 1.00 |
| ☐ 607 | Fost/Hein/Ros/Taveras RC | .40 | 1.00 |
| ☐ 608A | Apod/Ban/D'Acq/Wall ERR | .75 | 2.00 |
| ☐ 608B | Apod/Ban/D'Acq/Wall RC | 2.00 | 5.00 |
| ☐ 609 | Rico Petrocelli | .40 | 1.00 |
| ☐ 610 | Dave Kingman | .75 | 2.00 |
| ☐ 611 | Rich Stelmaszek | .20 | .50 |
| ☐ 612 | Luke Walker | .20 | .50 |
| ☐ 613 | Dan Monzon | .20 | .50 |
| ☐ 614 | Adrian Devine RC | .20 | .50 |
| ☐ 615 | Johnny Jeter UER | .20 | .50 |
| ☐ 616 | Larry Gura | .20 | .50 |
| ☐ 617 | Ted Ford | .20 | .50 |
| ☐ 618 | Jim Mason | .20 | .50 |
| ☐ 619 | Mike Anderson | .20 | .50 |
| ☐ 620 | Al Downing | .20 | .50 |
| ☐ 621 | Bernie Carbo | .20 | .50 |
| ☐ 622 | Phil Gagliano | .20 | .50 |
| ☐ 623 | Celerino Sanchez | .20 | .50 |
| ☐ 624 | Bob Miller | .20 | .50 |
| ☐ 625 | Ollie Brown | .20 | .50 |
| ☐ 626 | Pittsburgh Pirates TC | .40 | 1.00 |
| ☐ 627 | Carl Taylor | .20 | .50 |
| ☐ 628 | Ivan Murrell | .20 | .50 |
| ☐ 629 | Rusty Staub | .75 | 2.00 |
| ☐ 630 | Tommie Agee | .40 | 1.00 |
| ☐ 631 | Steve Barber | .20 | .50 |
| ☐ 632 | George Culver | .20 | .50 |
| ☐ 633 | Dave Hamilton | .20 | .50 |
| ☐ 634 | Eddie Mathews MG | 1.25 | 3.00 |
| ☐ 635 | Johnny Edwards | .20 | .50 |
| ☐ 636 | Dave Goltz | .20 | .50 |
| ☐ 637 | Checklist 529-660 | 1.25 | 3.00 |
| ☐ 638 | Ken Sanders | .20 | .50 |
| ☐ 639 | Joe Lovitto | .20 | .50 |
| ☐ 640 | Milt Pappas | .40 | 1.00 |
| ☐ 641 | Chuck Brinkman | .20 | .50 |
| ☐ 642 | Terry Harmon | .20 | .50 |
| ☐ 643 | Los Angeles Dodgers TC | .40 | 1.00 |
| ☐ 644 | Wayne Granger | .20 | .50 |
| ☐ 645 | Ken Boswell | .20 | .50 |
| ☐ 646 | George Foster | .75 | 2.00 |
| ☐ 647 | Juan Beniquez RC | .20 | .50 |
| ☐ 648 | Terry Crowley | .20 | .50 |
| ☐ 649 | Fernando Gonzalez RC | .20 | .50 |
| ☐ 650 | Mike Epstein | .20 | .50 |
| ☐ 651 | Leron Lee | .20 | .50 |
| ☐ 652 | Gail Hopkins | .20 | .50 |
| ☐ 653 | Bob Stinson | .20 | .50 |
| ☐ 654A | Jesus Alou NPOF | 1.50 | 4.00 |
| ☐ 654B | Jesus Alou COR | .40 | 1.00 |
| ☐ 655 | Mike Tyson RC | .20 | .50 |
| ☐ 656 | Adrian Garrett | .20 | .50 |
| ☐ 657 | Jim Shellenback | .20 | .50 |
| ☐ 658 | Lee Lacy | .20 | .50 |
| ☐ 659 | Joe Lis | .20 | .50 |
| ☐ 660 | Larry Dierker | .75 | 2.00 |

## 1975 Topps

RED SOX

CARL YASTRZEMSKI

| | | |
|---|---|---|
| COMPLETE SET (660) | 300.00 | 600.00 |
| WRAPPER (15-CENT) | | 8.00 |
| 1 Hank Aaron HL | 12.50 | 30.00 |
| 2 Lou Brock HL | 1.25 | 3.00 |
| 3 Bob Gibson HL | 1.25 | 3.00 |
| 4 Al Kaline HL | 2.50 | 6.00 |
| 5 Nolan Ryan HL | 6.00 | 15.00 |
| 6 Mike Marshall HL | .40 | 1.00 |
| 7 Ryan/Busby/Bosman HL | 3.00 | 8.00 |
| 8 Rogelio Moret | .20 | .50 |
| 9 Frank Tepedino | .40 | 1.00 |
| 10 Willie Davis | .40 | 1.00 |
| 11 Bill Melton | .20 | .50 |
| 12 David Clyde | .20 | .50 |
| 13 Gene Locklear RC | .40 | 1.00 |
| 14 Milt Wilcox | .40 | 1.00 |
| 15 Jose Cardenal | .40 | 1.00 |
| 16 Frank Tanana | .75 | 2.00 |
| 17 Dave Concepcion | .75 | 2.00 |
| 18 Detroit Tigers CL/Houk | .75 | 2.00 |
| 19 Jerry Koosman | .40 | 1.00 |
| 20 Thurman Munson | 3.00 | 8.00 |
| 21 Rollie Fingers | 1.25 | 3.00 |
| 22 Dave Cash | .20 | .50 |
| 23 Bill Russell | .40 | 1.00 |
| 24 Al Fitzmorris | .20 | .50 |
| 25 Lee May | .40 | 1.00 |
| 26 Dave McNally | .40 | 1.00 |
| 27 Ken Reitz | .20 | .50 |
| 28 Tom Murphy | .20 | .50 |
| 29 Dave Parker | 1.25 | 3.00 |
| 30 Bert Blyleven | .75 | 2.00 |
| 31 Dave Rader | .20 | .50 |
| 32 Reggie Cleveland | .20 | .50 |
| 33 Dusty Baker | .75 | 2.00 |
| 34 Steve Renko | .20 | .50 |
| 35 Ron Santo | .40 | 1.00 |
| 36 Joe Lovitto | .20 | .50 |
| 37 Dave Freisleben | .20 | .50 |
| 38 Buddy Bell | .75 | 2.00 |
| 39 Andre Thornton | .40 | 1.00 |
| 40 Bill Singer | .20 | .50 |
| 41 Cesar Geronimo | .40 | 1.00 |
| 42 Joe Coleman | .20 | .50 |
| 43 Cleon Jones | .40 | 1.00 |
| 44 Pat Dobson | .20 | .50 |
| 45 Joe Rudi | .40 | 1.00 |
| 46 Philadelphia Phillies CL/Ozark | .75 | 2.00 |
| 47 Tommy John | .75 | 2.00 |
| 48 Freddie Patek | .40 | 1.00 |
| 49 Larry Dierker | .40 | 1.00 |
| 50 Brooks Robinson | 3.00 | 8.00 |
| 51 Bob Forsch RC | .40 | 1.00 |
| 52 Darrell Porter | .40 | 1.00 |
| 53 Dave Giusti | .20 | .50 |
| 54 Eric Soderholm | .20 | .50 |
| 55 Bobby Bonds | .75 | 2.00 |
| 56 Rick Wise | .40 | 1.00 |
| 57 Dave Johnson | .40 | 1.00 |
| 58 Chuck Taylor | .20 | .50 |
| 59 Ken Henderson | .20 | .50 |
| 60 Fergie Jenkins | 1.25 | 3.00 |
| 61 Dave Winfield | 6.00 | 15.00 |
| 62 Fritz Peterson | .20 | .50 |
| 63 Steve Swisher RC | .20 | .50 |
| 64 Dave Chalk | .20 | .50 |
| 65 Don Gullett | .40 | 1.00 |
| 66 Willie Horton | .40 | 1.00 |
| 67 Tug McGraw | .40 | 1.00 |
| 68 Ron Blomberg | .20 | .50 |
| 69 John Odom | .20 | .50 |
| 70 Mike Schmidt | 8.00 | 20.00 |

| | | |
|---|---|---|
| 71 Charlie Hough | .40 | 1.00 |
| 72 Kansas City Royals CL/McKeon | .75 | 2.00 |
| 73 J.R. Richard | .40 | 1.00 |
| 74 Mark Belanger | .40 | 1.00 |
| 75 Ted Simmons | .75 | 2.00 |
| 76 Ed Sprague | .20 | .50 |
| 77 Richie Zisk | .40 | 1.00 |
| 78 Ray Corbin | .20 | .50 |
| 79 Gary Matthews | .40 | 1.00 |
| 80 Carlton Fisk | 3.00 | 8.00 |
| 81 Ron Reed | .20 | .50 |
| 82 Pat Kelly | .20 | .50 |
| 83 Jim Merritt | .20 | .50 |
| 84 Enzo Hernandez | .20 | .50 |
| 85 Bill Bonham | .20 | .50 |
| 86 Joe Lis | .20 | .50 |
| 87 George Foster | .75 | 2.00 |
| 88 Tom Egan | .20 | .50 |
| 89 Jim Ray | .20 | .50 |
| 90 Rusty Staub | .75 | 2.00 |
| 91 Dick Green | .20 | .50 |
| 92 Cecil Upshaw | .20 | .50 |
| 93 Davey Lopes | .75 | 2.00 |
| 94 Jim Lonborg | .40 | 1.00 |
| 95 John Mayberry | .40 | 1.00 |
| 96 Mike Cosgrove RC | .20 | .50 |
| 97 Earl Williams | .20 | .50 |
| 98 Rich Folkers | .20 | .50 |
| 99 Mike Hegan | .20 | .50 |
| 100 Willie Stargell | 1.50 | 4.00 |
| 101 Montreal Expos CL/Mauch | .75 | 2.00 |
| 102 Joe Decker | .20 | .50 |
| 103 Rick Miller | .20 | .50 |
| 104 Bill Madlock | .75 | 2.00 |
| 105 Buzz Capra | .20 | .50 |
| 106 Mike Hargrove UER RC | 1.25 | 3.00 |
| 107 Jim Barr | .20 | .50 |
| 108 Tom Hall | .20 | .50 |
| 109 George Hendrick | .40 | 1.00 |
| 110 Wilbur Wood | .20 | .50 |
| 111 Wayne Garrett | .20 | .50 |
| 112 Larry Hardy RC | .20 | .50 |
| 113 Elliott Maddox | .20 | .50 |
| 114 Dick Lange | .20 | .50 |
| 115 Joe Ferguson | .20 | .50 |
| 116 Lerrin LaGrow | .20 | .50 |
| 117 Baltimore Orioles CL/Weaver | 1.25 | 3.00 |
| 118 Mike Anderson | .20 | .50 |
| 119 Tommy Helms | .20 | .50 |
| 120 Steve Busby UER | .40 | 1.00 |
| 121 Bill North | .20 | .50 |
| 122 Al Hrabosky | .40 | 1.00 |
| 123 Johnny Briggs | .20 | .50 |
| 124 Jerry Reuss | .40 | 1.00 |
| 125 Ken Singleton | .40 | 1.00 |
| 126 Checklist 1-132 | 1.25 | 3.00 |
| 127 Glenn Borgmann | .20 | .50 |
| 128 Bill Lee | .40 | 1.00 |
| 129 Rick Monday | .40 | 1.00 |
| 130 Phil Niekro | 1.25 | 3.00 |
| 131 Toby Harrah | .40 | 1.00 |
| 132 Randy Moffitt | .20 | .50 |
| 133 Dan Driessen | .40 | 1.00 |
| 134 Ron Hodges | .20 | .50 |
| 135 Charlie Spikes | .20 | .50 |
| 136 Jim Mason | .20 | .50 |
| 137 Terry Forster | .40 | 1.00 |
| 138 Del Unser | .20 | .50 |
| 139 Horacio Pina | .20 | .50 |
| 140 Steve Garvey | 1.25 | 3.00 |
| 141 Mickey Stanley | .40 | 1.00 |
| 142 Bob Reynolds | .20 | .50 |
| 143 Cliff Johnson RC | .40 | 1.00 |
| 144 Jim Wohlford | .20 | .50 |
| 145 Ken Holtzman | .40 | 1.00 |
| 146 San Diego Padres CL/McNamara | .75 | 2.00 |
| 147 Pedro Garcia | .20 | .50 |
| 148 Jim Rooker | .20 | .50 |
| 149 Tim Foli | .20 | .50 |
| 150 Bob Gibson | 2.50 | 6.00 |
| 151 Steve Brye | .20 | .50 |
| 152 Mario Guerrero | .20 | .50 |
| 153 Rick Reuschel | .40 | 1.00 |
| 154 Mike Lum | .20 | .50 |
| 155 Jim Bibby | .20 | .50 |
| 156 Dave Kingman | .75 | 2.00 |
| 157 Pedro Borbon | .20 | .50 |
| 158 Jerry Grote | .20 | .50 |

| | | |
|---|---|---|
| 159 Steve Arlin | .20 | .50 |
| 160 Graig Nettles | .75 | 2.00 |
| 161 Stan Bahnsen | .20 | .50 |
| 162 Willie Montanez | .20 | .50 |
| 163 Jim Brewer | .20 | .50 |
| 164 Mickey Rivers | .40 | 1.00 |
| 165 Doug Rader | .40 | 1.00 |
| 166 Woodie Fryman | .20 | .50 |
| 167 Rich Coggins | .20 | .50 |
| 168 Bill Greif | .20 | .50 |
| 169 Cookie Rojas | .20 | .50 |
| 170 Bert Campaneris | .40 | 1.00 |
| 171 Ed Kirkpatrick | .20 | .50 |
| 172 Boston Red Sox CL/Johnson | 1.25 | 3.00 |
| 173 Steve Rogers | .40 | 1.00 |
| 174 Bake McBride | .40 | 1.00 |
| 175 Don Money | .40 | 1.00 |
| 176 Burt Hooton | .40 | 1.00 |
| 177 Vic Correll RC | .20 | .50 |
| 178 Cesar Tovar | .20 | .50 |
| 179 Tom Bradley | .20 | .50 |
| 180 Joe Morgan | 2.50 | 6.00 |
| 181 Fred Beene | .20 | .50 |
| 182 Don Hahn | .20 | .50 |
| 183 Mel Stottlemyre | .40 | 1.00 |
| 184 Jorge Orta | .20 | .50 |
| 185 Steve Carlton | 3.00 | 8.00 |
| 186 Willie Crawford | .20 | .50 |
| 187 Denny Doyle | .20 | .50 |
| 188 Tom Griffin | .20 | .50 |
| 189 T.Berra/Campanella MVP | 1.50 | 4.00 |
| 190 B.Shantz/H.Sauer MVP | .75 | 2.00 |
| 191 Al Rosen/H.Campanella MVP | .75 | 2.00 |
| 192 Y.Berra/W.Mays MVP | 1.50 | 4.00 |
| 193 Y.Berra/Campanella MVP | 1.25 | 3.00 |
| 194 M.Mantle/D.Newcombe MVP | 4.00 | 10.00 |
| 195 M.Mantle/H.Aaron MVP | 5.00 | 12.00 |
| 196 J.Jensen/E.Banks MVP | 1.25 | 3.00 |
| 197 N.Fox/E.Banks MVP | .75 | 2.00 |
| 198 R.Maris/D.Groat MVP | .75 | 2.00 |
| 199 R.Maris/F.Robinson MVP | 1.25 | 3.00 |
| 200 M.Mantle/M.Wills MVP | 4.00 | 10.00 |
| 201 E.Howard/S.Koufax MVP | .75 | 2.00 |
| 202 B.Robinson/K.Boyer MVP | .40 | 1.00 |
| 203 Z.Versailes/W.Mays MVP | .75 | 2.00 |
| 204 F.Robinson/B.Clemente MVP | 2.50 | 6.00 |
| 205 C.Yastrzemski/O.Cepeda MVP | .75 | 2.00 |
| 206 D.McLain/D.Gibson MVP | .75 | 2.00 |
| 207 H.Killebrew/W.McCovey MVP | .40 | 1.00 |
| 208 B.Powell/J.Bench MVP | .75 | 2.00 |
| 209 V.Blue/J.Torre MVP | .75 | 2.00 |
| 210 R.Allen/J.Bench MVP | .75 | 2.00 |
| 211 R.Jackson/P.Rose MVP | 2.00 | 5.00 |
| 212 J.Burroughs/S.Garvey MVP | .75 | 2.00 |
| 213 Oscar Gamble | .40 | 1.00 |
| 214 Harry Parker | .20 | .50 |
| 215 Bobby Valentine | .40 | 1.00 |
| 216 San Francisco Giants CL/Westrum | .75 | 2.00 |
| 217 Lou Piniella | .75 | 2.00 |
| 218 Jerry Johnson | .20 | .50 |
| 219 Ed Herrmann | .20 | .50 |
| 220 Don Sutton | 1.25 | 3.00 |
| 221 Aurelio Rodriguez | .20 | .50 |
| 222 Dan Spillner RC | .20 | .50 |
| 223 Robin Yount RC | 20.00 | 50.00 |
| 224 Ramon Hernandez | .20 | .50 |
| 225 Bob Grich | .40 | 1.00 |
| 226 Bill Campbell | .20 | .50 |
| 227 Bob Watson | .40 | 1.00 |
| 228 George Brett RC | 40.00 | 80.00 |
| 229 Barry Foote | .20 | .50 |
| 230 Jim Hunter | 1.50 | 4.00 |
| 231 Mike Tyson | .20 | .50 |
| 232 Diego Segui | .20 | .50 |
| 233 Billy Grabarkewitz | .20 | .50 |
| 234 Tom Grieve | .40 | 1.00 |
| 235 Jack Billingham | .40 | 1.00 |
| 236 California Angels CL/Williams | .75 | 2.00 |
| 237 Carl Morton | .40 | 1.00 |
| 238 Dave Duncan | .40 | 1.00 |
| 239 George Stone | .20 | .50 |
| 240 Garry Maddox | .40 | 1.00 |
| 241 Dick Tidrow | .20 | .50 |
| 242 Jay Johnstone | .40 | 1.00 |
| 243 Jim Kaat | .75 | 2.00 |
| 244 Bill Buckner | .40 | 1.00 |
| 245 Mickey Lolich | .40 | 1.00 |
| 246 St. Louis Cardinals CL/Schoen | .75 | 2.00 |

|  |  | | |
|---|---|---|---|
| 247 | Enos Cabell | .20 | .50 |
| 248 | Randy Jones | .75 | 2.00 |
| 249 | Danny Thompson | .20 | .50 |
| 250 | Ken Brett | .20 | .50 |
| 251 | Fran Healy | .20 | .50 |
| 252 | Fred Scherman | .20 | .50 |
| 253 | Jesus Alou | .20 | .50 |
| 254 | Mike Torrez | .40 | 1.00 |
| 255 | Dwight Evans | .75 | 2.00 |
| 256 | Billy Champion | .20 | .50 |
| 257 | Checklist: 133-264 | 1.25 | 3.00 |
| 258 | Dave LaRoche | .20 | .50 |
| 259 | Len Randle | .20 | .50 |
| 260 | Johnny Bench | 6.00 | 15.00 |
| 261 | Andy Hassler RC | .20 | .50 |
| 262 | Rowland Office RC | .20 | .50 |
| 263 | Jim Perry | .40 | 1.00 |
| 264 | John Milner | .20 | .50 |
| 265 | Ron Bryant | .20 | .50 |
| 266 | Sandy Alomar | .40 | 1.00 |
| 267 | Dick Ruthven | .20 | .50 |
| 268 | Hal McRae | .40 | 1.00 |
| 269 | Doug Rau | .20 | .50 |
| 270 | Ron Fairly | .40 | 1.00 |
| 271 | Gerry Moses | .20 | .50 |
| 272 | Lynn McGlothen | .20 | .50 |
| 273 | Steve Braun | .20 | .50 |
| 274 | Vicente Romo | .20 | .50 |
| 275 | Paul Blair | .40 | 1.00 |
| 276 | Chicago White Sox CL/Tanner | .75 | 2.00 |
| 277 | Frank Taveras | .20 | .50 |
| 278 | Paul Lindblad | .20 | .50 |
| 279 | Milt May | .20 | .50 |
| 280 | Carl Yastrzemski | 5.00 | 12.00 |
| 281 | Jim Slaton | .20 | .50 |
| 282 | Jerry Morales | .20 | .50 |
| 283 | Steve Foucault | .20 | .50 |
| 284 | Ken Griffey Sr. | 1.50 | 4.00 |
| 285 | Ellie Rodriguez | .20 | .50 |
| 286 | Mike Jorgensen | .20 | .50 |
| 287 | Roric Harrison | .20 | .50 |
| 288 | Bruce Ellingsen RC | .20 | .50 |
| 289 | Ken Rudolph | .20 | .50 |
| 290 | Jon Matlack | .20 | .50 |
| 291 | Bill Sudakis | .20 | .50 |
| 292 | Ron Schueler | .20 | .50 |
| 293 | Dick Sharon | .20 | .50 |
| 294 | Geoff Zahn RC | .20 | .50 |
| 295 | Vada Pinson | .75 | 2.00 |
| 296 | Alan Foster | .20 | .50 |
| 297 | Craig Kusick RC | .20 | .50 |
| 298 | Johnny Grubb | .20 | .50 |
| 299 | Bucky Dent | .75 | 2.00 |
| 300 | Reggie Jackson | 6.00 | 15.00 |
| 301 | Dave Roberts | .20 | .50 |
| 302 | Rick Burleson RC | .40 | 1.00 |
| 303 | Grant Jackson | .20 | .50 |
| 304 | Pittsburgh Pirates CL/Murtaugh | .75 | 2.00 |
| 305 | Jim Colborn | .20 | .50 |
| 306 | R.Carew/R.Garr LL | .75 | 2.00 |
| 307 | D.Allen/M.Schmidt LL | 1.50 | 4.00 |
| 308 | J.Burroughs/J.Bench LL | .75 | 2.00 |
| 309 | B.North/L.Brock LL | .75 | 2.00 |
| 310 | N.Hunter/Jenk/Mess/Niek LL | .75 | 2.00 |
| 311 | J.Hunter/B.Capra LL | .75 | 2.00 |
| 312 | N.Ryan/S.Carlton LL | 5.00 | 12.00 |
| 313 | T.Forster/M.Marshall LL | .40 | 1.00 |
| 314 | Buck Martinez | .20 | .50 |
| 315 | Don Kessinger | .40 | 1.00 |
| 316 | Jackie Brown | .20 | .50 |
| 317 | Joe Lahoud | .20 | .50 |
| 318 | Ernie McAnally | .20 | .50 |
| 319 | Johnny Oates | .40 | 1.00 |
| 320 | Pete Rose | 12.50 | 30.00 |
| 321 | Rudy May | .20 | .50 |
| 322 | Ed Goodson | .20 | .50 |
| 323 | Fred Holdsworth | .20 | .50 |
| 324 | Ed Kranepool | .40 | 1.00 |
| 325 | Tony Oliva | .75 | 2.00 |
| 326 | Wayne Twitchell | .20 | .50 |
| 327 | Jerry Hairston | .20 | .50 |
| 328 | Sonny Siebert | .20 | .50 |
| 329 | Ted Kubiak | .20 | .50 |
| 330 | Mike Marshall | .40 | 1.00 |
| 331 | Cleveland Indians CL/Robinson | .75 | 2.00 |
| 332 | Fred Kendall | .20 | .50 |
| 333 | Dick Drago | .20 | .50 |
| 334 | Greg Gross RC | .20 | .50 |
| 335 | Jim Palmer | 2.50 | 6.00 |
| 336 | Rennie Stennett | .20 | .50 |
| 337 | Kevin Kobel | .20 | .50 |
| 338 | Rich Stelmaszek | .20 | .50 |
| 339 | Jim Fregosi | .40 | 1.00 |
| 340 | Paul Splittorff | .20 | .50 |
| 341 | Hal Breeden | .20 | .50 |
| 342 | Leroy Stanton | .20 | .50 |
| 343 | Danny Frisella | .20 | .50 |
| 344 | Ben Oglivie | .40 | 1.00 |
| 345 | Clay Carroll | .40 | 1.00 |
| 346 | Bobby Darwin | .20 | .50 |
| 347 | Mike Caldwell | .20 | .50 |
| 348 | Tony Muser | .20 | .50 |
| 349 | Ray Sadecki | .20 | .50 |
| 350 | Bobby Murcer | .40 | 1.00 |
| 351 | Bob Boone | .75 | 2.00 |
| 352 | Darold Knowles | .20 | .50 |
| 353 | Luis Melendez | .20 | .50 |
| 354 | Dick Bosman | .20 | .50 |
| 355 | Chris Cannizzaro | .20 | .50 |
| 356 | Rico Petrocelli | .40 | 1.00 |
| 357 | Ken Forsch UER | .20 | .50 |
| 358 | Al Bumbry | .40 | 1.00 |
| 359 | Paul Popovich | .20 | .50 |
| 360 | George Scott | .40 | 1.00 |
| 361 | Los Angeles Dodgers CL/Alston | .75 | 2.00 |
| 362 | Steve Hargan | .20 | .50 |
| 363 | Carmen Fanzone | .20 | .50 |
| 364 | Doug Bird | .20 | .50 |
| 365 | Bob Bailey | .20 | .50 |
| 366 | Ken Sanders | .20 | .50 |
| 367 | Craig Robinson | .20 | .50 |
| 368 | Vic Albury | .20 | .50 |
| 369 | Merv Rettenmund | .20 | .50 |
| 370 | Tom Seaver | 5.00 | 12.00 |
| 371 | Gates Brown | .20 | .50 |
| 372 | John D'Acquisto | .20 | .50 |
| 373 | Bill Sharp | .20 | .50 |
| 374 | Eddie Watt | .20 | .50 |
| 375 | Roy White | .40 | 1.00 |
| 376 | Steve Yeager | .40 | 1.00 |
| 377 | Tom Hilgendorf | .20 | .50 |
| 378 | Derrel Thomas | .20 | .50 |
| 379 | Bernie Carbo | .20 | .50 |
| 380 | Sal Bando | .40 | 1.00 |
| 381 | John Curtis | .20 | .50 |
| 382 | Don Baylor | .75 | 2.00 |
| 383 | Jim York | .20 | .50 |
| 384 | Milwaukee Brewers CL/Crandall | .75 | 2.00 |
| 385 | Dock Ellis | .20 | .50 |
| 386 | Checklist: 265-396 UER | 1.25 | 3.00 |
| 387 | Jim Spencer | .20 | .50 |
| 388 | Steve Stone | .40 | 1.00 |
| 389 | Tony Solaita RC | .20 | .50 |
| 390 | Ron Cey | .75 | 2.00 |
| 391 | Don DeMola RC | .20 | .50 |
| 392 | Bruce Bochte RC | .40 | 1.00 |
| 393 | Gary Gentry | .20 | .50 |
| 394 | Larvell Blanks | .20 | .50 |
| 395 | Bud Harrelson | .40 | 1.00 |
| 396 | Fred Norman | .20 | .50 |
| 397 | Bill Freehan | .40 | 1.00 |
| 398 | Elias Sosa | .20 | .50 |
| 399 | Terry Harmon | .20 | .50 |
| 400 | Dick Allen | .75 | 2.00 |
| 401 | Mike Wallace | .20 | .50 |
| 402 | Bob Tolan | .20 | .50 |
| 403 | Tom Buskey RC | .20 | .50 |
| 404 | Ted Sizemore | .20 | .50 |
| 405 | John Montague RC | .20 | .50 |
| 406 | Bob Gallagher | .20 | .50 |
| 407 | Herb Washington RC | .75 | 2.00 |
| 408 | Clyde Wright UER | .20 | .50 |
| 409 | Bob Robertson | .20 | .50 |
| 410 | Mike Cuellar UER | .40 | 1.00 |
| 411 | George Mitterwald | .20 | .50 |
| 412 | Bill Hands | .20 | .50 |
| 413 | Marty Pattin | .20 | .50 |
| 414 | Manny Mota | .40 | 1.00 |
| 415 | John Hiller | .40 | 1.00 |
| 416 | Larry Lintz | .20 | .50 |
| 417 | Skip Lockwood | .20 | .50 |
| 418 | Leo Foster | .20 | .50 |
| 419 | Dave Goltz | .20 | .50 |
| 420 | Larry Bowa | .75 | 2.00 |
| 421 | New York Mets CL/Berra | 1.25 | 3.00 |
| 422 | Brian Downing | .40 | 1.00 |
| 423 | Clay Kirby | .20 | .50 |
| 424 | John Lowenstein | .20 | .50 |
| 425 | Tito Fuentes | .20 | .50 |
| 426 | George Medich | .20 | .50 |
| 427 | Clarence Gaston | .40 | 1.00 |
| 428 | Dave Hamilton | .20 | .50 |
| 429 | Jim Dwyer RC | .20 | .50 |
| 430 | Luis Tiant | .75 | 2.00 |
| 431 | Rod Gilbreath | .20 | .50 |
| 432 | Ken Berry | .20 | .50 |
| 433 | Larry Demery RC | .20 | .50 |
| 434 | Bob Locker | .20 | .50 |
| 435 | Dave Nelson | .20 | .50 |
| 436 | Ken Frailing | .20 | .50 |
| 437 | Al Cowens RC | .40 | 1.00 |
| 438 | Don Carrithers | .20 | .50 |
| 439 | Ed Brinkman | .20 | .50 |
| 440 | Andy Messersmith | .40 | 1.00 |
| 441 | Bobby Heise | .20 | .50 |
| 442 | Maximino Leon RC | .20 | .50 |
| 443 | Minnesota Twins CL/Quilici | .75 | 2.00 |
| 444 | Gene Garber | .40 | 1.00 |
| 445 | Felix Millan | .20 | .50 |
| 446 | Bart Johnson | .20 | .50 |
| 447 | Terry Crowley | .20 | .50 |
| 448 | Frank Duffy | .20 | .50 |
| 449 | Charlie Williams | .20 | .50 |
| 450 | Willie McCovey | 2.50 | 6.00 |
| 451 | Rick Dempsey | .40 | 1.00 |
| 452 | Angel Mangual | .20 | .50 |
| 453 | Claude Osteen | .40 | 1.00 |
| 454 | Doug Griffin | .20 | .50 |
| 455 | Don Wilson | .20 | .50 |
| 456 | Bob Coluccio | .20 | .50 |
| 457 | Mario Mendoza RC | .20 | .50 |
| 458 | Ross Grimsley | .20 | .50 |
| 459 | 1974 AL Championships | .40 | 1.00 |
| 460 | 1974 NL Championships | .75 | 2.00 |
| 461 | Reggie Jackson WS1 | 2.00 | 5.00 |
| 462 | W.Alston/J.Ferguson WS2 | .40 | 1.00 |
| 463 | Rollie Fingers WS3 | .75 | 2.00 |
| 464 | A's Batter WS4 | .40 | 1.00 |
| 465 | Joe Rudi WS5 | .40 | 1.00 |
| 466 | A's Do it Again WS | .75 | 2.00 |
| 467 | Ed Halicki RC | .20 | .50 |
| 468 | Bobby Mitchell | .20 | .50 |
| 469 | Tom Dettore RC | .20 | .50 |
| 470 | Jeff Burroughs | .40 | 1.00 |
| 471 | Bob Stinson | .20 | .50 |
| 472 | Bruce Dal Canton | .20 | .50 |
| 473 | Ken McMullen | .20 | .50 |
| 474 | Luke Walker | .20 | .50 |
| 475 | Darrell Evans | .40 | 1.00 |
| 476 | Ed Figueroa RC | .20 | .50 |
| 477 | Tom Hutton | .20 | .50 |
| 478 | Tom Burgmeier | .20 | .50 |
| 479 | Ken Boswell | .20 | .50 |
| 480 | Carlos May | .20 | .50 |
| 481 | Will McEnaney RC | .40 | 1.00 |
| 482 | Tom McCraw | .20 | .50 |
| 483 | Steve Ontiveros | .20 | .50 |
| 484 | Glenn Beckert | .40 | 1.00 |
| 485 | Sparky Lyle | .40 | 1.00 |
| 486 | Ray Fosse | .20 | .50 |
| 487 | Houston Astros CL/Gomez | .75 | 2.00 |
| 488 | Bill Travers RC | .20 | .50 |
| 489 | Cecil Cooper | .75 | 2.00 |
| 490 | Reggie Smith | .40 | 1.00 |
| 491 | Doyle Alexander | .40 | 1.00 |
| 492 | Rich Hebner | .40 | 1.00 |
| 493 | Don Stanhouse | .20 | .50 |
| 494 | Pete LaCock RC | .20 | .50 |
| 495 | Nelson Briles | .40 | 1.00 |
| 496 | Pepe Frias | .20 | .50 |
| 497 | Jim Nettles | .20 | .50 |
| 498 | Al Downing | .20 | .50 |
| 499 | Marty Perez | .20 | .50 |
| 500 | Nolan Ryan | 20.00 | 50.00 |
| 501 | Bill Robinson | .40 | 1.00 |
| 502 | Pat Bourque | .20 | .50 |
| 503 | Fred Stanley | .20 | .50 |
| 504 | Buddy Bradford | .20 | .50 |
| 505 | Chris Speier | .20 | .50 |
| 506 | Leron Lee | .20 | .50 |
| 507 | Tom Carroll RC | .20 | .50 |
| 508 | Bob Hansen RC | .20 | .50 |
| 509 | Dave Hilton | .20 | .50 |
| 510 | Vida Blue | .40 | 1.00 |

| # | Player | Low | High |
|---|--------|-----|------|
| 511 | Texas Rangers CL/Martin | .75 | 2.00 |
| 512 | Larry Milbourne RC | .20 | .50 |
| 513 | Dick Pole | .20 | .50 |
| 514 | Jose Cruz | .75 | 2.00 |
| 515 | Manny Sanguillen | .40 | 1.00 |
| 516 | Don Hood | .20 | .50 |
| 517 | Checklist: 397-528 | 1.25 | 3.00 |
| 518 | Leo Cardenas | .20 | .50 |
| 519 | Jim Todd RC | .20 | .50 |
| 520 | Amos Otis | .40 | 1.00 |
| 521 | Dennis Blair RC | .20 | .50 |
| 522 | Gary Sutherland | .20 | .50 |
| 523 | Tom Paciorek | .40 | 1.00 |
| 524 | John Doherty RC | .20 | .50 |
| 525 | Tom House | .20 | .50 |
| 526 | Larry Hisle | .40 | 1.00 |
| 527 | Mac Scarce | .20 | .50 |
| 528 | Eddie Leon | .20 | .50 |
| 529 | Gary Thomasson | .20 | .50 |
| 530 | Gaylord Perry | 1.25 | 3.00 |
| 531 | Cincinnati Reds CL/Anderson | 2.00 | 5.00 |
| 532 | Gorman Thomas | .40 | 1.00 |
| 533 | Rudy Meoli | .20 | .50 |
| 534 | Alex Johnson | .20 | .50 |
| 535 | Gene Tenace | .40 | 1.00 |
| 536 | Bob Moose | .20 | .50 |
| 537 | Tommy Harper | .40 | 1.00 |
| 538 | Duffy Dyer | .20 | .50 |
| 539 | Jesse Jefferson | .20 | .50 |
| 540 | Lou Brock | 2.50 | 6.00 |
| 541 | Roger Metzger | .20 | .50 |
| 542 | Pete Broberg | .20 | .50 |
| 543 | Larry Biittner | .20 | .50 |
| 544 | Steve Mingori | .20 | .50 |
| 545 | Billy Williams | 1.25 | 3.00 |
| 546 | John Knox | .20 | .50 |
| 547 | Von Joshua | .20 | .50 |
| 548 | Charlie Sands | .20 | .50 |
| 549 | Bill Butler | .20 | .50 |
| 550 | Ralph Garr | .40 | 1.00 |
| 551 | Larry Christenson | .20 | .50 |
| 552 | Jack Brohamer | .20 | .50 |
| 553 | John Boccabella | .20 | .50 |
| 554 | Goose Gossage | .75 | 2.00 |
| 555 | Al Oliver | .40 | 1.00 |
| 556 | Tim Johnson | .20 | .50 |
| 557 | Larry Gura | .20 | .50 |
| 558 | Dave Roberts | .20 | .50 |
| 559 | Bob Montgomery | .20 | .50 |
| 560 | Tony Perez | 1.50 | 4.00 |
| 561 | Oakland Athletics CL/Dark | .75 | 2.00 |
| 562 | Gary Nolan | .40 | 1.00 |
| 563 | Wilbur Howard | .20 | .50 |
| 564 | Tommy Davis | .40 | 1.00 |
| 565 | Joe Torre | .75 | 2.00 |
| 566 | Ray Burris | .20 | .50 |
| 567 | Jim Sundberg RC | .40 | 1.00 |
| 568 | Dale Murray RC | .20 | .50 |
| 569 | Frank White | .40 | 1.00 |
| 570 | Jim Wynn | .40 | 1.00 |
| 571 | Dave Lemanczyk RC | .20 | .50 |
| 572 | Roger Nelson | .20 | .50 |
| 573 | Orlando Pena | .20 | .50 |
| 574 | Tony Taylor | .20 | .50 |
| 575 | Gene Clines | .20 | .50 |
| 576 | Phil Roof | .20 | .50 |
| 577 | John Morris | .20 | .50 |
| 578 | Dave Tomlin RC | .20 | .50 |
| 579 | Skip Pitlock | .20 | .50 |
| 580 | Frank Robinson | 2.50 | 6.00 |
| 581 | Darrel Chaney | .20 | .50 |
| 582 | Eduardo Rodriguez | .20 | .50 |
| 583 | Andy Etchebarren | .20 | .50 |
| 584 | Mike Garman | .20 | .50 |
| 585 | Chris Chambliss | .40 | 1.00 |
| 586 | Tim McCarver | .75 | 2.00 |
| 587 | Chris Ward RC | .20 | .50 |
| 588 | Rick Auerbach | .20 | .50 |
| 589 | Atlanta Braves CL/King | .75 | 2.00 |
| 590 | Cesar Cedeno | .40 | 1.00 |
| 591 | Glenn Abbott | .20 | .50 |
| 592 | Balor Moore | .20 | .50 |
| 593 | Gene Lamont | .20 | .50 |
| 594 | Jim Fuller | .20 | .50 |
| 595 | Joe Niekro | .40 | 1.00 |
| 596 | Ollie Brown | .20 | .50 |
| 597 | Winston Llenas | .20 | .50 |
| 598 | Bruce Kison | .20 | .50 |
| 599 | Nate Colbert | .20 | .50 |
| 600 | Rod Carew | 3.00 | 8.00 |
| 601 | Juan Beniquez | .20 | .50 |
| 602 | John Vukovich | .20 | .50 |
| 603 | Lew Krausse | .20 | .50 |
| 604 | Oscar Zamora RC | .20 | .50 |
| 605 | John Ellis | .20 | .50 |
| 606 | Bruce Miller RC | .20 | .50 |
| 607 | Jim Holt | .20 | .50 |
| 608 | Gene Michael | .20 | .50 |
| 609 | Elrod Hendricks | .20 | .50 |
| 610 | Ron Hunt | .20 | .50 |
| 611 | New York Yankees CL/Virdon | .75 | 2.00 |
| 612 | Terry Hughes | .20 | .50 |
| 613 | Bill Parsons | .20 | .50 |
| 614 | Kuc/Mill/Ruhle/Sieb RC | .40 | 1.00 |
| 615 | Darcy/Leonard/Und/Webb RC | .75 | 2.00 |
| 616 | Jim Rice RC | 10.00 | 25.00 |
| 617 | Cubb/DeCinces/Sand/Trillo RC | .75 | 2.00 |
| 618 | East/John/McGregor/Rhoden RC | .40 | 1.00 |
| 619 | Ayala/Nyman/Smith Turner RC | .40 | 1.00 |
| 620 | Gary Carter RC | 6.00 | 15.00 |
| 621 | Denny/Eastwick/Kem/Vein RC | .75 | 2.00 |
| 622 | Fred Lynn RC | 3.00 | 8.00 |
| 623 | K.Kern RC/P.Garner RC | 4.00 | 10.00 |
| 624 | Kon/Lansde/Otten/Sol RC | .40 | 1.00 |
| 625 | Boog Powell | .75 | 2.00 |
| 626 | Larry Haney UER | .20 | .50 |
| 627 | Tom Walker | .20 | .50 |
| 628 | Ron LeFlore RC | .40 | 1.00 |
| 629 | Joe Hoerner | .20 | .50 |
| 630 | Greg Luzinski | .75 | 2.00 |
| 631 | Lee Lacy | .20 | .50 |
| 632 | Morris Nettles RC | .20 | .50 |
| 633 | Paul Casanova | .20 | .50 |
| 634 | Cy Acosta | .20 | .50 |
| 635 | Chuck Dobson | .20 | .50 |
| 636 | Charlie Moore | .20 | .50 |
| 637 | Ted Martinez | .20 | .50 |
| 638 | Chicago Cubs CL/Marshall | .75 | 2.00 |
| 639 | Steve Kline | .20 | .50 |
| 640 | Harmon Killebrew | 2.50 | 6.00 |
| 641 | Jim Northrup | .40 | 1.00 |
| 642 | Mike Phillips | .20 | .50 |
| 643 | Brent Strom | .20 | .50 |
| 644 | Bill Fahey | .20 | .50 |
| 645 | Danny Cater | .20 | .50 |
| 646 | Checklist: 529-660 | 1.25 | 3.00 |
| 647 | Claudell Washington RC | .75 | 2.00 |
| 648 | Dave Pagan RC | .20 | .50 |
| 649 | Jack Heidemann | .20 | .50 |
| 650 | Dave May | .20 | .50 |
| 651 | John Morlan RC | .20 | .50 |
| 652 | Lindy McDaniel | .40 | 1.00 |
| 653 | Lee Richard UER | .20 | .50 |
| 654 | Jerry Terrell | .20 | .50 |
| 655 | Rico Carty | .40 | 1.00 |
| 656 | Bill Plummer | .20 | .50 |
| 657 | Bob Oliver | .20 | .50 |
| 658 | Vic Harris | .20 | .50 |
| 659 | Bob Apodaca | .20 | .50 |
| 660 | Hank Aaron | 12.50 | 30.00 |

## 1976 Topps

MIKE SCHMIDT PHILLIES

| # | Player | Low | High |
|---|--------|-----|------|
| | COMPLETE SET (660) | 125.00 | 250.00 |
| 1 | Hank Aaron RB | 6.00 | 15.00 |
| 2 | Bobby Bonds RB | .60 | 1.50 |
| 3 | Mickey Lolich RB | .30 | .75 |
| 4 | Dave Lopes RB | .30 | .75 |
| 5 | Tom Seaver RB | 2.00 | 5.00 |
| 6 | Rennie Stennett RB | .30 | .75 |
| 7 | Jim Umbarger RB | .15 | .40 |
| 8 | Tito Fuentes RB | .15 | .40 |
| 9 | Paul Lindblad | .15 | .40 |
| 10 | Lou Brock | 2.00 | 5.00 |
| 11 | Jim Hughes | .15 | .40 |
| 12 | Richie Zisk | .30 | .75 |
| 13 | John Wockenfuss RC | .15 | .40 |
| 14 | Gene Garber | .30 | .75 |
| 15 | George Scott | .30 | .75 |
| 16 | Bob Apodaca | .15 | .40 |
| 17 | New York Yankees CL/Martin | .60 | 1.50 |
| 18 | Dale Murray | .15 | .40 |
| 19 | George Brett | 12.50 | 30.00 |
| 20 | Bob Watson | .30 | .75 |
| 21 | Dave LaRoche | .15 | .40 |
| 22 | Bill Russell | .30 | .75 |
| 23 | Brian Downing | .15 | .40 |
| 24 | Cesar Geronimo | .30 | .75 |
| 25 | Mike Torrez | .30 | .75 |
| 26 | Andre Thornton | .30 | .75 |
| 27 | Ed Figueroa | .15 | .40 |
| 28 | Dusty Baker | .60 | 1.50 |
| 29 | Rick Burleson | .30 | .75 |
| 30 | John Montefusco RC | .30 | .75 |
| 31 | Len Randle | .15 | .40 |
| 32 | Danny Frisella | .15 | .40 |
| 33 | Bill North | .15 | .40 |
| 34 | Mike Garman | .15 | .40 |
| 35 | Tony Oliva | .60 | 1.50 |
| 36 | Frank Tavares | .15 | .40 |
| 37 | John Hiller | .30 | .75 |
| 38 | Garry Maddox | .30 | .75 |
| 39 | Pete Broberg | .15 | .40 |
| 40 | Dave Kingman | .60 | 1.50 |
| 41 | Tippy Martinez RC | .30 | .75 |
| 42 | Barry Foote | .15 | .40 |
| 43 | Paul Splittorff | .15 | .40 |
| 44 | Doug Rader | .30 | .75 |
| 45 | Boog Powell | .60 | 1.50 |
| 46 | Los Angeles Dodgers CL/Alston | .60 | 1.50 |
| 47 | Jesse Jefferson | .15 | .40 |
| 48 | Dave Concepcion | .60 | 1.50 |
| 49 | Dave Duncan | .30 | .75 |
| 50 | Fred Lynn | .60 | 1.50 |
| 51 | Ray Burris | .15 | .40 |
| 52 | Dave Chalk | .15 | .40 |
| 53 | Mike Beard RC | .15 | .40 |
| 54 | Dave Rader | .15 | .40 |
| 55 | Gaylord Perry | 1.00 | 2.50 |
| 56 | Bob Tolan | .15 | .40 |
| 57 | Phil Garner | .30 | .75 |
| 58 | Ron Reed | .15 | .40 |
| 59 | Larry Hisle | .30 | .75 |
| 60 | Jerry Reuss | .30 | .75 |
| 61 | Ron LeFlore | .30 | .75 |
| 62 | Johnny Oates | .15 | .40 |
| 63 | Bobby Darwin | .15 | .40 |
| 64 | Jerry Koosman | .30 | .75 |
| 65 | Chris Chambliss | .30 | .75 |
| 66 | Gus/Buddy Bell FS | .30 | .75 |
| 67 | Bob/Ray Boone FS | .30 | .75 |
| 68 | Joe/Joe Jr. Coleman FS | .15 | .40 |
| 69 | Jim/Mike Hegan FS | .15 | .40 |
| 70 | Roy/Roy Jr. Smalley FS | .15 | .40 |
| 71 | Steve Rogers | .30 | .75 |
| 72 | Hal McRae | .30 | .75 |
| 73 | Baltimore Orioles CL/Weaver | .60 | 1.50 |
| 74 | Oscar Gamble | .30 | .75 |
| 75 | Larry Dierker | .30 | .75 |
| 76 | Willie Crawford | .15 | .40 |
| 77 | Pedro Borbon | .15 | .40 |
| 78 | Cecil Cooper | .30 | .75 |
| 79 | Jerry Morales | .15 | .40 |
| 80 | Jim Kaat | .60 | 1.50 |
| 81 | Darrell Evans | .30 | .75 |
| 82 | Von Joshua | .15 | .40 |
| 83 | Jim Spencer | .15 | .40 |
| 84 | Brent Strom | .15 | .40 |
| 85 | Mickey Rivers | .30 | .75 |
| 86 | Mike Tyson | .15 | .40 |
| 87 | Tom Burgmeier | .15 | .40 |
| 88 | Duffy Dyer | .15 | .40 |
| 89 | Vern Ruhle | .15 | .40 |
| 90 | Sal Bando | .30 | .75 |
| 91 | Tom Hutton | .15 | .40 |
| 92 | Eduardo Rodriguez | .15 | .40 |
| 93 | Mike Phillips | .15 | .40 |
| 94 | Jim Dwyer RC | .15 | .40 |
| 95 | Brooks Robinson | 2.50 | 6.00 |
| 96 | Doug Bird | .15 | .40 |
| 97 | Wilbur Howard | .15 | .40 |

| # | Player | Price 1 | Price 2 |
|---|--------|--------|--------|
| ❑ 98 | Dennis Eckersley RC | 12.50 | 30.00 |
| ❑ 99 | Lee Lacy | .15 | .40 |
| ❑ 100 | Jim Hunter | 1.25 | 3.00 |
| ❑ 101 | Pete LaCock | .15 | .40 |
| ❑ 102 | Jim Willoughby | .15 | .40 |
| ❑ 103 | Biff Pocoroba RC | .15 | .40 |
| ❑ 104 | Cincinnati Reds CL/Anderson | 1.00 | 2.50 |
| ❑ 105 | Gary Lavelle | .15 | .40 |
| ❑ 106 | Tom Grieve | .30 | .75 |
| ❑ 107 | Dave Roberts | .15 | .40 |
| ❑ 108 | Don Kirkwood RC | .15 | .40 |
| ❑ 109 | Larry Lintz | .15 | .40 |
| ❑ 110 | Carlos May | .15 | .40 |
| ❑ 111 | Danny Thompson | .15 | .40 |
| ❑ 112 | Kent Tekulve RC | .60 | 1.50 |
| ❑ 113 | Gary Sutherland | .15 | .40 |
| ❑ 114 | Jay Johnstone | .30 | .75 |
| ❑ 115 | Ken Holtzman | .30 | .75 |
| ❑ 116 | Charlie Moore | .15 | .40 |
| ❑ 117 | Mike Jorgensen | .15 | .40 |
| ❑ 118 | Boston Red Sox CL/Johnson | .60 | 1.50 |
| ❑ 119 | Checklist 1-132 | .60 | 1.50 |
| ❑ 120 | Rusty Staub | .15 | .40 |
| ❑ 121 | Tony Solaita | .15 | .40 |
| ❑ 122 | Mike Cosgrove | .15 | .40 |
| ❑ 123 | Walt Williams | .15 | .40 |
| ❑ 124 | Doug Rau | .15 | .40 |
| ❑ 125 | Don Baylor | .60 | 1.50 |
| ❑ 126 | Tom Dettore | .15 | .40 |
| ❑ 127 | Larvell Blanks | .15 | .40 |
| ❑ 128 | Ken Griffey Sr. | 1.00 | 2.50 |
| ❑ 129 | Andy Etchebarren | .15 | .40 |
| ❑ 130 | Luis Tiant | .60 | 1.50 |
| ❑ 131 | Bill Stein RC | .15 | .40 |
| ❑ 132 | Don Hood | .15 | .40 |
| ❑ 133 | Gary Matthews | .30 | .75 |
| ❑ 134 | Mike Ivie | .15 | .40 |
| ❑ 135 | Bake McBride | .30 | .75 |
| ❑ 136 | Dave Goltz | .15 | .40 |
| ❑ 137 | Bill Robinson | .30 | .75 |
| ❑ 138 | Lerrin LaGrow | .15 | .40 |
| ❑ 139 | Gorman Thomas | .30 | .75 |
| ❑ 140 | Vida Blue | .30 | .75 |
| ❑ 141 | Larry Parrish RC | .60 | 1.50 |
| ❑ 142 | Dick Drago | .15 | .40 |
| ❑ 143 | Jerry Grote | .15 | .40 |
| ❑ 144 | Al Fitzmorris | .15 | .40 |
| ❑ 145 | Larry Bowa | .30 | .75 |
| ❑ 146 | George Medich | .15 | .40 |
| ❑ 147 | Houston Astros CL/Virdon | .60 | 1.50 |
| ❑ 148 | Stan Thomas RC | .15 | .40 |
| ❑ 149 | Tommy Davis | .30 | .75 |
| ❑ 150 | Steve Garvey | 1.00 | 2.50 |
| ❑ 151 | Bill Bonham | .15 | .40 |
| ❑ 152 | Leroy Stanton | .15 | .40 |
| ❑ 153 | Buzz Capra | .15 | .40 |
| ❑ 154 | Bucky Dent | .30 | .75 |
| ❑ 155 | Jack Billingham | .30 | .75 |
| ❑ 156 | Rico Carty | .15 | .40 |
| ❑ 157 | Mike Caldwell | .15 | .40 |
| ❑ 158 | Ken Reitz | .15 | .40 |
| ❑ 159 | Jerry Terrell | .15 | .40 |
| ❑ 160 | Dave Winfield | 4.00 | 10.00 |
| ❑ 161 | Bruce Kison | .15 | .40 |
| ❑ 162 | Jack Pierce RC | .15 | .40 |
| ❑ 163 | Jim Slaton | .15 | .40 |
| ❑ 164 | Pepe Mangual | .15 | .40 |
| ❑ 165 | Gene Tenace | .30 | .75 |
| ❑ 166 | Skip Lockwood | .15 | .40 |
| ❑ 167 | Freddie Patek | .15 | .40 |
| ❑ 168 | Tom Hilgendorf | .15 | .40 |
| ❑ 169 | Graig Nettles | .60 | 1.50 |
| ❑ 170 | Rick Wise | .15 | .40 |
| ❑ 171 | Greg Gross | .15 | .40 |
| ❑ 172 | Texas Rangers CL/Lucchesi | .60 | 1.50 |
| ❑ 173 | Steve Swisher | .15 | .40 |
| ❑ 174 | Charlie Hough | .30 | .75 |
| ❑ 175 | Ken Singleton | .30 | .75 |
| ❑ 176 | Dick Lange | .15 | .40 |
| ❑ 177 | Marty Perez | .15 | .40 |
| ❑ 178 | Tom Buskey | .15 | .40 |
| ❑ 179 | George Foster | .60 | 1.50 |
| ❑ 180 | Goose Gossage | .60 | 1.50 |
| ❑ 181 | Willie Montanez | .15 | .40 |
| ❑ 182 | Harry Rasmussen | .15 | .40 |
| ❑ 183 | Steve Braun | .15 | .40 |
| ❑ 184 | Bill Greif | .15 | .40 |
| ❑ 185 | Dave Parker | .60 | 1.50 |
| ❑ 186 | Tom Walker | .15 | .40 |
| ❑ 187 | Pedro Garcia | .15 | .40 |
| ❑ 188 | Fred Scherman | .15 | .40 |
| ❑ 189 | Claudell Washington | .30 | .75 |
| ❑ 190 | Jon Matlack | .15 | .40 |
| ❑ 191 | Madlock/Simm/Maug.LL | .30 | .75 |
| ❑ 192 | Carew/Lynn/Munson LL | 1.00 | 2.50 |
| ❑ 193 | Schmidt/King/Luz LL | 1.25 | 3.00 |
| ❑ 194 | Reggie/Scott/Mayb LL | 1.25 | 3.00 |
| ❑ 195 | Luz/Bench/Perez LL | .60 | 1.50 |
| ❑ 196 | Scott/Mayb/Lynn LL | .30 | .75 |
| ❑ 197 | Lopes/Morgan/Brock LL | .60 | 1.50 |
| ❑ 198 | Rivers/Wash/Otis LL | .30 | .75 |
| ❑ 199 | Seaver/Jones/Mess LL | 1.00 | 2.50 |
| ❑ 200 | Hunter/Palmer/Blue LL | .60 | 1.50 |
| ❑ 201 | Jones/Mess/Seaver LL | .60 | 1.50 |
| ❑ 202 | Palmer/Hunter/Eck LL | 1.25 | 3.00 |
| ❑ 203 | Seaver/Mont/Mess LL | 1.00 | 2.50 |
| ❑ 204 | Tanana/Blyleven/Perry LL | .30 | .75 |
| ❑ 205 | A.Hrabosky/G.Gossage LL | .30 | .75 |
| ❑ 206 | Manny Trillo | .15 | .40 |
| ❑ 207 | Andy Hassler | .15 | .40 |
| ❑ 208 | Mike Lum | .15 | .40 |
| ❑ 209 | Alan Ashby RC | .15 | .40 |
| ❑ 210 | Lee May | .30 | .75 |
| ❑ 211 | Clay Carroll | .15 | .40 |
| ❑ 212 | Pat Kelly | .15 | .40 |
| ❑ 213 | Dave Heaverlo RC | .15 | .40 |
| ❑ 214 | Eric Soderholm | .15 | .40 |
| ❑ 215 | Reggie Smith | .30 | .75 |
| ❑ 216 | Montreal Expos CL/Kuehl | .60 | 1.50 |
| ❑ 217 | Dave Freisleben | .15 | .40 |
| ❑ 218 | John Knox | .15 | .40 |
| ❑ 219 | Tom Murphy | .15 | .40 |
| ❑ 220 | Manny Sanguillen | .30 | .75 |
| ❑ 221 | Jim Todd | .15 | .40 |
| ❑ 222 | Wayne Garrett | .15 | .40 |
| ❑ 223 | Ollie Brown | .15 | .40 |
| ❑ 224 | Jim York | .15 | .40 |
| ❑ 225 | Roy White | .30 | .75 |
| ❑ 226 | Jim Sundberg | .30 | .75 |
| ❑ 227 | Oscar Zamora | .15 | .40 |
| ❑ 228 | John Hale RC | .15 | .40 |
| ❑ 229 | Jerry Remy RC | .15 | .40 |
| ❑ 230 | Carl Yastrzemski | 4.00 | 10.00 |
| ❑ 231 | Tom House | .15 | .40 |
| ❑ 232 | Frank Duffy | .15 | .40 |
| ❑ 233 | Grant Jackson | .15 | .40 |
| ❑ 234 | Mike Sadek | .15 | .40 |
| ❑ 235 | Bert Blyleven | .60 | 1.50 |
| ❑ 236 | Kansas City Royals CL/Herzog | .60 | 1.50 |
| ❑ 237 | Dave Hamilton | .15 | .40 |
| ❑ 238 | Larry Biittner | .15 | .40 |
| ❑ 239 | John Curtis | .15 | .40 |
| ❑ 240 | Pete Rose | 10.00 | 25.00 |
| ❑ 241 | Hector Torres | .15 | .40 |
| ❑ 242 | Dan Meyer | .15 | .40 |
| ❑ 243 | Jim Rooker | .15 | .40 |
| ❑ 244 | Bill Sharp | .15 | .40 |
| ❑ 245 | Felix Millan | .15 | .40 |
| ❑ 246 | Cesar Tovar | .15 | .40 |
| ❑ 247 | Terry Harmon | .15 | .40 |
| ❑ 248 | Dick Tidrow | .15 | .40 |
| ❑ 249 | Cliff Johnson | .30 | .75 |
| ❑ 250 | Fergie Jenkins | 1.00 | 2.50 |
| ❑ 251 | Rick Monday | .30 | .75 |
| ❑ 252 | Tim Nordbrook RC | .15 | .40 |
| ❑ 253 | Bill Buckner | .30 | .75 |
| ❑ 254 | Rudy Meoli | .15 | .40 |
| ❑ 255 | Fritz Peterson | .15 | .40 |
| ❑ 256 | Rowland Office | .15 | .40 |
| ❑ 257 | Ross Grimsley | .15 | .40 |
| ❑ 258 | Nyls Nyman | .15 | .40 |
| ❑ 259 | Darrel Chaney | .15 | .40 |
| ❑ 260 | Steve Busby | .30 | .75 |
| ❑ 261 | Gary Thomasson | .15 | .40 |
| ❑ 262 | Checklist 133-264 | .60 | 1.50 |
| ❑ 263 | Lyman Bostock RC | .60 | 1.50 |
| ❑ 264 | Steve Renko | .15 | .40 |
| ❑ 265 | Willie Davis | .30 | .75 |
| ❑ 266 | Alan Foster | .15 | .40 |
| ❑ 267 | Aurelio Rodriguez | .15 | .40 |
| ❑ 268 | Del Unser | .15 | .40 |
| ❑ 269 | Rick Austin | .15 | .40 |
| ❑ 270 | Willie Stargell | 1.25 | 3.00 |
| ❑ 271 | Jim Lonborg | .30 | .75 |
| ❑ 272 | Rick Dempsey | .30 | .75 |
| ❑ 273 | Joe Niekro | .30 | .75 |
| ❑ 274 | Tommy Harper | .30 | .75 |
| ❑ 275 | Rick Manning RC | .15 | .40 |
| ❑ 276 | Mickey Scott | .15 | .40 |
| ❑ 277 | Chicago Cubs CL/Marshall | .60 | 1.50 |
| ❑ 278 | Bernie Carbo | .15 | .40 |
| ❑ 279 | Roy Howell RC | .15 | .40 |
| ❑ 280 | Burt Hooton | .30 | .75 |
| ❑ 281 | Dave May | .15 | .40 |
| ❑ 282 | Dan Osborn RC | .15 | .40 |
| ❑ 283 | Merv Rettenmund | .15 | .40 |
| ❑ 284 | Steve Ontiveros | .15 | .40 |
| ❑ 285 | Mike Cuellar | .30 | .75 |
| ❑ 286 | Jim Wohlford | .15 | .40 |
| ❑ 287 | Pete Mackanin | .15 | .40 |
| ❑ 288 | Bill Campbell | .15 | .40 |
| ❑ 289 | Enzo Hernandez | .15 | .40 |
| ❑ 290 | Ted Simmons | .30 | .75 |
| ❑ 291 | Ken Sanders | .15 | .40 |
| ❑ 292 | Leon Roberts | .15 | .40 |
| ❑ 293 | Bill Castro RC | .15 | .40 |
| ❑ 294 | Ed Kirkpatrick | .15 | .40 |
| ❑ 295 | Dave Cash | .15 | .40 |
| ❑ 296 | Pat Dobson | .15 | .40 |
| ❑ 297 | Roger Metzger | .15 | .40 |
| ❑ 298 | Dick Bosman | .15 | .40 |
| ❑ 299 | Champ Summers RC | .15 | .40 |
| ❑ 300 | Johnny Bench | 5.00 | 12.00 |
| ❑ 301 | Jackie Brown | .15 | .40 |
| ❑ 302 | Rick Miller | .15 | .40 |
| ❑ 303 | Steve Foucault | .15 | .40 |
| ❑ 304 | California Angels CL/Williams | .60 | 1.50 |
| ❑ 305 | Andy Messersmith | .30 | .75 |
| ❑ 306 | Rod Gilbreath | .15 | .40 |
| ❑ 307 | Al Bumbry | .30 | .75 |
| ❑ 308 | Jim Barr | .15 | .40 |
| ❑ 309 | Bill Melton | .15 | .40 |
| ❑ 310 | Randy Jones | .30 | .75 |
| ❑ 311 | Cookie Rojas | .15 | .40 |
| ❑ 312 | Don Carrithers | .15 | .40 |
| ❑ 313 | Dan Ford RC | .15 | .40 |
| ❑ 314 | Ed Kranepool | .15 | .40 |
| ❑ 315 | Al Hrabosky | .30 | .75 |
| ❑ 316 | Robin Yount | 6.00 | 15.00 |
| ❑ 317 | John Candelaria RC | .60 | 1.50 |
| ❑ 318 | Bob Boone | .60 | 1.50 |
| ❑ 319 | Larry Gura | .15 | .40 |
| ❑ 320 | Willie Horton | .30 | .75 |
| ❑ 321 | Jose Cruz | .60 | 1.50 |
| ❑ 322 | Glenn Abbott | .15 | .40 |
| ❑ 323 | Rob Sperring RC | .15 | .40 |
| ❑ 324 | Jim Bibby | .15 | .40 |
| ❑ 325 | Tony Perez | 1.25 | 3.00 |
| ❑ 326 | Dick Pole | .15 | .40 |
| ❑ 327 | Dave Moates RC | .15 | .40 |
| ❑ 328 | Carl Morton | .15 | .40 |
| ❑ 329 | Joe Ferguson | .15 | .40 |
| ❑ 330 | Nolan Ryan | 10.00 | 25.00 |
| ❑ 331 | San Diego Padres CL/McNamara | .60 | 1.50 |
| ❑ 332 | Charlie Williams | .15 | .40 |
| ❑ 333 | Bob Coluccio | .15 | .40 |
| ❑ 334 | Dennis Leonard | .30 | .75 |
| ❑ 335 | Bob Grich | .30 | .75 |
| ❑ 336 | Vic Albury | .15 | .40 |
| ❑ 337 | Bud Harrelson | .30 | .75 |
| ❑ 338 | Bob Bailey | .15 | .40 |
| ❑ 339 | John Denny | .30 | .75 |
| ❑ 340 | Jim Rice | 1.50 | 4.00 |
| ❑ 341 | Lou Gehrig ATG | 5.00 | 12.00 |
| ❑ 342 | Rogers Hornsby ATG | 1.25 | 3.00 |
| ❑ 343 | Pie Traynor ATG | .60 | 1.50 |
| ❑ 344 | Honus Wagner ATG | 2.00 | 5.00 |
| ❑ 345 | Babe Ruth ATG | 6.00 | 15.00 |
| ❑ 346 | Ty Cobb ATG | 5.00 | 12.00 |
| ❑ 347 | Ted Williams ATG | 5.00 | 12.00 |
| ❑ 348 | Mickey Cochrane ATG | .60 | 1.50 |
| ❑ 349 | Walter Johnson ATG | 2.00 | 5.00 |
| ❑ 350 | Lefty Grove ATG | .60 | 1.50 |
| ❑ 351 | Randy Hundley | .30 | .75 |
| ❑ 352 | Dave Giusti | .15 | .40 |
| ❑ 353 | Sixto Lezcano RC | .15 | .40 |
| ❑ 354 | Ron Blomberg | .15 | .40 |
| ❑ 355 | Steve Carlton | 2.50 | 6.00 |
| ❑ 356 | Ted Martinez | .15 | .40 |
| ❑ 357 | Ken Forsch | .15 | .40 |
| ❑ 358 | Buddy Bell | .30 | .75 |
| ❑ 359 | Rick Reuschel | .30 | .75 |
| ❑ 360 | Jeff Burroughs | .30 | .75 |
| ❑ 361 | Detroit Tigers CL/Houk | .60 | 1.50 |

|  |  | | |
|---|------|------|------|
| 362 | Will McEnaney | .30 | .75 |
| 363 | Dave Collins RC | .30 | .75 |
| 364 | Elias Sosa | .15 | .40 |
| 365 | Carlton Fisk | 2.50 | 6.00 |
| 366 | Bobby Valentine | .30 | .75 |
| 367 | Bruce Miller | .15 | .40 |
| 368 | Wilbur Wood | .15 | .40 |
| 369 | Frank White | .30 | .75 |
| 370 | Ron Cey | .30 | .75 |
| 371 | Elrod Hendricks | .15 | .40 |
| 372 | Rick Baldwin RC | .15 | .40 |
| 373 | Johnny Briggs | .15 | .40 |
| 374 | Dan Warthen RC | .15 | .40 |
| 375 | Ron Fairly | .30 | .75 |
| 376 | Rich Hebner | .30 | .75 |
| 377 | Mike Hegan | .15 | .40 |
| 378 | Steve Stone | .30 | .75 |
| 379 | Ken Boswell | .15 | .40 |
| 380 | Bobby Bonds | .60 | 1.50 |
| 381 | Denny Doyle | .15 | .40 |
| 382 | Matt Alexander RC | .15 | .40 |
| 383 | John Ellis | .15 | .40 |
| 384 | Philadelphia Phillies CL/Ozark | .60 | 1.50 |
| 385 | Mickey Lolich | .30 | .75 |
| 386 | Ed Goodson | .15 | .40 |
| 387 | Mike Miley RC | .15 | .40 |
| 388 | Stan Perzanowski RC | .15 | .40 |
| 389 | Glenn Adams RC | .15 | .40 |
| 390 | Don Gullett | .30 | .75 |
| 391 | Jerry Hairston | .15 | .40 |
| 392 | Checklist 265-396 | .60 | 1.50 |
| 393 | Paul Mitchell RC | .15 | .40 |
| 394 | Fran Healy | .15 | .40 |
| 395 | Jim Wynn | .30 | .75 |
| 396 | Bill Lee | .15 | .40 |
| 397 | Tim Foli | .15 | .40 |
| 398 | Dave Tomlin | .15 | .40 |
| 399 | Luis Melendez | .15 | .40 |
| 400 | Rod Carew | 2.50 | 6.00 |
| 401 | Ken Brett | .15 | .40 |
| 402 | Don Money | .30 | .75 |
| 403 | Geoff Zahn | .15 | .40 |
| 404 | Enos Cabell | .15 | .40 |
| 405 | Rollie Fingers | 1.00 | 2.50 |
| 406 | Ed Hermann | .15 | .40 |
| 407 | Tom Underwood | .15 | .40 |
| 408 | Charlie Spikes | .15 | .40 |
| 409 | Dave Lemanczyk | .15 | .40 |
| 410 | Ralph Garr | .30 | .75 |
| 411 | Bill Singer | .15 | .40 |
| 412 | Toby Harrah | .30 | .75 |
| 413 | Pete Varney RC | .15 | .40 |
| 414 | Wayne Garland | .15 | .40 |
| 415 | Vada Pinson | .60 | 1.50 |
| 416 | Tommy John | .60 | 1.50 |
| 417 | Gene Clines | .15 | .40 |
| 418 | Jose Morales RC | .15 | .40 |
| 419 | Reggie Cleveland | .15 | .40 |
| 420 | Joe Morgan | 2.00 | 5.00 |
| 421 | Oakland Athletics CL | .60 | 1.50 |
| 422 | Johnny Grubb | .15 | .40 |
| 423 | Ed Halicki | .15 | .40 |
| 424 | Phil Roof | .15 | .40 |
| 425 | Rennie Stennett | .15 | .40 |
| 426 | Bob Forsch | .15 | .40 |
| 427 | Kurt Bevacqua | .15 | .40 |
| 428 | Jim Crawford | .15 | .40 |
| 429 | Fred Stanley | .15 | .40 |
| 430 | Jose Cardenal | .30 | .75 |
| 431 | Dick Ruthven | .15 | .40 |
| 432 | Tom Veryzer | .15 | .40 |
| 433 | Rick Waits RC | .15 | .40 |
| 434 | Morris Nettles | .15 | .40 |
| 435 | Phil Niekro | 1.00 | 2.50 |
| 436 | Bill Fahey | .15 | .40 |
| 437 | Terry Forster | .15 | .40 |
| 438 | Doug DeCinces | .30 | .75 |
| 439 | Rick Rhoden | .30 | .75 |
| 440 | John Mayberry | .30 | .75 |
| 441 | Gary Carter | 1.50 | 4.00 |
| 442 | Hank Webb | .15 | .40 |
| 443 | San Francisco Giants CL | .60 | 1.50 |
| 444 | Gary Nolan | .30 | .75 |
| 445 | Rico Petrocelli | .30 | .75 |
| 446 | Larry Haney | .15 | .40 |
| 447 | Gene Locklear | .15 | .40 |
| 448 | Tom Johnson | .15 | .40 |
| 449 | Bob Robertson | .15 | .40 |
| 450 | Jim Palmer | 2.00 | 5.00 |
| 451 | Buddy Bradford | .15 | .40 |
| 452 | Tom Hausman RC | .15 | .40 |
| 453 | Lou Piniella | .60 | 1.50 |
| 454 | Tom Griffin | .15 | .40 |
| 455 | Dick Allen | .60 | 1.50 |
| 456 | Joe Coleman | .15 | .40 |
| 457 | Ed Crosby | .15 | .40 |
| 458 | Earl Williams | .15 | .40 |
| 459 | Jim Brewer | .15 | .40 |
| 460 | Cesar Cedeno | .30 | .75 |
| 461 | NL/AL Champs | .30 | .75 |
| 462 | 1975 WS/Reds Champs | .30 | .75 |
| 463 | Steve Hargan | .15 | .40 |
| 464 | Ken Henderson | .15 | .40 |
| 465 | Mike Marshall | .30 | .75 |
| 466 | Bob Stinson | .15 | .40 |
| 467 | Woodie Fryman | .15 | .40 |
| 468 | Jesus Alou | .15 | .40 |
| 469 | Rawly Eastwick | .30 | .75 |
| 470 | Bobby Murcer | .30 | .75 |
| 471 | Jim Burton | .15 | .40 |
| 472 | Bob Davis RC | .15 | .40 |
| 473 | Paul Blair | .30 | .75 |
| 474 | Ray Corbin | .15 | .40 |
| 475 | Joe Rudi | .30 | .75 |
| 476 | Bob Moose | .15 | .40 |
| 477 | Cleveland Indians CL/Robinson | .60 | 1.50 |
| 478 | Lynn McGlothen | .15 | .40 |
| 479 | Bobby Mitchell | .15 | .40 |
| 480 | Mike Schmidt | 6.00 | 15.00 |
| 481 | Rudy May | .15 | .40 |
| 482 | Tim Hosley | .15 | .40 |
| 483 | Mickey Stanley | .15 | .40 |
| 484 | Eric Raich RC | .15 | .40 |
| 485 | Mike Hargrove | .30 | .75 |
| 486 | Bruce Dal Canton | .15 | .40 |
| 487 | Leron Lee | .15 | .40 |
| 488 | Claude Osteen | .30 | .75 |
| 489 | Skip Jutze | .15 | .40 |
| 490 | Frank Tanana | .30 | .75 |
| 491 | Terry Crowley | .15 | .40 |
| 492 | Marty Pattin | .15 | .40 |
| 493 | Derrel Thomas | .15 | .40 |
| 494 | Craig Swan | .30 | .75 |
| 495 | Nate Colbert | .15 | .40 |
| 496 | Juan Beniquez | .15 | .40 |
| 497 | Joe McIntosh RC | .15 | .40 |
| 498 | Glenn Borgmann | .15 | .40 |
| 499 | Mario Guerrero | .15 | .40 |
| 500 | Reggie Jackson | 5.00 | 12.00 |
| 501 | Billy Champion | .15 | .40 |
| 502 | Tim McCarver | .60 | 1.50 |
| 503 | Elliott Maddox | .15 | .40 |
| 504 | Pittsburgh Pirates CL/Murtaugh | .60 | 1.50 |
| 505 | Mark Belanger | .30 | .75 |
| 506 | George Mitterwald | .15 | .40 |
| 507 | Ray Bare RC | .15 | .40 |
| 508 | Duane Kuiper RC | .30 | .75 |
| 509 | Bill Hands | .15 | .40 |
| 510 | Amos Otis | .30 | .75 |
| 511 | Jamie Easterley | .15 | .40 |
| 512 | Ellie Rodriguez | .15 | .40 |
| 513 | Bart Johnson | .15 | .40 |
| 514 | Dan Driessen | .30 | .75 |
| 515 | Steve Yeager | .30 | .75 |
| 516 | Wayne Granger | .15 | .40 |
| 517 | John Milner | .15 | .40 |
| 518 | Doug Flynn RC | .15 | .40 |
| 519 | Steve Brye | .15 | .40 |
| 520 | Willie McCovey | 2.00 | 5.00 |
| 521 | Jim Colborn | .15 | .40 |
| 522 | Ted Sizemore | .15 | .40 |
| 523 | Bob Montgomery | .15 | .40 |
| 524 | Pete Falcone RC | .15 | .40 |
| 525 | Billy Williams | 1.00 | 2.50 |
| 526 | Checklist 397-528 | .60 | 1.50 |
| 527 | Mike Anderson | .15 | .40 |
| 528 | Dock Ellis | .15 | .40 |
| 529 | Deron Johnson | .15 | .40 |
| 530 | Don Sutton | 1.00 | 2.50 |
| 531 | New York Mets CL/Frazier | .60 | 1.50 |
| 532 | Milt May | .15 | .40 |
| 533 | Lee Richard | .15 | .40 |
| 534 | Stan Bahnsen | .15 | .40 |
| 535 | Dave Nelson | .15 | .40 |
| 536 | Mike Thompson | .15 | .40 |
| 537 | Tony Muser | .15 | .40 |
| 538 | Pat Darcy | .15 | .40 |
| 539 | John Balaz RC | .15 | .40 |
| 540 | Bill Freehan | .30 | .75 |
| 541 | Steve Mingori | .15 | .40 |
| 542 | Keith Hernandez | .30 | .75 |
| 543 | Wayne Twitchell | .15 | .40 |
| 544 | Pepe Frias | .15 | .40 |
| 545 | Sparky Lyle | .30 | .75 |
| 546 | Dave Rosello | .15 | .40 |
| 547 | Roric Harrison | .15 | .40 |
| 548 | Manny Mota | .30 | .75 |
| 549 | Randy Tate RC | .15 | .40 |
| 550 | Hank Aaron | 10.00 | 25.00 |
| 551 | Jerry DaVanon | .15 | .40 |
| 552 | Terry Humphrey | .15 | .40 |
| 553 | Randy Moffitt | .15 | .40 |
| 554 | Ray Fosse | .15 | .40 |
| 555 | Dyar Miller | .15 | .40 |
| 556 | Minnesota Twins CL/Mauch | .60 | 1.50 |
| 557 | Dan Spillner | .15 | .40 |
| 558 | Clarence Gaston | .30 | .75 |
| 559 | Clyde Wright | .15 | .40 |
| 560 | Jorge Orta | .15 | .40 |
| 561 | Tom Carroll | .15 | .40 |
| 562 | Adrian Garrett | .15 | .40 |
| 563 | Larry Demery | .15 | .40 |
| 564 | Kurt Bevacqua GUM | .60 | 1.50 |
| 565 | Tug McGraw | .30 | .75 |
| 566 | Ken McMullen | .15 | .40 |
| 567 | George Stone | .15 | .40 |
| 568 | Rob Andrews RC | .15 | .40 |
| 569 | Nelson Briles | .30 | .75 |
| 570 | George Hendrick | .30 | .75 |
| 571 | Don DeMola | .15 | .40 |
| 572 | Rich Coggins | .15 | .40 |
| 573 | Bill Travers | .15 | .40 |
| 574 | Don Kessinger | .30 | .75 |
| 575 | Dwight Evans | .60 | 1.50 |
| 576 | Maximino Leon | .15 | .40 |
| 577 | Marc Hill | .15 | .40 |
| 578 | Ted Kubiak | .15 | .40 |
| 579 | Clay Kirby | .15 | .40 |
| 580 | Bert Campaneris | .30 | .75 |
| 581 | St. Louis Cardinals CL/Schoendienst | .60 | 1.50 |
| 582 | Mike Kekich | .15 | .40 |
| 583 | Tommy Helms | .15 | .40 |
| 584 | Stan Wall RC | .15 | .40 |
| 585 | Joe Torre | .60 | 1.50 |
| 586 | Ron Schueler | .15 | .40 |
| 587 | Leo Cardenas | .15 | .40 |
| 588 | Kevin Kobel | .15 | .40 |
| 589 | Alo/Flanagan/Pac/Torr RC | .60 | 1.50 |
| 590 | Cruz/Lemon/Valen/Whit RC | .30 | .75 |
| 591 | Grilli/Mitch/Sosa/Throop RC | .30 | .75 |
| 592 | Randolph/McK/Roy/Sta RC | 2.00 | 5.00 |
| 593 | And/Crosby/Litell/Metzger RC | .30 | .75 |
| 594 | Mer/Oh/Still/White RC | .30 | .75 |
| 595 | DeFil/Lerch/Monge/Barr RC | .30 | .75 |
| 596 | Rey/John/LeMas/Manuel RC | .30 | .75 |
| 597 | Aase/Kucek/LaCorte/Pazik RC | .30 | .75 |
| 598 | Cruz/Quirk/Turner/Wallis RC | .30 | .75 |
| 599 | Dres/Guidry/McCl/Zach RC | 3.00 | 8.00 |
| 600 | Tom Seaver | 4.00 | 10.00 |
| 601 | Ken Rudolph | .15 | .40 |
| 602 | Doug Konieczny | .15 | .40 |
| 603 | Jim Holt | .15 | .40 |
| 604 | Joe Lovitto | .15 | .40 |
| 605 | Al Downing | .15 | .40 |
| 606 | Milwaukee Brewers CL/Grammas | .60 | 1.50 |
| 607 | Rich Hinton | .15 | .40 |
| 608 | Vic Correll | .15 | .40 |
| 609 | Fred Norman | .15 | .40 |
| 610 | Greg Luzinski | .60 | 1.50 |
| 611 | Rich Folkers | .15 | .40 |
| 612 | Joe Lahoud | .15 | .40 |
| 613 | Tim Johnson | .15 | .40 |
| 614 | Fernando Arroyo RC | .15 | .40 |
| 615 | Mike Cubbage | .15 | .40 |
| 616 | Buck Martinez | .15 | .40 |
| 617 | Darold Knowles | .15 | .40 |
| 618 | Jack Brohamer | .15 | .40 |
| 619 | Bill Butler | .15 | .40 |
| 620 | Al Oliver | .30 | .75 |
| 621 | Tom Hall | .15 | .40 |
| 622 | Rick Auerbach | .15 | .40 |
| 623 | Bob Allietta RC | .15 | .40 |
| 624 | Tony Taylor | .15 | .40 |
| 625 | J.R. Richard | .30 | .75 |

| | | |
|---|---|---|
| ❏ 626 Bob Sheldon | .15 | .40 |
| ❏ 627 Bill Plummer | .15 | .40 |
| ❏ 628 John D'Acquisto | .15 | .40 |
| ❏ 629 Sandy Alomar | .30 | .75 |
| ❏ 630 Chris Speier | .15 | .40 |
| ❏ 631 Atlanta Braves CL/Bristol | .60 | 1.50 |
| ❏ 632 Rogelio Moret | .15 | .40 |
| ❏ 633 John Stearns RC | .30 | .75 |
| ❏ 634 Larry Christenson | .15 | .40 |
| ❏ 635 Jim Fregosi | .30 | .75 |
| ❏ 636 Joe Decker | .15 | .40 |
| ❏ 637 Bruce Bochte | .15 | .40 |
| ❏ 638 Doyle Alexander | .30 | .75 |
| ❏ 639 Fred Kendall | .15 | .40 |
| ❏ 640 Bill Madlock | .60 | 1.50 |
| ❏ 641 Tom Paciorek | .30 | .75 |
| ❏ 642 Dennis Blair | .15 | .40 |
| ❏ 643 Checklist 529-660 | .60 | 1.50 |
| ❏ 644 Tom Bradley | .15 | .40 |
| ❏ 645 Darrell Porter | .30 | .75 |
| ❏ 646 John Lowenstein | .15 | .40 |
| ❏ 647 Ramon Hernandez | .15 | .40 |
| ❏ 648 Al Cowens | .30 | .75 |
| ❏ 649 Dave Roberts | .15 | .40 |
| ❏ 650 Thurman Munson | 2.50 | 6.00 |
| ❏ 651 John Odom | .15 | .40 |
| ❏ 652 Ed Armbrister | .15 | .40 |
| ❏ 653 Mike Norris RC | .30 | .75 |
| ❏ 654 Doug Griffin | .15 | .40 |
| ❏ 655 Mike Vail RC | .15 | .40 |
| ❏ 656 Chicago White Sox CL/Tanner | .60 | 1.50 |
| ❏ 657 Roy Smalley RC | .30 | .75 |
| ❏ 658 Jerry Johnson | .15 | .40 |
| ❏ 659 Ben Oglivie | .30 | .75 |
| ❏ 660 Davey Lopes | .60 | 1.50 |

## 1977 Topps

ROYALS
GEORGE BRETT
A.L. ALL STARS

| | | |
|---|---|---|
| ❏ COMPLETE SET (660) | 125.00 | 250.00 |
| ❏ 1 G.Brett/B.Madlock LL | 3.00 | 8.00 |
| ❏ 2 G.Nettles/M.Schmidt LL | 1.00 | 2.50 |
| ❏ 3 L.May/G.Foster LL | .60 | 1.50 |
| ❏ 4 B.North/D.Lopes LL | .30 | .75 |
| ❏ 5 J.Palmer/R.Jones LL | .60 | 1.50 |
| ❏ 6 N.Ryan/T.Seaver LL | 6.00 | 15.00 |
| ❏ 7 M.Fidrych/J.Denny LL | .30 | .75 |
| ❏ 8 B.Campbell/R.Eastwick LL | .30 | .75 |
| ❏ 9 Doug Rader | .12 | .30 |
| ❏ 10 Reggie Jackson | 4.00 | 10.00 |
| ❏ 11 Rob Dressler | .12 | .30 |
| ❏ 12 Larry Haney | .12 | .30 |
| ❏ 13 Luis Gomez RC | .12 | .30 |
| ❏ 14 Tommy Smith | .12 | .30 |
| ❏ 15 Don Gullett | .30 | .75 |
| ❏ 16 Bob Jones RC | .12 | .30 |
| ❏ 17 Steve Stone | .30 | .75 |
| ❏ 18 Cleveland Indians CL/Robinson | .60 | 1.50 |
| ❏ 19 John D'Acquisto | .12 | .30 |
| ❏ 20 Graig Nettles | .60 | 1.50 |
| ❏ 21 Ken Forsch | .12 | .30 |
| ❏ 22 Bill Freehan | .30 | .75 |
| ❏ 23 Dan Driessen | .12 | .30 |
| ❏ 24 Carl Morton | .12 | .30 |
| ❏ 25 Dwight Evans | .60 | 1.50 |
| ❏ 26 Ray Sadecki | .12 | .30 |
| ❏ 27 Bill Buckner | .30 | .75 |
| ❏ 28 Woodie Fryman | .12 | .30 |
| ❏ 29 Bucky Dent | .30 | .75 |
| ❏ 30 Greg Luzinski | .60 | 1.50 |
| ❏ 31 Jim Todd | .12 | .30 |
| ❏ 32 Checklist 1-132 | .60 | 1.50 |
| ❏ 33 Wayne Garland | .12 | .30 |
| ❏ 34 California Angels CL/Sherry | .60 | 1.50 |
| ❏ 35 Rennie Stennett | .12 | .30 |
| ❏ 36 John Ellis | .12 | .30 |
| ❏ 37 Steve Hargan | .12 | .30 |
| ❏ 38 Craig Kusick | .12 | .30 |
| ❏ 39 Tom Griffin | .12 | .30 |
| ❏ 40 Bobby Murcer | .30 | .75 |
| ❏ 41 Jim Kern | .12 | .30 |
| ❏ 42 Jose Cruz | .30 | .75 |
| ❏ 43 Ray Bare | .12 | .30 |
| ❏ 44 Bud Harrelson | .30 | .75 |
| ❏ 45 Rawly Eastwick | .30 | .75 |
| ❏ 46 Buck Martinez | .12 | .30 |
| ❏ 47 Lynn McGlothen | .12 | .30 |
| ❏ 48 Tom Paciorek | .30 | .75 |
| ❏ 49 Grant Jackson | .12 | .30 |
| ❏ 50 Ron Cey | .30 | .75 |
| ❏ 51 Milwaukee Brewers CL/Grammas | .60 | 1.50 |
| ❏ 52 Ellis Valentine | .12 | .30 |
| ❏ 53 Paul Mitchell | .12 | .30 |
| ❏ 54 Sandy Alomar | .30 | .75 |
| ❏ 55 Jeff Burroughs | .30 | .75 |
| ❏ 56 Rudy May | .12 | .30 |
| ❏ 57 Marc Hill | .12 | .30 |
| ❏ 58 Chet Lemon | .30 | .75 |
| ❏ 59 Larry Christenson | .12 | .30 |
| ❏ 60 Jim Rice | 1.00 | 2.50 |
| ❏ 61 Manny Sanguillen | .30 | .75 |
| ❏ 62 Eric Raich | .12 | .30 |
| ❏ 63 Tito Fuentes | .12 | .30 |
| ❏ 64 Larry Biittner | .12 | .30 |
| ❏ 65 Skip Lockwood | .12 | .30 |
| ❏ 66 Roy Smalley | .30 | .75 |
| ❏ 67 Joaquin Andujar RC | .30 | .75 |
| ❏ 68 Bruce Bochte | .12 | .30 |
| ❏ 69 Jim Crawford | .12 | .30 |
| ❏ 70 Johnny Bench | 4.00 | 10.00 |
| ❏ 71 Dock Ellis | .12 | .30 |
| ❏ 72 Mike Anderson | .12 | .30 |
| ❏ 73 Charlie Williams | .12 | .30 |
| ❏ 74 Oakland Athletics CL/McKeon | .60 | 1.50 |
| ❏ 75 Dennis Leonard | .30 | .75 |
| ❏ 76 Tim Foli | .12 | .30 |
| ❏ 77 Dyar Miller | .12 | .30 |
| ❏ 78 Bob Davis | .12 | .30 |
| ❏ 79 Don Money | .30 | .75 |
| ❏ 80 Andy Messersmith | .30 | .75 |
| ❏ 81 Juan Beniquez | .12 | .30 |
| ❏ 82 Jim Rooker | .12 | .30 |
| ❏ 83 Kevin Bell RC | .12 | .30 |
| ❏ 84 Ollie Brown | .12 | .30 |
| ❏ 85 Duane Kuiper | .12 | .30 |
| ❏ 86 Pat Zachry | .12 | .30 |
| ❏ 87 Glenn Borgmann | .12 | .30 |
| ❏ 88 Stan Wall | .12 | .30 |
| ❏ 89 Butch Hobson RC | .30 | .75 |
| ❏ 90 Cesar Cedeno | .30 | .75 |
| ❏ 91 John Verhoeven RC | .12 | .30 |
| ❏ 92 Dave Rosello | .12 | .30 |
| ❏ 93 Tom Poquette | .12 | .30 |
| ❏ 94 Craig Swan | .12 | .30 |
| ❏ 95 Keith Hernandez | .30 | .75 |
| ❏ 96 Lou Piniella | .30 | .75 |
| ❏ 97 Dave Heaverlo | .12 | .30 |
| ❏ 98 Milt May | .12 | .30 |
| ❏ 99 Tom Hausman | .12 | .30 |
| ❏ 100 Joe Morgan | 1.50 | 4.00 |
| ❏ 101 Dick Bosman | .12 | .30 |
| ❏ 102 Jose Morales | .12 | .30 |
| ❏ 103 Mike Bacsik RC | .12 | .30 |
| ❏ 104 Omar Moreno RC | .30 | .75 |
| ❏ 105 Steve Yeager | .30 | .75 |
| ❏ 106 Mike Flanagan | .30 | .75 |
| ❏ 107 Bill Melton | .12 | .30 |
| ❏ 108 Alan Foster | .12 | .30 |
| ❏ 109 Jorge Orta | .12 | .30 |
| ❏ 110 Steve Carlton | 2.00 | 5.00 |
| ❏ 111 Rico Petrocelli | .30 | .75 |
| ❏ 112 Bill Greif | .12 | .30 |
| ❏ 113 Toronto Blue Jays CL/Hartsfield | .60 | 1.50 |
| ❏ 114 Bruce Dal Canton | .12 | .30 |
| ❏ 115 Rick Manning | .12 | .30 |
| ❏ 116 Joe Niekro | .30 | .75 |
| ❏ 117 Frank White | .30 | .75 |
| ❏ 118 Rick Jones RC | .12 | .30 |
| ❏ 119 John Stearns | .12 | .30 |
| ❏ 120 Rod Carew | 2.00 | 5.00 |
| ❏ 121 Gary Nolan | .12 | .30 |
| ❏ 122 Ben Oglivie | .30 | .75 |
| ❏ 123 Fred Stanley | .12 | .30 |
| ❏ 124 George Mitterwald | .12 | .30 |
| ❏ 125 Bill Travers | .12 | .30 |
| ❏ 126 Rod Gilbreath | .12 | .30 |
| ❏ 127 Ron Fairly | .30 | .75 |
| ❏ 128 Tommy John | .60 | 1.50 |
| ❏ 129 Mike Sadek | .12 | .30 |
| ❏ 130 Al Oliver | .30 | .75 |
| ❏ 131 Orlando Ramirez RC | .12 | .30 |
| ❏ 132 Chip Lang RC | .12 | .30 |
| ❏ 133 Ralph Garr | .30 | .75 |
| ❏ 134 San Diego Padres CL/McNamara | .60 | 1.50 |
| ❏ 135 Mark Belanger | .30 | .75 |
| ❏ 136 Jerry Mumphrey RC | .30 | .75 |
| ❏ 137 Jeff Terpko RC | .12 | .30 |
| ❏ 138 Bob Stinson | .12 | .30 |
| ❏ 139 Fred Norman | .12 | .30 |
| ❏ 140 Mike Schmidt | 5.00 | 12.00 |
| ❏ 141 Mark Littell | .12 | .30 |
| ❏ 142 Steve Dillard RC | .12 | .30 |
| ❏ 143 Ed Herrmann | .12 | .30 |
| ❏ 144 Bruce Sutter RC | 6.00 | 15.00 |
| ❏ 145 Tom Veryzer | .12 | .30 |
| ❏ 146 Dusty Baker | .60 | 1.50 |
| ❏ 147 Jackie Brown | .12 | .30 |
| ❏ 148 Fran Healy | .12 | .30 |
| ❏ 149 Mike Cubbage | .12 | .30 |
| ❏ 150 Tom Seaver | 3.00 | 8.00 |
| ❏ 151 Johnny LeMaster | .12 | .30 |
| ❏ 152 Gaylord Perry | 1.00 | 2.50 |
| ❏ 153 Ron Jackson RC | .12 | .30 |
| ❏ 154 Dave Giusti | .12 | .30 |
| ❏ 155 Joe Rudi | .30 | .75 |
| ❏ 156 Pete Mackanin | .12 | .30 |
| ❏ 157 Ken Brett | .12 | .30 |
| ❏ 158 Ted Kubiak | .12 | .30 |
| ❏ 159 Bernie Carbo | .12 | .30 |
| ❏ 160 Will McEnaney | .12 | .30 |
| ❏ 161 Garry Templeton RC | .60 | 1.50 |
| ❏ 162 Mike Cuellar | .30 | .75 |
| ❏ 163 Dave Hilton | .12 | .30 |
| ❏ 164 Tug McGraw | .30 | .75 |
| ❏ 165 Jim Wynn | .30 | .75 |
| ❏ 166 Bill Campbell | .12 | .30 |
| ❏ 167 Rich Hebner | .30 | .75 |
| ❏ 168 Charlie Spikes | .12 | .30 |
| ❏ 169 Darold Knowles | .12 | .30 |
| ❏ 170 Thurman Munson | 2.00 | 5.00 |
| ❏ 171 Ken Sanders | .12 | .30 |
| ❏ 172 John Milner | .12 | .30 |
| ❏ 173 Chuck Scrivener RC | .12 | .30 |
| ❏ 174 Nelson Briles | .30 | .75 |
| ❏ 175 Butch Wynegar RC | .30 | .75 |
| ❏ 176 Bob Robertson | .12 | .30 |
| ❏ 177 Bart Johnson | .12 | .30 |
| ❏ 178 Bombo Rivera RC | .12 | .30 |
| ❏ 179 Paul Hartzell RC | .12 | .30 |
| ❏ 180 Dave Lopes | .30 | .75 |
| ❏ 181 Ken McMullen | .12 | .30 |
| ❏ 182 Dan Spillner | .12 | .30 |
| ❏ 183 St.Louis Cardinals CL/V.Rapp | .60 | 1.50 |
| ❏ 184 Bo McLaughlin RC | .12 | .30 |
| ❏ 185 Sixto Lezcano | .12 | .30 |
| ❏ 186 Doug Flynn | .12 | .30 |
| ❏ 187 Dick Pole | .12 | .30 |
| ❏ 188 Bob Tolan | .12 | .30 |
| ❏ 189 Rick Dempsey | .30 | .75 |
| ❏ 190 Ray Burris | .12 | .30 |
| ❏ 191 Doug Griffin | .12 | .30 |
| ❏ 192 Clarence Gaston | .30 | .75 |
| ❏ 193 Larry Gura | .12 | .30 |
| ❏ 194 Gary Matthews | .30 | .75 |
| ❏ 195 Ed Figueroa | .12 | .30 |
| ❏ 196 Len Randle | .12 | .30 |
| ❏ 197 Ed Ott | .12 | .30 |
| ❏ 198 Wilbur Wood | .12 | .30 |
| ❏ 199 Pepe Frias | .12 | .30 |
| ❏ 200 Frank Tanana | .30 | .75 |
| ❏ 201 Ed Kranepool | .30 | .75 |
| ❏ 202 Tom Johnson | .12 | .30 |
| ❏ 203 Ed Armbrister | .12 | .30 |
| ❏ 204 Jeff Newman RC | .12 | .30 |
| ❏ 205 Pete Falcone | .12 | .30 |
| ❏ 206 Boog Powell | .60 | 1.50 |
| ❏ 207 Glenn Abbott | .12 | .30 |
| ❏ 208 Checklist 133-264 | .60 | 1.50 |
| ❏ 209 Rob Andrews | .12 | .30 |
| ❏ 210 Fred Lynn | .30 | .75 |
| ❏ 211 San Francisco Giants CL/Altobelli | .60 | 1.50 |
| ❏ 212 Jim Mason | .12 | .30 |

|  |  | | |
|---|---|---|---|
| 213 | Maximino Leon | .12 | .30 |
| 214 | Darrell Porter | .30 | .75 |
| 215 | Butch Metzger | .12 | .30 |
| 216 | Doug DeCinces | .30 | .75 |
| 217 | Tom Underwood | .12 | .30 |
| 218 | John Wathan RC | .30 | .75 |
| 219 | Joe Coleman | .12 | .30 |
| 220 | Chris Chambliss | .30 | .75 |
| 221 | Bob Bailey | .12 | .30 |
| 222 | Francisco Barrios RC | .12 | .30 |
| 223 | Earl Williams | .12 | .30 |
| 224 | Rusty Torres | .12 | .30 |
| 225 | Bob Apodaca | .12 | .30 |
| 226 | Leroy Stanton | .12 | .30 |
| 227 | Joe Sambito RC | .12 | .30 |
| 228 | Minnesota Twins CL/Mauch | .60 | 1.50 |
| 229 | Don Kessinger | .30 | .75 |
| 230 | Vida Blue | .30 | .75 |
| 231 | George Brett RB | 3.00 | 8.00 |
| 232 | Minnie Minoso RB | .30 | .75 |
| 233 | Jose Morales RB | .12 | .30 |
| 234 | Nolan Ryan RB | 6.00 | 15.00 |
| 235 | Cecil Cooper | .30 | .75 |
| 236 | Tom Buskey | .12 | .30 |
| 237 | Gene Clines | .12 | .30 |
| 238 | Tippy Martinez | .12 | .30 |
| 239 | Bill Plummer | .12 | .30 |
| 240 | Ron LeFlore | .30 | .75 |
| 241 | Dave Tomlin | .12 | .30 |
| 242 | Ken Henderson | .12 | .30 |
| 243 | Ron Reed | .12 | .30 |
| 244 | John Mayberry | .30 | .75 |
| 245 | Rick Rhoden | .30 | .75 |
| 246 | Mike Vail | .12 | .30 |
| 247 | Chris Knapp RC | .12 | .30 |
| 248 | Wilbur Howard | .12 | .30 |
| 249 | Pete Redfern RC | .12 | .30 |
| 250 | Bill Madlock | .30 | .75 |
| 251 | Tony Muser | .12 | .30 |
| 252 | Dale Murray | .12 | .30 |
| 253 | John Hale | .12 | .30 |
| 254 | Doyle Alexander | .12 | .30 |
| 255 | George Scott | .30 | .75 |
| 256 | Joe Hoerner | .12 | .30 |
| 257 | Mike Miley | .12 | .30 |
| 258 | Luis Tiant | .30 | .75 |
| 259 | New York Mets CL/Frazier | .60 | 1.50 |
| 260 | J.R. Richard | .30 | .75 |
| 261 | Phil Garner | .30 | .75 |
| 262 | Al Cowens | .30 | .75 |
| 263 | Mike Marshall | .30 | .75 |
| 264 | Tom Hutton | .12 | .30 |
| 265 | Mark Fidrych RC | 1.25 | 3.00 |
| 266 | Derrel Thomas | .12 | .30 |
| 267 | Ray Fosse | .12 | .30 |
| 268 | Rick Sawyer RC | .12 | .30 |
| 269 | Joe Lis | .12 | .30 |
| 270 | Dave Parker | .60 | 1.50 |
| 271 | Terry Forster | .12 | .30 |
| 272 | Lee Lacy | .12 | .30 |
| 273 | Eric Soderholm | .12 | .30 |
| 274 | Don Stanhouse | .12 | .30 |
| 275 | Mike Hargrove | .30 | .75 |
| 276 | Chris Chambliss ALCS | .60 | 1.50 |
| 277 | Pete Rose NLCS | 2.00 | 5.00 |
| 278 | Danny Frisella | .12 | .30 |
| 279 | Joe Wallis | .12 | .30 |
| 280 | Jim Hunter | 1.00 | 2.50 |
| 281 | Roy Staiger | .12 | .30 |
| 282 | Sid Monge | .12 | .30 |
| 283 | Jerry DaVanon | .12 | .30 |
| 284 | Mike Norris | .12 | .30 |
| 285 | Brooks Robinson | 2.00 | 5.00 |
| 286 | Johnny Grubb | .12 | .30 |
| 287 | Cincinnati Reds CL/Anderson | .60 | 1.50 |
| 288 | Bob Montgomery | .12 | .30 |
| 289 | Gene Garber | .30 | .75 |
| 290 | Amos Otis | .30 | .75 |
| 291 | Jason Thompson RC | .30 | .75 |
| 292 | Rogelio Moret | .12 | .30 |
| 293 | Jack Brohamer | .12 | .30 |
| 294 | George Medich | .12 | .30 |
| 295 | Gary Carter | 1.00 | 2.50 |
| 296 | Don Hood | .12 | .30 |
| 297 | Ken Reitz | .12 | .30 |
| 298 | Charlie Hough | .30 | .75 |
| 299 | Otto Velez | .12 | .30 |
| 300 | Jerry Koosman | .30 | .75 |
| 301 | Toby Harrah | .30 | .75 |
| 302 | Mike Garman | .12 | .30 |
| 303 | Gene Tenace | .30 | .75 |
| 304 | Jim Hughes | .12 | .30 |
| 305 | Mickey Rivers | .30 | .75 |
| 306 | Rick Waits | .12 | .30 |
| 307 | Gary Sutherland | .12 | .30 |
| 308 | Gene Pentz RC | .12 | .30 |
| 309 | Boston Red Sox CL/Zimmer | .60 | 1.50 |
| 310 | Larry Bowa | .30 | .75 |
| 311 | Vern Ruhle | .12 | .30 |
| 312 | Rob Belloir RC | .12 | .30 |
| 313 | Paul Blair | .30 | .75 |
| 314 | Steve Mingori | .12 | .30 |
| 315 | Dave Chalk | .12 | .30 |
| 316 | Steve Rogers | .12 | .30 |
| 317 | Kurt Bevacqua | .12 | .30 |
| 318 | Duffy Dyer | .12 | .30 |
| 319 | Goose Gossage | .60 | 1.50 |
| 320 | Ken Griffey Sr. | .60 | 1.50 |
| 321 | Dave Goltz | .12 | .30 |
| 322 | Bill Russell | .30 | .75 |
| 323 | Larry Lintz | .12 | .30 |
| 324 | John Curtis | .12 | .30 |
| 325 | Mike Ivie | .12 | .30 |
| 326 | Jesse Jefferson | .12 | .30 |
| 327 | Houston Astros CL/Virdon | .60 | 1.50 |
| 328 | Tommy Boggs RC | .12 | .30 |
| 329 | Ron Hodges | .12 | .30 |
| 330 | George Hendrick | .30 | .75 |
| 331 | Jim Colborn | .12 | .30 |
| 332 | Elliott Maddox | .12 | .30 |
| 333 | Paul Reuschel RC | .12 | .30 |
| 334 | Bill Stein | .12 | .30 |
| 335 | Bill Robinson | .30 | .75 |
| 336 | Denny Doyle | .12 | .30 |
| 337 | Ron Schueler | .12 | .30 |
| 338 | Dave Duncan | .30 | .75 |
| 339 | Adrian Devine | .12 | .30 |
| 340 | Hal McRae | .30 | .75 |
| 341 | Joe Kerrigan RC | .12 | .30 |
| 342 | Jerry Remy | .12 | .30 |
| 343 | Ed Halicki | .12 | .30 |
| 344 | Brian Downing | .30 | .75 |
| 345 | Reggie Smith | .30 | .75 |
| 346 | Bill Singer | .12 | .30 |
| 347 | George Foster | .60 | 1.50 |
| 348 | Brent Strom | .12 | .30 |
| 349 | Jim Holt | .12 | .30 |
| 350 | Larry Dierker | .30 | .75 |
| 351 | Jim Sundberg | .30 | .75 |
| 352 | Mike Phillips | .12 | .30 |
| 353 | Stan Thomas | .12 | .30 |
| 354 | Pittsburgh Pirates CL/Tanner | .60 | 1.50 |
| 355 | Lou Brock | 1.50 | 4.00 |
| 356 | Checklist 265-396 | .60 | 1.50 |
| 357 | Tim McCarver | .60 | 1.50 |
| 358 | Tom House | .12 | .30 |
| 359 | Willie Randolph | .60 | 1.50 |
| 360 | Rick Monday | .30 | .75 |
| 361 | Eduardo Rodriguez | .12 | .30 |
| 362 | Tommy Davis | .30 | .75 |
| 363 | Dave Roberts | .12 | .30 |
| 364 | Vic Correll | .12 | .30 |
| 365 | Mike Torrez | .30 | .75 |
| 366 | Ted Sizemore | .12 | .30 |
| 367 | Dave Hamilton | .12 | .30 |
| 368 | Mike Jorgensen | .12 | .30 |
| 369 | Terry Humphrey | .12 | .30 |
| 370 | John Montefusco | .30 | .75 |
| 371 | Kansas City Royals CL/Herzog | .60 | 1.50 |
| 372 | Rich Folkers | .12 | .30 |
| 373 | Bert Campaneris | .30 | .75 |
| 374 | Kent Tekulve | .30 | .75 |
| 375 | Larry Hisle | .30 | .75 |
| 376 | Nino Espinosa RC | .12 | .30 |
| 377 | Dave McKay | .12 | .30 |
| 378 | Jim Umbarger | .12 | .30 |
| 379 | Larry Cox RC | .12 | .30 |
| 380 | Lee May | .30 | .75 |
| 381 | Bob Forsch | .12 | .30 |
| 382 | Charlie Moore | .12 | .30 |
| 383 | Stan Bahnsen | .12 | .30 |
| 384 | Darrel Chaney | .12 | .30 |
| 385 | Dave LaRoche | .12 | .30 |
| 386 | Manny Mota | .30 | .75 |
| 387 | New York Yankees CL/Martin | 1.00 | 2.50 |
| 388 | Terry Harmon | .12 | .30 |
| 389 | Ken Kravec RC | .12 | .30 |
| 390 | Dave Winfield | 2.50 | 6.00 |
| 391 | Dan Warthen | .12 | .30 |
| 392 | Phil Roof | .12 | .30 |
| 393 | John Lowenstein | .12 | .30 |
| 394 | Bill Laxton RC | .12 | .30 |
| 395 | Manny Trillo | .12 | .30 |
| 396 | Tom Murphy | .12 | .30 |
| 397 | Larry Herndon RC | .30 | .75 |
| 398 | Tom Burgmeier | .12 | .30 |
| 399 | Bruce Boisclair RC | .12 | .30 |
| 400 | Steve Garvey | 1.00 | 2.50 |
| 401 | Mickey Stanley | .12 | .30 |
| 402 | Tommy Helms | .12 | .30 |
| 403 | Tom Grieve | .30 | .75 |
| 404 | Eric Rasmussen RC | .12 | .30 |
| 405 | Claudell Washington | .30 | .75 |
| 406 | Tim Johnson | .12 | .30 |
| 407 | Dave Freisleben | .12 | .30 |
| 408 | Cesar Tovar | .12 | .30 |
| 409 | Pete Broberg | .12 | .30 |
| 410 | Willie Montanez | .12 | .30 |
| 411 | J.Morgan/J.Bench WS | 1.00 | 2.50 |
| 412 | Johnny Bench WS | 1.00 | 2.50 |
| 413 | Cincy Wins WS | .30 | .75 |
| 414 | Tommy Harper | .30 | .75 |
| 415 | Jay Johnstone | .30 | .75 |
| 416 | Chuck Hartenstein | .12 | .30 |
| 417 | Wayne Garrett | .12 | .30 |
| 418 | Chicago White Sox CL/Lemon | .60 | 1.50 |
| 419 | Steve Swisher | .12 | .30 |
| 420 | Rusty Staub | .60 | 1.50 |
| 421 | Doug Rau | .12 | .30 |
| 422 | Freddie Patek | .30 | .75 |
| 423 | Gary Lavelle | .12 | .30 |
| 424 | Steve Brye | .12 | .30 |
| 425 | Joe Torre | .60 | 1.50 |
| 426 | Dick Drago | .12 | .30 |
| 427 | Dave Rader | .12 | .30 |
| 428 | Texas Rangers CL/Lucchesi | .60 | 1.50 |
| 429 | Ken Boswell | .12 | .30 |
| 430 | Fergie Jenkins | 1.00 | 2.50 |
| 431 | Dave Collins UER | .30 | .75 |
| 432 | Buzz Capra | .12 | .30 |
| 433 | Nate Colbert TBC | .12 | .30 |
| 434 | Carl Yastrzemski TBC | .60 | 1.50 |
| 435 | Maury Wills TBC | .30 | .75 |
| 436 | Bob Keegan TBC | .12 | .30 |
| 437 | Ralph Kiner TBC | .60 | 1.50 |
| 438 | Marty Perez | .12 | .30 |
| 439 | Gorman Thomas | .30 | .75 |
| 440 | Jon Matlack | .30 | .75 |
| 441 | Larvell Blanks | .12 | .30 |
| 442 | Atlanta Braves CL/Bristol | .60 | 1.50 |
| 443 | Lamar Johnson | .12 | .30 |
| 444 | Wayne Twitchell | .12 | .30 |
| 445 | Ken Singleton | .30 | .75 |
| 446 | Bill Bonham | .12 | .30 |
| 447 | Jerry Turner | .12 | .30 |
| 448 | Ellie Rodriguez | .12 | .30 |
| 449 | Al Fitzmorris | .12 | .30 |
| 450 | Pete Rose | 8.00 | 20.00 |
| 451 | Checklist 397-528 | .60 | 1.50 |
| 452 | Mike Caldwell | .12 | .30 |
| 453 | Pedro Garcia | .12 | .30 |
| 454 | Andy Etchebarren | .12 | .30 |
| 455 | Rick Wise | .12 | .30 |
| 456 | Leon Roberts | .12 | .30 |
| 457 | Steve Luebber | .12 | .30 |
| 458 | Leo Foster | .12 | .30 |
| 459 | Steve Foucault | .12 | .30 |
| 460 | Willie Stargell | 1.00 | 2.50 |
| 461 | Dick Tidrow | .12 | .30 |
| 462 | Don Baylor | .60 | 1.50 |
| 463 | Jamie Quirk | .12 | .30 |
| 464 | Randy Moffitt | .12 | .30 |
| 465 | Rico Carty | .30 | .75 |
| 466 | Fred Holdsworth | .12 | .30 |
| 467 | Philadelphia Phillies CL/Ozark | .60 | 1.50 |
| 468 | Ramon Hernandez | .12 | .30 |
| 469 | Pat Kelly | .12 | .30 |
| 470 | Ted Simmons | .30 | .75 |
| 471 | Del Unser | .12 | .30 |
| 472 | Aase/McCl/Patt/Wehr RC | .12 | .30 |
| 473 | Andre Dawson RC | 8.00 | 20.00 |
| 474 | Bailor/Garr/Reyn/Tav RC | .30 | .75 |
| 475 | Batt/Camp/McGr/Sarm RC | .30 | .75 |
| 476 | Dale Murphy RC | 6.00 | 15.00 |

| Card | Low | High |
|---|---|---|
| 477 Ault/Dauer/Gonz/Mank RC | .30 | .75 |
| 478 Gid/Hoot/John/Lemong RC | .30 | .75 |
| 479 Assel/Gross/Meij/Woods RC | .30 | .75 |
| 480 Carl Yastrzemski | 3.00 | 8.00 |
| 481 Roger Metzger | .12 | .30 |
| 482 Tony Solaita | .12 | .30 |
| 483 Richie Zisk | .12 | .30 |
| 484 Burt Hooton | .30 | .75 |
| 485 Roy White | .30 | .75 |
| 486 Ed Bane | .12 | .30 |
| 487 And/Glynn/Hend/Terl RC | .30 | .75 |
| 488 J.Clark/L.Mazzilli RC | 1.25 | 3.00 |
| 489 Barker/Ler/Mint/Overy RC | .30 | .75 |
| 490 Almon/Klutts/McM/Wag RC | .30 | .75 |
| 491 Dennis Martinez RC | 1.25 | 3.00 |
| 492 Armas/Kemp/Lop/Woods RC | .30 | .75 |
| 493 Krukow/Ott/Wheel/Will RC | .30 | .75 |
| 494 J.Gantner/B.Wills RC | .60 | 1.50 |
| 495 Al Hrabosky | .30 | .75 |
| 496 Gary Thomasson | .12 | .30 |
| 497 Clay Carroll | .12 | .30 |
| 498 Sal Bando | .30 | .75 |
| 499 Pablo Torrealba | .12 | .30 |
| 500 Dave Kingman | .60 | 1.50 |
| 501 Jim Bibby | .12 | .30 |
| 502 Randy Hundley | .12 | .30 |
| 503 Bill Lee | .12 | .30 |
| 504 Los Angeles Dodgers CL/Lasorda | .60 | 1.50 |
| 505 Oscar Gamble | .30 | .75 |
| 506 Steve Grilli | .12 | .30 |
| 507 Mike Hegan | .12 | .30 |
| 508 Dave Pagan | .12 | .30 |
| 509 Cookie Rojas | .30 | .75 |
| 510 John Candelaria | .12 | .30 |
| 511 Bill Fahey | .12 | .30 |
| 512 Jack Billingham | .12 | .30 |
| 513 Jerry Terrell | .12 | .30 |
| 514 Cliff Johnson | .12 | .30 |
| 515 Chris Speier | .12 | .30 |
| 516 Bake McBride | .30 | .75 |
| 517 Pete Vuckovich RC | .30 | .75 |
| 518 Chicago Cubs CL/Franks | .60 | 1.50 |
| 519 Don Kirkwood | .12 | .30 |
| 520 Garry Maddox | .12 | .30 |
| 521 Bob Grich | .30 | .75 |
| 522 Enzo Hernandez | .12 | .30 |
| 523 Rollie Fingers | 1.00 | 2.50 |
| 524 Rowland Office | .12 | .30 |
| 525 Dennis Eckersley | 2.00 | 5.00 |
| 526 Larry Parrish | .30 | .75 |
| 527 Dan Meyer | .30 | .75 |
| 528 Bill Castro | .12 | .30 |
| 529 Jim Essian RC | .30 | .75 |
| 530 Rick Reuschel | .30 | .75 |
| 531 Lyman Bostock | .30 | .75 |
| 532 Jim Willoughby | .12 | .30 |
| 533 Mickey Stanley | .30 | .75 |
| 534 Paul Splittorff | .12 | .30 |
| 535 Cesar Geronimo | .12 | .30 |
| 536 Vic Albury | .12 | .30 |
| 537 Dave Roberts | .12 | .30 |
| 538 Frank Taveras | .12 | .30 |
| 539 Mike Wallace | .12 | .30 |
| 540 Bob Watson | .30 | .75 |
| 541 John Denny | .30 | .75 |
| 542 Frank Duffy | .12 | .30 |
| 543 Ron Blomberg | .12 | .30 |
| 544 Gary Ross | .10 | .25 |
| 545 Bob Boone | .30 | .75 |
| 546 Baltimore Orioles CL/Weaver | .60 | 1.50 |
| 547 Willie McCovey | 1.50 | 4.00 |
| 548 Joel Youngblood RC | .12 | .30 |
| 549 Jerry Royster | .12 | .30 |
| 550 Randy Jones | .12 | .30 |
| 551 Bill North | .12 | .30 |
| 552 Pepe Mangual | .12 | .30 |
| 553 Jack Heidemann | .12 | .30 |
| 554 Bruce Kimm RC | .12 | .30 |
| 555 Dan Ford | .12 | .30 |
| 556 Doug Bird | .12 | .30 |
| 557 Jerry White | .12 | .30 |
| 558 Elias Sosa | .12 | .30 |
| 559 Alan Bannister RC | .12 | .30 |
| 560 Dave Concepcion | .60 | 1.50 |
| 561 Pete LaCock | .12 | .30 |
| 562 Checklist 529-660 | .60 | 1.50 |
| 563 Bruce Kison | .12 | .30 |
| 564 Alan Ashby | .12 | .30 |
| 565 Mickey Lolich | .30 | .75 |
| 566 Rick Miller | .12 | .30 |
| 567 Enos Cabell | .12 | .30 |
| 568 Carlos May | .12 | .30 |
| 569 Jim Lonborg | .30 | .75 |
| 570 Bobby Bonds | .60 | 1.50 |
| 571 Darrell Evans | .30 | .75 |
| 572 Ross Grimsley | .12 | .30 |
| 573 Joe Ferguson | .12 | .30 |
| 574 Aurelio Rodriguez | .12 | .30 |
| 575 Dick Ruthven | .12 | .30 |
| 576 Fred Kendall | .12 | .30 |
| 577 Jerry Augustine RC | .12 | .30 |
| 578 Bob Randall RC | .12 | .30 |
| 579 Don Carrithers | .12 | .30 |
| 580 George Brett | 6.00 | 15.00 |
| 581 Pedro Borbon | .12 | .30 |
| 582 Ed Kirkpatrick | .12 | .30 |
| 583 Paul Lindblad | .12 | .30 |
| 584 Ed Goodson | .12 | .30 |
| 585 Rick Burleson | .30 | .75 |
| 586 Steve Renko | .12 | .30 |
| 587 Rick Baldwin | .12 | .30 |
| 588 Dave Moales | .12 | .30 |
| 589 Mika Cosgrove | .12 | .30 |
| 590 Buddy Bell | .30 | .75 |
| 591 Chris Arnold | .12 | .30 |
| 592 Dan Briggs RC | .12 | .30 |
| 593 Dennis Blair | .12 | .30 |
| 594 Biff Pocoroba | .12 | .30 |
| 595 John Hiller | .12 | .30 |
| 596 Jerry Martin RC | .12 | .30 |
| 597 Seattle Mariners CL/Johnson | .60 | 1.50 |
| 598 Sparky Lyle | .30 | .75 |
| 599 Mike Tyson | .12 | .30 |
| 600 Jim Palmer | 1.50 | 4.00 |
| 601 Mike Lum | .12 | .30 |
| 602 Andy Hassler | .12 | .30 |
| 603 Willie Davis | .30 | .75 |
| 604 Jim Slaton | .12 | .30 |
| 605 Felix Millan | .12 | .30 |
| 606 Steve Braun | .12 | .30 |
| 607 Larry Demery | .12 | .30 |
| 608 Roy Howell | .12 | .30 |
| 609 Jim Barr | .12 | .30 |
| 610 Jose Cardenal | .30 | .75 |
| 611 Dave Lemanczyk | .12 | .30 |
| 612 Barry Foote | .12 | .30 |
| 613 Reggie Cleveland | .12 | .30 |
| 614 Greg Gross | .12 | .30 |
| 615 Phil Niekro | 1.00 | 2.50 |
| 616 Tommy Sandt RC | .12 | .30 |
| 617 Bobby Darwin | .12 | .30 |
| 618 Pat Dobson | .12 | .30 |
| 619 Johnny Oates | .30 | .75 |
| 620 Don Sutton | 1.00 | 2.50 |
| 621 Detroit Tigers CL/Houk | .60 | 1.50 |
| 622 Jim Wohlford | .12 | .30 |
| 623 Jack Kucek | .12 | .30 |
| 624 Hector Cruz | .12 | .30 |
| 625 Ken Holtzman | .30 | .75 |
| 626 Al Bumbry | .30 | .75 |
| 627 Bob Myrick RC | .12 | .30 |
| 628 Mario Guerrero | .12 | .30 |
| 629 Bobby Valentine | .30 | .75 |
| 630 Bert Blyleven | .60 | 1.50 |
| 631 Brett Brothers | 2.50 | 6.00 |
| 632 Forsch Brothers | 2.50 | 6.00 |
| 633 May Brothers | .30 | .75 |
| 634 Reuschel Brothers UER | 3.00 | 8.00 |
| 635 Robin Yount | 3.00 | 8.00 |
| 636 Santo Alcala | .12 | .30 |
| 637 Alex Johnson | .12 | .30 |
| 638 Jim Kaat | .60 | 1.50 |
| 639 Jerry Morales | .12 | .30 |
| 640 Carlton Fisk | 2.00 | 5.00 |
| 641 Dan Larson RC | .12 | .30 |
| 642 Willie Crawford | .12 | .30 |
| 643 Mike Pazik | .12 | .30 |
| 644 Matt Alexander | .12 | .30 |
| 645 Jerry Reuss | .30 | .75 |
| 646 Andres Mora RC | .12 | .30 |
| 647 Montreal Expos CL/Williams | .60 | 1.50 |
| 648 Jim Spencer | .12 | .30 |
| 649 Dave Cash | .12 | .30 |
| 650 Nolan Ryan | 12.50 | 30.00 |
| 651 Von Joshua | .12 | .30 |
| 652 Tom Walker | .12 | .30 |
| 653 Diego Segui | .30 | .75 |
| 654 Ron Pruitt RC | .12 | .30 |
| 655 Tony Perez | 1.00 | 2.50 |
| 656 Ron Guidry | .60 | 1.50 |
| 657 Mick Kelleher RC | .12 | .30 |
| 658 Marty Pattin | .12 | .30 |
| 659 Merv Rettenmund | .12 | .30 |
| 660 Willie Horton | .60 | 1.50 |

## 1978 Topps

Bruce Sutter — Cubs

| Card | Low | High |
|---|---|---|
| COMPLETE SET (726) | 100.00 | 200.00 |
| COMMON CARD (1-726) | .10 | .25 |
| COMMON CARD DP | .08 | .20 |
| 1 Lou Brock RB | 1.25 | 3.00 |
| 2 Sparky Lyle RB | .25 | .60 |
| 3 Willie McCovey RB | 1.00 | 2.50 |
| 4 Brooks Robinson RB | .50 | 1.25 |
| 5 Pete Rose RB | 3.00 | 8.00 |
| 6 Nolan Ryan RB | 6.00 | 15.00 |
| 7 Reggie Jackson RB | 1.50 | 4.00 |
| 8 Mike Sadek | .10 | .25 |
| 9 Doug DeCinces | .25 | .60 |
| 10 Phil Niekro | 1.00 | 2.50 |
| 11 Rick Manning | .10 | .25 |
| 12 Don Aase | .10 | .25 |
| 13 Art Howe RC | .25 | .60 |
| 14 Lerrin LaGrow | .10 | .25 |
| 15 Tony Perez DP | .50 | 1.25 |
| 16 Roy White | .10 | .25 |
| 17 Mike Krukow | .10 | .25 |
| 18 Bob Grich | .25 | .60 |
| 19 Darrell Porter | .25 | .60 |
| 20 Pete Rose DP | 5.00 | 12.00 |
| 21 Steve Kemp | .25 | .60 |
| 22 Charlie Hough | .25 | .60 |
| 23 Bump Wills | .10 | .25 |
| 24 Don Money DP | .08 | .20 |
| 25 Jon Matlack | .10 | .25 |
| 26 Rich Hebner | .10 | .25 |
| 27 Geoff Zahn | .10 | .25 |
| 28 Ed Ott | .10 | .25 |
| 29 Bob Lacey RC | .10 | .25 |
| 30 George Hendrick | .25 | .60 |
| 31 Glenn Abbott | .10 | .25 |
| 32 Garry Templeton | .25 | .60 |
| 33 Dave Lemanczyk | .10 | .25 |
| 34 Willie McCovey | 1.25 | 3.00 |
| 35 Sparky Lyle | .25 | .60 |
| 36 Eddie Murray RC | 40.00 | 80.00 |
| 37 Rick Waits | .10 | .25 |
| 38 Willie Montanez | .10 | .25 |
| 39 Floyd Bannister RC | .10 | .25 |
| 40 Carl Yastrzemski | 2.50 | 6.00 |
| 41 Burt Hooton | .25 | .60 |
| 42 Jorge Orta | .10 | .25 |
| 43 Bill Atkinson RC | .10 | .25 |
| 44 Toby Harrah | .25 | .60 |
| 45 Mark Fidrych | 1.00 | 2.50 |
| 46 Al Cowens | .25 | .60 |
| 47 Jack Billingham | .10 | .25 |
| 48 Don Baylor | .50 | 1.25 |
| 49 Ed Kranepool | .25 | .60 |
| 50 Rick Reuschel | .25 | .60 |
| 51 Charlie Moore DP | .08 | .20 |
| 52 Jim Lonborg | .10 | .25 |
| 53 Phil Garner DP | .10 | .25 |
| 54 Tom Johnson | .10 | .25 |
| 55 Mitchell Page RC | .10 | .25 |
| 56 Randy Jones | .10 | .25 |
| 57 Dan Meyer | .10 | .25 |
| 58 Bob Forsch | .10 | .25 |
| 59 Otto Velez | .10 | .25 |
| 60 Thurman Munson | 1.50 | 4.00 |
| 61 Larvell Blanks | .10 | .25 |

| Card | Price | Price | | Card | Price | Price | | Card | Price | Price |
|---|---|---|---|---|---|---|---|---|---|---|
| 62 Jim Barr | .10 | .25 | | 150 Bobby Bonds | .50 | 1.25 | | 238 Juan Beniquez | .10 | .25 |
| 63 Don Zimmer MG | .25 | .60 | | 151 Milt Wilcox | .10 | .25 | | 239 Dyar Miller | .10 | .25 |
| 64 Gene Pentz | .10 | .25 | | 152 Ivan DeJesus RC | .10 | .25 | | 240 Gene Tenace | .25 | .60 |
| 65 Ken Singleton | .25 | .60 | | 153 Steve Stone | .25 | .60 | | 241 Pete Vuckovich | .25 | .60 |
| 66 Chicago White Sox CL | .50 | 1.25 | | 154 Cecil Cooper DP | .25 | .60 | | 242 Barry Bonnell DP RC | .08 | .20 |
| 67 Claudell Washington | .25 | .60 | | 155 Butch Hobson | .25 | .60 | | 243 Bob McClure | .10 | .25 |
| 68 Steve Foucault DP | .08 | .20 | | 156 Andy Messersmith | .25 | .60 | | 244 Montreal Expos CL DP | .25 | .60 |
| 69 Mike Vail | .10 | .25 | | 157 Pete LaCock DP | .08 | .20 | | 245 Rick Burleson | .25 | .60 |
| 70 Goose Gossage | .50 | 1.25 | | 158 Joaquin Andujar | .25 | .60 | | 246 Dan Driessen | .10 | .25 |
| 71 Terry Humphrey | .10 | .25 | | 159 Lou Piniella | .25 | .60 | | 247 Larry Christenson | .10 | .25 |
| 72 Andre Dawson | 1.50 | 4.00 | | 160 Jim Palmer | 1.25 | 3.00 | | 248 Frank White DP | .25 | .60 |
| 73 Andy Hassler | .10 | .25 | | 161 Bob Boone | .50 | 1.25 | | 249 Dave Goltz DP | .08 | .20 |
| 74 Checklist 1-121 | .50 | 1.25 | | 162 Paul Thormodsgard RC | .10 | .25 | | 250 Graig Nettles DP | .25 | .60 |
| 75 Dick Ruthven | .10 | .25 | | 163 Bill North | .10 | .25 | | 251 Don Kirkwood | .10 | .25 |
| 76 Steve Ontiveros | .10 | .25 | | 164 Bob Owchinko RC | .10 | .25 | | 252 Steve Swisher DP | .08 | .20 |
| 77 Ed Kirkpatrick | .10 | .25 | | 165 Rennie Stennett | .10 | .25 | | 253 Jim Kern | .10 | .25 |
| 78 Pablo Torrealba | .10 | .25 | | 166 Carlos Lopez | .10 | .25 | | 254 Dave Collins | .25 | .60 |
| 79 Darrell Johnson MG DP | .08 | .20 | | 167 Tim Foli | .10 | .25 | | 255 Jerry Reuss | .25 | .60 |
| 80 Ken Griffey Sr. | .50 | 1.25 | | 168 Reggie Smith | .25 | .60 | | 256 Joe Altobelli MG RC | .10 | .25 |
| 81 Pete Redfern | .10 | .25 | | 169 Jerry Johnson | .10 | .25 | | 257 Hector Cruz | .10 | .25 |
| 82 San Francisco Giants CL | .50 | 1.25 | | 170 Lou Brock | 1.25 | 3.00 | | 258 John Hiller | .10 | .25 |
| 83 Bob Montgomery | .10 | .25 | | 171 Pat Zachry | .10 | .25 | | 259 Los Angeles Dodgers CL | .50 | 1.25 |
| 84 Kent Tekulve | .25 | .60 | | 172 Mike Hargrove | .25 | .60 | | 260 Bert Campaneris | .25 | .60 |
| 85 Ron Fairly | .25 | .60 | | 173 Robin Yount | 2.00 | 5.00 | | 261 Tim Hosley | .10 | .25 |
| 86 Dave Tomlin | .10 | .25 | | 174 Wayne Garland | .10 | .25 | | 262 Rudy May | .10 | .25 |
| 87 John Lowenstein | .10 | .25 | | 175 Jerry Morales | .10 | .25 | | 263 Danny Walton | .10 | .25 |
| 88 Mike Phillips | .10 | .25 | | 176 Milt May | .10 | .25 | | 264 Jamie Easterly | .10 | .25 |
| 89 Ken Clay RC | .10 | .25 | | 177 Gene Garber DP | .10 | .25 | | 265 Sal Bando DP | .25 | .60 |
| 90 Larry Bowa | .50 | 1.25 | | 178 Dave Chalk | .10 | .25 | | 266 Bob Shirley RC | .10 | .25 |
| 91 Oscar Zamora | .10 | .25 | | 179 Dick Tidrow | .10 | .25 | | 267 Doug Ault | .10 | .25 |
| 92 Adrian Devine | .10 | .25 | | 180 Dave Concepcion | .50 | 1.25 | | 268 Gil Flores RC | .10 | .25 |
| 93 Bobby Cox DP | .08 | .20 | | 181 Ken Forsch | .10 | .25 | | 269 Wayne Twitchell | .10 | .25 |
| 94 Chuck Scrivener | .10 | .25 | | 182 Jim Spencer | .10 | .25 | | 270 Carlton Fisk | 1.50 | 4.00 |
| 95 Jamie Quirk | .10 | .25 | | 183 Doug Bird | .10 | .25 | | 271 Randy Lerch DP | .08 | .20 |
| 96 Baltimore Orioles CL | .50 | 1.25 | | 184 Checklist 122-242 | .50 | 1.25 | | 272 Royle Stillman | .10 | .25 |
| 97 Stan Bahnsen | .10 | .25 | | 185 Ellis Valentine | .10 | .25 | | 273 Fred Norman | .10 | .25 |
| 98 Jim Essian | .25 | .60 | | 186 Bob Stanley DP RC | .08 | .20 | | 274 Freddie Patek | .25 | .60 |
| 99 Willie Hernandez RC | .50 | 1.25 | | 187 Jerry Royster DP | .08 | .20 | | 275 Dan Ford | .10 | .25 |
| 100 George Brett | 6.00 | 15.00 | | 188 Al Bumbry | .25 | .60 | | 276 Bill Bonham DP | .08 | .20 |
| 101 Sid Monge | .10 | .25 | | 189 Tom Lasorda MG DP | 1.00 | 2.50 | | 277 Bruce Boisclair | .10 | .25 |
| 102 Matt Alexander | .10 | .25 | | 190 John Candelaria | .25 | .60 | | 278 Enrique Romo RC | .10 | .25 |
| 103 Tom Murphy | .10 | .25 | | 191 Rodney Scott RC | .10 | .25 | | 279 Bill Virdon DP | .10 | .25 |
| 104 Lee Lacy | .10 | .25 | | 192 San Diego Padres CL | .50 | 1.25 | | 280 Buddy Bell | .25 | .60 |
| 105 Reggie Cleveland | .10 | .25 | | 193 Rich Chiles | .10 | .25 | | 281 Eric Rasmussen DP | .08 | .20 |
| 106 Bill Plummer | .10 | .25 | | 194 Derrel Thomas | .10 | .25 | | 282 New York Yankees CL | 1.00 | 2.50 |
| 107 Ed Halicki | .10 | .25 | | 195 Larry Dierker | .25 | .60 | | 283 Omar Moreno | .10 | .25 |
| 108 Von Joshua | .10 | .25 | | 196 Bob Bailor | .10 | .25 | | 284 Randy Moffitt | .10 | .25 |
| 109 Joe Torre MG | .25 | .60 | | 197 Nino Espinosa | .10 | .25 | | 285 Steve Yeager DP | .25 | .60 |
| 110 Richie Zisk | .10 | .25 | | 198 Ron Pruitt | .10 | .25 | | 286 Ben Oglivie | .25 | .60 |
| 111 Mike Tyson | .10 | .25 | | 199 Craig Reynolds | .10 | .25 | | 287 Kiko Garcia | .10 | .25 |
| 112 Houston Astros CL | .50 | 1.25 | | 200 Reggie Jackson | 3.00 | 8.00 | | 288 Dave Hamilton | .10 | .25 |
| 113 Don Carrithers | .10 | .25 | | 201 D.Parker/R.Carew LL | .50 | 1.25 | | 289 Checklist 243-363 | .50 | 1.25 |
| 114 Paul Blair | .25 | .60 | | 202 G.Foster/J.Rice LL DP | .25 | .60 | | 290 Willie Horton | .25 | .60 |
| 115 Gary Nolan | .10 | .25 | | 203 G.Foster/L.Hisle LL | .25 | .60 | | 291 Gary Ross | .10 | .25 |
| 116 Tucker Ashford RC | .10 | .25 | | 204 F.Taveras/F.Patek LL DP | .10 | .25 | | 292 Gene Richards | .10 | .25 |
| 117 John Montague | .10 | .25 | | 205 Carlton/Gol/Leon/Palm LL | 1.00 | 2.50 | | 293 Mike Willis | .10 | .25 |
| 118 Terry Harmon | .10 | .25 | | 206 P.Niekro/N.Ryan LL DP | 2.50 | 6.00 | | 294 Larry Parrish | .25 | .60 |
| 119 Dennis Martinez | 1.00 | 2.50 | | 207 J.Cand/F.Tanana LL DP | .25 | .60 | | 295 Bill Lee | .10 | .25 |
| 120 Gary Carter | 1.00 | 2.50 | | 208 R.Fingers/B.Campbell LL | .50 | 1.25 | | 296 Biff Pocoroba | .10 | .25 |
| 121 Alvis Woods | .10 | .25 | | 209 Dock Ellis | .10 | .25 | | 297 Warren Brusstar DP RC | .08 | .20 |
| 122 Dennis Eckersley | 1.25 | 3.00 | | 210 Jose Cardenal | .10 | .25 | | 298 Tony Armas | .25 | .60 |
| 123 Manny Trillo | .10 | .25 | | 211 Earl Weaver MG DP | .50 | 1.25 | | 299 Whitey Herzog MG | .25 | .60 |
| 124 Dave Rozema RC | .10 | .25 | | 212 Mike Caldwell | .10 | .25 | | 300 Joe Morgan | 1.25 | 3.00 |
| 125 George Scott | .25 | .60 | | 213 Alan Bannister | .10 | .25 | | 301 Buddy Schultz RC | .10 | .25 |
| 126 Paul Moskau RC | .10 | .25 | | 214 California Angels CL | .50 | 1.25 | | 302 Chicago Cubs CL | .50 | 1.25 |
| 127 Chet Lemon | .25 | .60 | | 215 Darrell Evans | .25 | .60 | | 303 Sam Hinds RC | .10 | .25 |
| 128 Bill Russell | .25 | .60 | | 216 Mike Paxton RC | .10 | .25 | | 304 John Milner | .10 | .25 |
| 129 Jim Colborn | .10 | .25 | | 217 Rod Gilbreath | .10 | .25 | | 305 Rico Carty | .25 | .60 |
| 130 Jeff Burroughs | .25 | .60 | | 218 Marty Pattin | .10 | .25 | | 306 Joe Niekro | .25 | .60 |
| 131 Bert Blyleven | .50 | 1.25 | | 219 Mike Cubbage | .10 | .25 | | 307 Glenn Borgmann | .10 | .25 |
| 132 Enos Cabell | .10 | .25 | | 220 Pedro Borbon | .10 | .25 | | 308 Jim Rooker | .10 | .25 |
| 133 Jerry Augustine | .10 | .25 | | 221 Chris Speier | .10 | .25 | | 309 Cliff Johnson | .10 | .25 |
| 134 Steve Henderson RC | .10 | .25 | | 222 Jerry Martin | .10 | .25 | | 310 Don Sutton | 1.00 | 2.50 |
| 135 Ron Guidry DP | .50 | 1.25 | | 223 Bruce Kison | .10 | .25 | | 311 Jose Baez DP RC | .08 | .20 |
| 136 Ted Sizemore | .10 | .25 | | 224 Jerry Tabb RC | .10 | .25 | | 312 Greg Minton | .10 | .25 |
| 137 Craig Kusick | .10 | .25 | | 225 Don Gullett DP | .10 | .25 | | 313 Andy Etchebarren | .10 | .25 |
| 138 Larry Demery | .10 | .25 | | 226 Joe Ferguson | .10 | .25 | | 314 Paul Lindblad | .10 | .25 |
| 139 Wayne Gross | .10 | .25 | | 227 Al Fitzmorris | .10 | .25 | | 315 Mark Belanger | .25 | .60 |
| 140 Rollie Fingers | 1.00 | 2.50 | | 228 Manny Mota DP | .10 | .25 | | 316 Henry Cruz DP | .08 | .20 |
| 141 Ruppert Jones | .10 | .25 | | 229 Leo Foster | .10 | .25 | | 317 Dave Johnson | .10 | .25 |
| 142 John Montefusco | .10 | .25 | | 230 Al Hrabosky | .25 | .60 | | 318 Tom Griffin | .10 | .25 |
| 143 Keith Hernandez | .25 | .60 | | 231 Wayne Nordhagen RC | .10 | .25 | | 319 Alan Ashby | .10 | .25 |
| 144 Jesse Jefferson | .10 | .25 | | 232 Mickey Stanley | .10 | .25 | | 320 Fred Lynn | .25 | .60 |
| 145 Rick Monday | .25 | .60 | | 233 Dick Pole | .10 | .25 | | 321 Santo Alcala | .10 | .25 |
| 146 Doyle Alexander | .25 | .60 | | 234 Herman Franks MG | .10 | .25 | | 322 Tom Paciorek | .25 | .60 |
| 147 Lee Mazzilli | .10 | .25 | | 235 Tim McCarver | .25 | .60 | | 323 Jim Fregosi DP | .10 | .25 |
| 148 Andre Thornton | .25 | .60 | | 236 Terry Whitfield | .10 | .25 | | 324 Vern Rapp MG RC | .10 | .25 |
| 149 Dale Murray | .10 | .25 | | 237 Rich Dauer | .10 | .25 | | 325 Bruce Sutter | 1.25 | 3.00 |

|  |  | | |
|---|---|---|---|
| 326 | Mike Lum DP | .08 | .20 |
| 327 | Rick Langford DP RC | .08 | .20 |
| 328 | Milwaukee Brewers CL | .50 | 1.25 |
| 329 | John Verhoeven | .10 | .25 |
| 330 | Bob Watson | .25 | .60 |
| 331 | Mark Littell | .10 | .25 |
| 332 | Duane Kuiper | .10 | .25 |
| 333 | Jim Todd | .10 | .25 |
| 334 | John Stearns | .10 | .25 |
| 335 | Bucky Dent | .25 | .60 |
| 336 | Steve Busby | .10 | .25 |
| 337 | Tom Grieve | .25 | .60 |
| 338 | Dave Heaverlo | .10 | .25 |
| 339 | Mario Guerrero | .10 | .25 |
| 340 | Bake McBride | .25 | .60 |
| 341 | Mike Flanagan | .25 | .60 |
| 342 | Aurelio Rodriguez | .10 | .25 |
| 343 | John Wathan DP | .08 | .20 |
| 344 | Sam Ewing RC | .10 | .25 |
| 345 | Luis Tiant | .25 | .60 |
| 346 | Larry Biittner | .10 | .25 |
| 347 | Terry Forster | .25 | .60 |
| 348 | Del Unser | .10 | .25 |
| 349 | Rick Camp DP | .08 | .20 |
| 350 | Steve Garvey | 1.00 | 2.50 |
| 351 | Jeff Torborg | .25 | .60 |
| 352 | Tony Scott RC | .10 | .25 |
| 353 | Doug Bair RC | .10 | .25 |
| 354 | Cesar Geronimo | .10 | .25 |
| 355 | Bill Travers | .10 | .25 |
| 356 | New York Mets CL | .50 | 1.25 |
| 357 | Tom Poquette | .10 | .25 |
| 358 | Mark Lemongello | .10 | .25 |
| 359 | Marc Hill | .10 | .25 |
| 360 | Mike Schmidt | 4.00 | 10.00 |
| 361 | Chris Knapp | .10 | .25 |
| 362 | Dave Nye | .10 | .25 |
| 363 | Bob Randall | .10 | .25 |
| 364 | Jerry Turner | .10 | .25 |
| 365 | Ed Figueroa | .10 | .25 |
| 366 | Larry Milbourne DP | .08 | .20 |
| 367 | Rick Dempsey | .25 | .60 |
| 368 | Balor Moore | .10 | .25 |
| 369 | Tim Nordbrook | .10 | .25 |
| 370 | Rusty Staub | .50 | 1.25 |
| 371 | Ray Burris | .10 | .25 |
| 372 | Brian Asselstine | .10 | .25 |
| 373 | Jim Willoughby | .10 | .25 |
| 374 | Jose Morales | .10 | .25 |
| 375 | Tommy John | .50 | 1.25 |
| 376 | Jim Wohlford | .10 | .25 |
| 377 | Manny Sarmiento | .10 | .25 |
| 378 | Bobby Winkles MG | .10 | .25 |
| 379 | Skip Lockwood | .10 | .25 |
| 380 | Ted Simmons | .25 | .60 |
| 381 | Philadelphia Phillies CL | .50 | 1.25 |
| 382 | Joe Lahoud | .10 | .25 |
| 383 | Mario Mendoza | .10 | .25 |
| 384 | Jack Clark | .50 | 1.25 |
| 385 | Tito Fuentes | .10 | .25 |
| 386 | Bob Gorinski RC | .10 | .25 |
| 387 | Ken Holtzman | .25 | .60 |
| 388 | Bill Fahey DP | .08 | .20 |
| 389 | Julio Gonzalez RC | .10 | .25 |
| 390 | Oscar Gamble | .25 | .60 |
| 391 | Larry Haney | .10 | .25 |
| 392 | Billy Almon | .10 | .25 |
| 393 | Tippy Martinez | .25 | .60 |
| 394 | Roy Howell DP | .08 | .20 |
| 395 | Jim Hughes | .10 | .25 |
| 396 | Bob Stinson DP | .08 | .20 |
| 397 | Greg Gross | .10 | .25 |
| 398 | Don Hood | .10 | .25 |
| 399 | Pete Mackanin | .10 | .25 |
| 400 | Nolan Ryan | 10.00 | 25.00 |
| 401 | Sparky Anderson MG | .25 | .60 |
| 402 | Dave Campbell | .10 | .25 |
| 403 | Bud Harrelson | .25 | .60 |
| 404 | Detroit Tigers CL | .50 | 1.25 |
| 405 | Rawly Eastwick | .10 | .25 |
| 406 | Mike Jorgensen | .10 | .25 |
| 407 | Odell Jones RC | .10 | .25 |
| 408 | Joe Zdeb RC | .10 | .25 |
| 409 | Ron Schueler | .10 | .25 |
| 410 | Bill Madlock | .25 | .60 |
| 411 | Mickey Rivers ALCS | .25 | .60 |
| 412 | Davey Lopes NLCS | .25 | .60 |
| 413 | Reggie Jackson WS | 1.50 | 4.00 |
| 414 | Darold Knowles DP | .08 | .20 |
| 415 | Ray Fosse | .10 | .25 |
| 416 | Jack Brohamer | .10 | .25 |
| 417 | Mike Garman DP | .08 | .20 |
| 418 | Tony Muser | .10 | .25 |
| 419 | Jerry Garvin RC | .10 | .25 |
| 420 | Greg Luzinski | .50 | 1.25 |
| 421 | Junior Moore RC | .10 | .25 |
| 422 | Steve Braun | .10 | .25 |
| 423 | Dave Rosello | .10 | .25 |
| 424 | Boston Red Sox CL | .50 | 1.25 |
| 425 | Steve Rogers DP | .10 | .25 |
| 426 | Fred Kendall | .10 | .25 |
| 427 | Mario Soto RC | .25 | .60 |
| 428 | Joel Youngblood | .10 | .25 |
| 429 | Mike Barlow RC | .10 | .25 |
| 430 | Al Oliver | .25 | .60 |
| 431 | Butch Metzger | .10 | .25 |
| 432 | Terry Bulling RC | .10 | .25 |
| 433 | Fernando Gonzalez | .10 | .25 |
| 434 | Mike Norris | .10 | .25 |
| 435 | Checklist 364-484 | .50 | 1.25 |
| 436 | Vic Harris DP | .08 | .20 |
| 437 | Bo McLaughlin | .10 | .25 |
| 438 | John Ellis | .10 | .25 |
| 439 | Ken Kravec | .10 | .25 |
| 440 | Dave Lopes | .25 | .60 |
| 441 | Larry Gura | .10 | .25 |
| 442 | Elliott Maddox | .10 | .25 |
| 443 | Darrel Chaney | .10 | .25 |
| 444 | Roy Hartsfield MG | .10 | .25 |
| 445 | Mike Ivie | .10 | .25 |
| 446 | Tug McGraw | .25 | .60 |
| 447 | Leroy Stanton | .10 | .25 |
| 448 | Bill Castro | .10 | .25 |
| 449 | Tim Blackwell DP RC | .08 | .20 |
| 450 | Tom Seaver | 2.50 | 6.00 |
| 451 | Minnesota Twins CL | .50 | 1.25 |
| 452 | Jerry Mumphrey | .10 | .25 |
| 453 | Doug Flynn | .10 | .25 |
| 454 | Dave LaRoche | .10 | .25 |
| 455 | Bill Robinson | .25 | .60 |
| 456 | Vern Ruhle | .10 | .25 |
| 457 | Bob Bailey | .10 | .25 |
| 458 | Jeff Newman | .10 | .25 |
| 459 | Charlie Spikes | .10 | .25 |
| 460 | Jim Hunter | 1.00 | 2.50 |
| 461 | Rob Andrews DP | .08 | .20 |
| 462 | Rogelio Moret | .10 | .25 |
| 463 | Kevin Bell | .10 | .25 |
| 464 | Jerry Grote | .10 | .25 |
| 465 | Hal McRae | .25 | .60 |
| 466 | Dennis Blair | .10 | .25 |
| 467 | Alvin Dark MG | .25 | .60 |
| 468 | Warren Cromartie RC | .25 | .60 |
| 469 | Rick Cerone | .25 | .60 |
| 470 | J.R. Richard | .25 | .60 |
| 471 | Roy Smalley | .25 | .60 |
| 472 | Ron Reed | .10 | .25 |
| 473 | Bill Buckner | .25 | .60 |
| 474 | Jim Slaton | .10 | .25 |
| 475 | Gary Matthews | .25 | .60 |
| 476 | Bill Stein | .10 | .25 |
| 477 | Doug Capilla RC | .10 | .25 |
| 478 | Jerry Remy | .10 | .25 |
| 479 | St. Louis Cardinals CL | .50 | 1.25 |
| 480 | Ron LeFlore | .25 | .60 |
| 481 | Jackson Todd RC | .10 | .25 |
| 482 | Rick Miller | .10 | .25 |
| 483 | Ken Macha RC | .10 | .25 |
| 484 | Jim Norris RC | .10 | .25 |
| 485 | Chris Chambliss | .25 | .60 |
| 486 | John Curtis | .10 | .25 |
| 487 | Jim Tyrone | .10 | .25 |
| 488 | Dan Spillner | .10 | .25 |
| 489 | Rudy Meoli | .10 | .25 |
| 490 | Amos Otis | .25 | .60 |
| 491 | Scott McGregor | .25 | .60 |
| 492 | Jim Sundberg | .25 | .60 |
| 493 | Steve Renko | .10 | .25 |
| 494 | Chuck Tanner MG | .25 | .60 |
| 495 | Dave Cash | .10 | .25 |
| 496 | Jim Clancy DP RC | .08 | .20 |
| 497 | Glenn Adams | .10 | .25 |
| 498 | Joe Sambito | .10 | .25 |
| 499 | Seattle Mariners CL | .50 | 1.25 |
| 500 | George Foster | .50 | 1.25 |
| 501 | Dave Roberts | .10 | .25 |
| 502 | Pat Rockett RC | .10 | .25 |
| 503 | Ike Hampton RC | .10 | .25 |
| 504 | Roger Freed | .10 | .25 |
| 505 | Felix Millan | .10 | .25 |
| 506 | Ron Blomberg | .10 | .25 |
| 507 | Willie Crawford | .10 | .25 |
| 508 | Johnny Oates | .25 | .60 |
| 509 | Brent Strom | .10 | .25 |
| 510 | Willie Stargell | 1.00 | 2.50 |
| 511 | Frank Duffy | .10 | .25 |
| 512 | Larry Herndon | .10 | .25 |
| 513 | Barry Foote | .10 | .25 |
| 514 | Rob Sperring | .10 | .25 |
| 515 | Tim Corcoran RC | .10 | .25 |
| 516 | Gary Beare RC | .10 | .25 |
| 517 | Andres Mora | .10 | .25 |
| 518 | Tommy Boggs DP | .10 | .25 |
| 519 | Brian Downing | .25 | .60 |
| 520 | Larry Hisle | .25 | .60 |
| 521 | Steve Staggs RC | .10 | .25 |
| 522 | Dick Williams MG | .25 | .60 |
| 523 | Donnie Moore RC | .10 | .25 |
| 524 | Bernie Carbo | .10 | .25 |
| 525 | Jerry Terrell | .10 | .25 |
| 526 | Cincinnati Reds CL | .50 | 1.25 |
| 527 | Vic Correll | .10 | .25 |
| 528 | Rob Picciolo RC | .10 | .25 |
| 529 | Paul Hartzell | .10 | .25 |
| 530 | Dave Winfield | 1.50 | 4.00 |
| 531 | Tom Underwood | .10 | .25 |
| 532 | Skip Jutze | .10 | .25 |
| 533 | Sandy Alomar | .25 | .60 |
| 534 | Wilbur Howard | .10 | .25 |
| 535 | Checklist 485-605 | .50 | 1.25 |
| 536 | Roric Harrison | .10 | .25 |
| 537 | Bruce Bochte | .10 | .25 |
| 538 | Johnny LeMaster | .10 | .25 |
| 539 | Vic Davalillo DP | .08 | .20 |
| 540 | Steve Carlton | 1.50 | 4.00 |
| 541 | Larry Cox | .10 | .25 |
| 542 | Tim Johnson | .10 | .25 |
| 543 | Larry Harlow DP RC | .08 | .20 |
| 544 | Len Randle DP | .08 | .20 |
| 545 | Bill Campbell | .10 | .25 |
| 546 | Ted Martinez | .10 | .25 |
| 547 | John Scott | .10 | .25 |
| 548 | Billy Hunter MG DP | .08 | .20 |
| 549 | Joe Kerrigan | .10 | .25 |
| 550 | John Mayberry | .25 | .60 |
| 551 | Atlanta Braves CL | .50 | 1.25 |
| 552 | Francisco Barrios | .10 | .25 |
| 553 | Terry Puhl RC | .25 | .60 |
| 554 | Joe Coleman | .10 | .25 |
| 555 | Butch Wynegar | .25 | .60 |
| 556 | Ed Armbrister | .10 | .25 |
| 557 | Tony Solaita | .10 | .25 |
| 558 | Paul Mitchell | .10 | .25 |
| 559 | Phil Mankowski | .10 | .25 |
| 560 | Dave Parker | .50 | 1.25 |
| 561 | Charlie Williams | .10 | .25 |
| 562 | Glenn Burke RC | .10 | .25 |
| 563 | Dave Hader | .10 | .25 |
| 564 | Mick Kelleher | .10 | .25 |
| 565 | Jerry Koosman | .25 | .60 |
| 566 | Merv Rettenmund | .10 | .25 |
| 567 | Dick Drago | .10 | .25 |
| 568 | Tom Hutton | .10 | .25 |
| 569 | Lary Sorensen RC | .10 | .25 |
| 570 | Dave Kingman | .25 | 1.25 |
| 571 | Buck Martinez | .10 | .25 |
| 572 | Rick Wise | .10 | .25 |
| 573 | Luis Gomez | .10 | .25 |
| 574 | Bob Lemon MG | .50 | 1.25 |
| 575 | Pat Dobson | .10 | .25 |
| 576 | Sam Mejias | .10 | .25 |
| 577 | Oakland Athletics CL | .50 | 1.25 |
| 578 | Buzz Capra | .10 | .25 |
| 579 | Rance Mulliniks RC | .10 | .25 |
| 580 | Rod Carew | 1.50 | 4.00 |
| 581 | Lynn McGlothen | .10 | .25 |
| 582 | Fran Healy | .10 | .25 |
| 583 | George Medich | .10 | .25 |
| 584 | John Hale | .10 | .25 |
| 585 | Woodie Fryman DP | .08 | .20 |
| 586 | Ed Goodson | .10 | .25 |
| 587 | John Urrea RC | .10 | .25 |
| 588 | Jim Mason | .10 | .25 |
| 589 | Bob Knepper RC | .10 | .25 |

| | | |
|---|---|---|
| 590 Bobby Murcer | .25 | .60 |
| 591 George Zeber RC | .10 | .25 |
| 592 Bob Apodaca | .10 | .25 |
| 593 Dave Skaggs RC | .10 | .25 |
| 594 Dave Freisleben | .10 | .25 |
| 595 Sixto Lezcano | .10 | .25 |
| 596 Gary Wheelock | .10 | .25 |
| 597 Steve Dillard | .10 | .25 |
| 598 Eddie Solomon | .10 | .25 |
| 599 Gary Woods | .10 | .25 |
| 600 Frank Tanana | .25 | .60 |
| 601 Gene Mauch MG | .25 | .60 |
| 602 Eric Soderholm | .10 | .25 |
| 603 Will McEnaney | .10 | .25 |
| 604 Earl Williams | .10 | .25 |
| 605 Rick Rhoden | .25 | .60 |
| 606 Pittsburgh Pirates CL | .50 | 1.25 |
| 607 Fernando Arroyo | .10 | .25 |
| 608 Johnny Grubb | .10 | .25 |
| 609 John Denny | .10 | .25 |
| 610 Garry Maddox | .25 | .60 |
| 611 Pat Scanlon RC | .10 | .25 |
| 612 Ken Henderson | .10 | .25 |
| 613 Marty Perez | .10 | .25 |
| 614 Joe Wallis | .10 | .25 |
| 615 Clay Carroll | .10 | .25 |
| 616 Pat Kelly | .10 | .25 |
| 617 Joe Nolan RC | .10 | .25 |
| 618 Tommy Helms | .10 | .25 |
| 619 Thad Bosley DP RC | .08 | .20 |
| 620 Willie Randolph | .50 | 1.25 |
| 621 Craig Swan DP | .08 | .20 |
| 622 Champ Summers | .10 | .25 |
| 623 Eduardo Rodriguez | .10 | .25 |
| 624 Gary Alexander DP | .08 | .20 |
| 625 Jose Cruz | .25 | .60 |
| 626 Toronto Blue Jays CL DP | .50 | 1.25 |
| 627 David Johnson | .10 | .25 |
| 628 Ralph Garr | .25 | .60 |
| 629 Don Stanhouse | .10 | .25 |
| 630 Ron Cey | .50 | 1.25 |
| 631 Danny Ozark MG | .10 | .25 |
| 632 Rowland Office | .10 | .25 |
| 633 Tom Veryzer | .10 | .25 |
| 634 Len Barker | .10 | .25 |
| 635 Joe Rudi | .25 | .60 |
| 636 Jim Bibby | .10 | .25 |
| 637 Duffy Dyer | .10 | .25 |
| 638 Paul Splittorff | .10 | .25 |
| 639 Gene Clines | .10 | .25 |
| 640 Lee May DP | .10 | .25 |
| 641 Doug Rau | .10 | .25 |
| 642 Denny Doyle | .10 | .25 |
| 643 Tom House | .10 | .25 |
| 644 Jim Dwyer | .10 | .25 |
| 645 Mike Torrez | .25 | .60 |
| 646 Rick Auerbach DP | .08 | .20 |
| 647 Steve Dunning | .10 | .25 |
| 648 Gary Thomasson | .10 | .25 |
| 649 Moose Haas RC | .10 | .25 |
| 650 Cesar Cedeno | .25 | .60 |
| 651 Doug Rader | .10 | .25 |
| 652 Checklist 606-726 | .50 | 1.25 |
| 653 Ron Hodges DP | .08 | .20 |
| 654 Pepe Frias | .10 | .25 |
| 655 Lyman Bostock | .25 | .60 |
| 656 Dave Garcia MG RC | .10 | .25 |
| 657 Bombo Rivera | .10 | .25 |
| 658 Manny Sanguillen | .25 | .60 |
| 659 Texas Rangers CL | .50 | 1.25 |
| 660 Jason Thompson | .25 | .60 |
| 661 Grant Jackson | .10 | .25 |
| 662 Paul Dade RC | .10 | .25 |
| 663 Paul Reuschel | .10 | .25 |
| 664 Fred Stanley | .10 | .25 |
| 665 Dennis Leonard | .25 | .60 |
| 666 Billy Smith RC | .10 | .25 |
| 667 Jeff Byrd RC | .10 | .25 |
| 668 Dusty Baker | .50 | 1.25 |
| 669 Pete Falcone | .10 | .25 |
| 670 Jim Rice | .50 | 1.25 |
| 671 Gary Lavelle | .10 | .25 |
| 672 Don Kessinger | .25 | .60 |
| 673 Steve Brye | .10 | .25 |
| 674 Ray Knight RC | 1.00 | 2.50 |

| | | |
|---|---|---|
| 675 Jay Johnstone | .25 | .60 |
| 676 Bob Myrick | .10 | .25 |
| 677 Ed Herrmann | .10 | .25 |
| 678 Tom Burgmeier | .10 | .25 |
| 679 Wayne Garrett | .10 | .25 |
| 680 Vida Blue | .25 | .60 |
| 681 Rob Belloir | .10 | .25 |
| 682 Ken Brett | .10 | .25 |
| 683 Mike Champion | .10 | .25 |
| 684 Ralph Houk MG | .25 | .60 |
| 685 Frank Taveras | .10 | .25 |
| 686 Gaylord Perry | 1.00 | 2.50 |
| 687 Julio Cruz RC | .10 | .25 |
| 688 George Mitterwald | .10 | .25 |
| 689 Cleveland Indians CL | .50 | 1.25 |
| 690 Mickey Rivers | .25 | .60 |
| 691 Ross Grimsley | .10 | .25 |
| 692 Ken Reitz | .10 | .25 |
| 693 Lamar Johnson | .10 | .25 |
| 694 Elias Sosa | .10 | .25 |
| 695 Dwight Evans | .50 | 1.25 |
| 696 Steve Mingori | .10 | .25 |
| 697 Roger Metzger | .10 | .25 |
| 698 Juan Bernhardt | .10 | .25 |
| 699 Jackie Brown | .10 | .25 |
| 700 Johnny Bench | 3.00 | 8.00 |
| 701 Hume/Land/McC/Tay RC | .25 | .60 |
| 702 Nah/Pas/Sweet/Wer RC | .25 | .60 |
| 703 Jack Morris DP RC | 2.00 | 5.00 |
| 704 Lou Whitaker RC | 3.00 | 8.00 |
| 705 Berg/Milone/Hurdle/Nor RC | .50 | 1.25 |
| 706 Cage/Cox/Put/Rev RC | .25 | .60 |
| 707 P.Molitor RC/A.Trammell RC | 20.00 | 50.00 |
| 708 D.Murphy/L.Parrish RC | 1.50 | 4.00 |
| 709 Burke/Keough/Rau/Schat RC | .25 | .60 |
| 710 Alston/Bos/Easler/Smith RC | .50 | 1.25 |
| 711 Camp/Lamp/Mit/Tho DP RC | .10 | .25 |
| 712 Bobby Valentine | .25 | .60 |
| 713 Bob Davis | .10 | .25 |
| 714 Mike Anderson | .10 | .25 |
| 715 Jim Kaat | .50 | 1.25 |
| 716 Clarence Gaston | .25 | .60 |
| 717 Nelson Briles | .10 | .25 |
| 718 Ron Jackson | .10 | .25 |
| 719 Randy Elliott RC | .10 | .25 |
| 720 Fergie Jenkins | 1.00 | 2.50 |
| 721 Billy Martin MG | .50 | 1.25 |
| 722 Pete Broberg | .10 | .25 |
| 723 John Wockenfuss | .10 | .25 |
| 724 Kansas City Royals CL | .50 | 1.25 |
| 725 Kurt Bevacqua | .10 | .25 |
| 726 Wilbur Wood | .50 | 1.25 |

### 1979 Topps

JACK MORRIS P
TIGERS

| | | |
|---|---|---|
| COMPLETE SET (726) | 100.00 | 200.00 |
| COMMON CARD (1-726) | .10 | .25 |
| COMMON CARD 727... | .08 | .20 |
| 1 R.Carew/D.Parker LL | 1.00 | 2.50 |
| 2 J.Rice/G.Foster LL | .60 | 1.50 |
| 3 J.Rice/G.Foster LL | .60 | 1.50 |
| 4 R.LeFlore/O.Moreno LL | .30 | .75 |
| 5 R.Guidry/G.Perry LL | .30 | .75 |
| 6 N.Ryan/J.Richard LL | 2.00 | 5.00 |
| 7 R.Guidry/C.Swan LL | .30 | .75 |
| 8 R.Gossage/R.Fingers LL | .60 | 1.50 |
| 9 Dave Campbell | .10 | .25 |
| 10 Lee May | .30 | .75 |
| 11 Marc Hill | .10 | .25 |
| 12 Dick Drago | .10 | .25 |
| 13 Paul Dade | .10 | .25 |
| 14 Rafael Landestoy RC | .10 | .25 |

| | | |
|---|---|---|
| 15 Ross Grimsley | .10 | .25 |
| 16 Fred Stanley | .10 | .25 |
| 17 Donnie Moore | .10 | .25 |
| 18 Tony Solaita | .10 | .25 |
| 19 Larry Gura DP | .08 | .20 |
| 20 Joe Morgan DP | 1.00 | 2.50 |
| 21 Kevin Kobel | .10 | .25 |
| 22 Mike Jorgensen | .10 | .25 |
| 23 Terry Forster | .10 | .25 |
| 24 Paul Molitor | 4.00 | 10.00 |
| 25 Steve Carlton | 1.25 | 3.00 |
| 26 Jamie Quirk | .10 | .25 |
| 27 Dave Goltz | .10 | .25 |
| 28 Steve Brye | .10 | .25 |
| 29 Rick Langford | .10 | .25 |
| 30 Dave Winfield | 1.50 | 4.00 |
| 31 Tom House DP | .08 | .20 |
| 32 Jerry Mumphrey | .10 | .25 |
| 33 Dave Rozema | .10 | .25 |
| 34 Rob Andrews | .10 | .25 |
| 35 Ed Figueroa | .10 | .25 |
| 36 Alan Ashby | .10 | .25 |
| 37 Joe Kerrigan DP | .08 | .20 |
| 38 Bernie Carbo | .10 | .25 |
| 39 Dale Murphy | 1.25 | 3.00 |
| 40 Dennis Eckersley | 1.00 | 2.50 |
| 41 Minnesota Twins CL/Mauch | .60 | 1.50 |
| 42 Ron Blomberg | .10 | .25 |
| 43 Wayne Twitchell | .10 | .25 |
| 44 Kurt Bevacqua | .10 | .25 |
| 45 Al Hrabosky | .30 | .75 |
| 46 Ron Hodges | .10 | .25 |
| 47 Fred Norman | .10 | .25 |
| 48 Merv Rettenmund | .10 | .25 |
| 49 Vern Ruhle | .10 | .25 |
| 50 Steve Garvey DP | .60 | 1.50 |
| 51 Ray Fosse DP | .08 | .20 |
| 52 Randy Lerch | .10 | .25 |
| 53 Mick Kelleher | .10 | .25 |
| 54 Dell Alston DP | .08 | .20 |
| 55 Willie Stargell | 1.00 | 2.50 |
| 56 John Hale | .10 | .25 |
| 57 Eric Rasmussen | .10 | .25 |
| 58 Bob Randall DP | .08 | .20 |
| 59 John Denny DP | .10 | .25 |
| 60 Mickey Rivers | .30 | .75 |
| 61 Bo Diaz | .10 | .25 |
| 62 Randy Moffitt | .10 | .25 |
| 63 Jack Brohamer | .10 | .25 |
| 64 Tom Underwood | .10 | .25 |
| 65 Mark Belanger | .30 | .75 |
| 66 Detroit Tigers CL/Moss | .60 | 1.50 |
| 67 Jim Mason DP | .08 | .20 |
| 68 Joe Niekro DP | .10 | .25 |
| 69 Elliott Maddox | .10 | .25 |
| 70 John Candelaria | .30 | .75 |
| 71 Brian Downing | .30 | .75 |
| 72 Steve Mingori | .10 | .25 |
| 73 Ken Henderson | .10 | .25 |
| 74 Shane Rawley RC | .10 | .25 |
| 75 Steve Yeager | .30 | .75 |
| 76 Warren Cromartie | .30 | .75 |
| 77 Dan Briggs DP | .08 | .20 |
| 78 Elias Sosa | .10 | .25 |
| 79 Ted Cox | .10 | .25 |
| 80 Jason Thompson | .30 | .75 |
| 81 Roger Erickson RC | .10 | .25 |
| 82 New York Mets CL/Torre | .60 | 1.50 |
| 83 Fred Kendall | .10 | .25 |
| 84 Greg Minton | .10 | .25 |
| 85 Gary Matthews | .30 | .75 |
| 86 Rodney Scott | .10 | .25 |
| 87 Pete Falcone | .10 | .25 |
| 88 Bob Molinaro RC | .10 | .25 |
| 89 Dick Tidrow | .10 | .25 |
| 90 Bob Boone | .60 | 1.50 |
| 91 Terry Crowley | .10 | .25 |
| 92 Jim Bibby | .10 | .25 |
| 93 Phil Mankowski | .10 | .25 |
| 94 Len Barker | .10 | .25 |
| 95 Robin Yount | 2.00 | 5.00 |
| 96 Cleveland Indians CL/Torborg | .60 | 1.50 |
| 97 Sam Mejias | .10 | .25 |
| 98 Ray Burris | .10 | .25 |
| 99 John Wathan | .30 | .75 |

|  |  | | |
|---|---|---|---|
| 100 | Tom Seaver DP | 1.50 | 4.00 |
| 101 | Roy Howell | .10 | .25 |
| 102 | Mike Anderson | .10 | .25 |
| 103 | Jim Todd | .10 | .25 |
| 104 | Johnny Oates DP | .10 | .25 |
| 105 | Rick Camp DP | .08 | .20 |
| 106 | Frank Duffy | .10 | .25 |
| 107 | Jesus Alou DP | .08 | .20 |
| 108 | Eduardo Rodriguez | .10 | .25 |
| 109 | Joel Youngblood | .10 | .25 |
| 110 | Vida Blue | .30 | .75 |
| 111 | Roger Freed | .10 | .25 |
| 112 | Philadelphia Phillies CL/Ozark | .60 | 1.50 |
| 113 | Pete Redfern | .10 | .25 |
| 114 | Cliff Johnson | .10 | .25 |
| 115 | Nolan Ryan | 8.00 | 20.00 |
| 116 | Ozzie Smith RC | 30.00 | 60.00 |
| 117 | Grant Jackson | .10 | .25 |
| 118 | Bud Harrelson | .30 | .75 |
| 119 | Don Stanhouse | .10 | .25 |
| 120 | Jim Sundberg | .30 | .75 |
| 121 | Checklist 1-121 DP | .30 | .75 |
| 122 | Mike Paxton | .10 | .25 |
| 123 | Lou Whitaker | 1.00 | 2.50 |
| 124 | Dan Schatzeder | .10 | .25 |
| 125 | Rick Burleson | .10 | .25 |
| 126 | Doug Bair | .10 | .25 |
| 127 | Thad Bosley | .10 | .25 |
| 128 | Ted Martinez | .10 | .25 |
| 129 | Marty Pattin DP | .08 | .20 |
| 130 | Bob Watson DP | .10 | .25 |
| 131 | Jim Clancy | .10 | .25 |
| 132 | Rowland Office | .10 | .25 |
| 133 | Bill Castro | .10 | .25 |
| 134 | Alan Bannister | .10 | .25 |
| 135 | Bobby Murcer | .30 | .75 |
| 136 | Jim Kaat | .30 | .75 |
| 137 | Larry Wolfe DP RC | .08 | .20 |
| 138 | Mark Lee RC | .10 | .25 |
| 139 | Luis Pujols RC | .10 | .25 |
| 140 | Don Gullett | .30 | .75 |
| 141 | Tom Paciorek | .10 | .25 |
| 142 | Charlie Williams | .10 | .25 |
| 143 | Tony Scott | .10 | .25 |
| 144 | Sandy Alomar | .10 | .25 |
| 145 | Rick Rhoden | .10 | .25 |
| 146 | Duane Kuiper | .10 | .25 |
| 147 | Dave Hamilton | .10 | .25 |
| 148 | Bruce Boisclair | .10 | .25 |
| 149 | Manny Sarmiento | .10 | .25 |
| 150 | Wayne Cage | .10 | .25 |
| 151 | John Hiller | .10 | .25 |
| 152 | Rick Cerone | .10 | .25 |
| 153 | Dennis Lamp | .10 | .25 |
| 154 | Jim Gantner DP | .10 | .25 |
| 155 | Dwight Evans | .60 | 1.50 |
| 156 | Buddy Solomon RC | .10 | .25 |
| 157 | U.L. Washington UER | .10 | .25 |
| 158 | Joe Sambito | .10 | .25 |
| 159 | Roy White | .30 | .75 |
| 160 | Mike Flanagan | .60 | 1.50 |
| 161 | Barry Foote | .10 | .25 |
| 162 | Tom Johnson | .10 | .25 |
| 163 | Glenn Burke | .10 | .25 |
| 164 | Mickey Lolich | .30 | .75 |
| 165 | Frank Taveras | .10 | .25 |
| 166 | Leon Roberts | .10 | .25 |
| 167 | Roger Metzger DP | .08 | .20 |
| 168 | Dave Freisleben | .10 | .25 |
| 169 | Bill Nahorodny | .10 | .25 |
| 170 | Don Sutton | 1.00 | 2.50 |
| 171 | Gene Clines | .10 | .25 |
| 172 | Mike Bruhert RC | .10 | .25 |
| 173 | John Lowenstein | .10 | .25 |
| 174 | Rick Auerbach | .10 | .25 |
| 175 | George Hendrick | .60 | 1.50 |
| 176 | Aurelio Rodriguez | .10 | .25 |
| 177 | Ron Reed | .10 | .25 |
| 178 | Alvis Woods | .10 | .25 |
| 179 | Jim Beattie DP RC | .08 | .20 |
| 180 | Larry Hisle | .10 | .25 |
| 181 | Mike Garman | .10 | .25 |
| 182 | Tim Johnson | .10 | .25 |
| 183 | Paul Splittorff | .10 | .25 |
| 184 | Darrel Chaney | .10 | .25 |
| 185 | Mike Torrez | .30 | .75 |
| 186 | Eric Soderholm | .10 | .25 |
| 187 | Mark Lemongello | .10 | .25 |
| 188 | Pat Kelly | .10 | .25 |
| 189 | Ed Whitson RC | .10 | .25 |
| 190 | Ron Cey | .30 | .75 |
| 191 | Mike Norris | .10 | .25 |
| 192 | St. Louis Cardinals CL/Boyer | .60 | 1.50 |
| 193 | Glenn Adams | .10 | .25 |
| 194 | Randy Jones | .10 | .25 |
| 195 | Bill Madlock | .30 | .75 |
| 196 | Steve Kemp DP | .10 | .25 |
| 197 | Bob Apodaca | .10 | .25 |
| 198 | Johnny Grubb | .10 | .25 |
| 199 | Larry Milbourne | .10 | .25 |
| 200 | Johnny Bench DP | 2.00 | 5.00 |
| 201 | Mike Edwards RB | .10 | .25 |
| 202 | Ron Guidry RB | .30 | .75 |
| 203 | J.R. Richard RB | .10 | .25 |
| 204 | Pete Rose RB | 2.00 | 5.00 |
| 205 | John Stearns RB | .10 | .25 |
| 206 | Sammy Stewart RB | .10 | .25 |
| 207 | Dave Lemanczyk | .10 | .25 |
| 208 | Clarence Gaston | .10 | .25 |
| 209 | Reggie Cleveland | .10 | .25 |
| 210 | Larry Bowa | .30 | .75 |
| 211 | Dennis Martinez | .30 | .75 |
| 212 | Carney Lansford RC | .60 | 1.50 |
| 213 | Bill Travers | .10 | .25 |
| 214 | Boston Red Sox CL/Zimmer | .60 | 1.50 |
| 215 | Willie McCovey | 1.00 | 2.50 |
| 216 | Wilbur Wood | .10 | .25 |
| 217 | Steve Dillard | .10 | .25 |
| 218 | Dennis Leonard | .10 | .25 |
| 219 | Roy Smalley | .30 | .75 |
| 220 | Cesar Geronimo | .10 | .25 |
| 221 | Jesse Jefferson | .10 | .25 |
| 222 | Bob Beall RC | .10 | .25 |
| 223 | Kent Tekulve | .30 | .75 |
| 224 | Dave Revering | .10 | .25 |
| 225 | Goose Gossage | .60 | 1.50 |
| 226 | Ron Pruitt | .10 | .25 |
| 227 | Steve Stone | .30 | .75 |
| 228 | Vic Davalillo | .10 | .25 |
| 229 | Doug Flynn | .10 | .25 |
| 230 | Bob Forsch | .10 | .25 |
| 231 | John Wockenfuss | .10 | .25 |
| 232 | Jimmy Sexton RC | .10 | .25 |
| 233 | Paul Mitchell | .10 | .25 |
| 234 | Toby Harrah | .30 | .75 |
| 235 | Steve Rogers | .10 | .25 |
| 236 | Jim Dwyer | .10 | .25 |
| 237 | Billy Smith | .10 | .25 |
| 238 | Balor Moore | .10 | .25 |
| 239 | Willie Horton | .30 | .75 |
| 240 | Rick Reuschel | .30 | .75 |
| 241 | Checklist 122-242 DP | .30 | .75 |
| 242 | Pablo Torrealba | .10 | .25 |
| 243 | Buck Martinez DP | .10 | .25 |
| 244 | Pittsburgh Pirates CL/Tanner | .60 | 1.50 |
| 245 | Jeff Burroughs | .30 | .75 |
| 246 | Darrell Jackson RC | .10 | .25 |
| 247 | Tucker Ashford DP | .08 | .20 |
| 248 | Pete LaCock | .10 | .25 |
| 249 | Paul Thormodsgard | .10 | .25 |
| 250 | Willie Randolph | .30 | .75 |
| 251 | Jack Morris | 1.00 | 2.50 |
| 252 | Bob Stinson | .10 | .25 |
| 253 | Rick Wise | .10 | .25 |
| 254 | Luis Gomez | .10 | .25 |
| 255 | Tommy John | .60 | 1.50 |
| 256 | Mike Sadek | .10 | .25 |
| 257 | Adrian Devine | .10 | .25 |
| 258 | Mike Phillips | .10 | .25 |
| 259 | Cincinnati Reds CL/Anderson | .60 | 1.50 |
| 260 | Richie Zisk | .10 | .25 |
| 261 | Mario Guerrero | .10 | .25 |
| 262 | Nelson Briles | .10 | .25 |
| 263 | Oscar Gamble | .30 | .75 |
| 264 | Don Robinson RC | .10 | .25 |
| 265 | Don Money | .10 | .25 |
| 266 | Jim Willoughby | .10 | .25 |
| 267 | Joe Rudi | .30 | .75 |
| 268 | Julio Gonzalez | .10 | .25 |
| 269 | Woodie Fryman | .10 | .25 |
| 270 | Butch Hobson | .30 | .75 |
| 271 | Rawly Eastwick | .10 | .25 |
| 272 | Tim Corcoran | .10 | .25 |
| 273 | Jerry Terrell | .10 | .25 |
| 274 | Willie Norwood | .10 | .25 |
| 275 | Junior Moore | .10 | .25 |
| 276 | Jim Colborn | .10 | .25 |
| 277 | Tom Grieve | .30 | .75 |
| 278 | Andy Messersmith | .30 | .75 |
| 279 | Jerry Grote DP | .08 | .20 |
| 280 | Andre Thornton | .30 | .75 |
| 281 | Vic Correll DP | .08 | .20 |
| 282 | Toronto Blue Jays CL/Hartsfield | .30 | .75 |
| 283 | Ken Kravec | .10 | .25 |
| 284 | Johnnie LeMaster | .10 | .25 |
| 285 | Bobby Bonds | .60 | 1.50 |
| 286 | Duffy Dyer | .10 | .25 |
| 287 | Andres Mora | .10 | .25 |
| 288 | Milt Wilcox | .10 | .25 |
| 289 | Jose Cruz | .60 | 1.50 |
| 290 | Dave Lopes | .30 | .75 |
| 291 | Tom Griffin | .10 | .25 |
| 292 | Don Reynolds RC | .10 | .25 |
| 293 | Jerry Garvin | .10 | .25 |
| 294 | Pepe Frias | .10 | .25 |
| 295 | Mitchell Page | .10 | .25 |
| 296 | Preston Hanna RC | .10 | .25 |
| 297 | Ted Sizemore | .10 | .25 |
| 298 | Rich Gale RC | .10 | .25 |
| 299 | Steve Ontiveros | .10 | .25 |
| 300 | Rod Carew | 1.25 | 3.00 |
| 301 | Tom Hume | .10 | .25 |
| 302 | Atlanta Braves CL/Cox | .60 | 1.50 |
| 303 | Lary Sorensen DP | .08 | .20 |
| 304 | Steve Swisher | .10 | .25 |
| 305 | Willie Montanez | .10 | .25 |
| 306 | Floyd Bannister | .10 | .25 |
| 307 | Larvell Blanks | .10 | .25 |
| 308 | Bert Blyleven | .60 | 1.50 |
| 309 | Ralph Garr | .30 | .75 |
| 310 | Thurman Munson | 1.25 | 3.00 |
| 311 | Gary Lavelle | .10 | .25 |
| 312 | Bob Robertson | .10 | .25 |
| 313 | Dyar Miller | .10 | .25 |
| 314 | Larry Harlow | .10 | .25 |
| 315 | Jon Matlack | .30 | .75 |
| 316 | Milt May | .10 | .25 |
| 317 | Jose Cardenal | .30 | .75 |
| 318 | Bob Welch RC | 1.00 | 2.50 |
| 319 | Wayne Garrett | .10 | .25 |
| 320 | Carl Yastrzemski | 2.00 | 5.00 |
| 321 | Gaylord Perry | 1.00 | 2.50 |
| 322 | Danny Goodwin RC | .10 | .25 |
| 323 | Lynn McGlothen | .10 | .25 |
| 324 | Mike Tyson | .10 | .25 |
| 325 | Cecil Cooper | .30 | .75 |
| 326 | Pedro Borbon | .10 | .25 |
| 327 | Art Howe DP | .10 | .25 |
| 328 | Oakland Athletics CL/McKeon | .60 | 1.50 |
| 329 | Joe Coleman | .10 | .25 |
| 330 | George Brett | 4.00 | 10.00 |
| 331 | Mickey Mahler | .10 | .25 |
| 332 | Gary Alexander | .10 | .25 |
| 333 | Chet Lemon | .30 | .75 |
| 334 | Craig Swan | .10 | .25 |
| 335 | Chris Chambliss | .30 | .75 |
| 336 | Bobby Thompson RC | .10 | .25 |
| 337 | John Montague | .10 | .25 |
| 338 | Vic Harris | .10 | .25 |
| 339 | Ron Jackson | .10 | .25 |
| 340 | Jim Palmer | 1.00 | 2.50 |
| 341 | Willie Upshaw RC | .30 | .75 |
| 342 | Dave Roberts | .10 | .25 |
| 343 | Ed Glynn | .10 | .25 |
| 344 | Jerry Royster | .10 | .25 |
| 345 | Tug McGraw | .30 | .75 |
| 346 | Bill Buckner | .30 | .75 |
| 347 | Doug Rau | .10 | .25 |
| 348 | Andre Dawson | 1.25 | 3.00 |
| 349 | Jim Wright RC | .10 | .25 |
| 350 | Garry Templeton | .30 | .75 |
| 351 | Wayne Nordhagen DP | .08 | .20 |
| 352 | Steve Renko | .10 | .25 |
| 353 | Checklist 243-363 | .60 | 1.50 |
| 354 | Bill Bonham | .10 | .25 |
| 355 | Lee Mazzilli | .10 | .25 |
| 356 | San Francisco Giants CL/Altobelli | .60 | 1.50 |
| 357 | Jerry Augustine | .10 | .25 |
| 358 | Alan Trammell | 1.25 | 3.00 |
| 359 | Dan Spillner DP | .08 | .20 |
| 360 | Amos Otis | .30 | .75 |
| 361 | Tom Dixon RC | .10 | .25 |
| 362 | Mike Cubbage | .10 | .25 |
| 363 | Craig Skok RC | .10 | .25 |

|  |  | | |
|---|---|---|---|
| ☐ 364 | Gene Richards | .10 | .25 |
| ☐ 365 | Sparky Lyle | .30 | .75 |
| ☐ 366 | Juan Bernhardt | .10 | .25 |
| ☐ 367 | Dave Skaggs | .10 | .25 |
| ☐ 368 | Don Aase | .10 | .25 |
| ☐ 369A | Bump Wills ERR | 1.25 | 3.00 |
| ☐ 369B | Bump Wills COR | 1.25 | 3.00 |
| ☐ 370 | Dave Kingman | .60 | 1.50 |
| ☐ 371 | Jeff Holly RC | .10 | .25 |
| ☐ 372 | Lamar Johnson | .10 | .25 |
| ☐ 373 | Lance Rautzhan | .10 | .25 |
| ☐ 374 | Ed Herrmann | .10 | .25 |
| ☐ 375 | Bill Campbell | .10 | .25 |
| ☐ 376 | Gorman Thomas | .30 | .75 |
| ☐ 377 | Paul Moskau | .10 | .25 |
| ☐ 378 | Rob Picciolo DP | .08 | .20 |
| ☐ 379 | Dale Murray | .10 | .25 |
| ☐ 380 | Jim Mayberry | .30 | .75 |
| ☐ 381 | Houston Astros CL/Virdon | .60 | 1.50 |
| ☐ 382 | Jerry Martin | .10 | .25 |
| ☐ 383 | Phil Garner | .30 | .75 |
| ☐ 384 | Tommy Boggs | .10 | .25 |
| ☐ 385 | Dan Ford | .10 | .25 |
| ☐ 386 | Francisco Barrios | .10 | .25 |
| ☐ 387 | Gary Thomasson | .10 | .25 |
| ☐ 388 | Jack Billingham | .10 | .25 |
| ☐ 389 | Joe Zdeb | .10 | .25 |
| ☐ 390 | Rollie Fingers | 1.00 | 2.50 |
| ☐ 391 | Al Oliver | .30 | .75 |
| ☐ 392 | Doug Ault | .10 | .25 |
| ☐ 393 | Scott McGregor | .30 | .75 |
| ☐ 394 | Randy Stein RC | .10 | .25 |
| ☐ 395 | Dave Cash | .10 | .25 |
| ☐ 396 | Bill Plummer | .10 | .25 |
| ☐ 397 | Sergio Ferrer RC | .10 | .25 |
| ☐ 398 | Ivan DeJesus | .10 | .25 |
| ☐ 399 | David Clyde | .10 | .25 |
| ☐ 400 | Jim Rice | .60 | 1.50 |
| ☐ 401 | Ray Knight | .30 | .75 |
| ☐ 402 | Paul Hartzell | .10 | .25 |
| ☐ 403 | Tim Foli | .10 | .25 |
| ☐ 404 | Chicago White Sox CL/Kessinger | .60 | 1.50 |
| ☐ 405 | Butch Wynegar DP | .08 | .20 |
| ☐ 406 | Joe Wallis DP | .08 | .20 |
| ☐ 407 | Pete Vuckovich | .30 | .75 |
| ☐ 408 | Charlie Moore DP | .08 | .20 |
| ☐ 409 | Willie Wilson RC | .60 | 1.50 |
| ☐ 410 | Darrell Evans | .60 | 1.50 |
| ☐ 411 | G.Sisler/T.Cobb ATL | 1.00 | 2.50 |
| ☐ 412 | H.Wilson/H.Aaron ATL | 1.00 | 2.50 |
| ☐ 413 | R.Maris/H.Aaron ATL | 1.50 | 4.00 |
| ☐ 414 | H.Hornsby/T.Cobb ATL | 1.00 | 2.50 |
| ☐ 415 | L.Brock/L.Brock ATL | .60 | 1.50 |
| ☐ 416 | J.Chesbro/C.Young ATL | .30 | .75 |
| ☐ 417 | N.Ryan/W.Johnson ATL DP | 2.00 | 5.00 |
| ☐ 418 | D.Leonard/W.Johnson ATL DP | .10 | .25 |
| ☐ 419 | Dick Ruthven | .10 | .25 |
| ☐ 420 | Ken Griffey Sr. | .30 | .75 |
| ☐ 421 | Doug DeCinces | .30 | .75 |
| ☐ 422 | Ruppert Jones | .10 | .25 |
| ☐ 423 | Bob Montgomery | .10 | .25 |
| ☐ 424 | California Angels CL/Fregosi | .60 | 1.50 |
| ☐ 425 | Rick Manning | .10 | .25 |
| ☐ 426 | Chris Speier | .10 | .25 |
| ☐ 427 | Andy Replogle RC | .10 | .25 |
| ☐ 428 | Bobby Valentine | .30 | .75 |
| ☐ 429 | John Urrea DP | .08 | .20 |
| ☐ 430 | Dave Parker | .30 | .75 |
| ☐ 431 | Glenn Borgmann | .10 | .25 |
| ☐ 432 | Dave Heaverlo | .10 | .25 |
| ☐ 433 | Larry Biittner | .10 | .25 |
| ☐ 434 | Ken Clay | .10 | .25 |
| ☐ 435 | Gene Tenace | .30 | .75 |
| ☐ 436 | Hector Cruz | .10 | .25 |
| ☐ 437 | Rick Williams RC | .10 | .25 |
| ☐ 438 | Horace Speed RC | .10 | .25 |
| ☐ 439 | Frank White | .30 | .75 |
| ☐ 440 | Rusty Staub | .60 | 1.50 |
| ☐ 441 | Lee Lacy | .10 | .25 |
| ☐ 442 | Doyle Alexander | .10 | .25 |
| ☐ 443 | Bruce Bochte | .10 | .25 |
| ☐ 444 | Aurelio Lopez RC | .10 | .25 |
| ☐ 445 | Steve Henderson | .10 | .25 |
| ☐ 446 | Jim Lonborg | .30 | .75 |
| ☐ 447 | Manny Sanguillen | .30 | .75 |
| ☐ 448 | Moose Haas | .10 | .25 |
| ☐ 449 | Bombo Rivera | .10 | .25 |
| ☐ 450 | Dave Concepcion | .60 | 1.50 |
| ☐ 451 | Kansas City Royals CL/Herzog | .60 | 1.50 |
| ☐ 452 | Jerry Morales | .10 | .25 |
| ☐ 453 | Chris Knapp | .10 | .25 |
| ☐ 454 | Len Randle | .10 | .25 |
| ☐ 455 | Bill Lee DP | .08 | .20 |
| ☐ 456 | Chuck Baker RC | .10 | .25 |
| ☐ 457 | Bruce Sutter | 1.00 | 2.50 |
| ☐ 458 | Jim Essian | .10 | .25 |
| ☐ 459 | Sid Monge | .10 | .25 |
| ☐ 460 | Graig Nettles | .60 | 1.50 |
| ☐ 461 | Jim Barr DP | .08 | .20 |
| ☐ 462 | Otto Velez | .10 | .25 |
| ☐ 463 | Steve Comer RC | .10 | .25 |
| ☐ 464 | Joe Nolan | .10 | .25 |
| ☐ 465 | Reggie Smith | .30 | .75 |
| ☐ 466 | Mark Littell | .10 | .25 |
| ☐ 467 | Don Kessinger DP | .10 | .25 |
| ☐ 468 | Stan Bahnsen DP | .08 | .20 |
| ☐ 469 | Lance Parrish | .60 | 1.50 |
| ☐ 470 | Garry Maddox DP | .10 | .25 |
| ☐ 471 | Joaquin Andujar | .30 | .75 |
| ☐ 472 | Craig Kusick | .10 | .25 |
| ☐ 473 | Dave Roberts | .10 | .25 |
| ☐ 474 | Dick Davis RC | .10 | .25 |
| ☐ 475 | Dan Driessen | .10 | .25 |
| ☐ 476 | Tom Poquette | .10 | .25 |
| ☐ 477 | Bob Grich | .30 | .75 |
| ☐ 478 | Juan Beniquez | .10 | .25 |
| ☐ 479 | San Diego Padres CL/Craig | .60 | 1.50 |
| ☐ 480 | Fred Lynn | .30 | .75 |
| ☐ 481 | Skip Lockwood | .10 | .25 |
| ☐ 482 | Craig Reynolds | .10 | .25 |
| ☐ 483 | Checklist 364-484 DP | .30 | .75 |
| ☐ 484 | Rick Waits | .10 | .25 |
| ☐ 485 | Bucky Dent | .30 | .75 |
| ☐ 486 | Bob Knepper | .10 | .25 |
| ☐ 487 | Miguel Dilone | .10 | .25 |
| ☐ 488 | Bob Owchinko | .10 | .25 |
| ☐ 489 | Larry Cox UER | .10 | .25 |
| ☐ 490 | Al Cowens | .30 | .75 |
| ☐ 491 | Tippy Martinez | .10 | .25 |
| ☐ 492 | Bob Bailor | .10 | .25 |
| ☐ 493 | Larry Christenson | .10 | .25 |
| ☐ 494 | Jerry White | .10 | .25 |
| ☐ 495 | Tony Perez | 1.00 | 2.50 |
| ☐ 496 | Barry Bonnell DP | .08 | .20 |
| ☐ 497 | Glenn Abbott | .10 | .25 |
| ☐ 498 | Rich Chiles | .10 | .25 |
| ☐ 499 | Texas Rangers CL/Corrales | .60 | 1.50 |
| ☐ 500 | Ron Guidry | .30 | .75 |
| ☐ 501 | Junior Kennedy RC | .10 | .25 |
| ☐ 502 | Steve Braun | .10 | .25 |
| ☐ 503 | Terry Humphrey | .10 | .25 |
| ☐ 504 | Larry McWilliams RC | .10 | .25 |
| ☐ 505 | Ed Kranepool | .10 | .25 |
| ☐ 506 | John D'Acquisto | .10 | .25 |
| ☐ 507 | Tony Armas | .30 | .75 |
| ☐ 508 | Charlie Hough | .30 | .75 |
| ☐ 509 | Mario Mendoza UER | .10 | .25 |
| ☐ 510 | Ted Simmons | .60 | 1.50 |
| ☐ 511 | Paul Reuschel DP | .08 | .20 |
| ☐ 512 | Jack Clark | .30 | .75 |
| ☐ 513 | Dave Johnson | .30 | .75 |
| ☐ 514 | Mike Proly RC | .10 | .25 |
| ☐ 515 | Enos Cabell | .10 | .25 |
| ☐ 516 | Champ Summers DP | .08 | .20 |
| ☐ 517 | Al Bumbry | .30 | .75 |
| ☐ 518 | Jim Umbarger | .10 | .25 |
| ☐ 519 | Ben Oglivie | .30 | .75 |
| ☐ 520 | Gary Carter | .60 | 1.50 |
| ☐ 521 | Sam Ewing | .10 | .25 |
| ☐ 522 | Ken Holtzman | .30 | .75 |
| ☐ 523 | John Milner | .10 | .25 |
| ☐ 524 | Tom Burgmeier | .10 | .25 |
| ☐ 525 | Freddie Patek | .10 | .25 |
| ☐ 526 | Los Angeles Dodgers CL/Lasorda | .60 | 1.50 |
| ☐ 527 | Lerrin LaGrow | .10 | .25 |
| ☐ 528 | Wayne Gross DP | .08 | .20 |
| ☐ 529 | Brian Asselstine | .10 | .25 |
| ☐ 530 | Frank Tanana | .30 | .75 |
| ☐ 531 | Fernando Gonzalez | .10 | .25 |
| ☐ 532 | Buddy Schultz | .10 | .25 |
| ☐ 533 | Leroy Stanton | .10 | .25 |
| ☐ 534 | Ken Forsch | .10 | .25 |
| ☐ 535 | Ellis Valentine | .10 | .25 |
| ☐ 536 | Jerry Reuss | .30 | .75 |
| ☐ 537 | Tom Veryzer | .10 | .25 |
| ☐ 538 | Mike Ivie DP | .08 | .20 |
| ☐ 539 | John Ellis | .10 | .25 |
| ☐ 540 | Greg Luzinski | .30 | .75 |
| ☐ 541 | Jim Slaton | .10 | .25 |
| ☐ 542 | Rick Bosetti | .10 | .25 |
| ☐ 543 | Kiko Garcia | .10 | .25 |
| ☐ 544 | Fergie Jenkins | 1.00 | 2.50 |
| ☐ 545 | John Stearns | .10 | .25 |
| ☐ 546 | Bill Russell | .30 | .75 |
| ☐ 547 | Clint Hurdle | .10 | .25 |
| ☐ 548 | Enrique Romo | .10 | .25 |
| ☐ 549 | Bob Bailey | .10 | .25 |
| ☐ 550 | Sal Bando | .30 | .75 |
| ☐ 551 | Chicago Cubs CL/Franks | .60 | 1.50 |
| ☐ 552 | Jose Morales | .10 | .25 |
| ☐ 553 | Denny Walling | .10 | .25 |
| ☐ 554 | Matt Keough | .10 | .25 |
| ☐ 555 | Biff Pocoroba | .10 | .25 |
| ☐ 556 | Mike Lum | .10 | .25 |
| ☐ 557 | Ken Brett | .10 | .25 |
| ☐ 558 | Jay Johnstone | .30 | .75 |
| ☐ 559 | Greg Pryor RC | .10 | .25 |
| ☐ 560 | John Montefusco | .10 | .25 |
| ☐ 561 | Ed Ott | .10 | .25 |
| ☐ 562 | Dusty Baker | .60 | 1.50 |
| ☐ 563 | Roy Thomas | .10 | .25 |
| ☐ 564 | Jerry Turner | .10 | .25 |
| ☐ 565 | Rico Carty | .30 | .75 |
| ☐ 566 | Nino Espinosa | .10 | .25 |
| ☐ 567 | Richie Hebner | .10 | .25 |
| ☐ 568 | Carlos Lopez | .10 | .25 |
| ☐ 569 | Bob Sykes | .10 | .25 |
| ☐ 570 | Cesar Cedeno | .30 | .75 |
| ☐ 571 | Darrel Porter | .30 | .75 |
| ☐ 572 | Rod Gilbreath | .10 | .25 |
| ☐ 573 | Jim Kern | .10 | .25 |
| ☐ 574 | Claudell Washington | .30 | .75 |
| ☐ 575 | Luis Tiant | .30 | .75 |
| ☐ 576 | Mike Parrott RC | .10 | .25 |
| ☐ 577 | Milwaukee Brewers CL/Bamberger | .60 | 1.50 |
| ☐ 578 | Pete Broberg | .10 | .25 |
| ☐ 579 | Greg Gross | .10 | .25 |
| ☐ 580 | Ron Fairly | .30 | .75 |
| ☐ 581 | Darrold Knowles | .10 | .25 |
| ☐ 582 | Paul Blair | .30 | .75 |
| ☐ 583 | Julio Cruz | .10 | .25 |
| ☐ 584 | Jim Rooker | .10 | .25 |
| ☐ 585 | Hal McRae | .60 | 1.50 |
| ☐ 586 | Bob Horner RC | .60 | 1.50 |
| ☐ 587 | Ken Reitz | .10 | .25 |
| ☐ 588 | Tom Murphy | .10 | .25 |
| ☐ 589 | Terry Whitfield | .10 | .25 |
| ☐ 590 | J.R. Richard | .30 | .75 |
| ☐ 591 | Mike Hargrove | .30 | .75 |
| ☐ 592 | Mike Krukow | .30 | .75 |
| ☐ 593 | Rick Dempsey | .30 | .75 |
| ☐ 594 | Bob Shirley | .10 | .25 |
| ☐ 595 | Phil Niekro | 1.00 | 2.50 |
| ☐ 596 | Jim Wohlford | .10 | .25 |
| ☐ 597 | Bob Stanley | .10 | .25 |
| ☐ 598 | Mark Wagner | .10 | .25 |
| ☐ 599 | Jim Spencer | .10 | .25 |
| ☐ 600 | George Foster | .30 | .75 |
| ☐ 601 | Dave LaRoche | .10 | .25 |
| ☐ 602 | Checklist 485-605 | .60 | 1.50 |
| ☐ 603 | Rudy May | .10 | .25 |
| ☐ 604 | Jeff Newman | .10 | .25 |
| ☐ 605 | Rick Monday DP | .10 | .25 |
| ☐ 606 | Montreal Expos CL/Williams | .60 | 1.50 |
| ☐ 607 | Omar Moreno | .10 | .25 |
| ☐ 608 | Dave McKay | .10 | .25 |
| ☐ 609 | Silvio Martinez RC | .10 | .25 |
| ☐ 610 | Mike Schmidt | 3.00 | 8.00 |
| ☐ 611 | Jim Norris | .10 | .25 |
| ☐ 612 | Rick Honeycutt RC | .30 | .75 |
| ☐ 613 | Mike Edwards RC | .10 | .25 |
| ☐ 614 | Willie Hernandez | .30 | .75 |
| ☐ 615 | Ken Singleton | .30 | .75 |
| ☐ 616 | Billy Almon | .10 | .25 |
| ☐ 617 | Terry Puhl | .10 | .25 |
| ☐ 618 | Jerry Remy | .10 | .25 |
| ☐ 619 | Ken Landreaux RC | .30 | .75 |
| ☐ 620 | Bert Campaneris | .30 | .75 |
| ☐ 621 | Pat Zachry | .10 | .25 |
| ☐ 622 | Dave Collins | .10 | .25 |
| ☐ 623 | Bob McClure | .10 | .25 |
| ☐ 624 | Larry Herndon | .10 | .25 |
| ☐ 625 | Mark Fidrych | 1.00 | 2.50 |
| ☐ 626 | New York Yankees CL/Lemon | .60 | 1.50 |

| | | |
|---|---|---|
| ❏ 627 Gary Serum RC | .10 | .25 |
| ❏ 628 Del Unser | .10 | .25 |
| ❏ 629 Gene Garber | .10 | .25 |
| ❏ 630 Bake McBride | .30 | .75 |
| ❏ 631 Jorge Orta | .10 | .25 |
| ❏ 632 Don Kirkwood | .10 | .25 |
| ❏ 633 Rob Wilfong DP RC | .08 | .20 |
| ❏ 634 Paul Lindblad | .10 | .25 |
| ❏ 635 Don Baylor | .60 | 1.50 |
| ❏ 636 Wayne Garland | .10 | .25 |
| ❏ 637 Bill Robinson | .30 | .75 |
| ❏ 638 Al Fitzmorris | .10 | .25 |
| ❏ 639 Manny Trillo | .10 | .25 |
| ❏ 640 Eddie Murray | 5.00 | 12.00 |
| ❏ 641 Bobby Castillo RC | .10 | .25 |
| ❏ 642 Wilbur Howard DP | .08 | .20 |
| ❏ 643 Tom Hausman | .10 | .25 |
| ❏ 644 Manny Mota | .30 | .75 |
| ❏ 645 George Scott DP | .10 | .25 |
| ❏ 646 Rick Sweet | .10 | .25 |
| ❏ 647 Bob Lacey | .10 | .25 |
| ❏ 648 Lou Piniella | .30 | .75 |
| ❏ 649 John Curtis | .10 | .25 |
| ❏ 650 Pete Rose | 5.00 | 12.00 |
| ❏ 651 Mike Caldwell | .10 | .25 |
| ❏ 652 Stan Papi RC | .10 | .25 |
| ❏ 653 Warren Brusstar DP | .08 | .20 |
| ❏ 654 Rick Miller | .10 | .25 |
| ❏ 655 Jerry Koosman | .30 | .75 |
| ❏ 656 Hosken Powell RC | .10 | .25 |
| ❏ 657 George Medich | .10 | .25 |
| ❏ 658 Taylor Duncan RC | .10 | .25 |
| ❏ 659 Seattle Mariners CL/Johnson | .60 | 1.50 |
| ❏ 660 Ron LeFlore DP | .10 | .25 |
| ❏ 661 Bruce Kison | .10 | .25 |
| ❏ 662 Kevin Bell | .10 | .25 |
| ❏ 663 Mike Vail | .10 | .25 |
| ❏ 664 Doug Bird | .10 | .25 |
| ❏ 665 Lou Brock | 1.00 | 2.50 |
| ❏ 666 Rich Dauer | .10 | .25 |
| ❏ 667 Don Hood | .10 | .25 |
| ❏ 668 Bill North | .10 | .25 |
| ❏ 669 Checklist 606-726 | .60 | 1.50 |
| ❏ 670 Jim Hunter DP | .60 | 1.50 |
| ❏ 671 Joe Ferguson DP | .08 | .20 |
| ❏ 672 Ed Halicki | .10 | .25 |
| ❏ 673 Tom Hutton | .10 | .25 |
| ❏ 674 Dave Tomlin | .10 | .25 |
| ❏ 675 Tim McCarver | .60 | 1.50 |
| ❏ 676 Johnny Sutton RC | .10 | .25 |
| ❏ 677 Larry Parrish | .30 | .75 |
| ❏ 678 Geoff Zahn | .10 | .25 |
| ❏ 679 Derrel Thomas | .10 | .25 |
| ❏ 680 Carlton Fisk | 1.25 | 3.00 |
| ❏ 681 John Henry Johnson RC | .10 | .25 |
| ❏ 682 Dave Chalk | .10 | .25 |
| ❏ 683 Dan Meyer DP | .08 | .20 |
| ❏ 684 Jamie Easterly DP | .08 | .20 |
| ❏ 685 Sixto Lezcano | .10 | .25 |
| ❏ 686 Ron Schueler DP | .08 | .20 |
| ❏ 687 Rennie Stennett | .10 | .25 |
| ❏ 688 Mike Willis | .10 | .25 |
| ❏ 689 Baltimore Orioles CL/Weaver | .60 | 1.50 |
| ❏ 690 Buddy Bell DP | .10 | .25 |
| ❏ 691 Dock Ellis DP | .08 | .20 |
| ❏ 692 Mickey Stanley | .10 | .25 |
| ❏ 693 Dave Rader | .10 | .25 |
| ❏ 694 Burt Hooton | .10 | .25 |
| ❏ 695 Keith Hernandez | .30 | .75 |
| ❏ 696 Andy Hassler | .10 | .25 |
| ❏ 697 Dave Bergman | .10 | .25 |
| ❏ 698 Bill Stein | .10 | .25 |
| ❏ 699 Hal Dues RC | .10 | .25 |
| ❏ 700 Reggie Jackson | 2.00 | 5.00 |
| ❏ 701 Corey/Flinn/Stewart DP | .30 | .75 |
| ❏ 702 Finch/Hancock/Ripley RC | .30 | .75 |
| ❏ 703 Anderson/Frost/Slater RC | .30 | .75 |
| ❏ 704 Baumgarten/Colbern/Squires RC | .30 | .75 |
| ❏ 705 Griffin/Norrid/Oliver RC | .60 | 1.50 |
| ❏ 706 Stegman/Tobik/Young RC | .30 | .75 |
| ❏ 707 Bass/Gaudet/McGilberry RC | .60 | 1.50 |
| ❏ 708 Bass/Romero/Yost RC | .60 | 1.50 |
| ❏ 709 Perkozzo/Sofield/Stanfield RC | .30 | .75 |
| ❏ 710 Doyle/Heath/Rajsich RC | .30 | .75 |
| ❏ 711 Murphy/Robinson/Wirth RC | .60 | 1.50 |
| ❏ 712 Anderson/Biercevicz/McLaughlin RC | .30 | .75 |
| ❏ 713 Darwin/Putnam/Sample RC | .60 | 1.50 |
| ❏ 714 Cruz/Kelly/Whitt RC | .30 | .75 |

| | | |
|---|---|---|
| ❏ 715 Benedict/Hubbard/Whisenton RC | .60 | 1.50 |
| ❏ 716 Geisel/Pagel/Thompson RC | .30 | .75 |
| ❏ 717 LaCoss/Oester/Spilman RC | .30 | .75 |
| ❏ 718 Bochy/Fischlin/Pisker RC | .30 | .75 |
| ❏ 719 Guerrero/Law/Simpson RC | .60 | 1.50 |
| ❏ 720 Fry/Pirtle/Sanderson RC | .60 | 1.50 |
| ❏ 721 Berenguer/Bernard/Norman RC | .60 | 1.50 |
| ❏ 722 Morrison/Smith/Wright RC | .60 | 1.50 |
| ❏ 723 Berra/Cotes/Wiltbank RC | .30 | .75 |
| ❏ 724 Bruno/Frazier/Kennedy RC | .60 | 1.50 |
| ❏ 725 Beswick/Mura/Perkins RC | .30 | .75 |
| ❏ 726 Johnston/Strain/Tamargo RC | .30 | .75 |

## 1980 Topps

| | | |
|---|---|---|
| ❏ COMPLETE SET (726) | 70.00 | 120.00 |
| ❏ COMMON CARD (1-726) | .08 | .25 |
| ❏ COMMON DP | .08 | .25 |
| ❏ 1 L.Brock/C.Yastrzemski HL | 1.00 | 2.50 |
| ❏ 2 Willie McCovey HL | .30 | .75 |
| ❏ 3 Manny Mota HL | .08 | .25 |
| ❏ 4 Pete Rose HL | 1.25 | 3.00 |
| ❏ 5 Garry Templeton HL | .08 | .25 |
| ❏ 6 Del Unser HL | .08 | .25 |
| ❏ 7 Mike Lum | .08 | .25 |
| ❏ 8 Craig Swan | .08 | .25 |
| ❏ 9 Steve Braun | .08 | .25 |
| ❏ 10 Dennis Martinez | .30 | .75 |
| ❏ 11 Jimmy Sexton | .08 | .25 |
| ❏ 12 John Curtis DP | .08 | .25 |
| ❏ 13 Ron Pruitt | .08 | .25 |
| ❏ 14 Dave Cash | .30 | .75 |
| ❏ 15 Bill Campbell | .08 | .25 |
| ❏ 16 Jerry Narron RC | .08 | .25 |
| ❏ 17 Bruce Sutter | .60 | 1.50 |
| ❏ 18 Ron Jackson | .08 | .25 |
| ❏ 19 Balor Moore | .08 | .25 |
| ❏ 20 Dan Ford | .08 | .25 |
| ❏ 21 Manny Sarmiento | .08 | .25 |
| ❏ 22 Pat Putnam | .08 | .25 |
| ❏ 23 Derrel Thomas | .08 | .25 |
| ❏ 24 Jim Slaton | .08 | .25 |
| ❏ 25 Lee Mazzilli | .30 | .75 |
| ❏ 26 Marty Pattin | .08 | .25 |
| ❏ 27 Del Unser | .08 | .25 |
| ❏ 28 Bruce Kison | .08 | .25 |
| ❏ 29 Mark Wagner | .08 | .25 |
| ❏ 30 Vida Blue | .30 | .75 |
| ❏ 31 Jay Johnstone | .30 | .75 |
| ❏ 32 Julio Cruz DP | .08 | .25 |
| ❏ 33 Tony Scott | .08 | .25 |
| ❏ 34 Jeff Newman DP | .08 | .25 |
| ❏ 35 Luis Tiant | .30 | .75 |
| ❏ 36 Rusty Torres | .08 | .25 |
| ❏ 37 Kiko Garcia | .08 | .25 |
| ❏ 38 Dan Spillner DP | .08 | .25 |
| ❏ 39 Rowland Office | .08 | .25 |
| ❏ 40 Carlton Fisk | 1.00 | 2.50 |
| ❏ 41 Texas Rangers CL/Corrales | .30 | .75 |
| ❏ 42 David Palmer RC | .08 | .25 |
| ❏ 43 Bombo Rivera | .08 | .25 |
| ❏ 44 Bill Fahey | .08 | .25 |
| ❏ 45 Frank White | .30 | .75 |
| ❏ 46 Rico Carty | .30 | .75 |
| ❏ 47 Bill Bonham DP | .08 | .25 |
| ❏ 48 Rick Miller | .08 | .25 |
| ❏ 49 Mario Guerrero | .08 | .25 |
| ❏ 50 J.R. Richard | .30 | .75 |
| ❏ 51 Joe Ferguson DP | .08 | .25 |
| ❏ 52 Warren Brusstar | .08 | .25 |
| ❏ 53 Ben Oglivie | .30 | .75 |
| ❏ 54 Dennis Lamp | .08 | .25 |
| ❏ 55 Bill Madlock | .30 | .75 |
| ❏ 56 Bobby Valentine | .30 | .75 |
| ❏ 57 Pete Vuckovich | .08 | .25 |

| | | |
|---|---|---|
| ❏ 58 Doug Flynn | .08 | .25 |
| ❏ 59 Eddy Putman RC | .08 | .25 |
| ❏ 60 Bucky Dent | .30 | .75 |
| ❏ 61 Gary Serum | .08 | .25 |
| ❏ 62 Mike Ivie | .08 | .25 |
| ❏ 63 Bob Stanley | .08 | .25 |
| ❏ 64 Joe Nolan | .08 | .25 |
| ❏ 65 Al Bumbry | .08 | .25 |
| ❏ 66 Kansas City Royals CL/Frey | .30 | .75 |
| ❏ 67 Doyle Alexander | .08 | .25 |
| ❏ 68 Larry Harlow | .08 | .25 |
| ❏ 69 Rick Williams | .08 | .25 |
| ❏ 70 Gary Carter | .60 | 1.50 |
| ❏ 71 John Milner DP | .08 | .25 |
| ❏ 72 Fred Howard DP RC | .08 | .25 |
| ❏ 73 Dave Collins | .08 | .25 |
| ❏ 74 Sid Monge | .08 | .25 |
| ❏ 75 Bill Russell | .30 | .75 |
| ❏ 76 John Stearns | .08 | .25 |
| ❏ 77 Dave Stieb RC | .60 | 1.50 |
| ❏ 78 Ruppert Jones | .08 | .25 |
| ❏ 79 Bob Owchinko | .08 | .25 |
| ❏ 80 Ron LeFlore | .30 | .75 |
| ❏ 81 Ted Sizemore | .08 | .25 |
| ❏ 82 Houston Astros CL/Virdon | .30 | .75 |
| ❏ 83 Steve Trout RC | .08 | .25 |
| ❏ 84 Gary Lavelle | .08 | .25 |
| ❏ 85 Ted Simmons | .30 | .75 |
| ❏ 86 Dave Hamilton | .08 | .25 |
| ❏ 87 Pepe Frias | .08 | .25 |
| ❏ 88 Ken Landreaux | .08 | .25 |
| ❏ 89 Don Hood | .08 | .25 |
| ❏ 90 Manny Trillo | .30 | .75 |
| ❏ 91 Rick Dempsey | .08 | .25 |
| ❏ 92 Rick Rhoden | .08 | .25 |
| ❏ 93 Dave Roberts DP | .08 | .25 |
| ❏ 94 Neil Allen RC | .30 | .75 |
| ❏ 95 Cecil Cooper | .30 | .75 |
| ❏ 96 Oakland Athletics CL/Marshall | .30 | .75 |
| ❏ 97 Bill Lee | .30 | .75 |
| ❏ 98 Jerry Terrell | .08 | .25 |
| ❏ 99 Victor Cruz | .08 | .25 |
| ❏ 100 Johnny Bench | 1.25 | 3.00 |
| ❏ 101 Aurelio Lopez | .08 | .25 |
| ❏ 102 Rich Dauer | .08 | .25 |
| ❏ 103 Bill Caudill RC | .08 | .25 |
| ❏ 104 Manny Mota | .30 | .75 |
| ❏ 105 Frank Tanana | .30 | .75 |
| ❏ 106 Jeff Leonard RC | .60 | 1.50 |
| ❏ 107 Francisco Barrios | .08 | .25 |
| ❏ 108 Bob Horner | .30 | .75 |
| ❏ 109 Bill Travers | .08 | .25 |
| ❏ 110 Fred Lynn DP | .20 | .50 |
| ❏ 111 Bob Knepper | .08 | .25 |
| ❏ 112 Chicago White Sox CL/LaRussa | .30 | .75 |
| ❏ 113 Geoff Zahn | .08 | .25 |
| ❏ 114 Juan Beniquez | .08 | .25 |
| ❏ 115 Sparky Lyle | .30 | .75 |
| ❏ 116 Larry Cox | .08 | .25 |
| ❏ 117 Dock Ellis | .08 | .25 |
| ❏ 118 Phil Garner | .30 | .75 |
| ❏ 119 Sammy Stewart | .08 | .25 |
| ❏ 120 Greg Luzinski | .30 | .75 |
| ❏ 121 Checklist 1-121 | .30 | .75 |
| ❏ 122 Dave Rosello DP | .08 | .25 |
| ❏ 123 Lynn Jones RC | .08 | .25 |
| ❏ 124 Dave Lemanczyk | .08 | .25 |
| ❏ 125 Tony Perez | .30 | .75 |
| ❏ 126 Dave Tomlin | .08 | .25 |
| ❏ 127 Gary Thomasson | .08 | .25 |
| ❏ 128 Tom Burgmeier | .08 | .25 |
| ❏ 129 Craig Reynolds | .08 | .25 |
| ❏ 130 Amos Otis | .30 | .75 |
| ❏ 131 Paul Mitchell | .08 | .25 |
| ❏ 132 Biff Pocoroba | .08 | .25 |
| ❏ 133 Jerry Turner | .08 | .25 |
| ❏ 134 Matt Keough | .08 | .25 |
| ❏ 135 Bill Buckner | .30 | .75 |
| ❏ 136 Dick Ruthven | .08 | .25 |
| ❏ 137 John Castino RC | .08 | .25 |
| ❏ 138 Ross Baumgarten | .08 | .25 |
| ❏ 139 Dane Iorg RC | .08 | .25 |
| ❏ 140 Rich Gossage | .30 | .75 |
| ❏ 141 Gary Alexander | .08 | .25 |
| ❏ 142 Phil Huffman RC | .08 | .25 |
| ❏ 143 Bruce Bochte DP | .08 | .25 |
| ❏ 144 Steve Comer | .08 | .25 |
| ❏ 145 Darrell Evans | .30 | .75 |

|  |  | | |
|---|--------|---|---|
| 146 | Bob Welch | .30 | .75 |
| 147 | Terry Puhl | .08 | .25 |
| 148 | Manny Sanguillen | .30 | .75 |
| 149 | Tom Hume | .08 | .25 |
| 150 | Jason Thompson | .08 | .25 |
| 151 | Tom Hausman DP | .08 | .25 |
| 152 | John Fulgham RC | .08 | .25 |
| 153 | Tim Blackwell | .08 | .25 |
| 154 | Lary Sorensen | .08 | .25 |
| 155 | Jerry Remy | .08 | .25 |
| 156 | Tony Brizzolara DP | .08 | .25 |
| 157 | Willie Wilson DP | .20 | .50 |
| 158 | Rob Picciolo DP | .08 | .25 |
| 159 | Ken Clay | .08 | .25 |
| 160 | Eddie Murray | 2.00 | 5.00 |
| 161 | Larry Christenson | .08 | .25 |
| 162 | Bob Randall | .08 | .25 |
| 163 | Steve Swisher | .08 | .25 |
| 164 | Greg Pryor | .08 | .25 |
| 165 | Omar Moreno | .08 | .25 |
| 166 | Glenn Abbott | .08 | .25 |
| 167 | Jack Clark | .30 | .75 |
| 168 | Rick Waits | .08 | .25 |
| 169 | Luis Gomez | .08 | .25 |
| 170 | Burt Hooton | .30 | .75 |
| 171 | Fernando Gonzalez | .08 | .25 |
| 172 | Ron Hodges | .08 | .25 |
| 173 | John Henry Johnson | .08 | .25 |
| 174 | Ray Knight | .30 | .75 |
| 175 | Rick Reuschel | .30 | .75 |
| 176 | Champ Summers | .08 | .25 |
| 177 | Dave Heaverlo | .08 | .25 |
| 178 | Tim McCarver | .30 | .75 |
| 179 | Ron Davis RC | .08 | .25 |
| 180 | Warren Cromartie | .08 | .25 |
| 181 | Moose Haas | .08 | .25 |
| 182 | Ken Reitz | .08 | .25 |
| 183 | Jim Anderson DP | .08 | .25 |
| 184 | Steve Renko DP | .08 | .25 |
| 185 | Hal McRae | .30 | .75 |
| 186 | Junior Moore | .08 | .25 |
| 187 | Alan Ashby | .08 | .25 |
| 188 | Terry Crowley | .08 | .25 |
| 189 | Kevin Kobel | .08 | .25 |
| 190 | Buddy Bell | .30 | .75 |
| 191 | Ted Martinez | .08 | .25 |
| 192 | Atlanta Braves CL/Cox | .30 | .75 |
| 193 | Dave Goltz | .08 | .25 |
| 194 | Mike Easler | .08 | .25 |
| 195 | John Montefusco | .08 | .25 |
| 196 | Lance Parrish | .30 | .75 |
| 197 | Byron McLaughlin | .08 | .25 |
| 198 | Del Alston DP | .08 | .25 |
| 199 | Mike LaCoss | .08 | .25 |
| 200 | Jim Rice | .30 | .75 |
| 201 | K.Hernandez/F.Lynn LL | .30 | .75 |
| 202 | D.Kingman/G.Thomas LL | .60 | 1.50 |
| 203 | D.Winfield/D.Baylor LL | .60 | 1.50 |
| 204 | O.Moreno/W.Wilson LL | .30 | .75 |
| 205 | Niekro/Niekro/Flan LL | .30 | .75 |
| 206 | J.Richard/N.Ryan LL | 2.00 | 5.00 |
| 207 | J.Richard/R.Guidry LL | .30 | .75 |
| 208 | Wayne Cage | .08 | .25 |
| 209 | Von Joshua | .08 | .25 |
| 210 | Steve Carlton | .60 | 1.50 |
| 211 | Dave Skaggs DP | .08 | .25 |
| 212 | Dave Roberts | .08 | .25 |
| 213 | Mike Jorgensen DP | .08 | .25 |
| 214 | California Angels CL/Fregosi | .30 | .75 |
| 215 | Sixto Lezcano | .08 | .25 |
| 216 | Phil Mankowski | .08 | .25 |
| 217 | Ed Halicki | .08 | .25 |
| 218 | Jose Morales | .08 | .25 |
| 219 | Steve Mingori | .08 | .25 |
| 220 | Dave Concepcion | .30 | .75 |
| 221 | Joe Cannon RC | .08 | .25 |
| 222 | Ron Hassey RC | .08 | .25 |
| 223 | Bob Sykes | .08 | .25 |
| 224 | Willie Montanez | .08 | .25 |
| 225 | Lou Piniella | .30 | .75 |
| 226 | Bill Stein | .08 | .25 |
| 227 | Len Barker | .08 | .25 |
| 228 | Johnny Oates | .08 | .25 |
| 229 | Jim Bibby | .08 | .25 |
| 230 | Dave Winfield | .60 | 1.50 |
| 231 | Steve McCatty | .08 | .25 |
| 232 | Alan Trammell | .60 | 1.50 |
| 233 | LaRue Washington RC | .08 | .25 |
| 234 | Vern Ruhle | .08 | .25 |
| 235 | Andre Dawson | .60 | 1.50 |
| 236 | Marc Hill | .08 | .25 |
| 237 | Scott McGregor | .30 | .75 |
| 238 | Rob Wilfong | .08 | .25 |
| 239 | Don Aase | .08 | .25 |
| 240 | Dave Kingman | .30 | .75 |
| 241 | Checklist 122-242 | .30 | .75 |
| 242 | Lamar Johnson | .08 | .25 |
| 243 | Jerry Augustine | .08 | .25 |
| 244 | St. Louis Cardinals CL/Boyer | .30 | .75 |
| 245 | Phil Niekro | .30 | .75 |
| 246 | Tim Foli DP | .08 | .25 |
| 247 | Frank Riccelli | .08 | .25 |
| 248 | Jamie Quirk | .08 | .25 |
| 249 | Jim Clancy | .08 | .25 |
| 250 | Jim Kaat | .30 | .75 |
| 251 | Kip Young | .08 | .25 |
| 252 | Ted Cox | .08 | .25 |
| 253 | John Montague | .08 | .25 |
| 254 | Paul Dade DP | .08 | .25 |
| 255 | Dusty Baker DP | .20 | .50 |
| 256 | Roger Erickson | .08 | .25 |
| 257 | Larry Herndon | .08 | .25 |
| 258 | Paul Moskau | .08 | .25 |
| 259 | New York Mets CL/Torre | .60 | 1.50 |
| 260 | Al Oliver | .30 | .75 |
| 261 | Dave Chalk | .08 | .25 |
| 262 | Benny Ayala | .08 | .25 |
| 263 | Dave LaRoche DP | .08 | .25 |
| 264 | Bill Robinson | .08 | .25 |
| 265 | Robin Yount | 1.25 | 3.00 |
| 266 | Bernie Carbo | .08 | .25 |
| 267 | Dan Schatzeder | .08 | .25 |
| 268 | Rafael Landestoy | .08 | .25 |
| 269 | Dave Tobik | .08 | .25 |
| 270 | Mike Schmidt DP | 1.25 | 3.00 |
| 271 | Dick Drago DP | .08 | .25 |
| 272 | Ralph Garr | .30 | .75 |
| 273 | Eduardo Rodriguez | .08 | .25 |
| 274 | Dale Murphy | 1.00 | 2.50 |
| 275 | Jerry Koosman | .30 | .75 |
| 276 | Tom Veryzer | .08 | .25 |
| 277 | Rick Bosetti | .08 | .25 |
| 278 | Jim Spencer | .08 | .25 |
| 279 | Rob Andrews | .08 | .25 |
| 280 | Gaylord Perry | .30 | .75 |
| 281 | Paul Blair | .30 | .75 |
| 282 | Seattle Mariners CL/Johnson | .30 | .75 |
| 283 | John Ellis | .08 | .25 |
| 284 | Larry Murray DP RC | .08 | .25 |
| 285 | Don Baylor | .30 | .75 |
| 286 | Darold Knowles DP | .08 | .25 |
| 287 | John Lowenstein | .08 | .25 |
| 288 | Dave Rozema | .08 | .25 |
| 289 | Bruce Bochy | .08 | .25 |
| 290 | Steve Garvey | .60 | 1.50 |
| 291 | Randy Scarberry RC | .08 | .25 |
| 292 | Dale Berra | .08 | .25 |
| 293 | Elias Sosa | .08 | .25 |
| 294 | Charlie Spikes | .08 | .25 |
| 295 | Larry Gura | .08 | .25 |
| 296 | Dave Rader | .08 | .25 |
| 297 | Tim Johnson | .08 | .25 |
| 298 | Ken Holtzman | .30 | .75 |
| 299 | Steve Henderson | .08 | .25 |
| 300 | Ron Guidry | .30 | .75 |
| 301 | Mike Edwards | .08 | .25 |
| 302 | Los Angeles Dodgers CL/Lasorda | .60 | 1.50 |
| 303 | Bill Castro | .08 | .25 |
| 304 | Butch Wynegar | .08 | .25 |
| 305 | Randy Jones | .30 | .75 |
| 306 | Denny Walling | .08 | .25 |
| 307 | Rick Honeycutt | .08 | .25 |
| 308 | Mike Hargrove | .30 | .75 |
| 309 | Larry McWilliams | .08 | .25 |
| 310 | Dave Parker | .30 | .75 |
| 311 | Roger Metzger | .08 | .25 |
| 312 | Mike Barlow | .08 | .25 |
| 313 | Johnny Grubb | .08 | .25 |
| 314 | Tim Stoddard RC | .08 | .25 |
| 315 | Steve Kemp | .30 | .75 |
| 316 | Bob Lacey | .08 | .25 |
| 317 | Mike Anderson RC | .08 | .25 |
| 318 | Jerry Reuss | .30 | .75 |
| 319 | Chris Speier | .08 | .25 |
| 320 | Dennis Eckersley | .60 | 1.50 |
| 321 | Keith Hernandez | .30 | .75 |
| 322 | Claudell Washington | .08 | .25 |
| 323 | Mick Kelleher | .08 | .25 |
| 324 | Tom Underwood | .08 | .25 |
| 325 | Dan Driessen | .08 | .25 |
| 326 | Bo McLaughlin | .08 | .25 |
| 327 | Ray Fosse DP | .20 | .50 |
| 328 | Minnesota Twins CL/Mauch | .30 | .75 |
| 329 | Bert Roberge RC | .08 | .25 |
| 330 | Al Cowens | .30 | .75 |
| 331 | Richie Hebner | .08 | .25 |
| 332 | Enrique Romo | .08 | .25 |
| 333 | Jim Norris DP | .08 | .25 |
| 334 | Jim Beattie | .08 | .25 |
| 335 | Willie McCovey | .60 | 1.50 |
| 336 | George Medich | .08 | .25 |
| 337 | Carney Lansford | .30 | .75 |
| 338 | John Wockenfuss | .08 | .25 |
| 339 | John D'Acquisto | .08 | .25 |
| 340 | Ken Singleton | .30 | .75 |
| 341 | Jim Essian | .08 | .25 |
| 342 | Odell Jones | .08 | .25 |
| 343 | Mike Vail | .08 | .25 |
| 344 | Randy Lerch | .08 | .25 |
| 345 | Larry Parrish | .30 | .75 |
| 346 | Buddy Solomon | .08 | .25 |
| 347 | Harry Chappas RC | .08 | .25 |
| 348 | Checklist 243-363 | .30 | .75 |
| 349 | Jack Brohamer | .08 | .25 |
| 350 | George Hendrick | .30 | .75 |
| 351 | Bob Davis | .08 | .25 |
| 352 | Dan Briggs | .08 | .25 |
| 353 | Andy Hassler | .08 | .25 |
| 354 | Rick Auerbach | .08 | .25 |
| 355 | Gary Matthews | .30 | .75 |
| 356 | San Diego Padres CL/Coleman | .30 | .75 |
| 357 | Bob McClure | .08 | .25 |
| 358 | Lou Whitaker | .30 | .75 |
| 359 | Randy Moffitt | .08 | .25 |
| 360 | Darrell Porter DP | .20 | .50 |
| 361 | Wayne Garland | .08 | .25 |
| 362 | Danny Goodwin | .08 | .25 |
| 363 | Wayne Gross | .08 | .25 |
| 364 | Ray Burris | .08 | .25 |
| 365 | Bobby Murcer | .30 | .75 |
| 366 | Rob Dressler | .08 | .25 |
| 367 | Billy Smith | .08 | .25 |
| 368 | Willie Aikens RC | .08 | .25 |
| 369 | Jim Kern | .08 | .25 |
| 370 | Cesar Cedeno | .30 | .75 |
| 371 | Jack Morris | .30 | .75 |
| 372 | Joel Youngblood | .08 | .25 |
| 373 | Dan Petry DP RC | .30 | .75 |
| 374 | Jim Gantner | .08 | .25 |
| 375 | Ross Grimsley | .08 | .25 |
| 376 | Gary Allenson RC | .08 | .25 |
| 377 | Junior Kennedy | .08 | .25 |
| 378 | Jerry Mumphrey | .08 | .25 |
| 379 | Kevin Bell | .08 | .25 |
| 380 | Garry Maddox | .30 | .75 |
| 381 | Chicago Cubs CL/Gomez | .30 | .75 |
| 382 | Dave Freisleben | .08 | .25 |
| 383 | Ed Ott | .08 | .25 |
| 384 | Joey McLaughlin RC | .08 | .25 |
| 385 | Enos Cabell | .08 | .25 |
| 386 | Darrell Jackson | .08 | .25 |
| 387A | F.Stanley Yellow | .75 | 2.00 |
| 387B | F.Stanley Red Name | .08 | .25 |
| 388 | Mike Paxton | .08 | .25 |
| 389 | Pete LaCock | .08 | .25 |
| 390 | Fergie Jenkins | .30 | .75 |
| 391 | Tony Armas DP | .20 | .50 |
| 392 | Milt Wilcox | .08 | .25 |
| 393 | Ozzie Smith | 4.00 | 10.00 |
| 394 | Reggie Cleveland | .08 | .25 |
| 395 | Ellis Valentine | .08 | .25 |
| 396 | Dan Meyer | .08 | .25 |
| 397 | Roy Thomas DP | .08 | .25 |
| 398 | Barry Foote | .08 | .25 |
| 399 | Mike Proly DP | .08 | .25 |
| 400 | George Foster | .30 | .75 |
| 401 | Pete Falcone | .08 | .25 |
| 402 | Merv Rettenmund | .08 | .25 |
| 403 | Pete Redfern DP | .08 | .25 |
| 404 | Baltimore Orioles CL/Weaver | .30 | .75 |
| 405 | Dwight Evans | .60 | 1.50 |
| 406 | Paul Molitor | 1.50 | 4.00 |
| 407 | Tony Solaita | .08 | .25 |
| 408 | Bill North | .08 | .25 |

|  |  | | |
|---|---|---|---|
| 409 | Paul Splittorff | .08 | .25 |
| 410 | Bobby Bonds | .30 | .75 |
| 411 | Frank LaCorte | .08 | .25 |
| 412 | Thad Bosley | .08 | .25 |
| 413 | Allen Ripley | .08 | .25 |
| 414 | George Scott | .30 | .75 |
| 415 | Bill Atkinson | .08 | .25 |
| 416 | Tom Brookens RC | .08 | .25 |
| 417 | Craig Chamberlain DP RC | .08 | .25 |
| 418 | Roger Freed DP | .08 | .25 |
| 419 | Vic Correll | .08 | .25 |
| 420 | Butch Hobson | .08 | .25 |
| 421 | Doug Bird | .08 | .25 |
| 422 | Larry Milbourne | .08 | .25 |
| 423 | Dave Frost | .08 | .25 |
| 424 | New York Yankees CL/Howser | .30 | .75 |
| 424A | New York Yankees CL/Martin | | |
| 425 | Mark Belanger | .30 | .75 |
| 426 | Grant Jackson | .08 | .25 |
| 427 | Tom Hutton DP | .08 | .25 |
| 428 | Pat Zachry | .08 | .25 |
| 429 | Duane Kuiper | .08 | .25 |
| 430 | Larry Hisle DP | .08 | .25 |
| 431 | Mike Krukow | .08 | .25 |
| 432 | Willie Norwood | .08 | .25 |
| 433 | Rich Gale | .08 | .25 |
| 434 | Johnnie LeMaster | .08 | .25 |
| 435 | Don Gullett | .30 | .75 |
| 436 | Billy Almon | .08 | .25 |
| 437 | Joe Niekro | .30 | .75 |
| 438 | Dave Revering | .08 | .25 |
| 439 | Mike Phillips | .08 | .25 |
| 440 | Don Sutton | .30 | .75 |
| 441 | Eric Soderholm | .08 | .25 |
| 442 | Jorge Orta | .08 | .25 |
| 443 | Mike Parrott | .08 | .25 |
| 444 | Alvis Woods | .08 | .25 |
| 445 | Mark Fidrych | .30 | .75 |
| 446 | Duffy Dyer | .08 | .25 |
| 447 | Nino Espinosa | .08 | .25 |
| 448 | Jim Wohlford | .08 | .25 |
| 449 | Doug Bair | .08 | .25 |
| 450 | George Brett | 3.00 | 8.00 |
| 451 | Cleveland Indians CL/Garcia | .30 | .75 |
| 452 | Steve Dillard | .08 | .25 |
| 453 | Mike Bacsik | .08 | .25 |
| 454 | Tom Donohue RC | .08 | .25 |
| 455 | Mike Torrez | .30 | .75 |
| 456 | Frank Taveras | .08 | .25 |
| 457 | Bert Blyleven | .30 | .75 |
| 458 | Billy Sample | .08 | .25 |
| 459 | Mickey Lolich DP | .20 | .50 |
| 460 | Willie Randolph | .30 | .75 |
| 461 | Dwayne Murphy | .08 | .25 |
| 462 | Mike Sadek DP | .08 | .25 |
| 463 | Jerry Royster | .08 | .25 |
| 464 | John Denny | .30 | .75 |
| 465 | Rick Monday | .30 | .75 |
| 466 | Mike Squires | .08 | .25 |
| 467 | Jesse Jefferson | .08 | .25 |
| 468 | Aurelio Rodriguez | .08 | .25 |
| 469 | Randy Niemann DP RC | .08 | .25 |
| 470 | Bob Boone | .30 | .75 |
| 471 | Hosken Powell DP | .08 | .25 |
| 472 | Willie Hernandez | .30 | .75 |
| 473 | Bump Wills | .08 | .25 |
| 474 | Steve Busby | .08 | .25 |
| 475 | Cesar Geronimo | .08 | .25 |
| 476 | Bob Shirley | .08 | .25 |
| 477 | Buck Martinez | .08 | .25 |
| 478 | Gil Flores | .08 | .25 |
| 479 | Montreal Expos CL/Williams | .30 | .75 |
| 480 | Bob Watson | .30 | .75 |
| 481 | Tom Paciorek | .08 | .25 |
| 482 | Rickey Henderson RC | 30.00 | 60.00 |
| 483 | Bo Diaz | .08 | .25 |
| 484 | Checklist 364-484 | .30 | .75 |
| 485 | Mickey Rivers | .30 | .75 |
| 486 | Mike Tyson DP | .08 | .25 |
| 487 | Wayne Nordhagen | .08 | .25 |
| 488 | Roy Howell | .08 | .25 |
| 489 | Preston Hanna DP | .08 | .25 |
| 490 | Lee May | .30 | .75 |
| 491 | Steve Mura DP | .08 | .25 |
| 492 | Todd Cruz RC | .08 | .25 |
| 493 | Jerry Martin | .08 | .25 |
| 494 | Craig Minetto RC | .08 | .25 |
| 495 | Bake McBride | .30 | .75 |
| 496 | Silvio Martinez | .08 | .25 |
| 497 | Jim Mason | .08 | .25 |
| 498 | Danny Darwin | .08 | .25 |
| 499 | San Francisco Giants CL/Bristol | .30 | .75 |
| 500 | Tom Seaver | 1.25 | 3.00 |
| 501 | Rennie Stennett | .08 | .25 |
| 502 | Rich Wortham DP RC | .08 | .25 |
| 503 | Mike Cubbage | .08 | .25 |
| 504 | Gene Garber | .08 | .25 |
| 505 | Bert Campaneris | .30 | .75 |
| 506 | Tom Buskey | .08 | .25 |
| 507 | Leon Roberts | .08 | .25 |
| 508 | U.L. Washington | .08 | .25 |
| 509 | Ed Glynn | .08 | .25 |
| 510 | Ron Cey | .30 | .75 |
| 511 | Eric Wilkins RC | .08 | .25 |
| 512 | Jose Cardenal | .08 | .25 |
| 513 | Tom Dixon DP | .08 | .25 |
| 514 | Steve Ontiveros | .08 | .25 |
| 515 | Mike Caldwell UER | .08 | .25 |
| 516 | Hector Cruz | .08 | .25 |
| 517 | Don Stanhouse | .08 | .25 |
| 518 | Nelson Norman RC | .08 | .25 |
| 519 | Steve Nicosia RC | .08 | .25 |
| 520 | Steve Rogers | .30 | .75 |
| 521 | Ken Brett | .08 | .25 |
| 522 | Jim Morrison | .08 | .25 |
| 523 | Ken Henderson | .08 | .25 |
| 524 | Jim Wright DP | .08 | .25 |
| 525 | Clint Hurdle | .08 | .25 |
| 526 | Philadelphia Phillies CL/Green | .30 | .75 |
| 527 | Doug Rau DP | .08 | .25 |
| 528 | Adrian Devine | .08 | .25 |
| 529 | Jim Barr | .08 | .25 |
| 530 | Jim Sundberg DP | .20 | .50 |
| 531 | Eric Rasmussen | .08 | .25 |
| 532 | Willie Horton | .30 | .75 |
| 533 | Checklist 485-605 | .30 | .75 |
| 534 | Andre Thornton | .30 | .75 |
| 535 | Bob Forsch | .30 | .75 |
| 536 | Lee Lacy | .08 | .25 |
| 537 | Alex Trevino RC | .08 | .25 |
| 538 | Joe Strain | .08 | .25 |
| 539 | Rudy May | .08 | .25 |
| 540 | Pete Rose | 3.00 | 8.00 |
| 541 | Miguel Dilone | .06 | .25 |
| 542 | Joe Coleman | .08 | .25 |
| 543 | Pat Kelly | .08 | .25 |
| 544 | Rick Sutcliffe RC | .60 | 1.50 |
| 545 | Jeff Burroughs | .30 | .75 |
| 546 | Rick Langford | .08 | .25 |
| 547 | John Wathan | .08 | .25 |
| 548 | Dave Rajsich | .08 | .25 |
| 549 | Larry Wolfe | .08 | .25 |
| 550 | Ken Griffey Sr. | .30 | .75 |
| 551 | Pittsburgh Pirates CL/Tanner | .30 | .75 |
| 552 | Bill Nahorodny | .08 | .25 |
| 553 | Dick Davis | .08 | .25 |
| 554 | Art Howe | .30 | .75 |
| 555 | Ed Figueroa | .08 | .25 |
| 556 | Joe Rudi | .30 | .75 |
| 557 | Mark Lee | .08 | .25 |
| 558 | Alfredo Griffin | .30 | .75 |
| 559 | Dale Murray | .08 | .25 |
| 560 | Dave Lopes | .30 | .75 |
| 561 | Eddie Whitson | .30 | .75 |
| 562 | Joe Wallis | .08 | .25 |
| 563 | Will McEnaney | .08 | .25 |
| 564 | Rick Manning | .08 | .25 |
| 565 | Dennis Leonard | .30 | .75 |
| 566 | Bud Harrelson | .30 | .75 |
| 567 | Skip Lockwood | .08 | .25 |
| 568 | Gary Roenicke RC | .08 | .25 |
| 569 | Terry Kennedy | .30 | .75 |
| 570 | Roy Smalley | .30 | .75 |
| 571 | Joe Sambito | .08 | .25 |
| 572 | Jerry Morales DP | .08 | .25 |
| 573 | Kent Tekulve | .30 | .75 |
| 574 | Scot Thompson | .08 | .25 |
| 575 | Ken Kravec | .08 | .25 |
| 576 | Jim Dwyer | .08 | .25 |
| 577 | Toronto Blue Jays CL/Mattick | .30 | .75 |
| 578 | Scott Sanderson | .08 | .25 |
| 579 | Charlie Moore | .06 | .25 |
| 580 | Nolan Ryan | 6.00 | 15.00 |
| 581 | Bob Bailor | .08 | .25 |
| 582 | Brian Doyle | .08 | .25 |
| 583 | Bob Stinson | .08 | .25 |
| 584 | Kurt Bevacqua | .08 | .25 |
| 585 | Al Hrabosky | .30 | .75 |
| 586 | Mitchell Page | .08 | .25 |
| 587 | Garry Templeton | .30 | .75 |
| 588 | Greg Minton | .08 | .25 |
| 589 | Chet Lemon | .30 | .75 |
| 590 | Jim Palmer | .60 | 1.50 |
| 591 | Rick Cerone | .08 | .25 |
| 592 | Jon Matlack | .30 | .75 |
| 593 | Jesus Alou | .08 | .25 |
| 594 | Dick Tidrow | .08 | .25 |
| 595 | Don Money | .08 | .25 |
| 596 | Rick Matula RC | .08 | .25 |
| 597 | Tom Poquette | .08 | .25 |
| 598 | Fred Kendall DP | .08 | .25 |
| 599 | Mike Norris | .08 | .25 |
| 600 | Reggie Jackson | 1.25 | 3.00 |
| 601 | Buddy Schultz | .08 | .25 |
| 602 | Brian Downing | .30 | .75 |
| 603 | Jack Billingham DP | .08 | .25 |
| 604 | Glenn Adams | .08 | .25 |
| 605 | Terry Forster | .30 | .75 |
| 606 | Cincinnati Reds CL/McNamara | .30 | .75 |
| 607 | Woodie Fryman | .08 | .25 |
| 608 | Alan Bannister | .08 | .25 |
| 609 | Ron Reed | .08 | .25 |
| 610 | Willie Stargell | .60 | 1.50 |
| 611 | Jerry Garvin DP | .08 | .25 |
| 612 | Cliff Johnson | .08 | .25 |
| 613 | Randy Stein | .08 | .25 |
| 614 | John Hiller | .30 | .75 |
| 615 | Doug DeCinces | .30 | .75 |
| 616 | Gene Richards | .08 | .25 |
| 617 | Joaquin Andujar | .30 | .75 |
| 618 | Bob Montgomery DP | .08 | .25 |
| 619 | Sergio Ferrer | .08 | .25 |
| 620 | Richie Zisk | .30 | .75 |
| 621 | Bob Grich | .30 | .75 |
| 622 | Mario Soto | .30 | .75 |
| 623 | Gorman Thomas | .30 | .75 |
| 624 | Lerrin LaGrow | .08 | .25 |
| 625 | Chris Chambliss | .30 | .75 |
| 626 | Detroit Tigers CL/Anderson | .30 | .75 |
| 627 | Pedro Borbon | .08 | .25 |
| 628 | Doug Capilla | .08 | .25 |
| 629 | Jim Todd | .08 | .25 |
| 630 | Larry Bowa | .30 | .75 |
| 631 | Mark Littell | .08 | .25 |
| 632 | Barry Bonnell | .08 | .25 |
| 633 | Bob Apodaca | .08 | .25 |
| 634 | Glenn Borgmann DP | .08 | .25 |
| 635 | John Candelaria | .30 | .75 |
| 636 | Toby Harrah | .30 | .75 |
| 637 | Joe Simpson | .08 | .25 |
| 638 | Mark Clear RC | .08 | .25 |
| 639 | Larry Biittner | .08 | .25 |
| 640 | Mike Flanagan | .30 | .75 |
| 641 | Ed Kranepool | .30 | .75 |
| 642 | Ken Forsch DP | .08 | .25 |
| 643 | John Mayberry | .30 | .75 |
| 644 | Charlie Hough | .30 | .75 |
| 645 | Rick Burleson | .30 | .75 |
| 646 | Checklist 606-726 | .30 | .75 |
| 647 | Milt May | .08 | .25 |
| 648 | Roy White | .30 | .75 |
| 649 | Tom Griffin | .08 | .25 |
| 650 | Joe Morgan | .60 | 1.50 |
| 651 | Rollie Fingers | .30 | .75 |
| 652 | Mario Mendoza | .08 | .25 |
| 653 | Stan Bahnsen | .08 | .25 |
| 654 | Bruce Boisclair DP | .08 | .25 |
| 655 | Tug McGraw | .30 | .75 |
| 656 | Larvell Blanks | .08 | .25 |
| 657 | Dave Edwards RC | .08 | .25 |
| 658 | Chris Knapp | .08 | .25 |
| 659 | Milwaukee Brewers CL/Bamberger | .30 | .75 |
| 660 | Rusty Staub | .30 | .75 |
| 661 | Corey/Ford/Krenchki RC | .08 | .25 |
| 662 | Finch/O'Berry/Rainey RC | .08 | .25 |
| 663 | Botting/Clark/Thon RC | .08 | .25 |
| 664 | Colbern/Hoffman/Robinson RC | .08 | .25 |
| 665 | Andersen/Cuellar/Whitol RC | .08 | .25 |
| 666 | Chris/Greene/Robbins RC | .08 | .25 |
| 667 | Mart/Paschl/Quisenberry RC | .30 | .75 |
| 668 | Baltzan/Mueller/Sakata RC | .08 | .25 |
| 669 | Graham/Sofield/Ward RC | .08 | .25 |
| 670 | Brown/Gulden/Jones RC | .08 | .25 |
| 671 | Bryant/Ragan/Morgan RC | .30 | .75 |

| | | |
|---|---|---|
| 672 Beamon/Craig/Vasquez RC | .08 | .25 |
| 673 Allard/Gleaton/Mahlberg RC | .08 | .25 |
| 674 Edge/Kelly/Wilborn RC | .08 | .25 |
| 675 Benedict/Bradford/Miller RC | .08 | .25 |
| 676 Geisel/Macko/Pagel RC | .08 | .25 |
| 677 DeFreites/Pastore/Spilman RC | .08 | .25 |
| 678 Baldwin/Knicaly/Ladd RC | .08 | .25 |
| 679 Beckwith/Hatcher/Patterson RC | .30 | .75 |
| 680 Bernazard/Miller/Tamargo RC | .08 | .25 |
| 681 Norman/Orosco/Scott RC | .60 | 1.50 |
| 682 Aviles/Noles/Saucier RC | .08 | .25 |
| 683 Boyland/Lois/Salenght RC | .08 | .25 |
| 684 Frazier/Herr/O'Brian RC | .30 | .75 |
| 685 Flannery/Greer/Wilhelm RC | .08 | .25 |
| 686 Johnston/Littlejohn/Nastu RC | .08 | .25 |
| 687 Mike Heath DP | .08 | .25 |
| 688 Steve Stone | .30 | .75 |
| 689 Boston Red Sox CL/Zimmer | .30 | .75 |
| 690 Tommy John | .30 | .75 |
| 691 Ivan DeJesus | .08 | .25 |
| 692 Rawly Eastwick DP | .20 | .50 |
| 693 Craig Kusick | .08 | .25 |
| 694 Jim Rooker | .08 | .25 |
| 695 Reggie Smith | .30 | .75 |
| 696 Julio Gonzalez | .08 | .25 |
| 697 David Clyde | .08 | .25 |
| 698 Oscar Gamble | .30 | .75 |
| 699 Floyd Bannister | .08 | .25 |
| 700 Rod Carew DP | .30 | .75 |
| 701 Ken Oberkfell RC | .08 | .25 |
| 702 Ed Farmer | .08 | .25 |
| 703 Otto Velez | .08 | .25 |
| 704 Gene Tenace | .15 | .40 |
| 705 Freddie Patek | .30 | .75 |
| 706 Tippy Martinez | .08 | .25 |
| 707 Elliott Maddox | .08 | .25 |
| 708 Bob Tolan | .08 | .25 |
| 709 Pat Underwood RC | .08 | .25 |
| 710 Graig Nettles | .30 | .75 |
| 711 Bob Galasso RC | .08 | .25 |
| 712 Rodney Scott | .08 | .25 |
| 713 Terry Whitfield | .08 | .25 |
| 714 Fred Norman | .08 | .25 |
| 715 Sal Bando | .30 | .75 |
| 716 Lynn McGlothen | .08 | .25 |
| 717 Mickey Klutts DP | .08 | .25 |
| 718 Greg Gross | .08 | .25 |
| 719 Don Robinson | .30 | .75 |
| 720 Carl Yastrzemski DP | .75 | 2.00 |
| 721 Paul Hartzell | .08 | .25 |
| 722 Jose Cruz | .30 | .75 |
| 723 Shane Rawley | .08 | .25 |
| 724 Jerry White | .08 | .25 |
| 725 Rick Wise | .08 | .25 |
| 726 Steve Yeager | .30 | .75 |

## 1981 Topps

| | | |
|---|---|---|
| COMPLETE SET (726) | 30.00 | 60.00 |
| COMMON CARD (1-726) | .05 | .15 |
| COMMON CARD DP | .05 | .15 |
| 1 G.Brett/B.Buckner LL | 1.25 | 3.00 |
| 2 Reggie/Ogliv/Schmidt LL | .60 | 1.50 |
| 3 C.Cooper/M.Schmidt LL | .60 | 1.50 |
| 4 R.Henderson/LeFlore LL | 1.25 | 3.00 |
| 5 S.Stone/S.Carlton LL | .15 | .40 |
| 6 Len Barker/S.Carlton LL | .15 | .40 |
| 7 R.May/D.Sutton LL | .15 | .40 |
| 8 Quis/Fingers/Hume LL | .15 | .40 |
| 9 Pete LaCock DP | .05 | .15 |
| 10 Mike Flanagan | .05 | .15 |
| 11 Jim Wohlford DP | .05 | .15 |
| 12 Mark Clear | .05 | .15 |
| 13 Joe Charboneau RC | .60 | 1.50 |
| 14 John Tudor RC | .60 | 1.50 |

| | | |
|---|---|---|
| 15 Larry Parrish | .05 | .15 |
| 16 Ron Davis | .05 | .15 |
| 17 Cliff Johnson | .05 | .15 |
| 18 Glenn Adams | .05 | .15 |
| 19 Jim Clancy | .05 | .15 |
| 20 Jeff Burroughs | .15 | .40 |
| 21 Ron Oester | .05 | .15 |
| 22 Danny Darwin | .05 | .15 |
| 23 Alex Trevino | .05 | .15 |
| 24 Don Stanhouse | .05 | .15 |
| 25 Sixto Lezcano | .05 | .15 |
| 26 U.L. Washington | .05 | .15 |
| 27 Champ Summers DP | .05 | .15 |
| 28 Enrique Romo | .05 | .15 |
| 29 Gene Tenace | .15 | .40 |
| 30 Jack Clark | .15 | .40 |
| 31 Checklist 1-121 DP | .08 | .25 |
| 32 Ken Oberkfell | .05 | .15 |
| 33 Rick Honeycutt | .05 | .15 |
| 34 Aurelio Rodriguez | .05 | .15 |
| 35 Mitchell Page | .05 | .15 |
| 36 Ed Farmer | .05 | .15 |
| 37 Gary Roenicke | .05 | .15 |
| 38 Win Remmerswaal RC | .05 | .15 |
| 39 Tom Veryzer | .05 | .15 |
| 40 Tug McGraw | .15 | .40 |
| 41 Babcock/Butcher/Gleaton RC | .08 | .25 |
| 42 Jerry White DP | .05 | .15 |
| 43 Jose Morales | .05 | .15 |
| 44 Larry McWilliams | .05 | .15 |
| 45 Enos Cabell | .05 | .15 |
| 46 Rick Bosetti | .05 | .15 |
| 47 Ken Brett | .05 | .15 |
| 48 Dave Skaggs | .05 | .15 |
| 49 Bob Shirley | .05 | .15 |
| 50 Dave Lopes | .15 | .40 |
| 51 Bill Robinson DP | .05 | .15 |
| 52 Hector Cruz | .05 | .15 |
| 53 Kevin Saucier | .05 | .15 |
| 54 Ivan DeJesus | .05 | .15 |
| 55 Mike Norris | .05 | .15 |
| 56 Buck Martinez | .05 | .15 |
| 57 Dave Roberts | .05 | .15 |
| 58 Joel Youngblood | .05 | .15 |
| 59 Dan Petry | .05 | .15 |
| 60 Willie Randolph | .15 | .40 |
| 61 Butch Wynegar | .05 | .15 |
| 62 Joe Pettini RC | .05 | .15 |
| 63 Steve Renko DP | .05 | .15 |
| 64 Brian Asselstine | .05 | .15 |
| 65 Scott McGregor | .05 | .15 |
| 66 Castillo/Ireland/M.Jones RC | .08 | .25 |
| 67 Ken Kravec | .05 | .15 |
| 68 Matt Alexander DP | .05 | .15 |
| 69 Ed Halicki | .05 | .15 |
| 70 Al Oliver DP | .08 | .25 |
| 71 Hal Dues | .05 | .15 |
| 72 Barry Evans DP RC | .05 | .15 |
| 73 Doug Bair | .05 | .15 |
| 74 Mike Hargrove | .05 | .15 |
| 75 Reggie Smith | .15 | .40 |
| 76 Mario Mendoza | .05 | .15 |
| 77 Mike Barlow | .05 | .15 |
| 78 Steve Dillard | .05 | .15 |
| 79 Bruce Robbins | .05 | .15 |
| 80 Rusty Staub | .15 | .40 |
| 81 Dave Stapleton RC | .05 | .15 |
| 82 Heep/Knicely/Sprowl RC | .08 | .25 |
| 83 Mike Proly | .05 | .15 |
| 84 Johnnie LeMaster | .05 | .15 |
| 85 Mike Caldwell | .05 | .15 |
| 86 Wayne Gross | .05 | .15 |
| 87 Rick Camp | .05 | .15 |
| 88 Joe Lefebvre RC | .05 | .15 |
| 89 Darrell Jackson | .05 | .15 |
| 90 Bake McBride | .15 | .40 |
| 91 Tim Stoddard DP | .05 | .15 |
| 92 Mike Easler | .05 | .15 |
| 93 Ed Glynn DP | .05 | .15 |
| 94 Harry Spilman DP | .05 | .15 |
| 95 Jim Sundberg | .05 | .15 |
| 96 Beard/Camacho/Dempsey RC | .08 | .25 |
| 97 Chris Speier | .05 | .15 |
| 98 Clint Hurdle | .05 | .15 |
| 99 Eric Wilkins | .05 | .15 |
| 100 Rod Carew | .30 | .75 |
| 101 Benny Ayala | .05 | .15 |
| 102 Dave Tobik | .05 | .15 |

| | | |
|---|---|---|
| 103 Jerry Martin | .05 | .15 |
| 104 Terry Forster | .15 | .40 |
| 105 Jose Cruz | .15 | .40 |
| 106 Don Money | .05 | .15 |
| 107 Rich Wortham | .05 | .15 |
| 108 Bruce Benedict | .05 | .15 |
| 109 Mike Scott | .15 | .40 |
| 110 Carl Yastrzemski | 1.00 | 2.50 |
| 111 Greg Minton | .05 | .15 |
| 112 Kurtz/Mullins/Sutherland RC | .08 | .25 |
| 113 Mike Phillips | .05 | .15 |
| 114 Tom Underwood | .05 | .15 |
| 115 Roy Smalley | .15 | .40 |
| 116 Joe Simpson | .05 | .15 |
| 117 Pete Falcone | .05 | .15 |
| 118 Kurt Bevacqua | .05 | .15 |
| 119 Tippy Martinez | .05 | .15 |
| 120 Larry Bowa | .15 | .40 |
| 121 Larry Harlow | .05 | .15 |
| 122 John Denny | .05 | .15 |
| 123 Al Cowens | .05 | .15 |
| 124 Jerry Garvin | .05 | .15 |
| 125 Andre Dawson | .30 | .75 |
| 126 Charlie Leibrandt RC | .30 | .75 |
| 127 Rudy Law | .05 | .15 |
| 128 Gary Allenson DP | .05 | .15 |
| 129 Art Howe | .05 | .15 |
| 130 Larry Gura | .05 | .15 |
| 131 Keith Moreland RC | .05 | .15 |
| 132 Tommy Boggs | .05 | .15 |
| 133 Jeff Cox RC | .05 | .15 |
| 134 Steve Mura | .05 | .15 |
| 135 Gorman Thomas | .15 | .40 |
| 136 Doug Capilla | .05 | .15 |
| 137 Hosken Powell | .05 | .15 |
| 138 Rich Dotson DP RC | .05 | .15 |
| 139 Oscar Gamble | .05 | .15 |
| 140 Bob Forsch | .05 | .15 |
| 141 Miguel Dilone | .05 | .15 |
| 142 Jackson Todd | .05 | .15 |
| 143 Dan Meyer | .05 | .15 |
| 144 Allen Ripley | .05 | .15 |
| 145 Mickey Rivers | .05 | .15 |
| 146 Bobby Castillo | .05 | .15 |
| 147 Dale Berra | .05 | .15 |
| 148 Randy Niemann | .05 | .15 |
| 149 Joe Nolan RC | .05 | .15 |
| 150 Mark Fidrych | .15 | .40 |
| 151 Claudell Washington | .05 | .15 |
| 152 John Urrea | .05 | .15 |
| 153 Tom Poquette | .05 | .15 |
| 154 Rick Langford | .05 | .15 |
| 155 Chris Chambliss | .15 | .40 |
| 156 Bob McClure | .05 | .15 |
| 157 John Wathan | .05 | .15 |
| 158 Fergie Jenkins | .15 | .40 |
| 159 Brian Doyle | .05 | .15 |
| 160 Garry Maddox | .05 | .15 |
| 161 Dan Graham | .05 | .15 |
| 162 Doug Corbett RC | .05 | .15 |
| 163 Bill Almon RC | .05 | .15 |
| 164 LaMarr Hoyt RC | .30 | .75 |
| 165 Tony Scott | .05 | .15 |
| 166 Floyd Bannister | .05 | .15 |
| 167 Terry Whitfield | .05 | .15 |
| 168 Don Robinson DP | .05 | .15 |
| 169 John Mayberry | .05 | .15 |
| 170 Ross Grimsley | .05 | .15 |
| 171 Gene Richards | .05 | .15 |
| 172 Gary Woods | .05 | .15 |
| 173 Bump Wills | .05 | .15 |
| 174 Doug Rau | .05 | .15 |
| 175 Dave Collins | .15 | .40 |
| 176 Mike Krukow RC | .15 | .40 |
| 177 Rick Peters RC | .05 | .15 |
| 178 Jim Essian DP | .05 | .15 |
| 179 Rudy May | .05 | .15 |
| 180 Pete Rose | 2.00 | 5.00 |
| 181 Elias Sosa | .05 | .15 |
| 182 Bob Grich | .15 | .40 |
| 183 Dick Davis DP | .05 | .15 |
| 184 Jim Dwyer | .05 | .15 |
| 185 Dennis Leonard | .15 | .40 |
| 186 Wayne Nordhagen | .05 | .15 |
| 187 Mike Parrott | .05 | .15 |
| 188 Doug DeCinces | .15 | .40 |
| 189 Craig Swan | .05 | .15 |
| 190 Cesar Cedeno | .15 | .40 |

|  |  | | |
|---|--------|------|------|
| 191 | Rick Sutcliffe | .15 | .40 |
| 192 | Harper/Miller/Ramirez RC | .08 | .25 |
| 193 | Pete Vuckovich | .05 | .15 |
| 194 | Rod Scurry RC | .05 | .15 |
| 195 | Rich Murray RC | .05 | .15 |
| 196 | Duffy Dyer | .05 | .15 |
| 197 | Jim Kern | .05 | .15 |
| 198 | Jerry Dybzinski RC | .05 | .15 |
| 199 | Chuck Rainey | .05 | .15 |
| 200 | George Foster | .15 | .40 |
| 201 | Johnny Bench RB | .30 | .75 |
| 202 | Steve Carlton RB | .15 | .40 |
| 203 | Bill Gullickson RB | .05 | .15 |
| 204 | R.LeFlore/R.Scott RB | .05 | .15 |
| 205 | Pete Rose RB | .60 | 1.50 |
| 206 | Mike Schmidt RB | .60 | 1.50 |
| 207 | Ozzie Smith RB | .75 | 2.00 |
| 208 | Willie Wilson RB | .05 | .15 |
| 209 | Dickie Thon DP | .05 | .15 |
| 210 | Jim Palmer | .30 | .75 |
| 211 | Derrel Thomas | .05 | .15 |
| 212 | Steve Nicosia | .05 | .15 |
| 213 | Al Holland RC | .05 | .15 |
| 214 | Botting/Dorsey/J.Harris RC | .08 | .25 |
| 215 | Larry Hisle | .05 | .15 |
| 216 | John Henry Johnson | .05 | .15 |
| 217 | Rich Hebner | .05 | .15 |
| 218 | Paul Splittorff | .05 | .15 |
| 219 | Ken Landreaux | .05 | .15 |
| 220 | Tom Seaver | .60 | 1.50 |
| 221 | Bob Davis | .05 | .15 |
| 222 | Jorge Orta | .05 | .15 |
| 223 | Roy Lee Jackson RC | .05 | .15 |
| 224 | Pat Zachry | .05 | .15 |
| 225 | Ruppert Jones | .05 | .15 |
| 226 | Manny Sanguillen DP | .08 | .25 |
| 227 | Fred Martinez RC | .05 | .15 |
| 228 | Tom Paciorek | .05 | .15 |
| 229 | Rollie Fingers | .15 | .40 |
| 230 | George Hendrick | .15 | .40 |
| 231 | Joe Beckwith | .05 | .15 |
| 232 | Mickey Klutts | .05 | .15 |
| 233 | Skip Lockwood | .05 | .15 |
| 234 | Lou Whitaker | .30 | .75 |
| 235 | Scott Sanderson | .05 | .15 |
| 236 | Mike Ivie | .05 | .15 |
| 237 | Charlie Moore | .05 | .15 |
| 238 | Willie Hernandez | .05 | .15 |
| 239 | Rick Miller DP | .05 | .15 |
| 240 | Nolan Ryan | 3.00 | 8.00 |
| 241 | Checklist 122-242 DP | .08 | .25 |
| 242 | Chet Lemon | .05 | .15 |
| 243 | Sal Butera RC | .05 | .15 |
| 244 | Landrum/Olmsted/Rincon RC | .08 | .25 |
| 245 | Ed Figueroa | .05 | .15 |
| 246 | Ed Ott DP | .05 | .15 |
| 247 | Glenn Hubbard DP | .05 | .15 |
| 248 | Joey McLaughlin | .05 | .15 |
| 249 | Larry Cox | .05 | .15 |
| 250 | Ron Guidry | .15 | .40 |
| 251 | Tom Brookens | .05 | .15 |
| 252 | Victor Cruz | .05 | .15 |
| 253 | Dave Bergman | .05 | .15 |
| 254 | Ozzie Smith | 2.00 | 5.00 |
| 255 | Mark Littell | .05 | .15 |
| 256 | Bombo Rivera | .05 | .15 |
| 257 | Rennie Stennett | .05 | .15 |
| 258 | Joe Price RC | .05 | .15 |
| 259 | M.Wilson/H.Brooks RC | 2.00 | 5.00 |
| 260 | Ron Cey | .15 | .40 |
| 261 | Rickey Henderson | 4.00 | 10.00 |
| 262 | Sammy Stewart | .05 | .15 |
| 263 | Brian Downing | .15 | .40 |
| 264 | Jim Norris | .05 | .15 |
| 265 | John Candelaria | .15 | .40 |
| 266 | Tom Herr | .05 | .15 |
| 267 | Stan Bahnsen | .05 | .15 |
| 268 | Jerry Royster | .05 | .15 |
| 269 | Ken Forsch | .05 | .15 |
| 270 | Greg Luzinski | .15 | .40 |
| 271 | Bill Castro | .05 | .15 |
| 272 | Bruce Kimm | .05 | .15 |
| 273 | Stan Papi | .05 | .15 |
| 274 | Craig Chamberlain | .05 | .15 |
| 275 | Dwight Evans | .30 | .75 |
| 276 | Dan Spillner | .05 | .15 |
| 277 | Alfredo Griffin | .05 | .15 |
| 278 | Rick Sofield | .05 | .15 |
| 279 | Bob Knepper | .05 | .15 |
| 280 | Ken Griffey | .15 | .40 |
| 281 | Fred Stanley | .05 | .15 |
| 282 | Anderson/Biercevicz/Craig RC | .08 | .25 |
| 283 | Billy Sample | .05 | .15 |
| 284 | Brian Kingman | .05 | .15 |
| 285 | Jerry Turner | .05 | .15 |
| 286 | Dave Frost | .05 | .15 |
| 287 | Lenn Sakata | .05 | .15 |
| 288 | Bob Clark | .05 | .15 |
| 289 | Mickey Hatcher | .05 | .15 |
| 290 | Bob Boone DP | .08 | .25 |
| 291 | Aurelio Lopez | .05 | .15 |
| 292 | Mike Squires | .05 | .15 |
| 293 | Charlie Lea RC | .15 | .40 |
| 294 | Mike Tyson DP | .05 | .15 |
| 295 | Hal McRae | .15 | .40 |
| 296 | Bill Nahorodny DP | .05 | .15 |
| 297 | Bob Bailor | .05 | .15 |
| 298 | Buddy Solomon | .05 | .15 |
| 299 | Elliott Maddox | .05 | .15 |
| 300 | Paul Molitor | .60 | 1.50 |
| 301 | Matt Keough | .05 | .15 |
| 302 | F.Valenzuela/M.Scioscia RC | 3.00 | 8.00 |
| 303 | Johnny Oates | .15 | .40 |
| 304 | John Castino | .05 | .15 |
| 305 | Ken Clay | .05 | .15 |
| 306 | Juan Beniquez DP | .05 | .15 |
| 307 | Gene Garber | .05 | .15 |
| 308 | Rick Manning | .05 | .15 |
| 309 | Luis Salazar RC | .30 | .75 |
| 310 | Vida Blue DP | .08 | .25 |
| 311 | Freddie Patek | .05 | .15 |
| 312 | Rick Rhoden | .05 | .15 |
| 313 | Luis Pujols | .05 | .15 |
| 314 | Rich Dauer | .05 | .15 |
| 315 | Kirk Gibson RC | 3.00 | 8.00 |
| 316 | Craig Minetto | .05 | .15 |
| 317 | Lonnie Smith | .15 | .40 |
| 318 | Steve Yeager | .05 | .15 |
| 319 | Rowland Office | .05 | .15 |
| 320 | Tom Burgmeier | .05 | .15 |
| 321 | Leon Durham RC | .30 | .75 |
| 322 | Neil Allen | .05 | .15 |
| 323 | Jim Morrison DP | .05 | .15 |
| 324 | Mike Willis | .05 | .15 |
| 325 | Ray Knight | .15 | .40 |
| 326 | Biff Pocoroba | .05 | .15 |
| 327 | Moose Haas | .05 | .15 |
| 328 | Engle/Johnston/G.Ward | .08 | .25 |
| 329 | Joaquin Andujar | .15 | .40 |
| 330 | Frank White | .15 | .40 |
| 331 | Dennis Lamp | .05 | .15 |
| 332 | Lee Lacy DP | .05 | .15 |
| 333 | Sid Monge | .05 | .15 |
| 334 | Dane Iorg | .05 | .15 |
| 335 | Rick Cerone | .05 | .15 |
| 336 | Eddie Whitson | .05 | .15 |
| 337 | Lynn Jones | .05 | .15 |
| 338 | Checklist 243-363 | .15 | .40 |
| 339 | John Ellis | .05 | .15 |
| 340 | Bruce Kison | .05 | .15 |
| 341 | Dwayne Murphy | .05 | .15 |
| 342 | Eric Rasmussen DP | .05 | .15 |
| 343 | Frank Taveras | .05 | .15 |
| 344 | Byron McLaughlin | .05 | .15 |
| 345 | Warren Cromartie | .05 | .15 |
| 346 | Larry Christenson DP | .05 | .15 |
| 347 | Harold Baines RC | 1.25 | 3.00 |
| 348 | Bob Sykes | .05 | .15 |
| 349 | Glenn Hoffman RC | .15 | .40 |
| 350 | J.R. Richard | .15 | .40 |
| 351 | Otto Velez | .05 | .15 |
| 352 | Dick Tidrow DP | .05 | .15 |
| 353 | Terry Kennedy | .05 | .15 |
| 354 | Mario Soto | .15 | .40 |
| 355 | Bob Horner | .15 | .40 |
| 356 | Stablein/Stimac/Tellmann RC | .08 | .25 |
| 357 | Jim Slaton | .05 | .15 |
| 358 | Mark Wagner | .05 | .15 |
| 359 | Tom Hausman | .05 | .15 |
| 360 | Willie Wilson | .15 | .40 |
| 361 | Joe Strain | .05 | .15 |
| 362 | Bo Diaz | .05 | .15 |
| 363 | Geoff Zahn | .05 | .15 |
| 364 | Mike Davis RC | .08 | .25 |
| 365 | Graig Nettles DP | .15 | .40 |
| 366 | Mike Ramsey RC | .08 | .25 |
| 367 | Dennis Martinez | .15 | .40 |
| 368 | Leon Roberts | .15 | .15 |
| 369 | Frank Tanana | .15 | .40 |
| 370 | Dave Winfield | .30 | .75 |
| 371 | Charlie Hough | .15 | .40 |
| 372 | Jay Johnstone | .05 | .15 |
| 373 | Pat Underwood | .05 | .15 |
| 374 | Tommy Hutton | .05 | .15 |
| 375 | Dave Concepcion | .15 | .40 |
| 376 | Ron Reed | .05 | .15 |
| 377 | Jerry Morales | .05 | .15 |
| 378 | Dave Rader | .05 | .15 |
| 379 | Lary Sorensen | .05 | .15 |
| 380 | Willie Stargell | .30 | .75 |
| 381 | Lezcano/Macko/Martz RC | .08 | .25 |
| 382 | Paul Mirabella RC | .05 | .15 |
| 383 | Eric Soderholm DP | .05 | .15 |
| 384 | Mike Sadek | .05 | .15 |
| 385 | Joe Sambito | .05 | .15 |
| 386 | Dave Edwards | .05 | .15 |
| 387 | Phil Niekro | .15 | .40 |
| 388 | Andre Thornton | .15 | .40 |
| 389 | Marty Pattin | .05 | .15 |
| 390 | Cesar Geronimo | .05 | .15 |
| 391 | Dave Lemanczyk DP | .05 | .15 |
| 392 | Lance Parrish | .15 | .40 |
| 393 | Broderick Perkins | .05 | .15 |
| 394 | Steve Woodie Fryman | .05 | .15 |
| 395 | Scot Thompson | .05 | .15 |
| 396 | Bill Campbell | .05 | .15 |
| 397 | Julio Cruz | .05 | .15 |
| 398 | Ross Baumgarten | .05 | .15 |
| 399 | Boddicker/Corey/Rayford RC | .30 | .75 |
| 400 | Reggie Jackson | .60 | 1.50 |
| 401 | George Brett ALCS | 1.00 | 2.50 |
| 402 | NL Champs | .30 | .75 |
| 403 | Larry Bowa WS | .30 | .75 |
| 404 | Tug McGraw WS | .15 | .40 |
| 405 | Nino Espinosa | .05 | .15 |
| 406 | Dickie Noles | .05 | .15 |
| 407 | Ernie Whitt | .05 | .15 |
| 408 | Fernando Arroyo | .05 | .15 |
| 409 | Larry Herndon | .05 | .15 |
| 410 | Bert Campaneris | .15 | .40 |
| 411 | Terry Puhl | .05 | .15 |
| 412 | Britt Burns RC | .05 | .15 |
| 413 | Tony Bernazard | .05 | .15 |
| 414 | John Pacella DP RC | .05 | .15 |
| 415 | Ben Oglivie | .15 | .40 |
| 416 | Gary Alexander | .05 | .15 |
| 417 | Dan Schatzeder | .05 | .15 |
| 418 | Bobby Brown | .05 | .15 |
| 419 | Tom Hume | .05 | .15 |
| 420 | Keith Hernandez | .15 | .40 |
| 421 | Bob Stanley | .05 | .15 |
| 422 | Dan Ford | .05 | .15 |
| 423 | Shane Rawley | .05 | .15 |
| 424 | Lollar/Robinson/Werth RC | .08 | .25 |
| 425 | Al Bumbry | .05 | .15 |
| 426 | Warren Brusstar | .05 | .15 |
| 427 | John D'Acquisto | .05 | .15 |
| 428 | John Stearns | .05 | .15 |
| 429 | Mick Kelleher | .05 | .15 |
| 430 | Jim Bibby | .05 | .15 |
| 431 | Dave Roberts | .05 | .15 |
| 432 | Len Barker | .15 | .40 |
| 433 | Rance Mulliniks | .05 | .15 |
| 434 | Roger Erickson | .05 | .15 |
| 435 | Jim Spencer | .05 | .15 |
| 436 | Gary Lucas RC | .05 | .15 |
| 437 | Mike Heath DP | .05 | .15 |
| 438 | John Montefusco | .05 | .15 |
| 439 | Denny Walling | .05 | .15 |
| 440 | Jerry Reuss | .15 | .40 |
| 441 | Ken Reitz | .05 | .15 |
| 442 | Ron Pruitt | .05 | .15 |
| 443 | Jim Beattie DP | .05 | .15 |
| 444 | Garth Iorg | .05 | .15 |
| 445 | Ellis Valentine | .05 | .15 |
| 446 | Checklist 364-484 | .15 | .40 |
| 447 | Junior Kennedy DP | .05 | .15 |
| 448 | Tim Corcoran | .05 | .15 |
| 449 | Paul Mitchell | .05 | .15 |
| 450 | Dave Kingman DP | .08 | .25 |
| 451 | Bando/Brennan/Wihtol RC | .08 | .25 |
| 452 | Renie Martin | .05 | .15 |
| 453 | Rob Wilfong DP | .05 | .15 |
| 454 | Andy Hassler | .05 | .15 |

|  | | |
|---|---|---|
| 455 Rick Burleson | .05 | .15 |
| 456 Jeff Reardon RC | .60 | 1.50 |
| 457 Mike Lum | .05 | .15 |
| 458 Randy Jones | .15 | .40 |
| 459 Greg Gross | .05 | .15 |
| 460 Rich Gossage | .15 | .40 |
| 461 Dave McKay RC | .05 | .15 |
| 462 Jack Brohamer | .05 | .15 |
| 463 Milt May | .05 | .15 |
| 464 Adrian Devine | .05 | .15 |
| 465 Bill Russell | .15 | .40 |
| 466 Bob Molinaro | .05 | .15 |
| 467 Dave Stieb | .15 | .40 |
| 468 John Wockenfuss | .05 | .15 |
| 469 Jeff Leonard | .15 | .40 |
| 470 Manny Trillo | .05 | .15 |
| 471 Mike Vail | .05 | .15 |
| 472 Dyar Miller DP | .05 | .15 |
| 473 Jose Cardenal | .05 | .15 |
| 474 Mike LaCoss | .05 | .15 |
| 475 Buddy Bell | .15 | .40 |
| 476 Jerry Koosman | .15 | .40 |
| 477 Luis Gomez | .05 | .15 |
| 478 Juan Eichelberger RC | .05 | .15 |
| 479 Tim Raines RC | 1.50 | 4.00 |
| 480 Carlton Fisk | .30 | .75 |
| 481 Bob Lacey DP | .05 | .15 |
| 482 Jim Gantner | .08 | .25 |
| 483 Mike Griffin RC | .05 | .15 |
| 484 Max Venable DP RC | .05 | .15 |
| 485 Garry Templeton | .15 | .40 |
| 486 Mark Hill | .05 | .15 |
| 487 Dewey Robinson | .05 | .15 |
| 488 Damaso Garcia RC | .05 | .15 |
| 489 John Littlefield RC | .05 | .15 |
| 490 Eddie Murray | 1.00 | 2.50 |
| 491 Gordy Pladson RC | .05 | .15 |
| 492 Barry Foote | .05 | .15 |
| 493 Dan Quisenberry | .05 | .15 |
| 494 Bob Walk RC | .30 | .75 |
| 495 Dusty Baker | .15 | .40 |
| 496 Paul Dade | .05 | .15 |
| 497 Fred Norman | .05 | .15 |
| 498 Pat Putnam | .05 | .15 |
| 499 Frank Pastore | .05 | .15 |
| 500 Jim Rice | .15 | .40 |
| 501 Tim Foli DP | .05 | .15 |
| 502 Bourjos/Hargesheimer/Rowland RC | .08 | .25 |
| 503 Steve McCatty | .05 | .15 |
| 504 Dale Murphy | .30 | .75 |
| 505 Jason Thompson | .05 | .15 |
| 506 Phil Huffman | .05 | .15 |
| 507 Jamie Quirk | .05 | .15 |
| 508 Rob Dressler | .05 | .15 |
| 509 Pete Mackanin | .05 | .15 |
| 510 Lee Mazzilli | .15 | .40 |
| 511 Wayne Garland | .05 | .15 |
| 512 Gary Thomasson | .05 | .15 |
| 513 Frank LaCorte | .05 | .15 |
| 514 George Riley RC | .05 | .15 |
| 515 Robin Yount | 1.00 | 2.50 |
| 516 Doug Bird | .05 | .15 |
| 517 Richie Zisk | .05 | .15 |
| 518 Grant Jackson | .05 | .15 |
| 519 John Tamargo DP | .05 | .15 |
| 520 Steve Stone | .15 | .40 |
| 521 Sam Mejias | .05 | .15 |
| 522 Mike Colbern | .05 | .15 |
| 523 John Fulgham | .05 | .15 |
| 524 Willie Aikens | .05 | .15 |
| 525 Mike Torrez | .05 | .15 |
| 526 Bystrom/Loviglio/Wright RC | .08 | .25 |
| 527 Danny Goodwin | .05 | .15 |
| 528 Gary Matthews | .15 | .40 |
| 529 Dave LaRoche | .05 | .15 |
| 530 Steve Garvey | .30 | .75 |
| 531 John Curtis | .05 | .15 |
| 532 Bill Stein | .05 | .15 |
| 533 Jesus Figueroa RC | .05 | .15 |
| 534 Dave Smith RC | .30 | .75 |
| 535 Omar Moreno | .05 | .15 |
| 536 Bob Owchinko DP | .05 | .15 |
| 537 Ron Hodges | .05 | .15 |
| 538 Tom Griffin | .05 | .15 |
| 539 Rodney Scott | .05 | .15 |
| 540 Mike Schmidt DP | .75 | 2.00 |
| 541 Steve Swisher | .05 | .15 |
| 542 Larry Bradford DP | .05 | .15 |
| 543 Terry Crowley | .05 | .15 |
| 544 Rich Gale | .05 | .15 |
| 545 Johnny Grubb | .05 | .15 |
| 546 Paul Moskau | .05 | .15 |
| 547 Mario Guerrero | .05 | .15 |
| 548 Dave Goltz | .05 | .15 |
| 549 Jerry Remy | .05 | .15 |
| 550 Tommy John | .15 | .40 |
| 551 Law/Pena/Perez RC | .60 | .75 |
| 552 Steve Trout | .05 | .15 |
| 553 Tim Blackwell | .05 | .15 |
| 554 Bert Blyleven | .15 | .40 |
| 555 Cecil Cooper | .15 | .40 |
| 556 Jerry Mumphrey | .05 | .15 |
| 557 Chris Knapp | .05 | .15 |
| 558 Barry Bonnell | .05 | .15 |
| 559 Willie Montanez | .05 | .15 |
| 560 Joe Morgan | .30 | .75 |
| 561 Dennis Littlejohn | .05 | .15 |
| 562 Checklist 485-605 | .15 | .40 |
| 563 Jim Kaat | .15 | .40 |
| 564 Ron Hassey DP | .05 | .15 |
| 565 Burt Hooton | .05 | .15 |
| 566 Del Unser | .05 | .15 |
| 567 Mark Bomback RC | .05 | .15 |
| 568 Dave Revering | .05 | .15 |
| 569 Al Williams DP RC | .05 | .15 |
| 570 Ken Singleton | .15 | .40 |
| 571 Todd Cruz | .05 | .15 |
| 572 Jack Morris | .30 | .75 |
| 573 Phil Garner | .15 | .40 |
| 574 Bill Caudill | .05 | .15 |
| 575 Tony Perez | .30 | .75 |
| 576 Reggie Cleveland | .05 | .15 |
| 577 Leal/Milner/Schrom RC | .08 | .25 |
| 578 Bill Gullickson RC | .30 | .75 |
| 579 Tim Flannery | .05 | .15 |
| 580 Don Baylor | .15 | .40 |
| 581 Roy Howell | .05 | .15 |
| 582 Gaylord Perry | .30 | .75 |
| 583 Larry Milbourne | .05 | .15 |
| 584 Randy Lerch | .05 | .15 |
| 585 Amos Otis | .15 | .40 |
| 586 Silvio Martinez | .05 | .15 |
| 587 Jeff Newman | .05 | .15 |
| 588 Gary Lavelle | .05 | .15 |
| 589 Lamar Johnson | .05 | .15 |
| 590 Bruce Sutter | .30 | .75 |
| 591 John Lowenstein | .05 | .15 |
| 592 Steve Comer | .05 | .15 |
| 593 Steve Kemp | .05 | .15 |
| 594 Preston Hanna DP | .05 | .15 |
| 595 Butch Hobson | .05 | .15 |
| 596 Jerry Augustine | .05 | .15 |
| 597 Rafael Landestoy | .05 | .15 |
| 598 George Vukovich DP RC | .05 | .15 |
| 599 Dennis Kinney RC | .05 | .15 |
| 600 Johnny Bench | .60 | 1.50 |
| 601 Don Aase | .05 | .15 |
| 602 Bobby Murcer | .15 | .40 |
| 603 John Verhoeven | .05 | .15 |
| 604 Rob Picciolo | .05 | .15 |
| 605 Don Sutton | .15 | .40 |
| 606 Berenyi/Combe/Householder DP RC | .08 | .25 |
| 607 David Palmer | .05 | .15 |
| 608 Greg Pryor | .05 | .15 |
| 609 Lynn McGlothen | .05 | .15 |
| 610 Darrell Porter | .05 | .15 |
| 611 Rick Matula DP | .05 | .15 |
| 612 Duane Kuiper | .05 | .15 |
| 613 Jim Anderson | .05 | .15 |
| 614 Dave Rozema | .05 | .15 |
| 615 Rick Dempsey | .15 | .40 |
| 616 Rick Wise | .05 | .15 |
| 617 Craig Reynolds | .05 | .15 |
| 618 John Milner | .05 | .15 |
| 619 Steve Henderson | .05 | .15 |
| 620 Dennis Eckersley | .30 | .75 |
| 621 Tom Donohue | .05 | .15 |
| 622 Randy Moffitt | .05 | .15 |
| 623 Sal Bando | .15 | .40 |
| 624 Bob Welch | .15 | .40 |
| 625 Bill Buckner | .15 | .40 |
| 626 Steffen/Ujdur/Weaver RC | .08 | .25 |
| 627 Luis Tiant | .15 | .40 |
| 628 Vic Correll | .05 | .15 |
| 629 Tony Armas | .15 | .40 |
| 630 Steve Carlton | .30 | .75 |
| 631 Ron Jackson | .05 | .15 |
| 632 Alan Bannister | .05 | .15 |
| 633 Bill Lee | .15 | .40 |
| 634 Doug Flynn | .05 | .15 |
| 635 Bobby Bonds | .15 | .40 |
| 636 Al Hrabosky | .15 | .40 |
| 637 Jerry Narron | .05 | .15 |
| 638 Checklist 606-726 | .15 | .40 |
| 639 Carney Lansford | .15 | .40 |
| 640 Dave Parker | .15 | .40 |
| 641 Mark Belanger | .15 | .40 |
| 642 Vern Ruhle | .05 | .15 |
| 643 Lloyd Moseby RC | .30 | .75 |
| 644 Ramon Aviles DP | .05 | .15 |
| 645 Rick Reuschel | .15 | .40 |
| 646 Marvis Foley RC | .05 | .15 |
| 647 Dick Drago | .05 | .15 |
| 648 Darrell Evans | .15 | .40 |
| 649 Manny Sarmiento | .05 | .15 |
| 650 Bucky Dent | .15 | .40 |
| 651 Pedro Guerrero | .15 | .40 |
| 652 John Montague | .05 | .15 |
| 653 Bill Fahey | .05 | .15 |
| 654 Ray Burris | .05 | .15 |
| 655 Dan Driessen | .15 | .40 |
| 656 Jon Matlack | .05 | .15 |
| 657 Mike Cubbage DP | .05 | .15 |
| 658 Milt Wilcox | .05 | .15 |
| 659 Flinn/Romero/Yost | .30 | .75 |
| 660 Gary Carter | .30 | .75 |
| 661 Orioles Team CL — Earl Weaver MG | .15 | .40 |
| 662 Red Sox Team CL — Ralph Houk MG | .15 | .40 |
| 663 Angels Team CL — Jim Fregosi MG | .15 | .40 |
| 664 White Sox Team/Mgr. — Tony LaRussa (Checklist back) | .15 | .40 |
| 665 Indians Team CL — Dave Garcia MG | .15 | .40 |
| 666 Tigers Team/Mgr. — Sparky Anderson (Checklist back) | .15 | .40 |
| 667 Royals Team CL — Jim Frey MG | .15 | .40 |
| 668 Brewers Team CL — Bob Rodgers MG | .15 | .40 |
| 669 Twins Team CL — John Goryl MG | .15 | .40 |
| 670 Yankees Team CL — Gene Michael MG | .15 | .40 |
| 671 A's Team CL — Billy Martin MG | .30 | .75 |
| 672 Mariners Team CL — Maury Wills MG | .15 | .40 |
| 673 Rangers Team CL — Don Zimmer MG | .15 | .40 |
| 674 Blue Jays Team/Mgr. — Bobby Mattick (Checklist bac) | .15 | .40 |
| 675 Braves Team CL — Bobby Cox MG | .15 | .40 |
| 676 Cubs Team CL — Joe Amalfitano MG | .15 | .40 |
| 677 Reds Team CL — John McNamara MG | .15 | .40 |
| 678 Astros Team CL — Bill Virdon MG | .15 | .40 |
| 679 Dodgers Team CL — Tom Lasorda MG | .30 | .75 |
| 680 Expos Team CL — Dick Williams MG | .15 | .40 |
| 681 Mets Team CL — Joe Torre MG | .30 | .75 |
| 682 Phillies Team CL — Dallas Green MG | .15 | .40 |
| 683 Pirates Team CL — Chuck Tanner MG | .15 | .40 |
| 684 Cardinals Team/Mgr. — Whitey Herzog (Checklist bac) | .15 | .40 |
| 685 Padres Team CL — Frank Howard MG | .15 | .40 |
| 686 Giants Team CL — Dave Bristol MG | .15 | .40 |
| 687 Jeff Jones RC | .05 | .15 |
| 688 Kiko Garcia | .05 | .15 |

|  |  | | |
|---|---|---|---|
| ❑ 689 | Bruce Hurst RC | .30 | .75 |
| ❑ 690 | Bob Watson | .05 | .15 |
| ❑ 691 | Dick Ruthven | .05 | .15 |
| ❑ 692 | Lenny Randle | .05 | .15 |
| ❑ 693 | Steve Howe RC | .08 | .25 |
| ❑ 694 | Bud Harrelson DP | .08 | .25 |
| ❑ 695 | Kent Tekulve | .05 | .15 |
| ❑ 696 | Alan Ashby | .05 | .15 |
| ❑ 697 | Rick Waits | .05 | .15 |
| ❑ 698 | Mike Jorgensen | .05 | .15 |
| ❑ 699 | Glenn Abbott | .05 | .15 |
| ❑ 700 | George Brett | 1.50 | 4.00 |
| ❑ 701 | Joe Rudi | .15 | .40 |
| ❑ 702 | George Medich | .05 | .15 |
| ❑ 703 | Alvis Woods | .05 | .15 |
| ❑ 704 | Bill Travers DP | .05 | .15 |
| ❑ 705 | Ted Simmons | .15 | .40 |
| ❑ 706 | Dave Ford RC | .05 | .15 |
| ❑ 707 | Dave Cash | .05 | .15 |
| ❑ 708 | Doyle Alexander | .05 | .15 |
| ❑ 709 | Alan Trammell DP | .20 | .50 |
| ❑ 710 | Ron LeFlore DP | .08 | .25 |
| ❑ 711 | Joe Ferguson | .05 | .15 |
| ❑ 712 | Bill Bonham | .05 | .15 |
| ❑ 713 | Bill North | .05 | .15 |
| ❑ 714 | Pete Redfern | .05 | .15 |
| ❑ 715 | Bill Madlock | .15 | .40 |
| ❑ 716 | Glenn Borgmann | .05 | .15 |
| ❑ 717 | Jim Barr DP | .05 | .15 |
| ❑ 718 | Larry Biittner | .05 | .15 |
| ❑ 719 | Sparky Lyle | .15 | .40 |
| ❑ 720 | Fred Lynn | .15 | .40 |
| ❑ 721 | Toby Harrah | .15 | .40 |
| ❑ 722 | Joe Niekro | .05 | .15 |
| ❑ 723 | Bruce Bochte | .05 | .15 |
| ❑ 724 | Lou Piniella | .15 | .40 |
| ❑ 725 | Steve Rogers | .15 | .40 |
| ❑ 726 | Rick Monday | .15 | .40 |

## 1982 Topps

|  |  | | |
|---|---|---|---|
| ❑ | COMPLETE SET (792) | 40.00 | 80.00 |
| ❑ 1 | Steve Carlton HL | .10 | .30 |
| ❑ 2 | Ron Davis HL Fans 8 straight in relief | .05 | .15 |
| ❑ 3 | Tim Raines HL | .10 | .30 |
| ❑ 4 | Pete Rose HL | .25 | .60 |
| ❑ 5 | Nolan Ryan HL | 1.25 | 3.00 |
| ❑ 6 | Fernando Valenzuela HL 8 shutouts as rookie | .25 | .60 |
| ❑ 7 | Scott Sanderson | .05 | .15 |
| ❑ 8 | Rich Dauer | .05 | .15 |
| ❑ 9 | Ron Guidry | .10 | .30 |
| ❑ 10 | Ron Guidry SA | .05 | .15 |
| ❑ 11 | Gary Alexander | .05 | .15 |
| ❑ 12 | Moose Haas | .05 | .15 |
| ❑ 13 | Lamar Johnson | .05 | .15 |
| ❑ 14 | Steve Howe | .05 | .15 |
| ❑ 15 | Ellis Valentine | .05 | .15 |
| ❑ 16 | Steve Comer | .05 | .15 |
| ❑ 17 | Darrell Evans | .10 | .30 |
| ❑ 18 | Fernando Arroyo | .05 | .15 |
| ❑ 19 | Ernie Whitt | .05 | .15 |
| ❑ 20 | Garry Maddox | .05 | .15 |
| ❑ 21 | Cal Ripken RC | 15.00 | 40.00 |
| ❑ 22 | Jim Beattie | .05 | .15 |
| ❑ 23 | Willie Hernandez | .05 | .15 |
| ❑ 24 | Dave Frost | .05 | .15 |
| ❑ 25 | Jerry Remy | .05 | .15 |
| ❑ 26 | Jorge Orta | .05 | .15 |
| ❑ 27 | Tom Herr | .05 | .15 |
| ❑ 28 | John Urrea | .05 | .15 |
| ❑ 29 | Dwayne Murphy | .05 | .15 |
| ❑ 30 | Tom Seaver | .50 | 1.25 |

|  |  | | |
|---|---|---|---|
| ❑ 31 | Tom Seaver SA | .10 | .30 |
| ❑ 32 | Gene Garber | .05 | .15 |
| ❑ 33 | Jerry Morales | .05 | .15 |
| ❑ 34 | Joe Sambito | .05 | .15 |
| ❑ 35 | Willie Aikens | .05 | .15 |
| ❑ 36 | Rangers TL BA: Al Oliver Pitching: Doc Medich ( | .25 | .60 |
| ❑ 37 | Dan Graham | .05 | .15 |
| ❑ 38 | Charlie Lea | .05 | .15 |
| ❑ 39 | Lou Whitaker | .10 | .30 |
| ❑ 40 | Dave Parker | .10 | .30 |
| ❑ 41 | Dave Parker SA | .05 | .15 |
| ❑ 42 | Rick Sofield | .05 | .15 |
| ❑ 43 | Mike Cubbage | .05 | .15 |
| ❑ 44 | Britt Burns | .05 | .15 |
| ❑ 45 | Rick Cerone | .05 | .15 |
| ❑ 46 | Jerry Augustine | .05 | .15 |
| ❑ 47 | Jeff Leonard | .05 | .15 |
| ❑ 48 | Bobby Castillo | .05 | .15 |
| ❑ 49 | Alvis Woods | .05 | .15 |
| ❑ 50 | Buddy Bell | .10 | .30 |
| ❑ 51 | Howell/Lezcano/Waller RC | .30 | .75 |
| ❑ 52 | Larry Andersen | .05 | .15 |
| ❑ 53 | Greg Gross | .05 | .15 |
| ❑ 54 | Ron Hassey | .05 | .15 |
| ❑ 55 | Rick Burleson | .05 | .15 |
| ❑ 56 | Mark Littell | .05 | .15 |
| ❑ 57 | Craig Reynolds | .05 | .15 |
| ❑ 58 | John D'Acquisto | .05 | .15 |
| ❑ 59 | Rich Gedman | .30 | .75 |
| ❑ 60 | Tony Armas | .10 | .30 |
| ❑ 61 | Tommy Boggs | .05 | .15 |
| ❑ 62 | Mike Tyson | .05 | .15 |
| ❑ 63 | Mario Soto | .10 | .30 |
| ❑ 64 | Lynn Jones | .05 | .15 |
| ❑ 65 | Terry Kennedy | .05 | .15 |
| ❑ 66 | Astros TL/Nolan Ryan | .75 | 2.00 |
| ❑ 67 | Rich Gale | .05 | .15 |
| ❑ 68 | Roy Howell | .05 | .15 |
| ❑ 69 | Al Williams | .05 | .15 |
| ❑ 70 | Tim Raines | .25 | .60 |
| ❑ 71 | Roy Lee Jackson | .05 | .15 |
| ❑ 72 | Rick Auerbach | .05 | .15 |
| ❑ 73 | Buddy Solomon | .05 | .15 |
| ❑ 74 | Bob Clark | .05 | .15 |
| ❑ 75 | Tommy John | .10 | .30 |
| ❑ 76 | Greg Pryor | .05 | .15 |
| ❑ 77 | Miguel Dilone | .05 | .15 |
| ❑ 78 | George Medich | .05 | .15 |
| ❑ 79 | Bob Bailor | .05 | .15 |
| ❑ 80 | Jim Palmer | .10 | .30 |
| ❑ 81 | Jim Palmer SA | .05 | .15 |
| ❑ 82 | Bob Welch | .10 | .30 |
| ❑ 83 | Bdlorn/McGaf/Rob RC | .30 | .75 |
| ❑ 84 | Rennie Stennett | .05 | .15 |
| ❑ 85 | Lynn McGlothen | .05 | .15 |
| ❑ 86 | Dane Iorg | .05 | .15 |
| ❑ 87 | Matt Keough | .05 | .15 |
| ❑ 88 | Biff Pocoroba | .05 | .15 |
| ❑ 89 | Steve Henderson | .05 | .15 |
| ❑ 90 | Nolan Ryan | 2.50 | 6.00 |
| ❑ 91 | Carney Lansford | .10 | .30 |
| ❑ 92 | Brad Havens | .05 | .15 |
| ❑ 93 | Larry Hisle | .05 | .15 |
| ❑ 94 | Andy Hassler | .05 | .15 |
| ❑ 95 | Ozzie Smith | 1.00 | 2.50 |
| ❑ 96 | Royals TL/George Brett | .50 | 1.25 |
| ❑ 97 | Paul Moskau | .05 | .15 |
| ❑ 98 | Terry Bulling | .05 | .15 |
| ❑ 99 | Barry Bonnell | .05 | .15 |
| ❑ 100 | Mike Schmidt | 1.25 | 3.00 |
| ❑ 101 | Mike Schmidt SA | .50 | 1.25 |
| ❑ 102 | Dan Briggs | .05 | .15 |
| ❑ 103 | Bob Lacey | .05 | .15 |
| ❑ 104 | Rance Mulliniks | .05 | .15 |
| ❑ 105 | Kirk Gibson | .50 | 1.25 |
| ❑ 106 | Enrique Romo | .05 | .15 |
| ❑ 107 | Wayne Krenchicki | .05 | .15 |
| ❑ 108 | Bob Sykes | .05 | .15 |
| ❑ 109 | Dave Revering | .05 | .15 |
| ❑ 110 | Carlton Fisk | .25 | .60 |
| ❑ 111 | Carlton Fisk SA | .10 | .30 |
| ❑ 112 | Billy Sample | .05 | .15 |
| ❑ 113 | Steve McCatty | .05 | .15 |
| ❑ 114 | Ken Landreaux | .05 | .15 |
| ❑ 115 | Gaylord Perry | .10 | .30 |

|  |  | | |
|---|---|---|---|
| ❑ 116 | Jim Wohlford | .05 | .15 |
| ❑ 117 | Rawly Eastwick | .10 | .30 |
| ❑ 118 | Francona/Mills/Smith RC | 2.00 | 5.00 |
| ❑ 119 | Joe Pittman | .05 | .15 |
| ❑ 120 | Gary Lucas | .05 | .15 |
| ❑ 121 | Ed Lynch | .05 | .15 |
| ❑ 122 | Jamie Easterly UER (Photo actually Reggie Clevel | .05 | .15 |
| ❑ 123 | Danny Goodwin | .05 | .15 |
| ❑ 124 | Reid Nichols | .05 | .15 |
| ❑ 125 | Danny Ainge | .10 | .30 |
| ❑ 126 | Braves TL BA: Claudell Washington Pitching: Rick | .25 | .60 |
| ❑ 127 | Lonnie Smith | .05 | .15 |
| ❑ 128 | Frank Pastore | .05 | .15 |
| ❑ 129 | Checklist 1-132 | .10 | .30 |
| ❑ 130 | Julio Cruz | .05 | .15 |
| ❑ 131 | Stan Bahnsen | .05 | .15 |
| ❑ 132 | Lee May | .05 | .15 |
| ❑ 133 | Pat Underwood | .05 | .15 |
| ❑ 134 | Dan Ford | .05 | .15 |
| ❑ 135 | Andy Rincon | .05 | .15 |
| ❑ 136 | Lenn Sakata | .05 | .15 |
| ❑ 137 | George Cappuzzello | .05 | .15 |
| ❑ 138 | Tony Pena | .10 | .30 |
| ❑ 139 | Jeff Jones | .05 | .15 |
| ❑ 140 | Ron LeFlore | .10 | .30 |
| ❑ 141 | Bando/Brennan/Hayes RC | .30 | .75 |
| ❑ 142 | Dave LaRoche | .05 | .15 |
| ❑ 143 | Mookie Wilson | .10 | .30 |
| ❑ 144 | Fred Breining | .05 | .15 |
| ❑ 145 | Bob Horner | .10 | .30 |
| ❑ 146 | Mike Griffin | .05 | .15 |
| ❑ 147 | Denny Walling | .05 | .15 |
| ❑ 148 | Mickey Klutts | .05 | .15 |
| ❑ 149 | Pat Putnam | .05 | .15 |
| ❑ 150 | Ted Simmons | .10 | .30 |
| ❑ 151 | Dave Edwards | .05 | .15 |
| ❑ 152 | Ramon Aviles | .05 | .15 |
| ❑ 153 | Roger Erickson | .05 | .15 |
| ❑ 154 | Dennis Werth | .05 | .15 |
| ❑ 155 | Otto Velez | .05 | .15 |
| ❑ 156 | A's TL/Rickey Henderson | .50 | 1.25 |
| ❑ 157 | Steve Crawford | .05 | .15 |
| ❑ 158 | Brian Downing | .10 | .30 |
| ❑ 159 | Larry Biittner | .05 | .15 |
| ❑ 160 | Luis Tiant | .10 | .30 |
| ❑ 161 | Bill Madlock Carney Lansford LL | .10 | .30 |
| ❑ 162 | Schmidt/Armas/Murray LL | .50 | 1.25 |
| ❑ 163 | Mike Schmidt/C. Murray LL | .50 | 1.25 |
| ❑ 164 | T. Raines/R.Henderson LL | .50 | 1.25 |
| ❑ 165 | Seav/Martinez/Morris LL | .10 | .30 |
| ❑ 166 | Strikeout Leaders Fernando Valenzuela Len Barker | .10 | .30 |
| ❑ 167 | N.Ryan/S.McCatty LL | .75 | 2.00 |
| ❑ 168 | B.Sutter/R.Fingers LL | .10 | .30 |
| ❑ 169 | Charlie Leibrandt | .05 | .15 |
| ❑ 170 | Jim Bibby | .05 | .15 |
| ❑ 171 | Brenly/Davis/Tufts RC | .60 | 1.50 |
| ❑ 172 | Bill Gullickson | .05 | .15 |
| ❑ 173 | Jamie Quirk | .05 | .15 |
| ❑ 174 | Dave Ford | .05 | .15 |
| ❑ 175 | Jerry Mumphrey | .05 | .15 |
| ❑ 176 | Dewey Robinson | .05 | .15 |
| ❑ 177 | John Ellis | .05 | .15 |
| ❑ 178 | Dyar Miller | .05 | .15 |
| ❑ 179 | Steve Garvey | .10 | .30 |
| ❑ 180 | Steve Garvey SA | .05 | .15 |
| ❑ 181 | Silvio Martinez | .05 | .15 |
| ❑ 182 | Larry Herndon | .05 | .15 |
| ❑ 183 | Mike Proly | .05 | .15 |
| ❑ 184 | Mick Kelleher | .05 | .15 |
| ❑ 185 | Phil Niekro | .10 | .30 |
| ❑ 186 | Cardinals TL BA: Keith Hernandez Pitching: Bob F | .10 | .30 |
| ❑ 187 | Jeff Newman | .05 | .15 |
| ❑ 188 | Randy Martz | .05 | .15 |
| ❑ 189 | Glenn Hoffman | .05 | .15 |
| ❑ 190 | J.R. Richard | .10 | .30 |
| ❑ 191 | Tim Wallach RC | .60 | 1.50 |
| ❑ 192 | Broderick Perkins | .05 | .15 |
| ❑ 193 | Darrell Jackson | .05 | .15 |
| ❑ 194 | Mike Vail | .05 | .15 |

|  |  | | |
|---|---|---|---|
| ☐ 195 | Paul Molitor | .10 | .30 |
| ☐ 196 | Willie Upshaw | .30 | .75 |
| ☐ 197 | Shane Rawley | .05 | .15 |
| ☐ 198 | Chris Speier | .05 | .15 |
| ☐ 199 | Don Aase | .05 | .15 |
| ☐ 200 | George Brett | 1.25 | 3.00 |
| ☐ 201 | George Brett SA | .60 | 1.50 |
| ☐ 202 | Rick Manning | .05 | .15 |
| ☐ 203 | Barfield/Miln/Wells RC | .60 | 1.50 |
| ☐ 204 | Gary Roenicke | .05 | .15 |
| ☐ 205 | Neil Allen | .05 | .15 |
| ☐ 206 | Tony Bernazard | .05 | .15 |
| ☐ 207 | Rod Scurry | .05 | .15 |
| ☐ 208 | Bobby Murcer | .10 | .30 |
| ☐ 209 | Gary Lavelle | .05 | .15 |
| ☐ 210 | Keith Hernandez | .10 | .30 |
| ☐ 211 | Dan Petry | .05 | .15 |
| ☐ 212 | Mario Mendoza | .05 | .15 |
| ☐ 213 | Dave Stewart RC | 1.00 | 2.50 |
| ☐ 214 | Brian Asselstine | .05 | .15 |
| ☐ 215 | Mike Krukow | .05 | .15 |
| ☐ 216 | White Sox TL BA: Chet Lemon Pitching: Dennis Lam | .25 | .60 |
| ☐ 217 | Bo McLaughlin | .05 | .15 |
| ☐ 218 | Dave Roberts | .05 | .15 |
| ☐ 219 | John Curtis | .05 | .15 |
| ☐ 220 | Manny Trillo | .05 | .15 |
| ☐ 221 | Jim Slaton | .05 | .15 |
| ☐ 222 | Butch Wynegar | .05 | .15 |
| ☐ 223 | Lloyd Moseby | .05 | .15 |
| ☐ 224 | Bruce Bochte | .05 | .15 |
| ☐ 225 | Mike Torrez | .05 | .15 |
| ☐ 226 | Checklist 133-264 | .25 | .60 |
| ☐ 227 | Ray Burris | .05 | .15 |
| ☐ 228 | Sam Mejias | .05 | .15 |
| ☐ 229 | Geoff Zahn | .05 | .15 |
| ☐ 230 | Willie Wilson | .10 | .30 |
| ☐ 231 | Davis/Demier/Virgil RC | .30 | .75 |
| ☐ 232 | Terry Crowley | .05 | .15 |
| ☐ 233 | Duane Kuiper | .05 | .15 |
| ☐ 234 | Ron Hodges | .05 | .15 |
| ☐ 235 | Mike Easler | .05 | .15 |
| ☐ 236 | John Martin RC | .08 | .25 |
| ☐ 237 | Rusty Kuntz | .05 | .15 |
| ☐ 238 | Kevin Saucier | .05 | .15 |
| ☐ 239 | Jon Matlack | .05 | .15 |
| ☐ 240 | Bucky Dent | .10 | .30 |
| ☐ 241 | Bucky Dent SA | .05 | .15 |
| ☐ 242 | Milt May | .05 | .15 |
| ☐ 243 | Bob Owchinko | .05 | .15 |
| ☐ 244 | Rufino Linares | .05 | .15 |
| ☐ 245 | Ken Reitz | .05 | .15 |
| ☐ 246 | New York Mets TL BA: Hubie Brooks Pitching: Mike | .25 | .60 |
| ☐ 247 | Pedro Guerrero | .10 | .30 |
| ☐ 248 | Frank LaCorte | .05 | .15 |
| ☐ 249 | Tim Flannery | .05 | .15 |
| ☐ 250 | Tug McGraw | .10 | .30 |
| ☐ 251 | Fred Lynn | .10 | .30 |
| ☐ 252 | Fred Lynn SA | .05 | .15 |
| ☐ 253 | Chuck Baker | .05 | .15 |
| ☐ 254 | George Bell RC | .60 | 1.50 |
| ☐ 255 | Tony Perez | .25 | .60 |
| ☐ 256 | Tony Perez SA | .10 | .30 |
| ☐ 257 | Larry Harlow | .05 | .15 |
| ☐ 258 | Bo Diaz | .05 | .15 |
| ☐ 259 | Rodney Scott | .05 | .15 |
| ☐ 260 | Bruce Sutter | .25 | .60 |
| ☐ 261 | Bailey/Castillo/Rucker RC | .05 | .15 |
| ☐ 262 | Doug Bair | .05 | .15 |
| ☐ 263 | Victor Cruz | .05 | .15 |
| ☐ 264 | Dan Quisenberry | .05 | .15 |
| ☐ 265 | Al Bumbry | .05 | .15 |
| ☐ 266 | Rick Leach | .05 | .15 |
| ☐ 267 | Kurt Bevacqua | .05 | .15 |
| ☐ 268 | Rickey Keeton | .05 | .15 |
| ☐ 269 | Jim Essian | .05 | .15 |
| ☐ 270 | Rusty Staub | .10 | .30 |
| ☐ 271 | Larry Bradford | .05 | .15 |
| ☐ 272 | Bump Wills | .05 | .15 |
| ☐ 273 | Doug Bird | .05 | .15 |
| ☐ 274 | Bob Ojeda RC | .30 | .75 |
| ☐ 275 | Bob Watson | .05 | .15 |
| ☐ 276 | Angels TL/Rod Carew | .25 | .60 |
| ☐ 277 | Terry Puhl | .05 | .15 |
| ☐ 278 | John Littlefield | .05 | .15 |
| ☐ 279 | Bill Russell | .10 | .30 |
| ☐ 280 | Ben Oglivie | .10 | .30 |
| ☐ 281 | John Verhoeven | .05 | .15 |
| ☐ 282 | Ken Macha | .05 | .15 |
| ☐ 283 | Brian Allard | .05 | .15 |
| ☐ 284 | Bob Grich | .10 | .30 |
| ☐ 285 | Sparky Lyle | .10 | .30 |
| ☐ 286 | Bill Fahey | .05 | .15 |
| ☐ 287 | Alan Bannister | .05 | .15 |
| ☐ 288 | Garry Templeton | .10 | .30 |
| ☐ 289 | Bob Stanley | .05 | .15 |
| ☐ 290 | Ken Singleton | .05 | .15 |
| ☐ 291 | Law/Long/Ray RC | .10 | .30 |
| ☐ 292 | David Palmer | .05 | .15 |
| ☐ 293 | Rob Picciolo | .05 | .15 |
| ☐ 294 | Mike LaCoss | .05 | .15 |
| ☐ 295 | Jason Thompson | .05 | .15 |
| ☐ 296 | Bob Walk | .05 | .15 |
| ☐ 297 | Clint Hurdle | .05 | .15 |
| ☐ 298 | Danny Darwin | .05 | .15 |
| ☐ 299 | Steve Trout | .05 | .15 |
| ☐ 300 | Reggie Jackson | .25 | .60 |
| ☐ 301 | Reggie Jackson SA | .10 | .30 |
| ☐ 302 | Doug Flynn | .05 | .15 |
| ☐ 303 | Bill Caudill | .05 | .15 |
| ☐ 304 | Johnnie LeMaster | .05 | .15 |
| ☐ 305 | Don Sutton | .10 | .30 |
| ☐ 306 | Don Sutton SA | .05 | .15 |
| ☐ 307 | Randy Bass | .30 | .75 |
| ☐ 308 | Charlie Moore | .05 | .15 |
| ☐ 309 | Pete Redfern | .05 | .15 |
| ☐ 310 | Mike Hargrove | .05 | .15 |
| ☐ 311 | Dusty Baker Burt Hooton TL | .10 | .30 |
| ☐ 312 | Lenny Randle | .05 | .15 |
| ☐ 313 | John Harris | .05 | .15 |
| ☐ 314 | Buck Martinez | .05 | .15 |
| ☐ 315 | Burt Hooton | .05 | .15 |
| ☐ 316 | Steve Braun | .05 | .15 |
| ☐ 317 | Dick Ruthven | .05 | .15 |
| ☐ 318 | Mike Heath | .05 | .15 |
| ☐ 319 | Dave Rozema | .05 | .15 |
| ☐ 320 | Chris Chambliss | .10 | .30 |
| ☐ 321 | Chris Chambliss SA | .05 | .15 |
| ☐ 322 | Garry Hancock | .05 | .15 |
| ☐ 323 | Bill Lee | .10 | .30 |
| ☐ 324 | Steve Dillard | .05 | .15 |
| ☐ 325 | Jose Cruz | .10 | .30 |
| ☐ 326 | Pete Falcone | .05 | .15 |
| ☐ 327 | Joe Nolan | .05 | .15 |
| ☐ 328 | Ed Farmer | .05 | .15 |
| ☐ 329 | U.L. Washington | .05 | .15 |
| ☐ 330 | Rick Wise | .05 | .15 |
| ☐ 331 | Benny Ayala | .05 | .15 |
| ☐ 332 | Don Robinson | .05 | .15 |
| ☐ 333 | DiPino/Edwards/Porter RC | .05 | .15 |
| ☐ 334 | Aurelio Rodriguez | .05 | .15 |
| ☐ 335 | Jim Sundberg | .10 | .30 |
| ☐ 336 | Mariners TL BA: Tom Paciorek Pitching: Glenn Abb | .25 | .60 |
| ☐ 337 | Pete Rose AS | .25 | .60 |
| ☐ 338 | Dave Lopes AS | .05 | .15 |
| ☐ 339 | Mike Schmidt AS | .50 | 1.25 |
| ☐ 340 | Dave Concepcion AS | .05 | .15 |
| ☐ 341 | Andre Dawson AS | .05 | .15 |
| ☐ 342A | George Foster AS (With autograph) | .10 | .30 |
| ☐ 342B | G.Foster AS ERR NO AU | .50 | 1.25 |
| ☐ 343 | Dave Parker AS | .05 | .15 |
| ☐ 344 | Gary Carter AS | .25 | .60 |
| ☐ 345 | Fernando Valenzuela AS | .25 | .60 |
| ☐ 346 | Tom Seaver AS | .10 | .30 |
| ☐ 346B | Tom Seaver AS COR | .10 | .30 |
| ☐ 347 | Bruce Sutter AS | .10 | .30 |
| ☐ 348 | Derrel Thomas | .05 | .15 |
| ☐ 349 | George Frazier | .05 | .15 |
| ☐ 350 | Thad Bosley | .05 | .15 |
| ☐ 351 | Brown/Comb/House RC | .05 | .15 |
| ☐ 352 | Dick Davis | .05 | .15 |
| ☐ 353 | Jack O'Connor | .05 | .15 |
| ☐ 354 | Roberto Ramos | .05 | .15 |
| ☐ 355 | Dwight Evans | .25 | .60 |
| ☐ 356 | Denny Lewallyn | .05 | .15 |
| ☐ 357 | Butch Hobson | .05 | .15 |
| ☐ 358 | Mike Parrott | .05 | .15 |
| ☐ 359 | Jim Dwyer | .05 | .15 |
| ☐ 360 | Len Barker | .05 | .15 |
| ☐ 361 | Rafael Landestoy | .05 | .15 |
| ☐ 362 | Jim Wright UER (Wrong Jim Wright pictured) | | |
| ☐ 363 | Bob Molinaro | .05 | .15 |
| ☐ 364 | Doyle Alexander | .05 | .15 |
| ☐ 365 | Bill Madlock | .10 | .30 |
| ☐ 366 | Padres TL BA: Luis Salazar Pitching: Juan Eiche | .25 | .60 |
| ☐ 367 | Jim Kaat | .10 | .30 |
| ☐ 368 | Alex Trevino | .05 | .15 |
| ☐ 369 | Champ Summers | .05 | .15 |
| ☐ 370 | Mike Norris | .05 | .15 |
| ☐ 371 | Jerry Don Gleaton | .05 | .15 |
| ☐ 372 | Luis Gomez | .05 | .15 |
| ☐ 373 | Gene Nelson | .05 | .15 |
| ☐ 374 | Tim Blackwell | .05 | .15 |
| ☐ 375 | Dusty Baker | .10 | .30 |
| ☐ 376 | Chris Welsh | .05 | .15 |
| ☐ 377 | Kiko Garcia | .05 | .15 |
| ☐ 378 | Mike Caldwell | .05 | .15 |
| ☐ 379 | Rob Wilfong | .05 | .15 |
| ☐ 380 | Dave Stieb | .10 | .30 |
| ☐ 381 | Bruce Hurst Dave Schmidt RC Julio Valdez RC | .05 | .15 |
| ☐ 382 | Joe Simpson | .05 | .15 |
| ☐ 383A | Pascual Perez ERR NPO | 15.00 | 40.00 |
| ☐ 383B | Pascual Perez COR | .10 | .30 |
| ☐ 384 | Keith Moreland | .05 | .15 |
| ☐ 385 | Ken Forsch | .05 | .15 |
| ☐ 386 | Jerry White | .05 | .15 |
| ☐ 387 | Tom Veryzer | .05 | .15 |
| ☐ 388 | Joe Rudi | .10 | .30 |
| ☐ 389 | George Vukovich | .05 | .15 |
| ☐ 390 | Eddie Murray | .50 | 1.25 |
| ☐ 391 | Dave Tobik | .05 | .15 |
| ☐ 392 | Rick Bosetti | .05 | .15 |
| ☐ 393 | Al Hrabosky | .05 | .15 |
| ☐ 394 | Checklist 265-396 | .25 | .60 |
| ☐ 395 | Omar Moreno | .05 | .15 |
| ☐ 396 | Twins TL BA: John Castino Pitching: Fernando Ar | .25 | .60 |
| ☐ 397 | Ken Brett | .05 | .15 |
| ☐ 398 | Mike Squires | .05 | .15 |
| ☐ 399 | Pat Zachry | .05 | .15 |
| ☐ 400 | Johnny Bench | .50 | 1.25 |
| ☐ 401 | Johnny Bench SA | .25 | .60 |
| ☐ 402 | Bill Stein | .05 | .15 |
| ☐ 403 | Jim Tracy | .10 | .30 |
| ☐ 404 | Dickie Thon | .10 | .30 |
| ☐ 405 | Rick Reuschel | .10 | .30 |
| ☐ 406 | Al Holland | .05 | .15 |
| ☐ 407 | Danny Boone | .05 | .15 |
| ☐ 408 | Ed Romero | .05 | .15 |
| ☐ 409 | Don Cooper | .05 | .15 |
| ☐ 410 | Ron Cey | .10 | .30 |
| ☐ 411 | Ron Cey SA | .05 | .15 |
| ☐ 412 | Luis Leal | .05 | .15 |
| ☐ 413 | Dan Meyer | .05 | .15 |
| ☐ 414 | Elias Sosa | .05 | .15 |
| ☐ 415 | Don Baylor | .10 | .30 |
| ☐ 416 | Marty Bystrom | .05 | .15 |
| ☐ 417 | Pat Kelly | .05 | .15 |
| ☐ 418 | Butcher/John/Schmidt RC | .05 | .15 |
| ☐ 419 | Steve Stone | .05 | .15 |
| ☐ 420 | George Hendrick | .10 | .30 |
| ☐ 421 | Mark Clear | .05 | .15 |
| ☐ 422 | Cliff Johnson | .05 | .15 |
| ☐ 423 | Stan Papi | .05 | .15 |
| ☐ 424 | Bruce Benedict | .05 | .15 |
| ☐ 425 | John Candelaria | .05 | .15 |
| ☐ 426 | Orioles TL/Eddie Murray | .25 | .60 |
| ☐ 427 | Ron Oester | .05 | .15 |
| ☐ 428 | LaMarr Hoyt | .05 | .15 |
| ☐ 429 | John Wathan | .05 | .15 |
| ☐ 430 | Vida Blue | .10 | .30 |
| ☐ 431 | Vida Blue SA | .05 | .15 |
| ☐ 432 | Mike Scott | .10 | .30 |
| ☐ 433 | Alan Ashby | .05 | .15 |
| ☐ 434 | Joe Lefebvre | .05 | .15 |
| ☐ 435 | Robin Yount | .75 | 2.00 |
| ☐ 436 | Joe Strain | .05 | .15 |
| ☐ 437 | Juan Berenguer | .05 | .15 |

|  |  | | |
|---|------|------|------|
| ☐ 438 | Pete Mackanin | .05 | .15 |
| ☐ 439 | Dave Righetti RC | 1.00 | 2.50 |
| ☐ 440 | Jeff Burroughs | .05 | .15 |
| ☐ 441 | Heep/Smith/Sprowl RC | .05 | .15 |
| ☐ 442 | Bruce Kison | .05 | .15 |
| ☐ 443 | Mark Wagner | .05 | .15 |
| ☐ 444 | Terry Forster | .10 | .30 |
| ☐ 445 | Larry Parrish | .05 | .15 |
| ☐ 446 | Wayne Garland | .05 | .15 |
| ☐ 447 | Darrell Porter | .05 | .15 |
| ☐ 448 | Darrell Porter SA | .05 | .15 |
| ☐ 449 | Luis Aguayo | .05 | .15 |
| ☐ 450 | Jack Morris | .10 | .30 |
| ☐ 451 | Ed Miller | .05 | .15 |
| ☐ 452 | Lee Smith RC | 1.25 | 3.00 |
| ☐ 453 | Art Howe | .05 | .15 |
| ☐ 454 | Rick Langford | .05 | .15 |
| ☐ 455 | Tom Burgmeier | .05 | .15 |
| ☐ 456 | Chicago Cubs TL | | |
| | BA: Bill Buckner | | |
| | Pitching: Randy | .10 | .30 |
| ☐ 457 | Tim Stoddard | .05 | .15 |
| ☐ 458 | Willie Montanez | .05 | .15 |
| ☐ 459 | Bruce Berenyi | .05 | .15 |
| ☐ 460 | Jack Clark | .10 | .30 |
| ☐ 461 | Rich Dotson | .05 | .15 |
| ☐ 462 | Dave Chalk | .05 | .15 |
| ☐ 463 | Jim Kern | .05 | .15 |
| ☐ 464 | Juan Bonilla RC | .08 | .25 |
| ☐ 465 | Lee Mazzilli | .10 | .30 |
| ☐ 466 | Randy Lerch | .05 | .15 |
| ☐ 467 | Mickey Hatcher | .05 | .15 |
| ☐ 468 | Floyd Bannister | .05 | .15 |
| ☐ 469 | Ed Ott | .05 | .15 |
| ☐ 470 | John Mayberry | .05 | .15 |
| ☐ 471 | Hammaker/Jones/Motley RC | .05 | .15 |
| ☐ 472 | Oscar Gamble | .05 | .15 |
| ☐ 473 | Mike Stanton | .05 | .15 |
| ☐ 474 | Ken Oberkfell | .05 | .15 |
| ☐ 475 | Alan Trammell | .10 | .30 |
| ☐ 476 | Brian Kingman | .05 | .15 |
| ☐ 477 | Steve Yeager | .10 | .30 |
| ☐ 478 | Ray Searage | .05 | .15 |
| ☐ 479 | Rowland Office | .05 | .15 |
| ☐ 480 | Steve Carlton | .25 | .60 |
| ☐ 481 | Steve Carlton SA | .05 | .15 |
| ☐ 482 | Glenn Hubbard | .05 | .15 |
| ☐ 483 | Gary Woods | .05 | .15 |
| ☐ 484 | Ivan DeJesus | .05 | .15 |
| ☐ 485 | Kent Tekulve | .05 | .15 |
| ☐ 486 | Yankees TL | | |
| | BA: Jerry Mumphrey | | |
| | Pitching: Tommy Jo | .10 | .30 |
| ☐ 487 | Bob McClure | .05 | .15 |
| ☐ 488 | Ron Jackson | .05 | .15 |
| ☐ 489 | Rick Dempsey | .05 | .15 |
| ☐ 490 | Dennis Eckersley | .25 | .60 |
| ☐ 491 | Checklist 397-528 | .25 | .60 |
| ☐ 492 | Joe Price | .05 | .15 |
| ☐ 493 | Chet Lemon | .10 | .30 |
| ☐ 494 | Hubie Brooks | .05 | .15 |
| ☐ 495 | Dennis Leonard | .05 | .15 |
| ☐ 496 | Johnny Grubb | .05 | .15 |
| ☐ 497 | Jim Anderson | .05 | .15 |
| ☐ 498 | Dave Bergman | .05 | .15 |
| ☐ 499 | Paul Mirabella | .05 | .15 |
| ☐ 500 | Rod Carew | .25 | .60 |
| ☐ 501 | Rod Carew SA | .10 | .30 |
| ☐ 502 | Brett Butler RC | .60 | 1.50 |
| ☐ 503 | Julio Gonzalez | .05 | .15 |
| ☐ 504 | Rick Peters | .05 | .15 |
| ☐ 505 | Graig Nettles | .10 | .30 |
| ☐ 506 | Graig Nettles SA | .05 | .15 |
| ☐ 507 | Terry Harper | .05 | .15 |
| ☐ 508 | Jody Davis | .05 | .15 |
| ☐ 509 | Harry Spilman | .05 | .15 |
| ☐ 510 | Fernando Valenzuela | .50 | 1.25 |
| ☐ 511 | Ruppert Jones | .05 | .15 |
| ☐ 512 | Jerry Dybzinski | .05 | .15 |
| ☐ 513 | Rick Rhoden | .05 | .15 |
| ☐ 514 | Joe Ferguson | .05 | .15 |
| ☐ 515 | Larry Bowa | .10 | .30 |
| ☐ 516 | Larry Bowa SA | .05 | .15 |
| ☐ 517 | Mark Brouhard | .05 | .15 |
| ☐ 518 | Garth Iorg | .05 | .15 |
| ☐ 519 | Glenn Adams | .05 | .15 |
| ☐ 520 | Mike Flanagan | .05 | .15 |
| ☐ 521 | Bill Almon | .05 | .15 |
| ☐ 522 | Chuck Rainey | .05 | .15 |
| ☐ 523 | Gary Gray | .05 | .15 |
| ☐ 524 | Tom Hausman | .05 | .15 |
| ☐ 525 | Ray Knight | .10 | .30 |
| ☐ 526 | Expos TL | | |
| | BA: Warren Cromartie | | |
| | Pitching: Bill Gul | .25 | .60 |
| ☐ 527 | John Henry Johnson | .05 | .15 |
| ☐ 528 | Matt Alexander | .05 | .15 |
| ☐ 529 | Allen Ripley | .05 | .15 |
| ☐ 530 | Dickie Noles | .05 | .15 |
| ☐ 531 | Bordi/Budaska/Moore RC | .05 | .15 |
| ☐ 532 | Toby Harrah | .10 | .30 |
| ☐ 533 | Joaquin Andujar | .10 | .30 |
| ☐ 534 | Dave McKay | .05 | .15 |
| ☐ 535 | Lance Parrish | .10 | .30 |
| ☐ 536 | Rafael Ramirez | .05 | .15 |
| ☐ 537 | Doug Capilla | .05 | .15 |
| ☐ 538 | Lou Piniella | .10 | .30 |
| ☐ 539 | Vern Ruhle | .05 | .15 |
| ☐ 540 | Andre Dawson | .10 | .30 |
| ☐ 541 | Barry Evans | .05 | .15 |
| ☐ 542 | Ned Yost | .05 | .15 |
| ☐ 543 | Bill Robinson | .05 | .15 |
| ☐ 544 | Larry Christenson | .05 | .15 |
| ☐ 545 | Reggie Smith | .10 | .30 |
| ☐ 546 | Reggie Smith SA | .05 | .15 |
| ☐ 547 | Rod Carew AS | .10 | .30 |
| ☐ 548 | Willie Randolph AS | .05 | .15 |
| ☐ 549 | George Brett AS | .60 | 1.50 |
| ☐ 550 | Bucky Dent AS | .05 | .15 |
| ☐ 551 | Reggie Jackson AS | .10 | .30 |
| ☐ 552 | Ken Singleton AS | .05 | .15 |
| ☐ 553 | Dave Winfield AS | .05 | .15 |
| ☐ 554 | Carlton Fisk AS | .10 | .30 |
| ☐ 555 | Scott McGregor AS | .05 | .15 |
| ☐ 556 | Jack Morris AS | .05 | .15 |
| ☐ 557 | Rich Gossage AS | .05 | .15 |
| ☐ 558 | John Tudor | .10 | .30 |
| ☐ 559 | Indians TL | | |
| | BA: Mike Hargrove | | |
| | Pitching: Bert Blyl | .10 | .30 |
| ☐ 560 | Doug Corbett | .05 | .15 |
| ☐ 561 | Brum/DeLeon/Roof RC | .05 | .15 |
| ☐ 562 | Mike O'Berry | .05 | .15 |
| ☐ 563 | Ross Baumgarten | .05 | .15 |
| ☐ 564 | Doug DeCinces | .05 | .15 |
| ☐ 565 | Jackson Todd | .05 | .15 |
| ☐ 566 | Mike Jorgensen | .05 | .15 |
| ☐ 567 | Bob Babcock | .05 | .15 |
| ☐ 568 | Joe Pettini | .05 | .15 |
| ☐ 569 | Willie Randolph | .10 | .30 |
| ☐ 570 | Willie Randolph SA | .05 | .15 |
| ☐ 571 | Glenn Abbott | .05 | .15 |
| ☐ 572 | Juan Beniquez | .05 | .15 |
| ☐ 573 | Rick Waits | .05 | .15 |
| ☐ 574 | Mike Ramsey | .05 | .15 |
| ☐ 575 | Al Cowens | .05 | .15 |
| ☐ 576 | Giants TL | | |
| | BA: Milt May | | |
| | Pitching: Vida Blue | | |
| | (Che | .25 | .60 |
| ☐ 577 | Rick Monday | .10 | .30 |
| ☐ 578 | Shooty Babitt | .05 | .15 |
| ☐ 579 | Rick Mahler | .05 | .15 |
| ☐ 580 | Bobby Bonds | .10 | .30 |
| ☐ 581 | Ron Reed | .05 | .15 |
| ☐ 582 | Luis Pujols | .05 | .15 |
| ☐ 583 | Tippy Martinez | .05 | .15 |
| ☐ 584 | Hosken Powell | .05 | .15 |
| ☐ 585 | Rollie Fingers | .10 | .30 |
| ☐ 586 | Rollie Fingers SA | .05 | .15 |
| ☐ 587 | Tim Lollar | .05 | .15 |
| ☐ 588 | Dale Berra | .05 | .15 |
| ☐ 589 | Dave Stapleton | .05 | .15 |
| ☐ 590 | Al Oliver | .10 | .30 |
| ☐ 591 | Al Oliver SA | .05 | .15 |
| ☐ 592 | Craig Swan | .05 | .15 |
| ☐ 593 | Billy Smith | .05 | .15 |
| ☐ 594 | Renie Martin | .05 | .15 |
| ☐ 595 | Dave Collins | .05 | .15 |
| ☐ 596 | Damaso Garcia | .05 | .15 |
| ☐ 597 | Wayne Nordhagen | .05 | .15 |
| ☐ 598 | Bob Galasso | .05 | .15 |
| ☐ 599 | Lovig/Patt/Suth RC | .05 | .15 |
| ☐ 600 | Dave Winfield | .10 | .30 |
| ☐ 601 | Sid Monge | .05 | .15 |
| ☐ 602 | Freddie Patek | .05 | .15 |
| ☐ 603 | Rich Hebner | .05 | .15 |
| ☐ 604 | Orlando Sanchez | .05 | .15 |
| ☐ 605 | Steve Rogers | .10 | .30 |
| ☐ 606 | Blue Jays TL | | |
| | BA: John Mayberry | | |
| | Pitching: Dave St | .10 | .30 |
| ☐ 607 | Leon Durham | .05 | .15 |
| ☐ 608 | Jerry Royster | .05 | .15 |
| ☐ 609 | Rick Sutcliffe | .10 | .30 |
| ☐ 610 | Rickey Henderson | 1.50 | 4.00 |
| ☐ 611 | Joe Niekro | .05 | .15 |
| ☐ 612 | Gary Ward | .05 | .15 |
| ☐ 613 | Jim Gantner | .05 | .15 |
| ☐ 614 | Juan Eichelberger | .05 | .15 |
| ☐ 615 | Bob Boone | .10 | .30 |
| ☐ 616 | Bob Boone SA | .05 | .15 |
| ☐ 617 | Scott McGregor | .05 | .15 |
| ☐ 618 | Tim Foli | .05 | .15 |
| ☐ 619 | Bill Campbell | .05 | .15 |
| ☐ 620 | Ken Griffey | .10 | .30 |
| ☐ 621 | Ken Griffey SA | .05 | .15 |
| ☐ 622 | Dennis Lamp | .05 | .15 |
| ☐ 623 | Gardenhire/Leach/Leary RC | .30 | .75 |
| ☐ 624 | Fergie Jenkins | .10 | .30 |
| ☐ 625 | Hal McRae | .10 | .30 |
| ☐ 626 | Randy Jones | .05 | .15 |
| ☐ 627 | Enos Cabell | .05 | .15 |
| ☐ 628 | Bill Travers | .05 | .15 |
| ☐ 629 | John Wockenfuss | .05 | .15 |
| ☐ 630 | Joe Charboneau | .10 | .30 |
| ☐ 631 | Gene Tenace | .10 | .30 |
| ☐ 632 | Bryan Clark RC | .08 | .25 |
| ☐ 633 | Mitchell Page | .05 | .15 |
| ☐ 634 | Checklist 529-660 | .25 | .60 |
| ☐ 635 | Ron Davis | .05 | .15 |
| ☐ 636 | Phillies TL/Rose/Carlton | .50 | 1.25 |
| ☐ 637 | Rick Camp | .05 | .15 |
| ☐ 638 | John Milner | .05 | .15 |
| ☐ 639 | Ken Kravec | .05 | .15 |
| ☐ 640 | Cesar Cedeno | .10 | .30 |
| ☐ 641 | Steve Mura | .05 | .15 |
| ☐ 642 | Mike Scioscia | .10 | .30 |
| ☐ 643 | Pete Vuckovich | .05 | .15 |
| ☐ 644 | John Castino | .05 | .15 |
| ☐ 645 | Frank White | .10 | .30 |
| ☐ 646 | Frank White SA | .05 | .15 |
| ☐ 647 | Warren Brusstar | .05 | .15 |
| ☐ 648 | Jose Morales | .05 | .15 |
| ☐ 649 | Ken Clay | .05 | .15 |
| ☐ 650 | Carl Yastrzemski | .75 | 2.00 |
| ☐ 651 | Carl Yastrzemski SA | .50 | 1.25 |
| ☐ 652 | Steve Nicosia | .05 | .15 |
| ☐ 653 | Brunansky/Sanch/Scon RC | .60 | 1.50 |
| ☐ 654 | Jim Morrison | .05 | .15 |
| ☐ 655 | Joel Youngblood | .05 | .15 |
| ☐ 656 | Eddie Whitson | .05 | .15 |
| ☐ 657 | Tom Poquette | .05 | .15 |
| ☐ 658 | Tito Landrum | .05 | .15 |
| ☐ 659 | Fred Martinez | .05 | .15 |
| ☐ 660 | Dave Concepcion | .10 | .30 |
| ☐ 661 | Dave Concepcion SA | .05 | .15 |
| ☐ 662 | Luis Salazar | .05 | .15 |
| ☐ 663 | Hector Cruz | .05 | .15 |
| ☐ 664 | Dan Spillner | .05 | .15 |
| ☐ 665 | Jim Clancy | .05 | .15 |
| ☐ 666 | Tigers TL | | |
| | BA: Steve Kemp | | |
| | Pitching: Dan Petry | | |
| | (C | .25 | .60 |
| ☐ 667 | Jeff Reardon | .10 | .30 |
| ☐ 668 | Dale Murphy | .25 | .60 |
| ☐ 669 | Larry Milbourne | .05 | .15 |
| ☐ 670 | Steve Kemp | .05 | .15 |
| ☐ 671 | Mike Davis | .05 | .15 |
| ☐ 672 | Bob Knepper | .05 | .15 |
| ☐ 673 | Keith Drumwright | .05 | .15 |
| ☐ 674 | Dave Goltz | .05 | .15 |
| ☐ 675 | Cecil Cooper | .10 | .30 |
| ☐ 676 | Sal Butera | .05 | .15 |
| ☐ 677 | Alfredo Griffin | .05 | .15 |
| ☐ 678 | Tom Paciorek | .05 | .15 |
| ☐ 679 | Sammy Stewart | .05 | .15 |
| ☐ 680 | Gary Matthews | .10 | .30 |
| ☐ 681 | Marshall/Roen/Sax RC | .60 | 1.50 |
| ☐ 682 | Jesse Jefferson | .05 | .15 |
| ☐ 683 | Phil Garner | .10 | .30 |
| ☐ 684 | Harold Baines | .10 | .30 |
| ☐ 685 | Bert Blyleven | .10 | .30 |

|  |  | | |
|---|---|---|---|
| 686 | Gary Allenson | .05 | .15 |
| 687 | Greg Minton | .05 | .15 |
| 688 | Leon Roberts | .05 | .15 |
| 689 | Lary Sorensen | .05 | .15 |
| 690 | Dave Kingman | .10 | .30 |
| 691 | Dan Schatzeder | .05 | .15 |
| 692 | Wayne Gross | .05 | .15 |
| 693 | Cesar Geronimo | .05 | .15 |
| 694 | Dave Wehrmeister | .05 | .15 |
| 695 | Warren Cromartie | .05 | .15 |
| 696 | Pirates TL BA: Bill Madlock Pitching: Eddie Solo | .25 | .60 |
| 697 | John Montefusco | .05 | .15 |
| 698 | Tony Scott | .05 | .15 |
| 699 | Dick Tidrow | .05 | .15 |
| 700 | George Foster | .10 | .30 |
| 701 | George Foster SA | .05 | .15 |
| 702 | Steve Renko | .05 | .15 |
| 703 | Brewers TL BA: Cecil Cooper Pitching: Pete Vucko | .25 | .60 |
| 704 | Mickey Rivers | .05 | .15 |
| 705 | Mickey Rivers SA | .05 | .15 |
| 706 | Barry Foote | .05 | .15 |
| 707 | Mark Bomback | .05 | .15 |
| 708 | Gene Richards | .05 | .15 |
| 709 | Don Money | .05 | .15 |
| 710 | Jerry Reuss | .05 | .15 |
| 711 | Edler/Henderson/Walton RC | .30 | .75 |
| 712 | Dennis Martinez | .10 | .30 |
| 713 | Del Unser | .05 | .15 |
| 714 | Jerry Koosman | .10 | .30 |
| 715 | Willie Stargell | .25 | .60 |
| 716 | Willie Stargell SA | .10 | .30 |
| 717 | Rick Miller | .05 | .15 |
| 718 | Charlie Hough | .10 | .30 |
| 719 | Jerry Narron | .05 | .15 |
| 720 | Greg Luzinski | .10 | .30 |
| 721 | Greg Luzinski SA | .05 | .15 |
| 722 | Jerry Martin | .05 | .15 |
| 723 | Junior Kennedy | .05 | .15 |
| 724 | Dave Rosello | .05 | .15 |
| 725 | Amos Otis | .10 | .30 |
| 726 | Amos Otis SA | .05 | .15 |
| 727 | Sixto Lezcano | .05 | .15 |
| 728 | Aurelio Lopez | .05 | .15 |
| 729 | Jim Spencer | .05 | .15 |
| 730 | Gary Carter | .10 | .30 |
| 731 | Armstrong/Gwosdz/Kuhaulua RC | .05 | .15 |
| 732 | Mike Lum | .05 | .15 |
| 733 | Larry McWilliams | .05 | .15 |
| 734 | Mike Ivie | .05 | .15 |
| 735 | Rudy May | .05 | .15 |
| 736 | Jerry Turner | .05 | .15 |
| 737 | Reggie Cleveland | .05 | .15 |
| 738 | Dave Engle | .05 | .15 |
| 739 | Joey McLaughlin | .05 | .15 |
| 740 | Dave Lopes | .10 | .30 |
| 741 | Dave Lopes SA | .05 | .15 |
| 742 | Dick Drago | .05 | .15 |
| 743 | John Stearns | .05 | .15 |
| 744 | Mike Witt | .30 | .75 |
| 745 | Bake McBride | .10 | .30 |
| 746 | Andre Thornton | .05 | .15 |
| 747 | John Lowenstein | .05 | .15 |
| 748 | Marc Hill | .05 | .15 |
| 749 | Bob Shirley | .05 | .15 |
| 750 | Jim Rice | .10 | .30 |
| 751 | Rick Honeycutt | .05 | .15 |
| 752 | Lee Lacy | .05 | .15 |
| 753 | Tom Brookens | .05 | .15 |
| 754 | Joe Morgan | .10 | .30 |
| 755 | Joe Morgan SA | .05 | .15 |
| 756 | Reds TL/Griffey/Seaver | .10 | .30 |
| 757 | Tom Underwood | .05 | .15 |
| 758 | Claudell Washington | .05 | .15 |
| 759 | Paul Splittorff | .05 | .15 |
| 760 | Bill Buckner | .10 | .30 |
| 761 | Dave Smith | .05 | .15 |
| 762 | Mike Phillips | .05 | .15 |
| 763 | Tom Hume | .05 | .15 |
| 764 | Steve Swisher | .05 | .15 |
| 765 | Gorman Thomas | .10 | .30 |
| 766 | Faedo/Hrbek/Laudner RC | .60 | 1.50 |
| 767 | Roy Smalley | .05 | .15 |
| 768 | Jerry Garvin | .05 | .15 |
| 769 | Richie Zisk | .05 | .15 |
| 770 | Rich Gossage | .10 | .30 |
| 771 | Rich Gossage SA | .05 | .15 |
| 772 | Bert Campaneris | .10 | .30 |
| 773 | John Denny | .05 | .15 |
| 774 | Jay Johnstone | .05 | .15 |
| 775 | Bob Forsch | .05 | .15 |
| 776 | Mark Belanger | .05 | .15 |
| 777 | Tom Griffin | .05 | .15 |
| 778 | Kevin Hickey RC | .08 | .25 |
| 779 | Grant Jackson | .05 | .15 |
| 780 | Pete Rose | 1.50 | 4.00 |
| 781 | Pete Rose SA | .50 | 1.25 |
| 782 | Frank Taveras | .05 | .15 |
| 783 | Greg Harris RC | .08 | .25 |
| 784 | Milt Wilcox | .05 | .15 |
| 785 | Dan Driessen | .05 | .15 |
| 786 | Red Sox TL BA: Carney Lansford Pitching: Mike To... | .25 | .60 |
| 787 | Fred Stanley | .05 | .15 |
| 788 | Woodie Fryman | .05 | .15 |
| 789 | Checklist 661-792 | .25 | .60 |
| 790 | Larry Gura | .05 | .15 |
| 791 | Bobby Brown | .05 | .15 |
| 792 | Frank Tanana | .10 | .30 |

## 1983 Topps

|  |  | | |
|---|---|---|---|
| | COMPLETE SET (792) | 40.00 | 80.00 |
| 1 | Tony Armas RB | .10 | .30 |
| 2 | Rickey Henderson RB | .50 | 1.25 |
| 3 | Greg Minton RB | .05 | .15 |
| 4 | Lance Parrish RB | .05 | .15 |
| 5 | Manny Trillo RB | .05 | .15 |
| 6 | John Wathan RB | .05 | .15 |
| 7 | Gene Richards | .05 | .15 |
| 8 | Steve Balboni | .05 | .15 |
| 9 | Joey McLaughlin | .05 | .15 |
| 10 | Gorman Thomas | .10 | .30 |
| 11 | Billy Gardner MG | .05 | .15 |
| 12 | Paul Mirabella | .05 | .15 |
| 13 | Larry Herndon | .05 | .15 |
| 14 | Frank LaCorte | .05 | .15 |
| 15 | Ron Cey | .10 | .30 |
| 16 | George Vukovich | .05 | .15 |
| 17 | Kent Tekulve | .05 | .15 |
| 18 | Kent Tekulve SV | .05 | .15 |
| 19 | Oscar Gamble | .05 | .15 |
| 20 | Carlton Fisk | .25 | .60 |
| 21 | Orioles TL/Murray/Palmer | .25 | .60 |
| 22 | Randy Martz | .05 | .15 |
| 23 | Mike Heath | .05 | .15 |
| 24 | Steve Mura | .05 | .15 |
| 25 | Hal McRae | .10 | .30 |
| 26 | Jerry Royster | .05 | .15 |
| 27 | Doug Corbett | .05 | .15 |
| 28 | Bruce Bochte | .05 | .15 |
| 29 | Randy Jones | .05 | .15 |
| 30 | Jim Rice | .10 | .30 |
| 31 | Bill Gullickson | .05 | .15 |
| 32 | Dave Bergman | .05 | .15 |
| 33 | Jack O'Connor | .05 | .15 |
| 34 | Paul Householder | .05 | .15 |
| 35 | Rollie Fingers | .10 | .30 |
| 36 | Rollie Fingers SV | .05 | .15 |
| 37 | Darrell Johnson MG | .05 | .15 |
| 38 | Tim Flannery | .05 | .15 |
| 39 | Terry Puhl | .05 | .15 |
| 40 | Fernando Valenzuela | .10 | .30 |
| 41 | Jerry Turner | .05 | .15 |
| 42 | Dale Murray | .05 | .15 |
| 43 | Bob Demier | .05 | .15 |
| 44 | Don Robinson | .05 | .15 |
| 45 | John Mayberry | .05 | .15 |
| 46 | Richard Dotson | .05 | .15 |
| 47 | Dave McKay | .05 | .15 |
| 48 | Lary Sorensen | .05 | .15 |
| 49 | Willie McGee RC | 1.00 | 2.50 |
| 50 | Bob Homer UER | .10 | .30 |
| 51 | Cubs TL/F.Jenkins | .05 | .15 |
| 52 | Onix Concepcion | .05 | .15 |
| 53 | Mike Witt | .05 | .15 |
| 54 | Jim Maler | .05 | .15 |
| 55 | Mookie Wilson | .10 | .30 |
| 56 | Chuck Rainey | .05 | .15 |
| 57 | Tim Blackwell | .05 | .15 |
| 58 | Al Holland | .05 | .15 |
| 59 | Benny Ayala | .05 | .15 |
| 60 | Johnny Bench | .50 | 1.25 |
| 61 | Johnny Bench SV | .25 | .60 |
| 62 | Bob McClure | .05 | .15 |
| 63 | Rick Monday | .10 | .30 |
| 64 | Bill Stein | .05 | .15 |
| 65 | Jack Morris | .10 | .30 |
| 66 | Bob Lillis MG | .05 | .15 |
| 67 | Sal Butera | .05 | .15 |
| 68 | Eric Show RC | .30 | .75 |
| 69 | Lee Lacy | .05 | .15 |
| 70 | Steve Carlton | .25 | .60 |
| 71 | Steve Carlton SV | .10 | .30 |
| 72 | Tom Paciorek | .05 | .15 |
| 73 | Allen Ripley | .05 | .15 |
| 74 | Julio Gonzalez | .05 | .15 |
| 75 | Amos Otis | .10 | .30 |
| 76 | Rick Mahler | .05 | .15 |
| 77 | Hosken Powell | .05 | .15 |
| 78 | Bill Caudill | .05 | .15 |
| 79 | Mick Kelleher | .05 | .15 |
| 80 | George Foster | .10 | .30 |
| 81 | J.Mumphrey/D.Righetti TL | .10 | .30 |
| 82 | Bruce Hurst | .05 | .15 |
| 83 | Ryne Sandberg RC | 8.00 | 20.00 |
| 84 | Milt May | .05 | .15 |
| 85 | Ken Singleton | .10 | .30 |
| 86 | Tom Hume | .05 | .15 |
| 87 | Joe Rudi | .10 | .30 |
| 88 | Jim Gantner | .05 | .15 |
| 89 | Leon Roberts | .05 | .15 |
| 90 | Jerry Reuss | .05 | .15 |
| 91 | Larry Milbourne | .05 | .15 |
| 92 | Mike LaCoss | .05 | .15 |
| 93 | John Castino | .05 | .15 |
| 94 | Dave Edwards | .05 | .15 |
| 95 | Alan Trammell | .10 | .30 |
| 96 | Dick Howser MG | .05 | .15 |
| 97 | Ross Baumgarten | .05 | .15 |
| 98 | Vance Law | .05 | .15 |
| 99 | Dickie Noles | .05 | .15 |
| 100 | Pete Rose | 1.50 | 4.00 |
| 101 | Pete Rose SV | .50 | 1.25 |
| 102 | Dave Beard | .05 | .15 |
| 103 | Darrell Porter | .05 | .15 |
| 104 | Bob Walk | .05 | .15 |
| 105 | Don Baylor | .10 | .30 |
| 106 | Gene Nelson | .05 | .15 |
| 107 | Mike Jorgensen | .05 | .15 |
| 108 | Glenn Hoffman | .05 | .15 |
| 109 | Luis Leal | .05 | .15 |
| 110 | Ken Griffey | .10 | .30 |
| 111 | Montreal Expos TL BA: Al Oliver ERA: Steve Roger... | .10 | .30 |
| 112 | Bob Shirley | .05 | .15 |
| 113 | Ron Roenicke | .05 | .15 |
| 114 | Jim Slaton | .05 | .15 |
| 115 | Chili Davis | .10 | .30 |
| 116 | Dave Schmidt | .05 | .15 |
| 117 | Alan Knicely | .05 | .15 |
| 118 | Chris Welsh | .05 | .15 |
| 119 | Tom Brookens | .05 | .15 |
| 120 | Len Barker | .05 | .15 |
| 121 | Mickey Hatcher | .05 | .15 |
| 122 | Jimmy Smith | .05 | .15 |
| 123 | George Frazier | .05 | .15 |
| 124 | Marc Hill | .05 | .15 |
| 125 | Leon Durham | .05 | .15 |
| 126 | Joe Torre MG | .10 | .30 |
| 127 | Preston Hanna | .05 | .15 |
| 128 | Mike Ramsey | .05 | .15 |
| 129 | Checklist: 1-132 | .10 | .30 |
| 130 | Dave Stieb | .10 | .30 |
| 131 | Ed Ott | .05 | .15 |
| 132 | Todd Cruz | .05 | .15 |

|  |  | | |
|---|---|---|---|
| ☐ 133 | Jim Barr | .05 | .15 |
| ☐ 134 | Hubie Brooks | .05 | .15 |
| ☐ 135 | Dwight Evans | .25 | .60 |
| ☐ 136 | Willie Aikens | .05 | .15 |
| ☐ 137 | Woodie Fryman | .05 | .15 |
| ☐ 138 | Rick Dempsey | .05 | .15 |
| ☐ 139 | Bruce Berenyi | .05 | .15 |
| ☐ 140 | Willie Randolph | .10 | .30 |
| ☐ 141 | Indians TL | | |
| | BA: Toby Harrah | | |
| | ERA: Rick Sutcliffe | | |
| ☐ 142 | Mike Caldwell | .10 | .30 |
| ☐ 143 | Joe Pettini | .05 | .15 |
| ☐ 144 | Mark Wagner | .05 | .15 |
| ☐ 145 | Don Sutton | .10 | .30 |
| ☐ 146 | Don Sutton SV | .05 | .15 |
| ☐ 147 | Rick Leach | .05 | .15 |
| ☐ 148 | Dave Roberts | .05 | .15 |
| ☐ 149 | Johnny Ray | .05 | .15 |
| ☐ 150 | Bruce Sutter | .25 | .60 |
| ☐ 151 | Bruce Sutter SV | .10 | .30 |
| ☐ 152 | Jay Johnstone | .05 | .15 |
| ☐ 153 | Jerry Koosman | .10 | .30 |
| ☐ 154 | Johnnie LeMaster | .05 | .15 |
| ☐ 155 | Dan Quisenberry | .25 | .60 |
| ☐ 156 | Billy Martin MG | .25 | .60 |
| ☐ 157 | Steve Bedrosian | .05 | .15 |
| ☐ 158 | Rob Wilfong | .05 | .15 |
| ☐ 159 | Mike Stanton | .05 | .15 |
| ☐ 160 | Dave Kingman | .10 | .30 |
| ☐ 161 | Dave Kingman SV | .05 | .15 |
| ☐ 162 | Mark Clear | .05 | .15 |
| ☐ 163 | Cal Ripken | 4.00 | 10.00 |
| ☐ 164 | David Palmer | .05 | .15 |
| ☐ 165 | Dan Driessen | .05 | .15 |
| ☐ 166 | John Pacella | .05 | .15 |
| ☐ 167 | Mark Brouhard | .05 | .15 |
| ☐ 168 | Juan Eichelberger | .05 | .15 |
| ☐ 169 | Doug Flynn | .05 | .15 |
| ☐ 170 | Steve Howe | .05 | .15 |
| ☐ 171 | Giants TL/Joe Morgan | .10 | .30 |
| ☐ 172 | Vern Ruhle | .05 | .15 |
| ☐ 173 | Jim Morrison | .05 | .15 |
| ☐ 174 | Jerry Ujdur | .05 | .15 |
| ☐ 175 | Bo Diaz | .05 | .15 |
| ☐ 176 | Dave Righetti | .10 | .30 |
| ☐ 177 | Harold Baines | .10 | .30 |
| ☐ 178 | Luis Tiant | .10 | .30 |
| ☐ 179 | Luis Tiant SV | .05 | .15 |
| ☐ 180 | Rickey Henderson | 1.00 | 2.50 |
| ☐ 181 | Terry Felton | .05 | .15 |
| ☐ 182 | Mike Fischlin | .05 | .15 |
| ☐ 183 | Ed VandeBerg | .05 | .15 |
| ☐ 184 | Bob Clark | .05 | .15 |
| ☐ 185 | Tim Lollar | .05 | .15 |
| ☐ 186 | Whitey Herzog MG | .10 | .30 |
| ☐ 187 | Terry Leach | .05 | .15 |
| ☐ 188 | Rick Miller | .05 | .15 |
| ☐ 189 | Dan Schatzeder | .05 | .15 |
| ☐ 190 | Cecil Cooper | .10 | .30 |
| ☐ 191 | Joe Price | .05 | .15 |
| ☐ 192 | Floyd Rayford | .05 | .15 |
| ☐ 193 | Harry Spilman | .05 | .15 |
| ☐ 194 | Cesar Geronimo | .05 | .15 |
| ☐ 195 | Bob Stoddard | .05 | .15 |
| ☐ 196 | Bill Fahey | .05 | .15 |
| ☐ 197 | Jim Eisenreich RC | .30 | .75 |
| ☐ 198 | Kiko Garcia | .05 | .15 |
| ☐ 199 | Marty Bystrom | .05 | .15 |
| ☐ 200 | Rod Carew | .25 | .60 |
| ☐ 201 | Rod Carew SV | .10 | .30 |
| ☐ 202 | Blue Jays TL | | |
| | BA: Damaso Garcia | | |
| | ERA: Dave Stieb | | |
| ☐ 203 | Mike Morgan | .10 | .30 |
| ☐ 204 | Junior Kennedy | .05 | .15 |
| ☐ 205 | Dave Parker | .10 | .30 |
| ☐ 206 | Ken Oberkfell | .05 | .15 |
| ☐ 207 | Rick Camp | .05 | .15 |
| ☐ 208 | Dan Meyer | .05 | .15 |
| ☐ 209 | Mike Moore RC | .30 | .75 |
| ☐ 210 | Jack Clark | .10 | .30 |
| ☐ 211 | John Denny | .05 | .15 |
| ☐ 212 | John Stearns | .05 | .15 |
| ☐ 213 | Tom Burgmeier | .05 | .15 |
| ☐ 214 | Jerry White | .05 | .15 |
| ☐ 215 | Mario Soto | .10 | .30 |
| ☐ 216 | Tony LaRussa MG | .10 | .30 |
| ☐ 217 | Tim Stoddard | .05 | .15 |
| ☐ 218 | Roy Howell | .05 | .15 |
| ☐ 219 | Mike Armstrong | .05 | .15 |
| ☐ 220 | Dusty Baker | .10 | .30 |
| ☐ 221 | Joe Niekro | .05 | .15 |
| ☐ 222 | Damaso Garcia | .05 | .15 |
| ☐ 223 | John Montefusco | .05 | .15 |
| ☐ 224 | Mickey Rivers | .05 | .15 |
| ☐ 225 | Enos Cabell | .05 | .15 |
| ☐ 226 | Enrique Romo | .05 | .15 |
| ☐ 227 | Chris Bando | .05 | .15 |
| ☐ 228 | Joaquin Andujar | .10 | .30 |
| ☐ 229 | Phillies TL/S.Carlton | .05 | .15 |
| ☐ 230 | Fergie Jenkins | .10 | .30 |
| ☐ 231 | Fergie Jenkins SV | .05 | .15 |
| ☐ 232 | Tom Brunansky | .10 | .30 |
| ☐ 233 | Wayne Gross | .05 | .15 |
| ☐ 234 | Larry Andersen | .05 | .15 |
| ☐ 235 | Claudell Washington | .05 | .15 |
| ☐ 236 | Steve Renko | .05 | .15 |
| ☐ 237 | Dan Norman | .05 | .15 |
| ☐ 238 | Bud Black RC | .30 | .75 |
| ☐ 239 | Dave Stapleton | .05 | .15 |
| ☐ 240 | Rich Gossage | .10 | .30 |
| ☐ 241 | Rich Gossage SV | .05 | .15 |
| ☐ 242 | Joe Nolan | .05 | .15 |
| ☐ 243 | Duane Walker | .05 | .15 |
| ☐ 244 | Dwight Bernard | .05 | .15 |
| ☐ 245 | Steve Sax | .10 | .30 |
| ☐ 246 | George Bamberger MG | .05 | .15 |
| ☐ 247 | Dave Smith | .05 | .15 |
| ☐ 248 | Bake McBride | .10 | .30 |
| ☐ 249 | Checklist: 133-264 | .10 | .30 |
| ☐ 250 | Bill Buckner | .10 | .30 |
| ☐ 251 | Alan Wiggins | .05 | .15 |
| ☐ 252 | Luis Aguayo | .05 | .15 |
| ☐ 253 | Larry McWilliams | .05 | .15 |
| ☐ 254 | Rick Cerone | .05 | .15 |
| ☐ 255 | Gene Garber | .05 | .15 |
| ☐ 256 | Gene Garber SV | .05 | .15 |
| ☐ 257 | Jesse Barfield | .10 | .30 |
| ☐ 258 | Manny Castillo | .05 | .15 |
| ☐ 259 | Jeff Jones | .05 | .15 |
| ☐ 260 | Steve Kemp | .05 | .15 |
| ☐ 261 | Tigers TL | | |
| | BA: Larry Herndon | | |
| | ERA: Dan Petry | | |
| | (Che | | |
| ☐ 262 | Ron Jackson | .10 | .30 |
| ☐ 263 | Renie Martin | .05 | .15 |
| ☐ 264 | Jamie Quirk | .05 | .15 |
| ☐ 265 | Joel Youngblood | .05 | .15 |
| ☐ 266 | Paul Boris | .05 | .15 |
| ☐ 267 | Terry Francona | .10 | .30 |
| ☐ 268 | Storm Davis RC | .30 | .75 |
| ☐ 269 | Ron Oester | .05 | .15 |
| ☐ 270 | Dennis Eckersley | .25 | .60 |
| ☐ 271 | Ed Romero | .05 | .15 |
| ☐ 272 | Frank Tanana | .10 | .30 |
| ☐ 273 | Mark Belanger | .05 | .15 |
| ☐ 274 | Terry Kennedy | .05 | .15 |
| ☐ 275 | Ray Knight | .10 | .30 |
| ☐ 276 | Gene Mauch MG | .05 | .15 |
| ☐ 277 | Rance Mulliniks | .05 | .15 |
| ☐ 278 | Kevin Hickey | .05 | .15 |
| ☐ 279 | Greg Gross | .05 | .15 |
| ☐ 280 | Bert Blyleven | .10 | .30 |
| ☐ 281 | Andre Robertson | .05 | .15 |
| ☐ 282 | R.Smith w/Sandberg | .50 | 1.25 |
| ☐ 283 | Reggie Smith SV | .05 | .15 |
| ☐ 284 | Jeff Lahti | .05 | .15 |
| ☐ 285 | Lance Parrish | .10 | .30 |
| ☐ 286 | Rick Langford | .05 | .15 |
| ☐ 287 | Bobby Brown | .05 | .15 |
| ☐ 288 | Joe Cowley | .05 | .15 |
| ☐ 289 | Jerry Dybzinski | .05 | .15 |
| ☐ 290 | Jeff Reardon | .10 | .30 |
| ☐ 291 | Bill Madlock | .10 | .30 |
| | John Candelaria TL | | |
| ☐ 292 | Craig Swan | .05 | .15 |
| ☐ 293 | Glenn Gulliver | .05 | .15 |
| ☐ 294 | Dave Engle | .05 | .15 |
| ☐ 295 | Jerry Remy | .05 | .15 |
| ☐ 296 | Greg Harris | .05 | .15 |
| ☐ 297 | Ned Yost | .05 | .15 |
| ☐ 298 | Floyd Chiffer | .05 | .15 |
| ☐ 299 | George Wright RC | .30 | .75 |
| ☐ 300 | Mike Schmidt | 1.25 | 3.00 |
| ☐ 301 | Mike Schmidt SV | .50 | 1.25 |
| ☐ 302 | Ernie Whitt | .05 | .15 |
| ☐ 303 | Miguel Dilone | .05 | .15 |
| ☐ 304 | Dave Rucker | .05 | .15 |
| ☐ 305 | Larry Bowa | .10 | .30 |
| ☐ 306 | Tom Lasorda MG | .25 | .60 |
| ☐ 307 | Lou Piniella | .10 | .30 |
| ☐ 308 | Jesus Vega | .05 | .15 |
| ☐ 309 | Jeff Leonard | .05 | .15 |
| ☐ 310 | Greg Luzinski | .10 | .30 |
| ☐ 311 | Glenn Brummer | .05 | .15 |
| ☐ 312 | Brian Kingman | .05 | .15 |
| ☐ 313 | Gary Gray | .05 | .15 |
| ☐ 314 | Ken Dayley | .05 | .15 |
| ☐ 315 | Rick Burleson | .05 | .15 |
| ☐ 316 | Paul Splittorff | .05 | .15 |
| ☐ 317 | Gary Rajsich | .05 | .15 |
| ☐ 318 | John Tudor | .05 | .15 |
| ☐ 319 | Lenn Sakata | .05 | .15 |
| ☐ 320 | Steve Rogers | .10 | .30 |
| ☐ 321 | Brewers TL/Robin Yount | .50 | 1.25 |
| ☐ 322 | Dave Van Gorder | .05 | .15 |
| ☐ 323 | Luis DeLeon | .05 | .15 |
| ☐ 324 | Mike Marshall | .05 | .15 |
| ☐ 325 | Von Hayes | .05 | .15 |
| ☐ 326 | Garth Iorg | .05 | .15 |
| ☐ 327 | Bobby Castillo | .05 | .15 |
| ☐ 328 | Craig Reynolds | .05 | .15 |
| ☐ 329 | Randy Niemann | .05 | .15 |
| ☐ 330 | Buddy Bell | .10 | .30 |
| ☐ 331 | Mike Krukow | .05 | .15 |
| ☐ 332 | Glenn Wilson | .30 | .75 |
| ☐ 333 | Dave LaRoche | .05 | .15 |
| ☐ 334 | Dave LaRoche SV | .05 | .15 |
| ☐ 335 | Steve Henderson | .05 | .15 |
| ☐ 336 | Rene Lachemann MG | .05 | .15 |
| ☐ 337 | Tito Landrum | .05 | .15 |
| ☐ 338 | Bob Owchinko | .05 | .15 |
| ☐ 339 | Terry Harper | .05 | .15 |
| ☐ 340 | Larry Gura | .05 | .15 |
| ☐ 341 | Doug DeCinces | .10 | .30 |
| ☐ 342 | Atlee Hammaker | .05 | .15 |
| ☐ 343 | Bob Bailor | .05 | .15 |
| ☐ 344 | Roger LaFrancois | .05 | .15 |
| ☐ 345 | Jim Clancy | .05 | .15 |
| ☐ 346 | Joe Pittman | .05 | .15 |
| ☐ 347 | Sammy Stewart | .05 | .15 |
| ☐ 348 | Alan Bannister | .05 | .15 |
| ☐ 349 | Checklist: 265-396 | .10 | .30 |
| ☐ 350 | Robin Yount | .75 | 2.00 |
| ☐ 351 | Reds TL | | |
| | BA: Cesar Cedeno | | |
| | ERA: Mario Soto | | |
| | (Check | | |
| ☐ 352 | Mike Scioscia | .10 | .30 |
| ☐ 353 | Steve Comer | .05 | .15 |
| ☐ 354 | Randy Johnson | .05 | .15 |
| ☐ 355 | Jim Bibby | .05 | .15 |
| ☐ 356 | Gary Woods | .05 | .15 |
| ☐ 357 | Len Matuszek | .05 | .15 |
| ☐ 358 | Jerry Garvin | .05 | .15 |
| ☐ 359 | Dave Collins | .05 | .15 |
| ☐ 360 | Nolan Ryan | 2.50 | 6.00 |
| ☐ 361 | Nolan Ryan SV | 1.25 | 3.00 |
| ☐ 362 | Bill Almon | .05 | .15 |
| ☐ 363 | John Stuper | .05 | .15 |
| ☐ 364 | Brett Butler | .10 | .30 |
| ☐ 365 | Dave Lopes | .10 | .30 |
| ☐ 366 | Dick Williams MG | .05 | .15 |
| ☐ 367 | Bud Anderson | .05 | .15 |
| ☐ 368 | Richie Zisk | .05 | .15 |
| ☐ 369 | Jesse Orosco | .05 | .15 |
| ☐ 370 | Gary Carter | .10 | .30 |
| ☐ 371 | Mike Richardt | .05 | .15 |
| ☐ 372 | Terry Crowley | .05 | .15 |
| ☐ 373 | Kevin Saucier | .05 | .15 |
| ☐ 374 | Wayne Krenchicki | .05 | .15 |
| ☐ 375 | Pete Vuckovich | .05 | .15 |
| ☐ 376 | Ken Landreaux | .05 | .15 |
| ☐ 377 | Lee May | .05 | .15 |
| ☐ 378 | Lee May SV | .05 | .15 |
| ☐ 379 | Guy Sularz | .05 | .15 |
| ☐ 380 | Ron Davis | .05 | .15 |
| ☐ 381 | Red Sox TL | | |
| | BA: Jim Rice | | |
| | ERA: Bob Stanley | | |

|  |  | | |
|---|---|---|---|
| | (Check | | |
| 382 | Bob Knepper | .10 | .30 |
| 383 | Ozzie Virgil | .05 | .15 |
| 384 | Dave Dravecky RC | .60 | 1.50 |
| 385 | Mike Easler | .05 | .15 |
| 386 | Rod Carew AS | .10 | .30 |
| 387 | Bob Grich AS | .05 | .15 |
| 388 | George Brett AS | .60 | 1.50 |
| 389 | Robin Yount AS | .50 | 1.25 |
| 390 | Reggie Jackson AS | .10 | .30 |
| 391 | Rickey Henderson AS | .50 | 1.25 |
| 392 | Fred Lynn AS | .05 | .15 |
| 393 | Carlton Fisk AS | .05 | .15 |
| 394 | Pete Vuckovich AS | .05 | .15 |
| 395 | Larry Gura AS | .05 | .15 |
| 396 | Dan Quisenberry AS | .05 | .15 |
| 397 | Pete Rose AS | .25 | .60 |
| 398 | Manny Trillo AS | .05 | .15 |
| 399 | Mike Schmidt AS | .50 | 1.25 |
| 400 | Dave Concepcion AS | .05 | .15 |
| 401 | Dale Murphy AS | .10 | .30 |
| 402 | Andre Dawson AS | .05 | .15 |
| 403 | Tim Raines AS | .05 | .15 |
| 404 | Gary Carter AS | .05 | .15 |
| 405 | Steve Rogers AS | .05 | .15 |
| 406 | Steve Carlton AS | .10 | .30 |
| 407 | Bruce Sutter AS | .10 | .30 |
| 408 | Rudy May | .05 | .15 |
| 409 | Marvis Foley | .05 | .15 |
| 410 | Phil Niekro | .10 | .30 |
| 411 | Phil Niekro SV | .05 | .15 |
| 412 | Rangers TL BA: Buddy Bell ERA: Charlie Hough (C | .10 | .30 |
| 413 | Matt Keough | .05 | .15 |
| 414 | Julio Cruz | .05 | .15 |
| 415 | Bob Forsch | .05 | .15 |
| 416 | Joe Ferguson | .05 | .15 |
| 417 | Tom Hausman | .05 | .15 |
| 418 | Greg Pryor | .05 | .15 |
| 419 | Steve Crawford | .05 | .15 |
| 420 | Al Oliver | .10 | .30 |
| 421 | Al Oliver SV | .05 | .15 |
| 422 | George Cappuzzello | .05 | .15 |
| 423 | Tom Lawless | .05 | .15 |
| 424 | Jerry Augustine | .05 | .15 |
| 425 | Pedro Guerrero | .10 | .30 |
| 426 | Earl Weaver MG | .10 | .30 |
| 427 | Roy Lee Jackson | .05 | .15 |
| 428 | Champ Summers | .05 | .15 |
| 429 | Eddie Whitson | .05 | .15 |
| 430 | Kirk Gibson | .10 | .30 |
| 431 | Gary Gaetti RC | .60 | 1.50 |
| 432 | Porfirio Altamirano | .05 | .15 |
| 433 | Dale Berra | .05 | .15 |
| 434 | Dennis Lamp | .05 | .15 |
| 435 | Tony Armas | .10 | .30 |
| 436 | Bill Campbell | .05 | .15 |
| 437 | Rick Sweet | .05 | .15 |
| 438 | Dave LaPoint | .05 | .15 |
| 439 | Rafael Ramirez | .05 | .15 |
| 440 | Ron Guidry | .10 | .30 |
| 441 | Astros TL BA: Ray Knight ERA: Joe Niekro (Check | .10 | .30 |
| 442 | Brian Downing | .10 | .30 |
| 443 | Don Hood | .05 | .15 |
| 444 | Wally Backman | .05 | .15 |
| 445 | Mike Flanagan | .05 | .15 |
| 446 | Reid Nichols | .05 | .15 |
| 447 | Bryn Smith | .05 | .15 |
| 448 | Darrell Evans | .05 | .15 |
| 449 | Eddie Milner | .05 | .15 |
| 450 | Ted Simmons | .10 | .30 |
| 451 | Ted Simmons SV | .05 | .15 |
| 452 | Lloyd Moseby | .05 | .15 |
| 453 | Lamar Johnson | .05 | .15 |
| 454 | Bob Welch | .10 | .30 |
| 455 | Sixto Lezcano | .05 | .15 |
| 456 | Lee Elia MG | .05 | .15 |
| 457 | Milt Wilcox | .05 | .15 |
| 458 | Ron Washington | .05 | .15 |
| 459 | Ed Farmer | .05 | .15 |
| 460 | Roy Smalley | .05 | .15 |
| 461 | Steve Trout | .05 | .15 |
| 462 | Steve Nicosia | .05 | .15 |
| 483 | Gaylord Perry | .10 | .30 |
| 464 | Gaylord Perry SV | .05 | .15 |
| 465 | Lonnie Smith | .05 | .15 |
| 466 | Tom Underwood | .05 | .15 |
| 467 | Rufino Linares | .05 | .15 |
| 468 | Dave Goltz | .05 | .15 |
| 469 | Ron Gardenhire | .05 | .15 |
| 470 | Greg Minton | .05 | .15 |
| 471 | Kansas City Royals TL BA: Willie Wilson ERA: Vid | .10 | .30 |
| 472 | Gary Allenson | .05 | .15 |
| 473 | John Lowenstein | .05 | .15 |
| 474 | Ray Burris | .05 | .15 |
| 475 | Cesar Cedeno | .10 | .30 |
| 476 | Rob Picciolo | .05 | .15 |
| 477 | Tom Niedenfuer | .05 | .15 |
| 478 | Phil Garner | .05 | .15 |
| 479 | Charlie Hough | .10 | .30 |
| 480 | Toby Harrah | .05 | .15 |
| 481 | Scot Thompson | .05 | .15 |
| 482 | Tony Gwynn RC | 8.00 | 20.00 |
| 483 | Lynn Jones | .05 | .15 |
| 484 | Dick Ruthven | .05 | .15 |
| 485 | Omar Moreno | .05 | .15 |
| 486 | Clyde King MG | .05 | .15 |
| 487 | Jerry Hairston | .05 | .15 |
| 488 | Alfredo Griffin | .05 | .15 |
| 489 | Tom Herr | .05 | .15 |
| 490 | Jim Palmer | .10 | .30 |
| 491 | Jim Palmer SV | .05 | .15 |
| 492 | Paul Serna | .05 | .15 |
| 493 | Steve McCatty | .05 | .15 |
| 494 | Bob Brenly | .05 | .15 |
| 495 | Warren Cromartie | .05 | .15 |
| 496 | Tom Veryzer | .05 | .15 |
| 497 | Rick Sutcliffe | .10 | .30 |
| 498 | Wade Boggs RC | 6.00 | 15.00 |
| 499 | Jeff Little | .05 | .15 |
| 500 | Reggie Jackson | .25 | .60 |
| 501 | Reggie Jackson SV | .10 | .30 |
| 502 | Braves TL:Murphy/Niekro | .25 | .60 |
| 503 | Moose Haas | .05 | .15 |
| 504 | Don Werner | .05 | .15 |
| 505 | Garry Templeton | .10 | .30 |
| 506 | Jim Gott RC | .30 | .75 |
| 507 | Tony Scott | .05 | .15 |
| 508 | Tom Filer | .05 | .15 |
| 509 | Lou Whitaker | .10 | .30 |
| 510 | Tug McGraw | .10 | .30 |
| 511 | Tug McGraw SV | .05 | .15 |
| 512 | Doyle Alexander | .05 | .15 |
| 513 | Fred Stanley | .05 | .15 |
| 514 | Rudy Law | .05 | .15 |
| 515 | Gene Tenace | .10 | .30 |
| 516 | Bill Virdon MG | .05 | .15 |
| 517 | Gary Ward | .05 | .15 |
| 518 | Bill Laskey | .05 | .15 |
| 519 | Terry Bulling | .05 | .15 |
| 520 | Fred Lynn | .10 | .30 |
| 521 | Bruce Benedict | .05 | .15 |
| 522 | Pat Zachry | .05 | .15 |
| 523 | Carney Lansford | .10 | .30 |
| 524 | Tom Brennan | .05 | .15 |
| 525 | Frank White | .10 | .30 |
| 526 | Checklist: 397-528 | .10 | .30 |
| 527 | Larry Biittner | .05 | .15 |
| 528 | Jamie Easterly | .05 | .15 |
| 529 | Tim Laudner | .05 | .15 |
| 530 | Eddie Murray | .50 | 1.25 |
| 531 | A's TL/Rickey Henderson | .50 | 1.25 |
| 532 | Dave Stewart | .10 | .30 |
| 533 | Luis Salazar | .05 | .15 |
| 534 | John Butcher | .05 | .15 |
| 535 | Manny Trillo | .05 | .15 |
| 536 | John Wockenfuss | .05 | .15 |
| 537 | Rod Scurry | .05 | .15 |
| 538 | Danny Heep | .05 | .15 |
| 539 | Roger Erickson | .05 | .15 |
| 540 | Ozzie Smith | .75 | 2.00 |
| 541 | Britt Burns | .05 | .15 |
| 542 | Jody Davis | .05 | .15 |
| 543 | Alan Fowlkes | .05 | .15 |
| 544 | Larry Whisenton | .05 | .15 |
| 545 | Floyd Bannister | .05 | .15 |
| 546 | Dave Garcia MG | .05 | .15 |
| 547 | Geoff Zahn | .05 | .15 |
| 548 | Brian Giles | .05 | .15 |
| 548 | Charlie Puleo | .05 | .15 |
| 550 | Carl Yastrzemski | .75 | 2.00 |
| 551 | Carl Yastrzemski SV | .50 | 1.25 |
| 552 | Tim Wallach | .10 | .30 |
| 553 | Dennis Martinez | .10 | .30 |
| 554 | Mike Vail | .05 | .15 |
| 555 | Steve Yeager | .10 | .30 |
| 556 | Willie Upshaw | .05 | .15 |
| 557 | Rick Honeycutt | .05 | .15 |
| 558 | Dickie Thon | .05 | .15 |
| 559 | Pete Redfern | .05 | .15 |
| 560 | Ron LaFlore | .10 | .30 |
| 561 | Cardinals TL BA: Lonnie Smith ERA: Joaquin Anduj | .10 | .30 |
| 562 | Dave Rozema | .05 | .15 |
| 563 | Juan Bonilla | .05 | .15 |
| 564 | Sid Monge | .05 | .15 |
| 565 | Bucky Dent | .10 | .30 |
| 566 | Manny Sarmiento | .05 | .15 |
| 567 | Joe Simpson | .05 | .15 |
| 568 | Willie Hernandez | .05 | .15 |
| 569 | Jack Perconte | .05 | .15 |
| 570 | Vida Blue | .10 | .30 |
| 571 | Mickey Klutts | .05 | .15 |
| 572 | Bob Watson | .05 | .15 |
| 573 | Andy Hassler | .05 | .15 |
| 574 | Glenn Adams | .05 | .15 |
| 575 | Neil Allen | .05 | .15 |
| 576 | Frank Robinson MG | .25 | .60 |
| 577 | Luis Aponte | .05 | .15 |
| 578 | David Green RC | .30 | .75 |
| 579 | Rich Dauer | .05 | .15 |
| 580 | Tom Seaver | .50 | 1.25 |
| 581 | Tom Seaver SV | .10 | .30 |
| 582 | Marshall Edwards | .05 | .15 |
| 583 | Terry Forster | .10 | .30 |
| 584 | Dave Hostetler | .05 | .15 |
| 585 | Jose Cruz | .10 | .30 |
| 586 | Frank Viola RC | 1.00 | 2.50 |
| 587 | Ivan DeJesus | .05 | .15 |
| 588 | Pat Underwood | .05 | .15 |
| 589 | Alvis Woods | .05 | .15 |
| 590 | Tony Pena | .05 | .15 |
| 591 | White Sox TL BA: Greg Luzinski ERA: LaMarr Hoyt# | .10 | .30 |
| 592 | Shane Rawley | .05 | .15 |
| 593 | Broderick Perkins | .05 | .15 |
| 594 | Eric Rasmussen | .05 | .15 |
| 595 | Tim Raines | .10 | .30 |
| 596 | Randy Johnson | .05 | .15 |
| 597 | Mike Proly | .05 | .15 |
| 598 | Dwayne Murphy | .05 | .15 |
| 599 | Don Aase | .05 | .15 |
| 600 | George Brett | 1.25 | 3.00 |
| 601 | Ed Lynch | .05 | .15 |
| 602 | Rich Gedman | .05 | .15 |
| 603 | Joe Morgan | .10 | .30 |
| 604 | Joe Morgan SV | .05 | .15 |
| 605 | Gary Roenicke | .05 | .15 |
| 606 | Bobby Cox MG | .10 | .30 |
| 607 | Charlie Leibrandt | .05 | .15 |
| 608 | Don Money | .05 | .15 |
| 609 | Danny Darwin | .05 | .15 |
| 610 | Steve Garvey | .10 | .30 |
| 611 | Bert Roberge | .05 | .15 |
| 612 | Steve Swisher | .05 | .15 |
| 613 | Mike Ivie | .05 | .15 |
| 614 | Ed Glynn | .05 | .15 |
| 615 | Garry Maddox | .05 | .15 |
| 616 | Bill Nahorodny | .05 | .15 |
| 617 | Butch Wynegar | .05 | .15 |
| 618 | LaMarr Hoyt | .05 | .15 |
| 619 | Keith Moreland | .05 | .15 |
| 620 | Mike Norris | .05 | .15 |
| 621 | New York Mets TL BA: Mookie Wilson ERA: Craig Sw | .10 | .30 |
| 622 | Dave Edler | .05 | .15 |
| 623 | Luis Sanchez | .05 | .15 |
| 624 | Glenn Hubbard | .05 | .15 |
| 625 | Ken Forsch | .05 | .15 |
| 626 | Jerry Martin | .05 | .15 |
| 627 | Doug Bair | .05 | .15 |
| 628 | Julio Valdez | .05 | .15 |
| 629 | Charlie Lea | .05 | .15 |
| 630 | Paul Molitor | .10 | .30 |

|  |  | | |
|---|---|---|---|
| 631 | Tippy Martinez | .05 | .15 |
| 632 | Alex Trevino | .05 | .15 |
| 633 | Vicente Romo | .05 | .15 |
| 634 | Max Venable | .05 | .15 |
| 635 | Graig Nettles | .10 | .30 |
| 636 | Graig Nettles SV | .05 | .15 |
| 637 | Pat Corrales MG | .05 | .15 |
| 638 | Dan Petry | .05 | .15 |
| 639 | Art Howe | .05 | .15 |
| 640 | Andre Thornton | .05 | .15 |
| 641 | Billy Sample | .05 | .15 |
| 642 | Checklist: 529-660 | .10 | .30 |
| 643 | Bump Wills | .05 | .15 |
| 644 | Joe Lefebvre | .05 | .15 |
| 645 | Bill Madlock | .10 | .30 |
| 646 | Jim Essian | .05 | .15 |
| 647 | Bobby Mitchell | .05 | .15 |
| 648 | Jeff Burroughs | .05 | .15 |
| 649 | Tommy Boggs | .05 | .15 |
| 650 | George Hendrick | .10 | .30 |
| 651 | Angels TL/Rod Carew | .10 | .30 |
| 652 | Butch Hobson | .05 | .15 |
| 653 | Ellis Valentine | .05 | .15 |
| 654 | Bob Ojeda | .05 | .15 |
| 655 | Al Bumbry | .05 | .15 |
| 656 | Dave Frost | .05 | .15 |
| 657 | Mike Gates | .05 | .15 |
| 658 | Frank Pastore | .05 | .15 |
| 659 | Charlie Moore | .05 | .15 |
| 660 | Mike Hargrove | .05 | .15 |
| 661 | Bill Russell | .10 | .30 |
| 662 | Joe Sambito | .05 | .15 |
| 663 | Tom O'Malley | .05 | .15 |
| 664 | Bob Molinaro | .05 | .15 |
| 665 | Jim Sundberg | .10 | .30 |
| 666 | Sparky Anderson MG | .10 | .30 |
| 667 | Dick Davis | .05 | .15 |
| 668 | Larry Christenson | .05 | .15 |
| 669 | Mike Squires | .05 | .15 |
| 670 | Jerry Mumphrey | .05 | .15 |
| 671 | Lenny Faedo | .05 | .15 |
| 672 | Jim Kaat | .10 | .30 |
| 673 | Jim Kaat SV | .05 | .15 |
| 674 | Kurt Bevacqua | .05 | .15 |
| 675 | Jim Beattie | .05 | .15 |
| 676 | Biff Pocoroba | .05 | .15 |
| 677 | Dave Revering | .05 | .15 |
| 678 | Juan Beniquez | .05 | .15 |
| 679 | Mike Scott | .10 | .30 |
| 680 | Andre Dawson | .10 | .30 |
| 681 | Dodgers Leaders BA: Pedro Guerrero ERA: Fernando | .10 | .30 |
| 682 | Bob Stanley | .05 | .15 |
| 683 | Dan Ford | .05 | .15 |
| 684 | Rafael Landestoy | .05 | .15 |
| 685 | Lee Mazzilli | .10 | .30 |
| 686 | Randy Lerch | .05 | .15 |
| 687 | U.L. Washington | .05 | .15 |
| 688 | Jim Wohlford | .05 | .15 |
| 689 | Ron Hassey | .05 | .15 |
| 690 | Kent Hrbek | .10 | .30 |
| 691 | Dave Tobik | .05 | .15 |
| 692 | Denny Walling | .05 | .15 |
| 693 | Sparky Lyle | .10 | .30 |
| 694 | Sparky Lyle SV | .05 | .15 |
| 695 | Ruppert Jones | .05 | .15 |
| 696 | Chuck Tanner MG | .05 | .15 |
| 697 | Barry Foote | .05 | .15 |
| 698 | Tony Bernazard | .05 | .15 |
| 699 | Lee Smith | .25 | .60 |
| 700 | Keith Hernandez | .10 | .30 |
| 701 | Willie Wilson Al Oliver LL | .10 | .30 |
| 702 | Reggie/Thomas/Kingman LL | .10 | .30 |
| 703 | RBI Leaders AL: Hal McRae NL: Dale Murphy NL: R. | .25 | .60 |
| 704 | R.Henderson/T.Raines LL | .50 | 1.25 |
| 705 | L.Hoyt/S.Carlton LL | .10 | .30 |
| 706 | F.Bannister/Carlton LL | .10 | .30 |
| 707 | Rick Sutcliffe Steve Rogers LL | .10 | .30 |
| 708 | Leading Firemen AL: Dan Quisenberry NL: Bruce Su | .10 | .30 |
| 709 | Jimmy Sexton | .05 | .15 |
| 710 | Willie Wilson | .10 | .30 |
| 711 | Mariners TL BA: Bruce Bochte ERA: Jim Beattie ( | .10 | .30 |
| 712 | Bruce Kison | .05 | .15 |
| 713 | Ron Hodges | .05 | .15 |
| 714 | Wayne Nordhagen | .05 | .15 |
| 715 | Tony Perez | .25 | .60 |
| 716 | Tony Perez SV | .10 | .30 |
| 717 | Scott Sanderson | .05 | .15 |
| 718 | Jim Dwyer | .05 | .15 |
| 719 | Rich Gale | .05 | .15 |
| 720 | Dave Concepcion | .10 | .30 |
| 721 | John Martin | .05 | .15 |
| 722 | Jorge Orta | .05 | .15 |
| 723 | Randy Moffitt | .05 | .15 |
| 724 | Johnny Grubb | .05 | .15 |
| 725 | Dan Spillner | .05 | .15 |
| 726 | Harvey Kuenn MG | .05 | .15 |
| 727 | Chet Lemon | .10 | .30 |
| 728 | Ron Reed | .05 | .15 |
| 729 | Jerry Morales | .05 | .15 |
| 730 | Jason Thompson | .05 | .15 |
| 731 | Al Williams | .05 | .15 |
| 732 | Dave Henderson | .05 | .15 |
| 733 | Buck Martinez | .05 | .15 |
| 734 | Steve Braun | .05 | .15 |
| 735 | Tommy John | .10 | .30 |
| 736 | Tommy John SV | .05 | .15 |
| 737 | Mitchell Page | .05 | .15 |
| 738 | Tim Foli | .05 | .15 |
| 739 | Rick Ownbey | .05 | .15 |
| 740 | Rusty Staub | .10 | .30 |
| 741 | Rusty Staub SV | .05 | .15 |
| 742 | Padres TL BA: Terry Kennedy ERA: Tim Lollar (Ch | .10 | .30 |
| 743 | Mike Torrez | .05 | .15 |
| 744 | Brad Mills | .05 | .15 |
| 745 | Scott McGregor | .05 | .15 |
| 746 | John Wathan | .05 | .15 |
| 747 | Fred Breining | .05 | .15 |
| 748 | Derrel Thomas | .05 | .15 |
| 749 | Jon Matlack | .05 | .15 |
| 750 | Ben Oglivie | .10 | .30 |
| 751 | Brad Havens | .05 | .15 |
| 752 | Luis Pujols | .05 | .15 |
| 753 | Elias Sosa | .05 | .15 |
| 754 | Bill Robinson | .05 | .15 |
| 755 | John Candelaria | .05 | .15 |
| 756 | Russ Nixon MG | .05 | .15 |
| 757 | Rick Manning | .05 | .15 |
| 758 | Aurelio Rodriguez | .05 | .15 |
| 759 | Doug Bird | .05 | .15 |
| 760 | Dale Murphy | .25 | .60 |
| 761 | Gary Lucas | .05 | .15 |
| 762 | Cliff Johnson | .05 | .15 |
| 763 | Al Cowens | .05 | .15 |
| 764 | Pete Falcone | .05 | .15 |
| 765 | Bob Boone | .10 | .30 |
| 766 | Barry Bonnell | .05 | .15 |
| 767 | Duane Kuiper | .05 | .15 |
| 768 | Chris Speier | .05 | .15 |
| 769 | Checklist: 661-792 | .10 | .30 |
| 770 | Dave Winfield | .10 | .30 |
| 771 | Twins TL BA: Kent Hrbek ERA: Bobby Castillo (Ch | .10 | .30 |
| 772 | Jim Kern | .05 | .15 |
| 773 | Larry Hisle | .05 | .15 |
| 774 | Alan Ashby | .05 | .15 |
| 775 | Burt Hooton | .05 | .15 |
| 776 | Larry Parrish | .05 | .15 |
| 777 | John Curtis | .05 | .15 |
| 778 | Rich Hebner | .05 | .15 |
| 779 | Rick Waits | .05 | .15 |
| 780 | Gary Matthews | .10 | .30 |
| 781 | Rick Rhoden | .05 | .15 |
| 782 | Bobby Murcer | .10 | .30 |
| 783 | Bobby Murcer SV | .05 | .15 |
| 784 | Jeff Newman | .05 | .15 |
| 785 | Dennis Leonard | .05 | .15 |
| 786 | Ralph Houk MG | .05 | .15 |
| 787 | Dick Tidrow | .05 | .15 |
| 788 | Dane Iorg | .05 | .15 |
| 789 | Bryan Clark | .05 | .15 |
| 790 | Bob Grich | .10 | .30 |
| 791 | Gary Lavelle | .10 | .30 |
| 792 | Chris Chambliss | .10 | .30 |
| XX | Game Insert Card | .02 | .10 |

## 1984 Topps

|  |  | | |
|---|---|---|---|
| | COMPLETE SET (792) | 20.00 | 50.00 |
| 1 | Steve Carlton HL | .08 | .25 |
| 2 | Rickey Henderson HL | .25 | .60 |
| 3 | Dan Quisenberry HL Sets save record | .05 | .15 |
| 4 | N.Ryan/Carlton/Perry HL | .40 | 1.00 |
| 5 | Dave Righetti& Bob Forsch& and Mike Warren HL ( | .08 | .25 |
| 6 | J.Bench/G.Perry/C.Yaz HL | .15 | .40 |
| 7 | Gary Lucas | .05 | .15 |
| 8 | Don Mattingly RC | 6.00 | 15.00 |
| 9 | Jim Gott | .05 | .15 |
| 10 | Robin Yount | .40 | 1.00 |
| 11 | Minnesota Twins TL Kent Hrbek Ken Schrom (Check | .08 | .25 |
| 12 | Billy Sample | .05 | .15 |
| 13 | Scott Holman | .05 | .15 |
| 14 | Tom Brookens | .08 | .25 |
| 15 | Burt Hooton | .05 | .15 |
| 16 | Omar Moreno | .05 | .15 |
| 17 | John Denny | .05 | .15 |
| 18 | Dale Berra | .05 | .15 |
| 19 | Ray Fontenot | .05 | .15 |
| 20 | Greg Luzinski | .08 | .25 |
| 21 | Joe Altobelli MG | .05 | .15 |
| 22 | Bryan Clark | .05 | .15 |
| 23 | Keith Moreland | .05 | .15 |
| 24 | John Martin | .05 | .15 |
| 25 | Glenn Hubbard | .05 | .15 |
| 26 | Bud Black | .05 | .15 |
| 27 | Daryl Sconiers | .05 | .15 |
| 28 | Frank Viola | .15 | .40 |
| 29 | Danny Heep | .05 | .15 |
| 30 | Wade Boggs | .60 | 1.50 |
| 31 | Andy McGaffigan | .05 | .15 |
| 32 | Bobby Ramos | .05 | .15 |
| 33 | Tom Burgmeier | .05 | .15 |
| 34 | Eddie Milner | .05 | .15 |
| 35 | Don Sutton | .08 | .25 |
| 36 | Denny Walling | .05 | .15 |
| 37 | Texas Rangers TL Buddy Bell Rick Honeycutt (Che | .08 | .25 |
| 38 | Luis DeLeon | .05 | .15 |
| 39 | Garth Iorg | .05 | .15 |
| 40 | Dusty Baker | .08 | .25 |
| 41 | Tony Bernazard | .05 | .15 |
| 42 | Johnny Grubb | .05 | .15 |
| 43 | Ron Reed | .05 | .15 |
| 44 | Jim Morrison | .05 | .15 |
| 45 | Jerry Mumphrey | .05 | .15 |
| 46 | Ray Smith | .05 | .15 |
| 47 | Rudy Law | .05 | .15 |
| 48 | Julio Franco | .08 | .25 |
| 49 | John Stuper | .05 | .15 |
| 50 | Chris Chambliss | .08 | .25 |
| 51 | Jim Frey MG | .05 | .15 |
| 52 | Paul Splittorff | .05 | .15 |
| 53 | Juan Beniquez | .05 | .15 |
| 54 | Jesse Orosco | .05 | .15 |
| 55 | Dave Concepcion | .08 | .25 |
| 56 | Gary Allenson | .05 | .15 |

|  |  | | |
|---|---|---|---|
| 57 | Dan Schatzeder | .05 | .15 |
| 58 | Max Venable | .05 | .15 |
| 59 | Sammy Stewart | .05 | .15 |
| 60 | Paul Molitor | .08 | .25 |
| 61 | Chris Codiroli | .05 | .15 |
| 62 | Dave Hostetler | .05 | .15 |
| 63 | Ed VandeBerg | .05 | .15 |
| 64 | Mike Scioscia | .08 | .25 |
| 65 | Kirk Gibson | .25 | .60 |
| 66 | Astros TU/Nolan Ryan | .40 | 1.00 |
| 67 | Gary Ward | .05 | .15 |
| 68 | Luis Salazar | .05 | .15 |
| 69 | Rod Scurry | .05 | .15 |
| 70 | Gary Matthews | .08 | .25 |
| 71 | Leo Hernandez | .05 | .15 |
| 72 | Mike Squires | .05 | .15 |
| 73 | Jody Davis | .05 | .15 |
| 74 | Jerry Martin | .05 | .15 |
| 75 | Bob Forsch | .05 | .15 |
| 76 | Alfredo Griffin | .05 | .15 |
| 77 | Brett Butler | .08 | .25 |
| 78 | Mike Torrez | .05 | .15 |
| 79 | Rob Wilfong | .05 | .15 |
| 80 | Steve Rogers | .08 | .25 |
| 81 | Billy Martin MG | .15 | .40 |
| 82 | Doug Bird | .05 | .15 |
| 83 | Richie Zisk | .05 | .15 |
| 84 | Lenny Faedo | .05 | .15 |
| 85 | Atlee Hammaker | .05 | .15 |
| 86 | John Shelby | .05 | .15 |
| 87 | Frank Pastore | .05 | .15 |
| 88 | Rob Picciolo | .05 | .15 |
| 89 | Mike Smithson | .05 | .15 |
| 90 | Pedro Guerrero | .08 | .25 |
| 91 | Dan Spillner | .05 | .15 |
| 92 | Lloyd Moseby | .05 | .15 |
| 93 | Bob Knepper | .05 | .15 |
| 94 | Mario Ramirez | .05 | .15 |
| 95 | Aurelio Lopez | .08 | .25 |
| 96 | Kansas City Royals TL | | |
| | Hal McRae | | |
| | Larry Gura | | |
| | (Che | .08 | .25 |
| 97 | LaMarr Hoyt | .08 | .25 |
| 98 | Steve Nicosia | .05 | .15 |
| 99 | Craig Lefferts RC | .15 | .40 |
| 100 | Reggie Jackson | .15 | .40 |
| 101 | Porfirio Altamirano | .05 | .15 |
| 102 | Ken Oberkfell | .05 | .15 |
| 103 | Dwayne Murphy | .05 | .15 |
| 104 | Ken Dayley | .05 | .15 |
| 105 | Tony Armas | .08 | .25 |
| 106 | Tim Stoddard | .05 | .15 |
| 107 | Ned Yost | .05 | .15 |
| 108 | Randy Moffitt | .05 | .15 |
| 109 | Brad Wellman | .05 | .15 |
| 110 | Ron Guidry | .08 | .25 |
| 111 | Bill Virdon MG | .05 | .15 |
| 112 | Tom Niedenfuer | .05 | .15 |
| 113 | Kelly Paris | .05 | .15 |
| 114 | Checklist 1-132 | .08 | .25 |
| 115 | Andre Thornton | .05 | .15 |
| 116 | George Bjorkman | .05 | .15 |
| 117 | Tom Veryzer | .05 | .15 |
| 118 | Charlie Hough | .08 | .25 |
| 119 | John Wockenfuss | .05 | .15 |
| 120 | Keith Hernandez | .08 | .25 |
| 121 | Pat Sheridan | .05 | .15 |
| 122 | Cecilio Guante | .05 | .15 |
| 123 | Butch Wynegar | .05 | .15 |
| 124 | Damaso Garcia | .05 | .15 |
| 125 | Britt Burns | .05 | .15 |
| 126 | Braves TL/Dale Murphy | .15 | .40 |
| 127 | Mike Madden | .05 | .15 |
| 128 | Rick Manning | .05 | .15 |
| 129 | Bill Laskey | .05 | .15 |
| 130 | Ozzie Smith | .40 | 1.00 |
| 131 | W.Boggs/B.Madlock LL | .25 | .60 |
| 132 | Mike Schmidt/J.Rice LL | .25 | .60 |
| 133 | D.Murphy/Coop.Dice LL | .15 | .40 |
| 134 | T.Raines/R.Henderson LL | .25 | .60 |
| 135 | John Denny | .05 | .15 |
| | LaMarr Hoyt LL | | |
| 136 | S.Carlton/J.Morris LL | .08 | .25 |
| 137 | A.Hammaker/R.Honeycutt LL | .08 | .25 |
| 138 | Al Holland | .05 | .15 |
| | Dan Quisenberry LL | | |
| 139 | Bert Campaneris | .08 | .25 |
| 140 | Storm Davis | .05 | .15 |
| 141 | Pat Corrales MG | .05 | .15 |
| 142 | Rich Gale | .05 | .15 |
| 143 | Jose Morales | .05 | .15 |
| 144 | Brian Harper RC | .15 | .40 |
| 145 | Gary Lavelle | .05 | .15 |
| 146 | Ed Romero | .05 | .15 |
| 147 | Dan Petry | .08 | .25 |
| 148 | Joe Lefebvre | .05 | .15 |
| 149 | Jon Matlack | .05 | .15 |
| 150 | Dale Murphy | .15 | .40 |
| 151 | Steve Trout | .05 | .15 |
| 152 | Glenn Brummer | .05 | .15 |
| 153 | Dick Tidrow | .05 | .15 |
| 154 | Dave Henderson | .05 | .15 |
| 155 | Frank White | .08 | .25 |
| 156 | A's TL/Rickey Henderson | .25 | .60 |
| 157 | Gary Gaetti | .15 | .40 |
| 158 | John Curtis | .05 | .15 |
| 159 | Darryl Cias | .05 | .15 |
| 160 | Mario Soto | .08 | .25 |
| 161 | Junior Ortiz | .05 | .15 |
| 162 | Bob Ojeda | .05 | .15 |
| 163 | Lorenzo Gray | .05 | .15 |
| 164 | Scott Sanderson | .05 | .15 |
| 165 | Ken Singleton | .08 | .25 |
| 166 | Jamie Nelson | .05 | .15 |
| 167 | Marshall Edwards | .05 | .15 |
| 168 | Juan Bonilla | .05 | .15 |
| 169 | Larry Parrish | .05 | .15 |
| 170 | Jerry Reuss | .05 | .15 |
| 171 | Frank Robinson MG | .15 | .40 |
| 172 | Frank DiPino | .05 | .15 |
| 173 | Marvell Wynne | .15 | .40 |
| 174 | Juan Berenguer | .05 | .15 |
| 175 | Graig Nettles | .08 | .25 |
| 176 | Lee Smith | .08 | .25 |
| 177 | Jerry Hairston | .05 | .15 |
| 178 | Bill Krueger RC | .05 | .15 |
| 179 | Buck Martinez | .05 | .15 |
| 180 | Manny Trillo | .05 | .15 |
| 181 | Roy Thomas | .05 | .15 |
| 182 | Darryl Strawberry RC | 1.25 | 3.00 |
| 183 | Al Williams | .05 | .15 |
| 184 | Mike O'Berry | .05 | .15 |
| 185 | Sixto Lezcano | .05 | .15 |
| 186 | Cardinal TL | .05 | .15 |
| | Lonnie Smith | | |
| | John Stuper | | |
| | (Checklist) | | |
| 187 | Luis Aponte | .08 | .25 |
| 188 | Bryan Little | .05 | .15 |
| 189 | Tim Conroy | .05 | .15 |
| 190 | Ben Oglivie | .08 | .25 |
| 191 | Mike Boddicker | .08 | .25 |
| 192 | Nick Esasky RC | .15 | .40 |
| 193 | Darrell Brown | .05 | .15 |
| 194 | Domingo Ramos | .05 | .15 |
| 195 | Jack Morris | .08 | .25 |
| 196 | Don Slaught | .08 | .25 |
| 197 | Garry Hancock | .05 | .15 |
| 198 | Bill Doran RC* | .15 | .40 |
| 199 | Willie Hernandez | .05 | .15 |
| 200 | Andre Dawson | .08 | .25 |
| 201 | Bruce Kison | .05 | .15 |
| 202 | Bobby Cox MG | .08 | .25 |
| 203 | Matt Keough | .05 | .15 |
| 204 | Bobby Meacham | .05 | .15 |
| 205 | Greg Minton | .05 | .15 |
| 206 | Andy Van Slyke RC | .60 | 1.50 |
| 207 | Donnie Moore | .05 | .15 |
| 208 | Jose Oquendo RC | .15 | .40 |
| 209 | Manny Sarmiento | .05 | .15 |
| 210 | Joe Morgan | .08 | .25 |
| 211 | Rick Sweet | .05 | .15 |
| 212 | Broderick Perkins | .05 | .15 |
| 213 | Bruce Hurst | .05 | .15 |
| 214 | Paul Householder | .05 | .15 |
| 215 | Tippy Martinez | .05 | .15 |
| 216 | White Sox TL/C.Fisk | .08 | .25 |
| 217 | Alan Ashby | .05 | .15 |
| 218 | Rick Waits | .05 | .15 |
| 219 | Joe Simpson | .05 | .15 |
| 220 | Fernando Valenzuela | .08 | .25 |
| 221 | Cliff Johnson | .05 | .15 |
| 222 | Rick Honeycutt | .05 | .15 |
| 223 | Wayne Krenchicki | .05 | .15 |
| 224 | Sid Monge | .05 | .15 |
| 225 | Lee Mazzilli | .08 | .25 |
| 226 | Juan Eichelberger | .05 | .15 |
| 227 | Steve Braun | .05 | .15 |
| 228 | John Rabb | .05 | .15 |
| 229 | Paul Owens MG | .05 | .15 |
| 230 | Rickey Henderson | .40 | 1.00 |
| 231 | Gary Woods | .05 | .15 |
| 232 | Tim Wallach | .08 | .25 |
| 233 | Checklist 133-264 | .08 | .25 |
| 234 | Rafael Ramirez | .05 | .15 |
| 235 | Matt Young RC | .15 | .40 |
| 236 | Ellis Valentine | .05 | .15 |
| 237 | John Castino | .05 | .15 |
| 238 | Reid Nichols | .05 | .15 |
| 239 | Jay Howell | .05 | .15 |
| 240 | Eddie Murray | .25 | .60 |
| 241 | Bill Almon | .05 | .15 |
| 242 | Alex Trevino | .05 | .15 |
| 243 | Pete Ladd | .05 | .15 |
| 244 | Candy Maldonado | .05 | .15 |
| 245 | Rick Sutcliffe | .08 | .25 |
| 246 | Mets TL/Tom Seaver | .08 | .25 |
| 247 | Onix Concepcion | .05 | .15 |
| 248 | Bill Dawley | .05 | .15 |
| 249 | Jay Johnstone | .05 | .15 |
| 250 | Bill Madlock | .08 | .25 |
| 251 | Tony Gwynn | 1.00 | 2.50 |
| 252 | Larry Christenson | .05 | .15 |
| 253 | Jim Wohlford | .05 | .15 |
| 254 | Shane Rawley | .05 | .15 |
| 255 | Bruce Benedict | .05 | .15 |
| 256 | Dave Geisel | .05 | .15 |
| 257 | Julio Cruz | .05 | .15 |
| 258 | Luis Sanchez | .05 | .15 |
| 259 | Sparky Anderson MG | .08 | .25 |
| 260 | Scott McGregor | .05 | .15 |
| 261 | Bobby Brown | .05 | .15 |
| 262 | Tom Candiotti RC | .30 | .75 |
| 263 | Jack Fimple | .05 | .15 |
| 264 | Doug Frobel RC | .05 | .15 |
| 265 | Donnie Hill | .05 | .15 |
| 266 | Steve Lubratich | .05 | .15 |
| 267 | Carmelo Martinez | .05 | .15 |
| 268 | Jack O'Connor | .05 | .15 |
| 269 | Aurelio Rodriguez | .05 | .15 |
| 270 | Jeff Russell RC | .15 | .40 |
| 271 | Moose Haas | .05 | .15 |
| 272 | Rick Dempsey | .05 | .15 |
| 273 | Charlie Puleo | .05 | .15 |
| 274 | Rick Monday | .08 | .25 |
| 275 | Len Matuszek | .05 | .15 |
| 276 | Angels TL/Rod Carew | .08 | .25 |
| 277 | Eddie Whitson | .05 | .15 |
| 278 | George Bell | .08 | .25 |
| 279 | Ivan DeJesus | .05 | .15 |
| 280 | Floyd Bannister | .05 | .15 |
| 281 | Larry Milbourne | .05 | .15 |
| 282 | Jim Barr | .05 | .15 |
| 283 | Larry Biittner | .05 | .15 |
| 284 | Howard Bailey | .05 | .15 |
| 285 | Darrell Porter | .05 | .15 |
| 286 | Lary Sorensen | .05 | .15 |
| 287 | Warren Cromartie | .05 | .15 |
| 288 | Jim Beattie | .05 | .15 |
| 289 | Randy Johnson | .05 | .15 |
| 290 | Dave Dravecky | .05 | .15 |
| 291 | Chuck Tanner MG | .05 | .15 |
| 292 | Tony Scott | .05 | .15 |
| 293 | Ed Lynch | .05 | .15 |
| 294 | U.L. Washington | .05 | .15 |
| 295 | Mike Flanagan | .05 | .15 |
| 296 | Jeff Newman | .05 | .15 |
| 297 | Bruce Berenyi | .05 | .15 |
| 298 | Jim Gantner | .05 | .15 |
| 299 | John Butcher | .05 | .15 |
| 300 | Pete Rose | .75 | 2.00 |
| 301 | Frank LaCorte | .05 | .15 |
| 302 | Barry Bonnell | .05 | .15 |
| 303 | Marty Castillo | .05 | .15 |
| 304 | Warren Brusstar | .05 | .15 |
| 305 | Roy Smalley | .05 | .15 |
| 306 | Dodgers TL | .05 | .15 |
| | Pedro Guerrero | | |
| | Bob Welch | | |
| | (Checklist) | | |
| 307 | Bobby Mitchell | .08 | .25 |
| 308 | Ron Hassey | .05 | .15 |
| 309 | Tony Phillips RC | .30 | .75 |

|  |  | | |
|---|---|---|---|
| ☐ 310 | Willie McGee | .08 | .25 |
| ☐ 311 | Jerry Koosman | .08 | .25 |
| ☐ 312 | Jorge Orta | .05 | .15 |
| ☐ 313 | Mike Jorgensen | .05 | .15 |
| ☐ 314 | Orlando Mercado | .05 | .15 |
| ☐ 315 | Bob Grich | .08 | .25 |
| ☐ 316 | Mark Bradley | .05 | .15 |
| ☐ 317 | Greg Pryor | .05 | .15 |
| ☐ 318 | Bill Gullickson | .05 | .15 |
| ☐ 319 | Al Bumbry | .05 | .15 |
| ☐ 320 | Bob Stanley | .05 | .15 |
| ☐ 321 | Harvey Kuenn MG | .08 | .25 |
| ☐ 322 | Ken Schrom | .05 | .15 |
| ☐ 323 | Alan Knicely | .05 | .15 |
| ☐ 324 | Alejandro Pena RC* | .30 | .75 |
| ☐ 325 | Darrell Evans | .08 | .25 |
| ☐ 326 | Bob Kearney | .05 | .15 |
| ☐ 327 | Ruppert Jones | .05 | .15 |
| ☐ 328 | Vern Ruhle | .05 | .15 |
| ☐ 329 | Pat Tabler | .05 | .15 |
| ☐ 330 | John Candelaria | .05 | .15 |
| ☐ 331 | Bucky Dent | .08 | .25 |
| ☐ 332 | Kevin Gross RC | .15 | .40 |
| ☐ 333 | Larry Herndon | .08 | .25 |
| ☐ 334 | Chuck Rainey | .05 | .15 |
| ☐ 335 | Don Baylor | .08 | .25 |
| ☐ 336 | Seattle Mariners TL | | |
| | Pat Putnam | | |
| | Matt Young | | |
| | (Chec | .08 | .25 |
| ☐ 337 | Kevin Hagen | .05 | .15 |
| ☐ 338 | Mike Warren | .05 | .15 |
| ☐ 339 | Roy Lee Jackson | .05 | .15 |
| ☐ 340 | Hal McRae | .08 | .25 |
| ☐ 341 | Dave Tobik | .05 | .15 |
| ☐ 342 | Tim Foli | .05 | .15 |
| ☐ 343 | Mark Davis | .05 | .15 |
| ☐ 344 | Rick Miller | .05 | .15 |
| ☐ 345 | Kent Hrbek | .08 | .25 |
| ☐ 346 | Kurt Bevacqua | .05 | .15 |
| ☐ 347 | Allan Ramirez | .05 | .15 |
| ☐ 348 | Toby Harrah | .08 | .25 |
| ☐ 349 | Bob L. Gibson RC | .05 | .15 |
| ☐ 350 | George Foster | .08 | .25 |
| ☐ 351 | Russ Nixon MG | .05 | .15 |
| ☐ 352 | Dave Stewart | .08 | .25 |
| ☐ 353 | Jim Anderson | .05 | .15 |
| ☐ 354 | Jeff Burroughs | .05 | .15 |
| ☐ 355 | Jason Thompson | .05 | .15 |
| ☐ 356 | Glenn Abbott | .05 | .15 |
| ☐ 357 | Ron Cey | .08 | .25 |
| ☐ 358 | Bob Demier | .05 | .15 |
| ☐ 359 | Jim Acker | .05 | .15 |
| ☐ 360 | Willie Randolph | .08 | .25 |
| ☐ 361 | Dave Smith | .05 | .15 |
| ☐ 362 | David Green | .05 | .15 |
| ☐ 363 | Tim Laudner | .05 | .15 |
| ☐ 364 | Scott Fletcher | .05 | .15 |
| ☐ 365 | Steve Bedrosian | .05 | .15 |
| ☐ 366 | Padres TL | | |
| | Terry Kennedy | | |
| | Dave Dravecky | | |
| | (Checkli | .08 | .25 |
| ☐ 367 | Jamie Easterly | .05 | .15 |
| ☐ 368 | Hubie Brooks | .05 | .15 |
| ☐ 369 | Steve McCatty | .05 | .15 |
| ☐ 370 | Tim Raines | .08 | .25 |
| ☐ 371 | Dave Gumpert | .05 | .15 |
| ☐ 372 | Gary Roenicke | .05 | .15 |
| ☐ 373 | Bill Scherrer | .05 | .15 |
| ☐ 374 | Don Money | .05 | .15 |
| ☐ 375 | Dennis Leonard | .05 | .15 |
| ☐ 376 | Dave Anderson RC | .05 | .15 |
| ☐ 377 | Danny Darwin | .05 | .15 |
| ☐ 378 | Bob Brenly | .05 | .15 |
| ☐ 379 | Checklist 265-396 | .08 | .25 |
| ☐ 380 | Steve Garvey | .08 | .25 |
| ☐ 381 | Ralph Houk MG | .05 | .15 |
| ☐ 382 | Chris Nyman | .05 | .15 |
| ☐ 383 | Terry Puhl | .05 | .15 |
| ☐ 384 | Lee Tunnell | .05 | .15 |
| ☐ 385 | Tony Perez | .15 | .40 |
| ☐ 386 | George Hendrick AS | .05 | .15 |
| ☐ 387 | Johnny Ray AS | .05 | .15 |
| ☐ 388 | Mike Schmidt AS | .25 | .60 |
| ☐ 389 | Ozzie Smith AS | .25 | .60 |
| ☐ 390 | Tim Raines AS | .15 | .40 |
| ☐ 391 | Dale Murphy AS | .08 | .25 |
| ☐ 392 | Andre Dawson AS | .05 | .15 |
| ☐ 393 | Gary Carter AS | .05 | .15 |
| ☐ 394 | Steve Rogers AS | .05 | .15 |
| ☐ 395 | Steve Carlton AS | .08 | .25 |
| ☐ 396 | Jesse Orosco AS | .05 | .15 |
| ☐ 397 | Eddie Murray AS | .15 | .40 |
| ☐ 398 | Lou Whitaker AS | .05 | .15 |
| ☐ 399 | George Brett AS | .25 | .60 |
| ☐ 400 | Cal Ripken AS | .75 | 2.00 |
| ☐ 401 | Jim Rice AS | .05 | .15 |
| ☐ 402 | Dave Winfield AS | .05 | .15 |
| ☐ 403 | Lloyd Moseby AS | .05 | .15 |
| ☐ 404 | Ted Simmons AS | .05 | .15 |
| ☐ 405 | LaMarr Hoyt AS | .05 | .15 |
| ☐ 406 | Ron Guidry AS | .05 | .15 |
| ☐ 407 | Dan Quisenberry AS | .05 | .15 |
| ☐ 408 | Lou Piniella | .08 | .25 |
| ☐ 409 | Juan Agosto | .05 | .15 |
| ☐ 410 | Claudell Washington | .05 | .15 |
| ☐ 411 | Houston Jimenez | .05 | .15 |
| ☐ 412 | Doug Rader MG | .05 | .15 |
| ☐ 413 | Spike Owen RC | .15 | .40 |
| ☐ 414 | Mitchell Page | .05 | .15 |
| ☐ 415 | Tommy John | .08 | .25 |
| ☐ 416 | Dane Iorg | .05 | .15 |
| ☐ 417 | Mike Armstrong | .05 | .15 |
| ☐ 418 | Ron Hodges | .05 | .15 |
| ☐ 419 | John Henry Johnson | .05 | .15 |
| ☐ 420 | Cecil Cooper | .08 | .25 |
| ☐ 421 | Charlie Lea | .05 | .15 |
| ☐ 422 | Jose Cruz | .08 | .25 |
| ☐ 423 | Mike Morgan | .05 | .15 |
| ☐ 424 | Dann Bilardello | .05 | .15 |
| ☐ 425 | Steve Howe | .05 | .15 |
| ☐ 426 | Orioles TL/Cal Ripken | .60 | 1.50 |
| ☐ 427 | Rick Leach | .05 | .15 |
| ☐ 428 | Fred Breining | .05 | .15 |
| ☐ 429 | Randy Bush | .05 | .15 |
| ☐ 430 | Rusty Staub | .08 | .25 |
| ☐ 431 | Chris Bando | .05 | .15 |
| ☐ 432 | Charles Hudson | .05 | .15 |
| ☐ 433 | Rich Hebner | .05 | .15 |
| ☐ 434 | Harold Baines | .08 | .25 |
| ☐ 435 | Neil Allen | .05 | .15 |
| ☐ 436 | Rick Peters | .05 | .15 |
| ☐ 437 | Mike Proly | .05 | .15 |
| ☐ 438 | Biff Pocoroba | .05 | .15 |
| ☐ 439 | Bob Stoddard | .05 | .15 |
| ☐ 440 | Steve Kemp | .05 | .15 |
| ☐ 441 | Bob Lillis MG | .05 | .15 |
| ☐ 442 | Byron McLaughlin | .05 | .15 |
| ☐ 443 | Benny Ayala | .05 | .15 |
| ☐ 444 | Steve Renko | .05 | .15 |
| ☐ 445 | Jerry Remy | .05 | .15 |
| ☐ 446 | Luis Pujols | .05 | .15 |
| ☐ 447 | Tom Brunansky | .05 | .15 |
| ☐ 448 | Ben Hayes | .05 | .15 |
| ☐ 449 | Joe Pettini | .05 | .15 |
| ☐ 450 | Gary Carter | .08 | .25 |
| ☐ 451 | Bob Jones | .05 | .15 |
| ☐ 452 | Chuck Porter | .05 | .15 |
| ☐ 453 | Willie Upshaw | .05 | .15 |
| ☐ 454 | Joe Beckwith | .05 | .15 |
| ☐ 455 | Terry Kennedy | .05 | .15 |
| ☐ 456 | Cubs TL/F.Jenkins | .08 | .25 |
| ☐ 457 | Dave Rozema | .05 | .15 |
| ☐ 458 | Kiko Garcia | .05 | .15 |
| ☐ 459 | Kevin Hickey | .05 | .15 |
| ☐ 460 | Dave Winfield | .08 | .25 |
| ☐ 461 | Jim Maler | .05 | .15 |
| ☐ 462 | Lee Lacy | .05 | .15 |
| ☐ 463 | Dave Engle | .05 | .15 |
| ☐ 464 | Jeff A. Jones | .05 | .15 |
| ☐ 465 | Mookie Wilson | .08 | .25 |
| ☐ 466 | Gene Garber | .05 | .15 |
| ☐ 467 | Mike Ramsey | .05 | .15 |
| ☐ 468 | Geoff Zahn | .05 | .15 |
| ☐ 469 | Tom O'Malley | .05 | .15 |
| ☐ 470 | Nolan Ryan | 1.25 | 3.00 |
| ☐ 471 | Dick Howser MG | .05 | .15 |
| ☐ 472 | Mike G. Brown RC | .05 | .15 |
| ☐ 473 | Jim Dwyer | .05 | .15 |
| ☐ 474 | Greg Bargar | .05 | .15 |
| ☐ 475 | Gary Redus RC* | .15 | .40 |
| ☐ 476 | Tom Tellmann | .05 | .15 |
| ☐ 477 | Rafael Landestoy | .05 | .15 |
| ☐ 478 | Alan Bannister | .05 | .15 |
| ☐ 479 | Frank Tanana | .08 | .25 |
| ☐ 480 | Ron Kittle | .05 | .15 |
| ☐ 481 | Mark Thurmond | .05 | .15 |
| ☐ 482 | Enos Cabell | .05 | .15 |
| ☐ 483 | Fergie Jenkins | .08 | .25 |
| ☐ 484 | Ozzie Virgil | .05 | .15 |
| ☐ 485 | Rick Rhoden | .05 | .15 |
| ☐ 486 | D.Baylor/R.Guidry TL | .08 | .25 |
| ☐ 487 | Ricky Adams | .05 | .15 |
| ☐ 488 | Jesse Barfield | .08 | .25 |
| ☐ 489 | Dave Von Ohlen | .05 | .15 |
| ☐ 490 | Cal Ripken | 1.50 | 4.00 |
| ☐ 491 | Bobby Castillo | .05 | .15 |
| ☐ 492 | Tucker Ashford | .05 | .15 |
| ☐ 493 | Mike Norris | .05 | .15 |
| ☐ 494 | Chili Davis | .08 | .25 |
| ☐ 495 | Rollie Fingers | .08 | .25 |
| ☐ 496 | Terry Francona | .08 | .25 |
| ☐ 497 | Bud Anderson | .05 | .15 |
| ☐ 498 | Rich Gedman | .05 | .15 |
| ☐ 499 | Mike Witt | .05 | .15 |
| ☐ 500 | George Brett | .60 | 1.50 |
| ☐ 501 | Steve Henderson | .05 | .15 |
| ☐ 502 | Joe Torre MG | .08 | .25 |
| ☐ 503 | Elias Sosa | .05 | .15 |
| ☐ 504 | Mickey Rivers | .05 | .15 |
| ☐ 505 | Pete Vuckovich | .05 | .15 |
| ☐ 506 | Ernie Whitt | .05 | .15 |
| ☐ 507 | Mike LaCoss | .05 | .15 |
| ☐ 508 | Mel Hall | .08 | .25 |
| ☐ 509 | Brad Havens | .05 | .15 |
| ☐ 510 | Alan Trammell | .08 | .25 |
| ☐ 511 | Marty Bystrom | .05 | .15 |
| ☐ 512 | Oscar Gamble | .05 | .15 |
| ☐ 513 | Dave Beard | .05 | .15 |
| ☐ 514 | Floyd Rayford | .05 | .15 |
| ☐ 515 | Gorman Thomas | .08 | .25 |
| ☐ 516 | Montreal Expos TL | | |
| | Al Oliver | | |
| | Charlie Lea | | |
| | (Checkl | .08 | .25 |
| ☐ 517 | John Moses | .05 | .15 |
| ☐ 518 | Greg Walker | .15 | .40 |
| ☐ 519 | Ron Davis | .05 | .15 |
| ☐ 520 | Bob Boone | .08 | .25 |
| ☐ 521 | Pete Falcone | .05 | .15 |
| ☐ 522 | Dave Bergman | .05 | .15 |
| ☐ 523 | Glenn Hoffman | .05 | .15 |
| ☐ 524 | Carlos Diaz | .05 | .15 |
| ☐ 525 | Willie Wilson | .08 | .25 |
| ☐ 526 | Ron Oester | .05 | .15 |
| ☐ 527 | Checklist 397-528 | .08 | .25 |
| ☐ 528 | Mark Brouhard | .05 | .15 |
| ☐ 529 | Keith Atherton | .05 | .15 |
| ☐ 530 | Dan Ford | .05 | .15 |
| ☐ 531 | Steve Boros MG | .05 | .15 |
| ☐ 532 | Eric Show | .05 | .15 |
| ☐ 533 | Ken Landreaux | .05 | .15 |
| ☐ 534 | Pete O'Brien RC* | .15 | .40 |
| ☐ 535 | Bo Diaz | .05 | .15 |
| ☐ 536 | Doug Bair | .05 | .15 |
| ☐ 537 | Johnny Ray | .05 | .15 |
| ☐ 538 | Kevin Bass | .05 | .15 |
| ☐ 539 | George Frazier | .05 | .15 |
| ☐ 540 | George Hendrick | .08 | .25 |
| ☐ 541 | Dennis Lamp | .05 | .15 |
| ☐ 542 | Duane Kuiper | .05 | .15 |
| ☐ 543 | Craig McMurtry | .05 | .15 |
| ☐ 544 | Cesar Geronimo | .05 | .15 |
| ☐ 545 | Bill Buckner | .08 | .25 |
| ☐ 546 | Indians TL | | |
| | Mike Hargrove | | |
| | Lary Sorensen | | |
| | (Checkl | .08 | .25 |
| ☐ 547 | Mike Moore | .08 | .25 |
| ☐ 548 | Ron Jackson | .05 | .15 |
| ☐ 549 | Walt Terrell | .05 | .15 |
| ☐ 550 | Jim Rice | .08 | .25 |
| ☐ 551 | Scott Ullger | .05 | .15 |
| ☐ 552 | Ray Burris | .05 | .15 |
| ☐ 553 | Joe Nolan | .05 | .15 |
| ☐ 554 | Ted Power | .05 | .15 |
| ☐ 555 | Greg Brock | .05 | .15 |
| ☐ 556 | Joey McLaughlin | .05 | .15 |
| ☐ 557 | Wayne Tolleson | .05 | .15 |
| ☐ 558 | Mike Davis | .05 | .15 |
| ☐ 559 | Mike Scott | .08 | .25 |
| ☐ 560 | Carlton Fisk | .15 | .40 |
| ☐ 561 | Whitey Herzog MG | .08 | .25 |

| Card | Name | Val1 | Val2 |
|---|---|---|---|
| ☐ 562 | Manny Castillo | .05 | .15 |
| ☐ 563 | Glenn Wilson | .08 | .25 |
| ☐ 564 | Al Holland | .05 | .15 |
| ☐ 565 | Leon Durham | .05 | .15 |
| ☐ 566 | Jim Bibby | .05 | .15 |
| ☐ 567 | Mike Heath | .05 | .15 |
| ☐ 568 | Pete Filson | .05 | .15 |
| ☐ 569 | Bake McBride | .08 | .25 |
| ☐ 570 | Dan Quisenberry | .05 | .15 |
| ☐ 571 | Bruce Bochy | .05 | .15 |
| ☐ 572 | Jerry Royster | .05 | .15 |
| ☐ 573 | Dave Kingman | .08 | .25 |
| ☐ 574 | Brian Downing | .08 | .25 |
| ☐ 575 | Jim Clancy | .05 | .15 |
| ☐ 576 | Giants TL | | |
| | Jeff Leonard | | |
| | Atlee Hammaker | | |
| | (Checklist | .08 | .25 |
| ☐ 577 | Mark Clear | .05 | .15 |
| ☐ 578 | Lenn Sakata | .05 | .15 |
| ☐ 579 | Bob James | .05 | .15 |
| ☐ 580 | Lonnie Smith | .05 | .15 |
| ☐ 581 | Jose DeLeon RC | .15 | .40 |
| ☐ 582 | Bob McClure | .05 | .15 |
| ☐ 583 | Derrel Thomas | .05 | .15 |
| ☐ 584 | Dave Schmidt | .05 | .15 |
| ☐ 585 | Dan Driessen | .05 | .15 |
| ☐ 586 | Joe Niekro | .08 | .25 |
| ☐ 587 | Von Hayes | .05 | .15 |
| ☐ 588 | Milt Wilcox | .05 | .15 |
| ☐ 589 | Mike Easler | .05 | .15 |
| ☐ 590 | Dave Stieb | .08 | .25 |
| ☐ 591 | Tony LaRussa MG | .08 | .25 |
| ☐ 592 | Andre Robertson | .05 | .15 |
| ☐ 593 | Jeff Lahti | .05 | .15 |
| ☐ 594 | Gene Richards | .05 | .15 |
| ☐ 595 | Jeff Reardon | .08 | .25 |
| ☐ 596 | Ryne Sandberg | 1.00 | 2.50 |
| ☐ 597 | Rick Camp | .05 | .15 |
| ☐ 598 | Rusty Kuntz | .05 | .15 |
| ☐ 599 | Doug Sisk | .05 | .15 |
| ☐ 600 | Rod Carew | .15 | .40 |
| ☐ 601 | John Tudor | .08 | .25 |
| ☐ 602 | John Wathan | .05 | .15 |
| ☐ 603 | Renie Martin | .05 | .15 |
| ☐ 604 | John Lowenstein | .05 | .15 |
| ☐ 605 | Mike Caldwell | .05 | .15 |
| ☐ 606 | Blue Jays TL | | |
| | Lloyd Moseby | | |
| | Dave Stieb | | |
| | (Checklist | .08 | .25 |
| ☐ 607 | Tom Hume | .05 | .15 |
| ☐ 608 | Bobby Johnson | .05 | .15 |
| ☐ 609 | Dan Meyer | .05 | .15 |
| ☐ 610 | Steve Sax | .05 | .15 |
| ☐ 611 | Chet Lemon | .08 | .25 |
| ☐ 612 | Harry Spilman | .05 | .15 |
| ☐ 613 | Greg Gross | .05 | .15 |
| ☐ 614 | Len Barker | .05 | .15 |
| ☐ 615 | Garry Templeton | .08 | .25 |
| ☐ 616 | Don Robinson | .05 | .15 |
| ☐ 617 | Rick Cerone | .05 | .15 |
| ☐ 618 | Dickie Noles | .05 | .15 |
| ☐ 619 | Jerry Dybzinski | .05 | .15 |
| ☐ 620 | Al Oliver | .08 | .25 |
| ☐ 621 | Frank Howard MG | .08 | .25 |
| ☐ 622 | Al Cowens | .05 | .15 |
| ☐ 623 | Ron Washington | .05 | .15 |
| ☐ 624 | Terry Harper | .05 | .15 |
| ☐ 625 | Larry Gura | .05 | .15 |
| ☐ 626 | Bob Clark | .05 | .15 |
| ☐ 627 | Dave LaPoint | .05 | .15 |
| ☐ 628 | Ed Jurak | .05 | .15 |
| ☐ 629 | Rick Langford | .05 | .15 |
| ☐ 630 | Ted Simmons | .08 | .25 |
| ☐ 631 | Dennis Martinez | .08 | .25 |
| ☐ 632 | Tom Foley | .05 | .15 |
| ☐ 633 | Mike Krukow | .05 | .15 |
| ☐ 634 | Mike Marshall | .05 | .15 |
| ☐ 635 | Dave Righetti | .08 | .25 |
| ☐ 636 | Pat Putnam | .05 | .15 |
| ☐ 637 | Phillies TL | | |
| | Gary Matthews | | |
| | John Denny | | |
| | (Checklist | .08 | .25 |
| ☐ 638 | George Vukovich | .05 | .15 |
| ☐ 639 | Rick Lysander | .05 | .15 |
| ☐ 640 | Lance Parrish | .15 | .40 |

| Card | Name | Val1 | Val2 |
|---|---|---|---|
| ☐ 641 | Mike Richardt | .05 | .15 |
| ☐ 642 | Tom Underwood | .05 | .15 |
| ☐ 643 | Mike C. Brown | .05 | .15 |
| ☐ 644 | Tim Lollar | .05 | .15 |
| ☐ 645 | Tony Pena | .05 | .15 |
| ☐ 646 | Checklist 529-660 | .08 | .25 |
| ☐ 647 | Ron Roenicke | .05 | .15 |
| ☐ 648 | Len Whitehouse | .05 | .15 |
| ☐ 649 | Tom Herr | .08 | .25 |
| ☐ 650 | Phil Niekro | .08 | .25 |
| ☐ 651 | John McNamara MG | .05 | .15 |
| ☐ 652 | Rudy May | .05 | .15 |
| ☐ 653 | Dave Stapleton | .05 | .15 |
| ☐ 654 | Bob Bailor | .05 | .15 |
| ☐ 655 | Amos Otis | .08 | .25 |
| ☐ 656 | Bryn Smith | .05 | .15 |
| ☐ 657 | Thad Bosley | .05 | .15 |
| ☐ 658 | Jerry Augustine | .05 | .15 |
| ☐ 659 | Duane Walker | .05 | .15 |
| ☐ 660 | Ray Knight | .08 | .25 |
| ☐ 661 | Steve Yeager | .05 | .15 |
| ☐ 662 | Tom Brennan | .05 | .15 |
| ☐ 663 | Johnnie LeMaster | .05 | .15 |
| ☐ 664 | Dave Stegman | .05 | .15 |
| ☐ 665 | Buddy Bell | .08 | .25 |
| ☐ 666 | Tigers TL/Morris/Whitak | .05 | .15 |
| ☐ 667 | Vance Law | .05 | .15 |
| ☐ 668 | Larry McWilliams | .05 | .15 |
| ☐ 669 | Dave Lopes | .08 | .25 |
| ☐ 670 | Rich Gossage | .08 | .25 |
| ☐ 671 | Jamie Quirk | .05 | .15 |
| ☐ 672 | Ricky Nelson | .05 | .15 |
| ☐ 673 | Mike Walters | .05 | .15 |
| ☐ 674 | Tim Flannery | .05 | .15 |
| ☐ 675 | Pascual Perez | .05 | .15 |
| ☐ 676 | Brian Giles | .05 | .15 |
| ☐ 677 | Doyle Alexander | .05 | .15 |
| ☐ 678 | Chris Speier | .05 | .15 |
| ☐ 679 | Art Howe | .05 | .15 |
| ☐ 680 | Fred Lynn | .08 | .25 |
| ☐ 681 | Tom Lasorda MG | .15 | .40 |
| ☐ 682 | Dan Morogiello | .15 | .40 |
| ☐ 683 | Marty Barrett RC | .15 | .40 |
| ☐ 684 | Bob Shirley | .05 | .15 |
| ☐ 685 | Willie Aikens | .05 | .15 |
| ☐ 686 | Joe Price | .05 | .15 |
| ☐ 687 | Roy Howell | .05 | .15 |
| ☐ 688 | George Wright | .05 | .15 |
| ☐ 689 | Mike Fischlin | .05 | .15 |
| ☐ 690 | Jack Clark | .08 | .25 |
| ☐ 691 | Steve Lake | .05 | .15 |
| ☐ 692 | Dickie Thon | .05 | .15 |
| ☐ 693 | Alan Wiggins | .05 | .15 |
| ☐ 694 | Mike Stanton | .05 | .15 |
| ☐ 695 | Lou Whitaker | .08 | .25 |
| ☐ 696 | Pirates TL | | |
| | Bill Madlock | | |
| | Rick Rhoden | | |
| | (Checklist | .08 | .25 |
| ☐ 697 | Dale Murray | .05 | .15 |
| ☐ 698 | Marc Hill | .05 | .15 |
| ☐ 699 | Dave Rucker | .05 | .15 |
| ☐ 700 | Mike Schmidt | .60 | 1.50 |
| ☐ 701 | Madlock/Rose/Parker LL | .25 | .60 |
| ☐ 702 | Rose/Staub/Perez LL | .25 | .60 |
| ☐ 703 | Schmidt/Perez/Kingm LL | .25 | .60 |
| ☐ 704 | Tony Perez | | |
| | Rusty Staub | | |
| | Al Oliver LL | .08 | .25 |
| ☐ 705 | Morgan/Cedeno/Bowa LL | .15 | .40 |
| ☐ 706 | S.Carlton/Jenk/Seaver LL | .15 | .40 |
| ☐ 707 | N.Ryan/Seaver/Carlton LL | .60 | 1.50 |
| ☐ 708 | Seaver/Carlton/Rog LL | .15 | .40 |
| ☐ 709 | NL Active Save | | |
| | Bruce Sutter | | |
| | Tug McGraw | | |
| | Gene Garr | .08 | .25 |
| ☐ 710 | Carew/Brett/Cooper LL | .15 | .40 |
| ☐ 711 | Carew/Camp/Reggie LL | .08 | .25 |
| ☐ 712 | Reggie/Nettles/Luz LL | .08 | .25 |
| ☐ 713 | Reggie/Simmons/Nett LL | .08 | .25 |
| ☐ 714 | AL Active Steals | | |
| | Bert Campaneris | | |
| | Dave Lopes | | |
| | Oma | .08 | .25 |
| ☐ 715 | Palmer/Sutton/John LL | .08 | .25 |
| ☐ 716 | AL Active Strikeout | | |
| | Don Sutton | | |

| Card | Name | Val1 | Val2 |
|---|---|---|---|
| | Bert Blyleven | | |
| | Je | .15 | .40 |
| ☐ 717 | Jim Palmer/Fingers LL | .15 | .40 |
| ☐ 718 | Fingers/Goose/Quis LL | .08 | .25 |
| ☐ 719 | Andy Hassler | .05 | .15 |
| ☐ 720 | Dwight Evans | .15 | .40 |
| ☐ 721 | Del Crandall MG | .05 | .15 |
| ☐ 722 | Bob Welch | .08 | .25 |
| ☐ 723 | Rich Dauer | .05 | .15 |
| ☐ 724 | Eric Rasmussen | .05 | .15 |
| ☐ 725 | Cesar Cedeno | .08 | .25 |
| ☐ 726 | Brewers TL | | |
| | Ted Simmons | | |
| | Moose Haas | | |
| | (Checklist on | .08 | .25 |
| ☐ 727 | Joel Youngblood | .05 | .15 |
| ☐ 728 | Tug McGraw | .08 | .25 |
| ☐ 729 | Gene Tenace | .08 | .25 |
| ☐ 730 | Bruce Sutter | .15 | .40 |
| ☐ 731 | Lynn Jones | .05 | .15 |
| ☐ 732 | Terry Crowley | .05 | .15 |
| ☐ 733 | Dave Collins | .05 | .15 |
| ☐ 734 | Odell Jones | .05 | .15 |
| ☐ 735 | Rick Burleson | .05 | .15 |
| ☐ 736 | Dick Ruthven | .05 | .15 |
| ☐ 737 | Jim Essian | .05 | .15 |
| ☐ 738 | Bill Schroeder | .05 | .15 |
| ☐ 739 | Bob Watson | .05 | .15 |
| ☐ 740 | Tom Seaver | .25 | .60 |
| ☐ 741 | Wayne Gross | .05 | .15 |
| ☐ 742 | Dick Williams MG | .05 | .15 |
| ☐ 743 | Don Hood | .05 | .15 |
| ☐ 744 | Jamie Allen | .05 | .15 |
| ☐ 745 | Dennis Eckersley | .15 | .40 |
| ☐ 746 | Mickey Hatcher | .05 | .15 |
| ☐ 747 | Pat Zachry | .05 | .15 |
| ☐ 748 | Jeff Leonard | .05 | .15 |
| ☐ 749 | Doug Flynn | .05 | .15 |
| ☐ 750 | Jim Palmer | .08 | .25 |
| ☐ 751 | Charlie Moore | .05 | .15 |
| ☐ 752 | Phil Garner | .08 | .25 |
| ☐ 753 | Doug Gwosdz | .05 | .15 |
| ☐ 754 | Kent Tekulve | .05 | .15 |
| ☐ 755 | Garry Maddox | .05 | .15 |
| ☐ 756 | Reds TL | | |
| | Ron Oester | | |
| | Mario Soto | | |
| | (Checklist on bac | .08 | .25 |
| ☐ 757 | Larry Bowa | .08 | .25 |
| ☐ 758 | Bill Stein | .05 | .15 |
| ☐ 759 | Richard Dotson | .05 | .15 |
| ☐ 760 | Bob Horner | .08 | .25 |
| ☐ 761 | John Montefusco | .05 | .15 |
| ☐ 762 | Rance Muliniks | .05 | .15 |
| ☐ 763 | Craig Swan | .05 | .15 |
| ☐ 764 | Mike Hargrove | .05 | .15 |
| ☐ 765 | Ken Forsch | .05 | .15 |
| ☐ 766 | Mike Vail | .05 | .15 |
| ☐ 767 | Carney Lansford | .08 | .25 |
| ☐ 768 | Champ Summers | .05 | .15 |
| ☐ 769 | Bill Caudill | .05 | .15 |
| ☐ 770 | Ken Griffey | .08 | .25 |
| ☐ 771 | Billy Gardner MG | .05 | .15 |
| ☐ 772 | Jim Slaton | .05 | .15 |
| ☐ 773 | Todd Cruz | .05 | .15 |
| ☐ 774 | Tom Gorman | .05 | .15 |
| ☐ 775 | Dave Parker | .08 | .25 |
| ☐ 776 | Craig Reynolds | .05 | .15 |
| ☐ 777 | Tom Paciorek | .05 | .15 |
| ☐ 778 | Andy Hawkins | .05 | .15 |
| ☐ 779 | Jim Sundberg | .08 | .25 |
| ☐ 780 | Steve Carlton | .15 | .40 |
| ☐ 781 | Checklist 661-792 | .08 | .25 |
| ☐ 782 | Steve Balboni | .05 | .15 |
| ☐ 783 | Luis Leal | .05 | .15 |
| ☐ 784 | Leon Roberts | .05 | .15 |
| ☐ 785 | Joaquin Andujar | .08 | .25 |
| ☐ 786 | Red Sox TL/Boggs/Ojeda | .15 | .40 |
| ☐ 787 | Bill Campbell | .05 | .15 |
| ☐ 788 | Milt May | .05 | .15 |
| ☐ 789 | Bert Blyleven | .05 | .15 |
| ☐ 790 | Doug DeCinces | .05 | .15 |
| ☐ 791 | Terry Forster | .08 | .25 |
| ☐ 792 | Bill Russell | .08 | .25 |

## 1985 Topps

| Card | Price | Price |
|---|---|---|
| COMPLETE SET (792) | 40.00 | 80.00 |
| COMP.FACT.SET (792) | 100.00 | 175.00 |
| 1 Carlton Fisk RB | .08 | .25 |
| 2 Steve Garvey RB | .05 | .15 |
| 3 Dwight Gooden RB | .25 | .60 |
| 4 Cliff Johnson RB | .05 | .15 |
| 5 Joe Morgan RB | .05 | .15 |
| 6 Pete Rose RB | .15 | .40 |
| 7 Nolan Ryan RB | .60 | 1.50 |
| 8 Juan Samuel RB | .05 | .15 |
| 9 Bruce Sutter RB | .05 | .15 |
| 10 Don Sutton RB | .05 | .15 |
| 11 Ralph Houk MG | .05 | .15 |
| 12 Dave Lopes | .08 | .25 |
| 13 Tim Lollar | .05 | .15 |
| 14 Chris Bando | .05 | .15 |
| 15 Jerry Koosman | .08 | .25 |
| 16 Bobby Meacham | .05 | .15 |
| 17 Mike Scott | .08 | .25 |
| 18 Mickey Hatcher | .05 | .15 |
| 19 George Frazier | .05 | .15 |
| 20 Chet Lemon | .08 | .25 |
| 21 Lee Tunnell | .05 | .15 |
| 22 Duane Kuiper | .05 | .15 |
| 23 Bret Saberhagen RC | .40 | 1.00 |
| 24 Jesse Barfield | .08 | .25 |
| 25 Steve Bedrosian | .05 | .15 |
| 26 Roy Smalley | .05 | .15 |
| 27 Bruce Berenyi | .05 | .15 |
| 28 Dann Bilardello | .05 | .15 |
| 29 Odell Jones | .05 | .15 |
| 30 Cal Ripken | 1.00 | 2.50 |
| 31 Terry Whitfield | .05 | .15 |
| 32 Chuck Porter | .05 | .15 |
| 33 Tito Landrum | .05 | .15 |
| 34 Ed Nunez | .05 | .15 |
| 35 Graig Nettles | .08 | .25 |
| 36 Fred Breining | .05 | .15 |
| 37 Reid Nichols | .05 | .15 |
| 38 Jackie Moore MG | .05 | .15 |
| 39 John Wockenfuss | .05 | .15 |
| 40 Phil Niekro | .08 | .25 |
| 41 Mike Fischlin | .05 | .15 |
| 42 Luis Sanchez | .05 | .15 |
| 43 Andre David | .05 | .15 |
| 44 Dickie Thon | .05 | .15 |
| 45 Greg Minton | .05 | .15 |
| 46 Gary Woods | .05 | .15 |
| 47 Dave Rozema | .05 | .15 |
| 48 Tony Fernandez | .25 | .60 |
| 49 Butch Davis | .05 | .15 |
| 50 John Candelaria | .05 | .15 |
| 51 Bob Watson | .08 | .25 |
| 52 Jerry Dybzinski | .05 | .15 |
| 53 Tom Gorman | .05 | .15 |
| 54 Cesar Cedeno | .08 | .25 |
| 55 Frank Tanana | .08 | .25 |
| 56 Jim Dwyer | .05 | .15 |
| 57 Pat Zachry | .05 | .15 |
| 58 Orlando Mercado | .05 | .15 |
| 59 Rick Waits | .05 | .15 |
| 60 George Hendrick | .08 | .25 |
| 61 Curt Kaufman | .05 | .15 |
| 62 Mike Ramsey | .05 | .15 |
| 63 Steve McCatty | .05 | .15 |
| 64 Mark Bailey | .05 | .15 |
| 65 Bill Buckner | .08 | .25 |
| 66 Dick Williams MG | .05 | .15 |
| 67 Rafael Santana | .05 | .15 |
| 68 Von Hayes | .08 | .25 |
| 69 Jim Winn | .05 | .15 |
| 70 Don Baylor | .08 | .25 |
| 71 Tim Laudner | .05 | .15 |
| 72 Rick Sutcliffe | .08 | .25 |
| 73 Rusty Kuntz | .05 | .15 |
| 74 Mike Krukow | .05 | .15 |
| 75 Willie Upshaw | .05 | .15 |
| 76 Alan Bannister | .05 | .15 |
| 77 Joe Beckwith | .05 | .15 |
| 78 Scott Fletcher | .05 | .15 |
| 79 Rick Mahler | .05 | .15 |
| 80 Keith Hernandez | .08 | .25 |
| 81 Lenn Sakata | .05 | .15 |
| 82 Joe Price | .05 | .15 |
| 83 Charlie Moore | .05 | .15 |
| 84 Spike Owen | .05 | .15 |
| 85 Mike Marshall | .05 | .15 |
| 86 Don Aase | .05 | .15 |
| 87 David Green | .05 | .15 |
| 88 Bryn Smith | .05 | .15 |
| 89 Jackie Gutierrez | .05 | .15 |
| 90 Rich Gossage | .08 | .25 |
| 91 Jeff Burroughs | .05 | .15 |
| 92 Paul Owens MG | .05 | .15 |
| 93 Don Schulze | .05 | .15 |
| 94 Toby Harrah | .08 | .25 |
| 95 Jose Cruz | .08 | .25 |
| 96 Johnny Ray | .05 | .15 |
| 97 Pete Filson | .05 | .15 |
| 98 Steve Lake | .05 | .15 |
| 99 Milt Wilcox | .05 | .15 |
| 100 George Brett | .60 | 1.50 |
| 101 Jim Acker | .05 | .15 |
| 102 Tommy Dunbar | .05 | .15 |
| 103 Randy Lerch | .05 | .15 |
| 104 Mike Fitzgerald | .05 | .15 |
| 105 Ron Kittle | .08 | .25 |
| 106 Pascual Perez | .05 | .15 |
| 107 Tom Foley | .05 | .15 |
| 108 Darnell Coles | .05 | .15 |
| 109 Gary Roenicke | .05 | .15 |
| 110 Alejandro Pena | .05 | .15 |
| 111 Doug DeCinces | .05 | .15 |
| 112 Tom Tellmann | .05 | .15 |
| 113 Tom Herr | .05 | .15 |
| 114 Bob James | .05 | .15 |
| 115 Rickey Henderson | .30 | .75 |
| 116 Dennis Boyd | .05 | .15 |
| 117 Greg Gross | .05 | .15 |
| 118 Eric Show | .05 | .15 |
| 119 Pat Corrales MG | .05 | .15 |
| 120 Steve Kemp | .05 | .15 |
| 121 Checklist: 1-132 | .08 | .25 |
| 122 Tom Brunansky | .08 | .25 |
| 123 Dave Smith | .05 | .15 |
| 124 Rich Hebner | .05 | .15 |
| 125 Kent Tekulve | .05 | .15 |
| 126 Ruppert Jones | .05 | .15 |
| 127 Mark Gubicza RC* | .15 | .40 |
| 128 Ernie Whitt | .05 | .15 |
| 129 Gene Garber | .05 | .15 |
| 130 Al Oliver | .08 | .25 |
| 131 Buddy/Gus Bell FS | .08 | .25 |
| 132 Yogi/Dale Berra FS | .25 | .60 |
| 133 Bob/Ray Boone FS | .08 | .25 |
| 134 Terry/Tito Francona FS | .08 | .25 |
| 135 Terry/Bob Kennedy FS | .05 | .15 |
| 136 Jeff/Bill Kunkel FS | .05 | .15 |
| 137 Vance/Vern Law FS | .08 | .25 |
| 138 Dick/Dick Schofield FS | .05 | .15 |
| 139 Joel/Bob Skinner FS | .05 | .15 |
| 140 Roy/Roy Smalley FS | .05 | .15 |
| 141 Mike/Dave Stenhouse FS | .05 | .15 |
| 142 Steve/Dizzy Trout FS | .05 | .15 |
| 143 Ozzie/Ossie Virgil FS | .05 | .15 |
| 144 Ron Gardenhire | .05 | .15 |
| 145 Alvin Davis RC* | .15 | .40 |
| 146 Gary Redus | .05 | .15 |
| 147 Bill Swaggerty | .05 | .15 |
| 148 Steve Yeager | .08 | .25 |
| 149 Dickie Noles | .05 | .15 |
| 150 Jim Rice | .08 | .25 |
| 151 Moose Haas | .05 | .15 |
| 152 Steve Braun | .05 | .15 |
| 153 Frank LaCorte | .05 | .15 |
| 154 Angel Salazar | .05 | .15 |
| 155 Yogi Berra MG/TC | .25 | .60 |
| 156 Craig Reynolds | .05 | .15 |
| 157 Tug McGraw | .08 | .25 |
| 158 Pat Tabler | .05 | .15 |
| 159 Carlos Diaz | .05 | .15 |
| 160 Lance Parrish | .08 | .25 |
| 161 Ken Schrom | .05 | .15 |
| 162 Benny Distefano | .05 | .15 |
| 163 Dennis Eckersley | .15 | .40 |
| 164 Jorge Orta | .05 | .15 |
| 165 Dusty Baker | .08 | .25 |
| 166 Keith Atherton | .05 | .15 |
| 167 Rufino Linares | .05 | .15 |
| 168 Garth Iorg | .05 | .15 |
| 169 Dan Spillner | .05 | .15 |
| 170 George Foster | .08 | .25 |
| 171 Bill Stein | .05 | .15 |
| 172 Jack Perconte | .05 | .15 |
| 173 Mike Young | .05 | .15 |
| 174 Rick Honeycutt | .05 | .15 |
| 175 Dave Parker | .08 | .25 |
| 176 Bill Schroeder | .05 | .15 |
| 177 Dave Von Ohlen | .05 | .15 |
| 178 Miguel Dilone | .05 | .15 |
| 179 Tommy John | .08 | .25 |
| 180 Dave Winfield | .08 | .25 |
| 181 Roger Clemens RC | 6.00 | 15.00 |
| 182 Tim Flannery | .05 | .15 |
| 183 Larry McWilliams | .05 | .15 |
| 184 Carmen Castillo | .05 | .15 |
| 185 Al Holland | .05 | .15 |
| 186 Bob Lillis MG | .05 | .15 |
| 187 Mike Walters | .05 | .15 |
| 188 Greg Pryor | .05 | .15 |
| 189 Warren Brusstar | .05 | .15 |
| 190 Rusty Staub | .08 | .25 |
| 191 Steve Nicosia | .05 | .15 |
| 192 Howard Johnson | .08 | .25 |
| 193 Jimmy Key RC | .30 | .75 |
| 194 Dave Stegman | .05 | .15 |
| 195 Glenn Hubbard | .05 | .15 |
| 196 Pete O'Brien | .05 | .15 |
| 197 Mike Warren | .05 | .15 |
| 198 Eddie Milner | .05 | .15 |
| 199 Dennis Martinez | .08 | .25 |
| 200 Reggie Jackson | .15 | .40 |
| 201 Burt Hooton | .05 | .15 |
| 202 Gorman Thomas | .08 | .25 |
| 203 Bob McClure | .05 | .15 |
| 204 Art Howe | .05 | .15 |
| 205 Steve Rogers | .05 | .15 |
| 206 Phil Garner | .08 | .25 |
| 207 Mark Clear | .05 | .15 |
| 208 Champ Summers | .05 | .15 |
| 209 Bill Campbell | .05 | .15 |
| 210 Gary Matthews | .08 | .25 |
| 211 Clay Christiansen | .05 | .15 |
| 212 George Vukovich | .05 | .15 |
| 213 Billy Gardner MG | .05 | .15 |
| 214 John Tudor | .05 | .15 |
| 215 Bob Brenly | .05 | .15 |
| 216 Jerry Don Gleaton | .05 | .15 |
| 217 Leon Roberts | .05 | .15 |
| 218 Doyle Alexander | .05 | .15 |
| 219 Gerald Perry | .08 | .25 |
| 220 Fred Lynn | .08 | .25 |
| 221 Ron Reed | .05 | .15 |
| 222 Hubie Brooks | .05 | .15 |
| 223 Tom Hume | .05 | .15 |
| 224 Al Cowens | .05 | .15 |
| 225 Mike Boddicker | .05 | .15 |
| 226 Juan Beniquez | .05 | .15 |
| 227 Danny Darwin | .05 | .15 |
| 228 Dion James | .05 | .15 |
| 229 Dave LaPoint | .05 | .15 |
| 230 Gary Carter | .08 | .25 |
| 231 Dwayne Murphy | .05 | .15 |
| 232 Dave Beard | .05 | .15 |
| 233 Ed Jurak | .05 | .15 |
| 234 Jerry Narron | .05 | .15 |
| 235 Garry Maddox | .05 | .15 |
| 236 Mark Thurmond | .05 | .15 |
| 237 Julio Franco | .08 | .25 |
| 238 Jose Rijo RC | .30 | .75 |
| 239 Tim Teufel | .05 | .15 |
| 240 Dave Stieb | .08 | .25 |
| 241 Jim Frey MG | .05 | .15 |
| 242 Greg Harris | .05 | .15 |
| 243 Barbaro Garbey | .05 | .15 |
| 244 Mike Jones | .05 | .15 |
| 245 Chili Davis | .08 | .25 |
| 246 Mike Norris | .05 | .15 |

|  |  | | |
|---|---|---|---|
| ❏ 247 | Wayne Tolleson | .05 | .15 |
| ❏ 248 | Terry Forster | .08 | .25 |
| ❏ 249 | Harold Baines | .08 | .25 |
| ❏ 250 | Jesse Orosco | .05 | .15 |
| ❏ 251 | Brad Gulden | .05 | .15 |
| ❏ 252 | Dan Ford | .05 | .15 |
| ❏ 253 | Sid Bream RC | .15 | .40 |
| ❏ 254 | Pete Vuckovich | .05 | .15 |
| ❏ 255 | Lonnie Smith | .05 | .15 |
| ❏ 256 | Mike Stanton | .05 | .15 |
| ❏ 257 | Bryan Little | .05 | .15 |
| ❏ 258 | Mike C. Brown | .05 | .15 |
| ❏ 259 | Gary Allenson | .05 | .15 |
| ❏ 260 | Dave Righetti | .08 | .25 |
| ❏ 261 | Checklist: 133-264 | .05 | .15 |
| ❏ 262 | Greg Booker | .05 | .15 |
| ❏ 263 | Mel Hall | .05 | .15 |
| ❏ 264 | Joe Sambito | .05 | .15 |
| ❏ 265 | Juan Samuel | .05 | .15 |
| ❏ 266 | Frank Viola | .08 | .25 |
| ❏ 267 | Henry Cotto RC | .05 | .15 |
| ❏ 268 | Chuck Tanner MG | .05 | .15 |
| ❏ 269 | Doug Baker | .05 | .15 |
| ❏ 270 | Dan Quisenberry | .05 | .15 |
| ❏ 271 | Tim Foli FDP | .05 | .15 |
| ❏ 272 | Jeff Burroughs FDP | .05 | .15 |
| ❏ 273 | Bill Almon FDP | .05 | .15 |
| ❏ 274 | Floyd Bannister FDP | .05 | .15 |
| ❏ 275 | Harold Baines FDP | .05 | .15 |
| ❏ 276 | Bob Horner FDP | .05 | .15 |
| ❏ 277 | Al Chambers FDP | .05 | .15 |
| ❏ 278 | Darryl Strawberry FDP | .15 | .40 |
| ❏ 279 | Mike Moore FDP | .05 | .15 |
| ❏ 280 | Shawon Dunston FDP RC | .30 | .75 |
| ❏ 281 | Tim Belcher FDP RC | .15 | .40 |
| ❏ 282 | Shawn Abner FDP RC | .05 | .15 |
| ❏ 283 | Fran Mullins | .05 | .15 |
| ❏ 284 | Marty Bystrom | .05 | .15 |
| ❏ 285 | Dan Driessen | .05 | .15 |
| ❏ 286 | Rudy Law | .05 | .15 |
| ❏ 287 | Walt Terrell | .05 | .15 |
| ❏ 288 | Jeff Kunkel | .05 | .15 |
| ❏ 289 | Tom Underwood | .05 | .15 |
| ❏ 290 | Cecil Cooper | .08 | .25 |
| ❏ 291 | Bob Welch | .08 | .25 |
| ❏ 292 | Brad Komminsk | .05 | .15 |
| ❏ 293 | Curt Young | .05 | .15 |
| ❏ 294 | Tom Nieto | .05 | .15 |
| ❏ 295 | Joe Niekro | .05 | .15 |
| ❏ 296 | Ricky Nelson | .05 | .15 |
| ❏ 297 | Gary Lucas | .05 | .15 |
| ❏ 298 | Marty Barrett | .05 | .15 |
| ❏ 299 | Andy Hawkins | .05 | .15 |
| ❏ 300 | Rod Carew | .15 | .40 |
| ❏ 301 | John Montefusco | .05 | .15 |
| ❏ 302 | Tim Corcoran | .05 | .15 |
| ❏ 303 | Mike Jeffcoat | .05 | .15 |
| ❏ 304 | Gary Gaetti | .08 | .25 |
| ❏ 305 | Dale Berra | .05 | .15 |
| ❏ 306 | Rick Reuschel | .05 | .15 |
| ❏ 307 | Sparky Anderson MG | .08 | .25 |
| ❏ 308 | John Wathan | .05 | .15 |
| ❏ 309 | Mike Witt | .05 | .15 |
| ❏ 310 | Manny Trillo | .05 | .15 |
| ❏ 311 | Jim Gott | .05 | .15 |
| ❏ 312 | Marc Hill | .05 | .15 |
| ❏ 313 | Dave Schmidt | .05 | .15 |
| ❏ 314 | Ron Oester | .05 | .15 |
| ❏ 315 | Doug Sisk | .05 | .15 |
| ❏ 316 | John Lowenstein | .05 | .15 |
| ❏ 317 | Jack Lazorko | .05 | .15 |
| ❏ 318 | Ted Simmons | .08 | .25 |
| ❏ 319 | Jeff Jones | .05 | .15 |
| ❏ 320 | Dale Murphy | .15 | .40 |
| ❏ 321 | Ricky Horton | .05 | .15 |
| ❏ 322 | Dave Stapleton | .05 | .15 |
| ❏ 323 | Andy McGaffigan | .05 | .15 |
| ❏ 324 | Bruce Bochy | .05 | .15 |
| ❏ 325 | John Denny | .05 | .15 |
| ❏ 326 | Kevin Bass | .05 | .15 |
| ❏ 327 | Brook Jacoby | .05 | .15 |
| ❏ 328 | Bob Shirley | .05 | .15 |
| ❏ 329 | Ron Washington | .05 | .15 |
| ❏ 330 | Leon Durham | .05 | .15 |
| ❏ 331 | Bill Laskey | .05 | .15 |
| ❏ 332 | Brian Harper | .05 | .15 |
| ❏ 333 | Willie Hernandez | .05 | .15 |
| ❏ 334 | Dick Howser MG | .05 | .15 |
| ❏ 335 | Bruce Benedict | .05 | .15 |
| ❏ 336 | Rance Mulliniks | .05 | .15 |
| ❏ 337 | Billy Sample | .05 | .15 |
| ❏ 338 | Britt Burns | .05 | .15 |
| ❏ 339 | Danny Heep | .05 | .15 |
| ❏ 340 | Robin Yount | .40 | 1.00 |
| ❏ 341 | Floyd Rayford | .05 | .15 |
| ❏ 342 | Ted Power | .05 | .15 |
| ❏ 343 | Bill Russell | .08 | .25 |
| ❏ 344 | Dave Henderson | .05 | .15 |
| ❏ 345 | Charlie Lea | .05 | .15 |
| ❏ 346 | Terry Pendleton RC | .30 | .75 |
| ❏ 347 | Rick Langford | .05 | .15 |
| ❏ 348 | Bob Boone | .08 | .25 |
| ❏ 349 | Domingo Ramos | .05 | .15 |
| ❏ 350 | Wade Boggs | .25 | .60 |
| ❏ 351 | Juan Agosto | .05 | .15 |
| ❏ 352 | Joe Morgan | .08 | .25 |
| ❏ 353 | Julio Solano | .05 | .15 |
| ❏ 354 | Andre Robertson | .05 | .15 |
| ❏ 355 | Bert Blyleven | .08 | .25 |
| ❏ 356 | Dave Meier | .05 | .15 |
| ❏ 357 | Rich Bordi | .05 | .15 |
| ❏ 358 | Tony Pena | .05 | .15 |
| ❏ 359 | Pat Sheridan | .05 | .15 |
| ❏ 360 | Steve Carlton | .08 | .25 |
| ❏ 361 | Alfredo Griffin | .05 | .15 |
| ❏ 362 | Craig McMurtry | .05 | .15 |
| ❏ 363 | Ron Hodges | .05 | .15 |
| ❏ 364 | Richard Dotson | .05 | .15 |
| ❏ 365 | Danny Ozark MG | .05 | .15 |
| ❏ 366 | Todd Cruz | .05 | .15 |
| ❏ 367 | Keefe Cato | .05 | .15 |
| ❏ 368 | Dave Bergman | .05 | .15 |
| ❏ 369 | R.J. Reynolds | .05 | .15 |
| ❏ 370 | Bruce Sutter | .08 | .25 |
| ❏ 371 | Mickey Rivers | .05 | .15 |
| ❏ 372 | Roy Howell | .05 | .15 |
| ❏ 373 | Mike Moore | .05 | .15 |
| ❏ 374 | Brian Downing | .08 | .25 |
| ❏ 375 | Jeff Reardon | .08 | .25 |
| ❏ 376 | Jeff Newman | .05 | .15 |
| ❏ 377 | Checklist: 265-396 | .05 | .15 |
| ❏ 378 | Alan Wiggins | .05 | .15 |
| ❏ 379 | Charles Hudson | .05 | .15 |
| ❏ 380 | Ken Griffey | .08 | .25 |
| ❏ 381 | Roy Smith | .05 | .15 |
| ❏ 382 | Denny Walling | .05 | .15 |
| ❏ 383 | Rick Lysander | .05 | .15 |
| ❏ 384 | Jody Davis | .05 | .15 |
| ❏ 385 | Jose DeLeon | .05 | .15 |
| ❏ 386 | Dan Gladden RC | .15 | .40 |
| ❏ 387 | Buddy Biancalana | .05 | .15 |
| ❏ 388 | Bert Roberge | .05 | .15 |
| ❏ 389 | Rod Dedeaux OLY CO RC | .08 | .25 |
| ❏ 390 | Sid Akins OLY RC | .05 | .15 |
| ❏ 391 | Flavio Alfaro OLY RC | .05 | .15 |
| ❏ 392 | Don August OLY RC | .05 | .15 |
| ❏ 393 | Scott Bankhead OLY RC | .05 | .15 |
| ❏ 394 | Bob Caffrey OLY RC | .05 | .15 |
| ❏ 395 | Mike Dunne OLY RC | .05 | .15 |
| ❏ 396 | Gary Green OLY RC | .05 | .15 |
| ❏ 397 | John Hoover OLY RC | .05 | .15 |
| ❏ 398 | Shane Mack OLY RC | .15 | .40 |
| ❏ 399 | John Marzano OLY RC | .05 | .15 |
| ❏ 400 | Oddibe McDowell OLY RC | .15 | .40 |
| ❏ 401 | Mark McGwire OLY RC | 12.50 | 30.00 |
| ❏ 402 | Pat Pacillo OLY RC | .05 | .15 |
| ❏ 403 | Cory Snyder OLY RC | .30 | .75 |
| ❏ 404 | Bill Swift OLY RC | .15 | .40 |
| ❏ 405 | Tom Veryzer | .05 | .15 |
| ❏ 406 | Len Whitehouse | .05 | .15 |
| ❏ 407 | Bobby Ramos | .05 | .15 |
| ❏ 408 | Sid Monge | .05 | .15 |
| ❏ 409 | Brad Wellman | .05 | .15 |
| ❏ 410 | Bob Horner | .08 | .25 |
| ❏ 411 | Bobby Cox MG | .08 | .25 |
| ❏ 412 | Bud Black | .05 | .15 |
| ❏ 413 | Vance Law | .05 | .15 |
| ❏ 414 | Gary Ward | .05 | .15 |
| ❏ 415 | Ron Darling UER | .08 | .25 |
| ❏ 416 | Wayne Gross | .05 | .15 |
| ❏ 417 | John Franco RC | .30 | .75 |
| ❏ 418 | Ken Landreaux | .05 | .15 |
| ❏ 419 | Mike Caldwell | .05 | .15 |
| ❏ 420 | Andre Dawson | .08 | .25 |
| ❏ 421 | Dave Rucker | .05 | .15 |
| ❏ 422 | Carney Lansford | .08 | .25 |
| ❏ 423 | Barry Bonnell | .05 | .15 |
| ❏ 424 | Al Nipper | .05 | .15 |
| ❏ 425 | Mike Hargrove | .05 | .15 |
| ❏ 426 | Vern Ruhle | .05 | .15 |
| ❏ 427 | Mario Ramirez | .05 | .15 |
| ❏ 428 | Larry Andersen | .05 | .15 |
| ❏ 429 | Rick Cerone | .05 | .15 |
| ❏ 430 | Ron Davis | .05 | .15 |
| ❏ 431 | U.L. Washington | .05 | .15 |
| ❏ 432 | Thad Bosley | .05 | .15 |
| ❏ 433 | Jim Morrison | .05 | .15 |
| ❏ 434 | Gene Richards | .05 | .15 |
| ❏ 435 | Dan Petry | .05 | .15 |
| ❏ 436 | Willie Aikens | .05 | .15 |
| ❏ 437 | Al Jones | .05 | .15 |
| ❏ 438 | Joe Torre MG | .08 | .25 |
| ❏ 439 | Junior Ortiz | .05 | .15 |
| ❏ 440 | Fernando Valenzuela | .08 | .25 |
| ❏ 441 | Duane Walker | .05 | .15 |
| ❏ 442 | Ken Forsch | .05 | .15 |
| ❏ 443 | George Wright | .05 | .15 |
| ❏ 444 | Tony Phillips | .05 | .15 |
| ❏ 445 | Tippy Martinez | .05 | .15 |
| ❏ 446 | Jim Sundberg | .08 | .25 |
| ❏ 447 | Jeff Lahti | .05 | .15 |
| ❏ 448 | Derrel Thomas | .05 | .15 |
| ❏ 449 | Phil Bradley | .15 | .40 |
| ❏ 450 | Steve Garvey | .08 | .25 |
| ❏ 451 | Bruce Hurst | .05 | .15 |
| ❏ 452 | John Castino | .05 | .15 |
| ❏ 453 | Tom Waddell | .05 | .15 |
| ❏ 454 | Glenn Wilson | .05 | .15 |
| ❏ 455 | Bob Knepper | .05 | .15 |
| ❏ 456 | Tim Foli | .05 | .15 |
| ❏ 457 | Cecilio Guante | .05 | .15 |
| ❏ 458 | Randy Johnson | .05 | .15 |
| ❏ 459 | Charlie Leibrandt | .05 | .15 |
| ❏ 460 | Ryne Sandberg | .50 | 1.25 |
| ❏ 461 | Marty Castillo | .05 | .15 |
| ❏ 462 | Gary Lavelle | .05 | .15 |
| ❏ 463 | Dave Collins | .05 | .15 |
| ❏ 464 | Mike Mason RC | .05 | .15 |
| ❏ 465 | Bob Grich | .08 | .25 |
| ❏ 466 | Tony LaRussa MG | .08 | .25 |
| ❏ 467 | Ed Lynch | .05 | .15 |
| ❏ 468 | Wayne Krenchicki | .05 | .15 |
| ❏ 469 | Sammy Stewart | .05 | .15 |
| ❏ 470 | Steve Sax | .08 | .25 |
| ❏ 471 | Pete Ladd | .05 | .15 |
| ❏ 472 | Jim Essian | .05 | .15 |
| ❏ 473 | Tim Wallach | .08 | .25 |
| ❏ 474 | Kurt Kepshire | .05 | .15 |
| ❏ 475 | Andre Thornton | .05 | .15 |
| ❏ 476 | Jeff Stone RC | .05 | .15 |
| ❏ 477 | Bob Ojeda | .05 | .15 |
| ❏ 478 | Kurt Bevacqua | .05 | .15 |
| ❏ 479 | Mike Madden | .05 | .15 |
| ❏ 480 | Lou Whitaker | .08 | .25 |
| ❏ 481 | Dale Murray | .05 | .15 |
| ❏ 482 | Harry Spilman | .05 | .15 |
| ❏ 483 | Mike Smithson | .05 | .15 |
| ❏ 484 | Larry Bowa | .08 | .25 |
| ❏ 485 | Matt Young | .05 | .15 |
| ❏ 486 | Steve Balboni | .05 | .15 |
| ❏ 487 | Frank Williams | .05 | .15 |
| ❏ 488 | Joel Skinner | .05 | .15 |
| ❏ 489 | Bryan Clark | .05 | .15 |
| ❏ 490 | Jason Thompson | .05 | .15 |
| ❏ 491 | Rick Camp | .05 | .15 |
| ❏ 492 | Dave Johnson MG | .05 | .15 |
| ❏ 493 | Orel Hershiser RC | .75 | 2.00 |
| ❏ 494 | Rich Dauer | .05 | .15 |
| ❏ 495 | Mario Soto | .08 | .25 |
| ❏ 496 | Donnie Scott | .05 | .15 |
| ❏ 497 | Gary Pettis UER | .05 | .15 |
| ❏ 498 | Ed Romero | .05 | .15 |
| ❏ 499 | Danny Cox | .05 | .15 |
| ❏ 500 | Mike Schmidt | .60 | 1.50 |
| ❏ 501 | Dan Schatzeder | .05 | .15 |
| ❏ 502 | Rick Miller | .05 | .15 |
| ❏ 503 | Tim Conroy | .05 | .15 |
| ❏ 504 | Jerry Willard | .05 | .15 |
| ❏ 505 | Jim Beattie | .05 | .15 |
| ❏ 506 | Franklin Stubbs | .05 | .15 |
| ❏ 507 | Ray Fontenot | .05 | .15 |
| ❏ 508 | John Shelby | .05 | .15 |
| ❏ 509 | Milt May | .05 | .15 |
| ❏ 510 | Kent Hrbek | .08 | .25 |

| Card | Price 1 | Price 2 |
|---|---|---|
| 511 Lee Smith | .08 | .25 |
| 512 Tom Brookens | .05 | .15 |
| 513 Lynn Jones | .05 | .15 |
| 514 Jeff Cornell | .05 | .15 |
| 515 Dave Concepcion | .08 | .25 |
| 516 Roy Lee Jackson | .05 | .15 |
| 517 Jerry Martin | .05 | .15 |
| 518 Chris Chambliss | .08 | .25 |
| 519 Doug Rader MG | .05 | .15 |
| 520 LaMarr Hoyt | .05 | .15 |
| 521 Rick Dempsey | .05 | .15 |
| 522 Paul Molitor | .08 | .25 |
| 523 Candy Maldonado | .05 | .15 |
| 524 Rob Wilfong | .05 | .15 |
| 525 Darrell Porter | .05 | .15 |
| 526 David Palmer | .05 | .15 |
| 527 Checklist: 397-528 | .05 | .15 |
| 528 Bill Krueger | .05 | .15 |
| 529 Rich Gedman | .05 | .15 |
| 530 Dave Dravecky | .08 | .25 |
| 531 Joe Lefebvre | .05 | .15 |
| 532 Frank DiPino | .05 | .15 |
| 533 Tony Bernazard | .05 | .15 |
| 534 Brian Dayett | .05 | .15 |
| 535 Pat Putnam | .05 | .15 |
| 536 Kirby Puckett RC | 5.00 | 12.00 |
| 537 Don Robinson | .05 | .15 |
| 538 Keith Moreland | .05 | .15 |
| 539 Aurelio Lopez | .05 | .15 |
| 540 Claudell Washington | .05 | .15 |
| 541 Mark Davis | .05 | .15 |
| 542 Don Slaught | .05 | .15 |
| 543 Mike Squires | .05 | .15 |
| 544 Bruce Kison | .05 | .15 |
| 545 Lloyd Moseby | .05 | .15 |
| 546 Brent Gaff | .05 | .15 |
| 547 Pete Rose MG/TC | .15 | .40 |
| 548 Larry Parrish | .05 | .15 |
| 549 Mike Scioscia | .08 | .25 |
| 550 Scott McGregor | .15 | .40 |
| 551 Andy Van Slyke | .15 | .40 |
| 552 Chris Codiroli | .05 | .15 |
| 553 Bob Clark | .05 | .15 |
| 554 Doug Flynn | .05 | .15 |
| 555 Bob Stanley | .05 | .15 |
| 556 Sixto Lezcano | .05 | .15 |
| 557 Len Barker | .05 | .15 |
| 558 Carmelo Martinez | .05 | .15 |
| 559 Jay Howell | .05 | .15 |
| 560 Bill Madlock | .08 | .25 |
| 561 Darryl Motley | .05 | .15 |
| 562 Houston Jimenez | .05 | .15 |
| 563 Dick Ruthven | .05 | .15 |
| 564 Alan Ashby | .05 | .15 |
| 565 Kirk Gibson | .08 | .25 |
| 566 Ed VandeBerg | .05 | .15 |
| 567 Joel Youngblood | .05 | .15 |
| 568 Cliff Johnson | .05 | .15 |
| 569 Ken Oberkfell | .05 | .15 |
| 570 Darryl Strawberry | .25 | .60 |
| 571 Charlie Hough | .08 | .25 |
| 572 Tom Paciorek | .05 | .15 |
| 573 Jay Tibbs | .05 | .15 |
| 574 Joe Altobelli MG | .05 | .15 |
| 575 Pedro Guerrero | .08 | .25 |
| 576 Jaime Cocanower | .05 | .15 |
| 577 Chris Speier | .05 | .15 |
| 578 Terry Francona | .08 | .25 |
| 579 Ron Romanick | .05 | .15 |
| 580 Dwight Evans | .15 | .40 |
| 581 Mark Wagner | .05 | .15 |
| 582 Ken Phelps | .05 | .15 |
| 583 Bobby Brown | .05 | .15 |
| 584 Kevin Gross | .05 | .15 |
| 585 Butch Wynegar | .05 | .15 |
| 586 Bill Scherrer | .05 | .15 |
| 587 Doug Frobel | .05 | .15 |
| 588 Bobby Castillo | .05 | .15 |
| 589 Bob Dernier | .05 | .15 |
| 590 Ray Knight | .08 | .25 |
| 591 Larry Herndon | .05 | .15 |
| 592 Jeff D. Robinson | .05 | .15 |
| 593 Rick Leach | .05 | .15 |
| 594 Curt Wilkerson | .05 | .15 |
| 595 Gary Gura | .05 | .15 |
| 596 Jerry Hairston | .05 | .15 |
| 597 Brad Lesley | .05 | .15 |
| 598 Jose Oquendo | .05 | .15 |
| 599 Storm Davis | .05 | .15 |
| 600 Pete Rose | .50 | 1.50 |
| 601 Tom Lasorda MG | .15 | .40 |
| 602 Jeff Dedmon | .05 | .15 |
| 603 Rick Manning | .05 | .15 |
| 604 Daryl Sconiers | .05 | .15 |
| 605 Ozzie Smith | .40 | 1.00 |
| 606 Rich Gale | .05 | .15 |
| 607 Bill Almon | .05 | .15 |
| 608 Craig Lefferts | .05 | .15 |
| 609 Broderick Perkins | .05 | .15 |
| 610 Jack Morris | .08 | .25 |
| 611 Ozzie Virgil | .05 | .15 |
| 612 Mike Armstrong | .05 | .15 |
| 613 Terry Puhl | .05 | .15 |
| 614 Al Williams | .05 | .15 |
| 615 Marvell Wynne | .05 | .15 |
| 616 Scott Sanderson | .05 | .15 |
| 617 Willie Wilson | .08 | .25 |
| 618 Pete Falcone | .05 | .15 |
| 619 Jeff Leonard | .05 | .15 |
| 620 Dwight Gooden RC | .75 | 2.00 |
| 621 Marvis Foley | .05 | .15 |
| 622 Luis Leal | .05 | .15 |
| 623 Greg Walker | .05 | .15 |
| 624 Benny Ayala | .05 | .15 |
| 625 Mark Langston RC | .30 | .75 |
| 626 German Rivera | .05 | .15 |
| 627 Eric Davis RC | .75 | 2.00 |
| 628 Rene Lachemann MG | .05 | .15 |
| 629 Dick Schofield | .05 | .15 |
| 630 Tim Raines | .08 | .25 |
| 631 Bob Forsch | .05 | .15 |
| 632 Bruce Bochte | .05 | .15 |
| 633 Glenn Hoffman | .05 | .15 |
| 634 Bill Dawley | .05 | .15 |
| 635 Terry Kennedy | .05 | .15 |
| 636 Shane Rawley | .05 | .15 |
| 637 Brett Butler | .08 | .25 |
| 638 Mike Pagliarulo | .05 | .15 |
| 639 Ed Hodge | .05 | .15 |
| 640 Steve Henderson | .05 | .15 |
| 641 Rod Scurry | .05 | .15 |
| 642 Dave Owen | .05 | .15 |
| 643 Johnny Grubb | .05 | .15 |
| 644 Mark Huismann | .05 | .15 |
| 645 Damaso Garcia | .05 | .15 |
| 646 Scot Thompson | .05 | .15 |
| 647 Rafael Ramirez | .05 | .15 |
| 648 Bob Jones | .05 | .15 |
| 649 Sid Fernandez | .08 | .25 |
| 650 Greg Luzinski | .08 | .25 |
| 651 Jeff Russell | .05 | .15 |
| 652 Joe Nolan | .05 | .15 |
| 653 Mark Brouhard | .05 | .15 |
| 654 Dave Anderson | .05 | .15 |
| 655 Joaquin Andujar | .08 | .25 |
| 656 Chuck Cottier MG | .05 | .15 |
| 657 Jim Slaton | .05 | .15 |
| 658 Mike Stenhouse | .05 | .15 |
| 659 Checklist: 529-660 | .05 | .15 |
| 660 Tony Gwynn | .50 | 1.25 |
| 661 Steve Crawford | .05 | .15 |
| 662 Mike Heath | .05 | .15 |
| 663 Luis Aguayo | .05 | .15 |
| 664 Steve Farr RC | .15 | .40 |
| 665 Don Mattingly | 1.00 | 2.50 |
| 666 Mike LaCoss | .05 | .15 |
| 667 Dave Engle | .05 | .15 |
| 668 Steve Trout | .05 | .15 |
| 669 Lee Lacy | .05 | .15 |
| 670 Tom Seaver | .15 | .40 |
| 671 Dane Iorg | .05 | .15 |
| 672 Juan Berenguer | .05 | .15 |
| 673 Buck Martinez | .05 | .15 |
| 674 Atlee Hammaker | .05 | .15 |
| 675 Tony Perez | .15 | .40 |
| 676 Albert Hall | .05 | .15 |
| 677 Wally Backman | .05 | .15 |
| 678 Joey McLaughlin | .05 | .15 |
| 679 Bob Kearney | .05 | .15 |
| 680 Jerry Reuss | .05 | .15 |
| 681 Ben Oglivie | .05 | .15 |
| 682 Doug Corbett | .05 | .15 |
| 683 Whitey Herzog MG | .05 | .15 |
| 684 Bill Doran | .05 | .15 |
| 685 Bill Caudill | .05 | .15 |
| 686 Mike Easler | .05 | .15 |
| 687 Bill Gullickson | .05 | .15 |
| 688 Len Matuszek | .05 | .15 |
| 689 Luis DeLeon | .05 | .15 |
| 690 Alan Trammell | .08 | .25 |
| 691 Dennis Rasmussen | .05 | .15 |
| 692 Randy Bush | .05 | .15 |
| 693 Tim Stoddard | .05 | .15 |
| 694 Joe Carter | .25 | .60 |
| 695 Rick Rhoden | .05 | .15 |
| 696 John Rabb | .05 | .15 |
| 697 Onix Concepcion | .05 | .15 |
| 698 George Bell | .08 | .25 |
| 699 Donnie Moore | .05 | .15 |
| 700 Eddie Murray | .25 | .60 |
| 701 Eddie Murray AS | .15 | .40 |
| 702 Damaso Garcia AS | .05 | .15 |
| 703 George Brett AS | .25 | .60 |
| 704 Cal Ripken AS | .60 | 1.50 |
| 705 Dave Winfield AS | .15 | .40 |
| 706 Rickey Henderson AS | .15 | .40 |
| 707 Tony Armas AS | .05 | .15 |
| 708 Lance Parrish AS | .08 | .25 |
| 709 Mike Boddicker AS | .05 | .15 |
| 710 Frank Viola AS | .05 | .15 |
| 711 Dan Quisenberry AS | .05 | .15 |
| 712 Keith Hernandez AS | .05 | .15 |
| 713 Ryne Sandberg AS | .25 | .60 |
| 714 Mike Schmidt AS | .25 | .60 |
| 715 Ozzie Smith AS | .05 | .15 |
| 716 Dale Murphy AS | .08 | .25 |
| 717 Tony Gwynn AS | .40 | 1.00 |
| 718 Jeff Leonard AS | .05 | .15 |
| 719 Gary Carter AS | .15 | .40 |
| 720 Rick Sutcliffe AS | .05 | .15 |
| 721 Bob Knepper AS | .05 | .15 |
| 722 Bruce Sutter AS | .05 | .15 |
| 723 Dave Stewart | .08 | .25 |
| 724 Oscar Gamble | .05 | .15 |
| 725 Floyd Bannister | .05 | .15 |
| 726 Al Bumbry | .05 | .15 |
| 727 Frank Pastore | .05 | .15 |
| 728 Bob Bailor | .05 | .15 |
| 729 Don Sutton | .08 | .25 |
| 730 Dave Kingman | .08 | .25 |
| 731 Neil Allen | .05 | .15 |
| 732 John McNamara MG | .05 | .15 |
| 733 Tony Scott | .05 | .15 |
| 734 John Henry Johnson | .05 | .15 |
| 735 Garry Templeton | .08 | .25 |
| 736 Jerry Mumphrey | .05 | .15 |
| 737 Bo Diaz | .05 | .15 |
| 738 Omar Moreno | .05 | .15 |
| 739 Ernie Camacho | .05 | .15 |
| 740 Jack Clark | .08 | .25 |
| 741 John Butcher | .05 | .15 |
| 742 Ron Hassey | .05 | .15 |
| 743 Frank White | .08 | .25 |
| 744 Doug Bair | .05 | .15 |
| 745 Buddy Bell | .08 | .25 |
| 746 Jim Clancy | .05 | .15 |
| 747 Alex Trevino | .05 | .15 |
| 748 Lee Mazzilli | .05 | .15 |
| 749 Julio Cruz | .05 | .15 |
| 750 Rollie Fingers | .15 | .40 |
| 751 Kelvin Chapman | .05 | .15 |
| 752 Bob Owchinko | .05 | .15 |
| 753 Greg Brock | .05 | .15 |
| 754 Larry Milbourne | .05 | .15 |
| 755 Ken Singleton | .08 | .25 |
| 756 Rob Picciolo | .05 | .15 |
| 757 Willie McGee | .08 | .25 |
| 758 Ray Burris | .05 | .15 |
| 759 Jim Fanning MG | .05 | .15 |
| 760 Nolan Ryan | 1.25 | 3.00 |
| 761 Jerry Remy | .05 | .15 |
| 762 Eddie Whitson | .05 | .15 |
| 763 Kiko Garcia | .05 | .15 |
| 764 Jamie Easterly | .05 | .15 |
| 765 Willie Randolph | .08 | .25 |
| 766 Paul Mirabella | .05 | .15 |
| 767 Darrell Brown | .05 | .15 |
| 768 Ron Cey | .08 | .25 |
| 769 Joe Cowley | .05 | .15 |
| 770 Carlton Fisk | .15 | .40 |
| 771 Geoff Zahn | .05 | .15 |
| 772 Johnnie LeMaster | .05 | .15 |
| 773 Hal McRae | .08 | .25 |
| 774 Dennis Lamp | .05 | .15 |

| | | |
|---|---|---|
| ☐ 775 Mookie Wilson | .08 | .25 |
| ☐ 776 Jerry Royster | .05 | .15 |
| ☐ 777 Ned Yost | .05 | .15 |
| ☐ 778 Mike Davis | .05 | .15 |
| ☐ 779 Nick Esasky | .05 | .15 |
| ☐ 780 Mike Flanagan | .05 | .15 |
| ☐ 781 Jim Gantner | .05 | .15 |
| ☐ 782 Tom Niedenfuer | .05 | .15 |
| ☐ 783 Mike Jorgensen | .05 | .15 |
| ☐ 784 Checklist: 661-792 | .05 | .15 |
| ☐ 785 Tony Armas | .08 | .25 |
| ☐ 786 Enos Cabell | .05 | .15 |
| ☐ 787 Jim Wohlford | .05 | .15 |
| ☐ 788 Steve Comer | .05 | .15 |
| ☐ 789 Luis Salazar | .05 | .15 |
| ☐ 790 Ron Guidry | .08 | .25 |
| ☐ 791 Ivan DeJesus | .05 | .15 |
| ☐ 792 Darrell Evans | .08 | .25 |

### 1986 Topps

VINCE COLEMAN

| | | |
|---|---|---|
| ☐ COMPLETE SET (792) | 10.00 | 25.00 |
| ☐ COMP.X-MAS.SET (792) | 75.00 | 150.00 |
| ☐ 1 Pete Rose | .75 | 2.00 |
| ☐ 2 Rose Special: '63-'66 | .08 | .25 |
| ☐ 3 Rose Special: '67-'70 | .08 | .25 |
| ☐ 4 Rose Special: '71-'74 | .08 | .25 |
| ☐ 5 Rose Special: '75-'78 | .08 | .25 |
| ☐ 6 Rose Special: '79-'82 | .08 | .25 |
| ☐ 7 Rose Special: '83-'85 | .08 | .25 |
| ☐ 8 Dwayne Murphy | .02 | .10 |
| ☐ 9 Roy Smith | .02 | .10 |
| ☐ 10 Tony Gwynn | .25 | .60 |
| ☐ 11 Bob Ojeda | .02 | .10 |
| ☐ 12 Jose Uribe | .02 | .10 |
| ☐ 13 Bob Kearney | .02 | .10 |
| ☐ 14 Julio Cruz | .02 | .10 |
| ☐ 15 Eddie Whitson | .02 | .10 |
| ☐ 16 Rick Schu | .02 | .10 |
| ☐ 17 Mike Stenhouse | .02 | .10 |
| ☐ 18 Brent Gaff | .02 | .10 |
| ☐ 19 Rich Hebner | .02 | .10 |
| ☐ 20 Lou Whitaker | .05 | .15 |
| ☐ 21 George Bamberger MG | .02 | .10 |
| ☐ 22 Duane Walker | .02 | .10 |
| ☐ 23 Manuel Lee RC* | .02 | .10 |
| ☐ 24 Len Barker | .02 | .10 |
| ☐ 25 Willie Wilson | .05 | .15 |
| ☐ 26 Frank DiPino | .02 | .10 |
| ☐ 27 Ray Knight | .05 | .15 |
| ☐ 28 Eric Davis | .15 | .40 |
| ☐ 29 Tony Phillips | .15 | .40 |
| ☐ 30 Eddie Murray | .15 | .40 |
| ☐ 31 Jamie Easterly | .02 | .10 |
| ☐ 32 Steve Yeager | .05 | .15 |
| ☐ 33 Jeff Lahti | .02 | .10 |
| ☐ 34 Ken Phelps | .02 | .10 |
| ☐ 35 Jeff Reardon | .05 | .15 |
| ☐ 36 Tigers Leaders Lance Parrish | .05 | .15 |
| ☐ 37 Mark Thurmond | .02 | .10 |
| ☐ 38 Glenn Hoffman | .02 | .10 |
| ☐ 39 Dave Rucker | .02 | .10 |
| ☐ 40 Ken Griffey | .05 | .15 |
| ☐ 41 Brad Wellman | .02 | .10 |
| ☐ 42 Geoff Zahn | .02 | .10 |
| ☐ 43 Dave Engle | .02 | .10 |
| ☐ 44 Lance McCullers | .02 | .10 |
| ☐ 45 Damaso Garcia | .02 | .10 |
| ☐ 46 Billy Hatcher | .02 | .10 |
| ☐ 47 Juan Berenguer | .02 | .10 |
| ☐ 48 Bill Almon | .02 | .10 |
| ☐ 49 Rick Manning | .02 | .10 |
| ☐ 50 Dan Quisenberry | .02 | .10 |
| ☐ 51 Bobby Wine MG ERR | .02 | .10 |

| | | |
|---|---|---|
| (Checklist back) (Number of ca | .02 | .10 |
| ☐ 52 Chris Welsh | .02 | .10 |
| ☐ 53 Len Dykstra RC | .30 | .75 |
| ☐ 54 John Franco | .05 | .15 |
| ☐ 55 Fred Lynn | .05 | .15 |
| ☐ 56 Tom Niedenfuer | .02 | .10 |
| ☐ 57 Bill Doran (See also 51) | | |
| ☐ 58 Bill Krueger | .02 | .10 |
| ☐ 59 Andre Thornton | .02 | .10 |
| ☐ 60 Dwight Evans | .08 | .25 |
| ☐ 61 Karl Best | .02 | .10 |
| ☐ 62 Bob Boone | .05 | .15 |
| ☐ 63 Ron Roenicke | .02 | .10 |
| ☐ 64 Floyd Bannister | .02 | .10 |
| ☐ 65 Dan Driessen | .02 | .10 |
| ☐ 66 Cardinals Leaders Bob Forsch | .02 | .10 |
| ☐ 67 Carmelo Martinez | .02 | .10 |
| ☐ 68 Ed Lynch | .02 | .10 |
| ☐ 69 Luis Aguayo | .02 | .10 |
| ☐ 70 Dave Winfield | .05 | .15 |
| ☐ 71 Ken Schrom | .02 | .10 |
| ☐ 72 Shawon Dunston | .05 | .15 |
| ☐ 73 Randy O'Neal | .02 | .10 |
| ☐ 74 Rance Mulliniks | .02 | .10 |
| ☐ 75 Jose DeLeon | .02 | .10 |
| ☐ 76 Dion James | .02 | .10 |
| ☐ 77 Charlie Leibrandt | .02 | .10 |
| ☐ 78 Bruce Benedict | .02 | .10 |
| ☐ 79 Dave Schmidt | .02 | .10 |
| ☐ 80 Daryl Strawberry | .08 | .25 |
| ☐ 81 Gene Mauch MG | .02 | .10 |
| ☐ 82 Tippy Martinez | .02 | .10 |
| ☐ 83 Phil Garner | .05 | .15 |
| ☐ 84 Curt Young | .02 | .10 |
| ☐ 85 Tony Perez w/E.Davis | .05 | .15 |
| ☐ 86 Tom Waddell | .02 | .10 |
| ☐ 87 Candy Maldonado | .02 | .10 |
| ☐ 88 Tom Nieto | .02 | .10 |
| ☐ 89 Randy St.Claire | .02 | .10 |
| ☐ 90 Garry Templeton | .05 | .15 |
| ☐ 91 Steve Crawford | .02 | .10 |
| ☐ 92 Al Cowens | .02 | .10 |
| ☐ 93 Scot Thompson | .02 | .10 |
| ☐ 94 Rich Bordi | .02 | .10 |
| ☐ 95 Ozzie Virgil | .02 | .10 |
| ☐ 96 Blue Jays Leaders Jim Clancy | .02 | .10 |
| ☐ 97 Gary Gaetti | .05 | .15 |
| ☐ 98 Dick Ruthven | .02 | .10 |
| ☐ 99 Buddy Biancalana | .02 | .10 |
| ☐ 100 Nolan Ryan | .75 | 2.00 |
| ☐ 101 Dave Bergman | .02 | .10 |
| ☐ 102 Joe Orsulak RC* | .08 | .25 |
| ☐ 103 Luis Salazar | .02 | .10 |
| ☐ 104 Sid Fernandez | .02 | .10 |
| ☐ 105 Gary Ward | .02 | .10 |
| ☐ 106 Ray Burris | .02 | .10 |
| ☐ 107 Rafael Ramirez | .02 | .10 |
| ☐ 108 Ted Power | .02 | .10 |
| ☐ 109 Len Matuszek | .02 | .10 |
| ☐ 110 Scott McGregor | .02 | .10 |
| ☐ 111 Roger Craig MG | .05 | .15 |
| ☐ 112 Bill Campbell | .02 | .10 |
| ☐ 113 U.L. Washington | .02 | .10 |
| ☐ 114 Mike C. Brown | .02 | .10 |
| ☐ 115 Jay Howell | .02 | .10 |
| ☐ 116 Brook Jacoby | .02 | .10 |
| ☐ 117 Bruce Kison | .02 | .10 |
| ☐ 118 Jerry Royster | .02 | .10 |
| ☐ 119 Barry Bonnell | .02 | .10 |
| ☐ 120 Steve Carlton | .05 | .15 |
| ☐ 121 Nelson Simmons | .02 | .10 |
| ☐ 122 Pete Filson | .02 | .10 |
| ☐ 123 Greg Walker | .02 | .10 |
| ☐ 124 Luis Sanchez | .02 | .10 |
| ☐ 125 Dave Lopes | .05 | .15 |
| ☐ 126 Mets Leaders Mookie Wilson | .02 | .10 |
| ☐ 127 Jack Howell | .02 | .10 |
| ☐ 128 John Wathan | .02 | .10 |
| ☐ 129 Jeff Dedmon | .02 | .10 |
| ☐ 130 Alan Trammell | .05 | .15 |
| ☐ 131 Checklist: 1-132 | .05 | .15 |
| ☐ 132 Razor Shines | .02 | .10 |
| ☐ 133 Andy McGaffigan | .02 | .10 |

| | | |
|---|---|---|
| ☐ 134 Carney Lansford | .05 | .15 |
| ☐ 135 Joe Niekro | .02 | .10 |
| ☐ 136 Mike Hargrove | .02 | .10 |
| ☐ 137 Charlie Moore | .02 | .10 |
| ☐ 138 Mark Davis | .02 | .10 |
| ☐ 139 Daryl Boston | .02 | .10 |
| ☐ 140 John Candelaria | .02 | .10 |
| ☐ 141 Chuck Cottier MG See also 171 | .02 | .10 |
| ☐ 142 Bob Jones | .02 | .10 |
| ☐ 143 Dave Van Gorder | .02 | .10 |
| ☐ 144 Doug Sisk | .02 | .10 |
| ☐ 145 Pedro Guerrero | .05 | .15 |
| ☐ 146 Jack Perconte | .02 | .10 |
| ☐ 147 Larry Sheets | .02 | .10 |
| ☐ 148 Mike Heath | .02 | .10 |
| ☐ 149 Brett Butler | .05 | .15 |
| ☐ 150 Joaquin Andujar | .05 | .15 |
| ☐ 151 Dave Stapleton | .02 | .10 |
| ☐ 152 Mike Morgan | .02 | .10 |
| ☐ 153 Ricky Adams | .02 | .10 |
| ☐ 154 Bert Roberge | .02 | .10 |
| ☐ 155 Bob Grich | .05 | .15 |
| ☐ 156 White Sox Leaders Richard Dotson | .02 | .10 |
| ☐ 157 Ron Hassey | .02 | .10 |
| ☐ 158 Derrel Thomas | .02 | .10 |
| ☐ 159 Orel Hershiser UER | .15 | .40 |
| ☐ 160 Chet Lemon | .05 | .15 |
| ☐ 161 Lee Tunnell | .02 | .10 |
| ☐ 162 Greg Gagne | .02 | .10 |
| ☐ 163 Pete Ladd | .02 | .10 |
| ☐ 164 Steve Balboni | .02 | .10 |
| ☐ 165 Mike Davis | .02 | .10 |
| ☐ 166 Dickie Thon | .02 | .10 |
| ☐ 167 Zane Smith | .02 | .10 |
| ☐ 168 Jeff Burroughs | .02 | .10 |
| ☐ 169 George Wright | .02 | .10 |
| ☐ 170 Gary Carter | .05 | .15 |
| ☐ 171 Bob Rodgers MG ERR (Checklist back) (Number of ca | .02 | .10 |
| ☐ 172 Jerry Reed | .02 | .10 |
| ☐ 173 Wayne Gross | .02 | .10 |
| ☐ 174 Brian Snyder | .02 | .10 |
| ☐ 175 Steve Sax | .05 | .15 |
| ☐ 176 Jay Tibbs | .02 | .10 |
| ☐ 177 Joel Youngblood | .02 | .10 |
| ☐ 178 Ivan DeJesus | .02 | .10 |
| ☐ 179 Stu Cliburn | .02 | .10 |
| ☐ 180 Don Mattingly | .50 | 1.25 |
| ☐ 181 Al Nipper | .02 | .10 |
| ☐ 182 Bobby Brown | .02 | .10 |
| ☐ 183 Larry Andersen | .02 | .10 |
| ☐ 184 Tim Laudner | .02 | .10 |
| ☐ 185 Rollie Fingers | .05 | .15 |
| ☐ 186 Astros Leaders Jose Cruz | .02 | .10 |
| ☐ 187 Scott Fletcher | .02 | .10 |
| ☐ 188 Bob Dernier | .02 | .10 |
| ☐ 189 Mike Mason | .02 | .10 |
| ☐ 190 George Hendrick | .05 | .15 |
| ☐ 191 Wally Backman | .02 | .10 |
| ☐ 192 Milt Wilcox | .02 | .10 |
| ☐ 193 Daryl Sconiers | .02 | .10 |
| ☐ 194 Craig McMurtry | .02 | .10 |
| ☐ 195 Dave Concepcion | .05 | .15 |
| ☐ 196 Doyle Alexander | .02 | .10 |
| ☐ 197 Enos Cabell | .02 | .10 |
| ☐ 198 Ken Dixon | .02 | .10 |
| ☐ 199 Dick Howser MG | .02 | .10 |
| ☐ 200 Mike Schmidt | .40 | 1.00 |
| ☐ 201 Vince Coleman RB Most stolen bases& seasons rook | | |
| ☐ 202 Dwight Gooden RB | .05 | .15 |
| ☐ 203 Keith Hernandez RB | .08 | .25 |
| ☐ 204 Phil Niekro RB Oldest shutout pitcher | | |
| ☐ 205 Tony Perez RB Oldest grand slammer | .05 | .15 |
| ☐ 206 Pete Rose RB | .15 | .40 |
| ☐ 207 Fernando Valenzuela RB Most cons. innings& start | .02 | .10 |
| ☐ 208 Ramon Romero | .02 | .10 |
| ☐ 209 Randy Ready | .02 | .10 |
| ☐ 210 Calvin Schiraldi | .02 | .10 |

|  |  | | |
|---|--------|---|---|
| 211 | Ed Wojna | .02 | .10 |
| 212 | Chris Speier | .02 | .10 |
| 213 | Bob Shirley | .02 | .10 |
| 214 | Randy Bush | .02 | .10 |
| 215 | Frank White | .05 | .15 |
| 216 | A's Leaders | | |
| | Dwayne Murphy | .02 | .10 |
| 217 | Bill Scherrer | .02 | .10 |
| 218 | Randy Hunt | .02 | .10 |
| 219 | Dennis Lamp | .02 | .10 |
| 220 | Bob Horner | .05 | .15 |
| 221 | Dave Henderson | .02 | .10 |
| 222 | Craig Gerber | .02 | .10 |
| 223 | Atlee Hammaker | .02 | .10 |
| 224 | Cesar Cedeno | .05 | .15 |
| 225 | Ron Darling | .05 | .15 |
| 226 | Lee Lacy | .02 | .10 |
| 227 | Al Jones | .02 | .10 |
| 228 | Tom Lawless | .02 | .10 |
| 229 | Bill Gullickson | .02 | .10 |
| 230 | Terry Kennedy | .02 | .10 |
| 231 | Jim Frey MG | .02 | .10 |
| 232 | Rick Rhoden | .02 | .10 |
| 233 | Steve Lyons | .02 | .10 |
| 234 | Doug Corbett | .02 | .10 |
| 235 | Butch Wynegar | .02 | .10 |
| 236 | Frank Eufemia | .02 | .10 |
| 237 | Ted Simmons | .05 | .15 |
| 238 | Larry Parrish | .02 | .10 |
| 239 | Joel Skinner | .02 | .10 |
| 240 | Tommy John | .05 | .15 |
| 241 | Tony Fernandez | .05 | .15 |
| 242 | Rich Thompson | .02 | .10 |
| 243 | Johnny Grubb | .02 | .10 |
| 244 | Craig Lefferts | .02 | .10 |
| 245 | Jim Sundberg | .02 | .10 |
| 246 | Steve Carlton TL | .05 | .15 |
| 247 | Terry Harper | .02 | .10 |
| 248 | Spike Owen | .02 | .10 |
| 249 | Rob Deer | .05 | .15 |
| 250 | Dwight Gooden | .15 | .40 |
| 251 | Rich Dauer | .02 | .10 |
| 252 | Bobby Castillo | .02 | .10 |
| 253 | Dann Bilardello | .02 | .10 |
| 254 | Ozzie Guillen RC | .60 | 1.50 |
| 255 | Tony Armas | .05 | .15 |
| 256 | Kurt Kepshire | .02 | .10 |
| 257 | Doug DeCinces | .02 | .10 |
| 258 | Tim Burke | .02 | .10 |
| 259 | Dan Pasqua | .02 | .10 |
| 260 | Tony Pena | .05 | .15 |
| 261 | Bobby Valentine MG | .05 | .15 |
| 262 | Mario Ramirez | .02 | .10 |
| 263 | Checklist: 133-264 | .05 | .15 |
| 264 | Darren Daulton RC | .20 | .50 |
| 265 | Ron Davis | .02 | .10 |
| 266 | Keith Moreland | .02 | .10 |
| 267 | Paul Molitor | .05 | .15 |
| 268 | Mike Scott | .05 | .15 |
| 269 | Dane Iorg | .02 | .10 |
| 270 | Jack Morris | .05 | .15 |
| 271 | Dave Collins | .02 | .10 |
| 272 | Tim Tolman | .02 | .10 |
| 273 | Jerry Willard | .02 | .10 |
| 274 | Ron Gardenhire | .05 | .15 |
| 275 | Charlie Hough | .05 | .15 |
| 276 | Yankees Leaders | | |
| | Willie Randolph | .05 | .15 |
| 277 | Jaime Cocanower | .02 | .10 |
| 278 | Sixto Lezcano | .02 | .10 |
| 279 | Al Pardo | .02 | .10 |
| 280 | Tim Raines | .05 | .15 |
| 281 | Steve Mura | .02 | .10 |
| 282 | Jerry Mumphrey | .02 | .10 |
| 283 | Mike Fischlin | .02 | .10 |
| 284 | Brian Dayett | .02 | .10 |
| 285 | Buddy Bell | .05 | .15 |
| 286 | Luis DeLeon | .02 | .10 |
| 287 | John Christensen | .02 | .10 |
| 288 | Don Aase | .02 | .10 |
| 289 | Johnnie LeMaster | .02 | .10 |
| 290 | Carlton Fisk | .08 | .25 |
| 291 | Tom Lasorda MG | .08 | .25 |
| 292 | Chuck Porter | .02 | .10 |
| 293 | Chris Chambliss | .05 | .15 |
| 294 | Danny Cox | .02 | .10 |
| 295 | Kirk Gibson | .08 | .25 |
| 296 | Geno Petralli | .02 | .10 |
| 297 | Tim Lollar | .02 | .10 |
| 298 | Craig Reynolds | .02 | .10 |
| 299 | Bryn Smith | .02 | .10 |
| 300 | George Brett | .40 | 1.00 |
| 301 | Dennis Rasmussen | .02 | .10 |
| 302 | Greg Gross | .02 | .10 |
| 303 | Curt Wardle | .02 | .10 |
| 304 | Mike Gallego RC | .02 | .10 |
| 305 | Phil Bradley | .02 | .10 |
| 306 | Padres Leaders | | |
| | Terry Kennedy | .02 | .10 |
| 307 | Dave Sax | .02 | .10 |
| 308 | Ray Fontenot | .02 | .10 |
| 309 | John Shelby | .02 | .10 |
| 310 | Greg Minton | .02 | .10 |
| 311 | Dick Schofield | .02 | .10 |
| 312 | Tom Filer | .02 | .10 |
| 313 | Joe DeSa | .02 | .10 |
| 314 | Frank Pastore | .02 | .10 |
| 315 | Mookie Wilson | .05 | .15 |
| 316 | Sammy Khalifa | .02 | .10 |
| 317 | Ed Romero | .02 | .10 |
| 318 | Terry Whitfield | .02 | .10 |
| 319 | Rick Camp | .02 | .10 |
| 320 | Jim Rice | .05 | .15 |
| 321 | Earl Weaver MG | .05 | .15 |
| 322 | Bob Forsch | .02 | .10 |
| 323 | Jerry Davis | .02 | .10 |
| 324 | Dan Schatzeder | .02 | .10 |
| 325 | Juan Beniquez | .02 | .10 |
| 326 | Kent Tekulve | .02 | .10 |
| 327 | Mike Pagliarulo | .05 | .15 |
| 328 | Pete O'Brien | .02 | .10 |
| 329 | Kirby Puckett | .40 | 1.00 |
| 330 | Rick Sutcliffe | .05 | .15 |
| 331 | Alan Ashby | .02 | .10 |
| 332 | Darryl Motley | .02 | .10 |
| 333 | Tom Henke | .05 | .15 |
| 334 | Ken Oberkfell | .02 | .10 |
| 335 | Don Sutton | .05 | .15 |
| 336 | Indians Leaders | | |
| | Andre Thornton | .05 | .15 |
| 337 | Darnell Coles | .05 | .15 |
| 338 | Jorge Bell | .05 | .15 |
| 339 | Bruce Berenyi | .02 | .10 |
| 340 | Cal Ripken | .60 | 1.50 |
| 341 | Frank Williams | .02 | .10 |
| 342 | Gary Redus | .02 | .10 |
| 343 | Carlos Diaz | .02 | .10 |
| 344 | Jim Wohlford | .02 | .10 |
| 345 | Donnie Moore | .02 | .10 |
| 346 | Bryan Little | .02 | .10 |
| 347 | Teddy Higuera RC* | .08 | .25 |
| 348 | Cliff Johnson | .02 | .10 |
| 349 | Mark Clear | .02 | .10 |
| 350 | Jack Clark | .05 | .15 |
| 351 | Chuck Tanner MG | .02 * | .10 |
| 352 | Harry Spilman | .02 | .10 |
| 353 | Keith Atherton | .02 | .10 |
| 354 | Tony Bernazard | .02 | .10 |
| 355 | Lee Smith | .05 | .15 |
| 356 | Mickey Hatcher | .02 | .10 |
| 357 | Ed VandeBerg | .02 | .10 |
| 358 | Rick Dempsey | .02 | .10 |
| 359 | Mike LaCoss | .02 | .10 |
| 360 | Lloyd Moseby | .02 | .10 |
| 361 | Shane Rawley | .02 | .10 |
| 362 | Tom Paciorek | .02 | .10 |
| 363 | Terry Forster | .05 | .15 |
| 364 | Reid Nichols | .02 | .10 |
| 365 | Mike Flanagan | .02 | .10 |
| 366 | Reds Leaders | | |
| | Dave Concepcion | .05 | .15 |
| 367 | Aurelio Lopez | .02 | .10 |
| 368 | Greg Brock | .02 | .10 |
| 369 | Al Holland | .02 | .10 |
| 370 | Vince Coleman RC | .20 | .50 |
| 371 | Bill Stein | .02 | .10 |
| 372 | Ben Oglivie | .05 | .15 |
| 373 | Urbano Lugo | .02 | .10 |
| 374 | Terry Francona | .02 | .10 |
| 375 | Rich Gedman | .02 | .10 |
| 376 | Bill Dawley | .02 | .10 |
| 377 | Joe Carter | .05 | .15 |
| 378 | Bruce Bochte | .02 | .10 |
| 379 | Bobby Meacham | .02 | .10 |
| 380 | LaMarr Hoyt | .02 | .10 |
| 381 | Ray Miller MG | .02 | .10 |
| 382 | Ivan Calderon RC* | .08 | .25 |
| 383 | Chris Brown RC | .02 | .10 |
| 384 | Steve Trout | .02 | .10 |
| 385 | Cecil Cooper | .05 | .15 |
| 386 | Cecil Fielder RC | .40 | 1.00 |
| 387 | Steve Kemp | .02 | .10 |
| 388 | Dickie Noles | .02 | .10 |
| 389 | Glenn Davis | .02 | .10 |
| 390 | Tom Seaver | .08 | .25 |
| 391 | Julio Franco | .05 | .15 |
| 392 | John Russell | .02 | .10 |
| 393 | Chris Pittaro | .02 | .10 |
| 394 | Checklist: 265-396 | .05 | .15 |
| 395 | Scott Garrelts | .02 | .10 |
| 396 | Red Sox Leaders | | |
| | Dwight Evans | .08 | .25 |
| 397 | Steve Buechele RC | .08 | .25 |
| 398 | Earnie Riles | .02 | .10 |
| 399 | Bill Swift | .02 | .10 |
| 400 | Rod Carew | .08 | .25 |
| 401 | Fernando Valenzuela | | |
| | | .02 | .10 |
| | TBC '81 | | |
| 402 | Tom Seaver TBC | .05 | .15 |
| 403 | Willie Mays TBC | .15 | .40 |
| 404 | Frank Robinson TBC | .05 | .15 |
| 405 | Roger Maris TBC | .15 | .40 |
| 406 | Scott Sanderson | .02 | .10 |
| 407 | Sal Butera | .02 | .10 |
| 408 | Dave Smith | .02 | .10 |
| 409 | Paul Runge RC | .02 | .10 |
| 410 | Dave Kingman | .05 | .15 |
| 411 | Sparky Anderson MG | .05 | .15 |
| 412 | Jim Clancy | .02 | .10 |
| 413 | Tim Flannery | .02 | .10 |
| 414 | Tom Gorman | .02 | .10 |
| 415 | Hal McRae | .05 | .15 |
| 416 | Dennis Martinez | .05 | .15 |
| 417 | R.J. Reynolds | .02 | .10 |
| 418 | Alan Knicely | .02 | .10 |
| 419 | Frank Wills | .02 | .10 |
| 420 | Von Hayes | .02 | .10 |
| 421 | David Palmer | .02 | .10 |
| 422 | Mike Jorgensen | .02 | .10 |
| 423 | Dan Spillner | .02 | .10 |
| 424 | Rick Miller | .02 | .10 |
| 425 | Larry McWilliams | .02 | .10 |
| 426 | Brewers Leaders | | |
| | Charlie Moore | .02 | .10 |
| 427 | Joe Cowley | .02 | .10 |
| 428 | Max Venable | .02 | .10 |
| 429 | Greg Booker | .02 | .10 |
| 430 | Kent Hrbek | .05 | .15 |
| 431 | George Frazier | .02 | .10 |
| 432 | Mark Bailey | .02 | .10 |
| 433 | Chris Codiroli | .02 | .10 |
| 434 | Curt Wilkerson | .02 | .10 |
| 435 | Bill Caudill | .02 | .10 |
| 436 | Doug Flynn | .02 | .10 |
| 437 | Rick Mahler | .02 | .10 |
| 438 | Clint Hurdle | .02 | .10 |
| 439 | Rick Honeycutt | .02 | .10 |
| 440 | Alvin Davis | .02 | .10 |
| 441 | Whitey Herzog MG | .08 | .25 |
| 442 | Ron Robinson | .02 | .10 |
| 443 | Bill Buckner | .05 | .15 |
| 444 | Alex Trevino | .02 | .10 |
| 445 | Bert Blyleven | .05 | .15 |
| 446 | Lenn Sakata | .02 | .10 |
| 447 | Jerry Don Gleaton | .02 | .10 |
| 448 | Herm Winningham | .02 | .10 |
| 449 | Rod Scurry | .02 | .10 |
| 450 | Graig Nettles | .05 | .15 |
| 451 | Mark Brown | .02 | .10 |
| 452 | Bob Clark | .02 | .10 |
| 453 | Steve Jeltz | .02 | .10 |
| 454 | Burt Hooton | .02 | .10 |
| 455 | Willie Randolph | .05 | .15 |
| 456 | Braves Leaders | | |
| | Dale Murphy | .08 | .25 |
| 457 | Mickey Tettleton RC | .08 | .25 |
| 458 | Kevin Bass | .02 | .10 |
| 459 | Luis Leal | .02 | .10 |
| 460 | Leon Durham | .02 | .10 |
| 461 | Walt Terrell | .02 | .10 |
| 462 | Domingo Ramos | .02 | .10 |
| 463 | Jim Gott | .02 | .10 |
| 464 | Ruppert Jones | .02 | .10 |
| 465 | Jesse Orosco | .02 | .10 |

|  |  | | |
|---|---|---|---|
| 466 | Tom Foley | .02 | .10 |
| 467 | Bob James | .02 | .10 |
| 468 | Mike Scioscia | .05 | .15 |
| 469 | Storm Davis | .02 | .10 |
| 470 | Bill Madlock | .05 | .15 |
| 471 | Bobby Cox MG | .05 | .15 |
| 472 | Joe Hesketh | .02 | .10 |
| 473 | Mark Brouhard | .02 | .10 |
| 474 | John Tudor | .05 | .15 |
| 475 | Juan Samuel | .02 | .10 |
| 476 | Ron Mathis | .02 | .10 |
| 477 | Mike Easler | .02 | .10 |
| 478 | Andy Hawkins | .02 | .10 |
| 479 | Bob Melvin | .02 | .10 |
| 480 | Oddibe McDowell | .02 | .10 |
| 481 | Scott Bradley | .02 | .10 |
| 482 | Rick Lysander | .02 | .10 |
| 483 | George Vukovich | .02 | .10 |
| 484 | Donnie Hill | .02 | .10 |
| 485 | Gary Matthews | .05 | .15 |
| 486 | Angels Leaders Bobby Grich | .02 | .10 |
| 487 | Bret Saberhagen | .05 | .15 |
| 488 | Lou Thornton | .02 | .10 |
| 489 | Jim Winn | .02 | .10 |
| 490 | Jeff Leonard | .02 | .10 |
| 491 | Pascual Perez | .02 | .10 |
| 492 | Kelvin Chapman | .02 | .10 |
| 493 | Gene Nelson | .02 | .10 |
| 494 | Gary Roenicke | .02 | .10 |
| 495 | Mark Langston | .05 | .15 |
| 496 | Jay Johnstone | .02 | .10 |
| 497 | John Stuper | .02 | .10 |
| 498 | Tito Landrum | .02 | .10 |
| 499 | Bob L. Gibson | .02 | .10 |
| 500 | Rickey Henderson | .15 | .40 |
| 501 | Dave Johnson MG | .02 | .10 |
| 502 | Glen Cook | .02 | .10 |
| 503 | Mike Fitzgerald | .02 | .10 |
| 504 | Denny Walling | .02 | .10 |
| 505 | Jerry Koosman | .05 | .15 |
| 506 | Bill Russell | .05 | .15 |
| 507 | Steve Ontiveros RC | .02 | .10 |
| 508 | Alan Wiggins | .02 | .10 |
| 509 | Ernie Camacho | .02 | .10 |
| 510 | Wade Boggs | .08 | .25 |
| 511 | Ed Nunez | .02 | .10 |
| 512 | Thad Bosley | .02 | .10 |
| 513 | Ron Washington | .02 | .10 |
| 514 | Mike Jones | .02 | .10 |
| 515 | Darrell Evans | .05 | .15 |
| 516 | Giants Leaders Greg Minton | | |
| 517 | Milt Thompson RC | .08 | .25 |
| 518 | Buck Martinez | .02 | .10 |
| 519 | Danny Darwin | .02 | .10 |
| 520 | Keith Hernandez | .05 | .15 |
| 521 | Nate Snell | .02 | .10 |
| 522 | Bob Bailor | .02 | .10 |
| 523 | Joe Price | .02 | .10 |
| 524 | Darrell Miller | .02 | .10 |
| 525 | Marvell Wynne | .02 | .10 |
| 526 | Charlie Lea | .02 | .10 |
| 527 | Checklist: 397-528 | .05 | .15 |
| 528 | Terry Pendleton | .05 | .15 |
| 529 | Marc Sullivan | .02 | .10 |
| 530 | Rich Gossage | .05 | .15 |
| 531 | Tony LaRussa MG | .05 | .15 |
| 532 | Don Carman | .02 | .10 |
| 533 | Billy Sample | .02 | .10 |
| 534 | Jeff Calhoun | .02 | .10 |
| 535 | Toby Harrah | .05 | .15 |
| 536 | Jose Rijo | .05 | .15 |
| 537 | Mark Salas | .02 | .10 |
| 538 | Dennis Eckersley | .08 | .25 |
| 539 | Glenn Hubbard | .02 | .10 |
| 540 | Dan Petry | .02 | .10 |
| 541 | Jorge Orta | .02 | .10 |
| 542 | Don Schulze | .02 | .10 |
| 543 | Jerry Narron | .02 | .10 |
| 544 | Eddie Milner | .02 | .10 |
| 545 | Jimmy Key | .05 | .15 |
| 546 | Mariners Leaders Dave Henderson | | |
| 547 | Roger McDowell RC* | .08 | .25 |
| 548 | Mike Young | .02 | .10 |
| 549 | Bob Welch | .05 | .15 |
| 550 | Tom Herr | .02 | .10 |
| 551 | Dave LaPoint | .02 | .10 |
| 552 | Marc Hill | .02 | .10 |
| 553 | Jim Morrison | .02 | .10 |
| 554 | Paul Householder | .02 | .10 |
| 555 | Hubie Brooks | .02 | .10 |
| 556 | John Denny | .02 | .10 |
| 557 | Gerald Perry | .02 | .10 |
| 558 | Tim Stoddard | .02 | .10 |
| 559 | Tommy Dunbar | .02 | .10 |
| 560 | Dave Righetti | .05 | .15 |
| 561 | Bob Lillis MG | .02 | .10 |
| 562 | Joe Beckwith | .02 | .10 |
| 563 | Alejandro Sanchez | .02 | .10 |
| 564 | Warren Brusstar | .02 | .10 |
| 565 | Tom Brunansky | .02 | .10 |
| 566 | Alfredo Griffin | .02 | .10 |
| 567 | Jeff Barkley | .02 | .10 |
| 568 | Donnie Scott | .02 | .10 |
| 569 | Jim Acker | .02 | .10 |
| 570 | Rusty Staub | .05 | .15 |
| 571 | Mike Jeffcoat | .02 | .10 |
| 572 | Paul Zuvella | .02 | .10 |
| 573 | Tom Hume | .02 | .10 |
| 574 | Ron Kittle | .02 | .10 |
| 575 | Mike Boddicker | .02 | .10 |
| 576 | Andre Dawson TL | .02 | .10 |
| 577 | Jerry Reuss | .02 | .10 |
| 578 | Lee Mazzilli | .05 | .15 |
| 579 | Jim Slaton | .02 | .10 |
| 580 | Willie McGee | .05 | .15 |
| 581 | Bruce Hurst | .02 | .10 |
| 582 | Jim Gantner | .02 | .10 |
| 583 | Al Bumbry | .02 | .10 |
| 584 | Brian Fisher RC | .02 | .10 |
| 585 | Garry Maddox | .02 | .10 |
| 586 | Greg Harris | .02 | .10 |
| 587 | Rafael Santana | .02 | .10 |
| 588 | Steve Lake | .02 | .10 |
| 589 | Sid Bream | .02 | .10 |
| 590 | Bob Knepper | .02 | .10 |
| 591 | Jackie Moore MG | .02 | .10 |
| 592 | Frank Tanana | .05 | .15 |
| 593 | Jesse Barfield | .05 | .15 |
| 594 | Chris Bando | .02 | .10 |
| 595 | Dave Parker | .05 | .15 |
| 596 | Onix Concepcion | .02 | .10 |
| 597 | Sammy Stewart | .02 | .10 |
| 598 | Jim Presley | .02 | .10 |
| 599 | Rick Aguilera RC | .08 | .25 |
| 600 | Dale Murphy | .08 | .25 |
| 601 | Gary Lucas | .02 | .10 |
| 602 | Mariano Duncan RC | .08 | .25 |
| 603 | Bill Laskey | .02 | .10 |
| 604 | Gary Pettis | .02 | .10 |
| 605 | Dennis Boyd | .02 | .10 |
| 606 | Royals Leaders Hal McRae | | |
| 607 | Ken Dayley | .05 | .15 |
| 608 | Bruce Bochy | .02 | .10 |
| 609 | Barbaro Garbey | .02 | .10 |
| 610 | Ron Guidry | .05 | .15 |
| 611 | Gary Woods | .02 | .10 |
| 612 | Richard Dotson | .02 | .10 |
| 613 | Roy Smalley | .02 | .10 |
| 614 | Rick Waits | .02 | .10 |
| 615 | Johnny Ray | .02 | .10 |
| 616 | Glenn Brummer | .02 | .10 |
| 617 | Lonnie Smith | .02 | .10 |
| 618 | Jim Pankovits | .02 | .10 |
| 619 | Danny Heep | .02 | .10 |
| 620 | Bruce Sutter | .05 | .15 |
| 621 | John Felske MG | .02 | .10 |
| 622 | Gary Lavelle | .02 | .10 |
| 623 | Floyd Rayford | .02 | .10 |
| 624 | Steve McCatty | .02 | .10 |
| 625 | Bob Brenly | .02 | .10 |
| 626 | Roy Thomas | .02 | .10 |
| 627 | Ron Oester | .02 | .10 |
| 628 | Kirk McCaskill RC | .08 | .25 |
| 629 | Mitch Webster | .02 | .10 |
| 630 | Fernando Valenzuela | .05 | .15 |
| 631 | Steve Braun | .02 | .10 |
| 632 | Dave Von Ohlen | .02 | .10 |
| 633 | Jackie Gutierrez | .02 | .10 |
| 634 | Roy Lee Jackson | .02 | .10 |
| 635 | Jason Thompson | .02 | .10 |
| 636 | Lee Smith TL | .02 | .10 |
| 637 | Rudy Law | .02 | .10 |
| 638 | John Butcher | .02 | .10 |
| 639 | Bo Diaz | .02 | .10 |
| 640 | Jose Cruz | .05 | .15 |
| 641 | Wayne Tolleson | .02 | .10 |
| 642 | Ray Searage | .02 | .10 |
| 643 | Tom Brookens | .02 | .10 |
| 644 | Mark Gubicza | .02 | .10 |
| 645 | Dusty Baker | .05 | .15 |
| 646 | Mike Moore | .02 | .10 |
| 647 | Mel Hall | .02 | .10 |
| 648 | Steve Bedrosian | .02 | .10 |
| 649 | Ronn Reynolds | .02 | .10 |
| 650 | Dave Stieb | .05 | .15 |
| 651 | Billy Martin MG/TC | .08 | .25 |
| 652 | Tom Browning | .02 | .10 |
| 653 | Jim Dwyer | .02 | .10 |
| 654 | Ken Howell | .02 | .10 |
| 655 | Manny Trillo | .02 | .10 |
| 656 | Brian Harper | .02 | .10 |
| 657 | Juan Agosto | .02 | .10 |
| 658 | Rob Wilfong | .02 | .10 |
| 659 | Checklist: 529-660 | .05 | .15 |
| 660 | Steve Garvey | .05 | .15 |
| 661 | Roger Clemens | 1.50 | 4.00 |
| 662 | Bill Schroeder | .02 | .10 |
| 663 | Neil Allen | .02 | .10 |
| 664 | Tim Corcoran | .02 | .10 |
| 665 | Alejandro Pena | .02 | .10 |
| 666 | Rangers Leaders Charlie Hough | .05 | .15 |
| 667 | Tim Teufel | .02 | .10 |
| 668 | Cecilio Guante | .02 | .10 |
| 669 | Ron Cey | .05 | .15 |
| 670 | Willie Hernandez | .02 | .10 |
| 671 | Lynn Jones | .02 | .10 |
| 672 | Rob Picciolo | .02 | .10 |
| 673 | Ernie Whitt | .02 | .10 |
| 674 | Pat Tabler | .02 | .10 |
| 675 | Claudell Washington | .02 | .10 |
| 676 | Matt Young | .02 | .10 |
| 677 | Nick Esasky | .02 | .10 |
| 678 | Dan Gladden | .02 | .10 |
| 679 | Britt Burns | .02 | .10 |
| 680 | George Foster | .05 | .15 |
| 681 | Dick Williams MG | .02 | .10 |
| 682 | Junior Ortiz | .02 | .10 |
| 683 | Andy Van Slyke | .08 | .25 |
| 684 | Bob McClure | .02 | .10 |
| 685 | Tim Wallach | .02 | .10 |
| 686 | Jeff Stone | .02 | .10 |
| 687 | Mike Trujillo | .02 | .10 |
| 688 | Larry Herndon | .02 | .10 |
| 689 | Dave Stewart | .05 | .15 |
| 690 | Ryne Sandberg | .30 | .75 |
| 691 | Mike Madden | .02 | .10 |
| 692 | Dale Berra | .02 | .10 |
| 693 | Tom Tellmann | .02 | .10 |
| 694 | Garth Iorg | .02 | .10 |
| 695 | Mike Smithson | .02 | .10 |
| 696 | Dodgers Leaders Bill Russell | .05 | .15 |
| 697 | Bud Black | .02 | .10 |
| 698 | Brad Komminsk | .02 | .10 |
| 699 | Pat Corrales MG | .02 | .10 |
| 700 | Reggie Jackson | .08 | .25 |
| 701 | Keith Hernandez AS | .02 | .10 |
| 702 | Tom Herr AS | .02 | .10 |
| 703 | Tim Wallach AS | .02 | .10 |
| 704 | Ozzie Smith AS | .15 | .40 |
| 705 | Dale Murphy AS | .05 | .15 |
| 706 | Pedro Guerrero AS | .02 | .10 |
| 707 | Willie McGee AS | .02 | .10 |
| 708 | Gary Carter AS | .02 | .10 |
| 709 | Dwight Gooden AS | .08 | .25 |
| 710 | John Tudor AS | .02 | .10 |
| 711 | Jeff Reardon AS | .02 | .10 |
| 712 | Don Mattingly AS | .25 | .60 |
| 713 | Damaso Garcia AS | .02 | .10 |
| 714 | George Brett AS | .15 | .40 |
| 715 | Cal Ripken AS | .15 | .40 |
| 716 | Rickey Henderson AS | .08 | .25 |
| 717 | Dave Winfield AS | .02 | .10 |
| 718 | George Bell AS | .02 | .10 |
| 719 | Carlton Fisk AS | .05 | .15 |
| 720 | Bret Saberhagen AS | .02 | .10 |
| 721 | Ron Guidry AS | .02 | .10 |
| 722 | Dan Quisenberry AS | .02 | .10 |
| 723 | Marty Bystrom | .02 | .10 |

| | | |
|---|---|---|
| ❑ 724 Tim Hulett | .02 | .10 |
| ❑ 725 Mario Soto | .05 | .15 |
| ❑ 726 Orioles Leaders | | |
| Rick Dempsey | .05 | .15 |
| ❑ 727 David Green | .02 | .10 |
| ❑ 728 Mike Marshall | .02 | .10 |
| ❑ 729 Jim Beattie | .02 | .10 |
| ❑ 730 Ozzie Smith | .25 | .60 |
| ❑ 731 Don Robinson | .02 | .10 |
| ❑ 732 Floyd Youmans | .02 | .10 |
| ❑ 733 Ron Romanick | .02 | .10 |
| ❑ 734 Marty Barrett | .02 | .10 |
| ❑ 735 Dave Dravecky | .02 | .10 |
| ❑ 736 Glenn Wilson | .02 | .10 |
| ❑ 737 Pete Vuckovich | .02 | .10 |
| ❑ 738 Andre Robertson | .02 | .10 |
| ❑ 739 Dave Rozema | .02 | .10 |
| ❑ 740 Lance Parrish | .05 | .15 |
| ❑ 741 Pete Rose MG/TC | .15 | .40 |
| ❑ 742 Frank Viola | .05 | .15 |
| ❑ 743 Pat Sheridan | .02 | .10 |
| ❑ 744 Lary Sorensen | .02 | .10 |
| ❑ 745 Willie Upshaw | .02 | .10 |
| ❑ 746 Denny Gonzalez | .02 | .10 |
| ❑ 747 Rick Cerone | .02 | .10 |
| ❑ 748 Steve Henderson | .02 | .10 |
| ❑ 749 Ed Jurak | .02 | .10 |
| ❑ 750 Gorman Thomas | .05 | .15 |
| ❑ 751 Howard Johnson | .05 | .15 |
| ❑ 752 Mike Krukow | .02 | .10 |
| ❑ 753 Dan Ford | .02 | .10 |
| ❑ 754 Pat Clements | .02 | .10 |
| ❑ 755 Harold Baines | .05 | .15 |
| ❑ 756 Pirates Leaders | | |
| Rick Rhoden | .02 | .10 |
| ❑ 757 Darrell Porter | .02 | .10 |
| ❑ 758 Dave Anderson | .02 | .10 |
| ❑ 759 Moose Haas | .02 | .10 |
| ❑ 760 Andre Dawson | .05 | .15 |
| ❑ 761 Don Slaught | .02 | .10 |
| ❑ 762 Eric Show | .02 | .10 |
| ❑ 763 Terry Puhl | .02 | .10 |
| ❑ 764 Kevin Gross | .02 | .10 |
| ❑ 765 Don Baylor | .05 | .15 |
| ❑ 766 Rick Langford | .02 | .10 |
| ❑ 767 Jody Davis | .02 | .10 |
| ❑ 768 Vern Ruhle | .02 | .10 |
| ❑ 769 Harold Reynolds RC | .30 | .75 |
| ❑ 770 Vida Blue | .05 | .15 |
| ❑ 771 John McNamara MG | .02 | .10 |
| ❑ 772 Brian Downing | .05 | .15 |
| ❑ 773 Greg Pryor | .02 | .10 |
| ❑ 774 Terry Leach | .02 | .10 |
| ❑ 775 Al Oliver | .05 | .15 |
| ❑ 776 Gene Garber | .02 | .10 |
| ❑ 777 Wayne Krenchicki | .02 | .10 |
| ❑ 778 Jerry Hairston | .02 | .10 |
| ❑ 779 Rick Reuschel | .05 | .15 |
| ❑ 780 Robin Yount | .25 | .60 |
| ❑ 781 Joe Nolan | .02 | .10 |
| ❑ 782 Ken Landreaux | .02 | .10 |
| ❑ 783 Ricky Horton | .02 | .10 |
| ❑ 784 Alan Bannister | .02 | .10 |
| ❑ 785 Bob Stanley | .02 | .10 |
| ❑ 786 Twins Leaders | | |
| Mickey Hatcher | .02 | .10 |
| ❑ 787 Vance Law | .02 | .10 |
| ❑ 788 Marty Castillo | .02 | .10 |
| ❑ 789 Kurt Bevacqua | .02 | .10 |
| ❑ 790 Phil Niekro | .05 | .15 |
| ❑ 791 Checklist: 661-792 | .05 | .15 |
| ❑ 792 Charles Hudson | .02 | .10 |

**1987 Topps**

| | | |
|---|---|---|
| ❑ COMPLETE SET (792) | 10.00 | 25.00 |
| ❑ COMP.FACT SET (792) | 15.00 | 40.00 |
| ❑ COMP.HOBBY SET (792) | 15.00 | 40.00 |
| ❑ COMP.X-MAS SET (792) | 15.00 | 40.00 |
| ❑ 1 Roger Clemens RB | .40 | 1.00 |
| ❑ 2 Jim Deshaies RB | | |
| Most cons. K's& | | |
| start of game | .01 | .05 |
| ❑ 3 Dwight Evans RB | | |
| Earliest home run& | | |
| season | .05 | .15 |
| ❑ 4 Davey Lopes RB | | |
| Most steals/season& | | |
| 40-year-old | .01 | .05 |
| ❑ 5 Dave Righetti RB | | |
| Most saves&season | .01 | .05 |
| ❑ 6 Ruben Sierra RB | .08 | .25 |
| ❑ 7 Todd Worrell RB | | |
| Most saves& | | |
| season& rookie | .01 | .05 |
| ❑ 8 Terry Pendleton | .01 | .10 |
| ❑ 9 Jay Tibbs | .01 | .05 |
| ❑ 10 Cecil Cooper | .02 | .10 |
| ❑ 11 Indians Team | | |
| (Mound conference) | .01 | .05 |
| ❑ 12 Jeff Sellers | .01 | .05 |
| ❑ 13 Nick Esasky | .01 | .05 |
| ❑ 14 Dave Stewart | .02 | .10 |
| ❑ 15 Claudell Washington | .01 | .05 |
| ❑ 16 Pat Clements | .01 | .05 |
| ❑ 17 Pete O'Brien | .01 | .05 |
| ❑ 18 Dick Howser MG | .01 | .05 |
| ❑ 19 Matt Young | .01 | .05 |
| ❑ 20 Gary Carter | .02 | .10 |
| ❑ 21 Mark Davis | .01 | .05 |
| ❑ 22 Doug DeCinces | .01 | .05 |
| ❑ 23 Lee Smith | .02 | .10 |
| ❑ 24 Tony Walker | .01 | .05 |
| ❑ 25 Bert Blyleven | .02 | .10 |
| ❑ 26 Greg Brock | .01 | .05 |
| ❑ 27 Joe Cowley | .01 | .05 |
| ❑ 28 Rick Dempsey | .01 | .05 |
| ❑ 29 Jimmy Key | .02 | .10 |
| ❑ 30 Tim Raines | .02 | .10 |
| ❑ 31 Braves Team | | |
| (Glenn Hubbard and | | |
| Rafael Ramirez) | .01 | .05 |
| ❑ 32 Tim Leary | .01 | .05 |
| ❑ 33 Andy Van Slyke | .05 | .15 |
| ❑ 34 Jose Rijo | .02 | .10 |
| ❑ 35 Sid Bream | .01 | .05 |
| ❑ 36 Eric King | .01 | .05 |
| ❑ 37 Marvell Wynne | .01 | .05 |
| ❑ 38 Dennis Leonard | .01 | .05 |
| ❑ 39 Marty Barrett | .01 | .05 |
| ❑ 40 Dave Righetti | .02 | .10 |
| ❑ 41 Bo Diaz | .01 | .05 |
| ❑ 42 Gary Redus | .01 | .05 |
| ❑ 43 Gene Michael MG | .01 | .05 |
| ❑ 44 Greg Harris | .01 | .05 |
| ❑ 45 Jim Presley | .01 | .05 |
| ❑ 46 Dan Gladden | .01 | .05 |
| ❑ 47 Dennis Powell | .01 | .05 |
| ❑ 48 Wally Backman | .01 | .05 |
| ❑ 49 Terry Harper | .01 | .05 |
| ❑ 50 Dave Smith | .01 | .05 |
| ❑ 51 Mel Hall | .01 | .05 |
| ❑ 52 Keith Atherton | .01 | .05 |
| ❑ 53 Ruppert Jones | .01 | .05 |
| ❑ 54 Bill Dawley | .01 | .05 |
| ❑ 55 Tim Wallach | .01 | .05 |
| ❑ 56 Brewers Team | | |
| (Mound conference) | .02 | .10 |
| ❑ 57 Scott Nielsen | .01 | .05 |
| ❑ 58 Thad Bosley | .01 | .05 |
| ❑ 59 Ken Dayley | .01 | .05 |
| ❑ 60 Tony Pena | .01 | .05 |
| ❑ 61 Bobby Thigpen RC | .08 | .25 |
| ❑ 62 Bobby Meacham | .01 | .05 |
| ❑ 63 Fred Toliver | .01 | .05 |
| ❑ 64 Harry Spilman | .01 | .05 |
| ❑ 65 Tom Browning | .01 | .05 |
| ❑ 66 Marc Sullivan | .01 | .05 |
| ❑ 67 Bill Swift | .01 | .05 |
| ❑ 68 Tony LaRussa MG | .02 | .10 |
| ❑ 69 Lonnie Smith | .01 | .05 |
| ❑ 70 Charlie Hough | .02 | .10 |
| ❑ 71 Mike Aldrete | .01 | .05 |

| | | |
|---|---|---|
| ❑ 72 Walt Terrell | .01 | .05 |
| ❑ 73 Dave Anderson | .01 | .05 |
| ❑ 74 Dan Pasqua | .01 | .05 |
| ❑ 75 Ron Darling | .02 | .10 |
| ❑ 76 Rafael Ramirez | .01 | .05 |
| ❑ 77 Bryan Oelkers | .01 | .05 |
| ❑ 78 Tom Foley | .01 | .05 |
| ❑ 79 Juan Nieves | .01 | .05 |
| ❑ 80 Wally Joyner RC | .15 | .40 |
| ❑ 81 Padres Team | | |
| (Andy Hawkins and | | |
| Terry Kennedy) | .01 | .05 |
| ❑ 82 Rob Murphy | .01 | .05 |
| ❑ 83 Mike Davis | .01 | .05 |
| ❑ 84 Steve Lake | .01 | .05 |
| ❑ 85 Kevin Bass | .01 | .05 |
| ❑ 86 Nate Snell | .01 | .05 |
| ❑ 87 Mark Salas | .01 | .05 |
| ❑ 88 Ed Wojna | .01 | .05 |
| ❑ 89 Ozzie Guillen | .05 | .15 |
| ❑ 90 Dave Stieb | .02 | .10 |
| ❑ 91 Harold Reynolds | .02 | .10 |
| ❑ 92A Urbano Lugo | | |
| ERR (no trademark) | .05 | .15 |
| ❑ 92B Urbano Lugo COR | .05 | .15 |
| ❑ 93 Jim Leyland MG/TC RC * | .08 | .25 |
| ❑ 94 Calvin Schiraldi | .01 | .05 |
| ❑ 95 Oddibe McDowell | .01 | .05 |
| ❑ 96 Frank Williams | .01 | .05 |
| ❑ 97 Glenn Wilson | .01 | .05 |
| ❑ 98 Bill Scherrer | .01 | .05 |
| ❑ 99 Darryl Motley | | |
| (Now with Braves | | |
| on card front) | .01 | .05 |
| ❑ 100 Steve Garvey | .01 | .05 |
| ❑ 101 Carl Willis RC | .02 | .10 |
| ❑ 102 Paul Zuvella | .01 | .05 |
| ❑ 103 Rick Aguilera | .04 | .10 |
| ❑ 104 Billy Sample | .01 | .05 |
| ❑ 105 Floyd Youmans | .01 | .05 |
| ❑ 106 Blue Jays Team | | |
| (George Bell and | | |
| Jesse Barfield) | .01 | .05 |
| ❑ 107 John Butcher | .01 | .05 |
| ❑ 108 Jim Gantner UER | | |
| (Brewers logo | | |
| reversed) | .01 | .05 |
| ❑ 109 R.J. Reynolds | .01 | .05 |
| ❑ 110 John Tudor | .02 | .10 |
| ❑ 111 Alfredo Griffin | .01 | .05 |
| ❑ 112 Alan Ashby | .01 | .05 |
| ❑ 113 Neil Allen | .01 | .05 |
| ❑ 114 Billy Beane | .02 | .10 |
| ❑ 115 Donnie Moore | .01 | .05 |
| ❑ 116 Bill Russell | .02 | .10 |
| ❑ 117 Jim Beattie | .01 | .05 |
| ❑ 118 Bobby Valentine MG | .02 | .10 |
| ❑ 119 Ron Robinson | .01 | .05 |
| ❑ 120 Eddie Murray | .08 | .25 |
| ❑ 121 Kevin Romine | .01 | .05 |
| ❑ 122 Jim Clancy | .01 | .05 |
| ❑ 123 John Kruk RC | .20 | .50 |
| ❑ 124 Ray Fontenot | .01 | .05 |
| ❑ 125 Bob Brenly | .01 | .05 |
| ❑ 126 Mike Loynd RC | .02 | .10 |
| ❑ 127 Vance Law | .01 | .05 |
| ❑ 128 Checklist 1-132 | .01 | .05 |
| ❑ 129 Rick Cerone | .01 | .05 |
| ❑ 130 Dwight Gooden | .05 | .15 |
| ❑ 131 Pirates Team | | |
| (Sid Bream and | | |
| Tony Pena) | .01 | .05 |
| ❑ 132 Paul Assenmacher | .08 | .25 |
| ❑ 133 Jose Oquendo | .01 | .05 |
| ❑ 134 Rich Yett | .01 | .05 |
| ❑ 135 Mike Easler | .01 | .05 |
| ❑ 136 Ron Romanick | .01 | .05 |
| ❑ 137 Jerry Willard | .01 | .05 |
| ❑ 138 Roy Lee Jackson | .01 | .05 |
| ❑ 139 Devon White RC | .15 | .40 |
| ❑ 140 Bret Saberhagen | .02 | .10 |
| ❑ 141 Herm Winningham | .01 | .05 |
| ❑ 142 Rick Sutcliffe | .02 | .10 |
| ❑ 143 Steve Boros MG | .01 | .05 |
| ❑ 144 Mike Scioscia | .02 | .10 |
| ❑ 145 Charlie Kerfeld | .01 | .05 |
| ❑ 146 Tracy Jones | .01 | .05 |
| ❑ 147 Randy Niemann | .01 | .05 |

|  |  | | |
|---|---|---|---|
| ❏ 148 | Dave Collins | .01 | .05 |
| ❏ 149 | Ray Searage | .01 | .05 |
| ❏ 150 | Wade Boggs | .05 | .15 |
| ❏ 151 | Mike LaCoss | .01 | .05 |
| ❏ 152 | Toby Harrah | .02 | .10 |
| ❏ 153 | Duane Ward RC * | .08 | .25 |
| ❏ 154 | Tom O'Malley | .01 | .05 |
| ❏ 155 | Eddie Whitson | .01 | .05 |
| ❏ 156 | Mariners Team (Mound conference) | | |
| ❏ 157 | Danny Darwin | .01 | .05 |
| ❏ 158 | Tim Teufel | .01 | .05 |
| ❏ 159 | Ed Olwine | .01 | .05 |
| ❏ 160 | Julio Franco | .02 | .10 |
| ❏ 161 | Steve Ontiveros | .01 | .05 |
| ❏ 162 | Mike LaValliere RC * | .08 | .25 |
| ❏ 163 | Kevin Gross | .01 | .05 |
| ❏ 164 | Sammy Khalifa | .01 | .05 |
| ❏ 165 | Jeff Reardon | .02 | .10 |
| ❏ 166 | Bob Boone | .02 | .10 |
| ❏ 167 | Jim Deshaies RC * | .02 | .10 |
| ❏ 168 | Lou Piniella MG | .01 | .05 |
| ❏ 169 | Ron Washington | .01 | .05 |
| ❏ 170 | Bo Jackson RC | 1.25 | 3.00 |
| ❏ 171 | Chuck Cary | .01 | .05 |
| ❏ 172 | Ron Oester | .01 | .05 |
| ❏ 173 | Alex Trevino | .01 | .05 |
| ❏ 174 | Henry Cotto | .01 | .05 |
| ❏ 175 | Bob Stanley | .01 | .05 |
| ❏ 176 | Steve Buechele | .01 | .05 |
| ❏ 177 | Keith Moreland | .01 | .05 |
| ❏ 178 | Cecil Fielder | .02 | .10 |
| ❏ 179 | Bill Wegman | .01 | .05 |
| ❏ 180 | Chris Brown | .01 | .05 |
| ❏ 181 | Cardinals Team (Mound conference) | | |
| ❏ 182 | Lee Lacy | .01 | .05 |
| ❏ 183 | Andy Hawkins | .01 | .05 |
| ❏ 184 | Bobby Bonilla RC | .15 | .40 |
| ❏ 185 | Roger McDowell | .01 | .05 |
| ❏ 186 | Bruce Benedict | .01 | .05 |
| ❏ 187 | Mark Huismann | .01 | .05 |
| ❏ 188 | Tony Phillips | .01 | .05 |
| ❏ 189 | Joe Hesketh | .01 | .05 |
| ❏ 190 | Jim Sundberg | .02 | .10 |
| ❏ 191 | Charles Hudson | .01 | .05 |
| ❏ 192 | Cory Snyder | .01 | .05 |
| ❏ 193 | Roger Craig MG | .02 | .10 |
| ❏ 194 | Kirk McCaskill | .01 | .05 |
| ❏ 195 | Mike Pagliarulo | .01 | .05 |
| ❏ 196 | Randy O'Neal UER (Wrong ML career W-L totals) | | |
| ❏ 197 | Mark Bailey | .01 | .05 |
| ❏ 198 | Lee Mazzilli | .02 | .10 |
| ❏ 199 | Mariano Duncan | .01 | .05 |
| ❏ 200 | Pete Rose | .25 | .60 |
| ❏ 201 | John Cangelosi | .01 | .05 |
| ❏ 202 | Ricky Wright | .01 | .05 |
| ❏ 203 | Mike Kingery RC | .02 | .10 |
| ❏ 204 | Sammy Stewart | .01 | .05 |
| ❏ 205 | Graig Nettles | .02 | .10 |
| ❏ 206 | Twins Team (Frank Viola and Tim Laudner) | | |
| ❏ 207 | George Frazier | .01 | .05 |
| ❏ 208 | John Shelby | .01 | .05 |
| ❏ 209 | Rick Schu | .01 | .05 |
| ❏ 210 | Lloyd Moseby | .01 | .05 |
| ❏ 211 | John Morris | .01 | .05 |
| ❏ 212 | Mike Fitzgerald | .01 | .05 |
| ❏ 213 | Randy Myers RC | .15 | .40 |
| ❏ 214 | Omar Moreno | .01 | .05 |
| ❏ 215 | Mark Langston | .01 | .05 |
| ❏ 216 | B.J. Surhoff RC | .15 | .40 |
| ❏ 217 | Chris Codiroli | .01 | .05 |
| ❏ 218 | Sparky Anderson MG | .02 | .10 |
| ❏ 219 | Cecilio Guante | .01 | .05 |
| ❏ 220 | Joe Carter | .02 | .10 |
| ❏ 221 | Vern Ruhle | .01 | .05 |
| ❏ 222 | Denny Walling | .01 | .05 |
| ❏ 223 | Charlie Leibrandt | .01 | .05 |
| ❏ 224 | Wayne Tolleson | .01 | .05 |
| ❏ 225 | Mike Smithson | .01 | .05 |
| ❏ 226 | Max Venable | .01 | .05 |
| ❏ 227 | Jamie Moyer RC | .20 | .50 |
| ❏ 228 | Curt Wilkerson | .01 | .05 |
| ❏ 229 | Mike Birkbeck | .02 | .10 |
| ❏ 230 | Don Baylor | .02 | .10 |
| ❏ 231 | Giants Team (Bob Brenly and Jim Gott) | | |
| ❏ 232 | Reggie Williams | .01 | .05 |
| ❏ 233 | Russ Morman | .01 | .05 |
| ❏ 234 | Pat Sheridan | .01 | .05 |
| ❏ 235 | Alvin Davis | .01 | .05 |
| ❏ 236 | Tommy John | .02 | .10 |
| ❏ 237 | Jim Morrison | .01 | .05 |
| ❏ 238 | Bill Krueger | .01 | .05 |
| ❏ 239 | Juan Espino | .01 | .05 |
| ❏ 240 | Steve Balboni | .01 | .05 |
| ❏ 241 | Danny Heep | .01 | .05 |
| ❏ 242 | Rick Mahler | .01 | .05 |
| ❏ 243 | Whitey Herzog MG | .02 | .10 |
| ❏ 244 | Dickie Noles | .01 | .05 |
| ❏ 245 | Willie Upshaw | .01 | .05 |
| ❏ 246 | Jim Dwyer | .01 | .05 |
| ❏ 247 | Jeff Reed | .01 | .05 |
| ❏ 248 | Gene Walter | .01 | .05 |
| ❏ 249 | Jim Pankovits | .01 | .05 |
| ❏ 250 | Teddy Higuera | .01 | .05 |
| ❏ 251 | Rob Wilfong | .01 | .05 |
| ❏ 252 | Dennis Martinez | .02 | .10 |
| ❏ 253 | Eddie Milner | .01 | .05 |
| ❏ 254 | Bob Tewksbury RC * | .08 | .25 |
| ❏ 255 | Juan Samuel | .01 | .05 |
| ❏ 256 | Royals TL/George Brett | .05 | .15 |
| ❏ 257 | Bob Forsch | .01 | .05 |
| ❏ 258 | Steve Yeager | .02 | .10 |
| ❏ 259 | Mike Greenwell RC | .08 | .25 |
| ❏ 260 | Vida Blue | .01 | .05 |
| ❏ 261 | Ruben Sierra RC | .20 | .50 |
| ❏ 262 | Jim Winn | .01 | .05 |
| ❏ 263 | Stan Javier | .01 | .05 |
| ❏ 264 | Checklist 133-264 | .02 | .10 |
| ❏ 265 | Darrell Evans | .02 | .10 |
| ❏ 266 | Jeff Hamilton | .01 | .05 |
| ❏ 267 | Howard Johnson | .02 | .10 |
| ❏ 268 | Pat Corrales MG | .01 | .05 |
| ❏ 269 | Cliff Speck | .01 | .05 |
| ❏ 270 | Jody Davis | .01 | .05 |
| ❏ 271 | Mike G. Brown | .01 | .05 |
| ❏ 272 | Andres Galarraga | .02 | .10 |
| ❏ 273 | Gene Nelson | .01 | .05 |
| ❏ 274 | Jeff Hearron UER (Duplicate 1986 stat line on ba | .01 | .05 |
| ❏ 275 | LaMarr Hoyt | .01 | .05 |
| ❏ 276 | Jackie Gutierrez | .01 | .05 |
| ❏ 277 | Juan Agosto | .01 | .05 |
| ❏ 278 | Gary Pettis | .01 | .05 |
| ❏ 279 | Dan Plesac | .01 | .05 |
| ❏ 280 | Jeff Leonard | .01 | .05 |
| ❏ 281 | Reds TL/Rose | .08 | .25 |
| ❏ 282 | Jeff Calhoun | .01 | .05 |
| ❏ 283 | Doug Drabek RC | .15 | .40 |
| ❏ 284 | John Moses | .01 | .05 |
| ❏ 285 | Dennis Boyd | .01 | .05 |
| ❏ 286 | Mike Woodard | .01 | .05 |
| ❏ 287 | Dave Von Ohlen | .01 | .05 |
| ❏ 288 | Tito Landrum | .01 | .05 |
| ❏ 289 | Bob Kipper | .01 | .05 |
| ❏ 290 | Leon Durham | .01 | .05 |
| ❏ 291 | Mitch Williams RC * | .08 | .25 |
| ❏ 292 | Franklin Stubbs | .01 | .05 |
| ❏ 293 | Bob Rodgers MG (Checklist back& inconsistent des | | |
| ❏ 294 | Steve Jeltz | .01 | .05 |
| ❏ 295 | Len Dykstra | .02 | .10 |
| ❏ 296 | Andres Thomas | .01 | .05 |
| ❏ 297 | Don Schulze | .01 | .05 |
| ❏ 298 | Larry Herndon | .01 | .05 |
| ❏ 299 | Joel Davis | .01 | .05 |
| ❏ 300 | Reggie Jackson | .05 | .15 |
| ❏ 301 | Luis Aquino UER (No trademark never corrected) | .01 | .05 |
| ❏ 302 | Bill Schroeder | .01 | .05 |
| ❏ 303 | Juan Berenguer | .01 | .05 |
| ❏ 304 | Phil Garner | .02 | .10 |
| ❏ 305 | John Franco | .02 | .10 |
| ❏ 306 | Red Sox TL/Seaver | .02 | .10 |
| ❏ 307 | Lee Guetterman | .01 | .05 |
| ❏ 308 | Don Slaught | .01 | .05 |
| ❏ 309 | Mike Young | .01 | .05 |
| ❏ 310 | Frank Viola | .02 | .10 |
| ❏ 311 | Rickey Henderson TBC | .05 | .15 |
| ❏ 312 | Reggie Jackson TBC | .02 | .10 |
| ❏ 313 | Roberto Clemente TBC | .08 | .25 |
| ❏ 314 | Carl Yastrzemski TBC | .08 | .25 |
| ❏ 315 | Maury Wills TBC '82 | .02 | .10 |
| ❏ 316 | Brian Fisher | .01 | .05 |
| ❏ 317 | Clint Hurdle | .01 | .05 |
| ❏ 318 | Jim Fregosi MG | .01 | .05 |
| ❏ 319 | Greg Swindell RC | .08 | .25 |
| ❏ 320 | Barry Bonds RC | 3.00 | 8.00 |
| ❏ 321 | Mike Laga | .01 | .05 |
| ❏ 322 | Chris Bando | .01 | .05 |
| ❏ 323 | Al Newman RC | .01 | .05 |
| ❏ 324 | David Palmer | .01 | .05 |
| ❏ 325 | Garry Templeton | .02 | .10 |
| ❏ 326 | Mark Gubicza | .01 | .05 |
| ❏ 327 | Dale Sveum | .01 | .05 |
| ❏ 328 | Bob Welch | .02 | .10 |
| ❏ 329 | Ron Roenicke | .01 | .05 |
| ❏ 330 | Mike Scott | .02 | .10 |
| ❏ 331 | Mets TL/Carter/Straw | .05 | .15 |
| ❏ 332 | Joe Price | .01 | .05 |
| ❏ 333 | Ken Phelps | .01 | .05 |
| ❏ 334 | Ed Correa | .01 | .05 |
| ❏ 335 | Candy Maldonado | .01 | .05 |
| ❏ 336 | Allan Anderson RC | .01 | .05 |
| ❏ 337 | Darrell Miller | .01 | .05 |
| ❏ 338 | Tim Conroy | .01 | .05 |
| ❏ 339 | Donnie Hill | .01 | .05 |
| ❏ 340 | Roger Clemens | .60 | 1.50 |
| ❏ 341 | Mike C. Brown | .01 | .05 |
| ❏ 342 | Bob James | .01 | .05 |
| ❏ 343 | Hal Lanier MG | .01 | .05 |
| ❏ 344A | Joe Niekro (Copyright inside righthand border) | | |
| ❏ 344B | Joe Niekro (Copyright outside righthand border) | .01 | .05 |
| ❏ 345 | Andre Dawson | .02 | .10 |
| ❏ 346 | Shawon Dunston | .01 | .05 |
| ❏ 347 | Mickey Brantley | .01 | .05 |
| ❏ 348 | Carmelo Martinez | .01 | .05 |
| ❏ 349 | Storm Davis | .01 | .05 |
| ❏ 350 | Keith Hernandez | .02 | .10 |
| ❏ 351 | Gene Garber | .01 | .05 |
| ❏ 352 | Mike Felder | .01 | .05 |
| ❏ 353 | Ernie Camacho | .01 | .05 |
| ❏ 354 | Jamie Quirk | .01 | .05 |
| ❏ 355 | Don Carman | .01 | .05 |
| ❏ 356 | White Sox Team (Mound conference) | | |
| ❏ 357 | Steve Fireovid | .01 | .05 |
| ❏ 358 | Sal Butera | .01 | .05 |
| ❏ 359 | Doug Corbett | .01 | .05 |
| ❏ 360 | Pedro Guerrero | .02 | .10 |
| ❏ 361 | Mark Thurmond | .01 | .05 |
| ❏ 362 | Luis Quinones | .01 | .05 |
| ❏ 363 | Jose Guzman | .01 | .05 |
| ❏ 364 | Randy Bush | .01 | .05 |
| ❏ 365 | Rick Rhoden | .01 | .05 |
| ❏ 366 | Mark McGwire | 1.50 | 4.00 |
| ❏ 367 | Jeff Lahti | .01 | .05 |
| ❏ 368 | John McNamara MG | .01 | .05 |
| ❏ 369 | Brian Dayett | .01 | .05 |
| ❏ 370 | Fred Lynn | .02 | .10 |
| ❏ 371 | Mark Eichhorn | .01 | .05 |
| ❏ 372 | Jerry Mumphrey | .01 | .05 |
| ❏ 373 | Jeff Dedmon | .01 | .05 |
| ❏ 374 | Glenn Hoffman | .01 | .05 |
| ❏ 375 | Ron Guidry | .02 | .10 |
| ❏ 376 | Scott Bradley | .01 | .05 |
| ❏ 377 | John Henry Johnson | .01 | .05 |
| ❏ 378 | Rafael Santana | .01 | .05 |
| ❏ 379 | John Russell | .01 | .05 |
| ❏ 380 | Rich Gossage | .02 | .10 |
| ❏ 381 | Expos Team (Mound conference) | | |
| ❏ 382 | Rudy Law | .01 | .05 |
| ❏ 383 | Ron Davis | .01 | .05 |
| ❏ 384 | Johnny Grubb | .01 | .05 |
| ❏ 385 | Orel Hershiser | .05 | .15 |
| ❏ 386 | Dickie Thon | .01 | .05 |
| ❏ 387 | T.R. Bryden | .01 | .05 |
| ❏ 388 | Geno Petralli | .01 | .05 |
| ❏ 389 | Jeff D. Robinson | .01 | .05 |
| ❏ 390 | Gary Matthews | .02 | .10 |

|  |  | | |
|---|---|---|---|
| ☐ 391 | Jay Howell | .01 | .05 |
| ☐ 392 | Checklist 265-396 | .05 | .05 |
| ☐ 393 | Pete Rose MG/TC | .05 | .15 |
| ☐ 394 | Mike Bielecki | .01 | .05 |
| ☐ 395 | Damaso Garcia | .01 | .05 |
| ☐ 396 | Tim Lollar | .01 | .05 |
| ☐ 397 | Greg Walker | .01 | .05 |
| ☐ 398 | Brad Havens | .01 | .05 |
| ☐ 399 | Curt Ford | .01 | .05 |
| ☐ 400 | George Brett | .25 | .60 |
| ☐ 401 | Billy Joe Robidoux | .01 | .05 |
| ☐ 402 | Mike Trujillo | .01 | .05 |
| ☐ 403 | Jerry Royster | .01 | .05 |
| ☐ 404 | Doug Sisk | .01 | .05 |
| ☐ 405 | Brook Jacoby | .01 | .05 |
| ☐ 406 | Yankees TL/Hend/Matt | .20 | .50 |
| ☐ 407 | Jim Acker | .01 | .05 |
| ☐ 408 | John Mizerock | .01 | .05 |
| ☐ 409 | Milt Thompson | .01 | .05 |
| ☐ 410 | Fernando Valenzuela | .02 | .10 |
| ☐ 411 | Darnell Coles | .01 | .05 |
| ☐ 412 | Eric Davis | .05 | .15 |
| ☐ 413 | Moose Haas | .01 | .05 |
| ☐ 414 | Joe Orsulak | .01 | .05 |
| ☐ 415 | Bobby Witt RC | .08 | .25 |
| ☐ 416 | Tom Nieto | .01 | .05 |
| ☐ 417 | Pat Perry | .01 | .05 |
| ☐ 418 | Dick Williams MG | .01 | .05 |
| ☐ 419 | Mark Portugal RC * | .08 | .25 |
| ☐ 420 | Will Clark RC | .40 | 1.00 |
| ☐ 421 | Jose DeLeon | .01 | .05 |
| ☐ 422 | Jack Howell | .01 | .05 |
| ☐ 423 | Jaime Cocanower | .01 | .05 |
| ☐ 424 | Chris Speier | .01 | .05 |
| ☐ 425 | Tom Seaver | .05 | .15 |
| ☐ 426 | Floyd Rayford | .01 | .05 |
| ☐ 427 | Edwin Nunez | .01 | .05 |
| ☐ 428 | Bruce Bochy | .01 | .05 |
| ☐ 429 | Tim Pyznarski | .01 | .05 |
| ☐ 430 | Mike Schmidt | .20 | .50 |
| ☐ 431 | Dodgers Team (Mound conference) | .01 | .05 |
| ☐ 432 | Jim Slaton | .01 | .05 |
| ☐ 433 | Ed Hearn RC | .01 | .05 |
| ☐ 434 | Mike Fischlin | .01 | .05 |
| ☐ 435 | Bruce Sutter | .02 | .10 |
| ☐ 436 | Andy Allanson RC | .01 | .05 |
| ☐ 437 | Ted Power | .01 | .05 |
| ☐ 438 | Kelly Downs RC | .02 | .10 |
| ☐ 439 | Karl Best | .01 | .05 |
| ☐ 440 | Willie McGee | .02 | .10 |
| ☐ 441 | Dave Leiper | .01 | .05 |
| ☐ 442 | Mitch Webster | .01 | .05 |
| ☐ 443 | John Felske MG | .01 | .05 |
| ☐ 444 | Jeff Russell | .01 | .05 |
| ☐ 445 | Dave Lopes | .02 | .10 |
| ☐ 446 | Chuck Finley RC | .15 | .40 |
| ☐ 447 | Bill Almon | .01 | .05 |
| ☐ 448 | Chris Bosio RC | .08 | .25 |
| ☐ 449 | Pat Dodson | .02 | .10 |
| ☐ 450 | Kirby Puckett | .20 | .50 |
| ☐ 451 | Joe Sambito | .01 | .05 |
| ☐ 452 | Dave Henderson | .01 | .05 |
| ☐ 453 | Scott Terry RC | .02 | .10 |
| ☐ 454 | Luis Salazar | .01 | .05 |
| ☐ 455 | Mike Boddicker | .01 | .05 |
| ☐ 456 | A's Team (Mound conference) | .01 | .05 |
| ☐ 457 | Len Matuszek | .01 | .05 |
| ☐ 458 | Kelly Gruber | .01 | .05 |
| ☐ 459 | Dennis Eckersley | .05 | .15 |
| ☐ 460 | Darryl Strawberry | .02 | .10 |
| ☐ 461 | Craig McMurtry | .01 | .05 |
| ☐ 462 | Scott Fletcher | .01 | .05 |
| ☐ 463 | Tom Candiotti | .01 | .05 |
| ☐ 464 | Butch Wynegar | .01 | .05 |
| ☐ 465 | Todd Worrell | .01 | .05 |
| ☐ 466 | Kal Daniels | .01 | .05 |
| ☐ 467 | Randy St.Claire | .01 | .05 |
| ☐ 468 | George Bamberger MG | .01 | .05 |
| ☐ 469 | Mike Diaz | .01 | .05 |
| ☐ 470 | Dave Dravecky | .01 | .05 |
| ☐ 471 | Ronn Reynolds | .01 | .05 |
| ☐ 472 | Bill Doran | .01 | .05 |
| ☐ 473 | Steve Farr | .01 | .05 |
| ☐ 474 | Jerry Narron | .01 | .05 |
| ☐ 475 | Scott Garrelts | .01 | .05 |
| ☐ 476 | Danny Tartabull | .01 | .05 |
| ☐ 477 | Ken Howell | .01 | .05 |
| ☐ 478 | Tim Laudner | .01 | .05 |
| ☐ 479 | Bob Sebra | .01 | .05 |
| ☐ 480 | Jim Rice | .02 | .10 |
| ☐ 481 | Phillies Team (Glenn Wilson& Juan Samuel& and V | .01 | .05 |
| ☐ 482 | Daryl Boston | .01 | .05 |
| ☐ 483 | Dwight Lowry | .01 | .05 |
| ☐ 484 | Jim Traber | .01 | .05 |
| ☐ 485 | Tony Fernandez | .01 | .05 |
| ☐ 486 | Otis Nixon | .01 | .05 |
| ☐ 487 | Dave Gumpert | .01 | .05 |
| ☐ 488 | Ray Knight | .02 | .10 |
| ☐ 489 | Bill Gullickson | .01 | .05 |
| ☐ 490 | Dale Murphy | .05 | .15 |
| ☐ 491 | Ron Karkovice RC | .08 | .25 |
| ☐ 492 | Mike Heath | .01 | .05 |
| ☐ 493 | Tom Lasorda MG | .05 | .15 |
| ☐ 494 | Barry Jones | .01 | .05 |
| ☐ 495 | Gorman Thomas | .02 | .10 |
| ☐ 496 | Bruce Bochte | .01 | .05 |
| ☐ 497 | Dale Mohorcic | .01 | .05 |
| ☐ 498 | Bob Kearney | .01 | .05 |
| ☐ 499 | Bruce Ruffin RC | .02 | .10 |
| ☐ 500 | Don Mattingly | .25 | .60 |
| ☐ 501 | Craig Lefferts | .01 | .05 |
| ☐ 502 | Dick Schofield | .01 | .05 |
| ☐ 503 | Larry Andersen | .01 | .05 |
| ☐ 504 | Mickey Hatcher | .01 | .05 |
| ☐ 505 | Bryn Smith | .01 | .05 |
| ☐ 506 | Orioles Team (Mound conference) | .01 | .05 |
| ☐ 507 | Dave L. Stapleton | .01 | .05 |
| ☐ 508 | Scott Bankhead | .01 | .05 |
| ☐ 509 | Enos Cabell | .01 | .05 |
| ☐ 510 | Tom Henke | .01 | .05 |
| ☐ 511 | Steve Lyons | .01 | .05 |
| ☐ 512 | Dave Magadan RC | .08 | .25 |
| ☐ 513 | Carmen Castillo | .01 | .05 |
| ☐ 514 | Orlando Mercado | .01 | .05 |
| ☐ 515 | Willie Hernandez | .01 | .05 |
| ☐ 516 | Ted Simmons | .02 | .10 |
| ☐ 517 | Mario Soto | .01 | .05 |
| ☐ 518 | Gene Mauch MG | .01 | .05 |
| ☐ 519 | Curt Young | .01 | .05 |
| ☐ 520 | Jack Clark | .02 | .10 |
| ☐ 521 | Rick Reuschel | .02 | .10 |
| ☐ 522 | Checklist 397-528 | .05 | .05 |
| ☐ 523 | Earnie Riles | .01 | .05 |
| ☐ 524 | Bob Shirley | .01 | .05 |
| ☐ 525 | Phil Bradley | .01 | .05 |
| ☐ 526 | Roger Mason | .01 | .05 |
| ☐ 527 | Jim Wohlford | .01 | .05 |
| ☐ 528 | Ken Dixon | .01 | .05 |
| ☐ 529 | Alvaro Espinoza RC | .05 | .15 |
| ☐ 530 | Tony Gwynn | .10 | .30 |
| ☐ 531 | Astros TL/Y.Berra | .01 | .05 |
| ☐ 532 | Jeff Stone | .01 | .05 |
| ☐ 533 | Angel Salazar | .01 | .05 |
| ☐ 534 | Scott Sanderson | .01 | .05 |
| ☐ 535 | Tony Armas | .02 | .10 |
| ☐ 536 | Terry Mulholland RC | .08 | .25 |
| ☐ 537 | Rance Mulliniks | .01 | .05 |
| ☐ 538 | Tom Niedenfuer | .01 | .05 |
| ☐ 539 | Reid Nichols | .01 | .05 |
| ☐ 540 | Terry Kennedy | .01 | .05 |
| ☐ 541 | Rafael Belliard RC | .08 | .25 |
| ☐ 542 | Ricky Horton | .01 | .05 |
| ☐ 543 | Dave Johnson MG | .01 | .05 |
| ☐ 544 | Zane Smith | .01 | .05 |
| ☐ 545 | Buddy Bell | .02 | .10 |
| ☐ 546 | Mike Morgan | .01 | .05 |
| ☐ 547 | Rob Deer | .02 | .10 |
| ☐ 548 | Bill Mooneyham | .01 | .05 |
| ☐ 549 | Bob Melvin | .01 | .05 |
| ☐ 550 | Pete Incaviglia RC * | .08 | .25 |
| ☐ 551 | Frank Wills | .01 | .05 |
| ☐ 552 | Larry Sheets | .01 | .05 |
| ☐ 553 | Mike Maddux RC | .05 | .15 |
| ☐ 554 | Buddy Biancalana | .01 | .05 |
| ☐ 555 | Dennis Rasmussen | .01 | .05 |
| ☐ 556 | Angels Team (Rene Lachemann CO& Mike Witt& and | .01 | .05 |
| ☐ 557 | John Cerutti | .01 | .05 |
| ☐ 558 | Greg Gagne | .01 | .05 |
| ☐ 559 | Lance McCullers | .01 | .05 |
| ☐ 560 | Glenn Davis | .01 | .05 |
| ☐ 561 | Rey Quinones | .01 | .05 |
| ☐ 562 | Bryan Clutterbuck | .01 | .05 |
| ☐ 563 | John Stefero | .01 | .05 |
| ☐ 564 | Larry McWilliams | .01 | .05 |
| ☐ 565 | Dusty Baker | .02 | .10 |
| ☐ 566 | Tim Hulett | .01 | .05 |
| ☐ 567 | Greg Mathews | .01 | .05 |
| ☐ 568 | Earl Weaver MG | .02 | .10 |
| ☐ 569 | Wade Rowdon | .01 | .05 |
| ☐ 570 | Sid Fernandez | .01 | .05 |
| ☐ 571 | Ozzie Virgil | .01 | .05 |
| ☐ 572 | Pete Ladd | .01 | .05 |
| ☐ 573 | Hal McRae | .02 | .10 |
| ☐ 574 | Manny Lee | .01 | .05 |
| ☐ 575 | Pat Tabler | .01 | .05 |
| ☐ 576 | Frank Pastore | .01 | .05 |
| ☐ 577 | Dann Bilardello | .01 | .05 |
| ☐ 578 | Billy Hatcher | .01 | .05 |
| ☐ 579 | Rick Burleson | .01 | .05 |
| ☐ 580 | Mike Krukow | .01 | .05 |
| ☐ 581 | Cubs Team (Ron Cey and Steve Trout) | .01 | .05 |
| ☐ 582 | Bruce Berenyi | .01 | .05 |
| ☐ 583 | Junior Ortiz | .01 | .05 |
| ☐ 584 | Ron Kittle | .01 | .05 |
| ☐ 585 | Scott Bailes | .01 | .05 |
| ☐ 586 | Ben Oglivie | .02 | .10 |
| ☐ 587 | Eric Plunk | .01 | .05 |
| ☐ 588 | Wallace Johnson | .01 | .05 |
| ☐ 589 | Steve Crawford | .01 | .05 |
| ☐ 590 | Vince Coleman | .01 | .05 |
| ☐ 591 | Spike Owen | .01 | .05 |
| ☐ 592 | Chris Welsh | .01 | .05 |
| ☐ 593 | Chuck Tanner MG | .01 | .05 |
| ☐ 594 | Rick Anderson | .01 | .05 |
| ☐ 595 | Keith Hernandez AS | .01 | .05 |
| ☐ 596 | Steve Sax AS | .01 | .05 |
| ☐ 597 | Mike Schmidt AS | .08 | .25 |
| ☐ 598 | Ozzie Smith AS | .08 | .25 |
| ☐ 599 | Tony Gwynn AS | .05 | .15 |
| ☐ 600 | Dave Parker AS | .01 | .05 |
| ☐ 601 | Darryl Strawberry AS | .01 | .05 |
| ☐ 602 | Gary Carter AS | .01 | .05 |
| ☐ 603A | Dwight Gooden AS NoTM | .02 | .10 |
| ☐ 603B | Dwight Gooden AS TM | .02 | .10 |
| ☐ 604 | Fernando Valenzuela AS | .01 | .05 |
| ☐ 605 | Todd Worrell AS | .01 | .05 |
| ☐ 606 | Don Mattingly AS | .10 | .30 |
| ☐ 606A | Don Mattingly AS NoTM | .40 | 1.00 |
| ☐ 607 | Tony Bernazard AS | .01 | .05 |
| ☐ 608 | Wade Boggs AS | .02 | .10 |
| ☐ 609 | Cal Ripken AS | .08 | .25 |
| ☐ 610 | Jim Rice AS | .01 | .05 |
| ☐ 611 | Kirby Puckett AS | .08 | .25 |
| ☐ 612 | George Bell AS | .01 | .05 |
| ☐ 613 | Lance Parrish AS UER (Pitcher heading on back) | .01 | .05 |
| ☐ 614 | Roger Clemens AS | .40 | 1.00 |
| ☐ 615 | Teddy Higuera AS | .01 | .05 |
| ☐ 616 | Dave Righetti AS | .01 | .05 |
| ☐ 617 | Al Nipper | .01 | .05 |
| ☐ 618 | Tom Kelly MG | .01 | .05 |
| ☐ 619 | Jerry Reed | .01 | .05 |
| ☐ 620 | Jose Canseco | .40 | 1.00 |
| ☐ 621 | Danny Cox | .01 | .05 |
| ☐ 622 | Glenn Braggs RC | .02 | .10 |
| ☐ 623 | Kurt Stillwell | .01 | .05 |
| ☐ 624 | Tim Burke | .01 | .05 |
| ☐ 625 | Mookie Wilson | .02 | .10 |
| ☐ 626 | Joel Skinner | .01 | .05 |
| ☐ 627 | Ken Oberkfell | .01 | .05 |
| ☐ 628 | Bob Walk | .01 | .05 |
| ☐ 629 | Larry Parrish | .01 | .05 |
| ☐ 630 | John Candelaria | .01 | .05 |
| ☐ 631 | Tigers Team (Mound conference) | .01 | .05 |
| ☐ 632 | Rob Woodward | .01 | .05 |
| ☐ 633 | Jose Uribe | .01 | .05 |
| ☐ 634 | Rafael Palmeiro RC | .50 | 1.50 |
| ☐ 635 | Ken Schrom | .01 | .05 |
| ☐ 636 | Darren Daulton | .02 | .10 |
| ☐ 637 | Bip Roberts RC | .08 | .25 |
| ☐ 638 | Rich Bordi | .01 | .05 |

|  |  | | |
|---|---|---|---|
| 639 | Gerald Perry | .01 | .05 |
| 640 | Mark Clear | .01 | .05 |
| 641 | Domingo Ramos | .01 | .05 |
| 642 | Al Pulido | .01 | .05 |
| 643 | Ron Shepherd | .01 | .05 |
| 644 | John Denny | .01 | .05 |
| 645 | Dwight Evans | .05 | .15 |
| 646 | Mike Mason | .01 | .05 |
| 647 | Tom Lawless | .01 | .05 |
| 648 | Barry Larkin RC | .40 | 1.00 |
| 649 | Mickey Tettleton | .01 | .05 |
| 650 | Hubie Brooks | .01 | .05 |
| 651 | Benny Distefano | .01 | .05 |
| 652 | Terry Forster | .02 | .10 |
| 653 | Kevin Mitchell RC * | .15 | .40 |
| 654 | Checklist 529-660 | .02 | .10 |
| 655 | Jesse Barfield | .02 | .10 |
| 656 | Rangers Team (Bobby Valentine MG and Ricky Wrigh) | | |
| 657 | Tom Waddell | .01 | .05 |
| 658 | Robby Thompson RC * | .08 | .25 |
| 659 | Aurelio Lopez | .01 | .05 |
| 660 | Bob Horner | .02 | .10 |
| 661 | Lou Whitaker | .02 | .10 |
| 662 | Frank DiPino | .01 | .05 |
| 663 | Cliff Johnson | .01 | .05 |
| 664 | Mike Marshall | .01 | .05 |
| 665 | Rod Scurry | .01 | .05 |
| 666 | Von Hayes | .01 | .05 |
| 667 | Ron Hassey | .01 | .05 |
| 668 | Juan Bonilla | .01 | .05 |
| 669 | Bud Black | .01 | .05 |
| 670 | Jose Cruz | .02 | .10 |
| 671A | Ray Soff ERR (No D* before copyright line) | .01 | .05 |
| 671B | Ray Soff COR (D* before copyright line) | .01 | .05 |
| 672 | Chili Davis | .02 | .10 |
| 673 | Don Sutton | .02 | .10 |
| 674 | Bill Campbell | .01 | .05 |
| 675 | Ed Romero | .01 | .05 |
| 676 | Charlie Moore | .01 | .05 |
| 677 | Bob Grich | .02 | .10 |
| 678 | Carney Lansford | .02 | .10 |
| 679 | Kent Hrbek | .02 | .10 |
| 680 | Ryne Sandberg | .15 | .40 |
| 681 | George Bell | .02 | .10 |
| 682 | Jerry Reuss | .01 | .05 |
| 683 | Gary Roenicke | .01 | .05 |
| 684 | Kent Tekulve | .01 | .05 |
| 685 | Jerry Hairston | .01 | .05 |
| 686 | Doyle Alexander | .01 | .05 |
| 687 | Alan Trammell | .02 | .10 |
| 688 | Juan Beniquez | .01 | .05 |
| 689 | Darrell Porter | .01 | .05 |
| 690 | Dane Iorg | .01 | .05 |
| 691 | Dave Parker | .02 | .10 |
| 692 | Frank White | .02 | .10 |
| 693 | Terry Puhl | .01 | .05 |
| 694 | Phil Niekro | .02 | .10 |
| 695 | Chico Walker | .01 | .05 |
| 696 | Gary Lucas | .01 | .05 |
| 697 | Ed Lynch | .01 | .05 |
| 698 | Ernie Whitt | .01 | .05 |
| 699 | Ken Landreaux | .01 | .05 |
| 700 | Dave Bergman | .01 | .05 |
| 701 | Willie Randolph | .02 | .10 |
| 702 | Greg Gross | .01 | .05 |
| 703 | Dave Schmidt | .01 | .05 |
| 704 | Jesse Orosco | .01 | .05 |
| 705 | Bruce Hurst | .01 | .05 |
| 706 | Rick Manning | .01 | .05 |
| 707 | Bob McClure | .01 | .05 |
| 708 | Scott McGregor | .01 | .05 |
| 709 | Dave Kingman | .02 | .10 |
| 710 | Gary Gaetti | .02 | .10 |
| 711 | Ken Griffey | .02 | .10 |
| 712 | Don Robinson | .01 | .05 |
| 713 | Tom Brookens | .01 | .05 |
| 714 | Dan Quisenberry | .01 | .05 |
| 715 | Bob Dernier | .01 | .05 |
| 716 | Rick Leach | .01 | .05 |
| 717 | Ed VandeBerg | .01 | .05 |
| 718 | Steve Carlton | .02 | .10 |
| 719 | Tom Hume | .01 | .05 |
| 720 | Richard Dotson | .01 | .05 |
| 721 | Tom Herr | .01 | .05 |
| 722 | Bob Knepper | .01 | .05 |
| 723 | Brett Butler | .02 | .10 |
| 724 | Greg Minton | .01 | .05 |
| 725 | George Hendrick | .02 | .10 |
| 726 | Frank Tanana | .02 | .10 |
| 727 | Mike Moore | .01 | .05 |
| 728 | Tippy Martinez | .01 | .05 |
| 729 | Tom Paciorek | .01 | .05 |
| 730 | Eric Show | .01 | .05 |
| 731 | Dave Concepcion | .02 | .10 |
| 732 | Manny Trillo | .01 | .05 |
| 733 | Bill Caudill | .01 | .05 |
| 734 | Bill Madlock | .02 | .10 |
| 735 | Rickey Henderson | .08 | .25 |
| 736 | Steve Bedrosian | .01 | .05 |
| 737 | Floyd Bannister | .01 | .05 |
| 738 | Jorge Orta | .01 | .05 |
| 739 | Chet Lemon | .02 | .10 |
| 740 | Rich Gedman | .01 | .05 |
| 741 | Paul Molitor | .02 | .10 |
| 742 | Andy McGaffigan | .01 | .05 |
| 743 | Dwayne Murphy | .01 | .05 |
| 744 | Roy Smalley | .01 | .05 |
| 745 | Glenn Hubbard | .01 | .05 |
| 746 | Bob Ojeda | .01 | .05 |
| 747 | Johnny Ray | .01 | .05 |
| 748 | Mike Flanagan | .01 | .05 |
| 749 | Ozzie Smith | .15 | .40 |
| 750 | Steve Trout | .01 | .05 |
| 751 | Garth Iorg | .01 | .05 |
| 752 | Dan Petry | .01 | .05 |
| 753 | Rick Honeycutt | .01 | .05 |
| 754 | Dave LaPoint | .01 | .05 |
| 755 | Luis Aguayo | .01 | .05 |
| 756 | Carlton Fisk | .05 | .15 |
| 757 | Nolan Ryan | .40 | 1.00 |
| 758 | Tony Bernazard | .01 | .05 |
| 759 | Joel Youngblood | .01 | .05 |
| 760 | Mike Witt | .01 | .05 |
| 761 | Greg Pryor | .01 | .05 |
| 762 | Gary Ward | .01 | .05 |
| 763 | Tim Flannery | .01 | .05 |
| 764 | Bill Buckner | .02 | .10 |
| 765 | Kirk Gibson | .02 | .10 |
| 766 | Don Aase | .01 | .05 |
| 767 | Ron Cey | .02 | .10 |
| 768 | Dennis Lamp | .01 | .05 |
| 769 | Steve Sax | .02 | .10 |
| 770 | Dave Winfield | .02 | .10 |
| 771 | Shane Rawley | .01 | .05 |
| 772 | Harold Baines | .02 | .10 |
| 773 | Robin Yount | .15 | .40 |
| 774 | Wayne Krenchicki | .01 | .05 |
| 775 | Joaquin Andujar | .02 | .10 |
| 776 | Tom Brunansky | .01 | .05 |
| 777 | Chris Chambliss | .02 | .10 |
| 778 | Jack Morris | .02 | .10 |
| 779 | Craig Reynolds | .01 | .05 |
| 780 | Andre Thornton | .01 | .05 |
| 781 | Atlee Hammaker | .01 | .05 |
| 782 | Brian Downing | .02 | .10 |
| 783 | Willie Wilson | .02 | .10 |
| 784 | Cal Ripken | .30 | .75 |
| 785 | Terry Francona | .02 | .10 |
| 786 | Jimy Williams MG | .01 | .05 |
| 787 | Alejandro Pena | .01 | .05 |
| 788 | Tim Stoddard | .01 | .05 |
| 789 | Dan Schatzeder | .01 | .05 |
| 790 | Julio Cruz | .01 | .05 |
| 791 | Lance Parrish UER (No trademark& never corrected) | .02 | .10 |
| 792 | Checklist 661-792 | .01 | .05 |

## 1988 Topps

PIRATES

| | | | |
|---|---|---|---|
| COMPLETE SET (792) | | 6.00 | 15.00 |
| COMP.FACT SET (792) | | 6.00 | 15.00 |
| COMP.X-MAS SET (792) | | 15.00 | 40.00 |
| 1 | Vince Coleman RB / 100 Steals for Third Cons. Seas | .01 | .05 |
| 2 | Don Mattingly RB | .10 | .30 |
| 3 | Mark McGwire RB | .30 | .75 |
| 3A | Mark McGwire ERR RB | .30 | .75 |
| 4 | Eddie Murray RB | .05 | .15 |
| 4A | Eddie Murray ERR RB | .20 | .50 |
| 5 | Phil Niekro / Joe Niekro RB / Brothers Win Record | .02 | .10 |
| 6 | Nolan Ryan RB | .15 | .40 |
| 7 | Benito Santiago RB | .01 | .05 |
| 8 | Kevin Elster RB | .01 | .05 |
| 9 | Andy Hawkins RB | .01 | .05 |
| 10 | Ryne Sandberg | .15 | .40 |
| 11 | Mike Young | .01 | .05 |
| 12 | Bill Schroeder | .01 | .05 |
| 13 | Andres Thomas | .01 | .05 |
| 14 | Sparky Anderson MG | .02 | .10 |
| 15 | Chili Davis | .02 | .10 |
| 16 | Kirk McCaskill | .01 | .05 |
| 17 | Ron Oester | .01 | .05 |
| 18A | Al Leiter ERR RC | .20 | .50 |
| 18B | Al Leiter RC | .20 | .50 |
| 19 | Mark Davidson | .01 | .05 |
| 20 | Kevin Gross | .01 | .05 |
| 21 | Wade Boggs / Spike Owen TL | .02 | .10 |
| 22 | Greg Swindell | .01 | .05 |
| 23 | Ken Landreaux | .01 | .05 |
| 24 | Jim Deshaies | .01 | .05 |
| 25 | Andres Galarraga | .02 | .10 |
| 26 | Mitch Williams | .01 | .05 |
| 27 | R.J. Reynolds | .01 | .05 |
| 28 | Jose Nunez | .01 | .05 |
| 29 | Angel Salazar | .01 | .05 |
| 30 | Sid Fernandez | .01 | .05 |
| 31 | Bruce Bochy | .01 | .05 |
| 32 | Mike Morgan | .01 | .05 |
| 33 | Rob Deer | .01 | .05 |
| 34 | Ricky Horton | .01 | .05 |
| 35 | Harold Baines | .02 | .10 |
| 36 | Jamie Moyer | .02 | .10 |
| 37 | Ed Romero | .01 | .05 |
| 38 | Jeff Calhoun | .01 | .05 |
| 39 | Gerald Perry | .01 | .05 |
| 40 | Orel Hershiser | .02 | .10 |
| 41 | Bob Melvin | .01 | .05 |
| 42 | Bill Landrum | .01 | .05 |
| 43 | Dick Schofield | .01 | .05 |
| 44 | Lou Piniella MG | .02 | .10 |
| 45 | Kent Hrbek | .02 | .10 |
| 46 | Darnell Coles | .01 | .05 |
| 47 | Joaquin Andujar | .02 | .10 |
| 48 | Alan Ashby | .01 | .05 |
| 49 | Dave Clark | .01 | .05 |
| 50 | Hubie Brooks | .01 | .05 |
| 51 | C.Ripken/E.Murray TL | .15 | .40 |
| 52 | Don Robinson | .01 | .05 |
| 53 | Curt Wilkerson | .01 | .05 |
| 54 | Jim Clancy | .01 | .05 |
| 55 | Phil Bradley | .01 | .05 |
| 56 | Ed Hearn | .01 | .05 |
| 57 | Tim Crews RC | .08 | .25 |
| 58 | Dave Magadan | .01 | .05 |
| 59 | Danny Cox | .01 | .05 |
| 60 | Rickey Henderson | .07 | .20 |
| 61 | Mark Knudson | .01 | .05 |

|  | | |
|---|---|---|
| ☐ 318 Mel Hall | .01 | .05 |
| ☐ 319 Mike Loynd | .01 | .05 |
| ☐ 320 Alan Trammell | .02 | .10 |
| ☐ 321 Harold Baines | | |
| Carlton Fisk TL | .02 | .10 |
| ☐ 322 Vicente Palacios | .01 | .05 |
| ☐ 323 Rick Leach | .01 | .05 |
| ☐ 324 Danny Jackson | .01 | .05 |
| ☐ 325 Glenn Hubbard | .01 | .05 |
| ☐ 326 Al Nipper | .01 | .05 |
| ☐ 327 Larry Sheets | .01 | .05 |
| ☐ 328 Greg Cadaret | .01 | .05 |
| ☐ 329 Chris Speier | .01 | .05 |
| ☐ 330 Eddie Whitson | .01 | .05 |
| ☐ 331 Brian Downing | .02 | .10 |
| ☐ 332 Jerry Reed | .01 | .05 |
| ☐ 333 Wally Backman | .01 | .05 |
| ☐ 334 Dave LaPoint | .01 | .05 |
| ☐ 335 Claudell Washington | .01 | .05 |
| ☐ 336 Ed Lynch | .01 | .05 |
| ☐ 337 Jim Gantner | .01 | .05 |
| ☐ 338 Brian Holton UER | | |
| (1987 ERA .389& | | |
| should be 3.89) | .01 | .05 |
| ☐ 339 Kurt Stillwell | .01 | .05 |
| ☐ 340 Jack Morris | .02 | .10 |
| ☐ 341 Carmen Castillo | .01 | .05 |
| ☐ 342 Larry Andersen | .01 | .05 |
| ☐ 343 Greg Gagne | .01 | .05 |
| ☐ 344 Tony LaRussa MG | .02 | .10 |
| ☐ 345 Scott Fletcher | .01 | .05 |
| ☐ 346 Vance Law | .01 | .05 |
| ☐ 347 Joe Johnson | .01 | .05 |
| ☐ 348 Jim Eisenreich | .01 | .05 |
| ☐ 349 Bob Walk | .01 | .05 |
| ☐ 350 Will Clark | .07 | .20 |
| ☐ 351 Red Schoendienst CO | | |
| Tony Pena TL | .02 | .10 |
| ☐ 352 Bill Ripken RC* | .01 | .05 |
| ☐ 353 Ed Olwine | .01 | .05 |
| ☐ 354 Marc Sullivan | .01 | .05 |
| ☐ 355 Roger McDowell | .01 | .05 |
| ☐ 356 Luis Aguayo | .01 | .05 |
| ☐ 357 Floyd Bannister | .01 | .05 |
| ☐ 358 Rey Quinones | .01 | .05 |
| ☐ 359 Tim Stoddard | .01 | .05 |
| ☐ 360 Tony Gwynn | .10 | .30 |
| ☐ 361 Greg Maddux | .40 | 1.00 |
| ☐ 362 Juan Castillo | .01 | .05 |
| ☐ 363 Willie Fraser | .01 | .05 |
| ☐ 364 Nick Esasky | .01 | .05 |
| ☐ 365 Floyd Youmans | .01 | .05 |
| ☐ 366 Chet Lemon | .02 | .10 |
| ☐ 367 Tim Leary | .01 | .05 |
| ☐ 368 Gerald Young | .01 | .05 |
| ☐ 369 Greg Harris | .01 | .05 |
| ☐ 370 Jose Canseco | .20 | .50 |
| ☐ 371 Joe Hesketh | .01 | .05 |
| ☐ 372 Matt Williams RC | .30 | .75 |
| ☐ 373 Checklist 265-396 | .01 | .05 |
| ☐ 374 Doc Edwards MG | .01 | .05 |
| ☐ 375 Tom Brunansky | .01 | .05 |
| ☐ 376 Bill Wilkinson | .01 | .05 |
| ☐ 377 Sam Horn RC | .02 | .10 |
| ☐ 378 Todd Frohwirth | .01 | .05 |
| ☐ 379 Rafael Ramirez | .01 | .05 |
| ☐ 380 Joe Magrane RC* | .01 | .05 |
| ☐ 381 Wally Joyner | | |
| Jack Howell TL | .02 | .10 |
| ☐ 382 Keith Miller RC | .08 | .25 |
| ☐ 383 Eric Bell | .01 | .05 |
| ☐ 384 Neil Allen | .01 | .05 |
| ☐ 385 Carlton Fisk | .05 | .15 |
| ☐ 386 Don Mattingly AS | .10 | .30 |
| ☐ 387 Willie Randolph AS | .01 | .05 |
| ☐ 388 Wade Boggs AS | .02 | .10 |
| ☐ 389 Alan Trammell AS | .01 | .05 |
| ☐ 390 George Bell AS | .01 | .05 |
| ☐ 391 Kirby Puckett AS | .05 | .15 |
| ☐ 392 Dave Winfield AS | .01 | .05 |
| ☐ 393 Matt Nokes AS | .01 | .05 |
| ☐ 394 Roger Clemens AS | .20 | .50 |
| ☐ 395 Jimmy Key AS | .01 | .05 |
| ☐ 396 Tom Henke AS | .01 | .05 |
| ☐ 397 Jack Clark AS | .01 | .05 |
| ☐ 398 Juan Samuel AS | .01 | .05 |
| ☐ 399 Tim Wallach AS | .01 | .05 |
| ☐ 400 Ozzie Smith AS | .07 | .20 |
| ☐ 401 Andre Dawson AS | .01 | .05 |
| ☐ 402 Tony Gwynn AS | .05 | .15 |
| ☐ 403 Tim Raines AS | .01 | .05 |
| ☐ 404 Benny Santiago AS | .01 | .05 |
| ☐ 405 Dwight Gooden AS | .01 | .05 |
| ☐ 406 Shane Rawley AS | .01 | .05 |
| ☐ 407 Steve Bedrosian AS | .01 | .05 |
| ☐ 408 Dion James | .01 | .05 |
| ☐ 409 Joel McKeon | .01 | .05 |
| ☐ 410 Tony Pena | .01 | .05 |
| ☐ 411 Wayne Tolleson | .01 | .05 |
| ☐ 412 Randy Myers | .02 | .10 |
| ☐ 413 John Christensen | .01 | .05 |
| ☐ 414 John McNamara MG | .01 | .05 |
| ☐ 415 Don Carman | .01 | .05 |
| ☐ 416 Keith Moreland | .01 | .05 |
| ☐ 417 Mark Ciardi | .01 | .05 |
| ☐ 418 Joel Youngblood | .01 | .05 |
| ☐ 419 Scott McGregor | .01 | .05 |
| ☐ 420 Wally Joyner | .02 | .10 |
| ☐ 421 Ed VandeBerg | .01 | .05 |
| ☐ 422 Dave Concepcion | .02 | .10 |
| ☐ 423 John Smiley RC* | .06 | .25 |
| ☐ 424 Dwayne Murphy | .01 | .05 |
| ☐ 425 Jeff Reardon | .02 | .10 |
| ☐ 426 Randy Ready | .01 | .05 |
| ☐ 427 Paul Kilgus | .01 | .05 |
| ☐ 428 John Shelby | .01 | .05 |
| ☐ 429 A.Trammell/K.Gibson TL | .02 | .10 |
| ☐ 430 Glenn Davis | .01 | .05 |
| ☐ 431 Casey Candaele | .01 | .05 |
| ☐ 432 Mike Moore | .01 | .05 |
| ☐ 433 Bill Pecota RC* | .01 | .05 |
| ☐ 434 Rick Aguilera | .01 | .05 |
| ☐ 435 Mike Pagliarulo | .01 | .05 |
| ☐ 436 Mike Bielecki | .01 | .05 |
| ☐ 437 Fred Manrique | .01 | .05 |
| ☐ 438 Rob Ducey | .01 | .05 |
| ☐ 439 Dave Martinez | .01 | .05 |
| ☐ 440 Steve Bedrosian | .01 | .05 |
| ☐ 441 Rick Manning | .01 | .05 |
| ☐ 442 Tom Bolton | .01 | .05 |
| ☐ 443 Ken Griffey | .02 | .10 |
| ☐ 444 Cal Ripken&Sr. MG | | |
| (Checklist back) | | |
| UER (two cop) | .01 | .05 |
| ☐ 445 Mike Krukow | .01 | .05 |
| ☐ 446 Doug DeCinces | | |
| (Now with Cardinals | | |
| on card front) | .01 | .05 |
| ☐ 447 Jeff Montgomery RC | .08 | .25 |
| ☐ 448 Mike Davis | .01 | .05 |
| ☐ 449 Jeff M. Robinson | .01 | .05 |
| ☐ 450 Barry Bonds | .75 | 2.00 |
| ☐ 451 Keith Atherton | .01 | .05 |
| ☐ 452 Willie Wilson | .02 | .10 |
| ☐ 453 Dennis Powell | .01 | .05 |
| ☐ 454 Marvell Wynne | .01 | .05 |
| ☐ 455 Shawn Hillegas | .01 | .05 |
| ☐ 456 Dave Anderson | .01 | .05 |
| ☐ 457 Terry Leach | .01 | .05 |
| ☐ 458 Ron Hassey | .01 | .05 |
| ☐ 459 Dave Winfield | | |
| Willie Randolph TL | .01 | .05 |
| ☐ 460 Ozzie Smith | .10 | .30 |
| ☐ 461 Danny Darwin | .01 | .05 |
| ☐ 462 Don Slaught | .01 | .05 |
| ☐ 463 Fred McGriff | .07 | .20 |
| ☐ 464 Jay Tibbs | .01 | .05 |
| ☐ 465 Paul Molitor | .02 | .10 |
| ☐ 466 Jerry Mumphrey | .01 | .05 |
| ☐ 467 Don Aase | .01 | .05 |
| ☐ 468 Darren Daulton | .02 | .10 |
| ☐ 469 Jeff Dedmon | .01 | .05 |
| ☐ 470 Dwight Evans | .05 | .15 |
| ☐ 471 Donnie Moore | .01 | .05 |
| ☐ 472 Robby Thompson | .01 | .05 |
| ☐ 473 Joe Niekro | .01 | .05 |
| ☐ 474 Tom Brookens | .01 | .05 |
| ☐ 475 Pete Rose MG/TC | .20 | .50 |
| ☐ 476 Dave Stewart | .02 | .10 |
| ☐ 477 Jamie Quirk | .01 | .05 |
| ☐ 478 Sid Bream | .01 | .05 |
| ☐ 479 Brett Butler | .02 | .10 |
| ☐ 480 Dwight Gooden | .02 | .10 |
| ☐ 481 Mariano Duncan | .01 | .05 |
| ☐ 482 Mark Davis | .01 | .05 |
| ☐ 483 Rod Booker | .01 | .05 |
| ☐ 484 Pat Clements | .01 | .05 |
| ☐ 485 Harold Reynolds | .02 | .10 |
| ☐ 486 Pat Keedy | .01 | .05 |
| ☐ 487 Jim Pankovits | .01 | .05 |
| ☐ 488 Andy McGaffigan | .01 | .05 |
| ☐ 489 Dodgers TL | | |
| Pedro Guerrero and | | |
| Fernando Valenzuel | .01 | .05 |
| ☐ 490 Larry Parrish | .01 | .05 |
| ☐ 491 B.J. Surhoff | .02 | .10 |
| ☐ 492 Doyle Alexander | .01 | .05 |
| ☐ 493 Mike Greenwell | .01 | .05 |
| ☐ 494 Wally Ritchie | .01 | .05 |
| ☐ 495 Eddie Murray | .07 | .20 |
| ☐ 496 Guy Hoffman | .01 | .05 |
| ☐ 497 Kevin Mitchell | .02 | .10 |
| ☐ 498 Bob Boone | .02 | .10 |
| ☐ 499 Eric King | .01 | .05 |
| ☐ 500 Andre Dawson | .02 | .10 |
| ☐ 501 Tim Birtsas | .01 | .05 |
| ☐ 502 Dan Gladden | .01 | .05 |
| ☐ 503 Junior Noboa | .01 | .05 |
| ☐ 504 Bob Rodgers MG | .01 | .05 |
| ☐ 505 Willie Upshaw | .01 | .05 |
| ☐ 506 John Cangelosi | .01 | .05 |
| ☐ 507 Mark Gubicza | .01 | .05 |
| ☐ 508 Tim Teufel | .01 | .05 |
| ☐ 509 Bill Dawley | .01 | .05 |
| ☐ 510 Dave Winfield | .02 | .10 |
| ☐ 511 Joel Davis | .01 | .05 |
| ☐ 512 Alex Trevino | .01 | .05 |
| ☐ 513 Tim Flannery | .01 | .05 |
| ☐ 514 Pat Sheridan | .01 | .05 |
| ☐ 515 Juan Nieves | .01 | .05 |
| ☐ 516 Jim Sundberg | .02 | .10 |
| ☐ 517 Ron Robinson | .01 | .05 |
| ☐ 518 Greg Gross | .01 | .05 |
| ☐ 519 Harold Reynolds | | |
| Phil Bradley TL | .01 | .05 |
| ☐ 520 Dave Smith | .01 | .05 |
| ☐ 521 Jim Dwyer | .01 | .05 |
| ☐ 522 Bob Patterson | .01 | .05 |
| ☐ 523 Gary Roenicke | .01 | .05 |
| ☐ 524 Gary Lucas | .01 | .05 |
| ☐ 525 Marty Barrett | .01 | .05 |
| ☐ 526 Juan Berenguer | .01 | .05 |
| ☐ 527 Steve Henderson | .01 | .05 |
| ☐ 528A Checklist 397-528 | | |
| ERR (455 S. Carlton) | .05 | .15 |
| ☐ 528B Checklist 397-528 | | |
| COR (455 S. Hillegas) | .02 | .10 |
| ☐ 529 Tim Burke | .01 | .05 |
| ☐ 530 Gary Carter | .02 | .10 |
| ☐ 531 Rich Yett | .01 | .05 |
| ☐ 532 Mike Kingery | .01 | .05 |
| ☐ 533 John Farrell RC | .02 | .10 |
| ☐ 534 John Wathan MG | .01 | .05 |
| ☐ 535 Ron Guidry | .02 | .10 |
| ☐ 536 John Morris | .01 | .05 |
| ☐ 537 Steve Buechele | .01 | .05 |
| ☐ 538 Bill Wegman | .01 | .05 |
| ☐ 539 Mike LaValliere | .01 | .05 |
| ☐ 540 Bret Saberhagen | .02 | .10 |
| ☐ 541 Juan Beniquez | .01 | .05 |
| ☐ 542 Paul Noce | .01 | .05 |
| ☐ 543 Kent Tekulve | .01 | .05 |
| ☐ 544 Jim Traber | .01 | .05 |
| ☐ 545 Don Baylor | .02 | .10 |
| ☐ 546 John Candelaria | .01 | .05 |
| ☐ 547 Felix Fermin | .01 | .05 |
| ☐ 548 Shane Mack | .01 | .05 |
| ☐ 549 Braves TL | | |
| Albert Hall& | | |
| Dale Murphy& | | |
| Ken Griffey | | |
| ☐ 550 Pedro Guerrero | .02 | .10 |
| ☐ 551 Terry Steinbach | .01 | .05 |
| ☐ 552 Mark Thurmond | .01 | .05 |
| ☐ 553 Tracy Jones | .01 | .05 |
| ☐ 554 Mike Smithson | .01 | .05 |
| ☐ 555 Brook Jacoby | .01 | .05 |
| ☐ 556 Stan Clarke | .01 | .05 |
| ☐ 557 Craig Reynolds | .01 | .05 |
| ☐ 558 Bob Ojeda | .01 | .05 |
| ☐ 559 Ken Williams | .01 | .05 |
| ☐ 560 Tim Wallach | .01 | .05 |
| ☐ 561 Rick Cerone | .01 | .05 |
| ☐ 562 Jim Lindeman | .01 | .05 |

| # | Player | Lo | Hi |
|---|--------|----|----|
| ☐ 563 | Jose Guzman | .01 | .05 |
| ☐ 564 | Frank Lucchesi MG | .01 | .05 |
| ☐ 565 | Lloyd Moseby | .01 | .05 |
| ☐ 566 | Charlie O'Brien | .01 | .05 |
| ☐ 567 | Mike Diaz | .01 | .05 |
| ☐ 568 | Chris Brown | .01 | .05 |
| ☐ 569 | Charlie Leibrandt | .01 | .05 |
| ☐ 570 | Jeffrey Leonard | .01 | .05 |
| ☐ 571 | Mark Williamson | .01 | .05 |
| ☐ 572 | Chris James | .01 | .05 |
| ☐ 573 | Bob Stanley | .01 | .05 |
| ☐ 574 | Graig Nettles | .02 | .10 |
| ☐ 575 | Don Sutton | .02 | .10 |
| ☐ 576 | Tommy Hinzo | .01 | .05 |
| ☐ 577 | Tom Browning | .01 | .05 |
| ☐ 578 | Gary Gaetti | .02 | .10 |
| ☐ 579 | Gary Carter / Kevin McReynolds TL | .01 | .05 |
| ☐ 580 | Mark McGwire | .60 | 1.50 |
| ☐ 581 | Tito Landrum | .01 | .05 |
| ☐ 582 | Mike Henneman RC* | .08 | .25 |
| ☐ 583 | Dave Valle | .01 | .05 |
| ☐ 584 | Steve Trout | .01 | .05 |
| ☐ 585 | Ozzie Guillen | .02 | .10 |
| ☐ 586 | Bob Forsch | .01 | .05 |
| ☐ 587 | Terry Puhl | .01 | .05 |
| ☐ 588 | Jeff Parrett | .01 | .05 |
| ☐ 589 | Geno Petralli | .01 | .05 |
| ☐ 590 | George Bell | .02 | .10 |
| ☐ 591 | Doug Drabek | .01 | .05 |
| ☐ 592 | Dale Sveum | .01 | .05 |
| ☐ 593 | Bob Tewksbury | .01 | .05 |
| ☐ 594 | Bobby Valentine MG | .02 | .10 |
| ☐ 595 | Frank White | .02 | .10 |
| ☐ 596 | John Kruk | .02 | .10 |
| ☐ 597 | Gene Garber | .01 | .05 |
| ☐ 598 | Lee Lacy | .01 | .05 |
| ☐ 599 | Calvin Schiraldi | .01 | .05 |
| ☐ 600 | Mike Schmidt | .20 | .50 |
| ☐ 601 | Jack Lazorko | .01 | .05 |
| ☐ 602 | Mike Aldrete | .01 | .05 |
| ☐ 603 | Rob Murphy | .01 | .05 |
| ☐ 604 | Chris Bando | .01 | .05 |
| ☐ 605 | Kirk Gibson | .07 | .20 |
| ☐ 606 | Moose Haas | .01 | .05 |
| ☐ 607 | Mickey Hatcher | .01 | .05 |
| ☐ 608 | Charlie Kerfeld | .01 | .05 |
| ☐ 609 | Gary Gaetti / Kent Hrbek TL | .02 | .10 |
| ☐ 610 | Keith Hernandez | .02 | .10 |
| ☐ 611 | Tommy John | .02 | .10 |
| ☐ 612 | Curt Ford | .01 | .05 |
| ☐ 613 | Bobby Thigpen | .01 | .05 |
| ☐ 614 | Herm Winningham | .01 | .05 |
| ☐ 615 | Jody Davis | .01 | .05 |
| ☐ 616 | Jay Aldrich | .01 | .05 |
| ☐ 617 | Oddibe McDowell | .01 | .05 |
| ☐ 618 | Cecil Fielder | .02 | .10 |
| ☐ 619 | Mike Dunne (inconsistent design & black name on f | .01 | .05 |
| ☐ 620 | Cory Snyder | .01 | .05 |
| ☐ 621 | Gene Nelson | .01 | .05 |
| ☐ 622 | Kal Daniels | .01 | .05 |
| ☐ 623 | Mike Flanagan | .01 | .05 |
| ☐ 624 | Jim Leyland MG | .02 | .10 |
| ☐ 625 | Frank Viola | .02 | .10 |
| ☐ 626 | Glenn Wilson | .01 | .05 |
| ☐ 627 | Joe Boever | .01 | .05 |
| ☐ 628 | Dave Henderson | .01 | .05 |
| ☐ 629 | Kelly Downs | .01 | .05 |
| ☐ 630 | Darrell Evans | .02 | .10 |
| ☐ 631 | Jack Howell | .01 | .05 |
| ☐ 632 | Steve Shields | .01 | .05 |
| ☐ 633 | Barry Lyons | .01 | .05 |
| ☐ 634 | Jose DeLeon | .01 | .05 |
| ☐ 635 | Terry Pendleton | .02 | .10 |
| ☐ 636 | Charles Hudson | .01 | .05 |
| ☐ 637 | Jay Bell RC | .15 | .40 |
| ☐ 638 | Steve Balboni | .01 | .05 |
| ☐ 639 | Glenn Braggs / Tony Muser CO TL | .01 | .05 |
| ☐ 640 | Gary Templeton (inconsistent design & green bord | | |
| ☐ 641 | Rick Honeycutt | .02 | .10 |
| ☐ 642 | Bob Dernier | .01 | .05 |
| ☐ 643 | Rocky Childress | .01 | .05 |
| ☐ 644 | Terry McGriff | .01 | .05 |
| ☐ 645 | Matt Nokes RC* | .08 | .25 |
| ☐ 646 | Checklist 529-660 | .01 | .05 |
| ☐ 647 | Pascual Perez | .01 | .05 |
| ☐ 648 | Al Newman | .01 | .05 |
| ☐ 649 | DeWayne Buice | .01 | .05 |
| ☐ 650 | Cal Ripken | .30 | .75 |
| ☐ 651 | Mike Jackson RC* | .08 | .25 |
| ☐ 652 | Bruce Benedict | .01 | .05 |
| ☐ 653 | Jeff Sellers | .01 | .05 |
| ☐ 654 | Roger Craig MG | .02 | .10 |
| ☐ 655 | Len Dykstra | .02 | .10 |
| ☐ 656 | Lee Guetterman | .01 | .05 |
| ☐ 657 | Gary Redus | .01 | .05 |
| ☐ 658 | Tim Conroy (Inconsistent design, name in white) | .01 | .05 |
| ☐ 659 | Bobby Meacham | .01 | .05 |
| ☐ 660 | Rick Reuschel | .02 | .10 |
| ☐ 661 | Nolan Ryan TBC | .20 | .50 |
| ☐ 663 | Ron Blomberg TBC | .01 | .05 |
| ☐ 664 | Bob Gibson TBC | .08 | .25 |
| ☐ 665 | Stan Musial TBC | .07 | .20 |
| ☐ 666 | Mario Soto | .01 | .05 |
| ☐ 667 | Luis Quinones | .01 | .05 |
| ☐ 668 | Walt Terrell | .01 | .05 |
| ☐ 669 | Lance Parrish / Mike Ryan CO TL | .01 | .05 |
| ☐ 670 | Dan Plesac | .01 | .05 |
| ☐ 671 | Tim Laudner | .01 | .05 |
| ☐ 672 | John Davis | .01 | .05 |
| ☐ 673 | Tony Phillips | .01 | .05 |
| ☐ 674 | Mike Fitzgerald | .01 | .05 |
| ☐ 675 | Jim Rice | .02 | .10 |
| ☐ 676 | Ken Dixon | .01 | .05 |
| ☐ 677 | Eddie Milner | .01 | .05 |
| ☐ 678 | Jim Acker | .01 | .05 |
| ☐ 679 | Darrell Miller | .01 | .05 |
| ☐ 680 | Charlie Hough | .02 | .10 |
| ☐ 681 | Bobby Bonilla | .02 | .10 |
| ☐ 682 | Jimmy Key | .02 | .10 |
| ☐ 683 | Julio Franco | .02 | .10 |
| ☐ 684 | Hal Lanier MG | .01 | .05 |
| ☐ 685 | Ron Darling | .02 | .10 |
| ☐ 686 | Terry Francona | .01 | .05 |
| ☐ 687 | Mickey Brantley | .01 | .05 |
| ☐ 688 | Jim Winn | .01 | .05 |
| ☐ 689 | Tom Pagnozzi RC | .02 | .10 |
| ☐ 690 | Jay Howell | .01 | .05 |
| ☐ 691 | Dan Pasqua | .01 | .05 |
| ☐ 692 | Mike Birkbeck | .01 | .05 |
| ☐ 693 | Benito Santiago | .10 | .25 |
| ☐ 694 | Eric Nolte | .01 | .05 |
| ☐ 695 | Shawon Dunston | .02 | .10 |
| ☐ 696 | Duane Ward | .01 | .05 |
| ☐ 697 | Steve Lombardozzi | .01 | .05 |
| ☐ 698 | Brad Havens | .01 | .05 |
| ☐ 699 | B.Santiago/T.Gwynn TL | .02 | .10 |
| ☐ 700 | George Brett | .20 | .50 |
| ☐ 701 | Sammy Stewart | .01 | .05 |
| ☐ 702 | Mike Gallego | .01 | .05 |
| ☐ 703 | Bob Brenly | .01 | .05 |
| ☐ 704 | Dennis Boyd | .01 | .05 |
| ☐ 705 | Juan Samuel | .01 | .05 |
| ☐ 706 | Rick Mahler | .01 | .05 |
| ☐ 707 | Fred Lynn | .02 | .10 |
| ☐ 708 | Gus Polidor | .01 | .05 |
| ☐ 709 | George Frazier | .01 | .05 |
| ☐ 710 | Darryl Strawberry | .02 | .10 |
| ☐ 711 | Bill Gullickson | .01 | .05 |
| ☐ 712 | John Moses | .01 | .05 |
| ☐ 713 | Willie Hernandez | .01 | .05 |
| ☐ 714 | Jim Fregosi MG | .02 | .10 |
| ☐ 715 | Todd Worrell | .02 | .10 |
| ☐ 716 | Lenn Sakata | .01 | .05 |
| ☐ 717 | Jay Baller | .01 | .05 |
| ☐ 718 | Mike Felder | .01 | .05 |
| ☐ 719 | Denny Walling | .01 | .05 |
| ☐ 720 | Tim Raines | .02 | .10 |
| ☐ 721 | Pete O'Brien | .01 | .05 |
| ☐ 722 | Manny Lee | .01 | .05 |
| ☐ 723 | Bob Kipper | .01 | .05 |
| ☐ 724 | Danny Tartabull | .02 | .10 |
| ☐ 725 | Mike Boddicker | .01 | .05 |
| ☐ 726 | Alfredo Griffin | .01 | .05 |
| ☐ 727 | Greg Booker | .01 | .05 |
| ☐ 728 | Andy Allanson | .01 | .05 |
| ☐ 729 | G.Bell/F.McGriff TL | .02 | .10 |
| ☐ 730 | John Franco | .02 | .10 |
| ☐ 731 | Rick Schu | .01 | .05 |
| ☐ 732 | David Palmer | .01 | .05 |
| ☐ 733 | Spike Owen | .01 | .05 |
| ☐ 734 | Craig Lefferts | .01 | .05 |
| ☐ 735 | Kevin McReynolds | .01 | .05 |
| ☐ 736 | Matt Young | .01 | .05 |
| ☐ 737 | Butch Wynegar | .01 | .05 |
| ☐ 738 | Scott Bankhead | .01 | .05 |
| ☐ 739 | Daryl Boston | .01 | .05 |
| ☐ 740 | Rick Sutcliffe | .02 | .10 |
| ☐ 741 | Mike Easler | .01 | .05 |
| ☐ 742 | Mark Clear | .01 | .05 |
| ☐ 743 | Larry Herndon | .01 | .05 |
| ☐ 744 | Whitey Herzog MG | .02 | .10 |
| ☐ 745 | Bill Doran | .01 | .05 |
| ☐ 746 | Gene Larkin RC* | .08 | .25 |
| ☐ 747 | Bobby Witt | .01 | .05 |
| ☐ 748 | Reid Nichols | .01 | .05 |
| ☐ 749 | Mark Eichhorn | .01 | .05 |
| ☐ 750 | Bo Jackson | .07 | .20 |
| ☐ 751 | Jim Morrison | .01 | .05 |
| ☐ 752 | Mark Grant | .01 | .05 |
| ☐ 753 | Danny Heep | .01 | .05 |
| ☐ 754 | Mike LaCoss | .01 | .05 |
| ☐ 755 | Ozzie Virgil | .01 | .05 |
| ☐ 756 | Mike Maddux | .01 | .05 |
| ☐ 757 | John Mazzano | .01 | .05 |
| ☐ 758 | Eddie Williams RC | .02 | .10 |
| ☐ 759 | M.McGwire/J.Canseco TL | .40 | 1.00 |
| ☐ 760 | Mike Scott | .02 | .10 |
| ☐ 761 | Tony Armas | .02 | .10 |
| ☐ 762 | Scott Bradley | .01 | .05 |
| ☐ 763 | Doug Sisk | .01 | .05 |
| ☐ 764 | Greg Walker | .01 | .05 |
| ☐ 765 | Neal Heaton | .01 | .05 |
| ☐ 766 | Henry Cotto | .01 | .05 |
| ☐ 767 | Jose Lind RC | .08 | .25 |
| ☐ 768 | Dickie Noles (Now with Tigers on card front) | .01 | .05 |
| ☐ 769 | Cecil Cooper | .02 | .10 |
| ☐ 770 | Lou Whitaker | .02 | .10 |
| ☐ 771 | Ruben Sierra | .02 | .10 |
| ☐ 772 | Sal Butera | .01 | .05 |
| ☐ 773 | Frank Williams | .01 | .05 |
| ☐ 774 | Gene Mauch MG | .01 | .05 |
| ☐ 775 | Dave Steib | .02 | .10 |
| ☐ 776 | Checklist 661-792 | .01 | .05 |
| ☐ 777 | Lonnie Smith | .01 | .05 |
| ☐ 778A | Keith Comstock ERR WL | .75 | 2.00 |
| ☐ 778B | Keith Comstock COR (Blue Padres) | .01 | .05 |
| ☐ 779 | Tom Glavine RC | 1.00 | 2.50 |
| ☐ 780 | Fernando Valenzuela | .02 | .10 |
| ☐ 781 | Keith Hughes | .01 | .05 |
| ☐ 782 | Jeff Ballard | .01 | .05 |
| ☐ 783 | Ron Roenicke | .01 | .05 |
| ☐ 784 | Joe Sambito | .01 | .05 |
| ☐ 785 | Alvin Davis | .01 | .05 |
| ☐ 786 | Joe Price (inconsistent design & orange team name | .01 | .05 |
| ☐ 787 | Bill Almon | .01 | .05 |
| ☐ 788 | Ray Searage | .01 | .05 |
| ☐ 789 | Joe Carter TL | .01 | .05 |
| ☐ 790 | Dave Righetti | .02 | .10 |
| ☐ 791 | Ted Simmons | .02 | .10 |
| ☐ 792 | John Tudor | .02 | .10 |

### 1989 Topps

ERIC DAVIS

| | | Lo | Hi |
|---|---|----|----|
| ☐ COMPLETE SET (792) | | 8.00 | 20.00 |
| ☐ COMP.FACT SET (792) | | 10.00 | 25.00 |

# 438 / 1989 Topps

|  |  | | |
|---|---|---|---|
| | COMP.X-MAS.SET (792) | 10.00 | 25.00 |
| | FS SUBSET VARIATIONS EXIST | | |
| | FS PHOTOS ARE PLACED HIGHER/LOWER | | |
| 1 | George Bell RB | .01 | .05 |
| 2 | Wade Boggs RB | .02 | .10 |
| 3 | Gary Carter RB | .01 | .05 |
| 4 | Andre Dawson RB | .01 | .05 |
| 5 | Orel Hershiser RB | .01 | .05 |
| 6 | Doug Jones RB UER | .01 | .05 |
| 7 | Kevin McReynolds RB | .01 | .05 |
| 8 | Dave Eiland | .01 | .05 |
| 9 | Tim Teufel | .01 | .05 |
| 10 | Andre Dawson | .02 | .10 |
| 11 | Bruce Sutter | .02 | .10 |
| 12 | Dale Sveum | .01 | .05 |
| 13 | Doug Sisk | .01 | .05 |
| 14 | Tom Kelly MG | .01 | .05 |
| 15 | Robby Thompson | .01 | .05 |
| 16 | Ron Robinson | .01 | .05 |
| 17 | Brian Downing | .02 | .10 |
| 18 | Rick Rhoden | .01 | .05 |
| 19 | Greg Gagne | .01 | .05 |
| 20 | Steve Bedrosian | .01 | .05 |
| 21 | Greg Walker TL | .01 | .05 |
| 22 | Tim Crews | .01 | .05 |
| 23 | Mike Fitzgerald | .01 | .05 |
| 24 | Larry Andersen | .01 | .05 |
| 25 | Frank White | .02 | .10 |
| 26 | Dale Mohorcic | .01 | .05 |
| 27A | Orestes Destrade RC * | .02 | .10 |
| 27B | Orestes Destrade VAR | .02 | .10 |
| 28 | Mike Moore | .01 | .05 |
| 29 | Kelly Gruber | .01 | .05 |
| 30 | Dwight Gooden | .02 | .10 |
| 31 | Terry Francona | .02 | .10 |
| 32 | Dennis Rasmussen | .01 | .05 |
| 33 | B.J. Surhoff | .02 | .10 |
| 34 | Ken Williams | .01 | .05 |
| 35 | John Tudor UER | .02 | .10 |
| | (With Red Sox in '84,should be Pir | | |
| 36 | Mitch Webster | .01 | .05 |
| 37 | Bob Stanley | .01 | .05 |
| 38 | Paul Runge | .01 | .05 |
| 39 | Mike Maddux | .01 | .05 |
| 40 | Steve Sax | .02 | .10 |
| 41 | Terry Mulholland | .01 | .05 |
| 42 | Jim Eppard | .01 | .05 |
| 43 | Guillermo Hernandez | .01 | .05 |
| 44 | Jim Snyder MG | .01 | .05 |
| 45 | Kal Daniels | .01 | .05 |
| 46 | Mark Portugal | .01 | .05 |
| 47 | Carney Lansford | .02 | .10 |
| 48 | Tim Burke | .01 | .05 |
| 49 | Craig Biggio RC | 1.25 | 3.00 |
| 50 | George Bell | .02 | .10 |
| 51 | Mark McLemore TL | .01 | .05 |
| 52 | Bob Brenly | .01 | .05 |
| 53 | Ruben Sierra | .02 | .10 |
| 54 | Steve Trout | .01 | .05 |
| 55 | Julio Franco | .02 | .10 |
| 56 | Pat Tabler | .01 | .05 |
| 57 | Alejandro Pena | .01 | .05 |
| 58 | Lee Mazzilli | .01 | .05 |
| 59 | Mark Davis | .01 | .05 |
| 60 | Tom Brunansky | .02 | .10 |
| 61 | Neil Allen | .01 | .05 |
| 62 | Alfredo Griffin | .01 | .05 |
| 63 | Mark Clear | .01 | .05 |
| 64 | Alex Trevino | .01 | .05 |
| 65 | Rick Reuschel | .02 | .10 |
| 66 | Manny Trillo | .01 | .05 |
| 67 | Dave Palmer | .01 | .05 |
| 68 | Darrell Miller | .01 | .05 |
| 69 | Jeff Ballard | .01 | .05 |
| 70 | Mark McGwire | .40 | 1.00 |
| 71 | Mike Boddicker | .01 | .05 |
| 72 | John Moses | .01 | .05 |
| 73 | Pascual Perez | .01 | .05 |
| 74 | Nick Leyva MG | .01 | .05 |
| 75 | Tom Henke | .01 | .05 |
| 76 | Terry Blocker | .01 | .05 |
| 77 | Doyle Alexander | .01 | .05 |
| 78 | Jim Sundberg | .02 | .10 |
| 79 | Scott Bankhead | .01 | .05 |
| 80 | Cory Snyder | .01 | .05 |
| 81 | Tim Raines TL | .01 | .05 |
| 82 | Dave Leiper | .01 | .05 |
| 83 | Jeff Blauser | .01 | .05 |
| 84 | Bill Bene FDP | .01 | .05 |
| 85 | Kevin McReynolds | .01 | .05 |
| 86 | Al Nipper | .01 | .05 |
| 87 | Larry Owen | .01 | .05 |
| 88 | Darryl Hamilton RC * | .08 | .25 |
| 89 | Dave LaPoint | .01 | .05 |
| 90 | Vince Coleman UER | .01 | .05 |
| | (Wrong birth year) | | |
| 91 | Floyd Youmans | .01 | .05 |
| 92 | Jeff Kunkel | .01 | .05 |
| 93 | Ken Howell | .01 | .05 |
| 94 | Chris Speier | .01 | .05 |
| 95 | Gerald Young | .01 | .05 |
| 96 | Rick Cerone | .01 | .05 |
| 97 | Greg Mathews | .01 | .05 |
| 98 | Larry Sheets | .01 | .05 |
| 99 | Sherman Corbett | .01 | .05 |
| 100 | Mike Schmidt | .20 | .50 |
| 101 | Les Straker | .01 | .05 |
| 102 | Mike Gallego | .01 | .05 |
| 103 | Tim Birtsas | .01 | .05 |
| 104 | Dallas Green MG | .01 | .05 |
| 105 | Ron Darling | .02 | .10 |
| 106 | Willie Upshaw | .01 | .05 |
| 107 | Jose DeLeon | .01 | .05 |
| 108 | Fred Manrique | .01 | .05 |
| 109 | Hipolito Pena | .01 | .05 |
| 110 | Paul Molitor | .02 | .10 |
| 111 | Eric Davis TL | .01 | .05 |
| 112 | Jim Presley | .01 | .05 |
| 113 | Lloyd Moseby | .01 | .05 |
| 114 | Bob Kipper | .01 | .05 |
| 115 | Jody Davis | .01 | .05 |
| 116 | Jeff Montgomery | .01 | .05 |
| 117 | Dave Anderson | .01 | .05 |
| 118 | Checklist 1-132 | .01 | .05 |
| 119 | Terry Puhl | .01 | .05 |
| 120 | Frank Viola | .02 | .10 |
| 121 | Garry Templeton | .01 | .05 |
| 122 | Lance Johnson | .01 | .05 |
| 123 | Spike Owen | .01 | .05 |
| 124 | Jim Traber | .01 | .05 |
| 125 | Mike Krukow | .01 | .05 |
| 126 | Sid Bream | .01 | .05 |
| 127 | Walt Terrell | .01 | .05 |
| 128 | Milt Thompson | .01 | .05 |
| 129 | Terry Clark | .01 | .05 |
| 130 | Gerald Perry | .01 | .05 |
| 131 | Dave Otto | .01 | .05 |
| 132 | Curt Ford | .01 | .05 |
| 133 | Bill Long | .01 | .05 |
| 134 | Don Zimmer MG | .01 | .05 |
| 135 | Jose Rijo | .02 | .10 |
| 136 | Joey Meyer | .01 | .05 |
| 137 | Geno Petralli | .01 | .05 |
| 138 | Wallace Johnson | .01 | .05 |
| 139 | Mike Flanagan | .01 | .05 |
| 140 | Shawon Dunston | .02 | .10 |
| 141 | Brook Jacoby TL | .01 | .05 |
| 142 | Mike Diaz | .01 | .05 |
| 143 | Mike Campbell | .01 | .05 |
| 144 | Jay Bell | .02 | .10 |
| 145 | Dave Stewart | .02 | .10 |
| 146 | Gary Pettis | .01 | .05 |
| 147 | DeWayne Buice | .01 | .05 |
| 148 | Bill Pecota | .01 | .05 |
| 149 | Doug Dascenzo | .01 | .05 |
| 150 | Fernando Valenzuela | .02 | .10 |
| 151 | Terry McGriff | .01 | .05 |
| 152 | Mark Thurmond | .01 | .05 |
| 153 | Jim Pankovits | .01 | .05 |
| 154 | Don Carman | .01 | .05 |
| 155 | Marty Barrett | .01 | .05 |
| 156 | Dave Gallagher | .01 | .05 |
| 157 | Tom Glavine | .08 | .25 |
| 158 | Mike Aldrete | .01 | .05 |
| 159 | Pat Clements | .01 | .05 |
| 160 | Jeffrey Leonard | .01 | .05 |
| 161 | Gregg Olson UER RC | .08 | .25 |
| 162 | John Davis | .01 | .05 |
| 163 | Bob Forsch | .01 | .05 |
| 164 | Hal Lanier MG | .01 | .05 |
| 165 | Mike Dunne | .01 | .05 |
| 166 | Doug Jennings | .01 | .05 |
| 167 | Steve Searcy FS | .01 | .05 |
| 168 | Willie Wilson | .02 | .10 |
| 169 | Mike Jackson | .01 | .05 |
| 170 | Tony Fernandez | .01 | .05 |
| 171 | Andres Thomas TL | .01 | .05 |
| 172 | Frank Williams | .01 | .05 |
| 173 | Mel Hall | .01 | .05 |
| 174 | Todd Burns | .01 | .05 |
| 175 | John Shelby | .01 | .05 |
| 176 | Jeff Parrett | .01 | .05 |
| 177 | Monty Fariss FDP | .01 | .05 |
| 178 | Mark Grant | .01 | .05 |
| 179 | Ozzie Virgil | .01 | .05 |
| 180 | Mike Scott | .02 | .10 |
| 181 | Craig Worthington | .01 | .05 |
| 182 | Bob McClure | .01 | .05 |
| 183 | Oddibe McDowell | .01 | .05 |
| 184 | John Costello | .01 | .05 |
| 185 | Claudell Washington | .01 | .05 |
| 186 | Pat Perry | .01 | .05 |
| 187 | Darren Daulton | .02 | .10 |
| 188 | Dennis Lamp | .01 | .05 |
| 189 | Kevin Mitchell | .02 | .10 |
| 190 | Mike Witt | .01 | .05 |
| 191 | Sil Campusano | .01 | .05 |
| 192 | Paul Mirabella | .01 | .05 |
| 193 | Sparky Anderson MG | .01 | .05 |
| | (Team checklist back) | | |
| | UER | .02 | .10 |
| 194 | Greg W.Harris RC | .02 | .10 |
| 195 | Ozzie Guillen | .01 | .05 |
| 196 | Denny Walling | .01 | .05 |
| 197 | Neal Heaton | .01 | .05 |
| 198 | Danny Heep | .01 | .05 |
| 199 | Mike Schooler RC * | .02 | .10 |
| 200 | George Brett | .25 | .60 |
| 201 | Kelly Gruber TL | .01 | .05 |
| 202 | Brad Moore | .01 | .05 |
| 203 | Rob Ducey | .01 | .05 |
| 204 | Brad Havens | .01 | .05 |
| 205 | Dwight Evans | .05 | .15 |
| 206 | Roberto Alomar | .08 | .25 |
| 207 | Terry Leach | .01 | .05 |
| 208 | Tom Pagnozzi | .01 | .05 |
| 209 | Jeff Bittiger | .01 | .05 |
| 210 | Dale Murphy | .05 | .15 |
| 211 | Mike Pagliarulo | .01 | .05 |
| 212 | Scott Sanderson | .01 | .05 |
| 213 | Rene Gonzales | .01 | .05 |
| 214 | Charlie O'Brien | .01 | .05 |
| 215 | Kevin Gross | .01 | .05 |
| 216 | Jack Howell | .01 | .05 |
| 217 | Joe Price | .01 | .05 |
| 218 | Mike LaValliere | .01 | .05 |
| 219 | Jim Clancy | .01 | .05 |
| 220 | Gary Gaetti | .02 | .10 |
| 221 | Cecil Espy | .01 | .05 |
| 222 | Mark Lewis RC | .08 | .25 |
| 223 | Jay Buhner | .02 | .10 |
| 224 | Tony LaRussa MG | .02 | .10 |
| 225 | Ramon Martinez | .08 | .25 |
| 226 | Bill Doran | .01 | .05 |
| 227 | John Farrell | .01 | .05 |
| 228 | Nelson Santovenia | .01 | .05 |
| 229 | Jimmy Key | .02 | .10 |
| 230 | Ozzie Smith | .15 | .40 |
| 231 | Padres TL/R.Alomar | .08 | .25 |
| 232 | Ricky Horton | .01 | .05 |
| 233 | Gregg Jefferies | .01 | .05 |
| 234 | Tom Browning | .01 | .05 |
| 235 | John Kruk | .02 | .10 |
| 236 | Charles Hudson | .01 | .05 |
| 237 | Glenn Hubbard | .01 | .05 |
| 238 | Eric King | .01 | .05 |
| 239 | Tim Laudner | .01 | .05 |
| 240 | Greg Maddux | .20 | .50 |
| 241 | Brett Butler | .02 | .10 |
| 242 | Ed VandeBerg | .01 | .05 |
| 243 | Bob Boone | .02 | .10 |
| 244 | Jim Acker | .01 | .05 |
| 245 | Jim Rice | .02 | .10 |
| 246 | Rey Quinones | .01 | .05 |
| 247 | Shawn Hillegas | .01 | .05 |
| 248 | Tony Phillips | .01 | .05 |
| 249 | Tim Leary | .01 | .05 |
| 250 | Cal Ripken | .30 | .75 |
| 251 | John Dopson | .01 | .05 |
| 252 | Billy Hatcher | .01 | .05 |
| 253 | Jose Alvarez | .02 | .10 |
| 254 | Tom Lasorda MG | .05 | .15 |
| 255 | Ron Guidry | .02 | .10 |
| 256 | Benny Santiago | .02 | .10 |

|  | | |
|---|---|---|
| 257 Rick Aguilera | .01 | .05 |
| 258 Checklist 133-264 | .01 | .05 |
| 259 Larry McWilliams | .01 | .05 |
| 260 Dave Winfield | .02 | .10 |
| 261 St.Louis Cardinals TL Tom Brunansky (With Luis A | | |
| 262 Jeff Pico | .01 | .05 |
| 263 Mike Felder | .01 | .05 |
| 264 Rob Dibble RC | .15 | .40 |
| 265 Kent Hrbek | .02 | .10 |
| 266 Luis Aquino | .01 | .05 |
| 267 Jeff M. Robinson | .01 | .05 |
| 268 Keith Miller RC | .08 | .25 |
| 269 Tom Bolton | .01 | .05 |
| 270 Wally Joyner | .02 | .10 |
| 271 Jay Tibbs | .01 | .05 |
| 272 Ron Hassey | .01 | .05 |
| 273 Jose Lind | .01 | .05 |
| 274 Mark Eichhorn | .01 | .05 |
| 275 Danny Tartabull UER (Born San Juan& PR should be | | |
| 276 Paul Kilgus | .01 | .05 |
| 277 Mike Davis | .01 | .05 |
| 278 Andy McGaffigan | .01 | .05 |
| 279 Scott Bradley | .01 | .05 |
| 280 Bob Knepper | .01 | .05 |
| 281 Gary Redus | .01 | .05 |
| 282 Cris Carpenter RC * | .02 | .10 |
| 283 Andy Allanson | .01 | .05 |
| 284 Jim Leyland MG | .02 | .10 |
| 285 John Candelaria | .01 | .05 |
| 286 Darrin Jackson | .02 | .10 |
| 287 Juan Nieves | .01 | .05 |
| 288 Pat Sheridan | .01 | .05 |
| 289 Ernie Whitt | .01 | .05 |
| 290 John Franco | .02 | .10 |
| 291 New York Mets TL Darryl Strawberry (With Keith H | | |
| 292 Jim Corsi | .01 | .05 |
| 293 Glenn Wilson | .01 | .05 |
| 294 Juan Berenguer | .01 | .05 |
| 295 Scott Fletcher | .01 | .05 |
| 296 Ron Gant | .02 | .10 |
| 297 Oswald Peraza | .01 | .05 |
| 298 Chris James | .01 | .05 |
| 299 Steve Ellsworth | .01 | .05 |
| 300 Darryl Strawberry | .02 | .10 |
| 301 Charlie Leibrandt | .01 | .05 |
| 302 Gary Ward | .01 | .05 |
| 303 Felix Fermin | .01 | .05 |
| 304 Joel Youngblood | .01 | .05 |
| 305 Dave Smith | .01 | .05 |
| 306 Tracy Woodson | .01 | .05 |
| 307 Lance McCullers | .01 | .05 |
| 308 Ron Karkovice | .01 | .05 |
| 309 Mario Diaz | .01 | .05 |
| 310 Rafael Palmeiro | .08 | .25 |
| 311 Chris Bosio | .01 | .05 |
| 312 Tom Lawless | .01 | .05 |
| 313 Dennis Martinez | .02 | .10 |
| 314 Bobby Valentine MG | .02 | .10 |
| 315 Greg Swindell | .01 | .05 |
| 316 Walt Weiss | .01 | .05 |
| 317 Jack Armstrong RC * | .08 | .25 |
| 318 Gene Larkin | .01 | .05 |
| 319 Greg Booker | .01 | .05 |
| 320 Lou Whitaker | .02 | .10 |
| 321 Jody Reed TL | .01 | .05 |
| 322 John Smiley | .01 | .05 |
| 323 Gary Thurman | .01 | .05 |
| 324 Bob Milacki | .01 | .05 |
| 325 Jesse Barfield | .02 | .10 |
| 326 Dennis Boyd | .01 | .05 |
| 327 Mark Lemke RC | .15 | .40 |
| 328 Rick Honeycutt | .01 | .05 |
| 329 Bob Melvin | .01 | .05 |
| 330 Eric Davis | .02 | .10 |
| 331 Curt Wilkerson | .01 | .05 |
| 332 Tony Armas | .02 | .10 |
| 333 Bob Ojeda | .01 | .05 |
| 334 Steve Lyons | .01 | .05 |
| 335 Dave Righetti | .02 | .10 |
| 336 Steve Balboni | .01 | .05 |
| 337 Calvin Schiraldi | .01 | .05 |
| 338 Jim Adduci | .01 | .05 |
| 339 Scott Bailes | .01 | .05 |
| 340 Kirk Gibson | .02 | .10 |
| 341 Jim Deshaies | .01 | .05 |
| 342 Tom Brookens | .01 | .05 |
| 343 Gary Sheffield RC | .60 | 1.50 |
| 344 Tom Trebelhorn MG | .01 | .05 |
| 345 Charlie Hough | .02 | .10 |
| 346 Rex Hudler | .01 | .05 |
| 347 John Cerutti | .01 | .05 |
| 348 Ed Hearn | .01 | .05 |
| 349 Ron Jones | .02 | .10 |
| 350 Andy Van Slyke | .05 | .15 |
| 351 San Fran. Giants TL Bob Melvin (With Bill Fahey | .01 | .05 |
| 352 Rick Schu | .01 | .05 |
| 353 Marvell Wynne | .01 | .05 |
| 354 Larry Parrish | .01 | .05 |
| 355 Mark Langston | .01 | .05 |
| 356 Kevin Elster | .01 | .05 |
| 357 Jerry Reuss | .01 | .05 |
| 358 Ricky Jordan RC | .08 | .25 |
| 359 Tommy John | .02 | .10 |
| 360 Ryne Sandberg | .15 | .40 |
| 361 Kelly Downs | .01 | .05 |
| 362 Jack Lazorko | .01 | .05 |
| 363 Rich Yett | .01 | .05 |
| 364 Rob Deer | .01 | .05 |
| 365 Mike Henneman | .01 | .05 |
| 366 Herm Winningham | .01 | .05 |
| 367 Johnny Paredes | .01 | .05 |
| 368 Brian Holton | .01 | .05 |
| 369 Ken Caminiti | .05 | .15 |
| 370 Dennis Eckersley | .05 | .15 |
| 371 Manny Lee | .01 | .05 |
| 372 Craig Lefferts | .01 | .05 |
| 373 Tracy Jones | .01 | .05 |
| 374 John Wathan MG | .01 | .05 |
| 375 Terry Pendleton | .02 | .10 |
| 376 Steve Lombardozzi | .01 | .05 |
| 377 Mike Smithson | .01 | .05 |
| 378 Checklist 265-396 | .01 | .05 |
| 379 Tim Flannery | .01 | .05 |
| 380 Rickey Henderson | .08 | .25 |
| 381 Larry Sheets TL | .01 | .05 |
| 382 John Smoltz RC | .60 | 1.50 |
| 383 Howard Johnson | .02 | .10 |
| 384 Mark Salas | .01 | .05 |
| 385 Von Hayes | .01 | .05 |
| 386 Andres Galarraga AS | .01 | .05 |
| 387 Ryne Sandberg AS | .08 | .25 |
| 388 Bobby Bonilla AS | .01 | .05 |
| 389 Ozzie Smith AS | .08 | .25 |
| 390 Darryl Strawberry AS | .05 | .15 |
| 391 Andre Dawson AS | .05 | .15 |
| 392 Andy Van Slyke AS | .02 | .10 |
| 393 Gary Carter AS | .05 | .15 |
| 394 Orel Hershiser AS | .01 | .05 |
| 395 Danny Jackson AS | .01 | .05 |
| 396 Kirk Gibson AS | .02 | .10 |
| 397 Don Mattingly AS | .10 | .30 |
| 398 Julio Franco AS | .01 | .05 |
| 399 Wade Boggs AS | .02 | .10 |
| 400 Alan Trammell AS | .05 | .15 |
| 401 Jose Canseco AS | .05 | .15 |
| 402 Mike Greenwell AS | .01 | .05 |
| 403 Kirby Puckett AS | .05 | .15 |
| 404 Bob Boone AS | .01 | .05 |
| 405 Roger Clemens AS | .20 | .50 |
| 406 Frank Viola AS | .01 | .05 |
| 407 Dave Winfield AS | .01 | .05 |
| 408 Greg Walker | .01 | .05 |
| 409 Ken Dayley | .01 | .05 |
| 410 Jack Clark | .02 | .10 |
| 411 Mitch Williams | .01 | .05 |
| 412 Barry Lyons | .01 | .05 |
| 413 Mike Kingery | .01 | .05 |
| 414 Jim Fregosi MG | .01 | .05 |
| 415 Rich Gossage | .02 | .10 |
| 416 Fred Lynn | .02 | .10 |
| 417 Mike LaCoss | .01 | .05 |
| 418 Bob Dernier | .01 | .05 |
| 419 Tom Filer | .01 | .05 |
| 420 Joe Carter | .02 | .10 |
| 421 Kirk McCaskill | .01 | .05 |
| 422 Bo Diaz | .01 | .05 |
| 423 Brian Fisher | .01 | .05 |
| 424 Luis Polonia UER | .01 | .05 |
| (Wrong birthdate) | | |
| 425 Jay Howell | .01 | .05 |
| 426 Dan Gladden | .01 | .05 |
| 427 Eric Show | .01 | .05 |
| 428 Craig Reynolds | .01 | .05 |
| 429 Minnesota Twins TL Greg Gagne (Taking throw at 2 | .01 | .05 |
| 430 Mark Gubicza | .01 | .05 |
| 431 Luis Rivera | .01 | .05 |
| 432 Chad Kreuter RC | .08 | .25 |
| 433 Albert Hall | .01 | .05 |
| 434 Ken Patterson | .01 | .05 |
| 435 Len Dykstra | .02 | .10 |
| 436 Bobby Meacham | .01 | .05 |
| 437 Andy Benes RC * | .15 | .40 |
| 438 Greg Gross | .01 | .05 |
| 439 Frank DiPino | .01 | .05 |
| 440 Bobby Bonilla | .02 | .10 |
| 441 Jerry Reed | .01 | .05 |
| 442 Jose Oquendo | .01 | .05 |
| 443 Rod Nichols | .01 | .05 |
| 444 Moose Stubing MG | .01 | .05 |
| 445 Matt Nokes | .01 | .05 |
| 446 Rob Murphy | .01 | .05 |
| 447 Donell Nixon | .01 | .05 |
| 448 Eric Plunk | .01 | .05 |
| 449 Carmelo Martinez | .01 | .05 |
| 450 Roger Clemens | .40 | 1.00 |
| 451 Mark Davidson | .01 | .05 |
| 452 Israel Sanchez | .01 | .05 |
| 453 Tom Prince | .01 | .05 |
| 454 Paul Assenmacher | .01 | .05 |
| 455 Johnny Ray | .01 | .05 |
| 456 Tim Belcher | .01 | .05 |
| 457 Mackey Sasser | .01 | .05 |
| 458 Donn Pall | .01 | .05 |
| 459 Dave Valle TL | .01 | .05 |
| 460 Dave Steib | .02 | .10 |
| 461 Buddy Bell | .02 | .10 |
| 462 Jose Guzman | .01 | .05 |
| 463 Steve Lake | .01 | .05 |
| 464 Bryn Smith | .01 | .05 |
| 465 Mark Grace | .08 | .25 |
| 466 Chuck Crim | .01 | .05 |
| 467 Jim Walewander | .01 | .05 |
| 468 Henry Cotto | .01 | .05 |
| 469 Jose Bautista RC | .02 | .10 |
| 470 Lance Parrish | .02 | .10 |
| 471 Steve Curry | .01 | .05 |
| 472 Brian Harper | .01 | .05 |
| 473 Don Robinson | .01 | .05 |
| 474 Bob Rodgers MG | .01 | .05 |
| 475 Dave Parker | .02 | .10 |
| 476 Jon Perlman | .01 | .05 |
| 477 Dick Schofield | .01 | .05 |
| 478 Doug Drabek | .01 | .05 |
| 479 Mike Macfarlane RC * | .08 | .25 |
| 480 Keith Hernandez | .02 | .10 |
| 481 Chris Brown | .01 | .05 |
| 482 Steve Peters | .01 | .05 |
| 483 Mickey Hatcher | .01 | .05 |
| 484 Steve Shields | .01 | .05 |
| 485 Hubie Brooks | .01 | .05 |
| 486 Jack McDowell | .02 | .10 |
| 487 Scott Lusader | .01 | .05 |
| 488 Kevin Coffman (%%Now with Cubs~ | .01 | .05 |
| 489 Phillies TL/M.Schmidt | .05 | .15 |
| 490 Chris Sabo RC * | .15 | .40 |
| 491 Mike Birkbeck | .01 | .05 |
| 492 Alan Ashby | .01 | .05 |
| 493 Todd Benzinger | .01 | .05 |
| 494 Shane Rawley | .01 | .05 |
| 495 Candy Maldonado | .01 | .05 |
| 496 Dwayne Henry | .01 | .05 |
| 497 Pete Stanicek | .01 | .05 |
| 498 Dave Valle | .01 | .05 |
| 499 Don Heinkel | .01 | .05 |
| 500 Jose Canseco | .08 | .25 |
| 501 Vance Law | .01 | .05 |
| 502 Duane Ward | .01 | .05 |
| 503 Al Newman | .01 | .05 |
| 504 Bob Walk | .01 | .05 |
| 505 Pete Rose MG/TC | .20 | .50 |
| 506 Kirt Manwaring | .01 | .05 |
| 507 Steve Farr | .01 | .05 |
| 508 Wally Backman | .01 | .05 |

|  |  | | |
|---|------|---|---|
| ☐ 509 | Bud Black | .01 | .05 |
| ☐ 510 | Bob Horner | .02 | .10 |
| ☐ 511 | Richard Dotson | .01 | .05 |
| ☐ 512 | Donnie Hill | .01 | .05 |
| ☐ 513 | Jesse Orosco | .01 | .05 |
| ☐ 514 | Chet Lemon | .02 | .10 |
| ☐ 515 | Barry Larkin | .05 | .15 |
| ☐ 516 | Eddie Whitson | .01 | .05 |
| ☐ 517 | Greg Brock | .01 | .05 |
| ☐ 518 | Bruce Ruffin | .01 | .05 |
| ☐ 519 | Willie Randolph TL | .01 | .05 |
| ☐ 520 | Rick Sutcliffe | .02 | .10 |
| ☐ 521 | Mickey Tettleton | .01 | .05 |
| ☐ 522 | Randy Kramer | .01 | .05 |
| ☐ 523 | Andres Thomas | .01 | .05 |
| ☐ 524 | Checklist 397-528 | .01 | .05 |
| ☐ 525 | Chili Davis | .02 | .10 |
| ☐ 526 | Wes Gardner | .01 | .05 |
| ☐ 527 | Dave Henderson | .01 | .05 |
| ☐ 528 | Luis Medina (Lower left front has white triangle | .01 | .05 |
| ☐ 529 | Tom Foley | .01 | .05 |
| ☐ 530 | Nolan Ryan | .40 | 1.00 |
| ☐ 531 | Dave Hengel | .01 | .05 |
| ☐ 532 | Jerry Browne | .01 | .05 |
| ☐ 533 | Andy Hawkins | .01 | .05 |
| ☐ 534 | Doc Edwards MG | .01 | .05 |
| ☐ 535 | Todd Worrell UER (4 wins in '88, should be 5) | .01 | .05 |
| ☐ 536 | Joel Skinner | .01 | .05 |
| ☐ 537 | Pete Smith | .01 | .05 |
| ☐ 538 | Juan Castillo | .01 | .05 |
| ☐ 539 | Barry Jones | .01 | .05 |
| ☐ 540 | Bo Jackson | .08 | .25 |
| ☐ 541 | Cecil Fielder | .02 | .10 |
| ☐ 542 | Todd Frohwirth | .01 | .05 |
| ☐ 543 | Damon Berryhill | .01 | .05 |
| ☐ 544 | Jeff Sellers | .01 | .05 |
| ☐ 545 | Mookie Wilson | .02 | .10 |
| ☐ 546 | Mark Williamson | .01 | .05 |
| ☐ 547 | Mark McLemore | .01 | .05 |
| ☐ 548 | Bobby Witt | .01 | .05 |
| ☐ 549 | Jamie Moyer TL | .01 | .05 |
| ☐ 550 | Orel Hershiser | .02 | .10 |
| ☐ 551 | Randy Ready | .01 | .05 |
| ☐ 552 | Greg Cadaret | .01 | .05 |
| ☐ 553 | Luis Salazar | .01 | .05 |
| ☐ 554 | Nick Esasky | .01 | .05 |
| ☐ 555 | Bert Blyleven | .02 | .10 |
| ☐ 556 | Bruce Fields | .01 | .05 |
| ☐ 557 | Keith A. Miller | .01 | .05 |
| ☐ 558 | Dan Pasqua | .01 | .05 |
| ☐ 559 | Juan Agosto | .01 | .05 |
| ☐ 560 | Tim Raines | .02 | .10 |
| ☐ 561 | Luis Aguayo | .01 | .05 |
| ☐ 562 | Danny Cox | .01 | .05 |
| ☐ 563 | Bill Schroeder | .01 | .05 |
| ☐ 564 | Russ Nixon MG | .01 | .05 |
| ☐ 565 | Jeff Russell | .01 | .05 |
| ☐ 566 | Al Pedrique | .01 | .05 |
| ☐ 567 | David Wells UER | .02 | .10 |
| ☐ 568 | Mickey Brantley | .01 | .05 |
| ☐ 569 | German Jimenez | .01 | .05 |
| ☐ 570 | Tony Gwynn | .10 | .30 |
| ☐ 571 | Billy Ripken | .01 | .05 |
| ☐ 572 | Atlee Hammaker | .01 | .05 |
| ☐ 573 | Jim Abbott RC | .40 | 1.00 |
| ☐ 574 | Dave Clark | .01 | .05 |
| ☐ 575 | Juan Samuel | .01 | .05 |
| ☐ 576 | Greg Minton | .01 | .05 |
| ☐ 577 | Randy Bush | .01 | .05 |
| ☐ 578 | John Morris | .01 | .05 |
| ☐ 579 | Glenn Davis TL | .01 | .05 |
| ☐ 580 | Harold Reynolds | .01 | .05 |
| ☐ 581 | Gene Nelson | .01 | .05 |
| ☐ 582 | Mike Marshall | .01 | .05 |
| ☐ 583 | Paul Gibson | .01 | .05 |
| ☐ 584 | Randy Velarde UER (Signed 1935& should be 1985) | .01 | .05 |
| ☐ 585 | Harold Baines | .02 | .10 |
| ☐ 586 | Joe Boever | .01 | .05 |
| ☐ 587 | Mike Stanley | .01 | .05 |
| ☐ 588 | Luis Alicea RC * | .08 | .25 |
| ☐ 589 | Dave Meads | .01 | .05 |
| ☐ 590 | Andres Galarraga | .02 | .10 |
| ☐ 591 | Jeff Musselman | .01 | .05 |
| ☐ 592 | John Cangelosi | .01 | .05 |
| ☐ 593 | Drew Hall | .01 | .05 |
| ☐ 594 | Jimy Williams MG | .01 | .05 |
| ☐ 595 | Teddy Higuera | .01 | .05 |
| ☐ 596 | Kurt Stillwell | .01 | .05 |
| ☐ 597 | Terry Taylor RC | .02 | .10 |
| ☐ 598 | Ken Gerhart | .01 | .05 |
| ☐ 599 | Tom Candiotti | .01 | .05 |
| ☐ 600 | Wade Boggs | .05 | .15 |
| ☐ 601 | Dave Dravecky | .01 | .05 |
| ☐ 602 | Devon White | .02 | .10 |
| ☐ 603 | Frank Tanana | .02 | .10 |
| ☐ 604 | Paul O'Neill | .02 | .10 |
| ☐ 605A | Bob Welch ML Line ERR | 4.00 | 10.00 |
| ☐ 605B | Bob Welch COR | .02 | .10 |
| ☐ 606 | Rick Dempsey | .01 | .05 |
| ☐ 607 | Willie Ansley RC | .02 | .10 |
| ☐ 608 | Phil Bradley | .01 | .05 |
| ☐ 609 | Detroit Tigers TL Frank Tanana (With Alan Trammel) | .01 | .05 |
| ☐ 610 | Randy Myers | .02 | .10 |
| ☐ 611 | Don Slaught | .01 | .05 |
| ☐ 612 | Dan Quisenberry | .01 | .05 |
| ☐ 613 | Gary Varsho | .01 | .05 |
| ☐ 614 | Joe Hesketh | .01 | .05 |
| ☐ 615 | Robin Yount | .15 | .40 |
| ☐ 616 | Steve Rosenberg | .01 | .05 |
| ☐ 617 | Mark Parent | .01 | .05 |
| ☐ 618 | Rance Mulliniks | .01 | .05 |
| ☐ 619 | Checklist 529-660 | .01 | .05 |
| ☐ 620 | Barry Bonds | .60 | 1.50 |
| ☐ 621 | Rick Mahler | .01 | .05 |
| ☐ 622 | Stan Javier | .01 | .05 |
| ☐ 623 | Fred Toliver | .01 | .05 |
| ☐ 624 | Jack McKeon MG | .02 | .10 |
| ☐ 625 | Eddie Murray | .08 | .25 |
| ☐ 626 | Jeff Reed | .01 | .05 |
| ☐ 627 | Greg A. Harris | .01 | .05 |
| ☐ 628 | Matt Williams | .08 | .25 |
| ☐ 629 | Pete O'Brien | .01 | .05 |
| ☐ 630 | Mike Greenwell | .01 | .05 |
| ☐ 631 | Dave Bergman | .01 | .05 |
| ☐ 632 | Bryan Harvey RC * | .08 | .25 |
| ☐ 633 | Daryl Boston | .01 | .05 |
| ☐ 634 | Marvin Freeman | .01 | .05 |
| ☐ 635 | Willie Randolph | .02 | .10 |
| ☐ 636 | Bill Wilkinson | .01 | .05 |
| ☐ 637 | Carmen Castillo | .01 | .05 |
| ☐ 638 | Floyd Bannister | .01 | .05 |
| ☐ 639 | Walt Weiss TL | .01 | .05 |
| ☐ 640 | Willie McGee | .02 | .10 |
| ☐ 641 | Curt Young | .01 | .05 |
| ☐ 642 | Angel Salazar | .01 | .05 |
| ☐ 643 | Louie Meadows | .01 | .05 |
| ☐ 644 | Lloyd McClendon | .01 | .05 |
| ☐ 645 | Jack Morris | .02 | .10 |
| ☐ 646 | Kevin Bass | .01 | .05 |
| ☐ 647 | Randy Johnson RC | .75 | 2.00 |
| ☐ 648 | Sandy Alomar Jr. RC | .15 | .40 |
| ☐ 649 | Stu Cliburn | .01 | .05 |
| ☐ 650 | Kirby Puckett | .08 | .25 |
| ☐ 651 | Tom Niedenfuer | .01 | .05 |
| ☐ 652 | Rich Gedman | .01 | .05 |
| ☐ 653 | Tommy Barrett | .01 | .05 |
| ☐ 654 | Whitey Herzog MG | .02 | .10 |
| ☐ 655 | Dave Magadan | .01 | .05 |
| ☐ 656 | Ivan Calderon | .01 | .05 |
| ☐ 657 | Joe Magrane | .01 | .05 |
| ☐ 658 | R.J. Reynolds | .01 | .05 |
| ☐ 659 | Al Leiter | .08 | .25 |
| ☐ 660 | Will Clark | .05 | .15 |
| ☐ 661 | Dwight Gooden TBC 84 | .05 | .15 |
| ☐ 662 | Lou Brock TBC | .02 | .10 |
| ☐ 663 | Hank Aaron TBC | .08 | .25 |
| ☐ 664 | Gil Hodges TBC 69 | .02 | .10 |
| ☐ 665A | T.John TBC Copyright ERR | .01 | .05 |
| ☐ 665B | Tony Oliva TBC 64 COR (fabricated card) | | |
| ☐ 666 | Randy St.Claire | .02 | .10 |
| ☐ 667 | Dwayne Murphy | .01 | .05 |
| ☐ 668 | Mike Bielecki | .01 | .05 |
| ☐ 669 | L.A. Dodgers TL Orel Hershiser (Mound conference | .02 | .10 |
| ☐ 670 | Kevin Seitzer | .01 | .05 |
| ☐ 671 | Jim Gantner | .01 | .05 |
| ☐ 672 | Allan Anderson | .01 | .05 |
| ☐ 673 | Don Baylor | .02 | .10 |
| ☐ 674 | Otis Nixon | .01 | .05 |
| ☐ 675 | Bruce Hurst | .01 | .05 |
| ☐ 676 | Ernie Riles | .01 | .05 |
| ☐ 677 | Dave Schmidt | .01 | .05 |
| ☐ 678 | Dion James | .01 | .05 |
| ☐ 679 | Willie Fraser | .01 | .05 |
| ☐ 680 | Gary Carter | .02 | .10 |
| ☐ 681 | Jeff D. Robinson | .01 | .05 |
| ☐ 682 | Rick Leach | .01 | .05 |
| ☐ 683 | Jose Cecena | .01 | .05 |
| ☐ 684 | Dave Johnson MG | .01 | .05 |
| ☐ 685 | Jeff Treadway | .01 | .05 |
| ☐ 686 | Scott Terry | .01 | .05 |
| ☐ 687 | Alvin Davis | .01 | .05 |
| ☐ 688 | Zane Smith | .01 | .05 |
| ☐ 689A | Stan Jefferson Pink ERR | 4.00 | 10.00 |
| ☐ 689B | Stan Jefferson (Violet triangle on front bottom | .01 | .05 |
| ☐ 690 | Doug Jones | .01 | .05 |
| ☐ 691 | Roberto Kelly UER | .01 | .05 |
| ☐ 692 | Steve Ontiveros | .01 | .05 |
| ☐ 693 | Pat Borders RC * | .08 | .25 |
| ☐ 694 | Les Lancaster | .01 | .05 |
| ☐ 695 | Carlton Fisk | .05 | .15 |
| ☐ 696 | Don August | .01 | .05 |
| ☐ 697A | Franklin Stubbs White ERR | 4.00 | 10.00 |
| ☐ 697B | Franklin Stubbs (Team name on front in gray) | .01 | .05 |
| ☐ 698 | Keith Atherton | .01 | .05 |
| ☐ 699 | Pittsburgh Pirates TL Al Pedrique (Tony Gwynn sl | .01 | .05 |
| ☐ 700 | Don Mattingly | .25 | .60 |
| ☐ 701 | Storm Davis | .01 | .05 |
| ☐ 702 | Jamie Quirk | .01 | .05 |
| ☐ 703 | Scott Garrelts | .01 | .05 |
| ☐ 704 | Carlos Quintana RC | .02 | .10 |
| ☐ 705 | Terry Kennedy | .01 | .05 |
| ☐ 706 | Pete Incaviglia | .01 | .05 |
| ☐ 707 | Steve Jeltz | .02 | .10 |
| ☐ 708 | Chuck Finley | .02 | .10 |
| ☐ 709 | Tom Herr | .01 | .05 |
| ☐ 710 | David Cone | .02 | .10 |
| ☐ 711 | Candy Sierra | .01 | .05 |
| ☐ 712 | Bill Swift | .01 | .05 |
| ☐ 713 | Ty Griffin FDP | .01 | .05 |
| ☐ 714 | Joe Morgan MG | .02 | .10 |
| ☐ 715 | Tony Pena | .01 | .05 |
| ☐ 716 | Wayne Tolleson | .01 | .05 |
| ☐ 717 | Jamie Moyer | .02 | .10 |
| ☐ 718 | Glenn Braggs | .01 | .05 |
| ☐ 719 | Danny Darwin | .01 | .05 |
| ☐ 720 | Tim Wallach | .01 | .05 |
| ☐ 721 | Ron Tingley | .01 | .05 |
| ☐ 722 | Todd Stottlemyre | .01 | .05 |
| ☐ 723 | Rafael Belliard | .01 | .05 |
| ☐ 724 | Jerry Don Gleaton | .01 | .05 |
| ☐ 725 | Terry Steinbach | .02 | .10 |
| ☐ 726 | Dickie Thon | .01 | .05 |
| ☐ 727 | Joe Orsulak | .01 | .05 |
| ☐ 728 | Charlie Puleo | .01 | .05 |
| ☐ 729 | Texas Rangers TL Steve Buechele (Inconsistent & | .01 | .05 |
| ☐ 730 | Danny Jackson | .01 | .05 |
| ☐ 731 | Mike Young | .01 | .05 |
| ☐ 732 | Steve Buechele | .01 | .05 |
| ☐ 733 | Randy Bockus | .01 | .05 |
| ☐ 734 | Jody Reed | .01 | .05 |
| ☐ 735 | Roger McDowell | .01 | .05 |
| ☐ 736 | Jeff Hamilton | .01 | .05 |
| ☐ 737 | Norm Charlton RC | .08 | .25 |
| ☐ 738 | Darnell Coles | .01 | .05 |
| ☐ 739 | Brook Jacoby | .01 | .05 |
| ☐ 740 | Dan Plesac | .01 | .05 |
| ☐ 741 | Ken Phelps | .01 | .05 |
| ☐ 742 | Mike Harkey RC | .02 | .10 |
| ☐ 743 | Mike Heath | .01 | .05 |
| ☐ 744 | Roger Craig MG | .02 | .10 |
| ☐ 745 | Fred McGriff | .05 | .15 |
| ☐ 746 | German Gonzalez UER (Wrong birthdate) | .01 | .05 |
| ☐ 747 | Wil Tejada | .01 | .05 |

|  |  | | |
|---|------|---|---|
| 748 | Jimmy Jones | .01 | .05 |
| 749 | Rafael Ramirez | .01 | .05 |
| 750 | Bret Saberhagen | .02 | .10 |
| 751 | Ken Oberkfell | .01 | .05 |
| 752 | Jim Gott | .01 | .05 |
| 753 | Jose Uribe | .01 | .05 |
| 754 | Bob Brower | .01 | .05 |
| 755 | Mike Scioscia | .02 | .10 |
| 756 | Scott Medvin | .01 | .05 |
| 757 | Brady Anderson RC | .15 | .40 |
| 758 | Gene Walter | .01 | .05 |
| 759 | Milwaukee Brewers TL Rob Deer | .01 | .05 |
| 760 | Lee Smith | .02 | .10 |
| 761 | Dante Bichette RC | .15 | .40 |
| 762 | Bobby Thigpen | .01 | .05 |
| 763 | Dave Martinez | .01 | .05 |
| 764 | Robin Ventura RC | .30 | .75 |
| 765 | Glenn Davis | .01 | .05 |
| 766 | Cecilio Guante | .01 | .05 |
| 767 | Mike Capel | .01 | .05 |
| 768 | Bill Wegman | .01 | .05 |
| 769 | Junior Ortiz | .01 | .05 |
| 770 | Alan Trammell | .02 | .10 |
| 771 | Ron Kittle | .01 | .05 |
| 772 | Ron Oester | .01 | .05 |
| 773 | Keith Moreland | .01 | .05 |
| 774 | Frank Robinson MG/TC | .05 | .15 |
| 775 | Jeff Reardon | .02 | .10 |
| 776 | Nelson Liriano | .01 | .05 |
| 777 | Ted Power | .01 | .05 |
| 778 | Bruce Benedict | .01 | .05 |
| 779 | Craig McMurtry | .01 | .05 |
| 780 | Pedro Guerrero | .02 | .10 |
| 781 | Greg Briley | .02 | .10 |
| 782 | Checklist 661-792 | .01 | .05 |
| 783 | Trevor Wilson RC | .01 | .05 |
| 784 | Steve Avery RC | .08 | .25 |
| 785 | Ellis Burks | .02 | .10 |
| 786 | Melido Perez | .01 | .05 |
| 787 | Dave West RC | .02 | .10 |
| 788 | Mike Morgan | .01 | .05 |
| 789 | Royals TU/Bo Jackson | .08 | .25 |
| 790 | Sid Fernandez | .01 | .05 |
| 791 | Jim Lindeman | .01 | .05 |
| 792 | Rafael Santana | .01 | .05 |

**1990 Topps**

| | | | |
|---|------|---|---|
| COMPLETE SET (792) | | 8.00 | 20.00 |
| COMP.FACT.SET (792) | | 10.00 | 25.00 |
| COMP.X-MAS.SET (792) | | 15.00 | 40.00 |
| 1 | Nolan Ryan | .40 | 1.00 |
| 2 | Nolan Ryan Salute New York Mets | .20 | .50 |
| 3 | Nolan Ryan Salute California Angels | .20 | .50 |
| 4 | Nolan Ryan Salute Houston Astros | .20 | .50 |
| 5 | Nolan Ryan Salute Texas Rangers UER (Says Texas) | .20 | .50 |
| 6 | Vince Coleman RB (50 consecutive stolen bases) | .01 | .05 |
| 7 | Rickey Henderson RB | .05 | .15 |
| 8 | Cal Ripken RB | .08 | .25 |
| 9 | Eric Plunk | .01 | .05 |
| 10 | Barry Larkin | .05 | .15 |
| 11 | Paul Gibson | .01 | .05 |
| 12 | Joe Girardi | .05 | .15 |
| 13 | Mark Williamson | .01 | .05 |
| 14 | Mike Fetters RC | .08 | .25 |
| 15 | Teddy Higuera | .01 | .05 |
| 16 | Kent Anderson | .01 | .05 |
| 17 | Kelly Downs | .01 | .05 |
| 18 | Carlos Quintana | .01 | .05 |
| 19 | Al Newman | .01 | .05 |
| 20 | Mark Gubicza | .01 | .05 |
| 21 | Jeff Torborg MG | .01 | .05 |
| 22 | Bruce Ruffin | .01 | .05 |
| 23 | Randy Velarde | .01 | .05 |
| 24 | Joe Hesketh | .01 | .05 |
| 25 | Willie Randolph | .02 | .10 |
| 26 | Don Slaught | .01 | .05 |
| 27 | Rick Leach | .01 | .05 |
| 28 | Duane Ward | .01 | .05 |
| 29 | John Cangelosi | .01 | .05 |
| 30 | David Cone | .02 | .10 |
| 31 | Henry Cotto | .01 | .05 |
| 32 | John Farrell | .01 | .05 |
| 33 | Greg Walker | .01 | .05 |
| 34 | Tony Fossas RC | .01 | .05 |
| 35 | Benito Santiago | .02 | .10 |
| 36 | John Costello | .01 | .05 |
| 37 | Domingo Ramos | .01 | .05 |
| 38 | Wes Gardner | .01 | .05 |
| 39 | Curt Ford | .01 | .05 |
| 40 | Jay Howell | .01 | .05 |
| 41 | Matt Williams | .02 | .10 |
| 42 | Jeff M. Robinson | .01 | .05 |
| 43 | Dante Bichette | .02 | .10 |
| 44 | Roger Salkeld FDP RC | .02 | .10 |
| 45 | Dave Parker UER | .02 | .10 |
| 46 | Rob Dibble | .02 | .10 |
| 47 | Brian Harper | .01 | .05 |
| 48 | Zane Smith | .01 | .05 |
| 49 | Tom Lawless | .01 | .05 |
| 50 | Glenn Davis | .01 | .05 |
| 51 | Doug Rader MG | .01 | .05 |
| 52 | Jack Daugherty RC | .01 | .05 |
| 53 | Mike LaCoss | .01 | .05 |
| 54 | Joel Skinner | .01 | .05 |
| 55 | Darrell Evans UER (HR total should be 414 & not 4 | .02 | .10 |
| 56 | Franklin Stubbs | .01 | .05 |
| 57 | Greg Vaughn | .01 | .05 |
| 58 | Keith Miller | .01 | .05 |
| 59 | Ted Power | .01 | .05 |
| 60 | George Brett | .25 | .60 |
| 61 | Deion Sanders | .08 | .25 |
| 62 | Ramon Martinez | .01 | .05 |
| 63 | Mike Pagliarulo | .01 | .05 |
| 64 | Danny Darwin | .01 | .05 |
| 65 | Devon White | .02 | .10 |
| 66 | Greg Litton | .01 | .05 |
| 67 | Scott Sanderson | .01 | .05 |
| 68 | Dave Henderson | .01 | .05 |
| 69 | Todd Frohwirth | .01 | .05 |
| 70 | Mike Greenwell | .02 | .10 |
| 71 | Allan Anderson | .01 | .05 |
| 72 | Jeff Huson RC | .02 | .10 |
| 73 | Bob Milacki | .01 | .05 |
| 74 | Jeff Jackson FDP RC | .02 | .10 |
| 75 | Doug Jones | .01 | .05 |
| 76 | Dave Valle | .01 | .05 |
| 77 | Dave Bergman | .01 | .05 |
| 78 | Mike Flanagan | .01 | .05 |
| 79 | Ron Kittle | .01 | .05 |
| 80 | Jeff Russell | .01 | .05 |
| 81 | Bob Rodgers MG | .01 | .05 |
| 82 | Scott Terry | .01 | .05 |
| 83 | Hensley Meulens | .01 | .05 |
| 84 | Ray Searage | .01 | .05 |
| 85 | Juan Samuel | .01 | .05 |
| 86 | Paul Kilgus | .01 | .05 |
| 87 | Rick Luecken RC | .01 | .05 |
| 88 | Glenn Braggs | .01 | .05 |
| 89 | Clint Zavaras RC | .01 | .05 |
| 90 | Jack Clark | .02 | .10 |
| 91 | Steve Frey RC | .01 | .05 |
| 92 | Mike Stanley | .01 | .05 |
| 93 | Shawn Hillegas | .01 | .05 |
| 94 | Herm Winningham | .01 | .05 |
| 95 | Todd Worrell | .01 | .05 |
| 96 | Jody Reed | .01 | .05 |
| 97 | Curt Schilling | .40 | 1.00 |
| 98 | Jose Gonzalez | .01 | .05 |
| 99 | Rich Monteleone | .01 | .05 |
| 100 | Will Clark | .05 | .15 |
| 101 | Shane Rawley | .01 | .05 |
| 102 | Stan Javier | .01 | .05 |
| 103 | Marvin Freeman | .01 | .05 |
| 104 | Bob Knepper | .01 | .05 |
| 105 | Randy Myers | .02 | .10 |
| 106 | Charlie O'Brien | .01 | .05 |
| 107 | Fred Lynn | .01 | .05 |
| 108 | Rod Nichols | .01 | .05 |
| 109 | Roberto Kelly | .01 | .05 |
| 110 | Tommy Helms MG | .01 | .05 |
| 111 | Ed Whited RC | .01 | .05 |
| 112 | Glenn Wilson | .01 | .05 |
| 113 | Manny Lee | .01 | .05 |
| 114 | Mike Bielecki | .01 | .05 |
| 115 | Tony Pena | .01 | .05 |
| 116 | Floyd Bannister | .01 | .05 |
| 117 | Mike Sharperson | .01 | .05 |
| 118 | Erik Hanson | .01 | .05 |
| 119 | Billy Hatcher | .01 | .05 |
| 120 | John Kruk | .02 | .10 |
| 121 | Robin Ventura | .08 | .25 |
| 122 | Shawn Abner | .01 | .05 |
| 123 | Rich Gedman | .01 | .05 |
| 124 | Dave Dravecky | .02 | .10 |
| 125 | Kent Hrbek | .02 | .10 |
| 126 | Randy Kramer | .01 | .05 |
| 127 | Mike Devereaux | .01 | .05 |
| 128 | Checklist 1 | .01 | .05 |
| 129 | Ron Jones | .01 | .05 |
| 130 | Bert Blyleven | .02 | .10 |
| 131 | Matt Nokes | .01 | .05 |
| 132 | Lance Blankenship | .01 | .05 |
| 133 | Ricky Horton | .01 | .05 |
| 134 | Earl Cunningham FDP RC | .02 | .10 |
| 135 | Dave Magadan | .01 | .05 |
| 136 | Kevin Brown | .02 | .10 |
| 137 | Marty Pevey RC | .01 | .05 |
| 138 | Al Leiter | .08 | .25 |
| 139 | Greg Brock | .01 | .05 |
| 140 | Andre Dawson | .02 | .10 |
| 141 | John Hart MG RC | .01 | .05 |
| 142 | Jeff Wetherby RC | .01 | .05 |
| 143 | Rafael Belliard | .01 | .05 |
| 144 | Bud Black | .01 | .05 |
| 145 | Terry Steinbach | .02 | .10 |
| 146 | Rob Richie RC | .01 | .05 |
| 147 | Chuck Finley | .02 | .10 |
| 148 | Edgar Martinez | .05 | .15 |
| 149 | Steve Farr | .01 | .05 |
| 150 | Kirk Gibson | .02 | .10 |
| 151 | Rick Mahler | .01 | .05 |
| 152 | Lonnie Smith | .01 | .05 |
| 153 | Randy Milligan | .01 | .05 |
| 154 | Mike Maddux | .01 | .05 |
| 155 | Ellis Burks | .01 | .05 |
| 156 | Ken Patterson | .01 | .05 |
| 157 | Craig Biggio | .08 | .25 |
| 158 | Craig Lefferts | .01 | .05 |
| 159 | Mike Felder | .01 | .05 |
| 160 | Dave Righetti | .01 | .05 |
| 161 | Harold Reynolds | .02 | .10 |
| 162 | Todd Zeile | .02 | .10 |
| 163 | Phil Bradley | .01 | .05 |
| 164 | Jeff Juden FDP RC | .02 | .10 |
| 165 | Walt Weiss | .01 | .05 |
| 166 | Bobby Witt | .01 | .05 |
| 167 | Kevin Appier | .02 | .10 |
| 168 | Jose Lind | .01 | .05 |
| 169 | Richard Dotson | .01 | .05 |
| 170 | George Bell | .02 | .10 |
| 171 | Russ Nixon MG | .01 | .05 |
| 172 | Tom Lampkin | .01 | .05 |
| 173 | Tim Belcher | .01 | .05 |
| 174 | Jeff Kunkel | .01 | .05 |
| 175 | Mike Moore | .01 | .05 |
| 176 | Luis Quinones | .01 | .05 |
| 177 | Mike Henneman | .01 | .05 |
| 178 | Chris James | .01 | .05 |
| 179 | Brian Holton | .01 | .05 |
| 180 | Tim Raines | .02 | .10 |
| 181 | Juan Agosto | .01 | .05 |
| 182 | Mookie Wilson | .01 | .05 |
| 183 | Steve Lake | .01 | .05 |
| 184 | Danny Cox | .01 | .05 |
| 185 | Ruben Sierra | .02 | .10 |
| 186 | Dave LaPoint | .01 | .05 |
| 187 | Rick Wrona | .01 | .05 |
| 188 | Mike Smithson | .01 | .05 |
| 189 | Dick Schofield | .01 | .05 |
| 190 | Rick Reuschel | .01 | .05 |

|  |  | | |
|---|---|---|---|
| ☐ 191 | Pat Borders | .01 | .05 |
| ☐ 192 | Don August | .01 | .05 |
| ☐ 193 | Andy Benes | .02 | .10 |
| ☐ 194 | Glenallen Hill | .01 | .05 |
| ☐ 195 | Tim Burke | .01 | .05 |
| ☐ 196 | Gerald Young | .01 | .05 |
| ☐ 197 | Doug Drabek | .01 | .05 |
| ☐ 198 | Mike Marshall | .01 | .05 |
| ☐ 199 | Sergio Valdez RC | .01 | .05 |
| ☐ 200 | Don Mattingly | .25 | .60 |
| ☐ 201 | Cito Gaston MG | .01 | .05 |
| ☐ 202 | Mike Macfarlane | .01 | .05 |
| ☐ 203 | Mike Roesler RC | .01 | .05 |
| ☐ 204 | Bob Dernier | .01 | .05 |
| ☐ 205 | Mark Davis | .01 | .05 |
| ☐ 206 | Nick Esasky | .01 | .05 |
| ☐ 207 | Bob Ojeda | .01 | .05 |
| ☐ 208 | Brook Jacoby | .01 | .05 |
| ☐ 209 | Greg Mathews | .01 | .05 |
| ☐ 210 | Ryne Sandberg | .15 | .40 |
| ☐ 211 | John Cerutti | .01 | .05 |
| ☐ 212 | Joe Orsulak | .01 | .05 |
| ☐ 213 | Scott Bankhead | .01 | .05 |
| ☐ 214 | Terry Francona | .02 | .10 |
| ☐ 215 | Kirk McCaskill | .01 | .05 |
| ☐ 216 | Ricky Jordan | .01 | .05 |
| ☐ 217 | Don Robinson | .01 | .05 |
| ☐ 218 | Wally Backman | .01 | .05 |
| ☐ 219 | Donn Pall | .01 | .05 |
| ☐ 220 | Barry Bonds | .40 | 1.00 |
| ☐ 221 | Gary Mielke RC | .01 | .05 |
| ☐ 222 | Kurt Stillwell UER (Graduate misspelled as gradu | .01 | .05 |
| ☐ 223 | Tommy Gregg | .01 | .05 |
| ☐ 224 | Delino DeShields RC | .08 | .25 |
| ☐ 225 | Jim Deshaies | .01 | .05 |
| ☐ 226 | Mickey Hatcher | .01 | .05 |
| ☐ 227 | Kevin Tapani RC | .08 | .25 |
| ☐ 228 | Dave Martinez | .01 | .05 |
| ☐ 229 | David Wells | .02 | .10 |
| ☐ 230 | Keith Hernandez | .02 | .10 |
| ☐ 231 | Jack McKeon MG | .01 | .05 |
| ☐ 232 | Darnell Coles | .01 | .05 |
| ☐ 233 | Ken Hill | .02 | .10 |
| ☐ 234 | Mariano Duncan | .01 | .05 |
| ☐ 235 | Jeff Reardon | .02 | .10 |
| ☐ 236 | Hal Morris | .01 | .05 |
| ☐ 237 | Kevin Ritz RC | .01 | .05 |
| ☐ 238 | Felix Jose | .01 | .05 |
| ☐ 239 | Eric Show | .01 | .05 |
| ☐ 240 | Mark Grace | .05 | .15 |
| ☐ 241 | Mike Krukow | .01 | .05 |
| ☐ 242 | Fred Manrique | .01 | .05 |
| ☐ 243 | Barry Jones | .01 | .05 |
| ☐ 244 | Bill Schroeder | .01 | .05 |
| ☐ 245 | Roger Clemens | .40 | 1.00 |
| ☐ 246 | Jim Eisenreich | .01 | .05 |
| ☐ 247 | Jerry Reed | .01 | .05 |
| ☐ 248 | Dave Anderson | .01 | .05 |
| ☐ 249 | Mike (Texas) Smith RC | .01 | .05 |
| ☐ 250 | Jose Canseco | .05 | .15 |
| ☐ 251 | Jeff Blauser | .01 | .05 |
| ☐ 252 | Otis Nixon | .05 | .15 |
| ☐ 253 | Mark Portugal | .01 | .05 |
| ☐ 254 | Francisco Cabrera | .01 | .05 |
| ☐ 255 | Bobby Thigpen | .01 | .05 |
| ☐ 256 | Marvell Wynne | .01 | .05 |
| ☐ 257 | Jose DeLeon | .01 | .05 |
| ☐ 258 | Barry Lyons | .01 | .05 |
| ☐ 259 | Lance McCullers | .01 | .05 |
| ☐ 260 | Eric Davis | .01 | .05 |
| ☐ 261 | Whitey Herzog MG | .02 | .10 |
| ☐ 262 | Checklist 2 | .02 | .10 |
| ☐ 263 | Mel Stottlemyre Jr. | .01 | .05 |
| ☐ 264 | Bryan Clutterbuck | .01 | .05 |
| ☐ 265 | Pete O'Brien | .01 | .05 |
| ☐ 266 | German Gonzalez | .01 | .05 |
| ☐ 267 | Mark Davidson | .01 | .05 |
| ☐ 268 | Rob Murphy | .01 | .05 |
| ☐ 269 | Dickie Thon | .01 | .05 |
| ☐ 270 | Dave Stewart | .02 | .10 |
| ☐ 271 | Chet Lemon | .01 | .05 |
| ☐ 272 | Bryan Harvey | .01 | .05 |
| ☐ 273 | Bobby Bonilla | .02 | .10 |
| ☐ 274 | Mauro Gozzo RC | .01 | .05 |
| ☐ 275 | Mickey Tettleton | .01 | .05 |
| ☐ 276 | Gary Thurman | .01 | .05 |

|  |  | | |
|---|---|---|---|
| ☐ 277 | Lenny Harris | .01 | .05 |
| ☐ 278 | Pascual Perez | .01 | .05 |
| ☐ 279 | Steve Buechele | .01 | .05 |
| ☐ 280 | Lou Whitaker | .02 | .10 |
| ☐ 281 | Kevin Bass | .01 | .05 |
| ☐ 282 | Derek Lilliquist | .01 | .05 |
| ☐ 283 | Joey Belle | .08 | .25 |
| ☐ 284 | Mark Gardner RC | .02 | .10 |
| ☐ 285 | Willie McGee | .02 | .10 |
| ☐ 286 | Lee Guetterman | .01 | .05 |
| ☐ 287 | Vance Law | .01 | .05 |
| ☐ 288 | Greg Briley | .01 | .05 |
| ☐ 289 | Norm Charlton | .01 | .05 |
| ☐ 290 | Robin Yount | .15 | .40 |
| ☐ 291 | Dave Johnson MG | .02 | .10 |
| ☐ 292 | Jim Gott | .01 | .05 |
| ☐ 293 | Mike Gallego | .01 | .05 |
| ☐ 294 | Craig McMurtry | .01 | .05 |
| ☐ 295 | Fred McGriff | .08 | .25 |
| ☐ 296 | Jeff Ballard | .01 | .05 |
| ☐ 297 | Tommy Herr | .01 | .05 |
| ☐ 298 | Dan Gladden | .01 | .05 |
| ☐ 299 | Adam Peterson | .01 | .05 |
| ☐ 300 | Bo Jackson | .08 | .25 |
| ☐ 301 | Don Aase | .01 | .05 |
| ☐ 302 | Marcus Lawton RC | .01 | .05 |
| ☐ 303 | Rick Cerone | .01 | .05 |
| ☐ 304 | Marty Clary | .01 | .05 |
| ☐ 305 | Eddie Murray | .08 | .25 |
| ☐ 306 | Tom Niedenfuer | .01 | .05 |
| ☐ 307 | Bip Roberts | .01 | .05 |
| ☐ 308 | Jose Guzman | .01 | .05 |
| ☐ 309 | Eric Yelding RC | .01 | .05 |
| ☐ 310 | Steve Bedrosian | .01 | .05 |
| ☐ 311 | Dwight Smith | .01 | .05 |
| ☐ 312 | Dan Quisenberry | .01 | .05 |
| ☐ 313 | Gus Polidor | .01 | .05 |
| ☐ 314 | Donald Harris FDP RC | .01 | .05 |
| ☐ 315 | Bruce Hurst | .01 | .05 |
| ☐ 316 | Carney Lansford | .02 | .10 |
| ☐ 317 | Mark Guthrie RC | .01 | .05 |
| ☐ 318 | Wallace Johnson | .01 | .05 |
| ☐ 319 | Dion James | .01 | .05 |
| ☐ 320 | Dave Stieb | .02 | .10 |
| ☐ 321 | Joe Morgan MG | .01 | .05 |
| ☐ 322 | Junior Ortiz | .01 | .05 |
| ☐ 323 | Willie Wilson | .01 | .05 |
| ☐ 324 | Pete Harnisch | .01 | .05 |
| ☐ 325 | Robby Thompson | .01 | .05 |
| ☐ 326 | Tom McCarthy | .01 | .05 |
| ☐ 327 | Ken Williams | .01 | .05 |
| ☐ 328 | Curt Young | .01 | .05 |
| ☐ 329 | Oddibe McDowell | .01 | .05 |
| ☐ 330 | Ron Darling | .01 | .05 |
| ☐ 331 | Juan Gonzalez RC | .40 | 1.00 |
| ☐ 332 | Paul O'Neill | .05 | .15 |
| ☐ 333 | Bill Wegman | .01 | .05 |
| ☐ 334 | Johnny Ray | .01 | .05 |
| ☐ 335 | Andy Hawkins | .01 | .05 |
| ☐ 336 | Ken Griffey Jr. | .30 | .75 |
| ☐ 337 | Lloyd McClendon | .01 | .05 |
| ☐ 338 | Dennis Lamp | .01 | .05 |
| ☐ 339 | Dave Clark | .01 | .05 |
| ☐ 340 | Fernando Valenzuela | .02 | .10 |
| ☐ 341 | Tom Foley | .01 | .05 |
| ☐ 342 | Alex Trevino | .01 | .05 |
| ☐ 343 | Frank Tanana | .01 | .05 |
| ☐ 344 | George Canale RC | .01 | .05 |
| ☐ 345 | Harold Baines | .02 | .10 |
| ☐ 346 | Jim Presley | .01 | .05 |
| ☐ 347 | Junior Felix | .01 | .05 |
| ☐ 348 | Gary Wayne | .01 | .05 |
| ☐ 349 | Steve Finley | .02 | .10 |
| ☐ 350 | Bret Saberhagen | .02 | .10 |
| ☐ 351 | Roger Craig MG | .01 | .05 |
| ☐ 352 | Bryn Smith | .01 | .05 |
| ☐ 353 | Sandy Alomar Jr. (Not listed as Jr. on card fron | | |
| ☐ 354 | Stan Belinda RC | .02 | .10 |
| ☐ 355 | Marty Barrett | .01 | .05 |
| ☐ 356 | Randy Ready | .01 | .05 |
| ☐ 357 | Dave West | .01 | .05 |
| ☐ 358 | Andres Thomas | .01 | .05 |
| ☐ 359 | Jimmy Jones | .01 | .05 |
| ☐ 360 | Paul Molitor | .02 | .10 |
| ☐ 361 | Randy McCament RC | .01 | .05 |
| ☐ 362 | Damon Berryhill | .01 | .05 |

|  |  | | |
|---|---|---|---|
| ☐ 363 | Dan Petry | .01 | .05 |
| ☐ 364 | Rolando Roomes | .01 | .05 |
| ☐ 365 | Ozzie Guillen | .02 | .10 |
| ☐ 366 | Mike Heath | .01 | .05 |
| ☐ 367 | Mike Morgan | .01 | .05 |
| ☐ 368 | Bill Doran | .01 | .05 |
| ☐ 369 | Todd Burns | .01 | .05 |
| ☐ 370 | Tim Wallach | .01 | .05 |
| ☐ 371 | Jimmy Key | .02 | .10 |
| ☐ 372 | Terry Kennedy | .01 | .05 |
| ☐ 373 | Alvin Davis | .01 | .05 |
| ☐ 374 | Steve Cummings RC | .01 | .05 |
| ☐ 375 | Dwight Evans | .05 | .15 |
| ☐ 376 | Checklist 3 UER (Higuera misalphabet- ized in B | .01 | .05 |
| ☐ 377 | Mickey Weston RC | .01 | .05 |
| ☐ 378 | Luis Salazar | .01 | .05 |
| ☐ 379 | Steve Rosenberg | .01 | .05 |
| ☐ 380 | Dave Winfield | .02 | .10 |
| ☐ 381 | Frank Robinson MG | .01 | .05 |
| ☐ 382 | Jeff Musselman | .01 | .05 |
| ☐ 383 | John Morris | .01 | .05 |
| ☐ 384 | Pat Combs | .01 | .05 |
| ☐ 385 | Fred McGriff AS | .02 | .10 |
| ☐ 386 | Julio Franco AS | .01 | .05 |
| ☐ 387 | Wade Boggs AS | .02 | .10 |
| ☐ 388 | Cal Ripken AS | .15 | .40 |
| ☐ 389 | Robin Yount AS | .08 | .25 |
| ☐ 390 | Ruben Sierra AS | .01 | .05 |
| ☐ 391 | Kirby Puckett AS | .05 | .15 |
| ☐ 392 | Carlton Fisk AS | .02 | .10 |
| ☐ 393 | Bret Saberhagen AS | .01 | .05 |
| ☐ 394 | Jeff Ballard AS | .01 | .05 |
| ☐ 395 | Jeff Russell AS | .01 | .05 |
| ☐ 396 | Bart Giamatti MEM | .08 | .25 |
| ☐ 397 | Will Clark AS | .02 | .10 |
| ☐ 398 | Ryne Sandberg AS | .08 | .25 |
| ☐ 399 | Howard Johnson AS | .01 | .05 |
| ☐ 400 | Ozzie Smith AS | .08 | .25 |
| ☐ 401 | Kevin Mitchell AS | .01 | .05 |
| ☐ 402 | Eric Davis AS | .01 | .05 |
| ☐ 403 | Tony Gwynn AS | .05 | .15 |
| ☐ 404 | Craig Biggio AS | .08 | .25 |
| ☐ 405 | Mike Scott AS | .01 | .05 |
| ☐ 406 | Joe Magrane AS | .01 | .05 |
| ☐ 407 | Mark Davis AS | .01 | .05 |
| ☐ 408 | Trevor Wilson | .01 | .05 |
| ☐ 409 | Tom Brunansky | .01 | .05 |
| ☐ 410 | Joe Boever | .01 | .05 |
| ☐ 411 | Ken Phelps | .01 | .05 |
| ☐ 412 | Jamie Moyer | .02 | .10 |
| ☐ 413 | Brian DuBois RC | .01 | .05 |
| ☐ 414A | Frank Thomas NNOF ! | 400.00 | 700.00 |
| ☐ 414B | Frank Thomas RC | .75 | 2.00 |
| ☐ 415 | Shawon Dunston | .01 | .05 |
| ☐ 416 | Dave Wayne Johnson RC | .01 | .05 |
| ☐ 417 | Jim Gantner | .01 | .05 |
| ☐ 418 | Tom Browning | .01 | .05 |
| ☐ 419 | Beau Allred RC | .01 | .05 |
| ☐ 420 | Carlton Fisk | .05 | .15 |
| ☐ 421 | Greg Minton | .01 | .05 |
| ☐ 422 | Pat Sheridan | .01 | .05 |
| ☐ 423 | Fred Toliver | .01 | .05 |
| ☐ 424 | Jerry Reuss | .01 | .05 |
| ☐ 425 | Bill Landrum | .01 | .05 |
| ☐ 426 | Jeff Hamilton UER (Stats say he fanned 197 times | .01 | .05 |
| ☐ 427 | Carmen Castillo | .01 | .05 |
| ☐ 428 | Steve Davis RC | .01 | .05 |
| ☐ 429 | Tom Kelly MG | .01 | .05 |
| ☐ 430 | Pete Incaviglia | .01 | .05 |
| ☐ 431 | Randy Johnson | .20 | .50 |
| ☐ 432 | Damaso Garcia | .01 | .05 |
| ☐ 433 | Steve Olin RC | .08 | .25 |
| ☐ 434 | Mark Carreon | .01 | .05 |
| ☐ 435 | Kevin Seitzer | .01 | .05 |
| ☐ 436 | Mel Hall | .01 | .05 |
| ☐ 437 | Les Lancaster | .01 | .05 |
| ☐ 438 | Greg Myers | .01 | .05 |
| ☐ 439 | Jeff Parrett | .01 | .05 |
| ☐ 440 | Alan Trammell | .02 | .10 |
| ☐ 441 | Bob Kipper | .01 | .05 |
| ☐ 442 | Jerry Browne | .01 | .05 |
| ☐ 443 | Cris Carpenter | .01 | .05 |
| ☐ 444 | Kyle Abbott FDP RC | .01 | .05 |
| ☐ 445 | Danny Jackson | .01 | .05 |

|  | | |
|---|---|---|
| 446 Dan Pasqua | .01 | .05 |
| 447 Atlee Hammaker | .01 | .05 |
| 448 Greg Gagne | .01 | .05 |
| 449 Dennis Rasmussen | .01 | .05 |
| 450 Rickey Henderson | .08 | .25 |
| 451 Mark Lemke | .01 | .05 |
| 452 Luis DeLosSantos | .01 | .05 |
| 453 Jody Davis | .01 | .05 |
| 455 Jeff King | .01 | .05 |
| 455 Jeffrey Leonard | .01 | .05 |
| 456 Chris Gwynn | .01 | .05 |
| 457 Gregg Jefferies | .02 | .10 |
| 458 Bob McClure | .01 | .05 |
| 459 Jim Lefebvre MG | .01 | .05 |
| 460 Mike Scott | .01 | .05 |
| 461 Carlos Martinez | .01 | .05 |
| 462 Denny Walling | .01 | .05 |
| 463 Drew Hall | .01 | .05 |
| 464 Jerome Walton | .01 | .05 |
| 465 Kevin Gross | .01 | .05 |
| 466 Rance Mulliniks | .01 | .05 |
| 467 Juan Nieves | .01 | .05 |
| 468 Bill Ripken | .01 | .05 |
| 469 John Kruk | .02 | .10 |
| 470 Frank Viola | .01 | .05 |
| 471 Mike Brumley | .01 | .05 |
| 472 Jose Uribe | .01 | .05 |
| 473 Joe Price | .01 | .05 |
| 474 Rich Thompson | .01 | .05 |
| 475 Bob Welch | .01 | .05 |
| 476 Brad Komminsk | .01 | .05 |
| 477 Willie Fraser | .01 | .05 |
| 478 Mike LaValliere | .01 | .05 |
| 479 Frank White | .02 | .10 |
| 480 Sid Fernandez | .01 | .05 |
| 481 Garry Templeton | .01 | .05 |
| 482 Steve Carter | .01 | .05 |
| 483 Alejandro Pena | .01 | .05 |
| 484 Mike Fitzgerald | .01 | .05 |
| 485 John Candelaria | .01 | .05 |
| 486 Jeff Treadway | .01 | .05 |
| 487 Steve Searcy | .01 | .05 |
| 488 Ken Oberkfell | .01 | .05 |
| 489 Nick Leyva MG | .01 | .05 |
| 490 Dan Plesac | .01 | .05 |
| 491 Dave Cochrane RC | .01 | .05 |
| 492 Ron Oester | .01 | .05 |
| 493 Jason Grimsley RC | .02 | .10 |
| 494 Terry Puhl | .01 | .05 |
| 495 Lee Smith | .02 | .10 |
| 496 Cecil Espy UER | | |
| ('88 stats have 3 | | |
| SB's should be | | |
| 497 Dave Schmidt | .01 | .05 |
| 498 Rick Schu | .01 | .05 |
| 499 Bill Long | .01 | .05 |
| 500 Kevin Mitchell | .05 | .15 |
| 501 Matt Young | .01 | .05 |
| 502 Mitch Webster | .01 | .05 |
| 503 Randy St.Claire | .01 | .05 |
| 504 Tom O'Malley | .01 | .05 |
| 505 Kelly Gruber | .01 | .05 |
| 506 Tom Glavine | .05 | .15 |
| 507 Gary Redus | .01 | .05 |
| 508 Terry Leach | .01 | .05 |
| 509 Tom Pagnozzi | .01 | .05 |
| 510 Dwight Gooden | .02 | .10 |
| 511 Clay Parker | .01 | .05 |
| 512 Gary Pettis | .01 | .05 |
| 513 Mark Eichhorn | .01 | .05 |
| 514 Andy Allanson | .01 | .05 |
| 515 Len Dykstra | .02 | .10 |
| 516 Tim Leary | .01 | .05 |
| 517 Roberto Alomar | .05 | .15 |
| 518 Bill Krueger | .01 | .05 |
| 519 Bucky Dent MG | .01 | .05 |
| 520 Mitch Williams | .01 | .05 |
| 521 Craig Worthington | .01 | .05 |
| 522 Mike Dunne | .01 | .05 |
| 523 Jay Bell | .02 | .10 |
| 524 Daryl Boston | .01 | .05 |
| 525 Wally Joyner | .02 | .10 |
| 526 Checklist 4 | .01 | .05 |
| 527 Ron Hassey | .01 | .05 |
| 528 Kevin Wickander UER | | |
| (Monthly scoreboard | | |
| strikeou | | |
| 529 Greg A. Harris | .01 | .05 |
| 530 Mark Langston | .01 | .05 |
| 531 Ken Caminiti | .02 | .10 |
| 532 Cecilio Guante | .01 | .05 |
| 533 Tim Jones | .01 | .05 |
| 534 Louie Meadows | .01 | .05 |
| 535 John Smoltz | .08 | .25 |
| 536 Bob Geren | .01 | .05 |
| 537 Mark Grant | .01 | .05 |
| 538 Bill Spiers UER | | |
| (Photo actually | | |
| George Canale) | | |
| 539 Neal Heaton | .01 | .05 |
| 540 Danny Tartabull | .02 | .10 |
| 541 Pat Perry | .01 | .05 |
| 542 Darren Daulton | .02 | .10 |
| 543 Nelson Liriano | .01 | .05 |
| 544 Dennis Boyd | .01 | .05 |
| 545 Kevin McReynolds | .01 | .05 |
| 546 Kevin Hickey | .01 | .05 |
| 547 Jack Howell | .01 | .05 |
| 548 Pat Clements | .01 | .05 |
| 549 Don Zimmer MG | .02 | .10 |
| 550 Julio Franco | .02 | .10 |
| 551 Tim Crews | .01 | .05 |
| 552 Mike (Miss.) Smith RC | .01 | .05 |
| 553 Scott Scudder UER | | |
| (Cedar Rapids) | | |
| 554 Jay Buhner | .02 | .10 |
| 555 Jack Morris | .02 | .10 |
| 556 Gene Larkin | .01 | .05 |
| 557 Jeff Innis RC | .01 | .05 |
| 558 Rafael Ramirez | .01 | .05 |
| 559 Andy McGaffigan | .01 | .05 |
| 560 Steve Sax | .01 | .05 |
| 561 Ken Dayley | .01 | .05 |
| 562 Chad Kreuter | .01 | .05 |
| 563 Alex Sanchez | .01 | .05 |
| 564 Tyler Houston FDP RC | .08 | .25 |
| 565 Scott Fletcher | .01 | .05 |
| 566 Mark Knudson | .01 | .05 |
| 567 Ron Gant | .02 | .10 |
| 568 John Smiley | .01 | .05 |
| 569 Ivan Calderon | .01 | .05 |
| 570 Cal Ripken | .30 | .75 |
| 571 Brett Butler | .02 | .10 |
| 572 Greg W. Harris | .01 | .05 |
| 573 Danny Heep | .01 | .05 |
| 574 Bill Swift | .01 | .05 |
| 575 Lance Parrish | .01 | .05 |
| 576 Mike Dyer RC | .01 | .05 |
| 577 Charlie Hayes | .01 | .05 |
| 578 Joe Magrane | .01 | .05 |
| 579 Art Howe MG | .01 | .05 |
| 580 Joe Carter | .02 | .10 |
| 581 Ken Griffey Sr. | .01 | .05 |
| 582 Rick Honeycutt | .01 | .05 |
| 583 Bruce Benedict | .01 | .05 |
| 584 Phil Stephenson | .01 | .05 |
| 585 Kal Daniels | .01 | .05 |
| 586 Edwin Nunez | .01 | .05 |
| 587 Lance Johnson | .01 | .05 |
| 588 Rick Rhoden | .01 | .05 |
| 589 Mike Aldrete | .01 | .05 |
| 590 Ozzie Smith | .15 | .40 |
| 591 Todd Stottlemyre | .02 | .10 |
| 592 R.J. Reynolds | .01 | .05 |
| 593 Scott Bradley | .01 | .05 |
| 594 Luis Sojo RC | .01 | .05 |
| 595 Greg Swindell | .01 | .05 |
| 596 Jose DeJesus | .01 | .05 |
| 597 Chris Bosio | .01 | .05 |
| 598 Brady Anderson | .02 | .10 |
| 599 Frank Williams | .01 | .05 |
| 600 Darryl Strawberry | .02 | .10 |
| 601 Luis Rivera | .01 | .05 |
| 602 Scott Garrelts | .01 | .05 |
| 603 Tony Armas | .01 | .05 |
| 604 Ron Robinson | .01 | .05 |
| 605 Mike Scioscia | .01 | .05 |
| 606 Storm Davis | .01 | .05 |
| 607 Steve Jeltz | .01 | .05 |
| 608 Eric Anthony RC | .10 | .25 |
| 609 Sparky Anderson MG | .02 | .10 |
| 610 Pedro Guerrero | .01 | .05 |
| 611 Walt Terrell | .01 | .05 |
| 612 Dave Gallagher | .01 | .05 |
| 613 Jeff Pico | .01 | .05 |
| 614 Nelson Santovenia | .01 | .05 |
| 615 Rob Deer | .01 | .05 |
| 616 Brian Holman | .01 | .05 |
| 617 Geronimo Berroa | .01 | .05 |
| 618 Ed Whitson | .01 | .05 |
| 619 Rob Ducey | .01 | .05 |
| 620 Tony Castillo | .01 | .05 |
| 621 Melido Perez | .01 | .05 |
| 622 Sid Bream | .01 | .05 |
| 623 Jim Corsi | .01 | .05 |
| 624 Darrin Jackson | .01 | .05 |
| 625 Roger McDowell | .01 | .05 |
| 626 Bob Melvin | .01 | .05 |
| 627 Jose Rijo | .01 | .05 |
| 628 Candy Maldonado | .01 | .05 |
| 629 Eric Hetzel | .01 | .05 |
| 630 Gary Gaetti | .02 | .10 |
| 631 John Wetteland | .08 | .25 |
| 632 Scott Lusader | .01 | .05 |
| 633 Dennis Cook | .01 | .05 |
| 634 Luis Polonia | .01 | .05 |
| 635 Brian Downing | .01 | .05 |
| 636 Jesse Orosco | .01 | .05 |
| 637 Craig Reynolds | .01 | .05 |
| 638 Jeff Montgomery | .02 | .10 |
| 639 Tony LaRussa MG | .02 | .10 |
| 640 Rick Sutcliffe | .02 | .10 |
| 641 Doug Strange RC | .01 | .05 |
| 642 Jack Armstrong | .01 | .05 |
| 643 Alfredo Griffin | .01 | .05 |
| 644 Paul Assenmacher | .01 | .05 |
| 645 Jose Oquendo | .01 | .05 |
| 646 Checklist 5 | .01 | .05 |
| 647 Rex Hudler | .01 | .05 |
| 648 Jim Clancy | .01 | .05 |
| 649 Dan Murphy RC | .02 | .10 |
| 650 Mike Witt | .01 | .05 |
| 651 Rafael Santana | .01 | .05 |
| 652 Mike Boddicker | .01 | .05 |
| 653 John Moses | .01 | .05 |
| 654 Paul Coleman FDP RC | .02 | .10 |
| 655 Gregg Olson | .02 | .10 |
| 656 Mackey Sasser | .01 | .05 |
| 657 Terry Mulholland | .01 | .05 |
| 658 Donell Nixon | .01 | .05 |
| 659 Greg Cadaret | .01 | .05 |
| 660 Vince Coleman | .01 | .05 |
| 661 Dick Howser TBC'85 | | |
| (Seaver's 300th | | |
| on 7/11/8 | .01 | .05 |
| 662 Mike Schmidt TBC | .08 | .25 |
| 663 Fred Lynn TBC'75 | .05 | .15 |
| 664 Johnny Bench TBC | .05 | .15 |
| 665 Sandy Koufax TBC | .20 | .50 |
| 666 Brian Fisher | .01 | .05 |
| 667 Curt Wilkerson | .01 | .05 |
| 668 Joe Oliver | .01 | .05 |
| 669 Tom Lasorda MG | .08 | .25 |
| 670 Dennis Eckersley | .02 | .10 |
| 671 Bob Boone | .02 | .10 |
| 672 Roy Smith | .01 | .05 |
| 673 Joey Meyer | .01 | .05 |
| 674 Spike Owen | .01 | .05 |
| 675 Jim Abbott | .05 | .15 |
| 676 Randy Kutcher | .01 | .05 |
| 677 Jay Tibbs | .01 | .05 |
| 678 Kirt Manwaring UER | | |
| ('88 Phoenix stats | | |
| repeated) | | |
| 679 Gary Ward | .01 | .05 |
| 680 Howard Johnson | .01 | .05 |
| 681 Mike Schooler | .01 | .05 |
| 682 Dann Bilardello | .01 | .05 |
| 683 Kenny Rogers | .02 | .10 |
| 684 Julio Machado RC | .01 | .05 |
| 685 Tony Fernandez | .01 | .05 |
| 686 Carmelo Martinez | .01 | .05 |
| 687 Tim Birtsas | .01 | .05 |
| 688 Milt Thompson | .01 | .05 |
| 689 Rich Yett | .01 | .05 |
| 690 Mark McGwire | .25 | .60 |
| 691 Chuck Cary | .01 | .05 |
| 692 Sammy Sosa RC | 1.00 | 2.50 |
| 693 Calvin Schiraldi | .01 | .05 |
| 694 Mike Stanton RC | .08 | .25 |
| 695 Tom Henke | .01 | .05 |
| 696 B.J. Surhoff | .02 | .10 |
| 697 Mike Davis | .01 | .05 |
| 698 Omar Vizquel | .08 | .25 |

|  | | |
|---|---|---|
| 699 Jim Leyland MG | .01 | .05 |
| 700 Kirby Puckett | .08 | .25 |
| 701 Bernie Williams RC | .60 | 1.50 |
| 702 Tony Phillips | .01 | .05 |
| 703 Jeff Brantley | .01 | .05 |
| 704 Chip Hale RC | .01 | .05 |
| 705 Claudell Washington | .01 | .05 |
| 706 Geno Petralli | .01 | .05 |
| 707 Luis Aquino | .01 | .05 |
| 708 Larry Sheets | .01 | .05 |
| 709 Juan Berenguer | .01 | .05 |
| 710 Von Hayes | .01 | .05 |
| 711 Rick Aguilera | .02 | .10 |
| 712 Todd Benzinger | .01 | .05 |
| 713 Tim Drummond RC | .01 | .05 |
| 714 Marquis Grissom RC | .15 | .40 |
| 715 Greg Maddux | .15 | .40 |
| 716 Steve Balboni | .01 | .05 |
| 717 Ron Karkovice | .01 | .05 |
| 718 Gary Sheffield | .08 | .25 |
| 719 Wally Whitehurst | .01 | .05 |
| 720 Andres Galarraga | .02 | .10 |
| 721 Lee Mazzilli | .01 | .05 |
| 722 Felix Fermin | .01 | .05 |
| 723 Jeff D. Robinson | .01 | .05 |
| 724 Juan Bell | .01 | .05 |
| 725 Terry Pendleton | .02 | .10 |
| 726 Gene Nelson | .01 | .05 |
| 727 Pat Tabler | .01 | .05 |
| 728 Jim Acker | .01 | .05 |
| 729 Bobby Valentine MG | .01 | .05 |
| 730 Tony Gwynn | .10 | .30 |
| 731 Don Carman | .01 | .05 |
| 732 Ernest Riles | .01 | .05 |
| 733 John Dopson | .01 | .05 |
| 734 Kevin Elster | .01 | .05 |
| 735 Charlie Hough | .02 | .10 |
| 736 Rick Dempsey | .01 | .05 |
| 737 Chris Sabo | .01 | .05 |
| 738 Gene Harris | .01 | .05 |
| 739 Dale Sveum | .01 | .05 |
| 740 Jesse Barfield | .01 | .05 |
| 741 Steve Wilson | .01 | .05 |
| 742 Ernie Whitt | .01 | .05 |
| 743 Tom Candiotti | .01 | .05 |
| 744 Kelly Mann RC | .01 | .05 |
| 745 Hubie Brooks | .01 | .05 |
| 746 Dave Smith | .01 | .05 |
| 747 Randy Bush | .01 | .05 |
| 748 Doyle Alexander | .01 | .05 |
| 749 Mark Parent UER ('87 BA .80, should be .080) | .01 | .05 |
| 750 Dale Murphy | .05 | .15 |
| 751 Steve Lyons | .01 | .05 |
| 752 Tom Gordon | .02 | .10 |
| 753 Chris Speier | .01 | .05 |
| 754 Bob Walk | .01 | .05 |
| 755 Rafael Palmeiro | .05 | .15 |
| 756 Ken Howell | .01 | .05 |
| 757 Larry Walker RC | .40 | 1.00 |
| 758 Mark Thurmond | .01 | .05 |
| 759 Tom Trebelhorn MG | .01 | .05 |
| 760 Wade Boggs | .05 | .15 |
| 761 Mike Jackson | .01 | .05 |
| 762 Doug Dascenzo | .01 | .05 |
| 763 Dennis Martinez | .02 | .10 |
| 764 Tim Teufel | .01 | .05 |
| 765 Chili Davis | .02 | .10 |
| 766 Brian Meyer | .01 | .05 |
| 767 Tracy Jones | .01 | .05 |
| 768 Chuck Crim | .01 | .05 |
| 769 Greg Hibbard RC | .02 | .10 |
| 770 Cory Snyder | .01 | .05 |
| 771 Pete Smith | .01 | .05 |
| 772 Jeff Reed | .01 | .05 |
| 773 Dave Leiper | .01 | .05 |
| 774 Ben McDonald RC | .08 | .25 |
| 775 Andy Van Slyke | .05 | .15 |
| 776 Charlie Leibrandt | .01 | .05 |
| 777 Tim Laudner | .01 | .05 |
| 778 Mike Jeffcoat | .01 | .05 |
| 779 Lloyd Moseby | .01 | .05 |
| 780 Orel Hershiser | .02 | .10 |
| 781 Mario Diaz | .01 | .05 |
| 782 Jose Alvarez | .01 | .05 |
| 783 Checklist 6 | .01 | .05 |
| 784 Scott Bailes | .01 | .05 |

|  | | |
|---|---|---|
| 785 Jim Rice | .02 | .10 |
| 786 Eric King | .01 | .05 |
| 787 Bernie Gonzales | .01 | .05 |
| 788 Frank DiPino | .01 | .05 |
| 789 John Wathan MG | .01 | .05 |
| 790 Gary Carter | .02 | .10 |
| 791 Alvaro Espinoza | .01 | .05 |
| 792 Gerald Perry | .01 | .05 |
| NNO George Bush PRES | | |

### 1991 Topps

|  | | |
|---|---|---|
| COMPLETE SET (792) | 8.00 | 20.00 |
| COMP.FACT.SET (792) | 10.00 | 25.00 |
| 1 Nolan Ryan | .50 | 1.50 |
| 2 George Brett RB | .10 | .30 |
| 3 Carlton Fisk RB | .02 | .10 |
| 4 Kevin Maas RB | .01 | .05 |
| 5 Cal Ripken RB | .15 | .40 |
| 6 Nolan Ryan RB | .20 | .50 |
| 7 Ryne Sandberg RB | .08 | .25 |
| 8 Bobby Thigpen RB | .01 | .05 |
| 9 Darrin Fletcher | .01 | .05 |
| 10 Gregg Olson | .01 | .05 |
| 11 Roberto Kelly | .01 | .05 |
| 12 Paul Assenmacher | .01 | .05 |
| 13 Mariano Duncan | .01 | .05 |
| 14 Dennis Lamp | .01 | .05 |
| 15 Von Hayes | .01 | .05 |
| 16 Mike Heath | .01 | .05 |
| 17 Jeff Brantley | .01 | .05 |
| 18 Nelson Liriano | .01 | .05 |
| 19 Jeff D. Robinson | .01 | .05 |
| 20 Pedro Guerrero | .02 | .10 |
| 21 Joe Morgan MG | .01 | .05 |
| 22 Storm Davis | .01 | .05 |
| 23 Jim Gantner | .01 | .05 |
| 24 Dave Martinez | .01 | .05 |
| 25 Tim Belcher | .01 | .05 |
| 26 Luis Sojo UER (Born in Barquisimiento& not Carqui) | .01 | .05 |
| 27 Bobby Witt | .01 | .05 |
| 28 Alvaro Espinoza | .01 | .05 |
| 29 Bob Walk | .01 | .05 |
| 30 Gregg Jefferies | .01 | .05 |
| 31 Colby Ward RC | .01 | .05 |
| 32 Mike Simms RC | .01 | .05 |
| 33 Barry Jones | .01 | .05 |
| 34 Atlee Hammaker | .01 | .05 |
| 35 Greg Maddux | .15 | .40 |
| 36 Donnie Hill | .01 | .05 |
| 37 Tom Bolton | .01 | .05 |
| 38 Scott Bradley | .01 | .05 |
| 39 Jim Neidlinger RC | .01 | .05 |
| 40 Kevin Mitchell | .01 | .05 |
| 41 Ken Dayley | .01 | .05 |
| 42 Chris Hoiles | .01 | .05 |
| 43 Roger McDowell | .01 | .05 |
| 44 Mike Felder | .01 | .05 |
| 45 Chris Sabo | .01 | .05 |
| 46 Tim Drummond | .01 | .05 |
| 47 Brook Jacoby | .01 | .05 |
| 48 Dennis Boyd | .01 | .05 |
| 49A Pat Borders ERR (40 steals at Kinston in '86) | .08 | .25 |
| 49B Pat Borders COR (0 steals at Kinston in '86) | .01 | .05 |
| 50 Bob Welch | .01 | .05 |
| 51 Art Howe MG | .01 | .05 |
| 52 Francisco Oliveras | .01 | .05 |
| 53 Mike Sharperson UER (Born in 1961, not 1960) | .01 | .05 |

|  | | |
|---|---|---|
| 54 Gary Mielke | .01 | .05 |
| 55 Jeffrey Leonard | .01 | .05 |
| 56 Jeff Parrett | .01 | .05 |
| 57 Jack Howell | .01 | .05 |
| 58 Mel Stottlemyre Jr. | .01 | .05 |
| 59 Eric Yelding | .01 | .05 |
| 60 Frank Viola | .02 | .10 |
| 61 Stan Javier | .01 | .05 |
| 62 Lee Guetterman | .01 | .05 |
| 63 Milt Thompson | .01 | .05 |
| 64 Tom Herr | .01 | .05 |
| 65 Bruce Hurst | .01 | .05 |
| 66 Terry Kennedy | .01 | .05 |
| 67 Rick Honeycutt | .01 | .05 |
| 68 Gary Sheffield | .02 | .10 |
| 69 Steve Wilson | .01 | .05 |
| 70 Ellis Burks | .02 | .10 |
| 71 Jim Acker | .01 | .05 |
| 72 Junior Ortiz | .01 | .05 |
| 73 Craig Worthington | .01 | .05 |
| 74 Shane Andrews RC | .08 | .25 |
| 75 Jack Morris | .02 | .10 |
| 76 Jerry Browne | .01 | .05 |
| 77 Drew Hall | .01 | .05 |
| 78 Geno Petralli | .01 | .05 |
| 79 Frank Thomas | .08 | .25 |
| 80A Fernando Valenzuela ERR | .15 | .40 |
| 80B Fernando Valenzuela COR | .02 | .10 |
| 81 Cito Gaston MG | .01 | .05 |
| 82 Tom Glavine | .05 | .15 |
| 83 Daryl Boston | .01 | .05 |
| 84 Bob McClure | .01 | .05 |
| 85 Jesse Barfield | .01 | .05 |
| 86 Les Lancaster | .01 | .05 |
| 87 Tracy Jones | .01 | .05 |
| 88 Bob Tewksbury | .01 | .05 |
| 89 Darren Daulton | .02 | .10 |
| 90 Danny Tartabull | .02 | .10 |
| 91 Greg Colbrunn RC | .08 | .25 |
| 92 Danny Jackson | .01 | .05 |
| 93 Ivan Calderon | .01 | .05 |
| 94 John Dopson | .01 | .05 |
| 95 Paul Molitor | .02 | .10 |
| 96 Trevor Wilson | .01 | .05 |
| 97A Brady Anderson ERR | .15 | .40 |
| 97B Brady Anderson COR | .02 | .10 |
| 98 Sergio Valdez | .01 | .05 |
| 99 Chris Gwynn | .01 | .05 |
| 100 Don Mattingly | .25 | .60 |
| 100A Don Mattingly ERR | .75 | 2.00 |
| 101 Rob Ducey | .01 | .05 |
| 102 Gene Larkin | .01 | .05 |
| 103 Tim Costo RC | .01 | .05 |
| 104 Don Robinson | .01 | .05 |
| 105 Kevin McReynolds | .01 | .05 |
| 106 Ed Nunez | .01 | .05 |
| 107 Luis Polonia | .01 | .05 |
| 108 Matt Young | .01 | .05 |
| 109 Greg Riddoch MG | .01 | .05 |
| 110 Tom Henke | .01 | .05 |
| 111 Andres Thomas | .01 | .05 |
| 112 Frank DiPino | .01 | .05 |
| 113 Carl Everett RC | .20 | .50 |
| 114 Lance Dickson RC | .02 | .10 |
| 115 Hubie Brooks | .01 | .05 |
| 116 Mark Davis | .01 | .05 |
| 117 Dion James | .01 | .05 |
| 118 Tom Edens RC | .01 | .05 |
| 119 Carl Nichols | .01 | .05 |
| 120 Joe Carter | .02 | .10 |
| 121 Eric King | .01 | .05 |
| 122 Paul O'Neill | .05 | .15 |
| 123 Greg A. Harris | .01 | .05 |
| 124 Randy Bush | .01 | .05 |
| 125 Steve Bedrosian | .01 | .05 |
| 126 Bernard Gilkey | .01 | .05 |
| 127 Joe Price | .01 | .05 |
| 128 Travis Fryman | .02 | .10 |
| 129 Mark Eichhorn | .01 | .05 |
| 130 Ozzie Smith | .15 | .40 |
| 131A Checklist 1 ERR 727 Phil Bradley | .08 | .25 |
| 131B Checklist 1 COR 717 Phil Bradley | | |
| 132 Jamie Quirk | .01 | .05 |
| 133 Greg Briley | .01 | .05 |
| 134 Kevin Elster | .01 | .05 |
| 135 Jerome Walton | .01 | .05 |

|  |  | | |
|---|---|---|---|
| ☐ 136 | Dave Schmidt | .01 | .05 |
| ☐ 137 | Randy Ready | .01 | .05 |
| ☐ 138 | Jamie Moyer | .02 | .10 |
| ☐ 139 | Jeff Treadway | .01 | .05 |
| ☐ 140 | Fred McGriff | .05 | .15 |
| ☐ 141 | Nick Leyva MG | .01 | .05 |
| ☐ 142 | Curt Wilkerson | .01 | .05 |
| ☐ 143 | John Smiley | .01 | .05 |
| ☐ 144 | Dave Henderson | .01 | .05 |
| ☐ 145 | Lou Whitaker | .02 | .10 |
| ☐ 146 | Dan Plesac | .01 | .05 |
| ☐ 147 | Carlos Baerga | .01 | .05 |
| ☐ 148 | Rey Palacios | .01 | .05 |
| ☐ 149 | Al Osuna UER RC | .02 | .10 |
| ☐ 150 | Cal Ripken | .30 | .75 |
| ☐ 151 | Tom Browning | .01 | .05 |
| ☐ 152 | Mickey Hatcher | .01 | .05 |
| ☐ 153 | Bryan Harvey | .01 | .05 |
| ☐ 154 | Jay Buhner | .02 | .10 |
| ☐ 155A | Dwight Evans ERR | .20 | .50 |
| ☐ 155B | Dwight Evans COR | .05 | .15 |
| ☐ 156 | Carlos Martinez | .01 | .05 |
| ☐ 157 | John Smoltz | .05 | .15 |
| ☐ 158 | Jose Uribe | .01 | .05 |
| ☐ 159 | Joe Boever | .01 | .05 |
| ☐ 160 | Vince Coleman UER (Wrong birth year& born 9/22/6) | | |
| ☐ 161 | Tim Leary | .01 | .05 |
| ☐ 162 | Ozzie Canseco | .01 | .05 |
| ☐ 163 | Dave Johnson | .01 | .05 |
| ☐ 164 | Edgar Diaz | .01 | .05 |
| ☐ 165 | Sandy Alomar Jr. | .01 | .05 |
| ☐ 166 | Harold Baines | .02 | .10 |
| ☐ 167A | Randy Tomlin ERR | .08 | .25 |
| ☐ 167B | Randy Tomlin COR RC | .01 | .05 |
| ☐ 168 | John Olerud | .02 | .10 |
| ☐ 169 | Luis Aquino | .01 | .05 |
| ☐ 170 | Carlton Fisk | .05 | .15 |
| ☐ 171 | Tony LaRussa MG | .02 | .10 |
| ☐ 172 | Pete Incaviglia | .01 | .05 |
| ☐ 173 | Jason Grimsley | .01 | .05 |
| ☐ 174 | Ken Caminiti | .02 | .10 |
| ☐ 175 | Jack Armstrong | .01 | .05 |
| ☐ 176 | John Orton | .01 | .05 |
| ☐ 177 | Reggie Harris | .01 | .05 |
| ☐ 178 | Dave Valle | .01 | .05 |
| ☐ 179 | Pete Harnisch | .01 | .05 |
| ☐ 180 | Tony Gwynn | .10 | .30 |
| ☐ 181 | Duane Ward | .01 | .05 |
| ☐ 182 | Junior Noboa | .01 | .05 |
| ☐ 183 | Clay Parker | .01 | .05 |
| ☐ 184 | Gary Green | .01 | .05 |
| ☐ 185 | Joe Magrane | .01 | .05 |
| ☐ 186 | Rod Booker | .01 | .05 |
| ☐ 187 | Greg Cadaret | .01 | .05 |
| ☐ 188 | Damon Berryhill | .01 | .05 |
| ☐ 189 | Daryl Irvine RC | .01 | .05 |
| ☐ 190 | Matt Williams | .02 | .10 |
| ☐ 191 | Willie Blair | .01 | .05 |
| ☐ 192 | Rob Deer | .01 | .05 |
| ☐ 193 | Felix Fermin | .01 | .05 |
| ☐ 194 | Xavier Hernandez | .01 | .05 |
| ☐ 195 | Wally Joyner | .02 | .10 |
| ☐ 196 | Jim Vatcher RC | .01 | .05 |
| ☐ 197 | Chris Nabholz | .01 | .05 |
| ☐ 198 | R.J. Reynolds | .01 | .05 |
| ☐ 199 | Mike Hartley | .01 | .05 |
| ☐ 200 | Darryl Strawberry | .02 | .10 |
| ☐ 201 | Tom Kelly MG | .01 | .05 |
| ☐ 202 | Jim Leyritz | .01 | .05 |
| ☐ 203 | Gene Harris | .01 | .05 |
| ☐ 204 | Herm Winningham | .01 | .05 |
| ☐ 205 | Mike Perez RC | .02 | .10 |
| ☐ 206 | Carlos Quintana | .01 | .05 |
| ☐ 207 | Gary Wayne | .01 | .05 |
| ☐ 208 | Willie Wilson | .01 | .05 |
| ☐ 209 | Ken Howell | .01 | .05 |
| ☐ 210 | Lance Parrish | .02 | .10 |
| ☐ 211 | Brian Barnes RC | .01 | .05 |
| ☐ 212 | Steve Finley | .01 | .05 |
| ☐ 213 | Frank Wills | .01 | .05 |
| ☐ 214 | Joe Girardi | .01 | .05 |
| ☐ 215 | Dave Smith | .01 | .05 |
| ☐ 216 | Greg Gagne | .01 | .05 |
| ☐ 217 | Chris Bosio | .01 | .05 |
| ☐ 218 | Rick Parker | .01 | .05 |
| ☐ 219 | Jack McDowell | .01 | .05 |
| ☐ 220 | Tim Wallach | .01 | .05 |
| ☐ 221 | Don Slaught | .01 | .05 |
| ☐ 222 | Brian McRae RC | .08 | .25 |
| ☐ 223 | Allan Anderson | .01 | .05 |
| ☐ 224 | Juan Gonzalez | .08 | .25 |
| ☐ 225 | Randy Johnson | .10 | .30 |
| ☐ 226 | Alfredo Griffin | .01 | .05 |
| ☐ 227 | Steve Avery UER | .05 | .15 |
| ☐ 228 | Rex Hudler | .01 | .05 |
| ☐ 229 | Rance Mulliniks | .01 | .05 |
| ☐ 230 | Sid Fernandez | .01 | .05 |
| ☐ 231 | Doug Rader MG | .01 | .05 |
| ☐ 232 | Jose DeJesus | .01 | .05 |
| ☐ 233 | Al Leiter | .01 | .05 |
| ☐ 234 | Scott Erickson | .02 | .10 |
| ☐ 235 | Dave Parker | .02 | .10 |
| ☐ 236A | Frank Tanana ERR (Tied for lead with 269 K's in | .08 | .25 |
| ☐ 236B | Frank Tanana COR (Led league with 269 K's in '75 | .01 | .05 |
| ☐ 237 | Rick Cerone | .01 | .05 |
| ☐ 238 | Mike Dunne | .01 | .05 |
| ☐ 239 | Darren Lewis FTC | .01 | .05 |
| ☐ 240 | Mike Scott | .01 | .05 |
| ☐ 241 | Dave Clark UER (Career totals 19 HR and 5 3B& sh | .01 | .05 |
| ☐ 242 | Mike LaCoss | .01 | .05 |
| ☐ 243 | Lance Johnson | .01 | .05 |
| ☐ 244 | Mike Jeffcoat | .01 | .05 |
| ☐ 245 | Kal Daniels | .01 | .05 |
| ☐ 246 | Kevin Wickander | .01 | .05 |
| ☐ 247 | Jody Reed | .01 | .05 |
| ☐ 248 | Tom Gordon | .01 | .05 |
| ☐ 249 | Bob Melvin | .01 | .05 |
| ☐ 250 | Dennis Eckersley | .02 | .10 |
| ☐ 251 | Mark Lemke | .01 | .05 |
| ☐ 252 | Mel Rojas | .01 | .05 |
| ☐ 253 | Garry Templeton | .01 | .05 |
| ☐ 254 | Shawn Boskie | .01 | .05 |
| ☐ 255 | Brian Downing | .01 | .05 |
| ☐ 256 | Greg Hibbard | .01 | .05 |
| ☐ 257 | Tom O'Malley | .01 | .05 |
| ☐ 258 | Chris Hammond FTC | .01 | .05 |
| ☐ 259 | Hensley Meulens | .01 | .05 |
| ☐ 260 | Harold Reynolds | .02 | .10 |
| ☐ 261 | Bud Harrelson MG | .01 | .05 |
| ☐ 262 | Tim Jones | .01 | .05 |
| ☐ 263 | Checklist 2 | .01 | .05 |
| ☐ 264 | Dave Hollins | .05 | .15 |
| ☐ 265 | Mark Gubicza | .01 | .05 |
| ☐ 266 | Carmelo Castillo | .01 | .05 |
| ☐ 267 | Mark Knudson | .01 | .05 |
| ☐ 268 | Tom Brookens | .01 | .05 |
| ☐ 269 | Joe Hesketh | .01 | .05 |
| ☐ 270 | Mark McGwire | .15 | .40 |
| ☐ 270A | Mark McGwire ERR | .75 | 2.00 |
| ☐ 271 | Omar Olivares RC | .02 | .10 |
| ☐ 272 | Jeff King | .01 | .05 |
| ☐ 273 | Johnny Ray | .01 | .05 |
| ☐ 274 | Ken Williams | .01 | .05 |
| ☐ 275 | Alan Trammell | .02 | .10 |
| ☐ 276 | Bill Swift | .01 | .05 |
| ☐ 277 | Scott Coolbaugh | .01 | .05 |
| ☐ 278 | Alex Fernandez UER | .01 | .05 |
| ☐ 279A | Jose Gonzalez ERR (Photo actually Billy Bean) | .08 | .25 |
| ☐ 279B | Jose Gonzalez COR | .01 | .05 |
| ☐ 280 | Bret Saberhagen | .01 | .05 |
| ☐ 281 | Larry Sheets | .01 | .05 |
| ☐ 282 | Don Carman | .01 | .05 |
| ☐ 283 | Marquis Grissom | .02 | .10 |
| ☐ 284 | Billy Spiers | .01 | .05 |
| ☐ 285 | Jim Abbott | .05 | .15 |
| ☐ 286 | Ken Oberkfell | .01 | .05 |
| ☐ 287 | Mark Grant | .01 | .05 |
| ☐ 288 | Derrick May | .01 | .05 |
| ☐ 289 | Tim Birtsas | .01 | .05 |
| ☐ 290 | Steve Sax | .01 | .05 |
| ☐ 291 | John Wathan MG | .01 | .05 |
| ☐ 292 | Bud Black | .01 | .05 |
| ☐ 293 | Jay Bell | .02 | .10 |
| ☐ 294 | Mike Moore | .01 | .05 |
| ☐ 295 | Rafael Palmeiro | .05 | .15 |
| ☐ 296 | Mark Williamson | .01 | .05 |
| ☐ 297 | Manny Lee | .01 | .05 |
| ☐ 298 | Omar Vizquel | .05 | .15 |
| ☐ 299 | Scott Radinsky | .01 | .05 |
| ☐ 300 | Kirby Puckett | .08 | .25 |
| ☐ 301 | Steve Farr | .01 | .05 |
| ☐ 302 | Tim Teufel | .01 | .05 |
| ☐ 303 | Mike Boddicker | .01 | .05 |
| ☐ 304 | Kevin Reimer | .01 | .05 |
| ☐ 305 | Mike Scioscia | .01 | .05 |
| ☐ 306A | Lonnie Smith ERR (136 games in '90) | .15 | .40 |
| ☐ 306B | Lonnie Smith COR (135 games in '90) | .01 | .05 |
| ☐ 307 | Andy Benes | .01 | .05 |
| ☐ 308 | Tom Pagnozzi | .01 | .05 |
| ☐ 309 | Norm Charlton | .01 | .05 |
| ☐ 310 | Gary Carter | .02 | .10 |
| ☐ 311 | Jeff Pico | .01 | .05 |
| ☐ 312 | Charlie Hayes | .01 | .05 |
| ☐ 313 | Ron Robinson | .01 | .05 |
| ☐ 314 | Gary Pettis | .01 | .05 |
| ☐ 315 | Roberto Alomar | .05 | .15 |
| ☐ 316 | Gene Nelson | .01 | .05 |
| ☐ 317 | Mike Fitzgerald | .01 | .05 |
| ☐ 318 | Rick Aguilera | .02 | .10 |
| ☐ 319 | Jeff McKnight | .01 | .05 |
| ☐ 320 | Tony Fernandez | .01 | .05 |
| ☐ 321 | Bob Rodgers MG | .01 | .05 |
| ☐ 322 | Terry Shumpert | .01 | .05 |
| ☐ 323 | Cory Snyder | .01 | .05 |
| ☐ 324A | Ron Kittle ERR (Set another standard ... | .15 | .40 |
| ☐ 324B | Ron Kittle COR (Tied another standard ... | .01 | .05 |
| ☐ 325 | Brett Butler | .02 | .10 |
| ☐ 326 | Ken Patterson | .01 | .05 |
| ☐ 327 | Ron Hassey | .01 | .05 |
| ☐ 328 | Walt Terrell | .01 | .05 |
| ☐ 329 | David Justice UER | .02 | .10 |
| ☐ 330 | Dwight Gooden | .02 | .10 |
| ☐ 331 | Eric Anthony | .01 | .05 |
| ☐ 332 | Kenny Rogers | .02 | .10 |
| ☐ 333 | Chipper Jones RC | 1.50 | 4.00 |
| ☐ 334 | Todd Benzinger | .01 | .05 |
| ☐ 335 | Mitch Williams | .01 | .05 |
| ☐ 336 | Matt Nokes | .01 | .05 |
| ☐ 337A | Keith Comstock ERR (Cubs logo on front) | .08 | .25 |
| ☐ 337B | Keith Comstock COR (Mariners logo on front) | .01 | .05 |
| ☐ 338 | Luis Rivera | .01 | .05 |
| ☐ 339 | Larry Walker | .08 | .25 |
| ☐ 340 | Ramon Martinez | .02 | .10 |
| ☐ 341 | John Moses | .01 | .05 |
| ☐ 342 | Mickey Morandini | .01 | .05 |
| ☐ 343 | Jose Oquendo | .01 | .05 |
| ☐ 344 | Jeff Russell | .01 | .05 |
| ☐ 345 | Len Dykstra | .02 | .10 |
| ☐ 346 | Jesse Orosco | .01 | .05 |
| ☐ 347 | Greg Vaughn | .01 | .05 |
| ☐ 348 | Todd Stottlemyre | .01 | .05 |
| ☐ 349 | Dave Gallagher | .01 | .05 |
| ☐ 350 | Glenn Davis | .01 | .05 |
| ☐ 351 | Joe Torre MG | .02 | .10 |
| ☐ 352 | Frank White | .01 | .05 |
| ☐ 353 | Tony Castillo | .01 | .05 |
| ☐ 354 | Sid Bream | .01 | .05 |
| ☐ 355 | Chili Davis | .02 | .10 |
| ☐ 356 | Mike Marshall | .01 | .05 |
| ☐ 357 | Jack Savage | .01 | .05 |
| ☐ 358 | Mark Parent | .01 | .05 |
| ☐ 359 | Chuck Cary | .01 | .05 |
| ☐ 360 | Tim Raines | .02 | .10 |
| ☐ 361 | Scott Garrelts | .01 | .05 |
| ☐ 362 | Hector Villenueva | .01 | .05 |
| ☐ 363 | Rick Mahler | .01 | .05 |
| ☐ 364 | Dan Pasqua | .01 | .05 |
| ☐ 365 | Mike Schooler | .01 | .05 |
| ☐ 366A | Checklist 3 ERR | .08 | .25 |
| | 19 Carl Nichols | | |
| ☐ 366B | Checklist 3 COR | | |
| | 119 Carl Nichols | .01 | .05 |
| ☐ 367 | Dave Walsh RC | .01 | .05 |
| ☐ 368 | Felix Jose | .02 | .10 |
| ☐ 369 | Steve Searcy | .01 | .05 |
| ☐ 370 | Kelly Gruber | .01 | .05 |

|  | | |
|---|---|---|
| ❑ 371 Jeff Montgomery | .01 | .05 |
| ❑ 372 Spike Owen | .01 | .05 |
| ❑ 373 Darrin Jackson | .01 | .05 |
| ❑ 374 Larry Casian RC | .01 | .05 |
| ❑ 375 Tony Pena | .01 | .05 |
| ❑ 376 Mike Harkey | .01 | .05 |
| ❑ 377 Rene Gonzales | .01 | .05 |
| ❑ 378A Wilson Alvarez ERR | .08 | .25 |
| ❑ 378B Wilson Alvarez FTC COR | | |
| ❑ 379 Randy Velarde | .01 | .05 |
| ❑ 380 Willie McGee | .02 | .10 |
| ❑ 381 Jim Leyland MG | .01 | .05 |
| ❑ 382 Mackey Sasser | .01 | .05 |
| ❑ 383 Pete Smith | .01 | .05 |
| ❑ 384 Gerald Perry | .01 | .05 |
| ❑ 385 Mickey Tettleton | .01 | .05 |
| ❑ 386 Cecil Fielder AS | .01 | .05 |
| ❑ 387 Julio Franco AS | .01 | .05 |
| ❑ 388 Kelly Gruber AS | .01 | .05 |
| ❑ 389 Alan Trammell AS | .02 | .10 |
| ❑ 390 Jose Canseco AS | .05 | .15 |
| ❑ 391 Rickey Henderson AS | .05 | .15 |
| ❑ 392 Ken Griffey Jr. AS | .15 | .40 |
| ❑ 393 Carlton Fisk AS | .02 | .10 |
| ❑ 394 Bob Welch AS | .01 | .05 |
| ❑ 395 Chuck Finley AS | .01 | .05 |
| ❑ 396 Bobby Thigpen AS | .01 | .05 |
| ❑ 397 Eddie Murray AS | .05 | .15 |
| ❑ 398 Ryne Sandberg AS | .08 | .25 |
| ❑ 399 Matt Williams AS | .05 | .15 |
| ❑ 400 Barry Larkin AS | .02 | .10 |
| ❑ 401 Barry Bonds AS | .20 | .50 |
| ❑ 402 Darryl Strawberry AS | .05 | .15 |
| ❑ 403 Bobby Bonilla AS | .05 | .15 |
| ❑ 404 Mike Scioscia AS | .01 | .05 |
| ❑ 405 Doug Drabek AS | .01 | .05 |
| ❑ 406 Frank Viola AS | .01 | .05 |
| ❑ 407 John Franco AS | .01 | .05 |
| ❑ 408 Earnest Riles | .01 | .05 |
| ❑ 409 Mike Stanley | .01 | .05 |
| ❑ 410 Dave Righetti | .02 | .10 |
| ❑ 411 Lance Blankenship | .01 | .05 |
| ❑ 412 Dave Bergman | .01 | .05 |
| ❑ 413 Terry Mulholland | .01 | .05 |
| ❑ 414 Sammy Sosa | .08 | .25 |
| ❑ 415 Rick Sutcliffe | .02 | .10 |
| ❑ 416 Randy Milligan | .01 | .05 |
| ❑ 417 Bill Krueger | .01 | .05 |
| ❑ 418 Nick Esasky | .01 | .05 |
| ❑ 419 Jeff Reed | .01 | .05 |
| ❑ 420 Bobby Thigpen | .01 | .05 |
| ❑ 421 Alex Cole | .01 | .05 |
| ❑ 422 Rick Reuschel | .01 | .05 |
| ❑ 423 Rafael Ramirez UER (Born 1959, not 1958) | .01 | .05 |
| ❑ 424 Calvin Schiraldi | .01 | .05 |
| ❑ 425 Andy Van Slyke | .05 | .15 |
| ❑ 426 Joe Grahe RC | .02 | .10 |
| ❑ 427 Rick Dempsey | .01 | .05 |
| ❑ 428 John Barfield | .01 | .05 |
| ❑ 429 Stump Merrill MG | .01 | .05 |
| ❑ 430 Gary Gaetti | .02 | .10 |
| ❑ 431 Paul Gibson | .01 | .05 |
| ❑ 432 Delino DeShields | .02 | .10 |
| ❑ 433 Pat Tabler | .01 | .05 |
| ❑ 434 Julio Machado | .01 | .05 |
| ❑ 435 Kevin Maas | .01 | .05 |
| ❑ 436 Scott Bankhead | .01 | .05 |
| ❑ 437 Doug Dascenzo | .01 | .05 |
| ❑ 438 Vicente Palacios | .01 | .05 |
| ❑ 439 Dickie Thon | .01 | .05 |
| ❑ 440 George Bell | .05 | .15 |
| ❑ 441 Zane Smith | .01 | .05 |
| ❑ 442 Charlie O'Brien | .01 | .05 |
| ❑ 443 Jeff Innis | .01 | .05 |
| ❑ 444 Glenn Braggs | .01 | .05 |
| ❑ 445 Greg Swindell | .01 | .05 |
| ❑ 446 Craig Grebeck | .01 | .05 |
| ❑ 447 John Burkett | .01 | .05 |
| ❑ 448 Craig Lefferts | .01 | .05 |
| ❑ 449 Juan Berenguer | .01 | .05 |
| ❑ 450 Wade Boggs | .05 | .15 |
| ❑ 451 Neal Heaton | .01 | .05 |
| ❑ 452 Bill Schroeder | .01 | .05 |
| ❑ 453 Lenny Harris | .01 | .05 |
| ❑ 454A Kevin Appier ERR | .15 | .40 |
| ❑ 454B Kevin Appier COR | .02 | .10 |
| ❑ 455 Walt Weiss | .01 | .05 |
| ❑ 456 Charlie Leibrandt | .01 | .05 |
| ❑ 457 Todd Hundley | .01 | .05 |
| ❑ 458 Brian Holman | .01 | .05 |
| ❑ 459 Tom Trebelhorn MG UER (Pitching and batting blu) | .01 | .05 |
| ❑ 460 Dave Stieb | .01 | .05 |
| ❑ 461 Robin Ventura | .02 | .10 |
| ❑ 462 Steve Frey | .01 | .05 |
| ❑ 463 Dwight Smith | .01 | .05 |
| ❑ 464 Steve Buechele | .01 | .05 |
| ❑ 465 Ken Griffey Sr. | .02 | .10 |
| ❑ 466 Charles Nagy | .01 | .05 |
| ❑ 467 Dennis Cook | .01 | .05 |
| ❑ 468 Tim Hulett | .01 | .05 |
| ❑ 469 Chet Lemon | .01 | .05 |
| ❑ 470 Howard Johnson | .01 | .05 |
| ❑ 471 Mike Lieberthal RC | .15 | .40 |
| ❑ 472 Kirt Manwaring | .01 | .05 |
| ❑ 473 Curt Young | .01 | .05 |
| ❑ 474 Phil Plantier RC | .02 | .10 |
| ❑ 475 Ted Higuera | .01 | .05 |
| ❑ 476 Glenn Wilson | .01 | .05 |
| ❑ 477 Mike Fetters | .01 | .05 |
| ❑ 478 Kurt Stillwell | .01 | .05 |
| ❑ 479 Bob Patterson UER (Has a decimal point between 7 | | |
| ❑ 480 Dave Magadan | .01 | .05 |
| ❑ 481 Eddie Whitson | .01 | .05 |
| ❑ 482 Tino Martinez | .08 | .25 |
| ❑ 483 Mike Aldrete | .01 | .05 |
| ❑ 484 Dave LaPoint | .01 | .05 |
| ❑ 485 Terry Pendleton | .02 | .10 |
| ❑ 486 Tommy Greene | .01 | .05 |
| ❑ 487 Rafael Belliard | .01 | .05 |
| ❑ 488 Jeff Manto | .01 | .05 |
| ❑ 489 Bobby Valentine MG | .01 | .05 |
| ❑ 490 Kirk Gibson | .02 | .10 |
| ❑ 491 Kurt Miller RC | .01 | .05 |
| ❑ 492 Ernie Whitt | .01 | .05 |
| ❑ 493 Jose Rijo | .01 | .05 |
| ❑ 494 Chris James | .01 | .05 |
| ❑ 495 Charlie Hough | .02 | .10 |
| ❑ 496 Marty Barrett | .01 | .05 |
| ❑ 497 Ben McDonald | .01 | .05 |
| ❑ 498 Mark Salas | .01 | .05 |
| ❑ 499 Melido Perez | .01 | .05 |
| ❑ 500 Will Clark | .05 | .15 |
| ❑ 501 Mike Bielecki | .01 | .05 |
| ❑ 502 Carney Lansford | .02 | .10 |
| ❑ 503 Roy Smith | .01 | .05 |
| ❑ 504 Julio Valera | .01 | .05 |
| ❑ 505 Chuck Finley | .02 | .10 |
| ❑ 506 Darnell Coles | .01 | .05 |
| ❑ 507 Steve Jeltz | .01 | .05 |
| ❑ 508 Mike York RC | .01 | .05 |
| ❑ 509 Glenallen Hill | .01 | .05 |
| ❑ 510 John Franco | .02 | .10 |
| ❑ 511 Steve Balboni | .01 | .05 |
| ❑ 512 Jose Mesa | .01 | .05 |
| ❑ 513 Jerald Clark | .01 | .05 |
| ❑ 514 Mike Stanton | .01 | .05 |
| ❑ 515 Alvin Davis | .01 | .05 |
| ❑ 516 Karl Rhodes | .01 | .05 |
| ❑ 517 Joe Oliver | .01 | .05 |
| ❑ 518 Cris Carpenter | .01 | .05 |
| ❑ 519 Sparky Anderson MG | .02 | .10 |
| ❑ 520 Mark Grace | .05 | .15 |
| ❑ 521 Joe Orsulak | .01 | .05 |
| ❑ 522 Stan Belinda | .01 | .05 |
| ❑ 523 Rodney McCray RC | .01 | .05 |
| ❑ 524 Darrel Akerfelds | .01 | .05 |
| ❑ 525 Willie Randolph | .02 | .10 |
| ❑ 526A Moises Alou ERR | .15 | .40 |
| ❑ 526B Moises Alou COR | .02 | .10 |
| ❑ 527A Checklist 4 ERR 105 Keith Miller 719 Kevin McRey | .08 | .25 |
| ❑ 527B Checklist 4 COR 105 Keith McReynolds 719 Keith M | .01 | .05 |
| ❑ 528 Dennis Martinez | .02 | .10 |
| ❑ 529 Marc Newfield RC | .02 | .10 |
| ❑ 530 Roger Clemens | .30 | .75 |
| ❑ 531 Dave Rohde | .01 | .05 |
| ❑ 532 Kirk McCaskill | .01 | .05 |
| ❑ 533 Oddibe McDowell | .01 | .05 |
| ❑ 534 Mike Jackson | .01 | .05 |
| ❑ 535 Ruben Sierra UER | .02 | .10 |
| ❑ 536 Mike Witt | .01 | .05 |
| ❑ 537 Jose Lind | .01 | .05 |
| ❑ 538 Bip Roberts | .01 | .05 |
| ❑ 539 Scott Terry | .01 | .05 |
| ❑ 540 George Brett | .25 | .60 |
| ❑ 541 Domingo Ramos | .01 | .05 |
| ❑ 542 Rob Murphy | .01 | .05 |
| ❑ 543 Junior Felix | .01 | .05 |
| ❑ 544 Alejandro Pena | .01 | .05 |
| ❑ 545 Dale Murphy | .05 | .15 |
| ❑ 546 Jeff Ballard | .01 | .05 |
| ❑ 547 Mike Pagliarulo | .01 | .05 |
| ❑ 548 Jaime Navarro | .01 | .05 |
| ❑ 549 John McNamara MG | .01 | .05 |
| ❑ 550 Eric Davis | .02 | .10 |
| ❑ 551 Bob Kipper | .01 | .05 |
| ❑ 552 Jeff Hamilton | .01 | .05 |
| ❑ 553 Joe Klink | .01 | .05 |
| ❑ 554 Brian Harper | .01 | .05 |
| ❑ 555 Turner Ward RC | .02 | .10 |
| ❑ 556 Gary Ward | .01 | .05 |
| ❑ 557 Wally Whitehurst | .01 | .05 |
| ❑ 558 Otis Nixon | .01 | .05 |
| ❑ 559 Adam Peterson | .01 | .05 |
| ❑ 560 Greg Smith | .01 | .05 |
| ❑ 561 Tim McIntosh | .01 | .05 |
| ❑ 562 Jeff Kunkel | .01 | .05 |
| ❑ 563 Brent Knackert | .01 | .05 |
| ❑ 564 Dante Bichette | .02 | .10 |
| ❑ 565 Craig Biggio | .05 | .15 |
| ❑ 566 Craig Wilson RC | .01 | .05 |
| ❑ 567 Dwayne Henry | .01 | .05 |
| ❑ 568 Ron Karkovice | .01 | .05 |
| ❑ 569 Curt Schilling | .08 | .25 |
| ❑ 570 Barry Bonds | .40 | 1.00 |
| ❑ 571 Pat Combs | .01 | .05 |
| ❑ 572 Dave Anderson | .01 | .05 |
| ❑ 573 Rich Rodriguez UER RC | .01 | .05 |
| ❑ 574 John Marzano | .01 | .05 |
| ❑ 575 Robin Yount | .15 | .40 |
| ❑ 576 Jeff Kaiser | .01 | .05 |
| ❑ 577 Bill Doran | .01 | .05 |
| ❑ 578 Dave West | .01 | .05 |
| ❑ 579 Roger Craig MG | .02 | .10 |
| ❑ 580 Dave Stewart | .02 | .10 |
| ❑ 581 Luis Quinones | .01 | .05 |
| ❑ 582 Marty Clary | .01 | .05 |
| ❑ 583 Tony Phillips | .01 | .05 |
| ❑ 584 Kevin Brown | .02 | .10 |
| ❑ 585 Pete O'Brien | .01 | .05 |
| ❑ 586 Fred Lynn | .01 | .05 |
| ❑ 587 Jose Offerman UER | .05 | .15 |
| ❑ 588 Mark Whiten FTC | .01 | .05 |
| ❑ 589 Scott Ruskin | .01 | .05 |
| ❑ 590 Eddie Murray | .08 | .25 |
| ❑ 591 Ken Hill | .01 | .05 |
| ❑ 592 B.J. Surhoff | .02 | .10 |
| ❑ 593A Mike Walker ERR ('90 Canton-Akron stat line omit) | .08 | .25 |
| ❑ 593B Mike Walker COR | .01 | .05 |
| ❑ 594 Rich Garces RC | .02 | .10 |
| ❑ 595 Bill Landrum | .01 | .05 |
| ❑ 596 Ronnie Walden RC | .02 | .10 |
| ❑ 597 Jerry Don Gleaton | .01 | .05 |
| ❑ 598 Sam Horn | .01 | .05 |
| ❑ 599A Greg Myers ERR ('90 Syracuse stat line omitted) | .08 | .25 |
| ❑ 599B Greg Myers COR | .01 | .05 |
| ❑ 600 Bo Jackson | .08 | .25 |
| ❑ 601 Bob Ojeda | .01 | .05 |
| ❑ 602 Casey Candaele | .01 | .05 |
| ❑ 603A Wes Chamberlain ERR | .15 | .40 |
| ❑ 603B Wes Chamberlain COR RC | .02 | .10 |
| ❑ 604 Billy Hatcher | .01 | .05 |
| ❑ 605 Jeff Reardon | .02 | .10 |
| ❑ 606 Jim Gott | .01 | .05 |
| ❑ 607 Edgar Martinez | .05 | .15 |
| ❑ 608 Todd Burns | .01 | .05 |
| ❑ 609 Jeff Torborg MG | .01 | .05 |
| ❑ 610 Andres Galarraga | .01 | .05 |
| ❑ 611 Dave Eiland | .01 | .05 |
| ❑ 612 Steve Lyons | .01 | .05 |
| ❑ 613 Eric Show | .01 | .05 |
| ❑ 614 Luis Salazar | .01 | .05 |

|  |  | | |
|---|---|---|---|
| 615 | Bert Blyleven | .02 | .10 |
| 616 | Todd Zeile | .01 | .05 |
| 617 | Bill Wegman | .01 | .05 |
| 618 | Sil Campusano | .01 | .05 |
| 619 | David Wells | .02 | .10 |
| 620 | Ozzie Guillen | .02 | .10 |
| 621 | Ted Power | .01 | .05 |
| 622 | Jack Daugherty | .01 | .05 |
| 623 | Jeff Blauser | .01 | .05 |
| 624 | Tom Candiotti | .01 | .05 |
| 625 | Terry Steinbach | .01 | .05 |
| 626 | Gerald Young | .01 | .05 |
| 627 | Tim Layana | .01 | .05 |
| 628 | Greg Litton | .01 | .05 |
| 629 | Wes Gardner | .01 | .05 |
| 630 | Dave Winfield | .02 | .10 |
| 631 | Mike Morgan | .01 | .05 |
| 632 | Lloyd Moseby | .01 | .05 |
| 633 | Kevin Tapani | .01 | .05 |
| 634 | Henry Cotto | .01 | .05 |
| 635 | Andy Hawkins | .01 | .05 |
| 636 | Geronimo Pena | .01 | .05 |
| 637 | Bruce Ruffin | .01 | .05 |
| 638 | Mike Macfarlane | .01 | .05 |
| 639 | Frank Robinson MG | .05 | .15 |
| 640 | Andre Dawson | .02 | .10 |
| 641 | Mike Henneman | .01 | .05 |
| 642 | Hal Morris | .01 | .05 |
| 643 | Jim Presley | .01 | .05 |
| 644 | Chuck Crim | .01 | .05 |
| 645 | Juan Samuel | .01 | .05 |
| 646 | Andujar Cedeno | .01 | .05 |
| 647 | Mark Portugal | .01 | .05 |
| 648 | Lee Stevens | .01 | .05 |
| 649 | Bill Sampen | .01 | .05 |
| 650 | Jack Clark | .02 | .10 |
| 651 | Allan Mills | .01 | .05 |
| 652 | Kevin Romine | .01 | .05 |
| 653 | Anthony Telford RC | .01 | .05 |
| 654 | Paul Sorrento | .01 | .05 |
| 655 | Erik Hanson | .01 | .05 |
| 656a | Checklist 5 ERR 348 Vicente Palacios 381 Jose Li | .08 | .25 |
| 656b | Checklist 5 ERR 433 Vicente Palacios (Palacios s | .08 | .25 |
| 656c | Checklist 5 COR 438 Vicente Palacios 537 Jose Li | .01 | .05 |
| 657 | Mike Kingery | .01 | .05 |
| 658 | Scott Aldred | .01 | .05 |
| 659 | Oscar Azocar | .01 | .05 |
| 660 | Lee Smith | .02 | .10 |
| 661 | Steve Lake | .01 | .05 |
| 662 | Ron Dibble | .02 | .10 |
| 663 | Greg Brock | .01 | .05 |
| 664 | John Farrell | .01 | .05 |
| 665 | Mike LaValliere | .01 | .05 |
| 666 | Danny Darwin | .01 | .05 |
| 667 | Kent Anderson | .01 | .05 |
| 668 | Bill Long | .01 | .05 |
| 669 | Lou Piniella MG | .02 | .10 |
| 670 | Rickey Henderson | .08 | .25 |
| 671 | Andy McGaffigan | .01 | .05 |
| 672 | Shane Mack | .01 | .05 |
| 673 | Greg Olson UER (6 RBI in '88 at Tide-water and | .01 | .05 |
| 674a | Kevin Gross ERR (89 BB with Phillies in '88 tied | .08 | .25 |
| 674b | Kevin Gross COR (89 BB with Phillies in '88 led | .01 | .05 |
| 675 | Tom Brunansky | .01 | .05 |
| 676 | Scott Chiamparino | .01 | .05 |
| 677 | Billy Ripken | .01 | .05 |
| 678 | Mark Davidson | .01 | .05 |
| 679 | Bill Bathe | .01 | .05 |
| 680 | David Cone | .02 | .10 |
| 681 | Jeff Schaefer | .01 | .05 |
| 682 | Ray Lankford | .02 | .10 |
| 683 | Derek Lilliquist | .01 | .05 |
| 684 | Milt Cuyler | .01 | .05 |
| 685 | Doug Drabek | .01 | .05 |
| 686 | Mike Gallego | .01 | .05 |
| 687a | John Cerutti ERR (4.46 ERA in '90) | .08 | .25 |
| 687b | John Cerutti COR (4.78 ERA in '90) | .01 | .05 |
| 688 | Rosario Rodriguez RC | .01 | .05 |
| 689 | John Kruk | .02 | .10 |
| 690 | Orel Hershiser | .02 | .10 |
| 691 | Mike Blowers | .01 | .05 |
| 692a | Efrain Valdez ERR | .08 | .25 |
| 692b | Efrain Valdez COR RC | .01 | .05 |
| 693 | Francisco Cabrera | .01 | .05 |
| 694 | Randy Veres | .01 | .05 |
| 695 | Kevin Seitzer | .01 | .05 |
| 696 | Steve Olin | .01 | .05 |
| 697 | Shawn Abner | .01 | .05 |
| 698 | Mark Guthrie | .01 | .05 |
| 699 | Jim Lefebvre MG | .01 | .05 |
| 700 | Jose Canseco | .05 | .15 |
| 701 | Pascual Perez | .01 | .05 |
| 702 | Tim Naehring | .01 | .05 |
| 703 | Juan Agosto | .01 | .05 |
| 704 | Devon White | .02 | .10 |
| 705 | Robby Thompson | .01 | .05 |
| 706a | Brad Arnsberg ERR | .08 | .25 |
| 706b | Brad Arnsberg COR | .01 | .05 |
| 707 | Jim Eisenreich | .01 | .05 |
| 708 | John Mitchell | .01 | .05 |
| 709 | Matt Sinatro | .01 | .05 |
| 710 | Kent Hrbek | .02 | .10 |
| 711 | Jose DeLeon | .01 | .05 |
| 712 | Ricky Jordan | .01 | .05 |
| 713 | Scott Scudder | .01 | .05 |
| 714 | Marvell Wynne | .01 | .05 |
| 715 | Tim Burke | .01 | .05 |
| 716 | Bob Geren | .01 | .05 |
| 717 | Phil Bradley | .01 | .05 |
| 718 | Steve Crawford | .01 | .05 |
| 719 | Keith Miller | .01 | .05 |
| 720 | Cecil Fielder | .02 | .10 |
| 721 | Mark Lee RC | .01 | .05 |
| 722 | Wally Backman | .01 | .05 |
| 723 | Candy Maldonado | .01 | .05 |
| 724 | David Segui | .01 | .05 |
| 725 | Ron Gant | .02 | .10 |
| 726 | Phil Stephenson | .01 | .05 |
| 727 | Mookie Wilson | .01 | .05 |
| 728 | Scott Sanderson | .01 | .05 |
| 729 | Don Zimmer MG | .02 | .10 |
| 730 | Barry Larkin | .05 | .15 |
| 731 | Jeff Gray RC | .01 | .05 |
| 732 | Franklin Stubbs | .01 | .05 |
| 733 | Kelly Downs | .01 | .05 |
| 734 | John Russell | .01 | .05 |
| 735 | Ron Darling | .01 | .05 |
| 736 | Dick Schofield | .01 | .05 |
| 737 | Tim Crews | .01 | .05 |
| 738 | Mel Hall | .01 | .05 |
| 739 | Russ Swan | .01 | .05 |
| 740 | Ryne Sandberg | .15 | .40 |
| 741 | Jimmy Key | .01 | .05 |
| 742 | Tommy Gregg | .01 | .05 |
| 743 | Bryn Smith | .01 | .05 |
| 744 | Nelson Santovenia | .01 | .05 |
| 745 | Doug Jones | .01 | .05 |
| 746 | John Shelby | .01 | .05 |
| 747 | Tony Fossas | .01 | .05 |
| 748 | Al Newman | .01 | .05 |
| 749 | Greg W. Harris | .01 | .05 |
| 750 | Bobby Bonilla | .02 | .10 |
| 751 | Wayne Edwards | .01 | .05 |
| 752 | Kevin Bass | .01 | .05 |
| 753 | Paul Marak UER RC | .01 | .05 |
| 754 | Bill Pecota | .01 | .05 |
| 755 | Mark Langston | .01 | .05 |
| 756 | Jeff Huson | .01 | .05 |
| 757 | Mark Gardner | .01 | .05 |
| 758 | Mike Devereaux | .01 | .05 |
| 759 | Bobby Cox MG | .01 | .05 |
| 760 | Benny Santiago | .02 | .10 |
| 761 | Larry Andersen | .01 | .05 |
| 762 | Mitch Webster | .01 | .05 |
| 763 | Dana Kiecker | .01 | .05 |
| 764 | Mark Carreon | .01 | .05 |
| 765 | Shawon Dunston | .01 | .05 |
| 766 | Jeff Robinson | .01 | .05 |
| 767 | Dan Wilson RC | .08 | .25 |
| 768 | Don Pall | .01 | .05 |
| 769 | Tim Sherrill | .01 | .05 |
| 770 | Jay Howell | .01 | .05 |
| 771 | Gary Redus UER (Born in Tanner's should say Athen | .01 | .05 |
| 772 | Kent Mercker (Born in Indianapolis, should say D | .01 | .05 |
| 773 | Tom Foley | .01 | .05 |
| 774 | Dennis Rasmussen | .01 | .05 |
| 775 | Julio Franco | .02 | .10 |
| 776 | Brent Mayne | .01 | .05 |
| 777 | John Candelaria | .01 | .05 |
| 778 | Dan Gladden | .01 | .05 |
| 779 | Carmelo Martinez | .01 | .05 |
| 780a | Randy Myers ERR (15 career losses) | .15 | .40 |
| 780b | Randy Myers COR (19 career losses) | .01 | .05 |
| 781 | Darryl Hamilton | .01 | .05 |
| 782 | Jim Deshaies | .01 | .05 |
| 783 | Joel Skinner | .01 | .05 |
| 784 | Willie Fraser | .01 | .05 |
| 785 | Scott Fletcher | .01 | .05 |
| 786 | Eric Plunk | .01 | .05 |
| 787 | Checklist 6 | .01 | .05 |
| 788 | Bob Milacki | .01 | .05 |
| 789 | Tom Lasorda MG | .08 | .25 |
| 790 | Ken Griffey Jr. | .30 | .75 |
| 791 | Mike Benjamin | .01 | .05 |
| 792 | Greg Greenwell | .01 | .05 |

## 1992 Topps

| | | | |
|---|---|---|---|
| | COMPLETE SET (792) | 10.00 | 25.00 |
| | COMP.FACT.SET (802) | 10.00 | 25.00 |
| | COMP.HOLIDAY SET (811) | 15.00 | 40.00 |
| 1 | Nolan Ryan | .40 | 1.00 |
| 2 | Rickey Henderson RB | .05 | .15 |
| 3 | Jeff Reardon RB | .01 | .05 |
| 4 | Nolan Ryan RB | .20 | .50 |
| 5 | Dave Winfield RB | .01 | .05 |
| 6 | Brien Taylor RC | .08 | .25 |
| 7 | Jim Olander | .01 | .05 |
| 8 | Bryan Hickerson RC | .02 | .10 |
| 9 | Jon Farrell RC | .02 | .10 |
| 10 | Wade Boggs | .05 | .15 |
| 11 | Jack McDowell | .02 | .10 |
| 12 | Luis Gonzalez | .02 | .10 |
| 13 | Mike Scioscia | .01 | .05 |
| 14 | Wes Chamberlain | .02 | .10 |
| 15 | Dennis Martinez | .02 | .10 |
| 16 | Jeff Montgomery | .01 | .05 |
| 17 | Randy Milligan | .01 | .05 |
| 18 | Greg Cadaret | .01 | .05 |
| 19 | Jamie Quirk | .01 | .05 |
| 20 | Bip Roberts | .01 | .05 |
| 21 | Buck Rodgers MG | .01 | .05 |
| 22 | Bill Wegman | .01 | .05 |
| 23 | Chuck Knoblauch | .02 | .10 |
| 24 | Randy Myers | .01 | .05 |
| 25 | Ron Gant | .02 | .10 |
| 26 | Mike Bielecki | .01 | .05 |
| 27 | Juan Gonzalez | .05 | .15 |
| 28 | Mike Schooler | .01 | .05 |
| 29 | Mickey Tettleton | .01 | .05 |
| 30 | John Kruk | .02 | .10 |
| 31 | Bryn Smith | .01 | .05 |
| 32 | Chris Nabholz | .01 | .05 |
| 33 | Carlos Baerga | .04 | .10 |
| 34 | Jeff Juden | .01 | .05 |
| 35 | Dave Righetti | .02 | .10 |
| 36 | Scott Ruffcorn RC | .02 | .10 |
| 37 | Luis Polonia | .01 | .05 |
| 38 | Tom Candiotti | .01 | .05 |
| 39 | Greg Olson | .01 | .05 |
| 40 | Cal Ripken/Gehrig | .75 | 2.00 |

|  |  | | |
|---|--------|------|------|
| 41 | Craig Lefferts | .01 | .05 |
| 42 | Mike Macfarlane | .01 | .05 |
| 43 | Jose Lind | .01 | .05 |
| 44 | Rick Aguilera | .02 | .10 |
| 45 | Gary Carter | .02 | .10 |
| 46 | Steve Farr | .01 | .05 |
| 47 | Rex Hudler | .01 | .05 |
| 48 | Scott Scudder | .01 | .05 |
| 49 | Damon Berryhill | .01 | .05 |
| 50 | Ken Griffey Jr. | .15 | .40 |
| 51 | Tom Runnells MG | .01 | .05 |
| 52 | Juan Bell | .01 | .05 |
| 53 | Tommy Gregg | .01 | .05 |
| 54 | David Wells | .02 | .10 |
| 55 | Rafael Palmeiro | .05 | .15 |
| 56 | Charlie O'Brien | .01 | .05 |
| 57 | Donn Pall | .01 | .05 |
| 58 | Brad Ausmus RC | .60 | 1.50 |
| 59 | Mo Vaughn | .02 | .10 |
| 60 | Tony Fernandez | .01 | .05 |
| 61 | Paul O'Neill | .05 | .15 |
| 62 | Gene Nelson | .01 | .05 |
| 63 | Randy Ready | .01 | .05 |
| 64 | Bob Kipper | .01 | .05 |
| 65 | Willie McGee | .02 | .10 |
| 66 | Scott Stahoviak RC | .02 | .10 |
| 67 | Luis Salazar | .01 | .05 |
| 68 | Marvin Freeman | .01 | .05 |
| 69 | Kenny Lofton | .05 | .15 |
| 70 | Gary Gaetti | .02 | .10 |
| 71 | Erik Hanson | .01 | .05 |
| 72 | Eddie Zosky | .01 | .05 |
| 73 | Brian Barnes | .01 | .05 |
| 74 | Scott Leius | .01 | .05 |
| 75 | Brel Saberhagen | .02 | .10 |
| 76 | Mike Gallego | .01 | .05 |
| 77 | Jack Armstrong | .01 | .05 |
| 78 | Ivan Rodriguez | .08 | .25 |
| 79 | Jesse Orosco | .01 | .05 |
| 80 | David Justice | .02 | .10 |
| 81 | Ced Landrum | .01 | .05 |
| 82 | Doug Simons | .01 | .05 |
| 83 | Tommy Greene | .01 | .05 |
| 84 | Leo Gomez | .01 | .05 |
| 85 | Jose DeLeon | .01 | .05 |
| 86 | Steve Finley | .02 | .10 |
| 87 | Bob MacDonald | .01 | .05 |
| 88 | Darrin Jackson | .01 | .05 |
| 89 | Neal Heaton | .01 | .05 |
| 90 | Robin Yount | .15 | .40 |
| 91 | Jeff Reed | .01 | .05 |
| 92 | Lenny Harris | .01 | .05 |
| 93 | Reggie Jefferson | .01 | .05 |
| 94 | Sammy Sosa | .08 | .25 |
| 95 | Scott Bailes | .01 | .05 |
| 96 | Tom McKinnon RC | .02 | .10 |
| 97 | Luis Rivera | .01 | .05 |
| 98 | Mike Harkey | .01 | .05 |
| 99 | Jeff Treadway | .01 | .05 |
| 100 | Jose Canseco | .05 | .15 |
| 101 | Omar Vizquel | .05 | .15 |
| 102 | Scott Kamieniecki | .01 | .05 |
| 103 | Ricky Jordan | .01 | .05 |
| 104 | Jeff Ballard | .01 | .05 |
| 105 | Felix Jose | .01 | .05 |
| 106 | Mike Boddicker | .01 | .05 |
| 107 | Dan Pasqua | .01 | .05 |
| 108 | Mike Timlin | .01 | .05 |
| 109 | Roger Craig MG | .01 | .05 |
| 110 | Ryne Sandberg | .15 | .40 |
| 111 | Mark Carreon | .01 | .05 |
| 112 | Oscar Azocar | .01 | .05 |
| 113 | Mike Greenwell | .01 | .05 |
| 114 | Mark Portugal | .01 | .05 |
| 115 | Terry Pendleton | .02 | .10 |
| 116 | Willie Randolph | .02 | .10 |
| 117 | Scott Terry | .01 | .05 |
| 118 | Chili Davis | .02 | .10 |
| 119 | Mark Gardner | .01 | .05 |
| 120 | Alan Trammell | .02 | .10 |
| 121 | Derek Bell | .02 | .10 |
| 122 | Gary Varsho | .01 | .05 |
| 123 | Bob Ojeda | .01 | .05 |
| 124 | Shawn Livsey RC | .02 | .10 |
| 125 | Chris Hoiles | .01 | .05 |
| 126 | Klesko/Jaha/Brogna/Staton | .08 | .25 |
| 127 | Carlos Quintana | .01 | .05 |
| 128 | Kurt Stillwell | .01 | .05 |
| 129 | Melido Perez | .01 | .05 |
| 130 | Alvin Davis | .01 | .05 |
| 131 | Checklist 1-132 | .01 | .05 |
| 132 | Eric Show | .01 | .05 |
| 133 | Rance Mulliniks | .01 | .05 |
| 134 | Darryl Kile | .02 | .10 |
| 135 | Von Hayes | .01 | .05 |
| 136 | Bill Doran | .01 | .05 |
| 137 | Jeff D. Robinson | .01 | .05 |
| 138 | Monty Fariss | .01 | .05 |
| 139 | Jeff Innis | .01 | .05 |
| 140 | Mark Grace UER | .05 | .15 |
| 141 | Jim Leyland MG UER (No closed parenthesis after | .02 | .10 |
| 142 | Todd Van Poppel | .02 | .10 |
| 143 | Paul Gibson | .01 | .05 |
| 144 | Bill Swift | .01 | .05 |
| 145 | Danny Tartabull | .01 | .05 |
| 146 | Al Newman | .01 | .05 |
| 147 | Cris Carpenter | .01 | .05 |
| 148 | Anthony Young | .01 | .05 |
| 149 | Brian Bohanon | .01 | .05 |
| 150 | Roger Clemens | .20 | .50 |
| 151 | Jeff Hamilton | .01 | .05 |
| 152 | Charlie Leibrandt | .01 | .05 |
| 153 | Ron Karkovice | .01 | .05 |
| 154 | Hensley Meulens | .01 | .05 |
| 155 | Scott Bankhead | .01 | .05 |
| 156 | Manny Ramirez RC | 2.00 | 5.00 |
| 157 | Keith Miller | .01 | .05 |
| 158 | Todd Frohwirth | .01 | .05 |
| 159 | Darrin Fletcher | .01 | .05 |
| 160 | Bobby Bonilla | .02 | .10 |
| 161 | Casey Candaele | .01 | .05 |
| 162 | Paul Faries | .01 | .05 |
| 163 | Dana Kiecker | .01 | .05 |
| 164 | Shane Mack | .01 | .05 |
| 165 | Mark Langston | .01 | .05 |
| 166 | Geronimo Pena | .01 | .05 |
| 167 | Andy Allanson | .01 | .05 |
| 168 | Dwight Smith | .01 | .05 |
| 169 | Chuck Crim | .01 | .05 |
| 170 | Alex Cole | .01 | .05 |
| 171 | Bill Plummer MG | .01 | .05 |
| 172 | Juan Berenguer | .01 | .05 |
| 173 | Brian Downing | .01 | .05 |
| 174 | Steve Frey | .01 | .05 |
| 175 | Orel Hershiser | .02 | .10 |
| 176 | Ramon Garcia | .01 | .05 |
| 177 | Dan Gladden | .01 | .05 |
| 178 | Jim Acker | .01 | .05 |
| 179 | DeJard/Bem/Moreno/Stank | .01 | .05 |
| 180 | Kevin Mitchell | .02 | .10 |
| 181 | Hector Villanueva | .01 | .05 |
| 182 | Jeff Reardon | .02 | .10 |
| 183 | Brent Mayne | .01 | .05 |
| 184 | Jimmy Jones | .01 | .05 |
| 185 | Benito Santiago | .02 | .10 |
| 186 | Cliff Floyd RC | .30 | .75 |
| 187 | Ernie Riles | .01 | .05 |
| 188 | Jose Guzman | .01 | .05 |
| 189 | Junior Felix | .01 | .05 |
| 190 | Glenn Davis | .01 | .05 |
| 191 | Charlie Hough | .02 | .10 |
| 192 | Dave Fleming | .01 | .05 |
| 193 | Omar Olivares | .01 | .05 |
| 194 | Eric Karros | .02 | .10 |
| 195 | David Cone | .02 | .10 |
| 196 | Frank Castillo | .01 | .05 |
| 197 | Glenn Braggs | .01 | .05 |
| 198 | Scott Aldred | .01 | .05 |
| 199 | Jeff Blauser | .01 | .05 |
| 200 | Len Dykstra | .02 | .10 |
| 201 | Buck Showalter MG RC | .08 | .25 |
| 202 | Rick Honeycutt | .01 | .05 |
| 203 | Greg Myers | .01 | .05 |
| 204 | Trevor Wilson | .01 | .05 |
| 205 | Jay Howell | .01 | .05 |
| 206 | Luis Sojo | .01 | .05 |
| 207 | Jack Clark | .02 | .10 |
| 208 | Julio Machado | .01 | .05 |
| 209 | Lloyd McClendon | .01 | .05 |
| 210 | Ozzie Guillen | .02 | .10 |
| 211 | Jeremy Hernandez RC | .02 | .10 |
| 212 | Randy Velarde | .01 | .05 |
| 213 | Les Lancaster | .01 | .05 |
| 214 | Andy Mota | .01 | .05 |
| 215 | Rich Gossage | .02 | .10 |
| 216 | Brent Gates RC | .02 | .10 |
| 217 | Brian Harper | .01 | .05 |
| 218 | Mike Flanagan | .01 | .05 |
| 219 | Jerry Browne | .01 | .05 |
| 220 | Jose Rijo | .01 | .05 |
| 221 | Skeeter Barnes | .01 | .05 |
| 222 | Jaime Navarro | .01 | .05 |
| 223 | Mel Hall | .01 | .05 |
| 224 | Bret Barberie | .01 | .05 |
| 225 | Roberto Alomar | .05 | .15 |
| 226 | Pete Smith | .01 | .05 |
| 227 | Daryl Boston | .01 | .05 |
| 228 | Eddie Whitson | .01 | .05 |
| 229 | Shawn Boskie | .01 | .05 |
| 230 | Dick Schofield | .01 | .05 |
| 231 | Brian Drahman | .01 | .05 |
| 232 | John Smiley | .01 | .05 |
| 233 | Mitch Webster | .01 | .05 |
| 234 | Terry Steinbach | .01 | .05 |
| 235 | Jack Morris | .02 | .10 |
| 236 | Bill Pecota | .01 | .05 |
| 237 | Jose Hernandez RC | .08 | .25 |
| 238 | Greg Litton | .01 | .05 |
| 239 | Brian Holman | .01 | .05 |
| 240 | Andres Galarraga | .02 | .10 |
| 241 | Gerald Young | .01 | .05 |
| 242 | Mike Mussina | .08 | .25 |
| 243 | Alvaro Espinoza | .01 | .05 |
| 244 | Darren Daulton | .05 | .15 |
| 245 | John Smoltz | .05 | .15 |
| 246 | Jason Pruitt RC | .02 | .10 |
| 247 | Chuck Finley | .02 | .10 |
| 248 | Jim Gantner | .01 | .05 |
| 249 | Tony Fossas | .01 | .05 |
| 250 | Ken Griffey Sr. | .02 | .10 |
| 251 | Kevin Elster | .01 | .05 |
| 252 | Dennis Rasmussen | .01 | .05 |
| 253 | Terry Kennedy | .01 | .05 |
| 254 | Ryan Bowen | .01 | .05 |
| 255 | Robin Ventura | .05 | .15 |
| 256 | Mike Aldrete | .01 | .05 |
| 257 | Jeff Russell | .01 | .05 |
| 258 | Jim Lindeman | .01 | .05 |
| 259 | Ron Darling | .01 | .05 |
| 260 | Devon White | .02 | .10 |
| 261 | Tom Lasorda MG | .02 | .10 |
| 262 | Terry Lee | .01 | .05 |
| 263 | Bob Patterson | .01 | .05 |
| 264 | Checklist 133-264 | .01 | .05 |
| 265 | Teddy Higuera | .01 | .05 |
| 266 | Roberto Kelly | .01 | .05 |
| 267 | Steve Bedrosian | .01 | .05 |
| 268 | Brady Anderson | .02 | .10 |
| 269 | Ruben Amaro | .01 | .05 |
| 270 | Tony Gwynn | .10 | .30 |
| 271 | Tracy Jones | .01 | .05 |
| 272 | Jerry Don Gleaton | .01 | .05 |
| 273 | Craig Grebeck | .01 | .05 |
| 274 | Bob Scanlan | .01 | .05 |
| 275 | Todd Zeile | .01 | .05 |
| 276 | Shawn Green RC | .40 | 1.00 |
| 277 | Scott Chiamparino | .01 | .05 |
| 278 | Darryl Hamilton | .01 | .05 |
| 279 | Jim Clancy | .01 | .05 |
| 280 | Carlos Martinez | .01 | .05 |
| 281 | Kevin Appier | .02 | .10 |
| 282 | John Wehner | .01 | .05 |
| 283 | Reggie Sanders | .02 | .10 |
| 284 | Gene Larkin | .01 | .05 |
| 285 | Bob Welch | .01 | .05 |
| 286 | Gilberto Reyes | .01 | .05 |
| 287 | Pete Schourek | .01 | .05 |
| 288 | Andujar Cedeno | .01 | .05 |
| 289 | Mike Morgan | .01 | .05 |
| 290 | Bo Jackson | .08 | .25 |
| 291 | Phil Garner MG | .02 | .10 |
| 292 | Ray Lankford | .02 | .10 |
| 293 | Mike Henneman | .01 | .05 |
| 294 | Dave Valle | .01 | .05 |
| 295 | Alonzo Powell | .01 | .05 |
| 296 | Tom Brunansky | .02 | .10 |
| 297 | Kevin Brown | .02 | .10 |
| 298 | Kelly Gruber | .01 | .05 |
| 299 | Charles Nagy | .05 | .15 |
| 300 | Don Mattingly | .25 | .60 |
| 301 | Kirk McCaskill | .01 | .05 |
| 302 | Joey Cora | .01 | .05 |

|  |  | | |
|---|--------|----|----|
| 303 | Dan Plesac | .01 | .05 |
| 304 | Joe Oliver | .01 | .05 |
| 305 | Tom Glavine | .05 | .15 |
| 306 | Al Shirley RC | .02 | .10 |
| 307 | Bruce Ruffin | .01 | .05 |
| 308 | Craig Shipley | .01 | .05 |
| 309 | Dave Martinez | .01 | .05 |
| 310 | Jose Mesa | .01 | .05 |
| 311 | Henry Cotto | .01 | .05 |
| 312 | Mike LaValliere | .01 | .05 |
| 313 | Kevin Tapani | .01 | .05 |
| 314 | Jeff Huson | .01 | .05 |
| 315 | Juan Samuel | .01 | .05 |
| 316 | Curt Schilling | .05 | .15 |
| 317 | Mike Bordick | .01 | .05 |
| 318 | Steve Howe | .01 | .05 |
| 319 | Tony Phillips | .01 | .05 |
| 320 | George Bell | .01 | .05 |
| 321 | Lou Piniella MG | .02 | .10 |
| 322 | Tim Burke | .01 | .05 |
| 323 | Milt Thompson | .01 | .05 |
| 324 | Danny Darwin | .01 | .05 |
| 325 | Joe Orsulak | .01 | .05 |
| 326 | Eric King | .01 | .05 |
| 327 | Jay Buhner | .02 | .10 |
| 328 | Joel Johnston | .01 | .05 |
| 329 | Franklin Stubbs | .01 | .05 |
| 330 | Will Clark | .05 | .15 |
| 331 | Steve Lake | .01 | .05 |
| 332 | Chris Jones | .01 | .05 |
| 333 | Pat Tabler | .01 | .05 |
| 334 | Kevin Gross | .01 | .05 |
| 335 | Dave Henderson | .01 | .05 |
| 336 | Greg Anthony RC | .02 | .10 |
| 337 | Alejandro Pena | .01 | .05 |
| 338 | Shawn Abner | .01 | .05 |
| 339 | Tom Browning | .01 | .05 |
| 340 | Otis Nixon | .01 | .05 |
| 341 | Bob Geren | .01 | .05 |
| 342 | Tim Spehr | .01 | .05 |
| 343 | John Vander Wal | .01 | .05 |
| 344 | Jack Daugherty | .01 | .05 |
| 345 | Zane Smith | .01 | .05 |
| 346 | Rheal Cormier | .01 | .05 |
| 347 | Kent Hrbek | .02 | .10 |
| 348 | Rick Wilkins | .01 | .05 |
| 349 | Steve Lyons | .01 | .05 |
| 350 | Gregg Olson | .01 | .05 |
| 351 | Greg Riddoch MG | .01 | .05 |
| 352 | Ed Nunez | .01 | .05 |
| 353 | Braulio Castillo | .01 | .05 |
| 354 | Dave Bergman | .01 | .05 |
| 355 | Warren Newson | .01 | .05 |
| 356 | Luis Quinones | .01 | .05 |
| 357 | Mike Witt | .01 | .05 |
| 358 | Ted Wood | .01 | .05 |
| 359 | Mike Moore | .01 | .05 |
| 360 | Lance Parrish | .02 | .10 |
| 361 | Barry Jones | .01 | .05 |
| 362 | Javier Ortiz | .01 | .05 |
| 363 | John Candelaria | .01 | .05 |
| 364 | Glenallen Hill | .01 | .05 |
| 365 | Duane Ward | .01 | .05 |
| 366 | Checklist 265-396 | .01 | .05 |
| 367 | Rafael Belliard | .01 | .05 |
| 368 | Bill Krueger | .01 | .05 |
| 369 | Steve Whitaker RC | .02 | .10 |
| 370 | Shawon Dunston | .01 | .05 |
| 371 | Dante Bichette | .02 | .10 |
| 372 | Kip Gross | .01 | .05 |
| 373 | Don Robinson | .01 | .05 |
| 374 | Bernie Williams | .05 | .15 |
| 375 | Bert Blyleven | .02 | .10 |
| 376 | Chris Donnels | .01 | .05 |
| 377 | Bob Zupcic RC | .02 | .10 |
| 378 | Joel Skinner | .01 | .05 |
| 379 | Steve Chitren | .01 | .05 |
| 380 | Barry Bonds | .40 | 1.00 |
| 381 | Sparky Anderson MG | .02 | .10 |
| 382 | Sid Fernandez | .01 | .05 |
| 383 | Dave Hollins | .05 | .15 |
| 384 | Mark Lee | .01 | .05 |
| 385 | Tim Wallach | .01 | .05 |
| 386 | Will Clark AS | .02 | .10 |
| 387 | Ryne Sandberg AS | .08 | .25 |
| 388 | Howard Johnson AS | .01 | .05 |
| 389 | Barry Larkin AS | .02 | .10 |
| 390 | Barry Bonds AS | .20 | .50 |
| 391 | Ron Gant AS | .01 | .05 |
| 392 | Bobby Bonilla AS | .01 | .05 |
| 393 | Craig Biggio AS | .02 | .10 |
| 394 | Dennis Martinez AS | .01 | .05 |
| 395 | Tom Glavine AS | .02 | .10 |
| 396 | Lee Smith AS | .01 | .05 |
| 397 | Cecil Fielder AS | .01 | .05 |
| 398 | Julio Franco AS | .01 | .05 |
| 399 | Wade Boggs AS | .02 | .10 |
| 400 | Cal Ripken AS | .15 | .40 |
| 401 | Jose Canseco AS | .05 | .15 |
| 402 | Joe Carter AS | .05 | .15 |
| 403 | Ruben Sierra AS | .01 | .05 |
| 404 | Matt Nokes AS | .01 | .05 |
| 405 | Roger Clemens AS | .08 | .25 |
| 406 | Jim Abbott AS | .02 | .10 |
| 407 | Bryan Harvey AS | .01 | .05 |
| 408 | Bob Milacki | .01 | .05 |
| 409 | Geno Petralli | .01 | .05 |
| 410 | Dave Stewart | .02 | .10 |
| 411 | Mike Jackson | .01 | .05 |
| 412 | Luis Aquino | .01 | .05 |
| 413 | Tim Teufel | .01 | .05 |
| 414 | Jeff Ware | .01 | .05 |
| 415 | Jim Deshaies | .01 | .05 |
| 416 | Ellis Burks | .02 | .10 |
| 417 | Allan Anderson | .01 | .05 |
| 418 | Alfredo Griffin | .01 | .05 |
| 419 | Wally Whitehurst | .01 | .05 |
| 420 | Sandy Alomar Jr. | .01 | .05 |
| 421 | Juan Agosto | .01 | .05 |
| 422 | Sam Horn | .01 | .05 |
| 423 | Jeff Fassero | .01 | .05 |
| 424 | Paul McClellan | .01 | .05 |
| 425 | Cecil Fielder | .05 | .15 |
| 426 | Tim Raines | .02 | .10 |
| 427 | Eddie Taubensee RC | .08 | .25 |
| 428 | Dennis Boyd | .01 | .05 |
| 429 | Tony LaRussa MG | .02 | .10 |
| 430 | Steve Sax | .01 | .05 |
| 431 | Tom Gordon | .01 | .05 |
| 432 | Billy Hatcher | .01 | .05 |
| 433 | Cal Eldred | .01 | .05 |
| 434 | Wally Backman | .01 | .05 |
| 435 | Mark Eichhorn | .01 | .05 |
| 436 | Mookie Wilson | .02 | .10 |
| 437 | Scott Servais | .01 | .05 |
| 438 | Mike Maddux | .01 | .05 |
| 439 | Chico Walker | .01 | .05 |
| 440 | Doug Drabek | .01 | .05 |
| 441 | Rob Deer | .01 | .05 |
| 442 | Dave West | .01 | .05 |
| 443 | Spike Owen | .01 | .05 |
| 444 | Tyrone Hill RC | .02 | .10 |
| 445 | Matt Williams | .02 | .10 |
| 446 | Mark Lewis | .01 | .05 |
| 447 | David Segui | .01 | .05 |
| 448 | Tom Pagnozzi | .01 | .05 |
| 449 | Jeff Johnson | .01 | .05 |
| 450 | Mark McGwire | .25 | .60 |
| 451 | Tom Henke | .01 | .05 |
| 452 | Wilson Alvarez | .01 | .05 |
| 453 | Gary Redus | .01 | .05 |
| 454 | Darren Holmes | .01 | .05 |
| 455 | Pete O'Brien | .01 | .05 |
| 456 | Pat Combs | .01 | .05 |
| 457 | Hubie Brooks | .01 | .05 |
| 458 | Frank Tanana | .01 | .05 |
| 459 | Tom Kelly MG | .01 | .05 |
| 460 | Andre Dawson | .02 | .10 |
| 461 | Doug Jones | .01 | .05 |
| 462 | Rich Rodriguez | .01 | .05 |
| 463 | Mike Simms | .01 | .05 |
| 464 | Mike Jeffcoat | .01 | .05 |
| 465 | Barry Larkin | .05 | .15 |
| 466 | Stan Belinda | .01 | .05 |
| 467 | Lonnie Smith | .01 | .05 |
| 468 | Greg Harris | .01 | .05 |
| 469 | Jim Eisenreich | .01 | .05 |
| 470 | Pedro Guerrero | .02 | .10 |
| 471 | Jose DeJesus | .01 | .05 |
| 472 | Rich Rowland RC | .02 | .10 |
| 473 | Bolick/Paquette/Red/Russo | .02 | .10 |
| 474 | Mike Rossiter RC | .02 | .10 |
| 475 | Robby Thompson | .01 | .05 |
| 476 | Randy Bush | .01 | .05 |
| 477 | Greg Hibbard | .01 | .05 |
| 478 | Dale Sveum | .01 | .05 |
| 479 | Chito Martinez | .01 | .05 |
| 480 | Scott Sanderson | .01 | .05 |
| 481 | Tino Martinez | .05 | .15 |
| 482 | Jimmy Key | .02 | .10 |
| 483 | Terry Shumpert | .01 | .05 |
| 484 | Mike Hartley | .01 | .05 |
| 485 | Chris Sabo | .01 | .05 |
| 486 | Bob Walk | .01 | .05 |
| 487 | John Cerutti | .01 | .05 |
| 488 | Scott Cooper | .01 | .05 |
| 489 | Bobby Cox MG | .02 | .10 |
| 490 | Julio Franco | .02 | .10 |
| 491 | Jeff Brantley | .01 | .05 |
| 492 | Mike Devereaux | .01 | .05 |
| 493 | Jose Offerman | .01 | .05 |
| 494 | Gary Thurman | .01 | .05 |
| 495 | Carney Lansford | .02 | .10 |
| 496 | Joe Grahe | .01 | .05 |
| 497 | Andy Ashby | .01 | .05 |
| 498 | Gerald Perry | .01 | .05 |
| 499 | Dave Otto | .01 | .05 |
| 500 | Vince Coleman | .01 | .05 |
| 501 | Rob Mallicoat | .01 | .05 |
| 502 | Greg Briley | .01 | .05 |
| 503 | Pascual Perez | .01 | .05 |
| 504 | Aaron Sele RC | .08 | .25 |
| 505 | Bobby Thigpen | .01 | .05 |
| 506 | Todd Benzinger | .01 | .05 |
| 507 | Candy Maldonado | .01 | .05 |
| 508 | Bill Gullickson | .01 | .05 |
| 509 | Doug Dascenzo | .01 | .05 |
| 510 | Frank Viola | .02 | .10 |
| 511 | Kenny Rogers | .02 | .10 |
| 512 | Mike Heath | .01 | .05 |
| 513 | Kevin Bass | .01 | .05 |
| 514 | Kim Batiste | .01 | .05 |
| 515 | Delino DeShields | .01 | .05 |
| 516 | Ed Sprague | .01 | .05 |
| 517 | Jim Gott | .01 | .05 |
| 518 | Jose Melendez | .01 | .05 |
| 519 | Hal McRae MG | .02 | .10 |
| 520 | Jeff Bagwell | .08 | .25 |
| 521 | Joe Hesketh | .01 | .05 |
| 522 | Milt Cuyler | .01 | .05 |
| 523 | Shawn Hillegas | .01 | .05 |
| 524 | Don Slaught | .01 | .05 |
| 525 | Randy Johnson | .08 | .25 |
| 526 | Doug Piatt | .01 | .05 |
| 527 | Checklist 397-528 | .01 | .05 |
| 528 | Steve Foster | .01 | .05 |
| 529 | Joe Girardi | .01 | .05 |
| 530 | Jim Abbott | .05 | .15 |
| 531 | Larry Walker | .05 | .15 |
| 532 | Mike Huff | .01 | .05 |
| 533 | Mackey Sasser | .01 | .05 |
| 534 | Benji Gil RC | .08 | .25 |
| 535 | Dave Stieb | .01 | .05 |
| 536 | Willie Wilson | .01 | .05 |
| 537 | Mark Leiter | .01 | .05 |
| 538 | Jose Uribe | .01 | .05 |
| 539 | Thomas Howard | .01 | .05 |
| 540 | Ben McDonald | .01 | .05 |
| 541 | Jose Tolentino | .01 | .05 |
| 542 | Keith Mitchell | .01 | .05 |
| 543 | Jerome Walton | .01 | .05 |
| 544 | Cliff Brantley | .01 | .05 |
| 545 | Andy Van Slyke | .05 | .15 |
| 546 | Paul Sorrento | .01 | .05 |
| 547 | Herm Winningham | .01 | .05 |
| 548 | Mark Guthrie | .01 | .05 |
| 549 | Joe Torre MG | .02 | .10 |
| 550 | Darryl Strawberry | .02 | .10 |
| 551 | Chipper Jones | .08 | .25 |
| 552 | Dave Gallagher | .01 | .05 |
| 553 | Edgar Martinez | .05 | .15 |
| 554 | Donald Harris | .01 | .05 |
| 555 | Frank Thomas | .08 | .25 |
| 556 | Storm Davis | .01 | .05 |
| 557 | Dickie Thon | .01 | .05 |
| 558 | Scott Garrelts | .01 | .05 |
| 559 | Steve Olin | .01 | .05 |
| 560 | Rickey Henderson | .08 | .25 |
| 561 | Jose Vizcaino | .01 | .05 |
| 562 | Wade Taylor | .01 | .05 |
| 563 | Pat Borders | .01 | .05 |
| 564 | Jimmy Gonzalez RC | .02 | .10 |
| 565 | Lee Smith | .02 | .10 |
| 566 | Bill Sampen | .01 | .05 |

|  |  | | |
|---|--------|----|----|
| ❑ 567 | Dean Palmer | .02 | .10 |
| ❑ 568 | Bryan Harvey | .01 | .05 |
| ❑ 569 | Tony Pena | .01 | .05 |
| ❑ 570 | Lou Whitaker | .02 | .10 |
| ❑ 571 | Randy Tomlin | .01 | .05 |
| ❑ 572 | Greg Vaughn | .01 | .05 |
| ❑ 573 | Kelly Downs | .01 | .05 |
| ❑ 574 | Steve Avery UER | .01 | .05 |
| ❑ 575 | Kirby Puckett | .08 | .25 |
| ❑ 576 | Heathcliff Slocumb | .01 | .05 |
| ❑ 577 | Kevin Seitzer | .01 | .05 |
| ❑ 578 | Lee Guetterman | .01 | .05 |
| ❑ 579 | Johnny Oates MG | .01 | .05 |
| ❑ 580 | Greg Maddux | .15 | .40 |
| ❑ 581 | Stan Javier | .01 | .05 |
| ❑ 582 | Vicente Palacios | .01 | .05 |
| ❑ 583 | Mel Rojas | .01 | .05 |
| ❑ 584 | Wayne Rosenthal RC | .02 | .10 |
| ❑ 585 | Lenny Webster | .01 | .05 |
| ❑ 586 | Rod Nichols | .01 | .05 |
| ❑ 587 | Mickey Morandini | .01 | .05 |
| ❑ 588 | Russ Swan | .01 | .05 |
| ❑ 589 | Mariano Duncan | .01 | .05 |
| ❑ 590 | Howard Johnson | .01 | .05 |
| ❑ 591 | Sid Bumitz/Brum/Coc/Dozier | .02 | .10 |
| ❑ 592 | Denny Neagle | .02 | .10 |
| ❑ 593 | Steve Decker | .01 | .05 |
| ❑ 594 | Brian Barber RC | .02 | .10 |
| ❑ 595 | Bruce Hurst | .01 | .05 |
| ❑ 596 | Kent Mercker | .01 | .05 |
| ❑ 597 | Mike Magnante RC | .02 | .10 |
| ❑ 598 | Jody Reed | .01 | .05 |
| ❑ 599 | Steve Searcy | .01 | .05 |
| ❑ 600 | Paul Molitor | .05 | .15 |
| ❑ 601 | Dave Smith | .01 | .05 |
| ❑ 602 | Mike Fetters | .01 | .05 |
| ❑ 603 | Luis Mercedes | .01 | .05 |
| ❑ 604 | Chris Gwynn | .01 | .05 |
| ❑ 605 | Scott Erickson | .01 | .05 |
| ❑ 606 | Brook Jacoby | .01 | .05 |
| ❑ 607 | Todd Stottlemyre | .01 | .05 |
| ❑ 608 | Scott Bradley | .01 | .05 |
| ❑ 609 | Mike Hargrove MG | .02 | .10 |
| ❑ 610 | Eric Davis | .02 | .10 |
| ❑ 611 | Brian Hunter | .01 | .05 |
| ❑ 612 | Pat Kelly | .01 | .05 |
| ❑ 613 | Pedro Munoz | .01 | .05 |
| ❑ 614 | Al Osuna | .01 | .05 |
| ❑ 615 | Matt Merullo | .01 | .05 |
| ❑ 616 | Larry Andersen | .01 | .05 |
| ❑ 617 | Junior Ortiz | .01 | .05 |
| ❑ 618 | Hosey/McNeely/Pelt | .05 | .15 |
| ❑ 619 | Danny Jackson | .01 | .05 |
| ❑ 620 | George Brett | .25 | .60 |
| ❑ 621 | Dan Gakeler | .01 | .05 |
| ❑ 622 | Steve Buechele | .01 | .05 |
| ❑ 623 | Bob Tewksbury | .01 | .05 |
| ❑ 624 | Shawn Estes RC | .08 | .25 |
| ❑ 625 | Kevin McReynolds | .01 | .05 |
| ❑ 626 | Chris Haney | .01 | .05 |
| ❑ 627 | Mike Sharperson | .01 | .05 |
| ❑ 628 | Mark Williamson | .01 | .05 |
| ❑ 629 | Wally Joyner | .02 | .10 |
| ❑ 630 | Carlton Fisk | .05 | .15 |
| ❑ 631 | Armando Reynoso RC | .08 | .25 |
| ❑ 632 | Felix Fermin | .01 | .05 |
| ❑ 633 | Mitch Williams | .01 | .05 |
| ❑ 634 | Manuel Lee | .01 | .05 |
| ❑ 635 | Harold Baines | .02 | .10 |
| ❑ 636 | Greg Harris | .01 | .05 |
| ❑ 637 | Orlando Merced | .01 | .05 |
| ❑ 638 | Chris Bosio | .01 | .05 |
| ❑ 639 | Wayne Housie | .01 | .05 |
| ❑ 640 | Xavier Hernandez | .01 | .05 |
| ❑ 641 | David Howard | .01 | .05 |
| ❑ 642 | Tim Crews | .01 | .05 |
| ❑ 643 | Rick Cerone | .01 | .05 |
| ❑ 644 | Terry Leach | .01 | .05 |
| ❑ 645 | Deion Sanders | .05 | .15 |
| ❑ 646 | Craig Wilson | .01 | .05 |
| ❑ 647 | Marquis Grissom | .02 | .10 |
| ❑ 648 | Scott Fletcher | .01 | .05 |
| ❑ 649 | Norm Charlton | .01 | .05 |
| ❑ 650 | Jesse Barfield | .01 | .05 |
| ❑ 651 | Joe Slusarski | .01 | .05 |
| ❑ 652 | Bobby Rose | .01 | .05 |
| ❑ 653 | Dennis Lamp | .01 | .05 |
| ❑ 654 | Allen Watson RC | .02 | .10 |

|  |  | | |
|---|--------|----|----|
| ❑ 655 | Brett Butler | .02 | .10 |
| ❑ 656 | Pem/H.Rod/Tinsley/G.Will | .02 | .10 |
| ❑ 657 | Dave Johnson | .01 | .05 |
| ❑ 658 | Checklist 529-660 | .01 | .05 |
| ❑ 659 | Brian McRae | .01 | .05 |
| ❑ 660 | Fred McGriff | .05 | .15 |
| ❑ 661 | Bill Landrum | .01 | .05 |
| ❑ 662 | Juan Guzman | .05 | .15 |
| ❑ 663 | Greg Gagne | .01 | .05 |
| ❑ 664 | Ken Hill | .01 | .05 |
| ❑ 665 | Dave Haas | .01 | .05 |
| ❑ 666 | Tom Foley | .01 | .05 |
| ❑ 667 | Roberto Hernandez | .01 | .05 |
| ❑ 668 | Dwayne Henry | .01 | .05 |
| ❑ 669 | Jim Fregosi MG | .02 | .10 |
| ❑ 670 | Harold Reynolds | .01 | .05 |
| ❑ 671 | Mark Whiten | .01 | .05 |
| ❑ 672 | Eric Plunk | .01 | .05 |
| ❑ 673 | Todd Hundley | .01 | .05 |
| ❑ 674 | Mo Sanford | .01 | .05 |
| ❑ 675 | Bobby Witt | .01 | .05 |
| ❑ 676 | Mill/Mahomes/Wendell/Salk | .08 | .25 |
| ❑ 677 | John Marzano | .01 | .05 |
| ❑ 678 | Joe Klink | .01 | .05 |
| ❑ 679 | Pete Incaviglia | .01 | .05 |
| ❑ 680 | Dale Murphy | .05 | .15 |
| ❑ 681 | Rene Gonzales | .01 | .05 |
| ❑ 682 | Andy Benes | .01 | .05 |
| ❑ 683 | Jim Poole | .01 | .05 |
| ❑ 684 | Trever Miller RC | .02 | .10 |
| ❑ 685 | Scott Livingstone | .01 | .05 |
| ❑ 686 | Rich DeLucia | .01 | .05 |
| ❑ 687 | Harvey Pulliam | .01 | .05 |
| ❑ 688 | Tim Belcher | .01 | .05 |
| ❑ 689 | Mark Lemke | .01 | .05 |
| ❑ 690 | John Franco | .02 | .10 |
| ❑ 691 | Walt Weiss | .01 | .05 |
| ❑ 692 | Scott Ruskin | .01 | .05 |
| ❑ 693 | Jeff King | .01 | .05 |
| ❑ 694 | Mike Gardiner | .01 | .05 |
| ❑ 695 | Gary Sheffield | .02 | .10 |
| ❑ 696 | Joe Boever | .01 | .05 |
| ❑ 697 | Mike Felder | .01 | .05 |
| ❑ 698 | John Habyan | .01 | .05 |
| ❑ 699 | Cito Gaston MG | .01 | .05 |
| ❑ 700 | Ruben Sierra | .02 | .10 |
| ❑ 701 | Scott Radinsky | .01 | .05 |
| ❑ 702 | Lee Stevens | .01 | .05 |
| ❑ 703 | Mark Wohlers | .01 | .05 |
| ❑ 704 | Curt Young | .01 | .05 |
| ❑ 705 | Dwight Evans | .05 | .15 |
| ❑ 706 | Rob Murphy | .01 | .05 |
| ❑ 707 | Gregg Jefferies | .01 | .05 |
| ❑ 708 | Tom Bolton | .01 | .05 |
| ❑ 709 | Chris James | .01 | .05 |
| ❑ 710 | Kevin Maas | .01 | .05 |
| ❑ 711 | Ricky Bones | .01 | .05 |
| ❑ 712 | Curt Wilkerson | .01 | .05 |
| ❑ 713 | Roger McDowell | .01 | .05 |
| ❑ 714 | Pokey Reese RC | .08 | .25 |
| ❑ 715 | Craig Biggio | .05 | .15 |
| ❑ 716 | Kirk Dressendorfer | .01 | .05 |
| ❑ 717 | Ken Dayley | .01 | .05 |
| ❑ 718 | B.J. Surhoff | .02 | .10 |
| ❑ 719 | Terry Mulholland | .01 | .05 |
| ❑ 720 | Kirk Gibson | .02 | .10 |
| ❑ 721 | Mike Pagliarulo | .01 | .05 |
| ❑ 722 | Walt Terrell | .01 | .05 |
| ❑ 723 | Jose Oquendo | .01 | .05 |
| ❑ 724 | Kevin Morton | .01 | .05 |
| ❑ 725 | Dwight Gooden | .02 | .10 |
| ❑ 726 | Ken Mamearing | .01 | .05 |
| ❑ 727 | Chuck McElroy | .01 | .05 |
| ❑ 728 | Dave Burba | .01 | .05 |
| ❑ 729 | Art Howe MG | .01 | .05 |
| ❑ 730 | Ramon Martinez | .01 | .05 |
| ❑ 731 | Donnie Hill | .01 | .05 |
| ❑ 732 | Nelson Santovenia | .01 | .05 |
| ❑ 733 | Bob Melvin | .01 | .05 |
| ❑ 734 | Scott Hatteberg RC | .08 | .25 |
| ❑ 735 | Greg Swindell | .01 | .05 |
| ❑ 736 | Lance Johnson | .01 | .05 |
| ❑ 737 | Kevin Reimer | .01 | .05 |
| ❑ 738 | Dennis Eckersley | .02 | .10 |
| ❑ 739 | Rob Ducey | .01 | .05 |
| ❑ 740 | Ken Caminiti | .02 | .10 |
| ❑ 741 | Mark Gubicza | .01 | .05 |
| ❑ 742 | Bill Spiers | .01 | .05 |

|  |  | | |
|---|--------|----|----|
| ❑ 743 | Darren Lewis | .01 | .05 |
| ❑ 744 | Chris Hammond | .01 | .05 |
| ❑ 745 | Dave Magadan | .01 | .05 |
| ❑ 746 | Bernard Gilkey | .01 | .05 |
| ❑ 747 | Willie Banks | .01 | .05 |
| ❑ 748 | Matt Nokes | .01 | .05 |
| ❑ 749 | Jerald Clark | .01 | .05 |
| ❑ 750 | Travis Fryman | .02 | .10 |
| ❑ 751 | Steve Wilson | .01 | .05 |
| ❑ 752 | Billy Ripken | .01 | .05 |
| ❑ 753 | Paul Assenmacher | .01 | .05 |
| ❑ 754 | Charlie Hayes | .01 | .05 |
| ❑ 755 | Alex Fernandez | .01 | .05 |
| ❑ 756 | Gary Pettis | .01 | .05 |
| ❑ 757 | Rob Dibble | .02 | .10 |
| ❑ 758 | Tim Naehring | .01 | .05 |
| ❑ 759 | Jeff Torborg MG | .01 | .05 |
| ❑ 760 | Ozzie Smith | .15 | .40 |
| ❑ 761 | Mike Fitzgerald | .01 | .05 |
| ❑ 762 | John Burkett | .01 | .05 |
| ❑ 763 | Kyle Abbott | .01 | .05 |
| ❑ 764 | Tyler Green RC | .02 | .10 |
| ❑ 765 | Pete Harnisch | .01 | .05 |
| ❑ 766 | Mark Davis | .01 | .05 |
| ❑ 767 | Kal Daniels | .01 | .05 |
| ❑ 768 | Jim Thome | .08 | .25 |
| ❑ 769 | Jack Howell | .01 | .05 |
| ❑ 770 | Sid Bream | .01 | .05 |
| ❑ 771 | Arthur Rhodes | .01 | .05 |
| ❑ 772 | Garry Templeton UER<br>(Stat heading in for pitchers | .01 | .05 |
| ❑ 773 | Hal Morris | .01 | .05 |
| ❑ 774 | Bud Black | .01 | .05 |
| ❑ 775 | Ivan Calderon | .01 | .05 |
| ❑ 776 | Doug Henry RC | .02 | .10 |
| ❑ 777 | John Olerud | .02 | .10 |
| ❑ 778 | Tim Leary | .01 | .05 |
| ❑ 779 | Jay Bell | .02 | .10 |
| ❑ 780 | Eddie Murray | .08 | .25 |
| ❑ 781 | Paul Abbott | .01 | .05 |
| ❑ 782 | Phil Plantier | .01 | .05 |
| ❑ 783 | Joe Magrane | .01 | .05 |
| ❑ 784 | Ken Patterson | .01 | .05 |
| ❑ 785 | Albert Belle | .02 | .10 |
| ❑ 786 | Royce Clayton | .01 | .05 |
| ❑ 787 | Checklist 661-792 | .01 | .05 |
| ❑ 788 | Mike Stanton | .01 | .05 |
| ❑ 789 | Bobby Valentine MG | .01 | .05 |
| ❑ 790 | Joe Carter | .02 | .10 |
| ❑ 791 | Danny Cox | .01 | .05 |
| ❑ 792 | Dave Winfield | .02 | .10 |

## 1993 Topps

|  | | |
|-----|----|----|
| ❑ COMPLETE SET (825) | 20.00 | 50.00 |
| ❑ COMP.HOBBY SET (847) | 30.00 | 60.00 |
| ❑ COMP.RETAIL SET (838) | 20.00 | 50.00 |
| ❑ COMPLETE SERIES 1 (396) | 10.00 | 25.00 |
| ❑ COMPLETE SERIES 2 (429) | 10.00 | 25.00 |
| ❑ 1 Robin Yount | .30 | .75 |
| ❑ 2 Barry Bonds | .60 | 1.50 |
| ❑ 3 Ryne Sandberg | .30 | .75 |
| ❑ 4 Roger Clemens | .40 | 1.00 |
| ❑ 5 Tony Gwynn | .25 | .60 |
| ❑ 6 Jeff Tackett | .02 | .10 |
| ❑ 7 Pete Incaviglia | .02 | .10 |
| ❑ 8 Mark Wohlers | .02 | .10 |
| ❑ 9 Kent Hrbek | .07 | .20 |
| ❑ 10 Will Clark | .10 | .30 |
| ❑ 11 Eric Karros | .07 | .20 |
| ❑ 12 Lee Smith | .07 | .20 |
| ❑ 13 Esteban Beltre | .02 | .10 |
| ❑ 14 Greg Briley | .02 | .10 |
| ❑ 15 Marquis Grissom | .07 | .20 |
| ❑ 16 Dan Plesac | .02 | .10 |

|  |  | | |
|---|---|---|---|
| ❑ 17 | Dave Hollins | .02 | .10 |
| ❑ 18 | Terry Steinbach | .02 | .10 |
| ❑ 19 | Ed Nunez | .02 | .10 |
| ❑ 20 | Tim Salmon | .10 | .30 |
| ❑ 21 | Luis Salazar | .02 | .10 |
| ❑ 22 | Jim Eisenreich | .02 | .10 |
| ❑ 23 | Todd Stottlemyre | .02 | .10 |
| ❑ 24 | Tim Naehring | .07 | .20 |
| ❑ 25 | John Franco | .02 | .10 |
| ❑ 26 | Skeeter Barnes | .02 | .10 |
| ❑ 27 | Carlos Garcia | .02 | .10 |
| ❑ 28 | Joe Orsulak | .02 | .10 |
| ❑ 29 | Dwayne Henry | .02 | .10 |
| ❑ 30 | Fred McGriff | .10 | .30 |
| ❑ 31 | Derek Lilliquist | .02 | .10 |
| ❑ 32 | Don Mattingly | .50 | 1.25 |
| ❑ 33 | B.J. Wallace | .02 | .10 |
| ❑ 34 | Juan Gonzalez | .07 | .20 |
| ❑ 35 | John Smoltz | .10 | .30 |
| ❑ 36 | Scott Servais | .02 | .10 |
| ❑ 37 | Lenny Webster | .02 | .10 |
| ❑ 38 | Chris James | .02 | .10 |
| ❑ 39 | Roger McDowell | .02 | .10 |
| ❑ 40 | Ozzie Smith | .30 | .75 |
| ❑ 41 | Alex Fernandez | .02 | .10 |
| ❑ 42 | Spike Owen | .02 | .10 |
| ❑ 43 | Ruben Amaro | .02 | .10 |
| ❑ 44 | Kevin Seitzer | .02 | .10 |
| ❑ 45 | Dave Fleming | .02 | .10 |
| ❑ 46 | Eric Fox | .02 | .10 |
| ❑ 47 | Bob Scanlan | .07 | .20 |
| ❑ 48 | Bert Blyleven | .07 | .20 |
| ❑ 49 | Brian McRae | .02 | .10 |
| ❑ 50 | Roberto Alomar | .10 | .30 |
| ❑ 51 | Mo Vaughn | .07 | .20 |
| ❑ 52 | Bobby Bonilla | .07 | .20 |
| ❑ 53 | Frank Tanana | .02 | .10 |
| ❑ 54 | Mike LaValliere | .02 | .10 |
| ❑ 55 | Mark McLemore | .02 | .10 |
| ❑ 56 | Chad Mottola RC | .10 | .30 |
| ❑ 57 | Norm Charlton | .02 | .10 |
| ❑ 58 | Jose Melendez | .02 | .10 |
| ❑ 59 | Carlos Martinez | .02 | .10 |
| ❑ 60 | Roberto Kelly | .07 | .20 |
| ❑ 61 | Gene Larkin | .02 | .10 |
| ❑ 62 | Rafael Belliard | .02 | .10 |
| ❑ 63 | Al Osuna | .02 | .10 |
| ❑ 64 | Scott Chiamparino | .02 | .10 |
| ❑ 65 | Brett Butler | .07 | .20 |
| ❑ 66 | John Burkett | .02 | .10 |
| ❑ 67 | Felix Jose | .02 | .10 |
| ❑ 68 | Omar Vizquel | .10 | .30 |
| ❑ 69 | John Vander Wal | .02 | .10 |
| ❑ 70 | Roberto Hernandez | .02 | .10 |
| ❑ 71 | Ricky Bones | .02 | .10 |
| ❑ 72 | Jeff Grotewold | .02 | .10 |
| ❑ 73 | Mike Moore | .02 | .10 |
| ❑ 74 | Steve Buechele | .02 | .10 |
| ❑ 75 | Juan Guzman | .07 | .20 |
| ❑ 76 | Kevin Appier | .07 | .20 |
| ❑ 77 | Junior Felix | .02 | .10 |
| ❑ 78 | Greg W. Harris | .02 | .10 |
| ❑ 79 | Dick Schofield | .02 | .10 |
| ❑ 80 | Cecil Fielder | .07 | .20 |
| ❑ 81 | Lloyd McClendon | .02 | .10 |
| ❑ 82 | David Segui | .02 | .10 |
| ❑ 83 | Reggie Sanders | .07 | .20 |
| ❑ 84 | Kurt Stillwell | .02 | .10 |
| ❑ 85 | Sandy Alomar Jr. | .02 | .10 |
| ❑ 86 | John Habyan | .02 | .10 |
| ❑ 87 | Kevin Reimer | .02 | .10 |
| ❑ 88 | Mike Stanton | .02 | .10 |
| ❑ 89 | Eric Anthony | .02 | .10 |
| ❑ 90 | Scott Erickson | .02 | .10 |
| ❑ 91 | Craig Colbert | .02 | .10 |
| ❑ 92 | Tom Pagnozzi | .02 | .10 |
| ❑ 93 | Pedro Astacio | .07 | .20 |
| ❑ 94 | Lance Johnson | .02 | .10 |
| ❑ 95 | Larry Walker | .07 | .20 |
| ❑ 96 | Russ Swan | .02 | .10 |
| ❑ 97 | Scott Fletcher | .02 | .10 |
| ❑ 98 | Derek Jeter RC | 6.00 | 15.00 |
| ❑ 99 | Mike Williams | .02 | .10 |
| ❑ 100 | Mark McGwire | .50 | 1.25 |
| ❑ 101 | Jim Bullinger | .02 | .10 |
| ❑ 102 | Brian Hunter | .02 | .10 |
| ❑ 103 | Jody Reed | .02 | .10 |
| ❑ 104 | Mike Butcher | .02 | .10 |
| ❑ 105 | Gregg Jefferies | .02 | .10 |
| ❑ 106 | Howard Johnson | .02 | .10 |
| ❑ 107 | John Kiely | .02 | .10 |
| ❑ 108 | Jose Lind | .02 | .10 |
| ❑ 109 | Sam Horn | .02 | .10 |
| ❑ 110 | Barry Larkin | .10 | .30 |
| ❑ 111 | Bruce Hurst | .02 | .10 |
| ❑ 112 | Brian Barnes | .02 | .10 |
| ❑ 113 | Thomas Howard | .02 | .10 |
| ❑ 114 | Mel Hall | .02 | .10 |
| ❑ 115 | Robby Thompson | .02 | .10 |
| ❑ 116 | Mark Lemke | .02 | .10 |
| ❑ 117 | Eddie Taubensee | .02 | .10 |
| ❑ 118 | David Hulse RC | .02 | .10 |
| ❑ 119 | Pedro Munoz | .02 | .10 |
| ❑ 120 | Ramon Martinez | .02 | .10 |
| ❑ 121 | Todd Worrell | .02 | .10 |
| ❑ 122 | Joey Cora | .02 | .10 |
| ❑ 123 | Moises Alou | .07 | .20 |
| ❑ 124 | Franklin Stubbs | .02 | .10 |
| ❑ 125 | Pete O'Brien | .02 | .10 |
| ❑ 126 | Bob Ayrault | .02 | .10 |
| ❑ 127 | Carney Lansford | .07 | .20 |
| ❑ 128 | Kal Daniels | .02 | .10 |
| ❑ 129 | Joe Grahe | .02 | .10 |
| ❑ 130 | Jeff Montgomery | .02 | .10 |
| ❑ 131 | Dave Winfield | .07 | .20 |
| ❑ 132 | Preston Wilson RC | .30 | .75 |
| ❑ 133 | Steve Wilson | .02 | .10 |
| ❑ 134 | Lee Guetterman | .02 | .10 |
| ❑ 135 | Mickey Tettleton | .02 | .10 |
| ❑ 136 | Jeff King | .02 | .10 |
| ❑ 137 | Alan Mills | .02 | .10 |
| ❑ 138 | Joe Oliver | .02 | .10 |
| ❑ 139 | Gary Gaetti | .02 | .10 |
| ❑ 140 | Gary Sheffield | .07 | .20 |
| ❑ 141 | Dennis Cook | .02 | .10 |
| ❑ 142 | Charlie Hayes | .02 | .10 |
| ❑ 143 | Jeff Huson | .02 | .10 |
| ❑ 144 | Kent Mercker | .02 | .10 |
| ❑ 145 | Eric Young | .02 | .10 |
| ❑ 146 | Scott Leius | .02 | .10 |
| ❑ 147 | Bryan Hickerson | .02 | .10 |
| ❑ 148 | Steve Finley | .07 | .20 |
| ❑ 149 | Rheal Cormier | .02 | .10 |
| ❑ 150 | Frank Thomas | .20 | .50 |
| ❑ 151 | Archi Cianfrocco | .02 | .10 |
| ❑ 152 | Rich DeLucia | .02 | .10 |
| ❑ 153 | Greg Vaughn | .02 | .10 |
| ❑ 154 | Wes Chamberlain | .02 | .10 |
| ❑ 155 | Dennis Eckersley | .07 | .20 |
| ❑ 156 | Sammy Sosa | .20 | .50 |
| ❑ 157 | Gary DiSarcina | .02 | .10 |
| ❑ 158 | Kevin Koslofski | .02 | .10 |
| ❑ 159 | Doug Linton | .02 | .10 |
| ❑ 160 | Lou Whitaker | .07 | .20 |
| ❑ 161 | Chad McConnell | .02 | .10 |
| ❑ 162 | Joe Hesketh | .02 | .10 |
| ❑ 163 | Tim Wakefield | .20 | .50 |
| ❑ 164 | Leo Gomez | .02 | .10 |
| ❑ 165 | Jose Rijo | .02 | .10 |
| ❑ 166 | Tim Scott | .02 | .10 |
| ❑ 167 | Steve Olin UER | .02 | .10 |
| ❑ 168 | Kevin Maas | .02 | .10 |
| ❑ 169 | Kenny Rogers | .07 | .20 |
| ❑ 170 | David Justice | .07 | .20 |
| ❑ 171 | Doug Jones | .02 | .10 |
| ❑ 172 | Jeff Reboulet | .02 | .10 |
| ❑ 173 | Andres Galarraga | .07 | .20 |
| ❑ 174 | Randy Velarde | .02 | .10 |
| ❑ 175 | Kirk McCaskill | .02 | .10 |
| ❑ 176 | Darren Lewis | .02 | .10 |
| ❑ 177 | Lenny Harris | .02 | .10 |
| ❑ 178 | Jeff Fassero | .02 | .10 |
| ❑ 179 | Ken Griffey Jr. | .30 | .75 |
| ❑ 180 | Darren Daulton | .07 | .20 |
| ❑ 181 | John Jaha | .02 | .10 |
| ❑ 182 | Ron Darling | .02 | .10 |
| ❑ 183 | Greg Maddux | .30 | .75 |
| ❑ 184 | Damion Easley | .02 | .10 |
| ❑ 185 | Jack Morris | .07 | .20 |
| ❑ 186 | Mike Magnante | .02 | .10 |
| ❑ 187 | John Dopson | .02 | .10 |
| ❑ 188 | Sid Fernandez | .02 | .10 |
| ❑ 189 | Tony Phillips | .02 | .10 |
| ❑ 190 | Doug Drabek | .02 | .10 |
| ❑ 191 | Sam Lowe RC | .02 | .10 |
| ❑ 192 | Bob Milacki | .02 | .10 |
| ❑ 193 | Steve Foster | .02 | .10 |
| ❑ 194 | Jerald Clark | .02 | .10 |
| ❑ 195 | Pete Harnisch | .02 | .10 |
| ❑ 196 | Pat Kelly | .02 | .10 |
| ❑ 197 | Jeff Frye | .02 | .10 |
| ❑ 198 | Alejandro Pena | .02 | .10 |
| ❑ 199 | Junior Ortiz | .02 | .10 |
| ❑ 200 | Kirby Puckett | .20 | .50 |
| ❑ 201 | Jose Uribe | .02 | .10 |
| ❑ 202 | Mike Scioscia | .02 | .10 |
| ❑ 203 | Bernard Gilkey | .02 | .10 |
| ❑ 204 | Dan Pasqua | .02 | .10 |
| ❑ 205 | Gary Carter | .07 | .20 |
| ❑ 206 | Henry Cotto | .02 | .10 |
| ❑ 207 | Paul Molitor | .07 | .20 |
| ❑ 208 | Mike Hartley | .02 | .10 |
| ❑ 209 | Jeff Parrett | .02 | .10 |
| ❑ 210 | Mark Langston | .02 | .10 |
| ❑ 211 | Doug Dascenzo | .02 | .10 |
| ❑ 212 | Rick Reed | .02 | .10 |
| ❑ 213 | Candy Maldonado | .02 | .10 |
| ❑ 214 | Danny Darwin | .02 | .10 |
| ❑ 215 | Pat Howell | .02 | .10 |
| ❑ 216 | Mark Leiter | .02 | .10 |
| ❑ 217 | Kevin Mitchell | .02 | .10 |
| ❑ 218 | Ben McDonald | .02 | .10 |
| ❑ 219 | Bip Roberts | .02 | .10 |
| ❑ 220 | Benny Santiago | .07 | .20 |
| ❑ 221 | Carlos Baerga | .02 | .10 |
| ❑ 222 | Bernie Williams | .10 | .30 |
| ❑ 223 | Roger Pavlik | .02 | .10 |
| ❑ 224 | Sid Bream | .02 | .10 |
| ❑ 225 | Matt Williams | .07 | .20 |
| ❑ 226 | Willie Banks | .02 | .10 |
| ❑ 227 | Jeff Bagwell | .10 | .30 |
| ❑ 228 | Tom Goodwin | .02 | .10 |
| ❑ 229 | Mike Perez | .02 | .10 |
| ❑ 230 | Carlton Fisk | .10 | .30 |
| ❑ 231 | John Wetteland | .07 | .20 |
| ❑ 232 | Tino Martinez | .10 | .30 |
| ❑ 233 | Rick Greene | .02 | .10 |
| ❑ 234 | Tim McIntosh | .02 | .10 |
| ❑ 235 | Mitch Williams | .02 | .10 |
| ❑ 236 | Kevin Campbell | .02 | .10 |
| ❑ 237 | Jose Vizcaino | .02 | .10 |
| ❑ 238 | Chris Donnels | .02 | .10 |
| ❑ 239 | Mike Boddicker | .02 | .10 |
| ❑ 240 | John Olerud | .07 | .20 |
| ❑ 241 | Mike Gardiner | .02 | .10 |
| ❑ 242 | Charlie O'Brien | .02 | .10 |
| ❑ 243 | Rob Deer | .02 | .10 |
| ❑ 244 | Denny Neagle | .07 | .20 |
| ❑ 245 | Chris Sabo | .02 | .10 |
| ❑ 246 | Gregg Olson | .02 | .10 |
| ❑ 247 | Frank Seminara UER | .02 | .10 |
| ❑ 248 | Scott Scudder | .02 | .10 |
| ❑ 249 | Tim Burke | .02 | .10 |
| ❑ 250 | Chuck Knoblauch | .07 | .20 |
| ❑ 251 | Mike Bielecki | .02 | .10 |
| ❑ 252 | Xavier Hernandez | .02 | .10 |
| ❑ 253 | Jose Guzman | .02 | .10 |
| ❑ 254 | Cory Snyder | .02 | .10 |
| ❑ 255 | Orel Hershiser | .07 | .20 |
| ❑ 256 | Wil Cordero | .02 | .10 |
| ❑ 257 | Luis Alicea | .02 | .10 |
| ❑ 258 | Mike Schooler | .02 | .10 |
| ❑ 259 | Craig Grebeck | .02 | .10 |
| ❑ 260 | Duane Ward | .02 | .10 |
| ❑ 261 | Bill Wegman | .02 | .10 |
| ❑ 262 | Mickey Morandini | .02 | .10 |
| ❑ 263 | Vince Horsman | .02 | .10 |
| ❑ 264 | Paul Sorrento | .02 | .10 |
| ❑ 265 | Andre Dawson | .07 | .20 |
| ❑ 266 | Rene Gonzales | .02 | .10 |
| ❑ 267 | Keith Miller | .02 | .10 |
| ❑ 268 | Derek Bell | .02 | .10 |
| ❑ 269 | Todd Steverson RC | .07 | .20 |
| ❑ 270 | Frank Viola | .07 | .20 |
| ❑ 271 | Wally Whitehurst | .02 | .10 |
| ❑ 272 | Kurt Knudsen | .02 | .10 |
| ❑ 273 | Dan Walters | .02 | .10 |
| ❑ 274 | Rick Sutcliffe | .07 | .20 |
| ❑ 275 | Andy Van Slyke | .10 | .30 |
| ❑ 276 | Paul O'Neill | .10 | .30 |
| ❑ 277 | Mark Whiten | .02 | .10 |
| ❑ 278 | Chris Nabholz | .02 | .10 |
| ❑ 279 | Todd Burns | .02 | .10 |
| ❑ 280 | Tom Glavine | .10 | .30 |

|  |  | | |
|---|---|---|---|
| 281 | Butch Henry | .02 | .10 |
| 282 | Shane Mack | .02 | .10 |
| 283 | Mike Jackson | .02 | .10 |
| 284 | Henry Rodriguez | .02 | .10 |
| 285 | Bob Tewksbury | .02 | .10 |
| 286 | Ron Karkovice | .02 | .10 |
| 287 | Mike Gallego | .02 | .10 |
| 288 | Dave Cochrane | .02 | .10 |
| 289 | Jesse Orosco | .02 | .10 |
| 290 | Dave Stewart | .07 | .20 |
| 291 | Tommy Greene | .02 | .10 |
| 292 | Rey Sanchez | .02 | .10 |
| 293 | Rob Ducey | .02 | .10 |
| 294 | Brent Mayne | .02 | .10 |
| 295 | Dave Stieb | .02 | .10 |
| 296 | Luis Rivera | .02 | .10 |
| 297 | Jeff Innis | .02 | .10 |
| 298 | Scott Livingstone | .02 | .10 |
| 299 | Bob Patterson | .02 | .10 |
| 300 | Cal Ripken | .60 | 1.50 |
| 301 | Cesar Hernandez | .02 | .10 |
| 302 | Randy Myers | .02 | .10 |
| 303 | Brook Jacoby | .02 | .10 |
| 304 | Melido Perez | .02 | .10 |
| 305 | Rafael Palmeiro | .10 | .30 |
| 306 | Damon Berryhill | .02 | .10 |
| 307 | Dan Serafini RC | .10 | .30 |
| 308 | Darryl Kile | .07 | .20 |
| 309 | J.T. Bruett | .02 | .10 |
| 310 | Dave Righetti | .07 | .20 |
| 311 | Jay Howell | .02 | .10 |
| 312 | Geronimo Pena | .02 | .10 |
| 313 | Greg Hibbard | .02 | .10 |
| 314 | Mark Gardner | .02 | .10 |
| 315 | Edgar Martinez | .10 | .30 |
| 316 | Dave Nilsson | .02 | .10 |
| 317 | Kyle Abbott | .02 | .10 |
| 318 | Willie Wilson | .02 | .10 |
| 319 | Paul Assenmacher | .02 | .10 |
| 320 | Tim Fortugno | .02 | .10 |
| 321 | Rusty Meacham | .02 | .10 |
| 322 | Pat Borders | .02 | .10 |
| 323 | Mike Greenwell | .02 | .10 |
| 324 | Willie Randolph | .07 | .20 |
| 325 | Bill Gullickson | .02 | .10 |
| 326 | Gary Varsho | .02 | .10 |
| 327 | Tim Hulett | .02 | .10 |
| 328 | Scott Ruskin | .02 | .10 |
| 329 | Mike Maddux | .02 | .10 |
| 330 | Danny Tartabull | .02 | .10 |
| 331 | Kenny Lofton | .07 | .20 |
| 332 | Geno Petralli | .02 | .10 |
| 333 | Otis Nixon | .02 | .10 |
| 334 | Jason Kendall RC | .40 | 1.00 |
| 335 | Mark Portugal | .02 | .10 |
| 336 | Mike Pagliarulo | .02 | .10 |
| 337 | Kirt Manwaring | .02 | .10 |
| 338 | Bob Ojeda | .02 | .10 |
| 339 | Mark Clark | .02 | .10 |
| 340 | John Kruk | .07 | .20 |
| 341 | Mel Rojas | .02 | .10 |
| 342 | Erik Hanson | .02 | .10 |
| 343 | Doug Henry | .02 | .10 |
| 344 | Jack McDowell | .07 | .20 |
| 345 | Harold Baines | .07 | .20 |
| 346 | Chuck McElroy | .02 | .10 |
| 347 | Luis Sojo | .02 | .10 |
| 348 | Andy Stankiewicz | .02 | .10 |
| 349 | Hipolito Pichardo | .02 | .10 |
| 350 | Joe Carter | .07 | .20 |
| 351 | Ellis Burks | .07 | .20 |
| 352 | Pete Schourek | .02 | .10 |
| 353 | Buddy Groom | .02 | .10 |
| 354 | Jay Bell | .07 | .20 |
| 355 | Brady Anderson | .07 | .20 |
| 356 | Freddie Benavides | .02 | .10 |
| 357 | Phil Stephenson | .02 | .10 |
| 358 | Kevin Wickander | .02 | .10 |
| 359 | Mike Stanley | .02 | .10 |
| 360 | Ivan Rodriguez | .10 | .30 |
| 361 | Scott Bankhead | .02 | .10 |
| 362 | Luis Gonzalez | .02 | .10 |
| 363 | John Smiley | .02 | .10 |
| 364 | Trevor Wilson | .02 | .10 |
| 365 | Tom Candiotti | .02 | .10 |
| 366 | Craig Wilson | .02 | .10 |
| 367 | Steve Sax | .02 | .10 |
| 368 | Delino DeShields | .02 | .10 |
| 369 | Jaime Navarro | .02 | .10 |
| 370 | Dave Valle | .02 | .10 |
| 371 | Mariano Duncan | .02 | .10 |
| 372 | Rod Nichols | .02 | .10 |
| 373 | Mike Morgan | .02 | .10 |
| 374 | Julio Valera | .02 | .10 |
| 375 | Wally Joyner | .07 | .20 |
| 376 | Tom Henke | .02 | .10 |
| 377 | Herm Winningham | .02 | .10 |
| 378 | Orlando Merced | .02 | .10 |
| 379 | Mike Munoz | .02 | .10 |
| 380 | Todd Hundley | .02 | .10 |
| 381 | Mike Flanagan | .02 | .10 |
| 382 | Tim Belcher | .02 | .10 |
| 383 | Jerry Browne | .02 | .10 |
| 384 | Mike Benjamin | .02 | .10 |
| 385 | Jim Leyritz | .02 | .10 |
| 386 | Ray Lankford | .07 | .20 |
| 387 | Devon White | .07 | .20 |
| 388 | Jeremy Hernandez | .02 | .10 |
| 389 | Brian Harper | .02 | .10 |
| 390 | Wade Boggs | .10 | .30 |
| 391 | Derrick May | .02 | .10 |
| 392 | Travis Fryman | .07 | .20 |
| 393 | Ron Gant | .07 | .20 |
| 394 | Checklist 1-132 | .02 | .10 |
| 395 | Checklist 133-264 UER | .02 | .10 |
| 396 | Checklist 265-396 | .02 | .10 |
| 397 | George Brett | .50 | 1.25 |
| 398 | Bobby Witt | .02 | .10 |
| 399 | Daryl Boston | .02 | .10 |
| 400 | Bo Jackson | .20 | .50 |
| 401 | F.McGriff/F.Thomas AS | .10 | .30 |
| 402 | R.Sandberg/C.Baerga AS | .07 | .20 |
| 403 | G.Sheffield/E.Martinez AS | .07 | .20 |
| 404 | B.Larkin/T.Fryman AS | .07 | .20 |
| 405 | K.Griffey Jr./J.A.Van Slyke AS | .20 | .50 |
| 406 | L.Walker/K.Puckett AS | .10 | .30 |
| 407 | B.Bonds/J.Carter AS | .30 | .75 |
| 408 | D.Daulton/B.Harper AS | .07 | .20 |
| 409 | G.Maddux/R.Clemens AS | .20 | .50 |
| 410 | T.Glavine/D.Fleming AS | .07 | .20 |
| 411 | L.Smith/D.Eckersley AS | .07 | .20 |
| 412 | Jamie McAndrew | .02 | .10 |
| 413 | Pete Smith | .02 | .10 |
| 414 | Juan Guerrero | .02 | .10 |
| 415 | Todd Frohwirth | .02 | .10 |
| 416 | Randy Tomlin | .02 | .10 |
| 417 | B.J. Surhoff | .02 | .10 |
| 418 | Jim Gott | .02 | .10 |
| 419 | Mark Thompson RC | .07 | .20 |
| 420 | Kevin Tapani | .02 | .10 |
| 421 | Curt Schilling | .07 | .20 |
| 422 | J.T.Snow RC | .20 | .50 |
| 423 | Ryan Klesko | .20 | .50 |
| 424 | John Valentin | .02 | .10 |
| 425 | Joe Girardi | .02 | .10 |
| 426 | Nigel Wilson | .02 | .10 |
| 427 | Bob MacDonald | .02 | .10 |
| 428 | Todd Zeile | .02 | .10 |
| 429 | Milt Cuyler | .02 | .10 |
| 430 | Eddie Murray | .20 | .50 |
| 431 | Rich Amaral | .02 | .10 |
| 432 | Pete Young | .02 | .10 |
| 433 | Tom Schmidt RC | .02 | .10 |
| 434 | Jack Armstrong | .02 | .10 |
| 435 | Willie McGee | .07 | .20 |
| 436 | Greg W. Harris | .02 | .10 |
| 437 | Chris Hammond | .02 | .10 |
| 438 | Ritchie Moody RC | .02 | .10 |
| 439 | Bryan Harvey | .02 | .10 |
| 440 | Ruben Sierra | .07 | .20 |
| 441 | Todd Pridy RC | .02 | .10 |
| 442 | Kevin McReynolds | .02 | .10 |
| 443 | Terry Leach | .02 | .10 |
| 444 | David Nied | .02 | .10 |
| 445 | Dale Murphy | .10 | .30 |
| 446 | Luis Mercedes | .02 | .10 |
| 447 | Keith Shepherd RC | .02 | .10 |
| 448 | Ken Caminiti | .07 | .20 |
| 449 | Jim Austin | .02 | .10 |
| 450 | Darryl Strawberry | .07 | .20 |
| 451 | Quinton McCracken RC | .08 | .25 |
| 452 | Bob Wickman | .02 | .10 |
| 453 | Victor Cole | .02 | .10 |
| 454 | John Johnstone RC | .02 | .10 |
| 455 | Chili Davis | .02 | .10 |
| 456 | Scott Taylor | .02 | .10 |
| 457 | Tracy Woodson | .02 | .10 |
| 458 | David Wells | .07 | .20 |
| 459 | Derek Wallace RC | .02 | .10 |
| 460 | Randy Johnson | .20 | .50 |
| 461 | Steve Reed RC | .02 | .10 |
| 462 | Felix Fermin | .02 | .10 |
| 463 | Scott Aldred | .02 | .10 |
| 464 | Greg Colbrunn | .02 | .10 |
| 465 | Tony Fernandez | .02 | .10 |
| 466 | Mike Felder | .02 | .10 |
| 467 | Lee Stevens | .02 | .10 |
| 468 | Matt Whiteside RC | .02 | .10 |
| 469 | Dave Hansen | .02 | .10 |
| 470 | Rob Dibble | .07 | .20 |
| 471 | Dave Gallagher | .02 | .10 |
| 472 | Chris Gwynn | .02 | .10 |
| 473 | Dave Henderson | .02 | .10 |
| 474 | Ozzie Guillen | .02 | .10 |
| 475 | Jeff Reardon | .07 | .20 |
| 476 | Will Scalzitti RC | .02 | .10 |
| 477 | Jimmy Jones | .02 | .10 |
| 478 | Greg Cadaret | .02 | .10 |
| 479 | Todd Pratt RC | .02 | .10 |
| 480 | Pat Listach | .02 | .10 |
| 481 | Ryan Luzinski RC | .02 | .10 |
| 482 | Darren Reed | .02 | .10 |
| 483 | Brian Griffiths RC | .02 | .10 |
| 484 | John Wehner | .02 | .10 |
| 485 | Glenn Davis | .02 | .10 |
| 486 | Eric Wedge RC | .02 | .10 |
| 487 | Jesse Hollins | .02 | .10 |
| 488 | Manuel Lee | .02 | .10 |
| 489 | Scott Fredrickson RC | .02 | .10 |
| 490 | Omar Olivares | .02 | .10 |
| 491 | Shawn Hare | .02 | .10 |
| 492 | Tom Lampkin | .02 | .10 |
| 493 | Jeff Nelson | .02 | .10 |
| 494 | L.Lucca RC/E.Perez | .02 | .10 |
| 495 | Ken Hill | .02 | .10 |
| 496 | Reggie Jefferson | .02 | .10 |
| 497 | Willie Brown RC | .02 | .10 |
| 498 | Bud Black | .02 | .10 |
| 499 | Chuck Crim | .02 | .10 |
| 500 | Jose Canseco | .10 | .30 |
| 501 | Johnny Oates MG | | |
| | Bobby Cox MG | .07 | .20 |
| 502 | Butch Hobson MG | | |
| | Jim Lefebvre MG | .02 | .10 |
| 503 | Buck Rodgers MG | | |
| | Tony Perez MG | .07 | .20 |
| 504 | Gene Lamont MG | | |
| | Don Baylor MG | .07 | .20 |
| 505 | Mike Hargrove MG | | |
| | Rene Lachemann MG | .07 | .20 |
| 506 | Sparky Anderson MG | | |
| | Art Howe MG | .07 | .20 |
| 507 | Hal McRae MG | | |
| | Tom Lasorda MG | .07 | .20 |
| 508 | Phil Garner MG | | |
| | Felipe Alou MG | .07 | .20 |
| 509 | Tom Kelly MG | | |
| | Jeff Torborg MG | .02 | .10 |
| 510 | Buck Showalter MG | | |
| | Jim Fregosi MG | .02 | .10 |
| 511 | Tony LaRussa MG | | |
| | Jim Leyland MG | .02 | .10 |
| 512 | Lou Piniella MG | | |
| | Joe Torre MG | .07 | .20 |
| 513 | Kevin Kennedy MG | | |
| | Jim Riggleman MG | .02 | .10 |
| 514 | Cito Gaston MG | | |
| | Dusty Baker MG | .07 | .20 |
| 515 | Greg Swindell | .07 | .20 |
| 516 | Alex Arias | .02 | .10 |
| 517 | Bill Pecota | .02 | .10 |
| 518 | Benji Grigsby RC | .02 | .10 |
| 519 | David Howard | .02 | .10 |
| 520 | Charlie Hough | .07 | .20 |
| 521 | Kevin Flora | .02 | .10 |
| 522 | Shane Reynolds | .02 | .10 |
| 523 | Doug Bochtler RC | .02 | .10 |
| 524 | Chris Hoiles | .02 | .10 |
| 525 | Scott Sanderson | .02 | .10 |
| 526 | Mike Sharperson | .02 | .10 |
| 527 | Mike Fetters | .02 | .10 |
| 528 | Paul Quantrill | .02 | .10 |
| 529 | Chipper Jones | .20 | .50 |
| 530 | Sterling Hitchcock RC | .08 | .25 |

|  |  | | |
|---|---|---|---|
| 531 | Joe Millette | .02 | .10 |
| 532 | Tom Brunansky | .02 | .10 |
| 533 | Frank Castillo | .02 | .10 |
| 534 | Randy Knorr | .02 | .10 |
| 535 | Jose Oquendo | .02 | .10 |
| 536 | Dave Haas | .02 | .10 |
| 537 | Jason Hutchins RC | .02 | .10 |
| 538 | Jimmy Baron RC | .02 | .10 |
| 539 | Kerry Woodson | .02 | .10 |
| 540 | Ivan Calderon | .02 | .10 |
| 541 | Denis Boucher | .02 | .10 |
| 542 | Royce Clayton | .02 | .10 |
| 543 | Reggie Williams | .02 | .10 |
| 544 | Steve Decker | .02 | .10 |
| 545 | Dean Palmer | .07 | .20 |
| 546 | Hal Morris | .02 | .10 |
| 547 | Ryan Thompson | .02 | .10 |
| 548 | Lance Blankenship | .02 | .10 |
| 549 | Hensley Meulens | .02 | .10 |
| 550 | Scott Radinsky | .02 | .10 |
| 551 | Eric Young | .02 | .10 |
| 552 | Jeff Blauser | .02 | .10 |
| 553 | Andujar Cedeno | .02 | .10 |
| 554 | Arthur Rhodes | .02 | .10 |
| 555 | Terry Mulholland | .02 | .10 |
| 556 | Darryl Hamilton | .02 | .10 |
| 557 | Pedro Martinez | .40 | 1.00 |
| 558 | Ryan Whitman RC | .02 | .10 |
| 559 | Jamie Arnold RC | .02 | .10 |
| 560 | Zane Smith | .02 | .10 |
| 561 | Matt Nokes | .02 | .10 |
| 562 | Bob Zupcic | .02 | .10 |
| 563 | Shawn Boskie | .02 | .10 |
| 564 | Mike Timlin | .02 | .10 |
| 565 | Jerald Clark | .02 | .10 |
| 566 | Rod Brewer | .02 | .10 |
| 567 | Mark Carreon | .02 | .10 |
| 568 | Andy Benes | .02 | .10 |
| 569 | Shawn Barton RC | .02 | .10 |
| 570 | Tim Wallach | .02 | .10 |
| 571 | Dave Mlicki | .02 | .10 |
| 572 | Trevor Hoffman | .20 | .50 |
| 573 | John Patterson | .02 | .10 |
| 574 | DeShawn Warren RC | .02 | .10 |
| 575 | Monty Fariss | .02 | .10 |
| 576 | Cliff Floyd | .07 | .20 |
| 577 | Tim Costo | .02 | .10 |
| 578 | Dave Magadan | .02 | .10 |
| 579 | Jason Bates RC | .02 | .10 |
| 580 | Walt Weiss | .02 | .10 |
| 581 | Chris Haney | .02 | .10 |
| 582 | Shawn Abner | .02 | .10 |
| 583 | Marvin Freeman | .02 | .10 |
| 584 | Casey Candaele | .02 | .10 |
| 585 | Ricky Jordan | .02 | .10 |
| 586 | Jeff Tabaka RC | .02 | .10 |
| 587 | Manny Alexander | .02 | .10 |
| 588 | Mike Trombley | .02 | .10 |
| 589 | Carlos Hernandez | .02 | .10 |
| 590 | Cal Eldred | .10 | .30 |
| 591 | Alex Cole | .02 | .10 |
| 592 | Phil Plantier | .02 | .10 |
| 593 | Brett Merriman RC | .02 | .10 |
| 594 | Jerry Nielsen | .02 | .10 |
| 595 | Shawon Dunston | .02 | .10 |
| 596 | Jimmy Key | .07 | .20 |
| 597 | Gerald Perry | .02 | .10 |
| 598 | Rico Brogna | .07 | .20 |
| 599 | Clemente Nunez | .02 | .10 |
| 600 | Bret Saberhagen | .07 | .20 |
| 601 | Craig Shipley | .02 | .10 |
| 602 | Henry Mercedes | .02 | .10 |
| 603 | Jim Thome | .10 | .30 |
| 604 | Rod Beck | .02 | .10 |
| 605 | Chuck Finley | .07 | .20 |
| 606 | Jayhawk Owens RC | .02 | .10 |
| 607 | Dan Smith | .02 | .10 |
| 608 | Bill Doran | .02 | .10 |
| 609 | Lance Parrish | .07 | .20 |
| 610 | Dennis Martinez | .07 | .20 |
| 611 | Tom Gordon | .02 | .10 |
| 612 | Byron Mathews RC | .02 | .10 |
| 613 | Joel Adamson RC | .02 | .10 |
| 614 | Brian Williams | .02 | .10 |
| 615 | Steve Avery | .07 | .20 |
| 616 | Midre Cummings RC | .02 | .10 |
| 617 | Craig Lefferts | .02 | .10 |
| 618 | Tony Pena | .02 | .10 |
| 619 | Billy Spiers | .02 | .10 |
| 620 | Todd Benzinger | .02 | .10 |
| 621 | Greg Boyd RC | .02 | .10 |
| 622 | Ben Rivera | .02 | .10 |
| 623 | Al Martin | .02 | .10 |
| 624 | Sam Militello UER | .02 | .10 |
| 625 | Rick Aguilera | .02 | .10 |
| 626 | Dan Gladden | .02 | .10 |
| 627 | Andres Berumen RC | .02 | .10 |
| 628 | Kelly Gruber | .02 | .10 |
| 629 | Cris Carpenter | .02 | .10 |
| 630 | Mark Grace | .10 | .30 |
| 631 | Jeff Brantley | .02 | .10 |
| 632 | Chris Widger RC | .08 | .25 |
| 633 | Three Russians | .02 | .10 |
| 634 | Mo Sanford | .02 | .10 |
| 635 | Albert Belle | .07 | .20 |
| 636 | Tim Teufel | .02 | .10 |
| 637 | Greg Myers | .02 | .10 |
| 638 | Brian Bohanon | .02 | .10 |
| 639 | Mike Bordick | .02 | .10 |
| 640 | Dwight Gooden | .07 | .20 |
| 641 | P.Leahy/G.Baugh RC | .02 | .10 |
| 642 | Milt Hill | .02 | .10 |
| 643 | Luis Aquino | .02 | .10 |
| 644 | Dante Bichette | .07 | .20 |
| 645 | Bobby Thigpen | .02 | .10 |
| 646 | Rich Scheid RC | .02 | .10 |
| 647 | Brian Sackinsky RC | .02 | .10 |
| 648 | Ryan Hawblitzel | .02 | .10 |
| 649 | Tom Marsh | .02 | .10 |
| 650 | Terry Pendleton | .07 | .20 |
| 651 | Rafael Bournigal | .02 | .10 |
| 652 | Dave West | .02 | .10 |
| 653 | Steve Hosey | .02 | .10 |
| 654 | Gerald Williams | .02 | .10 |
| 655 | Scott Cooper | .02 | .10 |
| 656 | Gary Scott | .02 | .10 |
| 657 | Mike Harkey | .02 | .10 |
| 658 | J.Burnitz/S.Walker RC | .07 | .20 |
| 659 | Ed Sprague | .02 | .10 |
| 660 | Alan Trammell | .07 | .20 |
| 661 | Garvin Alston RC | .02 | .10 |
| 662 | Donovan Osborne | .02 | .10 |
| 663 | Jeff Gardner | .02 | .10 |
| 664 | Calvin Jones | .02 | .10 |
| 665 | Darrin Fletcher | .02 | .10 |
| 666 | Glenallen Hill | .02 | .10 |
| 667 | Jim Rosenbohm RC | .02 | .10 |
| 668 | Scott Lewis | .02 | .10 |
| 669 | Kip Yaughn RC | .02 | .10 |
| 670 | Julio Franco | .07 | .20 |
| 671 | Dave Martinez | .02 | .10 |
| 672 | Kevin Bass | .02 | .10 |
| 673 | Todd Van Poppel | .02 | .10 |
| 674 | Mark Gubicza | .02 | .10 |
| 675 | Tim Raines | .07 | .20 |
| 676 | Rudy Seanez | .02 | .10 |
| 677 | Charlie Leibrandt | .02 | .10 |
| 678 | Randy Milligan | .02 | .10 |
| 679 | Kim Batiste | .02 | .10 |
| 680 | Craig Biggio | .10 | .30 |
| 681 | Darren Holmes | .02 | .10 |
| 682 | John Candelaria | .02 | .10 |
| 683 | Eddie Christian RC | .02 | .10 |
| 684 | Pat Mahomes | .02 | .10 |
| 685 | Bob Walk | .02 | .10 |
| 686 | Russ Springer | .02 | .10 |
| 687 | Tony Sheffield UER | .02 | .10 |
| 688 | Dwight Smith | .02 | .10 |
| 689 | Eddie Zosky | .02 | .10 |
| 690 | Bien Figueroa | .02 | .10 |
| 691 | Jim Tatum RC | .02 | .10 |
| 692 | Chad Kreuter | .02 | .10 |
| 693 | Rich Rodriguez | .02 | .10 |
| 694 | Shane Turner | .02 | .10 |
| 695 | Kent Bottenfield | .02 | .10 |
| 696 | Jose Mesa | .02 | .10 |
| 697 | Darrell Whitmore RC | .02 | .10 |
| 698 | Ted Wood | .02 | .10 |
| 699 | Chad Curtis | .02 | .10 |
| 700 | Nolan Ryan | .75 | 2.00 |
| 701 | M.Piazza/C.Delgado | 1.50 | 4.00 |
| 702 | Tim Pugh RC | .02 | .10 |
| 703 | Jeff Kent | .20 | .50 |
| 704 | J.Goodrich/D.Figueroa RC | .02 | .10 |
| 705 | Bob Welch | .02 | .10 |
| 706 | Sherard Clinkscales RC | .02 | .10 |
| 707 | Donn Pall | .02 | .10 |
| 708 | Greg Olson | .02 | .10 |
| 709 | Jeff Juden | .02 | .10 |
| 710 | Mike Mussina | .10 | .30 |
| 711 | Scott Chiamparino | .02 | .10 |
| 712 | Stan Javier | .02 | .10 |
| 713 | John Doherty | .02 | .10 |
| 714 | Kevin Gross | .02 | .10 |
| 715 | Greg Gagne | .02 | .10 |
| 716 | Steve Cooke | .02 | .10 |
| 717 | Steve Farr | .02 | .10 |
| 718 | Jay Buhner | .07 | .20 |
| 719 | Butch Henry | .02 | .10 |
| 720 | David Cone | .07 | .20 |
| 721 | Rick Wilkins | .02 | .10 |
| 722 | Chuck Carr | .02 | .10 |
| 723 | Kenny Felder RC | .02 | .10 |
| 724 | Guillermo Velasquez | .02 | .10 |
| 725 | Billy Hatcher | .02 | .10 |
| 726 | Mike Veneziale RC | .02 | .10 |
| 727 | Jonathan Hurst | .02 | .10 |
| 728 | Steve Frey | .02 | .10 |
| 729 | Mark Leonard | .02 | .10 |
| 730 | Charles Nagy | .02 | .10 |
| 731 | Donald Harris | .02 | .10 |
| 732 | Travis Buckley RC | .02 | .10 |
| 733 | Tom Browning | .02 | .10 |
| 734 | Anthony Young | .02 | .10 |
| 735 | Steve Shifflett | .02 | .10 |
| 736 | Jeff Russell | .02 | .10 |
| 737 | Wilson Alvarez | .02 | .10 |
| 738 | Lance Painter RC | .02 | .10 |
| 739 | Dave Weathers | .02 | .10 |
| 740 | Len Dykstra | .07 | .20 |
| 741 | Mike Devereaux | .02 | .10 |
| 742 | R.Arrocha RC/A.Embree | .08 | .25 |
| 743 | Dave Landaker RC | .02 | .10 |
| 744 | Chris George | .02 | .10 |
| 745 | Eric Davis | .07 | .20 |
| 746 | Lamar Rogers RC | .02 | .10 |
| 747 | Carl Willis | .02 | .10 |
| 748 | Stan Belinda | .02 | .10 |
| 749 | Scott Kamieniecki | .02 | .10 |
| 750 | Rickey Henderson | .20 | .50 |
| 751 | Eric Hillman | .02 | .10 |
| 752 | Pat Hentgen | .02 | .10 |
| 753 | Jim Corsi | .02 | .10 |
| 754 | Brian Jordan | .07 | .20 |
| 755 | Bill Swift | .02 | .10 |
| 756 | Mike Henneman | .02 | .10 |
| 757 | Harold Reynolds | .07 | .20 |
| 758 | Sean Berry | .02 | .10 |
| 759 | Charlie Hayes | .02 | .10 |
| 760 | Luis Polonia | .02 | .10 |
| 761 | Darrin Jackson | .02 | .10 |
| 762 | Mark Lewis | .02 | .10 |
| 763 | Rob Maurer | .02 | .10 |
| 764 | Willie Greene | .02 | .10 |
| 765 | Vince Coleman | .02 | .10 |
| 766 | Todd Revenig | .02 | .10 |
| 767 | Rich Ireland RC | .02 | .10 |
| 768 | Mike Macfarlane | .02 | .10 |
| 769 | Francisco Cabrera | .02 | .10 |
| 770 | Robin Ventura | .07 | .20 |
| 771 | Kevin Ritz | .02 | .10 |
| 772 | Chito Martinez | .02 | .10 |
| 773 | Cliff Brantley | .02 | .10 |
| 774 | Curt Leskanic RC | .08 | .25 |
| 775 | Chris Bosio | .02 | .10 |
| 776 | Jose Offerman | .02 | .10 |
| 777 | Mark Guthrie | .02 | .10 |
| 778 | Don Slaught | .02 | .10 |
| 779 | Rich Monteleone | .02 | .10 |
| 780 | Jim Abbott | .10 | .30 |
| 781 | Jack Clark | .07 | .20 |
| 782 | R.Mendoza/D.Roman RC | .02 | .10 |
| 783 | Heathcliff Slocumb | .02 | .10 |
| 784 | Jeff Branson | .02 | .10 |
| 785 | Kevin Brown | .07 | .20 |
| 786 | K.Ryan/Gandarillas RC | .02 | .10 |
| 787 | Matt Matthews RC | .02 | .10 |
| 788 | Mackey Sasser | .02 | .10 |
| 789 | Jeff Conine UER | .07 | .20 |
| 790 | George Bell | .02 | .10 |
| 791 | Pat Rapp | .02 | .10 |
| 792 | Joe Boever | .02 | .10 |
| 793 | Jim Poole | .02 | .10 |
| 794 | Andy Ashby | .02 | .10 |

| | | |
|---|---|---|
| ❑ 795 Deion Sanders | .10 | .30 |
| ❑ 796 Scott Brosius | .07 | .20 |
| ❑ 797 Brad Pennington | .02 | .10 |
| ❑ 798 Greg Blosser | .02 | .10 |
| ❑ 799 Jim Edmonds RC | .75 | 2.00 |
| ❑ 800 Shawn Jeter | .02 | .10 |
| ❑ 801 Jesse Levis | .02 | .10 |
| ❑ 802 Phil Clark UER | .02 | .10 |
| ❑ 803 Eddie Pierce RC | .02 | .10 |
| ❑ 804 Jose Valentin RC | .08 | .25 |
| ❑ 805 Terry Jorgensen | .02 | .10 |
| ❑ 806 Mark Hutton | .02 | .10 |
| ❑ 807 Troy Neel | .02 | .10 |
| ❑ 808 Bret Boone | .07 | .20 |
| ❑ 809 Cris Colon | .02 | .10 |
| ❑ 810 Domingo Martinez RC | .02 | .10 |
| ❑ 811 Javier Lopez | .10 | .30 |
| ❑ 812 Matt Walbeck RC | .02 | .10 |
| ❑ 813 Dan Wilson | .07 | .20 |
| ❑ 814 Scooter Tucker | .02 | .10 |
| ❑ 815 Billy Ashley | .02 | .10 |
| ❑ 816 Tim Laker RC | .02 | .10 |
| ❑ 817 Bobby Jones | .07 | .20 |
| ❑ 818 Brad Brink | .02 | .10 |
| ❑ 819 William Pennyfeather | .02 | .10 |
| ❑ 820 Stan Royer | .02 | .10 |
| ❑ 821 Doug Brocail | .02 | .10 |
| ❑ 822 Kevin Rogers | .02 | .10 |
| ❑ 823 Checklist 397-540 | .02 | .10 |
| ❑ 824 Checklist 541-691 | .02 | .10 |
| ❑ 825 Checklist 692-825 | .02 | .10 |

## 1994 Topps

| | | |
|---|---|---|
| ❑ COMPLETE SET (792) | 20.00 | 50.00 |
| ❑ COMP.FACT.SET (808) | 40.00 | 80.00 |
| ❑ COMP.BAKER SET (817) | 40.00 | 80.00 |
| ❑ COMPLETE SERIES 1 (396) | 10.00 | 25.00 |
| ❑ COMPLETE SERIES 2 (396) | 10.00 | 25.00 |
| ❑ 1 Mike Piazza | .40 | 1.00 |
| ❑ 2 Bernie Williams | .10 | .30 |
| ❑ 3 Kevin Rogers | .02 | .10 |
| ❑ 4 Paul Carey | .02 | .10 |
| ❑ 5 Ozzie Guillen | .07 | .20 |
| ❑ 6 Derrick May | .02 | .10 |
| ❑ 7 Jose Mesa | .02 | .10 |
| ❑ 8 Todd Hundley | .02 | .10 |
| ❑ 9 Chris Haney | .02 | .10 |
| ❑ 10 John Olerud | .07 | .20 |
| ❑ 11 Andujar Cedeno | .02 | .10 |
| ❑ 12 John Smiley | .02 | .10 |
| ❑ 13 Phil Plantier | .02 | .10 |
| ❑ 14 Willie Banks | .02 | .10 |
| ❑ 15 Jay Bell | .07 | .20 |
| ❑ 16 Doug Henry | .02 | .10 |
| ❑ 17 Lance Blankenship | .02 | .10 |
| ❑ 18 Greg W. Harris | .02 | .10 |
| ❑ 19 Scott Livingstone | .02 | .10 |
| ❑ 20 Bryan Harvey | .02 | .10 |
| ❑ 21 Wil Cordero | .02 | .10 |
| ❑ 22 Roger Pavlik | .02 | .10 |
| ❑ 23 Mark Lemke | .02 | .10 |
| ❑ 24 Jeff Nelson | .02 | .10 |
| ❑ 25 Todd Zeile | .07 | .20 |
| ❑ 26 Billy Hatcher | .02 | .10 |
| ❑ 27 Joe Magrane | .02 | .10 |
| ❑ 28 Tony Longmire | .02 | .10 |
| ❑ 29 Omar Daal | .02 | .10 |
| ❑ 30 Kirt Manwaring | .02 | .10 |
| ❑ 31 Melido Perez | .02 | .10 |
| ❑ 32 Tim Hulett | .02 | .10 |
| ❑ 33 Jeff Schwarz | .02 | .10 |
| ❑ 34 Nolan Ryan | .75 | 2.00 |
| ❑ 35 Jose Guzman | .02 | .10 |
| ❑ 36 Felix Fermin | .02 | .10 |

| | | |
|---|---|---|
| ❑ 37 Jeff Innis | .02 | .10 |
| ❑ 38 Brett Mayne | .02 | .10 |
| ❑ 39 Huck Flener RC | .02 | .10 |
| ❑ 40 Jeff Bagwell | .10 | .30 |
| ❑ 41 Kevin Wickander | .02 | .10 |
| ❑ 42 Ricky Gutierrez | .02 | .10 |
| ❑ 43 Pat Mahomes | .02 | .10 |
| ❑ 44 Jeff King | .02 | .10 |
| ❑ 45 Cal Eldred | .02 | .10 |
| ❑ 46 Craig Paquette | .02 | .10 |
| ❑ 47 Richie Lewis | .02 | .10 |
| ❑ 48 Tony Phillips | .02 | .10 |
| ❑ 49 Armando Reynoso | .02 | .10 |
| ❑ 50 Moises Alou | .07 | .20 |
| ❑ 51 Manuel Lee | .02 | .10 |
| ❑ 52 Otis Nixon | .02 | .10 |
| ❑ 53 Billy Ashley | .02 | .10 |
| ❑ 54 Mark Whiten | .02 | .10 |
| ❑ 55 Jeff Russell | .02 | .10 |
| ❑ 56 Chad Curtis | .02 | .10 |
| ❑ 57 Kevin Stocker | .02 | .10 |
| ❑ 58 Mike Jackson | .02 | .10 |
| ❑ 59 Matt Nokes | .02 | .10 |
| ❑ 60 Chris Bosio | .02 | .10 |
| ❑ 61 Damon Buford | .02 | .10 |
| ❑ 62 Tim Belcher | .02 | .10 |
| ❑ 63 Glenallen Hill | .02 | .10 |
| ❑ 64 Bill Wertz | .02 | .10 |
| ❑ 65 Eddie Murray | .20 | .50 |
| ❑ 66 Tom Gordon | .02 | .10 |
| ❑ 67 Alex Gonzalez | .02 | .10 |
| ❑ 68 Eddie Taubensee | .02 | .10 |
| ❑ 69 Jacob Brumfield | .02 | .10 |
| ❑ 70 Andy Benes | .02 | .10 |
| ❑ 71 Rich Becker | .02 | .10 |
| ❑ 72 Steve Cooke | .02 | .10 |
| ❑ 73 Billy Spiers | .02 | .10 |
| ❑ 74 Scott Brosius | .07 | .20 |
| ❑ 75 Alan Trammell | .07 | .20 |
| ❑ 76 Luis Aquino | .02 | .10 |
| ❑ 77 Jerald Clark | .02 | .10 |
| ❑ 78 Mel Rojas | .02 | .10 |
| ❑ 79 Craig McClure RC | .02 | .10 |
| ❑ 80 Jose Canseco | .10 | .30 |
| ❑ 81 Greg McMichael | .02 | .10 |
| ❑ 82 Brian Turang RC | .02 | .10 |
| ❑ 83 Tom Urbani | .02 | .10 |
| ❑ 84 Garret Anderson | .20 | .50 |
| ❑ 85 Tony Pena | .02 | .10 |
| ❑ 86 Ricky Jordan | .02 | .10 |
| ❑ 87 Jim Gott | .02 | .10 |
| ❑ 88 Pat Kelly | .02 | .10 |
| ❑ 89 Bud Black | .02 | .10 |
| ❑ 90 Robin Ventura | .07 | .20 |
| ❑ 91 Rick Sutcliffe | .02 | .10 |
| ❑ 92 Jose Bautista | .02 | .10 |
| ❑ 93 Bob Ojeda | .02 | .10 |
| ❑ 94 Phil Hiatt | .02 | .10 |
| ❑ 95 Tim Pugh | .02 | .10 |
| ❑ 96 Randy Knorr | .02 | .10 |
| ❑ 97 Todd Jones | .02 | .10 |
| ❑ 98 Ryan Thompson | .02 | .10 |
| ❑ 99 Tim Mauser | .02 | .10 |
| ❑ 100 Kirby Puckett | .20 | .50 |
| ❑ 101 Mark Dewey | .02 | .10 |
| ❑ 102 B.J. Surhoff | .07 | .20 |
| ❑ 103 Sterling Hitchcock | .02 | .10 |
| ❑ 104 Alex Arias | .02 | .10 |
| ❑ 105 David Wells | .07 | .20 |
| ❑ 106 Daryl Boston | .02 | .10 |
| ❑ 107 Mike Stanton | .02 | .10 |
| ❑ 108 Gary Redus | .02 | .10 |
| ❑ 109 Delino DeShields | .07 | .20 |
| ❑ 110 Lee Smith | .07 | .20 |
| ❑ 111 Greg Litton | .02 | .10 |
| ❑ 112 Frankie Rodriguez | .02 | .10 |
| ❑ 113 Russ Springer | .02 | .10 |
| ❑ 114 Mitch Williams | .02 | .10 |
| ❑ 115 Eric Karros | .07 | .20 |
| ❑ 116 Jeff Brantley | .02 | .10 |
| ❑ 117 Jack Voigt | .02 | .10 |
| ❑ 118 Jason Bere | .02 | .10 |
| ❑ 119 Kevin Roberson | .02 | .10 |
| ❑ 120 Jimmy Key | .07 | .20 |
| ❑ 121 Reggie Jefferson | .02 | .10 |
| ❑ 122 Jeromy Burnitz | .07 | .20 |
| ❑ 123 Billy Brewer | .02 | .10 |
| ❑ 124 Willie Canate | .02 | .10 |

| | | |
|---|---|---|
| ❑ 125 Greg Swindell | .02 | .10 |
| ❑ 126 Hal Morris | .02 | .10 |
| ❑ 127 Brad Ausmus | .10 | .30 |
| ❑ 128 George Tsamis | .02 | .10 |
| ❑ 129 Denny Neagle | .07 | .20 |
| ❑ 130 Pat Listach | .02 | .10 |
| ❑ 131 Steve Karsay | .02 | .10 |
| ❑ 132 Bret Barberie | .02 | .10 |
| ❑ 133 Mark Leiter | .02 | .10 |
| ❑ 134 Greg Colbrunn | .02 | .10 |
| ❑ 135 David Nied | .02 | .10 |
| ❑ 136 Dean Palmer | .07 | .20 |
| ❑ 137 Steve Avery | .02 | .10 |
| ❑ 138 Bill Haselman | .02 | .10 |
| ❑ 139 Tripp Cromer | .02 | .10 |
| ❑ 140 Frank Viola | .07 | .20 |
| ❑ 141 Rene Gonzales | .02 | .10 |
| ❑ 142 Curt Schilling | .07 | .20 |
| ❑ 143 Tim Wallach | .02 | .10 |
| ❑ 144 Bobby Munoz | .02 | .10 |
| ❑ 145 Brady Anderson | .07 | .20 |
| ❑ 146 Rod Beck | .02 | .10 |
| ❑ 147 Mike LaValliere | .02 | .10 |
| ❑ 148 Greg Hibbard | .02 | .10 |
| ❑ 149 Kenny Lofton | .07 | .20 |
| ❑ 150 Dwight Gooden | .07 | .20 |
| ❑ 151 Greg Gagne | .02 | .10 |
| ❑ 152 Ray McDavid | .02 | .10 |
| ❑ 153 Chris Donnels | .02 | .10 |
| ❑ 154 Dan Wilson | .02 | .10 |
| ❑ 155 Todd Stottlemyre | .02 | .10 |
| ❑ 156 David McCarty | .02 | .10 |
| ❑ 157 Paul Wagner | .02 | .10 |
| ❑ 158 Derek Jeter | .60 | 1.50 |
| ❑ 159 Mike Fetters | .02 | .10 |
| ❑ 160 Scott Lydy | .02 | .10 |
| ❑ 161 Darrell Whitmore | .02 | .10 |
| ❑ 162 Bob MacDonald | .02 | .10 |
| ❑ 163 Vinny Castilla | .07 | .20 |
| ❑ 164 Denis Boucher | .02 | .10 |
| ❑ 165 Ivan Rodriguez | .10 | .30 |
| ❑ 166 Ron Gant | .07 | .20 |
| ❑ 167 Tim Davis | .02 | .10 |
| ❑ 168 Steve Dixon | .02 | .10 |
| ❑ 169 Scott Fletcher | .02 | .10 |
| ❑ 170 Terry Mulholland | .02 | .10 |
| ❑ 171 Greg Myers | .02 | .10 |
| ❑ 172 Brett Butler | .07 | .20 |
| ❑ 173 Bob Wickman | .02 | .10 |
| ❑ 174 Dave Martinez | .02 | .10 |
| ❑ 175 Fernando Valenzuela | .07 | .20 |
| ❑ 176 Craig Grebeck | .02 | .10 |
| ❑ 177 Shawn Boskie | .02 | .10 |
| ❑ 178 Albie Lopez | .02 | .10 |
| ❑ 179 Butch Huskey | .02 | .10 |
| ❑ 180 George Brett | .50 | 1.25 |
| ❑ 181 Juan Guzman | .07 | .20 |
| ❑ 182 Eric Anthony | .02 | .10 |
| ❑ 183 Rob Dibble | .07 | .20 |
| ❑ 184 Craig Shipley | .02 | .10 |
| ❑ 185 Kevin Tapani | .02 | .10 |
| ❑ 186 Marcus Moore | .02 | .10 |
| ❑ 187 Graeme Lloyd | .02 | .10 |
| ❑ 188 Mike Bordick | .02 | .10 |
| ❑ 189 Chris Hammond | .02 | .10 |
| ❑ 190 Cecil Fielder | .07 | .20 |
| ❑ 191 Curt Leskanic | .02 | .10 |
| ❑ 192 Lou Frazier | .02 | .10 |
| ❑ 193 Steve Dreyer RC | .02 | .10 |
| ❑ 194 Javier Lopez | .07 | .20 |
| ❑ 195 Edgar Martinez | .10 | .30 |
| ❑ 196 Allen Watson | .02 | .10 |
| ❑ 197 John Flaherty | .02 | .10 |
| ❑ 198 Kurt Stillwell | .02 | .10 |
| ❑ 199 Danny Jackson | .02 | .10 |
| ❑ 200 Cal Ripken | .60 | 1.50 |
| ❑ 201 Mike Bell RC | .02 | .10 |
| ❑ 202 Alan Benes RC | .08 | .25 |
| ❑ 203 Matt Farmer RC | .02 | .10 |
| ❑ 204 Jeff Granger | .02 | .10 |
| ❑ 205 Brooks Kieschnick RC | .02 | .10 |
| ❑ 206 Jeremy Lee RC | .02 | .10 |
| ❑ 207 Charles Peterson RC | .02 | .10 |
| ❑ 208 Andy Rice RC | .02 | .10 |
| ❑ 209 Billy Wagner RC | .60 | 1.50 |
| ❑ 210 Kelly Wunsch RC | .08 | .25 |
| ❑ 211 Tom Candiotti | .02 | .10 |
| ❑ 212 Domingo Jean | .02 | .10 |

|  | | |
|---|---|---|
| 213 John Burkett | .02 | .10 |
| 214 George Bell | .02 | .10 |
| 215 Dan Plesac | .02 | .10 |
| 216 Manny Ramirez | .20 | .50 |
| 217 Mike Maddux | .02 | .10 |
| 218 Kevin McReynolds | .02 | .10 |
| 219 Pat Borders | .02 | .10 |
| 220 Doug Drabek | .02 | .10 |
| 221 Larry Luebbers RC | .02 | .10 |
| 222 Trevor Hoffman | .10 | .30 |
| 223 Pat Meares | .02 | .10 |
| 224 Danny Miceli | .02 | .10 |
| 225 Greg Vaughn | .02 | .10 |
| 226 Scott Hemond | .02 | .10 |
| 227 Pat Rapp | .02 | .10 |
| 228 Kirk Gibson | .07 | .20 |
| 229 Lance Painter | .02 | .10 |
| 230 Larry Walker | .07 | .20 |
| 231 Benji Gil | .02 | .10 |
| 232 Mark Wohlers | .02 | .10 |
| 233 Rich Amaral | .02 | .10 |
| 234 Eric Pappas | .02 | .10 |
| 235 Scott Cooper | .02 | .10 |
| 236 Mike Butcher | .02 | .10 |
| 237 Pride RC/Green/Sweeney RC | .20 | .50 |
| 238 Kim Batiste | .02 | .10 |
| 239 Paul Assenmacher | .02 | .10 |
| 240 Will Clark | .10 | .30 |
| 241 Jose Offerman | .02 | .10 |
| 242 Todd Frohwirth | .02 | .10 |
| 243 Tim Raines | .07 | .20 |
| 244 Rick Wilkins | .02 | .10 |
| 245 Bret Saberhagen | .07 | .20 |
| 246 Thomas Howard | .02 | .10 |
| 247 Stan Belinda | .02 | .10 |
| 248 Rickey Henderson | .20 | .50 |
| 249 Brian Williams | .02 | .10 |
| 250 Barry Larkin | .10 | .30 |
| 251 Jose Valentin | .02 | .10 |
| 252 Lenny Webster | .02 | .10 |
| 253 Blas Minor | .02 | .10 |
| 254 Tim Teufel | .02 | .10 |
| 255 Bobby Witt | .02 | .10 |
| 256 Walt Weiss | .02 | .10 |
| 257 Chad Kreuter | .02 | .10 |
| 258 Roberto Mejia | .02 | .10 |
| 259 Cliff Floyd | .07 | .20 |
| 260 Julio Franco | .07 | .20 |
| 261 Rafael Belliard | .02 | .10 |
| 262 Marc Newfield | .02 | .10 |
| 263 Gerald Perry | .02 | .10 |
| 264 Ken Ryan | .02 | .10 |
| 265 Chili Davis | .07 | .20 |
| 266 Dave West | .02 | .10 |
| 267 Royce Clayton | .02 | .10 |
| 268 Pedro Martinez | .20 | .50 |
| 269 Mark Hutton | .02 | .10 |
| 270 Frank Thomas | .20 | .50 |
| 271 Brad Pennington | .02 | .10 |
| 272 Mike Harkey | .02 | .10 |
| 273 Sandy Alomar Jr. | .02 | .10 |
| 274 Dave Gallagher | .02 | .10 |
| 275 Wally Joyner | .07 | .20 |
| 276 Ricky Trlicek | .02 | .10 |
| 277 Al Osuna | .02 | .10 |
| 278 Pokey Reese | .02 | .10 |
| 279 Kevin Higgins | .02 | .10 |
| 280 Rick Aguilera | .02 | .10 |
| 281 Orlando Merced | .02 | .10 |
| 282 Mike Mohler | .02 | .10 |
| 283 John Jaha | .02 | .10 |
| 284 Robb Nen | .02 | .10 |
| 285 Travis Fryman | .07 | .20 |
| 286 Mark Thompson | .02 | .10 |
| 287 Mike Lansing | .02 | .10 |
| 288 Craig Lefferts | .02 | .10 |
| 289 Damon Berryhill | .02 | .10 |
| 290 Randy Johnson | .20 | .50 |
| 291 Jeff Reed | .02 | .10 |
| 292 Danny Darwin | .02 | .10 |
| 293 J.T. Snow | .07 | .20 |
| 294 Tyler Green | .02 | .10 |
| 295 Chris Hoiles | .07 | .20 |
| 296 Roger McDowell | .02 | .10 |
| 297 Spike Owen | .02 | .10 |
| 298 Salomon Torres | .02 | .10 |
| 299 Wilson Alvarez | .02 | .10 |
| 300 Ryne Sandberg | .30 | .75 |
| 301 Derek Lilliquist | .02 | .10 |
| 302 Howard Johnson | .02 | .10 |
| 303 Greg Cadaret | .02 | .10 |
| 304 Pat Hentgen | .02 | .10 |
| 305 Craig Biggio | .10 | .30 |
| 306 Scott Service | .02 | .10 |
| 307 Melvin Nieves | .02 | .10 |
| 308 Mike Trombley | .02 | .10 |
| 309 Carlos Garcia | .02 | .10 |
| 310 Robin Yount | .30 | .75 |
| 311 Marcos Armas | .02 | .10 |
| 312 Rich Rodriguez | .02 | .10 |
| 313 Justin Thompson | .02 | .10 |
| 314 Danny Sheaffer | .02 | .10 |
| 315 Ken Hill | .02 | .10 |
| 316 Terrell Wade RC | .02 | .10 |
| 317 Cris Carpenter | .02 | .10 |
| 318 Jeff Blauser | .02 | .10 |
| 319 Ted Power | .02 | .10 |
| 320 Ozzie Smith | .30 | .75 |
| 321 John Dopson | .02 | .10 |
| 322 Chris Turner | .02 | .10 |
| 323 Pete Incaviglia | .02 | .10 |
| 324 Alan Mills | .02 | .10 |
| 325 Jody Reed | .02 | .10 |
| 326 Rich Monteleone | .02 | .10 |
| 327 Mark Carreon | .02 | .10 |
| 328 Donn Pall | .02 | .10 |
| 329 Matt Walbeck | .02 | .10 |
| 330 Charley Nagy | .02 | .10 |
| 331 Jeff McKnight | .02 | .10 |
| 332 Jose Lind | .02 | .10 |
| 333 Mike Timlin | .02 | .10 |
| 334 Doug Jones | .02 | .10 |
| 335 Kevin Mitchell | .07 | .20 |
| 336 Luis Lopez | .02 | .10 |
| 337 Shane Mack | .02 | .10 |
| 338 Randy Tomlin | .02 | .10 |
| 339 Matt Mieske | .02 | .10 |
| 340 Mark McGwire | .50 | 1.25 |
| 341 Nigel Wilson | .02 | .10 |
| 342 Danny Gladden | .02 | .10 |
| 343 Mo Sanford | .02 | .10 |
| 344 Sean Berry | .02 | .10 |
| 345 Kevin Brown | .07 | .20 |
| 346 Greg Olson | .02 | .10 |
| 347 Dave Magadan | .02 | .10 |
| 348 Rene Arocha | .02 | .10 |
| 349 Carlos Quintana | .02 | .10 |
| 350 Jim Abbott | .10 | .30 |
| 351 Gary DiSarcina | .02 | .10 |
| 352 Ben Rivera | .02 | .10 |
| 353 Carlos Hernandez | .02 | .10 |
| 354 Darren Lewis | .02 | .10 |
| 355 Harold Reynolds | .07 | .20 |
| 356 Scott Ruffcorn | .02 | .10 |
| 357 Mark Gubicza | .02 | .10 |
| 358 Paul Sorrento | .02 | .10 |
| 359 Anthony Young | .02 | .10 |
| 360 Mark Grace | .10 | .30 |
| 361 Rob Butler | .02 | .10 |
| 362 Kevin Bass | .02 | .10 |
| 363 Eric Helfand | .02 | .10 |
| 364 Derek Bell | .02 | .10 |
| 365 Scott Erickson | .02 | .10 |
| 366 Al Martin | .02 | .10 |
| 367 Ricky Bones | .02 | .10 |
| 368 Jeff Branson | .02 | .10 |
| 369 J.Giambi/D.Bell RC | .20 | .50 |
| 370 Benito Santiago | .07 | .20 |
| 371 John Doherty | .02 | .10 |
| 372 Joe Girardi | .02 | .10 |
| 373 Tim Scott | .02 | .10 |
| 374 Marvin Freeman | .02 | .10 |
| 375 Deion Sanders | .10 | .30 |
| 376 Roger Salkeld | .02 | .10 |
| 377 Bernard Gilkey | .02 | .10 |
| 378 Tony Fossas | .02 | .10 |
| 379 Mark McLemore UER | .02 | .10 |
| 380 Darren Daulton | .07 | .20 |
| 381 Chuck Finley | .02 | .10 |
| 382 Mitch Webster | .02 | .10 |
| 383 Gerald Williams | .02 | .10 |
| 384 F.Thomas/F.McGriff AS | .10 | .30 |
| 385 R.Alomar/R.Thompson AS | .07 | .20 |
| 386 W.Boggs/M.Williams AS | .07 | .20 |
| 387 C.Ripken/J.Blauser AS | .20 | .50 |
| 388 K.Griffey/L.Dykstra AS | .20 | .50 |
| 389 J.Gonzalez/D.Justice AS | .07 | .20 |
| 390 A.Belle/B.Bonds AS | .30 | .75 |
| 391 M.Stanley/M.Piazza AS | .20 | .50 |
| 392 J.McDowell/G.Maddux AS | .10 | .30 |
| 393 J.Key/T.Glavine AS | .07 | .20 |
| 394 J.Montgomery/R.Myers AS | .02 | .10 |
| 395 Checklist 1-198 | .02 | .10 |
| 396 Checklist 199-396 | .02 | .10 |
| 397 Tim Salmon | .10 | .30 |
| 398 Todd Benzinger | .02 | .10 |
| 399 Frank Castillo | .02 | .10 |
| 400 Ken Griffey Jr. | .30 | .75 |
| 401 John Kruk | .07 | .20 |
| 402 Dave Telgheder | .02 | .10 |
| 403 Gary Gaetti | .07 | .20 |
| 404 Jim Edmonds | .20 | .50 |
| 405 Don Slaught | .02 | .10 |
| 406 Jose Oquendo | .02 | .10 |
| 407 Bruce Ruffin | .02 | .10 |
| 408 Phil Clark | .02 | .10 |
| 409 Joe Klink | .02 | .10 |
| 410 Lou Whitaker | .07 | .20 |
| 411 Kevin Seitzer | .02 | .10 |
| 412 Darrin Fletcher | .02 | .10 |
| 413 Kenny Rogers | .07 | .20 |
| 414 Bill Pecota | .02 | .10 |
| 415 Dave Fleming | .02 | .10 |
| 416 Luis Alicea | .02 | .10 |
| 417 Paul Quantrill | .02 | .10 |
| 418 Damion Easley | .02 | .10 |
| 419 Wes Chamberlain | .02 | .10 |
| 420 Harold Baines | .07 | .20 |
| 421 Scott Radinsky | .02 | .10 |
| 422 Rey Sanchez | .02 | .10 |
| 423 Junior Ortiz | .02 | .10 |
| 424 Jeff Kent | .10 | .30 |
| 425 Brian McRae | .02 | .10 |
| 426 Ed Sprague | .02 | .10 |
| 427 Tom Edens | .02 | .10 |
| 428 Willie Greene | .02 | .10 |
| 429 Bryan Hickerson | .02 | .10 |
| 430 Dave Winfield | .07 | .20 |
| 431 Pedro Astacio | .02 | .10 |
| 432 Mike Gallego | .02 | .10 |
| 433 Dave Burba | .02 | .10 |
| 434 Bob Walk | .02 | .10 |
| 435 Darryl Hamilton | .02 | .10 |
| 436 Vince Horsman | .02 | .10 |
| 437 Bob Natal | .02 | .10 |
| 438 Mike Henneman | .02 | .10 |
| 439 Willie Blair | .02 | .10 |
| 440 Dennis Martinez | .07 | .20 |
| 441 Dan Peltier | .02 | .10 |
| 442 Tony Tarasco | .02 | .10 |
| 443 John Cummings | .02 | .10 |
| 444 Geronimo Pena | .02 | .10 |
| 445 Aaron Sele | .07 | .20 |
| 446 Stan Javier | .02 | .10 |
| 447 Mike Williams | .02 | .10 |
| 448 D.J. Boston RC | .02 | .10 |
| 449 Jim Poole | .02 | .10 |
| 450 Carlos Baerga | .10 | .30 |
| 451 Bob Scanlan | .02 | .10 |
| 452 Lance Johnson | .02 | .10 |
| 453 Eric Hillman | .02 | .10 |
| 454 Keith Miller | .02 | .10 |
| 455 Dave Stewart | .07 | .20 |
| 456 Pete Harnisch | .02 | .10 |
| 457 Roberto Kelly | .07 | .20 |
| 458 Tim Worrell | .02 | .10 |
| 459 Pedro Munoz | .02 | .10 |
| 460 Orel Hershiser | .07 | .20 |
| 461 Randy Velarde | .02 | .10 |
| 462 Trevor Wilson | .02 | .10 |
| 463 Jerry Goff | .02 | .10 |
| 464 Bill Wegman | .02 | .10 |
| 465 Dennis Eckersley | .10 | .30 |
| 466 Jeff Conine | .07 | .20 |
| 467 Joe Boever | .02 | .10 |
| 468 Dante Bichette | .07 | .20 |
| 469 Jeff Shaw | .02 | .10 |
| 470 Rafael Palmeiro | .10 | .30 |
| 471 Phil Leftwich RC | .02 | .10 |
| 472 Jay Buhner | .07 | .20 |
| 473 Bob Tewksbury | .02 | .10 |
| 474 Tim Naehring | .02 | .10 |
| 475 Tom Glavine | .10 | .30 |
| 476 Dave Hollins | .07 | .20 |

|  |  | | |
|---|---|---|---|
| 477 | Arthur Rhodes | .02 | .10 |
| 478 | Joey Cora | .02 | .10 |
| 479 | Mike Morgan | .02 | .10 |
| 480 | Albert Belle | .07 | .20 |
| 481 | John Franco | .07 | .20 |
| 482 | Hipolito Pichardo | .02 | .10 |
| 483 | Duane Ward | .02 | .10 |
| 484 | Luis Gonzalez | .07 | .20 |
| 485 | Joe Oliver | .02 | .10 |
| 486 | Wally Whitehurst | .02 | .10 |
| 487 | Mike Benjamin | .02 | .10 |
| 488 | Eric Davis | .07 | .20 |
| 489 | Scott Kamieniecki | .02 | .10 |
| 490 | Kent Hrbek | .07 | .20 |
| 491 | John Hope RC | .07 | .20 |
| 492 | Jesse Orosco | .02 | .10 |
| 493 | Troy Neel | .02 | .10 |
| 494 | Ryan Bowen | .02 | .10 |
| 495 | Mickey Tettleton | .07 | .20 |
| 496 | Chris Jones | .02 | .10 |
| 497 | John Wetteland | .07 | .20 |
| 498 | David Hulse | .02 | .10 |
| 499 | Greg Maddux | .30 | .75 |
| 500 | Bo Jackson | .20 | .50 |
| 501 | Donovan Osborne | .02 | .10 |
| 502 | Mike Greenwell | .07 | .20 |
| 503 | Steve Frey | .02 | .10 |
| 504 | Jim Eisenreich | .02 | .10 |
| 505 | Robby Thompson | .02 | .10 |
| 506 | Leo Gomez | .02 | .10 |
| 507 | Dave Staton | .02 | .10 |
| 508 | Wayne Kirby | .02 | .10 |
| 509 | Tim Bogar | .02 | .10 |
| 510 | David Cone | .07 | .20 |
| 511 | Devon White | .07 | .20 |
| 512 | Xavier Hernandez | .02 | .10 |
| 513 | Tim Costo | .02 | .10 |
| 514 | Gene Harris | .02 | .10 |
| 515 | Jack McDowell | .07 | .20 |
| 516 | Kevin Gross | .02 | .10 |
| 517 | Scott Leius | .02 | .10 |
| 518 | Lloyd McClendon | .02 | .10 |
| 519 | Alex Diaz RC | .02 | .10 |
| 520 | Wade Boggs | .10 | .30 |
| 521 | Bob Welch | .02 | .10 |
| 522 | Henry Cotto | .02 | .10 |
| 523 | Mike Moore | .02 | .10 |
| 524 | Tim Laker | .02 | .10 |
| 525 | Andres Galarraga | .07 | .20 |
| 526 | Jamie Moyer | .02 | .10 |
| 527 | J.Hardtke RC/C.Sexton RC | .02 | .10 |
| 528 | Sid Bream | .02 | .10 |
| 529 | Erik Hanson | .02 | .10 |
| 530 | Ray Lankford | .07 | .20 |
| 531 | Rob Deer | .02 | .10 |
| 532 | Rod Correia | .02 | .10 |
| 533 | Roger Mason | .02 | .10 |
| 534 | Mike Devereaux | .02 | .10 |
| 535 | Jeff Montgomery | .02 | .10 |
| 536 | Dwight Smith | .02 | .10 |
| 537 | Jeremy Hernandez | .02 | .10 |
| 538 | Ellis Burks | .07 | .20 |
| 539 | Bobby Jones | .02 | .10 |
| 540 | Paul Molitor | .07 | .20 |
| 541 | Jeff Juden | .02 | .10 |
| 542 | Chris Sabo | .02 | .10 |
| 543 | Larry Casian | .02 | .10 |
| 544 | Jeff Gardner | .02 | .10 |
| 545 | Ramon Martinez | .02 | .10 |
| 546 | Paul O'Neill | .10 | .30 |
| 547 | Steve Hosey | .02 | .10 |
| 548 | Dave Nilsson | .02 | .10 |
| 549 | Ron Darling | .02 | .10 |
| 550 | Matt Williams | .07 | .20 |
| 551 | Jack Armstrong | .02 | .10 |
| 552 | Bill Krueger | .02 | .10 |
| 553 | Freddie Benavides | .02 | .10 |
| 554 | Jeff Fassero | .02 | .10 |
| 555 | Chuck Knoblauch | .07 | .20 |
| 556 | Guillermo Velasquez | .02 | .10 |
| 557 | Joel Johnston | .02 | .10 |
| 558 | Tom Lampkin | .02 | .10 |
| 559 | Todd Van Poppel | .02 | .10 |
| 560 | Gary Sheffield | .07 | .20 |
| 561 | Skeeter Barnes | .02 | .10 |
| 562 | Darren Holmes | .02 | .10 |
| 563 | John Vander Wal | .02 | .10 |
| 564 | Mike Ignasiak | .02 | .10 |
| 565 | Fred McGriff | .10 | .30 |
| 566 | Luis Polonia | .02 | .10 |
| 567 | Mike Perez | .02 | .10 |
| 568 | John Valentin | .02 | .10 |
| 569 | Mike Felder | .02 | .10 |
| 570 | Tommy Greene | .02 | .10 |
| 571 | David Segui | .02 | .10 |
| 572 | Roberto Hernandez | .02 | .10 |
| 573 | Steve Wilson | .02 | .10 |
| 574 | Willie McGee | .07 | .20 |
| 575 | Randy Myers | .02 | .10 |
| 576 | Darrin Jackson | .02 | .10 |
| 577 | Eric Plunk | .02 | .10 |
| 578 | Mike Macfarlane | .02 | .10 |
| 579 | Doug Brocail | .02 | .10 |
| 580 | Steve Finley | .07 | .20 |
| 581 | John Roper | .02 | .10 |
| 582 | Darryl Cox | .02 | .10 |
| 583 | Chip Hale | .02 | .10 |
| 584 | Scott Bullett | .02 | .10 |
| 585 | Kevin Reimer | .02 | .10 |
| 586 | Brent Gates | .02 | .10 |
| 587 | Matt Turner | .02 | .10 |
| 588 | Rich Rowland | .02 | .10 |
| 589 | Kent Bottenfield | .02 | .10 |
| 590 | Marquis Grissom | .07 | .20 |
| 591 | Doug Strange | .02 | .10 |
| 592 | Jay Howell | .02 | .10 |
| 593 | Omar Vizquel | .10 | .30 |
| 594 | Rheal Cormier | .02 | .10 |
| 595 | Andre Dawson | .07 | .20 |
| 596 | Hilly Hathaway | .02 | .10 |
| 597 | Todd Pratt | .02 | .10 |
| 598 | Mike Mussina | .10 | .30 |
| 599 | Alex Fernandez | .02 | .10 |
| 600 | Don Mattingly | .50 | 1.25 |
| 601 | Frank Thomas MOG | .10 | .30 |
| 602 | Ryne Sandberg MOG | .20 | .50 |
| 603 | Wade Boggs MOG | .10 | .30 |
| 604 | Cal Ripken MOG | .30 | .75 |
| 605 | Barry Bonds MOG | .30 | .75 |
| 606 | Ken Griffey Jr. MOG | .20 | .50 |
| 607 | Kirby Puckett MOG | .10 | .30 |
| 608 | Darren Daulton MOG | .02 | .10 |
| 609 | Paul Molitor MOG | .02 | .10 |
| 610 | Terry Steinbach | .02 | .10 |
| 611 | Todd Worrell | .02 | .10 |
| 612 | Jim Thome | .10 | .30 |
| 613 | Chuck McElroy | .02 | .10 |
| 614 | John Habyan | .02 | .10 |
| 615 | Sid Fernandez | .02 | .10 |
| 616 | Jermaine Allensworth RC | .02 | .10 |
| 617 | Steve Bedrosian | .02 | .10 |
| 618 | Rob Ducey | .02 | .10 |
| 619 | Tom Browning | .02 | .10 |
| 620 | Tony Gwynn | .25 | .60 |
| 621 | Carl Willis | .02 | .10 |
| 622 | Kevin Young | .02 | .10 |
| 623 | Rafael Novoa | .02 | .10 |
| 624 | Jerry Browne | .02 | .10 |
| 625 | Charlie Hough | .07 | .20 |
| 626 | Chris Gomez | .02 | .10 |
| 627 | Steve Reed | .02 | .10 |
| 628 | Kirk Rueter | .02 | .10 |
| 629 | Matt Whiteside | .02 | .10 |
| 630 | David Justice | .07 | .20 |
| 631 | Brad Holman | .02 | .10 |
| 632 | Brian Jordan | .07 | .20 |
| 633 | Scott Bankhead | .02 | .10 |
| 634 | Torey Lovullo | .02 | .10 |
| 635 | Len Dykstra | .07 | .20 |
| 636 | Ben McDonald | .02 | .10 |
| 637 | Steve Howe | .02 | .10 |
| 638 | Jose Vizcaino | .02 | .10 |
| 639 | Bill Swift | .02 | .10 |
| 640 | Darryl Strawberry | .07 | .20 |
| 641 | Steve Farr | .02 | .10 |
| 642 | Tom Kramer | .02 | .10 |
| 643 | Joe Orsulak | .02 | .10 |
| 644 | Tom Henke | .02 | .10 |
| 645 | Joe Carter | .07 | .20 |
| 646 | Ken Caminiti | .07 | .20 |
| 647 | Reggie Sanders | .07 | .20 |
| 648 | Andy Ashby | .02 | .10 |
| 649 | Derek Parks | .02 | .10 |
| 650 | Andy Van Slyke | .10 | .30 |
| 651 | Juan Bell | .02 | .10 |
| 652 | Roger Smithberg | .02 | .10 |
| 653 | Chuck Carr | .02 | .10 |
| 654 | Bill Gullickson | .02 | .10 |
| 655 | Charlie Hayes | .02 | .10 |
| 656 | Chris Nabholz | .02 | .10 |
| 657 | Karl Rhodes | .02 | .10 |
| 658 | Pete Smith | .02 | .10 |
| 659 | Bret Boone | .07 | .20 |
| 660 | Gregg Jefferies | .02 | .10 |
| 661 | Bob Zupcic | .02 | .10 |
| 662 | Steve Sax | .02 | .10 |
| 663 | Mariano Duncan | .02 | .10 |
| 664 | Jeff Tackett | .02 | .10 |
| 665 | Mark Langston | .02 | .10 |
| 666 | Candy Maldonado | .02 | .10 |
| 667 | Candy Maldonado | .02 | .10 |
| 668 | Woody Williams | .07 | .20 |
| 669 | Tim Wakefield | .10 | .30 |
| 670 | Danny Tartabull | .02 | .10 |
| 671 | Charlie O'Brien | .02 | .10 |
| 672 | Felix Jose | .02 | .10 |
| 673 | Bobby Ayala | .02 | .10 |
| 674 | Scott Servais | .02 | .10 |
| 675 | Roberto Alomar | .10 | .30 |
| 676 | Pedro A.Martinez RC | .02 | .10 |
| 677 | Eddie Guardado | .07 | .20 |
| 678 | Mark Lewis | .02 | .10 |
| 679 | Jaime Navarro | .02 | .10 |
| 680 | Ruben Sierra | .07 | .20 |
| 681 | Rick Renteria | .02 | .10 |
| 682 | Storm Davis | .02 | .10 |
| 683 | Cory Snyder | .02 | .10 |
| 684 | Ron Karkovice | .02 | .10 |
| 685 | Juan Gonzalez | .07 | .20 |
| 686 | Carlos Delgado | .10 | .30 |
| 687 | John Smoltz | .10 | .30 |
| 688 | Brian Dorsett | .02 | .10 |
| 689 | Omar Olivares | .02 | .10 |
| 690 | Mo Vaughn | .07 | .20 |
| 691 | Joe Grahe | .02 | .10 |
| 692 | Mickey Morandini | .02 | .10 |
| 693 | Tino Martinez | .10 | .30 |
| 694 | Brian Barnes | .02 | .10 |
| 695 | Mike Stanley | .02 | .10 |
| 696 | Mark Clark | .02 | .10 |
| 697 | Dave Hansen | .02 | .10 |
| 698 | Willie Wilson | .02 | .10 |
| 699 | Pete Schourek | .02 | .10 |
| 700 | Barry Bonds | .60 | 1.50 |
| 701 | Kevin Appier | .07 | .20 |
| 702 | Tony Fernandez | .02 | .10 |
| 703 | Darryl Kile | .07 | .20 |
| 704 | Archi Cianfrocco | .02 | .10 |
| 705 | Jose Rijo | .02 | .10 |
| 706 | Brian Harper | .02 | .10 |
| 707 | Zane Smith | .02 | .10 |
| 708 | Dave Henderson | .02 | .10 |
| 709 | Angel Miranda UER | .02 | .10 |
| 710 | Orestes Destrade | .02 | .10 |
| 711 | Greg Gohr | .02 | .10 |
| 712 | Eric Young | .02 | .10 |
| 713 | Bullinger/Will/Wat/Welch | .02 | .10 |
| 714 | Tim Spehr | .02 | .10 |
| 715 | Hank Aaron 715 HR | .20 | .50 |
| 716 | Nate Minchey | .02 | .10 |
| 717 | Mike Blowers | .02 | .10 |
| 718 | Kent Mercker | .02 | .10 |
| 719 | Tom Pagnozzi | .02 | .10 |
| 720 | Roger Clemens | .40 | 1.00 |
| 721 | Eduardo Perez | .02 | .10 |
| 722 | Milt Thompson | .02 | .10 |
| 723 | Gregg Olson | .02 | .10 |
| 724 | Kirk McCaskill | .02 | .10 |
| 725 | Sammy Sosa | .20 | .50 |
| 726 | Alvaro Espinoza | .02 | .10 |
| 727 | Henry Rodriguez | .02 | .10 |
| 728 | Jim Leyritz | .02 | .10 |
| 729 | Steve Scarsone | .02 | .10 |
| 730 | Bobby Bonilla | .07 | .20 |
| 731 | Chris Gwynn | .02 | .10 |
| 732 | Al Leiter | .07 | .20 |
| 733 | Bip Roberts | .02 | .10 |
| 734 | Mark Portugal | .02 | .10 |
| 735 | Terry Pendleton | .07 | .20 |
| 736 | Dave Valle | .02 | .10 |
| 737 | Paul Kilgus | .02 | .10 |
| 738 | Greg A. Harris | .02 | .10 |
| 739 | Jon Ratliff RC | .02 | .10 |
| 740 | Kirk Presley RC | .02 | .10 |

| | | |
|---|---|---|
| 741 Josue Estrada RC | .02 | .10 |
| 742 Wayne Gomes RC | .02 | .10 |
| 743 Pat Watkins RC | .02 | .10 |
| 744 Jamey Wright RC | .08 | .25 |
| 745 Jay Powell RC | .02 | .10 |
| 746 Ryan McGuire RC | .02 | .10 |
| 747 Marc Barcelo RC | .02 | .10 |
| 748 Sloan Smith RC | .02 | .10 |
| 749 John Wasdin RC | .02 | .10 |
| 750 Marc Valdes | .02 | .10 |
| 751 Dan Ehler RC | .02 | .10 |
| 752 Andre King RC | .02 | .10 |
| 753 Greg Keagle RC | .02 | .10 |
| 754 Jason Myers RC | .02 | .10 |
| 755 Dax Winslett RC | .02 | .10 |
| 756 Casey Whitten RC | .02 | .10 |
| 757 Tony Fuduric RC | .02 | .10 |
| 758 Greg Norton RC | .08 | .25 |
| 759 Jeff D'Amico RC | .08 | .25 |
| 760 Ryan Hancock RC | .02 | .10 |
| 761 David Cooper RC | .02 | .10 |
| 762 Kevin Orie RC | .02 | .10 |
| 763 J.O'Donoghue/M.Oquist | .02 | .10 |
| 764 C.Bailey RC/S.Hattleberg | .02 | .10 |
| 765 M.Holzemer/P.Swingle RC | .02 | .10 |
| 766 J.Baldwin/R.Bolton | .02 | .10 |
| 767 J.Tavarez RCU.DiPoto | .08 | .25 |
| 768 D.Bautista/S.Bergman | .02 | .10 |
| 769 B.Hamelin/J.Vitiello | .02 | .10 |
| 770 M.Kiefer/T.O'Leary | .02 | .10 |
| 771 D.Hocking/O.Munoz RC | .02 | .10 |
| 772 Russ Davis/B.Taylor | .02 | .10 |
| 773 K.Abbott/M.Jimenez | .08 | .25 |
| 774 K.King RC/Plantenberg RC | .02 | .10 |
| 775 J.Shave/D.Wilson | .02 | .10 |
| 776 D.D.Cedeno/P.Spoljaric | .02 | .10 |
| 777 C.Jones/R.Klesko | .20 | .50 |
| 778 S.Trachsel/T.Wendell | .02 | .10 |
| 779 J.Spradlin RC/J.Ruffin | .02 | .10 |
| 780 J.Bates/J.Burke | .02 | .10 |
| 781 C.Everett/D.Weathers | .07 | .20 |
| 782 J.Mouton/G.Mota | .07 | .20 |
| 783 R.Mondesi/B.Van Ryn | .07 | .20 |
| 784 R.White/G.White | .07 | .20 |
| 785 B.Pulsipher/B.Fordyce | .07 | .20 |
| 786 K.Foster RC/G.Schall | .02 | .10 |
| 787 Rich Aude RC/M.Cummings | .02 | .10 |
| 788 B.Barber/R.Batchelor | .02 | .10 |
| 789 B.Johnson RC/S.Sanders | .02 | .10 |
| 790 J.Phillips/R.Faneyte | .02 | .10 |
| 791 Checklist 3 | .02 | .10 |
| 792 Checklist 4 | .02 | .10 |

## 1995 Topps

| | | |
|---|---|---|
| COMPLETE SET (660) | 50.00 | 80.00 |
| COMP.HOBBY SET (677) | 60.00 | 120.00 |
| COMP.RETAIL SET (677) | 60.00 | 120.00 |
| COMPLETE SERIES 1 (396) | 25.00 | 40.00 |
| COMPLETE SERIES 2 (264) | 25.00 | 40.00 |
| 1 Frank Thomas | .30 | .75 |
| 2 Mickey Morandini | .05 | .15 |
| 3 Babe Ruth 100th B-Day | .75 | 2.00 |
| 4 Scott Cooper | .05 | .15 |
| 5 David Cone | .10 | .30 |
| 6 Jacob Shumate | .05 | .15 |
| 7 Trevor Hoffman | .10 | .30 |
| 8 Shane Mack | .05 | .15 |
| 9 Delino DeShields | .05 | .15 |
| 10 Matt Williams | .10 | .30 |
| 11 Sammy Sosa | .30 | .75 |
| 12 Gary DiSarcina | .05 | .15 |
| 13 Kenny Rogers | .10 | .30 |
| 14 Jose Vizcaino | .05 | .15 |
| 15 Lou Whitaker | .10 | .30 |

| | | |
|---|---|---|
| 16 Ron Darling | .05 | .15 |
| 17 Dave Nilsson | .05 | .15 |
| 18 Chris Hammond | .05 | .15 |
| 19 Sid Bream | .05 | .15 |
| 20 Denny Martinez | .10 | .30 |
| 21 Orlando Merced | .05 | .15 |
| 22 John Wetteland | .10 | .30 |
| 23 Mike Devereaux | .05 | .15 |
| 24 Rene Arocha | .05 | .15 |
| 25 Jay Buhner | .10 | .30 |
| 26 Darren Holmes | .05 | .15 |
| 27 Hal Morris | .05 | .15 |
| 28 Brian Buchanan RC | .05 | .15 |
| 29 Keith Miller | .05 | .15 |
| 30 Paul Molitor | .10 | .30 |
| 31 Dave West | .05 | .15 |
| 32 Tony Tarasco | .05 | .15 |
| 33 Scott Sanders | .05 | .15 |
| 34 Eddie Zambrano | .05 | .15 |
| 35 Ricky Bones | .05 | .15 |
| 36 John Valentin | .05 | .15 |
| 37 Kevin Tapani | .05 | .15 |
| 38 Tim Wallach | .05 | .15 |
| 39 Darren Lewis | .05 | .15 |
| 40 Travis Fryman | .10 | .30 |
| 41 Mark Leiter | .05 | .15 |
| 42 Jose Bautista | .05 | .15 |
| 43 Pete Smith | .05 | .15 |
| 44 Bret Barberie | .05 | .15 |
| 45 Dennis Eckersley | .10 | .30 |
| 46 Ken Hill | .05 | .15 |
| 47 Chad Ogea | .05 | .15 |
| 48 Pete Harnisch | .05 | .15 |
| 49 James Baldwin | .05 | .15 |
| 50 Mike Mussina | .20 | .50 |
| 51 Al Martin | .05 | .15 |
| 52 Mark Thompson | .05 | .15 |
| 53 Matt Smith | .05 | .15 |
| 54 Joey Hamilton | .10 | .30 |
| 55 Edgar Martinez | .20 | .50 |
| 56 John Smiley | .05 | .15 |
| 57 Rey Sanchez | .05 | .15 |
| 58 Mike Timlin | .05 | .15 |
| 59 Ricky Bottalico | .05 | .15 |
| 60 Jim Abbott | .20 | .50 |
| 61 Mike Kelly | .05 | .15 |
| 62 Brian Jordan | .10 | .30 |
| 63 Ken Ryan | .05 | .15 |
| 64 Matt Mieske | .05 | .15 |
| 65 Rick Aguilera | .05 | .15 |
| 66 Ismael Valdes | .05 | .15 |
| 67 Royce Clayton | .05 | .15 |
| 68 Junior Felix | .05 | .15 |
| 69 Harold Reynolds | .05 | .15 |
| 70 Juan Gonzalez | .10 | .30 |
| 71 Kelly Stinnett | .05 | .15 |
| 72 Carlos Reyes | .05 | .15 |
| 73 Dave Weathers | .05 | .15 |
| 74 Mel Rojas | .05 | .15 |
| 75 Doug Drabek | .05 | .15 |
| 76 Charles Nagy | .05 | .15 |
| 77 Tim Raines | .10 | .30 |
| 78 Midre Cummings | .05 | .15 |
| 79 Ray Brown RC | .05 | .15 |
| 80 Rafael Palmeiro | .20 | .50 |
| 81 Charlie Hayes | .05 | .15 |
| 82 Ray Lankford | .10 | .30 |
| 83 Tom Davis | .05 | .15 |
| 84 C.J. Nitkowski | .05 | .15 |
| 85 Andy Ashby | .05 | .15 |
| 86 Gerald Williams | .05 | .15 |
| 87 Terry Shumpert | .05 | .15 |
| 88 Heathcliff Slocumb | .05 | .15 |
| 89 Domingo Cedeno | .05 | .15 |
| 90 Mark Grace | .20 | .50 |
| 91 Brad Woodall RC | .05 | .15 |
| 92 Gar Finnvold | .05 | .15 |
| 93 Jaime Navarro | .05 | .15 |
| 94 Carlos Hernandez | .05 | .15 |
| 95 Mark Langston | .05 | .15 |
| 96 Chuck Carr | .05 | .15 |
| 97 Mike Gardiner | .05 | .15 |
| 98 Dave McCarty | .05 | .15 |
| 99 Cris Carpenter | .05 | .15 |
| 100 Barry Bonds | .75 | 2.00 |
| 101 David Segui | .05 | .15 |
| 102 Scott Brosius | .10 | .30 |
| 103 Mariano Duncan | .05 | .15 |

| | | |
|---|---|---|
| 104 Kenny Lofton | .10 | .30 |
| 105 Ken Caminiti | .10 | .30 |
| 106 Darrin Jackson | .05 | .15 |
| 107 Jim Poole | .05 | .15 |
| 108 Wil Cordero | .05 | .15 |
| 109 Danny Miceli | .05 | .15 |
| 110 Walt Weiss | .05 | .15 |
| 111 Tom Pagnozzi | .05 | .15 |
| 112 Terrence Long | .05 | .15 |
| 113 Bret Boone | .10 | .30 |
| 114 Daryl Boston | .05 | .15 |
| 115 Wally Joyner | .10 | .30 |
| 116 Rob Butler | .05 | .15 |
| 117 Rafael Belliard | .05 | .15 |
| 118 Luis Lopez | .05 | .15 |
| 119 Tony Fossas | .05 | .15 |
| 120 Len Dykstra | .10 | .30 |
| 121 Mike Morgan | .05 | .15 |
| 122 Denny Hocking | .05 | .15 |
| 123 Kevin Gross | .05 | .15 |
| 124 Todd Benzinger | .05 | .15 |
| 125 John Doherty | .05 | .15 |
| 126 Eduardo Perez | .05 | .15 |
| 127 Dan Smith | .05 | .15 |
| 128 Joe Orsulak | .05 | .15 |
| 129 Brent Gates | .05 | .15 |
| 130 Jeff Conine | .10 | .30 |
| 131 Doug Henry | .05 | .15 |
| 132 Paul Sorrento | .05 | .15 |
| 133 Mike Hampton | .10 | .30 |
| 134 Tim Spehr | .05 | .15 |
| 135 Julio Franco | .10 | .30 |
| 136 Mike Dyer | .05 | .15 |
| 137 Chris Sabo | .05 | .15 |
| 138 Rheal Cormier | .05 | .15 |
| 139 Paul Konerko | .40 | 1.00 |
| 140 Dante Bichette | .10 | .30 |
| 141 Chuck McElroy | .05 | .15 |
| 142 Mike Stanley | .05 | .15 |
| 143 Bob Hamelin | .05 | .15 |
| 144 Tommy Greene | .05 | .15 |
| 145 John Smoltz | .20 | .50 |
| 146 Ed Sprague | .05 | .15 |
| 147 Ray McDavid | .05 | .15 |
| 148 Otis Nixon | .05 | .15 |
| 149 Turk Wendell | .05 | .15 |
| 150 Chris James | .05 | .15 |
| 151 Derek Parks | .05 | .15 |
| 152 Jose Offerman | .05 | .15 |
| 153 Tony Clark | .05 | .15 |
| 154 Chad Curtis | .05 | .15 |
| 155 Mark Portugal | .05 | .15 |
| 156 Bill Pulsipher | .20 | .50 |
| 157 Trey Neel | .05 | .15 |
| 158 Dave Winfield | .10 | .30 |
| 159 Bill Wegman | .05 | .15 |
| 160 Benito Santiago | .05 | .15 |
| 161 Jose Mesa | .05 | .15 |
| 162 Luis Gonzalez | .10 | .30 |
| 163 Alex Fernandez | .05 | .15 |
| 164 Freddie Benavides | .05 | .15 |
| 165 Ben McDonald | .05 | .15 |
| 166 Blas Minor | .05 | .15 |
| 167 Bret Wagner | .05 | .15 |
| 168 Mac Suzuki | .05 | .15 |
| 169 Roberto Mejia | .05 | .15 |
| 170 Wade Boggs | .20 | .50 |
| 171 Pokey Reese | .05 | .15 |
| 172 Hipolito Pichardo | .05 | .15 |
| 173 Kim Batiste | .05 | .15 |
| 174 Darren Hall | .05 | .15 |
| 175 Tom Glavine | .20 | .50 |
| 176 Phil Plantier | .05 | .15 |
| 177 Chris Howard | .05 | .15 |
| 178 Karl Rhodes | .05 | .15 |
| 179 LaTroy Hawkins | .05 | .15 |
| 180 Raul Mondesi | .10 | .30 |
| 181 Jeff Reed | .05 | .15 |
| 182 Milt Cuyler | .05 | .15 |
| 183 Jim Edmonds | .20 | .50 |
| 184 Hector Fajardo | .05 | .15 |
| 185 Jeff Kent | .10 | .30 |
| 186 Wilson Alvarez | .05 | .15 |
| 187 Geronimo Berroa | .05 | .15 |
| 188 Billy Spiers | .05 | .15 |
| 189 Derek Lilliquist | .05 | .15 |
| 190 Craig Biggio | .20 | .50 |
| 191 Roberto Hernandez | .05 | .15 |

| Card | .05 | .15 |
|---|---|---|
| ❏ 192 Bob Natal | .05 | .15 |
| ❏ 193 Bobby Ayala | .05 | .15 |
| ❏ 194 Travis Miller RC | .05 | .15 |
| ❏ 195 Bob Tewksbury | .05 | .15 |
| ❏ 196 Rondell White | .10 | .30 |
| ❏ 197 Steve Cooke | .05 | .15 |
| ❏ 198 Jeff Branson | .05 | .15 |
| ❏ 199 Derek Jeter | .75 | 2.00 |
| ❏ 200 Tim Salmon | .20 | .50 |
| ❏ 201 Steve Frey | .05 | .15 |
| ❏ 202 Kent Mercker | .05 | .15 |
| ❏ 203 Randy Johnson | .30 | .75 |
| ❏ 204 Todd Worrell | .05 | .15 |
| ❏ 205 Mo Vaughn | .10 | .30 |
| ❏ 206 Howard Johnson | .05 | .15 |
| ❏ 207 John Wasdin | .05 | .15 |
| ❏ 208 Eddie Williams | .05 | .15 |
| ❏ 209 Tim Belcher | .05 | .15 |
| ❏ 210 Jeff Montgomery | .05 | .15 |
| ❏ 211 Kirt Manwaring | .05 | .15 |
| ❏ 212 Ben Grieve | .20 | .50 |
| ❏ 213 Pat Hentgen | .05 | .15 |
| ❏ 214 Shawon Dunston | .05 | .15 |
| ❏ 215 Mike Greenwell | .05 | .15 |
| ❏ 216 Alex Diaz | .05 | .15 |
| ❏ 217 Pat Mahomes | .05 | .15 |
| ❏ 218 Dave Hansen | .05 | .15 |
| ❏ 219 Kevin Rogers | .05 | .15 |
| ❏ 220 Cecil Fielder | .10 | .30 |
| ❏ 221 Andrew Lorraine | .05 | .15 |
| ❏ 222 Jack Armstrong | .05 | .15 |
| ❏ 223 Todd Hundley | .05 | .15 |
| ❏ 224 Mark Acre | .05 | .15 |
| ❏ 225 Darrell Whitmore | .05 | .15 |
| ❏ 226 Randy Milligan | .05 | .15 |
| ❏ 227 Wayne Kirby | .05 | .15 |
| ❏ 228 Darryl Kile | .10 | .30 |
| ❏ 229 Bob Zupcic | .05 | .15 |
| ❏ 230 Jay Bell | .10 | .30 |
| ❏ 231 Dustin Hermanson | .05 | .15 |
| ❏ 232 Harold Baines | .10 | .30 |
| ❏ 233 Alan Benes | .05 | .15 |
| ❏ 234 Felix Fermin | .05 | .15 |
| ❏ 235 Ellis Burks | .10 | .30 |
| ❏ 236 Jeff Brantley | .05 | .15 |
| ❏ 237 Karim Garcia RC | .05 | .15 |
| ❏ 238 Matt Nokes | .05 | .15 |
| ❏ 239 Ben Rivera | .05 | .15 |
| ❏ 240 Joe Carter | .10 | .30 |
| ❏ 241 Jeff Granger | .05 | .15 |
| ❏ 242 Terry Pendleton | .10 | .30 |
| ❏ 243 Melvin Nieves | .05 | .15 |
| ❏ 244 Frankie Rodriguez | .05 | .15 |
| ❏ 245 Darryl Hamilton | .05 | .15 |
| ❏ 246 Brooks Kieschnick | .05 | .15 |
| ❏ 247 Todd Hollandsworth | .05 | .15 |
| ❏ 248 Joe Rosselli | .05 | .15 |
| ❏ 249 Bill Gullickson | .05 | .15 |
| ❏ 250 Chuck Knoblauch | .10 | .30 |
| ❏ 251 Kurt Miller | .05 | .15 |
| ❏ 252 Bobby Jones | .05 | .15 |
| ❏ 253 Lance Blankenship | .05 | .15 |
| ❏ 254 Matt Whiteside | .05 | .15 |
| ❏ 255 Darrin Fletcher | .05 | .15 |
| ❏ 256 Eric Plunk | .05 | .15 |
| ❏ 257 Shane Reynolds | .05 | .15 |
| ❏ 258 Norberto Martin | .05 | .15 |
| ❏ 259 Mike Thurman | .05 | .15 |
| ❏ 260 Andy Van Slyke | .20 | .50 |
| ❏ 261 Dwight Smith | .05 | .15 |
| ❏ 262 Allen Watson | .05 | .15 |
| ❏ 263 Dan Wilson | .05 | .15 |
| ❏ 264 Brent Mayne | .05 | .15 |
| ❏ 265 Bip Roberts | .05 | .15 |
| ❏ 266 Sterling Hitchcock | .05 | .15 |
| ❏ 267 Alex Gonzalez | .05 | .15 |
| ❏ 268 Greg Harris | .05 | .15 |
| ❏ 269 Ricky Jordan | .05 | .15 |
| ❏ 270 Johnny Ruffin | .05 | .15 |
| ❏ 271 Mike Stanton | .05 | .15 |
| ❏ 272 Rich Rowland | .05 | .15 |
| ❏ 273 Steve Trachsel | .05 | .15 |
| ❏ 274 Pedro Munoz | .05 | .15 |
| ❏ 275 Ramon Martinez | .05 | .15 |
| ❏ 276 Dave Henderson | .05 | .15 |
| ❏ 277 Chris Gomez | .05 | .15 |
| ❏ 278 Joe Grahe | .05 | .15 |
| ❏ 279 Rusty Greer | .10 | .30 |
| ❏ 280 John Franco | .10 | .30 |
| ❏ 281 Mike Bordick | .05 | .15 |
| ❏ 282 Jeff D'Amico | .05 | .15 |
| ❏ 283 Dave Magadan | .05 | .15 |
| ❏ 284 Tony Pena | .05 | .15 |
| ❏ 285 Greg Swindell | .05 | .15 |
| ❏ 286 Doug Million | .05 | .15 |
| ❏ 287 Gabe White | .05 | .15 |
| ❏ 288 Trey Beamon | .05 | .15 |
| ❏ 289 Arthur Rhodes | .05 | .15 |
| ❏ 290 Juan Guzman | .05 | .15 |
| ❏ 291 Jose Oquendo | .05 | .15 |
| ❏ 292 Willie Blair | .05 | .15 |
| ❏ 293 Eddie Taubensee | .05 | .15 |
| ❏ 294 Steve Howe | .05 | .15 |
| ❏ 295 Greg Maddux | .50 | 1.25 |
| ❏ 296 Mike Macfarlane | .05 | .15 |
| ❏ 297 Curt Schilling | .10 | .30 |
| ❏ 298 Phil Clark | .05 | .15 |
| ❏ 299 Woody Williams | .05 | .15 |
| ❏ 300 Jose Canseco | .20 | .50 |
| ❏ 301 Aaron Sele | .05 | .15 |
| ❏ 302 Carl Willis | .05 | .15 |
| ❏ 303 Steve Buechele | .05 | .15 |
| ❏ 304 Dave Burba | .05 | .15 |
| ❏ 305 Orel Hershiser | .10 | .30 |
| ❏ 306 Damion Easley | .05 | .15 |
| ❏ 307 Mike Henneman | .05 | .15 |
| ❏ 308 Josias Manzanillo | .05 | .15 |
| ❏ 309 Kevin Seitzer | .05 | .15 |
| ❏ 310 Ruben Sierra | .10 | .30 |
| ❏ 311 Bryan Harvey | .05 | .15 |
| ❏ 312 Jim Thome | .20 | .50 |
| ❏ 313 Ramon Castro RC | .15 | .40 |
| ❏ 314 Lance Johnson | .05 | .15 |
| ❏ 315 Marquis Grissom | .10 | .30 |
| ❏ 316 Eddie Priest RC | .05 | .15 |
| ❏ 317 Paul Wagner | .05 | .15 |
| ❏ 318 Jamie Moyer | .10 | .30 |
| ❏ 319 Todd Zeile | .05 | .15 |
| ❏ 320 Chris Bosio | .05 | .15 |
| ❏ 321 Steve Reed | .05 | .15 |
| ❏ 322 Erik Hanson | .05 | .15 |
| ❏ 323 Luis Polonia | .05 | .15 |
| ❏ 324 Ryan Klesko | .10 | .30 |
| ❏ 325 Kevin Appier | .10 | .30 |
| ❏ 326 Jim Eisenreich | .05 | .15 |
| ❏ 327 Randy Knorr | .05 | .15 |
| ❏ 328 Craig Shipley | .05 | .15 |
| ❏ 329 Tim Naehring | .05 | .15 |
| ❏ 330 Randy Myers | .05 | .15 |
| ❏ 331 Alex Cole | .05 | .15 |
| ❏ 332 Jim Gott | .05 | .15 |
| ❏ 333 Mike Jackson | .05 | .15 |
| ❏ 334 John Flaherty | .05 | .15 |
| ❏ 335 Chili Davis | .05 | .15 |
| ❏ 336 Benji Gil | .05 | .15 |
| ❏ 337 Jason Jacome | .05 | .15 |
| ❏ 338 Stan Javier | .05 | .15 |
| ❏ 339 Mike Fetters | .05 | .15 |
| ❏ 340 Rich Renteria | .05 | .15 |
| ❏ 341 Kevin Witt | .05 | .15 |
| ❏ 342 Scott Servais | .05 | .15 |
| ❏ 343 Craig Grebeck | .05 | .15 |
| ❏ 344 Kirk Rueter | .05 | .15 |
| ❏ 345 Don Slaught | .05 | .15 |
| ❏ 346 Armando Benitez | .05 | .15 |
| ❏ 347 Ozzie Smith | .50 | 1.25 |
| ❏ 348 Mike Blowers | .05 | .15 |
| ❏ 349 Armando Reynoso | .05 | .15 |
| ❏ 350 Barry Larkin | .20 | .50 |
| ❏ 351 Mike Williams | .05 | .15 |
| ❏ 352 Scott Kamieniecki | .05 | .15 |
| ❏ 353 Gary Gaetti | .10 | .30 |
| ❏ 354 Todd Stottlemyre | .05 | .15 |
| ❏ 355 Fred McGriff | .20 | .50 |
| ❏ 356 Tim Mauser | .05 | .15 |
| ❏ 357 Chris Gwynn | .05 | .15 |
| ❏ 358 Frank Castillo | .05 | .15 |
| ❏ 359 Jeff Reboulet | .05 | .15 |
| ❏ 360 Roger Clemens | .60 | 1.50 |
| ❏ 361 Mark Carreon | .05 | .15 |
| ❏ 362 Chad Kreuter | .05 | .15 |
| ❏ 363 Mark Farris | .05 | .15 |
| ❏ 364 Bob Welch | .05 | .15 |
| ❏ 365 Dean Palmer | .10 | .30 |
| ❏ 366 Jeromy Burnitz | .10 | .30 |
| ❏ 367 B.J. Surhoff | .10 | .30 |
| ❏ 368 Mike Butcher | .05 | .15 |
| ❏ 369 B.Buckles RC/B.Clontz | .05 | .15 |
| ❏ 370 Eddie Murray | .30 | .75 |
| ❏ 371 Orlando Miller | .05 | .15 |
| ❏ 372 Ron Karkovice | .05 | .15 |
| ❏ 373 Richie Lewis | .05 | .15 |
| ❏ 374 Lenny Webster | .05 | .15 |
| ❏ 375 Jeff Tackett | .05 | .15 |
| ❏ 376 Tom Urbani | .05 | .15 |
| ❏ 377 Tino Martinez | .20 | .50 |
| ❏ 378 Mark Dewey | .05 | .15 |
| ❏ 379 Charles O'Brien | .05 | .15 |
| ❏ 380 Terry Mulholland | .05 | .15 |
| ❏ 381 Thomas Howard | .05 | .15 |
| ❏ 382 Chris Haney | .05 | .15 |
| ❏ 383 Billy Hatcher | .05 | .15 |
| ❏ 384 T.Thomas/J.Bagwell AS | .20 | .50 |
| ❏ 385 B.Boone/C.Baerga AS | .10 | .30 |
| ❏ 386 M.Williams/W.Boggs AS | .10 | .30 |
| ❏ 387 C.Ripken/W.Cordero AS | .30 | .75 |
| ❏ 388 K.Griffey Jr./B.Bonds AS | .40 | 1.00 |
| ❏ 389 T.Gwynn/A.Belle AS | .10 | .30 |
| ❏ 390 D.Bichette/K.Puckett AS | .20 | .50 |
| ❏ 391 M.Piazza/M.Stanley AS | .30 | .75 |
| ❏ 392 G.Maddux/D.Cone AS | .30 | .75 |
| ❏ 393 D.Jackson/J.Key AS | .05 | .15 |
| ❏ 394 J.Franco/L.Smith AS | .05 | .15 |
| ❏ 395 Checklist 1-198 | .05 | .15 |
| ❏ 396 Checklist 199-396 | .05 | .15 |
| ❏ 397 Ken Griffey Jr. | .50 | 1.25 |
| ❏ 398 Rick Heiserman RC | .05 | .15 |
| ❏ 399 Don Mattingly | .75 | 2.00 |
| ❏ 400 Henry Rodriguez | .05 | .15 |
| ❏ 401 Lenny Harris | .05 | .15 |
| ❏ 402 Ryan Thompson | .05 | .15 |
| ❏ 403 Darren Oliver | .05 | .15 |
| ❏ 404 Omar Vizquel | .20 | .50 |
| ❏ 405 Jeff Bagwell | .20 | .50 |
| ❏ 406 Doug Webb RC | .05 | .15 |
| ❏ 407 Todd Van Poppel | .05 | .15 |
| ❏ 408 Leo Gomez | .05 | .15 |
| ❏ 409 Mark Whiten | .05 | .15 |
| ❏ 410 Pedro A.Martinez | .05 | .15 |
| ❏ 411 Reggie Sanders | .10 | .30 |
| ❏ 412 Kevin Foster | .05 | .15 |
| ❏ 413 Danny Tartabull | .05 | .15 |
| ❏ 414 Jeff Blauser | .05 | .15 |
| ❏ 415 Mike Magnante | .05 | .15 |
| ❏ 416 Tom Candiotti | .05 | .15 |
| ❏ 417 Rod Beck | .05 | .15 |
| ❏ 418 Jody Reed | .05 | .15 |
| ❏ 419 Vince Coleman | .05 | .15 |
| ❏ 420 Danny Jackson | .05 | .15 |
| ❏ 421 Ryan Nye RC | .05 | .15 |
| ❏ 422 Larry Walker | .10 | .30 |
| ❏ 423 Russ Johnson DP | .05 | .15 |
| ❏ 424 Pat Borders | .05 | .15 |
| ❏ 425 Lee Smith | .10 | .30 |
| ❏ 426 Paul O'Neill | .20 | .50 |
| ❏ 427 Devon White | .05 | .15 |
| ❏ 428 Jim Bullinger | .05 | .15 |
| ❏ 429 Rob Welch RC | .05 | .15 |
| ❏ 430 Steve Avery | .05 | .15 |
| ❏ 431 Tony Gwynn | .40 | 1.00 |
| ❏ 432 Pat Meares | .05 | .15 |
| ❏ 433 Bill Swift | .05 | .15 |
| ❏ 434 David Wells | .10 | .30 |
| ❏ 435 John Briscoe | .05 | .15 |
| ❏ 436 Roger Pavlik | .05 | .15 |
| ❏ 437 Jayson Peterson RC | .05 | .15 |
| ❏ 438 Roberto Alomar | .20 | .50 |
| ❏ 439 Billy Brewer | .05 | .15 |
| ❏ 440 Gary Sheffield | .10 | .30 |
| ❏ 441 Lou Frazier | .05 | .15 |
| ❏ 442 Terry Steinbach | .05 | .15 |
| ❏ 443 Jay Payton RC | .30 | .75 |
| ❏ 444 Jason Bere | .05 | .15 |
| ❏ 445 Denny Neagle | .10 | .30 |
| ❏ 446 Andres Galarraga | .10 | .30 |
| ❏ 447 Hector Carrasco | .05 | .15 |
| ❏ 448 Bill Risley | .05 | .15 |
| ❏ 449 Andy Benes | .05 | .15 |
| ❏ 450 Jim Leyritz | .05 | .15 |
| ❏ 451 Jose Oliva | .05 | .15 |
| ❏ 452 Greg Vaughn | .05 | .15 |
| ❏ 453 Rich Monteleone | .05 | .15 |
| ❏ 454 Tony Eusebio | .05 | .15 |
| ❏ 455 Chuck Finley | .10 | .30 |

|  |  | | |
|---|---|---|---|
| ❑ 456 | Kevin Brown | .10 | .30 |
| ❑ 457 | Joe Boever | .05 | .15 |
| ❑ 458 | Bobby Munoz | .05 | .15 |
| ❑ 459 | Bret Saberhagen | .10 | .30 |
| ❑ 460 | Kurt Abbott | .05 | .15 |
| ❑ 461 | Bobby Witt | .05 | .15 |
| ❑ 462 | Cliff Floyd | .10 | .30 |
| ❑ 463 | Mark Clark | .05 | .15 |
| ❑ 464 | Andujar Cedeno | .05 | .15 |
| ❑ 465 | Marvin Freeman | .05 | .15 |
| ❑ 466 | Mike Piazza | .50 | 1.25 |
| ❑ 467 | Willie Greene | .05 | .15 |
| ❑ 468 | Pat Kelly | .05 | .15 |
| ❑ 469 | Carlos Delgado | .10 | .30 |
| ❑ 470 | Willie Banks | .05 | .15 |
| ❑ 471 | Matt Walbeck | .05 | .15 |
| ❑ 472 | Mark McGwire | .75 | 2.00 |
| ❑ 473 | McKay Christensen RC | .05 | .15 |
| ❑ 474 | Alan Trammell | .10 | .30 |
| ❑ 475 | Tom Gordon | .05 | .15 |
| ❑ 476 | Greg Colbrunn | .05 | .15 |
| ❑ 477 | Darren Daulton | .10 | .30 |
| ❑ 478 | Albie Lopez | .05 | .15 |
| ❑ 479 | Robin Ventura | .10 | .30 |
| ❑ 480 | Eddie Perez RC | .15 | .40 |
| ❑ 481 | Bryan Eversgerd | .05 | .15 |
| ❑ 482 | Dave Fleming | .05 | .15 |
| ❑ 483 | Scott Livingstone | .05 | .15 |
| ❑ 484 | Pete Schourek | .05 | .15 |
| ❑ 485 | Bernie Williams | .20 | .50 |
| ❑ 486 | Mark Lemke | .05 | .15 |
| ❑ 487 | Eric Karros | .10 | .30 |
| ❑ 488 | Scott Ruffcorn | .05 | .15 |
| ❑ 489 | Billy Ashley | .05 | .15 |
| ❑ 490 | Rico Brogna | .05 | .15 |
| ❑ 491 | John Burkett | .05 | .15 |
| ❑ 492 | Cade Gaspar RC | .05 | .15 |
| ❑ 493 | Jorge Fabregas | .05 | .15 |
| ❑ 494 | Greg Gagne | .05 | .15 |
| ❑ 495 | Doug Jones | .05 | .15 |
| ❑ 496 | Troy O'Leary | .05 | .15 |
| ❑ 497 | Pat Rapp | .05 | .15 |
| ❑ 498 | Butch Henry | .05 | .15 |
| ❑ 499 | John Olerud | .10 | .30 |
| ❑ 500 | John Hudek | .05 | .15 |
| ❑ 501 | Jeff King | .05 | .15 |
| ❑ 502 | Bobby Bonilla | .10 | .30 |
| ❑ 503 | Albert Belle | .10 | .30 |
| ❑ 504 | Rick Wilkins | .05 | .15 |
| ❑ 505 | John Jaha | .05 | .15 |
| ❑ 506 | Nigel Wilson | .05 | .15 |
| ❑ 507 | Sid Fernandez | .05 | .15 |
| ❑ 508 | Deion Sanders | .20 | .50 |
| ❑ 509 | Gil Heredia | .05 | .15 |
| ❑ 510 | Scott Elarton RC | .15 | .40 |
| ❑ 511 | Melido Perez | .05 | .15 |
| ❑ 512 | Greg McMichael | .05 | .15 |
| ❑ 513 | Rusty Meacham | .05 | .15 |
| ❑ 514 | Shawn Green | .10 | .30 |
| ❑ 515 | Carlos Garcia | .05 | .15 |
| ❑ 516 | Dave Stevens | .05 | .15 |
| ❑ 517 | Eric Young | .05 | .15 |
| ❑ 518 | Omar Daal | .05 | .15 |
| ❑ 519 | Kirk Gibson | .10 | .30 |
| ❑ 520 | Spike Owen | .05 | .15 |
| ❑ 521 | Jacob Cruz RC | .10 | .30 |
| ❑ 522 | Sandy Alomar Jr. | .05 | .15 |
| ❑ 523 | Steve Bedrosian | .05 | .15 |
| ❑ 524 | Ricky Gutierrez | .05 | .15 |
| ❑ 525 | Dave Veres | .05 | .15 |
| ❑ 526 | Gregg Jefferies | .05 | .15 |
| ❑ 527 | Jose Valentin | .05 | .15 |
| ❑ 528 | Robb Nen | .10 | .30 |
| ❑ 529 | Jose Rijo | .05 | .15 |
| ❑ 530 | Sean Berry | .05 | .15 |
| ❑ 531 | Mike Gallego | .05 | .15 |
| ❑ 532 | Roberto Kelly | .05 | .15 |
| ❑ 533 | Kevin Stocker | .05 | .15 |
| ❑ 534 | Kirby Puckett | .30 | .75 |
| ❑ 535 | Chipper Jones | .30 | .75 |
| ❑ 536 | Russ Davis | .05 | .15 |
| ❑ 537 | Jon Lieber | .05 | .15 |
| ❑ 538 | Trey Moore RC | .05 | .15 |
| ❑ 539 | Joe Girardi | .05 | .15 |
| ❑ 540 | Miguel Cairo RC | .05 | .15 |
| ❑ 541 | Tony Phillips | .05 | .15 |
| ❑ 542 | Brian Anderson | .05 | .15 |
| ❑ 543 | Ivan Rodriguez | .20 | .50 |

|  |  | | |
|---|---|---|---|
| ❑ 544 | Jeff Cirillo | .05 | .15 |
| ❑ 545 | Joey Cora | .05 | .15 |
| ❑ 546 | Chris Hoiles | .05 | .15 |
| ❑ 547 | Bernard Gilkey | .05 | .15 |
| ❑ 548 | Mike Lansing | .05 | .15 |
| ❑ 549 | Jimmy Key | .10 | .30 |
| ❑ 550 | Mark Wohlers | .05 | .15 |
| ❑ 551 | Chris Clemons RC | .05 | .15 |
| ❑ 552 | Vinny Castilla | .10 | .30 |
| ❑ 553 | Mark Guthrie | .05 | .15 |
| ❑ 554 | Mike Lieberthal | .10 | .30 |
| ❑ 555 | Tommy Davis RC | .05 | .15 |
| ❑ 556 | Robby Thompson | .05 | .15 |
| ❑ 557 | Danny Bautista | .05 | .15 |
| ❑ 558 | Will Clark | .20 | .50 |
| ❑ 559 | Rickey Henderson | .30 | .75 |
| ❑ 560 | Todd Jones | .05 | .15 |
| ❑ 561 | Jack McDowell | .05 | .15 |
| ❑ 562 | Carlos Rodriguez | .05 | .15 |
| ❑ 563 | Mark Eichhorn | .05 | .15 |
| ❑ 564 | Jeff Nelson | .05 | .15 |
| ❑ 565 | Eric Anthony | .05 | .15 |
| ❑ 566 | Randy Velarde | .05 | .15 |
| ❑ 567 | Javier Lopez | .10 | .30 |
| ❑ 568 | Kevin Mitchell | .05 | .15 |
| ❑ 569 | Steve Karsay | .05 | .15 |
| ❑ 570 | Brian Meadows RC | .15 | .40 |
| ❑ 571 | Rey Ordonez RC | .30 | .75 |
| ❑ 572 | John Kruk | .10 | .30 |
| ❑ 573 | Scott Leius | .05 | .15 |
| ❑ 574 | John Patterson | .05 | .15 |
| ❑ 575 | Kevin Brown | .10 | .30 |
| ❑ 576 | Mike Moore | .05 | .15 |
| ❑ 577 | Manny Ramirez | .20 | .50 |
| ❑ 578 | Jose Lind | .05 | .15 |
| ❑ 579 | Derrick May | .05 | .15 |
| ❑ 580 | Cal Eldred | .05 | .15 |
| ❑ 581 | A.Boone RC/D.Bell | .30 | .75 |
| ❑ 582 | J.T. Snow | .10 | .30 |
| ❑ 583 | Luis Sojo | .05 | .15 |
| ❑ 584 | Moises Alou | .10 | .30 |
| ❑ 585 | Dave Clark | .05 | .15 |
| ❑ 586 | Dave Hollins | .05 | .15 |
| ❑ 587 | Nomar Garciaparra | .75 | 2.00 |
| ❑ 588 | Cal Ripken | 1.00 | 2.50 |
| ❑ 589 | Pedro Astacio | .05 | .15 |
| ❑ 590 | J.R. Phillips | .05 | .15 |
| ❑ 591 | Jeff Frye | .05 | .15 |
| ❑ 592 | Bo Jackson | .30 | .75 |
| ❑ 593 | Steve Ontiveros | .05 | .15 |
| ❑ 594 | David Nied | .05 | .15 |
| ❑ 595 | Brad Ausmus | .10 | .30 |
| ❑ 596 | Carlos Baerga | .10 | .30 |
| ❑ 597 | James Mouton | .05 | .15 |
| ❑ 598 | Ozzie Guillen | .10 | .30 |
| ❑ 599 | Johnny Damon | .30 | .75 |
| ❑ 600 | Yorkis Perez | .05 | .15 |
| ❑ 601 | Rich Rodriguez | .05 | .15 |
| ❑ 602 | Mark McLemore | .05 | .15 |
| ❑ 603 | Jeff Fassero | .05 | .15 |
| ❑ 604 | John Roper | .05 | .15 |
| ❑ 605 | Mark Johnson RC | .15 | .40 |
| ❑ 606 | Wes Chamberlain | .05 | .15 |
| ❑ 607 | Felix Jose | .05 | .15 |
| ❑ 608 | Tony Longmire | .05 | .15 |
| ❑ 609 | Duane Ward | .05 | .15 |
| ❑ 610 | Brett Butler | .10 | .30 |
| ❑ 611 | William VanLandingham | .05 | .15 |
| ❑ 612 | Mickey Tettleton | .05 | .15 |
| ❑ 613 | Brady Anderson | .10 | .30 |
| ❑ 614 | Reggie Jefferson | .05 | .15 |
| ❑ 615 | Mike Kingery | .05 | .15 |
| ❑ 616 | Derek Bell | .05 | .15 |
| ❑ 617 | Scott Erickson | .05 | .15 |
| ❑ 618 | Bob Wickman | .05 | .15 |
| ❑ 619 | Phil Leftwich | .05 | .15 |
| ❑ 620 | David Justice | .10 | .30 |
| ❑ 621 | Paul Wilson | .05 | .15 |
| ❑ 622 | Pedro Martinez | .20 | .50 |
| ❑ 623 | Terry Mathews | .05 | .15 |
| ❑ 624 | Brian McRae | .05 | .15 |
| ❑ 625 | Bruce Ruffin | .05 | .15 |
| ❑ 626 | Steve Finley | .10 | .30 |
| ❑ 627 | Ron Gant | .10 | .30 |
| ❑ 628 | Rafael Bournigal | .05 | .15 |
| ❑ 629 | Darryl Strawberry | .10 | .30 |
| ❑ 630 | Luis Alicea | .05 | .15 |
| ❑ 631 | Mark Smith | .05 | .15 |

|  |  | | |
|---|---|---|---|
| ❑ 632 | C.Bailey/S.Hatteberg | .05 | .15 |
| ❑ 633 | Todd Greene | .10 | .30 |
| ❑ 634 | Rod Bolton | .05 | .15 |
| ❑ 635 | Herbert Perry | .05 | .15 |
| ❑ 636 | Sean Bergman | .05 | .15 |
| ❑ 637 | J.Randa/J.Vitiello | .10 | .30 |
| ❑ 638 | Jose Mercedes | .05 | .15 |
| ❑ 639 | Marty Cordova | .05 | .15 |
| ❑ 640 | R.Rivera/A.Pettitte | .10 | .30 |
| ❑ 641 | W.Adams/S.Spiezio | .05 | .15 |
| ❑ 642 | Eddy Diaz RC | .05 | .15 |
| ❑ 643 | Jon Shave | .05 | .15 |
| ❑ 644 | Paul Spoljaric | .05 | .15 |
| ❑ 645 | Damon Hollins | .05 | .15 |
| ❑ 646 | Doug Glanville | .05 | .15 |
| ❑ 647 | Tim Belk | .05 | .15 |
| ❑ 648 | Rod Pedraza | .05 | .15 |
| ❑ 649 | Marc Valdes | .05 | .15 |
| ❑ 650 | Rick Huisman | .05 | .15 |
| ❑ 651 | Ron Coomer RC | .15 | .40 |
| ❑ 652 | Carlos Perez | .05 | .15 |
| ❑ 653 | Jason Isringhausen | .10 | .30 |
| ❑ 654 | Kevin Jordan | .05 | .15 |
| ❑ 655 | Esteban Loaiza | .05 | .15 |
| ❑ 656 | John Frascatore | .05 | .15 |
| ❑ 657 | Bryce Florie | .05 | .15 |
| ❑ 658 | Keith Williams | .05 | .15 |
| ❑ 659 | Checklist | .05 | .15 |
| ❑ 660 | Checklist | .05 | .15 |

## 1996 Topps

|  |  | | |
|---|---|---|---|
| ❑ | COMPLETE SET (440) | 15.00 | 40.00 |
| ❑ | COMP.HOBBY SET (449) | 15.00 | 40.00 |
| ❑ | COMP.CEREAL SET (444) | 25.00 | 50.00 |
| ❑ | COMPLETE SERIES 1 (220) | 8.00 | 20.00 |
| ❑ | COMPLETE SERIES 2 (220) | 8.00 | 20.00 |
| ❑ | COMMON CARD (1-440) | .07 | .15 |
| ❑ | COMMON RC | .08 | .25 |
| ❑ 1 | Tony Gwynn STP | .10 | .30 |
| ❑ 2 | Mike Piazza STP | .20 | .50 |
| ❑ 3 | Greg Maddux STP | .20 | .50 |
| ❑ 4 | Jeff Bagwell STP | .07 | .20 |
| ❑ 5 | Larry Walker STP | .07 | .20 |
| ❑ 6 | Barry Larkin STP | .07 | .20 |
| ❑ 7 | Mickey Mantle | 1.50 | 4.00 |
| ❑ 8 | Tom Glavine STP | .07 | .20 |
| ❑ 9 | Craig Biggio STP | .07 | .20 |
| ❑ 10 | Barry Bonds STP | .30 | .75 |
| ❑ 11 | Heathcliff Slocumb STP | .07 | .20 |
| ❑ 12 | Matt Williams STP | .07 | .20 |
| ❑ 13 | Todd Helton | .40 | 1.00 |
| ❑ 14 | Mark Redman | .08 | .25 |
| ❑ 15 | Michael Barrett | .08 | .25 |
| ❑ 16 | Ben Davis | .08 | .25 |
| ❑ 17 | Juan LeBron | .08 | .25 |
| ❑ 18 | Tony McKnight | .08 | .25 |
| ❑ 19 | Ryan Jaroncyk | .08 | .25 |
| ❑ 20 | Corey Jenkins | .08 | .25 |
| ❑ 21 | Jim Scharrer | .08 | .25 |
| ❑ 22 | Mark Bellhorn RC | .40 | 1.00 |
| ❑ 23 | Jarrod Washburn RC | .30 | .75 |
| ❑ 24 | Geoff Jenkins RC | .30 | .75 |
| ❑ 25 | Sean Casey RC | 1.50 | 4.00 |
| ❑ 26 | Brett Tomko RC | .15 | .40 |
| ❑ 27 | Tony Fernandez | .07 | .20 |
| ❑ 28 | Rich Becker | .07 | .20 |
| ❑ 29 | Andujar Cedeno | .07 | .20 |
| ❑ 30 | Paul Molitor | .07 | .20 |
| ❑ 31 | Brent Gates | .07 | .20 |
| ❑ 32 | Glenallen Hill | .07 | .20 |
| ❑ 33 | Mike Macfarlane | .07 | .20 |
| ❑ 34 | Manny Alexander | .07 | .20 |
| ❑ 35 | Todd Zeile | .07 | .20 |
| ❑ 36 | Joe Girardi | .07 | .20 |

|  |  | | |
|---|--------|----|----|
| ☐ 37 | Tony Tarasco | .07 | .20 |
| ☐ 38 | Tim Belcher | .07 | .20 |
| ☐ 39 | Tom Goodwin | .07 | .20 |
| ☐ 40 | Orel Hershiser | .07 | .20 |
| ☐ 41 | Tripp Cromer | .07 | .20 |
| ☐ 42 | Sean Bergman | .07 | .20 |
| ☐ 43 | Troy Percival | .07 | .20 |
| ☐ 44 | Kevin Stocker | .07 | .20 |
| ☐ 45 | Albert Belle | .07 | .20 |
| ☐ 46 | Tony Eusebio | .07 | .20 |
| ☐ 47 | Sid Roberson | .07 | .20 |
| ☐ 48 | Todd Hollandsworth | .07 | .20 |
| ☐ 49 | Mark Wohlers | .07 | .20 |
| ☐ 50 | Kirby Puckett | .20 | .50 |
| ☐ 51 | Darren Holmes | .07 | .20 |
| ☐ 52 | Ron Karkovice | .07 | .20 |
| ☐ 53 | Al Martin | .07 | .20 |
| ☐ 54 | Pat Rapp | .07 | .20 |
| ☐ 55 | Mark Grace | .10 | .30 |
| ☐ 56 | Greg Gagne | .07 | .20 |
| ☐ 57 | Stan Javier | .07 | .20 |
| ☐ 58 | Scott Sanders | .07 | .20 |
| ☐ 59 | J.T. Snow | .07 | .20 |
| ☐ 60 | David Justice | .07 | .20 |
| ☐ 61 | Royce Clayton | .07 | .20 |
| ☐ 62 | Kevin Foster | .07 | .20 |
| ☐ 63 | Tim Naehring | .07 | .20 |
| ☐ 64 | Orlando Miller | .07 | .20 |
| ☐ 65 | Mike Mussina | .10 | .30 |
| ☐ 66 | Jim Eisenreich | .07 | .20 |
| ☐ 67 | Felix Fermin | .07 | .20 |
| ☐ 68 | Bernie Williams | .10 | .30 |
| ☐ 69 | Robb Nen | .07 | .20 |
| ☐ 70 | Ron Gant | .07 | .20 |
| ☐ 71 | Felipe Lira | .07 | .20 |
| ☐ 72 | Jacob Brumfield | .07 | .20 |
| ☐ 73 | John Mabry | .07 | .20 |
| ☐ 74 | Mark Carreon | .07 | .20 |
| ☐ 75 | Carlos Baerga | .07 | .20 |
| ☐ 76 | Jim Dougherty | .07 | .20 |
| ☐ 77 | Ryan Thompson | .07 | .20 |
| ☐ 78 | Scott Leius | .07 | .20 |
| ☐ 79 | Roger Pavlik | .07 | .20 |
| ☐ 80 | Gary Sheffield | .07 | .20 |
| ☐ 81 | Julian Tavarez | .07 | .20 |
| ☐ 82 | Andy Ashby | .07 | .20 |
| ☐ 83 | Mark Lemke | .07 | .20 |
| ☐ 84 | Omar Vizquel | .10 | .30 |
| ☐ 85 | Darren Daulton | .07 | .20 |
| ☐ 86 | Mike Lansing | .07 | .20 |
| ☐ 87 | Rusty Greer | .07 | .20 |
| ☐ 88 | Dave Stevens | .07 | .20 |
| ☐ 89 | Jose Offerman | .07 | .20 |
| ☐ 90 | Tom Henke | .07 | .20 |
| ☐ 91 | Troy O'Leary | .07 | .20 |
| ☐ 92 | Michael Tucker | .07 | .20 |
| ☐ 93 | Marvin Freeman | .07 | .20 |
| ☐ 94 | Alex Diaz | .07 | .20 |
| ☐ 95 | John Wetteland | .07 | .20 |
| ☐ 96 | Cal Ripken 2131 | .75 | 2.00 |
| ☐ 97 | Mike Mimbs | .07 | .20 |
| ☐ 98 | Bobby Higginson | .07 | .20 |
| ☐ 99 | Edgardo Alfonzo | .07 | .20 |
| ☐ 100 | Frank Thomas | .20 | .50 |
| ☐ 101 | Bob Abreu | .20 | .50 |
| ☐ 102 | B.Givens/T.J.Mathews | .08 | .25 |
| ☐ 103 | C.Pritchett/T.Hubbard | .08 | .25 |
| ☐ 104 | E.Owens/B.Huskey | .08 | .25 |
| ☐ 105 | Doug Drabek | .07 | .20 |
| ☐ 106 | Tomas Perez | .07 | .20 |
| ☐ 107 | Mark Lelter | .07 | .20 |
| ☐ 108 | Joe Oliver | .07 | .20 |
| ☐ 109 | Tony Castillo | .07 | .20 |
| ☐ 110 | Checklist (1-110) | .07 | .20 |
| ☐ 111 | Kevin Seitzer | .07 | .20 |
| ☐ 112 | Pete Schourek | .07 | .20 |
| ☐ 113 | Sean Berry | .07 | .20 |
| ☐ 114 | Todd Stottlemyre | .07 | .20 |
| ☐ 115 | Joe Carter | .07 | .20 |
| ☐ 116 | Jeff King | .07 | .20 |
| ☐ 117 | Dan Wilson | .07 | .20 |
| ☐ 118 | Kurt Abbott | .07 | .20 |
| ☐ 119 | Lyle Mouton | .07 | .20 |
| ☐ 120 | Jose Rijo | .07 | .20 |
| ☐ 121 | Curtis Goodwin | .07 | .20 |
| ☐ 122 | Jose Valentin | .07 | .20 |
| ☐ 123 | Ellis Burks | .07 | .20 |
| ☐ 124 | David Cone | .07 | .20 |
| ☐ 125 | Eddie Murray | .20 | .50 |
| ☐ 126 | Brian Jordan | .07 | .20 |
| ☐ 127 | Darrin Fletcher | .07 | .20 |
| ☐ 128 | Curt Schilling | .07 | .20 |
| ☐ 129 | Ozzie Guillen | .07 | .20 |
| ☐ 130 | Kenny Rogers | .07 | .20 |
| ☐ 131 | Tom Pagnozzi | .07 | .20 |
| ☐ 132 | Garret Anderson | .07 | .20 |
| ☐ 133 | Bobby Jones | .07 | .20 |
| ☐ 134 | Chris Gomez | .07 | .20 |
| ☐ 135 | Mike Stanley | .07 | .20 |
| ☐ 136 | Hideo Nomo | .20 | .50 |
| ☐ 137 | Jon Nunnally | .07 | .20 |
| ☐ 138 | Tim Wakefield | .07 | .20 |
| ☐ 139 | Steve Finley | .07 | .20 |
| ☐ 140 | Ivan Rodriguez | .10 | .30 |
| ☐ 141 | Quilvio Veras | .07 | .20 |
| ☐ 142 | Mike Fetters | .07 | .20 |
| ☐ 143 | Mike Greenwell | .07 | .20 |
| ☐ 144 | Bill Pulsipher | .07 | .20 |
| ☐ 145 | Mark McGwire | .50 | 1.25 |
| ☐ 146 | Frank Castillo | .07 | .20 |
| ☐ 147 | Greg Vaughn | .07 | .20 |
| ☐ 148 | Pat Hentgen | .07 | .20 |
| ☐ 149 | Walt Weiss | .07 | .20 |
| ☐ 150 | Randy Johnson | .20 | .50 |
| ☐ 151 | David Segui | .07 | .20 |
| ☐ 152 | Benji Gil | .07 | .20 |
| ☐ 153 | Tom Candiotti | .07 | .20 |
| ☐ 154 | Geronimo Berroa | .07 | .20 |
| ☐ 155 | John Franco | .07 | .20 |
| ☐ 156 | Jay Bell | .07 | .20 |
| ☐ 157 | Mark Gubicza | .07 | .20 |
| ☐ 158 | Hal Morris | .07 | .20 |
| ☐ 159 | Wilson Alvarez | .07 | .20 |
| ☐ 160 | Derek Bell | .07 | .20 |
| ☐ 161 | Ricky Bottalico | .07 | .20 |
| ☐ 162 | Bret Boone | .07 | .20 |
| ☐ 163 | Brad Radke | .07 | .20 |
| ☐ 164 | John Valentin | .07 | .20 |
| ☐ 165 | Steve Avery | .07 | .20 |
| ☐ 166 | Mark McLemore | .07 | .20 |
| ☐ 167 | Danny Jackson | .07 | .20 |
| ☐ 168 | Tino Martinez | .10 | .30 |
| ☐ 169 | Shane Reynolds | .07 | .20 |
| ☐ 170 | Terry Pendleton | .07 | .20 |
| ☐ 171 | Jim Edmonds | .07 | .20 |
| ☐ 172 | Esteban Loaiza | .07 | .20 |
| ☐ 173 | Ray Durham | .07 | .20 |
| ☐ 174 | Carlos Perez | .07 | .20 |
| ☐ 175 | Raul Mondesi | .07 | .20 |
| ☐ 176 | Steve Ontiveros | .07 | .20 |
| ☐ 177 | Chipper Jones | .20 | .50 |
| ☐ 178 | Otis Nixon | .07 | .20 |
| ☐ 179 | John Burkett | .07 | .20 |
| ☐ 180 | Gregg Jefferies | .07 | .20 |
| ☐ 181 | Denny Martinez | .07 | .20 |
| ☐ 182 | Ken Caminiti | .07 | .20 |
| ☐ 183 | Doug Jones | .07 | .20 |
| ☐ 184 | Brian McRae | .07 | .20 |
| ☐ 185 | Don Mattingly | .50 | 1.25 |
| ☐ 186 | Mel Rojas | .07 | .20 |
| ☐ 187 | Marty Cordova | .07 | .20 |
| ☐ 188 | Vinny Castilla | .07 | .20 |
| ☐ 189 | John Smoltz | .10 | .30 |
| ☐ 190 | Travis Fryman | .07 | .20 |
| ☐ 191 | Chris Hoiles | .07 | .20 |
| ☐ 192 | Chuck Finley | .07 | .20 |
| ☐ 193 | Ryan Klesko | .07 | .20 |
| ☐ 194 | Alex Fernandez | .07 | .20 |
| ☐ 195 | Dante Bichette | .07 | .20 |
| ☐ 196 | Eric Karros | .07 | .20 |
| ☐ 197 | Roger Clemens | .40 | 1.00 |
| ☐ 198 | Randy Myers | .07 | .20 |
| ☐ 199 | Tony Phillips | .07 | .20 |
| ☐ 200 | Cal Ripken | .60 | 1.50 |
| ☐ 201 | Rod Beck | .07 | .20 |
| ☐ 202 | Chad Curtis | .07 | .20 |
| ☐ 203 | Jack McDowell | .07 | .20 |
| ☐ 204 | Gary Gaetti | .07 | .20 |
| ☐ 205 | Ken Griffey Jr. | .30 | .75 |
| ☐ 206 | Ramon Martinez | .07 | .20 |
| ☐ 207 | Jeff Kent | .07 | .20 |
| ☐ 208 | Brad Ausmus | .07 | .20 |
| ☐ 209 | Devon White | .07 | .20 |
| ☐ 210 | Jason Giambi | .07 | .20 |
| ☐ 211 | Nomar Garciaparra | .30 | .75 |
| ☐ 212 | Billy Wagner | .07 | .20 |
| ☐ 213 | Todd Greene | .07 | .20 |
| ☐ 214 | Paul Wilson | .07 | .20 |
| ☐ 215 | Johnny Damon | .10 | .30 |
| ☐ 216 | Alan Benes | .07 | .20 |
| ☐ 217 | Karim Garcia | .07 | .20 |
| ☐ 218 | Dustin Hermanson | .07 | .20 |
| ☐ 219 | Derek Jeter | .50 | 1.25 |
| ☐ 220 | Checklist (111-220) | .07 | .20 |
| ☐ 221 | Kirby Puckett STP | .10 | .30 |
| ☐ 222 | Cal Ripken STP | .30 | .75 |
| ☐ 223 | Albert Belle STP | .07 | .20 |
| ☐ 224 | Randy Johnson STP | .10 | .30 |
| ☐ 225 | Wade Boggs STP | .07 | .20 |
| ☐ 226 | Carlos Baerga STP | .07 | .20 |
| ☐ 227 | Ivan Rodriguez STP | .07 | .20 |
| ☐ 228 | Mike Mussina STP | .07 | .20 |
| ☐ 229 | Frank Thomas STP | .10 | .30 |
| ☐ 230 | Ken Griffey Jr. STP | .20 | .50 |
| ☐ 231 | Jose Mesa STP | .07 | .20 |
| ☐ 232 | Matt Morris RC | .60 | 1.50 |
| ☐ 233 | Craig Wilson RC | .30 | .75 |
| ☐ 234 | Alvie Shepherd | .08 | .25 |
| ☐ 235 | Randy Winn RC | .30 | .75 |
| ☐ 236 | David Yocum RC | .08 | .25 |
| ☐ 237 | Jason Brester RC | .08 | .25 |
| ☐ 238 | Shane Monahan RC | .08 | .25 |
| ☐ 239 | Brian McNichol RC | .08 | .25 |
| ☐ 240 | Reggie Taylor | .08 | .25 |
| ☐ 241 | Garrett Long | .08 | .25 |
| ☐ 242 | Jonathan Johnson | .08 | .25 |
| ☐ 243 | Jeff Liefer RC | .08 | .25 |
| ☐ 244 | Brian Powell | .08 | .25 |
| ☐ 245 | Brian Buchanan RC | .08 | .25 |
| ☐ 246 | Mike Piazza | .30 | .75 |
| ☐ 247 | Edgar Martinez | .10 | .30 |
| ☐ 248 | Chuck Knoblauch | .07 | .20 |
| ☐ 249 | Andres Galarraga | .07 | .20 |
| ☐ 250 | Tony Gwynn | .25 | .60 |
| ☐ 251 | Lee Smith | .07 | .20 |
| ☐ 252 | Sammy Sosa | .20 | .50 |
| ☐ 253 | Jim Thome | .10 | .30 |
| ☐ 254 | Frank Rodriguez | .07 | .20 |
| ☐ 255 | Charlie Hayes | .07 | .20 |
| ☐ 256 | Bernard Gilkey | .07 | .20 |
| ☐ 257 | John Smiley | .07 | .20 |
| ☐ 258 | Brady Anderson | .07 | .20 |
| ☐ 259 | Rico Brogna | .07 | .20 |
| ☐ 260 | Kirt Manwaring | .07 | .20 |
| ☐ 261 | Len Dykstra | .07 | .20 |
| ☐ 262 | Tom Glavine | .10 | .30 |
| ☐ 263 | Vince Coleman | .07 | .20 |
| ☐ 264 | John Olerud | .07 | .20 |
| ☐ 265 | Orlando Merced | .07 | .20 |
| ☐ 266 | Kent Mercker | .07 | .20 |
| ☐ 267 | Terry Steinbach | .07 | .20 |
| ☐ 268 | Brian L. Hunter | .07 | .20 |
| ☐ 269 | Jeff Fassero | .07 | .20 |
| ☐ 270 | Jay Buhner | .07 | .20 |
| ☐ 271 | Jeff Brantley | .07 | .20 |
| ☐ 272 | Tim Raines | .07 | .20 |
| ☐ 273 | Jimmy Key | .07 | .20 |
| ☐ 274 | Mo Vaughn | .07 | .20 |
| ☐ 275 | Andre Dawson | .07 | .20 |
| ☐ 276 | Jose Mesa | .07 | .20 |
| ☐ 277 | Brett Butler | .07 | .20 |
| ☐ 278 | Luis Gonzalez | .07 | .20 |
| ☐ 279 | Steve Sparks | .07 | .20 |
| ☐ 280 | Chili Davis | .07 | .20 |
| ☐ 281 | Carl Everett | .07 | .20 |
| ☐ 282 | Alex Cirillo | .07 | .20 |
| ☐ 283 | Thomas Howard | .07 | .20 |
| ☐ 284 | Paul O'Neill | .10 | .30 |
| ☐ 285 | Pat Meares | .07 | .20 |
| ☐ 286 | Mickey Tettleton | .07 | .20 |
| ☐ 287 | Rey Sanchez | .07 | .20 |
| ☐ 288 | Bip Roberts | .07 | .20 |
| ☐ 289 | Roberto Alomar | .10 | .30 |
| ☐ 290 | Ruben Sierra | .07 | .20 |
| ☐ 291 | John Flaherty | .07 | .20 |
| ☐ 292 | Bret Saberhagen | .07 | .20 |
| ☐ 293 | Barry Larkin | .10 | .30 |
| ☐ 294 | Sandy Alomar Jr. | .07 | .20 |
| ☐ 295 | Ed Sprague | .07 | .20 |
| ☐ 296 | Gary DiSarcina | .07 | .20 |
| ☐ 297 | Marquis Grissom | .07 | .20 |
| ☐ 298 | John Frascatore | .07 | .20 |
| ☐ 299 | Will Clark | .10 | .30 |
| ☐ 300 | Barry Bonds | .60 | 1.50 |

| Card | Lo | Hi |
|---|---|---|
| 301 Ozzie Smith | .30 | .75 |
| 302 Dave Nilsson | .07 | .20 |
| 303 Pedro Martinez | .10 | .30 |
| 304 Joey Cora | .07 | .20 |
| 305 Rick Aguilera | .07 | .20 |
| 306 Craig Biggio | .10 | .30 |
| 307 Jose Vizcaino | .07 | .20 |
| 308 Jeff Montgomery | .07 | .20 |
| 309 Moises Alou | .07 | .20 |
| 310 Robin Ventura | .07 | .20 |
| 311 David Wells | .07 | .20 |
| 312 Delino DeShields | .07 | .20 |
| 313 Trevor Hoffman | .07 | .20 |
| 314 Andy Benes | .07 | .20 |
| 315 Deion Sanders | .10 | .30 |
| 316 Jim Bullinger | .07 | .20 |
| 317 John Jaha | .07 | .20 |
| 318 Greg Maddux | .30 | .75 |
| 319 Tim Salmon | .10 | .30 |
| 320 Ben McDonald | .07 | .20 |
| 321 Sandy Martinez | .07 | .20 |
| 322 Dan Miceli | .07 | .20 |
| 323 Wade Boggs | .10 | .30 |
| 324 Ismael Valdes | .07 | .20 |
| 325 Juan Gonzalez | .20 | .50 |
| 326 Charles Nagy | .07 | .20 |
| 327 Ray Lankford | .07 | .20 |
| 328 Mark Portugal | .07 | .20 |
| 329 Bobby Bonilla | .07 | .20 |
| 330 Reggie Sanders | .07 | .20 |
| 331 Jamie Brewington RC | .08 | .25 |
| 332 Aaron Sele | .07 | .20 |
| 333 Pete Harnisch | .07 | .20 |
| 334 Cliff Floyd | .07 | .20 |
| 335 Cal Eldred | .07 | .20 |
| 336 Jason Bates | .07 | .20 |
| 337 Tony Clark | .07 | .20 |
| 338 Jose Herrera | .07 | .20 |
| 339 Alex Ochoa | .07 | .20 |
| 340 Mark Loretta | .07 | .20 |
| 341 Donne Wall | .07 | .20 |
| 342 Jason Kendall | .07 | .20 |
| 343 Shannon Stewart | .07 | .20 |
| 344 Brooks Kieschnick | .07 | .20 |
| 345 Chris Snopek | .07 | .20 |
| 346 Ruben Rivera | .07 | .20 |
| 347 Jeff Suppan | .07 | .20 |
| 348 Phil Nevin | .07 | .20 |
| 349 John Wasdin | .07 | .20 |
| 350 Jay Payton | .07 | .20 |
| 351 Tim Crabtree | .07 | .20 |
| 352 Rick Krivda | .07 | .20 |
| 353 Bob Wolcott | .07 | .20 |
| 354 Jimmy Haynes | .07 | .20 |
| 355 Herb Perry | .07 | .20 |
| 356 Ryne Sandberg | .30 | .75 |
| 357 Harold Baines | .07 | .20 |
| 358 Chad Ogea | .07 | .20 |
| 359 Lee Tinsley | .07 | .20 |
| 360 Matt Williams | .07 | .20 |
| 361 Randy Velarde | .07 | .20 |
| 362 Jose Canseco | .10 | .30 |
| 363 Larry Walker | .07 | .20 |
| 364 Kevin Appier | .07 | .20 |
| 365 Darryl Hamilton | .07 | .20 |
| 366 Jose Lima | .07 | .20 |
| 367 Javy Lopez | .07 | .20 |
| 368 Dennis Eckersley | .07 | .20 |
| 369 Jason Isringhausen | .07 | .20 |
| 370 Mickey Morandini | .07 | .20 |
| 371 Scott Cooper | .07 | .20 |
| 372 Jim Abbott | .10 | .30 |
| 373 Paul Sorrento | .07 | .20 |
| 374 Chris Hammond | .07 | .20 |
| 375 Lance Johnson | .07 | .20 |
| 376 Kevin Brown | .07 | .20 |
| 377 Luis Alicea | .07 | .20 |
| 378 Andy Pettitte | .10 | .30 |
| 379 Dean Palmer | .07 | .20 |
| 380 Jeff Bagwell | .10 | .30 |
| 381 Jaime Navarro | .07 | .20 |
| 382 Rondell White | .07 | .20 |
| 383 Erik Hanson | .07 | .20 |
| 384 Pedro Munoz | .07 | .20 |
| 385 Heathcliff Slocumb | .07 | .20 |
| 386 Wally Joyner | .07 | .20 |
| 387 Bob Tewksbury | .07 | .20 |
| 388 David Bell | .07 | .20 |
| 389 Fred McGriff | .10 | .30 |
| 390 Mike Henneman | .07 | .20 |
| 391 Robby Thompson | .07 | .20 |
| 392 Norm Charlton | .07 | .20 |
| 393 Cecil Fielder | .07 | .20 |
| 394 Benito Santiago | .07 | .20 |
| 395 Rafael Palmeiro | .10 | .30 |
| 396 Ricky Bones | .07 | .20 |
| 397 Rickey Henderson | .20 | .50 |
| 398 C.J. Nitkowski | .07 | .20 |
| 399 Shawon Dunston | .07 | .20 |
| 400 Manny Ramirez | .10 | .30 |
| 401 Bill Swift | .07 | .20 |
| 402 Chad Fonville | .07 | .20 |
| 403 Joey Hamilton | .07 | .20 |
| 404 Alex Gonzalez | .07 | .20 |
| 405 Roberto Hernandez | .07 | .20 |
| 406 Jeff Blauser | .07 | .20 |
| 407 LaTroy Hawkins | .07 | .20 |
| 408 Greg Colbrunn | .07 | .20 |
| 409 Todd Hundley | .07 | .20 |
| 410 Glenn Dishman | .07 | .20 |
| 411 Joe Vitiello | .07 | .20 |
| 412 Todd Worrell | .07 | .20 |
| 413 Wil Cordero | .07 | .20 |
| 414 Ken Hill | .07 | .20 |
| 415 Carlos Garcia | .07 | .20 |
| 416 Bryan Rekar | .07 | .20 |
| 417 Shawn Green | .07 | .20 |
| 418 Tyler Green | .07 | .20 |
| 419 Mike Blowers | .07 | .20 |
| 420 Kenny Lofton | .20 | .50 |
| 421 Denny Neagle | .07 | .20 |
| 422 Jeff Conine | .07 | .20 |
| 423 Mark Langston | .07 | .20 |
| 424 Ron Wright RC/D.Lee | .30 | .75 |
| 425 D.Ward RC/R.Sexson | .40 | 1.00 |
| 426 Adam Riggs RC | .08 | .25 |
| 427 N.Perez/E.Wilson | .08 | .25 |
| 428 Bartolo Colon | .20 | .50 |
| 429 Marty Janzen RC | .08 | .25 |
| 430 Rich Hunter RC | .06 | .20 |
| 431 Dave Coggin RC | .08 | .25 |
| 432 R.Ibanez RC/P.Konerko | .60 | 1.50 |
| 433 Marc Kroon | .07 | .20 |
| 434 S.Rolen/S.Spiezio | .20 | .50 |
| 435 V.Guerrero/A.Jones | 1.00 | 2.50 |
| 436 Shane Spencer RC | .15 | .40 |
| 437 A.French/D.Stovall RC | .08 | .25 |
| 438 M.Coleman RC/R.Hidalgo | .08 | .25 |
| 439 Jermaine Dye | .07 | .20 |
| 440 Checklist | .07 | .20 |
| F7 Mickey Mantle Last Day | 2.00 | 5.00 |
| NNO Mickey Mantle Tribute Card, promotes the Mantle F | 1.25 | 3.00 |

### 1997 Topps

| Card | Lo | Hi |
|---|---|---|
| COMPLETE SET (495) | 40.00 | 80.00 |
| COMPLETE SERIES 1 (276) | 20.00 | 40.00 |
| COMPLETE SERIES 2 (220) | 20.00 | 40.00 |
| 1 Barry Bonds | .60 | 1.50 |
| 2 Tom Pagnozzi | .07 | .20 |
| 3 Terrell Wade | .07 | .20 |
| 4 Jose Valentin | .07 | .20 |
| 5 Mark Clark | .07 | .20 |
| 6 Brady Anderson | .07 | .20 |
| 7 Wade Boggs | .10 | .30 |
| 8 Scott Stahoviak | .07 | .20 |
| 9 Andres Galarraga | .07 | .20 |
| 10 Steve Avery | .07 | .20 |
| 11 Rusty Greer | .07 | .20 |
| 12 Derek Jeter | .50 | 1.25 |
| 13 Derek Jeter | .50 | 1.25 |
| 14 Ricky Bottalico | .07 | .20 |
| 15 Andy Ashby | .07 | .20 |
| 16 Paul Shuey | .07 | .20 |
| 17 F.P. Santangelo | .07 | .20 |
| 18 Royce Clayton | .07 | .20 |
| 19 Mike Mohler | .07 | .20 |
| 20 Mike Piazza | .30 | .75 |
| 21 Jaime Navarro | .07 | .20 |
| 22 Billy Wagner | .07 | .20 |
| 23 Mike Timlin | .07 | .20 |
| 24 Garret Anderson | .07 | .20 |
| 25 Ben McDonald | .07 | .20 |
| 26 Mel Rojas | .07 | .20 |
| 27 John Burkett | .07 | .20 |
| 28 Jeff King | .07 | .20 |
| 29 Reggie Jefferson | .07 | .20 |
| 30 Kevin Appier | .07 | .20 |
| 31 Felipe Lira | .07 | .20 |
| 32 Kevin Tapani | .07 | .20 |
| 33 Mark Portugal | .07 | .20 |
| 34 Carlos Garcia | .07 | .20 |
| 35 Joey Cora | .07 | .20 |
| 36 David Segui | .07 | .20 |
| 37 Mark Grace | .10 | .30 |
| 38 Erik Hanson | .07 | .20 |
| 39 Jeff D'Amico | .07 | .20 |
| 40 Jay Buhner | .07 | .20 |
| 41 B.J. Surhoff | .07 | .20 |
| 42 Jackie Robinson TRIB | .20 | .50 |
| 43 Roger Pavlik | .07 | .20 |
| 44 Hal Morris | .07 | .20 |
| 45 Mariano Duncan | .07 | .20 |
| 46 Harold Baines | .07 | .20 |
| 47 Jorge Fabregas | .07 | .20 |
| 48 Jose Herrera | .07 | .20 |
| 49 Jeff Cirillo | .07 | .20 |
| 50 Tom Glavine | .10 | .30 |
| 51 Pedro Astacio | .07 | .20 |
| 52 Mark Gardner | .07 | .20 |
| 53 Arthur Rhodes | .07 | .20 |
| 54 Troy O'Leary | .07 | .20 |
| 55 Bip Roberts | .07 | .20 |
| 56 Mike Lieberthal | .07 | .20 |
| 57 Shane Andrews | .07 | .20 |
| 58 Scott Karl | .07 | .20 |
| 59 Gary DiSarcina | .07 | .20 |
| 60 Andy Pettitte | .10 | .30 |
| 61 Kevin Elster | .07 | .20 |
| 61B Mike Fetters UER | .07 | .20 |
| 62 Mark McGwire | .50 | 1.25 |
| 63 Dan Wilson | .07 | .20 |
| 64 Mickey Morandini | .07 | .20 |
| 65 Chuck Knoblauch | .07 | .20 |
| 66 Tim Wakefield | .07 | .20 |
| 67 Raul Mondesi | .07 | .20 |
| 68 Todd Jones | .07 | .20 |
| 69 Albert Belle | .20 | .50 |
| 70 Trevor Hoffman | .07 | .20 |
| 71 Eric Young | .07 | .20 |
| 72 Robert Perez | .07 | .20 |
| 73 Butch Huskey | .07 | .20 |
| 74 Brian McRae | .07 | .20 |
| 75 Jim Edmonds | .07 | .20 |
| 76 Mike Henneman | .07 | .20 |
| 77 Frank Rodriguez | .07 | .20 |
| 78 Danny Tartabull | .07 | .20 |
| 79 Robb Nen | .07 | .20 |
| 80 Reggie Sanders | .07 | .20 |
| 81 Ron Karkovice | .07 | .20 |
| 82 Benito Santiago | .07 | .20 |
| 83 Mike Lansing | .07 | .20 |
| 85 Craig Biggio | .10 | .30 |
| 86 Mike Bordick | .07 | .20 |
| 87 Ray Lankford | .07 | .20 |
| 88 Charles Nagy | .07 | .20 |
| 89 Paul Wilson | .07 | .20 |
| 90 John Wetteland | .07 | .20 |
| 91 Tom Candiotti | .07 | .20 |
| 92 Carlos Delgado | .07 | .20 |
| 93 Derek Bell | .07 | .20 |
| 94 Mark Lemke | .07 | .20 |
| 95 Edgar Martinez | .10 | .30 |
| 96 Rickey Henderson | .20 | .50 |
| 97 Greg Myers | .07 | .20 |
| 98 Jim Leyritz | .07 | .20 |
| 99 Mark Johnson | .07 | .20 |
| 100 Dwight Gooden HL | .07 | .20 |
| 101 Al Leiter HL | .07 | .20 |
| 102 John Mabry HL | .07 | .20 |
| 103 Alex Ochoa HL | .07 | .20 |

| Card | .. | .. |
|---|---|---|
| ❑ 104 Mike Piazza HL | .20 | .50 |
| ❑ 105 Jim Thome | .10 | .30 |
| ❑ 106 Ricky Otero | .07 | .20 |
| ❑ 107 Jamey Wright | .07 | .20 |
| ❑ 108 Frank Thomas | .20 | .50 |
| ❑ 109 Jody Reed | .07 | .20 |
| ❑ 110 Orel Hershiser | .07 | .20 |
| ❑ 111 Terry Steinbach | .07 | .20 |
| ❑ 112 Mark Loretta | .07 | .20 |
| ❑ 113 Turk Wendell | .07 | .20 |
| ❑ 114 Marvin Benard | .07 | .20 |
| ❑ 115 Kevin Brown | .07 | .20 |
| ❑ 116 Robert Person | .07 | .20 |
| ❑ 117 Joey Hamilton | .07 | .20 |
| ❑ 118 Francisco Cordova | .07 | .20 |
| ❑ 119 John Smiley | .07 | .20 |
| ❑ 120 Travis Fryman | .07 | .20 |
| ❑ 121 Jimmy Key | .07 | .20 |
| ❑ 122 Tom Goodwin | .07 | .20 |
| ❑ 123 Mike Greenwell | .07 | .20 |
| ❑ 124 Juan Gonzalez | .20 | .50 |
| ❑ 125 Pete Harnisch | .07 | .20 |
| ❑ 126 Roger Cedeno | .07 | .20 |
| ❑ 127 Ron Gant | .07 | .20 |
| ❑ 128 Mark Langston | .07 | .20 |
| ❑ 129 Tim Crabtree | .07 | .20 |
| ❑ 130 Greg Maddux | .30 | .75 |
| ❑ 131 William VanLandingham | .07 | .20 |
| ❑ 132 Wally Joyner | .07 | .20 |
| ❑ 133 Randy Myers | .07 | .20 |
| ❑ 134 John Valentin | .07 | .20 |
| ❑ 135 Bret Boone | .07 | .20 |
| ❑ 136 Bruce Ruffin | .07 | .20 |
| ❑ 137 Chris Snopek | .07 | .20 |
| ❑ 138 Paul Molitor | .07 | .20 |
| ❑ 139 Mark McLemore | .07 | .20 |
| ❑ 140 Rafael Palmeiro | .10 | .30 |
| ❑ 141 Herb Perry | .07 | .20 |
| ❑ 142 Luis Gonzalez | .07 | .20 |
| ❑ 143 Doug Drabek | .07 | .20 |
| ❑ 144 Ken Ryan | .07 | .20 |
| ❑ 145 Todd Hundley | .07 | .20 |
| ❑ 146 Ellis Burks | .07 | .20 |
| ❑ 147 Ozzie Guillen | .07 | .20 |
| ❑ 148 Rich Becker | .07 | .20 |
| ❑ 149 Sterling Hitchcock | .07 | .20 |
| ❑ 150 Bernie Williams | .10 | .30 |
| ❑ 151 Mike Stanley | .07 | .20 |
| ❑ 152 Roberto Alomar | .10 | .30 |
| ❑ 153 Jose Mesa | .07 | .20 |
| ❑ 154 Steve Trachsel | .07 | .20 |
| ❑ 155 Alex Gonzalez | .07 | .20 |
| ❑ 156 Troy Percival | .07 | .20 |
| ❑ 157 John Smoltz | .10 | .30 |
| ❑ 158 Pedro Martinez | .10 | .30 |
| ❑ 159 Jeff Conine | .07 | .20 |
| ❑ 160 Bernard Gilkey | .07 | .20 |
| ❑ 161 Jim Eisenreich | .07 | .20 |
| ❑ 162 Mickey Tettleton | .07 | .20 |
| ❑ 163 Justin Thompson | .07 | .20 |
| ❑ 164 Jose Offerman | .07 | .20 |
| ❑ 165 Tony Phillips | .07 | .20 |
| ❑ 166 Ismael Valdes | .07 | .20 |
| ❑ 167 Ryne Sandberg | .30 | .75 |
| ❑ 168 Matt Mieske | .07 | .20 |
| ❑ 169 Geronimo Berroa | .07 | .20 |
| ❑ 170 Otis Nixon | .07 | .20 |
| ❑ 171 John Mabry | .07 | .20 |
| ❑ 172 Shawon Dunston | .07 | .20 |
| ❑ 173 Omar Vizquel | .10 | .30 |
| ❑ 174 Chris Holles | .07 | .20 |
| ❑ 175 Dwight Gooden | .07 | .20 |
| ❑ 176 Wilson Alvarez | .07 | .20 |
| ❑ 177 Todd Hollandsworth | .07 | .20 |
| ❑ 178 Roger Salkeld | .07 | .20 |
| ❑ 179 Rey Sanchez | .07 | .20 |
| ❑ 180 Rey Ordonez | .10 | .30 |
| ❑ 181 Denny Martinez | .07 | .20 |
| ❑ 182 Ramon Martinez | .07 | .20 |
| ❑ 183 Dave Nilsson | .07 | .20 |
| ❑ 184 Marquis Grissom | .07 | .20 |
| ❑ 185 Randy Velarde | .07 | .20 |
| ❑ 186 Ron Coomer | .07 | .20 |
| ❑ 187 Tino Martinez | .10 | .30 |
| ❑ 188 Jeff Brantley | .07 | .20 |
| ❑ 189 Steve Finley | .07 | .20 |
| ❑ 190 Andy Benes | .07 | .20 |
| ❑ 191 Terry Adams | .07 | .20 |
| ❑ 192 Mike Blowers | .07 | .20 |
| ❑ 193 Russ Davis | .07 | .20 |
| ❑ 194 Darryl Hamilton | .07 | .20 |
| ❑ 195 Jason Kendall | .07 | .20 |
| ❑ 196 Johnny Damon | .10 | .30 |
| ❑ 197 Dave Martinez | .07 | .20 |
| ❑ 198 Mike Macfarlane | .07 | .20 |
| ❑ 199 Norm Charlton | .07 | .20 |
| ❑ 200 Damian Moss | .08 | .25 |
| ❑ 201 Jenkins/Ibanez/Cameron | .07 | .20 |
| ❑ 202 Sean Casey | .10 | .30 |
| ❑ 203 J.Hansen/H.Bush/F.Crespo | .07 | .20 |
| ❑ 204 K.Orie/G.Alvarez/A.Boone | .07 | .20 |
| ❑ 205 B.Davis/K.Brown/B.Estalella | .07 | .20 |
| ❑ 206 Bubba Trammell RC | .15 | .40 |
| ❑ 207 Jarrod Washburn | .07 | .20 |
| ❑ 208 Brian Hunter | .07 | .20 |
| ❑ 209 Jason Giambi | .07 | .20 |
| ❑ 210 Henry Rodriguez | .07 | .20 |
| ❑ 211 Edgar Renteria | .07 | .20 |
| ❑ 212 Edgardo Alfonzo | .07 | .20 |
| ❑ 213 Fernando Vina | .07 | .20 |
| ❑ 214 Shawn Green | .07 | .20 |
| ❑ 215 Ray Durham | .07 | .20 |
| ❑ 216 Joe Randa | .07 | .20 |
| ❑ 217 Armando Reynoso | .07 | .20 |
| ❑ 218 Eric Davis | .07 | .20 |
| ❑ 219 Bob Tewksbury | .07 | .20 |
| ❑ 220 Jacob Cruz | .07 | .20 |
| ❑ 221 Glenallen Hill | .07 | .20 |
| ❑ 222 Gary Gaetti | .07 | .20 |
| ❑ 223 Donne Wall | .07 | .20 |
| ❑ 224 Brad Clontz | .07 | .20 |
| ❑ 225 Marty Janzen | .07 | .20 |
| ❑ 226 Todd Worrell | .07 | .20 |
| ❑ 227 John Franco | .07 | .20 |
| ❑ 228 David Wells | .07 | .20 |
| ❑ 229 Gregg Jefferies | .07 | .20 |
| ❑ 230 Tim Naehring | .07 | .20 |
| ❑ 231 Thomas Howard | .07 | .20 |
| ❑ 232 Roberto Hernandez | .07 | .20 |
| ❑ 233 Kevin Ritz | .07 | .20 |
| ❑ 234 Julian Tavarez | .07 | .20 |
| ❑ 235 Ken Hill | .07 | .20 |
| ❑ 236 Greg Gagne | .07 | .20 |
| ❑ 237 Bobby Chouinard | .07 | .20 |
| ❑ 238 Joe Carter | .10 | .30 |
| ❑ 239 Jermaine Dye | .07 | .20 |
| ❑ 240 Antonio Osuna | .07 | .20 |
| ❑ 241 Julio Franco | .07 | .20 |
| ❑ 242 Mike Grace | .07 | .20 |
| ❑ 243 Aaron Sele | .07 | .20 |
| ❑ 244 David Justice | .07 | .20 |
| ❑ 245 Sandy Alomar Jr. | .07 | .20 |
| ❑ 246 Jose Canseco | .10 | .30 |
| ❑ 247 Paul O'Neill | .10 | .30 |
| ❑ 248 Sean Berry | .07 | .20 |
| ❑ 249 N.Bierbrodt/K.Sweeney RC | .08 | .25 |
| ❑ 250 Vladimir Nunez RC | .08 | .25 |
| ❑ 251 R.Hartman/D.Hayman RC | .08 | .25 |
| ❑ 252 A.Sanchez/M.Quatraro RC | .15 | .40 |
| ❑ 253 Ronni Seberino RC | .08 | .25 |
| ❑ 254 Rex Hudler | .07 | .20 |
| ❑ 255 Orlando Miller | .07 | .20 |
| ❑ 256 Mariano Rivera | .20 | .50 |
| ❑ 257 Brad Radke | .07 | .20 |
| ❑ 258 Bobby Higginson | .07 | .20 |
| ❑ 259 Jay Bell | .07 | .20 |
| ❑ 260 Mark Grudzielanek | .07 | .20 |
| ❑ 261 Lance Johnson | .07 | .20 |
| ❑ 262 Ken Caminiti | .07 | .20 |
| ❑ 263 J.T. Snow | .07 | .20 |
| ❑ 264 Gary Sheffield | .10 | .30 |
| ❑ 265 Darren Fletcher | .07 | .20 |
| ❑ 266 Eric Owens | .07 | .20 |
| ❑ 267 Luis Castillo | .07 | .20 |
| ❑ 268 Scott Rolen | .10 | .30 |
| ❑ 269 T.Noel/J.Oliver RC | .08 | .25 |
| ❑ 270 Robert Stratton RC | .15 | .40 |
| ❑ 271 Gil Meche RC | .40 | 1.00 |
| ❑ 272 E.Milton/D.Brown RC | .15 | .40 |
| ❑ 273 Chris Reitsma RC | .07 | .20 |
| ❑ 274 J.Marquis/A.J.Zapp RC | .30 | .75 |
| ❑ 275 Checklist | .07 | .20 |
| ❑ 276 Checklist | .07 | .20 |
| ❑ 277 Chipper Jones UER276 | .20 | .50 |
| ❑ 278 Orlando Merced | .07 | .20 |
| ❑ 279 Ariel Prieto | .07 | .20 |
| ❑ 280 Al Leiter | .07 | .20 |
| ❑ 281 Pat Meares | .07 | .20 |
| ❑ 282 Darryl Strawberry | .07 | .20 |
| ❑ 283 Jamie Moyer | .07 | .20 |
| ❑ 284 Scott Servais | .07 | .20 |
| ❑ 285 Delino DeShields | .07 | .20 |
| ❑ 286 Danny Graves | .07 | .20 |
| ❑ 287 Gerald Williams | .07 | .20 |
| ❑ 288 Todd Greene | .07 | .20 |
| ❑ 289 Rico Brogna | .07 | .20 |
| ❑ 290 Derrick Gibson | .07 | .20 |
| ❑ 291 Joe Girardi | .07 | .20 |
| ❑ 292 Darren Lewis | .07 | .20 |
| ❑ 293 Nomar Garciaparra | .30 | .75 |
| ❑ 294 Greg Colbrunn | .07 | .20 |
| ❑ 295 Jeff Bagwell | .10 | .30 |
| ❑ 296 Brent Gates | .07 | .20 |
| ❑ 297 Jose Vizcaino | .07 | .20 |
| ❑ 298 Alex Ochoa | .07 | .20 |
| ❑ 299 Sid Fernandez | .07 | .20 |
| ❑ 300 Ken Griffey Jr. | .30 | .75 |
| ❑ 301 Chris Gomez | .07 | .20 |
| ❑ 302 Wendell Magee | .07 | .20 |
| ❑ 303 Darren Oliver | .07 | .20 |
| ❑ 304 Mel Nieves | .07 | .20 |
| ❑ 305 Sammy Sosa | .20 | .50 |
| ❑ 306 George Arias | .07 | .20 |
| ❑ 307 Jack McDowell | .07 | .20 |
| ❑ 308 Stan Javier | .07 | .20 |
| ❑ 309 Kimera Bartee | .07 | .20 |
| ❑ 310 James Baldwin | .07 | .20 |
| ❑ 311 Rocky Coppinger | .07 | .20 |
| ❑ 312 Keith Lockhart | .07 | .20 |
| ❑ 313 C.J. Nitkowski | .07 | .20 |
| ❑ 314 Allen Watson | .07 | .20 |
| ❑ 315 Darryl Kile | .07 | .20 |
| ❑ 316 Amaury Telemaco | .07 | .20 |
| ❑ 317 Jason Isringhausen | .07 | .20 |
| ❑ 318 Manny Ramirez | .10 | .30 |
| ❑ 319 Terry Pendleton | .07 | .20 |
| ❑ 320 Tim Salmon | .10 | .30 |
| ❑ 321 Eric Karros | .07 | .20 |
| ❑ 322 Mark Whiten | .07 | .20 |
| ❑ 323 Rick Krivda | .07 | .20 |
| ❑ 324 Brett Butler | .07 | .20 |
| ❑ 325 Randy Johnson | .20 | .50 |
| ❑ 326 Eddie Taubensee | .07 | .20 |
| ❑ 327 Mark Leiter | .07 | .20 |
| ❑ 328 Kevin Gross | .07 | .20 |
| ❑ 329 Ernie Young | .07 | .20 |
| ❑ 330 Pat Hentgen | .07 | .20 |
| ❑ 331 Rondell White | .07 | .20 |
| ❑ 332 Bobby Witt | .07 | .20 |
| ❑ 333 Eddie Murray | .20 | .50 |
| ❑ 334 Tim Raines | .10 | .30 |
| ❑ 335 Jeff Fassero | .07 | .20 |
| ❑ 336 Chuck Finley | .07 | .20 |
| ❑ 337 Willie Adams | .07 | .20 |
| ❑ 338 Chan Ho Park | .07 | .20 |
| ❑ 339 Jay Powell | .07 | .20 |
| ❑ 340 Ivan Rodriguez | .10 | .30 |
| ❑ 341 Jermaine Allensworth | .07 | .20 |
| ❑ 342 Jay Payton | .07 | .20 |
| ❑ 343 T.J. Mathews | .07 | .20 |
| ❑ 344 Tony Batista | .07 | .20 |
| ❑ 345 Ed Sprague | .07 | .20 |
| ❑ 346 Jeff Kent | .07 | .20 |
| ❑ 347 Scott Erickson | .07 | .20 |
| ❑ 348 Jeff Suppan | .07 | .20 |
| ❑ 349 Pete Schourek | .07 | .20 |
| ❑ 350 Kenny Lofton | .10 | .30 |
| ❑ 351 Alan Benes | .07 | .20 |
| ❑ 352 Fred McGriff | .10 | .30 |
| ❑ 353 Charlie O'Brien | .07 | .20 |
| ❑ 354 Darren Bragg | .07 | .20 |
| ❑ 355 Alex Fernandez | .07 | .20 |
| ❑ 356 Al Martin | .07 | .20 |
| ❑ 357 Bob Wells | .07 | .20 |
| ❑ 358 Chad Mottola | .07 | .20 |
| ❑ 359 Devon White | .07 | .20 |
| ❑ 360 David Cone | .10 | .30 |
| ❑ 361 Bobby Jones | .07 | .20 |
| ❑ 362 Scott Sanders | .07 | .20 |
| ❑ 363 Karim Garcia | .07 | .20 |
| ❑ 364 Kirt Manwaring | .07 | .20 |
| ❑ 365 Chili Davis | .07 | .20 |
| ❑ 366 Mike Hampton | .07 | .20 |
| ❑ 367 Chad Ogea | .07 | .20 |

|  |  | | |
|---|---|---|---|
| 368 | Curt Schilling | .07 | .20 |
| 369 | Phil Nevin | .07 | .20 |
| 370 | Roger Clemens | .40 | 1.00 |
| 371 | Willie Greene | .07 | .20 |
| 372 | Kenny Rogers | .07 | .20 |
| 373 | Jose Rijo | .07 | .20 |
| 374 | Bobby Bonilla | .07 | .20 |
| 375 | Mike Mussina | .10 | .30 |
| 376 | Curtis Pride | .07 | .20 |
| 377 | Todd Walker | .07 | .20 |
| 378 | Jason Bere | .07 | .20 |
| 379 | Heathcliff Slocumb | .07 | .20 |
| 380 | Dante Bichette | .07 | .20 |
| 381 | Carlos Baerga | .07 | .20 |
| 382 | Livan Hernandez | .07 | .20 |
| 383 | Jason Schmidt | .07 | .20 |
| 384 | Kevin Stocker | .07 | .20 |
| 385 | Matt Williams | .07 | .20 |
| 386 | Bartolo Colon | .07 | .20 |
| 387 | Will Clark | .10 | .30 |
| 388 | Dennis Eckersley | .07 | .20 |
| 389 | Brooks Kieschnick | .07 | .20 |
| 390 | Ryan Klesko | .07 | .20 |
| 391 | Mark Carreon | .07 | .20 |
| 392 | Tim Worrell | .07 | .20 |
| 393 | Dean Palmer | .07 | .20 |
| 394 | Wil Cordero | .07 | .20 |
| 395 | Javy Lopez | .07 | .20 |
| 396 | Rich Aurilia | .07 | .20 |
| 397 | Greg Vaughn | .07 | .20 |
| 398 | Vinny Castilla | .07 | .20 |
| 399 | Jeff Montgomery | .07 | .20 |
| 400 | Cal Ripken | .60 | 1.50 |
| 401 | Walt Weiss | .07 | .20 |
| 402 | Brad Ausmus | .07 | .20 |
| 403 | Ruben Rivera | .07 | .20 |
| 404 | Mark Wohlers | .07 | .20 |
| 405 | Rick Aguilera | .07 | .20 |
| 406 | Tony Clark | .07 | .20 |
| 407 | Lyle Mouton | .07 | .20 |
| 408 | Bill Pulsipher | .07 | .20 |
| 409 | Jose Rosado | .07 | .20 |
| 410 | Tony Gwynn | .25 | .60 |
| 411 | Cecil Fielder | .07 | .20 |
| 412 | John Flaherty | .07 | .20 |
| 413 | Lenny Dykstra | .07 | .20 |
| 414 | Ugueth Urbina | .07 | .20 |
| 415 | Brian Jordan | .07 | .20 |
| 416 | Bob Abreu | .10 | .30 |
| 417 | Craig Paquette | .07 | .20 |
| 418 | Sandy Martinez | .07 | .20 |
| 419 | Jeff Blauser | .07 | .20 |
| 420 | Barry Larkin | .10 | .30 |
| 421 | Kevin Seitzer | .07 | .20 |
| 422 | Tim Belcher | .07 | .20 |
| 423 | Paul Sorrento | .07 | .20 |
| 424 | Cal Eldred | .07 | .20 |
| 425 | Robin Ventura | .07 | .20 |
| 426 | John Olerud | .07 | .20 |
| 427 | Bob Wolcott | .07 | .20 |
| 428 | Matt Lawton | .07 | .20 |
| 429 | Rod Beck | .07 | .20 |
| 430 | Shane Reynolds | .07 | .20 |
| 431 | Mike James | .07 | .20 |
| 432 | Steve Wojciechowski | .07 | .20 |
| 433 | Vladimir Guerrero | .20 | .50 |
| 434 | Dustin Hermanson | .07 | .20 |
| 435 | Marty Cordova | .07 | .20 |
| 436 | Marc Newfield | .07 | .20 |
| 437 | Todd Stottlemyre | .07 | .20 |
| 438 | Jeffrey Hammonds | .07 | .20 |
| 439 | Dave Stevens | .07 | .20 |
| 440 | Hideo Nomo | .20 | .50 |
| 441 | Mark Thompson | .07 | .20 |
| 442 | Mark Lewis | .07 | .20 |
| 443 | Quinton McCracken | .07 | .20 |
| 444 | Cliff Floyd | .07 | .20 |
| 445 | Denny Neagle | .07 | .20 |
| 446 | John Jaha | .07 | .20 |
| 447 | Mike Sweeney | .07 | .20 |
| 448 | John Wasdin | .07 | .20 |
| 449 | Chad Curtis | .07 | .20 |
| 450 | Mo Vaughn | .20 | .50 |
| 451 | Donovan Osborne | .07 | .20 |
| 452 | Ruben Sierra | .07 | .20 |
| 453 | Michael Tucker | .07 | .20 |
| 454 | Kurt Abbott | .07 | .20 |
| 455 | Andruw Jones UER | .10 | .30 |
| 456 | Shannon Stewart | .07 | .20 |
| 457 | Scott Brosius | .07 | .20 |
| 458 | Juan Guzman | .07 | .20 |
| 459 | Ron Villone | .07 | .20 |
| 460 | Moises Alou | .07 | .20 |
| 461 | Larry Walker | .07 | .20 |
| 462 | Eddie Murray SH | .10 | .30 |
| 463 | Paul Molitor SH | .07 | .20 |
| 464 | Hideo Nomo SH | .07 | .20 |
| 465 | Barry Bonds SH | .30 | .75 |
| 466 | Todd Hundley SH | .07 | .20 |
| 467 | Rheal Cormier | .07 | .20 |
| 468 | J.Sandoval/J.Conti RC | .08 | .25 |
| 469 | R.Barajas/J.Rexrode RC | .60 | 1.50 |
| 470 | Jared Sandberg RC | .08 | .25 |
| 471 | P.Wilder/C.Gunner RC | .08 | .25 |
| 472 | M.DeCelle/M.McCain RC | .08 | .25 |
| 473 | Todd Zeile | .07 | .20 |
| 474 | Neifi Perez | .07 | .20 |
| 475 | Jeromy Burnitz | .07 | .20 |
| 476 | Trey Beamon | .07 | .20 |
| 477 | J.Patterson/B.Looper RC | .30 | .75 |
| 478 | Jake Westbrook RC | .20 | .50 |
| 479 | E.Chavez/A.Eaton RC | .75 | 2.00 |
| 480 | P.Tuccii/Lawrence RC | .08 | .25 |
| 481 | K.Benson/B.Koch RC | .20 | .50 |
| 482 | J.Nicholson/A.Prater RC | .08 | .25 |
| 483 | M.Kotsay/W.Johnson RC | .30 | .75 |
| 484 | Armando Benitez | .07 | .20 |
| 485 | Mike Matheny | .07 | .20 |
| 486 | Jeff Reed | .07 | .20 |
| 487 | M.Bellhorn/R.Johnson/E.Wilson | .07 | .20 |
| 488 | R.Hidalgo/B.Grieve | .07 | .20 |
| 489 | Konerko/D.Lee/Wright | .10 | .30 |
| 490 | Bill Mueller | .50 | 1.25 |
| 491 | J.Abbott/S.Monahan/E.Velazquez | .07 | .20 |
| 492 | Jimmy Anderson RC | .08 | .25 |
| 493 | Carl Pavano | .07 | .20 |
| 494 | Nelson Figueroa RC | .08 | .25 |
| 495 | Checklist (277-400) | .07 | .20 |
| 496 | Checklist (401-496) | .07 | .20 |
| NNO | Derek Jeter AU | 75.00 | 150.00 |

# 1998 Topps

| | | | |
|---|---|---|---|
| COMPLETE SET (503) | | 40.00 | 80.00 |
| COMP.HOBBY SET (511) | | 60.00 | 120.00 |
| COMP.RETAIL SET (511) | | 60.00 | 120.00 |
| COMPLETE SERIES 1 (282) | | 20.00 | 40.00 |
| COMPLETE SERIES 2 (221) | | 20.00 | 40.00 |
| 1 | Tony Gwynn | .25 | .60 |
| 2 | Larry Walker | .07 | .20 |
| 3 | Billy Wagner | .07 | .20 |
| 4 | Denny Neagle | .07 | .20 |
| 5 | Vladimir Guerrero | .20 | .50 |
| 6 | Kevin Brown | .10 | .30 |
| 7 | Tony Clark | .20 | .50 |
| 8 | Deion Sanders | .10 | .30 |
| 9 | Francisco Cordova | .07 | .20 |
| 10 | Matt Williams | .07 | .20 |
| 11 | Carlos Baerga | .07 | .20 |
| 12 | Mo Vaughn | .20 | .50 |
| 13 | Bobby Witt | .07 | .20 |
| 14 | Matt Stairs | .07 | .20 |
| 15 | Chan Ho Park | .07 | .20 |
| 16 | Mike Bordick | .07 | .20 |
| 17 | Michael Tucker | .07 | .20 |
| 18 | Mike Lieberthal | .07 | .20 |
| 19 | Michael Tucker | .07 | .20 |
| 20 | Frank Thomas | .20 | .50 |
| 21 | Roberto Clemente | .40 | 1.00 |
| 22 | Dmitri Young | .07 | .20 |
| 23 | Steve Trachsel | .07 | .20 |
| 24 | Jeff Kent | .07 | .20 |
| 25 | Scott Rolen | .10 | .30 |
| 26 | John Thomson | .07 | .20 |

|  |  | | |
|---|---|---|---|
| 27 | Joe Vitiello | .07 | .20 |
| 28 | Eddie Guardado | .07 | .20 |
| 29 | Charlie Hayes | .07 | .20 |
| 30 | Juan Gonzalez | .07 | .20 |
| 31 | Garret Anderson | .07 | .20 |
| 32 | John Jaha | .07 | .20 |
| 33 | Omar Vizquel | .10 | .30 |
| 34 | Brian Hunter | .07 | .20 |
| 35 | Jeff Bagwell | .10 | .30 |
| 36 | Mark Lemke | .07 | .20 |
| 37 | Doug Glanville | .07 | .20 |
| 38 | Dan Wilson | .07 | .20 |
| 39 | Steve Cooke | .07 | .20 |
| 40 | Chili Davis | .07 | .20 |
| 41 | Mike Cameron | .07 | .20 |
| 42 | F.P. Santangelo | .07 | .20 |
| 43 | Brad Ausmus | .07 | .20 |
| 44 | Gary DiSarcina | .07 | .20 |
| 45 | Pat Hentgen | .07 | .20 |
| 46 | Wilton Guerrero | .07 | .20 |
| 47 | Devon White | .07 | .20 |
| 48 | Danny Patterson | .07 | .20 |
| 49 | Pat Meares | .07 | .20 |
| 50 | Rafael Palmeiro | .10 | .30 |
| 51 | Mark Gardner | .07 | .20 |
| 52 | Jeff Blauser | .07 | .20 |
| 53 | Dave Hollins | .07 | .20 |
| 54 | Carlos Garcia | .07 | .20 |
| 55 | Ben McDonald | .07 | .20 |
| 56 | John Mabry | .07 | .20 |
| 57 | Trevor Hoffman | .07 | .20 |
| 58 | Tony Fernandez | .07 | .20 |
| 59 | Rich Loiselle | .07 | .20 |
| 60 | Mark Leiter | .07 | .20 |
| 61 | Pat Kelly | .07 | .20 |
| 62 | John Flaherty | .07 | .20 |
| 63 | Roger Bailey | .07 | .20 |
| 64 | Tom Gordon | .07 | .20 |
| 65 | Ryan Klesko | .07 | .20 |
| 66 | Darryl Hamilton | .07 | .20 |
| 67 | Jim Eisenreich | .07 | .20 |
| 68 | Butch Huskey | .07 | .20 |
| 69 | Mark Grudzielanek | .07 | .20 |
| 70 | Marquis Grissom | .07 | .20 |
| 71 | Mark McLemore | .07 | .20 |
| 72 | Gary Gaetti | .07 | .20 |
| 73 | Greg Gagne | .07 | .20 |
| 74 | Lyle Mouton | .07 | .20 |
| 75 | Jim Edmonds | .07 | .20 |
| 76 | Shawn Green | .07 | .20 |
| 77 | Greg Vaughn | .07 | .20 |
| 78 | Terry Adams | .07 | .20 |
| 79 | Kevin Polcovich | .07 | .20 |
| 80 | Troy O'Leary | .07 | .20 |
| 81 | Jeff Shaw | .07 | .20 |
| 82 | Rich Becker | .07 | .20 |
| 83 | David Wells | .07 | .20 |
| 84 | Steve Karsay | .07 | .20 |
| 85 | Charles Nagy | .07 | .20 |
| 86 | B.J. Surhoff | .07 | .20 |
| 87 | Jamey Wright | .07 | .20 |
| 88 | James Baldwin | .07 | .20 |
| 89 | Edgardo Alfonzo | .07 | .20 |
| 90 | Jay Buhner | .07 | .20 |
| 91 | Brady Anderson | .07 | .20 |
| 92 | Scott Servais | .07 | .20 |
| 93 | Edgar Renteria | .07 | .20 |
| 94 | Mike Lieberthal | .07 | .20 |
| 95 | Rick Aguilera | .07 | .20 |
| 96 | Walt Weiss | .07 | .20 |
| 97 | Deivi Cruz | .07 | .20 |
| 98 | Kurt Abbott | .07 | .20 |
| 99 | Henry Rodriguez | .07 | .20 |
| 100 | Mike Piazza | .30 | .75 |
| 101 | Bill Taylor | .07 | .20 |
| 102 | Todd Zeile | .07 | .20 |
| 103 | Rey Ordonez | .07 | .20 |
| 104 | Willie Greene | .07 | .20 |
| 105 | Tony Womack | .07 | .20 |
| 106 | Mike Sweeney | .07 | .20 |
| 107 | Jeffrey Hammonds | .07 | .20 |
| 108 | Kevin Orie | .07 | .20 |
| 109 | Alex Gonzalez | .07 | .20 |
| 110 | Jose Canseco | .10 | .30 |
| 111 | Paul Sorrento | .07 | .20 |
| 112 | Joey Hamilton | .07 | .20 |
| 113 | Brad Radke | .07 | .20 |
| 114 | Steve Avery | .07 | .20 |

|  |  | | |
|---|--------|------|------|
| ☐ 115 | Esteban Loaiza | .07 | .20 |
| ☐ 116 | Stan Javier | .07 | .20 |
| ☐ 117 | Chris Gomez | .07 | .20 |
| ☐ 118 | Royce Clayton | .07 | .20 |
| ☐ 119 | Orlando Merced | .07 | .20 |
| ☐ 120 | Kevin Appier | .07 | .20 |
| ☐ 121 | Mel Nieves | .07 | .20 |
| ☐ 122 | Joe Girardi | .07 | .20 |
| ☐ 123 | Rico Brogna | .07 | .20 |
| ☐ 124 | Kent Mercker | .07 | .20 |
| ☐ 125 | Manny Ramirez | .10 | .30 |
| ☐ 126 | Jeromy Burnitz | .07 | .20 |
| ☐ 127 | Kevin Foster | .07 | .20 |
| ☐ 128 | Matt Morris | .07 | .20 |
| ☐ 129 | Jason Dickson | .07 | .20 |
| ☐ 130 | Tom Glavine | .10 | .30 |
| ☐ 131 | Wally Joyner | .07 | .20 |
| ☐ 132 | Rick Reed | .07 | .20 |
| ☐ 133 | Todd Jones | .07 | .20 |
| ☐ 134 | Dave Martinez | .07 | .20 |
| ☐ 135 | Sandy Alomar Jr. | .07 | .20 |
| ☐ 136 | Mike Lansing | .07 | .20 |
| ☐ 137 | Sean Berry | .07 | .20 |
| ☐ 138 | Doug Jones | .07 | .20 |
| ☐ 139 | Todd Stottlemyre | .07 | .20 |
| ☐ 140 | Jay Bell | .07 | .20 |
| ☐ 141 | Jaime Navarro | .07 | .20 |
| ☐ 142 | Chris Hoiles | .07 | .20 |
| ☐ 143 | Joey Cora | .07 | .20 |
| ☐ 144 | Scott Spiezio | .07 | .20 |
| ☐ 145 | Joe Carter | .10 | .30 |
| ☐ 146 | Jose Guillen | .07 | .20 |
| ☐ 147 | Damion Easley | .07 | .20 |
| ☐ 148 | Lee Stevens | .07 | .20 |
| ☐ 149 | Alex Fernandez | .07 | .20 |
| ☐ 150 | Randy Johnson | .20 | .50 |
| ☐ 151 | J.T. Snow | .07 | .20 |
| ☐ 152 | Chuck Finley | .07 | .20 |
| ☐ 153 | Bernard Gilkey | .07 | .20 |
| ☐ 154 | David Segui | .07 | .20 |
| ☐ 155 | Dante Bichette | .07 | .20 |
| ☐ 156 | Kevin Stocker | .07 | .20 |
| ☐ 157 | Carl Everett | .07 | .20 |
| ☐ 158 | Jose Valentin | .07 | .20 |
| ☐ 159 | Pokey Reese | .07 | .20 |
| ☐ 160 | Derek Jeter | .50 | 1.25 |
| ☐ 161 | Roger Pavlik | .07 | .20 |
| ☐ 162 | Mark Wohlers | .07 | .20 |
| ☐ 163 | Ricky Bottalico | .07 | .20 |
| ☐ 164 | Ozzie Guillen | .07 | .20 |
| ☐ 165 | Mike Mussina | .10 | .30 |
| ☐ 166 | Gary Sheffield | .07 | .20 |
| ☐ 167 | Hideo Nomo | .20 | .50 |
| ☐ 168 | Mark Grace | .10 | .30 |
| ☐ 169 | Aaron Sele | .07 | .20 |
| ☐ 170 | Darryl Kile | .07 | .20 |
| ☐ 171 | Shawn Estes | .07 | .20 |
| ☐ 172 | Vinny Castilla | .07 | .20 |
| ☐ 173 | Ron Coomer | .07 | .20 |
| ☐ 174 | Jose Rosado | .07 | .20 |
| ☐ 175 | Kenny Lofton | .07 | .20 |
| ☐ 176 | Jason Giambi | .07 | .20 |
| ☐ 177 | Hal Morris | .07 | .20 |
| ☐ 178 | Darren Bragg | .07 | .20 |
| ☐ 179 | Orel Hershiser | .07 | .20 |
| ☐ 180 | Ray Lankford | .07 | .20 |
| ☐ 181 | Hideki Irabu | .07 | .20 |
| ☐ 182 | Kevin Young | .07 | .20 |
| ☐ 183 | Javy Lopez | .07 | .20 |
| ☐ 184 | Jeff Montgomery | .07 | .20 |
| ☐ 185 | Mike Holtz | .07 | .20 |
| ☐ 186 | George Williams | .07 | .20 |
| ☐ 187 | Cal Eldred | .07 | .20 |
| ☐ 188 | Tom Candiotti | .07 | .20 |
| ☐ 189 | Glenallen Hill | .07 | .20 |
| ☐ 190 | Brian Giles | .07 | .20 |
| ☐ 191 | Dave Mlicki | .07 | .20 |
| ☐ 192 | Garrett Stephenson | .07 | .20 |
| ☐ 193 | Jeff Frye | .07 | .20 |
| ☐ 194 | Joe Oliver | .07 | .20 |
| ☐ 195 | Bob Hamelin | .07 | .20 |
| ☐ 196 | Luis Sojo | .07 | .20 |
| ☐ 197 | LaTroy Hawkins | .07 | .20 |
| ☐ 198 | Kevin Elster | .07 | .20 |
| ☐ 199 | Jeff Reed | .07 | .20 |
| ☐ 200 | Dennis Eckersley | .07 | .20 |
| ☐ 201 | Bill Mueller | .07 | .20 |
| ☐ 202 | Russ Davis | .07 | .20 |
| ☐ 203 | Armando Benitez | .07 | .20 |
| ☐ 204 | Quilvio Veras | .07 | .20 |
| ☐ 205 | Tim Naehring | .07 | .20 |
| ☐ 206 | Quinton McCracken | .07 | .20 |
| ☐ 207 | Raul Casanova | .07 | .20 |
| ☐ 208 | Matt Lawton | .07 | .20 |
| ☐ 209 | Luis Alicea | .07 | .20 |
| ☐ 210 | Luis Gonzalez | .07 | .20 |
| ☐ 211 | Allen Watson | .07 | .20 |
| ☐ 212 | Gerald Williams | .07 | .20 |
| ☐ 213 | David Bell | .07 | .20 |
| ☐ 214 | Todd Hollandsworth | .07 | .20 |
| ☐ 215 | Wade Boggs | .10 | .30 |
| ☐ 216 | Jose Mesa | .07 | .20 |
| ☐ 217 | Jamie Moyer | .07 | .20 |
| ☐ 218 | Darren Daulton | .07 | .20 |
| ☐ 219 | Mickey Morandini | .07 | .20 |
| ☐ 220 | Rusty Greer | .07 | .20 |
| ☐ 221 | Jim Bullinger | .07 | .20 |
| ☐ 222 | Jose Offerman | .07 | .20 |
| ☐ 223 | Matt Karchner | .07 | .20 |
| ☐ 224 | Woody Williams | .07 | .20 |
| ☐ 225 | Mark Loretta | .07 | .20 |
| ☐ 226 | Mike Hampton | .07 | .20 |
| ☐ 227 | Willie Adams | .07 | .20 |
| ☐ 228 | Scott Hatteberg | .07 | .20 |
| ☐ 229 | Rich Amaral | .07 | .20 |
| ☐ 230 | Terry Steinbach | .07 | .20 |
| ☐ 231 | Glendon Rusch | .07 | .20 |
| ☐ 232 | Bret Boone | .07 | .20 |
| ☐ 233 | Robert Person | .07 | .20 |
| ☐ 234 | Jose Hernandez | .07 | .20 |
| ☐ 235 | Doug Drabek | .07 | .20 |
| ☐ 236 | Jason McDonald | .07 | .20 |
| ☐ 237 | Chris Widger | .07 | .20 |
| ☐ 238 | Tom Martin | .07 | .20 |
| ☐ 239 | Dave Burba | .07 | .20 |
| ☐ 240 | Pete Rose Jr. | .07 | .20 |
| ☐ 241 | Bobby Ayala | .07 | .20 |
| ☐ 242 | Tim Wakefield | .07 | .20 |
| ☐ 243 | Dennis Springer | .07 | .20 |
| ☐ 244 | Tim Belcher | .07 | .20 |
| ☐ 245 | J.Garland/G.Goetz | .10 | .30 |
| ☐ 246 | L.Berkman/G.Davis | .10 | .30 |
| ☐ 247 | V.Wells/A.Akin | .10 | .30 |
| ☐ 248 | A.Kennedy/J.Romano | .07 | .20 |
| ☐ 249 | J.Dellaero/T.Cameron | .07 | .20 |
| ☐ 250 | J.Sandberg/A.Sanchez | .07 | .20 |
| ☐ 251 | P.Ortega/J.Manias | .07 | .20 |
| ☐ 252 | Mike Stoner RC | .07 | .20 |
| ☐ 253 | J.Patterson/L.Rodriguez | .07 | .20 |
| ☐ 254 | R.Minor RC/A.Beltre | .10 | .30 |
| ☐ 255 | B.Grieve/D.Brown | .07 | .20 |
| ☐ 256 | Wood/Pavano/Mack | .10 | .30 |
| ☐ 257 | D.Ortiz/Sexson/Ward | 1.00 | 2.50 |
| ☐ 258 | J.Encarn/Winn/Vessel | .07 | .20 |
| ☐ 259 | Bens/T.Smith RC/C.Dunc RC | .07 | .20 |
| ☐ 260 | Warren Morris RC | .07 | .20 |
| ☐ 261 | R.Hernandez/B.Davis/E.Marrero | .07 | .20 |
| ☐ 262 | E.Chavez/R.Branyan | .10 | .30 |
| ☐ 263 | Ryan Jackson RC | .07 | .20 |
| ☐ 264 | B.Fuentes RC/Clement/Halladay | .10 | .30 |
| ☐ 265 | Randy Johnson SH | .10 | .30 |
| ☐ 266 | Kevin Brown SH | .07 | .20 |
| ☐ 267 | R.Rincon/F.Cordova SH | .07 | .20 |
| ☐ 268 | Nomar Garciaparra SH | .20 | .50 |
| ☐ 269 | Tino Martinez SH | .07 | .20 |
| ☐ 270 | Chuck Knoblauch IL | .07 | .20 |
| ☐ 271 | Pedro Martinez IL | .10 | .30 |
| ☐ 272 | Denny Neagle IL | .07 | .20 |
| ☐ 273 | Juan Gonzalez IL | .07 | .20 |
| ☐ 274 | Andres Galarraga IL | .07 | .20 |
| ☐ 275 | Checklist (1-195) | .07 | .20 |
| ☐ 276 | Checklist (196-283/inserts) | .07 | .20 |
| ☐ 277 | Moises Alou WS | .07 | .20 |
| ☐ 278 | Sandy Alomar Jr. WS | .07 | .20 |
| ☐ 279 | Gary Sheffield WS | .07 | .20 |
| ☐ 280 | Matt Williams WS | .07 | .20 |
| ☐ 281 | Livan Hernandez WS | .07 | .20 |
| ☐ 282 | Chad Ogea WS | .07 | .20 |
| ☐ 283 | Marlins Champs | .07 | .20 |
| ☐ 284 | Tino Martinez | .10 | .30 |
| ☐ 285 | Roberto Alomar | .10 | .30 |
| ☐ 286 | Jeff King | .07 | .20 |
| ☐ 287 | Brian Jordan | .07 | .20 |
| ☐ 288 | Darin Erstad | .07 | .20 |
| ☐ 289 | Ken Caminiti | .07 | .20 |
| ☐ 290 | Jim Thome | .10 | .30 |
| ☐ 291 | Paul Molitor | .07 | .20 |
| ☐ 292 | Ivan Rodriguez | .10 | .30 |
| ☐ 293 | Bernie Williams | .10 | .30 |
| ☐ 294 | Todd Hundley | .07 | .20 |
| ☐ 295 | Andres Galarraga | .07 | .20 |
| ☐ 296 | Greg Maddux | .30 | .75 |
| ☐ 297 | Edgar Martinez | .07 | .20 |
| ☐ 298 | Ron Gant | .07 | .20 |
| ☐ 299 | Derek Bell | .07 | .20 |
| ☐ 300 | Roger Clemens | .40 | 1.00 |
| ☐ 301 | Rondell White | .07 | .20 |
| ☐ 302 | Barry Larkin | .10 | .30 |
| ☐ 303 | Robin Ventura | .07 | .20 |
| ☐ 304 | Jason Kendall | .07 | .20 |
| ☐ 305 | Chipper Jones | .20 | .50 |
| ☐ 306 | John Franco | .07 | .20 |
| ☐ 307 | Sammy Sosa | .20 | .50 |
| ☐ 308 | Troy Percival | .07 | .20 |
| ☐ 309 | Chuck Knoblauch | .07 | .20 |
| ☐ 310 | Ellis Burks | .07 | .20 |
| ☐ 311 | Al Martin | .07 | .20 |
| ☐ 312 | Tim Salmon | .10 | .30 |
| ☐ 313 | Moises Alou | .07 | .20 |
| ☐ 314 | Lance Johnson | .07 | .20 |
| ☐ 315 | Justin Thompson | .07 | .20 |
| ☐ 316 | Will Clark | .10 | .30 |
| ☐ 317 | Barry Bonds | .60 | 1.50 |
| ☐ 318 | Craig Biggio | .10 | .30 |
| ☐ 319 | John Smoltz | .10 | .30 |
| ☐ 320 | Cal Ripken | .60 | 1.50 |
| ☐ 321 | Ken Griffey Jr. | .30 | .75 |
| ☐ 322 | Paul O'Neill | .10 | .30 |
| ☐ 323 | Todd Helton | .10 | .30 |
| ☐ 324 | John Olerud | .07 | .20 |
| ☐ 325 | Mark McGwire | .50 | 1.25 |
| ☐ 326 | Jose Cruz Jr. | .07 | .20 |
| ☐ 327 | Jeff Cirillo | .07 | .20 |
| ☐ 328 | Dean Palmer | .07 | .20 |
| ☐ 329 | John Wetteland | .07 | .20 |
| ☐ 330 | Steve Finley | .07 | .20 |
| ☐ 331 | Albert Belle | .10 | .30 |
| ☐ 332 | Curt Schilling | .07 | .20 |
| ☐ 333 | Raul Mondesi | .07 | .20 |
| ☐ 334 | Andruw Jones | .10 | .30 |
| ☐ 335 | Nomar Garciaparra | .30 | .75 |
| ☐ 336 | David Justice | .07 | .20 |
| ☐ 337 | Andy Pettitte | .10 | .30 |
| ☐ 338 | Pedro Martinez | .10 | .30 |
| ☐ 339 | Travis Miller | .07 | .20 |
| ☐ 340 | Chris Stynes | .07 | .20 |
| ☐ 341 | Gregg Jefferies | .07 | .20 |
| ☐ 342 | Jeff Fassero | .07 | .20 |
| ☐ 343 | Craig Counsell | .07 | .20 |
| ☐ 344 | Wilson Alvarez | .07 | .20 |
| ☐ 345 | Bip Roberts | .07 | .20 |
| ☐ 346 | Kelvim Escobar | .07 | .20 |
| ☐ 347 | Mark Bellhorn | .07 | .20 |
| ☐ 348 | Cory Lidle RC | .60 | 1.50 |
| ☐ 349 | Fred McGriff | .10 | .30 |
| ☐ 350 | Chuck Carr | .07 | .20 |
| ☐ 351 | Bob Abreu | .07 | .20 |
| ☐ 352 | Juan Guzman | .07 | .20 |
| ☐ 353 | Fernando Vina | .07 | .20 |
| ☐ 354 | Andy Benes | .07 | .20 |
| ☐ 355 | Dave Nilsson | .07 | .20 |
| ☐ 356 | Bobby Bonilla | .07 | .20 |
| ☐ 357 | Ismael Valdes | .07 | .20 |
| ☐ 358 | Carlos Perez | .07 | .20 |
| ☐ 359 | Kirk Rueter | .07 | .20 |
| ☐ 360 | Bartolo Colon | .07 | .20 |
| ☐ 361 | Mel Rojas | .07 | .20 |
| ☐ 362 | Johnny Damon | .10 | .30 |
| ☐ 363 | Geronimo Berroa | .07 | .20 |
| ☐ 364 | Reggie Sanders | .07 | .20 |
| ☐ 365 | Jermaine Allensworth | .07 | .20 |
| ☐ 366 | Orlando Cabrera | .07 | .20 |
| ☐ 367 | Jorge Fabregas | .07 | .20 |
| ☐ 368 | Scott Stahoviak | .07 | .20 |
| ☐ 369 | Ken Cloude | .07 | .20 |
| ☐ 370 | Donovan Osborne | .07 | .20 |
| ☐ 371 | Roger Cedeno | .07 | .20 |
| ☐ 372 | Neifi Perez | .07 | .20 |
| ☐ 373 | Chris Holt | .07 | .20 |
| ☐ 374 | Cecil Fielder | .07 | .20 |
| ☐ 375 | Marty Cordova | .07 | .20 |
| ☐ 376 | Tom Goodwin | .07 | .20 |
| ☐ 377 | Jeff Suppan | .07 | .20 |
| ☐ 378 | Jeff Brantley | .07 | .20 |

|  |  | | |
|---|---|---|---|
| 379 | Mark Langston | .07 | .20 |
| 380 | Shane Reynolds | .07 | .20 |
| 381 | Mike Fetters | .07 | .20 |
| 382 | Todd Greene | .07 | .20 |
| 383 | Ray Durham | .07 | .20 |
| 384 | Carlos Delgado | .07 | .20 |
| 385 | Jeff D'Amico | .07 | .20 |
| 386 | Brian McRae | .07 | .20 |
| 387 | Alan Benes | .07 | .20 |
| 388 | Heathcliff Slocumb | .07 | .20 |
| 389 | Eric Young | .07 | .20 |
| 390 | Travis Fryman | .07 | .20 |
| 391 | David Cone | .07 | .20 |
| 392 | Otis Nixon | .07 | .20 |
| 393 | Jeremi Gonzalez | .07 | .20 |
| 394 | Jeff Juden | .07 | .20 |
| 395 | Jose Vizcaino | .07 | .20 |
| 396 | Ugueth Urbina | .07 | .20 |
| 397 | Ramon Martinez | .07 | .20 |
| 398 | Robb Nen | .07 | .20 |
| 399 | Harold Baines | .07 | .20 |
| 400 | Delino DeShields | .07 | .20 |
| 401 | John Burkett | .07 | .20 |
| 402 | Sterling Hitchcock | .07 | .20 |
| 403 | Mark Clark | .07 | .20 |
| 404 | Terrell Wade | .07 | .20 |
| 405 | Scott Brosius | .07 | .20 |
| 406 | Chad Curtis | .07 | .20 |
| 407 | Brian Johnson | .07 | .20 |
| 408 | Roberto Kelly | .07 | .20 |
| 409 | Dave Dellucci RC | .15 | .40 |
| 410 | Michael Tucker | .07 | .20 |
| 411 | Mark Kotsay | .07 | .20 |
| 412 | Mark Lewis | .07 | .20 |
| 413 | Ryan McGuire | .07 | .20 |
| 414 | Shawon Dunston | .07 | .20 |
| 415 | Brad Rigby | .07 | .20 |
| 416 | Scott Erickson | .07 | .20 |
| 417 | Bobby Jones | .07 | .20 |
| 418 | Darren Oliver | .07 | .20 |
| 419 | John Smiley | .07 | .20 |
| 420 | T.J. Mathews | .07 | .20 |
| 421 | Dustin Hermanson | .07 | .20 |
| 422 | Mike Timlin | .07 | .20 |
| 423 | Willie Blair | .07 | .20 |
| 424 | Manny Alexander | .07 | .20 |
| 425 | Bob Tewksbury | .07 | .20 |
| 426 | Pete Schourek | .07 | .20 |
| 427 | Reggie Jefferson | .07 | .20 |
| 428 | Ed Sprague | .07 | .20 |
| 429 | Jeff Conine | .07 | .20 |
| 430 | Roberto Hernandez | .07 | .20 |
| 431 | Tom Pagnozzi | .07 | .20 |
| 432 | Jaret Wright | .07 | .20 |
| 433 | Livan Hernandez | .07 | .20 |
| 434 | Andy Ashby | .07 | .20 |
| 435 | Todd Dunn | .07 | .20 |
| 436 | Bobby Higginson | .07 | .20 |
| 437 | Rod Beck | .07 | .20 |
| 438 | Jim Leyritz | .07 | .20 |
| 439 | Matt Williams | .07 | .20 |
| 440 | Brett Tomko | .07 | .20 |
| 441 | Joe Randa | .07 | .20 |
| 442 | Chris Carpenter | .07 | .20 |
| 443 | Dennis Reyes | .07 | .20 |
| 444 | Al Leiter | .07 | .20 |
| 445 | Jason Schmidt | .07 | .20 |
| 446 | Ken Hill | .07 | .20 |
| 447 | Shannon Stewart | .07 | .20 |
| 448 | Enrique Wilson | .07 | .20 |
| 449 | Fernando Tatis | .07 | .20 |
| 450 | Jimmy Key | .07 | .20 |
| 451 | Darrin Fletcher | .07 | .20 |
| 452 | John Valentin | .07 | .20 |
| 453 | Kevin Tapani | .07 | .20 |
| 454 | Eric Karros | .07 | .20 |
| 455 | Jay Bell | .07 | .20 |
| 456 | Walt Weiss | .07 | .20 |
| 457 | Devon White | .07 | .20 |
| 458 | Carl Pavano | .07 | .20 |
| 459 | Mike Lansing | .07 | .20 |
| 460 | John Flaherty | .07 | .20 |
| 461 | Richard Hidalgo | .07 | .20 |
| 462 | Quinton McCracken | .07 | .20 |
| 463 | Karim Garcia | .07 | .20 |
| 464 | Miguel Cairo | .07 | .20 |
| 465 | Edwin Diaz | .07 | .20 |
| 466 | Bobby Smith | .07 | .20 |
| 467 | Yamil Benitez | .07 | .20 |
| 468 | Rich Butler | .07 | .20 |
| 469 | Ben Ford RC | .07 | .20 |
| 470 | Bubba Trammell | .07 | .20 |
| 471 | Brent Brede | .07 | .20 |
| 472 | Brooks Kieschnick | .07 | .20 |
| 473 | Carlos Castillo | .07 | .20 |
| 474 | Brad Radke SH | .07 | .20 |
| 475 | Roger Clemens SH | .20 | .50 |
| 476 | Curt Schilling SH | .07 | .20 |
| 477 | John Olerud SH | .07 | .20 |
| 478 | Mark McGwire SH | .25 | .60 |
| 479 | M.Piazza/K.Griffey Jr. IL | .20 | .50 |
| 480 | J.Bagwell/F.Thomas IL | .10 | .30 |
| 481 | C.Jones/N.Garciaparra IL | .10 | .30 |
| 482 | L.Walker/J.Gonzalez IL | .07 | .20 |
| 483 | G.Sheffield/T.Martinez IL | .07 | .20 |
| 484 | D.Gib/M.Colem/Hutchins | .07 | .20 |
| 485 | B.Rose/Looper/Politte | .07 | .20 |
| 486 | E.Milton/Marquis/C.Lee | .07 | .20 |
| 487 | Robert Fick RC | .10 | .30 |
| 488 | A.Ramirez/A.Gonz/Casey | .10 | .30 |
| 489 | D.Bridges/T.Drew RC | .07 | .20 |
| 490 | D.McDonald/N.Ndungidi RC | .07 | .20 |
| 491 | Ryan Anderson RC | .07 | .20 |
| 492 | Troy Glaus RC | .50 | 1.25 |
| 493 | J.Werth/D.Reichert RC | .07 | .20 |
| 494 | Michael Cuddyer RC | .30 | .75 |
| 495 | Jack Cust RC | .20 | .50 |
| 496 | Brian Anderson | .07 | .20 |
| 497 | Tony Saunders | .07 | .20 |
| 498 | J.Sandoval/V.Nunez | .07 | .20 |
| 499 | B.Penny/N.Bierbrodt | .10 | .30 |
| 500 | D.Carr/L.Cruz RC | .07 | .20 |
| 501 | C.Bowers/M.McCain | .07 | .20 |
| 502 | Checklist | .07 | .20 |
| 503 | Checklist | .07 | .20 |
| 504 | Alex Rodriguez | .75 | 2.00 |

# 1999 Topps

| # | Set / Player | | |
|---|---|---|---|
| | COMPLETE SET (462) | 30.00 | 80.00 |
| | COMP.HOBBY SET (462) | 40.00 | 80.00 |
| | COMP.X-MAS SET (463) | 40.00 | 80.00 |
| | COMPLETE SERIES 1 (241) | 15.00 | 40.00 |
| | COMPLETE SERIES 2 (221) | 15.00 | 40.00 |
| | COMP.MAC HR SET (70) | 250.00 | 500.00 |
| | COMP.SOSA HR SET (66) | 100.00 | 250.00 |
| 1 | Roger Clemens | .40 | 1.00 |
| 2 | Andres Galarraga | .07 | .20 |
| 3 | Scott Brosius | .07 | .20 |
| 4 | John Flaherty | .07 | .20 |
| 5 | Jim Leyritz | .07 | .20 |
| 6 | Ray Durham | .07 | .20 |
| 7 | Jose Vizcaino | .07 | .20 |
| 8 | Jose Vizcaino | .07 | .20 |
| 9 | Will Clark | .10 | .30 |
| 10 | David Wells | .07 | .20 |
| 11 | Jose Guillen | .07 | .20 |
| 12 | Scott Hatteberg | .07 | .20 |
| 13 | Edgardo Alfonzo | .07 | .20 |
| 14 | Mike Bordick | .07 | .20 |
| 15 | Manny Ramirez | .10 | .30 |
| 16 | Greg Maddux | .30 | .75 |
| 17 | David Segui | .07 | .20 |
| 18 | Darryl Strawberry | .07 | .20 |
| 19 | Brad Radke | .07 | .20 |
| 20 | Kerry Wood | .40 | 1.00 |
| 21 | Matt Anderson | .07 | .20 |
| 22 | Derrek Lee | .10 | .30 |
| 23 | Mickey Morandini | .07 | .20 |
| 24 | Paul Konerko | .20 | .50 |
| 25 | Travis Lee | .07 | .20 |
| 26 | Ken Hill | .07 | .20 |
| 27 | Kenny Rogers | .07 | .20 |
| 28 | Paul Sorrento | .07 | .20 |
| 29 | Quilvio Veras | .07 | .20 |
| 30 | Todd Walker | .07 | .20 |
| 31 | Ryan Jackson | .07 | .20 |
| 32 | John Olerud | .07 | .20 |
| 33 | Doug Glanville | .07 | .20 |
| 34 | Nolan Ryan | .75 | 2.00 |
| 35 | Ray Lankford | .07 | .20 |
| 36 | Mark Loretta | .07 | .20 |
| 37 | Jason Dickson | .07 | .20 |
| 38 | Sean Bergman | .07 | .20 |
| 39 | Quinton McCracken | .07 | .20 |
| 40 | Bartolo Colon | .07 | .20 |
| 41 | Brady Anderson | .07 | .20 |
| 42 | Chris Stynes | .07 | .20 |
| 43 | Jorge Posada | .10 | .30 |
| 44 | Justin Thompson | .07 | .20 |
| 45 | Johnny Damon | .10 | .30 |
| 46 | Armando Benitez | .07 | .20 |
| 47 | Brant Brown | .07 | .20 |
| 48 | Charlie Hayes | .07 | .20 |
| 49 | Darren Dreifort | .07 | .20 |
| 50 | Juan Gonzalez | .20 | .50 |
| 51 | Chuck Knoblauch | .10 | .30 |
| 52 | Todd Helton | .10 | .30 |
| 53 | Rick Reed | .07 | .20 |
| 54 | Chris Gomez | .07 | .20 |
| 55 | Gary Sheffield | .07 | .20 |
| 56 | Rod Beck | .07 | .20 |
| 57 | Rey Sanchez | .07 | .20 |
| 58 | Garret Anderson | .07 | .20 |
| 59 | Jimmy Haynes | .07 | .20 |
| 60 | Steve Woodard | .07 | .20 |
| 61 | Rondell White | .07 | .20 |
| 62 | Vladimir Guerrero | .20 | .50 |
| 63 | Eric Karros | .07 | .20 |
| 64 | Russ Davis | .07 | .20 |
| 65 | Mo Vaughn | .07 | .20 |
| 66 | Sammy Sosa | .20 | .50 |
| 67 | Troy Percival | .07 | .20 |
| 68 | Kenny Lofton | .07 | .20 |
| 69 | Bill Taylor | .07 | .20 |
| 70 | Mark McGwire | .50 | 1.25 |
| 71 | Roger Cedeno | .07 | .20 |
| 72 | Javy Lopez | .07 | .20 |
| 73 | Damion Easley | .07 | .20 |
| 74 | Andy Pettitte | .10 | .30 |
| 75 | Tony Gwynn | .25 | .60 |
| 76 | Ricardo Rincon | .07 | .20 |
| 77 | F.P. Santangelo | .07 | .20 |
| 78 | Jay Bell | .07 | .20 |
| 79 | Scott Servais | .07 | .20 |
| 80 | Jose Canseco | .10 | .30 |
| 81 | Roberto Hernandez | .07 | .20 |
| 82 | Todd Dunwoody | .07 | .20 |
| 83 | John Wetteland | .07 | .20 |
| 84 | Mike Caruso | .07 | .20 |
| 85 | Derek Jeter | .50 | 1.25 |
| 86 | Aaron Sele | .07 | .20 |
| 87 | Jose Lima | .07 | .20 |
| 88 | Ryan Christenson | .07 | .20 |
| 89 | Jeff Cirillo | .07 | .20 |
| 90 | Jose Hernandez | .07 | .20 |
| 91 | Mark Kotsay | .07 | .20 |
| 92 | Darren Bragg | .07 | .20 |
| 93 | Albert Belle | .07 | .20 |
| 94 | Matt Lawton | .07 | .20 |
| 95 | Pedro Martinez | .10 | .30 |
| 96 | Greg Vaughn | .07 | .20 |
| 97 | Neifi Perez | .07 | .20 |
| 98 | Gerald Williams | .07 | .20 |
| 99 | Derek Bell | .07 | .20 |
| 100 | Ken Griffey Jr. | .30 | .75 |
| 101 | David Cone | .07 | .20 |
| 102 | Brian Johnson | .07 | .20 |
| 103 | Dean Palmer | .07 | .20 |
| 104 | Javier Valentin | .07 | .20 |
| 105 | Trevor Hoffman | .07 | .20 |
| 106 | Butch Huskey | .07 | .20 |
| 107 | Dave Martinez | .07 | .20 |
| 108 | Billy Wagner | .07 | .20 |
| 109 | Shawn Green | .07 | .20 |
| 110 | Ben Grieve | .07 | .20 |
| 111 | Tom Goodwin | .07 | .20 |
| 112 | Jaret Wright | .07 | .20 |
| 113 | Aramis Ramirez | .07 | .20 |
| 114 | Dmitri Young | .07 | .20 |
| 115 | Hideki Irabu | .07 | .20 |
| 116 | Roberto Kelly | .07 | .20 |

|  |  | | |
|---|---|---|---|
| 117 | Jeff Fassero | .07 | .20 |
| 118 | Mark Clark | .07 | .20 |
| 119 | Jason McDonald | .07 | .20 |
| 120 | Matt Williams | .07 | .20 |
| 121 | Dave Burba | .07 | .20 |
| 122 | Bret Saberhagen | .07 | .20 |
| 123 | Deivi Cruz | .07 | .20 |
| 124 | Chad Curtis | .07 | .20 |
| 125 | Scott Rolen | .10 | .30 |
| 126 | Lee Stevens | .07 | .20 |
| 127 | J.T. Snow | .07 | .20 |
| 128 | Rusty Greer | .07 | .20 |
| 129 | Brian Meadows | .07 | .20 |
| 130 | Jim Edmonds | .07 | .20 |
| 131 | Ron Gant | .07 | .20 |
| 132 | A.J. Hinch | .07 | .20 |
| 133 | Shannon Stewart | .07 | .20 |
| 134 | Brad Fullmer | .07 | .20 |
| 135 | Cal Eldred | .07 | .20 |
| 136 | Matt Walbeck | .07 | .20 |
| 137 | Carl Everett | .07 | .20 |
| 138 | Walt Weiss | .07 | .20 |
| 139 | Fred McGriff | .10 | .30 |
| 140 | Darin Erstad | .07 | .20 |
| 141 | Dave Nilsson | .07 | .20 |
| 142 | Eric Young | .07 | .20 |
| 143 | Dan Wilson | .07 | .20 |
| 144 | Jeff Reed | .07 | .20 |
| 145 | Brett Tomko | .07 | .20 |
| 146 | Terry Steinbach | .07 | .20 |
| 147 | Seth Greisinger | .07 | .20 |
| 148 | Pat Meares | .07 | .20 |
| 149 | Livan Hernandez | .07 | .20 |
| 150 | Jeff Bagwell | .10 | .30 |
| 151 | Bob Wickman | .07 | .20 |
| 152 | Omar Vizquel | .10 | .30 |
| 153 | Eric Davis | .07 | .20 |
| 154 | Larry Sutton | .07 | .20 |
| 155 | Magglio Ordonez | .07 | .20 |
| 156 | Eric Milton | .07 | .20 |
| 157 | Darren Lewis | .07 | .20 |
| 158 | Rick Aguilera | .07 | .20 |
| 159 | Mike Lieberthal | .07 | .20 |
| 160 | Robb Nen | .07 | .20 |
| 161 | Brian Giles | .07 | .20 |
| 162 | Jeff Brantley | .07 | .20 |
| 163 | Gary DiSarcina | .07 | .20 |
| 164 | John Valentin | .07 | .20 |
| 165 | David Dellucci | .07 | .20 |
| 166 | Chan Ho Park | .07 | .20 |
| 167 | Masato Yoshii | .07 | .20 |
| 168 | Jason Schmidt | .07 | .20 |
| 169 | LaTroy Hawkins | .07 | .20 |
| 170 | Bret Boone | .07 | .20 |
| 171 | Jerry DiPoto | .07 | .20 |
| 172 | Mariano Rivera | .20 | .50 |
| 173 | Mike Cameron | .07 | .20 |
| 174 | Scott Erickson | .07 | .20 |
| 175 | Charles Johnson | .07 | .20 |
| 176 | Bobby Jones | .07 | .20 |
| 177 | Francisco Cordova | .07 | .20 |
| 178 | Todd Jones | .07 | .20 |
| 179 | Jeff Montgomery | .07 | .20 |
| 180 | Mike Mussina | .10 | .30 |
| 181 | Bob Abreu | .07 | .20 |
| 182 | Ismael Valdes | .07 | .20 |
| 183 | Andy Fox | .07 | .20 |
| 184 | Woody Williams | .07 | .20 |
| 185 | Denny Neagle | .07 | .20 |
| 186 | Jose Valentin | .07 | .20 |
| 187 | Darrin Fletcher | .07 | .20 |
| 188 | Gabe Alvarez | .07 | .20 |
| 189 | Eddie Taubensee | .07 | .20 |
| 190 | Edgar Martinez | .10 | .30 |
| 191 | Jason Kendall | .07 | .20 |
| 192 | Darryl Kile | .07 | .20 |
| 193 | Jeff King | .07 | .20 |
| 194 | Rey Ordonez | .07 | .20 |
| 195 | Andruw Jones | .10 | .30 |
| 196 | Tony Fernandez | .07 | .20 |
| 197 | Jamey Wright | .07 | .20 |
| 198 | B.J. Surhoff | .07 | .20 |
| 199 | Vinny Castilla | .07 | .20 |
| 200 | David Wells HL | .07 | .20 |
| 201 | Mark McGwire HL | .25 | .60 |
| 202 | Sammy Sosa HL | .10 | .30 |
| 203 | Roger Clemens HL | .20 | .50 |
| 204 | Kerry Wood HL | .07 | .20 |
| 205 | L.Berkman/G.Kapler | .15 | .40 |
| 206 | Alex Escobar RC | .15 | .40 |
| 207 | Peter Bergeron RC | .08 | .25 |
| 208 | M.Barrett/B.Davis/R.Fick | .08 | .25 |
| 209 | P.Cline/R.Hernandez/J.Werth | .08 | .25 |
| 210 | R.Anderson/Chen/Enochs | .08 | .25 |
| 211 | B.Penny/Dotel/Lincoln | .08 | .25 |
| 212 | Chuck Abbott RC | .08 | .25 |
| 213 | C.Jones/J.Urban RC | .08 | .25 |
| 214 | T.Torcato/A.McDowell RC | .08 | .25 |
| 215 | J.Tyner/J.McKinley RC | .08 | .25 |
| 216 | M.Burch/S.Etherton RC | .08 | .25 |
| 217 | R.Elder/M.Tucker RC | .08 | .25 |
| 218 | J.M.Gold/R.Mills RC | .08 | .25 |
| 219 | A.Brown/C.Freeman RC | .08 | .25 |
| 220A | Mark McGwire HR 1 | 15.00 | 40.00 |
| 220B | Mark McGwire HR 2 | 6.00 | 15.00 |
| 220C | Mark McGwire HR 3 | 6.00 | 15.00 |
| 220D | Mark McGwire HR 4 | 6.00 | 15.00 |
| 220E | Mark McGwire HR 5 | 6.00 | 15.00 |
| 220F | Mark McGwire HR 6 | 6.00 | 15.00 |
| 220G | Mark McGwire HR 7 | 6.00 | 15.00 |
| 220H | Mark McGwire HR 8 | 6.00 | 15.00 |
| 220I | Mark McGwire HR 9 | 6.00 | 15.00 |
| 220J | Mark McGwire HR 10 | 6.00 | 15.00 |
| 220K | Mark McGwire HR 11 | 6.00 | 15.00 |
| 220L | Mark McGwire HR 12 | 6.00 | 15.00 |
| 220M | Mark McGwire HR 13 | 6.00 | 15.00 |
| 220N | Mark McGwire HR 14 | 6.00 | 15.00 |
| 220O | Mark McGwire HR 15 | 6.00 | 15.00 |
| 220P | Mark McGwire HR 16 | 6.00 | 15.00 |
| 220Q | Mark McGwire HR 17 | 6.00 | 15.00 |
| 220R | Mark McGwire HR 18 | 6.00 | 15.00 |
| 220S | Mark McGwire HR 19 | 6.00 | 15.00 |
| 220T | Mark McGwire HR 20 | 6.00 | 15.00 |
| 220U | Mark McGwire HR 21 | 6.00 | 15.00 |
| 220V | Mark McGwire HR 22 | 6.00 | 15.00 |
| 220W | Mark McGwire HR 23 | 6.00 | 15.00 |
| 220X | Mark McGwire HR 24 | 6.00 | 15.00 |
| 220Y | Mark McGwire HR 25 | 6.00 | 15.00 |
| 220Z | Mark McGwire HR 26 | 6.00 | 15.00 |
| 220AA | Mark McGwire HR 27 | 6.00 | 15.00 |
| 220AB | Mark McGwire HR 28 | 6.00 | 15.00 |
| 220AC | Mark McGwire HR 29 | 6.00 | 15.00 |
| 220AD | Mark McGwire HR 30 | 6.00 | 15.00 |
| 220AE | Mark McGwire HR 31 | 6.00 | 15.00 |
| 220AF | Mark McGwire HR 32 | 6.00 | 15.00 |
| 220AG | Mark McGwire HR 33 | 6.00 | 15.00 |
| 220AH | Mark McGwire HR 34 | 6.00 | 15.00 |
| 220AI | Mark McGwire HR 35 | 6.00 | 15.00 |
| 220AJ | Mark McGwire HR 36 | 6.00 | 15.00 |
| 220AK | Mark McGwire HR 37 | 6.00 | 15.00 |
| 220AL | Mark McGwire HR 38 | 6.00 | 15.00 |
| 220AM | Mark McGwire HR 39 | 6.00 | 15.00 |
| 220AN | Mark McGwire HR 40 | 6.00 | 15.00 |
| 220AO | Mark McGwire HR 41 | 6.00 | 15.00 |
| 220AP | Mark McGwire HR 42 | 6.00 | 15.00 |
| 220AQ | Mark McGwire HR 43 | 6.00 | 15.00 |
| 220AR | Mark McGwire HR 44 | 6.00 | 15.00 |
| 220AS | Mark McGwire HR 45 | 6.00 | 15.00 |
| 220AT | Mark McGwire HR 46 | 6.00 | 15.00 |
| 220AU | Mark McGwire HR 47 | 6.00 | 15.00 |
| 220AV | Mark McGwire HR 48 | 6.00 | 15.00 |
| 220AW | Mark McGwire HR 49 | 6.00 | 15.00 |
| 220AX | Mark McGwire HR 50 | 6.00 | 15.00 |
| 220AY | Mark McGwire HR 51 | 6.00 | 15.00 |
| 220AZ | Mark McGwire HR 52 | 6.00 | 15.00 |
| 220BB | Mark McGwire HR 53 | 6.00 | 15.00 |
| 220CC | Mark McGwire HR 54 | 6.00 | 15.00 |
| 220DD | Mark McGwire HR 55 | 6.00 | 15.00 |
| 220EE | Mark McGwire HR 56 | 6.00 | 15.00 |
| 220FF | Mark McGwire HR 57 | 6.00 | 15.00 |
| 220GG | Mark McGwire HR 58 | 6.00 | 15.00 |
| 220HH | Mark McGwire HR 59 | 6.00 | 15.00 |
| 220II | Mark McGwire HR 60 | 6.00 | 15.00 |
| 220JJ | Mark McGwire HR 61 | 12.50 | 30.00 |
| 220KK | Mark McGwire HR 62 | 15.00 | 40.00 |
| 220LL | Mark McGwire HR 63 | 6.00 | 15.00 |
| 220MM | Mark McGwire HR 64 | 6.00 | 15.00 |
| 220NN | Mark McGwire HR 65 | 6.00 | 15.00 |
| 220OO | Mark McGwire HR 66 | 6.00 | 15.00 |
| 220PP | Mark McGwire HR 67 | 6.00 | 15.00 |
| 220QQ | Mark McGwire HR 68 | 6.00 | 15.00 |
| 220RR | Mark McGwire HR 69 | 6.00 | 15.00 |
| 220SS | Mark McGwire HR 70 | 50.00 | 100.00 |
| 221 | Larry Walker LL | .07 | .20 |
| 222 | Bernie Williams LL | .07 | .20 |
| 223 | Mark McGwire LL | .25 | .60 |
| 224 | Ken Griffey Jr. LL | .20 | .50 |
| 225 | Sammy Sosa LL | .10 | .30 |
| 226 | Juan Gonzalez LL | .07 | .20 |
| 227 | Dante Bichette LL | .07 | .20 |
| 228 | Alex Rodriguez LL | .20 | .50 |
| 229 | Sammy Sosa LL | .10 | .30 |
| 230 | Derek Jeter LL | .25 | .60 |
| 231 | Greg Maddux LL | .20 | .50 |
| 232 | Roger Clemens LL | .20 | .50 |
| 233 | Ricky Ledee WS | .07 | .20 |
| 234 | Chuck Knoblauch WS | .07 | .20 |
| 235 | Bernie Williams WS | .07 | .20 |
| 236 | Tino Martinez WS | .07 | .20 |
| 237 | Orlando Hernandez WS | .07 | .20 |
| 238 | Scott Brosius WS | .07 | .20 |
| 239 | Andy Pettitte WS | .07 | .20 |
| 240 | Mariano Rivera WS | .10 | .30 |
| 241 | Checklist 1 | .07 | .20 |
| 242 | Checklist 2 | .07 | .20 |
| 243 | Tom Glavine | .10 | .30 |
| 244 | Andy Benes | .07 | .20 |
| 245 | Sandy Alomar Jr. | .07 | .20 |
| 246 | Wilton Guerrero | .07 | .20 |
| 247 | Alex Gonzalez | .07 | .20 |
| 248 | Roberto Alomar | .10 | .30 |
| 249 | Ruben Rivera | .07 | .20 |
| 250 | Eric Chavez | .07 | .20 |
| 251 | Ellis Burks | .07 | .20 |
| 252 | Richie Sexson | .07 | .20 |
| 253 | Steve Finley | .07 | .20 |
| 254 | Dwight Gooden | .07 | .20 |
| 255 | Dustin Hermanson | .07 | .20 |
| 256 | Kirk Rueter | .07 | .20 |
| 257 | Steve Trachsel | .07 | .20 |
| 258 | Gregg Jefferies | .07 | .20 |
| 259 | Matt Stairs | .07 | .20 |
| 260 | Shane Reynolds | .07 | .20 |
| 261 | Gregg Olson | .07 | .20 |
| 262 | Kevin Tapani | .07 | .20 |
| 263 | Matt Morris | .07 | .20 |
| 264 | Carl Pavano | .07 | .20 |
| 265 | Nomar Garciaparra | .30 | .75 |
| 266 | Kevin Young | .07 | .20 |
| 267 | Rick Helling | .07 | .20 |
| 268 | Matt Franco | .07 | .20 |
| 269 | Brian McRae | .07 | .20 |
| 270 | Cal Ripken | .60 | 1.50 |
| 271 | Jeff Abbott | .07 | .20 |
| 272 | Tony Batista | .07 | .20 |
| 273 | Bill Simas | .07 | .20 |
| 274 | Brian Hunter | .07 | .20 |
| 275 | John Franco | .07 | .20 |
| 276 | Devon White | .07 | .20 |
| 277 | Rickey Henderson | .20 | .50 |
| 278 | Chuck Finley | .07 | .20 |
| 279 | Mike Blowers | .07 | .20 |
| 280 | Mark Grace | .10 | .30 |
| 281 | Randy Winn | .07 | .20 |
| 282 | Bobby Bonilla | .07 | .20 |
| 283 | David Justice | .07 | .20 |
| 284 | Shane Monahan | .07 | .20 |
| 285 | Kevin Brown | .10 | .30 |
| 286 | Todd Zeile | .07 | .20 |
| 287 | Al Martin | .07 | .20 |
| 288 | Troy O'Leary | .07 | .20 |
| 289 | Darryl Hamilton | .07 | .20 |
| 290 | Tino Martinez | .10 | .30 |
| 291 | David Ortiz | .20 | .50 |
| 292 | Tony Clark | .07 | .20 |
| 293 | Ryan Minor | .07 | .20 |
| 294 | Mark Leiter | .07 | .20 |
| 295 | Wally Joyner | .07 | .20 |
| 296 | Cliff Floyd | .07 | .20 |
| 297 | Shawn Estes | .07 | .20 |
| 298 | Pat Hentgen | .07 | .20 |
| 299 | Scott Elarton | .07 | .20 |
| 300 | Alex Rodriguez | .30 | .75 |
| 301 | Ozzie Guillen | .07 | .20 |
| 302 | Hideo Nomo | .20 | .50 |
| 303 | Ryan McGuire | .07 | .20 |
| 304 | Brad Ausmus | .07 | .20 |
| 305 | Alex Gonzalez | .07 | .20 |
| 306 | Brian Jordan | .07 | .20 |
| 307 | John Jaha | .07 | .20 |
| 308 | Mark Grudzielanek | .07 | .20 |
| 309 | Juan Guzman | .07 | .20 |
| 310 | Tony Womack | .07 | .20 |
| 311 | Dennis Reyes | .07 | .20 |

| | | |
|---|---|---|
| ❑ 312 Marty Cordova | .07 | .20 |
| ❑ 313 Ramiro Mendoza | .07 | .20 |
| ❑ 314 Robin Ventura | .07 | .20 |
| ❑ 315 Rafael Palmeiro | .10 | .30 |
| ❑ 316 Ramon Martinez | .07 | .20 |
| ❑ 317 Pedro Astacio | .07 | .20 |
| ❑ 318 Dave Hollins | .07 | .20 |
| ❑ 319 Tom Candiotti | .07 | .20 |
| ❑ 320 Al Leiter | .07 | .20 |
| ❑ 321 Rico Brogna | .07 | .20 |
| ❑ 322 Reggie Jefferson | .07 | .20 |
| ❑ 323 Bernard Gilkey | .07 | .20 |
| ❑ 324 Jason Giambi | .07 | .20 |
| ❑ 325 Craig Biggio | .10 | .30 |
| ❑ 326 Troy Glaus | .10 | .30 |
| ❑ 327 Delino DeShields | .07 | .20 |
| ❑ 328 Fernando Vina | .07 | .20 |
| ❑ 329 John Smoltz | .10 | .30 |
| ❑ 330 Jeff Kent | .07 | .20 |
| ❑ 331 Roy Halladay | .07 | .20 |
| ❑ 332 Andy Ashby | .07 | .20 |
| ❑ 333 Tim Wakefield | .07 | .20 |
| ❑ 334 Roger Clemens | .40 | 1.00 |
| ❑ 335 Bernie Williams | .10 | .30 |
| ❑ 336 Desi Relaford | .07 | .20 |
| ❑ 337 John Burkett | .07 | .20 |
| ❑ 338 Mike Hampton | .07 | .20 |
| ❑ 339 Royce Clayton | .07 | .20 |
| ❑ 340 Mike Piazza | .30 | .75 |
| ❑ 341 Jaren Gonzalez | .07 | .20 |
| ❑ 342 Mike Lansing | .07 | .20 |
| ❑ 343 Jamie Moyer | .07 | .20 |
| ❑ 344 Ron Coomer | .07 | .20 |
| ❑ 345 Barry Larkin | .10 | .30 |
| ❑ 346 Fernando Tatis | .07 | .20 |
| ❑ 347 Chili Davis | .07 | .20 |
| ❑ 348 Bobby Higginson | .07 | .20 |
| ❑ 349 Hal Morris | .07 | .20 |
| ❑ 350 Larry Walker | .07 | .20 |
| ❑ 351 Carlos Guillen | .07 | .20 |
| ❑ 352 Miguel Tejada | .07 | .20 |
| ❑ 353 Travis Fryman | .07 | .20 |
| ❑ 354 Jarrod Washburn | .07 | .20 |
| ❑ 355 Chipper Jones | .20 | .50 |
| ❑ 356 Todd Stottlemyre | .07 | .20 |
| ❑ 357 Henry Rodriguez | .07 | .20 |
| ❑ 358 Eli Marrero | .07 | .20 |
| ❑ 359 Alan Benes | .07 | .20 |
| ❑ 360 Tim Salmon | .10 | .30 |
| ❑ 361 Luis Gonzalez | .07 | .20 |
| ❑ 362 Scott Spiezio | .07 | .20 |
| ❑ 363 Chris Carpenter | .07 | .20 |
| ❑ 364 Bobby Howry | .07 | .20 |
| ❑ 365 Raul Mondesi | .07 | .20 |
| ❑ 366 Ugueth Urbina | .07 | .20 |
| ❑ 367 Tom Evans | .07 | .20 |
| ❑ 368 Kerry Ligtenberg RC | .08 | .25 |
| ❑ 369 Adrian Beltre | .07 | .20 |
| ❑ 370 Ryan Klesko | .07 | .20 |
| ❑ 371 Wilson Alvarez | .07 | .20 |
| ❑ 372 John Thomson | .07 | .20 |
| ❑ 373 Tony Saunders | .07 | .20 |
| ❑ 374 Dave Mlicki | .07 | .20 |
| ❑ 375 Ken Caminiti | .07 | .20 |
| ❑ 376 Jay Buhner | .07 | .20 |
| ❑ 377 Bill Mueller | .07 | .20 |
| ❑ 378 Jeff Blauser | .07 | .20 |
| ❑ 379 Edgar Renteria | .07 | .20 |
| ❑ 380 Jim Thome | .10 | .30 |
| ❑ 381 Joey Hamilton | .07 | .20 |
| ❑ 382 Calvin Pickering | .07 | .20 |
| ❑ 383 Marquis Grissom | .07 | .20 |
| ❑ 384 Omar Daal | .07 | .20 |
| ❑ 385 Curt Schilling | .07 | .20 |
| ❑ 386 Jose Cruz Jr. | .07 | .20 |
| ❑ 387 Chris Widger | .07 | .20 |
| ❑ 388 Pete Harnisch | .07 | .20 |
| ❑ 389 Charles Nagy | .07 | .20 |
| ❑ 390 Tom Gordon | .07 | .20 |
| ❑ 391 Bobby Smith | .07 | .20 |
| ❑ 392 Derrick Gibson | .07 | .20 |
| ❑ 393 Jeff Conine | .07 | .20 |
| ❑ 394 Carlos Perez | .07 | .20 |
| ❑ 395 Barry Bonds | .60 | 1.50 |
| ❑ 396 Mark McLemore | .07 | .20 |
| ❑ 397 Juan Encarnacion | .07 | .20 |
| ❑ 398 Wade Boggs | .10 | .30 |
| ❑ 399 Ivan Rodriguez | .10 | .30 |

| | | |
|---|---|---|
| ❑ 400 Moises Alou | .07 | .20 |
| ❑ 401 Jeromy Burnitz | .07 | .20 |
| ❑ 402 Sean Casey | .07 | .20 |
| ❑ 403 Jose Offerman | .07 | .20 |
| ❑ 404 Joe Fontenot | .07 | .20 |
| ❑ 405 Kevin Millwood | .07 | .20 |
| ❑ 406 Lance Johnson | .07 | .20 |
| ❑ 407 Richard Hidalgo | .07 | .20 |
| ❑ 408 Mike Jackson | .07 | .20 |
| ❑ 409 Brian Anderson | .07 | .20 |
| ❑ 410 Jeff Shaw | .07 | .20 |
| ❑ 411 Preston Wilson | .07 | .20 |
| ❑ 412 Todd Hundley | .07 | .20 |
| ❑ 413 Jim Parque | .07 | .20 |
| ❑ 414 Justin Baughman | .07 | .20 |
| ❑ 415 Dante Bichette | .07 | .20 |
| ❑ 416 Paul O'Neill | .10 | .30 |
| ❑ 417 Miguel Cairo | .07 | .20 |
| ❑ 418 Randy Johnson | .20 | .50 |
| ❑ 419 Jesus Sanchez | .07 | .20 |
| ❑ 420 Carlos Delgado | .07 | .20 |
| ❑ 421 Ricky Ledee | .07 | .20 |
| ❑ 422 Orlando Hernandez | .07 | .20 |
| ❑ 423 Frank Thomas | .20 | .50 |
| ❑ 424 Pokey Reese | .07 | .20 |
| ❑ 425 C.Lee/M.Lowell | .15 | .40 |
| ❑ 426 M.Cuddyer/DeRosa/Hairston | .08 | .25 |
| ❑ 427 M.Anderson/Belliard/Cabrera | .15 | .40 |
| ❑ 428 M.Bowie/P.Norton RC/Woll | .08 | .25 |
| ❑ 429 J.Cressend RC/Rocker | .15 | .40 |
| ❑ 430 R.Mateo/M.Zywica RC | .08 | .25 |
| ❑ 431 J.LaRue/Le.Croy/Meluskey | .08 | .25 |
| ❑ 432 Gabe Kapler | .15 | .40 |
| ❑ 433 A.Kennedy/M.Lopez RC | .08 | .25 |
| ❑ 434 Jose Fernandez RC/C.Truby | .08 | .25 |
| ❑ 435 Doug Mientkiewicz RC | .20 | .50 |
| ❑ 436 R.Brown RC/V.Wells | .20 | .50 |
| ❑ 437 A.J. Burnett RC | .30 | .75 |
| ❑ 438 M.Belisle/M.Roney RC | .08 | .25 |
| ❑ 439 A.Kearns/C.George RC | .60 | 1.50 |
| ❑ 440 N.Comejo/N.Bump RC | .08 | .25 |
| ❑ 441 B.Lidge/M.Nannini RC | .60 | 1.50 |
| ❑ 442 M.Holliday/J.Winchester RC | 1.50 | 4.00 |
| ❑ 443 A.Everett/C.Ambres RC | .20 | .50 |
| ❑ 444 P.Burrell/E.Valent RC | .60 | 1.50 |
| ❑ 445 Roger Clemens SK | .20 | .50 |
| ❑ 446 Kerry Wood SK | .07 | .20 |
| ❑ 447 Curt Schilling SK | .07 | .20 |
| ❑ 448 Randy Johnson SK | .10 | .30 |
| ❑ 449 Pedro Martinez SK | .10 | .30 |
| ❑ 450 Bagwell/Galar/McGwire AT | .20 | .50 |
| ❑ 451 Olerud/Thome/Martinez AT | .20 | .50 |
| ❑ 452 ARod/Nomar/Jeter AT | .25 | .60 |
| ❑ 453 Castilla/Jones/Rolen AT | .10 | .30 |
| ❑ 454 Sosa/Griffey/Gonzalez AT | .20 | .50 |
| ❑ 455 Bonds/Ramirez/Walker AT | .30 | .75 |
| ❑ 456 Thomas/Salmon/Justice AT | .20 | .50 |
| ❑ 457 Lee/Helton/Grieve AT | .07 | .20 |
| ❑ 458 Guerrero/Vaughn/B.Will AT | .20 | .50 |
| ❑ 459 Piazza/IRod/Kendall AT | .20 | .50 |
| ❑ 460 Clemens/Wood/Maddux AT | .20 | .50 |
| ❑ 461A Sammy Sosa HR 1 | 6.00 | 15.00 |
| ❑ 461B Sammy Sosa HR 2 | 2.50 | 6.00 |
| ❑ 461C Sammy Sosa HR 3 | 2.50 | 6.00 |
| ❑ 461D Sammy Sosa HR 4 | 2.50 | 6.00 |
| ❑ 461E Sammy Sosa HR 5 | 2.50 | 6.00 |
| ❑ 461F Sammy Sosa HR 6 | 2.50 | 6.00 |
| ❑ 461G Sammy Sosa HR 7 | 2.50 | 6.00 |
| ❑ 461H Sammy Sosa HR 8 | 2.50 | 6.00 |
| ❑ 461I Sammy Sosa HR 9 | 2.50 | 6.00 |
| ❑ 461J Sammy Sosa HR 10 | 2.50 | 6.00 |
| ❑ 461K Sammy Sosa HR 11 | 2.50 | 6.00 |
| ❑ 461L Sammy Sosa HR 12 | 2.50 | 6.00 |
| ❑ 461M Sammy Sosa HR 13 | 2.50 | 6.00 |
| ❑ 461N Sammy Sosa HR 14 | 2.50 | 6.00 |
| ❑ 461O Sammy Sosa HR 15 | 2.50 | 6.00 |
| ❑ 461P Sammy Sosa HR 16 | 2.50 | 6.00 |
| ❑ 461Q Sammy Sosa HR 17 | 2.50 | 6.00 |
| ❑ 461R Sammy Sosa HR 18 | 2.50 | 6.00 |
| ❑ 461S Sammy Sosa HR 19 | 2.50 | 6.00 |
| ❑ 461T Sammy Sosa HR 20 | 2.50 | 6.00 |
| ❑ 461U Sammy Sosa HR 21 | 2.50 | 6.00 |
| ❑ 461V Sammy Sosa HR 22 | 2.50 | 6.00 |
| ❑ 461W Sammy Sosa HR 23 | 2.50 | 6.00 |
| ❑ 461X Sammy Sosa HR 24 | 2.50 | 6.00 |
| ❑ 461Y Sammy Sosa HR 25 | 2.50 | 6.00 |
| ❑ 461Z Sammy Sosa HR 26 | 2.50 | 6.00 |
| ❑ 461AA Sammy Sosa HR 27 | 2.50 | 6.00 |

| | | |
|---|---|---|
| ❑ 461AB Sammy Sosa HR 28 | 2.50 | 6.00 |
| ❑ 461AC Sammy Sosa HR 29 | 2.50 | 6.00 |
| ❑ 461AD Sammy Sosa HR 30 | 2.50 | 6.00 |
| ❑ 461AE Sammy Sosa HR 31 | 2.50 | 6.00 |
| ❑ 461AF Sammy Sosa HR 32 | 2.50 | 6.00 |
| ❑ 461AG Sammy Sosa HR 33 | 2.50 | 6.00 |
| ❑ 461AH Sammy Sosa HR 34 | 2.50 | 6.00 |
| ❑ 461AI Sammy Sosa HR 35 | 2.50 | 6.00 |
| ❑ 461AJ Sammy Sosa HR 36 | 2.50 | 6.00 |
| ❑ 461AK Sammy Sosa HR 37 | 2.50 | 6.00 |
| ❑ 461AL Sammy Sosa HR 38 | 2.50 | 6.00 |
| ❑ 461AM Sammy Sosa HR 39 | 2.50 | 6.00 |
| ❑ 461AN Sammy Sosa HR 40 | 2.50 | 6.00 |
| ❑ 461AO Sammy Sosa HR 41 | 2.50 | 6.00 |
| ❑ 461AP Sammy Sosa HR 42 | 2.50 | 6.00 |
| ❑ 461AQ Sammy Sosa HR 43 | 2.50 | 6.00 |
| ❑ 461AR Sammy Sosa HR 44 | 2.50 | 6.00 |
| ❑ 461AS Sammy Sosa HR 45 | 2.50 | 6.00 |
| ❑ 461AT Sammy Sosa HR 46 | 2.50 | 6.00 |
| ❑ 461AU Sammy Sosa HR 47 | 2.50 | 6.00 |
| ❑ 461AV Sammy Sosa HR 48 | 2.50 | 6.00 |
| ❑ 461AW Sammy Sosa HR 49 | 2.50 | 6.00 |
| ❑ 461AX Sammy Sosa HR 50 | 2.50 | 6.00 |
| ❑ 461AY Sammy Sosa HR 50 | 2.50 | 6.00 |
| ❑ 461AZ Sammy Sosa HR 51 | 2.50 | 6.00 |
| ❑ 461BB Sammy Sosa HR 52 | 2.50 | 6.00 |
| ❑ 461CC Sammy Sosa HR 53 | 2.50 | 6.00 |
| ❑ 461DD Sammy Sosa HR 54 | 2.50 | 6.00 |
| ❑ 461EE Sammy Sosa HR 55 | 2.50 | 6.00 |
| ❑ 461FF Sammy Sosa HR 56 | 2.50 | 6.00 |
| ❑ 461GG Sammy Sosa HR 57 | 2.50 | 6.00 |
| ❑ 461HH Sammy Sosa HR 58 | 2.50 | 6.00 |
| ❑ 461II Sammy Sosa HR 59 | 2.50 | 6.00 |
| ❑ 461JJ Sammy Sosa HR 60 | 2.50 | 6.00 |
| ❑ 461KK Sammy Sosa HR 61 | 6.00 | 15.00 |
| ❑ 461LL Sammy Sosa HR 62 | 8.00 | 20.00 |
| ❑ 461MM Sammy Sosa HR 63 | 3.00 | 8.00 |
| ❑ 461NN Sammy Sosa HR 64 | 3.00 | 8.00 |
| ❑ 461OO Sammy Sosa HR 65 | 3.00 | 8.00 |
| ❑ 461PP Sammy Sosa HR 66 | 10.00 | 25.00 |
| ❑ 462 Checklist | .07 | .20 |
| ❑ 463 Checklist | .07 | .20 |

## 2000 Topps

| | | |
|---|---|---|
| ❑ COMPLETE SET (478) | 20.00 | 50.00 |
| ❑ COMP.HOBBY SET (478) | 30.00 | 60.00 |
| ❑ COMPLETE SERIES 1 (239) | 10.00 | 25.00 |
| ❑ COMPLETE SERIES 2 (240) | 10.00 | 25.00 |
| ❑ MCGWIRE MM SET (5) | 5.00 | 12.00 |
| ❑ AARON MM SET (5) | 4.00 | 10.00 |
| ❑ RIPKEN MM SET (5) | 6.00 | 15.00 |
| ❑ BOGGS MM SET (5) | 1.25 | 3.00 |
| ❑ GWYNN MM SET (5) | 3.00 | 8.00 |
| ❑ GRIFFEY MM SET (5) | 3.00 | 8.00 |
| ❑ BONDS MM SET (5) | 5.00 | 12.00 |
| ❑ JETER MM SET (5) | 3.00 | 8.00 |
| ❑ A.ROD MM SET (5) | 3.00 | 8.00 |
| ❑ 1 Mark McGwire | .50 | 1.25 |
| ❑ 2 Tony Gwynn | .25 | .60 |
| ❑ 3 Wade Boggs | .10 | .30 |
| ❑ 4 Cal Ripken | .60 | 1.50 |
| ❑ 5 Matt Williams | .07 | .20 |
| ❑ 6 Jay Buhner | .07 | .20 |
| ❑ 7 Jeff Conine | .07 | .20 |
| ❑ 8 Todd Greene | .07 | .20 |
| ❑ 9 Charles Nagy | .07 | .20 |
| ❑ 10 Mike Lieberthal | .07 | .20 |
| ❑ 11 Steve Avery | .07 | .20 |
| ❑ 12 Bret Saberhagen | .07 | .20 |
| ❑ 13 Magglio Ordonez | .07 | .20 |
| ❑ 14 Brad Radke | .07 | .20 |
| ❑ 15 Derek Jeter | .50 | 1.25 |
| ❑ 16 Javy Lopez | .07 | .20 |
| ❑ 17 Russ Davis | .07 | .20 |
| ❑ 18 Armando Benitez | .07 | .20 |

| Card | | |
|---|---|---|
| ❏ 19 B.J. Surhoff | .07 | .20 |
| ❏ 20 Darryl Kile | .07 | .20 |
| ❏ 21 Mark Lewis | .07 | .20 |
| ❏ 22 Mike Williams | .07 | .20 |
| ❏ 23 Mark McLemore | .07 | .20 |
| ❏ 24 Sterling Hitchcock | .07 | .20 |
| ❏ 25 Darin Erstad | .07 | .20 |
| ❏ 26 Ricky Gutierrez | .07 | .20 |
| ❏ 27 John Jaha | .07 | .20 |
| ❏ 28 Homer Bush | .07 | .20 |
| ❏ 29 Darrin Fletcher | .07 | .20 |
| ❏ 30 Mark Grace | .10 | .30 |
| ❏ 31 Fred McGriff | .10 | .30 |
| ❏ 32 Omar Daal | .07 | .20 |
| ❏ 33 Eric Karros | .07 | .20 |
| ❏ 34 Orlando Cabrera | .07 | .20 |
| ❏ 35 J.T. Snow | .07 | .20 |
| ❏ 36 Luis Castillo | .07 | .20 |
| ❏ 37 Rey Ordonez | .07 | .20 |
| ❏ 38 Bob Abreu | .07 | .20 |
| ❏ 39 Warren Morris | .07 | .20 |
| ❏ 40 Juan Gonzalez | .20 | .50 |
| ❏ 41 Mike Lansing | .07 | .20 |
| ❏ 42 Chili Davis | .07 | .20 |
| ❏ 43 Dean Palmer | .07 | .20 |
| ❏ 44 Hank Aaron | .30 | .75 |
| ❏ 45 Jeff Bagwell | .10 | .30 |
| ❏ 46 Jose Valentin | .07 | .20 |
| ❏ 47 Shannon Stewart | .07 | .20 |
| ❏ 48 Kent Bottenfield | .07 | .20 |
| ❏ 49 Jeff Shaw | .07 | .20 |
| ❏ 50 Sammy Sosa | .20 | .50 |
| ❏ 51 Randy Johnson | .20 | .50 |
| ❏ 52 Benny Agbayani | .07 | .20 |
| ❏ 53 Dante Bichette | .07 | .20 |
| ❏ 54 Pete Harnisch | .07 | .20 |
| ❏ 55 Frank Thomas | .20 | .50 |
| ❏ 56 Jorge Posada | .10 | .30 |
| ❏ 57 Todd Walker | .07 | .20 |
| ❏ 58 Juan Encarnacion | .07 | .20 |
| ❏ 59 Mike Sweeney | .07 | .20 |
| ❏ 60 Pedro Martinez | .10 | .30 |
| ❏ 61 Lee Stevens | .07 | .20 |
| ❏ 62 Brian Giles | .07 | .20 |
| ❏ 63 Chad Ogea | .07 | .20 |
| ❏ 64 Ivan Rodriguez | .10 | .30 |
| ❏ 65 Roger Cedeno | .07 | .20 |
| ❏ 66 David Justice | .07 | .20 |
| ❏ 67 Steve Trachsel | .07 | .20 |
| ❏ 68 Eli Marrero | .07 | .20 |
| ❏ 69 Dave Nilsson | .07 | .20 |
| ❏ 70 Ken Caminiti | .07 | .20 |
| ❏ 71 Tim Raines | .07 | .20 |
| ❏ 72 Brian Jordan | .07 | .20 |
| ❏ 73 Jeff Blauser | .07 | .20 |
| ❏ 74 Bernard Gilkey | .07 | .20 |
| ❏ 75 John Flaherty | .07 | .20 |
| ❏ 76 Brent Mayne | .07 | .20 |
| ❏ 77 Jose Vidro | .07 | .20 |
| ❏ 78 David Bell | .07 | .20 |
| ❏ 79 Bruce Aven | .07 | .20 |
| ❏ 80 John Olerud | .07 | .20 |
| ❏ 81 Pokey Reese | .07 | .20 |
| ❏ 82 Woody Williams | .07 | .20 |
| ❏ 83 Ed Sprague | .07 | .20 |
| ❏ 84 Joe Girardi | .07 | .20 |
| ❏ 85 Barry Larkin | .10 | .30 |
| ❏ 86 Mike Caruso | .07 | .20 |
| ❏ 87 Bobby Higginson | .07 | .20 |
| ❏ 88 Roberto Kelly | .07 | .20 |
| ❏ 89 Edgar Martinez | .10 | .30 |
| ❏ 90 Mark Kotsay | .07 | .20 |
| ❏ 91 Paul Sorrento | .07 | .20 |
| ❏ 92 Eric Young | .07 | .20 |
| ❏ 93 Carlos Delgado | .07 | .20 |
| ❏ 94 Troy Glaus | .07 | .20 |
| ❏ 95 Ben Grieve | .07 | .20 |
| ❏ 96 Jose Lima | .07 | .20 |
| ❏ 97 Garret Anderson | .07 | .20 |
| ❏ 98 Luis Gonzalez | .07 | .20 |
| ❏ 99 Carl Pavano | .07 | .20 |
| ❏ 100 Alex Rodriguez | .30 | .75 |
| ❏ 101 Preston Wilson | .07 | .20 |
| ❏ 102 Ron Gant | .07 | .20 |
| ❏ 103 Brady Anderson | .07 | .20 |
| ❏ 104 Rickey Henderson | .20 | .50 |
| ❏ 105 Gary Sheffield | .07 | .20 |
| ❏ 106 Mickey Morandini | .07 | .20 |
| ❏ 107 Jim Edmonds | .07 | .20 |
| ❏ 108 Kris Benson | .07 | .20 |
| ❏ 109 Adrian Beltre | .07 | .20 |
| ❏ 110 Alex Fernandez | .07 | .20 |
| ❏ 111 Dan Wilson | .07 | .20 |
| ❏ 112 Mark Clark | .07 | .20 |
| ❏ 113 Greg Vaughn | .07 | .20 |
| ❏ 114 Neifi Perez | .07 | .20 |
| ❏ 115 Paul O'Neill | .10 | .30 |
| ❏ 116 Jermaine Dye | .07 | .20 |
| ❏ 117 Todd Jones | .07 | .20 |
| ❏ 118 Terry Steinbach | .07 | .20 |
| ❏ 119 Greg Norton | .07 | .20 |
| ❏ 120 Curt Schilling | .07 | .20 |
| ❏ 121 Todd Zeile | .07 | .20 |
| ❏ 122 Edgardo Alfonzo | .07 | .20 |
| ❏ 123 Ryan McGuire | .07 | .20 |
| ❏ 124 Rich Aurilia | .07 | .20 |
| ❏ 125 John Smoltz | .10 | .30 |
| ❏ 126 Bob Wickman | .07 | .20 |
| ❏ 127 Richard Hidalgo | .07 | .20 |
| ❏ 128 Chuck Finley | .07 | .20 |
| ❏ 129 Billy Wagner | .07 | .20 |
| ❏ 130 Todd Hundley | .07 | .20 |
| ❏ 131 Dwight Gooden | .07 | .20 |
| ❏ 132 Russ Ortiz | .07 | .20 |
| ❏ 133 Mike Lowell | .07 | .20 |
| ❏ 134 Reggie Sanders | .07 | .20 |
| ❏ 135 John Valentin | .07 | .20 |
| ❏ 136 Brad Ausmus | .07 | .20 |
| ❏ 137 Chad Kreuter | .07 | .20 |
| ❏ 138 David Cone | .07 | .20 |
| ❏ 139 Brook Fordyce | .07 | .20 |
| ❏ 140 Roberto Alomar | .10 | .30 |
| ❏ 141 Charles Nagy | .07 | .20 |
| ❏ 142 Brian Hunter | .07 | .20 |
| ❏ 143 Mike Mussina | .10 | .30 |
| ❏ 144 Robin Ventura | .10 | .30 |
| ❏ 145 Kevin Brown | .10 | .30 |
| ❏ 146 Pat Hentgen | .07 | .20 |
| ❏ 147 Ryan Klesko | .07 | .20 |
| ❏ 148 Derek Bell | .07 | .20 |
| ❏ 149 Andy Sheets | .07 | .20 |
| ❏ 150 Larry Walker | .07 | .20 |
| ❏ 151 Scott Williamson | .07 | .20 |
| ❏ 152 Jose Offerman | .07 | .20 |
| ❏ 153 Doug Mientkiewicz | .07 | .20 |
| ❏ 154 John Snyder RC | .15 | .40 |
| ❏ 155 Sandy Alomar Jr. | .07 | .20 |
| ❏ 156 Joe Nathan | .07 | .20 |
| ❏ 157 Lance Johnson | .07 | .20 |
| ❏ 158 Odalis Perez | .07 | .20 |
| ❏ 159 Hideo Nomo | .20 | .50 |
| ❏ 160 Steve Finley | .07 | .20 |
| ❏ 161 Dave Martinez | .07 | .20 |
| ❏ 162 Matt Walbeck | .07 | .20 |
| ❏ 163 Bill Spiers | .07 | .20 |
| ❏ 164 Fernando Tatis | .07 | .20 |
| ❏ 165 Kenny Lofton | .07 | .20 |
| ❏ 166 Paul Byrd | .07 | .20 |
| ❏ 167 Aaron Sele | .07 | .20 |
| ❏ 168 Eddie Taubensee | .07 | .20 |
| ❏ 169 Reggie Jefferson | .07 | .20 |
| ❏ 170 Roger Clemens | .40 | 1.00 |
| ❏ 171 Francisco Cordova | .07 | .20 |
| ❏ 172 Mike Bordick | .07 | .20 |
| ❏ 173 Wally Joyner | .07 | .20 |
| ❏ 174 Marvin Benard | .07 | .20 |
| ❏ 175 Jason Kendall | .07 | .20 |
| ❏ 176 Mike Stanley | .07 | .20 |
| ❏ 177 Chad Allen | .07 | .20 |
| ❏ 178 Carlos Beltran | .07 | .20 |
| ❏ 179 Deivi Cruz | .07 | .20 |
| ❏ 180 Chipper Jones | .50 | 1.25 |
| ❏ 181 Vladimir Guerrero | .20 | .50 |
| ❏ 182 Dave Burba | .07 | .20 |
| ❏ 183 Tom Goodwin | .07 | .20 |
| ❏ 184 Brian Daubach | .07 | .20 |
| ❏ 185 Jay Bell | .07 | .20 |
| ❏ 186 Roy Halladay | .07 | .20 |
| ❏ 187 Miguel Tejada | .07 | .20 |
| ❏ 188 Armando Rios | .07 | .20 |
| ❏ 189 Fernando Vina | .07 | .20 |
| ❏ 190 Eric Davis | .07 | .20 |
| ❏ 191 Henry Rodriguez | .07 | .20 |
| ❏ 192 Joe McEwing | .07 | .20 |
| ❏ 193 Jeff Kent | .07 | .20 |
| ❏ 194 Mike Jackson | .07 | .20 |
| ❏ 195 Mike Morgan | .07 | .20 |
| ❏ 196 Jeff Montgomery | .07 | .20 |
| ❏ 197 Jeff Zimmerman | .07 | .20 |
| ❏ 198 Tony Fernandez | .07 | .20 |
| ❏ 199 Jason Giambi | .07 | .20 |
| ❏ 200 Jose Canseco | .10 | .30 |
| ❏ 201 Alex Gonzalez | .07 | .20 |
| ❏ 202 J.Cust/Colangelo/D.Brown | .15 | .40 |
| ❏ 203 A.Soriano/F.Lopez | .20 | .50 |
| ❏ 204 Durazo/Burrell/Johnson | .15 | .40 |
| ❏ 205 John Sneed RC/K.Wells | .15 | .40 |
| ❏ 206 Kalinowski/Tejera/Mears RC | .15 | .40 |
| ❏ 207 L.Berkman/C.Patterson | .15 | .40 |
| ❏ 208 K.Pellow/K.Barker/R.Branyan | .15 | .40 |
| ❏ 209 B.Garbe/L.Bigbie RC | .20 | .50 |
| ❏ 210 B.Bradley RC/E.Munson | .15 | .40 |
| ❏ 211 J.Girdley/K.Snyder | .15 | .40 |
| ❏ 212 Chance Caple RC/J.Jennings | .15 | .40 |
| ❏ 213 B.Myers/R.Christianson RC | .40 | 1.00 |
| ❏ 214 J.Stumm/R.Purvis RC | .15 | .40 |
| ❏ 215 D.Walling/M.Paradis | .15 | .40 |
| ❏ 216 C.Ortiz/J.Gehrke | .15 | .40 |
| ❏ 217 David Cone HL | .07 | .20 |
| ❏ 218 Jose Jimenez HL | .07 | .20 |
| ❏ 219 Chris Singleton HL | .07 | .20 |
| ❏ 220 Fernando Tatis HL | .07 | .20 |
| ❏ 221 Todd Helton HL | .07 | .20 |
| ❏ 222 Kevin Millwood DIV | .07 | .20 |
| ❏ 223 Todd Pratt DIV | .07 | .20 |
| ❏ 224 Orlando Hernandez DIV | .07 | .20 |
| ❏ 225 Pedro Martinez DIV | .10 | .30 |
| ❏ 226 Tom Glavine LCS | .07 | .20 |
| ❏ 227 Bernie Williams LCS | .07 | .20 |
| ❏ 228 Mariano Rivera WS | .10 | .30 |
| ❏ 229 Tony Gwynn 20CB | .25 | .60 |
| ❏ 230 Wade Boggs 20CB | .10 | .30 |
| ❏ 231 Lance Johnson CB | .07 | .20 |
| ❏ 232 Mark McGwire 20CB | .50 | 1.25 |
| ❏ 233 Rickey Henderson 20CB | .20 | .50 |
| ❏ 234 Rickey Henderson 20CB | .20 | .50 |
| ❏ 235 Roger Clemens 20CB | .40 | 1.00 |
| ❏ 236A M.McGwire MM 1st HR | .75 | 2.00 |
| ❏ 236B M.McGwire MM 1987 ROY | .75 | 2.00 |
| ❏ 236C M.McGwire MM 62nd HR | .75 | 2.00 |
| ❏ 236D M.McGwire MM 70th HR | .75 | 2.00 |
| ❏ 236E M.McGwire MM 500th HR | .75 | 2.00 |
| ❏ 237A H.Aaron MM 1st Career HR | .75 | 2.00 |
| ❏ 237B H.Aaron MM 1957 MVP | .75 | 2.00 |
| ❏ 237C H.Aaron MM 3000th Hit | .75 | 2.00 |
| ❏ 237D H.Aaron MM 715th Hit | .75 | 2.00 |
| ❏ 237E H.Aaron MM 755th Hit | .75 | 2.00 |
| ❏ 238A C.Ripken MM 1982 ROY | 1.50 | 4.00 |
| ❏ 238B C.Ripken MM 1991 MVP | 1.50 | 4.00 |
| ❏ 238C C.Ripken MM 2131 Game | 1.50 | 4.00 |
| ❏ 238D C.Ripken MM Streak Ends | 1.50 | 4.00 |
| ❏ 238E C.Ripken MM 400th Hit | 1.50 | 4.00 |
| ❏ 239A W.Boggs MM 1983 Batting | .30 | .75 |
| ❏ 239B W.Boggs MM 1988 Batting | .30 | .75 |
| ❏ 239C W.Boggs MM 2000th Hit | .30 | .75 |
| ❏ 239D W.Boggs MM 1996 Champs | .30 | .75 |
| ❏ 239E W.Boggs MM 3000th Hit | .30 | .75 |
| ❏ 240A T.Gwynn MM 1984 Batting | .60 | 1.50 |
| ❏ 240B T.Gwynn MM 1984 NLCS | .60 | 1.50 |
| ❏ 240C T.Gwynn MM 1995 Batting | .60 | 1.50 |
| ❏ 240D T.Gwynn MM 1998 NLCS | .60 | 1.50 |
| ❏ 240E T.Gwynn MM 3000th Hit | .60 | 1.50 |
| ❏ 241 Tom Glavine | .10 | .30 |
| ❏ 242 David Wells | .07 | .20 |
| ❏ 243 Kevin Appier | .07 | .20 |
| ❏ 244 Troy Percival | .07 | .20 |
| ❏ 245 Ray Lankford | .07 | .20 |
| ❏ 246 Marquis Grissom | .07 | .20 |
| ❏ 247 Randy Winn | .07 | .20 |
| ❏ 248 Miguel Batista | .07 | .20 |
| ❏ 249 Darren Dreifort | .07 | .20 |
| ❏ 250 Barry Bonds | .60 | 1.50 |
| ❏ 251 Harold Baines | .07 | .20 |
| ❏ 252 Cliff Floyd | .07 | .20 |
| ❏ 253 Freddy Garcia | .07 | .20 |
| ❏ 254 Kenny Rogers | .07 | .20 |
| ❏ 255 Ben Davis | .07 | .20 |
| ❏ 256 Charles Johnson | .07 | .20 |
| ❏ 257 Bubba Trammell | .07 | .20 |
| ❏ 258 Desi Relaford | .07 | .20 |
| ❏ 259 Al Martin | .07 | .20 |
| ❏ 260 Andy Pettitte | .10 | .30 |
| ❏ 261 Carlos Lee | .07 | .20 |
| ❏ 262 Matt Lawton | .07 | .20 |

|  |  | | |
|---|---|---|---|
| 263 | Andy Fox | .07 | .20 |
| 264 | Chan Ho Park | .07 | .20 |
| 265 | Billy Koch | .07 | .20 |
| 266 | Dave Roberts | .07 | .20 |
| 267 | Carl Everett | .07 | .20 |
| 268 | Orel Hershiser | .07 | .20 |
| 269 | Trot Nixon | .07 | .20 |
| 270 | Rusty Greer | .07 | .20 |
| 271 | Will Clark | .10 | .30 |
| 272 | Quivio Veras | .07 | .20 |
| 273 | Rico Brogna | .07 | .20 |
| 274 | Devon White | .07 | .20 |
| 275 | Tim Hudson | .07 | .20 |
| 276 | Mike Hampton | .07 | .20 |
| 277 | Miguel Cairo | .07 | .20 |
| 278 | Darren Oliver | .07 | .20 |
| 279 | Jeff Cirillo | .07 | .20 |
| 280 | Al Leiter | .07 | .20 |
| 281 | Shane Andrews | .07 | .20 |
| 282 | Carlos Febles | .07 | .20 |
| 283 | Pedro Astacio | .07 | .20 |
| 284 | Juan Guzman | .07 | .20 |
| 285 | Orlando Hernandez | .07 | .20 |
| 286 | Paul Konerko | .07 | .20 |
| 287 | Tony Clark | .07 | .20 |
| 288 | Aaron Boone | .07 | .20 |
| 289 | Ismael Valdes | .07 | .20 |
| 290 | Moises Alou | .07 | .20 |
| 291 | Kevin Tapani | .07 | .20 |
| 292 | John Franco | .07 | .20 |
| 293 | Todd Zeile | .07 | .20 |
| 294 | Jason Schmidt | .07 | .20 |
| 295 | Johnny Damon | .10 | .30 |
| 296 | Scott Brosius | .07 | .20 |
| 297 | Travis Fryman | .07 | .20 |
| 298 | Jose Vizcaino | .07 | .20 |
| 299 | Eric Chavez | .07 | .20 |
| 300 | Mike Piazza | .30 | .75 |
| 301 | Matt Clement | .07 | .20 |
| 302 | Cristian Guzman | .07 | .20 |
| 303 | C.J. Nitkowski | .07 | .20 |
| 304 | Michael Tucker | .07 | .20 |
| 305 | Brett Tomko | .07 | .20 |
| 306 | Mike Lansing | .07 | .20 |
| 307 | Eric Owens | .07 | .20 |
| 308 | Livan Hernandez | .07 | .20 |
| 309 | Rondell White | .07 | .20 |
| 310 | Todd Stottlemyre | .07 | .20 |
| 311 | Chris Carpenter | .07 | .20 |
| 312 | Ken Hill | .07 | .20 |
| 313 | Mark Loretta | .07 | .20 |
| 314 | John Rocker | .07 | .20 |
| 315 | Richie Sexson | .07 | .20 |
| 316 | Ruben Mateo | .07 | .20 |
| 317 | Joe Randa | .07 | .20 |
| 318 | Mike Sirotka | .07 | .20 |
| 319 | Jose Rosado | .07 | .20 |
| 320 | Matt Mantei | .07 | .20 |
| 321 | Kevin Millwood | .07 | .20 |
| 322 | Gary Disarcina | .07 | .20 |
| 323 | Dustin Hermanson | .07 | .20 |
| 324 | Mike Stanton | .07 | .20 |
| 325 | Kirk Rueter | .07 | .20 |
| 326 | Damian Miller RC | .15 | .40 |
| 327 | Doug Glanville | .07 | .20 |
| 328 | Scott Rolen | .10 | .30 |
| 329 | Ray Durham | .07 | .20 |
| 330 | Butch Huskey | .07 | .20 |
| 331 | Mariano Rivera | .20 | .50 |
| 332 | Darren Lewis | .07 | .20 |
| 333 | Mike Timlin | .07 | .20 |
| 334 | Mark Grudzielanek | .07 | .20 |
| 335 | Mike Cameron | .07 | .20 |
| 336 | Kelvim Escobar | .07 | .20 |
| 337 | Bret Boone | .07 | .20 |
| 338 | Mo Vaughn | .07 | .20 |
| 339 | Craig Biggio | .10 | .30 |
| 340 | Michael Barrett | .07 | .20 |
| 341 | Marlon Anderson | .07 | .20 |
| 342 | Bobby Jones | .07 | .20 |
| 343 | John Halama | .07 | .20 |
| 344 | Todd Ritchie | .07 | .20 |
| 345 | Chuck Knoblauch | .07 | .20 |
| 346 | Rick Reed | .07 | .20 |
| 347 | Kelly Stinnett | .07 | .20 |
| 348 | Tim Salmon | .10 | .30 |
| 349 | A.J. Hinch | .07 | .20 |
| 350 | Jose Cruz Jr. | .07 | .20 |
| 351 | Roberto Hernandez | .07 | .20 |
| 352 | Edgar Renteria | .07 | .20 |
| 353 | Jose Hernandez | .07 | .20 |
| 354 | Brad Fullmer | .07 | .20 |
| 355 | Trevor Hoffman | .07 | .20 |
| 356 | Troy O'Leary | .07 | .20 |
| 357 | Justin Thompson | .07 | .20 |
| 358 | Kevin Young | .07 | .20 |
| 359 | Hideki Irabu | .07 | .20 |
| 360 | Jim Thome | .10 | .30 |
| 361 | Steve Karsay | .07 | .20 |
| 362 | Octavio Dotel | .07 | .20 |
| 363 | Omar Vizquel | .10 | .30 |
| 364 | Raul Mondesi | .07 | .20 |
| 365 | Shane Reynolds | .07 | .20 |
| 366 | Bartolo Colon | .07 | .20 |
| 367 | Chris Widger | .07 | .20 |
| 368 | Gabe Kapler | .07 | .20 |
| 369 | Bill Simas | .07 | .20 |
| 370 | Tino Martinez | .10 | .30 |
| 371 | John Thomson | .07 | .20 |
| 372 | Delino Deshields | .07 | .20 |
| 373 | Carlos Perez | .07 | .20 |
| 374 | Eddie Perez | .07 | .20 |
| 375 | Jeromy Burnitz | .07 | .20 |
| 376 | Jimmy Haynes | .07 | .20 |
| 377 | Travis Lee | .07 | .20 |
| 378 | Darryl Hamilton | .07 | .20 |
| 379 | Jamie Moyer | .07 | .20 |
| 380 | Alex Gonzalez | .07 | .20 |
| 381 | John Wetteland | .07 | .20 |
| 382 | Vinny Castilla | .07 | .20 |
| 383 | Jeff Suppan | .07 | .20 |
| 384 | Jim Leyritz | .07 | .20 |
| 385 | Robb Nen | .07 | .20 |
| 386 | Wilson Alvarez | .07 | .20 |
| 387 | Andres Galarraga | .10 | .30 |
| 388 | Mike Remlinger | .07 | .20 |
| 389 | Geoff Jenkins | .07 | .20 |
| 390 | Matt Stairs | .07 | .20 |
| 391 | Bill Mueller | .07 | .20 |
| 392 | Mike Lowell | .07 | .20 |
| 393 | Andy Ashby | .07 | .20 |
| 394 | Ruben Rivera | .07 | .20 |
| 395 | Todd Helton | .10 | .30 |
| 396 | Bernie Williams | .10 | .30 |
| 397 | Royce Clayton | .07 | .20 |
| 398 | Manny Ramirez | .10 | .30 |
| 399 | Kerry Wood | .07 | .20 |
| 400 | Ken Griffey Jr. | .30 | .75 |
| 401 | Enrique Wilson | .07 | .20 |
| 402 | Joey Hamilton | .07 | .20 |
| 403 | Shawn Estes | .07 | .20 |
| 404 | Ugueth Urbina | .07 | .20 |
| 405 | Albert Belle | .07 | .20 |
| 406 | Rick Helling | .07 | .20 |
| 407 | Steve Parris | .07 | .20 |
| 408 | Eric Milton | .07 | .20 |
| 409 | Dave Mlicki | .07 | .20 |
| 410 | Shawn Green | .10 | .30 |
| 411 | Jaret Wright | .07 | .20 |
| 412 | Tony Womack | .07 | .20 |
| 413 | Vernon Wells | .07 | .20 |
| 414 | Ron Belliard | .07 | .20 |
| 415 | Ellis Burks | .07 | .20 |
| 416 | Scott Erickson | .07 | .20 |
| 417 | Rafael Palmeiro | .10 | .30 |
| 418 | Damion Easley | .07 | .20 |
| 419 | Jamey Wright | .07 | .20 |
| 420 | Corey Koskie | .07 | .20 |
| 421 | Bobby Howry | .07 | .20 |
| 422 | Ricky Ledee | .07 | .20 |
| 423 | Dmitri Young | .07 | .20 |
| 424 | David Segui | .07 | .20 |
| 425 | Greg Maddux | .30 | .75 |
| 426 | Jose Guillen | .07 | .20 |
| 427 | Jon Lieber | .07 | .20 |
| 428 | Andy Benes | .07 | .20 |
| 429 | Randy Velarde | .07 | .20 |
| 430 | Sean Casey | .07 | .20 |
| 431 | Torii Hunter | .07 | .20 |
| 432 | Ryan Rupe | .07 | .20 |
| 433 | David Segui | .07 | .20 |
| 434 | Todd Pratt | .07 | .20 |
| 435 | Nomar Garciaparra | .30 | .75 |
| 436 | Denny Neagle | .07 | .20 |
| 437 | Ron Coomer | .07 | .20 |
| 438 | Chris Singleton | .07 | .20 |
| 439 | Tony Batista | .07 | .20 |
| 440 | Andruw Jones | .10 | .30 |
| 441 | Burroughs/Platt/Huff | .07 | .20 |
| 442 | Rafael Furcal | .15 | .40 |
| 443 | M.Lamb RC/J.Crede- | .40 | 1.00 |
| 444 | Julio Zuleta RC | .15 | .40 |
| 445 | Garry Maddox Jr. RC | .15 | .40 |
| 446 | Riley/Sabathia/Mulder | .15 | .40 |
| 447 | Scott Downs RC | .15 | .40 |
| 448 | D.Mirabelli/B.Patrick/J.Werth | .15 | .40 |
| 449 | C.Myers RC/J.Hamilton | .20 | .50 |
| 450 | B.Christensen/R.Stahl RC | .15 | .40 |
| 451 | B.Zito/B.Sheets RC | 1.00 | 2.50 |
| 452 | K.Ainsworth/Howington RC | .15 | .40 |
| 453 | R.Asadoorian/V.Faison RC | .15 | .40 |
| 454 | K.Reed/J.Heaverlo RC | .15 | .40 |
| 455 | M.MacDougal/B.Baker RC | .15 | .40 |
| 456 | Mark McGwire SH | .25 | .60 |
| 457 | Cal Ripken SH | .30 | .75 |
| 458 | Wade Boggs SH | .07 | .20 |
| 459 | Tony Gwynn SH | .10 | .30 |
| 460 | Jesse Orosco SH | .07 | .20 |
| 461 | L.Walker/N.Garciaparra LL | .10 | .30 |
| 462 | K.Griffey Jr./M.McGwire LL | .20 | .50 |
| 463 | M.Ramirez/M.McGwire LL | .20 | .50 |
| 464 | P.Martinez/R.Johnson LL | .10 | .30 |
| 465 | P.Martinez/R.Johnson LL | .10 | .30 |
| 466 | D.Jeter/L.Gonzalez LL | .20 | .50 |
| 467 | L.Walker/M.Ramirez LL | .10 | .30 |
| 468 | Tony Gwynn 20CB | .25 | .60 |
| 469 | Mark McGwire 20CB | .50 | 1.25 |
| 470 | Frank Thomas 20CB | .10 | .30 |
| 471 | Harold Baines 20CB | .07 | .20 |
| 472 | Roger Clemens 20CB | .40 | 1.00 |
| 473 | John Franco 20CB | .07 | .20 |
| 474 | John Franco 20CB | .07 | .20 |
| 475A | K.Griffey Jr. MM 350th HR | .75 | 2.00 |
| 475B | K.Griffey Jr. MM 1997 MVP | .75 | 2.00 |
| 475C | K.Griffey Jr. MM HR Dad | .75 | 2.00 |
| 475D | K.Griffey Jr. MM 1992 AS MVP | .75 | 2.00 |
| 475E | K.Griffey Jr. MM 50 HR 1997 | .75 | 2.00 |
| 476A | B.Bonds MM 400HR/400SB | 1.25 | 3.00 |
| 476B | B.Bonds MM 40HR/40SB | 1.25 | 3.00 |
| 476C | B.Bonds MM 1993 MVP | 1.25 | 3.00 |
| 476D | B.Bonds MM 1990 MVP | 1.25 | 3.00 |
| 476E | B.Bonds MM 1992 MVP | 1.25 | 3.00 |
| 477A | S.Sosa MM 20 HR June | .75 | 2.00 |
| 477B | S.Sosa MM 66 HR 1998 | .75 | 2.00 |
| 477C | S.Sosa MM 60 HR 1999 | .75 | 2.00 |
| 477D | S.Sosa MM 1998 MVP | .75 | 2.00 |
| 477E | S.Sosa MM HR's 61/62 | .75 | 2.00 |
| 478A | D.Jeter MM 1996 ROY | 1.25 | 3.00 |
| 478B | D.Jeter MM Wins 1999 WS | 1.25 | 3.00 |
| 478C | D.Jeter MM Wins 1998 WS | 1.25 | 3.00 |
| 478D | D.Jeter MM Wins 1996 WS | 1.25 | 3.00 |
| 478E | D.Jeter MM 17 GM Hit Streak | 1.25 | 3.00 |
| 479A | A.Rodriguez MM 40HR/40SB | .75 | 2.00 |
| 479B | A.Rodriguez MM 100th Hit | .75 | 2.00 |
| 479C | A.Rodriguez MM 1996 POY | .75 | 2.00 |
| 479D | A.Rodriguez MM Wins 1 Million | .75 | 2.00 |
| 479E | A.Rodriguez MM 1996 Batting Leader | .75 | 2.00 |
| NNO | McGwire 85 Reprint | 2.00 | 5.00 |

## 2001 Topps

| | | |
|---|---|---|
| COMPLETE SET (790) | 40.00 | 80.00 |
| COMP.FACT.BLUE SET (795) | 60.00 | 120.00 |
| COMPLETE SERIES 1 (405) | 20.00 | 40.00 |
| COMPLETE SERIES 2 (385) | 20.00 | 40.00 |
| COMMON CARD (1-6/6-791) | .07 | .20 |
| COMMON (352-376/727-751) | .08 | .25 |
| 1 Cal Ripken | .60 | 1.50 |
| 2 Chipper Jones | .20 | .50 |
| 3 Roger Cedeno | .07 | .20 |
| 4 Garret Anderson | .07 | .20 |

|  |  | | |
|---|--------|---|---|
| 5 | Robin Ventura | .07 | .20 |
| 6 | Daryle Ward | .07 | .20 |
| 7 | Does Not Exist | | |
| 8 | Craig Paquette | .07 | .20 |
| 9 | Phil Nevin | .07 | .20 |
| 10 | Jermaine Dye | .07 | .20 |
| 11 | Chris Singleton | .07 | .20 |
| 12 | Mike Stanton | .07 | .20 |
| 13 | Brian Hunter | .07 | .20 |
| 14 | Mike Redmond | .07 | .20 |
| 15 | Jim Thome | .10 | .30 |
| 16 | Brian Jordan | .07 | .20 |
| 17 | Joe Girardi | .07 | .20 |
| 18 | Steve Woodard | .07 | .20 |
| 19 | Dustin Hermanson | .07 | .20 |
| 20 | Shawn Green | .07 | .20 |
| 21 | Todd Stottlemyre | .07 | .20 |
| 22 | Dan Wilson | .07 | .20 |
| 23 | Todd Pratt | .07 | .20 |
| 24 | Derek Lowe | .07 | .20 |
| 25 | Juan Gonzalez | .07 | .20 |
| 26 | Clay Bellinger | .07 | .20 |
| 27 | Jeff Fassero | .07 | .20 |
| 28 | Pat Meares | .07 | .20 |
| 29 | Eddie Taubensee | .07 | .20 |
| 30 | Paul O'Neill | .10 | .30 |
| 31 | Jeffrey Hammonds | .07 | .20 |
| 32 | Pokey Reese | .07 | .20 |
| 33 | Mike Mussina | .10 | .30 |
| 34 | Rico Brogna | .07 | .20 |
| 35 | Jay Buhner | .07 | .20 |
| 36 | Steve Cox | .07 | .20 |
| 37 | Quilvio Veras | .07 | .20 |
| 38 | Marquis Grissom | .07 | .20 |
| 39 | Shigetoshi Hasegawa | .07 | .20 |
| 40 | Shane Reynolds | .07 | .20 |
| 41 | Adam Piatt | .07 | .20 |
| 42 | Luis Polonia | .07 | .20 |
| 43 | Brook Fordyce | .07 | .20 |
| 44 | Preston Wilson | .07 | .20 |
| 45 | Ellis Burks | .07 | .20 |
| 46 | Armando Rios | .07 | .20 |
| 47 | Chuck Finley | .07 | .20 |
| 48 | Dan Plesac | .07 | .20 |
| 49 | Shannon Stewart | .07 | .20 |
| 50 | Mark McGwire | .50 | 1.25 |
| 51 | Mark Loretta | .07 | .20 |
| 52 | Gerald Williams | .07 | .20 |
| 53 | Eric Young | .07 | .20 |
| 54 | Peter Bergeron | .07 | .20 |
| 55 | Dave Hansen | .07 | .20 |
| 56 | Arthur Rhodes | .07 | .20 |
| 57 | Bobby Jones | .07 | .20 |
| 58 | Matt Clement | .07 | .20 |
| 59 | Mike Benjamin | .07 | .20 |
| 60 | Pedro Martinez | .10 | .30 |
| 61 | Jose Canseco | .10 | .30 |
| 62 | Matt Anderson | .07 | .20 |
| 63 | Torii Hunter | .07 | .20 |
| 64 | Carlos Lee | .07 | .20 |
| 65 | David Cone | .07 | .20 |
| 66 | Rey Sanchez | .07 | .20 |
| 67 | Eric Chavez | .07 | .20 |
| 68 | Rick Helling | .07 | .20 |
| 69 | Manny Alexander | .07 | .20 |
| 70 | John Franco | .07 | .20 |
| 71 | Mike Bordick | .07 | .20 |
| 72 | Andres Galarraga | .07 | .20 |
| 73 | Jose Cruz Jr. | .07 | .20 |
| 74 | Mike Matheny | .07 | .20 |
| 75 | Randy Johnson | .20 | .50 |
| 76 | Richie Sexson | .07 | .20 |
| 77 | Vladimir Nunez | .07 | .20 |
| 78 | Harold Baines | .07 | .20 |
| 79 | Aaron Boone | .07 | .20 |
| 80 | Darin Erstad | .07 | .20 |
| 81 | Alex Gonzalez | .07 | .20 |
| 82 | Gil Heredia | .07 | .20 |
| 83 | Shane Andrews | .07 | .20 |
| 84 | Todd Hundley | .07 | .20 |
| 85 | Bill Mueller | .07 | .20 |
| 86 | Mark McLemore | .07 | .20 |
| 87 | Scott Spiezio | .07 | .20 |
| 88 | Kevin McGlinchy | .07 | .20 |
| 89 | Bubba Trammell | .07 | .20 |
| 90 | Manny Ramirez | .10 | .30 |
| 91 | Mike Lamb | .07 | .20 |
| 92 | Scott Karl | .07 | .20 |
| 93 | Brian Buchanan | .07 | .20 |
| 94 | Chris Turner | .07 | .20 |
| 95 | Mike Sweeney | .07 | .20 |
| 96 | John Wetteland | .07 | .20 |
| 97 | Rob Bell | .07 | .20 |
| 98 | Pat Rapp | .07 | .20 |
| 99 | John Burkett | .07 | .20 |
| 100 | Derek Jeter | .50 | 1.25 |
| 101 | J.D. Drew | .07 | .20 |
| 102 | Jose Offerman | .07 | .20 |
| 103 | Rick Reed | .07 | .20 |
| 104 | Will Clark | .10 | .30 |
| 105 | Rickey Henderson | .20 | .50 |
| 106 | Dave Berg | .07 | .20 |
| 107 | Kirk Rueter | .07 | .20 |
| 108 | Lee Stevens | .07 | .20 |
| 109 | Jay Bell | .07 | .20 |
| 110 | Fred McGriff | .10 | .30 |
| 111 | Julio Zuleta | .07 | .20 |
| 112 | Brian Anderson | .07 | .20 |
| 113 | Orlando Cabrera | .07 | .20 |
| 114 | Alex Fernandez | .07 | .20 |
| 115 | Derek Bell | .07 | .20 |
| 116 | Eric Owens | .07 | .20 |
| 117 | Brian Bohanon | .07 | .20 |
| 118 | Dennys Reyes | .07 | .20 |
| 119 | Mike Stanley | .07 | .20 |
| 120 | Jorge Posada | .10 | .30 |
| 121 | Rich Becker | .07 | .20 |
| 122 | Paul Konerko | .07 | .20 |
| 123 | Mike Remlinger | .07 | .20 |
| 124 | Travis Lee | .07 | .20 |
| 125 | Ken Caminiti | .07 | .20 |
| 126 | Kevin Barker | .07 | .20 |
| 127 | Paul Quantrill | .07 | .20 |
| 128 | Ozzie Guillen | .07 | .20 |
| 129 | Kevin Tapani | .07 | .20 |
| 130 | Mark Johnson | .07 | .20 |
| 131 | Randy Wolf | .07 | .20 |
| 132 | Michael Tucker | .07 | .20 |
| 133 | Darren Lewis | .07 | .20 |
| 134 | Joe Randa | .07 | .20 |
| 135 | Jeff Cirillo | .07 | .20 |
| 136 | David Ortiz | .20 | .50 |
| 137 | Herb Perry | .07 | .20 |
| 138 | Jeff Nelson | .07 | .20 |
| 139 | Chris Stynes | .07 | .20 |
| 140 | Johnny Damon | .10 | .30 |
| 141 | Jeff Reboulet | .07 | .20 |
| 142 | Jason Schmidt | .07 | .20 |
| 143 | Charles Johnson | .07 | .20 |
| 144 | Pat Burrell | .07 | .20 |
| 145 | Gary Sheffield | .07 | .20 |
| 146 | Tom Glavine | .10 | .30 |
| 147 | Jason Isringhausen | .07 | .20 |
| 148 | Chris Carpenter | .07 | .20 |
| 149 | Jeff Suppan | .07 | .20 |
| 150 | Ivan Rodriguez | .10 | .30 |
| 151 | Luis Sojo | .07 | .20 |
| 152 | Ron Villone | .07 | .20 |
| 153 | Mike Sirotka | .07 | .20 |
| 154 | Chuck Knoblauch | .07 | .20 |
| 155 | Jason Kendall | .07 | .20 |
| 156 | Dennis Cook | .07 | .20 |
| 157 | Bobby Estalella | .07 | .20 |
| 158 | Jose Guillen | .07 | .20 |
| 159 | Thomas Howard | .07 | .20 |
| 160 | Carlos Delgado | .07 | .20 |
| 161 | Benji Gil | .07 | .20 |
| 162 | Tim Bogar | .07 | .20 |
| 163 | Kevin Elster | .07 | .20 |
| 164 | Einar Diaz | .07 | .20 |
| 165 | Andy Benes | .07 | .20 |
| 166 | Adrian Beltre | .07 | .20 |
| 167 | David Bell | .07 | .20 |
| 168 | Turk Wendell | .07 | .20 |
| 169 | Pete Harnisch | .07 | .20 |
| 170 | Roger Clemens | .40 | 1.00 |
| 171 | Scott Williamson | .07 | .20 |
| 172 | Kevin Jordan | .07 | .20 |
| 173 | Brad Penny | .07 | .20 |
| 174 | John Flaherty | .07 | .20 |
| 175 | Troy Glaus | .07 | .20 |
| 176 | Kevin Appier | .07 | .20 |
| 177 | Walt Weiss | .07 | .20 |
| 178 | Tyler Houston | .07 | .20 |
| 179 | Michael Barrett | .07 | .20 |
| 180 | Mike Hampton | .07 | .20 |
| 181 | Francisco Cordova | .07 | .20 |
| 182 | Mike Jackson | .07 | .20 |
| 183 | David Segui | .07 | .20 |
| 184 | Carlos Febles | .07 | .20 |
| 185 | Roy Halladay | .07 | .20 |
| 186 | Seth Etherton | .07 | .20 |
| 187 | Charlie Hayes | .07 | .20 |
| 188 | Fernando Tatis | .07 | .20 |
| 189 | Steve Trachsel | .07 | .20 |
| 190 | Livan Hernandez | .07 | .20 |
| 191 | Joe Oliver | .07 | .20 |
| 192 | Stan Javier | .07 | .20 |
| 193 | B.J. Surhoff | .07 | .20 |
| 194 | Rob Ducey | .07 | .20 |
| 195 | Barry Larkin | .10 | .30 |
| 196 | Danny Patterson | .07 | .20 |
| 197 | Bobby Howry | .07 | .20 |
| 198 | Dmitri Young | .07 | .20 |
| 199 | Brian Hunter | .07 | .20 |
| 200 | Alex Rodriguez | .30 | .75 |
| 201 | Hideo Nomo | .20 | .50 |
| 202 | Luis Alicea | .07 | .20 |
| 203 | Warren Morris | .07 | .20 |
| 204 | Antonio Alfonseca | .07 | .20 |
| 205 | Edgardo Alfonzo | .07 | .20 |
| 206 | Mark Grudzielanek | .07 | .20 |
| 207 | Fernando Vina | .07 | .20 |
| 208 | Willie Greene | .07 | .20 |
| 209 | Homer Bush | .07 | .20 |
| 210 | Jason Giambi | .07 | .20 |
| 211 | Mike Morgan | .07 | .20 |
| 212 | Steve Karsay | .07 | .20 |
| 213 | Matt Lawton | .07 | .20 |
| 214 | Wendell Magee Jr. | .07 | .20 |
| 215 | Rusty Greer | .07 | .20 |
| 216 | Keith Lockhart | .07 | .20 |
| 217 | Billy Koch | .07 | .20 |
| 218 | Todd Hollandsworth | .07 | .20 |
| 219 | Raul Ibanez | .07 | .20 |
| 220 | Tony Gwynn | .25 | .60 |
| 221 | Carl Everett | .07 | .20 |
| 222 | Hector Carrasco | .07 | .20 |
| 223 | Jose Valentin | .07 | .20 |
| 224 | Deivi Cruz | .07 | .20 |
| 225 | Bret Boone | .07 | .20 |
| 226 | Kurt Abbott | .07 | .20 |
| 227 | Melvin Mora | .07 | .20 |
| 228 | Danny Graves | .07 | .20 |
| 229 | Jose Jimenez | .07 | .20 |
| 230 | James Baldwin | .07 | .20 |
| 231 | C.J. Nitkowski | .07 | .20 |
| 232 | Jeff Zimmerman | .07 | .20 |
| 233 | Mike Lowell | .07 | .20 |
| 234 | Hideki Irabu | .07 | .20 |
| 235 | Greg Vaughn | .07 | .20 |
| 236 | Omar Daal | .07 | .20 |
| 237 | Darren Dreifort | .07 | .20 |
| 238 | Gil Meche | .07 | .20 |
| 239 | Damian Jackson | .07 | .20 |
| 240 | Frank Thomas | .20 | .50 |
| 241 | Travis Miller | .07 | .20 |
| 242 | Jeff Frye | .07 | .20 |
| 243 | Dave Magadan | .07 | .20 |
| 244 | Luis Castillo | .07 | .20 |
| 245 | Bartolo Colon | .07 | .20 |
| 246 | Steve Kline | .07 | .20 |
| 247 | Shawon Dunston | .07 | .20 |
| 248 | Rick Aguilera | .07 | .20 |
| 249 | Omar Olivares | .07 | .20 |
| 250 | Craig Biggio | .10 | .30 |
| 251 | Scott Schoeneweis | .07 | .20 |
| 252 | Dave Veres | .07 | .20 |
| 253 | Ramon Martinez | .07 | .20 |
| 254 | Jose Vidro | .07 | .20 |
| 255 | Todd Helton | .10 | .30 |
| 256 | Greg Norton | .07 | .20 |
| 257 | Jacque Jones | .07 | .20 |
| 258 | Jason Grimsley | .07 | .20 |
| 259 | Dan Reichert | .07 | .20 |
| 260 | Robb Nen | .07 | .20 |
| 261 | Mark Clark | .07 | .20 |
| 262 | Scott Hatteberg | .07 | .20 |
| 263 | Doug Brocail | .07 | .20 |
| 264 | Mark Johnson | .07 | .20 |
| 265 | Eric Davis | .07 | .20 |
| 266 | Terry Shumpert | .07 | .20 |
| 267 | Kevin Millar | .07 | .20 |
| 268 | Ismael Valdes | .07 | .20 |

| # | Card | Price | Price |
|---|------|-------|-------|
| 269 | Richard Hidalgo | .07 | .20 |
| 270 | Randy Velarde | .07 | .20 |
| 271 | Bengie Molina | .07 | .20 |
| 272 | Tony Womack | .07 | .20 |
| 273 | Enrique Wilson | .07 | .20 |
| 274 | Jeff Brantley | .07 | .20 |
| 275 | Rick Ankiel | .07 | .20 |
| 276 | Terry Mulholland | .07 | .20 |
| 277 | Ron Belliard | .07 | .20 |
| 278 | Terrence Long | .07 | .20 |
| 279 | Alberto Castillo | .07 | .20 |
| 280 | Royce Clayton | .07 | .20 |
| 281 | Joe McEwing | .07 | .20 |
| 282 | Jason McDonald | .07 | .20 |
| 283 | Ricky Bottalico | .07 | .20 |
| 284 | Keith Foulke | .07 | .20 |
| 285 | Brad Radke | .07 | .20 |
| 286 | Gabe Kapler | .07 | .20 |
| 287 | Pedro Astacio | .07 | .20 |
| 288 | Armando Reynoso | .07 | .20 |
| 289 | Darryl Kile | .07 | .20 |
| 290 | Reggie Sanders | .07 | .20 |
| 291 | Esteban Yan | .07 | .20 |
| 292 | Joe Nathan | .07 | .20 |
| 293 | Jay Payton | .07 | .20 |
| 294 | Francisco Cordero | .07 | .20 |
| 295 | Gregg Jefferies | .07 | .20 |
| 296 | LaTroy Hawkins | .07 | .20 |
| 297 | Jeff Tam RC | .15 | .40 |
| 298 | Jacob Cruz | .07 | .20 |
| 299 | Chris Holt | .07 | .20 |
| 300 | Vladimir Guerrero | .20 | .50 |
| 301 | Marvin Benard | .07 | .20 |
| 302 | Alex Ramirez | .07 | .20 |
| 303 | Mike Williams | .07 | .20 |
| 304 | Sean Bergman | .07 | .20 |
| 305 | Juan Encarnacion | .07 | .20 |
| 306 | Russ Davis | .07 | .20 |
| 307 | Hanley Frias | .07 | .20 |
| 308 | Ramon Hernandez | .07 | .20 |
| 309 | Matt Walbeck | .07 | .20 |
| 310 | Bill Spiers | .07 | .20 |
| 311 | Bob Wickman | .07 | .20 |
| 312 | Sandy Alomar Jr. | .07 | .20 |
| 313 | Eddie Guardado | .07 | .20 |
| 314 | Shane Halter | .07 | .20 |
| 315 | Geoff Jenkins | .07 | .20 |
| 316 | Brian Meadows | .07 | .20 |
| 317 | Damian Miller | .07 | .20 |
| 318 | Darrin Fletcher | .07 | .20 |
| 319 | Rafael Furcal | .07 | .20 |
| 320 | Mark Grace | .10 | .30 |
| 321 | Mark Mulder | .07 | .20 |
| 322 | Joe Torre MG | .10 | .30 |
| 323 | Bobby Cox MG | .07 | .20 |
| 324 | Mike Scioscia MG | .07 | .20 |
| 325 | Mike Hargrove MG | .07 | .20 |
| 326 | Jimy Williams MG | .07 | .20 |
| 327 | Jerry Manuel MG | .07 | .20 |
| 328 | Buck Showalter MG | .07 | .20 |
| 329 | Charlie Manuel MG | .07 | .20 |
| 330 | Don Baylor MG | .07 | .20 |
| 331 | Phil Garner MG | .07 | .20 |
| 332 | Jack McKeon MG | .07 | .20 |
| 333 | Tony Muser MG | .07 | .20 |
| 334 | Buddy Bell MG | .07 | .20 |
| 335 | Tom Kelly MG | .07 | .20 |
| 336 | John Boles MG | .07 | .20 |
| 337 | Art Howe MG | .07 | .20 |
| 338 | Larry Dierker MG | .07 | .20 |
| 339 | Lou Piniella MG | .07 | .20 |
| 340 | Davey Johnson MG | .07 | .20 |
| 341 | Larry Rothschild MG | .07 | .20 |
| 342 | Davey Lopes MG | .07 | .20 |
| 343 | Johnny Oates MG | .07 | .20 |
| 344 | Felipe Alou MG | .07 | .20 |
| 345 | Jim Fregosi MG | .07 | .20 |
| 346 | Bobby Valentine MG | .07 | .20 |
| 347 | Terry Francona MG | .07 | .20 |
| 348 | Gene Lamont MG | .07 | .20 |
| 349 | Tony LaRussa MG | .07 | .20 |
| 350 | Bruce Bochy MG | .07 | .20 |
| 351 | Dusty Baker MG | .07 | .20 |
| 352 | A.Gonzalez/C.Johnson | .08 | .25 |
| 353 | M.Wheatland/B.Digby | .07 | .20 |
| 354 | T.Johnson/S.Thorman | .08 | .25 |
| 355 | P.Dumatrait/A.Wainwright | .20 | .50 |
| 356 | David Parrish RC | .08 | .25 |
| 357 | M.Folsom RC/R.Baldelli | .15 | .40 |
| 358 | Dominic Rich RC | .08 | .25 |
| 359 | M.Stodolka/S.Burnett | .08 | .25 |
| 360 | D.Thompson/C.Smith | .08 | .25 |
| 361 | D.Borrell RC/J.Bourgeois RC | .08 | .25 |
| 362 | Chen/Patterson/Hamilton | .20 | .50 |
| 363 | B.Zito/C.Sabathia | .20 | .50 |
| 364 | Ben Sheets | .20 | .50 |
| 365 | Howington/Kalinowski/Girdley | .20 | .50 |
| 366 | Hee Seop Choi RC | .20 | .50 |
| 367 | Bradley/Ainsworth/Tsao | .15 | .40 |
| 368 | Glendenning/Kelly/Silvestre | .08 | .25 |
| 369 | J.R. House | .08 | .25 |
| 370 | Rafael Soriano RC | .15 | .40 |
| 371 | T.Hafner RC/B.Jacobsen | 1.50 | 4.00 |
| 372 | Conti/Wakeland/Cole | .08 | .25 |
| 373 | Seabol/Huff/Crede | .30 | .75 |
| 374 | Everett/Ortiz/Ginter | .08 | .25 |
| 375 | Hernandez/Guzman/Eaton | .08 | .25 |
| 376 | Kielty/Bradley/J.Rivera | .15 | .40 |
| 377 | Mark McGwire GM | .25 | .60 |
| 378 | Don Larsen GM | .07 | .20 |
| 379 | Bobby Thomson GM | .07 | .20 |
| 380 | Bill Mazeroski GM | .07 | .20 |
| 381 | Reggie Jackson GM | .10 | .30 |
| 382 | Kirk Gibson GM | .07 | .20 |
| 383 | Roger Maris GM | .10 | .30 |
| 384 | Cal Ripken GM | .30 | .75 |
| 385 | Hank Aaron GM | .20 | .50 |
| 386 | Joe Carter GM | .07 | .20 |
| 387 | Cal Ripken SH | .60 | 1.50 |
| 388 | Randy Johnson SH | .10 | .30 |
| 389 | Ken Griffey Jr. SH | .30 | .75 |
| 390 | Troy Glaus SH | .07 | .20 |
| 391 | Kazuhiro Sasaki SH | .07 | .20 |
| 392 | S.Sosa/T.Glaus LL | .10 | .30 |
| 393 | T.Helton/E.Martinez LL | .07 | .20 |
| 394 | T.Helton/N.Garciaparra LL | .20 | .50 |
| 395 | B.Bonds/J.Giambi LL | .30 | .75 |
| 396 | T.Helton/M.Ramirez LL | .20 | .50 |
| 397 | T.Helton/D.Erstad LL | .07 | .20 |
| 398 | K.Brown/P.Martinez LL | .10 | .30 |
| 399 | R.Johnson/P.Martinez LL | .10 | .30 |
| 400 | Will Clark HL | .10 | .30 |
| 401 | New York Mets HL | .20 | .50 |
| 402 | New York Yankees HL | .30 | .75 |
| 403 | Seattle Mariners HL | .07 | .20 |
| 404 | Mike Hampton HL | .07 | .20 |
| 405 | New York Yankees HL | .40 | 1.00 |
| 406 | New York Yankees Champs | .75 | 2.00 |
| 407 | Jeff Bagwell | .10 | .30 |
| 408 | Brant Brown | .07 | .20 |
| 409 | Brad Fullmer | .07 | .20 |
| 410 | Dean Palmer | .07 | .20 |
| 411 | Greg Zaun | .07 | .20 |
| 412 | Jose Vizcaino | .07 | .20 |
| 413 | Jeff Abbott | .07 | .20 |
| 414 | Travis Fryman | .07 | .20 |
| 415 | Mike Cameron | .07 | .20 |
| 416 | Matt Mantei | .07 | .20 |
| 417 | Alan Benes | .07 | .20 |
| 418 | Mickey Morandini | .07 | .20 |
| 419 | Troy Percival | .07 | .20 |
| 420 | Eddie Perez | .07 | .20 |
| 421 | Vernon Wells | .07 | .20 |
| 422 | Ricky Gutierrez | .07 | .20 |
| 423 | Carlos Hernandez | .07 | .20 |
| 424 | Chan Ho Park | .07 | .20 |
| 425 | Armando Benitez | .07 | .20 |
| 426 | Sidney Ponson | .07 | .20 |
| 427 | Adrian Brown | .07 | .20 |
| 428 | Ruben Mateo | .07 | .20 |
| 429 | Alex Ochoa | .07 | .20 |
| 430 | Jose Rosado | .07 | .20 |
| 431 | Masato Yoshii | .07 | .20 |
| 432 | Corey Koskie | .07 | .20 |
| 433 | Andy Pettitte | .10 | .30 |
| 434 | Brian Daubach | .07 | .20 |
| 435 | Sterling Hitchcock | .07 | .20 |
| 436 | Timo Perez | .07 | .20 |
| 437 | Shawn Estes | .07 | .20 |
| 438 | Tony Armas Jr. | .07 | .20 |
| 439 | Danny Bautista | .07 | .20 |
| 440 | Randy Winn | .07 | .20 |
| 441 | Wilson Alvarez | .07 | .20 |
| 442 | Rondell White | .07 | .20 |
| 443 | Jeromy Burnitz | .07 | .20 |
| 444 | Kelvim Escobar | .07 | .20 |
| 445 | Paul Bako | .07 | .20 |
| 446 | Javier Vazquez | .07 | .20 |
| 447 | Eric Gagne | .07 | .20 |
| 448 | Kenny Lofton | .07 | .20 |
| 449 | Mark Kotsay | .07 | .20 |
| 450 | Jamie Moyer | .07 | .20 |
| 451 | Delino DeShields | .07 | .20 |
| 452 | Rey Ordonez | .07 | .20 |
| 453 | Russ Ortiz | .07 | .20 |
| 454 | Dave Burba | .07 | .20 |
| 455 | Eric Karros | .07 | .20 |
| 456 | Felix Martinez | .07 | .20 |
| 457 | Tony Batista | .07 | .20 |
| 458 | Bobby Higginson | .07 | .20 |
| 459 | Jeff D'Amico | .07 | .20 |
| 460 | Shane Spencer | .07 | .20 |
| 461 | Brent Mayne | .07 | .20 |
| 462 | Glendon Rusch | .07 | .20 |
| 463 | Chris Gomez | .07 | .20 |
| 464 | Jeff Shaw | .07 | .20 |
| 465 | Damon Buford | .07 | .20 |
| 466 | Mike DiFelice | .07 | .20 |
| 467 | Jimmy Haynes | .07 | .20 |
| 468 | Billy Wagner | .07 | .20 |
| 469 | A.J. Hinch | .07 | .20 |
| 470 | Gary DiSarcina | .07 | .20 |
| 471 | Tom Lampkin | .07 | .20 |
| 472 | Adam Eaton | .07 | .20 |
| 473 | Brian Giles | .07 | .20 |
| 474 | John Thomson | .07 | .20 |
| 475 | Cal Eldred | .07 | .20 |
| 476 | Ramiro Mendoza | .07 | .20 |
| 477 | Scott Sullivan | .07 | .20 |
| 478 | Scott Rolen | .10 | .30 |
| 479 | Todd Ritchie | .07 | .20 |
| 480 | Pablo Ozuna | .07 | .20 |
| 481 | Carl Pavano | .07 | .20 |
| 482 | Matt Morris | .07 | .20 |
| 483 | Matt Stairs | .07 | .20 |
| 484 | Tim Belcher | .07 | .20 |
| 485 | Lance Berkman | .07 | .20 |
| 486 | Brian Meadows | .07 | .20 |
| 487 | Bob Abreu | .07 | .20 |
| 488 | John VanderWal | .07 | .20 |
| 489 | Donnie Sadler | .07 | .20 |
| 490 | Damion Easley | .07 | .20 |
| 491 | David Justice | .07 | .20 |
| 492 | Ray Durham | .07 | .20 |
| 493 | Todd Zeile | .07 | .20 |
| 494 | Desi Relaford | .07 | .20 |
| 495 | Cliff Floyd | .07 | .20 |
| 496 | Scott Downs | .07 | .20 |
| 497 | Barry Bonds | .50 | 1.25 |
| 498 | Jeff D'Amico | .07 | .20 |
| 499 | Octavio Dotel | .07 | .20 |
| 500 | Kent Mercker | .07 | .20 |
| 501 | Craig Grebeck | .07 | .20 |
| 502 | Roberto Hernandez | .07 | .20 |
| 503 | Matt Williams | .07 | .20 |
| 504 | Bruce Aven | .07 | .20 |
| 505 | Brett Tomko | .07 | .20 |
| 506 | Kris Benson | .07 | .20 |
| 507 | Neifi Perez | .07 | .20 |
| 508 | Alfonso Soriano | .10 | .30 |
| 509 | Keith Osik | .07 | .20 |
| 510 | Matt Franco | .07 | .20 |
| 511 | Steve Finley | .07 | .20 |
| 512 | Olmedo Saenz | .07 | .20 |
| 513 | Esteban Loaiza | .07 | .20 |
| 514 | Adam Kennedy | .07 | .20 |
| 515 | Scott Elarton | .07 | .20 |
| 516 | Moises Alou | .07 | .20 |
| 517 | Bryan Rekar | .07 | .20 |
| 518 | Darryl Hamilton | .07 | .20 |
| 519 | Osvaldo Fernandez | .07 | .20 |
| 520 | Kip Wells | .07 | .20 |
| 521 | Bernie Williams | .10 | .30 |
| 522 | Mike Darr | .07 | .20 |
| 523 | Marlon Anderson | .07 | .20 |
| 524 | Derrek Lee | .10 | .30 |
| 525 | Ugueth Urbina | .07 | .20 |
| 526 | Vinny Castilla | .07 | .20 |
| 527 | David Wells | .07 | .20 |
| 528 | Jason Marquis | .07 | .20 |
| 529 | Orlando Palmeiro | .07 | .20 |
| 530 | Carlos Perez | .07 | .20 |
| 531 | J.T. Snow | .07 | .20 |
| 532 | Al Leiter | .07 | .20 |

|  |  | | |
|---|--------|------|------|
| 533 | Jimmy Anderson | .07 | .20 |
| 534 | Brett Laxton | .07 | .20 |
| 535 | Burch Huskey | .07 | .20 |
| 536 | Orlando Hernandez | .07 | .20 |
| 537 | Magglio Ordonez | .07 | .20 |
| 538 | Willie Blair | .07 | .20 |
| 539 | Kevin Selcik | .07 | .20 |
| 540 | Chad Curtis | .07 | .20 |
| 541 | John Halama | .07 | .20 |
| 542 | Andy Fox | .07 | .20 |
| 543 | Juan Guzman | .07 | .20 |
| 544 | Frank Menechino RC | .07 | .20 |
| 545 | Raul Mondesi | .07 | .20 |
| 546 | Tim Salmon | .10 | .30 |
| 547 | Ryan Rupe | .07 | .20 |
| 548 | Jeff Reed | .07 | .20 |
| 549 | Mike Mordecai | .07 | .20 |
| 550 | Jeff Kent | .20 | .50 * |
| 551 | Wiki Gonzalez | .07 | .20 |
| 552 | Kenny Rogers | .07 | .20 |
| 553 | Kevin Young | .07 | .20 |
| 554 | Brian Johnson | .07 | .20 |
| 555 | Tom Goodwin | .07 | .20 |
| 556 | Tony Clark | .07 | .20 |
| 557 | Mac Suzuki | .07 | .20 |
| 558 | Brian Moehler | .07 | .20 |
| 559 | Jim Parque | .07 | .20 |
| 560 | Mariano Rivera | .20 | .50 |
| 561 | Trot Nixon | .07 | .20 |
| 562 | Mike Mussina | .10 | .30 |
| 563 | Nelson Figueroa | .07 | .20 |
| 564 | Alex Gonzalez | .07 | .20 |
| 565 | Benny Agbayani | .07 | .20 |
| 566 | Ed Sprague | .07 | .20 |
| 567 | Scott Erickson | .07 | .20 |
| 568 | Abraham Nunez | .07 | .20 |
| 569 | Jerry DiPoto | .07 | .20 |
| 570 | Sean Casey | .07 | .20 |
| 571 | Wilton Veras | .07 | .20 |
| 572 | Joe Mays | .07 | .20 |
| 573 | Bill Simas | .07 | .20 |
| 574 | Doug Glanville | .07 | .20 |
| 575 | Scott Sauerbeck | .07 | .20 |
| 576 | Ben Davis | .07 | .20 |
| 577 | Jesus Sanchez | .07 | .20 |
| 578 | Ricardo Rincon | .07 | .20 |
| 579 | John Olerud | .07 | .20 |
| 580 | Curt Schilling | .07 | .20 |
| 581 | Alex Cora | .07 | .20 |
| 582 | Pat Hentgen | .07 | .20 |
| 583 | Javy Lopez | .07 | .20 |
| 584 | Ben Grieve | .07 | .20 |
| 585 | Frank Castillo | .07 | .20 |
| 586 | Kevin Stocker | .07 | .20 |
| 587 | Mark Sweeney | .07 | .20 |
| 588 | Ray Lankford | .07 | .20 |
| 589 | Turner Ward | .07 | .20 |
| 590 | Felipe Crespo | .07 | .20 |
| 591 | Omar Vizquel | .10 | .30 |
| 592 | Mike Lieberthal | .07 | .20 |
| 593 | Ken Griffey Jr. | .30 | .75 |
| 594 | Troy O'Leary | .07 | .20 |
| 595 | Dave Mlicki | .07 | .20 |
| 596 | Manny Ramirez Sox | .10 | .30 |
| 597 | Mike Lansing | .07 | .20 |
| 598 | Rich Aurilia | .07 | .20 |
| 599 | Russell Branyan | .07 | .20 |
| 600 | Russ Johnson | .07 | .20 |
| 601 | Greg Colbrunn | .07 | .20 |
| 602 | Andruw Jones | .10 | .30 |
| 603 | Henry Blanco | .07 | .20 |
| 604 | Jarrod Washburn | .07 | .20 |
| 605 | Tony Eusebio | .07 | .20 |
| 606 | Aaron Sele | .07 | .20 |
| 607 | Charles Nagy | .07 | .20 |
| 608 | Ryan Klesko | .07 | .20 |
| 609 | Dante Bichette | .07 | .20 |
| 610 | Bill Haselman | .07 | .20 |
| 611 | Jerry Spradlin | .07 | .20 |
| 612 | Alex Rodriguez Rangers | .30 | .75 |
| 613 | Jose Silva | .07 | .20 |
| 614 | Darren Oliver | .07 | .20 |
| 615 | Pat Mahomes | .07 | .20 |
| 616 | Roberto Alomar | .10 | .30 |
| 617 | Edgar Renteria | .07 | .20 |
| 618 | Jon Lieber | .07 | .20 |
| 619 | John Rocker | .07 | .20 |
| 620 | Miguel Tejada | .07 | .20 |
| 621 | Mo Vaughn | .07 | .20 |
| 622 | Jose Lima | .07 | .20 |
| 623 | Kerry Wood | .07 | .20 |
| 624 | Mike Timlin | .07 | .20 |
| 625 | Wil Cordero | .07 | .20 |
| 626 | Albert Belle | .07 | .20 |
| 627 | Bobby Jones | .07 | .20 |
| 628 | Doug Mirabelli | .07 | .20 |
| 629 | Jason Tyner | .07 | .20 |
| 630 | Andy Ashby | .07 | .20 |
| 631 | Jose Hernandez | .07 | .20 |
| 632 | Devon White | .07 | .20 |
| 633 | Ruben Rivera | .07 | .20 |
| 634 | Steve Parris | .07 | .20 |
| 635 | David McCarty | .07 | .20 |
| 636 | Jose Canseco | .10 | .30 |
| 637 | Todd Walker | .07 | .20 |
| 638 | Stan Spencer | .07 | .20 |
| 639 | Wayne Gomes | .07 | .20 |
| 640 | Freddy Garcia | .07 | .20 |
| 641 | Jeremy Giambi | .07 | .20 |
| 642 | Luis Lopez | .07 | .20 |
| 643 | John Smoltz | .10 | .30 |
| 644 | Kelly Stinnett | .07 | .20 |
| 645 | Kevin Brown | .07 | .20 |
| 646 | Wilton Guerrero | .07 | .20 |
| 647 | Al Martin | .07 | .20 |
| 648 | Woody Williams | .07 | .20 |
| 649 | Brian Rose | .07 | .20 |
| 650 | Rafael Palmeiro | .10 | .30 |
| 651 | Pete Schourek | .07 | .20 |
| 652 | Kevin Jarvis | .07 | .20 |
| 653 | Mark Redman | .07 | .20 |
| 654 | Ricky Ledee | .07 | .20 |
| 655 | Larry Walker | .07 | .20 |
| 656 | Paul Byrd | .07 | .20 |
| 657 | Jason Bere | .07 | .20 |
| 658 | Rick White | .07 | .20 |
| 659 | Calvin Murray | .07 | .20 |
| 660 | Greg Maddux | .30 | .75 |
| 661 | Ron Gant | .07 | .20 |
| 662 | Eli Marrero | .07 | .20 |
| 663 | Graeme Lloyd | .07 | .20 |
| 664 | Trevor Hoffman | .07 | .20 |
| 665 | Nomar Garciaparra | .30 | .75 |
| 666 | Glenallen Hill | .07 | .20 |
| 667 | Matt LeCroy | .07 | .20 |
| 668 | Justin Thompson | .07 | .20 |
| 669 | Brady Anderson | .07 | .20 |
| 670 | Miguel Batista | .07 | .20 |
| 671 | Erubiel Durazo | .07 | .20 |
| 672 | Kevin Millwood | .07 | .20 |
| 673 | Mitch Meluskey | .07 | .20 |
| 674 | Luis Gonzalez | .07 | .20 |
| 675 | Edgar Martinez | .10 | .30 |
| 676 | Robert Person | .07 | .20 |
| 677 | Benito Santiago | .07 | .20 |
| 678 | Todd Jones | .07 | .20 |
| 679 | Tino Martinez | .10 | .30 |
| 680 | Carlos Beltran | .07 | .20 |
| 681 | Gabe White | .07 | .20 |
| 682 | Bret Saberhagen | .07 | .20 |
| 683 | Jeff Conine | .07 | .20 |
| 684 | Jaret Wright | .07 | .20 |
| 685 | Bernard Gilkey | .07 | .20 |
| 686 | Garrett Stephenson | .07 | .20 |
| 687 | Jamey Wright | .07 | .20 |
| 688 | Sammy Sosa | .20 | .50 |
| 689 | John Jaha | .07 | .20 |
| 690 | Ramon Martinez | .07 | .20 |
| 691 | Robert Fick | .07 | .20 |
| 692 | Eric Milton | .07 | .20 |
| 693 | Denny Neagle | .07 | .20 |
| 694 | Ron Coomer | .07 | .20 |
| 695 | John Valentin | .07 | .20 |
| 696 | Placido Polanco | .07 | .20 |
| 697 | Tim Hudson | .07 | .20 |
| 698 | Marty Cordova | .07 | .20 |
| 699 | Chad Kreuter | .07 | .20 |
| 700 | Frank Catalanotto | .07 | .20 |
| 701 | Tim Wakefield | .07 | .20 |
| 702 | Jim Edmonds | .07 | .20 |
| 703 | Michael Tucker | .07 | .20 |
| 704 | Cristian Guzman | .07 | .20 |
| 705 | Joey Hamilton | .07 | .20 |
| 706 | Mike Piazza | .30 | .75 |
| 707 | Dave Martinez | .07 | .20 |
| 708 | Mike Hampton | .07 | .20 |
| 709 | Bobby Bonilla | .07 | .20 |
| 710 | Juan Pierre | .07 | .20 |
| 711 | John Parrish | .07 | .20 |
| 712 | Kory DeHaan | .07 | .20 |
| 713 | Brian Tollberg | .07 | .20 |
| 714 | Chris Truby | .07 | .20 |
| 715 | Emil Brown | .07 | .20 |
| 716 | Ryan Dempster | .07 | .20 |
| 717 | Rich Garces | .07 | .20 |
| 718 | Mike Myers | .07 | .20 |
| 719 | Luis Ordaz | .07 | .20 |
| 720 | Kazuhiro Sasaki | .07 | .20 |
| 721 | Mark Quinn | .07 | .20 |
| 722 | Ramon Ortiz | .07 | .20 |
| 723 | Kerry Ligtenberg | .07 | .20 |
| 724 | Rolando Arrojo | .07 | .20 |
| 725 | Tsuyoshi Shinjo RC | .20 | .50 * |
| 726 | Ichiro Suzuki RC | 5.00 | 12.00 |
| 727 | Oswalt/Strange/Rauch | .30 | .75 |
| 728 | Jake Peavy RC | 1.40 | 4.00 |
| 729 | S.Smyth RC/Bynum/Haynes | .08 | .25 |
| 730 | Cuddyer/Lawrence/Freeman | .08 | .25 |
| 731 | C.Pena/Barnes/Wise | .08 | .25 |
| 732 | Dawkins/Almonte/Lopez | .08 | .25 |
| 733 | Escobar/Valent/Wilkerson | .08 | .25 |
| 734 | Hall/Barajas/Goldbach | .08 | .25 |
| 735 | Romano/Giles/Ozuna | .15 | .40 |
| 736 | D.Brown/Cust/V.Wells | .08 | .25 |
| 737 | L.Montanez RC/D.Espinosa | .08 | .25 |
| 738 | J.Wayne RC/A.Pluta RC | .08 | .25 |
| 739 | J.Axelson RC/C.Cali RC | .08 | .25 |
| 740 | S.Boyd RC/C.Morris RC | .08 | .25 |
| 741 | T.Arko RC/D.Moylan RC | .08 | .25 |
| 742 | L.Cotto RC/L.Escobar | .08 | .25 |
| 743 | B.Mims RC/B.Williams RC | .08 | .25 |
| 744 | C.Russ RC/B.Edwards | .08 | .25 |
| 745 | J.Torres/B.Diggins | .08 | .25 |
| 746 | Edwin Encarnacion RC | 1.25 | 3.00 |
| 747 | B.Bass RC/O.Ayala RC | .08 | .25 |
| 748 | M.Matthews RC/J.Kaanoi | .08 | .25 |
| 749 | S.McFarland RC/A.Sterrett RC | .08 | .25 |
| 750 | D.Krynzel/G.Sizemore | .60 | 1.50 |
| 751 | K.Buckfrot/D.Sandberg | .08 | .25 |
| 752 | Anaheim Angels TC | .07 | .20 |
| 753 | Arizona Diamondbacks TC | .07 | .20 |
| 754 | Atlanta Braves TC | .07 | .20 |
| 755 | Baltimore Orioles TC | .07 | .20 |
| 756 | Boston Red Sox TC | .07 | .20 |
| 757 | Chicago Cubs TC | .07 | .20 |
| 758 | Chicago White Sox TC | .07 | .20 |
| 759 | Cincinnati Reds TC | .07 | .20 |
| 760 | Cleveland Indians TC | .07 | .20 |
| 761 | Colorado Rockies TC | .07 | .20 |
| 762 | Detroit Tigers TC | .07 | .20 |
| 763 | Florida Marlins TC | .07 | .20 |
| 764 | Houston Astros TC | .07 | .20 |
| 765 | Kansas City Royals TC | .07 | .20 |
| 766 | Los Angeles Dodgers TC | .07 | .20 |
| 767 | Milwaukee Brewers TC | .07 | .20 |
| 768 | Minnesota Twins TC | .07 | .20 |
| 769 | Montreal Expos TC | .07 | .20 |
| 770 | New York Mets TC | .07 | .20 |
| 771 | New York Yankees TC | .40 | 1.00 |
| 772 | Oakland Athletics TC | .07 | .20 |
| 773 | Philadelphia Phillies TC | .07 | .20 |
| 774 | Pittsburgh Pirates TC | .07 | .20 |
| 775 | San Diego Padres TC | .07 | .20 |
| 776 | San Francisco Giants TC | .07 | .20 |
| 777 | Seattle Mariners TC | .07 | .20 |
| 778 | St. Louis Cardinals TC | .07 | .20 |
| 779 | Tampa Bay Devil Rays TC | .07 | .20 |
| 780 | Texas Rangers TC | .07 | .20 |
| 781 | Toronto Blue Jays TC | .07 | .20 |
| 782 | Bucky Dent GM | .07 | .20 |
| 783 | Jackie Robinson GM | .20 | .50 |
| 784 | Roberto Clemente GM | .25 | .60 |
| 785 | Nolan Ryan GM | .30 | .75 |
| 786 | Kerry Wood GM | .07 | .20 |
| 787 | Rickey Henderson GM | .07 | .20 |
| 788 | Lou Brock GM | .10 | .30 |
| 789 | David Wells GM | .07 | .20 |
| 790 | Andruw Jones GM | .07 | .20 |
| 791 | Carlton Fisk GM | .07 | .20 |
| TK | B.Jackson/D.Sanders Bat | 60.00 | 120.00 |
| NNO | B.Thomson/R.Branca AU | 30.00 | 60.00 |

## 2002 Topps

| | | |
|---|---|---|
| ❑ COMPLETE SET (718) | 30.00 | 80.00 |
| ❑ COMP.FACT.BROWN SET (723) | 40.00 | 80.00 |
| ❑ COMP.FACT.GREEN SET (723) | 40.00 | 80.00 |
| ❑ COMPLETE SERIES 1 (364) | 15.00 | 40.00 |
| ❑ COMPLETE SERIES 2 (354) | 15.00 | 40.00 |
| ❑ COMMON CARD (1-6/8-719) | .07 | .20 |
| ❑ COMMON (307-331/671-695) | .20 | .50 |
| ❑ COMMON (332-364) | .20 | .50 |
| ❑ 1 Pedro Martinez | .10 | .30 |
| ❑ 2 Mike Stanton | .07 | .20 |
| ❑ 3 Brad Penny | .07 | .20 |
| ❑ 4 Mike Matheny | .07 | .20 |
| ❑ 5 Johnny Damon | .10 | .30 |
| ❑ 6 Bret Boone | .07 | .20 |
| ❑ 7 Does Not Exist | | |
| ❑ 8 Chris Truby | .07 | .20 |
| ❑ 9 B.J. Surhoff | .07 | .20 |
| ❑ 10 Mike Hampton | .07 | .20 |
| ❑ 11 Juan Pierre | .07 | .20 |
| ❑ 12 Mark Buehrle | .07 | .20 |
| ❑ 13 Bob Abreu | .07 | .20 |
| ❑ 14 David Cone | .07 | .20 |
| ❑ 15 Aaron Sele | .07 | .20 |
| ❑ 16 Fernando Tatis | .07 | .20 |
| ❑ 17 Bobby Jones | .07 | .20 |
| ❑ 18 Rick Helling | .07 | .20 |
| ❑ 19 Dmitri Young | .07 | .20 |
| ❑ 20 Mike Mussina | .10 | .30 |
| ❑ 21 Mike Sweeney | .07 | .20 |
| ❑ 22 Cristian Guzman | .07 | .20 |
| ❑ 23 Ryan Kohlmeier | .07 | .20 |
| ❑ 24 Adam Kennedy | .07 | .20 |
| ❑ 25 Larry Walker | .07 | .20 |
| ❑ 26 Eric Davis | .07 | .20 |
| ❑ 27 Jason Tyner | .07 | .20 |
| ❑ 28 Eric Young | .07 | .20 |
| ❑ 29 Jason Marquis | .07 | .20 |
| ❑ 30 Luis Gonzalez | .07 | .20 |
| ❑ 31 Kevin Tapani | .07 | .20 |
| ❑ 32 Orlando Cabrera | .07 | .20 |
| ❑ 33 Marty Cordova | .07 | .20 |
| ❑ 34 Brad Ausmus | .07 | .20 |
| ❑ 35 Livan Hernandez | .07 | .20 |
| ❑ 36 Alex Gonzalez | .07 | .20 |
| ❑ 37 Edgar Renteria | .07 | .20 |
| ❑ 38 Bengie Molina | .07 | .20 |
| ❑ 39 Frank Menechino | .07 | .20 |
| ❑ 40 Rafael Palmeiro | .10 | .30 |
| ❑ 41 Brad Fullmer | .07 | .20 |
| ❑ 42 Julio Zuleta | .07 | .20 |
| ❑ 43 Darren Dreifort | .07 | .20 |
| ❑ 44 Trot Nixon | .07 | .20 |
| ❑ 45 Trevor Hoffman | .07 | .20 |
| ❑ 46 Vladimir Nunez | .07 | .20 |
| ❑ 47 Mark Kotsay | .07 | .20 |
| ❑ 48 Kenny Rogers | .07 | .20 |
| ❑ 49 Ben Petrick | .07 | .20 |
| ❑ 50 Jeff Bagwell | .10 | .30 |
| ❑ 51 Juan Encarnacion | .07 | .20 |
| ❑ 52 Ramiro Mendoza | .07 | .20 |
| ❑ 53 Brian Meadows | .07 | .20 |
| ❑ 54 Chad Curtis | .07 | .20 |
| ❑ 55 Aramis Ramirez | .07 | .20 |
| ❑ 56 Mark McLemore | .07 | .20 |
| ❑ 57 Dante Bichette | .07 | .20 |
| ❑ 58 Scott Schoeneweis | .07 | .20 |
| ❑ 59 Jose Cruz Jr. | .07 | .20 |
| ❑ 60 Roger Clemens | .40 | 1.00 |
| ❑ 61 Jose Guillen | .07 | .20 |
| ❑ 62 Darren Oliver | .07 | .20 |
| ❑ 63 Chris Reitsma | .07 | .20 |
| ❑ 64 Jeff Abbott | .07 | .20 |

| | | |
|---|---|---|
| ❑ 65 Robin Ventura | .07 | .20 |
| ❑ 66 Denny Neagle | .07 | .20 |
| ❑ 67 Al Martin | .07 | .20 |
| ❑ 68 Benito Santiago | .07 | .20 |
| ❑ 69 Roy Oswalt | .07 | .20 |
| ❑ 70 Juan Gonzalez | .07 | .20 |
| ❑ 71 Garret Anderson | .07 | .20 |
| ❑ 72 Bobby Bonilla | .07 | .20 |
| ❑ 73 Danny Bautista | .07 | .20 |
| ❑ 74 J.T. Snow | .07 | .20 |
| ❑ 75 Derek Jeter | .50 | 1.25 |
| ❑ 76 John Olerud | .07 | .20 |
| ❑ 77 Kevin Appier | .07 | .20 |
| ❑ 78 Phil Nevin | .07 | .20 |
| ❑ 79 Sean Casey | .07 | .20 |
| ❑ 80 Troy Glaus | .07 | .20 |
| ❑ 81 Joe Randa | .07 | .20 |
| ❑ 82 Jose Valentin | .07 | .20 |
| ❑ 83 Ricky Bottalico | .07 | .20 |
| ❑ 84 Todd Zeile | .07 | .20 |
| ❑ 85 Barry Larkin | .10 | .30 |
| ❑ 86 Bob Wickman | .07 | .20 |
| ❑ 87 Jeff Shaw | .07 | .20 |
| ❑ 88 Greg Vaughn | .07 | .20 |
| ❑ 89 Fernando Vina | .07 | .20 |
| ❑ 90 Mark Mulder | .07 | .20 |
| ❑ 91 Paul Bako | .07 | .20 |
| ❑ 92 Aaron Boone | .07 | .20 |
| ❑ 93 Esteban Loaiza | .07 | .20 |
| ❑ 94 Richie Sexson | .07 | .20 |
| ❑ 95 Alfonso Soriano | .07 | .20 |
| ❑ 96 Tony Womack | .07 | .20 |
| ❑ 97 Paul Shuey | .07 | .20 |
| ❑ 98 Melvin Mora | .07 | .20 |
| ❑ 99 Tony Gwynn | .25 | .60 |
| ❑ 100 Vladimir Guerrero | .20 | .50 |
| ❑ 101 Keith Osik | .07 | .20 |
| ❑ 102 Bud Smith | .07 | .20 |
| ❑ 103 Scott Williamson | .07 | .20 |
| ❑ 104 Daryle Ward | .07 | .20 |
| ❑ 105 Doug Mientkiewicz | .07 | .20 |
| ❑ 106 Stan Javier | .07 | .20 |
| ❑ 107 Russ Ortiz | .07 | .20 |
| ❑ 108 Wade Miller | .07 | .20 |
| ❑ 109 Luke Prokopec | .07 | .20 |
| ❑ 110 Andruw Jones | .10 | .30 |
| ❑ 111 Ron Coomer | .07 | .20 |
| ❑ 112 Dan Wilson | .07 | .20 |
| ❑ 113 Luis Castillo | .07 | .20 |
| ❑ 114 Derek Bell | .07 | .20 |
| ❑ 115 Gary Sheffield | .07 | .20 |
| ❑ 116 Ruben Rivera | .07 | .20 |
| ❑ 117 Paul O'Neill | .10 | .30 |
| ❑ 118 Craig Paquette | .07 | .20 |
| ❑ 119 Kelvim Escobar | .07 | .20 |
| ❑ 120 Brad Radke | .07 | .20 |
| ❑ 121 Jorge Fabregas | .07 | .20 |
| ❑ 122 Randy Winn | .07 | .20 |
| ❑ 123 Tom Goodwin | .07 | .20 |
| ❑ 124 Jaret Wright | .07 | .20 |
| ❑ 125 Manny Ramirez | .10 | .30 |
| ❑ 126 Al Leiter | .07 | .20 |
| ❑ 127 Ben Davis | .07 | .20 |
| ❑ 128 Frank Catalanotto | .07 | .20 |
| ❑ 129 Jose Cabrera | .07 | .20 |
| ❑ 130 Magglio Ordonez | .07 | .20 |
| ❑ 131 Jose Macias | .07 | .20 |
| ❑ 132 Ted Lilly | .07 | .20 |
| ❑ 133 Chris Holt | .07 | .20 |
| ❑ 134 Eric Milton | .07 | .20 |
| ❑ 135 Shannon Stewart | .07 | .20 |
| ❑ 136 Omar Olivares | .07 | .20 |
| ❑ 137 David Segui | .07 | .20 |
| ❑ 138 Jeff Nelson | .07 | .20 |
| ❑ 139 Matt Williams | .07 | .20 |
| ❑ 140 Ellis Burks | .07 | .20 |
| ❑ 141 Jason Bere | .07 | .20 |
| ❑ 142 Jimmy Haynes | .07 | .20 |
| ❑ 143 Ramon Hernandez | .07 | .20 |
| ❑ 144 Craig Counsell | .07 | .20 |
| ❑ 145 John Smoltz | .10 | .30 |
| ❑ 146 Homer Bush | .07 | .20 |
| ❑ 147 Quilvio Veras | .07 | .20 |
| ❑ 148 Esteban Yan | .07 | .20 |
| ❑ 149 Ramon Ortiz | .07 | .20 |
| ❑ 150 Carlos Delgado | .07 | .20 |
| ❑ 151 Lee Stevens | .07 | .20 |
| ❑ 152 Wil Cordero | .07 | .20 |

| | | |
|---|---|---|
| ❑ 153 Mike Bordick | .07 | .20 |
| ❑ 154 John Flaherty | .07 | .20 |
| ❑ 155 Omar Daal | .07 | .20 |
| ❑ 156 Todd Ritchie | .07 | .20 |
| ❑ 157 Carl Everett | .07 | .20 |
| ❑ 158 Scott Sullivan | .07 | .20 |
| ❑ 159 Deivi Cruz | .07 | .20 |
| ❑ 160 Albert Pujols | .40 | 1.00 |
| ❑ 160A Albert Pujols COR | | |
| ❑ 161 Royce Clayton | .07 | .20 |
| ❑ 162 Jeff Suppan | .07 | .20 |
| ❑ 163 C.C. Sabathia | .07 | .20 |
| ❑ 164 Jimmy Rollins | .07 | .20 |
| ❑ 165 Rickey Henderson | .20 | .50 |
| ❑ 166 Rey Ordonez | .07 | .20 |
| ❑ 167 Shawn Estes | .07 | .20 |
| ❑ 168 Reggie Sanders | .07 | .20 |
| ❑ 169 Jon Lieber | .07 | .20 |
| ❑ 170 Armando Benitez | .07 | .20 |
| ❑ 171 Mike Remlinger | .07 | .20 |
| ❑ 172 Billy Wagner | .07 | .20 |
| ❑ 173 Troy Percival | .07 | .20 |
| ❑ 174 Devon White | .07 | .20 |
| ❑ 175 Ivan Rodriguez | .10 | .30 |
| ❑ 176 Dustin Hermanson | .07 | .20 |
| ❑ 177 Brian Anderson | .07 | .20 |
| ❑ 178 Graeme Lloyd | .07 | .20 |
| ❑ 179 Russell Branyan | .07 | .20 |
| ❑ 180 Bobby Higginson | .07 | .20 |
| ❑ 181 Alex Gonzalez | .07 | .20 |
| ❑ 182 John Franco | .07 | .20 |
| ❑ 183 Sidney Ponson | .07 | .20 |
| ❑ 184 Jose Mesa | .07 | .20 |
| ❑ 185 Todd Hollandsworth | .07 | .20 |
| ❑ 186 Kevin Young | .07 | .20 |
| ❑ 187 Tim Wakefield | .07 | .20 |
| ❑ 188 Craig Biggio | .10 | .30 |
| ❑ 189 Jason Isringhausen | .07 | .20 |
| ❑ 190 Mark Quinn | .07 | .20 |
| ❑ 191 Glendon Rusch | .07 | .20 |
| ❑ 192 Damian Miller | .07 | .20 |
| ❑ 193 Sandy Alomar Jr. | .07 | .20 |
| ❑ 194 Scott Brosius | .07 | .20 |
| ❑ 195 Dave Martinez | .07 | .20 |
| ❑ 196 Danny Graves | .07 | .20 |
| ❑ 197 Shea Hillenbrand | .07 | .20 |
| ❑ 198 Jimmy Anderson | .07 | .20 |
| ❑ 199 Travis Lee | .07 | .20 |
| ❑ 200 Randy Johnson | .20 | .50 |
| ❑ 201 Carlos Beltran | .07 | .20 |
| ❑ 202 Jerry Hairston | .07 | .20 |
| ❑ 203 Jesus Sanchez | .07 | .20 |
| ❑ 204 Eddie Taubensee | .07 | .20 |
| ❑ 205 David Wells | .07 | .20 |
| ❑ 206 Russ Davis | .07 | .20 |
| ❑ 207 Michael Barrett | .07 | .20 |
| ❑ 208 Marquis Grissom | .07 | .20 |
| ❑ 209 Byung-Hyun Kim | .07 | .20 |
| ❑ 210 Hideo Nomo | .20 | .50 |
| ❑ 211 Ryan Rupe | .07 | .20 |
| ❑ 212 Ricky Gutierrez | .07 | .20 |
| ❑ 213 Darryl Kile | .07 | .20 |
| ❑ 214 Rico Brogna | .07 | .20 |
| ❑ 215 Terrence Long | .07 | .20 |
| ❑ 216 Mike Jackson | .07 | .20 |
| ❑ 217 Jamey Wright | .07 | .20 |
| ❑ 218 Adrian Beltre | .07 | .20 |
| ❑ 219 Benny Agbayani | .07 | .20 |
| ❑ 220 Chuck Knoblauch | .07 | .20 |
| ❑ 221 Randy Wolf | .07 | .20 |
| ❑ 222 Andy Ashby | .07 | .20 |
| ❑ 223 Corey Koskie | .07 | .20 |
| ❑ 224 Roger Cedeno | .07 | .20 |
| ❑ 225 Ichiro Suzuki | .40 | 1.00 |
| ❑ 226 Keith Foulke | .07 | .20 |
| ❑ 227 Ryan Minor | .07 | .20 |
| ❑ 228 Shawon Dunston | .07 | .20 |
| ❑ 229 Alex Cora | .07 | .20 |
| ❑ 230 Jeromy Burnitz | .07 | .20 |
| ❑ 231 Mark Grace | .10 | .30 |
| ❑ 232 Kanye Huff | .07 | .20 |
| ❑ 233 Jeffrey Hammonds | .07 | .20 |
| ❑ 234 Olmedo Saenz | .07 | .20 |
| ❑ 235 Brian Jordan | .07 | .20 |
| ❑ 236 Jeremy Giambi | .07 | .20 |
| ❑ 237 Joe Girardi | .07 | .20 |
| ❑ 238 Eric Gagne | .07 | .20 |
| ❑ 239 Masato Yoshii | .07 | .20 |

| # | Card | | |
|---|------|---|---|
| ❏ 240 | Greg Maddux | .30 | .75 |
| ❏ 241 | Bryan Rekar | .07 | .20 |
| ❏ 242 | Ray Durham | .07 | .20 |
| ❏ 243 | Torii Hunter | .07 | .20 |
| ❏ 244 | Derrek Lee | .10 | .30 |
| ❏ 245 | Jim Edmonds | .07 | .20 |
| ❏ 246 | Einar Diaz | .07 | .20 |
| ❏ 247 | Brian Bohanon | .07 | .20 |
| ❏ 248 | Ron Belliard | .07 | .20 |
| ❏ 249 | Mike Lowell | .07 | .20 |
| ❏ 250 | Sammy Sosa | .20 | .50 |
| ❏ 251 | Richard Hidalgo | .07 | .20 |
| ❏ 252 | Bartolo Colon | .07 | .20 |
| ❏ 253 | Jorge Posada | .10 | .30 |
| ❏ 254 | LaTroy Hawkins | .07 | .20 |
| ❏ 255 | Paul LoDuca | .07 | .20 |
| ❏ 256 | Carlos Febles | .07 | .20 |
| ❏ 257 | Nelson Cruz | .07 | .20 |
| ❏ 258 | Edgardo Alfonzo | .07 | .20 |
| ❏ 259 | Joey Hamilton | .07 | .20 |
| ❏ 260 | Cliff Floyd | .07 | .20 |
| ❏ 261 | Wes Helms | .07 | .20 |
| ❏ 262 | Jay Bell | .07 | .20 |
| ❏ 263 | Mike Cameron | .07 | .20 |
| ❏ 264 | Paul Konerko | .07 | .20 |
| ❏ 265 | Jeff Kent | .07 | .20 |
| ❏ 266 | Robert Fick | .07 | .20 |
| ❏ 267 | Allen Levrault | .07 | .20 |
| ❏ 268 | Placido Polanco | .07 | .20 |
| ❏ 269 | Marlon Anderson | .07 | .20 |
| ❏ 270 | Mariano Rivera | .20 | .50 |
| ❏ 271 | Chan Ho Park | .07 | .20 |
| ❏ 272 | Jose Vizcaino | .07 | .20 |
| ❏ 273 | Jeff D'Amico | .07 | .20 |
| ❏ 274 | Mark Gardner | .07 | .20 |
| ❏ 275 | Travis Fryman | .07 | .20 |
| ❏ 276 | Darren Lewis | .07 | .20 |
| ❏ 277 | Bruce Bochy MG | .07 | .20 |
| ❏ 278 | Jerry Manuel MG | .07 | .20 |
| ❏ 279 | Bob Brenly MG | .07 | .20 |
| ❏ 280 | Don Baylor MG | .07 | .20 |
| ❏ 281 | Davey Lopes MG | .07 | .20 |
| ❏ 282 | Jerry Narron MG | .07 | .20 |
| ❏ 283 | Tony Muser MG | .07 | .20 |
| ❏ 284 | Hal McRae MG | .07 | .20 |
| ❏ 285 | Bobby Cox MG | .07 | .20 |
| ❏ 286 | Larry Dierker MG | .07 | .20 |
| ❏ 287 | Phil Garner MG | .07 | .20 |
| ❏ 288 | Joe Kerrigan MG | .07 | .20 |
| ❏ 289 | Bobby Valentine MG | .07 | .20 |
| ❏ 290 | Dusty Baker MG | .07 | .20 |
| ❏ 291 | Lloyd McClendon MG | .07 | .20 |
| ❏ 292 | Mike Scioscia MG | .07 | .20 |
| ❏ 293 | Buck Martinez MG | .07 | .20 |
| ❏ 294 | Larry Bowa MG | .07 | .20 |
| ❏ 295 | Tony LaRussa MG | .07 | .20 |
| ❏ 296 | Jeff Torborg MG | .07 | .20 |
| ❏ 297 | Tom Kelly MG | .07 | .20 |
| ❏ 298 | Mike Hargrove MG | .07 | .20 |
| ❏ 299 | Art Howe MG | .07 | .20 |
| ❏ 300 | Lou Piniella MG | .07 | .20 |
| ❏ 301 | Charlie Manuel MG | .07 | .20 |
| ❏ 302 | Buddy Bell MG | .07 | .20 |
| ❏ 303 | Tony Perez MG | .07 | .20 |
| ❏ 304 | Bob Boone MG | .07 | .20 |
| ❏ 305 | Joe Torre MG | .10 | .30 |
| ❏ 306 | Jim Tracy MG | .07 | .20 |
| ❏ 307 | Jason Lane PROS | .20 | .50 |
| ❏ 308 | Chris George PROS | .20 | .50 |
| ❏ 309 | Hank Blalock PROS | .40 | 1.00 |
| ❏ 310 | Joe Borchard PROS | .20 | .50 |
| ❏ 311 | Marlon Byrd PROS | .20 | .50 |
| ❏ 312 | Raymond Cabrera PROS RC | .20 | .50 |
| ❏ 313 | Freddy Sanchez PROS RC | .75 | 2.00 |
| ❏ 314 | Scott Wiggins PROS RC | .20 | .50 |
| ❏ 315 | Jason Maule PROS RC | .20 | .50 |
| ❏ 316 | Dionys Cesar PROS RC | .20 | .50 |
| ❏ 317 | Boof Bonser PROS | .20 | .50 |
| ❏ 318 | Juan Tolentino PROS RC | .20 | .50 |
| ❏ 319 | Earl Snyder PROS RC | .20 | .50 |
| ❏ 320 | Travis Wade PROS RC | .20 | .50 |
| ❏ 321 | Napoleon Calzado PROS RC | .20 | .50 |
| ❏ 322 | Eric Glaser PROS RC | .20 | .50 |
| ❏ 323 | Craig Kuzmic PROS RC | .20 | .50 |
| ❏ 324 | Nic Jackson PROS RC | .20 | .50 |
| ❏ 325 | Mike Rivera PROS | .20 | .50 |
| ❏ 326 | Jason Bay PROS RC | 1.50 | 4.00 |
| ❏ 327 | Chris Smith DP | .20 | .50 |
| ❏ 328 | Jake Gautreau DP | .20 | .50 |
| ❏ 329 | Gabe Gross DP | .20 | .50 |
| ❏ 330 | Kenny Baugh DP | .20 | .50 |
| ❏ 331 | J.D. Martin DP | .20 | .50 |
| ❏ 332 | Barry Bonds HL | .50 | 1.25 |
| ❏ 333 | Rickey Henderson HL | .20 | .50 |
| ❏ 334 | Bud Smith HL | .20 | .50 |
| ❏ 335 | Rickey Henderson HL | .20 | .50 |
| ❏ 336 | Barry Bonds HL | .50 | 1.25 |
| ❏ 337 | Ichiro/Giambi/Alomar LL | .20 | .50 |
| ❏ 338 | A.Rod/Ichiro/Boone LL | .20 | .50 |
| ❏ 339 | A.Rod/Thome/Palmeiro LL | .20 | .50 |
| ❏ 340 | Boone/J.Gonz/A.Rod LL | .20 | .50 |
| ❏ 341 | Garcia/Mussina/Mays LL | .20 | .50 |
| ❏ 342 | Nomo/Mussina/Clemens LL | .20 | .50 |
| ❏ 343 | Walker/Helton/Alou/Berk LL | .20 | .50 |
| ❏ 344 | Sosa/Helton/Bonds LL | .30 | .75 |
| ❏ 345 | Bonds/Sosa/L.Gonz LL | .30 | .75 |
| ❏ 346 | Sosa/Helton/L.Gonz LL | .20 | .50 |
| ❏ 347 | R.John/Schilling/Burkett LL | .20 | .50 |
| ❏ 348 | R.John/Schilling/Park LL | .20 | .50 |
| ❏ 349 | Seattle Mariners PB | .20 | .50 |
| ❏ 350 | Oakland Athletics PB | .20 | .50 |
| ❏ 351 | New York Yankees PB | .20 | .50 |
| ❏ 352 | Cleveland Indians PB | .20 | .50 |
| ❏ 353 | Arizona Diamondbacks PB | .20 | .50 |
| ❏ 354 | Atlanta Braves PB | .20 | .50 |
| ❏ 355 | St. Louis Cardinals PB | .20 | .50 |
| ❏ 356 | Houston Astros PB | .20 | .50 |
| ❏ 357 | Diamondbacks-Astros UWS | .20 | .50 |
| ❏ 358 | Mike Piazza UWS | .20 | .50 |
| ❏ 359 | Braves-Phillies UWS ~ | .20 | .50 |
| ❏ 360 | Curt Schilling UWS | .20 | .50 |
| ❏ 361 | R.Clemens/L.Mazzilli UWS | .20 | .50 |
| ❏ 362 | Sammy Sosa UWS | .10 | .30 |
| ❏ 363 | Lampkin/Ichiro/Boone UWS | .20 | .50 |
| ❏ 364 | B.Bonds/J.Bagwell UWS | .30 | .75 |
| ❏ 365 | Barry Bonds HR 1 | 6.00 | 15.00 |
| ❏ 365 | Barry Bonds HR 2 | 4.00 | 10.00 |
| ❏ 365 | Barry Bonds HR 3 | 4.00 | 10.00 |
| ❏ 365 | Barry Bonds HR 4 | 4.00 | 10.00 |
| ❏ 365 | Barry Bonds HR 5 | 4.00 | 10.00 |
| ❏ 365 | Barry Bonds HR 6 | 4.00 | 10.00 |
| ❏ 365 | Barry Bonds HR 7 | 4.00 | 10.00 |
| ❏ 365 | Barry Bonds HR 8 | 4.00 | 10.00 |
| ❏ 365 | Barry Bonds HR 9 | 4.00 | 10.00 |
| ❏ 365 | Barry Bonds HR 10 | 4.00 | 10.00 |
| ❏ 365 | Barry Bonds HR 11 | 4.00 | 10.00 |
| ❏ 365 | Barry Bonds HR 12 | 4.00 | 10.00 |
| ❏ 365 | Barry Bonds HR 13 | 4.00 | 10.00 |
| ❏ 365 | Barry Bonds HR 14 | 4.00 | 10.00 |
| ❏ 365 | Barry Bonds HR 15 | 4.00 | 10.00 |
| ❏ 365 | Barry Bonds HR 16 | 4.00 | 10.00 |
| ❏ 365 | Barry Bonds HR 17 | 4.00 | 10.00 |
| ❏ 365 | Barry Bonds HR 18 | 4.00 | 10.00 |
| ❏ 365 | Barry Bonds HR 19 | 4.00 | 10.00 |
| ❏ 365 | Barry Bonds HR 20 | 4.00 | 10.00 |
| ❏ 365 | Barry Bonds HR 21 | 4.00 | 10.00 |
| ❏ 365 | Barry Bonds HR 22 | 4.00 | 10.00 |
| ❏ 365 | Barry Bonds HR 23 | 4.00 | 10.00 |
| ❏ 365 | Barry Bonds HR 24 | 4.00 | 10.00 |
| ❏ 365 | Barry Bonds HR 25 | 4.00 | 10.00 |
| ❏ 365 | Barry Bonds HR 26 | 4.00 | 10.00 |
| ❏ 365 | Barry Bonds HR 27 | 4.00 | 10.00 |
| ❏ 365 | Barry Bonds HR 28 | 4.00 | 10.00 |
| ❏ 365 | Barry Bonds HR 29 | 4.00 | 10.00 |
| ❏ 365 | Barry Bonds HR 30 | 4.00 | 10.00 |
| ❏ 365 | Barry Bonds HR 31 | 4.00 | 10.00 |
| ❏ 365 | Barry Bonds HR 32 | 4.00 | 10.00 |
| ❏ 365 | Barry Bonds HR 33 | 4.00 | 10.00 |
| ❏ 365 | Barry Bonds HR 34 | 4.00 | 10.00 |
| ❏ 365 | Barry Bonds HR 35 | 4.00 | 10.00 |
| ❏ 365 | Barry Bonds HR 36 | 4.00 | 10.00 |
| ❏ 365 | Barry Bonds HR 37 | 4.00 | 10.00 |
| ❏ 365 | Barry Bonds HR 38 | 4.00 | 10.00 |
| ❏ 365 | Barry Bonds HR 39 | 4.00 | 10.00 |
| ❏ 365 | Barry Bonds HR 40 | 4.00 | 10.00 |
| ❏ 365 | Barry Bonds HR 41 | 4.00 | 10.00 |
| ❏ 365 | Barry Bonds HR 42 | 4.00 | 10.00 |
| ❏ 365 | Barry Bonds HR 43 | 4.00 | 10.00 |
| ❏ 365 | Barry Bonds HR 44 | 4.00 | 10.00 |
| ❏ 365 | Barry Bonds HR 45 | 4.00 | 10.00 |
| ❏ 365 | Barry Bonds HR 46 | 4.00 | 10.00 |
| ❏ 365 | Barry Bonds HR 47 | 4.00 | 10.00 |
| ❏ 365 | Barry Bonds HR 48 | 4.00 | 10.00 |
| ❏ 365 | Barry Bonds HR 49 | 4.00 | 10.00 |
| ❏ 365 | Barry Bonds HR 50 | 4.00 | 10.00 |
| ❏ 365 | Barry Bonds HR 51 | 4.00 | 10.00 |
| ❏ 365 | Barry Bonds HR 52 | 4.00 | 10.00 |
| ❏ 365 | Barry Bonds HR 53 | 4.00 | 10.00 |
| ❏ 365 | Barry Bonds HR 54 | 4.00 | 10.00 |
| ❏ 365 | Barry Bonds HR 55 | 4.00 | 10.00 |
| ❏ 365 | Barry Bonds HR 56 | 4.00 | 10.00 |
| ❏ 365 | Barry Bonds HR 57 | 4.00 | 10.00 |
| ❏ 365 | Barry Bonds HR 58 | 4.00 | 10.00 |
| ❏ 365 | Barry Bonds HR 59 | 4.00 | 10.00 |
| ❏ 365 | Barry Bonds HR 60 | 4.00 | 10.00 |
| ❏ 365 | Barry Bonds HR 61 | 6.00 | 15.00 |
| ❏ 365 | Barry Bonds HR 62 | 4.00 | 10.00 |
| ❏ 365 | Barry Bonds HR 63 | 4.00 | 10.00 |
| ❏ 365 | Barry Bonds HR 64 | 4.00 | 10.00 |
| ❏ 365 | Barry Bonds HR 65 | 4.00 | 10.00 |
| ❏ 365 | Barry Bonds HR 66 | 4.00 | 10.00 |
| ❏ 365 | Barry Bonds HR 67 | 4.00 | 10.00 |
| ❏ 365 | Barry Bonds HR 68 | 4.00 | 10.00 |
| ❏ 365 | Barry Bonds HR 69 | 4.00 | 10.00 |
| ❏ 365 | Barry Bonds HR 70 | 6.00 | 15.00 |
| ❏ 365 | Barry Bonds HR 71 | 4.00 | 10.00 |
| ❏ 365 | Barry Bonds HR 72 | 4.00 | 10.00 |
| ❏ 365 | Barry Bonds HR 73 | 20.00 | 50.00 |
| ❏ 366 | Pat Meares | .07 | .20 |
| ❏ 367 | Mike Lieberthal | .07 | .20 |
| ❏ 368 | Larry Bigbie | .07 | .20 |
| ❏ 369 | Ron Gant | .07 | .20 |
| ❏ 370 | Moises Alou | .07 | .20 |
| ❏ 371 | Chad Kreuter | .07 | .20 |
| ❏ 372 | Willis Roberts | .07 | .20 |
| ❏ 373 | Toby Hall | .07 | .20 |
| ❏ 374 | Miguel Batista | .07 | .20 |
| ❏ 375 | John Burkett | .07 | .20 |
| ❏ 376 | Cory Lidle | .07 | .20 |
| ❏ 377 | Nick Neugebauer | .07 | .20 |
| ❏ 378 | Jay Payton | .07 | .20 |
| ❏ 379 | Steve Karsay | .07 | .20 |
| ❏ 380 | Eric Chavez | .07 | .20 |
| ❏ 381 | Kelly Stinnett | .07 | .20 |
| ❏ 382 | Jarrod Washburn | .07 | .20 |
| ❏ 383 | Rick White | .07 | .20 |
| ❏ 384 | Jeff Conine | .07 | .20 |
| ❏ 385 | Fred McGriff | .10 | .30 |
| ❏ 386 | Marvin Benard | .07 | .20 |
| ❏ 387 | Joe Crede | .07 | .20 |
| ❏ 388 | Dennis Cook | .07 | .20 |
| ❏ 389 | Rick Reed | .07 | .20 |
| ❏ 390 | Tom Glavine | .10 | .30 |
| ❏ 391 | Rondell White | .07 | .20 |
| ❏ 392 | Matt Morris | .07 | .20 |
| ❏ 393 | Pat Rapp | .07 | .20 |
| ❏ 394 | Robert Person | .07 | .20 |
| ❏ 395 | Omar Vizquel | .10 | .30 |
| ❏ 396 | Jeff Cirillo | .07 | .20 |
| ❏ 397 | Dave Mlicki | .07 | .20 |
| ❏ 398 | Jose Ortiz | .07 | .20 |
| ❏ 399 | Ryan Dempster | .07 | .20 |
| ❏ 400 | Curt Schilling | .20 | .50 |
| ❏ 401 | Peter Bergeron | .07 | .20 |
| ❏ 402 | Kyle Lohse | .07 | .20 |
| ❏ 403 | Craig Wilson | .07 | .20 |
| ❏ 404 | David Justice | .20 | .50 |
| ❏ 405 | Darin Erstad | .10 | .30 |
| ❏ 406 | Jose Mercedes | .07 | .20 |
| ❏ 407 | Carl Pavano | .07 | .20 |
| ❏ 408 | Albie Lopez | .07 | .20 |
| ❏ 409 | Alex Ochoa | .07 | .20 |
| ❏ 410 | Chipper Jones | .20 | .50 |
| ❏ 411 | Tyler Houston | .07 | .20 |
| ❏ 412 | Dean Palmer | .07 | .20 |
| ❏ 413 | Damian Jackson | .07 | .20 |
| ❏ 414 | Josh Towers | .07 | .20 |
| ❏ 415 | Rafael Furcal | .07 | .20 |
| ❏ 416 | Mike Morgan | .07 | .20 |
| ❏ 417 | Herb Perry | .07 | .20 |
| ❏ 418 | Mike Sirotka | .07 | .20 |
| ❏ 419 | Mark Wohlers | .07 | .20 |
| ❏ 420 | Nomar Garciaparra | .30 | .75 |
| ❏ 421 | Felipe Lopez | .07 | .20 |
| ❏ 422 | Joe McEwing | .07 | .20 |
| ❏ 423 | Jacque Jones | .07 | .20 |
| ❏ 424 | Julio Franco | .07 | .20 |
| ❏ 425 | Frank Thomas | .20 | .50 |
| ❏ 426 | So Taguchi RC | .30 | .75 |
| ❏ 427 | Kazuhisa Ishii RC | .20 | .50 |
| ❏ 428 | D'Angelo Jimenez | .07 | .20 |
| ❏ 429 | Chris Stynes | .07 | .20 |
| ❏ 430 | Kerry Wood | .07 | .20 |
| ❏ 431 | Chris Singleton | .07 | .20 |

|  |  | | |
|---|---|---|---|
| 432 | Erubiel Durazo | .07 | .20 |
| 433 | Matt Lawton | .07 | .20 |
| 434 | Bill Mueller | .07 | .20 |
| 435 | Jose Canseco | .10 | .30 |
| 436 | Ben Grieve | .07 | .20 |
| 437 | Terry Mulholland | .07 | .20 |
| 438 | David Bell | .07 | .20 |
| 439 | A.J. Pierzynski | .07 | .20 |
| 440 | Adam Dunn | .07 | .20 |
| 441 | Jon Garland | .07 | .20 |
| 442 | Jeff Fassero | .07 | .20 |
| 443 | Julio Lugo | .07 | .20 |
| 444 | Carlos Guillen | .07 | .20 |
| 445 | Orlando Hernandez | .07 | .20 |
| 446 | M.Loretta UER Leskanic | .07 | .20 |
| 447 | Scott Spiezio | .07 | .20 |
| 448 | Kevin Millwood | .07 | .20 |
| 449 | Jamie Moyer | .07 | .20 |
| 450 | Todd Helton | .10 | .30 |
| 451 | Todd Walker | .07 | .20 |
| 452 | Jose Lima | .07 | .20 |
| 453 | Brook Fordyce | .07 | .20 |
| 454 | Aaron Rowand | .07 | .20 |
| 455 | Barry Zito | .07 | .20 |
| 456 | Eric Owens | .07 | .20 |
| 457 | Charles Nagy | .07 | .20 |
| 458 | Raul Ibanez | .07 | .20 |
| 459 | Joe Mays | .07 | .20 |
| 460 | Jim Thome | .10 | .30 |
| 461 | Adam Eaton | .07 | .20 |
| 462 | Felix Martinez | .07 | .20 |
| 463 | Vernon Wells | .07 | .20 |
| 464 | Donnie Sadler | .07 | .20 |
| 465 | Tony Clark | .07 | .20 |
| 466 | Jose Hernandez | .07 | .20 |
| 467 | Ramon Martinez | .07 | .20 |
| 468 | Rusty Greer | .07 | .20 |
| 469 | Rod Barajas | .07 | .20 |
| 470 | Lance Berkman | .07 | .20 |
| 471 | Brady Anderson | .07 | .20 |
| 472 | Pedro Astacio | .07 | .20 |
| 473 | Shane Halter | .07 | .20 |
| 474 | Bret Prinz | .07 | .20 |
| 475 | Edgar Martinez | .10 | .30 |
| 476 | Steve Trachsel | .07 | .20 |
| 477 | Gary Matthews Jr. | .07 | .20 |
| 478 | Ismael Valdes | .07 | .20 |
| 479 | Juan Uribe | .07 | .20 |
| 480 | Shawn Green | .07 | .20 |
| 481 | Kirk Rueter | .07 | .20 |
| 482 | Damion Easley | .07 | .20 |
| 483 | Chris Carpenter | .07 | .20 |
| 484 | Kris Benson | .07 | .20 |
| 485 | Antonio Alfonseca | .07 | .20 |
| 486 | Kyle Farnsworth | .07 | .20 |
| 487 | Brandon Lyon | .07 | .20 |
| 488 | Hideki Irabu | .07 | .20 |
| 489 | David Ortiz | .20 | .50 |
| 490 | Mike Piazza | .30 | .75 |
| 491 | Derek Lowe | .07 | .20 |
| 492 | Chris Gomez | .07 | .20 |
| 493 | Mark Johnson | .07 | .20 |
| 494 | John Rocker | .07 | .20 |
| 495 | Eric Karros | .07 | .20 |
| 496 | Bill Haselman | .07 | .20 |
| 497 | Dave Veres | .07 | .20 |
| 498 | Pete Harnisch | .07 | .20 |
| 499 | Tomokazu Ohka | .07 | .20 |
| 500 | Barry Bonds | .50 | 1.25 |
| 501 | David Dellucci | .07 | .20 |
| 502 | Wendell Magee | .07 | .20 |
| 503 | Tom Gordon | .07 | .20 |
| 504 | Javier Vazquez | .07 | .20 |
| 505 | Ben Sheets | .07 | .20 |
| 506 | Wilton Guerrero | .07 | .20 |
| 507 | John Halama | .07 | .20 |
| 508 | Mark Redman | .07 | .20 |
| 509 | Jack Wilson | .07 | .20 |
| 510 | Bernie Williams | .10 | .30 |
| 511 | Miguel Cairo | .07 | .20 |
| 512 | Denny Hocking | .07 | .20 |
| 513 | Tony Batista | .07 | .20 |
| 514 | Mark Grudzielanek | .07 | .20 |
| 515 | Jose Vidro | .07 | .20 |
| 516 | Sterling Hitchcock | .07 | .20 |
| 517 | Billy Koch | .07 | .20 |
| 518 | Matt Clement | .07 | .20 |
| 519 | Bruce Chen | .07 | .20 |
| 520 | Roberto Alomar | .10 | .30 |
| 521 | Orlando Palmeiro | .07 | .20 |
| 522 | Steve Finley | .07 | .20 |
| 523 | Danny Patterson | .07 | .20 |
| 524 | Terry Adams | .07 | .20 |
| 525 | Tino Martinez | .10 | .30 |
| 526 | Tony Armas Jr. | .07 | .20 |
| 527 | Geoff Jenkins | .07 | .20 |
| 528 | Kerry Robinson | .07 | .20 |
| 529 | Corey Patterson | .07 | .20 |
| 530 | Brian Giles | .07 | .20 |
| 531 | Jose Jimenez | .07 | .20 |
| 532 | Joe Kennedy | .07 | .20 |
| 533 | Armando Rios | .07 | .20 |
| 534 | Osvaldo Fernandez | .07 | .20 |
| 535 | Ruben Sierra | .07 | .20 |
| 536 | Octavio Dotel | .07 | .20 |
| 537 | Luis Sojo | .07 | .20 |
| 538 | Brent Butler | .07 | .20 |
| 539 | Pablo Ozuna | .07 | .20 |
| 540 | Freddy Garcia | .07 | .20 |
| 541 | Chad Durbin | .07 | .20 |
| 542 | Orlando Merced | .07 | .20 |
| 543 | Michael Tucker | .07 | .20 |
| 544 | Roberto Hernandez | .07 | .20 |
| 545 | Pat Burrell | .07 | .20 |
| 546 | A.J. Burnett | .07 | .20 |
| 547 | Bubba Trammell | .07 | .20 |
| 548 | Scott Elarton | .07 | .20 |
| 549 | Mike Darr | .07 | .20 |
| 550 | Ken Griffey Jr. | .30 | .75 |
| 551 | Ugueth Urbina | .07 | .20 |
| 552 | Todd Jones | .07 | .20 |
| 553 | Delino Deshields | .07 | .20 |
| 554 | Adam Piatt | .07 | .20 |
| 555 | Jason Kendall | .07 | .20 |
| 556 | Hector Ortiz | .07 | .20 |
| 557 | Turk Wendell | .07 | .20 |
| 558 | Rob Bell | .07 | .20 |
| 559 | Sun Woo Kim | .07 | .20 |
| 560 | Raul Mondesi | .07 | .20 |
| 561 | Brent Abernathy | .07 | .20 |
| 562 | Seth Etherton | .07 | .20 |
| 563 | Shawn Wooten | .07 | .20 |
| 564 | Jay Buhner | .07 | .20 |
| 565 | Andres Galarraga | .07 | .20 |
| 566 | Shane Reynolds | .07 | .20 |
| 567 | Rod Beck | .07 | .20 |
| 568 | Dee Brown | .07 | .20 |
| 569 | Pedro Feliz | .07 | .20 |
| 570 | Ryan Klesko | .07 | .20 |
| 571 | John Vander Wal | .07 | .20 |
| 572 | Nick Bierbrodt | .07 | .20 |
| 573 | Joe Nathan | .07 | .20 |
| 574 | James Baldwin | .07 | .20 |
| 575 | J.D. Drew | .07 | .20 |
| 576 | Greg Colbrunn | .07 | .20 |
| 577 | Doug Glanville | .07 | .20 |
| 578 | Brandon Duckworth | .07 | .20 |
| 579 | Shawn Chacon | .07 | .20 |
| 580 | Rich Aurilia | .07 | .20 |
| 581 | Chuck Finley | .07 | .20 |
| 582 | Abraham Nunez | .07 | .20 |
| 583 | Kenny Lofton | .07 | .20 |
| 584 | Brian Daubach | .07 | .20 |
| 585 | Miguel Tejada | .07 | .20 |
| 586 | Nate Cornejo | .07 | .20 |
| 587 | Kazuhiro Sasaki | .07 | .20 |
| 588 | Chris Richard | .07 | .20 |
| 589 | Armando Reynoso | .07 | .20 |
| 590 | Tim Hudson | .07 | .20 |
| 591 | Neifi Perez | .07 | .20 |
| 592 | Steve Cox | .07 | .20 |
| 593 | Henry Blanco | .07 | .20 |
| 594 | Ricky Ledee | .07 | .20 |
| 595 | Tim Salmon | .10 | .30 |
| 596 | Luis Rivas | .07 | .20 |
| 597 | Jeff Zimmerman | .07 | .20 |
| 598 | Matt Stairs | .07 | .20 |
| 599 | Preston Wilson | .07 | .20 |
| 600 | Mark McGwire | .50 | 1.25 |
| 601 | Timo Perez | .07 | .20 |
| 602 | Matt Anderson | .07 | .20 |
| 603 | Todd Hundley | .07 | .20 |
| 604 | Rick Ankiel | .07 | .20 |
| 605 | Tsuyoshi Shinjo | .07 | .20 |
| 606 | Woody Williams | .07 | .20 |
| 607 | Jason LaRue | .07 | .20 |
| 608 | Carlos Lee | .07 | .20 |
| 609 | Russ Johnson | .07 | .20 |
| 610 | Scott Rolen | .10 | .30 |
| 611 | Brent Mayne | .07 | .20 |
| 612 | Darrin Fletcher | .07 | .20 |
| 613 | Ray Lankford | .07 | .20 |
| 614 | Troy O'Leary | .07 | .20 |
| 615 | Javier Lopez | .07 | .20 |
| 616 | Randy Velarde | .07 | .20 |
| 617 | Vinny Castilla | .07 | .20 |
| 618 | Milton Bradley | .07 | .20 |
| 619 | Ruben Mateo | .07 | .20 |
| 620 | Jason Giambi Yankees | .20 | .50 |
| 621 | Andy Benes | .07 | .20 |
| 622 | Joe Mauer RC | 4.00 | 10.00 |
| 623 | Andy Pettitte | .10 | .30 |
| 624 | Jose Offerman | .07 | .20 |
| 625 | Mo Vaughn | .07 | .20 |
| 626 | Steve Sparks | .07 | .20 |
| 627 | Mike Matthews | .07 | .20 |
| 628 | Robb Nen | .07 | .20 |
| 629 | Kip Wells | .07 | .20 |
| 630 | Kevin Brown | .07 | .20 |
| 631 | Arthur Rhodes | .07 | .20 |
| 632 | Gabe Kapler | .07 | .20 |
| 633 | Jermaine Dye | .07 | .20 |
| 634 | Josh Beckett | .07 | .20 |
| 635 | Pokey Reese | .07 | .20 |
| 636 | Benji Gil | .07 | .20 |
| 637 | Marcus Giles | .07 | .20 |
| 638 | Julian Tavarez | .07 | .20 |
| 639 | Jason Schmidt | .07 | .20 |
| 640 | Alex Rodriguez | .30 | .75 |
| 641 | Anaheim Angels TC | .07 | .20 |
| 642 | Arizona Diamondbacks TC | .10 | .30 |
| 643 | Atlanta Braves TC | .07 | .20 |
| 644 | Baltimore Orioles TC | .07 | .20 |
| 645 | Boston Red Sox TC | .07 | .20 |
| 646 | Chicago Cubs TC | .07 | .20 |
| 647 | Chicago White Sox TC | .07 | .20 |
| 648 | Cincinnati Reds TC | .07 | .20 |
| 649 | Cleveland Indians TC | .07 | .20 |
| 650 | Colorado Rockies TC | .07 | .20 |
| 651 | Detroit Tigers TC | .07 | .20 |
| 652 | Florida Marlins TC | .07 | .20 |
| 653 | Houston Astros TC | .07 | .20 |
| 654 | Kansas City Royals TC | .07 | .20 |
| 655 | Los Angeles Dodgers TC | .07 | .20 |
| 656 | Milwaukee Brewers TC | .07 | .20 |
| 657 | Minnesota Twins TC | .07 | .20 |
| 658 | Montreal Expos TC | .07 | .20 |
| 659 | New York Mets TC | .07 | .20 |
| 660 | New York Yankees TC | .20 | .50 |
| 661 | Oakland Athletics TC | .07 | .20 |
| 662 | Philadelphia Phillies TC | .07 | .20 |
| 663 | Pittsburgh Pirates TC | .07 | .20 |
| 664 | San Diego Padres TC | .07 | .20 |
| 665 | San Francisco Giants TC | .07 | .20 |
| 666 | Seattle Mariners TC | .10 | .30 |
| 667 | St. Louis Cardinals TC | .07 | .20 |
| 668 | Tampa Bay Devil Rays TC | .07 | .20 |
| 669 | Texas Rangers TC | .07 | .20 |
| 670 | Toronto Blue Jays TC | .07 | .20 |
| 671 | Juan Cruz PROS | .20 | .50 |
| 672 | Kevin Cash PROS RC | .20 | .50 |
| 673 | Jimmy Gobble PROS RC | .20 | .50 |
| 674 | Mike Hill PROS RC | .20 | .50 |
| 675 | Taylor Buchholz PROS RC | .20 | .50 |
| 676 | Bill Hall PROS | .20 | .50 |
| 677 | Brett Roneberg PROS RC | .20 | .50 |
| 678 | Royce Huffman PROS RC | .20 | .50 |
| 679 | Chris Tritle PROS RC | .20 | .50 |
| 680 | Nate Espy PROS RC | .20 | .50 |
| 681 | Nick Alvarez PROS RC | .20 | .50 |
| 682 | Jason Botts PROS RC | .20 | .50 |
| 683 | Ryan Gripp PROS RC | .20 | .50 |
| 684 | Dan Phillips PROS RC | .20 | .50 |
| 685 | Pablo Arias PROS RC | .20 | .50 |
| 686 | John Rodriguez PROS RC | .20 | .50 |
| 687 | Rich Harden PROS RC | 1.25 | 3.00 |
| 688 | Neal Frendling PROS RC | .20 | .50 |
| 689 | Rich Thompson PROS RC | .20 | .50 |
| 690 | Greg Montalbano PROS RC | .20 | .50 |
| 691 | Len Dinardo DP RC | .20 | .50 |
| 692 | Ryan Rabum DP RC | .20 | .50 |
| 693 | Josh Barfield DP RC | 1.00 | 2.50 |
| 694 | David Bacani DP RC | .20 | .50 |
| 695 | Dan Johnson DP RC | .40 | 1.00 |

| | | |
|---|---|---|
| 696 Mike Mussina GG | .07 | .20 |
| 697 Ivan Rodriguez GG | .10 | .30 |
| 698 Doug Mientkiewicz GG | .07 | .20 |
| 699 Roberto Alomar GG | .07 | .20 |
| 700 Eric Chavez GG | .07 | .20 |
| 701 Omar Vizquel GG | .07 | .20 |
| 702 Mike Cameron GG | .07 | .20 |
| 703 Torii Hunter GG | .07 | .20 |
| 704 Ichiro Suzuki GG | .20 | .50 |
| 705 Greg Maddux GG | .20 | .50 |
| 706 Brad Ausmus GG | .07 | .20 |
| 707 Todd Helton GG | .07 | .20 |
| 708 Fernando Vina GG | .07 | .20 |
| 709 Scott Rolen GG | .07 | .20 |
| 710 Orlando Cabrera GG | .07 | .20 |
| 711 Andruw Jones GG | .07 | .20 |
| 712 Jim Edmonds GG | .07 | .20 |
| 713 Larry Walker GG | .07 | .20 |
| 714 Roger Clemens CY | .20 | .50 |
| 715 Randy Johnson CY | .10 | .30 |
| 716 Ichiro Suzuki MVP | .20 | .50 |
| 717 Barry Bonds MVP | .30 | .75 |
| 718 Ichiro Suzuki ROY | .20 | .50 |
| 719 Albert Pujols ROY | .20 | .50 |

## 2003 Topps

| | | |
|---|---|---|
| COMPLETE SET (720) | 40.00 | 80.00 |
| COMPLETE SERIES 1 (366) | 20.00 | 40.00 |
| COMPLETE SERIES 2 (354) | 20.00 | 40.00 |
| COMMON CARD (1-6/8-721) | .07 | .20 |
| COMMON (292-331/660-684) | .20 | .50 |
| 1 Alex Rodriguez | .30 | .75 |
| 2 Dan Wilson | .07 | .20 |
| 3 Jimmy Rollins | .07 | .20 |
| 4 Jermaine Dye | .07 | .20 |
| 5 Steve Karsay | .07 | .20 |
| 6 Timo Perez | .07 | .20 |
| 7 Jose Vidro | .07 | .20 |
| 8 Eddie Guardado | .07 | .20 |
| 9 Mark Prior | .10 | .30 |
| 10 Curt Schilling | .07 | .20 |
| 11 Dennis Cook | .07 | .20 |
| 12 Andruw Jones | .10 | .30 |
| 13 David Segui | .07 | .20 |
| 14 Trot Nixon | .07 | .20 |
| 15 Kerry Wood | .07 | .20 |
| 16 Magglio Ordonez | .07 | .20 |
| 17 Jason LaRue | .07 | .20 |
| 18 Danys Baez | .07 | .20 |
| 20 Todd Helton | .10 | .30 |
| 21 Denny Neagle | .07 | .20 |
| 22 Dave Mlicki | .07 | .20 |
| 23 Roberto Hernandez | .07 | .20 |
| 24 Odalis Perez | .07 | .20 |
| 25 Nick Neugebauer | .07 | .20 |
| 26 David Ortiz | .20 | .50 |
| 27 Andres Galarraga | .20 | .50 |
| 28 Edgardo Alfonzo | .07 | .20 |
| 29 Chad Bradford | .07 | .20 |
| 30 Jason Giambi | .20 | .50 |
| 31 Brian Giles | .07 | .20 |
| 32 Delvi Cruz | .07 | .20 |
| 33 Robb Nen | .07 | .20 |
| 34 Jeff Nelson | .07 | .20 |
| 35 Edgar Renteria | .07 | .20 |
| 36 Aubrey Huff | .07 | .20 |
| 37 Brandon Duckworth | .07 | .20 |
| 38 Juan Gonzalez | .20 | .50 |
| 39 Sidney Ponson | .07 | .20 |
| 40 Eric Hinske | .07 | .20 |
| 41 Kevin Appier | .07 | .20 |
| 42 Danny Bautista | .07 | .20 |
| 43 Javier Lopez | .07 | .20 |
| 44 Jeff Conine | .07 | .20 |
| 45 Carlos Baerga | .07 | .20 |
| 46 Ugueth Urbina | .07 | .20 |
| 47 Mark Buehrle | .07 | .20 |
| 48 Aaron Boone | .07 | .20 |
| 49 Jason Simontacchi | .07 | .20 |
| 50 Sammy Sosa | .20 | .50 |
| 51 Jose Jimenez | .07 | .20 |
| 52 Bobby Higginson | .07 | .20 |
| 53 Luis Castillo | .07 | .20 |
| 54 Orlando Merced | .07 | .20 |
| 55 Brian Jordan | .07 | .20 |
| 56 Eric Young | .07 | .20 |
| 57 Bobby Kielty | .07 | .20 |
| 58 Luis Rivas | .07 | .20 |
| 59 Brad Wilkerson | .07 | .20 |
| 60 Roberto Alomar | .10 | .30 |
| 61 Roger Clemens | .40 | 1.00 |
| 62 Scott Hatteberg | .07 | .20 |
| 63 Andy Ashby | .07 | .20 |
| 64 Mike Williams | .07 | .20 |
| 65 Ron Gant | .07 | .20 |
| 66 Benito Santiago | .07 | .20 |
| 67 Bret Boone | .07 | .20 |
| 68 Matt Morris | .07 | .20 |
| 69 Troy Glaus | .07 | .20 |
| 70 Austin Kearns | .07 | .20 |
| 71 Jim Thome | .10 | .30 |
| 72 Rickey Henderson | .20 | .50 |
| 73 Luis Gonzalez | .20 | .50 |
| 74 Brad Fullmer | .07 | .20 |
| 75 Herbert Perry | .07 | .20 |
| 76 Randy Wolf | .07 | .20 |
| 77 Miguel Tejada | .07 | .20 |
| 78 Jimmy Anderson | .07 | .20 |
| 79 Ramon Martinez | .07 | .20 |
| 80 Ivan Rodriguez | .10 | .30 |
| 81 John Flaherty | .07 | .20 |
| 82 Shannon Stewart | .07 | .20 |
| 83 Orlando Palmeiro | .07 | .20 |
| 84 Rafael Furcal | .07 | .20 |
| 85 Kenny Rogers | .07 | .20 |
| 86 Terry Adams | .07 | .20 |
| 87 Mo Vaughn | .07 | .20 |
| 88 Jose Cruz Jr. | .07 | .20 |
| 89 Mike Matheny | .07 | .20 |
| 90 Alfonso Soriano | .20 | .50 |
| 91 Orlando Cabrera | .07 | .20 |
| 92 Jeffrey Hammonds | .07 | .20 |
| 93 Hideo Nomo | .20 | .50 |
| 94 Carlos Febles | .07 | .20 |
| 95 Billy Wagner | .07 | .20 |
| 96 Alex Gonzalez | .07 | .20 |
| 97 Todd Zeile | .07 | .20 |
| 98 Omar Vizquel | .10 | .30 |
| 99 Jose Rijo | .07 | .20 |
| 100 Ichiro Suzuki | .40 | 1.00 |
| 101 Steve Cox | .07 | .20 |
| 102 Hideki Irabu | .07 | .20 |
| 103 Roy Halladay | .07 | .20 |
| 104 David Eckstein | .07 | .20 |
| 105 Greg Maddux | .30 | .75 |
| 106 Jay Gibbons | .07 | .20 |
| 107 Travis Driskill | .07 | .20 |
| 108 Fred McGriff | .10 | .30 |
| 109 Frank Thomas | .20 | .50 |
| 110 Shawn Green | .20 | .50 |
| 111 Ruben Quevedo | .07 | .20 |
| 112 Jacque Jones | .07 | .20 |
| 113 Tomo Ohka | .07 | .20 |
| 114 Joe McEwing | .07 | .20 |
| 115 Ramiro Mendoza | .07 | .20 |
| 116 Mark Mulder | .07 | .20 |
| 117 Mike Lieberthal | .07 | .20 |
| 118 Jack Wilson | .07 | .20 |
| 119 Randall Simon | .07 | .20 |
| 120 Bernie Williams | .10 | .30 |
| 121 Marvin Benard | .07 | .20 |
| 122 Jamie Moyer | .07 | .20 |
| 123 Andy Benes | .07 | .20 |
| 124 Tino Martinez | .10 | .30 |
| 125 Esteban Yan | .07 | .20 |
| 126 Juan Uribe | .07 | .20 |
| 127 Jason Isringhausen | .07 | .20 |
| 128 Chris Carpenter | .07 | .20 |
| 129 Mike Cameron | .07 | .20 |
| 130 Gary Sheffield | .20 | .50 |
| 131 Geronimo Gil | .07 | .20 |
| 132 Brian Daubach | .07 | .20 |
| 133 Corey Patterson | .07 | .20 |
| 134 Aaron Rowand | .07 | .20 |
| 135 Chris Reitsma | .07 | .20 |
| 136 Bob Wickman | .07 | .20 |
| 137 Cesar Izturis | .07 | .20 |
| 138 Jason Jennings | .07 | .20 |
| 139 Brandon Inge | .07 | .20 |
| 140 Larry Walker | .07 | .20 |
| 141 Ramon Santiago | .07 | .20 |
| 142 Vladimir Nunez | .07 | .20 |
| 143 Jose Vizcaino | .07 | .20 |
| 144 Mark Quinn | .07 | .20 |
| 145 Michael Tucker | .07 | .20 |
| 146 Darren Dreifort | .07 | .20 |
| 147 Ben Sheets | .07 | .20 |
| 148 Corey Koskie | .07 | .20 |
| 149 Tony Armas Jr. | .07 | .20 |
| 150 Kazuhisa Ishii | .07 | .20 |
| 151 Al Leiter | .07 | .20 |
| 152 Steve Trachsel | .07 | .20 |
| 153 Mike Stanton | .07 | .20 |
| 154 David Justice | .07 | .20 |
| 155 Marlon Anderson | .07 | .20 |
| 156 Jason Kendall | .07 | .20 |
| 157 Brian Lawrence | .07 | .20 |
| 158 J.T. Snow | .07 | .20 |
| 159 Edgar Martinez | .10 | .30 |
| 160 Pat Burrell | .20 | .50 |
| 161 Kerry Robinson | .07 | .20 |
| 162 Greg Vaughn | .07 | .20 |
| 163 Carl Everett | .07 | .20 |
| 164 Vernon Wells | .07 | .20 |
| 165 Jose Mesa | .07 | .20 |
| 166 Troy Percival | .07 | .20 |
| 167 Eruibel Durazo | .07 | .20 |
| 168 Jason Marquis | .07 | .20 |
| 169 Jerry Hairston Jr. | .07 | .20 |
| 170 Vladimir Guerrero | .20 | .50 |
| 171 Byung-Hyun Kim | .07 | .20 |
| 172 Marcus Giles | .07 | .20 |
| 173 Johnny Damon | .10 | .30 |
| 174 Jon Lieber | .07 | .20 |
| 175 Terrence Long | .07 | .20 |
| 176 Sean Casey | .07 | .20 |
| 177 Adam Dunn | .07 | .20 |
| 178 Juan Pierre | .07 | .20 |
| 179 Wendell Magee | .07 | .20 |
| 180 Barry Zito | .07 | .20 |
| 181 Aramis Ramirez | .07 | .20 |
| 182 Pokey Reese | .07 | .20 |
| 183 Jeff Kent | .07 | .20 |
| 184 Russ Ortiz | .07 | .20 |
| 185 Ruben Sierra | .07 | .20 |
| 186 Brent Abernathy | .07 | .20 |
| 187 Ismael Valdes | .07 | .20 |
| 188 Tom Wilson | .07 | .20 |
| 189 Craig Counsell | .07 | .20 |
| 190 Mike Mussina | .10 | .30 |
| 191 Ramon Hernandez | .07 | .20 |
| 192 Adam Kennedy | .07 | .20 |
| 193 Tony Womack | .07 | .20 |
| 194 Wes Helms | .07 | .20 |
| 195 Tony Batista | .07 | .20 |
| 196 Rolando Arrojo | .07 | .20 |
| 197 Kyle Farnsworth | .07 | .20 |
| 198 Gary Bennett | .07 | .20 |
| 199 Scott Sullivan | .07 | .20 |
| 200 Albert Pujols | .40 | 1.00 |
| 201 Kirk Rueter | .07 | .20 |
| 202 Phil Nevin | .07 | .20 |
| 203 Kip Wells | .07 | .20 |
| 204 Ron Coomer | .07 | .20 |
| 205 Jeromy Burnitz | .07 | .20 |
| 206 Kyle Lohse | .07 | .20 |
| 207 Mike DeJean | .07 | .20 |
| 208 Paul Lo Duca | .07 | .20 |
| 209 Carlos Beltran | .07 | .20 |
| 210 Roy Oswalt | .07 | .20 |
| 211 Mike Lowell | .07 | .20 |
| 212 Robert Fick | .07 | .20 |
| 213 Todd Jones | .07 | .20 |
| 214 C.C. Sabathia | .07 | .20 |
| 215 Denny Graves | .07 | .20 |
| 216 Todd Hundley | .07 | .20 |
| 217 Tim Wakefield | .07 | .20 |
| 218 Derek Lowe | .07 | .20 |
| 219 Kevin Millwood | .07 | .20 |
| 220 Jorge Posada | .10 | .30 |

|  |  | | |
|---|---|---|---|
| 221 | Bobby J. Jones | .07 | .20 |
| 222 | Carlos Guillen | .07 | .20 |
| 223 | Fernando Vina | .07 | .20 |
| 224 | Ryan Rupe | .07 | .20 |
| 225 | Kelvim Escobar | .07 | .20 |
| 226 | Ramon Ortiz | .07 | .20 |
| 227 | Junior Spivey | .07 | .20 |
| 228 | Juan Cruz | .07 | .20 |
| 229 | Melvin Mora | .07 | .20 |
| 230 | Lance Berkman | .07 | .20 |
| 231 | Brent Butler | .07 | .20 |
| 232 | Shane Halter | .07 | .20 |
| 233 | Derrek Lee | .10 | .30 |
| 234 | Matt Lawton | .07 | .20 |
| 235 | Chuck Knoblauch | .07 | .20 |
| 236 | Eric Gagne | .07 | .20 |
| 237 | Alex Sanchez | .07 | .20 |
| 238 | Denny Hocking | .07 | .20 |
| 239 | Eric Milton | .07 | .20 |
| 240 | Rey Ordonez | .07 | .20 |
| 241 | Orlando Hernandez | .07 | .20 |
| 242 | Robert Person | .07 | .20 |
| 243 | Sean Burroughs | .07 | .20 |
| 244 | Jeff Cirillo | .07 | .20 |
| 245 | Mike Lamb | .07 | .20 |
| 246 | Jose Valentin | .07 | .20 |
| 247 | Ellis Burks | .07 | .20 |
| 248 | Shawn Chacon | .07 | .20 |
| 249 | Josh Beckett | .07 | .20 |
| 250 | Nomar Garciaparra | .30 | .75 |
| 251 | Craig Biggio | .10 | .30 |
| 252 | Joe Randa | .07 | .20 |
| 253 | Mark Grudzielanek | .07 | .20 |
| 254 | Glendon Rusch | .07 | .20 |
| 255 | Michael Barrett | .07 | .20 |
| 256 | Omar Daal | .07 | .20 |
| 257 | Elmer Dessens | .07 | .20 |
| 258 | Wade Miller | .07 | .20 |
| 259 | Adrian Beltre | .07 | .20 |
| 260 | Vicente Padilla | .07 | .20 |
| 261 | Kazuhiro Sasaki | .07 | .20 |
| 262 | Mike Scioscia MG | .07 | .20 |
| 263 | Bobby Cox MG | .07 | .20 |
| 264 | Mike Hargrove MG | .07 | .20 |
| 265 | Grady Little MG RC | .07 | .20 |
| 266 | Alex Gonzalez | .07 | .20 |
| 267 | Jerry Manuel MG | .07 | .20 |
| 268 | Bob Boone MG | .07 | .20 |
| 269 | Joel Skinner MG | .07 | .20 |
| 270 | Clint Hurdle MG | .07 | .20 |
| 271 | Miguel Batista | .07 | .20 |
| 272 | Bob Brenly MG | .07 | .20 |
| 273 | Jeff Torborg MG | .07 | .20 |
| 274 | Jimy Williams MG | .07 | .20 |
| 275 | Tony Pena MG | .07 | .20 |
| 276 | Jim Tracy MG | .07 | .20 |
| 277 | Jerry Royster MG | .07 | .20 |
| 278 | Ron Gardenhire MG | .07 | .20 |
| 279 | Frank Robinson MG | .10 | .30 |
| 280 | John Halama | .07 | .20 |
| 281 | Joe Torre MG | .10 | .30 |
| 282 | Art Howe MG | .07 | .20 |
| 283 | Larry Bowa MG | .07 | .20 |
| 284 | Lloyd McClendon MG | .07 | .20 |
| 285 | Bruce Bochy MG | .07 | .20 |
| 286 | Dusty Baker MG | .07 | .20 |
| 287 | Lou Piniella MG | .07 | .20 |
| 288 | Tony LaRussa MG | .07 | .20 |
| 289 | Todd Walker | .07 | .20 |
| 290 | Jerry Narron MG | .07 | .20 |
| 291 | Carlos Tosca MG | .07 | .20 |
| 292 | Chris Duncan FY RC | 1.25 | 3.00 |
| 293 | Franklin Gutierrez FY RC | .40 | 1.00 |
| 294 | Adam LaRoche FY | .20 | .50 |
| 295 | Manuel Ramirez FY RC | .20 | .50 |
| 296 | Il Kim FY RC | .20 | .50 |
| 297 | Wayne Lydon FY RC | .20 | .50 |
| 298 | Daryl Clark FY RC | .20 | .50 |
| 299 | Sean Pierce FY | .20 | .50 |
| 300 | Andy Marte FY RC | 1.25 | 3.00 |
| 301 | Matthew Peterson FY RC | .20 | .50 |
| 302 | Gonzalo Lopez FY RC | .20 | .50 |
| 303 | Bernie Castro FY RC | .20 | .50 |
| 304 | Cliff Lee FY | .20 | .50 |
| 305 | Jason Perry FY RC | .20 | .50 |
| 306 | Jaime Bubela FY RC | .20 | .50 |
| 307 | Alexis Rios FY | .40 | 1.00 |
| 308 | Brendan Harris FY RC | .20 | .50 |
| 309 | Ramon Nivar-Martinez FY RC | .20 | .50 |
| 310 | Terry Tiffee FY RC | .20 | .50 |
| 311 | Kevin Youkilis FY RC | .75 | 2.00 |
| 312 | Ruddy Lugo FY RC | .20 | .50 |
| 313 | C.J. Wilson FY | .20 | .50 |
| 314 | Mike McNutt FY RC | .20 | .50 |
| 315 | Jeff Clark FY RC | .20 | .50 |
| 316 | Mark Malaska FY RC | .20 | .50 |
| 317 | Doug Waechter FY RC | .20 | .50 |
| 318 | Derell McCall FY RC | .20 | .50 |
| 319 | Scott Tyler FY RC | .20 | .50 |
| 320 | Craig Brazell FY RC | .20 | .50 |
| 321 | Walter Young FY | .20 | .50 |
| 322 | M.Byrd/J.Padilla FS | .20 | .50 |
| 323 | C.Snelling/S.Choo FS | .20 | .50 |
| 324 | H.Blalock/M.Teixeira FS | .20 | .50 |
| 325 | J.Hamilton/C.Crawford FS | .40 | 1.00 |
| 326 | O.Hudson/J.Phelps FS | .20 | .50 |
| 327 | J.Cust/R.Reyes FS | .20 | .50 |
| 328 | A.Berroa/A.Gomez FS | .20 | .50 |
| 329 | M.Cuddyer/M.Restovich FS | .20 | .50 |
| 330 | J.Rivera/M.Thames FS | .20 | .50 |
| 331 | B.Pufier/J.Bong FS | .20 | .50 |
| 332 | Mike Cameron SH | .07 | .20 |
| 333 | Shawn Green SH | .07 | .20 |
| 334 | Oakland A's SH | .07 | .20 |
| 335 | Jason Giambi SH | .07 | .20 |
| 336 | Derek Lowe SH | .07 | .20 |
| 337 | AL Batting Average LL | .10 | .30 |
| 338 | AL Runs Scored LL | .07 | .20 |
| 339 | AL Home Runs LL | .10 | .30 |
| 340 | AL RBI's LL | .20 | .50 |
| 341 | AL ERA LL | .07 | .20 |
| 342 | AL Strikeouts LL | .10 | .30 |
| 343 | NL Batting Average LL | .20 | .50 |
| 344 | NL Runs Scored LL | .07 | .20 |
| 345 | NL Home Runs LL | .20 | .50 |
| 346 | NL RBI's LL | .20 | .50 |
| 347 | NL ERA LL | .10 | .30 |
| 348 | NL Strikeouts LL | .10 | .30 |
| 349 | AL Division Angels | .07 | .20 |
| 350 | AL/NL Division Twins/Cards | .10 | .30 |
| 351 | AL/NL Division Angels/Giants | .10 | .30 |
| 352 | NL Division Cardinals | .10 | .30 |
| 353 | Adam Kennedy ALCS | .07 | .20 |
| 354 | J.T. Snow WS | .10 | .30 |
| 355 | David Bell NLCS | .10 | .30 |
| 356 | Jason Giambi ALCS | .07 | .20 |
| 357 | Alfonso Soriano AS | .07 | .20 |
| 358 | Alex Rodriguez AS | .20 | .50 |
| 359 | Eric Chavez AS | .07 | .20 |
| 360 | Torii Hunter AS | .07 | .20 |
| 361 | Bernie Williams AS | .07 | .20 |
| 362 | Garret Anderson AS | .07 | .20 |
| 363 | Jorge Posada AS | .07 | .20 |
| 364 | Derek Lowe AS | .07 | .20 |
| 365 | Barry Zito AS | .07 | .20 |
| 366 | Manny Ramirez AS | .10 | .30 |
| 367 | Mike Scioscia AS | .07 | .20 |
| 368 | Francisco Rodriguez AS | .20 | .50 |
| 369 | Chris Hammond | .07 | .20 |
| 370 | Chipper Jones AS | .20 | .50 |
| 371 | Chris Singleton | .07 | .20 |
| 372 | Cliff Floyd | .07 | .20 |
| 373 | Bobby Hill | .07 | .20 |
| 374 | Antonio Osuna | .07 | .20 |
| 375 | Barry Larkin | .10 | .30 |
| 376 | Charles Nagy | .07 | .20 |
| 377 | Denny Stark | .07 | .20 |
| 378 | Dean Palmer | .07 | .20 |
| 379 | Eric Owens | .07 | .20 |
| 380 | Randy Johnson | .20 | .50 |
| 381 | Jeff Suppan | .07 | .20 |
| 382 | Eric Karros | .07 | .20 |
| 383 | Luis Vizcaino | .07 | .20 |
| 384 | Johan Santana | .30 | .75 |
| 385 | Javier Vazquez | .07 | .20 |
| 386 | John Thomson | .07 | .20 |
| 387 | Nick Johnson | .07 | .20 |
| 388 | Mark Ellis | .07 | .20 |
| 389 | Doug Glanville | .07 | .20 |
| 390 | Ken Griffey Jr. | .30 | .75 |
| 391 | Bubba Trammell | .07 | .20 |
| 392 | Livan Hernandez | .07 | .20 |
| 393 | Desi Relaford | .07 | .20 |
| 394 | Eli Marrero | .07 | .20 |
| 395 | Jared Sandberg | .07 | .20 |
| 396 | Barry Bonds | .50 | 1.25 |
| 397 | Esteban Loaiza | .07 | .20 |
| 398 | Aaron Sele | .07 | .20 |
| 399 | Geoff Blum | .07 | .20 |
| 400 | Derek Jeter | .50 | 1.25 |
| 401 | Eric Byrnes | .07 | .20 |
| 402 | Mike Timlin | .07 | .20 |
| 403 | Mark Kotsay | .07 | .20 |
| 404 | Rich Aurilia | .07 | .20 |
| 405 | Joel Pineiro | .07 | .20 |
| 406 | Chuck Finley | .07 | .20 |
| 407 | Bengie Molina | .07 | .20 |
| 408 | Steve Finley | .07 | .20 |
| 409 | Julio Franco | .07 | .20 |
| 410 | Marty Cordova | .07 | .20 |
| 411 | Shea Hillenbrand | .07 | .20 |
| 412 | Mark Bellhorn | .07 | .20 |
| 413 | Jon Garland | .07 | .20 |
| 414 | Reggie Taylor | .07 | .20 |
| 415 | Milton Bradley | .07 | .20 |
| 416 | Carlos Pena | .07 | .20 |
| 417 | Andy Fox | .07 | .20 |
| 418 | Brad Ausmus | .07 | .20 |
| 419 | Brent Mayne | .07 | .20 |
| 420 | Paul Quantrill | .07 | .20 |
| 421 | Carlos Delgado | .07 | .20 |
| 422 | Kevin Mench | .07 | .20 |
| 423 | Joe Kennedy | .07 | .20 |
| 424 | Mike Crudale | .07 | .20 |
| 425 | Mark McLemore | .07 | .20 |
| 426 | Bill Mueller | .07 | .20 |
| 427 | Rob Mackowiak | .07 | .20 |
| 428 | Ricky Ledee | .07 | .20 |
| 429 | Ted Lilly | .07 | .20 |
| 430 | Sterling Hitchcock | .07 | .20 |
| 431 | Scott Strickland | .07 | .20 |
| 432 | Damion Easley | .07 | .20 |
| 433 | Torii Hunter | .07 | .20 |
| 434 | Brad Radke | .07 | .20 |
| 435 | Geoff Jenkins | .07 | .20 |
| 436 | Paul Byrd | .07 | .20 |
| 437 | Morgan Ensberg | .07 | .20 |
| 438 | Mike Maroth | .07 | .20 |
| 439 | Mike Hampton | .07 | .20 |
| 440 | Adam Hyzdu | .07 | .20 |
| 441 | Vance Wilson | .07 | .20 |
| 442 | Todd Ritchie | .07 | .20 |
| 443 | Tom Gordon | .07 | .20 |
| 444 | John Burkett | .07 | .20 |
| 445 | Rodrigo Lopez | .07 | .20 |
| 446 | Tim Spooneybarger | .07 | .20 |
| 447 | Quinton Mccracken | .07 | .20 |
| 448 | Tim Salmon | .10 | .30 |
| 449 | Jarrod Washburn | .07 | .20 |
| 450 | Pedro Martinez | .10 | .30 |
| 451 | Dustan Mohr | .07 | .20 |
| 452 | Julio Lugo | .07 | .20 |
| 453 | Scott Stewart | .07 | .20 |
| 454 | Armando Benitez | .07 | .20 |
| 455 | Raul Mondesi | .07 | .20 |
| 456 | Robin Ventura | .07 | .20 |
| 457 | Bobby Abreu | .07 | .20 |
| 458 | Josh Fogg | .07 | .20 |
| 459 | Ryan Klesko | .07 | .20 |
| 460 | Tsuyoshi Shinjo | .07 | .20 |
| 461 | Jim Edmonds | .07 | .20 |
| 462 | Cliff Politte | .07 | .20 |
| 463 | Chan Ho Park | .07 | .20 |
| 464 | John Mabry | .07 | .20 |
| 465 | Woody Williams | .07 | .20 |
| 466 | Jason Michaels | .07 | .20 |
| 467 | Scott Schoeneweis | .07 | .20 |
| 468 | Brian Anderson | .07 | .20 |
| 469 | Brett Tomko | .07 | .20 |
| 470 | Scott Erickson | .07 | .20 |
| 471 | Kevin Millar Sox | .07 | .20 |
| 472 | Danny Wright | .07 | .20 |
| 473 | Jason Schmidt | .07 | .20 |
| 474 | Scott Williamson | .07 | .20 |
| 475 | Einar Diaz | .07 | .20 |
| 476 | Jay Payton | .07 | .20 |
| 477 | Juan Acevedo | .07 | .20 |
| 478 | Ben Grieve | .07 | .20 |
| 479 | Raul Ibanez | .07 | .20 |
| 480 | Richie Sexson | .07 | .20 |
| 481 | Rick Reed | .07 | .20 |
| 482 | Pedro Astacio | .07 | .20 |
| 483 | Adam Piatt | .07 | .20 |
| 484 | Bud Smith | .07 | .20 |

| | | |
|---|---|---|
| ☐ 485 Tomas Perez | .07 | .20 |
| ☐ 486 Adam Eaton | .07 | .20 |
| ☐ 487 Rafael Palmeiro | .10 | .30 |
| ☐ 488 Jason Tyner | .07 | .20 |
| ☐ 489 Scott Rolen | .10 | .30 |
| ☐ 490 Randy Winn | .07 | .20 |
| ☐ 491 Ryan Jensen | .07 | .20 |
| ☐ 492 Trevor Hoffman | .07 | .20 |
| ☐ 493 Craig Wilson | .07 | .20 |
| ☐ 494 Jeremy Giambi | .07 | .20 |
| ☐ 495 Daryle Ward | .07 | .20 |
| ☐ 496 Shane Spencer | .07 | .20 |
| ☐ 497 Andy Pettitte | .10 | .30 |
| ☐ 498 John Franco | .07 | .20 |
| ☐ 499 Felipe Lopez | .07 | .20 |
| ☐ 500 Mike Piazza | .30 | .75 |
| ☐ 501 Cristian Guzman | .07 | .20 |
| ☐ 502 Jose Hernandez | .07 | .20 |
| ☐ 503 Octavio Dotel | .07 | .20 |
| ☐ 504 Brad Penny | .07 | .20 |
| ☐ 505 Dave Veres | .07 | .20 |
| ☐ 506 Ryan Dempster | .07 | .20 |
| ☐ 507 Joe Crede | .07 | .20 |
| ☐ 508 Chad Hermanson | .07 | .20 |
| ☐ 509 Gary Matthews Jr. | .07 | .20 |
| ☐ 510 Matt Franco | .07 | .20 |
| ☐ 511 Ben Weber | .07 | .20 |
| ☐ 512 Dave Berg | .07 | .20 |
| ☐ 513 Michael Young | .10 | .30 |
| ☐ 514 Frank Catalanotto | .07 | .20 |
| ☐ 515 Darin Erstad | .07 | .20 |
| ☐ 516 Matt Williams | .07 | .20 |
| ☐ 517 B.J. Surhoff | .07 | .20 |
| ☐ 518 Kerry Ligtenberg | .07 | .20 |
| ☐ 519 Mike Bordick | .07 | .20 |
| ☐ 520 Arthur Rhodes | .07 | .20 |
| ☐ 521 Joe Girardi | .07 | .20 |
| ☐ 522 D'Angelo Jimenez | .07 | .20 |
| ☐ 523 Paul Konerko | .07 | .20 |
| ☐ 524 Jose Macias | .07 | .20 |
| ☐ 525 Joe Mays | .07 | .20 |
| ☐ 526 Marquis Grissom | .07 | .20 |
| ☐ 527 Neifi Perez | .07 | .20 |
| ☐ 528 Preston Wilson | .07 | .20 |
| ☐ 529 Jeff Weaver | .07 | .20 |
| ☐ 530 Eric Chavez | .07 | .20 |
| ☐ 531 Placido Polanco | .07 | .20 |
| ☐ 532 Matt Mantei | .07 | .20 |
| ☐ 533 James Baldwin | .07 | .20 |
| ☐ 534 Toby Hall | .07 | .20 |
| ☐ 535 Brendan Donnelly | .07 | .20 |
| ☐ 536 Benji Gil | .07 | .20 |
| ☐ 537 Damian Moss | .07 | .20 |
| ☐ 538 Jorge Julio | .07 | .20 |
| ☐ 539 Matt Clement | .07 | .20 |
| ☐ 540 Brian Moehler | .07 | .20 |
| ☐ 541 Lee Stevens | .07 | .20 |
| ☐ 542 Jimmy Haynes | .07 | .20 |
| ☐ 543 Terry Mulholland | .07 | .20 |
| ☐ 544 Dave Roberts | .07 | .20 |
| ☐ 545 J.C. Romero | .07 | .20 |
| ☐ 546 Bartolo Colon | .07 | .20 |
| ☐ 547 Roger Cedeno | .07 | .20 |
| ☐ 548 Mariano Rivera | .20 | .50 |
| ☐ 549 Billy Koch | .07 | .20 |
| ☐ 550 Manny Ramirez | .10 | .30 |
| ☐ 551 Travis Lee | .07 | .20 |
| ☐ 552 Oliver Perez | .07 | .20 |
| ☐ 553 Tim Worrell | .07 | .20 |
| ☐ 554 Rafael Soriano | .07 | .20 |
| ☐ 555 Damian Miller | .07 | .20 |
| ☐ 556 John Smoltz | .10 | .30 |
| ☐ 557 Willis Roberts | .07 | .20 |
| ☐ 558 Tim Hudson | .07 | .20 |
| ☐ 559 Moises Alou | .07 | .20 |
| ☐ 560 Gary Glover | .07 | .20 |
| ☐ 561 Corky Miller | .07 | .20 |
| ☐ 562 Ben Broussard | .07 | .20 |
| ☐ 563 Gabe Kapler | .07 | .20 |
| ☐ 564 Chris Woodward | .07 | .20 |
| ☐ 565 Paul Wilson | .07 | .20 |
| ☐ 566 Todd Hollandsworth | .07 | .20 |
| ☐ 567 So Taguchi | .07 | .20 |
| ☐ 568 John Olerud | .07 | .20 |
| ☐ 569 Reggie Sanders | .07 | .20 |
| ☐ 570 Jake Peavy | .07 | .20 |
| ☐ 571 Kris Benson | .07 | .20 |
| ☐ 572 Todd Pratt | .07 | .20 |

| | | |
|---|---|---|
| ☐ 573 Ray Durham | .07 | .20 |
| ☐ 574 Boomer Wells | .07 | .20 |
| ☐ 575 Chris Widger | .07 | .20 |
| ☐ 576 Shawn Wooten | .07 | .20 |
| ☐ 577 Tom Glavine | .10 | .30 |
| ☐ 578 Antonio Alfonseca | .07 | .20 |
| ☐ 579 Keith Foulke | .07 | .20 |
| ☐ 580 Shawn Estes | .07 | .20 |
| ☐ 581 Mark Grace | .10 | .30 |
| ☐ 582 Dmitri Young | .07 | .20 |
| ☐ 583 A.J. Burnett | .07 | .20 |
| ☐ 584 Richard Hidalgo | .07 | .20 |
| ☐ 585 Mike Sweeney | .07 | .20 |
| ☐ 586 Alex Cora | .07 | .20 |
| ☐ 587 Matt Stairs | .07 | .20 |
| ☐ 588 Doug Mientkiewicz | .07 | .20 |
| ☐ 589 Fernando Tatis | .07 | .20 |
| ☐ 590 David Weathers | .07 | .20 |
| ☐ 591 Cory Lidle | .07 | .20 |
| ☐ 592 Dan Plesac | .07 | .20 |
| ☐ 593 Jeff Bagwell | .10 | .30 |
| ☐ 594 Steve Sparks | .07 | .20 |
| ☐ 595 Sandy Alomar Jr. | .07 | .20 |
| ☐ 596 John Lackey | .07 | .20 |
| ☐ 597 Rick Helling | .07 | .20 |
| ☐ 598 Mark DeRosa | .07 | .20 |
| ☐ 599 Carlos Lee | .07 | .20 |
| ☐ 600 Garret Anderson | .07 | .20 |
| ☐ 601 Vinny Castilla | .07 | .20 |
| ☐ 602 Ryan Drese | .07 | .20 |
| ☐ 603 LaTroy Hawkins | .07 | .20 |
| ☐ 604 David Bell | .07 | .20 |
| ☐ 605 Freddy Garcia | .07 | .20 |
| ☐ 606 Miguel Cairo | .07 | .20 |
| ☐ 607 Scott Spiezio | .07 | .20 |
| ☐ 608 Mike Remlinger | .07 | .20 |
| ☐ 609 Tony Graffanino | .07 | .20 |
| ☐ 610 Russell Branyan | .07 | .20 |
| ☐ 611 Chris Magruder | .07 | .20 |
| ☐ 612 Jose Contreras RC | .40 | 1.00 |
| ☐ 613 Carl Pavano | .07 | .20 |
| ☐ 614 Kevin Brown | .07 | .20 |
| ☐ 615 Tyler Houston | .07 | .20 |
| ☐ 616 A.J. Pierzynski | .07 | .20 |
| ☐ 617 Tony Fiore | .07 | .20 |
| ☐ 618 Peter Bergeron | .07 | .20 |
| ☐ 619 Rondell White | .07 | .20 |
| ☐ 620 Brett Myers | .07 | .20 |
| ☐ 621 Kevin Young | .07 | .20 |
| ☐ 622 Kenny Lofton | .07 | .20 |
| ☐ 623 Ben Davis | .07 | .20 |
| ☐ 624 J.D. Drew | .07 | .20 |
| ☐ 625 Chris Gomez | .07 | .20 |
| ☐ 626 Karim Garcia | .07 | .20 |
| ☐ 627 Ricky Gutierrez | .07 | .20 |
| ☐ 628 Mark Redman | .07 | .20 |
| ☐ 629 Juan Encarnacion | .07 | .20 |
| ☐ 630 Anaheim Angels TC | .10 | .30 |
| ☐ 631 Arizona Diamondbacks TC | .07 | .20 |
| ☐ 632 Atlanta Braves TC | .07 | .20 |
| ☐ 633 Baltimore Orioles TC | .07 | .20 |
| ☐ 634 Boston Red Sox TC | .07 | .20 |
| ☐ 635 Chicago Cubs TC | .07 | .20 |
| ☐ 636 Chicago White Sox TC | .07 | .20 |
| ☐ 637 Cincinnati Reds TC | .07 | .20 |
| ☐ 638 Cleveland Indians TC | .07 | .20 |
| ☐ 639 Colorado Rockies TC | .07 | .20 |
| ☐ 640 Detroit Tigers TC | .07 | .20 |
| ☐ 641 Florida Marlins TC | .07 | .20 |
| ☐ 642 Houston Astros TC | .07 | .20 |
| ☐ 643 Kansas City Royals TC | .07 | .20 |
| ☐ 644 Los Angeles Dodgers TC | .07 | .20 |
| ☐ 645 Milwaukee Brewers TC | .07 | .20 |
| ☐ 646 Minnesota Twins TC | .07 | .20 |
| ☐ 647 Montreal Expos TC | .07 | .20 |
| ☐ 648 New York Mets TC | .07 | .20 |
| ☐ 649 New York Yankees TC | .10 | .30 |
| ☐ 650 Oakland Athletics TC | .07 | .20 |
| ☐ 651 Philadelphia Phillies TC | .07 | .20 |
| ☐ 652 Pittsburgh Pirates TC | .07 | .20 |
| ☐ 653 San Diego Padres TC | .07 | .20 |
| ☐ 654 San Francisco Giants TC | .07 | .20 |
| ☐ 655 Seattle Mariners TC | .07 | .20 |
| ☐ 656 St. Louis Cardinals TC | .07 | .20 |
| ☐ 657 Tampa Bay Devil Rays TC | .07 | .20 |
| ☐ 658 Texas Rangers TC | .07 | .20 |
| ☐ 659 Toronto Blue Jays TC | .07 | .20 |
| ☐ 660 Bryan Bullington DP RC | .20 | .50 |

| | | |
|---|---|---|
| ☐ 661 Jeremy Guthrie DP | .20 | .50 |
| ☐ 662 Joey Gomes DP RC | .20 | .50 |
| ☐ 663 Evel Bastide-Martinez DP RC | .20 | .50 |
| ☐ 664 Brian Wright DP RC | .20 | .50 |
| ☐ 665 B.J. Upton DP | .30 | .75 |
| ☐ 666 Jeff Francis DP | .20 | .50 |
| ☐ 667 Drew Meyer DP | .20 | .50 |
| ☐ 668 Jeremy Hermida DP | .30 | .75 |
| ☐ 669 Khalil Greene DP | .30 | .75 |
| ☐ 670 Darrell Rasner DP RC | .20 | .50 |
| ☐ 671 Cole Hamels DP | .75 | 2.00 |
| ☐ 672 James Loney DP | .25 | .60 |
| ☐ 673 Sergio Santos DP | .20 | .50 |
| ☐ 674 Jason Pride DP | .20 | .50 |
| ☐ 675 B.Phillips/V.Martinez | .20 | .50 |
| ☐ 676 H.Choi/N.Jackson | .20 | .50 |
| ☐ 677 D.Willis/J.Stokes | .30 | .75 |
| ☐ 678 C.Tracy/L.Overbay | .20 | .50 |
| ☐ 679 J.Borchard/C.Malone | .20 | .50 |
| ☐ 680 J.Mauer/J.Morneau | .30 | .75 |
| ☐ 681 D.Henson/B.Claussen | .20 | .50 |
| ☐ 682 C.Utley/G.Floyd | .30 | .75 |
| ☐ 683 T.Bozied/X.Nady | .20 | .50 |
| ☐ 684 A.Heilman/J.Reyes | .20 | .50 |
| ☐ 685 Kenny Rogers AW | .07 | .20 |
| ☐ 686 Bengie Molina AW | .07 | .20 |
| ☐ 687 John Olerud AW | .07 | .20 |
| ☐ 688 Bret Boone AW | .07 | .20 |
| ☐ 689 Eric Chavez AW | .07 | .20 |
| ☐ 690 Alex Rodriguez AW | .20 | .50 |
| ☐ 691 Darin Erstad AW | .07 | .20 |
| ☐ 692 Ichiro Suzuki AW | .20 | .50 |
| ☐ 693 Torii Hunter AW | .07 | .20 |
| ☐ 694 Greg Maddux AW | .20 | .50 |
| ☐ 695 Brad Ausmus AW | .07 | .20 |
| ☐ 696 Todd Helton AW | .07 | .20 |
| ☐ 697 Fernando Vina AW | .07 | .20 |
| ☐ 698 Scott Rolen AW | .07 | .20 |
| ☐ 699 Edgar Renteria AW | .07 | .20 |
| ☐ 700 Andruw Jones AW | .07 | .20 |
| ☐ 701 Larry Walker AW | .07 | .20 |
| ☐ 702 Jim Edmonds AW | .07 | .20 |
| ☐ 703 Barry Zito AW | .07 | .20 |
| ☐ 704 Randy Johnson AW | .10 | .30 |
| ☐ 705 Miguel Tejada AW | .07 | .20 |
| ☐ 706 Barry Bonds AW | .30 | .75 |
| ☐ 707 Eric Hinske AW | .07 | .20 |
| ☐ 708 Jason Jennings AW | .07 | .20 |
| ☐ 709 Todd Helton AS | .07 | .20 |
| ☐ 710 Jeff Kent AS | .07 | .20 |
| ☐ 711 Edgar Renteria AS | .07 | .20 |
| ☐ 712 Scott Rolen AS | .07 | .20 |
| ☐ 713 Barry Bonds AS | .30 | .75 |
| ☐ 714 Sammy Sosa AS | .10 | .30 |
| ☐ 715 Vladimir Guerrero AS | .10 | .30 |
| ☐ 716 Mike Piazza AS | .20 | .50 |
| ☐ 717 Curt Schilling AS | .07 | .20 |
| ☐ 718 Randy Johnson AS | .10 | .30 |
| ☐ 719 Bobby Cox AS | .07 | .20 |
| ☐ 720 Anaheim Angels WS | .10 | .30 |
| ☐ 721 Anaheim Angels WS | .20 | .50 |

## 2004 Topps

| | | |
|---|---|---|
| ☐ COMP.HOBBY SET (737) | 40.00 | 80.00 |
| ☐ COMP.HOLIDAY SET (742) | 40.00 | 80.00 |
| ☐ COMP.RETAIL SET (737) | 40.00 | 80.00 |
| ☐ COMP.ASTROS SET (737) | 40.00 | 80.00 |
| ☐ COMP.CUBS SET (737) | 40.00 | 80.00 |
| ☐ COMP.RED SOX SET (737) | 40.00 | 80.00 |
| ☐ COMP.YANKEES SET (737) | 40.00 | 80.00 |
| ☐ COMPLETE SET (732) | 30.00 | 80.00 |
| ☐ COMPLETE SERIES 1 (366) | 15.00 | 40.00 |
| ☐ COMPLETE SERIES 2 (366) | 15.00 | 40.00 |
| ☐ COMMON CARD (1-6/8-732) | .07 | .20 |

|  |  | | |
|---|---|---|---|
| ❑ | COMMON (297-326/668-687) | .20 | .50 |
| ❑ | COMMON (327-331/688-692) | .20 | .50 |
| ❑ 1 | Jim Thome | .10 | .30 |
| ❑ 2 | Reggie Sanders | .07 | .20 |
| ❑ 3 | Mark Kotsay | .07 | .20 |
| ❑ 4 | Edgardo Alfonzo | .07 | .20 |
| ❑ 5 | Ben Davis | .07 | .20 |
| ❑ 6 | Mike Matheny | .07 | .20 |
| ❑ 7 | Marlon Anderson | .07 | .20 |
| ❑ 8 | Chan Ho Park | .07 | .20 |
| ❑ 9 | Ichiro Suzuki | .40 | 1.00 |
| ❑ 11 | Kevin Millwood | .07 | .20 |
| ❑ 12 | Bengie Molina | .07 | .20 |
| ❑ 13 | Tom Glavine | .10 | .30 |
| ❑ 14 | Junior Spivey | .07 | .20 |
| ❑ 15 | Marcus Giles | .07 | .20 |
| ❑ 16 | David Segui | .07 | .20 |
| ❑ 17 | Kevin Millar | .07 | .20 |
| ❑ 18 | Corey Patterson | .07 | .20 |
| ❑ 19 | Aaron Rowand | .07 | .20 |
| ❑ 20 | Derek Jeter | .40 | 1.00 |
| ❑ 21 | Jason LaRue | .07 | .20 |
| ❑ 22 | Chris Hammond | .07 | .20 |
| ❑ 23 | Jay Payton | .07 | .20 |
| ❑ 24 | Bobby Higginson | .07 | .20 |
| ❑ 25 | Lance Berkman | .07 | .20 |
| ❑ 26 | Juan Pierre | .07 | .20 |
| ❑ 27 | Brent Mayne | .07 | .20 |
| ❑ 28 | Fred McGriff | .10 | .30 |
| ❑ 29 | Richie Sexson | .07 | .20 |
| ❑ 30 | Tim Hudson | .07 | .20 |
| ❑ 31 | Mike Piazza | .30 | .75 |
| ❑ 32 | Brad Radke | .07 | .20 |
| ❑ 33 | Jeff Weaver | .07 | .20 |
| ❑ 34 | Ramon Hernandez | .07 | .20 |
| ❑ 35 | David Bell | .07 | .20 |
| ❑ 36 | Craig Wilson | .07 | .20 |
| ❑ 37 | Jake Peavy | .07 | .20 |
| ❑ 38 | Tim Worrell | .07 | .20 |
| ❑ 39 | Gil Meche | .07 | .20 |
| ❑ 40 | Albert Pujols | .40 | 1.00 |
| ❑ 41 | Michael Young | .07 | .20 |
| ❑ 42 | Josh Phelps | .07 | .20 |
| ❑ 43 | Brendan Donnelly | .07 | .20 |
| ❑ 44 | Steve Finley | .07 | .20 |
| ❑ 45 | John Smoltz | .10 | .30 |
| ❑ 46 | Jay Gibbons | .07 | .20 |
| ❑ 47 | Trot Nixon | .07 | .20 |
| ❑ 48 | Carl Pavano | .07 | .20 |
| ❑ 49 | Frank Thomas | .20 | .50 |
| ❑ 50 | Mark Prior | .10 | .30 |
| ❑ 51 | Danny Graves | .07 | .20 |
| ❑ 52 | Milton Bradley UER | .07 | .20 |
| ❑ 53 | Jose Jimenez | .07 | .20 |
| ❑ 54 | Shane Halter | .07 | .20 |
| ❑ 55 | Mike Lowell | .07 | .20 |
| ❑ 56 | Geoff Blum | .07 | .20 |
| ❑ 57 | Michael Tucker UER | .07 | .20 |
| ❑ 58 | Paul Lo Duca | .07 | .20 |
| ❑ 59 | Vicente Padilla | .07 | .20 |
| ❑ 60 | Jacque Jones | .07 | .20 |
| ❑ 61 | Fernando Tatis | .07 | .20 |
| ❑ 62 | Ty Wigginton | .07 | .20 |
| ❑ 63 | Pedro Astacio | .07 | .20 |
| ❑ 64 | Andy Pettitte | .10 | .30 |
| ❑ 65 | Terrence Long | .07 | .20 |
| ❑ 66 | Cliff Floyd | .07 | .20 |
| ❑ 67 | Mariano Rivera | .20 | .50 |
| ❑ 68 | Carlos Silva | .07 | .20 |
| ❑ 69 | Marlon Byrd | .07 | .20 |
| ❑ 70 | Mark Mulder | .07 | .20 |
| ❑ 71 | Kerry Ligtenberg | .07 | .20 |
| ❑ 72 | Carlos Guillen | .07 | .20 |
| ❑ 73 | Fernando Vina | .07 | .20 |
| ❑ 74 | Lance Carter | .07 | .20 |
| ❑ 75 | Hank Blalock | .07 | .20 |
| ❑ 76 | Jimmy Rollins | .07 | .20 |
| ❑ 77 | Francisco Rodriguez | .07 | .20 |
| ❑ 78 | Javy Lopez | .07 | .20 |
| ❑ 79 | Jerry Hairston Jr. | .07 | .20 |
| ❑ 80 | Andruw Jones | .10 | .30 |
| ❑ 81 | Rodrigo Lopez | .07 | .20 |
| ❑ 82 | Johnny Damon | .10 | .30 |
| ❑ 83 | Hee Seop Choi | .07 | .20 |
| ❑ 84 | Miguel Olivo | .07 | .20 |
| ❑ 85 | Jon Garland | .07 | .20 |
| ❑ 86 | Matt Lawton | .07 | .20 |
| ❑ 87 | Juan Uribe | .07 | .20 |
| ❑ 88 | Steve Sparks | .07 | .20 |
| ❑ 89 | Tim Spooneybarger | .07 | .20 |
| ❑ 90 | Jose Vidro | .07 | .20 |
| ❑ 91 | Luis Rivas | .07 | .20 |
| ❑ 92 | Hideo Nomo | .20 | .50 |
| ❑ 93 | Javier Vazquez | .07 | .20 |
| ❑ 94 | Al Leiter | .07 | .20 |
| ❑ 95 | Darren Dreifort | .07 | .20 |
| ❑ 96 | Alex Cintron | .07 | .20 |
| ❑ 97 | Zach Day | .07 | .20 |
| ❑ 98 | Jorge Posada | .10 | .30 |
| ❑ 99 | John Halama | .07 | .20 |
| ❑ 100 | Alex Rodriguez | .30 | .75 |
| ❑ 101 | Orlando Palmeiro | .07 | .20 |
| ❑ 102 | Dave Berg | .07 | .20 |
| ❑ 103 | Brad Fullmer | .07 | .20 |
| ❑ 104 | Mike Hampton | .07 | .20 |
| ❑ 105 | Willis Roberts | .07 | .20 |
| ❑ 106 | Ramiro Mendoza | .07 | .20 |
| ❑ 107 | Juan Cruz | .07 | .20 |
| ❑ 108 | Esteban Loaiza | .07 | .20 |
| ❑ 109 | Russell Branyan | .07 | .20 |
| ❑ 110 | Todd Helton | .10 | .30 |
| ❑ 111 | Braden Looper | .07 | .20 |
| ❑ 112 | Octavio Dotel | .07 | .20 |
| ❑ 113 | Mike MacDougal | .07 | .20 |
| ❑ 114 | Cesar Izturis | .07 | .20 |
| ❑ 115 | Johan Santana | .20 | .50 |
| ❑ 116 | Jose Contreras | .07 | .20 |
| ❑ 117 | Placido Polanco | .07 | .20 |
| ❑ 118 | Jason Phillips | .07 | .20 |
| ❑ 119 | Adam Eaton | .07 | .20 |
| ❑ 120 | Vernon Wells | .07 | .20 |
| ❑ 121 | Ben Grieve | .07 | .20 |
| ❑ 122 | Randy Winn | .07 | .20 |
| ❑ 123 | Ismael Valdes | .07 | .20 |
| ❑ 124 | Eric Owens | .07 | .20 |
| ❑ 125 | Curt Schilling | .20 | .50 |
| ❑ 126 | Russ Ortiz | .07 | .20 |
| ❑ 127 | Mark Buehrle | .07 | .20 |
| ❑ 128 | Danys Baez | .07 | .20 |
| ❑ 129 | Dmitri Young | .07 | .20 |
| ❑ 130 | Kazuhisa Ishii | .07 | .20 |
| ❑ 131 | A.J. Pierzynski | .07 | .20 |
| ❑ 132 | Michael Barrett | .07 | .20 |
| ❑ 133 | Joe McEwing | .07 | .20 |
| ❑ 134 | Alex Cora | .07 | .20 |
| ❑ 135 | Tom Wilson | .07 | .20 |
| ❑ 136 | Carlos Zambrano | .07 | .20 |
| ❑ 137 | Brett Tomko | .07 | .20 |
| ❑ 138 | Shigetoshi Hasegawa | .07 | .20 |
| ❑ 139 | Jarrod Washburn | .07 | .20 |
| ❑ 140 | Greg Maddux | .30 | .75 |
| ❑ 141 | Craig Counsell | .07 | .20 |
| ❑ 142 | Reggie Taylor | .07 | .20 |
| ❑ 143 | Omar Vizquel | .10 | .30 |
| ❑ 144 | Alex Gonzalez | .07 | .20 |
| ❑ 145 | Billy Wagner | .07 | .20 |
| ❑ 146 | Brian Jordan | .07 | .20 |
| ❑ 147 | Wes Helms | .07 | .20 |
| ❑ 148 | Kyle Lohse | .07 | .20 |
| ❑ 149 | Timo Perez | .07 | .20 |
| ❑ 150 | Jason Giambi | .07 | .20 |
| ❑ 151 | Erubiel Durazo | .07 | .20 |
| ❑ 152 | Mike Lieberthal | .07 | .20 |
| ❑ 153 | Jason Kendall | .07 | .20 |
| ❑ 154 | Xavier Nady | .07 | .20 |
| ❑ 155 | Kirk Rueter | .07 | .20 |
| ❑ 156 | Mike Cameron | .07 | .20 |
| ❑ 157 | Miguel Cairo | .07 | .20 |
| ❑ 158 | Woody Williams | .07 | .20 |
| ❑ 159 | Toby Hall | .07 | .20 |
| ❑ 160 | Bernie Williams | .10 | .30 |
| ❑ 161 | Darin Erstad | .07 | .20 |
| ❑ 162 | Matt Mantei | .07 | .20 |
| ❑ 163 | Geronimo Gil | .07 | .20 |
| ❑ 164 | Bill Mueller | .07 | .20 |
| ❑ 165 | Damian Miller | .07 | .20 |
| ❑ 166 | Tony Graffanino | .07 | .20 |
| ❑ 167 | Sean Casey | .07 | .20 |
| ❑ 168 | Brandon Phillips | .07 | .20 |
| ❑ 169 | Mike Remlinger | .07 | .20 |
| ❑ 170 | Adam Dunn | .07 | .20 |
| ❑ 171 | Carlos Lee | .07 | .20 |
| ❑ 172 | Juan Encarnacion | .07 | .20 |
| ❑ 173 | Angel Berroa | .07 | .20 |
| ❑ 174 | Desi Relaford | .07 | .20 |
| ❑ 175 | Paul Quantrill | .07 | .20 |
| ❑ 176 | Ben Sheets | .07 | .20 |
| ❑ 177 | Eddie Guardado | .07 | .20 |
| ❑ 178 | Rocky Biddle | .07 | .20 |
| ❑ 179 | Mike Stanton | .07 | .20 |
| ❑ 180 | Eric Chavez | .07 | .20 |
| ❑ 181 | Jason Michaels | .07 | .20 |
| ❑ 182 | Terry Adams | .07 | .20 |
| ❑ 183 | Kip Wells | .07 | .20 |
| ❑ 184 | Brian Lawrence | .07 | .20 |
| ❑ 185 | Bret Boone | .07 | .20 |
| ❑ 186 | Tino Martinez | .10 | .30 |
| ❑ 187 | Aubrey Huff | .07 | .20 |
| ❑ 188 | Kevin Mench | .07 | .20 |
| ❑ 189 | Tim Salmon | .10 | .30 |
| ❑ 190 | Carlos Delgado | .07 | .20 |
| ❑ 191 | John Lackey | .07 | .20 |
| ❑ 192 | Oscar Villarreal | .07 | .20 |
| ❑ 193 | Luis Matos | .07 | .20 |
| ❑ 194 | Derek Lowe | .07 | .20 |
| ❑ 195 | Mark Grudzielanek | .07 | .20 |
| ❑ 196 | Tom Gordon | .07 | .20 |
| ❑ 197 | Matt Clement | .07 | .20 |
| ❑ 198 | Byung-Hyun Kim | .07 | .20 |
| ❑ 199 | Brandon Inge | .07 | .20 |
| ❑ 200 | Nomar Garciaparra | .30 | .75 |
| ❑ 201 | Antonio Osuna | .07 | .20 |
| ❑ 202 | Jose Mesa | .07 | .20 |
| ❑ 203 | Bo Hart | .07 | .20 |
| ❑ 204 | Jack Wilson | .07 | .20 |
| ❑ 205 | Ray Durham | .07 | .20 |
| ❑ 206 | Freddy Garcia | .07 | .20 |
| ❑ 207 | J.D. Drew | .07 | .20 |
| ❑ 208 | Einar Diaz | .07 | .20 |
| ❑ 209 | Roy Halladay | .07 | .20 |
| ❑ 210 | David Eckstein UER | .07 | .20 |
| ❑ 211 | Jason Marquis | .07 | .20 |
| ❑ 212 | Jorge Julio | .07 | .20 |
| ❑ 213 | Tim Wakefield | .07 | .20 |
| ❑ 214 | Moises Alou | .07 | .20 |
| ❑ 215 | Bartolo Colon | .07 | .20 |
| ❑ 216 | Jimmy Haynes | .07 | .20 |
| ❑ 217 | Preston Wilson | .07 | .20 |
| ❑ 218 | Luis Castillo | .07 | .20 |
| ❑ 219 | Richard Hidalgo | .07 | .20 |
| ❑ 220 | Manny Ramirez | .10 | .30 |
| ❑ 221 | Mike Mussina | .10 | .30 |
| ❑ 222 | Randy Wolf | .07 | .20 |
| ❑ 223 | Kris Benson | .07 | .20 |
| ❑ 224 | Ryan Klesko | .07 | .20 |
| ❑ 225 | Rich Aurilia | .07 | .20 |
| ❑ 226 | Kelvim Escobar | .07 | .20 |
| ❑ 227 | Francisco Cordero | .07 | .20 |
| ❑ 228 | Kazuhiro Sasaki | .07 | .20 |
| ❑ 229 | Danny Bautista | .07 | .20 |
| ❑ 230 | Rafael Furcal | .07 | .20 |
| ❑ 231 | Travis Driskill | .07 | .20 |
| ❑ 232 | Kyle Farnsworth | .07 | .20 |
| ❑ 233 | Jose Valentin | .07 | .20 |
| ❑ 234 | Felipe Lopez | .07 | .20 |
| ❑ 235 | C.C. Sabathia | .07 | .20 |
| ❑ 236 | Brad Penny | .07 | .20 |
| ❑ 237 | Brad Ausmus | .07 | .20 |
| ❑ 238 | Raul Ibanez | .07 | .20 |
| ❑ 239 | Adrian Beltre | .07 | .20 |
| ❑ 240 | Rocco Baldelli | .07 | .20 |
| ❑ 241 | Orlando Hudson | .07 | .20 |
| ❑ 242 | Dave Roberts | .07 | .20 |
| ❑ 243 | Doug Mientkiewicz | .07 | .20 |
| ❑ 244 | Brad Wilkerson | .07 | .20 |
| ❑ 245 | Scott Strickland | .07 | .20 |
| ❑ 246 | Ryan Franklin | .07 | .20 |
| ❑ 247 | Chad Bradford | .07 | .20 |
| ❑ 248 | Gary Bennett | .07 | .20 |
| ❑ 249 | Jose Cruz Jr. | .07 | .20 |
| ❑ 250 | Jeff Kent | .07 | .20 |
| ❑ 251 | Josh Beckett | .07 | .20 |
| ❑ 252 | Ramon Ortiz | .07 | .20 |
| ❑ 253 | Miguel Batista | .07 | .20 |
| ❑ 254 | Jung Bong | .07 | .20 |
| ❑ 255 | Deivi Cruz | .07 | .20 |
| ❑ 256 | Alex Gonzalez | .07 | .20 |
| ❑ 257 | Shawn Chacon | .07 | .20 |
| ❑ 258 | Runelvys Hernandez | .07 | .20 |
| ❑ 259 | Joe Mays | .07 | .20 |
| ❑ 260 | Eric Gagne | .07 | .20 |
| ❑ 261 | Dustan Mohr | .07 | .20 |
| ❑ 262 | Tomokazu Ohka | .07 | .20 |
| ❑ 263 | Eric Byrnes | .07 | .20 |

| # | Card | | |
|---|---|---|---|
| ❑ 264 | Frank Catalanotto | .07 | .20 |
| ❑ 265 | Cristian Guzman | .07 | .20 |
| ❑ 266 | Orlando Cabrera | .07 | .20 |
| ❑ 267A | Juan Castro | .07 | .20 |
| ❑ 267B | Mike Scioscia MG UER 274 | .07 | .20 |
| ❑ 268 | Bob Brenly MG | .07 | .20 |
| ❑ 269 | Bobby Cox MG | .07 | .20 |
| ❑ 270 | Mike Hargrove MG | .07 | .20 |
| ❑ 271 | Grady Little MG | .07 | .20 |
| ❑ 272 | Dusty Baker MG | .07 | .20 |
| ❑ 273 | Jerry Manuel MG | .07 | .20 |
| ❑ 275 | Eric Wedge MG | .07 | .20 |
| ❑ 276 | Clint Hurdle MG | .07 | .20 |
| ❑ 277 | Alan Trammell MG | .07 | .20 |
| ❑ 278 | Jack McKeon MG | .07 | .20 |
| ❑ 279 | Jimy Williams MG | .07 | .20 |
| ❑ 280 | Tony Pena MG | .07 | .20 |
| ❑ 281 | Jim Tracy MG | .07 | .20 |
| ❑ 282 | Ned Yost MG | .07 | .20 |
| ❑ 283 | Ron Gardenhire MG | .07 | .20 |
| ❑ 284 | Frank Robinson MG | .07 | .20 |
| ❑ 285 | Art Howe MG | .07 | .20 |
| ❑ 286 | Joe Torre MG | .10 | .30 |
| ❑ 287 | Ken Macha MG | .07 | .20 |
| ❑ 288 | Larry Bowa MG | .07 | .20 |
| ❑ 289 | Lloyd McClendon MG | .07 | .20 |
| ❑ 290 | Bruce Bochy MG | .07 | .20 |
| ❑ 291 | Felipe Alou MG | .07 | .20 |
| ❑ 292 | Bob Melvin MG | .07 | .20 |
| ❑ 293 | Tony LaRussa MG | .07 | .20 |
| ❑ 294 | Lou Piniella MG | .07 | .20 |
| ❑ 295 | Buck Showalter MG | .07 | .20 |
| ❑ 296 | Carlos Tosca MG | .07 | .20 |
| ❑ 297 | Anthony Acevedo FY RC | .20 | .50 |
| ❑ 298 | Anthony Lerew FY RC | .30 | .75 |
| ❑ 299 | Blake Hawksworth FY RC | .20 | .50 |
| ❑ 300 | Brayan Pena FY RC | .20 | .50 |
| ❑ 301 | Casey Myers FY RC | .20 | .50 |
| ❑ 302 | Craig Ansman FY RC | .20 | .50 |
| ❑ 303 | David Murphy FY RC | .30 | .75 |
| ❑ 304 | Dave Crouthers FY RC | .20 | .50 |
| ❑ 305 | Dioner Navarro FY RC | .30 | .75 |
| ❑ 306 | Donald Levinski FY RC | .20 | .50 |
| ❑ 307 | Jesse Roman FY RC | .20 | .50 |
| ❑ 308 | Sung Jung FY RC | .20 | .50 |
| ❑ 309 | Jon Knott FY RC | .20 | .50 |
| ❑ 310 | Josh Labandeira FY RC | .20 | .50 |
| ❑ 311 | Kenny Perez FY RC | .20 | .50 |
| ❑ 312 | Khalid Ballouli FY RC | .20 | .50 |
| ❑ 313 | Kyle Davies FY RC | 1.00 | 2.50 |
| ❑ 314 | Marcus McBeth FY RC | .20 | .50 |
| ❑ 315 | Matt Creighton FY RC | .20 | .50 |
| ❑ 316 | Chris O'Riordan FY RC | .20 | .50 |
| ❑ 317 | Mike Gosling FY RC | .20 | .50 |
| ❑ 318 | Nic Ungs FY RC | .20 | .50 |
| ❑ 319 | Omar Falcon FY RC | .20 | .50 |
| ❑ 320 | Rodney Choy Foo FY RC | .20 | .50 |
| ❑ 321 | Tim Frend FY RC | .20 | .50 |
| ❑ 322 | Todd Sell FY RC | .20 | .50 |
| ❑ 323 | Tydus Meadows FY RC | .20 | .50 |
| ❑ 324 | Yadier Molina FY RC | .75 | 2.00 |
| ❑ 325 | Zach Duke FY RC | .75 | 2.00 |
| ❑ 326 | Zach Miner FY RC | .50 | 1.25 |
| ❑ 327 | B.Castro/K.Greene FS | .20 | .50 |
| ❑ 328 | R.Madson/E.Ramirez FS | .20 | .50 |
| ❑ 329 | R.Harden/B.Crosby FS | .20 | .50 |
| ❑ 330 | Z.Greinke/J.Gobble FS | .20 | .50 |
| ❑ 331 | B.Jenks/C.Kotchman FS | .20 | .50 |
| ❑ 332 | Sammy Sosa HL | .10 | .30 |
| ❑ 333 | Kevin Millwood HL | .07 | .20 |
| ❑ 334 | Rafael Palmeiro HL | .20 | .50 |
| ❑ 335 | Roger Clemens HL | .20 | .50 |
| ❑ 336 | Eric Gagne HL | .07 | .20 |
| ❑ 337 | Mueller/Manny/Jeter LL | .10 | .30 |
| ❑ 338 | V.Wells/Ichiro/M.Young LL | .20 | .50 |
| ❑ 339 | A-Rod/Thomas/Delgado LL | .20 | .50 |
| ❑ 340 | Delgado/A-Rod/Boone LL | .20 | .50 |
| ❑ 341 | Pedro/Hudson/Loaiza LL | .10 | .30 |
| ❑ 342 | Loaiza/Pedro/Halladay LL | .10 | .30 |
| ❑ 343 | Pujols/Helton/Renteria LL | .20 | .50 |
| ❑ 344 | Pujols/Helton/Pierre LL | .20 | .50 |
| ❑ 345 | Thome/Sexson/J.Lopez LL | .07 | .20 |
| ❑ 346 | P.Wilson/Sheff/Thome LL | .07 | .20 |
| ❑ 347 | Schmidt/K.Brown/Prior LL | .10 | .30 |
| ❑ 348 | Wood/Prior/Vazquez LL | .10 | .30 |
| ❑ 349 | R.Clemens/D.Wells ALDS | .20 | .50 |
| ❑ 350 | K.Wood/M.Prior NLDS | .10 | .30 |
| ❑ 351 | Beckett/Cabrera/I.Rod NLCS | .20 | .50 |
| ❑ 352 | Giambi/Rivera/Boone ALCS | .20 | .50 |
| ❑ 353 | D.Lowe/I.Rod AL/NLDS | .20 | .50 |
| ❑ 354 | Pedro/Posa/Clemens ALCS | .20 | .50 |
| ❑ 355 | Juan Pierre WS | .07 | .20 |
| ❑ 356 | Carlos Delgado AS | .07 | .20 |
| ❑ 357 | Bret Boone AS | .07 | .20 |
| ❑ 358 | Alex Rodriguez AS | .20 | .50 |
| ❑ 359 | Bill Mueller AS | .07 | .20 |
| ❑ 360 | Vernon Wells AS | .07 | .20 |
| ❑ 361 | Garret Anderson AS | .07 | .20 |
| ❑ 362 | Magglio Ordonez AS | .07 | .20 |
| ❑ 363 | Jorge Posada AS | .07 | .20 |
| ❑ 364 | Roy Halladay AS | .07 | .20 |
| ❑ 365 | Andy Pettitte AS | .07 | .20 |
| ❑ 366 | Frank Thomas AS | .10 | .30 |
| ❑ 367 | Jody Gerut AS | .07 | .20 |
| ❑ 368 | Sammy Sosa | .20 | .50 |
| ❑ 369 | Joe Crede | .07 | .20 |
| ❑ 370 | Gary Sheffield | .07 | .20 |
| ❑ 371 | Coco Crisp | .07 | .20 |
| ❑ 372 | Torii Hunter | .07 | .20 |
| ❑ 373 | Derrek Lee | .10 | .30 |
| ❑ 374 | Adam Everett | .07 | .20 |
| ❑ 375 | Miguel Tejada | .07 | .20 |
| ❑ 376 | Jeremy Affeldt | .07 | .20 |
| ❑ 377 | Robin Ventura | .07 | .20 |
| ❑ 378 | Scott Podsednik | .07 | .20 |
| ❑ 379 | Matthew LeCroy | .07 | .20 |
| ❑ 380 | Vladimir Guerrero | .20 | .50 |
| ❑ 381 | Tike Redman | .07 | .20 |
| ❑ 382 | Jeff Nelson | .07 | .20 |
| ❑ 383 | Cliff Lee | .07 | .20 |
| ❑ 384 | Bobby Abreu | .07 | .20 |
| ❑ 385 | Josh Fogg | .07 | .20 |
| ❑ 386 | Trevor Hoffman | .07 | .20 |
| ❑ 387 | Jesse Foppert | .07 | .20 |
| ❑ 388 | Edgar Martinez | .10 | .30 |
| ❑ 389 | Edgar Renteria | .07 | .20 |
| ❑ 390 | Chipper Jones | .20 | .50 |
| ❑ 391 | Eric Munson | .07 | .20 |
| ❑ 392 | Dewon Brazelton | .07 | .20 |
| ❑ 393 | John Thomson | .07 | .20 |
| ❑ 394 | Chris Woodward | .07 | .20 |
| ❑ 395 | Adam LaRoche | .07 | .20 |
| ❑ 396 | Elmer Dessens | .07 | .20 |
| ❑ 397 | Johnny Estrada | .07 | .20 |
| ❑ 398 | Damian Moss | .07 | .20 |
| ❑ 399 | Gabe Kapler | .07 | .20 |
| ❑ 400 | Dontrelle Willis | .10 | .30 |
| ❑ 401 | Troy Glaus | .07 | .20 |
| ❑ 402 | Raul Mondesi | .07 | .20 |
| ❑ 403 | Shane Reynolds | .07 | .20 |
| ❑ 404 | Kurt Ainsworth | .07 | .20 |
| ❑ 405 | Pedro Martinez | .10 | .30 |
| ❑ 406 | Eric Karros | .07 | .20 |
| ❑ 407 | Billy Koch | .07 | .20 |
| ❑ 408 | Scott Schoeneweis | .07 | .20 |
| ❑ 409 | Paul Wilson | .07 | .20 |
| ❑ 410 | Mike Sweeney | .07 | .20 |
| ❑ 411 | Jason Bay | .07 | .20 |
| ❑ 412 | Mark Redman | .07 | .20 |
| ❑ 413 | Jason Jennings | .07 | .20 |
| ❑ 414 | Rondell White | .07 | .20 |
| ❑ 415 | Todd Hundley | .07 | .20 |
| ❑ 416 | Shannon Stewart | .07 | .20 |
| ❑ 417 | Jae Weong Seo | .07 | .20 |
| ❑ 418 | Livan Hernandez | .07 | .20 |
| ❑ 419 | Mark Ellis | .07 | .20 |
| ❑ 420 | Pat Burrell | .07 | .20 |
| ❑ 421 | Mark Loretta | .07 | .20 |
| ❑ 422 | Robb Nen | .07 | .20 |
| ❑ 423 | Joel Pineiro | .07 | .20 |
| ❑ 424 | Jason Simontacchi | .07 | .20 |
| ❑ 425 | Sterling Hitchcock | .07 | .20 |
| ❑ 426 | Rey Ordonez | .07 | .20 |
| ❑ 427 | Greg Myers | .07 | .20 |
| ❑ 428 | Shane Spencer | .07 | .20 |
| ❑ 429 | Carlos Baerga | .07 | .20 |
| ❑ 430 | Garret Anderson | .07 | .20 |
| ❑ 431 | Horacio Ramirez | .07 | .20 |
| ❑ 432 | Brian Roberts | .07 | .20 |
| ❑ 433 | Damian Jackson | .07 | .20 |
| ❑ 434 | Doug Glanville | .07 | .20 |
| ❑ 435 | Brian Daubach | .07 | .20 |
| ❑ 436 | Alex Escobar | .07 | .20 |
| ❑ 437 | Alex Sanchez | .07 | .20 |
| ❑ 438 | Jeff Bagwell | .10 | .30 |
| ❑ 439 | Darrell May | .07 | .20 |
| ❑ 440 | Shawn Green | .07 | .20 |
| ❑ 441 | Geoff Jenkins | .07 | .20 |
| ❑ 442 | Endy Chavez | .07 | .20 |
| ❑ 443 | Nick Johnson | .07 | .20 |
| ❑ 444 | Jose Guillen | .07 | .20 |
| ❑ 445 | Tomas Perez | .07 | .20 |
| ❑ 446 | Phil Nevin | .07 | .20 |
| ❑ 447 | Jason Schmidt | .07 | .20 |
| ❑ 448 | Julio Mateo | .07 | .20 |
| ❑ 449 | So Taguchi | .07 | .20 |
| ❑ 450 | Randy Johnson | .20 | .50 |
| ❑ 451 | Paul Byrd | .07 | .20 |
| ❑ 452 | Chone Figgins | .07 | .20 |
| ❑ 453 | Larry Bigbie | .07 | .20 |
| ❑ 454 | Scott Williamson | .07 | .20 |
| ❑ 455 | Ramon Martinez | .07 | .20 |
| ❑ 456 | Roberto Alomar | .10 | .30 |
| ❑ 457 | Ryan Dempster | .07 | .20 |
| ❑ 458 | Ryan Ludwick | .07 | .20 |
| ❑ 459 | Ramon Santiago | .07 | .20 |
| ❑ 460 | Jeff Conine | .07 | .20 |
| ❑ 461 | Brad Lidge | .07 | .20 |
| ❑ 462 | Ken Harvey | .07 | .20 |
| ❑ 463 | Guillermo Mota | .07 | .20 |
| ❑ 464 | Rick Reed | .07 | .20 |
| ❑ 465 | Joey Eischen | .07 | .20 |
| ❑ 466 | Wade Miller | .07 | .20 |
| ❑ 467 | Steve Karsay | .07 | .20 |
| ❑ 468 | Chase Utley | .10 | .30 |
| ❑ 469 | Matt Stairs | .07 | .20 |
| ❑ 470 | Yorvit Torrealba | .07 | .20 |
| ❑ 471 | Joe Kennedy | .07 | .20 |
| ❑ 472 | Reed Johnson | .07 | .20 |
| ❑ 473 | Victor Zambrano | .07 | .20 |
| ❑ 474 | Jeff Davanon | .07 | .20 |
| ❑ 475 | Luis Gonzalez | .07 | .20 |
| ❑ 476 | Eli Marrero | .07 | .20 |
| ❑ 477 | Ray King | .07 | .20 |
| ❑ 478 | Jack Cust | .07 | .20 |
| ❑ 479 | Omar Daal | .07 | .20 |
| ❑ 480 | Todd Walker | .07 | .20 |
| ❑ 481 | Shawn Estes | .07 | .20 |
| ❑ 482 | Chris Reitsma | .07 | .20 |
| ❑ 483 | Jake Westbrook | .07 | .20 |
| ❑ 484 | Jeremy Bonderman | .70 | .20 |
| ❑ 485 | A.J. Burnett | .07 | .20 |
| ❑ 486 | Roy Oswalt | .07 | .20 |
| ❑ 487 | Kevin Brown | .07 | .20 |
| ❑ 488 | Eric Milton | .07 | .20 |
| ❑ 489 | Claudio Vargas | .07 | .20 |
| ❑ 490 | Roger Cedeno | .07 | .20 |
| ❑ 491 | David Wells | .07 | .20 |
| ❑ 492 | Scott Hatteberg | .07 | .20 |
| ❑ 493 | Ricky Ledee | .07 | .20 |
| ❑ 494 | Eric Young | .07 | .20 |
| ❑ 495 | Armando Benitez | .07 | .20 |
| ❑ 496 | Dan Haren | .07 | .20 |
| ❑ 497 | Carl Crawford | .07 | .20 |
| ❑ 498 | Laynce Nix | .07 | .20 |
| ❑ 499 | Eric Hinske | .07 | .20 |
| ❑ 500 | Ivan Rodriguez | .10 | .30 |
| ❑ 501 | Scot Shields | .07 | .20 |
| ❑ 502 | Brandon Webb | .07 | .20 |
| ❑ 503 | Mark DeRosa | .07 | .20 |
| ❑ 504 | Jhonny Peralta | .07 | .20 |
| ❑ 505 | Adam Kennedy | .07 | .20 |
| ❑ 506 | Tony Batista | .07 | .20 |
| ❑ 507 | Jeff Suppan | .07 | .20 |
| ❑ 508 | Kenny Lofton | .07 | .20 |
| ❑ 509 | Scott Sullivan | .07 | .20 |
| ❑ 510 | Ken Griffey Jr. | .30 | .75 |
| ❑ 511 | Billy Traber | .07 | .20 |
| ❑ 512 | Larry Walker | .07 | .20 |
| ❑ 513 | Mike Maroth | .07 | .20 |
| ❑ 514 | Todd Hollandsworth | .07 | .20 |
| ❑ 515 | Kirk Saarloos | .07 | .20 |
| ❑ 516 | Carlos Beltran | .07 | .20 |
| ❑ 517 | Juan Rivera | .07 | .20 |
| ❑ 518 | Roger Clemens | .40 | 1.00 |
| ❑ 519 | Karim Garcia | .07 | .20 |
| ❑ 520 | Jose Reyes | .07 | .20 |
| ❑ 521 | Brandon Duckworth | .07 | .20 |
| ❑ 522 | Brian Giles | .07 | .20 |
| ❑ 523 | J.T. Snow | .07 | .20 |
| ❑ 524 | Jamie Moyer | .07 | .20 |
| ❑ 525 | Jason Isringhausen | .07 | .20 |
| ❑ 526 | Julio Lugo | .07 | .20 |
| ❑ 527 | Mark Teixeira | .10 | .30 |

| # | Card | | |
|---|---|---|---|
| ☐ 528 | Cory Lidle | .07 | .20 |
| ☐ 529 | Lyle Overbay | .07 | .20 |
| ☐ 530 | Troy Percival | .07 | .20 |
| ☐ 531 | Robby Hammock | .07 | .20 |
| ☐ 532 | Robert Fick | .07 | .20 |
| ☐ 533 | Jason Johnson | .07 | .20 |
| ☐ 534 | Brandon Lyon | .07 | .20 |
| ☐ 535 | Antonio Alfonseca | .07 | .20 |
| ☐ 536 | Tom Goodwin | .07 | .20 |
| ☐ 537 | Paul Konerko | .07 | .20 |
| ☐ 538 | D'Angelo Jimenez | .07 | .20 |
| ☐ 539 | Ben Broussard | .07 | .20 |
| ☐ 540 | Magglio Ordonez | .07 | .20 |
| ☐ 541 | Ellis Burks | .07 | .20 |
| ☐ 542 | Carlos Pena | .07 | .20 |
| ☐ 543 | Chad Fox | .07 | .20 |
| ☐ 544 | Jeriome Robertson | .07 | .20 |
| ☐ 545 | Travis Hafner | .07 | .20 |
| ☐ 546 | Joe Randa | .07 | .20 |
| ☐ 547 | Wil Cordero | .07 | .20 |
| ☐ 548 | Brady Clark | .07 | .20 |
| ☐ 549 | Ruben Sierra | .07 | .20 |
| ☐ 550 | Barry Zito | .07 | .20 |
| ☐ 551 | Brett Myers | .07 | .20 |
| ☐ 552 | Oliver Perez | .07 | .20 |
| ☐ 553 | Trey Hodges | .07 | .20 |
| ☐ 554 | Benito Santiago | .07 | .20 |
| ☐ 555 | David Ross | .07 | .20 |
| ☐ 556 | Ramon Vazquez | .07 | .20 |
| ☐ 557 | Joe Nathan | .07 | .20 |
| ☐ 558 | Dan Wilson | .07 | .20 |
| ☐ 559 | Joe Mauer | .20 | .50 |
| ☐ 560 | Jim Edmonds | .07 | .20 |
| ☐ 561 | Shawn Wooten | .07 | .20 |
| ☐ 562 | Matt Kata | .07 | .20 |
| ☐ 563 | Vinny Castilla | .07 | .20 |
| ☐ 564 | Marty Cordova | .07 | .20 |
| ☐ 565 | Aramis Ramirez | .07 | .20 |
| ☐ 566 | Carl Everett | .07 | .20 |
| ☐ 567 | Ryan Freel | .07 | .20 |
| ☐ 568 | Jason Davis | .07 | .20 |
| ☐ 569 | Mark Bellhorn Sox | .07 | .20 |
| ☐ 570 | Craig Monroe | .07 | .20 |
| ☐ 571 | Roberto Hernandez | .07 | .20 |
| ☐ 572 | Tim Redding | .07 | .20 |
| ☐ 573 | Kevin Appier | .07 | .20 |
| ☐ 574 | Jeromy Burnitz | .07 | .20 |
| ☐ 575 | Miguel Cabrera | .10 | .30 |
| ☐ 576 | Ramon Nivar | .07 | .20 |
| ☐ 577 | Casey Blake | .07 | .20 |
| ☐ 578 | Aaron Boone | .07 | .20 |
| ☐ 579 | Jermaine Dye | .07 | .20 |
| ☐ 580 | Jerome Williams | .07 | .20 |
| ☐ 581 | John Olerud | .07 | .20 |
| ☐ 582 | Scott Rolen | .10 | .30 |
| ☐ 583 | Bobby Kielty | .07 | .20 |
| ☐ 584 | Travis Lee | .07 | .20 |
| ☐ 585 | Jeff Cirillo | .07 | .20 |
| ☐ 586 | Scott Spiezio | .07 | .20 |
| ☐ 587 | Spanky Randolph | .07 | .20 |
| ☐ 588 | Melvin Mora | .07 | .20 |
| ☐ 589 | Mike Timlin | .07 | .20 |
| ☐ 590 | Kerry Wood | .07 | .20 |
| ☐ 591 | Tony Womack | .07 | .20 |
| ☐ 592 | Jody Gerut | .07 | .20 |
| ☐ 593 | Franklyn German | .07 | .20 |
| ☐ 594 | Morgan Ensberg | .07 | .20 |
| ☐ 595 | Odalis Perez | .07 | .20 |
| ☐ 596 | Michael Cuddyer | .07 | .20 |
| ☐ 597 | Jon Lieber | .07 | .20 |
| ☐ 598 | Mike Williams | .07 | .20 |
| ☐ 599 | Jose Hernandez | .07 | .20 |
| ☐ 600 | Alfonso Soriano | .07 | .20 |
| ☐ 601 | Marquis Grissom | .07 | .20 |
| ☐ 602 | Matt Morris | .07 | .20 |
| ☐ 603 | Damian Rolls | .07 | .20 |
| ☐ 604 | Juan Gonzalez | .07 | .20 |
| ☐ 605 | Aquilino Lopez | .07 | .20 |
| ☐ 606 | Jose Valverde | .07 | .20 |
| ☐ 607 | Kenny Rogers | .07 | .20 |
| ☐ 608 | Joe Borowski | .07 | .20 |
| ☐ 609 | Josh Bard | .07 | .20 |
| ☐ 610 | Austin Kearns | .07 | .20 |
| ☐ 611 | Chin-Hui Tsao | .07 | .20 |
| ☐ 612 | Wil Ledezma | .07 | .20 |
| ☐ 613 | Aaron Guiel | .07 | .20 |
| ☐ 614 | LaTroy Hawkins | .07 | .20 |
| ☐ 615 | Tony Armas Jr. | .07 | .20 |

| # | Card | | |
|---|---|---|---|
| ☐ 616 | Steve Trachsel | .07 | .20 |
| ☐ 617 | Ted Lilly | .07 | .20 |
| ☐ 618 | Todd Pratt | .07 | .20 |
| ☐ 619 | Sean Burroughs | .07 | .20 |
| ☐ 620 | Rafael Palmeiro | .10 | .30 |
| ☐ 621 | Jeremi Gonzalez | .07 | .20 |
| ☐ 622 | Quinton McCracken | .07 | .20 |
| ☐ 623 | David Ortiz | .20 | .50 |
| ☐ 624 | Randall Simon | .07 | .20 |
| ☐ 625 | Wily Mo Pena | .07 | .20 |
| ☐ 626 | Nate Cornejo | .07 | .20 |
| ☐ 627 | Brian Anderson | .07 | .20 |
| ☐ 628 | Corey Koskie | .07 | .20 |
| ☐ 629 | Keith Foulke | .07 | .20 |
| ☐ 630 | Rheal Cormier | .07 | .20 |
| ☐ 631 | Sidney Ponson | .07 | .20 |
| ☐ 632 | Gary Matthews Jr. | .07 | .20 |
| ☐ 633 | Herbert Perry | .07 | .20 |
| ☐ 634 | Shea Hillenbrand | .07 | .20 |
| ☐ 635 | Craig Biggio | .10 | .30 |
| ☐ 636 | Barry Larkin | .10 | .30 |
| ☐ 637 | Arthur Rhodes | .07 | .20 |
| ☐ 638 | Anaheim Angels TC | .07 | .20 |
| ☐ 639 | Arizona Diamondbacks TC | .07 | .20 |
| ☐ 640 | Atlanta Braves TC | .07 | .20 |
| ☐ 641 | Baltimore Orioles TC | .07 | .20 |
| ☐ 642 | Boston Red Sox TC | .10 | .30 |
| ☐ 643 | Chicago Cubs TC | .07 | .20 |
| ☐ 644 | Chicago White Sox TC | .07 | .20 |
| ☐ 645 | Cincinnati Reds TC | .07 | .20 |
| ☐ 646 | Cleveland Indians TC | .07 | .20 |
| ☐ 647 | Colorado Rockies TC | .07 | .20 |
| ☐ 648 | Detroit Tigers TC | .07 | .20 |
| ☐ 649 | Florida Marlins TC | .07 | .20 |
| ☐ 650 | Houston Astros TC | .07 | .20 |
| ☐ 651 | Kansas City Royals TC | .07 | .20 |
| ☐ 652 | Los Angeles Dodgers TC | .07 | .20 |
| ☐ 653 | Milwaukee Brewers TC | .07 | .20 |
| ☐ 654 | Minnesota Twins TC | .07 | .20 |
| ☐ 655 | Montreal Expos TC | .07 | .20 |
| ☐ 656 | New York Mets TC | .07 | .20 |
| ☐ 657 | New York Yankees TC | .20 | .50 |
| ☐ 658 | Oakland Athletics TC | .07 | .20 |
| ☐ 659 | Philadelphia Phillies TC | .07 | .20 |
| ☐ 660 | Pittsburgh Pirates TC | .07 | .20 |
| ☐ 661 | San Diego Padres TC | .07 | .20 |
| ☐ 662 | San Francisco Giants TC | .07 | .20 |
| ☐ 663 | Seattle Mariners TC | .07 | .20 |
| ☐ 664 | St. Louis Cardinals TC | .07 | .20 |
| ☐ 665 | Tampa Bay Devil Rays TC | .07 | .20 |
| ☐ 666 | Texas Rangers TC | .07 | .20 |
| ☐ 667 | Toronto Blue Jays TC | .07 | .20 |
| ☐ 668 | Kyle Sleeth DP RC | .20 | .50 |
| ☐ 669 | Bradley Sullivan DP RC | .20 | .50 |
| ☐ 670 | Carlos Quentin DP RC | 1.00 | 2.50 |
| ☐ 671 | Conor Jackson DP RC | 1.25 | 3.00 |
| ☐ 672 | Jeffrey Allison DP RC | .20 | .50 |
| ☐ 673 | Matthew Moses DP RC | .40 | 1.00 |
| ☐ 674 | Tim Stauffer DP RC | .30 | .75 |
| ☐ 675 | Estee Harris DP RC | .20 | .50 |
| ☐ 676 | David Aardsma DP RC | .20 | .50 |
| ☐ 677 | Omar Quintanilla DP RC | .20 | .50 |
| ☐ 678 | Aaron Hill DP | .20 | .50 |
| ☐ 679 | Tony Richie DP RC | .20 | .50 |
| ☐ 680 | Lastings Milledge DP RC | 1.50 | 4.00 |
| ☐ 681 | Brad Snyder DP RC | .20 | .50 |
| ☐ 682 | Jason Hirsh DP RC | .60 | 1.50 |
| ☐ 683 | Logan Kensing DP RC | .20 | .50 |
| ☐ 684 | Chris Lubanski DP | .20 | .50 |
| ☐ 685 | Ryan Harvey DP | .20 | .50 |
| ☐ 686 | Ryan Wagner DP | .20 | .50 |
| ☐ 687 | Rickie Weeks DP | .20 | .50 |
| ☐ 688 | G.Szemanol/J.Guthrie | .20 | .50 |
| ☐ 689 | E.Jackson/G.Miller | .20 | .50 |
| ☐ 690 | J.Reed/N.Cotts | .20 | .50 |
| ☐ 691 | A.Loewen/N.Markakis | .20 | .50 |
| ☐ 692 | B.Upton/D.Young | .20 | .50 |
| ☐ 693 | A.Rodriguez/D.Jeter | .60 | 1.50 |
| ☐ 694 | I.Suzuki/A.Pujols | .40 | 1.00 |
| ☐ 695 | J.Thome/M.Schmidt | .40 | 1.00 |
| ☐ 696 | Mike Mussina GG | .07 | .20 |
| ☐ 697 | Bengie Molina GG | .07 | .20 |
| ☐ 698 | John Olerud GG | .07 | .20 |
| ☐ 699 | Bret Boone GG | .07 | .20 |
| ☐ 700 | Eric Chavez GG | .07 | .20 |
| ☐ 701 | Alex Rodriguez GG | .20 | .50 |
| ☐ 702 | Mike Cameron GG | .07 | .20 |
| ☐ 703 | Ichiro Suzuki GG | .20 | .50 |

| # | Card | | |
|---|---|---|---|
| ☐ 704 | Torii Hunter GG | .07 | .20 |
| ☐ 705 | Mike Hampton GG | .07 | .20 |
| ☐ 706 | Mike Matheny GG | .07 | .20 |
| ☐ 707 | Derrek Lee GG | .07 | .20 |
| ☐ 708 | Luis Castillo GG | .07 | .20 |
| ☐ 709 | Scott Rolen GG | .07 | .20 |
| ☐ 710 | Edgar Renteria GG | .07 | .20 |
| ☐ 711 | Andruw Jones GG | .07 | .20 |
| ☐ 712 | Jose Cruz Jr. GG | .07 | .20 |
| ☐ 713 | Jim Edmonds GG | .07 | .20 |
| ☐ 714 | Roy Halladay CY | .07 | .20 |
| ☐ 715 | Eric Gagne CY | .07 | .20 |
| ☐ 716 | Alex Rodriguez MVP | .20 | .50 |
| ☐ 717 | Angel Berroa ROY | .07 | .20 |
| ☐ 718 | Dontrelle Willis ROY | .07 | .20 |
| ☐ 719 | Todd Helton AS | .07 | .20 |
| ☐ 720 | Marcus Giles AS | .07 | .20 |
| ☐ 721 | Edgar Renteria AS | .07 | .20 |
| ☐ 722 | Scott Rolen AS | .07 | .20 |
| ☐ 723 | Albert Pujols AS | .20 | .50 |
| ☐ 724 | Gary Sheffield AS | .07 | .20 |
| ☐ 725 | Javy Lopez AS | .07 | .20 |
| ☐ 726 | Eric Gagne AS | .07 | .20 |
| ☐ 727 | Randy Wolf AS | .07 | .20 |
| ☐ 728 | Bobby Cox AS | .07 | .20 |
| ☐ 729 | Scott Podsednik AS | .07 | .20 |
| ☐ 730 | Alex Gonzalez WS | .10 | .30 |
| ☐ 731 | Brad Penny WS | .10 | .30 |
| ☐ 732 | Beckett/I.Fod/A.Gonz WS | .10 | .30 |
| ☐ 733 | Josh Beckett WS MVP | .10 | .30 |

## 2005 Topps

| | | |
|---|---|---|
| ☐ COMP.HOBBY SET (737) | 40.00 | 80.00 |
| ☐ COMP.HOLIDAY SET (742) | 40.00 | 80.00 |
| ☐ COMP.CUBS SET (737) | 40.00 | 80.00 |
| ☐ COMP.GIANTS SET (737) | 40.00 | 80.00 |
| ☐ COMP.NATIONALS SET (737) | 40.00 | 80.00 |
| ☐ COMP.RED SOX SET (737) | 40.00 | 80.00 |
| ☐ COMP.TIGERS SET (737) | 40.00 | 80.00 |
| ☐ COMP.YANKEES SET (737) | 40.00 | 80.00 |
| ☐ COMPLETE SET (732) | 40.00 | 80.00 |
| ☐ COMPLETE SERIES 1 (366) | 20.00 | 40.00 |
| ☐ COMPLETE SERIES 2 (366) | 20.00 | 40.00 |
| ☐ COMMON CARD (1-6/8-734) | .07 | .20 |
| ☐ COMMON (297-326/668-687) | .20 | .50 |
| ☐ COMMON (327-331/688-692) | .20 | .50 |
| ☐ COMMON (349-355/368/731-734) | .40 | 1.00 |
| ☐ CARD NUMBER 7 DOES NOT EXIST | | |
| ☐ OVERALL PLATE SER.1 ODDS 1:154 HTA | | |
| ☐ OVERALL PLATE SER.2 ODDS 1:112 HTA | | |
| ☐ PLATE PRINT RUN 1 SET PER COLOR | | |
| ☐ BLACK-CYAN-MAGENTA-YELLOW ISSUED | | |
| ☐ NO PLATE PRICING DUE TO SCARCITY | | |
| ☐ 1 Alex Rodriguez | .40 | 1.00 |
| ☐ 2 Placido Polanco | .07 | .20 |
| ☐ 3 Torii Hunter | .07 | .20 |
| ☐ 4 Lyle Overbay | .07 | .20 |
| ☐ 5 Johnny Damon | .10 | .30 |
| ☐ 6 Johnny Estrada | .07 | .20 |
| ☐ 8 Francisco Rodriguez | .07 | .20 |
| ☐ 9 Jason LaRue | .07 | .20 |
| ☐ 10 Sammy Sosa | .20 | .50 |
| ☐ 11 Randy Wolf | .07 | .20 |
| ☐ 12 Jason Bay | .20 | .50 |
| ☐ 13 Tom Glavine | .10 | .30 |
| ☐ 14 Michael Tucker | .07 | .20 |
| ☐ 15 Brian Giles | .07 | .20 |
| ☐ 16 Dan Wilson | .07 | .20 |
| ☐ 17 Jim Edmonds | .07 | .20 |
| ☐ 18 Danys Baez | .07 | .20 |
| ☐ 19 Roy Halladay | .07 | .20 |
| ☐ 20 Hank Blalock | .07 | .20 |
| ☐ 21 Darin Erstad | .07 | .20 |
| ☐ 22 Robby Hammock | .07 | .20 |

|  |  | | |
|---|--------|---|---|
| ☐ 23 | Mike Hampton | .07 | .20 |
| ☐ 24 | Mark Bellhorn | .07 | .20 |
| ☐ 25 | Jim Thome | .10 | .30 |
| ☐ 26 | Scott Schoeneweis | .07 | .20 |
| ☐ 27 | Jody Gerut | .07 | .20 |
| ☐ 28 | Vinny Castilla | .07 | .20 |
| ☐ 29 | Luis Castillo | .07 | .20 |
| ☐ 30 | Ivan Rodriguez | .10 | .30 |
| ☐ 31 | Craig Biggio | .10 | .30 |
| ☐ 32 | Joe Randa | .07 | .20 |
| ☐ 33 | Adrian Beltre | .07 | .20 |
| ☐ 34 | Scott Podsednik | .07 | .20 |
| ☐ 35 | Cliff Floyd | .07 | .20 |
| ☐ 36 | Livan Hernandez | .07 | .20 |
| ☐ 37 | Eric Byrnes | .07 | .20 |
| ☐ 38 | Gabe Kapler | .07 | .20 |
| ☐ 39 | Jack Wilson | .07 | .20 |
| ☐ 40 | Gary Sheffield | .07 | .20 |
| ☐ 41 | Chan Ho Park | .07 | .20 |
| ☐ 42 | Carl Crawford | .07 | .20 |
| ☐ 43 | Miguel Batista | .07 | .20 |
| ☐ 44 | David Bell | .07 | .20 |
| ☐ 45 | Jeff DaVanon | .07 | .20 |
| ☐ 46 | Brandon Webb | .07 | .20 |
| ☐ 47 | Bronson Arroyo | .07 | .20 |
| ☐ 48 | Melvin Mora | .07 | .20 |
| ☐ 49 | David Ortiz | .20 | .50 |
| ☐ 50 | Andruw Jones | .10 | .30 |
| ☐ 51 | Chone Figgins | .07 | .20 |
| ☐ 52 | Danny Graves | .07 | .20 |
| ☐ 53 | Preston Wilson | .07 | .20 |
| ☐ 54 | Jeremy Bonderman | .07 | .20 |
| ☐ 55 | Chad Fox | .07 | .20 |
| ☐ 56 | Dan Miceli | .07 | .20 |
| ☐ 57 | Jimmy Gobble | .07 | .20 |
| ☐ 58 | Darren Dreifort | .07 | .20 |
| ☐ 59 | Matt LeCroy | .07 | .20 |
| ☐ 60 | Jose Vidro | .07 | .20 |
| ☐ 61 | Al Leiter | .07 | .20 |
| ☐ 62 | Javier Vazquez | .07 | .20 |
| ☐ 63 | Erubiel Durazo | .07 | .20 |
| ☐ 64 | Doug Glanville | .07 | .20 |
| ☐ 65 | Scot Shields | .07 | .20 |
| ☐ 66 | Edgardo Alfonzo | .07 | .20 |
| ☐ 67 | Ryan Franklin | .07 | .20 |
| ☐ 68 | Francisco Cordero | .07 | .20 |
| ☐ 69 | Brett Myers | .07 | .20 |
| ☐ 70 | Curt Schilling | .10 | .30 |
| ☐ 71 | Matt Kata | .07 | .20 |
| ☐ 72 | Mark DeRosa | .07 | .20 |
| ☐ 73 | Rodrigo Lopez | .07 | .20 |
| ☐ 74 | Tim Wakefield | .10 | .30 |
| ☐ 75 | Frank Thomas | .20 | .50 |
| ☐ 76 | Jimmy Rollins | .07 | .20 |
| ☐ 77 | Barry Zito | .07 | .20 |
| ☐ 78 | Hideo Nomo | .20 | .50 |
| ☐ 79 | Brad Wilkerson | .07 | .20 |
| ☐ 80 | Adam Dunn | .07 | .20 |
| ☐ 81 | Billy Traber | .07 | .20 |
| ☐ 82 | Fernando Vina | .07 | .20 |
| ☐ 83 | Nate Robertson | .07 | .20 |
| ☐ 84 | Brad Ausmus | .07 | .20 |
| ☐ 85 | Mike Sweeney | .07 | .20 |
| ☐ 86 | Kip Wells | .07 | .20 |
| ☐ 87 | Chris Reitsma | .07 | .20 |
| ☐ 88 | Zach Day | .07 | .20 |
| ☐ 89 | Tony Clark | .07 | .20 |
| ☐ 90 | Bret Boone | .07 | .20 |
| ☐ 91 | Mark Loretta | .07 | .20 |
| ☐ 92 | Jerome Williams | .07 | .20 |
| ☐ 93 | Randy Wirin | .07 | .20 |
| ☐ 94 | Marlon Anderson | .07 | .20 |
| ☐ 95 | Aubrey Huff | .07 | .20 |
| ☐ 96 | Kevin Mench | .07 | .20 |
| ☐ 97 | Frank Catalanotto | .07 | .20 |
| ☐ 98 | Flash Gordon | .07 | .20 |
| ☐ 99 | Scott Hatteberg | .07 | .20 |
| ☐ 100 | Albert Pujols | .40 | 1.00 |
| ☐ 101 | Jose/Bengie Molina | .20 | .50 |
| ☐ 102 | Oscar Villarreal | .07 | .20 |
| ☐ 103 | Jay Gibbons | .07 | .20 |
| ☐ 104 | Byung-Hyun Kim | .10 | .30 |
| ☐ 105 | Joe Borowski | .07 | .20 |
| ☐ 106 | Mark Grudzielanek | .07 | .20 |
| ☐ 107 | Mark Buehrle | .07 | .20 |
| ☐ 108 | Paul Wilson | .07 | .20 |
| ☐ 109 | Ronnie Belliard | .07 | .20 |
| ☐ 110 | Reggie Sanders | .07 | .20 |
| ☐ 111 | Tim Redding | .07 | .20 |
| ☐ 112 | Brian Lawrence | .07 | .20 |
| ☐ 113 | Darrell May | .07 | .20 |
| ☐ 114 | Jose Hernandez | .07 | .20 |
| ☐ 115 | Ben Sheets | .07 | .20 |
| ☐ 116 | Johan Santana | .20 | .50 |
| ☐ 117 | Billy Wagner | .07 | .20 |
| ☐ 118 | Mariano Rivera | .20 | .50 |
| ☐ 119 | Steve Trachsel | .07 | .20 |
| ☐ 120 | Akinori Otsuka | .07 | .20 |
| ☐ 121 | Bobby Kielty | .07 | .20 |
| ☐ 122 | Orlando Hernandez | .07 | .20 |
| ☐ 123 | Raul Ibanez | .07 | .20 |
| ☐ 124 | Mike Matheny | .07 | .20 |
| ☐ 125 | Vernon Wells | .07 | .20 |
| ☐ 126 | Jason Isringhausen | .07 | .20 |
| ☐ 127 | Jose Guillen | .07 | .20 |
| ☐ 128 | Danny Bautista | .07 | .20 |
| ☐ 129 | Marcus Giles | .07 | .20 |
| ☐ 130 | Javy Lopez | .07 | .20 |
| ☐ 131 | Kevin Millar | .07 | .20 |
| ☐ 132 | Kyle Farnsworth | .07 | .20 |
| ☐ 133 | Carl Pavano | .07 | .20 |
| ☐ 134 | D'Angelo Jimenez | .07 | .20 |
| ☐ 135 | Casey Blake | .07 | .20 |
| ☐ 136 | Matt Holliday | .08 | .25 |
| ☐ 137 | Bobby Higginson | .07 | .20 |
| ☐ 138 | Nate Field | .07 | .20 |
| ☐ 139 | Alex Gonzalez | .07 | .20 |
| ☐ 140 | Jeff Kent | .07 | .20 |
| ☐ 141 | Aaron Guiel | .07 | .20 |
| ☐ 142 | Shawn Green | .07 | .20 |
| ☐ 143 | Bill Hall | .07 | .20 |
| ☐ 144 | Shannon Stewart | .07 | .20 |
| ☐ 145 | Juan Rivera | .07 | .20 |
| ☐ 146 | Coco Crisp | .07 | .20 |
| ☐ 147 | Mike Mussina | .10 | .30 |
| ☐ 148 | Eric Chavez | .07 | .20 |
| ☐ 149 | Jon Lieber | .07 | .20 |
| ☐ 150 | Vladimir Guerrero | .20 | .50 |
| ☐ 151 | Alex Cintron | .07 | .20 |
| ☐ 152 | Horacio Ramirez | .07 | .20 |
| ☐ 153 | Sidney Ponson | .07 | .20 |
| ☐ 154 | Trot Nixon | .10 | .30 |
| ☐ 155 | Greg Maddux | .30 | .75 |
| ☐ 156 | Edgar Renteria | .07 | .20 |
| ☐ 157 | Ryan Freel | .07 | .20 |
| ☐ 158 | Matt Lawton | .07 | .20 |
| ☐ 159 | Shawn Chacon | .07 | .20 |
| ☐ 160 | Josh Beckett | .07 | .20 |
| ☐ 161 | Ken Harvey | .07 | .20 |
| ☐ 162 | Juan Cruz | .07 | .20 |
| ☐ 163 | Juan Encarnacion | .07 | .20 |
| ☐ 164 | Wes Helms | .07 | .20 |
| ☐ 165 | Brad Radke | .07 | .20 |
| ☐ 166 | Claudio Vargas | .07 | .20 |
| ☐ 167 | Mike Cameron | .07 | .20 |
| ☐ 168 | Billy Koch | .07 | .20 |
| ☐ 169 | Bobby Crosby | .07 | .20 |
| ☐ 170 | Mike Lieberthal | .07 | .20 |
| ☐ 171 | Rob Mackowiak | .07 | .20 |
| ☐ 172 | Sean Burroughs | .07 | .20 |
| ☐ 173 | J.T. Snow Jr. | .07 | .20 |
| ☐ 174 | Paul Konerko | .07 | .20 |
| ☐ 175 | Luis Gonzalez | .07 | .20 |
| ☐ 176 | John Lackey | .07 | .20 |
| ☐ 177 | Antonio Alfonseca | .07 | .20 |
| ☐ 178 | Brian Roberts | .07 | .20 |
| ☐ 179 | Bill Mueller | .07 | .20 |
| ☐ 180 | Carlos Lee | .07 | .20 |
| ☐ 181 | Corey Patterson | .07 | .20 |
| ☐ 182 | Sean Casey | .07 | .20 |
| ☐ 183 | Cliff Lee | .07 | .20 |
| ☐ 184 | Jason Jennings | .07 | .20 |
| ☐ 185 | Dmitri Young | .07 | .20 |
| ☐ 186 | Juan Uribe | .07 | .20 |
| ☐ 187 | Andy Pettitte | .10 | .30 |
| ☐ 188 | Juan Gonzalez | .20 | .50 |
| ☐ 189 | Pokey Reese | .07 | .20 |
| ☐ 190 | Jason Phillips | .07 | .20 |
| ☐ 191 | Rocky Biddle | .07 | .20 |
| ☐ 192 | Lew Ford | .07 | .20 |
| ☐ 193 | Mark Mulder | .07 | .20 |
| ☐ 194 | Bobby Abreu | .07 | .20 |
| ☐ 195 | Jason Kendall | .07 | .20 |
| ☐ 196 | Terrence Long | .07 | .20 |
| ☐ 197 | A.J. Pierzynski | .07 | .20 |
| ☐ 198 | Eddie Guardado | .07 | .20 |
| ☐ 199 | So Taguchi | .07 | .20 |
| ☐ 200 | Jason Giambi | .07 | .20 |
| ☐ 201 | Tony Batista | .07 | .20 |
| ☐ 202 | Kyle Lohse | .07 | .20 |
| ☐ 203 | Trevor Hoffman | .07 | .20 |
| ☐ 204 | Tike Redman | .07 | .20 |
| ☐ 205 | Matt Herges | .07 | .20 |
| ☐ 206 | Gil Meche | .07 | .20 |
| ☐ 207 | Chris Carpenter | .07 | .20 |
| ☐ 208 | Ben Broussard | .07 | .20 |
| ☐ 209 | Eric Young | .07 | .20 |
| ☐ 210 | Doug Waechter | .07 | .20 |
| ☐ 211 | Jarrod Washburn | .07 | .20 |
| ☐ 212 | Chad Tracy | .07 | .20 |
| ☐ 213 | John Smoltz | .10 | .30 |
| ☐ 214 | Jorge Julio | .07 | .20 |
| ☐ 215 | Todd Walker | .07 | .20 |
| ☐ 216 | Shingo Takatsu | .07 | .20 |
| ☐ 217 | Jose Acevedo | .07 | .20 |
| ☐ 218 | David Riske | .07 | .20 |
| ☐ 219 | Shawn Estes | .07 | .20 |
| ☐ 220 | Lance Berkman | .07 | .20 |
| ☐ 221 | Carlos Guillen | .07 | .20 |
| ☐ 222 | Jeremy Affeldt | .07 | .20 |
| ☐ 223 | Cesar Izturis | .07 | .20 |
| ☐ 224 | Scott Sullivan | .07 | .20 |
| ☐ 225 | Kazuo Matsui | .07 | .20 |
| ☐ 226 | Josh Fogg | .07 | .20 |
| ☐ 227 | Jason Schmidt | .07 | .20 |
| ☐ 228 | Jason Marquis | .07 | .20 |
| ☐ 229 | Scott Spiezio | .07 | .20 |
| ☐ 230 | Miguel Tejada | .07 | .20 |
| ☐ 231 | Bartolo Colon | .07 | .20 |
| ☐ 232 | Jose Valverde | .07 | .20 |
| ☐ 233 | Derrek Lee | .10 | .30 |
| ☐ 234 | Scott Williamson | .07 | .20 |
| ☐ 235 | Joe Crede | .07 | .20 |
| ☐ 236 | John Thomson | .07 | .20 |
| ☐ 237 | Mike MacDougal | .07 | .20 |
| ☐ 238 | Eric Gagne | .07 | .20 |
| ☐ 239 | Alex Sanchez | .07 | .20 |
| ☐ 240 | Miguel Cabrera | .10 | .30 |
| ☐ 241 | Luis Rivas | .07 | .20 |
| ☐ 242 | Adam Everett | .07 | .20 |
| ☐ 243 | Jason Johnson | .07 | .20 |
| ☐ 244 | Travis Hafner | .07 | .20 |
| ☐ 245 | Jose Valentin | .07 | .20 |
| ☐ 246 | Stephen Randolph | .07 | .20 |
| ☐ 247 | Rafael Furcal | .07 | .20 |
| ☐ 248 | Adam Kennedy | .07 | .20 |
| ☐ 249 | Luis Matos | .07 | .20 |
| ☐ 250 | Mark Prior | .10 | .30 |
| ☐ 251 | Angel Berroa | .07 | .20 |
| ☐ 252 | Phil Nevin | .07 | .20 |
| ☐ 253 | Oliver Perez | .07 | .20 |
| ☐ 254 | Orlando Hudson | .07 | .20 |
| ☐ 255 | Braden Looper | .07 | .20 |
| ☐ 256 | Khalil Greene | .10 | .30 |
| ☐ 257 | Tim Worrell | .07 | .20 |
| ☐ 258 | Carlos Zambrano | .07 | .20 |
| ☐ 259 | Odalis Perez | .07 | .20 |
| ☐ 260 | Gerald Laird | .07 | .20 |
| ☐ 261 | Jose Cruz Jr. | .07 | .20 |
| ☐ 262 | Michael Barrett | .07 | .20 |
| ☐ 263 | Michael Young UER | .07 | .20 |
| ☐ 264 | Toby Hall | .07 | .20 |
| ☐ 265 | Woody Williams | .07 | .20 |
| ☐ 266 | Rich Harden | .07 | .20 |
| ☐ 267 | Mike Scioscia MG | .07 | .20 |
| ☐ 268 | Al Pedrique MG | .07 | .20 |
| ☐ 269 | Bobby Cox MG | .07 | .20 |
| ☐ 270 | Lee Mazzilli MG | .07 | .20 |
| ☐ 271 | Terry Francona MG | .10 | .30 |
| ☐ 272 | Dusty Baker MG | .07 | .20 |
| ☐ 273 | Ozzie Guillen MG | .20 | .50 |
| ☐ 274 | Dave Miley MG | .07 | .20 |
| ☐ 275 | Eric Wedge MG | .07 | .20 |
| ☐ 276 | Clint Hurdle MG | .07 | .20 |
| ☐ 277 | Alan Trammell MG | .07 | .20 |
| ☐ 278 | Jack McKeon MG | .07 | .20 |
| ☐ 279 | Phil Garner MG | .07 | .20 |
| ☐ 280 | Tony Pena MG | .07 | .20 |
| ☐ 281 | Jim Tracy MG | .07 | .20 |
| ☐ 282 | Ned Yost MG | .07 | .20 |
| ☐ 283 | Ron Gardenhire MG | .07 | .20 |
| ☐ 284 | Frank Robinson MG | .07 | .20 |
| ☐ 285 | Art Howe MG | .07 | .20 |
| ☐ 286 | Joe Torre MG | .10 | .30 |

| # | Card | | |
|---|---|---|---|
| 287 | Ken Macha MG | .07 | .20 |
| 288 | Larry Bowa MG | .07 | .20 |
| 289 | Lloyd McClendon MG | .07 | .20 |
| 290 | Bruce Bochy MG | .07 | .20 |
| 291 | Felipe Alou MG | .07 | .20 |
| 292 | Bob Melvin MG | .07 | .20 |
| 293 | Tony LaRussa MG | .07 | .20 |
| 294 | Lou Piniella MG | .07 | .20 |
| 295 | Buck Showalter MG | .07 | .20 |
| 296 | John Gibbons MG | .07 | .20 |
| 297 | Steve Doetsch FY RC | .30 | .75 |
| 298 | Melky Cabrera FY RC | .75 | 2.00 |
| 299 | Luis Ramirez FY RC | .20 | .50 |
| 300 | Chris Seddon FY RC | .20 | .50 |
| 301 | Nate Schierholtz FY | .30 | .75 |
| 302 | Ian Kinsler FY RC | 1.50 | 4.00 |
| 303 | Brandon Moss FY RC | .60 | 1.50 |
| 304 | Chadd Blasko FY RC | .30 | .75 |
| 305 | Jeremy West FY | .30 | .75 |
| 306 | Sean Marshall FY RC | .60 | 1.50 |
| 307 | Matt DeSalvo FY RC | .30 | .75 |
| 308 | Ryan Sweeney FY RC | .40 | 1.00 |
| 309 | Matthew Lindstrom FY RC | .20 | .50 |
| 310 | Ryan Goleski FY RC | .30 | .75 |
| 311 | Brett Harper FY RC | .30 | .75 |
| 312 | Chris Roberson FY RC | .20 | .50 |
| 313 | Andre Ethier FY RC | 2.00 | 5.00 |
| 314 | Chris Denorfia FY RC | .40 | 1.00 |
| 315 | Ian Bladergroen FY RC | .30 | .75 |
| 316 | Darren Fenster FY RC | .20 | .50 |
| 317 | Kevin West FY RC | .20 | .50 |
| 318 | Chaz Lytle FY RC | .30 | .75 |
| 319 | James Jurries FY RC | .30 | .75 |
| 320 | Matt Rogelstad FY RC | .20 | .50 |
| 321 | Wade Robinson FY RC | .20 | .50 |
| 322 | Jake Dittler FY | .20 | .50 |
| 323 | Brian Stavisky FY RC | .20 | .50 |
| 324 | Kole Strayhorn FY RC | .20 | .50 |
| 325 | Jose Vaquedano FY RC | .20 | .50 |
| 326 | Elvys Quezada FY RC | .20 | .50 |
| 327 | J.Maine/V.Majewski FS | .20 | .50 |
| 328 | R.Weeks/J.Hardy FS | .20 | .50 |
| 329 | G.Gross/G.Quinz FS | .20 | .50 |
| 330 | D.Wright/C.Brazell FS | 1.25 | 3.00 |
| 331 | D.McPherson/J.Mathis FS | .20 | .50 |
| 332 | Randy Johnson SH | .10 | .30 |
| 333 | Randy Johnson SH | .10 | .30 |
| 334 | Ichiro Suzuki SH | .20 | .50 |
| 335 | Ken Griffey Jr. SH | .20 | .50 |
| 336 | Greg Maddux SH | .20 | .50 |
| 337 | Ichiro/Mora/Guerrero LL | .20 | .50 |
| 338 | Ichiro/Young/Guerrero LL | .20 | .50 |
| 339 | Manny/Konerko/Ortiz LL | .10 | .30 |
| 340 | Tejada/Ortiz/Manny LL | .20 | .50 |
| 341 | Johan/Schill/West LL | .10 | .30 |
| 342 | Johan/Pedro/Schill LL | .10 | .30 |
| 343 | Helton/Loretta/Beltre LL | .07 | .20 |
| 344 | Pierre/Loretta/Wilson LL | .07 | .20 |
| 345 | Beltre/Dunn/Pujols LL | .20 | .50 |
| 346 | Castilla/Rolen/Pujols LL | .20 | .50 |
| 347 | Peavy/Johnson/Sheets LL | .10 | .30 |
| 348 | Johnson/Sheets/Schmidt LL | .10 | .30 |
| 349 | A.Rodriguez/R.Sierra ALDS | .40 | 1.00 |
| 350 | L.Walker/A.Pujols NLDS | .40 | 1.00 |
| 351 | C.Schilling/D.Ortiz ALDS | .40 | 1.00 |
| 352 | Curt Schilling WS2 | .40 | 1.00 |
| 353 | Sox Celeb/Ortiz-Schil ALCS | .40 | 1.00 |
| 354 | Cards Celeb/Puj-Edm NLCS | .40 | 1.00 |
| 355 | Mark Bellhorn WS1 | .40 | 1.00 |
| 356 | Paul Konerko AS | .07 | .20 |
| 357 | Alfonso Soriano AS | .07 | .20 |
| 358 | Miguel Tejada AS | .07 | .20 |
| 359 | Melvin Mora AS | .07 | .20 |
| 360 | Vladimir Guerrero AS | .10 | .30 |
| 361 | Ichiro Suzuki AS | .20 | .50 |
| 362 | Manny Ramirez AS | .10 | .30 |
| 363 | Ivan Rodriguez AS | .07 | .20 |
| 364 | Johan Santana AS | .10 | .30 |
| 365 | Paul Konerko AS | .07 | .20 |
| 366 | David Ortiz AS | .10 | .30 |
| 367 | Bobby Crosby AS | .07 | .20 |
| 368 | Sox Celeb/Ram-Lowe WS4 | .60 | 1.50 |
| 369 | Garret Anderson | .20 | .50 |
| 370 | Randy Johnson | .20 | .50 |
| 371 | Charles Thomas | .07 | .20 |
| 372 | Rafael Palmeiro | .10 | .30 |
| 373 | Kevin Youkilis | .20 | .50 |
| 374 | Freddy Garcia | .07 | .20 |
| 375 | Maggio Ordonez | .07 | .20 |
| 376 | Aaron Harang | .07 | .20 |
| 377 | Grady Sizemore | .10 | .30 |
| 378 | Chin-Hui Tsao | .07 | .20 |
| 379 | Eric Munson | .07 | .20 |
| 380 | Juan Pierre | .07 | .20 |
| 381 | Brad Lidge | .07 | .20 |
| 382 | Brian Anderson | .07 | .20 |
| 383 | Alex Cora | .07 | .20 |
| 384 | Brady Clark | .07 | .20 |
| 385 | Todd Helton | .10 | .30 |
| 386 | Chad Cordero | .07 | .20 |
| 387 | Kris Benson | .07 | .20 |
| 388 | Brad Halsey | .07 | .20 |
| 389 | Jermaine Dye | .07 | .20 |
| 390 | Manny Ramirez | .10 | .30 |
| 391 | Daryle Ward | .07 | .20 |
| 392 | Adam Eaton | .07 | .20 |
| 393 | Brett Tomko | .07 | .20 |
| 394 | Bucky Jacobsen | .07 | .20 |
| 395 | Dontrelle Willis | .07 | .20 |
| 396 | B.J. Upton | .20 | .50 |
| 397 | Rocco Baldelli | .07 | .20 |
| 398 | Ted Lilly | .07 | .20 |
| 399 | Ryan Drese | .07 | .20 |
| 400 | Ichiro Suzuki | .40 | 1.00 |
| 401 | Brendan Donnelly | .07 | .20 |
| 402 | Brandon Lyon | .07 | .20 |
| 403 | Nick Green | .07 | .20 |
| 404 | Jerry Hairston Jr. | .07 | .20 |
| 405 | Mike Lowell | .07 | .20 |
| 406 | Kerry Wood | .07 | .20 |
| 407 | Carl Everett | .07 | .20 |
| 408 | Hideki Matsui | .30 | .75 |
| 409 | Omar Vizquel | .10 | .30 |
| 410 | Joe Kennedy | .07 | .20 |
| 411 | Carlos Pena | .07 | .20 |
| 412 | Armando Benitez | .07 | .20 |
| 413 | Carlos Beltran | .20 | .50 |
| 414 | Kevin Appier | .07 | .20 |
| 415 | Jeff Weaver | .07 | .20 |
| 416 | Chad Moeller | .07 | .20 |
| 417 | Joe Mays | .07 | .20 |
| 418 | Termel Sledge | .07 | .20 |
| 419 | Richard Hidalgo | .07 | .20 |
| 420 | Kenny Lofton | .07 | .20 |
| 421 | Justin Duchscherer | .07 | .20 |
| 422 | Eric Milton | .07 | .20 |
| 423 | Jose Mesa | .07 | .20 |
| 424 | Ramon Hernandez | .07 | .20 |
| 425 | Jose Reyes | .07 | .20 |
| 426 | Joel Pineiro | .07 | .20 |
| 427 | Matt Morris | .07 | .20 |
| 428 | John Halama | .07 | .20 |
| 429 | Gary Matthews Jr. | .07 | .20 |
| 430 | Ryan Madson | .07 | .20 |
| 431 | Mark Kotsay | .07 | .20 |
| 432 | Carlos Delgado | .07 | .20 |
| 433 | Casey Kotchman | .07 | .20 |
| 434 | Greg Aquino | .07 | .20 |
| 435 | Eli Marrero | .07 | .20 |
| 436 | David Newhan | .07 | .20 |
| 437 | Mike Timlin | .07 | .20 |
| 438 | LaTroy Hawkins | .07 | .20 |
| 439 | Jose Contreras | .07 | .20 |
| 440 | Ken Griffey Jr. | .30 | .75 |
| 441 | C.C. Sabathia | .07 | .20 |
| 442 | Brandon Inge | .07 | .20 |
| 443 | Pete Munro | .07 | .20 |
| 444 | John Buck | .07 | .20 |
| 445 | Hee Seop Choi | .07 | .20 |
| 446 | Chris Capuano | .07 | .20 |
| 447 | Jesse Crain | .07 | .20 |
| 448 | Geoff Jenkins | .07 | .20 |
| 449 | Brian Schneider | .07 | .20 |
| 450 | Mike Piazza | .20 | .50 |
| 451 | Jorge Posada | .10 | .30 |
| 452 | Nick Swisher | .07 | .20 |
| 453 | Kevin Millwood | .07 | .20 |
| 454 | Mike Gonzalez | .07 | .20 |
| 455 | Jake Peavy | .07 | .20 |
| 456 | Dustin Hermanson | .07 | .20 |
| 457 | Jeremy Reed | .07 | .20 |
| 458 | Julian Tavarez | .07 | .20 |
| 459 | Geoff Blum | .07 | .20 |
| 460 | Alfonso Soriano | .07 | .20 |
| 461 | Alexis Rios | .07 | .20 |
| 462 | David Eckstein | .07 | .20 |
| 463 | Shea Hillenbrand | .07 | .20 |
| 464 | Russ Ortiz | .07 | .20 |
| 465 | Kurt Ainsworth | .07 | .20 |
| 466 | Orlando Cabrera | .07 | .20 |
| 467 | Carlos Silva | .07 | .20 |
| 468 | Ross Gload | .07 | .20 |
| 469 | Josh Phelps | .07 | .20 |
| 470 | Marquis Grissom | .07 | .20 |
| 471 | Mike Maroth | .07 | .20 |
| 472 | Guillermo Mota | .07 | .20 |
| 473 | Chris Burke | .07 | .20 |
| 474 | David DeJesus | .07 | .20 |
| 475 | Jose Lima | .07 | .20 |
| 476 | Cristian Guzman | .07 | .20 |
| 477 | Nick Johnson | .07 | .20 |
| 478 | Victor Zambrano | .07 | .20 |
| 479 | Rod Barajas | .07 | .20 |
| 480 | Damian Miller | .07 | .20 |
| 481 | Chase Utley | .10 | .30 |
| 482 | Todd Pratt | .07 | .20 |
| 483 | Sean Burnett | .07 | .20 |
| 484 | Boomer Wells | .07 | .20 |
| 485 | Dustin Mohr | .07 | .20 |
| 486 | Bobby Madritsch | .07 | .20 |
| 487 | Ray King | .07 | .20 |
| 488 | Reed Johnson | .07 | .20 |
| 489 | R.A. Dickey | .07 | .20 |
| 490 | Scott Kazmir | .07 | .20 |
| 491 | Tony Womack | .07 | .20 |
| 492 | Tomas Perez | .07 | .20 |
| 493 | Esteban Loaiza | .07 | .20 |
| 494 | Tomo Ohka | .07 | .20 |
| 495 | Mike Lamb | .07 | .20 |
| 496 | Ramon Ortiz | .07 | .20 |
| 497 | Richie Sexson | .07 | .20 |
| 498 | J.D. Drew | .07 | .20 |
| 499 | David Segui | .07 | .20 |
| 500 | Barry Bonds | .75 | 2.00 |
| 501 | Aramis Ramirez | .07 | .20 |
| 502 | Wily Mo Pena | .07 | .20 |
| 503 | Jeromy Burnitz | .07 | .20 |
| 504 | Craig Monroe | .07 | .20 |
| 505 | Nomar Garciaparra | .20 | .50 |
| 506 | Brandon Backe | .07 | .20 |
| 507 | Marcus Thames | .07 | .20 |
| 508 | Derek Lowe | .07 | .20 |
| 509 | Doug Davis | .07 | .20 |
| 510 | Joe Mauer | .20 | .50 |
| 511 | Endy Chavez | .07 | .20 |
| 512 | Bernie Williams | .10 | .30 |
| 513 | Mark Redman | .07 | .20 |
| 514 | Jason Michaels | .07 | .20 |
| 515 | Craig Wilson | .07 | .20 |
| 516 | Ryan Klesko | .07 | .20 |
| 517 | Ray Durham | .07 | .20 |
| 518 | Jose Lopez | .07 | .20 |
| 519 | Jeff Suppan | .07 | .20 |
| 520 | Julio Lugo | .07 | .20 |
| 521 | Mike Wood | .07 | .20 |
| 522 | David Bush | .07 | .20 |
| 523 | Juan Rincon | .07 | .20 |
| 524 | Paul Quantrill | .07 | .20 |
| 525 | Marlon Byrd | .07 | .20 |
| 526 | Roy Oswalt | .07 | .20 |
| 527 | Rondell White | .07 | .20 |
| 528 | Troy Glaus | .07 | .20 |
| 529 | Scott Hairston | .20 | .50 |
| 530 | Chipper Jones | .20 | .50 |
| 531 | Daniel Cabrera | .07 | .20 |
| 532 | Doug Mientkiewicz | .07 | .20 |
| 533 | Glendon Rusch | .07 | .20 |
| 534 | Jon Garland | .07 | .20 |
| 535 | Austin Kearns | .07 | .20 |
| 536 | Jake Westbrook | .07 | .20 |
| 537 | Aaron Miles | .07 | .20 |
| 538 | Omar Infante | .07 | .20 |
| 539 | Paul Lo Duca | .07 | .20 |
| 540 | Morgan Ensberg | .07 | .20 |
| 541 | Tony Graffanino | .07 | .20 |
| 542 | Milton Bradley | .07 | .20 |
| 543 | Keith Ginter | .07 | .20 |
| 544 | Justin Morneau | .20 | .50 |
| 545 | Tony Armas Jr. | .07 | .20 |
| 546 | Mike Stanton | .07 | .20 |
| 547 | Kevin Brown | .07 | .20 |
| 548 | Marco Scutaro | .07 | .20 |
| 549 | Tim Hudson | .07 | .20 |
| 550 | Pat Burrell | .07 | .20 |

|  |  | | |
|---|--------|------|------|
| ☐ 551 | Ty Wigginton | .07 | .20 |
| ☐ 552 | Jeff Cirillo | .07 | .20 |
| ☐ 553 | Jim Brower | .07 | .20 |
| ☐ 554 | Jamie Moyer | .07 | .20 |
| ☐ 555 | Larry Walker | .10 | .30 |
| ☐ 556 | Dewon Brazelton | .07 | .20 |
| ☐ 557 | Brian Jordan | .07 | .20 |
| ☐ 558 | Josh Towers | .07 | .20 |
| ☐ 559 | Shigetoshi Hasegawa | .07 | .20 |
| ☐ 560 | Octavio Dotel | .07 | .20 |
| ☐ 561 | Travis Lee | .07 | .20 |
| ☐ 562 | Michael Cuddyer | .07 | .20 |
| ☐ 563 | Junior Spivey | .07 | .20 |
| ☐ 564 | Zack Greinke | .07 | .20 |
| ☐ 565 | Roger Clemens | .30 | .75 |
| ☐ 566 | Chris Shelton | .10 | .30 |
| ☐ 567 | Ugueth Urbina | .07 | .20 |
| ☐ 568 | Rafael Betancourt | .07 | .20 |
| ☐ 569 | Willie Harris | .07 | .20 |
| ☐ 570 | Todd Hollandsworth | .07 | .20 |
| ☐ 571 | Keith Foulke | .07 | .20 |
| ☐ 572 | Larry Bigbie | .07 | .20 |
| ☐ 573 | Paul Byrd | .07 | .20 |
| ☐ 574 | Troy Percival | .07 | .20 |
| ☐ 575 | Pedro Martinez | .10 | .30 |
| ☐ 576 | Matt Clement | .07 | .20 |
| ☐ 577 | Ryan Wagner | .07 | .20 |
| ☐ 578 | Jeff Francis | .07 | .20 |
| ☐ 579 | Jeff Conine | .07 | .20 |
| ☐ 580 | Wade Miller | .07 | .20 |
| ☐ 581 | Matt Stairs | .07 | .20 |
| ☐ 582 | Gavin Floyd | .20 | .50 |
| ☐ 583 | Kazuhisa Ishii | .07 | .20 |
| ☐ 584 | Victor Santos | .07 | .20 |
| ☐ 585 | Jacque Jones | .07 | .20 |
| ☐ 586 | Sunny Kim | .07 | .20 |
| ☐ 587 | Dan Kolb | .07 | .20 |
| ☐ 588 | Cory Lidle | .07 | .20 |
| ☐ 589 | Jose Castillo | .07 | .20 |
| ☐ 590 | Alex Gonzalez | .07 | .20 |
| ☐ 591 | Kirk Rueter | .07 | .20 |
| ☐ 592 | Jolbert Cabrera | .07 | .20 |
| ☐ 593 | Erik Bedard | .07 | .20 |
| ☐ 594 | Ben Grieve | .07 | .20 |
| ☐ 595 | Ricky Ledee | .07 | .20 |
| ☐ 596 | Mark Hendrickson | .07 | .20 |
| ☐ 597 | Laynce Nix | .07 | .20 |
| ☐ 598 | Jason Frasor | .07 | .20 |
| ☐ 599 | Kevin Gregg | .07 | .20 |
| ☐ 600 | Derek Jeter | .40 | 1.00 |
| ☐ 601 | Luis Terrero | .07 | .20 |
| ☐ 602 | Jaret Wright | .07 | .20 |
| ☐ 603 | Edwin Jackson | .07 | .20 |
| ☐ 604 | Dave Roberts | .07 | .20 |
| ☐ 605 | Moises Alou | .07 | .20 |
| ☐ 606 | Aaron Rowand | .07 | .20 |
| ☐ 607 | Kazuhito Tadano | .07 | .20 |
| ☐ 608 | Luis A. Gonzalez | .07 | .20 |
| ☐ 609 | A.J. Burnett | .07 | .20 |
| ☐ 610 | Jeff Bagwell | .10 | .30 |
| ☐ 611 | Brad Penny | .07 | .20 |
| ☐ 612 | Craig Counsell | .07 | .20 |
| ☐ 613 | Corey Koskie | .07 | .20 |
| ☐ 614 | Mark Ellis | .07 | .20 |
| ☐ 615 | Felix Rodriguez | .07 | .20 |
| ☐ 616 | Jay Payton | .07 | .20 |
| ☐ 617 | Hector Luna | .07 | .20 |
| ☐ 618 | Miguel Olivo | .07 | .20 |
| ☐ 619 | Rob Bell | .07 | .20 |
| ☐ 620 | Scott Rolen | .10 | .30 |
| ☐ 621 | Ricardo Rodriguez | .07 | .20 |
| ☐ 622 | Eric Hinske | .07 | .20 |
| ☐ 623 | Tim Salmon | .10 | .30 |
| ☐ 624 | Adam LaRoche | .07 | .20 |
| ☐ 625 | B.J. Ryan | .07 | .20 |
| ☐ 626 | Roberto Alomar | .10 | .30 |
| ☐ 627 | Steve Finley | .07 | .20 |
| ☐ 628 | Joe Nathan | .07 | .20 |
| ☐ 629 | Scott Linebrink | .07 | .20 |
| ☐ 630 | Vicente Padilla | .07 | .20 |
| ☐ 631 | Raul Mondesi | .07 | .20 |
| ☐ 632 | Yadier Molina | .07 | .20 |
| ☐ 633 | Tino Martinez | .10 | .30 |
| ☐ 634 | Mark Teixeira | .10 | .30 |
| ☐ 635 | Kelvim Escobar | .07 | .20 |
| ☐ 636 | Pedro Feliz | .07 | .20 |
| ☐ 637 | Rich Aurilia | .07 | .20 |
| ☐ 638 | Los Angeles Angels TC | .07 | .20 |
| ☐ 639 | Arizona Diamondbacks TC | .07 | .20 |
| ☐ 640 | Atlanta Braves TC | .10 | .30 |
| ☐ 641 | Baltimore Orioles TC | .07 | .20 |
| ☐ 642 | Boston Red Sox TC | .20 | .50 |
| ☐ 643 | Chicago Cubs TC | .10 | .30 |
| ☐ 644 | Chicago White Sox TC | .07 | .20 |
| ☐ 645 | Cincinnati Reds TC | .07 | .20 |
| ☐ 646 | Cleveland Indians TC | .07 | .20 |
| ☐ 647 | Colorado Rockies TC | .07 | .20 |
| ☐ 648 | Detroit Tigers TC | .07 | .20 |
| ☐ 649 | Florida Marlins TC | .07 | .20 |
| ☐ 650 | Houston Astros TC | .07 | .20 |
| ☐ 651 | Kansas City Royals TC | .07 | .20 |
| ☐ 652 | Los Angeles Dodgers TC | .07 | .20 |
| ☐ 653 | Milwaukee Brewers TC | .07 | .20 |
| ☐ 654 | Minnesota Twins TC | .07 | .20 |
| ☐ 655 | Montreal Expos TC | .07 | .20 |
| ☐ 656 | New York Mets TC | .07 | .20 |
| ☐ 657 | New York Yankees TC | .20 | .50 |
| ☐ 658 | Oakland Athletics TC | .07 | .20 |
| ☐ 659 | Philadelphia Phillies TC | .07 | .20 |
| ☐ 660 | Pittsburgh Pirates TC | .07 | .20 |
| ☐ 661 | San Diego Padres TC | .07 | .20 |
| ☐ 662 | San Francisco Giants TC | .07 | .20 |
| ☐ 663 | Seattle Mariners TC | .07 | .20 |
| ☐ 664 | St. Louis Cardinals TC | .10 | .30 |
| ☐ 665 | Tampa Bay Devil Rays TC | .07 | .20 |
| ☐ 666 | Texas Rangers TC | .07 | .20 |
| ☐ 667 | Toronto Blue Jays TC | .07 | .20 |
| ☐ 668 | Billy Butler FY RC | 1.50 | 4.00 |
| ☐ 669 | Wes Swackhamer FY RC | .20 | .50 |
| ☐ 670 | Matt Campbell FY RC | .20 | .50 |
| ☐ 671 | Ryan Mullins FY RC | .20 | .50 |
| ☐ 672 | Glen Perkins FY RC | .30 | .75 |
| ☐ 673 | Michael Rogers FY RC | .20 | .50 |
| ☐ 674 | Kevin Melillo FY RC | .30 | .75 |
| ☐ 675 | Erik Cordier FY RC | .20 | .50 |
| ☐ 676 | Landon Powell FY RC | .30 | .75 |
| ☐ 677 | Justin Verlander FY RC | 1.50 | 4.00 |
| ☐ 678 | Eric Nielsen FY RC | .20 | .50 |
| ☐ 679 | Alexander Smit FY RC | .20 | .50 |
| ☐ 680 | Ryan Garko FY RC | .60 | 1.50 |
| ☐ 681 | Bobby Livingston FY RC | .20 | .50 |
| ☐ 682 | Jeff Niemann FY RC | .30 | .75 |
| ☐ 683 | Wladimir Balentien FY RC | .30 | .75 |
| ☐ 684 | Chip Cannon FY RC | .30 | .75 |
| ☐ 685 | Yorman Bazardo FY RC | .20 | .50 |
| ☐ 686 | Mike Bourn FY RC | .30 | .75 |
| ☐ 687 | Andy LaRoche FY RC | 1.25 | 3.00 |
| ☐ 688 | F.Hernandez/J.Leone | .20 | .50 |
| ☐ 689 | R.Howard/C.Hamels | 2.00 | 5.00 |
| ☐ 690 | M.Cain/M.Valdez | .40 | 1.00 |
| ☐ 691 | A.Marte/J.Francoeur | .75 | 2.00 |
| ☐ 692 | C.Billingsley/J.Guzman | .20 | .50 |
| ☐ 693 | J.Hairston Jr./S.Hairston | .07 | .20 |
| ☐ 694 | M.Tejada/L.Berkman | .10 | .30 |
| ☐ 695 | Kenny Rogers GG | .07 | .20 |
| ☐ 696 | Ivan Rodriguez GG | .07 | .20 |
| ☐ 697 | Darin Erstad GG | .07 | .20 |
| ☐ 698 | Bret Boone GG | .07 | .20 |
| ☐ 699 | Eric Chavez GG | .07 | .20 |
| ☐ 700 | Derek Jeter GG | .20 | .50 |
| ☐ 701 | Vernon Wells GG | .07 | .20 |
| ☐ 702 | Ichiro Suzuki GG | .20 | .50 |
| ☐ 703 | Torii Hunter GG | .07 | .20 |
| ☐ 704 | Greg Maddux GG | .20 | .50 |
| ☐ 705 | Mike Matheny GG | .07 | .20 |
| ☐ 706 | Todd Helton GG | .07 | .20 |
| ☐ 707 | Luis Castillo GG | .07 | .20 |
| ☐ 708 | Scott Rolen GG | .07 | .20 |
| ☐ 709 | Cesar Izturis GG | .07 | .20 |
| ☐ 710 | Jim Edmonds GG | .07 | .20 |
| ☐ 711 | Andruw Jones GG | .07 | .20 |
| ☐ 712 | Steve Finley GG | .07 | .20 |
| ☐ 713 | Johan Santana CY | .10 | .30 |
| ☐ 714 | Roger Clemens CY | .20 | .50 |
| ☐ 715 | Vladimir Guerrero MVP | .20 | .50 |
| ☐ 716 | Barry Bonds MVP | .40 | 1.00 |
| ☐ 717 | Bobby Crosby ROY | .07 | .20 |
| ☐ 718 | Jason Bay ROY | .07 | .20 |
| ☐ 719 | Albert Pujols AS | .20 | .50 |
| ☐ 720 | Mark Loretta AS | .07 | .20 |
| ☐ 721 | Edgar Renteria AS | .07 | .20 |
| ☐ 722 | Scott Rolen AS | .07 | .20 |
| ☐ 723 | J.D. Drew AS | .07 | .20 |
| ☐ 724 | Jim Edmonds AS | .07 | .20 |
| ☐ 725 | Johnny Estrada AS | .07 | .20 |
| ☐ 726 | Jason Schmidt AS | .07 | .20 |
| ☐ 727 | Chris Carpenter AS | .07 | .20 |
| ☐ 728 | Eric Gagne AS | .07 | .20 |
| ☐ 729 | Jason Bay AS | .07 | .20 |
| ☐ 730 | Bobby Cox MG AS | .07 | .20 |
| ☐ 731 | D.Ortiz/M.Bellhorn WS1 | .40 | 1.00 |
| ☐ 732 | Curt Schilling WS2 | .40 | 1.00 |
| ☐ 733 | M.Ramirez/P.Martinez WS3 | .40 | 1.00 |
| ☐ 734 | Sox Win Damon/Lowe WS4 | .60 | 1.50 |

## 2005 Topps Update

| | | |
|---|------|------|
| ☐ COMPLETE SET (330) | 15.00 | 40.00 |
| ☐ COMP.FACT.SET (330) | 25.00 | 40.00 |
| ☐ COMMON CARD (1-330) | .07 | .20 |
| ☐ COM (30-110/203-220) | .20 | .50 |
| ☐ COMMON (116-134) | .20 | .50 |
| ☐ COM (14/66/221-310) | .20 | .50 |
| ☐ COMMON (311-330) | .20 | .50 |
| ☐ PLATE ODDS 1:2009 H, 1:582 HTA, 1:2009 R | | |
| ☐ PLATE PRINT RUN 1 SET PER COLOR | | |
| ☐ BLACK-CYAN-MAGENTA-YELLOW ISSUED | | |
| ☐ NO PLATE PRICING DUE TO SCARCITY | | |
| ☐ 1 | Sammy Sosa | .20 | .50 |
| ☐ 2 | Jeff Francoeur | .60 | 1.50 |
| ☐ 3 | Tony Clark | .07 | .20 |
| ☐ 4 | Michael Tucker | .07 | .20 |
| ☐ 5 | Mike Matheny | .07 | .20 |
| ☐ 6 | Eric Young | .07 | .20 |
| ☐ 7 | Jose Valentin | .07 | .20 |
| ☐ 8 | Matt Lawton | .07 | .20 |
| ☐ 9 | Juan Rivera | .07 | .20 |
| ☐ 10 | Shawn Green | .07 | .20 |
| ☐ 11 | Aaron Boone | .07 | .20 |
| ☐ 12 | Woody Williams | .07 | .20 |
| ☐ 13 | Brad Wilkerson | .07 | .20 |
| ☐ 14 | Anthony Reyes RC | .40 | 1.00 |
| ☐ 15 | Russ Adams | .07 | .20 |
| ☐ 16 | Gustavo Chacin | .07 | .20 |
| ☐ 17 | Michael Restovich | .07 | .20 |
| ☐ 18 | Humberto Quintero | .07 | .20 |
| ☐ 19 | Matt Ginter | .07 | .20 |
| ☐ 20 | Scott Podsednik | .07 | .20 |
| ☐ 21 | Byung-Hyun Kim | .07 | .20 |
| ☐ 22 | Orlando Hernandez | .07 | .20 |
| ☐ 23 | Mark Grudzielanek | .07 | .20 |
| ☐ 24 | Jody Gerut | .07 | .20 |
| ☐ 25 | Adrian Beltre | .07 | .20 |
| ☐ 26 | Scott Schoeneweis | .07 | .20 |
| ☐ 27 | Marlon Anderson | .07 | .20 |
| ☐ 28 | Jason Vargas | .07 | .20 |
| ☐ 29 | Claudio Vargas | .07 | .20 |
| ☐ 30 | Jason Kendall | .07 | .20 |
| ☐ 31 | Aaron Small | .07 | .20 |
| ☐ 32 | Juan Cruz | .07 | .20 |
| ☐ 33 | Placido Polanco | .07 | .20 |
| ☐ 34 | Jorge Sosa | .07 | .20 |
| ☐ 35 | John Olerud | .07 | .20 |
| ☐ 36 | Ryan Langerhans | .07 | .20 |
| ☐ 37 | Randy Winn | .07 | .20 |
| ☐ 38 | Zach Duke | .10 | .30 |
| ☐ 39 | Garrett Atkins | .07 | .20 |
| ☐ 40 | Al Leiter | .07 | .20 |
| ☐ 41 | Shawn Chacon | .07 | .20 |
| ☐ 42 | Mark DeRosa | .07 | .20 |
| ☐ 43 | Miguel Ojeda | .07 | .20 |
| ☐ 44 | A.J. Pierzynski | .07 | .20 |
| ☐ 45 | Carlos Lee | .07 | .20 |
| ☐ 46 | LaTroy Hawkins | .07 | .20 |
| ☐ 47 | Nick Green | .07 | .20 |
| ☐ 48 | Shawn Estes | .07 | .20 |
| ☐ 49 | Eli Marrero | .07 | .20 |
| ☐ 50 | Jeff Kent | .07 | .20 |
| ☐ 51 | Joe Randa | .07 | .20 |
| ☐ 52 | Jose Hernandez | .07 | .20 |
| ☐ 53 | Joe Blanton | .07 | .20 |

| Card | | |
|---|---|---|
| ❑ 54 Huston Street | .10 | .30 |
| ❑ 55 Marlon Byrd | .07 | .20 |
| ❑ 56 Alex Sanchez | .07 | .20 |
| ❑ 57 Livan Hernandez | .07 | .20 |
| ❑ 58 Chris Young | .07 | .20 |
| ❑ 59 Brad Eldred | .07 | .20 |
| ❑ 60 Terrence Long | .07 | .20 |
| ❑ 61 Phil Nevin | .07 | .20 |
| ❑ 62 Kyle Farnsworth | .07 | .20 |
| ❑ 63 Jon Lieber | .07 | .20 |
| ❑ 64 Antonio Alfonseca | .07 | .20 |
| ❑ 65 Tony Graffanino | .07 | .20 |
| ❑ 66 Tadahito Iguchi RC | .60 | 1.50 |
| ❑ 67 Brad Thompson | .07 | .20 |
| ❑ 68 Jose Vidro | .07 | .20 |
| ❑ 69 Jason Phillips | .07 | .20 |
| ❑ 70 Carl Pavano | .07 | .20 |
| ❑ 71 Pokey Reese | .07 | .20 |
| ❑ 72 Jerome Williams | .07 | .20 |
| ❑ 73 Kazuhisa Ishii | .07 | .20 |
| ❑ 74 Zach Day | .07 | .20 |
| ❑ 75 Edgar Renteria | .07 | .20 |
| ❑ 76 Mike Myers | .07 | .20 |
| ❑ 77 Jeff Cirillo | .07 | .20 |
| ❑ 78 Endy Chavez | .07 | .20 |
| ❑ 79 Jose Guillen | .07 | .20 |
| ❑ 80 Ugueth Urbina | .07 | .20 |
| ❑ 81 Vinny Castilla | .07 | .20 |
| ❑ 82 Javier Vazquez | .07 | .20 |
| ❑ 83 Willy Taveras | .07 | .20 |
| ❑ 84 Mark Mulder | .07 | .20 |
| ❑ 85 Mike Hargrove MG | .07 | .20 |
| ❑ 86 Buddy Bell MG | .07 | .20 |
| ❑ 87 Charlie Manuel MG | .07 | .20 |
| ❑ 88 Willie Randolph MG | .07 | .20 |
| ❑ 89 Bob Melvin MG | .07 | .20 |
| ❑ 90 Chris Lambert PROS | .20 | .50 |
| ❑ 91 Homer Bailey PROS | .20 | .50 |
| ❑ 92 Ervin Santana PROS | .20 | .50 |
| ❑ 93 Bill Bray PROS | .20 | .50 |
| ❑ 94 Thomas Diamond PROS | .20 | .50 |
| ❑ 95 Trevor Plouffe PROS | .20 | .50 |
| ❑ 96 James Houser PROS | .20 | .50 |
| ❑ 97 Jake Stevens PROS | .20 | .50 |
| ❑ 98 Anthony Whittington PROS | .20 | .50 |
| ❑ 99 Philip Hughes PROS | .20 | .50 |
| ❑ 100 Greg Golson PROS | .20 | .50 |
| ❑ 101 Paul Maholm PROS | .20 | .50 |
| ❑ 102 Carlos Quentin PROS | .20 | .50 |
| ❑ 103 Dan Johnson PROS | .20 | .50 |
| ❑ 104 Mark Rogers PROS | .20 | .50 |
| ❑ 105 Neil Walker PROS | .20 | .50 |
| ❑ 106 Omar Quintanilla PROS | .20 | .50 |
| ❑ 107 Blake DeWitt PROS | .20 | .50 |
| ❑ 108 Taylor Tankersley PROS | .20 | .50 |
| ❑ 109 David Murphy PROS | .20 | .50 |
| ❑ 110 Felix Hernandez PROS | .40 | 1.00 |
| ❑ 111 Craig Biggio HL | .07 | .20 |
| ❑ 112 Greg Maddux HL | .20 | .50 |
| ❑ 113 Bobby Abreu HL | .07 | .20 |
| ❑ 114 Alex Rodriguez HL | .20 | .50 |
| ❑ 115 Trevor Hoffman HL | .07 | .20 |
| ❑ 116 A.Pierzynski/J.Iguchi ALDS | .07 | .20 |
| ❑ 117 Reggie Sanders NLDS | .07 | .20 |
| ❑ 118 B.Molina/F.Santana ALDS | .20 | .50 |
| ❑ 119 Burke/Berkman/LaR NLDS | .20 | .50 |
| ❑ 120 Garret Anderson ALCS | .20 | .50 |
| ❑ 121 A.J. Pierzynski ALCS | .20 | .50 |
| ❑ 122 Paul Konerko ALCS | .20 | .50 |
| ❑ 123 Joe Crede ALCS | .20 | .50 |
| ❑ 124 M.Buehrle/J.Garland ALCS | .20 | .50 |
| ❑ 125 F.Garcia/J.Contreras ALCS | .20 | .50 |
| ❑ 126 Reggie Sanders NLCS | .07 | .20 |
| ❑ 127 Roy Oswalt NLCS | .40 | 1.00 |
| ❑ 128 Roger Clemens NLCS | .40 | 1.00 |
| ❑ 129 Albert Pujols NLCS | .40 | 1.00 |
| ❑ 130 Roy Oswalt NLCS | .20 | .50 |
| ❑ 131 J.Crede/B.Jenks WS | .30 | .75 |
| ❑ 132 P.Konerko/S.Podsed WS | .30 | .75 |
| ❑ 133 Geoff Blum WS | .20 | .50 |
| ❑ 134 White Sox Sweep WS | .40 | 1.00 |
| ❑ 135 ARod/Ortiz/Manny AL HR | .20 | .50 |
| ❑ 136 Young/ARod/Vlad AL BA | .10 | .30 |
| ❑ 137 Ortiz/Teix/Manny AL RBI | .10 | .30 |
| ❑ 138 Colon/Garland/Lee AL W | .07 | .20 |
| ❑ 139 Mill/Johan/Buehrle AL ERA | .10 | .30 |
| ❑ 140 Johan/Randy/Lackey AL K | .10 | .30 |
| ❑ 141 Andruw/Lee/Pujols NL HR | .20 | .50 |
| ❑ 142 Lee/Pujols/Cabrera NL BA | .20 | .50 |
| ❑ 143 Andruw/Pujols/Burr NL RBI | .20 | .50 |
| ❑ 144 Willis/Carp/Oswalt NL W | .20 | .50 |
| ❑ 145 Roger/Andy/Willis NL ERA | .20 | .50 |
| ❑ 146 Peavy/Carp/Pedro NL K | .20 | .50 |
| ❑ 147 Mark Teixeira AS | .07 | .20 |
| ❑ 148 Brian Roberts AS | .07 | .20 |
| ❑ 149 Michael Young AS | .07 | .20 |
| ❑ 150 Alex Rodriguez AS | .20 | .50 |
| ❑ 151 Johnny Damon AS | .07 | .20 |
| ❑ 152 Vladimir Guerrero AS | .10 | .30 |
| ❑ 153 Manny Ramirez AS | .20 | .50 |
| ❑ 154 David Ortiz AS | .10 | .30 |
| ❑ 155 Mariano Rivera AS | .10 | .30 |
| ❑ 156 Joe Nathan AS | .07 | .20 |
| ❑ 157 Albert Pujols AS | .20 | .50 |
| ❑ 158 Jeff Kent AS | .07 | .20 |
| ❑ 159 Felipe Lopez AS | .07 | .20 |
| ❑ 160 Morgan Ensberg AS | .07 | .20 |
| ❑ 161 Miguel Cabrera AS | .20 | .50 |
| ❑ 162 Ken Griffey Jr. AS | .20 | .50 |
| ❑ 163 Andruw Jones AS | .20 | .50 |
| ❑ 164 Paul Lo Duca AS | .07 | .20 |
| ❑ 165 Chad Cordero AS | .07 | .20 |
| ❑ 166 Ken Griffey Jr. Comeback | .20 | .50 |
| ❑ 167 Jason Giambi Comeback | .07 | .20 |
| ❑ 168 Willy Taveras ROY | .07 | .20 |
| ❑ 169 Huston Street ROY | .07 | .20 |
| ❑ 170 Chris Carpenter AS | .07 | .20 |
| ❑ 171 Bartolo Colon AS | .07 | .20 |
| ❑ 172 Bobby Cox AS MG | .07 | .20 |
| ❑ 173 Ozzie Guillen AS MG | .07 | .20 |
| ❑ 174 Andruw Jones POY | .07 | .20 |
| ❑ 175 Johnny Damon AS | .07 | .20 |
| ❑ 176 Alex Rodriguez AS | .20 | .50 |
| ❑ 177 David Ortiz AS | .10 | .30 |
| ❑ 178 Manny Ramirez AS | .07 | .20 |
| ❑ 179 Miguel Tejada AS | .07 | .20 |
| ❑ 180 Vladimir Guerrero AS | .10 | .30 |
| ❑ 181 Mark Teixeira AS | .07 | .20 |
| ❑ 182 Ivan Rodriguez AS | .07 | .20 |
| ❑ 183 Brian Roberts AS | .07 | .20 |
| ❑ 184 Mark Buehrle AS | .07 | .20 |
| ❑ 185 Bobby Abreu AS | .07 | .20 |
| ❑ 186 Carlos Beltran AS | .07 | .20 |
| ❑ 187 Albert Pujols AS | .20 | .50 |
| ❑ 188 Derrek Lee AS | .07 | .20 |
| ❑ 189 Jim Edmonds AS | .07 | .20 |
| ❑ 190 Aramis Ramirez AS | .07 | .20 |
| ❑ 191 Mike Piazza AS | .10 | .30 |
| ❑ 192 Jeff Kent AS | .07 | .20 |
| ❑ 193 David Eckstein AS | .07 | .20 |
| ❑ 194 Chris Carpenter AS | .07 | .20 |
| ❑ 195 Bobby Abreu HR | .07 | .20 |
| ❑ 196 Ivan Rodriguez HR | .07 | .20 |
| ❑ 197 Carlos Lee HR | .07 | .20 |
| ❑ 198 David Ortiz HR | .10 | .30 |
| ❑ 199 Hee-Seop Choi HR | .07 | .20 |
| ❑ 200 Andruw Jones HR | .07 | .20 |
| ❑ 201 Mark Teixeira HR | .07 | .20 |
| ❑ 202 Jason Bay HR | .07 | .20 |
| ❑ 203 Hanley Ramirez FUT | .20 | .50 |
| ❑ 204 Shin-Soo Choo FUT | .20 | .50 |
| ❑ 205 Justin Huber FUT | .20 | .50 |
| ❑ 206 Nelson Cruz FUT RC | .75 | 2.00 |
| ❑ 207 Edwin Encarnacion FUT | .20 | .50 |
| ❑ 208 Miguel Montero FUT RC | .50 | 1.25 |
| ❑ 209 William Bergolla FUT | .20 | .50 |
| ❑ 210 Luis Montanez FUT | .20 | .50 |
| ❑ 211 Francisco Liriano FUT | .60 | 1.50 |
| ❑ 212 Kevin Thompson FUT | .20 | .50 |
| ❑ 213 B.J. Upton FUT | .20 | .50 |
| ❑ 214 Conor Jackson FUT | .20 | .50 |
| ❑ 215 Delmon Young FUT | .20 | .50 |
| ❑ 216 Andy LaRoche FUT | .40 | 1.00 |
| ❑ 217 Ryan Garko FUT | .20 | .50 |
| ❑ 218 Josh Barfield FUT | .20 | .50 |
| ❑ 219 Chris B.Young FUT | .20 | .50 |
| ❑ 220 Justin Verlander FUT | .60 | 1.50 |
| ❑ 221 Drew Anderson FY RC | .20 | .50 |
| ❑ 222 Luis Hernandez FY RC | .20 | .50 |
| ❑ 223 Jim Burt FY RC | .20 | .50 |
| ❑ 224 Mike Morse FY RC | .20 | .50 |
| ❑ 225 Elliot Johnson FY RC | .20 | .50 |
| ❑ 226 C.J. Smith FY RC | .20 | .50 |
| ❑ 227 Casey McGehee FY RC | .20 | .50 |
| ❑ 228 Brian Miller FY RC | .20 | .50 |
| ❑ 229 Chris Vines FY RC | .20 | .50 |
| ❑ 230 D.J. Houlton FY RC | .20 | .50 |
| ❑ 231 Chuck Tiffany FY RC | .40 | 1.00 |
| ❑ 232 Humberto Sanchez FY RC | .75 | 2.00 |
| ❑ 233 Baltazar Lopez FY RC | .20 | .50 |
| ❑ 234 Russ Martin FY RC | 1.00 | 2.50 |
| ❑ 235 Dana Eveland FY RC | .20 | .50 |
| ❑ 236 Johan Silva FY RC | .20 | .50 |
| ❑ 237 Adam Harben FY RC | .30 | .75 |
| ❑ 238 Brian Bannister FY RC | .40 | 1.00 |
| ❑ 239 Adam Boeve FY RC | .20 | .50 |
| ❑ 240 Thomas Oldham FY RC | .20 | .50 |
| ❑ 241 Cody Haerther FY RC | .20 | .50 |
| ❑ 242 Dan Santin FY RC | .20 | .50 |
| ❑ 243 Daniel Haigwood FY RC | .30 | .75 |
| ❑ 244 Craig Tatum FY RC | .20 | .50 |
| ❑ 245 Martin Prado FY RC | .20 | .50 |
| ❑ 246 Errol Simonitsch FY RC | .30 | .75 |
| ❑ 247 Lorenzo Scott FY RC | .20 | .50 |
| ❑ 248 Hayden Penn FY RC | .30 | .75 |
| ❑ 249 Heath Totten FY RC | .20 | .50 |
| ❑ 250 Nick Masset FY RC | .20 | .50 |
| ❑ 251 Pedro Lopez FY RC | .20 | .50 |
| ❑ 252 Ben Harrison FY RC | .20 | .50 |
| ❑ 253 Mike Spidale FY RC | .20 | .50 |
| ❑ 254 Jeremy Harts FY RC | .20 | .50 |
| ❑ 255 Danny Zell FY RC | .20 | .50 |
| ❑ 256 Kevin Collins FY RC | .20 | .50 |
| ❑ 257 Tony Americh FY RC | .20 | .50 |
| ❑ 258 Matt Albers FY RC | .50 | 1.25 |
| ❑ 259 Ricky Barrett FY RC | .20 | .50 |
| ❑ 260 Hernan Iribarren FY RC | .30 | .75 |
| ❑ 261 Sean Tracey FY RC | .20 | .50 |
| ❑ 262 Jerry Owens FY RC | .20 | .50 |
| ❑ 263 Steve Nelson FY RC | .20 | .50 |
| ❑ 264 Brandon McCarthy FY RC | .40 | 1.00 |
| ❑ 265 David Shepard FY RC | .20 | .50 |
| ❑ 266 Steven Bondurant FY RC | .20 | .50 |
| ❑ 267 Billy Sadler FY RC | .20 | .50 |
| ❑ 268 Ryan Feierabend FY RC | .20 | .50 |
| ❑ 269 Stuart Pomeranz FY RC | .20 | .50 |
| ❑ 270 Shaun Marcum FY | .20 | .50 |
| ❑ 271 Erik Schindewolf FY RC | .20 | .50 |
| ❑ 272 Stefan Bailie FY RC | .20 | .50 |
| ❑ 273 Mike Esposito FY RC | .20 | .50 |
| ❑ 274 Buck Coats FY RC | .20 | .50 |
| ❑ 275 Andy Sides FY RC | .20 | .50 |
| ❑ 276 Micah Schnurstein FY RC | .20 | .50 |
| ❑ 277 Jesse Gutierrez FY RC | .20 | .50 |
| ❑ 278 Jake Postlewait FY RC | .20 | .50 |
| ❑ 279 Willy Mota FY RC | .20 | .50 |
| ❑ 280 Ryan Speier FY RC | .20 | .50 |
| ❑ 281 Frank Mata FY RC | .20 | .50 |
| ❑ 282 Jair Jurrjens FY RC | .60 | 1.50 |
| ❑ 283 Nick Touchstone FY RC | .20 | .50 |
| ❑ 284 Matthew Kemp FY RC | 1.25 | 3.00 |
| ❑ 285 Vinny Rottino FY RC | .20 | .50 |
| ❑ 286 J.B. Thurmond FY RC | .20 | .50 |
| ❑ 287 Kelvin Pichardo FY RC | .20 | .50 |
| ❑ 288 Scott Milchinson FY RC | .20 | .50 |
| ❑ 289 Darwinson Salazar FY RC | .20 | .50 |
| ❑ 290 George Kottaras FY RC | .30 | .75 |
| ❑ 291 Kenny Durost FY RC | .20 | .50 |
| ❑ 292 Jonathan Sanchez FY RC | .60 | 1.50 |
| ❑ 293 Brandon Moorhead FY RC | .20 | .50 |
| ❑ 294 Kennard Bibbs FY RC | .20 | .50 |
| ❑ 295 David Gassner FY RC | .20 | .50 |
| ❑ 296 Micah Furtado FY RC | .20 | .50 |
| ❑ 297 Ismael Ramirez FY RC | .20 | .50 |
| ❑ 298 Carlos Gonzalez FY RC | .60 | 1.50 |
| ❑ 299 Brandon Sing FY RC | .30 | .75 |
| ❑ 300 Jason Motte FY RC | .20 | .50 |
| ❑ 301 Chuck James FY RC | .50 | 1.25 |
| ❑ 302 Andy Santana FY RC | .20 | .50 |
| ❑ 303 Manny Parra FY RC | .15 | .40 |
| ❑ 304 Chris B.Young FY RC | .50 | 1.25 |
| ❑ 305 Juan Senreiso FY RC | .20 | .50 |
| ❑ 306 Franklin Morales FY RC | .30 | .75 |
| ❑ 307 Jared Gothreaux FY RC | .20 | .50 |
| ❑ 308 Jayce Tingler FY RC | .20 | .50 |
| ❑ 309 Matt Brown FY RC | .20 | .50 |
| ❑ 310 Frank Diaz FY RC | .20 | .50 |
| ❑ 311 Stephen Drew DP RC | 1.50 | 4.00 |
| ❑ 312 Jered Weaver DP RC | 1.50 | 4.00 |
| ❑ 313 Ryan Braun DP RC | 5.00 | 12.00 |
| ❑ 314 John Mayberry Jr. DP RC | .40 | 1.00 |
| ❑ 315 Aaron Thompson DP RC | .30 | .75 |
| ❑ 316 Cesar Carrillo DP RC | .40 | 1.00 |
| ❑ 317 Jacoby Ellsbury DP RC | 5.00 | 12.00 |

|  |  | | |
|---|---|---|---|
| 318 | Matt Garza DP RC | 1.00 | 2.50 |
| 319 | Cliff Pennington DP RC | .30 | .75 |
| 320 | Colby Rasmus DP RC | 1.50 | 4.00 |
| 321 | Chris Volstad DP RC | .40 | 1.00 |
| 322 | Ricky Romero DP RC | .30 | .75 |
| 323 | Ryan Zimmerman DP RC | 2.00 | 5.00 |
| 324 | C.J. Henry DP RC | .60 | 1.50 |
| 325 | Jay Bruce DP RC | 5.00 | 12.00 |
| 326 | Beau Jones DP RC | .40 | 1.00 |
| 327 | Mark McCormick DP RC | .30 | .75 |
| 328 | Eli Iorg DP RC | .30 | .75 |
| 329 | Andrew McCutchen DP RC | .75 | 2.00 |
| 330 | Mike Costanzo DP RC | .50 | 1.25 |

### 2006 Topps

| | | |
|---|---|---|
| COMP.HOBBY SET (664) | 50.00 | 80.00 |
| COMP.HOLIDAY SET (664) | 50.00 | 80.00 |
| COMP.CARDINALS SET (664) | 50.00 | 80.00 |
| COMP.CUBS SET (664) | 50.00 | 80.00 |
| COMP.PIRATES SET (664) | 50.00 | 80.00 |
| COMP.RED SOX SET (664) | 50.00 | 80.00 |
| COMP.YANKEES SET (664) | 50.00 | 80.00 |
| COMPLETE SET (659) | 30.00 | 80.00 |
| COMPLETE SERIES 1 (329) | 15.00 | 40.00 |
| COMPLETE SERIES 2 (330) | 15.00 | 40.00 |
| COMMON CARD (1-660) | .07 | .20 |

COMP.SER.1 SET EXCLUDES CARD 297
CARD 297 NOT INTENDED FOR RELEASE
CARDS 287b AND 312b ISSUED IN FACT.SET
2 TICKETS EXCH.CARD RANDOM IN PACKS
OVERALL PLATE SER.1 ODDS 1:246 HTA
OVERALL PLATE SER.2 ODDS 1:193 HTA
PLATE PRINT RUN 1 SET PER COLOR
BLACK-CYAN-MAGENTA-YELLOW ISSUED
NO PLATE PRICING DUE TO SCARCITY

|  |  | | |
|---|---|---|---|
| 1 | Alex Rodriguez | .30 | .75 |
| 2 | Jose Valentin | .07 | .20 |
| 3 | Garrett Atkins | .07 | .20 |
| 4 | Scott Hatteberg | .07 | .20 |
| 5 | Carl Crawford | .20 | .50 |
| 6 | Armando Benitez | .07 | .20 |
| 7 | Mickey Mantle | 3.00 | 6.00 |
| 8 | Mike Morse | .07 | .20 |
| 9 | Damian Miller | .07 | .20 |
| 10 | Clint Barmes | .07 | .20 |
| 11 | Michael Barrett | .07 | .20 |
| 12 | Coco Crisp | .07 | .20 |
| 13 | Tadahito Iguchi | .07 | .20 |
| 14 | Chris Snyder | .07 | .20 |
| 15 | Brian Roberts | .07 | .20 |
| 16 | David Wright | .30 | .75 |
| 17 | Victor Santos | .07 | .20 |
| 18 | Trevor Hoffman | .07 | .20 |
| 19 | Jeremy Reed | .07 | .20 |
| 20 | Bobby Abreu | .07 | .20 |
| 21 | Lance Berkman | .07 | .20 |
| 22 | Zach Day | .07 | .20 |
| 23 | Jonny Gomes | .07 | .20 |
| 24 | Jason Marquis | .07 | .20 |
| 25 | Chipper Jones | .20 | .50 |
| 26 | Scott Hairston | .07 | .20 |
| 27 | Ryan Dempster | .07 | .20 |
| 28 | Brandon Inge | .07 | .20 |
| 29 | Aaron Harang | .07 | .20 |
| 30 | Jon Garland | .07 | .20 |
| 31 | Pokey Reese | .07 | .20 |
| 32 | Mike MacDougal | .07 | .20 |
| 33 | Mike Lieberthal | .07 | .20 |
| 34 | Cesar Izturis | .07 | .20 |
| 35 | Brad Wilkerson | .07 | .20 |
| 36 | Jeff Suppan | .07 | .20 |
| 37 | Adam Everett | .07 | .20 |
| 38 | Bengie Molina | .07 | .20 |
| 39 | Rickie Weeks | .07 | .20 |
| 40 | Jorge Posada | .10 | .30 |
| 41 | Rheal Cormier | .07 | .20 |
| 42 | Reed Johnson | .07 | .20 |
| 43 | Laynce Nix | .07 | .20 |
| 44 | Carl Everett | .07 | .20 |
| 45 | Greg Maddux | .30 | .75 |
| 46 | Jeff Francis | .07 | .20 |
| 47 | Felipe Lopez | .07 | .20 |
| 48 | Dan Johnson | .07 | .20 |
| 49 | Humberto Cota | .07 | .20 |
| 50 | Manny Ramirez | .10 | .30 |
| 51 | Juan Uribe | .07 | .20 |
| 52 | Jaret Wright | .07 | .20 |
| 53 | Tomo Ohka | .07 | .20 |
| 54 | Mike Matheny | .07 | .20 |
| 55 | Joe Mauer | .20 | .50 |
| 56 | Jarrod Washburn | .07 | .20 |
| 57 | Randy Winn | .07 | .20 |
| 58 | Pedro Feliz | .07 | .20 |
| 59 | Kenny Rogers | .07 | .20 |
| 60 | Rocco Baldelli | .07 | .20 |
| 61 | Eric Hinske | .07 | .20 |
| 62 | Damaso Marte | .07 | .20 |
| 63 | Desi Relaford | .07 | .20 |
| 64 | Juan Encarnacion | .07 | .20 |
| 65 | Nomar Garciaparra | .20 | .50 |
| 66 | Shawn Estes | .07 | .20 |
| 67 | Brian Jordan | .07 | .20 |
| 68 | Steve Kline | .07 | .20 |
| 69 | Braden Looper | .07 | .20 |
| 70 | Carlos Lee | .07 | .20 |
| 71 | Tom Glavine | .10 | .30 |
| 72 | Craig Biggio | .10 | .30 |
| 73 | Steve Finley | .07 | .20 |
| 74 | David Newhan | .07 | .20 |
| 75 | Eric Gagne | .07 | .20 |
| 76 | Tony Graffanino | .07 | .20 |
| 77 | Dallas McPherson | .07 | .20 |
| 78 | Nick Punto | .07 | .20 |
| 79 | Mark Kotsay | .07 | .20 |
| 80 | Kerry Wood | .07 | .20 |
| 81 | Kyle Farnsworth | .07 | .20 |
| 82 | Huston Street | .07 | .20 |
| 83 | Endy Chavez | .07 | .20 |
| 84 | So Taguchi | .07 | .20 |
| 85 | Hank Blalock | .07 | .20 |
| 86 | Brad Radke | .07 | .20 |
| 87 | Chien-Ming Wang | .30 | .75 |
| 88 | B.J. Surhoff | .07 | .20 |
| 89 | Glendon Rusch | .07 | .20 |
| 90 | Mark Buehrle | .07 | .20 |
| 91 | Rafael Betancourt | .07 | .20 |
| 92 | Lance Cormier | .07 | .20 |
| 93 | Alex Gonzalez | .07 | .20 |
| 94 | Matt Stairs | .07 | .20 |
| 95 | Andy Pettitte | .10 | .30 |
| 96 | Jesse Crain | .07 | .20 |
| 97 | Kenny Lofton | .07 | .20 |
| 98 | Geoff Blum | .07 | .20 |
| 99 | Mark Redman | .07 | .20 |
| 100 | Barry Bonds | .40 | 1.00 |
| 101 | Chad Orvella | .07 | .20 |
| 102 | Xavier Nady | .07 | .20 |
| 103 | Junior Spivey | .07 | .20 |
| 104 | Bernie Williams | .10 | .30 |
| 105 | Victor Martinez | .07 | .20 |
| 106 | Nook Logan | .07 | .20 |
| 107 | Mark Teahen | .07 | .20 |
| 108 | Mike Lamb | .07 | .20 |
| 109 | Jayson Werth | .07 | .20 |
| 110 | Mariano Rivera | .20 | .50 |
| 111 | Erubiel Durazo | .07 | .20 |
| 112 | Ryan Vogelsong | .07 | .20 |
| 113 | Bobby Madritsch | .07 | .20 |
| 114 | Travis Lee | .07 | .20 |
| 115 | Adam Dunn | .07 | .20 |
| 116 | David Riske | .07 | .20 |
| 117 | Troy Percival | .07 | .20 |
| 118 | Chad Tracy | .07 | .20 |
| 119 | Andy Marte | .07 | .20 |
| 120 | Edgar Renteria | .07 | .20 |
| 121 | Jason Giambi | .07 | .20 |
| 122 | Justin Morneau | .07 | .20 |
| 123 | J.T. Snow | .07 | .20 |
| 124 | Danys Baez | .07 | .20 |
| 125 | Carlos Delgado | .07 | .20 |
| 126 | John Buck | .07 | .20 |
| 127 | Shannon Stewart | .07 | .20 |
| 128 | Mike Cameron | .07 | .20 |
| 129 | Joe McEwing | .07 | .20 |
| 130 | Richie Sexson | .07 | .20 |
| 131 | Rod Barajas | .07 | .20 |
| 132 | Russ Adams | .07 | .20 |
| 133 | J.D. Closser | .07 | .20 |
| 134 | Ramon Ortiz | .07 | .20 |
| 135 | Josh Beckett | .07 | .20 |
| 136 | Ryan Freel | .07 | .20 |
| 137 | Victor Zambrano | .07 | .20 |
| 138 | Ronnie Belliard | .07 | .20 |
| 139 | Jason Michaels | .07 | .20 |
| 140 | Brian Giles | .07 | .20 |
| 141 | Randy Wolf | .07 | .20 |
| 142 | Robinson Cano | .10 | .30 |
| 143 | Joe Blanton | .07 | .20 |
| 144 | Esteban Loaiza | .07 | .20 |
| 145 | Troy Glaus | .07 | .20 |
| 146 | Matt Clement | .07 | .20 |
| 147 | Geoff Jenkins | .07 | .20 |
| 148 | John Thomson | .07 | .20 |
| 149 | A.J. Pierzynski | .07 | .20 |
| 150 | Pedro Martinez | .10 | .30 |
| 151 | Roger Clemens | .40 | 1.00 |
| 152 | Jack Wilson | .07 | .20 |
| 153 | Ray King | .07 | .20 |
| 154 | Ryan Church | .07 | .20 |
| 155 | Paul Lo Duca | .07 | .20 |
| 156 | Dan Wheeler | .07 | .20 |
| 157 | Carlos Zambrano | .07 | .20 |
| 158 | Mike Timlin | .07 | .20 |
| 159 | Brandon Claussen | .07 | .20 |
| 160 | Travis Hafner | .07 | .20 |
| 161 | Chris Shelton | .07 | .20 |
| 162 | Rafael Furcal | .07 | .20 |
| 163 | Tom Gordon | .07 | .20 |
| 164 | Noah Lowry | .07 | .20 |
| 165 | Larry Walker | .10 | .30 |
| 166 | Dave Roberts | .07 | .20 |
| 167 | Scott Schoeneweis | .07 | .20 |
| 168 | Julian Tavarez | .07 | .20 |
| 169 | Jhonny Peralta | .07 | .20 |
| 170 | Vernon Wells | .07 | .20 |
| 171 | Jorge Cantu | .07 | .20 |
| 172 | Todd Greene | .07 | .20 |
| 173 | Willy Taveras | .07 | .20 |
| 174 | Corey Patterson | .07 | .20 |
| 175 | Ivan Rodriguez | .10 | .30 |
| 176 | Bobby Kielty | .07 | .20 |
| 177 | Jose Reyes | .07 | .20 |
| 178 | Barry Zito | .07 | .20 |
| 179 | Deivi Cruz | .07 | .20 |
| 180 | Mark Teixeira | .10 | .30 |
| 181 | Chone Figgins | .07 | .20 |
| 182 | Aaron Rowand | .07 | .20 |
| 183 | Tim Wakefield | .07 | .20 |
| 184 | Mike Maroth | .07 | .20 |
| 185 | Johnny Damon | .10 | .30 |
| 186 | Vicente Padilla | .07 | .20 |
| 187 | Ryan Klesko | .07 | .20 |
| 188 | Gary Matthews | .07 | .20 |
| 189 | Jose Mesa | .07 | .20 |
| 190 | Nick Johnson | .07 | .20 |
| 191 | Freddy Garcia | .07 | .20 |
| 192 | Larry Bigbie | .07 | .20 |
| 193 | Chris Ray | .07 | .20 |
| 194 | Torii Hunter | .07 | .20 |
| 195 | Mike Sweeney | .07 | .20 |
| 196 | Brad Penny | .07 | .20 |
| 197 | Jason Frasor | .07 | .20 |
| 198 | Kevin Mench | .07 | .20 |
| 199 | Adam Kennedy | .07 | .20 |
| 200 | Albert Pujols | .40 | 1.00 |
| 201 | Jody Gerut | .07 | .20 |
| 202 | Luis Gonzalez | .07 | .20 |
| 203 | Zack Greinke | .07 | .20 |
| 204 | Miguel Cairo | .07 | .20 |
| 205 | Jimmy Rollins | .07 | .20 |
| 206 | Edgardo Alfonzo | .07 | .20 |
| 207 | Billy Wagner | .07 | .20 |
| 208 | B.J. Ryan | .07 | .20 |
| 209 | Orlando Hudson | .07 | .20 |
| 210 | Preston Wilson | .07 | .20 |
| 211 | Melvin Mora | .07 | .20 |
| 212 | Bill Mueller | .07 | .20 |
| 213 | Javy Lopez | .07 | .20 |
| 214 | Wilson Betemit | .07 | .20 |
| 215 | Garret Anderson | .07 | .20 |

|  |  | | |
|---|---|---|---|
| 216 | Russell Branyan | .07 | .20 |
| 217 | Jeff Weaver | .07 | .20 |
| 218 | Doug Mientkiewicz | .07 | .20 |
| 219 | Mark Ellis | .07 | .20 |
| 220 | Jason Bay | .07 | .20 |
| 221 | Adam LaRoche | .07 | .20 |
| 222 | C.C. Sabathia | .07 | .20 |
| 223 | Humberto Quintero | .07 | .20 |
| 224 | Bartolo Colon | .07 | .20 |
| 225 | Ichiro Suzuki | .30 | .75 |
| 226 | Brett Tomko | .07 | .20 |
| 227 | Corey Koskie | .07 | .20 |
| 228 | David Eckstein | .07 | .20 |
| 229 | Cristian Guzman | .07 | .20 |
| 230 | Jeff Kent | .07 | .20 |
| 231 | Chris Capuano | .07 | .20 |
| 232 | Rodrigo Lopez | .07 | .20 |
| 233 | Jason Phillips | .07 | .20 |
| 234 | Luis Rivas | .07 | .20 |
| 235 | Cliff Floyd | .07 | .20 |
| 236 | Gil Meche | .07 | .20 |
| 237 | Adam Eaton | .07 | .20 |
| 238 | Matt Morris | .07 | .20 |
| 239 | Kyle Davies | .07 | .20 |
| 240 | David Wells | .07 | .20 |
| 241 | John Smoltz | .10 | .30 |
| 242 | Felix Hernandez | .20 | .50 |
| 243 | Kenny Rogers GG | .07 | .20 |
| 244 | Mark Teixeira GG | .07 | .20 |
| 245 | Orlando Hudson GG | .07 | .20 |
| 246 | Derek Jeter GG | .20 | .50 |
| 247 | Eric Chavez GG | .07 | .20 |
| 248 | Torii Hunter GG | .07 | .20 |
| 249 | Vernon Wells GG | .07 | .20 |
| 250 | Ichiro Suzuki GG | .20 | .50 |
| 251 | Greg Maddux GG | .20 | .50 |
| 252 | Mike Matheny GG | .07 | .20 |
| 253 | Derrek Lee GG | .07 | .20 |
| 254 | Luis Castillo GG | .07 | .20 |
| 255 | Omar Vizquel GG | .07 | .20 |
| 256 | Mike Lowell GG | .07 | .20 |
| 257 | Andruw Jones GG | .07 | .20 |
| 258 | Jim Edmonds GG | .07 | .20 |
| 259 | Bobby Abreu GG | .07 | .20 |
| 260 | Bartolo Colon CY | .07 | .20 |
| 261 | Chris Carpenter CY | .07 | .20 |
| 262 | Alex Rodriguez MVP | .20 | .50 |
| 263 | Albert Pujols MVP | .20 | .50 |
| 264 | Huston Street ROY | .07 | .20 |
| 265 | Ryan Howard ROY | .15 | .40 |
| 266 | Bobby Cox MG | .07 | .20 |
| 267 | Bobby Cox MG | .07 | .20 |
| 268 | Baltimore Orioles TC | .07 | .20 |
| 269 | Boston Red Sox TC | .20 | .50 |
| 270 | Chicago White Sox TC | .20 | .50 |
| 271 | Dusty Baker MG | .07 | .20 |
| 272 | Jerry Narron MG | .07 | .20 |
| 273 | Cleveland Indians TC | .07 | .20 |
| 274 | Clint Hurdle MG | .07 | .20 |
| 275 | Detroit Tigers TC | .07 | .20 |
| 276 | Jack McKeon MG | .07 | .20 |
| 277 | Phil Garner MG | .07 | .20 |
| 278 | Kansas City Royals TC | .07 | .20 |
| 279 | Jim Tracy MG | .07 | .20 |
| 280 | Los Angeles Angels TC | .07 | .20 |
| 281 | Milwaukee Brewers TC | .07 | .20 |
| 282 | Minnesota Twins TC | .07 | .20 |
| 283 | Willie Randolph MG | .07 | .20 |
| 284 | New York Yankees TC | .20 | .50 |
| 285 | Oakland Athletics TC | .07 | .20 |
| 286 | Charlie Manuel MG | .07 | .20 |
| 287a | Pete Mackanin MG ERR | .07 | .20 |
| 287b | Pete Mackanin MG COR | .07 | .20 |
| 288 | Bruce Bochy MG | .07 | .20 |
| 289 | Felipe Alou MG | .07 | .20 |
| 290 | Seattle Mariners TC | .07 | .20 |
| 291 | Tony LaRussa MG | .07 | .20 |
| 292 | Tampa Bay Devil Rays TC | .07 | .20 |
| 293 | Texas Rangers TC | .07 | .20 |
| 294 | Toronto Blue Jays TC | .07 | .20 |
| 295 | Frank Robinson MG | .10 | .30 |
| 296 | Anderson Hernandez (RC) | .20 | .50 |
| 297A | Alex Gordon (RC) Full | 250.00 | 500.00 |
| 297B | Alex Gordon Cut Out | 30.00 | 60.00 |
| 297C | Alex Gordon Blank Gold | 15.00 | 40.00 |
| 297D | Alex Gordon Blank Silver | | |
| 298 | Jason Botts (RC) | .20 | .50 |
| 299 | Jeff Mathis (RC) | .20 | .50 |
| 300 | Ryan Garko (RC) | .20 | .50 |
| 301 | Charlton Jimerson (RC) | .20 | .50 |
| 302 | Chris Denorfia (RC) | .20 | .50 |
| 303 | Anthony Reyes (RC) | .20 | .50 |
| 304 | Bryan Bullington (RC) | .20 | .50 |
| 305 | Chuck James (RC) | .20 | .50 |
| 306 | Danny Sandoval RC | .20 | .50 |
| 307 | Walter Young (RC) | .20 | .50 |
| 308 | Fausto Carmona (RC) | .20 | .50 |
| 309 | Francisco Liriano (RC) | .75 | 2.00 |
| 310 | Hong-Chih Kuo (RC) | .40 | 1.00 |
| 311 | Joe Saunders (RC) | .20 | .50 |
| 312a | John Koronka Cubs (RC) | .20 | .50 |
| 312b | John Koronka Rangers (RC) | .20 | .50 |
| 313 | Robert Andino (RC) | .20 | .50 |
| 314 | Shaun Marcum (RC) | .20 | .50 |
| 315 | Tom Gorzelanny (RC) | .20 | .50 |
| 316 | Craig Breslow RC | .20 | .50 |
| 317 | Chris DeMaria RC | .20 | .50 |
| 318 | Brayan Pena (RC) | .20 | .50 |
| 319 | Rich Hill (RC) | .20 | .50 |
| 320 | Rick Short (RC) | .20 | .50 |
| 321 | C.J. Wilson (RC) | .20 | .50 |
| 322 | Marshall McDougall (RC) | .20 | .50 |
| 323 | Darrell Rasner (RC) | .20 | .50 |
| 324 | Brandon Watson (RC) | .20 | .50 |
| 325 | Paul McAnulty (RC) | .20 | .50 |
| 326 | D.Jeter/A.Rodriguez TS | .40 | 1.00 |
| 327 | M.Tejada/M.Mora TS | .07 | .20 |
| 328 | M.Giles/C.Jones TS | .10 | .30 |
| 329 | M.Ramirez/D.Ortiz TS | .20 | .50 |
| 330 | M.Barrett/G.Maddux TS | .07 | .20 |
| 331 | Matt Holliday | .08 | .25 |
| 332 | Orlando Cabrera | .07 | .20 |
| 333 | Ryan Langerhans | .07 | .20 |
| 334 | Lew Ford | .07 | .20 |
| 335 | Mark Prior | .10 | .30 |
| 336 | Ted Lilly | .07 | .20 |
| 337 | Michael Young | .07 | .20 |
| 338 | Livan Hernandez | .07 | .20 |
| 339 | Yadier Molina | .07 | .20 |
| 340 | Eric Chavez | .07 | .20 |
| 341 | Miguel Batista | .07 | .20 |
| 342 | Bruce Chen | .07 | .20 |
| 343 | Sean Casey | .07 | .20 |
| 344 | Doug Davis | .07 | .20 |
| 345 | Andruw Jones | .10 | .30 |
| 346 | Hideki Matsui | .20 | .50 |
| 347 | Joe Randa | .07 | .20 |
| 348 | Reggie Sanders | .07 | .20 |
| 349 | Jason Jennings | .07 | .20 |
| 350 | Joe Nathan | .07 | .20 |
| 351 | Jose Lopez | .07 | .20 |
| 352 | John Lackey | .07 | .20 |
| 353 | Claudio Vargas | .07 | .20 |
| 354 | Grady Sizemore | .20 | .50 |
| 355 | Jon Papelbon (RC) | .75 | 2.00 |
| 356 | Luis Matos | .07 | .20 |
| 357 | Orlando Hernandez | .07 | .20 |
| 358 | Jamie Moyer | .07 | .20 |
| 359 | Chase Utley | .20 | .50 |
| 360 | Moises Alou | .07 | .20 |
| 361 | Chad Cordero | .07 | .20 |
| 362 | Brian McCann | .20 | .50 |
| 363 | Jermaine Dye | .07 | .20 |
| 364 | Ryan Madson | .07 | .20 |
| 365 | Aramis Ramirez | .07 | .20 |
| 366 | Matt Treanor | .07 | .20 |
| 367 | Ray Durham | .07 | .20 |
| 368 | Khalil Greene | .10 | .30 |
| 369 | Mike Hampton | .07 | .20 |
| 370 | Mike Mussina | .10 | .30 |
| 371 | Brad Hawpe | .07 | .20 |
| 372 | Marlon Byrd | .07 | .20 |
| 373 | Woody Williams | .07 | .20 |
| 374 | Victor Diaz | .07 | .20 |
| 375 | Brady Clark | .07 | .20 |
| 376 | Luis Gonzalez | .07 | .20 |
| 377 | Raul Ibanez | .07 | .20 |
| 378 | Tony Clark | .07 | .20 |
| 379 | Shawn Chacon | .07 | .20 |
| 380 | Marcus Giles | .07 | .20 |
| 381 | Odalis Perez | .07 | .20 |
| 382 | Steve Trachsel | .07 | .20 |
| 383 | Russ Ortiz | .07 | .20 |
| 384 | Toby Hall | .07 | .20 |
| 385 | Bill Hall | .07 | .20 |
| 386 | Luke Hudson | .07 | .20 |
| 387 | Ken Griffey Jr. | .30 | .75 |
| 388 | Tim Hudson | .07 | .20 |
| 389 | Brian Moehler | .07 | .20 |
| 390 | Jake Peavy | .07 | .20 |
| 391 | Casey Blake | .07 | .20 |
| 392 | Sidney Ponson | .07 | .20 |
| 393 | Brian Schneider | .07 | .20 |
| 394 | J.J. Hardy | .07 | .20 |
| 395 | Austin Kearns | .07 | .20 |
| 396 | Pat Burrell | .07 | .20 |
| 397 | Jason Vargas | .07 | .20 |
| 398 | Ryan Howard | .30 | .75 |
| 399 | Joe Crede | .07 | .20 |
| 400 | Vladimir Guerrero | .20 | .50 |
| 401 | Roy Halladay | .07 | .20 |
| 402 | David Dellucci | .07 | .20 |
| 403 | Brandon Webb | .07 | .20 |
| 404 | Marlon Anderson | .07 | .20 |
| 405 | Miguel Tejada | .07 | .20 |
| 406 | Ryan Doumit | .07 | .20 |
| 407 | Kevin Youkilis | .07 | .20 |
| 408 | Jon Lieber | .07 | .20 |
| 409 | Edwin Encarnacion | .07 | .20 |
| 410 | Miguel Cabrera | .10 | .30 |
| 411 | A.J. Burnett | .07 | .20 |
| 412 | David Bell | .07 | .20 |
| 413 | Gregg Zaun | .07 | .20 |
| 414 | Lance Niekro | .07 | .20 |
| 415 | Shawn Green | .07 | .20 |
| 416 | Roberto Hernandez | .07 | .20 |
| 417 | Jay Gibbons | .07 | .20 |
| 418 | Johnny Estrada | .07 | .20 |
| 419 | Omar Vizquel | .10 | .30 |
| 420 | Gary Sheffield | .07 | .20 |
| 421 | Brad Halsey | .07 | .20 |
| 422 | Aaron Cook | .07 | .20 |
| 423 | David Ortiz | .20 | .50 |
| 424 | Tony Womack | .07 | .20 |
| 425 | Joe Kennedy | .07 | .20 |
| 426 | Dustin McGowan | .07 | .20 |
| 427 | Carl Pavano | .07 | .20 |
| 428 | Nick Green | .07 | .20 |
| 429 | Francisco Cordero | .07 | .20 |
| 430 | Octavio Dotel | .07 | .20 |
| 431 | Julio Franco | .07 | .20 |
| 432 | Brett Myers | .07 | .20 |
| 433 | Casey Kotchman | .07 | .20 |
| 434 | Frank Catalanotto | .07 | .20 |
| 435 | Paul Konerko | .07 | .20 |
| 436 | Keith Foulke | .07 | .20 |
| 437 | Juan Rivera | .07 | .20 |
| 438 | Todd Pratt | .07 | .20 |
| 439 | Ben Broussard | .07 | .20 |
| 440 | Scott Kazmir | .10 | .30 |
| 441 | Rich Aurilia | .07 | .20 |
| 442 | Craig Monroe | .07 | .20 |
| 443 | Danny Kolb | .07 | .20 |
| 444 | Curtis Granderson | .20 | .50 |
| 445 | Jeff Francoeur | .20 | .50 |
| 446 | Dustin Hermanson | .07 | .20 |
| 447 | Jacque Jones | .07 | .20 |
| 448 | Bobby Crosby | .07 | .20 |
| 449 | Jason LaRue | .07 | .20 |
| 450 | Derrek Lee | .07 | .20 |
| 451 | Curt Schilling | .10 | .30 |
| 452 | Jake Westbrook | .07 | .20 |
| 453 | Daniel Cabrera | .07 | .20 |
| 454 | Bobby Jenks | .07 | .20 |
| 455 | Dontrelle Willis | .20 | .50 |
| 456 | Brad Lidge | .07 | .20 |
| 457 | Shea Hillenbrand | .07 | .20 |
| 458 | Luis Castillo | .07 | .20 |
| 459 | Mark Hendrickson | .07 | .20 |
| 460 | Randy Johnson | .20 | .50 |
| 461 | Placido Polanco | .07 | .20 |
| 462 | Aaron Boone | .07 | .20 |
| 463 | Todd Walker | .07 | .20 |
| 464 | Nick Swisher | .07 | .20 |
| 465 | Joel Pineiro | .07 | .20 |
| 466 | Jay Payton | .07 | .20 |
| 467 | Cliff Lee | .07 | .20 |
| 468 | Johan Santana | .10 | .30 |
| 469 | Josh Willingham | .07 | .20 |
| 470 | Jeremy Bonderman | .07 | .20 |
| 471 | Runelvys Hernandez | .07 | .20 |
| 472 | Duaner Sanchez | .07 | .20 |
| 473 | Jason Lane | .07 | .20 |
| 474 | Trot Nixon | .07 | .20 |

| | | |
|---|---|---|
| ❑ 475 Ramon Hernandez | .07 | .20 |
| ❑ 476 Mike Lowell | .07 | .20 |
| ❑ 477 Chan Ho Park | .07 | .20 |
| ❑ 478 Doug Waechter | .07 | .20 |
| ❑ 479 Carlos Silva | .07 | .20 |
| ❑ 480 Jose Contreras | .07 | .20 |
| ❑ 481 Vinny Castilla | .07 | .20 |
| ❑ 482 Chris Reitsma | .07 | .20 |
| ❑ 483 Jose Guillen | .07 | .20 |
| ❑ 484 Aaron Hill | .07 | .20 |
| ❑ 485 Kevin Millwood | .07 | .20 |
| ❑ 486 Wily Mo Pena | .07 | .20 |
| ❑ 487 Rich Harden | .07 | .20 |
| ❑ 488 Chris Carpenter | .07 | .20 |
| ❑ 489 Jason Bartlett | .07 | .20 |
| ❑ 490 Magglio Ordonez | .07 | .20 |
| ❑ 491 John Rodriguez | .07 | .20 |
| ❑ 492 Bob Wickman | .07 | .20 |
| ❑ 493 Eddie Guardado | .07 | .20 |
| ❑ 494 Kip Wells | .07 | .20 |
| ❑ 495 Adrian Beltre | .07 | .20 |
| ❑ 496 Jose Capellan (RC) | .20 | .50 |
| ❑ 497 Scott Podsednik | .07 | .20 |
| ❑ 498 Brad Thompson | .07 | .20 |
| ❑ 499 Aaron Heilman | .07 | .20 |
| ❑ 500 Derek Jeter | .50 | 1.25 |
| ❑ 501 Emil Brown | .07 | .20 |
| ❑ 502 Morgan Ensberg | .07 | .20 |
| ❑ 503 Nate Bump | .07 | .20 |
| ❑ 504 Phil Nevin | .07 | .20 |
| ❑ 505 Jason Schmidt | .07 | .20 |
| ❑ 506 Michael Cuddyer | .07 | .20 |
| ❑ 507 John Patterson | .07 | .20 |
| ❑ 508 Danny Haren | .07 | .20 |
| ❑ 509 Freddy Sanchez | .07 | .20 |
| ❑ 510 J.D. Drew | .07 | .20 |
| ❑ 511 Dmitri Young | .07 | .20 |
| ❑ 512 Eric Milton | .07 | .20 |
| ❑ 513 Ervin Santana | .10 | .30 |
| ❑ 514 Mark Loretta | .07 | .20 |
| ❑ 515 Mark Grudzielanek | .07 | .20 |
| ❑ 516 Derrick Turnbow | .07 | .20 |
| ❑ 517 Denny Bautista | .07 | .20 |
| ❑ 518 Lyle Overbay | .07 | .20 |
| ❑ 519 Julio Lugo | .07 | .20 |
| ❑ 520 Carlos Beltran | .07 | .20 |
| ❑ 521 Jose Cruz Jr. | .07 | .20 |
| ❑ 522 Jason Isringhausen | .07 | .20 |
| ❑ 523 Bronson Arroyo | .07 | .20 |
| ❑ 524 Ben Sheets | .07 | .20 |
| ❑ 525 Zach Duke | .07 | .20 |
| ❑ 526 Ryan Wagner | .07 | .20 |
| ❑ 527 Jose Vidro | .07 | .20 |
| ❑ 528 Doug Mirabelli | .07 | .20 |
| ❑ 529 Kris Benson | .07 | .20 |
| ❑ 530 Carlos Guillen | .07 | .20 |
| ❑ 531 Juan Pierre | .07 | .20 |
| ❑ 532 Scot Shields | .07 | .20 |
| ❑ 533 Scott Hatteberg | .07 | .20 |
| ❑ 534 Tim Stauffer | .07 | .20 |
| ❑ 535 Jim Edmonds | .10 | .30 |
| ❑ 536 Scot Eyre | .07 | .20 |
| ❑ 537 Ben Johnson | .07 | .20 |
| ❑ 538 Mark Mulder | .07 | .20 |
| ❑ 539 Juan Rincon | .07 | .20 |
| ❑ 540 Gustavo Chacin | .07 | .20 |
| ❑ 541 Oliver Perez | .07 | .20 |
| ❑ 542 Chris Young | .07 | .20 |
| ❑ 543 Edinson Volquez | .07 | .20 |
| ❑ 544 Mark Bellhorn | .07 | .20 |
| ❑ 545 Kelvim Escobar | .07 | .20 |
| ❑ 546 Andy Sisco | .07 | .20 |
| ❑ 547 Derek Lowe | .07 | .20 |
| ❑ 548 Sean Burroughs | .07 | .20 |
| ❑ 549 Erik Bedard | .07 | .20 |
| ❑ 550 Alfonso Soriano | .07 | .20 |
| ❑ 551 Matt Murton | .07 | .20 |
| ❑ 552 Eric Byrnes | .07 | .20 |
| ❑ 553 Chris Duffy | .07 | .20 |
| ❑ 554 Kazuo Matsui | .07 | .20 |
| ❑ 555 Scott Rolen | .10 | .30 |
| ❑ 556 Rob Mackowiak | .07 | .20 |
| ❑ 557 Chris Burke | .07 | .20 |
| ❑ 558 Jeromy Burnitz | .07 | .20 |
| ❑ 559 Jerry Hairston Jr. | .07 | .20 |
| ❑ 560 Jim Thome | .10 | .30 |
| ❑ 561 Miguel Olivo | .07 | .20 |
| ❑ 562 Jose Castillo | .07 | .20 |

| | | |
|---|---|---|
| ❑ 563 Brad Ausmus | .07 | .20 |
| ❑ 564 Yorvit Torrealba | .07 | .20 |
| ❑ 565 David DeJesus | .07 | .20 |
| ❑ 566 Paul Byrd | .07 | .20 |
| ❑ 567 Brandon Backe | .07 | .20 |
| ❑ 568 Aubrey Huff | .07 | .20 |
| ❑ 569 Mike Jacobs | .07 | .20 |
| ❑ 570 Todd Helton | .10 | .30 |
| ❑ 571 Angel Berroa | .07 | .20 |
| ❑ 572 Todd Jones | .07 | .20 |
| ❑ 573 Jeff Bagwell | .10 | .30 |
| ❑ 574 Darin Erstad | .07 | .20 |
| ❑ 575 Roy Oswalt | .07 | .20 |
| ❑ 576 Rondell White | .07 | .20 |
| ❑ 577 Alex Rios | .07 | .20 |
| ❑ 578 Wes Helms | .07 | .20 |
| ❑ 579 Javier Vazquez | .07 | .20 |
| ❑ 580 Frank Thomas | .20 | .50 |
| ❑ 581 Brian Fuentes | .07 | .20 |
| ❑ 582 Francisco Rodriguez | .07 | .20 |
| ❑ 583 Craig Counsell | .07 | .20 |
| ❑ 584 Jorge Sosa | .07 | .20 |
| ❑ 585 Mike Piazza | .20 | .50 |
| ❑ 586 Mike Scioscia MG | .07 | .20 |
| ❑ 587 Joe Torre MG | .10 | .30 |
| ❑ 588 Ken Macha MG | .07 | .20 |
| ❑ 589 John Gibbons MG | .07 | .20 |
| ❑ 590 Joe Maddon MG | .07 | .20 |
| ❑ 591 Eric Wedge MG | .07 | .20 |
| ❑ 592 Mike Hargrove MG | .07 | .20 |
| ❑ 593 Sam Perlozzo MG | .07 | .20 |
| ❑ 594 Buck Showalter MG | .07 | .20 |
| ❑ 595 Terry Francona MG | .07 | .20 |
| ❑ 596 Buddy Bell MG | .07 | .20 |
| ❑ 597 Jim Leyland MG | .07 | .20 |
| ❑ 598 Ron Gardenhire MG | .07 | .20 |
| ❑ 599 Ozzie Guillen MG | .07 | .20 |
| ❑ 600 Ned Yost MG | .07 | .20 |
| ❑ 601 Atlanta Braves TC | .10 | .30 |
| ❑ 602 Philadelphia Phillies TC | .07 | .20 |
| ❑ 603 New York Mets TC | .07 | .20 |
| ❑ 604 Washington Nationals TC | .07 | .20 |
| ❑ 605 Florida Marlins TC | .07 | .20 |
| ❑ 606 Houston Astros TC | .07 | .20 |
| ❑ 607 Chicago Cubs TC | .10 | .30 |
| ❑ 608 St. Louis Cardinals TC | .10 | .30 |
| ❑ 609 Pittsburgh Pirates TC | .07 | .20 |
| ❑ 610 Cincinnati Reds TC | .07 | .20 |
| ❑ 611 Colorado Rockies TC | .07 | .20 |
| ❑ 612 Los Angeles Dodgers TC | .07 | .20 |
| ❑ 613 San Francisco Giants TC | .07 | .20 |
| ❑ 614 San Diego Padres TC | .07 | .20 |
| ❑ 615 Arizona Diamondbacks TC | .07 | .20 |
| ❑ 616 Kenji Johjima RC | .75 | 2.00 |
| ❑ 617 Ryan Zimmerman (RC) | 1.00 | 2.50 |
| ❑ 618 Craig Hansen RC | .60 | 1.50 |
| ❑ 619 Joey Devine RC | .25 | .60 |
| ❑ 620 Hanley Ramirez (RC) | .25 | .60 |
| ❑ 621 Scott Olsen (RC) | .20 | .50 |
| ❑ 622 Jason Bergmann RC | .20 | .50 |
| ❑ 623 Geovany Soto (RC) | .20 | .50 |
| ❑ 624 J.J. Furmaniak (RC) | .20 | .50 |
| ❑ 625 Jeremy Accardo RC | .20 | .50 |
| ❑ 626 Mark Woodyard (RC) | .20 | .50 |
| ❑ 627 Matt Capps (RC) | .20 | .50 |
| ❑ 628 Tim Corcoran RC | .20 | .50 |
| ❑ 629 Ryan Jorgensen (RC) | .20 | .50 |
| ❑ 630 Ronny Paulino (RC) | .20 | .50 |
| ❑ 631 Dan Uggla (RC) | .40 | 1.00 |
| ❑ 632 Ian Kinsler (RC) | .25 | .60 |
| ❑ 633 Josh Barfield (RC) | .20 | .50 |
| ❑ 634 Reggie Abercrombie (RC) | .20 | .50 |
| ❑ 635 Joel Zumaya (RC) | .50 | 1.25 |
| ❑ 636 Matt Cain (RC) | .30 | .75 |
| ❑ 637 Conor Jackson (RC) | .30 | .75 |
| ❑ 638 Brian Anderson (RC) | .20 | .50 |
| ❑ 639 Prince Fielder (RC) | .60 | 1.50 |
| ❑ 640 Jeremy Hermida (RC) | .30 | .75 |
| ❑ 641 Justin Verlander (RC) | .60 | 1.50 |
| ❑ 642 Brian Bannister (RC) | .20 | .50 |
| ❑ 643 Willie Eyre (RC) | .20 | .50 |
| ❑ 644 Ricky Nolasco (RC) | .20 | .50 |
| ❑ 645 Paul Maholm (RC) | .20 | .50 |
| ❑ 646 J.Damon/J.Giambi | .10 | .30 |
| ❑ 647 R.White/L.Ford | .07 | .20 |
| ❑ 648 O.Hernandez/O.Hudson | .07 | .20 |
| ❑ 649 A.Soriano/K.Griffey Jr. | .30 | .75 |
| ❑ 650 P.Burrell/M.Lieberthal | .07 | .20 |

| | | |
|---|---|---|
| ❑ 651 J.Reyes/K.Matsui | .07 | .20 |
| ❑ 652 H.Blalock/M.Young | .07 | .20 |
| ❑ 653 P.Fielder/R.Weeks | .30 | .75 |
| ❑ 654 T.Lee/R.Baldelli | .07 | .20 |
| ❑ 655 D.Lee/A.Ramirez | .07 | .20 |
| ❑ 656 G.Sizemore/A.Boone | .10 | .30 |
| ❑ 657 Gonzalez/Green/Hill | .07 | .20 |
| ❑ 658 I.Rodriguez/C.Guillen | .10 | .30 |
| ❑ 659 A.Rodriguez/G.Sheffield | .30 | .75 |
| ❑ 660 E.Santana/F.Rodriguez | .07 | .20 |
| ❑ RC1 Alay Soler | 30.00 | 60.00 |
| ❑ NNO 2 Tickets EXCH | 8.00 | 20.00 |

## 2006 Topps Update

| | | |
|---|---|---|
| ❑ COMPLETE SET (330) | 20.00 | 50.00 |
| ❑ COMMON CARD (1-132) | .07 | .20 |
| ❑ SEMISTARS 1-132 | .12 | .30 |
| ❑ UNLISTED STARS 1-132 | .20 | .50 |
| ❑ COMMON ROOKIE (133-170) | .20 | .50 |
| ❑ RC SEMIS 133-170 | .30 | .75 |
| ❑ RC UNLISTED 133-170 | .50 | 1.25 |
| ❑ COMMON CARD (171-330) | .12 | .30 |
| ❑ SEMISTARS 171-330 | .20 | .50 |
| ❑ UNLISTED STARS 171-330 | .30 | .75 |
| ❑ 1-330 PLATE ODDS 1:85 HTA | | |
| ❑ PLATE PRINT RUN 1 SET PER COLOR | | |
| ❑ BLACK-CYAN-MAGENTA-YELLOW ISSUED | | |
| ❑ NO PLATE PRICING DUE TO SCARCITY | | |
| ❑ 1 Austin Kearns | .07 | .20 |
| ❑ 2 Adam Eaton | .07 | .20 |
| ❑ 3 Juan Encarnacion | .07 | .20 |
| ❑ 4 Jarrod Washburn | .07 | .20 |
| ❑ 5 Alex Gonzalez | .07 | .20 |
| ❑ 6 Toby Hall | .07 | .20 |
| ❑ 7 Preston Wilson | .07 | .20 |
| ❑ 8 Ramon Ortiz | .07 | .20 |
| ❑ 9 Jason Michaels | .07 | .20 |
| ❑ 10 Jeff Weaver | .07 | .20 |
| ❑ 11 Russell Branyan | .07 | .20 |
| ❑ 12 Brett Tomko | .07 | .20 |
| ❑ 13 Doug Mientkiewicz | .07 | .20 |
| ❑ 14 David Wells | .07 | .20 |
| ❑ 15 Corey Koskie | .07 | .20 |
| ❑ 16 Russ Ortiz | .07 | .20 |
| ❑ 17 Carlos Pena | .07 | .20 |
| ❑ 18 Mark Hendrickson | .07 | .20 |
| ❑ 19 Julian Tavarez | .07 | .20 |
| ❑ 20 Jeff Conine | .07 | .20 |
| ❑ 21 Dioner Navarro | .07 | .20 |
| ❑ 22 Bob Wickman | .07 | .20 |
| ❑ 23 Felipe Lopez | .07 | .20 |
| ❑ 24 Eddie Guardado | .07 | .20 |
| ❑ 25 David Dellucci | .07 | .20 |
| ❑ 26 Ryan Wagner | .07 | .20 |
| ❑ 27 Nick Green | .07 | .20 |
| ❑ 28 Gary Majewski | .07 | .20 |
| ❑ 29 Shea Hillenbrand | .07 | .20 |
| ❑ 30 Jae Seo | .07 | .20 |
| ❑ 31 Royce Clayton | .07 | .20 |
| ❑ 32 Dave Riske | .07 | .20 |
| ❑ 33 Joey Gathright | .07 | .20 |
| ❑ 34 Robinson Tejada | .07 | .20 |
| ❑ 35 Edwin Jackson | .07 | .20 |
| ❑ 36 Aubrey Huff | .07 | .20 |
| ❑ 37 Akinori Otsuka | .07 | .20 |
| ❑ 38 Juan Castro | .07 | .20 |
| ❑ 39 Zach Day | .07 | .20 |
| ❑ 40 Jeremy Accardo | .07 | .20 |
| ❑ 41 Shawn Green | .07 | .20 |
| ❑ 42 Kazuo Matsui | .07 | .20 |
| ❑ 43 J.J. Putz | .07 | .20 |
| ❑ 44 David Ross | .07 | .20 |
| ❑ 45 Scott Williamson | .07 | .20 |
| ❑ 46 Joe Borchard | .07 | .20 |

|  |  | | |
|---|---|---|---|
| ❑ 47 | Elmer Dessens | .07 | .20 |
| ❑ 48 | Odalis Perez | .07 | .20 |
| ❑ 49 | Kelly Shoppach | .07 | .20 |
| ❑ 50 | Brandon Phillips | .07 | .20 |
| ❑ 51 | Guillermo Mota | .07 | .20 |
| ❑ 52 | Alex Cintron | .07 | .20 |
| ❑ 53 | Denny Bautista | .07 | .20 |
| ❑ 54 | Josh Bard | .07 | .20 |
| ❑ 55 | Julio Lugo | .07 | .20 |
| ❑ 56 | Doug Mirabelli | .07 | .20 |
| ❑ 57 | Kip Wells | .07 | .20 |
| ❑ 58 | Adrian Gonzalez | .07 | .20 |
| ❑ 59 | Shawn Chacon | .07 | .20 |
| ❑ 60 | Marcus Thames | .07 | .20 |
| ❑ 61 | Craig Wilson | .07 | .20 |
| ❑ 62 | Cory Sullivan | .07 | .20 |
| ❑ 63 | Ben Broussard | .07 | .20 |
| ❑ 64 | Todd Walker | .07 | .20 |
| ❑ 65 | Greg Maddux | .30 | .75 |
| ❑ 66 | Xavier Nady | .07 | .20 |
| ❑ 67 | Oliver Perez | .07 | .20 |
| ❑ 68 | Sean Casey | .07 | .20 |
| ❑ 69 | Kyle Lohse | .07 | .20 |
| ❑ 70 | Carlos Lee | .07 | .20 |
| ❑ 71 | Rheal Cormier | .07 | .20 |
| ❑ 72 | Ronnie Belliard | .07 | .20 |
| ❑ 73 | Cory Lidle | 1.50 | 4.00 |
| ❑ 74 | David Bell | .07 | .20 |
| ❑ 75 | Wilson Betemit | .07 | .20 |
| ❑ 76 | Danys Baez | .07 | .20 |
| ❑ 77 | Mike Stanton | .07 | .20 |
| ❑ 78 | Kevin Mench | .07 | .20 |
| ❑ 79 | Sandy Alomar Jr. | .07 | .20 |
| ❑ 80 | Cesar Izturis | .07 | .20 |
| ❑ 81 | Jeremy Affeldt | .07 | .20 |
| ❑ 82 | Matt Stairs | .07 | .20 |
| ❑ 83 | Hector Luna | .07 | .20 |
| ❑ 84 | Tony Graffanino | .07 | .20 |
| ❑ 85 | J.P. Howell | .07 | .20 |
| ❑ 86 | Bengie Molina | .07 | .20 |
| ❑ 87 | Maicer Izturis | .07 | .20 |
| ❑ 88 | Marco Scutaro | .07 | .20 |
| ❑ 89 | Daryle Ward | .07 | .20 |
| ❑ 90 | Sal Fasano | .07 | .20 |
| ❑ 91 | Oscar Villarreal | .07 | .20 |
| ❑ 92 | Gabe Gross | .07 | .20 |
| ❑ 93 | Phil Nevin | .07 | .20 |
| ❑ 94 | Damon Hollins | .07 | .20 |
| ❑ 95 | Juan Cruz | .07 | .20 |
| ❑ 96 | Marlon Anderson | .07 | .20 |
| ❑ 97 | Jason Davis | .07 | .20 |
| ❑ 98 | Ryan Shealy | .07 | .20 |
| ❑ 99 | Francisco Cordero | .07 | .20 |
| ❑ 100 | Bobby Abreu | .07 | .20 |
| ❑ 101 | Roberto Hernandez | .07 | .20 |
| ❑ 102 | Gary Bennett | .07 | .20 |
| ❑ 103 | Aaron Sele | .07 | .20 |
| ❑ 104 | Nook Logan | .07 | .20 |
| ❑ 105 | Alfredo Amezaga | .07 | .20 |
| ❑ 106 | Chris Woodward | .07 | .20 |
| ❑ 107 | Kevin Jarvis | .07 | .20 |
| ❑ 108 | B.J. Upton | .07 | .20 |
| ❑ 109 | Alan Embree | .07 | .20 |
| ❑ 110 | Milton Bradley | .07 | .20 |
| ❑ 111 | Pete Orr | .07 | .20 |
| ❑ 112 | Jeff Cirillo | .07 | .20 |
| ❑ 113 | Corey Patterson | .07 | .20 |
| ❑ 114 | Josh Paul | .07 | .20 |
| ❑ 115 | Fernando Rodney | .07 | .20 |
| ❑ 116 | Jerry Hairston Jr. | .07 | .20 |
| ❑ 117 | Scott Proctor | .07 | .20 |
| ❑ 118 | Ambiorix Burgos | .07 | .20 |
| ❑ 119 | Jose Bautista | .07 | .20 |
| ❑ 120 | Livan Hernandez | .07 | .20 |
| ❑ 121 | John McDonald | .07 | .20 |
| ❑ 122 | Ronny Cedeno | .07 | .20 |
| ❑ 123 | Nate Robertson | .07 | .20 |
| ❑ 124 | Jamey Carroll | .07 | .20 |
| ❑ 125 | Alex Escobar | .07 | .20 |
| ❑ 126 | Endy Chavez | .07 | .20 |
| ❑ 127 | Jorge Julio | .07 | .20 |
| ❑ 128 | Kenny Lofton | .07 | .20 |
| ❑ 129 | Matt Diaz | .07 | .20 |
| ❑ 130 | Dave Bush | .07 | .20 |
| ❑ 131 | Jose Molina | .07 | .20 |
| ❑ 132 | Mike MacDougal | .07 | .20 |
| ❑ 133 | Ben Zobrist (RC) | .50 | 1.25 |
| ❑ 134 | Shane Komine RC | .30 | .75 |
| ❑ 135 | Casey Janssen RC | .30 | .75 |
| ❑ 136 | Kevin Frandsen (RC) | .30 | .75 |
| ❑ 137 | John Rheinecker (RC) | .20 | .50 |
| ❑ 138 | Matt Kemp (RC) | .50 | 1.25 |
| ❑ 139 | Scott Mathieson (RC) | .20 | .50 |
| ❑ 140 | Jered Weaver (RC) | 1.00 | 2.50 |
| ❑ 141 | Joel Guzman (RC) | .20 | .50 |
| ❑ 142 | Anibal Sanchez (RC) | .30 | .75 |
| ❑ 143 | Melky Cabrera (RC) | .30 | .75 |
| ❑ 144 | Howie Kendrick (RC) | 1.00 | 2.50 |
| ❑ 145 | Cole Hamels (RC) | .75 | 2.00 |
| ❑ 146 | Willy Aybar (RC) | .20 | .50 |
| ❑ 147 | Jamie Shields RC | .20 | .50 |
| ❑ 148 | Kevin Thompson (RC) | .20 | .50 |
| ❑ 149 | Jon Lester RC | 1.25 | 3.00 |
| ❑ 150 | Stephen Drew (RC) | .50 | 1.25 |
| ❑ 151 | Andre Ethier (RC) | .50 | 1.25 |
| ❑ 152 | Jordan Tata RC | .20 | .50 |
| ❑ 153 | Mike Napoli (RC) | .50 | 1.25 |
| ❑ 154 | Kason Gabbard (RC) | .20 | .50 |
| ❑ 155 | Lastings Milledge (RC) | .30 | .75 |
| ❑ 156 | Erick Aybar (RC) | .20 | .50 |
| ❑ 157 | Fausto Carmona (RC) | .30 | .75 |
| ❑ 158 | Russ Martin (RC) | .30 | .75 |
| ❑ 159 | David Pauley (RC) | .20 | .50 |
| ❑ 160 | Andy Marte (RC) | .20 | .50 |
| ❑ 161 | Carlos Quentin (RC) | .30 | .75 |
| ❑ 162 | Franklin Gutierrez (RC) | .20 | .50 |
| ❑ 163 | Taylor Buchholz (RC) | .30 | .75 |
| ❑ 164 | Josh Johnson (RC) | .30 | .75 |
| ❑ 165 | Chad Billingsley (RC) | .30 | .75 |
| ❑ 166 | Kendry Morales (RC) | .50 | 1.25 |
| ❑ 167 | Adam Loewen (RC) | .30 | .75 |
| ❑ 168 | Yusmeiro Petit (RC) | .20 | .50 |
| ❑ 169 | Matt Albers (RC) | .20 | .50 |
| ❑ 170 | John Maine (RC) | .30 | .75 |
| ❑ 171 | Alex Rodriguez SH | .50 | 1.25 |
| ❑ 172 | Mike Piazza SH | .12 | .30 |
| ❑ 173 | Cory Sullivan SH | .12 | .30 |
| ❑ 174 | Anibal Sanchez SH | .12 | .30 |
| ❑ 175 | Trevor Hoffman SH | .12 | .30 |
| ❑ 176 | Barry Bonds SH | .60 | 1.50 |
| ❑ 177 | Derek Jeter SH | .75 | 2.00 |
| ❑ 178 | Jose Reyes SH | .12 | .30 |
| ❑ 179 | Manny Ramirez SH | .20 | .50 |
| ❑ 180 | Vladimir Guerrero SH | .30 | .75 |
| ❑ 181 | Mariano Rivera SH | .30 | .75 |
| ❑ 182 | Mark Kotsay PH | .12 | .30 |
| ❑ 183 | Derek Jeter PH | .75 | 2.00 |
| ❑ 184 | Carlos Delgado PH | .12 | .30 |
| ❑ 185 | Frank Thomas PH | .30 | .75 |
| ❑ 186 | Albert Pujols PH | .60 | 1.50 |
| ❑ 187 | Magglio Ordonez PH | .12 | .30 |
| ❑ 188 | Carlos Delgado PH | .12 | .30 |
| ❑ 189 | Kenny Rogers PH | .12 | .30 |
| ❑ 190 | Tom Glavine PH | .20 | .50 |
| ❑ 191 | P.Polanco/J.Suppan PH | .12 | .30 |
| ❑ 192 | Jose Reyes PH | .30 | .75 |
| ❑ 193 | E.Chavez/Y.Molina PH | .12 | .30 |
| ❑ 194 | Craig Monroe PH | .12 | .30 |
| ❑ 195 | J.Verlander/J.Zumaya PH | .50 | 1.25 |
| ❑ 196 | P.LoDuca/C.Beltran PH | .12 | .30 |
| ❑ 197 | A.Pujols/J.Edmonds/S.Rolen PH | .60 | 1.50 |
| ❑ 198 | Anthony Reyes PH | .12 | .30 |
| ❑ 199 | Chris Carpenter PH | .12 | .30 |
| ❑ 200 | David Eckstein PH | .12 | .30 |
| ❑ 201 | Jered Weaver PH | .60 | 1.50 |
| ❑ 202 | D.Ortiz/J.Dye/T.Hafner LL | .20 | .50 |
| ❑ 203 | J.Mauer/D.Jeter/R.Cano LL | .30 | .75 |
| ❑ 204 | D.Ortiz/J.Morneau/R.Ibanez LL | .20 | .50 |
| ❑ 205 | Crawford/Figgins/Ichiro LL | .30 | .75 |
| ❑ 206 | J.Santana/C.Wang/J.Garland LL | .30 | .75 |
| ❑ 207 | J.Santana/R.Halladay/C.Sabathia LL | .30 | .75 |
| ❑ 208 | J.Santana/J.Bonderman/J.Lackey LL | .30 | .75 |
| ❑ 209 | F.Rodriguez/B.Jenks/B.Ryan LL | .12 | .30 |
| ❑ 210 | R.Howard/A.Pujols/A.Soriano LL | .60 | 1.50 |
| ❑ 211 | Sanch./Cabrera/Pujols LL | .60 | 1.50 |
| ❑ 212 | Howard/Pujols/Berk LL | .60 | 1.50 |
| ❑ 213 | J.Reyes/J.Pierre/H.Ramirez LL | .30 | .75 |
| ❑ 214 | D.Lowe/B.Webb/C.Zambrano LL | .12 | .30 |
| ❑ 215 | R.Oswalt/C.Carpenter/B.Webb LL | .12 | .30 |
| ❑ 216 | A.Harang/J.Peavy/J.Smoltz LL | .12 | .30 |
| ❑ 217 | T.Hoffman/B.Wagner/J.Borowski LL | .12 | .30 |
| ❑ 218 | Ichiro Suzuki AS | .50 | 1.25 |
| ❑ 219 | Derek Jeter AS | .75 | 2.00 |
| ❑ 220 | Alex Rodriguez AS | .50 | 1.25 |
| ❑ 221 | David Ortiz AS | .30 | .75 |
| ❑ 222 | Vladimir Guerrero AS | .30 | .75 |
| ❑ 223 | Ivan Rodriguez AS | .20 | .50 |
| ❑ 224 | Vernon Wells AS | .12 | .30 |
| ❑ 225 | Mark Loretta AS | .12 | .30 |
| ❑ 226 | Kenny Rogers AS | .12 | .30 |
| ❑ 227 | Alfonso Soriano AS | .12 | .30 |
| ❑ 228 | Carlos Beltran AS | .12 | .30 |
| ❑ 229 | Albert Pujols AS | .60 | 1.50 |
| ❑ 230 | Jason Bay AS | .12 | .30 |
| ❑ 231 | Edgar Renteria AS | .12 | .30 |
| ❑ 232 | David Wright AS | .50 | 1.25 |
| ❑ 233 | Chase Utley AS | .30 | .75 |
| ❑ 234 | Paul LoDuca AS | .12 | .30 |
| ❑ 235 | Brad Penny AS | .12 | .30 |
| ❑ 236 | Derrick Turnbow AS | .12 | .30 |
| ❑ 237 | Mark Redman AS | .12 | .30 |
| ❑ 238 | Francisco Liriano AS | .30 | .75 |
| ❑ 239 | A.J. Pierzynski AS | .12 | .30 |
| ❑ 240 | Grady Sizemore AS | .20 | .50 |
| ❑ 241 | Jose Contreras AS | .12 | .30 |
| ❑ 242 | Jermaine Dye AS | .12 | .30 |
| ❑ 243 | Jason Schmidt AS | .12 | .30 |
| ❑ 244 | Nomar Garciaparra AS | .30 | .75 |
| ❑ 245 | Scott Kazmir AS | .20 | .50 |
| ❑ 246 | Johan Santana AS | .20 | .50 |
| ❑ 247 | Chris Capuano AS | .12 | .30 |
| ❑ 248 | Magglio Ordonez AS | .12 | .30 |
| ❑ 249 | Gary Matthews Jr. AS | .12 | .30 |
| ❑ 250 | Carlos Lee AS | .12 | .30 |
| ❑ 251 | David Eckstein AS | .12 | .30 |
| ❑ 252 | Michael Young AS | .12 | .30 |
| ❑ 253 | Matt Holliday AS | .30 | .75 |
| ❑ 254 | Lance Berkman AS | .12 | .30 |
| ❑ 255 | Scott Rolen AS | .20 | .50 |
| ❑ 256 | Bronson Arroyo AS | .12 | .30 |
| ❑ 257 | Barry Zito AS | .12 | .30 |
| ❑ 258 | Brian McCann AS | .12 | .30 |
| ❑ 259 | Jose Lopez AS | .12 | .30 |
| ❑ 260 | Chris Carpenter AS | .12 | .30 |
| ❑ 261 | Roy Halladay AS | .12 | .30 |
| ❑ 262 | Jim Thome AS | .20 | .50 |
| ❑ 263 | Dan Uggla AS | .30 | .75 |
| ❑ 264 | Mariano Rivera AS | .30 | .75 |
| ❑ 265 | Roy Oswalt AS | .12 | .30 |
| ❑ 266 | Tom Gordon AS | .12 | .30 |
| ❑ 267 | Troy Glaus AS | .12 | .30 |
| ❑ 268 | Bobby Jenks AS | .12 | .30 |
| ❑ 269 | Freddy Sanchez AS | .12 | .30 |
| ❑ 270 | Paul Konerko AS | .12 | .30 |
| ❑ 271 | Joe Mauer AS | .30 | .75 |
| ❑ 272 | B.J. Ryan AS | .12 | .30 |
| ❑ 273 | Ryan Howard AS | .50 | 1.25 |
| ❑ 274 | Brian Fuentes AS | .12 | .30 |
| ❑ 275 | Miguel Cabrera AS | .20 | .50 |
| ❑ 276 | Brandon Webb AS | .12 | .30 |
| ❑ 277 | Mark Buehrle AS | .12 | .30 |
| ❑ 278 | Trevor Hoffman AS | .12 | .30 |
| ❑ 279 | Jonathan Papelbon AS | .60 | 1.50 |
| ❑ 280 | Andruw Jones AS | .20 | .50 |
| ❑ 281 | Miguel Tejada AS | .12 | .30 |
| ❑ 282 | Carlos Zambrano AS | .12 | .30 |
| ❑ 283 | Ryan Howard HRD | .50 | 1.25 |
| ❑ 284 | David Wright HRD | .50 | 1.25 |
| ❑ 285 | Miguel Cabrera HRD | .20 | .50 |
| ❑ 286 | David Ortiz HRD | .30 | .75 |
| ❑ 287 | Jermaine Dye HRD | .12 | .30 |
| ❑ 288 | Miguel Tejada HRD | .12 | .30 |
| ❑ 289 | Lance Berkman HRD | .12 | .30 |
| ❑ 290 | Troy Glaus HRD | .12 | .30 |
| ❑ 291 | D.Wright/T.Glavine TL | .50 | 1.25 |
| ❑ 292 | R.Howard/T.Gordon TL | .50 | 1.25 |
| ❑ 293 | M.Cabrera/D.Willis TL | .20 | .50 |
| ❑ 294 | A.Jones/J.Smoltz TL | .20 | .50 |
| ❑ 295 | A.Soriano/A.Soriano TL | .12 | .30 |
| ❑ 296 | A.Pujols/C.Carpenter TL | .60 | 1.50 |
| ❑ 297 | A.Dunn/B.Arroyo TL | .12 | .30 |
| ❑ 298 | L.Berkman/R.Oswalt TL | .12 | .30 |
| ❑ 299 | C.Capuano/P.Fielder TL | .50 | 1.25 |
| ❑ 300 | F.Sanchez/J.Bay TL | .12 | .30 |
| ❑ 301 | C.Zambrano/J.Pierre TL | .12 | .30 |
| ❑ 302 | A.Gonzalez/T.Hoffman TL | .12 | .30 |
| ❑ 303 | D.Lowe/R.Furcal TL | .12 | .30 |
| ❑ 304 | O.Vizquel/J.Schmidt TL | .20 | .50 |
| ❑ 305 | B.Webb/C.Tracy TL | .12 | .30 |
| ❑ 306 | M.Holliday/G.Atkins TL | .30 | .75 |
| ❑ 307 | A.Rodriguez/C.Wang TL | .50 | 1.25 |
| ❑ 308 | C.Schilling/D.Ortiz TL | .20 | .50 |
| ❑ 309 | R.Halladay/V.Wells TL | .12 | .30 |
| ❑ 310 | M.Tejada/E.Bedard TL | .12 | .30 |

| Card | | |
|---|---|---|
| ❑ 311 C.Crawford/S.Kazmir TL | .20 | .50 |
| ❑ 312 J.Bonderman/M.Ordonez TL | .12 | .30 |
| ❑ 313 J.Momeau/J.Santana TL | .20 | .50 |
| ❑ 314 J.Garland/J.Dye TL | .12 | .30 |
| ❑ 315 T.Hafner/C.Sabathia TL | .12 | .30 |
| ❑ 316 E.Brown/M.Grudzielanek TL | .12 | .30 |
| ❑ 317 F.Thomas/B.Zito TL | .30 | .75 |
| ❑ 318 J.Weaver/V.Guerrero TL | .60 | 1.50 |
| ❑ 319 M.Young/G.Matthews TL | .12 | .30 |
| ❑ 320 I.Suzuki/J.Putz TL | .50 | 1.25 |
| ❑ 321 D.Jeter/R.Cano TL | .75 | 2.00 |
| ❑ 322 C.Carpenter/M.Mulder CD | .12 | .30 |
| ❑ 323 J.Schmidt/T.Hoffman CD | .12 | .30 |
| ❑ 324 D.Wright/P.LoDuca CD | .50 | 1.25 |
| ❑ 325 L.Berkman/R.Oswalt CD | .12 | .30 |
| ❑ 326 D.Jeter/J.Reyes CD | .30 | .75 |
| ❑ 327 C.Floyd/D.Wright CD | .50 | 1.25 |
| ❑ 328 F.Liriano/J.Santana CD | .30 | .75 |
| ❑ 329 J.Drew/S.Drew CD | .30 | .75 |
| ❑ 330 J.Weaver/J.Weaver CD | .60 | 1.50 |

## 2007 Topps

| | | |
|---|---|---|
| ❑ COMP.HOBBY SET (661) | 40.00 | 80.00 |
| ❑ COMP.HOLIDAY SET (661) | 40.00 | 80.00 |
| ❑ COMP.CARDINALS SET (661) | 40.00 | 80.00 |
| ❑ COMP.CUBS SET (661) | 40.00 | 80.00 |
| ❑ COMP.DODGERS SET (661) | 40.00 | 80.00 |
| ❑ COMP.RED SOX SET (661) | 40.00 | 80.00 |
| ❑ COMP.YANKEES SET (661) | 40.00 | 80.00 |
| ❑ COMP.SET w/o VAR. (661) | 40.00 | 80.00 |
| ❑ COMPLETE SERIES 1 (330) | 15.00 | 30.00 |
| ❑ COMP.SERIES 1 w/#40 (329) | 10.00 | 25.00 |
| ❑ COMPLETE SERIES 2 (331) | 25.00 | 50.00 |
| ❑ COMMON CARD (1-330) | .07 | .20 |
| ❑ COMMON RC | .50 | |
| ❑ SER.1 VAR. ODDS 1:3700 WAL-MART | | |
| ❑ SER.2 VAR.ODDS 1:30 HOBBY | | |
| ❑ NO SER.1 VAR.PRICING DUE TO SCARTIY | | |
| ❑ OVERALL PLATE SER.1 ODDS 1:98 HTA | | |
| ❑ OVERALL PLATE SER.2 ODDS 1:139 HTA | | |
| ❑ PLATE PRINT RUN 1 SET PER COLOR | | |
| ❑ BLACK-CYAN-MAGENTA-YELLOW ISSUED | | |
| ❑ NO PLATE PRICING DUE TO SCARCITY | | |
| ❑ 1 John Lackey | .07 | .20 |
| ❑ 2 Nick Swisher | .07 | .20 |
| ❑ 3 Brad Lidge | .07 | .20 |
| ❑ 4 Bengie Molina | .07 | .20 |
| ❑ 5 Bobby Abreu | .07 | .20 |
| ❑ 6 Edgar Renteria | .07 | .20 |
| ❑ 7 Mickey Mantle | 1.00 | 2.50 |
| ❑ 8 Preston Wilson | .07 | .20 |
| ❑ 9 Ryan Dempster | .07 | .20 |
| ❑ 10 C.C. Sabathia | .07 | .20 |
| ❑ 11 Julio Lugo | .07 | .20 |
| ❑ 12 J.D. Drew | .07 | .20 |
| ❑ 13 Miguel Batista | .07 | .20 |
| ❑ 14 Eliezer Alfonzo | .07 | .20 |
| ❑ 15a Andrew Miller RC | 1.25 | 3.00 |
| ❑ 15b A.Miller Posed RC | 1.25 | 3.00 |
| ❑ 16 Jason Varitek | .20 | .50 |
| ❑ 17 Saul Rivera | .07 | .20 |
| ❑ 18 Orlando Hernandez | .07 | .20 |
| ❑ 19 Alfredo Amezaga | .07 | .20 |
| ❑ 20a D.Young Face Right (RC) | .30 | .75 |
| ❑ 20b D.Young Face Left (RC) | .30 | .75 |
| ❑ 21 Chris Britton | .07 | .20 |
| ❑ 22 Corey Patterson | .07 | .20 |
| ❑ 23 Josh Bard | .07 | .20 |
| ❑ 24 Tom Gordon | .07 | .20 |
| ❑ 25 Gary Matthews | .07 | .20 |
| ❑ 26 Jason Jennings | .07 | .20 |
| ❑ 27 Joey Gathright | .07 | .20 |
| ❑ 28 Brandon Inge | .07 | .20 |
| ❑ 29 Pat Neshek | .30 | .75 |

| | | |
|---|---|---|
| ❑ 30 Bronson Arroyo | .07 | .20 |
| ❑ 31 Jay Payton | .07 | .20 |
| ❑ 32 Andy Pettitte | .12 | .30 |
| ❑ 33 Ervin Santana | .07 | .20 |
| ❑ 34 Paul Konerko | .07 | .20 |
| ❑ 35 Joel Zumaya | .12 | .30 |
| ❑ 36 Gregg Zaun | .07 | .20 |
| ❑ 37 Tony Gwynn Jr. | .07 | .20 |
| ❑ 38 Adam LaRoche | .07 | .20 |
| ❑ 39 Jim Edmonds | .07 | .20 |
| ❑ 40a D.Jeter w/ Mantle/Bush | 5.00 | 12.00 |
| ❑ 40b Derek Jeter | .50 | 1.25 |
| ❑ 41 Rich Hill | .07 | .20 |
| ❑ 42 Livan Hernandez | .07 | .20 |
| ❑ 43 Aubrey Huff | .07 | .20 |
| ❑ 44 Todd Greene | .07 | .20 |
| ❑ 45 Andre Ethier | .12 | .30 |
| ❑ 46 Jeremy Sowers | .07 | .20 |
| ❑ 47 Ben Broussard | .07 | .20 |
| ❑ 48 Darren Oliver | .07 | .20 |
| ❑ 49 Nook Logan | .07 | .20 |
| ❑ 50 Miguel Cabrera | .12 | .30 |
| ❑ 51 Carlos Lee | .07 | .20 |
| ❑ 52 Jose Castillo | .07 | .20 |
| ❑ 53 Mike Piazza | .20 | .50 |
| ❑ 54 Daniel Cabrera | .07 | .20 |
| ❑ 55 Cole Hamels | .20 | .50 |
| ❑ 56 Mark Loretta | .07 | .20 |
| ❑ 57 Brian Fuentes | .07 | .20 |
| ❑ 58 Todd Coffey | .07 | .20 |
| ❑ 59 Brent Clevlen | .07 | .20 |
| ❑ 60 John Smoltz | .12 | .30 |
| ❑ 61 Jason Grilli | .07 | .20 |
| ❑ 62 Dan Wheeler | .07 | .20 |
| ❑ 63 Scott Proctor | .07 | .20 |
| ❑ 64 Bobby Kielty | .07 | .20 |
| ❑ 65 Dan Uggla | .12 | .30 |
| ❑ 66 Lyle Overbay | .07 | .20 |
| ❑ 67 Geoff Jenkins | .07 | .20 |
| ❑ 68 Michael Barrett | .07 | .20 |
| ❑ 69 Casey Fossum | .07 | .20 |
| ❑ 70 Ivan Rodriguez | .12 | .30 |
| ❑ 71 Jose Lopez | .07 | .20 |
| ❑ 72 Jake Westbrook | .07 | .20 |
| ❑ 73 Moises Alou | .07 | .20 |
| ❑ 74 Jose Valverde | .07 | .20 |
| ❑ 75 Jered Weaver | .12 | .30 |
| ❑ 76 Lastings Milledge | .12 | .30 |
| ❑ 77 Austin Kearns | .07 | .20 |
| ❑ 78 Adam Loewen | .07 | .20 |
| ❑ 79 Josh Barfield | .07 | .20 |
| ❑ 80 Johan Santana | .20 | .50 |
| ❑ 81 Ian Kinsler | .07 | .20 |
| ❑ 82 Ian Snell | .07 | .20 |
| ❑ 83 Mike Lowell | .07 | .20 |
| ❑ 84 Elizardo Ramirez | .07 | .20 |
| ❑ 85 Scott Rolen | .12 | .30 |
| ❑ 86 Shannon Stewart | .07 | .20 |
| ❑ 87 Alexis Gomez | .07 | .20 |
| ❑ 88 Jimmy Gobble | .07 | .20 |
| ❑ 89 Jamey Carroll | .07 | .20 |
| ❑ 90 Chipper Jones | .20 | .50 |
| ❑ 91 Carlos Silva | .07 | .20 |
| ❑ 92 Joe Crede | .07 | .20 |
| ❑ 93 Mike Napoli | .07 | .20 |
| ❑ 94 Willy Taveras | .07 | .20 |
| ❑ 95 Rafael Furcal | .07 | .20 |
| ❑ 96 Phil Nevin | .07 | .20 |
| ❑ 97 Dave Bush | .07 | .20 |
| ❑ 98 Marcus Giles | .07 | .20 |
| ❑ 99 Joe Blanton | .07 | .20 |
| ❑ 100 Dontrelle Willis | .12 | .30 |
| ❑ 101 Scott Kazmir | .12 | .30 |
| ❑ 102 Jeff Kent | .07 | .20 |
| ❑ 103 Pedro Feliz | .07 | .20 |
| ❑ 104 Johnny Estrada | .07 | .20 |
| ❑ 105 Travis Hafner | .07 | .20 |
| ❑ 106 Ryan Garko | .07 | .20 |
| ❑ 107 Rafael Soriano | .07 | .20 |
| ❑ 108 Wes Helms | .07 | .20 |
| ❑ 109 Billy Wagner | .07 | .20 |
| ❑ 110 Aaron Rowand | .07 | .20 |
| ❑ 111 Felipe Lopez | .07 | .20 |
| ❑ 112 Jeff Conine | .07 | .20 |
| ❑ 113 Nick Markakis | .12 | .30 |
| ❑ 114 John Koronka | .07 | .20 |
| ❑ 115 B.J. Ryan | .07 | .20 |
| ❑ 116 Tim Wakefield | .07 | .20 |

| | | |
|---|---|---|
| ❑ 117 David Ross | .07 | .20 |
| ❑ 118 Emil Brown | .07 | .20 |
| ❑ 119 Michael Cuddyer | .07 | .20 |
| ❑ 120 Jason Giambi | .07 | .20 |
| ❑ 121 Alex Cintron | .07 | .20 |
| ❑ 122 Luke Scott | .07 | .20 |
| ❑ 123 Chone Figgins | .07 | .20 |
| ❑ 124 Huston Street | .07 | .20 |
| ❑ 125 Carlos Delgado | .07 | .20 |
| ❑ 126 Daryle Ward | .07 | .20 |
| ❑ 127 Chris Duncan | .07 | .20 |
| ❑ 128 Damian Miller | .07 | .20 |
| ❑ 129 Aramis Ramirez | .07 | .20 |
| ❑ 130 Albert Pujols | .40 | 1.00 |
| ❑ 131 Chris Snyder | .07 | .20 |
| ❑ 132 Ray Durham | .07 | .20 |
| ❑ 133 Gary Sheffield | .07 | .20 |
| ❑ 134 Mike Jacobs | .07 | .20 |
| ❑ 135a Troy Tulowitzki (RC) | .50 | 1.25 |
| ❑ 135b T.Tulowitzki Throw (RC) | .50 | 1.25 |
| ❑ 136 Jon Rauch | .07 | .20 |
| ❑ 137 Jay Gibbons | .07 | .20 |
| ❑ 138 Adrian Gonzalez | .07 | .20 |
| ❑ 139 Prince Fielder | .20 | .50 |
| ❑ 140 Freddy Sanchez | .07 | .20 |
| ❑ 141 Rich Aurilia | .07 | .20 |
| ❑ 142 Trot Nixon | .07 | .20 |
| ❑ 143 Vicente Padilla | .07 | .20 |
| ❑ 144 Jack Wilson | .07 | .20 |
| ❑ 145 Jake Peavy | .07 | .20 |
| ❑ 146 Luke Hudson | .07 | .20 |
| ❑ 147 Javier Vazquez | .07 | .20 |
| ❑ 148 Scott Podsednik | .07 | .20 |
| ❑ 149 M.Ordonez/I.Rodriguez CC | .12 | .30 |
| ❑ 150 Todd Helton | .12 | .30 |
| ❑ 151 Kendry Morales | .12 | .30 |
| ❑ 152 Adam Everett | .07 | .20 |
| ❑ 153 Bob Wickman | .07 | .20 |
| ❑ 154 Bill Hall | .07 | .20 |
| ❑ 155 Jeremy Bonderman | .07 | .20 |
| ❑ 156 Ryan Theriot | .07 | .20 |
| ❑ 157 Rocco Baldelli | .07 | .20 |
| ❑ 158 Noah Lowry | .07 | .20 |
| ❑ 159 Jason Michaels | .07 | .20 |
| ❑ 160 Justin Verlander | .20 | .50 |
| ❑ 161 Eduardo Perez | .07 | .20 |
| ❑ 162 Chris Ray | .07 | .20 |
| ❑ 163 Brian Roberts | .07 | .20 |
| ❑ 164 Zach Duke | .07 | .20 |
| ❑ 165 Mark Buehrle | .07 | .20 |
| ❑ 166 Hank Blalock | .07 | .20 |
| ❑ 167 Royce Clayton | .07 | .20 |
| ❑ 168 Mark Teahen | .07 | .20 |
| ❑ 169 Todd Jones | .07 | .20 |
| ❑ 170 Chien-Ming Wang | .20 | .50 |
| ❑ 171 Nick Punto | .07 | .20 |
| ❑ 172 Morgan Ensberg | .07 | .20 |
| ❑ 173 Rob Mackowiak | .07 | .20 |
| ❑ 174 Frank Catalanotto | .07 | .20 |
| ❑ 175 Matt Murton | .07 | .20 |
| ❑ 176 A.Soriano/C.Beltran CC | .07 | .20 |
| ❑ 177 Francisco Cordero | .07 | .20 |
| ❑ 178 Jason Marquis | .07 | .20 |
| ❑ 179 Joe Nathan | .07 | .20 |
| ❑ 180 Roy Halladay | .07 | .20 |
| ❑ 181 Melvin Mora | .07 | .20 |
| ❑ 182 Ramon Ortiz | .07 | .20 |
| ❑ 183 Jose Valentin | .07 | .20 |
| ❑ 184 Gil Meche | .07 | .20 |
| ❑ 185 B.J. Upton | .07 | .20 |
| ❑ 186 Grady Sizemore | .12 | .30 |
| ❑ 187 Matt Cain | .12 | .30 |
| ❑ 188 Eric Byrnes | .07 | .20 |
| ❑ 189 Carl Crawford | .07 | .20 |
| ❑ 190 J.J. Putz | .07 | .20 |
| ❑ 191 Cla Meredith | .07 | .20 |
| ❑ 192 Matt Capps | .07 | .20 |
| ❑ 193 Rod Barajas | .07 | .20 |
| ❑ 194 Edwin Encarnacion | .07 | .20 |
| ❑ 195 James Loney | .12 | .30 |
| ❑ 196 Johnny Damon | .12 | .30 |
| ❑ 197 Freddy Garcia | .07 | .20 |
| ❑ 198 Mike Redmond | .07 | .20 |
| ❑ 199 Ryan Shealy | .07 | .20 |
| ❑ 200 Carlos Beltran | .07 | .20 |
| ❑ 201 Chuck James | .07 | .20 |
| ❑ 202 Mark Ellis | .07 | .20 |
| ❑ 203 Brad Ausmus | .07 | .20 |

|  |  | | |
|---|---|---|---|
| ❑ 204 | Juan Rivera | .07 | .20 |
| ❑ 205 | Cory Sullivan | .07 | .20 |
| ❑ 206 | Ben Sheets | .07 | .20 |
| ❑ 207 | Mark Mulder | .07 | .20 |
| ❑ 208 | Carlos Quentin | .07 | .20 |
| ❑ 209 | Jonathan Broxton | .07 | .20 |
| ❑ 210 | Kazuo Matsui | .07 | .20 |
| ❑ 211 | Armando Benitez | .07 | .20 |
| ❑ 212 | Richie Sexson | .07 | .20 |
| ❑ 213 | Josh Johnson | .07 | .20 |
| ❑ 214 | Brian Schneider | .07 | .20 |
| ❑ 215 | Craig Monroe | .07 | .20 |
| ❑ 216 | Chris Duffy | .07 | .20 |
| ❑ 217 | Chris Coste | .07 | .20 |
| ❑ 218 | Clay Hensley | .07 | .20 |
| ❑ 219 | Chris Gomez | .07 | .20 |
| ❑ 220 | Hideki Matsui | .20 | .50 |
| ❑ 221 | Robinson Tejada | .07 | .20 |
| ❑ 222 | Scott Hatteberg | .07 | .20 |
| ❑ 223 | Jeff Francis | .07 | .20 |
| ❑ 224 | Matt Thornton | .07 | .20 |
| ❑ 225 | Robinson Cano | .12 | .30 |
| ❑ 226 | Chicago White Sox | .07 | .20 |
| ❑ 227 | Oakland Athletics | .07 | .20 |
| ❑ 228 | St. Louis Cardinals | .07 | .20 |
| ❑ 229 | New York Mets | .07 | .20 |
| ❑ 230 | Barry Zito | .07 | .20 |
| ❑ 231 | Baltimore Orioles | .07 | .20 |
| ❑ 232 | Seattle Mariners | .07 | .20 |
| ❑ 233 | Houston Astros | .07 | .20 |
| ❑ 234 | Pittsburgh Pirates | .07 | .20 |
| ❑ 235 | Reed Johnson | .07 | .20 |
| ❑ 236 | Boston Red Sox | .30 | .75 |
| ❑ 237 | Cincinnati Reds | .07 | .20 |
| ❑ 238 | Philadelphia Phillies | .07 | .20 |
| ❑ 239 | New York Yankees | .20 | .50 |
| ❑ 240 | Chris Carpenter | .07 | .20 |
| ❑ 241 | Atlanta Braves | .12 | .30 |
| ❑ 242 | San Francisco Giants | .07 | .20 |
| ❑ 243 | Joe Torre MG | .12 | .30 |
| ❑ 244 | Tampa Bay Devil Rays | .07 | .20 |
| ❑ 245 | Chad Tracy | .07 | .20 |
| ❑ 246 | Clint Hurdle MG | .07 | .20 |
| ❑ 247 | Mike Scioscia MG | .07 | .20 |
| ❑ 248 | Ron Gardenhire MG | .07 | .20 |
| ❑ 249 | Tony LaRussa MG | .07 | .20 |
| ❑ 250 | Anibal Sanchez | .07 | .20 |
| ❑ 251 | Charlie Manuel MG | .07 | .20 |
| ❑ 252 | John Gibbons MG | .07 | .20 |
| ❑ 253 | Jim Tracy MG | .07 | .20 |
| ❑ 254 | Jerry Narron MG | .07 | .20 |
| ❑ 255 | Brad Penny | .20 | .50 |
| ❑ 256 | Bobby Cox MG | .07 | .20 |
| ❑ 257 | Bob Melvin MG | .07 | .20 |
| ❑ 258 | Mike Hargrove MG | .07 | .20 |
| ❑ 259 | Phil Garner MG | .07 | .20 |
| ❑ 260 | David Wright | .30 | .75 |
| ❑ 261 | Vinny Rottino (RC) | .20 | .50 |
| ❑ 262 | Ryan Braun RC | .20 | .50 |
| ❑ 263 | Kevin Kouzmanoff (RC) | .20 | .50 |
| ❑ 264 | David Murphy (RC) | .20 | .50 |
| ❑ 265 | Jimmy Rollins | .07 | .20 |
| ❑ 266 | Joe Maddon MG | .12 | .30 |
| ❑ 267 | Grady Little MG | .07 | .20 |
| ❑ 268 | Ryan Sweeney (RC) | .20 | .50 |
| ❑ 269 | Fred Lewis (RC) | .30 | .75 |
| ❑ 270 | Alfonso Soriano | .20 | .50 |
| ❑ 271a | Delwyn Young (RC) | .20 | .50 |
| ❑ 271b | D.Young Swing (RC) | .20 | .50 |
| ❑ 272 | Jeff Salazar (RC) | .20 | .50 |
| ❑ 273 | Miguel Montero (RC) | .20 | .50 |
| ❑ 274 | Shawn Riggans (RC) | .20 | .50 |
| ❑ 275 | Greg Maddux | .30 | .75 |
| ❑ 276 | Brian Stokes (RC) | .20 | .50 |
| ❑ 277 | Philip Humber (RC) | .20 | .50 |
| ❑ 278 | Scott Moore (RC) | .20 | .50 |
| ❑ 279 | Adam Lind (RC) | .20 | .50 |
| ❑ 280 | Curt Schilling | .12 | .30 |
| ❑ 281 | Chris Narveson (RC) | .20 | .50 |
| ❑ 282 | Oswaldo Navarro RC | .20 | .50 |
| ❑ 283 | Drew Anderson RC | .20 | .50 |
| ❑ 284 | Jerry Owens (RC) | .20 | .50 |
| ❑ 285 | Stephen Drew | .12 | .30 |
| ❑ 286 | Joaquin Arias (RC) | .20 | .50 |
| ❑ 287 | Jose Garcia RC | .20 | .50 |
| ❑ 288 | Shane Youman RC | .20 | .50 |
| ❑ 289 | Brian Burres (RC) | .20 | .50 |
| ❑ 290 | Matt Holliday | .20 | .50 |
| ❑ 291 | Ryan Feierabend (RC) | .20 | .50 |
| ❑ 292a | Josh Fields (RC) | .20 | .50 |
| ❑ 292b | J.Fields Running (RC) | .20 | .50 |
| ❑ 293 | Glen Perkins (RC) | .20 | .50 |
| ❑ 294 | Mike Rabelo RC | .20 | .50 |
| ❑ 295 | Jorge Posada | .12 | .30 |
| ❑ 296 | Ubaldo Jimenez (RC) | .20 | .50 |
| ❑ 297 | Brad Ausmus GG | .07 | .20 |
| ❑ 298 | Eric Chavez GG | .07 | .20 |
| ❑ 299 | Orlando Hudson GG | .07 | .20 |
| ❑ 300 | Vladimir Guerrero | .20 | .50 |
| ❑ 301 | Derek Jeter GG | .50 | 1.25 |
| ❑ 302 | Scott Rolen GG | .12 | .30 |
| ❑ 303 | Mark Grudzielanek GG | .07 | .20 |
| ❑ 304 | Kenny Rogers GG | .07 | .20 |
| ❑ 305 | Frank Thomas | .20 | .50 |
| ❑ 306 | Mike Cameron GG | .07 | .20 |
| ❑ 307 | Torii Hunter GG | .07 | .20 |
| ❑ 308 | Albert Pujols GG | .40 | 1.00 |
| ❑ 309 | Mark Teixeira GG | .20 | .50 |
| ❑ 310 | Jonathan Papelbon | .20 | .50 |
| ❑ 311 | Greg Maddux GG | .30 | .75 |
| ❑ 312 | Carlos Beltran GG | .07 | .20 |
| ❑ 313 | Ichiro Suzuki GG | .30 | .75 |
| ❑ 314 | Andruw Jones GG | .12 | .30 |
| ❑ 315 | Manny Ramirez | .20 | .50 |
| ❑ 316 | Vernon Wells GG | .07 | .20 |
| ❑ 317 | Omar Vizquel GG | .07 | .20 |
| ❑ 318 | Ivan Rodriguez GG | .12 | .30 |
| ❑ 319 | Brandon Webb CY | .20 | .50 |
| ❑ 320 | Magglio Ordonez | .07 | .20 |
| ❑ 321 | Johan Santana CY | .12 | .30 |
| ❑ 322 | Ryan Howard MVP | .30 | .75 |
| ❑ 323 | Justin Morneau MVP | .07 | .20 |
| ❑ 324 | Hanley Ramirez ROY | .12 | .30 |
| ❑ 325 | Joe Mauer | .20 | .50 |
| ❑ 326 | Justin Verlander ROY | .20 | .50 |
| ❑ 327 | B.Abreu/D.Jeter CC | .50 | 1.25 |
| ❑ 328 | C.Delgado/D.Wright CC | .30 | .75 |
| ❑ 329 | Y.Molina/A.Pujols CC | .40 | 1.00 |
| ❑ 330 | Ryan Howard | .30 | .75 |
| ❑ 331 | Kelly Johnson | .07 | .20 |
| ❑ 332 | Chris Young | .07 | .20 |
| ❑ 333 | Mark Kotsay | .07 | .20 |
| ❑ 334 | A.J. Burnett | .07 | .20 |
| ❑ 335 | Brian McCann | .20 | .50 |
| ❑ 336 | Woody Williams | .07 | .20 |
| ❑ 337 | Jason Isringhausen | .07 | .20 |
| ❑ 338 | Juan Pierre | .07 | .20 |
| ❑ 339 | Jonny Gomes | .07 | .20 |
| ❑ 340 | Roger Clemens | .50 | 1.25 |
| ❑ 341 | Akinori Iwamura RC | .50 | 1.25 |
| ❑ 342 | Bengie Molina | .07 | .20 |
| ❑ 343 | Shin-Soo Choo | .12 | .30 |
| ❑ 344 | Kenji Johjima | .20 | .50 |
| ❑ 345 | Joe Borowski | .07 | .20 |
| ❑ 346 | Shawn Green | .07 | .20 |
| ❑ 347 | Chicago Cubs | .12 | .30 |
| ❑ 348 | Rodrigo Lopez | .07 | .20 |
| ❑ 349 | Brian Giles | .07 | .20 |
| ❑ 350 | Chase Utley | .20 | .50 |
| ❑ 351 | Mark DeRosa | .07 | .20 |
| ❑ 352 | Carl Pavano | .07 | .20 |
| ❑ 353 | Kyle Lohse | .07 | .20 |
| ❑ 354 | Chris Iannetta | .07 | .20 |
| ❑ 355 | Oliver Perez | .07 | .20 |
| ❑ 356 | Curtis Granderson | .07 | .20 |
| ❑ 357 | Sean Casey | .07 | .20 |
| ❑ 358 | Jason Tyner | .07 | .20 |
| ❑ 359 | Jon Garland | .07 | .20 |
| ❑ 360 | David Ortiz | .12 | .30 |
| ❑ 361 | Adam Kennedy | .07 | .20 |
| ❑ 362 | Chris Burke | .07 | .20 |
| ❑ 363 | Bobby Crosby | .07 | .20 |
| ❑ 364 | Conor Jackson | .07 | .20 |
| ❑ 365 | Tim Hudson | .07 | .20 |
| ❑ 366 | Rickie Weeks | .07 | .20 |
| ❑ 367 | Cristian Guzman | .07 | .20 |
| ❑ 368 | Mark Prior | .12 | .30 |
| ❑ 369 | Ben Zobrist | .07 | .20 |
| ❑ 370 | Troy Glaus | .07 | .20 |
| ❑ 371 | Kenny Lofton | .07 | .20 |
| ❑ 372 | Shane Victorino | .07 | .20 |
| ❑ 373 | Cliff Lee | .07 | .20 |
| ❑ 374 | Adrian Beltre | .07 | .20 |
| ❑ 375 | Miguel Olivo | .07 | .20 |
| ❑ 376 | Endy Chavez | .07 | .20 |
| ❑ 377 | Zack Segovia (RC) | .20 | .50 |
| ❑ 378 | Ramon Hernandez | .07 | .20 |
| ❑ 379 | Chris Young | .07 | .20 |
| ❑ 380 | Jason Schmidt | .07 | .20 |
| ❑ 381 | Ronny Paulino | .07 | .20 |
| ❑ 382 | Kevin Millwood | .07 | .20 |
| ❑ 383 | Jon Lester | .12 | .30 |
| ❑ 384 | Alex Gonzalez | .07 | .20 |
| ❑ 385 | Brad Hawpe | .07 | .20 |
| ❑ 386 | Placido Polanco | .07 | .20 |
| ❑ 387 | Nate Robertson | .07 | .20 |
| ❑ 388 | Torii Hunter | .07 | .20 |
| ❑ 389 | Gavin Floyd | .07 | .20 |
| ❑ 390 | Roy Oswalt | .07 | .20 |
| ❑ 391 | Kelvim Escobar | .07 | .20 |
| ❑ 392 | Craig Wilson | .07 | .20 |
| ❑ 393 | Milton Bradley | .07 | .20 |
| ❑ 394 | Aaron Hill | .07 | .20 |
| ❑ 395 | Matt Diaz | .07 | .20 |
| ❑ 396 | Chris Capuano | .07 | .20 |
| ❑ 397 | Juan Encarnacion | .07 | .20 |
| ❑ 398 | Jacque Jones | .07 | .20 |
| ❑ 399 | James Shields | .07 | .20 |
| ❑ 400 | Ichiro Suzuki | .30 | .75 |
| ❑ 401 | Matt Kemp | .20 | .50 |
| ❑ 402 | Matt Morris | .07 | .20 |
| ❑ 403 | Casey Blake | .07 | .20 |
| ❑ 404 | Corey Hart | .07 | .20 |
| ❑ 405 | Josh Willingham | .07 | .20 |
| ❑ 406 | Ryan Madson | .07 | .20 |
| ❑ 407 | Nick Johnson | .07 | .20 |
| ❑ 408 | Kevin Millar | .07 | .20 |
| ❑ 409 | Khalil Greene | .12 | .30 |
| ❑ 410 | Tom Glavine | .12 | .30 |
| ❑ 411a | Jason Bay | .12 | .30 |
| ❑ 411b | Jason Bay No Sig | 2.00 | 5.00 |
| ❑ 412 | Gerald Laird | .07 | .20 |
| ❑ 413 | Coco Crisp | .07 | .20 |
| ❑ 414 | Brandon Phillips | .20 | .50 |
| ❑ 415 | Aaron Cook | .07 | .20 |
| ❑ 416 | Mark Redman | .07 | .20 |
| ❑ 417 | Mike Maroth | .07 | .20 |
| ❑ 418 | Boof Bonser | .07 | .20 |
| ❑ 419 | Jorge Cantu | .07 | .20 |
| ❑ 420 | Jeff Weaver | .07 | .20 |
| ❑ 421 | Melky Cabrera | .20 | .50 |
| ❑ 422 | Francisco Rodriguez | .07 | .20 |
| ❑ 423 | Mike Lamb | .07 | .20 |
| ❑ 424 | Dan Haren | .07 | .20 |
| ❑ 425 | Tomo Ohka | .07 | .20 |
| ❑ 426 | Jeff Francoeur | .20 | .50 |
| ❑ 427 | Randy Wolf | .07 | .20 |
| ❑ 428 | So Taguchi | .07 | .20 |
| ❑ 429 | Carlos Zambrano | .07 | .20 |
| ❑ 430 | Justin Morneau | .20 | .50 |
| ❑ 431 | Luis Gonzalez | .07 | .20 |
| ❑ 432 | Takashi Saito | .07 | .20 |
| ❑ 433 | Brandon Morrow RC | .50 | 1.25 |
| ❑ 434 | Victor Martinez | .07 | .20 |
| ❑ 435 | Felix Hernandez | .12 | .30 |
| ❑ 436 | Ricky Nolasco | .07 | .20 |
| ❑ 437 | Paul LoDuca | .07 | .20 |
| ❑ 437b | Paul LoDuca No Sig | 2.00 | 5.00 |
| ❑ 438 | Chad Cordero | .07 | .20 |
| ❑ 439 | Miguel Tejada | .07 | .20 |
| ❑ 440 | Mark Teixeira | .12 | .30 |
| ❑ 441 | Pat Burrell | .07 | .20 |
| ❑ 442 | Paul Maholm | .07 | .20 |
| ❑ 443 | Mike Cameron | .07 | .20 |
| ❑ 444 | Josh Beckett | .12 | .30 |
| ❑ 445 | Pablo Ozuna | .07 | .20 |
| ❑ 446 | Jaret Wright | .07 | .20 |
| ❑ 447 | Angel Berroa | .07 | .20 |
| ❑ 448 | Fernando Rodney | .07 | .20 |
| ❑ 449 | Francisco Liriano | .20 | .50 |
| ❑ 450 | Ken Griffey Jr. | .30 | .75 |
| ❑ 451 | Bobby Jenks | .07 | .20 |
| ❑ 452 | Mike Mussina | .12 | .30 |
| ❑ 453 | Howie Kendrick | .07 | .20 |
| ❑ 454 | Milwaukee Brewers | .07 | .20 |
| ❑ 455 | Dan Johnson | .07 | .20 |
| ❑ 456 | Ted Lilly | .07 | .20 |
| ❑ 457 | Mike Hampton | .07 | .20 |
| ❑ 458 | J.J. Hardy | .07 | .20 |
| ❑ 459 | Jeff Suppan | .07 | .20 |
| ❑ 460 | Jose Reyes | .20 | .50 |
| ❑ 461 | Jae Seo | .07 | .20 |
| ❑ 462 | Edgar Gonzalez | .07 | .20 |
| ❑ 463 | Russell Martin | .07 | .20 |

| | | | | | | | | | |
|---|---|---|---|---|---|---|---|---|---|
| 464 Omar Vizquel | .12 | .30 | 551 Ronnie Belliard | .07 | .20 | 636 Mike Rabelo RC | .20 | .50 |
| 465 Jhonny Peralta | .07 | .20 | 552 Chris Woodward | .07 | .20 | 637 Justin Hampson (RC) | .20 | .50 |
| 466 Raul Ibanez | .12 | .30 | 553 Ramon Martinez | .07 | .20 | 638 Cesar Jimenez RC | .20 | .50 |
| 467 Hanley Ramirez | .12 | .30 | 554 Elizardo Ramirez | .07 | .20 | 639 Joe Smith RC | .20 | .50 |
| 468 Kerry Wood | .07 | .20 | 555 Andy Marte | .07 | .20 | 640 Kei Igawa RC | .50 | 1.25 |
| 469 Ryan Church | .07 | .20 | 556 John Patterson | .07 | .20 | 641 Hideki Okajima RC | 1.00 | 2.50 |
| 470 Gary Sheffield | .07 | .20 | 557 Scott Olsen | .07 | .20 | 642 Sean Henn (RC) | .20 | .50 |
| 471 David Wells | .07 | .20 | 558 Steve Trachsel | .07 | .20 | 643 Jay Marshall RC | .20 | .50 |
| 472 David Dellucci | .07 | .20 | 559 Doug Mientkiewicz | .07 | .20 | 644 Jared Burton RC | .20 | .50 |
| 473 Xavier Nady | .07 | .20 | 560 Randy Johnson | .20 | .50 | 645 Angel Sanchez RC | .20 | .50 |
| 474 Michael Young | .07 | .20 | 561 Chan Ho Park | .07 | .20 | 646 Devern Hansack RC | .20 | .50 |
| 475 Kevin Youkilis | .07 | .20 | 562 Jamie Moyer | .07 | .20 | 647 Juan Morillo (RC) | .20 | .50 |
| 476 Aaron Harang | .07 | .20 | 563 Mike Gonzalez | .07 | .20 | 648 Hector Gimenez (RC) | .20 | .50 |
| 477 Brian Lawrence | .07 | .20 | 564 Nelson Cruz | .07 | .20 | 649 Brian Barden RC | .20 | .50 |
| 478 Octavio Dotel | .07 | .20 | 565 Alex Cora | .07 | .20 | 650 A.Rodriguez/J.Giambi CC | .30 | .75 |
| 479 Chris Shelton | .07 | .20 | 566 Ryan Freel | .07 | .20 | 651 J.Michaels/T.Hafner CC | .07 | .20 |
| 480 Matt Garza | .07 | .20 | 567 Chris Stewart RC | .20 | .50 | 652 J.Johnson/M.Olivo CC | .07 | .20 |
| 481a Jim Thome | .07 | .20 | 568 Carlos Guillen | .07 | .20 | 653 S.Casey/P.Polanco CC | .07 | .20 |
| 481b Jim Thome No Sig | 2.00 | 5.00 | 569 Jason Bartlett | .07 | .20 | 654 I.Rodriguez/F.Rodney CC | .12 | .30 |
| 482 Jose Contreras | .07 | .20 | 570 Mariano Rivera | .20 | .50 | 655 D.Uggla/H.Ramirez CC | .12 | .30 |
| 483 Kris Benson | .07 | .20 | 571 Norris Hopper | .07 | .20 | 656 C.Beltran/J.Reyes CC | .20 | .50 |
| 484 John Maine | .07 | .20 | 572 Alex Escobar | .07 | .20 | 657 A.Rodriguez/D.Jeter CC | .50 | 1.25 |
| 485 Tadahito Iguchi | .07 | .20 | 573 Gustavo Chacin | .07 | .20 | 658 A.Rowand/J.Rollins CC | .07 | .20 |
| 486 Wandy Rodriguez | .07 | .20 | 574 Brandon McCarthy | .07 | .20 | 659 A.Berroa/A.Blanco CC | .07 | .20 |
| 487 Eric Chavez | .07 | .20 | 575 Seth McClung | .07 | .20 | 660a Yadier Molina | .07 | .20 |
| 488 Vernon Wells | .07 | .20 | 576 Yuniesky Betancourt | .07 | .20 | 660b Yadier Molina No Sig | 2.00 | 5.00 |
| 489 Doug Davis | .07 | .20 | 577 Jason LaRue | .07 | .20 | 661 Barry Bonds | 4.00 | 10.00 |
| 490 Andruw Jones | .12 | .30 | 578 Dustin Pedroia | .25 | .60 | | | |
| 491 David Eckstein | .07 | .20 | 579 Taylor Tankersley | .07 | .20 | | | |
| 492 Michael Barrett | .07 | .20 | 580 Garret Anderson | .07 | .20 | | | |
| 493 Greg Norton | .07 | .20 | 581 Mike Sweeney | .07 | .20 | | | |
| 494 Orlando Hudson | .07 | .20 | 582 Scott Thorman | .07 | .20 | | | |
| 495 Wilson Betemit | .07 | .20 | 583 Joe Inglett | .07 | .20 | | | |
| 496 Ryan Klesko | .07 | .20 | 584 Clint Barmes | .07 | .20 | | | |
| 497 Fausto Carmona | .07 | .20 | 585 Willie Bloomquist | .07 | .20 | | | |
| 498 Jarrod Washburn | .07 | .20 | 586 Willy Aybar | .07 | .20 | | | |
| 499 Aaron Boone | .07 | .20 | 587 Brian Bannister | .07 | .20 | | | |
| 500 Pedro Martinez | .12 | .30 | 588 Jose Guillen UER | .07 | .20 | | | |
| 501 Mike O'Connor | .07 | .20 | 589 Brad Wilkerson | .07 | .20 | | | |
| 502 Brian Roberts | .07 | .20 | 590 Lance Berkman | .07 | .20 | | | |
| 503 Jeff Cirillo | .07 | .20 | 591 Toronto Blue Jays | .07 | .20 | | | |
| 504 Brett Myers | .07 | .20 | 592 Florida Marlins | .07 | .20 | | | |
| 505 Jose Bautista | .07 | .20 | 593 Washington Nationals | .07 | .20 | | | |
| 506 Akinori Otsuka | .07 | .20 | 594 Los Angeles Angels | .07 | .20 | | | |
| 507 Shea Hillenbrand | .07 | .20 | 595 Cleveland Indians | .07 | .20 | | | |
| 508 Ryan Langerhans | .07 | .20 | 596 Texas Rangers | .07 | .20 | | | |
| 509 Josh Fogg | .07 | .20 | 597 Detroit Tigers | .07 | .20 | | | |
| 510 Alex Rodriguez | .30 | .75 | 598 Arizona Diamondbacks | .07 | .20 | | | |
| 511 Kenny Rogers | .07 | .20 | 599 Kansas City Royals | .07 | .20 | | | |
| 512 Jason Kubel | .07 | .20 | 600 Ryan Zimmerman | .20 | .50 | | | |
| 513 Jermaine Dye | .07 | .20 | 601 Colorado Rockies | .07 | .20 | | | |
| 514 Mark Grudzielanek | .07 | .20 | 602 Minnesota Twins | .07 | .20 | | | |
| 515 Josh Phelps | .07 | .20 | 603 Los Angeles Dodgers | .07 | .20 | | | |
| 516 Bartolo Colon | .07 | .20 | 604 San Diego Padres | .07 | .20 | | | |
| 517 Craig Biggio | .12 | .30 | 605 Bruce Bochy MG | .07 | .20 | | | |
| 518 Esteban Loaiza | .07 | .20 | 606 Ron Washington MG | .07 | .20 | | | |
| 519 Alex Rios | .07 | .20 | 607 Manny Acta MG | .07 | .20 | | | |
| 520 Adam Dunn | .07 | .20 | 608 Sam Perlozzo MG | .07 | .20 | | | |
| 521 Derrick Turnbow | .07 | .20 | 609 Terry Francona MG | .07 | .20 | | | |
| 522 Anthony Reyes | .07 | .20 | 610 Jim Leyland MG | .07 | .20 | | | |
| 523 Derrek Lee | .07 | .20 | 611 Eric Wedge MG | .07 | .20 | | | |
| 524 Ty Wigginton | .07 | .20 | 612 Ozzie Guillen MG | .07 | .20 | | | |
| 525 Jeremy Hermida | .07 | .20 | 613 Buddy Bell MG | .07 | .20 | | | |
| 526 Derek Lowe | .07 | .20 | 614 Bob Geren MG | .07 | .20 | | | |
| 527 Randy Winn | .07 | .20 | 615 Lou Piniella MG | .07 | .20 | | | |
| 528 Paul Byrd | .07 | .20 | 616 Fredi Gonzalez MG | .07 | .20 | | | |
| 529 Chris Snelling | .07 | .20 | 617 Ned Yost MG | .07 | .20 | | | |
| 530 Brandon Webb | .07 | .20 | 618 Willie Randolph MG | .07 | .20 | | | |
| 531 Julio Franco | .07 | .20 | 619 Bud Black MG | .07 | .20 | | | |
| 532 Jose Vidro | .07 | .20 | 620 Garrett Atkins | .07 | .20 | | | |
| 533 Erik Bedard | .07 | .20 | 621 Alexi Casilla RC | .30 | .75 | | | |
| 534 Termel Sledge | .07 | .20 | 622 Matt Chico (RC) | .20 | .50 | | | |
| 535 Jon Lieber | .07 | .20 | 623 Alejandro De Aza RC | .30 | .75 | | | |
| 536 Tom Gorzelanny | .07 | .20 | 624 Jeremy Brown | .07 | .20 | | | |
| 537 Kip Wells | .07 | .20 | 625 Josh Hamilton (RC) | .50 | 1.25 | | | |
| 538 Willy Mo Pena | .07 | .20 | 626 Doug Slaten RC | .20 | .50 | | | |
| 539 Eric Milton | .07 | .20 | 627 Andy Cannizaro RC | .20 | .50 | | | |
| 540 Chad Billingsley | .07 | .20 | 628 Juan Salas (RC) | .20 | .50 | | | |
| 541 David DeJesus | .07 | .20 | 629 Levale Speigner RC | .20 | .50 | | | |
| 542 Omar Infante | .07 | .20 | 630a D.Matsuzaka English RC | 3.00 | 8.00 | | | |
| 543 Rondell White | .07 | .20 | 630b D.Matsuzaka Japanese RC | 4.00 | 10.00 | | | |
| 544 Juan Uribe | .07 | .20 | 630c Daisuke Matsuzaka No Sig | 4.00 | 10.00 | | | |
| 545 Miguel Cairo | .07 | .20 | 631 Elijah Dukes RC | .30 | .75 | | | |
| 546 Orlando Cabrera | .07 | .20 | 632 Kevin Cameron RC | .20 | .50 | | | |
| 547 Byung-Hyun Kim | .07 | .20 | 633 Juan Perez RC | .20 | .50 | | | |
| 548 Jason Kendall | .07 | .20 | 634a Alex Gordon RC | .75 | 2.00 | | | |
| 549 Horacio Ramirez | .07 | .20 | 634b A.Gordon No Sig | 3.00 | 8.00 | | | |
| 550 Trevor Hoffman | .07 | .20 | 635 Juan Lara RC | .20 | .50 | | | |

## 2007 Topps Update

| | | |
|---|---|---|
| COMP.SET w/o SPs (330) | 20.00 | 50.00 |
| COMMON CARD (1-330) | .12 | .30 |
| COMMON ROOKIE (1-330) | .20 | .50 |
| 1-330 PLATE ODDS 1:54 HTA | | |
| PLATE PRINT RUN 1 SET PER COLOR | | |
| BLACK-CYAN-MAGENTA-YELLOW ISSUED | | |
| NO PLATE PRICING DUE TO SCARCITY | | |
| 1 Tony Armas Jr. | .12 | .30 |
| 2 Shannon Stewart | .12 | .30 |
| 3 Jason Marquis | .12 | .30 |
| 4 Josh Wilson | .12 | .30 |
| 5 Steve Trachsel | .12 | .30 |
| 6 J.D. Drew | .12 | .30 |
| 7 Ronnie Belliard | .12 | .30 |
| 8 Trot Nixon | .12 | .30 |
| 9 Adam LaRoche | .12 | .30 |
| 10 Mark Loretta | .12 | .30 |
| 11 Matt Morris | .12 | .30 |
| 12 Marlon Anderson | .12 | .30 |
| 13 Jorge Julio | .12 | .30 |
| 14 Brady Clark | .12 | .30 |
| 15 David Wells | .12 | .30 |
| 16 Francisco Rosario | .12 | .30 |
| 17 Jason Ellison | .12 | .30 |
| 18 Adam Jones | .12 | .30 |
| 19 Russell Branyan | .12 | .30 |
| 20 Rob Bowen | .12 | .30 |
| 21 J.D. Durbin | .12 | .30 |
| 22 Jeff Salazar | .12 | .30 |
| 23 Tadahito Iguchi | .12 | .30 |
| 24 Brad Hennessey | .12 | .30 |
| 25 Mark Hendrickson | .12 | .30 |
| 26 Kameron Loe | .12 | .30 |
| 27 Yusmeiro Petit | .12 | .30 |
| 28 Olmedo Saenz | .12 | .30 |
| 29 Carlos Silva | .12 | .30 |
| 30 Kevin Frandsen | .12 | .30 |
| 31 Tony Pena | .12 | .30 |
| 32 Russ Ortiz | .12 | .30 |
| 33 Hong-Chih Kuo | .12 | .30 |
| 34 Paul McAnulty | .12 | .30 |
| 35 Hiram Bocachica | .12 | .30 |
| 36 Justin Germano | .12 | .30 |
| 37 Jason Simontacchi | .12 | .30 |
| 38 Jose Cruz | .12 | .30 |

|  |  | | |
|---|---|---|---|
| 39 | Wilfredo Ledezma | .12 | .30 |
| 40 | Chris Denorfia | .12 | .30 |
| 41 | Ryan Langerhans | .12 | .30 |
| 42 | Chris Snelling | .12 | .30 |
| 43 | Ubaldo Jimenez | .12 | .30 |
| 44 | Scott Spiezio | .12 | .30 |
| 45 | Byung-Hyun Kim | .12 | .30 |
| 46 | Brandon Lyon | .12 | .30 |
| 47 | Scott Hairston | .12 | .30 |
| 48 | Chad Durbin | .12 | .30 |
| 49 | Sammy Sosa | .30 | .75 |
| 50 | Jason Smith | .12 | .30 |
| 51 | Zack Greinke | .12 | .30 |
| 52 | Armando Benitez | .12 | .30 |
| 53 | Randy Messenger | .12 | .30 |
| 54 | Mark Teixeira | .20 | .50 |
| 55 | Mike Maroth | .12 | .30 |
| 56 | Jamie Burke | .12 | .30 |
| 57 | Carlos Marmol | .12 | .30 |
| 58 | David Weathers | .12 | .30 |
| 59 | Ryan Doumit | .12 | .30 |
| 60 | Michael Barrett | .12 | .30 |
| 61 | Shawn Chacon | .12 | .30 |
| 62 | Mike Fontenot | .12 | .30 |
| 63 | Cesar Izturis | .12 | .30 |
| 64 | Cliff Floyd | .12 | .30 |
| 65 | Angel Pagan | .12 | .30 |
| 66 | Aaron Miles | .12 | .30 |
| 67 | Tony Graffanino | .12 | .30 |
| 68 | Kevin Mench | .12 | .30 |
| 69 | Claudio Vargas | .12 | .30 |
| 70 | Jose Capellan | .12 | .30 |
| 71 | A.J. Pierzynski | .12 | .30 |
| 72 | Darin Erstad | .12 | .30 |
| 73 | Boone Logan | .12 | .30 |
| 74 | Luis Castillo | .12 | .30 |
| 75 | Marcus Thames | .12 | .30 |
| 76 | Neifi Perez | .12 | .30 |
| 77 | Esteban German | .12 | .30 |
| 78 | Tony Pena | .12 | .30 |
| 79 | Adam Wainwright | .20 | .50 |
| 80 | Reggie Sanders | .12 | .30 |
| 81 | Kelly Shoppach | .12 | .30 |
| 82 | Rafael Betancourt | .12 | .30 |
| 83 | Tom Mastny | .12 | .30 |
| 84 | Kyle Farnsworth | .12 | .30 |
| 85 | Rick Ankiel | .20 | .50 |
| 86 | Kevin Thompson | .12 | .30 |
| 87 | Jeff Karstens | .12 | .30 |
| 88 | Eric Hinske | .12 | .30 |
| 89 | Doug Mirabelli | .12 | .30 |
| 90 | Julian Tavarez | .12 | .30 |
| 91 | Carlos Pena | .12 | .30 |
| 92 | Brendan Harris | .12 | .30 |
| 93 | Chris Sampson | .12 | .30 |
| 94 | Al Reyes | .12 | .30 |
| 95 | Dmitri Young | .12 | .30 |
| 96 | Jason Bergmann | .12 | .30 |
| 97 | Shawn Hill | .12 | .30 |
| 98 | Greg Dobbs | .12 | .30 |
| 99 | Carlos Ruiz | .12 | .30 |
| 100a | Abraham Nunez | .12 | .30 |
| 100b | Jacoby Ellsbury (RC) | 60.00 | 120.00 |
| 101 | Jason Werth | .12 | .30 |
| 102 | Adam Eaton | .12 | .30 |
| 103 | Antonio Alfonseca | .12 | .30 |
| 104 | Jorge Sosa | .12 | .30 |
| 105 | Ramon Castro | .12 | .30 |
| 106 | Ruben Gotay | .12 | .30 |
| 107 | Damion Easley | .12 | .30 |
| 108 | David Newhan | .12 | .30 |
| 109 | Jason Wood | .12 | .30 |
| 110 | Reggie Abercrombie | .12 | .30 |
| 111 | Kevin Gregg | .12 | .30 |
| 112 | Henry Owens | .12 | .30 |
| 113 | Willie Harris | .12 | .30 |
| 114 | Pete Orr | .12 | .30 |
| 115 | Casey Janssen | .12 | .30 |
| 116 | Jason Frasor | .12 | .30 |
| 117 | Jeremy Accardo | .12 | .30 |
| 118 | John McDonald | .12 | .30 |
| 119 | Matt Stairs | .12 | .30 |
| 120 | Jason Phillips | .12 | .30 |
| 121 | Justin Duchscherer | .12 | .30 |
| 122 | Rich Harden | .12 | .30 |
| 123 | Jack Cust | .12 | .30 |
| 124 | Lenny DiNardo | .12 | .30 |
| 125 | Joe Kennedy | .12 | .30 |
| 126 | Chad Gaudin | .12 | .30 |
| 127 | Marco Scutaro | .12 | .30 |
| 128 | Brad Thompson | .12 | .30 |
| 129 | Dustin Moseley | .12 | .30 |
| 130 | Eric Gagne | .12 | .30 |
| 131 | Marlon Byrd | .12 | .30 |
| 132 | Scot Shields | .12 | .30 |
| 133 | Victor Diaz | .12 | .30 |
| 134 | Reggie Willits | .12 | .30 |
| 135 | Jose Molina | .12 | .30 |
| 136 | Ramon Vazquez | .12 | .30 |
| 137 | Erick Aybar | .12 | .30 |
| 138 | Sean Marshall | .12 | .30 |
| 139 | Casey Kotchman | .12 | .30 |
| 140 | Ryan Spilborghs | .12 | .30 |
| 141 | Cameron Maybin (RC) | 1.00 | 2.50 |
| 142 | Jeremy Guthrie | .12 | .30 |
| 143 | Jeff Baker | .12 | .30 |
| 144 | Edwin Jackson | .12 | .30 |
| 145 | Macay McBride | .12 | .30 |
| 146 | Freddie Bynum | .12 | .30 |
| 147 | Eric Patterson | .12 | .30 |
| 148 | Dustin McGowan | .12 | .30 |
| 149 | Homer Bailey (RC) | .30 | .75 |
| 150 | Ryan Braun (RC) | 1.25 | 3.00 |
| 151 | Tony Abreu RC | .50 | 1.25 |
| 152 | Tyler Clippard (RC) | .30 | .75 |
| 153 | Mark Reynolds RC | 1.25 | 3.00 |
| 154 | Jesse Litsch RC | .30 | .75 |
| 155 | Carlos Gomez RC | .30 | .75 |
| 156 | Matt DeSalvo (RC) | .20 | .50 |
| 157 | Andy LaRoche (RC) | .20 | .50 |
| 158 | Tim Lincecum RC | 2.50 | 6.00 |
| 159 | Jarrod Saltalamacchia (RC) | .30 | .75 |
| 160 | Hunter Pence (RC) | 1.00 | 2.50 |
| 161 | Brandon Wood | .20 | .50 |
| 162 | Phil Hughes (RC) | 1.00 | 2.50 |
| 163 | Rocky Cherry RC | .50 | 1.25 |
| 164 | Chase Wright RC | .30 | .75 |
| 165 | Dallas Braden RC | .30 | .75 |
| 166 | Felix Pie (RC) | .30 | .75 |
| 167 | Zach McClellan RC | .20 | .50 |
| 168 | Rick Vanden Hurk RC | .30 | .75 |
| 169 | Micah Owings (RC) | .20 | .50 |
| 170 | Jon Coutlangus (RC) | .20 | .50 |
| 171 | Andy Sonnanstine RC | .20 | .50 |
| 172 | Yunel Escobar (RC) | .20 | .50 |
| 173 | Kevin Slowey (RC) | .50 | 1.25 |
| 174 | Curtis Thigpen (RC) | .20 | .50 |
| 175 | Masumi Kuwata RC | 1.50 | 4.00 |
| 176 | Kurt Suzuki (RC) | .20 | .50 |
| 177 | Travis Buck (RC) | .20 | .50 |
| 178 | Matt Lindstrom (RC) | .20 | .50 |
| 179 | Jesus Flores RC | .20 | .50 |
| 180 | Joakim Soria RC | .20 | .50 |
| 181 | Nathan Haynes (RC) | .20 | .50 |
| 182 | Matthew Brown RC | .20 | .50 |
| 183 | Travis Metcalf RC | .30 | .75 |
| 184 | Yovani Gallardo (RC) | .60 | 1.50 |
| 185 | Nate Schierholtz (RC) | .20 | .50 |
| 186 | Kyle Kendrick RC | .50 | 1.25 |
| 187 | Kevin Melillo (RC) | .20 | .50 |
| 188 | Ryan Rowland-Smith | .12 | .30 |
| 189 | Lee Gronkiewicz RC | .12 | .30 |
| 190 | Eulogio De La Cruz (RC) | .20 | .50 |
| 191 | Brett Carroll RC | .20 | .50 |
| 192 | Terry Evans RC | .20 | .50 |
| 193 | Chase Headley (RC) | .30 | .75 |
| 194 | Guillermo Rodriguez RC | .20 | .50 |
| 195 | Marcus McBeth (RC) | .20 | .50 |
| 196 | Brian Wolfe (RC) | .20 | .50 |
| 197 | Troy Cate RC | .12 | .30 |
| 198 | Mike Zagurski RC | .20 | .50 |
| 199 | Yoel Hernandez RC | .12 | .30 |
| 200 | Brad Salmon RC | .20 | .50 |
| 201 | Alberto Arias RC | .20 | .50 |
| 202 | Danny Putnam (RC) | .20 | .50 |
| 203 | Jamie Vermilyea RC | .20 | .50 |
| 204 | Kyle Lohse | .12 | .30 |
| 205 | Sammy Sosa | .30 | .75 |
| 206 | Tom Glavine | .30 | .75 |
| 207 | Prince Fielder | .30 | .75 |
| 208 | Mark Buehrle | .12 | .30 |
| 209 | Troy Tulowitzki | .30 | .75 |
| 210 | Daisuke Matsuzaka RC | 1.50 | 4.00 |
| 211 | Randy Johnson | .30 | .75 |
| 212 | Justin Verlander | .30 | .75 |
| 213 | Trevor Hoffman | .12 | .30 |
| 214 | Alex Rodriguez | .50 | 1.25 |
| 215 | Ivan Rodriguez | .20 | .50 |
| 216 | David Ortiz | .20 | .50 |
| 217 | Placido Polanco | .12 | .30 |
| 218 | Derek Jeter | .75 | 2.00 |
| 219 | Alex Rodriguez | .50 | 1.25 |
| 220 | Vladimir Guerrero | .30 | .75 |
| 221 | Magglio Ordonez | .12 | .30 |
| 222 | Ichiro Suzuki | .50 | 1.25 |
| 223 | Russell Martin | .12 | .30 |
| 224 | Prince Fielder | .30 | .75 |
| 225 | Chase Utley | .30 | .75 |
| 226 | Jose Reyes | .30 | .75 |
| 227 | David Wright | .50 | 1.25 |
| 228 | Carlos Beltran | .12 | .30 |
| 229 | Barry Bonds | .60 | 1.50 |
| 230 | Ken Griffey Jr. | .50 | 1.25 |
| 231 | Torii Hunter | .12 | .30 |
| 232 | Jonathan Papelbon | .30 | .75 |
| 233 | J.J. Putz | .12 | .30 |
| 234 | Francisco Rodriguez | .12 | .30 |
| 235 | C.C. Sabathia | .12 | .30 |
| 236 | Johan Santana | .20 | .50 |
| 237 | Justin Verlander | .30 | .75 |
| 238 | Francisco Cordero | .12 | .30 |
| 239 | Mike Lowell | .12 | .30 |
| 240 | Cole Hamels | .30 | .75 |
| 241 | Trevor Hoffman | .12 | .30 |
| 242 | Manny Ramirez | .20 | .50 |
| 243 | Jake Peavy | .12 | .30 |
| 244 | Brad Penny | .12 | .30 |
| 245 | Takashi Saito | .12 | .30 |
| 246 | Ben Sheets | .12 | .30 |
| 247 | Hideki Okajima | .60 | 1.50 |
| 248 | Roy Oswalt | .12 | .30 |
| 249 | Billy Wagner | .12 | .30 |
| 250 | Carl Crawford | .12 | .30 |
| 251 | Chris Young | .12 | .30 |
| 252 | Brian McCann | .12 | .30 |
| 253 | Derrek Lee | .12 | .30 |
| 254 | Albert Pujols | .60 | 1.50 |
| 255 | Dmitri Young | .12 | .30 |
| 256 | Orlando Hudson | .12 | .30 |
| 257 | J.J. Hardy | .12 | .30 |
| 258 | Miguel Cabrera | .20 | .50 |
| 259 | Freddy Sanchez | .12 | .30 |
| 260 | Matt Holliday | .30 | .75 |
| 261 | Carlos Lee | .12 | .30 |
| 262 | Aaron Rowand | .12 | .30 |
| 263 | Alfonso Soriano | .20 | .50 |
| 264 | Victor Martinez | .12 | .30 |
| 265 | Jorge Posada | .20 | .50 |
| 266 | Justin Morneau | .12 | .30 |
| 267 | Brian Roberts | .12 | .30 |
| 268 | Carlos Guillen | .12 | .30 |
| 269 | Grady Sizemore | .20 | .50 |
| 270 | Josh Beckett | .20 | .50 |
| 271 | Dan Haren | .12 | .30 |
| 272 | Bobby Jenks | .12 | .30 |
| 273 | John Lackey | .12 | .30 |
| 274 | Gil Meche | .12 | .30 |
| 275 | M.Fontenot/K.Greene | .12 | .30 |
| 276 | A.Rodriguez/R.Martin | .50 | 1.25 |
| 277 | T.Tulowitzki/J.Reyes | .30 | .75 |
| 278 | Posada/Jeter/ARod | .75 | 2.00 |
| 279 | C.Utley/Ichiro | .50 | 1.25 |
| 280 | C.Crawford/C.Guillen | .12 | .30 |
| 281 | C.Hamels/R.Martin | .30 | .75 |
| 282 | J.Papelbon/J.Posada | .30 | .75 |
| 283 | C.Crawford/V.Martinez | .12 | .30 |
| 284 | A.Soriano/J.Hardy | .12 | .30 |
| 285 | Justin Morneau | .12 | .30 |
| 286 | Prince Fielder | .30 | .75 |
| 287 | Alex Rios | .12 | .30 |
| 288 | Vladimir Guerrero | .30 | .75 |
| 289 | Albert Pujols | .60 | 1.50 |
| 290 | Ryan Howard | .50 | 1.25 |
| 291 | Magglio Ordonez | .12 | .30 |
| 292 | Matt Holliday | .30 | .75 |
| 293 | Wilson Betemit | .12 | .30 |
| 294 | Todd Wellemeyer | .12 | .30 |
| 295 | Scott Baker | .12 | .30 |
| 296 | Edgar Gonzalez | .12 | .30 |
| 297 | J.P. Howell | .12 | .30 |
| 298 | Shaun Marcum | .12 | .30 |
| 299 | Edinson Volquez | .12 | .30 |
| 300 | Kason Gabbard | .12 | .30 |
| 301 | Bob Howry | .12 | .30 |

| | | |
|---|---|---|
| ☐ 302 J.A. Happ | .50 | 1.25 |
| ☐ 303 Scott Feldman | .20 | .50 |
| ☐ 304 D'Angelo Jimenez | .12 | .30 |
| ☐ 305 Orlando Palmeiro | .12 | .30 |
| ☐ 306 Paul Bako | .12 | .30 |
| ☐ 307 Kyle Davies | .12 | .30 |
| ☐ 308 Gabe Gross | .12 | .30 |
| ☐ 309 John Wasdin | .12 | .30 |
| ☐ 310 Jon Knott | .12 | .30 |
| ☐ 311 Josh Phelps | .12 | .30 |
| ☐ 312a J.Chamberlain RC | 4.00 | 10.00 |
| ☐ 312b J.Chamberlain Rev.Neg | 90.00 | 150.00 |
| ☐ 312c J.Chamberlain Hou UER | | |
| ☐ 313 Octavio Dotel | .12 | .30 |
| ☐ 314 Craig Monroe | .12 | .30 |
| ☐ 315 Edward Mujica | .12 | .30 |
| ☐ 316 Brandon Watson | .12 | .30 |
| ☐ 317 Chris Schroder | .12 | .30 |
| ☐ 318 Scott Proctor | .12 | .30 |
| ☐ 319 Ty Wigginton | .12 | .30 |
| ☐ 320 Troy Percival | .12 | .30 |
| ☐ 321 Scott Linebrink | .12 | .30 |
| ☐ 322 David Murphy | .12 | .30 |
| ☐ 323 Jorge Cantu | .12 | .30 |
| ☐ 324 Dan Wheeler | .12 | .30 |
| ☐ 325 Jason Kendall | .12 | .30 |
| ☐ 326 Milton Bradley | .12 | .30 |
| ☐ 327 Justin Upton RC | 1.25 | 3.00 |
| ☐ 328 Kenny Lofton | .12 | .30 |
| ☐ 329 Roger Clemens | .50 | 1.25 |
| ☐ 330 Brian Burres | .12 | .30 |
| ☐ SQ1 Poley Walnuts | 12.50 | 30.00 |

## 2008 Topps

| | | |
|---|---|---|
| ☐ COMP.HOBBY SET (660) | 40.00 | 80.00 |
| ☐ COMP.CUBS SET (660) | 40.00 | 80.00 |
| ☐ COMP.DODGERS SET (660) | 40.00 | 80.00 |
| ☐ COMP.METS SET (660) | 40.00 | 80.00 |
| ☐ COMP.RED SOX SET (680) | 40.00 | 80.00 |
| ☐ COMP.TIGERS SET (660) | 40.00 | 80.00 |
| ☐ COMP.YANKEES SET (660) | 40.00 | 80.00 |
| ☐ COMP.SET w/o VAR (660) | 40.00 | 80.00 |
| ☐ COMP.SERIES 1 (331) | 15.00 | 30.00 |
| ☐ COMP.SERIES 2 (330) | 15.00 | 30.00 |
| ☐ COMMON CARD (1-660) | .12 | .30 |
| ☐ COMMON RC (1-660) | .25 | .60 |
| ☐ SERIES 1 SET DOES NOT INCLUDE FS1 | | |
| ☐ SERIES 1 SET DOES NOT INCLUDE #234C | | |
| ☐ SER.2 SET DOES NOT INCLUDE #661 | | |
| ☐ SER.2 SET DOES NOT INCLUDE NNO CARDS | | |
| ☐ SER.1 PLATE ODDS 1:1348 HOBBY | | |
| ☐ SER.2 PLATE ODDS 1:900 HOBBY | | |
| ☐ PLATE PRINT RUN 1 SET PER COLOR | | |
| ☐ BLACK-CYAN-MAGENTA-YELLOW ISSUED | | |
| ☐ NO PLATE PRICING DUE TO SCARCITY | | |
| ☐ 1 Alex Rodriguez | .50 | 1.25 |
| ☐ 2 Barry Zito | .12 | .30 |
| ☐ 3 Jeff Suppan | .12 | .30 |
| ☐ 4 Rick Ankiel | .12 | .30 |
| ☐ 5 Scott Kazmir | .20 | .50 |
| ☐ 6 Felix Pie | .12 | .30 |
| ☐ 7 Mickey Mantle | 1.25 | 3.00 |
| ☐ 8 Stephen Drew | .12 | .30 |
| ☐ 9 Randy Wolf | .12 | .30 |
| ☐ 10 Miguel Cabrera | .20 | .50 |
| ☐ 11 Yorvit Torrealba | .12 | .30 |
| ☐ 12 Jason Bartlett | .12 | .30 |
| ☐ 13 Kendry Morales | .12 | .30 |
| ☐ 14 Lenny DiNardo | .12 | .30 |
| ☐ 15 Ordon/Suzuki/Polan | .50 | 1.25 |
| ☐ 16 Kevin Gregg | .12 | .30 |
| ☐ 17 Cristian Guzman | .12 | .30 |
| ☐ 18 J.D. Durbin | .12 | .30 |
| ☐ 19 Robinson Tejeda | .12 | .30 |

| | | |
|---|---|---|
| ☐ 20 Daisuke Matsuzaka | .40 | 1.00 |
| ☐ 21 Edwin Encarnacion | .12 | .30 |
| ☐ 22 Ron Washington MG | .12 | .30 |
| ☐ 23 Chin-Lung Hu (RC) | .40 | 1.00 |
| ☐ 24 ARod/Ordon/Vlad | .50 | 1.25 |
| ☐ 25 Kaz Matsui | .12 | .30 |
| ☐ 26 Manny Ramirez | .30 | .75 |
| ☐ 27 Bob Melvin MG | .12 | .30 |
| ☐ 28 Kyle Kendrick | .12 | .30 |
| ☐ 29 Anibal Sanchez | .12 | .30 |
| ☐ 30 Jimmy Rollins | .20 | .50 |
| ☐ 31 Ronny Paulino | .12 | .30 |
| ☐ 32 Howie Kendrick | .12 | .30 |
| ☐ 33 Joe Mauer | .30 | .75 |
| ☐ 34 Aaron Cook | .12 | .30 |
| ☐ 35 Cole Hamels | .30 | .75 |
| ☐ 36 Brendan Harris | .12 | .30 |
| ☐ 37 Jason Marquis | .12 | .30 |
| ☐ 38 Preston Wilson | .12 | .30 |
| ☐ 39 Yovanni Gallardo | .12 | .30 |
| ☐ 40 Miguel Tejada | .12 | .30 |
| ☐ 41 Rich Aurilia | .12 | .30 |
| ☐ 42 Corey Hart | .12 | .30 |
| ☐ 43 Ryan Dempster | .12 | .30 |
| ☐ 44 Jonathan Broxton | .12 | .30 |
| ☐ 45 Dontrelle Willis | .12 | .30 |
| ☐ 46 Zack Greinke | .12 | .30 |
| ☐ 47 Orlando Cabrera | .12 | .30 |
| ☐ 48 Zach Duke | .12 | .30 |
| ☐ 49 Orlando Hernandez | .12 | .30 |
| ☐ 50 Jake Peavy | .20 | .50 |
| ☐ 51 Erik Bedard | .12 | .30 |
| ☐ 52 Trevor Hoffman | .12 | .30 |
| ☐ 53 Hank Blalock | .12 | .30 |
| ☐ 54 Victor Martinez | .12 | .30 |
| ☐ 55 Chris Young | .12 | .30 |
| ☐ 56 Seth Smith (RC) | .25 | .60 |
| ☐ 57 Vladimir Balentien (RC) | .25 | .60 |
| ☐ 58 Holliday/Howard/Mig.Cabrera | .40 | 1.00 |
| ☐ 59 Grady Sizemore | .20 | .50 |
| ☐ 60 Jose Reyes | .20 | .50 |
| ☐ 61 ARod/Pena/Ortiz | .20 | .50 |
| ☐ 62 Rich Thompson RC | .40 | 1.00 |
| ☐ 63 Jason Michaels | .12 | .30 |
| ☐ 64 Mike Lowell | .12 | .30 |
| ☐ 65 Billy Wagner | .12 | .30 |
| ☐ 66 Brad Wilkerson | .12 | .30 |
| ☐ 67 Wes Helms | .12 | .30 |
| ☐ 68 Kevin Millar | .12 | .30 |
| ☐ 69 Bobby Cox MG | .12 | .30 |
| ☐ 70 Dan Uggla | .20 | .50 |
| ☐ 71 Jarrod Washburn | .12 | .30 |
| ☐ 72 Mike Piazza | .30 | .75 |
| ☐ 73 Mike Napoli | .12 | .30 |
| ☐ 74 Garrett Atkins | .12 | .30 |
| ☐ 75 Felix Hernandez | .20 | .50 |
| ☐ 76 Ivan Rodriguez | .20 | .50 |
| ☐ 77 Angel Guzman | .12 | .30 |
| ☐ 78 Radhames Liz RC | .40 | 1.00 |
| ☐ 79 Omar Vizquel | .12 | .30 |
| ☐ 80 Alex Rios | .12 | .30 |
| ☐ 81 Ray Durham | .12 | .30 |
| ☐ 82 So Taguchi | .12 | .30 |
| ☐ 83 Mark Reynolds | .12 | .30 |
| ☐ 84 Brian Fuentes | .12 | .30 |
| ☐ 85 Jason Bay | .20 | .50 |
| ☐ 86 Scott Podsednik | .12 | .30 |
| ☐ 87 Maicer Izturis | .12 | .30 |
| ☐ 88 Jack Cust | .12 | .30 |
| ☐ 89 Josh Willingham | .12 | .30 |
| ☐ 90 Vladimir Guerrero | .30 | .75 |
| ☐ 91 Marcus Giles | .12 | .30 |
| ☐ 92 Ross Detwiler RC | .60 | 1.50 |
| ☐ 93 Kenny Lofton | .12 | .30 |
| ☐ 94 Bud Black MG | .12 | .30 |
| ☐ 95 John Lackey | .12 | .30 |
| ☐ 96 Sam Fuld RC | .25 | .60 |
| ☐ 97 Clint Sammons (RC) | .40 | 1.00 |
| ☐ 98 R.Howard/C.Utley | .40 | 1.00 |
| ☐ 99 D.Ortiz/M.Ramirez | .20 | .50 |
| ☐ 100 Ryan Howard | .40 | 1.00 |
| ☐ 101 Ryan Braun ROY | .40 | 1.00 |
| ☐ 102 Ross Ohlendorf RC | .40 | 1.00 |
| ☐ 103 Jonathan Albaladejo RC | .40 | 1.00 |
| ☐ 104 Kevin Youkilis | .20 | .50 |
| ☐ 105 Roger Clemens | .40 | 1.00 |
| ☐ 106 Josh Bard | .12 | .30 |
| ☐ 107 Shawn Green | .12 | .30 |

| | | |
|---|---|---|
| ☐ 108 B.J. Ryan | .12 | .30 |
| ☐ 109 Joe Nathan | .12 | .30 |
| ☐ 110 Justin Morneau | .20 | .50 |
| ☐ 111 Ubaldo Jimenez | .12 | .30 |
| ☐ 112 Jacque Jones | .12 | .30 |
| ☐ 113 Kevin Frandsen | .12 | .30 |
| ☐ 114 Mike Fontenot | .12 | .30 |
| ☐ 115 Johan Santana | .20 | .50 |
| ☐ 116 Chuck James | .12 | .30 |
| ☐ 117 Rod Bonser | .12 | .30 |
| ☐ 118 Marco Scutaro | .12 | .30 |
| ☐ 119 Jeremy Hermida | .12 | .30 |
| ☐ 120 Andruw Jones | .12 | .30 |
| ☐ 121 Mike Cameron | .12 | .30 |
| ☐ 122 Jason Varitek | .30 | .75 |
| ☐ 123 Terry Francona MG | .12 | .30 |
| ☐ 124 Bob Geren MG | .12 | .30 |
| ☐ 125 Tim Hudson | .12 | .30 |
| ☐ 126 Brandon Jones RC | .60 | 1.50 |
| ☐ 127 Steve Pearce RC | .40 | 1.00 |
| ☐ 128 Kenny Lofton | .12 | .30 |
| ☐ 129 Kevin Hart (RC) | .25 | .60 |
| ☐ 130 Justin Upton | .30 | .75 |
| ☐ 131 Norris Hopper | .12 | .30 |
| ☐ 132 Ramon Vazquez | .12 | .30 |
| ☐ 133 Mike Bacsik | .12 | .30 |
| ☐ 134 Matt Stairs | .12 | .30 |
| ☐ 135 Brad Penny | .12 | .30 |
| ☐ 136 Robinson Cano | .20 | .50 |
| ☐ 137 Jamey Carroll | .12 | .30 |
| ☐ 138 Dan Wheeler | .12 | .30 |
| ☐ 139 Johnny Estrada | .12 | .30 |
| ☐ 140 Brandon Webb | .20 | .50 |
| ☐ 141 Ryan Klesko | .12 | .30 |
| ☐ 142 Chris Duncan | .12 | .30 |
| ☐ 143 Willie Harris | .12 | .30 |
| ☐ 144 Jerry Owens | .12 | .30 |
| ☐ 145 Magglio Ordonez | .20 | .50 |
| ☐ 146 Aaron Hill | .12 | .30 |
| ☐ 147 Marlon Anderson | .12 | .30 |
| ☐ 148 Gerald Laird | .12 | .30 |
| ☐ 149 Luke Hochevar RC | .40 | 1.00 |
| ☐ 150 Alfonso Soriano | .20 | .50 |
| ☐ 151 Adam Loewen | .12 | .30 |
| ☐ 152 Bronson Arroyo | .12 | .30 |
| ☐ 153 Luis Mendoza (RC) | .25 | .60 |
| ☐ 154 David Ross | .12 | .30 |
| ☐ 155 Carlos Zambrana | .20 | .50 |
| ☐ 156 Brandon McCarthy | .12 | .30 |
| ☐ 157 Tim Redding | .12 | .30 |
| ☐ 158 Jose Bautista | .12 | .30 |
| ☐ 159 Luke Scott | .12 | .30 |
| ☐ 160 Ben Sheets | .20 | .50 |
| ☐ 161 Matt Garza | .12 | .30 |
| ☐ 162 Andy Laroche | .12 | .30 |
| ☐ 163 Doug Davis | .12 | .30 |
| ☐ 164 Nate Schierholtz | .12 | .30 |
| ☐ 165 Tim Lincecum | .40 | 1.00 |
| ☐ 166 Andy Sonnanstine | .12 | .30 |
| ☐ 167 Jason Hirsh | .12 | .30 |
| ☐ 168 Phil Hughes | .30 | .75 |
| ☐ 169 Adam Lind | .12 | .30 |
| ☐ 170 Scott Rolen | .20 | .50 |
| ☐ 171 John Maine | .12 | .30 |
| ☐ 172 Chris Ray | .12 | .30 |
| ☐ 173 Jamie Moyer | .12 | .30 |
| ☐ 174 Julian Tavarez | .12 | .30 |
| ☐ 175 Delmon Young | .20 | .50 |
| ☐ 176 Troy Patton (RC) | .12 | .30 |
| ☐ 177 Josh Anderson RC | .25 | .60 |
| ☐ 178 Dustin Pedroia ROY | .40 | 1.00 |
| ☐ 179 Chris Young | .12 | .30 |
| ☐ 180 Jose Valverde | .12 | .30 |
| ☐ 181 Borowski/Jenks/Putz | .12 | .30 |
| ☐ 182 Billy Buckner (RC) | .25 | .60 |
| ☐ 183 Paul Byrd | .12 | .30 |
| ☐ 184 Tadahito Iguchi | .12 | .30 |
| ☐ 185 Yunel Escobar | .12 | .30 |
| ☐ 186 Lastings Milledge | .12 | .30 |
| ☐ 187 Dustin McGowan | .12 | .30 |
| ☐ 188 Kei Igawa | .12 | .30 |
| ☐ 189 Esteban German | .12 | .30 |
| ☐ 190 Russell Martin | .20 | .50 |
| ☐ 191 Orlando Hudson | .12 | .30 |
| ☐ 192 Jim Edmonds | .20 | .50 |
| ☐ 193 J.J. Hardy | .12 | .30 |
| ☐ 194 Chad Billingsley | .12 | .30 |
| ☐ 195 Todd Helton | .20 | .50 |

|  |  | | |
|---|---|---|---|
| 196 | Ross Gload | .12 | .30 |
| 197 | Melky Cabrera | .12 | .30 |
| 198 | Shannon Stewart | .12 | .30 |
| 199 | Adrian Beltre | .12 | .30 |
| 200 | Manny Ramirez | .30 | .75 |
| 201 | Matt Capps | .12 | .30 |
| 202 | Mike Lamb | .12 | .30 |
| 203 | Jason Tyner | .12 | .30 |
| 204 | Rafael Furcal | .12 | .30 |
| 205 | Gil Meche | .12 | .30 |
| 206 | Geoff Jenkins | .12 | .30 |
| 207 | Jeff Kent | .12 | .30 |
| 208 | David DeJesus | .12 | .30 |
| 209 | Andy Phillips | .12 | .30 |
| 210 | Mark Teahen | .12 | .30 |
| 211 | Lyle Overbay | .12 | .30 |
| 212 | Moises Alou | .12 | .30 |
| 213 | Michael Barrett | .12 | .30 |
| 214 | C.J. Wilson | .12 | .30 |
| 215 | Bobby Jenks | .12 | .30 |
| 216 | Ryan Garko | .12 | .30 |
| 217 | Josh Beckett | .20 | .50 |
| 218 | Clint Hurdle MG | .12 | .30 |
| 219 | Kevin Kouzmanoff | .12 | .30 |
| 220 | Roy Oswalt | .12 | .30 |
| 221 | Ian Snell | .12 | .30 |
| 222 | Mark Grudzielanek | .12 | .30 |
| 223 | Odalis Perez | .12 | .30 |
| 224 | Mark Buehrle | .12 | .30 |
| 225 | Hunter Pence | .30 | .75 |
| 226 | Kurt Suzuki | .12 | .30 |
| 227 | Alfredo Amezaga | .12 | .30 |
| 228 | Geoff Blum | .12 | .30 |
| 229 | Dustin Pedroia | .40 | 1.00 |
| 230 | Roy Halladay | .12 | .30 |
| 231 | Casey Blake | .12 | .30 |
| 232 | Clay Buchholz (RC) | .60 | 1.50 |
| 233 | Jimmy Rollins MVP | .20 | .50 |
| 234a | Boston Red Sox | .50 | 1.25 |
| 234b | Red Sox w/Giuliani | 3.00 | 8.00 |
| 234c | Red Sox w/Giuliani Red | 30.00 | 60.00 |
| 235 | Rich Harden | .12 | .30 |
| 236 | Joe Koshansky (RC) | .25 | .60 |
| 237 | Eric Wedge MG | .12 | .30 |
| 238 | Shane Victorino | .12 | .30 |
| 239 | Richie Sexson | .12 | .30 |
| 240 | Jim Thome | .20 | .50 |
| 241 | Ervin Santana | .12 | .30 |
| 242 | Manny Acta | .12 | .30 |
| 243 | Akinori Iwamura | .12 | .30 |
| 244 | Adam Wainwright | .20 | .50 |
| 245 | Dan Haren | .12 | .30 |
| 246 | Jason Isringhausen | .12 | .30 |
| 247 | Edgar Gonzalez | .12 | .30 |
| 248 | Jose Contreras | .12 | .30 |
| 249 | Chris Sampson | .12 | .30 |
| 250 | Jonathan Papelbon | .20 | .50 |
| 251 | Dan Johnson | .12 | .30 |
| 252 | Dmitri Young | .12 | .30 |
| 253 | Bronson Sardinha (RC) | .25 | .60 |
| 254 | David Murphy | .12 | .30 |
| 255 | Brandon Phillips | .12 | .30 |
| 256 | A.Rodriguez MVP | .50 | 1.25 |
| 257 | A.Kearns/D.Young | .12 | .30 |
| 258 | M.Ramirez/K.Youkilis | .30 | .75 |
| 259 | Emilio Bonifacio RC | .60 | 1.50 |
| 260 | Chad Cordero | .12 | .30 |
| 261 | Josh Barfield | .12 | .30 |
| 262 | Brett Myers | .12 | .30 |
| 263 | Nook Logan | .12 | .30 |
| 264 | Byung-Hyun Kim | .12 | .30 |
| 265 | Fredi Gonzalez | .12 | .30 |
| 266 | Ryan Doumit | .12 | .30 |
| 267 | Chris Burke | .12 | .30 |
| 268 | Daric Barton (RC) | .25 | .60 |
| 269 | James Loney | .20 | .50 |
| 270 | C.C. Sabathia | .12 | .30 |
| 271 | Chad Tracy | .12 | .30 |
| 272 | Anthony Reyes | .12 | .30 |
| 273 | Rafael Soriano | .12 | .30 |
| 274 | Jermaine Dye | .12 | .30 |
| 275 | C.C. Sabathia | .12 | .30 |
| 276 | Brad Ausmus | .12 | .30 |
| 277 | Aubrey Huff | .12 | .30 |
| 278 | Xavier Nady | .12 | .30 |
| 279 | Damion Easley | .12 | .30 |
| 280 | Willie Randolph MG | .12 | .30 |
| 281 | Carlos Ruiz | .12 | .30 |
| 282 | Jon Lester | .20 | .50 |
| 283 | Jorge Sosa | .12 | .30 |
| 284 | Lance Broadway (RC) | .25 | .60 |
| 285 | Tony LaRussa MG | .12 | .30 |
| 286 | Jeff Clement (RC) | .40 | 1.00 |
| 287 | Morneau/Santana/Mauer | .30 | .75 |
| 288 | I.Rodriguez/J.Verlander | .20 | .50 |
| 289 | Justin Ruggiano RC | .40 | 1.00 |
| 290 | Edgar Renteria | .12 | .30 |
| 291 | Eugenio Velez RC | .25 | .60 |
| 292 | Mark Loretta | .12 | .30 |
| 293 | Gavin Floyd | .12 | .30 |
| 294 | Brian McCann | .20 | .50 |
| 295 | Tim Wakefield | .12 | .30 |
| 296 | Paul Konerko | .12 | .30 |
| 297 | Jorge Posada | .20 | .50 |
| 298 | Fielder/Howard/Dunn | .40 | 1.00 |
| 299 | Cesar Izturis | .12 | .30 |
| 300 | Chien-Ming Wang | .30 | .75 |
| 301 | Chris Duffy | .12 | .30 |
| 302 | Horacio Ramirez | .12 | .30 |
| 303 | Jose Lopez | .12 | .30 |
| 304 | Jose Vidro | .12 | .30 |
| 305 | Carlos Delgado | .12 | .30 |
| 306 | Scott Olsen | .12 | .30 |
| 307 | Shawn Hill | .12 | .30 |
| 308 | Felipe Lopez | .12 | .30 |
| 309 | Ryan Church | .12 | .30 |
| 310 | Kelvim Escobar | .12 | .30 |
| 311 | Jeremy Guthrie | .12 | .30 |
| 312 | Ramon Hernandez | .12 | .30 |
| 313 | Kameron Loe | .12 | .30 |
| 314 | Ian Kinsler | .20 | .50 |
| 315 | David Weathers | .12 | .30 |
| 316 | Scott Hatteberg | .12 | .30 |
| 317 | Cliff Lee | .12 | .30 |
| 318 | Ned Yost MG | .12 | .30 |
| 319 | Joey Votto (RC) | .60 | 1.50 |
| 320 | Ichiro Suzuki | .50 | 1.25 |
| 321 | J.R. Towles RC | .40 | 1.00 |
| 322 | Kazmir/Santana/Bedard | .20 | .50 |
| 323 | Valverde/Cordero/Hoffman | .20 | .50 |
| 324 | Jake Peavy | .20 | .50 |
| 325 | Jim Leyland MG | .12 | .30 |
| 326 | Holliday/Chipper/Hanley | .40 | 1.00 |
| 327 | Peavy/Harang/Smoltz | .30 | .75 |
| 328 | Nyjer Morgan (RC) | .25 | .60 |
| 329 | Lou Piniella MG | .12 | .30 |
| 330 | Curtis Granderson | .20 | .50 |
| 331 | Dave Roberts | .12 | .30 |
| 332 | Grady Sizemore/Jhonny Peralta | .20 | .50 |
| 333 | Jayson Nix (RC) | .25 | .60 |
| 334 | Oliver Perez | .12 | .30 |
| 335 | Eric Byrnes | .12 | .30 |
| 336 | Jhonny Peralta | .12 | .30 |
| 337 | Livan Hernandez | .12 | .30 |
| 338 | Matt Diaz | .12 | .30 |
| 339 | Troy Percival | .12 | .30 |
| 340 | David Wright | .40 | 1.00 |
| 341 | Daniel Cabrera | .12 | .30 |
| 342 | Matt Belisle | .12 | .30 |
| 343 | Kason Gabbard | .12 | .30 |
| 344 | Mike Rabelo | .12 | .30 |
| 345 | Carl Crawford | .20 | .50 |
| 346 | Adam Everett | .12 | .30 |
| 347 | Chris Capuano | .12 | .30 |
| 348 | Craig Monroe | .12 | .30 |
| 349 | Mike Mussina | .20 | .50 |
| 350 | Mark Teixeira | .20 | .50 |
| 351 | Bobby Crosby | .12 | .30 |
| 352 | Miguel Batista | .12 | .30 |
| 353 | Brendan Ryan | .12 | .30 |
| 354 | Edwin Jackson | .12 | .30 |
| 355 | Brian Roberts | .20 | .50 |
| 356 | Manny Corpas | .12 | .30 |
| 357 | Jeremy Accardo | .12 | .30 |
| 358 | John Patterson | .12 | .30 |
| 359 | Evan Meek RC | .25 | .60 |
| 360 | David Ortiz | .20 | .50 |
| 361 | Wesley Wright RC | .25 | .60 |
| 362 | Fernando Hernandez RC | .25 | .60 |
| 363 | Brian Barton RC | .40 | 1.00 |
| 364 | Al Reyes | .12 | .30 |
| 365 | Derek Lee | .20 | .50 |
| 366 | Jeff Weaver | .12 | .30 |
| 367 | Khalil Greene | .20 | .50 |
| 368 | Michael Bourn | .12 | .30 |
| 369 | Luis Castillo | .12 | .30 |
| 370 | Adam Dunn | .12 | .30 |
| 371 | Rickie Weeks | .12 | .30 |
| 372 | Matt Kemp | .30 | .75 |
| 373 | Casey Kotchman | .12 | .30 |
| 374 | Jason Jennings | .12 | .30 |
| 375 | Fausto Carmona | .12 | .30 |
| 376 | Willy Taveras | .12 | .30 |
| 377 | Jake Westbrook | .12 | .30 |
| 378 | Ozzie Guillen | .12 | .30 |
| 379 | Hideki Okajima | .12 | .30 |
| 380 | Grady Sizemore | .20 | .50 |
| 381 | Jeff Francoeur | .20 | .50 |
| 382 | Micah Owings | .12 | .30 |
| 383 | Jered Weaver | .12 | .30 |
| 384 | Carlos Quentin | .12 | .30 |
| 385 | Troy Tulowitzki | .20 | .50 |
| 386 | Julio Lugo | .12 | .30 |
| 387 | Sean Marshall | .12 | .30 |
| 388 | Jorge Cantu | .12 | .30 |
| 389 | Callix Crabbe (RC) | .25 | .60 |
| 390 | Troy Glaus | .20 | .50 |
| 391 | Nick Markakis | .20 | .50 |
| 392 | Joey Gathright | .12 | .30 |
| 393 | Michael Cuddyer | .12 | .30 |
| 394 | Mark Ellis | .12 | .30 |
| 395 | Lance Berkman | .20 | .50 |
| 396 | Randy Johnson | .30 | .75 |
| 397 | Brian Wilson | .12 | .30 |
| 398 | Kenji Johjima | .12 | .30 |
| 399 | Jarrod Saltalamacchia | .12 | .30 |
| 400 | Matt Holliday | .20 | .50 |
| 401 | Scott Hairston | .12 | .30 |
| 402 | Taylor Buchholz | .12 | .30 |
| 403 | Nate Robertson | .12 | .30 |
| 404 | Cecil Cooper | .12 | .30 |
| 405 | Travis Hafner | .12 | .30 |
| 406 | Takashi Saito | .12 | .30 |
| 407 | Johnny Damon | .20 | .50 |
| 408 | Edinson Volquez | .12 | .30 |
| 409 | Jason Giambi | .20 | .50 |
| 410 | Alex Gordon | .20 | .50 |
| 411 | Jason Kubel | .12 | .30 |
| 412 | Joel Zumaya | .12 | .30 |
| 413 | Wandy Rodriguez | .12 | .30 |
| 414 | Andrew Miller | .20 | .50 |
| 415 | Derek Lowe | .12 | .30 |
| 416 | Elijah Dukes | .12 | .30 |
| 417 | Dioner Navarro | .12 | .30 |
| 418 | Bengie Molina | .12 | .30 |
| 419 | Nick Swisher | .20 | .50 |
| 420 | Brandon Backe | .12 | .30 |
| 421 | Erick Aybar | .12 | .30 |
| 422 | Mike Scioscia MG | .12 | .30 |
| 423 | Aaron Harang | .12 | .30 |
| 424 | Aaron Harang | .12 | .30 |
| 425 | Hanley Ramirez | .30 | .75 |
| 426 | Franklin Gutierrez | .12 | .30 |
| 427 | Carlos Guillen | .12 | .30 |
| 428 | Jair Jurrjens | .12 | .30 |
| 429 | Billy Butler | .12 | .30 |
| 430 | Ryan Braun | .40 | 1.00 |
| 431 | Delwyn Young | .12 | .30 |
| 432 | Jason Kendall | .12 | .30 |
| 433 | Carlos Silva | .12 | .30 |
| 434 | Ron Gardenhire MG | .12 | .30 |
| 435 | Torii Hunter | .12 | .30 |
| 436 | Joe Blanton | .12 | .30 |
| 437 | Brandon Wood | .12 | .30 |
| 438 | Jay Payton | .12 | .30 |
| 439 | Josh Hamilton | .40 | 1.00 |
| 440 | Pedro Martinez | .20 | .50 |
| 441 | Miguel Olivo | .12 | .30 |
| 442 | Luis Gonzalez | .12 | .30 |
| 443 | Greg Dobbs | .12 | .30 |
| 444 | Jack Wilson | .12 | .30 |
| 445 | Hideki Matsui | .30 | .75 |
| 446 | Randor Bierd RC | .25 | .60 |
| 447 | Chipper Jones/Mark Teixeira | .40 | 1.00 |
| 448 | Cameron Maybin | .20 | .50 |
| 449 | Braden Looper | .12 | .30 |
| 450 | Prince Fielder | .30 | .75 |
| 451 | Brian Giles | .12 | .30 |
| 452 | Kevin Slowey | .12 | .30 |
| 453 | Josh Fogg | .12 | .30 |
| 454 | Mike Hampton | .12 | .30 |
| 455 | Derek Jeter | .75 | 2.00 |
| 456 | Chone Figgins | .12 | .30 |
| 457 | Josh Fields | .12 | .30 |
| 458 | Brad Hawpe | .12 | .30 |

|  |  | | |
|---|--------|---|---|
| ❑ 459 | Mike Sweeney | .12 | .30 |
| ❑ 460 | Chase Utley | .30 | .75 |
| ❑ 461 | Jacoby Ellsbury | .50 | 1.25 |
| ❑ 462 | Freddy Sanchez | .12 | .30 |
| ❑ 463 | John McLaren | .12 | .30 |
| ❑ 464 | Rocco Baldelli | .12 | .30 |
| ❑ 465 | Huston Street | .12 | .30 |
| ❑ 466 | Miguel Cabrera/Ivan Rodriguez | .20 | .50 |
| ❑ 467 | Nick Blackburn RC | .40 | 1.00 |
| ❑ 468 | Gregor Blanco RC | .25 | .60 |
| ❑ 469 | Brian Bocock RC | .25 | .60 |
| ❑ 470 | Tom Gorzelanny | .12 | .30 |
| ❑ 471 | Brian Schneider | .12 | .30 |
| ❑ 472 | Shaun Marcum | .12 | .30 |
| ❑ 473 | Joe Maddon | .12 | .30 |
| ❑ 474 | Yuniesky Betancourt | .12 | .30 |
| ❑ 475 | Adrian Gonzalez | .20 | .50 |
| ❑ 477 | Ben Broussard | .12 | .30 |
| ❑ 478 | Geovany Soto | .30 | .75 |
| ❑ 479 | Bobby Abreu | .12 | .30 |
| ❑ 480 | Matt Cain | .12 | .30 |
| ❑ 481 | Manny Parra | .12 | .30 |
| ❑ 483 | Mike Jacobs | .12 | .30 |
| ❑ 484 | Todd Jones | .12 | .30 |
| ❑ 485 | J.J. Putz | .12 | .30 |
| ❑ 486 | Javier Vazquez | .12 | .30 |
| ❑ 487 | Corey Patterson | .12 | .30 |
| ❑ 488 | Mike Gonzalez | .12 | .30 |
| ❑ 489 | Joakim Soria | .12 | .30 |
| ❑ 490 | Albert Pujols | .60 | 1.50 |
| ❑ 491 | Cliff Floyd | .12 | .30 |
| ❑ 492 | Harvey Garcia (RC) | .25 | .60 |
| ❑ 493 | Steve Holm RC | .25 | .60 |
| ❑ 494 | Paul Maholm | .12 | .30 |
| ❑ 495 | James Shields | .12 | .30 |
| ❑ 496 | Brad Lidge | .12 | .30 |
| ❑ 497 | Cla Meredith | .12 | .30 |
| ❑ 498 | Matt Chico | .12 | .30 |
| ❑ 499 | Milton Bradley | .12 | .30 |
| ❑ 500 | Chipper Jones | .40 | 1.00 |
| ❑ 501 | Elliot Johnson (RC) | .25 | .60 |
| ❑ 502 | Alex Cora | .12 | .30 |
| ❑ 503 | Jeremy Bonderman | .12 | .30 |
| ❑ 504 | Conor Jackson | .12 | .30 |
| ❑ 505 | B.J. Upton | .20 | .50 |
| ❑ 506 | Jay Gibbons | .12 | .30 |
| ❑ 507 | Mark DeRosa | .12 | .30 |
| ❑ 508 | John Danks | .12 | .30 |
| ❑ 509 | Alex Gonzalez | .12 | .30 |
| ❑ 510 | Justin Verlander | .20 | .50 |
| ❑ 511 | Jeff Francis | .12 | .30 |
| ❑ 512 | Placido Polanco | .12 | .30 |
| ❑ 513 | Rick Vanden Hurk | .12 | .30 |
| ❑ 514 | Tony Pena | .12 | .30 |
| ❑ 515 | A.J. Burnett | .12 | .30 |
| ❑ 516 | Jason Schmidt | .12 | .30 |
| ❑ 517 | Bill Hall | .12 | .30 |
| ❑ 518 | Ian Stewart | .12 | .30 |
| ❑ 519 | Travis Buck | .12 | .30 |
| ❑ 520 | Vernon Wells | .12 | .30 |
| ❑ 521 | Jayson Werth | .12 | .30 |
| ❑ 522 | Nate McLouth | .12 | .30 |
| ❑ 523 | Noah Lowry | .12 | .30 |
| ❑ 524 | Raul Ibanez | .20 | .50 |
| ❑ 525 | Gary Matthews | .12 | .30 |
| ❑ 526 | Juan Encarnacion | .12 | .30 |
| ❑ 527 | Marlon Byrd | .12 | .30 |
| ❑ 528 | Paul Lo Duca | .12 | .30 |
| ❑ 529 | Masahide Kobayashi RC | .40 | 1.00 |
| ❑ 530 | Ryan Zimmerman | .20 | .50 |
| ❑ 531 | Hiroki Kuroda RC | .40 | 1.00 |
| ❑ 532 | Tim Lahey RC | .25 | .60 |
| ❑ 533 | Kyle McClellan RC | .25 | .60 |
| ❑ 534 | Matt Tuiasosopo RC | .25 | .60 |
| ❑ 535 | Francisco Rodriguez | .12 | .30 |
| ❑ 536 | A.Pujols/P.Fielder | .60 | 1.50 |
| ❑ 537 | Scott Moore | .12 | .30 |
| ❑ 538 | Alex Romero (RC) | .40 | 1.00 |
| ❑ 539 | Clete Thomas RC | .40 | 1.00 |
| ❑ 540 | John Smoltz | .30 | .75 |
| ❑ 541 | Adam Jones | .12 | .30 |
| ❑ 542 | Adam Kennedy | .12 | .30 |
| ❑ 543 | Carlos Lee | .12 | .30 |
| ❑ 544 | Chad Gaudin | .12 | .30 |
| ❑ 545 | Chris Young | .12 | .30 |
| ❑ 546 | Francisco Liriano | .20 | .50 |
| ❑ 547 | Fred Lewis | .12 | .30 |
| ❑ 548 | Garrett Olson | .12 | .30 |

|  |  | | |
|---|--------|---|---|
| ❑ 549 | Gregg Zaun | .12 | .30 |
| ❑ 550 | Curt Schilling | .20 | .50 |
| ❑ 551 | Erick Threets (RC) | .25 | .60 |
| ❑ 552 | J.D. Drew | .12 | .30 |
| ❑ 553 | Jo-Jo Reyes | .12 | .30 |
| ❑ 554 | Joe Borowski | .12 | .30 |
| ❑ 555 | Josh Beckett | .20 | .50 |
| ❑ 556 | John Gibbons | .12 | .30 |
| ❑ 557 | John McDonald | .12 | .30 |
| ❑ 558 | John Russell | .12 | .30 |
| ❑ 559 | Jonny Gomes | .12 | .30 |
| ❑ 560 | Aramis Ramirez | .12 | .30 |
| ❑ 561 | Matt Tolbert RC | .40 | 1.00 |
| ❑ 562 | Ronnie Belliard | .12 | .30 |
| ❑ 563 | Ramon Troncoso RC | .25 | .60 |
| ❑ 564 | Frank Catalanotto | .12 | .30 |
| ❑ 565 | A.J. Pierzynski | .12 | .30 |
| ❑ 566 | Kevin Millwood | .12 | .30 |
| ❑ 567 | David Eckstein | .12 | .30 |
| ❑ 568 | Jose Guillen | .12 | .30 |
| ❑ 569 | Brad Hennessey | .12 | .30 |
| ❑ 570 | Homer Bailey | .20 | .50 |
| ❑ 571 | Eric Gagne | .12 | .30 |
| ❑ 572 | Adam Eaton | .12 | .30 |
| ❑ 573 | Tom Gordon | .12 | .30 |
| ❑ 574 | Scott Baker | .12 | .30 |
| ❑ 575 | Ty Wigginton | .12 | .30 |
| ❑ 576 | Dave Bush | .12 | .30 |
| ❑ 577 | John Buck | .12 | .30 |
| ❑ 578 | Ricky Nolasco | .12 | .30 |
| ❑ 579 | Jesse Litsch | .12 | .30 |
| ❑ 580 | Ken Griffey Jr. | .50 | 1.25 |
| ❑ 581 | Kazuo Matsui | .12 | .30 |
| ❑ 582 | Dusty Baker | .12 | .30 |
| ❑ 583 | Nick Punto | .12 | .30 |
| ❑ 584 | Ryan Theriot | .12 | .30 |
| ❑ 585 | Brian Bannister | .12 | .30 |
| ❑ 586 | Coco Crisp | .12 | .30 |
| ❑ 587 | Jim Snyder | .12 | .30 |
| ❑ 588 | Tony Gwynn | .12 | .30 |
| ❑ 589 | Dave Trembley | .12 | .30 |
| ❑ 590 | Mariano Rivera | .30 | .75 |
| ❑ 591 | Rico Washington (RC) | .25 | .60 |
| ❑ 592 | Matt Morris | .12 | .30 |
| ❑ 593 | Randy Wells RC | .40 | 1.00 |
| ❑ 594 | Mike Morse | .12 | .30 |
| ❑ 595 | Francisco Cordero | .12 | .30 |
| ❑ 596 | Joba Chamberlain | .40 | 1.00 |
| ❑ 597 | Kyle Davies | .12 | .30 |
| ❑ 598 | Bruce Bochy | .12 | .30 |
| ❑ 599 | Austin Kearns | .12 | .30 |
| ❑ 600 | Tom Glavine | .20 | .50 |
| ❑ 601 | Felipe Paulino RC | .40 | 1.00 |
| ❑ 602 | Lyle Overbay/Vernon Wells | .12 | .30 |
| ❑ 603 | Blake DeWitt (RC) | .60 | 1.50 |
| ❑ 604 | Wily Mo Pena | .12 | .30 |
| ❑ 605 | Andre Ethier | .20 | .50 |
| ❑ 606 | Jason Bergmann | .12 | .30 |
| ❑ 607 | Ryan Spilborghs | .12 | .30 |
| ❑ 608 | Brian Burres | .12 | .30 |
| ❑ 609 | Ted Lilly | .12 | .30 |
| ❑ 610 | Carlos Beltran | .20 | .50 |
| ❑ 611 | Garret Anderson | .12 | .30 |
| ❑ 612 | Kelly Johnson | .12 | .30 |
| ❑ 613 | Melvin Mora | .12 | .30 |
| ❑ 614 | Rich Hill | .12 | .30 |
| ❑ 615 | Pat Burrell | .12 | .30 |
| ❑ 616 | Jon Garland | .12 | .30 |
| ❑ 617 | Asdrubal Cabrera | .12 | .30 |
| ❑ 618 | Pat Neshek | .12 | .30 |
| ❑ 619 | Sergio Mitre | .12 | .30 |
| ❑ 620 | Gary Sheffield | .20 | .50 |
| ❑ 621 | Denard Span | .20 | .50 |
| ❑ 622 | Jorge De La Rosa | .12 | .30 |
| ❑ 623 | Trey Hillman MG | .12 | .30 |
| ❑ 624 | Joe Torre MG | .20 | .50 |
| ❑ 625 | Greg Maddux | .40 | 1.00 |
| ❑ 626 | Mike Redmond | .12 | .30 |
| ❑ 627 | Mike Pelfrey | .12 | .30 |
| ❑ 628 | Andy Pettitte | .20 | .50 |
| ❑ 629 | Eric Chavez | .12 | .30 |
| ❑ 630 | Chris Carpenter | .12 | .30 |
| ❑ 631 | Joe Girardi MG | .12 | .30 |
| ❑ 632 | Charlie Manuel MG | .12 | .30 |
| ❑ 633 | Adam LaRoche | .12 | .30 |
| ❑ 634 | Kenny Rogers | .12 | .30 |
| ❑ 635 | Michael Young | .12 | .30 |
| ❑ 636 | Rafael Betancourt | .12 | .30 |

|  |  | | |
|---|--------|---|---|
| ❑ 637 | Jose Castillo | .12 | .30 |
| ❑ 638 | Juan Pierre | .12 | .30 |
| ❑ 639 | Juan Uribe | .12 | .30 |
| ❑ 640 | Carlos Pena | .30 | .75 |
| ❑ 641 | Marcus Thames | .12 | .30 |
| ❑ 642 | Mark Kotsay | .12 | .30 |
| ❑ 643 | Matt Murton | .12 | .30 |
| ❑ 644 | Reggie Willits | .12 | .30 |
| ❑ 645 | Andy Marte | .12 | .30 |
| ❑ 646 | Rajai Davis | .12 | .30 |
| ❑ 647 | Randy Winn | .12 | .30 |
| ❑ 648 | Ryan Freel | .12 | .30 |
| ❑ 649 | Joe Crede | .12 | .30 |
| ❑ 650 | Frank Thomas | .30 | .75 |
| ❑ 651 | Martin Prado | .12 | .30 |
| ❑ 652 | Rod Barajas | .12 | .30 |
| ❑ 653 | Endy Chavez | .12 | .30 |
| ❑ 654 | Willy Aybar | .12 | .30 |
| ❑ 655 | Aaron Rowand | .12 | .30 |
| ❑ 656 | Darin Erstad | .12 | .30 |
| ❑ 657 | Jeff Keppinger | .12 | .30 |
| ❑ 658 | Kerry Wood | .12 | .30 |
| ❑ 659 | Vicente Padilla | .12 | .30 |
| ❑ 660 | Yadier Molina | .20 | .50 |
| ❑ 661 | Johan Santana NoNo | 150.00 | 250.00 |
| ❑ FS1 | Kazuo Uzuki | .75 | 2.00 |
| ❑ NNO | Alexei Ramirez | 50.00 | 100.00 |
| ❑ NNO | Kosuke Fukudome | 40.00 | 80.00 |
| ❑ NNO | Yasuhiko Yabuta | 40.00 | 80.00 |

## 2008 Topps Update

| | | | |
|---|---|---|---|
| ❑ COMP.SET w/o VAR (330) | | 20.00 | 50.00 |
| ❑ COMMON CARD (1-330) | | .12 | .30 |
| ❑ COMMON ROOKIE (1-330) | | .20 | .50 |
| ❑ 1-330 PLATE ODDS 1:457 HOBBY | | | |
| ❑ PLATE PRINT RUN 1 SET PER COLOR | | | |
| ❑ BLACK-CYAN-MAGENTA-YELLOW ISSUED | | | |
| ❑ NO PLATE PRICING DUE TO SCARCITY | | | |
| ❑ UH1A | Kosuke Fukudome RC | .60 | 1.50 |
| ❑ UH1B | Kosuke Fukudome VAR | 15.00 | 40.00 |
| ❑ UH2 | Sean Casey | .12 | .30 |
| ❑ UH3 | Freddie Bynum | .12 | .30 |
| ❑ UH4 | Brent Lillibridge (RC) | .20 | .50 |
| ❑ UH5 | Chipper Jones AS | .40 | 1.00 |
| ❑ UH6 | Yamid Haad | .12 | .30 |
| ❑ UH7 | Josh Anderson | .12 | .30 |
| ❑ UH8 | Jeff Mathis | .12 | .30 |
| ❑ UH9 | Shawn Riggans | .12 | .30 |
| ❑ UH10A | Evan Longoria RC | 2.00 | 5.00 |
| ❑ UH10B | Evan Longoria VAR | 40.00 | 80.00 |
| ❑ UH11 | Matt Holliday AS | .20 | .50 |
| ❑ UH12 | Trot Nixon | .12 | .30 |
| ❑ UH13 | Geoff Blum | .12 | .30 |
| ❑ UH14 | Bartolo Colon | .12 | .30 |
| ❑ UH15 | Kevin Cash | .12 | .30 |
| ❑ UH16 | Paul Janish (RC) | .20 | .50 |
| ❑ UH17 | Russell Martin AS | .12 | .30 |
| ❑ UH18 | Andy Phillips | .12 | .30 |
| ❑ UH19 | Johnny Estrada | .12 | .30 |
| ❑ UH20 | Justin Masterson RC | 1.00 | 2.50 |
| ❑ UH21 | Darrell Rasner | .12 | .30 |
| ❑ UH22 | Brian Moehler | .12 | .30 |
| ❑ UH23 | Cristian Guzman AS | .12 | .30 |
| ❑ UH24 | Tony Armas Jr. | .12 | .30 |
| ❑ UH25 | Lance Berkman AS | .20 | .50 |
| ❑ UH26 | Chris Iannetta | .12 | .30 |
| ❑ UH27 | Reid Brignac | .20 | .50 |
| ❑ UH28 | Miguel Tejada AS | .12 | .30 |
| ❑ UH29 | Ryan Ludwick AS | .12 | .30 |
| ❑ UH30 | Brendan Harris | .12 | .30 |
| ❑ UH31 | Marco Scutaro | .12 | .30 |
| ❑ UH32 | Cody Ross | .12 | .30 |
| ❑ UH33 | Carlos Marmol | .12 | .30 |
| ❑ UH34 | Nate McLouth AS | .12 | .30 |

|  | | |  | | |  | | |
|---|---|---|---|---|---|---|---|---|
| UH35 Hanley Ramirez AS | .30 | .75 | UH120 Angel Berroa | .12 | .30 | UH208 Kerry Wood AS | .12 | .30 |
| UH36 Xavier Nady | .12 | .30 | UH121 Jacque Jones | .12 | .30 | UH209 Carlos Guillen AS | .12 | .30 |
| UH37 Connor Robertson | .12 | .30 | UH122 DeWayne Wise | .12 | .30 | UH210 Joe Saunders | .12 | .30 |
| UH38 Carlos Villanueva | .12 | .30 | UH123 Matt Joyce RC | .50 | 1.25 | UH211 Brett Tomko | .12 | .30 |
| UH39 Jose Molina | .12 | .30 | UH124 A.Rodriguez/E.Longoria | 1.25 | 3.00 | UH212 Guillermo Mota | .12 | .30 |
| UH40 Jon Rauch | .12 | .30 | UH125 John Smoltz HL | .30 | .75 | UH213 German Duran RC | .30 | .75 |
| UH41 Joe Mauer AS | .30 | .75 | UH126 Morgan Ensberg | .12 | .30 | UH214 Carlos Zambrano AS | .12 | .30 |
| UH42 Chip Ambres | .12 | .30 | UH127 M.Young/D.Jeter | .75 | 2.00 | UH215 Josh Hamilton AS | .40 | 1.00 |
| UH43 Jason Bartlett | .12 | .30 | UH128 LaTroy Hawkins | .12 | .30 | UH216 Jason Bay | .20 | .50 |
| UH44 Ryan Sweeney | .12 | .30 | UH129 Nick Adenhart (RC) | .20 | .50 | UH217 Willy Aybar | .12 | .30 |
| UH45 Eric Hurley (RC) | .20 | .50 | UH130 Mike Cameron | .12 | .30 | UH218 Salomon Torres | .12 | .30 |
| UH46 Kevin Youkilis AS | .20 | .50 | UH131 Manny Ramirez HL | .30 | .75 | UH219 Damaso Marte | .12 | .30 |
| UH47 Dustin Pedroia AS | .40 | 1.00 | UH132 Jorge De La Rosa | .12 | .30 | UH220 Geoff Jenkins | .12 | .30 |
| UH48 Grant Balfour | .12 | .30 | UH133 Tadahito Iguchi | .12 | .30 | UH221 J.D. Drew AS | .12 | .30 |
| UH49 Ryan Ludwick | .12 | .30 | UH134 Joey Devine | .12 | .30 | UH222 Dave Borkowski | .12 | .30 |
| UH50 Matt Garza | .12 | .30 | UH135 Jose Arredondo RC | .30 | .75 | UH223 Jeff Ridgway RC | .30 | .75 |
| UH51 Fernando Tatis | .12 | .30 | UH136 H.Ramirez/A.Pujols | .60 | 1.50 | UH224 Angel Pagan | .12 | .30 |
| UH52 Derek Jeter AS | .75 | 2.00 | UH137 Evan Longoria HL | 1.25 | 3.00 | UH225 Ryan Tucker (RC) | .20 | .50 |
| UH53 Justin Duchscherer AS | .12 | .30 | UH138 T.J. Beam | .12 | .30 | UH226 Brian McCann AS | .20 | .50 |
| UH54 Matt Ginter | .12 | .30 | UH139 Jon Lieber | .12 | .30 | UH227 Carlos Quentin AS | .12 | .30 |
| UH55 Cesar Izturis | .12 | .30 | UH140 Dana Eveland | .12 | .30 | UH228 Joe Blanton | .12 | .30 |
| UH56 Roy Halladay AS | .30 | .75 | UH141 Michael Aubrey RC | .30 | .75 | UH229 Adrian Gonzalez AS | .20 | .50 |
| UH57 Ramon Castro | .12 | .30 | UH142 Adrian Gonzalez/Matt Holliday | .20 | .50 | UH230 Jason Jennings | .12 | .30 |
| UH58 Scott Kazmir AS | .20 | .50 | UH143 Chipper Jones HL | .40 | 1.00 | UH231 Chris Davis RC | .50 | 1.25 |
| UH59 Cliff Lee AS | .12 | .30 | UH144 Robinson Tejeda | .12 | .30 | UH232 Geovany Soto AS | .30 | .75 |
| UH60 Jim Edmonds | .20 | .50 | UH145 Kip Wells | .12 | .30 | UH233 Grady Sizemore AS | .20 | .50 |
| UH61 Randy Wolf | .12 | .30 | UH146 Carlos Gonzalez (RC) | .20 | .50 | UH234 Carl Pavano | .12 | .30 |
| UH62 Matt Albers | .12 | .30 | UH147 Josh Banks (RC) | .20 | .50 | UH235 Eddie Guardado | .12 | .30 |
| UH63 Eric Bruntlett | .12 | .30 | UH148 David Wright AS | .40 | 1.00 | UH236 Chris Snelling | .12 | .30 |
| UH64 Joe Nathan AS | .12 | .30 | UH149 Paul Hoover | .12 | .30 | UH237 Manny Ramirez | .30 | .75 |
| UH65 Alex Rodriguez AS | .50 | 1.25 | UH150 Jon Lester HL | .20 | .50 | UH238 Dan Uggla AS | .20 | .50 |
| UH66 Robinson Cancel | .12 | .30 | UH151 Darin Erstad | .12 | .30 | UH239 Milton Bradley AS | .12 | .30 |
| UH67 Jamey Carroll | .12 | .30 | UH152 Steve Trachsel | .12 | .30 | UH240 Clayton Kershaw RC | 1.00 | 2.50 |
| UH68 Jonathan Papelbon AS | .30 | .75 | UH153 Armando Galarraga RC | .30 | .75 | UH241 Chase Utley AS | .30 | .75 |
| UH69 Chad Moeller | .12 | .30 | UH154 Grady Sizemore HRD | .12 | .30 | UH242 Raul Chavez | .12 | .30 |
| UH70 George Sherrill | .12 | .30 | UH155 Jay Bruce HL | .50 | 1.25 | UH243 Joe Mather RC | .30 | .75 |
| UH71 Mariano Rivera AS | .30 | .75 | UH156 Juan Rincon | .12 | .30 | UH244 Brandon Webb AS | .20 | .50 |
| UH72 Pete Orr | .12 | .30 | UH157 Mark Hendrickson | .12 | .30 | UH245 Ryan Braun | .40 | 1.00 |
| UH73 Jonathan Albaladejo RC | .30 | .75 | UH158 Chad Durbin | .12 | .30 | UH246 Kelvim Jimenez | .12 | .30 |
| UH74 Corey Patterson | .12 | .30 | UH159 Mike Aviles RC | .30 | .75 | UH247 Scott Podsednik | .12 | .30 |
| UH75 Matt Treanor | .12 | .30 | UH160 Orlando Cabrera | .12 | .30 | UH248 Doug Mientkiewicz | .12 | .30 |
| UH76 Francisco Rodriguez AS | .12 | .30 | UH161 Asdrubal Cabrera HL | .12 | .30 | UH249 Chris Volstad (RC) | .20 | .50 |
| UH77 Ervin Santana AS | .12 | .30 | UH162 Eric Stults | .12 | .30 | UH250 Pedro Feliz | .12 | .30 |
| UH78 Dallas Braden | .12 | .30 | UH163 Miguel Cairo | .12 | .30 | UH251 Mark Redman | .12 | .30 |
| UH79 Willie Harris | .12 | .30 | UH164 Jason LaRue | .12 | .30 | UH252 Tony Clark | .12 | .30 |
| UH80 Erik Bedard | .12 | .30 | UH165 Burke Badenhop RC | .20 | .50 | UH253 Josh Johnson | .12 | .30 |
| UH81 J.C. Romero | .12 | .30 | UH166 Ryan Braun HRD | .40 | 1.00 | UH254 Jose Castillo | .12 | .30 |
| UH82 Joe Saunders AS | .12 | .30 | UH167 Justin Morneau HRD | .20 | .50 | UH255 Brian Horwitz RC | .20 | .50 |
| UH83 George Sherrill AS | .12 | .30 | UH168 Ben Zobrist | .12 | .30 | UH256 Aramis Ramirez AS | .12 | .30 |
| UH84 Julian Tavarez | .12 | .30 | UH169 Eulogio De La Cruz | .12 | .30 | UH257 Casey Blake | .12 | .30 |
| UH85 Chad Gaudin | .12 | .30 | UH170 Greg Smith (RC) | .20 | .50 | UH258 Arthur Rhodes | .12 | .30 |
| UH86 David Aardsma | .12 | .30 | UH171 Brian Bixler (RC) | .20 | .50 | UH259 Aaron Boone | .12 | .30 |
| UH87 Ryan Langerhans | .12 | .30 | UH172 Evan Longoria HRD | 1.25 | 3.00 | UH260 Emil Brown | .12 | .30 |
| UH88 Dan Haren | .12 | .30 | UH173 Randy Johnson HL | .30 | .75 | UH261 Matt Macri (RC) | .20 | .50 |
| Russell Martin | | | UH174 D.J. Carrasco | .12 | .30 | UH262 Brian Wilson AS | .12 | .30 |
| UH89 Joakim Soria AS | .12 | .30 | UH175 Luis Vizcaino | .12 | .30 | UH263 Eric Patterson | .12 | .30 |
| UH90 Dan Haren | .12 | .30 | UH176 Brad Wilkerson | .12 | .30 | UH264 David Ortiz | .20 | .50 |
| UH91 Billy Buckner | .12 | .30 | UH177 Emmanuel Burriss RC | .30 | .75 | UH265 Tony Abreu | .12 | .30 |
| UH92 Eric Hinske | .12 | .30 | UH178 Lance Berkman HRD | .20 | .50 | UH266 Rob Mackowiak | .12 | .30 |
| UH93 Chris Coste | .12 | .30 | UH179 Johnny Damon HL | .20 | .50 | UH267 Gregorio Petit RC | .30 | .75 |
| UH94 Edinson Volquez | .12 | .30 | UH180 Scott Rolen | .20 | .50 | UH268 Alfonso Soriano AS | .20 | .50 |
| Russell Martin | | | UH181 Runelvys Hernandez | .12 | .30 | UH269 Robert Andino | .12 | .30 |
| UH95 Ichiro Suzuki AS | .50 | 1.25 | UH182 Sidney Ponson | .12 | .30 | UH270 Justin Duchscherer | .12 | .30 |
| UH96 Vladimir Nunez | .12 | .30 | UH183 Greg Reynolds RC | .30 | .75 | UH271 Brad Thompson | .12 | .30 |
| UH97 Sean Gallagher | .12 | .30 | UH184 Chase Utley HRD | .30 | .75 | UH272 Guillermo Quiroz | .12 | .30 |
| UH98 Denny Bautista | .12 | .30 | UH185 Joey Votto HL | .12 | .30 | UH273 Chris Perez RC | .30 | .75 |
| UH99 Hanley Ramirez/David Ortiz | .30 | .75 | UH186 Wes Littleton | .12 | .30 | UH274 Albert Pujols AS | .60 | 1.50 |
| UH100 Jay Bruce (RC) | .75 | 2.00 | UH187 Rod Barajas | .12 | .30 | UH275 Rich Harden | .12 | .30 |
| UH100B Jay Bruce VAR | 20.00 | 50.00 | UH188 Ray Durham | .12 | .30 | UH276 Corey Hart AS | .12 | .30 |
| UH101 Dioner Navarro | .12 | .30 | UH189 Micah Hoffpauir RC | .60 | 1.50 | UH277 John Rheineckar | .12 | .30 |
| UH102 Matt Murton | .12 | .30 | UH190 Manny Ramirez AS | .30 | .75 | UH278 So Taguchi | .12 | .30 |
| UH103 Chris Burke | .12 | .30 | UH191 Ian Kinsler AS | .20 | .50 | UH279 Alex Hinshaw RC | .30 | .75 |
| UH104 Omar Infante | .12 | .30 | UH192 Craig Hansen | .12 | .30 | UH280 Max Scherzer RC | .50 | 1.25 |
| UH105 Dan Giese (RC) | .20 | .50 | UH193 Jeremy Affeldt | .12 | .30 | UH281 Chris Aguila | .12 | .30 |
| UH106 C.Guillen/J.Hamilton | .40 | 1.00 | UH194 Gary Bennett | .12 | .30 | UH282 Carlos Marmol RC | .12 | .30 |
| UH107 Jason Varitek AS | .30 | .75 | UH195 Chris Carter (RC) | .30 | .75 | UH283 Alex Cintron | .12 | .30 |
| UH108 Shin-Soo Choo | .12 | .30 | UH196 Dan Uggla HRD | .20 | .50 | UH284 Curtis Thigpen | .12 | .30 |
| UH109 Alberto Callaspo | .12 | .30 | UH197 Michael Young AS | .20 | .50 | UH285 Kosuke Fukudome AS | .40 | 1.00 |
| UH110 Jose Valverde | .12 | .30 | UH198 Andy LaRoche | .12 | .30 | UH286 Aaron Cook AS | .12 | .30 |
| UH111 Brandon Boggs (RC) | .30 | .75 | UH199 Lance Cormier | .12 | .30 | UH287 Chase Headley | .12 | .30 |
| UH112 J.Hamilton/J.Drew | .40 | 1.00 | UH200 Luke Scott | .12 | .30 | UH288 Evan Longoria AS | 1.25 | 3.00 |
| UH113 Justin Morneau AS | .20 | .50 | UH201 Travis Denker RC | .30 | .75 | UH289 Chris Gomez | .12 | .30 |
| UH114 Billy Traber | .12 | .30 | UH202 Josh Hamilton | .40 | 1.00 | UH290 Carlos Gomez | .12 | .30 |
| UH115 Mike Lamb | .12 | .30 | UH203 Joe Crede AS | .12 | .30 | UH291 Jonathan Herrera RC | .30 | .75 |
| UH116 Odalis Perez | .12 | .30 | UH204 Franquelis Osoria | .12 | .30 | UH292 Ryan Dempster AS | .12 | .30 |
| UH117 Jed Lowrie RC | .50 | 1.25 | UH205 Octavio Dotel | .12 | .30 | UH293 Adam Dunn | .12 | .30 |
| UH118 Justin Morneau/David Ortiz | .20 | .50 | UH206 Russell Branyan | .12 | .30 | UH294 Mark Teixeira AS | .20 | .50 |
| UH119 Ken Griffey Jr. HL | .50 | 1.25 | UH207 Alberto Gonzalez RC | .30 | .75 | UH295 Aaron Miles | .12 | .30 |

|  | | |
|---|---|---|
| UH296 Gabe Gross | .12 | .30 |
| UH297 Cory Wade (RC) | .20 | .50 |
| UH298 Dan Haren AS | .12 | .30 |
| UH299 Jolbert Cabrera | .12 | .30 |
| UH300 C.C. Sabathia | .12 | .30 |
| UH301 Tony Pena | .12 | .30 |
| UH302 Brandon Moss | .12 | .30 |
| UH303 Taylor Teagarden RC | .30 | .75 |
| UH304 Brad Lidge AS | .12 | .30 |
| UH305 Ben Francisco | .12 | .30 |
| UH306 Casey Kotchman | .12 | .30 |
| UH307 Greg Norton | .12 | .30 |
| UH308 Shelley Duncan | .12 | .30 |
| UH309 John Bowker (RC) | .20 | .50 |
| UH310 Kyle Lohse | .12 | .30 |
| UH311 Oscar Salazar | .12 | .30 |
| UH312 Ivan Rodriguez | .20 | .50 |
| UH313 Tim Lincecum AS | .40 | 1.00 |
| UH314 Wilson Betemit | .12 | .30 |
| UH315 Sean Rodriguez (RC) | .20 | .50 |
| UH316 Ben Sheets AS | .20 | .50 |
| UH317 Brian Buscher | .12 | .30 |
| UH318 Kyle Farnsworth | .12 | .30 |
| UH319 Ruben Gotay | .12 | .30 |
| UH320 Heath Bell | .12 | .30 |
| UH321 Jeff Niemann (RC) | .20 | .50 |
| UH322 Edinson Volquez AS | .12 | .30 |
| UH323 Jorge Velandia | .12 | .30 |
| UH324 Ken Griffey Jr. | .50 | 1.25 |
| UH325 Clay Hensley | .12 | .30 |
| UH326 Kevin Mench | .12 | .30 |
| UH327 Hernan Iribarren (RC) | .30 | .75 |
| UH328 Billy Wagner AS | .12 | .30 |
| UH329 Jeremy Sowers | .12 | .30 |
| UH330 Johan Santana | .20 | .50 |

## 2009 Topps

|  | | |
|---|---|---|
| COMP.HOBBY SET (660) | 40.00 | 80.00 |
| COMP.ALLSTAR.SET (660) | 40.00 | 80.00 |
| COMP.CUBS SET (660) | 40.00 | 80.00 |
| COMP.METS SET (660) | 40.00 | 80.00 |
| COMP.RED SOX SET (660) | 40.00 | 80.00 |
| COMP.YANKEES SET (660) | 40.00 | 80.00 |
| COMP.SET w/o SP's (660) | 40.00 | 80.00 |
| COMP.SER.1 SET w/o SP's (330) | 15.00 | 30.00 |
| COMP.SER.2 SET w/o SP's (330) | 15.00 | 30.00 |
| COMMON CARD (1-696) | .15 | .40 |
| SER.1 SP VAR ODDS 1:95 HOBBY | | |
| SER.2 SP VAR ODDS 1:82 HOBBY | | |
| COMMON RC (1-696) | .30 | .75 |
| SER.1 PLATE ODDS 1:925 HOBBY | | |
| SER.2 PLATE ODDS 1:1056 HOBBY | | |
| PLATE PRINT RUN 1 SET PER COLOR | | |
| BLACK-CYAN-MAGENTA-YELLOW ISSUED | | |
| NO PLATE PRICING DUE TO SCARCITY | | |
| 1a Alex Rodriguez | .60 | 1.50 |
| 1b Babe Ruth SP | 20.00 | 50.00 |
| 2a Omar Vizquel | .15 | .40 |
| 2b Pee Wee Reese SP | 6.00 | 15.00 |
| 3 Andy Marte | .15 | .40 |
| 4 Chipper/Pujols/Holliday LL | 1.00 | 2.50 |
| 5 John Lackey | .15 | .40 |
| 6 Raul Ibanez | .25 | .60 |
| 7 Mickey Mantle | 1.25 | 3.00 |
| 8 Terry Francona MG | .25 | .60 |
| 9 Dallas McPherson | .15 | .40 |
| 10a Dan Uggla | .15 | .40 |
| 10b Rogers Hornsby SP | 6.00 | 15.00 |
| 11 Fernando Tatis | .15 | .40 |
| 12 Andrew Carpenter RC | .50 | 1.25 |
| 13 Ryan Langerhans | .15 | .40 |
| 14 Jon Rauch | .15 | .40 |
| 15 Nate McLouth | .15 | .40 |
| 16 Evan Longoria HL | .60 | 1.50 |
| 17 Bobby Cox MG | .15 | .40 |
| 18 George Sherrill | .15 | .40 |
| 19 Edgar Gonzalez | .15 | .40 |
| 20 Brad Lidge | .15 | .40 |
| 21 Jack Wilson | .15 | .40 |
| 22 E. Longoria/D.Price CC | .50 | 1.25 |
| 23 Gerald Laird | .15 | .40 |
| 24 Frank Thomas | .40 | 1.00 |
| 25 Jon Lester | .25 | .60 |
| 26 Jason Giambi | .15 | .40 |
| 27 Jonathon Niese RC | .50 | 1.25 |
| 28 Mike Lowell | .15 | .40 |
| 29 Jerry Hairston | .15 | .40 |
| 30a Ken Griffey Jr. | .60 | 1.50 |
| 30b Jackie Robinson SP | 8.00 | 20.00 |
| 31 Ian Stewart | .15 | .40 |
| 32 Daric Barton | .15 | .40 |
| 33 Jose Guillen | .15 | .40 |
| 34 Brandon Inge | .15 | .40 |
| 35 David Price RC | 1.00 | 2.50 |
| 36 Kevin Slowey | .25 | .60 |
| 37 Erick Aybar | .15 | .40 |
| 38 Eric Wedge MG | .15 | .40 |
| 39 Stephen Drew | .15 | .40 |
| 40 Carl Crawford | .25 | .60 |
| 41 Mike Mussina | .25 | .60 |
| 42 Jeff Francoeur | .25 | .60 |
| 43 Joe Mauer/Dustin Pedroia/Milton Bradley LL | .50 | |
| 44a Geoff Jenkins | .15 | .40 |
| 44b Barack Obama SP | 12.50 | 30.00 |
| 45 Aubrey Huff | .15 | .40 |
| 46 Brad Ziegler | .15 | .40 |
| 47 Jose Valverde | .15 | .40 |
| 48 Mike Napoli | .15 | .40 |
| 49 Kazuo Matsui | .15 | .40 |
| 50 David Ortiz | .25 | .60 |
| 51 Will Venable RC | .30 | .75 |
| 52 Marco Scutaro | .15 | .40 |
| 53 Jonathan Sanchez | .15 | .40 |
| 54 Dusty Baker MG | .15 | .40 |
| 55 J.J. Hardy | .15 | .40 |
| 56 Edwin Encarnacion | .15 | .40 |
| 57 Jo-Jo Reyes | .15 | .40 |
| 58 Travis Snider RC | .75 | 2.00 |
| 59 Eric Gagne | .15 | .40 |
| 60a Mariano Rivera | .25 | .60 |
| 60b Cy Young SP | 5.00 | 12.00 |
| 61 Lance Berkman/Carlos Lee CC | .25 | .60 |
| 62 Brian Barton | .15 | .40 |
| 63 Josh Outman RC | .50 | 1.25 |
| 64 Miguel Montero | .15 | .40 |
| 65 Mike Pelfrey | .15 | .40 |
| 66a Dustin Pedroia | .50 | 1.25 |
| 66b Ty Cobb SP | 12.50 | 30.00 |
| 67 Andruw Jones | .15 | .40 |
| 68 Kyle Lohse | .15 | .40 |
| 69 Rich Aurilia | .15 | .40 |
| 70 Jermaine Dye | .15 | .40 |
| 71 Mat Gamel RC | .75 | 2.00 |
| 72 David Dellucci | .15 | .40 |
| 73 Shane Victorino | .15 | .40 |
| 74 Trey Hillman MG | .15 | .40 |
| 75 Rich Harden | .15 | .40 |
| 76 Marcus Thames | .15 | .40 |
| 77 Jed Lowrie | .25 | .60 |
| 78 Tim Lincecum | .50 | 1.25 |
| 79 David Eckstein | .15 | .40 |
| 80 Brian McCann | .25 | .60 |
| 81 Howard/Dunn/Delgado LL | .50 | 1.25 |
| 82 Miguel Cairo | .15 | .40 |
| 83 Ryan Garko | .15 | .40 |
| 84 Rod Barajas | .15 | .40 |
| 85 Justin Verlander | .25 | .60 |
| 86 Kila Kaaihue (RC) | .50 | 1.25 |
| 87 Brad Hawpe | .15 | .40 |
| 88 Fredi Gonzalez MG | .15 | .40 |
| 89 Jon Lester/Jason Bay HL | .25 | .60 |
| 90 Justin Morneau | .25 | .60 |
| 91 Cody Ross | .15 | .40 |
| 92 Luis Castillo | .15 | .40 |
| 93 James Parr (RC) | .30 | .75 |
| 94 Adam Lind | .15 | .40 |
| 95 Andrew Miller | .25 | .60 |
| 96 Dexter Fowler (RC) | .50 | 1.25 |
| 97 Willie Harris | .15 | .40 |
| 98 Akinori Iwamura | .15 | .40 |
| 99 Juan Castro | .15 | .40 |
| 100 David Wright | .50 | 1.25 |
| 101 Nick Hundley | .15 | .40 |
| 102 Garrett Atkins | .15 | .40 |
| 103 Kyle Kendrick | .15 | .40 |
| 104 Brandon Moss | .15 | .40 |
| 105 Francisco Liriano | .15 | .40 |
| 106 Marlon Byrd | .15 | .40 |
| 107 Pedro Feliz | .15 | .40 |
| 108 Alcides Escobar RC | .50 | 1.25 |
| 109 Tom Gorzelanny | .15 | .40 |
| 110 Hideki Matsui | .40 | 1.00 |
| 111 Troy Percival | .15 | .40 |
| 112 Hideki Okajima | .15 | .40 |
| 113 Chris Young | .15 | .40 |
| 114 Chris Dickerson | .15 | .40 |
| 115a Kevin Youkilis | .25 | .60 |
| 115b George Sisler SP | 8.00 | 20.00 |
| 116 Omar Infante | .15 | .40 |
| 117 Ron Gardenhire MG | .15 | .40 |
| 118 Josh Johnson | .15 | .40 |
| 119 Craig Counsell | .15 | .40 |
| 120 Mark Teixeira | .40 | 1.00 |
| 121 Greg Golson (RC) | .30 | .75 |
| 122 Joe Mather | .15 | .40 |
| 123 Casey Blake | .15 | .40 |
| 124 Reed Johnson | .15 | .40 |
| 125 Roy Oswalt | .25 | .60 |
| 126 Orlando Hudson | .15 | .40 |
| 127 M.Cabrera/Quentin/ARod LL | .60 | 1.50 |
| 128 Johnny Gusto | .15 | .40 |
| 129 Angel Berroa | .15 | .40 |
| 130 Vladimir Guerrero | .40 | 1.00 |
| 131 Joe Torre MG | .25 | .60 |
| 132 Juan Pierre | .15 | .40 |
| 133 Brandon Jones | .15 | .40 |
| 134 Evan Longoria | .60 | 1.50 |
| 135 Carlos Delgado | .15 | .40 |
| 136 Tim Hudson | .15 | .40 |
| 137 Angel Salome (RC) | .30 | .75 |
| 138 Ubaldo Jimenez | .15 | .40 |
| 139 Matt Stairs HL | .15 | .40 |
| 140 Brandon Webb | .25 | .60 |
| 141 Mark Teahen | .15 | .40 |
| 142 Brad Penny | .15 | .40 |
| 143 Matt Joyce | .15 | .40 |
| 144 Matt Tuiasosopo (RC) | .30 | .75 |
| 145 Alex Gordon | .25 | .60 |
| 146 Glen Perkins | .15 | .40 |
| 147 Howard/Wright/A.Gonzalez LL | .50 | 1.25 |
| 148 Ty Wigginton | .15 | .40 |
| 149 Juan Uribe | .15 | .40 |
| 150 Kosuke Fukudome | .40 | 1.00 |
| 151 Carl Pavano | .15 | .40 |
| 152 Cody Ransom | .15 | .40 |
| 153 Lastings Milledge | .15 | .40 |
| 154 A.J. Pierzynski | .15 | .40 |
| 155 Roy Halladay | .25 | .60 |
| 156 Carlos Pena | .25 | .60 |
| 157 Brandon Webb/Dan Haren CC | .25 | .60 |
| 158 Ray Durham | .15 | .40 |
| 159 Matt Antonelli RC | .50 | 1.25 |
| 160 Evan Longoria | .60 | 1.50 |
| 161 Brendan Harris | .15 | .40 |
| 162 Mike Cameron | .15 | .40 |
| 163 Ross Gload | .15 | .40 |
| 164 Bob Geren MG | .15 | .40 |
| 165 Matt Kemp | .40 | 1.00 |
| 166 Jeff Baker | .15 | .40 |
| 167 Aaron Harang | .15 | .40 |
| 168 Mark DeRosa | .15 | .40 |
| 169 Juan Miranda RC | .50 | 1.25 |
| 170a CC Sabathia | .25 | .60 |
| 170b CC Sabathia SP | 5.00 | 12.00 |
| 171 Jeff Bailey | .15 | .40 |
| 172 Yadier Molina | .25 | .60 |
| 173 Manny Delcarmen | .15 | .40 |
| 174 James Shields | .15 | .40 |
| 175 Jeff Samardzija | .25 | .60 |
| 176 Josh Hamilton/Justin Morneau/Miguel Cabrera LL | .40 | 1.00 |
| 177 Eric Hinske | .15 | .40 |
| 178 Frank Catalanotto | .15 | .40 |
| 179 Rafael Furcal | .15 | .40 |
| 180 Cliff Lee | .25 | .60 |
| 181 Jeff Manuel MG | .15 | .40 |
| 182 Daniel Murphy RC | .75 | 2.00 |
| 183 Jason Michaels | .15 | .40 |
| 184 Bobby Parnell RC | .50 | 1.25 |

|  |  | | |
|---|---|---|---|
| 185 | Randy Johnson | .40 | 1.00 |
| 186 | Ryan Madson | .15 | .40 |
| 187 | Jon Garland | .15 | .40 |
| 188 | Josh Bard | .15 | .40 |
| 189 | Jay Payton | .15 | .40 |
| 190 | Chien-Ming Wang | .40 | 1.00 |
| 191 | Shane Victorino HL | .15 | .40 |
| 192 | Collin Balester | .15 | .40 |
| 193 | Zack Greinke | .25 | .60 |
| 194 | Jeremy Guthrie | .15 | .40 |
| 195a | Tim Lincecum | .50 | 1.25 |
| 195b | Christy Mathewson SP | 8.00 | 20.00 |
| 196 | Jason Motte (RC) | .30 | .75 |
| 197 | Ronnie Belliard | .15 | .40 |
| 198 | Conor Jackson | .15 | .40 |
| 199 | Ramon Castro | .15 | .40 |
| 200a | Chase Utley | .40 | 1.00 |
| 200b | Jimmie Foxx SP | 6.00 | 15.00 |
| 201 | Jarrod Saltalamacchia/Josh Hamilton CC | .40 | 1.00 |
| 202 | Gaby Sanchez RC | .30 | .75 |
| 203 | Jair Jurrjens | .25 | .60 |
| 204 | Andy Sonnanstine | .15 | .40 |
| 205a | Miguel Tejada | .25 | .60 |
| 205b | Honus Wagner SP | 8.00 | 20.00 |
| 206 | Santana/Lincecum/Peavy LL | .50 | 1.25 |
| 207 | Joe Blanton | .15 | .40 |
| 208 | James McDonald RC | .75 | 2.00 |
| 209 | Alfredo Amezaga | .15 | .40 |
| 210a | Geovany Soto | .25 | .60 |
| 210b | Roy Campanella SP | 5.00 | 12.00 |
| 211 | Ryan Rowland-White | .15 | .40 |
| 212 | Denard Span | .25 | .60 |
| 213 | Jeremy Sowers | .15 | .40 |
| 214 | Scott Elbert (RC) | .30 | .75 |
| 215 | Ian Kinsler | .25 | .60 |
| 216 | Joe Maddon MG | .15 | .40 |
| 217 | Albert Pujols | 1.00 | 2.50 |
| 218 | Emmanuel Burriss | .15 | .40 |
| 219 | Shin-Soo Choo | .15 | .40 |
| 220 | Jay Bruce | .40 | 1.00 |
| 221 | C.Lee/Halladay/Matsuzaka LL | .60 | 1.50 |
| 222 | Mark Sweeney | .15 | .40 |
| 223 | Dave Roberts | .15 | .40 |
| 224 | Max Scherzer | .25 | .60 |
| 225 | Aaron Cook | .15 | .40 |
| 226 | Neal Cotts | .15 | .40 |
| 227 | Freddy Sandoval (RC) | .30 | .75 |
| 228 | Scott Rolen | .40 | 1.00 |
| 229 | Cesar Izturis | .15 | .40 |
| 230 | Justin Upton | .25 | .60 |
| 231 | Xavier Nady | .15 | .40 |
| 232 | Gabe Kapler | .15 | .40 |
| 233 | Erik Bedard | .15 | .40 |
| 234 | John Russell MG | .15 | .40 |
| 235 | Chad Billingsley | .15 | .40 |
| 236 | Kelly Johnson | .15 | .40 |
| 237 | Aaron Cunningham RC | .30 | .75 |
| 238 | Jorge Cantu | .15 | .40 |
| 239 | Brandon League | .15 | .40 |
| 240a | Ryan Braun | .50 | 1.25 |
| 240b | Mel Ott SP | 8.00 | 20.00 |
| 241 | David Newhan | .15 | .40 |
| 242 | Ricky Nolasco | .15 | .40 |
| 243 | Chase Headley | .15 | .40 |
| 244 | Sean Rodriguez | .25 | .60 |
| 245 | Pat Burrell | .15 | .40 |
| 246 | B.Upton/Crawford/Longoria HL | .60 | 1.50 |
| 247 | Yuniesky Betancourt | .15 | .40 |
| 248 | Scott Lewis (RC) | .30 | .75 |
| 249 | Jack Hannahan | .15 | .40 |
| 250 | Josh Hamilton | .40 | 1.00 |
| 251 | Greg Smith | .15 | .40 |
| 252 | Brandon Wood | .15 | .40 |
| 253 | Edgar Renteria | .15 | .40 |
| 254 | Cito Gaston MG | .15 | .40 |
| 255 | Joe Crede | .15 | .40 |
| 256 | Reggie Abercrombie | .15 | .40 |
| 257 | George Kottaras (RC) | .30 | .75 |
| 258 | Casey Kotchman | .15 | .40 |
| 259 | Lince/Haren/Santana LL | .50 | 1.25 |
| 260 | Manny Ramirez | .40 | 1.00 |
| 261 | Jose Bautista | .15 | .40 |
| 262 | Mike Gonzalez | .15 | .40 |
| 263 | Elijah Dukes | .15 | .40 |
| 264 | Dave Bush | .15 | .40 |
| 265 | Carlos Zambrano | .15 | .40 |
| 266 | Todd Wellemeyer | .15 | .40 |
| 267 | Michael Bowden (RC) | .50 | 1.25 |
| 268 | Chris Burke | .15 | .40 |
| 269 | Hunter Pence | .25 | .60 |
| 270a | Grady Sizemore | .25 | .60 |
| 270b | Tris Speaker SP | 8.00 | 20.00 |
| 271 | Cliff Lee | .25 | .60 |
| 272 | Chan Ho Park | .15 | .40 |
| 273 | Brian Roberts | .15 | .40 |
| 274 | Alex Hinshaw | .15 | .40 |
| 275 | Alex Rios | .15 | .40 |
| 276 | Geovany Soto | .25 | .60 |
| 277 | Asdrubal Cabrera | .15 | .40 |
| 278 | Philadelphia Phillies HL | .15 | .40 |
| 279 | Ryan Church | .15 | .40 |
| 280 | Joe Saunders | .15 | .40 |
| 281 | Tug Hulett | .15 | .40 |
| 282 | Chris Lambert (RC) | .30 | .75 |
| 283 | John Baker | .15 | .40 |
| 284 | Luis Ayala | .15 | .40 |
| 285 | Justin Duchscherer | .15 | .40 |
| 286 | Odalis Perez | .15 | .40 |
| 287a | Greg Maddux | .50 | 1.25 |
| 287b | Walter Johnson SP | 6.00 | 15.00 |
| 288 | Guillermo Quiroz | .15 | .40 |
| 289 | Josh Banks | .15 | .40 |
| 290a | Albert Pujols | 1.00 | 2.50 |
| 290b | Lou Gehrig SP | 12.50 | 30.00 |
| 291 | Chris Coste | .15 | .40 |
| 292 | Francisco Cervelli RC | .75 | 2.00 |
| 293 | Brian Bixler | .15 | .40 |
| 294 | Brandon Boggs | .15 | .40 |
| 295 | Derrek Lee | .25 | .60 |
| 296 | Reid Brignac | .15 | .40 |
| 297 | Bud Black MG | .15 | .40 |
| 298 | Jonathan Van Every | .15 | .40 |
| 299 | Cole Hamels HL | .40 | 1.00 |
| 300 | Ichiro Suzuki | .60 | 1.50 |
| 301 | Clint Barmes | .15 | .40 |
| 302 | Brian Giles | .15 | .40 |
| 303 | Zach Duke | .15 | .40 |
| 304 | Jason Kubel | .15 | .40 |
| 305a | Ivan Rodriguez | .25 | .60 |
| 305b | Thurman Munson SP | 10.00 | 25.00 |
| 306 | Javier Vazquez | .15 | .40 |
| 307 | A.J. Burnett/Ervin Santana/Roy Halladay LL | | .25 |
| 308 | Chris Duncan | .15 | .40 |
| 309 | Humberto Sanchez (RC) | .30 | .75 |
| 310 | Johan Santana | .40 | 1.00 |
| 311 | Kelly Shoppach | .15 | .40 |
| 312 | Ryan Sweeney | .15 | .40 |
| 313 | Jamey Carroll | .15 | .40 |
| 314 | Matt Treanor | .15 | .40 |
| 315 | Hiroki Kuroda | .15 | .40 |
| 316 | Brian Stokes | .15 | .40 |
| 317 | Jarrod Saltalamacchia | .15 | .40 |
| 318 | Manny Acta MG | .15 | .40 |
| 319 | Brian Fuentes | .15 | .40 |
| 320a | Miguel Cabrera | .25 | .60 |
| 320b | Johnny Mize SP | 5.00 | 12.00 |
| 321 | S.Kazmir/D.Price CC | .50 | 1.25 |
| 322 | John Buck | .15 | .40 |
| 323 | Vicente Padilla | .15 | .40 |
| 324 | Mark Reynolds | .15 | .40 |
| 325 | Dustin McGowan | .15 | .40 |
| 326 | Manny Ramirez HL | .40 | 1.00 |
| 327 | Phil Coke RC | .50 | 1.25 |
| 328 | Doug Mientkiewicz | .15 | .40 |
| 329 | Gil Meche | .15 | .40 |
| 330 | Daisuke Matsuzaka | .60 | 1.50 |
| 331 | Luke Scott | .15 | .40 |
| 332 | Chone Figgins | .15 | .40 |
| 333 | Jeremy Sowers/Aaron Laffey | .15 | .40 |
| 334 | Blake DeWitt | .25 | .60 |
| 335 | Chris Young | .15 | .40 |
| 336 | Jordan Schafer SP | .50 | 1.25 |
| 337 | Bobby Jenks | .15 | .40 |
| 338 | Daniel Cabrera | .15 | .40 |
| 339 | Jim Leyland MG | .15 | .40 |
| 340a | Joe Mauer | .40 | 1.00 |
| 340b | Wade Boggs SP | 6.00 | 15.00 |
| 341 | Willy Taveras | .15 | .40 |
| 342 | Gerald Laird | .15 | .40 |
| 343 | Ian Snell | .15 | .40 |
| 344 | J.R. Towles | .15 | .40 |
| 345 | Stephen Drew | .15 | .40 |
| 346 | Mike Cameron | .15 | .40 |
| 347 | Jason Bartlett | .15 | .40 |
| 348 | Tony Pena | .15 | .40 |
| 349 | Justin Masterson | .25 | .60 |
| 350a | Dustin Pedroia | .50 | 1.25 |
| 350b | Ryne Sandberg SP | 8.00 | 20.00 |
| 351 | Chris Snyder | .15 | .40 |
| 352 | Gregor Blanco | .15 | .40 |
| 353a | Derek Jeter | 1.00 | 2.50 |
| 353b | Cal Ripken Jr. SP | 8.00 | 20.00 |
| 354 | Mike Aviles | .15 | .40 |
| 355a | John Smoltz | .40 | 1.00 |
| 355b | Jim Palmer SP | 5.00 | 12.00 |
| 356 | Ervin Santana | .15 | .40 |
| 357 | Huston Street | .15 | .40 |
| 358 | Chad Tracy | .15 | .40 |
| 359 | Jason Varitek | .25 | .60 |
| 360 | Jorge Posada | .25 | .60 |
| 361 | Alex Rios/Vernon Wells | .15 | .40 |
| 362 | Luke Montz RC | .30 | .75 |
| 363 | Jhonny Peralta | .15 | .40 |
| 364 | Kevin Millwood | .15 | .40 |
| 365 | Mark Buehrle | .15 | .40 |
| 366 | Alexi Casilla | .15 | .40 |
| 367 | Bobby Abreu | .15 | .40 |
| 368 | Trevor Hoffman | .15 | .40 |
| 369 | Matt Harrison | .15 | .40 |
| 370 | Victor Martinez | .25 | .60 |
| 371 | Jeff Francis | .15 | .40 |
| 372 | Rickie Weeks | .15 | .40 |
| 373 | Joe Martinez RC | .50 | 1.25 |
| 374 | Kevin Kouzmanoff | .15 | .40 |
| 375 | Carlos Quentin | .15 | .40 |
| 376 | Rajai Davis | .15 | .40 |
| 377 | Trevor Crowe RC | .50 | 1.25 |
| 378 | Mark Hendrickson | .15 | .40 |
| 379 | Howie Kendrick | .15 | .40 |
| 380 | Aramis Ramirez | .15 | .40 |
| 381 | Sharon Martis RC | .50 | 1.25 |
| 382 | Wily Mo Pena | .15 | .40 |
| 383 | Everth Cabrera RC | .50 | 1.25 |
| 384 | Bob Melvin MG | .15 | .40 |
| 385 | Mike Jacobs | .15 | .40 |
| 386 | Jonathan Papelbon | .25 | .60 |
| 387 | Adam Everett | .15 | .40 |
| 388 | Humberto Quintero | .15 | .40 |
| 389 | Garrett Olson | .15 | .40 |
| 390 | Joey Votto | .25 | .60 |
| 391 | Jason Giambi | .25 | .60 |
| 392 | Brandon Phillips | .15 | .40 |
| 393 | Alex Cintron | .15 | .40 |
| 394 | Barry Zito | .15 | .40 |
| 395 | Magglio Ordonez | .15 | .40 |
| 396 | Alex Cora | .15 | .40 |
| 397 | Carlos Ruiz | .15 | .40 |
| 398 | Cameron Maybin | .25 | .60 |
| 399 | Wandy Rodriguez | .15 | .40 |
| 400a | Alfonso Soriano | .25 | .60 |
| 400b | Frank Robinson SP | 6.00 | 15.00 |
| 401 | Tony La Russa MG | .15 | .40 |
| 402 | Nick Blackburn | .15 | .40 |
| 403 | Trevor Cahill RC | .50 | 1.25 |
| 404 | Matt Capps | .15 | .40 |
| 405 | Todd Helton | .25 | .60 |
| 406 | Mark Ellis | .15 | .40 |
| 407 | Dave Trembley MG | .15 | .40 |
| 408 | Ronny Paulino | .15 | .40 |
| 409 | Jesse Chavez RC | .30 | .75 |
| 410 | Lou Piniella MG | .25 | .60 |
| 411 | Troy Tulowitzki | .25 | .60 |
| 412 | Taylor Teagarden | .25 | .60 |
| 413 | Ruben Gotay | .15 | .40 |
| 414 | Cha Seung Baek | .15 | .40 |
| 415a | Josh Beckett | .25 | .60 |
| 415b | Bob Gibson SP | 6.00 | 15.00 |
| 416 | Josh Whitesell RC | .50 | 1.25 |
| 417 | Jason Marquis | .15 | .40 |
| 418 | Andy Pettitte | .25 | .60 |
| 419 | Braden Looper | .15 | .40 |
| 420 | Scott Baker | .15 | .40 |
| 421 | B.J. Ryan | .15 | .40 |
| 422 | Hank Blalock | .15 | .40 |
| 423 | Melvin Mora | .15 | .40 |
| 424 | Jorge Campillo | .15 | .40 |
| 425 | Curtis Granderson | .40 | 1.00 |
| 426 | Pablo Sandoval | .50 | 1.25 |
| 427 | Brian Duensing RC | .50 | 1.25 |
| 428 | Jamie Moyer | .15 | .40 |
| 429 | Mike Hampton | .15 | .40 |
| 430 | Francisco Rodriguez | .25 | .60 |
| 431 | Ramon Hernandez | .15 | .40 |

|  |  | | |
|---|---|---|---|
| ☐ 432 | Wladimir Balentien | .15 | .40 |
| ☐ 433 | Coco Crisp | .15 | .40 |
| ☐ 434 | Carlos Guillen/Miguel Cabrera | .25 | .60 |
| ☐ 435 | Carlos Lee | .15 | .40 |
| ☐ 436 | Ryan Theriot | .15 | .40 |
| ☐ 437 | Austin Kearns | .15 | .40 |
| ☐ 438 | Mark Loretta | .15 | .40 |
| ☐ 439 | Ryan Spilborghs | .15 | .40 |
| ☐ 440 | Fausto Carmona | .15 | .40 |
| ☐ 441 | Andrew Bailey RC | .50 | 1.25 |
| ☐ 442 | Cliff Pennington | .15 | .40 |
| ☐ 443 | Gavin Floyd | .15 | .40 |
| ☐ 444 | Jody Gerut | .15 | .40 |
| ☐ 445 | Joe Nathan | .15 | .40 |
| ☐ 446 | Matt Holliday | .25 | .60 |
| ☐ 447 | Freddy Sanchez | .15 | .40 |
| ☐ 448 | Jeff Clement | .15 | .40 |
| ☐ 449 | Mike Fontenot | .15 | .40 |
| ☐ 450 | Hanley Ramirez | .40 | 1.00 |
| ☐ 451 | Ryan Perry RC | .75 | 2.00 |
| ☐ 452 | Orlando Cabrera | .15 | .40 |
| ☐ 453 | Javier Valentin | .15 | .40 |
| ☐ 454 | Carlos Silva | .15 | .40 |
| ☐ 455 | Adam Jones | .25 | .60 |
| ☐ 456 | Jason Kendall | .15 | .40 |
| ☐ 457 | John Maine | .15 | .40 |
| ☐ 458 | Jeremy Bonderman | .15 | .40 |
| ☐ 459 | Brian Bannister | .15 | .40 |
| ☐ 460 | Nick Markakis | .25 | .60 |
| ☐ 461 | Mike Scioscia MG | .15 | .40 |
| ☐ 462 | James Loney | .25 | .60 |
| ☐ 463 | Brian Wilson | .15 | .40 |
| ☐ 464 | Bobby Crosby | .15 | .40 |
| ☐ 465 | Troy Glaus | .15 | .40 |
| ☐ 466 | Wilson Betemit | .15 | .40 |
| ☐ 467 | Chris Volstad | .15 | .40 |
| ☐ 468 | Derek Lowe | .15 | .40 |
| ☐ 469 | Michael Cuddyer | .15 | .40 |
| ☐ 470 | Lance Berkman | .25 | .60 |
| ☐ 471 | Kerry Wood | .15 | .40 |
| ☐ 472 | Bill Hall | .15 | .40 |
| ☐ 473 | Jered Weaver | .15 | .40 |
| ☐ 474 | Franklin Gutierrez | .15 | .40 |
| ☐ 475a | Chipper Jones | .40 | 1.00 |
| ☐ 475b | Mike Schmidt SP | 8.00 | 20.00 |
| ☐ 476a | Edinson Volquez | .15 | .40 |
| ☐ 476b | Juan Marichal SP | 5.00 | 12.00 |
| ☐ 477 | Josh Willingham | .15 | .40 |
| ☐ 478 | Jose Molina | .15 | .40 |
| ☐ 479 | Brad Nelson (RC) | .30 | .75 |
| ☐ 480 | Prince Fielder | .40 | 1.00 |
| ☐ 481 | Nyjer Morgan | .15 | .40 |
| ☐ 482 | Jason Jaramillo (RC) | .30 | .75 |
| ☐ 483 | John Lannan | .15 | .40 |
| ☐ 484 | Chris Carpenter | .25 | .60 |
| ☐ 485 | Aaron Rowand | .15 | .40 |
| ☐ 486 | J.J. Putz | .15 | .40 |
| ☐ 487 | Travis Hafner | .15 | .40 |
| ☐ 488 | Ozzie Guillen MG | .15 | .40 |
| ☐ 489 | Matt Guerrier | .15 | .40 |
| ☐ 490a | Joba Chamberlain | .50 | 1.25 |
| ☐ 490b | Nolan Ryan SP | 8.00 | 20.00 |
| ☐ 491 | Paul Bako | .15 | .40 |
| ☐ 492 | Andre Ethier | .25 | .60 |
| ☐ 493 | Ramiro Pena RC | .50 | 1.25 |
| ☐ 494 | Gary Matthews | .15 | .40 |
| ☐ 495a | Eric Chavez | .15 | .40 |
| ☐ 495b | Brooks Robinson SP | 8.00 | 20.00 |
| ☐ 496 | Charlie Manuel MG | .15 | .40 |
| ☐ 497 | Clint Hurdle MG | .15 | .40 |
| ☐ 498 | Kyle Davies | .15 | .40 |
| ☐ 499 | Edwin Moreno (RC) | .30 | .75 |
| ☐ 500 | Ryan Howard | .50 | 1.25 |
| ☐ 501 | Jeff Suppan | .15 | .40 |
| ☐ 502 | Yovani Gallardo | .15 | .40 |
| ☐ 503 | Carlos Gonzalez | .15 | .40 |
| ☐ 504 | Felix Pie | .15 | .40 |
| ☐ 505 | Scott Olsen | .15 | .40 |
| ☐ 506 | Paul Konerko | .15 | .40 |
| ☐ 507 | Melky Cabrera | .15 | .40 |
| ☐ 508 | Kenji Johjima | .25 | .60 |
| ☐ 509 | Lou Montanez | .15 | .40 |
| ☐ 510 | Ryan Ludwick | .25 | .60 |
| ☐ 511 | Chad Qualls | .15 | .40 |
| ☐ 512 | Steve Pearce | .15 | .40 |
| ☐ 513 | Bronson Arroyo | .15 | .40 |
| ☐ 514 | Nick Hundley | .15 | .40 |
| ☐ 515a | Gary Sheffield | .15 | .40 |
| ☐ 515b | Reggie Jackson SP | 10.00 | 25.00 |
| ☐ 516 | Brian Anderson | .15 | .40 |
| ☐ 517 | Kevin Frandsen | .15 | .40 |
| ☐ 518 | Chris Perez | .15 | .40 |
| ☐ 519 | Dioner Navarro | .15 | .40 |
| ☐ 520a | Adrian Gonzalez | .25 | .60 |
| ☐ 520b | Tony Gwynn SP | 6.00 | 15.00 |
| ☐ 521 | Dana Eveland | .15 | .40 |
| ☐ 522 | Gio Gonzalez | .15 | .40 |
| ☐ 523 | Brandon Morrow | .15 | .40 |
| ☐ 524 | Andy LaRoche | .15 | .40 |
| ☐ 525 | Jimmy Rollins | .25 | .60 |
| ☐ 526 | Bruce Bochy MG | .15 | .40 |
| ☐ 527 | Jason Isringhausen | .15 | .40 |
| ☐ 528 | Nick Swisher | .15 | .40 |
| ☐ 529 | Fernando Rodney | .15 | .40 |
| ☐ 530 | Felix Hernandez | .25 | .60 |
| ☐ 531 | Frank Francisco | .15 | .40 |
| ☐ 532 | Garret Anderson | .15 | .40 |
| ☐ 533 | Darin Erstad | .15 | .40 |
| ☐ 534 | Skip Schumaker | .15 | .40 |
| ☐ 535 | Ryan Doumit | .15 | .40 |
| ☐ 536 | Khalil Greene | .15 | .40 |
| ☐ 537 | Anthony Reyes | .15 | .40 |
| ☐ 538 | Carlos Guillen | .15 | .40 |
| ☐ 539 | Miguel Olivo | .15 | .40 |
| ☐ 540 | Russell Martin | .25 | .60 |
| ☐ 541 | Jason Bay | .25 | .60 |
| ☐ 542 | Chris Ray | .15 | .40 |
| ☐ 543 | Travis Ishikawa | .15 | .40 |
| ☐ 544 | Pat Neshek | .15 | .40 |
| ☐ 545 | Matt Garza | .15 | .40 |
| ☐ 546 | Matt Cain | .15 | .40 |
| ☐ 547 | Jack Cust | .15 | .40 |
| ☐ 548 | John Danks | .15 | .40 |
| ☐ 549 | Randy Winn | .15 | .40 |
| ☐ 550 | Carlos Beltran | .15 | .40 |
| ☐ 551 | Tim Redding | .15 | .40 |
| ☐ 552 | Eric Byrnes | .15 | .40 |
| ☐ 553 | Jeff Karstens | .15 | .40 |
| ☐ 554 | Adam LaRoche | .15 | .40 |
| ☐ 555 | Joe Girardi MG | .25 | .60 |
| ☐ 556 | Brendan Ryan | .15 | .40 |
| ☐ 557 | Jayson Werth | .15 | .40 |
| ☐ 558 | Edgar Renteria | .15 | .40 |
| ☐ 559 | Esteban German | .15 | .40 |
| ☐ 560 | Adrian Beltre | .15 | .40 |
| ☐ 561 | Ryan Freel | .15 | .40 |
| ☐ 562 | Cecil Cooper MG | .15 | .40 |
| ☐ 563 | Francisco Cordero | .15 | .40 |
| ☐ 564 | Jesus Flores | .15 | .40 |
| ☐ 565 | Jose Lopez | .15 | .40 |
| ☐ 566 | Dontrelle Willis | .15 | .40 |
| ☐ 567 | Willy Aybar | .15 | .40 |
| ☐ 568 | Greg Reynolds | .15 | .40 |
| ☐ 569 | Ted Lilly | .15 | .40 |
| ☐ 570 | David DeJesus | .15 | .40 |
| ☐ 571 | Noah Lowry | .15 | .40 |
| ☐ 572 | Michael Bourn | .15 | .40 |
| ☐ 573 | Adam Wainwright | .15 | .40 |
| ☐ 574 | Nate Schierholtz | .15 | .40 |
| ☐ 575 | Clayton Kershaw | .40 | 1.00 |
| ☐ 576 | Don Wakamatsu MG | .15 | .40 |
| ☐ 577 | Jose Contreras | .15 | .40 |
| ☐ 578 | Adam Kennedy | .15 | .40 |
| ☐ 579 | Rocco Baldelli | .15 | .40 |
| ☐ 580 | Scott Kazmir | .25 | .60 |
| ☐ 581 | David Purcey | .15 | .40 |
| ☐ 582 | Yunel Escobar | .15 | .40 |
| ☐ 583 | Brett Anderson RC | .50 | 1.25 |
| ☐ 584 | Ron Washington MG | .15 | .40 |
| ☐ 585 | Alexei Ramirez | .25 | .60 |
| ☐ 586 | Nelson Cruz | .15 | .40 |
| ☐ 587 | Adam Dunn | .25 | .60 |
| ☐ 588 | Jorge De La Rosa | .15 | .40 |
| ☐ 589 | Rickey Romero (RC) | .30 | .75 |
| ☐ 590 | Johnny Damon | .15 | .40 |
| ☐ 591 | Elvis Andrus RC | .75 | 2.00 |
| ☐ 592 | Fred Lewis | .15 | .40 |
| ☐ 593 | Kenshin Kawakami RC | .75 | 2.00 |
| ☐ 594 | Milton Bradley | .15 | .40 |
| ☐ 595a | Vernon Wells | .15 | .40 |
| ☐ 595b | Robin Yount SP | 6.00 | 15.00 |
| ☐ 596 | Radhames Liz | .15 | .40 |
| ☐ 597 | Randy Wolf | .15 | .40 |
| ☐ 598 | Micah Owings | .15 | .40 |
| ☐ 599 | Placido Polanco | .15 | .40 |
| ☐ 600a | Jake Peavy | .25 | .60 |
| ☐ 600b | Greg Maddux SP | 10.00 | 25.00 |
| ☐ 601 | Ryan Howard/Jimmy Rollins | .50 | 1.25 |
| ☐ 602 | Carlos Gomez | .15 | .40 |
| ☐ 603 | Jose Reyes | .40 | 1.00 |
| ☐ 604 | Gregg Zaun | .15 | .40 |
| ☐ 605 | Rick Ankiel | .25 | .60 |
| ☐ 606 | Nick Johnson | .15 | .40 |
| ☐ 607 | Jarrod Washburn | .15 | .40 |
| ☐ 608 | Cristian Guzman | .15 | .40 |
| ☐ 609 | Juan Rivera | .15 | .40 |
| ☐ 610a | Michael Young | .25 | .60 |
| ☐ 610b | Paul Molitor SP | 6.00 | 15.00 |
| ☐ 611 | Jeremy Hermida | .15 | .40 |
| ☐ 612 | Joel Pineiro | .15 | .40 |
| ☐ 613 | Kendry Morales | .15 | .40 |
| ☐ 614 | David Murphy | .15 | .40 |
| ☐ 615 | Robinson Cano | .25 | .60 |
| ☐ 616 | Koji Uehara RC | .75 | 2.00 |
| ☐ 617 | Shaun Marcum | .15 | .40 |
| ☐ 618 | Brandon Backe | .15 | .40 |
| ☐ 619 | Chris Carter | .15 | .40 |
| ☐ 620 | Ryan Zimmerman | .25 | .60 |
| ☐ 621 | Oliver Perez | .15 | .40 |
| ☐ 622 | Kurt Suzuki | .15 | .40 |
| ☐ 623 | Aaron Hill | .15 | .40 |
| ☐ 624 | Ben Francisco | .15 | .40 |
| ☐ 625 | Jim Thome | .25 | .60 |
| ☐ 626 | Scott Hairston | .15 | .40 |
| ☐ 627 | Billy Butler | .15 | .40 |
| ☐ 628 | Justin Upton/Chris Young | .15 | .40 |
| ☐ 629 | Lyle Overbay | .15 | .40 |
| ☐ 630 | A.J. Burnett | .25 | .60 |
| ☐ 631 | Colby Rasmus (RC) | .50 | 1.25 |
| ☐ 632 | Brett Myers | .15 | .40 |
| ☐ 633 | David Patton RC | .50 | 1.25 |
| ☐ 634 | Chris Davis | .15 | .40 |
| ☐ 635 | Joakim Soria | .15 | .40 |
| ☐ 636 | Armando Galarraga | .15 | .40 |
| ☐ 637 | Donald Veal RC | .50 | 1.25 |
| ☐ 638 | Eugenio Velez | .15 | .40 |
| ☐ 639 | Corey Hart | .15 | .40 |
| ☐ 640 | B.J. Upton | .25 | .60 |
| ☐ 641 | Jesse Litsch | .15 | .40 |
| ☐ 642 | Ken Macha MG | .15 | .40 |
| ☐ 643 | David Freese RC | .75 | 2.00 |
| ☐ 644 | Alfredo Aceves RC | .50 | 1.25 |
| ☐ 645 | Paul Maholm | .15 | .40 |
| ☐ 646 | Chris Iannetta | .15 | .40 |
| ☐ 647 | Manny Parra | .15 | .40 |
| ☐ 648 | J.D. Drew | .15 | .40 |
| ☐ 649 | Luke Hochevar | .15 | .40 |
| ☐ 650a | Cole Hamels | .40 | 1.00 |
| ☐ 650b | Steve Carlton SP | 5.00 | 12.00 |
| ☐ 651 | Jake Westbrook | .15 | .40 |
| ☐ 652 | Doug Davis | .15 | .40 |
| ☐ 653 | Nick Evans | .15 | .40 |
| ☐ 654 | Brian Schneider | .15 | .40 |
| ☐ 655 | Bengie Molina | .15 | .40 |
| ☐ 656 | Delmon Young | .25 | .60 |
| ☐ 657 | Aaron Heilman | .15 | .40 |
| ☐ 658 | Rick Porcello RC | 1.25 | 3.00 |
| ☐ 659 | Torii Hunter | .15 | .40 |
| ☐ 660a | Jacoby Ellsbury | .40 | 1.00 |
| ☐ 660b | Carl Yastrzemski SP | 6.00 | 15.00 |

## 2003 Topps 205

| | | | |
|---|---|---|---|
| ☐ COMPLETE SERIES 1 (165) | | 15.00 | 40.00 |
| ☐ COMPLETE SERIES 2 (175) | | 75.00 | 125.00 |
| ☐ COMP.SERIES 2 w/o SP's (155) | | 15.00 | 40.00 |
| ☐ COM (1-130/161-169/193-315) | | .20 | .50 |
| ☐ COMMON (131-145/170-192) | | .20 | .50 |
| ☐ COMMON CARD (146-160) | | .40 | 1.00 |
| ☐ COMMON SP | | 1.00 | 2.50 |
| ☐ SERIES 2 SP STATED ODDS 1:5 | | | |

| Card | Low | High |
|---|---|---|
| 1A Barry Bonds w/Cap | 1.25 | 3.00 |
| 1B Barry Bonds w/Helmet | 1.25 | 3.00 |
| 2 Bret Boone | .20 | .50 |
| 3A Albert Pujols Clear Logo | 1.00 | 2.50 |
| 3B Albert Pujols White Logo | 1.00 | 2.50 |
| 4 Carl Crawford | .20 | .50 |
| 5 Bartolo Colon | .20 | .50 |
| 6 Cliff Floyd | .20 | .50 |
| 7 John Olerud | .20 | .50 |
| 8A Jason Giambi Full Jkt | .20 | .50 |
| 8B Jason Giambi Partial Jkt | .20 | .50 |
| 9 Edgardo Alfonzo | .20 | .50 |
| 10 Ivan Rodriguez | .30 | .75 |
| 11 Jim Edmonds | .20 | .50 |
| 12A Mike Piazza Orange | .75 | 2.00 |
| 12B Mike Piazza Yellow | .75 | 2.00 |
| 13 Greg Maddux | .75 | 2.00 |
| 14 Jose Vidro | .20 | .50 |
| 15A Vlad Guerrero Clear Logo | .50 | 1.25 |
| 15B Vlad Guerrero White Logo | .50 | 1.25 |
| 16 Bernie Williams | .30 | .75 |
| 17 Roger Clemens | 1.00 | 2.50 |
| 18A Miguel Tejada Blue | .20 | .50 |
| 18B Miguel Tejada Green | .20 | .50 |
| 19 Carlos Delgado | .20 | .50 |
| 20A Alfonso Soriano w/Bat | .50 | 1.25 |
| 20B Alfonso Soriano Sunglasses | .50 | 1.25 |
| 21 Bobby Cox MG | .20 | .50 |
| 22 Mike Scioscia | .20 | .50 |
| 23 John Smoltz | .30 | .75 |
| 24 Luis Gonzalez | .20 | .50 |
| 25 Shawn Green | .20 | .50 |
| 26 Raul Ibanez | .20 | .50 |
| 27 Andruw Jones | .30 | .75 |
| 28 Josh Beckett | .20 | .50 |
| 29 Derek Lowe | .20 | .50 |
| 30 Todd Helton | .30 | .75 |
| 31 Barry Larkin | .30 | .75 |
| 32 Jason Jennings | .20 | .50 |
| 33 Darin Erstad | .20 | .50 |
| 34 Magglio Ordonez | .20 | .50 |
| 35 Mike Sweeney | .20 | .50 |
| 36 Kazuhisa Ishii | .20 | .50 |
| 37 Ron Gardenhire MG | .20 | .50 |
| 38 Tim Hudson | .20 | .50 |
| 39 Tim Salmon | .20 | .50 |
| 40A Pat Burrell Black Bat | .20 | .50 |
| 40B Pat Burrell Brown Bat | .20 | .50 |
| 41 Manny Ramirez | .30 | .75 |
| 42 Nick Johnson | .20 | .50 |
| 43 Tom Glavine | .30 | .75 |
| 44 Mark Mulder | .20 | .50 |
| 45 Brian Jordan | .20 | .50 |
| 46 Rafael Palmeiro | .30 | .75 |
| 47 Vernon Wells | .20 | .50 |
| 48 Bob Brenly MG | .20 | .50 |
| 49 C.C. Sabathia | .20 | .50 |
| 50A Alex Rodriguez Look Ahead | .75 | 2.00 |
| 50B Alex Rodriguez Look Away | .75 | 2.00 |
| 51A Sammy Sosa Head Back | .50 | 1.25 |
| 51B Sammy Sosa Head Left | .50 | 1.25 |
| 52 Paul Konerko | .20 | .50 |
| 53 Craig Biggio | .30 | .75 |
| 54 Moises Alou | .20 | .50 |
| 55 Johnny Damon | .30 | .75 |
| 56 Torii Hunter | .20 | .50 |
| 57 Omar Vizquel | .30 | .75 |
| 58 Orlando Hernandez | .20 | .50 |
| 59 Barry Zito | .20 | .50 |
| 60 Lance Berkman | .20 | .50 |
| 61 Carlos Beltran | .20 | .50 |
| 62 Edgar Renteria | .20 | .50 |
| 63 Ben Sheets | .20 | .50 |
| 64 Doug Mientkiewicz | .20 | .50 |
| 65 Troy Glaus | .20 | .50 |
| 66 Preston Wilson | .20 | .50 |
| 67 Kerry Wood | .20 | .50 |
| 68 Frank Thomas | .50 | 1.25 |
| 69 Jimmy Rollins | .20 | .50 |
| 70 Brian Giles | .20 | .50 |
| 71 Bobby Higginson | .20 | .50 |
| 72 Larry Walker | .20 | .50 |
| 73 Randy Johnson | .50 | 1.25 |
| 74 Tony LaRussa MG | .20 | .50 |
| 75A Derek Jeter w/Gold Trim | 1.25 | 3.00 |
| 75B Derek Jeter w/o Gold Trim | 1.25 | 3.00 |
| 76 Bobby Abreu | .20 | .50 |
| 77A Adam Dunn Closed Mouth | .20 | .50 |
| 77B Adam Dunn Open Mouth | .20 | .50 |
| 78 Ryan Klesko | .20 | .50 |
| 79 Francisco Rodriguez | .20 | .50 |
| 80 Scott Rolen | .30 | .75 |
| 81 Roberto Alomar | .30 | .75 |
| 82 Joe Torre MG | .30 | .75 |
| 83 Jim Thome | .30 | .75 |
| 84 Kevin Millwood | .20 | .50 |
| 85 J.T. Snow | .20 | .50 |
| 86 Trevor Hoffman | .20 | .50 |
| 87 Jay Gibbons | .20 | .50 |
| 88A Mark Prior New Logo | .30 | .75 |
| 88B Mark Prior Old Logo | .30 | .75 |
| 89 Rich Aurilia | .20 | .50 |
| 90 Chipper Jones | .50 | 1.25 |
| 91 Richie Sexson | .20 | .50 |
| 92 Gary Sheffield | .20 | .50 |
| 93 Pedro Martinez | .30 | .75 |
| 94 Rodrigo Lopez | .20 | .50 |
| 95 Al Leiter | .20 | .50 |
| 96 Jorge Posada | .30 | .75 |
| 97 Luis Castillo | .20 | .50 |
| 98 Aubrey Huff | .20 | .50 |
| 99 A.J. Pierzynski | .20 | .50 |
| 100A Ichiro Suzuki Look Ahead | 1.00 | 2.50 |
| 100B Ichiro Suzuki Look Right | .20 | .50 |
| 101 Eric Chavez | .20 | .50 |
| 102 Brett Myers | .20 | .50 |
| 103 Jason Kendall | .20 | .50 |
| 104 Jeff Kent | .20 | .50 |
| 105 Eric Hinske | .20 | .50 |
| 106 Jacque Jones | .20 | .50 |
| 107 Phil Nevin | .20 | .50 |
| 108 Roy Oswalt | .20 | .50 |
| 109 Curt Schilling | .30 | .75 |
| 110A N.Garciaparra w/Gold Trim | .75 | 2.00 |
| 110B N.Garciaparra w/o Gold Trim | .75 | 2.00 |
| 111 Garret Anderson | .20 | .50 |
| 112 Eric Gagne | .20 | .50 |
| 113 Javier Vazquez | .20 | .50 |
| 114 Jeff Bagwell | .30 | .75 |
| 115 Mike Lowell | .20 | .50 |
| 116 Carlos Pena | .20 | .50 |
| 117 Ken Griffey Jr. | .75 | 2.00 |
| 118 Tony Batista | .20 | .50 |
| 119 Edgar Martinez | .30 | .75 |
| 120 Austin Kearns | .20 | .50 |
| 121 Jason Stokes PROS | .20 | .50 |
| 122 Jose Reyes PROS | .50 | 1.25 |
| 123 Rocco Baldelli PROS | .30 | .75 |
| 124 Joe Borchard PROS | .20 | .50 |
| 125 Joe Mauer PROS | .50 | 1.25 |
| 126 Gavin Floyd PROS | .30 | .75 |
| 127 Mark Teixeira PROS | .50 | 1.25 |
| 128 Jeremy Guthrie PROS | .20 | .50 |
| 129 B.J. Upton PROS | .50 | 1.25 |
| 130 Khalil Greene PROS | .50 | 1.25 |
| 131 Hanley Ramirez FY RC | 2.00 | 5.00 |
| 132 Andy Marte FY RC | 1.50 | 4.00 |
| 133 J.D. Durbin FY RC | .20 | .50 |
| 134 Jason Kubel FY RC | .20 | .50 |
| 135 Craig Brazell FY RC | .20 | .50 |
| 136 Bryan Bullington FY RC | .20 | .50 |
| 137 Jose Contreras FY RC | .40 | 1.00 |
| 138 Brian Burgamy FY RC | .20 | .50 |
| 139 Evel Bastida-Martinez FY RC | .40 | 1.00 |
| 140 Joey Gomes FY RC | .20 | .50 |
| 141 Ismael Castro FY RC | .25 | .60 |
| 142 Travis Wong FY RC | .25 | .60 |
| 143 Michael Garciaparra FY RC | .20 | .50 |
| 144 Arnaldo Munoz FY RC | .20 | .50 |
| 145 Louis Sockalexis FY XRC | .20 | .50 |
| 146 Chad Hoblitzell REP | .40 | 1.00 |
| 147 George Graham REP | .40 | 1.00 |
| 148 Hal Chase REP | .40 | 1.00 |
| 149 John McGraw REP | .60 | 1.50 |
| 150 Bobby Wallace REP | .40 | 1.00 |
| 151 David Shean REP | .40 | 1.00 |
| 152 Richard Hoblitzell REP SP | 1.00 | 2.50 |
| 153 Hal Chase REP | .40 | 1.00 |
| 154 Hooks Wiltse REP | .40 | 1.00 |
| 155 George Brett RET | 1.25 | 3.00 |
| 156 Willie Mays RET | 1.25 | 3.00 |
| 157 Honus Wagner RET SP | 4.00 | 10.00 |
| 158 Nolan Ryan RET | 1.50 | 4.00 |
| 159 Reggie Jackson RET | .60 | 1.50 |
| 160 Mike Schmidt RET | 1.25 | 3.00 |
| 161 Josh Barfield PROS | .20 | .50 |
| 162 Grady Sizemore PROS | .50 | 1.25 |
| 163 Justin Morneau PROS | .20 | .50 |
| 164 Laynce Nix PROS | .20 | .50 |
| 165 Zack Greinke PROS | .50 | 1.25 |
| 166 Victor Martinez PROS | .30 | .75 |
| 167 Jeff Mathis PROS | .20 | .50 |
| 168 Casey Kotchman PROS | .20 | .50 |
| 169 Gabe Gross PROS | .20 | .50 |
| 170 Edwin Jackson FY RC | .25 | .60 |
| 171 Delmon Young FY SP RC | 4.00 | 10.00 |
| 172 Eric Duncan FY SP RC | 2.50 | 6.00 |
| 173 Brian Snyder FY SP RC | 2.00 | 5.00 |
| 174 Chris Lubanski FY SP RC | 2.00 | 5.00 |
| 175 Ryan Harvey FY SP RC | 2.50 | 6.00 |
| 176 Nick Markakis FY SP RC | 3.00 | 8.00 |
| 177 Chad Billingsley FY SP RC | 3.00 | 8.00 |
| 178 Elizardo Ramirez FY RC | .25 | .60 |
| 179 Ben Francisco FY RC | .20 | .50 |
| 180 Franklin Gutierrez FY SP RC | 2.00 | 5.00 |
| 181 Aaron Hill FY SP RC | 2.00 | 5.00 |
| 182 Kevin Correia FY RC | .20 | .50 |
| 183 Kelly Shoppach FY RC | .40 | 1.00 |
| 184 Felix Pie FY SP RC | 3.00 | 8.00 |
| 185 Adam Loewen FY SP RC | 2.00 | 5.00 |
| 186 Danny Garcia FY RC | .20 | .50 |
| 187 Rickie Weeks FY SP RC | 3.00 | 8.00 |
| 188 Robby Hammock FY SP RC | 1.50 | 4.00 |
| 189 Ryan Wagner FY SP RC | 1.50 | 4.00 |
| 190 Matt Kata FY SP RC | 1.50 | 4.00 |
| 191 Bo Hart FY SP RC | 1.50 | 4.00 |
| 192 Brandon Webb FY SP RC | 2.50 | 6.00 |
| 193 Bengie Molina | .20 | .50 |
| 194 Junior Spivey | .20 | .50 |
| 195 Gary Sheffield | .20 | .50 |
| 196 Jason Johnson | .20 | .50 |
| 197 David Ortiz | .50 | 1.25 |
| 198 Roberto Alomar | .30 | .75 |
| 199 Wily Mo Pena | .20 | .50 |
| 200 Sammy Sosa | .50 | 1.25 |
| 201 Jay Payton | .20 | .50 |
| 202 Dmitri Young | .20 | .50 |
| 203 Derek Lee | .30 | .75 |
| 204A Jeff Bagwell w/Hat | .20 | .50 |
| 204B Jeff Bagwell w/o Hat | .20 | .50 |
| 205 Runelvys Hernandez | .20 | .50 |
| 206 Kevin Brown | .20 | .50 |
| 207 Wes Helms | .20 | .50 |
| 208 Eddie Guardado | .20 | .50 |
| 209 Orlando Cabrera | .20 | .50 |
| 210 Alfonso Soriano | .20 | .50 |
| 211 Ty Wigginton | .20 | .50 |
| 212A Rich Harden Look Left | .30 | .75 |
| 212B Rich Harden Look Right | .30 | .75 |
| 213 Mike Lieberthal | .20 | .50 |
| 214 Brian Giles | .20 | .50 |
| 215 Jason Schmidt | .20 | .50 |
| 216 Jamie Moyer | .20 | .50 |
| 217 Matt Morris | .20 | .50 |
| 218 Victor Zambrano | .20 | .50 |
| 219 Roy Halladay | .20 | .50 |
| 220 Mike Hampton | .20 | .50 |
| 221 Kevin Millar Sox | .20 | .50 |
| 222 Hideo Nomo | .50 | 1.25 |
| 223 Milton Bradley | .20 | .50 |
| 224 Tike Redman | .20 | .50 |
| 225 Derek Jeter | 1.25 | 3.00 |
| 226 Rondell White | .20 | .50 |
| 227A Hank Blalock Look Jsy | .30 | .75 |
| 227B Hank Blalock White Jsy | .30 | .75 |
| 228 Shigetoshi Hasegawa | .20 | .50 |
| 229 Mike Mussina | .30 | .75 |
| 230 Cristian Guzman | .20 | .50 |
| 231A Todd Helton Blue | .30 | .75 |
| 231B Todd Helton Green | .30 | .75 |
| 232 Kenny Lofton | .30 | .75 |
| 233 Carl Everett | .20 | .50 |
| 234 Shea Hillenbrand | .20 | .50 |
| 235 Brad Fullmer | .20 | .50 |
| 236 Bernie Williams | .30 | .75 |
| 237 Vicente Padilla | .20 | .50 |
| 238 Tim Worrell | .20 | .50 |
| 239 Juan Gonzalez | .20 | .50 |
| 240 Ichiro Suzuki | 1.00 | 2.50 |
| 241 Aaron Boone | .20 | .50 |
| 242 Shannon Stewart | .20 | .50 |
| 243A Barry Zito Blue | .20 | .50 |
| 243B Barry Zito Green | .20 | .50 |
| 244 Reggie Sanders | .20 | .50 |

**2002 Topps 206**

| | | |
|---|---|---|
| ☐ 245 Scott Podsednik | .20 | .50 |
| ☐ 246 Miguel Cabrera | .50 | 1.25 |
| ☐ 247 Angel Berroa | .20 | .50 |
| ☐ 248 Carlos Zambrano | .20 | .50 |
| ☐ 249 Marlon Byrd | .20 | .50 |
| ☐ 250 Mark Prior | .30 | .75 |
| ☐ 251 Esteban Loaiza | .20 | .50 |
| ☐ 252 David Eckstein | .20 | .50 |
| ☐ 253 Alex Cintron | .20 | .50 |
| ☐ 254 Melvin Mora | .20 | .50 |
| ☐ 255 Russ Ortiz | .20 | .50 |
| ☐ 256 Carlos Lee | .20 | .50 |
| ☐ 257 Tino Martinez | .30 | .75 |
| ☐ 258 Randy Wolf | .20 | .50 |
| ☐ 259 Jason Phillips | .20 | .50 |
| ☐ 260 Vladimir Guerrero | .50 | 1.25 |
| ☐ 261 Brad Wilkerson | .20 | .50 |
| ☐ 262 Ivan Rodriguez | .30 | .75 |
| ☐ 263 Matt Lawton | .20 | .50 |
| ☐ 264 Adam Dunn | .20 | .50 |
| ☐ 265 Joe Borowski | .20 | .50 |
| ☐ 266 Jody Gerut | .20 | .50 |
| ☐ 267 Alex Rodriguez | .75 | 2.00 |
| ☐ 268 Brendan Donnelly | .20 | .50 |
| ☐ 269A Randy Johnson Grey | .50 | 1.25 |
| ☐ 269B Randy Johnson Pink | .50 | 1.25 |
| ☐ 270 Nomar Garciaparra | .75 | 2.00 |
| ☐ 271 Javy Lopez | .20 | .50 |
| ☐ 272 Travis Hafner | .20 | .50 |
| ☐ 273 Juan Pierre | .20 | .50 |
| ☐ 274 Morgan Ensberg | .20 | .50 |
| ☐ 275 Albert Pujols | 1.00 | 2.50 |
| ☐ 276 Jason LaRue | .20 | .50 |
| ☐ 277 Paul Lo Duca | .20 | .50 |
| ☐ 278 Andy Pettitte | .30 | .75 |
| ☐ 279 Mike Piazza | .75 | 2.00 |
| ☐ 280A Jim Thome Blue | .30 | .75 |
| ☐ 280B Jim Thome Green | .30 | .75 |
| ☐ 281 Marquis Grissom | .20 | .50 |
| ☐ 282 Woody Williams | .20 | .50 |
| ☐ 283A Curt Schilling Look Ahead | .20 | .50 |
| ☐ 283B Curt Schilling Look Right | .20 | .50 |
| ☐ 284A Chipper Jones Blue | .50 | 1.25 |
| ☐ 284B Chipper Jones Yellow | .50 | 1.25 |
| ☐ 285 Deivi Cruz | .20 | .50 |
| ☐ 286 Johnny Damon | .30 | .75 |
| ☐ 287 Chin-Hui Tsao | .20 | .50 |
| ☐ 288 Alex Gonzalez | .20 | .50 |
| ☐ 289 Billy Wagner | .20 | .50 |
| ☐ 290 Jason Giambi | .20 | .50 |
| ☐ 291 Keith Foulke | .20 | .50 |
| ☐ 292 Jerome Williams | .20 | .50 |
| ☐ 293 Livan Hernandez | .20 | .50 |
| ☐ 294 Aaron Guiel | .20 | .50 |
| ☐ 295 Randall Simon | .20 | .50 |
| ☐ 296 Byung-Hyun Kim | .20 | .50 |
| ☐ 297 Jorge Julio | .20 | .50 |
| ☐ 298 Miguel Batista | .20 | .50 |
| ☐ 299 Rafael Furcal | .20 | .50 |
| ☐ 300A Dontrelle Willis No Smile | .50 | 1.25 |
| ☐ 300B Dontrelle Willis Smile SP | 1.50 | 4.00 |
| ☐ 301 Alex Sanchez | .20 | .50 |
| ☐ 302 Shawn Chacon | .20 | .50 |
| ☐ 303 Matt Clement | .20 | .50 |
| ☐ 304 Luis Matos | .20 | .50 |
| ☐ 305 Steve Finley | .20 | .50 |
| ☐ 306 Marcus Giles | .20 | .50 |
| ☐ 307 Boomer Wells | .20 | .50 |
| ☐ 308 Jeromy Burnitz | .20 | .50 |
| ☐ 309 Mike MacDougal | .20 | .50 |
| ☐ 310 Mariano Rivera | .50 | 1.25 |
| ☐ 311 Adrian Beltre | .20 | .50 |
| ☐ 312 Mark Loretta | .20 | .50 |
| ☐ 313 Ugueth Urbina | .20 | .50 |
| ☐ 314 Bill Mueller | .20 | .50 |
| ☐ 315 Johan Santana | .30 | .75 |
| ☐ NNO Vintage Buyback | | |

| | | |
|---|---|---|
| ☐ COMPLETE SET (525) | 110.00 | 220.00 |
| ☐ COMPLETE SERIES 1 (180) | 25.00 | 60.00 |
| ☐ COMPLETE SERIES 2 (180) | 25.00 | 60.00 |
| ☐ COMPLETE SERIES 3 (165) | 50.00 | 100.00 |
| ☐ COM(1-140/181-270/308-418) | .20 | .50 |
| ☐ COMMON (141-155/271-285) | .20 | .50 |
| ☐ COMMON RC (308-418) | .20 | .50 |
| ☐ COMMON SP (308-398) | .75 | 2.00 |
| ☐ COMMON FYP SP (419-432) | .40 | 1.00 |
| ☐ COMMON RET SP (433-447) | .75 | 2.00 |
| ☐ 1 Vladimir Guerrero | .50 | 1.25 |
| ☐ 2 Sammy Sosa | .50 | 1.25 |
| ☐ 3 Garret Anderson | .20 | .50 |
| ☐ 4 Rafael Palmeiro | .30 | .75 |
| ☐ 5 Juan Gonzalez | .20 | .50 |
| ☐ 6 John Smoltz | .30 | .75 |
| ☐ 7 Mark Mulder | .20 | .50 |
| ☐ 8 Jon Lieber | .20 | .50 |
| ☐ 9 Greg Maddux | .75 | 2.00 |
| ☐ 10 Moises Alou | .20 | .50 |
| ☐ 11 Joe Randa | .20 | .50 |
| ☐ 12 Bobby Abreu | .20 | .50 |
| ☐ 13 Juan Pierre | .20 | .50 |
| ☐ 14 Kerry Wood | .20 | .50 |
| ☐ 15 Craig Biggio | .30 | .75 |
| ☐ 16 Curt Schilling | .20 | .50 |
| ☐ 17 Brian Jordan | .20 | .50 |
| ☐ 18 Edgardo Alfonzo | .20 | .50 |
| ☐ 19 Darren Dreifort | .20 | .50 |
| ☐ 20 Todd Helton | .30 | .75 |
| ☐ 21 Ramon Ortiz | .20 | .50 |
| ☐ 22 Ichiro Suzuki | 1.00 | 2.50 |
| ☐ 23 Jimmy Rollins | .20 | .50 |
| ☐ 24 Darin Erstad | .20 | .50 |
| ☐ 25 Shawn Green | .20 | .50 |
| ☐ 26 Tino Martinez | .30 | .75 |
| ☐ 27 Bret Boone | .20 | .50 |
| ☐ 28 Alfonso Soriano | .20 | .50 |
| ☐ 29 Chan Ho Park | .20 | .50 |
| ☐ 30 Roger Clemens | 1.00 | 2.50 |
| ☐ 31 Cliff Floyd | .20 | .50 |
| ☐ 32 Johnny Damon | .30 | .75 |
| ☐ 33 Frank Thomas | .50 | 1.25 |
| ☐ 34 Barry Bonds | 1.25 | 3.00 |
| ☐ 35 Luis Gonzalez | .20 | .50 |
| ☐ 36 Carlos Lee | .20 | .50 |
| ☐ 37 Roberto Alomar | .30 | .75 |
| ☐ 38 Carlos Delgado | .20 | .50 |
| ☐ 39 Nomar Garciaparra | .75 | 2.00 |
| ☐ 40 Jason Kendall | .20 | .50 |
| ☐ 41 Scott Rolen | .30 | .75 |
| ☐ 42 Tom Glavine | .30 | .75 |
| ☐ 43 Ryan Klesko | .20 | .50 |
| ☐ 44 Brian Giles | .20 | .50 |
| ☐ 45 Bud Smith | .20 | .50 |
| ☐ 46 Charles Nagy | .20 | .50 |
| ☐ 47 Tony Gwynn | .60 | 1.50 |
| ☐ 48 C.C. Sabathia | .20 | .50 |
| ☐ 49 Frank Catalanotto | .20 | .50 |
| ☐ 50 Jerry Hairston | .20 | .50 |
| ☐ 51 Jimmy Burnitz | .20 | .50 |
| ☐ 52 David Justice | .20 | .50 |
| ☐ 53 Bartolo Colon | .20 | .50 |
| ☐ 54 Andres Galarraga | .20 | .50 |
| ☐ 55 Jeff Weaver | .20 | .50 |
| ☐ 56 Terrence Long | .20 | .50 |
| ☐ 57 Tsuyoshi Shinjo | .20 | .50 |
| ☐ 58 Barry Zito | .20 | .50 |
| ☐ 59 Mariano Rivera | .50 | 1.25 |
| ☐ 60 John Olerud | .20 | .50 |
| ☐ 61 Randy Johnson | .50 | 1.25 |
| ☐ 62 Kenny Lofton | .20 | .50 |

| | | |
|---|---|---|
| ☐ 63 Jermaine Dye | .20 | .50 |
| ☐ 64 Troy Glaus | .20 | .50 |
| ☐ 65 Larry Walker | .20 | .50 |
| ☐ 66 Hideo Nomo | .50 | 1.25 |
| ☐ 67 Mike Mussina | .30 | .75 |
| ☐ 68 Paul LoDuca | .20 | .50 |
| ☐ 69 Magglio Ordonez | .20 | .50 |
| ☐ 70 Paul O'Neill | .30 | .75 |
| ☐ 71 Sean Casey | .20 | .50 |
| ☐ 72 Lance Berkman | .20 | .50 |
| ☐ 73 Adam Dunn | .20 | .50 |
| ☐ 74 Aramis Ramirez | .20 | .50 |
| ☐ 75 Rafael Furcal | .20 | .50 |
| ☐ 76 Gary Sheffield | .20 | .50 |
| ☐ 77 Todd Hollandsworth | .20 | .50 |
| ☐ 78 Chipper Jones | .50 | 1.25 |
| ☐ 79 Bernie Williams | .30 | .75 |
| ☐ 80 Richard Hidalgo | .20 | .50 |
| ☐ 81 Eric Chavez | .20 | .50 |
| ☐ 82 Mike Piazza | .75 | 2.00 |
| ☐ 83 J.D. Drew | .20 | .50 |
| ☐ 84 Ken Griffey Jr. | .75 | 2.00 |
| ☐ 85 Joe Kennedy | .20 | .50 |
| ☐ 86 Joel Pineiro | .20 | .50 |
| ☐ 87 Josh Towers | .20 | .50 |
| ☐ 88 Andruw Jones | .30 | .75 |
| ☐ 89 Carlos Beltran | .20 | .50 |
| ☐ 90 Mike Cameron | .20 | .50 |
| ☐ 91 Albert Pujols | 1.00 | 2.50 |
| ☐ 92 Alex Rodriguez | .75 | 2.00 |
| ☐ 93 Omar Vizquel | .30 | .75 |
| ☐ 94 Juan Encarnacion | .20 | .50 |
| ☐ 95 Jeff Bagwell | .30 | .75 |
| ☐ 96 Jose Canseco | .30 | .75 |
| ☐ 97 Ben Sheets | .20 | .50 |
| ☐ 98 Mark Grace | .30 | .75 |
| ☐ 99 Mike Sweeney | .20 | .50 |
| ☐ 100 Mark McGwire | 1.25 | 3.00 |
| ☐ 101 Ivan Rodriguez | .30 | .75 |
| ☐ 102 Rich Aurilia | .20 | .50 |
| ☐ 103 Cristian Guzman | .20 | .50 |
| ☐ 104 Roy Oswalt | .20 | .50 |
| ☐ 105 Tim Hudson | .20 | .50 |
| ☐ 106 Brent Abernathy | .20 | .50 |
| ☐ 107 Mike Hampton | .20 | .50 |
| ☐ 108 Miguel Tejada | .20 | .50 |
| ☐ 109 Bobby Higginson | .20 | .50 |
| ☐ 110 Edgar Martinez | .20 | .50 |
| ☐ 111 Jorge Posada | .30 | .75 |
| ☐ 112 Jason Giambi Yankees | .20 | .50 |
| ☐ 113 Pedro Astacio | .20 | .50 |
| ☐ 114 Kazuhiro Sasaki | .20 | .50 |
| ☐ 115 Preston Wilson | .20 | .50 |
| ☐ 116 Jason Bere | .20 | .50 |
| ☐ 117 Mark Quinn | .20 | .50 |
| ☐ 118 Pokey Reese | .20 | .50 |
| ☐ 119 Derek Jeter | 1.25 | 3.00 |
| ☐ 120 Shannon Stewart | .20 | .50 |
| ☐ 121 Jeff Kent | .20 | .50 |
| ☐ 122 Jeremy Giambi | .20 | .50 |
| ☐ 123 Pat Burrell | .20 | .50 |
| ☐ 124 Jim Edmonds | .20 | .50 |
| ☐ 125 Mark Buehrle | .20 | .50 |
| ☐ 126 Kevin Brown | .20 | .50 |
| ☐ 127 Raul Mondesi | .20 | .50 |
| ☐ 128 Pedro Martinez | .30 | .75 |
| ☐ 129 Jim Thome | .30 | .75 |
| ☐ 130 Russ Ortiz | .20 | .50 |
| ☐ 131 Brandon Duckworth PROS | .20 | .50 |
| ☐ 132 Ryan Jamison PROS | .20 | .50 |
| ☐ 133 Brandon Inge PROS | .20 | .50 |
| ☐ 134 Felipe Lopez PROS | .20 | .50 |
| ☐ 135 Jason Lane PROS | .20 | .50 |
| ☐ 136 Forrest Johnson PROS RC | .20 | .50 |
| ☐ 137 Greg Nash PROS | .20 | .50 |
| ☐ 138 Coveli Crisp PROS | .75 | 2.00 |
| ☐ 139 Nick Neugebauer PROS | .20 | .50 |
| ☐ 140 Dustan Mohr PROS | .20 | .50 |
| ☐ 141 Freddy Sanchez FYP RC | .75 | 2.00 |
| ☐ 142 Justin Backsmeyer FYP RC | .20 | .50 |
| ☐ 143 Jorge Julio FYP | .20 | .50 |
| ☐ 144 Ryan Mottl FYP RC | .20 | .50 |
| ☐ 145 Chris Tritle FYP RC | .20 | .50 |
| ☐ 146 Noochie Varner FYP RC | .20 | .50 |
| ☐ 147 Brian Rogers FYP | .20 | .50 |
| ☐ 148 Michael Hill FYP RC | .20 | .50 |
| ☐ 149 Luis Pineda FYP | .20 | .50 |
| ☐ 150 Rich Thompson FYP RC | .20 | .50 |

|  | | |
|---|---|---|
| 151 Bill Hall FYP | .20 | .50 |
| 152 Juan Dominguez FYP RC | .20 | .50 |
| 153 Justin Woodrow FYP | .20 | .50 |
| 154 Nic Jackson FYP | .20 | .50 |
| 155 Laynce Nix FYP RC | .60 | 1.50 |
| 156 Hank Aaron RET | 2.00 | 5.00 |
| 157 Ernie Banks RET | 1.00 | 2.50 |
| 158 Johnny Bench RET | 1.00 | 2.50 |
| 159 George Brett RET | 2.00 | 5.00 |
| 160 Carlton Fisk RET | .60 | 1.50 |
| 161 Bob Gibson RET | .60 | 1.50 |
| 162 Reggie Jackson RET | .60 | 1.50 |
| 163 Don Mattingly RET | 2.00 | 5.00 |
| 164 Kirby Puckett RET | 1.00 | 2.50 |
| 165 Frank Robinson RET | .60 | 1.50 |
| 166 Nolan Ryan RET | 2.50 | 6.00 |
| 167 Tom Seaver RET | .60 | 1.50 |
| 168 Mike Schmidt RET | 2.00 | 5.00 |
| 169 Dave Winfield RET | .40 | 1.00 |
| 170 Carl Yastrzemski RET | 1.25 | 3.00 |
| 171 Frank Chance REP | .40 | 1.00 |
| 172 Ty Cobb REP | 2.00 | 5.00 |
| 173 Sam Crawford REP | .40 | 1.00 |
| 174 Johnny Evers REP | .40 | 1.00 |
| 175 John McGraw REP | .60 | 1.50 |
| 176 Eddie Plank REP | 1.00 | 2.50 |
| 177 Tris Speaker REP | 1.00 | 2.50 |
| 178 Joe Tinker REP | .40 | 1.00 |
| 179 H.Wagner Orange REP | 3.00 | 8.00 |
| 180 Cy Young REP | 1.00 | 2.50 |
| 181 Javier Vazquez | .20 | .50 |
| 182A Mark Mulder Green Jsy | .20 | .50 |
| 182B Mark Mulder White Jsy | .20 | .50 |
| 183A Roger Clemens Blue Jsy | 1.00 | 2.50 |
| 183B Roger Clemens Pinstripes | 1.00 | 2.50 |
| 184 Kazuhisa Ishii RC | .30 | .75 |
| 185 Roberto Alomar | .20 | .50 |
| 186 Lance Berkman | .20 | .50 |
| 187A Adam Dunn Arms Folded | .20 | .50 |
| 187B Adam Dunn w/Bat | .20 | .50 |
| 188A Aramis Ramirez w/Bat | .20 | .50 |
| 188B Aramis Ramirez w/o Bat | .20 | .50 |
| 189 Chuck Knoblauch | .20 | .50 |
| 190 Nomar Garciaparra | .75 | 2.00 |
| 191 Brad Penny | .20 | .50 |
| 192A Gary Sheffield w/Bat | .20 | .50 |
| 192B Gary Sheffield w/o Bat | .20 | .50 |
| 193 Alfonso Soriano | .20 | .50 |
| 194 Andruw Jones | .30 | .75 |
| 195A Randy Johnson Black Jsy | .50 | 1.25 |
| 195B Randy Johnson Purple Jsy | .50 | 1.25 |
| 196A Corey Patterson Blue Jsy | .20 | .50 |
| 196B Corey Patterson Pinstripes | .20 | .50 |
| 197 Milton Bradley | .20 | .50 |
| 198A J.Damon Blue Jsy/Cap | .30 | .75 |
| 198B J.Damon Blue Jsy/Hlmt | .30 | .75 |
| 198C J.Damon White Jsy | .30 | .75 |
| 199A Paul Lo Duca Blue Jsy | .20 | .50 |
| 199B Paul Lo Duca White Jsy | .20 | .50 |
| 200A Albert Pujols Red Jsy | 1.00 | 2.50 |
| 200B Albert Pujols Running | 1.00 | 2.50 |
| 200C Albert Pujols w/Bat | 1.00 | 2.50 |
| 201 Scott Rolen | .30 | .75 |
| 202A J.D. Drew Running | .20 | .50 |
| 202B J.D. Drew w/Bat | .20 | .50 |
| 202C J.D. Drew White Jsy | .20 | .50 |
| 203 Vladimir Guerrero | .50 | 1.25 |
| 204A Jason Giambi Blue Jsy | .20 | .50 |
| 204B Jason Giambi Grey Jsy | .20 | .50 |
| 204C Jason Giambi Pinstripes | .20 | .50 |
| 205A Moises Alou Grey Jsy | .20 | .50 |
| 205B Moises Alou Pinstripes | .20 | .50 |
| 206A Magglio Ordonez Signing | .20 | .50 |
| 206B Magglio Ordonez w/Bat | .20 | .50 |
| 207 Carlos Febles | .20 | .50 |
| 208 So Taguchi RC | .30 | .75 |
| 209A Rafael Palmeiro One Hand | .30 | .75 |
| 209B Rafael Palmeiro Two Hands | .30 | .75 |
| 210 David Wells | .20 | .50 |
| 211 Orlando Cabrera | .20 | .50 |
| 212 Sammy Sosa | .50 | 1.25 |
| 213 Armando Benitez | .20 | .50 |
| 214 Wes Helms | .20 | .50 |
| 215A Mariano Rivera Arms Folded | .50 | 1.25 |
| 215B Mariano Rivera Holding Ball | .50 | 1.25 |
| 216 Jimmy Rollins | .20 | .50 |
| 217 Matt Lawton | .20 | .50 |
| 218A Shawn Green w/Bat | .20 | .50 |
| 218B Shawn Green w/o Bat | .20 | .50 |
| 219A Bernie Williams w/Bat | .20 | .50 |
| 219B Bernie Williams w/o Bat | .30 | .75 |
| 220A Bret Boone Blue Jsy | .20 | .50 |
| 220B Bret Boone White Jsy | .20 | .50 |
| 221A Alex Rodriguez Blue Jsy | .75 | 2.00 |
| 221B Alex Rodriguez One Hand | .75 | 2.00 |
| 221C Alex Rodriguez Two Hands | .75 | 2.00 |
| 222 Roger Cedeno | .20 | .50 |
| 223 Marty Cordova | .20 | .50 |
| 224 Fred McGriff | .30 | .75 |
| 225A Chipper Jones Batting | .50 | 1.25 |
| 225B Chipper Jones Running | .50 | 1.25 |
| 226 Kerry Wood | .20 | .50 |
| 227A Larry Walker Grey Jsy | .20 | .50 |
| 227B Larry Walker Purple Jsy | .20 | .50 |
| 228 Robin Ventura | .20 | .50 |
| 229 Robert Fick | .20 | .50 |
| 230A Tino Martinez Black Glove | .30 | .75 |
| 230B Tino Martinez Throwing | .30 | .75 |
| 230C Tino Martinez w/Bat | .30 | .75 |
| 231 Ben Petrick | .20 | .50 |
| 232 Neifi Perez | .20 | .50 |
| 233 Steve Finley | .20 | .50 |
| 234A Brian Jordan Grey Jsy | .20 | .50 |
| 234B Brian Jordan White Jsy | .20 | .50 |
| 235 Freddy Garcia | .20 | .50 |
| 236A Derek Jeter Batting | 1.25 | 3.00 |
| 236B Derek Jeter Blue Jsy | 1.25 | 3.00 |
| 236C Derek Jeter Kneeling | 1.25 | 3.00 |
| 237 Ben Grieve | .20 | .50 |
| 238A Barry Bonds Black Jsy | 1.25 | 3.00 |
| 238B Barry Bonds w/Wrist Band | 1.25 | 3.00 |
| 238C B.Bonds w/o Wrist Band | 1.25 | 3.00 |
| 239 Luis Gonzalez | .20 | .50 |
| 240 Shane Halter | .20 | .50 |
| 241A Brian Giles Black Jsy | .20 | .50 |
| 241B Brian Giles Grey Jsy | .20 | .50 |
| 242 Bud Smith | .20 | .50 |
| 243 Richie Sexson | .20 | .50 |
| 244A Barry Zito Green Jsy | .20 | .50 |
| 244B Barry Zito Grey Jsy | .20 | .50 |
| 245 Eric Milton | .20 | .50 |
| 246A Ivan Rodriguez Blue Jsy | .30 | .75 |
| 246B Ivan Rodriguez Grey Jsy | .30 | .75 |
| 246C Ivan Rodriguez White Jsy | .30 | .75 |
| 247 Toby Hall | .20 | .50 |
| 248A Mike Piazza Black Jsy | .75 | 2.00 |
| 248B Mike Piazza Grey Jsy | .75 | 2.00 |
| 249 Ruben Sierra | .20 | .50 |
| 250A Tsuyoshi Shinjo Cap | .20 | .50 |
| 250B Tsuyoshi Shinjo Helmet | .20 | .50 |
| 251A Jermaine Dye Green Jsy | .20 | .50 |
| 251B Jermaine Dye White Jsy | .20 | .50 |
| 252 Roy Oswalt | .20 | .50 |
| 253 Todd Helton | .30 | .75 |
| 254 Adrian Beltre | .20 | .50 |
| 255 Doug Mientkiewicz | .20 | .50 |
| 256A Ichiro Suzuki Blue Jsy | 1.00 | 2.50 |
| 256B Ichiro Suzuki w/Bat | 1.00 | 2.50 |
| 256C Ichiro Suzuki White Jsy | .20 | .50 |
| 257A C.C. Sabathia Blue Jsy | .20 | .50 |
| 257B C.C. Sabathia White Jsy | .20 | .50 |
| 258 Paul Konerko | .20 | .50 |
| 259 Ken Griffey Jr. | .75 | 2.00 |
| 260A Jeromy Burnitz w/Bat | .20 | .50 |
| 260B Jeromy Burnitz w/o Bat | .20 | .50 |
| 261 Hank Blalock PROS | .30 | .75 |
| 262 Mark Prior PROS | .30 | .75 |
| 263 Josh Beckett PROS | .20 | .50 |
| 264 Carlos Pena PROS | .20 | .50 |
| 265 Sean Burroughs PROS | .20 | .50 |
| 266 Austin Kearns PROS | .20 | .50 |
| 267 Chin-Hui Tsao PROS | .20 | .50 |
| 268 Dewon Brazelton PROS | .20 | .50 |
| 269 J.D. Martin PROS | .20 | .50 |
| 270 Marlon Byrd PROS | .20 | .50 |
| 271 Joe Mauer FYP RC | 4.00 | 10.00 |
| 272 Jason Botts FYP RC | .20 | .50 |
| 273 Mauricio Lara FYP RC | .20 | .50 |
| 274 Jonny Gomes FYP RC | 1.00 | 2.50 |
| 275 Gavin Floyd FYP RC | .40 | 1.00 |
| 276 Alex Requena FYP RC | .20 | .50 |
| 277 Jimmy Gobble FYP RC | .20 | .50 |
| 278 Colt Griffin FYP RC | .20 | .50 |
| 279 Ryan Church FYP RC | .40 | 1.00 |
| 280 Ryan Church FYP RC | .40 | 1.00 |
| 281 Beltran Perez FYP RC | .20 | .50 |
| 282 Clint Nageotte FYP RC | .30 | .75 |
| 283 Justin Schuda FYP RC | .20 | .50 |
| 284 Scott Hairston FYP RC | .30 | .75 |
| 285 Mario Ramos FYP RC | .20 | .50 |
| 286A Tom Seaver White Sox RET | .60 | 1.50 |
| 286B Tom Seaver Mets RET | .60 | 1.50 |
| 287A Hank Aaron White Jsy RET | 2.00 | 5.00 |
| 287B Hank Aaron Blue Jsy RET | 2.00 | 5.00 |
| 288 Mike Schmidt RET | 2.00 | 5.00 |
| 289A Robin Yount Pinstripe RET | 1.00 | 2.50 |
| 289B Robin Yount P'stripes RET | 1.00 | 2.50 |
| 290 Joe Morgan RET | .40 | 1.00 |
| 291 Frank Robinson RET | .60 | 1.50 |
| 292A Reggie Jackson A's RET | .60 | 1.50 |
| 292B Reggie Jackson Yanks RET | .60 | 1.50 |
| 293A Nolan Ryan Astros RET | 2.50 | 6.00 |
| 293B Nolan Ryan Rangers RET | 2.50 | 6.00 |
| 294 Dave Winfield RET | .40 | 1.00 |
| 295 Willie Mays RET | 2.00 | 5.00 |
| 296 Brooks Robinson RET | .60 | 1.50 |
| 297A Mark McGwire A's RET | 2.50 | 6.00 |
| 297B Mark McGwire Cards RET | 2.50 | 6.00 |
| 298 Honus Wagner RET | 1.00 | 2.50 |
| 299A Sherry Magie REP | .40 | 1.00 |
| 299B Sherry Magie UER REP | .40 | 1.00 |
| 300 Frank Chance REP | .40 | 1.00 |
| 301A Joe Doyle NY REP | .60 | 1.50 |
| 301B Joe Doyle NY Nat'l REP | .60 | 1.50 |
| 302 John McGraw REP | .60 | 1.50 |
| 303 Jimmy Collins REP | .40 | 1.00 |
| 304 Buck Herzog REP | .40 | 1.00 |
| 305 Sam Crawford REP | .40 | 1.00 |
| 306 Cy Young REP | 1.00 | 2.50 |
| 307 Honus Wagner Blue REP | 3.00 | 8.00 |
| 308A A.Rodriguez Blue Jsy SP | 1.50 | 4.00 |
| 308B A.Rodriguez White Jsy | .75 | 2.00 |
| 309 Vernon Wells | .20 | .50 |
| 310A B.Bonds w/Elbow Pad | 1.25 | 3.00 |
| 310B B.Bonds w/o Elbow Pad SP | 2.50 | 6.00 |
| 311 Vicente Padilla | .20 | .50 |
| 312A A.Soriano w/Wristband | .20 | .50 |
| 312B A.Soriano w/o Wristband SP | .75 | 2.00 |
| 313 Mike Piazza | .75 | 2.00 |
| 314 Jacque Jones | .20 | .50 |
| 315 Shawn Green SP | .75 | 2.00 |
| 316 Paul Byrd | .20 | .50 |
| 317 Lance Berkman | .20 | .50 |
| 318 Larry Walker | .20 | .50 |
| 319 Ken Griffey Jr. SP | 1.50 | 4.00 |
| 320 Shea Hillenbrand | .20 | .50 |
| 321 Jay Gibbons | .20 | .50 |
| 322 Andruw Jones | .30 | .75 |
| 323 Luis Gonzalez SP | .75 | 2.00 |
| 324 Garret Anderson | .20 | .50 |
| 325 Roy Halladay | .20 | .50 |
| 326 Randy Winn | .20 | .50 |
| 327 Matt Morris | .20 | .50 |
| 328 Robb Nen | .20 | .50 |
| 329 Trevor Hoffman | .20 | .50 |
| 330 Kip Wells | .20 | .50 |
| 331 Orlando Hernandez | .20 | .50 |
| 332 Rey Ordonez | .20 | .50 |
| 333 Torii Hunter | .20 | .50 |
| 334 Geoff Jenkins | .20 | .50 |
| 335 Eric Karros | .20 | .50 |
| 336 Mike Lowell | .20 | .50 |
| 337 Nick Johnson | .20 | .50 |
| 338 Randall Simon | .20 | .50 |
| 339 Ellis Burks | .20 | .50 |
| 340A Sammy Sosa Blue Jsy SP | 1.00 | 2.50 |
| 340B Sammy Sosa White Jsy | .50 | 1.25 |
| 341 Pedro Martinez | .30 | .75 |
| 342 Junior Spivey | .20 | .50 |
| 343 Vinny Castilla | .20 | .50 |
| 344 Randy Johnson SP | 1.00 | 2.50 |
| 345 Chipper Jones SP | .75 | 2.00 |
| 346 Orlando Hudson | .20 | .50 |
| 347 Albert Pujols SP | 2.00 | 5.00 |
| 348 Rondell White | .20 | .50 |
| 349 Vladimir Guerrero | .50 | 1.25 |
| 350A Mark Prior Red SP | .60 | 1.50 |
| 350B Mark Prior Yellow | .30 | .75 |
| 351 Eric Gagne | .20 | .50 |
| 352 Todd Zeile | .20 | .50 |
| 353 Manny Ramirez SP | .75 | 2.00 |
| 354 Kevin Millwood | .20 | .50 |
| 355 Troy Percival | .20 | .50 |
| 356A Jason Giambi Batting SP | .75 | 2.00 |

| | | |
|---|---|---|
| 356B Jason Giambi Throwing | .20 | .50 |
| 357 Bartolo Colon | .20 | .50 |
| 358 Jeremy Giambi | .20 | .50 |
| 359 Jose Cruz Jr. | .20 | .50 |
| 360A I.Suzuki Blue Jsy SP | 2.00 | 5.00 |
| 360B I.Suzuki White Jsy | 1.00 | 2.50 |
| 361 Eddie Guardado | .20 | .50 |
| 362 Ivan Rodriguez | .30 | .75 |
| 363 Carl Crawford | .20 | .50 |
| 364 Jason Simontacchi RC | .20 | .50 |
| 365 Kenny Lofton | .20 | .50 |
| 366 Raul Mondesi | .20 | .50 |
| 367 A.J. Pierzynski | .20 | .50 |
| 368 Ugueth Urbina | .20 | .50 |
| 369 Rodrigo Lopez | .20 | .50 |
| 370A N.Garciaparra One Bat SP | 1.50 | 4.00 |
| 370B N.Garciaparra Two Bats | .75 | 2.00 |
| 371 Craig Counsell | .20 | .50 |
| 372 Barry Larkin | .30 | .75 |
| 373 Carlos Pena | .20 | .50 |
| 374 Luis Castillo | .20 | .50 |
| 375 Raul Ibanez | .20 | .50 |
| 376 Kazuhisa Ishii SP | .75 | 2.00 |
| 377 Derek Lowe | .20 | .50 |
| 378 Curt Schilling | .30 | .75 |
| 379 Jim Thome Phillies | .30 | .75 |
| 380A Derek Jeter Blue SP | 2.50 | 6.00 |
| 380B Derek Jeter Seats | 1.25 | 3.00 |
| 381 Pat Burrell | .20 | .50 |
| 382 Jamie Moyer | .20 | .50 |
| 383 Eric Hinske | .20 | .50 |
| 384 Scott Rolen | .30 | .75 |
| 385 Miguel Tejada SP | .75 | 2.00 |
| 386 Andy Pettitte | .30 | .75 |
| 387 Mike Lieberthal | .20 | .50 |
| 388 Al Leiter | .20 | .50 |
| 389 Todd Helton SP | .75 | 2.00 |
| 390A Adam Dunn Bat SP | .75 | 2.00 |
| 390B Adam Dunn Glove | .20 | .50 |
| 391 Cliff Floyd | .20 | .50 |
| 392 Tim Salmon | .30 | .75 |
| 393 Joe Torre MG | .30 | .75 |
| 394 Bobby Cox MG | .20 | .50 |
| 395 Tony LaRussa MG | .20 | .50 |
| 396 Art Howe MG | .20 | .50 |
| 397 Bob Brenly MG | .20 | .50 |
| 398 Ron Gardenhire MG | .20 | .50 |
| 399 Mike Cuddyer PROS | .20 | .50 |
| 400 Joe Mauer PROS | 4.00 | 10.00 |
| 401 Mark Teixeira PROS | .50 | 1.25 |
| 402 Hee Seop Choi PROS | .20 | .50 |
| 403 Angel Berroa PROS | .20 | .50 |
| 404 Jesse Foppert PROS RC | .20 | .75 |
| 405 Bobby Crosby PROS | .50 | 1.25 |
| 406 Jose Reyes PROS | .30 | .75 |
| 407 Casey Kotchman PROS RC | .40 | 1.00 |
| 408 Aaron Heilman PROS | .20 | .50 |
| 409 Adrian Gonzalez PROS | .20 | .50 |
| 410 Delwyn Young PROS RC | .40 | 1.00 |
| 411 Brett Myers PROS | .20 | .50 |
| 412 Justin Huber PROS RC | .20 | .50 |
| 413 Drew Henson PROS | .20 | .50 |
| 414 Taggert Bozied PROS RC | .30 | .75 |
| 415 Dontrelle Willis PROS RC | 2.00 | 5.00 |
| 416 Rocco Baldelli PROS | .20 | .50 |
| 417 Jason Stokes PROS RC | .20 | .50 |
| 418 Brandon Phillips PROS | .20 | .50 |
| 419 Jake Blalock FYP RC | .20 | .50 |
| 420 Micah Schilling FYP RC | .40 | 1.00 |
| 421 Denard Span FYP RC | .40 | 1.00 |
| 422A J.Loney Red FYP RC | 1.50 | 4.00 |
| 422B J.Loney w/Sky FYP RC | 1.50 | 4.00 |
| 423A W.Bankston Blue FYP RC | .75 | 2.00 |
| 423B W.Bankston w/Sky FYP RC | .75 | 2.00 |
| 424 Jeremy Hermida FYP RC | 2.00 | 5.00 |
| 425 Curtis Granderson FYP RC | 1.25 | 3.00 |
| 426A J.Pridie Red FYP RC | .40 | 1.00 |
| 426B J.Pridie w/Sky FYP RC | .40 | 1.00 |
| 427 Larry Broadway FYP RC | .20 | .50 |
| 428A K.Greene Green FYP RC | 3.00 | 8.00 |
| 428B K.Greene Red FYP RC | 3.00 | 8.00 |
| 429 Joey Votto FYP RC | 1.25 | 3.00 |
| 430A B.Upton Grey FYP RC | 2.00 | 5.00 |
| 430B B.Upton w/People FYP RC | 2.00 | 5.00 |
| 431A S.Santos Gold FYP RC | .40 | 1.00 |
| 431B B.Santos Grey FYP RC | .40 | 1.00 |
| 432 Brian Dopirak FYP RC | .40 | 1.00 |
| 433 Ozzie Smith RET SP | 1.50 | 4.00 |
| 434 Wade Boggs RET SP | 1.00 | 2.50 |
| 435 Yogi Berra RET SP | 1.50 | 4.00 |
| 436 Al Kaline RET SP | 1.50 | 4.00 |
| 437 Robin Roberts RET SP | .75 | 2.00 |
| 438 Roberto Clemente RET SP | 3.00 | 8.00 |
| 439 Gary Carter RET SP | .75 | 2.00 |
| 440 Fergie Jenkins RET SP | .75 | 2.00 |
| 441 Orlando Cepeda RET SP | .75 | 2.00 |
| 442 Rod Carew RET SP | 1.00 | 2.50 |
| 443 Harmon Killebrew RET SP | 1.50 | 4.00 |
| 444 Duke Snider RET SP | 1.00 | 2.50 |
| 445 Stan Musial RET SP | 2.50 | 6.00 |
| 446 Hank Greenberg RET SP | 1.50 | 4.00 |
| 447 Lou Brock RET SP | 1.00 | 2.50 |
| 448 Jim Palmer RET | .50 | 1.25 |
| 449 John McGraw REP | .60 | 1.50 |
| 450 Mordecai Brown REP | .60 | 1.50 |
| 451 Christy Mathewson REP | .60 | 1.50 |
| 452 Sam Crawford REP | .40 | 1.00 |
| 453 Bill O'Hara REP | .40 | 1.00 |
| 454 Joe Tinker REP | .40 | 1.00 |
| 455 Nap Lajoie REP | .60 | 1.50 |
| 456 Honus Wagner Red REP | 3.00 | 8.00 |
| NNO Repurchased Tobacco Card | | |

## 2006 Topps 52

| | | |
|---|---|---|
| COMP.SET w/o SPs (275) | 40.00 | 80.00 |
| COMMON CARD (1-275) | .20 | .50 |
| COMMON LOGO VAR. | 1.50 | 4.00 |
| COMMON SP | 2.50 | 6.00 |
| SP STATED ODDS 1:5 H, 1:5 R | | |
| 1 Howie Kendrick RC | .50 | 1.25 |
| 2 Enrique Gonzalez (RC) | .20 | .50 |
| 3 Chuck James RC | .30 | .75 |
| 4 Chris Britton RC | .20 | .50 |
| 5 David Pauley RC | .20 | .50 |
| 6 Angel Pagan (RC) | .20 | .50 |
| 7 Pat Neshek RC | 2.00 | 5.00 |
| 8 Walter Young (RC) | .20 | .50 |
| 9 Chris Denorfia (RC) | .20 | .50 |
| 10 Rafael Perez RC | .20 | .50 |
| 11 Ryan Spilborghs (RC) | .30 | .75 |
| 12 Jon Huber RC | .20 | .50 |
| 13 Jordan Tata RC | .20 | .50 |
| 14 Eric Reed (RC) | .20 | .50 |
| 15 Norris Hopper RC | .20 | .50 |
| 16 Scott Olsen (RC) | .20 | .50 |
| 17 Fernando Nieve (RC) | .20 | .50 |
| 18 Chris Booker (RC) | .20 | .50 |
| 19 Chad Billingsley (RC) | .30 | .75 |
| 20 Carlos Villanueva RC | .20 | .50 |
| 21 Craig Hansen RC | .75 | 2.00 |
| 22 Dave Gassner (RC) | .20 | .50 |
| 23 Mike Pelfrey RC | .75 | 2.00 |
| 24 Matt Smith RC | .20 | .50 |
| 25 Chris Roberson (RC) | .20 | .50 |
| 26 John Van Benschoten (RC) | .20 | .50 |
| 27 Kevin Frandsen (RC) | .20 | .50 |
| 28 Les Walrond (RC) | .20 | .50 |
| 29 James Shields RC | .20 | .50 |
| 30 Russell Martin (RC) | .30 | .75 |
| 31 Ben Zobrist (RC) | .30 | .75 |
| 32 John Rheinecker (RC) | .20 | .50 |
| 33 Francisco Rosario (RC) | .20 | .50 |
| 34 Santiago Ramirez (RC) | .20 | .50 |
| 35 Mike Napoli RC | .50 | 1.25 |
| 36 Tony Pena Jr. (RC) | .20 | .50 |
| 37A Jeff Karstens RC | .20 | .50 |
| 37B Jeff Karstens 52 Logo | 1.50 | 4.00 |
| 38 Phil Stockman (RC) | .20 | .50 |
| 39 Kurt Birkins RC | .20 | .50 |
| 40 Dustin Pedroia (RC) | 4.00 | 10.00 |
| 41 Buck Coats (RC) | .20 | .50 |
| 42 Jim Johnson RC | .20 | .50 |
| 43 Angel Guzman (RC) | .20 | .50 |
| 44 Kelly Shoppach (RC) | .20 | .50 |
| 45 Josh Wilson RC | .20 | .50 |
| 46 Jack Hannahan RC | .20 | .50 |
| 47 Ricky Nolasco (RC) | .20 | .50 |
| 48 T.J. Bohn (RC) | .20 | .50 |
| 49 Joel Zumaya (RC) | .50 | 1.25 |
| 50 Phil Barzilla RC | .20 | .50 |
| 51 Justin Huber (RC) | .20 | .50 |
| 52A Willy Aybar (RC) | .20 | .50 |
| 52B Willy Aybar 52 Logo | 1.50 | 4.00 |
| 53 Tony Gwynn Jr. (RC) | .50 | 1.25 |
| 54 Chris Barnwell RC | .20 | .50 |
| 55 Henry Owens RC | .30 | .75 |
| 56 Jeff Bajenaru (RC) | .20 | .50 |
| 57 Jonah Bayliss RC | .20 | .50 |
| 58 Josh Sharpless RC | .20 | .50 |
| 59 Eliezer Alfonzo RC | .20 | .50 |
| 60 Bobby Livingston (RC) | .20 | .50 |
| 61 John Gall (RC) | .20 | .50 |
| 62 Ruddy Lugo (RC) | .20 | .50 |
| 63 Fabio Castro RC | .20 | .50 |
| 64 Casey Janssen RC | .30 | .75 |
| 65 Mike O'Connor RC | .20 | .50 |
| 66 Kendry Morales (RC) | .50 | 1.25 |
| 67 James Hoey RC | .20 | .50 |
| 68 Dustin Moseley (RC) | .20 | .50 |
| 69 Peter Moylan RC | .20 | .50 |
| 70 Manny Delcarmen (RC) | .20 | .50 |
| 71 Rich Hill (RC) | .20 | .50 |
| 72 Boone Logan RC | .20 | .50 |
| 73 Cody Ross (RC) | .20 | .50 |
| 74 Fausto Carmona (RC) | .50 | .50 |
| 75 Ramon Ramirez (RC) | .20 | .50 |
| 76 Zach Miner (RC) | .20 | .50 |
| 77 Hanley Ramirez UER (RC) | .50 | 1.25 |
| 78 Josh Johnson (RC) | .30 | .75 |
| 79 Taylor Buchholz (RC) | .20 | .50 |
| 80 Joe Nelson (RC) | .20 | .50 |
| 81 Hong-Chih Kuo (RC) | .50 | 1.25 |
| 82 Chris Mabeus (RC) | .20 | .50 |
| 83 Willie Eyre (RC) | .20 | .50 |
| 84 John Maine (RC) | .30 | .75 |
| 85 Yurendell DeCaster (RC) | .20 | .50 |
| 86 Mike Thompson RC | .20 | .50 |
| 87 Brian Wilson RC | .20 | .50 |
| 88A Matt Cain (RC) | .75 | 2.00 |
| 88B Matt Cain 52 Logo | 2.00 | 5.00 |
| 89 Sean Green RC | .20 | .50 |
| 90 Tyler Johnson (RC) | .20 | .50 |
| 91 Jason Childers RC | .20 | .50 |
| 92 Wes Littleton (RC) | .20 | .50 |
| 93 Ty Taubenheim RC | .20 | .50 |
| 94 Saul Rivera (RC) | .20 | .50 |
| 95 Reggie Willits RC | .75 | 2.00 |
| 96 Carlos Quentin (RC) | .30 | .75 |
| 97 Macay McBride (RC) | .20 | .50 |
| 98 Brandon Fahey RC | .20 | .50 |
| 99 Sean Marshall (RC) | .20 | .50 |
| 100 Sean Tracey (RC) | .20 | .50 |
| 101 Brian Slocum (RC) | .20 | .50 |
| 102 Choo Freeman (RC) | .20 | .50 |
| 103 Brent Clevlen (RC) | .30 | .75 |
| 104 Josh Willingham (RC) | .20 | .50 |
| 105 Chris Resop (RC) | .20 | .50 |
| 106 Chris Sampson RC | .20 | .50 |
| 107A James Loney (RC) | .20 | .50 |
| 107B James Loney 52 Logo | 2.00 | 5.00 |
| 108 Matt Kemp (RC) | .30 | .75 |
| 109 Jason Kubel (RC) | .20 | .50 |
| 110 Brian Bannister (RC) | .20 | .50 |
| 111 Kevin Thompson (RC) | .20 | .50 |
| 112 Jeremy Brown (RC) | .20 | .50 |
| 113 Brian Sanches (RC) | .20 | .50 |
| 114 Nate McLouth (RC) | .20 | .50 |
| 115 Ben Johnson (RC) | .20 | .50 |
| 116 Jonathan Sanchez (RC) | .20 | .50 |
| 117 Mark Lowe (RC) | .20 | .50 |
| 118 Skip Schumaker (RC) | .20 | .50 |
| 119 Jason Hammel (RC) | .20 | .50 |
| 120 Drew Meyer (RC) | .20 | .50 |
| 121 Melvin Dorta RC | .20 | .50 |
| 122 Jeff Mathis (RC) | .20 | .50 |
| 123 Davis Romero (RC) | .20 | .50 |
| 124 Joey Devine RC | .20 | .50 |
| 125 Sendy Rleal RC | .20 | .50 |
| 126 Freddie Bynum (RC) | .20 | .50 |

|  | | |
|---|---|---|
| 127 Brian Anderson (RC) | .20 | .50 |
| 128 Jeremy Sowers (RC) | .20 | .50 |
| 129 Ryan Shealy (RC) | .20 | .50 |
| 130 Reggie Abercrombie (RC) | .20 | .50 |
| 131 Matt Albers (RC) | .20 | .50 |
| 132 Lastings Milledge (RC) | .30 | .75 |
| 133 Robert Andino RC | .20 | .50 |
| 134 Chris Demaria RC | .20 | .50 |
| 135 Boof Bonser (RC) | .30 | .75 |
| 136 Alay Soler RC | .20 | .50 |
| 137 Wil Nieves (RC) | .20 | .50 |
| 138 Mike Rouse (RC) | .20 | .50 |
| 139 Carlos Ruiz (RC) | .20 | .50 |
| 140 Matt Capps (RC) | .20 | .50 |
| 141 Travis Ishikawa (RC) | .20 | .50 |
| 142 Josh Kinney RC | .20 | .50 |
| 143 Josh Rupe (RC) | .20 | .50 |
| 144 Shaun Marcum (RC) | .20 | .50 |
| 145 Jason Bergmann RC | .20 | .50 |
| 146 Tommy Murphy (RC) | .20 | .50 |
| 147 Martin Prado (RC) | .20 | .50 |
| 148 Val Majewski (RC) | .20 | .50 |
| 149 Ian Kinsler (RC) | .30 | .75 |
| 150 Joe Winkelsas (RC) | .20 | .50 |
| 151 Agustin Montero (RC) | .20 | .50 |
| 152 Joe Inglett RC | .20 | .50 |
| 153 Manuel Corpas RC | .20 | .50 |
| 154 Yusmeiro Petit (RC) | .20 | .50 |
| 155 Mark Woodyard (RC) | .20 | .50 |
| 156 Jeff Fulchino RC | .20 | .50 |
| 157 Stephen Andrade (RC) | .20 | .50 |
| 158 Tim Hamulack (RC) | .20 | .50 |
| 159 Collier Bean (RC) | .20 | .50 |
| 160 Anderson Hernandez (RC) | .20 | .50 |
| 161 Kevin Reese (RC) | .20 | .50 |
| 162 Jason Windsor (RC) | .20 | .50 |
| 163A Paul Maholm (RC) | .20 | .50 |
| 163B Paul Maholm 52 Logo | 2.00 | 5.00 |
| 164 Jeremy Accardo RC | .25 | .50 |
| 165 Joel Guzman (RC) | .20 | .50 |
| 166 Erick Aybar (RC) | .20 | .50 |
| 167 Scott Thorman (RC) | .20 | .50 |
| 168 Adam Loewen (RC) | .20 | .50 |
| 169 Carlos Marmol RC | .20 | .50 |
| 170 Bill Bray (RC) | .20 | .50 |
| 171 Edward Mujica RC | .20 | .50 |
| 172 Jeremy Hermida (RC) | .20 | .50 |
| 173 Taylor Tankersley (RC) | .20 | .50 |
| 174 Bobby Keppel (RC) | .20 | .50 |
| 175 Chris B. Young (RC) | .20 | .50 |
| 176 Josh Rabe RC | .20 | .50 |
| 177 T.J. Beam (RC) | .20 | .50 |
| 178A Shane Komine RC | .30 | .75 |
| 178B Shane Komine 52 Logo | 2.00 | 5.00 |
| 179 Scott Mathieson (RC) | .20 | .50 |
| 180 Josh Barfield (RC) | .20 | .50 |
| 181 Justin Knoedler (RC) | .20 | .50 |
| 182 Emiliano Fruto RC | .20 | .50 |
| 183 Adam Wainwright (RC) | .30 | .75 |
| 184 Nick Masset (RC) | .20 | .50 |
| 185 Ryan Roberts (RC) | .20 | .50 |
| 186 Brandon Watson (RC) | .20 | .50 |
| 187 Chris Bootcheck (RC) | .20 | .50 |
| 188 Dan Ortmeier (RC) | .20 | .50 |
| 189 Kevin Barry (RC) | .20 | .50 |
| 190 Cory Morris RC | .20 | .50 |
| 191 Kason Gabbard (RC) | .20 | .50 |
| 192 Tom Mastny (RC) | .20 | .50 |
| 193 David Aardsma (RC) | .20 | .50 |
| 194 Anthony Reyes (RC) | .30 | .75 |
| 195 Mike Jacobs (RC) | .20 | .50 |
| 196 Conor Jackson (RC) | .30 | .75 |
| 197 Kenji Johjima RC | 1.00 | 2.50 |
| 198 Jack Taschner (RC) | .20 | .50 |
| 199 Renyel Pinto (RC) | .20 | .50 |
| 200 Chad Santos (RC) | .20 | .50 |
| 201 Aaron Rakers (RC) | .20 | .50 |
| 202 Franklin Gutierrez (RC) | .20 | .50 |
| 203 Chris Coste RC | .75 | 2.00 |
| 204 Chris Iannetta RC | .20 | .50 |
| 205 Mike Vento (RC) | .20 | .50 |
| 206 Ryan O'Malley RC | .20 | .50 |
| 207 Jason Botts RC | .20 | .50 |
| 208 John Hattig (RC) | .20 | .50 |
| 209 Brandon Harper RC | .20 | .50 |
| 210 Ryan Theriot RC | 2.00 | 5.00 |
| 211 Travis Hughes (RC) | .20 | .50 |
| 212 Paul Hoover (RC) | .20 | .50 |

|  | | |
|---|---|---|
| 213 Brayan Pena (RC) | .20 | .50 |
| 214 Craig Breslow RC | .26 | .50 |
| 215 Eude Brito (RC) | .20 | .50 |
| 216A Melky Cabrera (RC) | .30 | .75 |
| 216B Melky Cabrera 52 Logo | 2.00 | 5.00 |
| 217A Jonathan Broxton (RC) | .20 | .50 |
| 217B Jonathan Broxton 52 Logo | 1.50 | 4.00 |
| 218 Bryan Corey (RC) | .20 | .50 |
| 219 Ron Flores RC | .20 | .50 |
| 220 Andrew Brown (RC) | .20 | .50 |
| 221 Jaime Bubela (RC) | .20 | .50 |
| 222 Jason Bulger (RC) | .20 | .50 |
| 223 Alberto Callaspo (RC) | .20 | .50 |
| 224 Jose Capellan (RC) | .20 | .50 |
| 225A Cole Hamels (RC) | .50 | 1.25 |
| 225B Cole Hamels 52 Logo | 3.00 | 8.00 |
| 226 Bernie Castro (RC) | .20 | .50 |
| 227 Shin-Soo Choo (RC) | .30 | .75 |
| 228 Doug Clark (RC) | .20 | .50 |
| 229 Roy Corcoran RC | .20 | .50 |
| 230 Tim Corcoran RC | .20 | .50 |
| 231 Nelson Cruz (RC) | .30 | .75 |
| 232 Rajai Davis (RC) | .20 | .50 |
| 233A Chris Duncan (RC) | .30 | .75 |
| 233B Chris Duncan 52 Logo | 2.00 | 5.00 |
| 234 Scott Dunn (RC) | .20 | .50 |
| 235 Mike Esposito (RC) | .20 | .50 |
| 236 Scott Feldman RC | .20 | .50 |
| 237 Luis Figueroa RC | .20 | .50 |
| 238 Bartolome Fortunato (RC) | .20 | .50 |
| 239 Alejandro Freire RC | .20 | .50 |
| 240 J.J. Furmaniak (RC) | .20 | .50 |
| 241 Nick Markakis (RC) | .30 | .75 |
| 242 Matt Garza (RC) | .20 | .50 |
| 243 Justin Germano (RC) | .20 | .50 |
| 244 Alexis Gomez (RC) | .20 | .50 |
| 245 Tom Gorzelanny (RC) | .20 | .50 |
| 246 Dan Uggla (RC) | .50 | 1.25 |
| 247 Jeremy Guthrie (RC) | .20 | .50 |
| 248 Stephen Drew (RC) | .50 | 1.25 |
| 249 Brendan Harris (RC) | .20 | .50 |
| 250 Jeff Harris RC | .20 | .50 |
| 251 Corey Hart (RC) | .20 | .50 |
| 252 Chris Heintz RC | .20 | .50 |
| 253 Prince Fielder (RC) | .75 | 2.00 |
| 254 Francisco Liriano (RC) | 1.00 | 2.50 |
| 255 Jason Hirsh (RC) | .20 | .50 |
| 256 J.R. House (RC) | .20 | .50 |
| 257 Zach Jackson (RC) | .20 | .50 |
| 258 Charlton Jimerson (RC) | .20 | .50 |
| 259 Greg Jones (RC) | .20 | .50 |
| 260 Mitch Jones (RC) | .20 | .50 |
| 261 Ryan Jorgensen RC | .20 | .50 |
| 262 Logan Kensing (RC) | .20 | .50 |
| 263 John Koronka (RC) | .20 | .50 |
| 264 Anthony Lerew (RC) | .20 | .50 |
| 265 Anibal Sanchez (RC) | .30 | .75 |
| 266 Juan Mateo RC | .20 | .50 |
| 267 Paul McAnulty (RC) | .20 | .50 |
| 268 Dustin McGowan (RC) | .20 | .50 |
| 269 Marty McLeary (RC) | .20 | .50 |
| 270 Ryan Zimmerman (RC) | 1.25 | 3.00 |
| 271 Dustin Nippert (RC) | .20 | .50 |
| 272 Eric O'Flaherty RC | .20 | .50 |
| 273 Ronny Paulino (RC) | .20 | .50 |
| 274 Tony Pena (RC) | .20 | .50 |
| 275 Hayden Penn (RC) | .20 | .50 |
| 276 Miguel Perez SP (RC) | 2.50 | 6.00 |
| 277 Paul Phillips SP (RC) | 2.50 | 6.00 |
| 278 Omar Quintanilla SP (RC) | 2.50 | 6.00 |
| 279 Guillermo Quiroz SP (RC) | 2.50 | 6.00 |
| 280 Darrell Rasner SP (RC) | 2.50 | 6.00 |
| 281 Kenny Ray SP (RC) | 2.50 | 6.00 |
| 282 Royce Ring SP (RC) | 2.50 | 6.00 |
| 283 Brian Rogers SP RC | 3.00 | 8.00 |
| 284 Ed Rogers SP (RC) | 2.50 | 6.00 |
| 285 Danny Sandoval SP RC | 2.50 | 6.00 |
| 286 Joe Saunders SP (RC) | 2.50 | 6.00 |
| 287 Chris Schroder SP RC | 2.50 | 6.00 |
| 288 Mike Smith SP (RC) | 3.00 | 8.00 |
| 289 Travis Smith SP (RC) | 2.50 | 6.00 |
| 290 Geovany Soto SP (RC) | 2.50 | 6.00 |
| 291 Brian Sweeney SP (RC) | 2.50 | 6.00 |
| 292 Jon Switzer SP (RC) | 2.50 | 6.00 |
| 293 Joe Thurston SP (RC) | 2.50 | 6.00 |
| 294 Jermaine Van Buren SP (RC) | 2.50 | 6.00 |
| 295 Ryan Garko SP (RC) | 2.50 | 6.00 |
| 296 Cla Meredith SP (RC) | 3.00 | 8.00 |

|  | | |
|---|---|---|
| 297 Luke Scott SP (RC) | 2.50 | 6.00 |
| 298 Andy Marte SP (RC) | 2.50 | 6.00 |
| 299 Jered Weaver SP (RC) | 4.00 | 10.00 |
| 300 Freddy Guzman SP (RC) | 2.50 | 6.00 |
| 301 Jonathan Papelbon SP (RC) | 4.00 | 10.00 |
| 302 John-Ford Griffin SP (RC) | 2.50 | 6.00 |
| 303 Jon Lester SP RC | 4.00 | 10.00 |
| 304 Shawn Hill SP (RC) | 2.50 | 6.00 |
| 305 Brian Myrow SP RC | 2.50 | 6.00 |
| 306 Anderson Garcia SP RC | 2.50 | 6.00 |
| 307 Andre Ethier SP (RC) | 3.00 | 8.00 |
| 308 Ben Hendrickson SP (RC) | 2.50 | 6.00 |
| 309 Alejandro Machado SP RC | 2.50 | 6.00 |
| 310 Justin Verlander SP (RC) | 4.00 | 10.00 |
| 311A Mickey Mantle SP Blue | 20.00 | 50.00 |
| 311B Mickey Mantle Black | 4.00 | 10.00 |
| 311C Mickey Mantle Green | 4.00 | 10.00 |
| 311D Mickey Mantle Orange | 4.00 | 10.00 |
| 311E Mickey Mantle Red | 4.00 | 10.00 |
| 311F Mickey Mantle Yellow | 4.00 | 10.00 |
| 312 Steve Stemle SP RC | 2.50 | 6.00 |

## 2007 Topps 52

|  | | |
|---|---|---|
| COMP.SET w/o SPs (202) | 20.00 | 50.00 |
| COMMON CARD (1-227) | .25 | .60 |
| COMMON ACTION VARIATION | 2.00 | 5.00 |
| ACT.VAR.STATED ODDS 1:6 H, 1:6 R | | |
| COMMON SP | 2.00 | 5.00 |
| SP STATED ODDS 1:6 H, 1:6 R | | |
| 1 Akinori Iwamura RC | .60 | 1.50 |
| 2 Angel Sanchez RC | .25 | .60 |
| 3 Luis Hernandez (RC) | .25 | .60 |
| 4 Joaquin Arias (RC) | .25 | .60 |
| 5a Troy Tulowitzki (RC) | .60 | 1.50 |
| 5b T.Tulowitzki Action SP | 2.50 | 6.00 |
| 6 Jesus Flores RC | .25 | .60 |
| 7 Mickey Mantle | 2.50 | 6.00 |
| 8 Kory Casto (RC) | .25 | .60 |
| 9 Tony Abreu RC | .60 | 1.50 |
| 10 Kevin Kouzmanoff (RC) | .25 | .60 |
| 11 Travis Buck (RC) | .25 | .60 |
| 12 Kurt Suzuki (RC) | .25 | .60 |
| 13 Matt DeSalvo (RC) | .25 | .60 |
| 14 Jerry Owens (RC) | .25 | .60 |
| 15 Alex Gordon RC | 1.00 | 2.50 |
| 16 Jeff Baker (RC) | .25 | .60 |
| 17 Ben Francisco (RC) | .25 | .60 |
| 18 Nate Schierholtz (RC) | .25 | .60 |
| 19 Nathan Haynes (RC) | .25 | .60 |
| 20a Ryan Braun (RC) | 1.50 | 4.00 |
| 20b R.Braun Action SP | 3.00 | 8.00 |
| 21 Brian Barden RC | .25 | .60 |
| 22 Sean Barker RC | .25 | .60 |
| 23 Alejandro De Aza RC | .40 | 1.00 |
| 24 Jamie Burke (RC) | .25 | .60 |
| 25 Michael Bourn (RC) | .25 | .60 |
| 26 Jeff Salazar (RC) | .25 | .60 |
| 27 Chase Headley (RC) | .25 | .60 |
| 28 Chris Basak RC | .25 | .60 |
| 29 Mike Fontenot (RC) | .25 | .60 |
| 30a Hunter Pence (RC) | 1.25 | 3.00 |
| 30b H.Pence Action SP | 3.00 | 8.00 |
| 31 Masumi Kuwata RC | 2.00 | 5.00 |
| 32 Ryan Rowland-Smith RC | .25 | .60 |
| 33 Tyler Clippard (RC) | .40 | 1.00 |
| 34 Matt Lindstrom (RC) | .25 | .60 |
| 35 Fred Lewis (RC) | .40 | 1.00 |
| 36 Brett Carroll RC | .25 | .60 |
| 37 Alexi Casilla RC | .40 | 1.00 |
| 38 Nick Gorneault (RC) | .25 | .60 |
| 39 Dennis Sarfate (RC) | .25 | .60 |
| 40 Felix Pie (RC) | .25 | .60 |
| 41 Miguel Montero (RC) | .25 | .60 |
| 42 Danny Putnam (RC) | .25 | .60 |

|  |  | | |
|---|---|---|---|
| 43 | Shane Youman RC | .25 | .60 |
| 44 | Andy LaRoche RC | .25 | .60 |
| 45 | Jarrod Saltalamacchia (RC) | .40 | 1.00 |
| 46 | Kei Igawa RC | .60 | 1.50 |
| 47 | Don Kelly (RC) | .25 | .60 |
| 48 | Fernando Cortez (RC) | .25 | .60 |
| 49 | Travis Metcalf RC | .40 | 1.00 |
| 50a | Daisuke Matsuzaka RC | 2.00 | 5.00 |
| 50b | D.Matsuzaka Action SP | 3.00 | 8.00 |
| 51 | Edwar Ramirez RC | .60 | 1.50 |
| 52 | Ryan Sweeney (RC) | .25 | .60 |
| 53 | Shawn Riggans (RC) | .25 | .60 |
| 54 | Billy Sadler (RC) | .25 | .60 |
| 55 | Billy Butler (RC) | .40 | 1.00 |
| 56 | Andy Cavazos RC | .25 | .60 |
| 57 | Sean Henn (RC) | .25 | .60 |
| 58 | Brian Esposito (RC) | .25 | .60 |
| 59 | Brandon Morrow RC | .60 | 1.50 |
| 60 | Adam Lind (RC) | .25 | .60 |
| 61 | Joe Smith RC | .25 | .60 |
| 62 | Chris Stewart RC | .25 | .60 |
| 63 | Eulogio De La Cruz (RC) | .25 | .60 |
| 64 | Sean Gallagher (RC) | .25 | .60 |
| 65 | Carlos Gomez RC | .40 | 1.00 |
| 66 | Jailen Peguero RC | .25 | .60 |
| 67 | Juan Perez RC | .25 | .60 |
| 68 | Lavale Speigner RC | .25 | .60 |
| 69 | Jamie Vermilyea RC | .25 | .60 |
| 70a | Delmon Young (RC) | .40 | 1.00 |
| 70b | D.Young Action SP | 2.00 | 5.00 |
| 71 | Jo-Jo Reyes (RC) | .25 | .60 |
| 72 | Zack Segovia (RC) | .25 | .60 |
| 73 | Andy Sonnanstine RC | .25 | .60 |
| 74 | Chase Wright RC | .60 | 1.50 |
| 75 | Josh Fields (RC) | .25 | .60 |
| 76 | Jon Knott (RC) | .25 | .60 |
| 77 | Guillermo Rodriguez RC | .25 | .60 |
| 78 | Jon Coutlangus (RC) | .25 | .60 |
| 79 | Kevin Cameron RC | .25 | .60 |
| 80 | Mark Reynolds RC | 1.50 | 4.00 |
| 81 | Brian Stokes RC | .25 | .60 |
| 82 | Alberto Arias RC | .25 | .60 |
| 83 | Yoel Hernandez RC | .25 | .60 |
| 84 | David Murphy (RC) | .25 | .60 |
| 85 | Josh Hamilton (RC) | .60 | 1.50 |
| 86 | Justin Hampson (RC) | .25 | .60 |
| 87 | Doug Slaten RC | .25 | .60 |
| 88 | Joseph Bisenius RC | .25 | .60 |
| 89 | Troy Cate RC | .25 | .60 |
| 90 | Homer Bailey (RC) | .40 | 1.00 |
| 91 | Jacoby Ellsbury (RC) | 2.50 | 6.00 |
| 92 | Devern Hansack RC | .25 | .60 |
| 93 | Zach McClellan RC | .25 | .60 |
| 94 | Vinny Rottino (RC) | .25 | .60 |
| 95 | Elijah Dukes RC | .40 | 1.00 |
| 96 | Ryan Z. Braun UER RC | .60 | 1.50 |
| 97 | Lee Gardner (RC) | .25 | .60 |
| 98 | Joakim Soria RC | .25 | .60 |
| 99 | Jason Miller (RC) | .25 | .60 |
| 100a | Hideki Okajima RC | 1.25 | 3.00 |
| 100b | H.Okajima Action SP | 3.00 | 8.00 |
| 101 | John Danks RC | .25 | .60 |
| 102 | Garrett Jones (RC) | .60 | 1.50 |
| 103 | Jensen Lewis RC | .25 | .60 |
| 104 | Clay Rapada RC | .25 | .60 |
| 105 | Kyle Kendrick RC | .60 | 1.50 |
| 106 | Eric Stults RC | .25 | .60 |
| 107 | Jared Burton RC | .25 | .60 |
| 108 | Julio DePaula RC | .40 | 1.00 |
| 109 | Jesse Litsch RC | .40 | 1.00 |
| 110 | Micah Owings (RC) | .25 | .60 |
| 111 | Cory Doyne (RC) | .25 | .60 |
| 112 | Jay Marshall RC | .25 | .60 |
| 113 | Mike Schultz RC | .25 | .60 |
| 114 | Juan Salas (RC) | .25 | .60 |
| 115 | Matt Chico (RC) | .25 | .60 |
| 116 | Brad Salmon RC | .25 | .60 |
| 117 | Jeff Bailey RC | .25 | .60 |
| 118 | Gustavo Molina RC | .25 | .60 |
| 119 | Brian Burres (RC) | .25 | .60 |
| 120 | Yovani Gallardo (RC) | .75 | 2.00 |
| 121 | Hector Gimenez (RC) | .25 | .60 |
| 122 | Kelvin Jimenez RC | .25 | .60 |
| 123 | Rick Vanden Hurk RC | .40 | 1.00 |
| 124 | Billy Petrick (RC) | .25 | .60 |
| 125 | Andrew Miller RC | 1.50 | 4.00 |
| 126 | Rocky Cherry RC | .60 | 1.50 |
| 127 | Jordan De Jong RC | .25 | .60 |
| 128 | Eric Hull RC | .25 | .60 |
| 129 | Kevin Mahar RC | .25 | .60 |
| 130a | Tim Lincecum RC | 3.00 | 8.00 |
| 130b | T.Lincecum Action SP | 3.00 | 8.00 |
| 131 | Garrett Olson (RC) | .25 | .60 |
| 132 | Neal Musser RC | .25 | .60 |
| 133 | Mike Rabelo RC | .25 | .60 |
| 134 | Dennis Dove (RC) | .25 | .60 |
| 135 | J.D. Durbin (RC) | .25 | .60 |
| 136 | Jose Garcia RC | .25 | .60 |
| 137 | Marcus McBeth (RC) | .25 | .60 |
| 138 | Curtis Thigpen (RC) | .25 | .60 |
| 139 | Mike Zagurski RC | .25 | .60 |
| 140 | Kevin Slowey (RC) | .60 | 1.50 |
| 141 | Dewon Day RC | .25 | .60 |
| 142 | Glen Perkins (RC) | .25 | .60 |
| 143 | Brian Wolfe (RC) | .25 | .60 |
| 144 | Dallas Braden RC | .40 | 1.00 |
| 145 | J.A. Happ RC | 1.00 | 2.50 |
| 146 | Lee Gronkiewicz RC | .25 | .60 |
| 147 | Cesar Jimenez RC | .25 | .60 |
| 148 | Mark McLemore (RC) | .25 | .60 |
| 149 | Connor Robertson RC | .25 | .60 |
| 150a | Phil Hughes (RC) | 1.25 | 3.00 |
| 150b | P.Hughes Action SP | 3.00 | 8.00 |
| 151 | Matthew Brown RC | .25 | .60 |
| 152 | Ryan Feierabend (RC) | .25 | .60 |
| 153 | Brendan Ryan (RC) | .25 | .60 |
| 154 | Terry Evans RC | .25 | .60 |
| 155 | Eric Patterson (RC) | .25 | .60 |
| 156 | Patrick Misch (RC) | .25 | .60 |
| 157 | Darren Clarke RC | .25 | .60 |
| 158 | Kevin Melillo (RC) | .25 | .60 |
| 159 | Edwin Bellorin RC | .25 | .60 |
| 160 | Ubaldo Jimenez (RC) | .25 | .60 |
| 161 | Ryan Budde (RC) | .25 | .60 |
| 162 | Brian Buscher RC | .40 | 1.00 |
| 163 | Juan Gutierrez RC | .25 | .60 |
| 164 | Franklin Morales (RC) | .25 | .60 |
| 165 | Carmen Pignatiello (RC) | .25 | .60 |
| 166 | Jair Jurrjens (RC) | .25 | .60 |
| 167 | Manny Acosta (RC) | .25 | .60 |
| 168 | Ian Stewart RC | .25 | .60 |
| 169 | Daniel Barone (RC) | .25 | .60 |
| 170a | Justin Upton RC | 1.50 | 4.00 |
| 170b | J.Upton Action SP | 3.00 | 8.00 |
| 171 | Tommy Watkins RC | .40 | 1.00 |
| 172 | Ross Wolf RC | .25 | .60 |
| 173 | Jack Cassel RC | .25 | .60 |
| 174 | Asdrubal Cabrera RC | .60 | 1.50 |
| 175 | Mauro Zarate RC | .25 | .60 |
| 176 | Aaron Laffey RC | .60 | 1.50 |
| 177 | Marcus Gwyn RC | .25 | .60 |
| 178 | Danny Richar RC | .25 | .60 |
| 179 | Joel Hanrahan (RC) | .25 | .60 |
| 180 | Cameron Maybin RC | 1.25 | 3.00 |
| 181 | John Lannan RC | .25 | .60 |
| 182 | Shelley Duncan (RC) | .60 | 1.50 |
| 183 | Brandon Wood (RC) | .25 | .60 |
| 184 | Delwyn Young (RC) | .25 | .60 |
| 185 | Manny Parra (RC) | .25 | .60 |
| 186 | Ehren Wassermann RC | .25 | .60 |
| 187 | Jose A. Reyes RC | .25 | .60 |
| 188 | Jose Ascanio RC | .25 | .60 |
| 190a | Alvin Colina RC | .60 | 1.50 |
| 190b | J.Chamberlain Action SP | 5.00 | 12.00 |
| 191 | Yunel Escobar (RC) | .25 | .60 |
| 192 | Carlos Maldonado (RC) | .25 | .60 |
| 193 | Dan Meyer (RC) | .25 | .60 |
| 194 | Scott Moore (RC) | .25 | .60 |
| 195 | Romulo Sanchez RC | .25 | .60 |
| 196 | Tom Shearn (RC) | .25 | .60 |
| 197 | Craig Stansberry (RC) | .25 | .60 |
| 201 | Joba Chamberlain RC | 1.25 | 3.00 |
| 202 | John Nelson SP (RC) | 2.00 | 5.00 |
| 203 | Phil Dumatrait (RC) | .25 | .60 |
| 204 | Brandon Moss (RC) | .25 | .60 |
| 205 | Beltran Perez (RC) | .25 | .60 |
| 206 | Drew Anderson RC | .25 | .60 |
| 207 | Brett Campbell RC | .25 | .60 |
| 208 | Andy Cannizaro SP RC | 2.00 | 5.00 |
| 209 | Travis Chick SP (RC) | 2.00 | 5.00 |
| 210 | Francisco Cruceta SP (RC) | 2.00 | 5.00 |
| 211 | Jose Diaz SP (RC) | 2.00 | 5.00 |
| 212 | Jeff Fiorentino SP (RC) | 2.00 | 5.00 |
| 213 | Tim Gradoville SP RC | 2.00 | 5.00 |
| 214 | Kevin Hooper SP (RC) | 2.00 | 5.00 |
| 215 | Philip Humber SP (RC) | 2.00 | 5.00 |
| 216 | Juan Lara SP RC | 2.00 | 5.00 |
| 217 | Mitch Maier SP RC | 2.00 | 5.00 |
| 218 | Juan Morillo SP (RC) | 2.00 | 5.00 |
| 219 | A.J. Murray SP RC | 2.00 | 5.00 |
| 220 | Chris Narveson SP (RC) | 2.00 | 5.00 |
| 221 | Oswaldo Navarro SP RC | 2.00 | 5.00 |

## 2006 Topps Allen and Ginter

| | | |
|---|---|---|
| COMPLETE SET (350) | 60.00 | 120.00 |
| COMP.SET w/o SP's (300) | 15.00 | 40.00 |
| COMMON SP | 1.25 | 3.00 |

SP STATED ODDS 1:2 HOBBY, 1:2 RETAIL
SP CL: 5/15/25/35/45/50-59/65/85/105/115
SP CL: 125/135/145/150-159/165/175/185
SP CL: 205/215/235/245/251/255-256/265
SP CL: 285/295/305/315/325/335/345
FRAMED ORIGINALS ODDS 1:3227 H, 1:3227 R

|  |  | | |
|---|---|---|---|
| 1 | Albert Pujols | .75 | 2.00 |
| 2 | Aubrey Huff | .15 | .40 |
| 3 | Mark Teixeira | .25 | .60 |
| 4 | Vernon Wells | .15 | .40 |
| 5 | Ken Griffey Jr. SP | 2.00 | 5.00 |
| 6 | Nick Swisher | .15 | .40 |
| 7 | Jose Reyes | .40 | 1.00 |
| 8 | David Wright | .60 | 1.50 |
| 9 | Vladimir Guerrero | .40 | 1.00 |
| 10 | Andruw Jones | .25 | .60 |
| 11 | Ramon Hernandez | .15 | .40 |
| 12 | Miguel Tejada | .15 | .40 |
| 13 | Juan Pierre | .15 | .40 |
| 14 | Jim Thome | .25 | .60 |
| 15 | Austin Kearns SP | 1.25 | 3.00 |
| 16 | Jhonny Peralta | .15 | .40 |
| 17 | Clint Barmes | .15 | .40 |
| 18 | Angel Berroa | .15 | .40 |
| 19 | Nomar Garciaparra | .40 | 1.00 |
| 20 | Joe Nathan | .15 | .40 |
| 21 | Brandon Webb | .15 | .40 |
| 22 | Chad Tracy | .15 | .40 |
| 23 | Derek Jeter | 1.00 | 2.50 |
| 24 | Conor Jackson (RC) | .25 | .60 |
| 25 | Jason Giambi SP | 1.25 | 3.00 |
| 26 | Johnny Estrada | .15 | .40 |
| 27 | Luis Gonzalez | .15 | .40 |
| 28 | Javier Vazquez | .15 | .40 |
| 29 | Orlando Hudson | .15 | .40 |
| 30 | Shawn Green | .15 | .40 |
| 31 | Mark Buehrle | .15 | .40 |
| 32 | Wily Mo Pena | .15 | .40 |
| 33 | C.C. Sabathia | .15 | .40 |
| 34 | Ronnie Belliard | .15 | .40 |
| 35 | Travis Hafner SP | 1.25 | 3.00 |
| 36 | Mike Jacobs (RC) | .15 | .40 |
| 37 | Roy Oswalt | .15 | .40 |
| 38 | Zack Greinke | .15 | .40 |
| 39 | J.D. Drew | .15 | .40 |
| 40 | Jeff Kent | .15 | .40 |
| 41 | Ben Sheets | .15 | .40 |
| 42 | Luis Castillo | .15 | .40 |
| 43 | Carlos Delgado | .15 | .40 |
| 44 | Cliff Floyd | .15 | .40 |
| 45 | Danny Haren SP | 1.25 | 3.00 |
| 46 | Bobby Abreu | .15 | .40 |
| 47 | Jeromy Burnitz | .15 | .40 |
| 48 | Khalil Greene | .25 | .60 |
| 49 | Moises Alou | .15 | .40 |
| 50 | Alex Rodriguez SP | 2.00 | 5.00 |
| 51 | Ervin Santana SP | 1.25 | 3.00 |
| 52 | Bartolo Colon SP | 1.25 | 3.00 |
| 53 | John Smoltz SP | 1.25 | 3.00 |
| 54 | David Ortiz SP | 1.25 | 3.00 |
| 55 | Hideki Matsui SP | 1.25 | 3.00 |

|  | | |
|---|---|---|
| ❑ 56 Jermaine Dye SP | 1.25 | 3.00 |
| ❑ 57 Victor Martinez SP | 1.25 | 3.00 |
| ❑ 58 Willy Taveras SP | 1.25 | 3.00 |
| ❑ 59 Brady Clark SP | 1.25 | 3.00 |
| ❑ 60 Justin Morneau | .15 | .40 |
| ❑ 61 Xavier Nady | .15 | .40 |
| ❑ 62 Rich Harden | .15 | .40 |
| ❑ 63 Jack Wilson | .15 | .40 |
| ❑ 64 Brian Giles | .15 | .40 |
| ❑ 65 Jon Lieber SP | 1.25 | 3.00 |
| ❑ 66 Dan Johnson | .15 | .40 |
| ❑ 67 Billy Wagner | .15 | .40 |
| ❑ 68 Rickie Weeks | .15 | .40 |
| ❑ 69 Chris Ray (RC) | .15 | .40 |
| ❑ 70 Chris Shelton | .15 | .40 |
| ❑ 71 Dmitri Young | .15 | .40 |
| ❑ 72 Ivan Rodriguez | .25 | .60 |
| ❑ 73 Jeremy Bonderman | .15 | .40 |
| ❑ 74 Justin Verlander (RC) | .60 | 1.50 |
| ❑ 75 Randy Johnson | .40 | 1.00 |
| ❑ 76 Magglio Ordonez | .15 | .40 |
| ❑ 77 Brandon Inge | .15 | .40 |
| ❑ 78 Placido Polanco | .15 | .40 |
| ❑ 79 Ryan Howard | .60 | 1.50 |
| ❑ 80 Jason Bay | .15 | .40 |
| ❑ 81 Sean Casey | .15 | .40 |
| ❑ 82 Jeremy Hermida (RC) | .15 | .40 |
| ❑ 83 Mike Cameron | .15 | .40 |
| ❑ 84 Trevor Hoffman | .15 | .40 |
| ❑ 85 Mike Matheny SP | 1.25 | 3.00 |
| ❑ 86 Steve Finley | .15 | .40 |
| ❑ 87 Adam Everett | .15 | .40 |
| ❑ 88 Jason Isringhausen | .15 | .40 |
| ❑ 89 Jonny Gomes | .15 | .40 |
| ❑ 90 Barry Zito | .15 | .40 |
| ❑ 91 Bobby Crosby | .15 | .40 |
| ❑ 92 Eric Chavez | .15 | .40 |
| ❑ 93 Frank Thomas | .40 | 1.00 |
| ❑ 94 Huston Street | .15 | .40 |
| ❑ 95 Jorge Posada | .25 | .60 |
| ❑ 96 Casey Kotchman | .15 | .40 |
| ❑ 97 Darin Erstad | .15 | .40 |
| ❑ 98 Chipper Jones | .40 | 1.00 |
| ❑ 99 Jeff Francoeur | .40 | 1.00 |
| ❑ 100 Barry Bonds | .75 | 2.00 |
| ❑ 101 Alfonso Soriano | .15 | .40 |
| ❑ 102 Brandon Claussen | .15 | .40 |
| ❑ 103 Aaron Boone | .15 | .40 |
| ❑ 104 Roger Clemens | .60 | 1.50 |
| ❑ 105 Andy Pettitte SP | 1.25 | 3.00 |
| ❑ 106 Nick Johnson | .15 | .40 |
| ❑ 107 Tom Gordon | .15 | .40 |
| ❑ 108 Orlando Hernandez | .15 | .40 |
| ❑ 109 Francisco Rodriguez | .15 | .40 |
| ❑ 110 Orlando Cabrera | .15 | .40 |
| ❑ 111 Edgar Renteria | .15 | .40 |
| ❑ 112 Tim Hudson | .15 | .40 |
| ❑ 113 Coco Crisp | .15 | .40 |
| ❑ 114 Matt Clement | .15 | .40 |
| ❑ 115 Greg Maddux SP | 2.00 | 5.00 |
| ❑ 116 Paul Konerko | .15 | .40 |
| ❑ 117 Felipe Lopez | .15 | .40 |
| ❑ 118 Garrett Atkins | .15 | .40 |
| ❑ 119 Akinori Otsuka | .15 | .40 |
| ❑ 120 Craig Biggio | .25 | .60 |
| ❑ 121 Danys Baez | .15 | .40 |
| ❑ 122 Brad Penny | .15 | .40 |
| ❑ 123 Eric Gagne | .15 | .40 |
| ❑ 124 Lew Ford | .15 | .40 |
| ❑ 125 Mariano Rivera SP | 1.25 | 3.00 |
| ❑ 126 Carlos Beltran | .15 | .40 |
| ❑ 127 Pedro Martinez | .25 | .60 |
| ❑ 128 Todd Helton | .15 | .40 |
| ❑ 129 Aaron Rowand | .15 | .40 |
| ❑ 130 Mike Lieberthal | .15 | .40 |
| ❑ 131 Oliver Perez | .15 | .40 |
| ❑ 132 Ryan Klesko | .15 | .40 |
| ❑ 133 Randy Winn | .15 | .40 |
| ❑ 134 Yuniesky Betancourt | .15 | .40 |
| ❑ 135 David Eckstein SP | 1.25 | 3.00 |
| ❑ 136 Chad Orvella | .15 | .40 |
| ❑ 137 Toby Hall | .15 | .40 |
| ❑ 138 Hank Blalock | .15 | .40 |
| ❑ 139 B.J. Ryan | .15 | .40 |
| ❑ 140 Roy Halladay | .15 | .40 |
| ❑ 141 Livan Hernandez | .15 | .40 |
| ❑ 142 John Patterson | .15 | .40 |
| ❑ 143 Bengie Molina | .15 | .40 |
| ❑ 144 Brad Wilkerson | .15 | .40 |
| ❑ 145 Jorge Cantu SP | 1.25 | 3.00 |
| ❑ 146 Mark Mulder | .15 | .40 |
| ❑ 147 Felix Hernandez | .25 | .60 |
| ❑ 148 Paul Lo Duca | .15 | .40 |
| ❑ 149 Prince Fielder (RC) | .60 | 1.50 |
| ❑ 150 Johnny Damon SP | 1.25 | 3.00 |
| ❑ 151 Ryan Langerhans SP | 1.25 | 3.00 |
| ❑ 152 Kris Benson SP | 1.25 | 3.00 |
| ❑ 153 Curt Schilling SP | 1.25 | 3.00 |
| ❑ 154 Manny Ramirez SP | 1.25 | 3.00 |
| ❑ 155 Robinson Cano SP | 1.25 | 3.00 |
| ❑ 156 Derrek Lee SP | 1.25 | 3.00 |
| ❑ 157 A.J. Pierzynski SP | 1.25 | 3.00 |
| ❑ 158 Adam Dunn SP | 1.25 | 3.00 |
| ❑ 159 Cliff Lee SP | 1.25 | 3.00 |
| ❑ 160 Grady Sizemore | .25 | .60 |
| ❑ 161 Jeff Francis | .15 | .40 |
| ❑ 162 Dontrelle Willis | .15 | .40 |
| ❑ 163 Brad Ausmus | .15 | .40 |
| ❑ 164 Preston Wilson | .15 | .40 |
| ❑ 165 Derek Lowe SP | 1.25 | 3.00 |
| ❑ 166 Chris Capuano | .15 | .40 |
| ❑ 167 Joe Mauer | .40 | 1.00 |
| ❑ 168 Torii Hunter | .15 | .40 |
| ❑ 169 Chase Utley | .40 | 1.00 |
| ❑ 170 Zach Duke | .15 | .40 |
| ❑ 171 Jason Schmidt | .15 | .40 |
| ❑ 172 Adrian Beltre | .15 | .40 |
| ❑ 173 Eddie Guardado | .15 | .40 |
| ❑ 174 Richie Sexson | .15 | .40 |
| ❑ 175 Miguel Cabrera SP | 1.25 | 3.00 |
| ❑ 176 Julio Lugo | .15 | .40 |
| ❑ 177 Francisco Cordero | .15 | .40 |
| ❑ 178 Kevin Millwood | .15 | .40 |
| ❑ 179 A.J. Burnett | .15 | .40 |
| ❑ 180 Jose Guillen | .15 | .40 |
| ❑ 181 Larry Bigbie | .15 | .40 |
| ❑ 182 Raul Ibanez | .25 | .60 |
| ❑ 183 Jake Peavy | .15 | .40 |
| ❑ 184 Pat Burrell | .15 | .40 |
| ❑ 185 Tom Glavine SP | 1.25 | 3.00 |
| ❑ 186 J.J. Hardy | .15 | .40 |
| ❑ 187 Emil Brown | .15 | .40 |
| ❑ 188 Lance Berkman | .15 | .40 |
| ❑ 189 Marcus Giles | .15 | .40 |
| ❑ 190 Scott Podsednik | .15 | .40 |
| ❑ 191 Chone Figgins | .15 | .40 |
| ❑ 192 Melvin Mora | .15 | .40 |
| ❑ 193 Mark Loretta | .15 | .40 |
| ❑ 194 Carlos Zambrano | .15 | .40 |
| ❑ 195 Chien-Ming Wang | .40 | 1.00 |
| ❑ 196 Mark Prior | .25 | .60 |
| ❑ 197 Bobby Jenks | .15 | .40 |
| ❑ 198 Brian Fuentes | .15 | .40 |
| ❑ 199 Garret Anderson | .15 | .40 |
| ❑ 200 Ichiro Suzuki | .60 | 1.50 |
| ❑ 201 Brian Roberts | .15 | .40 |
| ❑ 202 Jason Kendall | .15 | .40 |
| ❑ 203 Milton Bradley | .15 | .40 |
| ❑ 204 Jimmy Rollins | .15 | .40 |
| ❑ 205 Brett Myers SP | 1.25 | 3.00 |
| ❑ 206 Joe Randa | .15 | .40 |
| ❑ 207 Mike Piazza | .40 | 1.00 |
| ❑ 208 Matt Morris | .15 | .40 |
| ❑ 209 Omar Vizquel | .25 | .60 |
| ❑ 210 Jeremy Reed | .15 | .40 |
| ❑ 211 Chris Carpenter | .15 | .40 |
| ❑ 212 Jim Edmonds | .25 | .60 |
| ❑ 213 Scott Kazmir | .25 | .60 |
| ❑ 214 Travis Lee | .15 | .40 |
| ❑ 215 Michael Young SP | 1.25 | 3.00 |
| ❑ 216 Rod Barajas | .15 | .40 |
| ❑ 217 Gustavo Chacin | .15 | .40 |
| ❑ 218 Lyle Overbay | .15 | .40 |
| ❑ 219 Troy Glaus | .15 | .40 |
| ❑ 220 Chad Cordero | .15 | .40 |
| ❑ 221 Jose Vidro | .15 | .40 |
| ❑ 222 Scott Rolen | .25 | .60 |
| ❑ 223 Carl Crawford | .15 | .40 |
| ❑ 224 Rocco Baldelli | .15 | .40 |
| ❑ 225 Mike Mussina | .25 | .60 |
| ❑ 226 Kelvim Escobar | .15 | .40 |
| ❑ 227 Corey Patterson | .15 | .40 |
| ❑ 228 Javy Lopez | .15 | .40 |
| ❑ 229 Jonathan Papelbon (RC) | .75 | 2.00 |
| ❑ 230 Aramis Ramirez | .15 | .40 |
| ❑ 231 Tadahito Iguchi | .15 | .40 |
| ❑ 232 Morgan Ensberg | .15 | .40 |
| ❑ 233 Mark Grudzielanek | .15 | .40 |
| ❑ 234 Mike Sweeney | .15 | .40 |
| ❑ 235 Shawn Chacon SP | 1.25 | 3.00 |
| ❑ 236 Nick Punto | .15 | .40 |
| ❑ 237 Geoff Jenkins | .15 | .40 |
| ❑ 238 Carlos Lee | .15 | .40 |
| ❑ 239 David DeJesus | .15 | .40 |
| ❑ 240 Brad Lidge | .15 | .40 |
| ❑ 241 Bob Wickman | .15 | .40 |
| ❑ 242 Jon Garland | .15 | .40 |
| ❑ 243 Kerry Wood | .15 | .40 |
| ❑ 244 Bronson Arroyo | .15 | .40 |
| ❑ 245 Matt Holliday SP | 1.50 | 4.00 |
| ❑ 246 Josh Beckett | .15 | .40 |
| ❑ 247 Johan Santana | .25 | .60 |
| ❑ 248 Rafael Furcal | .15 | .40 |
| ❑ 249 Shannon Stewart | .15 | .40 |
| ❑ 250 Gary Sheffield | .15 | .40 |
| ❑ 251 Josh Barfield SP (RC) | 1.25 | 3.00 |
| ❑ 252 Kenji Johjima RC | .75 | 2.00 |
| ❑ 253 Ian Kinsler (RC) | .50 | 1.25 |
| ❑ 254 Brian Anderson (RC) | .15 | .40 |
| ❑ 255 Matt Cain SP (RC) | 1.25 | 3.00 |
| ❑ 256 Josh Willingham SP (RC) | 1.25 | 3.00 |
| ❑ 257 John Koronka (RC) | .15 | .40 |
| ❑ 258 Chris Duffy (RC) | .15 | .40 |
| ❑ 259 Brian McCann (RC) | .15 | .40 |
| ❑ 260 Hanley Ramirez (RC) | .40 | 1.00 |
| ❑ 261 Hong-Chih Kuo (RC) | .40 | 1.00 |
| ❑ 262 Francisco Liriano (RC) | .40 | 1.00 |
| ❑ 263 Anderson Hernandez (RC) | .15 | .40 |
| ❑ 264 Ryan Zimmerman (RC) | .75 | 2.00 |
| ❑ 265 Brian Bannister SP (RC) | 1.25 | 3.00 |
| ❑ 266 Nolan Ryan | 1.00 | 2.50 |
| ❑ 267 Frank Robinson | .15 | .40 |
| ❑ 268 Roberto Clemente | 1.25 | 3.00 |
| ❑ 269 Hank Greenberg | .40 | 1.00 |
| ❑ 270 Napoleon Lajoie | .25 | .60 |
| ❑ 271 Lloyd Waner | .25 | .60 |
| ❑ 272 Paul Waner | .25 | .60 |
| ❑ 273 Frankie Frisch | .25 | .60 |
| ❑ 274 Moose Skowron | .15 | .40 |
| ❑ 275 Mickey Mantle | 2.00 | 5.00 |
| ❑ 276 Brooks Robinson | .25 | .60 |
| ❑ 277 Carl Yastrzemski | .60 | 1.50 |
| ❑ 278 Johnny Pesky | .15 | .40 |
| ❑ 279 Stan Musial | .60 | 1.50 |
| ❑ 280 Bill Mazeroski | .25 | .60 |
| ❑ 281 Harmon Killebrew | .40 | 1.00 |
| ❑ 282 Monte Irvin | .15 | .40 |
| ❑ 283 Bob Gibson | .25 | .60 |
| ❑ 284 Ted Williams | 1.00 | 2.50 |
| ❑ 285 Yogi Berra SP | 1.25 | 3.00 |
| ❑ 286 Ernie Banks | .40 | 1.00 |
| ❑ 287 Bobby Doerr | .15 | .40 |
| ❑ 288 Josh Gibson | .40 | 1.00 |
| ❑ 289 Bob Feller | .15 | .40 |
| ❑ 290 Cal Ripken | 1.50 | 4.00 |
| ❑ 291 Bobby Cox MG | .15 | .40 |
| ❑ 292 Terry Francona MG | .15 | .40 |
| ❑ 293 Dusty Baker MG | .15 | .40 |
| ❑ 294 Ozzie Guillen MG | .15 | .40 |
| ❑ 295 Jim Leyland MG SP | 1.25 | 3.00 |
| ❑ 296 Willie Randolph MG | .15 | .40 |
| ❑ 297 Joe Torre MG | .25 | .60 |
| ❑ 298 Felipe Alou MG | .15 | .40 |
| ❑ 299 Tony La Russa MG | .15 | .40 |
| ❑ 300 Frank Robinson MG | .15 | .40 |
| ❑ 301 Mike Styga | .60 | 1.50 |
| ❑ 302 Duke Paoa Kahanamoku | .15 | .40 |
| ❑ 303 Jennie Finch | 1.00 | 2.50 |
| ❑ 304 Brandi Chastain | .15 | .40 |
| ❑ 305 Danica Patrick SP | 3.00 | 8.00 |
| ❑ 306 Wendy Gulley | .15 | .40 |
| ❑ 307 Hulk Hogan | .50 | 1.25 |
| ❑ 308 Carl Lewis | .10 | .30 |
| ❑ 309 John Wooden | .25 | .60 |
| ❑ 310 Randy Couture | .75 | 2.00 |
| ❑ 311 Andy Irons | .15 | .40 |
| ❑ 312 Takeru Kobayashi | .50 | 1.25 |
| ❑ 313 Leon Spinks | .10 | .20 |
| ❑ 314 Jim Thorpe | .25 | .60 |
| ❑ 315 Jerry Bailey SP | 1.25 | 3.00 |
| ❑ 316 Adrian C. Anson REP | .25 | .60 |
| ❑ 317 John M. Ward REP | .15 | .40 |
| ❑ 318 Mike Kelly REP | | |
| ❑ 319 Capt. Jack Glasscock REP | .15 | .40 |

|  |  | | |
|---|---|---|---|
| 320 | Aaron Hill | .15 | .40 |
| 321 | Derrick Turnbow | .15 | .40 |
| 322 | Nick Markakis (RC) | .25 | .60 |
| 323 | Brad Hawpe | .15 | .40 |
| 324 | Kevin Mench | .15 | .40 |
| 325 | John Lackey SP | 1.25 | 3.00 |
| 326 | Chester A. Arthur | .07 | .20 |
| 327 | Ulysses S. Grant | .10 | .20 |
| 328 | Abraham Lincoln | .10 | .20 |
| 329 | Grover Cleveland | .10 | .20 |
| 330 | Benjamin Harrison | .10 | .20 |
| 331 | Theodore Roosevelt | .10 | .30 |
| 332 | Rutherford B. Hayes | .10 | .20 |
| 333 | Chancellor Otto Von Bismarck | .15 | .40 |
| 334 | Kaiser Wilhelm II | .15 | .40 |
| 335 | Queen Victoria SP | 1.25 | 3.00 |
| 336 | Pope Leo XIII | .15 | .40 |
| 337 | Thomas Edison | .10 | .20 |
| 338 | Orville Wright | .10 | .20 |
| 339 | Wilbur Wright | .10 | .20 |
| 340 | Nathaniel Hawthorne | .15 | .40 |
| 341 | Herman Melville | .15 | .40 |
| 342 | Stonewall Jackson | .10 | .20 |
| 343 | Robert E. Lee | .10 | .20 |
| 344 | Andrew Carnegie | | |
| 345 | John Rockefeller SP | 1.25 | 3.00 |
| 346 | Bob Fitzsimmons | .10 | .20 |
| 347 | Billy The Kid | | |
| 348 | Buffalo Bill | .15 | .40 |
| 349 | Jesse James | .10 | .20 |
| 350 | Statue Of Liberty | .15 | .40 |
| NNO | Framed Originals | 60.00 | 120.00 |

## 2007 Topps Allen and Ginter

| | | | |
|---|---|---|---|
| COMPLETE SET (350) | | 60.00 | 120.00 |
| COMP.SET w/o SP's (300) | | 20.00 | 50.00 |
| COMMON CARD | | .12 | .30 |
| COMMON RC | | .20 | .50 |
| COMMON SP | | 1.25 | 3.00 |

SP STATED ODDS 1:2 HOBBY, 1:2 RETAIL
SP C: 5/43/48/58/63/107/110/119/130/137
SP C: 152/159/178/193/194/203/219/222
SP C: 224/243/263/301/302/303/306/307
SP C: 308/309/310/316/317/318/319/320
SP C: 321/322/325/326/327/330/331/334
SP C: 335/336/339/340/345/348/349/350
FRAMED ORIGINALS ODDS 1:17,072 HOBBY
FRAMED ORIGINALS ODDS 1:34,654 RETAIL

|  |  | | |
|---|---|---|---|
| 1 | Ryan Howard | .50 | 1.25 |
| 2 | Mike Gonzalez | .12 | .30 |
| 3 | Austin Kearns | .12 | .30 |
| 4 | Josh Hamilton (RC) | .50 | 1.25 |
| 5 | Stephen Drew SP | 1.25 | 3.00 |
| 6 | Matt Murton | .12 | .30 |
| 7 | Mickey Mantle | 1.50 | 4.00 |
| 8 | Howie Kendrick | .30 | .75 |
| 9 | Alexander Graham Bell | .12 | .30 |
| 10 | Jason Bay | .20 | .50 |
| 11 | Hank Blalock | .12 | .30 |
| 12 | Johan Santana | .20 | .50 |
| 13 | Eleanor Roosevelt | .12 | .30 |
| 14 | Kei Igawa RC | .50 | 1.25 |
| 15 | Jeff Francoeur | .30 | .75 |
| 16 | Carl Crawford | .12 | .30 |
| 17 | Jhonny Peralta | .12 | .30 |
| 18 | Mariano Rivera | .30 | .75 |
| 19 | Mario Andretti | .30 | .75 |
| 20 | Vladimir Guerrero | .30 | .75 |
| 21 | Adam Wainwright | .20 | .50 |
| 22 | Huston Street | .12 | .30 |
| 23 | Cael Sanderson | .12 | .30 |
| 24 | Susan B. Anthony | .12 | .30 |
| 25 | Jay Payton | .12 | .30 |
| 26 | P.T. Barnum | .12 | .30 |
| 27 | Scott Podsednik | .12 | .30 |
| 28 | Willie Randolph | .12 | .30 |
| 29 | Sean Casey | .12 | .30 |
| 30 | Eiffel Tower | .12 | .30 |
| 31 | Kenji Johjima | .30 | .75 |
| 32 | Felix Hernandez | .20 | .50 |
| 33 | Elijah Dukes RC | .30 | .75 |
| 34 | Mark Grudzielanek | .12 | .30 |
| 35 | J.D. Drew | .12 | .30 |
| 36 | Kevin Kouzmanoff | .12 | .30 |
| 37 | Jonathan Papelbon | .30 | .75 |
| 38 | Bobby Crosby | .12 | .30 |
| 39 | Brooklyn Bridge | .12 | .30 |
| 40 | Adam Dunn | .12 | .30 |
| 41 | Lyle Overbay | .12 | .30 |
| 42 | Brian Fuentes | .12 | .30 |
| 43 | Scott Rolen SP | 1.25 | 3.00 |
| 44 | Matt Lindstrom (RC) | .20 | .50 |
| 45 | Carlos Zambrano | .12 | .30 |
| 46 | Cole Hamels | .30 | .75 |
| 47 | Matt Kemp | .30 | .75 |
| 48 | Gary Matthews SP | 1.25 | 3.00 |
| 49 | J.J. Putz | .12 | .30 |
| 50 | Albert Pujols | .60 | 1.50 |
| 51 | Dan Haren | .12 | .30 |
| 52 | Aaron Harang | .12 | .30 |
| 53 | Ferris Wheel | .12 | .30 |
| 54 | Juan Rivera | .12 | .30 |
| 55 | Ken Griffey Jr. | .50 | 1.25 |
| 56 | Chien-Ming Wang | .30 | .75 |
| 57 | Sean Henn (RC) | .20 | .50 |
| 58 | Mike Mussina SP | 1.25 | 3.00 |
| 59 | Ian Snell | .12 | .30 |
| 60 | Josh Barfield | .12 | .30 |
| 61 | Justin Morneau | .12 | .30 |
| 62 | Dwight D. Eisenhower | .12 | .30 |
| 63 | Bengie Molina SP | 1.25 | 3.00 |
| 64 | Brett Myers | .12 | .30 |
| 65 | Andy Marte | .12 | .30 |
| 66 | Bill Hall | .12 | .30 |
| 67 | Ryan Shealy | .12 | .30 |
| 68 | Joe B. Scott | .12 | .30 |
| 69 | Mike Rabelo RC | .20 | .50 |
| 70 | Jermaine Dye | .12 | .30 |
| 71 | Andre Ethier | .20 | .50 |
| 72 | Bruce Lee | .50 | 1.25 |
| 73 | Nick Punto | .12 | .30 |
| 74 | Ervin Santana | .12 | .30 |
| 75 | Troy Tulowitzki (RC) | .50 | 1.25 |
| 76 | Garret Anderson | .12 | .30 |
| 77 | Ryan Freel | .12 | .30 |
| 78 | Carlos Guillen | .12 | .30 |
| 79 | John Smoltz | .20 | .50 |
| 80 | Chase Utley | .30 | .75 |
| 81 | Mike Sweeney | .12 | .30 |
| 82 | Joe Frazier | .30 | .75 |
| 83 | Brad Lidge | .12 | .30 |
| 84 | Casey Blake | .12 | .30 |
| 85 | Ivan Rodriguez | .20 | .50 |
| 86 | Roy Oswalt | .12 | .30 |
| 87 | Akinori Iwamura RC | .50 | 1.25 |
| 88 | Francisco Rodriguez | .12 | .30 |
| 89 | John Lackey | .12 | .30 |
| 90 | Miguel Cabrera | .20 | .50 |
| 91 | Kevin Mench | .12 | .30 |
| 92 | Victor Martinez | .12 | .30 |
| 93 | Chad Tracy | .12 | .30 |
| 94 | Charlie Manuel | .12 | .30 |
| 95 | Hanley Ramirez | .20 | .50 |
| 96 | Dontrelle Willis | .12 | .30 |
| 97 | Doug Slaten RC | .20 | .50 |
| 98 | Noah Lowry | .12 | .30 |
| 99 | Shawn Green | .12 | .30 |
| 100 | David Ortiz | .20 | .50 |
| 101 | Mark Reynolds RC | 1.25 | 3.00 |
| 102 | Preston Wilson | .12 | .30 |
| 103 | Mohandas Gandhi | .12 | .30 |
| 104 | Jeff Kent | .12 | .30 |
| 105 | Lance Berkman | .12 | .30 |
| 106 | C.C. Sabathia | .12 | .30 |
| 107 | Jason Vantek SP | 1.25 | 3.00 |
| 108 | Mark Twain | .12 | .30 |
| 109 | Melvin Mora | .12 | .30 |
| 110 | Michael Young SP | 1.25 | 3.00 |
| 111 | Scott Hatteberg | .12 | .30 |
| 112 | Erik Bedard | .12 | .30 |
| 113 | Sitting Bull | .12 | .30 |
| 114 | Homer Bailey (RC) | .30 | .75 |
| 115 | Mark Teahen | .12 | .30 |
| 116 | Ryan Braun (RC) | 1.00 | 2.50 |
| 117 | John Miles | .12 | .30 |
| 118 | Coco Crisp | .12 | .30 |
| 119 | Hunter Pence SP (RC) | 2.00 | 5.00 |
| 120 | Delmon Young (RC) | .30 | .75 |
| 121 | Aramis Ramirez | .12 | .30 |
| 122 | Maggio Ordonez | .12 | .30 |
| 123 | Tadahito Iguchi | .12 | .30 |
| 124 | Mark Selby | .12 | .30 |
| 125 | Gil Meche | .12 | .30 |
| 126 | Curt Schilling | .20 | .50 |
| 127 | Brandon Phillips | .12 | .30 |
| 128 | Milton Bradley | .12 | .30 |
| 129 | Craig Monroe | .12 | .30 |
| 130 | Jason Schmidt SP | 1.25 | 3.00 |
| 131 | Nick Markakis | .20 | .50 |
| 132 | Paul Konerko | .12 | .30 |
| 133 | Carlos Gomez RC | .30 | .75 |
| 134 | Garrett Atkins | .12 | .30 |
| 135 | Jered Weaver | .20 | .50 |
| 136 | Edgar Renteria | .12 | .30 |
| 137 | Jason Isringhausen SP | 1.25 | 3.00 |
| 138 | Ray Durham | .12 | .30 |
| 139 | Bob Baffert | .12 | .30 |
| 140 | Nick Swisher | .12 | .30 |
| 141 | Brian McCann | .12 | .30 |
| 142 | Orlando Hudson | .12 | .30 |
| 143 | Brian Bannister | .12 | .30 |
| 144 | Manny Acta | .12 | .30 |
| 145 | Jose Vidro | .12 | .30 |
| 146 | Carlos Quentin | .12 | .30 |
| 147 | Billy Butler (RC) | .30 | .75 |
| 148 | Kenny Rogers | .12 | .30 |
| 149 | Tom Gordon | .12 | .30 |
| 150 | Derek Jeter | .75 | 2.00 |
| 151 | Bob Wickman | .12 | .30 |
| 152 | Carlos Lee SP | 1.25 | 3.00 |
| 153 | Willy Taveras | .12 | .30 |
| 154 | Paul LoDuca | .12 | .30 |
| 155 | Ben Sheets | .12 | .30 |
| 156 | Brian Roberts | .12 | .30 |
| 157 | Freddy Adu | .30 | .75 |
| 158 | Jason Kendall | .12 | .30 |
| 159 | Michael Barrett SP | 1.25 | 3.00 |
| 160 | Frank Thomas | .30 | .75 |
| 161 | Manny Ramirez | .20 | .50 |
| 162 | Stanley Glenn | .12 | .30 |
| 163 | Robinson Cano | .20 | .50 |
| 164 | Phil Hughes (RC) | 1.00 | 2.50 |
| 165 | Joe Mauer | .30 | .75 |
| 166 | Derrek Lee | .12 | .30 |
| 167 | Jeff Weaver | .12 | .30 |
| 168 | Joe Smith RC | .12 | .30 |
| 169 | Louis Pasteur | .12 | .30 |
| 170 | Gary Sheffield | .12 | .30 |
| 171 | Luis Castillo | .12 | .30 |
| 172 | Joe Torre | .20 | .50 |
| 173 | Andy LaRoche SP | .12 | .30 |
| 174 | Jamie Fischer | .12 | .30 |
| 175 | Carlos Beltran | .12 | .30 |
| 176 | Bronson Arroyo | .12 | .30 |
| 177 | Rafael Furcal | .12 | .30 |
| 178 | Juan Pierre SP | 1.25 | 3.00 |
| 179 | Matt Cain | .12 | .30 |
| 180 | Alfonso Soriano | .12 | .30 |
| 181 | Joe Borowski | .12 | .30 |
| 182 | Conor Jackson | .12 | .30 |
| 183 | Groundhog Day | .12 | .30 |
| 184 | Pat Burrell | .12 | .30 |
| 185 | Troy Glaus | .12 | .30 |
| 186 | Joel Zumaya | .20 | .50 |
| 187 | Russell Martin | .12 | .30 |
| 188 | Josh Willingham | .12 | .30 |
| 189 | Jason Saltalamacchia | .30 | .75 |
| 190 | Scott Kazmir | .20 | .50 |
| 191 | Jeremy Hermida | .12 | .30 |
| 192 | Tower Bridge | .12 | .30 |
| 193 | Rich Hill SP | 1.25 | 3.00 |
| 194 | Francisco Cordero SP | 1.25 | 3.00 |
| 195 | Mike Piazza | .30 | .75 |
| 196 | Brad Ausmus | .12 | .30 |
| 197 | Greg Lougarnis | .12 | .30 |
| 198 | Frank Catalanotto | .12 | .30 |
| 199 | Alejandro De Aza RC | .30 | .75 |
| 200 | David Wright | .50 | 1.25 |

|  |  | | |
|---|---|---|---|
| ❑ 201 | Freddy Sanchez | .12 | .30 |
| ❑ 202 | Shea Hillenbrand | .12 | .30 |
| ❑ 203 | Justin Verlander SP | 1.25 | 3.00 |
| ❑ 204 | Alex Gordon RC | .75 | 2.00 |
| ❑ 205 | Jimmy Rollins | .12 | .30 |
| ❑ 206 | Mike Napoli | .12 | .30 |
| ❑ 207 | Chris Burke | .12 | .30 |
| ❑ 208 | Chipper Jones | .30 | .75 |
| ❑ 209 | Randy Johnson | .30 | .75 |
| ❑ 210 | Daisuke Matsuzaka RC | 1.50 | 4.00 |
| ❑ 211 | Orlando Cabrera | .12 | .30 |
| ❑ 212 | B.J. Upton | .12 | .30 |
| ❑ 213 | Lou Piniella MG | .12 | .30 |
| ❑ 214 | Mike Cameron | .12 | .30 |
| ❑ 215 | Luis Gonzalez | .12 | .30 |
| ❑ 216 | Rickie Weeks | .12 | .30 |
| ❑ 217 | Hideki Okajima RC | 1.00 | 2.50 |
| ❑ 218 | Johnny Estrada | .12 | .30 |
| ❑ 219 | Dan Uggla SP | 1.25 | 3.00 |
| ❑ 220 | Ryan Zimmerman | .30 | .75 |
| ❑ 221 | Tony Gwynn Jr. | .12 | .30 |
| ❑ 222 | Rocco Baldelli SP | 1.25 | 3.00 |
| ❑ 223 | Xavier Nady | .12 | .30 |
| ❑ 224 | Josh Bard SP | 1.25 | 3.00 |
| ❑ 225 | Raul Ibanez | .20 | .50 |
| ❑ 226 | Chris Carpenter | .12 | .30 |
| ❑ 227 | Matt DeSalvo (RC) | .20 | .50 |
| ❑ 228 | Jack the Ripper | .12 | .30 |
| ❑ 229 | Eric Chavez | .12 | .30 |
| ❑ 230 | Jose Reyes | .30 | .75 |
| ❑ 231 | Glen Perkins (RC) | .20 | .50 |
| ❑ 232 | Gregg Zaun | .12 | .30 |
| ❑ 233 | Jim Thome | .20 | .50 |
| ❑ 234 | Joe Crede | .12 | .30 |
| ❑ 235 | Barry Zito | .12 | .30 |
| ❑ 236 | Yosi Hernandez RC | .20 | .50 |
| ❑ 237 | Kelly Johnson | .12 | .30 |
| ❑ 238 | Chris Young | .12 | .30 |
| ❑ 239 | Fyodor Dostoevsky | .12 | .30 |
| ❑ 240 | Miguel Tejada | .12 | .30 |
| ❑ 241 | Doug Mientkiewicz | .12 | .30 |
| ❑ 242 | Bobby Jenks | .12 | .30 |
| ❑ 243 | Brad Hawpe SP | 1.25 | 3.00 |
| ❑ 244 | Jay Marshall RC | .20 | .50 |
| ❑ 245 | Brad Penny | .12 | .30 |
| ❑ 246 | Johnny Damon | .20 | .50 |
| ❑ 247 | Dave Roberts | .12 | .30 |
| ❑ 248 | Ron Washington | .12 | .30 |
| ❑ 249 | Mike Aponte | .12 | .30 |
| ❑ 250 | Brandon Webb | .12 | .30 |
| ❑ 251 | Andy Pettitte | .20 | .50 |
| ❑ 252 | Bud Black | .12 | .30 |
| ❑ 253 | Michael Cuddyer | .12 | .30 |
| ❑ 254 | Chris Stewart RC | .20 | .50 |
| ❑ 255 | Mark Teixeira | .20 | .50 |
| ❑ 256 | Hideki Matsui | .30 | .75 |
| ❑ 257 | Curtis Granderson | .12 | .30 |
| ❑ 258 | A.J. Pierzynski | .12 | .30 |
| ❑ 259 | Tony La Russa | .12 | .30 |
| ❑ 260 | Andruw Jones | .20 | .50 |
| ❑ 261 | Torii Hunter | .12 | .30 |
| ❑ 262 | Mark Loretta | .12 | .30 |
| ❑ 263 | Jim Edmonds SP | 1.25 | 3.00 |
| ❑ 264 | Aaron Rowand | .12 | .30 |
| ❑ 265 | Roy Halladay | .12 | .30 |
| ❑ 266 | Freddy Garcia | .12 | .30 |
| ❑ 267 | Reggie Sanders | .12 | .30 |
| ❑ 268 | Washington Monument | .12 | .30 |
| ❑ 269 | Franklin D. Roosevelt | .12 | .30 |
| ❑ 270 | Alex Rodriguez | .50 | 1.25 |
| ❑ 271 | Wes Helms | .12 | .30 |
| ❑ 272 | Mia Hamm | .30 | .75 |
| ❑ 273 | Jorge Posada | .20 | .50 |
| ❑ 274 | Tim Lincecum RC | 2.50 | 6.00 |
| ❑ 275 | Bobby Abreu | .12 | .30 |
| ❑ 276 | Zach Duke | .12 | .30 |
| ❑ 277 | Carlos Delgado | .12 | .30 |
| ❑ 278 | Julio Juarez | .12 | .30 |
| ❑ 279 | Brandon Inge | .12 | .30 |
| ❑ 280 | Todd Helton | .20 | .50 |
| ❑ 281 | Marcus Giles | .12 | .30 |
| ❑ 282 | Josh Johnson | .12 | .30 |
| ❑ 283 | Chris Capuano | .12 | .30 |
| ❑ 284 | B.J. Ryan | .12 | .30 |
| ❑ 285 | Nick Johnson | .12 | .30 |
| ❑ 286 | Khalil Greene | .20 | .50 |
| ❑ 287 | Travis Hafner | .12 | .30 |
| ❑ 288 | Ted Lilly | .12 | .30 |
| ❑ 289 | Jim Leyland | .12 | .30 |
| ❑ 290 | Prince Fielder | .30 | .75 |
| ❑ 291 | Trevor Hoffman | .20 | .50 |
| ❑ 292 | Brian Giles | .12 | .30 |
| ❑ 293 | Omar Vizquel | .20 | .50 |
| ❑ 294 | Julio Lugo | .12 | .30 |
| ❑ 295 | Jake Peavy | .12 | .30 |
| ❑ 296 | Adrian Beltre | .12 | .30 |
| ❑ 297 | Josh Beckett | .20 | .50 |
| ❑ 298 | Harry S. Truman | .12 | .30 |
| ❑ 299 | Mark Buehrle | .12 | .30 |
| ❑ 300 | Ichiro Suzuki | .50 | 1.25 |
| ❑ 301 | Chris Duncan SP | 1.25 | 3.00 |
| ❑ 302 | Augie Garrido SP CO | 1.25 | 3.00 |
| ❑ 303 | Tyler Clippard SP (RC) | 1.25 | 3.00 |
| ❑ 304 | Ramon Hernandez | .12 | .30 |
| ❑ 305 | Jeremy Bonderman | .12 | .30 |
| ❑ 306 | Morgan Ensberg SP | 1.25 | 3.00 |
| ❑ 307 | J.J. Hardy SP | 1.25 | 3.00 |
| ❑ 308 | Mark Zupan SP | 1.25 | 3.00 |
| ❑ 309 | Laila Ali SP | 1.25 | 3.00 |
| ❑ 310 | Greg Maddux SP | 1.50 | 4.00 |
| ❑ 311 | David Ross | .12 | .30 |
| ❑ 312 | Chris Duffy | .12 | .30 |
| ❑ 313 | Moises Alou | .12 | .30 |
| ❑ 314 | Yadier Molina | .12 | .30 |
| ❑ 315 | Corey Patterson | .12 | .30 |
| ❑ 316 | Dan O'Brien SP | 1.25 | 3.00 |
| ❑ 317 | Michael Bourn SP (RC) | 1.25 | 3.00 |
| ❑ 318 | Jonny Gomes SP | 1.25 | 3.00 |
| ❑ 319 | Ken Jennings SP | 1.25 | 3.00 |
| ❑ 320 | Barry Bonds SP | 1.50 | 4.00 |
| ❑ 321 | Gary Hall Jr. SP | 1.25 | 3.00 |
| ❑ 322 | Kern Walsh SP | 1.25 | 3.00 |
| ❑ 323 | Craig Biggio | .20 | .50 |
| ❑ 324 | Ian Kinsler | .12 | .30 |
| ❑ 325 | Grady Sizemore SP | 1.25 | 3.00 |
| ❑ 326 | Alex Rios SP | 1.25 | 3.00 |
| ❑ 327 | Ted Toles SP | 1.25 | 3.00 |
| ❑ 328 | Jason Jennings | .12 | .30 |
| ❑ 329 | Vernon Wells | .12 | .30 |
| ❑ 330 | Bob Geren SP MG | 1.25 | 3.00 |
| ❑ 331 | Dennis Rodman SP | 1.25 | 3.00 |
| ❑ 332 | Tom Glavine | .20 | .50 |
| ❑ 333 | Pedro Martinez | .20 | .50 |
| ❑ 334 | Gustavo Molina SP (RC) | 1.25 | 3.00 |
| ❑ 335 | Bartolo Colon SP | 1.25 | 3.00 |
| ❑ 336 | Misty May-Treanor SP | 1.25 | 3.00 |
| ❑ 337 | Randy Winn | .12 | .30 |
| ❑ 338 | Eric Byrnes | .12 | .30 |
| ❑ 339 | Jason McElwain SP | 1.25 | 3.00 |
| ❑ 340 | Placido Polanco SP | 1.25 | 3.00 |
| ❑ 341 | Adrian Gonzalez | .12 | .30 |
| ❑ 342 | Chad Cordero | .12 | .30 |
| ❑ 343 | Jeff Francis | .12 | .30 |
| ❑ 344 | Lastings Milledge | .20 | .50 |
| ❑ 345 | Sammy Sosa SP | 1.25 | 3.00 |
| ❑ 346 | Jacque Jones | .12 | .30 |
| ❑ 347 | Anibal Sanchez | .12 | .30 |
| ❑ 348 | Roger Clemens SP | 1.50 | 4.00 |
| ❑ 349 | Jesse Litsch SP RC | 1.25 | 3.00 |
| ❑ 350 | Adam LaRoche SP | 1.25 | 3.00 |
| ❑ NNO | Framed Originals | 50.00 | 100.00 |

## 2008 Topps Allen and Ginter

| | | | |
|---|---|---|---|
| ❑ COMP.SET w/o FUKU.(350) | | 50.00 | 100.00 |
| ❑ COMP.SET w/o SPs (300) | | 15.00 | 40.00 |
| ❑ COMMON CARD (1-300) | | .15 | .40 |
| ❑ COMMON RC (1-300) | | .40 | 1.00 |
| ❑ COMMON SP (301-350) | | 1.25 | 3.00 |
| ❑ SP STATED ODDS 1:2 HOBBY | | | |
| ❑ FRAMED ORIG.ODDS 1:26,500 HOBBY | | | |

|  |  | | |
|---|---|---|---|
| ❑ 1 | Alex Rodriguez | .60 | 1.50 |
| ❑ 2 | Juan Pierre | .15 | .40 |
| ❑ 3 | Benjamin Franklin | .25 | .60 |
| ❑ 4 | Roy Halladay | .15 | .40 |
| ❑ 5 | C.C. Sabathia | .15 | .40 |
| ❑ 6 | Brian Barton RC | .60 | 1.50 |
| ❑ 7 | Mickey Mantle | 1.50 | 4.00 |
| ❑ 8 | Bran Bass (RC) | .40 | 1.00 |
| ❑ 9 | Ian Kinsler | .25 | .60 |
| ❑ 10 | Manny Ramirez | .40 | 1.00 |
| ❑ 11 | Michael Cuddyer | .15 | .40 |
| ❑ 12 | Ian Snell | .15 | .40 |
| ❑ 13 | Mike Lowell | .15 | .40 |
| ❑ 14 | Adrian Gonzalez | .25 | .60 |
| ❑ 15 | B.J. Upton | .25 | .60 |
| ❑ 16 | Hiroki Kuroda RC | .60 | 1.50 |
| ❑ 17 | Kenji Johjima | .15 | .40 |
| ❑ 18 | James Loney | .15 | .40 |
| ❑ 19 | Albert Einstein | .25 | .60 |
| ❑ 20 | Vladimir Guerrero | .40 | 1.00 |
| ❑ 21 | Miguel Tejada | .15 | .40 |
| ❑ 22 | Chin-Lung Hu (RC) | .60 | 1.50 |
| ❑ 23 | A.J. Burnett | .15 | .40 |
| ❑ 24 | Bobby Jenks | .15 | .40 |
| ❑ 25 | Aramis Ramirez | .15 | .40 |
| ❑ 26 | Corey Hart | .15 | .40 |
| ❑ 27 | Brad Hawpe | .15 | .40 |
| ❑ 28 | Adam LaRoche | .15 | .40 |
| ❑ 29 | Empire State Building | .25 | .60 |
| ❑ 30 | Miguel Cabrera | .25 | .60 |
| ❑ 31 | Ryan Zimmerman | .15 | .40 |
| ❑ 32 | Mark Ellis | .15 | .40 |
| ❑ 33 | Nick Swisher | .15 | .40 |
| ❑ 34 | Bill Hall | .15 | .40 |
| ❑ 35 | Eric Byrnes | .15 | .40 |
| ❑ 36 | Michael Young | .15 | .40 |
| ❑ 37 | Pedro Martinez | .25 | .60 |
| ❑ 38 | Andruw Jones | .15 | .40 |
| ❑ 39 | J.R. Towles RC | .60 | 1.50 |
| ❑ 40 | Justin Upton | .40 | 1.00 |
| ❑ 41 | Paul Konerko | .15 | .40 |
| ❑ 42 | Luke Scott | .15 | .40 |
| ❑ 43 | Rickie Weeks | .15 | .40 |
| ❑ 44 | Adam Wainwright | .25 | .60 |
| ❑ 45 | Justin Morneau | .25 | .60 |
| ❑ 46 | Chris Young | .15 | .40 |
| ❑ 47 | Chad Billingsley | .15 | .40 |
| ❑ 48 | Kazuo Matsui | .15 | .40 |
| ❑ 49 | Shane Victorino | .15 | .40 |
| ❑ 50 | Albert Pujols | .75 | 2.00 |
| ❑ 51 | Brian McCann | .25 | .60 |
| ❑ 52 | Carlos Delgado | .15 | .40 |
| ❑ 53 | Chien-Ming Wang | .40 | 1.00 |
| ❑ 54 | Takashi Saito | .15 | .40 |
| ❑ 55 | Josh Beckett | .25 | .60 |
| ❑ 56 | Nick Johnson | .15 | .40 |
| ❑ 57 | Ben Sheets | .15 | .40 |
| ❑ 58 | Johnny Damon | .25 | .60 |
| ❑ 59 | Nicky Hayden | .25 | .60 |
| ❑ 60 | Prince Fielder | .40 | 1.00 |
| ❑ 61 | Adam Dunn | .15 | .40 |
| ❑ 62 | Dustin Pedroia | .50 | 1.25 |
| ❑ 63 | Jacoby Ellsbury | .60 | 1.50 |
| ❑ 64 | Brad Penny | .15 | .40 |
| ❑ 65 | Victor Martinez | .15 | .40 |
| ❑ 66 | Joe Mauer | .40 | 1.00 |
| ❑ 67 | Kevin Kouzmanoff | .15 | .40 |
| ❑ 68 | Frank Thomas | .40 | 1.00 |
| ❑ 69 | Stevie Williams | .25 | .60 |
| ❑ 70 | Matt Holliday | .25 | .60 |
| ❑ 71 | Fausto Carmona | .15 | .40 |
| ❑ 72 | Clayton Kershaw RC | 2.00 | 5.00 |
| ❑ 73 | Tadahito Iguchi | .15 | .40 |
| ❑ 74 | Khalil Greene | .25 | .60 |
| ❑ 75 | Travis Hafner | .15 | .40 |
| ❑ 76 | Jim Thome | .25 | .60 |
| ❑ 77 | Joba Chamberlain | .50 | 1.25 |
| ❑ 78 | Ivan Rodriguez | .25 | .60 |
| ❑ 79 | Jose Guillen | .15 | .40 |
| ❑ 80 | Hanley Ramirez | .40 | 1.00 |
| ❑ 81 | Vernon Wells | .15 | .40 |
| ❑ 82 | Jayson Nix (RC) | .40 | 1.00 |
| ❑ 83 | Masahide Kobayashi RC | .60 | 1.50 |
| ❑ 84 | Bonnie Blair | .25 | .60 |
| ❑ 85 | Curtis Granderson | .25 | .60 |
| ❑ 86 | Kelvim Escobar | .15 | .40 |
| ❑ 87 | Aaron Rowand | .15 | .40 |
| ❑ 88 | Troy Glaus | .25 | .60 |

|  |  | | |
|---|---|---|---|
| 89 | Billy Wagner | .15 | .40 |
| 90 | Jose Reyes | .25 | .60 |
| 91 | Scott Rolen | .25 | .60 |
| 92 | Dan Jansen | .25 | .60 |
| 93 | David Eckstein | .15 | .40 |
| 94 | Tom Gorzelanny | .15 | .40 |
| 95 | Garrett Atkins | .15 | .40 |
| 96 | Carlos Zambrano | .15 | .40 |
| 97 | Jeff Francis | .15 | .40 |
| 98 | Kazuo Fukumori RC | .60 | 1.50 |
| 99 | John Bowker (RC) | .40 | 1.00 |
| 100 | David Wright | .50 | 1.25 |
| 101 | Adrian Beltre | .15 | .40 |
| 102 | Ray Durham | .15 | .40 |
| 103 | Kerri Strug | .25 | .60 |
| 104 | Orlando Hudson | .15 | .40 |
| 105 | Jonathan Papelbon | .25 | .60 |
| 106 | Brian Schneider | .15 | .40 |
| 107 | Matt Biondi | .25 | .60 |
| 108 | Alex Romero (RC) | .60 | 1.50 |
| 109 | Joey Chestnut | .25 | .60 |
| 110 | Chase Utley | .40 | 1.00 |
| 111 | Dan Uggla | .15 | .40 |
| 112 | Akinori Iwamura | .15 | .40 |
| 113 | Curt Schilling | .25 | .60 |
| 114 | Trevor Hoffman | .15 | .40 |
| 115 | Alex Rios | .15 | .40 |
| 116 | Mariano Rivera | .40 | 1.00 |
| 117 | Jeff Niemann (RC) | .40 | 1.00 |
| 118 | Geovany Soto | .40 | 1.00 |
| 119 | Billy Mitchell | .25 | .60 |
| 120 | Derek Jeter | 1.00 | 2.50 |
| 121 | Yovani Gallardo | .25 | .60 |
| 122 | The Gateway Arch | .25 | .60 |
| 123 | Josh Willingham | .15 | .40 |
| 124 | Greg Maddux | .50 | 1.25 |
| 125 | John Lackey | .15 | .40 |
| 126 | Chris Young | .15 | .40 |
| 127 | Billy Butler | .15 | .40 |
| 128 | Golden Gate Bridge | .25 | .60 |
| 129 | Joey Votto (RC) | 1.00 | 2.50 |
| 130 | Tim Wakefield | .15 | .40 |
| 131 | Todd Helton | .25 | .60 |
| 132 | Gary Matthews | .15 | .40 |
| 133 | Wild Bill Hickok | .25 | .60 |
| 134 | Jason Varitek | .40 | 1.00 |
| 135 | Robinson Cano | .25 | .60 |
| 136 | Javier Vazquez | .15 | .40 |
| 137 | Annie Oakley | .25 | .60 |
| 138 | Andy Pettitte | .25 | .60 |
| 139 | Greg Reynolds RC | .60 | 1.50 |
| 140 | Jimmy Rollins | .25 | .60 |
| 141 | Jermaine Dye | .15 | .40 |
| 142 | Eugenio Velez RC | .40 | 1.00 |
| 143 | J.J. Hardy | .15 | .40 |
| 144 | Grand Canyon | .25 | .60 |
| 145 | Bobby Abreu | .15 | .40 |
| 146 | Scott Kazmir | .25 | .60 |
| 147 | James Fenimore Cooper | .25 | .60 |
| 148 | Mark Buehrle | .15 | .40 |
| 149 | Freddy Sanchez | .15 | .40 |
| 150 | Johan Santana | .25 | .60 |
| 151 | Orlando Cabrera | .15 | .40 |
| 152 | Lyle Overbay | .15 | .40 |
| 153 | Clay Buchholz (RC) | 1.00 | 2.50 |
| 154 | Jesse Carlson RC | .60 | 1.50 |
| 155 | Troy Tulowitzki | .25 | .60 |
| 156 | Delmon Young | .25 | .60 |
| 157 | Ross Ohlendorf RC | .60 | 1.50 |
| 158 | Mary Shelley | .25 | .60 |
| 159 | James Shields | .15 | .40 |
| 160 | Alfonso Soriano | .25 | .60 |
| 161 | Randy Winn | .15 | .40 |
| 162 | Austin Kearns | .15 | .40 |
| 163 | Jeremy Hermida | .15 | .40 |
| 164 | Jorge Posada | .25 | .60 |
| 165 | Justin Verlander | .25 | .60 |
| 166 | Bram Stoker | .25 | .60 |
| 167 | Marie Curie | .25 | .60 |
| 168 | Melky Cabrera | .15 | .40 |
| 169 | Howie Kendrick | .15 | .40 |
| 170 | Jake Peavy | .25 | .60 |
| 171 | J.D. Drew | .15 | .40 |
| 172 | Pablo Picasso | .25 | .60 |
| 173 | Rick Ankiel | .15 | .40 |
| 174 | Jose Valverde | .15 | .40 |
| 175 | Chipper Jones | .50 | 1.25 |
| 176 | Claude Monet | .25 | .60 |
| 177 | Evan Longoria RC | 4.00 | 10.00 |
| 178 | Jose Vidro | .15 | .40 |
| 179 | Hideki Matsui | .40 | 1.00 |
| 180 | Ryan Braun | .50 | 1.25 |
| 181 | Moises Alou | .15 | .40 |
| 182 | Nate McLouth | .15 | .40 |
| 183 | Harriet Tubman | .25 | .60 |
| 184 | Felix Hernandez | .25 | .60 |
| 185 | Carlos Pena | .40 | 1.00 |
| 186 | Jarrod Saltalamacchia | .25 | .60 |
| 187 | Les Miles | .25 | .60 |
| 188 | Kelly Johnson | .15 | .40 |
| 189 | Rampage Jackson | .40 | 1.00 |
| 190 | Grady Sizemore | .25 | .60 |
| 191 | Francisco Cordero | .15 | .40 |
| 192 | Yunel Escobar | .15 | .40 |
| 193 | Edwin Encarnacion | .15 | .40 |
| 194 | Melvin Mora | .15 | .40 |
| 195 | Russ Martin | .25 | .60 |
| 196 | Edgar Renteria | .15 | .40 |
| 197 | Bigfoot | .40 | 1.00 |
| 198 | Steve Holm RC | .40 | 1.00 |
| 199 | Daric Barton (RC) | .40 | 1.00 |
| 200 | David Ortiz | .25 | .60 |
| 201 | Tim Lincecum | .50 | 1.25 |
| 202 | Jeff King | .25 | .60 |
| 203 | Jhonny Peralta | .15 | .40 |
| 204 | Julio Lugo | .15 | .40 |
| 205 | J.J. Putz | .15 | .40 |
| 206 | Jeff Francoeur | .25 | .60 |
| 207 | Yuniesky Betancourt | .15 | .40 |
| 208 | Bruce Jenner | .25 | .60 |
| 209 | Clete Thomas RC | .60 | 1.50 |
| 210 | Carlos Lee | .15 | .40 |
| 211 | Josh Hamilton | .50 | 1.25 |
| 212 | Pyotr Ilyich Tchaikovsky | .25 | .60 |
| 213 | Brendan Harris | .15 | .40 |
| 214 | Dustin McGowan | .15 | .40 |
| 215 | Aaron Harang | .15 | .40 |
| 216 | Brett Myers | .15 | .40 |
| 217 | Friedrich Nietzsche | .25 | .60 |
| 218 | John Maine | .15 | .40 |
| 219 | Charles Dickens | .25 | .60 |
| 220 | Erik Bedard | .15 | .40 |
| 221 | Tim Hudson | .15 | .40 |
| 222 | Jeremy Bonderman | .15 | .40 |
| 223 | Nyjer Morgan (RC) | .40 | 1.00 |
| 224 | Johnny Cueto RC | .60 | 1.50 |
| 225 | Roy Oswalt | .15 | .40 |
| 226 | Rich Hill | .15 | .40 |
| 227 | Frederick Douglass | .25 | .60 |
| 228 | Derek Lowe | .15 | .40 |
| 229 | Joe Blanton | .15 | .40 |
| 230 | Carlos Beltran | .25 | .60 |
| 231 | Huston Street | .15 | .40 |
| 232 | Davy Crockett | .25 | .60 |
| 233 | Pluto | .25 | .60 |
| 234 | Jered Weaver | .15 | .40 |
| 235 | Dan Haren | .15 | .40 |
| 236 | Alex Gordon | .25 | .60 |
| 237 | Zack Greinke | .15 | .40 |
| 238 | Todd Clever | .25 | .60 |
| 239 | Brian Bannister | .15 | .40 |
| 240 | Magglio Ordonez | .25 | .60 |
| 241 | Ryan Garko | .15 | .40 |
| 242 | Takudzwa Ngwenya | .25 | .60 |
| 243 | Gil Meche | .15 | .40 |
| 244 | Mark Teahen | .15 | .40 |
| 245 | Carlos Guillen | .15 | .40 |
| 246 | Jeff Kent | .15 | .40 |
| 247 | Lisa Leslie | .40 | 1.00 |
| 248 | Lastings Milledge | .15 | .40 |
| 249 | Serena Williams | .50 | 1.25 |
| 250 | Ichiro Suzuki | .60 | 1.50 |
| 251 | Matt Cain | .15 | .40 |
| 252 | Calix Crabbe (RC) | .40 | 1.00 |
| 253 | Nick Blackburn RC | .60 | 1.50 |
| 254 | Hunter Pence | .40 | 1.00 |
| 255 | Cole Hamels | .40 | 1.00 |
| 256 | Garret Anderson | .15 | .40 |
| 257 | Luis Gonzalez | .15 | .40 |
| 258 | Eric Chavez | .15 | .40 |
| 259 | Francisco Rodriguez | .15 | .40 |
| 260 | Mark Teixeira | .25 | .60 |
| 261 | Bob Motley | .25 | .60 |
| 262 | Mark Spitz | .25 | .60 |
| 263 | Yadier Molina | .15 | .40 |
| 264 | Adam Jones | .15 | .40 |
| 265 | Brian Roberts | .25 | .60 |
| 266 | Matt Kemp | .40 | 1.00 |
| 267 | Andrew Miller | .25 | .60 |
| 268 | Dean Karnazes | .25 | .60 |
| 269 | Gary Sheffield | .15 | .40 |
| 270 | Lance Berkman | .25 | .60 |
| 271 | Paul Lo Duca | .15 | .40 |
| 272 | Matt Tolbert RC | .60 | 1.50 |
| 273 | Jay Bruce (RC) | 1.50 | 4.00 |
| 274 | John Smoltz | .40 | 1.00 |
| 275 | Nick Markakis | .25 | .60 |
| 276 | Oscar Wilde | .25 | .60 |
| 277 | Dontrelle Willis | .15 | .40 |
| 278 | Kevin Van Dam | .25 | .60 |
| 279 | Jim Edmonds | .25 | .60 |
| 280 | Brandon Webb | .25 | .60 |
| 281 | Joe Nathan | .15 | .40 |
| 282 | Jeanette Lee | .25 | .60 |
| 283 | Andrew Litz | .25 | .60 |
| 284 | Daisuke Matsuzaka | .50 | 1.25 |
| 285 | Brandon Phillips | .15 | .40 |
| 286 | Pat Burrell | .15 | .40 |
| 287 | Chris Carpenter | .15 | .40 |
| 288 | Pete Weber | .25 | .60 |
| 289 | Derek Lee | .25 | .60 |
| 290 | Ken Griffey Jr. | .60 | 1.50 |
| 291 | Rich Thompson RC | .60 | 1.50 |
| 292 | Elijah Dukes | .15 | .40 |
| 293 | Pedro Feliz | .15 | .40 |
| 294 | Torii Hunter | .15 | .40 |
| 295 | Chone Figgins | .15 | .40 |
| 296 | Hideki Okajima | .15 | .40 |
| 297 | Max Scherzer RC | 1.00 | 2.50 |
| 298 | Greg Smith RC | .40 | 1.00 |
| 299 | Rafael Furcal | .15 | .40 |
| 300 | Ryan Howard | .50 | 1.25 |
| 301 | Felix Pie SP | 1.25 | 3.00 |
| 302 | Brad Lidge SP | 1.25 | 3.00 |
| 303 | Jason Bay SP | 1.25 | 3.00 |
| 304 | Victor Hugo SP | 1.25 | 3.00 |
| 305 | Randy Johnson SP | 1.25 | 3.00 |
| 306 | Carlos Gomez SP | 1.25 | 3.00 |
| 307 | Pat Neshek SP | 1.25 | 3.00 |
| 308 | Jed Lowrie SP (RC) | 1.25 | 3.00 |
| 309 | Ryan Church SP | 1.25 | 3.00 |
| 310 | Michael Bourn SP | 1.25 | 3.00 |
| 311 | B.J. Ryan SP | 1.25 | 3.00 |
| 312 | Brandon Wood SP | 1.25 | 3.00 |
| 313 | Harriet Beecher Stowe SP | 1.25 | 3.00 |
| 314 | Mike Cameron SP | 1.25 | 3.00 |
| 315 | Tom Glavine SP | 1.25 | 3.00 |
| 316 | Ervin Santana SP | 1.25 | 3.00 |
| 317 | Geoff Jenkins SP | 1.25 | 3.00 |
| 318 | Andre Ethier SP | 1.25 | 3.00 |
| 319 | Jason Giambi SP | 1.25 | 3.00 |
| 320 | Dmitri Young SP | 1.25 | 3.00 |
| 321 | Wily Mo Pena SP | 1.25 | 3.00 |
| 322 | Hank Blalock SP | 1.25 | 3.00 |
| 323 | James Bowie SP | 1.25 | 3.00 |
| 324 | Casey Kotchman SP | 1.25 | 3.00 |
| 325 | Stephen Drew SP | 1.25 | 3.00 |
| 326 | Adam Kennedy SP | 1.25 | 3.00 |
| 327 | A.J. Pierzynski SP | 1.25 | 3.00 |
| 328 | Richie Sexson SP | 1.25 | 3.00 |
| 329 | Jeff Clement SP (RC) | 1.25 | 3.00 |
| 330 | Luke Hochevar SP RC | 1.25 | 3.00 |
| 331 | Luis Castillo SP | 1.25 | 3.00 |
| 332 | Dave Roberts SP | 1.25 | 3.00 |
| 333 | Coco Crisp SP | 1.25 | 3.00 |
| 334 | Jo-Jo Reyes SP | 1.25 | 3.00 |
| 335 | Phil Hughes SP | 1.25 | 3.00 |
| 336 | Allen Fisher SP | 1.25 | 3.00 |
| 337 | Jason Schmidt SP | 1.25 | 3.00 |
| 338 | Placido Polanco SP | 1.25 | 3.00 |
| 339 | Jack Cust SP | 1.25 | 3.00 |
| 340 | Carl Crawford SP | 1.25 | 3.00 |
| 341 | Ty Wigginton SP | 1.25 | 3.00 |
| 342 | Aubrey Huff SP | 1.25 | 3.00 |
| 343 | Bengie Molina SP | 1.25 | 3.00 |
| 344 | Matt Diaz SP | 1.25 | 3.00 |
| 345 | Francisco Liriano SP | 1.25 | 3.00 |
| 346 | Brandon Boggs SP (RC) | 1.25 | 3.00 |
| 347 | David DeJesus SP | 1.25 | 3.00 |
| 348 | Justin Masterson SP RC | 1.50 | 4.00 |
| 349 | Frank Morris SP | 1.25 | 3.00 |
| 350 | Kevin Youkilis SP | 1.25 | 3.00 |
| NNO | Kosuke Fukudome | 10.00 | 25.00 |
| NNO | Framed Original | 50.00 | 100.00 |

## 2009 Topps Allen and Ginter

|  | | |
|---|---|---|
| COMPLETE SET (350) | 30.00 | 60.00 |
| COMP.SET w/o SP's (300) | 12.50 | 30.00 |
| COMMON CARD (1-300) | .15 | .40 |
| COMMON RC (1-300) | .40 | 1.00 |
| COMMON SP (301-350) | 1.25 | 3.00 |
| SP STATED ODDS 1:2 HOBBY | | |
| 1 Jay Bruce | .40 | 1.00 |
| 2 Zack Greinke | .25 | .60 |
| 3 Manny Parra | .15 | .40 |
| 4 Jorge Posada | .25 | .60 |
| 5 Luke Hochevar | .15 | .40 |
| 6 Adam Eaton | .15 | .40 |
| 7 John Smoltz | .40 | 1.00 |
| 8 Matt Cain | .15 | .40 |
| 9 Ryan Theriot | .15 | .40 |
| 10 Chone Figgins | .15 | .40 |
| 11 Jacoby Ellsbury | .40 | 1.00 |
| 12 Jermaine Dye | .15 | .40 |
| 13 Travis Hafner | .15 | .40 |
| 14 Troy Tulowitzki | .25 | .60 |
| 15 Alfred Nobel | .15 | .40 |
| 16 Josh Johnson | .15 | .40 |
| 17 Manny Ramirez | .40 | 1.00 |
| 18 Clyde Parris | .40 | 1.00 |
| 19 Mike Pelfrey | .15 | .40 |
| 20 Adam Jones | .25 | .60 |
| 21 Robinson Cano | .25 | .60 |
| 22 Mariano Rivera | .25 | .60 |
| 23 Kristin Armstrong | .15 | .40 |
| 24 Steve Wiebe | .15 | .40 |
| 25 Evan Longoria | .60 | 1.50 |
| 26 Charles Goodyear | .15 | .40 |
| 27 Chien-Ming Wang | .40 | 1.00 |
| 28 Ervin Santana | .15 | .40 |
| 29 Jonathan Papelbon | .25 | .60 |
| 30 Ryan Howard | .50 | 1.25 |
| 31 Nick Markakis | .25 | .60 |
| 32 Jeremy Bonderman | .15 | .40 |
| 33 Florence Nightingale | .15 | .40 |
| 34 Ryan Dempster | .15 | .40 |
| 35 Geovany Soto | .25 | .60 |
| 36 Joba Chamberlain | .50 | 1.25 |
| 37 Andre Ethier | .25 | .60 |
| 38 Troy Glaus | .15 | .40 |
| 39 Hanley Ramirez | .40 | 1.00 |
| 40 Jeremy Hermida | .15 | .40 |
| 41 Victor Martinez | .25 | .60 |
| 42 Mark Buehrle | .15 | .40 |
| 43 Koji Uehara RC | 1.00 | 2.50 |
| 44 Freddy Sanchez | .15 | .40 |
| 45 Derek Lee | .25 | .60 |
| 46 Brian Roberts | .15 | .40 |
| 47 J.J. Hardy | .15 | .40 |
| 48 Brigham Young | .15 | .40 |
| 49 Ubaldo Jimenez | .15 | .40 |
| 50 Pat Neshek | .25 | .60 |
| 51 Ryan Perry RC | 1.00 | 2.50 |
| 52 Aaron Hill | .15 | .40 |
| 53 Clayton Kershaw | .40 | 1.00 |
| 54 Carlos Guillen | .15 | .40 |
| 55 Alex Rios | .15 | .40 |
| 56 Daniel Murphy RC | 1.00 | 2.50 |
| 57 Frank Evans | .25 | .60 |
| 58 Brad Hawpe | .15 | .40 |
| 59 Mark Reynolds | .25 | .60 |
| 60 Matt Holliday | .25 | .60 |
| 61 Burke Kenny | .15 | .40 |
| 62 Dan Uggla | .15 | .40 |
| 63 Andrew Miller | .15 | .40 |
| 64 Jordan Zimmermann RC | 1.00 | 2.50 |
| 65 Dexter Fowler (RC) | .60 | 1.50 |
| 66 Alex Rodriguez | .60 | 1.50 |
| 67 Ian Kinsler | .25 | .60 |
| 68 Jamie Moyer | .15 | .40 |
| 69 James Loney | .25 | .60 |
| 70 Rick Ankiel | .15 | .40 |
| 71 Albert Pujols | 1.00 | 2.50 |
| 72 Carlos Lee | .15 | .40 |
| 73 Vernon Wells | .15 | .40 |
| 74 Matt Tuiasosopo (RC) | .40 | 1.00 |
| 75 David Wright | .50 | 1.25 |
| 76 Brandon Phillips | .15 | .40 |
| 77 Francisco Liriano | .15 | .40 |
| 78 Eric Byrnes | .15 | .40 |
| 79 Electron | .15 | .40 |
| 80 Joe Martinez RC | .60 | 1.50 |
| 81 Willie Williams | .40 | 1.00 |
| 82 Justin Verlander | .25 | .60 |
| 83 Ludwig van Beethoven | .15 | .40 |
| 84 Justin Upton | .25 | .60 |
| 85 Jason Jaramillo (RC) | .40 | 1.00 |
| 86 Michael Cuddyer | .15 | .40 |
| 87 Aaron Cook | .15 | .40 |
| 88 Brad Penny | .15 | .40 |
| 89 Elvis Andrus RC | 1.00 | 2.50 |
| 90 Bobby Crosby | .15 | .40 |
| 91 Alex Gordon | .25 | .60 |
| 92 Joe Mauer | .40 | 1.00 |
| 93 David DeJesus | .15 | .40 |
| 94 Paul Maholm | .15 | .40 |
| 95 David Patton RC | .60 | 1.50 |
| 96 Geronimo | .15 | .40 |
| 97 Art Pennington | .40 | 1.00 |
| 98 Josh Whitesell RC | .60 | 1.50 |
| 99 Chris Duncan | .15 | .40 |
| 100 Ichiro Suzuki | .60 | 1.50 |
| 101 Andrew Bailey RC | .60 | 1.50 |
| 102 Edinson Volquez | .15 | .40 |
| 103 Aaron Harang | .15 | .40 |
| 104 Jeff Francoeur | .25 | .60 |
| 105 Kurt Suzuki | .15 | .40 |
| 106 Mike Jacobs | .15 | .40 |
| 107 Bryan Berg | .15 | .40 |
| 108 Alamo | .15 | .40 |
| 109 Samuel Morse | .15 | .40 |
| 110 Kevin Youkilis | .25 | .60 |
| 111 Jason Giambi | .15 | .40 |
| 112 Milito Navarro | .40 | 1.00 |
| 113 Rafael Furcal | .15 | .40 |
| 114 Hideki Matsui | .40 | 1.00 |
| 115 Ryan Doumit | .15 | .40 |
| 116 Charles Darwin | .15 | .40 |
| 117 Blake DeWitt | .25 | .60 |
| 118 Scott Olsen | .15 | .40 |
| 119 Scott Lewis (RC) | .40 | 1.00 |
| 120 Edwin Moreno (RC) | .40 | 1.00 |
| 121 Ryan Church | .15 | .40 |
| 122 Dontrelle Willis | .15 | .40 |
| 123 Barry Zito | .15 | .40 |
| 124 Donald Veal RC | .60 | 1.50 |
| 125 Randy Johnson | .40 | 1.00 |
| 126 Trevor Crowe RC | .60 | 1.50 |
| 127 J.D. Drew | .15 | .40 |
| 128 Red Moore | .40 | 1.00 |
| 129 Brian Giles | .15 | .40 |
| 130 Johnny Damon | .25 | .60 |
| 131 Rickie Weeks | .15 | .40 |
| 132 Anna Tunnicliffe | .15 | .40 |
| 133 Roy Halladay | .25 | .60 |
| 134 Jered Weaver | .15 | .40 |
| 135 Jeff Suppan | .15 | .40 |
| 136 Mickey Mantle | 1.25 | 3.00 |
| 137 Mark Teixeira | .40 | 1.00 |
| 138 Garrett Atkins | .15 | .40 |
| 139 Daisuke Matsuzaka | .60 | 1.50 |
| 140 Loren Opstedahl | .40 | 1.00 |
| 141 Carlos Zambrano | .15 | .40 |
| 142 LaShawn Merritt | .15 | .40 |
| 143 Robbie Maddison | .15 | .40 |
| 144 Joakim Soria | .15 | .40 |
| 145 Todd Wellemeyer | .15 | .40 |
| 146 Rich Harden | .15 | .40 |
| 147 Coco Crisp | .15 | .40 |
| 148 Brad Lidge | .15 | .40 |
| 149 Chipper Jones | .40 | 1.00 |
| 150 Prince Fielder | .40 | 1.00 |
| 151 Cole Hamels | .25 | .60 |
| 152 Phil Coke RC | .60 | 1.50 |
| 153 CC Sabathia | .25 | .60 |
| 154 Corey Hart | .15 | .40 |
| 155 Yadier Molina | .25 | .60 |
| 156 Jayson Werth | .25 | .60 |
| 157 Jason Motte (RC) | .40 | 1.00 |
| 158 Sigmund Freud | .15 | .40 |
| 159 Denard Span | .25 | .60 |
| 160 Max Scherzer | .25 | .60 |
| 161 Justin Morneau | .25 | .60 |
| 162 Shane Victorino | .15 | .40 |
| 163 Matt Garza | .15 | .40 |
| 164 Erik Bedard | .15 | .40 |
| 165 Chase Utley | .40 | 1.00 |
| 166 Gil Meche | .15 | .40 |
| 167 Jim Thome | .25 | .60 |
| 168 Adrian Gonzalez | .25 | .60 |
| 169 Kazuo Matsui | .15 | .40 |
| 170 Lance Berkman | .25 | .60 |
| 171 Brett Anderson RC | .60 | 1.50 |
| 172 Jarrod Saltalamacchia | .15 | .40 |
| 173 Francisco Rodriguez | .25 | .60 |
| 174 John Lannan | .15 | .40 |
| 175 Alfonso Soriano | .25 | .60 |
| 176 Ramiro Pena RC | .60 | 1.50 |
| 177 David Freese RC | 1.00 | 2.50 |
| 178 Adam LaRoche | .15 | .40 |
| 179 Trevor Hoffman | .25 | .60 |
| 180 Russell Martin | .25 | .60 |
| 181 Aaron Rowand | .15 | .40 |
| 182 Jose Reyes | .40 | 1.00 |
| 183 Pedro Feliz | .15 | .40 |
| 184 Chris Young | .15 | .40 |
| 185 Dustin Pedroia | .50 | 1.25 |
| 186 Adrian Beltre | .15 | .40 |
| 187 Brett Myers | .15 | .40 |
| 188 Chris Davis | .25 | .60 |
| 189 Casey Kotchman | .15 | .40 |
| 190 B.J. Upton | .25 | .60 |
| 191 Hiroki Kuroda | .15 | .40 |
| 192 Ryan Zimmerman | .25 | .60 |
| 193 Khalil Greene | .15 | .40 |
| 194 Brandon Morrow | .15 | .40 |
| 195 Kevin Kouzmanoff | .15 | .40 |
| 196 Joey Votto | .25 | .60 |
| 197 Jhonny Peralta | .15 | .40 |
| 198 Raul Ibanez | .25 | .60 |
| 199 James McDonald RC | .60 | 1.50 |
| 200 Carlos Quentin | .15 | .40 |
| 201 Travis Snider RC | 1.00 | 2.50 |
| 202 Conor Jackson | .15 | .40 |
| 203 Scott Kazmir | .25 | .60 |
| 204 Casey Blake | .15 | .40 |
| 205 Ryan Braun | .50 | 1.25 |
| 206 Miguel Tejada | .15 | .40 |
| 207 Jack Cust | .15 | .40 |
| 208 Michael Young | .25 | .60 |
| 209 St. Patrick's Cathedral | .15 | .40 |
| 210 Johan Santana | .40 | 1.00 |
| 211 Kevin Millwood | .15 | .40 |
| 212 David Zagunis | .15 | .40 |
| 213 Stephanie Brown Trafton | .25 | .60 |
| 214 Adam Dunn | .25 | .60 |
| 215 Jed Lowrie | .15 | .40 |
| 216 Derek Lowe | .15 | .40 |
| 217 Jorge Cantu | .15 | .40 |
| 218 Bobby Parnell RC | .60 | 1.50 |
| 219 Nate McLouth | .15 | .40 |
| 220 Suez Canal | .15 | .40 |
| 221 Brandon Webb | .25 | .60 |
| 222 Akinori Iwamura | .15 | .40 |
| 223 Scott Rolen | .40 | 1.00 |
| 224 Tim Lincecum | .50 | 1.25 |
| 225 David Price RC | 1.25 | 3.00 |
| 226 Ricky Romero (RC) | .40 | 1.00 |
| 227 Nelson Cruz | .15 | .40 |
| 228 Will Simpson/Archie Bunker | .15 | .40 |
| 229 Mark Ellis | .15 | .40 |
| 230 Torii Hunter | .25 | .60 |
| 231 David Murphy | .15 | .40 |
| 232 Everth Cabrera RC | .60 | 1.50 |
| 233 John Lackey | .15 | .40 |
| 234 Wyatt Earp | .15 | .40 |
| 235 Roy Oswalt | .25 | .60 |
| 236 Edgar Renteria | .15 | .40 |
| 237 Walton Glenn Eller | .15 | .40 |
| 238 Vincent Van Gogh | .15 | .40 |
| 239 Chris Carpenter | .25 | .60 |
| 240 Hank Blalock | .15 | .40 |
| 241 Trevor Cahill RC | .60 | 1.50 |
| 242 Mark Teahen | .15 | .40 |
| 243 Alexander Cartwright | .15 | .40 |
| 244 Carlos Beltran | .15 | .40 |
| 245 Todd Helton | .25 | .60 |
| 246 General Custer | .15 | .40 |
| 247 Jeff Clement | .15 | .40 |
| 248 Colby Rasmus (RC) | .60 | 1.50 |
| 249 John Higby | .15 | .40 |
| 250 Grady Sizemore | .25 | .60 |
| 251 Carl Crawford | .25 | .60 |
| 252 Lastings Milledge | .15 | .40 |
| 253 Miguel Cabrera | .40 | 1.00 |
| 254 John Maine | .15 | .40 |
| 255 Aramis Ramirez | .15 | .40 |

| | | | | | | | | | | |
|---|---|---|---|---|---|---|---|---|---|---|
| ❑ 256 Jose Lopez | .15 | .40 | ❑ 344 Chris Young SP | 1.25 | 3.00 | ❑ 78 Corey Hart | | .10 | .25 |
| ❑ 257 Heinrich Hertz | .15 | .40 | ❑ 345 Carlos Delgado SP | 1.25 | 3.00 | ❑ 79 Brad Hawpe | | .10 | .25 |
| ❑ 258 Felix Hernandez | .25 | .60 | ❑ 346 Dominique Wilkins SP | 1.25 | 3.00 | ❑ 80 Todd Helton | | .15 | .40 |
| ❑ 259 Napoleon Bonaparte | .15 | .40 | ❑ 347 Yovani Gallardo SP | 1.25 | 3.00 | ❑ 81 Jeremy Hermida | | .10 | .25 |
| ❑ 260 Louis Braille | .15 | .40 | ❑ 348 Justin Masterson SP | 1.25 | 3.00 | ❑ 82 Ramon Hernandez | | .10 | .25 |
| ❑ 261 John Danks | .15 | .40 | ❑ 349 Aubrey Huff SP | 1.25 | 3.00 | ❑ 83 Felix Hernandez | | .15 | .40 |
| ❑ 262 Maggio Ordonez | .25 | .60 | ❑ 350 Jimmy Rollins SP | 1.25 | 3.00 | ❑ 84 Trevor Hoffman | | .10 | .25 |
| ❑ 263 Brian Duensing RC | .60 | 1.50 | **2009 Topps Attax** | | | ❑ 85 Orlando Hudson | | .10 | .25 |
| ❑ 264 Carlos Pena | .25 | .60 | | | | ❑ 86 Tim Hudson | | .10 | .25 |
| ❑ 265 Paul Konerko | .15 | .40 | ❑ COMPLETE SET (220) | 15.00 | 40.00 | ❑ 87 Aubrey Huff | | .10 | .25 |
| ❑ 266 Johnny Cueto | .15 | .40 | ❑ COMMON CARD | .10 | .25 | ❑ 88 Torii Hunter | | .10 | .25 |
| ❑ 267 Melvin Mora | .15 | .40 | ❑ 1 Bobby Abreu | .10 | .25 | ❑ 89 Chris Iannetta | | .10 | .25 |
| ❑ 268 Andy Pettitte | .25 | .60 | ❑ 2 Garret Anderson | .10 | .25 | ❑ 90 Raul Ibanez | | .15 | .40 |
| ❑ 269 Brian McCann | .25 | .60 | ❑ 3 Rick Ankiel | .15 | .40 | ❑ 91 Akinori Iwamura | | .15 | .40 |
| ❑ 270 Josh Outman RC | .60 | 1.50 | ❑ 4 Mike Aviles | .10 | .25 | ❑ 92 Conor Jackson | | .10 | .25 |
| ❑ 271 Jair Jurrjens | .25 | .60 | ❑ 5 Rocco Baldelli | .10 | .25 | ❑ 93 Bobby Jenks | | .10 | .25 |
| ❑ 272 Brad Nelson (RC) | .40 | 1.00 | ❑ 6 Jason Bay | .15 | .40 | ❑ 94 Derek Jeter | | .60 | 1.50 |
| ❑ 273 Jason Bay | .25 | .60 | ❑ 7 Josh Beckett | .15 | .40 | ❑ 95 Ubaldo Jimenez | | .10 | .25 |
| ❑ 274 Josh Hamilton | .40 | 1.00 | ❑ 8 Erik Bedard | .10 | .25 | ❑ 96 Kenji Johjima | | .15 | .40 |
| ❑ 275 Vladimir Guerrero | .40 | 1.00 | ❑ 9 Ronnie Belliard | .10 | .25 | ❑ 97 Kelly Johnson | | .10 | .25 |
| ❑ 276 Michael Phelps | .75 | 2.00 | ❑ 10 Carlos Beltran | .10 | .25 | ❑ 98 Randy Johnson | | .25 | .60 |
| ❑ 277 Kerry Wood | .15 | .40 | ❑ 11 Adrian Beltre | .10 | .25 | ❑ 99 Adam Jones | | .15 | .40 |
| ❑ 278 Herb Simpson | .40 | 1.00 | ❑ 12 Yuniesky Betancourt | .10 | .25 | ❑ 100 Scott Kazmir | | .15 | .40 |
| ❑ 279 Jon Lester | .25 | .60 | ❑ 13 Chad Billingsley | .10 | .25 | ❑ 101 Matt Kemp | | .25 | .60 |
| ❑ 280 Shin-Soo Choo | .15 | .40 | ❑ 14 Casey Blake | .10 | .25 | ❑ 102 Howie Kendrick | | .10 | .25 |
| ❑ 281 Jake Peavy | .25 | .60 | ❑ 15 Hank Blalock | .10 | .25 | ❑ 103 Jeff Kent | | .10 | .25 |
| ❑ 282 Eric Chavez | .15 | .40 | ❑ 16 Milton Bradley | .10 | .25 | ❑ 104 Clayton Kershaw | | .25 | .60 |
| ❑ 283 Mike Aviles | .15 | .40 | ❑ 17 Ryan Braun | .30 | .75 | ❑ 105 Ian Kinsler | | .15 | .40 |
| ❑ 284 Kenshin Kawakami RC | 1.00 | 2.50 | ❑ 18 Mark Buehrle | .10 | .25 | ❑ 106 Paul Konerko | | .10 | .25 |
| ❑ 285 George Kottaras (RC) | .40 | 1.00 | ❑ 19 A.J. Burnett | .15 | .40 | ❑ 107 Casey Kotchman | | .10 | .25 |
| ❑ 286 Matt Kemp | .40 | 1.00 | ❑ 20 Pat Burrell | .15 | .40 | ❑ 108 Kevin Kouzmanoff | | .10 | .25 |
| ❑ 287 James Shields | .15 | .40 | ❑ 21 Billy Butler | .10 | .25 | ❑ 109 Hiroki Kuroda | | .10 | .25 |
| ❑ 288 Joe Saunders | .15 | .40 | ❑ 22 Eric Byrnes | .10 | .25 | ❑ 110 Adam LaRoche | | .10 | .25 |
| ❑ 289 Milky Way | .15 | .40 | ❑ 23 Orlando Cabrera | .10 | .25 | ❑ 111 Derek Lee | | .15 | .40 |
| ❑ 290 Cal Osterman | .50 | 1.25 | ❑ 24 Daniel Cabrera | .10 | .25 | ❑ 112 Carlos Lee | | .10 | .25 |
| ❑ 291 Josh Beckett | .25 | .60 | ❑ 25 Mike Cameron | .10 | .25 | ❑ 113 Jon Lester | | .15 | .40 |
| ❑ 292 Oliver Perez | .15 | .40 | ❑ 26 Jorge Cantu | .10 | .25 | ❑ 114 Fred Lewis | | .10 | .25 |
| ❑ 293 Ian Snell | .15 | .40 | ❑ 27 Fausto Carmona | .10 | .25 | ❑ 115 Brad Lidge | | .10 | .25 |
| ❑ 294 Tim Hudson | .15 | .40 | ❑ 28 Joba Chamberlain | .30 | .75 | ❑ 116 Francisco Liriano | | .10 | .25 |
| ❑ 295 Brett Gardner | .15 | .40 | ❑ 29 Eric Chavez | .10 | .25 | ❑ 117 James Loney | | .15 | .40 |
| ❑ 296 Bobby Abreu | .15 | .40 | ❑ 30 Ryan Church | .10 | .25 | ❑ 118 Jose Lopez | | .10 | .25 |
| ❑ 297 Kolan McConiughey | .15 | .40 | ❑ 31 Carl Crawford | .15 | .40 | ❑ 119 Derek Lowe | | .10 | .25 |
| ❑ 298 Dan Haren | .15 | .40 | ❑ 32 Joe Crede | .10 | .25 | ❑ 120 Mike Lowell | | .10 | .25 |
| ❑ 299 Shairon Martis RC | .60 | 1.50 | ❑ 33 Bobby Crosby | .10 | .25 | ❑ 121 Jed Lowrie | | .15 | .40 |
| ❑ 300 David Ortiz | .25 | .60 | ❑ 34 Johnny Cueto | .10 | .25 | ❑ 122 Ryan Ludwick | | .10 | .25 |
| ❑ 301 Jonathan Sanchez SP | 1.25 | 3.00 | ❑ 35 Johnny Damon | .15 | .40 | ❑ 123 John Maine | | .10 | .25 |
| ❑ 302 Stephen Drew SP | 1.25 | 3.00 | ❑ 36 Chris Davis | .10 | .25 | ❑ 124 Victor Martinez | | .15 | .40 |
| ❑ 303 Rocco Baldelli SP | 1.25 | 3.00 | ❑ 37 David DeJesus | .10 | .25 | ❑ 125 Pedro Martinez | | .15 | .40 |
| ❑ 304 Yunel Escobar SP | 1.25 | 3.00 | ❑ 38 Carlos Delgado | .10 | .25 | ❑ 126 Justin Masterson | | .10 | .25 |
| ❑ 305 Javier Vazquez SP | 1.25 | 3.00 | ❑ 39 Ryan Dempster | .10 | .25 | ❑ 127 Kaz Matsui | | .10 | .25 |
| ❑ 306 Cliff Lee SP | 1.25 | 3.00 | ❑ 40 Mark DeRosa | .10 | .25 | ❑ 128 Hideki Matsui | | .25 | .60 |
| ❑ 307 Hunter Pence SP | 1.25 | 3.00 | ❑ 41 Matt Diaz | .10 | .25 | ❑ 129 Gary Matthews | | .10 | .25 |
| ❑ 308 Fausto Carmona SP | 1.25 | 3.00 | ❑ 42 Ryan Doumit | .10 | .25 | ❑ 130 Joe Mauer | | .25 | .60 |
| ❑ 309 Kosuke Fukudome SP | 1.25 | 3.00 | ❑ 43 Stephen Drew | .10 | .25 | ❑ 131 Cameron Maybin | | .10 | .25 |
| ❑ 310 Old Faithful SP | 1.25 | 3.00 | ❑ 44 J.D. Drew | .10 | .25 | ❑ 132 Brian McCann | | .15 | .40 |
| ❑ 311 Gavin Floyd SP | 1.25 | 3.00 | ❑ 45 Adam Dunn | .15 | .40 | ❑ 133 Lastings Milledge | | .10 | .25 |
| ❑ 312 A.J. Burnett SP | 1.25 | 3.00 | ❑ 46 Jermaine Dye | .10 | .25 | ❑ 134 Bengie Molina | | .10 | .25 |
| ❑ 313 Jeff Francis SP | 1.25 | 3.00 | ❑ 47 Jim Edmonds | .15 | .40 | ❑ 135 Yadier Molina | | .15 | .40 |
| ❑ 314 Chad Billingsley SP | 1.25 | 3.00 | ❑ 48 Jacoby Ellsbury | .25 | .60 | ❑ 136 Melvin Mora | | .10 | .25 |
| ❑ 315 Andy LaRoche SP | 1.25 | 3.00 | ❑ 49 Edwin Encarnacion | .10 | .25 | ❑ 137 David Murphy | | .10 | .25 |
| ❑ 316 Rick Porcello SP RC | 2.50 | 6.00 | ❑ 50 Yunel Escobar | .10 | .25 | ❑ 138 Brett Myers | | .10 | .25 |
| ❑ 317 John Baker SP | 1.25 | 3.00 | ❑ 51 Andre Ethier | .15 | .40 | ❑ 139 Xavier Nady | | .10 | .25 |
| ❑ 318 Delmon Young SP | 1.25 | 3.00 | ❑ 52 Pedro Feliz | .10 | .25 | ❑ 140 Joe Nathan | | .10 | .25 |
| ❑ 319 Gary Sheffield SP | 1.25 | 3.00 | ❑ 53 Chone Figgins | .10 | .25 | ❑ 141 Maggio Ordonez | | .15 | .40 |
| ❑ 320 B.J. Ryan SP | 1.25 | 3.00 | ❑ 54 Jeff Francoeur | .15 | .40 | ❑ 142 David Ortiz | | .15 | .40 |
| ❑ 321 Kelly Shoppach SP | 1.25 | 3.00 | ❑ 55 Kosuke Fukudome | .25 | .60 | ❑ 143 Roy Oswalt | | .15 | .40 |
| ❑ 322 Chris Volstad SP | 1.25 | 3.00 | ❑ 56 Rafael Furcal | .10 | .25 | ❑ 144 Lyle Overbay | | .10 | .25 |
| ❑ 323 Derek Jeter SP | 3.00 | 8.00 | ❑ 57 Ryan Garko | .10 | .25 | ❑ 145 Jonathan Papelbon | | .15 | .40 |
| ❑ 324 Wladimir Balentien SP | 1.25 | 3.00 | ❑ 58 Jon Garland | .10 | .25 | ❑ 146 Dustin Pedroia | | .30 | .75 |
| ❑ 325 Dioner Navarro SP | 1.25 | 3.00 | ❑ 59 Matt Garza | .10 | .25 | ❑ 147 Mike Pelfrey | | .10 | .25 |
| ❑ 326 Cameron Maybin SP | 1.25 | 3.00 | ❑ 60 Jason Giambi | .10 | .25 | ❑ 148 Carlos Pena | | .15 | .40 |
| ❑ 327 Kenji Johjima SP | 1.25 | 3.00 | ❑ 61 Brian Giles | .10 | .25 | ❑ 149 Hunter Pence | | .15 | .40 |
| ❑ 328 Matt LaPorta SP RC | 2.00 | 5.00 | ❑ 62 Troy Glaus | .10 | .25 | ❑ 150 Jhonny Peralta | | .10 | .25 |
| ❑ 329 Carlos Gomez SP | 1.25 | 3.00 | ❑ 63 Carlos Gomez | .10 | .25 | ❑ 151 Andy Pettitte | | .15 | .40 |
| ❑ 330 Cristian Guzman SP | 1.25 | 3.00 | ❑ 64 Adrian Gonzalez | .15 | .40 | ❑ 152 Brandon Phillips | | .10 | .25 |
| ❑ 331 Jeff Samardzija SP | 1.25 | 3.00 | ❑ 65 Curtis Granderson | .25 | .60 | ❑ 153 Juan Pierre | | .10 | .25 |
| ❑ 332 Curtis Granderson SP | 1.25 | 3.00 | ❑ 66 Ken Griffey Jr. | .40 | 1.00 | ❑ 154 A.J. Pierzynski | | .10 | .25 |
| ❑ 333 Nick Swisher SP | 1.25 | 3.00 | ❑ 67 Vladimir Guerrero | .25 | .60 | ❑ 155 Placido Polanco | | .10 | .25 |
| ❑ 334 Pat Burrell SP | 1.25 | 3.00 | ❑ 68 Carlos Guillen | .10 | .25 | ❑ 156 Jorge Posada | | .15 | .40 |
| ❑ 335 Justin Duchscherer SP | 1.25 | 3.00 | ❑ 69 Jose Guillen | .10 | .25 | ❑ 157 David Price | | .30 | .75 |
| ❑ 336 Ryan Ludwick SP | 1.25 | 3.00 | ❑ 70 Cristian Guzman | .10 | .25 | ❑ 158 J.J. Putz | | .10 | .25 |
| ❑ 337 Billy Butler SP | 1.25 | 3.00 | ❑ 71 Travis Hafner | .10 | .25 | ❑ 159 Aramis Ramirez | | .10 | .25 |
| ❑ 338 Jason Wong SP | 1.25 | 3.00 | ❑ 72 Bill Hall | .10 | .25 | ❑ 160 Manny Ramirez | | .25 | .60 |
| ❑ 339 Jordan Schafer SP (RC) | 1.25 | 3.00 | ❑ 73 Cole Hamels | .25 | .60 | ❑ 161 Edgar Renteria | | .10 | .25 |
| ❑ 340 Richard Gatling SP | 1.25 | 3.00 | ❑ 74 Rich Harden | .10 | .25 | ❑ 162 Jose Reyes | | .25 | .60 |
| ❑ 341 Edgar Gonzalez SP | 1.25 | 3.00 | ❑ 75 J.J. Hardy | .15 | .40 | ❑ 163 Mark Reynolds | | .10 | .25 |
| ❑ 342 Sitting Bull SP | 1.25 | 3.00 | ❑ 76 Dan Haren | .10 | .25 | ❑ 164 Alex Rios | | .10 | .25 |
| ❑ 343 Doc Holliday SP | 1.25 | 3.00 | ❑ 77 Brendan Harris | .10 | .25 | ❑ 165 Mariano Rivera | | .15 | .40 |

| | | |
|---|---|---|
| 166 Brian Roberts | .10 | .25 |
| 167 Francisco Rodriguez | .15 | .40 |
| 168 Ivan Rodriguez | .15 | .40 |
| 169 Scott Rolen | .25 | .60 |
| 170 Jimmy Rollins | .15 | .40 |
| 171 Aaron Rowand | .10 | .25 |
| 172 CC Sabathia | .15 | .40 |
| 173 Jarrod Saltalamacchia | .10 | .25 |
| 174 Jeff Samardzija | .15 | .40 |
| 175 Freddy Sanchez | .10 | .25 |
| 176 Max Scherzer | .15 | .40 |
| 177 Brian Schneider | .10 | .25 |
| 178 Luke Scott | .10 | .25 |
| 179 Ben Sheets | .10 | .25 |
| 180 Gary Sheffield | .10 | .25 |
| 181 James Shields | .10 | .25 |
| 182 Grady Sizemore | .15 | .40 |
| 183 Travis Snider | .25 | .60 |
| 184 Chris Snyder | .10 | .25 |
| 185 Geovany Soto | .15 | .40 |
| 186 Denard Span | .15 | .40 |
| 187 Kurt Suzuki | .10 | .25 |
| 188 Mark Teahen | .10 | .25 |
| 189 Mark Teixeira | .25 | .60 |
| 190 Miguel Tejada | .15 | .40 |
| 191 Ryan Theriot | .10 | .25 |
| 192 Jim Thome | .15 | .40 |
| 193 Troy Tulowitzki | .15 | .40 |
| 194 Dan Uggla | .10 | .25 |
| 195 Justin Upton | .15 | .40 |
| 196 B.J. Upton | .15 | .40 |
| 197 Chase Utley | .25 | .60 |
| 198 Jose Valverde | .10 | .25 |
| 199 Jason Varitek | .15 | .40 |
| 200 Javier Vazquez | .10 | .25 |
| 201 Justin Verlander | .15 | .40 |
| 202 Shane Victorino | .15 | .40 |
| 203 Edinson Volquez | .10 | .25 |
| 204 Joey Votto | .15 | .40 |
| 205 Tim Wakefield | .10 | .25 |
| 206 Chien-Ming Wang | .25 | .60 |
| 207 Jered Weaver | .15 | .40 |
| 208 Rickie Weeks | .10 | .25 |
| 209 Vernon Wells | .10 | .25 |
| 210 Jayson Werth | .10 | .25 |
| 211 Ty Wigginton | .10 | .25 |
| 212 Josh Willingham | .10 | .25 |
| 213 Dontrelle Willis | .10 | .25 |
| 214 Randy Winn | .10 | .25 |
| 215 David Wright | .30 | .75 |
| 216 Kevin Youkilis | .15 | .40 |
| 217 Chris Young | .10 | .25 |
| 218 Delmon Young | .15 | .40 |
| 219 Michael Young | .15 | .40 |
| 220 Carlos Zambrano | .10 | .25 |

### 1996 Topps Chrome

| | | |
|---|---|---|
| COMPLETE SET (165) | 20.00 | 50.00 |
| 1 Tony Gwynn STP | .50 | 1.25 |
| 2 Mike Piazza STP | .75 | 2.00 |
| 3 Greg Maddux STP | .75 | 2.00 |
| 4 Jeff Bagwell STP | .30 | .75 |
| 5 Larry Walker STP | .30 | .75 |
| 6 Barry Larkin STP | .30 | .75 |
| 7 Mickey Mantle COMM | 4.00 | 10.00 |
| 8 Tom Glavine STP | .30 | .75 |
| 9 Craig Biggio STP | .30 | .75 |
| 10 Barry Bonds STP | 1.00 | 2.50 |
| 11 Heathcliff Slocumb STP | .30 | .75 |
| 12 Matt Williams STP | .30 | .75 |
| 13 Todd Helton | 1.50 | 4.00 |
| 14 Paul Molitor | .30 | .75 |
| 15 Glenallen Hill | .30 | .75 |
| 16 Troy Percival | .30 | .75 |

| | | |
|---|---|---|
| 17 Albert Belle | .30 | .75 |
| 18 Mark Wohlers | .30 | .75 |
| 19 Kirby Puckett | .75 | 2.00 |
| 20 Mark Grace | .50 | 1.25 |
| 21 J.T. Snow | .30 | .75 |
| 22 David Justice | .30 | .75 |
| 23 Mike Mussina | .50 | 1.25 |
| 24 Bernie Williams | .50 | 1.25 |
| 25 Ron Gant | .30 | .75 |
| 26 Carlos Baerga | .30 | .75 |
| 27 Gary Sheffield | .30 | .75 |
| 28 Cal Ripken 2131 | 2.50 | 6.00 |
| 29 Frank Thomas | .75 | 2.00 |
| 30 Kevin Seitzer | .30 | .75 |
| 31 Joe Carter | .30 | .75 |
| 32 Jeff King | .30 | .75 |
| 33 David Cone | .30 | .75 |
| 34 Eddie Murray | .75 | 2.00 |
| 35 Brian Jordan | .30 | .75 |
| 36 Garret Anderson | .30 | .75 |
| 37 Hideo Nomo | .75 | 2.00 |
| 38 Steve Finley | .30 | .75 |
| 39 Ivan Rodriguez | .50 | 1.25 |
| 40 Quilvio Veras | .30 | .75 |
| 41 Mark McGwire | 2.00 | 5.00 |
| 42 Greg Vaughn | .30 | .75 |
| 43 Randy Johnson | .75 | 2.00 |
| 44 David Segui | .30 | .75 |
| 45 Derek Bell | .30 | .75 |
| 46 John Valentin | .30 | .75 |
| 47 Steve Avery | .30 | .75 |
| 48 Tino Martinez | .50 | 1.25 |
| 49 Shane Reynolds | .30 | .75 |
| 50 Jim Edmonds | .30 | .75 |
| 51 Raul Mondesi | .30 | .75 |
| 52 Chipper Jones | .75 | 2.00 |
| 53 Gregg Jefferies | .30 | .75 |
| 54 Ken Caminiti | .30 | .75 |
| 55 Brian McRae | .30 | .75 |
| 56 Don Mattingly | 2.00 | 5.00 |
| 57 Marty Cordova | .30 | .75 |
| 58 Vinny Castilla | .30 | .75 |
| 59 John Smoltz | .50 | 1.25 |
| 60 Travis Fryman | .30 | .75 |
| 61 Ryan Klesko | .30 | .75 |
| 62 Alex Fernandez | .30 | .75 |
| 63 Dante Bichette | .30 | .75 |
| 64 Eric Karros | .30 | .75 |
| 65 Roger Clemens | 1.50 | 4.00 |
| 66 Randy Myers | .30 | .75 |
| 67 Cal Ripken | 2.50 | 6.00 |
| 68 Rod Beck | .30 | .75 |
| 69 Jack McDowell | .30 | .75 |
| 70 Ken Griffey Jr. | 1.25 | 3.00 |
| 71 Ramon Martinez | .30 | .75 |
| 72 Jason Giambi | .30 | .75 |
| 73 Nomar Garciaparra | 1.25 | 3.00 |
| 74 Billy Wagner | .30 | .75 |
| 75 Todd Greene | .30 | .75 |
| 76 Paul Wilson | .30 | .75 |
| 77 Johnny Damon | .50 | 1.25 |
| 78 Alan Benes | .30 | .75 |
| 79 Karim Garcia | .30 | .75 |
| 80 Derek Jeter | 2.00 | 5.00 |
| 81 Kirby Puckett STP | .50 | 1.25 |
| 82 Cal Ripken STP | 1.25 | 3.00 |
| 83 Albert Belle STP | .30 | .75 |
| 84 Randy Johnson STP | .50 | 1.25 |
| 85 Wade Boggs STP | .50 | 1.25 |
| 86 Carlos Baerga STP | .30 | .75 |
| 87 Ivan Rodriguez STP | .30 | .75 |
| 88 Mike Mussina STP | .30 | .75 |
| 89 Frank Thomas STP | .75 | 2.00 |
| 90 Ken Griffey Jr. STP | .75 | 2.00 |
| 91 Jose Mesa STP | .30 | .75 |
| 92 Matt Morris RC | 2.00 | 5.00 |
| 93 Mike Piazza | 1.25 | 3.00 |
| 94 Edgar Martinez | .30 | .75 |
| 95 Chuck Knoblauch | .30 | .75 |
| 96 Andres Galarraga | .30 | .75 |
| 97 Tony Gwynn | 1.00 | 2.50 |
| 98 Lee Smith | .30 | .75 |
| 99 Sammy Sosa | .75 | 2.00 |
| 100 Jim Thome | .75 | 2.00 |
| 101 Bernard Gilkey | .30 | .75 |
| 102 Brady Anderson | .30 | .75 |
| 103 Rico Brogna | .30 | .75 |
| 104 Len Dykstra | .30 | .75 |

| | | |
|---|---|---|
| 105 Tom Glavine | .50 | 1.25 |
| 106 John Olerud | .30 | .75 |
| 107 Terry Steinbach | .30 | .75 |
| 108 Brian Hunter | .30 | .75 |
| 109 Jay Buhner | .30 | .75 |
| 110 Mo Vaughn | .30 | .75 |
| 111 Jose Mesa | .30 | .75 |
| 112 Brett Butler | .30 | .75 |
| 113 Chili Davis | .30 | .75 |
| 114 Paul O'Neill | .50 | 1.25 |
| 115 Roberto Alomar | .50 | 1.25 |
| 116 Barry Larkin | .50 | 1.25 |
| 117 Marquis Grissom | .30 | .75 |
| 118 Will Clark | .50 | 1.25 |
| 119 Barry Bonds | 2.00 | 5.00 |
| 120 Ozzie Smith | 1.25 | 3.00 |
| 121 Pedro Martinez | .50 | 1.25 |
| 122 Craig Biggio | .30 | .75 |
| 123 Moises Alou | .30 | .75 |
| 124 Robin Ventura | .30 | .75 |
| 125 Greg Maddux | 1.25 | 3.00 |
| 126 Tim Salmon | .50 | 1.25 |
| 127 Wade Boggs | .50 | 1.25 |
| 128 Ismael Valdes | .30 | .75 |
| 129 Juan Gonzalez | .30 | .75 |
| 130 Ray Lankford | .30 | .75 |
| 131 Bobby Bonilla | .30 | .75 |
| 132 Reggie Sanders | .30 | .75 |
| 133 Alex Ochoa | .30 | .75 |
| 134 Mark Loretta | .30 | .75 |
| 135 Jason Kendall | .30 | .75 |
| 136 Brooks Kieschnick | .30 | .75 |
| 137 Chris Snopek | .30 | .75 |
| 138 Ruben Rivera | .30 | .75 |
| 139 Jeff Suppan | .30 | .75 |
| 140 John Wasdin | .30 | .75 |
| 141 Jay Payton | .30 | .75 |
| 142 Rick Krivda | .30 | .75 |
| 143 Jimmy Haynes | .30 | .75 |
| 144 Ryne Sandberg | 1.25 | 3.00 |
| 145 Matt Williams | .30 | .75 |
| 146 Jose Canseco | .50 | 1.25 |
| 147 Larry Walker | .30 | .75 |
| 148 Kevin Appier | .30 | .75 |
| 149 Javy Lopez | .30 | .75 |
| 150 Dennis Eckersley | .30 | .75 |
| 151 Jason Isringhausen | .30 | .75 |
| 152 Dean Palmer | .30 | .75 |
| 153 Jeff Bagwell | .50 | 1.25 |
| 154 Rondell White | .30 | .75 |
| 155 Wally Joyner | .30 | .75 |
| 156 Fred McGriff | .50 | 1.25 |
| 157 Cecil Fielder | .30 | .75 |
| 158 Rafael Palmeiro | .50 | 1.25 |
| 159 Rickey Henderson | .75 | 2.00 |
| 160 Shawon Dunston | .30 | .75 |
| 161 Manny Ramirez | .50 | 1.25 |
| 162 Alex Gonzalez | .30 | .75 |
| 163 Shawn Green | .30 | .75 |
| 164 Kenny Lofton | .30 | .75 |
| 165 Jeff Conine | .30 | .75 |

### 1997 Topps Chrome

| | | |
|---|---|---|
| COMPLETE SET (165) | 20.00 | 50.00 |
| 1 Barry Bonds | 2.00 | 5.00 |
| 2 Jose Valentin | .30 | .75 |
| 3 Brady Anderson | .30 | .75 |
| 4 Wade Boggs | .50 | 1.25 |
| 5 Andres Galarraga | .30 | .75 |
| 6 Rusty Greer | .30 | .75 |
| 7 Derek Jeter | 2.00 | 5.00 |
| 8 Ricky Bottalico | .30 | .75 |
| 9 Mike Piazza | 1.25 | 3.00 |
| 10 Garret Anderson | .30 | .75 |

|  |  | | |
|---|--------|------|------|
| 11 | Jeff King | .30 | .75 |
| 12 | Kevin Appier | .30 | .75 |
| 13 | Mark Grace | .50 | 1.25 |
| 14 | Jeff D'Amico | .30 | .75 |
| 15 | Jay Buhner | .30 | .75 |
| 16 | Hal Morris | .30 | .75 |
| 17 | Harold Baines | .30 | .75 |
| 18 | Jeff Cirillo | .30 | .75 |
| 19 | Tom Glavine | .50 | 1.25 |
| 20 | Andy Pettitte | .50 | 1.25 |
| 21 | Mark McGwire | 2.00 | 5.00 |
| 22 | Chuck Knoblauch | .30 | .75 |
| 23 | Raul Mondesi | .30 | .75 |
| 24 | Albert Belle | .30 | .75 |
| 25 | Trevor Hoffman | .30 | .75 |
| 26 | Eric Young | .30 | .75 |
| 27 | Brian McRae | .30 | .75 |
| 28 | Jim Edmonds | .30 | .75 |
| 29 | Robb Nen | .30 | .75 |
| 30 | Reggie Sanders | .30 | .75 |
| 31 | Mike Lansing | .30 | .75 |
| 32 | Craig Biggio | .50 | 1.25 |
| 33 | Ray Lankford | .30 | .75 |
| 34 | Charles Nagy | .30 | .75 |
| 35 | Paul Wilson | .30 | .75 |
| 36 | John Wetteland | .30 | .75 |
| 37 | Derek Bell | .30 | .75 |
| 38 | Edgar Martinez | .50 | 1.25 |
| 39 | Rickey Henderson | .75 | 2.00 |
| 40 | Jim Thome | .75 | 2.00 |
| 41 | Frank Thomas | .75 | 2.00 |
| 42 | Jackie Robinson | .75 | 2.00 |
| 43 | Terry Steinbach | .30 | .75 |
| 44 | Kevin Brown | .30 | .75 |
| 45 | Joey Hamilton | .30 | .75 |
| 46 | Travis Fryman | .30 | .75 |
| 47 | Juan Gonzalez | .75 | 2.00 |
| 48 | Ron Gant | .30 | .75 |
| 49 | Greg Maddux | 1.25 | 3.00 |
| 50 | Wally Joyner | .30 | .75 |
| 51 | John Valentin | .30 | .75 |
| 52 | Bret Boone | .30 | .75 |
| 53 | Paul Molitor | .50 | 1.25 |
| 54 | Rafael Palmeiro | .50 | 1.25 |
| 55 | Todd Hundley | .30 | .75 |
| 56 | Ellis Burks | .30 | .75 |
| 57 | Bernie Williams | .50 | 1.25 |
| 58 | Roberto Alomar | .50 | 1.25 |
| 59 | Jose Mesa | .30 | .75 |
| 60 | Troy Percival | .30 | .75 |
| 61 | John Smoltz | .50 | 1.25 |
| 62 | Jeff Conine | .30 | .75 |
| 63 | Bernard Gilkey | .30 | .75 |
| 64 | Mickey Tettleton | .30 | .75 |
| 65 | Justin Thompson | .30 | .75 |
| 66 | Tony Phillips | .30 | .75 |
| 67 | Ryne Sandberg | 1.25 | 3.00 |
| 68 | Geronimo Berroa | .30 | .75 |
| 69 | Todd Hollandsworth | .30 | .75 |
| 70 | Rey Ordonez | .30 | .75 |
| 71 | Marquis Grissom | .30 | .75 |
| 72 | Tino Martinez | .50 | 1.25 |
| 73 | Steve Finley | .30 | .75 |
| 74 | Andy Benes | .30 | .75 |
| 75 | Jason Kendall | .30 | .75 |
| 76 | Johnny Damon | .50 | 1.25 |
| 77 | Jason Giambi | .30 | .75 |
| 78 | Henry Rodriguez | .30 | .75 |
| 79 | Edgar Renteria | .30 | .75 |
| 80 | Ray Durham | .30 | .75 |
| 81 | Gregg Jefferies | .30 | .75 |
| 82 | Roberto Hernandez | .30 | .75 |
| 83 | Joe Carter | .30 | .75 |
| 84 | Jermaine Dye | .30 | .75 |
| 85 | Julio Franco | .30 | .75 |
| 86 | David Justice | .30 | .75 |
| 87 | Jose Canseco | .50 | 1.25 |
| 88 | Paul O'Neill | .50 | 1.25 |
| 89 | Mariano Rivera | .75 | 2.00 |
| 90 | Bobby Higginson | .30 | .75 |
| 91 | Mark Grudzielanek | .30 | .75 |
| 92 | Lance Johnson | .30 | .75 |
| 93 | Ken Caminiti | .30 | .75 |
| 94 | Gary Sheffield | .30 | .75 |
| 95 | Luis Castillo | .30 | .75 |
| 96 | Scott Rolen | .50 | 1.25 |
| 97 | Chipper Jones | .75 | 2.00 |
| 98 | Darryl Strawberry | .30 | .75 |
| 99 | Nomar Garciaparra | 1.25 | 3.00 |
| 100 | Jeff Bagwell | .50 | 1.25 |
| 101 | Ken Griffey Jr. | 1.25 | 3.00 |
| 102 | Sammy Sosa | .75 | 2.00 |
| 103 | Jack McDowell | .30 | .75 |
| 104 | James Baldwin | .30 | .75 |
| 105 | Rocky Coppinger | .30 | .75 |
| 106 | Manny Ramirez | .50 | 1.25 |
| 107 | Tim Salmon | .50 | 1.25 |
| 108 | Eric Karros | .30 | .75 |
| 109 | Brett Butler | .30 | .75 |
| 110 | Randy Johnson | .75 | 2.00 |
| 111 | Pat Hentgen | .30 | .75 |
| 112 | Rondell White | .30 | .75 |
| 113 | Eddie Murray | .75 | 2.00 |
| 114 | Ivan Rodriguez | .50 | 1.25 |
| 115 | Jermaine Allensworth | .30 | .75 |
| 116 | Ed Sprague | .30 | .75 |
| 117 | Kenny Lofton | .30 | .75 |
| 118 | Alan Benes | .30 | .75 |
| 119 | Fred McGriff | .50 | 1.25 |
| 120 | Alex Fernandez | .30 | .75 |
| 121 | Al Martin | .30 | .75 |
| 122 | Devon White | .30 | .75 |
| 123 | David Cone | .30 | .75 |
| 124 | Karim Garcia | .30 | .75 |
| 125 | Chili Davis | .30 | .75 |
| 126 | Roger Clemens | 1.50 | 4.00 |
| 127 | Bobby Bonilla | .30 | .75 |
| 128 | Mike Mussina | .50 | 1.25 |
| 129 | Todd Walker | .30 | .75 |
| 130 | Dante Bichette | .30 | .75 |
| 131 | Carlos Baerga | .30 | .75 |
| 132 | Matt Williams | .30 | .75 |
| 133 | Will Clark | .50 | 1.25 |
| 134 | Dennis Eckersley | .30 | .75 |
| 135 | Ryan Klesko | .30 | .75 |
| 136 | Dean Palmer | .30 | .75 |
| 137 | Javy Lopez | .30 | .75 |
| 138 | Greg Vaughn | .30 | .75 |
| 139 | Vinny Castilla | .30 | .75 |
| 140 | Cal Ripken | 2.50 | 6.00 |
| 141 | Ruben Rivera | .30 | .75 |
| 142 | Mark Wohlers | .30 | .75 |
| 143 | Tony Clark | .30 | .75 |
| 144 | Jose Rosado | .30 | .75 |
| 145 | Tony Gwynn | 1.00 | 2.50 |
| 146 | Cecil Fielder | .30 | .75 |
| 147 | Brian Jordan | .30 | .75 |
| 148 | Bob Abreu | .50 | 1.25 |
| 149 | Barry Larkin | .50 | 1.25 |
| 150 | Robin Ventura | .30 | .75 |
| 151 | John Olerud | .30 | .75 |
| 152 | Rod Beck | .30 | .75 |
| 153 | Vladimir Guerrero | .75 | 2.00 |
| 154 | Marty Cordova | .30 | .75 |
| 155 | Todd Stottlemyre | .30 | .75 |
| 156 | Hideo Nomo | .75 | 2.00 |
| 157 | Denny Neagle | .30 | .75 |
| 158 | John Jaha | .30 | .75 |
| 159 | Mo Vaughn | .30 | .75 |
| 160 | Andruw Jones | .50 | 1.25 |
| 161 | Moises Alou | .30 | .75 |
| 162 | Larry Walker | .30 | .75 |
| 163 | Eddie Murray SH | .50 | 1.25 |
| 164 | Paul Molitor SH | .30 | .75 |
| 165 | Checklist | .30 | .75 |

## 1998 Topps Chrome

| | | | |
|---|---|------|------|
| COMPLETE SET (503) | | 60.00 | 150.00 |
| COMPLETE SERIES 1 (282) | | 30.00 | 80.00 |
| COMPLETE SERIES 2 (221) | | 30.00 | 80.00 |
| 1 | Tony Gwynn | 1.00 | 2.50 |
| 2 | Larry Walker | .30 | .75 |
| 3 | Billy Wagner | .30 | .75 |
| 4 | Denny Neagle | .30 | .75 |
| 5 | Vladimir Guerrero | .75 | 2.00 |
| 6 | Kevin Brown | .50 | 1.25 |
| 7 | Mariano Rivera | .75 | 2.00 |
| 8 | Tony Clark | .30 | .75 |
| 9 | Deion Sanders | .50 | 1.25 |
| 10 | Deion Sanders | .50 | 1.25 |
| 11 | Francisco Cordova | .30 | .75 |
| 12 | Matt Williams | .30 | .75 |
| 13 | Carlos Baerga | .30 | .75 |
| 14 | Mo Vaughn | .30 | .75 |
| 15 | Bobby Witt | .30 | .75 |
| 16 | Matt Stairs | .30 | .75 |
| 17 | Chan Ho Park | .30 | .75 |
| 18 | Mike Bordick | .30 | .75 |
| 19 | Michael Tucker | .30 | .75 |
| 20 | Frank Thomas | .75 | 2.00 |
| 21 | Roberto Clemente | 2.00 | 5.00 |
| 22 | Dmitri Young | .30 | .75 |
| 23 | Steve Trachsel | .30 | .75 |
| 24 | Jeff Kent | .30 | .75 |
| 25 | Scott Rolen | .50 | 1.25 |
| 26 | John Thomson | .30 | .75 |
| 27 | Joe Vitiello | .30 | .75 |
| 28 | Eddie Guardado | .30 | .75 |
| 29 | Charlie Hayes | .30 | .75 |
| 30 | Juan Gonzalez | .30 | .75 |
| 31 | Garret Anderson | .30 | .75 |
| 32 | John Jaha | .30 | .75 |
| 33 | Omar Vizquel | .50 | 1.25 |
| 34 | Brian Hunter | .30 | .75 |
| 35 | Jeff Bagwell | .50 | 1.25 |
| 36 | Mark Lemke | .30 | .75 |
| 37 | Doug Glanville | .30 | .75 |
| 38 | Dan Wilson | .30 | .75 |
| 39 | Steve Cooke | .30 | .75 |
| 40 | Chili Davis | .30 | .75 |
| 41 | Mike Cameron | .30 | .75 |
| 42 | F.P. Santangelo | .30 | .75 |
| 43 | Brad Ausmus | .30 | .75 |
| 44 | Gary DiSarcina | .30 | .75 |
| 45 | Pat Hentgen | .30 | .75 |
| 46 | Wilton Guerrero | .30 | .75 |
| 47 | Devon White | .30 | .75 |
| 48 | Danny Patterson | .30 | .75 |
| 49 | Pat Meares | .30 | .75 |
| 50 | Rafael Palmeiro | .50 | 1.25 |
| 51 | Mark Gardner | .30 | .75 |
| 52 | Jeff Blauser | .30 | .75 |
| 53 | Dave Hollins | .30 | .75 |
| 54 | Carlos Garcia | .30 | .75 |
| 55 | Ben McDonald | .30 | .75 |
| 56 | John Mabry | .30 | .75 |
| 57 | Trevor Hoffman | .30 | .75 |
| 58 | Tony Fernandez | .30 | .75 |
| 59 | Rich Loiselle RC | .30 | .75 |
| 60 | Mark Leiter | .30 | .75 |
| 61 | Pat Kelly | .30 | .75 |
| 62 | John Flaherty | .30 | .75 |
| 63 | Roger Bailey | .30 | .75 |
| 64 | Tom Gordon | .30 | .75 |
| 65 | Ryan Klesko | .30 | .75 |
| 66 | Darryl Hamilton | .30 | .75 |
| 67 | Jim Eisenreich | .30 | .75 |
| 68 | Butch Huskey | .30 | .75 |
| 69 | Mark Grudzielanek | .30 | .75 |
| 70 | Marquis Grissom | .30 | .75 |
| 71 | Mark McLemore | .30 | .75 |
| 72 | Gary Gaetti | .30 | .75 |
| 73 | Greg Gagne | .30 | .75 |
| 74 | Lyle Mouton | .30 | .75 |
| 75 | Jim Edmonds | .30 | .75 |
| 76 | Shawn Green | .30 | .75 |
| 77 | Greg Vaughn | .30 | .75 |
| 78 | Terry Adams | .30 | .75 |
| 79 | Kevin Polcovich | .30 | .75 |
| 80 | Troy O'Leary | .30 | .75 |
| 81 | Jeff Shaw | .30 | .75 |
| 82 | Rich Becker | .30 | .75 |
| 83 | David Wells | .30 | .75 |
| 84 | Steve Karsay | .30 | .75 |
| 85 | Charles Nagy | .30 | .75 |
| 86 | B.J. Surhoff | .30 | .75 |
| 87 | Jamey Wright | .30 | .75 |
| 88 | James Baldwin | .30 | .75 |
| 89 | Edgardo Alfonzo | .30 | .75 |
| 90 | Jay Buhner | .30 | .75 |
| 91 | Brady Anderson | .30 | .75 |

|  |  | | |
|---|---|---|---|
| ☐ 92 | Scott Servais | .30 | .75 |
| ☐ 93 | Edgar Renteria | .30 | .75 |
| ☐ 94 | Mike Lieberthal | .30 | .75 |
| ☐ 95 | Rick Aguilera | .30 | .75 |
| ☐ 96 | Walt Weiss | .30 | .75 |
| ☐ 97 | Deivi Cruz | .30 | .75 |
| ☐ 98 | Kurt Abbott | .30 | .75 |
| ☐ 99 | Henry Rodriguez | .30 | .75 |
| ☐ 100 | Mike Piazza | 1.25 | 3.00 |
| ☐ 101 | Billy Taylor | .30 | .75 |
| ☐ 102 | Todd Zeile | .30 | .75 |
| ☐ 103 | Rey Ordonez | .30 | .75 |
| ☐ 104 | Willie Greene | .30 | .75 |
| ☐ 105 | Tony Womack | .30 | .75 |
| ☐ 106 | Mike Sweeney | .30 | .75 |
| ☐ 107 | Jeffrey Hammonds | .30 | .75 |
| ☐ 108 | Kevin Orie | .30 | .75 |
| ☐ 109 | Alex Gonzalez | .30 | .75 |
| ☐ 110 | Jose Canseco | .50 | 1.25 |
| ☐ 111 | Paul Sorrento | .30 | .75 |
| ☐ 112 | Joey Hamilton | .30 | .75 |
| ☐ 113 | Brad Radke | .30 | .75 |
| ☐ 114 | Steve Avery | .30 | .75 |
| ☐ 115 | Esteban Loaiza | .30 | .75 |
| ☐ 116 | Stan Javier | .30 | .75 |
| ☐ 117 | Chris Gomez | .30 | .75 |
| ☐ 118 | Royce Clayton | .30 | .75 |
| ☐ 119 | Orlando Merced | .30 | .75 |
| ☐ 120 | Kevin Appier | .30 | .75 |
| ☐ 121 | Mel Nieves | .30 | .75 |
| ☐ 122 | Joe Girardi | .30 | .75 |
| ☐ 123 | Rico Brogna | .30 | .75 |
| ☐ 124 | Kent Mercker | .30 | .75 |
| ☐ 125 | Manny Ramirez | .50 | 1.25 |
| ☐ 126 | Jeromy Burnitz | .30 | .75 |
| ☐ 127 | Kevin Foster | .30 | .75 |
| ☐ 128 | Matt Morris | .30 | .75 |
| ☐ 129 | Jason Dickson | .30 | .75 |
| ☐ 130 | Tom Glavine | .50 | 1.25 |
| ☐ 131 | Wally Joyner | .30 | .75 |
| ☐ 132 | Rick Reed | .30 | .75 |
| ☐ 133 | Todd Jones | .30 | .75 |
| ☐ 134 | Dave Martinez | .30 | .75 |
| ☐ 135 | Sandy Alomar Jr. | .30 | .75 |
| ☐ 136 | Mike Lansing | .30 | .75 |
| ☐ 137 | Sean Berry | .30 | .75 |
| ☐ 138 | Doug Jones | .30 | .75 |
| ☐ 139 | Todd Stottlemyre | .30 | .75 |
| ☐ 140 | Jay Bell | .30 | .75 |
| ☐ 141 | Jaime Navarro | .30 | .75 |
| ☐ 142 | Chris Hoiles | .30 | .75 |
| ☐ 143 | Joey Cora | .30 | .75 |
| ☐ 144 | Scott Spiezio | .30 | .75 |
| ☐ 145 | Joe Carter | .30 | .75 |
| ☐ 146 | Jose Guillen | .30 | .75 |
| ☐ 147 | Damion Easley | .30 | .75 |
| ☐ 148 | Lee Stevens | .30 | .75 |
| ☐ 149 | Alex Fernandez | .30 | .75 |
| ☐ 150 | Randy Johnson | .75 | 2.00 |
| ☐ 151 | J.T. Snow | .30 | .75 |
| ☐ 152 | Chuck Finley | .30 | .75 |
| ☐ 153 | Bernard Gilkey | .30 | .75 |
| ☐ 154 | David Segui | .30 | .75 |
| ☐ 155 | Dante Bichette | .30 | .75 |
| ☐ 156 | Kevin Stocker | .30 | .75 |
| ☐ 157 | Carl Everett | .30 | .75 |
| ☐ 158 | Jose Valentin | .30 | .75 |
| ☐ 159 | Pokey Reese | .30 | .75 |
| ☐ 160 | Derek Jeter | 2.00 | 5.00 |
| ☐ 161 | Roger Pavlik | .30 | .75 |
| ☐ 162 | Mark Wohlers | .30 | .75 |
| ☐ 163 | Ricky Bottalico | .30 | .75 |
| ☐ 164 | Ozzie Guillen | .30 | .75 |
| ☐ 165 | Mike Mussina | .50 | 1.25 |
| ☐ 166 | Gary Sheffield | .30 | .75 |
| ☐ 167 | Hideo Nomo | .75 | 2.00 |
| ☐ 168 | Mark Grace | .50 | 1.25 |
| ☐ 169 | Aaron Sele | .30 | .75 |
| ☐ 170 | Darryl Kile | .30 | .75 |
| ☐ 171 | Shawn Estes | .30 | .75 |
| ☐ 172 | Vinny Castilla | .30 | .75 |
| ☐ 173 | Ron Coomer | .30 | .75 |
| ☐ 174 | Jose Rosado | .30 | .75 |
| ☐ 175 | Kenny Lofton | .50 | 1.25 |
| ☐ 176 | Jason Giambi | .30 | .75 |
| ☐ 177 | Hal Morris | .30 | .75 |
| ☐ 178 | Darren Bragg | .30 | .75 |
| ☐ 179 | Orel Hershiser | .30 | .75 |
| ☐ 180 | Ray Lankford | .30 | .75 |
| ☐ 181 | Hideki Irabu | .30 | .75 |
| ☐ 182 | Kevin Young | .30 | .75 |
| ☐ 183 | Javy Lopez | .30 | .75 |
| ☐ 184 | Jeff Montgomery | .30 | .75 |
| ☐ 185 | Mike Holtz | .30 | .75 |
| ☐ 186 | George Williams | .30 | .75 |
| ☐ 187 | Cal Eldred | .30 | .75 |
| ☐ 188 | Tom Candiotti | .30 | .75 |
| ☐ 189 | Glenallen Hill | .30 | .75 |
| ☐ 190 | Brian Giles | .30 | .75 |
| ☐ 191 | Dave Mlicki | .30 | .75 |
| ☐ 192 | Garrett Stephenson | .30 | .75 |
| ☐ 193 | Jeff Frye | .30 | .75 |
| ☐ 194 | Joe Oliver | .30 | .75 |
| ☐ 195 | Bob Hamelin | .30 | .75 |
| ☐ 196 | Luis Sojo | .30 | .75 |
| ☐ 197 | LaTroy Hawkins | .30 | .75 |
| ☐ 198 | Kevin Elster | .30 | .75 |
| ☐ 199 | Jeff Reed | .30 | .75 |
| ☐ 200 | Dennis Eckersley | .30 | .75 |
| ☐ 201 | Bill Mueller | .30 | .75 |
| ☐ 202 | Russ Davis | .30 | .75 |
| ☐ 203 | Armando Benitez | .30 | .75 |
| ☐ 204 | Quilvio Veras | .30 | .75 |
| ☐ 205 | Tim Naehring | .30 | .75 |
| ☐ 206 | Quinton McCracken | .30 | .75 |
| ☐ 207 | Raul Casanova | .30 | .75 |
| ☐ 208 | Matt Lawton | .30 | .75 |
| ☐ 209 | Luis Alicea | .30 | .75 |
| ☐ 210 | Luis Gonzalez | .30 | .75 |
| ☐ 211 | Allen Watson | .30 | .75 |
| ☐ 212 | Gerald Williams | .30 | .75 |
| ☐ 213 | David Bell | .30 | .75 |
| ☐ 214 | Todd Hollandsworth | .30 | .75 |
| ☐ 215 | Wade Boggs | .50 | 1.25 |
| ☐ 216 | Jose Mesa | .30 | .75 |
| ☐ 217 | Jamie Moyer | .30 | .75 |
| ☐ 218 | Darren Daulton | .30 | .75 |
| ☐ 219 | Mickey Morandini | .30 | .75 |
| ☐ 220 | Rusty Greer | .30 | .75 |
| ☐ 221 | Jim Bullinger | .30 | .75 |
| ☐ 222 | Jose Offerman | .30 | .75 |
| ☐ 223 | Matt Karchner | .30 | .75 |
| ☐ 224 | Woody Williams | .30 | .75 |
| ☐ 225 | Mark Loretta | .30 | .75 |
| ☐ 226 | Mike Hampton | .30 | .75 |
| ☐ 227 | Willie Adams | .30 | .75 |
| ☐ 228 | Scott Hatteberg | .30 | .75 |
| ☐ 229 | Rich Amaral | .30 | .75 |
| ☐ 230 | Terry Steinbach | .30 | .75 |
| ☐ 231 | Glendon Rusch | .30 | .75 |
| ☐ 232 | Bret Boone | .30 | .75 |
| ☐ 233 | Robert Person | .30 | .75 |
| ☐ 234 | Jose Hernandez | .30 | .75 |
| ☐ 235 | Doug Drabek | .30 | .75 |
| ☐ 236 | Jason McDonald | .30 | .75 |
| ☐ 237 | Chris Widger | .30 | .75 |
| ☐ 238 | Tom Martin | .30 | .75 |
| ☐ 239 | Dave Burba | .30 | .75 |
| ☐ 240 | Pete Rose Jr. RC | .30 | .75 |
| ☐ 241 | Bobby Ayala | .30 | .75 |
| ☐ 242 | Tim Wakefield | .30 | .75 |
| ☐ 243 | Dennis Springer | .30 | .75 |
| ☐ 244 | Tim Belcher | .30 | .75 |
| ☐ 245 | J.Garland/G.Goetz | .40 | 1.00 |
| ☐ 246 | L.Berkman/G.Davis | .40 | 1.00 |
| ☐ 247 | V.Wells/A.Akin | .40 | 1.00 |
| ☐ 248 | A.Kennedy/J.Romano | .40 | 1.00 |
| ☐ 249 | J.Dellaero/T.Cameron | .40 | 1.00 |
| ☐ 250 | J.Sandberg/A.Sanchez | .40 | 1.00 |
| ☐ 251 | P.Ortega/J.Manias | .40 | 1.00 |
| ☐ 252 | Mike Stoner RC | .40 | 1.00 |
| ☐ 253 | J.Patterson/L.Rodriguez | .40 | 1.00 |
| ☐ 254 | R.Minor RC/A.Beltre | .40 | 1.00 |
| ☐ 255 | B.Grieve/D.Brown | .40 | 1.00 |
| ☐ 256 | Wood/Pavano/Meche | .40 | 1.00 |
| ☐ 257 | D.Ortiz/Sexson/Ward | 2.00 | 5.00 |
| ☐ 258 | J.Encarnacion/Winn/Vess | .40 | 1.00 |
| ☐ 259 | Bens/T.Smith RC/C.Dunc RC | .40 | 1.00 |
| ☐ 260 | Warren Morris RC | .40 | 1.00 |
| ☐ 261 | B.Davis/Marrero/R.Hern. | .40 | 1.00 |
| ☐ 262 | E.Chavez/R.Branyan | .40 | 1.00 |
| ☐ 263 | Ryan Jackson RC | .40 | 1.00 |
| ☐ 264 | B.Fuentes RC/Clement/Halladay | .40 | 1.00 |
| ☐ 265 | Randy Johnson SH | .50 | 1.25 |
| ☐ 266 | Kevin Brown SH | .30 | .75 |
| ☐ 267 | Ricardo Rincon SH | .30 | .75 |
| ☐ 268 | Nomar Garciaparra SH | .75 | 2.00 |
| ☐ 269 | Tino Martinez SH | .30 | .75 |
| ☐ 270 | Chuck Knoblauch IL | .30 | .75 |
| ☐ 271 | Pedro Martinez IL | .50 | 1.25 |
| ☐ 272 | Denny Neagle IL | .30 | .75 |
| ☐ 273 | Juan Gonzalez IL | .50 | 1.25 |
| ☐ 274 | Andres Galarraga IL | .30 | .75 |
| ☐ 275 | Checklist | .30 | .75 |
| ☐ 276 | Checklist | .30 | .75 |
| ☐ 277 | Moises Alou WS | .30 | .75 |
| ☐ 278 | Sandy Alomar Jr. WS | .30 | .75 |
| ☐ 279 | Gary Sheffield WS | .30 | .75 |
| ☐ 280 | Matt Williams WS | .30 | .75 |
| ☐ 281 | Livan Hernandez WS | .30 | .75 |
| ☐ 282 | Chad Ogea WS | .30 | .75 |
| ☐ 283 | Marlins Champs | .30 | .75 |
| ☐ 284 | Tino Martinez | .30 | .75 |
| ☐ 285 | Roberto Alomar | .50 | 1.25 |
| ☐ 286 | Jeff King | .30 | .75 |
| ☐ 287 | Brian Jordan | .30 | .75 |
| ☐ 288 | Darin Erstad | .30 | .75 |
| ☐ 289 | Ken Caminiti | .30 | .75 |
| ☐ 290 | Jim Thome | .50 | 1.25 |
| ☐ 291 | Paul Molitor | .50 | * .75 |
| ☐ 292 | Ivan Rodriguez | .50 | 1.25 |
| ☐ 293 | Bernie Williams | .50 | 1.25 |
| ☐ 294 | Todd Hundley | .30 | .75 |
| ☐ 295 | Andres Galarraga | .30 | .75 |
| ☐ 296 | Greg Maddux | 1.25 | 3.00 |
| ☐ 297 | Edgar Martinez | .50 | 1.25 |
| ☐ 298 | Ron Gant | .30 | .75 |
| ☐ 299 | Derek Bell | .30 | .75 |
| ☐ 300 | Roger Clemens | 1.50 | 4.00 |
| ☐ 301 | Rondell White | .30 | .75 |
| ☐ 302 | Barry Larkin | .50 | 1.25 |
| ☐ 303 | Robin Ventura | .30 | .75 |
| ☐ 304 | Jason Kendall | .30 | .75 |
| ☐ 305 | Chipper Jones | .75 | 2.00 |
| ☐ 306 | John Franco | .30 | .75 |
| ☐ 307 | Sammy Sosa | .75 | 2.00 |
| ☐ 308 | Trey Percival | .30 | .75 |
| ☐ 309 | Chuck Knoblauch | .30 | .75 |
| ☐ 310 | Ellis Burks | .30 | .75 |
| ☐ 311 | Al Martin | .30 | .75 |
| ☐ 312 | Tim Salmon | .50 | 1.25 |
| ☐ 313 | Moises Alou | .30 | .75 |
| ☐ 314 | Lance Johnson | .30 | .75 |
| ☐ 315 | Justin Thompson | .30 | .75 |
| ☐ 316 | Will Clark | .50 | 1.25 |
| ☐ 317 | Barry Bonds | 2.00 | 5.00 |
| ☐ 318 | Craig Biggio | .50 | 1.25 |
| ☐ 319 | John Smoltz | .50 | 1.25 |
| ☐ 320 | Cal Ripken | 2.50 | 6.00 |
| ☐ 321 | Ken Griffey Jr. | 1.25 | 3.00 |
| ☐ 322 | Paul O'Neill | .50 | 1.25 |
| ☐ 323 | Todd Helton | .50 | 1.25 |
| ☐ 324 | John Olerud | .30 | .75 |
| ☐ 325 | Mark McGwire | 2.00 | 5.00 |
| ☐ 326 | Jose Cruz Jr. | .30 | .75 |
| ☐ 327 | Jeff Cirillo | .30 | .75 |
| ☐ 328 | Dean Palmer | .30 | .75 |
| ☐ 329 | John Wetteland | .30 | .75 |
| ☐ 330 | Steve Finley | .30 | .75 |
| ☐ 331 | Albert Belle | .30 | .75 |
| ☐ 332 | Curt Schilling | .30 | .75 |
| ☐ 333 | Raul Mondesi | .30 | .75 |
| ☐ 334 | Andruw Jones | .50 | 1.25 |
| ☐ 335 | Nomar Garciaparra | 1.25 | 3.00 |
| ☐ 336 | David Justice | .30 | .75 |
| ☐ 337 | Andy Pettitte | .50 | 1.25 |
| ☐ 338 | Pedro Martinez | .50 | 1.25 |
| ☐ 339 | Travis Miller | .30 | .75 |
| ☐ 340 | Chris Stynes | .30 | .75 |
| ☐ 341 | Gregg Jefferies | .30 | .75 |
| ☐ 342 | Jeff Fassero | .30 | .75 |
| ☐ 343 | Craig Counsell | .30 | .75 |
| ☐ 344 | Wilson Alvarez | .30 | .75 |
| ☐ 345 | Bip Roberts | .30 | .75 |
| ☐ 346 | Kelvim Escobar | .30 | .75 |
| ☐ 347 | Mark Bellhorn | .30 | .75 |
| ☐ 348 | Cory Lidle RC | 3.00 | 8.00 |
| ☐ 349 | Fred McGriff | .50 | 1.25 |
| ☐ 350 | Chuck Carr | .30 | .75 |
| ☐ 351 | Bob Abreu | .30 | .75 |
| ☐ 352 | Juan Guzman | .30 | .75 |
| ☐ 353 | Fernando Vina | .30 | .75 |
| ☐ 354 | Andy Benes | .30 | .75 |
| ☐ 355 | Dave Nilsson | .30 | .75 |

| | | |
|---|---|---|
| 356 Bobby Bonilla | .30 | .75 |
| 357 Ismael Valdes | .30 | .75 |
| 358 Carlos Perez | .30 | .75 |
| 359 Kirk Rueter | .30 | .75 |
| 360 Bartolo Colon | .30 | .75 |
| 361 Mel Rojas | .30 | .75 |
| 362 Johnny Damon | .50 | 1.25 |
| 363 Geronimo Berroa | .30 | .75 |
| 364 Reggie Sanders | .30 | .75 |
| 365 Jermaine Allensworth | .30 | .75 |
| 366 Orlando Cabrera | .30 | .75 |
| 367 Jorge Fabregas | .30 | .75 |
| 368 Scott Stahoviak | .30 | .75 |
| 369 Ken Cloude | .30 | .75 |
| 370 Donovan Osborne | .30 | .75 |
| 371 Roger Cedeno | .30 | .75 |
| 372 Neifi Perez | .30 | .75 |
| 373 Chris Holt | .30 | .75 |
| 374 Cecil Fielder | .30 | .75 |
| 375 Marty Cordova | .30 | .75 |
| 376 Tom Goodwin | .30 | .75 |
| 377 Jeff Suppan | .30 | .75 |
| 378 Jeff Brantley | .30 | .75 |
| 379 Mark Langston | .30 | .75 |
| 380 Shane Reynolds | .30 | .75 |
| 381 Mike Fetters | .30 | .75 |
| 382 Todd Greene | .30 | .75 |
| 383 Ray Durham | .30 | .75 |
| 384 Carlos Delgado | .30 | .75 |
| 385 Jeff D'Amico | .30 | .75 |
| 386 Brian McRae | .30 | .75 |
| 387 Alan Benes | .30 | .75 |
| 388 Heathcliff Slocumb | .30 | .75 |
| 389 Eric Young | .30 | .75 |
| 390 Travis Fryman | .30 | .75 |
| 391 David Cone | .30 | .75 |
| 392 Otis Nixon | .30 | .75 |
| 393 Jeremi Gonzalez | .30 | .75 |
| 394 Jeff Juden | .30 | .75 |
| 395 Jose Vizcaino | .30 | .75 |
| 396 Ugueth Urbina | .30 | .75 |
| 397 Ramon Martinez | .30 | .75 |
| 398 Robb Nen | .30 | .75 |
| 399 Harold Baines | .30 | .75 |
| 400 Delino DeShields | .30 | .75 |
| 401 John Burkett | .30 | .75 |
| 402 Sterling Hitchcock | .30 | .75 |
| 403 Mark Clark | .30 | .75 |
| 404 Terrell Wade | .30 | .75 |
| 405 Scott Brosius | .30 | .75 |
| 406 Chad Curtis | .30 | .75 |
| 407 Brian Johnson | .30 | .75 |
| 408 Roberto Kelly | .30 | .75 |
| 409 Dave Dellucci RC | .50 | 1.25 |
| 410 Michael Tucker | .30 | .75 |
| 411 Mark Kotsay | .30 | .75 |
| 412 Mark Lewis | .30 | .75 |
| 413 Ryan McGuire | .30 | .75 |
| 414 Shawon Dunston | .30 | .75 |
| 415 Brad Rigby | .30 | .75 |
| 416 Scott Erickson | .30 | .75 |
| 417 Bobby Jones | .30 | .75 |
| 418 Darren Oliver | .30 | .75 |
| 419 John Smiley | .30 | .75 |
| 420 T.J. Mathews | .30 | .75 |
| 421 Dustin Hermanson | .30 | .75 |
| 422 Mike Timlin | .30 | .75 |
| 423 Willie Blair | .30 | .75 |
| 424 Manny Alexander | .30 | .75 |
| 425 Bob Tewksbury | .30 | .75 |
| 426 Pete Schourek | .30 | .75 |
| 427 Reggie Jefferson | .30 | .75 |
| 428 Ed Sprague | .30 | .75 |
| 429 Jeff Conine | .30 | .75 |
| 430 Roberto Hernandez | .30 | .75 |
| 431 Tom Pagnozzi | .30 | .75 |
| 432 Jaret Wright | .30 | .75 |
| 433 Livan Hernandez | .30 | .75 |
| 434 Andy Ashby | .30 | .75 |
| 435 Todd Dunn | .30 | .75 |
| 436 Bobby Higginson | .30 | .75 |
| 437 Rod Beck | .30 | .75 |
| 438 Jim Leyritz | .30 | .75 |
| 439 Matt Williams | .30 | .75 |
| 440 Brett Tomko | .30 | .75 |
| 441 Joe Randa | .30 | .75 |
| 442 Chris Carpenter | .30 | .75 |
| 443 Dennis Reyes | .30 | .75 |
| 444 Al Leiter | .30 | .75 |
| 445 Jason Schmidt | .30 | .75 |
| 446 Ken Hill | .30 | .75 |
| 447 Shannon Stewart | .30 | .75 |
| 448 Enrique Wilson | .30 | .75 |
| 449 Fernando Tatis | .30 | .75 |
| 450 Jimmy Key | .30 | .75 |
| 451 Darrin Fletcher | .30 | .75 |
| 452 John Valentin | .30 | .75 |
| 453 Kevin Tapani | .30 | .75 |
| 454 Eric Karros | .30 | .75 |
| 455 Jay Bell | .30 | .75 |
| 456 Walt Weiss | .30 | .75 |
| 457 Devon White | .30 | .75 |
| 458 Carl Pavano | .30 | .75 |
| 459 Mike Lansing | .30 | .75 |
| 460 John Flaherty | .30 | .75 |
| 461 Richard Hidalgo | .30 | .75 |
| 462 Quinton McCracken | .30 | .75 |
| 463 Karim Garcia | .30 | .75 |
| 464 Miguel Cairo | .30 | .75 |
| 465 Edwin Diaz | .30 | .75 |
| 466 Bobby Smith | .30 | .75 |
| 467 Yamil Benitez | .30 | .75 |
| 468 Rich Butler RC | .30 | .75 |
| 469 Ben Ford RC | .30 | .75 |
| 470 Bubba Trammell | .30 | .75 |
| 471 Brent Brede | .30 | .75 |
| 472 Brooks Kieschnick | .30 | .75 |
| 473 Carlos Castillo | .30 | .75 |
| 474 Brad Radke SH | .30 | .75 |
| 475 Roger Clemens SH | .75 | 2.00 |
| 476 Curt Schilling SH | .30 | .75 |
| 477 John Olerud SH | .30 | .75 |
| 478 Mark McGwire SH | 1.00 | 2.50 |
| 479 M.Piazza/K.Griffey Jr. IL | .75 | 2.00 |
| 480 J.Bagwell/F.Thomas IL | .50 | 1.25 |
| 481 C.Jones/N.Garciaparra IL | .50 | 1.25 |
| 482 L.Walker/J.Gonzalez IL | .30 | .75 |
| 483 G.Sheffield/T.Martinez IL | .30 | .75 |
| 484 D.Gib/M.Colem/Hutchins | .30 | .75 |
| 485 B.Rose/Looper/Politte | .40 | 1.00 |
| 486 E.Milton/Marquis/C.Lee | .40 | 1.00 |
| 487 Rob Fick RC | .40 | 1.00 |
| 488 A.Ramirez/A.Gonz/Casey | .40 | 1.00 |
| 489 D.Bridges/T.Drew RC | .40 | 1.00 |
| 490 D.McDonald/N.Ndungidi RC | .40 | 1.00 |
| 491 Ryan Anderson RC | .40 | 1.00 |
| 492 Troy Glaus RC | 2.00 | 5.00 |
| 493 Dan Reichert RC | .40 | 1.00 |
| 494 Michael Cuddyer RC | 1.00 | 2.50 |
| 495 Jack Cust RC | .75 | 2.00 |
| 496 Brian Anderson | .40 | 1.00 |
| 497 Tony Saunders | .40 | 1.00 |
| 498 J.Sandoval/V.Nunez | .40 | 1.00 |
| 499 B.Penny/N.Bierbrodt | .40 | 1.00 |
| 500 D.Carr/L.Cruz RC | .40 | 1.00 |
| 501 C.Bowers/M.McCain | .40 | 1.00 |
| 502 Checklist | .30 | .75 |
| 503 Checklist | .30 | .75 |
| 504 Alex Rodriguez | 1.50 | 4.00 |

## 1999 Topps Chrome

| | | |
|---|---|---|
| COMPLETE SET (462) | 50.00 | 120.00 |
| COMPLETE SERIES 1 (241) | 25.00 | 60.00 |
| COMPLETE SERIES 2 (221) | 25.00 | 60.00 |
| COMMON CARD (1-6/8-463) | .20 | .50 |
| COMMON (205-212/425-437) | .40 | 1.00 |
| 1 Roger Clemens | 1.50 | 4.00 |
| 2 Andres Galarraga | .30 | .75 |
| 3 Scott Brosius | .20 | .50 |
| 4 John Flaherty | .20 | .50 |
| 5 Jim Leyritz | .20 | .50 |
| 6 Ray Durham | .30 | .75 |

| | | |
|---|---|---|
| 8 Jose Vizcaino | .20 | .50 |
| 9 Will Clark | .50 | 1.25 |
| 10 David Wells | .30 | .75 |
| 11 Jose Guillen | .30 | .75 |
| 12 Scott Hatteberg | .20 | .50 |
| 13 Edgardo Alfonzo | .20 | .50 |
| 14 Mike Bordick | .20 | .50 |
| 15 Manny Ramirez | .50 | 1.25 |
| 16 Greg Maddux | 1.25 | 3.00 |
| 17 David Segui | .20 | .50 |
| 18 Darryl Strawberry | .30 | .75 |
| 19 Brad Radke | .30 | .75 |
| 20 Kerry Wood | .30 | .75 |
| 21 Matt Anderson | .20 | .50 |
| 22 Derek Lee | .50 | 1.25 |
| 23 Mickey Morandini | .20 | .50 |
| 24 Paul Konerko | .30 | .75 |
| 25 Travis Lee | .20 | .50 |
| 26 Ken Hill | .20 | .50 |
| 27 Kenny Rogers | .20 | .50 |
| 28 Paul Sorrento | .20 | .50 |
| 29 Quilvio Veras | .20 | .50 |
| 30 Todd Walker | .20 | .50 |
| 31 Ryan Jackson | .20 | .50 |
| 32 John Olerud | .30 | .75 |
| 33 Doug Glanville | .20 | .50 |
| 34 Nolan Ryan | 2.50 | 6.00 |
| 35 Ray Lankford | .30 | .75 |
| 36 Mark Loretta | .20 | .50 |
| 37 Jason Dickson | .20 | .50 |
| 38 Sean Bergman | .20 | .50 |
| 39 Quinton McCracken | .20 | .50 |
| 40 Bartolo Colon | .20 | .50 |
| 41 Brady Anderson | .30 | .75 |
| 42 Chris Stynes | .20 | .50 |
| 43 Jorge Posada | .50 | 1.25 |
| 44 Justin Thompson | .20 | .50 |
| 45 Johnny Damon | .50 | 1.25 |
| 46 Armando Benitez | .20 | .50 |
| 47 Brant Brown | .20 | .50 |
| 48 Charlie Hayes | .20 | .50 |
| 49 Darren Dreifort | .20 | .50 |
| 50 Juan Gonzalez | .30 | .75 |
| 51 Chuck Knoblauch | .30 | .75 |
| 52 Todd Helton | .50 | 1.25 |
| 53 Rick Reed | .20 | .50 |
| 54 Chris Gomez | .20 | .50 |
| 55 Gary Sheffield | .30 | .75 |
| 56 Rod Beck | .20 | .50 |
| 57 Rey Sanchez | .20 | .50 |
| 58 Garret Anderson | .30 | .75 |
| 59 Jimmy Haynes | .20 | .50 |
| 60 Steve Woodard | .20 | .50 |
| 61 Rondell White | .20 | .50 |
| 62 Vladimir Guerrero | .75 | 2.00 |
| 63 Eric Karros | .30 | .75 |
| 64 Russ Davis | .20 | .50 |
| 65 Mo Vaughn | .30 | .75 |
| 66 Sammy Sosa | .75 | 2.00 |
| 67 Troy Percival | .30 | .75 |
| 68 Kenny Lofton | .30 | .75 |
| 69 Bill Taylor | .20 | .50 |
| 70 Mark McGwire | 2.00 | 5.00 |
| 71 Roger Cedeno | .20 | .50 |
| 72 Javy Lopez | .30 | .75 |
| 73 Damion Easley | .20 | .50 |
| 74 Andy Pettitte | .50 | 1.25 |
| 75 Tony Gwynn | 1.00 | 2.50 |
| 76 Ricardo Rincon | .20 | .50 |
| 77 F.P. Santangelo | .20 | .50 |
| 78 Jay Bell | .30 | .75 |
| 79 Scott Servais | .20 | .50 |
| 80 Jose Canseco | .50 | 1.25 |
| 81 Roberto Hernandez | .20 | .50 |
| 82 Todd Dunwoody | .20 | .50 |
| 83 John Wetteland | .30 | .75 |
| 84 Mike Caruso | .20 | .50 |
| 85 Derek Jeter | 2.00 | 5.00 |
| 86 Aaron Sele | .20 | .50 |
| 87 Jose Lima | .20 | .50 |
| 88 Ryan Christenson | .20 | .50 |
| 89 Jeff Cirillo | .30 | .75 |
| 90 Jose Hernandez | .20 | .50 |
| 91 Mark Kotsay | .30 | .75 |
| 92 Darren Bragg | .20 | .50 |
| 93 Albert Belle | .30 | .75 |
| 94 Matt Lawton | .20 | .50 |
| 95 Pedro Martinez | .50 | 1.25 |

|  |  | | |
|---|---|---|---|
| 96 | Greg Vaughn | .20 | .50 |
| 97 | Neifi Perez | .20 | .50 |
| 98 | Gerald Williams | .20 | .50 |
| 99 | Derek Bell | .20 | .50 |
| 100 | Ken Griffey Jr. | 1.25 | 3.00 |
| 101 | David Cone | .30 | .75 |
| 102 | Brian Johnson | .20 | .50 |
| 103 | Dean Palmer | .30 | .75 |
| 104 | Javier Valentin | .20 | .50 |
| 105 | Trevor Hoffman | .30 | .75 |
| 106 | Butch Huskey | .20 | .50 |
| 107 | Dave Martinez | .20 | .50 |
| 108 | Billy Wagner | .30 | .75 |
| 109 | Shawn Green | .30 | .75 |
| 110 | Ben Grieve | .20 | .50 |
| 111 | Tom Goodwin | .20 | .50 |
| 112 | Jaret Wright | .20 | .50 |
| 113 | Aramis Ramirez | .30 | .75 |
| 114 | Dmitri Young | .30 | .75 |
| 115 | Hideki Irabu | .20 | .50 |
| 116 | Roberto Kelly | .20 | .50 |
| 117 | Jeff Fassero | .20 | .50 |
| 118 | Mark Clark | .20 | .50 |
| 119 | Jason McDonald | .20 | .50 |
| 120 | Matt Williams | .30 | .75 |
| 121 | Dave Burba | .20 | .50 |
| 122 | Bret Saberhagen | .30 | .75 |
| 123 | Delvi Cruz | .20 | .50 |
| 124 | Chad Curtis | .20 | .50 |
| 125 | Scott Rolen | .50 | 1.25 |
| 126 | Lee Stevens | .20 | .50 |
| 127 | J.T. Snow | .30 | .75 |
| 128 | Rusty Greer | .30 | .75 |
| 129 | Brian Meadows | .20 | .50 |
| 130 | Jim Edmonds | .30 | .75 |
| 131 | Ron Gant | .30 | .75 |
| 132 | A.J. Hinch | .20 | .50 |
| 133 | Shannon Stewart | .30 | .75 |
| 134 | Brad Fullmer | .20 | .50 |
| 135 | Cal Eldred | .20 | .50 |
| 136 | Matt Walbeck | .20 | .50 |
| 137 | Carl Everett | .30 | .75 |
| 138 | Walt Weiss | .20 | .50 |
| 139 | Fred McGriff | .50 | 1.25 |
| 140 | Darin Erstad | .30 | .75 |
| 141 | Dave Nilsson | .20 | .50 |
| 142 | Eric Young | .20 | .50 |
| 143 | Dan Wilson | .20 | .50 |
| 144 | Jeff Reed | .20 | .50 |
| 145 | Brett Tomko | .20 | .50 |
| 146 | Terry Steinbach | .20 | .50 |
| 147 | Seth Greisinger | .20 | .50 |
| 148 | Pat Meares | .20 | .50 |
| 149 | Linen Hernandez | .30 | .75 |
| 150 | Jeff Bagwell | .50 | 1.25 |
| 151 | Bob Wickman | .20 | .50 |
| 152 | Omar Vizquel | .50 | 1.25 |
| 153 | Eric Davis | .30 | .75 |
| 154 | Larry Sutton | .20 | .50 |
| 155 | Magglio Ordonez | .30 | .75 |
| 156 | Eric Milton | .20 | .50 |
| 157 | Darren Lewis | .20 | .50 |
| 158 | Rick Aguilera | .20 | .50 |
| 159 | Mike Lieberthal | .30 | .75 |
| 160 | Robb Nen | .20 | .50 |
| 161 | Brian Giles | .30 | .75 |
| 162 | Jeff Brantley | .20 | .50 |
| 163 | Gary DiSarcina | .20 | .50 |
| 164 | John Valentin | .20 | .50 |
| 165 | Dave Dellucci | .20 | .50 |
| 166 | Chan Ho Park | .30 | .75 |
| 167 | Masato Yoshii | .20 | .50 |
| 168 | Jason Schmidt | .20 | .50 |
| 169 | LaTroy Hawkins | .20 | .50 |
| 170 | Bret Boone | .20 | .50 |
| 171 | Jerry DiPoto | .20 | .50 |
| 172 | Mariano Rivera | .75 | 2.00 |
| 173 | Mike Cameron | .20 | .50 |
| 174 | Scott Erickson | .20 | .50 |
| 175 | Charles Johnson | .30 | .75 |
| 176 | Bobby Jones | .20 | .50 |
| 177 | Francisco Cordova | .20 | .50 |
| 178 | Todd Jones | .20 | .50 |
| 179 | Jeff Montgomery | .20 | .50 |
| 180 | Mike Mussina | .50 | 1.25 |
| 181 | Bob Abreu | .30 | .75 |
| 182 | Ismael Valdes | .20 | .50 |
| 183 | Andy Fox | .20 | .50 |
| 184 | Woody Williams | .20 | .50 |
| 185 | Denny Neagle | .20 | .50 |
| 186 | Jose Valentin | .20 | .50 |
| 187 | Darrin Fletcher | .20 | .50 |
| 188 | Gabe Alvarez | .20 | .50 |
| 189 | Eddie Taubensee | .20 | .50 |
| 190 | Edgar Martinez | .50 | 1.25 |
| 191 | Jason Kendall | .30 | .75 |
| 192 | Darryl Kile | .30 | .75 |
| 193 | Jeff King | .20 | .50 |
| 194 | Rey Ordonez | .20 | .50 |
| 195 | Andruw Jones | .50 | 1.25 |
| 196 | Tony Fernandez | .20 | .50 |
| 197 | Jamey Wright | .20 | .50 |
| 198 | B.J. Surhoff | .30 | .75 |
| 199 | Vinny Castilla | .30 | .75 |
| 200 | David Wells HL | .20 | .50 |
| 201 | Mark McGwire HL | 1.00 | 2.50 |
| 202 | Sammy Sosa HL | .50 | 1.25 |
| 203 | Roger Clemens HL | .75 | 2.00 |
| 204 | Kerry Wood HL | .50 | 1.25 |
| 205 | L.Berkman/G.Kapler | .40 | 1.00 |
| 206 | Alex Escobar RC | .40 | 1.00 |
| 207 | Peter Bergeron RC | .40 | 1.00 |
| 208 | M.Barrett/B.Davis/R.Fick | .40 | 1.00 |
| 209 | J.Werth/Hernandez/Cline | .40 | 1.00 |
| 210 | Ryan Anderson | .40 | 1.00 |
| 211 | B.Penny/Dotel/Lincoln | .40 | 1.00 |
| 212 | Chuck Abbott RC | .40 | 1.00 |
| 213 | C.Jones/J.Urban RC | .40 | 1.00 |
| 214 | T.Torcato/A.McDowell RC | .40 | 1.00 |
| 215 | J.Tyner/J.McKinley RC | .40 | 1.00 |
| 216 | M.Burch/S.Etherton RC | .40 | 1.00 |
| 217 | R.Elder/M.Tucker RC | .40 | 1.00 |
| 218 | J.M.Gold/R.Mills RC | .40 | 1.00 |
| 219 | A.Brown/C.Freeman RC | .40 | 1.00 |
| 220A | Mark McGwire HR 1 | 20.00 | 50.00 |
| 220B | Mark McGwire HR 2 | 12.50 | 30.00 |
| 220C | Mark McGwire HR 3 | 12.50 | 30.00 |
| 220D | Mark McGwire HR 4 | 12.50 | 30.00 |
| 220E | Mark McGwire HR 5 | 12.50 | 30.00 |
| 220F | Mark McGwire HR 6 | 12.50 | 30.00 |
| 220G | Mark McGwire HR 7 | 12.50 | 30.00 |
| 220H | Mark McGwire HR 8 | 12.50 | 30.00 |
| 220I | Mark McGwire HR 9 | 12.50 | 30.00 |
| 220J | Mark McGwire HR 10 | 12.50 | 30.00 |
| 220K | Mark McGwire HR 11 | 12.50 | 30.00 |
| 220L | Mark McGwire HR 12 | 12.50 | 30.00 |
| 220M | Mark McGwire HR 13 | 12.50 | 30.00 |
| 220N | Mark McGwire HR 14 | 12.50 | 30.00 |
| 220O | Mark McGwire HR 15 | 12.50 | 30.00 |
| 220P | Mark McGwire HR 16 | 12.50 | 30.00 |
| 220Q | Mark McGwire HR 17 | 12.50 | 30.00 |
| 220R | Mark McGwire HR 18 | 12.50 | 30.00 |
| 220S | Mark McGwire HR 19 | 12.50 | 30.00 |
| 220T | Mark McGwire HR 20 | 12.50 | 30.00 |
| 220U | Mark McGwire HR 21 | 12.50 | 30.00 |
| 220V | Mark McGwire HR 22 | 12.50 | 30.00 |
| 220W | Mark McGwire HR 23 | 12.50 | 30.00 |
| 220X | Mark McGwire HR 24 | 12.50 | 30.00 |
| 220Y | Mark McGwire HR 25 | 12.50 | 30.00 |
| 220Z | Mark McGwire HR 26 | 12.50 | 30.00 |
| 220AA | Mark McGwire HR 27 | 12.50 | 30.00 |
| 220AB | Mark McGwire HR 28 | 12.50 | 30.00 |
| 220AC | Mark McGwire HR 29 | 12.50 | 30.00 |
| 220AD | Mark McGwire HR 30 | 12.50 | 30.00 |
| 220AE | Mark McGwire HR 31 | 12.50 | 30.00 |
| 220AF | Mark McGwire HR 32 | 12.50 | 30.00 |
| 220AG | Mark McGwire HR 33 | 12.50 | 30.00 |
| 220AH | Mark McGwire HR 34 | 12.50 | 30.00 |
| 220AI | Mark McGwire HR 35 | 12.50 | 30.00 |
| 220AJ | Mark McGwire HR 36 | 12.50 | 30.00 |
| 220AK | Mark McGwire HR 37 | 12.50 | 30.00 |
| 220AL | Mark McGwire HR 38 | 12.50 | 30.00 |
| 220AM | Mark McGwire HR 39 | 12.50 | 30.00 |
| 220AN | Mark McGwire HR 40 | 12.50 | 30.00 |
| 220AO | Mark McGwire HR 41 | 12.50 | 30.00 |
| 220AP | Mark McGwire HR 42 | 12.50 | 30.00 |
| 220AQ | Mark McGwire HR 43 | 12.50 | 30.00 |
| 220AR | Mark McGwire HR 44 | 12.50 | 30.00 |
| 220AS | Mark McGwire HR 45 | 12.50 | 30.00 |
| 220AT | Mark McGwire HR 46 | 12.50 | 30.00 |
| 220AU | Mark McGwire HR 47 | 12.50 | 30.00 |
| 220AV | Mark McGwire HR 48 | 12.50 | 30.00 |
| 220AW | Mark McGwire HR 49 | 12.50 | 30.00 |
| 220AX | Mark McGwire HR 50 | 12.50 | 30.00 |
| 220AY | Mark McGwire HR 51 | 12.50 | 30.00 |
| 220AZ | Mark McGwire HR 52 | 12.50 | 30.00 |
| 220BB | Mark McGwire HR 53 | 12.50 | 30.00 |
| 220CC | Mark McGwire HR 54 | 12.50 | 30.00 |
| 220DD | Mark McGwire HR 55 | 12.50 | 30.00 |
| 220EE | Mark McGwire HR 56 | 12.50 | 30.00 |
| 220FF | Mark McGwire HR 57 | 12.50 | 30.00 |
| 220GG | Mark McGwire HR 58 | 12.50 | 30.00 |
| 220HH | Mark McGwire HR 59 | 12.50 | 30.00 |
| 220II | Mark McGwire HR 60 | 12.50 | 30.00 |
| 220JJ | Mark McGwire HR 61 | 20.00 | 50.00 |
| 220KK | Mark McGwire HR 62 | 40.00 | 80.00 |
| 220LL | Mark McGwire HR 63 | 12.50 | 30.00 |
| 220MM | Mark McGwire HR 64 | 20.00 | 50.00 |
| 220NN | Mark McGwire HR 65 | 20.00 | 50.00 |
| 220OO | Mark McGwire HR 66 | 20.00 | 50.00 |
| 220PP | Mark McGwire HR 67 | 20.00 | 50.00 |
| 220QQ | Mark McGwire HR 68 | 20.00 | 50.00 |
| 220RR | Mark McGwire HR 69 | 20.00 | 50.00 |
| 220SS | Mark McGwire HR 70 | 60.00 | 120.00 |
| 221 | Larry Walker LL | .20 | .50 |
| 222 | Bernie Williams LL | .30 | .75 |
| 223 | Mark McGwire LL | 1.00 | 2.50 |
| 224 | Ken Griffey Jr. LL | .75 | 2.00 |
| 225 | Sammy Sosa LL | .50 | 1.25 |
| 226 | Juan Gonzalez LL | .20 | .50 |
| 227 | Dante Bichette LL | .20 | .50 |
| 228 | Alex Rodriguez LL | .75 | 2.00 |
| 229 | Sammy Sosa LL | .50 | 1.25 |
| 230 | Derek Jeter LL | 1.00 | 2.50 |
| 231 | Greg Maddux LL | .75 | 2.00 |
| 232 | Roger Clemens LL | .75 | 2.00 |
| 233 | Ricky Ledee WS | .20 | .50 |
| 234 | Chuck Knoblauch WS | .20 | .50 |
| 235 | Bernie Williams WS | .30 | .75 |
| 236 | Tino Martinez WS | .30 | .75 |
| 237 | Orlando Hernandez WS | .30 | .75 |
| 238 | Scott Brosius WS | .20 | .50 |
| 239 | Andy Pettitte WS | .30 | .75 |
| 240 | Mariano Rivera WS | .50 | 1.25 |
| 241 | Checklist | .20 | .50 |
| 242 | Checklist | .20 | .50 |
| 243 | Tom Glavine | .50 | 1.25 |
| 244 | Andy Benes | .20 | .50 |
| 245 | Sandy Alomar Jr. | .20 | .50 |
| 246 | Wilton Guerrero | .20 | .50 |
| 247 | Alex Gonzalez | .20 | .50 |
| 248 | Roberto Alomar | .50 | 1.25 |
| 249 | Ruben Rivera | .20 | .50 |
| 250 | Eric Chavez | .30 | .75 |
| 251 | Ellis Burks | .30 | .75 |
| 252 | Richie Sexson | .30 | .75 |
| 253 | Steve Finley | .30 | .75 |
| 254 | Dwight Gooden | .30 | .75 |
| 255 | Dustin Hermanson | .20 | .50 |
| 256 | Kirk Rueter | .20 | .50 |
| 257 | Steve Trachsel | .20 | .50 |
| 258 | Gregg Jefferies | .20 | .50 |
| 259 | Matt Stairs | .20 | .50 |
| 260 | Shane Reynolds | .20 | .50 |
| 261 | Gregg Olson | .20 | .50 |
| 262 | Kevin Tapani | .20 | .50 |
| 263 | Matt Morris | .30 | .75 |
| 264 | Carl Pavano | .20 | .50 |
| 265 | Nomar Garciaparra | 1.25 | 3.00 |
| 266 | Kevin Young | .30 | .75 |
| 267 | Rick Helling | .20 | .50 |
| 268 | Matt Franco | .20 | .50 |
| 269 | Brian McRae | .20 | .50 |
| 270 | Cal Ripken | 2.50 | 6.00 |
| 271 | Jeff Abbott | .20 | .50 |
| 272 | Tony Batista | .20 | .50 |
| 273 | Bill Simas | .20 | .50 |
| 274 | Brian Hunter | .20 | .50 |
| 275 | John Franco | .30 | .75 |
| 276 | Devon White | .30 | .75 |
| 277 | Rickey Henderson | .75 | 2.00 |
| 278 | Chuck Finley | .20 | .50 |
| 279 | Mike Blowers | .20 | .50 |
| 280 | Mark Grace | .50 | 1.25 |
| 281 | Randy Winn | .20 | .50 |
| 282 | Bobby Bonilla | .30 | .75 |
| 283 | David Justice | .30 | .75 |
| 284 | Shane Monahan | .20 | .50 |
| 285 | Kevin Brown | .50 | 1.25 |
| 286 | Todd Zeile | .30 | .75 |
| 287 | Al Martin | .20 | .50 |
| 288 | Troy O'Leary | .20 | .50 |
| 289 | Darryl Hamilton | .20 | .50 |
| 290 | Tino Martinez | .50 | 1.25 |

|  |  | | |
|---|---|---|---|
| □ 291 | David Ortiz | .75 | 2.00 |
| □ 292 | Tony Clark | .20 | .50 |
| □ 293 | Ryan Minor | .20 | .50 |
| □ 294 | Mark Leiter | .20 | .50 |
| □ 295 | Wally Joyner | .30 | .75 |
| □ 296 | Cliff Floyd | .30 | .75 |
| □ 297 | Shawn Estes | .20 | .50 |
| □ 298 | Pat Hentgen | .20 | .50 |
| □ 299 | Scott Elarton | .20 | .50 |
| □ 300 | Alex Rodriguez | 1.25 | 3.00 |
| □ 301 | Ozzie Guillen | .30 | .75 |
| □ 302 | Hideo Nomo | .75 | 2.00 |
| □ 303 | Ryan McGuire | .20 | .50 |
| □ 304 | Brad Ausmus | .30 | .75 |
| □ 305 | Alex Gonzalez | .20 | .50 |
| □ 306 | Brian Jordan | .30 | .75 |
| □ 307 | John Jaha | .20 | .50 |
| □ 308 | Mark Grudzielanek | .20 | .50 |
| □ 309 | Juan Guzman | .20 | .50 |
| □ 310 | Tony Womack | .20 | .50 |
| □ 311 | Dennis Reyes | .20 | .50 |
| □ 312 | Marty Cordova | .20 | .50 |
| □ 313 | Ramiro Mendoza | .20 | .50 |
| □ 314 | Robin Ventura | .30 | .75 |
| □ 315 | Rafael Palmeiro | .50 | 1.25 |
| □ 316 | Ramon Martinez | .20 | .50 |
| □ 317 | Pedro Astacio | .20 | .50 |
| □ 318 | Dave Hollins | .20 | .50 |
| □ 319 | Tom Candiotti | .20 | .50 |
| □ 320 | Al Leiter | .30 | .75 |
| □ 321 | Rico Brogna | .20 | .50 |
| □ 322 | Reggie Jefferson | .20 | .50 |
| □ 323 | Bernard Gilkey | .20 | .50 |
| □ 324 | Jason Giambi | .30 | .75 |
| □ 325 | Craig Biggio | .50 | 1.25 |
| □ 326 | Troy Glaus | .50 | 1.25 |
| □ 327 | Delino DeShields | .20 | .50 |
| □ 328 | Fernando Vina | .20 | .50 |
| □ 329 | John Smoltz | .50 | 1.25 |
| □ 330 | Jeff Kent | .30 | .75 |
| □ 331 | Roy Halladay | .30 | .75 |
| □ 332 | Andy Ashby | .20 | .50 |
| □ 333 | Tim Wakefield | .30 | .75 |
| □ 334 | Roger Clemens | 1.50 | 4.00 |
| □ 335 | Bernie Williams | .50 | 1.25 |
| □ 336 | Desi Relaford | .20 | .50 |
| □ 337 | John Burkett | .20 | .50 |
| □ 338 | Mike Hampton | .30 | .75 |
| □ 339 | Royce Clayton | .20 | .50 |
| □ 340 | Mike Piazza | 1.25 | 3.00 |
| □ 341 | Jeremi Gonzalez | .20 | .50 |
| □ 342 | Mike Lansing | .20 | .50 |
| □ 343 | Jamie Moyer | .30 | .75 |
| □ 344 | Ron Coomer | .20 | .50 |
| □ 345 | Barry Larkin | .50 | 1.25 |
| □ 346 | Fernando Tatis | .30 | .75 |
| □ 347 | Chili Davis | .30 | .75 |
| □ 348 | Bobby Higginson | .30 | .75 |
| □ 349 | Hal Morris | .20 | .50 |
| □ 350 | Larry Walker | .30 | .75 |
| □ 351 | Carlos Guillen | .20 | .50 |
| □ 352 | Miguel Tejada | .30 | .75 |
| □ 353 | Travis Fryman | .30 | .75 |
| □ 354 | Jarrod Washburn | .20 | .50 |
| □ 355 | Chipper Jones | .75 | 2.00 |
| □ 356 | Todd Stottlemyre | .20 | .50 |
| □ 357 | Henry Rodriguez | .20 | .50 |
| □ 358 | Eli Marrero | .20 | .50 |
| □ 359 | Alan Benes | .20 | .50 |
| □ 360 | Tim Salmon | .50 | 1.25 |
| □ 361 | Luis Gonzalez | .30 | .75 |
| □ 362 | Scott Spiezio | .20 | .50 |
| □ 363 | Chris Carpenter | .30 | .75 |
| □ 364 | Bobby Howry | .20 | .50 |
| □ 365 | Raul Mondesi | .30 | .75 |
| □ 366 | Ugueth Urbina | .20 | .50 |
| □ 367 | Tom Evans | .20 | .50 |
| □ 368 | Kerry Ligtenberg RC | .20 | .50 |
| □ 369 | Adrian Beltre | .30 | .75 |
| □ 370 | Ryan Klesko | .30 | .75 |
| □ 371 | Wilson Alvarez | .20 | .50 |
| □ 372 | John Thomson | .20 | .50 |
| □ 373 | Tony Saunders | .20 | .50 |
| □ 374 | Dave Milcki | .20 | .50 |
| □ 375 | Ken Caminiti | .30 | .75 |
| □ 376 | Jay Buhner | .30 | .75 |
| □ 377 | Bill Mueller | .30 | .75 |
| □ 378 | Jeff Blauser | .20 | .50 |

|  |  | | |
|---|---|---|---|
| □ 379 | Edgar Renteria | .30 | .75 |
| □ 380 | Jim Thome | .50 | 1.25 |
| □ 381 | Joey Hamilton | .20 | .50 |
| □ 382 | Calvin Pickering | .20 | .50 |
| □ 383 | Marquis Grissom | .30 | .75 |
| □ 384 | Omar Daal | .20 | .50 |
| □ 385 | Curt Schilling | .30 | .75 |
| □ 386 | Jose Cruz Jr. | .20 | .50 |
| □ 387 | Chris Widger | .20 | .50 |
| □ 388 | Pete Harnisch | .20 | .50 |
| □ 389 | Charles Nagy | .20 | .50 |
| □ 390 | Tom Gordon | .20 | .50 |
| □ 391 | Bobby Smith | .20 | .50 |
| □ 392 | Derrick Gibson | .20 | .50 |
| □ 393 | Jeff Conine | .30 | .75 |
| □ 394 | Carlos Perez | .20 | .50 |
| □ 395 | Barry Bonds | 2.00 | 5.00 |
| □ 396 | Mark McLemore | .20 | .50 |
| □ 397 | Juan Encarnacion | .20 | .50 |
| □ 398 | Wade Boggs | .50 | 1.25 |
| □ 399 | Ivan Rodriguez | .50 | 1.25 |
| □ 401 | Moises Alou | .30 | .75 |
| □ 402 | Jeromy Burnitz | .20 | .50 |
| □ 402 | Sean Casey | .30 | .75 |
| □ 403 | Jose Offerman | .20 | .50 |
| □ 404 | Joe Fontenot | .20 | .50 |
| □ 405 | Kevin Millwood | .30 | .75 |
| □ 406 | Lance Johnson | .20 | .50 |
| □ 407 | Richard Hidalgo | .20 | .50 |
| □ 408 | Mike Jackson | .20 | .50 |
| □ 409 | Brian Anderson | .20 | .50 |
| □ 410 | Jeff Shaw | .20 | .50 |
| □ 411 | Preston Wilson | .30 | .75 |
| □ 412 | Todd Hundley | .20 | .50 |
| □ 413 | Jim Parque | .20 | .50 |
| □ 414 | Justin Baughman | .20 | .50 |
| □ 415 | Dante Bichette | .30 | .75 |
| □ 416 | Paul O'Neill | .50 | 1.25 |
| □ 417 | Miguel Cairo | .20 | .50 |
| □ 418 | Randy Johnson | .75 | 2.00 |
| □ 419 | Jesus Sanchez | .20 | .50 |
| □ 420 | Carlos Delgado | .30 | .75 |
| □ 421 | Ricky Ledee | .20 | .50 |
| □ 422 | Orlando Hernandez | .30 | .75 |
| □ 423 | Frank Thomas | .75 | 2.00 |
| □ 424 | Pokey Reese | .20 | .50 |
| □ 425 | C.Lee/M.Lowell | .40 | 1.00 |
| □ 426 | A.Cuyidyen/DeRosa/Hairston | .40 | 1.00 |
| □ 427 | M.Anderson/Belliard/Cabrera | .40 | 1.00 |
| □ 428 | M.Bowie/P.Norton RC/Wolf | .40 | 1.00 |
| □ 429 | J.Cressend RC/Rocker | .40 | 1.00 |
| □ 430 | R.Mateo/M.Zywica RC | .40 | 1.00 |
| □ 431 | J.LaRue/LeCroy/Moluskey | .40 | 1.00 |
| □ 432 | Gabe Kapler | .40 | 1.00 |
| □ 433 | A.Kennedy/M.Lopez RC | .40 | 1.00 |
| □ 434 | Jose Fernandez RC/C.Truby | .40 | 1.00 |
| □ 435 | Doug Mientkiewicz RC | .60 | 1.50 |
| □ 436 | R.Brown RC/V.Wells | .40 | 1.00 |
| □ 437 | A.J. Burnett RC | .75 | 2.00 |
| □ 438 | M.Belisle/M.Roney RC | .40 | 1.00 |
| □ 439 | A.Kearns/C.George RC | 1.50 | 4.00 |
| □ 440 | N.Cornejo/N.Bump RC | .40 | 1.00 |
| □ 441 | B.Lidge/M.Nannini RC | 1.50 | 4.00 |
| □ 442 | M.Holliday/J.Winchester RC | 3.00 | 8.00 |
| □ 443 | A.Everett/C.Ambres RC | .60 | 1.50 |
| □ 444 | P.Burrell/E.Valent RC | 1.50 | 4.00 |
| □ 445 | Roger Clemens SK | .75 | 2.00 |
| □ 446 | Kerry Wood SK | .20 | .50 |
| □ 447 | Curt Schilling SK | .20 | .50 |
| □ 448 | Randy Johnson SK | .50 | 1.25 |
| □ 449 | Pedro Martinez SK | .50 | 1.25 |
| □ 450 | Bagwell/Galar/McGwire AT | 1.00 | 2.00 |
| □ 451 | Olerud/Thome/Martinez AT | .30 | .75 |
| □ 452 | ARod/Nomar/Jeter AT | 1.00 | 2.50 |
| □ 453 | Castilla/Jones/Rolen AT | .50 | 1.25 |
| □ 454 | Sosa/Griffey/Gonzalez AT | .75 | 2.00 |
| □ 455 | Bonds/Ramirez/Walker AT | 1.00 | 2.50 |
| □ 456 | Thomas/Salmon/Justice AT | .75 | 2.00 |
| □ 457 | Lee/Helton/Grieve AT | .30 | .75 |
| □ 458 | Guerrero/Vaughn/B.Will AT | .30 | .75 |
| □ 459 | Piazza/I.Rod/Kendall AT | .50 | 1.25 |
| □ 460 | Clemens/Wood/Maddux AT | .75 | 2.00 |
| □ 461A | Sammy Sosa HR 1 | 8.00 | 20.00 |
| □ 461B | Sammy Sosa HR 2 | 5.00 | 12.00 |
| □ 461C | Sammy Sosa HR 3 | 5.00 | 12.00 |
| □ 461D | Sammy Sosa HR 4 | 5.00 | 12.00 |
| □ 461E | Sammy Sosa HR 5 | 5.00 | 12.00 |
| □ 461F | Sammy Sosa HR 6 | 5.00 | 12.00 |

|  |  | | |
|---|---|---|---|
| □ 461G | Sammy Sosa HR 7 | 5.00 | 12.00 |
| □ 461H | Sammy Sosa HR 8 | 5.00 | 12.00 |
| □ 461I | Sammy Sosa HR 9 | 5.00 | 12.00 |
| □ 461J | Sammy Sosa HR 10 | 5.00 | 12.00 |
| □ 461K | Sammy Sosa HR 11 | 5.00 | 12.00 |
| □ 461L | Sammy Sosa HR 12 | 5.00 | 12.00 |
| □ 461M | Sammy Sosa HR 13 | 5.00 | 12.00 |
| □ 461N | Sammy Sosa HR 14 | 5.00 | 12.00 |
| □ 461O | Sammy Sosa HR 15 | 5.00 | 12.00 |
| □ 461P | Sammy Sosa HR 16 | 5.00 | 12.00 |
| □ 461Q | Sammy Sosa HR 17 | 5.00 | 12.00 |
| □ 461R | Sammy Sosa HR 18 | 5.00 | 12.00 |
| □ 461S | Sammy Sosa HR 19 | 5.00 | 12.00 |
| □ 461T | Sammy Sosa HR 20 | 5.00 | 12.00 |
| □ 461U | Sammy Sosa HR 21 | 5.00 | 12.00 |
| □ 461V | Sammy Sosa HR 22 | 5.00 | 12.00 |
| □ 461W | Sammy Sosa HR 23 | 5.00 | 12.00 |
| □ 461X | Sammy Sosa HR 24 | 5.00 | 12.00 |
| □ 461Y | Sammy Sosa HR 25 | 5.00 | 12.00 |
| □ 461Z | Sammy Sosa HR 26 | 5.00 | 12.00 |
| □ 461AA | Sammy Sosa HR 27 | 5.00 | 12.00 |
| □ 461AB | Sammy Sosa HR 28 | 5.00 | 12.00 |
| □ 461AC | Sammy Sosa HR 29 | 5.00 | 12.00 |
| □ 461AD | Sammy Sosa HR 30 | 5.00 | 12.00 |
| □ 461AE | Sammy Sosa HR 31 | 5.00 | 12.00 |
| □ 461AF | Sammy Sosa HR 32 | 5.00 | 12.00 |
| □ 461AG | Sammy Sosa HR 33 | 5.00 | 12.00 |
| □ 461AH | Sammy Sosa HR 34 | 5.00 | 12.00 |
| □ 461AI | Sammy Sosa HR 35 | 5.00 | 12.00 |
| □ 461AJ | Sammy Sosa HR 36 | 5.00 | 12.00 |
| □ 461AK | Sammy Sosa HR 37 | 5.00 | 12.00 |
| □ 461AL | Sammy Sosa HR 38 | 5.00 | 12.00 |
| □ 461AM | Sammy Sosa HR 39 | 5.00 | 12.00 |
| □ 461AN | Sammy Sosa HR 40 | 5.00 | 12.00 |
| □ 461AO | Sammy Sosa HR 41 | 5.00 | 12.00 |
| □ 461AP | Sammy Sosa HR 42 | 5.00 | 12.00 |
| □ 461AR | Sammy Sosa HR 43 | 5.00 | 12.00 |
| □ 461AS | Sammy Sosa HR 44 | 5.00 | 12.00 |
| □ 461AT | Sammy Sosa HR 45 | 5.00 | 12.00 |
| □ 461AU | Sammy Sosa HR 46 | 5.00 | 12.00 |
| □ 461AV | Sammy Sosa HR 47 | 5.00 | 12.00 |
| □ 461AW | Sammy Sosa HR 48 | 5.00 | 12.00 |
| □ 461AX | Sammy Sosa HR 49 | 5.00 | 12.00 |
| □ 461AY | Sammy Sosa HR 50 | 5.00 | 12.00 |
| □ 461BA | Sammy Sosa HR 51 | 5.00 | 12.00 |
| □ 461BB | Sammy Sosa HR 52 | 5.00 | 12.00 |
| □ 461CC | Sammy Sosa HR 53 | 5.00 | 12.00 |
| □ 461DD | Sammy Sosa HR 54 | 5.00 | 12.00 |
| □ 461EE | Sammy Sosa HR 55 | 5.00 | 12.00 |
| □ 461FF | Sammy Sosa HR 56 | 5.00 | 12.00 |
| □ 461GG | Sammy Sosa HR 57 | 5.00 | 12.00 |
| □ 461HH | Sammy Sosa HR 58 | 5.00 | 12.00 |
| □ 461II | Sammy Sosa HR 59 | 5.00 | 12.00 |
| □ 461JJ | Sammy Sosa HR 60 | 5.00 | 12.00 |
| □ 461KK | Sammy Sosa HR 61 | 8.00 | 20.00 |
| □ 461LL | Sammy Sosa HR 62 | 12.50 | 30.00 |
| □ 461MM | Sammy Sosa HR 63 | 8.00 | 20.00 |
| □ 461NN | Sammy Sosa HR 64 | 8.00 | 20.00 |
| □ 461OO | Sammy Sosa HR 65 | 8.00 | 20.00 |
| □ 461PP | Sammy Sosa HR 66 | 30.00 | 60.00 |
| □ 462 | Checklist | .20 | .50 |
| □ 463 | Checklist | .20 | .50 |

## 2000 Topps Chrome

| | | |
|---|---|---|
| □ COMPLETE SET (478) | 60.00 | 160.00 |
| □ COMPLETE SERIES 1 (239) | 30.00 | 80.00 |
| □ COMPLETE SERIES 2 (240) | 30.00 | 80.00 |
| □ MCGWIRE MM SET (5) | 20.00 | 50.00 |
| □ AARON MM SET (5) | 15.00 | 40.00 |
| □ RIPKEN MM SET (5) | 25.00 | 60.00 |
| □ BOGGS MM SET (5) | 5.00 | 12.00 |
| □ GWYNN MM SET (5) | 10.00 | 25.00 |
| □ GRIFFEY MM SET (5) | 12.50 | 30.00 |
| □ BONDS MM SET (5) | 20.00 | 50.00 |

| Card | Low | High |
|---|---|---|
| ☐ SOSA MM SET (5) | 12.50 | 30.00 |
| ☐ JETER MM SET (5) | 20.00 | 50.00 |
| ☐ A.ROD MM SET (5) | 15.00 | 40.00 |
| ☐ 1 Mark McGwire | 2.00 | 5.00 |
| ☐ 2 Tony Gwynn | 1.00 | 2.50 |
| ☐ 3 Wade Boggs | .50 | 1.25 |
| ☐ 4 Cal Ripken | 2.50 | 6.00 |
| ☐ 5 Matt Williams | .30 | .75 |
| ☐ 6 Jay Buhner | .30 | .75 |
| ☐ 7 Does Not Exist | | |
| ☐ 8 Jeff Conine | .30 | .75 |
| ☐ 9 Todd Greene | .30 | .75 |
| ☐ 10 Mike Lieberthal | .30 | .75 |
| ☐ 11 Steve Avery | .30 | .75 |
| ☐ 12 Bret Saberhagen | .30 | .75 |
| ☐ 13 Magglio Ordonez | .30 | .75 |
| ☐ 14 Brad Radke | .30 | .75 |
| ☐ 15 Derek Jeter | 2.00 | 5.00 |
| ☐ 16 Javy Lopez | .30 | .75 |
| ☐ 17 Russ Davis | .30 | .75 |
| ☐ 18 Armando Benitez | .30 | .75 |
| ☐ 19 B.J. Surhoff | .30 | .75 |
| ☐ 20 Darryl Kile | .30 | .75 |
| ☐ 21 Mark Lewis | .30 | .75 |
| ☐ 22 Mike Williams | .30 | .75 |
| ☐ 23 Mark McLemore | .30 | .75 |
| ☐ 24 Sterling Hitchcock | .30 | .75 |
| ☐ 25 Darin Erstad | .30 | .75 |
| ☐ 26 Ricky Gutierrez | .30 | .75 |
| ☐ 27 John Jaha | .30 | .75 |
| ☐ 28 Homer Bush | .30 | .75 |
| ☐ 29 Darrin Fletcher | .30 | .75 |
| ☐ 30 Mark Grace | .50 | 1.25 |
| ☐ 31 Fred McGriff | .50 | 1.25 |
| ☐ 32 Omar Daal | .30 | .75 |
| ☐ 33 Eric Karros | .30 | .75 |
| ☐ 34 Orlando Cabrera | .30 | .75 |
| ☐ 35 J.T. Snow | .30 | .75 |
| ☐ 36 Luis Castillo | .30 | .75 |
| ☐ 37 Rey Ordonez | .30 | .75 |
| ☐ 38 Bob Abreu | .30 | .75 |
| ☐ 39 Warren Morris | .30 | .75 |
| ☐ 40 Juan Gonzalez | .30 | .75 |
| ☐ 41 Mike Lansing | .30 | .75 |
| ☐ 42 Chili Davis | .30 | .75 |
| ☐ 43 Dean Palmer | .30 | .75 |
| ☐ 44 Hank Aaron | 1.50 | 4.00 |
| ☐ 45 Jeff Bagwell | .50 | 1.25 |
| ☐ 46 Jose Valentin | .30 | .75 |
| ☐ 47 Shannon Stewart | .30 | .75 |
| ☐ 48 Kent Bottenfield | .30 | .75 |
| ☐ 49 Jeff Shaw | .30 | .75 |
| ☐ 50 Sammy Sosa | .75 | 2.00 |
| ☐ 51 Randy Johnson | .75 | 2.00 |
| ☐ 52 Benny Agbayani | .30 | .75 |
| ☐ 53 Dante Bichette | .30 | .75 |
| ☐ 54 Pete Harnisch | .30 | .75 |
| ☐ 55 Frank Thomas | .75 | 2.00 |
| ☐ 56 Jorge Posada | .50 | 1.25 |
| ☐ 57 Todd Walker | .30 | .75 |
| ☐ 58 Juan Encarnacion | .30 | .75 |
| ☐ 59 Mike Sweeney | .30 | .75 |
| ☐ 60 Pedro Martinez | .75 | 1.25 |
| ☐ 61 Lee Stevens | .30 | .75 |
| ☐ 62 Brian Giles | .30 | .75 |
| ☐ 63 Chad Ogea | .30 | .75 |
| ☐ 64 Ivan Rodriguez | .50 | 1.25 |
| ☐ 65 Roger Cedeno | .30 | .75 |
| ☐ 66 David Justice | .30 | .75 |
| ☐ 67 Steve Trachsel | .30 | .75 |
| ☐ 68 Eli Marrero | .30 | .75 |
| ☐ 69 Dave Nilsson | .30 | .75 |
| ☐ 70 Ken Caminiti | .30 | .75 |
| ☐ 71 Tim Raines | .30 | .75 |
| ☐ 72 Brian Jordan | .30 | .75 |
| ☐ 73 Jeff Blauser | .30 | .75 |
| ☐ 74 Bernard Gilkey | .30 | .75 |
| ☐ 75 John Flaherty | .30 | .75 |
| ☐ 76 Brent Mayne | .30 | .75 |
| ☐ 77 Jose Vidro | .30 | .75 |
| ☐ 78 David Bell | .30 | .75 |
| ☐ 79 Bruce Aven | .30 | .75 |
| ☐ 80 John Olerud | .30 | .75 |
| ☐ 81 Pokey Reese | .30 | .75 |
| ☐ 82 Woody Williams | .30 | .75 |
| ☐ 83 Ed Sprague | .30 | .75 |
| ☐ 84 Joe Girardi | .30 | .75 |
| ☐ 85 Barry Larkin | .50 | 1.25 |
| ☐ 86 Mike Caruso | .30 | .75 |
| ☐ 87 Bobby Higginson | .30 | .75 |
| ☐ 88 Roberto Kelly | .30 | .75 |
| ☐ 89 Edgar Martinez | .50 | 1.25 |
| ☐ 90 Mark Kotsay | .30 | .75 |
| ☐ 91 Paul Sorrento | .30 | .75 |
| ☐ 92 Eric Young | .30 | .75 |
| ☐ 93 Carlos Delgado | .30 | .75 |
| ☐ 94 Troy Glaus | .30 | .75 |
| ☐ 95 Ben Grieve | .30 | .75 |
| ☐ 96 Jose Lima | .30 | .75 |
| ☐ 97 Garret Anderson | .30 | .75 |
| ☐ 98 Luis Gonzalez | .30 | .75 |
| ☐ 99 Carl Pavano | .30 | .75 |
| ☐ 100 Alex Rodriguez | 1.25 | 3.00 |
| ☐ 101 Preston Wilson | .30 | .75 |
| ☐ 102 Ron Gant | .30 | .75 |
| ☐ 103 Brady Anderson | .30 | .75 |
| ☐ 104 Rickey Henderson | .75 | 2.00 |
| ☐ 105 Gary Sheffield | .30 | .75 |
| ☐ 106 Mickey Morandini | .30 | .75 |
| ☐ 107 Jim Edmonds | .30 | .75 |
| ☐ 108 Kris Benson | .30 | .75 |
| ☐ 109 Adrian Beltre | .30 | .75 |
| ☐ 110 Alex Fernandez | .30 | .75 |
| ☐ 111 Dan Wilson | .30 | .75 |
| ☐ 112 Mark Clark | .30 | .75 |
| ☐ 113 Greg Vaughn | .30 | .75 |
| ☐ 114 Neifi Perez | .30 | .75 |
| ☐ 115 Paul O'Neill | .50 | 1.25 |
| ☐ 116 Jermaine Dye | .30 | .75 |
| ☐ 117 Todd Jones | .30 | .75 |
| ☐ 118 Terry Steinbach | .30 | .75 |
| ☐ 119 Greg Norton | .30 | .75 |
| ☐ 120 Curt Schilling | .30 | .75 |
| ☐ 121 Todd Zeile | .30 | .75 |
| ☐ 122 Edgardo Alfonzo | .30 | .75 |
| ☐ 123 Ryan McGuire | .30 | .75 |
| ☐ 124 Rich Aurilia | .30 | .75 |
| ☐ 125 John Smoltz | .50 | 1.25 |
| ☐ 126 Bob Wickman | .30 | .75 |
| ☐ 127 Richard Hidalgo | .30 | .75 |
| ☐ 128 Chuck Finley | .30 | .75 |
| ☐ 129 Billy Wagner | .30 | .75 |
| ☐ 130 Todd Hundley | .30 | .75 |
| ☐ 131 Dwight Gooden | .30 | .75 |
| ☐ 132 Russ Ortiz | .30 | .75 |
| ☐ 133 Mike Lowell | .30 | .75 |
| ☐ 134 Reggie Sanders | .30 | .75 |
| ☐ 135 John Valentin | .30 | .75 |
| ☐ 136 Brad Ausmus | .30 | .75 |
| ☐ 137 Chad Kreuter | .30 | .75 |
| ☐ 138 David Cone | .30 | .75 |
| ☐ 139 Brook Fordyce | .30 | .75 |
| ☐ 140 Roberto Alomar | .50 | 1.25 |
| ☐ 141 Charles Nagy | .30 | .75 |
| ☐ 142 Brian Hunter | .30 | .75 |
| ☐ 143 Mike Mussina | .50 | 1.25 |
| ☐ 144 Robin Ventura | .50 | 1.25 |
| ☐ 145 Kevin Brown | .30 | .75 |
| ☐ 146 Pat Hentgen | .30 | .75 |
| ☐ 147 Ryan Klesko | .30 | .75 |
| ☐ 148 Derek Bell | .30 | .75 |
| ☐ 149 Andy Sheets | .30 | .75 |
| ☐ 150 Larry Walker | .30 | .75 |
| ☐ 151 Scott Williamson | .30 | .75 |
| ☐ 152 Jose Offerman | .30 | .75 |
| ☐ 153 Doug Mientkiewicz | .30 | .75 |
| ☐ 154 John Snyder RC | .40 | 1.00 |
| ☐ 155 Sandy Alomar Jr. | .30 | .75 |
| ☐ 156 Joe Nathan | .30 | .75 |
| ☐ 157 Lance Johnson | .30 | .75 |
| ☐ 158 Odalis Perez | .30 | .75 |
| ☐ 159 Hideo Nomo | .75 | 2.00 |
| ☐ 160 Steve Finley | .30 | .75 |
| ☐ 161 Dave Martinez | .30 | .75 |
| ☐ 162 Matt Walbeck | .30 | .75 |
| ☐ 163 Bill Spiers | .30 | .75 |
| ☐ 164 Fernando Tatis | .30 | .75 |
| ☐ 165 Kenny Lofton | .30 | .75 |
| ☐ 166 Paul Byrd | .30 | .75 |
| ☐ 167 Aaron Sele | .30 | .75 |
| ☐ 168 Eddie Taubensee | .30 | .75 |
| ☐ 169 Reggie Jefferson | .30 | .75 |
| ☐ 170 Roger Clemens | 1.50 | 4.00 |
| ☐ 171 Francisco Cordova | .30 | .75 |
| ☐ 172 Mike Bordick | .30 | .75 |
| ☐ 173 Wally Joyner | .30 | .75 |
| ☐ 174 Marvin Benard | .30 | .75 |
| ☐ 175 Jason Kendall | .30 | .75 |
| ☐ 176 Mike Stanley | .30 | .75 |
| ☐ 177 Chad Allen | .30 | .75 |
| ☐ 178 Carlos Beltran | .30 | .75 |
| ☐ 179 Deivi Cruz | .30 | .75 |
| ☐ 180 Chipper Jones | .75 | 2.00 |
| ☐ 181 Vladimir Guerrero | .75 | 2.00 |
| ☐ 182 Dave Burba | .30 | .75 |
| ☐ 183 Tom Goodwin | .30 | .75 |
| ☐ 184 Brian Daubach | .30 | .75 |
| ☐ 185 Jay Bell | .30 | .75 |
| ☐ 186 Roy Halladay | .30 | .75 |
| ☐ 187 Miguel Tejada | .30 | .75 |
| ☐ 188 Armando Rios | .30 | .75 |
| ☐ 189 Fernando Vina | .30 | .75 |
| ☐ 190 Eric Davis | .30 | .75 |
| ☐ 191 Henry Rodriguez | .30 | .75 |
| ☐ 192 Joe McEwing | .30 | .75 |
| ☐ 193 Jeff Kent | .30 | .75 |
| ☐ 194 Mike Jackson | .30 | .75 |
| ☐ 195 Mike Morgan | .30 | .75 |
| ☐ 196 Jeff Montgomery | .30 | .75 |
| ☐ 197 Jeff Zimmerman | .30 | .75 |
| ☐ 198 Tony Fernandez | .30 | .75 |
| ☐ 199 Jason Giambi | .30 | .75 |
| ☐ 200 Jose Canseco | .50 | 1.25 |
| ☐ 201 Alex Gonzalez | .30 | .75 |
| ☐ 202 J.Cust/Colangelo/D.Brown | .40 | 1.00 |
| ☐ 203 A.Soriano/F.Lopez | .75 | 2.00 |
| ☐ 204 Durazo/Burrell/Johnson | .60 | 1.50 |
| ☐ 205 John Sneed RC/K.Wells | .40 | 1.00 |
| ☐ 206 Kalinowski/Tejera/Mears RC | .40 | 1.00 |
| ☐ 207 L.Berkman/C.Patterson | .60 | 1.50 |
| ☐ 208 K.Pellow/K.Barker/R.Branyan | .40 | 1.00 |
| ☐ 209 B.Garbel/L.Bigbie RC | 1.00 | 2.50 |
| ☐ 210 B.Bradley RC/E.Munson | .40 | 1.00 |
| ☐ 211 J.Girdley/K.Snyder | .40 | 1.00 |
| ☐ 212 Chance Caple RC/J.Jennings | .40 | 1.00 |
| ☐ 213 B.Myers/R.Christianson RC | 1.50 | 1.00 |
| ☐ 214 J.Stumm/R.Purvis RC | .40 | 1.00 |
| ☐ 215 D.Walling/M.Paradis | .40 | 1.00 |
| ☐ 216 O.Ortiz/J.Gehrke | .40 | 1.00 |
| ☐ 217 David Cone HL | .30 | .75 |
| ☐ 218 Jose Jimenez HL | .30 | .75 |
| ☐ 219 Chris Singleton HL | .30 | .75 |
| ☐ 220 Fernando Tatis HL | .30 | .75 |
| ☐ 221 Todd Helton HL | .30 | .75 |
| ☐ 222 Kevin Millwood DIV | .30 | .75 |
| ☐ 223 Todd Pratt DIV | .30 | .75 |
| ☐ 224 Orlando Hernandez DIV | .30 | .75 |
| ☐ 225 Pedro Martinez DIV | .50 | 1.25 |
| ☐ 226 Tom Glavine LCS | .30 | .75 |
| ☐ 227 Bernie Williams LCS | .30 | .75 |
| ☐ 228 Mariano Rivera WS | .50 | 1.25 |
| ☐ 229 Tony Gwynn 20CB | 1.00 | 2.50 |
| ☐ 230 Wade Boggs 20CB | .50 | 1.25 |
| ☐ 231 Lance Johnson CB | .30 | .75 |
| ☐ 232 Mark McGwire 20CB | 2.00 | 5.00 |
| ☐ 233 Rickey Henderson 20CB | .75 | 2.00 |
| ☐ 234 Rickey Henderson 20CB | .75 | 2.00 |
| ☐ 235 Roger Clemens 20CB | 1.50 | 4.00 |
| ☐ 236A M.McGwire MM 1st HR | 5.00 | 12.00 |
| ☐ 236B M.McGwire MM 1987 ROY | 5.00 | 12.00 |
| ☐ 236C M.McGwire MM 62nd HR | 5.00 | 12.00 |
| ☐ 236D M.McGwire MM 70th HR | 5.00 | 12.00 |
| ☐ 236E M.McGwire MM 500th HR | 5.00 | 12.00 |
| ☐ 237A H.Aaron MM 1st Career HR | 4.00 | 10.00 |
| ☐ 237B H.Aaron MM 1957 MVP | 4.00 | 10.00 |
| ☐ 237C H.Aaron MM 3000th Hit | 4.00 | 10.00 |
| ☐ 237D H.Aaron MM 715th HR | 4.00 | 10.00 |
| ☐ 237E H.Aaron MM 755th HR | 4.00 | 10.00 |
| ☐ 238A C.Ripken MM 1982 ROY | 6.00 | 15.00 |
| ☐ 238B C.Ripken MM 1991 MVP | 6.00 | 15.00 |
| ☐ 238C C.Ripken MM 2131 Game | 6.00 | 15.00 |
| ☐ 238D C.Ripken MM Streak Ends | 6.00 | 15.00 |
| ☐ 238E C.Ripken MM 400th HR | 6.00 | 15.00 |
| ☐ 239A W.Boggs MM 1983 Batting | 1.25 | 3.00 |
| ☐ 239B W.Boggs MM 1988 Batting | 1.25 | 3.00 |
| ☐ 239C W.Boggs MM 2000th Hit | 1.25 | 3.00 |
| ☐ 239D W.Boggs MM 1996 Champs | 1.25 | 3.00 |
| ☐ 239E W.Boggs MM 3000th Hit | 1.25 | 3.00 |
| ☐ 240A T.Gwynn MM 1984 Batting | 2.50 | 6.00 |
| ☐ 240B T.Gwynn MM 1984 NLCS | 2.50 | 6.00 |
| ☐ 240C T.Gwynn MM 1995 Batting | 2.50 | 6.00 |
| ☐ 240D T.Gwynn MM 1998 NLCS | 2.50 | 6.00 |
| ☐ 240E T.Gwynn MM 3000th Hit | 2.50 | 6.00 |
| ☐ 241 Tom Glavine | .50 | 1.25 |

|  |  | | |
|---|---|---|---|
| 242 | David Wells | .30 | .75 |
| 243 | Kevin Appier | .30 | .75 |
| 244 | Troy Percival | .30 | .75 |
| 245 | Ray Lankford | .30 | .75 |
| 246 | Marquis Grissom | .30 | .75 |
| 247 | Randy Winn | .30 | .75 |
| 248 | Miguel Batista | .30 | .75 |
| 249 | Darren Dreifort | .30 | .75 |
| 250 | Barry Bonds | 1.50 | 4.00 |
| 251 | Harold Baines | .30 | .75 |
| 252 | Cliff Floyd | .30 | .75 |
| 253 | Freddy Garcia | .30 | .75 |
| 254 | Kenny Rogers | .30 | .75 |
| 255 | Ben Davis | .30 | .75 |
| 256 | Charles Johnson | .30 | .75 |
| 257 | Bubba Trammell | .30 | .75 |
| 258 | Desi Relaford | .30 | .75 |
| 259 | Al Martin | .30 | .75 |
| 260 | Andy Pettitte | .50 | 1.25 |
| 261 | Carlos Lee | .30 | .75 |
| 262 | Matt Lawton | .30 | .75 |
| 263 | Andy Fox | .30 | .75 |
| 264 | Chan Ho Park | .30 | .75 |
| 265 | Billy Koch | .30 | .75 |
| 266 | Dave Roberts | .30 | .75 |
| 267 | Carl Everett | .30 | .75 |
| 268 | Orel Hershiser | .30 | .75 |
| 269 | Trot Nixon | .30 | .75 |
| 270 | Rusty Greer | .30 | .75 |
| 271 | Will Clark | .50 | 1.25 |
| 272 | Quilvio Veras | .30 | .75 |
| 273 | Rico Brogna | .30 | .75 |
| 274 | Devon White | .30 | .75 |
| 275 | Tim Hudson | .30 | .75 |
| 276 | Mike Hampton | .30 | .75 |
| 277 | Miguel Cairo | .30 | .75 |
| 278 | Darren Oliver | .30 | .75 |
| 279 | Jeff Cirillo | .30 | .75 |
| 280 | Al Leiter | .30 | .75 |
| 281 | Shane Andrews | .30 | .75 |
| 282 | Carlos Febles | .30 | .75 |
| 283 | Pedro Astacio | .30 | .75 |
| 284 | Juan Guzman | .30 | .75 |
| 285 | Orlando Hernandez | .30 | .75 |
| 286 | Paul Konerko | .30 | .75 |
| 287 | Tony Clark | .30 | .75 |
| 288 | Aaron Boone | .30 | .75 |
| 289 | Ismael Valdes | .30 | .75 |
| 290 | Moises Alou | .30 | .75 |
| 291 | Kevin Tapani | .30 | .75 |
| 292 | John Franco | .30 | .75 |
| 293 | Todd Zeile | .30 | .75 |
| 294 | Jason Schmidt | .30 | .75 |
| 295 | Johnny Damon | .50 | 1.25 |
| 296 | Scott Brosius | .30 | .75 |
| 297 | Travis Fryman | .30 | .75 |
| 298 | Jose Vizcaino | .30 | .75 |
| 299 | Eric Chavez | .30 | .75 |
| 300 | Mike Piazza | 1.25 | 3.00 |
| 301 | Matt Clement | .30 | .75 |
| 302 | Cristian Guzman | .30 | .75 |
| 303 | C.J. Nitkowski | .30 | .75 |
| 304 | Michael Tucker | .30 | .75 |
| 305 | Brett Tomko | .30 | .75 |
| 306 | Mike Lansing | .30 | .75 |
| 307 | Eric Owens | .30 | .75 |
| 308 | Livan Hernandez | .30 | .75 |
| 309 | Rondell White | .30 | .75 |
| 310 | Todd Stottlemyre | .30 | .75 |
| 311 | Chris Carpenter | .30 | .75 |
| 312 | Ken Hill | .30 | .75 |
| 313 | Mark Loretta | .30 | .75 |
| 314 | John Rocker | .30 | .75 |
| 315 | Richie Sexson | .30 | .75 |
| 316 | Ruben Mateo | .30 | .75 |
| 317 | Joe Randa | .30 | .75 |
| 318 | Mike Sirotka | .30 | .75 |
| 319 | Jose Rosado | .30 | .75 |
| 320 | Matt Mantei | .30 | .75 |
| 321 | Kevin Millwood | .30 | .75 |
| 322 | Gary Disarcina | .30 | .75 |
| 323 | Dustin Hermanson | .30 | .75 |
| 324 | Mike Stanton | .30 | .75 |
| 325 | Kirk Rueter | .30 | .75 |
| 326 | Damian Miller RC | .60 | 1.50 |
| 327 | Doug Glanville | .30 | .75 |
| 328 | Scott Rolen | .50 | 1.25 |
| 329 | Ray Durham | .30 | .75 |
| 330 | Butch Huskey | .30 | .75 |
| 331 | Mariano Rivera | .75 | 2.00 |
| 332 | Darren Lewis | .30 | .75 |
| 333 | Mike Timlin | .30 | .75 |
| 334 | Mark Grudzielanek | .30 | .75 |
| 335 | Mike Cameron | .30 | .75 |
| 336 | Kelvim Escobar | .30 | .75 |
| 337 | Bret Boone | .30 | .75 |
| 338 | Mo Vaughn | .30 | .75 |
| 339 | Craig Biggio | .50 | 1.25 |
| 340 | Michael Barrett | .30 | .75 |
| 341 | Marlon Anderson | .30 | .75 |
| 342 | Bobby Jones | .30 | .75 |
| 343 | John Halama | .30 | .75 |
| 344 | Todd Ritchie | .30 | .75 |
| 345 | Chuck Knoblauch | .30 | .75 |
| 346 | Rick Reed | .30 | .75 |
| 347 | Kelly Stinnett | .30 | .75 |
| 348 | Tim Salmon | .50 | 1.25 |
| 349 | A.J. Hinch | .30 | .75 |
| 350 | Jose Cruz Jr. | .30 | .75 |
| 351 | Roberto Hernandez | .30 | .75 |
| 352 | Edgar Renteria | .30 | .75 |
| 353 | Jose Hernandez | .30 | .75 |
| 354 | Brad Fullmer | .30 | .75 |
| 355 | Trevor Hoffman | .30 | .75 |
| 356 | Troy O'Leary | .30 | .75 |
| 357 | Justin Thompson | .30 | .75 |
| 358 | Kevin Young | .30 | .75 |
| 359 | Hideki Irabu | .30 | .75 |
| 360 | Jim Thome | .50 | 1.25 |
| 361 | Steve Karsay | .30 | .75 |
| 362 | Octavio Dotel | .30 | .75 |
| 363 | Omar Vizquel | .50 | 1.25 |
| 364 | Raul Mondesi | .30 | .75 |
| 365 | Shane Reynolds | .30 | .75 |
| 366 | Bartolo Colon | .30 | .75 |
| 367 | Chris Widger | .30 | .75 |
| 368 | Gabe Kapler | .30 | .75 |
| 369 | Bill Simas | .30 | .75 |
| 370 | Tino Martinez | .50 | 1.25 |
| 371 | John Thomson | .30 | .75 |
| 372 | Delino Deshields | .30 | .75 |
| 373 | Carlos Perez | .30 | .75 |
| 374 | Eddie Perez | .30 | .75 |
| 375 | Jeromy Burnitz | .30 | .75 |
| 376 | Jimmy Haynes | .30 | .75 |
| 377 | Travis Lee | .30 | .75 |
| 378 | Darryl Hamilton | .30 | .75 |
| 379 | Jamie Moyer | .30 | .75 |
| 380 | Alex Gonzalez | .30 | .75 |
| 381 | John Wetteland | .30 | .75 |
| 382 | Vinny Castilla | .30 | .75 |
| 383 | Jeff Suppan | .30 | .75 |
| 384 | Jim Leyritz | .30 | .75 |
| 385 | Robb Nen | .30 | .75 |
| 386 | Wilson Alvarez | .30 | .75 |
| 387 | Andres Galarraga | .30 | .75 |
| 388 | Mike Remlinger | .30 | .75 |
| 389 | Geoff Jenkins | .30 | .75 |
| 390 | Matt Stairs | .30 | .75 |
| 391 | Bill Mueller | .30 | .75 |
| 392 | Mike Lowell | .30 | .75 |
| 393 | Andy Ashby | .30 | .75 |
| 394 | Ruben Rivera | .30 | .75 |
| 395 | Todd Helton | .50 | 1.25 |
| 396 | Bernie Williams | .50 | 1.25 |
| 397 | Royce Clayton | .30 | .75 |
| 398 | Manny Ramirez | .50 | 1.25 |
| 399 | Kerry Wood | .30 | .75 |
| 400 | Ken Griffey Jr. | 1.25 | 3.00 |
| 401 | Enrique Wilson | .30 | .75 |
| 402 | Joey Hamilton | .30 | .75 |
| 403 | Shawn Estes | .30 | .75 |
| 404 | Ugueth Urbina | .30 | .75 |
| 405 | Albert Belle | .30 | .75 |
| 406 | Rick Helling | .30 | .75 |
| 407 | Steve Parris | .30 | .75 |
| 408 | Eric Milton | .30 | .75 |
| 409 | Dave Mlicki | .30 | .75 |
| 410 | Shawn Green | .30 | .75 |
| 411 | Jaret Wright | .30 | .75 |
| 412 | Tony Womack | .30 | .75 |
| 413 | Vernon Wells | .30 | .75 |
| 414 | Ron Belliard | .30 | .75 |
| 415 | Ellis Burks | .30 | .75 |
| 416 | Scott Erickson | .30 | .75 |
| 417 | Rafael Palmeiro | .50 | 1.25 |
| 418 | Damion Easley | .30 | .75 |
| 419 | Jamey Wright | .30 | .75 |
| 420 | Corey Koskie | .30 | .75 |
| 421 | Bobby Howry | .30 | .75 |
| 422 | Ricky Ledee | .30 | .75 |
| 423 | Dmitri Young | .30 | .75 |
| 424 | Sidney Ponson | .30 | .75 |
| 425 | Greg Maddux | 1.25 | 3.00 |
| 426 | Jose Guillen | .30 | .75 |
| 427 | Jon Lieber | .30 | .75 |
| 428 | Andy Benes | .30 | .75 |
| 429 | Randy Velarde | .30 | .75 |
| 430 | Sean Casey | .30 | .75 |
| 431 | Torii Hunter | .30 | .75 |
| 432 | Ryan Rupe | .30 | .75 |
| 433 | David Segui | .30 | .75 |
| 434 | Todd Pratt | .30 | .75 |
| 435 | Nomar Garciaparra | 1.25 | 3.00 |
| 436 | Denny Neagle | .30 | .75 |
| 437 | Ron Coomer | .30 | .75 |
| 438 | Chris Singleton | .30 | .75 |
| 439 | Tony Batista | .30 | .75 |
| 440 | Andruw Jones | .50 | 1.25 |
| 441 | Burroughs/Piatt/Huff | .30 | .75 |
| 442 | Rafael Furcal | .60 | 1.50 |
| 443 | M.Lamb RC/J.Crede | 1.50 | 4.00 |
| 444 | Julio Zuleta RC | .40 | 1.00 |
| 445 | Garry Maddux Jr. RC | .40 | 1.00 |
| 446 | Riley/Sabathia/Mulder | .60 | 1.50 |
| 447 | Scott Downs RC | .40 | 1.00 |
| 448 | D.Mirabelli/B.Petrick/J.Werth | .40 | 1.00 |
| 450 | B.Christensen/R.Stahl RC | .40 | 1.00 |
| 451 | B.Zito/B.Sheets RC | 4.00 | 10.00 |
| 452 | K.Ainsworth/Howington RC | .40 | 1.00 |
| 453 | A.Asadoorian/V.Faison RC | .60 | 1.50 |
| 454 | K.Reed/J.Heaverlo RC | .40 | 1.00 |
| 455 | M.MacDougal/B.Baker RC | .40 | 1.00 |
| 456 | Mark McGwire SH | 1.00 | 2.50 |
| 457 | Cal Ripken SH | 1.25 | 3.00 |
| 458 | Wade Boggs SH | .30 | .75 |
| 459 | Tony Gwynn SH | .50 | 1.25 |
| 460 | Jesse Orosco SH | .30 | .75 |
| 461 | L.Walker/N.Garciaparra LL | .50 | 1.25 |
| 462 | K.Griffey Jr./M.McGwire LL | .75 | 2.00 |
| 463 | M.Ramirez/M.McGwire LL | .75 | 2.00 |
| 464 | P.Martinez/R.Johnson LL | .50 | 1.25 |
| 465 | P.Martinez/R.Johnson LL | .50 | 1.25 |
| 466 | D.Jeter/L.Gonzalez LL | .75 | 2.00 |
| 467 | L.Walker/M.Ramirez LL | .50 | 1.25 |
| 468 | Tony Gwynn 20CB | 1.00 | 2.50 |
| 469 | Mark McGwire 20CB | 2.00 | 5.00 |
| 470 | Frank Thomas 20CB | .50 | 1.25 |
| 471 | Harold Baines 20CB | .30 | .75 |
| 472 | Roger Clemens 20CB | 1.50 | 4.00 |
| 473 | John Franco 20CB | .30 | .75 |
| 474 | John Franco 20CB | .30 | .75 |
| 475A | K.Griffey Jr. MM 350th HR | 3.00 | 8.00 |
| 475B | K.Griffey Jr. MM 1997 MVP | 3.00 | 8.00 |
| 475C | K.Griffey Jr. MM HR Dad | 3.00 | 8.00 |
| 475D | K.Griffey Jr. MM 1992 AS MVP | 3.00 | 8.00 |
| 475E | K.Griffey Jr. MM 50 HR 1997 | 3.00 | 8.00 |
| 476A | B.Bonds MM 400HR/400SB | 5.00 | 12.00 |
| 476B | B.Bonds MM 40HR/40SB | 5.00 | 12.00 |
| 476C | B.Bonds MM 1993 MVP | 5.00 | 12.00 |
| 476D | B.Bonds MM 1990 MVP | 5.00 | 12.00 |
| 476E | B.Bonds MM 1992 MVP | 5.00 | 12.00 |
| 477A | S.Sosa MM 20 HR June | 3.00 | 8.00 |
| 477B | S.Sosa MM 66 HR 1998 | 3.00 | 8.00 |
| 477C | S.Sosa MM 60 HR 1999 | 3.00 | 8.00 |
| 477D | S.Sosa MM 1998 MVP | 3.00 | 8.00 |
| 477E | S.Sosa MM HR's 61/62 | 3.00 | 8.00 |
| 478A | D.Jeter MM 1996 ROY | 5.00 | 12.00 |
| 478B | D.Jeter MM Wins 1999 WS | 5.00 | 12.00 |
| 478C | D.Jeter MM Wins 1998 WS | 5.00 | 12.00 |
| 478D | D.Jeter MM Wins 1996 WS | 5.00 | 12.00 |
| 478E | D.Jeter MM 17 GM Hit Streak | 5.00 | 12.00 |
| 479A | A.Rodriguez MM 40HR/40SB | 4.00 | 10.00 |
| 479B | A.Rodriguez MM 100th HR | 4.00 | 10.00 |
| 479C | A.Rodriguez MM 1998 POY | 4.00 | 10.00 |
| 479D | A.Rodriguez MM Wins 1 Million | 4.00 | 10.00 |
| 479E | A.Rodriguez MM 1996 Batting Leader | 4.00 | 10.00 |
| NNO | M.McGwire 85 Reprint | 3.00 | 8.00 |

## 2001 Topps Chrome

| | | |
|---|---|---|
| ☐ COMPLETE SET (661) | 150.00 | 300.00 |
| ☐ COMPLETE SERIES 1 (331) | 75.00 | 150.00 |
| ☐ COMPLETE SERIES 2 (330) | 75.00 | -150.00 |
| ☐ 1 Cal Ripken | 2.50 | 6.00 |
| ☐ 2 Chipper Jones | .75 | 2.00 |
| ☐ 3 Roger Cedeno | .20 | .50 |
| ☐ 4 Garret Anderson | .30 | .75 |
| ☐ 5 Robin Ventura | .30 | .75 |
| ☐ 6 Daryle Ward | .20 | .50 |
| ☐ 7 Does Not Exist | | |
| ☐ 8 Phil Nevin | .30 | .75 |
| ☐ 9 Jermaine Dye | .30 | .75 |
| ☐ 10 Chris Singleton | .20 | .50 |
| ☐ 11 Mike Redmond | .20 | .50 |
| ☐ 12 Jim Thome | .50 | 1.25 |
| ☐ 13 Brian Jordan | .30 | .75 |
| ☐ 14 Dustin Hermanson | .20 | .50 |
| ☐ 15 Shawn Green | .30 | .75 |
| ☐ 16 Todd Stottlemyre | .20 | .50 |
| ☐ 17 Dan Wilson | .20 | .50 |
| ☐ 18 Derek Lowe | .30 | .75 |
| ☐ 19 Juan Gonzalez | .30 | .75 |
| ☐ 20 Pat Meares | .20 | .50 |
| ☐ 21 Paul O'Neill | .50 | 1.25 |
| ☐ 22 Jeffrey Hammonds | .20 | .50 |
| ☐ 23 Pokey Reese | .20 | .50 |
| ☐ 24 Mike Mussina | .50 | 1.25 |
| ☐ 25 Rico Brogna | .20 | .50 |
| ☐ 26 Jay Buhner | .30 | .75 |
| ☐ 27 Steve Cox | .20 | .50 |
| ☐ 28 Quilvio Veras | .20 | .50 |
| ☐ 29 Marquis Grissom | .20 | .50 |
| ☐ 30 Shigetoshi Hasegawa | .30 | .75 |
| ☐ 31 Shane Reynolds | .20 | .50 |
| ☐ 32 Adam Piatt | .20 | .50 |
| ☐ 33 Preston Wilson | .30 | .75 |
| ☐ 34 Ellis Burks | .30 | .75 |
| ☐ 35 Armando Rios | .20 | .50 |
| ☐ 36 Chuck Finley | .30 | .75 |
| ☐ 37 Shannon Stewart | .30 | .75 |
| ☐ 38 Mark McGwire | 2.00 | 5.00 |
| ☐ 39 Gerald Williams | .20 | .50 |
| ☐ 40 Eric Young | .20 | .50 |
| ☐ 41 Peter Bergeron | .20 | .50 |
| ☐ 42 Arthur Rhodes | .20 | .50 |
| ☐ 43 Bobby Jones | .20 | .50 |
| ☐ 44 Matt Clement | .30 | .75 |
| ☐ 45 Pedro Martinez | .50 | 1.25 |
| ☐ 46 Jose Canseco | .50 | 1.25 |
| ☐ 47 Matt Anderson | .20 | .50 |
| ☐ 48 Torii Hunter | .30 | .75 |
| ☐ 49 Carlos Lee | .30 | .75 |
| ☐ 50 Eric Chavez | .30 | .75 |
| ☐ 51 Rick Helling | .20 | .50 |
| ☐ 52 John Franco | .30 | .75 |
| ☐ 53 Mike Bordick | .30 | .75 |
| ☐ 54 Andres Galarraga | .30 | .75 |
| ☐ 55 Jose Cruz Jr. | .20 | .50 |
| ☐ 56 Mike Matheny | .20 | .50 |
| ☐ 57 Randy Johnson | .75 | 2.00 |
| ☐ 58 Richie Sexson | .20 | .50 |
| ☐ 59 Vladimir Nunez | .20 | .50 |
| ☐ 60 Aaron Boone | .30 | .75 |
| ☐ 61 Darin Erstad | .30 | .75 |
| ☐ 62 Alex Gonzalez | .20 | .50 |
| ☐ 63 Gil Heredia | .20 | .50 |
| ☐ 64 Shane Andrews | .20 | .50 |
| ☐ 65 Todd Hundley | .20 | .50 |
| ☐ 66 Bill Mueller | .30 | .75 |
| ☐ 67 Mark McLemore | .20 | .50 |
| ☐ 68 Scott Spiezio | .20 | .50 |
| ☐ 69 Kevin McGlinchy | .20 | .50 |

| | | |
|---|---|---|
| ☐ 70 Manny Ramirez | .50 | 1.25 |
| ☐ 71 Mike Lamb | .20 | .50 |
| ☐ 72 Brian Buchanan | .20 | .50 |
| ☐ 73 Mike Sweeney | .30 | .75 |
| ☐ 74 John Wetteland | .30 | .75 |
| ☐ 75 Rob Bell | .20 | .50 |
| ☐ 76 John Burkett | .20 | .50 |
| ☐ 77 Derek Jeter | 2.00 | 5.00 |
| ☐ 78 J.D. Drew | .30 | .75 |
| ☐ 79 Jose Offerman | .20 | .50 |
| ☐ 80 Rick Reed | .20 | .50 |
| ☐ 81 Will Clark | .50 | 1.25 |
| ☐ 82 Rickey Henderson | .75 | 2.00 |
| ☐ 83 Kirk Rueter | .20 | .50 |
| ☐ 84 Lee Stevens | .20 | .50 |
| ☐ 85 Jay Bell | .30 | .75 |
| ☐ 86 Fred McGriff | .50 | 1.25 |
| ☐ 87 Julio Zuleta | .20 | .50 |
| ☐ 88 Brian Anderson | .20 | .50 |
| ☐ 89 Orlando Cabrera | .30 | .75 |
| ☐ 90 Alex Fernandez | .20 | .50 |
| ☐ 91 Derek Bell | .20 | .50 |
| ☐ 92 Eric Owens | .20 | .50 |
| ☐ 93 Dennys Reyes | .20 | .50 |
| ☐ 94 Mike Stanley | .20 | .50 |
| ☐ 95 Jorge Posada | .50 | 1.25 |
| ☐ 96 Paul Konerko | .30 | .75 |
| ☐ 97 Mike Remlinger | .20 | .50 |
| ☐ 98 Travis Lee | .20 | .50 |
| ☐ 99 Ken Caminiti | .30 | .75 |
| ☐ 100 Kevin Barker | .20 | .50 |
| ☐ 101 Ozzie Guillen | .30 | .75 |
| ☐ 102 Randy Wolf | .20 | .50 |
| ☐ 103 Michael Tucker | .20 | .50 |
| ☐ 104 Darren Lewis | .20 | .50 |
| ☐ 105 Joe Randa | .20 | .50 |
| ☐ 106 Jeff Cirillo | .20 | .50 |
| ☐ 107 David Ortiz | .75 | 2.00 |
| ☐ 108 Herb Perry | .20 | .50 |
| ☐ 109 Jeff Nelson | .20 | .50 |
| ☐ 110 Chris Stynes | .20 | .50 |
| ☐ 111 Johnny Damon | .50 | 1.25 |
| ☐ 112 Jason Schmidt | .30 | .75 |
| ☐ 113 Charles Johnson | .30 | .75 |
| ☐ 114 Pat Burrell | .30 | .75 |
| ☐ 115 Gary Sheffield | .50 | 1.25 |
| ☐ 116 Tom Glavine | .50 | 1.25 |
| ☐ 117 Jason Isringhausen | .30 | .75 |
| ☐ 118 Chris Carpenter | .20 | .50 |
| ☐ 119 Jeff Suppan | .20 | .50 |
| ☐ 120 Ivan Rodriguez | .50 | 1.25 |
| ☐ 121 Luis Sojo | .20 | .50 |
| ☐ 122 Ron Villone | .20 | .50 |
| ☐ 123 Mike Sirotka | .20 | .50 |
| ☐ 124 Chuck Knoblauch | .30 | .75 |
| ☐ 125 Jason Kendall | .30 | .75 |
| ☐ 126 Bobby Estalella | .20 | .50 |
| ☐ 127 Jose Guillen | .20 | .50 |
| ☐ 128 Carlos Delgado | .30 | .75 |
| ☐ 129 Benji Gil | .20 | .50 |
| ☐ 130 Einar Diaz | .20 | .50 |
| ☐ 131 Andy Benes | .20 | .50 |
| ☐ 132 Adrian Beltre | .30 | .75 |
| ☐ 133 Roger Clemens | 1.50 | 4.00 |
| ☐ 134 Scott Williamson | .20 | .50 |
| ☐ 135 Brad Penny | .20 | .50 |
| ☐ 136 Troy Glaus | .50 | 1.25 |
| ☐ 137 Kevin Appier | .30 | .75 |
| ☐ 138 Walt Weiss | .20 | .50 |
| ☐ 139 Michael Barrett | .20 | .50 |
| ☐ 140 Mike Hampton | .30 | .75 |
| ☐ 141 Francisco Cordova | .20 | .50 |
| ☐ 142 David Segui | .20 | .50 |
| ☐ 143 Carlos Febles | .20 | .50 |
| ☐ 144 Roy Halladay | .30 | .75 |
| ☐ 145 Seth Etherton | .20 | .50 |
| ☐ 146 Fernando Tatis | .20 | .50 |
| ☐ 147 Livan Hernandez | .30 | .75 |
| ☐ 148 B.J. Surhoff | .30 | .75 |
| ☐ 149 Barry Larkin | .50 | 1.25 |
| ☐ 150 Bobby Howry | .20 | .50 |
| ☐ 151 Dmitri Young | .20 | .50 |
| ☐ 152 Brian Hunter | .20 | .50 |
| ☐ 153 Alex Rodriguez | 1.25 | 3.00 |
| ☐ 154 Hideo Nomo | .75 | 2.00 |
| ☐ 155 Warren Morris | .20 | .50 |
| ☐ 156 Antonio Alfonseca | .20 | .50 |
| ☐ 157 Edgardo Alfonzo | .20 | .50 |

| | | |
|---|---|---|
| ☐ 158 Mark Grudzielanek | .20 | .50 |
| ☐ 159 Fernando Vina | .20 | .50 |
| ☐ 160 Homer Bush | .20 | .50 |
| ☐ 161 Jason Giambi | .30 | .75 |
| ☐ 162 Steve Karsay | .20 | .50 |
| ☐ 163 Matt Lawton | .20 | .50 |
| ☐ 164 Rusty Greer | .30 | .75 |
| ☐ 165 Billy Koch | .20 | .50 |
| ☐ 166 Todd Hollandsworth | .20 | .50 |
| ☐ 167 Raul Ibanez | .20 | .50 |
| ☐ 168 Tony Gwynn | 1.00 | 2.50 |
| ☐ 169 Carl Everett | .30 | .75 |
| ☐ 170 Hector Carrasco | .20 | .50 |
| ☐ 171 Jose Valentin | .20 | .50 |
| ☐ 172 Deivi Cruz | .20 | .50 |
| ☐ 173 Bret Boone | .30 | .75 |
| ☐ 174 Melvin Mora | .30 | .75 |
| ☐ 175 Danny Graves | .20 | .50 |
| ☐ 176 Jose Jimenez | .20 | .50 |
| ☐ 177 James Baldwin | .20 | .50 |
| ☐ 178 C.J. Nitkowski | .20 | .50 |
| ☐ 179 Jeff Zimmerman | .20 | .50 |
| ☐ 180 Mike Lowell | .30 | .75 |
| ☐ 181 Hideki Irabu | .20 | .50 |
| ☐ 182 Greg Vaughn | .20 | .50 |
| ☐ 183 Omar Daal | .20 | .50 |
| ☐ 184 Darren Dreifort | .20 | .50 |
| ☐ 185 Gil Meche | .20 | .50 |
| ☐ 186 Damian Jackson | .20 | .50 |
| ☐ 187 Frank Thomas | .75 | 2.00 |
| ☐ 188 Luis Castillo | .20 | .50 |
| ☐ 189 Bartolo Colon | .30 | .75 |
| ☐ 190 Craig Biggio | .50 | 1.25 |
| ☐ 191 Scott Schoeneweis | .20 | .50 |
| ☐ 192 Dave Veres | .20 | .50 |
| ☐ 193 Ramon Martinez | .20 | .50 |
| ☐ 194 Jose Vidro | .20 | .50 |
| ☐ 195 Todd Helton | .50 | 1.25 |
| ☐ 196 Greg Norton | .20 | .50 |
| ☐ 197 Jacque Jones | .30 | .75 |
| ☐ 198 Jason Grimsley | .20 | .50 |
| ☐ 199 Dan Reichert | .20 | .50 |
| ☐ 200 Robb Nen | .30 | .75 |
| ☐ 201 Scott Hatteberg | .20 | .50 |
| ☐ 202 Terry Shumpert | .20 | .50 |
| ☐ 203 Kevin Millar | .30 | .75 |
| ☐ 204 Ismael Valdes | .20 | .50 |
| ☐ 205 Richard Hidalgo | .20 | .50 |
| ☐ 206 Randy Velarde | .20 | .50 |
| ☐ 207 Bengie Molina | .20 | .50 |
| ☐ 208 Tony Womack | .20 | .50 |
| ☐ 209 Enrique Wilson | .20 | .50 |
| ☐ 210 Jeff Brantley | .20 | .50 |
| ☐ 211 Rick Ankiel | .20 | .50 |
| ☐ 212 Terry Mulholland | .20 | .50 |
| ☐ 213 Ron Belliard | .20 | .50 |
| ☐ 214 Terrence Long | .20 | .50 |
| ☐ 215 Alberto Castillo | .20 | .50 |
| ☐ 216 Royce Clayton | .20 | .50 |
| ☐ 217 Joe McEwing | .20 | .50 |
| ☐ 218 Jason McDonald | .20 | .50 |
| ☐ 219 Ricky Bottalico | .20 | .50 |
| ☐ 220 Keith Foulke | .30 | .75 |
| ☐ 221 Brad Radke | .30 | .75 |
| ☐ 222 Gabe Kapler | .30 | .75 |
| ☐ 223 Pedro Astacio | .20 | .50 |
| ☐ 224 Armando Reynoso | .20 | .50 |
| ☐ 225 Darryl Kile | .30 | .75 |
| ☐ 226 Reggie Sanders | .30 | .75 |
| ☐ 227 Esteban Yan | .20 | .50 |
| ☐ 228 Joe Nathan | .20 | .50 |
| ☐ 229 Jay Payton | .20 | .50 |
| ☐ 230 Francisco Cordero | .20 | .50 |
| ☐ 231 Gregg Jefferies | .20 | .50 |
| ☐ 232 LaTroy Hawkins | .20 | .50 |
| ☐ 233 Jacob Cruz | .20 | .50 |
| ☐ 234 Chris Holt | .20 | .50 |
| ☐ 235 Vladimir Guerrero | .75 | 2.00 |
| ☐ 236 Marvin Benard | .20 | .50 |
| ☐ 237 Alex Ramirez | .20 | .50 |
| ☐ 238 Mike Williams | .20 | .50 |
| ☐ 239 Sean Bergman | .20 | .50 |
| ☐ 240 Juan Encarnacion | .20 | .50 |
| ☐ 241 Russ Davis | .20 | .50 |
| ☐ 242 Ramon Hernandez | .20 | .50 |
| ☐ 243 Sandy Alomar Jr. | .20 | .50 |
| ☐ 244 Eddie Guardado | .20 | .50 |
| ☐ 245 Shane Halter | .20 | .50 |

|  |  | | |
|---|---|---|---|
| 246 | Geoff Jenkins | .20 | .50 |
| 247 | Brian Meadows | .20 | .50 |
| 248 | Damian Miller | .20 | .50 |
| 249 | Darrin Fletcher | .20 | .50 |
| 250 | Rafael Furcal | .30 | .75 |
| 251 | Mark Grace | .50 | 1.25 |
| 252 | Mark Mulder | .30 | .75 |
| 253 | Joe Torre MG | .50 | 1.25 |
| 254 | Bobby Cox MG | .20 | .50 |
| 255 | Mike Scioscia MG | .20 | .50 |
| 256 | Mike Hargrove MG | .20 | .50 |
| 257 | Jimy Williams MG | .20 | .50 |
| 258 | Jerry Manuel MG | .20 | .50 |
| 259 | Charlie Manuel MG | .20 | .50 |
| 260 | Don Baylor MG | .30 | .75 |
| 261 | Phil Garner MG | .30 | .75 |
| 262 | Tony Muser MG | .20 | .50 |
| 263 | Buddy Bell MG | .30 | .75 |
| 264 | Tom Kelly MG | .20 | .50 |
| 265 | John Boles MG | .20 | .50 |
| 266 | Art Howe MG | .20 | .50 |
| 267 | Larry Dierker MG | .20 | .50 |
| 268 | Lou Piniella MG | .30 | .75 |
| 269 | Larry Rothschild MG | .20 | .50 |
| 270 | Davey Lopes MG | .30 | .75 |
| 271 | Johnny Oates MG | .20 | .50 |
| 272 | Felipe Alou MG | .20 | .50 |
| 273 | Bobby Valentine MG | .20 | .50 |
| 274 | Tony LaRussa MG | .20 | .50 |
| 275 | Bruce Bochy MG | .20 | .50 |
| 276 | Dusty Baker MG | .30 | .75 |
| 277 | A.Gonzalez/A.Johnson | .40 | 1.00 |
| 278 | M.Wheatland/B.Digby | .40 | 1.00 |
| 279 | T.Johnson/S.Thorman | .40 | 1.00 |
| 280 | P.Dumatrait/A.Wainwright | .75 | 2.00 |
| 281 | David Parrish RC | .40 | 1.00 |
| 282 | M.Folsom RC/R.Baldelli | .60 | 1.50 |
| 283 | Dominic Rich RC | .40 | 1.00 |
| 284 | M.Stodolka/S.Burnett | .40 | 1.00 |
| 285 | D.Thompson/C.Smith | .40 | 1.00 |
| 286 | D.Borrell RC/J.Bourgeois RC | .40 | 1.00 |
| 287 | Chen/Patterson/Hamilton | .75 | 2.00 |
| 288 | B.Zito/C.Sabathia | .75 | 2.00 |
| 289 | Ben Sheets | .75 | 2.00 |
| 290 | Hoewing/Kalinowski/Girdley | .40 | 1.00 |
| 291 | Hee Seop Choi RC | .75 | 2.00 |
| 292 | Bradley/Ainsworth/Tsao | .60 | 1.50 |
| 293 | Glendenning/Kelly/Silvestre | .40 | 1.00 |
| 294 | J.R. House | .40 | 1.00 |
| 295 | Rafael Soriano RC | .40 | 1.00 |
| 296 | T.Hisher RC/B.Jacobsen | 4.00 | 10.00 |
| 297 | Conti/Wakeland/Cole | .40 | 1.00 |
| 298 | Seabol/Huff/Crede | 1.00 | 2.50 |
| 299 | Everett/Ortiz/Ginter | .40 | 1.00 |
| 300 | Hernandez/Guzman/Eaton | .60 | 1.50 |
| 301 | Kielty/Bradley/J.Rivera | .60 | 1.50 |
| 302 | Mark McGwire GM | 1.00 | 2.50 |
| 303 | Don Larsen GM | .30 | .75 |
| 304 | Bobby Thomson GM | .30 | .75 |
| 305 | Bill Mazeroski GM | .30 | .75 |
| 306 | Reggie Jackson GM | .50 | 1.25 |
| 307 | Kirk Gibson GM | .30 | .75 |
| 308 | Roger Maris GM | .50 | 1.25 |
| 309 | Cal Ripken GM | 1.25 | 3.00 |
| 310 | Hank Aaron GM | .75 | 2.00 |
| 311 | Joe Carter GM | .30 | .75 |
| 312 | Cal Ripken SH | 1.25 | 3.00 |
| 313 | Randy Johnson SH | .50 | 1.25 |
| 314 | Ken Griffey Jr. SH | .75 | 2.00 |
| 315 | Troy Glaus SH | .30 | .75 |
| 316 | Kazuhiro Sasaki SH | .30 | .75 |
| 317 | S.Sosa/T.Glaus LL | .50 | 1.25 |
| 318 | T.Helton/E.Martinez LL | .30 | .75 |
| 319 | T.Helton/N.Garicaparra LL | .75 | 2.00 |
| 320 | B.Bonds/J.Giambi LL | .75 | 2.00 |
| 321 | T.Helton/M.Ramirez LL | .30 | .75 |
| 322 | T.Helton/D.Erstad LL | .30 | .75 |
| 323 | K.Brown/P.Martinez LL | .50 | 1.25 |
| 324 | R.Johnson/P.Martinez LL | .50 | 1.25 |
| 325 | Will Clark HL | .50 | 1.25 |
| 326 | New York Mets HL | .75 | 2.00 |
| 327 | New York Yankees HL | 1.25 | 3.00 |
| 328 | Seattle Mariners HL | .30 | .75 |
| 329 | Mike Hampton HL | .30 | .75 |
| 330 | New York Yankees HL | 1.50 | 4.00 |
| 331 | New York Yankees Champs | 3.00 | 8.00 |
| 332 | Jeff Bagwell | .50 | 1.25 |
| 333 | Andy Pettitte | .50 | 1.25 |
| 334 | Tony Armas Jr. | .20 | .50 |
| 335 | Jeromy Burnitz | .30 | .75 |
| 336 | Javier Vazquez | .30 | .75 |
| 337 | Eric Karros | .30 | .75 |
| 338 | Brian Giles | .30 | .75 |
| 339 | Scott Rolen | .50 | 1.25 |
| 340 | David Justice | .30 | .75 |
| 341 | Ray Durham | .30 | .75 |
| 342 | Todd Zeile | .30 | .75 |
| 343 | Cliff Floyd | .30 | .75 |
| 344 | Barry Bonds | 2.00 | 5.00 |
| 345 | Matt Williams | .50 | 1.25 |
| 346 | Steve Finley | .30 | .75 |
| 347 | Scott Elarton | .20 | .50 |
| 348 | Bernie Williams | .50 | 1.25 |
| 349 | David Wells | .30 | .75 |
| 350 | J.T. Snow | .30 | .75 |
| 351 | Al Leiter | .30 | .75 |
| 352 | Magglio Ordonez | .30 | .75 |
| 353 | Raul Mondesi | .30 | .75 |
| 354 | Tim Salmon | .50 | 1.25 |
| 355 | Jeff Kent | .30 | .75 |
| 356 | Mariano Rivera | .75 | 2.00 |
| 357 | John Olerud | .30 | .75 |
| 358 | Jay Payton | .30 | .75 |
| 359 | Ben Grieve | .20 | .50 |
| 360 | Ray Lankford | .30 | .75 |
| 361 | Ken Griffey Jr. | 1.25 | 3.00 |
| 362 | Rich Aurilia | .20 | .50 |
| 363 | Andruw Jones | .50 | 1.25 |
| 364 | Ryan Klesko | .30 | .75 |
| 365 | Roberto Alomar | .50 | 1.25 |
| 366 | Miguel Tejada | .30 | .75 |
| 367 | Mo Vaughn | .30 | .75 |
| 368 | Albert Belle | .30 | .75 |
| 369 | Jose Canseco | .50 | 1.25 |
| 370 | Kevin Brown | .30 | .75 |
| 371 | Rafael Palmeiro | .50 | 1.25 |
| 372 | Mark Redman | .20 | .50 |
| 373 | Larry Walker | .30 | .75 |
| 374 | Greg Maddux | 1.25 | 3.00 |
| 375 | Nomar Garciaparra | 1.25 | 3.00 |
| 376 | Kevin Millwood | .30 | .75 |
| 377 | Edgar Martinez | .50 | 1.25 |
| 378 | Sammy Sosa | .75 | 2.00 |
| 379 | Tim Hudson | .30 | .75 |
| 380 | Jim Edmonds | .30 | .75 |
| 381 | Mike Piazza | 1.25 | 3.00 |
| 382 | Brant Brown | .20 | .50 |
| 383 | Brad Fullmer | .20 | .50 |
| 384 | Alan Benes | .20 | .50 |
| 385 | Mickey Morandini | .20 | .50 |
| 386 | Troy Percival | .30 | .75 |
| 387 | Eddie Perez | .20 | .50 |
| 388 | Vernon Wells | .30 | .75 |
| 389 | Ricky Gutierrez | .20 | .50 |
| 390 | Rondell White | .30 | .75 |
| 391 | Kelvim Escobar | .20 | .50 |
| 392 | Tony Batista | .20 | .50 |
| 393 | Jimmy Haynes | .20 | .50 |
| 394 | Billy Wagner | .30 | .75 |
| 395 | A.J. Hinch | .20 | .50 |
| 396 | Matt Morris | .20 | .50 |
| 397 | Lance Berkman | .30 | .75 |
| 398 | Jeff D'Amico | .20 | .50 |
| 399 | Octavio Dotel | .20 | .50 |
| 400 | Olmedo Saenz | .20 | .50 |
| 401 | Esteban Loaiza | .20 | .50 |
| 402 | Adam Kennedy | .20 | .50 |
| 403 | Moises Alou | .30 | .75 |
| 404 | Orlando Palmeiro | .20 | .50 |
| 405 | Kevin Young | .20 | .50 |
| 406 | Tom Goodwin | .20 | .50 |
| 407 | Mac Suzuki | .30 | .75 |
| 408 | Pat Hentgen | .20 | .50 |
| 409 | Kevin Stocker | .20 | .50 |
| 410 | Mark Sweeney | .20 | .50 |
| 411 | Tony Eusebio | .20 | .50 |
| 412 | Edgar Renteria | .30 | .75 |
| 413 | John Rocker | .20 | .50 |
| 414 | Jose Lima | .20 | .50 |
| 415 | Kerry Wood | .30 | .75 |
| 416 | Mike Timlin | .20 | .50 |
| 417 | Jose Hernandez | .20 | .50 |
| 418 | Jeremy Giambi | .20 | .50 |
| 419 | Luis Lopez | .20 | .50 |
| 420 | Mitch Meluskey | .20 | .50 |
| 421 | Garrett Stephenson | .20 | .50 |
| 422 | Jamey Wright | .20 | .50 |
| 423 | John Jaha | .20 | .50 |
| 424 | Placido Polanco | .20 | .50 |
| 425 | Marty Cordova | .20 | .50 |
| 426 | Joey Hamilton | .20 | .50 |
| 427 | Travis Fryman | .30 | .75 |
| 428 | Mike Cameron | .20 | .50 |
| 429 | Matt Mantei | .20 | .50 |
| 430 | Chan Ho Park | .30 | .75 |
| 431 | Shawn Estes | .20 | .50 |
| 432 | Danny Bautista | .20 | .50 |
| 433 | Wilson Alvarez | .20 | .50 |
| 434 | Kenny Lofton | .30 | .75 |
| 435 | Russ Ortiz | .20 | .50 |
| 436 | Dave Burba | .20 | .50 |
| 437 | Felix Martinez | .20 | .50 |
| 438 | Jeff Shaw | .20 | .50 |
| 439 | Mike DiFelice | .20 | .50 |
| 440 | Roberto Hernandez | .20 | .50 |
| 441 | Bryan Rekar | .20 | .50 |
| 442 | Ugueth Urbina | .20 | .50 |
| 443 | Vinny Castilla | .30 | .75 |
| 444 | Carlos Perez | .20 | .50 |
| 445 | Juan Guzman | .20 | .50 |
| 446 | Ryan Rupe | .20 | .50 |
| 447 | Mike Mordecai | .20 | .50 |
| 448 | Ricardo Rincon | .20 | .50 |
| 449 | Curt Schilling | .30 | .75 |
| 450 | Alex Cora | .20 | .50 |
| 451 | Turner Ward | .20 | .50 |
| 452 | Omar Vizquel | .50 | 1.25 |
| 453 | Russ Branyan | .20 | .50 |
| 454 | Russ Johnson | .20 | .50 |
| 455 | Greg Colbrunn | .20 | .50 |
| 456 | Charles Nagy | .20 | .50 |
| 457 | Wil Cordero | .20 | .50 |
| 458 | Jason Tyner | .20 | .50 |
| 459 | Devon White | .30 | .75 |
| 460 | Kelly Stinnett | .20 | .50 |
| 461 | Wilton Guerrero | .20 | .50 |
| 462 | Jason Bere | .20 | .50 |
| 463 | Calvin Murray | .20 | .50 |
| 464 | Miguel Batista | .20 | .50 |
| 465 | Luis Gonzalez | .30 | .75 |
| 466 | Jaret Wright | .20 | .50 |
| 467 | Chad Kreuter | .20 | .50 |
| 468 | Armando Benitez | .20 | .50 |
| 469 | Erubiel Durazo | .20 | .50 |
| 470 | Sidney Ponson | .20 | .50 |
| 471 | Adrian Brown | .20 | .50 |
| 472 | Sterling Hitchcock | .20 | .50 |
| 473 | Timo Perez | .20 | .50 |
| 474 | Jamie Moyer | .30 | .75 |
| 475 | Delino DeShields | .20 | .50 |
| 476 | Glendon Rusch | .20 | .50 |
| 477 | Chris Gomez | .20 | .50 |
| 478 | Adam Eaton | .20 | .50 |
| 479 | Pablo Ozuna | .20 | .50 |
| 480 | Bob Abreu | .30 | .75 |
| 481 | Kris Benson | .20 | .50 |
| 482 | Keith Osik | .20 | .50 |
| 483 | Darryl Hamilton | .20 | .50 |
| 484 | Marlon Anderson | .20 | .50 |
| 485 | Jimmy Anderson | .20 | .50 |
| 486 | John Halama | .20 | .50 |
| 487 | Nelson Figueroa | .20 | .50 |
| 488 | Alex Gonzalez | .20 | .50 |
| 489 | Benny Agbayani | .20 | .50 |
| 490 | Ed Sprague | .20 | .50 |
| 491 | Scott Erickson | .20 | .50 |
| 492 | Doug Glanville | .20 | .50 |
| 493 | Jesus Sanchez | .20 | .50 |
| 494 | Mike Lieberthal | .30 | .75 |
| 495 | Aaron Sele | .20 | .50 |
| 496 | Pat Mahomes | .20 | .50 |
| 497 | Ruben Rivera | .20 | .50 |
| 498 | Wayne Gomes | .20 | .50 |
| 499 | Freddy Garcia | .30 | .75 |
| 500 | Al Martin | .20 | .50 |
| 501 | Woody Williams | .20 | .50 |
| 502 | Paul Byrd | .20 | .50 |
| 503 | Rick White | .20 | .50 |
| 504 | Trevor Hoffman | .30 | .75 |
| 505 | Brady Anderson | .30 | .75 |
| 506 | Robert Person | .20 | .50 |
| 507 | Jeff Conine | .20 | .50 |
| 508 | Chris Truby | .20 | .50 |
| 509 | Emil Brown | .20 | .50 |

|  |  | | |
|---|---|---|---|
| 510 | Ryan Dempster | .20 | .50 |
| 511 | Ruben Mateo | .20 | .50 |
| 512 | Alex Ochoa | .20 | .50 |
| 513 | Jose Rosado | .20 | .50 |
| 514 | Masato Yoshii | .20 | .50 |
| 515 | Brian Daubach | .20 | .50 |
| 516 | Jeff D'Amico | .20 | .50 |
| 517 | Brent Mayne | .20 | .50 |
| 518 | John Thomson | .20 | .50 |
| 519 | Todd Ritchie | .20 | .50 |
| 520 | John VanderWal | .20 | .50 |
| 521 | Neifi Perez | .20 | .50 |
| 522 | Chad Curtis | .20 | .50 |
| 523 | Kenny Rogers | .30 | .75 |
| 524 | Trot Nixon | .30 | .75 |
| 525 | Sean Casey | .30 | .75 |
| 526 | Wilton Veras | .20 | .50 |
| 527 | Troy O'Leary | .20 | .50 |
| 528 | Dante Bichette | .30 | .75 |
| 529 | Jose Silva | .20 | .50 |
| 530 | Darren Oliver | .20 | .50 |
| 531 | Steve Parris | .20 | .50 |
| 532 | David McCarty | .20 | .50 |
| 533 | Todd Walker | .20 | .50 |
| 534 | Brian Rose | .20 | .50 |
| 535 | Pete Schourek | .20 | .50 |
| 536 | Ricky Ledee | .20 | .50 |
| 537 | Justin Thompson | .20 | .50 |
| 538 | Benito Santiago | .30 | .75 |
| 539 | Carlos Beltran | .30 | .75 |
| 540 | Gabe White | .20 | .50 |
| 541 | Bret Saberhagen | .20 | .50 |
| 542 | Ramon Martinez | .20 | .50 |
| 543 | John Valentin | .20 | .50 |
| 544 | Frank Catalanotto | .20 | .50 |
| 545 | Tim Wakefield | .30 | .75 |
| 546 | Michael Tucker | .20 | .50 |
| 547 | Juan Pierre | .30 | .75 |
| 548 | Rich Garces | .20 | .50 |
| 549 | Luis Ordaz | .20 | .50 |
| 550 | Jerry Spradlin | .20 | .50 |
| 551 | Corey Koskie | .20 | .50 |
| 552 | Cal Eldred | .20 | .50 |
| 553 | Alfonso Soriano | .50 | 1.25 |
| 554 | Kip Wells | .20 | .50 |
| 555 | Orlando Hernandez | .30 | .75 |
| 556 | Bill Simas | .20 | .50 |
| 557 | Jim Parque | .20 | .50 |
| 558 | Joe Mays | .20 | .50 |
| 559 | Tim Belcher | .20 | .50 |
| 560 | Shane Spencer | .20 | .50 |
| 561 | Glanallen Hill | .20 | .50 |
| 562 | Matt LeCroy | .20 | .50 |
| 563 | Tino Martinez | .50 | 1.25 |
| 564 | Eric Milton | .20 | .50 |
| 565 | Ron Coomer | .20 | .50 |
| 566 | Cristian Guzman | .20 | .50 |
| 567 | Kazuhiro Sasaki | .30 | .75 |
| 568 | Mark Quinn | .20 | .50 |
| 569 | Eric Gagne | .20 | .50 |
| 570 | Kerry Ligtenberg | .20 | .50 |
| 571 | Rolando Arrojo | .20 | .50 |
| 572 | Jon Lieber | .20 | .50 |
| 573 | Jose Vizcaino | .20 | .50 |
| 574 | Jeff Abbott | .20 | .50 |
| 575 | Carlos Hernandez | .20 | .50 |
| 576 | Scott Sullivan | .20 | .50 |
| 577 | Matt Stairs | .20 | .50 |
| 578 | Tom Lampkin | .20 | .50 |
| 579 | Donnie Sadler | .20 | .50 |
| 580 | Desi Relaford | .20 | .50 |
| 581 | Scott Downs | .20 | .50 |
| 582 | Mike Mussina | .50 | 1.25 |
| 583 | Ramon Ortiz | .20 | .50 |
| 584 | Mike Myers | .20 | .50 |
| 585 | Frank Castillo | .20 | .50 |
| 586 | Manny Ramirez Sox | .50 | 1.25 |
| 587 | Alex Rodriguez | 1.25 | 3.00 |
| 588 | Andy Ashby | .20 | .50 |
| 589 | Felipe Crespo | .20 | .50 |
| 590 | Bobby Bonilla | .30 | .75 |
| 591 | Denny Neagle | .20 | .50 |
| 592 | Dave Martinez | .20 | .50 |
| 593 | Mike Hampton | .30 | .75 |
| 594 | Gary DiSarcina | .20 | .50 |
| 595 | Tsuyoshi Shinjo RC | .75 | 2.00 |
| 596 | Albert Pujols RC | 30.00 | 60.00 |
| 597 | Oswalt/Strange/Rauch | 1.00 | 2.50 |
| 598 | Jake Peavy RC | 4.00 | 10.00 |
| 599 | S.Smyth RC/Bynum/Haynes | .40 | 1.00 |
| 600 | Cuddyer/Lawrence/Freeman | .40 | 1.00 |
| 601 | C.Pena/Barnes/Wise | .40 | 1.00 |
| 602 | E.Almonte RC/F.Lopez | .40 | 1.00 |
| 603 | Escobar/Valent/Wilkerson | .40 | 1.00 |
| 604 | Hall/Barajas/Goldbach | .40 | 1.00 |
| 605 | Romano/Giles/Ozuna | .60 | 1.50 |
| 606 | D.Brown/Cust/V.Wells | .40 | 1.00 |
| 607 | L.Montanez RC/D.Espinosa | .40 | 1.00 |
| 608 | J.Wayne RC/A.Pluta RC | .40 | 1.00 |
| 609 | J.Axelson RC/C.Cali RC | .40 | 1.00 |
| 610 | S.Boyd RC/C.Morris RC | .40 | 1.00 |
| 611 | T.Arko RC/O.Moylan RC | .40 | 1.00 |
| 612 | L.Cotto RC/L.Escobar | .40 | 1.00 |
| 613 | B.Mims RC/B.Williams RC | .40 | 1.00 |
| 614 | C.Russ RC/B.Edwards | .40 | 1.00 |
| 615 | J.Torres/B.Diggins | .40 | 1.00 |
| 616 | Edwin Encarnacion RC | 4.00 | 10.00 |
| 617 | B.Bass RC/O.Ayala RC | .40 | 1.00 |
| 618 | M.Matthews RC/J.Kanooi | .40 | 1.00 |
| 619 | S.McFarland RC/A.Sterrett RC | .40 | 1.00 |
| 620 | D.Krynzel/G.Sizemore | 2.00 | 5.00 |
| 621 | K.Bucktrot/D.Sardinha | .40 | 1.00 |
| 622 | Anaheim Angels TC | .30 | .75 |
| 623 | Arizona Diamondbacks TC | .30 | .75 |
| 624 | Atlanta Braves TC | .30 | .75 |
| 625 | Baltimore Orioles TC | .30 | .75 |
| 626 | Boston Red Sox TC | .30 | .75 |
| 627 | Chicago Cubs TC | .30 | .75 |
| 628 | Chicago White Sox TC | .30 | .75 |
| 629 | Cincinnati Reds TC | .30 | .75 |
| 630 | Cleveland Indians TC | .30 | .75 |
| 631 | Colorado Rockies TC | .30 | .75 |
| 632 | Detroit Tigers TC | .30 | .75 |
| 633 | Florida Marlins TC | .30 | .75 |
| 634 | Houston Astros TC | .30 | .75 |
| 635 | Kansas City Royals TC | .30 | .75 |
| 636 | Los Angeles Dodgers TC | .30 | .75 |
| 637 | Milwaukee Brewers TC | .30 | .75 |
| 638 | Minnesota Twins TC | .30 | .75 |
| 639 | Montreal Expos TC | .30 | .75 |
| 640 | New York Mets TC | .30 | .75 |
| 641 | New York Yankees TC | 1.50 | 4.00 |
| 642 | Oakland Athletics TC | .30 | .75 |
| 643 | Philadelphia Phillies TC | .30 | .75 |
| 644 | Pittsburgh Pirates TC | .30 | .75 |
| 645 | San Diego Padres TC | .30 | .75 |
| 646 | San Francisco Giants TC | .30 | .75 |
| 647 | Seattle Mariners TC | .30 | .75 |
| 648 | St. Louis Cardinals TC | .30 | .75 |
| 649 | Tampa Bay Devil Rays TC | .30 | .75 |
| 650 | Texas Rangers TC | .30 | .75 |
| 651 | Toronto Blue Jays TC | .30 | .75 |
| 652 | Bucky Dent GM | .20 | .50 |
| 653 | Jackie Robinson GM | .75 | 2.00 |
| 654 | Roberto Clemente GM | 1.00 | 2.50 |
| 655 | Nolan Ryan GM | 1.25 | 3.00 |
| 656 | Kerry Wood GM | .30 | .75 |
| 657 | Rickey Henderson GM | .75 | 2.00 |
| 658 | Lou Brock GM | .50 | 1.25 |
| 659 | David Wells GM | .20 | .50 |
| 660 | Andruw Jones GM | .30 | .75 |
| 661 | Carlton Fisk GM | .30 | .75 |

## 2002 Topps Chrome

| | | |
|---|---|---|
| COMPLETE SET (660) | 100.00 | 250.00 |
| COMPLETE SERIES 1 (330) | 50.00 | 125.00 |
| COMPLETE SERIES 2 (330) | 50.00 | 125.00 |
| COMMON (1-331/366-695) | .20 | .50 |
| COMMON (307-326/671-690) | .60 | 1.50 |
| COMMON (327-331/691-695) | .60 | 1.50 |

|  |  | | |
|---|---|---|---|
| 1 | Pedro Martinez | .60 | 1.50 |
| 2 | Mike Stanton | .20 | .50 |
| 3 | Brad Penny | .20 | .50 |
| 4 | Mike Matheny | .20 | .50 |
| 5 | Johnny Damon | .60 | 1.50 |
| 6 | Bret Boone | .40 | 1.00 |
| 7 | Does Not Exist | | |
| 8 | Chris Truby | .20 | .50 |
| 9 | B.J. Surhoff | .20 | .50 |
| 10 | Mike Hampton | .40 | 1.00 |
| 11 | Juan Pierre | .40 | 1.00 |
| 12 | Mark Buehrle | .40 | 1.00 |
| 13 | Bob Abreu | .40 | 1.00 |
| 14 | David Cone | .20 | .50 |
| 15 | Aaron Sele | .20 | .50 |
| 16 | Fernando Tatis | .20 | .50 |
| 17 | Bobby Jones | .20 | .50 |
| 18 | Rick Helling | .20 | .50 |
| 19 | Dmitri Young | .40 | 1.00 |
| 20 | Mike Mussina | .60 | 1.50 |
| 21 | Mike Sweeney | .40 | 1.00 |
| 22 | Cristian Guzman | .20 | .50 |
| 23 | Ryan Kohlmeier | .20 | .50 |
| 24 | Adam Kennedy | .20 | .50 |
| 25 | Larry Walker | .40 | 1.00 |
| 26 | Eric Davis | .40 | 1.00 |
| 27 | Jason Tyner | .20 | .50 |
| 28 | Eric Young | .20 | .50 |
| 29 | Jason Marquis | .20 | .50 |
| 30 | Luis Gonzalez | .40 | 1.00 |
| 31 | Kevin Tapani | .20 | .50 |
| 32 | Orlando Cabrera | .40 | 1.00 |
| 33 | Marty Cordova | .20 | .50 |
| 34 | Brad Ausmus | .20 | .50 |
| 35 | Livan Hernandez | .40 | 1.00 |
| 36 | Alex Gonzalez | .20 | .50 |
| 37 | Edgar Renteria | .40 | 1.00 |
| 38 | Bengie Molina | .20 | .50 |
| 39 | Frank Menechino | .20 | .50 |
| 40 | Rafael Palmeiro | .60 | 1.50 |
| 41 | Brad Fullmer | .20 | .50 |
| 42 | Julio Zuleta | .20 | .50 |
| 43 | Darren Dreifort | .20 | .50 |
| 44 | Trot Nixon | .40 | 1.00 |
| 45 | Trevor Hoffman | .40 | 1.00 |
| 46 | Vladimir Nunez | .20 | .50 |
| 47 | Mark Kotsay | .40 | 1.00 |
| 48 | Kenny Rogers | .40 | 1.00 |
| 49 | Ben Petrick | .20 | .50 |
| 50 | Jeff Bagwell | .60 | 1.50 |
| 51 | Juan Encarnacion | .20 | .50 |
| 52 | Ramiro Mendoza | .20 | .50 |
| 53 | Brian Meadows | .20 | .50 |
| 54 | Chad Curtis | .20 | .50 |
| 55 | Aramis Ramirez | .40 | 1.00 |
| 56 | Mark McLemore | .20 | .50 |
| 57 | Dante Bichette | .40 | 1.00 |
| 58 | Scott Schoeneweis | .20 | .50 |
| 59 | Jose Cruz Jr. | .20 | .50 |
| 60 | Roger Clemens | 2.00 | 5.00 |
| 61 | Jose Guillen | .40 | 1.00 |
| 62 | Darren Oliver | .20 | .50 |
| 63 | Chris Reitsma | .20 | .50 |
| 64 | Jeff Abbott | .20 | .50 |
| 65 | Robin Ventura | .40 | 1.00 |
| 66 | Denny Neagle | .20 | .50 |
| 67 | Al Martin | .20 | .50 |
| 68 | Benito Santiago | .40 | 1.00 |
| 69 | Roy Oswalt | .40 | 1.00 |
| 70 | Juan Gonzalez | .40 | 1.00 |
| 71 | Garret Anderson | .40 | 1.00 |
| 72 | Bobby Bonilla | .40 | 1.00 |
| 73 | Danny Bautista | .20 | .50 |
| 74 | J.T. Snow | .40 | 1.00 |
| 75 | Derek Jeter | 2.50 | 6.00 |
| 76 | John Olerud | .40 | 1.00 |
| 77 | Kevin Appier | .20 | .50 |
| 78 | Phil Nevin | .40 | 1.00 |
| 79 | Sean Casey | .40 | 1.00 |
| 80 | Troy Glaus | .40 | 1.00 |
| 81 | Joe Randa | .20 | .50 |
| 82 | Jose Valentin | .20 | .50 |
| 83 | Ricky Bottalico | .20 | .50 |
| 84 | Todd Zeile | .20 | .50 |
| 85 | Barry Larkin | .60 | 1.50 |
| 86 | Bob Wickman | .20 | .50 |
| 87 | Jeff Shaw | .20 | .50 |
| 88 | Greg Vaughn | .20 | .50 |
| 89 | Fernando Vina | .20 | .50 |
| 90 | Mark Mulder | .40 | 1.00 |

|  |  | | |
|---|---|---|---|
| 91 | Paul Bako | .20 | .50 |
| 92 | Aaron Boone | .40 | 1.00 |
| 93 | Esteban Loaiza | .20 | .50 |
| 94 | Richie Sexson | .40 | 1.00 |
| 95 | Alfonso Soriano | .20 | .50 |
| 96 | Tony Womack | .20 | .50 |
| 97 | Paul Shuey | .20 | .50 |
| 98 | Melvin Mora | .40 | 1.00 |
| 99 | Tony Gwynn | 1.25 | 3.00 |
| 100 | Vladimir Guerrero | 1.00 | 2.50 |
| 101 | Keith Osik | .20 | .50 |
| 102 | Bud Smith | .20 | .50 |
| 103 | Scott Williamson | .20 | .50 |
| 104 | Daryle Ward | .20 | .50 |
| 105 | Doug Mientkiewicz | .40 | 1.00 |
| 106 | Stan Javier | .20 | .50 |
| 107 | Russ Ortiz | .20 | .50 |
| 108 | Wade Miller | .20 | .50 |
| 109 | Luke Prokopec | .20 | .50 |
| 110 | Andruw Jones | .60 | 1.50 |
| 111 | Ron Coomer | .20 | .50 |
| 112 | Dan Wilson | .20 | .50 |
| 113 | Luis Castillo | .20 | .50 |
| 114 | Derek Bell | .20 | .50 |
| 115 | Gary Sheffield | .40 | 1.00 |
| 116 | Ruben Rivera | .20 | .50 |
| 117 | Paul O'Neill | .60 | 1.50 |
| 118 | Craig Paquette | .20 | .50 |
| 119 | Kelvim Escobar | .20 | .50 |
| 120 | Brad Radke | .20 | .50 |
| 121 | Jorge Fabregas | .20 | .50 |
| 122 | Randy Winn | .20 | .50 |
| 123 | Tom Goodwin | .20 | .50 |
| 124 | Jaret Wright | .20 | .50 |
| 125 | Barry Bonds HR 73 | 15.00 | 40.00 |
| 126 | Al Leiter | .20 | .50 |
| 127 | Ben Davis | .20 | .50 |
| 128 | Frank Catalanotto | .20 | .50 |
| 129 | Jose Cabrera | .20 | .50 |
| 130 | Magglio Ordonez | .40 | 1.00 |
| 131 | Jose Macias | .20 | .50 |
| 132 | Ted Lilly | .20 | .50 |
| 133 | Chris Holt | .20 | .50 |
| 134 | Eric Milton | .20 | .50 |
| 135 | Shannon Stewart | .40 | 1.00 |
| 136 | Omar Olivares | .20 | .50 |
| 137 | David Segui | .20 | .50 |
| 138 | Jeff Nelson | .20 | .50 |
| 139 | Matt Williams | .40 | 1.00 |
| 140 | Ellis Burks | .40 | 1.00 |
| 141 | Jason Bere | .20 | .50 |
| 142 | Jimmy Haynes | .20 | .50 |
| 143 | Ramon Hernandez | .20 | .50 |
| 144 | Craig Counsell | .20 | .50 |
| 145 | John Smoltz | .60 | 1.50 |
| 146 | Homer Bush | .20 | .50 |
| 147 | Quilvio Veras | .20 | .50 |
| 148 | Esteban Yan | .20 | .50 |
| 149 | Ramon Ortiz | .20 | .50 |
| 150 | Carlos Delgado | .40 | 1.00 |
| 151 | Lee Stevens | .20 | .50 |
| 152 | Wil Cordero | .20 | .50 |
| 153 | Mike Bordick | .40 | 1.00 |
| 154 | John Flaherty | .20 | .50 |
| 155 | Omar Daal | .20 | .50 |
| 156 | Todd Ritchie | .20 | .50 |
| 157 | Carl Everett | .40 | 1.00 |
| 158 | Scott Sullivan | .20 | .50 |
| 159 | Delvi Cruz | .20 | .50 |
| 160 | Albert Pujols | 2.00 | 5.00 |
| 161 | Royce Clayton | .20 | .50 |
| 162 | Jeff Suppan | .20 | .50 |
| 163 | C.C. Sabathia | .40 | 1.00 |
| 164 | Jimmy Rollins | .40 | 1.00 |
| 165 | Rickey Henderson | 1.00 | 2.50 |
| 166 | Rey Ordonez | .20 | .50 |
| 167 | Shawn Estes | .20 | .50 |
| 168 | Reggie Sanders | .40 | 1.00 |
| 169 | Jon Lieber | .20 | .50 |
| 170 | Armando Benitez | .20 | .50 |
| 171 | Mike Remlinger | .20 | .50 |
| 172 | Billy Wagner | .40 | 1.00 |
| 173 | Troy Percival | .40 | 1.00 |
| 174 | Devon White | .40 | 1.00 |
| 175 | Ivan Rodriguez | .60 | 1.50 |
| 176 | Dustin Hermanson | .20 | .50 |
| 177 | Brian Anderson | .20 | .50 |
| 178 | Graeme Lloyd | .20 | .50 |
| 179 | Russell Branyan | .20 | .50 |
| 180 | Bobby Higginson | .40 | 1.00 |
| 181 | Alex Gonzalez | .20 | .50 |
| 182 | John Franco | .40 | 1.00 |
| 183 | Sidney Ponson | .20 | .50 |
| 184 | Jose Mesa | .20 | .50 |
| 185 | Todd Hollandsworth | .20 | .50 |
| 186 | Kevin Young | .20 | .50 |
| 187 | Tim Wakefield | .40 | 1.00 |
| 188 | Craig Biggio | .60 | 1.50 |
| 189 | Jason Isringhausen | .40 | 1.00 |
| 190 | Mark Quinn | .20 | .50 |
| 191 | Glendon Rusch | .20 | .50 |
| 192 | Damian Miller | .20 | .50 |
| 193 | Sandy Alomar Jr. | .20 | .50 |
| 194 | Scott Brosius | .40 | 1.00 |
| 195 | Dave Martinez | .20 | .50 |
| 196 | Danny Graves | .20 | .50 |
| 197 | Shea Hillenbrand | .40 | 1.00 |
| 198 | Jimmy Anderson | .20 | .50 |
| 199 | Travis Lee | .20 | .50 |
| 200 | Randy Johnson | 1.00 | 2.50 |
| 201 | Carlos Beltran | .40 | 1.00 |
| 202 | Jerry Hairston | .20 | .50 |
| 203 | Jesus Sanchez | .20 | .50 |
| 204 | Eddie Taubensee | .20 | .50 |
| 205 | David Wells | .40 | 1.00 |
| 206 | Russ Davis | .20 | .50 |
| 207 | Michael Barrett | .20 | .50 |
| 208 | Marquis Grissom | .40 | 1.00 |
| 209 | Byung-Hyun Kim | .40 | 1.00 |
| 210 | Hideo Nomo | 1.00 | 2.50 |
| 211 | Ryan Rupe | .20 | .50 |
| 212 | Ricky Gutierrez | .20 | .50 |
| 213 | Darryl Kile | .40 | 1.00 |
| 214 | Rico Brogna | .20 | .50 |
| 215 | Terrence Long | .20 | .50 |
| 216 | Mike Jackson | .20 | .50 |
| 217 | Jamey Wright | .20 | .50 |
| 218 | Adrian Beltre | .40 | 1.00 |
| 219 | Benny Agbayani | .20 | .50 |
| 220 | Chuck Knoblauch | .40 | 1.00 |
| 221 | Randy Wolf | .20 | .50 |
| 222 | Andy Ashby | .20 | .50 |
| 223 | Corey Koskie | .40 | 1.00 |
| 224 | Roger Cedeno | .20 | .50 |
| 225 | Ichiro Suzuki | 2.00 | 5.00 |
| 226 | Keith Foulke | .40 | 1.00 |
| 227 | Ryan Minor | .20 | .50 |
| 228 | Shawon Dunston | .20 | .50 |
| 229 | Alex Cora | .20 | .50 |
| 230 | Jeromy Burnitz | .40 | 1.00 |
| 231 | Mark Grace | .60 | 1.50 |
| 232 | Aubrey Huff | .40 | 1.00 |
| 233 | Jeffrey Hammonds | .20 | .50 |
| 234 | Olmedo Saenz | .20 | .50 |
| 235 | Brian Jordan | .40 | 1.00 |
| 236 | Jeremy Giambi | .20 | .50 |
| 237 | Joe Girardi | .20 | .50 |
| 238 | Eric Gagne | .40 | 1.00 |
| 239 | Masato Yoshii | .20 | .50 |
| 240 | Greg Maddux | 1.50 | 4.00 |
| 241 | Bryan Rekar | .20 | .50 |
| 242 | Ray Durham | .40 | 1.00 |
| 243 | Torii Hunter | .40 | 1.00 |
| 244 | Derrek Lee | .60 | 1.50 |
| 245 | Jim Edmonds | .40 | 1.00 |
| 246 | Einar Diaz | .20 | .50 |
| 247 | Brian Bohanon | .20 | .50 |
| 248 | Ron Belliard | .20 | .50 |
| 249 | Mike Lowell | .40 | 1.00 |
| 250 | Sammy Sosa | 1.00 | 2.50 |
| 251 | Richard Hidalgo | .20 | .50 |
| 252 | Bartolo Colon | .40 | 1.00 |
| 253 | Jorge Posada | .60 | 1.50 |
| 254 | Latroy Hawkins | .20 | .50 |
| 255 | Paul LoDuca | .40 | 1.00 |
| 256 | Carlos Febles | .20 | .50 |
| 257 | Nelson Cruz | .20 | .50 |
| 258 | Edgardo Alfonzo | .20 | .50 |
| 259 | Joey Hamilton | .20 | .50 |
| 260 | Cliff Floyd | .40 | 1.00 |
| 261 | Wes Helms | .20 | .50 |
| 262 | Jay Bell | .20 | .50 |
| 263 | Mike Cameron | .20 | .50 |
| 264 | Paul Konerko | .40 | 1.00 |
| 265 | Jeff Kent | .40 | 1.00 |
| 266 | Robert Fick | .20 | .50 |
| 267 | Allen Levrault | .20 | .50 |
| 268 | Placido Polanco | .20 | .50 |
| 269 | Marlon Anderson | .20 | .50 |
| 270 | Mariano Rivera | 1.00 | 2.50 |
| 271 | Chan Ho Park | .40 | 1.00 |
| 272 | Jose Vizcaino | .20 | .50 |
| 273 | Jeff D'Amico | .20 | .50 |
| 274 | Mark Gardner | .20 | .50 |
| 275 | Travis Fryman | .40 | 1.00 |
| 276 | Darren Lewis | .20 | .50 |
| 277 | Bruce Bochy MG | .20 | .50 |
| 278 | Jerry Manuel MG | .20 | .50 |
| 279 | Bob Brenly MG | .40 | 1.00 |
| 280 | Don Baylor MG | .40 | 1.00 |
| 281 | Davey Lopes MG | .40 | 1.00 |
| 282 | Jerry Narron MG | .20 | .50 |
| 283 | Tony Muser MG | .20 | .50 |
| 284 | Hal McRae MG | .40 | 1.00 |
| 285 | Bobby Cox MG | .20 | .50 |
| 286 | Larry Dierker MG | .20 | .50 |
| 287 | Phil Garner MG | .20 | .50 |
| 288 | Joe Kerrigan MG | .20 | .50 |
| 289 | Bobby Valentine MG | .40 | 1.00 |
| 290 | Dusty Baker MG | .40 | 1.00 |
| 291 | Lloyd McClendon MG | .20 | .50 |
| 292 | Mike Scioscia MG | .20 | .50 |
| 293 | Buck Martinez MG | .20 | .50 |
| 294 | Larry Bowa MG | .40 | 1.00 |
| 295 | Tony LaRussa MG | .40 | 1.00 |
| 296 | Jeff Torborg MG | .20 | .50 |
| 297 | Tom Kelly MG | .20 | .50 |
| 298 | Mike Hargrove MG | .20 | .50 |
| 299 | Art Howe MG | .20 | .50 |
| 300 | Lou Piniella MG | .20 | .50 |
| 301 | Charlie Manuel MG | .20 | .50 |
| 302 | Buddy Bell MG | .40 | 1.00 |
| 303 | Tony Perez MG | .40 | 1.00 |
| 304 | Bob Boone MG | .40 | 1.00 |
| 305 | Joe Torre MG | .60 | 1.50 |
| 306 | Jim Tracy MG | .20 | .50 |
| 307 | Jason Lane PROS | .60 | 1.50 |
| 308 | Chris George PROS | .60 | 1.50 |
| 309 | Hank Blalock PROS | 1.00 | 2.50 |
| 310 | Joe Borchard PROS | .60 | 1.50 |
| 311 | Marlon Byrd PROS | .60 | 1.50 |
| 312 | Raymond Cabrera PROS RC | .60 | 1.50 |
| 313 | Freddy Sanchez PROS RC | 2.50 | 6.00 |
| 314 | Scott Wiggins PROS RC | .60 | 1.50 |
| 315 | Jason Maule PROS RC | .60 | 1.50 |
| 316 | Dionys Cesar PROS RC | .60 | 1.50 |
| 317 | Boof Bonser PROS | .60 | 1.50 |
| 318 | Juan Tolentino PROS RC | .60 | 1.50 |
| 319 | Earl Snyder PROS RC | .60 | 1.50 |
| 320 | Travis Wade PROS RC | .60 | 1.50 |
| 321 | Napoleon Calzado PROS RC | .60 | 1.50 |
| 322 | Eric Glaser PROS RC | .60 | 1.50 |
| 323 | Craig Kuzmic PROS RC | .60 | 1.50 |
| 324 | Nic Jackson PROS RC | .60 | 1.50 |
| 325 | Mike Rivera PROS | .60 | 1.50 |
| 326 | Jason Bay PROS RC | 3.00 | 8.00 |
| 327 | Chris Smith DP | .60 | 1.50 |
| 328 | Jake Gautreau DP | .60 | 1.50 |
| 329 | Gabe Gross DP | .60 | 1.50 |
| 330 | Kenny Baugh DP | .60 | 1.50 |
| 331 | J.D. Martin DP | .60 | 1.50 |
| 366 | Pat Meares | .20 | .50 |
| 367 | Mike Lieberthal | .40 | 1.00 |
| 368 | Larry Bigbie | .20 | .50 |
| 369 | Ron Gant | .40 | 1.00 |
| 370 | Moises Alou | .40 | 1.00 |
| 371 | Chad Kreuter | .20 | .50 |
| 372 | Willis Roberts | .20 | .50 |
| 373 | Toby Hall | .20 | .50 |
| 374 | Miguel Batista | .20 | .50 |
| 375 | John Burkett | .20 | .50 |
| 376 | Cory Lidle | .20 | .50 |
| 377 | Nick Neugebauer | .20 | .50 |
| 378 | Jay Payton | .20 | .50 |
| 379 | Steve Karsay | .20 | .50 |
| 380 | Eric Chavez | .40 | 1.00 |
| 381 | Kelly Stinnett | .20 | .50 |
| 382 | Jarrod Washburn | .20 | .50 |
| 383 | Rick White | .20 | .50 |
| 384 | Jeff Conine | .40 | 1.00 |
| 385 | Fred McGriff | .60 | 1.50 |
| 386 | Marvin Benard | .20 | .50 |
| 387 | Joe Crede | .40 | 1.00 |
| 388 | Dennis Cook | .20 | .50 |

|  |  | | |
|---|---|---|---|
| ❑ 389 | Rick Reed | .20 | .50 |
| ❑ 390 | Tom Glavine | .60 | 1.50 |
| ❑ 391 | Rondell White | .20 | .50 |
| ❑ 392 | Matt Morris | .40 | 1.00 |
| ❑ 393 | Pat Rapp | .20 | .50 |
| ❑ 394 | Robert Person | .20 | .50 |
| ❑ 395 | Omar Vizquel | .60 | 1.50 |
| ❑ 396 | Jeff Cirillo | .20 | .50 |
| ❑ 397 | Dave Mlicki | .20 | .50 |
| ❑ 398 | Jose Ortiz | .20 | .50 |
| ❑ 399 | Ryan Dempster | .20 | .50 |
| ❑ 400 | Curt Schilling | .40 | 1.00 |
| ❑ 401 | Peter Bergeron | .20 | .50 |
| ❑ 402 | Kyle Lohse | .20 | .50 |
| ❑ 403 | Craig Wilson | .20 | .50 |
| ❑ 404 | David Justice | .40 | 1.00 |
| ❑ 405 | Darin Erstad | .40 | 1.00 |
| ❑ 406 | Jose Mercedes | .20 | .50 |
| ❑ 407 | Carl Pavano | .40 | 1.00 |
| ❑ 408 | Albie Lopez | .20 | .50 |
| ❑ 409 | Alex Ochoa | .20 | .50 |
| ❑ 410 | Chipper Jones | 1.00 | 2.50 |
| ❑ 411 | Tyler Houston | .20 | .50 |
| ❑ 412 | Dean Palmer | .20 | .50 |
| ❑ 413 | Damian Jackson | .20 | .50 |
| ❑ 414 | Josh Towers | .20 | .50 |
| ❑ 415 | Rafael Furcal | .40 | 1.00 |
| ❑ 416 | Mike Morgan | .20 | .50 |
| ❑ 417 | Herb Perry | .20 | .50 |
| ❑ 418 | Mike Sirotka | .20 | .50 |
| ❑ 419 | Mark Wohlers | .20 | .50 |
| ❑ 420 | Nomar Garciaparra | 1.50 | 4.00 |
| ❑ 421 | Felipe Lopez | .20 | .50 |
| ❑ 422 | Joe McEwing | .20 | .50 |
| ❑ 423 | Jacque Jones | .40 | 1.00 |
| ❑ 424 | Julio Franco | .40 | 1.00 |
| ❑ 425 | Frank Thomas | 1.00 | 2.50 |
| ❑ 426 | So Taguchi RC | 1.00 | 2.50 |
| ❑ 427 | Kazuhisa Ishii RC | 1.00 | 2.50 |
| ❑ 428 | D'Angelo Jimenez | .20 | .50 |
| ❑ 429 | Chris Stynes | .20 | .50 |
| ❑ 430 | Kerry Wood | .40 | 1.00 |
| ❑ 431 | Chris Singleton | .20 | .50 |
| ❑ 432 | Enibel Durazo | .20 | .50 |
| ❑ 433 | Matt Lawton | .20 | .50 |
| ❑ 434 | Bill Mueller | .40 | 1.00 |
| ❑ 435 | Jose Canseco | .60 | 1.50 |
| ❑ 436 | Ben Grieve | .20 | .50 |
| ❑ 437 | Terry Mulholland | .20 | .50 |
| ❑ 438 | David Bell | .20 | .50 |
| ❑ 439 | A.J. Pierzynski | .40 | 1.00 |
| ❑ 440 | Adam Dunn | .40 | 1.00 |
| ❑ 441 | Jon Garland | .40 | 1.00 |
| ❑ 442 | Jeff Fassero | .20 | .50 |
| ❑ 443 | Julio Lugo | .20 | .50 |
| ❑ 444 | Carlos Guillen | .40 | 1.00 |
| ❑ 445 | Orlando Hernandez | .40 | 1.00 |
| ❑ 446 | Mark Loretta | .20 | .50 |
| ❑ 447 | Scott Spiezio | .20 | .50 |
| ❑ 448 | Kevin Millwood | .40 | 1.00 |
| ❑ 449 | Jamie Moyer | .40 | 1.00 |
| ❑ 450 | Todd Helton | .50 | 1.50 |
| ❑ 451 | Todd Walker | .20 | .50 |
| ❑ 452 | Jose Lima | .20 | .50 |
| ❑ 453 | Brook Fordyce | .20 | .50 |
| ❑ 454 | Aaron Rowand | .40 | 1.00 |
| ❑ 455 | Barry Zito | .40 | 1.00 |
| ❑ 456 | Eric Owens | .20 | .50 |
| ❑ 457 | Charles Nagy | .20 | .50 |
| ❑ 458 | Raul Ibanez | .20 | .50 |
| ❑ 459 | Jose Mays | .20 | .50 |
| ❑ 460 | Jim Thome | .60 | 1.50 |
| ❑ 461 | Adam Eaton | .20 | .50 |
| ❑ 462 | Felix Martinez | .20 | .50 |
| ❑ 463 | Vernon Wells | .40 | 1.00 |
| ❑ 464 | Donnie Sadler | .20 | .50 |
| ❑ 465 | Tony Clark | .20 | .50 |
| ❑ 466 | Jose Hernandez | .20 | .50 |
| ❑ 467 | Ramon Martinez | .20 | .50 |
| ❑ 468 | Rusty Greer | .40 | 1.00 |
| ❑ 469 | Rod Barajas | .20 | .50 |
| ❑ 470 | Lance Berkman | .40 | 1.00 |
| ❑ 471 | Brady Anderson | .40 | 1.00 |
| ❑ 472 | Pedro Astacio | .20 | .50 |
| ❑ 473 | Shane Halter | .20 | .50 |
| ❑ 474 | Bret Prinz | .20 | .50 |
| ❑ 475 | Edgar Martinez | .60 | 1.50 |
| ❑ 476 | Steve Trachsel | .20 | .50 |
| ❑ 477 | Gary Matthews Jr. | .20 | .50 |
| ❑ 478 | Ismael Valdes | .20 | .50 |
| ❑ 479 | Juan Uribe | .20 | .50 |
| ❑ 480 | Shawn Green | .40 | 1.00 |
| ❑ 481 | Kirk Rueter | .20 | .50 |
| ❑ 482 | Damion Easley | .20 | .50 |
| ❑ 483 | Chris Carpenter | .40 | 1.00 |
| ❑ 484 | Kris Benson | .20 | .50 |
| ❑ 485 | Antonio Alfonseca | .20 | .50 |
| ❑ 486 | Kyle Farnsworth | .20 | .50 |
| ❑ 487 | Brandon Lyon | .20 | .50 |
| ❑ 488 | Hideki Irabu | .20 | .50 |
| ❑ 489 | David Ortiz | 1.00 | 2.50 |
| ❑ 490 | Mike Piazza | 1.50 | 4.00 |
| ❑ 491 | Derek Lowe | .40 | 1.00 |
| ❑ 492 | Chris Gomez | .20 | .50 |
| ❑ 493 | Mark Johnson | .20 | .50 |
| ❑ 494 | John Rocker | .40 | 1.00 |
| ❑ 495 | Eric Karros | .40 | 1.00 |
| ❑ 496 | Bill Haselman | .20 | .50 |
| ❑ 497 | Dave Veres | .20 | .50 |
| ❑ 498 | Pete Harnisch | .20 | .50 |
| ❑ 499 | Tomokazu Ohka | .20 | .50 |
| ❑ 500 | Barry Bonds | 2.50 | 6.00 |
| ❑ 501 | David Dellucci | .20 | .50 |
| ❑ 502 | Wendell Magee | .20 | .50 |
| ❑ 503 | Tom Gordon | .20 | .50 |
| ❑ 504 | Javier Vazquez | .40 | 1.00 |
| ❑ 505 | Ben Sheets | .40 | 1.00 |
| ❑ 506 | Wilton Guerrero | .20 | .50 |
| ❑ 507 | John Halama | .20 | .50 |
| ❑ 508 | Mark Redman | .20 | .50 |
| ❑ 509 | Jack Wilson | .20 | .50 |
| ❑ 510 | Bernie Williams | .60 | 1.50 |
| ❑ 511 | Miguel Cairo | .20 | .50 |
| ❑ 512 | Denny Hocking | .20 | .50 |
| ❑ 513 | Tony Batista | .20 | .50 |
| ❑ 514 | Mark Grudzielanek | .20 | .50 |
| ❑ 515 | Jose Vidro | .20 | .50 |
| ❑ 516 | Sterling Hitchcock | .20 | .50 |
| ❑ 517 | Billy Koch | .20 | .50 |
| ❑ 518 | Matt Clement | .40 | 1.00 |
| ❑ 519 | Bruce Chen | .20 | .50 |
| ❑ 520 | Roberto Alomar | .60 | 1.50 |
| ❑ 521 | Orlando Palmeiro | .20 | .50 |
| ❑ 522 | Steve Finley | .40 | 1.00 |
| ❑ 523 | Danny Patterson | .20 | .50 |
| ❑ 524 | Terry Adams | .20 | .50 |
| ❑ 525 | Tino Martinez | .60 | 1.50 |
| ❑ 526 | Tony Armas Jr. | .20 | .50 |
| ❑ 527 | Geoff Jenkins | .20 | .50 |
| ❑ 528 | Kerry Robinson | .20 | .50 |
| ❑ 529 | Corey Patterson | .40 | 1.00 |
| ❑ 530 | Brian Giles | .40 | 1.00 |
| ❑ 531 | Jose Jimenez | .20 | .50 |
| ❑ 532 | Joe Kennedy | .20 | .50 |
| ❑ 533 | Armando Rios | .20 | .50 |
| ❑ 534 | Osvaldo Fernandez | .20 | .50 |
| ❑ 535 | Ruben Sierra | .40 | 1.00 |
| ❑ 536 | Octavio Dotel | .20 | .50 |
| ❑ 537 | Luis Sojo | .20 | .50 |
| ❑ 538 | Brent Butler | .20 | .50 |
| ❑ 539 | Pablo Ozuna | .20 | .50 |
| ❑ 540 | Freddy Garcia | .40 | 1.00 |
| ❑ 541 | Chad Durbin | .20 | .50 |
| ❑ 542 | Orlando Merced | .20 | .50 |
| ❑ 543 | Michael Tucker | .20 | .50 |
| ❑ 544 | Roberto Hernandez | .20 | .50 |
| ❑ 545 | Pat Burrell | .40 | 1.00 |
| ❑ 546 | A.J. Burnett | .40 | 1.00 |
| ❑ 547 | Bubba Trammell | .20 | .50 |
| ❑ 548 | Scott Elarton | .20 | .50 |
| ❑ 549 | Mike Darr | .20 | .50 |
| ❑ 550 | Ken Griffey Jr. | 1.50 | 4.00 |
| ❑ 551 | Ugueth Urbina | .20 | .50 |
| ❑ 552 | Todd Jones | .20 | .50 |
| ❑ 553 | Delino Deshields | .20 | .50 |
| ❑ 554 | Adam Piatt | .20 | .50 |
| ❑ 555 | Jason Kendall | .40 | 1.00 |
| ❑ 556 | Hector Ortiz | .20 | .50 |
| ❑ 557 | Turk Wendell | .20 | .50 |
| ❑ 558 | Rob Bell | .20 | .50 |
| ❑ 559 | Sun Woo Kim | .20 | .50 |
| ❑ 560 | Raul Mondesi | .40 | 1.00 |
| ❑ 561 | Brent Abernathy | .20 | .50 |
| ❑ 562 | Seth Etherton | .20 | .50 |
| ❑ 563 | Shawn Wooten | .20 | .50 |
| ❑ 564 | Jay Buhner | .40 | 1.00 |
| ❑ 565 | Andres Galarraga | .40 | 1.00 |
| ❑ 566 | Shane Reynolds | .20 | .50 |
| ❑ 567 | Rod Beck | .20 | .50 |
| ❑ 568 | Dee Brown | .20 | .50 |
| ❑ 569 | Pedro Feliz | .20 | .50 |
| ❑ 570 | Ryan Klesko | .40 | 1.00 |
| ❑ 571 | John Vander Wal | .20 | .50 |
| ❑ 572 | Nick Bierbrodt | .20 | .50 |
| ❑ 573 | Joe Nathan | .40 | 1.00 |
| ❑ 574 | James Baldwin | .20 | .50 |
| ❑ 575 | J.D. Drew | .40 | 1.00 |
| ❑ 576 | Greg Colbrunn | .20 | .50 |
| ❑ 577 | Doug Glanville | .20 | .50 |
| ❑ 578 | Brandon Duckworth | .20 | .50 |
| ❑ 579 | Shawn Chacon | .20 | .50 |
| ❑ 580 | Rich Aurilia | .20 | .50 |
| ❑ 581 | Chuck Finley | .40 | 1.00 |
| ❑ 582 | Abraham Nunez | .20 | .50 |
| ❑ 583 | Kenny Lofton | .40 | 1.00 |
| ❑ 584 | Brian Daubach | .20 | .50 |
| ❑ 585 | Miguel Tejada | .40 | 1.00 |
| ❑ 586 | Nate Cornejo | .20 | .50 |
| ❑ 587 | Kazuhiro Sasaki | .40 | 1.00 |
| ❑ 588 | Chris Richard | .20 | .50 |
| ❑ 589 | Armando Reynoso | .20 | .50 |
| ❑ 590 | Tim Hudson | .40 | 1.00 |
| ❑ 591 | Neifi Perez | .20 | .50 |
| ❑ 592 | Steve Cox | .20 | .50 |
| ❑ 593 | Henry Blanco | .20 | .50 |
| ❑ 594 | Ricky Ledee | .20 | .50 |
| ❑ 595 | Tim Salmon | .60 | 1.50 |
| ❑ 596 | Luis Rivas | .20 | .50 |
| ❑ 597 | Jeff Zimmerman | .20 | .50 |
| ❑ 598 | Matt Stairs | .20 | .50 |
| ❑ 599 | Preston Wilson | .20 | .50 |
| ❑ 600 | Mark McGwire | 2.50 | 6.00 |
| ❑ 601 | Timo Perez | .20 | .50 |
| ❑ 602 | Matt Anderson | .20 | .50 |
| ❑ 603 | Todd Hundley | .20 | .50 |
| ❑ 604 | Rick Ankiel | .20 | .50 |
| ❑ 605 | Tsuyoshi Shinjo | .40 | 1.00 |
| ❑ 606 | Woody Williams | .20 | .50 |
| ❑ 607 | Jason LaRue | .20 | .50 |
| ❑ 608 | Carlos Lee | .40 | 1.00 |
| ❑ 609 | Russ Johnson | .20 | .50 |
| ❑ 610 | Scott Rolen | .60 | 1.50 |
| ❑ 611 | Brent Mayne | .20 | .50 |
| ❑ 612 | Darrin Fletcher | .20 | .50 |
| ❑ 613 | Ray Lankford | .40 | 1.00 |
| ❑ 614 | Troy O'Leary | .20 | .50 |
| ❑ 615 | Javier Lopez | .20 | .50 |
| ❑ 616 | Randy Velarde | .20 | .50 |
| ❑ 617 | Vinny Castilla | .40 | 1.00 |
| ❑ 618 | Milton Bradley | .40 | 1.00 |
| ❑ 619 | Ruben Mateo | .20 | .50 |
| ❑ 620 | Jason Giambi Yankees | .40 | 1.00 |
| ❑ 621 | Andy Benes | .20 | .50 |
| ❑ 622 | Joe Mauer RC | 6.00 | 15.00 |
| ❑ 623 | Andy Pettitte | .60 | 1.50 |
| ❑ 624 | Jose Offerman | .20 | .50 |
| ❑ 625 | Mo Vaughn | .40 | 1.00 |
| ❑ 626 | Steve Sparks | .20 | .50 |
| ❑ 627 | Mike Matthews | .20 | .50 |
| ❑ 628 | Robb Nen | .40 | 1.00 |
| ❑ 629 | Kip Wells | .20 | .50 |
| ❑ 630 | Kevin Brown | .40 | 1.00 |
| ❑ 631 | Arthur Rhodes | .20 | .50 |
| ❑ 632 | Gabe Kapler | .20 | .50 |
| ❑ 633 | Jermaine Dye | .40 | 1.00 |
| ❑ 634 | Josh Beckett | .40 | 1.00 |
| ❑ 635 | Pokey Reese | .20 | .50 |
| ❑ 636 | Benji Gil | .20 | .50 |
| ❑ 637 | Marcus Giles | .20 | .50 |
| ❑ 638 | Julian Tavarez | .20 | .50 |
| ❑ 639 | Jason Schmidt | .40 | 1.00 |
| ❑ 640 | Alex Rodriguez | 1.50 | 4.00 |
| ❑ 641 | Anaheim Angels TC | .40 | 1.00 |
| ❑ 642 | Arizona Diamondbacks TC | .60 | 1.50 |
| ❑ 643 | Atlanta Braves TC | .40 | 1.00 |
| ❑ 644 | Baltimore Orioles TC | .40 | 1.00 |
| ❑ 645 | Boston Red Sox TC | .40 | 1.00 |
| ❑ 646 | Chicago Cubs TC | .40 | 1.00 |
| ❑ 647 | Chicago White Sox TC | .40 | 1.00 |
| ❑ 648 | Cincinnati Reds TC | .40 | 1.00 |
| ❑ 649 | Cleveland Indians TC | .40 | 1.00 |
| ❑ 650 | Colorado Rockies TC | .40 | 1.00 |
| ❑ 651 | Detroit Tigers TC | .40 | 1.00 |
| ❑ 652 | Florida Marlins TC | .40 | 1.00 |

| | | |
|---|---|---|
| 653 Houston Astros TC | .40 | 1.00 |
| 654 Kansas City Royals TC | .40 | 1.00 |
| 655 Los Angeles Dodgers TC | .40 | 1.00 |
| 656 Milwaukee Brewers TC | .40 | 1.00 |
| 657 Minnesota Twins TC | .40 | 1.00 |
| 658 Montreal Expos TC | .40 | 1.00 |
| 659 New York Mets TC | .40 | 1.00 |
| 660 New York Yankees TC | 1.00 | 2.50 |
| 661 Oakland Athletics TC | .40 | 1.00 |
| 662 Philadelphia Phillies TC | .40 | 1.00 |
| 663 Pittsburgh Pirates TC | .40 | 1.00 |
| 664 San Diego Padres TC | .40 | 1.00 |
| 665 San Francisco Giants TC | .40 | 1.00 |
| 666 Seattle Mariners TC | .60 | 1.50 |
| 667 St. Louis Cardinals TC | .40 | 1.00 |
| 668 Tampa Bay Devil Rays TC | .40 | 1.00 |
| 669 Texas Rangers TC | .40 | 1.00 |
| 670 Toronto Blue Jays TC | .40 | 1.00 |
| 671 Juan Cruz PROS | .60 | 1.50 |
| 672 Kevin Cash PROS RC | .60 | 1.50 |
| 673 Jimmy Gobble PROS RC | .60 | 1.50 |
| 674 Mike Hill PROS RC | .60 | 1.50 |
| 675 Taylor Buchholz PROS RC | .60 | 1.50 |
| 676 Bill Hall PROS | .60 | 1.50 |
| 677 Brett Roneberg PROS RC | .60 | 1.50 |
| 678 Royce Huffman PROS RC | .60 | 1.50 |
| 679 Chris Tritle PROS RC | .60 | 1.50 |
| 680 Nate Espy PROS | .60 | 1.50 |
| 681 Nick Alvarez PROS RC | .60 | 1.50 |
| 682 Jason Botts PROS RC | .60 | 1.50 |
| 683 Ryan Gripp PROS RC | .60 | 1.50 |
| 684 Dan Phillips PROS RC | .60 | 1.50 |
| 685 Pablo Arias PROS RC | .60 | 1.50 |
| 686 John Rodriguez PROS RC | 1.00 | 2.50 |
| 687 Rich Harden PROS RC | 3.00 | 8.00 |
| 688 Neal Frendling PROS RC | .60 | 1.50 |
| 689 Rich Thompson PROS RC | .60 | 1.50 |
| 690 Greg Montalbano PROS RC | .60 | 1.50 |
| 691 Len Dinardo DP RC | .60 | 1.50 |
| 692 Ryan Raburn DP RC | .50 | 1.50 |
| 693 Josh Barfield DP RC | 2.00 | 5.00 |
| 694 David Bacani DP RC | .40 | 1.00 |
| 695 Dan Johnson DP RC | 1.00 | 2.50 |

## 2003 Topps Chrome

| | | |
|---|---|---|
| COMPLETE SET (440) | 80.00 | 200.00 |
| COMPLETE SERIES 1 (220) | 40.00 | 100.00 |
| COMPLETE SERIES 2 (220) | 40.00 | 100.00 |
| COMMON (1-200/221-420) | .40 | 1.00 |
| COMMON (201-220/421-440) | .60 | 1.50 |
| 1 Alex Rodriguez | 1.50 | 4.00 |
| 2 Eddie Guardado | .40 | 1.00 |
| 3 Curt Schilling | .40 | 1.00 |
| 4 Andruw Jones | .60 | 1.50 |
| 5 Magglio Ordonez | .40 | 1.00 |
| 6 Todd Helton | .60 | 1.50 |
| 7 Odalis Perez | .40 | 1.00 |
| 8 Edgardo Alfonzo | .40 | 1.00 |
| 9 Eric Hinske | .40 | 1.00 |
| 10 Danny Bautista | .40 | 1.00 |
| 11 Sammy Sosa | 1.00 | 2.50 |
| 12 Roberto Alomar | .60 | 1.50 |
| 13 Roger Clemens | 2.00 | 5.00 |
| 14 Austin Kearns | .40 | 1.00 |
| 15 Luis Gonzalez | .40 | 1.00 |
| 16 Mo Vaughn | .40 | 1.00 |
| 17 Alfonso Soriano | .40 | 1.00 |
| 18 Orlando Cabrera | .40 | 1.00 |
| 19 Hideo Nomo | 1.00 | 2.50 |
| 20 Omar Vizquel | .60 | 1.50 |
| 21 Greg Maddux | 1.50 | 4.00 |
| 22 Fred McGriff | .60 | 1.50 |
| 23 Frank Thomas | 1.00 | 2.50 |
| 24 Shawn Green | .40 | 1.00 |

| | | |
|---|---|---|
| 25 Jacque Jones | .40 | 1.00 |
| 26 Bernie Williams | .60 | 1.50 |
| 27 Corey Patterson | .40 | 1.00 |
| 28 Cesar Izturis | .40 | 1.00 |
| 29 Larry Walker | .40 | 1.00 |
| 30 Darren Dreifort | .40 | 1.00 |
| 31 Al Leiter | .40 | 1.00 |
| 32 Jason Marquis | .40 | 1.00 |
| 33 Sean Casey | .40 | 1.00 |
| 34 Craig Counsell | .40 | 1.00 |
| 35 Albert Pujols | 2.00 | 5.00 |
| 36 Kyle Lohse | .40 | 1.00 |
| 37 Paul Lo Duca | .40 | 1.00 |
| 38 Roy Oswalt | .40 | 1.00 |
| 39 Danny Graves | .40 | 1.00 |
| 40 Kevin Millwood | .40 | 1.00 |
| 41 Lance Berkman | .40 | 1.00 |
| 42 Denny Hocking | .40 | 1.00 |
| 43 Jose Valentin | .40 | 1.00 |
| 44 Josh Beckett | .40 | 1.00 |
| 45 Nomar Garciaparra | 1.50 | 4.00 |
| 46 Craig Biggio | .60 | 1.50 |
| 47 Omar Daal | .40 | 1.00 |
| 48 Jimmy Rollins | .40 | 1.00 |
| 49 Jermaine Dye | .40 | 1.00 |
| 50 Edgar Renteria | .40 | 1.00 |
| 51 Brandon Duckworth | .40 | 1.00 |
| 52 Luis Castillo | .40 | 1.00 |
| 53 Andy Ashby | .40 | 1.00 |
| 54 Mike Williams | .40 | 1.00 |
| 55 Benito Santiago | .40 | 1.00 |
| 56 Bret Boone | .40 | 1.00 |
| 57 Randy Wolf | .40 | 1.00 |
| 58 Ivan Rodriguez | .60 | 1.50 |
| 59 Shannon Stewart | .40 | 1.00 |
| 60 Jose Cruz Jr. | .40 | 1.00 |
| 61 Billy Wagner | .40 | 1.00 |
| 62 Alex Gonzalez | .40 | 1.00 |
| 63 Ichiro Suzuki | 2.00 | 5.00 |
| 64 Joe McEwing | .40 | 1.00 |
| 65 Mark Mulder | .40 | 1.00 |
| 66 Mike Cameron | .40 | 1.00 |
| 67 Corey Koskie | .40 | 1.00 |
| 68 Marlon Anderson | .40 | 1.00 |
| 69 Jason Kendall | .40 | 1.00 |
| 70 J.T. Snow | .40 | 1.00 |
| 71 Edgar Martinez | .60 | 1.50 |
| 72 Vernon Wells | .40 | 1.00 |
| 73 Vladimir Guerrero | 1.00 | 2.50 |
| 74 Adam Dunn | .40 | 1.00 |
| 75 Barry Zito | .40 | 1.00 |
| 76 Jeff Kent | .40 | 1.00 |
| 77 Russ Ortiz | .40 | 1.00 |
| 78 Phil Nevin | .40 | 1.00 |
| 79 Carlos Beltran | .40 | 1.00 |
| 80 Mike Lowell | .40 | 1.00 |
| 81 Bob Wickman | .40 | 1.00 |
| 82 Junior Spivey | .40 | 1.00 |
| 83 Melvin Mora | .40 | 1.00 |
| 84 Derrek Lee | .60 | 1.50 |
| 85 Chuck Knoblauch | .40 | 1.00 |
| 86 Eric Gagne | 1.00 | 2.50 |
| 87 Orlando Hernandez | .40 | 1.00 |
| 88 Robert Person | .40 | 1.00 |
| 89 Elmer Dessens | .40 | 1.00 |
| 90 Wade Miller | .40 | 1.00 |
| 91 Adrian Beltre | .40 | 1.00 |
| 92 Kazuhiro Sasaki | .40 | 1.00 |
| 93 Timo Perez | .40 | 1.00 |
| 94 Jose Vidro | .40 | 1.00 |
| 95 Geronimo Gil | .40 | 1.00 |
| 96 Trot Nixon | .40 | 1.00 |
| 97 Denny Neagle | .40 | 1.00 |
| 98 Roberto Hernandez | .40 | 1.00 |
| 99 David Ortiz | 1.00 | 2.50 |
| 100 Robb Nen | .40 | 1.00 |
| 101 Sidney Ponson | .40 | 1.00 |
| 102 Kevin Appier | .40 | 1.00 |
| 103 Javier Lopez | .40 | 1.00 |
| 104 Jeff Conine | .40 | 1.00 |
| 105 Mark Buehrle | .40 | 1.00 |
| 106 Jason Simontacchi | .40 | 1.00 |
| 107 Jose Jimenez | .40 | 1.00 |
| 108 Brian Jordan | .40 | 1.00 |
| 109 Brad Wilkerson | .40 | 1.00 |
| 110 Scott Hatteberg | .40 | 1.00 |
| 111 Matt Morris | .40 | 1.00 |
| 112 Miguel Tejada | .40 | 1.00 |

| | | |
|---|---|---|
| 113 Rafael Furcal | .40 | 1.00 |
| 114 Steve Cox | .40 | 1.00 |
| 115 Roy Halladay | .40 | 1.00 |
| 116 David Eckstein | .40 | 1.00 |
| 117 Tomo Ohka | .40 | 1.00 |
| 118 Jack Wilson | .40 | 1.00 |
| 119 Randall Simon | .40 | 1.00 |
| 120 Jamie Moyer | .40 | 1.00 |
| 121 Andy Benes | .40 | 1.00 |
| 122 Tino Martinez | .60 | 1.50 |
| 123 Esteban Yan | .40 | 1.00 |
| 124 Jason Isringhausen | .40 | 1.00 |
| 125 Chris Carpenter | .40 | 1.00 |
| 126 Aaron Rowand | .40 | 1.00 |
| 127 Brandon Inge | .40 | 1.00 |
| 128 Jose Vizcaino | .40 | 1.00 |
| 129 Jose Mesa | .40 | 1.00 |
| 130 Troy Percival | .40 | 1.00 |
| 131 Jon Lieber | .40 | 1.00 |
| 132 Brian Giles | .40 | 1.00 |
| 133 Aaron Boone | .40 | 1.00 |
| 134 Bobby Higginson | .40 | 1.00 |
| 135 Luis Rivas | .40 | 1.00 |
| 136 Troy Glaus | .40 | 1.00 |
| 137 Jim Thome | .60 | 1.50 |
| 138 Ramon Martinez | .40 | 1.00 |
| 139 Jay Gibbons | .40 | 1.00 |
| 140 Mike Lieberthal | .40 | 1.00 |
| 141 Juan Uribe | .40 | 1.00 |
| 142 Gary Sheffield | .40 | 1.00 |
| 143 Ramon Santiago | .40 | 1.00 |
| 144 Ben Sheets | .40 | 1.00 |
| 145 Tony Armas Jr. | .40 | 1.00 |
| 146 Kazuhisa Ishii | .40 | 1.00 |
| 147 Erubiel Durazo | .40 | 1.00 |
| 148 Jerry Hairston Jr. | .40 | 1.00 |
| 149 Byung-Hyun Kim | .40 | 1.00 |
| 150 Marcus Giles | .40 | 1.00 |
| 151 Johnny Damon | .60 | 1.50 |
| 152 Terrence Long | .40 | 1.00 |
| 153 Juan Pierre | .40 | 1.00 |
| 154 Aramis Ramirez | .40 | 1.00 |
| 155 Brent Abernathy | .40 | 1.00 |
| 156 Ismael Valdes | .40 | 1.00 |
| 157 Mike Mussina | .60 | 1.50 |
| 158 Ramon Hernandez | .40 | 1.00 |
| 159 Adam Kennedy | .40 | 1.00 |
| 160 Tony Womack | .40 | 1.00 |
| 161 Tony Batista | .40 | 1.00 |
| 162 Kip Wells | .40 | 1.00 |
| 163 Jeromy Burnitz | .40 | 1.00 |
| 164 Todd Hundley | .40 | 1.00 |
| 165 Tim Wakefield | .40 | 1.00 |
| 166 Derek Lowe | .40 | 1.00 |
| 167 Jorge Posada | .60 | 1.50 |
| 168 Ramon Ortiz | .40 | 1.00 |
| 169 Brent Butler | .40 | 1.00 |
| 170 Shane Halter | .40 | 1.00 |
| 171 Matt Lawton | .40 | 1.00 |
| 172 Alex Sanchez | .40 | 1.00 |
| 173 Eric Milton | .40 | 1.00 |
| 174 Vicente Padilla | .40 | 1.00 |
| 175 Steve Karsay | .40 | 1.00 |
| 176 Mark Prior | .60 | 1.50 |
| 177 Kerry Wood | .60 | 1.50 |
| 178 Jason LaRue | .40 | 1.00 |
| 179 Danys Baez | .40 | 1.00 |
| 180 Nick Neugebauer | .40 | 1.00 |
| 181 Andres Galarraga | .40 | 1.00 |
| 182 Jason Giambi | .60 | 1.50 |
| 183 Aubrey Huff | .40 | 1.00 |
| 184 Juan Gonzalez | .60 | 1.50 |
| 185 Ugueth Urbina | .40 | 1.00 |
| 186 Rickey Henderson | 1.00 | 2.50 |
| 187 Brad Fullmer | .40 | 1.00 |
| 188 Todd Zeile | .40 | 1.00 |
| 189 Jason Jennings | .40 | 1.00 |
| 190 Vladimir Nunez | .40 | 1.00 |
| 191 David Justice | .40 | 1.00 |
| 192 Brian Lawrence | .40 | 1.00 |
| 193 Pat Burrell | .40 | 1.00 |
| 194 Pokey Reese | .40 | 1.00 |
| 195 Robert Fick | .40 | 1.00 |
| 196 C.C. Sabathia | .40 | 1.00 |
| 197 Fernando Vina | .40 | 1.00 |
| 198 Sean Burroughs | .40 | 1.00 |
| 199 Ellis Burks | .40 | 1.00 |
| 200 Joe Randa | .40 | 1.00 |

| # | Card | Low | High |
|---|------|-----|------|
| 201 | Chris Duncan FY RC | 1.50 | 4.00 |
| 202 | Franklin Gutierrez FY RC | 1.25 | 3.00 |
| 203 | Adam LaRoche FY | .60 | 1.50 |
| 204 | Manuel Ramirez FY RC | 1.00 | 2.50 |
| 205 | Il Kim FY RC | .60 | 1.50 |
| 206 | Daryl Clark FY RC | .60 | 1.50 |
| 207 | Sean Pierce FY | .60 | 1.50 |
| 208 | Andy Marte FY RC | 3.00 | 8.00 |
| 209 | Bernie Castro FY | .60 | 1.50 |
| 210 | Jason Perry FY RC | 1.00 | 2.50 |
| 211 | Jaime Bubela FY RC | .60 | 1.50 |
| 212 | Alexis Rios FY | 1.00 | 2.50 |
| 213 | Brendan Harris FY RC | 1.00 | 2.50 |
| 214 | Ramon Nivar-Martinez FY RC | .60 | 1.50 |
| 215 | Terry Tiffee FY RC | .60 | 1.50 |
| 216 | Kevin Youkilis FY RC | 1.50 | 4.00 |
| 217 | Derell McCall FY RC | .60 | 1.50 |
| 218 | Scott Tyler FY RC | 1.00 | 2.50 |
| 219 | Craig Brazell FY RC | .60 | 1.50 |
| 220 | Walter Young FY | .60 | 1.50 |
| 221 | Francisco Rodriguez | .40 | 1.00 |
| 222 | Chipper Jones | 1.00 | 2.50 |
| 223 | Chris Singleton | .40 | 1.00 |
| 224 | Cliff Floyd | .40 | 1.00 |
| 225 | Bobby Hill | .40 | 1.00 |
| 226 | Antonio Osuna | .40 | 1.00 |
| 227 | Barry Larkin | .60 | 1.50 |
| 228 | Dean Palmer | .40 | 1.00 |
| 229 | Eric Owens | .40 | 1.00 |
| 230 | Randy Johnson | 1.00 | 2.50 |
| 231 | Jeff Suppan | .40 | 1.00 |
| 232 | Eric Karros | .40 | 1.00 |
| 233 | Johan Santana | .60 | 1.50 |
| 234 | Javier Vazquez | .40 | 1.00 |
| 235 | John Thomson | .40 | 1.00 |
| 236 | Nick Johnson | .40 | 1.00 |
| 237 | Mark Ellis | .40 | 1.00 |
| 238 | Doug Glanville | .40 | 1.00 |
| 239 | Ken Griffey Jr. | 1.50 | 4.00 |
| 240 | Bubba Trammell | .40 | 1.00 |
| 241 | Livan Hernandez | .40 | 1.00 |
| 242 | Desi Relaford | .40 | 1.00 |
| 243 | Eli Marrero | .40 | 1.00 |
| 244 | Jared Sandberg | .40 | 1.00 |
| 245 | Barry Bonds | 2.50 | 6.00 |
| 246 | Aaron Sele | .40 | 1.00 |
| 247 | Derek Jeter | 2.50 | 6.00 |
| 248 | Eric Byrnes | .40 | 1.00 |
| 249 | Rich Aurilia | .40 | 1.00 |
| 250 | Joel Pineiro | .40 | 1.00 |
| 251 | Chuck Finley | .40 | 1.00 |
| 252 | Bengie Molina | .40 | 1.00 |
| 253 | Steve Finley | .40 | 1.00 |
| 254 | Marty Cordova | .40 | 1.00 |
| 255 | Shea Hillenbrand | .40 | 1.00 |
| 256 | Milton Bradley | .40 | 1.00 |
| 257 | Carlos Pena | .40 | 1.00 |
| 258 | Brad Ausmus | .40 | 1.00 |
| 259 | Carlos Delgado | .40 | 1.00 |
| 260 | Kevin Mench | .40 | 1.00 |
| 261 | Joe Kennedy | .40 | 1.00 |
| 262 | Mark McLemore | .40 | 1.00 |
| 263 | Bill Mueller | .40 | 1.00 |
| 264 | Ricky Ledee | .40 | 1.00 |
| 265 | Ted Lilly | .40 | 1.00 |
| 266 | Sterling Hitchcock | .40 | 1.00 |
| 267 | Scott Strickland | .40 | 1.00 |
| 268 | Damion Easley | .40 | 1.00 |
| 269 | Torii Hunter | .40 | 1.00 |
| 270 | Brad Radke | .40 | 1.00 |
| 271 | Geoff Jenkins | .40 | 1.00 |
| 272 | Paul Byrd | .40 | 1.00 |
| 273 | Morgan Ensberg | .40 | 1.00 |
| 274 | Mike Maroth | .40 | 1.00 |
| 275 | Mike Hampton | .40 | 1.00 |
| 276 | Flash Gordon | .40 | 1.00 |
| 277 | John Burkett | .40 | 1.00 |
| 278 | Rodrigo Lopez | .40 | 1.00 |
| 279 | Tim Spooneybarger | .40 | 1.00 |
| 280 | Quinton McCracken | .40 | 1.00 |
| 281 | Tim Salmon | .60 | 1.50 |
| 282 | Jarrod Washburn | .40 | 1.00 |
| 283 | Pedro Astacio | .60 | 1.50 |
| 284 | Julio Lugo | .40 | 1.00 |
| 285 | Armando Benitez | .40 | 1.00 |
| 286 | Raul Mondesi | .40 | 1.00 |
| 287 | Robin Ventura | .40 | 1.00 |
| 288 | Bobby Abreu | .40 | 1.00 |
| 289 | Josh Fogg | .40 | 1.00 |
| 290 | Ryan Klesko | .40 | 1.00 |
| 291 | Tsuyoshi Shinjo | .40 | 1.00 |
| 292 | Jim Edmonds | .60 | 1.50 |
| 293 | Chan Ho Park | .40 | 1.00 |
| 294 | John Mabry | .40 | 1.00 |
| 295 | Woody Williams | .40 | 1.00 |
| 296 | Scott Schoeneweis | .40 | 1.00 |
| 297 | Brian Anderson | .40 | 1.00 |
| 298 | Brett Tomko | .40 | 1.00 |
| 299 | Scott Erickson | .40 | 1.00 |
| 300 | Kevin Millar Sox | .40 | 1.00 |
| 301 | Danny Wright | .40 | 1.00 |
| 302 | Jason Schmidt | .40 | 1.00 |
| 303 | Scott Williamson | .40 | 1.00 |
| 304 | Einar Diaz | .40 | 1.00 |
| 305 | Jay Payton | .40 | 1.00 |
| 306 | Juan Acevedo | .40 | 1.00 |
| 307 | Ben Grieve | .40 | 1.00 |
| 308 | Raul Ibanez | .40 | 1.00 |
| 309 | Richie Sexson | .40 | 1.00 |
| 310 | Rick Reed | .40 | 1.00 |
| 311 | Pedro Astacio | .40 | 1.00 |
| 312 | Bud Smith | .40 | 1.00 |
| 313 | Tomas Perez | .40 | 1.00 |
| 314 | Rafael Palmeiro | .60 | 1.50 |
| 315 | Jason Tyner | .40 | 1.00 |
| 316 | Scott Rolen | .60 | 1.50 |
| 317 | Randy Winn | .40 | 1.00 |
| 318 | Ryan Jensen | .40 | 1.00 |
| 319 | Trevor Hoffman | .40 | 1.00 |
| 320 | Craig Wilson | .40 | 1.00 |
| 321 | Jeremy Giambi | .40 | 1.00 |
| 322 | Andy Pettitte | .60 | 1.50 |
| 323 | John Franco | .40 | 1.00 |
| 324 | Felipe Lopez | .40 | 1.00 |
| 325 | Mike Piazza | 1.50 | 4.00 |
| 326 | Cristian Guzman | .40 | 1.00 |
| 327 | Jose Hernandez | .40 | 1.00 |
| 328 | Octavio Dotel | .40 | 1.00 |
| 329 | Brad Penny | .40 | 1.00 |
| 330 | Dave Veres | .40 | 1.00 |
| 331 | Ryan Dempster | .40 | 1.00 |
| 332 | Joe Crede | .40 | 1.00 |
| 333 | Chad Hermansen | .40 | 1.00 |
| 334 | Gary Matthews Jr. | .40 | 1.00 |
| 335 | Frank Catalanotto | .40 | 1.00 |
| 336 | Darin Erstad | .40 | 1.00 |
| 337 | Matt Williams | .40 | 1.00 |
| 338 | B.J. Surhoff | .40 | 1.00 |
| 339 | Kerry Ligtenberg | .40 | 1.00 |
| 340 | Mike Bordick | .40 | 1.00 |
| 341 | Joe Girardi | .40 | 1.00 |
| 342 | D'Angelo Jimenez | .40 | 1.00 |
| 343 | Paul Konerko | .40 | 1.00 |
| 344 | Joe Mays | .40 | 1.00 |
| 345 | Marquis Grissom | .40 | 1.00 |
| 346 | Neifi Perez | .40 | 1.00 |
| 347 | Preston Wilson | .40 | 1.00 |
| 348 | Jeff Weaver | .40 | 1.00 |
| 349 | Eric Chavez | .40 | 1.00 |
| 350 | Placido Polanco | .40 | 1.00 |
| 351 | Matt Mantei | .40 | 1.00 |
| 352 | James Baldwin | .40 | 1.00 |
| 353 | Toby Hall | .40 | 1.00 |
| 354 | Benji Gil | .40 | 1.00 |
| 355 | Damian Moss | .40 | 1.00 |
| 356 | Syd Julio | .40 | 1.00 |
| 357 | Matt Clement | .40 | 1.00 |
| 358 | Lee Stevens | .40 | 1.00 |
| 359 | Dave Roberts | .40 | 1.00 |
| 360 | J.C. Romero | .40 | 1.00 |
| 361 | Bartolo Colon | .40 | 1.00 |
| 362 | Roger Cedeno | .40 | 1.00 |
| 363 | Mariano Rivera | 1.00 | 2.50 |
| 364 | Billy Koch | .40 | 1.00 |
| 365 | Manny Ramirez | .60 | 1.50 |
| 366 | Travis Lee | .40 | 1.00 |
| 367 | Oliver Perez | .40 | 1.00 |
| 368 | Tim Worrell | .40 | 1.00 |
| 369 | Damian Miller | .40 | 1.00 |
| 370 | John Smoltz | .60 | 1.50 |
| 371 | Willis Roberts | .40 | 1.00 |
| 372 | Tim Hudson | .40 | 1.00 |
| 373 | Moises Alou | .40 | 1.00 |
| 374 | Corky Miller | .40 | 1.00 |
| 375 | Ben Broussard | .40 | 1.00 |
| 376 | Gabe Kapler | .40 | 1.00 |
| 377 | Chris Woodward | .40 | 1.00 |
| 378 | Todd Hollandsworth | .40 | 1.00 |
| 379 | So Taguchi | .40 | 1.00 |
| 380 | John Olerud | .40 | 1.00 |
| 381 | Reggie Sanders | .40 | 1.00 |
| 382 | Jake Peavy | .40 | 1.00 |
| 383 | Kris Benson | .40 | 1.00 |
| 384 | Ray Durham | .40 | 1.00 |
| 385 | Boomer Wells | .40 | 1.00 |
| 386 | Tom Glavine | .60 | 1.50 |
| 387 | Antonio Alfonseca | .40 | 1.00 |
| 388 | Keith Foulke | .40 | 1.00 |
| 389 | Shawn Estes | .40 | 1.00 |
| 390 | Mark Grace | .60 | 1.50 |
| 391 | Dmitri Young | .40 | 1.00 |
| 392 | A.J. Burnett | .40 | 1.00 |
| 393 | Richard Hidalgo | .40 | 1.00 |
| 394 | Mike Sweeney | .40 | 1.00 |
| 395 | Doug Mientkiewicz | .40 | 1.00 |
| 396 | Cory Lidle | .40 | 1.00 |
| 397 | Jeff Bagwell | .60 | 1.50 |
| 398 | Steve Sparks | .40 | 1.00 |
| 399 | Sandy Alomar Jr. | .40 | 1.00 |
| 400 | John Lackey | .40 | 1.00 |
| 401 | Rick Helling | .40 | 1.00 |
| 402 | Carlos Lee | .40 | 1.00 |
| 403 | Garret Anderson | .40 | 1.00 |
| 404 | Vinny Castilla | .40 | 1.00 |
| 405 | David Bell | .40 | 1.00 |
| 406 | Freddy Garcia | .40 | 1.00 |
| 407 | Scott Spiezio | .40 | 1.00 |
| 408 | Russell Branyan | .40 | 1.00 |
| 409 | Jose Contreras RC | 1.25 | 3.00 |
| 410 | Kevin Brown | .40 | 1.00 |
| 411 | Tyler Houston | .40 | 1.00 |
| 412 | A.J. Pierzynski | .40 | 1.00 |
| 413 | Peter Bergeron | .40 | 1.00 |
| 414 | Brett Myers | .40 | 1.00 |
| 415 | Kenny Lofton | .40 | 1.00 |
| 416 | Ben Davis | .40 | 1.00 |
| 417 | J.D. Drew | .40 | 1.00 |
| 418 | Ricky Gutierrez | .40 | 1.00 |
| 419 | Mark Redman | .40 | 1.00 |
| 420 | Juan Encarnacion | .40 | 1.00 |
| 421 | Bryan Bullington DP RC | .60 | 1.50 |
| 422 | Jeremy Guthrie DP | .60 | 1.50 |
| 423 | Joey Gomes DP RC | .60 | 1.50 |
| 424 | Ever Bautista-Martinez DP RC | .60 | 1.50 |
| 425 | Brian Wright DP RC | .60 | 1.50 |
| 426 | B.J. Upton DP | 1.00 | 2.50 |
| 427 | Jeff Francis DP | .60 | 1.50 |
| 428 | Jeremy Hermida DP | 1.00 | 2.50 |
| 429 | Khalil Greene DP | 1.00 | 2.50 |
| 430 | Darrell Rasner DP RC | .60 | 1.50 |
| 431 | B.Phillips/V.Martinez | 1.00 | 2.50 |
| 432 | H.Choi/N.Jackson | .60 | 1.50 |
| 433 | D.Willis/J.Stokes | 1.00 | 2.50 |
| 434 | C.Tracy/L.Overbay | .60 | 1.50 |
| 435 | J.Borchard/C.Malone | .60 | 1.50 |
| 436 | J.Mauer/J.Morneau | 1.00 | 2.50 |
| 437 | D.Henson/B.Claussen | .60 | 1.50 |
| 438 | C.Utley/G.Floyd | 1.00 | 2.50 |
| 439 | T.Bozied/X.Nady | .60 | 1.50 |
| 440 | A.Heilman/J.Reyes | .60 | 1.50 |

## 2004 Topps Chrome

| | | | |
|---|---|---|---|
| COMP.SERIES 1 w/o SP's (220) | | 40.00 | 80.00 |
| COMP.SERIES 2 w/o SP's (220) | | 40.00 | 80.00 |
| COMMON (1-210/377-466) | | .40 | 1.00 |
| COMMON (211-220/247-256) | | .75 | 2.00 |
| COMMON AU (221-246) | | 4.00 | 10.00 |
| 1 | Jim Thome | .60 | 1.50 |
| 2 | Reggie Sanders | .40 | 1.00 |
| 3 | Mark Kotsay | .40 | 1.00 |

|  |  | | |
|---|---|---|---|
| 4 | Edgardo Alfonzo | .40 | 1.00 |
| 5 | Tim Wakefield | .40 | 1.00 |
| 6 | Moises Alou | .40 | 1.00 |
| 7 | Jorge Julio | .40 | 1.00 |
| 8 | Bartolo Colon | .40 | 1.00 |
| 9 | Chan Ho Park | .40 | 1.00 |
| 10 | Ichiro Suzuki | 2.00 | 5.00 |
| 11 | Kevin Millwood | .40 | 1.00 |
| 12 | Preston Wilson | .40 | 1.00 |
| 13 | Tom Glavine | .60 | 1.50 |
| 14 | Junior Spivey | .40 | 1.00 |
| 15 | Marcus Giles | .40 | 1.00 |
| 16 | David Segui | .40 | 1.00 |
| 17 | Kevin Millar | .40 | 1.00 |
| 18 | Corey Patterson | .40 | 1.00 |
| 19 | Aaron Rowand | .40 | 1.00 |
| 20 | Derek Jeter | 2.00 | 5.00 |
| 21 | Luis Castillo | .40 | 1.00 |
| 22 | Manny Ramirez | .60 | 1.50 |
| 23 | Jay Payton | .40 | 1.00 |
| 24 | Bobby Higginson | .40 | 1.00 |
| 25 | Lance Berkman | .40 | 1.00 |
| 26 | Juan Pierre | .40 | 1.00 |
| 27 | Mike Mussina | .60 | 1.50 |
| 28 | Fred McGriff | .60 | 1.50 |
| 29 | Richie Sexson | .40 | 1.00 |
| 30 | Tim Hudson | .40 | 1.00 |
| 31 | Mike Piazza | 1.50 | 4.00 |
| 32 | Brad Radke | .40 | 1.00 |
| 33 | Jeff Weaver | .40 | 1.00 |
| 34 | Ramon Hernandez | .40 | 1.00 |
| 35 | David Bell | .40 | 1.00 |
| 36 | Randy Wolf | .40 | 1.00 |
| 37 | Jake Peavy | .40 | 1.00 |
| 38 | Tim Worrell | .40 | 1.00 |
| 39 | Gil Meche | .40 | 1.00 |
| 40 | Albert Pujols | 2.00 | 5.00 |
| 41 | Michael Young | .40 | 1.00 |
| 42 | Josh Phelps | .40 | 1.00 |
| 43 | Brendan Donnelly | .40 | 1.00 |
| 44 | Steve Finley | .40 | 1.00 |
| 45 | John Smoltz | .60 | 1.50 |
| 46 | Jay Gibbons | .40 | 1.00 |
| 47 | Trot Nixon | .40 | 1.00 |
| 48 | Carl Pavano | .40 | 1.00 |
| 49 | Frank Thomas | 1.00 | 2.50 |
| 50 | Mark Prior | .60 | 1.50 |
| 51 | Danny Graves | .40 | 1.00 |
| 52 | Milton Bradley | .40 | 1.00 |
| 53 | Kris Benson | .40 | 1.00 |
| 54 | Ryan Klesko | .40 | 1.00 |
| 55 | Mike Lowell | .40 | 1.00 |
| 56 | Geoff Blum | .40 | 1.00 |
| 57 | Michael Tucker | .40 | 1.00 |
| 58 | Paul Lo Duca | .40 | 1.00 |
| 59 | Vicente Padilla | .40 | 1.00 |
| 60 | Jacque Jones | .40 | 1.00 |
| 61 | Fernando Tatis | .40 | 1.00 |
| 62 | Ty Wigginton | .40 | 1.00 |
| 63 | Rich Aurilia | .40 | 1.00 |
| 64 | Andy Pettitte | .60 | 1.50 |
| 65 | Terrence Long | .40 | 1.00 |
| 66 | Cliff Floyd | .40 | 1.00 |
| 67 | Mariano Rivera | 1.00 | 2.50 |
| 68 | Kelvim Escobar | .40 | 1.00 |
| 69 | Marlon Byrd | .40 | 1.00 |
| 70 | Mark Mulder | .40 | 1.00 |
| 71 | Francisco Cordero | .40 | 1.00 |
| 72 | Carlos Guillen | .40 | 1.00 |
| 73 | Fernando Vina | .40 | 1.00 |
| 74 | Lance Carter | .40 | 1.00 |
| 75 | Hank Blalock | .40 | 1.00 |
| 76 | Jimmy Rollins | .40 | 1.00 |
| 77 | Francisco Rodriguez | .40 | 1.00 |
| 78 | Javy Lopez | .40 | 1.00 |
| 79 | Jerry Hairston Jr. | .40 | 1.00 |
| 80 | Andruw Jones | .60 | 1.50 |
| 81 | Rodrigo Lopez | .40 | 1.00 |
| 82 | Johnny Damon | .60 | 1.50 |
| 83 | Hee Seop Choi | .40 | 1.00 |
| 84 | Kazuhiro Sasaki | .40 | 1.00 |
| 85 | Danny Bautista | .40 | 1.00 |
| 86 | Matt Lawton | .40 | 1.00 |
| 87 | Juan Uribe | .40 | 1.00 |
| 88 | Rafael Furcal | .40 | 1.00 |
| 89 | Kyle Farnsworth | .40 | 1.00 |
| 90 | Jose Vidro | .40 | 1.00 |
| 91 | Luis Rivas | .40 | 1.00 |
| 92 | Hideo Nomo | 1.00 | 2.50 |
| 93 | Javier Vazquez | .40 | 1.00 |
| 94 | Al Leiter | .40 | 1.00 |
| 95 | Jose Valentin | .40 | 1.00 |
| 96 | Alex Cintron | .40 | 1.00 |
| 97 | Zach Day | .40 | 1.00 |
| 98 | Jorge Posada | .60 | 1.50 |
| 99 | C.C. Sabathia | .40 | 1.00 |
| 100 | Alex Rodriguez | 1.50 | 4.00 |
| 101 | Brad Penny | .40 | 1.00 |
| 102 | Brad Ausmus | .40 | 1.00 |
| 103 | Raul Ibanez | .40 | 1.00 |
| 104 | Mike Hampton | .40 | 1.00 |
| 105 | Adrian Beltre | .40 | 1.00 |
| 106 | Ramiro Mendoza | .40 | 1.00 |
| 107 | Rocco Baldelli | .40 | 1.00 |
| 108 | Esteban Loaiza | .40 | 1.00 |
| 109 | Russell Branyan | .40 | 1.00 |
| 110 | Todd Helton | .60 | 1.50 |
| 111 | Braden Looper | .40 | 1.00 |
| 112 | Octavio Dotel | .40 | 1.00 |
| 113 | Mike MacDougal | .40 | 1.00 |
| 114 | Cesar Izturis | .40 | 1.00 |
| 115 | Johan Santana | 1.00 | 2.50 |
| 116 | Jose Contreras | .40 | 1.00 |
| 117 | Placido Polanco | .40 | 1.00 |
| 118 | Jason Phillips | .40 | 1.00 |
| 119 | Orlando Hudson | .40 | 1.00 |
| 120 | Vernon Wells | .40 | 1.00 |
| 121 | Ben Grieve | .40 | 1.00 |
| 122 | Dave Roberts | .40 | 1.00 |
| 123 | Ismael Valdes | .40 | 1.00 |
| 124 | Eric Owens | .40 | 1.00 |
| 125 | Curt Schilling | .40 | 1.00 |
| 126 | Russ Ortiz | .40 | 1.00 |
| 127 | Mark Buehrle | .40 | 1.00 |
| 128 | Doug Mientkiewicz | .40 | 1.00 |
| 129 | Dmitri Young | .40 | 1.00 |
| 130 | Kazuhisa Ishii | .40 | 1.00 |
| 131 | A.J. Pierzynski | .40 | 1.00 |
| 132 | Brad Wilkerson | .40 | 1.00 |
| 133 | Joe McEwing | .40 | 1.00 |
| 134 | Alex Cora | .40 | 1.00 |
| 135 | Jose Cruz Jr. | .40 | 1.00 |
| 136 | Carlos Zambrano | .40 | 1.00 |
| 137 | Jeff Kent | .40 | 1.00 |
| 138 | Shigetoshi Hasegawa | .40 | 1.00 |
| 139 | Jarrod Washburn | .40 | 1.00 |
| 140 | Greg Maddux | 1.50 | 4.00 |
| 141 | Josh Beckett | .40 | 1.00 |
| 142 | Miguel Batista | .40 | 1.00 |
| 143 | Omar Vizquel | .60 | 1.50 |
| 144 | Alex Gonzalez | .40 | 1.00 |
| 145 | Billy Wagner | .40 | 1.00 |
| 146 | Brian Jordan | .40 | 1.00 |
| 147 | Wes Helms | .40 | 1.00 |
| 148 | Deivi Cruz | .40 | 1.00 |
| 149 | Alex Gonzalez | .40 | 1.00 |
| 150 | Jason Giambi | .40 | 1.00 |
| 151 | Erubiel Durazo | .40 | 1.00 |
| 152 | Mike Lieberthal | .40 | 1.00 |
| 153 | Jason Kendall | .40 | 1.00 |
| 154 | Xavier Nady | .40 | 1.00 |
| 155 | Kirk Rueter | .40 | 1.00 |
| 156 | Mike Cameron | .40 | 1.00 |
| 157 | Miguel Cairo | .40 | 1.00 |
| 158 | Woody Williams | .40 | 1.00 |
| 159 | Toby Hall | .40 | 1.00 |
| 160 | Bernie Williams | .60 | 1.50 |
| 161 | Darin Erstad | .40 | 1.00 |
| 162 | Matt Mantei | .40 | 1.00 |
| 163 | Shawn Chacon | .40 | 1.00 |
| 164 | Bill Mueller | .40 | 1.00 |
| 165 | Damian Miller | .40 | 1.00 |
| 166 | Tony Graffanino | .40 | 1.00 |
| 167 | Sean Casey | .40 | 1.00 |
| 168 | Brandon Phillips | .40 | 1.00 |
| 169 | Runelvys Hernandez | .40 | 1.00 |
| 170 | Adam Dunn | .40 | 1.00 |
| 171 | Carlos Lee | .40 | 1.00 |
| 172 | Juan Encarnacion | .40 | 1.00 |
| 173 | Angel Berroa | .40 | 1.00 |
| 174 | Desi Relaford | .40 | 1.00 |
| 175 | Joe Mays | .40 | 1.00 |
| 176 | Ben Sheets | .40 | 1.00 |
| 177 | Eddie Guardado | .40 | 1.00 |
| 178 | Rocky Biddle | .40 | 1.00 |
| 179 | Eric Gagne | .40 | 1.00 |
| 180 | Eric Chavez | .40 | 1.00 |
| 181 | Jason Michaels | .40 | 1.00 |
| 182 | Dustan Mohr | .40 | 1.00 |
| 183 | Kip Wells | .40 | 1.00 |
| 184 | Brian Lawrence | .40 | 1.00 |
| 185 | Bret Boone | .40 | 1.00 |
| 186 | Tino Martinez | .60 | 1.50 |
| 187 | Aubrey Huff | .40 | 1.00 |
| 188 | Kevin Mench | .40 | 1.00 |
| 189 | Tim Salmon | .60 | 1.50 |
| 190 | Carlos Delgado | .40 | 1.00 |
| 191 | John Lackey | .40 | 1.00 |
| 192 | Eric Byrnes | .40 | 1.00 |
| 193 | Luis Matos | .40 | 1.00 |
| 194 | Derek Lowe | .40 | 1.00 |
| 195 | Mark Grudzielanek | .40 | 1.00 |
| 196 | Tom Gordon | .40 | 1.00 |
| 197 | Matt Clement | .40 | 1.00 |
| 198 | Byung-Hyun Kim | .40 | 1.00 |
| 199 | Brandon Inge | .40 | 1.00 |
| 200 | Nomar Garciaparra | 1.50 | 4.00 |
| 201 | Frank Catalanotto | .40 | 1.00 |
| 202 | Cristian Guzman | .40 | 1.00 |
| 203 | Bo Hart | .40 | 1.00 |
| 204 | Jack Wilson | .40 | 1.00 |
| 205 | Ray Durham | .40 | 1.00 |
| 206 | Freddy Garcia | .40 | 1.00 |
| 207 | J.D. Drew | .40 | 1.00 |
| 208 | Orlando Cabrera | .40 | 1.00 |
| 209 | Roy Halladay | .40 | 1.00 |
| 210 | David Eckstein | .40 | 1.00 |
| 211 | Omar Falcon FY RC | .75 | 2.00 |
| 212 | Todd Self FY RC | .75 | 2.00 |
| 213 | David Murphy FY RC | 1.25 | 3.00 |
| 214 | Dioner Navarro FY RC | 1.25 | 3.00 |
| 215 | Marcus McBeth FY RC | .75 | 2.00 |
| 216 | Chris O'Riordan FY RC | .75 | 2.00 |
| 217 | Rodney Choy Foo FY RC | .75 | 2.00 |
| 218 | Tim Frend FY RC | .75 | 2.00 |
| 219 | Yadier Molina FY RC | 2.50 | 6.00 |
| 220 | Zach Duke FY RC | 2.00 | 5.00 |
| 221 | Anthony Lerew FY AU RC | 6.00 | 15.00 |
| 222 | B.Hawksworth FY AU RC | 6.00 | 15.00 |
| 223 | Brayan Pena FY AU RC | 4.00 | 10.00 |
| 224 | Craig Brazell FY AU RC | 4.00 | 10.00 |
| 225 | Jon Knott FY AU RC | 4.00 | 10.00 |
| 226 | Josh Labandeira FY AU RC | 4.00 | 10.00 |
| 227 | Khalel Ballouli FY AU RC | 4.00 | 10.00 |
| 228 | Kyle Davies FY AU RC | 10.00 | 25.00 |
| 229 | Matt Creighton FY AU RC | 4.00 | 10.00 |
| 230 | Mike Gosling FY AU RC | 4.00 | 10.00 |
| 231 | Nic Ungs FY AU RC | 4.00 | 10.00 |
| 232 | Zach Miner FY AU RC | 10.00 | 25.00 |
| 233 | Donald Levinski FY AU RC | 4.00 | 10.00 |
| 234A | Bradley Sullivan FY AU RC | 6.00 | 15.00 |
| 234B | B.Sullivan FY AU ERR 345 | 10.00 | 25.00 |
| 235 | Carlos Quentin FY AU RC | 10.00 | 25.00 |
| 236 | Conor Jackson FY AU RC | 12.50 | 30.00 |
| 237 | Estee Harris FY AU RC | 6.00 | 15.00 |
| 238 | Jeffrey Allison FY AU RC | 4.00 | 10.00 |
| 239 | Kyle Sleeth FY AU RC | 6.00 | 15.00 |
| 240 | Matthew Moses FY AU RC | 6.00 | 15.00 |
| 241 | Tim Stauffer FY AU RC | 4.00 | 10.00 |
| 242 | Brad Snyder FY AU RC | 5.00 | 12.00 |
| 243 | Jason Hirsh FY AU RC | 10.00 | 25.00 |
| 244 | L.Milledge FY AU RC | 20.00 | 50.00 |
| 245 | Logan Kensing FY AU RC | 4.00 | 10.00 |
| 246 | Kory Casto FY AU RC | 6.00 | 15.00 |
| 247 | David Aardsma FY RC | 1.25 | 3.00 |
| 248 | Omar Quintanilla FY RC | 1.25 | 3.00 |
| 249 | Ervin Santana FY RC | 2.00 | 5.00 |
| 250 | Merkin Valdez FY RC | .75 | 2.00 |
| 251 | Vito Chiaravalloti FY RC | .75 | 2.00 |
| 252 | Travis Blackley FY RC | .75 | 2.00 |
| 253 | Chris Shelton FY RC | 1.25 | 3.00 |
| 254 | Rudy Guillen FY RC | 1.25 | 3.00 |
| 255 | Bobby Brownlie FY RC | 1.00 | 2.50 |
| 256 | Paul Maholm FY RC | 1.50 | 4.00 |
| 257 | Roger Clemens | 2.00 | 5.00 |
| 258 | Laynce Nix | .40 | 1.00 |
| 259 | Eric Hinske | .40 | 1.00 |
| 260 | Ivan Rodriguez | .60 | 1.50 |
| 261 | Brandon Webb | .40 | 1.00 |
| 262 | Jhonny Peralta | .40 | 1.00 |
| 263 | Adam Kennedy | .40 | 1.00 |
| 264 | Tony Batista | .40 | 1.00 |
| 265 | Jeff Suppan | .40 | 1.00 |
| 266 | Kenny Lofton | .40 | 1.00 |

| □ 267 Scott Sullivan | .40 | 1.00 |
| □ 268 Ken Griffey Jr. | 1.50 | 4.00 |
| □ 269 Juan Rivera | .40 | 1.00 |
| □ 270 Larry Walker | .40 | 1.00 |
| □ 271 Todd Hollandsworth | .40 | 1.00 |
| □ 272 Carlos Beltran | .40 | 1.00 |
| □ 273 Carl Crawford | .40 | 1.00 |
| □ 274 Karim Garcia | .40 | 1.00 |
| □ 275 Jose Reyes | .40 | 1.00 |
| □ 276 Brandon Duckworth | .40 | 1.00 |
| □ 277 Brian Giles | .60 | 1.50 |
| □ 278 J.T. Snow | .60 | 1.50 |
| □ 279 Jamie Moyer | .40 | 1.00 |
| □ 280 Julio Lugo | .40 | 1.00 |
| □ 281 Mark Teixeira | .60 | 1.50 |
| □ 282 Cory Lidle | .40 | 1.00 |
| □ 283 Lyle Overbay | .40 | 1.00 |
| □ 284 Troy Percival | .40 | 1.00 |
| □ 285 Robby Hammock | .40 | 1.00 |
| □ 286 Jason Johnson | .40 | 1.00 |
| □ 287 Damian Rolls | .40 | 1.00 |
| □ 288 Antonio Alfonseca | .40 | 1.00 |
| □ 289 Tom Goodwin | .40 | 1.00 |
| □ 290 Paul Konerko | .40 | 1.00 |
| □ 291 D'Angelo Jimenez | .40 | 1.00 |
| □ 292 Ben Broussard | .40 | 1.00 |
| □ 293 Magglio Ordonez | .40 | 1.00 |
| □ 294 Carlos Pena | .40 | 1.00 |
| □ 295 Chad Fox | .40 | 1.00 |
| □ 296 Jerome Robertson | .40 | 1.00 |
| □ 297 Travis Hafner | .40 | 1.00 |
| □ 298 Joe Randa | .40 | 1.00 |
| □ 299 Brady Clark | .40 | 1.00 |
| □ 300 Barry Zito | .40 | 1.00 |
| □ 301 Ruben Sierra | .40 | 1.00 |
| □ 302 Brett Myers | .40 | 1.00 |
| □ 303 Oliver Perez | .40 | 1.00 |
| □ 304 Benito Santiago | .40 | 1.00 |
| □ 305 David Ross | .40 | 1.00 |
| □ 306 Joe Nathan | .40 | 1.00 |
| □ 307 Jim Edmonds | .40 | 1.00 |
| □ 308 Matt Kata | .40 | 1.00 |
| □ 309 Vinny Castilla | .40 | 1.00 |
| □ 310 Marty Cordova | .40 | 1.00 |
| □ 311 Aramis Ramirez | .40 | 1.00 |
| □ 312 Carl Everett | .40 | 1.00 |
| □ 313 Ryan Freel | .40 | 1.00 |
| □ 314 Mark Bellhorn Sox | .40 | 1.00 |
| □ 315 Joe Mauer | 1.00 | 2.50 |
| □ 316 Tim Redding | .40 | 1.00 |
| □ 317 Jeromy Burnitz | .40 | 1.00 |
| □ 318 Miguel Cabrera | .60 | 1.50 |
| □ 319 Ramon Nivar | .40 | 1.00 |
| □ 320 Casey Blake | .40 | 1.00 |
| □ 321 Adam LaRoche | .40 | 1.00 |
| □ 322 Jermaine Dye | .40 | 1.00 |
| □ 323 Jerome Williams | .40 | 1.00 |
| □ 324 John Olerud | .40 | 1.00 |
| □ 325 Scott Rolen | .60 | 1.50 |
| □ 326 Bobby Kielty | .40 | 1.00 |
| □ 327 Travis Lee | .40 | 1.00 |
| □ 328 Jeff Cirillo | .40 | 1.00 |
| □ 329 Scott Spiezio | .40 | 1.00 |
| □ 330 Melvin Mora | .40 | 1.00 |
| □ 331 Mike Timlin | .40 | 1.00 |
| □ 332 Kerry Wood | .40 | 1.00 |
| □ 333 Tony Womack | .40 | 1.00 |
| □ 334 Jody Gerut | .40 | 1.00 |
| □ 335 Morgan Ensberg | .40 | 1.00 |
| □ 336 Odalis Perez | .40 | 1.00 |
| □ 337 Michael Cuddyer | .40 | 1.00 |
| □ 338 Jose Hernandez | .40 | 1.00 |
| □ 339 LaTroy Hawkins | .40 | 1.00 |
| □ 340 Marquis Grissom | .40 | 1.00 |
| □ 341 Matt Morris | .40 | 1.00 |
| □ 342 Juan Gonzalez | .40 | 1.00 |
| □ 343 Jose Valverde | .40 | 1.00 |
| □ 344 Joe Borowski | .40 | 1.00 |
| □ 345 Josh Bard | .40 | 1.00 |
| □ 346 Austin Kearns | .40 | 1.00 |
| □ 347 Chin-Hui Tsao | .40 | 1.00 |
| □ 348 Wil Ledezma | .40 | 1.00 |
| □ 349 Aaron Guiel | .40 | 1.00 |
| □ 350 Alfonso Soriano | .40 | 1.00 |
| □ 351 Ted Lilly | .40 | 1.00 |
| □ 352 Sean Burroughs | .40 | 1.00 |
| □ 353 Rafael Palmeiro | .60 | 1.50 |
| □ 354 Quinton McCracken | .40 | 1.00 |

| □ 355 David Ortiz | 1.00 | 2.50 |
| □ 356 Randall Simon | .40 | 1.00 |
| □ 357 Wily Mo Pena | .40 | 1.00 |
| □ 358 Brian Anderson | .40 | 1.00 |
| □ 359 Corey Koskie | .40 | 1.00 |
| □ 360 Keith Foulke Sox | .40 | 1.00 |
| □ 361 Sidney Ponson | .40 | 1.00 |
| □ 362 Gary Matthews Jr. | .40 | 1.00 |
| □ 363 Herbert Perry | .40 | 1.00 |
| □ 364 Shea Hillenbrand | .40 | 1.00 |
| □ 365 Craig Biggio | .60 | 1.50 |
| □ 366 Barry Larkin | .60 | 1.50 |
| □ 367 Arthur Rhodes | .40 | 1.00 |
| □ 368 Sammy Sosa | 1.00 | 2.50 |
| □ 369 Joe Crede | .40 | 1.00 |
| □ 370 Gary Sheffield | .40 | 1.00 |
| □ 371 Coco Crisp | .40 | 1.00 |
| □ 372 Torii Hunter | .40 | 1.00 |
| □ 373 Derrek Lee | .60 | 1.50 |
| □ 374 Adam Everett | .40 | 1.00 |
| □ 375 Miguel Tejada | .40 | 1.00 |
| □ 376 Jeremy Affeldt | .40 | 1.00 |
| □ 377 Robin Ventura | .40 | 1.00 |
| □ 378 Scott Podsednik | .40 | 1.00 |
| □ 379 Matthew LeCroy | .40 | 1.00 |
| □ 380 Vladimir Guerrero | 1.00 | 2.50 |
| □ 381 Steve Karsay | .40 | 1.00 |
| □ 382 Jeff Nelson | .40 | 1.00 |
| □ 383 Chase Utley | .60 | 1.50 |
| □ 384 Bobby Abreu | .40 | 1.00 |
| □ 385 Josh Fogg | .40 | 1.00 |
| □ 386 Trevor Hoffman | .40 | 1.00 |
| □ 387 Matt Stairs | .40 | 1.00 |
| □ 388 Edgar Martinez | .60 | 1.50 |
| □ 389 Edgar Renteria | .40 | 1.00 |
| □ 390 Chipper Jones | 1.00 | 2.50 |
| □ 391 Eric Munson | .40 | 1.00 |
| □ 392 Dewon Brazelton | .40 | 1.00 |
| □ 393 John Thomson | .40 | 1.00 |
| □ 394 Chris Woodward | .40 | 1.00 |
| □ 395 Jose Kennedy | .40 | 1.00 |
| □ 396 Reed Johnson | .40 | 1.00 |
| □ 397 Johnny Estrada | .40 | 1.00 |
| □ 398 Damian Moss | .40 | 1.00 |
| □ 399 Victor Zambrano | .40 | 1.00 |
| □ 400 Dontrelle Willis | .60 | 1.50 |
| □ 401 Troy Glaus | .40 | 1.00 |
| □ 402 Raul Mondesi | .40 | 1.00 |
| □ 403 Jeff Davanon | .40 | 1.00 |
| □ 404 Kurt Ainsworth | .40 | 1.00 |
| □ 405 Pedro Martinez | .60 | 1.50 |
| □ 406 Eric Karros | .40 | 1.00 |
| □ 407 Billy Koch | .40 | 1.00 |
| □ 408 Luis Gonzalez | .40 | 1.00 |
| □ 409 Jack Cust | .40 | 1.00 |
| □ 410 Mike Sweeney | .40 | 1.00 |
| □ 411 Jason Bay | .40 | 1.00 |
| □ 412 Mark Redman | .40 | 1.00 |
| □ 413 Jason Jennings | .40 | 1.00 |
| □ 414 Rondell White | .40 | 1.00 |
| □ 415 Todd Hundley | .40 | 1.00 |
| □ 416 Shannon Stewart | .40 | 1.00 |
| □ 417 Jae Weong Seo | .40 | 1.00 |
| □ 418 Livan Hernandez | .40 | 1.00 |
| □ 419 Mark Ellis | .40 | 1.00 |
| □ 420 Pat Burrell | .40 | 1.00 |
| □ 421 Mark Loretta | .40 | 1.00 |
| □ 422 Robb Nen | .40 | 1.00 |
| □ 423 Joel Pineiro | .40 | 1.00 |
| □ 424 Todd Walker | .40 | 1.00 |
| □ 425 Jeremy Bonderman | .40 | 1.00 |
| □ 426 A.J. Burnett | .40 | 1.00 |
| □ 427 Greg Myers | .40 | 1.00 |
| □ 428 Roy Oswalt | .40 | 1.00 |
| □ 429 Carlos Baerga | .40 | 1.00 |
| □ 430 Garret Anderson | .40 | 1.00 |
| □ 431 Horacio Ramirez | .40 | 1.00 |
| □ 432 Brian Roberts | .40 | 1.00 |
| □ 433 Kevin Brown | .40 | 1.00 |
| □ 434 Eric Milton | .40 | 1.00 |
| □ 435 Ramon Vazquez | .40 | 1.00 |
| □ 436 Alex Escobar | .40 | 1.00 |
| □ 437 Alex Sanchez | .40 | 1.00 |
| □ 438 Jeff Bagwell | .60 | 1.50 |
| □ 439 Claudio Vargas | .40 | 1.00 |
| □ 440 Shawn Green | .40 | 1.00 |
| □ 441 Geoff Jenkins | .40 | 1.00 |
| □ 442 David Wells | .40 | 1.00 |

| □ 443 Nick Johnson | .40 | 1.00 |
| □ 444 Jose Guillen | .40 | 1.00 |
| □ 445 Scott Hatteberg | .40 | 1.00 |
| □ 446 Phil Nevin | .40 | 1.00 |
| □ 447 Jason Schmidt | .40 | 1.00 |
| □ 448 Ricky Ledee | .40 | 1.00 |
| □ 449 So Taguchi | .40 | 1.00 |
| □ 450 Randy Johnson | 1.00 | 2.50 |
| □ 451 Eric Young | .40 | 1.00 |
| □ 452 Chone Figgins | .40 | 1.00 |
| □ 453 Larry Bigbie | .40 | 1.00 |
| □ 454 Scott Williamson | .40 | 1.00 |
| □ 455 Ramon Martinez | .40 | 1.00 |
| □ 456 Roberto Alomar | .60 | 1.50 |
| □ 457 Ryan Dempster | .40 | 1.00 |
| □ 458 Ryan Ludwick | .40 | 1.00 |
| □ 459 Ramon Santiago | .40 | 1.00 |
| □ 460 Jeff Conine | .40 | 1.00 |
| □ 461 Brad Lidge | .40 | 1.00 |
| □ 462 Ken Harvey | .40 | 1.00 |
| □ 463 Guillermo Mota | .40 | 1.00 |
| □ 464 Rick Reed | .40 | 1.00 |
| □ 465 Armando Benitez | .40 | 1.00 |
| □ 466 Wade Miller | .40 | 1.00 |

## 2005 Topps Chrome

| □ COMP.SET w/o AU'S (440) | 80.00 | 160.00 |
| □ COMP.SERIES 1 w/o AU'S (220) | 40.00 | 80.00 |
| □ COMP.SERIES 2 w/o AU'S (220) | 40.00 | 80.00 |
| □ COMMON (1-210/253-467) | .40 | 1.00 |
| □ COMMON (211-220/468-472) | .75 | 2.00 |
| □ 221-252 PRINT RUN PROVIDED BY TOPPS | | |
| □ EXCHANGE DEADLINE 05/31/07 | | |
| □ 1-234 PLATE ODDS 1:310 SER.1 HOBBY | | |
| □ 235-252 PLATE ODDS 1:350 SER.2 MINI BOX | | |
| □ 253-472 PLATE ODDS 1:29 SER.2 MINI BOX | | |
| □ PLATE PRINT RUN 1 SET PER COLOR | | |
| □ BLACK-CYAN-MAGENTA-YELLOW ISSUED | | |
| □ NO PLATE PRICING DUE TO SCARCITY | | |
| □ 1 Alex Rodriguez | 1.50 | 4.00 |
| □ 2 Placido Polanco | .40 | 1.00 |
| □ 3 Torii Hunter | .40 | 1.00 |
| □ 4 Lyle Overbay | .40 | 1.00 |
| □ 5 Johnny Damon | .60 | 1.50 |
| □ 6 Johnny Estrada | .40 | 1.00 |
| □ 7 Rich Harden | .40 | 1.00 |
| □ 8 Francisco Rodriguez | .40 | 1.00 |
| □ 9 Jarrod Washburn | .40 | 1.00 |
| □ 10 Sammy Sosa | 1.00 | 2.50 |
| □ 11 Randy Wolf | .40 | 1.00 |
| □ 12 Jason Bay | .40 | 1.00 |
| □ 13 Tom Glavine | .60 | 1.50 |
| □ 14 Michael Tucker | .40 | 1.00 |
| □ 15 Brian Giles | .60 | 1.50 |
| □ 16 Chad Tracy | .40 | 1.00 |
| □ 17 Jim Edmonds | .40 | 1.00 |
| □ 18 John Smoltz | .60 | 1.50 |
| □ 19 Roy Halladay | .40 | 1.00 |
| □ 20 Hank Blalock | .40 | 1.00 |
| □ 21 Darin Erstad | .40 | 1.00 |
| □ 22 Todd Walker | .40 | 1.00 |
| □ 23 Mike Hampton | .40 | 1.00 |
| □ 24 Mark Bellhorn | .40 | 1.00 |
| □ 25 Jim Thome | .60 | 1.50 |
| □ 26 Shingo Takatsu | .40 | 1.00 |
| □ 27 Jody Gerut | .40 | 1.00 |
| □ 28 Vinny Castilla | .40 | 1.00 |
| □ 29 Luis Castillo | .40 | 1.00 |
| □ 30 Ivan Rodriguez | .60 | 1.50 |
| □ 31 Craig Biggio | .60 | 1.50 |
| □ 32 Joe Randa | .40 | 1.00 |
| □ 33 Adrian Beltre | .40 | 1.00 |
| □ 34 Scott Podsednik | .40 | 1.00 |
| □ 35 Cliff Floyd | .40 | 1.00 |

| # | Player | Lo | Hi |
|---|--------|----|----|
| 36 | Livan Hernandez | .40 | 1.00 |
| 37 | Eric Byrnes | .40 | 1.00 |
| 38 | Jose Acevedo | .40 | 1.00 |
| 39 | Jack Wilson | .40 | 1.00 |
| 40 | Gary Sheffield | .40 | 1.00 |
| 41 | Chan Ho Park | .40 | 1.00 |
| 42 | Carl Crawford | .40 | 1.00 |
| 43 | Shawn Estes | .40 | 1.00 |
| 44 | David Bell | .40 | 1.00 |
| 45 | Jeff DaVanon | .40 | 1.00 |
| 46 | Brandon Webb | .40 | 1.00 |
| 47 | Lance Berkman | .40 | 1.00 |
| 48 | Melvin Mora | .40 | 1.00 |
| 49 | David Ortiz | 1.00 | 2.50 |
| 50 | Andruw Jones | .60 | 1.50 |
| 51 | Chone Figgins | .40 | 1.00 |
| 52 | Danny Graves | .40 | 1.00 |
| 53 | Preston Wilson | .40 | 1.00 |
| 54 | Jeremy Bonderman | .40 | 1.00 |
| 55 | Carlos Guillen | .40 | 1.00 |
| 56 | Cesar Izturis | .40 | 1.00 |
| 57 | Kazuo Matsui | .40 | 1.00 |
| 58 | Jason Schmidt | .40 | 1.00 |
| 59 | Jason Marquis | .40 | 1.00 |
| 60 | Jose Vidro | .40 | 1.00 |
| 61 | Al Leiter | .40 | 1.00 |
| 62 | Javier Vazquez | .40 | 1.00 |
| 63 | Enubel Durazo | .40 | 1.00 |
| 64 | Scott Spiezio | .40 | 1.00 |
| 65 | Scot Shields | .40 | 1.00 |
| 66 | Edgardo Alfonzo | .40 | 1.00 |
| 67 | Miguel Tejada | .40 | 1.00 |
| 68 | Francisco Cordero | .40 | 1.00 |
| 69 | Brett Myers | .40 | 1.00 |
| 70 | Curt Schilling | .60 | 1.50 |
| 71 | Matt Kata | .40 | 1.00 |
| 72 | Bartolo Colon | .40 | 1.00 |
| 73 | Rodrigo Lopez | .40 | 1.00 |
| 74 | Tim Wakefield | .40 | 1.00 |
| 75 | Frank Thomas | 1.00 | 2.50 |
| 76 | Jimmy Rollins | .40 | 1.00 |
| 77 | Barry Zito | .40 | 1.00 |
| 78 | Hideo Nomo | 1.00 | 2.50 |
| 79 | Brad Wilkerson | .40 | 1.00 |
| 80 | Adam Dunn | .40 | 1.00 |
| 81 | Derek Lee | .60 | 1.50 |
| 82 | Joe Crede | .40 | 1.00 |
| 83 | Nate Robertson | .40 | 1.00 |
| 84 | John Thomson | .40 | 1.00 |
| 85 | Mike Sweeney | .40 | 1.00 |
| 86 | Kip Wells | .40 | 1.00 |
| 87 | Eric Gagne | .40 | 1.00 |
| 88 | Zach Day | .40 | 1.00 |
| 89 | Alex Sanchez | .40 | 1.00 |
| 90 | Bret Boone | .40 | 1.00 |
| 91 | Mark Loretta | .40 | 1.00 |
| 92 | Miguel Cabrera | .60 | 1.50 |
| 93 | Randy Winn | .40 | 1.00 |
| 94 | Adam Everett | .40 | 1.00 |
| 95 | Aubrey Huff | .40 | 1.00 |
| 96 | Kevin Mench | .40 | 1.00 |
| 97 | Frank Catalanotto | .40 | 1.00 |
| 98 | Flash Gordon | .40 | 1.00 |
| 99 | Scott Hatteberg | .40 | 1.00 |
| 100 | Albert Pujols | 2.00 | 5.00 |
| 101 | J.Molina/B.Molina | .40 | 1.00 |
| 102 | Jason Johnson | .40 | 1.00 |
| 103 | Jay Gibbons | .40 | 1.00 |
| 104 | Byung-Hyun Kim | .40 | 1.00 |
| 105 | Joe Borowski | .40 | 1.00 |
| 106 | Mark Grudzielanek | .40 | 1.00 |
| 107 | Mark Buehrle | .40 | 1.00 |
| 108 | Paul Wilson | .40 | 1.00 |
| 109 | Ronnie Belliard | .40 | 1.00 |
| 110 | Reggie Sanders | .40 | 1.00 |
| 111 | Tim Redding | .40 | 1.00 |
| 112 | Brian Lawrence | .40 | 1.00 |
| 113 | Travis Hafner | .40 | 1.00 |
| 114 | Jose Hernandez | .40 | 1.00 |
| 115 | Ben Sheets | .40 | 1.00 |
| 116 | Johan Santana | 1.00 | 2.50 |
| 117 | Billy Wagner | .40 | 1.00 |
| 118 | Mariano Rivera | 1.00 | 2.50 |
| 119 | Steve Trachsel | .40 | 1.00 |
| 120 | Akinori Otsuka | .40 | 1.00 |
| 121 | Jose Valentin | .40 | 1.00 |
| 122 | Orlando Hernandez | .40 | 1.00 |
| 123 | Raul Ibanez | .40 | 1.00 |
| 124 | Mike Matheny | .40 | 1.00 |
| 125 | Vernon Wells | .40 | 1.00 |
| 126 | Jason Isringhausen | .40 | 1.00 |
| 127 | Jose Guillen | .40 | 1.00 |
| 128 | Danny Bautista | .40 | 1.00 |
| 129 | Marcus Giles | .40 | 1.00 |
| 130 | Javy Lopez | .40 | 1.00 |
| 131 | Kevin Millar | .40 | 1.00 |
| 132 | Kyle Farnsworth | .40 | 1.00 |
| 133 | Carl Pavano | .40 | 1.00 |
| 134 | Rafael Furcal | .40 | 1.00 |
| 135 | Casey Blake | .40 | 1.00 |
| 136 | Matt Holliday | .50 | 1.25 |
| 137 | Bobby Higginson | .40 | 1.00 |
| 138 | Adam Kennedy | .40 | 1.00 |
| 139 | Alex Gonzalez | .40 | 1.00 |
| 140 | Jeff Kent | .40 | 1.00 |
| 141 | Aaron Guiel | .40 | 1.00 |
| 142 | Shawn Green | .40 | 1.00 |
| 143 | Bill Hall | .40 | 1.00 |
| 144 | Shannon Stewart | .40 | 1.00 |
| 145 | Juan Rivera | .40 | 1.00 |
| 146 | Coco Crisp | .40 | 1.00 |
| 147 | Mike Mussina | .60 | 1.50 |
| 148 | Eric Chavez | .40 | 1.00 |
| 149 | Jon Lieber | .40 | 1.00 |
| 150 | Vladimir Guerrero | 1.00 | 2.50 |
| 151 | Alex Cintron | .40 | 1.00 |
| 152 | Luis Matos | .40 | 1.00 |
| 153 | Sidney Ponson | .40 | 1.00 |
| 154 | Trot Nixon | .40 | 1.00 |
| 155 | Greg Maddux | 1.50 | 4.00 |
| 156 | Edgar Renteria | .40 | 1.00 |
| 157 | Ryan Freel | .40 | 1.00 |
| 158 | Matt Lawton | .40 | 1.00 |
| 159 | Mark Prior | .60 | 1.50 |
| 160 | Josh Beckett | .40 | 1.00 |
| 161 | Ken Harvey | .40 | 1.00 |
| 162 | Angel Berroa | .40 | 1.00 |
| 163 | Juan Encarnacion | .40 | 1.00 |
| 164 | Wes Helms | .40 | 1.00 |
| 165 | Brad Radke | .40 | 1.00 |
| 166 | Phil Nevin | .40 | 1.00 |
| 167 | Mike Cameron | .40 | 1.00 |
| 168 | Billy Koch | .40 | 1.00 |
| 169 | Bobby Crosby | .40 | 1.00 |
| 170 | Mike Lieberthal | .40 | 1.00 |
| 171 | Rob Mackowiak | .40 | 1.00 |
| 172 | Sean Burroughs | .40 | 1.00 |
| 173 | J.T. Snow | .40 | 1.00 |
| 174 | Paul Konerko | .40 | 1.00 |
| 175 | Luis Gonzalez | .40 | 1.00 |
| 176 | John Lackey | .40 | 1.00 |
| 177 | Oliver Perez | .40 | 1.00 |
| 178 | Brian Roberts | .40 | 1.00 |
| 179 | Bill Mueller | .40 | 1.00 |
| 180 | Carlos Lee | .40 | 1.00 |
| 181 | Corey Patterson | .40 | 1.00 |
| 182 | Sean Casey | .40 | 1.00 |
| 183 | Cliff Lee | .40 | 1.00 |
| 184 | Jason Jennings | .40 | 1.00 |
| 185 | Dmitri Young | .40 | 1.00 |
| 186 | Juan Uribe | .40 | 1.00 |
| 187 | Andy Pettitte | .60 | 1.50 |
| 188 | Juan Gonzalez | .40 | 1.00 |
| 189 | Orlando Hudson | .40 | 1.00 |
| 190 | Jason Phillips | .40 | 1.00 |
| 191 | Braden Looper | .40 | 1.00 |
| 192 | Lew Ford | .40 | 1.00 |
| 193 | Mark Mulder | .40 | 1.00 |
| 194 | Bobby Abreu | .40 | 1.00 |
| 195 | Jason Kendall | .40 | 1.00 |
| 196 | Khalil Greene | .60 | 1.50 |
| 197 | A.J. Pierzynski | .40 | 1.00 |
| 198 | Tim Worrell | .40 | 1.00 |
| 199 | So Taguchi | .40 | 1.00 |
| 200 | Jason Giambi | .40 | 1.00 |
| 201 | Tony Batista | .40 | 1.00 |
| 202 | Carlos Zambrano | .40 | 1.00 |
| 203 | Trevor Hoffman | .40 | 1.00 |
| 204 | Odalis Perez | .40 | 1.00 |
| 205 | Jose Cruz Jr. | .40 | 1.00 |
| 206 | Michael Barrett | .40 | 1.00 |
| 207 | Chris Carpenter | .40 | 1.00 |
| 208 | Michael Young UER | .40 | 1.00 |
| 209 | Toby Hall | .40 | 1.00 |
| 210 | Woody Williams | .40 | 1.00 |
| 211 | Chris Denorfia FY RC | 1.25 | 3.00 |
| 212 | Darren Fenster FY RC | .75 | 2.00 |
| 213 | Elvys Quezada FY RC | .75 | 2.00 |
| 214 | Ian Kinsler FY RC | 2.00 | 5.00 |
| 215 | Matthew Lindstrom FY RC | .75 | 2.00 |
| 216 | Ryan Goleski FY RC | 1.25 | 3.00 |
| 217 | Ryan Sweeney FY RC | 1.50 | 4.00 |
| 218 | Sean Marshall FY RC | 2.00 | 5.00 |
| 219 | Steve Doetsch FY RC | 1.25 | 3.00 |
| 220 | Wade Robinson FY RC | .75 | 2.00 |
| 221 | Andre Ethier FY AU RC | 15.00 | 40.00 |
| 222 | Brandon Moss FY AU RC | 8.00 | 20.00 |
| 223 | Chadd Blasko FY AU RC | 6.00 | 15.00 |
| 224 | Chris Roberson FY AU RC | 4.00 | 10.00 |
| 225 | Chris Seddon FY AU RC | 4.00 | 10.00 |
| 226 | Ian Bladergroen FY AU RC | 6.00 | 15.00 |
| 227 | Jake Dittler FY AU | 4.00 | 10.00 |
| 228 | Jose Vaquedano FY AU RC | 4.00 | 10.00 |
| 229 | Jeremy West FY AU RC | 6.00 | 15.00 |
| 230 | Kole Strayhorn FY AU RC | 4.00 | 10.00 |
| 231 | Kevin West FY AU RC | 4.00 | 10.00 |
| 232 | Luis Ramirez FY AU RC | 4.00 | 10.00 |
| 233 | Melky Cabrera FY AU RC | 20.00 | 40.00 |
| 234 | Nate Schierholtz FY AU | 8.00 | 20.00 |
| 235 | Billy Butler FY AU RC | 20.00 | 50.00 |
| 236 | B.Szymanski FY AU EXCH | 4.00 | 10.00 |
| 237 | Chip Cannon FY AU RC | 8.00 | 20.00 |
| 238 | Eric Niesen FY AU RC | 4.00 | 10.00 |
| 239 | Erik Cordier FY AU RC | 4.00 | 10.00 |
| 240 | Glen Perkins FY AU RC | 8.00 | 20.00 |
| 241 | Justin Verlander FY AU RC | 20.00 | 50.00 |
| 242 | Kevin Melillo FY AU RC | 6.00 | 15.00 |
| 243 | Landon Powell FY AU RC | 6.00 | 15.00 |
| 244 | Matt Campbell FY AU RC | 6.00 | 15.00 |
| 245 | Michael Rogers FY AU RC | 4.00 | 10.00 |
| 246 | Nate McLouth FY AU RC | 8.00 | 20.00 |
| 247 | Scott Mathieson FY AU RC | 4.00 | 10.00 |
| 248 | Shane Costa FY AU RC | 4.00 | 10.00 |
| 249 | Tony Giarratano FY AU RC | 4.00 | 10.00 |
| 250 | Tony Pelland FY AU RC | 6.00 | 15.00 |
| 251 | Wes Swackhamer FY AU RC | 4.00 | 10.00 |
| 252 | Garret Anderson | .40 | 1.00 |
| 253 | Randy Johnson | 1.00 | 2.50 |
| 254 | Charles Thomas | .40 | 1.00 |
| 255 | Rafael Palmeiro | .60 | 1.50 |
| 256 | Kevin Youkilis | .40 | 1.00 |
| 257 | Freddy Garcia | .40 | 1.00 |
| 258 | Magglio Ordonez | .40 | 1.00 |
| 259 | Aaron Harang | .40 | 1.00 |
| 260 | Grady Sizemore | .60 | 1.50 |
| 261 | Chin-hui Tsao | .40 | 1.00 |
| 262 | Eric Munson | .40 | 1.00 |
| 263 | Juan Pierre | .40 | 1.00 |
| 264 | Brad Lidge | .40 | 1.00 |
| 265 | Brian Anderson | .40 | 1.00 |
| 266 | Todd Helton | .60 | 1.50 |
| 267 | Chad Cordero | .40 | 1.00 |
| 268 | Kris Benson | .40 | 1.00 |
| 269 | Brad Halsey | .40 | 1.00 |
| 270 | Jermaine Dye | .40 | 1.00 |
| 271 | Manny Ramirez | .60 | 1.50 |
| 272 | Adam Eaton | .40 | 1.00 |
| 273 | Brett Tomko | .40 | 1.00 |
| 274 | Bucky Jacobsen | .40 | 1.00 |
| 275 | Dontrelle Willis | .40 | 1.00 |
| 276 | B.J. Upton | .40 | 1.00 |
| 277 | Rocco Baldelli | .40 | 1.00 |
| 278 | Ryan Drese | .40 | 1.00 |
| 279 | Ichiro Suzuki | 2.00 | 5.00 |
| 280 | Brandon Lyon | .40 | 1.00 |
| 281 | Nick Green | .40 | 1.00 |
| 282 | Jerry Hairston Jr. | .40 | 1.00 |
| 283 | Mike Lowell | .40 | 1.00 |
| 284 | Kerry Wood | .40 | 1.00 |
| 285 | Omar Vizquel | .60 | 1.50 |
| 286 | Carlos Beltran | .40 | 1.00 |
| 287 | Carlos Pena | .40 | 1.00 |
| 288 | Jeff Weaver | .40 | 1.00 |
| 289 | Chad Moeller | .40 | 1.00 |
| 290 | Joe Mays | .40 | 1.00 |
| 291 | Termel Sledge | .40 | 1.00 |
| 292 | Richard Hidalgo | .40 | 1.00 |
| 293 | Justin Duchscherer | .40 | 1.00 |
| 294 | Eric Milton | .40 | 1.00 |
| 295 | Ramon Hernandez | .40 | 1.00 |
| 296 | Jose Reyes | .40 | 1.00 |
| 297 | Joel Pineiro | .40 | 1.00 |
| 298 | Matt Morris | .40 | 1.00 |
| 299 | Matt Morris | .40 | 1.00 |

| | | |
|---|---|---|
| ❑ 300 John Halama | .40 | 1.00 |
| ❑ 301 Gary Matthews Jr. | .40 | 1.00 |
| ❑ 302 Ryan Madson | .40 | 1.00 |
| ❑ 303 Mark Kotsay | .40 | 1.00 |
| ❑ 304 Carlos Delgado | .40 | 1.00 |
| ❑ 305 Casey Kotchman | .40 | 1.00 |
| ❑ 306 Greg Aquino | .40 | 1.00 |
| ❑ 307 LaTroy Hawkins | .40 | 1.00 |
| ❑ 308 Jose Contreras | .40 | 1.00 |
| ❑ 309 Ken Griffey Jr. | 1.50 | 4.00 |
| ❑ 310 C.C. Sabathia | .40 | 1.00 |
| ❑ 311 Brandon Inge | .40 | 1.00 |
| ❑ 312 John Buck | .40 | 1.00 |
| ❑ 313 Hee Seop Choi | .40 | 1.00 |
| ❑ 314 Chris Capuano | .40 | 1.00 |
| ❑ 315 Jesse Crain | .40 | 1.00 |
| ❑ 316 Geoff Jenkins | .40 | 1.00 |
| ❑ 317 Mike Piazza | 1.00 | 2.50 |
| ❑ 318 Jorge Posada | .60 | 1.50 |
| ❑ 319 Nick Swisher | .40 | 1.00 |
| ❑ 320 Kevin Millwood | .40 | 1.00 |
| ❑ 321 Mike Gonzalez | .40 | 1.00 |
| ❑ 322 Jake Peavy | .40 | 1.00 |
| ❑ 323 Dustin Hermanson | .40 | 1.00 |
| ❑ 324 Jeremy Reed | .40 | 1.00 |
| ❑ 325 Alfonso Soriano | .40 | 1.00 |
| ❑ 326 Alexis Rios | .40 | 1.00 |
| ❑ 327 David Eckstein | .40 | 1.00 |
| ❑ 328 Shea Hillenbrand | .40 | 1.00 |
| ❑ 329 Russ Ortiz | .40 | 1.00 |
| ❑ 330 Kurt Ainsworth | .40 | 1.00 |
| ❑ 331 Orlando Cabrera | .40 | 1.00 |
| ❑ 332 Carlos Silva | .40 | 1.00 |
| ❑ 333 Ross Gload | .40 | 1.00 |
| ❑ 334 Josh Phelps | .40 | 1.00 |
| ❑ 335 Mike Maroth | .40 | 1.00 |
| ❑ 336 Guillermo Mota | .40 | 1.00 |
| ❑ 337 Chris Burke | .40 | 1.00 |
| ❑ 338 David DeJesus | .40 | 1.00 |
| ❑ 339 Jose Lima | .40 | 1.00 |
| ❑ 340 Cristian Guzman | .40 | 1.00 |
| ❑ 341 Nick Johnson | .40 | 1.00 |
| ❑ 342 Victor Zambrano | .40 | 1.00 |
| ❑ 343 Rod Barajas | .40 | 1.00 |
| ❑ 344 Damian Miller | .40 | 1.00 |
| ❑ 345 Chase Utley | .60 | 1.50 |
| ❑ 346 Sean Burnett | .40 | 1.00 |
| ❑ 347 David Wells | .40 | 1.00 |
| ❑ 348 Dustan Mohr | .40 | 1.00 |
| ❑ 349 Bobby Madritsch | .40 | 1.00 |
| ❑ 350 Reed Johnson | .40 | 1.00 |
| ❑ 351 R.A. Dickey | .40 | 1.00 |
| ❑ 352 Scott Kazmir | .40 | 1.00 |
| ❑ 353 Tony Womack | .40 | 1.00 |
| ❑ 354 Tomas Perez | .40 | 1.00 |
| ❑ 355 Esteban Loaiza | .40 | 1.00 |
| ❑ 356 Tomokazu Ohka | .40 | 1.00 |
| ❑ 357 Ramon Ortiz | .40 | 1.00 |
| ❑ 358 Richie Sexson | .40 | 1.00 |
| ❑ 359 J.D. Drew | .40 | 1.00 |
| ❑ 360 Barry Bonds | 2.50 | 6.00 |
| ❑ 361 Aramis Ramirez | .40 | 1.00 |
| ❑ 362 Wily Mo Pena | .40 | 1.00 |
| ❑ 363 Jeromy Burnitz | .40 | 1.00 |
| ❑ 364 Nomar Garciaparra | 1.00 | 2.50 |
| ❑ 365 Brandon Backe | .40 | 1.00 |
| ❑ 366 Derek Lowe | .40 | 1.00 |
| ❑ 367 Doug Davis | .40 | 1.00 |
| ❑ 368 Joe Mauer | 1.00 | 2.50 |
| ❑ 369 Endy Chavez | .40 | 1.00 |
| ❑ 370 Bernie Williams | .60 | 1.50 |
| ❑ 371 Jason Michaels | .40 | 1.00 |
| ❑ 372 Craig Wilson | .40 | 1.00 |
| ❑ 373 Ryan Klesko | .40 | 1.00 |
| ❑ 374 Ray Durham | .40 | 1.00 |
| ❑ 375 Jose Lopez | .40 | 1.00 |
| ❑ 376 Jeff Suppan | .40 | 1.00 |
| ❑ 377 David Bush | .40 | 1.00 |
| ❑ 378 Marlon Byrd | .40 | 1.00 |
| ❑ 379 Roy Oswalt | .40 | 1.00 |
| ❑ 380 Rondell White | .40 | 1.00 |
| ❑ 381 Troy Glaus | .40 | 1.00 |
| ❑ 382 Scott Hairston | .40 | 1.00 |
| ❑ 383 Chipper Jones | 1.00 | 2.50 |
| ❑ 384 Daniel Cabrera | .40 | 1.00 |
| ❑ 385 Jon Garland | .40 | 1.00 |
| ❑ 386 Austin Kearns | .40 | 1.00 |
| ❑ 387 Jake Westbrook | .40 | 1.00 |

| | | |
|---|---|---|
| ❑ 388 Aaron Miles | .40 | 1.00 |
| ❑ 389 Omar Infante | .40 | 1.00 |
| ❑ 390 Paul Lo Duca | .40 | 1.00 |
| ❑ 391 Morgan Ensberg | .40 | 1.00 |
| ❑ 392 Tony Graffanino | .40 | 1.00 |
| ❑ 393 Milton Bradley | .40 | 1.00 |
| ❑ 394 Keith Ginter | .40 | 1.00 |
| ❑ 395 Justin Morneau | .40 | 1.00 |
| ❑ 396 Tony Armas Jr. | .40 | 1.00 |
| ❑ 397 Kevin Brown | .40 | 1.00 |
| ❑ 398 Marco Scutaro | .40 | 1.00 |
| ❑ 399 Tim Hudson | .60 | 1.50 |
| ❑ 400 Pat Burrell | .40 | 1.00 |
| ❑ 401 Jeff Cirillo | .40 | 1.00 |
| ❑ 402 Larry Walker | .60 | 1.50 |
| ❑ 403 Dewon Brazelton | .40 | 1.00 |
| ❑ 404 Shigetoshi Hasegawa | .40 | 1.00 |
| ❑ 405 Octavio Dotel | .40 | 1.00 |
| ❑ 406 Michael Cuddyer | .40 | 1.00 |
| ❑ 407 Junior Spivey | .40 | 1.00 |
| ❑ 408 Zack Greinke | .40 | 1.00 |
| ❑ 409 Roger Clemens | 1.50 | 4.00 |
| ❑ 410 Chris Shelton | .60 | 1.50 |
| ❑ 411 Ugueth Urbina | .40 | 1.00 |
| ❑ 412 Rafael Betancourt | .40 | 1.00 |
| ❑ 413 Willie Harris | .40 | 1.00 |
| ❑ 414 Keith Foulke | .40 | 1.00 |
| ❑ 415 Larry Bigbie | .40 | 1.00 |
| ❑ 416 Paul Byrd | .40 | 1.00 |
| ❑ 417 Troy Percival | .40 | 1.00 |
| ❑ 418 Pedro Martinez | .60 | 1.50 |
| ❑ 419 Matt Clement | .40 | 1.00 |
| ❑ 420 Ryan Wagner | .40 | 1.00 |
| ❑ 421 Jeff Francis | .40 | 1.00 |
| ❑ 422 Jeff Conine | .40 | 1.00 |
| ❑ 423 Wade Miller | .40 | 1.00 |
| ❑ 424 Gavin Floyd | .40 | 1.00 |
| ❑ 425 Kazuhisa Ishii | .40 | 1.00 |
| ❑ 426 Victor Santos | .40 | 1.00 |
| ❑ 427 Jacque Jones | .40 | 1.00 |
| ❑ 428 Hideki Matsui | 1.50 | 4.00 |
| ❑ 429 Cory Lidle | .40 | 1.00 |
| ❑ 430 Jose Castillo | .40 | 1.00 |
| ❑ 431 Alex Gonzalez | .40 | 1.00 |
| ❑ 432 Kirk Rueter | .40 | 1.00 |
| ❑ 433 Jolbert Cabrera | .40 | 1.00 |
| ❑ 434 Erik Bedard | .40 | 1.00 |
| ❑ 435 Ricky Ledee | .40 | 1.00 |
| ❑ 436 Mark Hendrickson | .40 | 1.00 |
| ❑ 437 Laynce Nix | .40 | 1.00 |
| ❑ 438 Jason Frasor | .40 | 1.00 |
| ❑ 439 Kevin Gregg | .40 | 1.00 |
| ❑ 440 Derek Jeter | 2.00 | 5.00 |
| ❑ 441 Jaret Wright | .40 | 1.00 |
| ❑ 442 Edwin Jackson | .40 | 1.00 |
| ❑ 443 Moises Alou | .40 | 1.00 |
| ❑ 444 Aaron Rowand | .40 | 1.00 |
| ❑ 445 Kazuhito Tadano | .40 | 1.00 |
| ❑ 446 Luis Gonzalez | .40 | 1.00 |
| ❑ 447 A.J. Burnett | .40 | 1.00 |
| ❑ 448 Jeff Bagwell | .60 | 1.50 |
| ❑ 449 Brad Penny | .40 | 1.00 |
| ❑ 450 Corey Koskie | .40 | 1.00 |
| ❑ 451 Mark Ellis | .40 | 1.00 |
| ❑ 452 Hector Luna | .40 | 1.00 |
| ❑ 453 Miguel Olivo | .40 | 1.00 |
| ❑ 454 Scott Rolen | .60 | 1.50 |
| ❑ 455 Ricardo Rodriguez | .40 | 1.00 |
| ❑ 456 Eric Hinske | .40 | 1.00 |
| ❑ 457 Tim Salmon | .60 | 1.50 |
| ❑ 458 Adam LaRoche | .40 | 1.00 |
| ❑ 459 B.J. Ryan | .40 | 1.00 |
| ❑ 460 Steve Finley | .40 | 1.00 |
| ❑ 461 Joe Nathan | .40 | 1.00 |
| ❑ 462 Vicente Padilla | .40 | 1.00 |
| ❑ 463 Yadier Molina | .40 | 1.00 |
| ❑ 464 Tino Martinez | .60 | 1.50 |
| ❑ 465 Mark Teixeira | .60 | 1.50 |
| ❑ 466 Kelvim Escobar | .40 | 1.00 |
| ❑ 467 Pedro Feliz | .40 | 1.00 |
| ❑ 468 Ryan Garko FY RC | 2.00 | 5.00 |
| ❑ 469 Bobby Livingston FY RC | .75 | 2.00 |
| ❑ 470 Yorman Bazardo FY RC | .75 | 2.00 |
| ❑ 471 Mike Boum FY RC | 1.25 | 3.00 |
| ❑ 472 Andy LaRoche FY RC | 3.00 | 8.00 |

## 2005 Topps Chrome Update

| | | |
|---|---|---|
| ❑ COMPLETE SET (237) | 200.00 | 300.00 |
| ❑ COMP.SET w/o SP's (220) | 40.00 | 80.00 |
| ❑ COM (1-85/216-220) | | .75 |
| ❑ COMMON (86-105) | | 1.00 |
| ❑ COM (14/85/106-215) | .40 | 1.00 |
| ❑ 221-237 GROUP A ODDS 1:25 H, 1:49 R | | |
| ❑ 221-237 GROUP B ODDS 1:29 H, 1:57 R | | |
| ❑ 1-220 PLATE ODDS 1:347 H | | |
| ❑ 221-237 PLATE AU ODDS 1:4857 H | | |
| ❑ PLATE PRINT RUN 1 SET PER COLOR | | |
| ❑ BLACK-CYAN-MAGENTA-YELLOW ISSUED | | |
| ❑ NO PLATE PRICING DUE TO SCARCITY | | |
| ❑ 1 Sammy Sosa | .75 | 2.00 |
| ❑ 2 Jeff Francoeur | 1.00 | 2.50 |
| ❑ 3 Tony Clark | .30 | .75 |
| ❑ 4 Michael Tucker | .30 | .75 |
| ❑ 5 Mike Matheny | .30 | .75 |
| ❑ 6 Eric Young | .30 | .75 |
| ❑ 7 Jose Valentin | .30 | .75 |
| ❑ 8 Matt Lawton | .30 | .75 |
| ❑ 9 Juan Rivera | .30 | .75 |
| ❑ 10 Shawn Green | .30 | .75 |
| ❑ 11 Aaron Boone | .30 | .75 |
| ❑ 12 Woody Williams | .30 | .75 |
| ❑ 13 Brad Wilkerson | .30 | .75 |
| ❑ 14 Anthony Reyes RC | 2.00 | 5.00 |
| ❑ 15 Gustavo Chacin | .30 | .75 |
| ❑ 16 Michael Restovich | .30 | .75 |
| ❑ 17 Humberto Quintero | .30 | .75 |
| ❑ 18 Matt Ginter | .30 | .75 |
| ❑ 19 Scott Podsednik | .30 | .75 |
| ❑ 20 Byung-Hyun Kim | .30 | .75 |
| ❑ 21 Orlando Hernandez | .30 | .75 |
| ❑ 22 Mark Grudzielanek | .30 | .75 |
| ❑ 23 Jody Gerut | .30 | .75 |
| ❑ 24 Adrian Beltre | .30 | .75 |
| ❑ 25 Scott Schoeneweis | .30 | .75 |
| ❑ 26 Marlon Anderson | .30 | .75 |
| ❑ 27 Jason Vargas | .30 | .75 |
| ❑ 28 Claudio Vargas | .30 | .75 |
| ❑ 29 Jason Kendall | .30 | .75 |
| ❑ 30 Aaron Small | .30 | .75 |
| ❑ 31 Juan Cruz | .30 | .75 |
| ❑ 32 Placido Polanco | .30 | .75 |
| ❑ 33 Jorge Sosa | .30 | .75 |
| ❑ 34 John Olerud | .30 | .75 |
| ❑ 35 Ryan Langerhans | .30 | .75 |
| ❑ 36 Randy Winn | .30 | .75 |
| ❑ 37 Zach Duke | .75 | 2.00 |
| ❑ 38 Garrett Atkins | .30 | .75 |
| ❑ 39 Al Leiter | .30 | .75 |
| ❑ 40 Shawn Chacon | .30 | .75 |
| ❑ 41 Mark DeRosa | .30 | .75 |
| ❑ 42 Miguel Ojeda | .30 | .75 |
| ❑ 43 A.J. Pierzynski | .30 | .75 |
| ❑ 44 Carlos Lee | .30 | .75 |
| ❑ 45 LaTroy Hawkins | .30 | .75 |
| ❑ 46 Nick Green | .30 | .75 |
| ❑ 47 Shawn Estes | .30 | .75 |
| ❑ 48 Eli Marrero | .30 | .75 |
| ❑ 49 Jeff Kent | .30 | .75 |
| ❑ 50 Joe Randa | .30 | .75 |
| ❑ 51 Jose Hernandez | .30 | .75 |
| ❑ 52 Joe Blanton | .30 | .75 |
| ❑ 53 Huston Street | .75 | 2.00 |
| ❑ 54 Marlon Byrd | .30 | .75 |
| ❑ 55 Alex Sanchez | .30 | .75 |
| ❑ 56 Livan Hernandez | .30 | .75 |
| ❑ 57 Chris Young | .30 | .75 |
| ❑ 58 Brad Eldred | .30 | .75 |
| ❑ 59 Terrence Long | .30 | .75 |

| | | |
|---|---|---|
| ❏ 60 Phil Nevin | .30 | .75 |
| ❏ 61 Kyle Farnsworth | .30 | .75 |
| ❏ 62 Jon Lieber | .30 | .75 |
| ❏ 63 Antonio Alfonseca | .30 | .75 |
| ❏ 64 Tony Graffanino | .30 | .75 |
| ❏ 65 Tadahito Iguchi RC | 1.25 | 3.00 |
| ❏ 66 Brad Thompson | .30 | .75 |
| ❏ 67 Jose Vidro | .30 | .75 |
| ❏ 68 Jason Phillips | .30 | .75 |
| ❏ 69 Carl Pavano | .30 | .75 |
| ❏ 70 Pokey Reese | .30 | .75 |
| ❏ 71 Jerome Williams | .30 | .75 |
| ❏ 72 Kazuhisa Ishii | .30 | .75 |
| ❏ 73 Felix Hernandez | 1.25 | 3.00 |
| ❏ 74 Edgar Renteria | .30 | .75 |
| ❏ 75 Mike Myers | .30 | .75 |
| ❏ 76 Jeff Cirillo | .30 | .75 |
| ❏ 77 Endy Chavez | .30 | .75 |
| ❏ 78 Jose Guillen | .30 | .75 |
| ❏ 79 Ugueth Urbina | .30 | .75 |
| ❏ 80 Zach Day | .30 | .75 |
| ❏ 81 Javier Vazquez | .30 | .75 |
| ❏ 82 Willy Taveras | .30 | .75 |
| ❏ 83 Mark Mulder | .30 | .75 |
| ❏ 84 Vinny Castilla | .30 | .75 |
| ❏ 85 Russ Adams | .30 | .75 |
| ❏ 86 Homer Bailey PROS | .30 | .75 |
| ❏ 87 Ervin Santana PROS | .30 | .75 |
| ❏ 88 Bill Bray PROS | .30 | .75 |
| ❏ 89 Thomas Diamond PROS | .30 | .75 |
| ❏ 90 Trevor Plouffe PROS | .30 | .75 |
| ❏ 91 James Houser PROS | .30 | .75 |
| ❏ 92 Jake Stevens PROS | .30 | .75 |
| ❏ 93 Anthony Whittington PROS | .30 | .75 |
| ❏ 94 Philip Hughes PROS | .30 | .75 |
| ❏ 95 Greg Golson PROS | .30 | .75 |
| ❏ 96 Paul Maholm PROS | .30 | .75 |
| ❏ 97 Carlos Quentin PROS | .30 | .75 |
| ❏ 98 Dan Johnson PROS | .30 | .75 |
| ❏ 99 Mark Rogers PROS | .30 | .75 |
| ❏ 100 Neil Walker PROS | .30 | .75 |
| ❏ 101 Omar Quintanilla PROS | .30 | .75 |
| ❏ 102 Blake DeWitt PROS | .30 | .75 |
| ❏ 103 Taylor Tankersley PROS | .30 | .75 |
| ❏ 104 David Murphy PROS | .30 | .75 |
| ❏ 105 Chris Lambert PROS | .30 | .75 |
| ❏ 106 Drew Anderson FY RC | .40 | 1.00 |
| ❏ 107 Luis Hernandez FY RC | .40 | 1.00 |
| ❏ 108 Jim Burt FY RC | .40 | 1.00 |
| ❏ 109 Mike Morse FY RC | .75 | 2.00 |
| ❏ 110 Elliot Johnson FY RC | .40 | 1.00 |
| ❏ 111 C.J. Smith FY RC | .40 | 1.00 |
| ❏ 112 Casey McGehee FY RC | .40 | 1.00 |
| ❏ 113 Brian Miller FY RC | .40 | 1.00 |
| ❏ 114 Chris Vines FY RC | .40 | 1.00 |
| ❏ 115 D.J. Houlton FY RC | .40 | 1.00 |
| ❏ 116 Chuck Tiffany FY RC | 1.25 | 3.00 |
| ❏ 117 Humberto Sanchez FY RC | 1.50 | 4.00 |
| ❏ 118 Baltazar Lopez FY RC | .40 | 1.00 |
| ❏ 119 Russ Martin FY RC | 1.25 | 3.00 |
| ❏ 120 Dana Eveland FY RC | .40 | 1.00 |
| ❏ 121 Johan Silva FY RC | .40 | 1.00 |
| ❏ 122 Adam Harben FY RC | .50 | 1.25 |
| ❏ 123 Brian Bannister FY RC | 1.25 | 3.00 |
| ❏ 124 Adam Boeve FY RC | .40 | 1.00 |
| ❏ 125 Thomas Oldham FY RC | .40 | 1.00 |
| ❏ 126 Cody Haerther FY RC | .40 | 1.00 |
| ❏ 127 Dan Santin FY RC | .40 | 1.00 |
| ❏ 128 Daniel Haigwood FY RC | .75 | 2.00 |
| ❏ 129 Craig Tatum FY RC | .40 | 1.00 |
| ❏ 130 Martin Prado FY RC | .40 | 1.00 |
| ❏ 131 Errol Simonitsch FY RC | .50 | 1.25 |
| ❏ 132 Lorenzo Scott FY RC | .40 | 1.00 |
| ❏ 133 Hayden Penn FY RC | .75 | 2.00 |
| ❏ 134 Heath Totten FY RC | .40 | 1.00 |
| ❏ 135 Nick Masset FY RC | .40 | 1.00 |
| ❏ 136 Pedro Lopez FY RC | .40 | 1.00 |
| ❏ 137 Ben Harrison FY RC | .40 | 1.00 |
| ❏ 138 Mike Spidale FY RC | .40 | 1.00 |
| ❏ 139 Jeremy Harts FY RC | .40 | 1.00 |
| ❏ 140 Danny Zell FY RC | .40 | 1.00 |
| ❏ 141 Kevin Collins FY RC | .40 | 1.00 |
| ❏ 142 Tony Americh FY RC | .40 | 1.00 |
| ❏ 143 Matt Albers FY RC | 1.00 | 2.50 |
| ❏ 144 Ricky Barrett FY RC | .40 | 1.00 |
| ❏ 145 Hernan Iribarren FY RC | .50 | 1.25 |
| ❏ 146 Sean Tracey FY RC | .40 | 1.00 |
| ❏ 147 Jerry Owens FY RC | .50 | 1.25 |

| | | |
|---|---|---|
| ❏ 148 Steve Nelson FY RC | .40 | 1.00 |
| ❏ 149 Brandon McCarthy FY RC | 1.00 | 2.50 |
| ❏ 150 David Shepard FY RC | .40 | 1.00 |
| ❏ 151 Steven Bondurant FY RC | .40 | 1.00 |
| ❏ 152 Billy Sadler FY RC | .40 | 1.00 |
| ❏ 153 Ryan Feierabend FY RC | .40 | 1.00 |
| ❏ 154 Stuart Pomeranz FY RC | .40 | 1.00 |
| ❏ 155 Shaun Marcum FY | .40 | 1.00 |
| ❏ 156 Erik Schindewolf FY RC | .40 | 1.00 |
| ❏ 157 Stefan Bailie FY RC | .40 | 1.00 |
| ❏ 158 Mike Esposito FY RC | .40 | 1.00 |
| ❏ 159 Buck Coats FY RC | .40 | 1.00 |
| ❏ 160 Andy Sides FY RC | .40 | 1.00 |
| ❏ 161 Micah Schnurstein FY RC | .40 | 1.00 |
| ❏ 162 Jesse Gutierrez FY RC | .40 | 1.00 |
| ❏ 163 Jake Postlewait FY RC | .40 | 1.00 |
| ❏ 164 Willy Mota FY RC | .40 | 1.00 |
| ❏ 165 Ryan Speier FY RC | .40 | 1.00 |
| ❏ 166 Frank Mata FY RC | .40 | 1.00 |
| ❏ 167 Jair Jurrjens FY RC | 1.00 | 2.50 |
| ❏ 168 Nick Touchstone FY RC | .40 | 1.00 |
| ❏ 169 Matthew Kemp FY RC | 3.00 | 8.00 |
| ❏ 170 Vinny Rottino FY RC | .40 | 1.00 |
| ❏ 171 J.B. Thurmond FY RC | .40 | 1.00 |
| ❏ 172 Kelvin Pichardo FY RC | .40 | 1.00 |
| ❏ 173 Scott Michinson FY RC | .40 | 1.00 |
| ❏ 174 Darwinson Salazar FY RC | .40 | 1.00 |
| ❏ 175 George Kottaras FY RC | .75 | 2.00 |
| ❏ 176 Kenny Durost FY RC | .40 | 1.00 |
| ❏ 177 Jonathan Sanchez FY RC | 1.50 | 4.00 |
| ❏ 178 Brandon Moorehead FY RC | .40 | 1.00 |
| ❏ 179 Kennard Bibbs FY RC | .40 | 1.00 |
| ❏ 180 David Gassner FY RC | .40 | 1.00 |
| ❏ 181 Micah Furtado FY RC | .40 | 1.00 |
| ❏ 182 Ismael Ramirez FY RC | .40 | 1.00 |
| ❏ 183 Carlos Gonzalez FY RC | 1.50 | 4.00 |
| ❏ 184 Brandon Sing FY RC | .50 | 1.25 |
| ❏ 185 Jason Motte FY RC | .40 | 1.00 |
| ❏ 186 Chuck James FY RC | 2.00 | 5.00 |
| ❏ 187 Andy Santana FY RC | .40 | 1.00 |
| ❏ 188 Manny Parra FY RC | 1.50 | 4.00 |
| ❏ 189 Chris B.Young FY RC | 1.50 | 4.00 |
| ❏ 190 Juan Senreso FY RC | .40 | 1.00 |
| ❏ 191 Franklin Morales FY RC | .75 | 2.00 |
| ❏ 192 Jared Gothreaux FY RC | .40 | 1.00 |
| ❏ 193 Jayce Tingler FY RC | .40 | 1.00 |
| ❏ 194 Matt Brown FY RC | .40 | 1.00 |
| ❏ 195 Frank Diaz FY RC | .40 | 1.00 |
| ❏ 196 Stephen Drew FY RC | 4.00 | 10.00 |
| ❏ 197 Jered Weaver FY RC | 4.00 | 10.00 |
| ❏ 198 Ryan Braun FY RC | 6.00 | 15.00 |
| ❏ 199 John Mayberry Jr. FY RC | 1.00 | 2.50 |
| ❏ 200 Aaron Thompson FY RC | .75 | 2.00 |
| ❏ 201 Ben Copeland FY RC | 1.50 | 4.00 |
| ❏ 202 Jacoby Ellsbury FY RC | 8.00 | 20.00 |
| ❏ 203 Garrett Olson FY RC | .75 | 2.00 |
| ❏ 204 Cliff Pennington FY RC | .75 | 2.00 |
| ❏ 205 Colby Rasmus FY RC | 4.00 | 10.00 |
| ❏ 206 Chris Volstad FY RC | 1.00 | 2.50 |
| ❏ 207 Ricky Romero FY RC | 1.25 | 3.00 |
| ❏ 208 Ryan Zimmerman FY RC | 5.00 | 12.00 |
| ❏ 209 C.J. Henry FY RC | 1.50 | 4.00 |
| ❏ 210 Nelson Cruz FY RC | 2.50 | 6.00 |
| ❏ 211 Josh Wall FY RC | .50 | 1.25 |
| ❏ 212 Nick Webber FY RC | .40 | 1.00 |
| ❏ 213 Paul Kelly FY RC | .50 | 1.25 |
| ❏ 214 Kyle Winters FY RC | .50 | 1.25 |
| ❏ 215 Mitch Boggs FY RC | .40 | 1.00 |
| ❏ 216 Craig Biggio HL | .30 | .75 |
| ❏ 217 Greg Maddux HL | .75 | 2.00 |
| ❏ 218 Bobby Abreu HL | .30 | .75 |
| ❏ 219 Alex Rodriguez HL | .75 | 2.00 |
| ❏ 220 Trevor Hoffman HL | .30 | .75 |
| ❏ 221 Trevor Bell FY AU A RC | 6.00 | 15.00 |
| ❏ 222 Jay Bruce FY AU A RC | 40.00 | 80.00 |
| ❏ 223 Travis Buck FY AU B RC | 6.00 | 15.00 |
| ❏ 224 Cesar Carrillo FY AU B RC | 6.00 | 15.00 |
| ❏ 225 Mike Costanzo FY AU A RC | 8.00 | 20.00 |
| ❏ 226 Brent Cox FY AU A RC | 4.00 | 10.00 |
| ❏ 227 Matt Garza FY AU A RC | 10.00 | 25.00 |
| ❏ 228 Josh Geer FY AU A RC | 4.00 | 10.00 |
| ❏ 229 Tyler Greene FY AU A RC | 6.00 | 15.00 |
| ❏ 230 Eli Iorg FY AU A RC | 4.00 | 10.00 |
| ❏ 231 Craig Italiano FY AU B RC | 4.00 | 10.00 |
| ❏ 232 Beau Jones FY AU A RC | 6.00 | 15.00 |
| ❏ 233 M.McCormick FY AU B RC | 4.00 | 10.00 |
| ❏ 234 A.McCutchen FY AU B RC | 20.00 | 50.00 |
| ❏ 235 Micah Owings FY AU B RC | 8.00 | 20.00 |

| | | |
|---|---|---|
| ❏ 236 Cesar Ramos FY AU B RC | 4.00 | 10.00 |
| ❏ 237 Chaz Roe FY AU A RC | 4.00 | 10.00 |

## 2006 Topps Chrome

| | | |
|---|---|---|
| ❏ COMP.SET w/o AU's (330) | 40.00 | 80.00 |
| ❏ COMMON CARD (1-252) | .25 | .60 |
| ❏ COMMON CARD (253-275) | .15 | .40 |
| ❏ COMMON ROOKIE (276-330) | .40 | 1.00 |
| ❏ COMMON AU (280b/331-354) | 4.00 | 10.00 |
| ❏ AU 331-354 ODDS 1:15 HOBBY | | |
| ❏ JOHJIMA AU ODDS 1:1650 HOBBY | | |
| ❏ 1-330 PLATES 1:25 HOBBY BOX LDR | | |
| ❏ 331-354 AU PLATES 1:324 HOBBY BOX LDR | | |
| ❏ PLATE PRINT RUN 1 SET PER COLOR | | |
| ❏ BLACK-CYAN-MAGENTA-YELLOW ISSUED | | |
| ❏ NO PLATE PRICING DUE TO SCARCITY | | |
| ❏ 1 Alex Rodriguez | 1.00 | 2.50 |
| ❏ 2 Garrett Atkins | .25 | .60 |
| ❏ 3 Carl Crawford | .25 | .60 |
| ❏ 4 Clint Barmes | .25 | .60 |
| ❏ 5 Tadahito Iguchi | .25 | .60 |
| ❏ 6 Brian Roberts | .25 | .60 |
| ❏ 7 Mickey Mantle | 3.00 | 8.00 |
| ❏ 8 David Wright | 1.00 | 2.50 |
| ❏ 9 Jeremy Reed | .25 | .60 |
| ❏ 10 Bobby Abreu | .25 | .60 |
| ❏ 11 Lance Berkman | .25 | .60 |
| ❏ 12 Jonny Gomes | .25 | .60 |
| ❏ 13 Jason Marquis | .25 | .60 |
| ❏ 14 Chipper Jones | .60 | 1.50 |
| ❏ 15 Jon Garland | .25 | .60 |
| ❏ 16 Brad Wilkerson | .25 | .60 |
| ❏ 17 Rickie Weeks | .25 | .60 |
| ❏ 18 Jorge Posada | .40 | 1.00 |
| ❏ 19 Greg Maddux | 1.00 | 2.50 |
| ❏ 20 Jeff Francis | .25 | .60 |
| ❏ 21 Felipe Lopez | .25 | .60 |
| ❏ 22 Dan Johnson | .25 | .60 |
| ❏ 23 Manny Ramirez | .40 | 1.00 |
| ❏ 24 Joe Mauer | .60 | 1.50 |
| ❏ 25 Randy Winn | .25 | .60 |
| ❏ 26 Pedro Feliz | .25 | .60 |
| ❏ 27 Kenny Rogers | .25 | .60 |
| ❏ 28 Rocco Baldelli | .25 | .60 |
| ❏ 29 Nomar Garciaparra | .60 | 1.50 |
| ❏ 30 Carlos Lee | .25 | .60 |
| ❏ 31 Tom Glavine | .40 | 1.00 |
| ❏ 32 Craig Biggio | .40 | 1.00 |
| ❏ 33 Steve Finley | .25 | .60 |
| ❏ 34 Eric Gagne | .25 | .60 |
| ❏ 35 Dallas McPherson | .25 | .60 |
| ❏ 36 Mark Kotsay | .25 | .60 |
| ❏ 37 Kerry Wood | .25 | .60 |
| ❏ 38 Huston Street | .25 | .60 |
| ❏ 39 Hank Blalock | .25 | .60 |
| ❏ 40 Brad Radke | .25 | .60 |
| ❏ 41 Chien-Ming Wang | .60 | 1.50 |
| ❏ 42 Mark Buehrle | .25 | .60 |
| ❏ 43 Andy Pettitte | .40 | 1.00 |
| ❏ 44 Bernie Williams | .40 | 1.00 |
| ❏ 45 Victor Martinez | .25 | .60 |
| ❏ 46 Darin Erstad | .25 | .60 |
| ❏ 47 Gustavo Chacin | .25 | .60 |
| ❏ 48 Carlos Guillen | .25 | .60 |
| ❏ 49 Lyle Overbay | .25 | .60 |
| ❏ 50 Barry Bonds | 1.25 | 3.00 |
| ❏ 51 Nook Logan | .25 | .60 |
| ❏ 52 Mark Teahen | .25 | .60 |
| ❏ 53 Mike Lamb | .25 | .60 |
| ❏ 54 Jayson Werth | .25 | .60 |
| ❏ 55 Mariano Rivera | .60 | 1.50 |
| ❏ 56 Julio Lugo | .25 | .60 |
| ❏ 57 Adam Dunn | .25 | .60 |
| ❏ 58 Troy Percival | .25 | .60 |

|  |  | | |
|---|---|---|---|
| ☐ 59 | Chad Tracy | .25 | .60 |
| ☐ 60 | Edgar Renteria | .25 | .60 |
| ☐ 61 | Jason Giambi | .25 | .60 |
| ☐ 62 | Justin Morneau | .25 | .60 |
| ☐ 63 | Carlos Delgado | .25 | .60 |
| ☐ 64 | John Buck | .25 | .60 |
| ☐ 65 | Shannon Stewart | .25 | .60 |
| ☐ 66 | Mike Cameron | .25 | .60 |
| ☐ 67 | Richie Sexson | .25 | .60 |
| ☐ 68 | Russ Adams | .25 | .60 |
| ☐ 69 | Josh Beckett | .25 | .60 |
| ☐ 70 | Ryan Freel | .25 | .60 |
| ☐ 71 | Victor Zambrano | .25 | .60 |
| ☐ 72 | Ronnie Belliard | .25 | .60 |
| ☐ 73 | Brian Giles | .25 | .60 |
| ☐ 74 | Randy Wolf | .25 | .60 |
| ☐ 75 | Robinson Cano | .40 | 1.00 |
| ☐ 76 | Joe Blanton | .25 | .60 |
| ☐ 77 | Esteban Loaiza | .25 | .60 |
| ☐ 78 | Troy Glaus | .25 | .60 |
| ☐ 79 | Matt Clement | .25 | .60 |
| ☐ 80 | Geoff Jenkins | .25 | .60 |
| ☐ 81 | Roy Oswalt | .25 | .60 |
| ☐ 82 | A.J. Pierzynski | .25 | .60 |
| ☐ 83 | Pedro Martinez | .40 | 1.00 |
| ☐ 84 | Roger Clemens | 1.25 | 3.00 |
| ☐ 85 | Jack Wilson | .25 | .60 |
| ☐ 86 | Mike Piazza | .60 | 1.50 |
| ☐ 87 | Paul Lo Duca | .25 | .60 |
| ☐ 88 | Jeff Bagwell | .40 | 1.00 |
| ☐ 89 | Carlos Zambrano | .25 | .60 |
| ☐ 90 | Brandon Claussen | .25 | .60 |
| ☐ 91 | Travis Hafner | .25 | .60 |
| ☐ 92 | Chris Shelton | .25 | .60 |
| ☐ 93 | Rafael Furcal | .25 | .60 |
| ☐ 94 | Frank Thomas | .60 | 1.50 |
| ☐ 95 | Noah Lowry | .25 | .60 |
| ☐ 96 | Jhonny Peralta | .25 | .60 |
| ☐ 97 | Vernon Wells | .25 | .60 |
| ☐ 98 | Jorge Cantu | .25 | .60 |
| ☐ 99 | Willy Taveras | .25 | .60 |
| ☐ 100 | Ivan Rodriguez | .40 | 1.00 |
| ☐ 101 | Jose Reyes | .60 | 1.50 |
| ☐ 102 | Barry Zito | .25 | .60 |
| ☐ 103 | Mark Teixeira | .40 | 1.00 |
| ☐ 104 | Chone Figgins | .25 | .60 |
| ☐ 105 | Todd Helton | .40 | 1.00 |
| ☐ 106 | Tim Wakefield | .25 | .60 |
| ☐ 107 | Mike Maroth | .25 | .60 |
| ☐ 108 | Johnny Damon | .40 | 1.00 |
| ☐ 109 | David DeJesus | .25 | .60 |
| ☐ 110 | Ryan Klesko | .25 | .60 |
| ☐ 111 | Nick Johnson | .25 | .60 |
| ☐ 112 | Freddy Garcia | .25 | .60 |
| ☐ 113 | Torii Hunter | .25 | .60 |
| ☐ 114 | Mike Sweeney | .25 | .60 |
| ☐ 115 | Scott Rolen | .40 | 1.00 |
| ☐ 116 | Jim Thome | .40 | 1.00 |
| ☐ 117 | Adam Kennedy | .25 | .60 |
| ☐ 118 | Albert Pujols | 1.25 | 3.00 |
| ☐ 119 | Kazuo Matsui | .25 | .60 |
| ☐ 120 | Zack Greinke | .25 | .60 |
| ☐ 121 | Jimmy Rollins | .25 | .60 |
| ☐ 122 | Edgardo Alfonzo | .25 | .60 |
| ☐ 123 | Billy Wagner | .25 | .60 |
| ☐ 124 | B.J. Ryan | .25 | .60 |
| ☐ 125 | Orlando Hudson | .25 | .60 |
| ☐ 126 | Preston Wilson | .25 | .60 |
| ☐ 127 | Melvin Mora | .25 | .60 |
| ☐ 128 | Alfonso Soriano | .40 | 1.00 |
| ☐ 129 | Javy Lopez | .25 | .60 |
| ☐ 130 | Wilson Betemit | .25 | .60 |
| ☐ 131 | Garret Anderson | .25 | .60 |
| ☐ 132 | Jason Bay | .25 | .60 |
| ☐ 133 | Adam LaRoche | .25 | .60 |
| ☐ 134 | C.C. Sabathia | .25 | .60 |
| ☐ 135 | Bartolo Colon | .25 | .60 |
| ☐ 136 | Ichiro Suzuki | 1.00 | 2.50 |
| ☐ 137 | Jim Edmonds | .40 | 1.00 |
| ☐ 138 | David Eckstein | .25 | .60 |
| ☐ 139 | Cristian Guzman | .25 | .60 |
| ☐ 140 | Jeff Kent | .25 | .60 |
| ☐ 141 | Chris Capuano | .25 | .60 |
| ☐ 142 | Cliff Floyd | .25 | .60 |
| ☐ 143 | Zach Duke | .25 | .60 |
| ☐ 144 | Matt Morris | .25 | .60 |
| ☐ 145 | Jose Vidro | .25 | .60 |
| ☐ 146 | David Wells | .25 | .60 |
| ☐ 147 | John Smoltz | .40 | 1.00 |
| ☐ 148 | Felix Hernandez | .60 | 1.50 |
| ☐ 149 | Orlando Cabrera | .25 | .60 |
| ☐ 150 | Mark Prior | .40 | 1.00 |
| ☐ 151 | Ted Lilly | .25 | .60 |
| ☐ 152 | Michael Young | .25 | .60 |
| ☐ 153 | Livan Hernandez | .25 | .60 |
| ☐ 154 | Yadier Molina | .25 | .60 |
| ☐ 155 | Eric Chavez | .25 | .60 |
| ☐ 156 | Miguel Batista | .25 | .60 |
| ☐ 157 | Ben Sheets | .25 | .60 |
| ☐ 158 | Oliver Perez | .25 | .60 |
| ☐ 159 | Doug Davis | .25 | .60 |
| ☐ 160 | Andruw Jones | .40 | 1.00 |
| ☐ 161 | Hideki Matsui | .60 | 1.50 |
| ☐ 162 | Reggie Sanders | .25 | .60 |
| ☐ 163 | Joe Nathan | .25 | .60 |
| ☐ 164 | John Lackey | .25 | .60 |
| ☐ 165 | Matt Murton | .25 | .60 |
| ☐ 166 | Grady Sizemore | .40 | 1.00 |
| ☐ 167 | Brad Thompson | .25 | .60 |
| ☐ 168 | Kevin Millwood | .25 | .60 |
| ☐ 169 | Orlando Hernandez | .25 | .60 |
| ☐ 170 | Mark Mulder | .25 | .60 |
| ☐ 171 | Chase Utley | .60 | 1.50 |
| ☐ 172 | Moises Alou | .25 | .60 |
| ☐ 173 | Wily Mo Pena | .25 | .60 |
| ☐ 174 | Brian McCann | .25 | .60 |
| ☐ 175 | Jermaine Dye | .25 | .60 |
| ☐ 176 | Ryan Madson | .25 | .60 |
| ☐ 177 | Aramis Ramirez | .25 | .60 |
| ☐ 178 | Khalil Greene | .40 | 1.00 |
| ☐ 179 | Mike Hampton | .25 | .60 |
| ☐ 180 | Mike Mussina | .40 | 1.00 |
| ☐ 181 | Rich Harden | .25 | .60 |
| ☐ 182 | Woody Williams | .25 | .60 |
| ☐ 183 | Chris Carpenter | .25 | .60 |
| ☐ 184 | Brady Clark | .25 | .60 |
| ☐ 185 | Luis Gonzalez | .25 | .60 |
| ☐ 186 | Raul Ibanez | .25 | .60 |
| ☐ 187 | Magglio Ordonez | .40 | 1.00 |
| ☐ 188 | Adrian Beltre | .25 | .60 |
| ☐ 189 | Marcus Giles | .25 | .60 |
| ☐ 190 | Odalis Perez | .25 | .60 |
| ☐ 191 | Derek Jeter | 1.50 | 4.00 |
| ☐ 192 | Jason Schmidt | .25 | .60 |
| ☐ 193 | Toby Hall | .25 | .60 |
| ☐ 194 | Danny Haren | .25 | .60 |
| ☐ 195 | Tim Hudson | .25 | .60 |
| ☐ 196 | Jake Peavy | .25 | .60 |
| ☐ 197 | Casey Blake | .25 | .60 |
| ☐ 198 | J.D. Drew | .25 | .60 |
| ☐ 199 | Ervin Santana | .25 | .60 |
| ☐ 200 | J.J. Hardy | .25 | .60 |
| ☐ 201 | Austin Kearns | .25 | .60 |
| ☐ 202 | Pat Burrell | .25 | .60 |
| ☐ 203 | Jason Vargas | .25 | .60 |
| ☐ 204 | Ryan Howard | 1.00 | 2.50 |
| ☐ 205 | Joe Crede | .25 | .60 |
| ☐ 206 | Vladimir Guerrero | .60 | 1.50 |
| ☐ 207 | Roy Halladay | .25 | .60 |
| ☐ 208 | David Dellucci | .25 | .60 |
| ☐ 209 | Brandon Webb | .25 | .60 |
| ☐ 210 | Ryan Church | .25 | .60 |
| ☐ 211 | Miguel Tejada | .25 | .60 |
| ☐ 212 | Mark Loretta | .25 | .60 |
| ☐ 213 | Kevin Youkilis | .25 | .60 |
| ☐ 214 | Jon Lieber | .25 | .60 |
| ☐ 215 | Miguel Cabrera | .40 | 1.00 |
| ☐ 216 | A.J. Burnett | .25 | .60 |
| ☐ 217 | David Bell | .25 | .60 |
| ☐ 218 | Eric Byrnes | .25 | .60 |
| ☐ 219 | Lance Niekro | .25 | .60 |
| ☐ 220 | Shawn Green | .25 | .60 |
| ☐ 221 | Ken Griffey Jr. | 1.00 | 2.50 |
| ☐ 222 | Johnny Estrada | .25 | .60 |
| ☐ 223 | Omar Vizquel | .40 | 1.00 |
| ☐ 224 | Gary Sheffield | .25 | .60 |
| ☐ 225 | Brad Halsey | .25 | .60 |
| ☐ 226 | Aaron Cook | .25 | .60 |
| ☐ 227 | David Ortiz | .60 | 1.50 |
| ☐ 228 | Scott Kazmir | .40 | 1.00 |
| ☐ 229 | Dustin McGowan | .25 | .60 |
| ☐ 230 | Gregg Zaun | .25 | .60 |
| ☐ 231 | Carlos Beltran | .25 | .60 |
| ☐ 232 | Bob Wickman | .25 | .60 |
| ☐ 233 | Brett Myers | .25 | .60 |
| ☐ 234 | Casey Kotchman | .25 | .60 |
| ☐ 235 | Jeff Francoeur | .60 | 1.50 |
| ☐ 236 | Paul Konerko | .25 | .60 |
| ☐ 237 | Juan Rivera | .25 | .60 |
| ☐ 238 | Bobby Crosby | .25 | .60 |
| ☐ 239 | Derrek Lee | .25 | .60 |
| ☐ 240 | Curt Schilling | .40 | 1.00 |
| ☐ 241 | Jake Westbrook | .25 | .60 |
| ☐ 242 | Dontrelle Willis | .25 | .60 |
| ☐ 243 | Brad Lidge | .25 | .60 |
| ☐ 244 | Randy Johnson | .60 | 1.50 |
| ☐ 245 | Nick Swisher | .25 | .60 |
| ☐ 246 | Johan Santana | .40 | 1.00 |
| ☐ 247 | Jeremy Bonderman | .25 | .60 |
| ☐ 248 | Ramon Hernandez | .25 | .60 |
| ☐ 249 | Mike Lowell | .25 | .60 |
| ☐ 250 | Javier Vazquez | .25 | .60 |
| ☐ 251 | Jose Contreras | .25 | .60 |
| ☐ 252 | Aubrey Huff | .25 | .60 |
| ☐ 253 | Kenny Rogers AW | .15 | .40 |
| ☐ 254 | Mark Teixeira AW | .25 | .60 |
| ☐ 255 | Orlando Hudson AW | .15 | .40 |
| ☐ 256 | Derek Jeter AW | 1.00 | 2.50 |
| ☐ 257 | Eric Chavez AW | .15 | .40 |
| ☐ 258 | Torii Hunter AW | .15 | .40 |
| ☐ 259 | Vernon Wells AW | .15 | .40 |
| ☐ 260 | Ichiro Suzuki AW | .60 | 1.50 |
| ☐ 261 | Greg Maddux AW | .60 | 1.50 |
| ☐ 262 | Mike Matheny AW | .15 | .40 |
| ☐ 263 | Derek Lee AW | .15 | .40 |
| ☐ 264 | Luis Castillo AW | .15 | .40 |
| ☐ 265 | Omar Vizquel AW | .25 | .60 |
| ☐ 266 | Mike Lowell AW | .15 | .40 |
| ☐ 267 | Andruw Jones AW | .25 | .60 |
| ☐ 268 | Jim Edmonds AW | .25 | .60 |
| ☐ 269 | Bobby Abreu AW | .15 | .40 |
| ☐ 270 | Bartolo Colon AW | .25 | .60 |
| ☐ 271 | Chris Carpenter AW | .15 | .40 |
| ☐ 272 | Alex Rodriguez AW | .60 | 1.50 |
| ☐ 273 | Albert Pujols AW | .75 | 2.00 |
| ☐ 274 | Huston Street AW | .15 | .40 |
| ☐ 275 | Ryan Howard AW | .60 | 1.50 |
| ☐ 276 | Chris Denorfia (RC) | .40 | 1.00 |
| ☐ 277 | John Van Benschoten (RC) | .40 | 1.00 |
| ☐ 278 | Russ Martin (RC) | .60 | 1.50 |
| ☐ 279 | Fausto Carmona (RC) | .40 | 1.00 |
| ☐ 280 | Freddie Bynum (RC) | .40 | 1.00 |
| ☐ 281 | Kelly Shoppach (RC) | .40 | 1.00 |
| ☐ 282 | Chris Demaria RC | .40 | 1.00 |
| ☐ 283 | Jordan Tata RC | .40 | 1.00 |
| ☐ 284 | Ryan Zimmerman (RC) | 2.00 | 5.00 |
| ☐ 285a | Kenji Johjima RC | 2.00 | 5.00 |
| ☐ 285b | Kenji Johjima AU | 50.00 | 100.00 |
| ☐ 286 | Ruddy Lugo (RC) | .40 | 1.00 |
| ☐ 287 | Tommy Murphy (RC) | .40 | 1.00 |
| ☐ 288 | Bobby Livingston (RC) | .40 | 1.00 |
| ☐ 289 | Anderson Hernandez (RC) | .40 | 1.00 |
| ☐ 290 | Brian Slocum (RC) | .40 | 1.00 |
| ☐ 291 | Sendy Rleal RC | .40 | 1.00 |
| ☐ 292 | Ryan Spilborghs (RC) | .60 | 1.50 |
| ☐ 293 | Brandon Fahey RC | .40 | 1.00 |
| ☐ 294 | Jason Kubel (RC) | .40 | 1.00 |
| ☐ 295 | James Loney (RC) | .60 | 1.50 |
| ☐ 296 | Jeremy Accardo RC | .40 | 1.00 |
| ☐ 297 | Fabio Castro RC | .40 | 1.00 |
| ☐ 298 | Matt Capps (RC) | .40 | 1.00 |
| ☐ 299 | Casey Janssen (RC) | .40 | 1.00 |
| ☐ 300 | Martin Prado (RC) | .40 | 1.00 |
| ☐ 301 | Ronny Paulino (RC) | .40 | 1.00 |
| ☐ 302 | Josh Barfield (RC) | .40 | 1.00 |
| ☐ 303 | Joel Zumaya (RC) | 1.00 | 2.50 |
| ☐ 304 | Matt Cain (RC) | .60 | 1.50 |
| ☐ 305 | Conor Jackson (RC) | .60 | 1.50 |
| ☐ 306 | Brian Anderson (RC) | .60 | 1.50 |
| ☐ 307 | Prince Fielder (RC) | 1.50 | 4.00 |
| ☐ 308 | Jeremy Hermida (RC) | .60 | 1.50 |
| ☐ 309 | Justin Verlander (RC) | 1.50 | 4.00 |
| ☐ 310 | Brian Bannister (RC) | .40 | 1.00 |
| ☐ 311 | Josh Willingham (RC) | .40 | 1.00 |
| ☐ 312 | John Rheinecker (RC) | .40 | 1.00 |
| ☐ 313 | Nick Markakis (RC) | .60 | 1.50 |
| ☐ 314 | Jonathan Papelbon (RC) | 2.00 | 5.00 |
| ☐ 315 | Mike Jacobs (RC) | .40 | 1.00 |
| ☐ 316 | Jose Capellan (RC) | .40 | 1.00 |
| ☐ 317 | Mike Napoli RC | 1.00 | 2.50 |
| ☐ 318 | Ricky Nolasco (RC) | .40 | 1.00 |
| ☐ 319 | Ben Johnson (RC) | .40 | 1.00 |
| ☐ 320 | Paul Maholm (RC) | .40 | 1.00 |
| ☐ 321 | Drew Meyer (RC) | .40 | 1.00 |

|  |  | | |
|---|--------|---|---|
| 322 | Jeff Mathis (RC) | .40 | 1.00 |
| 323 | Fernando Nieve (RC) | .40 | 1.00 |
| 324 | John Koronka (RC) | .40 | 1.00 |
| 325 | Wil Nieves (RC) | .40 | 1.00 |
| 326 | Nate McLouth (RC) | .40 | 1.00 |
| 327 | Howie Kendrick (RC) | 2.00 | 5.00 |
| 328 | Sean Marshall (RC) | .40 | 1.00 |
| 329 | Brandon Watson (RC) | .40 | 1.00 |
| 330 | Skip Schumaker (RC) | .40 | 1.00 |
| 331 | Ryan Garko AU (RC) | 4.00 | 10.00 |
| 332 | Jason Bergmann AU RC | 4.00 | 10.00 |
| 333 | Chuck James AU (RC) | 6.00 | 15.00 |
| 334 | Adam Wainwright AU (RC) | 10.00 | 25.00 |
| 335 | Dan Ortmeier AU (RC) | 4.00 | 10.00 |
| 336 | Francisco Liriano AU (RC) | 8.00 | 20.00 |
| 337 | Craig Breslow AU RC | 4.00 | 10.00 |
| 338 | Darrell Rasner AU (RC) | 4.00 | 10.00 |
| 339 | Jason Botts AU (RC) | 4.00 | 10.00 |
| 340 | Ian Kinsler AU (RC) | 10.00 | 25.00 |
| 341 | Joey Devine AU RC | 4.00 | 10.00 |
| 342 | Miguel Perez AU (RC) | 4.00 | 10.00 |
| 343 | Scott Olsen AU (RC) | 6.00 | 15.00 |
| 344 | Tyler Johnson AU (RC) | 4.00 | 10.00 |
| 345 | Anthony Lerew AU (RC) | 4.00 | 10.00 |
| 346 | Nelson Cruz AU (RC) | 6.00 | 15.00 |
| 347 | Willie Eyre AU (RC) | 4.00 | 10.00 |
| 348 | Josh Johnson AU (RC) | 8.00 | 20.00 |
| 349 | Shaun Marcum AU (RC) | 4.00 | 10.00 |
| 350 | Dustin Nippert AU (RC) | 4.00 | 10.00 |
| 351 | Josh Wilson AU (RC) | 4.00 | 10.00 |
| 352 | Hanley Ramirez AU (RC) | 15.00 | 40.00 |
| 353 | Reggie Abercrombie AU (RC) | 4.00 | 10.00 |
| 354 | Dan Uggla AU (RC) | 8.00 | 20.00 |

## 2007 Topps Chrome

CABRERA

| | | | |
|---|---|---|---|
| COMP.SET w/o AU's (330) | | 40.00 | 80.00 |
| COMMON CARD | | .20 | .50 |
| COMMON ROOKIE | | .40 | 1.00 |
| JAPANESE VARIATION ODDS 1:82 H | | | |
| COMMON AUTO | | 3.00 | 8.00 |
| AUTO ODDS 1:16 HOBBY, 1:122 RETAIL | | | |
| PRINT.PLATE ODDS 1:36 HOBBY LDR | | | |
| VAR.PLATES 1:1943 HOBBY BOX LDR | | | |
| AU PLATES 1:343 HOBBY BOX LDR | | | |
| PLATE PRINT RUN 1 SET PER COLOR | | | |
| BLACK-CYAN-MAGENTA-YELLOW ISSUED | | | |
| NO PLATE PRICING DUE TO SCARCITY | | | |
| EXCHANGE DEADLINE 07/31/09 | | | |

|  |  | | |
|---|--------|---|---|
| 1 | Nick Swisher | .20 | .50 |
| 2 | Bobby Abreu | .20 | .50 |
| 3 | Edgar Renteria | .20 | .50 |
| 4 | Mickey Mantle | 1.50 | 4.00 |
| 5 | Preston Wilson | .20 | .50 |
| 6 | C.C. Sabathia | .20 | .50 |
| 7 | Julio Lugo | .20 | .50 |
| 8 | J.D. Drew | .20 | .50 |
| 9 | Jason Varitek | .50 | 1.25 |
| 10 | Orlando Hernandez | .20 | .50 |
| 11 | Corey Patterson | .20 | .50 |
| 12 | Josh Bard | .20 | .50 |
| 13 | Gary Matthews | .20 | .50 |
| 14 | Jason Jennings | .20 | .50 |
| 15 | Bronson Arroyo | .20 | .50 |
| 16 | Andy Pettitte | .30 | .75 |
| 17 | Ervin Santana | .20 | .50 |
| 18 | Paul Konerko | .20 | .50 |
| 19 | Adam LaRoche | .20 | .50 |
| 20 | Jim Edmonds | .30 | .75 |
| 21 | Derek Jeter | 1.25 | 3.00 |
| 22 | Aubrey Huff | .20 | .50 |
| 23 | Andre Ethier | .30 | .75 |
| 24 | Jeremy Sowers | .20 | .50 |
| 25 | Miguel Cabrera | .30 | .75 |
| 26 | Carlos Lee | .20 | .50 |
| 27 | Mike Piazza | .50 | 1.25 |
| 28 | Cole Hamels | .50 | 1.25 |
| 29 | Mark Loretta | .20 | .50 |
| 30 | John Smoltz | .30 | .75 |
| 31 | Dan Uggla | .20 | .50 |
| 32 | Lyle Overbay | .20 | .50 |
| 33 | Michael Barrett | .20 | .50 |
| 34 | Ivan Rodriguez | .30 | .75 |
| 35 | Jake Westbrook | .20 | .50 |
| 36 | Moises Alou | .20 | .50 |
| 37 | Jered Weaver | .30 | .75 |
| 38 | Lastings Milledge | .20 | .50 |
| 39 | Austin Kearns | .20 | .50 |
| 40 | Adam Loewen | .20 | .50 |
| 41 | Josh Barfield | .20 | .50 |
| 42 | Johan Santana | .30 | .75 |
| 43 | Ian Kinsler | .20 | .50 |
| 44 | Mike Lowell | .20 | .50 |
| 45 | Scott Rolen | .30 | .75 |
| 46 | Chipper Jones | .50 | 1.25 |
| 47 | Joe Crede | .20 | .50 |
| 48 | Rafael Furcal | .20 | .50 |
| 49 | Dave Bush | .20 | .50 |
| 50 | Marcus Giles | .20 | .50 |
| 51 | Joe Blanton | .20 | .50 |
| 52 | Dontrelle Willis | .20 | .50 |
| 53 | Scott Kazmir | .30 | .75 |
| 54 | Jeff Kent | .20 | .50 |
| 55 | Travis Hafner | .20 | .50 |
| 56 | Ryan Garko | .20 | .50 |
| 57 | Nick Markakis | .30 | .75 |
| 58 | Michael Cuddyer | .20 | .50 |
| 59 | Jason Giambi | .20 | .50 |
| 60 | Chone Figgins | .20 | .50 |
| 61 | Carlos Delgado | .20 | .50 |
| 62 | Aramis Ramirez | .20 | .50 |
| 63 | Albert Pujols | 1.00 | 2.50 |
| 64 | Gary Sheffield | .20 | .50 |
| 65 | Adrian Gonzalez | .20 | .50 |
| 66 | Prince Fielder | .50 | 1.25 |
| 67 | Freddy Sanchez | .20 | .50 |
| 68 | Jack Wilson | .20 | .50 |
| 69 | Jake Peavy | .20 | .50 |
| 70 | Javier Vazquez | .20 | .50 |
| 71 | Todd Helton | .30 | .75 |
| 72 | Bill Hall | .20 | .50 |
| 73 | Jeremy Bonderman | .20 | .50 |
| 74 | Rocco Baldelli | .20 | .50 |
| 75 | Noah Lowry | .20 | .50 |
| 76 | Justin Verlander | .50 | 1.25 |
| 77 | Mark Buehrle | .20 | .50 |
| 78 | Hank Blalock | .20 | .50 |
| 79 | Mark Teahen | .20 | .50 |
| 80 | Chien-Ming Wang | .50 | 1.25 |
| 81 | Roy Halladay | .30 | .75 |
| 82 | Melvin Mora | .20 | .50 |
| 83 | Grady Sizemore | .30 | .75 |
| 84 | Matt Cain | .30 | .75 |
| 85 | Carl Crawford | .30 | .75 |
| 86 | Johnny Damon | .30 | .75 |
| 87 | Freddy Garcia | .20 | .50 |
| 88 | Ryan Shealy | .20 | .50 |
| 89 | Carlos Beltran | .30 | .75 |
| 90 | Chuck James | .20 | .50 |
| 91 | Ben Sheets | .20 | .50 |
| 92 | Mark Mulder | .20 | .50 |
| 93 | Carlos Quentin | .20 | .50 |
| 94 | Richie Sexson | .20 | .50 |
| 95 | Brian Schneider | .20 | .50 |
| 96a | Hideki Matsui | .50 | 1.25 |
| 96b | H.Matsui Japanese | 2.00 | 5.00 |
| 97 | Robinson Tejeda | .20 | .50 |
| 98 | Scott Hatteberg | .20 | .50 |
| 99 | Jeff Francis | .20 | .50 |
| 100 | Robinson Cano | .30 | .75 |
| 101 | Barry Zito | .20 | .50 |
| 102 | Reed Johnson | .20 | .50 |
| 103 | Chris Carpenter | .20 | .50 |
| 104 | Chad Tracy | .20 | .50 |
| 105 | Anibal Sanchez | .20 | .50 |
| 106 | Brad Penny | .20 | .50 |
| 107 | David Wright | .75 | 2.00 |
| 108 | Jimmy Rollins | .20 | .50 |
| 109 | Alfonso Soriano | .30 | .75 |
| 110 | Greg Maddux | .75 | 2.00 |
| 111 | Curt Schilling | .30 | .75 |
| 112 | Stephen Drew | .30 | .75 |
| 113 | Matt Holliday | .50 | 1.25 |
| 114 | Jorge Posada | .30 | .75 |
| 115 | Vladimir Guerrero | .50 | 1.25 |
| 116 | Frank Thomas | .50 | 1.25 |
| 117 | Jonathan Papelbon | .50 | 1.25 |
| 118 | Manny Ramirez | .30 | .75 |
| 119 | Magglio Ordonez | .30 | .75 |
| 120 | Joe Mauer | .50 | 1.25 |
| 121 | Ryan Howard | .75 | 2.00 |
| 122 | Chris Young | .20 | .50 |
| 123 | A.J. Burnett | .20 | .50 |
| 124 | Brian McCann | .20 | .50 |
| 125 | Juan Pierre | .20 | .50 |
| 126 | Jonny Gomes | .20 | .50 |
| 127 | Roger Clemens | .75 | 2.00 |
| 128 | Chad Billingsley | .20 | .50 |
| 129a | Kenji Johjima | .50 | 1.25 |
| 129b | Kenji Johjima Japanese | 2.00 | 5.00 |
| 130 | Brian Giles | .20 | .50 |
| 131 | Chase Utley | .50 | 1.25 |
| 132 | Carl Pavano | .20 | .50 |
| 133 | Curtis Granderson | .20 | .50 |
| 134 | Sean Casey | .20 | .50 |
| 135 | Jon Garland | .20 | .50 |
| 136 | David Ortiz | .30 | .75 |
| 137 | Bobby Crosby | .20 | .50 |
| 138 | Conor Jackson | .20 | .50 |
| 139 | Tim Hudson | .20 | .50 |
| 140 | Rickie Weeks | .20 | .50 |
| 141 | Mark Prior | .30 | .75 |
| 142 | Ben Zobrist | .20 | .50 |
| 143 | Troy Glaus | .20 | .50 |
| 144 | Cliff Lee | .20 | .50 |
| 145 | Adrian Beltre | .20 | .50 |
| 146 | Endy Chavez | .20 | .50 |
| 147 | Ramon Hernandez | .20 | .50 |
| 148 | Chris Young | .20 | .50 |
| 149 | Jason Schmidt | .20 | .50 |
| 150 | Kevin Millwood | .20 | .50 |
| 151 | Placido Polanco | .20 | .50 |
| 152 | Torii Hunter | .20 | .50 |
| 153 | Roy Oswalt | .20 | .50 |
| 154 | Kelvim Escobar | .20 | .50 |
| 155 | Milton Bradley | .20 | .50 |
| 156 | Chris Capuano | .20 | .50 |
| 157 | Juan Encarnacion | .20 | .50 |
| 158a | Ichiro Suzuki | .75 | 2.00 |
| 158b | Ichiro Suzuki Japanese | 3.00 | 8.00 |
| 159 | Matt Kemp | .50 | 1.25 |
| 160 | Matt Morris | .20 | .50 |
| 161 | Casey Blake | .20 | .50 |
| 162 | Josh Willingham | .20 | .50 |
| 163 | Nick Johnson | .20 | .50 |
| 164 | Khalil Greene | .20 | .50 |
| 165 | Tom Glavine | .30 | .75 |
| 166 | Jason Bay | .30 | .75 |
| 167 | Brandon Phillips | .20 | .50 |
| 168 | Jorge Cantu | .20 | .50 |
| 169 | Jeff Weaver | .20 | .50 |
| 170 | Melky Cabrera | .20 | .50 |
| 171 | Dan Haren | .20 | .50 |
| 172 | Jeff Francoeur | .50 | 1.25 |
| 173 | Randy Wolf | .20 | .50 |
| 174 | Carlos Zambrano | .20 | .50 |
| 175 | Justin Morneau | .20 | .50 |
| 176 | Takashi Saito | .20 | .50 |
| 177 | Victor Martinez | .20 | .50 |
| 178 | Felix Hernandez | .30 | .75 |
| 179 | Paul LoDuca | .20 | .50 |
| 180 | Miguel Tejada | .20 | .50 |
| 181 | Mark Teixeira | .30 | .75 |
| 182 | Pat Burrell | .20 | .50 |
| 183 | Mike Cameron | .20 | .50 |
| 184 | Josh Beckett | .30 | .75 |
| 185 | Francisco Liriano | .50 | 1.25 |
| 186 | Ken Griffey Jr. | .75 | 2.00 |
| 187 | Mike Mussina | .30 | .75 |
| 188 | Howie Kendrick | .20 | .50 |
| 189 | Ted Lilly | .20 | .50 |
| 190 | Mike Hampton | .20 | .50 |
| 191 | Jeff Suppan | .20 | .50 |
| 192 | Jose Reyes | .50 | 1.25 |
| 193 | Russell Martin | .20 | .50 |
| 194 | Jhonny Peralta | .20 | .50 |
| 195 | Raul Ibanez | .30 | .75 |
| 196 | Hanley Ramirez | .30 | .75 |
| 197 | Kerry Wood | .20 | .50 |
| 198 | Gary Sheffield | .20 | .50 |
| 199 | David Dellucci | .20 | .50 |

|  |  | | |
|---|--------|---|---|
| 200 | Xavier Nady | .20 | .50 |
| 201 | Michael Young | .20 | .50 |
| 202 | Kevin Youkilis | .20 | .50 |
| 203 | Aaron Harang | .20 | .50 |
| 204 | Matt Garza | .20 | .50 |
| 205 | Jim Thome | .30 | .75 |
| 206 | Jose Contreras | .20 | .50 |
| 207 | Tadahito Iguchi | .20 | .50 |
| 208 | Eric Chavez | .20 | .50 |
| 209 | Vernon Wells | .20 | .50 |
| 210 | Doug Davis | .20 | .50 |
| 211 | Andruw Jones | .30 | .75 |
| 212 | David Eckstein | .20 | .50 |
| 213 | J.J. Hardy | .20 | .50 |
| 214 | Orlando Hudson | .20 | .50 |
| 215 | Pedro Martinez | .30 | .75 |
| 216 | Brian Roberts | .20 | .50 |
| 217 | Brett Myers | .20 | .50 |
| 218 | Alex Rodriguez | .75 | 2.00 |
| 219 | Kenny Rogers | .20 | .50 |
| 220 | Jason Kubel | .20 | .50 |
| 221 | Jermaine Dye | .20 | .50 |
| 222 | Bartolo Colon | .20 | .50 |
| 223 | Craig Biggio | .30 | .75 |
| 224 | Alex Rios | .20 | .50 |
| 225 | Adam Dunn | .20 | .50 |
| 226 | Anthony Reyes | .20 | .50 |
| 227 | Derek Lee | .20 | .50 |
| 228 | Jeremy Hermida | .20 | .50 |
| 229 | Derek Lowe | .20 | .50 |
| 230 | Randy Winn | .20 | .50 |
| 231 | Brandon Webb | .20 | .50 |
| 232 | Jose Vidro | .20 | .50 |
| 233 | Erik Bedard | .20 | .50 |
| 234 | Jon Lieber | .20 | .50 |
| 235 | Wily Mo Pena | .20 | .50 |
| 236 | Kelly Johnson | .20 | .50 |
| 237 | David DeJesus | .20 | .50 |
| 238 | Andy Marte | .20 | .50 |
| 239 | Scott Olsen | .20 | .50 |
| 240 | Randy Johnson | .50 | 1.25 |
| 241 | Nelson Cruz | .20 | .50 |
| 242 | Carlos Guillen | .20 | .50 |
| 243 | Brandon McCarthy | .20 | .50 |
| 244 | Garret Anderson | .20 | .50 |
| 245 | Mike Sweeney | .20 | .50 |
| 246 | Brian Bannister | .20 | .50 |
| 247 | Jose Guillen | .20 | .50 |
| 248 | Brad Wilkerson | .20 | .50 |
| 249 | Lance Berkman | .20 | .50 |
| 250 | Ryan Zimmerman | .50 | 1.25 |
| 251 | Garrett Atkins | .20 | .50 |
| 252 | Johan Santana | .30 | .75 |
| 253 | Brandon Webb | .20 | .50 |
| 254 | Justin Verlander | .50 | 1.25 |
| 255 | Hanley Ramirez | .30 | .75 |
| 256 | Justin Morneau | .30 | .75 |
| 257 | Ryan Howard | .75 | 2.00 |
| 258 | Eric Chavez | .20 | .50 |
| 259 | Scott Rolen | .30 | .75 |
| 260 | Derek Jeter | 1.25 | 3.00 |
| 261 | Omar Vizquel | .30 | .75 |
| 262 | Mark Grudzielanek | .20 | .50 |
| 263 | Orlando Hudson | .20 | .50 |
| 264 | Mark Teixeira | .30 | .75 |
| 265 | Albert Pujols | 1.00 | 2.50 |
| 266 | Ivan Rodriguez | .30 | .75 |
| 267 | Brad Ausmus | .20 | .50 |
| 268 | Torii Hunter | .20 | .50 |
| 269 | Mike Cameron | .20 | .50 |
| 270 | Ichiro Suzuki | .75 | 2.00 |
| 271 | Carlos Beltran | .20 | .50 |
| 272 | Vernon Wells | .20 | .50 |
| 273 | Andruw Jones | .30 | .75 |
| 274 | Kenny Rogers | .20 | .50 |
| 275 | Greg Maddux | .75 | 2.00 |
| 276 | Danny Putnam (RC) | .40 | 1.00 |
| 277 | Chase Wright RC | 1.00 | 2.50 |
| 278 | Zach McClellan RC | .40 | 1.00 |
| 279 | Jamie Vermilyea RC | .40 | 1.00 |
| 280 | Felix Pie (RC) | .40 | 1.00 |
| 281 | Phil Hughes (RC) | 2.00 | 5.00 |
| 282 | Jon Knott (RC) | .40 | 1.00 |
| 283 | Micah Owings (RC) | .40 | 1.00 |
| 284 | Devern Hansack RC | .40 | 1.00 |
| 285 | Andy Cannizaro RC | .40 | 1.00 |
| 286 | Lee Gardner (RC) | .40 | 1.00 |
| 287 | Josh Hamilton (RC) | 1.00 | 2.50 |

|  |  | | |
|---|--------|---|---|
| 288a | Angel Sanchez RC | | |
| 288b | Angel Sanchez AU | 3.00 | 8.00 |
| 289 | J.D. Durbin (RC) | .40 | 1.00 |
| 290 | Jaime Burke (RC) | .40 | 1.00 |
| 291 | Joe Bisenius RC | .40 | 1.00 |
| 292 | Rick Vanden Hurk RC | .60 | 1.50 |
| 293 | Brian Barden RC | .40 | 1.00 |
| 294 | Levale Speigner RC | .40 | 1.00 |
| 295 | Kevin Cameron RC | .40 | 1.00 |
| 296 | Don Kelly (RC) | .40 | 1.00 |
| 297a | Hideki Okajima RC | 2.00 | 5.00 |
| 297b | Hideki Okajima Japanese | 3.00 | 8.00 |
| 298 | Andrew Miller RC | 2.50 | 6.00 |
| 299 | Delmon Young (RC) | 1.00 | 2.50 |
| 300 | Vinny Rottino (RC) | .40 | 1.00 |
| 301 | Philip Humber (RC) | .40 | 1.00 |
| 302 | Drew Anderson RC | .40 | 1.00 |
| 303 | Jerry Owens (RC) | .40 | 1.00 |
| 304 | Jose Garcia RC | .40 | 1.00 |
| 305 | Shane Youman RC | .40 | 1.00 |
| 306 | Ryan Feierabend (RC) | .40 | 1.00 |
| 307 | Mike Rabelo RC | .40 | 1.00 |
| 308 | Josh Fields (RC) | .40 | 1.00 |
| 309 | Jon Coutlangus (RC) | .40 | 1.00 |
| 310 | Travis Buck (RC) | .40 | 1.00 |
| 311 | Doug Slaten RC | .40 | 1.00 |
| 312 | Ryan Z. Braun RC | .40 | 1.00 |
| 313 | Juan Salas (RC) | .40 | 1.00 |
| 314 | Matt Lindstrom (RC) | .40 | 1.00 |
| 315 | Cesar Jimenez RC | .40 | 1.00 |
| 316 | Jay Marshall RC | .40 | 1.00 |
| 317 | Jared Burton RC | .40 | 1.00 |
| 318 | Juan Perez RC | .40 | 1.00 |
| 319 | Elijah Dukes RC | .60 | 1.50 |
| 320 | Juan Lara RC | .40 | 1.00 |
| 321 | Justin Hampson (RC) | .40 | 1.00 |
| 322a | Kei Igawa RC | 1.00 | 2.50 |
| 322b | Kei Igawa Japanese | 2.00 | 5.00 |
| 323 | Zack Segovia (RC) | .40 | 1.00 |
| 324 | Alejandro De Aza RC | .60 | 1.50 |
| 325 | Brandon Morrow RC | 1.00 | 2.50 |
| 326 | Gustavo Molina RC | .40 | 1.00 |
| 327 | Joe Smith RC | .40 | 1.00 |
| 328 | Jesus Flores RC | .40 | 1.00 |
| 329 | Jeff Baker (RC) | .40 | 1.00 |
| 330a | Daisuke Matsuzaka RC | 4.00 | 10.00 |
| 330b | Daisuke Matsuzaka Japanese | 4.00 | 10.00 |
| 331 | Troy Tulowitzki AU (RC) | 10.00 | 25.00 |
| 332 | John Danks AU RC | 4.00 | 10.00 |
| 333 | Kevin Kouzmanoff AU (RC) | 3.00 | 8.00 |
| 334 | David Murphy AU (RC) | 3.00 | 8.00 |
| 335 | Ryan Sweeney AU (RC) | 3.00 | 8.00 |
| 336 | Fred Lewis AU (RC) | 4.00 | 10.00 |
| 337 | Delwyn Young AU (RC) | 3.00 | 8.00 |
| 338 | Matt Chico AU (RC) | 3.00 | 8.00 |
| 339 | Miguel Montero AU (RC) | 3.00 | 8.00 |
| 340 | Shawn Riggans AU (RC) | 3.00 | 8.00 |
| 341 | Brian Stokes AU (RC) | 3.00 | 8.00 |
| 342 | Scott Moore AU (RC) | 3.00 | 8.00 |
| 343 | Adam Lind AU (RC) | 4.00 | 10.00 |
| 344 | Chris Narveson AU (RC) | 3.00 | 8.00 |
| 345 | Alex Gordon AU (RC) | 12.50 | 30.00 |
| 346 | Joaquin Arias AU (RC) | 3.00 | 8.00 |
| 347 | Brian Burres AU (RC) | 3.00 | 8.00 |
| 348 | Glen Perkins AU (RC) | 3.00 | 8.00 |
| 349 | Ubaldo Jimenez AU (RC) | 6.00 | 15.00 |
| 350 | Chris Stewart AU (RC) | 3.00 | 8.00 |
| 351 | Beltran Perez AU (RC) | 3.00 | 8.00 |
| 352 | Dennis Sarfate AU (RC) | 3.00 | 8.00 |
| 353 | Carlos Maldonado AU (RC) | 3.00 | 8.00 |
| 354 | Mitch Maier AU RC | 3.00 | 8.00 |
| 355 | Kory Casto AU (RC) | 3.00 | 8.00 |
| 356 | Juan Morillo AU (RC) | 3.00 | 8.00 |
| 357 | Hector Gimenez AU (RC) | 3.00 | 8.00 |
| 358 | Alexi Casilla AU RC | 4.00 | 10.00 |
| 359 | Michael Bourn AU (RC) | 4.00 | 10.00 |
| 360 | Sean Henn AU (RC) | 3.00 | 8.00 |
| 361 | Tim Gradoville AU RC | 3.00 | 8.00 |
| 362 | A.Iwamura AU RC EXCH | 8.00 | 20.00 |
| 363 | Oswaldo Navarro AU (RC) | 3.00 | 8.00 |

## 2008 Topps Chrome

| | | |
|---|---|---|
| COMP.SET w/o AU's (220) | 30.00 | 60.00 |
| COMMON CARD | .20 | .50 |
| COMMON ROOKIE | .60 | 1.50 |
| COMMON AUTO | 4.00 | 10.00 |
| AUTO ODDS 1:15 HOBBY | | |
| PRINT.PLATE ODDS 1:1896 HOBBY | | |
| AU PLATES 1:10,961 HOBBY | | |
| PLATE PRINT RUN 1 SET PER COLOR | | |
| BLACK-CYAN-MAGENTA-YELLOW ISSUED | | |
| NO PLATE PRICING DUE TO SCARCITY | | |
| EXCHANGE DEADLINE 6/30/2010 | | |

|  |  | | |
|---|--------|---|---|
| 1 | Alex Rodriguez | .75 | 2.00 |
| 2 | Barry Zito | .20 | .50 |
| 3 | Scott Kazmir | .30 | .75 |
| 4 | Stephen Drew | .20 | .50 |
| 5 | Miguel Cabrera | .30 | .75 |
| 6 | Daisuke Matsuzaka | .60 | 1.50 |
| 7 | Mickey Mantle | 2.00 | 5.00 |
| 8 | Jimmy Rollins | .30 | .75 |
| 9 | Joe Mauer | .50 | 1.25 |
| 10 | Cole Hamels | .50 | 1.25 |
| 11 | Yovani Gallardo | .20 | .50 |
| 12 | Miguel Tejada | .20 | .50 |
| 13 | Dontrelle Willis | .20 | .50 |
| 14 | Orlando Cabrera | .20 | .50 |
| 15 | Jake Peavy | .30 | .75 |
| 16 | Erik Bedard | .20 | .50 |
| 17 | Victor Martinez | .20 | .50 |
| 18 | Chris Young | .20 | .50 |
| 19 | Jose Reyes | .30 | .75 |
| 20 | Mike Lowell | .20 | .50 |
| 21 | Dan Uggla | .30 | .75 |
| 22 | Garrett Atkins | .20 | .50 |
| 23 | Felix Hernandez | .30 | .75 |
| 24 | Ivan Rodriguez | .30 | .75 |
| 25 | Alex Rios | .20 | .50 |
| 26 | Jason Bay | .30 | .75 |
| 27 | Vladimir Guerrero | .50 | 1.25 |
| 28 | John Lackey | .20 | .50 |
| 29 | Ryan Howard | .60 | 1.50 |
| 30 | Kevin Youkilis | .30 | .75 |
| 31 | Justin Morneau | .30 | .75 |
| 32 | Johan Santana | .30 | .75 |
| 33 | Jeremy Hermida | .20 | .50 |
| 34 | Andruw Jones | .20 | .50 |
| 35 | Mike Cameron | .20 | .50 |
| 36 | Jason Varitek | .50 | 1.25 |
| 37 | Tim Hudson | .20 | .50 |
| 38 | Justin Upton | .50 | 1.25 |
| 39 | Brad Penny | .20 | .50 |
| 40 | Robinson Cano | .30 | .75 |
| 41 | Brandon Webb | .30 | .75 |
| 42 | Magglio Ordonez | .30 | .75 |
| 43 | Aaron Hill | .20 | .50 |
| 44 | Alfonso Soriano | .30 | .75 |
| 45 | Carlos Zambrano | .20 | .50 |
| 46 | Ben Sheets | .20 | .50 |
| 47 | Tim Lincecum | .60 | 1.50 |
| 48 | Phil Hughes | .50 | 1.25 |
| 49 | Scott Rolen | .20 | .50 |
| 50 | John Maine | .20 | .50 |
| 51 | Delmon Young | .20 | .50 |
| 52 | Tadahito Iguchi | .20 | .50 |
| 53 | Yunel Escobar | .20 | .50 |
| 54 | Orlando Hudson | .20 | .50 |
| 55 | Jim Edmonds | .30 | .75 |
| 56 | Jim Edmonds | .30 | .75 |
| 57 | Todd Helton | .30 | .75 |
| 58 | Melky Cabrera | .20 | .50 |
| 59 | Adrian Beltre | .20 | .50 |
| 60 | Manny Ramirez | .50 | 1.25 |
| 61 | Gil Meche | .20 | .50 |

|  |  | | |
|---|---|---|---|
| 62 | David DeJesus | .20 | .50 |
| 63 | Roy Oswalt | .20 | .50 |
| 64 | Mark Buehrle | .20 | .50 |
| 65 | Hunter Pence | .50 | 1.25 |
| 66 | Dustin Pedroia | .60 | 1.50 |
| 67 | Roy Halladay | .20 | .50 |
| 68 | Rich Harden | .20 | .50 |
| 69 | Jim Thome | .30 | .75 |
| 70 | Akinori Iwamura | .20 | .50 |
| 71 | Dan Haren | .20 | .50 |
| 72 | Brandon Phillips | .20 | .50 |
| 73 | Brett Myers | .20 | .50 |
| 74 | James Loney | .30 | .75 |
| 75 | C.C. Sabathia | .20 | .50 |
| 76 | Jermaine Dye | .20 | .50 |
| 77 | Carlos Ruiz | .20 | .50 |
| 78 | Brian McCann | .30 | .75 |
| 79 | Paul Konerko | .20 | .50 |
| 80 | Jorge Posada | .30 | .75 |
| 81 | Chien-Ming Wang | .50 | 1.25 |
| 82 | Carlos Delgado | .20 | .50 |
| 83 | Ichiro Suzuki | .75 | 2.00 |
| 84 | Elijah Dukes | .20 | .50 |
| 85 | David Wright | .60 | 1.50 |
| 86 | Carl Crawford | .30 | .75 |
| 87 | Mark Teixeira | .30 | .75 |
| 88 | Bobby Crosby | .20 | .50 |
| 89 | Brian Roberts | .20 | .50 |
| 90 | David Ortiz | .30 | .75 |
| 91 | Derrek Lee | .30 | .75 |
| 92 | Adam Dunn | .20 | .50 |
| 93 | Fausto Carmona | .20 | .50 |
| 94 | Grady Sizemore | .30 | .75 |
| 95 | Jeff Francoeur | .20 | .50 |
| 96 | Jered Weaver | .20 | .50 |
| 97 | Troy Tulowitzki | .30 | .75 |
| 98 | Troy Glaus | .20 | .50 |
| 99 | Nick Markakis | .30 | .75 |
| 100 | Lance Berkman | .30 | .75 |
| 101 | Randy Johnson | .50 | 1.25 |
| 102 | Kenji Johjima | .20 | .50 |
| 103 | Jarrod Saltalamacchia | .20 | .50 |
| 104 | Matt Holliday | .30 | .75 |
| 105 | Travis Hafner | .20 | .50 |
| 106 | Johnny Damon | .30 | .75 |
| 107 | Alex Gordon | .30 | .75 |
| 108 | Derek Lowe | .20 | .50 |
| 109 | Nick Swisher | .20 | .50 |
| 110 | Aaron Harang | .20 | .50 |
| 111 | Hanley Ramirez | .50 | 1.25 |
| 112 | Carlos Guillen | .20 | .50 |
| 113 | Ryan Braun | .60 | 1.50 |
| 114 | Torii Hunter | .20 | .50 |
| 115 | Joe Blanton | .20 | .50 |
| 116 | Josh Hamilton | .60 | 1.50 |
| 117 | Pedro Martinez | .30 | .75 |
| 118 | Hideki Matsui | .50 | 1.25 |
| 119 | Cameron Maybin | .30 | .75 |
| 120 | Prince Fielder | .50 | 1.25 |
| 121 | Derek Jeter | 1.25 | 3.00 |
| 122 | Chone Figgins | .20 | .50 |
| 123 | Chase Utley | .50 | 1.25 |
| 124 | Jacoby Ellsbury | .75 | 2.00 |
| 125 | Freddy Sanchez | .20 | .50 |
| 126 | Rocco Baldelli | .20 | .50 |
| 127 | Tom Gorzelanny | .20 | .50 |
| 128 | Adrian Gonzalez | .30 | .75 |
| 129 | Geovany Soto | .50 | 1.25 |
| 130 | Bobby Abreu | .20 | .50 |
| 131 | Albert Pujols | 1.00 | 2.50 |
| 132 | Chipper Jones | .60 | 1.50 |
| 133 | Jeremy Bonderman | .20 | .50 |
| 134 | B.J. Upton | .30 | .75 |
| 135 | Justin Verlander | .30 | .75 |
| 136 | Jeff Francis | .20 | .50 |
| 137 | A.J. Burnett | .20 | .50 |
| 138 | Travis Buck | .20 | .50 |
| 139 | Vernon Wells | .30 | .75 |
| 140 | Raul Ibanez | .20 | .50 |
| 141 | Ryan Zimmerman | .30 | .75 |
| 142 | John Smoltz | .50 | 1.25 |
| 143 | Carlos Lee | .20 | .50 |
| 144 | Chris Young | .20 | .50 |
| 145 | Francisco Liriano | .30 | .75 |
| 146 | Curt Schilling | .30 | .75 |
| 147 | Josh Beckett | .30 | .75 |
| 148 | Aramis Ramirez | .20 | .50 |
| 149 | Ronnie Belliard | .20 | .50 |
| 150 | Homer Bailey | .30 | .75 |
| 151 | Curtis Granderson | .20 | .50 |
| 152 | Ken Griffey Jr. | .75 | 2.00 |
| 153 | Kazuo Matsui | .20 | .50 |
| 154 | Brian Bannister | .20 | .50 |
| 155 | Joba Chamberlain | .60 | 1.50 |
| 156 | Tom Glavine | .30 | .75 |
| 157 | Carlos Beltran | .20 | .50 |
| 158 | Kelly Johnson | .20 | .50 |
| 159 | Rich Hill | .20 | .50 |
| 160 | Pat Burrell | .20 | .50 |
| 161 | Asdrubal Cabrera | .20 | .50 |
| 162 | Gary Sheffield | .20 | .50 |
| 163 | Greg Maddux | .60 | 1.50 |
| 164 | Eric Chavez | .20 | .50 |
| 165 | Chris Carpenter | .20 | .50 |
| 166 | Michael Young | .20 | .50 |
| 167 | Carlos Pena | .50 | 1.25 |
| 168 | Frank Thomas | .50 | 1.25 |
| 169 | Aaron Rowand | .20 | .50 |
| 170 | Yadier Molina | .30 | .75 |
| 171 | Luis Castillo | .20 | .50 |
| 172 | Ryan Theriot | .20 | .50 |
| 173 | Andre Ethier | .30 | .75 |
| 174 | Casey Kotchman | .20 | .50 |
| 175 | Rickie Weeks | .20 | .50 |
| 176 | Milton Bradley | .20 | .50 |
| 177 | Daniel Cabrera | .20 | .50 |
| 178 | Jo-Jo Reyes | .20 | .50 |
| 179 | Livan Hernandez | .20 | .50 |
| 180 | Hideki Okajima | .20 | .50 |
| 181 | Matt Kemp | .50 | 1.25 |
| 182 | Jonny Gomes | .20 | .50 |
| 183 | Billy Butler | .20 | .50 |
| 184 | Adam LaRoche | .20 | .50 |
| 185 | Brad Hawpe | .20 | .50 |
| 186 | Paul Maholm | .20 | .50 |
| 187 | Placido Polanco | .20 | .50 |
| 188 | Noah Lowry | .20 | .50 |
| 189 | Gregg Zaun | .20 | .50 |
| 190 | Nate McLouth | .20 | .50 |
| 191 | Edinson Volquez | .20 | .50 |
| 192 | Jeff Niemann (RC) | .60 | 1.50 |
| 193 | Evan Longoria RC | 6.00 | 15.00 |
| 194 | Adam Jones | .20 | .50 |
| 195 | Eugenio Velez RC | .60 | 1.50 |
| 196 | Joey Votto (RC) | 1.50 | 4.00 |
| 197 | Nick Blackburn RC | 1.00 | 2.50 |
| 198 | Harvey Garcia (RC) | .60 | 1.50 |
| 199 | Hiroki Kuroda RC | 1.00 | 2.50 |
| 200 | Elliot Johnson (RC) | .60 | 1.50 |
| 201 | Luis Mendoza (RC) | .60 | 1.50 |
| 202 | Alex Romero (RC) | .60 | 1.50 |
| 203 | Gregor Blanco (RC) | .60 | 1.50 |
| 204 | Rico Washington (RC) | .60 | 1.50 |
| 205 | Brian Bocock RC | .60 | 1.50 |
| 206 | Evan Meek RC | .60 | 1.50 |
| 207 | Stephen Holm RC | .60 | 1.50 |
| 208 | Matt Tupman RC | .60 | 1.50 |
| 209 | Fernando Hernandez RC | .60 | 1.50 |
| 210 | Randor Bierd RC | .60 | 1.50 |
| 211 | Blake DeWitt (RC) | 1.50 | 4.00 |
| 212 | Randy Wells RC | 1.00 | 2.50 |
| 213 | Wesley Wright RC | .60 | 1.50 |
| 214 | Clete Thomas RC | 1.00 | 2.50 |
| 215 | Kyle McClellan RC | .60 | 1.50 |
| 216 | Brian Bixler (RC) | .60 | 1.50 |
| 217 | Kazuo Fukumori RC | 1.00 | 2.50 |
| 218 | Burke Badenhop RC | 1.00 | 2.50 |
| 219 | Denard Span (RC) | 1.00 | 2.50 |
| 220 | Brian Bass (RC) | .60 | 1.50 |
| 221 | J.R. Towles AU RC | 4.00 | 10.00 |
| 222 | Felipe Paulino AU RC | 4.00 | 10.00 |
| 223 | Sam Fuld AU RC | 4.00 | 10.00 |
| 224 | Kevin Hart AU (RC) | 4.00 | 10.00 |
| 225 | Nyjer Morgan AU (RC) | 4.00 | 10.00 |
| 226 | Daric Barton AU (RC) | 4.00 | 10.00 |
| 227 | Armando Galarraga AU RC | 8.00 | 20.00 |
| 228 | Chin-Lung Hu AU RC | 6.00 | 15.00 |
| 229 | Buchholz AU (RC) EXCH | 10.00 | 25.00 |
| 230 | Rich Thompson AU RC | 4.00 | 10.00 |
| 231 | Brian Barton AU RC | 5.00 | 12.00 |
| 232 | Ross Ohlendorf AU RC | 4.00 | 10.00 |
| 233 | Masahide Kobayashi AU RC | 5.00 | 12.00 |
| 234 | Callix Crabbe AU (RC) | 4.00 | 10.00 |
| 235 | Matt Tolbert AU RC | 4.00 | 10.00 |
| 236 | Jayson Nix AU (RC) | 4.00 | 10.00 |
| 237 | Johnny Cueto AU RC | 10.00 | 25.00 |
| 238 | Evan Meek AU RC | 4.00 | 10.00 |
| 239 | Randy Wells AU (RC) | 6.00 | 15.00 |

## 2009 Topps Chrome

| | | | |
|---|---|---|---|
| | COMP.SET w/o AU's (220) | 50.00 | 100.00 |
| | COMMON CARD | .20 | .50 |
| | COMMON ROOKIE | .60 | 1.50 |
| | COMMON AUTO | 4.00 | 10.00 |
| | AUTO ODDS 1:2 HOBBY | | |
| | PRINT.PLATE ODDS 1:383 HOBBY | | |
| | AU PLATES 1:5330 HOBBY | | |
| | PLATE PRINT RUN 1 SET PER COLOR | | |
| | BLACK-CYAN-MAGENTA-YELLOW ISSUED | | |
| | NO PLATE PRICING DUE TO SCARCITY | | |
| 1 | Alex Rodriguez | .75 | 2.00 |
| 2 | Kerry Wood | .20 | .50 |
| 3 | Dan Uggla | .20 | .50 |
| 4 | Nate McLouth | .20 | .50 |
| 5 | Brad Lidge | .20 | .50 |
| 6 | Jon Lester | .30 | .75 |
| 7 | Mickey Mantle | 1.50 | 4.00 |
| 8 | Jason Giambi | .20 | .50 |
| 9 | Mike Lowell | .20 | .50 |
| 10 | Ken Griffey Jr. | .75 | 2.00 |
| 11 | Erick Aybar | .20 | .50 |
| 12 | Stephen Drew | .20 | .50 |
| 13 | Geoff Jenkins | .20 | .50 |
| 14 | Aubrey Huff | .20 | .50 |
| 15 | Kazuo Matsui | .20 | .50 |
| 16 | David Ortiz | .30 | .75 |
| 17 | Mariano Rivera | .30 | .75 |
| 18 | Jermaine Dye | .20 | .50 |
| 19 | Rich Harden | .20 | .50 |
| 20 | Brian McCann | .30 | .75 |
| 21 | Brad Hawpe | .20 | .50 |
| 22 | Justin Morneau | .30 | .75 |
| 23 | Akinori Iwamura | .30 | .75 |
| 24 | David Wright | .60 | 1.50 |
| 25 | Garrett Atkins | .20 | .50 |
| 26 | David DeJesus | .20 | .50 |
| 27 | Francisco Liriano | .20 | .50 |
| 28 | George Sherrill | .20 | .50 |
| 29 | Hideki Matsui | .50 | 1.25 |
| 30 | Chris Young | .20 | .50 |
| 31 | Kevin Youkilis | .30 | .75 |
| 32 | Mark Teixeira | .50 | 1.25 |
| 33 | Roy Oswalt | .30 | .75 |
| 34 | Orlando Hudson | .20 | .50 |
| 35 | Vladimir Guerrero | .50 | 1.25 |
| 36 | Juan Pierre | .20 | .50 |
| 37 | Carlos Delgado | .20 | .50 |
| 38 | Tim Hudson | .20 | .50 |
| 39 | Brandon Webb | .30 | .75 |
| 40 | Alex Gordon | .20 | .50 |
| 41 | Glen Perkins | .20 | .50 |
| 42 | Kosuke Fukudome | .50 | 1.25 |
| 43 | Ian Stewart | .20 | .50 |
| 44a | A.J. Pierzynski | .20 | .50 |
| 44b | Barack Obama SP | 6.00 | 15.00 |
| 45 | Roy Halladay | .30 | .75 |
| 46 | Carlos Pena | .30 | .75 |
| 47 | Evan Longoria | .75 | 2.00 |
| 48 | Matt Kemp | .50 | 1.25 |
| 49 | CC Sabathia | .30 | .75 |
| 50 | Yadier Molina | .30 | .75 |
| 51 | James Shields | .20 | .50 |
| 52 | Jeff Samardzija | .20 | .50 |
| 53 | Rafael Furcal | .20 | .50 |
| 54 | Cliff Lee | .30 | .75 |
| 55 | Daniel Murphy RC | 1.50 | 4.00 |
| 56 | Randy Johnson | .50 | 1.25 |
| 57 | Dan Uggla | .20 | .50 |
| 58 | Chien-Ming Wang | .50 | 1.25 |
| 59 | Zack Greinke | .30 | .75 |
| 60 | Tim Lincecum | .60 | 1.50 |
| 61 | Connor Jackson | .20 | .50 |
| 62 | Chase Utley | .50 | 1.25 |
| 63 | Andy Sonnanstine | .20 | .50 |
| 64 | Miguel Tejada | .30 | .75 |
| 65 | Geovany Soto | .30 | .75 |
| 66 | Jeremy Sowers | .20 | .50 |
| 67 | Ian Kinsler | .30 | .75 |
| 68 | Jay Bruce | .50 | 1.25 |
| 69 | Max Scherzer | .30 | .75 |
| 70 | Scott Rolen | .50 | 1.25 |
| 71 | Justin Upton | .30 | .75 |
| 72 | Xavier Nady | .20 | .50 |
| 73 | Erik Bedard | .20 | .50 |

|  |  | | |
|---|---|---|---|
| 74 | Chad Billingsley | .20 | .50 |
| 75 | Ryan Braun | .60 | 1.50 |
| 76 | Pat Burrell | .30 | .75 |
| 77 | Edgar Renteria | .20 | .50 |
| 78 | Joe Crede | .20 | .50 |
| 79 | Manny Ramirez | .50 | 1.25 |
| 80 | Carlos Zambrano | .20 | .50 |
| 81 | Hunter Pence | .30 | .75 |
| 82 | Grady Sizemore | .30 | .75 |
| 83 | Brian Roberts | .20 | .50 |
| 84 | Alex Rios | .20 | .50 |
| 85 | Joe Saunders | .20 | .50 |
| 86 | Albert Pujols | 1.25 | 3.00 |
| 87 | Derrek Lee | .30 | .75 |
| 88 | Ichiro Suzuki | .75 | 2.00 |
| 89 | Javier Vazquez | .20 | .50 |
| 90 | Johan Santana | .50 | 1.25 |
| 91 | Miguel Cabrera | .30 | .75 |
| 92 | Daisuke Matsuzaka | .75 | 2.00 |
| 93 | Chris Young | .20 | .50 |
| 94 | Joe Mauer | .50 | 1.25 |
| 95 | Stephen Drew | .20 | .50 |
| 96 | Justin Masterson | .30 | .75 |
| 97 | Dustin Pedroia | .60 | 1.50 |
| 98 | Derek Jeter | 1.25 | 3.00 |
| 99 | John Smoltz | .50 | 1.25 |
| 100 | Jason Varitek | .30 | .75 |
| 101 | Jorge Posada | .30 | .75 |
| 102 | Mark Buehrle | .20 | .50 |
| 103 | Bobby Abreu | .20 | .50 |
| 104 | Victor Martinez | .30 | .75 |
| 105 | Jeff Francis | .20 | .50 |
| 106 | Rickie Weeks | .20 | .50 |
| 107 | Carlos Quentin | .20 | .50 |
| 108 | Howie Kendrick | .20 | .50 |
| 109 | Aramis Ramirez | .20 | .50 |
| 110 | Jonathan Papelbon | .30 | .75 |
| 111 | Dan Haren | .20 | .50 |
| 112 | Barry Zito | .20 | .50 |
| 113 | Magglio Ordonez | .30 | .75 |
| 114 | Alfonso Soriano | .30 | .75 |
| 115 | Todd Helton | .30 | .75 |
| 116 | Troy Tulowitzki | .30 | .75 |
| 117 | Josh Beckett | .30 | .75 |
| 118 | Andy Pettitte | .30 | .75 |
| 119 | Hank Blalock | .20 | .50 |
| 120 | Curtis Granderson | .50 | 1.25 |
| 121 | Francisco Rodriguez | .30 | .75 |
| 122 | Carlos Lee | .20 | .50 |
| 123 | Gavin Floyd | .20 | .50 |
| 124 | Joe Nathan | .20 | .50 |
| 125 | Matt Holliday | .30 | .75 |
| 126 | Hanley Ramirez | .50 | 1.25 |
| 127 | Javier Valentin | .20 | .50 |
| 128 | John Maine | .20 | .50 |
| 129 | Jeremy Bonderman | .20 | .50 |
| 130 | Nick Markakis | .30 | .75 |
| 131 | Troy Glaus | .20 | .50 |
| 132 | Derek Lowe | .20 | .50 |
| 133 | Lance Berkman | .30 | .75 |
| 134 | Jered Weaver | .20 | .50 |
| 135 | Chipper Jones | .50 | 1.25 |
| 136 | Prince Fielder | .50 | 1.25 |
| 137 | Travis Hafner | .20 | .50 |
| 138 | Joba Chamberlain | .60 | 1.50 |
| 139 | Ryan Howard | .60 | 1.50 |
| 140 | Paul Konerko | .20 | .50 |
| 141 | Kenji Johjima | .30 | .75 |
| 142 | Yovani Gallardo | .30 | .75 |
| 143 | Adrian Gonzalez | .30 | .75 |
| 144 | Jimmy Rollins | .30 | .75 |
| 145 | Nick Swisher | .20 | .50 |
| 146 | Felix Hernandez | .30 | .75 |
| 147 | Garret Anderson | .20 | .50 |
| 148 | Russell Martin | .30 | .75 |
| 149 | Jason Bay | .30 | .75 |
| 150 | Fausto Carmona | .20 | .50 |
| 151 | Matt Garza | .20 | .50 |
| 152 | Matt Cain | .20 | .50 |
| 153 | Ryan Freel | .20 | .50 |
| 154 | Rocco Baldelli | .20 | .50 |
| 155 | Scott Kazmir | .30 | .75 |
| 156 | Alexei Ramirez | .30 | .75 |
| 157 | Adam Dunn | .30 | .75 |
| 158 | Johnny Damon | .30 | .75 |
| 159 | Jake Peavy | .30 | .75 |
| 160 | Jose Reyes | .50 | 1.25 |
| 161 | Rick Ankiel | .30 | .75 |
| 162 | Michael Young | .30 | .75 |
| 163 | Robinson Cano | .30 | .75 |
| 164 | Ryan Zimmerman | .30 | .75 |
| 165 | Jim Thome | .30 | .75 |
| 166 | A.J. Burnett | .30 | .75 |
| 167 | Joakim Soria | .20 | .50 |
| 168 | J.D. Drew | .20 | .50 |
| 169 | Cole Hamels | .50 | 1.25 |
| 170 | Jacoby Ellsbury | .50 | 1.25 |
| 171 | Travis Snider RC | 1.50 | 4.00 |
| 172 | Josh Outman RC | 1.00 | 2.50 |
| 173 | Dexter Fowler (RC) | 1.00 | 2.50 |
| 174 | Matt Tuiasosopo (RC) | .60 | 1.50 |
| 175 | Bobby Parnell RC | 1.00 | 2.50 |
| 176 | Jason Motte (RC) | .60 | 1.50 |
| 177 | James McDonald RC | 1.50 | 4.00 |
| 178 | Scott Lewis (RC) | .60 | 1.50 |
| 179 | George Kottaras (RC) | .60 | 1.50 |
| 180 | Phil Coke RC | 1.00 | 2.50 |
| 181 | Jordan Schafer (RC) | 1.00 | 2.50 |
| 182 | Joe Martinez RC | 1.00 | 2.50 |
| 183 | Trevor Crowe RC | 1.00 | 2.50 |
| 184 | Shairon Martis RC | 1.00 | 2.50 |
| 185 | Everth Cabrera RC | 1.00 | 2.50 |
| 186 | Trevor Cahill RC | 1.00 | 2.50 |
| 187 | Jesse Chavez RC | .60 | 1.50 |
| 188 | Josh Whitesell RC | 1.00 | 2.50 |
| 189 | Brian Duensing RC | 1.00 | 2.50 |
| 190 | Andrew Bailey RC | 1.00 | 2.50 |
| 191 | Ryan Perry RC | 1.50 | 4.00 |
| 192 | Brett Anderson RC | 1.00 | 2.50 |
| 193 | Ricky Romero (RC) | .60 | 1.50 |
| 194 | Elvis Andrus RC | 1.50 | 4.00 |
| 195 | Kenshin Kawakami RC | 1.50 | 4.00 |
| 196 | Colby Rasmus RC | 1.00 | 2.50 |
| 197 | David Patton RC | .60 | 1.50 |
| 198 | David Hernandez RC | 1.00 | 2.50 |
| 199 | David Freese RC | 1.50 | 4.00 |
| 200 | Rick Porcello RC | 2.50 | 6.00 |
| 201 | Fernando Martinez RC | 1.50 | 4.00 |
| 202 | Edwin Moreno (RC) | .60 | 1.50 |
| 203 | Koji Uehara RC | 1.50 | 4.00 |
| 204 | Jason Jaramillo RC | .60 | 1.50 |
| 205 | Ramiro Pena RC | 1.00 | 2.50 |
| 206 | Brad Nelson (RC) | .60 | 1.50 |
| 207 | Michael Hinckley (RC) | .60 | 1.50 |
| 208 | Ronald Belisario (RC) | .60 | 1.50 |
| 209 | Chris Jakubauskas RC | 1.00 | 2.50 |
| 210 | Hunter Jones RC | 1.00 | 2.50 |
| 211 | Walter Silva RC | 1.00 | 2.50 |
| 212 | Jordan Zimmermann RC | 1.50 | 4.00 |
| 213 | Andrew McCutchen (RC) | 1.50 | 4.00 |
| 214 | Gordon Beckham RC | 5.00 | 12.00 |
| 215 | Anthony Claggett RC | 1.00 | 2.50 |
| 216 | Mark Melancon RC | .60 | 1.50 |
| 217 | Brett Cecil RC | 1.00 | 2.50 |
| 218 | Derek Holland RC | 1.50 | 4.00 |
| 219 | Greg Golson (RC) | .60 | 1.50 |
| 220 | Bobby Scales RC | 1.00 | 2.50 |
| 221 | Jordan Schafer AU | 5.00 | 12.00 |
| 222 | Trevor Crowe AU | 4.00 | 10.00 |
| 223 | Ramiro Pena AU | 6.00 | 15.00 |
| 224 | Trevor Cahill AU | 6.00 | 15.00 |
| 225 | Ryan Perry AU | 8.00 | 20.00 |
| 226 | Brett Anderson AU | 8.00 | 20.00 |
| 227 | Elvis Andrus AU | 8.00 | 20.00 |
| 229 | Michael Bowden AU (RC) | 6.00 | 15.00 |
| 230 | David Freese AU | 4.00 | 10.00 |
| 231 | Nolan Reimold AU (RC) | 8.00 | 20.00 |
| 233 | Jason Jaramillo AU | 4.00 | 10.00 |
| 234 | Ricky Romero AU | 4.00 | 10.00 |
| 235 | Jordan Zimmermann AU | 5.00 | 12.00 |
| 236 | Derek Holland AU | 8.00 | 20.00 |
| 237 | George Kottaras AU | 4.00 | 10.00 |
| 239 | Sergio Escalona AU RC | 4.00 | 10.00 |
| 240 | Brian Duensing AU | 4.00 | 10.00 |
| 241 | Everth Cabrera AU | 6.00 | 15.00 |
| 242 | Andrew Bailey AU | 4.00 | 10.00 |
| 243 | Chris Jakubauskas AU | 4.00 | 10.00 |
| CL1 | Checklist Card | .20 | .50 |
| CL2 | Checklist Card | .20 | .50 |
| CL3 | Checklist Card | .20 | .50 |
| NNO1 | Tommy Hanson AU RC | 20.00 | 50.00 |
| NNO2 | Mark Melancon AU | 6.00 | 15.00 |
| NNO3 | Will Venable AU RC | 4.00 | 10.00 |

## 2004 Topps Cracker Jack

|  |  | | |
|---|---|---|---|
| | COMPLETE SET (250) | 125.00 | 200.00 |
| | COMP.SET w/o SP's (200) | 15.00 | 40.00 |
| | COMMON CARD | .15 | .40 |
| | COMMON SP | 1.50 | 4.00 |
| | COMMON SP RC | 1.50 | 4.00 |
| | SP STATED ODDS 1:3 | | |
| | SP CL: 226/229B/232/236A-236B | | |
| 1 | Jose Reyes SP | 1.50 | 4.00 |
| 2 | Edgar Renteria | .15 | .40 |
| 3A | Albert Pujols Portrait | .75 | 2.00 |
| 3B | Albert Pujols Swinging SP | 3.00 | 8.00 |
| 4 | Garret Anderson | .15 | .40 |
| 5 | Bobby Abreu | .15 | .40 |
| 6 | Andruw Jones | .25 | .60 |
| 7 | Jeff Kent | .15 | .40 |
| 8 | Magglio Ordonez | .15 | .40 |
| 9 | Kris Benson | .15 | .40 |
| 10 | Luis Gonzalez | .15 | .40 |
| 11 | Corey Patterson | .15 | .40 |
| 12 | Connie Mack MG | .15 | .40 |
| 13 | Vernon Wells SP | 1.50 | 4.00 |
| 14 | Jim Edmonds | .15 | .40 |
| 15 | Bret Boone | .15 | .40 |
| 16 | Travis Lee | .15 | .40 |
| 17 | Alex Rodriguez Yanks SP | 3.00 | 8.00 |
| 18 | Erubiel Durazo | .15 | .40 |
| 19 | Brett Myers | .15 | .40 |
| 20 | Scott Rolen SP | 2.00 | 5.00 |
| 21 | Paul Lo Duca | .15 | .40 |
| 22 | Geoff Jenkins | .15 | .40 |
| 23 | Charles Comiskey | .15 | .40 |
| 24 | Cliff Floyd | .15 | .40 |
| 25A | Jim Thome Batting | .25 | .60 |
| 25B | Jim Thome Fielding SP | 2.00 | 5.00 |
| 26 | Russ Ortiz | .15 | .40 |
| 27 | Bill Mueller | .15 | .40 |
| 28 | Kenny Lofton | .15 | .40 |
| 29 | Jay Gibbons | .15 | .40 |
| 30 | Ken Griffey Jr. | .60 | 1.50 |
| 31 | Jeff Bagwell | .25 | .60 |
| 32 | Jose Lima | .15 | .40 |
| 33 | Brad Radke | .15 | .40 |
| 34 | Ramon Hernandez | .15 | .40 |
| 35 | Brian Giles SP | 1.50 | 4.00 |
| 36 | Jeremy Bonderman | .15 | .40 |
| 37 | Jerome Williams | .15 | .40 |
| 38 | Rafael Palmeiro | .25 | .60 |
| 39 | Scott Podsednik | .15 | .40 |
| 40 | Rafael Furcal | .15 | .40 |
| 41 | Roy Oswalt | .15 | .40 |
| 42 | Orlando Hudson | .15 | .40 |
| 43 | Todd Helton | .25 | .60 |
| 44 | Kerry Wood | .15 | .40 |
| 45 | Tom Glavine | .25 | .60 |
| 46 | David Eckstein | .15 | .40 |
| 47 | Trot Nixon | .15 | .40 |
| 48 | Preston Wilson | .15 | .40 |
| 49 | Bernie Williams | .25 | .60 |
| 50 | Eric Gagne SP | 1.50 | 4.00 |
| 51 | Ichiro Suzuki SP | 3.00 | 8.00 |
| 52 | Juan Gonzalez | .25 | .60 |
| 53 | Torii Hunter | .15 | .40 |
| 54 | Bartolo Colon | .15 | .40 |
| 55A | Dick Hoblitzel ERR | .15 | .40 |
| 55B | Dick Hoblitzell COR | .15 | .40 |
| 56 | Al Leiter | .15 | .40 |
| 57 | Johnny Damon | .25 | .60 |
| 58 | Larry Walker | .15 | .40 |
| 59 | Brian Jordan | .15 | .40 |
| 60 | Richie Sexson SP | 1.50 | 4.00 |
| 61 | Orlando Cabrera | .15 | .40 |

| Card | Lo | Hi |
|---|---|---|
| 62 Jason Phillips | .15 | .40 |
| 63 Phil Nevin | .15 | .40 |
| 64 John Olerud | .15 | .40 |
| 65 Miguel Tejada | .15 | .40 |
| 66A Nap La Joie ERR | .40 | 1.00 |
| 66B Nap Lajoie COR | .40 | 1.00 |
| 67 C.C. Sabathia | .15 | .40 |
| 68 Ty Wigginton | .15 | .40 |
| 69 Troy Glaus | .15 | .40 |
| 70 Mike Piazza | .40 | 1.50 |
| 71 Craig Biggio | .25 | .60 |
| 72 Cristian Guzman | .15 | .40 |
| 73 Dmitri Young | .15 | .40 |
| 74 Roger Clemens | .60 | 1.50 |
| 75 Runelvys Hernandez | .15 | .40 |
| 76 Nomar Garciaparra | .60 | 1.50 |
| 77 Mark Mulder | .15 | .40 |
| 78 Derek Lowe | .15 | .40 |
| 79 Paul Konerko | .15 | .40 |
| 80A Sammy Sosa SP | 2.00 | 5.00 |
| 80B Felix Pie SP | 2.00 | 5.00 |
| 81 Vladimir Guerrero | .40 | 1.00 |
| 82 Xavier Nady | .15 | .40 |
| 83 Joel Pineiro | .15 | .40 |
| 84 Chipper Jones | .40 | 1.00 |
| 85 Manny Ramirez | .25 | .60 |
| 86A Burt Shotten ERR | .15 | .40 |
| 86B Burt Shotten COR | .15 | .40 |
| 87 Raul Ibanez SP | 1.50 | 4.00 |
| 88 Eric Chavez | .15 | .40 |
| 89 Frank Catalanotto | .15 | .40 |
| 90 Dontrelle Willis | .25 | .80 |
| 91 Roy Halladay | .15 | .40 |
| 92 Jermaine Dye | .15 | .40 |
| 93 Jason Kendall | .15 | .40 |
| 94 Jacque Jones | .15 | .40 |
| 95A Gary Sheffield Braves | .15 | .40 |
| 95B Gary Sheffield Yanks SP | 2.00 | 5.00 |
| 96 Mike Lieberthal | .15 | .40 |
| 97 Adam Dunn | .15 | .40 |
| 98 Carl Crawford | .15 | .40 |
| 99 Reggie Sanders | .15 | .40 |
| 100 Mark Prior SP | 2.00 | 5.00 |
| 101 Luis Matos | .15 | .40 |
| 102 Barry Zito | .15 | .40 |
| 103 Randy Johnson | .40 | 1.00 |
| 104A Kevin Brown | .15 | .40 |
| 104B Edwin Jackson SP | 1.50 | 4.00 |
| 105 Pat Burrell | .15 | .40 |
| 106 Steve Finley | .15 | .40 |
| 107 Moises Alou | .15 | .40 |
| 108 David Ortiz SP | 2.50 | 6.00 |
| 109 Austin Kearns SP | 1.50 | 4.00 |
| 110 Carlos Beltran | .15 | .40 |
| 111 Shawn Green | .15 | .40 |
| 112 Javier Vazquez | .15 | .40 |
| 113 Hideo Nomo | .40 | 1.00 |
| 114 Kazuhisa Ishii | .15 | .40 |
| 115 Corey Koskie | .15 | .40 |
| 116 Kevin Millwood | .15 | .40 |
| 117 Randy Wolf | .15 | .40 |
| 118 Darin Erstad | .15 | .40 |
| 119 Fernando Vina | .15 | .40 |
| 120 Pedro Martinez | .25 | .60 |
| 121 Melvin Mora | .15 | .40 |
| 122 Carl Everett | .15 | .40 |
| 123 Matt Morris | .15 | .40 |
| 124 Greg Maddux | .60 | 1.50 |
| 125 Jason Schmidt | .15 | .40 |
| 126 Mark Teixeira SP | 2.00 | 5.00 |
| 127 Randy Winn | .15 | .40 |
| 128 Rich Aurilia | .15 | .40 |
| 129 Vicente Padilla | .15 | .40 |
| 130 Tim Hudson | .15 | .40 |
| 131 Marlon Byrd | .15 | .40 |
| 132 Jae Weong Seo | .15 | .40 |
| 133 Branch Rickey MG | .15 | .40 |
| 134 A.J. Pierzynski | .15 | .40 |
| 135 Ryan Klesko | .15 | .40 |
| 136 Eric Hinske | .15 | .40 |
| 137 Mike Cameron | .15 | .40 |
| 138 Roberto Alomar | .25 | .60 |
| 139 Jarrod Washburn | .15 | .40 |
| 140A Curt Schilling D'backs | .15 | .40 |
| 140B Curt Schilling Sox SP | 2.00 | 5.00 |
| 141 Omar Vizquel | .25 | .60 |
| 142 Mike Sweeney | .15 | .40 |
| 143 Wade Miller | .15 | .40 |
| 144 Jose Vidro | .15 | .40 |
| 145 Rich Harden SP | 1.50 | 4.00 |
| 146 Eric Munson | .15 | .40 |
| 147 Lance Berkman | .15 | .40 |
| 148 Mark Buehrle | .15 | .40 |
| 149 Carlos Delgado | .15 | .40 |
| 150 Sean Burroughs | .15 | .40 |
| 151 Kevin Millar | .15 | .40 |
| 152 Frank Thomas | .40 | 1.00 |
| 153 Adrian Beltre | .15 | .40 |
| 154 Shannon Stewart | .15 | .40 |
| 155 Johan Santana | .40 | 1.00 |
| 156 Edgardo Alfonzo | .15 | .40 |
| 157 Jose Cruz Jr. | .15 | .40 |
| 158 Sidney Ponson | .15 | .40 |
| 159 Edgar Martinez | .25 | .60 |
| 160 Jamie Moyer | .15 | .40 |
| 161 Tony Batista | .15 | .40 |
| 162 Wes Helms | .15 | .40 |
| 163 Brandon Webb SP | 1.50 | 4.00 |
| 164 Gil Meche | .15 | .40 |
| 165 Marcus Giles SP | 1.50 | 4.00 |
| 166 Angel Berroa SP | 1.50 | 4.00 |
| 167 Rocco Baldelli SP | 1.50 | 4.00 |
| 168 Michael Young | .15 | .40 |
| 169 Esteban Loaiza | .15 | .40 |
| 170 Casey Blake | .15 | .40 |
| 171 Jody Gerut | .15 | .40 |
| 172 Bo Hart SP | 1.50 | 4.00 |
| 173 Kelvim Escobar | .15 | .40 |
| 174 Aaron Guiel | .15 | .40 |
| 175 Javy Lopez SP | 1.50 | 4.00 |
| 176 Aubry Huff | .15 | .40 |
| 177 Hank Blalock | .15 | .40 |
| 178 Edwin Jackson | .15 | .40 |
| 179 Delmon Young SP | 2.00 | 5.00 |
| 180 Bobby Jenks | .15 | .40 |
| 181 Felix Pie | .25 | .60 |
| 182 Jeremy Reed SP | 1.50 | 4.00 |
| 183 Aaron Hill | .15 | .40 |
| 184 Casey Kotchman SP | 1.50 | 4.00 |
| 185 Grady Sizemore | .40 | 1.00 |
| 186 Joe Mauer SP | 2.00 | 5.00 |
| 187 Ryan Harvey | .15 | .40 |
| 188 Neal Cotts | .15 | .40 |
| 189 Victor Martinez | .15 | .40 |
| 190 Rene Reyes | .15 | .40 |
| 191 Eric Duncan | .15 | .40 |
| 192 B.J. Upton SP | 2.00 | 5.00 |
| 193 Khalil Greene SP | 2.00 | 5.00 |
| 194 Bobby Crosby | .15 | .40 |
| 195 Rickie Weeks SP | 1.50 | 4.00 |
| 196 Zack Greinke SP | 1.50 | 4.00 |
| 197 Laynce Nix | .15 | .40 |
| 198 Vito Chiaravalloti SP RC | 1.50 | 4.00 |
| 199 Estee Harris RC | .40 | 1.00 |
| 200 Jon Knott SP RC | 1.50 | 4.00 |
| 201 Dioner Navarro RC | .30 | .75 |
| 202 Craig Ansman RC | .30 | .75 |
| 203 Travis Blackley RC | .75 | .75 |
| 204 Yadier Molina RC | .75 | 2.00 |
| 205 Rodney Choy Foo RC | .20 | .50 |
| 206 Kyle Sleeth SP RC | 2.00 | 5.00 |
| 207 Jeff Allison RC | .30 | .75 |
| 208 Josh Labandeira RC | .30 | .75 |
| 209 Lastings Milledge SP RC | 3.00 | 8.00 |
| 210 Rudy Guillen SP RC | 2.00 | 5.00 |
| 211 Blake Hawksworth SP RC | 2.00 | 5.00 |
| 212 David Aardsma RC | .40 | 1.00 |
| 213 Shawn Hill RC | .30 | .75 |
| 214 Erick Aybar RC | 2.00 | 5.00 |
| 215 Ervin Santana RC | .75 | 2.00 |
| 216 Tim Stauffer SP RC | 2.00 | 5.00 |
| 217 Merkin Valdez RC | .40 | 1.00 |
| 218 Jack McKeon MG | .15 | .40 |
| 219 Jeff Conine | .15 | .40 |
| 220 Josh Beckett SP | 1.50 | 4.00 |
| 221 Luis Castillo | .15 | .40 |
| 222 Mike Lowell | .15 | .40 |
| 223 Juan Pierre | .15 | .40 |
| 224A Ivan Rodriguez Marlins | .25 | .60 |
| 224B Ivan Rodriguez Tigers SP | 1.50 | 4.00 |
| 225 A.J. Burnett | .15 | .40 |
| 226 Miguel Cabrera SP | 2.00 | 5.00 |
| 227 Jeffrey Loria | .15 | .40 |
| 228 Jose Torre MG | .25 | .60 |
| 229A Jason Giambi Portrait | .15 | .40 |
| 229B Jason Giambi Fielding SP | 1.50 | 4.00 |
| 230 Aaron Boone | .15 | .40 |
| 231 Jose Contreras | .15 | .40 |
| 232 Derek Jeter SP | 3.00 | 8.00 |
| 233 Ruben Sierra | .15 | .40 |
| 234 Mike Mussina | .25 | .60 |
| 235 Mariano Rivera | .40 | 1.00 |
| 236A Jorge Posada SP | 2.00 | 5.00 |
| 236B Dioner Navarro SP | 2.00 | 5.00 |
| 237 Alfonso Soriano | .15 | .40 |
| NNO Alex Rodriguez Yanks | 1.25 | 3.00 |
| VB Vintage Buyback | | |

## 2005 Topps Cracker Jack

ALEX RODRIGUEZ

| | Lo | Hi |
|---|---|---|
| COMPLETE SET (250) | 100.00 | 200.00 |
| COMP SET w/o SP's (200) | 15.00 | 40.00 |
| SP STATED ODDS 1:3 HOBBY/RETAIL | | |
| SP CL: 1/38/4/6/11/13/21/26/30/31/41/51 | | |
| SP CL: 56/60B/71/75A/75B/84/85B/106/110 | | |
| SP CL: 111/112/126/135A/135B/146/151/156 | | |
| SP CL: 164B/166/176/181/186/191/196/201 | | |
| SP CL: 211/216/221A/221B/225/226/228B | | |
| SP CL: 231/235/236A/236B | | |
| 1 David Wright SP | 3.00 | 8.00 |
| 2 Rafael Furcal | .15 | .40 |
| 3A Alex Rodriguez Portrait | .60 | 1.50 |
| 3B Alex Rodriguez Fielding SP | 2.50 | 6.00 |
| 4 Victor Martinez SP | 1.50 | 4.00 |
| 5 Ken Griffey Jr. | .60 | 1.50 |
| 6 Bobby Crosby SP | 1.50 | 4.00 |
| 7 Ivan Rodriguez | .25 | .60 |
| 8 Darin Erstad | .15 | .40 |
| 9 Javy Lopez | .15 | .40 |
| 10 Brian Giles | .15 | .40 |
| 11 Aaron Rowand SP | 1.50 | 4.00 |
| 12 Joe Torre MG | .25 | .60 |
| 13 Zack Greinke SP | 1.50 | 4.00 |
| 14 Shannon Stewart | .15 | .40 |
| 15 Jack Wilson | .15 | .40 |
| 16 Jose Vidro | .15 | .40 |
| 17 Josh Beckett | .15 | .40 |
| 18 Barry Zito | .15 | .40 |
| 19 Bret Boone | .15 | .40 |
| 20 Greg Maddux | .60 | 1.50 |
| 21 Carl Crawford SP | 1.50 | 4.00 |
| 22 Mark Teixeira | .25 | .60 |
| 23 Jason Schmidt | .15 | .40 |
| 24 Kazuhisa Ishii | .15 | .40 |
| 25 Mike Piazza | .40 | 1.00 |
| 26 Daniel Cabrera SP | 1.50 | 4.00 |
| 27 Mike Lieberthal | .15 | .40 |
| 28 Gil Meche | .15 | .40 |
| 29 Phil Nevin | .15 | .40 |
| 30 Adrian Beltre SP | 1.50 | 4.00 |
| 31 Chipper Jones SP | 2.00 | 5.00 |
| 32 Zach Day | .15 | .40 |
| 33 Ben Sheets | .15 | .40 |
| 34 Carlos Zambrano | .15 | .40 |
| 35 Melvin Mora | .15 | .40 |
| 36 Joe Mauer | .40 | 1.00 |
| 37 Ken Harvey | .15 | .40 |
| 38 Bernie Williams | .15 | .40 |
| 39 Mike Maroth | .15 | .40 |
| 40 Eric Chavez | .15 | .40 |
| 41 Matt Lawton SP | 1.50 | 4.00 |
| 42 Ray Durham | .15 | .40 |
| 43 Vernon Wells | .15 | .40 |
| 44 Mike Lowell | .15 | .40 |
| 45 Jim Thome | .25 | .60 |
| 46 Joel Pineiro | .15 | .40 |
| 47 Lance Berkman | .15 | .40 |
| 48 Ryan Klesko | .15 | .40 |
| 49 Adam Dunn | .15 | .40 |

|  |  | | |
|---|---|---|---|
| 50 | Vladimir Guerrero | .40 | 1.00 |
| 51 | Eric Gagne SP | 1.50 | 4.00 |
| 52 | Richie Sexson | .15 | .40 |
| 53 | Javier Vazquez | .15 | .40 |
| 54 | Roy Oswalt | .15 | .40 |
| 55 | Carlos Delgado | .15 | .40 |
| 56 | John Buck SP | 1.50 | 4.00 |
| 57 | Kenny Rogers | .15 | .40 |
| 58 | Sidney Ponson | .15 | .40 |
| 59 | Vicente Padilla | .15 | .40 |
| 60A | Mark Prior Leg Up | .25 | .60 |
| 60B | Mark Prior Portrait SP | 2.00 | 5.00 |
| 61 | A.J. Pierzynski | .15 | .40 |
| 62 | Aubrey Huff | .15 | .40 |
| 63 | Shea Hillenbrand | .15 | .40 |
| 64 | Carlos Guillen | .15 | .40 |
| 65 | Lyle Overbay | .15 | .40 |
| 66 | Al Leiter | .15 | .40 |
| 67 | Eric Hinske | .15 | .40 |
| 68 | Laynce Nix | .15 | .40 |
| 69 | Scott Hairston | .15 | .40 |
| 70 | Roger Clemens | .60 | 1.50 |
| 71 | Cesar Izturis SP | 1.50 | 4.00 |
| 72 | Shawn Green | .15 | .40 |
| 73 | Marcus Giles | .15 | .40 |
| 74 | Rafael Palmeiro | .25 | .60 |
| 75A | Gary Sheffield SP | 1.50 | 4.00 |
| 75B | Melky Cabrera SP | 3.00 | 8.00 |
| 76 | Juan Pierre | .15 | .40 |
| 77 | Pat Burrell | .15 | .40 |
| 78 | Sean Burroughs | .15 | .40 |
| 79 | Frank Thomas | .40 | 1.00 |
| 80 | Andruw Jones | .25 | .50 |
| 81 | C.C. Sabathia | .15 | .40 |
| 82 | Jeff Bagwell | .25 | .60 |
| 83 | Tom Glavine | .15 | .40 |
| 84 | Craig Wilson SP | 1.50 | 4.00 |
| 85A | Johan Santana Throwing | .40 | 1.00 |
| 85B | Johan Santana Portrait SP | 2.50 | 6.00 |
| 86 | Raul Ibanez | .15 | .40 |
| 87 | Sean Casey | .15 | .40 |
| 88 | Bucky Jacobsen | .15 | .40 |
| 89 | B.J. Upton | .25 | .60 |
| 90 | Bobby Abreu | .15 | .40 |
| 91 | Geoff Jenkins | .15 | .40 |
| 92 | Troy Glaus | .15 | .40 |
| 93 | Dontrelle Willis | .15 | .40 |
| 94 | Jose Lima | .15 | .40 |
| 95 | Rocco Baldelli | .15 | .40 |
| 96 | Aramis Ramirez | .15 | .40 |
| 97 | Paul Lo Duca | .15 | .40 |
| 98 | Torii Hunter | .15 | .40 |
| 99 | Jay Payton | .15 | .40 |
| 100 | Carlos Beltran | .15 | .40 |
| 101 | Jarel Wright | .15 | .40 |
| 102 | Jason Bay | .15 | .40 |
| 103 | Cliff Floyd | .15 | .40 |
| 104 | Mike Sweeney | .15 | .40 |
| 105 | Sammy Sosa | .40 | 1.00 |
| 106 | Khalil Greene SP | 2.00 | 5.00 |
| 107 | David DeJesus | .15 | .40 |
| 108 | Jermaine Dye | .15 | .40 |
| 109 | Miguel Cabrera | .25 | .60 |
| 110 | Miguel Tejada SP | 1.50 | 4.00 |
| 111 | Johnny Estrada SP | 1.50 | 4.00 |
| 112 | Ronnie Belliard SP | 1.50 | 4.00 |
| 113 | Austin Kearns | .15 | .40 |
| 114 | Erubiel Durazo | .15 | .40 |
| 115 | Preston Wilson | .15 | .40 |
| 116 | Hideo Nomo | .40 | 1.00 |
| 117 | Dmitri Young | .15 | .40 |
| 118 | Jon Lieber | .15 | .40 |
| 119 | Derrek Lee | .25 | .60 |
| 120 | Todd Helton | .25 | .60 |
| 121 | Omar Vizquel | .25 | .60 |
| 122 | Wily Mo Pena | .15 | .40 |
| 123 | J.D. Drew | .15 | .40 |
| 124 | Matt Holliday | .20 | .50 |
| 125 | Ichiro Suzuki | .75 | 2.00 |
| 126 | Mark Buehrle SP | 1.50 | 4.00 |
| 127 | Barry Bonds | 1.00 | 2.50 |
| 128 | Jeff Kent | .15 | .40 |
| 129 | Kerry Wood | .15 | .40 |
| 130 | Mariano Rivera | .40 | 1.00 |
| 131 | Nick Johnson | .15 | .40 |
| 132 | Randy Winn | .15 | .40 |
| 133 | Phil Garner MG | .15 | .40 |
| 134 | Jose Reyes | .15 | .40 |

|  |  | | |
|---|---|---|---|
| 135A | Michael Young SP | 1.50 | 4.00 |
| 135B | Ian Kinsler SP | 4.00 | 10.00 |
| 136 | Jose Contreras | .15 | .40 |
| 137 | Oliver Perez | .15 | .40 |
| 138 | Roy Halladay | .15 | .40 |
| 139 | Kevin Millwood | .15 | .40 |
| 140 | Jorge Posada | .25 | .60 |
| 141 | Mike Cameron | .15 | .40 |
| 142 | Edgardo Alfonzo | .15 | .40 |
| 143 | Chris Shelton | .25 | .60 |
| 144 | Luis Castillo | .15 | .40 |
| 145 | Alfonso Soriano | .15 | .40 |
| 146 | Ryan Drese SP | 1.50 | 4.00 |
| 147 | Mark Mulder | .15 | .40 |
| 148 | Jason Giambi | .15 | .40 |
| 149 | Travis Hafner | .15 | .40 |
| 150 | Randy Johnson | .40 | 1.00 |
| 151 | Paul Konerko SP | 1.50 | 4.00 |
| 152 | Mike Mussina | .25 | .60 |
| 153 | Brad Wilkerson | .15 | .40 |
| 154 | Tim Hudson | .15 | .40 |
| 155 | Garret Anderson | .15 | .40 |
| 156 | Chase Utley SP | 2.00 | 5.00 |
| 157 | Jamie Moyer | .15 | .40 |
| 158 | Scott Kazmir | .15 | .40 |
| 159 | Brett Myers | .15 | .40 |
| 160 | Kazuo Matsui | .15 | .40 |
| 161 | Orlando Hudson | .15 | .40 |
| 162 | Luis Gonzalez | .15 | .40 |
| 163 | Kevin Youkilis | .15 | .40 |
| 164A | Jason Kendall | .15 | .40 |
| 164B | Landon Powell SP | 2.00 | 5.00 |
| 165 | Hank Blalock | .15 | .40 |
| 166 | Mark Loretta SP | 1.50 | 4.00 |
| 167 | Miguel Cairo | .15 | .40 |
| 168 | Corey Patterson | .15 | .40 |
| 169 | Victor Zambrano | .15 | .40 |
| 170 | Magglio Ordonez | .15 | .40 |
| 171 | J.T. Snow | .15 | .40 |
| 172 | Randy Wolf | .15 | .40 |
| 173 | Rich Harden | .15 | .40 |
| 174 | Bartolo Colon | .15 | .40 |
| 175 | Derek Jeter | .75 | 2.00 |
| 176 | Casey Kotchman SP | 1.50 | 4.00 |
| 177 | Val Majewski | .15 | .40 |
| 178 | Grady Sizemore | .25 | .60 |
| 179 | Rickie Weeks | .15 | .40 |
| 180 | Robinson Cano | .25 | .60 |
| 181 | Nick Swisher SP | 1.50 | 4.00 |
| 182 | Ryan Howard | 1.00 | 2.50 |
| 183 | John Van Benschoten | .15 | .40 |
| 184 | Delmon Young | .25 | .60 |
| 185 | Aaron Hill | .15 | .40 |
| 186 | Chris Burke SP | 1.50 | 4.00 |
| 187 | Merkin Valdez | .15 | .40 |
| 188 | Jeremy Reed | .15 | .40 |
| 189 | Conor Jackson | .25 | .60 |
| 190 | Mark Teahen | .15 | .40 |
| 191 | Joey Gathright SP | 1.50 | 4.00 |
| 192 | Gavin Floyd | .15 | .40 |
| 193 | Joe Blanton | .15 | .40 |
| 194 | Jason Kubel | .15 | .40 |
| 195 | Jeff Francis | .15 | .40 |
| 196 | Angel Guzman SP | 1.50 | 4.00 |
| 197 | Dallas McPherson | .15 | .40 |
| 198 | Melky Cabrera RC | .75 | 2.00 |
| 199 | Jake Dittler | .20 | .50 |
| 200 | Elvys Quezada RC | .30 | .75 |
| 201 | Ian Kinsler SP RC | 4.00 | 10.00 |
| 202 | Nate McLouth RC | .40 | 1.00 |
| 203 | Chris Seddon RC | .30 | .75 |
| 204 | Chad Orvella RC | .30 | .75 |
| 205 | Ian Bladergroen RC | .40 | 1.00 |
| 206 | James Jurries SP RC | 2.00 | 5.00 |
| 207 | Landon Powell RC | .40 | 1.00 |
| 208 | Eric Nielsen RC | .30 | .75 |
| 209 | Chris Roberson RC | .30 | .75 |
| 210 | Andre Ethier RC | 2.00 | 5.00 |
| 211 | Chris Denorfia SP RC | 2.00 | 5.00 |
| 212 | Darren Fenster RC | .30 | .75 |
| 213 | Jeremy West RC | .40 | 1.00 |
| 214 | Sean Marshall RC | 1.00 | 2.50 |
| 215 | Ryan Sweeney RC | .50 | 1.25 |
| 216 | Steve Doetsch SP RC | 2.00 | 5.00 |
| 217 | Kevin Melillo RC | .40 | 1.00 |
| 218 | Chip Cannon RC | .40 | 1.00 |
| 219 | Tony La Russa MG | .15 | .40 |
| 220 | Chris Carpenter | .15 | .40 |

|  |  | | |
|---|---|---|---|
| 221A | Edgar Renteria Sox SP | 1.50 | 4.00 |
| 221B | Edgar Renteria Cards SP | 1.50 | 4.00 |
| 222 | Albert Pujols | .75 | 2.00 |
| 223 | Jim Edmonds | .15 | .40 |
| 224 | Jason Marquis | .15 | .40 |
| 225 | Scott Rolen SP | 2.00 | 5.00 |
| 226 | Larry Walker SP | 2.00 | 5.00 |
| 227 | Matt Morris | .15 | .40 |
| 228A | Mike Matheny Giants | .15 | .40 |
| 228B | Mike Matheny Cards SP | 1.50 | 4.00 |
| 229 | Jeromy Burnitz | .15 | .40 |
| 230 | Terry Francona MG | .25 | .60 |
| 231 | Johnny Damon SP | 2.00 | 5.00 |
| 232 | Keith Foulke | .15 | .40 |
| 233 | Trot Nixon | .15 | .40 |
| 234 | Manny Ramirez | .25 | .60 |
| 235 | David Ortiz SP | 2.00 | 5.00 |
| 236A | Pedro Martinez Sox SP | 2.00 | 5.00 |
| 236B | Pedro Martinez Mets SP | 2.00 | 5.00 |
| 237 | Curt Schilling | .25 | .60 |
| 238 | Kevin Millar | .15 | .40 |
| 239 | Bill Mueller | .15 | .40 |
| 240 | Mark Bellhorn | .15 | .40 |
| NNO | Josh Beckett NNO SP | 1.50 | 4.00 |

### 2001 Topps Heritage

| | | |
|---|---|---|
| COMP. MASTER SET (487) | 350.00 | 500.00 |
| COMPLETE SET (407) | 250.00 | 400.00 |
| COMP. BASIC SET (230) | 40.00 | 80.00 |
| COMMON CARD (81-310) | .20 | .50 |
| COMMON CARD (1-80) | 1.00 | 2.50 |
| COMMON CARD (311-407) | 1.00 | 2.50 |
| 1 | Kris Benson | 1.00 | 2.50 |
| 1 | Kris Benson Black | 1.00 | 2.50 |
| 2 | Brian Jordan | 1.00 | 2.50 |
| 2 | Brian Jordan Black | 1.00 | 2.50 |
| 3 | Fernando Vina | 1.00 | 2.50 |
| 3 | Fernando Vina Black | 1.00 | 2.50 |
| 4 | Mike Sweeney | 1.00 | 2.50 |
| 4 | Mike Sweeney Black | 1.00 | 2.50 |
| 5 | Rafael Palmeiro | 1.00 | 2.50 |
| 5 | Rafael Palmeiro Black | 1.00 | 2.50 |
| 6 | Paul O'Neill | 1.00 | 2.50 |
| 6 | Paul O'Neill Black | 1.00 | 2.50 |
| 7 | Todd Helton | 1.00 | 2.50 |
| 7 | Todd Helton Black | 1.00 | 2.50 |
| 8 | Ramiro Mendoza | 1.00 | 2.50 |
| 8 | Ramiro Mendoza Black | 1.00 | 2.50 |
| 9 | Kevin Millwood | 1.00 | 2.50 |
| 9 | Kevin Millwood Black | 1.00 | 2.50 |
| 10 | Chuck Knoblauch | 1.00 | 2.50 |
| 10 | Chuck Knoblauch Black | 1.00 | 2.50 |
| 11 | Derek Jeter | 4.00 | 10.00 |
| 11 | Derek Jeter Black | 4.00 | 10.00 |
| 12 | Alex Rodriguez Rangers | 2.50 | 6.00 |
| 12A | Rod Black Rangers | 2.50 | 6.00 |
| 13 | Geoff Jenkins | 1.00 | 2.50 |
| 13 | Geoff Jenkins Black | 1.00 | 2.50 |
| 14 | David Justice | 1.00 | 2.50 |
| 14 | David Justice Black | 1.00 | 2.50 |
| 15 | David Cone | 1.00 | 2.50 |
| 15 | David Cone Black | 1.00 | 2.50 |
| 16 | Andres Galarraga | 1.00 | 2.50 |
| 16 | Andres Galarraga Black | 1.00 | 2.50 |
| 17 | Garret Anderson | 1.00 | 2.50 |
| 17 | Garret Anderson Black | 1.00 | 2.50 |
| 18 | Roger Cedeno | 1.00 | 2.50 |
| 18 | Roger Cedeno Black | 1.00 | 2.50 |
| 19 | Randy Velarde | 1.00 | 2.50 |
| 19 | Randy Velarde Black | 1.00 | 2.50 |
| 20 | Carlos Delgado | 1.00 | 2.50 |
| 20 | Carlos Delgado Black | 1.00 | 2.50 |
| 21 | Quilvio Veras | 1.00 | 2.50 |
| 21 | Quilvio Veras Black | 1.00 | 2.50 |

|  | | |  | | |  | | |
|---|---|---|---|---|---|---|---|---|
| 22 Jose Vidro | 1.00 | 2.50 | 66 Cliff Floyd | 1.00 | 2.50 | 139 Mike Stodolka | .20 | .50 |
| 22 Jose Vidro Black | 1.00 | 2.50 | 66 Cliff Floyd Black | 1.00 | 2.50 | 140 Milton Bradley | .25 | .60 |
| 23 Corey Patterson | 1.00 | 2.50 | 67 Tony Batista | 1.00 | 2.50 | 141 Curt Schilling | .25 | .60 |
| 23 Corey Patterson Black | 1.00 | 2.50 | 67 Tony Batista Black | 1.00 | 2.50 | 142 Sandy Alomar Jr. | .20 | .50 |
| 24 Jorge Posada | 1.00 | 2.50 | 68 Jeff Bagwell | 1.00 | 2.50 | 143 Brent Mayne | .20 | .50 |
| 24 Jorge Posada Black | 1.00 | 2.50 | 68 Jeff Bagwell Black | 1.00 | 2.50 | 144 Todd Jones | .20 | .50 |
| 25 Eddie Perez | 1.00 | 2.50 | 69 Billy Wagner | 1.00 | 2.50 | 145 Charles Johnson | .25 | .60 |
| 25 Eddie Perez Black | 1.00 | 2.50 | 69 Billy Wagner Black | 1.00 | 2.50 | 146 Dean Palmer | .25 | .60 |
| 26 Jack Cust | 1.00 | 2.50 | 70 Eric Chavez | 1.00 | 2.50 | 147 Masato Yoshii | .20 | .50 |
| 26 Jack Cust Black | 1.00 | 2.50 | 70 Eric Chavez Black | 1.00 | 2.50 | 148 Edgar Renteria | .25 | .60 |
| 27 Sean Burroughs | 1.00 | 2.50 | 71 Troy Percival | 1.00 | 2.50 | 149 Joe Randa | .20 | .50 |
| 27 Sean Burroughs Black | 1.00 | 2.50 | 71 Troy Percival Black | 1.00 | 2.50 | 150 Adam Johnson | .20 | .50 |
| 28 Randy Wolf | 1.00 | 2.50 | 72 Andruw Jones | 1.00 | 2.50 | 151 Greg Vaughn | .20 | .50 |
| 28 Randy Wolf Black | 1.00 | 2.50 | 72 Andruw Jones Black | 1.00 | 2.50 | 152 Adrian Beltre | .25 | .60 |
| 29 Mike Lamb | 1.00 | 2.50 | 73 Shane Reynolds | 1.00 | 2.50 | 153 Glenallen Hill | .20 | .50 |
| 29 Mike Lamb Black | 1.00 | 2.50 | 73 Shane Reynolds Black | 1.00 | 2.50 | 154 David Parrish RC | .20 | .50 |
| 30 Rafael Furcal | 1.00 | 2.50 | 74 Barry Zito | 1.00 | 2.50 | 155 Neifi Perez | .20 | .50 |
| 30 Rafael Furcal Black | 1.00 | 2.50 | 74 Barry Zito Black | 1.00 | 2.50 | 156 Pete Harnisch | .20 | .50 |
| 31 Barry Bonds | 4.00 | 10.00 | 75 Roy Halladay | 1.00 | 2.50 | 157 Paul Konerko | .25 | .60 |
| 31 Barry Bonds Black | 4.00 | 10.00 | 75 Roy Halladay Black | 1.00 | 2.50 | 158 Dennys Reyes | .20 | .50 |
| 32 Tim Hudson | 1.00 | 2.50 | 76 David Wells | 1.00 | 2.50 | 159 Jose Lima Black | .20 | .50 |
| 32 Tim Hudson Black | 1.00 | 2.50 | 76 David Wells Black | 1.00 | 2.50 | 160 Eddie Taubensee | .20 | .50 |
| 33 Tom Glavine | 1.00 | 2.50 | 77 Jason Giambi | 1.00 | 2.50 | 161 Miguel Cairo | .20 | .50 |
| 33 Tom Glavine Black | 1.00 | 2.50 | 77 Jason Giambi Black | 1.00 | 2.50 | 162 Jeff Kent | .25 | .60 |
| 34 Javy Lopez | 1.00 | 2.50 | 78 Scott Elarton | 1.00 | 2.50 | 163 Dustin Hermanson | .20 | .50 |
| 34 Javy Lopez Black | 1.00 | 2.50 | 78 Scott Elarton Black | 1.00 | 2.50 | 164 Alex Gonzalez | .20 | .50 |
| 35 Aubrey Huff | 1.00 | 2.50 | 79 Moises Alou | 1.00 | 2.50 | 165 Hideo Nomo | .60 | 1.50 |
| 35 Aubrey Huff Black | 1.00 | 2.50 | 79 Moises Alou Black | 1.00 | 2.50 | 166 Sammy Sosa | .60 | 1.50 |
| 36 Wally Joyner | 1.00 | 2.50 | 80 Adam Piatt | 1.00 | 2.50 | 167 C.J. Nitkowski | .20 | .50 |
| 36 Wally Joyner Black | 1.00 | 2.50 | 80 Adam Piatt Black | 1.00 | 2.50 | 168 Cal Eldred | .20 | .50 |
| 37 Magglio Ordonez | 1.00 | 2.50 | 81 Wilton Veras | .20 | .50 | 169 Jeff Abbott | .20 | .50 |
| 37 Magglio Ordonez Black | 1.00 | 2.50 | 82 Darryl Kile | .25 | .60 | 170 Jim Edmonds | .25 | .60 |
| 38 Matt Lawton | 1.00 | 2.50 | 83 Johnny Damon | .40 | 1.00 | 171 Mark Mulder Black | .25 | .60 |
| 38 Matt Lawton Black | 1.00 | 2.50 | 84 Tony Armas Jr. | .25 | .60 | 172 Dominic Rich RC | .20 | .50 |
| 39 Mariano Rivera | 1.50 | 4.00 | 85 Ellis Burks | .25 | .60 | 173 Ray Lankford | .25 | .60 |
| 39 Mariano Rivera Black | 1.50 | 4.00 | 86 Jamey Wright | .20 | .50 | 174 Danny Borrell RC | .20 | .50 |
| 40 Andy Ashby | 1.00 | 2.50 | 87 Jose Vizcaino | .20 | .50 | 175 Rick Aguilera | .20 | .50 |
| 40 Andy Ashby Black | 1.00 | 2.50 | 88 Bartolo Colon | .25 | .60 | 176 Shannon Stewart Black | .25 | .60 |
| 41 Mark Buehrle | 1.00 | 2.50 | 89 Carmen Cali RC | .20 | .50 | 177 Steve Finley | .25 | .60 |
| 41 Mark Buehrle Black | 1.00 | 2.50 | 90 Kevin Brown | .25 | .60 | 178 Jim Parque | .20 | .50 |
| 42 Esteban Loaiza | 1.00 | 2.50 | 91 Josh Hamilton | .40 | 1.00 | 179 Kevin Appier Black | .20 | .50 |
| 42 Esteban Loaiza Black | 1.00 | 2.50 | 92 Jay Buhner | .25 | .60 | 180 Adrian Gonzalez | .20 | .50 |
| 43 Mark Redman | 1.00 | 2.50 | 93 Scott Pratt RC | .25 | .60 | 181 Tom Goodwin | .20 | .50 |
| 43 Mark Redman Black | 1.00 | 2.50 | 94 Alex Cora | .20 | .50 | 182 Kevin Tapani | .20 | .50 |
| 44 Mark Quinn | 1.00 | 2.50 | 95 Luis Montanez RC | .25 | .60 | 183 Fernando Tatis | .20 | .50 |
| 44 Mark Quinn Black | 1.00 | 2.50 | 96 Dmitri Young | .20 | .50 | 184 Mark Grudzielanek | .20 | .50 |
| 45 Tino Martinez | 1.00 | 2.50 | 97 J.T. Snow | .25 | .60 | 185 Ryan Anderson | .20 | .50 |
| 45 Tino Martinez Black | 1.00 | 2.50 | 98 Damion Easley | .20 | .50 | 186 Jeffrey Hammonds | .20 | .50 |
| 46 Joe Mays | 1.00 | 2.50 | 99 Greg Norton | .20 | .50 | 187 Corey Koskie | .20 | .50 |
| 46 Joe Mays Black | 1.00 | 2.50 | 100 Matt Wheatland | .20 | .50 | 188 Brad Fullmer Black | .20 | .50 |
| 47 Walt Weiss | 1.00 | 2.50 | 101 Chin-Feng Chen | .25 | .60 | 189 Rey Sanchez | .20 | .50 |
| 47 Walt Weiss Black | 1.00 | 2.50 | 102 Tony Womack | .20 | .50 | 190 Michael Barrett | .20 | .50 |
| 48 Roger Clemens | 3.00 | 8.00 | 103 Adam Kennedy Black | .25 | .60 | 191 Rickey Henderson | .60 | 1.50 |
| 48 Roger Clemens Black | 3.00 | 8.00 | 104 J.D. Drew | .25 | .60 | 192 Jermaine Dye | .25 | .60 |
| 49 Greg Maddux | 2.50 | 6.00 | 105 Carlos Febles | .20 | .50 | 193 Scott Brosius | .20 | .50 |
| 49 Greg Maddux Black | 2.50 | 6.00 | 106 Jim Thome | .40 | 1.00 | 194 Matt Anderson | .20 | .50 |
| 50 Richard Hidalgo | 1.00 | 2.50 | 107 Danny Graves | .20 | .50 | 195 Brian Buchanan | .20 | .50 |
| 50 Richard Hidalgo Black | 1.00 | 2.50 | 108 Dave Mlicki | .20 | .50 | 196 Derrek Lee | .40 | 1.00 |
| 51 Orlando Hernandez | 1.00 | 2.50 | 109 Ron Coomer | .20 | .50 | 197 Larry Walker | .25 | .60 |
| 51 Orlando Hernandez Black | 1.00 | 2.50 | 110 James Baldwin | .20 | .50 | 198 Dan Moylan RC | .20 | .50 |
| 52 Chipper Jones | 1.50 | 4.00 | 111 Shaun Boyd RC | .20 | .50 | 199 Vinny Castilla | .25 | .60 |
| 52 Chipper Jones Black | 1.50 | 4.00 | 112 Brian Bohanon | .20 | .50 | 200 Ken Griffey Jr. | 1.00 | 2.50 |
| 53 Ben Grieve | 1.00 | 2.50 | 113 Jacque Jones | .25 | .60 | 201 Matt Stairs Black | .20 | .50 |
| 53 Ben Grieve Black | 1.00 | 2.50 | 114 Alfonso Soriano | .40 | 1.00 | 202 Ty Howington | .20 | .50 |
| 54 Jimmy Haynes | 1.00 | 2.50 | 115 Tony Clark | .20 | .50 | 203 Andy Benes | .20 | .50 |
| 54 Jimmy Haynes Black | 1.00 | 2.50 | 116 Terrence Long | .20 | .50 | 204 Luis Gonzalez | .25 | .60 |
| 55 Ken Caminiti | 1.00 | 2.50 | 117 Todd Hundley | .20 | .50 | 205 Brian Moehler | .20 | .50 |
| 55 Ken Caminiti Black | 1.00 | 2.50 | 118 Kazuhiro Sasaki | .25 | .60 | 206 Harold Baines | .25 | .60 |
| 56 Tim Salmon | 1.00 | 2.50 | 119 Brian Sellier RC | .20 | .50 | 207 Pedro Astacio | .20 | .50 |
| 56 Tim Salmon Black | 1.00 | 2.50 | 120 John Olerud | .25 | .60 | 208 Cristian Guzman | .20 | .50 |
| 57 Andy Pettitte | 1.00 | 2.50 | 121 Javier Vazquez | .20 | .50 | 209 Kip Wells | .20 | .50 |
| 57 Andy Pettitte Black | 1.00 | 2.50 | 122 Sean Burnett | .20 | .50 | 210 Frank Thomas | .60 | 1.50 |
| 58 Darin Erstad | 1.00 | 2.50 | 123 Matt LeCroy | .20 | .50 | 211 Jose Rosado | .20 | .50 |
| 58 Darin Erstad Black | 1.00 | 2.50 | 124 Enubiel Durazo | .20 | .50 | 212 Vernon Wells Black | .25 | .60 |
| 59 Marquis Grissom | 1.00 | 2.50 | 125 Juan Encarnacion | .20 | .50 | 213 Bobby Higginson | .20 | .50 |
| 59 Marquis Grissom Black | 1.00 | 2.50 | 126 Pablo Ozuna | .20 | .50 | 214 Juan Gonzalez | .25 | .60 |
| 60 Raul Mondesi | 1.00 | 2.50 | 127 Russ Ortiz | .20 | .50 | 215 Omar Vizquel | .40 | 1.00 |
| 60 Raul Mondesi Black | 1.00 | 2.50 | 128 David Segui | .20 | .50 | 216 Bernie Williams | .40 | 1.00 |
| 61 Bengie Molina | 1.00 | 2.50 | 129 Mark McGwire | 1.50 | 4.00 | 217 Aaron Sele | .20 | .50 |
| 61 Bengie Molina Black | 1.00 | 2.50 | 130 Mark Grace | .40 | 1.00 | 218 Shawn Estes | .20 | .50 |
| 62 Miguel Tejada | 1.00 | 2.50 | 131 Fred McGriff | .40 | 1.00 | 219 Roberto Alomar | .40 | 1.00 |
| 62 Miguel Tejada Black | 1.00 | 2.50 | 132 Carl Pavano | .25 | .60 | 220 Rick Ankiel | .20 | .50 |
| 63 Jose Cruz Jr. | 1.00 | 2.50 | 133 Derek Thompson | .20 | .50 | 221 Josh Kalinowski | .20 | .50 |
| 63 Jose Cruz Jr. Black | 1.00 | 2.50 | 134 Shawn Green | .25 | .60 | 222 David Bell | .20 | .50 |
| 64 Billy Koch | 1.00 | 2.50 | 135 B.J. Surhoff | .25 | .60 | 223 Keith Foulke | .20 | .50 |
| 64 Billy Koch Black | 1.00 | 2.50 | 136 Michael Tucker | .20 | .50 | 224 Craig Biggio Black | .40 | 1.00 |
| 65 Troy Glaus | 1.00 | 2.50 | 137 Jason Isringhausen | .25 | .60 | 225 Josh Axelson RC | .20 | .50 |
| 65 Troy Glaus Black | 1.00 | 2.50 | 138 Eric Milton | .20 | .50 | 226 Scott Williamson | .20 | .50 |

| | | |
|---|---|---|
| ☐ 227 Ron Belliard | .20 | .50 |
| ☐ 228 Chris Singleton | .20 | .50 |
| ☐ 229 Alex Serrano RC | .20 | .50 |
| ☐ 230 Deivi Cruz | .20 | .50 |
| ☐ 231 Eric Munson | .20 | .50 |
| ☐ 232 Luis Castillo | .20 | .50 |
| ☐ 233 Edgar Martinez | .40 | 1.00 |
| ☐ 234 Jeff Shaw | .20 | .50 |
| ☐ 235 Jeromy Burnitz | .25 | .60 |
| ☐ 236 Richie Sexson | .25 | .60 |
| ☐ 237 Will Clark | .40 | 1.00 |
| ☐ 238 Ron Villone | .20 | .50 |
| ☐ 239 Kerry Wood | .25 | .60 |
| ☐ 240 Rich Aurilia | .20 | .50 |
| ☐ 241 Mo Vaughn Black | .25 | .60 |
| ☐ 242 Travis Fryman | .25 | .60 |
| ☐ 243 Manny Ramirez Sox | .40 | 1.00 |
| ☐ 244 Chris Stynes | .20 | .50 |
| ☐ 245 Ray Durham | .25 | .60 |
| ☐ 246 Juan Uribe RC | .40 | 1.00 |
| ☐ 247 Juan Guzman | .20 | .50 |
| ☐ 248 Lee Stevens | .20 | .50 |
| ☐ 249 Devon White | .25 | .60 |
| ☐ 250 Kyle Lohse RC | .40 | 1.00 |
| ☐ 251 Bryan Wolff | .20 | .50 |
| ☐ 252 Matt Galante RC | .25 | .60 |
| ☐ 253 Eric Young | .25 | .60 |
| ☐ 254 Freddy Garcia | .25 | .60 |
| ☐ 255 Jay Bell | .20 | .50 |
| ☐ 256 Steve Cox | .20 | .50 |
| ☐ 257 Torii Hunter | .25 | .60 |
| ☐ 258 Jose Canseco | .40 | 1.00 |
| ☐ 259 Brad Ausmus | .20 | .50 |
| ☐ 260 Jeff Cirillo | .20 | .50 |
| ☐ 261 Brad Penny | .20 | .50 |
| ☐ 262 Antonio Alfonseca | .20 | .50 |
| ☐ 263 Russ Branyan | .20 | .50 |
| ☐ 264 Chris Morris RC | .20 | .50 |
| ☐ 265 John Lackey | .20 | .50 |
| ☐ 266 Justin Wayne RC | .25 | .60 |
| ☐ 267 Brad Radke | .20 | .50 |
| ☐ 268 Todd Stottlemyre | .20 | .50 |
| ☐ 269 Mark Loretta | .20 | .50 |
| ☐ 270 Matt Williams | .25 | .60 |
| ☐ 271 Kenny Lofton | .25 | .60 |
| ☐ 272 Jeff D'Amico | .20 | .50 |
| ☐ 273 Jamie Moyer | .20 | .50 |
| ☐ 274 Darren Dreifort | .20 | .50 |
| ☐ 275 Denny Neagle | .20 | .50 |
| ☐ 276 Orlando Cabrera | .20 | .50 |
| ☐ 277 Chuck Finley | .25 | .60 |
| ☐ 278 Miguel Batista | .20 | .50 |
| ☐ 279 Carlos Beltran | .25 | .60 |
| ☐ 280 Eric Karros | .25 | .60 |
| ☐ 281 Mark Kotsay | .25 | .60 |
| ☐ 282 Ryan Dempster | .20 | .50 |
| ☐ 283 Barry Larkin | .40 | 1.00 |
| ☐ 284 Jeff Suppan | .20 | .50 |
| ☐ 285 Gary Sheffield | .25 | .60 |
| ☐ 286 Jose Valentin | .20 | .50 |
| ☐ 287 Robb Nen | .25 | .60 |
| ☐ 288 Chan Ho Park | .25 | .60 |
| ☐ 289 John Halama | .20 | .50 |
| ☐ 290 Steve Smyth RC | .20 | .50 |
| ☐ 291 Gerald Williams | .20 | .50 |
| ☐ 292 Preston Wilson | .25 | .60 |
| ☐ 293 Victor Hall RC | .25 | .60 |
| ☐ 294 Ben Sheets | .40 | 1.00 |
| ☐ 295 Eric Davis | .25 | .60 |
| ☐ 296 Kirk Rueter | .20 | .50 |
| ☐ 297 Chad Petty RC | .20 | .50 |
| ☐ 298 Kevin Millar | .25 | .60 |
| ☐ 299 Marvin Benard | .20 | .50 |
| ☐ 300 Vladimir Guerrero | .60 | 1.50 |
| ☐ 301 Livan Hernandez | .25 | .60 |
| ☐ 302 Travis Baptist RC | .20 | .50 |
| ☐ 303 Bill Mueller | .20 | .50 |
| ☐ 304 Mike Cameron | .20 | .50 |
| ☐ 305 Randy Johnson | .60 | 1.50 |
| ☐ 306 Alan Mahaffey RC | .20 | .50 |
| ☐ 307 Timo Perez UER | .20 | .50 |
| ☐ 308 Pokey Reese | .20 | .50 |
| ☐ 309 Ryan Rupe | .20 | .50 |
| ☐ 310 Carlos Lee | .25 | .60 |
| ☐ 311 Doug Glanville SP | 2.00 | 5.00 |
| ☐ 312 Jay Payton SP | 2.00 | 5.00 |
| ☐ 313 Troy O'Leary SP | 2.00 | 5.00 |
| ☐ 314 Francisco Cordero SP | 2.00 | 5.00 |

| | | |
|---|---|---|
| ☐ 315 Rusty Greer SP | 2.00 | 5.00 |
| ☐ 316 Cal Ripken SP | 10.00 | 25.00 |
| ☐ 317 Ricky Ledee SP | 2.00 | 5.00 |
| ☐ 318 Brian Daubach SP | 2.00 | 5.00 |
| ☐ 319 Robin Ventura SP | 2.00 | 5.00 |
| ☐ 320 Todd Zeile SP | 2.00 | 5.00 |
| ☐ 321 Francisco Cordova SP | 2.00 | 5.00 |
| ☐ 322 Henry Rodriguez SP | 2.00 | 5.00 |
| ☐ 323 Pat Meares SP | 2.00 | 5.00 |
| ☐ 324 Glendon Rusch SP | 2.00 | 5.00 |
| ☐ 325 Keith Osik SP | 2.00 | 5.00 |
| ☐ 326 Robert Keppel SP RC | 2.00 | 5.00 |
| ☐ 327 Bobby Jones SP | 2.00 | 5.00 |
| ☐ 328 Alex Ramirez SP | 2.00 | 5.00 |
| ☐ 329 Robert Person SP | 2.00 | 5.00 |
| ☐ 330 Ruben Mateo SP | 2.00 | 5.00 |
| ☐ 331 Rob Bell SP | 2.00 | 5.00 |
| ☐ 332 Carl Everett SP | 2.00 | 5.00 |
| ☐ 333 Jason Schmidt SP | 2.00 | 5.00 |
| ☐ 334 Scott Rolen SP | 3.00 | 8.00 |
| ☐ 335 Jimmy Anderson SP | 2.00 | 5.00 |
| ☐ 336 Bret Boone SP | 2.00 | 5.00 |
| ☐ 337 Delino DeShields SP | 2.00 | 5.00 |
| ☐ 338 Trevor Hoffman SP | 2.00 | 5.00 |
| ☐ 339 Bob Abreu SP | 2.00 | 5.00 |
| ☐ 340 Mike Williams SP | 2.00 | 5.00 |
| ☐ 341 Mike Hampton SP | 2.00 | 5.00 |
| ☐ 342 John Wetteland SP | 2.00 | 5.00 |
| ☐ 343 Scott Erickson SP | 2.00 | 5.00 |
| ☐ 344 Enrique Wilson SP | 2.00 | 5.00 |
| ☐ 345 Tim Wakefield SP | 2.00 | 5.00 |
| ☐ 346 Mike Lowell SP | 2.00 | 5.00 |
| ☐ 347 Todd Pratt SP | 2.00 | 5.00 |
| ☐ 348 Brook Fordyce SP | 2.00 | 5.00 |
| ☐ 349 Benny Agbayani SP | 2.00 | 5.00 |
| ☐ 350 Gabe Kapler SP | 2.00 | 5.00 |
| ☐ 351 Sean Casey SP | 2.00 | 5.00 |
| ☐ 352 Darren Oliver SP | 2.00 | 5.00 |
| ☐ 353 Todd Ritchie SP | 2.00 | 5.00 |
| ☐ 354 Kenny Rogers SP | 2.00 | 5.00 |
| ☐ 355 Jason Kendall SP | 2.00 | 5.00 |
| ☐ 356 John Vander Wal SP | 2.00 | 5.00 |
| ☐ 357 Ramon Martinez SP | 2.00 | 5.00 |
| ☐ 358 Edgardo Alfonzo SP | 2.00 | 5.00 |
| ☐ 359 Phil Nevin SP | 2.00 | 5.00 |
| ☐ 360 Albert Belle SP | 2.00 | 5.00 |
| ☐ 361 Ruben Rivera SP | 2.00 | 5.00 |
| ☐ 362 Pedro Martinez SP | 3.00 | 8.00 |
| ☐ 363 Derek Lowe SP | 2.00 | 5.00 |
| ☐ 364 Pat Burrell SP | 2.00 | 5.00 |
| ☐ 365 Mike Mussina SP | 3.00 | 8.00 |
| ☐ 366 Brady Anderson SP | 2.00 | 5.00 |
| ☐ 367 Darren Lewis SP | 2.00 | 5.00 |
| ☐ 368 Sidney Ponson SP | 2.00 | 5.00 |
| ☐ 369 Adam Eaton SP | 2.00 | 5.00 |
| ☐ 370 Eric Owens SP | 2.00 | 5.00 |
| ☐ 371 Aaron Boone SP | 2.00 | 5.00 |
| ☐ 372 Matt Clement SP | 2.00 | 5.00 |
| ☐ 373 Derek Bell SP | 2.00 | 5.00 |
| ☐ 374 Trot Nixon SP | 2.00 | 5.00 |
| ☐ 375 Travis Lee SP | 2.00 | 5.00 |
| ☐ 376 Mike Benjamin SP | 2.00 | 5.00 |
| ☐ 377 Jeff Zimmerman SP | 2.00 | 5.00 |
| ☐ 378 Mike Lieberthal SP | 2.00 | 5.00 |
| ☐ 379 Rick Reed SP | 2.00 | 5.00 |
| ☐ 380 Nomar Garciaparra SP | 5.00 | 12.00 |
| ☐ 381 Omar Daal SP | 2.00 | 5.00 |
| ☐ 382 Ryan Klesko SP | 2.00 | 5.00 |
| ☐ 383 Rey Ordonez SP | 2.00 | 5.00 |
| ☐ 384 Kevin Young SP | 2.00 | 5.00 |
| ☐ 385 Rick Helling SP | 2.00 | 5.00 |
| ☐ 386 Brian Giles SP | 2.00 | 5.00 |
| ☐ 387 Tony Gwynn SP | 4.00 | 10.00 |
| ☐ 388 Ed Sprague SP | 2.00 | 5.00 |
| ☐ 389 J.R. House SP | 2.00 | 5.00 |
| ☐ 390 Scott Hatteberg SP | 2.00 | 5.00 |
| ☐ 391 John Valentin SP | 2.00 | 5.00 |
| ☐ 392 Melvin Mora SP | 2.00 | 5.00 |
| ☐ 393 Royce Clayton SP | 2.00 | 5.00 |
| ☐ 394 Jeff Fassero SP | 2.00 | 5.00 |
| ☐ 395 Manny Alexander SP | 2.00 | 5.00 |
| ☐ 396 John Franco SP | 2.00 | 5.00 |
| ☐ 397 Luis Alicea SP | 2.00 | 5.00 |
| ☐ 398 Ivan Rodriguez SP | 3.00 | 8.00 |
| ☐ 399 Kevin Jordan SP | 2.00 | 5.00 |
| ☐ 400 Jose Offerman SP | 2.00 | 5.00 |
| ☐ 401 Jeff Conine SP | 2.00 | 5.00 |
| ☐ 402 Seth Etherton SP | 2.00 | 5.00 |

| | | |
|---|---|---|
| ☐ 403 Mike Bordick SP | 2.00 | 5.00 |
| ☐ 404 Al Leiter SP | 2.00 | 5.00 |
| ☐ 405 Mike Piazza SP | 5.00 | 12.00 |
| ☐ 406 Armando Benitez SP | 2.00 | 5.00 |
| ☐ 407 Warren Morris SP | 2.00 | 5.00 |
| ☐ NNO 1952 Card Redemption EXCH | | |
| ☐ NNO Replica Hat-Jsy EXCH | | |

## 2002 Topps Heritage

PEDRO MARTINEZ

| | | |
|---|---|---|
| ☐ COMPLETE SET (440) | 200.00 | 400.00 |
| ☐ COMP.SET w/o SP's (350) | 40.00 | 80.00 |
| ☐ COMMON CARD (1-363) | .20 | .50 |
| ☐ COMMON SP (364-446) | 2.00 | 5.00 |
| ☐ 1 Ichiro Suzuki SP | 6.00 | 15.00 |
| ☐ 2 Darin Erstad | .25 | .60 |
| ☐ 3 Rod Beck | .25 | .60 |
| ☐ 4 Doug Mientkiewicz | .25 | .60 |
| ☐ 5 Mike Sweeney | .25 | .60 |
| ☐ 6 Roger Clemens | 1.25 | 3.00 |
| ☐ 7 Jason Tyner | .20 | .50 |
| ☐ 8 Alex Gonzalez | .20 | .50 |
| ☐ 9 Eric Young | .20 | .50 |
| ☐ 10 Randy Johnson | .60 | 1.50 |
| ☐ 10N Randy Johnson Night SP | 3.00 | 8.00 |
| ☐ 11 Aaron Sele | .20 | .50 |
| ☐ 12 Tony Clark | .20 | .50 |
| ☐ 13 C.C. Sabathia | .25 | .60 |
| ☐ 14 Melvin Mora | .25 | .60 |
| ☐ 15 Tim Hudson | .25 | .60 |
| ☐ 16 Ben Petrick | .20 | .50 |
| ☐ 17 Tom Glavine | .40 | 1.00 |
| ☐ 18 Jason Lane | .25 | .60 |
| ☐ 19 Larry Walker | .25 | .60 |
| ☐ 20 Mark Mulder | .25 | .60 |
| ☐ 21 Steve Finley | .25 | .60 |
| ☐ 22 Bengie Molina | .20 | .50 |
| ☐ 23 Rob Bell | .20 | .50 |
| ☐ 24 Nathan Haynes | .20 | .50 |
| ☐ 25 Rafael Furcal | .25 | .60 |
| ☐ 25N Rafael Furcal Night SP | 2.00 | 5.00 |
| ☐ 26 Mike Mussina | .40 | 1.00 |
| ☐ 27 Paul LoDuca | .25 | .60 |
| ☐ 28 Torii Hunter | .25 | .60 |
| ☐ 29 Carlos Lee | .25 | .60 |
| ☐ 30 Jimmy Rollins | .20 | .50 |
| ☐ 31 Arthur Rhodes | .20 | .50 |
| ☐ 32 Ivan Rodriguez | .40 | 1.00 |
| ☐ 33 Wes Helms | .20 | .50 |
| ☐ 34 Cliff Floyd | .20 | .50 |
| ☐ 35 Julian Tavarez | .20 | .50 |
| ☐ 36 Mark McGwire | 1.50 | 4.00 |
| ☐ 37 Chipper Jones SP | 3.00 | 8.00 |
| ☐ 38 Denny Neagle | .20 | .50 |
| ☐ 39 Odalis Perez | .20 | .50 |
| ☐ 40 Antonio Alfonseca | .20 | .50 |
| ☐ 41 Edgar Renteria | .25 | .60 |
| ☐ 42 Troy Glaus | .25 | .60 |
| ☐ 43 Scott Brosius | .25 | .60 |
| ☐ 44 Abraham Nunez | .20 | .50 |
| ☐ 45 Jamey Wright | .20 | .50 |
| ☐ 46 Bobby Bonilla | .25 | .60 |
| ☐ 47 Ismael Valdes | .20 | .50 |
| ☐ 48 Chris Reitsma | .20 | .50 |
| ☐ 49 Neifi Perez | .20 | .50 |
| ☐ 50 Juan Cruz | .20 | .50 |
| ☐ 51 Kevin Brown | .25 | .60 |
| ☐ 52 Ben Grieve | .20 | .50 |
| ☐ 53 Alex Rodriguez SP | 5.00 | 12.00 |
| ☐ 54 Charles Nagy | .20 | .50 |
| ☐ 55 Reggie Sanders | .20 | .50 |
| ☐ 56 Nelson Figueroa | .20 | .50 |
| ☐ 57 Felipe Lopez | .20 | .50 |
| ☐ 58 Bill Ortega | .20 | .50 |
| ☐ 59 Jeffrey Hammonds | .25 | .60 |

|  |  | | |
|---|---|---|---|
| 60 | Johnny Estrada | .20 | .50 |
| 61 | Bob Wickman | .20 | .50 |
| 62 | Doug Glanville | .20 | .50 |
| 63 | Jeff Cirillo | .20 | .50 |
| 63N | Jeff Cirillo Night SP | 2.00 | 5.00 |
| 64 | Corey Patterson | .20 | .50 |
| 65 | Aaron Myette | .20 | .50 |
| 66 | Magglio Ordonez | .20 | .50 |
| 67 | Ellis Burks | .25 | .60 |
| 68 | Miguel Tejada | .25 | .60 |
| 69 | John Olerud | .25 | .60 |
| 69N | John Olerud Night SP | 2.00 | 5.00 |
| 70 | Greg Vaughn | .20 | .50 |
| 71 | Andy Pettitte | .40 | 1.00 |
| 72 | Mike Matheny | .20 | .50 |
| 73 | Brandon Duckworth | .20 | .50 |
| 74 | Scott Schoeneweis | .20 | .50 |
| 75 | Mike Lowell | .25 | .60 |
| 76 | Einar Diaz | .20 | .50 |
| 77 | Tino Martinez | .40 | 1.00 |
| 78 | Matt Williams | .25 | .60 |
| 79 | Jason Young RC | .40 | 1.00 |
| 80 | Nate Cornejo | .20 | .50 |
| 81 | Andres Galarraga | .25 | .60 |
| 82 | Bernie Williams SP | 3.00 | 8.00 |
| 83 | Ryan Klesko | .25 | .60 |
| 84 | Dan Wilson | .20 | .50 |
| 85 | Henry Pichardo RC | .40 | 1.00 |
| 86 | Ray Durham | .25 | .60 |
| 87 | Omar Daal | .20 | .50 |
| 88 | Derrek Lee | .40 | 1.00 |
| 89 | Al Leiter | .25 | .60 |
| 90 | Darrin Fletcher | .20 | .50 |
| 91 | Josh Beckett | .25 | .60 |
| 92 | Johnny Damon | .40 | 1.00 |
| 92N | Johnny Damon Night SP | 3.00 | 8.00 |
| 93 | Abraham Nunez | .20 | .50 |
| 94 | Ricky Ledee | .20 | .50 |
| 95 | Richie Sexson | .25 | .60 |
| 96 | Adam Kennedy | .20 | .50 |
| 97 | Raul Mondesi | .25 | .60 |
| 98 | John Burkett | .20 | .50 |
| 99 | Ben Sheets | .25 | .60 |
| 99N | Ben Sheets Night SP | 2.00 | 5.00 |
| 100 | Preston Wilson | .20 | .50 |
| 100N | Preston Wilson Night SP | 2.00 | 5.00 |
| 101 | Bool Bonser | .20 | .50 |
| 102 | Shigetoshi Hasegawa | .25 | .60 |
| 103 | Carlos Febles | .20 | .50 |
| 104 | Jorge Posada SP | 3.00 | 8.00 |
| 105 | Michael Tucker | .20 | .50 |
| 106 | Roberto Hernandez | .20 | .50 |
| 107 | John Rodriguez RC | .40 | 1.00 |
| 108 | Danny Graves | .20 | .50 |
| 109 | Rich Aurilia | .20 | .50 |
| 110 | Jon Lieber | .20 | .50 |
| 111 | Tim Hummel RC | .40 | 1.00 |
| 112 | J.T. Snow | .25 | .60 |
| 113 | Kris Benson | .20 | .50 |
| 114 | Derek Jeter | 1.50 | 4.00 |
| 115 | John Franco | .25 | .60 |
| 116 | Matt Stairs | .20 | .50 |
| 117 | Ben Davis | .20 | .50 |
| 118 | Darryl Kile | .25 | .60 |
| 119 | Mike Peeples RC | .40 | 1.00 |
| 120 | Kevin Tapani | .20 | .50 |
| 121 | Armando Benitez | .20 | .50 |
| 122 | Damian Miller | .20 | .50 |
| 123 | Jose Jimenez | .20 | .50 |
| 124 | Pedro Astacio | .20 | .50 |
| 125 | Marlyn Tisdale RC | .40 | 1.00 |
| 126 | Calvi Cruz | .20 | .50 |
| 127 | Paul O'Neill | .40 | 1.00 |
| 128 | Jermaine Dye | .25 | .60 |
| 129 | Marcus Giles | .20 | .50 |
| 130 | Mark Loretta | .20 | .50 |
| 131 | Garret Anderson | .25 | .60 |
| 132 | Todd Ritchie | .20 | .50 |
| 133 | Joe Crede | .20 | .50 |
| 134 | Kevin Millwood | .25 | .60 |
| 135 | Shane Reynolds | .20 | .50 |
| 136 | Mark Grace | .40 | 1.00 |
| 137 | Shannon Stewart | .25 | .60 |
| 138 | Nick Neugebauer | .20 | .50 |
| 139 | Nic Jackson RC | .40 | 1.00 |
| 140 | Robb Nen UER | .25 | .60 |
| 141 | Dmitri Young | .20 | .50 |
| 142 | Kevin Appier | .25 | .60 |
| 143 | Jack Cust | .20 | .50 |
| 144 | Andres Torres | .20 | .50 |
| 145 | Frank Thomas | .60 | 1.50 |
| 146 | Jason Kendall | .25 | .60 |
| 147 | Greg Maddux | 1.00 | 2.50 |
| 148 | David Justice | .25 | .60 |
| 149 | Hideo Nomo | .60 | 1.50 |
| 150 | Bret Boone | .25 | .60 |
| 151 | Wade Miller | .20 | .50 |
| 152 | Jeff Kent | .25 | .60 |
| 153 | Scott Williamson | .20 | .50 |
| 154 | Julio Lugo | .20 | .50 |
| 155 | Bobby Higginson | .20 | .50 |
| 156 | Geoff Jenkins | .20 | .50 |
| 157 | Darren Dreifort | .20 | .50 |
| 158 | Freddy Sanchez RC | 1.25 | 3.00 |
| 159 | Bud Smith | .20 | .50 |
| 160 | Phil Nevin | .25 | .60 |
| 161 | Cesar Izturis | .20 | .50 |
| 162 | Sean Casey | .25 | .60 |
| 163 | Jose Ortiz | .20 | .50 |
| 164 | Brent Abernathy | .20 | .50 |
| 165 | Kevin Young | .20 | .50 |
| 166 | Daryle Ward | .20 | .50 |
| 167 | Trevor Hoffman | .25 | .60 |
| 168 | Rondell White | .20 | .50 |
| 169 | Kip Wells | .20 | .50 |
| 170 | John Vander Wal | .20 | .50 |
| 171 | Jose Lima | .20 | .50 |
| 172 | Wilton Guerrero | .20 | .50 |
| 173 | Aaron Dean RC | .40 | 1.00 |
| 174 | Rick Helling | .20 | .50 |
| 175 | Juan Pierre | .25 | .60 |
| 176 | Jay Bell | .20 | .50 |
| 177 | Craig House | .20 | .50 |
| 178 | David Bell | .20 | .50 |
| 179 | Pat Burrell | .25 | .60 |
| 180 | Eric Gagne | .25 | .60 |
| 181 | Adam Pettyjohn | .20 | .50 |
| 182 | Ugueth Urbina | .20 | .50 |
| 183 | Peter Bergeron | .20 | .50 |
| 184 | Adrian Gonzalez | .20 | .50 |
| 184N | Adrian Gonzalez Night SP | 2.00 | 5.00 |
| 185 | Damion Easley | .20 | .50 |
| 186 | Gookie Dawkins | .20 | .50 |
| 187 | Matt Lawton | .20 | .50 |
| 188 | Frank Catalanotto | .20 | .50 |
| 189 | David Wells | .25 | .60 |
| 190 | Roger Cedeno | .20 | .50 |
| 191 | Brian Giles | .25 | .60 |
| 192 | Julio Zuleta | .20 | .50 |
| 193 | Timo Perez | .20 | .50 |
| 194 | Billy Wagner | .25 | .60 |
| 195 | Craig Counsell | .20 | .50 |
| 196 | Bart Miadich | .20 | .50 |
| 197 | Gary Sheffield | .25 | .60 |
| 198 | Richard Hidalgo | .20 | .50 |
| 199 | Juan Uribe | .20 | .50 |
| 200 | Curt Schilling | .25 | .60 |
| 201 | Javy Lopez | .25 | .60 |
| 202 | Jimmy Haynes | .20 | .50 |
| 203 | Jim Edmonds | .25 | .60 |
| 204 | Pokey Reese | .20 | .50 |
| 204N | Pokey Reese Night SP | 2.00 | 5.00 |
| 205 | Matt Clement | .20 | .50 |
| 206 | Dean Palmer | .20 | .50 |
| 207 | Nick Johnson | .25 | .60 |
| 208 | Nate Espy RC | .40 | 1.00 |
| 209 | Pedro Feliz | .20 | .50 |
| 210 | Aaron Rowand | .25 | .60 |
| 211 | Masato Yoshii | .20 | .50 |
| 212 | Jose Cruz Jr. | .25 | .60 |
| 213 | Paul Byrd | .20 | .50 |
| 214 | Mark Phillips RC | .40 | 1.00 |
| 215 | Benny Agbayani | .20 | .50 |
| 216 | Frank Menechino | .20 | .50 |
| 217 | John Flaherty | .20 | .50 |
| 218 | Brian Boehringer | .20 | .50 |
| 219 | Todd Hollandsworth | .20 | .50 |
| 220 | Sammy Sosa SP | 3.00 | 8.00 |
| 221 | Steve Sparks | .20 | .50 |
| 222 | Homer Bush | .20 | .50 |
| 223 | Mike Hampton | .25 | .60 |
| 224 | Bobby Abreu | .25 | .60 |
| 225 | Barry Larkin | .40 | 1.00 |
| 226 | Ryan Rupe | .20 | .50 |
| 227 | Bubba Trammell | .20 | .50 |
| 228 | Todd Zeile | .25 | .60 |
| 229 | Jeff Shaw | .20 | .50 |
| 230 | Alex Ochoa | .20 | .50 |
| 231 | Orlando Cabrera | .25 | .60 |
| 232 | Jeremy Giambi | .20 | .50 |
| 233 | Tomo Ohka | .20 | .50 |
| 234 | Luis Castillo | .20 | .50 |
| 235 | Chris Holt | .20 | .50 |
| 236 | Shawn Green | .25 | .60 |
| 237 | Sidney Ponson | .20 | .50 |
| 238 | Lee Stevens | .20 | .50 |
| 239 | Hank Blalock | .40 | 1.00 |
| 240 | Randy Winn | .20 | .50 |
| 241 | Pedro Martinez | .40 | 1.00 |
| 242 | Vinny Castilla | .25 | .60 |
| 243 | Steve Karsay | .20 | .50 |
| 244 | Barry Bonds SP | 8.00 | 20.00 |
| 245 | Jason Bere | .20 | .50 |
| 246 | Scott Rolen | .40 | 1.00 |
| 246N | Scott Rolen Night SP | 3.00 | 8.00 |
| 247 | Ryan Kohlmeier | .20 | .50 |
| 248 | Kerry Wood | .25 | .60 |
| 249 | Aramis Ramirez | .25 | .60 |
| 250 | Lance Berkman | .25 | .60 |
| 251 | Omar Vizquel | .40 | 1.00 |
| 252 | Juan Encarnacion | .20 | .50 |
| 253 | Does Not Exist | | |
| 254 | David Segui | .20 | .50 |
| 255 | Brian Anderson | .20 | .50 |
| 256 | Jay Payton | .20 | .50 |
| 257 | Mark Grudzielanek | .20 | .50 |
| 258 | Jimmy Anderson | .20 | .50 |
| 259 | Eric Valent | .20 | .50 |
| 260 | Chad Durbin | .20 | .50 |
| 261 | Does Not Exist | | |
| 262 | Alex Gonzalez | .20 | .50 |
| 263 | Scott Dunn | .20 | .50 |
| 264 | Scott Elarton | .20 | .50 |
| 265 | Tom Gordon | .20 | .50 |
| 266 | Moises Alou | .25 | .60 |
| 267 | Does Not Exist | | |
| 268 | Does Not Exist | | |
| 269 | Mark Buehrle | .25 | .60 |
| 270 | Jerry Hairston | .20 | .50 |
| 271 | Does Not Exist | | |
| 272 | Luke Prokopec | .20 | .50 |
| 273 | Graeme Lloyd | .20 | .50 |
| 274 | Bret Prinz | .20 | .50 |
| 275 | Does Not Exist | | |
| 276 | Chris Carpenter | .25 | .60 |
| 277 | Ryan Minor | .20 | .50 |
| 278 | Jeff D'Amico | .20 | .50 |
| 279 | Raul Ibanez | .20 | .50 |
| 280 | Joe Mays | .20 | .50 |
| 281 | Livan Hernandez | .20 | .50 |
| 282 | Robin Ventura | .25 | .60 |
| 283 | Gabe Kapler | .20 | .50 |
| 284 | Tony Batista | .20 | .50 |
| 285 | Ramon Hernandez | .20 | .50 |
| 286 | Craig Paquette | .20 | .50 |
| 287 | Mark Kotsay | .25 | .60 |
| 288 | Mike Lieberthal | .20 | .50 |
| 289 | Joe Borchard | .25 | .60 |
| 290 | Cristian Guzman | .20 | .50 |
| 291 | Craig Biggio | .40 | 1.00 |
| 292 | Joaquin Benoit | .20 | .50 |
| 293 | Ken Caminiti | .25 | .60 |
| 294 | Sean Burroughs | .25 | .60 |
| 295 | Eric Karros | .25 | .60 |
| 296 | Eric Chavez | .25 | .60 |
| 297 | LaTroy Hawkins | .20 | .50 |
| 298 | Alfonso Soriano | .25 | .60 |
| 299 | John Smoltz | .40 | 1.00 |
| 300 | Adam Dunn | .25 | .60 |
| 301 | Ryan Dempster | .20 | .50 |
| 302 | Travis Hafner | .20 | .50 |
| 303 | Russell Branyan | .20 | .50 |
| 304 | Dustin Hermanson | .20 | .50 |
| 305 | Jim Thome | .40 | 1.00 |
| 306 | Carlos Beltran | .25 | .60 |
| 307 | Jason Botts RC | .25 | .60 |
| 308 | David Cone | .25 | .60 |
| 309 | Ivanon Coffie | .20 | .50 |
| 310 | Brian Jordan | .25 | .60 |
| 311 | Todd Walker | .20 | .50 |
| 312 | Jeromy Burnitz | .20 | .50 |
| 313 | Tony Armas Jr. | .20 | .50 |
| 314 | Jeff Conine | .20 | .50 |
| 315 | Todd Jones | .20 | .50 |

|  |  | | |
|---|---|---|---|
| 316 | Roy Oswalt | .25 | .60 |
| 317 | Aubrey Huff | .25 | .60 |
| 318 | Josh Fogg | .20 | .50 |
| 319 | Jose Vidro | .20 | .50 |
| 320 | Jace Brewer | .20 | .50 |
| 321 | Mike Redmond | .20 | .50 |
| 322 | Noochie Varner RC | .40 | 1.00 |
| 323 | Russ Ortiz | .20 | .50 |
| 324 | Edgardo Alfonzo | .20 | .50 |
| 325 | Ruben Sierra | .25 | .60 |
| 326 | Calvin Murray | .20 | .50 |
| 327 | Marlon Anderson | .20 | .50 |
| 328 | Albie Lopez | .20 | .50 |
| 329 | Chris Gomez | .20 | .50 |
| 330 | Fernando Tatis | .20 | .50 |
| 331 | Stubby Clapp | .20 | .50 |
| 332 | Rickey Henderson | .60 | 1.50 |
| 333 | Brad Radke | .25 | .60 |
| 334 | Brent Mayne | .20 | .50 |
| 335 | Cory Lidle | .20 | .50 |
| 336 | Edgar Martinez | .40 | 1.00 |
| 337 | Aaron Boone | .25 | .60 |
| 338 | Jay Witasick | .20 | .50 |
| 339 | Benito Santiago | .20 | .50 |
| 340 | Jose Mercedes | .20 | .50 |
| 341 | Fernando Vina | .20 | .50 |
| 342 | A.J. Pierzynski | .25 | .60 |
| 343 | Jeff Bagwell | .40 | 1.00 |
| 344 | Brian Bohanon | .20 | .50 |
| 345 | Adrian Beltre | .25 | .60 |
| 346 | Troy Percival | .25 | .60 |
| 347 | Napoleon Calzado RC | .40 | 1.00 |
| 348 | Ruben Rivera | .20 | .50 |
| 349 | Rafael Soriano | .20 | .50 |
| 350 | Damian Jackson | .20 | .50 |
| 351 | Joe Randa | .20 | .50 |
| 352 | Chan Ho Park | .25 | .60 |
| 353 | Dante Bichette | .20 | .50 |
| 354 | Bartolo Colon | .20 | .50 |
| 355 | Jason Bay RC | 2.00 | 5.00 |
| 356 | Shea Hillenbrand | .25 | .60 |
| 357 | Matt Morris | .25 | .60 |
| 358 | Brad Penny | .20 | .50 |
| 359 | Mark Quinn | .20 | .50 |
| 360 | Marquis Grissom | .25 | .60 |
| 361 | Henry Blanco | .20 | .50 |
| 362 | Billy Koch | .20 | .50 |
| 363 | Mike Cameron | .20 | .50 |
| 364 | Albert Pujols SP | 6.00 | 15.00 |
| 365 | Paul Konerko SP | 2.00 | 5.00 |
| 366 | Eric Milton SP | 2.00 | 5.00 |
| 367 | Nick Bierbrodt SP | 2.00 | 5.00 |
| 368 | Rafael Palmeiro SP | 3.00 | 8.00 |
| 369 | Jorge Padilla SP RC | 2.00 | 5.00 |
| 370 | Jason Giambi Yankees SP | 2.00 | 5.00 |
| 371 | Mike Piazza SP | 5.00 | 12.00 |
| 372 | Alex Cora SP | 2.00 | 5.00 |
| 373 | Todd Helton SP | 3.00 | 8.00 |
| 374 | Juan Gonzalez SP | 2.00 | 5.00 |
| 375 | Mariano Rivera SP | 3.00 | 8.00 |
| 376 | Jason LaRue SP | 2.00 | 5.00 |
| 377 | Tony Gwynn SP | 4.00 | 10.00 |
| 378 | Wilson Betemit SP | 2.00 | 5.00 |
| 379 | J.J. Trujillo SP RC | 2.00 | 5.00 |
| 380 | Brad Ausmus SP | 2.00 | 5.00 |
| 381 | Chris George SP | 2.00 | 5.00 |
| 382 | Jose Canseco SP | 3.00 | 8.00 |
| 383 | Ramon Ortiz SP | 2.00 | 5.00 |
| 384 | John Rocker SP | 2.00 | 5.00 |
| 385 | Rey Ordonez SP | 2.00 | 5.00 |
| 386 | Ken Griffey Jr. SP | 5.00 | 12.00 |
| 387 | Juan Pena SP | 2.00 | 5.00 |
| 388 | Michael Barrett SP | 2.00 | 5.00 |
| 389 | J.D. Drew SP | 2.00 | 5.00 |
| 390 | Corey Koskie SP | 2.00 | 5.00 |
| 391 | Vernon Wells SP | 2.00 | 5.00 |
| 392 | Juan Tolentino SP RC | 2.00 | 5.00 |
| 393 | Luis Gonzalez SP | 2.00 | 5.00 |
| 394 | Terrence Long SP | 2.00 | 5.00 |
| 395 | Travis Lee SP | 2.00 | 5.00 |
| 396 | Earl Snyder SP RC | 2.00 | 5.00 |
| 397 | Nomar Garciaparra SP | 5.00 | 12.00 |
| 398 | Jason Schmidt SP | 2.00 | 5.00 |
| 399 | David Espinosa SP | 2.00 | 5.00 |
| 400 | Steve Green SP | 2.00 | 5.00 |
| 401 | Jack Wilson SP | 2.00 | 5.00 |
| 402 | Chris Tritle SP RC | 2.00 | 5.00 |
| 403 | Angel Berroa SP | 2.00 | 5.00 |
| 404 | Josh Towers SP | 2.00 | 5.00 |
| 405 | Andruw Jones SP | 3.00 | 8.00 |
| 406 | Brent Butler SP | 2.00 | 5.00 |
| 407 | Craig Kuzmic SP | 2.00 | 5.00 |
| 408 | Derek Bell SP | 2.00 | 5.00 |
| 409 | Eric Glaser SP RC | 2.00 | 5.00 |
| 410 | Joel Pineiro SP | 2.00 | 5.00 |
| 411 | Alexis Gomez SP | 2.00 | 5.00 |
| 412 | Mike Rivera SP | 2.00 | 5.00 |
| 413 | Shawn Estes SP | 2.00 | 5.00 |
| 414 | Milton Bradley SP | 2.00 | 5.00 |
| 415 | Carl Everett SP | 2.00 | 5.00 |
| 416 | Kazuhiro Sasaki SP | 2.00 | 5.00 |
| 417 | Tony Fontana SP RC | 2.00 | 5.00 |
| 418 | Josh Pearce SP | 2.00 | 5.00 |
| 419 | Gary Matthews Jr. SP | 2.00 | 5.00 |
| 420 | Raymond Cabrera SP RC | 2.00 | 5.00 |
| 421 | Joe Kennedy SP | 2.00 | 5.00 |
| 422 | Jason Maule SP RC | 2.00 | 5.00 |
| 423 | Casey Fossum SP | 2.00 | 5.00 |
| 424 | Christian Parker SP | 2.00 | 5.00 |
| 425 | Laynce Nix SP RC | 4.00 | 10.00 |
| 426 | Byung-Hyun Kim SP | 2.00 | 5.00 |
| 427 | Freddy Garcia SP | 2.00 | 5.00 |
| 428 | Herbert Perry SP | 2.00 | 5.00 |
| 429 | Jason Marquis SP | 2.00 | 5.00 |
| 430 | Sandy Alomar Jr. SP | 2.00 | 5.00 |
| 431 | Roberto Alomar SP | 3.00 | 8.00 |
| 432 | Tsuyoshi Shinjo SP | 2.00 | 5.00 |
| 433 | Tim Wakefield SP | 2.00 | 5.00 |
| 434 | Robert Fick SP | 2.00 | 5.00 |
| 435 | Vladimir Guerrero SP | 3.00 | 8.00 |
| 436 | Jose Mesa SP | 2.00 | 5.00 |
| 437 | Scott Spiezio SP | 2.00 | 5.00 |
| 438 | Jose Hernandez SP | 2.00 | 5.00 |
| 439 | Jose Acevedo SP | 2.00 | 5.00 |
| 440 | Brian West SP RC | 2.00 | 5.00 |
| 441 | Barry Zito SP | 2.00 | 5.00 |
| 442 | Luis Maza SP | 2.00 | 5.00 |
| 443 | Marlon Byrd SP | 2.00 | 5.00 |
| 444 | A.J. Burnett SP | 2.00 | 5.00 |
| 445 | Dee Brown SP | 2.00 | 5.00 |
| 446 | Carlos Delgado SP | 2.00 | 5.00 |
| NNO | 1953 Repurchased EXCH. | | |

**2003 Topps Heritage**

| | | | |
|---|---|---|---|
| COMPLETE SET (450) | | 175.00 | 300.00 |
| COMP.SET w/o SP's (350) | | 40.00 | 80.00 |
| COMMON CARD | | .20 | .50 |
| COMMON RC | | .40 | 1.00 |
| COMMON SP | | 2.00 | 5.00 |
| COMMON SP RC | | 2.00 | 5.00 |
| 1A | Alex Rodriguez Red | 1.00 | 2.50 |
| 1B | Alex Rodriguez Black SP | 5.00 | 12.00 |
| 2 | Jose Cruz Jr. | .20 | .50 |
| 3 | Ichiro Suzuki SP | 6.00 | 15.00 |
| 4 | Rich Aurilia | .25 | .60 |
| 5 | Trevor Hoffman | .25 | .60 |
| 6A | Brian Giles New Logo | .25 | .60 |
| 6B | Brian Giles Old Logo SP | 2.00 | 5.00 |
| 7A | Albert Pujols Orange | 1.25 | 3.00 |
| 7B | Albert Pujols Black SP | 6.00 | 15.00 |
| 8 | Vicente Padilla | .20 | .50 |
| 9 | Bobby Crosby | .25 | .60 |
| 10A | Derek Jeter New Logo | 1.50 | 4.00 |
| 10B | Derek Jeter Old Logo SP | 6.00 | 15.00 |
| 11A | Pat Burrell New Logo | .25 | .60 |
| 11B | Pat Burrell Old Logo SP | 2.00 | 5.00 |
| 12 | Armando Benitez | .20 | .50 |
| 13 | Javier Vazquez | .25 | .60 |
| 14 | Justin Morneau | .25 | .60 |
| 15 | Doug Mientkiewicz | .25 | .60 |
| 16 | Kevin Brown | .25 | .60 |
| 17 | Alexis Gomez | .20 | .50 |
| 18A | Lance Berkman Blue | .25 | .60 |
| 18B | Lance Berkman Black SP | 2.00 | 5.00 |
| 19 | Adrian Gonzalez | .20 | .50 |
| 20A | Todd Helton Green | .40 | 1.00 |
| 20B | Todd Helton Black SP | 3.00 | 8.00 |
| 21 | Carlos Pena | .20 | .50 |
| 22 | Matt Lawton | .20 | .50 |
| 23 | Omer Deesens | .20 | .50 |
| 24 | Hee Seop Choi | .20 | .50 |
| 25 | Chris Duncan SP RC | 5.00 | 12.00 |
| 26 | Ugueth Urbina | .20 | .50 |
| 27A | Rodrigo Lopez New Logo | .20 | .50 |
| 27B | Rodrigo Lopez Old Logo SP | 2.00 | 5.00 |
| 28 | Damian Moss | .20 | .50 |
| 29 | Steve Finley | .25 | .60 |
| 30A | Sammy Sosa New Logo | .60 | 1.50 |
| 30B | Sammy Sosa Old Logo SP | 3.00 | 8.00 |
| 31 | Kevin Cash | .20 | .50 |
| 32 | Kenny Rogers | .25 | .60 |
| 33 | Ben Grieve | .20 | .50 |
| 34 | Jason Simontacchi | .20 | .50 |
| 35 | Shin-Soo Choo | .20 | .50 |
| 36 | Freddy Garcia | .25 | .60 |
| 37 | Jesse Foppert | .25 | .60 |
| 38 | Tony LaRussa MG | .20 | .50 |
| 39 | Mark Kotsay | .25 | .60 |
| 40 | Barry Zito | .25 | .60 |
| 41 | Josh Fogg | .20 | .50 |
| 42 | Marlon Byrd | .20 | .50 |
| 43 | Marcus Thames | .20 | .50 |
| 44 | Al Leiter | .20 | .50 |
| 45 | Michael Barrett | .20 | .50 |
| 46 | Jake Peavy | .25 | .60 |
| 47 | Dustan Mohr | .20 | .50 |
| 48 | Alex Sanchez | .20 | .50 |
| 49 | Chin-Feng Chen | .25 | .60 |
| 50A | Kazuhisa Ishii Blue | .25 | .60 |
| 50B | Kazuhisa Ishii Black SP | 2.00 | 5.00 |
| 51 | Carlos Beltran | .25 | .60 |
| 52 | Franklin Gutierrez RC | .40 | 1.00 |
| 53 | Miguel Cabrera | .60 | 1.50 |
| 54 | Roger Clemens | 1.25 | 3.00 |
| 55 | Juan Cruz | .20 | .50 |
| 56 | Jason Young | .20 | .50 |
| 57 | Alex Herrera | .20 | .50 |
| 58 | Aaron Boone | .20 | .50 |
| 59 | Mark Buehrle | .25 | .60 |
| 60 | Larry Walker | .25 | .60 |
| 61 | Morgan Ensberg | .25 | .60 |
| 62 | Barry Larkin | .40 | 1.00 |
| 63 | Joe Borchard | .20 | .50 |
| 64 | Jason Dubois | .20 | .50 |
| 65 | Shea Hillenbrand | .20 | .50 |
| 66 | Jay Gibbons | .20 | .50 |
| 67 | Vinny Castilla | .20 | .50 |
| 68 | Jeff Mathis | .25 | .60 |
| 69 | Curt Schilling | .25 | .60 |
| 70 | Garret Anderson | .25 | .60 |
| 71 | Josh Phelps | .25 | .60 |
| 72 | Chan Ho Park | .25 | .60 |
| 73 | Edgar Renteria | .25 | .60 |
| 74 | Kazuhiro Sasaki | .25 | .60 |
| 75 | Lloyd McClendon MG | .20 | .50 |
| 76 | Jon Lieber | .20 | .50 |
| 77 | Rolando Viera | .20 | .50 |
| 78 | Jon Corenie | .25 | .60 |
| 79 | Kevin Millwood | .25 | .60 |
| 80A | Randy Johnson Green | .60 | 1.50 |
| 80B | Randy Johnson Black SP | 5.00 | 12.00 |
| 81 | Troy Percival | .25 | .60 |
| 82 | Cliff Floyd | .25 | .60 |
| 83 | Tony Graffanino | .20 | .50 |
| 84 | Austin Kearns | .20 | .50 |
| 85 | Manuel Ramirez SP RC | 3.00 | 8.00 |
| 86 | Jim Tracy MG | .20 | .50 |
| 87 | Rondell White | .25 | .60 |
| 88 | Trot Nixon | .25 | .60 |
| 89 | Carlos Lee | .25 | .60 |
| 90 | Mike Lowell | .25 | .60 |
| 91 | Raul Ibanez | .25 | .60 |
| 92 | Ricardo Rodriguez | .20 | .50 |
| 93 | Ben Sheets | .25 | .60 |
| 94 | Jason Perry SP RC | 3.00 | 8.00 |
| 95 | Mark Teixeira | .40 | 1.00 |
| 96 | Brad Fullmer | .20 | .50 |
| 97 | Casey Kotchman | .25 | .60 |
| 98 | Craig Counsell | .20 | .50 |
| 99 | Jason Marquis | .20 | .50 |

|  |  | | |
|---|---|---|---|
| 100A | N.Garciaparra New Logo | 1.00 | 2.50 |
| 100B | N.Garciaparra Old Logo SP | 5.00 | 12.00 |
| 101 | Ed Rogers | .20 | .50 |
| 102 | Wilson Betemit | .20 | .50 |
| 103 | Wayne Lydon RC | .40 | 1.00 |
| 104 | Jack Cust | .20 | .50 |
| 105 | Derrek Lee | .40 | 1.00 |
| 106 | Jim Kavourias | .20 | .50 |
| 107 | Joe Randa | .25 | .60 |
| 108 | Taylor Buchholz | .20 | .50 |
| 109 | Gabe Kapler | .25 | .60 |
| 110 | Preston Wilson | .25 | .60 |
| 111 | Craig Biggio | .40 | 1.00 |
| 112 | Paul Lo Duca | .25 | .60 |
| 113 | Eddie Guardado | .20 | .50 |
| 114 | Andres Galarraga | .40 | 1.00 |
| 115 | Edgardo Alfonzo | .25 | .60 |
| 116 | Robin Ventura | .25 | .60 |
| 117 | Jeremy Giambi | .20 | .50 |
| 118 | Ray Durham | .25 | .60 |
| 119 | Mariano Rivera | .60 | 1.50 |
| 120 | Jimmy Rollins | .25 | .60 |
| 121 | Dennis Tankersley | .20 | .50 |
| 122 | Jason Schmidt | .25 | .60 |
| 123 | Bret Boone | .25 | .60 |
| 124 | Josh Hamilton | .40 | 1.00 |
| 125 | Scott Rolen | .40 | 1.00 |
| 126 | Steve Cox | .20 | .50 |
| 127 | Larry Bowa MG | .25 | .60 |
| 128 | Adam LaRoche SP | 2.00 | 5.00 |
| 129 | Ryan Klesko | .25 | .60 |
| 130 | Tim Hudson | .25 | .60 |
| 131 | Brandon Claussen | .20 | .50 |
| 132 | Craig Brazell SP RC | 2.00 | 5.00 |
| 133 | Grady Little MG | .20 | .50 |
| 134 | Jarrod Washburn | .20 | .50 |
| 135 | Lyle Overbay | .20 | .50 |
| 136 | John Burkett | .20 | .50 |
| 137 | Daryl Clark RC | .40 | 1.00 |
| 138 | Kirk Rueter | .20 | .50 |
| 139A | Mauer Brothers Green | .60 | 1.50 |
| 139B | Mauer Brothers Black SP | 4.00 | 10.00 |
| 140 | Troy Glaus | .25 | .60 |
| 141 | Trey Hodges SP | 2.00 | 5.00 |
| 142 | Dallas McPherson | .25 | .60 |
| 143 | Art Howe MG | .20 | .50 |
| 144 | Jesus Cota | .20 | .50 |
| 145 | J.R. House | .20 | .50 |
| 146 | Reggie Sanders | .25 | .60 |
| 147 | Clint Nageotte | .20 | .50 |
| 148 | Jim Edmonds | .25 | .60 |
| 149 | Carl Crawford | .25 | .60 |
| 150A | Mike Piazza Blue | 1.00 | 2.50 |
| 150B | Mike Piazza Black SP | 5.00 | 12.00 |
| 151 | Seung Song | .20 | .50 |
| 152 | Roberto Hernandez | .20 | .50 |
| 153 | Marquis Grissom | .25 | .60 |
| 154 | Billy Wagner | .25 | .60 |
| 155 | Josh Beckett | .25 | .60 |
| 156A | Randall Simon New Logo | .20 | .50 |
| 156B | Randall Simon Old Logo SP | 2.00 | 5.00 |
| 157 | Ben Broussard | .20 | .50 |
| 158 | Russell Branyan | .20 | .50 |
| 159 | Frank Thomas | .60 | 1.50 |
| 160 | Alex Escobar | .20 | .50 |
| 161 | Mark Bellhorn | .25 | .60 |
| 162 | Melvin Mora | .25 | .60 |
| 163 | Andruw Jones | .40 | 1.00 |
| 164 | Danny Bautista | .20 | .50 |
| 165 | Ramon Ortiz | .20 | .50 |
| 166 | Wily Mo Pena | .25 | .60 |
| 167 | Jose Jimenez | .20 | .50 |
| 168 | Mark Redman | .20 | .50 |
| 169 | Angel Berroa | .20 | .50 |
| 170 | Andy Marte SP RC | 5.00 | 12.00 |
| 171 | Juan Gonzalez | .25 | .60 |
| 172 | Fernando Vina | .20 | .50 |
| 173 | Joel Pineiro | .20 | .50 |
| 174 | Boof Bonser | .20 | .50 |
| 175 | Bernie Castro SP RC | 2.00 | 5.00 |
| 176 | Bobby Cox MG | .20 | .50 |
| 177 | Jeff Kent | .25 | .60 |
| 178 | Oliver Perez | .25 | .60 |
| 179 | Chase Utley | .60 | 1.50 |
| 180 | Mark Mulder | .25 | .60 |
| 181 | Bobby Abreu | .25 | .60 |
| 182 | Ramiro Mendoza | .20 | .50 |
| 183 | Aaron Heilman | .20 | .50 |
| 184 | A.J. Pierzynski | .25 | .60 |
| 185 | Eric Gagne | .25 | .60 |
| 186 | Kirk Saarloos | .20 | .50 |
| 187 | Ron Gardenhire MG | .20 | .50 |
| 188 | Dmitri Young | .25 | .60 |
| 189 | Todd Zeile | .25 | .60 |
| 190A | Jim Thome New Logo | .40 | 1.00 |
| 190B | Jim Thome Old Logo SP | 3.00 | 8.00 |
| 191 | Cliff Lee | .25 | .60 |
| 192 | Matt Morris | .25 | .60 |
| 193 | Robert Fick | .25 | .60 |
| 194 | C.C. Sabathia | .25 | .60 |
| 195 | Alexis Rios | .25 | .60 |
| 196 | D'Angelo Jimenez | .20 | .50 |
| 197 | Edgar Martinez | .40 | 1.00 |
| 198 | Robb Nen | .25 | .60 |
| 199 | Taggert Bozied | .25 | .60 |
| 200 | Vladimir Guerrero SP | 3.00 | 8.00 |
| 201 | Walter Young SP | 2.00 | 5.00 |
| 202 | Brendan Harris RC | .40 | 1.00 |
| 203 | Mike Hargrove MG | .20 | .50 |
| 204 | Vernon Wells | .25 | .60 |
| 205 | Hank Blalock | .20 | .50 |
| 206 | Mike Cameron | .20 | .50 |
| 207 | Tony Batista | .20 | .50 |
| 208 | Matt Williams | .25 | .60 |
| 209 | Tony Womack | .20 | .50 |
| 210 | Ramon Nivar-Martinez RC | .40 | 1.00 |
| 211 | Aaron Sele | .20 | .50 |
| 212 | Mark Grace | .40 | 1.00 |
| 213 | Joe Crede | .25 | .60 |
| 214 | Ryan Dempster | .20 | .50 |
| 215 | Omar Vizquel | .40 | 1.00 |
| 216 | Juan Pierre | .25 | .60 |
| 217 | Denny Bautista | .20 | .50 |
| 218 | Chuck Knoblauch | .25 | .60 |
| 219 | Eric Karros | .25 | .60 |
| 220 | Victor Diaz | .25 | .60 |
| 221 | Jacque Jones | .25 | .60 |
| 222 | Jose Vidro | .20 | .50 |
| 223 | Joe McEwing | .20 | .50 |
| 224 | Nick Johnson | .20 | .50 |
| 225 | Eric Chavez | .25 | .60 |
| 226 | Jose Mesa | .20 | .50 |
| 227 | Aramis Ramirez | .20 | .50 |
| 228 | John Lackey | .20 | .50 |
| 229 | David Bell | .20 | .50 |
| 230 | John Olerud | .25 | .60 |
| 231 | Tino Martinez | .40 | 1.00 |
| 232 | Randy Winn | .20 | .50 |
| 233 | Todd Hollandsworth | .20 | .50 |
| 234 | Ruddy Lugo RC | .40 | 1.00 |
| 235 | Carlos Delgado | .25 | .60 |
| 236 | Chris Narveson | .20 | .50 |
| 237 | Tim Salmon | .40 | 1.00 |
| 238 | Orlando Palmeiro | .20 | .50 |
| 239 | Jeff Clark SP RC | 2.00 | 5.00 |
| 240 | Byung-Hyun Kim | .25 | .60 |
| 241 | Mike Remlinger | .20 | .50 |
| 242 | Johnny Damon | .40 | 1.00 |
| 243 | Corey Patterson | .25 | .60 |
| 244 | Paul Konerko | .25 | .60 |
| 245 | Danny Graves | .20 | .50 |
| 246 | Ellis Burks | .20 | .50 |
| 247 | Gavin Floyd | .25 | .60 |
| 248 | Jaime Bubela RC | .40 | 1.00 |
| 249 | Sean Burroughs | .20 | .50 |
| 250 | Alex Rodriguez SP | 5.00 | 12.00 |
| 251 | Gabe Gross | .25 | .60 |
| 252 | Rafael Palmeiro | .40 | 1.00 |
| 253 | Dewon Brazelton | .20 | .50 |
| 254 | Jimmy Journell | .20 | .50 |
| 255 | Rafael Soriano | .20 | .50 |
| 256 | Jerome Williams | .20 | .50 |
| 257 | Xavier Nady | .25 | .60 |
| 258 | Mike Williams | .20 | .50 |
| 259 | Randy Wolf | .20 | .50 |
| 260A | Miguel Tejada Orange | .25 | .60 |
| 260B | Miguel Tejada Black SP | 2.00 | 5.00 |
| 261 | Juan Rivera | .20 | .50 |
| 262 | Rey Ordonez | .20 | .50 |
| 263 | Bartolo Colon | .20 | .50 |
| 264 | Eric Milton | .20 | .50 |
| 265 | Jeffrey Hammonds | .20 | .50 |
| 266 | Odalis Perez | .20 | .50 |
| 267 | Mike Sweeney | .25 | .60 |
| 268 | Richard Hidalgo | .20 | .50 |
| 269 | Alex Gonzalez | .20 | .50 |
| 270 | Aaron Cook | .20 | .50 |
| 271 | Earl Snyder | .20 | .50 |
| 272 | Todd Walker | .20 | .50 |
| 273 | Aaron Rowand | .25 | .60 |
| 274 | Matt Clement | .20 | .50 |
| 275 | Anastacio Martinez | .20 | .50 |
| 276 | Mike Bordick | .25 | .60 |
| 277 | John Smoltz | .40 | 1.00 |
| 278 | Scott Hairston | .20 | .50 |
| 279 | David Eckstein | .25 | .60 |
| 280 | Shannon Stewart | .25 | .60 |
| 281 | Carl Everett | .25 | .60 |
| 282 | Aubrey Huff | .25 | .60 |
| 283 | Mike Mussina | .40 | 1.00 |
| 284 | Ruben Sierra | .20 | .50 |
| 285 | Russ Ortiz | .20 | .50 |
| 286 | Brian Lawrence | .20 | .50 |
| 287 | Kip Wells | .20 | .50 |
| 288 | Placido Polanco | .20 | .50 |
| 289 | Ted Lilly | .20 | .50 |
| 290 | Andy Pettitte | .40 | 1.00 |
| 291 | John Buck | .20 | .50 |
| 292 | Orlando Cabrera | .25 | .60 |
| 293 | Cristian Guzman | .20 | .50 |
| 294 | Ruben Quevedo | .20 | .50 |
| 295 | Cesar Izturis | .20 | .50 |
| 296 | Ryan Ludwick | .20 | .50 |
| 297 | Roy Oswalt | .25 | .60 |
| 298 | Jason Stokes | .20 | .50 |
| 299 | Mike Hampton | .25 | .60 |
| 300 | Pedro Martinez | .40 | 1.00 |
| 301 | Nic Jackson | .20 | .50 |
| 302A | Magglio Ordonez New Logo | .20 | .50 |
| 302B | Magglio Ordonez Old Logo SP | 2.00 | 5.00 |
| 303 | Manny Ramirez | .40 | 1.00 |
| 304 | Jorge Julio | .20 | .50 |
| 305 | Javy Lopez | .25 | .60 |
| 306 | Roy Halladay | .25 | .60 |
| 307 | Kevin Mench | .20 | .50 |
| 308 | Jason Isringhausen | .20 | .50 |
| 309 | Carlos Guillen | .20 | .50 |
| 310 | Tsuyoshi Shinjo | .25 | .60 |
| 311 | Phil Nevin | .25 | .60 |
| 312 | Pokey Reese | .20 | .50 |
| 313 | Jorge Padilla | .20 | .50 |
| 314 | Jermaine Dye | .25 | .60 |
| 315 | David Wells | .25 | .60 |
| 316 | Mo Vaughn | .25 | .60 |
| 317 | Bernie Williams | .40 | 1.00 |
| 318 | Michael Restovich | .20 | .50 |
| 319 | Jose Hernandez | .20 | .50 |
| 320 | Richie Sexson | .25 | .60 |
| 321 | Dontrelle Ward | .20 | .50 |
| 322 | Luis Castillo | .25 | .60 |
| 323 | Rene Reyes | .20 | .50 |
| 324 | Victor Martinez | .40 | 1.00 |
| 325A | Adam Dunn New Logo | .40 | 1.00 |
| 325B | Adam Dunn Old Logo SP | 2.00 | 5.00 |
| 326 | Corwin Malone | .20 | .50 |
| 327 | Kerry Wood | .25 | .60 |
| 328 | Rickey Henderson | .60 | 1.50 |
| 329 | Marty Cordova | .20 | .50 |
| 330 | Greg Maddux | 1.00 | 2.50 |
| 331 | Miguel Batista | .20 | .50 |
| 332 | Chris Bootcheck | .20 | .50 |
| 333 | Carlos Baerga | .20 | .50 |
| 334 | Antonio Alfonseca | .20 | .50 |
| 335 | Shane Halter | .20 | .50 |
| 336 | Juan Encarnacion | .20 | .50 |
| 337 | Tom Gordon | .20 | .50 |
| 338 | Hideo Nomo | .60 | 1.50 |
| 339 | Torii Hunter | .25 | .60 |
| 340A | Alfonso Soriano Yellow | .25 | .60 |
| 340B | Alfonso Soriano Black SP | 2.00 | 5.00 |
| 341 | Roberto Alomar | .40 | 1.00 |
| 342 | David Justice | .25 | .60 |
| 343 | Mike Lieberthal | .25 | .60 |
| 344 | Jeff Weaver | .20 | .50 |
| 345 | Timo Perez | .20 | .50 |
| 346 | Travis Lee | .20 | .50 |
| 347 | Sean Casey | .25 | .60 |
| 348 | Willie Harris | .20 | .50 |
| 349 | Derek Lowe | .25 | .60 |
| 350 | Tom Glavine | .40 | 1.00 |
| 351 | Eric Hinske | .25 | .60 |
| 352 | Rocco Baldelli | .25 | .60 |
| 353 | J.D. Drew | .25 | .60 |
| 354 | Jamie Moyer | .25 | .60 |

|  | | |
|---|---|---|
| 355 Todd Linden | .20 | .50 |
| 356 Benito Santiago | .25 | .60 |
| 357 Brad Baker | .20 | .50 |
| 358 Alex Gonzalez | .20 | .50 |
| 359 Brandon Duckworth | .20 | .50 |
| 360 John Rheinecker | .20 | .50 |
| 361 Orlando Hernandez | .25 | .60 |
| 362 Pedro Astacio | .20 | .50 |
| 363 Brad Wilkerson | .20 | .50 |
| 364 David Ortiz SP | 3.00 | 8.00 |
| 365 Geoff Jenkins SP | 2.00 | 5.00 |
| 366 Brian Jordan SP | 2.00 | 5.00 |
| 367 Paul Byrd SP | 2.00 | 5.00 |
| 368 Jason Lane SP | 2.00 | 5.00 |
| 369 Jeff Bagwell SP | 3.00 | 8.00 |
| 370 Bobby Higginson SP | 2.00 | 5.00 |
| 371 Juan Uribe SP | 2.00 | 5.00 |
| 372 Lee Stevens SP | 2.00 | 5.00 |
| 373 Jimmy Haynes SP | 2.00 | 5.00 |
| 374 Jose Valentin SP | 2.00 | 5.00 |
| 375 Ken Griffey Jr. SP | 5.00 | 12.00 |
| 376 Barry Bonds SP | 8.00 | 20.00 |
| 377 Gary Matthews Jr. SP | 2.00 | 5.00 |
| 378 Gary Sheffield SP | 2.00 | 5.00 |
| 379 Rick Helling SP | 2.00 | 5.00 |
| 380 Junior Spivey SP | 2.00 | 5.00 |
| 381 Francisco Rodriguez SP | 2.00 | 5.00 |
| 382 Chipper Jones SP | 3.00 | 8.00 |
| 383 Orlando Hudson SP | 2.00 | 5.00 |
| 384 Ivan Rodriguez SP | 3.00 | 8.00 |
| 385 Chris Snelling SP | 2.00 | 5.00 |
| 386 Kenny Lofton SP | 2.00 | 5.00 |
| 387 Eric Cyr SP | 2.00 | 5.00 |
| 388 Jason Kendall SP | 2.00 | 5.00 |
| 389 Marlon Anderson SP | 2.00 | 5.00 |
| 390 Billy Koch SP | 2.00 | 5.00 |
| 392 Jose Reyes SP | 2.00 | 5.00 |
| 393 Fernando Tatis SP | 2.00 | 5.00 |
| 394 Michael Cuddyer SP | 2.00 | 5.00 |
| 395 Mark Prior SP | 3.00 | 8.00 |
| 396 Dontrelle Willis SP | 3.00 | 8.00 |
| 397 Jay Payton SP | 2.00 | 5.00 |
| 398 Brandon Phillips SP | 2.00 | 5.00 |
| 399 Dustin Moseley SP RC | 2.00 | 5.00 |
| 400 Jason Giambi SP | 2.00 | 5.00 |
| 401 John Mabry SP | 2.00 | 5.00 |
| 402 Ron Gant SP | 2.00 | 5.00 |
| 403 J.T. Snow SP | 2.00 | 5.00 |
| 404 Jeff Cirillo SP | 2.00 | 5.00 |
| 405 Darin Erstad SP | 2.00 | 5.00 |
| 406 Luis Gonzalez SP | 2.00 | 5.00 |
| 407 Marcus Giles SP | 2.00 | 5.00 |
| 408 Brian Daubach SP | 2.00 | 5.00 |
| 409 Moises Alou SP | 2.00 | 5.00 |
| 410 Raul Mondesi SP | 2.00 | 5.00 |
| 411 Adrian Beltre SP | 2.00 | 5.00 |
| 412 A.J. Burnett SP | 2.00 | 5.00 |
| 413 Jason Jennings SP | 2.00 | 5.00 |
| 414 Edwin Almonte SP | 2.00 | 5.00 |
| 415 Fred McGriff SP | 3.00 | 8.00 |
| 416 Tim Raines Jr. SP | 2.00 | 5.00 |
| 417 Rafael Furcal SP | 2.00 | 5.00 |
| 418 Erubiel Durazo SP | 2.00 | 5.00 |
| 419 Drew Henson SP | 2.00 | 5.00 |
| 420 Kevin Appier SP | 2.00 | 5.00 |
| 421 Chad Tracy SP | 2.00 | 5.00 |
| 422 Adam Wainwright SP | 2.00 | 5.00 |
| 423 Choo Freeman SP | 2.00 | 5.00 |
| 424 Sandy Alomar Jr. SP | 2.00 | 5.00 |
| 425 Corey Koskie SP | 2.00 | 5.00 |
| 426 Jeromy Burnitz SP | 2.00 | 5.00 |
| 427 Jorge Posada SP | 3.00 | 8.00 |
| 428 Jason Arnold SP | 2.00 | 5.00 |
| 429 Brett Myers SP | 2.00 | 5.00 |
| 430 Shawn Green SP | 2.00 | 5.00 |

## 2004 Topps Heritage

| | | |
|---|---|---|
| COMPLETE SET (495) | 200.00 | 350.00 |
| COMP.SET w/o SP's (385) | 30.00 | 60.00 |
| 1A Jim Thome Fielding | .40 | 1.00 |
| 1B Jim Thome Hitting SP | 3.00 | 8.00 |
| 2 Nomar Garciaparra SP | 4.00 | 10.00 |
| 3 Aramis Ramirez | .25 | .60 |
| 4 Rafael Palmeiro SP | 3.00 | 8.00 |
| 5 Danny Graves | .20 | .50 |
| 6 Casey Blake | .20 | .50 |
| 7 Juan Uribe | .20 | .50 |
| 8A Dmitri Young New Logo | .25 | .60 |

| | | |
|---|---|---|
| 8B Dmitri Young Old Logo SP | 2.00 | 5.00 |
| 9 Billy Wagner | .25 | .60 |
| 10A Jason Giambi Swinging | .25 | .60 |
| 10B Jason Giambi Btg Stance SP | 2.00 | 5.00 |
| 11 Carlos Beltran | .25 | .60 |
| 12 Chad Hermansen | .20 | .50 |
| 13 B.J. Upton | .40 | 1.00 |
| 14 Dustan Mohr | .20 | .50 |
| 15 Endy Chavez | .20 | .50 |
| 16 Cliff Floyd | .25 | .60 |
| 17 Bernie Williams | .40 | 1.00 |
| 18 Eric Chavez | .25 | .60 |
| 19 Chase Utley | .40 | 1.00 |
| 20 Randy Johnson | .60 | 1.50 |
| 21 Vernon Wells | .25 | .60 |
| 22 Juan Gonzalez | .25 | .60 |
| 23 Joe Kennedy | .20 | .50 |
| 24 Bengie Molina | .20 | .50 |
| 25 Carlos Lee | .25 | .60 |
| 26 Horacio Ramirez | .20 | .50 |
| 27 Anthony Acevedo RC | .30 | .75 |
| 28 Sammy Sosa SP | 3.00 | 8.00 |
| 29 Jon Garland | .25 | .60 |
| 30A Adam Dunn Fielding | .25 | .60 |
| 30B Adam Dunn Hitting SP | 2.00 | 5.00 |
| 31 Aaron Rowand | .25 | .60 |
| 32 Jody Gerut | .20 | .50 |
| 33 Chin-Hui Tsao | .25 | .60 |
| 34 Alex Sanchez | .20 | .50 |
| 35 A.J. Burnett | .25 | .60 |
| 36 Brad Ausmus | .25 | .60 |
| 37 Blake Hawksworth RC | .40 | 1.00 |
| 38 Francisco Rodriguez | .25 | .60 |
| 39 Alex Cintron | .20 | .50 |
| 40A Chipper Jones Pointing | .60 | 1.50 |
| 40B Chipper Jones Fielding SP | 3.00 | 8.00 |
| 41 Deivi Cruz | .20 | .50 |
| 42 Bill Mueller | .25 | .60 |
| 43 Joe Borowski | .20 | .50 |
| 44 Jimmy Haynes | .20 | .50 |
| 45 Mark Loretta | .20 | .50 |
| 46 Jerome Williams | .20 | .50 |
| 47 Gary Sheffield Yanks SP | 3.00 | 8.00 |
| 48 Richard Hidalgo | .20 | .50 |
| 49A Jason Kendall New Logo | .25 | .60 |
| 49B Jason Kendall Old Logo SP | 2.00 | 5.00 |
| 50 Ichiro Suzuki SP | 5.00 | 12.00 |
| 51 Jim Edmonds | .25 | .60 |
| 52 Frank Catalanotto | .20 | .50 |
| 53 Jose Contreras | .20 | .50 |
| 54 Mo Vaughn | .25 | .60 |
| 55 Brendan Donnelly | .20 | .50 |
| 56 Luis Gonzalez | .25 | .60 |
| 57 Robert Fick | .20 | .50 |
| 58 Laynce Nix | .40 | 1.00 |
| 59 Johnny Damon | .40 | 1.00 |
| 60A Maggio Ordonez Running | .25 | .60 |
| 60B Maggio Ordonez Hitting SP | 2.00 | 5.00 |
| 61 Matt Clement | .25 | .60 |
| 62 Ryan Ludwick | .20 | .50 |
| 63 Luis Castillo | .20 | .50 |
| 64 Dave Crouthers RC | .30 | .75 |
| 65 Dave Berg | .20 | .50 |
| 66 Kyle Davies RC | 1.50 | 4.00 |
| 67 Tim Salmon | .25 | .60 |
| 68 Marcus Giles | .25 | .60 |
| 69 Marty Cordova | .20 | .50 |
| 70A Todd Helton White Jsy | .40 | 1.00 |
| 70B Todd Helton Purple Jsy SP | 3.00 | 8.00 |
| 71 Jeff Kent | .25 | .60 |
| 72 Michael Tucker | .20 | .50 |
| 73 Cesar Izturis | .20 | .50 |
| 74 Paul Quantrill | .20 | .50 |
| 75 Conor Jackson RC | 1.25 | 3.00 |

| | | |
|---|---|---|
| 76 Placido Polanco | .20 | .50 |
| 77 Adam Eaton | .20 | .50 |
| 78 Ramon Hernandez | .25 | .60 |
| 79 Edgardo Alfonzo | .20 | .50 |
| 80 Dioner Navarro RC | .40 | 1.00 |
| 81 Woody Williams | .20 | .50 |
| 82 Rey Ordonez | .20 | .50 |
| 83 Randy Winn | .20 | .50 |
| 84 Casey Myers RC | .30 | .75 |
| 85A R.Choy Foo New Logo RC | .30 | .75 |
| 85B R.Choy Foo Old Logo SP | 2.00 | 5.00 |
| 86 Ray Durham | .25 | .60 |
| 87 Sean Burroughs | .20 | .50 |
| 88 Tim Frend RC | .30 | .75 |
| 89 Shigetoshi Hasegawa | .25 | .60 |
| 90 Jeffrey Allison RC | .30 | .75 |
| 91 Orlando Hudson | .20 | .50 |
| 92 Matt Creighton SP RC | 2.00 | 5.00 |
| 93 Tim Worrell | .20 | .50 |
| 94 Kris Benson | .20 | .50 |
| 95 Mike Lieberthal | .25 | .60 |
| 96 David Wells | .25 | .60 |
| 97 Jason Phillips | .20 | .50 |
| 98 Bobby Cox MGR | .20 | .50 |
| 99 Johan Santana | .60 | 1.50 |
| 100A Alex Rodriguez Hitting | 1.00 | 2.50 |
| 100B Alex Rodriguez Throwing SP | 4.00 | 10.00 |
| 101 John Vander Wal | .20 | .50 |
| 102 Orlando Cabrera | .25 | .60 |
| 103 Hideo Nomo | .60 | 1.50 |
| 104 Todd Walker | .20 | .50 |
| 105 Jason Johnson | .20 | .50 |
| 106 Matt Mantei | .20 | .50 |
| 107 Jarrod Washburn | .20 | .50 |
| 108 Preston Wilson | .25 | .60 |
| 109 Carl Pavano | .25 | .60 |
| 110 Geoff Blum | .20 | .50 |
| 111 Eric Gagne | .20 | .50 |
| 112 Geoff Jenkins | .20 | .50 |
| 113 Joe Torre MG | .40 | 1.00 |
| 114 Jon Knott RC | .30 | .75 |
| 115 Hank Blalock | .25 | .60 |
| 116 John Olerud | .25 | .60 |
| 117A Pat Burrell New Logo | .25 | .60 |
| 117B Pat Burrell Old Logo SP | 2.00 | 5.00 |
| 118 Aaron Boone | .25 | .60 |
| 119 Zach Day | .20 | .50 |
| 120A Frank Thomas New Logo | .60 | 1.50 |
| 120B Frank Thomas Old Logo SP | 3.00 | 8.00 |
| 121 Kyle Farnsworth | .20 | .50 |
| 122 Derek Lowe | .25 | .60 |
| 123 Zach Minor SP RC | 3.00 | 8.00 |
| 124 Matthew Moses SP RC | 3.00 | 8.00 |
| 125 Jesse Roman RC | .30 | .75 |
| 126 Josh Phelps | .20 | .50 |
| 127 Nic Ungs RC | .30 | .75 |
| 128 Dan Haren | .25 | .60 |
| 129 Kirk Rueter | .20 | .50 |
| 130 Jack McKeon MGR | .20 | .50 |
| 131 Keith Foulke | .25 | .60 |
| 132 Garrett Stephenson | .20 | .50 |
| 133 Wes Helms | .20 | .50 |
| 134 Raul Ibanez | .25 | .60 |
| 135 Morgan Ensberg | .25 | .60 |
| 136 Jay Payton | .20 | .50 |
| 137 Billy Koch | .20 | .50 |
| 138 Mark Grudzielanek | .20 | .50 |
| 139 Rodrigo Lopez | .20 | .50 |
| 140 Corey Patterson | .20 | .50 |
| 141 Troy Percival | .25 | .60 |
| 142 Shea Hillenbrand | .25 | .60 |
| 143 Brad Fullmer | .20 | .50 |
| 144 Ricky Nolasco RC | .60 | 1.50 |
| 145 Mark Teixeira | .40 | 1.00 |
| 146 Tydus Meadows RC | .30 | .75 |
| 147 Toby Hall | .20 | .50 |
| 148 Orlando Palmeiro | .20 | .50 |
| 149 Khalid Ballouli RC | .30 | .75 |
| 150 Grady Little MGR | .20 | .50 |
| 151 David Eckstein | .25 | .60 |
| 152 Kenny Perez RC | .30 | .75 |
| 153 Ben Grieve | .20 | .50 |
| 154 Ismael Valdes | .20 | .50 |
| 155 Bret Boone | .25 | .60 |
| 156 Jesse Foppert | .20 | .50 |
| 157 Vicente Padilla | .20 | .50 |
| 158 Bobby Abreu | .25 | .60 |
| 159 Scott Hatteberg | .20 | .50 |

|  |  | | |
|---|---|---|---|
| 160 | Carlos Quentin RC | 1.00 | 2.50 |
| 161 | Anthony Lerew RC | .40 | 1.00 |
| 162 | Lance Carter | .20 | .50 |
| 163 | Robb Nen | .25 | .60 |
| 164 | Zach Duke SP RC | 4.00 | 10.00 |
| 165 | Xavier Nady | .20 | .50 |
| 166 | Kip Wells | .20 | .50 |
| 167 | Kevin Millwood | .25 | .60 |
| 168 | Jon Lieber | .20 | .50 |
| 169 | Jose Reyes | .20 | .50 |
| 170 | Eric Byrnes | .20 | .50 |
| 171 | Paul Konerko | .25 | .60 |
| 172 | Chris Lubanski | .25 | .60 |
| 173 | Jae Weong Seo | .20 | .50 |
| 174 | Corey Koskie | .20 | .50 |
| 175 | Tim Stauffer RC | 4.00 | 1.00 |
| 176 | John Lackey | .20 | .50 |
| 177 | Danny Bautista | .20 | .50 |
| 178 | Shane Reynolds | .20 | .50 |
| 179 | Jorge Julio | .20 | .50 |
| 180A | Manny Ramirez New Logo | .40 | 1.00 |
| 180B | Manny Ramirez Old Logo SP | 3.00 | 8.00 |
| 181 | Alex Gonzalez | .20 | .50 |
| 182A | Moises Alou New Logo | .25 | .60 |
| 182B | Moises Alou Old Logo SP | 2.00 | 5.00 |
| 183 | Mark Buehrle | .25 | .60 |
| 184 | Carlos Guillen | .25 | .60 |
| 185 | Nate Cornejo | .20 | .50 |
| 186 | Billy Traber | .20 | .50 |
| 187 | Jason Jennings | .20 | .50 |
| 188 | Eric Munson | .20 | .50 |
| 189 | Braden Looper | .20 | .50 |
| 190 | Juan Encarnacion | .20 | .50 |
| 191 | Dusty Baker MGR | .25 | .60 |
| 192 | Travis Lee | .20 | .50 |
| 193 | Miguel Cairo | .20 | .50 |
| 194 | Rich Aurilia SP | 2.00 | 5.00 |
| 195 | Tom Gordon | .20 | .50 |
| 196 | Freddy Garcia | .25 | .60 |
| 197 | Brian Lawrence | .20 | .50 |
| 198 | Jorge Posada SP | 3.00 | 8.00 |
| 199 | Javier Vazquez | .25 | .60 |
| 200A | Albert Pujols New Logo | 1.25 | 3.00 |
| 200B | Albert Pujols Old Logo SP | 5.00 | 12.00 |
| 201 | Victor Zambrano | .20 | .50 |
| 202 | Eli Marrero | .20 | .50 |
| 203 | Joel Pineiro | .25 | .60 |
| 204 | Rondell White | .20 | .50 |
| 205 | Craig Ansman RC | .30 | .75 |
| 206 | Michael Young | .25 | .60 |
| 207 | Carlos Baerga | .20 | .50 |
| 208 | Andruw Jones | .40 | 1.00 |
| 209 | Jerry Hairston Jr. | .20 | .50 |
| 210 | Shawn Green SP | 2.00 | 5.00 |
| 211 | Ron Gardenhire MGR | .20 | .50 |
| 212 | Darin Erstad | .25 | .60 |
| 213A | Brandon Webb Glove Chest | .20 | .50 |
| 213B | Brandon Webb Glove Out SP | 2.00 | 5.00 |
| 214 | Greg Maddux | 1.00 | 2.50 |
| 215 | Reed Johnson | .20 | .50 |
| 216 | John Thomson | .20 | .50 |
| 217 | Tino Martinez | .40 | 1.00 |
| 218 | Mike Cameron | .20 | .50 |
| 219 | Edgar Martinez | .40 | 1.00 |
| 220 | Eric Young | .20 | .50 |
| 221 | Reggie Sanders | .25 | .60 |
| 222 | Randy Wolf | .20 | .50 |
| 223 | Enribel Durazo | .20 | .50 |
| 224 | Mike Mussina | .40 | 1.00 |
| 225 | Tom Glavine | .40 | 1.00 |
| 226 | Troy Glaus | .25 | .60 |
| 227 | Oscar Villarreal | .20 | .50 |
| 228 | David Segui | .20 | .50 |
| 229 | Jeff Suppan | .20 | .50 |
| 230 | Kenny Lofton | .25 | .60 |
| 231 | Esteban Loaiza | .20 | .50 |
| 232 | Felipe Lopez | .20 | .50 |
| 233 | Matt Lawton | .20 | .50 |
| 234 | Mark Bellhorn | .20 | .50 |
| 235 | Wili Ledezma | .20 | .50 |
| 236 | Todd Hollandsworth | .20 | .50 |
| 237 | Octavio Dotel | .20 | .50 |
| 238 | Darren Dreifort | .20 | .50 |
| 239 | Paul Lo Duca | .25 | .60 |
| 240 | Richie Sexson | .25 | .60 |
| 241 | Doug Mientkiewicz | .25 | .60 |
| 242 | Luis Rivas | .20 | .50 |
| 243 | Claudio Vargas | .20 | .50 |
| 244 | Mark Ellis | .20 | .50 |
| 245 | Brett Myers | .20 | .50 |
| 246 | Jake Peavy | .25 | .60 |
| 247 | Marquis Grissom | .20 | .50 |
| 248 | Armando Benitez | .20 | .50 |
| 249 | Ryan Franklin | .20 | .50 |
| 250A | Alfonso Soriano Throwing | .25 | .60 |
| 250B | Alfonso Soriano Fielding SP | - 2.00 | 5.00 |
| 251 | Tim Hudson | .25 | .60 |
| 252 | Shannon Stewart | .25 | .60 |
| 253 | A.J. Pierzynski | .25 | .60 |
| 254 | Runelvys Hernandez | .20 | .50 |
| 255 | Roy Oswalt | .25 | .60 |
| 256 | Shawn Chacon | .20 | .50 |
| 257 | Tony Graffanino | .20 | .50 |
| 258 | Tim Wakefield | .25 | .60 |
| 259 | Damian Miller | .20 | .50 |
| 260 | Joe Crede | .25 | .60 |
| 261 | Jason LaRue | .20 | .50 |
| 262 | Jose Jimenez | .20 | .50 |
| 263 | Juan Pierre | .25 | .60 |
| 264 | Wade Miller | .20 | .50 |
| 265 | Odalis Perez | .20 | .50 |
| 266 | Eddie Guardado | .20 | .50 |
| 267 | Rocky Biddle | .20 | .50 |
| 268 | Jeff Nelson | .20 | .50 |
| 269 | Terrence Long | .20 | .50 |
| 270 | Ramon Ortiz | .20 | .50 |
| 271 | Raul Mondesi | .25 | .60 |
| 272 | Ugueth Urbina | .20 | .50 |
| 273 | Jeromy Burnitz | .25 | .60 |
| 274 | Brad Radke | .20 | .50 |
| 275 | Jose Vidro | .25 | .60 |
| 276 | Bobby Jenks | .25 | .60 |
| 277 | Ty Wigginton | .20 | .50 |
| 278 | Jose Guillen | .25 | .60 |
| 279 | Delmon Young | .40 | 1.00 |
| 280 | Brian Giles | .25 | .60 |
| 281 | Jason Schmidt | .25 | .60 |
| 282 | Nick Markakis | .25 | .60 |
| 283 | Felipe Alou MGR | .25 | .60 |
| 284 | Carl Crawford | .25 | .60 |
| 285 | Neifi Perez | .20 | .50 |
| 286 | Miguel Tejada | .25 | .60 |
| 287 | Victor Martinez | .25 | .60 |
| 288 | Adam Kennedy | .20 | .50 |
| 289 | Kerry Lightenberg | .20 | .50 |
| 290 | Scott Williamson | .20 | .50 |
| 291 | Tony Womack | .20 | .50 |
| 292 | Travis Hafner | .25 | .60 |
| 293 | Bobby Crosby | .25 | .60 |
| 294 | Chad Billingsley | .25 | .60 |
| 295 | Russ Ortiz | .20 | .50 |
| 296 | John Burkett | .20 | .50 |
| 297 | Carlos Zambrano | .20 | .50 |
| 298 | Randall Simon | .20 | .50 |
| 299 | Juan Castro | .20 | .50 |
| 300 | Mike Lowell | .25 | .60 |
| 301 | Fred McGriff | .40 | 1.00 |
| 302 | Glendon Rusch | .20 | .50 |
| 303 | Sung Jung RC | .30 | .75 |
| 304 | Rocco Baldelli | .25 | .60 |
| 305 | Fernando Vina | .20 | .50 |
| 306 | Gil Meche | .20 | .50 |
| 307 | Jose Cruz Jr. | .20 | .50 |
| 308 | Bernie Castro | .20 | .50 |
| 309 | Scott Spiezio | .20 | .50 |
| 310 | Paul Byrd | .20 | .50 |
| 311A | Jay Gibbons New Logo | .20 | .50 |
| 311B | Jay Gibbons Old Logo SP | 2.00 | 5.00 |
| 312 | Trot Nixon | .25 | .60 |
| 313 | Chris O'Riordan RC | .30 | .75 |
| 314 | Julio Lugo | .20 | .50 |
| 315 | Ben Davis | .20 | .50 |
| 316 | Mike Williams | .20 | .50 |
| 317 | Trevor Hoffman | .25 | .60 |
| 318 | Andy Pettitte | .40 | 1.00 |
| 319 | Orlando Hernandez | .20 | .50 |
| 320 | Juan Rivera | .20 | .50 |
| 321 | Elizardo Ramirez | .20 | .50 |
| 322 | Junior Spivey | .20 | .50 |
| 323 | Tony Batista | .20 | .50 |
| 324 | Mike Remlinger | .20 | .50 |
| 325 | Alex Gonzalez | .20 | .50 |
| 326 | Aaron Hill | .20 | .50 |
| 327 | Steve Finley | .25 | .60 |
| 328 | Vinny Castilla | .25 | .60 |
| 329 | Eric Duncan | .20 | .50 |
| 330 | Mike Gosling RC | .30 | .75 |
| 331 | Eric Hinske | .20 | .50 |
| 332 | Scott Rolen | .40 | 1.00 |
| 333 | Benito Santiago | .20 | .50 |
| 334 | Jimmy Gobble | .20 | .50 |
| 335 | Bobby Higginson | .25 | .60 |
| 336 | Kelvim Escobar | .20 | .50 |
| 337 | Mike DeJean | .20 | .50 |
| 338 | Sidney Ponson | .20 | .50 |
| 339 | Todd Sell RC | .40 | 1.00 |
| 340 | Jeff Cirillo | .20 | .50 |
| 341 | Jimmy Rollins | .25 | .60 |
| 342A | Barry Zito White Jsy | .25 | .60 |
| 342B | Barry Zito Green Jsy SP | 2.00 | 5.00 |
| 343 | Felix Pie | .40 | 1.00 |
| 344 | Matt Morris | .25 | .60 |
| 345 | Kazuhiro Sasaki | .25 | .60 |
| 346 | Jack Wilson | .20 | .50 |
| 347 | Nick Johnson | .20 | .50 |
| 348 | Wil Cordero | .20 | .50 |
| 349 | Ryan Madson | .20 | .50 |
| 350 | Toni Hunter | .20 | .50 |
| 351 | Andy Ashby | .20 | .50 |
| 352 | Aubrey Huff | .20 | .50 |
| 353 | Brad Lidge | .20 | .50 |
| 354 | Derrek Lee | .40 | 1.00 |
| 355 | Yadier Molina RC | 1.00 | 2.50 |
| 356 | Paul Wilson | .20 | .50 |
| 357 | Omar Vizquel | .40 | 1.00 |
| 358 | Rene Reyes | .20 | .50 |
| 359 | Marlon Anderson | .20 | .50 |
| 360 | Bobby Kielty | .20 | .50 |
| 361A | Ryan Wagner New Logo | .20 | .50 |
| 361B | Ryan Wagner Old Logo SP | 2.00 | 5.00 |
| 362 | Justin Morneau | .25 | .60 |
| 363 | Shane Spencer | .25 | .60 |
| 364 | David Bell | .20 | .50 |
| 365 | Matt Stairs | .20 | .50 |
| 366 | Joe Borchard | .20 | .50 |
| 367 | Mark Redman | .20 | .50 |
| 368 | Dave Roberts | .20 | .50 |
| 369 | Desi Relaford | .20 | .50 |
| 370 | Rich Harden | .25 | .60 |
| 371 | Fernando Tatis | .25 | .60 |
| 372 | Eric Karros | .25 | .60 |
| 373 | Eric Milton | .20 | .50 |
| 374 | Mike Sweeney | .25 | .60 |
| 375 | Brian Daubach | .20 | .50 |
| 376 | Brian Snyder | .20 | .50 |
| 377 | Chris Reitsma | .20 | .50 |
| 378 | Kyle Lohse | .20 | .50 |
| 379 | Livan Hernandez | .20 | .50 |
| 380 | Robin Ventura | .25 | .60 |
| 381 | Jacque Jones | .20 | .50 |
| 382 | Danny Kolb | .20 | .50 |
| 383 | Casey Kotchman | .20 | .50 |
| 384 | Cristian Guzman | .20 | .50 |
| 385 | Josh Beckett | .25 | .60 |
| 386 | Khalil Greene | .40 | 1.00 |
| 387 | Greg Myers | .20 | .50 |
| 388 | Francisco Cordero | .20 | .50 |
| 389 | Donald Levinski RC | .30 | .75 |
| 390 | Roy Halladay | .25 | .60 |
| 391 | J.D. Drew | .25 | .60 |
| 392 | Jamie Moyer | .25 | .60 |
| 393 | Ken Macha MGR | .20 | .50 |
| 394 | Jeff Davanon | .20 | .50 |
| 395 | Matt Kata | .20 | .50 |
| 396 | Jack Cust | .20 | .50 |
| 397 | Mike Timlin | .20 | .50 |
| 398 | Zack Greinke SP | 2.00 | 5.00 |
| 399 | Byung-Hyun Kim SP | 2.00 | 5.00 |
| 400 | Kazuhisa Ishii SP | 2.00 | 5.00 |
| 401 | Brayan Pena SP RC | 2.00 | 5.00 |
| 402 | Garret Anderson SP | 2.00 | 5.00 |
| 403 | Kyle Sleeth SP RC | 3.00 | 8.00 |
| 404 | Jany Lopez SP | 2.00 | 5.00 |
| 405 | Damian Moss SP | 2.00 | 5.00 |
| 406 | David Ortiz SP | 3.00 | 8.00 |
| 407 | Pedro Martinez SP | 3.00 | 8.00 |
| 408 | Hee Seop Choi SP | 2.00 | 5.00 |
| 409 | Carl Everett SP | 2.00 | 5.00 |
| 410 | Dontrelle Willis SP | 3.00 | 8.00 |
| 411 | Ryan Harvey SP | 2.00 | 5.00 |
| 412 | Russell Branyan SP | 2.00 | 5.00 |
| 413 | Milton Bradley SP | 2.00 | 5.00 |
| 414 | Marcus McBeth SP RC | 2.00 | 5.00 |
| 415 | Carlos Pena SP | 2.00 | 5.00 |

| | | |
|---|---|---|
| 416 Ivan Rodriguez SP | 3.00 | 8.00 |
| 417 Craig Biggio SP | 3.00 | 8.00 |
| 418 Angel Berroa SP | 2.00 | 5.00 |
| 419 Brian Jordan SP | 2.00 | 5.00 |
| 420 Scott Podsednik SP | 2.00 | 5.00 |
| 421 Omar Falcon SP RC | 2.00 | 5.00 |
| 422 Joe Mays SP | 2.00 | 5.00 |
| 423 Brad Wilkerson SP | 2.00 | 5.00 |
| 424 Al Leiter SP | 2.00 | 5.00 |
| 425 Derek Jeter SP | 5.00 | 12.00 |
| 426 Mark Mulder SP | 2.00 | 5.00 |
| 427 Marlon Byrd SP | 2.00 | 5.00 |
| 428 David Murphy SP RC | 3.00 | 8.00 |
| 429 Phil Nevin SP | 2.00 | 5.00 |
| 430 J.T. Snow SP | 2.00 | 5.00 |
| 431 Brad Sullivan SP RC | 3.00 | 8.00 |
| 432 Bo Hart SP | 2.00 | 5.00 |
| 433 Josh Labandeira SP RC | 2.00 | 5.00 |
| 434 Chan Ho Park SP | 2.00 | 5.00 |
| 435 Carlos Delgado SP | 2.00 | 5.00 |
| 436 Curt Schilling Sox SP | 3.00 | 8.00 |
| 437 John Smoltz SP | 3.00 | 8.00 |
| 438 Luis Matos SP | 2.00 | 5.00 |
| 439 Mark Prior SP | 5.00 | 12.00 |
| 440 Roberto Alomar SP | 3.00 | 8.00 |
| 441 Coco Crisp SP | 2.00 | 5.00 |
| 442 Austin Kearns SP | 2.00 | 5.00 |
| 443 Larry Walker SP | 2.00 | 5.00 |
| 444 Neal Cotts SP | 2.00 | 5.00 |
| 445 Jeff Bagwell SP | 3.00 | 8.00 |
| 446 Adrian Beltre SP | 2.00 | 5.00 |
| 447 Grady Sizemore SP | 3.00 | 8.00 |
| 448 Keith Ginter SP | 2.00 | 5.00 |
| 449 Vladimir Guerrero SP | 3.00 | 8.00 |
| 450 Lyle Overbay SP | 2.00 | 5.00 |
| 451 Rafael Furcal SP | 2.00 | 5.00 |
| 452 Melvin Mora SP | 2.00 | 5.00 |
| 453 Kerry Wood SP | 2.00 | 5.00 |
| 454 Jose Valentin SP | 2.00 | 5.00 |
| 455 Ken Griffey Jr. SP | 4.00 | 10.00 |
| 456 Brandon Phillips SP | 2.00 | 5.00 |
| 457 Miguel Cabrera SP | 3.00 | 8.00 |
| 458 Edwin Jackson SP | 2.00 | 5.00 |
| 459 Eric Owens SP | 2.00 - | 5.00 |
| 460 Miguel Batista SP | 2.00 | 5.00 |
| 461 Mike Hampton SP | 2.00 | 5.00 |
| 462 Kevin Millar SP | 2.00 | 5.00 |
| 463 Bartolo Colon SP | 2.00 | 5.00 |
| 464 Sean Casey SP | 2.00 | 5.00 |
| 465 C.C. Sabathia SP | 2.00 | 5.00 |
| 466 Rickie Weeks SP | 2.00 | 5.00 |
| 467 Brad Penny SP | 2.00 | 5.00 |
| 468 Mike MacDougal SP | 2.00 | 5.00 |
| 469 Kevin Brown SP | 2.00 | 5.00 |
| 470 Lance Berkman SP | 2.00 | 5.00 |
| 471 Ben Sheets SP | 2.00 | 5.00 |
| 472 Mariano Rivera SP | 3.00 | 8.00 |
| 473 Mike Piazza SP | 4.00 | 10.00 |
| 474 Ryan Klesko SP | 2.00 | 5.00 |
| 475 Edgar Renteria SP | 2.00 | 5.00 |

## 2005 Topps Heritage

| | | |
|---|---|---|
| COMPLETE SET (495) | 250.00 | 400.00 |
| COMP.SET w/o SP's (385) | 30.00 | 60.00 |
| COMMON CARD | .20 | .50 |
| COMMON RC | .20 | .50 |
| COMMON TEAM CARD | .20 | .50 |
| COMMON SP | .20 | .50 |
| COMMON SP RC | 3.00 | 8.00 |
| SP STATED ODDS 1:2 HOBBY/RETAIL | | |
| BASIC SP: 5/20/30/31/33/79/101/110/130 | | |
| BASIC SP: 135/260/292/398-475 | | |
| VARIATION SP: 3/6/7/51/50/69/78/82/118 | | |
| VARIATION SP: 125/135/155/261/273/286 | | |

| | | |
|---|---|---|
| VARIATION SP: 296/300/312/353/389 | | |
| SEE BECKETT.COM FOR VAR.DESCRIPTIONS | | |
| 1 Will Harridge | .20 | .50 |
| 2 Warren Giles | .20 | .50 |
| 3A Alfonso Soriano Fldg | .20 | .50 |
| 3B Alfonso Soriano Running SP | 3.00 | 8.00 |
| 4 Mark Mulder | .20 | .50 |
| 5 Todd Helton SP | 3.00 | 8.00 |
| 6A Jason Bay Black Cap | .20 | .50 |
| 6B Jason Bay Yellow Cap SP | 3.00 | 8.00 |
| 7A Ichiro Suzuki Running | .60 | 1.50 |
| 7B Ichiro Suzuki Crouch SP | 4.00 | 10.00 |
| 8 Jim Tracy MG | .20 | .50 |
| 9 Gavin Floyd | .20 | .50 |
| 10 John Smoltz | .30 | .75 |
| 11 Chicago Cubs TC | .20 | .50 |
| 12 Darin Erstad | .20 | .50 |
| 13 Chad Tracy | .20 | .50 |
| 14 Charles Thomas | .20 | .50 |
| 15 Miguel Tejada | .20 | .50 |
| 16 Andre Ethier RC | 2.00 | 5.00 |
| 17 Jeff Francis | .20 | .50 |
| 18 Derrek Lee | .30 | .75 |
| 19 Juan Uribe | .20 | .50 |
| 20 Jim Edmonds SP | 3.00 | 8.00 |
| 21 Kenny Lofton | .20 | .50 |
| 22 Brad Ausmus | .20 | .50 |
| 23 Jon Garland | .20 | .50 |
| 24 Edwin Jackson | .20 | .50 |
| 25 Joe Mauer | .40 | 1.00 |
| 26 Wes Helms | .20 | .50 |
| 27 Brian Schneider | .20 | .50 |
| 28 Kazuo Matsui | .20 | .50 |
| 29 Flash Gordon | .20 | .50 |
| 30 Hideo Nomo SP | 3.00 | 8.00 |
| 31A Albert Pujols Red Hat SP | 5.00 | 12.00 |
| 31B Albert Pujols Blue Hat SP | 5.00 | 12.00 |
| 32 Carl Crawford | .20 | .50 |
| 33 Vladimir Guerrero SP | 3.00 | 8.00 |
| 34 Nick Green | .20 | .50 |
| 35 Jay Gibbons | .20 | .50 |
| 36 Kevin Youkilis | .20 | .50 |
| 37 Billy Wagner | .20 | .50 |
| 38 Terrence Long | .20 | .50 |
| 39 Kevin Mench | .20 | .50 |
| 40 Garret Anderson | .20 | .50 |
| 41 Reed Johnson | .20 | .50 |
| 42 Reggie Sanders | .20 | .50 |
| 43 Kirk Rueter | .20 | .50 |
| 44 Jay Payton | .20 | .50 |
| 45 Tike Redman | .20 | .50 |
| 46 Mike Lieberthal | .20 | .50 |
| 47 Damian Miller | .20 | .50 |
| 48 Zach Day | .20 | .50 |
| 49 Juan Rincon | .20 | .50 |
| 50A Jim Thome At Bat | .30 | .75 |
| 50B Jim Thome Fldg SP | 3.00 | 8.00 |
| 51 Jose Guillen | .20 | .50 |
| 52 Richie Sexson | .20 | .50 |
| 53 Juan Cruz | .20 | .50 |
| 54 Byung-Hyun Kim | .20 | .50 |
| 55 Carlos Zambrano | .20 | .50 |
| 56 Carlos Lee | .20 | .50 |
| 57 Adam Dunn | .20 | .50 |
| 58 David Riske | .20 | .50 |
| 59 Carlos Guillen | .20 | .50 |
| 60 Larry Bowa MG | .20 | .50 |
| 61 Barry Bonds | 3.00 | 8.00 |
| 62 Chris Woodward | .20 | .50 |
| 63 Matt DeSalvo RC | .30 | .75 |
| 64 Brian Stavisky RC | .20 | .50 |
| 65 Scot Shields | .20 | .50 |
| 66 J.D. Drew | .20 | .50 |
| 67 Erik Bedard | .20 | .50 |
| 68 Scott Williamson | .20 | .50 |
| 69A M.Prior New C on Cap | .20 | .50 |
| 69B M.Prior Old C on Cap SP | 3.00 | 8.00 |
| 70 Ken Griffey Jr. | .60 | 1.50 |
| 71 Kazuhito Tadano | .20 | .50 |
| 72 Philadelphia Phillies TC | .20 | .50 |
| 73 Jeremy Reed | .20 | .50 |
| 74 Ricardo Rodriguez | .20 | .50 |
| 75 Carlos Delgado | .20 | .50 |
| 76 Eric Milton | .20 | .50 |
| 77 Miguel Olivo | .20 | .50 |
| 78A E.Alfonzo No Socks | .20 | .50 |
| 78B E.Alfonzo Black Socks SP | 3.00 | 8.00 |
| 79 Kazuhisa Ishii SP | 3.00 | 8.00 |

| | | |
|---|---|---|
| 80 Jason Giambi | .20 | .50 |
| 81 Cliff Floyd | .20 | .50 |
| 82A Torii Hunter Twins Cap | .20 | .50 |
| 82B Torii Hunter Wash Cap SP | 3.00 | 8.00 |
| 83 Odalis Perez | .20 | .50 |
| 84 Scott Podsednik | .20 | .50 |
| 85 Cleveland Indians TC | .20 | .50 |
| 86 Jeff Suppan | .20 | .50 |
| 87 Ray Durham | .20 | .50 |
| 88 Tyler Clippard RC | 8.00 | 20.00 |
| 89 Ryan Howard | 1.00 | 2.50 |
| 90 Cincinnati Reds TC | .20 | .50 |
| 91 Bengie Molina | .20 | .50 |
| 92 Danny Bautista | .20 | .50 |
| 93 Eli Marrero | .20 | .50 |
| 94 Larry Bigbie | .20 | .50 |
| 95 Atlanta Braves TC | .20 | .50 |
| 96 Merkin Valdez | .20 | .50 |
| 97 Rocco Baldelli | .20 | .50 |
| 98 Woody Williams | .20 | .50 |
| 99 Jason Frasor | .20 | .50 |
| 100 Baltimore Orioles TC | .20 | .50 |
| 101 Ivan Rodriguez SP | 3.00 | 8.00 |
| 102 Joe Kennedy | .20 | .50 |
| 103 Mike Lowell | .20 | .50 |
| 104 Armando Benitez | .20 | .50 |
| 105 Craig Biggio | .30 | .75 |
| 106 David DeJesus | .20 | .50 |
| 107 Adrian Beltre | .20 | .50 |
| 108 Phil Nevin | .20 | .50 |
| 109 Cristian Guzman | .20 | .50 |
| 110 Jorge Posada SP | 3.00 | 8.00 |
| 111 Boston Red Sox TC | .40 | 1.00 |
| 112 Jeff Mathis | .20 | .50 |
| 113 Bartolo Colon | .20 | .50 |
| 114 Alex Cintron | .20 | .50 |
| 115 Russ Ortiz | .20 | .50 |
| 116 Doug Mientkiewicz | .20 | .50 |
| 117 Placido Polanco | .20 | .50 |
| 118A M.Ordonez Black Uni | .20 | .50 |
| 118B M.Ordonez White Uni SP | 3.00 | 8.00 |
| 119 Chris Seddon RC | .20 | .50 |
| 120 Bobby Abreu | .20 | .50 |
| 121 Pittsburgh Pirates TC | .20 | .50 |
| 122 Dallas McPherson | .20 | .50 |
| 123 Rodrigo Lopez | .20 | .50 |
| 124 Mark Bellhorn | .20 | .50 |
| 125A N.Garciaparra Red Cap | .40 | 1.00 |
| 125B N.Garciaparra Blue Cap SP | 3.00 | 8.00 |
| 126 Sean Casey | .20 | .50 |
| 127 Ronnie Belliard | .20 | .50 |
| 128 Tom Goodwin | .20 | .50 |
| 129 Preston Wilson | .20 | .50 |
| 130 Andruw Jones SP | 3.00 | 8.00 |
| 131 Roberto Alomar | .30 | .75 |
| 132 John Buck | .20 | .50 |
| 133 Jason LaRue | .20 | .50 |
| 134 St. Louis Cardinals TC | .30 | .75 |
| 135A Alex Rodriguez Fldg SP | 4.00 | 10.00 |
| 135B Alex Rodriguez At Bat SP | 4.00 | 10.00 |
| 136 Nate Robertson | .20 | .50 |
| 137 Juan Pierre | .20 | .50 |
| 138 Morgan Ensberg | .20 | .50 |
| 139 Vinny Castilla | .20 | .50 |
| 140 Jake Dittler | .20 | .50 |
| 141 Chan Ho Park | .20 | .50 |
| 142 Felix Hernandez | 1.25 | 3.00 |
| 143 Jason Isringhausen | .20 | .50 |
| 144 Dustan Mohr | .20 | .50 |
| 145 Khalil Greene | .30 | .75 |
| 146 Minnesota Twins TC | .20 | .50 |
| 147 Vicente Padilla | .20 | .50 |
| 148 Oliver Perez | .20 | .50 |
| 149 Brian Giles | .20 | .50 |
| 150 Shawn Green | .20 | .50 |
| 151 Matt Lawton | .20 | .50 |
| 152 Casey Blake | .20 | .50 |
| 153 Frank Thomas | .40 | 1.00 |
| 154 Orlando Hernandez | .20 | .50 |
| 155A Eric Chavez Green Cap | .20 | .50 |
| 155B Eric Chavez Blue Cap SP | 3.00 | 8.00 |
| 156 Chase Utley | .30 | .75 |
| 157 John Olerud | .20 | .50 |
| 158 Adam Eaton | .20 | .50 |
| 159 Josh Fogg | .20 | .50 |
| 160 Michael Tucker | .20 | .50 |
| 161 Kevin Brown | .20 | .50 |
| 162 Bobby Crosby | .20 | .50 |

|  |  | | |
|---|---|---|---|
| 163 | Jason Schmidt | .20 | .50 |
| 164 | Shannon Stewart | .20 | .50 |
| 165 | Tony Womack | .20 | .50 |
| 166 | Los Angeles Dodgers TC | .30 | .75 |
| 167 | Franklin Gutierrez | .20 | .50 |
| 168 | Ted Lilly | .20 | .50 |
| 169 | Mark Teixeira | .30 | .75 |
| 170 | Matt Morris | .20 | .50 |
| 171 | Bucky Jacobsen | .20 | .50 |
| 172 | Steve Doetsch RC | .30 | .75 |
| 173 | Jeff Weaver | .20 | .50 |
| 174 | Tony Graffanino | .20 | .50 |
| 175 | Jeff Bagwell | .30 | .75 |
| 176 | Carl Pavano | .20 | .50 |
| 177 | Junior Spivey | .20 | .50 |
| 178 | Carlos Silva | .20 | .50 |
| 179 | Tim Redding | .20 | .50 |
| 180 | Brett Myers | .20 | .50 |
| 181 | Mike Mussina | .30 | .75 |
| 182 | Richard Hidalgo | .20 | .50 |
| 183 | Nick Johnson | .20 | .50 |
| 184 | Lew Ford | .20 | .50 |
| 185 | Barry Zito | .20 | .50 |
| 186 | Jimmy Rollins | .20 | .50 |
| 187 | Jack Wilson | .20 | .50 |
| 188 | Chicago White Sox TC | .20 | .50 |
| 189 | Guillermo Quiroz | .20 | .50 |
| 190 | Mark Hendrickson | .20 | .50 |
| 191 | Jeremy Bonderman | .20 | .50 |
| 192 | Jason Jennings | .20 | .50 |
| 193 | Paul Lo Duca | .20 | .50 |
| 194 | A.J. Burnett | .20 | .50 |
| 195 | Ken Harvey | .20 | .50 |
| 196 | Geoff Jenkins | .20 | .50 |
| 197 | Joe Mays | .20 | .50 |
| 198 | Jose Vidro | .20 | .50 |
| 199 | David Wright | .75 | 2.00 |
| 200 | Randy Johnson | .40 | 1.00 |
| 201 | Jeff DaVanon | .20 | .50 |
| 202 | Paul Byrd | .20 | .50 |
| 203 | David Ortiz | .40 | 1.00 |
| 204 | Kyle Farnsworth | .20 | .50 |
| 205 | Keith Foulke | .20 | .50 |
| 206 | Joe Crede | .20 | .50 |
| 207 | Austin Kearns | .20 | .50 |
| 208 | Jody Gerut | .20 | .50 |
| 209 | Shawn Chacon | .20 | .50 |
| 210 | Carlos Pena | .20 | .50 |
| 211 | Luis Castillo | .20 | .50 |
| 212 | Chris Denorfia RC | .40 | 1.00 |
| 213 | Detroit Tigers TC | .20 | .50 |
| 214 | Aubrey Huff | .20 | .50 |
| 215 | Brad Fullmer | .20 | .50 |
| 216 | Frank Catalanotto | .20 | .50 |
| 217 | Raul Ibanez | .20 | .50 |
| 218 | Ryan Klesko | .20 | .50 |
| 219 | Octavio Dotel | .20 | .50 |
| 220 | Rob Mackowiak | .20 | .50 |
| 221 | Scott Hatteberg | .20 | .50 |
| 222 | Pat Burrell | .20 | .50 |
| 223 | Bernie Williams | .30 | .75 |
| 224 | Kris Benson | .20 | .50 |
| 225 | Eric Gagne | .20 | .50 |
| 226 | San Francisco Giants TC | .30 | .75 |
| 227 | Roy Oswalt | .20 | .50 |
| 228 | Josh Beckett | .20 | .50 |
| 229 | Lee Mazzilli MG | .20 | .50 |
| 230 | Rickie Weeks | .20 | .50 |
| 231 | Troy Glaus | .20 | .50 |
| 232 | Chone Figgins | .20 | .50 |
| 233 | John Thomson | .20 | .50 |
| 234 | Trot Nixon | .20 | .50 |
| 235 | Brad Penny | .20" | .50 |
| 236 | Oakland A's TC | .20 | .50 |
| 237 | Miguel Batista | .20 | .50 |
| 238 | Ryan Drese | .20 | .50 |
| 239 | Aaron Miles | .20 | .50 |
| 240 | Randy Wolf | .20 | .50 |
| 241 | Brian Lawrence | .20 | .50 |
| 242 | A.J. Pierzynski | .20 | .50 |
| 243 | Jamie Moyer | .20 | .50 |
| 244 | Chris Carpenter | .20 | .50 |
| 245 | So Taguchi | .20 | .50 |
| 246 | Rob Bell | .20 | .50 |
| 247 | Francisco Cordero | .20 | .50 |
| 248 | Tom Glavine | .30 | .75 |
| 249 | Jermaine Dye | .20 | .50 |
| 250 | Cliff Lee | .20 | .50 |
| 251 | New York Yankees TC | .40 | 1.00 |
| 252 | Vernon Wells | .20 | .50 |
| 253 | R.A. Dickey | .20 | .50 |
| 254 | Larry Walker | .30 | .75 |
| 255 | Randy Winn | .20 | .50 |
| 256 | Pedro Feliz | .20 | .50 |
| 257 | Mark Loretta | .20 | .50 |
| 258 | Tim Worrell | .20 | .50 |
| 259 | Kip Wells | .20 | .50 |
| 260 | Cesar Izturis SP | 3.00 | 8.00 |
| 261A | Carlos Beltran Fldg | .20 | .50 |
| 261B | Carlos Beltran At Bat SP | 3.00 | 8.00 |
| 262 | Juan Encarnacion | .20 | .50 |
| 263 | Luis A. Gonzalez | .20 | .50 |
| 264 | Grady Sizemore | .30 | .75 |
| 265 | Paul Wilson | .20 | .50 |
| 266 | Mark Buehrle | .20 | .50 |
| 267 | Todd Hollandsworth | .20 | .50 |
| 268 | Orlando Cabrera | .20 | .50 |
| 269 | Sidney Ponson | .20 | .50 |
| 270 | Mike Hampton | .20 | .50 |
| 271 | Luis Gonzalez | .20 | .50 |
| 272 | Brendan Donnelly | .20 | .50 |
| 273A | Chipper Jones Slide | .40 | 1.00 |
| 273B | Chipper Jones Fldg SP | 3.00 | 8.00 |
| 274 | Brandon Webb | .20 | .50 |
| 275 | Marty Cordova | .20 | .50 |
| 276 | Greg Maddux | .60 | 1.50 |
| 277 | Jose Contreras | .20 | .50 |
| 278 | Aaron Harang | .20 | .50 |
| 279 | Coco Crisp | .20 | .50 |
| 280 | Bobby Higginson | .20 | .50 |
| 281 | Guillermo Mota | .20 | .50 |
| 282 | Andy Pettitte | .30 | .75 |
| 283 | Jeremy West RC | .30 | .75 |
| 284 | Craig Brazell | .20 | .50 |
| 285 | Eric Hinske | .20 | .50 |
| 286A | Hank Blalock Hitting | .20 | .50 |
| 286B | Hank Blalock Fldg SP | 3.00 | 8.00 |
| 287 | B.J. Upton | .30 | .75 |
| 288 | Jason Marquis | .20 | .50 |
| 289 | Matt Herges | .20 | .50 |
| 290 | Ramon Hernandez | .20 | .50 |
| 291 | Marlon Byrd | .20 | .50 |
| 292 | Ryan Sweeney SP RC | 3.00 | 8.00 |
| 293 | Esteban Loaiza | .20 | .50 |
| 294 | Al Leiter | .20 | .50 |
| 295 | Alex Gonzalez | .20 | .50 |
| 296A | J.Santana Twins Cap | .40 | 1.00 |
| 296B | J.Santana Wash Cap SP | 3.00 | 8.00 |
| 297 | Milton Bradley | .20 | .50 |
| 298 | Mike Sweeney | .20 | .50 |
| 299 | Wade Miller | .20 | .50 |
| 300A | Sammy Sosa Hitting | .40 | 1.00 |
| 300B | Sammy Sosa Standing SP | 3.00 | 8.00 |
| 301 | Wily Mo Pena | .20 | .50 |
| 302 | Tim Wakefield | .20 | .50 |
| 303 | Rafael Palmeiro | .30 | .75 |
| 304 | Rafael Furcal | .20 | .50 |
| 305 | David Eckstein | .20 | .50 |
| 306 | David Segui | .20 | .50 |
| 307 | Kevin Millar | .20 | .50 |
| 308 | Matt Clement | .20 | .50 |
| 309 | Wade Robinson RC | .20 | .50 |
| 310 | Brad Radke | .20 | .50 |
| 311 | Steve Finley | .20 | .50 |
| 312A | Lance Berkman Hitting | .20 | .50 |
| 312B | Lance Berkman Fldg SP | 3.00 | 8.00 |
| 313 | Joe Randa | .20 | .50 |
| 314 | Miguel Cabrera | .30 | .75 |
| 315 | Billy Koch | .20 | .50 |
| 316 | Alex Sanchez | .20 | .50 |
| 317 | Chin-Hui Tsao | .20 | .50 |
| 318 | Omar Vizquel | .30 | .75 |
| 319 | Ryan Freel | .20 | .50 |
| 320 | LaTroy Hawkins | .20 | .50 |
| 321 | Aaron Rowand | .20 | .50 |
| 322 | Paul Konerko | .20 | .50 |
| 323 | Joe Borowski | .20 | .50 |
| 324 | Jarrod Washburn | .20 | .50 |
| 325 | Jaret Wright | .20 | .50 |
| 326 | Johnny Damon | .30 | .75 |
| 327 | Corey Patterson | .20 | .50 |
| 328 | Travis Hafner | .20 | .50 |
| 329 | Shingo Takatsu | .20 | .50 |
| 330 | Dmitri Young | .20 | .50 |
| 331 | Matt Holliday | .25 | .60 |
| 332 | Jeff Kent | .20 | .50 |
| 333 | Desi Relaford | .20 | .50 |
| 334 | Jose Hernandez | .20 | .50 |
| 335 | Lyle Overbay | .20 | .50 |
| 336 | Jacque Jones | .20 | .50 |
| 337 | Termel Sledge | .20 | .50 |
| 338 | Victor Zambrano | .20 | .50 |
| 339 | Gary Sheffield | .20 | .50 |
| 340 | Brad Wilkerson | .20 | .50 |
| 341 | Ian Kinsler RC | 1.25 | 3.00 |
| 342 | Jesse Crain | .20 | .50 |
| 343 | Orlando Hudson | .20 | .50 |
| 344 | Laynce Nix | .20 | .50 |
| 345 | Jose Cruz Jr. | .20 | .50 |
| 346 | Edgar Renteria | .20 | .50 |
| 347 | Eddie Guardado | .20 | .50 |
| 348 | Jerome Williams | .20 | .50 |
| 349 | Trevor Hoffman | .20 | .50 |
| 350 | Mike Piazza | .40 | 1.00 |
| 351 | Jason Kendall | .20 | .50 |
| 352 | Kevin Millwood | .20 | .50 |
| 353A | Tim Hudson Atl Cap | .20 | .50 |
| 353B | Tim Hudson Milw Cap SP | 3.00 | 8.00 |
| 354 | Paul Quantrill | .20 | .50 |
| 355 | Jon Lieber | .20 | .50 |
| 356 | Braden Looper | .20 | .50 |
| 357 | Chad Cordero | .20 | .50 |
| 358 | Joe Nathan | .20 | .50 |
| 359 | Doug Davis | .20 | .50 |
| 360 | Ian Sladegroen RC | .30 | .75 |
| 361 | Val Majewski | .20 | .50 |
| 362 | Francisco Rodriguez | .20 | .50 |
| 363 | Kelvim Escobar | .20 | .50 |
| 364 | Marcus Giles | .20 | .50 |
| 365 | Darren Fenster RC | .30 | .75 |
| 366 | David Bell | .20 | .50 |
| 367 | Shea Hillenbrand | .20 | .50 |
| 368 | Manny Ramirez | .30 | .75 |
| 369 | Ben Broussard | .20 | .50 |
| 370 | Luis Ramirez RC | .30 | .75 |
| 371 | Dustin Hermanson | .20 | .50 |
| 372 | Akinori Otsuka | .20 | .50 |
| 373 | Chadd Blasko RC | .30 | .75 |
| 374 | Delmon Young | .30 | .75 |
| 375 | Michael Young | .30 | .75 |
| 376 | Bret Boone | .20 | .50 |
| 377 | Jake Peavy | .20 | .50 |
| 378 | Matthew Lindstrom RC | .30 | .75 |
| 379 | Sean Burroughs | .20 | .50 |
| 380 | Rich Harden | .20 | .50 |
| 381 | Chris Roberson RC | .30 | .75 |
| 382 | John Lackey | .20 | .50 |
| 383 | Johnny Estrada | .20 | .50 |
| 384 | Matt Rogelstad RC | .30 | .75 |
| 385 | Toby Hall | .20 | .50 |
| 386 | Adam LaRoche | .20 | .50 |
| 387 | Bill Hall | .20 | .50 |
| 388 | Tim Salmon | .20 | .50 |
| 389A | Curt Schilling Throw | .30 | .75 |
| 389B | Curt Schilling Glove Up SP | 3.00 | 8.00 |
| 390 | Michael Barrett | .20 | .50 |
| 391 | Jose Acevedo | .20 | .50 |
| 392 | Nate Schierholtz | .30 | .75 |
| 393 | J.T. Snow Jr. | .20 | .50 |
| 394 | Mark Redman | .20 | .50 |
| 395 | Ryan Madson | .20 | .50 |
| 396 | Kevin West RC | .20 | .50 |
| 397 | Ramon Ortiz | .20 | .50 |
| 398 | Derek Lowe SP | 3.00 | 8.00 |
| 399 | Kerry Wood SP | 3.00 | 8.00 |
| 400 | Derek Jeter SP | 5.00 | 12.00 |
| 401 | Livan Hernandez SP | 3.00 | 8.00 |
| 402 | Casey Kotchman SP | 3.00 | 8.00 |
| 403 | Chaz Lytle SP RC | 3.00 | 8.00 |
| 404 | Alexis Rios SP | 3.00 | 8.00 |
| 405 | Scott Spiezio SP | 3.00 | 8.00 |
| 406 | Craig Wilson SP | 3.00 | 8.00 |
| 407 | Felix Rodriguez SP | 3.00 | 8.00 |
| 408 | D'Angelo Jimenez SP | 3.00 | 8.00 |
| 409 | Rondell White SP | 3.00 | 8.00 |
| 410 | Shawn Estes SP | 3.00 | 8.00 |
| 411 | Troy Percival SP | 3.00 | 8.00 |
| 412 | Melvin Mora SP | 3.00 | 8.00 |
| 413 | Aramis Ramirez SP | 3.00 | 8.00 |
| 414 | Carl Everett SP | 3.00 | 8.00 |
| 415 | Elvys Quezada SP RC | 3.00 | 8.00 |
| 416 | Ben Sheets SP | 3.00 | 8.00 |
| 417 | Matt Stairs SP | 3.00 | 8.00 |
| 418 | Adam Everett SP | 3.00 | 8.00 |

| | | |
|---|---|---|
| ❑ 419 Jason Johnson SP | 3.00 | 8.00 |
| ❑ 420 Billy Butler SP RC | 4.00 | 10.00 |
| ❑ 421 Justin Morneau SP | 3.00 | 8.00 |
| ❑ 422 Jose Reyes SP | 3.00 | 8.00 |
| ❑ 423 Mariano Rivera SP | 3.00 | 8.00 |
| ❑ 424 Jose Vaquedano SP RC | 3.00 | 8.00 |
| ❑ 425 Gabe Gross SP | 3.00 | 8.00 |
| ❑ 426 Scott Rolen SP | 3.00 | 8.00 |
| ❑ 427 Ty Wigginton SP | 3.00 | 8.00 |
| ❑ 428 James Jurries SP RC | 3.00 | 8.00 |
| ❑ 429 Pedro Martinez SP | 3.00 | 8.00 |
| ❑ 430 Mark Grudzielanek SP | 3.00 | 8.00 |
| ❑ 431 Josh Phelps SP | 3.00 | 8.00 |
| ❑ 432 Ryan Goleski SP RC | 3.00 | 8.00 |
| ❑ 433 Mike Matheny SP | 3.00 | 8.00 |
| ❑ 434 Bobby Kielty SP | 3.00 | 8.00 |
| ❑ 435 Tony Batista SP | 3.00 | 8.00 |
| ❑ 436 Corey Koskie SP | 3.00 | 8.00 |
| ❑ 437 Brad Lidge SP | 3.00 | 8.00 |
| ❑ 438 Dontrelle Willis SP | 3.00 | 8.00 |
| ❑ 439 Angel Berroa SP | 3.00 | 8.00 |
| ❑ 440 Jason Kubel SP | 3.00 | 8.00 |
| ❑ 441 Roy Halladay SP | 3.00 | 8.00 |
| ❑ 442 Brian Roberts SP | 3.00 | 8.00 |
| ❑ 443 Bill Mueller SP | 3.00 | 8.00 |
| ❑ 444 Adam Kennedy SP | 3.00 | 8.00 |
| ❑ 445 Brandon Moss SP RC | 3.00 | 8.00 |
| ❑ 446 Sean Burnett SP | 3.00 | 8.00 |
| ❑ 447 Eric Byrnes SP | 3.00 | 8.00 |
| ❑ 448 Matt Campbell SP RC | 3.00 | 8.00 |
| ❑ 449 Ryan Webb SP | 3.00 | 8.00 |
| ❑ 450 Jose Valentin SP | 3.00 | 8.00 |
| ❑ 451 Jake Westbrook SP | 3.00 | 8.00 |
| ❑ 452 Glen Perkins SP RC | 3.00 | 8.00 |
| ❑ 453 Alex Gonzalez SP | 3.00 | 8.00 |
| ❑ 454 Jeromy Burnitz SP | 3.00 | 8.00 |
| ❑ 455 Zack Greinke SP | 3.00 | 8.00 |
| ❑ 456 Sean Marshall SP RC | 2.50 | 6.00 |
| ❑ 457 Enubiel Durazo SP | 3.00 | 8.00 |
| ❑ 458 Michael Cuddyer SP | 3.00 | 8.00 |
| ❑ 459 Hee Seop Choi SP | 3.00 | 8.00 |
| ❑ 460 Melky Cabrera SP RC | 4.00 | 10.00 |
| ❑ 461 Jerry Hairston Jr. SP | 3.00 | 8.00 |
| ❑ 462 Moises Alou SP | 3.00 | 8.00 |
| ❑ 463 Michael Rogers SP RC | 3.00 | 8.00 |
| ❑ 464 Javy Lopez SP | 3.00 | 8.00 |
| ❑ 465 Freddy Garcia SP | 3.00 | 8.00 |
| ❑ 466 Brett Harper SP RC | 3.00 | 8.00 |
| ❑ 467 Juan Gonzalez SP | 3.00 | 8.00 |
| ❑ 468 Kevin Melillo SP RC | 3.00 | 8.00 |
| ❑ 469 Todd Walker SP | 3.00 | 8.00 |
| ❑ 470 C.C. Sabathia SP | 3.00 | 8.00 |
| ❑ 471 Kole Strayhorn SP RC | 3.00 | 8.00 |
| ❑ 472 Mark Kotsay SP | 3.00 | 8.00 |
| ❑ 473 Javier Vazquez SP | 3.00 | 8.00 |
| ❑ 474 Mike Cameron SP | 3.00 | 8.00 |
| ❑ 475 Wes Swackhamer SP RC | 3.00 | 8.00 |

## 2006 Topps Heritage

| | | |
|---|---|---|
| ❑ COMPLETE SET (494) | 250.00 | 400.00 |
| ❑ COMP SET w/o SP's (384) | 30.00 | 60.00 |
| ❑ COMMON CARD | .20 | .50 |
| ❑ COMMON RC | .20 | .50 |
| ❑ COMMON TEAM CARD | .20 | .50 |
| ❑ COMMON SP | 3.00 | 8.00 |
| ❑ SP STATED ODDS 1:2 HOBBY/RETAIL | | |
| ❑ SP CL: 1/2/10/12/8/20B/23B/25/35/55 | | |
| ❑ SP CL: 70/76/80B/91/95A/95B/99/106 | | |
| ❑ SP CL: 123/127/165B/200B/212B/265-269 | | |
| ❑ SP CL: 271-274/276-316/318-323/325A | | |
| ❑ SP CL: 325B/326-328/330-349/350A/350B | | |
| ❑ SP CL: 351-352/400/407/475 | | |
| ❑ VARIATION CL: 20/23/80/95/165/200 | | |
| ❑ VARIATION CL: 212/325/350/475 | | |

| | | |
|---|---|---|
| ❑ TWO VERSIONS OF EACH VARIATION EXIST | | |
| ❑ SEE BECKETT.COM FOR VAR.DESCRIPTIONS | | |
| ❑ CARD 255 NOT INTENDED FOR RELEASE | | |
| ❑ COMP SET EXCLUDES CARD 255 CUT OUT | | |
| ❑ 1 David Ortiz SP | 3.00 | 8.00 |
| ❑ 2 Mike Piazza SP | 4.00 | 10.00 |
| ❑ 3 Daryle Ward | .20 | .50 |
| ❑ 4 Rafael Furcal | .20 | .50 |
| ❑ 5 Derek Lowe | .20 | .50 |
| ❑ 6 Eric Chavez | .20 | .50 |
| ❑ 7 Juan Uribe | .20 | .50 |
| ❑ 8 C.C. Sabathia | .20 | .50 |
| ❑ 9 Sean Casey | .20 | .50 |
| ❑ 10 Barry Bonds SP | 5.00 | 12.00 |
| ❑ 11 Gary Sheffield | .20 | .50 |
| ❑ 12 Ted Lilly | .20 | .50 |
| ❑ 13 Lew Ford | .20 | .50 |
| ❑ 14 Tom Gordon | .20 | .50 |
| ❑ 15 Curt Schilling | .40 | 1.00 |
| ❑ 16 Jason Kendall | .20 | .50 |
| ❑ 17 Frank Catalanotto | .20 | .50 |
| ❑ 18 Pedro Martinez SP | 3.00 | 8.00 |
| ❑ 19 David Dellucci | .20 | .50 |
| ❑ 20A A.Jones w/o Seats | .40 | 1.00 |
| ❑ 20B A.Jones w/Seats SP | 3.00 | 8.00 |
| ❑ 21 Brad Halsey | .20 | .50 |
| ❑ 22 Vernon Wells | .20 | .50 |
| ❑ 23A D.Jeter Yellow/White Ltr | 1.50 | 4.00 |
| ❑ 23B D.Jeter Blue Ltr SP | 5.00 | 12.00 |
| ❑ 24 Todd Helton | .40 | 1.00 |
| ❑ 25 Randy Johnson SP | 4.00 | 10.00 |
| ❑ 26 Jay Gibbons | .20 | .50 |
| ❑ 27 Joe Mays | .20 | .50 |
| ❑ 28 Paul Konerko | .20 | .50 |
| ❑ 29 Lyle Overbay | .20 | .50 |
| ❑ 30 Jorge Posada | .40 | 1.00 |
| ❑ 31 Brandon Webb | .20 | .50 |
| ❑ 32 Marcus Giles | .20 | .50 |
| ❑ 33 J.T. Snow | .20 | .50 |
| ❑ 34 Todd Walker | .20 | .50 |
| ❑ 35 Wily Mo Pena SP | 3.00 | 8.00 |
| ❑ 36 Carlos Delgado | .20 | .50 |
| ❑ 37 David Wright | .60 | 1.50 |
| ❑ 38 Shea Hillenbrand | .20 | .50 |
| ❑ 39 Daniel Cabrera | .20 | .50 |
| ❑ 40 Trevor Hoffman | .20 | .50 |
| ❑ 41 Matt Morris | .20 | .50 |
| ❑ 42 Mariano Rivera | .60 | 1.50 |
| ❑ 43 Jeff Bagwell | .40 | 1.00 |
| ❑ 44 J.D. Drew | .20 | .50 |
| ❑ 45 Carl Pavano | .20 | .50 |
| ❑ 46 Placido Polanco | .20 | .50 |
| ❑ 47 Adrian Beltre | .20 | .50 |
| ❑ 48 J.D. Closser | .20 | .50 |
| ❑ 49 Paul Lo Duca | .20 | .50 |
| ❑ 50 Scott Rolen | .20 | .50 |
| ❑ 51 Bernie Williams | .40 | 1.00 |
| ❑ 52 Jose Guillen | .20 | .50 |
| ❑ 53 Aubrey Huff | .20 | .50 |
| ❑ 54 Greg Maddux | 1.00 | 2.50 |
| ❑ 55 Derrek Lee SP | 3.00 | 8.00 |
| ❑ 56 Hideki Matsui | .60 | 1.50 |
| ❑ 57 Jose Bautista | .20 | .50 |
| ❑ 58 Kyle Farnsworth | .20 | .50 |
| ❑ 59 Nate Robertson | .20 | .50 |
| ❑ 60 Sammy Sosa | .60 | 1.50 |
| ❑ 61 Javier Vazquez | .20 | .50 |
| ❑ 62 Jeff Mathis | .20 | .50 |
| ❑ 63 Mark Buehrle | .20 | .50 |
| ❑ 64 Orlando Hernandez | .20 | .50 |
| ❑ 65 Brandon Claussen | .20 | .50 |
| ❑ 66 Miguel Batista | .20 | .50 |
| ❑ 67 Eddie Guardado | .20 | .50 |
| ❑ 68 Alex Gonzalez | .20 | .50 |
| ❑ 69 Kris Benson | .20 | .50 |
| ❑ 70 Bobby Abreu SP | 3.00 | 8.00 |
| ❑ 71 Vinny Castilla | .20 | .50 |
| ❑ 72 Ben Broussard | .20 | .50 |
| ❑ 73 Travis Hafner | .20 | .50 |
| ❑ 74 Dmitri Young | .20 | .50 |
| ❑ 75 Alex S. Gonzalez | .20 | .50 |
| ❑ 76 Jason Bay SP | 3.00 | 8.00 |
| ❑ 77 Charlton Jimerson | .20 | .50 |
| ❑ 78 Ryan Garko | .20 | .50 |
| ❑ 79 Lance Berkman | .20 | .50 |
| ❑ 80A T.Hudson Red/Blue Ltr | .20 | .50 |
| ❑ 80B T.Hudson Blue Ltr SP | 3.00 | 8.00 |
| ❑ 81 Guillermo Mota | .20 | .50 |

| | | |
|---|---|---|
| ❑ 82 Chris B. Young | .20 | .50 |
| ❑ 83 Brad Lidge | .20 | .50 |
| ❑ 84 A.J. Pierzynski | .20 | .50 |
| ❑ 85 Maicer Izturis | .20 | .50 |
| ❑ 86 Vladimir Guerrero | .60 | 1.50 |
| ❑ 87 J.J. Hardy | .20 | .50 |
| ❑ 88 Cesar Izturis | .20 | .50 |
| ❑ 89 Mark Ellis | .20 | .50 |
| ❑ 90 Chipper Jones | .60 | 1.50 |
| ❑ 91 Chris Snelling SP | 3.00 | 8.00 |
| ❑ 92 Jose Reyes | .20 | .50 |
| ❑ 93 Mike Lieberthal | .20 | .50 |
| ❑ 94 Octavio Dotel | .20 | .50 |
| ❑ 95A A.Rodriguez Fielding SP | 4.00 | 10.00 |
| ❑ 95B A.Rodriguez w/Bat SP | 4.00 | 10.00 |
| ❑ 96 Brett Myers | .20 | .50 |
| ❑ 97 New York Yankees TC | .40 | 1.00 |
| ❑ 98 Ryan Klesko | .20 | .50 |
| ❑ 99 Brian Jordan SP | 3.00 | 8.00 |
| ❑ 100 W.Harridge/W.Giles | .20 | .50 |
| ❑ 101 Adam Eaton | .20 | .50 |
| ❑ 102 Aaron Boone | .20 | .50 |
| ❑ 103 Alex Rios | .20 | .50 |
| ❑ 104 Andy Pettitte | .40 | 1.00 |
| ❑ 105 Barry Zito | .20 | .50 |
| ❑ 106 Bengie Molina SP | 3.00 | 8.00 |
| ❑ 107 Austin Kearns | .20 | .50 |
| ❑ 108 Adam Everett | .20 | .50 |
| ❑ 109 A.J. Burnett | .20 | .50 |
| ❑ 110 Mark Prior | .40 | 1.00 |
| ❑ 111 Russ Ortiz | .20 | .50 |
| ❑ 112 Adam Dunn | .20 | .50 |
| ❑ 113 Byung-Hyun Kim | .20 | .50 |
| ❑ 114 Atlanta Braves TC | .20 | .50 |
| ❑ 115 Carlos Silva | .20 | .50 |
| ❑ 116 Chad Cordero | .20 | .50 |
| ❑ 117 Chone Figgins | .20 | .50 |
| ❑ 118 Chris Reitsma | .20 | .50 |
| ❑ 119 Coco Crisp | .20 | .50 |
| ❑ 120 David DeJesus | .20 | .50 |
| ❑ 121 Chris Snyder | .20 | .50 |
| ❑ 122 Brad Eldred | .20 | .50 |
| ❑ 123 Humberto Cota SP | 3.00 | 8.00 |
| ❑ 124 Erubiel Durazo | .20 | .50 |
| ❑ 125 Josh Beckett | .20 | .50 |
| ❑ 126 Kenny Lofton | .20 | .50 |
| ❑ 127 Joe Nathan SP | 3.00 | 8.00 |
| ❑ 128 Bryan Bullington | .20 | .50 |
| ❑ 129 Jim Thome | .40 | 1.00 |
| ❑ 130 Shawn Green | .20 | .50 |
| ❑ 131 LaTroy Hawkins | .20 | .50 |
| ❑ 132 Mark Kotsay | .20 | .50 |
| ❑ 133 Matt Lawton | .20 | .50 |
| ❑ 134 Luis Castillo | .20 | .50 |
| ❑ 135 Michael Barrett | .20 | .50 |
| ❑ 136 Preston Wilson | .20 | .50 |
| ❑ 137 Orlando Cabrera | .20 | .50 |
| ❑ 138 Chuck James | .20 | .50 |
| ❑ 139 Raul Ibanez | .20 | .50 |
| ❑ 140 Frank Thomas | .60 | 1.50 |
| ❑ 141 Orlando Hudson | .20 | .50 |
| ❑ 142 Scott Kazmir | .20 | .50 |
| ❑ 143 Steve Finley | .20 | .50 |
| ❑ 144 Danny Sandoval RC | .20 | .50 |
| ❑ 145 Javy Lopez | .20 | .50 |
| ❑ 146 Tony Giarratano | .20 | .50 |
| ❑ 147 Terrence Long | .20 | .50 |
| ❑ 148 Victor Martinez | .20 | .50 |
| ❑ 149 Toby Hall | .20 | .50 |
| ❑ 150 Fausto Carmona | .20 | .50 |
| ❑ 151 Tim Wakefield | .20 | .50 |
| ❑ 152 Troy Percival | .20 | .50 |
| ❑ 153 Chris Denorfia | .20 | .50 |
| ❑ 154 Junior Spivey | .20 | .50 |
| ❑ 155 Desi Relaford | .20 | .50 |
| ❑ 156 Francisco Liriano | 1.25 | 3.00 |
| ❑ 157 Corey Koskie | .20 | .50 |
| ❑ 158 Chris Carpenter | .20 | .50 |
| ❑ 159 Robert Andino RC | .20 | .50 |
| ❑ 160 Cliff Floyd | .20 | .50 |
| ❑ 161 Pittsburgh Pirates TC | .20 | .50 |
| ❑ 162 Anderson Hernandez | .20 | .50 |
| ❑ 163 Mike Maroth | .20 | .50 |
| ❑ 164 Aaron Rowand | .20 | .50 |
| ❑ 165A A.Pujols Grey Shirt | 1.25 | 3.00 |
| ❑ 165B A.Pujols Red Shirt SP | 5.00 | 12.00 |
| ❑ 166 David Bell | .20 | .50 |
| ❑ 167 Angel Berroa | .20 | .50 |

|  |  | | |  |  | | |  |  | | |
|---|---|---|---|---|---|---|---|---|---|---|---|
| 168 | B.J. Ryan | .20 | .50 | 254 | Carlos Lee | .20 | .50 | 341 | Jason Giambi SP | 3.00 | 8.00 |
| 169 | Bartolo Colon | .20 | .50 | 255 | Alex Gordon Cut Out | 100.00 | 200.00 | 342 | Bill Hall SP | 3.00 | 8.00 |
| 170 | Hong-Chih Kuo | .60 | 1.50 | 256 | Gustavo Chacin | .20 | .50 | 343 | Jon Garland SP | 3.00 | 8.00 |
| 171 | Cincinnati Reds TC | .20 | .50 | 257 | Jermaine Dye | .20 | .50 | 344 | Dontrelle Willis SP | 3.00 | 8.00 |
| 172 | Bill Mueller | .20 | .50 | 258 | Jose Mesa | .20 | .50 | 345 | Danny Haren SP | 3.00 | 8.00 |
| 173 | John Koronka | .20 | .50 | 259 | Julio Lugo | .20 | .50 | 346 | Brian Giles SP | 3.00 | 8.00 |
| 174 | Billy Wagner | .20 | .50 | 260 | Mark Redman | .20 | .50 | 347 | Brad Penny SP | 3.00 | 8.00 |
| 175 | Zack Greinke | .20 | .50 | 261 | Brandon Watson | .20 | .50 | 348 | Brandon McCarthy SP | 3.00 | 8.00 |
| 176 | Rick Short | .20 | .50 | 262 | Pedro Feliz | .20 | .50 | 349 | Chien-Ming Wang SP | 4.00 | 10.00 |
| 177 | Yadier Molina | .20 | .50 | 263 | Esteban Loaiza | .20 | .50 | 350A | T.Hunter Red/Blue Ltr SP | 3.00 | 8.00 |
| 178 | Willy Taveras | .20 | .50 | 264 | Anthony Reyes | .40 | 1.00 | 350B | T.Hunter Blue Ltr SP | 3.00 | 8.00 |
| 179 | Wes Helms | .20 | .50 | 265 | Jose Contreras SP | 3.00 | 8.00 | 351 | Yhency Brazoban SP | 3.00 | 8.00 |
| 180 | Wade Miller | .20 | .50 | 266 | Tadahito Iguchi SP | 3.00 | 8.00 | 352 | Rodrigo Lopez SP | 3.00 | 8.00 |
| 181 | Luis Gonzalez | .20 | .50 | 267 | Mark Loretta SP | 3.00 | 8.00 | 353 | Paul McAnulty | .20 | .50 |
| 182 | Victor Zambrano | .20 | .50 | 268 | Ray Durham SP | 3.00 | 8.00 | 354 | Francisco Cordero | .20 | .50 |
| 183 | Chicago Cubs TC | .20 | .50 | 269 | Neifi Perez SP | 3.00 | 8.00 | 355 | Brandon Inge | .20 | .50 |
| 184 | Victor Santos | .20 | .50 | 270 | Washington Nationals TC | .20 | .50 | 356 | Jason Lane | .20 | .50 |
| 185 | Tyler Walker | .20 | .50 | 271 | Troy Glaus SP | 3.00 | 8.00 | 357 | Brian Schneider | .20 | .50 |
| 186 | Bobby Crosby | .20 | .50 | 272 | Matt Holliday SP | 4.00 | 10.00 | 358 | Dustin Hermanson | .20 | .50 |
| 187 | Trot Nixon | .20 | .50 | 273 | Kevin Millwood SP | 3.00 | 8.00 | 359 | Eric Hinske | .20 | .50 |
| 188 | Nick Johnson | .20 | .50 | 274 | Jon Lieber SP | 3.00 | 8.00 | 360 | Jarrod Washburn | .20 | .50 |
| 189 | Nick Swisher | .20 | .50 | 275 | Cleveland Indians TC | .20 | .50 | 361 | Jayson Werth | .20 | .50 |
| 190 | Brian Roberts | .20 | .50 | 276 | Jeremy Reed SP | 3.00 | 8.00 | 362 | Craig Breslow RC | .20 | .50 |
| 191 | Nomar Garciaparra | .60 | 1.50 | 277 | Garrett Atkins SP | 3.00 | 8.00 | 363 | Jeff Weaver | .20 | .50 |
| 192 | Oliver Perez | .20 | .50 | 278 | Geoff Jenkins SP | 3.00 | 8.00 | 364 | Jeromy Burnitz | .20 | .50 |
| 193 | Ramon Hernandez | .20 | .50 | 279 | Joey Gathright SP | 3.00 | 8.00 | 365 | Jhonny Peralta | .20 | .50 |
| 194 | Randy Winn | .20 | .50 | 280 | Ben Sheets SP | 3.00 | 8.00 | 366 | Joe Crede | .20 | .50 |
| 195 | Ryan Church | .20 | .50 | 281 | Melvin Mora SP | 3.00 | 8.00 | 367 | Johan Santana | .60 | 1.50 |
| 196 | Ryan Wagner | .20 | .50 | 282 | Jonathan Papelbon SP | 4.00 | 10.00 | 368 | Jose Valentin | .20 | .50 |
| 197 | Todd Hollandsworth | .20 | .50 | 283 | John Smoltz SP | 3.00 | 8.00 | 369 | Keith Foulke | .20 | .50 |
| 198 | Detroit Tigers TC | .20 | .50 | 284 | Jake Peavy SP | 3.00 | 8.00 | 370 | Larry Bigbie | .20 | .50 |
| 199 | Tino Martinez | .40 | 1.00 | 285 | Felix Hernandez SP | 3.00 | 8.00 | 371 | Manny Ramirez | .40 | 1.00 |
| 200A | R.Clemens On Mound | 1.25 | 3.00 | 286 | Alfonso Soriano SP | 3.00 | 8.00 | 372 | Jim Edmonds | .20 | .50 |
| 200B | R.Clemens Red Shirt SP | 4.00 | 10.00 | 287 | Bronson Arroyo SP | 3.00 | 8.00 | 373 | Horacio Ramirez | .20 | .50 |
| 201 | Shawn Estes | .20 | .50 | 288 | Adam LaRoche SP | 3.00 | 8.00 | 374 | Garret Anderson | .20 | .50 |
| 202 | Justin Morneau | .20 | .50 | 289 | Aramis Ramirez SP | 3.00 | 8.00 | 375 | Felipe Lopez | .20 | .50 |
| 203 | Jeff Francis | .20 | .50 | 290 | Brad Hennessey SP | 3.00 | 8.00 | 376 | Eric Byrnes | .20 | .50 |
| 204 | Oakland Athletics TC | .20 | .50 | 291 | Conor Jackson SP | 3.00 | 8.00 | 377 | Darin Erstad | .20 | .50 |
| 205 | Jeff Francoeur | .60 | 1.50 | 292 | Rod Barajas SP | 3.00 | 8.00 | 378 | Carlos Zambrano | .20 | .50 |
| 206 | C.J. Wilson | .20 | .50 | 293 | Chris R. Young SP | 3.00 | 8.00 | 379 | Craig Biggio | .40 | 1.00 |
| 207 | Francisco Rodriguez | .20 | .50 | 294 | Jeremy Bonderman SP | 3.00 | 8.00 | 380 | Darrell Rasner | .20 | .50 |
| 208 | Edgardo Alfonzo | .20 | .50 | 295 | Jack Wilson SP | 3.00 | 8.00 | 381 | Dave Roberts | .20 | .50 |
| 209 | David Eckstein | .20 | .50 | 296 | Jay Payton SP | 3.00 | 8.00 | 382 | Hanley Ramirez | .20 | .50 |
| 210 | Cory Lidle | .20 | .50 | 297 | Danys Baez SP | 3.00 | 8.00 | 383 | Geoff Blum | .20 | .50 |
| 211 | Chase Utley | .40 | 1.00 | 298 | Jose Lima SP | 3.00 | 8.00 | 384 | Joel Pineiro | .20 | .50 |
| 212A | R.Baldelli Yellow/White Ltr | .20 | .50 | 299 | Luis A. Gonzalez SP | 3.00 | 8.00 | 385 | Kip Wells | .20 | .50 |
| 212B | R.Baldelli Blue Ltr SP | 3.00 | 8.00 | 300 | Mike Sweeney SP | 3.00 | 8.00 | 386 | Kelvim Escobar | .20 | .50 |
| 213 | So Taguchi | .20 | .50 | 301 | Nelson Cruz SP | 3.00 | 8.00 | 387 | John Patterson | .20 | .50 |
| 214 | Philadelphia Phillies TC | .20 | .50 | 302 | Eric Gagne SP | 3.00 | 8.00 | 388 | Jody Gerut | .20 | .50 |
| 215 | Brad Hawpe | .20 | .50 | 303 | Juan Castro SP | 3.00 | 8.00 | 389 | Marshall McDougall | .20 | .50 |
| 216 | Walter Young | .20 | .50 | 304 | Joe Mauer SP | 3.00 | 8.00 | 390 | Mike MacDougal | .20 | .50 |
| 217 | Tom Gorzelanny | .20 | .50 | 305 | Richie Sexson SP | 3.00 | 8.00 | 391 | Orlando Palmeiro | .20 | .50 |
| 218 | Shaun Marcum | .20 | .50 | 306 | Roy Oswalt SP | 3.00 | 8.00 | 392 | Rich Aurilia | .20 | .50 |
| 219 | Ryan Howard | 1.00 | 2.50 | 307 | Rickie Weeks SP | 3.00 | 8.00 | 393 | Ronnie Belliard | .20 | .50 |
| 220 | Damian Jackson | .20 | .50 | 308 | Pat Borders SP | 3.00 | 8.00 | 394 | Rich Hill | .20 | .50 |
| 221 | Craig Counsell | .20 | .50 | 309 | Mike Morse SP | 3.00 | 8.00 | 395 | Scott Hatteberg | .20 | .50 |
| 222 | Damian Miller | .20 | .50 | 310 | Matt Stairs SP | 3.00 | 8.00 | 396 | Ryan Langerhans | .20 | .50 |
| 223 | Derrick Turnbow | .20 | .50 | 311 | Chad Tracy SP | 3.00 | 8.00 | 397 | Richard Hidalgo | .20 | .50 |
| 224 | Hank Blalock | .20 | .50 | 312 | Matt Cain SP | 3.00 | 8.00 | 398 | Omar Vizquel | .40 | 1.00 |
| 225 | Brayan Pena | .20 | .50 | 313 | Mark Mulder SP | 3.00 | 8.00 | 399 | Mike Lowell | .20 | .50 |
| 226 | Grady Sizemore | .40 | 1.00 | 314 | Mark Grudzielanek SP | 3.00 | 8.00 | 400 | Astros Aces SP | 3.00 | 8.00 |
| 227 | Ivan Rodriguez | .40 | 1.00 | 315 | Johnny Damon Yanks SP | 4.00 | 10.00 | 401 | Mike Cameron | .20 | .50 |
| 228 | Jason Isringhausen | .20 | .50 | 316 | Casey Kotchman SP | 3.00 | 8.00 | 402 | Matt Clement | .20 | .50 |
| 229 | Brian Fuentes | .20 | .50 | 317 | San Francisco Giants TC | .20 | .50 | 403 | Miguel Cabrera | .40 | 1.00 |
| 230 | Jason Phillips | .20 | .50 | 318 | Chris Burke SP | 3.00 | 8.00 | 404 | Milton Bradley | .20 | .50 |
| 231 | Jason Schmidt | .20 | .50 | 319 | Carl Crawford SP | 3.00 | 8.00 | 405 | Laynce Nix | .20 | .50 |
| 232 | Javier Valentin | .20 | .50 | 320 | Edgar Renteria SP | 3.00 | 8.00 | 406 | Rob Mackowiak | .20 | .50 |
| 233 | Jeff Kent | .20 | .50 | 321 | Chan Ho Park SP | 3.00 | 8.00 | 407 | White Sox Power Hitters SP | 3.00 | 8.00 |
| 234 | John Buck | .20 | .50 | 322 | Boston Red Sox TC SP | 3.00 | 8.00 | 408 | Mark Teixeira | .40 | 1.00 |
| 235 | Mike Matheny | .20 | .50 | 323 | Robinson Cano SP | 3.00 | 8.00 | 409 | Brady Clark | .20 | .50 |
| 236 | Jorge Cantu | .20 | .50 | 324 | Los Angeles Dodgers TC | .20 | .50 | 410 | Johnny Estrada | .20 | .50 |
| 237 | Jose Castillo | .20 | .50 | 325A | M.Tejada w/Bat SP | 3.00 | 8.00 | 411 | Juan Encarnacion | .20 | .50 |
| 238 | Kenny Rogers | .20 | .50 | 325B | M.Tejada Hand Up SP | 3.00 | 8.00 | 412 | Morgan Ensberg | .20 | .50 |
| 239 | Kerry Wood | .20 | .50 | 326 | Jimmy Rollins SP | 3.00 | 8.00 | 413 | Nook Logan | .20 | .50 |
| 240 | Kevin Mench | .20 | .50 | 327 | Juan Pierre SP | 3.00 | 8.00 | 414 | Phil Nevin | .20 | .50 |
| 241 | Tim Stauffer | .20 | .50 | 328 | Dan Johnson SP | 3.00 | 8.00 | 415 | Reggie Sanders | .20 | .50 |
| 242 | Eric Milton | .20 | .50 | 329 | Chicago White Sox TC | .40 | 1.00 | 416 | Roy Halladay | .20 | .50 |
| 243 | St. Louis Cardinals TC | .20 | .50 | 330 | Pat Burrell SP | 3.00 | 8.00 | 417 | Livan Hernandez | .20 | .50 |
| 244 | Shawn Chacon | .20 | .50 | 331 | Ramon Ortiz SP | 3.00 | 8.00 | 418 | Jose Vidro | .20 | .50 |
| 245 | Mike Jacobs | .20 | .50 | 332 | Rondell White SP | 3.00 | 8.00 | 419 | Shannon Stewart | .20 | .50 |
| 246 | Ryan Dempster | .20 | .50 | 333 | David Wells SP | 3.00 | 8.00 | 420 | Brian Bruney | .20 | .50 |
| 247 | Todd Jones | .20 | .50 | 334 | Michael Young SP | 3.00 | 8.00 | 421 | Royce Clayton | .20 | .50 |
| 248 | Tom Glavine | .40 | 1.00 | 335 | Mike Mussina SP | 3.00 | 8.00 | 422 | Chris Demaria RC | .20 | .50 |
| 249 | Tony Graffanino | .20 | .50 | 336 | Moises Alou SP | 3.00 | 8.00 | 423 | Eduardo Perez | .20 | .50 |
| 250 | Ichiro Suzuki | 1.00 | 2.50 | 337 | Scott Podsednik SP | 3.00 | 8.00 | 424 | Jeff Suppan | .20 | .50 |
| 251 | Baltimore Orioles TC | .20 | .50 | 338 | Rich Harden SP | 3.00 | 8.00 | 425 | Jaret Wright | .20 | .50 |
| 252 | Brad Radke | .20 | .50 | 339 | Mark Teahen SP | 3.00 | 8.00 | 426 | Joe Randa | .20 | .50 |
| 253 | Brad Wilkerson | .20 | .50 | 340 | Jacque Jones SP | 3.00 | 8.00 | 427 | Bobby Kielty | .20 | .50 |

|  | | |
|---|---|---|
| 428 Jason Ellison | .20 | .50 |
| 429 Gregg Zaun | .20 | .50 |
| 430 Runelvys Hernandez | .20 | .50 |
| 431 Joe McEwing | .20 | .50 |
| 432 Jason LaRue | .20 | .50 |
| 433 Aaron Miles | .20 | .50 |
| 434 Adam Kennedy | .20 | .50 |
| 435 Ambiorix Burgos | .20 | .50 |
| 436 Armando Benitez | .20 | .50 |
| 437 Brad Ausmus | .20 | .50 |
| 438 Brandon Backe | .20 | .50 |
| 439 Brian James Anderson | .20 | .50 |
| 440 Bruce Chen | .20 | .50 |
| 441 Carlos Guillen | .20 | .50 |
| 442 Casey Blake | .20 | .50 |
| 443 Chris Capuano | .20 | .50 |
| 444 Chris Duffy | .20 | .50 |
| 445 Chris Ray | .20 | .50 |
| 446 Clint Barmes | .20 | .50 |
| 447 Andrew Sisco | .20 | .50 |
| 448 Dallas McPherson | .20 | .50 |
| 449 Tanyon Sturtze | .20 | .50 |
| 450 Carlos Beltran | .20 | .50 |
| 451 Jason Vargas | .20 | .50 |
| 452 Ervin Santana | .20 | .50 |
| 453 Jason Marquis | .20 | .50 |
| 454 Juan Rivera | .20 | .50 |
| 455 Jake Westbrook | .20 | .50 |
| 456 Jason Johnson | .20 | .50 |
| 457 Joe Blanton | .20 | .50 |
| 458 Kevin Millar | .20 | .50 |
| 459 John Thomson | .20 | .50 |
| 460 J.P. Howell | .20 | .50 |
| 461 Justin Verlander | 1.00 | 2.50 |
| 462 Kelly Johnson | .20 | .50 |
| 463 Kyle Davies | .20 | .50 |
| 464 Lance Niekro | .20 | .50 |
| 465 Magglio Ordonez | .20 | .50 |
| 466 Melky Cabrera | .20 | .50 |
| 467 Nick Punto | .20 | .50 |
| 468 Paul Byrd | .20 | .50 |
| 469 Randy Wolf | .20 | .50 |
| 470 Ruben Gotay | .20 | .50 |
| 471 Ryan Madson | .20 | .50 |
| 472 Victor Diaz | .20 | .50 |
| 473 Xavier Nady | .20 | .50 |
| 474 Zach Duke | .20 | .50 |
| 475A H.Street Yellow/White Ltr | .20 | .50 |
| 475B H.Street Blue Ltr SP | 3.00 | 8.00 |
| 476 Brad Thompson | .20 | .50 |
| 477 Jonny Gomes | .20 | .50 |
| 478 B.J. Upton | .20 | .50 |
| 479 Jamey Carroll | .20 | .50 |
| 480 Mike Hampton | .20 | .50 |
| 481 Tony Clark | .20 | .50 |
| 482 Antonio Alfonseca | .20 | .50 |
| 483 Justin Duchscherer | .20 | .50 |
| 484 Mike Timlin | .20 | .50 |
| 485 Joe Saunders | .20 | .50 |

## 2007 Topps Heritage

Andrew Miller

DETROIT TIGERS

| | | |
|---|---|---|
| COMPLETE SET (527) | 250.00 | 400.00 |
| COMP SET w/o SP's (384) | 30.00 | 60.00 |
| COMMON CARD | .20 | .50 |
| COMMON RC | .20 | .50 |
| COMMON TEAM CARD | .20 | .50 |
| COMMON SP | 2.50 | 6.00 |
| SP STATED ODDS 1:2 HOBBY/RETAIL | | |
| SEE BECKETT.COM FOR SP CHECKLIST | | |
| COMMON YELLOW | 2.00 | 5.00 |
| YELLOW STATED ODDS 1:6 HOBBY/RETAIL | | |
| SEE BECKETT.COM FOR YELLOW CL | | |
| CARD 145 DOES NOT EXIST | | |
| 1 David Ortiz | .30 | .75 |

|  | | |
|---|---|---|
| 2a Roger Clemens | .75 | 2.00 |
| 2b Roger Clemens YT | 3.00 | 8.00 |
| 3 David Wells | .20 | .50 |
| 4 Ronny Paulino SP | 2.50 | 6.00 |
| 5 Derek Jeter SP | 6.00 | 15.00 |
| 6 Felix Hernandez | .30 | .75 |
| 7 Todd Helton | .30 | .75 |
| 8a David Eckstein | .20 | .50 |
| 8b David Eckstein YN | 2.00 | 5.00 |
| 9 Craig Wilson | .20 | .50 |
| 10 John Smoltz | .30 | .75 |
| 11a Rob Mackowiak | .20 | .50 |
| 11b Rob Mackowiak YT | 2.00 | 5.00 |
| 12 Scott Hatteberg | .20 | .50 |
| 13a Wilfredo Ledezma SP | 2.50 | 6.00 |
| 13b Wilfredo Ledezma YT | 2.00 | 5.00 |
| 14 Bobby Abreu SP | 2.50 | 6.00 |
| 15 Mike Stanton | .20 | .50 |
| 16 Wilson Betemit | .20 | .50 |
| 17 Darren Oliver | .20 | .50 |
| 18 Josh Beckett | .30 | .75 |
| 19 San Francisco Giants TC | .20 | .50 |
| 20a Robinson Cano | .20 | .50 |
| 20b Robinson Cano YT | 2.50 | 6.00 |
| 21 Matt Cain | .30 | .75 |
| 22 Jason Kendall SP | 2.50 | 6.00 |
| 23a Mark Kotsay SP | 2.50 | 6.00 |
| 23b Mark Kotsay YN | 2.00 | 5.00 |
| 24a Yadier Molina | .20 | .50 |
| 24b Yadier Molina YN | 2.00 | 5.00 |
| 25 Brad Penny | .20 | .50 |
| 26 Adrian Gonzalez | .20 | .50 |
| 27 Danny Haren | .20 | .50 |
| 28 Brian Giles | .20 | .50 |
| 29 Jose Lopez | .20 | .50 |
| 30a Ichiro Suzuki | .75 | 2.00 |
| 30b Ichiro Suzuki YN | 3.00 | 8.00 |
| 31 Beltran Perez SP (RC) | .20 | .50 |
| 32 Brad Hawpe SP | 2.50 | 6.00 |
| 33a Jim Thome | .30 | .75 |
| 33b Jim Thome YT | 2.50 | 6.00 |
| 34 Mark DeRosa | .20 | .50 |
| 35a Woody Williams | .20 | .50 |
| 35b Woody Williams YT | 2.00 | 5.00 |
| 36 Luis Gonzalez | .20 | .50 |
| 37 Billy Sadler (RC) | .20 | .50 |
| 38 Dave Roberts | .20 | .50 |
| 39 Mitch Maier RC | .20 | .50 |
| 40 Francisco Cordero SP | 2.50 | 6.00 |
| 41 Anthony Reyes SP | 2.50 | 6.00 |
| 42 Russell Martin | .20 | .50 |
| 43 Scott Proctor | .20 | .50 |
| 44 Washington Nationals TC | .20 | .50 |
| 45 Shane Victorino | .20 | .50 |
| 46a Joel Zumaya | .30 | .75 |
| 46b Joel Zumaya YT | 2.50 | 6.00 |
| 47 Delmon Young (RC) | .50 | 1.25 |
| 48 Alex Rios | .20 | .50 |
| 49 Willy Taveras SP | 2.50 | 6.00 |
| 50a Mark Buehrle SP | 2.50 | 6.00 |
| 50b Mark Buehrle YT | 2.00 | 5.00 |
| 51 Livan Hernandez | .20 | .50 |
| 52a Jason Bay | .30 | .75 |
| 52b Jason Bay YT | 2.00 | 5.00 |
| 53a Jose Valentin | .20 | .50 |
| 53b Jose Valentin YN | 2.00 | 5.00 |
| 54 Kevin Reese | .20 | .50 |
| 55 Felipe Lopez | .20 | .50 |
| 56 Ryan Sweeney (RC) | .20 | .50 |
| 57a Kelvim Escobar | .20 | .50 |
| 57b Kelvim Escobar YN | 2.00 | 5.00 |
| 58a N.Swisher Sm.Print SP | 2.50 | 6.00 |
| 58b N.Swisher Lg.Print YT | 2.00 | 5.00 |
| 59 Kevin Millwood SP | 2.50 | 6.00 |
| 60a Preston Wilson | .20 | .50 |
| 60b Preston Wilson YN | 2.00 | 5.00 |
| 61a Mariano Rivera | .50 | 1.25 |
| 61b Mariano Rivera YN | 2.50 | 6.00 |
| 62 Josh Barfield | .20 | .50 |
| 63 Ryan Freel | .20 | .50 |
| 64 Tim Hudson | .20 | .50 |
| 65a Chris Narveson (RC) | .20 | .50 |
| 65b Chris Narveson YN (RC) | 2.00 | 5.00 |
| 66 Matt Murton | .20 | .50 |
| 67 Melvin Mora SP | 2.50 | 6.00 |
| 68 Jason Jennings SP | 2.50 | 6.00 |
| 69 Emil Brown | .20 | .50 |
| 70a Magglio Ordonez | .20 | .50 |

|  | | |
|---|---|---|
| 70b Magglio Ordonez YN | 2.00 | 5.00 |
| 71 Los Angeles Dodgers TC | .20 | .50 |
| 72 Ross Gload | .20 | .50 |
| 73 David Ross | .20 | .50 |
| 74 Juan Uribe | .20 | .50 |
| 75 Scott Podsednik | .20 | .50 |
| 76a Cole Hamels SP | 3.00 | 8.00 |
| 76b Cole Hamels YT | 2.50 | 6.00 |
| 77a Rafael Furcal SP | 2.50 | 6.00 |
| 77b Rafael Furcal YN | 2.00 | 5.00 |
| 78a Ryan Theriot | .20 | .50 |
| 78b Ryan Theriot YN | 2.00 | 5.00 |
| 79a Corey Patterson | .20 | .50 |
| 79b Corey Patterson YN | 2.00 | 5.00 |
| 80 Jered Weaver | .30 | .75 |
| 81a Stephen Drew | .30 | .75 |
| 81b Stephen Drew YT | 2.50 | 6.00 |
| 82 Adam Kennedy | .20 | .50 |
| 83 Tony Gwynn Jr. | .20 | .50 |
| 84 Kazuo Matsui | .20 | .50 |
| 85a Omar Vizquel SP | 3.00 | 8.00 |
| 85b Omar Vizquel YT | 2.50 | 6.00 |
| 86 Fred Lewis SP (RC) | 2.50 | 6.00 |
| 87a Shawn Chacon | .20 | .50 |
| 87b Shawn Chacon YT | 2.00 | 5.00 |
| 88 Frank Catalanotto | .20 | .50 |
| 89 Orlando Hudson | .20 | .50 |
| 90 Pat Burrell | .20 | .50 |
| 91 David DeJesus | .20 | .50 |
| 92a David Wright | .75 | 2.00 |
| 92b David Wright YN | 3.00 | 8.00 |
| 93 Conor Jackson | .20 | .50 |
| 94 Xavier Nady SP | 2.50 | 6.00 |
| 95 Bill Hall SP | 2.50 | 6.00 |
| 96 Kip Wells | .20 | .50 |
| 97a Jeff Suppan | .20 | .50 |
| 97b Jeff Suppan YN | 2.00 | 5.00 |
| 98a Ryan Zimmerman | .50 | 1.25 |
| 98b Ryan Zimmerman YN | 2.50 | 6.00 |
| 99 Wes Helms | .20 | .50 |
| 100a Jose Contreras | .20 | .50 |
| 100b Jose Contreras YT | 2.00 | 5.00 |
| 101a Miguel Cairo | .20 | .50 |
| 101b Miguel Cairo YN | 2.00 | 5.00 |
| 102 Brian Roberts | .20 | .50 |
| 103 Carl Crawford SP | 2.50 | 6.00 |
| 104 Mike Lamb SP | 2.50 | 6.00 |
| 105 Mark Ellis | .20 | .50 |
| 106 Scott Rolen | .30 | .75 |
| 107 Garrett Atkins | .20 | .50 |
| 108a Hanley Ramirez | .30 | .75 |
| 108b Hanley Ramirez YT | 2.50 | 6.00 |
| 109 Trot Nixon | .20 | .50 |
| 110 Edgar Renteria | .20 | .50 |
| 111 Jeff Francis | .20 | .50 |
| 112 Marcus Thames SP | 2.50 | 6.00 |
| 113 Brian Burres SP (RC) | 2.50 | 6.00 |
| 114 Brian Schneider | .20 | .50 |
| 115 Jeremy Bonderman | .20 | .50 |
| 116 Ryan Madson | .20 | .50 |
| 117 Gerald Laird | .20 | .50 |
| 118 Roy Halladay | .20 | .50 |
| 119 Victor Martinez | .20 | .50 |
| 120 Greg Maddux | .75 | 2.00 |
| 121 Jay Payton SP | 2.50 | 6.00 |
| 122 Jacque Jones SP | 2.50 | 6.00 |
| 123 Juan Lara RC | .20 | .50 |
| 124 Derrick Turnbow | .20 | .50 |
| 125 Adam Everett | .20 | .50 |
| 126 Michael Cuddyer | .20 | .50 |
| 127 Gil Meche | .20 | .50 |
| 128 Willy Aybar | .20 | .50 |
| 129 Jerry Owens (RC) | .20 | .50 |
| 130 Manny Ramirez SP | 3.00 | 8.00 |
| 131 Howie Kendrick SP | 2.50 | 6.00 |
| 132 Byung-Hyun Kim | .20 | .50 |
| 133 Kevin Kouzmanoff (RC) | .20 | .50 |
| 134 Philadelphia Phillies TC | .20 | .50 |
| 135 Joe Blanton | .20 | .50 |
| 136 Ray Durham | .20 | .50 |
| 137 Luke Hudson | .20 | .50 |
| 138 Eric Byrnes | .20 | .50 |
| 139 Ryan Braun SP RC | 2.50 | 6.00 |
| 140 Johnny Damon SP | 3.00 | 8.00 |
| 141 Ambiorix Burgos | .20 | .50 |
| 142 Hideki Matsui | .50 | 1.25 |
| 143 Josh Johnson | .20 | .50 |
| 144 Miguel Cabrera | .30 | .75 |

| Card | Lo | Hi |
|---|---|---|
| ❑ 146 Delwyn Young (RC) | .20 | .50 |
| ❑ 147 Chuck James | .20 | .50 |
| ❑ 148 Morgan Ensberg | .20 | .50 |
| ❑ 149 Jose Vidro SP | 2.50 | 6.00 |
| ❑ 150 Alex Rodriguez SP | 5.00 | 12.00 |
| ❑ 151 Carlos Maldonado (RC) | .20 | .50 |
| ❑ 152 Jason Schmidt | .20 | .50 |
| ❑ 153 Alex Escobar | .20 | .50 |
| ❑ 154 Chris Gomez | .20 | .50 |
| ❑ 155 Endy Chavez | .20 | .50 |
| ❑ 156 Kris Benson | .20 | .50 |
| ❑ 157 Bronson Arroyo | .20 | .50 |
| ❑ 158 Cleveland Indians TC SP | 2.50 | 6.00 |
| ❑ 159 Chris Ray SP | 2.50 | 6.00 |
| ❑ 160 Richie Sexson | .20 | .50 |
| ❑ 161 Huston Street | .20 | .50 |
| ❑ 162 Kevin Youkilis | .20 | .50 |
| ❑ 163 Armando Benitez | .20 | .50 |
| ❑ 164 Vinny Rottino (RC) | .20 | .50 |
| ❑ 165 Garret Anderson | .20 | .50 |
| ❑ 166 Todd Greene | .20 | .50 |
| ❑ 167 Brian Stokes SP (RC) | 2.50 | 6.00 |
| ❑ 168 Albert Pujols SP | 6.00 | 15.00 |
| ❑ 169 Todd Coffey | .20 | .50 |
| ❑ 170 Jason Michaels | .20 | .50 |
| ❑ 171 David Dellucci | .20 | .50 |
| ❑ 172 Eric Milton | .20 | .50 |
| ❑ 173 Austin Kearns | .20 | .50 |
| ❑ 174 Oakland Athletics TC | .20 | .50 |
| ❑ 175 Andy Cannizaro RC | .20 | .50 |
| ❑ 176 David Weathers SP | 2.50 | 6.00 |
| ❑ 177 Jermaine Dye SP | 2.50 | 6.00 |
| ❑ 178 Wily Mo Pena | .20 | .50 |
| ❑ 179 Chris Burke | .20 | .50 |
| ❑ 180 Jeff Weaver | .20 | .50 |
| ❑ 181 Edwin Encarnacion | .20 | .50 |
| ❑ 182 Jeremy Hermida | .20 | .50 |
| ❑ 183 Tim Wakefield | .20 | .50 |
| ❑ 184 Rich Hill | .20 | .50 |
| ❑ 185 Aaron Hill SP | 2.50 | 6.00 |
| ❑ 186 Scot Shields SP | 2.50 | 6.00 |
| ❑ 187 Randy Johnson | .50 | 1.25 |
| ❑ 188 Dan Johnson | .20 | .50 |
| ❑ 189 Sean Marshall | .20 | .50 |
| ❑ 190 Marcus Giles | .20 | .50 |
| ❑ 191 Jonathan Broxton | .20 | .50 |
| ❑ 192 Mike Piazza | .50 | 1.25 |
| ❑ 193 Carlos Quentin | .20 | .50 |
| ❑ 194 Derek Lowe SP | 2.50 | 6.00 |
| ❑ 195 Russell Branyan SP | 2.50 | 6.00 |
| ❑ 196 Jason Marquis | .20 | .50 |
| ❑ 197 Khalil Greene | .30 | .75 |
| ❑ 198 Ryan Dempster | .20 | .50 |
| ❑ 199 Ronnie Belliard | .20 | .50 |
| ❑ 200 Josh Fogg | .20 | .50 |
| ❑ 201 Carlos Lee | .20 | .50 |
| ❑ 202 Chris Denorfia | .20 | .50 |
| ❑ 203 Kendry Morales SP | 3.00 | 8.00 |
| ❑ 204 Rafael Soriano SP | 2.50 | 6.00 |
| ❑ 205 Brandon Phillips | .20 | .50 |
| ❑ 206 Andrew Miller RC | 1.25 | 3.00 |
| ❑ 207 John Koronka | .20 | .50 |
| ❑ 208 Luis Castillo | .20 | .50 |
| ❑ 209 Angel Guzman | .20 | .50 |
| ❑ 210 Jim Edmonds | .30 | .75 |
| ❑ 211 Patrick Misch (RC) | .20 | .50 |
| ❑ 212 Ty Wigginton SP | 2.50 | 6.00 |
| ❑ 213 Brandon Inge SP | 2.50 | 6.00 |
| ❑ 214 Royce Clayton | .20 | .50 |
| ❑ 215 Ben Broussard | .20 | .50 |
| ❑ 216 St. Louis Cardinals TC | .20 | .50 |
| ❑ 217 Mark Mulder | .20 | .50 |
| ❑ 218 Kenji Johjima | .50 | 1.25 |
| ❑ 219 Joe Crede | .20 | .50 |
| ❑ 220 Shea Hillenbrand | .20 | .50 |
| ❑ 221 Josh Fields SP (RC) | 2.50 | 6.00 |
| ❑ 222 Pat Neshek SP | 3.00 | 8.00 |
| ❑ 223 Reed Johnson | .20 | .50 |
| ❑ 224 Mike Mussina | .30 | .75 |
| ❑ 225 Randy Winn | .20 | .50 |
| ❑ 226 Brian Rogers | .20 | .50 |
| ❑ 227 Juan Rivera | .20 | .50 |
| ❑ 228 Shawn Green | .20 | .50 |
| ❑ 229 Mike Napoli | .20 | .50 |
| ❑ 230 Chase Utley SP | 3.00 | 8.00 |
| ❑ 231 John Nelson SP (RC) | 2.50 | 6.00 |
| ❑ 232 Casey Blake | .20 | .50 |
| ❑ 233 Lyle Overbay | .20 | .50 |
| ❑ 234 Adam LaRoche | .20 | .50 |
| ❑ 235 Julio Lugo | .20 | .50 |
| ❑ 236 Johnny Estrada | .20 | .50 |
| ❑ 237 James Shields | .20 | .50 |
| ❑ 238 Jose Castillo | .20 | .50 |
| ❑ 239 Doug Davis SP | 2.50 | 6.00 |
| ❑ 240 Jason Giambi SP | 2.50 | 6.00 |
| ❑ 241 Mike Gonzalez | .20 | .50 |
| ❑ 242 Scott Downs | .20 | .50 |
| ❑ 243 Joe Inglett | .20 | .50 |
| ❑ 244 Matt Kemp | .50 | 1.25 |
| ❑ 245 Ted Lilly | .20 | .50 |
| ❑ 246 New York Yankees TC | .50 | 1.25 |
| ❑ 247 Jamey Carroll | .20 | .50 |
| ❑ 248 Adam Wainwright SP | 2.50 | 6.00 |
| ❑ 249 Matt Thornton SP | 2.50 | 6.00 |
| ❑ 250 Alfonso Soriano | .20 | .50 |
| ❑ 251 Tom Gordon | .20 | .50 |
| ❑ 252 Dennis Sarfate (RC) | .20 | .50 |
| ❑ 253 Zach Duke | .20 | .50 |
| ❑ 254 Hank Blalock | .20 | .50 |
| ❑ 255 John Santana | .30 | .75 |
| ❑ 256 Chicago White Sox TC | .20 | .50 |
| ❑ 257 Aaron Cook SP | 2.50 | 6.00 |
| ❑ 258 Cliff Lee SP | 2.50 | 6.00 |
| ❑ 259 Miguel Tejada | .20 | .50 |
| ❑ 260 Mike Lowell | .20 | .50 |
| ❑ 261 Ian Snell | .20 | .50 |
| ❑ 262 Jason Tyner | .20 | .50 |
| ❑ 263 Troy Tulowitzki (RC) | .50 | 1.25 |
| ❑ 264 Ervin Santana | .20 | .50 |
| ❑ 265 Jon Lester | .30 | .75 |
| ❑ 266 Andy Pettitte SP | 3.00 | 8.00 |
| ❑ 267 A.J. Pierzynski SP | 2.50 | 6.00 |
| ❑ 268 Rich Aurilia | .20 | .50 |
| ❑ 269 Phil Nevin | .20 | .50 |
| ❑ 270 Tom Glavine | .30 | .75 |
| ❑ 271 Chris Coste | .20 | .50 |
| ❑ 272 Moises Alou | .20 | .50 |
| ❑ 273 J.D. Drew | .20 | .50 |
| ❑ 274 Abraham Nunez | .20 | .50 |
| ❑ 275 Jorge Posada SP | 3.00 | 8.00 |
| ❑ 276 Jeff Conine SP | 2.50 | 6.00 |
| ❑ 277 Chad Cordero | .20 | .50 |
| ❑ 278 Nick Johnson | .20 | .50 |
| ❑ 279 Kevin Millar | .20 | .50 |
| ❑ 280 Mark Grudzielanek | .20 | .50 |
| ❑ 281 Chris Stewart RC | .20 | .50 |
| ❑ 282 Nate Robertson | .20 | .50 |
| ❑ 283 Drew Anderson RC | .20 | .50 |
| ❑ 284 Doug Mientkiewicz SP | 2.50 | 6.00 |
| ❑ 285 Ken Griffey Jr. SP | 4.00 | 10.00 |
| ❑ 286 Cory Sullivan | .20 | .50 |
| ❑ 287 Chris Carpenter | .20 | .50 |
| ❑ 288 Gary Matthews | .20 | .50 |
| ❑ 289 J.Verlander/Jef.Weaver | .50 | 1.25 |
| ❑ 290 Vicente Padilla | .20 | .50 |
| ❑ 291 Chris Roberson | .20 | .50 |
| ❑ 292 Chris R. Young | .20 | .50 |
| ❑ 293 Ryan Garko SP | 2.50 | 6.00 |
| ❑ 294 Miguel Batista SP | 2.50 | 6.00 |
| ❑ 295 B.J. Upton | .50 | 1.25 |
| ❑ 296 Justin Verlander | .50 | 1.25 |
| ❑ 297 Ben Zobrist | .20 | .50 |
| ❑ 298 Ben Sheets | .20 | .50 |
| ❑ 299 Eric Chavez | .20 | .50 |
| ❑ 300 Scott Schoeneweis | .20 | .50 |
| ❑ 301 Placido Polanco | .20 | .50 |
| ❑ 302 Angel Sanchez SP RC | 2.50 | 6.00 |
| ❑ 303 Freddy Sanchez SP | 2.50 | 6.00 |
| ❑ 304 M.Ordonez/C.Monroe | .20 | .50 |
| ❑ 305 A.J. Burnett | .20 | .50 |
| ❑ 306 Juan Perez RC | .20 | .50 |
| ❑ 307 Chris Britton | .20 | .50 |
| ❑ 308 Jon Garland | .20 | .50 |
| ❑ 309 Pedro Feliz | .20 | .50 |
| ❑ 310 Ryan Howard | .75 | 2.00 |
| ❑ 311 Aaron Harang SP | 2.50 | 6.00 |
| ❑ 312 Boston Red Sox TC SP | 3.00 | 8.00 |
| ❑ 313 Chad Billingsley | .20 | .50 |
| ❑ 314 C.Jones/B.Cox MG | .50 | 1.25 |
| ❑ 315 Bengie Molina | .20 | .50 |
| ❑ 316 Juan Pierre | .20 | .50 |
| ❑ 317 Luke Scott | .20 | .50 |
| ❑ 318 Javier Valentin | .20 | .50 |
| ❑ 319 Mark Loretta | .20 | .50 |
| ❑ 320 Kenny Lofton SP | 2.50 | 6.00 |
| ❑ 321 V.Guerrero/I.Rodriguez SP | 3.00 | 8.00 |
| ❑ 322 Josh Willingham | .20 | .50 |
| ❑ 323 Lance Berkman | .20 | .50 |
| ❑ 324 Anibal Sanchez | .20 | .50 |
| ❑ 325 Maicer Izturis | .20 | .50 |
| ❑ 326 Brett Myers | .20 | .50 |
| ❑ 327 Chicago Cubs TC | .30 | .75 |
| ❑ 328 Francisco Liriano | .50 | 1.25 |
| ❑ 329 Craig Monroe SP | 2.50 | 6.00 |
| ❑ 330 Paul LoDuca SP | 2.50 | 6.00 |
| ❑ 331 Steve Trachsel | .20 | .50 |
| ❑ 332 Bernie Williams | .30 | .75 |
| ❑ 333 Carlos Guillen | .20 | .50 |
| ❑ 334 C.Wang/M.Mussina | .50 | 1.25 |
| ❑ 335 Dave Bush | .20 | .50 |
| ❑ 336 Carlos Beltran | .20 | .50 |
| ❑ 337 Jason Isringhausen | .20 | .50 |
| ❑ 338 Todd Walker SP | 2.50 | 6.00 |
| ❑ 339 Jarrod Washburn SP | 2.50 | 6.00 |
| ❑ 340 Brandon Webb | .20 | .50 |
| ❑ 341 Pittsburgh Pirates TC | .20 | .50 |
| ❑ 342 Daryle Ward | .20 | .50 |
| ❑ 343 Chad Santos | .20 | .50 |
| ❑ 344 Brad Lidge | .20 | .50 |
| ❑ 345 Brad Ausmus | .20 | .50 |
| ❑ 346 Carlos Delgado | .20 | .50 |
| ❑ 347 Boone Logan SP | 2.50 | 6.00 |
| ❑ 348 Jimmy Rollins SP | 2.50 | 6.00 |
| ❑ 349 Orlando Hernandez | .20 | .50 |
| ❑ 350 Gary Sheffield | .20 | .50 |
| ❑ 351 Pujols/Duncan/Edmonds/Molina | 1.00 | 2.50 |
| ❑ 352 Jake Peavy | .20 | .50 |
| ❑ 353 Jason Varitek | .50 | 1.25 |
| ❑ 354 Freddy Garcia | .20 | .50 |
| ❑ 355 Matt Diaz | .20 | .50 |
| ❑ 356 Bernie Castro SP | 2.50 | 6.00 |
| ❑ 357 Eric Stults SP RC | 2.50 | 6.00 |
| ❑ 358 John Lackey | .20 | .50 |
| ❑ 359 Bobby Jenks | .20 | .50 |
| ❑ 360 Mark Teixeira | .30 | .75 |
| ❑ 361 Jonathan Papelbon | .50 | 1.25 |
| ❑ 362 Paul Konerko | .20 | .50 |
| ❑ 363 Erik Bedard | .20 | .50 |
| ❑ 364 Eliezer Alfonzo | .20 | .50 |
| ❑ 365 Fernando Rodney | 2.50 | 6.00 |
| ❑ 366 Chris Duncan SP | 2.50 | 6.00 |
| ❑ 367 Jose Diaz (RC) | .20 | .50 |
| ❑ 368 Travis Hafner | .20 | .50 |
| ❑ 369 Matt Capps | .20 | .50 |
| ❑ 370 Ivan Rodriguez | .30 | .75 |
| ❑ 371 David Murphy (RC) | .20 | .50 |
| ❑ 372 Carlos Zambrano | .20 | .50 |
| ❑ 373 Chris Iannetta | .20 | .50 |
| ❑ 374 Jose Mesa SP | 2.50 | 6.00 |
| ❑ 375 Michael Young SP | 2.50 | 6.00 |
| ❑ 376 Bill Bray | .20 | .50 |
| ❑ 377 Atlanta Braves TC | .30 | .75 |
| ❑ 378 Jeff Cirillo | .20 | .50 |
| ❑ 379 Barry Zito | .20 | .50 |
| ❑ 380 Clay Hensley | .20 | .50 |
| ❑ 381 J.J. Putz | .20 | .50 |
| ❑ 382 C.C. Sabathia | .20 | .50 |
| ❑ 383 Eduardo Perez SP | 2.50 | 6.00 |
| ❑ 384 Scott Moore SP (RC) | 2.50 | 6.00 |
| ❑ 385 Scott Olsen | .20 | .50 |
| ❑ 386 R.Howard/C.Utley | .75 | 2.00 |
| ❑ 387 Aaron Rowand | .20 | .50 |
| ❑ 388 Mike Rouse | .20 | .50 |
| ❑ 389 Alexis Gomez | .20 | .50 |
| ❑ 390 Brian McCann | .20 | .50 |
| ❑ 391 Ryan Shealy | .20 | .50 |
| ❑ 392 Shane Youman SP RC | 2.50 | 6.00 |
| ❑ 393 Melky Cabrera SP | 2.50 | 6.00 |
| ❑ 394 Jeremy Sowers | .20 | .50 |
| ❑ 395 Casey Janssen | .20 | .50 |
| ❑ 396 Travis Chick (RC) | .20 | .50 |
| ❑ 397 Detroit Tigers TC | .50 | 1.25 |
| ❑ 398 Reggie Abercrombie | .20 | .50 |
| ❑ 399 Ricky Nolasco | .20 | .50 |
| ❑ 400 Tadahito Iguchi | .20 | .50 |
| ❑ 401 Jose Reyes SP | 2.50 | 6.00 |
| ❑ 402 Juan Encarnacion SP | 2.50 | 6.00 |
| ❑ 403 Brandon Harper | .20 | .50 |
| ❑ 404 Torii Hunter | .20 | .50 |
| ❑ 405 Dan Uggla | .30 | .75 |
| ❑ 406 Orlando Cabrera | .20 | .50 |
| ❑ 407 Jose Capellan | .20 | .50 |
| ❑ 408 Baltimore Orioles TC | .20 | .50 |
| ❑ 409 Frank Thomas | .50 | 1.25 |

|  |  | | |
|---|------|------|------|
| 410 | Francisco Rodriguez SP | 2.50 | 6.00 |
| 411 | Ian Kinsler SP | 3.00 | 8.00 |
| 412 | Billy Wagner | .20 | .50 |
| 413 | Andy Marte | .20 | .50 |
| 414 | Mike Jacobs | .20 | .50 |
| 415 | Raul Ibanez | .30 | .75 |
| 416 | Jhonny Peralta | .20 | .50 |
| 417 | Chris B. Young | .20 | .50 |
| 418 | A.Pujols/M.Ordonez | 1.00 | 2.50 |
| 419 | Scott Kazmir SP | 3.00 | 8.00 |
| 420 | Norris Hopper SP | 2.50 | 6.00 |
| 421 | Chris Capuano | .20 | .50 |
| 422 | Troy Glaus | .20 | .50 |
| 423 | Roy Oswalt | .20 | .50 |
| 424 | Grady Sizemore | .30 | .75 |
| 425 | Chone Figgins | .20 | .50 |
| 426 | Chad Tracy | .20 | .50 |
| 427 | Brian Fuentes | .20 | .50 |
| 428 | Cincinnati Reds TC SP | 2.50 | 6.00 |
| 429 | Ramon Hernandez SP | 2.50 | 6.00 |
| 430 | Mike Cameron | .20 | .50 |
| 431 | Dontrelle Willis | .20 | .50 |
| 432 | Josh Sharpless | .20 | .50 |
| 433 | Adrian Beltre | .20 | .50 |
| 434 | Curtis Granderson | .20 | .50 |
| 435 | B.J. Ryan | .20 | .50 |
| 436 | D.Wright/R.Howard | .75 | 2.00 |
| 437 | Vernon Wells SP | 2.50 | 6.00 |
| 438 | Vladimir Guerrero SP | 3.00 | 8.00 |
| 439 | Jake Westbrook | .20 | .50 |
| 440 | Chipper Jones | .50 | 1.25 |
| 441 | James Loney | .30 | .75 |
| 442 | Nook Logan | .20 | .50 |
| 443 | Oswaldo Navarro RC | .20 | .50 |
| 444 | Joe Mauer | .50 | 1.25 |
| 445 | Miguel Montero (RC) | .20 | .50 |
| 446 | Franklin Gutierrez SP | 2.50 | 6.00 |
| 447 | Mark Redman SP | 2.50 | 6.00 |
| 448 | Mike Rabelo RC | .20 | .50 |
| 449 | Philip Humber (RC) | .30 | .75 |
| 450 | Justin Morneau | .20 | .50 |
| 451 | Hector Gimenez (RC) | .20 | .50 |
| 452 | Matt Holliday | .50 | 1.25 |
| 453 | Akinori Otsuka | .20 | .50 |
| 454 | Prince Fielder | .50 | 1.25 |
| 455 | Chien-Ming Wang SP | 4.00 | 10.00 |
| 456 | Shawn Riggans SP | 2.50 | 6.00 |
| 457 | John Maine | .20 | .50 |
| 458 | Adam Lind (RC) | .20 | .50 |
| 459 | Ubaldo Jimenez (RC) | .20 | .50 |
| 460 | Jaret Wright | .20 | .50 |
| 461 | Cla Meredith | .20 | .50 |
| 462 | Joaquin Arias (RC) | .20 | .50 |
| 463 | Kenny Rogers | .20 | .50 |
| 464 | Jose Garcia SP RC | 2.50 | 6.00 |
| 465 | Pedro Martinez SP | 3.00 | 8.00 |
| 466 | Jeff Salazar (RC) | .20 | .50 |
| 467 | Glen Perkins | .20 | .50 |
| 468 | Travis Ishikawa | .20 | .50 |
| 469 | Joe Borowski | .20 | .50 |
| 470 | Jeremy Brown | .20 | .50 |
| 471 | Andre Ethier | .30 | .75 |
| 472 | Taylor Tankersley | .20 | .50 |
| 473 | Lastings Milledge SP | 3.00 | 8.00 |
| 474 | Brian Sanches SP | 2.50 | 6.00 |
| 475 | O.Guillen AS MG/P.Garner AS MG | | |
| 476 | Albert Pujols AS | 1.00 | 2.50 |
| 477 | David Ortiz AS | .30 | .75 |
| 478 | Chase Utley AS | .50 | 1.25 |
| 479 | Mark Loretta AS | .20 | .50 |
| 480 | David Wright AS | .75 | 2.00 |
| 481 | Alex Rodriguez AS | .75 | 2.00 |
| 482 | Edgar Renteria AS | 2.50 | 6.00 |
| 483 | Derek Jeter AS SP | 5.00 | 12.00 |
| 484 | Alfonso Soriano AS | .20 | .50 |
| 485 | Vladimir Guerrero AS | .50 | 1.25 |
| 486 | Carlos Beltran AS | .20 | .50 |
| 487 | Vernon Wells AS | .20 | .50 |
| 488 | Jason Bay AS | .30 | .75 |
| 489 | Ichiro Suzuki AS | .75 | 2.00 |
| 490 | Paul LoDuca AS | .20 | .50 |
| 491 | Ivan Rodriguez AS SP | 3.00 | 8.00 |
| 492 | Brad Penny AS SP | 2.50 | 6.00 |
| 493 | Roy Halladay AS | .20 | .50 |
| 494 | Brian Fuentes AS | .20 | .50 |
| 495 | Kenny Rogers AS | .20 | .50 |

## 2008 Topps Heritage

ichiro

SEATTLE MARINERS
OUTFIELDER

| | | | |
|---|------|------|------|
| | COMP.SET w/o SP's (425) | 40.00 | 80.00 |
| | COMP.HN SET (220) | 125.00 | 200.00 |
| | COMP.HN SET w/ SP's (150) | 12.50 | 30.00 |
| | COMMON CARD | .15 | .40 |
| | COMMON SP | .40 | 1.00 |
| | COMMON TEAM CARD | .15 | .40 |
| | COMMON GB SP | .40 | 1.00 |
| | COMMON SP | 2.50 | 6.00 |
| | SP STATED ODDS 1:3 HOBBY/RETAIL | | |
| | HN SP ODDS 1:3 HOBBY/RETAIL | | |
| 1 | Vladimir Guerrero | .40 | 1.00 |
| 2 | Placido Polanco GB SP | .40 | 1.00 |
| 3 | Eric Byrnes GB SP | .40 | 1.00 |
| 4 | Mark Teixeira | .25 | .60 |
| 5 | Javier Vazquez GB SP | .40 | 1.00 |
| 6 | Jacoby Ellsbury | .60 | 1.50 |
| 7 | Joey Gathright GB SP | .40 | 1.00 |
| 8 | Philadelphia Phillies GB SP | .40 | 1.00 |
| 9 | Andre Ethier GB SP | .60 | 1.50 |
| 10 | Alex Rodriguez | .60 | 1.50 |
| 11 | Luke Scott SP | 2.50 | 6.00 |
| 12 | Curt Schilling GB SP | .60 | 1.50 |
| 13 | Billy Wagner GB SP | .40 | 1.00 |
| 14 | Gary Matthews GB SP | .40 | 1.00 |
| 15 | Sean Marshall | .15 | .40 |
| 16 | I.Suzuki GB SP | 1.50 | 4.00 |
| 17 | Wilson/Bay/Sanchez | .25 | .60 |
| 18 | Dontrelle Willis GB SP | .40 | 1.00 |
| 19 | Josh Willingham | .15 | .40 |
| 20 | Jeff Kent | .15 | .40 |
| 21 | Troy Tulowitzki GB SP | .60 | 1.50 |
| 22 | Brian Fuentes GB SP | .40 | 1.00 |
| 23 | Robinson Cano GB SP | .60 | 1.50 |
| 24 | Felix Hernandez GB SP | .60 | 1.50 |
| 25 | Edwin Encarnacion | .15 | .40 |
| 26 | Fausto Carmona | .15 | .40 |
| 27 | Greg Maddux | .50 | 1.25 |
| 28 | Ivan Rodriguez GB SP | .60 | 1.50 |
| 29 | Joe Nathan | .15 | .40 |
| 30 | Paul Konerko | .15 | .40 |
| 31 | Nook Logan | .15 | .40 |
| 32 | Derek Lowe | .15 | .40 |
| 33 | Jose Lopez | .15 | .40 |
| 34 | Ordonez/Granderson GB SP | .60 | 1.50 |
| 35 | Adam LaRoche GB SP | .40 | 1.00 |
| 36 | Kenny Lofton | .15 | .40 |
| 37 | Matt Capps | .15 | .40 |
| 38 | Mark Reynolds | .15 | .40 |
| 39 | Joe Mauer | .40 | 1.00 |
| 40 | Tim Hudson GB SP | .40 | 1.00 |
| 41 | Kelvim Escobar GB SP | .40 | 1.00 |
| 42 | Jason Jennings GB SP | .40 | 1.00 |
| 43 | Victor Martinez | .15 | .40 |
| 44 | Jason Kendall | .15 | .40 |
| 45 | Chris Ray GB SP | .40 | 1.00 |
| 46 | Jason Bergmann | .15 | .40 |
| 47 | Jason Marquis | .15 | .40 |
| 48 | Baltimore Orioles | .15 | .40 |
| 49 | Bill Hall GB SP | .40 | 1.00 |
| 50 | Ken Griffey Jr. | .60 | 1.50 |
| 51 | Chad Cordero | .15 | .40 |
| 52 | Omar Vizquel GB SP | .40 | 1.00 |
| 53 | Jim Edmonds | .25 | .60 |
| 54 | Justin Upton GB SP | 1.00 | 2.50 |
| 55 | Josh Beckett | .25 | .60 |
| 56 | Jeff Francis | .15 | .40 |
| 57 | Brad Lidge GB SP | .40 | 1.00 |
| 58 | Paul Lo Duca GB SP | .40 | 1.00 |
| 59 | John Patterson | .15 | .40 |
| 60 | Andy Pettitte GB SP | .60 | 1.50 |
| 61 | Brendan Harris SP | .40 | 1.00 |
| 62 | Chris Young GB SP | .40 | 1.00 |

|  |  | | |
|---|------|------|------|
| 63 | Eric Chavez | .15 | .40 |
| 64 | Francisco Rodriguez | .15 | .40 |
| 65 | Jason Giambi GB SP | .60 | 1.50 |
| 66 | B.J. Ryan | .15 | .40 |
| 67 | Rich Hill GB SP | .40 | 1.00 |
| 68 | Derek Jeter | 1.00 | 2.50 |
| 69 | San Francisco Giants GB SP | .40 | 1.00 |
| 70 | Carlos Guillen | .15 | .40 |
| 71 | Trevor Hoffman GB SP | .40 | 1.00 |
| 72 | Zach Duke | .15 | .40 |
| 73 | Dustin Pedroia | .50 | 1.25 |
| 74 | D.Young/R.Zimmerman | .25 | .60 |
| 75 | Cole Hamels | .15 | .40 |
| 76 | Carlos Delgado | .15 | .40 |
| 77 | Jonathan Broxton | .15 | .40 |
| 78 | Josh Hamilton GB SP | 1.25 | 3.00 |
| 79 | Mark Loretta GB SP | .40 | 1.00 |
| 80 | Grady Sizemore | .25 | .60 |
| 81 | Torii Hunter GB SP | .40 | 1.00 |
| 82 | Carlos Beltran GB SP | .40 | 1.00 |
| 83 | Jason Isringhausen GB SP | .40 | 1.00 |
| 84 | Brad Penny GB SP | .40 | 1.00 |
| 85 | Jayson Werth | .15 | .40 |
| 86 | Alex Gordon | .25 | .60 |
| 87 | David DeJesus | .15 | .40 |
| 88 | Clay Buchholz | .40 | 1.00 |
| 89 | Conor Jackson | .15 | .40 |
| 90 | Hideki Matsui GB SP | 1.00 | 2.50 |
| 91 | Matt Garza GB SP | .40 | 1.00 |
| 92 | P.Hughes GB SP | 1.00 | 2.50 |
| 93 | Mike Piazza | .40 | 1.00 |
| 94 | Chicago White Sox GB SP | .40 | 1.00 |
| 95 | Buddy Carlyle | .15 | .40 |
| 96 | Mark DeRosa | .15 | .40 |
| 97 | Brandon Webb | .25 | .60 |
| 98 | Jon Garland GB SP | .40 | 1.00 |
| 99 | Mariano Rivera | .40 | 1.00 |
| 100 | Jack Cust | .15 | .40 |
| 101 | Carlos Ruiz | .15 | .40 |
| 102 | Moises Alou GB SP | .40 | 1.00 |
| 103 | Bengie Molina | .15 | .40 |
| 104 | Adam Jones | .15 | .40 |
| 105 | Alfonso Soriano | .25 | .60 |
| 106 | Troy Glaus | .15 | .40 |
| 107 | John Maine | .15 | .40 |
| 108 | Pat Burrell | .15 | .40 |
| 109 | David Eckstein | .15 | .40 |
| 110 | Homer Bailey | .25 | .60 |
| 111 | Cincinnati Reds | .15 | .40 |
| 112 | Corey Hart | .15 | .40 |
| 113 | Orlando Hernandez | .15 | .40 |
| 114 | Orlando Cabrera | .15 | .40 |
| 115 | Ryan Garko | .15 | .40 |
| 116 | Wladimir Balentien GB SP (RC) | .40 | 1.00 |
| 117 | Daric Barton GB SP | .40 | 1.00 |
| 118 | Emilio Bonifacio RC | 1.00 | 2.50 |
| 119 | Lance Broadway (RC) | .40 | 1.00 |
| 120 | Jeff Clement (RC) | .60 | 1.50 |
| 121 | Dave Davidson RC | .40 | 1.00 |
| 122 | Ross Detwiler GB SP RC | 1.00 | 2.50 |
| 123 | Sam Fuld RC | .60 | 1.50 |
| 124 | Armando Galarraga RC | .60 | 1.50 |
| 125 | Harvey Garcia (RC) | .40 | 1.00 |
| 126 | Dan Giese GB SP (RC) | .40 | 1.00 |
| 127 | Alberto Gonzalez GB SP RC | .60 | 1.50 |
| 128 | Kevin Hart (RC) | .40 | 1.00 |
| 129 | Luke Hochevar GB SP RC | .60 | 1.50 |
| 130 | Chin-Lung Hu GB SP (RC) | .60 | 1.50 |
| 131 | Brandon Jones RC | 1.00 | 2.50 |
| 132 | Joe Koshansky (RC) | .40 | 1.00 |
| 133 | Radhames Liz RC | .60 | 1.50 |
| 134 | Donny Lucy (RC) | .40 | 1.00 |
| 135 | Mitch Slatter GB SP RC | .60 | 1.50 |
| 136 | Nyjer Morgan (RC) | .60 | 1.50 |
| 137 | Ross Ohlendorf RC | .60 | 1.50 |
| 138 | Steve Pearce RC | .60 | 1.50 |
| 139 | Jeff Ridgway RC | .60 | 1.50 |
| 140 | Bronson Sardinha (RC) | .60 | 1.50 |
| 141 | Seth Smith (RC) | .40 | 1.00 |
| 142 | Rich Thompson RC | .40 | 1.00 |
| 143 | Erick Threets (RC) | .40 | 1.00 |
| 144 | J.R. Towles RC | .60 | 1.50 |
| 145 | Eugenio Velez RC | .40 | 1.00 |
| 146 | Joey Votto (RC) | 1.00 | 2.50 |
| 147 | Soriano/A.Ramirez/D.Lee | .25 | .60 |
| 148 | Hunter Pence | .40 | 1.00 |
| 149 | Barry Zito | .15 | .40 |
| 150 | Albert Pujols | 2.00 | 5.00 |

|  |  | | |
|---|--------|------|------|
| 151 | Sammy Sosa | .25 | .60 |
| 152 | Brian Bannister | .15 | .40 |
| 153 | Reggie Willits | .15 | .40 |
| 154 | Bobby Abreu | .15 | .40 |
| 155 | Johnny Damon GB SP | .60 | 1.50 |
| 156 | B.Webb/J.Peavy | .25 | .60 |
| 157 | Aramis Ramirez | .15 | .40 |
| 158 | Aaron Cook | .15 | .40 |
| 159 | David Weathers | .15 | .40 |
| 160 | Jack Wilson | .15 | .40 |
| 161 | Josh Fogg | .15 | .40 |
| 162 | Garrett Atkins | .15 | .40 |
| 163 | Brad Ausmus | .15 | .40 |
| 164 | Gil Meche | .15 | .40 |
| 165 | Jeff Francoeur | .25 | .60 |
| 166 | V.Marti/Hafner/Sizemore | .25 | .60 |
| 167 | Juan Pierre | .15 | .40 |
| 168 | Rafael Furcal | .15 | .40 |
| 169 | J.J. Hardy | .25 | .60 |
| 170 | Nick Markakis | .25 | .60 |
| 171 | Delmon Young | .25 | .60 |
| 172 | Oakland Athletics | .15 | .40 |
| 173 | Ronny Paulino GB SP | .40 | 1.00 |
| 174 | Mike Cameron GB SP | .40 | 1.00 |
| 175 | Jeff Weaver GB SP | .40 | 1.00 |
| 176 | Preston Wilson GB SP | .40 | 1.00 |
| 177 | Robinson Tejeda GB SP | .40 | 1.00 |
| 178 | Adam Lind GB SP | .40 | 1.00 |
| 179 | Austin Kearns GB SP | .40 | 1.00 |
| 180 | Jorge Posada GB SP | .60 | 1.50 |
| 181 | Tadahito Iguchi | .15 | .40 |
| 182 | Matt Cain | .15 | .40 |
| 183 | Yuniesky Betancourt | .15 | .40 |
| 184 | Bronson Arroyo | .15 | .40 |
| 185 | Brad Hawpe GB SP | .40 | 1.00 |
| 186 | Rickie Weeks GB SP | .40 | 1.00 |
| 187 | Carlos Silva GB SP | .40 | 1.00 |
| 188 | Adrian Gonzalez | .25 | .60 |
| 189 | Kenji Johjima | .15 | .40 |
| 190 | Chris Duncan | .15 | .40 |
| 191 | James Shields | .15 | .40 |
| 192 | Akinori Iwamura | .15 | .40 |
| 193 | David Murphy | .15 | .40 |
| 194 | Alex Rios | .15 | .40 |
| 195 | Carlos Quentin GB SP | .40 | 1.00 |
| 196 | Jose Valverde GB SP | .40 | 1.00 |
| 197 | Dernek Lee GB SP | .40 | 1.00 |
| 198 | Jerry Owens GB SP | .40 | 1.00 |
| 199 | Russell Martin | .15 | .40 |
| 200 | Yovani Gallardo | .15 | .40 |
| 201a | Johan Santana Twins | .40 | 1.00 |
| 201b | J.Santana Mets | 60.00 | 120.00 |
| 202 | Nick Swisher | .15 | .40 |
| 203 | So Taguchi | .15 | .40 |
| 204 | Justin Morneau | .25 | .60 |
| 205 | Milton Bradley | .15 | .40 |
| 206 | Jake Westbrook | .15 | .40 |
| 207 | Dave Roberts | .15 | .40 |
| 208 | Billy Butler | .15 | .40 |
| 209 | Lance Berkman | .25 | .60 |
| 210 | J.J. Putz GB SP | .40 | 1.00 |
| 211 | Mike Sweeney GB SP | .40 | 1.00 |
| 212 | A.Jones/C.Jones | .50 | 1.25 |
| 213 | Ricky Nolasco | .15 | .40 |
| 214 | Andy LaRoche | .15 | .40 |
| 215 | Ray Durham | .15 | .40 |
| 216 | Francisco Cordero | .15 | .40 |
| 217 | Jered Weaver | .15 | .40 |
| 218 | Rafael Soriano | .15 | .40 |
| 219 | Orlando Hudson | .15 | .40 |
| 220 | Mike Lowell | .15 | .40 |
| 221 | Chris Snyder | .15 | .40 |
| 222 | Cesar Izturis | .15 | .40 |
| 223 | St. Louis Cardinals | .15 | .40 |
| 224 | D.Wright GB SP | 1.25 | 3.00 |
| 225 | Pedro Martinez GB SP | .60 | 1.50 |
| 226 | Rich Harden GB SP | .40 | 1.00 |
| 227 | Shane Victorino GB SP | .40 | 1.00 |
| 228 | Andrew Miller GB SP | .60 | 1.50 |
| 229 | Chris Young | .15 | .40 |
| 230 | Andruw Jones | .15 | .40 |
| 231 | Kevin Gregg SP | 2.50 | 6.00 |
| 232 | C.C. Sabathia | .25 | .60 |
| 233 | Hanley Ramirez | .40 | 1.00 |
| 234 | Wandy Rodriguez | .15 | .40 |
| 235 | Roy Oswalt | .15 | .40 |
| 236 | Mark Grudzielanek | .15 | .40 |
| 237 | Jeter/Wang/Cano | .40 | 1.00 |
| 238 | Todd Helton | .25 | .60 |
| 239 | Zack Greinke | .15 | .40 |
| 240 | Carlos Gomez | .15 | .40 |
| 241 | Lastings Milledge | .15 | .40 |
| 242 | Huston Street | .15 | .40 |
| 243 | Dan Haren | .15 | .40 |
| 244 | Carlos Pena | .40 | 1.00 |
| 245 | Brad Wilkerson | .15 | .40 |
| 246 | Roy Halladay | .40 | 1.00 |
| 247 | Dmitri Young | .15 | .40 |
| 248 | Boston Red Sox | .60 | 1.50 |
| 249 | Jonathan Papelbon | .25 | .60 |
| 250 | Felix Pie | .15 | .40 |
| 251 | Alex Gonzalez | .15 | .40 |
| 252 | Bobby Crosby | .15 | .40 |
| 253 | Justin Ruggiano RC | .60 | 1.50 |
| 254 | Freddy Garcia | .15 | .40 |
| 255 | Khalil Greene | .25 | .60 |
| 256 | Rich Aurilia | .15 | .40 |
| 257 | Jarrod Washburn | .15 | .40 |
| 258 | B.J. Upton | .25 | .60 |
| 259 | Michael Young | .15 | .40 |
| 260 | Carlos Zambrano | .15 | .40 |
| 261 | Livan Hernandez | .15 | .40 |
| 262 | Billingsley/Lowe/Penny GB SP | .40 | 1.00 |
| 263 | Melky Cabrera GB SP | .40 | 1.00 |
| 264 | Shannon Stewart GB SP | .40 | 1.00 |
| 265 | Aaron Rowand GB SP | .40 | 1.00 |
| 266 | Matt Morris GB SP | .40 | 1.00 |
| 267 | Xavier Nady GB SP | .40 | 1.00 |
| 268 | Jim Thome | .25 | .60 |
| 269 | Horacio Ramirez | .15 | .40 |
| 270 | Prince Fielder | .40 | 1.00 |
| 271 | Andy Phillips | .15 | .40 |
| 272 | Aaron Harang | .15 | .40 |
| 273 | Josh Barfield | .15 | .40 |
| 274 | Ubaldo Jimenez | .15 | .40 |
| 275 | Anibal Sanchez | .15 | .40 |
| 276 | Carlos Lee | .15 | .40 |
| 277 | Mark Teahen | .15 | .40 |
| 278 | Delwyn Young | .15 | .40 |
| 279 | Kurt Suzuki | .15 | .40 |
| 280 | Nate Schierholtz | .15 | .40 |
| 281 | Raul Ibanez | .25 | .60 |
| 282 | Jose Vidro | .15 | .40 |
| 283 | Miguel Cabrera GB SP | .60 | 1.50 |
| 284 | Luis Gonzalez GB SP | .40 | 1.00 |
| 285 | Chad Billingsley GB SP | .40 | 1.00 |
| 286 | Tony Gwynn GB SP | .40 | 1.00 |
| 287 | Matt Kemp | .40 | 1.00 |
| 288 | James Loney | .25 | .60 |
| 289 | Brett Myers | .15 | .40 |
| 290 | Nate McLouth | .15 | .40 |
| 291 | M.Chico/J.Bergmann GB SP | .40 | 1.00 |
| 292 | Chad Tracy | .15 | .40 |
| 293 | Edgar Renteria | .15 | .40 |
| 294 | Jay Payton | .15 | .40 |
| 295 | Josh Johnson | .15 | .40 |
| 296 | Josh Banks (RC) | .40 | 1.00 |
| 297 | Bill Murphy (RC) | .40 | 1.00 |
| 298 | Ben Sheets | .15 | .40 |
| 299 | Jose Reyes | .25 | .60 |
| 300 | Chase Utley | .40 | 1.00 |
| 301 | Ronnie Belliard GB SP | .40 | 1.00 |
| 302 | Willy Mo Pena | .15 | .40 |
| 303 | Tim Lincecum | .50 | 1.25 |
| 304 | Chicago Cubs | .25 | .60 |
| 305 | John Lackey | .15 | .40 |
| 306 | Stephen Drew | .15 | .40 |
| 307 | Kelly Johnson | .15 | .40 |
| 308 | Daisuke Matsuzaka | .50 | 1.25 |
| 309 | Craig Monroe | .15 | .40 |
| 310 | Jerry Owens | .15 | .40 |
| 311 | Jeff Suppan | .15 | .40 |
| 312 | Tom Glavine | .25 | .60 |
| 313 | Kei Igawa | .15 | .40 |
| 314 | Mark Kotsay | .15 | .40 |
| 315 | Jacque Jones SP | 2.50 | 6.00 |
| 316 | Melvin Mora | .15 | .40 |
| 317 | M.Holliday/H.Ramirez | .40 | 1.00 |
| 318 | Jarrod Saltalamacchia | .15 | .40 |
| 319 | A.J. Burnett | .15 | .40 |
| 320 | Casey Kotchman | .15 | .40 |
| 321 | Randy Winn GB SP | .40 | 1.00 |
| 322 | Richie Sexson GB SP | .40 | 1.00 |
| 323 | Juan Encarnacion GB SP | .40 | 1.00 |
| 324 | Rick Ankiel GB SP | .40 | 1.00 |
| 325 | Dan Wheeler GB SP | .40 | 1.00 |
| 326 | Brian Roberts | .25 | .60 |
| 327 | David Ortiz | .25 | .60 |
| 328 | Garret Anderson | .15 | .40 |
| 329 | Detroit Tigers | .15 | .40 |
| 330 | Ty Wigginton GB SP | .40 | 1.00 |
| 331 | Travis Hafner | .15 | .40 |
| 332 | Howie Kendrick GB SP | .40 | 1.00 |
| 333 | Kevin Kouzmanoff GB SP | .40 | 1.00 |
| 334 | Matt Holliday GB SP | .60 | 1.50 |
| 335 | Brandon Phillips GB SP | .40 | 1.00 |
| 336 | Ian Kinsler GB SP | .60 | 1.50 |
| 337 | Lyle Overbay GB SP | .40 | 1.00 |
| 338 | Justin Verlander GB SP | .60 | 1.50 |
| 339 | Ian Snell | .15 | .40 |
| 340 | Hank Blalock | .15 | .40 |
| 341 | Vernon Wells | .40 | 1.00 |
| 342 | Matt Chico | .15 | .40 |
| 343 | Tim Wakefield | .15 | .40 |
| 344 | Michael Bourn | .15 | .40 |
| 345 | Chris Carpenter | .15 | .40 |
| 346 | Matsuzaka/Beckett | .50 | 1.25 |
| 347 | Chuck James GB SP | .40 | 1.00 |
| 348 | Joba Chamberlain | .50 | 1.25 |
| 349 | Erik Bedard | .15 | .40 |
| 350 | Jimmy Rollins GB SP | .60 | 1.50 |
| 351 | Andruw Reyes | .15 | .40 |
| 352 | Carl Crawford | .15 | .40 |
| 353 | Jeremy Hermida | .15 | .40 |
| 354 | Ervin Santana | .15 | .40 |
| 355 | Edgar Gonzalez | .15 | .40 |
| 356 | Yunel Escobar | .15 | .40 |
| 357 | Yorvit Torrealba | .15 | .40 |
| 358 | Hideki Okajima | .15 | .40 |
| 359 | Paul Byrd | .15 | .40 |
| 360 | Magglio Ordonez GB SP | .60 | 1.50 |
| 361 | Joe Borowski | .15 | .40 |
| 362 | Clint Sammons (RC) | .40 | 1.00 |
| 363 | Chris Duffy | .15 | .40 |
| 364 | Fred Lewis | .15 | .40 |
| 365 | Adrian Beltre | .15 | .40 |
| 366 | Alex Rodriguez BT | .60 | 1.50 |
| 367 | Troy Tulowitzki BT | .25 | .60 |
| 368 | Prince Fielder BT | .40 | 1.00 |
| 369 | Clay Buchholz BT | .40 | 1.00 |
| 370 | Justin Verlander BT GB SP | .60 | 1.50 |
| 371 | Dan Haren/Peavy BT GB SP | .60 | 1.50 |
| 372 | R.Howard BT GB SP | 1.25 | 3.00 |
| 373 | Ichiro Suzuki BT | .60 | 1.50 |
| 374 | Kenny Lofton BT | .15 | .40 |
| 375 | Manny Ramirez BT | .40 | 1.00 |
| 376 | Randy Johnson | .40 | 1.00 |
| 377 | Chris Capuano | .15 | .40 |
| 378 | Johnny Estrada | .15 | .40 |
| 379 | Franklin Morales | .15 | .40 |
| 380 | Ryan Howard | .50 | 1.25 |
| 381 | Casey Blake SP | 2.50 | 6.00 |
| 382 | Coco Crisp | .15 | .40 |
| 383 | J.Maine/W.Randolph MG | .15 | .40 |
| 384 | Jeremy Guthrie | .15 | .40 |
| 385 | Geoff Jenkins | .15 | .40 |
| 386 | Marlon Byrd | .15 | .40 |
| 387 | Jeremy Bonderman | .15 | .40 |
| 388 | Jason Varitek | .40 | 1.00 |
| 389 | Joe Girardi MG | .15 | .40 |
| 390 | Ryan Braun | .50 | 1.25 |
| 391 | Ryan Zimmerman | .25 | .60 |
| 392 | Lowell/Youkilis/Pedroia | .50 | 1.25 |
| 393 | Pittsburgh Pirates | .15 | .40 |
| 394 | Ryan Spilborghs | .15 | .40 |
| 395 | Eric Gagne | .15 | .40 |
| 396 | Joe Blanton | .15 | .40 |
| 397 | Washington Nationals | .15 | .40 |
| 398 | Ryan Church | .15 | .40 |
| 399 | Ted Lilly | .15 | .40 |
| 400 | Manny Ramirez | .40 | 1.00 |
| 401 | Chad Gaudin | .15 | .40 |
| 402 | Dustin McGowan | .15 | .40 |
| 403 | Scott Baker | .15 | .40 |
| 404 | Franklin Gutierrez | .15 | .40 |
| 405 | Dave Bush | .15 | .40 |
| 406 | Aubrey Huff | .15 | .40 |
| 407 | Jermaine Dye | .15 | .40 |
| 408 | C.Utley/J.Rollins | .40 | 1.00 |
| 409 | Jon Lester SP | 3.00 | 8.00 |
| 410 | Mark Buehrle | .15 | .40 |
| 411 | Sergio Mitre | .15 | .40 |
| 412 | Jason Bartlett | .15 | .40 |
| 413 | Edwin Jackson | .15 | .40 |

| | | |
|---|---|---|
| ❏ 414 J.D. Drew | .15 | .40 |
| ❏ 415 Freddy Sanchez GB SP | .40 | 1.00 |
| ❏ 416 Asdrubal Cabrera | .15 | .40 |
| ❏ 417 Nate Robertson | .15 | .40 |
| ❏ 418 Shaun Marcum | .15 | .40 |
| ❏ 419 Atlanta Braves | .25 | .60 |
| ❏ 420 Noah Lowry | .15 | .40 |
| ❏ 421 Jamie Moyer | .15 | .40 |
| ❏ 422 Michael Cuddyer | .15 | .40 |
| ❏ 423 Randy Wolf | .15 | .40 |
| ❏ 424 Juan Uribe | .15 | .40 |
| ❏ 425 Brian McCann | .25 | .60 |
| ❏ 426 Kyle Lohse SP | 2.50 | 6.00 |
| ❏ 427 Doug Davis SP | 2.50 | 6.00 |
| ❏ 428 Snell/Capps/Gorz/Maholm SP | 2.50 | 6.00 |
| ❏ 429 Miguel Batista SP | 2.50 | 6.00 |
| ❏ 430 C.Wang SP | 4.00 | 10.00 |
| ❏ 431 Jeff Salazar SP | 2.50 | 6.00 |
| ❏ 432 Yadier Molina SP | 2.50 | 6.00 |
| ❏ 433 Adam Wainwright SP | 2.50 | 6.00 |
| ❏ 434 Scott Kazmir SP | 2.50 | 6.00 |
| ❏ 435 Adam Dunn SP | 2.50 | 6.00 |
| ❏ 436 Ryan Freel SP | 2.50 | 6.00 |
| ❏ 437 Jhonny Peralta SP | 2.50 | 6.00 |
| ❏ 438 Kazuo Matsui SP | 2.50 | 6.00 |
| ❏ 439 Daniel Cabrera | .15 | .40 |
| ❏ 440a John Smoltz | .40 | 1.00 |
| ❏ 440b J.Smoltz Jon Var | 50.00 | 100.00 |
| ❏ 441 Emil Brown SP | 2.50 | 6.00 |
| ❏ 442 Gary Sheffield SP | 2.50 | 6.00 |
| ❏ 443 Jake Peavy SP | 3.00 | 8.00 |
| ❏ 444 Scott Rolen SP | 3.00 | 8.00 |
| ❏ 445 Kason Gabbard SP | 2.50 | 6.00 |
| ❏ 446 Aaron Hill SP | 2.50 | 6.00 |
| ❏ 447 Felipe Lopez SP | 2.50 | 6.00 |
| ❏ 448 Dan Uggla SP | 2.50 | 6.00 |
| ❏ 449 Willy Taveras SP | 2.50 | 6.00 |
| ❏ 450 Chipper Jones SP | 3.00 | 8.00 |
| ❏ 451 Josh Anderson SP (RC) | 3.00 | 8.00 |
| ❏ 452 Young/Upton/Byrnes SP | 3.00 | 8.00 |
| ❏ 453 Braden Looper SP | 2.50 | 6.00 |
| ❏ 454 Brandon Inge SP | 2.50 | 6.00 |
| ❏ 455 Brian Giles SP | 2.50 | 6.00 |
| ❏ 456 Corey Patterson SP | 2.50 | 6.00 |
| ❏ 457 Los Angeles Dodgers SP | 3.00 | 8.00 |
| ❏ 458 Sean Casey SP | 2.50 | 6.00 |
| ❏ 459 Pedro Feliz SP | 2.50 | 6.00 |
| ❏ 460 Tom Gorzelanny | .15 | .40 |
| ❏ 461 Chone Figgins SP | 2.50 | 6.00 |
| ❏ 462 Kyle Kendrick SP | 2.50 | 6.00 |
| ❏ 463 Tony Pena SP | 2.50 | 6.00 |
| ❏ 464 Marcus Giles SP | 2.50 | 6.00 |
| ❏ 465 Augie Ojeda SP | 2.50 | 6.00 |
| ❏ 466 Micah Owings SP | 2.50 | 6.00 |
| ❏ 467 Ryan Theriot SP | 2.50 | 6.00 |
| ❏ 468 Shawn Green SP | 2.50 | 6.00 |
| ❏ 469 Frank Thomas SP | 3.00 | 8.00 |
| ❏ 470 Lenny DiNardo SP | 2.50 | 6.00 |
| ❏ 471 Jose Bautista SP | 2.50 | 6.00 |
| ❏ 472 Manny Corpas SP | 2.50 | 6.00 |
| ❏ 473 Kevin Millwood SP | 2.50 | 6.00 |
| ❏ 474 Kevin Youkilis SP | 2.50 | 6.00 |
| ❏ 475 Jose Contreras SP | 2.50 | 6.00 |
| ❏ 476 Cleveland Indians | .15 | .40 |
| ❏ 477 Julio Lugo SP | 2.50 | 6.00 |
| ❏ 478 Jason Bay | .25 | .60 |
| ❏ 479 Tony LaRussa AS MG SP | 2.50 | 6.00 |
| ❏ 480 Jim Leyland AS MG SP | 2.50 | 6.00 |
| ❏ 481 Derek Lee AS SP | 2.50 | 6.00 |
| ❏ 482 Justin Morneau AS SP | 2.50 | 6.00 |
| ❏ 483 Orlando Hudson AS SP | 2.50 | 6.00 |
| ❏ 484 Brian Roberts AS SP | 2.50 | 6.00 |
| ❏ 485 Miguel Cabrera AS SP | 3.00 | 8.00 |
| ❏ 486 Mike Lowell AS SP | 2.50 | 6.00 |
| ❏ 487 J.J. Hardy AS SP | 2.50 | 6.00 |
| ❏ 488 Carlos Guillen AS SP | 2.50 | 6.00 |
| ❏ 489 K.Griffey Jr. AS SP | 4.00 | 10.00 |
| ❏ 490 Vladimir Guerrero AS SP | 3.00 | 8.00 |
| ❏ 491 Alfonso Soriano AS SP | 3.00 | 8.00 |
| ❏ 492 I.Suzuki AS SP | 4.00 | 10.00 |
| ❏ 493 Matt Holliday AS SP | 3.00 | 8.00 |
| ❏ 494 Magglio Ordonez AS SP | 3.00 | 8.00 |
| ❏ 495 Brian McCann AS SP | 2.50 | 6.00 |
| ❏ 496 Victor Martinez AS SP | 2.50 | 6.00 |
| ❏ 497 Brad Penny AS SP | 2.50 | 6.00 |
| ❏ 498 Josh Beckett AS SP | 3.00 | 8.00 |
| ❏ 499 Cole Hamels AS SP | 3.00 | 8.00 |
| ❏ 500 Justin Verlander AS SP | 3.00 | 8.00 |

| | | |
|---|---|---|
| ❏ 501 John Danks | .15 | .40 |
| ❏ 502 Jamey Wright | .15 | .40 |
| ❏ 503 Johnny Cueto RC | .60 | 1.50 |
| ❏ 504 Todd Wellemeyer | .15 | .40 |
| ❏ 505 Chase Headley | .15 | .40 |
| ❏ 506 Takashi Saito | .15 | .40 |
| ❏ 507 Skip Schumaker | .15 | .40 |
| ❏ 508 Tampa Bay Rays | .15 | .40 |
| ❏ 509 Marcus Thames | .15 | .40 |
| ❏ 510 Joe Saunders | .15 | .40 |
| ❏ 511 Jair Jurrjens | .15 | .40 |
| ❏ 512 Ryan Sweeney | .15 | .40 |
| ❏ 513 Darin Erstad | .15 | .40 |
| ❏ 514 Brandon Backe GB SP | .40 | 1.00 |
| ❏ 515 Chris Volstad (RC) | .40 | 1.00 |
| ❏ 516 Salomon Torres | .15 | .40 |
| ❏ 517 Brian Burres | .15 | .40 |
| ❏ 518 Brandon Boggs (RC) | .60 | 1.50 |
| ❏ 519 Max Scherzer SP | 1.00 | 2.50 |
| ❏ 520 Cliff Lee | .15 | .40 |
| ❏ 521 Angel Pagan | .15 | .40 |
| ❏ 522 Jason Kubel | .15 | .40 |
| ❏ 523 Jose Molina GB SP | .40 | 1.00 |
| ❏ 524 Hiroki Kuroda RC | .60 | 1.50 |
| ❏ 525 Matt Harrison (RC) | .40 | 1.00 |
| ❏ 526 C.J. Wilson | .15 | .40 |
| ❏ 527 Robb Quinlan | .15 | .40 |
| ❏ 528 Darrell Rasner | .40 | 1.00 |
| ❏ 529 Frank Catalanotto GB SP | .40 | 1.00 |
| ❏ 530 Mike Mussina | .15 | .40 |
| ❏ 531 Ryan Doumit GB SP | .40 | 1.00 |
| ❏ 532 Willie Bloomquist GB SP | .40 | 1.00 |
| ❏ 533 Jonny Gomes | .15 | .40 |
| ❏ 534 Jesse Litsch | .15 | .40 |
| ❏ 535 Curtis Granderson | .15 | .40 |
| ❏ 536 A.J. Pierzynski | .15 | .40 |
| ❏ 537 Toronto Blue Jays | .15 | .40 |
| ❏ 538 Brian Buscher GB SP | .40 | 1.00 |
| ❏ 539 Kelly Shoppach GB SP | .40 | 1.00 |
| ❏ 540 Edinson Volquez | .15 | .40 |
| ❏ 541 Jon Rauch GB SP | .40 | 1.00 |
| ❏ 542 Ramon Castro GB SP | .40 | 1.00 |
| ❏ 543 Greg Smith RC | .40 | 1.00 |
| ❏ 544 Sean Gallagher | .15 | .40 |
| ❏ 545 Justin Masterson GB SP RC | 2.00 | 5.00 |
| ❏ 546 Milwaukee Brewers | .15 | .40 |
| ❏ 547 Jay Bruce (RC) | 1.50 | 4.00 |
| ❏ 548 Glendon Rusch | .15 | .40 |
| ❏ 549 Jeremy Sowers GB SP | .40 | 1.00 |
| ❏ 550 Ryan Dempster | .15 | .40 |
| ❏ 551 Ciete Thomas RC | .60 | 1.50 |
| ❏ 552 Jose Castillo | .15 | .40 |
| ❏ 553 Brandon Lyon | .15 | .40 |
| ❏ 554 Vicente Padilla | .15 | .40 |
| ❏ 555 Jeff Keppinger | .15 | .40 |
| ❏ 556 Colorado Rockies | .15 | .40 |
| ❏ 557 Dallas Braden SP | .40 | 1.00 |
| ❏ 558 Adam Kennedy | .15 | .40 |
| ❏ 559 Luis Mendoza (RC) | .40 | 1.00 |
| ❏ 560 Justin Duchscherer | .15 | .40 |
| ❏ 561 Mike Aviles RC | .60 | 1.50 |
| ❏ 562 Jed Lowrie (RC) | 1.00 | 2.50 |
| ❏ 563 Doug Mientkiewicz GB SP | .40 | 1.00 |
| ❏ 564 Chris Burke | .15 | .40 |
| ❏ 565 Dana Eveland | .15 | .40 |
| ❏ 566 Bryan Lahair RC | .40 | 1.00 |
| ❏ 567 Denard Span (RC) | .60 | 1.50 |
| ❏ 568 Damion Easley | .15 | .40 |
| ❏ 569 Josh Fields | .15 | .40 |
| ❏ 570 Geovany Soto | .40 | 1.00 |
| ❏ 571 Gerald Laird UER | .15 | .40 |
| ❏ 572 Bobby Jenks | .15 | .40 |
| ❏ 573 Andy Marte | .15 | .40 |
| ❏ 574 Mike Pelfrey | .15 | .40 |
| ❏ 575 Jerry Hairston | .15 | .40 |
| ❏ 576 Mike Lamb | .15 | .40 |
| ❏ 577 Ben Zobrist | .15 | .40 |
| ❏ 578 Carlos Gonzalez (RC) | .40 | 1.00 |
| ❏ 579 Carlos Guillen GB SP | .40 | 1.00 |
| ❏ 580 Kosuke Fukudome SP | 1.25 | 3.00 |
| ❏ 581 Gabe Kapler GB SP | .40 | 1.00 |
| ❏ 582 Florida Marlins | .15 | .40 |
| ❏ 583 Ramon Vazquez GB SP | .40 | 1.00 |
| ❏ 584 Wes Helms GB SP | .40 | 1.00 |
| ❏ 585 Minnesota Twins | .15 | .40 |
| ❏ 586 Cody Ross | .15 | .40 |
| ❏ 587 Mike Napoli | .15 | .40 |
| ❏ 588 Alexi Casilla | .15 | .40 |

| | | |
|---|---|---|
| ❏ 589 Emmanuel Burriss RC | .60 | 1.50 |
| ❏ 590 Brian Wilson | .15 | .40 |
| ❏ 591 Rod Barajas | .15 | .40 |
| ❏ 592 Mike Hampton GB SP | .40 | 1.00 |
| ❏ 593 Nick Blackburn RC | .60 | 1.50 |
| ❏ 594 Joe Mather RC | .60 | 1.50 |
| ❏ 595 Clayton Kershaw GB SP RC | 2.00 | 5.00 |
| ❏ 596 Cliff Floyd GB SP | .40 | 1.00 |
| ❏ 597 Sidney Ponson GB SP | .40 | 1.00 |
| ❏ 598 Brian Anderson | .15 | .40 |
| ❏ 599 Joe Inglett | .15 | .40 |
| ❏ 600 Miguel Tejada | .15 | .40 |
| ❏ 601 San Diego Padres | .15 | .40 |
| ❏ 602 Scott Hairston GB SP | .40 | 1.00 |
| ❏ 603 Joel Pineiro | .15 | .40 |
| ❏ 604 Fernando Tatis | .15 | .40 |
| ❏ 605 Greg Reynolds RC | .60 | 1.50 |
| ❏ 606 Brian Moehler | .15 | .40 |
| ❏ 607 Kevin Millar GB SP | .40 | 1.00 |
| ❏ 608 Ben Francisco | .15 | .40 |
| ❏ 609 Troy Percival | .15 | .40 |
| ❏ 610 Kerry Wood | .15 | .40 |
| ❏ 611 Max Ramirez RC | .40 | 1.00 |
| ❏ 612 Jeff Baker | .15 | .40 |
| ❏ 613 Houston Astros | .15 | .40 |
| ❏ 614 Russell Branyan | .15 | .40 |
| ❏ 615 Todd Jones | .15 | .40 |
| ❏ 616 Brian Schneider | .15 | .40 |
| ❏ 617 Gregorio Petit RC | .60 | 1.50 |
| ❏ 618 Matt Diaz | .15 | .40 |
| ❏ 619 Blake DeWitt GB SP (RC) | 1.00 | 2.50 |
| ❏ 620 Cristian Guzman | .15 | .40 |
| ❏ 621 Jeff Samardzija GB SP RC | 1.25 | 3.00 |
| ❏ 622 John Baker (RC) | .40 | 1.00 |
| ❏ 623 Eric Hinske | .15 | .40 |
| ❏ 624 Scott Olsen | .15 | .40 |
| ❏ 625 Greg Dobbs | .15 | .40 |
| ❏ 626 Carlos Marmol GB SP | .40 | 1.00 |
| ❏ 627 Kansas City Royals | .15 | .40 |
| ❏ 628 Esteban German | .15 | .40 |
| ❏ 629 Dennis Sarfate | .15 | .40 |
| ❏ 630 Ryan Ludwick | .15 | .40 |
| ❏ 631 Mike Jacobs | .15 | .40 |
| ❏ 632 Tyler Yates | .15 | .40 |
| ❏ 633 Joel Hanrahan | .15 | .40 |
| ❏ 634 Manny Parra | .15 | .40 |
| ❏ 635 Maicer Izturis | .15 | .40 |
| ❏ 636 Juan Rivera | .15 | .40 |
| ❏ 637 Tim Redding | .15 | .40 |
| ❏ 638 Jose Arredondo RC | .60 | 1.50 |
| ❏ 639 Mike Redmond GB SP | .40 | 1.00 |
| ❏ 640 Joe Crede | .15 | .40 |
| ❏ 641 Omar Infante | .15 | .40 |
| ❏ 642 Nick Punto | .15 | .40 |
| ❏ 643 Jeff Mathis | .15 | .40 |
| ❏ 644 Andy Sonnanstine | .15 | .40 |
| ❏ 645 Masahide Kobayashi RC | .60 | 1.50 |
| ❏ 646 Marco Scutaro | .15 | .40 |
| ❏ 647 Matt Macri (RC) | .40 | 1.00 |
| ❏ 648 Ian Stewart SP | 2.50 | 6.00 |
| ❏ 649 David Dellucci GB SP | .40 | 1.00 |
| ❏ 650 Evan Longoria RC | 4.00 | 10.00 |
| ❏ 651 Martin Prado GB SP | .40 | 1.00 |
| ❏ 652 Glen Perkins | .15 | .40 |
| ❏ 653 Alfredo Amezaga GB SP | .40 | 1.00 |
| ❏ 654 Brett Gardner (RC) | 1.00 | 2.50 |
| ❏ 655 Angel Berroa GB SP | .40 | 1.00 |
| ❏ 656 Pablo Sandoval RC | 2.50 | 6.00 |
| ❏ 657 Jody Gerut | .15 | .40 |
| ❏ 658 Arizona Diamondbacks | .15 | 4.00 |
| ❏ 659 Ryan Freel GB SP | .40 | 1.00 |
| ❏ 660 Dioner Navarro | .15 | .40 |
| ❏ 661 Endy Chavez GB SP | .40 | 1.00 |
| ❏ 662 Jorge Campillo | .15 | .40 |
| ❏ 663 Mark Ellis | .15 | .40 |
| ❏ 664 John Buck | .15 | .40 |
| ❏ 665 Texas Rangers | .15 | .40 |
| ❏ 666 Jason Michaels | .15 | .40 |
| ❏ 667 Chris Dickerson RC | .60 | 1.50 |
| ❏ 668 Kevin Mench | .15 | .40 |
| ❏ 669 Aaron Miles | .15 | .40 |
| ❏ 670 Joakim Soria | .15 | .40 |
| ❏ 671 Chris Davis RC | 1.00 | 2.50 |
| ❏ 672 Taylor Teagarden GB SP RC | .60 | 1.50 |
| ❏ 673 Willy Aybar | .15 | .40 |
| ❏ 674 Paul Maholm | .15 | .40 |
| ❏ 675 Miguel Gonzalez | .15 | .40 |
| ❏ 676 Seattle Mariners | .15 | .40 |

| # | Card | Lo | Hi |
|---|------|----|----|
| ❏ 677 | Ryan Langerhans SP | 2.50 | 6.00 |
| ❏ 678 | Alex Romero (RC) | .60 | 1.50 |
| ❏ 679 | Erick Aybar | .15 | .40 |
| ❏ 680 | George Sherrill | .15 | .40 |
| ❏ 681 | John Bowker (RC) | .40 | 1.00 |
| ❏ 682 | Zach Miner GB SP | .40 | 1.00 |
| ❏ 683 | Jorge Cantu | .15 | .40 |
| ❏ 684 | Jo-Jo Reyes | .15 | .40 |
| ❏ 685 | Ryan Raburn | .15 | .40 |
| ❏ 686 | Gavin Floyd SP | 2.50 | 6.00 |
| ❏ 687 | Kevin Slowey SP | 2.50 | 6.00 |
| ❏ 688 | Gio Gonzalez SP (RC) | 2.50 | 6.00 |
| ❏ 689 | Eric Patterson SP | 2.50 | 6.00 |
| ❏ 690 | Jonathan Sanchez SP | 2.50 | 6.00 |
| ❏ 691 | Oliver Perez SP | 2.50 | 6.00 |
| ❏ 692 | John Lannan SP | 2.50 | 6.00 |
| ❏ 693 | Ramon Hernandez SP | 2.50 | 6.00 |
| ❏ 694 | Mike Fontenot SP | 2.50 | 6.00 |
| ❏ 695 | Ross Gload SP | 2.50 | 6.00 |
| ❏ 696 | Mark Sweeney SP | 2.50 | 6.00 |
| ❏ 697 | Nick Hundley SP (RC) | 2.50 | 6.00 |
| ❏ 698 | Kevin Correia SP | 2.50 | 6.00 |
| ❏ 699 | Jeremy Reed SP | 2.50 | 6.00 |
| ❏ 700 | Eddie Kunz SP RC | 2.50 | 6.00 |
| ❏ 701 | Miguel Montero SP | 2.50 | 6.00 |
| ❏ 702 | Gabe Gross SP | 2.50 | 6.00 |
| ❏ 703 | Matt Stairs SP | 2.50 | 6.00 |
| ❏ 704 | Kenny Rogers SP | 2.50 | 6.00 |
| ❏ 705 | Mark Hendrickson SP | 2.50 | 6.00 |
| ❏ 706 | Heath Bell SP | 2.50 | 6.00 |
| ❏ 707 | Wilson Betemit SP | 2.50 | 6.00 |
| ❏ 708 | Brandon Morrow SP | 2.50 | 6.00 |
| ❏ 709 | Brendan Ryan SP | 2.50 | 6.00 |
| ❏ 710 | Eric Hurley SP (RC) | 2.50 | 6.00 |
| ❏ 711 | Los Angeles Angels SP | 2.50 | 6.00 |
| ❏ 712 | Jack Hannahan SP | 2.50 | 6.00 |
| ❏ 713 | Seth McClung SP | 2.50 | 6.00 |
| ❏ 714 | New York Mets SP | 2.50 | 6.00 |
| ❏ 715 | Chris Perez SP RC | 2.50 | 6.00 |
| ❏ 716 | Clayton Richard SP (RC) | 2.50 | 6.00 |
| ❏ 717 | Jaime Garcia SP RC | 2.50 | 6.00 |
| ❏ 718 | Matt Joyce SP RC | 2.50 | 6.00 |
| ❏ 719 | Brad Ziegler SP RC | 2.50 | 6.00 |
| ❏ 720 | Ivan Ochoa (RC) | .60 | 1.50 |

## 2009 Topps Heritage

| # | Card | Lo | Hi |
|---|------|----|----|
| ❏ | COMPLETE SET (500) | 250.00 | 350.00 |
| ❏ | COMP SET w/o SP's (425) | 30.00 | 60.00 |
| ❏ | COMMON CARD (1-500) | .15 | .40 |
| ❏ | COMMON ROOKIE | .40 | 1.00 |
| ❏ | COMMON SP (426-500) | 2.50 | 6.00 |
| ❏ | SP ODDS XXX | | |
| ❏ 1 | Mark Buehrle | .15 | .40 |
| ❏ 2 | Nyjer Morgan | .15 | .40 |
| ❏ 3 | Casey Kotchman | .15 | .40 |
| ❏ 4 | Edinson Volquez | .15 | .40 |
| ❏ 5 | Andre Ethier | .25 | .60 |
| ❏ 6 | Brandon Inge | .15 | .40 |
| ❏ 7 | T.Lincecum/B.Bochy | .50 | 1.25 |
| ❏ 8 | Gil Meche | .15 | .40 |
| ❏ 9 | Brad Hawpe | .15 | .40 |
| ❏ 10 | Hanley Ramirez | .40 | 1.00 |
| ❏ 11 | Ross Gload | .15 | .40 |
| ❏ 12 | Jeremy Guthrie | .15 | .40 |
| ❏ 13 | Garret Anderson | .15 | .40 |
| ❏ 14 | Jeremy Sowers | .15 | .40 |
| ❏ 15 | Dustin Pedroia | .50 | 1.25 |
| ❏ 16 | Chris Perez | .15 | .40 |
| ❏ 17 | Adam Lind | .15 | .40 |
| ❏ 18 | Los Angeles Dodgers TC | .15 | .40 |
| ❏ 19 | Stephen Drew | .15 | .40 |
| ❏ 20 | Matt Capps | .15 | .40 |
| ❏ 21 | Mike Napoli | .15 | .40 |
| ❏ 22 | Khalil Greene | .15 | .40 |
| ❏ 23 | Andy Sonnanstine | .15 | .40 |
| ❏ 24 | Marco Scutaro | .15 | .40 |
| ❏ 25 | Paul Konerko | .15 | .40 |
| ❏ 26 | Miguel Tejada | .25 | .60 |
| ❏ 27 | Nick Blackburn | .15 | .40 |
| ❏ 28 | Nick Markakis | .25 | .60 |
| ❏ 29 | Johan Santana | .40 | 1.00 |
| ❏ 30 | Grady Sizemore | .25 | .60 |
| ❏ 31 | Raul Ibanez | .25 | .60 |
| ❏ 32 | Jay Bruce/Johnny Cueto | .40 | 1.00 |
| ❏ 33 | Randy Johnson | .40 | 1.00 |
| ❏ 34 | Ian Kinsler | .25 | .60 |
| ❏ 35 | Andy Pettitte | .40 | 1.00 |
| ❏ 36 | Lyle Overbay | .15 | .40 |
| ❏ 37 | Jeff Francoeur | .25 | .60 |
| ❏ 38 | Justin Duchscherer | .15 | .40 |
| ❏ 39 | Mike Cameron | .15 | .40 |
| ❏ 40 | Ryan Ludwick | .25 | .60 |
| ❏ 41 | Dave Bush | .15 | .40 |
| ❏ 42 | Pablo Sandoval (RC) | 1.25 | 3.00 |
| ❏ 43 | Washington Nationals TC | .15 | .40 |
| ❏ 44 | Dana Eveland | .15 | .40 |
| ❏ 45 | Jeff Keppinger | .15 | .40 |
| ❏ 46 | Brandon Backe | .15 | .40 |
| ❏ 47 | Ryan Theriot | .15 | .40 |
| ❏ 48 | Vernon Wells | .15 | .40 |
| ❏ 49 | Doug Davis | .15 | .40 |
| ❏ 50 | Curtis Granderson | .40 | 1.00 |
| ❏ 51 | Aaron Laffey | .15 | .40 |
| ❏ 52 | Chris Young | .15 | .40 |
| ❏ 53 | Adam Jones | .25 | .60 |
| ❏ 54 | Jonathan Papelbon | .25 | .60 |
| ❏ 55 | Nate McLouth | .15 | .40 |
| ❏ 56 | Hunter Pence | .25 | .60 |
| ❏ 57 | Scot Shields/Francisco Rodriguez | .25 | .60 |
| ❏ 58a | Conor Jackson ARI | .15 | .40 |
| ❏ 59 | John Maine | .15 | .40 |
| ❏ 60 | Ramon Hernandez | .15 | .40 |
| ❏ 61 | Jorge De La Rosa | .15 | .40 |
| ❏ 62 | Greg Maddux | .50 | 1.25 |
| ❏ 63 | Carlos Beltran | .15 | .40 |
| ❏ 64 | Matt Harrison (RC) | .40 | 1.00 |
| ❏ 65 | Ivan Rodriguez | .25 | .60 |
| ❏ 66 | Jesse Litsch | .15 | .40 |
| ❏ 67 | Omar Vizquel | .15 | .40 |
| ❏ 68 | Edwin Jackson | .15 | .40 |
| ❏ 69 | Ray Durham | .15 | .40 |
| ❏ 70a | Tom Glavine | .25 | .60 |
| ❏ 70b | Tom Glavine UER SP | 20.00 | 50.00 |
| ❏ 71 | Darin Erstad | .15 | .40 |
| ❏ 72 | Detroit Tigers TC | .15 | .40 |
| ❏ 73 | David Price SP | 1.25 | 3.00 |
| ❏ 74 | Marlon Byrd | .15 | .40 |
| ❏ 75 | Ryan Garko | .15 | .40 |
| ❏ 76 | Jered Weaver | .15 | .40 |
| ❏ 77 | Kelly Shoppach | .15 | .40 |
| ❏ 78 | Joe Saunders | .15 | .40 |
| ❏ 79 | Carlos Pena | .25 | .60 |
| ❏ 80 | Brian Wilson | .15 | .40 |
| ❏ 81 | Carlos Gonzalez | .15 | .40 |
| ❏ 82 | Scott Baker | .15 | .40 |
| ❏ 83 | Derek Jeter | 1.00 | 2.50 |
| ❏ 84 | Yadier Molina | .25 | .60 |
| ❏ 85 | Justin Verlander | .25 | .60 |
| ❏ 86 | Jose Lopez | .15 | .40 |
| ❏ 87 | Jarrod Washburn | .15 | .40 |
| ❏ 88 | Russell Martin | .25 | .60 |
| ❏ 89 | Garrett Olson | .15 | .40 |
| ❏ 90 | Erick Aybar | .15 | .40 |
| ❏ 91 | Kevin Millwood | .15 | .40 |
| ❏ 92 | Jose Guillen | .15 | .40 |
| ❏ 93 | Rickie Weeks | .15 | .40 |
| ❏ 94 | Yovani Gallardo | .15 | .40 |
| ❏ 95 | Aramis Ramirez | .15 | .40 |
| ❏ 96 | Phil Hughes | .25 | .60 |
| ❏ 97 | Kevin Kouzmanoff | .15 | .40 |
| ❏ 98 | Shaun Marcum | .15 | .40 |
| ❏ 99 | Lastings Milledge | .15 | .40 |
| ❏ 100 | Jair Jurrjens | .25 | .60 |
| ❏ 101 | Gio Gonzalez | .15 | .40 |
| ❏ 102a | Adrian Gonzalez | .25 | .60 |
| ❏ 102b | A.Gonzalez Flgr Logo | 20.00 | 50.00 |
| ❏ 103 | Brad Lidge | .15 | .40 |
| ❏ 104 | Chris Davis | .15 | .40 |
| ❏ 105 | Brad Penny | .15 | .40 |
| ❏ 106 | David Eckstein | .15 | .40 |
| ❏ 107 | Jo-Jo Reyes | .15 | .40 |
| ❏ 108 | John Buck | .15 | .40 |
| ❏ 109 | Delmon Young | .25 | .60 |
| ❏ 110 | Johnny Cueto | .15 | .40 |
| ❏ 111 | Kevin Youkilis | .25 | .60 |
| ❏ 112 | Scott Lewis (RC) | .40 | 1.00 |
| ❏ 113 | Brandon Moss | .15 | .40 |
| ❏ 114 | Alexi Casilla | .15 | .40 |
| ❏ 115 | Jonathan Papelbon/Tim Wakefield | .25 | .60 |
| ❏ 116 | Emil Brown | .15 | .40 |
| ❏ 117 | Michael Bowden (RC) | .60 | 1.50 |
| ❏ 118 | Chris Lambert (RC) | .40 | 1.00 |
| ❏ 119 | Wilkin Castillo RC | .60 | 1.50 |
| ❏ 120 | Fernando Perez (RC) | .40 | 1.00 |
| ❏ 121 | Angel Salome (RC) | .40 | 1.00 |
| ❏ 122 | Dexter Fowler (RC) | .60 | 1.50 |
| ❏ 123 | Will Venable RC | .40 | 1.00 |
| ❏ 124 | Jason Motte (RC) | .40 | 1.00 |
| ❏ 125 | Jesus Delgado RC | .60 | 1.50 |
| ❏ 126 | Alfredo Simon (RC) | .40 | 1.00 |
| ❏ 127 | Gaby Sanchez RC | .40 | 1.00 |
| ❏ 128 | Scott Elbert (RC) | .40 | 1.00 |
| ❏ 129 | James Parr (RC) | .40 | 1.00 |
| ❏ 130 | Greg Golson (RC) | .40 | 1.00 |
| ❏ 131 | Jonathon Niese RC | .60 | 1.50 |
| ❏ 132 | Mat Gamel RC | 1.00 | 2.50 |
| ❏ 133 | Luis Cruz RC | .40 | 1.00 |
| ❏ 134 | Phil Coke RC | .60 | 1.50 |
| ❏ 135 | Devon Lowery (RC) | .40 | 1.00 |
| ❏ 136 | Matt Tuiasosopo (RC) | .40 | 1.00 |
| ❏ 137 | Kila Ka'aihue (RC) | .60 | 1.50 |
| ❏ 138 | Andrew Carpenter RC | .60 | 1.50 |
| ❏ 139 | Jensen Lewis (RC) | .40 | 1.00 |
| ❏ 140 | Lou Marson (RC) | .40 | 1.00 |
| ❏ 141 | Wade LeBlanc RC | .60 | 1.50 |
| ❏ 142 | Juan Miranda (RC) | .60 | 1.50 |
| ❏ 143 | Alcides Escobar RC | .60 | 1.50 |
| ❏ 144 | Matt Antonelli RC | .40 | 1.00 |
| ❏ 145 | Jesse Chavez RC | .40 | 1.00 |
| ❏ 146 | Ramon Ramirez (RC) | .40 | 1.00 |
| ❏ 147 | Aaron Cunningham RC | .40 | 1.00 |
| ❏ 148 | Travis Snider RC | 1.00 | 2.50 |
| ❏ 149 | Adam Dunn | .25 | .60 |
| ❏ 150 | John Danks | .15 | .40 |
| ❏ 151 | San Francisco Giants TC | .15 | .40 |
| ❏ 152 | Jorge Cantu | .15 | .40 |
| ❏ 153 | Jacoby Ellsbury | .40 | 1.00 |
| ❏ 154 | Rich Aurilia | .15 | .40 |
| ❏ 155 | Jeff Kent | .15 | .40 |
| ❏ 156 | Salomon Torres | .15 | .40 |
| ❏ 157 | Juan Uribe | .15 | .40 |
| ❏ 158 | Gregor Blanco | .15 | .40 |
| ❏ 159 | Shin-Soo Choo | .15 | .40 |
| ❏ 160 | D.Wright/A.Rodriguez AS | .60 | 1.50 |
| ❏ 161 | Jose Valverde | .15 | .40 |
| ❏ 162 | B.J. Upton | .25 | .60 |
| ❏ 163 | Johnny Damon | .25 | .60 |
| ❏ 164 | Cincinnati Reds TC | .15 | .40 |
| ❏ 165 | Tim Lincecum | .50 | 1.25 |
| ❏ 166 | Carl Crawford | .25 | .60 |
| ❏ 167 | Jeff Mathis | .15 | .40 |
| ❏ 168 | Felipe Lopez | .15 | .40 |
| ❏ 169 | Joe Nathan | .15 | .40 |
| ❏ 170 | Brian McCann | .25 | .60 |
| ❏ 171 | Matt Joyce | .15 | .40 |
| ❏ 172 | Cameron Maybin | .25 | .60 |
| ❏ 173 | Brandon Phillips | .15 | .40 |
| ❏ 174 | Cleveland Indians TC | .15 | .40 |
| ❏ 175 | Tim Redding | .15 | .40 |
| ❏ 176 | Corey Patterson | .15 | .40 |
| ❏ 177 | Joakim Soria | .15 | .40 |
| ❏ 178 | Jhonny Peralta | .15 | .40 |
| ❏ 179 | Daniel Murphy RC | 1.00 | 2.50 |
| ❏ 180 | Ryan Church | .15 | .40 |
| ❏ 181 | Josh Johnson | .15 | .40 |
| ❏ 182 | Carlos Zambrano | .15 | .40 |
| ❏ 183 | Pittsburgh Pirates TC | .15 | .40 |
| ❏ 184 | Boston Red Sox TC | .25 | .60 |
| ❏ 185 | Kyle Kendrick | .15 | .40 |
| ❏ 186 | Joel Zumaya | .15 | .40 |
| ❏ 187 | Bronson Arroyo | .15 | .40 |
| ❏ 188 | Joey Gathright | .15 | .40 |
| ❏ 189 | Mike Lowell | .15 | .40 |
| ❏ 190 | Luke Scott | .15 | .40 |
| ❏ 191 | Jonathan Broxton | .15 | .40 |
| ❏ 192 | Jeff Baker | .15 | .40 |
| ❏ 193 | Brian Fuentes | .15 | .40 |
| ❏ 194 | Pat Burrell | .25 | .60 |
| ❏ 195 | Ryan Franklin | .15 | .40 |
| ❏ 196 | Alex Gordon | .25 | .60 |
| ❏ 197 | Orlando Hudson | .15 | .40 |
| ❏ 198 | Chris Dickerson | .15 | .40 |
| ❏ 199 | David Purcey | .15 | .40 |
| ❏ 200 | Ken Griffey Jr. | .60 | 1.50 |
| ❏ 201 | Chad Tracy | .15 | .40 |
| ❏ 202 | Troy Percival | .15 | .40 |
| ❏ 203 | Chris Iannetta | .15 | .40 |
| ❏ 204 | Baltimore Orioles TC | .15 | .40 |
| ❏ 205 | Yunel Escobar | .15 | .40 |
| ❏ 206 | Dan Haren | .25 | .60 |
| ❏ 207 | Aubrey Huff | .15 | .40 |
| ❏ 208 | Chicago White Sox TC | .15 | .40 |
| ❏ 209 | Randy Wolf | .15 | .40 |
| ❏ 210 | Ryan Zimmerman | .25 | .60 |

|  |  | | |
|---|---|---|---|
| ❏ 211 | Manny Parra | .15 | .40 |
| ❏ 212 | Manny Acta MG | .15 | .40 |
| ❏ 213 | Dusty Baker MG | .15 | .40 |
| ❏ 214 | Bruce Bochy MG | .15 | .40 |
| ❏ 215 | Bobby Cox MG | .15 | .40 |
| ❏ 216 | Terry Francona MG | .25 | .60 |
| ❏ 217 | Joe Girardi MG | .25 | .60 |
| ❏ 218 | Ozzie Guillen MG | .15 | .40 |
| ❏ 219 | Bob Geren MG | .15 | .40 |
| ❏ 220 | Tony La Russa MG | .25 | .60 |
| ❏ 221 | Jim Leyland MG | .15 | .40 |
| ❏ 222 | Charlie Manuel MG | .15 | .40 |
| ❏ 223 | Lou Piniella MG | .15 | .40 |
| ❏ 224 | John Russell MG | .15 | .40 |
| ❏ 225 | Joe Torre MG | .25 | .60 |
| ❏ 226 | Dave Trembley MG | .15 | .40 |
| ❏ 227 | Eric Wedge MG | .15 | .40 |
| ❏ 228 | Jeff Suppan | .15 | .40 |
| ❏ 229 | Kaz Matsui | .15 | .40 |
| ❏ 230 | Beckett/Lester/Matsuzaka | .60 | 1.50 |
| ❏ 231 | Mark Reynolds | .15 | .40 |
| ❏ 232 | Jay Payton | .15 | .40 |
| ❏ 233 | Kerry Wood | .15 | .40 |
| ❏ 234 | Juan Pierre | .15 | .40 |
| ❏ 235 | Ryan Freel | .15 | .40 |
| ❏ 236 | Ryan Feierabend | .15 | .40 |
| ❏ 237 | Xavier Nady | .15 | .40 |
| ❏ 238 | Ronny Paulino | .15 | .40 |
| ❏ 239 | A.J. Burnett | .25 | .60 |
| ❏ 240 | Orlando Cabrera | .15 | .40 |
| ❏ 241 | Corey Hart | .15 | .40 |
| ❏ 242 | St. Louis Cardinals TC | .15 | .40 |
| ❏ 243 | Andy Marte | .15 | .40 |
| ❏ 244 | Trevor Hoffman | .25 | .60 |
| ❏ 245 | Carlos Guillen | .15 | .40 |
| ❏ 246 | Brandon Jones | .15 | .40 |
| ❏ 247 | Hideki Matsui | .40 | 1.00 |
| ❏ 248 | Henry Blanco | .15 | .40 |
| ❏ 249 | Jon Lester | .25 | .60 |
| ❏ 250 | Albert Pujols | 1.00 | 2.50 |
| ❏ 251 | Manny Ramirez | .40 | 1.00 |
| ❏ 252 | Brian Bannister | .15 | .40 |
| ❏ 253 | Alex Cintron | .15 | .40 |
| ❏ 254 | Brandon Lyon | .15 | .40 |
| ❏ 255 | Blake DeWitt | .25 | .60 |
| ❏ 256 | Luis Castillo | .15 | .40 |
| ❏ 257 | Mark Teixeira | .40 | 1.00 |
| ❏ 258 | Jack Wilson | .15 | .40 |
| ❏ 259 | Kosuke Fukudome | .40 | 1.00 |
| ❏ 260 | Manny Ramirez/Andre Ethier | .40 | 1.00 |
| ❏ 261 | Scott Kazmir | .25 | .60 |
| ❏ 262 | Mark Teahen | .15 | .40 |
| ❏ 263 | Dioner Navarro | .15 | .40 |
| ❏ 264 | Cole Hamels | .40 | 1.00 |
| ❏ 265 | Justin Upton | .25 | .60 |
| ❏ 266 | Ricky Nolasco | .15 | .40 |
| ❏ 267 | Hank Blalock | .15 | .40 |
| ❏ 268 | John Lackey | .15 | .40 |
| ❏ 269 | Jeremy Hermida | .15 | .40 |
| ❏ 270 | Chien-Ming Wang | .40 | 1.00 |
| ❏ 271 | Lance Berkman | .25 | .60 |
| ❏ 272 | Scott Olsen | .15 | .40 |
| ❏ 273 | Alex Rios | .15 | .40 |
| ❏ 274 | Matt Garza | .15 | .40 |
| ❏ 275 | Skip Schumaker | .15 | .40 |
| ❏ 276 | Greg Smith | .15 | .40 |
| ❏ 277 | Bobby Crosby | .15 | .40 |
| ❏ 278 | Hiroki Kuroda | .15 | .40 |
| ❏ 279 | Gary Matthews | .15 | .40 |
| ❏ 280 | Tim Wakefield | .15 | .40 |
| ❏ 281 | Mike Jacobs | .15 | .40 |
| ❏ 282 | Chris Volstad | .15 | .40 |
| ❏ 283 | Jeff Clement | .15 | .40 |
| ❏ 284 | Max Scherzer | .25 | .60 |
| ❏ 285 | Chase Headley | .15 | .40 |
| ❏ 286 | Francisco Rodriguez | .25 | .60 |
| ❏ 287 | Moises Alou | .15 | .40 |
| ❏ 288 | Jeff Francis | .15 | .40 |
| ❏ 289 | Carlos Delgado | .15 | .40 |
| ❏ 290 | Jose Reyes | .40 | 1.00 |
| ❏ 291 | Ubaldo Jimenez | .15 | .40 |
| ❏ 292 | Kelly Shoppach/Victor Martinez | .25 | .60 |
| ❏ 293 | Joe Blanton | .15 | .40 |
| ❏ 294 | Mark DeRosa | .15 | .40 |
| ❏ 295 | Casey Blake | .15 | .40 |
| ❏ 296 | Mike Pelfrey | .15 | .40 |
| ❏ 297 | Aaron Boone | .15 | .40 |
| ❏ 298 | Aaron Cook | .15 | .40 |

|  |  | | |
|---|---|---|---|
| ❏ 299 | Daric Barton | .15 | .40 |
| ❏ 300 | Ryan Howard | .50 | 1.25 |
| ❏ 301 | Ty Wigginton | .15 | .40 |
| ❏ 302 | Philadelphia Phillies TC | .15 | .40 |
| ❏ 303 | Barry Zito | .15 | .40 |
| ❏ 304 | Jake Peavy | .25 | .60 |
| ❏ 305 | Alfonso Soriano | .15 | .40 |
| ❏ 306 | Scott Linebrink | .15 | .40 |
| ❏ 307 | Torii Hunter | .25 | .60 |
| ❏ 308 | Zack Greinke | .25 | .60 |
| ❏ 309 | Ryan Sweeney | .15 | .40 |
| ❏ 310 | Mike Lowell | .15 | .40 |
| ❏ 311 | Jason Marquis | .15 | .40 |
| ❏ 312 | Aaron Rowand | .15 | .40 |
| ❏ 313 | Brandon Morrow | .15 | .40 |
| ❏ 314 | Edgar Renteria | .15 | .40 |
| ❏ 315 | Mariano Rivera | .25 | .60 |
| ❏ 316 | Wilson Betemit | .15 | .40 |
| ❏ 317 | Joey Votto | .15 | .40 |
| ❏ 318 | Evan Longoria | .60 | 1.50 |
| ❏ 319 | Mike Aviles | .15 | .40 |
| ❏ 320 | Jay Bruce | .40 | 1.00 |
| ❏ 321 | Denard Span | .15 | .40 |
| ❏ 322 | David Murphy | .15 | .40 |
| ❏ 323 | Geovany Soto | .25 | .60 |
| ❏ 324 | John Lannan | .15 | .40 |
| ❏ 325 | Brad Ziegler | .15 | .40 |
| ❏ 326 | Ichiro Suzuki | .60 | 1.50 |
| ❏ 327 | Kyle Lohse | .15 | .40 |
| ❏ 328 | Jesus Flores | .15 | .40 |
| ❏ 329 | Edwin Encarnacion | .15 | .40 |
| ❏ 330 | Franklin Gutierrez | .15 | .40 |
| ❏ 331 | Troy Glaus | .15 | .40 |
| ❏ 332 | David Ortiz | .25 | .60 |
| ❏ 333 | Anibal Sanchez | .15 | .40 |
| ❏ 334 | Jimmy Rollins | .25 | .60 |
| ❏ 335 | Kelly Johnson | .15 | .40 |
| ❏ 336 | Paul Byrd | .15 | .40 |
| ❏ 337 | Akinori Iwamura | .15 | .40 |
| ❏ 338 | Milton Bradley | .15 | .40 |
| ❏ 339 | Miguel Olivo | .15 | .40 |
| ❏ 340 | Ian Snell | .15 | .40 |
| ❏ 341 | Vladimir Guerrero | .40 | 1.00 |
| ❏ 342 | Asdrubal Cabrera | .15 | .40 |
| ❏ 343 | Clayton Kershaw | .40 | 1.00 |
| ❏ 344 | Rafael Furcal | .15 | .40 |
| ❏ 345 | Aaron Harang | .15 | .40 |
| ❏ 346a | Fred Lewis | .15 | .40 |
| ❏ 346b | F.Lewis UER Winn SP | 20.00 | 50.00 |
| ❏ 347 | Jack Cust | .15 | .40 |
| ❏ 348 | Todd Helton | .25 | .60 |
| ❏ 349 | Steve Pearce | .15 | .40 |
| ❏ 350 | Javier Vazquez | .15 | .40 |
| ❏ 351 | Ben Sheets | .15 | .40 |
| ❏ 352 | Joey Votto/Edwin Encarnacion/Jay Bruce | .40 | 1.00 |
| ❏ 353 | Luke Hochevar | .15 | .40 |
| ❏ 354 | Chris Snyder | .15 | .40 |
| ❏ 355 | Rick Ankiel | .25 | .60 |
| ❏ 356 | Emmanuel Burriss | .15 | .40 |
| ❏ 357 | Vicente Padilla | .15 | .40 |
| ❏ 358 | Yuniesky Betancourt | .15 | .40 |
| ❏ 359 | Willy Taveras | .15 | .40 |
| ❏ 360 | Gavin Floyd | .15 | .40 |
| ❏ 361 | Gerald Laird | .15 | .40 |
| ❏ 362 | Roy Oswalt | .25 | .60 |
| ❏ 363 | Coco Crisp | .15 | .40 |
| ❏ 364 | Felix Hernandez | .25 | .60 |
| ❏ 365 | Carlos Quentin | .15 | .40 |
| ❏ 366 | Ervin Santana | .15 | .40 |
| ❏ 367 | David DeJesus | .15 | .40 |
| ❏ 368 | Aaron Miles | .15 | .40 |
| ❏ 369 | B.J. Ryan | .15 | .40 |
| ❏ 370 | Jason Giambi | .15 | .40 |
| ❏ 371 | J.J. Putz | .15 | .40 |
| ❏ 372 | Brian Schneider | .15 | .40 |
| ❏ 373 | Andy LaRoche | .15 | .40 |
| ❏ 374 | Tim Hudson | .15 | .40 |
| ❏ 375 | Garrett Atkins | .15 | .40 |
| ❏ 376 | James Shields | .15 | .40 |
| ❏ 377 | Alex Rodriguez | .60 | 1.50 |
| ❏ 378 | J.J. Hardy | .15 | .40 |
| ❏ 379 | Michael Young | .25 | .60 |
| ❏ 380 | Prince Fielder | .40 | 1.00 |
| ❏ 381 | Atlanta Braves TC | .15 | .40 |
| ❏ 382 | Chone Figgins | .15 | .40 |
| ❏ 383 | David Wright | .50 | 1.25 |
| ❏ 384 | Brian Giles | .15 | .40 |
| ❏ 385 | Chase Utley WS | .40 | 1.00 |

|  |  | | |
|---|---|---|---|
| ❏ 386 | Eric Bruntlett WS | .15 | .40 |
| ❏ 387 | Carlos Ruiz WS | .15 | .40 |
| ❏ 388 | Ryan Howard WS | .50 | 1.25 |
| ❏ 389 | Jayson Werth WS | .15 | .40 |
| ❏ 390 | B.J. Upton WS | .25 | .60 |
| ❏ 391 | Brad Lidge | .15 | .40 |
| ❏ 392 | Chad Cordero | .15 | .40 |
| ❏ 393 | Ryan Doumit | .15 | .40 |
| ❏ 394 | James Loney | .25 | .60 |
| ❏ 395 | George Sherrill | .15 | .40 |
| ❏ 396 | Gary Sheffield | .15 | .40 |
| ❏ 397 | Chicago Cubs TC | .15 | .40 |
| ❏ 398 | Rich Harden | .15 | .40 |
| ❏ 399 | Kazmir/Price/Shields | .50 | 1.25 |
| ❏ 400 | Magglio Ordonez | .25 | .60 |
| ❏ 401 | Dan Uggla | .15 | .40 |
| ❏ 402 | Adam LaRoche | .15 | .40 |
| ❏ 403 | Taylor Teagarden | .15 | .40 |
| ❏ 404 | Chris Young | .15 | .40 |
| ❏ 405 | Robinson Cano | .25 | .60 |
| ❏ 406 | Dustin McGowan | .15 | .40 |
| ❏ 407a | Randy Winn | .15 | .40 |
| ❏ 407b | Winn UER Lewis SP | 20.00 | 50.00 |
| ❏ 408 | Carlos Lee | .15 | .40 |
| ❏ 409 | Kurt Suzuki | .15 | .40 |
| ❏ 410 | Matt Cain | .15 | .40 |
| ❏ 411 | Paul Bako | .15 | .40 |
| ❏ 412 | Ted Lilly | .15 | .40 |
| ❏ 413 | Kansas City Royals TC | .15 | .40 |
| ❏ 414 | Miguel Cabrera | .25 | .60 |
| ❏ 415 | Jayson Werth | .15 | .40 |
| ❏ 416 | J.C. Romero | .15 | .40 |
| ❏ 417 | Martin Prado | .15 | .40 |
| ❏ 418 | Armando Galarraga | .15 | .40 |
| ❏ 419 | Brian Roberts | .15 | .40 |
| ❏ 420 | Chipper Jones | .40 | 1.00 |
| ❏ 421 | Bengie Molina | .15 | .40 |
| ❏ 422 | Matt Kemp | .40 | 1.00 |
| ❏ 423 | Brian Buscher | .15 | .40 |
| ❏ 424 | Erik Bedard | .15 | .40 |
| ❏ 425 | Chad Billingsley | .15 | .40 |
| ❏ 426 | Scott Rolen SP | 3.00 | 8.00 |
| ❏ 427 | Ben Francisco SP | 2.50 | 6.00 |
| ❏ 428 | Jermaine Dye SP | 2.50 | 6.00 |
| ❏ 429 | Dustin Pedroia/Ichiro Suzuki SP | 4.00 | 10.00 |
| ❏ 430 | Kevin Slowey SP | 3.00 | 8.00 |
| ❏ 431 | Jason Bartlett SP | 2.50 | 6.00 |
| ❏ 432 | Glen Perkins SP | 2.50 | 6.00 |
| ❏ 433 | Carlos Gomez SP | 2.50 | 6.00 |
| ❏ 434 | Jon Garland SP | 2.50 | 6.00 |
| ❏ 435 | Joe Crede SP | 2.50 | 6.00 |
| ❏ 436 | Billy Butler SP | 2.50 | 6.00 |
| ❏ 437 | Zach Duke SP | 2.50 | 6.00 |
| ❏ 438 | Chris Coste SP | 2.50 | 6.00 |
| ❏ 439 | Daisuke Matsuzaka SP | 4.00 | 10.00 |
| ❏ 440 | Elijah Dukes SP | 2.50 | 6.00 |
| ❏ 441 | Fausto Carmona SP | 2.50 | 6.00 |
| ❏ 442 | Joe Mauer SP | 5.00 | 12.00 |
| ❏ 443 | Marcus Thames SP | 2.50 | 6.00 |
| ❏ 444 | Mike Fontenot SP | 2.50 | 6.00 |
| ❏ 445a | J.Smoltz ATL SP | 3.00 | 8.00 |
| ❏ 445b | J.Smoltz BOS SP | 30.00 | 60.00 |
| ❏ 446 | Pedro Martinez SP | 3.00 | 8.00 |
| ❏ 447 | Adrian Beltre SP | 2.50 | 6.00 |
| ❏ 448 | Kevin Millar SP | 2.50 | 6.00 |
| ❏ 449 | Nick Swisher SP | 2.50 | 6.00 |
| ❏ 450 | Justin Morneau SP | 3.00 | 8.00 |
| ❏ 451 | Shane Victorino SP | 2.50 | 6.00 |
| ❏ 452 | Placido Polanco SP | 2.50 | 6.00 |
| ❏ 453 | Ryan Dempster SP | 2.50 | 6.00 |
| ❏ 454 | Frank Thomas SP | 3.00 | 8.00 |
| ❏ 455 | Dave Jauss/Juan Samuel /John Shelby CO SP | 2.50 | 6.00 |
| ❏ 456 | Brad Mills/John Farrell /Dave Magadan CO SP | 2.50 | 6.00 |
| ❏ 457 | Alan Trammell/Larry Rothschild /Matt Sinatro CO SP | 2.50 | 6.00 |
| ❏ 458 | Joey Cora/Harold Baines/Jeff Cox CO SP | 2.50 | 6.00 |
| ❏ 459 | Chris Speier/Billy Hatcher/Dick Pole CO SP | 2.50 | 6.00 |
| ❏ 460 | Jeff Datz/Luis Rivera/Carl Willis /Joel Skinner CO SP | 2.50 | 6.00 |
| ❏ 461 | Lloyd McClendon/Andy Van Slyke /Rafael Belliard CO SP | 2.50 | 6.00 |
| ❏ 462 | Jim Hickey/Steve Henderson /Tom Foley CO SP | 2.50 | 6.00 |
| ❏ 463 | Larry Bowa/Rick Honeycutt/Mariano Duncan | | |

| | | |
|---|---|---|
| ☐ /Bob Schaefer CO SP | 2.50 | 6.00 |
| ☐ 464 Roger McDowell/Terry Pendleton/Chino Cadahia | | |
| /Glenn Hubbard CO SP | 2.50 | 6.00 |
| ☐ 465 Rob Thomson/Tony Pena/Kevin Long | | |
| /Dave Eiland CO SP | 2.50 | 6.00 |
| ☐ 466 Milt Thompson/Rich Dubee | | |
| /Davey Lopes CO SP | 2.50 | 6.00 |
| ☐ 467 Tony Beasley/Joe Kerrigan | | |
| /Don Long CO SP | 2.50 | 6.00 |
| ☐ 468 Dave Duncan/Hal McRae/Jose Oquendo | | |
| /Dave McKay CO SP | 2.50 | 6.00 |
| ☐ 469 Sandy Alomar Sr./Howard Johnson | | |
| /Dan Warthen CO SP | 2.50 | 6.00 |
| ☐ 470 Randy St. Claire/Marquis Grissom | | |
| Jim Riggleman CO SP | 2.50 | 6.00 |
| ☐ 471 Brad Ausmus SP | 2.50 | 6.00 |
| ☐ 472 Melvin Mora SP | 2.50 | 6.00 |
| ☐ 473 Austin Kearns SP | 2.50 | 6.00 |
| ☐ 474 Josh Willingham SP | 2.50 | 6.00 |
| ☐ 475 Derek Lowe SP | 2.50 | 6.00 |
| ☐ 476 Nick Punto SP | 2.50 | 6.00 |
| ☐ 477 A.J. Pierzynski SP | 2.50 | 6.00 |
| ☐ 478 Troy Tulowitzki SP | 3.00 | 8.00 |
| ☐ 479 CC Sabathia SP | 3.00 | 8.00 |
| ☐ 480 Jorge Posada SP | 3.00 | 8.00 |
| ☐ 481 Kevin Youkilis AS SP | 3.00 | 8.00 |
| ☐ 482 Lance Berkman AS SP | 3.00 | 8.00 |
| ☐ 483 Dustin Pedroia AS SP | 4.00 | 10.00 |
| ☐ 484 Chase Utley AS SP | 3.00 | 8.00 |
| ☐ 485 Alex Rodriguez AS SP | 4.00 | 10.00 |
| ☐ 486 Chipper Jones AS SP | 3.00 | 8.00 |
| ☐ 487 Derek Jeter AS SP | 5.00 | 12.00 |
| ☐ 488a H.Ramirez AS FLA SP | 3.00 | 8.00 |
| ☐ 488b H.Ramirez AS BOS SP | 40.00 | 80.00 |
| ☐ 489 Josh Hamilton AS SP | 3.00 | 8.00 |
| ☐ 490 Ryan Braun AS SP | 4.00 | 10.00 |
| ☐ 491 Manny Ramirez AS SP | 3.00 | 8.00 |
| ☐ 492 Kosuke Fukudome AS SP | 4.00 | 10.00 |
| ☐ 493 Ichiro Suzuki AS SP | 4.00 | 10.00 |
| ☐ 494 Matt Holliday AS SP | 3.00 | 8.00 |
| ☐ 495 Joe Mauer AS SP | 5.00 | 12.00 |
| ☐ 496 Geovany Soto AS SP | 3.00 | 8.00 |
| ☐ 497 Roy Halladay AS SP | 4.00 | 10.00 |
| ☐ 498 Ben Sheets AS SP | 2.50 | 6.00 |
| ☐ 499 Cliff Lee AS SP | 3.00 | 8.00 |
| ☐ 500 Billy Wagner AS SP | 2.50 | 6.00 |

## 2005 Topps Opening Day

| | | |
|---|---|---|
| ☐ COMPLETE SET (165) | 15.00 | 40.00 |
| ☐ COMMON CARD (1-165) | .15 | .40 |
| ☐ ISSUED IN OPENING DAY PACKS | | |
| ☐ 1 Alex Rodriguez | .60 | 1.50 |
| ☐ 2 Placido Polanco | .15 | .40 |
| ☐ 3 Torii Hunter | .15 | .40 |
| ☐ 4 Lyle Overbay | .15 | .40 |
| ☐ 5 Johnny Damon | .25 | .60 |
| ☐ 6 Mike Cameron | .15 | .40 |
| ☐ 7 Ichiro Suzuki | .75 | 2.00 |
| ☐ 8 Francisco Rodriguez | .15 | .40 |
| ☐ 9 Bobby Crosby | .15 | .40 |
| ☐ 10 Sammy Sosa | .40 | 1.00 |
| ☐ 11 Randy Wolf | .15 | .40 |
| ☐ 12 Jason Bay | .15 | .40 |
| ☐ 13 Mike Lieberthal | .15 | .40 |
| ☐ 14 Paul Konerko | .15 | .40 |
| ☐ 15 Brian Giles | .15 | .40 |
| ☐ 16 Luis Gonzalez | .15 | .40 |
| ☐ 17 Jim Edmonds | .15 | .40 |
| ☐ 18 Carlos Lee | .15 | .40 |
| ☐ 19 Corey Patterson | .15 | .40 |
| ☐ 20 Hank Blalock | .15 | .40 |
| ☐ 21 Sean Casey | .15 | .40 |
| ☐ 22 Dmitri Young | .15 | .40 |
| ☐ 23 Mark Mulder | .15 | .40 |

| | | |
|---|---|---|
| ☐ 24 Bobby Abreu | .15 | .40 |
| ☐ 25 Jim Thome | .25 | .60 |
| ☐ 26 Jason Kendall | .15 | .40 |
| ☐ 27 Jason Giambi | .15 | .40 |
| ☐ 28 Vinny Castilla | .15 | .40 |
| ☐ 29 Tony Batista | .15 | .40 |
| ☐ 30 Ivan Rodriguez | .25 | .60 |
| ☐ 31 Craig Biggio | .25 | .60 |
| ☐ 32 Chris Carpenter | .15 | .40 |
| ☐ 33 Adrian Beltre | .15 | .40 |
| ☐ 34 Scott Podsednik | .15 | .40 |
| ☐ 35 Cliff Floyd | .15 | .40 |
| ☐ 36 Chad Tracy | .15 | .40 |
| ☐ 37 John Smoltz | .25 | .60 |
| ☐ 38 Shingo Takatsu | .15 | .40 |
| ☐ 39 Jack Wilson | .15 | .40 |
| ☐ 40 Gary Sheffield | .15 | .40 |
| ☐ 41 Lance Berkman | .15 | .40 |
| ☐ 42 Carl Crawford | .15 | .40 |
| ☐ 43 Carlos Guillen | .15 | .40 |
| ☐ 44 David Bell | .15 | .40 |
| ☐ 45 Kazuo Matsui | .15 | .40 |
| ☐ 46 Jason Schmidt | .15 | .40 |
| ☐ 47 Jason Marquis | .15 | .40 |
| ☐ 48 Melvin Mora | .15 | .40 |
| ☐ 49 David Ortiz | .40 | 1.00 |
| ☐ 50 Andruw Jones | .25 | .60 |
| ☐ 51 Miguel Tejada | .15 | .40 |
| ☐ 52 Bartolo Colon | .15 | .40 |
| ☐ 53 Derrek Lee | .25 | .60 |
| ☐ 54 Eric Gagne | .15 | .40 |
| ☐ 55 Miguel Cabrera | .25 | .60 |
| ☐ 56 Travis Hafner | .15 | .40 |
| ☐ 57 Jose Valentin | .15 | .40 |
| ☐ 58 Mark Prior | .25 | .60 |
| ☐ 59 Phil Nevin | .15 | .40 |
| ☐ 60 Jose Vidro | .15 | .40 |
| ☐ 61 Khalil Greene | .25 | .60 |
| ☐ 62 Carlos Zambrano | .15 | .40 |
| ☐ 63 Erubiel Durazo | .15 | .40 |
| ☐ 64 Michael Young UER | .15 | .40 |
| ☐ 65 Woody Williams | .15 | .40 |
| ☐ 66 Edgardo Alfonzo | .15 | .40 |
| ☐ 67 Troy Glaus | .15 | .40 |
| ☐ 68 Garret Anderson | .15 | .40 |
| ☐ 69 Richie Sexson | .15 | .40 |
| ☐ 70 Curt Schilling | .25 | .60 |
| ☐ 71 Randy Johnson | .40 | 1.00 |
| ☐ 72 Chipper Jones | .40 | 1.00 |
| ☐ 73 J.D. Drew | .15 | .40 |
| ☐ 74 Russ Ortiz | .15 | .40 |
| ☐ 75 Frank Thomas | .40 | 1.00 |
| ☐ 76 Jimmy Rollins | .15 | .40 |
| ☐ 77 Barry Zito | .15 | .40 |
| ☐ 78 Rafael Palmeiro | .15 | .40 |
| ☐ 79 Brad Wilkerson | .15 | .40 |
| ☐ 80 Adam Dunn | .15 | .40 |
| ☐ 81 Doug Mientkiewicz | .15 | .40 |
| ☐ 82 Manny Ramirez | .25 | .60 |
| ☐ 83 Pedro Martinez | .25 | .60 |
| ☐ 84 Moises Alou | .15 | .40 |
| ☐ 85 Mike Sweeney | .15 | .40 |
| ☐ 86 Boston Red Sox WC | .40 | 1.00 |
| ☐ 87 Matt Clement | .15 | .40 |
| ☐ 88 Nomar Garciaparra | .40 | 1.00 |
| ☐ 89 Magglio Ordonez | .15 | .40 |
| ☐ 90 Bret Boone | .15 | .40 |
| ☐ 91 Mark Loretta | .15 | .40 |
| ☐ 92 Jose Contreras | .15 | .40 |
| ☐ 93 Randy Winn | .15 | .40 |
| ☐ 94 Austin Kearns | .15 | .40 |
| ☐ 95 Ken Griffey Jr. | .60 | 1.50 |
| ☐ 96 Jake Westbrook | .15 | .40 |
| ☐ 97 Kazuhito Tadano | .15 | .40 |
| ☐ 98 C.C. Sabathia | .15 | .40 |
| ☐ 99 Todd Helton | .25 | .60 |
| ☐ 100 Albert Pujols | .75 | 2.00 |
| ☐ 101 Jose Molina | | |
| Bengie Molina | .15 | .40 |
| ☐ 102 Aaron Miles | .15 | .40 |
| ☐ 103 Mike Lowell | .15 | .40 |
| ☐ 104 Paul Lo Duca | .15 | .40 |
| ☐ 105 Juan Pierre | .15 | .40 |
| ☐ 106 Dontrelle Willis | .15 | .40 |
| ☐ 107 Jeff Bagwell | .25 | .60 |
| ☐ 108 Carlos Beltran | .15 | .40 |
| ☐ 109 Ronnie Belliard | .15 | .40 |
| ☐ 110 Roy Oswalt | .15 | .40 |

| | | |
|---|---|---|
| ☐ 111 Zack Greinke | .15 | .40 |
| ☐ 112 Steve Finley | .15 | .40 |
| ☐ 113 Kazuhisa Ishii | .15 | .40 |
| ☐ 114 Justin Morneau | .15 | .40 |
| ☐ 115 Ben Sheets | .15 | .40 |
| ☐ 116 Johan Santana | .40 | 1.00 |
| ☐ 117 Billy Wagner | .15 | .40 |
| ☐ 118 Mariano Rivera | .40 | 1.00 |
| ☐ 119 Corey Koskie | .15 | .40 |
| ☐ 120 Akinori Otsuka | .15 | .40 |
| ☐ 121 Joe Mauer | .40 | 1.00 |
| ☐ 122 Jacque Jones | .15 | .40 |
| ☐ 123 Joe Nathan | .15 | .40 |
| ☐ 124 Nick Johnson | .15 | .40 |
| ☐ 125 Vernon Wells | .15 | .40 |
| ☐ 126 Mike Piazza | .40 | 1.00 |
| ☐ 127 Jose Guillen | .15 | .40 |
| ☐ 128 Jose Reyes | .15 | .40 |
| ☐ 129 Marcus Giles | .15 | .40 |
| ☐ 130 Javy Lopez | .15 | .40 |
| ☐ 131 Kevin Millar | .15 | .40 |
| ☐ 132 Jorge Posada | .25 | .60 |
| ☐ 133 Carl Pavano | .15 | .40 |
| ☐ 134 Bernie Williams | .25 | .60 |
| ☐ 135 Kerry Wood | .15 | .40 |
| ☐ 136 Matt Holliday | .20 | .50 |
| ☐ 137 Kevin Brown | .15 | .40 |
| ☐ 138 Derek Jeter | .75 | 2.00 |
| ☐ 139 Barry Bonds | 1.00 | 2.50 |
| ☐ 140 Jeff Kent | .15 | .40 |
| ☐ 141 Mark Kotsay | .15 | .40 |
| ☐ 142 Shawn Green | .15 | .40 |
| ☐ 143 Tim Hudson | .15 | .40 |
| ☐ 144 Shannon Stewart | .15 | .40 |
| ☐ 145 Pat Burrell | .15 | .40 |
| ☐ 146 Ryan Freel | .15 | .40 |
| ☐ 147 Mike Mussina | .25 | .60 |
| ☐ 148 Eric Chavez | .15 | .40 |
| ☐ 149 Jon Lieber | .15 | .40 |
| ☐ 150 Vladimir Guerrero | .40 | 1.00 |
| ☐ 151 Vicente Padilla | .15 | .40 |
| ☐ 152 Ryan Klesko | .15 | .40 |
| ☐ 153 Jake Peavy | .15 | .40 |
| ☐ 154 Scott Rolen | .25 | .60 |
| ☐ 155 Greg Maddux | .60 | 1.50 |
| ☐ 156 Edgar Renteria | .15 | .40 |
| ☐ 157 Larry Walker | .25 | .60 |
| ☐ 158 Scott Kazmir | .15 | .40 |
| ☐ 159 B.J. Upton | .25 | .60 |
| ☐ 160 Mark Teixeira | .25 | .60 |
| ☐ 161 Ken Harvey | .15 | .40 |
| ☐ 162 Alfonso Soriano | .15 | .40 |
| ☐ 163 Carlos Delgado | .15 | .40 |
| ☐ 164 Alexis Rios | .15 | .40 |
| ☐ 165 Checklist | .15 | .40 |

## 2006 Topps Opening Day

| | | |
|---|---|---|
| ☐ COMPLETE SET (165) | 15.00 | 40.00 |
| ☐ COMMON CARD (1-165) | .15 | .40 |
| ☐ OVERALL PLATE SER.1 ODDS 1:246 HTA | | |
| ☐ PLATE PRINT RUN 1 SET PER COLOR | | |
| ☐ BLACK-CYAN-MAGENTA-YELLOW ISSUED | | |
| ☐ NO PLATE PRICING DUE TO SCARCITY | | |
| ☐ 1 Alex Rodriguez | .60 | 1.50 |
| ☐ 2 Jhonny Peralta | .20 | .50 |
| ☐ 3 Garrett Atkins | .15 | .40 |
| ☐ 4 Vernon Wells | .15 | .40 |
| ☐ 5 Carl Crawford | .15 | .40 |
| ☐ 6 Josh Beckett | .15 | .40 |
| ☐ 7 Mickey Mantle | 3.00 | 8.00 |
| ☐ 8 Willy Taveras | .15 | .40 |
| ☐ 9 Ivan Rodriguez | .25 | .60 |
| ☐ 10 Clint Barmes | .15 | .40 |
| ☐ 11 Jose Reyes | .40 | 1.00 |

|  |  | | |
|---|---|---|---|
| 12 | Travis Hafner | .15 | .40 |
| 13 | Tadahito Iguchi | .15 | .40 |
| 14 | Barry Zito | .15 | .40 |
| 15 | Brian Roberts | .15 | .40 |
| 16 | David Wright | .60 | 1.50 |
| 17 | Mark Teixeira | .25 | .60 |
| 18 | Roy Halladay | .15 | .40 |
| 19 | Scott Rolen | .25 | .60 |
| 20 | Bobby Abreu | .15 | .40 |
| 21 | Lance Berkman | .15 | .40 |
| 22 | Moises Alou | .15 | .40 |
| 23 | Chone Figgins | .15 | .40 |
| 24 | Aaron Rowand | .15 | .40 |
| 25 | Chipper Jones | .40 | 1.00 |
| 26 | Johnny Damon | .25 | .60 |
| 27 | Matt Clement | .15 | .40 |
| 28 | Nick Johnson | .15 | .40 |
| 29 | Freddy Garcia | .15 | .40 |
| 30 | Jon Garland | .15 | .40 |
| 31 | Torii Hunter | .15 | .40 |
| 32 | Mike Sweeney | .15 | .40 |
| 33 | Mike Lieberthal | .15 | .40 |
| 34 | Rafael Furcal | .15 | .40 |
| 35 | Brad Wilkerson | .15 | .40 |
| 36 | Brad Penny | .15 | .40 |
| 37 | Jorge Cantu | .15 | .40 |
| 38 | Paul Konerko | .15 | .40 |
| 39 | Rickie Weeks | .15 | .40 |
| 40 | Jorge Posada | .25 | .60 |
| 41 | Albert Pujols | .75 | 2.00 |
| 42 | Zack Greinke | .15 | .40 |
| 43 | Jimmy Rollins | .15 | .40 |
| 44 | Mark Prior | .25 | .60 |
| 45 | Greg Maddux | .60 | 1.50 |
| 46 | Jeff Francis | .15 | .40 |
| 47 | Felipe Lopez | .15 | .40 |
| 48 | Dan Johnson | .15 | .40 |
| 49 | B.J. Ryan | .15 | .40 |
| 50 | Manny Ramirez | .25 | .60 |
| 51 | Melvin Mora | .15 | .40 |
| 52 | Javy Lopez | .15 | .40 |
| 53 | Garret Anderson | .15 | .40 |
| 54 | Jason Bay | .25 | .60 |
| 55 | Joe Mauer | .40 | 1.00 |
| 56 | C.C. Sabathia | .15 | .40 |
| 57 | Bartolo Colon | .15 | .40 |
| 58 | Ichiro Suzuki | .60 | 1.50 |
| 59 | Andruw Jones | .25 | .60 |
| 60 | Rocco Baldelli | .15 | .40 |
| 61 | Jeff Kent | .15 | .40 |
| 62 | Cliff Floyd | .15 | .40 |
| 63 | John Smoltz | .25 | .60 |
| 64 | Shawn Green | .15 | .40 |
| 65 | Nomar Garciaparra | .40 | 1.00 |
| 66 | Miguel Cabrera | .25 | .60 |
| 67 | Vladimir Guerrero | .40 | 1.00 |
| 68 | Gary Sheffield | .15 | .40 |
| 69 | Jake Peavy | .15 | .40 |
| 70 | Carlos Lee | .15 | .40 |
| 71 | Tom Glavine | .25 | .60 |
| 72 | Craig Biggio | .25 | .60 |
| 73 | Steve Finley | .15 | .40 |
| 74 | Adrian Beltre | .15 | .40 |
| 75 | Eric Gagne | .15 | .40 |
| 76 | Aubrey Huff | .15 | .40 |
| 77 | Livan Hernandez | .15 | .40 |
| 78 | Scott Podsednik | .15 | .40 |
| 79 | Todd Helton | .25 | .60 |
| 80 | Kerry Wood | .15 | .40 |
| 81 | Randy Johnson | .40 | 1.00 |
| 82 | Huston Street | .15 | .40 |
| 83 | Pedro Martinez | .25 | .60 |
| 84 | Roger Clemens | .75 | 2.00 |
| 85 | Hank Blalock | .15 | .40 |
| 86 | Carlos Beltran | .15 | .40 |
| 87 | Chien-Ming Wang | .40 | 1.00 |
| 88 | Rich Harden | .15 | .40 |
| 89 | Mike Mussina | .25 | .60 |
| 90 | Mark Buehrle | .15 | .40 |
| 91 | Michael Young | .15 | .40 |
| 92 | Mark Mulder | .15 | .40 |
| 93 | Khalil Greene | .25 | .60 |
| 94 | Johan Santana | .25 | .60 |
| 95 | Andy Pettitte | .25 | .60 |
| 96 | Derek Jeter | 1.00 | 2.50 |
| 97 | Jack Wilson | .15 | .40 |
| 98 | Ben Sheets | .15 | .40 |
| 99 | Miguel Tejada | .15 | .40 |
| 100 | Barry Bonds | 1.00 | 2.50 |
| 101 | Dontrelle Willis | .15 | .40 |
| 102 | Curt Schilling | .25 | .60 |
| 103 | Jose Contreras | .15 | .40 |
| 104 | Jeremy Bonderman | .15 | .40 |
| 105 | David Ortiz | .25 | .60 |
| 106 | Lyle Overbay | .15 | .40 |
| 107 | Robinson Cano | .25 | .60 |
| 108 | Tim Hudson | .15 | .40 |
| 109 | Paul Lo Duca | .15 | .40 |
| 110 | Mariano Rivera | .25 | .60 |
| 111 | Derrek Lee | .15 | .40 |
| 112 | Morgan Ensberg | .15 | .40 |
| 113 | Wily Mo Pena | .15 | .40 |
| 114 | Roy Oswalt | .15 | .40 |
| 115 | Adam Dunn | .15 | .40 |
| 116 | Hideki Matsui | .60 | 1.50 |
| 117 | Pat Burrell | .15 | .40 |
| 118 | Jason Schmidt | .15 | .40 |
| 119 | Alfonso Soriano | .15 | .40 |
| 120 | Aramis Ramirez | .15 | .40 |
| 121 | Jason Giambi | .15 | .40 |
| 122 | Orlando Hernandez | .15 | .40 |
| 123 | Magglio Ordonez | .15 | .40 |
| 124 | Troy Glaus | .15 | .40 |
| 125 | Carlos Delgado | .15 | .40 |
| 126 | Kevin Millwood | .15 | .40 |
| 127 | Shannon Stewart | .15 | .40 |
| 128 | Luis Castillo | .15 | .40 |
| 129 | Jim Edmonds | .25 | .60 |
| 130 | Richie Sexson | .15 | .40 |
| 131 | Dmitri Young | .15 | .40 |
| 132 | Russ Adams | .15 | .40 |
| 133 | Nick Swisher | .15 | .40 |
| 134 | Jermaine Dye | .15 | .40 |
| 135 | Anderson Hernandez (RC) | .15 | .40 |
| 136 | Justin Huber (RC) | .15 | .40 |
| 137 | Jason Botts (RC) | .15 | .40 |
| 138 | Jeff Mathis (RC) | .15 | .40 |
| 139 | Ryan Garko (RC) | .15 | .40 |
| 140 | Charlton Jimerson (RC) | .15 | .40 |
| 141 | Chris Denorfia (RC) | .15 | .40 |
| 142 | Anthony Reyes (RC) | .15 | .40 |
| 143 | Bryan Bullington (RC) | .15 | .40 |
| 144 | Chuck James (RC) | .25 | .60 |
| 145 | Danny Sandoval RC | .15 | .40 |
| 146 | Walter Young (RC) | .15 | .40 |
| 147 | Fausto Carmona (RC) | .15 | .40 |
| 148 | Francisco Liriano (RC) | .40 | 1.00 |
| 149 | Hong-Chih Kuo (RC) | .40 | 1.00 |
| 150 | Joe Saunders (RC) | .15 | .40 |
| 151 | John Koronka (RC) | .15 | .40 |
| 152 | Robert Andino RC | .15 | .40 |
| 153 | Shaun Marcum (RC) | .15 | .40 |
| 154 | Tom Gorzelanny (RC) | .15 | .40 |
| 155 | Craig Breslow RC | .15 | .40 |
| 156 | Chris Demaria RC | .15 | .40 |
| 157 | Brayan Pena (RC) | .15 | .40 |
| 158 | Rich Hill (RC) | .15 | .40 |
| 159 | Rick Short (RC) | .15 | .40 |
| 160 | Darrell Rasner (RC) | .15 | .40 |
| 161 | C.J. Wilson (RC) | .15 | .40 |
| 162 | Brandon Watson (RC) | .15 | .40 |
| 163 | Paul McAnulty (RC) | .15 | .40 |
| 164 | Marshall McDougall (RC) | .15 | .40 |
| 165 | Checklist | .15 | .40 |

## 2007 Topps Opening Day

| | | | |
|---|---|---|---|
| COMPLETE SET (220) | | 20.00 | 50.00 |
| COMMON CARD (1-220) | | .20 | .50 |
| COMMON RC | | .20 | .50 |
| 1 | Bobby Abreu | .15 | .40 |
| 2 | Mike Piazza | .40 | 1.00 |
| 3 | Jake Westbrook | .15 | .40 |
| 4 | Zach Duke | .15 | .40 |
| 5 | David Wright | .60 | 1.50 |
| 6 | Adrian Gonzalez | .15 | .40 |
| 7 | Mickey Mantle | 2.00 | 5.00 |
| 8 | Bill Hall | .15 | .40 |
| 9 | Robinson Cano | .25 | .60 |
| 10 | Dontrelle Willis | .15 | .40 |
| 11 | J.D. Drew | .15 | .40 |
| 12 | Paul Konerko | .15 | .40 |
| 13 | Austin Kearns | .15 | .40 |
| 14 | Mike Lowell | .15 | .40 |
| 15 | Magglio Ordonez | .15 | .40 |
| 16 | Rafael Furcal | .15 | .40 |
| 17 | Matt Cain | .15 | .40 |
| 18 | Craig Monroe | .15 | .40 |
| 19 | Matt Holliday | .20 | .50 |
| 20 | Edgar Renteria | .15 | .40 |
| 21 | Mark Reynolds | .15 | .40 |
| 22 | Carlos Quentin | .15 | .40 |
| 23 | C.C. Sabathia | .15 | .40 |
| 24 | Nick Markakis | .25 | .60 |
| 25 | Chipper Jones | .40 | 1.00 |
| 26 | Jason Giambi | .15 | .40 |
| 27 | Barry Zito | .15 | .40 |
| 28 | Jake Peavy | .15 | .40 |
| 29 | Hank Blalock | .15 | .40 |
| 30 | Johnny Damon | .25 | .60 |
| 31 | Chad Tracy | .15 | .40 |
| 32 | Nick Swisher | .15 | .40 |
| 33 | Willy Taveras | .15 | .40 |
| 34 | Chuck James | .15 | .40 |
| 35 | Carlos Delgado | .15 | .40 |
| 36 | Livan Hernandez | .15 | .40 |
| 37 | Freddy Garcia | .15 | .40 |
| 38 | Bronson Arroyo | .15 | .40 |
| 39 | Jack Wilson | .15 | .40 |
| 40 | Dan Uggla | .25 | .60 |
| 41 | Chris Carpenter | .15 | .40 |
| 42 | Jorge Posada | .25 | .60 |
| 43 | Joe Mauer | .25 | .60 |
| 44 | Corey Patterson | .15 | .40 |
| 45 | Chien-Ming Wang | .60 | 1.50 |
| 46 | Derek Jeter | 6.00 | 15.00 |
| 47 | Carlos Beltran | .15 | .40 |
| 48 | Jim Edmonds | .25 | .60 |
| 49 | Jeremy Sowers | .15 | .40 |
| 50 | Randy Johnson | .40 | 1.00 |
| 51 | Jered Weaver | .25 | .60 |
| 52 | Josh Barfield | .15 | .40 |
| 53 | Scott Rolen | .25 | .60 |
| 54 | Ryan Shealy | .15 | .40 |
| 55 | Freddy Sanchez | .15 | .40 |
| 56 | Javier Vazquez | .15 | .40 |
| 57 | Jeremy Bonderman | .15 | .40 |
| 58 | Miguel Cabrera | .25 | .60 |
| 59 | Kazuo Matsui | .15 | .40 |
| 60 | Curt Schilling | .25 | .60 |
| 61 | Alfonso Soriano | .15 | .40 |
| 62 | Orlando Hernandez | .15 | .40 |
| 63 | Joe Blanton | .15 | .40 |
| 64 | Aramis Ramirez | .15 | .40 |
| 65 | Ben Sheets | .15 | .40 |
| 66 | Jimmy Rollins | .15 | .40 |
| 67 | Mark Loretta | .15 | .40 |
| 68 | Cole Hamels | .25 | .60 |
| 69 | Albert Pujols | .75 | 2.00 |
| 70 | Moises Alou | .15 | .40 |
| 71 | Mark Teahen | .15 | .40 |
| 72 | Roy Halladay | .15 | .40 |
| 73 | Cory Sullivan | .15 | .40 |
| 74 | Frank Thomas | .40 | 1.00 |
| 75 | Ryan Howard | .60 | 1.50 |
| 76 | Rocco Baldelli | .15 | .40 |
| 77 | Manny Ramirez | .25 | .60 |
| 78 | Ray Durham | .15 | .40 |
| 79 | Gary Sheffield | .15 | .40 |
| 80 | Jay Gibbons | .15 | .40 |
| 81 | Todd Helton | .25 | .60 |
| 82 | Gary Matthews | .15 | .40 |
| 83 | Brandon Inge | .15 | .40 |
| 84 | Jonathan Papelbon | .40 | 1.00 |
| 85 | John Smoltz | .25 | .60 |
| 86 | Chone Figgins | .15 | .40 |
| 87 | Hideki Matsui | .40 | 1.00 |
| 88 | Carlos Lee | .15 | .40 |
| 89 | Jose Reyes | .15 | .40 |
| 90 | Lyle Overbay | .15 | .40 |
| 91 | Johan Santana | .25 | .60 |

|  |  | | |
|----|--------|---|---|
| 92 | Ian Kinsler | .15 | .40 |
| 93 | Scott Kazmir | .25 | .60 |
| 94 | Hanley Ramirez | .25 | .60 |
| 95 | Greg Maddux | .60 | 1.50 |
| 96 | Johnny Estrada | .15 | .40 |
| 97 | B.J. Upton | .15 | .40 |
| 98 | Francisco Liriano | .40 | 1.00 |
| 99 | Chase Utley | .40 | 1.00 |
| 100 | Preston Wilson | .15 | .40 |
| 101 | Marcus Giles | .15 | .40 |
| 102 | Jeff Kent | .15 | .40 |
| 103 | Grady Sizemore | .25 | .60 |
| 104 | Ken Griffey | .60 | 1.50 |
| 105 | Garret Anderson | .15 | .40 |
| 106 | Brian McCann | .15 | .40 |
| 107 | Jon Garland | .15 | .40 |
| 108 | Troy Glaus | .15 | .40 |
| 109 | Brandon Webb | .15 | .40 |
| 110 | Jason Schmidt | .15 | .40 |
| 111 | Ramon Hernandez | .15 | .40 |
| 112 | Justin Morneau | .15 | .40 |
| 113 | Mike Cameron | .15 | .40 |
| 114 | Andruw Jones | .25 | .60 |
| 115 | Russell Martin | .15 | .40 |
| 116 | Vernon Wells | .15 | .40 |
| 117 | Orlando Hudson | .15 | .40 |
| 118 | Derek Lowe | .15 | .40 |
| 119 | Alex Rodriguez | .60 | 1.50 |
| 120 | Chad Billingsley | .15 | .40 |
| 121 | Kenji Johjima | .40 | 1.00 |
| 122 | Nick Johnson | .15 | .40 |
| 123 | Dan Haren | .15 | .40 |
| 124 | Mark Teixeira | .25 | .60 |
| 125 | Jeff Francoeur | .40 | 1.00 |
| 126 | Ted Lilly | .15 | .40 |
| 127 | Jhonny Peralta | .15 | .40 |
| 128 | Aaron Harang | .15 | .40 |
| 129 | Ryan Zimmerman | .40 | 1.00 |
| 130 | Jermaine Dye | .15 | .40 |
| 131 | Orlando Cabrera | .15 | .40 |
| 132 | Juan Pierre | .15 | .40 |
| 133 | Brian Giles | .15 | .40 |
| 134 | Jason Bay | .15 | .40 |
| 135 | David Ortiz | .40 | 1.00 |
| 136 | Chris Capuano | .15 | .40 |
| 137 | Carlos Zambrano | .15 | .40 |
| 138 | Luis Gonzalez | .15 | .40 |
| 139 | Jeff Weaver | .15 | .40 |
| 140 | Lance Berkman | .15 | .40 |
| 141 | Raul Ibanez | .15 | .40 |
| 142 | Jim Thome | .25 | .60 |
| 143 | Jose Contreras | .15 | .40 |
| 144 | David Eckstein | .15 | .40 |
| 145 | Adam Dunn | .15 | .40 |
| 146 | Alex Rios | .15 | .40 |
| 147 | Garrett Atkins | .15 | .40 |
| 148 | A.J. Burnett | .15 | .40 |
| 149 | Jeremy Hermida | .15 | .40 |
| 150 | Conor Jackson | .15 | .40 |
| 151 | Adrian Beltre | .15 | .40 |
| 152 | Torii Hunter | .15 | .40 |
| 153 | Andrew Miller RC | 1.50 | 4.00 |
| 154 | Ichiro Suzuki | .60 | 1.50 |
| 155 | Mark Redman | .15 | .40 |
| 156 | Paul LoDuca | .15 | .40 |
| 157 | Xavier Nady | .15 | .40 |
| 158 | Stephen Drew | .25 | .60 |
| 159 | Eric Chavez | .15 | .40 |
| 160 | Pedro Martinez | .25 | .60 |
| 161 | Derrek Lee | .15 | .40 |
| 162 | David DeJesus | .15 | .40 |
| 163 | Troy Tulowitzki (RC) | .50 | 1.25 |
| 164 | Vinny Rottino (RC) | .20 | .50 |
| 165 | Philip Humber (RC) | .20 | .75 |
| 166 | Jerry Owens (RC) | .20 | .50 |
| 167 | Ubaldo Jimenez (RC) | .20 | .50 |
| 168 | Michael Young | .15 | .40 |
| 169 | Ryan Braun RC | .20 | .50 |
| 170 | Kevin Kouzmanoff (RC) | .20 | .50 |
| 171 | Oswaldo Navarro RC | .20 | .50 |
| 172 | Miguel Montero (RC) | .20 | .50 |
| 173 | Roy Oswalt | .15 | .40 |
| 174 | Shane Youman RC | .20 | .50 |
| 175 | Josh Fields (RC) | .20 | .50 |
| 176 | Adam Lind (RC) | .20 | .50 |
| 177 | Miguel Tejada | .15 | .40 |
| 178 | Delwyn Young (RC) | .20 | .50 |
| 179 | Scott Moore (RC) | .20 | .50 |
| 180 | Fred Lewis (RC) | .20 | .50 |
| 181 | Glen Perkins (RC) | .20 | .50 |
| 182 | Vladimir Guerrero | .40 | 1.00 |
| 183 | Drew Anderson RC | .20 | .50 |
| 184 | Jeff Salazar (RC) | .20 | .50 |
| 185 | Tom Gordon | .15 | .40 |
| 186 | The Bird | .15 | .40 |
| 187 | Justin Verlander | .40 | 1.00 |
| 188 | Delmon Young (RC) | .50 | 1.25 |
| 189 | Homer | .15 | .40 |
| 190 | Wally the Green Monster | .15 | .40 |
| 191 | Southpaw | .15 | .40 |
| 192 | Dinger | .15 | .40 |
| 193 | Carl Crawford | .15 | .40 |
| 194 | Slider | .15 | .40 |
| 195 | Gapper | .15 | .40 |
| 196 | Paws | .15 | .40 |
| 197 | Billy the Marlin | .15 | .40 |
| 198 | Ivan Rodriguez | .25 | .60 |
| 199 | Slugger | .15 | .40 |
| 200 | Junction Jack | .15 | .40 |
| 201 | Bernie Brewer | .15 | .40 |
| 202 | Travis Hafner | .15 | .40 |
| 203 | Stomper | .15 | .40 |
| 204 | Mr. Met | .15 | .40 |
| 205 | The Moose | .15 | .40 |
| 206 | Phillie Phanatic | .15 | .40 |
| 207 | Prince Fielder | .40 | 1.00 |
| 208 | Julio Lugo | .15 | .40 |
| 209 | Pirate Parrot | .15 | .40 |
| 210 | Joel Zumaya | .25 | .60 |
| 211 | Swinging Friar | .15 | .40 |
| 212 | Jay Payton | .15 | .40 |
| 213 | Lou Seal | .15 | .40 |
| 214 | Fredbird | .15 | .40 |
| 215 | Screech | .15 | .40 |
| 216 | TC Bear | .15 | .40 |
| 217 | Andre Ethier | .25 | .60 |
| 218 | Ervin Santana | .15 | .40 |
| 219 | Melvin Mora | .15 | .40 |
| 220 | Checklist | .15 | .40 |

## 2008 Topps Opening Day

| | | |
|---|---|---|
| COMPLETE SET (220) | 15.00 | 40.00 |
| COMMON CARD (1-194) | .12 | .30 |
| COMMON CARD (195-220) | .20 | .50 |
| OVERALL PLATE ODDS 1:546 HOBBY | | |
| PLATE PRINT RUN 1 SET PER COLOR | | |
| BLACK-CYAN-MAGENTA-YELLOW ISSUED | | |
| NO PLATE PRICING DUE TO SCARCITY | | |

|  |  | | |
|----|--------|---|---|
| 1 | Alex Rodriguez | .50 | 1.25 |
| 2 | Barry Zito | .12 | .30 |
| 3 | Jeff Suppan | .12 | .30 |
| 4 | Placido Polanco | .12 | .30 |
| 5 | Scott Kazmir | .20 | .50 |
| 6 | Ivan Rodriguez | .20 | .50 |
| 7 | Mickey Mantle | 1.25 | 3.00 |
| 8 | Stephen Drew | .12 | .30 |
| 9 | Ken Griffey Jr. | .50 | 1.25 |
| 10 | Miguel Cabrera | .20 | .50 |
| 11 | Yorvit Torrealba | .12 | .30 |
| 12 | Daisuke Matsuzaka | .40 | 1.00 |
| 13 | Kyle Kendrick | .12 | .30 |
| 14 | Jimmy Rollins | .12 | .30 |
| 15 | Joe Mauer | .30 | .75 |
| 16 | Cole Hamels | .20 | .50 |
| 17 | Yovani Gallardo | .20 | .50 |
| 18 | Miguel Tejada | .12 | .30 |
| 19 | Corey Hart | .12 | .30 |
| 20 | Nick Markakis | .20 | .50 |
| 21 | Zack Greinke | .12 | .30 |
| 22 | Orlando Cabrera | .12 | .30 |
| 23 | Jake Peavy | .20 | .50 |
| 24 | Erik Bedard | .12 | .30 |
| 25 | Trevor Hoffman | .12 | .30 |
| 26 | Derrek Lee | .20 | .50 |
| 27 | Hank Blalock | .12 | .30 |
| 28 | Victor Martinez | .12 | .30 |
| 29 | Chris Young | .12 | .30 |
| 30 | Jose Reyes | .20 | .50 |
| 31 | Mike Lowell | .12 | .30 |
| 32 | Curtis Granderson | .12 | .30 |
| 33 | Dan Uggla | .20 | .50 |
| 34 | Mike Piazza | .30 | .75 |
| 35 | Garrett Atkins | .12 | .30 |
| 36 | Felix Hernandez | .20 | .50 |
| 37 | Alex Rios | .12 | .30 |
| 38 | Mark Reynolds | .12 | .30 |
| 39 | Jason Bay | .20 | .50 |
| 40 | Josh Beckett | .20 | .50 |
| 41 | Jack Cust | .12 | .30 |
| 42 | Vladimir Guerrero | .30 | .75 |
| 43 | Marcus Giles | .12 | .30 |
| 44 | Kenny Lofton | .12 | .30 |
| 45 | John Lackey | .12 | .30 |
| 46 | Ryan Howard | .40 | 1.00 |
| 47 | Kevin Youkilis | .20 | .50 |
| 48 | Gary Sheffield | .12 | .30 |
| 49 | Justin Morneau | .12 | .30 |
| 50 | Albert Pujols | .60 | 1.50 |
| 51 | Ubaldo Jimenez | .20 | .50 |
| 52 | Johan Santana | .20 | .50 |
| 53 | Chuck James | .12 | .30 |
| 54 | Jeremy Hermida | .12 | .30 |
| 55 | Andruw Jones | .12 | .30 |
| 56 | Jason Varitek | .30 | .75 |
| 57 | Tim Hudson | .12 | .30 |
| 58 | Justin Upton | .30 | .75 |
| 59 | Brad Penny | .12 | .30 |
| 60 | Robinson Cano | .20 | .50 |
| 61 | Johnny Estrada | .12 | .30 |
| 62 | Brandon Webb | .12 | .30 |
| 63 | Chris Duncan | .12 | .30 |
| 64 | Aaron Hill | .12 | .30 |
| 65 | Alfonso Soriano | .20 | .50 |
| 66 | Carlos Zambrano | .20 | .50 |
| 67 | Ben Sheets | .20 | .50 |
| 68 | Andy LaRoche | .12 | .30 |
| 69 | Tim Lincecum | .40 | 1.00 |
| 70 | Phil Hughes | .40 | 1.00 |
| 71 | Magglio Ordonez | .20 | .50 |
| 72 | Scott Rolen | .20 | .50 |
| 73 | John Maine | .12 | .30 |
| 74 | Delmon Young | .20 | .50 |
| 75 | Chase Utley | .30 | .75 |
| 76 | Jose Valverde | .12 | .30 |
| 77 | Tadahito Iguchi | .12 | .30 |
| 78 | Checklist | .12 | .30 |
| 79 | Russell Martin | .12 | .30 |
| 80 | B.J. Upton | .20 | .50 |
| 81 | Orlando Hudson | .12 | .30 |
| 82 | Jim Edmonds | .20 | .50 |
| 83 | J.J. Hardy | .20 | .50 |
| 84 | Todd Helton | .20 | .50 |
| 85 | Melky Cabrera | .12 | .30 |
| 86 | Adrian Beltre | .12 | .30 |
| 87 | Manny Ramirez | .30 | .75 |
| 88 | Rafael Furcal | .12 | .30 |
| 89 | Gil Meche | .12 | .30 |
| 90 | Grady Sizemore | .20 | .50 |
| 91 | Jeff Kent | .12 | .30 |
| 92 | David DeJesus | .12 | .30 |
| 93 | Lyle Overbay | .12 | .30 |
| 94 | Moises Alou | .12 | .30 |
| 95 | Frank Thomas | .30 | .75 |
| 96 | Ryan Garko | .12 | .30 |
| 97 | Kevin Kouzmanoff | .12 | .30 |
| 98 | Roy Oswalt | .12 | .30 |
| 99 | Mark Buehrle | .12 | .30 |
| 100 | David Ortiz | .20 | .50 |
| 101 | Hunter Pence | .30 | .75 |
| 102 | David Wright | .40 | 1.00 |
| 103 | Dustin Pedroia | .40 | 1.00 |
| 104 | Roy Halladay | .12 | .30 |
| 105 | Derek Jeter | .75 | 2.00 |
| 106 | Casey Blake | .12 | .30 |
| 107 | Rich Harden | .12 | .30 |
| 108 | Shane Victorino | .12 | .30 |
| 109 | Richie Sexson | .12 | .30 |
| 110 | Jim Thome | .20 | .50 |
| 111 | Akinori Iwamura | .12 | .30 |
| 112 | Dan Haren | .12 | .30 |

|  |  | | |
|---|---|---|---|
| ☐ 113 | Jose Contreras | .12 | .30 |
| ☐ 114 | Jonathan Papelbon | .20 | .50 |
| ☐ 115 | Prince Fielder | .30 | .75 |
| ☐ 116 | Dan Johnson | .12 | .30 |
| ☐ 117 | Dmitri Young | .12 | .30 |
| ☐ 118 | Brandon Phillips | .12 | .30 |
| ☐ 119 | Brett Myers | .12 | .30 |
| ☐ 120 | James Loney | .20 | .50 |
| ☐ 121 | C.C. Sabathia | .12 | .30 |
| ☐ 122 | Jermaine Dye | .12 | .30 |
| ☐ 123 | Aubrey Huff | .12 | .30 |
| ☐ 124 | Carlos Ruiz | .12 | .30 |
| ☐ 125 | Hanley Ramirez | .30 | .75 |
| ☐ 126 | Edgar Renteria | .12 | .30 |
| ☐ 127 | Mark Loretta | .12 | .30 |
| ☐ 128 | Brian McCann | .20 | .50 |
| ☐ 129 | Paul Konerko | .12 | .30 |
| ☐ 130 | Jorge Posada | .20 | .50 |
| ☐ 131 | Chien-Ming Wang | .30 | .75 |
| ☐ 132 | Jose Vidro | .12 | .30 |
| ☐ 133 | Carlos Delgado | .12 | .30 |
| ☐ 134 | Kelvim Escobar | .12 | .30 |
| ☐ 135 | Pedro Martinez | .20 | .50 |
| ☐ 136 | Jeremy Guthrie | .12 | .30 |
| ☐ 137 | Ramon Hernandez | .12 | .30 |
| ☐ 138 | Ian Kinsler | .20 | .50 |
| ☐ 139 | Ichiro Suzuki | .50 | 1.25 |
| ☐ 140 | Garret Anderson | .12 | .30 |
| ☐ 141 | Tom Gorzelanny | .12 | .30 |
| ☐ 142 | Bobby Crosby | .12 | .30 |
| ☐ 143 | Jeff Francoeur | .20 | .50 |
| ☐ 144 | Josh Hamilton | .40 | 1.00 |
| ☐ 145 | Mark Teixeira | .20 | .50 |
| ☐ 146 | Fausto Carmona | .12 | .30 |
| ☐ 147 | Alex Gordon | .20 | .50 |
| ☐ 148 | Nick Swisher | .12 | .30 |
| ☐ 149 | Justin Verlander | .20 | .50 |
| ☐ 150 | Pat Burrell | .12 | .30 |
| ☐ 151 | Chris Carpenter | .12 | .30 |
| ☐ 152 | Matt Holliday | .20 | .50 |
| ☐ 153 | Adam Dunn | .12 | .30 |
| ☐ 154 | Curt Schilling | .20 | .50 |
| ☐ 155 | Kelly Johnson | .12 | .30 |
| ☐ 156 | Aaron Rowand | .12 | .30 |
| ☐ 157 | Brian Roberts | .20 | .50 |
| ☐ 158 | Bobby Abreu | .12 | .30 |
| ☐ 159 | Carlos Beltran | .12 | .30 |
| ☐ 160 | Lance Berkman | .12 | .30 |
| ☐ 161 | Gary Matthews | .12 | .30 |
| ☐ 162 | Jeff Francis | .12 | .30 |
| ☐ 163 | Vernon Wells | .12 | .30 |
| ☐ 164 | Dontrelle Willis | .12 | .30 |
| ☐ 165 | Travis Hafner | .12 | .30 |
| ☐ 166 | Brian Bannister | .12 | .30 |
| ☐ 167 | Carlos Pena | .30 | .75 |
| ☐ 168 | Raul Ibanez | .20 | .50 |
| ☐ 169 | Aramis Ramirez | .12 | .30 |
| ☐ 170 | Eric Byrnes | .12 | .30 |
| ☐ 171 | Greg Maddux | .40 | 1.00 |
| ☐ 172 | John Smoltz | .30 | .75 |
| ☐ 173 | Jarrod Saltalamacchia | .12 | .30 |
| ☐ 174 | Hideki Okajima | .20 | .50 |
| ☐ 175 | Javier Vazquez | .12 | .30 |
| ☐ 176 | Aaron Harang | .12 | .30 |
| ☐ 177 | Jhonny Peralta | .12 | .30 |
| ☐ 178 | Carlos Lee | .12 | .30 |
| ☐ 179 | Ryan Braun | .40 | 1.00 |
| ☐ 180 | Torii Hunter | .12 | .30 |
| ☐ 181 | Hideki Matsui | .30 | .75 |
| ☐ 182 | Eric Chavez | .12 | .30 |
| ☐ 183 | Freddy Sanchez | .12 | .30 |
| ☐ 184 | Adrian Gonzalez | .20 | .50 |
| ☐ 185 | Bengie Molina | .12 | .30 |
| ☐ 186 | Kenji Johjima | .12 | .30 |
| ☐ 187 | Carl Crawford | .12 | .30 |
| ☐ 188 | Chipper Jones | .40 | 1.00 |
| ☐ 189 | Chris Young | .12 | .30 |
| ☐ 190 | Michael Young | .12 | .30 |
| ☐ 191 | Troy Glaus | .20 | .50 |
| ☐ 192 | Ryan Zimmerman | .20 | .50 |
| ☐ 193 | Brian Giles | .12 | .30 |
| ☐ 194 | Troy Tulowitzki | .20 | .50 |
| ☐ 195 | Chin-Lung Hu (RC) | .30 | .75 |
| ☐ 196 | Seth Smith (RC) | .20 | .50 |
| ☐ 197 | Wladimir Balentien (RC) | .20 | .50 |
| ☐ 198 | Rich Thompson RC | .30 | .75 |
| ☐ 199 | Radhames Liz RC | .30 | .75 |
| ☐ 200 | Ross Detwiler RC | .50 | 1.25 |
| ☐ 201 | Sam Fuld RC | .20 | .50 |
| ☐ 202 | Clint Sammons (RC) | .20 | .50 |
| ☐ 203 | Ross Ohlendorf RC | .30 | .75 |
| ☐ 204 | Jonathan Albaladejo RC | .30 | .75 |
| ☐ 205 | Brandon Jones RC | .50 | 1.25 |
| ☐ 206 | Steve Pearce RC | .30 | .75 |
| ☐ 207 | Kevin Hart (RC) | .20 | .50 |
| ☐ 208 | Luke Hochevar RC | .30 | .75 |
| ☐ 209 | Troy Patton (RC) | .20 | .50 |
| ☐ 210 | Josh Anderson (RC) | .20 | .50 |
| ☐ 211 | Clay Buchholz (RC) | .50 | 1.25 |
| ☐ 212 | Joe Koshansky (RC) | .20 | .50 |
| ☐ 213 | Bronson Sardinha (RC) | .20 | .50 |
| ☐ 214 | Emilio Bonifacio RC | .50 | 1.25 |
| ☐ 215 | Daric Barton (RC) | .30 | .75 |
| ☐ 216 | Lance Broadway (RC) | .20 | .50 |
| ☐ 217 | Jeff Clement (RC) | .30 | .75 |
| ☐ 218 | Joey Votto (RC) | .50 | 1.25 |
| ☐ 219 | J.R. Towles RC | .30 | .75 |
| ☐ 220 | Nyjer Morgan (RC) | .20 | .50 |

## 2002 Topps Total

|  |  | | |
|---|---|---|---|
| ☐ | COMPLETE SET (990) | 75.00 | 150.00 |
| ☐ 1 | Joe Mauer RC | 4.00 | 10.00 |
| ☐ 2 | Derek Jeter | .75 | 2.00 |
| ☐ 3 | Shawn Green | .10 | .30 |
| ☐ 4 | Vladimir Guerrero | .30 | .75 |
| ☐ 5 | Mike Piazza | .50 | 1.25 |
| ☐ 6 | Brandon Duckworth | .07 | .20 |
| ☐ 7 | Aramis Ramirez | .10 | .30 |
| ☐ 8 | Josh Barfield RC | 1.00 | 2.50 |
| ☐ 9 | Troy Glaus | .10 | .30 |
| ☐ 10 | Sammy Sosa | .30 | .75 |
| ☐ 11 | Rod Barajas | .07 | .20 |
| ☐ 12 | Tsuyoshi Shinjo | .10 | .30 |
| ☐ 13 | Larry Bigbie | .07 | .20 |
| ☐ 14 | Tino Martinez | .20 | .50 |
| ☐ 15 | Craig Biggio | .20 | .50 |
| ☐ 16 | Anastacio Martinez RC | .15 | .40 |
| ☐ 17 | John McDonald | .07 | .20 |
| ☐ 18 | Kyle Kane RC | .08 | .25 |
| ☐ 19 | Aubrey Huff | .07 | .20 |
| ☐ 20 | Juan Cruz | .07 | .20 |
| ☐ 21 | Doug Creek | .07 | .20 |
| ☐ 22 | Luther Hackman | .07 | .20 |
| ☐ 23 | Rafael Furcal | .10 | .30 |
| ☐ 24 | Andres Torres | .07 | .20 |
| ☐ 25 | Jason Giambi | .10 | .30 |
| ☐ 26 | Jose Paniagua | .07 | .20 |
| ☐ 27 | Jose Offerman | .07 | .20 |
| ☐ 28 | Alex Arias | .07 | .20 |
| ☐ 29 | J.M. Gold | .07 | .20 |
| ☐ 30 | Jeff Bagwell | .20 | .50 |
| ☐ 31 | Brent Cookson | .07 | .20 |
| ☐ 32 | Kelly Wunsch | .07 | .20 |
| ☐ 33 | Larry Walker | .07 | .20 |
| ☐ 34 | Luis Gonzalez | .10 | .30 |
| ☐ 35 | John Franco | .10 | .30 |
| ☐ 36 | Roy Oswalt | .20 | .50 |
| ☐ 37 | Tom Glavine | .20 | .50 |
| ☐ 38 | C.C. Sabathia | .10 | .30 |
| ☐ 39 | Jay Gibbons | .07 | .20 |
| ☐ 40 | Wilson Betemit | .07 | .20 |
| ☐ 41 | Tony Armas Jr. | .07 | .20 |
| ☐ 42 | Mo Vaughn | .10 | .30 |
| ☐ 43 | Gerard Oakes RC | .15 | .40 |
| ☐ 44 | Dmitri Young | .10 | .30 |
| ☐ 45 | Tim Salmon | .20 | .50 |
| ☐ 46 | Barry Zito | .10 | .30 |
| ☐ 47 | Adrian Gonzalez | .20 | .50 |
| ☐ 48 | Jose Davenport | .07 | .20 |
| ☐ 49 | Adrian Hernandez | .07 | .20 |
| ☐ 50 | Randy Johnson | .30 | .75 |
| ☐ 52 | Adam Pettyjohn | .07 | .20 |
| ☐ 53 | Alex Escobar | .07 | .20 |
| ☐ 54 | Stevenson Agosto RC | .08 | .25 |
| ☐ 55 | Omar Daal | .07 | .20 |
| ☐ 56 | Mike Buddie | .07 | .20 |
| ☐ 57 | Dave Williams | .07 | .20 |
| ☐ 58 | Marquis Grissom | .10 | .30 |
| ☐ 59 | Pat Burrell | .10 | .30 |
| ☐ 60 | Mark Prior | .20 | .50 |
| ☐ 61 | Mike Bynum | .07 | .20 |
| ☐ 62 | Mike Hill RC | .15 | .40 |
| ☐ 63 | Brandon Backe RC | .20 | .50 |
| ☐ 64 | Dan Wilson | .07 | .20 |
| ☐ 65 | Nick Johnson | .10 | .30 |
| ☐ 66 | Jason Grimsley | .07 | .20 |
| ☐ 67 | Russ Johnson | .07 | .20 |
| ☐ 68 | Todd Walker | .07 | .20 |
| ☐ 69 | Kyle Farnsworth | .07 | .20 |
| ☐ 70 | Ben Broussard | .07 | .20 |
| ☐ 71 | Garrett Guzman RC | .15 | .40 |
| ☐ 72 | Terry Mulholland | .07 | .20 |
| ☐ 73 | Tyler Houston | .07 | .20 |
| ☐ 74 | Jace Brewer | .07 | .20 |
| ☐ 75 | Chris Baker | .15 | .40 |
| ☐ 76 | Frank Catalanotto | .07 | .20 |
| ☐ 77 | Mike Redmond | .07 | .20 |
| ☐ 78 | Matt Wise | .07 | .20 |
| ☐ 79 | Fernando Vina | .07 | .20 |
| ☐ 80 | Kevin Brown | .10 | .30 |
| ☐ 81 | Grant Balfour | .07 | .20 |
| ☐ 82 | Clint Nageotte RC | .20 | .50 |
| ☐ 83 | Jeff Tam | .07 | .20 |
| ☐ 84 | Steve Trachsel | .07 | .20 |
| ☐ 85 | Tomo Ohka | .07 | .20 |
| ☐ 86 | Keith McDonald | .07 | .20 |
| ☐ 87 | Jose Ortiz | .07 | .20 |
| ☐ 88 | Rusty Greer | .10 | .30 |
| ☐ 89 | Jeff Suppan | .07 | .20 |
| ☐ 90 | Moises Alou | .10 | .30 |
| ☐ 91 | Juan Encarnacion | .07 | .20 |
| ☐ 92 | Tyler Yates RC | .15 | .40 |
| ☐ 93 | Scott Strickland | .07 | .20 |
| ☐ 94 | Brent Butler | .07 | .20 |
| ☐ 95 | Jon Rauch | .07 | .20 |
| ☐ 96 | Brian Mallette RC | .08 | .25 |
| ☐ 97 | Joe Randa | .10 | .30 |
| ☐ 98 | Cesar Crespo | .07 | .20 |
| ☐ 99 | Felix Rodriguez | .07 | .20 |
| ☐ 100 | Chipper Jones | .30 | .75 |
| ☐ 101 | Victor Martinez | .20 | .50 |
| ☐ 102 | Danny Graves | .07 | .20 |
| ☐ 103 | Brandon Berger | .07 | .20 |
| ☐ 104 | Carlos Garcia | .07 | .20 |
| ☐ 105 | Alfonso Soriano | .10 | .30 |
| ☐ 106 | Allan Simpson RC | .08 | .25 |
| ☐ 107 | Brad Thomas | .07 | .20 |
| ☐ 108 | Devon White | .10 | .30 |
| ☐ 109 | Scott Chiasson | .07 | .20 |
| ☐ 110 | Cliff Floyd | .10 | .30 |
| ☐ 111 | Scott Williamson | .07 | .20 |
| ☐ 112 | Julio Zuleta | .07 | .20 |
| ☐ 113 | Terry Adams | .07 | .20 |
| ☐ 114 | Zach Day | .07 | .20 |
| ☐ 115 | Ben Grieve | .07 | .20 |
| ☐ 116 | Mark Ellis | .07 | .20 |
| ☐ 117 | Bobby Jenks RC | .60 | 1.50 |
| ☐ 118 | LaTroy Hawkins | .07 | .20 |
| ☐ 119 | Tim Raines Jr. | .07 | .20 |
| ☐ 120 | Juan Uribe | .07 | .20 |
| ☐ 121 | Bob Scanlan | .07 | .20 |
| ☐ 122 | Brad Nelson RC | .15 | .40 |
| ☐ 123 | Adam Johnson | .07 | .20 |
| ☐ 124 | Raul Casanova | .07 | .20 |
| ☐ 125 | Jeff D'Amico | .07 | .20 |
| ☐ 126 | Aaron Cook RC | .15 | .40 |
| ☐ 127 | Alan Benes | .07 | .20 |
| ☐ 128 | Mark Little | .07 | .20 |
| ☐ 129 | Randy Wolf | .07 | .20 |
| ☐ 130 | Phil Nevin | .10 | .30 |
| ☐ 131 | Guillermo Mota | .07 | .20 |
| ☐ 132 | Nick Neugebauer | .07 | .20 |
| ☐ 133 | Pedro Borbon Jr. | .07 | .20 |
| ☐ 134 | Doug Mientkiewicz | .10 | .30 |
| ☐ 135 | Edgardo Alfonzo | .07 | .20 |
| ☐ 136 | Dustan Mohr | .07 | .20 |
| ☐ 137 | Dan Reichert | .07 | .20 |
| ☐ 138 | Dewon Brazelton | .10 | .30 |
| ☐ 139 | Orlando Cabrera | .10 | .30 |
| ☐ 140 | Todd Hollandsworth | .07 | .20 |

|  |  | | |
|---|---|---|---|
| ❏ 141 Darren Dreifort | .07 | .20 |
| ❏ 142 Jose Valentin | .07 | .20 |
| ❏ 143 Josh Kalinowski | .07 | .20 |
| ❏ 144 Randy Keisler | .07 | .20 |
| ❏ 145 Bret Boone | .10 | .30 |
| ❏ 146 Roosevelt Brown | .07 | .20 |
| ❏ 147 Brent Abernathy | .07 | .20 |
| ❏ 148 Jorge Julio | .07 | .20 |
| ❏ 149 Alex Gonzalez | .07 | .20 |
| ❏ 150 Juan Pierre | .10 | .30 |
| ❏ 151 Roger Cedeno | .07 | .20 |
| ❏ 152 Javier Vazquez | .10 | .30 |
| ❏ 153 Armando Benitez | .07 | .20 |
| ❏ 154 Dave Burba | .07 | .20 |
| ❏ 155 Brad Penny | .07 | .20 |
| ❏ 156 Ryan Jensen | .07 | .20 |
| ❏ 157 Jeromy Burnitz | .10 | .30 |
| ❏ 158 Matt Childers RC | .15 | .40 |
| ❏ 159 Wilmy Caceres | .07 | .20 |
| ❏ 160 Roger Clemens | .60 | 1.50 |
| ❏ 161 Jamie Cerda RC | .15 | .40 |
| ❏ 162 Jason Christiansen | .07 | .20 |
| ❏ 163 Pokey Reese | .07 | .20 |
| ❏ 164 Ivanon Coffie | .07 | .20 |
| ❏ 165 Joaquin Benoit | .07 | .20 |
| ❏ 166 Mike Matheny | .07 | .20 |
| ❏ 167 Eric Cammack | .07 | .20 |
| ❏ 168 Alex Graman | .07 | .20 |
| ❏ 169 Brook Fordyce | .07 | .20 |
| ❏ 170 Mike Lieberthal | .10 | .30 |
| ❏ 171 Giovanni Carrara | .07 | .20 |
| ❏ 172 Antonio Perez | .07 | .20 |
| ❏ 173 Fernando Tatis | .07 | .20 |
| ❏ 174 Jason Bay RC | 2.00 | 5.00 |
| ❏ 175 Jason Botts RC | .20 | .50 |
| ❏ 176 Danys Baez | .07 | .20 |
| ❏ 177 Shea Hillenbrand | .10 | .30 |
| ❏ 178 Jack Cust | .07 | .20 |
| ❏ 179 Clay Bellinger | .07 | .20 |
| ❏ 180 Roberto Alomar | .20 | .50 |
| ❏ 181 Graeme Lloyd | .07 | .20 |
| ❏ 182 Clint Weibl RC | .08 | .25 |
| ❏ 183 Royce Clayton | .07 | .20 |
| ❏ 184 Ben Davis | .07 | .20 |
| ❏ 185 Brian Adams RC | .08 | .25 |
| ❏ 186 Jack Wilson | .07 | .20 |
| ❏ 187 David Coggin | .07 | .20 |
| ❏ 188 Derrick Turnbow | .07 | .20 |
| ❏ 189 Vladimir Nunez | .07 | .20 |
| ❏ 190 Mariano Rivera | .30 | .75 |
| ❏ 191 Wilson Guzman | .07 | .20 |
| ❏ 192 Michael Barrett | .07 | .20 |
| ❏ 193 Corey Patterson | .07 | .20 |
| ❏ 194 Luis Sojo | .07 | .20 |
| ❏ 195 Scott Elarton | .07 | .20 |
| ❏ 196 Charles Thomas RC | .15 | .40 |
| ❏ 197 Ricky Bottalico | .07 | .20 |
| ❏ 198 Wilfredo Rodriguez | .07 | .20 |
| ❏ 199 Ricardo Rincon | .07 | .20 |
| ❏ 200 John Smoltz | .20 | .50 |
| ❏ 201 Travis Miller | .07 | .20 |
| ❏ 202 Ben Weber | .07 | .20 |
| ❏ 203 T.J. Tucker | .07 | .20 |
| ❏ 204 Terry Shumpert | .07 | .20 |
| ❏ 205 Bernie Williams | .20 | .50 |
| ❏ 206 Russ Ortiz | .07 | .20 |
| ❏ 207 Nate Rolison | .07 | .20 |
| ❏ 208 Jose Cruz Jr. | .07 | .20 |
| ❏ 209 Bill Ortega | .07 | .20 |
| ❏ 210 Carl Everett | .10 | .30 |
| ❏ 211 Luis Lopez | .07 | .20 |
| ❏ 212 Brian Wolfe RC | .15 | .40 |
| ❏ 213 Doug Davis | .07 | .20 |
| ❏ 214 Troy Mattes | .07 | .20 |
| ❏ 215 Al Leiter | .10 | .30 |
| ❏ 216 Joe Mays | .07 | .20 |
| ❏ 217 Bobby Smith | .07 | .20 |
| ❏ 218 J.J. Trujillo RC | .15 | .40 |
| ❏ 219 Hideo Nomo | .30 | .75 |
| ❏ 220 Jimmy Rollins | .10 | .30 |
| ❏ 221 Bobby Seay | .07 | .20 |
| ❏ 222 Mike Thurman | .07 | .20 |
| ❏ 223 Bartolo Colon | .10 | .30 |
| ❏ 224 Jesus Sanchez | .07 | .20 |
| ❏ 225 Ray Durham | .10 | .30 |
| ❏ 226 Juan Diaz | .07 | .20 |
| ❏ 227 Lee Stevens | .07 | .20 |
| ❏ 228 Ben Howard RC | .15 | .40 |
| ❏ 229 James Mouton | .07 | .20 |
| ❏ 230 Paul Quantrill | .07 | .20 |
| ❏ 231 Randy Knorr | .07 | .20 |
| ❏ 232 Abraham Nunez | .07 | .20 |
| ❏ 233 Mike Fetters | .07 | .20 |
| ❏ 234 Mario Encarnacion | .07 | .20 |
| ❏ 235 Jeremy Fikac | .07 | .20 |
| ❏ 236 Travis Lee | .07 | .20 |
| ❏ 237 Bob File | .07 | .20 |
| ❏ 238 Pete Harnisch | .07 | .20 |
| ❏ 239 Randy Galvez RC | .15 | .40 |
| ❏ 240 Geoff Goetz | .07 | .20 |
| ❏ 241 Gary Glover | .07 | .20 |
| ❏ 242 Troy Percival | .10 | .30 |
| ❏ 243 Len Dinardo RC | .15 | .40 |
| ❏ 244 Jonny Gomes RC | 1.00 | 2.50 |
| ❏ 245 Jesus Medrano RC | .15 | .40 |
| ❏ 246 Rey Ordonez | .07 | .20 |
| ❏ 247 Juan Gonzalez | .10 | .30 |
| ❏ 248 Jose Guillen | .07 | .20 |
| ❏ 249 Franklyn German RC | .15 | .40 |
| ❏ 250 Mike Mussina | .20 | .50 |
| ❏ 251 Ugueth Urbina | .07 | .20 |
| ❏ 252 Melvin Mora | .10 | .30 |
| ❏ 253 Gerald Williams | .07 | .20 |
| ❏ 254 Jared Sandberg | .07 | .20 |
| ❏ 255 Darrin Fletcher | .07 | .20 |
| ❏ 256 A.J. Pierzynski | .10 | .30 |
| ❏ 257 Lenny Harris | .07 | .20 |
| ❏ 258 Blaine Neal | .07 | .20 |
| ❏ 259 Denny Neagle | .07 | .20 |
| ❏ 260 Jason Hart | .07 | .20 |
| ❏ 261 Henry Mateo | .07 | .20 |
| ❏ 262 Rheal Cormier | .07 | .20 |
| ❏ 263 Luis Terrero | .07 | .20 |
| ❏ 264 Shigetoshi Hasegawa | .10 | .30 |
| ❏ 265 Bill Haselman | .07 | .20 |
| ❏ 266 Scott Hatteberg | .07 | .20 |
| ❏ 267 Adam Hyzdu | .07 | .20 |
| ❏ 268 Mike Williams | .07 | .20 |
| ❏ 269 Marlon Anderson | .07 | .20 |
| ❏ 270 Bruce Chen | .07 | .20 |
| ❏ 271 Eli Marrero | .07 | .20 |
| ❏ 272 Jimmy Haynes | .07 | .20 |
| ❏ 273 Bronson Arroyo | .10 | .30 |
| ❏ 274 Kevin Jordan | .07 | .20 |
| ❏ 275 Rick Helling | .07 | .20 |
| ❏ 276 Mark Loretta | .07 | .20 |
| ❏ 277 Dustin Hermanson | .07 | .20 |
| ❏ 278 Pablo Ozuna | .07 | .20 |
| ❏ 279 Keto Anderson RC | .15 | .40 |
| ❏ 280 Jermaine Dye | .10 | .30 |
| ❏ 281 Will Smith | .07 | .20 |
| ❏ 282 Brian Daubach | .07 | .20 |
| ❏ 283 Eric Hinske | .07 | .20 |
| ❏ 284 Joe Jiannetti RC | .15 | .40 |
| ❏ 285 Chan Ho Park | .10 | .30 |
| ❏ 286 Curtis Legendre RC | .15 | .40 |
| ❏ 287 Jeff Reboulet | .07 | .20 |
| ❏ 288 Scott Rolen | .20 | .50 |
| ❏ 289 Chris Richard | .07 | .20 |
| ❏ 290 Eric Chavez | .10 | .30 |
| ❏ 291 Scot Shields | .07 | .20 |
| ❏ 292 Donnie Sadler | .07 | .20 |
| ❏ 293 Dave Veres | .07 | .20 |
| ❏ 294 Craig Counsell | .07 | .20 |
| ❏ 295 Armando Reynoso | .07 | .20 |
| ❏ 296 Kyle Lohse | .07 | .20 |
| ❏ 297 Arthur Rhodes | .07 | .20 |
| ❏ 298 Sidney Ponson | .07 | .20 |
| ❏ 299 Trevor Hoffman | .10 | .30 |
| ❏ 300 Kerry Wood | .10 | .30 |
| ❏ 301 Danny Bautista | .07 | .20 |
| ❏ 302 Scott Sauerbeck | .07 | .20 |
| ❏ 303 Johnny Estrada | .07 | .20 |
| ❏ 304 Mike Timlin | .07 | .20 |
| ❏ 305 Orlando Hernandez | .10 | .30 |
| ❏ 306 Tony Clark | .07 | .20 |
| ❏ 307 Tomas Perez | .07 | .20 |
| ❏ 308 Marcus Giles | .10 | .30 |
| ❏ 309 Mike Bordick | .10 | .30 |
| ❏ 310 Jorge Posada | .20 | .50 |
| ❏ 311 Jason Conti | .07 | .20 |
| ❏ 312 Kevin Millar | .10 | .30 |
| ❏ 313 Paul Shuey | .07 | .20 |
| ❏ 314 Jake Mauer RC | .15 | .40 |
| ❏ 315 Luke Hudson | .07 | .20 |
| ❏ 316 Angel Berroa | .07 | .20 |
| ❏ 317 Fred Bastardo RC | .15 | .40 |
| ❏ 318 Shawn Estes | .07 | .20 |
| ❏ 319 Andy Ashby | .07 | .20 |
| ❏ 320 Ryan Klecko | .10 | .30 |
| ❏ 321 Kevin Appier | .10 | .30 |
| ❏ 322 Juan Pena | .07 | .20 |
| ❏ 323 Alex Herrera | .07 | .20 |
| ❏ 324 Robb Nen | .10 | .30 |
| ❏ 325 Orlando Hudson | .07 | .20 |
| ❏ 326 Lyle Overbay | .07 | .20 |
| ❏ 327 Ben Sheets | .10 | .30 |
| ❏ 328 Mike DiFelice | .07 | .20 |
| ❏ 329 Pablo Arias RC | .15 | .40 |
| ❏ 330 Mike Sweeney | .10 | .30 |
| ❏ 331 Rick Ankiel | .07 | .20 |
| ❏ 332 Tomas De La Rosa | .07 | .20 |
| ❏ 333 Kazuhisa Ishii RC | .20 | .50 |
| ❏ 334 Jose Reyes | .20 | .50 |
| ❏ 335 Jeremy Giambi | .07 | .20 |
| ❏ 336 Jose Mesa | .07 | .20 |
| ❏ 337 Ralph Roberts RC | .15 | .40 |
| ❏ 338 Jose Nunez | .07 | .20 |
| ❏ 339 Curt Schilling | .10 | .30 |
| ❏ 340 Sean Casey | .10 | .30 |
| ❏ 341 Bob Wells | .07 | .20 |
| ❏ 342 Carlos Beltran | .10 | .30 |
| ❏ 343 Alexis Gomez | .07 | .20 |
| ❏ 344 Brandon Claussen | .07 | .20 |
| ❏ 345 Buddy Groom | .07 | .20 |
| ❏ 346 Mark Phillips RC | .15 | .40 |
| ❏ 347 Francisco Cordova | .07 | .20 |
| ❏ 348 Joe Oliver | .07 | .20 |
| ❏ 349 Danny Patterson | .07 | .20 |
| ❏ 350 Joel Pineiro | .07 | .20 |
| ❏ 351 J.R. House | .07 | .20 |
| ❏ 352 Benny Agbayani | .07 | .20 |
| ❏ 353 Jose Vidro | .07 | .20 |
| ❏ 354 Reed Johnson RC | .40 | 1.00 |
| ❏ 355 Mike Lowell | .10 | .30 |
| ❏ 356 Scott Schoeneweis | .07 | .20 |
| ❏ 357 Brian Jordan | .07 | .20 |
| ❏ 358 Steve Finley | .10 | .30 |
| ❏ 359 Randy Choate | .07 | .20 |
| ❏ 360 Jose Lima | .07 | .20 |
| ❏ 361 Miguel Olivo | .07 | .20 |
| ❏ 362 Kenny Rogers | .10 | .30 |
| ❏ 363 David Justice | .10 | .30 |
| ❏ 364 Brandon Knight | .07 | .20 |
| ❏ 365 Joe Kennedy | .07 | .20 |
| ❏ 366 Eric Valent | .07 | .20 |
| ❏ 367 Nelson Cruz | .07 | .20 |
| ❏ 368 Brian Giles | .10 | .30 |
| ❏ 369 Charles Gipson RC | .08 | .25 |
| ❏ 370 Juan Pena | .07 | .20 |
| ❏ 371 Mark Redman | .07 | .20 |
| ❏ 372 Billy Koch | .07 | .20 |
| ❏ 373 Ted Lilly | .07 | .20 |
| ❏ 374 Craig Paquette | .07 | .20 |
| ❏ 375 Kevin Jarvis | .07 | .20 |
| ❏ 376 Scott Erickson | .07 | .20 |
| ❏ 377 Josh Paul | .07 | .20 |
| ❏ 378 Darwin Cubillan | .07 | .20 |
| ❏ 379 Nelson Figueroa | .07 | .20 |
| ❏ 380 Darin Erstad | .10 | .30 |
| ❏ 381 Jeremy Hill RC | .15 | .40 |
| ❏ 382 Elvin Nina | .07 | .20 |
| ❏ 383 David Wells | .10 | .30 |
| ❏ 384 Jay Caligiuri RC | .15 | .40 |
| ❏ 385 Freddy Garcia | .07 | .20 |
| ❏ 386 Damian Miller | .07 | .20 |
| ❏ 387 Bobby Higginson | .10 | .30 |
| ❏ 388 Alejandro Giron RC | .15 | .40 |
| ❏ 389 Ivan Rodriguez | .20 | .50 |
| ❏ 390 Ed Rogers | .07 | .20 |
| ❏ 391 Andy Benes | .07 | .20 |
| ❏ 392 Matt Blank | .07 | .20 |
| ❏ 393 Ryan Vogelsong | .07 | .20 |
| ❏ 394 Kelly Ramos RC | .08 | .25 |
| ❏ 395 Eric Karros | .10 | .30 |
| ❏ 396 Bobby J. Jones | .07 | .20 |
| ❏ 397 Omar Vizquel | .20 | .50 |
| ❏ 398 Matt Perisho | .07 | .20 |
| ❏ 399 Delino DeShields | .07 | .20 |
| ❏ 400 Carlos Hernandez | .07 | .20 |
| ❏ 401 Derek Lee | .20 | .50 |
| ❏ 402 Kirk Rueter | .07 | .20 |
| ❏ 403 David Wright RC | 12.50 | 30.00 |
| ❏ 404 Paul LoDuca | .10 | .30 |

|  |  | | |
|---|---|---|---|
| ☐ 405 | Brian Schneider | .07 | .20 |
| ☐ 406 | Milton Bradley | .10 | .30 |
| ☐ 407 | Daryle Ward | .07 | .20 |
| ☐ 408 | Cody Ransom | .07 | .20 |
| ☐ 409 | Fernando Rodney | .07 | .20 |
| ☐ 410 | John Suomi RC | .15 | .40 |
| ☐ 411 | Joe Girardi | .07 | .20 |
| ☐ 412 | Demetrius Heath RC | .15 | .40 |
| ☐ 413 | John Foster RC | .15 | .40 |
| ☐ 414 | Doug Glanville | .07 | .20 |
| ☐ 415 | Ryan Kohlmeier | .07 | .20 |
| ☐ 416 | Mike Matthews | .07 | .20 |
| ☐ 417 | Craig Wilson | .07 | .20 |
| ☐ 418 | Jay Witasick | .07 | .20 |
| ☐ 419 | Jay Payton | .07 | .20 |
| ☐ 420 | Andruw Jones | .20 | .50 |
| ☐ 421 | Benji Gil | .07 | .20 |
| ☐ 422 | Jeff Liefer | .07 | .20 |
| ☐ 423 | Kevin Young | .07 | .20 |
| ☐ 424 | Richie Sexson | .10 | .30 |
| ☐ 425 | Cory Lidle | .07 | .20 |
| ☐ 426 | Shane Halter | .07 | .20 |
| ☐ 427 | Jesse Foppert RC | .20 | .50 |
| ☐ 428 | Jose Molina | .07 | .20 |
| ☐ 429 | Nick Alvarez RC | .15 | .40 |
| ☐ 430 | Brian L. Hunter | .07 | .20 |
| ☐ 431 | Cliff Bartosh RC | .15 | .40 |
| ☐ 432 | Junior Spivey | .07 | .20 |
| ☐ 433 | Eric Good RC | .15 | .40 |
| ☐ 434 | Chin-Feng Chen | .10 | .30 |
| ☐ 435 | T.J. Mathews | .07 | .20 |
| ☐ 436 | Rich Rodriguez | .07 | .20 |
| ☐ 437 | Bobby Abreu | .10 | .30 |
| ☐ 438 | Joe McEwing | .07 | .20 |
| ☐ 439 | Michael Tucker | .07 | .20 |
| ☐ 440 | Preston Wilson | .10 | .30 |
| ☐ 441 | Mike MacDougal | .07 | .20 |
| ☐ 442 | Shannon Stewart | .10 | .30 |
| ☐ 443 | Bob Howry | .07 | .20 |
| ☐ 444 | Mike Benjamin | .07 | .20 |
| ☐ 445 | Erik Hiljus | .07 | .20 |
| ☐ 446 | Ryan Gripp RC | .15 | .40 |
| ☐ 447 | Jose Vizcaino | .07 | .20 |
| ☐ 448 | Shawn Wooten | .07 | .20 |
| ☐ 449 | Steve Kent RC | .15 | .40 |
| ☐ 450 | Ramiro Mendoza | .07 | .20 |
| ☐ 451 | Jake Westbrook | .07 | .20 |
| ☐ 452 | Joe Lawrence | .07 | .20 |
| ☐ 453 | Jae Seo | .07 | .20 |
| ☐ 454 | Ryan Fry RC | .15 | .40 |
| ☐ 455 | Darren Lewis | .07 | .20 |
| ☐ 456 | Brad Wilkerson | .07 | .20 |
| ☐ 457 | Gustavo Chacin RC | .40 | 1.00 |
| ☐ 458 | Adrian Brown | .07 | .20 |
| ☐ 459 | Mike Cameron | .07 | .20 |
| ☐ 460 | Bud Smith | .07 | .20 |
| ☐ 461 | Derrick Lewis | .07 | .20 |
| ☐ 462 | Derek Lowe | .10 | .30 |
| ☐ 463 | Matt Williams | .10 | .30 |
| ☐ 464 | Jason Jennings | .07 | .20 |
| ☐ 465 | Albie Lopez | .07 | .20 |
| ☐ 466 | Felipe Lopez | .07 | .20 |
| ☐ 467 | Luke Allen | .07 | .20 |
| ☐ 468 | Brian Anderson | .07 | .20 |
| ☐ 469 | Matt Riley | .07 | .20 |
| ☐ 470 | Ryan Dempster | .07 | .20 |
| ☐ 471 | Matt Ginter | .07 | .20 |
| ☐ 472 | David Ortiz | .30 | .75 |
| ☐ 473 | Cole Barthel RC | .08 | .25 |
| ☐ 474 | Damian Jackson | .07 | .20 |
| ☐ 475 | Andy Van Hekken | .07 | .20 |
| ☐ 476 | Doug Brocail | .07 | .20 |
| ☐ 477 | Denny Hocking | .07 | .20 |
| ☐ 478 | Sean Douglass | .07 | .20 |
| ☐ 479 | Eric Owens | .07 | .20 |
| ☐ 480 | Ryan Ludwick | .07 | .20 |
| ☐ 481 | Todd Pratt | .07 | .20 |
| ☐ 482 | Aaron Sele | .07 | .20 |
| ☐ 483 | Edgar Renteria | .10 | .30 |
| ☐ 484 | Raymond Cabrera RC | .15 | .40 |
| ☐ 485 | Brandon Lyon | .07 | .20 |
| ☐ 486 | Chase Utley RC | 1.00 | 2.50 |
| ☐ 487 | Robert Fick | .07 | .20 |
| ☐ 488 | Wilfredo Cordero | .07 | .20 |
| ☐ 489 | Octavio Dotel | .07 | .20 |
| ☐ 490 | Paul Abbott | .07 | .20 |
| ☐ 491 | Jason Kendall | .10 | .30 |
| ☐ 492 | Jarrod Washburn | .07 | .20 |
| ☐ 493 | Dane Sardinha | .07 | .20 |
| ☐ 494 | Jung Bong | .07 | .20 |
| ☐ 495 | J.D. Drew | .10 | .30 |
| ☐ 496 | Jason Schmidt | .10 | .30 |
| ☐ 497 | Mike Magnante | .07 | .20 |
| ☐ 498 | Jorge Padilla RC | .15 | .40 |
| ☐ 499 | Eric Gagne | .10 | .30 |
| ☐ 500 | Todd Helton | .20 | .50 |
| ☐ 501 | Jeff Weaver | .07 | .20 |
| ☐ 502 | Alex Sanchez | .07 | .20 |
| ☐ 503 | Ken Griffey Jr. | .50 | 1.25 |
| ☐ 504 | Abraham Nunez | .07 | .20 |
| ☐ 505 | Reggie Sanders | .10 | .30 |
| ☐ 506 | Casey Kotchman RC | .40 | 1.00 |
| ☐ 507 | Jim Mann | .07 | .20 |
| ☐ 508 | Matt LeCroy | .07 | .20 |
| ☐ 509 | Frank Castillo | .07 | .20 |
| ☐ 510 | Geoff Jenkins | .07 | .20 |
| ☐ 511 | Jayson Durocher | .08 | .25 |
| ☐ 512 | Ellis Burks | .07 | .20 |
| ☐ 513 | Aaron Fultz | .07 | .20 |
| ☐ 514 | Hiram Bocachica | .07 | .20 |
| ☐ 515 | Nate Espy RC | .15 | .40 |
| ☐ 516 | Placido Polanco | .07 | .20 |
| ☐ 517 | Kerry Ligtenberg | .07 | .20 |
| ☐ 518 | Doug Nickle | .07 | .20 |
| ☐ 519 | Ramon Ortiz | .07 | .20 |
| ☐ 520 | Greg Swindell | .07 | .20 |
| ☐ 521 | J.J. Davis | .07 | .20 |
| ☐ 522 | Sandy Alomar Jr. | .07 | .20 |
| ☐ 523 | Chris Carpenter | .10 | .30 |
| ☐ 524 | Vance Wilson | .07 | .20 |
| ☐ 525 | Nomar Garciaparra | .50 | 1.25 |
| ☐ 526 | Jim Mecir | .07 | .20 |
| ☐ 527 | Taylor Buchholz RC | .20 | .50 |
| ☐ 528 | Brent Mayne | .07 | .20 |
| ☐ 529 | John Rodriguez RC | .20 | .50 |
| ☐ 530 | David Segui | .07 | .20 |
| ☐ 531 | Nate Cornejo | .07 | .20 |
| ☐ 532 | Gil Heredia | .07 | .20 |
| ☐ 533 | Esteban Loaiza | .07 | .20 |
| ☐ 534 | Pat Mahomes | .07 | .20 |
| ☐ 535 | Matt Morris | .10 | .30 |
| ☐ 536 | Todd Stottlemyre | .07 | .20 |
| ☐ 537 | Brian Lesher | .07 | .20 |
| ☐ 538 | Arturo McDowell | .07 | .20 |
| ☐ 539 | Felix Diaz | .07 | .20 |
| ☐ 540 | Mark Mulder | .10 | .30 |
| ☐ 541 | Kevin Frederick RC | .15 | .40 |
| ☐ 542 | Andy Fox | .07 | .20 |
| ☐ 543 | Dionys Cesar RC | .08 | .25 |
| ☐ 544 | Justin Miller | .07 | .20 |
| ☐ 545 | Keith Osik | .07 | .20 |
| ☐ 546 | Shane Reynolds | .07 | .20 |
| ☐ 547 | Mike Myers | .07 | .20 |
| ☐ 548 | Raul Chavez RC | .08 | .25 |
| ☐ 549 | Joe Nathan | .10 | .30 |
| ☐ 550 | Rayan Anderson | .07 | .20 |
| ☐ 551 | Jason Marquis | .07 | .20 |
| ☐ 552 | Marty Cordova | .07 | .20 |
| ☐ 553 | Kevin Tapani | .07 | .20 |
| ☐ 554 | Jimmy Anderson | .07 | .20 |
| ☐ 555 | Pedro Martinez | .20 | .50 |
| ☐ 556 | Rocky Biddle | .07 | .20 |
| ☐ 557 | Alex Ochoa | .07 | .20 |
| ☐ 558 | D'Angelo Jimenez | .07 | .20 |
| ☐ 559 | Wilkin Ruan | .07 | .20 |
| ☐ 560 | Terrence Long | .07 | .20 |
| ☐ 561 | Mark Lukasiewicz | .07 | .20 |
| ☐ 562 | Jose Santiago | .07 | .20 |
| ☐ 563 | Brad Fullmer | .07 | .20 |
| ☐ 564 | Corky Miller | .07 | .20 |
| ☐ 565 | Matt White | .07 | .20 |
| ☐ 566 | Mark Grace | .20 | .50 |
| ☐ 567 | Raul Ibanez | .07 | .20 |
| ☐ 568 | Josh Towers | .07 | .20 |
| ☐ 569 | Juan M. Gonzalez RC | .15 | .40 |
| ☐ 570 | Brian Buchanan | .07 | .20 |
| ☐ 571 | Ken Harvey | .07 | .20 |
| ☐ 572 | Jeffrey Hammonds | .07 | .20 |
| ☐ 573 | Wade Miller | .07 | .20 |
| ☐ 574 | Elpidio Guzman | .07 | .20 |
| ☐ 575 | Kevin Olsen | .07 | .20 |
| ☐ 576 | Austin Kearns | .07 | .20 |
| ☐ 577 | Tim Kalita RC | .15 | .40 |
| ☐ 578 | David Dellucci | .07 | .20 |
| ☐ 579 | Alex Gonzalez | .07 | .20 |
| ☐ 580 | Joe Orloski RC | .15 | .40 |
| ☐ 581 | Gary Matthews Jr. | .07 | .20 |
| ☐ 582 | Ryan Mills | .07 | .20 |
| ☐ 583 | Erick Almonte | .07 | .20 |
| ☐ 584 | Jeremy Affeldt | .07 | .20 |
| ☐ 585 | Chris Tritle RC | .08 | .25 |
| ☐ 586 | Michael Cuddyer | .07 | .20 |
| ☐ 587 | Kris Foster | .07 | .20 |
| ☐ 588 | Russell Branyan | .07 | .20 |
| ☐ 589 | Darren Oliver | .07 | .20 |
| ☐ 590 | Frankie Money RC | .15 | .40 |
| ☐ 591 | Carlos Lee | .10 | .30 |
| ☐ 592 | Tim Wakefield | .10 | .30 |
| ☐ 593 | Bubba Trammell | .07 | .20 |
| ☐ 594 | John Koronka RC | .40 | 1.00 |
| ☐ 595 | Geoff Blum | .07 | .20 |
| ☐ 596 | Darryl Kile | .10 | .30 |
| ☐ 597 | Neifi Perez | .07 | .20 |
| ☐ 598 | Torii Hunter | .10 | .30 |
| ☐ 599 | Luis Castillo | .07 | .20 |
| ☐ 600 | Mark Buehrle | .10 | .30 |
| ☐ 601 | Jeff Zimmerman | .07 | .20 |
| ☐ 602 | Mike DeJean | .07 | .20 |
| ☐ 603 | Julio Lugo | .07 | .20 |
| ☐ 604 | Chad Hermansen | .07 | .20 |
| ☐ 605 | Keith Foulke | .10 | .30 |
| ☐ 606 | Lance Davis | .07 | .20 |
| ☐ 607 | Jeff Austin RC | .15 | .40 |
| ☐ 608 | Brandon Inge | .07 | .20 |
| ☐ 609 | Orlando Merced | .07 | .20 |
| ☐ 610 | Johnny Damon Sox | .20 | .50 |
| ☐ 611 | Doug Henry | .07 | .20 |
| ☐ 612 | Adam Kennedy | .07 | .20 |
| ☐ 613 | Wiki Gonzalez | .07 | .20 |
| ☐ 614 | Brian West RC | .15 | .40 |
| ☐ 615 | Andy Pettitte | .20 | .50 |
| ☐ 616 | Chone Figgins RC | .60 | 1.50 |
| ☐ 617 | Matt Lawton | .07 | .20 |
| ☐ 618 | Paul Rigdon | .07 | .20 |
| ☐ 619 | Keith Lockhart | .07 | .20 |
| ☐ 620 | Tim Redding | .07 | .20 |
| ☐ 621 | John Parrish | .07 | .20 |
| ☐ 622 | Homer Bush | .07 | .20 |
| ☐ 623 | Todd Greene | .07 | .20 |
| ☐ 624 | David Eckstein | .10 | .30 |
| ☐ 625 | Greg Montalbano RC | .15 | .40 |
| ☐ 626 | Joe Beimel | .07 | .20 |
| ☐ 627 | Adrian Beltre | .10 | .30 |
| ☐ 628 | Charles Nagy | .07 | .20 |
| ☐ 629 | Cristian Guzman | .07 | .20 |
| ☐ 630 | Toby Hall | .07 | .20 |
| ☐ 631 | Jose Hernandez | .07 | .20 |
| ☐ 632 | Jose Macias | .07 | .20 |
| ☐ 633 | Jarat Wright | .07 | .20 |
| ☐ 634 | Steve Parris | .07 | .20 |
| ☐ 635 | Gene Kingsale | .07 | .20 |
| ☐ 636 | Tim Worrell | .07 | .20 |
| ☐ 637 | Billy Martin | .07 | .20 |
| ☐ 638 | Jovanny Cedeno | .07 | .20 |
| ☐ 639 | Curtis Leskanic | .07 | .20 |
| ☐ 640 | Tim Hudson | .07 | .20 |
| ☐ 641 | Juan Castro | .07 | .20 |
| ☐ 642 | Rafael Soriano | .07 | .20 |
| ☐ 643 | Juan Rincon | .07 | .20 |
| ☐ 644 | Mark DeRosa | .07 | .20 |
| ☐ 645 | Carlos Pena | .20 | .50 |
| ☐ 646 | Robin Ventura | .10 | .30 |
| ☐ 647 | Odalis Perez | .07 | .20 |
| ☐ 648 | Damion Easley | .07 | .20 |
| ☐ 649 | Benito Santiago | .10 | .30 |
| ☐ 650 | Alex Rodriguez | .50 | 1.25 |
| ☐ 651 | Aaron Rowand | .10 | .30 |
| ☐ 652 | Alex Cora | .07 | .20 |
| ☐ 653 | Bobby Kielty | .07 | .20 |
| ☐ 654 | Jose Rodriguez RC | .15 | .40 |
| ☐ 655 | Herbert Perry | .07 | .20 |
| ☐ 656 | Jeff Urban | .07 | .20 |
| ☐ 657 | Paul Bako | .07 | .20 |
| ☐ 658 | Shane Spencer | .07 | .20 |
| ☐ 659 | Pat Hentgen | .07 | .20 |
| ☐ 660 | Jeff Kent | .10 | .30 |
| ☐ 661 | Mark McLemore | .10 | .30 |
| ☐ 662 | Chuck Knoblauch | .10 | .30 |
| ☐ 663 | Blake Stein | .07 | .20 |
| ☐ 664 | Brett Roneberg RC | .15 | .40 |
| ☐ 665 | Josh Phelps | .07 | .20 |
| ☐ 666 | Byung-Hyun Kim | .10 | .30 |
| ☐ 667 | Dave Martinez | .07 | .20 |
| ☐ 668 | Mike Maroth | .07 | .20 |

|  |  | | |  |  | | |  |  | | |
|---|---|---|---|---|---|---|---|---|---|---|---|
| 669 | Shawn Chacon | .07 | .20 | 757 | Yorvit Torrealba | .07 | .20 | 845 | Mike Sirotka | .07 | .20 |
| 670 | Billy Wagner | .10 | .30 | 758 | Jason Standridge | .07 | .20 | 846 | Garret Anderson | .10 | .30 |
| 671 | Luis Alicea | .07 | .20 | 759 | Desi Relaford | .07 | .20 | 847 | James Shanks RC | .15 | .40 |
| 672 | Sterling Hitchcock | .07 | .20 | 760 | Jolbert Cabrera | .07 | .20 | 848 | Trot Nixon | .10 | .30 |
| 673 | Adam Piatt | .07 | .20 | 761 | Chris George | .07 | .20 | 849 | Keith Ginter | .07 | .20 |
| 674 | Ryan Franklin | .07 | .20 | 762 | Erubiel Durazo | .07 | .20 | 850 | Tim Spooneybarger | .07 | .20 |
| 675 | Luke Prokopec | .07 | .20 | 763 | Paul Konerko | .10 | .30 | 851 | Matt Stairs | .07 | .20 |
| 676 | Alfredo Amezaga | .07 | .20 | 764 | Tike Redman | .07 | .20 | 852 | Chris Stynes | .07 | .20 |
| 677 | Gookie Dawkins | .07 | .20 | 765 | Chad Ricketts RC | .08 | .25 | 853 | Marvin Benard | .07 | .20 |
| 678 | Eric Byrnes | .07 | .20 | 766 | Roberto Hernandez | .07 | .20 | 854 | Raul Mondesi | .10 | .30 |
| 679 | Barry Larkin | .20 | .50 | 767 | Mark Lewis | .07 | .20 | 855 | Jeremy Owens | .07 | .20 |
| 680 | Albert Pujols | .60 | 1.50 | 768 | Livan Hernandez | .10 | .30 | 856 | Jon Garland | .10 | .30 |
| 681 | Edwards Guzman | .07 | .20 | 769 | Carlos Brackley RC | .15 | .40 | 857 | Mitch Meluskey | .07 | .20 |
| 682 | Jason Bere | .07 | .20 | 770 | Kazuhiro Sasaki | .10 | .30 | 858 | Chad Durbin | .07 | .20 |
| 683 | Adam Everett | .07 | .20 | 771 | Bill Hall | .10 | .30 | 859 | John Burkett | .07 | .20 |
| 684 | Greg Colbrunn | .07 | .20 | 772 | Nelson Castro RC | .15 | .40 | 860 | Jon Switzer RC | .15 | .40 |
| 685 | Brandon Puffer RC | .15 | .40 | 773 | Eric Milton | .07 | .20 | 861 | Peter Bergeron | .07 | .20 |
| 686 | Mark Kotsay | .10 | .30 | 774 | Tom Davey | .07 | .20 | 862 | Jesus Colome | .07 | .20 |
| 687 | Willie Bloomquist | .10 | .30 | 775 | Todd Ritchie | .07 | .20 | 863 | Todd Hundley | .07 | .20 |
| 688 | Hank Blalock | .20 | .50 | 776 | Seth Etherton | .07 | .20 | 864 | Ben Petrick | .07 | .20 |
| 689 | Travis Hafner | .10 | .30 | 777 | Chris Singleton | .07 | .20 | 865 | So Taguchi RC | .20 | .50 |
| 690 | Lance Berkman | .10 | .30 | 778 | Robert Averette RC | .08 | .25 | 866 | Ryan Drese | .07 | .20 |
| 691 | Joe Crede | .10 | .30 | 779 | Robert Person | .07 | .20 | 867 | Mike Trombley | .07 | .20 |
| 692 | Chuck Finley | .10 | .30 | 780 | Fred McGriff | .20 | .50 | 868 | Rick Reed | .07 | .20 |
| 693 | John Grabow | .07 | .20 | 781 | Richard Hidalgo | .07 | .20 | 869 | Mark Teixeira | .30 | .75 |
| 694 | Randy Winn | .07 | .20 | 782 | Kris Wilson | .07 | .20 | 870 | Corey Thurman RC | .15 | .40 |
| 695 | Mike James | .07 | .20 | 783 | John Rocker | .10 | .30 | 871 | Brian Roberts | .10 | .30 |
| 696 | Kris Benson | .07 | .20 | 784 | Justin Kaye | .07 | .20 | 872 | Mike Timlin | .07 | .20 |
| 697 | Bret Prinz | .07 | .20 | 785 | Glendon Rusch | .07 | .20 | 873 | Chris Reitsma | .07 | .20 |
| 698 | Jeff Williams | .07 | .20 | 786 | Greg Vaughn | .07 | .20 | 874 | Jeff Fassero | .07 | .20 |
| 699 | Eric Munson | .07 | .20 | 787 | Mike Lamb | .07 | .20 | 875 | Carlos Valderrama | .07 | .20 |
| 700 | Mike Hampton | .10 | .30 | 788 | Greg Myers | .07 | .20 | 876 | John Lackey | .20 | .50 |
| 701 | Ramon E. Martinez | .07 | .20 | 789 | Nate Field RC | .15 | .40 | 877 | Travis Fryman | .10 | .30 |
| 702 | Hansel Izquierdo RC | .15 | .40 | 790 | Jim Edmonds | .10 | .30 | 878 | Ismael Valdes | .07 | .20 |
| 703 | Nathan Haynes | .07 | .20 | 791 | Olmedo Saenz | .07 | .20 | 879 | Rick White | .07 | .20 |
| 704 | Eddie Taubensee | .07 | .20 | 792 | Jason Johnson | .07 | .20 | 880 | Edgar Martinez | .20 | .50 |
| 705 | Esteban German | .07 | .20 | 793 | Mike Lincoln | .07 | .20 | 881 | Dean Palmer | .10 | .30 |
| 706 | Ross Gload | .07 | .20 | 794 | Todd Coffey RC | .15 | .40 | 882 | Matt Allegra RC | .15 | .40 |
| 707 | Matt Merricks RC | .15 | .40 | 795 | Jesus Sanchez | .07 | .20 | 883 | Greg Sain RC | .15 | .40 |
| 708 | Chris Piersoll RC | .08 | .25 | 796 | Aaron Myette | .07 | .20 | 884 | Carlos Silva | .07 | .20 |
| 709 | Seth Greisinger | .07 | .20 | 797 | Tony Womack | .07 | .20 | 885 | Jose Valverde RC | .15 | .40 |
| 710 | Ichiro Suzuki | .60 | 1.50 | 798 | Chad Kreuter | .07 | .20 | 886 | Demeli Stenson | .07 | .20 |
| 711 | Cesar Izturis | .07 | .20 | 799 | Brady Clark | .07 | .20 | 887 | Todd Van Poppel | .07 | .20 |
| 712 | Brad Cresse | .07 | .20 | 800 | Adam Dunn | .10 | .30 | 888 | Wes Anderson | .07 | .20 |
| 713 | Carl Pavano | .10 | .30 | 801 | Jacque Jones | .10 | .30 | 889 | Bill Mueller | .10 | .30 |
| 714 | Steve Sparks | .07 | .20 | 802 | Kevin Millwood | .10 | .30 | 890 | Morgan Ensberg | .10 | .30 |
| 715 | Dennis Tankersley | .07 | .20 | 803 | Mike Rivera | .07 | .20 | 891 | Marcus Thames | .07 | .20 |
| 716 | Kelvim Escobar | .07 | .20 | 804 | Jim Thome | .20 | .50 | 892 | Adam Walker RC | .15 | .40 |
| 717 | Jason LaRue | .07 | .20 | 805 | Jeff Conine | .10 | .30 | 893 | John Halama | .07 | .20 |
| 718 | Corey Koskie | .07 | .20 | 806 | Elmer Dessens | .07 | .20 | 894 | Frank Menechino | .07 | .20 |
| 719 | Vinny Castilla | .10 | .30 | 807 | Randy Velarde | .07 | .20 | 895 | Greg Maddux | .50 | 1.25 |
| 720 | Tim Drew | .07 | .20 | 808 | Carlos Delgado | .10 | .30 | 896 | Gary Bennett | .07 | .20 |
| 721 | Chin-Hui Tsao | .10 | .30 | 809 | Steve Karsay | .07 | .20 | 897 | Mauricio Lara RC | .15 | .40 |
| 722 | Paul Byrd | .07 | .20 | 810 | Casey Fossum | .07 | .20 | 898 | Mike Young | .30 | .75 |
| 723 | Alex Cintron | .07 | .20 | 811 | J.C. Romero | .07 | .20 | 899 | Travis Phelps | .07 | .20 |
| 724 | Orlando Palmeiro | .07 | .20 | 812 | Chris Truby | .07 | .20 | 900 | Rich Aurilia | .07 | .20 |
| 725 | Ramon Hernandez | .07 | .20 | 813 | Tony Graffanino | .07 | .20 | 901 | Henry Blanco | .07 | .20 |
| 726 | Mark Johnson | .07 | .20 | 814 | Wascar Serrano | .07 | .20 | 902 | Carlos Febles | .07 | .20 |
| 727 | B.J. Ryan | .07 | .20 | 815 | Delvin James | .07 | .20 | 903 | Scott MacRae | .07 | .20 |
| 728 | Wendell Magee | .07 | .20 | 816 | Pedro Feliz | .07 | .20 | 904 | Lou Merloni | .07 | .20 |
| 729 | Michael Coleman | .07 | .20 | 817 | Damian Rolls | .07 | .20 | 905 | Dicky Gonzalez | .07 | .20 |
| 730 | Mario Ramos RC | .15 | .40 | 818 | Scott Linebrink | .07 | .20 | 906 | Jeff DaVanon | .07 | .20 |
| 731 | Mike Stanton | .07 | .20 | 819 | Rafael Palmeiro | .20 | .50 | 907 | A.J. Burnett | .10 | .30 |
| 732 | Dee Brown | .07 | .20 | 820 | Javy Lopez | .10 | .30 | 908 | Einar Diaz | .07 | .20 |
| 733 | Brad Ausmus | .07 | .20 | 821 | Larry Barnes | .07 | .20 | 909 | Julio Franco | .10 | .30 |
| 734 | Napoleon Calzado RC | .15 | .40 | 822 | Brian Lawrence | .07 | .20 | 910 | John Olerud | .10 | .30 |
| 735 | Woody Williams | .07 | .20 | 823 | Scotty Layfield RC | .15 | .40 | 911 | Mark Hamilton RC | .15 | .40 |
| 736 | Paxton Crawford | .07 | .20 | 824 | Jeff Cirillo | .07 | .20 | 912 | David Riske | .07 | .20 |
| 737 | Jason Kamuth | .07 | .20 | 825 | Willis Roberts | .07 | .20 | 913 | Jason Tyner | .07 | .20 |
| 738 | Michael Restovich | .07 | .20 | 826 | Rich Harden RC | 1.25 | 3.00 | 914 | Britt Reames | .07 | .20 |
| 739 | Ramon Castro | .07 | .20 | 827 | Chris Snelling RC | .25 | .60 | 915 | Vernon Wells | .10 | .30 |
| 740 | Magglio Ordonez | .10 | .30 | 828 | Gary Sheffield | .10 | .30 | 916 | Eddie Perez | .07 | .20 |
| 741 | Tom Gordon | .07 | .20 | 829 | Jeff Heaverlo | .07 | .20 | 917 | Edwin Almonte RC | .15 | .40 |
| 742 | Mark Grudzielanek | .07 | .20 | 830 | Matt Clement | .10 | .30 | 918 | Enrique Wilson | .07 | .20 |
| 743 | Jaime Moyer | .10 | .30 | 831 | Rich Garces | .07 | .20 | 919 | Chris Gomez | .07 | .20 |
| 744 | Marlyn Tisdale RC | .15 | .40 | 832 | Rondell White | .10 | .30 | 920 | Jayson Werth | .20 | .50 |
| 745 | Steve Kline | .07 | .20 | 833 | Henry Pichardo RC | .15 | .40 | 921 | Jeff Nelson | .07 | .20 |
| 746 | Adam Eaton | .07 | .20 | 834 | Aaron Boone | .10 | .30 | 922 | Freddy Sanchez RC | .75 | 2.00 |
| 747 | Eric Glaser RC | .15 | .40 | 835 | Ruben Sierra | .10 | .30 | 923 | John Vander Wal | .07 | .20 |
| 748 | Sean DePaula | .07 | .20 | 836 | Deivis Santos | .07 | .20 | 924 | Chad Qualls RC | .20 | .50 |
| 749 | Greg Norton | .07 | .20 | 837 | Tony Batista | .07 | .20 | 925 | Gabe White | .07 | .20 |
| 750 | Steve Reed | .07 | .20 | 838 | Rob Bell | .07 | .20 | 926 | Chad Harville | .07 | .20 |
| 751 | Ricardo Arambeles | .07 | .20 | 839 | Frank Thomas | .30 | .75 | 927 | Ricky Gutierrez | .07 | .20 |
| 752 | Matt Mantei | .07 | .20 | 840 | Jose Silva | .07 | .20 | 928 | Carlos Guillen | .10 | .30 |
| 753 | Gene Stechschulte | .07 | .20 | 841 | Dan Johnson RC | .40 | 1.00 | 929 | B.J. Surhoff | .10 | .30 |
| 754 | Chuck McElroy | .07 | .20 | 842 | Steve Cox | .07 | .20 | 930 | Chris Woodward | .07 | .20 |
| 755 | Barry Bonds | .75 | 2.00 | 843 | Jose Acevedo | .07 | .20 | 931 | Ricardo Rodriguez | .07 | .20 |
| 756 | Matt Anderson | .07 | .20 | 844 | Jay Bell | .10 | .30 | 932 | Jimmy Gobble RC | .15 | .40 |

|  |  | | |
|---|---|---|---|
| 933 | Jon Lieber | .07 | .20 |
| 934 | Craig Kuzmic RC | .15 | .40 |
| 935 | Eric Young | .07 | .20 |
| 936 | Greg Zaun | .07 | .20 |
| 937 | Miguel Batista | .07 | .20 |
| 938 | Danny Wright | .07 | .20 |
| 939 | Todd Zeile | .10 | .30 |
| 940 | Chad Zerbe | .07 | .20 |
| 941 | Jason Young RC | .08 | .25 |
| 942 | Ronnie Belliard | .07 | .20 |
| 943 | John Ennis RC | .15 | .40 |
| 944 | John Flaherty | .07 | .20 |
| 945 | Jerry Hairston Jr. | .07 | .20 |
| 946 | Al Levine | .07 | .20 |
| 947 | Antonio Alfonseca | .07 | .20 |
| 948 | Brian Moehler | .07 | .20 |
| 949 | Calvin Murray | .07 | .20 |
| 950 | Nick Bierbrodt | .07 | .20 |
| 951 | Sun Woo Kim | .07 | .20 |
| 952 | Noochie Varner RC | .15 | .40 |
| 953 | Luis Rivas | .07 | .20 |
| 954 | Donnie Bridges | .07 | .20 |
| 955 | Ramon Vazquez | .07 | .20 |
| 956 | Luis Garcia | .07 | .20 |
| 957 | Mark Quinn | .07 | .20 |
| 958 | Armando Rios | .07 | .20 |
| 959 | Chad Fox | .07 | .20 |
| 960 | Hee Seop Choi | .07 | .20 |
| 961 | Turk Wendell | .07 | .20 |
| 962 | Adam Roller RC | .15 | .40 |
| 963 | Grant Roberts | .07 | .20 |
| 964 | Ben Molina | .07 | .20 |
| 965 | Juan Rivera | .07 | .20 |
| 966 | Matt Kinney | .07 | .20 |
| 967 | Rod Beck | .07 | .20 |
| 968 | Xavier Nady | .07 | .20 |
| 969 | Masato Yoshii | .07 | .20 |
| 970 | Miguel Tejada | .10 | .30 |
| 971 | Danny Kolb | .07 | .20 |
| 972 | Mike Remlinger | .07 | .20 |
| 973 | Ray Lankford | .10 | .30 |
| 974 | Ryan Minor | .07 | .20 |
| 975 | J.T. Snow | .10 | .30 |
| 976 | Brad Radke | .10 | .30 |
| 977 | Jason Lane | .10 | .30 |
| 978 | Jamey Wright | .07 | .20 |
| 979 | Tom Goodwin | .07 | .20 |
| 980 | Erik Bedard | .10 | .30 |
| 981 | Gabe Kapler | .10 | .30 |
| 982 | Brian Reith | .07 | .20 |
| 983 | Nic Jackson RC | .15 | .40 |
| 984 | Kurt Ainsworth | .07 | .20 |
| 985 | Jason Isringhausen | .10 | .30 |
| 986 | Willie Harris | .07 | .20 |
| 987 | David Cone | .10 | .30 |
| 988 | Bob Wickman | .07 | .20 |
| 989 | Wes Helms | .07 | .20 |
| 990 | Josh Beckett | .10 | .30 |

## 2003 Topps Total

|  |  | | |
|---|---|---|---|
| | COMPLETE SET (990) | 100.00 | 200.00 |
| | COMMON CARD (1-990) | .07 | .20 |
| | COMMON RC | .08 | .25 |
| 1 | Brent Abernathy | .07 | .20 |
| 2 | Bobby Hill | .07 | .20 |
| 3 | Victor Martinez | .20 | .50 |
| 4 | Chip Ambres | .07 | .20 |
| 5 | Matt Anderson | .07 | .20 |
| 6 | Ricardo Aramboles | .07 | .20 |
| 7 | Carlos Pena | .07 | .20 |
| 8 | Aaron Guiel | .07 | .20 |
| 9 | Luke Allen | .07 | .20 |
| 10 | Francisco Rodriguez | .10 | .30 |
| 11 | Jason Marquis | .07 | .20 |

|  |  | | |
|---|---|---|---|
| 12 | Edwin Almonte | .07 | .20 |
| 13 | Grant Balfour | .07 | .20 |
| 14 | Adam Platt | .07 | .20 |
| 15 | Andy Phillips | .07 | .20 |
| 16 | Adrian Beltre | .10 | .30 |
| 17 | Brandon Backe | .07 | .20 |
| 18 | Dave Berg | .07 | .20 |
| 19 | Brett Myers | .10 | .30 |
| 20 | Brian Meadows | .07 | .20 |
| 21 | Chin-Feng Chen | .10 | .30 |
| 22 | Blake Williams | .07 | .20 |
| 23 | Josh Bard | .07 | .20 |
| 24 | Josh Beckett | .10 | .30 |
| 25 | Tommy Whiteman | .07 | .20 |
| 26 | Matt Childers | .07 | .20 |
| 27 | Adam Everett | .07 | .20 |
| 28 | Mike Bordick | .10 | .30 |
| 29 | Antonio Alfonseca | .07 | .20 |
| 30 | Doug Creek | .07 | .20 |
| 31 | J.D. Drew | .10 | .30 |
| 32 | Milton Bradley | .10 | .30 |
| 33 | David Wells | .07 | .20 |
| 34 | Vance Wilson | .07 | .20 |
| 35 | Jeff Fassero | .07 | .20 |
| 36 | Sandy Alomar Jr. | .07 | .20 |
| 37 | Ryan Vogelsong | .07 | .20 |
| 38 | Roger Clemens | .60 | 1.50 |
| 39 | Juan Gonzalez | .10 | .30 |
| 40 | Dustin Hermanson | .07 | .20 |
| 41 | Andy Ashby | .07 | .20 |
| 42 | Adam Hyzdu | .07 | .20 |
| 43 | Ben Broussard | .07 | .20 |
| 44 | Ryan Klesko | .10 | .30 |
| 45 | Chris Buglovsky FY RC | .15 | .40 |
| 46 | Bud Smith | .07 | .20 |
| 47 | Aaron Boone | .10 | .30 |
| 48 | Cliff Floyd | .10 | .30 |
| 49 | Alex Cora | .07 | .20 |
| 50 | Curt Schilling | .20 | .50 |
| 51 | Michael Cuddyer | .07 | .20 |
| 52 | Joe Valentine FY RC | .15 | .40 |
| 53 | Carlos Guillen | .10 | .30 |
| 54 | Angel Berroa | .07 | .20 |
| 55 | Eli Marrero | .07 | .20 |
| 56 | A.J. Burnett | .10 | .30 |
| 57 | Oliver Perez | .10 | .30 |
| 58 | Matt Morris | .10 | .30 |
| 59 | Valerio De Los Santos | .07 | .20 |
| 60 | Austin Kearns | .07 | .20 |
| 61 | Darren Dreifort | .07 | .20 |
| 62 | Jason Standridge | .07 | .20 |
| 63 | Carlos Silva | .07 | .20 |
| 64 | Moises Alou | .10 | .30 |
| 65 | Jason Anderson | .07 | .20 |
| 66 | Russell Branyan | .07 | .20 |
| 67 | B.J. Ryan | .07 | .20 |
| 68 | Cory Aldridge | .07 | .20 |
| 69 | Ellis Burks | .10 | .30 |
| 70 | Troy Glaus | .10 | .30 |
| 71 | Kelly Wunsch | .07 | .20 |
| 72 | Brad Wilkerson | .07 | .20 |
| 73 | Jayson Durocher | .07 | .20 |
| 74 | Tony Fiore | .07 | .20 |
| 75 | Brian Giles | .10 | .30 |
| 76 | Billy Wagner | .10 | .30 |
| 77 | Neifi Perez | .07 | .20 |
| 78 | Jose Valverde | .07 | .20 |
| 79 | Brent Butler | .07 | .20 |
| 80 | Mario Ramos | .07 | .20 |
| 81 | Kerry Robinson | .07 | .20 |
| 82 | Brent Mayne | .07 | .20 |
| 83 | Sean Casey | .10 | .30 |
| 84 | Danys Baez | .07 | .20 |
| 85 | Chase Utley | .30 | .75 |
| 86 | Jared Sandberg | .07 | .20 |
| 87 | Terrence Long | .07 | .20 |
| 88 | Kevin Walker | .07 | .20 |
| 89 | Royce Clayton | .07 | .20 |
| 90 | Shea Hillenbrand | .10 | .30 |
| 91 | Brad Lidge | .07 | .20 |
| 92 | Shawn Chacon | .07 | .20 |
| 93 | Kenny Rogers | .10 | .30 |
| 94 | Chris Snelling | .07 | .20 |
| 95 | Omar Vizquel | .20 | .50 |
| 96 | Joe Borchard | .07 | .20 |
| 97 | Matt Belisle | .07 | .20 |
| 98 | Steve Smyth | .07 | .20 |
| 99 | Raul Mondesi | .10 | .30 |

|  |  | | |
|---|---|---|---|
| 100 | Chipper Jones | .30 | .75 |
| 101 | Victor Alvarez | .07 | .20 |
| 102 | J.M. Gold | .07 | .20 |
| 103 | Willis Roberts | .07 | .20 |
| 104 | Eddie Guardado | .07 | .20 |
| 105 | Brad Voyles | .07 | .20 |
| 106 | Bronson Arroyo | .10 | .30 |
| 107 | Juan Castro | .07 | .20 |
| 108 | Dan Plesac | .07 | .20 |
| 109 | Ramon Castro | .07 | .20 |
| 110 | Tim Salmon | .20 | .50 |
| 111 | Gene Kingsale | .07 | .20 |
| 112 | J.D. Closser | .07 | .20 |
| 113 | Mark Buehrle | .10 | .30 |
| 114 | Steve Karsay | .07 | .20 |
| 115 | Cristian Guerrero | .07 | .20 |
| 116 | Brad Ausmus | .10 | .30 |
| 117 | Cristian Guzman | .07 | .20 |
| 118 | Dan Wilson | .07 | .20 |
| 119 | Jake Westbrook | .07 | .20 |
| 120 | Manny Ramirez | .20 | .50 |
| 121 | Jason Giambi | .10 | .30 |
| 122 | Bob Wickman | .07 | .20 |
| 123 | Aaron Cook | .07 | .20 |
| 124 | Alfredo Amezaga | .07 | .20 |
| 125 | Corey Thurman | .07 | .20 |
| 126 | Brandon Puffer | .07 | .20 |
| 127 | Hee Seop Choi | .07 | .20 |
| 128 | Javier Vazquez | .10 | .30 |
| 129 | Carlos Valderrama | .07 | .20 |
| 130 | Jerome Williams | .07 | .20 |
| 131 | Wilson Betemit | .07 | .20 |
| 132 | Luke Prokopec | .07 | .20 |
| 133 | Esteban Yan | .07 | .20 |
| 134 | Brandon Berger | .07 | .20 |
| 135 | Bill Hall | .07 | .20 |
| 136 | LaTroy Hawkins | .07 | .20 |
| 137 | Nate Cornejo | .07 | .20 |
| 138 | Jim Mecir | .07 | .20 |
| 139 | Joe Crede | .10 | .30 |
| 140 | Andres Galarraga | .20 | .50 |
| 141 | Reggie Sanders | .10 | .30 |
| 142 | Joey Eischen | .07 | .20 |
| 143 | Mike Timlin | .07 | .20 |
| 144 | Jose Cruz Jr. | .07 | .20 |
| 145 | Wes Helms | .07 | .20 |
| 146 | Brian Roberts | .10 | .30 |
| 147 | Bret Prinz | .07 | .20 |
| 148 | Brian Hunter | .07 | .20 |
| 149 | Chad Hermansen | .07 | .20 |
| 150 | Andruw Jones | .20 | .50 |
| 151 | Kurt Ainsworth | .07 | .20 |
| 152 | Cliff Bartosh | .07 | .20 |
| 153 | Kyle Lohse | .07 | .20 |
| 154 | Brian Jordan | .10 | .30 |
| 155 | Coco Crisp | .20 | .50 |
| 156 | Tomas Perez | .07 | .20 |
| 157 | Keith Foulke | .10 | .30 |
| 158 | Chris Carpenter | .10 | .30 |
| 159 | Mike Remlinger | .07 | .20 |
| 160 | Dewon Brazelton | .07 | .20 |
| 161 | Brook Fordyce | .07 | .20 |
| 162 | Rusty Greer | .10 | .30 |
| 163 | Scott Downs | .07 | .20 |
| 164 | Jason Dubois | .07 | .20 |
| 165 | David Coggin | .07 | .20 |
| 166 | Mike DeJean | .07 | .20 |
| 167 | Carlos Hernandez | .07 | .20 |
| 168 | Matt Williams | .10 | .30 |
| 169 | Rheal Cormier | .07 | .20 |
| 170 | Duaner Sanchez | .07 | .20 |
| 171 | Craig Counsell | .07 | .20 |
| 172 | Edgar Martinez | .20 | .50 |
| 173 | Zack Greinke | .10 | .30 |
| 174 | Pedro Feliz | .07 | .20 |
| 175 | Randy Choate | .07 | .20 |
| 176 | Jon Garland | .10 | .30 |
| 177 | Keith Ginter | .07 | .20 |
| 178 | Carlos Febles | .07 | .20 |
| 179 | Kerry Wood | .10 | .30 |
| 180 | Jack Cust | .07 | .20 |
| 181 | Koyie Hill | .07 | .20 |
| 182 | Ricky Gutierrez | .07 | .20 |
| 183 | Ben Grieve | .07 | .20 |
| 184 | Scott Eyre | .07 | .20 |
| 185 | Jason Isringhausen | .10 | .30 |
| 186 | Gookie Dawkins | .07 | .20 |
| 187 | Roberto Alomar | .20 | .50 |

|  |  | | |
|---|--------|---|---|
| 188 | Eric Junge | .07 | .20 |
| 189 | Carlos Beltran | .10 | .30 |
| 190 | Denny Hocking | .07 | .20 |
| 191 | Jason Schmidt | .10 | .30 |
| 192 | Cory Lidle | .07 | .20 |
| 193 | Rob Mackowiak | .07 | .20 |
| 194 | Charlton Jimerson RC | .15 | .40 |
| 195 | Darin Erstad | .10 | .30 |
| 196 | Jason Davis | .07 | .20 |
| 197 | Luis Castillo | .07 | .20 |
| 198 | Juan Encarnacion | .07 | .20 |
| 199 | Jeffrey Hammonds | .07 | .20 |
| 200 | Nomar Garciaparra | .50 | 1.25 |
| 201 | Ryan Christianson | .07 | .20 |
| 202 | Robert Person | .07 | .20 |
| 203 | Damian Moss | .07 | .20 |
| 204 | Chris Richard | .07 | .20 |
| 205 | Todd Hundley | .07 | .20 |
| 206 | Paul Bako | .07 | .20 |
| 207 | Adam Kennedy | .07 | .20 |
| 208 | Scott Hatteberg | .07 | .20 |
| 209 | Andy Pratt | .07 | .20 |
| 210 | Ken Griffey Jr. | .50 | 1.25 |
| 211 | Chris George | .07 | .20 |
| 212 | Lance Niekro | .07 | .20 |
| 213 | Greg Colbrunn | .07 | .20 |
| 214 | Herbert Perry | .07 | .20 |
| 215 | Cody Ransom | .07 | .20 |
| 216 | Craig Biggio | .20 | .50 |
| 217 | Miguel Batista | .07 | .20 |
| 218 | Alex Escobar | .07 | .20 |
| 219 | Willie Harris | .07 | .20 |
| 220 | Scott Strickland | .07 | .20 |
| 221 | Felix Rodriguez | .07 | .20 |
| 222 | Toni Hunter | .10 | .30 |
| 223 | Tyler Houston | .07 | .20 |
| 224 | Darrell May | .07 | .20 |
| 225 | Benito Santiago | .10 | .30 |
| 226 | Ryan Dempster | .07 | .20 |
| 227 | Andy Fox | .07 | .20 |
| 228 | Jung Bong | .07 | .20 |
| 229 | Jose Macias | .07 | .20 |
| 230 | Shannon Stewart | .10 | .30 |
| 231 | Buddy Groom | .07 | .20 |
| 232 | Eric Valent | .07 | .20 |
| 233 | Scott Schoeneweis | .07 | .20 |
| 234 | Corey Hart | .07 | .20 |
| 235 | Brett Tomko | .07 | .20 |
| 236 | Shane Bazzell RC | .15 | .40 |
| 237 | Tim Hummel | .07 | .20 |
| 238 | Matt Stairs | .07 | .20 |
| 239 | Pete Munro | .07 | .20 |
| 240 | Ismael Valdes | .07 | .20 |
| 241 | Brian Fuentes | .07 | .20 |
| 242 | Cesar Izturis | .07 | .20 |
| 243 | Mark Bellhorn | .10 | .30 |
| 244 | Geoff Jenkins | .07 | .20 |
| 245 | Derek Jeter | .75 | 2.00 |
| 246 | Anderson Machado | .07 | .20 |
| 247 | Dave Roberts | .07 | .20 |
| 248 | Jaime Cerda | .07 | .20 |
| 249 | Woody Williams | .07 | .20 |
| 250 | Vernon Wells | .10 | .30 |
| 251 | Jon Lieber | .07 | .20 |
| 252 | Franklyn German | .07 | .20 |
| 253 | David Segui | .07 | .20 |
| 254 | Freddy Garcia | .10 | .30 |
| 255 | James Baldwin | .07 | .20 |
| 256 | Tony Alvarez | .07 | .20 |
| 257 | Walter Young | .07 | .20 |
| 258 | Alex Herrera | .07 | .20 |
| 259 | Robert Fick | .07 | .20 |
| 260 | Rob Bell | .07 | .20 |
| 261 | Ben Petrick | .07 | .20 |
| 262 | Dee Brown | .07 | .20 |
| 263 | Mike Bacsik | .07 | .20 |
| 264 | Corey Patterson | .07 | .20 |
| 265 | Marvin Benard | .07 | .20 |
| 266 | Eddie Rogers | .07 | .20 |
| 267 | Elio Serrano | .07 | .20 |
| 268 | D'Angelo Jimenez | .07 | .20 |
| 269 | Adam Johnson | .07 | .20 |
| 270 | Gregg Zaun | .07 | .20 |
| 271 | Nick Johnson | .10 | .30 |
| 272 | Geoff Goetz | .07 | .20 |
| 273 | Ryan Drese | .07 | .20 |
| 274 | Eric Dubose | .07 | .20 |
| 275 | Barry Zito | .10 | .30 |
| 276 | Mike Crudale | .07 | .20 |
| 277 | Paul Byrd | .07 | .20 |
| 278 | Eric Gagne | .10 | .30 |
| 279 | Aramis Ramirez | .10 | .30 |
| 280 | Ray Durham | .10 | .30 |
| 281 | Tony Graffanino | .07 | .20 |
| 282 | Jeremy Guthrie | .07 | .20 |
| 283 | Erik Bedard | .07 | .20 |
| 284 | Vince Faison | .07 | .20 |
| 285 | Bobby Kielty | .07 | .20 |
| 286 | Francis Beltran | .07 | .20 |
| 287 | Alexis Gomez | .07 | .20 |
| 288 | Vladimir Guerrero | .30 | .75 |
| 289 | Kevin Appier | .10 | .30 |
| 290 | Gil Meche | .07 | .20 |
| 291 | Marquis Grissom | .10 | .30 |
| 292 | John Burkett | .07 | .20 |
| 293 | Vinny Castilla | .10 | .30 |
| 294 | Tyler Walker | .07 | .20 |
| 295 | Shane Halter | .07 | .20 |
| 296 | Geronimo Gil | .07 | .20 |
| 297 | Eric Hinske | .07 | .20 |
| 298 | Adam Dunn | .10 | .30 |
| 299 | Mike Kinkade | .07 | .20 |
| 300 | Mark Prior | .20 | .50 |
| 301 | Corey Koskie | .07 | .20 |
| 302 | David Dellucci | .07 | .20 |
| 303 | Todd Helton | .20 | .50 |
| 304 | Greg Miller | .07 | .20 |
| 305 | Delvin James | .07 | .20 |
| 306 | Humberto Cota | .07 | .20 |
| 307 | Aaron Harang | .07 | .20 |
| 308 | Jeremy Hill | .07 | .20 |
| 309 | Billy Koch | .07 | .20 |
| 310 | Brandon Claussen | .07 | .20 |
| 311 | Matt Ginter | .07 | .20 |
| 312 | Jason Lane | .07 | .20 |
| 313 | Ben Weber | .07 | .20 |
| 314 | Alan Benes | .07 | .20 |
| 315 | Matt Walbeck | .07 | .20 |
| 316 | Danny Graves | .07 | .20 |
| 317 | Jason Johnson | .07 | .20 |
| 318 | Jason Grimsley | .07 | .20 |
| 319 | Steve Kline | .07 | .20 |
| 320 | Johnny Damon | .20 | .50 |
| 321 | Jay Gibbons | .07 | .20 |
| 322 | J.J. Putz | .07 | .20 |
| 323 | Stephen Randolph RC | .15 | .40 |
| 324 | Bobby Higginson | .10 | .30 |
| 325 | Kazuhisa Ishii | .10 | .30 |
| 326 | Carlos Lee | .10 | .30 |
| 327 | J.R. House | .07 | .20 |
| 328 | Mark Loretta | .07 | .20 |
| 329 | Mike Matheny | .07 | .20 |
| 330 | Ben Diggins | .07 | .20 |
| 331 | Seth Etherton | .07 | .20 |
| 332 | Eli Whiteside FY RC | .15 | .40 |
| 333 | Juan Rivera | .07 | .20 |
| 334 | Jeff Conine | .10 | .30 |
| 335 | John McDonald | .07 | .20 |
| 336 | Erik Hiljus | .07 | .20 |
| 337 | David Eckstein | .10 | .30 |
| 338 | Jeff Bagwell | .20 | .50 |
| 339 | Matt Holliday | .08 | .25 |
| 340 | Jeff Liefer | .07 | .20 |
| 341 | Greg Myers | .07 | .20 |
| 342 | Scott Sauerbeck | .07 | .20 |
| 343 | Omar Infante | .07 | .20 |
| 344 | Ryan Langerhans | .10 | .30 |
| 345 | Abraham Nunez | .07 | .20 |
| 346 | Mike MacDougal | .07 | .20 |
| 347 | Travis Phelps | .07 | .20 |
| 348 | Terry Shumpert | .07 | .20 |
| 349 | Alex Rodriguez | .50 | 1.25 |
| 350 | Bobby Seay | .07 | .20 |
| 351 | Ichiro Suzuki | .60 | 1.50 |
| 352 | Brandon Inge | .07 | .20 |
| 353 | Jack Wilson | .07 | .20 |
| 354 | John Ennis | .07 | .20 |
| 355 | Jamal Strong | .07 | .20 |
| 356 | Jason Jennings | .07 | .20 |
| 357 | Jeff Kent | .10 | .30 |
| 358 | Scott Chiasson | .07 | .20 |
| 359 | Jeremy Griffiths | .15 | .40 |
| 360 | Paul Konerko | .10 | .30 |
| 361 | Jeff Austin | .07 | .20 |
| 362 | Todd Van Poppel | .07 | .20 |
| 363 | Sun Woo Kim | .07 | .20 |
| 364 | Jerry Hairston Jr. | .07 | .20 |
| 365 | Tony Torcato | .07 | .20 |
| 366 | Arthur Rhodes | .07 | .20 |
| 367 | Jose Jimenez | .07 | .20 |
| 368 | Matt LeCroy | .07 | .20 |
| 369 | Curtis Leskanic | .07 | .20 |
| 370 | Ramon Vazquez | .07 | .20 |
| 371 | Joe Randa | .10 | .30 |
| 372 | John Franco | .10 | .30 |
| 373 | Bobby Estalella | .07 | .20 |
| 374 | Craig Wilson | .07 | .20 |
| 375 | Michael Young | .20 | .50 |
| 376 | Mark Ellis | .07 | .20 |
| 377 | Joe Mauer | .30 | .75 |
| 378 | Checklist 1 | .07 | .20 |
| 379 | Jason Kendall | .10 | .30 |
| 380 | Checklist 2 | .07 | .20 |
| 381 | Alex Gonzalez | .07 | .20 |
| 382 | Tom Gordon | .07 | .20 |
| 383 | John Buck | .07 | .20 |
| 384 | Shigetoshi Hasegawa | .10 | .30 |
| 385 | Scott Stewart | .07 | .20 |
| 386 | Luke Hudson | .07 | .20 |
| 387 | Todd Jones | .07 | .20 |
| 388 | Fred McGriff | .20 | .50 |
| 389 | Mike Sweeney | .10 | .30 |
| 390 | Marlon Anderson | .07 | .20 |
| 391 | Terry Adams | .07 | .20 |
| 392 | Mark DeRosa | .07 | .20 |
| 393 | Doug Mientkiewicz | .10 | .30 |
| 394 | Miguel Cairo | .07 | .20 |
| 395 | Jamie Moyer | .10 | .30 |
| 396 | Jose Leon | .07 | .20 |
| 397 | Matt Clement | .10 | .30 |
| 398 | Bengie Molina | .07 | .20 |
| 399 | Marcus Thames | .07 | .20 |
| 400 | Nick Bierbrodt | .07 | .20 |
| 401 | Tim Kalita | .07 | .20 |
| 402 | Corwin Malone | .07 | .20 |
| 403 | Jesse Orosco | .07 | .20 |
| 404 | Brandon Phillips | .07 | .20 |
| 405 | Eric Cyr | .07 | .20 |
| 406 | Jason Michaels | .07 | .20 |
| 407 | Julio Lugo | .07 | .20 |
| 408 | Gabe Kapler | .10 | .30 |
| 409 | Mark Mulder | .10 | .30 |
| 410 | Adam Eaton | .07 | .20 |
| 411 | Ken Harvey | .07 | .20 |
| 412 | Jolbert Cabrera | .07 | .20 |
| 413 | Eric Milton | .07 | .20 |
| 414 | Josh Hall RC | .15 | .40 |
| 415 | Bob File | .07 | .20 |
| 416 | Brett Evert | .07 | .20 |
| 417 | Ron Chiavacci | .07 | .20 |
| 418 | Jorge De La Rosa | .07 | .20 |
| 419 | Quinton McCracken | .07 | .20 |
| 420 | Luther Hackman | .07 | .20 |
| 421 | Gary Knotts | .07 | .20 |
| 422 | Kevin Brown | .10 | .30 |
| 423 | Jeff Cirillo | .07 | .20 |
| 424 | Damaso Marte | .07 | .20 |
| 425 | Chan Ho Park | .10 | .30 |
| 426 | Nathan Haynes | .07 | .20 |
| 427 | Matt Lawton | .07 | .20 |
| 428 | Mike Stanton | .07 | .20 |
| 429 | Bernie Williams | .20 | .50 |
| 430 | Kevin Jarvis | .07 | .20 |
| 431 | Joe McEwing | .07 | .20 |
| 432 | Mark Kotsay | .10 | .30 |
| 433 | Juan Cruz | .07 | .20 |
| 434 | Russ Ortiz | .07 | .20 |
| 435 | Jeff Nelson | .07 | .20 |
| 436 | Alan Embree | .07 | .20 |
| 437 | Miguel Tejada | .10 | .30 |
| 438 | Kirk Saarloos | .07 | .20 |
| 439 | Cliff Lee | .07 | .20 |
| 440 | Ryan Ludwick | .07 | .20 |
| 441 | Derrek Lee | .20 | .50 |
| 442 | Bobby Abreu | .10 | .30 |
| 443 | Dustan Mohr | .07 | .20 |
| 444 | Nook Logan RC | .20 | .50 |
| 445 | Seth McClung | .07 | .20 |
| 446 | Miguel Olivo | .07 | .20 |
| 447 | Henry Blanco | .07 | .20 |
| 448 | Seung Song | .07 | .20 |
| 449 | Kris Wilson | .07 | .20 |
| 450 | Xavier Nady | .07 | .20 |
| 451 | Corky Miller | .07 | .20 |

|  |  | | |
|---|---|---|---|
| ☐ 716 | Steve Sparks | .07 | .20 |
| ☐ 717 | Glendon Rusch | .07 | .20 |
| ☐ 718 | Ricky Stone | .07 | .20 |
| ☐ 719 | Benji Gil | .07 | .20 |
| ☐ 720 | Pete Walker | .07 | .20 |
| ☐ 721 | Tim Worrell | .07 | .20 |
| ☐ 722 | Michael Tejera | .07 | .20 |
| ☐ 723 | David Kelton | .07 | .20 |
| ☐ 724 | Britt Reames | .07 | .20 |
| ☐ 725 | John Stephens | .07 | .20 |
| ☐ 726 | Mark McLemore | .07 | .20 |
| ☐ 727 | Jeff Zimmerman | .07 | .20 |
| ☐ 728 | Checklist 3 | .07 | .20 |
| ☐ 729 | Andres Torres | .07 | .20 |
| ☐ 730 | Checklist 4 | .07 | .20 |
| ☐ 731 | Johan Santana | .20 | .50 |
| ☐ 732 | Dane Sardinha | .07 | .20 |
| ☐ 733 | Rodrigo Rosario | .07 | .20 |
| ☐ 734 | Frank Thomas | .30 | .75 |
| ☐ 735 | Tom Glavine | .20 | .50 |
| ☐ 736 | Doug Mirabelli | .07 | .20 |
| ☐ 737 | Juan Uribe | .07 | .20 |
| ☐ 738 | Ryan Anderson | .07 | .20 |
| ☐ 739 | Sean Burroughs | .07 | .20 |
| ☐ 740 | Eric Chavez | .10 | .30 |
| ☐ 741 | Enrique Wilson | .07 | .20 |
| ☐ 742 | Elmer Dessens | .07 | .20 |
| ☐ 743 | Marlon Byrd | .07 | .20 |
| ☐ 744 | Brendan Donnelly | .07 | .20 |
| ☐ 745 | Gary Bennett | .07 | .20 |
| ☐ 746 | Roy Oswalt | .10 | .30 |
| ☐ 747 | Andy Van Hekken | .07 | .20 |
| ☐ 748 | Jesus Colome | .07 | .20 |
| ☐ 749 | Erick Almonte | .07 | .20 |
| ☐ 750 | Frank Catalanotto | .07 | .20 |
| ☐ 751 | Kenny Lofton | .10 | .30 |
| ☐ 752 | Carlos Delgado | .10 | .30 |
| ☐ 753 | Ryan Franklin | .07 | .20 |
| ☐ 754 | Wilkin Ruan | .07 | .20 |
| ☐ 755 | Kelvim Escobar | .07 | .20 |
| ☐ 756 | Tim Drew | .07 | .20 |
| ☐ 757 | Jarrod Washburn | .07 | .20 |
| ☐ 758 | Runelvys Hernandez | .07 | .20 |
| ☐ 759 | Cory Vance | .07 | .20 |
| ☐ 760 | Doug Glanville | .07 | .20 |
| ☐ 761 | Ryan Rupe | .07 | .20 |
| ☐ 762 | Jermaine Dye | .10 | .30 |
| ☐ 763 | Mike Cameron | .07 | .20 |
| ☐ 764 | Scott Erickson | .07 | .20 |
| ☐ 765 | Richie Sexson | .10 | .30 |
| ☐ 766 | Jose Vidro | .07 | .20 |
| ☐ 767 | Brian West | .07 | .20 |
| ☐ 768 | Shawn Estes | .07 | .20 |
| ☐ 769 | Brian Tallet | .07 | .20 |
| ☐ 770 | Larry Walker | .10 | .30 |
| ☐ 771 | Josh Hamilton | .15 | .40 |
| ☐ 772 | Orlando Hudson | .07 | .20 |
| ☐ 773 | Justin Morneau | .10 | .30 |
| ☐ 774 | Ryan Bukvich | .07 | .20 |
| ☐ 775 | Mike Gonzalez | .07 | .20 |
| ☐ 776 | Tsuyoshi Shinjo | .10 | .30 |
| ☐ 777 | Matt Mantei | .07 | .20 |
| ☐ 778 | Jimmy Journell | .07 | .20 |
| ☐ 779 | Brian Lawrence | .07 | .20 |
| ☐ 780 | Mike Lieberthal | .10 | .30 |
| ☐ 781 | Scott Mullen | .07 | .20 |
| ☐ 782 | Zach Day | .07 | .20 |
| ☐ 783 | John Thomson | .07 | .20 |
| ☐ 784 | Ben Sheets | .10 | .30 |
| ☐ 785 | Damon Minor | .07 | .20 |
| ☐ 786 | Jose Valentin | .07 | .20 |
| ☐ 787 | Armando Benitez | .07 | .20 |
| ☐ 788 | Jamie Walker RC | .08 | .25 |
| ☐ 789 | Preston Wilson | .07 | .20 |
| ☐ 790 | Josh Wilson | .07 | .20 |
| ☐ 791 | Phil Nevin | .10 | .30 |
| ☐ 792 | Roberto Hernandez | .07 | .20 |
| ☐ 793 | Mike Williams | .07 | .20 |
| ☐ 794 | Jake Peavy | .10 | .30 |
| ☐ 795 | Paul Shuey | .07 | .20 |
| ☐ 796 | Chad Bradford | .07 | .20 |
| ☐ 797 | Bobby Jenks | .10 | .30 |
| ☐ 798 | Sean Douglass | .07 | .20 |
| ☐ 799 | Damian Miller | .07 | .20 |
| ☐ 800 | Mark Wohlers | .07 | .20 |
| ☐ 801 | Ty Wigginton | .07 | .20 |
| ☐ 802 | Alfonso Soriano | .10 | .30 |
| ☐ 803 | Randy Johnson | .30 | .75 |
| ☐ 804 | Placido Polanco | .07 | .20 |
| ☐ 805 | Drew Henson | .07 | .20 |
| ☐ 806 | Tony Womack | .07 | .20 |
| ☐ 807 | Pokey Reese | .07 | .20 |
| ☐ 808 | Albert Pujols | .60 | 1.50 |
| ☐ 809 | Henri Stanley | .07 | .20 |
| ☐ 810 | Mike Rivera | .07 | .20 |
| ☐ 811 | John Lackey | .07 | .20 |
| ☐ 812 | Brian Wright FY RC | .15 | .40 |
| ☐ 813 | Eric Good | .07 | .20 |
| ☐ 814 | Demell Stenson | .07 | .20 |
| ☐ 815 | Kirk Rueter | .07 | .20 |
| ☐ 816 | Todd Zeile | .07 | .20 |
| ☐ 817 | Brad Thomas | .07 | .20 |
| ☐ 818 | Shawn Sedlacek | .07 | .20 |
| ☐ 819 | Garrett Stephenson | .07 | .20 |
| ☐ 820 | Mark Teixeira | .20 | .50 |
| ☐ 821 | Tim Hudson | .10 | .30 |
| ☐ 822 | Mike Koplove | .07 | .20 |
| ☐ 823 | Chris Reitsma | .07 | .20 |
| ☐ 824 | Rafael Soriano | .07 | .20 |
| ☐ 825 | Ugueth Urbina | .07 | .20 |
| ☐ 826 | Lance Carter | .07 | .20 |
| ☐ 827 | Colin Young | .07 | .20 |
| ☐ 828 | Pat Strange | .07 | .20 |
| ☐ 829 | Juan Pena | .07 | .20 |
| ☐ 830 | Joe Thurston | .07 | .20 |
| ☐ 831 | Shawn Green | .10 | .30 |
| ☐ 832 | Pedro Astacio | .07 | .20 |
| ☐ 833 | Danny Wright | .07 | .20 |
| ☐ 834 | Wes O'Brien FY RC | .15 | .40 |
| ☐ 835 | Luis Lopez | .07 | .20 |
| ☐ 836 | Randall Simon | .07 | .20 |
| ☐ 837 | Jaret Wright | .07 | .20 |
| ☐ 838 | Jayson Werth | .07 | .20 |
| ☐ 839 | Endy Chavez | .07 | .20 |
| ☐ 840 | Checklist 5 | .07 | .20 |
| ☐ 841 | Chad Paronto | .07 | .20 |
| ☐ 842 | Randy Winn | .07 | .20 |
| ☐ 843 | Sidney Ponson | .07 | .20 |
| ☐ 844 | Robin Ventura | .10 | .30 |
| ☐ 845 | Rich Aurilia | .07 | .20 |
| ☐ 846 | Joaquin Benoit | .07 | .20 |
| ☐ 847 | Barry Bonds | .75 | 2.00 |
| ☐ 848 | Carl Crawford | .10 | .30 |
| ☐ 849 | Jeromy Burnitz | .10 | .30 |
| ☐ 850 | Orlando Cabrera | .10 | .30 |
| ☐ 851 | Luis Vizcaino | .07 | .20 |
| ☐ 852 | Randy Wolf | .07 | .20 |
| ☐ 853 | Todd Walker | .07 | .20 |
| ☐ 854 | Jeremy Affeldt | .07 | .20 |
| ☐ 855 | Einar Diaz | .07 | .20 |
| ☐ 856 | Carl Everett | .10 | .30 |
| ☐ 857 | Wiki Gonzalez | .07 | .20 |
| ☐ 858 | Mike Paradis | .07 | .20 |
| ☐ 859 | Travis Harper | .07 | .20 |
| ☐ 860 | Mike Piazza | .50 | 1.25 |
| ☐ 861 | Will Ohman | .07 | .20 |
| ☐ 862 | Eric Young | .07 | .20 |
| ☐ 863 | Jason Grabowski | .07 | .20 |
| ☐ 864 | Rett Johnson RC | .15 | .40 |
| ☐ 865 | Aubrey Huff | .10 | .30 |
| ☐ 866 | John Smoltz | .20 | .50 |
| ☐ 867 | Mickey Callaway | .07 | .20 |
| ☐ 868 | Joe Kennedy | .07 | .20 |
| ☐ 869 | Tim Redding | .07 | .20 |
| ☐ 870 | Colby Lewis | .07 | .20 |
| ☐ 871 | Salomon Torres | .07 | .20 |
| ☐ 872 | Marco Scutaro | .07 | .20 |
| ☐ 873 | Tony Batista | .07 | .20 |
| ☐ 874 | Dmitri Young | .10 | .30 |
| ☐ 875 | Scott Williamson | .07 | .20 |
| ☐ 876 | Scott Spiezio | .07 | .20 |
| ☐ 877 | John Webb | .07 | .20 |
| ☐ 878 | Jose Acevedo | .07 | .20 |
| ☐ 879 | Kevin One | .07 | .20 |
| ☐ 880 | Jacque Jones | .10 | .30 |
| ☐ 881 | Ben Francisco FY RC | .15 | .40 |
| ☐ 882 | Bobby Basham FY RC | .15 | .40 |
| ☐ 883 | Corey Shafer FY RC | .15 | .40 |
| ☐ 884 | J.D. Durbin FY RC | .15 | .40 |
| ☐ 885 | Chien-Ming Wang FY RC | 3.00 | 8.00 |
| ☐ 886 | Adam Stern FY RC | .08 | .25 |
| ☐ 887 | Wayne Lydon FY RC | .15 | .40 |
| ☐ 888 | Derell McCall FY RC | .15 | .40 |
| ☐ 889 | Jon Nelson FY RC | .20 | .50 |
| ☐ 890 | Willie Eyre FY RC | .15 | .40 |
| ☐ 891 | Ramon Nivar-Martinez FY RC | .15 | .40 |
| ☐ 892 | Adrian Myers FY RC | .08 | .25 |
| ☐ 893 | Jamie Athas FY RC | .15 | .40 |
| ☐ 894 | Ismael Castro FY RC | .20 | .50 |
| ☐ 895 | David Martinez FY RC | .15 | .40 |
| ☐ 896 | Terry Tiffee FY RC | .15 | .40 |
| ☐ 897 | Nathan Panther FY RC | .15 | .40 |
| ☐ 898 | Kyle Roat FY RC | .15 | .40 |
| ☐ 899 | Kason Gabbard FY RC | .15 | .40 |
| ☐ 900 | Hanley Ramirez FY RC | 2.00 | 5.00 |
| ☐ 901 | Bryan Grace FY RC | .15 | .40 |
| ☐ 902 | B.J. Barns FY RC | .15 | .40 |
| ☐ 903 | Greg Bruso FY RC | .15 | .40 |
| ☐ 904 | Mike Neu FY RC | .15 | .40 |
| ☐ 905 | Dustin Yount FY RC | .20 | .50 |
| ☐ 906 | Shane Victorino FY RC | .40 | 1.00 |
| ☐ 907 | Brian Burgamy FY RC | .15 | .40 |
| ☐ 908 | Beau Kemp FY RC | .15 | .40 |
| ☐ 909 | David Corrente FY RC | .15 | .40 |
| ☐ 910 | Dexter Cooper FY RC | .15 | .40 |
| ☐ 911 | Chris Colton FY RC | .15 | .40 |
| ☐ 912 | David Cash FY RC | .15 | .40 |
| ☐ 913 | Bernie Castro FY RC | .15 | .40 |
| ☐ 914 | Luis Hodge FY RC | .15 | .40 |
| ☐ 915 | Jeff Clark FY RC | .15 | .40 |
| ☐ 916 | Jason Kubel FY RC | .40 | 1.00 |
| ☐ 917 | T.J. Bohn FY RC | .15 | .40 |
| ☐ 918 | Luke Steidlmayer FY RC | .15 | .40 |
| ☐ 919 | Matthew Peterson FY RC | .15 | .40 |
| ☐ 920 | Darrell Rasner FY RC | .15 | .40 |
| ☐ 921 | Scott Tyler FY RC | .20 | .50 |
| ☐ 922 | Gary Schneidmiller FY RC | .15 | .40 |
| ☐ 923 | Gregor Blanco FY RC | .15 | .40 |
| ☐ 924 | Ryan Cameron FY RC | .15 | .40 |
| ☐ 925 | Wilfredo Rodriguez FY | .07 | .20 |
| ☐ 926 | Rajai Davis FY RC | .15 | .40 |
| ☐ 927 | Evel Bastida-Martinez FY RC | .15 | .40 |
| ☐ 928 | Chris Duncan FY RC | 1.50 | 4.00 |
| ☐ 929 | Dave Pember FY RC | .15 | .40 |
| ☐ 930 | Branden Florence FY RC | .15 | .40 |
| ☐ 931 | Eric Eckenstahler FY | .07 | .20 |
| ☐ 932 | Hong-Chih Kuo FY RC | 2.00 | 5.00 |
| ☐ 933 | Il Kim FY RC | .15 | .40 |
| ☐ 934 | Michael Garciaparra FY RC | .15 | .40 |
| ☐ 935 | Kip Bouknight FY RC | .20 | .50 |
| ☐ 936 | Gary Harris FY RC | .15 | .40 |
| ☐ 937 | Derry Hammond FY RC | .15 | .40 |
| ☐ 938 | Joey Gomes FY RC | .15 | .40 |
| ☐ 939 | Donnie Hood FY RC | .20 | .50 |
| ☐ 940 | Clay Hensley FY RC | .15 | .40 |
| ☐ 941 | David Pahucki FY RC | .15 | .40 |
| ☐ 942 | Wilton Reynolds FY RC | .15 | .40 |
| ☐ 943 | Michael Hinckley FY RC | .20 | .50 |
| ☐ 944 | Josh Willingham FY RC | .40 | 1.00 |
| ☐ 945 | Pete LaForest FY RC | .15 | .40 |
| ☐ 946 | Pete Smart FY RC | .15 | .40 |
| ☐ 947 | Jay Sitzman FY RC | .15 | .40 |
| ☐ 948 | Mark Malaska FY RC | .15 | .40 |
| ☐ 949 | Mike Gallo FY RC | .15 | .40 |
| ☐ 950 | Matt Diaz FY RC | .30 | .75 |
| ☐ 951 | Brennan King FY RC | .15 | .40 |
| ☐ 952 | Ryan Howard FY RC | 8.00 | 20.00 |
| ☐ 953 | Daryl Clark FY RC | .15 | .40 |
| ☐ 954 | Dayton Buller FY RC | .15 | .40 |
| ☐ 955 | Rylan Reed FY RC | .15 | .40 |
| ☐ 956 | Chris Booker FY RC | .07 | .20 |
| ☐ 957 | Brandon Watson FY RC | .15 | .40 |
| ☐ 958 | Matt DeMarco FY RC | .15 | .40 |
| ☐ 959 | Doug Waechter FY RC | .20 | .50 |
| ☐ 960 | Callix Crabbe FY RC | .20 | .50 |
| ☐ 961 | Jairo Garcia FY RC | .20 | .50 |
| ☐ 962 | Jason Perry FY RC | .15 | .40 |
| ☐ 963 | Eric Riggs FY RC | .20 | .50 |
| ☐ 964 | Travis Ishikawa FY RC | .30 | .75 |
| ☐ 965 | Simon Pond FY RC | .15 | .40 |
| ☐ 966 | Manuel Ramirez FY RC | .20 | .50 |
| ☐ 967 | Tyler Johnson FY RC | .15 | .40 |
| ☐ 968 | Jaime Bubela FY RC | .15 | .40 |
| ☐ 969 | Haj Turay FY RC | .08 | .25 |
| ☐ 970 | Tyson Graham FY RC | .15 | .40 |
| ☐ 971 | David DeJesus FY RC | .30 | .75 |
| ☐ 972 | Franklin Gutierrez FY RC | .40 | 1.00 |
| ☐ 973 | Craig Brazell FY RC | .15 | .40 |
| ☐ 974 | Keith Stamler FY RC | .15 | .40 |
| ☐ 975 | Jemel Spearman FY RC | .15 | .40 |
| ☐ 976 | Ozzie Chavez FY RC | .15 | .40 |
| ☐ 977 | Nick Trzesniak FY RC | .15 | .40 |
| ☐ 978 | Bill Simon FY RC | .15 | .40 |
| ☐ 979 | Matthew Hagen FY RC | .15 | .40 |

- ☐ 980 Chris Kroski FY RC .15 .40
- ☐ 981 Prentice Redman FY RC .15 .40
- ☐ 982 Kevin Randel FY RC .15 .40
- ☐ 983 Thomari Story-Harden FY RC .15 .40
- ☐ 984 Brian Shackelford FY RC .15 .40
- ☐ 985 Mike Adams FY RC .15 .40
- ☐ 986 Brian McCann FY RC 2.00 5.00
- ☐ 987 Mike McNutt FY RC .15 .40
- ☐ 988 Aron Weston FY RC .15 .40
- ☐ 989 Dustin Moseley FY RC .15 .40
- ☐ 990 Bryan Bullington FY RC .15 .40

## 2004 Topps Total

- ☐ COMPLETE SET (880) 75.00 150.00
- ☐ OVERALL PRESS PLATES ODDS 1:159
- ☐ PLATES PRINT RUN 1 #'d SET PER COLOR
- ☐ PLATES: BLACK, CYAN, MAGENTA & YELLOW
- ☐ NO PLATES PRICING DUE TO SCARCITY
- ☐ 1 Kevin Brown .10 .30
- ☐ 2 Mike Mordecai .10 .30
- ☐ 3 Seung Song .10 .30
- ☐ 4 Mike Maroth .10 .30
- ☐ 5 Mike Lieberthal .10 .30
- ☐ 6 Billy Koch .10 .30
- ☐ 7 Mike Stanton .10 .30
- ☐ 8 Brad Penny .10 .30
- ☐ 9 Brooks Kieschnick .10 .30
- ☐ 10 Carlos Delgado .10 .30
- ☐ 11 Brady Clark .10 .30
- ☐ 12 Ramon Martinez .10 .30
- ☐ 13 Dan Wilson .10 .30
- ☐ 14 Guillermo Mota .10 .30
- ☐ 15 Trevor Hoffman .10 .30
- ☐ 16 Tony Batista .10 .30
- ☐ 17 Rusty Greer .10 .30
- ☐ 18 David Weathers .10 .30
- ☐ 19 Horacio Ramirez .10 .30
- ☐ 20 Aubrey Huff .10 .30
- ☐ 21 Casey Blake .10 .30
- ☐ 22 Ryan Bukvich .10 .30
- ☐ 23 Garrett Atkins .10 .30
- ☐ 24 Jose Contreras .10 .30
- ☐ 25 Chipper Jones .30 .75
- ☐ 26 Neifi Perez .10 .30
- ☐ 27 Scott Linebrink .10 .30
- ☐ 28 Matt Kinney .10 .30
- ☐ 29 Michael Restovich .10 .30
- ☐ 30 Scott Rolen .20 .50
- ☐ 31 John Franco .10 .30
- ☐ 32 Toby Hall .10 .30
- ☐ 33 Willy Mo Pena .10 .30
- ☐ 34 Dennis Tankersley .10 .30
- ☐ 35 Robb Nen .10 .30
- ☐ 36 Jose Valverde .10 .30
- ☐ 37 Chin-Feng Chen .10 .30
- ☐ 38 Gary Knotts .10 .30
- ☐ 39 Mark Sweeney .10 .30
- ☐ 40 Bret Boone .10 .30
- ☐ 41 Josh Phelps .10 .30
- ☐ 42 Jason LaRue .10 .30
- ☐ 43 Tim Redding .10 .30
- ☐ 44 Greg Myers .10 .30
- ☐ 45 Darin Erstad .10 .30
- ☐ 46 Kip Wells .10 .30
- ☐ 47 Matt Ford .10 .30
- ☐ 48 Jerome Williams .10 .30
- ☐ 49 Brian Meadows .10 .30
- ☐ 50 Albert Pujols .60 1.50
- ☐ 51 Kirk Saarloos .10 .30
- ☐ 52 Scott Eyre .10 .30
- ☐ 53 John Flaherty .10 .30
- ☐ 54 Rafael Soriano .10 .30
- ☐ 55 Shea Hillenbrand .10 .30
- ☐ 56 Kyle Farnsworth .10 .30
- ☐ 57 Nate Cornejo .10 .30
- ☐ 58 Julian Tavarez .10 .30
- ☐ 59 Ryan Vogelsong .10 .30
- ☐ 60 Ryan Klesko .10 .30
- ☐ 61 Luke Hudson .10 .30
- ☐ 62 Justin Morneau .10 .30
- ☐ 63 Frank Catalanotto .10 .30
- ☐ 64 Derrick Turnbow .10 .30
- ☐ 65 Marcus Giles .10 .30
- ☐ 66 Mark Mulder .10 .30
- ☐ 67 Matt Anderson .10 .30
- ☐ 68 Mike Matheny .10 .30
- ☐ 69 Brian Lawrence .10 .30
- ☐ 70 Bobby Abreu .10 .30
- ☐ 71 Damian Moss .10 .30
- ☐ 72 Richard Hidalgo .10 .30
- ☐ 73 Mark Kotsay .10 .30
- ☐ 74 Mike Cameron .10 .30
- ☐ 75 Troy Glaus .10 .30
- ☐ 76 Matt Holliday .15 .40
- ☐ 77 Byung-Hyun Kim .10 .30
- ☐ 78 Aaron Sele .10 .30
- ☐ 79 Danny Graves .10 .30
- ☐ 80 Barry Zito .10 .30
- ☐ 81 Matt LeCroy .10 .30
- ☐ 82 Jason Isringhausen .10 .30
- ☐ 83 Colby Lewis .10 .30
- ☐ 84 Franklyn German .10 .30
- ☐ 85 Luis Matos .10 .30
- ☐ 86 Mike Timlin .10 .30
- ☐ 87 Miguel Batista .10 .30
- ☐ 88 John McDonald .10 .30
- ☐ 89 Joey Eischen .10 .30
- ☐ 90 Mike Mussina .20 .50
- ☐ 91 Jack Wilson .10 .30
- ☐ 92 Aaron Cook .10 .30
- ☐ 93 John Parrish .10 .30
- ☐ 94 Jose Valentin .10 .30
- ☐ 95 Johnny Damon .20 .50
- ☐ 96 Pat Burrell .10 .30
- ☐ 97 Brendan Donnelly .10 .30
- ☐ 98 Lance Carter .10 .30
- ☐ 99 Omar Daal .10 .30
- ☐ 100 Ichiro Suzuki .60 1.50
- ☐ 101 Robin Ventura .10 .30
- ☐ 102 Brian Shouse .10 .30
- ☐ 103 Kevin Jarvis .10 .30
- ☐ 104 Jason Young .10 .30
- ☐ 105 Moises Alou .10 .30
- ☐ 106 Wes Obermueller .10 .30
- ☐ 107 David Segui .10 .30
- ☐ 108 Mike MacDougal .10 .30
- ☐ 109 John Buck .10 .30
- ☐ 110 Gary Sheffield .10 .30
- ☐ 111 Yorvit Torrealba .10 .30
- ☐ 112 Matt Kata .10 .30
- ☐ 113 David Bell .10 .30
- ☐ 114 Juan Gonzalez .10 .30
- ☐ 115 Kelvim Escobar .10 .30
- ☐ 116 Ruben Sierra .10 .30
- ☐ 117 Todd Wellemeyer .10 .30
- ☐ 118 Jamie Walker .10 .30
- ☐ 119 Will Cunnane .10 .30
- ☐ 120 Cliff Floyd .10 .30
- ☐ 121 Aramis Ramirez .10 .30
- ☐ 122 Damian Marte .10 .30
- ☐ 123 Juan Castro .10 .30
- ☐ 124 Chris Woodward .10 .30
- ☐ 125 Andruw Jones .20 .50
- ☐ 126 Ben Weber .10 .30
- ☐ 127 Dee Brown .10 .30
- ☐ 128 Steve Reed .10 .30
- ☐ 129 Gabe Kapler .10 .30
- ☐ 130 Melvin Cabrera .20 .50
- ☐ 131 Billy McMillon .10 .30
- ☐ 132 Julio Mateo .10 .30
- ☐ 133 Preston Wilson .10 .30
- ☐ 134 Tony Clark .10 .30
- ☐ 135 Carlos Lee .10 .30
- ☐ 136 Carlos Baerga .10 .30
- ☐ 137 Mike Crudale .10 .30
- ☐ 138 David Ross .10 .30
- ☐ 139 Josh Fogg .10 .30
- ☐ 140 Dmitri Young .10 .30
- ☐ 141 Cliff Lee .10 .30
- ☐ 142 Mike Lowell .10 .30
- ☐ 143 Jason Lane .10 .30
- ☐ 144 Pedro Feliz .10 .30
- ☐ 145 Ken Griffey Jr. .50 1.25
- ☐ 146 Dustin Hermanson .10 .30
- ☐ 147 Scott Hodges .10 .30
- ☐ 148 Aquilino Lopez .10 .30
- ☐ 149 Wes Helms .10 .30
- ☐ 150 Jason Giambi .10 .30
- ☐ 151 Erasmo Ramirez .10 .30
- ☐ 152 Sean Burroughs .10 .30
- ☐ 153 J.T. Snow .10 .30
- ☐ 154 Eddie Guardado .10 .30
- ☐ 155 C.C. Sabathia .10 .30
- ☐ 156 Kyle Lohse .10 .30
- ☐ 157 Roberto Hernandez .10 .30
- ☐ 158 Jason Simontacchi .10 .30
- ☐ 159 Tim Spooneybarger .10 .30
- ☐ 160 Alfonso Soriano .10 .30
- ☐ 161 Mike Gonzalez .10 .30
- ☐ 162 Alex Cora .10 .30
- ☐ 163 Kevin Gryboski .10 .30
- ☐ 164 Mike Lincoln .10 .30
- ☐ 165 Luis Castillo .10 .30
- ☐ 166 Odalis Perez .10 .30
- ☐ 167 Alex Sanchez .10 .30
- ☐ 168 Rob Mackowiak .10 .30
- ☐ 169 Francisco Rodriguez .10 .30
- ☐ 170 Roy Oswalt .10 .30
- ☐ 171 Omar Infante .10 .30
- ☐ 172 Ryan Jensen .10 .30
- ☐ 173 Ben Broussard .10 .30
- ☐ 174 Mark Hendrickson .10 .30
- ☐ 175 Manny Ramirez .20 .50
- ☐ 176 Rob Bell .10 .30
- ☐ 177 Adam Everett .10 .30
- ☐ 178 Chris George .10 .30
- ☐ 179 Ronnie Belliard .10 .30
- ☐ 180 Eric Gagne .10 .30
- ☐ 181 Scott Schoeneweis .10 .30
- ☐ 182 Kris Benson .10 .30
- ☐ 183 Amaury Telemaco .10 .30
- ☐ 184 John Riedling .10 .30
- ☐ 185 Juan Pierre .10 .30
- ☐ 186 Ramon Ortiz .10 .30
- ☐ 187 Luis Rivas .10 .30
- ☐ 188 Larry Bigbie .10 .30
- ☐ 189 Robby Hammock .10 .30
- ☐ 190 Geoff Jenkins .10 .30
- ☐ 191 Chad Cordero .10 .30
- ☐ 192 Mark Ellis .10 .30
- ☐ 193 Mark Loretta .10 .30
- ☐ 194 Ryan Drese .10 .30
- ☐ 195 Lance Berkman .10 .30
- ☐ 196 Kevin Appier .10 .30
- ☐ 197 Kiko Calero .10 .30
- ☐ 198 Mickey Callaway .10 .30
- ☐ 199 Chase Utley .20 .50
- ☐ 200 Nomar Garciaparra .50 1.25
- ☐ 201 Kevin Cash .10 .30
- ☐ 202 Ramiro Mendoza .10 .30
- ☐ 203 Shane Reynolds .10 .30
- ☐ 204 Chris Spurling .10 .30
- ☐ 205 Aaron Guiel .10 .30
- ☐ 206 Mark DeRosa .10 .30
- ☐ 207 Adam Kennedy .10 .30
- ☐ 208 Andy Pettitte .20 .50
- ☐ 209 Rafael Palmeiro .20 .50
- ☐ 210 Luis Gonzalez .10 .30
- ☐ 211 Ryan Franklin .10 .30
- ☐ 212 Bob Wickman .10 .30
- ☐ 213 Ron Calloway .10 .30
- ☐ 214 Jae Weong Seo .10 .30
- ☐ 215 Kazuhisa Ishii .10 .30
- ☐ 216 Sterling Hitchcock .10 .30
- ☐ 217 Jimmy Gobble .10 .30
- ☐ 218 Chad Moeller .10 .30
- ☐ 219 Jake Peavy .10 .30
- ☐ 220 John Smoltz .20 .50
- ☐ 221 Donovan Osborne .10 .30
- ☐ 222 David Wells .10 .30
- ☐ 223 Brad Lidge .10 .30
- ☐ 224 Carlos Zambrano .10 .30
- ☐ 225 Kerry Wood .10 .30
- ☐ 226 Alex Cintron .10 .30
- ☐ 227 Javier A. Lopez .10 .30
- ☐ 228 Jeremy Griffiths .10 .30
- ☐ 229 Jon Garland .10 .30
- ☐ 230 Curt Schilling .20 .50
- ☐ 231 Alex Scott Gonzalez .10 .30
- ☐ 232 Jay Gibbons .10 .30

|  |  | | |
|---|---|---|---|
| 233 | Aaron Miles | .10 | .30 |
| 234 | Mike Gallo | .10 | .30 |
| 235 | Johan Santana | .30 | .75 |
| 236 | Jose Guillen | .10 | .30 |
| 237 | Jeff Conine | .10 | .30 |
| 238 | Matt Roney | .10 | .30 |
| 239 | Desi Relaford | .10 | .30 |
| 240 | Frank Thomas | .30 | .75 |
| 241 | Danny Patterson | .10 | .30 |
| 242 | Kevin Mench | .10 | .30 |
| 243 | Mike Redmond | .10 | .30 |
| 244 | Jeff Suppan | .10 | .30 |
| 245 | Carl Everett | .10 | .30 |
| 246 | Jack Cressend | .10 | .30 |
| 247 | Matt Mantei | .10 | .30 |
| 248 | Enrique Wilson | .10 | .30 |
| 249 | Craig Counsell | .10 | .30 |
| 250 | Mark Prior | .20 | .50 |
| 251 | Jared Sandberg | .10 | .30 |
| 252 | Scott Strickland | .10 | .30 |
| 253 | Lew Ford | .10 | .30 |
| 254 | Hee Seop Choi | .10 | .30 |
| 255 | Jason Phillips | .10 | .30 |
| 256 | Jason Jennings | .10 | .30 |
| 257 | Todd Pratt | .10 | .30 |
| 258 | Matt Herges | .10 | .30 |
| 259 | Kerry Ligtenberg | .10 | .30 |
| 260 | Austin Kearns | .10 | .30 |
| 261 | Jay Witasick | .10 | .30 |
| 262 | Tony Armas Jr. | .10 | .30 |
| 263 | Tom Martin | .10 | .30 |
| 264 | Oliver Perez | .10 | .30 |
| 265 | Jorge Posada | .20 | .50 |
| 266 | Jason Boyd | .10 | .30 |
| 267 | Ben Hendrickson | .10 | .30 |
| 268 | Reggie Sandels | .10 | .30 |
| 269 | Julio Lugo | .10 | .30 |
| 270 | Pedro Martinez | .20 | .50 |
| 271 | Kyle Snyder | .10 | .30 |
| 272 | Felipe Lopez | .10 | .30 |
| 273 | Kevin Millar | .10 | .30 |
| 274 | Travis Hafner | .10 | .30 |
| 275 | Magglio Ordonez | .10 | .30 |
| 276 | Marlon Byrd | .10 | .30 |
| 277 | Scott Spiezio | .10 | .30 |
| 278 | Mark Corey | .10 | .30 |
| 279 | Tim Salmon | .20 | .50 |
| 280 | Alex Gonzalez | .10 | .30 |
| 281 | Marquis Grissom | .10 | .30 |
| 282 | Miguel Olivo | .10 | .30 |
| 283 | Orlando Hudson | .10 | .30 |
| 284 | Rondell White | .10 | .30 |
| 285 | Jermaine Dye | .10 | .30 |
| 286 | Paul Shuey | .10 | .30 |
| 287 | Brandon Inge | .10 | .30 |
| 288 | B.J. Surhoff | .10 | .30 |
| 289 | Edgar Gonzalez | .10 | .30 |
| 290 | Angel Berroa | .10 | .30 |
| 291 | Claudio Vargas | .10 | .30 |
| 292 | Cesar Izturis | .10 | .30 |
| 293 | Brandon Phillips | .10 | .30 |
| 294 | Jeff Duncan | .10 | .30 |
| 295 | Randy Wolf | .10 | .30 |
| 296 | Barry Larkin | .20 | .50 |
| 297 | Felix Rodriguez | .10 | .30 |
| 298 | Robb Quinlan | .10 | .30 |
| 299 | Brian Jordan | .10 | .30 |
| 300 | Dontrelle Willis | .20 | .50 |
| 301 | Doug Davis | .10 | .30 |
| 302 | Ricky Stone | .10 | .30 |
| 303 | Travis Harper | .10 | .30 |
| 304 | Jaret Wright | .10 | .30 |
| 305 | Edgardo Alfonzo | .10 | .30 |
| 306 | Quinton McCracken | .10 | .30 |
| 307 | Jason Bay | .10 | .30 |
| 308 | Joe Randa | .10 | .30 |
| 309 | Steve Sparks | .10 | .30 |
| 310 | Roy Halladay | .10 | .30 |
| 311 | Antonio Alfonseca | .10 | .30 |
| 312 | Michael Cuddyer | .10 | .30 |
| 313 | John Patterson | .10 | .30 |
| 314 | Chris Widger | .10 | .30 |
| 315 | Shigetoshi Hasegawa | .10 | .30 |
| 316 | Tim Wakefield | .10 | .30 |
| 317 | Scott Hatteberg | .10 | .30 |
| 318 | Mike Remlinger | .10 | .30 |
| 319 | Jose Vizcaino | .10 | .30 |
| 320 | Rocco Baldelli | .10 | .30 |
| 321 | David Riske | .10 | .30 |
| 322 | Steve Karsay | .10 | .30 |
| 323 | Peter Bergeron | .10 | .30 |
| 324 | Jeff Weaver | .10 | .30 |
| 325 | Larry Walker | .10 | .30 |
| 326 | Jack Cust | .10 | .30 |
| 327 | Bo Hart | .10 | .30 |
| 328 | Rod Beck | .10 | .30 |
| 329 | Jose Acevedo | .10 | .30 |
| 330 | Hank Blalock | .10 | .30 |
| 331 | Tom Gordon | .10 | .30 |
| 332 | Brian Fuentes | .10 | .30 |
| 333 | Tomas Perez | .10 | .30 |
| 334 | Lenny Harris | .10 | .30 |
| 335 | Matt Morris | .10 | .30 |
| 336 | Jeremi Gonzalez | .10 | .30 |
| 337 | David Eckstein | .10 | .30 |
| 338 | Aaron Rowand | .10 | .30 |
| 339 | Rick Bauer | .10 | .30 |
| 340 | Jim Edmonds | .10 | .30 |
| 341 | Joe Borowski | .10 | .30 |
| 342 | Eric DuBose | .10 | .30 |
| 343 | D'Angelo Jimenez | .10 | .30 |
| 344 | Tomo Ohka | .10 | .30 |
| 345 | Victor Zambrano | .10 | .30 |
| 346 | Joe McEwing | .10 | .30 |
| 347 | Jorge Sosa | .10 | .30 |
| 348 | Keith Ginter | .10 | .30 |
| 349 | A.J. Pierzynski | .10 | .30 |
| 350 | Mike Sweeney | .10 | .30 |
| 351 | Shawn Chacon | .10 | .30 |
| 352 | Matt Clement | .10 | .30 |
| 353 | Vance Wilson | .10 | .30 |
| 354 | Benito Santiago | .10 | .30 |
| 355 | Eric Hinske | .10 | .30 |
| 356 | Vladimir Guerrero | .30 | .75 |
| 357 | Kenny Rogers | .10 | .30 |
| 358 | Travis Lee | .10 | .30 |
| 359 | Jay Powell | .10 | .30 |
| 360 | Phil Nevin | .10 | .30 |
| 361 | Willie Harris | .10 | .30 |
| 362 | Ty Wigginton | .10 | .30 |
| 363 | Chad Fox | .10 | .30 |
| 364 | Junior Spivey | .10 | .30 |
| 365 | Brandon Webb | .10 | .30 |
| 366 | Brett Myers | .10 | .30 |
| 367 | Alexis Gomez | .10 | .30 |
| 368 | Dave Roberts | .10 | .30 |
| 369 | LaTroy Hawkins | .10 | .30 |
| 370 | Kevin Millwood | .10 | .30 |
| 371 | Brian Schneider | .10 | .30 |
| 372 | Blaine Neal | .10 | .30 |
| 373 | Jeromy Burnitz | .10 | .30 |
| 374 | Ted Lilly | .10 | .30 |
| 375 | Shawn Green | .10 | .30 |
| 376 | Carlos Pena | .10 | .30 |
| 377 | Gil Meche | .10 | .30 |
| 378 | Jeff Bagwell | .20 | .50 |
| 379 | Alex Escobar | .10 | .30 |
| 380 | Erubiel Durazo | .10 | .30 |
| 381 | Cristian Guzman | .10 | .30 |
| 382 | Rocky Biddle | .10 | .30 |
| 383 | Craig Wilson | .10 | .30 |
| 384 | Rey Sanchez | .10 | .30 |
| 385 | Russ Ortiz | .10 | .30 |
| 386 | Freddy Garcia | .10 | .30 |
| 387 | Luis Vizcaino | .10 | .30 |
| 388 | David Ortiz | .30 | .75 |
| 389 | Jose Molina | .10 | .30 |
| 390 | Edgar Martinez | .20 | .50 |
| 391 | Nate Bump | .10 | .30 |
| 392 | Brent Mayne | .10 | .30 |
| 393 | Ray King | .10 | .30 |
| 394 | Paul Wilson | .10 | .30 |
| 395 | Melvin Mora | .10 | .30 |
| 396 | Morgan Ensberg | .10 | .30 |
| 397 | Ramon Hernandez | .10 | .30 |
| 398 | Juan Rincon | .10 | .30 |
| 399 | Ron Mahay | .10 | .30 |
| 400 | Jeff Kent | .10 | .30 |
| 401 | Cal Eldred | .10 | .30 |
| 402 | Mike Difelice | .10 | .30 |
| 403 | Valerio De Los Santos | .10 | .30 |
| 404 | Steve Finley | .10 | .30 |
| 405 | Trot Nixon | .10 | .30 |
| 406 | Akinori Otsuka RC | .15 | .40 |
| 407 | Ryan Freel | .10 | .30 |
| 408 | Ray Durham | .10 | .30 |
| 409 | Aaron Heilman | .10 | .30 |
| 410 | Edgar Renteria | .10 | .30 |
| 411 | Mike Hampton | .10 | .30 |
| 412 | Kirk Rueter | .10 | .30 |
| 413 | Jim Mecir | .10 | .30 |
| 414 | Brian Roberts | .10 | .30 |
| 415 | Paul Konerko | .10 | .30 |
| 416 | Reed Johnson | .10 | .30 |
| 417 | Roger Clemens | .60 | 1.50 |
| 418 | Coco Crisp | .10 | .30 |
| 419 | Carlos Hernandez | .10 | .30 |
| 420 | Scott Podsednik | .10 | .30 |
| 421 | Miguel Cairo | .10 | .30 |
| 422 | Abraham Nunez | .10 | .30 |
| 423 | Endy Chavez | .10 | .30 |
| 424 | Eric Munson | .10 | .30 |
| 425 | Torii Hunter | .10 | .30 |
| 426 | Ben Howard | .10 | .30 |
| 427 | Chris Gomez | .10 | .30 |
| 428 | Francisco Cordero | .10 | .30 |
| 429 | Jeffrey Hammonds | .10 | .30 |
| 430 | Shannon Stewart | .10 | .30 |
| 431 | Einar Diaz | .10 | .30 |
| 432 | Eric Byrnes | .10 | .30 |
| 433 | Marty Cordova | .10 | .30 |
| 434 | Matt Ginter | .10 | .30 |
| 435 | Victor Martinez | .10 | .30 |
| 436 | Geronimo Gil | .10 | .30 |
| 437 | Grant Balfour | .10 | .30 |
| 438 | Ramon Vazquez | .10 | .30 |
| 439 | Jose Cruz Jr. | .10 | .30 |
| 440 | Orlando Cabrera | .10 | .30 |
| 441 | Joe Kennedy | .10 | .30 |
| 442 | Scott Williamson | .10 | .30 |
| 443 | Troy Percival | .10 | .30 |
| 444 | Derrek Lee | .20 | .50 |
| 445 | Runelvys Hernandez | .10 | .30 |
| 446 | Mark Grudzielanek | .10 | .30 |
| 447 | Trey Hodges | .10 | .30 |
| 448 | Jimmy Haynes | .10 | .30 |
| 449 | Eric Milton | .10 | .30 |
| 450 | Todd Helton | .20 | .50 |
| 451 | Greg Zaun | .10 | .30 |
| 452 | Woody Williams | .10 | .30 |
| 453 | Todd Walker | .10 | .30 |
| 454 | Juan Cruz | .10 | .30 |
| 455 | Fernando Vina | .10 | .30 |
| 456 | Omar Vizquel | .20 | .50 |
| 457 | Roberto Alomar | .20 | .50 |
| 458 | Bill Hall | .10 | .30 |
| 459 | Juan Rivera | .10 | .30 |
| 460 | Tom Glavine | .20 | .50 |
| 461 | Ramon Castro | .10 | .30 |
| 462 | Cory Vance | .10 | .30 |
| 463 | Dan Miceli | .10 | .30 |
| 464 | Lyle Overbay | .10 | .30 |
| 465 | Craig Biggio | .20 | .50 |
| 466 | Ricky Ledee | .10 | .30 |
| 467 | Michael Barrett | .10 | .30 |
| 468 | Jason Anderson | .10 | .30 |
| 469 | Matt Stairs | .10 | .30 |
| 470 | Jarrod Washburn | .10 | .30 |
| 471 | Todd Hundley | .10 | .30 |
| 472 | Grant Roberts | .10 | .30 |
| 473 | Randy Winn | .10 | .30 |
| 474 | Pat Hentgen | .10 | .30 |
| 475 | Jose Vidro | .10 | .30 |
| 476 | Tony Torcato | .10 | .30 |
| 477 | Jeremy Affeldt | .10 | .30 |
| 478 | Carlos Gallon | .10 | .30 |
| 479 | Paul Quantrill | .10 | .30 |
| 480 | Rafael Furcal | .10 | .30 |
| 481 | Adam Melhuse | .10 | .30 |
| 482 | Jerry Hairston Jr. | .10 | .30 |
| 483 | Adam Bernero | .10 | .30 |
| 484 | Terrence Long | .10 | .30 |
| 485 | Paul Lo Duca | .10 | .30 |
| 486 | Corey Koskie | .10 | .30 |
| 487 | John Lackey | .10 | .30 |
| 488 | Chad Zerbe | .10 | .30 |
| 489 | Vinny Castilla | .10 | .30 |
| 490 | Corey Patterson | .10 | .30 |
| 491 | John Olerud | .10 | .30 |
| 492 | Josh Bard | .10 | .30 |
| 493 | Darren Dreifort | .10 | .30 |
| 494 | Jason Standridge | .10 | .30 |
| 495 | Ben Sheets | .10 | .30 |
| 496 | Jose Castillo | .10 | .30 |

|  |  | | |
|---|---|---|---|
| 497 | Jay Payton | .10 | .30 |
| 498 | Rob Bowen | .10 | .30 |
| 499 | Bobby Higginson | .10 | .30 |
| 500 | Alex Rodriguez Yanks | .50 | 1.25 |
| 501 | Octavio Dotel | .10 | .30 |
| 502 | Rheal Cormier | .10 | .30 |
| 503 | Felix Heredia | .10 | .30 |
| 504 | Dan Wright | .10 | .30 |
| 505 | Michael Young | .10 | .30 |
| 506 | Wilfredo Ledezma | .10 | .30 |
| 507 | Sun Woo Kim | .10 | .30 |
| 508 | Michael Tejera | .10 | .30 |
| 509 | Herbert Perry | .10 | .30 |
| 510 | Esteban Loaiza | .10 | .30 |
| 511 | Alan Embree | .10 | .30 |
| 512 | Ben Davis | .10 | .30 |
| 513 | Greg Colbrunn | .10 | .30 |
| 514 | Josh Hall | .10 | .30 |
| 515 | Raul Ibanez | .10 | .30 |
| 516 | Jason Kershner | .10 | .30 |
| 517 | Corky Miller | .10 | .30 |
| 518 | Jason Marquis | .10 | .30 |
| 519 | Roger Cedeno | .10 | .30 |
| 520 | Adam Dunn | .10 | .30 |
| 521 | Paul Byrd | .10 | .30 |
| 522 | Sandy Alomar Jr. | .10 | .30 |
| 523 | Salomon Torres | .10 | .30 |
| 524 | John Halama | .10 | .30 |
| 525 | Mike Piazza | .50 | 1.25 |
| 526 | Buddy Groom | .10 | .30 |
| 527 | Adrian Beltre | .10 | .30 |
| 528 | Chad Harville | .10 | .30 |
| 529 | Javier Vazquez | .10 | .30 |
| 530 | Jody Gerut | .10 | .30 |
| 531 | Elmer Dessens | .10 | .30 |
| 532 | B.J. Ryan | .10 | .30 |
| 533 | Chad Durbin | .10 | .30 |
| 534 | Doug Mirabelli | .10 | .30 |
| 535 | Bernie Williams | .20 | .50 |
| 536 | Jeff DaVanon | .10 | .30 |
| 537 | Dave Berg | .10 | .30 |
| 538 | Geoff Blum | .10 | .30 |
| 539 | John Thomson | .10 | .30 |
| 540 | Jeremy Bonderman | .10 | .30 |
| 541 | Jeff Zimmerman | .10 | .30 |
| 542 | Derek Lowe | .10 | .30 |
| 543 | Scot Shields | .10 | .30 |
| 544 | Michael Tucker | .10 | .30 |
| 545 | Tim Hudson | .10 | .30 |
| 546 | Ryan Ludwick | .10 | .30 |
| 547 | Rick Reed | .10 | .30 |
| 548 | Placido Polanco | .10 | .30 |
| 549 | Tony Graffanino | .10 | .30 |
| 550 | Garret Anderson | .10 | .30 |
| 551 | Timo Perez | .10 | .30 |
| 552 | Jesus Colome | .10 | .30 |
| 553 | R.A. Dickey | .10 | .30 |
| 554 | Tim Worrell | .10 | .30 |
| 555 | Jason Kendall | .10 | .30 |
| 556 | Tom Goodwin | .10 | .30 |
| 557 | Joaquin Benoit | .10 | .30 |
| 558 | Stephen Randolph | .10 | .30 |
| 559 | Miguel Tejada | .10 | .30 |
| 560 | A.J. Burnett | .10 | .30 |
| 561 | Ben Diggins | .10 | .30 |
| 562 | Kent Mercker | .10 | .30 |
| 563 | Zach Day | .10 | .30 |
| 564 | Antonio Perez | .10 | .30 |
| 565 | Jason Schmidt | .10 | .30 |
| 566 | Armando Benitez | .10 | .30 |
| 567 | Denny Neagle | .10 | .30 |
| 568 | Eric Eckenstahler | .10 | .30 |
| 569 | Chan Ho Park | .10 | .30 |
| 570 | Carlos Beltran | .10 | .30 |
| 571 | Brett Tomko | .10 | .30 |
| 572 | Henry Mateo | .10 | .30 |
| 573 | Ken Harvey | .10 | .30 |
| 574 | Matt Lawton | .10 | .30 |
| 575 | Mariano Rivera | .30 | .75 |
| 576 | Darrell May | .10 | .30 |
| 577 | Jamie Moyer | .10 | .30 |
| 578 | Paul Bako | .10 | .30 |
| 579 | Cory Lidle | .10 | .30 |
| 580 | Jacque Jones | .10 | .30 |
| 581 | Jolbert Cabrera | .10 | .30 |
| 582 | Jason Grimsley | .10 | .30 |
| 583 | Danny Kolb | .10 | .30 |
| 584 | Billy Wagner | .10 | .30 |
| 585 | Rich Aurilia | .10 | .30 |
| 586 | Vicente Padilla | .10 | .30 |
| 587 | Oscar Villarreal | .10 | .30 |
| 588 | Rene Reyes | .10 | .30 |
| 589 | Jon Lieber | .10 | .30 |
| 590 | Nick Johnson | .10 | .30 |
| 591 | Bobby Crosby | .10 | .50 |
| 592 | Steve Trachsel | .10 | .30 |
| 593 | Brian Boehringer | .10 | .30 |
| 594 | Juan Uribe | .10 | .30 |
| 595 | Bartolo Colon | .10 | .30 |
| 596 | Bobby Hill | .10 | .30 |
| 597 | Chris Shelton RC | .40 | 1.00 |
| 598 | Carl Pavano | .10 | .30 |
| 599 | Kurt Ainsworth | .10 | .30 |
| 600 | Derek Jeter | .60 | 1.50 |
| 601 | Doug Mientkiewicz | .10 | .30 |
| 602 | Orlando Palmeiro | .10 | .30 |
| 603 | J.C. Romero | .10 | .30 |
| 604 | Scott Sullivan | .10 | .30 |
| 605 | Brad Radke | .10 | .30 |
| 606 | Fernando Rodney | .10 | .30 |
| 607 | Jim Brower | .10 | .30 |
| 608 | Josh Towers | .10 | .30 |
| 609 | Brad Fullmer | .10 | .30 |
| 610 | Jose Reyes | .10 | .30 |
| 611 | Ryan Wagner | .10 | .30 |
| 612 | Joe Mays | .10 | .30 |
| 613 | Jung Bong | .10 | .30 |
| 614 | Curtis Leskanic | .10 | .30 |
| 615 | Al Leiter | .10 | .30 |
| 616 | Wade Miller | .10 | .30 |
| 617 | Keith Foulke Sox | .10 | .30 |
| 618 | Casey Fossum | .10 | .30 |
| 619 | Craig Monroe | .10 | .30 |
| 620 | Hideo Nomo | .30 | .75 |
| 621 | Bob File | .10 | .30 |
| 622 | Steve Kline | .10 | .30 |
| 623 | Bobby Kielty | .10 | .30 |
| 624 | Dewon Brazelton | .10 | .30 |
| 625 | Eric Chavez | .10 | .30 |
| 626 | Chris Carpenter | .10 | .30 |
| 627 | Alexis Rios | .10 | .30 |
| 628 | Jason Davis | .10 | .30 |
| 629 | Jose Jimenez | .10 | .30 |
| 630 | Vernon Wells | .10 | .30 |
| 631 | Kenny Lofton | .10 | .30 |
| 632 | Chad Bradford | .10 | .30 |
| 633 | Brad Wilkerson | .10 | .30 |
| 634 | Pokey Reese | .10 | .30 |
| 635 | Richie Sexson | .10 | .30 |
| 636 | Chin-Hui Tsao | .10 | .30 |
| 637 | Eli Marrero | .10 | .30 |
| 638 | Chris Reitsma | .10 | .30 |
| 639 | Daryle Ward | .10 | .30 |
| 640 | Mark Teixeira | .20 | .50 |
| 641 | Corwin Malone | .10 | .30 |
| 642 | Adam Eaton | .10 | .30 |
| 643 | Jimmy Rollins | .10 | .30 |
| 644 | Brian Anderson | .10 | .30 |
| 645 | Bill Mueller | .10 | .30 |
| 646 | Jake Westbrook | .10 | .30 |
| 647 | Bengie Molina | .10 | .30 |
| 648 | Jorge Julio | .10 | .30 |
| 649 | Billy Traber | .10 | .30 |
| 650 | Randy Johnson | .30 | .75 |
| 651 | Javy Lopez | .10 | .30 |
| 652 | Doug Glanville | .10 | .30 |
| 653 | Jeff Cirillo | .10 | .30 |
| 654 | Tino Martinez | .20 | .50 |
| 655 | Mark Buehrle | .10 | .30 |
| 656 | Jason Michaels | .10 | .30 |
| 657 | Damian Rolls | .10 | .30 |
| 658 | Rosman Garcia | .10 | .30 |
| 659 | Scott Hairston | .10 | .30 |
| 660 | Carl Crawford | .10 | .30 |
| 661 | Luis Hernandez | .10 | .30 |
| 662 | Danny Bautista | .10 | .30 |
| 663 | Brad Ausmus | .10 | .30 |
| 664 | Juan Acevedo | .10 | .30 |
| 665 | Sean Casey | .10 | .30 |
| 666 | Josh Beckett | .10 | .30 |
| 667 | Milton Bradley | .10 | .30 |
| 668 | Braden Looper | .10 | .30 |
| 669 | Paul Abbott | .10 | .30 |
| 670 | Joel Pineiro | .10 | .30 |
| 671 | Luis Terrero | .10 | .30 |
| 672 | Rodrigo Lopez | .10 | .30 |
| 673 | Joe Crede | .10 | .30 |
| 674 | Mike Koplove | .10 | .30 |
| 675 | Brian Giles | .10 | .30 |
| 676 | Jeff Nelson | .10 | .30 |
| 677 | Russell Branyan | .10 | .30 |
| 678 | Mike DeJean | .10 | .30 |
| 679 | Brian Daubach | .10 | .30 |
| 680 | Ellis Burks | .10 | .30 |
| 681 | Ryan Dempster | .10 | .30 |
| 682 | Cliff Politte | .10 | .30 |
| 683 | Brian Reith | .10 | .30 |
| 684 | Scott Stewart | .10 | .30 |
| 685 | Allan Simpson | .10 | .30 |
| 686 | Shawn Estes | .10 | .30 |
| 687 | Jason Johnson | .10 | .30 |
| 688 | Wil Cordero | .10 | .30 |
| 689 | Kelly Stinnett | .10 | .30 |
| 690 | Jose Lima | .10 | .30 |
| 691 | Gary Bennett | .10 | .30 |
| 692 | T.J. Tucker | .10 | .30 |
| 693 | Shane Spencer | .10 | .30 |
| 694 | Chris Hammond | .10 | .30 |
| 695 | Raul Mondesi | .10 | .30 |
| 696 | Xavier Nady | .10 | .30 |
| 697 | Cody Ransom | .10 | .30 |
| 698 | Ron Villone | .10 | .30 |
| 699 | Brook Fordyce | .10 | .30 |
| 700 | Sammy Sosa | .30 | .75 |
| 701 | Terry Adams | .10 | .30 |
| 702 | Ricardo Rincon | .10 | .30 |
| 703 | Tike Redman | .10 | .30 |
| 704 | Chris Stynes | .10 | .30 |
| 705 | Mark Redman | .10 | .30 |
| 706 | Juan Encarnacion | .10 | .30 |
| 707 | Jhonny Peralta | .10 | .30 |
| 708 | Denny Hocking | .10 | .30 |
| 709 | Ivan Rodriguez | .20 | .50 |
| 710 | Jose Hernandez | .10 | .30 |
| 711 | Brandon Duckworth | .10 | .30 |
| 712 | Dave Burba | .10 | .30 |
| 713 | Joe Nathan | .10 | .30 |
| 714 | Dan Smith | .10 | .30 |
| 715 | Karim Garcia | .10 | .30 |
| 716 | Arthur Rhodes | .10 | .30 |
| 717 | Shawn Wooten | .10 | .30 |
| 718 | Ramon Santiago | .10 | .30 |
| 719 | Luis Ugueto | .10 | .30 |
| 720 | Danys Baez | .10 | .30 |
| 721 | Alfredo Amezaga PROS | .10 | .30 |
| 722 | Sidney Ponson | .10 | .30 |
| 723 | Joe Mauer PROS | .30 | .75 |
| 724 | Jesse Foppert PROS | .10 | .30 |
| 725 | Todd Greene | .10 | .30 |
| 726 | Dan Haren PROS | .10 | .30 |
| 727 | Brandon Larson PROS | .10 | .30 |
| 728 | Bobby Jenks PROS | .10 | .30 |
| 729 | Grady Sizemore PROS | .30 | .75 |
| 730 | Ben Grieve | .10 | .30 |
| 731 | Khalil Greene PROS | .20 | .50 |
| 732 | Chad Gaudin PROS | .10 | .30 |
| 733 | Johnny Estrada PROS | .10 | .30 |
| 734 | Joe Valentine PROS | .10 | .30 |
| 735 | Tim Raines Jr. PROS | .10 | .30 |
| 736 | Brandon Claussen PROS | .10 | .30 |
| 737 | Sam Marsonek PROS | .10 | .30 |
| 738 | Delmon Young PROS | .20 | .50 |
| 739 | David Dellucci | .10 | .30 |
| 740 | Sergio Mitre PROS | .10 | .30 |
| 741 | Nick Neugebauer PROS | .10 | .30 |
| 742 | Laynce Nix PROS | .10 | .30 |
| 743 | Joe Thurston PROS | .10 | .30 |
| 744 | Ryan Langerhans PROS | .10 | .30 |
| 745 | Pete LaForest PROS | .10 | .30 |
| 746 | Arnie Munoz PROS | .10 | .30 |
| 747 | Rickie Weeks PROS | .10 | .30 |
| 748 | Neal Cotts PROS | .10 | .30 |
| 749 | Jonny Gomes PROS | .10 | .30 |
| 750 | Jim Thome | .20 | .50 |
| 751 | Jon Rauch PROS | .10 | .30 |
| 752 | Edwin Jackson PROS | .10 | .30 |
| 753 | Ryan Madson PROS | .10 | .30 |
| 754 | Andrew Good PROS | .10 | .30 |
| 755 | Eddie Perez | .10 | .30 |
| 756 | Joe Borchard PROS | .10 | .30 |
| 757 | Jeremy Guthrie PROS | .10 | .30 |
| 758 | Jose Mesa | .10 | .30 |
| 759 | Doug Waechter PROS | .10 | .30 |
| 760 | J.D. Drew | .10 | .30 |

|  |  | | |
|---|---|---|---|
| 761 | Adam LaRoche PROS | .10 | .30 |
| 762 | Rich Harden PROS | .10 | .30 |
| 763 | Justin Speier | .10 | .30 |
| 764 | Todd Zeile | .10 | .30 |
| 765 | Turk Wendell | .10 | .30 |
| 766 | Mark Bellhorn Sox | .10 | .30 |
| 767 | Mike Jackson | .10 | .30 |
| 768 | Chone Figgins | .10 | .30 |
| 769 | Mike Neu | .10 | .30 |
| 770 | Greg Maddux | .50 | 1.25 |
| 771 | Frank Menechino | .10 | .30 |
| 772 | Alec Zumwalt RC | .10 | .30 |
| 773 | Eric Young | .10 | .30 |
| 774 | Dustan Mohr | .10 | .30 |
| 775 | Shane Halter | .10 | .30 |
| 776 | Brian Buchanan | .10 | .30 |
| 777 | So Taguchi | .10 | .30 |
| 778 | Eric Karros | .10 | .30 |
| 779 | Ramon Nivar | .10 | .30 |
| 780 | Marlon Anderson | .10 | .30 |
| 781 | Brayan Pena FY RC | .15 | .40 |
| 782 | Chris O'Riordan FY RC | .15 | .40 |
| 783 | Dioner Navarro FY RC | .30 | .75 |
| 784 | Alberto Callaspo FY RC | .30 | .75 |
| 785 | Hector Gimenez FY RC | .10 | .30 |
| 786 | Yadier Molina FY RC | .75 | 2.00 |
| 787 | Kevin Richardson FY RC | .15 | .40 |
| 788 | Brian Pilkington FY RC | .10 | .30 |
| 789 | Adam Greenberg FY RC | .30 | .75 |
| 790 | Ervin Santana FY RC | .75 | 2.00 |
| 791 | Brant Colamarino FY RC | .30 | .75 |
| 792 | Ben Himes FY RC | .10 | .30 |
| 793 | Todd Sell FY RC | .20 | .50 |
| 794 | Brad Vericker FY RC | .15 | .40 |
| 795 | Donald Kelly FY RC | .15 | .40 |
| 796 | Brock Jacobsen FY RC | .10 | .30 |
| 797 | Brock Peterson FY RC | .15 | .40 |
| 798 | Carlos Sosa FY RC | .15 | .40 |
| 799 | Chad Chop FY RC | .15 | .40 |
| 800 | Matt Moses FY RC | .40 | 1.00 |
| 801 | Chris Aguila FY RC | .15 | .40 |
| 802 | David Murphy FY RC | .30 | .75 |
| 803 | Don Sutton FY RC | .40 | 1.00 |
| 804 | Jereme Milons FY RC | .20 | .50 |
| 805 | Jon Coutlangus FY RC | .15 | .40 |
| 806 | Greg Thissen FY RC | .15 | .40 |
| 807 | Ismael Casillas FY RC | .20 | .50 |
| 808 | Chad Santos FY RC | .15 | .40 |
| 809 | Wardell Starling FY RC | .15 | .40 |
| 810 | Kevin Kouzmanoff FY RC | .75 | 2.00 |
| 811 | Kevin Davidson FY RC | .10 | .30 |
| 812 | Michael Mooney FY RC | .15 | .40 |
| 813 | Rodney Choy Foo FY RC | .10 | .30 |
| 814 | Reid Gorecki FY RC | .15 | .40 |
| 815 | Rudy Guillen FY RC | .30 | .75 |
| 816 | Harvey Garcia FY RC | .10 | .30 |
| 817 | Wanner Madrigal FY RC | .30 | .75 |
| 818 | Kenny Perez FY RC | .15 | .40 |
| 819 | Joaquin Arias FY RC | .30 | .75 |
| 820 | Benji DeQuin FY RC | .10 | .30 |
| 821 | Lastings Milledge FY RC | 2.00 | 5.00 |
| 822 | Blake Hawksworth FY RC | .20 | .50 |
| 823 | Estee Harris FY RC | .20 | .50 |
| 824 | Bobby Brownlie FY RC | .40 | 1.00 |
| 825 | Wanel Severino FY RC | .10 | .30 |
| 826 | Bobby Madritsch FY | .10 | .30 |
| 827 | Travis Hanson FY RC | .20 | .50 |
| 828 | Brandon Medders FY RC | .15 | .40 |
| 829 | Kevin Howard FY RC | .20 | .50 |
| 830 | Brian Sleffek FY RC | .10 | .30 |
| 831 | Terry Jones FY RC | .20 | .50 |
| 832 | Anthony Acevedo FY RC | .15 | .40 |
| 833 | Kory Casto FY RC | .20 | .50 |
| 834 | Brooks Conrad FY RC | .15 | .40 |
| 835 | Juan Gutierrez FY RC | .15 | .40 |
| 836 | Charlie Zink FY RC | .15 | .40 |
| 837 | David Aardsma FY RC | .20 | .50 |
| 838 | Carl Loadenthal FY RC | .20 | .50 |
| 839 | Donald Levinski FY RC | .10 | .30 |
| 840 | Dustin Nippert FY RC | .20 | .50 |
| 841 | Calvin Hayes FY RC | .20 | .50 |
| 842 | Felix Hernandez FY RC | 3.00 | 8.00 |
| 843 | Tyler Davidson FY RC | .20 | .50 |
| 844 | George Sherrill FY RC | .15 | .40 |
| 845 | Craig Ansman FY RC | .15 | .40 |
| 846 | Jeff Allison FY RC | .15 | .40 |
| 847 | Tommy Murphy FY RC | .15 | .40 |
| 848 | Jerome Gamble FY RC | .10 | .30 |
| 849 | Jesse English FY RC | .15 | .40 |
| 850 | Alex Romero FY RC | .15 | .40 |
| 851 | Joel Zumaya FY RC | 1.25 | 3.00 |
| 852 | Carlos Quentin FY RC | 1.00 | 2.50 |
| 853 | Jose Valdez FY RC | .15 | .40 |
| 854 | J.J. Furmaniak FY RC | .30 | .75 |
| 855 | Juan Cedeno FY RC | .15 | .40 |
| 856 | Kyle Sleeth FY RC | .20 | .50 |
| 857 | Josh Labandeira FY RC | .15 | .40 |
| 858 | Lee Gwaltney FY RC | .10 | .30 |
| 859 | Lincoln Holtzkom FY RC | .15 | .40 |
| 860 | Ivan Ochoa FY RC | .15 | .40 |
| 861 | Luke Anderson FY RC | .10 | .30 |
| 862 | Conor Jackson FY RC | 1.25 | 3.00 |
| 863 | Matt Capps FY RC | .15 | .40 |
| 864 | Merkin Valdez FY RC | .20 | .50 |
| 865 | Paul Bacot FY RC | .20 | .50 |
| 866 | Erick Aybar FY RC | .40 | 1.00 |
| 867 | Scott Proctor FY RC | .20 | .50 |
| 868 | Tim Stauffer FY RC | .40 | 1.00 |
| 869 | Matt Creighton FY RC | .15 | .40 |
| 870 | Zach Miner FY RC | .50 | 1.25 |
| 871 | Danny Gonzalez FY RC | .10 | .30 |
| 872 | Tom Farmer FY RC | .15 | .40 |
| 873 | John Santor FY RC | .10 | .30 |
| 874 | Logan Kensing FY RC | .15 | .40 |
| 875 | Vito Chiaravalloti FY RC | .15 | .40 |
| 876 | Checklist | .10 | .30 |
| 877 | Checklist | .10 | .30 |
| 878 | Checklist | .10 | .30 |
| 879 | Checklist | .10 | .30 |
| 880 | Checklist | .10 | .30 |

## 2005 Topps Total

|  | | |
|---|---|---|
| COMPLETE SET (770) | 75.00 | 150.00 |
| COMMON (1-575/666) | .10 | .30 |
| COMMON CARD (576-690) | .10 | .30 |
| COM (269/589/691-765) | .10 | .30 |
| COMMON CL (766-770) | .10 | .30 |
| OVERALL PLATE ODDS 1:85 HOBBY | | |
| PLATE PRINT RUN 1 SET PER COLOR | | |
| BLACK-CYAN-MAGENTA-YELLOW ISSUED | | |
| FRONT AND BACK PLATES PRODUCED | | |
| NO PLATE PRICING DUE TO SCARCITY | | |

|  |  | | |
|---|---|---|---|
| 1 | Rafael Furcal | .12 | .30 |
| 2 | Tony Clark | .12 | .30 |
| 3 | Hideki Matsui | .50 | 1.25 |
| 4 | Zach Day | .12 | .30 |
| 5 | Garret Anderson | .12 | .30 |
| 6 | B.J. Surhoff | .12 | .30 |
| 7 | Trevor Hoffman | .12 | .30 |
| 8 | Kenny Lofton | .12 | .30 |
| 9 | Ross Gload | .12 | .30 |
| 10 | Jorge Cantu | .12 | .30 |
| 11 | Joel Pineiro | .12 | .30 |
| 12 | Alex Cintron | .12 | .30 |
| 13 | Mike Matheny | .12 | .30 |
| 14 | Rod Barajas | .12 | .30 |
| 15 | Ray Durham | .12 | .30 |
| 16 | Danys Baez | .12 | .30 |
| 17 | Brian Schneider | .12 | .30 |
| 18 | Tike Redman | .12 | .30 |
| 19 | Ricardo Rodriguez | .12 | .30 |
| 20 | Mike Sweeney | .12 | .30 |
| 21 | Greg Myers | .12 | .30 |
| 22 | Chone Figgins | .12 | .30 |
| 23 | Brian Lawrence | .12 | .30 |
| 24 | Joe Mauer | .30 | .75 |
| 25 | Placido Polanco | .12 | .30 |
| 26 | Yadier Molina | .12 | .30 |
| 27 | Gary Bennett | .12 | .30 |
| 28 | Yorvit Torrealba | .12 | .30 |
| 29 | Javier Valentin | .12 | .30 |
| 30 | Jason Giambi | .12 | .30 |
| 31 | Brandon Claussen | .12 | .30 |
| 32 | Miguel Olivo | .12 | .30 |
| 33 | Josh Bard | .12 | .30 |
| 34 | Ramon Hernandez | .12 | .30 |
| 35 | Geoff Jenkins | .12 | .30 |
| 36 | Bobby Kielty | .12 | .30 |
| 37 | Luis A. Gonzalez | .12 | .30 |
| 38 | Benito Santiago | .12 | .30 |
| 39 | Brandon Inge | .12 | .30 |
| 40 | Mark Prior | .20 | .50 |
| 41 | Mike Lieberthal | .12 | .30 |
| 42 | Toby Hall | .12 | .30 |
| 43 | Brad Ausmus | .12 | .30 |
| 44 | Damian Miller | .12 | .30 |
| 45 | Mark Kotsay | .12 | .30 |
| 46 | John Buck | .12 | .30 |
| 47 | Oliver Perez | .12 | .30 |
| 48 | Matt Morris | .12 | .30 |
| 49 | Raul Chavez | .12 | .30 |
| 50 | Randy Johnson | .30 | .75 |
| 51 | Dave Bush | .12 | .30 |
| 52 | Jose Macias | .12 | .30 |
| 53 | Paul Wilson | .12 | .30 |
| 54 | Wilfredo Ledezma | .12 | .30 |
| 55 | J.D. Drew | .12 | .30 |
| 56 | Pedro Martinez | .20 | .50 |
| 57 | Josh Towers | .12 | .30 |
| 58 | Jamie Moyer | .12 | .30 |
| 59 | Scott Elarton | .12 | .30 |
| 60 | Ken Griffey Jr. | .50 | 1.25 |
| 61 | Steve Trachsel | .12 | .30 |
| 62 | Bubba Crosby | .12 | .30 |
| 63 | Michael Barrett | .12 | .30 |
| 64 | Odalis Perez | .12 | .30 |
| 65 | B.J. Upton | .20 | .50 |
| 66 | Eric Brunlfett | .12 | .30 |
| 67 | Victor Zambrano | .12 | .30 |
| 68 | Brandon League | .12 | .30 |
| 69 | Carlos Silva | .12 | .30 |
| 70 | Lyle Overbay | .12 | .30 |
| 71 | Runelvys Hernandez | .12 | .30 |
| 72 | Brad Penny | .12 | .30 |
| 73 | Ty Wigginton | .12 | .30 |
| 74 | Orlando Hudson | .12 | .30 |
| 75 | Roy Oswalt | .12 | .30 |
| 76 | Jason LaRue | .12 | .30 |
| 77 | Ismael Valdez | .12 | .30 |
| 78 | Calvin Pickering | .12 | .30 |
| 79 | Bill Hall | .12 | .30 |
| 80 | Carl Crawford | .12 | .30 |
| 81 | Tomas Perez | .12 | .30 |
| 82 | Joe Kennedy | .12 | .30 |
| 83 | Chris Woodward | .12 | .30 |
| 84 | Jason Lane | .12 | .30 |
| 85 | Steve Finley | .12 | .30 |
| 86 | Jeff Francis | .12 | .30 |
| 87 | Felipe Lopez | .12 | .30 |
| 88 | Chan Ho Park | .12 | .30 |
| 89 | Joe Crede | .12 | .30 |
| 90 | Jose Vidro | .12 | .30 |
| 91 | Casey Kotchman | .12 | .30 |
| 92 | Brandon Backe | .12 | .30 |
| 93 | Mike Hampton | .12 | .30 |
| 94 | Ryan Dempster | .12 | .30 |
| 95 | Wily Mo Pena | .12 | .30 |
| 96 | Matt Holliday | .20 | .50 |
| 97 | A.J. Pierzynski | .12 | .30 |
| 98 | Jason Jennings | .12 | .30 |
| 99 | Eli Marrero | .12 | .30 |
| 100 | Carlos Beltran | .30 | .75 |
| 101 | Scott Kazmir | .30 | .75 |
| 102 | Kenny Rogers | .12 | .30 |
| 103 | Roy Halladay | .12 | .30 |
| 104 | Alex Cora | .12 | .30 |
| 105 | Richie Sexson | .12 | .30 |
| 106 | Ben Sheets | .12 | .30 |
| 107 | Bartolo Colon | .12 | .30 |
| 108 | Eddie Perez | .12 | .30 |
| 109 | Vicente Padilla | .12 | .30 |
| 110 | Sammy Sosa | .30 | .75 |
| 111 | Mark Ellis | .12 | .30 |
| 112 | Woody Williams | .12 | .30 |
| 113 | Todd Greene | .12 | .30 |
| 114 | Nook Logan | .12 | .30 |
| 115 | Francisco Rodriguez | .12 | .30 |
| 116 | Miguel Batista | .12 | .30 |
| 117 | Livan Hernandez | .12 | .30 |
| 118 | Chris Aguila | .12 | .30 |

|  |  | | |
|---|--------|---|---|
| ☐ 119 | Coco Crisp | .12 | .30 |
| ☐ 120 | Jose Reyes | .30 | .75 |
| ☐ 121 | Ricky Ledee | .12 | .30 |
| ☐ 122 | Brad Radke | .12 | .30 |
| ☐ 123 | Carlos Guillen | .12 | .30 |
| ☐ 124 | Paul Bako | .12 | .30 |
| ☐ 125 | Tom Glavine | .20 | .50 |
| ☐ 126 | Chad Moeller | .12 | .30 |
| ☐ 127 | Mark Buehrle | .12 | .30 |
| ☐ 128 | Casey Blake | .12 | .30 |
| ☐ 129 | Juan Rivera | .12 | .30 |
| ☐ 130 | Preston Wilson | .12 | .30 |
| ☐ 131 | Nate Robertson | .12 | .30 |
| ☐ 132 | Julio Franco | .12 | .30 |
| ☐ 133 | Derek Lowe | .12 | .30 |
| ☐ 134 | Rob Bell | .12 | .30 |
| ☐ 135 | Javy Lopez | .12 | .30 |
| ☐ 136 | Javier Vazquez | .12 | .30 |
| ☐ 137 | Desi Relaford | .12 | .30 |
| ☐ 138 | Danny Graves | .12 | .30 |
| ☐ 139 | Josh Fogg | .12 | .30 |
| ☐ 140 | Bobby Crosby | .12 | .30 |
| ☐ 141 | Ramon Castro | .12 | .30 |
| ☐ 142 | Jerry Hairston Jr. | .12 | .30 |
| ☐ 143 | Morgan Ensberg | .12 | .30 |
| ☐ 144 | Brandon Webb | .12 | .30 |
| ☐ 145 | Jack Wilson | .12 | .30 |
| ☐ 146 | Bill Mueller | .12 | .30 |
| ☐ 147 | Troy Glaus | .12 | .30 |
| ☐ 148 | Armando Benitez | .12 | .30 |
| ☐ 149 | Adam LaRoche | .12 | .30 |
| ☐ 150 | Hank Blalock | .12 | .30 |
| ☐ 151 | Ryan Franklin | .12 | .30 |
| ☐ 152 | Kevin Millwood | .12 | .30 |
| ☐ 153 | Jason Marquis | .12 | .30 |
| ☐ 154 | Dewon Brazelton | .12 | .30 |
| ☐ 155 | Al Leiter | .12 | .30 |
| ☐ 156 | Garrett Atkins | .12 | .30 |
| ☐ 157 | Todd Walker | .12 | .30 |
| ☐ 158 | Kris Benson | .12 | .30 |
| ☐ 159 | Eric Milton | .12 | .30 |
| ☐ 160 | Bret Boone | .12 | .30 |
| ☐ 161 | Matt LeCroy | .12 | .30 |
| ☐ 162 | Chris Widger | .12 | .30 |
| ☐ 163 | Ruben Gotay | .12 | .30 |
| ☐ 164 | Craig Monroe | .12 | .30 |
| ☐ 165 | Travis Hafner | .12 | .30 |
| ☐ 166 | Vance Wilson | .12 | .30 |
| ☐ 167 | Jason Grabowski | .12 | .30 |
| ☐ 168 | Tim Salmon | .12 | .30 |
| ☐ 169 | Henry Blanco | .12 | .30 |
| ☐ 170 | Josh Beckett | .12 | .30 |
| ☐ 171 | Jake Westbrook | .12 | .30 |
| ☐ 172 | Paul Lo Duca | .12 | .30 |
| ☐ 173 | Julio Lugo | .12 | .30 |
| ☐ 174 | Juan Cruz | .12 | .30 |
| ☐ 175 | Mark Mulder | .12 | .30 |
| ☐ 176 | Juan Castro | .12 | .30 |
| ☐ 177 | Damion Easley | .12 | .30 |
| ☐ 178 | LaTroy Hawkins | .12 | .30 |
| ☐ 179 | Jon Lieber | .12 | .30 |
| ☐ 180 | Vernon Wells | .12 | .30 |
| ☐ 181 | Jeff DaVanon | .12 | .30 |
| ☐ 182 | Dustan Mohr | .12 | .30 |
| ☐ 183 | Ryan Freel | .12 | .30 |
| ☐ 184 | Doug Davis | .12 | .30 |
| ☐ 185 | Sean Casey | .12 | .30 |
| ☐ 186 | Robb Quinlan | .12 | .30 |
| ☐ 187 | J.D. Closser | .12 | .30 |
| ☐ 188 | Tim Wakefield | .12 | .30 |
| ☐ 189 | Brian Jordan | .12 | .30 |
| ☐ 190 | Adam Dunn | .12 | .30 |
| ☐ 191 | Antonio Perez | .12 | .30 |
| ☐ 192 | Brett Tomko | .12 | .30 |
| ☐ 193 | John Flaherty | .12 | .30 |
| ☐ 194 | Michael Cuddyer | .12 | .30 |
| ☐ 195 | Ronnie Belliard | .12 | .30 |
| ☐ 196 | Tony Womack | .12 | .30 |
| ☐ 197 | Jason Johnson | .12 | .30 |
| ☐ 198 | Victor Santos | .12 | .30 |
| ☐ 199 | Danny Haren | .12 | .30 |
| ☐ 200 | Derek Jeter | .75 | 2.00 |
| ☐ 201 | Brian Anderson | .12 | .30 |
| ☐ 202 | Carlos Pena | .12 | .30 |
| ☐ 203 | Jaret Wright | .12 | .30 |
| ☐ 204 | Paul Byrd | .12 | .30 |
| ☐ 205 | Shannon Stewart | .12 | .30 |
| ☐ 206 | Chris Carpenter | .12 | .30 |
| ☐ 207 | Matt Stairs | .12 | .30 |
| ☐ 208 | Brad Hawpe | .12 | .30 |
| ☐ 209 | Bobby Higginson | .12 | .30 |
| ☐ 210 | Torii Hunter | .12 | .30 |
| ☐ 211 | Shawn Green | .12 | .30 |
| ☐ 212 | Todd Hollandsworth | .12 | .30 |
| ☐ 213 | Scott Erickson | .12 | .30 |
| ☐ 214 | C.C. Sabathia | .12 | .30 |
| ☐ 215 | Mike Mussina | .20 | .50 |
| ☐ 216 | Jason Kendall | .12 | .30 |
| ☐ 217 | Todd Pratt | .12 | .30 |
| ☐ 218 | Danny Kolb | .12 | .30 |
| ☐ 219 | Tony Armas | .12 | .30 |
| ☐ 220 | Edgar Renteria | .12 | .30 |
| ☐ 221 | Dave Roberts | .12 | .30 |
| ☐ 222 | Luis Rivas | .12 | .30 |
| ☐ 223 | Adam Everett | .12 | .30 |
| ☐ 224 | Jeff Cirillo | .12 | .30 |
| ☐ 225 | Orlando Hernandez | .12 | .30 |
| ☐ 226 | Ken Harvey | .12 | .30 |
| ☐ 227 | Corey Patterson | .12 | .30 |
| ☐ 228 | Humberto Cota | .12 | .30 |
| ☐ 229 | A.J. Burnett | .12 | .30 |
| ☐ 230 | Roger Clemens | .50 | 1.25 |
| ☐ 231 | Joe Randa | .12 | .30 |
| ☐ 232 | David Dellucci | .12 | .30 |
| ☐ 233 | Troy Percival | .12 | .30 |
| ☐ 234 | Dustin Hermanson | .12 | .30 |
| ☐ 235 | Eric Gagne | .12 | .30 |
| ☐ 236 | Terry Tiffee | .12 | .30 |
| ☐ 237 | Tony Graffanino | .12 | .30 |
| ☐ 238 | Jayson Werth | .12 | .30 |
| ☐ 239 | Mark Sweeney | .12 | .30 |
| ☐ 240 | Chipper Jones | .30 | .75 |
| ☐ 241 | Aramis Ramirez | .12 | .30 |
| ☐ 242 | Frank Catalanotto | .12 | .30 |
| ☐ 243 | Mike Maroth | .12 | .30 |
| ☐ 244 | Kelvim Escobar | .12 | .30 |
| ☐ 245 | Bobby Abreu | .12 | .30 |
| ☐ 246 | Kyle Lohse | .12 | .30 |
| ☐ 247 | Jason Isringhausen | .12 | .30 |
| ☐ 248 | Jose Lima | .12 | .30 |
| ☐ 249 | Adrian Gonzalez | .12 | .30 |
| ☐ 250 | Alex Rodriguez | .50 | 1.25 |
| ☐ 251 | Ramon Ortiz | .12 | .30 |
| ☐ 252 | Frank Menechino | .12 | .30 |
| ☐ 253 | Keith Ginter | .12 | .30 |
| ☐ 254 | Kip Wells | .12 | .30 |
| ☐ 255 | Dmitri Young | .12 | .30 |
| ☐ 256 | Craig Biggio | .20 | .50 |
| ☐ 257 | Ramon E. Martinez | .12 | .30 |
| ☐ 258 | Jason Bartlett | .12 | .30 |
| ☐ 259 | Brad Lidge | .12 | .30 |
| ☐ 260 | Brian Giles | .12 | .30 |
| ☐ 261 | Luis Terrero | .12 | .30 |
| ☐ 262 | Miguel Ojeda | .12 | .30 |
| ☐ 263 | Rich Harden | .12 | .30 |
| ☐ 264 | Jacque Jones | .12 | .30 |
| ☐ 265 | Marcus Giles | .12 | .30 |
| ☐ 266 | Carlos Zambrano | .12 | .30 |
| ☐ 267 | Michael Tucker | .12 | .30 |
| ☐ 268 | Wes Obermueller | .12 | .30 |
| ☐ 269 | Pete Orr RC | .20 | .50 |
| ☐ 270 | Jim Thome | .20 | .50 |
| ☐ 271 | Omar Vizquel | .12 | .30 |
| ☐ 272 | Jose Valentin | .12 | .30 |
| ☐ 273 | Juan Uribe | .12 | .30 |
| ☐ 274 | Doug Mirabelli | .12 | .30 |
| ☐ 275 | Jeff Kent | .12 | .30 |
| ☐ 276 | Brad Wilkerson | .12 | .30 |
| ☐ 277 | Chris Burke | .12 | .30 |
| ☐ 278 | Endy Chavez | .12 | .30 |
| ☐ 279 | Richard Hidalgo | .12 | .30 |
| ☐ 280 | John Smoltz | .20 | .50 |
| ☐ 281 | Jarrod Washburn | .12 | .30 |
| ☐ 282 | Larry Bigbie | .12 | .30 |
| ☐ 283 | Edgardo Alfonzo | .12 | .30 |
| ☐ 284 | Cliff Lee | .12 | .30 |
| ☐ 285 | Carlos Lee | .12 | .30 |
| ☐ 286 | Olmedo Saenz | .12 | .30 |
| ☐ 287 | Tomo Ohka | .12 | .30 |
| ☐ 288 | Ruben Sierra | .12 | .30 |
| ☐ 289 | Nick Swisher | .20 | .50 |
| ☐ 290 | Frank Thomas | .30 | .75 |
| ☐ 291 | Aaron Cook | .12 | .30 |
| ☐ 292 | Cody McKay | .12 | .30 |
| ☐ 293 | Hee-Seop Choi | .12 | .30 |
| ☐ 294 | Carl Pavano | .12 | .30 |
| ☐ 295 | Scott Rolen | .20 | .50 |
| ☐ 296 | Matt Kata | .12 | .30 |
| ☐ 297 | Terrence Long | .12 | .30 |
| ☐ 298 | Jimmy Gobble | .12 | .30 |
| ☐ 299 | Jason Repko | .12 | .30 |
| ☐ 300 | Manny Ramirez | .20 | .50 |
| ☐ 301 | Dan Wilson | .12 | .30 |
| ☐ 302 | Jhonny Peralta | .12 | .30 |
| ☐ 303 | John Mabry | .12 | .30 |
| ☐ 304 | Adam Melhuse | .12 | .30 |
| ☐ 305 | Kerry Wood | .12 | .30 |
| ☐ 306 | Ryan Langerhans | .12 | .30 |
| ☐ 307 | Antonio Alfonseca | .12 | .30 |
| ☐ 308 | Marco Scutaro | .12 | .30 |
| ☐ 309 | Jamey Carroll | .12 | .30 |
| ☐ 310 | Lance Berkman | .12 | .30 |
| ☐ 311 | Willie Harris | .12 | .30 |
| ☐ 312 | Phil Nevin | .12 | .30 |
| ☐ 313 | Gregg Zaun | .12 | .30 |
| ☐ 314 | Michael Ryan | .12 | .30 |
| ☐ 315 | Zack Greinke | .12 | .30 |
| ☐ 316 | Ted Lilly | .12 | .30 |
| ☐ 317 | David Eckstein | .12 | .30 |
| ☐ 318 | Tony Torcato | .12 | .30 |
| ☐ 319 | Rob Mackowiak | .12 | .30 |
| ☐ 320 | Mark Teixeira | .20 | .50 |
| ☐ 321 | Jason Phillips | .12 | .30 |
| ☐ 322 | Jeremy Reed | .12 | .30 |
| ☐ 323 | Bengie Molina | .12 | .30 |
| ☐ 324 | Termel Sledge | .12 | .30 |
| ☐ 325 | Justin Morneau | .12 | .30 |
| ☐ 326 | Sandy Alomar Jr. | .12 | .30 |
| ☐ 327 | Jon Garland | .12 | .30 |
| ☐ 328 | Jay Payton | .12 | .30 |
| ☐ 329 | Tino Martinez | .20 | .50 |
| ☐ 330 | Jason Bay | .12 | .30 |
| ☐ 331 | Jeff Conine | .12 | .30 |
| ☐ 332 | Shawn Chacon | .12 | .30 |
| ☐ 333 | Angel Berroa | .12 | .30 |
| ☐ 334 | Reggie Sanders | .12 | .30 |
| ☐ 335 | Kevin Brown | .12 | .30 |
| ☐ 336 | Brady Clark | .12 | .30 |
| ☐ 337 | Casey Fossum | .12 | .30 |
| ☐ 338 | Raul Ibanez | .12 | .30 |
| ☐ 339 | Derrek Lee | .20 | .50 |
| ☐ 340 | Victor Martinez | .12 | .30 |
| ☐ 341 | Kazuhisa Ishii | .12 | .30 |
| ☐ 342 | Royce Clayton | .12 | .30 |
| ☐ 343 | Trot Nixon | .12 | .30 |
| ☐ 344 | Eric Young | .12 | .30 |
| ☐ 345 | Aubrey Huff | .12 | .30 |
| ☐ 346 | Brett Myers | .12 | .30 |
| ☐ 347 | Joey Gathright | .12 | .30 |
| ☐ 348 | Mark Grudzielanek | .12 | .30 |
| ☐ 349 | Scott Spiezio | .12 | .30 |
| ☐ 350 | Eric Chavez | .12 | .30 |
| ☐ 351 | Einar Diaz | .12 | .30 |
| ☐ 352 | Dallas McPherson | .12 | .30 |
| ☐ 353 | John Thomson | .12 | .30 |
| ☐ 354 | Neifi Perez | .12 | .30 |
| ☐ 355 | Larry Walker | .20 | .50 |
| ☐ 356 | Billy Wagner | .12 | .30 |
| ☐ 357 | Mike Cameron | .12 | .30 |
| ☐ 358 | Jimmy Rollins | .12 | .30 |
| ☐ 359 | Kevin Mench | .12 | .30 |
| ☐ 360 | Joe Mauer | .30 | .75 |
| ☐ 361 | Jose Molina | .12 | .30 |
| ☐ 362 | Joe Borchard | .12 | .30 |
| ☐ 363 | Kevin Cash | .12 | .30 |
| ☐ 364 | Jay Gibbons | .12 | .30 |
| ☐ 365 | Khalil Greene | .20 | .50 |
| ☐ 366 | Justin Leone | .12 | .30 |
| ☐ 367 | Eddie Guardado | .12 | .30 |
| ☐ 368 | Mike Lamb | .12 | .30 |
| ☐ 369 | Matt Riley | .12 | .30 |
| ☐ 370 | Luis Gonzalez | .12 | .30 |
| ☐ 371 | Alfredo Amezaga | .12 | .30 |
| ☐ 372 | J.J. Hardy | .12 | .30 |
| ☐ 373 | Hector Luna | .12 | .30 |
| ☐ 374 | Greg Aquino | .12 | .30 |
| ☐ 375 | Jim Edmonds | .20 | .50 |
| ☐ 376 | Joe Blanton | .12 | .30 |
| ☐ 377 | Russell Branyan | .12 | .30 |
| ☐ 378 | J.T. Snow | .12 | .30 |
| ☐ 379 | Magglio Ordonez | .12 | .30 |
| ☐ 380 | Rafael Palmeiro | .20 | .50 |
| ☐ 381 | Andruw Jones | .20 | .50 |
| ☐ 382 | David DeJesus | .12 | .30 |

|  |  | | |
|---|---|---|---|
| 383 | Marquis Grissom | .12 | .30 |
| 384 | Bobby Hill | .12 | .30 |
| 385 | Kazuo Matsui | .12 | .30 |
| 386 | Mark Loretta | .12 | .30 |
| 387 | Chris Shelton | .12 | .30 |
| 388 | Johnny Estrada | .12 | .30 |
| 389 | Adam Hyzdu | .12 | .30 |
| 390 | Nomar Garciaparra | .30 | .75 |
| 391 | Mark Teahen | .12 | .30 |
| 392 | Chris Capuano | .12 | .30 |
| 393 | Ben Broussard | .12 | .30 |
| 394 | Daniel Cabrera | .12 | .30 |
| 395 | Jeremy Bonderman | .12 | .30 |
| 396 | Darin Erstad | .12 | .30 |
| 397 | Alex S. Gonzalez | .12 | .30 |
| 398 | Kevin Millar | .12 | .30 |
| 399 | Freddy Garcia | .12 | .30 |
| 400 | Alfonso Soriano | .12 | .30 |
| 401 | Koyie Hill | .12 | .30 |
| 402 | Omar Infante | .12 | .30 |
| 403 | Alex Gonzalez | .12 | .30 |
| 404 | Pat Burrell | .12 | .30 |
| 405 | Wes Helms | .12 | .30 |
| 406 | Junior Spivey | .12 | .30 |
| 407 | Joe Mays | .12 | .30 |
| 408 | Jason Stanford | .12 | .30 |
| 409 | Gil Meche | .12 | .30 |
| 410 | Tim Hudson | .12 | .30 |
| 411 | Chase Utley | .20 | .50 |
| 412 | Matt Clement | .12 | .30 |
| 413 | Nick Green | .12 | .30 |
| 414 | Jose Vizcaino | .12 | .30 |
| 415 | Ryan Klesko | .12 | .30 |
| 416 | Vinny Castilla | .12 | .30 |
| 417 | Brian Roberts | .12 | .30 |
| 418 | Geronimo Gil | .12 | .30 |
| 419 | Gary Matthews | .12 | .30 |
| 420 | Jeff Weaver | .12 | .30 |
| 421 | Jerome Williams | .12 | .30 |
| 422 | Andy Pettitte | .20 | .50 |
| 423 | Randy Wolf | .12 | .30 |
| 424 | D'Angelo Jimenez | .12 | .30 |
| 425 | Moises Alou | .12 | .30 |
| 426 | Eric Byrnes | .12 | .30 |
| 427 | Mark Redman | .12 | .30 |
| 428 | Jermaine Dye | .12 | .30 |
| 429 | Cory Lidle | .12 | .30 |
| 430 | Jason Schmidt | .12 | .30 |
| 431 | Jason W. Smith | .12 | .30 |
| 432 | Jose Castillo | .12 | .30 |
| 433 | Pokey Reese | .12 | .30 |
| 434 | Matt Lawton | .12 | .30 |
| 435 | Jose Guillen | .12 | .30 |
| 436 | Craig Counsell | .12 | .30 |
| 437 | Jose Hernandez | .12 | .30 |
| 438 | Braden Looper | .12 | .30 |
| 439 | Scott Hatteberg | .12 | .30 |
| 440 | Gary Sheffield | .12 | .30 |
| 441 | Gabe Gross | .12 | .30 |
| 442 | Chris Gomez | .12 | .30 |
| 443 | Dontrelle Willis | .12 | .30 |
| 444 | Jamey Wright | .12 | .30 |
| 445 | Rocco Baldelli | .12 | .30 |
| 446 | Bernie Williams | .20 | .50 |
| 447 | Sean Burroughs | .12 | .30 |
| 448 | Willie Bloomquist | .12 | .30 |
| 449 | Luis Castillo | .12 | .30 |
| 450 | Mike Piazza | .30 | .75 |
| 451 | Ryan Drese | .12 | .30 |
| 452 | Pedro Feliz | .12 | .30 |
| 453 | Horacio Ramirez | .12 | .30 |
| 454 | Luis Matos | .12 | .30 |
| 455 | Craig Wilson | .12 | .30 |
| 456 | Russ Ortiz | .12 | .30 |
| 457 | Xavier Nady | .12 | .30 |
| 458 | Hideo Nomo | .30 | .75 |
| 459 | Miguel Cairo | .12 | .30 |
| 460 | Mike Lowell | .12 | .30 |
| 461 | Corky Miller | .12 | .30 |
| 462 | Bobby Madritsch | .12 | .30 |
| 463 | Jose Contreras | .12 | .30 |
| 464 | Johnny Damon | .20 | .50 |
| 465 | Miguel Cabrera | .20 | .50 |
| 466 | Eric Hinske | .12 | .30 |
| 467 | Mark Byrd | .12 | .30 |
| 468 | Aaron Miles | .12 | .30 |
| 469 | Ramon Vazquez | .12 | .30 |
| 470 | Michael Young | .12 | .30 |
| 471 | Alex Sanchez | .12 | .30 |
| 472 | Shea Hillenbrand | .12 | .30 |
| 473 | Jeff Bagwell | .20 | .50 |
| 474 | Erik Bedard | .12 | .30 |
| 475 | Jake Peavy | .20 | .50 |
| 476 | Jody Gerut | .12 | .30 |
| 477 | Randy Winn | .12 | .30 |
| 478 | Kevin Youkilis | .12 | .30 |
| 479 | Eric Dubose | .12 | .30 |
| 480 | David Wright | .50 | 1.25 |
| 481 | Wilson Valdez | .12 | .30 |
| 482 | Cliff Floyd | .12 | .30 |
| 483 | Jose Mesa | .12 | .30 |
| 484 | Doug Mientkiewicz | .12 | .30 |
| 485 | Jorge Posada | .20 | .50 |
| 486 | Sidney Ponson | .12 | .30 |
| 487 | Dave Krynzel | .12 | .30 |
| 488 | Octavio Dotel | .12 | .30 |
| 489 | Matt Treanor | .12 | .30 |
| 490 | Johan Santana | .30 | .75 |
| 491 | John Patterson | .12 | .30 |
| 492 | So Taguchi | .12 | .30 |
| 493 | Carl Everett | .12 | .30 |
| 494 | Jason Dubois | .12 | .30 |
| 495 | Albert Pujols | .75 | 2.00 |
| 496 | Kirk Rueter | .12 | .30 |
| 497 | Geoff Blum | .12 | .30 |
| 498 | Juan Encarnacion | .12 | .30 |
| 499 | Mark Hendrickson | .12 | .30 |
| 500 | Barry Bonds | .75 | 2.00 |
| 501 | Cesar Izturis | .12 | .30 |
| 502 | David Wells | .12 | .30 |
| 503 | Jorge Julio | .12 | .30 |
| 504 | Cristian Guzman | .12 | .30 |
| 505 | Juan Pierre | .12 | .30 |
| 506 | Adam Eaton | .12 | .30 |
| 507 | Nick Johnson | .12 | .30 |
| 508 | Mike Redmond | .12 | .30 |
| 509 | Daryle Ward | .12 | .30 |
| 510 | Adrian Beltre | .12 | .30 |
| 511 | Laynce Nix | .12 | .30 |
| 512 | Reed Johnson | .12 | .30 |
| 513 | Jeremy Affeldt | .12 | .30 |
| 514 | R.A. Dickey | .12 | .30 |
| 515 | Alex Rios | .12 | .30 |
| 516 | Orlando Palmeiro | .12 | .30 |
| 517 | Mark Bellhorn | .12 | .30 |
| 518 | Adam Kennedy | .12 | .30 |
| 519 | Curtis Granderson | .12 | .30 |
| 520 | Todd Helton | .20 | .50 |
| 521 | Aaron Boone | .12 | .30 |
| 522 | Milton Bradley | .12 | .30 |
| 523 | Timo Perez | .12 | .30 |
| 524 | Jeff Suppan | .12 | .30 |
| 525 | Austin Kearns | .12 | .30 |
| 526 | Charles Thomas | .12 | .30 |
| 527 | Bronson Arroyo | .12 | .30 |
| 528 | Roger Cedeno | .12 | .30 |
| 529 | Russ Adams | .12 | .30 |
| 530 | Barry Zito | .12 | .30 |
| 531 | Bob Wickman | .12 | .30 |
| 532 | Deivi Cruz | .12 | .30 |
| 533 | Mariano Rivera | .30 | .75 |
| 534 | J.J. Davis | .12 | .30 |
| 535 | Greg Maddux | .12 | .30 |
| 536 | Ryan Vogelsong | .12 | .30 |
| 537 | Josh Phelps | .12 | .30 |
| 538 | Scott Hairston | .12 | .30 |
| 539 | Vladimir Guerrero | .30 | .75 |
| 540 | Ivan Rodriguez | .20 | .50 |
| 541 | David Newhan | .12 | .30 |
| 542 | David Bell | .12 | .30 |
| 543 | Lew Ford | .12 | .30 |
| 544 | Grady Sizemore | .20 | .50 |
| 545 | David Ortiz | .30 | .75 |
| 546 | Jose Cruz Jr. | .12 | .30 |
| 547 | Aaron Rowand | .12 | .30 |
| 548 | Marcus Thames | .12 | .30 |
| 549 | Scott Podsednik | .12 | .30 |
| 550 | Ichiro Suzuki | .50 | 1.25 |
| 551 | Eduardo Perez | .12 | .30 |
| 552 | Chris Snyder | .12 | .30 |
| 553 | Corey Koskie | .12 | .30 |
| 554 | Miguel Tejada | .12 | .30 |
| 555 | Orlando Cabrera | .12 | .30 |
| 556 | Rondell White | .12 | .30 |
| 557 | Wade Miller | .12 | .30 |
| 558 | Rodrigo Lopez | .12 | .30 |
| 559 | Chad Tracy | .12 | .30 |
| 560 | Paul Konerko | .12 | .30 |
| 561 | Wil Cordero | .12 | .30 |
| 562 | John McDonald | .12 | .30 |
| 563 | Jason Ellison | .12 | .30 |
| 564 | Jason Michaels | .12 | .30 |
| 565 | Melvin Mora | .12 | .30 |
| 566 | Ryan Church | .12 | .30 |
| 567 | Ryan Ludwick | .12 | .30 |
| 568 | Erubiel Durazo | .12 | .30 |
| 569 | Noah Lowry | .12 | .30 |
| 570 | Curt Schilling | .20 | .50 |
| 571 | Esteban Loaiza | .12 | .30 |
| 572 | Freddy Sanchez | .12 | .30 |
| 573 | Rich Aurilia | .12 | .30 |
| 574 | Travis Lee | .12 | .30 |
| 575 | Nick Punto | .12 | .30 |
| 576 | J.Christiansen/K.Correia | .12 | .30 |
| 577 | B.Baker/T.Redding | .12 | .30 |
| 578 | T.Adams/G.Floyd | .12 | .30 |
| 579 | S.Etherton/D.Meyer | .12 | .30 |
| 580 | J.Lehr/D.Turnbow | .12 | .30 |
| 581 | M.Gosling/B.Halsey | .12 | .30 |
| 582 | J.Meciri/L.Kensing | .12 | .30 |
| 583 | B.Hennessey/J.Fassero | .12 | .30 |
| 584 | J.Adkins/F.Diaz | .12 | .30 |
| 585 | J.Crain/J.Rincon | .12 | .30 |
| 586 | J.Cerda/N.Field | .12 | .30 |
| 587 | B.Fortunato/J.Seo | .12 | .30 |
| 588 | S.Schmoll RC/Y.Brazoban | .12 | .30 |
| 589 | U.Urbina/J.Walker | .12 | .30 |
| 590 | J.De Paula/S.Proctor | .12 | .30 |
| 591 | J.Davis/B.Howry | .12 | .30 |
| 592 | T.Worrell/P.Liriano | .12 | .30 |
| 593 | J.Acevedo/K.Mercker | .12 | .30 |
| 594 | C.Hammond/S.Linebrink | .12 | .30 |
| 595 | F.Nieve/J.Franco | .12 | .30 |
| 596 | R.Flores/M.LaRocca | .12 | .30 |
| 597 | J.Borowski/S.Mitre | .12 | .30 |
| 598 | L.Carter/J.Colome | .12 | .30 |
| 599 | J.Halama/L.DiNardo | .12 | .30 |
| 600 | C.Bradford/K.Calero | .12 | .30 |
| 601 | D.Aardsma/J.Brower | .12 | .30 |
| 602 | G.Geary/R.Madson | .12 | .30 |
| 603 | B.Moehler/N.Bump | .12 | .30 |
| 604 | C.Tsao/R.Speier | .12 | .30 |
| 605 | R.Wagner/A.Harang | .12 | .30 |
| 606 | S.Kline/R.Bauer | .12 | .30 |
| 607 | L.Cormier/R.Choate | .12 | .30 |
| 608 | J.Leicester/T.Wellemeyer | .12 | .30 |
| 609 | V.Chulk/J.Frasor | .12 | .30 |
| 610 | S.Dohmann/B.Fuentes | .12 | .30 |
| 611 | S.Colyer/R.Hernandez | .12 | .30 |
| 612 | I.Snell/S.Torres | .12 | .30 |
| 613 | C.Eldred/A.Wainwright | .20 | .50 |
| 614 | R.Bukvich/D.Brocail | .12 | .30 |
| 615 | J.Putz/A.Sele | .12 | .30 |
| 616 | B.Chen/T.Williams | .12 | .30 |
| 617 | D.Weathers/B.Weber | .12 | .30 |
| 618 | D.Reyes/R.Soriano | .12 | .30 |
| 619 | T.Hanrkkala/R.Rincon | .12 | .30 |
| 620 | S.Camp/D.Bautista | .12 | .30 |
| 621 | J.Lopez/A.Simpson | .12 | .30 |
| 622 | M.Remlinger/G.Rusch | .12 | .30 |
| 623 | R.Colon/K.Gryboski | .12 | .30 |
| 624 | T.Martin/C.Reitsma | .12 | .30 |
| 625 | C.Qualls/D.Wheeler | .12 | .30 |
| 626 | T.Phelps/M.Wise | .12 | .30 |
| 627 | S.Schoeneweis/J.Speier | .12 | .30 |
| 628 | F.Cordero/F.Francisco | .12 | .30 |
| 629 | R.Soriano/M.Thornton | .12 | .30 |
| 630 | M.Stanton/S.Karsay | .12 | .30 |
| 631 | M.MacDougal/S.Sullivan | .12 | .30 |
| 632 | B.Bruney/O.Villarreal | .12 | .30 |
| 633 | M.Adams/R.Bottalico | .12 | .30 |
| 634 | E.Rodriguez/D.Borkowski | .12 | .30 |
| 635 | R.Betancourt/D.Riske | .12 | .30 |
| 636 | J.De La Rosa/G.Glover | .12 | .30 |
| 637 | M.Perisho/B.Howard | .12 | .30 |
| 638 | J.Bajenaru/L.Vizcaino | .12 | .30 |
| 639 | R.Mahay/E.Ramirez | .12 | .30 |
| 640 | J.Grabow/M.Gonzalez | .12 | .30 |
| 641 | J.Romero/M.Guerrier | .12 | .30 |
| 642 | C.Hernandez/B.Duckworth | .12 | .30 |
| 643 | T.Harper/S.McClung | .12 | .30 |
| 644 | M.Herges/T.Walker | .12 | .30 |
| 645 | K.Wunsch/E.Dessens | .12 | .30 |
| 646 | M.Malaska/M.Myers | .12 | .30 |

| | | |
|---|---|---|
| ☐ 647 K.Farnsworth/G.Knotts | .12 | .30 |
| ☐ 648 J.Duchscherer/J. Garcia | .12 | .30 |
| ☐ 649 A.Rakers/S.Reed | .12 | .30 |
| ☐ 650 T.Gordon/P.Quantrill | .12 | .30 |
| ☐ 651 B.Lyon/S.Estes | .12 | .30 |
| ☐ 652 P.Walker/G.Chacin | .12 | .30 |
| ☐ 653 J.Lackey/S.Shields | .12 | .30 |
| ☐ 654 D.Waechter/T.Miller | .12 | .30 |
| ☐ 655 L.Ayala/C.Cordero | .12 | .30 |
| ☐ 656 R.Villone/J.Mateo | .12 | .30 |
| ☐ 657 M.Mantei/B.Neal | .12 | .30 |
| ☐ 658 D.Marte/C.Pollitte | .12 | .30 |
| ☐ 659 J.Valentine/L.Hudson | .12 | .30 |
| ☐ 660 T.Jones/J.Riedling | .12 | .30 |
| ☐ 661 H.Bell/A.Heilman | .12 | .30 |
| ☐ 662 D.May/A.Otsuka | .12 | .30 |
| ☐ 663 J.Eischen/J.Horgan | .12 | .30 |
| ☐ 664 A.Sisco/M.Wood | .12 | .30 |
| ☐ 665 A.Embree/M.Timlin | .12 | .30 |
| ☐ 666 Keith Foulke | .12 | .30 |
| ☐ 667 R.Cormier/A.Fultz | .12 | .30 |
| ☐ 668 J.Woods/K.Gregg | .12 | .30 |
| ☐ 669 M.Grier/F.German | .12 | .30 |
| ☐ 670 S.Eyre/M.Valdez | .12 | .30 |
| ☐ 671 B.Meadows/R.White | .12 | .30 |
| ☐ 672 G.Mota/T.Spooneybarger | .12 | .30 |
| ☐ 673 J.Grimsley/B.Ryan | .12 | .30 |
| ☐ 674 N.Cotts/S.Takatsu | .12 | .30 |
| ☐ 675 M.DeJean/F.Heredia | .12 | .30 |
| ☐ 676 M.Belisle/J.Hancock | .12 | .30 |
| ☐ 677 J.Rauch/T.Tucker | .12 | .30 |
| ☐ 678 N.Regilio/B.Shouse | .12 | .30 |
| ☐ 679 J.Tavarez/R.King | .12 | .30 |
| ☐ 680 C.Fox/M.Wuertz | .12 | .30 |
| ☐ 681 J.Sosa/A.Bernero | .12 | .30 |
| ☐ 682 J.Valverde/M.Koplove | .12 | .30 |
| ☐ 683 A.Rhodes/S.Sauerbeck | .12 | .30 |
| ☐ 684 F.Rodriguez/T.Sturtze | .12 | .30 |
| ☐ 685 G.Carrara/D.Sanchez | .12 | .30 |
| ☐ 686 M.Gallo/C.Harville | .12 | .30 |
| ☐ 687 M.Johnston/S.Burnett | .12 | .30 |
| ☐ 688 J.Nelson/S.Hasegawa | .12 | .30 |
| ☐ 689 C.Vargas/A.Osuna | .12 | .30 |
| ☐ 690 B.Donnelly/E.Yan | .12 | .30 |
| ☐ 691 J.Mathis/E.Santana | .20 | .50 |
| ☐ 692 C.Everts/B.Bray | .12 | .30 |
| ☐ 693 J.Kubel/T.Plouffe | .12 | .30 |
| ☐ 694 J.Stevens/A.Marte | .20 | .50 |
| ☐ 695 A.Hill/C.Gaudin | .20 | .50 |
| ☐ 696 C.Quentin/J.Cota | .20 | .50 |
| ☐ 697 T.Diamond/C.Young | .20 | .50 |
| ☐ 698 O.Quintanilla/D.Johnson | .12 | .30 |
| ☐ 699 J.Maine/W.Majewski | .12 | .30 |
| ☐ 700 J.Houser/J.Gomes | .12 | .30 |
| ☐ 701 D.Murphy/H.Ramirez | .20 | .50 |
| ☐ 702 C.Lambert/R.Ankiel | .20 | .50 |
| ☐ 703 F.Pie/A.Guzman | .12 | .30 |
| ☐ 704 F.Lewis/N.Schierholtz | .20 | .50 |
| ☐ 705 A.Munoz/G.Gonzalez | .20 | .50 |
| ☐ 706 F.Hernandez/T.Blackley | .50 | 1.25 |
| ☐ 707 R.Olmedo/E.Encarnacion | .20 | .50 |
| ☐ 708 T.Stauffer/J.Germano | .12 | .30 |
| ☐ 709 J.Guthrie/J.Sowers | .20 | .50 |
| ☐ 710 J.Cortes/T.Gorzelanny | .20 | .50 |
| ☐ 711 T.Tankersley/E.Reed | .20 | .50 |
| ☐ 712 N.Walker/P.Maholm | .20 | .50 |
| ☐ 713 W.Taveras/L.Scott | .30 | .75 |
| ☐ 714 R.Howard/G.Golson | .60 | 1.50 |
| ☐ 715 B.DeWitt/E.Jackson | .12 | .30 |
| ☐ 716 H.Street/D.Putnam | .12 | .30 |
| ☐ 717 R.Weeks/M.Rogers | .12 | .30 |
| ☐ 718 R.Cano/P.Hughes | .20 | .50 |
| ☐ 719 K.Waldrop/J.Rainville | .12 | .30 |
| ☐ 720 C.Brazell/Y.Petit | .20 | .50 |
| ☐ 721 B.Lopez/N.Brown RC | .12 | .30 |
| ☐ 722 D.Thomp RC/E.Chavez RC | .12 | .30 |
| ☐ 723 D.Uggla RC/E.Sch'wolf RC | 6.00 | 15.00 |
| ☐ 724 I.Ramirez RC/J.Tingler RC | .12 | .30 |
| ☐ 725 T.G'tano RC/E.de la Cruz RC | .12 | .30 |
| ☐ 726 M.Campbell RC/S.Costa RC | .12 | .30 |
| ☐ 727 M.Prado RC/B.McCarthy RC | .12 | .30 |
| ☐ 728 I.Kinsler RC/J.Senreiso RC | 1.00 | 2.50 |
| ☐ 729 L.Ramirez RC/Lo.Scott RC | .12 | .30 |
| ☐ 730 C.Seddon RC/E.Johnson RC | .12 | .30 |
| ☐ 731 C.Tatum RC/J.Moran RC | .12 | .30 |
| ☐ 732 S.Pomeranz RC/J.Motte RC | .12 | .30 |
| ☐ 733 J.Vaguedano RC/S.Bailie RC | .12 | .30 |
| ☐ 734 M.Albers RC/W.Robinson RC | .12 | .30 |

| | | |
|---|---|---|
| ☐ 735 M.DeSalvo RC/Me.Cabr RC | .20 | .50 |
| ☐ 736 B.Slavisky RC/L.Powell RC | .12 | .30 |
| ☐ 737 S.Mathieson RC/S.Mitch RC | .20 | .50 |
| ☐ 738 S.Marshall RC/B.Bay RC | .50 | 1.25 |
| ☐ 739 B.McCarthy RC/P.Lopez RC | .12 | .30 |
| ☐ 740 A.Smit RC/R.Barrett RC | .12 | .30 |
| ☐ 741 M.P'stad RC/R.Fbend RC | .12 | .30 |
| ☐ 742 N.McLouth RC/A.Boeve RC | .20 | .50 |
| ☐ 743 K.Melillo RC/M.Rogers RC | .20 | .50 |
| ☐ 744 M.Kemp RC/H.Totten RC | 1.00 | 2.50 |
| ☐ 745 J.Miller RC/T.Americh RC | .12 | .30 |
| ☐ 746 T.Pelland RC/J.Gutierrez RC | .12 | .30 |
| ☐ 747 J.West RC/W.Mota RC | .20 | .50 |
| ☐ 748 R.Goleski RC/R.Garko RC | .12 | .30 |
| ☐ 749 B.Triplett RC/J.Gothreaux RC | .12 | .30 |
| ☐ 750 K.West RC/G.Perkins RC | .20 | .50 |
| ☐ 751 M.Esposito RC/Z.Parker RC | .12 | .30 |
| ☐ 752 R.Sweeney RC/B.Miller RC | .30 | .75 |
| ☐ 753 A.McGehee RC/B.Coats RC | .12 | .30 |
| ☐ 754 M.Bourn RC/K.Pichardo RC | .30 | .75 |
| ☐ 755 M.Morse RC/B.Livingston RC | .20 | .50 |
| ☐ 756 W.Swack RC/B.Ryan RC | .12 | .30 |
| ☐ 757 M.Furtado RC/N.Massett RC | .12 | .30 |
| ☐ 758 P.Ramos RC/G.Kottaras RC | .30 | .75 |
| ☐ 759 E.Quezada RC/T.Beam RC | .20 | .50 |
| ☐ 760 D.Eveland RC/T.Hinton RC | .12 | .30 |
| ☐ 761 J.Jurries RC/C.Vines RC | .20 | .50 |
| ☐ 762 H.Sanch RC/J.Verlander RC | .60 | 1.50 |
| ☐ 763 P.Humber RC/S.Bowman RC | .30 | .75 |
| ☐ 764 P.Misch RC/J.Thurmond RC | .12 | .30 |
| ☐ 765 C.Colonel RC/N.Wilson RC | .12 | .30 |
| ☐ 766 Checklist 1 | .10 | .30 |
| ☐ 767 Checklist 2 | .10 | .30 |
| ☐ 768 Checklist 3 | .10 | .30 |
| ☐ 769 Checklist 4 | .10 | .30 |
| ☐ 770 Checklist 5 | .10 | .30 |

## 2005 Topps Turkey Red

| | | |
|---|---|---|
| ☐ COMPLETE SET (330) | 200.00 | 300.00 |
| ☐ COMP.SET w/o SP's (275) | 20.00 | 50.00 |
| ☐ COMMON CARD (1-270) | .15 | .40 |
| ☐ COMMON SP (1-270) | 3.00 | 8.00 |
| ☐ SP CL: 160A/160B/170/175/181/184/185/193 | | |
| ☐ COMMON REPRINT | .30 | .75 |
| ☐ COMMON RC (271-300) | .40 | 1.00 |
| ☐ COMMON RET (301-315) | .40 | 1.00 |
| ☐ VAR CL: 1/5/10/16/75/83/100/102/120/125 | | |
| ☐ VAR CL: 130/160/225/230/270 | | |
| ☐ TWO VERSIONS OF EACH VARIATION EXIST | | |
| ☐ 1A B.Bonds Grey Uni SP | 6.00 | 15.00 |
| ☐ 1B B.Bonds White Uni | 1.00 | 2.50 |
| ☐ 2 Michael Young | .15 | .40 |
| ☐ 3 Jim Edmonds | .15 | .40 |
| ☐ 4 Cliff Floyd | .15 | .40 |
| ☐ 5A R.Clemens Blue Sky SP | 4.00 | 10.00 |
| ☐ 5B R.Clemens Yellow Sky SP | 4.00 | 10.00 |
| ☐ 6 Hal Chase REP | .30 | .75 |
| ☐ 7 Shannon Stewart | .15 | .40 |
| ☐ 8 Fred Clarke REP | .30 | .75 |
| ☐ 9 Travis Hafner | .15 | .40 |
| ☐ 10A S.Sosa w/Name SP | 3.00 | 8.00 |
| ☐ 10B S.Sosa w/o Name SP | 3.00 | 8.00 |
| ☐ 11 Jermaine Dye | .15 | .40 |
| ☐ 12 Lyle Overbay | .15 | .40 |
| ☐ 13 Oliver Perez | .15 | .40 |
| ☐ 14 Red Dooin REP | .30 | .75 |
| ☐ 15 Kid Elberfald REP | .30 | .75 |
| ☐ 16A M.Piazza Blue Uni SP | 3.00 | 8.00 |
| ☐ 16B M.Piazza Pinstripe | .40 | 1.00 |
| ☐ 17 Bret Boone | .15 | .40 |
| ☐ 18 Hughie Jennings REP | .30 | .75 |
| ☐ 19 Jeff Francis | .15 | .40 |
| ☐ 20 Manny Ramirez SP | 3.00 | 8.00 |
| ☐ 21 Russ Ortiz | .15 | .40 |

| | | |
|---|---|---|
| ☐ 22 Carlos Zambrano | .15 | .40 |
| ☐ 23 Luis Castillo | .15 | .40 |
| ☐ 24 David DeJesus | .15 | .40 |
| ☐ 25 Carlos Beltran SP | 3.00 | 8.00 |
| ☐ 26 Doug Davis | .15 | .40 |
| ☐ 27 Bobby Abreu | .15 | .40 |
| ☐ 28 Rich Harden SP | 3.00 | 8.00 |
| ☐ 29 Brian Giles | .15 | .40 |
| ☐ 30 Richie Sexson SP | 3.00 | 8.00 |
| ☐ 31 Nick Johnson | .15 | .40 |
| ☐ 32 Roy Halladay | .15 | .40 |
| ☐ 33 Andy Pettitte | .25 | .60 |
| ☐ 34 Miguel Cabrera | .25 | .60 |
| ☐ 35 Jeff Kent | .15 | .40 |
| ☐ 36 Chone Figgins | .15 | .40 |
| ☐ 37 Carlos Lee | .15 | .40 |
| ☐ 38 Greg Maddux | .60 | 1.50 |
| ☐ 39 Preston Wilson | .15 | .40 |
| ☐ 40 Chipper Jones | .40 | 1.00 |
| ☐ 41 Coco Crisp | .15 | .40 |
| ☐ 42 Adam Dunn | .15 | .40 |
| ☐ 43 Out at Second M.Tejada CL | .15 | .40 |
| ☐ 44 Sheffield At Bat CL | .15 | .40 |
| ☐ 45 Play at the Plate J.Lopez CL | .15 | .40 |
| ☐ 46 Rolen Diggin' In CL | .15 | .40 |
| ☐ 47 Helton With the Slap Tag CL | .15 | .40 |
| ☐ 48 Clemens Bringing Heat CL | .40 | 1.00 |
| ☐ 49 A Close Play J.Rollins CL | .15 | .40 |
| ☐ 50 Ichiro At Bat CL | .40 | 1.00 |
| ☐ 51 Can of Corn C.Floyd CL | .15 | .40 |
| ☐ 52 Pulling String J.Santana CL | .40 | 1.00 |
| ☐ 53 Mark Teixeira | .25 | .60 |
| ☐ 54 Chris Carpenter | .15 | .40 |
| ☐ 55 Roy Oswalt SP | 3.00 | 8.00 |
| ☐ 56 Casey Kotchman | .15 | .40 |
| ☐ 57 Torii Hunter | .15 | .40 |
| ☐ 58 Jose Reyes | .15 | .40 |
| ☐ 59 Wily Mo Pena SP | 3.00 | 8.00 |
| ☐ 60 Maggilo Ordonez SP | 3.00 | 8.00 |
| ☐ 61 Aaron Miles | .15 | .40 |
| ☐ 62 Dallas McPherson | .15 | .40 |
| ☐ 63 Javy Lopez | .15 | .40 |
| ☐ 64 Luis Gonzalez | .15 | .40 |
| ☐ 65 David Ortiz | .40 | 1.00 |
| ☐ 66 Jorge Posada | .25 | .60 |
| ☐ 67 Xavier Nady | .15 | .40 |
| ☐ 68 Larry Walker | .25 | .60 |
| ☐ 69 Mark Loretta | .15 | .40 |
| ☐ 70 Jim Thome SP | 3.00 | 8.00 |
| ☐ 71 Livan Hernandez | .15 | .40 |
| ☐ 72 Garrett Atkins | .15 | .40 |
| ☐ 73 Milton Bradley | .15 | .40 |
| ☐ 74 B.J. Upton | .15 | .40 |
| ☐ 75A I.Suzuki w/Name SP | 4.00 | 10.00 |
| ☐ 75B I.Suzuki w/o Name SP | 4.00 | 10.00 |
| ☐ 76 Aramis Ramirez | .15 | .40 |
| ☐ 77 Eric Milton | .15 | .40 |
| ☐ 78 Troy Glaus SP | 3.00 | 8.00 |
| ☐ 79 David Newhan | .15 | .40 |
| ☐ 80 Delmon Young | .25 | .60 |
| ☐ 81 Justin Morneau | .15 | .40 |
| ☐ 82 Ramon Ortiz | .15 | .40 |
| ☐ 83A E.Chavez Blue Sky | .15 | .40 |
| ☐ 83B E.Chavez Purple Sky SP | 3.00 | 8.00 |
| ☐ 84 Sean Burroughs | .15 | .40 |
| ☐ 85 Scott Rolen SP | 3.00 | 8.00 |
| ☐ 86 Rocco Baldelli | .15 | .40 |
| ☐ 87 Joe Mauer SP | 4.00 | 10.00 |
| ☐ 88 Tony Womack | .15 | .40 |
| ☐ 89 Ken Griffey Jr. | .60 | 1.50 |
| ☐ 90 Alfonso Soriano SP | 3.00 | 8.00 |
| ☐ 91 Paul Konerko | .15 | .40 |
| ☐ 92 Guillermo Mota | .15 | .40 |
| ☐ 93 Lance Berkman | .15 | .40 |
| ☐ 94 Mark Buehrle | .15 | .40 |
| ☐ 95 Matt Clement | .15 | .40 |
| ☐ 96 Melvin Mora | .15 | .40 |
| ☐ 97 Khalil Greene | .25 | .60 |
| ☐ 98 David Wright | .60 | 1.50 |
| ☐ 99 Jack Wilson | .15 | .40 |
| ☐ 100A A.Rodriguez w/Bat SP | 4.00 | 10.00 |
| ☐ 100B A.Rodriguez w/Glove SP | 4.00 | 10.00 |
| ☐ 101 Joe Nathan | .15 | .40 |
| ☐ 102A A.Beltre Grey Uni SP | 3.00 | 8.00 |
| ☐ 102B A.Beltre White Uni | .15 | .40 |
| ☐ 103 Mike Sweeney | .15 | .40 |
| ☐ 104 Brad Lidge | .15 | .40 |
| ☐ 105 Shawn Green | .15 | .40 |

|  |  | | |
|---|---|---|---|
| 106 | Miguel Tejada SP | 3.00 | 8.00 |
| 107 | Derrek Lee | .25 | .60 |
| 108 | Eric Hinske | .15 | .40 |
| 109 | Eric Byrnes | .15 | .40 |
| 110 | Hideki Matsui SP | 3.00 | 8.00 |
| 111 | Tom Glavine | .25 | .60 |
| 112 | Jimmy Rollins | .15 | .40 |
| 113 | Ryan Drese | .15 | .40 |
| 114 | Josh Beckett | .15 | .40 |
| 115 | Curt Schilling SP | 3.00 | 8.00 |
| 116 | Jeremy Bonderman | .15 | .40 |
| 117 | Kazuo Matsui | .15 | .40 |
| 118 | Chase Utley | .25 | .60 |
| 119 | Troy Percival | .15 | .40 |
| 120A | V.Guerrero w/Bat SP | 3.00 | 8.00 |
| 120B | V.Guerrero w/Glove SP | 3.00 | 8.00 |
| 121 | Gary Sheffield | .15 | .40 |
| 122 | Jeromy Burnitz | .15 | .40 |
| 123 | Javier Vazquez | .15 | .40 |
| 124 | Kevin Millar | .15 | .40 |
| 125A | R.Johnson Blue Sky | .40 | 1.00 |
| 125B | R.Johnson Purple Sky SP | 3.00 | 8.00 |
| 126 | Pat Burrell | .15 | .40 |
| 127 | Jason Schmidt | .15 | .40 |
| 128 | Jose Vidro | .15 | .40 |
| 129 | Kip Wells | .15 | .40 |
| 130A | I.Rodriguez w/Cap | .25 | .60 |
| 130B | I.Rodriguez w/Helmet SP | 3.00 | 8.00 |
| 131 | C.C. Sabathia | .15 | .40 |
| 132 | Carlos Delgado SP | 3.00 | 8.00 |
| 133 | Bartolo Colon | .15 | .40 |
| 134 | Andruw Jones | .25 | .60 |
| 135 | Kerry Wood | .15 | .40 |
| 136 | Sidney Ponson | .15 | .40 |
| 137 | Eric Gagne | .15 | .40 |
| 138 | Rickie Weeks | .15 | .40 |
| 139 | Mariano Rivera | .40 | 1.00 |
| 140 | Bobby Crosby | .15 | .40 |
| 141 | Jamie Moyer | .15 | .40 |
| 142 | Corey Koskie | .15 | .40 |
| 143 | John Smoltz | .25 | .60 |
| 144 | Frank Thomas | .40 | 1.00 |
| 145 | Cristian Guzman | .15 | .40 |
| 146 | Paul Lo Duca | .15 | .40 |
| 147 | Geoff Jenkins | .15 | .40 |
| 148 | Nick Swisher | .15 | .40 |
| 149 | Jason Bay SP | 3.00 | 8.00 |
| 150 | Albert Pujols SP | 6.00 | 15.00 |
| 151 | Edwin Jackson | .15 | .40 |
| 152 | Carl Crawford | .15 | .40 |
| 153 | Mark Mulder | .15 | .40 |
| 154 | Rafael Palmeiro | .25 | .60 |
| 155 | Pedro Martinez SP | 3.00 | 8.00 |
| 156 | Jake Westbrook | .15 | .40 |
| 157 | Sean Casey | .15 | .40 |
| 158 | Aaron Rowand | .15 | .40 |
| 159 | J.D. Drew | .15 | .40 |
| 160A | J.Sant Glove on Knee SP | 3.00 | 8.00 |
| 160B | J.Santana Throwing SP | 3.00 | 8.00 |
| 161 | Gavin Floyd | .15 | .40 |
| 162 | Vernon Wells | .15 | .40 |
| 163 | Aubrey Huff | .15 | .40 |
| 164 | Jeff Bagwell | .25 | .60 |
| 165 | Boomer Wells | .15 | .40 |
| 166 | Brad Penny | .15 | .40 |
| 167 | Austin Kearns | .15 | .40 |
| 168 | Mike Mussina | .25 | .60 |
| 169 | Randy Wolf | .15 | .40 |
| 170 | Tim Hudson SP | 3.00 | 8.00 |
| 171 | Casey Blake | .15 | .40 |
| 172 | Edgar Renteria | .15 | .40 |
| 173 | Ben Sheets | .15 | .40 |
| 174 | Kevin Brown | .15 | .40 |
| 175 | Nomar Garciaparra SP | 3.00 | 8.00 |
| 176 | Armando Benitez | .15 | .40 |
| 177 | Jody Gerut | .15 | .40 |
| 178 | Craig Biggio | .25 | .60 |
| 179 | Omar Vizquel | .25 | .60 |
| 180 | Jake Peavy | .15 | .40 |
| 181 | Gustavo Chacin SP | 3.00 | 8.00 |
| 182 | Johnny Damon | .25 | .60 |
| 183 | Mike Lieberthal | .15 | .40 |
| 184 | Felix Hernandez SP | 6.00 | 15.00 |
| 185 | Zach Day SP | 3.00 | 8.00 |
| 186 | Matt Cain | .40 | 1.00 |
| 187 | Erubiel Durazo | .15 | .40 |
| 188 | Zack Greinke | .15 | .40 |
| 189 | Matt Morris | .15 | .40 |
| 190 | Billy Wagner | .15 | .40 |
| 191 | Al Leiter | .15 | .40 |
| 192 | Miguel Olivo | .15 | .40 |
| 193 | Jose Capellan SP | 3.00 | 8.00 |
| 194 | Adam Eaton | .15 | .40 |
| 195 | Steven While SP RC | 3.00 | 8.00 |
| 196 | Joe Randa | .15 | .40 |
| 197 | Richard Hidalgo | .15 | .40 |
| 198 | Orlando Cabrera | .15 | .40 |
| 199 | Joel Guzman SP | 3.00 | 8.00 |
| 200 | Garret Anderson | .15 | .40 |
| 201 | Endy Chavez | .15 | .40 |
| 202 | Andy Marte | .15 | .40 |
| 203 | Jose Guillen | .15 | .40 |
| 204 | Victor Martinez | .15 | .40 |
| 205 | Johnny Estrada | .15 | .40 |
| 206 | Damian Miller | .15 | .40 |
| 207 | Ken Harvey | .15 | .40 |
| 208 | Ronnie Belliard | .15 | .40 |
| 209 | Chan Ho Park | .15 | .40 |
| 210 | Laynce Nix | .15 | .40 |
| 211 | Lew Ford | .15 | .40 |
| 212 | Moises Alou | .15 | .40 |
| 213 | Kris Benson | .15 | .40 |
| 214 | Mike Gonzalez SP | 3.00 | 8.00 |
| 215 | Chris Burke | .15 | .40 |
| 216 | Juan Pierre | .15 | .40 |
| 217 | Phil Nevin | .15 | .40 |
| 218 | Jerry Hairston Jr. | .15 | .40 |
| 219 | Jeremy Reed | .15 | .40 |
| 220 | Scott Kazmir SP | 3.00 | 8.00 |
| 221 | Mike Maroth | .15 | .40 |
| 222 | Alex Rios | .15 | .40 |
| 223 | Esteban Loaiza | .15 | .40 |
| 224 | Termmel Sledge | .15 | .40 |
| 225A | M.Prior Blue Sky SP | 3.00 | 8.00 |
| 225B | M.Prior Yellow Sky SP | 3.00 | 8.00 |
| 226 | Hank Blalock | .15 | .40 |
| 227 | Craig Wilson | .15 | .40 |
| 228 | Cesar Izturis | .15 | .40 |
| 229 | Dmitri Young | .15 | .40 |
| 230A | D.Jeter Blue Sky SP | 6.00 | 15.00 |
| 230B | D.Jeter Purple Sky SP | 6.00 | 15.00 |
| 231 | Mark Kotsay | .15 | .40 |
| 232 | Darin Erstad | .15 | .40 |
| 233 | Brandon Backe SP | 3.00 | 8.00 |
| 234 | Mike Lowell | .15 | .40 |
| 235 | Scott Podsednik | .15 | .40 |
| 236 | Michael Barrett | .15 | .40 |
| 237 | Chad Tracy | .15 | .40 |
| 238 | David Dellucci | .15 | .40 |
| 239 | Brady Clark | .15 | .40 |
| 240 | Jorge Cantu | .15 | .40 |
| 241 | Wil Ledezma | .15 | .40 |
| 242 | Morgan Ensberg | .15 | .40 |
| 243 | Omar Infante | .15 | .40 |
| 244 | Corey Patterson | .15 | .40 |
| 245 | Matt Holliday | .20 | .50 |
| 246 | Vinny Castilla | .15 | .40 |
| 247 | Jason Bartlett | .15 | .40 |
| 248 | Noah Lowry | .15 | .40 |
| 249 | Huston Street | .25 | .60 |
| 250 | Russell Branyan | .15 | .40 |
| 251 | Juan Uribe | .15 | .40 |
| 252 | Larry Bigbie | .15 | .40 |
| 253 | Grady Sizemore | .25 | .60 |
| 254 | Pedro Feliz | .15 | .40 |
| 255 | Brad Wilkerson | .15 | .40 |
| 256 | Brandon Inge | .15 | .40 |
| 257 | Dewon Brazelton | .15 | .40 |
| 258 | Rodrigo Lopez | .15 | .40 |
| 259 | Jacque Jones | .15 | .40 |
| 260 | Jason Giambi | .15 | .40 |
| 261 | Clint Barmes | .15 | .40 |
| 262 | Willy Taveras | .15 | .40 |
| 263 | Marcus Giles | .15 | .40 |
| 264 | Joe Blanton | .15 | .40 |
| 265 | John Thomson | .15 | .40 |
| 266 | Steve Finley SP | 3.00 | 8.00 |
| 267 | Kevin Millwood | .15 | .40 |
| 268 | David Eckstein | .15 | .40 |
| 269 | Barry Zito | .15 | .40 |
| 270A | T.Helton Purple Sky SP | 3.00 | 8.00 |
| 270B | T.Helton Yellow Sky SP | 3.00 | 8.00 |
| 271 | Landon Powell RC | .15 | .40 |
| 272 | Justin Verlander RC | 1.50 | 4.00 |
| 273 | Wes Swackhamer RC | .40 | 1.00 |
| 274 | Wladimir Balentien RC | .40 | 1.00 |
| 275 | Philip Humber RC | .40 | 1.00 |
| 276 | Kevin Melillo RC | .40 | 1.00 |
| 277 | Billy Butler RC | 1.50 | 4.00 |
| 278 | Michael Rogers RC | .40 | 1.00 |
| 279 | Bobby Livingston RC | .40 | 1.00 |
| 280 | Glen Perkins RC | .40 | 1.00 |
| 281 | Mike Bourn RC | .40 | 1.00 |
| 282 | Tyler Pelland RC | .40 | 1.00 |
| 283 | Jeremy West RC | .40 | 1.00 |
| 284 | Brandon McCarthy RC | .60 | 1.50 |
| 285 | Ian Kinsler RC | 1.00 | 2.50 |
| 286 | Chris Robinson RC | .40 | 1.00 |
| 287 | Melky Cabrera RC | .75 | 2.00 |
| 288 | Ryan Sweeney RC | .40 | 1.00 |
| 289 | Chip Cannon RC | .50 | 1.25 |
| 290 | Andy LaRoche RC | 1.50 | 4.00 |
| 291 | Chuck Tiffany RC | .50 | 1.25 |
| 292 | Ian Bladergroen RC | .40 | 1.00 |
| 293 | Bear Bay RC | .40 | 1.00 |
| 294 | Hernan Iribarren RC | .50 | 1.25 |
| 295 | Stuart Pomeranz RC | .40 | 1.00 |
| 296 | Luke Scott RC | .75 | 2.00 |
| 297 | Chuck James RC | .75 | 2.00 |
| 298 | Kennard Bibbs RC | .40 | 1.00 |
| 299 | Steven Bondurant RC | .40 | 1.00 |
| 300 | Thomas Oldham RC | .40 | 1.00 |
| 301 | Nolan Ryan RET | 2.00 | 5.00 |
| 302 | Reggie Jackson RET | .50 | 1.25 |
| 303 | Tom Seaver RET | .50 | 1.25 |
| 304 | Al Kaline RET | .75 | 2.00 |
| 305 | Cal Ripken RET | 2.50 | 6.00 |
| 306 | Josh Gibson RET | .75 | 2.00 |
| 307 | Frank Robinson RET | .40 | 1.00 |
| 308 | Duke Snider RET | .50 | 1.25 |
| 309 | Wade Boggs RET | .50 | 1.25 |
| 310 | Tony Gwynn RET | 1.00 | 2.50 |
| 311 | Carl Yastrzemski RET | .75 | 2.00 |
| 312 | Ryne Sandberg RET | 1.25 | 3.00 |
| 313 | Gary Carter RET | .40 | 1.00 |
| 314 | Brooks Robinson RET | .50 | 1.25 |
| 315 | Ernie Banks RET | .75 | 2.00 |

## 2006 Topps Turkey Red

| | | | |
|---|---|---|---|
| COMPLETE SET (330) | | 150.00 | 250.00 |
| COMP.SET w/o SP's (275) | | 15.00 | 40.00 |
| COMMON CARD (316-580) | | .15 | .40 |
| COMMON SP (316-580) | | 3.00 | 8.00 |
| SP STATED ODDS 1:4 HOBBY, 1:4 RETAIL | | | |
| SEE BECKETT.COM FOR SP CHECKLIST | | | |
| COMMON CL (571-580) | | .07 | .20 |
| CL SEMIS 571-580 | | .12 | .30 |
| COMMON RET (581-590) | | .30 | .75 |
| COMMON RC (591-630) | | .40 | 1.00 |
| OVERALL PLATE ODDS 1:477 H | | | |
| PLATE PRINT RUN 1 SET PER COLOR | | | |
| BLACK-CYAN-MAGENTA-YELLOW ISSUED | | | |
| NO PLATE PRICING DUE TO SCARCITY | | | |
| 316A | A.Rodriguez Yanks | .60 | 1.50 |
| 316B | A.Rodriguez Rangers SP | 4.00 | 10.00 |
| 316C | Alex Rodriguez M's SP | 4.00 | 10.00 |
| 317 | Jeff Francoeur SP | 3.00 | 8.00 |
| 318 | Shawn Green | .15 | .40 |
| 319 | Daniel Cabrera | .15 | .40 |
| 320 | Craig Biggio | .25 | .60 |
| 321 | Jeremy Bonderman | .15 | .40 |
| 322 | Mark Kotsay | .15 | .40 |
| 323 | Cliff Floyd | .15 | .40 |
| 324 | Jimmy Rollins | .15 | .40 |
| 325A | M.Ordonez Tigers | .15 | .40 |
| 325B | M.Ordonez W.Sox SP | 3.00 | 8.00 |
| 326 | C.C. Sabathia | .15 | .40 |
| 327 | Oliver Perez | .15 | .40 |
| 328 | Orlando Hudson | .15 | .40 |
| 329 | Chris Ray | .15 | .40 |

|  |  | | |
|---|---|---|---|
| 330 | Manny Ramirez | .25 | .60 |
| 331 | Paul Konerko | .15 | .40 |
| 332 | Joe Mauer SP | 3.00 | 8.00 |
| 333 | Jorge Posada | .25 | .60 |
| 334 | Mark Ellis | .15 | .40 |
| 335 | A.J. Burnett | .15 | .40 |
| 336 | Mike Sweeney | .15 | .40 |
| 337 | Shannon Stewart | .15 | .40 |
| 338 | Jake Peavy SP | 3.00 | 8.00 |
| 339A | C.Delgado Mets SP | 3.00 | 8.00 |
| 339B | C.Delgado B.Jays SP | 3.00 | 8.00 |
| 340 | Brian Roberts | .15 | .40 |
| 341 | Dontrelle Willis | .15 | .40 |
| 342 | Aaron Rowand | .15 | .40 |
| 343A | R.Sexson M's | .15 | .40 |
| 343B | R.Sexson Brewers SP | 3.00 | 8.00 |
| 344 | Chris Carpenter | .15 | .40 |
| 345 | Carlos Zambrano | .15 | .40 |
| 346 | Nomar Garciaparra | .40 | 1.00 |
| 347 | Carlos Lee | .15 | .40 |
| 348A | P.Wilson Astros | .15 | .40 |
| 348B | P.Wilson Marlins SP | 3.00 | 8.00 |
| 349 | Mariano Rivera | .40 | 1.00 |
| 350 | Ichiro Suzuki SP | 4.00 | 10.00 |
| 351A | M.Piazza Padres | .40 | 1.00 |
| 351B | Mike Piazza Mets SP | 3.00 | 8.00 |
| 352 | Jason Schmidt | .15 | .40 |
| 353 | Jeff Weaver | .15 | .40 |
| 354 | Rocco Baldelli | .15 | .40 |
| 355 | Adam Dunn | .15 | .40 |
| 356 | Jeromy Burnitz | .15 | .40 |
| 357 | Chris Shelton SP | 3.00 | 8.00 |
| 358 | Chone Figgins SP | 3.00 | 8.00 |
| 359 | Javier Vazquez | .15 | .40 |
| 360 | Chipper Jones | .40 | 1.00 |
| 361 | Frank Thomas | .40 | 1.00 |
| 362 | Mark Loretta | .15 | .40 |
| 363 | Hideki Matsui | .40 | 1.00 |
| 364 | J.J. Hardy SP | 3.00 | 8.00 |
| 365 | Todd Helton | .25 | .60 |
| 366 | Reggie Sanders | .15 | .40 |
| 367 | Jay Gibbons | .15 | .40 |
| 368 | Johnny Estrada | .15 | .40 |
| 369 | Grady Sizemore | .25 | .60 |
| 370 | Jim Thome | .25 | .60 |
| 371 | Ivan Rodriguez | .25 | .60 |
| 372 | Jason Bay | .15 | .40 |
| 373 | Carl Crawford | .15 | .40 |
| 374 | Adrian Beltre | .15 | .40 |
| 375 | Derrek Lee SP | 3.00 | 8.00 |
| 376 | Miguel Olivo | .15 | .40 |
| 377 | Roy Oswalt | .15 | .40 |
| 378 | Coco Crisp | .15 | .40 |
| 379 | Moises Alou | .15 | .40 |
| 380 | Kevin Millwood | .15 | .40 |
| 381 | Mark Grudzielanek | .15 | .40 |
| 382 | Justin Morneau | .15 | .40 |
| 383 | Austin Kearns | .15 | .40 |
| 384 | Brad Penny | .15 | .40 |
| 385 | Troy Glaus | .15 | .40 |
| 386 | Cliff Lee | .15 | .40 |
| 387 | Armando Benitez | .15 | .40 |
| 388 | Clint Barmes | .15 | .40 |
| 389 | Orlando Cabrera | .15 | .40 |
| 390 | Jim Edmonds SP | 3.00 | 8.00 |
| 391 | Jermaine Dye | .15 | .40 |
| 392 | Morgan Ensberg SP | 3.00 | 8.00 |
| 393 | Paul LoDuca | .15 | .40 |
| 394 | Eric Chavez | .15 | .40 |
| 395 | Greg Maddux SP | 4.00 | 10.00 |
| 396 | Jack Wilson | .15 | .40 |
| 397 | Omar Vizquel | .25 | .60 |
| 398 | Joe Nathan | .15 | .40 |
| 399 | Bobby Abreu | .15 | .40 |
| 400 | Barry Bonds SP | 6.00 | 15.00 |
| 401 | Gary Sheffield | .15 | .40 |
| 402 | John Patterson | .15 | .40 |
| 403 | J.D. Drew | .15 | .40 |
| 404 | Bruce Chen | .15 | .40 |
| 405 | Johnny Damon SP | 3.00 | 8.00 |
| 406 | Aubrey Huff | .15 | .40 |
| 407 | Mark Mulder | .15 | .40 |
| 408 | Jamie Moyer | .15 | .40 |
| 409 | Carlos Guillen | .15 | .40 |
| 410 | Andruw Jones SP | 3.00 | 8.00 |
| 411 | Jhonny Peralta SP | 3.00 | 8.00 |
| 412 | Doug Davis | .15 | .40 |
| 413 | Aaron Miles | .15 | .40 |
| 414 | Jon Lieber | .15 | .40 |
| 415 | Aaron Hill | .15 | .40 |
| 416 | Josh Beckett SP | 3.00 | 8.00 |
| 417 | Bobby Crosby | .15 | .40 |
| 418 | Noah Lowry SP | 3.00 | 8.00 |
| 419 | Sidney Ponson | .15 | .40 |
| 420 | Luis Castillo | .15 | .40 |
| 421 | Brad Wilkerson | .15 | .40 |
| 422 | Felix Hernandez SP | 3.00 | 8.00 |
| 423 | Vinny Castilla | .15 | .40 |
| 424 | Tom Glavine | .25 | .60 |
| 425 | Vladimir Guerrero | .40 | 1.00 |
| 426 | Javy Lopez | .15 | .40 |
| 427 | Ronnie Belliard | .15 | .40 |
| 428 | Dmitri Young | .15 | .40 |
| 429 | Johan Santana | .25 | .60 |
| 430A | D.Ortiz Red Sox SP | 3.00 | 8.00 |
| 430B | D.Ortiz Twins SP | 3.00 | 8.00 |
| 431 | Ben Sheets | .15 | .40 |
| 432 | Matt Holliday | .40 | 1.00 |
| 433 | Brian McCann | .15 | .40 |
| 434 | Joe Blanton | .15 | .40 |
| 435 | Sean Casey | .15 | .40 |
| 436 | Brad Lidge | .15 | .40 |
| 437 | Chad Tracy | .15 | .40 |
| 438 | Brett Myers | .15 | .40 |
| 439 | Matt Morris | .15 | .40 |
| 440 | Brian Giles | .15 | .40 |
| 441 | Zach Duke | .15 | .40 |
| 442 | Jose Lopez | .15 | .40 |
| 443 | Kris Benson | .15 | .40 |
| 444 | Jose Reyes SP | 3.00 | 8.00 |
| 445 | Travis Hafner | .15 | .40 |
| 446 | Orlando Hernandez | .15 | .40 |
| 447 | Edgar Renteria | .15 | .40 |
| 448 | Scott Podsednik | .15 | .40 |
| 449 | Nick Swisher SP | 3.00 | 8.00 |
| 450 | Derek Jeter SP | 6.00 | 15.00 |
| 451 | Scott Kazmir SP | 3.00 | 8.00 |
| 452 | Hank Blalock | .15 | .40 |
| 453 | Jake Westbrook | .15 | .40 |
| 454 | Miguel Cabrera | .25 | .60 |
| 455A | K.Griffey Jr. Reds | .60 | 1.50 |
| 455B | K.Griffey Jr. M's SP | 4.00 | 10.00 |
| 456 | Rafael Furcal | .15 | .40 |
| 457 | Lance Berkman | .15 | .40 |
| 458 | Aramis Ramirez | .15 | .40 |
| 459A | X.Nady Mets | .15 | .40 |
| 459B | X.Nady Padres SP | 3.00 | 8.00 |
| 460A | R.Johnson Yanks | .40 | 1.00 |
| 460B | R.Johnson Astros SP | 3.00 | 8.00 |
| 461 | Khalil Greene | .25 | .60 |
| 462 | Bartolo Colon | .15 | .40 |
| 463 | Mike Lowell | .15 | .40 |
| 464 | David DeJesus | .15 | .40 |
| 465 | Ryan Howard SP | 4.00 | 10.00 |
| 466 | Tim Salmon SP | 3.00 | 8.00 |
| 467 | Mark Buehrle SP | 3.00 | 8.00 |
| 468 | Curtis Granderson | .15 | .40 |
| 469 | Kerry Wood | .15 | .40 |
| 470 | Miguel Tejada | .15 | .40 |
| 471 | Geoff Jenkins | .15 | .40 |
| 472 | Jeremy Reed | .15 | .40 |
| 473 | David Eckstein | .15 | .40 |
| 474 | Lyle Overbay | .15 | .40 |
| 475 | Michael Young | .15 | .40 |
| 476A | N.Johnson Nats SP | 3.00 | 8.00 |
| 476B | N.Johnson Yanks SP | 3.00 | 8.00 |
| 477 | Carlos Beltran | .15 | .40 |
| 478 | Huston Street | .15 | .40 |
| 479 | Brandon Webb | .15 | .40 |
| 480 | Phil Nevin | .15 | .40 |
| 481 | Ryan Madson SP | 3.00 | 8.00 |
| 482 | Jason Giambi | .15 | .40 |
| 483 | Angel Berroa | .15 | .40 |
| 484 | Casey Blake | .15 | .40 |
| 485 | Pat Burrell | .15 | .40 |
| 486 | B.J. Ryan | .15 | .40 |
| 487 | Torii Hunter | .15 | .40 |
| 488 | Garret Anderson | .15 | .40 |
| 489 | Chase Utley SP | 3.00 | 8.00 |
| 490 | Matt Murton | .15 | .40 |
| 491 | Rich Harden | .15 | .40 |
| 492 | Garrett Atkins | .15 | .40 |
| 493 | Tadahito Iguchi SP | 3.00 | 8.00 |
| 494 | Jarrod Washburn | .15 | .40 |
| 495 | Carl Everett | .15 | .40 |
| 496 | Kameron Loe | .15 | .40 |
| 497 | Jorge Cantu SP | 3.00 | 8.00 |
| 498 | Chris Young | .15 | .40 |
| 499 | Marcus Giles | .15 | .40 |
| 500 | Albert Pujols | .75 | 2.00 |
| 501A | A.Soriano Nats SP | 3.00 | 8.00 |
| 501B | A.Soriano Yanks SP | 3.00 | 8.00 |
| 502 | Randy Winn | .15 | .40 |
| 503 | Roy Halladay | .15 | .40 |
| 504 | Victor Martinez | .15 | .40 |
| 505 | Pedro Martinez | .25 | .60 |
| 506 | Rickie Weeks | .15 | .40 |
| 507 | Dan Johnson | .15 | .40 |
| 508A | T.Hudson Braves | .15 | .40 |
| 508B | T.Hudson A's SP | 3.00 | 8.00 |
| 509 | Mark Prior | .25 | .60 |
| 510 | Melvin Mora | .15 | .40 |
| 511 | Matt Clement | .15 | .40 |
| 512 | Brandon Inge | .15 | .40 |
| 513 | Mike Mussina | .25 | .60 |
| 514 | Mike Cameron | .15 | .40 |
| 515 | Barry Zito | .15 | .40 |
| 516 | Luis Gonzalez | .15 | .40 |
| 517 | Jose Castillo | .15 | .40 |
| 518 | Andy Pettitte | .25 | .60 |
| 519 | Wily Mo Pena | .15 | .40 |
| 520 | Billy Wagner | .15 | .40 |
| 521 | Ervin Santana SP | 3.00 | 8.00 |
| 522 | Juan Pierre | .15 | .40 |
| 523 | Dan Haren | .15 | .40 |
| 524 | Adrian Gonzalez SP | 3.00 | 8.00 |
| 525 | Robinson Cano | .25 | .60 |
| 526 | Jeff Kent | .15 | .40 |
| 527 | Cory Sullivan | .15 | .40 |
| 528 | Joe Crede SP | 3.00 | 8.00 |
| 529 | John Smoltz | .25 | .60 |
| 530 | David Wright | .60 | 1.50 |
| 531 | Chad Cordero | .15 | .40 |
| 532 | Scott Rolen SP | 3.00 | 8.00 |
| 533 | Edwin Jackson | .15 | .40 |
| 534 | Doug Mientkiewicz | .15 | .40 |
| 535 | Mark Teixeira SP | 3.00 | 8.00 |
| 536 | Kelvim Escobar | .15 | .40 |
| 537 | Alex Rios | .15 | .40 |
| 538 | Jose Vidro | .15 | .40 |
| 539 | Alex Gonzalez | .15 | .40 |
| 540 | Yadier Molina | .15 | .40 |
| 541 | Ronny Cedeno SP | 3.00 | 8.00 |
| 542 | Mark Hendrickson | .15 | .40 |
| 543 | Russ Adams | .15 | .40 |
| 544 | Chris Capuano | .15 | .40 |
| 545 | Raul Ibanez | .25 | .60 |
| 546 | Vicente Padilla | .15 | .40 |
| 547 | Chris Duffy | .15 | .40 |
| 548 | Bengie Molina | .15 | .40 |
| 549 | Chien-Ming Wang | .40 | 1.00 |
| 550 | Curt Schilling | .25 | .60 |
| 551 | Craig Wilson | .15 | .40 |
| 552 | Mike Lieberthal | .15 | .40 |
| 553 | Kazuo Matsui | .15 | .40 |
| 554 | Jeff Francis | .15 | .40 |
| 555 | Brady Clark | .15 | .40 |
| 556 | Willy Taveras | .15 | .40 |
| 557 | Mike Maroth | .15 | .40 |
| 558 | Bernie Williams | .25 | .60 |
| 559 | Edwin Encarnacion | .15 | .40 |
| 560 | Vernon Wells | .15 | .40 |
| 561A | L.Hernandez Nats | .15 | .40 |
| 561B | L.Hernandez Giants SP | 3.00 | 8.00 |
| 562 | Kenny Rogers | .15 | .40 |
| 563 | Steve Finley | .15 | .40 |
| 564 | Trot Nixon | .15 | .40 |
| 565 | Jonny Gomes SP | 3.00 | 8.00 |
| 566 | Brandon Phillips | .15 | .40 |
| 567 | Shawn Chacon | .15 | .40 |
| 568 | Dave Bush | .15 | .40 |
| 569 | Jose Guillen | .15 | .40 |
| 570 | Gustavo Chacin | .15 | .40 |
| 571 | A.Rod Safe at the Plate CL | .30 | .75 |
| 572 | Pujols At Bat CL | .40 | 1.00 |
| 573 | Bonds On Deck CL | .40 | 1.00 |
| 574 | Breaking Up Two CL | .20 | .50 |
| 575 | Conference On The Mound CL | .20 | .50 |
| 576 | Touch Em All CL | .30 | .75 |
| 577 | Avoiding The Runner CL | .07 | .20 |
| 578 | Bunting The Runner Over CL | .07 | .20 |
| 579 | In The Hole CL | .07 | .20 |
| 580 | Jeter Steals Third CL | .50 | 1.25 |
| 581 | Nolan Ryan RET | 2.00 | 5.00 |

| Card | Lo | Hi |
|---|---|---|
| ☐ 582 Cal Ripken RET | 3.00 | 8.00 |
| ☐ 583 Carl Yastrzemski RET | 1.25 | 3.00 |
| ☐ 584 Duke Snider RET | .50 | 1.25 |
| ☐ 585 Tom Seaver RET | .50 | 1.25 |
| ☐ 586 Mickey Mantle RET | 4.00 | 10.00 |
| ☐ 587 Jim Palmer RET | .30 | .75 |
| ☐ 588 Gary Carter RET | .30 | .75 |
| ☐ 589 Stan Musial RET | 1.25 | 3.00 |
| ☐ 590 Luis Aparicio RET | .30 | .75 |
| ☐ 591 Prince Fielder (RC) | 1.50 | 4.00 |
| ☐ 592 Conor Jackson (RC) | .60 | 1.50 |
| ☐ 593 Jeremy Hermida (RC) | .40 | 1.00 |
| ☐ 594 Jeff Mathis (RC) | .40 | 1.00 |
| ☐ 595 Alay Soler RC | .40 | 1.00 |
| ☐ 596 Ryan Spilborghs (RC) | .60 | 1.50 |
| ☐ 597 Chuck James (RC) | .60 | 1.50 |
| ☐ 598 Josh Barfield (RC) | .40 | 1.00 |
| ☐ 599 Ian Kinsler (RC) | 1.25 | 3.00 |
| ☐ 600 Val Majewski (RC) | .40 | 1.00 |
| ☐ 601 Brian Slocum (RC) | .40 | 1.00 |
| ☐ 602 Matt Kemp (RC) | 1.00 | 2.50 |
| ☐ 603 Nate McLouth (RC) | .40 | 1.00 |
| ☐ 604 Sean Marshall RC | .40 | 1.00 |
| ☐ 605 Brian Bannister (RC) | .40 | 1.00 |
| ☐ 606 Ryan Zimmerman (RC) | 2.00 | 5.00 |
| ☐ 607 Kendry Morales (RC) | 1.00 | 2.50 |
| ☐ 608 Jonathan Papelbon (RC) | 2.00 | 5.00 |
| ☐ 609 Matt Cain (RC) | .60 | 1.50 |
| ☐ 610 Anderson Hernandez (RC) | .40 | 1.00 |
| ☐ 611 Jose Capellan (RC) | .40 | 1.00 |
| ☐ 612 Lastings Milledge (RC) | .60 | 1.50 |
| ☐ 613 Francisco Liriano (RC) | 2.00 | 5.00 |
| ☐ 614 Hanley Ramirez (RC) | 1.00 | 2.50 |
| ☐ 615 Brian Anderson (RC) | .40 | 1.00 |
| ☐ 616 Reggie Abercrombie (RC) | .40 | 1.00 |
| ☐ 617 Erick Aybar (RC) | .40 | 1.00 |
| ☐ 618 James Loney (RC) | .60 | 1.50 |
| ☐ 619 Joel Zumaya (RC) | 1.00 | 2.50 |
| ☐ 620 Travis Ishikawa (RC) | .40 | 1.00 |
| ☐ 621 Jason Kubel (RC) | .40 | 1.00 |
| ☐ 622 Drew Meyer (RC) | .40 | 1.00 |
| ☐ 623 Kenji Johjima RC | 2.00 | 5.00 |
| ☐ 624 Fausto Carmona (RC) | .40 | 1.00 |
| ☐ 625 Nick Markakis (RC) | .60 | 1.50 |
| ☐ 626 John Rheinecker (RC) | .40 | 1.00 |
| ☐ 627 Melky Cabrera (RC) | .60 | 1.50 |
| ☐ 628 Michael Pelfrey RC | 1.50 | 4.00 |
| ☐ 629 Dan Uggla (RC) | 1.00 | 2.50 |
| ☐ 630 Justin Verlander (RC) | 1.50 | 4.00 |

## 2007 Topps Turkey Red

| Item | Lo | Hi |
|---|---|---|
| ☐ COMPLETE SET (200) | 150.00 | 200.00 |
| ☐ COMP SET w/o SP's (150) | 12.50 | 30.00 |
| ☐ COMMON CARD (1-186) | .12 | .30 |
| ☐ COMMON RC (1-186) | .15 | .40 |
| ☐ COMMON SP (1-186) | 2.50 | 6.00 |
| ☐ SP ODDS 1:4 HOBBY, 1:4 RETAIL | | |
| ☐ COMMON AD BACK (1-186) | 2.50 | 6.00 |
| ☐ AD ODDS 1:4 HOBBY,1:4 RETAIL | | |
| ☐ 1 Ryan Howard | .50 | 1.25 |
| ☐ 1b R.Howard Ad Back SP | 4.00 | 10.00 |
| ☐ 2 Dontrelle Willis | .12 | .30 |
| ☐ 3 Matt Cain | .20 | .50 |
| ☐ 4 John Maine | .12 | .30 |
| ☐ 5 Cole Hamels | .20 | .50 |
| ☐ 6 Corey Patterson | .12 | .30 |
| ☐ 7 Mickey Mantle SP | 10.00 | 25.00 |
| ☐ 8 Servin Up Strikes Joham Santana CL | .20 | .50 |
| ☐ 9 Josh Beckett | .12 | .30 |
| ☐ 10 Jimmy Rollins | .12 | .30 |
| ☐ 11 Kenji Johjima | .30 | .75 |
| ☐ 12 Orlando Hernandez | .12 | .30 |
| ☐ 13 Jorge Posada Play at the Plate CL | .20 | .50 |
| ☐ 14 Ivan Rodriguez | .20 | .50 |
| ☐ 15 Ichiro Suzuki | .50 | 1.25 |
| ☐ 15b I.Suzuki Ad Back SP | 4.00 | 10.00 |
| ☐ 16 Double Griffey CL | .50 | 1.25 |
| ☐ 17 Stephen Drew | .20 | .50 |
| ☐ 18 B.J. Upton | .12 | .30 |
| ☐ 19 Mickey Mantle | 1.00 | 2.50 |
| ☐ 20b A.Rod Ad Back SP | 4.00 | 10.00 |
| ☐ 21 Adam Dunn | .12 | .30 |
| ☐ 22 Adam Lind SP (RC) | 2.50 | 6.00 |
| ☐ 23 Adrian Gonzalez | .12 | .30 |
| ☐ 24 Akinori Iwamura RC | .40 | 1.00 |
| ☐ 25 Albert Pujols | .60 | 1.50 |
| ☐ 25b A.Pujols Ad Back SP | 4.00 | 10.00 |
| ☐ 26 Frank Thomas | .30 | .75 |
| ☐ 27 Roy Halladay | .12 | .30 |
| ☐ 28 Alejandro De Aza RC | .25 | .60 |
| ☐ 29 Alex Gordon RC | .75 | 2.00 |
| ☐ 30 Barry Bonds | .60 | 1.50 |
| ☐ 31 Andrew Miller RC | 1.00 | 2.50 |
| ☐ 32 Andruw Jones | .20 | .50 |
| ☐ 33 Karl Suzuki SP (RC) | 2.50 | 6.00 |
| ☐ 34 Mickey Mantle | 1.00 | 2.50 |
| ☐ 35 Andy Pettitte | .20 | .50 |
| ☐ 36 Tadahito Iguchi | .12 | .30 |
| ☐ 37 Edgar Renteria | .12 | .30 |
| ☐ 38 Tim Hudson | .12 | .30 |
| ☐ 39 Micah Owings (RC) | .15 | .40 |
| ☐ 40 Chipper Jones | .30 | .75 |
| ☐ 40b C.Jones Ad Back SP | 3.00 | 8.00 |
| ☐ 41 Barry Zito | .12 | .30 |
| ☐ 42 Dice-K CL | 1.25 | 3.00 |
| ☐ 43 Jarrod Saltalamacchia SP (RC) | 2.50 | 6.00 |
| ☐ 44 Bill Hall | .12 | .30 |
| ☐ 45 Billy Butler (RC) | .25 | .60 |
| ☐ 46 Billy Wagner | .12 | .30 |
| ☐ 47 Rich Harden SP | 2.50 | 6.00 |
| ☐ 48 Prince Albert CL | .60 | 1.50 |
| ☐ 49 Brandon Inge | .12 | .30 |
| ☐ 50 Jason Giambi | .12 | .30 |
| ☐ 51 Brandon Webb | .12 | .30 |
| ☐ 52 Brandon Wood (RC) | .15 | .40 |
| ☐ 53 Swiping Second Carl Crawford CL | .12 | .30 |
| ☐ 54 Brian Giles | .12 | .30 |
| ☐ 55 Josh Hamilton (RC) | .75 | 2.00 |
| ☐ 56 C.Utley Ad Back SP | 3.00 | 8.00 |
| ☐ 57 Miguel Montero (RC) | .15 | .40 |
| ☐ 58 Carl Crawford | .12 | .30 |
| ☐ 59 Carlos Beltran | .12 | .30 |
| ☐ 60 Mariano Rivera | .30 | .75 |
| ☐ 61 Carlos Delgado | .12 | .30 |
| ☐ 62 Carlos Lee SP | 2.50 | 6.00 |
| ☐ 63 Carlos Zambrano SP | 2.50 | 6.00 |
| ☐ 64 Miguel Tejada | .12 | .30 |
| ☐ 65 Mike Cameron | .12 | .30 |
| ☐ 66 Chase Utley SP | 3.00 | 8.00 |
| ☐ 67 Chase Wright RC | .40 | 1.00 |
| ☐ 68 Chien-Ming Wang | .50 | 1.25 |
| ☐ 69 Nick Swisher | .12 | .30 |
| ☐ 70 David Wright | .50 | 1.25 |
| ☐ 71 Mike Piazza SP | 3.00 | 8.00 |
| ☐ 72 Chris Carpenter | .12 | .30 |
| ☐ 73 Mark Buehrle SP | 2.50 | 6.00 |
| ☐ 74 Torii Hunter SP | 2.50 | 6.00 |
| ☐ 75 Tyler Clippard (RC) | .25 | .60 |
| ☐ 76 Nick Markakis | .20 | .50 |
| ☐ 77 Mickey Mantle SP | 1.00 | 2.50 |
| ☐ 78 Curt Schilling | .20 | .50 |
| ☐ 79 Curtis Granderson | .20 | .50 |
| ☐ 80 Craig Biggio | .20 | .50 |
| ☐ 81 Juan Pierre | .12 | .30 |
| ☐ 82 Dallas Braden SP RC | 2.50 | 6.00 |
| ☐ 83 Dan Haren SP | 3.00 | 8.00 |
| ☐ 84 Dan Uggla | .20 | .50 |
| ☐ 85 Danny Putnam (RC) | .15 | .40 |
| ☐ 86 David DeJesus | .12 | .30 |
| ☐ 87 David Eckstein | .12 | .30 |
| ☐ 88 Tim Lincecum RC | 1.25 | 3.00 |
| ☐ 89 Johnny Damon SP | 2.50 | 6.00 |
| ☐ 90 Justin Morneau | .12 | .30 |
| ☐ 91 Delmon Young (RC) | .25 | .60 |
| ☐ 92 Homer Bailey (RC) | .25 | .60 |
| ☐ 93 Carlos Gomez RC | .25 | .60 |
| ☐ 94 Josh Fields SP (RC) | 2.50 | 6.00 |
| ☐ 95 Derek Jeter | .75 | 2.00 |
| ☐ 95b D.Jeter Ad Back SP | 6.00 | 15.00 |
| ☐ 96 Derek Lee | .12 | .30 |
| ☐ 97 Don Kelly (RC) | .15 | .40 |
| ☐ 98 Doug Slaten RC | .15 | .40 |
| ☐ 99 Dustin Moseley | .12 | .30 |
| ☐ 100 Gary Sheffield | .12 | .30 |
| ☐ 101 Orlando Hudson SP | 2.50 | 6.00 |
| ☐ 102 Elijah Dukes RC | .25 | .60 |
| ☐ 103 Eric Byrnes SP | 2.50 | 6.00 |
| ☐ 104 Eric Chavez | .12 | .30 |
| ☐ 105 Phil Hughes (RC) | .75 | 2.00 |
| ☐ 105b Hughes Ad Back SP (RC) | 4.00 | 10.00 |
| ☐ 106 Felix Hernandez SP | 2.50 | 6.00 |
| ☐ 106b Felix Hernandez Ad Back SP | | |
| ☐ 107 Mickey Mantle | 1.00 | 2.50 |
| ☐ 108 Felix Pie (RC) | .15 | .40 |
| ☐ 109 Captain Jeter CL | .75 | 2.00 |
| ☐ 110 Daisuke Matsuzaka RC | 1.50 | 4.00 |
| ☐ 110b Dice-K Ad Back SP RC | 6.00 | 15.00 |
| ☐ 111 Francisco Rodriguez | .12 | .30 |
| ☐ 112 Ramon Hernandez | .12 | .30 |
| ☐ 113 Randy Johnson | .30 | .75 |
| ☐ 114 Gary Matthews | .12 | .30 |
| ☐ 115 Prince Fielder | .30 | .75 |
| ☐ 116 Vladdy Yard CL | .30 | .75 |
| ☐ 117 Mickey Mantle | 1.00 | 2.50 |
| ☐ 118 Hideki Matsui | .30 | .75 |
| ☐ 119 Hideki Okajima RC | .75 | 2.00 |
| ☐ 120 Manny Ramirez | .20 | .50 |
| ☐ 121 H.Pence SP (RC) | 6.00 | 15.00 |
| ☐ 122 Roy Oswalt | .12 | .30 |
| ☐ 123 Josh Willingham SP | 2.50 | 6.00 |
| ☐ 124 Tom Gordon SP | 2.50 | 6.00 |
| ☐ 125 Michael Young | .12 | .30 |
| ☐ 126 J.D. Drew | .12 | .30 |
| ☐ 127 Ryan Zimmerman | .30 | .75 |
| ☐ 128 James Shields SP | 3.00 | 8.00 |
| ☐ 129 Jack Wilson | .12 | .30 |
| ☐ 130 David Ortiz | .30 | .75 |
| ☐ 130b D.Ortiz Ad Back SP | 3.00 | 8.00 |
| ☐ 131 Jose Reyes CL | .30 | .75 |
| ☐ 132 Jamie Vermilyea RC | .15 | .40 |
| ☐ 133 Jason Bay | .12 | .30 |
| ☐ 134 Scott Kazmir SP | 2.50 | 6.00 |
| ☐ 135 Jason Isringhausen SP | 3.00 | 8.00 |
| ☐ 136 Jason Marquis SP | 2.50 | 6.00 |
| ☐ 137 Jason Schmidt | .12 | .30 |
| ☐ 138 Shawn Green | .12 | .30 |
| ☐ 139 Jeff Francoeur SP | 3.00 | 8.00 |
| ☐ 140 Alfonso Soriano | .12 | .30 |
| ☐ 141 Kevin Kouzmanoff (RC) | .15 | .40 |
| ☐ 142 Jered Weaver | .20 | .50 |
| ☐ 143 Todd Helton SP | 2.50 | 6.00 |
| ☐ 144 Jermaine Dye | .12 | .30 |
| ☐ 145 Jim Thome | .20 | .50 |
| ☐ 146 Tom Glavine SP | 2.50 | 6.00 |
| ☐ 147 Joe Mauer | .20 | .50 |
| ☐ 148 Joe Nathan | .12 | .30 |
| ☐ 149 Joe Smith RC | .15 | .40 |
| ☐ 150 Ken Griffey Jr. | .50 | 1.25 |
| ☐ 150b Griffey Ad Back SP | 4.00 | 10.00 |
| ☐ 151 Grady Sizemore | .20 | .50 |
| ☐ 152 Sammy Sosa SP | 3.00 | 8.00 |
| ☐ 153 Andy LaRoche (RC) | .15 | .40 |
| ☐ 154 Travis Buck (RC) | .15 | .40 |
| ☐ 155 Alex Rios | .12 | .30 |
| ☐ 156 Travis Hafner | .12 | .30 |
| ☐ 157 Jake Peavy | .12 | .30 |
| ☐ 158 Jeff Kent | .12 | .30 |
| ☐ 159 Johan Santana | .20 | .50 |
| ☐ 159b Johan Santana Ad Back SP | 2.50 | 6.00 |
| ☐ 160 Ivan Rodriguez | .20 | .50 |
| ☐ 161 Trevor Hoffman | .12 | .30 |
| ☐ 162 Troy Glaus | .12 | .30 |
| ☐ 163 Troy Tulowitzki (RC) | .40 | 1.00 |
| ☐ 164 Jorge Posada | .20 | .50 |
| ☐ 165 Kei Igawa SP RC | 3.00 | 8.00 |
| ☐ 166 Jose Reyes | .30 | .75 |
| ☐ 167 Mickey Mantle | 1.00 | 2.50 |
| ☐ 168 Utley Streak CL | .30 | .75 |
| ☐ 169 Justin Verlander | .30 | .75 |
| ☐ 170 Hanley Ramirez | .20 | .50 |
| ☐ 171 Kelly Johnson SP | 2.50 | 6.00 |
| ☐ 172 Kelvin Jimenez RC | .15 | .40 |
| ☐ 173 Roger Clemens | .60 | 1.50 |
| ☐ 174 Khalil Greene SP | 2.50 | 6.00 |
| ☐ 175 Lance Berkman | .12 | .30 |
| ☐ 176 Turning Two Hanley Ramirez CL | .20 | .50 |
| ☐ 177 Kyle Kendrick RC | .40 | 1.00 |
| ☐ 178 Magglio Ordonez | .20 | .50 |
| ☐ 179 Marcus Giles SP | 2.50 | 6.00 |

|  | | |
|---|---|---|
| □ 180 Miguel Cabrera SP | .20 | .50 |
| □ 180b Miguel Cabrera Ad Back SP | 2.50 | 6.00 |
| □ 181 Mark Teahen | .12 | .30 |
| □ 182 Mark Teixeira SP | 2.50 | 6.00 |
| □ 183 Matt Chico SP (RC) | 2.50 | 6.00 |
| □ 184 Matt Holliday | .15 | .40 |
| □ 185 Vladimir Guerrero | .30 | .75 |
| □ 185b V. Guerrero Ad Back SP | 3.00 | 8.00 |
| □ 186 Yovani Gallardo (RC) | .40 | 1.00 |

## 2008 UD A Piece of History

|  | | |
|---|---|---|
| □ COMPLETE SET (200) | 15.00 | 40.00 |
| □ COMMON CARD (1-100) | .20 | .50 |
| □ COMMON ROOKIE (101-150) | .40 | 1.00 |
| □ COMMON HM (151-200) | .20 | .50 |
| □ 1 Brandon Webb | .30 | .75 |
| □ 2 Dan Haren | .20 | .50 |
| □ 3 Justin Upton | .50 | 1.25 |
| □ 4 Chris B. Young | .20 | .50 |
| □ 5 Mark Teixeira | .30 | .75 |
| □ 6 Jeff Francoeur | .30 | .75 |
| □ 7 John Smoltz | .50 | 1.25 |
| □ 8 Tom Glavine | .30 | .75 |
| □ 9 Brian McCann | .30 | .75 |
| □ 10 Chipper Jones | .60 | 1.50 |
| □ 11 Erik Bedard | .20 | .50 |
| □ 12 Nick Markakis | .30 | .75 |
| □ 13 Josh Beckett | .30 | .75 |
| □ 14 David Ortiz | .50 | 1.25 |
| □ 15 Manny Ramirez | .50 | 1.25 |
| □ 16 Dustin Pedroia | .60 | 1.50 |
| □ 17 Grady Sizemore | .30 | .75 |
| □ 18 Jonathan Papelbon | .30 | .75 |
| □ 19 Daisuke Matsuzaka | .60 | 1.50 |
| □ 20 Curt Schilling | .30 | .75 |
| □ 21 Alfonso Soriano | .30 | .75 |
| □ 22 Aramis Ramirez | .20 | .50 |
| □ 23 Carlos Zambrano | .20 | .50 |
| □ 24 Nick Swisher | .20 | .50 |
| □ 25 Jim Thome | .30 | .75 |
| □ 26 Ken Griffey Jr. | .75 | 2.00 |
| □ 27 Adam Dunn | .20 | .50 |
| □ 28 Aaron Harang | .20 | .50 |
| □ 29 Matt Holliday | .30 | .75 |
| □ 30 Troy Tulowitzki | .30 | .75 |
| □ 31 Todd Helton | .30 | .75 |
| □ 32 Magglio Ordonez | .30 | .75 |
| □ 33 Justin Verlander | .30 | .75 |
| □ 34 Miguel Cabrera | .50 | 1.25 |
| □ 35 Gary Sheffield | .20 | .50 |
| □ 36 Ivan Rodriguez | .30 | .75 |
| □ 37 Dontrelle Willis | .20 | .50 |
| □ 38 Hanley Ramirez | .50 | 1.25 |
| □ 39 Andrew Miller | .30 | .75 |
| □ 40 Lance Berkman | .30 | .75 |
| □ 41 Roy Oswalt | .20 | .50 |
| □ 42 Carlos Lee | .20 | .50 |
| □ 43 Hunter Pence | .50 | 1.25 |
| □ 44 Alex Gordon | .30 | .75 |
| □ 45 Mark Teahen | .20 | .50 |
| □ 46 Torii Hunter | .20 | .50 |
| □ 47 Vladimir Guerrero | .50 | 1.25 |
| □ 48 Victor Martinez | .20 | .50 |
| □ 49 Andruw Jones | .20 | .50 |
| □ 50 James Loney | .30 | .75 |
| □ 51 Russell Martin | .20 | .50 |
| □ 52 Jeff Kent | .20 | .50 |
| □ 53 Ryan Braun | .60 | 1.50 |
| □ 54 Prince Fielder | .50 | 1.25 |
| □ 55 Joe Mauer | .50 | 1.25 |
| □ 56 Justin Morneau | .30 | .75 |
| □ 57 Delmon Young | .30 | .75 |
| □ 58 Jose Reyes | .30 | .75 |
| □ 59 David Wright | .60 | 1.50 |
| □ 60 Carlos Beltran | .20 | .50 |
| □ 61 Johan Santana | .30 | .75 |
| □ 62 Pedro Martinez | .30 | .75 |
| □ 63 Alex Rodriguez | .75 | 2.00 |
| □ 64 Derek Jeter | 1.25 | 3.00 |
| □ 65 Hideki Matsui | .50 | 1.25 |
| □ 66 Robinson Cano | .60 | 1.50 |
| □ 67 Joba Chamberlain | .50 | 1.25 |
| □ 68 Phil Hughes | .50 | 1.25 |
| □ 69 Mariano Rivera | .50 | 1.25 |
| □ 70 Rich Harden | .20 | .50 |
| □ 71 Joe Blanton | .20 | .50 |
| □ 72 Cole Hamels | .50 | 1.25 |
| □ 73 Ryan Howard | .60 | 1.50 |
| □ 74 Jimmy Rollins | .30 | .75 |
| □ 75 Chase Utley | .50 | 1.25 |
| □ 76 Jason Bay | .30 | .75 |
| □ 77 Freddy Sanchez | .20 | .50 |
| □ 78 Jake Peavy | .30 | .75 |
| □ 79 Greg Maddux | .60 | 1.50 |
| □ 80 Trevor Hoffman | .20 | .50 |
| □ 81 Barry Zito | .20 | .50 |
| □ 82 Tim Lincecum | .60 | 1.50 |
| □ 83 Travis Hafner | .20 | .50 |
| □ 84 C.C. Sabathia | .20 | .50 |
| □ 85 Felix Hernandez | .30 | .75 |
| □ 86 Ichiro Suzuki | .75 | 2.00 |
| □ 87 Troy Glaus | .20 | .50 |
| □ 88 Albert Pujols | 1.00 | 2.50 |
| □ 89 Chris Carpenter | .20 | .50 |
| □ 90 Scott Kazmir | .30 | .75 |
| □ 91 Carl Crawford | .30 | .75 |
| □ 92 B.J. Upton | .30 | .75 |
| □ 93 Michael Young | .30 | .75 |
| □ 94 Josh Hamilton | .60 | 1.50 |
| □ 95 Vernon Wells | .20 | .50 |
| □ 96 Alex Rios | .20 | .50 |
| □ 97 Scott Rolen | .30 | .75 |
| □ 98 Frank Thomas | .50 | 1.25 |
| □ 99 Chad Cordero | .20 | .50 |
| □ 100 Ryan Zimmerman | .30 | .75 |
| □ 101 Emilio Bonifacio RC | 1.00 | 2.50 |
| □ 102 Bill Murphy (RC) | .40 | 1.00 |
| □ 103 Billy Buckner (RC) | .40 | 1.00 |
| □ 104 Brandon Jones RC | 1.00 | 2.50 |
| □ 105 Clint Sammons (RC) | .40 | 1.00 |
| □ 106 Clay Buchholz (RC) | 1.00 | 2.50 |
| □ 107 Kevin Hart (RC) | .40 | 1.00 |
| □ 108 Lance Broadway (RC) | .40 | 1.00 |
| □ 109 Donny Lucy (RC) | .40 | 1.00 |
| □ 110 Heath Phillips RC | .60 | 1.50 |
| □ 111 Ryan Hanigan RC | .60 | 1.50 |
| □ 112 Joey Votto (RC) | 1.00 | 2.50 |
| □ 113 Joe Koshansky (RC) | .40 | 1.00 |
| □ 114 Josh Newman RC | .60 | 1.50 |
| □ 115 Seth Smith (RC) | .40 | 1.00 |
| □ 116 Harvey Garcia (RC) | .40 | 1.00 |
| □ 117 Chris Seddon (RC) | .40 | 1.00 |
| □ 118 Josh Anderson (RC) | .40 | 1.00 |
| □ 119 Troy Patton RC | .60 | 1.50 |
| □ 120 Felipe Paulino RC | .60 | 1.50 |
| □ 121 J.R. Towles RC | .60 | 1.50 |
| □ 122 Luke Hochevar RC | .60 | 1.50 |
| □ 123 Chin-Lung Hu (RC) | .40 | 1.00 |
| □ 124 Jonathan Meloan RC | .60 | 1.50 |
| □ 125 Sam Fuld RC | .40 | 1.00 |
| □ 126 Mitch Stetter RC | .40 | 1.00 |
| □ 127 Jose Morales (RC) | .40 | 1.00 |
| □ 128 Carlos Muniz RC | .40 | 1.00 |
| □ 129 Alberto Gonzalez RC | .40 | 1.00 |
| □ 130 Ian Kennedy RC | 1.00 | 2.50 |
| □ 131 Ross Ohlendorf RC | .60 | 1.50 |
| □ 132 Jonathan Albaladejo RC | .40 | 1.00 |
| □ 133 Daric Barton (RC) | .40 | 1.00 |
| □ 134 Jerry Blevins RC | .60 | 1.50 |
| □ 135 Dave Davidson RC | .40 | 1.00 |
| □ 136 Nyjer Morgan (RC) | .40 | 1.00 |
| □ 137 Steve Pearce RC | .60 | 1.50 |
| □ 138 Colt Morton RC | .60 | 1.50 |
| □ 139 Eugenio Velez RC | .60 | 1.50 |
| □ 140 Erick Threets (RC) | .40 | 1.00 |
| □ 141 Bronson Sardinha (RC) | .40 | 1.00 |
| □ 142 Wladimir Balentien (RC) | .40 | 1.00 |
| □ 143 Jeff Clement (RC) | .40 | 1.00 |
| □ 144 Rob Johnson (RC) | .40 | 1.00 |
| □ 145 Jeff Ridgway RC | .40 | 1.00 |
| □ 146 Justin Ruggiano (RC) | .60 | 1.50 |
| □ 147 Luis Mendoza (RC) | .40 | 1.00 |
| □ 148 Bill White RC | .40 | 1.00 |
| □ 149 Ross Detwiler RC | 1.00 | 2.50 |
| □ 150 Justin Maxwell RC | .60 | 1.50 |
| □ 151 Fall of the Berlin Wall | .20 | .50 |
| □ 152 Wright Brothers 1st Flight | .20 | .50 |
| □ 153 Signing of Declaration of Independence | .20 | .50 |
| □ 154 Columbus Discovers America | .20 | .50 |
| □ 155 First Space Shuttle launch | .20 | .50 |
| □ 156 Hawaii becomes 50th state | .20 | .50 |
| □ 157 Statue of Liberty given to U.S. | .20 | .50 |
| □ 158 Gettysburg Address | .20 | .50 |
| □ 159 Completion of Transcontinental Railroad | .20 | .50 |
| □ 160 Opening of Panama Canal | .20 | .50 |
| □ 161 U.S. enters World War 1 | .20 | .50 |
| □ 162 Treaty of Versailles | .20 | .50 |
| □ 163 Television invented | .20 | .50 |
| □ 164 Geneva Summit | .20 | .50 |
| □ 165 Woodstock | .20 | .50 |
| □ 166 Invention of Cotton Gin | .20 | .50 |
| □ 167 Eiffel Tower | .20 | .50 |
| □ 168 Suez Canal opens | .20 | .50 |
| □ 169 New York City Subway opens | .20 | .50 |
| □ 170 Polio Vaccine invented | .20 | .50 |
| □ 171 Bell X-1 Breaks Sound Barrier | .20 | .50 |
| □ 172 USS Enterprise Aircraft Carrier launched | .20 | .50 |
| □ 173 Hubble Telescope launches | .20 | .50 |
| □ 174 N.A.T.O. created | .20 | .50 |
| □ 175 Sputnik launched by Russia | .20 | .50 |
| □ 176 U.S.S.R. Crumbles | .20 | .50 |
| □ 177 Boston Tea Party | .20 | .50 |
| □ 178 Paul Revere's Ride | .20 | .50 |
| □ 179 Civil Rights Act Passes | .20 | .50 |
| □ 180 Hindenburg blows up | .20 | .50 |
| □ 181 Franklin discovers electricity | .20 | .50 |
| □ 182 Creation of the Internet | .20 | .50 |
| □ 183 1st World's Fair - 1851 London | .20 | .50 |
| □ 184 Pope John Paul II | .20 | .50 |
| □ 185 1st Heart Transplant | .20 | .50 |
| □ 186 California Gold Rush | .20 | .50 |
| □ 187 Creation of the personal computer | .20 | .50 |
| □ 188 Louisiana Purchase | .20 | .50 |
| □ 189 1st Dictionary published | .20 | .50 |
| □ 190 Steam Engine invented | .20 | .50 |
| □ 191 History of Nobel Prize | .20 | .50 |
| □ 192 Liberty Bell | .20 | .50 |
| □ 193 International Space Station | .20 | .50 |
| □ 194 Human Genome Project | .20 | .50 |
| □ 195 The Supreme Court | .20 | .50 |
| □ 196 Lewis and Clark | .20 | .50 |
| □ 197 Battle of the Alamo | .20 | .50 |
| □ 198 The creation of baseball | .20 | .50 |
| □ 199 Ponce De Leon | .20 | .50 |
| □ 200 Jamestown - 1607 | .20 | .50 |

## 2009 UD A Piece of History

|  | | |
|---|---|---|
| □ COMPLETE SET (200) | 20.00 | 50.00 |
| □ COMMON CARD | .20 | .50 |
| □ COMMON ROOKIE | .40 | 1.00 |
| □ 1 Brandon Webb | .30 | .75 |
| □ 2 Randy Johnson | .50 | 1.25 |
| □ 3 Dan Haren | .20 | .50 |
| □ 4 Adam Dunn | .30 | .75 |
| □ 5 Chipper Jones | .50 | 1.25 |
| □ 6 John Smoltz | .30 | .75 |
| □ 7 Tom Glavine | .30 | .75 |
| □ 8 Brian Roberts | .20 | .50 |
| □ 9 Nick Markakis | .30 | .75 |
| □ 10 Josh Beckett | .30 | .75 |
| □ 11 David Ortiz | .30 | .75 |
| □ 12 Daisuke Matsuzaka | .75 | 2.00 |
| □ 13 Jacoby Ellsbury | .50 | 1.25 |
| □ 14 Jonathan Papelbon | .30 | .75 |
| □ 15 Alfonso Soriano | .30 | .75 |
| □ 16 Derek Lee | .30 | .75 |
| □ 17 Kosuke Fukudome | .50 | 1.25 |
| □ 18 Carlos Zambrano | .20 | .50 |
| □ 19 Aramis Ramirez | .20 | .50 |
| □ 20 Rich Harden | .20 | .50 |
| □ 21 Carlos Quentin | .30 | .75 |
| □ 22 Jim Thome | .30 | .75 |
| □ 23 Ken Griffey Jr. | .75 | 2.00 |
| □ 24 Jay Bruce | .50 | 1.25 |
| □ 25 Edinson Volquez | .30 | .75 |
| □ 26 Brandon Phillips | .20 | .50 |

|  |  | | |
|---|---|---|---|
| 27 | Victor Martinez | .30 | .75 |
| 28 | Grady Sizemore | .30 | .75 |
| 29 | Travis Hafner | .20 | .50 |
| 30 | Matt Holliday | .30 | .75 |
| 31 | Troy Tulowitzki | .30 | .75 |
| 32 | Garrett Atkins | .20 | .50 |
| 33 | Miguel Cabrera | .30 | .75 |
| 34 | Magglio Ordonez | .30 | .75 |
| 35 | Justin Verlander | .30 | .75 |
| 36 | Hanley Ramirez | .50 | 1.25 |
| 37 | Dan Uggla | .30 | .75 |
| 38 | Lance Berkman | .30 | .75 |
| 39 | Carlos Lee | .20 | .50 |
| 40 | Kevin Youkilis | .30 | .75 |
| 41 | Miguel Tejada | .30 | .75 |
| 42 | Alex Gordon | .30 | .75 |
| 43 | Zack Greinke | .30 | .75 |
| 44 | Mark Teixeira | .50 | 1.25 |
| 45 | Vladimir Guerrero | .50 | 1.25 |
| 46 | Torii Hunter | .20 | .50 |
| 47 | Manny Ramirez | .50 | 1.25 |
| 48 | Russell Martin | .30 | .75 |
| 49 | Matt Kemp | .50 | 1.25 |
| 50 | Clayton Kershaw | .50 | 1.25 |
| 51 | CC Sabathia | .30 | .75 |
| 52 | Corey Hart | .20 | .50 |
| 53 | Prince Fielder | .50 | 1.25 |
| 54 | Ryan Braun | .60 | 1.50 |
| 55 | Joe Mauer | .50 | 1.25 |
| 56 | Justin Morneau | .30 | .75 |
| 57 | Jose Reyes | .50 | 1.25 |
| 58 | David Wright | .60 | 1.50 |
| 59 | Johan Santana | .50 | 1.25 |
| 60 | Carlos Beltran | .20 | .50 |
| 61 | Pedro Martinez | .30 | .75 |
| 62 | Alex Rodriguez | .75 | 2.00 |
| 63 | Derek Jeter | 1.25 | 3.00 |
| 64 | Chien-Ming Wang | .50 | 1.25 |
| 65 | Hideki Matsui | .50 | 1.25 |
| 66 | Joba Chamberlain | .60 | 1.50 |
| 67 | Mariano Rivera | .30 | .75 |
| 68 | Xavier Nady | .20 | .50 |
| 69 | Frank Thomas | .50 | 1.25 |
| 70 | Jason Giambi | .20 | .50 |
| 71 | Chase Utley | .50 | 1.25 |
| 72 | Ryan Howard | .60 | 1.50 |
| 73 | Jimmy Rollins | .30 | .75 |
| 74 | Ryan Doumit | .20 | .50 |
| 75 | Nate McLouth | .20 | .50 |
| 76 | Adrian Gonzalez | .30 | .75 |
| 77 | Chris Young | | |
| 78 | Jake Peavy | .30 | .75 |
| 79 | Brian Giles | .20 | .50 |
| 80 | Tim Lincecum | .60 | 1.50 |
| 81 | Matt Cain | .20 | .50 |
| 82 | Felix Hernandez | .30 | .75 |
| 83 | Ichiro Suzuki | .75 | 2.00 |
| 84 | Erik Bedard | .20 | .50 |
| 85 | Ryan Ludwick | .30 | .75 |
| 86 | Albert Pujols | 1.25 | 3.00 |
| 87 | Chris Carpenter | .30 | .75 |
| 88 | Rick Ankiel | .30 | .75 |
| 89 | B.J. Upton | .30 | .75 |
| 90 | Evan Longoria | .75 | 2.00 |
| 91 | Scott Kazmir | .30 | .75 |
| 92 | Carl Crawford | .30 | .75 |
| 93 | Josh Hamilton | .50 | 1.25 |
| 94 | Ian Kinsler | .30 | .75 |
| 95 | Michael Young | .30 | .75 |
| 96 | Roy Halladay | .30 | .75 |
| 97 | Vernon Wells | .20 | .50 |
| 98 | Alex Rios | .30 | .75 |
| 99 | Ryan Zimmerman | .30 | .75 |
| 100 | Lastings Milledge | .20 | .50 |
| 101 | David Price RC | 1.25 | 3.00 |
| 102 | Conor Gillaspie RC | 1.00 | 2.50 |
| 103 | Josh Roenicke RC | .40 | 1.00 |
| 104 | Jeff Baisley RC | .40 | 1.00 |
| 105 | Alfredo Aceves RC | .60 | 1.50 |
| 106 | Matt Antonelli (RC) | .60 | 1.50 |
| 107 | Michael Bowden (RC) | .60 | 1.50 |
| 108 | Josh Whitesell RC | .60 | 1.50 |
| 109 | Wilkin Castillo RC | .60 | 1.50 |
| 110 | Francisco Cervelli RC | 1.00 | 2.50 |
| 111 | Phil Coke RC | .60 | 1.50 |
| 112 | Luis Cruz RC | .60 | 1.50 |
| 113 | Jesus Delgado RC | .60 | 1.50 |
| 114 | Scott Elbert (RC) | .40 | 1.00 |
| 115 | Alcides Escobar RC | .60 | 1.50 |
| 116 | Dexter Fowler (RC) | .60 | 1.50 |
| 117 | Mat Gamel RC | 1.00 | 2.50 |
| 118 | Josh Geer (RC) | .40 | 1.00 |
| 119 | Greg Golson (RC) | .40 | 1.00 |
| 120 | Kila Ka'aihue (RC) | .60 | 1.50 |
| 121 | Chris Lambert (RC) | .40 | 1.00 |
| 122 | Wade LeBlanc RC | .60 | 1.50 |
| 123 | Scott Lewis (RC) | .40 | 1.00 |
| 124 | Lou Marson (RC) | .40 | 1.00 |
| 125 | Shairon Martis RC | .60 | 1.50 |
| 126 | James McDonald RC | .60 | 1.50 |
| 127 | Juan Miranda RC | .60 | 1.50 |
| 128 | Luke Montz RC | .40 | 1.00 |
| 129 | Jonathon Niese RC | .60 | 1.50 |
| 130 | Josh Outman RC | .60 | 1.50 |
| 131 | James Parr (RC) | .40 | 1.00 |
| 132 | Dusty Ryan RC | .40 | 1.00 |
| 133 | Angel Salome (RC) | .40 | 1.00 |
| 134 | Travis Snider RC | 1.00 | 2.50 |
| 135 | Matt Tuiasosopo (RC) | .40 | 1.00 |
| 136 | Will Venable RC | .40 | 1.00 |
| 137 | Aaron Cunningham RC | .40 | 1.00 |
| 138 | George Kottaras (RC) | .40 | 1.00 |
| 139 | Devon Lowery (RC) | .40 | 1.00 |
| 140 | Jose Mijares RC | 1.00 | 2.50 |
| 141 | Jason Motte RC | .60 | 1.50 |
| 142 | Bobby Parnell RC | .60 | 1.50 |
| 143 | Fernando Perez RC | .40 | 1.00 |
| 144 | Jason Pridie (RC) | .40 | 1.00 |
| 145 | Ramon Ramirez (RC) | .40 | 1.00 |
| 146 | Justin Thomas (RC) | .40 | 1.00 |
| 147 | Luis Valbuena RC | .60 | 1.50 |
| 148 | Gaby Sanchez RC | .40 | 1.00 |
| 149 | Mike Hinckley (RC) | .40 | 1.00 |
| 150 | Mitch Talbot (RC) | .40 | 1.00 |
| 151 | Star Spangled Banner | .20 | .50 |
| 152 | Dwight D. Eisenhower | .20 | .50 |
| 153 | First Atomic Submarine Launched | .20 | .50 |
| 154 | Alaska Becomes 49th State | .20 | .50 |
| 155 | I Have A Dream Speech | .20 | .50 |
| 156 | 18th Amendment Adopted | .20 | .50 |
| 157 | Discovery of Penicilin | .20 | .50 |
| 158 | Germany Leaves League of Nations | .20 | .50 |
| 159 | Attack on Pearl Harbor | .20 | .50 |
| 160 | U.S.A. Enters World War II | .20 | .50 |
| 161 | D-Day Invasion | .20 | .50 |
| 162 | NATO Organized | .20 | .50 |
| 163 | 1970 Earth Day | .20 | .50 |
| 164 | 1989 San Francisco Earthquake | .20 | .50 |
| 165 | Warsaw Pact | .20 | .50 |
| 166 | NAFTA | .20 | .50 |
| 167 | Boy Scouts of America Launches | .20 | .50 |
| 168 | New Zealand Pioneers Women's Voting Rights | .20 | .50 |
| 169 | First Moving Assembly Line | .20 | .50 |
| 170 | Hollywood Sign Debuts | .20 | .50 |
| 171 | Taj Mahal Completed | .20 | .50 |
| 172 | United States Constitution Signed | .20 | .50 |
| 173 | Empire State Building Built | .20 | .50 |
| 174 | Golden Gate Bridge Completed | .20 | .50 |
| 175 | Smallpox Eradicated | .20 | .50 |
| 176 | Elevator Invented | .20 | .50 |
| 177 | Microwave Oven Invented | .20 | .50 |
| 178 | E-Mail Invented | .20 | .50 |
| 179 | Eiffel Tower Erected | .20 | .50 |
| 180 | Pilgrims Land at Plymouth Rock | .20 | .50 |
| 181 | First Photograph Taken | .20 | .50 |
| 182 | First Anesthetic Used | .20 | .50 |
| 183 | First Kentucky Derby | .20 | .50 |
| 184 | Brooklyn Bridge Completed | .20 | .50 |
| 185 | X-Ray Invented | .20 | .50 |
| 186 | Pluto Recategorized as Dwarf Planet | .20 | .50 |
| 187 | Mount Rushmore Finished | .20 | .50 |
| 188 | Thanksgiving Adopted as Holiday | .20 | .50 |
| 189 | Chicago Cubs | .20 | .50 |
| 190 | Baseball Hall of Fame Opens | .20 | .50 |
| 191 | National League Established | .20 | .50 |
| 192 | Olympic Games Begin | .20 | .50 |
| 193 | Voyager 2 | .20 | .50 |
| 194 | New Orleans Founded | .20 | .50 |
| 195 | Discovery of New York | .20 | .50 |
| 196 | Debut of the New York Times | .20 | .50 |
| 197 | Republican Party Founded | .20 | .50 |
| 198 | City of Boston Founded | .20 | .50 |
| 199 | Introduction of EURO Currency | .20 | .50 |
| 200 | Czechoslavakia Splits in Two | .20 | .50 |

### 2007 UD Masterpieces

| | | | |
|---|---|---|---|
| COMPLETE SET (90) | | 15.00 | 40.00 |
| COMMON CARD (1-90) | | .25 | .60 |
| COMMON ROOKIE (1-90) | | .25 | .60 |
| PRINTING PLATES RANDOMLY INSERTED | | | |
| PLATE PRINT RUN 1 SET PER COLOR | | | |
| BLACK-CYAN-MAGENTA-YELLOW ISSUED | | | |
| NO PLATE PRICING DUE TO SCARCITY | | | |
| 1 | Babe Ruth | 1.50 | 4.00 |
| 2 | Babe Ruth | 1.50 | 4.00 |
| 3 | Bobby Thomson | .40 | 1.00 |
| 4 | Bill Mazeroski | .40 | 1.00 |
| 5 | Carlton Fisk | .40 | 1.00 |
| 6 | Kirk Gibson | .25 | .60 |
| 7 | Don Larsen | .25 | .60 |
| 8 | Lou Gehrig | 1.25 | 3.00 |
| 9 | Roger Maris | .60 | 1.50 |
| 10 | Cal Ripken Jr. | 2.50 | 6.00 |
| 11 | Bucky Dent | .25 | .60 |
| 12 | Ryan Howard | 1.00 | 2.50 |
| 13 | Brooks Robinson | .40 | 1.00 |
| 14 | David Ortiz | .40 | 1.00 |
| 15 | Hideki Matsui | .60 | 1.50 |
| 16 | Roger Clemens | 1.00 | 2.50 |
| 17 | Sandy Koufax | 2.00 | 5.00 |
| 18 | Reggie Jackson | .40 | 1.00 |
| 19 | Ozzie Smith | 1.00 | 2.50 |
| 20 | Ty Cobb | 1.00 | 2.50 |
| 21 | Walter Johnson | .60 | 1.50 |
| 22 | Babe Ruth | 1.50 | 4.00 |
| 23 | Roy Campanella | .60 | 1.50 |
| 24 | Jackie Robinson | .60 | 1.50 |
| 25 | Carl Yastrzemski | 1.00 | 2.50 |
| 26 | Sandy Koufax | 2.00 | 5.00 |
| 27 | Daisuke Matsuzaka RC | 2.00 | 5.00 |
| 28 | Kei Igawa RC | .60 | 1.50 |
| 29 | Ken Griffey Jr. | 1.00 | 2.50 |
| 30 | Derek Jeter | 1.50 | 4.00 |
| 31 | David Ortiz | .40 | 1.00 |
| 32 | Vladimir Guerrero | .60 | 1.50 |
| 33 | Chase Utley | .60 | 1.50 |
| 34 | Troy Tulowitzki RC | .60 | 1.50 |
| 35 | Joe Mauer | .60 | 1.50 |
| 36 | Travis Hafner | .25 | .60 |
| 37 | Miguel Cabrera | .40 | 1.00 |
| 38 | Albert Pujols | 1.25 | 3.00 |
| 39 | Frank Thomas | .60 | 1.50 |
| 40 | Mike Piazza | .60 | 1.50 |
| 41 | Josh Hamilton | .60 | 1.50 |
| 42 | T.Gwynn/C.Ripken Jr. | 2.50 | 6.00 |
| 43 | Ichiro Suzuki | 1.00 | 2.50 |
| 44 | Hideki Matsui | .60 | 1.50 |
| 45 | Ken Griffey Jr. | 1.00 | 2.50 |
| 46 | Michael Jordan | 1.50 | 4.00 |
| 47 | John F. Kennedy | 1.00 | 2.50 |
| 48 | Randy Johnson | .60 | 1.50 |
| 49 | Albert Pujols | 1.25 | 3.00 |
| 50 | Carlos Beltran | .25 | .60 |
| 51 | Delmon Young RC | .40 | 1.00 |
| 52 | Johan Santana | .40 | 1.00 |
| 53 | Cal Ripken Jr. | 2.50 | 6.00 |
| 54 | Y Berra/J.Robinson | .60 | 1.50 |
| 55 | Cal Ripken Jr. | 2.50 | 6.00 |
| 56 | Hanley Ramirez | .60 | 1.50 |
| 57 | Victor Martinez | .25 | .60 |
| 58 | Cole Hamels | .60 | 1.50 |
| 59 | Bobby Doerr | .25 | .60 |
| 60 | Bruce Sutter | .25 | .60 |
| 61 | Jason Bay | .40 | 1.00 |
| 62 | Luis Aparicio | .25 | .60 |
| 63 | Stephen Drew | .40 | 1.00 |
| 64 | Jered Weaver | .40 | 1.00 |
| 65 | Alex Gordon RC | 1.00 | 2.50 |

☐ 66 Howie Kendrick .25 .60
☐ 67 Ryan Zimmerman .60 1.50
☐ 68 Akinori Iwamura RC .60 1.50
☐ 69 Chien-Ming Wang .60 1.50
☐ 70 David Wright 1.00 2.50
☐ 71 Ryan Howard 1.00 2.50
☐ 72 Alex Rodriguez 1.00 2.50
☐ 73 Justin Morneau .25 .60
☐ 74 Andrew Miller RC 1.50 4.00
☐ 75 Richard Nixon .60 1.50
☐ 76 Bill Clinton 1.00 2.50
☐ 77 Phil Hughes (RC) 1.25 3.00
☐ 78 Tom Glavine .40 1.00
☐ 79 Chipper Jones .60 1.50
☐ 80 Craig Biggio .40 1.00
☐ 81 Chris Chambliss .25 .60
☐ 82 Tim Lincecum RC 3.00 8.00
☐ 83 Billy Butler (RC) .40 1.00
☐ 84 Andy LaRoche (RC) .25 .60
☐ 85 1969 New York Mets .25 .60
☐ 86 2004 Boston Red Sox 1.00 2.50
☐ 87 Roberto Clemente 2.00 5.00
☐ 88 Chase Utley .60 1.50
☐ 89 Reggie Jackson .40 1.00
☐ 90 Curt Schilling .40 1.00

## 2008 UD Masterpieces

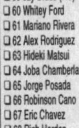

☐ COMPLETE SET (120) 60.00 120.00
☐ COMP.SET w/o SPs (90) 12.50 30.00
☐ COMMON CARD (1-90) .20 .50
☐ COMMON ROOKIE (1-90) .40 1.00
☐ COMMON SP (91-120) .50 1.25
☐ SP ODDS 1:2 HOBBY
☐ 1 Brandon Webb .30 .75
☐ 2 Justin Upton .50 1.25
☐ 3 Randy Johnson .50 1.25
☐ 4 Chipper Jones .60 1.50
☐ 5 Max Scherzer RC 1.00 2.50
☐ 6 Mark Teixeira .30 .75
☐ 7 Evan Longoria RC 4.00 10.00
☐ 8 Jim Palmer .20 .50
☐ 9 Brooks Robinson .30 .75
☐ 10 Nick Markakis .30 .75
☐ 11 Carl Yastrzemski .75 2.00
☐ 12 Wade Boggs .30 .75
☐ 13 Curt Schilling .30 .75
☐ 14 Daisuke Matsuzaka .60 1.50
☐ 15 David Ortiz .30 .75
☐ 16 Jonathan Papelbon .30 .75
☐ 17 Manny Ramirez .50 1.25
☐ 18 Alfonso Soriano .30 .75
☐ 19 Ryne Sandberg 1.00 2.50
☐ 20 Carlos Zambrano .20 .50
☐ 21 Derrek Lee .30 .75
☐ 22 Kosuke Fukudome RC 1.25 3.00
☐ 23 Jim Thome .30 .75
☐ 24 Adam Dunn .20 .50
☐ 25 Joe Morgan .20 .50
☐ 26 Grady Sizemore .30 .75
☐ 27 Victor Martinez .20 .50
☐ 28 Travis Hafner .20 .50
☐ 29 Troy Tulowitzki .30 .75
☐ 30 Matt Holliday .30 .75
☐ 31 Todd Helton .30 .75
☐ 32 Justin Verlander .30 .75
☐ 33 Asdrubal Cabrera .20 .50
☐ 34 Gary Sheffield .20 .50
☐ 35 Magglio Ordonez .30 .75
☐ 36 Miguel Cabrera .50 1.25
☐ 37 Hanley Ramirez .50 1.25
☐ 38 Lance Berkman .30 .75
☐ 39 Roy Oswalt .20 .50
☐ 40 Alex Gordon .30 .75
☐ 41 Vladimir Guerrero .50 1.25

☐ 42 Andruw Jones .20 .50
☐ 43 Chin-Lung Hu (RC) .60 1.50
☐ 44 James Loney .30 .75
☐ 45 Hunter Pence .50 1.25
☐ 46 Robin Yount .50 1.25
☐ 47 Prince Fielder .50 1.25
☐ 48 Ryan Braun .60 1.50
☐ 49 Harmon Killebrew .50 1.25
☐ 50 Joe Mauer .50 1.25
☐ 51 Justin Morneau .30 .75
☐ 52 Ken Griffey Jr. .75 2.00
☐ 53 Carlos Beltran .20 .50
☐ 54 David Wright .60 1.50
☐ 55 Johan Santana .30 .75
☐ 56 Jose Reyes .30 .75
☐ 57 Pedro Martinez .30 .75
☐ 58 Ian Kennedy RC 1.00 2.50
☐ 59 Jay Bruce RC 1.50 4.00
☐ 60 Whitey Ford .50 1.25
☐ 61 Mariano Rivera .50 1.25
☐ 62 Alex Rodriguez .75 2.00
☐ 63 Hideki Matsui .50 1.25
☐ 64 Joba Chamberlain .60 1.50
☐ 65 Jorge Posada .30 .75
☐ 66 Robinson Cano .30 .75
☐ 67 Eric Chavez .20 .50
☐ 68 Rich Harden .20 .50
☐ 69 Chase Utley .50 1.25
☐ 70 Jimmy Rollins .30 .75
☐ 71 Ryan Howard .60 1.50
☐ 72 Bill Mazeroski .20 .50
☐ 73 Freddy Sanchez .20 .50
☐ 74 Luke Hochevar RC .60 1.50
☐ 75 Tony Gwynn .60 1.50
☐ 76 Greg Maddux .60 1.50
☐ 77 Jake Peavy .30 .75
☐ 78 Barry Zito .20 .50
☐ 79 Russell Martin .30 .75
☐ 80 Tim Lincecum .60 1.50
☐ 81 Ichiro Suzuki .75 2.00
☐ 82 Felix Hernandez .30 .75
☐ 83 Ozzie Smith .75 2.00
☐ 84 Jason Varitek .50 1.25
☐ 85 Chris Carpenter .20 .50
☐ 86 Carl Crawford .30 .75
☐ 87 Michael Young .20 .50
☐ 88 Frank Thomas .50 1.25
☐ 89 Roy Halladay .20 .50
☐ 90 Ryan Zimmerman .30 .75
☐ 91 Eddie Murray SP 1.25 3.00
☐ 92 Cal Ripken Jr. SP 5.00 12.00
☐ 93 Frank Robinson SP .50 1.25
☐ 94 Ryne Sandberg SP 2.50 6.00
☐ 95 Warren Spahn SP .75 2.00
☐ 96 Ernie Banks SP 1.25 3.00
☐ 97 Carlton Fisk SP .75 2.00
☐ 98 Johnny Bench SP 1.25 3.00
☐ 99 Ken Griffey Jr. SP 2.00 5.00
☐ 100 Al Kaline SP 1.00 2.50
☐ 101 Cal Ripken Jr. SP 5.00 12.00
☐ 102 Nolan Ryan SP 4.00 10.00
☐ 103 Jack Morris SP .50 1.25
☐ 104 Rod Carew SP .75 2.00
☐ 105 Tom Seaver SP .75 2.00
☐ 106 Don Mattingly SP 2.50 6.00
☐ 107 Lou Brock SP .75 2.00
☐ 108 Joe DiMaggio SP 3.00 8.00
☐ 109 Derek Jeter SP 3.00 8.00
☐ 110 Yogi Berra SP 1.25 3.00
☐ 111 Reggie Jackson SP .75 2.00
☐ 112 Mike Schmidt SP 2.00 5.00
☐ 113 Steve Carlton SP .50 1.25
☐ 114 Willie Stargell SP .50 1.25
☐ 115 Roberto Clemente SP 2.50 6.00
☐ 116 Albert Pujols SP 2.00 5.00
☐ 117 Stan Musial SP 2.00 5.00
☐ 118 Bob Gibson SP .75 2.00
☐ 119 Dave Winfield SP .50 1.25
☐ 120 Joe Carter SP .50 1.25

## 2001 Ultra

☐ COMPLETE SET (275) 60.00 120.00
☐ COMP.SET w/o SP's (250) 10.00 25.00
☐ COMMON CARD (1-250) .10 .30
☐ COMMON CARD (251-275) 1.25 3.00
☐ COMMON CARD (276-280) 2.00 5.00
☐ 1 Pedro Martinez .20 .50
☐ 2 Derek Jeter .75 2.00
☐ 3 Cal Ripken 1.00 2.50
☐ 4 Alex Rodriguez .50 1.25
☐ 5 Vladimir Guerrero .30 .75
☐ 6 Troy Glaus .10 .30
☐ 7 Sammy Sosa .30 .75
☐ 8 Mike Piazza .50 1.25
☐ 9 Tony Gwynn .40 1.00
☐ 10 Tim Hudson .10 .30
☐ 11 John Flaherty .10 .30
☐ 12 Jeff Cirillo .10 .30
☐ 13 Ellis Burks .10 .30
☐ 14 Carlos Lee .10 .30
☐ 15 Carlos Beltran .10 .30
☐ 16 Ruben Rivera .10 .30
☐ 17 Richard Hidalgo .10 .30
☐ 18 Omar Vizquel .20 .50
☐ 19 Michael Barrett .10 .30
☐ 20 Jose Canseco .20 .50
☐ 21 Jason Giambi .20 .50
☐ 22 Greg Maddux .50 1.25
☐ 23 Charles Johnson .10 .30
☐ 24 Sandy Alomar Jr. .10 .30
☐ 25 Rick Ankiel .10 .30
☐ 26 Richie Sexson .10 .30
☐ 27 Matt Williams .10 .30
☐ 28 Joe Girardi .10 .30
☐ 29 Jason Kendall .10 .30
☐ 30 Brad Fullmer .10 .30
☐ 31 Alex Gonzalez .10 .30
☐ 32 Rick Helling .10 .30
☐ 33 Mike Mussina .20 .50
☐ 34 Joe Randa .10 .30
☐ 35 J.T. Snow .10 .30
☐ 36 Edgardo Alfonzo .10 .30
☐ 37 Dante Bichette .10 .30
☐ 38 Brad Ausmus .10 .30
☐ 39 Bobby Abreu .10 .30
☐ 40 Warren Morris .10 .30
☐ 41 Tony Womack .10 .30
☐ 42 Russell Branyan .10 .30
☐ 43 Mike Lowell .10 .30
☐ 44 Mark Grace .20 .50
☐ 45 Jeromy Burnitz .10 .30
☐ 46 J.D. Drew .10 .30
☐ 47 David Justice .10 .30
☐ 48 Alex Gonzalez .10 .30
☐ 49 Tino Martinez .20 .50
☐ 50 Raul Mondesi .10 .30
☐ 51 Rafael Furcal .10 .30
☐ 52 Marquis Grissom .10 .30
☐ 53 Kevin Young .10 .30
☐ 54 Jon Lieber .10 .30
☐ 55 Henry Rodriguez .10 .30
☐ 56 Dave Burba .10 .30
☐ 57 Shannon Stewart .10 .30
☐ 58 Preston Wilson .10 .30
☐ 59 Paul O'Neill .20 .50
☐ 60 Jimmy Haynes .10 .30
☐ 61 Darryl Kile .10 .30
☐ 62 Bret Boone .10 .30
☐ 63 Bartolo Colon .10 .30
☐ 64 Andres Galarraga .10 .30
☐ 65 Trot Nixon .10 .30
☐ 66 Steve Finley .10 .30

|  | | |
|---|---|---|
| 67 Shawn Green | .10 | .30 |
| 68 Robert Person | .10 | .30 |
| 69 Kenny Rogers | .10 | .30 |
| 70 Bobby Higginson | .10 | .30 |
| 71 Barry Larkin | .20 | .50 |
| 72 Al Martin | .10 | .30 |
| 73 Tom Glavine | .20 | .50 |
| 74 Rondell White | .10 | .30 |
| 75 Ray Lankford | .10 | .30 |
| 76 Moises Alou | .10 | .30 |
| 77 Matt Clement | .10 | .30 |
| 78 Geoff Jenkins | .10 | .30 |
| 79 David Wells | .10 | .30 |
| 80 Chuck Finley | .10 | .30 |
| 81 Andy Pettitte | .20 | .50 |
| 82 Travis Fryman | .10 | .30 |
| 83 Ron Coomer | .10 | .30 |
| 84 Mark McGwire | .75 | 2.00 |
| 85 Kerry Wood | .10 | .30 |
| 86 Jorge Posada | .20 | .50 |
| 87 Jeff Bagwell | .20 | .50 |
| 88 Andruw Jones | .20 | .50 |
| 89 Ryan Klesko | .10 | .30 |
| 90 Mariano Rivera | .30 | .75 |
| 91 Lance Berkman | .10 | .30 |
| 92 Kenny Lofton | .10 | .30 |
| 93 Jacque Jones | .10 | .30 |
| 94 Eric Young | .10 | .30 |
| 95 Edgar Renteria | .10 | .30 |
| 96 Chipper Jones | .30 | .75 |
| 97 Todd Helton | .20 | .50 |
| 98 Shawn Estes | .10 | .30 |
| 99 Mark Mulder | .10 | .30 |
| 100 Lee Stevens | .10 | .30 |
| 101 Jermaine Dye | .10 | .30 |
| 102 Greg Vaughn | .10 | .30 |
| 103 Chris Singleton | .10 | .30 |
| 104 Brady Anderson | .10 | .30 |
| 105 Terrence Long | .10 | .30 |
| 106 Quilvio Veras | .10 | .30 |
| 107 Magglio Ordonez | .10 | .30 |
| 108 Johnny Damon | .20 | .50 |
| 109 Jeffrey Hammonds | .10 | .30 |
| 110 Fred McGriff | .20 | .50 |
| 111 Carl Pavano | .10 | .30 |
| 112 Bobby Estalella | .10 | .30 |
| 113 Todd Hundley | .10 | .30 |
| 114 Scott Rolen | .20 | .50 |
| 115 Robin Ventura | .10 | .30 |
| 116 Pokey Reese | .10 | .30 |
| 117 Luis Gonzalez | .10 | .30 |
| 118 Jose Offerman | .10 | .30 |
| 119 Edgar Martinez | .20 | .50 |
| 120 Dean Palmer | .10 | .30 |
| 121 David Segui | .10 | .30 |
| 122 Troy O'Leary | .10 | .30 |
| 123 Tony Batista | .10 | .30 |
| 124 Todd Zeile | .10 | .30 |
| 125 Randy Johnson | .30 | .75 |
| 126 Luis Castillo | .10 | .30 |
| 127 Kris Benson | .10 | .30 |
| 128 John Olerud | .10 | .30 |
| 129 Eric Karros | .10 | .30 |
| 130 Eddie Taubensee | .10 | .30 |
| 131 Neifi Perez | .10 | .30 |
| 132 Matt Stairs | .10 | .30 |
| 133 Luis Alicea | .10 | .30 |
| 134 Jeff Kent | .10 | .30 |
| 135 Javier Vazquez | .10 | .30 |
| 136 Garret Anderson | .10 | .30 |
| 137 Frank Thomas | .30 | .75 |
| 138 Carlos Febles | .10 | .30 |
| 139 Albert Belle | .10 | .30 |
| 140 Tony Clark | .10 | .30 |
| 141 Pat Burrell | .10 | .30 |
| 142 Mike Sweeney | .10 | .30 |
| 143 Jay Buhner | .10 | .30 |
| 144 Gabe Kapler | .10 | .30 |
| 145 Derek Bell | .10 | .30 |
| 146 B.J. Surhoff | .10 | .30 |
| 147 Adam Kennedy | .10 | .30 |
| 148 Aaron Boone | .10 | .30 |
| 149 Todd Stottlemyre | .10 | .30 |
| 150 Roberto Alomar | .20 | .50 |
| 151 Orlando Hernandez | .10 | .30 |
| 152 Jason Varitek | .30 | .75 |
| 153 Gary Sheffield | .10 | .30 |
| 154 Cliff Floyd | .10 | .30 |
| 155 Chad Hermansen | .10 | .30 |
| 156 Carlos Delgado | .10 | .30 |
| 157 Aaron Sele | .10 | .30 |
| 158 Sean Casey | .10 | .30 |
| 159 Ruben Mateo | .10 | .30 |
| 160 Mike Bordick | .10 | .30 |
| 161 Mike Cameron | .10 | .30 |
| 162 Doug Glanville | .10 | .30 |
| 163 Damion Easley | .10 | .30 |
| 164 Carl Everett | .10 | .30 |
| 165 Bengie Molina | .10 | .30 |
| 166 Adrian Beltre | .10 | .30 |
| 167 Tom Goodwin | .10 | .30 |
| 168 Rickey Henderson | .30 | .75 |
| 169 Mo Vaughn | .10 | .30 |
| 170 Mike Lieberthal | .10 | .30 |
| 171 Ken Griffey Jr. | .50 | 1.25 |
| 172 Juan Gonzalez | .10 | .30 |
| 173 Ivan Rodriguez | .20 | .50 |
| 174 Al Leiter | .10 | .30 |
| 175 Vinny Castilla | .10 | .30 |
| 176 Peter Bergeron | .10 | .30 |
| 177 Pedro Astacio | .10 | .30 |
| 178 Paul Konerko | .10 | .30 |
| 179 Mitch Meluskey | .10 | .30 |
| 180 Kevin Millwood | .10 | .30 |
| 181 Ben Grieve | .10 | .30 |
| 182 Barry Bonds | .75 | 2.00 |
| 183 Rusty Greer | .10 | .30 |
| 184 Miguel Tejada | .10 | .30 |
| 185 Mark Quinn | .10 | .30 |
| 186 Larry Walker | .10 | .30 |
| 187 Jose Valentin | .10 | .30 |
| 188 Jose Vidro | .10 | .30 |
| 189 Delino DeShields | .10 | .30 |
| 190 Darin Erstad | .10 | .30 |
| 191 Bill Mueller | .10 | .30 |
| 192 Ray Durham | .10 | .30 |
| 193 Ken Caminiti | .10 | .30 |
| 194 Jim Thome | .20 | .50 |
| 195 Javy Lopez | .10 | .30 |
| 196 Fernando Vina | .10 | .30 |
| 197 Eric Chavez | .10 | .30 |
| 198 Eric Owens | .10 | .30 |
| 199 Brad Radke | .10 | .30 |
| 200 Travis Lee | .10 | .30 |
| 201 Tim Salmon | .20 | .50 |
| 202 Rafael Palmeiro | .20 | .50 |
| 203 Nomar Garciaparra | .50 | 1.25 |
| 204 Mike Hampton | .10 | .30 |
| 205 Kevin Brown | .10 | .30 |
| 206 Juan Encarnacion | .10 | .30 |
| 207 Danny Graves | .10 | .30 |
| 208 Carlos Guillen | .10 | .30 |
| 209 Phil Nevin | .10 | .30 |
| 210 Matt Lawton | .10 | .30 |
| 211 Manny Ramirez | .20 | .50 |
| 212 James Baldwin | .10 | .30 |
| 213 Fernando Tatis | .10 | .30 |
| 214 Craig Biggio | .20 | .50 |
| 215 Brian Jordan | .10 | .30 |
| 216 Bernie Williams | .20 | .50 |
| 217 Ryan Dempster | .10 | .30 |
| 218 Roger Clemens | .60 | 1.50 |
| 219 Jose Cruz Jr. | .10 | .30 |
| 220 John Valentin | .10 | .30 |
| 221 Dmitri Young | .10 | .30 |
| 222 Curt Schilling | .10 | .30 |
| 223 Jim Edmonds | .10 | .30 |
| 224 Chan Ho Park | .10 | .30 |
| 225 Brian Giles | .10 | .30 |
| 226 J.Anderson/T.Redman | .10 | .30 |
| 227 A.Piatt/J.Ortiz | .10 | .30 |
| 228 K.Kelly/A.Huff | .10 | .30 |
| 229 R.Choate/C.Dingman | .10 | .30 |
| 230 E.Cammack/G.Roberts | .10 | .30 |
| 231 Y.Lara/A.Tracy | .10 | .30 |
| 232 W.Franklin/S.Linebrink | .10 | .30 |
| 233 C.Cairncross/C.Perry | .10 | .30 |
| 234 J.Romero/M.LaCroy | .10 | .30 |
| 235 G.Guzman/J.Conti | .10 | .30 |
| 236 M.Burkhart/P.Crawford | .10 | .30 |
| 237 P.Coco/L.Estrella | .10 | .30 |
| 238 J.Parrish/F.Lunar | .10 | .30 |
| 239 C.Casimiro/I.Coffie | .10 | .30 |
| 240 C.Casimiro/I.Coffie | .10 | .30 |
| 241 D.Garibay/R.Quevedo | .10 | .30 |
| 242 S.Lee/T.Ohka | .10 | .30 |
| 243 H.Ortiz/J.D'Amico | .10 | .30 |
| 244 J.Sparks/T.Harper | .10 | .30 |
| 245 J.Boyd/D.Coggin | .10 | .30 |
| 246 M.Buehrlel/L.Barcelo | .20 | .50 |
| 247 A.Melhuse/B.Petrick | .10 | .30 |
| 248 K.Davis/P.Rigdon | .10 | .30 |
| 249 M.Darr/K.DeHaan | .10 | .30 |
| 250 V.Padilla/M.Brownson | 1.25 | 3.00 |
| 251 Barry Zito PROS | 2.00 | 5.00 |
| 252 Tim Drew PROS | 1.25 | 3.00 |
| 253 Luis Matos PROS | 1.25 | 3.00 |
| 254 Alex Cabrera PROS | 1.25 | 3.00 |
| 255 Jon Garland PROS | 1.25 | 3.00 |
| 256 Milton Bradley PROS | 1.25 | 3.00 |
| 257 Juan Pierre PROS | 1.25 | 3.00 |
| 258 Ismael Villegas PROS | 1.25 | 3.00 |
| 259 Eric Munson PROS | 1.25 | 3.00 |
| 260 Tomas De la Rosa PROS | 1.25 | 3.00 |
| 261 Chris Richard PROS | 1.25 | 3.00 |
| 262 Jason Tyner PROS | 1.25 | 3.00 |
| 263 B.J. Waszgis PROS | 1.25 | 3.00 |
| 264 Jason Marquis PROS | 1.25 | 3.00 |
| 265 Dusty Allen PROS | 1.25 | 3.00 |
| 266 Corey Patterson PROS | 1.25 | 3.00 |
| 267 Eric Byrnes PROS | 1.25 | 3.00 |
| 268 Xavier Nady PROS | 1.25 | 3.00 |
| 269 George Lombard PROS | 1.25 | 3.00 |
| 270 Timo Perez PROS | 1.25 | 3.00 |
| 271 Gary Matthews Jr. PROS | 1.25 | 3.00 |
| 272 Chad Durbin PROS | 1.25 | 3.00 |
| 273 Tony Armas Jr. PROS | 1.25 | 3.00 |
| 274 Francisco Cordero PROS | 1.25 | 3.00 |
| 275 Alfonso Soriano PROS | 2.00 | 5.00 |
| 276 J.Spivey RC/J.Uribe RC | 3.00 | 8.00 |
| 277 A.Pujols RC/B.Smith RC | 30.00 | 60.00 |
| 278 I.Suzuki RC/T.Shinjo RC | 12.50 | 30.00 |
| 279 D.Henson RC/J.Melian RC | 1.25 | 3.00 |
| 280 M.White RC/A.Hernandez RC | 2.00 | 5.00 |

## 2002 Ultra

| | | |
|---|---|---|
| COMPLETE SET (285) | 80.00 | 200.00 |
| COMP.SET w/o SP's (200) | 10.00 | 25.00 |
| COMMON CARD (1-200) | .10 | .30 |
| COMMON CARD (201-250) | .40 | 1.00 |
| COMMON CARD (251-285) | 1.25 | 3.00 |
| 1 Jeff Bagwell | .20 | .50 |
| 2 Derek Jeter | .75 | 2.00 |
| 3 Alex Rodriguez | .50 | 1.25 |
| 4 Eric Chavez | .10 | .30 |
| 5 Tsuyoshi Shinjo | .10 | .30 |
| 6 Chris Stynes | .10 | .30 |
| 7 Ivan Rodriguez | .20 | .50 |
| 8 Cal Ripken | 1.00 | 2.50 |
| 9 Freddy Garcia | .10 | .30 |
| 10 Chipper Jones | .30 | .75 |
| 11 Hideo Nomo | .30 | .75 |
| 12 Rafael Furcal | .10 | .30 |
| 13 Preston Wilson | .10 | .30 |
| 14 Jimmy Rollins | .10 | .30 |
| 15 Cristian Guzman | .10 | .30 |
| 16 Garret Anderson | .10 | .30 |
| 17 Todd Helton | .20 | .50 |
| 18 Moises Alou | .10 | .30 |
| 19 Tony Gwynn | .40 | 1.00 |
| 20 Jorge Posada | .20 | .50 |
| 21 Sean Casey | .10 | .30 |
| 22 Ray Lankford | .10 | .30 |
| 23 Manny Ramirez | .20 | .50 |
| 24 Barry Bonds | .75 | 2.00 |
| 25 Fred McGriff | .10 | .30 |
| 26 Vladimir Guerrero | .30 | .75 |
| 27 Todd Helton | .10 | .30 |
| 28 Jermaine Dye | .10 | .30 |

|  |  | | |
|---|--------|------|------|
| 29 | Adrian Beltre | .10 | .30 |
| 30 | Ken Griffey Jr. | .50 | 1.25 |
| 31 | Ramon Hernandez | .10 | .30 |
| 32 | Kerry Wood | .10 | .30 |
| 33 | Greg Maddux | .50 | 1.25 |
| 34 | Rondell White | .10 | .30 |
| 35 | Mike Mussina | .20 | .50 |
| 36 | Jim Edmonds | .10 | .30 |
| 37 | Scott Rolen | .20 | .50 |
| 38 | Mike Lowell | .10 | .30 |
| 39 | Al Leiter | .10 | .30 |
| 40 | Tony Clark | .10 | .30 |
| 41 | Joe Mays | .10 | .30 |
| 42 | Mo Vaughn | .10 | .30 |
| 43 | Geoff Jenkins | .10 | .30 |
| 44 | Curt Schilling | .10 | .30 |
| 45 | Pedro Martinez | .20 | .50 |
| 46 | Andy Pettitte | .20 | .50 |
| 47 | Tim Salmon | .10 | .30 |
| 48 | Carl Everett | .10 | .30 |
| 49 | Lance Berkman | .10 | .30 |
| 50 | Troy Glaus | .10 | .30 |
| 51 | Ichiro Suzuki | .60 | 1.50 |
| 52 | Alfonso Soriano | .10 | .30 |
| 53 | Tomo Ohka | .10 | .30 |
| 54 | Dean Palmer | .10 | .30 |
| 55 | Kevin Brown | .10 | .30 |
| 56 | Albert Pujols | .60 | 1.50 |
| 57 | Homer Bush | .10 | .30 |
| 58 | Tim Hudson | .10 | .30 |
| 59 | Frank Thomas | .30 | .75 |
| 60 | Joe Randa | .10 | .30 |
| 61 | Chan Ho Park | .10 | .30 |
| 62 | Bobby Higginson | .10 | .30 |
| 63 | Bartolo Colon | .10 | .30 |
| 64 | Aramis Ramirez | .10 | .30 |
| 65 | Jeff Cirillo | .10 | .30 |
| 66 | Roberto Alomar | .20 | .50 |
| 67 | Mark Kotsay | .10 | .30 |
| 68 | Mike Cameron | .10 | .30 |
| 69 | Mike Hampton | .10 | .30 |
| 70 | Trot Nixon | .10 | .30 |
| 71 | Juan Gonzalez | .10 | .30 |
| 72 | Damian Rolls | .10 | .30 |
| 73 | Brad Fullmer | .10 | .30 |
| 74 | David Ortiz | .30 | .75 |
| 75 | Brandon Inge | .10 | .30 |
| 76 | Orlando Hernandez | .10 | .30 |
| 77 | Matt Stairs | .10 | .30 |
| 78 | Jay Gibbons | .10 | .30 |
| 79 | Greg Vaughn | .10 | .30 |
| 80 | Brady Anderson | .10 | .30 |
| 81 | Jim Thome | .20 | .50 |
| 82 | Ben Sheets | .10 | .30 |
| 83 | Rafael Palmeiro | .20 | .50 |
| 84 | Edgar Renteria | .10 | .30 |
| 85 | Doug Mientkiewicz | .10 | .30 |
| 86 | Raul Mondesi | .10 | .30 |
| 87 | Shane Reynolds | .10 | .30 |
| 88 | Steve Finley | .10 | .30 |
| 89 | Jose Cruz Jr. | .10 | .30 |
| 90 | Edgardo Alfonzo | .10 | .30 |
| 91 | Jose Valentin | .10 | .30 |
| 92 | Mark McGwire | .75 | 2.00 |
| 93 | Mark Grace | .20 | .50 |
| 94 | Mike Lieberthal | .10 | .30 |
| 95 | Barry Larkin | .20 | .50 |
| 96 | Chuck Knoblauch | .10 | .30 |
| 97 | Deivi Cruz | .10 | .30 |
| 98 | Jeromy Burnitz | .10 | .30 |
| 99 | Shannon Stewart | .10 | .30 |
| 100 | David Wells | .10 | .30 |
| 101 | Brook Fordyce | .10 | .30 |
| 102 | Rusty Greer | .10 | .30 |
| 103 | Andruw Jones | .20 | .50 |
| 104 | Jason Kendall | .10 | .30 |
| 105 | Nomar Garciaparra | .50 | 1.25 |
| 106 | Shawn Green | .20 | .50 |
| 107 | Craig Biggio | .20 | .50 |
| 108 | Masato Yoshii | .10 | .30 |
| 109 | Ben Petrick | .10 | .30 |
| 110 | Gary Sheffield | .10 | .30 |
| 111 | Travis Lee | .10 | .30 |
| 112 | Matt Williams | .10 | .30 |
| 113 | Billy Wagner | .10 | .30 |
| 114 | Robin Ventura | .10 | .30 |
| 115 | Jerry Hairston | .10 | .30 |
| 116 | Paul LoDuca | .10 | .30 |
| 117 | Darin Erstad | .10 | .30 |
| 118 | Ruben Sierra | .10 | .30 |
| 119 | Ricky Gutierrez | .10 | .30 |
| 120 | Bret Boone | .10 | .30 |
| 121 | John Rocker | .10 | .30 |
| 122 | Roger Clemens | .60 | 1.50 |
| 123 | Eric Karros | .10 | .30 |
| 124 | J.D. Drew | .10 | .30 |
| 125 | Carlos Delgado | .10 | .30 |
| 126 | Jeffrey Hammonds | .10 | .30 |
| 127 | Jeff Kent | .10 | .30 |
| 128 | David Justice | .10 | .30 |
| 129 | Cliff Floyd | .10 | .30 |
| 130 | Omar Vizquel | .20 | .50 |
| 131 | Matt Morris | .10 | .30 |
| 132 | Rich Aurilia | .10 | .30 |
| 133 | Larry Walker | .10 | .30 |
| 134 | Miguel Tejada | .10 | .30 |
| 135 | Eric Young | .10 | .30 |
| 136 | Aaron Sele | .10 | .30 |
| 137 | Eric Milton | .10 | .30 |
| 138 | Travis Fryman | .10 | .30 |
| 139 | Magglio Ordonez | .10 | .30 |
| 140 | Sammy Sosa | .30 | .75 |
| 141 | Pokey Reese | .10 | .30 |
| 142 | Adam Eaton | .10 | .30 |
| 143 | Adam Kennedy | .10 | .30 |
| 144 | Mike Piazza | .50 | 1.25 |
| 145 | Larry Barnes | .10 | .30 |
| 146 | Darryl Kile | .10 | .30 |
| 147 | Tom Glavine | .20 | .50 |
| 148 | Ryan Klesko | .10 | .30 |
| 149 | Jose Vidro | .10 | .30 |
| 150 | Joe Kennedy | .10 | .30 |
| 151 | Bernie Williams | .20 | .50 |
| 152 | C.C. Sabathia | .10 | .30 |
| 153 | Alex Ochoa | .10 | .30 |
| 154 | A.J. Pierzynski | .10 | .30 |
| 155 | Johnny Damon | .20 | .50 |
| 156 | Omar Daal | .10 | .30 |
| 157 | A.J. Burnett | .10 | .30 |
| 158 | Eric Munson | .10 | .30 |
| 159 | Fernando Vina | .10 | .30 |
| 160 | Chris Singleton | .10 | .30 |
| 161 | Juan Pierre | .10 | .30 |
| 162 | John Olerud | .10 | .30 |
| 163 | Randy Johnson | .30 | .75 |
| 164 | Paul Konerko | .10 | .30 |
| 165 | Tino Martinez | .20 | .50 |
| 166 | Richard Hidalgo | .10 | .30 |
| 167 | Luis Gonzalez | .10 | .30 |
| 168 | Ben Grieve | .10 | .30 |
| 169 | Matt Lawton | .10 | .30 |
| 170 | Gabe Kapler | .10 | .30 |
| 171 | Mariano Rivera | .30 | .75 |
| 172 | Kenny Lofton | .10 | .30 |
| 173 | Brian Jordan | .10 | .30 |
| 174 | Brian Giles | .10 | .30 |
| 175 | Mark Quinn | .10 | .30 |
| 176 | Neifi Perez | .10 | .30 |
| 177 | Ellis Burks | .10 | .30 |
| 178 | Bobby Abreu | .10 | .30 |
| 179 | Jeff Weaver | .10 | .30 |
| 180 | Andres Galarraga | .10 | .30 |
| 181 | Javy Lopez | .10 | .30 |
| 182 | Todd Walker | .10 | .30 |
| 183 | Fernando Tatis | .10 | .30 |
| 184 | Charles Johnson | .10 | .30 |
| 185 | Pat Burrell | .10 | .30 |
| 186 | Jay Bell | .10 | .30 |
| 187 | Aaron Boone | .10 | .30 |
| 188 | Jason Giambi | .20 | .50 |
| 189 | Jay Payton | .10 | .30 |
| 190 | Carlos Lee | .10 | .30 |
| 191 | Phil Nevin | .10 | .30 |
| 192 | Mike Sweeney | .10 | .30 |
| 193 | J.T. Snow | .10 | .30 |
| 194 | Dmitri Young | .10 | .30 |
| 195 | Richie Sexson | .10 | .30 |
| 196 | Derrek Lee | .20 | .50 |
| 197 | Corey Koskie | .10 | .30 |
| 198 | Edgar Martinez | .20 | .50 |
| 199 | Wade Miller | .10 | .30 |
| 200 | Tony Batista | .10 | .30 |
| 201 | John Olerud AS | .40 | 1.00 |
| 202 | Bret Boone AS | .40 | 1.00 |
| 203 | Cal Ripken AS | 2.00 | 5.00 |
| 204 | Alex Rodriguez AS | 1.00 | 2.50 |
| 205 | Ichiro Suzuki AS | 1.25 | 3.00 |
| 206 | Manny Ramirez AS | .20 | .50 |
| 207 | Juan Gonzalez AS | .40 | 1.00 |
| 208 | Ivan Rodriguez AS | .60 | 1.50 |
| 209 | Roger Clemens AS | 1.25 | 3.00 |
| 210 | Edgar Martinez AS | .60 | 1.50 |
| 211 | Todd Helton AS | .60 | 1.50 |
| 212 | Jeff Kent AS | .40 | 1.00 |
| 213 | Chipper Jones AS | .60 | 1.50 |
| 214 | Rich Aurilia AS | .40 | 1.00 |
| 215 | Barry Bonds AS | 1.50 | 4.00 |
| 216 | Sammy Sosa AS | .60 | 1.50 |
| 217 | Luis Gonzalez AS | .40 | 1.00 |
| 218 | Mike Piazza AS | 1.00 | 2.50 |
| 219 | Randy Johnson AS | .60 | 1.50 |
| 220 | Larry Walker AS | .40 | 1.00 |
| 221 | T.Helton/J.Uribe | .40 | 1.00 |
| 222 | P.Burrell/E.Valent | .40 | 1.00 |
| 223 | E.Martinez/I.Suzuki | 1.25 | 3.00 |
| 224 | B.Grieve/J.Tyner | .40 | 1.00 |
| 225 | M.Quinn/D.Brown | .40 | 1.00 |
| 226 | C.Ripken/B.Roberts | 2.00 | 5.00 |
| 227 | C.Floyd/A.Nunez | .40 | 1.00 |
| 228 | J.Bagwell/A.Everett | .40 | 1.00 |
| 229 | M.McGwire/A.Pujols | 1.50 | 4.00 |
| 230 | D.Mientkewicz/L.Rivas | .40 | 1.00 |
| 231 | J.Gonzalez/D.Peoples | .40 | 1.00 |
| 232 | K.Brown/L.Prokopec | .40 | 1.00 |
| 233 | R.Sexson/B.Sheets | .40 | 1.00 |
| 234 | J.Giambi/J.Hart | .40 | 1.00 |
| 235 | B.Bonds/C.Valderrama | 1.50 | 4.00 |
| 236 | T.Gwynn/C.Crespo | .75 | 2.00 |
| 237 | K.Griffey Jr./A.Dunn | 1.00 | 2.50 |
| 238 | F.Thomas/J.Crede | .60 | 1.50 |
| 239 | D.Jeter/D.Henson | 1.50 | 4.00 |
| 240 | C.Jones/W.Betemit | .60 | 1.50 |
| 241 | L.Gonzalez/J.Spivey | .40 | 1.00 |
| 242 | B.Higginson/A.Torres | .40 | 1.00 |
| 243 | C.Delgado/V.Wells | .40 | 1.00 |
| 244 | S.Sosa/C.Patterson | .60 | 1.50 |
| 245 | N.Garciaparra/S.Hillenbrand | 1.00 | 2.50 |
| 246 | A.Rodriguez/J.Romano | 1.00 | 2.50 |
| 247 | T.Glaus/D.Eckstein | .40 | 1.00 |
| 248 | M.Piazza/A.Escobar | 1.00 | 2.50 |
| 249 | B.Giles/J.Wilson | .40 | 1.00 |
| 250 | V.Guerrero/S.Hodges | .60 | 1.50 |
| 251 | Bud Smith PROS | 1.25 | 3.00 |
| 252 | Juan Diaz PROS | 1.25 | 3.00 |
| 253 | Wilkin Ruan PROS | 1.25 | 3.00 |
| 254 | Chris Spurling PROS RC | 1.25 | 3.00 |
| 255 | Toby Hall PROS | 1.25 | 3.00 |
| 256 | Jason Jennings PROS | 1.25 | 3.00 |
| 257 | George Perez PROS | 1.25 | 3.00 |
| 258 | D'Angelo Jimenez PROS | 1.25 | 3.00 |
| 259 | Jose Acevedo PROS | 1.25 | 3.00 |
| 260 | Josue Perez PROS | 1.25 | 3.00 |
| 261 | Brian Rogers PROS | 1.25 | 3.00 |
| 262 | Carlos Maldonado PROS RC | 1.25 | 3.00 |
| 263 | Travis Phelps PROS | 1.25 | 3.00 |
| 264 | Rob Mackowiak PROS | 1.25 | 3.00 |
| 265 | Ryan Drese PROS | 1.25 | 3.00 |
| 266 | Carlos Garcia PROS | 1.25 | 3.00 |
| 267 | Alexis Gomez PROS | 1.25 | 3.00 |
| 268 | Jeremy Affeldt PROS | 1.25 | 3.00 |
| 269 | Scott Podsednik PROS | 1.50 | 4.00 |
| 270 | Adam Johnson PROS | 1.25 | 3.00 |
| 271 | Pedro Santana PROS | 1.25 | 3.00 |
| 272 | Les Walrond PROS | 1.25 | 3.00 |
| 273 | Jackson Melian PROS | 1.25 | 3.00 |
| 274 | Carlos Hernandez PROS | 1.25 | 3.00 |
| 275 | Mark Nussbeck PROS RC | 1.25 | 3.00 |
| 276 | Cory Aldridge PROS | 1.25 | 3.00 |
| 277 | Troy Mattes PROS | 1.25 | 3.00 |
| 278 | Brent Abernathy PROS | 1.25 | 3.00 |
| 279 | J.J. Davis PROS | 1.25 | 3.00 |
| 280 | Brandon Duckworth PROS | 1.25 | 3.00 |
| 281 | Kyle Lohse PROS | 1.25 | 3.00 |
| 282 | Justin Kaye PROS | 1.25 | 3.00 |
| 283 | Cody Ransom PROS | 1.25 | 3.00 |
| 284 | Dave Williams PROS | 1.25 | 3.00 |
| 285 | Luis Lopez PROS | 1.25 | 3.00 |

# 2003 Ultra

|  |  | | |
|---|---|---|---|
| | COMP LO SET (250) | 40.00 | 100.00 |
| | COMP LO SET w/o SP's (200) | 10.00 | 25.00 |
| | COMMON CARD (201-220) | .60 | 1.50 |
| | COMMON CARD (221-250) | .75 | 2.00 |
| | COMMON CARD (251-265) | 1.25 | 3.00 |
| 1 | Barry Bonds | .75 | 2.00 |
| 2 | Derek Jeter | .75 | 2.00 |
| 3 | Ichiro Suzuki | .60 | 1.50 |
| 4 | Mike Lowell | .10 | .30 |
| 5 | Hideo Nomo | .30 | .75 |
| 6 | Javier Vazquez | .10 | .30 |
| 7 | Jeremy Giambi | .10 | .30 |
| 8 | Jamie Moyer | .10 | .30 |
| 9 | Rafael Palmeiro | .20 | .50 |
| 10 | Magglio Ordonez | .20 | .50 |
| 11 | Trot Nixon | .10 | .30 |
| 12 | Luis Castillo | .10 | .30 |
| 13 | Paul Byrd | .10 | .30 |
| 14 | Adam Kennedy | .10 | .30 |
| 15 | Trevor Hoffman | .10 | .30 |
| 16 | Matt Morris | .10 | .30 |
| 17 | Nomar Garciaparra | .50 | 1.25 |
| 18 | Matt Lawton | .10 | .30 |
| 19 | Carlos Beltran | .10 | .30 |
| 20 | Jason Giambi | .30 | .75 |
| 21 | Brian Giles | .10 | .30 |
| 22 | Jim Edmonds | .10 | .30 |
| 23 | Garret Anderson | .10 | .30 |
| 24 | Tony Batista | .10 | .30 |
| 25 | Aaron Boone | .10 | .30 |
| 26 | Mike Hampton | .10 | .30 |
| 27 | Billy Wagner | .10 | .30 |
| 28 | Kazuhisa Ishii | .10 | .30 |
| 29 | Al Leiter | .10 | .30 |
| 30 | Pat Burrell | .10 | .30 |
| 31 | Jeff Kent | .10 | .30 |
| 32 | Randy Johnson | .30 | .75 |
| 33 | Ray Durham | .10 | .30 |
| 34 | Josh Beckett | .10 | .30 |
| 35 | Cristian Guzman | .10 | .30 |
| 36 | Roger Clemens | .60 | 1.50 |
| 37 | Freddy Garcia | .10 | .30 |
| 38 | Roy Halladay | .10 | .30 |
| 39 | David Eckstein | .10 | .30 |
| 40 | Jerry Hairston | .10 | .30 |
| 41 | Barry Larkin | .20 | .50 |
| 42 | Larry Walker | .10 | .30 |
| 43 | Craig Biggio | .20 | .50 |
| 44 | Edgardo Alfonzo | .10 | .30 |
| 45 | Marlon Byrd | .10 | .30 |
| 46 | J.T. Snow | .10 | .30 |
| 47 | Juan Gonzalez | .10 | .30 |
| 48 | Ramon Ortiz | .10 | .30 |
| 49 | Jay Gibbons | .10 | .30 |
| 50 | Adam Dunn | .10 | .30 |
| 51 | Juan Pierre | .10 | .30 |
| 52 | Jeff Bagwell | .20 | .50 |
| 53 | Kevin Brown | .10 | .30 |
| 54 | Pedro Astacio | .10 | .30 |
| 55 | Mike Lieberthal | .10 | .30 |
| 56 | Johnny Damon | .20 | .50 |
| 57 | Tim Salmon | .20 | .50 |
| 58 | Mike Bordick | .10 | .30 |
| 59 | Ken Griffey Jr. | .50 | 1.25 |
| 60 | Jason Jennings | .10 | .30 |
| 61 | Lance Berkman | .20 | .50 |
| 62 | Jeromy Burnitz | .10 | .30 |
| 63 | Jimmy Rollins | .10 | .30 |
| 64 | Tsuyoshi Shinjo | .10 | .30 |
| 65 | Alex Rodriguez | .50 | 1.25 |
| 66 | Greg Maddux | .50 | 1.25 |
| 67 | Mark Prior | .20 | .50 |
| 68 | Mike Maroth | .10 | .30 |
| 69 | Geoff Jenkins | .10 | .30 |
| 70 | Tony Armas Jr. | .10 | .30 |
| 71 | Jermaine Dye | .10 | .30 |
| 72 | Albert Pujols | .60 | 1.50 |
| 73 | Shannon Stewart | .10 | .30 |
| 74 | Troy Glaus | .10 | .30 |
| 75 | Brook Fordyce | .10 | .30 |
| 76 | Juan Encarnacion | .10 | .30 |
| 77 | Todd Hollandsworth | .10 | .30 |
| 78 | Roy Oswalt | .10 | .30 |
| 79 | Paul Lo Duca | .10 | .30 |
| 80 | Mike Piazza | .50 | 1.25 |
| 81 | Bobby Abreu | .10 | .30 |
| 82 | Sean Burroughs | .10 | .30 |
| 83 | Randy Winn | .10 | .30 |
| 84 | Curt Schilling | .10 | .30 |
| 85 | Chris Singleton | .10 | .30 |
| 86 | Sean Casey | .10 | .30 |
| 87 | Todd Zeile | .10 | .30 |
| 88 | Richard Hidalgo | .10 | .30 |
| 89 | Roberto Alomar | .20 | .50 |
| 90 | Tim Hudson | .10 | .30 |
| 91 | Ryan Klesko | .10 | .30 |
| 92 | Greg Vaughn | .10 | .30 |
| 93 | Tony Womack | .10 | .30 |
| 94 | Fred McGriff | .20 | .50 |
| 95 | Tom Glavine | .20 | .50 |
| 96 | Todd Walker | .10 | .30 |
| 97 | Travis Fryman | .10 | .30 |
| 98 | Shane Reynolds | .10 | .30 |
| 99 | Shawn Green | .10 | .30 |
| 100 | Mo Vaughn | .10 | .30 |
| 101 | Adam Piatt | .10 | .30 |
| 102 | Deivi Cruz | .10 | .30 |
| 103 | Steve Cox | .10 | .30 |
| 104 | Luis Gonzalez | .10 | .30 |
| 105 | Russell Branyan | .10 | .30 |
| 106 | Danyle Ward | .10 | .30 |
| 107 | Mariano Rivera | .30 | .75 |
| 108 | Phil Nevin | .10 | .30 |
| 109 | Ben Grieve | .10 | .30 |
| 110 | Moises Alou | .10 | .30 |
| 111 | Omar Vizquel | .20 | .50 |
| 112 | Joe Randa | .10 | .30 |
| 113 | Jorge Posada | .20 | .50 |
| 114 | Mark Kotsay | .10 | .30 |
| 115 | Ryan Rupe | .10 | .30 |
| 116 | Javy Lopez | .10 | .30 |
| 117 | Corey Patterson | .10 | .30 |
| 118 | Bobby Higginson | .10 | .30 |
| 119 | Jose Vidro | .10 | .30 |
| 120 | Barry Zito | .10 | .30 |
| 121 | Scott Rolen | .20 | .50 |
| 122 | Gary Sheffield | .10 | .30 |
| 123 | Kerry Wood | .10 | .30 |
| 124 | Brandon Inge | .10 | .30 |
| 125 | Jose Hernandez | .10 | .30 |
| 126 | Michael Barrett | .10 | .30 |
| 127 | Miguel Tejada | .10 | .30 |
| 128 | Edgar Renteria | .10 | .30 |
| 129 | Junior Spivey | .10 | .30 |
| 130 | Jose Valentin | .10 | .30 |
| 131 | Derrek Lee | .20 | .50 |
| 132 | A.J. Pierzynski | .10 | .30 |
| 133 | Mike Mussina | .20 | .50 |
| 134 | Bret Boone | .10 | .30 |
| 135 | Chan Ho Park | .10 | .30 |
| 136 | Steve Finley | .10 | .30 |
| 137 | Mark Buehrle | .10 | .30 |
| 138 | A.J. Burnett | .10 | .30 |
| 139 | Ben Sheets | .10 | .30 |
| 140 | David Ortiz | .30 | .75 |
| 141 | Nick Johnson | .10 | .30 |
| 142 | Randall Simon | .10 | .30 |
| 143 | Carlos Delgado | .20 | .50 |
| 144 | Darin Erstad | .10 | .30 |
| 145 | Shea Hillenbrand | .10 | .30 |
| 146 | Todd Helton | .20 | .50 |
| 147 | Preston Wilson | .10 | .30 |
| 148 | Eric Gagne | .10 | .30 |
| 149 | Vladimir Guerrero | .30 | .75 |
| 150 | Brandon Duckworth | .10 | .30 |
| 151 | Rich Aurilia | .10 | .30 |
| 152 | Ivan Rodriguez | .20 | .50 |
| 153 | Andruw Jones | .20 | .50 |
| 154 | Carlos Lee | .10 | .30 |
| 155 | Robert Fick | .10 | .30 |
| 156 | Jacque Jones | .10 | .30 |
| 157 | Bernie Williams | .20 | .50 |
| 158 | John Olerud | .10 | .30 |
| 159 | Eric Hinske | .10 | .30 |
| 160 | Matt Clement | .10 | .30 |
| 161 | Dmitri Young | .10 | .30 |
| 162 | Torii Hunter | .10 | .30 |
| 163 | Carlos Pena | .10 | .30 |
| 164 | Mike Cameron | .10 | .30 |
| 165 | Raul Mondesi | .10 | .30 |
| 166 | Pedro Martinez | .20 | .50 |
| 167 | Bob Wickman | .10 | .30 |
| 168 | Mike Sweeney | .10 | .30 |
| 169 | David Wells | .10 | .30 |
| 170 | Jason Kendall | .10 | .30 |
| 171 | Tino Martinez | .20 | .50 |
| 172 | Matt Williams | .10 | .30 |
| 173 | Frank Thomas | .30 | .75 |
| 174 | Cliff Floyd | .10 | .30 |
| 175 | Corey Koskie | .10 | .30 |
| 176 | Orlando Hernandez | .10 | .30 |
| 177 | Edgar Martinez | .20 | .50 |
| 178 | Richie Sexson | .10 | .30 |
| 179 | Manny Ramirez | .20 | .50 |
| 180 | Jim Thome | .20 | .50 |
| 181 | Andy Pettitte | .20 | .50 |
| 182 | Aramis Ramirez | .10 | .30 |
| 183 | J.D. Drew | .10 | .30 |
| 184 | Brian Jordan | .10 | .30 |
| 185 | Sammy Sosa | .30 | .75 |
| 186 | Jeff Weaver | .10 | .30 |
| 187 | Jeffrey Hammonds | .10 | .30 |
| 188 | Eric Milton | .10 | .30 |
| 189 | Eric Chavez | .10 | .30 |
| 190 | Kazuhiro Sasaki | .10 | .30 |
| 191 | Jose Cruz Jr. | .10 | .30 |
| 192 | Derek Lowe | .10 | .30 |
| 193 | C.C. Sabathia | .10 | .30 |
| 194 | Adrian Beltre | .10 | .30 |
| 195 | Alfonso Soriano | .10 | .30 |
| 196 | Jack Wilson | .10 | .30 |
| 197 | Fernando Vina | .10 | .30 |
| 198 | Chipper Jones | .30 | .75 |
| 199 | Paul Konerko | .10 | .30 |
| 200 | Rusty Greer | .10 | .30 |
| 201 | Jason Giambi AS | .60 | 1.50 |
| 202 | Alfonso Soriano AS | .60 | 1.50 |
| 203 | Shea Hillenbrand AS | .60 | 1.50 |
| 204 | Alex Rodriguez AS | 1.00 | 2.50 |
| 205 | Jorge Posada AS | .60 | 1.50 |
| 206 | Ichiro Suzuki AS | 1.25 | 3.00 |
| 207 | Manny Ramirez AS | .60 | 1.50 |
| 208 | Torii Hunter AS | .60 | 1.50 |
| 209 | Todd Helton AS | .60 | 1.50 |
| 210 | Jose Vidro AS | .60 | 1.50 |
| 211 | Scott Rolen AS | .60 | 1.50 |
| 212 | Jimmy Rollins AS | .60 | 1.50 |
| 213 | Mike Piazza AS | 1.00 | 2.50 |
| 214 | Barry Bonds AS | 1.50 | 4.00 |
| 215 | Sammy Sosa AS | .60 | 1.50 |
| 216 | Vladimir Guerrero AS | .60 | 1.50 |
| 217 | Lance Berkman AS | .60 | 1.50 |
| 218 | Derek Jeter AS | 1.50 | 4.00 |
| 219 | Nomar Garciaparra AS | 1.00 | 2.50 |
| 220 | Luis Gonzalez AS | .60 | 1.50 |
| 221 | Kazuhisa Ishii 02R | .75 | 2.00 |
| 222 | Satoru Komiyama 02R | .75 | 2.00 |
| 223 | So Taguchi 02R | .75 | 2.00 |
| 224 | Jorge Padilla 02R | .75 | 2.00 |
| 225 | Ben Howard 02R | .75 | 2.00 |
| 226 | Jason Simontacchi 02R | .75 | 2.00 |
| 227 | Ramy Wesson 02R | .75 | 2.00 |
| 228 | Howie Clark 02R | .75 | 2.00 |
| 229 | Aaron Guiel 02R | .75 | 2.00 |
| 230 | Oliver Perez 02R | .75 | 2.00 |
| 231 | David Ross 02R | .75 | 2.00 |
| 232 | Julius Matos 02R | .75 | 2.00 |
| 233 | Chris Snelling 02R | .75 | 2.00 |
| 234 | Rodrigo Lopez 02R | .75 | 2.00 |
| 235 | Will Nieves 02R | .75 | 2.00 |
| 236 | Joe Borchard 02R | .75 | 2.00 |
| 237 | Aaron Cook 02R | .75 | 2.00 |
| 238 | Anderson Machado 02R | .75 | 2.00 |
| 239 | Corey Thurman 02R | .75 | 2.00 |
| 240 | Tyler Yates 02R | .75 | 2.00 |
| 241 | Coco Crisp 03R | 1.25 | 3.00 |
| 242 | Andy Van Hekken 03R | .75 | 2.00 |
| 243 | Jim Rushford 03R | .75 | 2.00 |

| | | | |
|---|---|---|---|
| ❑ 244 Jeriome Robertson 03R | .75 | 2.00 |
| ❑ 245 Shane Nance 03R | .75 | 2.00 |
| ❑ 246 Kevin Cash 03R | .75 | 2.00 |
| ❑ 247 Kirk Saarloos 03R | .75 | 2.00 |
| ❑ 248 Josh Bard 03R | .75 | 2.00 |
| ❑ 249 Dave Pember 03R RC | .75 | 2.00 |
| ❑ 250 Freddy Sanchez 03R | .75 | 2.00 |
| ❑ 251 Chien-Ming Wang PROS RC | 8.00 | 20.00 |
| ❑ 252 Rickie Weeks PROS RC | 2.50 | 6.00 |
| ❑ 253 Brandon Webb PROS RC | 3.00 | 8.00 |
| ❑ 254 Hideki Matsui PROS RC | 4.00 | 10.00 |
| ❑ 255 Michael Hessman PROS RC | 1.25 | 3.00 |
| ❑ 256 Ryan Wagner PROS RC | 1.25 | 3.00 |
| ❑ 257 Matt Kata PROS RC | 1.25 | 3.00 |
| ❑ 258 Edwin Jackson PROS RC | 1.50 | 4.00 |
| ❑ 259 Jose Contreras PROS RC | 1.50 | 4.00 |
| ❑ 260 Delmon Young PROS RC | 4.00 | 10.00 |
| ❑ 261 Bo Hart PROS RC | 1.25 | 3.00 |
| ❑ 262 Jeff Duncan PROS RC | 1.25 | 3.00 |
| ❑ 263 Robby Hammock PROS RC | 1.25 | 3.00 |
| ❑ 264 Jeremy Bonderman PROS RC | 4.00 | 10.00 |
| ❑ 265 Clint Barmes PROS RC | 1.00 | 2.50 |

## 2004 Ultra

| | | |
|---|---|---|
| ❑ COMPLETE SERIES 1 (220) | 30.00 | 60.00 |
| ❑ COMP.SERIES 1 w/o SP's (200) | 10.00 | 25.00 |
| ❑ COMP.SERIES 2 w/o SP's (75) | 10.00 | 25.00 |
| ❑ COMP.SERIES 2 w/o L13 (162) | 50.00 | 100.00 |
| ❑ COMMON CARD (1-200) | .10 | .30 |
| ❑ COMMON CARD (201-220) | .50 | 1.25 |
| ❑ 201-220 APPROXIMATE ODDS 1:2 HOBBY | | |
| ❑ 201-220 RANDOM IN RETAIL PACKS | | |
| ❑ COMMON CARD (296-382) | .75 | 2.00 |
| ❑ 296-382 ODDS TWO PER HOBBY/RETAIL | | |
| ❑ COMMON CARD (383-395) | 5.00 | 12.00 |
| ❑ 383-395 ODDS 1:28 HOBBY, 1:2000 RETAIL | | |
| ❑ 383-395 PRINT RUN 500 SERIAL #'d SETS | | |
| ❑ 1 Magglio Ordonez | .10 | .30 |
| ❑ 2 Bobby Abreu | .10 | .30 |
| ❑ 3 Eric Munson | .10 | .30 |
| ❑ 4 Eric Byrnes | .10 | .30 |
| ❑ 5 Bartolo Colon | .10 | .30 |
| ❑ 6 Juan Encarnacion | .10 | .30 |
| ❑ 7 Jody Gerut | .10 | .30 |
| ❑ 8 Eddie Guardado | .10 | .30 |
| ❑ 9 Shea Hillenbrand | .10 | .30 |
| ❑ 10 Andruw Jones | .20 | .50 |
| ❑ 11 Carlos Lee | .10 | .30 |
| ❑ 12 Pedro Martinez | .20 | .50 |
| ❑ 13 Barry Larkin | .20 | .50 |
| ❑ 14 Angel Berroa | .10 | .30 |
| ❑ 15 Edgar Martinez | .20 | .50 |
| ❑ 16 Sidney Ponson | .10 | .30 |
| ❑ 17 Mariano Rivera | .30 | .75 |
| ❑ 18 Richie Sexson | .10 | .30 |
| ❑ 19 Frank Thomas | .30 | .75 |
| ❑ 20 Jerome Williams | .10 | .30 |
| ❑ 21 Barry Zito | .10 | .30 |
| ❑ 22 Roberto Alomar | .20 | .50 |
| ❑ 23 Rocky Biddle | .10 | .30 |
| ❑ 24 Orlando Cabrera | .10 | .30 |
| ❑ 25 Placido Polanco | .10 | .30 |
| ❑ 26 Morgan Ensberg | .10 | .30 |
| ❑ 27 Jason Giambi | .10 | .30 |
| ❑ 28 Jim Thome | .20 | .50 |
| ❑ 29 Vladimir Guerrero | .30 | .75 |
| ❑ 30 Tim Hudson | .10 | .30 |
| ❑ 31 Jacque Jones | .10 | .30 |
| ❑ 32 Derek Lee | .20 | .50 |
| ❑ 33 Rafael Palmeiro | .20 | .50 |
| ❑ 34 Mike Mussina | .20 | .50 |
| ❑ 35 Corey Patterson | .10 | .30 |
| ❑ 36 Mike Cameron | .10 | .30 |
| ❑ 37 Ivan Rodriguez | .20 | .50 |

| | | |
|---|---|---|
| ❑ 38 Ben Sheets | .10 | .30 |
| ❑ 39 Woody Williams | .10 | .30 |
| ❑ 40 Ichiro Suzuki | .60 | 1.50 |
| ❑ 41 Moises Alou | .10 | .30 |
| ❑ 42 Craig Biggio | .20 | .50 |
| ❑ 43 Jorge Posada | .20 | .50 |
| ❑ 44 Craig Monroe | .10 | .30 |
| ❑ 45 Darin Erstad | .10 | .30 |
| ❑ 46 Jay Gibbons | .10 | .30 |
| ❑ 47 Aaron Guiel | .10 | .30 |
| ❑ 48 Travis Lee | .10 | .30 |
| ❑ 49 Jorge Julio | .10 | .30 |
| ❑ 50 Torii Hunter | .10 | .30 |
| ❑ 51 Luis Matos | .10 | .30 |
| ❑ 52 Brett Myers | .10 | .30 |
| ❑ 53 Sean Casey | .10 | .30 |
| ❑ 54 Mark Prior | .20 | .50 |
| ❑ 55 Alex Rodriguez | .50 | 1.25 |
| ❑ 56 Gary Sheffield | .10 | .30 |
| ❑ 57 Jason Varitek | .30 | .75 |
| ❑ 58 Dontrelle Willis | .10 | .30 |
| ❑ 59 Garret Anderson | .10 | .30 |
| ❑ 60 Casey Blake | .10 | .30 |
| ❑ 61 Jay Payton | .10 | .30 |
| ❑ 62 Carl Crawford | .10 | .30 |
| ❑ 63 Carl Everett | .10 | .30 |
| ❑ 64 Marcus Giles | .10 | .30 |
| ❑ 65 Jose Guillen | .10 | .30 |
| ❑ 66 Eric Karros | .10 | .30 |
| ❑ 67 Mike Lieberthal | .10 | .30 |
| ❑ 68 Hideki Matsui | .50 | 1.25 |
| ❑ 69 Xavier Nady | .10 | .30 |
| ❑ 70 Hank Blalock | .10 | .30 |
| ❑ 71 Albert Pujols | .60 | 1.50 |
| ❑ 72 Jose Cruz Jr. | .10 | .30 |
| ❑ 73 Randall Simon | .10 | .30 |
| ❑ 74 Javier Vazquez | .10 | .30 |
| ❑ 75 Preston Wilson | .10 | .30 |
| ❑ 76 Danys Baez | .10 | .30 |
| ❑ 77 Alex Cintron | .10 | .30 |
| ❑ 78 Jake Peavy | .10 | .30 |
| ❑ 79 Scott Rolen | .20 | .50 |
| ❑ 80 Robert Fick | .10 | .30 |
| ❑ 81 Brian Giles | .10 | .30 |
| ❑ 82 Roy Halladay | .10 | .30 |
| ❑ 83 Kazuhisa Ishii | .10 | .30 |
| ❑ 84 Austin Kearns | .10 | .30 |
| ❑ 85 Paul Lo Duca | .10 | .30 |
| ❑ 86 Darrell May | .10 | .30 |
| ❑ 87 Phil Nevin | .10 | .30 |
| ❑ 88 Carlos Pena | .10 | .30 |
| ❑ 89 Manny Ramirez | .20 | .50 |
| ❑ 90 C.C. Sabathia | .10 | .30 |
| ❑ 91 John Smoltz | .20 | .50 |
| ❑ 92 Jose Vidro | .10 | .30 |
| ❑ 93 Randy Wolf | .10 | .30 |
| ❑ 94 Jeff Bagwell | .20 | .50 |
| ❑ 95 Barry Bonds | .75 | 2.00 |
| ❑ 96 Frank Catalanotto | .10 | .30 |
| ❑ 97 Zach Day | .10 | .30 |
| ❑ 98 David Ortiz | .30 | .75 |
| ❑ 99 Troy Glaus | .10 | .30 |
| ❑ 100 Bo Hart | .10 | .30 |
| ❑ 101 Geoff Jenkins | .10 | .30 |
| ❑ 102 Jason Kendall | .10 | .30 |
| ❑ 103 Esteban Loaiza | .10 | .30 |
| ❑ 104 Doug Mientkiewicz | .10 | .30 |
| ❑ 105 Trot Nixon | .10 | .30 |
| ❑ 106 Troy Percival | .10 | .30 |
| ❑ 107 Aramis Ramirez | .10 | .30 |
| ❑ 108 Alex Sanchez | .10 | .30 |
| ❑ 109 Alfonso Soriano | .10 | .30 |
| ❑ 110 Omar Vizquel | .20 | .50 |
| ❑ 111 Kerry Wood | .10 | .30 |
| ❑ 112 Rocco Baldelli | .10 | .30 |
| ❑ 113 Bret Boone | .10 | .30 |
| ❑ 114 Shawn Chacon | .10 | .30 |
| ❑ 115 Carlos Delgado | .10 | .30 |
| ❑ 116 Shawn Green | .10 | .30 |
| ❑ 117 Tim Worrell | .10 | .30 |
| ❑ 118 Tom Glavine | .20 | .50 |
| ❑ 119 Shigetoshi Hasegawa | .10 | .30 |
| ❑ 120 Derek Jeter | .60 | 1.50 |
| ❑ 121 Jeff Kent | .20 | .50 |
| ❑ 122 Braden Looper | .10 | .30 |
| ❑ 123 Kevin Millwood | .10 | .30 |
| ❑ 124 Hideo Nomo | .30 | .75 |
| ❑ 125 Jason Phillips | .10 | .30 |

| | | |
|---|---|---|
| ❑ 126 Tim Redding | .10 | .30 |
| ❑ 127 Reggie Sanders | .10 | .30 |
| ❑ 128 Sammy Sosa | .30 | .75 |
| ❑ 129 Billy Wagner | .10 | .30 |
| ❑ 130 Miguel Batista | .10 | .30 |
| ❑ 131 Milton Bradley | .10 | .30 |
| ❑ 132 Eric Chavez | .10 | .30 |
| ❑ 133 J.D. Drew | .10 | .30 |
| ❑ 134 Keith Foulke | .10 | .30 |
| ❑ 135 Luis Gonzalez | .10 | .30 |
| ❑ 136 LaTroy Hawkins | .10 | .30 |
| ❑ 137 Randy Johnson | .30 | .75 |
| ❑ 138 Byung-Hyun Kim | .10 | .30 |
| ❑ 139 Javy Lopez | .10 | .30 |
| ❑ 140 Melvin Mora | .10 | .30 |
| ❑ 141 Aubrey Huff | .10 | .30 |
| ❑ 142 Mike Piazza | .50 | 1.25 |
| ❑ 143 Mark Redman | .10 | .30 |
| ❑ 144 Kazuhiro Sasaki | .10 | .30 |
| ❑ 145 Shannon Stewart | .10 | .30 |
| ❑ 146 Larry Walker | .10 | .30 |
| ❑ 147 Dmitri Young | .10 | .30 |
| ❑ 148 Josh Beckett | .10 | .30 |
| ❑ 149 Jae Woong Seo | .10 | .30 |
| ❑ 150 Hee Seop Choi | .10 | .30 |
| ❑ 151 Adam Dunn | .10 | .30 |
| ❑ 152 Rafael Furcal | .10 | .30 |
| ❑ 153 Juan Gonzalez | .10 | .30 |
| ❑ 154 Todd Helton | .20 | .50 |
| ❑ 155 Carlos Zambrano | .10 | .30 |
| ❑ 156 Ryan Klesko | .10 | .30 |
| ❑ 157 Mike Lowell | .10 | .30 |
| ❑ 158 Jamie Moyer | .10 | .30 |
| ❑ 159 Russ Ortiz | .10 | .30 |
| ❑ 160 Juan Pierre | .10 | .30 |
| ❑ 161 Edgar Renteria | .10 | .30 |
| ❑ 162 Curt Schilling | .10 | .30 |
| ❑ 163 Mike Sweeney | .10 | .30 |
| ❑ 164 Brandon Webb | .10 | .30 |
| ❑ 165 Michael Young | .10 | .30 |
| ❑ 166 Carlos Beltran | .10 | .30 |
| ❑ 167 Sean Burroughs | .10 | .30 |
| ❑ 168 Luis Castillo | .10 | .30 |
| ❑ 169 David Eckstein | .10 | .30 |
| ❑ 170 Eric Gagne | .10 | .30 |
| ❑ 171 Chipper Jones | .30 | .75 |
| ❑ 172 Livan Hernandez | .10 | .30 |
| ❑ 173 Nick Johnson | .10 | .30 |
| ❑ 174 Corey Koskie | .10 | .30 |
| ❑ 175 Jason Schmidt | .10 | .30 |
| ❑ 176 Bill Mueller | .10 | .30 |
| ❑ 177 Steve Finley | .10 | .30 |
| ❑ 178 A.J. Pierzynski | .10 | .30 |
| ❑ 179 Rene Reyes | .10 | .30 |
| ❑ 180 Jason Johnson | .10 | .30 |
| ❑ 181 Mark Teixeira | .20 | .50 |
| ❑ 182 Kip Wells | .10 | .30 |
| ❑ 183 Mike MacDougal | .10 | .30 |
| ❑ 184 Lance Berkman | .10 | .30 |
| ❑ 185 Victor Zambrano | .10 | .30 |
| ❑ 186 Roger Clemens | .60 | 1.50 |
| ❑ 187 Jim Edmonds | .10 | .30 |
| ❑ 188 Nomar Garciaparra | .50 | 1.25 |
| ❑ 189 Ken Griffey Jr. | .50 | 1.25 |
| ❑ 190 Richard Hidalgo | .10 | .30 |
| ❑ 191 Cliff Floyd | .10 | .30 |
| ❑ 192 Greg Maddux | .50 | 1.25 |
| ❑ 193 Mark Mulder | .10 | .30 |
| ❑ 194 Roy Oswalt | .10 | .30 |
| ❑ 195 Marlon Byrd | .10 | .30 |
| ❑ 196 Jose Reyes | .10 | .30 |
| ❑ 197 Kevin Brown | .10 | .30 |
| ❑ 198 Miguel Tejada | .10 | .30 |
| ❑ 199 Vernon Wells | .10 | .30 |
| ❑ 200 Joel Pineiro | .10 | .30 |
| ❑ 201 Rickie Weeks AR | .75 | 2.00 |
| ❑ 202 Chad Gaudin AR | .50 | 1.25 |
| ❑ 203 Ryan Wagner AR | .50 | 1.25 |
| ❑ 204 Chris Bootcheck AR | .50 | 1.25 |
| ❑ 205 Koyie Hill AR | .50 | 1.25 |
| ❑ 206 Jeff Duncan AR | .50 | 1.25 |
| ❑ 207 Rich Harden AR | .75 | 2.00 |
| ❑ 208 Edwin Jackson AR | .50 | 1.25 |
| ❑ 209 Robby Hammock AR | .50 | 1.25 |
| ❑ 210 Khalil Greene AR | 1.25 | 3.00 |
| ❑ 211 Chien-Ming Wang AR | 2.00 | 5.00 |
| ❑ 212 Prentice Redman AR | .50 | 1.25 |
| ❑ 213 Todd Wellemeyer AR | .50 | 1.25 |

|  |  | | |
|---|---|---|---|
| 214 | Clint Barnes AR | .75 | 2.00 |
| 215 | Matt Kata AR | .50 | 1.25 |
| 216 | Jon Leicester AR | .50 | 1.25 |
| 217 | Jeremy Guthrie AR | .50 | 1.25 |
| 218 | Chin-Hui Tsao AR | .75 | 2.00 |
| 219 | Dan Haren AR | .50 | 1.25 |
| 220 | Delmon Young AR | 1.25 | 3.00 |
| 221 | Vladimir Guerrero | .50 | 1.25 |
| 222 | Andy Pettitte | .30 | .75 |
| 223 | Gary Sheffield | .20 | .50 |
| 224 | Javier Vazquez | .20 | .50 |
| 225 | Alex Rodriguez | .75 | 2.00 |
| 226 | Billy Wagner | .20 | .50 |
| 227 | Miguel Tejada | .20 | .50 |
| 228 | Greg Maddux | .75 | 2.00 |
| 229 | Ivan Rodriguez | .30 | .75 |
| 230 | Roger Clemens | 1.00 | 2.50 |
| 231 | Alfonso Soriano | .20 | .50 |
| 232 | Miguel Cabrera | .30 | .75 |
| 233 | Javy Lopez | .20 | .50 |
| 234 | David Wells | .20 | .50 |
| 235 | Eric Milton | .20 | .50 |
| 236 | Armando Benitez | .20 | .50 |
| 237 | Mike Cameron | .20 | .50 |
| 238 | J.D. Drew | .20 | .50 |
| 239 | Carlos Beltran | .20 | .50 |
| 240 | Bartolo Colon | .20 | .50 |
| 241 | Jose Guillen | .20 | .50 |
| 242 | Kevin Brown | .20 | .50 |
| 243 | Carlos Guillen | .20 | .50 |
| 244 | Kenny Lofton | .20 | .50 |
| 245 | Pokey Reese | .20 | .50 |
| 246 | Rafael Palmeiro | .30 | .75 |
| 247 | Nomar Garciaparra | .75 | 2.00 |
| 248 | Juan Uribe | .20 | .50 |
| 249 | Hee Seop Choi | .20 | .50 |
| 250 | Nick Johnson | .20 | .50 |
| 251 | Scott Podsednik | .20 | .50 |
| 252 | Richie Sexson | .20 | .50 |
| 253 | Keith Foulke Sox | .20 | .50 |
| 254 | Jaret Wright | .20 | .50 |
| 255 | Johnny Estrada | .20 | .50 |
| 256 | Michael Barrett | .20 | .50 |
| 257 | Bernie Williams | .30 | .75 |
| 258 | Octavio Dotel | .20 | .50 |
| 259 | Jeromy Burnitz | .20 | .50 |
| 260 | Kevin Youkilis | .20 | .50 |
| 261 | Derrek Lee | .30 | .75 |
| 262 | Jack Wilson | .20 | .50 |
| 263 | Craig Wilson | .20 | .50 |
| 264 | Richard Hidalgo | .20 | .50 |
| 265 | Royce Clayton | .20 | .50 |
| 266 | Curt Schilling | .30 | .75 |
| 267 | Joe Mauer | .30 | .75 |
| 268 | Bobby Crosby | .20 | .50 |
| 269 | Zack Greinke | .20 | .50 |
| 270 | Victor Martinez | .20 | .50 |
| 271 | Pedro Feliz | .20 | .50 |
| 272 | Tony Batista | .20 | .50 |
| 273 | Casey Kotchman | .20 | .50 |
| 274 | Freddy Garcia | .20 | .50 |
| 275 | Adam Everett | .20 | .50 |
| 276 | Alexis Rios | .20 | .50 |
| 277 | Lew Ford | .20 | .50 |
| 278 | Adam LaRoche | .20 | .50 |
| 279 | Lyle Overbay | .20 | .50 |
| 280 | Juan Gonzalez | .20 | .50 |
| 281 | A.J. Pierzynski | .20 | .50 |
| 282 | Scott Hairston | .20 | .50 |
| 283 | Danny Bautista | .20 | .50 |
| 284 | Brad Penny | .20 | .50 |
| 285 | Paul Konerko | .20 | .50 |
| 286 | Matt Lawton | .20 | .50 |
| 287 | Carl Pavano | .20 | .50 |
| 288 | Pat Burrell | .20 | .50 |
| 289 | Kenny Rogers | .20 | .50 |
| 290 | Laynce Nix | .20 | .50 |
| 291 | Johnny Damon | .30 | .75 |
| 292 | Paul Wilson | .20 | .50 |
| 293 | Vinny Castilla | .20 | .50 |
| 294 | Aaron Miles | .20 | .50 |
| 295 | Ken Harvey | .20 | .50 |
| 296 | Onil Joseph RC | .75 | 2.00 |
| 297 | Kazuhito Tadano RC | 1.25 | 3.00 |
| 298 | Jeff Bennett RC | .75 | 2.00 |
| 299 | Chad Bentz RC | .75 | 2.00 |
| 300 | Akinori Otsuka RC | .75 | 2.00 |
| 301 | Jon Knott RC | .75 | 2.00 |
| 302 | Ian Snell RC | 1.25 | 3.00 |
| 303 | Fernando Nieve RC | 1.25 | 3.00 |
| 304 | Mike Rouse RC | .75 | 2.00 |
| 305 | Dennis Sarfate RC | .75 | 2.00 |
| 306 | Josh Labandeira RC | .75 | 2.00 |
| 307 | Chris Oxspring RC | .75 | 2.00 |
| 308 | Alfredo Simon RC | .75 | 2.00 |
| 309 | Rusty Tucker RC | 1.25 | 3.00 |
| 310 | Lincoln Holdzkom RC | .75 | 2.00 |
| 311 | Justin Leone RC | 1.25 | 3.00 |
| 312 | Jorge Sequea RC | .75 | 2.00 |
| 313 | Brian Dallimore RC | .75 | 2.00 |
| 314 | Tim Bittner RC | .75 | 2.00 |
| 315 | Ronny Cedeno RC | 1.25 | 3.00 |
| 316 | Justin Hampson RC | .75 | 2.00 |
| 317 | Ryan Wing RC | .75 | 2.00 |
| 318 | Mariano Gomez RC | .75 | 2.00 |
| 319 | Carlos Vasquez RC | 1.25 | 3.00 |
| 320 | Casey Daigle RC | .75 | 2.00 |
| 321 | Renyel Pinto RC | .75 | 2.00 |
| 322 | Chris Shelton RC | 1.25 | 3.00 |
| 323 | Mike Gosling RC | .75 | 2.00 |
| 324 | Aaron Baldiris RC | 1.25 | 3.00 |
| 325 | Ramon Ramirez RC | .75 | 2.00 |
| 326 | Roberto Novoa RC | 1.25 | 3.00 |
| 327 | Sean Henn RC | .75 | 2.00 |
| 328 | Nick Regilio RC | .75 | 2.00 |
| 329 | Dave Crouthers RC | .75 | 2.00 |
| 330 | Greg Dobbs RC | .75 | 2.00 |
| 331 | Angel Chavez RC | .75 | 2.00 |
| 332 | Luis A. Gonzalez RC | .75 | 2.00 |
| 333 | Justin Knoedler RC | .75 | 2.00 |
| 334 | Jason Frasor RC | .75 | 2.00 |
| 335 | Jerry Gil RC | .75 | 2.00 |
| 336 | Carlos Hines RC | .75 | 2.00 |
| 337 | Ivan Ochoa RC | .75 | 2.00 |
| 338 | Jose Capellan RC | 1.25 | 3.00 |
| 339 | Hector Gimenez RC | .75 | 2.00 |
| 340 | Shawn Hill RC | .75 | 2.00 |
| 341 | Freddy Guzman RC | .75 | 2.00 |
| 342 | Scott Proctor RC | .75 | 2.00 |
| 343 | Frank Francisco RC | .75 | 2.00 |
| 344 | Brandon Medders RC | .75 | 2.00 |
| 345 | Andy Green RC | .75 | 2.00 |
| 346 | Eddy Rodriguez RC | 1.25 | 3.00 |
| 347 | Tim Harmulack RC | .75 | 2.00 |
| 348 | Michael Wuertz RC | .75 | 2.00 |
| 349 | Amie Munoz RC | .75 | 2.00 |
| 350 | Enemencio Pacheco RC | .75 | 2.00 |
| 351 | Dusty Bergman RC | .75 | 2.00 |
| 352 | Charles Thomas RC | .75 | 2.00 |
| 353 | William Bergolla RC | .75 | 2.00 |
| 354 | Ramon Castro RC | .75 | 2.00 |
| 355 | Justin Lehr RC | .75 | 2.00 |
| 356 | Lino Urdaneta RC | .75 | 2.00 |
| 357 | Donnie Kelly RC | .75 | 2.00 |
| 358 | Kevin Cave RC | .75 | 2.00 |
| 359 | Franklyn Gracesqui RC | .75 | 2.00 |
| 360 | Chris Aguila RC | .75 | 2.00 |
| 361 | Jorge Vasquez RC | .75 | 2.00 |
| 362 | Andres Blanco RC | .75 | 2.00 |
| 363 | Orlando Rodriguez RC | .75 | 2.00 |
| 364 | Colby Miller RC | .75 | 2.00 |
| 365 | Shawn Camp RC | .75 | 2.00 |
| 366 | Jake Woods RC | .75 | 2.00 |
| 367 | George Sherrill RC | .75 | 2.00 |
| 368 | Justin Huisman RC | .75 | 2.00 |
| 369 | Johnny Serrano RC | .75 | 2.00 |
| 370 | Mike Johnston RC | .75 | 2.00 |
| 371 | Ryan Meaux RC | .75 | 2.00 |
| 372 | Scott Dohmann RC | .75 | 2.00 |
| 373 | Brad Halsey RC | 1.25 | 3.00 |
| 374 | Joey Gathright RC | 1.50 | 4.00 |
| 375 | Yadier Molina RC | 2.00 | 5.00 |
| 376 | Travis Blackley RC | .75 | 2.00 |
| 377 | Steve Andrade RC | .75 | 2.00 |
| 378 | Phil Stockman RC | .75 | 2.00 |
| 379 | Roman Colon RC | .75 | 2.00 |
| 380 | Jesse Crain RC | 1.25 | 3.00 |
| 381 | Edwardo Sierra RC | 1.25 | 3.00 |
| 382 | Justin Germano RC | .75 | 2.00 |
| 383 | Kaz Matsui L13 RC | 4.00 | 10.00 |
| 384 | Shingo Takatsu L13 RC | 4.00 | 10.00 |
| 385 | John Gall L13 RC | 5.00 | 12.00 |
| 386 | Chris Saenz L13 RC | 5.00 | 12.00 |
| 387 | Merkin Valdez L13 RC | 4.00 | 10.00 |
| 388 | Jamie Brown L13 RC | 5.00 | 12.00 |
| 389 | Jason Bartlett L13 RC | 5.00 | 12.00 |
| 390 | David Aardsma L13 RC | 5.00 | 12.00 |
| 391 | Scott Kazmir L13 RC | 12.50 | 30.00 |
| 392 | David Wright L13 | 12.50 | 30.00 |
| 393 | Dioner Navarro L13 RC | 4.00 | 10.00 |
| 394 | B.J. Upton L13 | 5.00 | 12.00 |
| 395 | Gavin Floyd L13 | 5.00 | 12.00 |

## 2005 Ultra

| | | | |
|---|---|---|---|
| COMPLETE SET (220) | | 40.00 | 100.00 |
| COMP.SET w/o SP's (200) | | 15.00 | 40.00 |
| COMMON CARD (1-200) | | .10 | .25 |
| COMMON CARD (201-220) | | .75 | 2.00 |
| 201-220 ODDS 1:4 HOBBY, 1:5 RETAIL | | | |
| 1 | Andy Pettitte | .20 | .50 |
| 2 | Jose Cruz Jr. | .10 | .30 |
| 3 | Cliff Floyd | .10 | .30 |
| 4 | Paul Konerko | .10 | .30 |
| 5 | Joe Mauer | .30 | .75 |
| 6 | Scott Spiezio | .10 | .30 |
| 7 | Ben Sheets | .10 | .30 |
| 8 | Kerry Wood | .10 | .30 |
| 9 | Carl Pavano | .10 | .30 |
| 10 | Matt Morris | .10 | .30 |
| 11 | Kaz Matsui | .20 | .50 |
| 12 | Ivan Rodriguez | .20 | .50 |
| 13 | Victor Martinez | .10 | .30 |
| 14 | Justin Morneau | .10 | .30 |
| 15 | Adam Everett | .10 | .30 |
| 16 | Carl Crawford | .20 | .50 |
| 17 | David Ortiz | .30 | .75 |
| 18 | Jason Giambi | .10 | .30 |
| 19 | Derrek Lee | .20 | .50 |
| 20 | Magglio Ordonez | .10 | .30 |
| 21 | Bobby Abreu | .10 | .30 |
| 22 | Milton Bradley | .10 | .30 |
| 23 | Jeff Bagwell | .20 | .50 |
| 24 | Jim Edmonds | .10 | .30 |
| 25 | Garret Anderson | .10 | .30 |
| 26 | Jacque Jones | .10 | .30 |
| 27 | Ted Lilly | .10 | .30 |
| 28 | Greg Maddux | .50 | 1.25 |
| 29 | Jermaine Dye | .10 | .30 |
| 30 | Bill Mueller | .10 | .30 |
| 31 | Roy Oswalt | .20 | .50 |
| 32 | Tony Womack | .10 | .30 |
| 33 | Andruw Jones | .20 | .50 |
| 34 | Tom Glavine | .20 | .50 |
| 35 | Mariano Rivera | .30 | .75 |
| 36 | Sean Casey | .10 | .30 |
| 37 | Edgardo Alfonzo | .10 | .30 |
| 38 | Brad Penny | .10 | .30 |
| 39 | Johan Santana | .30 | .75 |
| 40 | Mark Teixeira | .20 | .50 |
| 41 | Manny Ramirez | .20 | .50 |
| 42 | Gary Sheffield | .10 | .30 |
| 43 | Matt Lawton | .10 | .30 |
| 44 | Troy Percival | .10 | .30 |
| 45 | Rocco Baldelli | .10 | .30 |
| 46 | Doug Mientkiewicz | .10 | .30 |
| 47 | Corey Patterson | .10 | .30 |
| 48 | Austin Kearns | .10 | .30 |
| 49 | Edgar Martinez | .10 | .30 |
| 50 | Brad Radke | .10 | .30 |
| 51 | Barry Larkin | .20 | .50 |
| 52 | Chone Figgins | .10 | .30 |
| 53 | Alex Rodriguez | .50 | 1.25 |
| 54 | Vinny Castilla | .10 | .30 |
| 55 | Javier Vazquez | .10 | .30 |
| 56 | Javy Lopez | .10 | .30 |
| 57 | Mike Cameron | .10 | .30 |
| 58 | Brian Giles | .10 | .30 |
| 60 | Dontrelle Willis | .10 | .30 |
| 61 | Rafael Furcal | .10 | .30 |

|  |  | | |
|---|---|---|---|
| 62 | Trot Nixon | .10 | .30 |
| 63 | Mark Mulder | .10 | .30 |
| 64 | Josh Beckett | .10 | .30 |
| 65 | J.D. Drew | .10 | .30 |
| 66 | Brandon Webb | .10 | .30 |
| 67 | Wade Miller | .10 | .30 |
| 68 | Lyle Overbay | .10 | .30 |
| 69 | Pedro Martinez | .20 | .50 |
| 70 | Rich Harden | .10 | .30 |
| 71 | Al Leiter | .10 | .30 |
| 72 | Adam Eaton | .10 | .30 |
| 73 | Mike Sweeney | .10 | .30 |
| 74 | Steve Finley | .10 | .30 |
| 75 | Kris Benson | .10 | .30 |
| 76 | Jim Thome | .20 | .50 |
| 77 | Juan Pierre | .10 | .30 |
| 78 | Bartolo Colon | .10 | .30 |
| 79 | Carlos Delgado | .10 | .30 |
| 80 | Jack Wilson | .10 | .30 |
| 81 | Ken Harvey | .10 | .30 |
| 82 | Nomar Garciaparra | .30 | .75 |
| 83 | Paul Lo Duca | .10 | .30 |
| 84 | Cesar Izturis | .10 | .30 |
| 85 | Adrian Beltre | .10 | .30 |
| 86 | Brian Roberts | .10 | .30 |
| 87 | David Eckstein | .10 | .30 |
| 88 | Jimmy Rollins | .10 | .30 |
| 89 | Roger Clemens | .50 | 1.25 |
| 90 | Randy Johnson | .30 | .75 |
| 91 | Orlando Hudson | .10 | .30 |
| 92 | Tim Hudson | .10 | .30 |
| 93 | Dmitri Young | .10 | .30 |
| 94 | Chipper Jones | .30 | .75 |
| 95 | John Smoltz | .20 | .50 |
| 96 | Billy Wagner | .10 | .30 |
| 97 | Hideo Nomo | .30 | .75 |
| 98 | Sammy Sosa | .30 | .75 |
| 99 | Darin Erstad | .10 | .30 |
| 100 | Todd Helton | .20 | .50 |
| 101 | Aubrey Huff | .10 | .30 |
| 102 | Alfonso Soriano | .10 | .30 |
| 103 | Jose Vidro | .10 | .30 |
| 104 | Carlos Lee | .10 | .30 |
| 105 | Corey Koskie | .10 | .30 |
| 106 | Bret Boone | .10 | .30 |
| 107 | Torii Hunter | .10 | .30 |
| 108 | Aramis Ramirez | .10 | .30 |
| 109 | Chase Utley | .20 | .50 |
| 110 | Reggie Sanders | .10 | .30 |
| 111 | Livan Hernandez | .10 | .30 |
| 112 | Jeromy Burnitz | .10 | .30 |
| 113 | Carlos Zambrano | .10 | .30 |
| 114 | Hank Blalock | .10 | .30 |
| 115 | Sidney Ponson | .10 | .30 |
| 116 | Zack Greinke | .10 | .30 |
| 117 | Trevor Hoffman | .10 | .30 |
| 118 | Jeff Kent | .10 | .30 |
| 119 | Richie Sexson | .10 | .30 |
| 120 | Melvin Mora | .10 | .30 |
| 121 | Eric Chavez | .10 | .30 |
| 122 | Miguel Cabrera | .20 | .50 |
| 123 | Ryan Freel | .10 | .30 |
| 124 | Russ Ortiz | .10 | .30 |
| 125 | Craig Wilson | .10 | .30 |
| 126 | Craig Biggio | .20 | .50 |
| 127 | Curt Schilling | .20 | .50 |
| 128 | Kaz Ishii | .10 | .30 |
| 129 | Marquis Grissom | .10 | .30 |
| 130 | Bernie Williams | .20 | .50 |
| 131 | Travis Hafner | .10 | .30 |
| 132 | Hee Seop Choi | .10 | .30 |
| 133 | Scott Rolen | .20 | .50 |
| 134 | Tony Batista | .10 | .30 |
| 135 | Frank Thomas | .30 | .75 |
| 136 | Jason Varitek | .30 | .75 |
| 137 | Ichiro Suzuki | .60 | 1.50 |
| 138 | Junior Spivey | .10 | .30 |
| 139 | Adam Dunn | .10 | .30 |
| 140 | Jorge Posada | .20 | .50 |
| 141 | Edgar Renteria | .10 | .30 |
| 142 | Hideki Matsui | .50 | 1.25 |
| 143 | Carlos Guillen | .10 | .30 |
| 144 | Jody Gerut | .10 | .30 |
| 145 | Wily Mo Pena | .10 | .30 |
| 146 | Derek Jeter | .60 | 1.50 |
| 147 | C.C. Sabathia | .10 | .30 |
| 148 | Geoff Jenkins | .10 | .30 |
| 149 | Albert Pujols | .60 | 1.50 |
| 150 | Eric Munson | .10 | .30 |
| 151 | Moises Alou | .10 | .30 |
| 152 | Jerry Hairston | .10 | .30 |
| 153 | Ray Durham | .10 | .30 |
| 154 | Mike Piazza | .30 | .75 |
| 155 | Omar Vizquel | .10 | .30 |
| 156 | A.J. Pierzynski | .10 | .30 |
| 157 | Michael Young | .10 | .30 |
| 158 | Jason Bay | .10 | .30 |
| 159 | Mark Loretta | .10 | .30 |
| 160 | Shawn Green | .10 | .30 |
| 161 | Luis Gonzalez | .10 | .30 |
| 162 | Johnny Damon | .20 | .50 |
| 163 | Eric Milton | .10 | .30 |
| 164 | Mike Lowell | .10 | .30 |
| 165 | Jose Guillen | .10 | .30 |
| 166 | Eric Hinske | .10 | .30 |
| 167 | Jason Kendall | .10 | .30 |
| 168 | Carlos Beltran | .10 | .30 |
| 169 | Johnny Estrada | .10 | .30 |
| 170 | Scott Hatteberg | .10 | .30 |
| 171 | Laynce Nix | .10 | .30 |
| 172 | Eric Gagne | .10 | .30 |
| 173 | Richard Hidalgo | .10 | .30 |
| 174 | Bobby Crosby | .10 | .30 |
| 175 | Woody Williams | .10 | .30 |
| 176 | Justin Leone | .10 | .30 |
| 177 | Orlando Cabrera | .10 | .30 |
| 178 | Mark Prior | .20 | .50 |
| 179 | Jorge Julio | .10 | .30 |
| 180 | Jamie Moyer | .10 | .30 |
| 181 | Jose Reyes | .20 | .50 |
| 182 | Ken Griffey Jr. | .50 | 1.25 |
| 183 | Mike Lieberthal | .10 | .30 |
| 184 | Kenny Rogers | .10 | .30 |
| 185 | Mike Mussina | .20 | .50 |
| 186 | Preston Wilson | .10 | .30 |
| 187 | Khalil Greene | .20 | .50 |
| 188 | Angel Berroa | .10 | .30 |
| 189 | Miguel Tejada | .10 | .30 |
| 190 | Freddy Garcia | .10 | .30 |
| 191 | Pat Burrell | .10 | .30 |
| 192 | Luis Castillo | .10 | .30 |
| 193 | Vladimir Guerrero | .30 | .75 |
| 194 | Roy Halladay | .10 | .30 |
| 195 | Barry Zito | .10 | .30 |
| 196 | Lance Berkman | .20 | .50 |
| 197 | Rafael Palmeiro | .20 | .50 |
| 198 | Nate Robertson | .10 | .30 |
| 199 | Jason Schmidt | .10 | .30 |
| 200 | Scott Podsednik | .10 | .30 |
| 201 | Casey Kotchman AR | 1.25 | 3.00 |
| 202 | Scott Kazmir AR | 2.00 | 5.00 |
| 203 | Bucky Jacobsen AR | .75 | 2.00 |
| 204 | Jeff Keppinger AR | .75 | 2.00 |
| 205 | Dave Bush AR | .75 | 2.00 |
| 206 | Gavin Floyd AR | .75 | 2.00 |
| 207 | David Wright AR | 3.00 | 8.00 |
| 208 | B.J. Upton AR | 2.00 | 5.00 |
| 209 | David Aardsma AR | .75 | 2.00 |
| 210 | Jason Bartlett AR | .75 | 2.00 |
| 211 | Dioner Navarro AR | 1.25 | 3.00 |
| 212 | Jason Kubel AR | .75 | 2.00 |
| 213 | Ryan Howard AR | 3.00 | 8.00 |
| 214 | Charles Thomas AR | .75 | 2.00 |
| 215 | Freddy Guzman AR | .75 | 2.00 |
| 216 | Brad Halsey AR | .75 | 2.00 |
| 217 | Joey Gathright AR | 1.25 | 3.00 |
| 218 | Jeff Francis AR | .75 | 2.00 |
| 219 | Terry Tiffee AR | .75 | 2.00 |
| 220 | Nick Swisher AR | 2.00 | 5.00 |

**2006 Ultra**

| | | | |
|---|---|---|---|
| COMP.SET w/o RL13 (200) | | 15.00 | 40.00 |
| COMMON CARD (1-180) | | .15 | .40 |
| RL13 201-250 ODDS 1:4 HOBBY, 1:4 RETAIL | | | |
| 251 PRINT RUN 5000 CARDS | | | |
| 251 JOHJIMA IS NOT SERIAL NUMBERED | | | |
| 251 PRINT RUN INFO PROVIDED BY UD | | | |
| 251 JOHJIMA EXCH. DEADLINE 05/25/08 | | | |
| 1 | Vladimir Guerrero | .40 | 1.00 |
| 2 | Bartolo Colon | .15 | .40 |
| 3 | Francisco Rodriguez | .15 | .40 |
| 4 | Darin Erstad | .15 | .40 |
| 5 | Chone Figgins | .15 | .40 |
| 6 | Bengie Molina | .15 | .40 |
| 7 | Roger Clemens | .75 | 2.00 |
| 8 | Lance Berkman | .15 | .40 |
| 9 | Morgan Ensberg | .15 | .40 |
| 10 | Roy Oswalt | .15 | .40 |
| 11 | Andy Pettitte | .25 | .60 |
| 12 | Craig Biggio | .25 | .60 |
| 13 | Eric Chavez | .15 | .40 |
| 14 | Barry Zito | .15 | .40 |
| 15 | Huston Street | .15 | .40 |
| 16 | Bobby Crosby | .15 | .40 |
| 17 | Nick Swisher | .15 | .40 |
| 18 | Rich Harden | .15 | .40 |
| 19 | Vernon Wells | .15 | .40 |
| 20 | Roy Halladay | .15 | .40 |
| 21 | Alex Rios | .15 | .40 |
| 22 | Orlando Hudson | .15 | .40 |
| 23 | Shea Hillenbrand | .15 | .40 |
| 24 | Gustavo Chacin | .15 | .40 |
| 25 | Chipper Jones | .40 | 1.00 |
| 26 | Andruw Jones | .25 | .60 |
| 27 | Jeff Francoeur | .40 | 1.00 |
| 28 | John Smoltz | .25 | .60 |
| 29 | Tim Hudson | .15 | .40 |
| 30 | Marcus Giles | .15 | .40 |
| 31 | Carlos Lee | .15 | .40 |
| 32 | Ben Sheets | .15 | .40 |
| 33 | Rickie Weeks | .15 | .40 |
| 34 | Chris Capuano | .15 | .40 |
| 35 | Geoff Jenkins | .15 | .40 |
| 36 | Brady Clark | .15 | .40 |
| 37 | Albert Pujols | .75 | 2.00 |
| 38 | Jim Edmonds | .25 | .60 |
| 39 | Chris Carpenter | .15 | .40 |
| 40 | Mark Mulder | .15 | .40 |
| 41 | Yadier Molina | .15 | .40 |
| 42 | Scott Rolen | .25 | .60 |
| 43 | Derek Lee | .15 | .40 |
| 44 | Mark Prior | .25 | .60 |
| 45 | Aramis Ramirez | .15 | .40 |
| 46 | Carlos Zambrano | .15 | .40 |
| 47 | Greg Maddux | .60 | 1.50 |
| 48 | Nomar Garciaparra | .40 | 1.00 |
| 49 | Jonny Gomes | .15 | .40 |
| 50 | Carl Crawford | .15 | .40 |
| 51 | Scott Kazmir | .25 | .60 |
| 52 | Jorge Cantu | .15 | .40 |
| 53 | Julio Lugo | .15 | .40 |
| 54 | Aubrey Huff | .15 | .40 |
| 55 | Luis Gonzalez | .15 | .40 |
| 56 | Brandon Webb | .15 | .40 |
| 57 | Troy Glaus | .15 | .40 |
| 58 | Shawn Green | .15 | .40 |
| 59 | Craig Counsell | .15 | .40 |
| 60 | Conor Jackson (RC) | .60 | 1.50 |
| 61 | Jeff Kent | .15 | .40 |
| 62 | Eric Gagne | .15 | .40 |
| 63 | J.D. Drew | .15 | .40 |
| 64 | Milton Bradley | .15 | .40 |
| 65 | Jeff Weaver | .15 | .40 |
| 66 | Cesar Izturis | .15 | .40 |
| 67 | Jason Schmidt | .15 | .40 |
| 68 | Moises Alou | .15 | .40 |
| 69 | Pedro Feliz | .15 | .40 |
| 70 | Randy Winn | .15 | .40 |
| 71 | Omar Vizquel | .25 | .60 |
| 72 | Noah Lowry | .15 | .40 |
| 73 | Travis Hafner | .15 | .40 |
| 74 | Victor Martinez | .15 | .40 |
| 75 | C.C. Sabathia | .15 | .40 |
| 76 | Grady Sizemore | .25 | .60 |
| 77 | Coco Crisp | .15 | .40 |
| 78 | Cliff Lee | .15 | .40 |
| 79 | Raul Ibañez | .25 | .60 |
| 80 | Ichiro Suzuki | .60 | 1.50 |
| 81 | Richie Sexson | .15 | .40 |

|  |  | | |
|---|--------|---|---|
| ☐ 82 | Felix Hernandez | .25 | .60 |
| ☐ 83 | Adrian Beltre | .15 | .40 |
| ☐ 84 | Jamie Moyer | .15 | .40 |
| ☐ 85 | Miguel Cabrera | .25 | .60 |
| ☐ 86 | A.J. Burnett | .15 | .40 |
| ☐ 87 | Juan Pierre | .15 | .40 |
| ☐ 88 | Carlos Delgado | .15 | .40 |
| ☐ 89 | Dontrelle Willis | .15 | .40 |
| ☐ 90 | Juan Encarnacion | .15 | .40 |
| ☐ 91 | Carlos Beltran | .15 | .40 |
| ☐ 92 | Jose Reyes | .40 | 1.00 |
| ☐ 93 | David Wright | .60 | 1.50 |
| ☐ 94 | Tom Glavine | .25 | .60 |
| ☐ 95 | Mike Piazza | .40 | 1.00 |
| ☐ 96 | Pedro Martinez | .25 | .60 |
| ☐ 97 | Ryan Zimmerman (RC) | 2.00 | 5.00 |
| ☐ 98 | Nick Johnson | .15 | .40 |
| ☐ 99 | Jose Vidro | .15 | .40 |
| ☐ 100 | Jose Guillen | .15 | .40 |
| ☐ 101 | Livan Hernandez | .15 | .40 |
| ☐ 102 | John Patterson | .15 | .40 |
| ☐ 103 | Miguel Tejada | .15 | .40 |
| ☐ 104 | Melvin Mora | .15 | .40 |
| ☐ 105 | Brian Roberts | .15 | .40 |
| ☐ 106 | Erik Bedard | .15 | .40 |
| ☐ 107 | Javy Lopez | .15 | .40 |
| ☐ 108 | Rodrigo Lopez | .15 | .40 |
| ☐ 109 | Jake Peavy | .15 | .40 |
| ☐ 110 | Mike Cameron | .15 | .40 |
| ☐ 111 | Mark Loretta | .15 | .40 |
| ☐ 112 | Brian Giles | .15 | .40 |
| ☐ 113 | Trevor Hoffman | .15 | .40 |
| ☐ 114 | Ramon Hernandez | .15 | .40 |
| ☐ 115 | Bobby Abreu | .15 | .40 |
| ☐ 116 | Chase Utley | .40 | 1.00 |
| ☐ 117 | Pat Burrell | .15 | .40 |
| ☐ 118 | Jimmy Rollins | .15 | .40 |
| ☐ 119 | Ryan Howard | .60 | 1.50 |
| ☐ 120 | Billy Wagner | .15 | .40 |
| ☐ 121 | Jason Bay | .15 | .40 |
| ☐ 122 | Oliver Perez | .15 | .40 |
| ☐ 123 | Jack Wilson | .15 | .40 |
| ☐ 124 | Zach Duke | .15 | .40 |
| ☐ 125 | Rob Mackowiak | .15 | .40 |
| ☐ 126 | Freddy Sanchez | .15 | .40 |
| ☐ 127 | Mark Teixeira | .25 | .60 |
| ☐ 128 | Michael Young | .15 | .40 |
| ☐ 129 | Alfonso Soriano | .15 | .40 |
| ☐ 130 | Hank Blalock | .15 | .40 |
| ☐ 131 | Kenny Rogers | .15 | .40 |
| ☐ 132 | Kevin Mench | .15 | .40 |
| ☐ 133 | Manny Ramirez | .25 | .60 |
| ☐ 134 | Josh Beckett | .15 | .40 |
| ☐ 135 | David Ortiz | .25 | .60 |
| ☐ 136 | Johnny Damon | .25 | .60 |
| ☐ 137 | Edgar Renteria | .15 | .40 |
| ☐ 138 | Curt Schilling | .25 | .60 |
| ☐ 139 | Ken Griffey Jr. | .60 | 1.50 |
| ☐ 140 | Adam Dunn | .15 | .40 |
| ☐ 141 | Felipe Lopez | .15 | .40 |
| ☐ 142 | Wily Mo Pena | .15 | .40 |
| ☐ 143 | Aaron Harang | .15 | .40 |
| ☐ 144 | Sean Casey | .15 | .40 |
| ☐ 145 | Todd Helton | .25 | .60 |
| ☐ 146 | Garrett Atkins | .15 | .40 |
| ☐ 147 | Matt Holliday | .40 | 1.00 |
| ☐ 148 | Jeff Francis | .15 | .40 |
| ☐ 149 | Clint Barmes | .15 | .40 |
| ☐ 150 | Luis Gonzalez | .15 | .40 |
| ☐ 151 | Mike Sweeney | .15 | .40 |
| ☐ 152 | Zack Greinke | .15 | .40 |
| ☐ 153 | Angel Berroa | .15 | .40 |
| ☐ 154 | Emil Brown | .15 | .40 |
| ☐ 155 | David DeJesus | .15 | .40 |
| ☐ 156 | Ivan Rodriguez | .25 | .60 |
| ☐ 157 | Jeremy Bonderman | .15 | .40 |
| ☐ 158 | Brandon Inge | .15 | .40 |
| ☐ 159 | Craig Monroe | .15 | .40 |
| ☐ 160 | Chris Shelton | .15 | .40 |
| ☐ 161 | Dmitri Young | .15 | .40 |
| ☐ 162 | Johan Santana | .25 | .60 |
| ☐ 163 | Joe Mauer | .40 | 1.00 |
| ☐ 164 | Torii Hunter | .15 | .40 |
| ☐ 165 | Shannon Stewart | .15 | .40 |
| ☐ 166 | Scott Baker | .15 | .40 |
| ☐ 167 | Brad Radke | .15 | .40 |
| ☐ 168 | Jon Garland | .15 | .40 |
| ☐ 169 | Tadahito Iguchi | .15 | .40 |
| ☐ 170 | Paul Konerko | .15 | .40 |
| ☐ 171 | Scott Podsednik | .15 | .40 |
| ☐ 172 | Mark Buehrle | .15 | .40 |
| ☐ 173 | Joe Crede | .15 | .40 |
| ☐ 174 | Derek Jeter | 1.00 | 2.50 |
| ☐ 175 | Alex Rodriguez | .60 | 1.50 |
| ☐ 176 | Hideki Matsui | .40 | 1.00 |
| ☐ 177 | Randy Johnson | .40 | 1.00 |
| ☐ 178 | Gary Sheffield | .15 | .40 |
| ☐ 179 | Mariano Rivera | .40 | 1.00 |
| ☐ 180 | Jason Giambi | .15 | .40 |
| ☐ 181 | Joey Devine RC | .40 | 1.00 |
| ☐ 182 | Alejandro Freire RC | .40 | 1.00 |
| ☐ 183 | Craig Hansen RC | .75 | 2.00 |
| ☐ 184 | Robert Andino RC | .40 | 1.00 |
| ☐ 185 | Ryan Jorgensen RC | .40 | 1.00 |
| ☐ 186 | Chris Demaria RC | .40 | 1.00 |
| ☐ 187 | Jonah Bayliss RC | .40 | 1.00 |
| ☐ 188 | Ryan Theriot RC | .30 | .75 |
| ☐ 189 | Steve Stemle RC | .40 | 1.00 |
| ☐ 190 | Brian Myrow RC | .40 | 1.00 |
| ☐ 191 | Chris Heintz RC | .40 | 1.00 |
| ☐ 192 | Ron Flores RC | .40 | 1.00 |
| ☐ 193 | Danny Sandoval RC | .40 | 1.00 |
| ☐ 194 | Craig Breslow RC | .40 | 1.00 |
| ☐ 195 | Jeremy Accardo RC | .40 | 1.00 |
| ☐ 196 | Jeff Harris RC | .40 | 1.00 |
| ☐ 197 | Tim Corcoran RC | .40 | 1.00 |
| ☐ 198 | Scott Feldman RC | .60 | 1.50 |
| ☐ 199 | Robinson Cano | .25 | .60 |
| ☐ 200 | Jason Bergmann RC | .75 | 2.00 |
| ☐ 201 | Ken Griffey Jr. RL13 | 3.00 | 8.00 |
| ☐ 202 | Frank Thomas RL13 | 2.00 | 5.00 |
| ☐ 203 | Chipper Jones RL13 | 2.00 | 5.00 |
| ☐ 204 | Tony Clark RL13 | .75 | 2.00 |
| ☐ 205 | Mike Lieberthal RL13 | .75 | 2.00 |
| ☐ 206 | Manny Ramirez RL13 | 1.25 | 3.00 |
| ☐ 207 | Phil Nevin RL13 | .75 | 2.00 |
| ☐ 208 | Derek Jeter RL13 | 4.00 | 10.00 |
| ☐ 209 | Preston Wilson RL13 | .75 | 2.00 |
| ☐ 210 | Billy Wagner RL13 | .75 | 2.00 |
| ☐ 211 | Alex Rodriguez RL13 | 3.00 | 8.00 |
| ☐ 212 | Trot Nixon RL13 | .75 | 2.00 |
| ☐ 213 | Jaret Wright RL13 | .75 | 2.00 |
| ☐ 214 | Nomar Garciaparra RL13 | 2.00 | 5.00 |
| ☐ 215 | Paul Konerko RL13 | .75 | 2.00 |
| ☐ 216 | Paul Wilson RL13 | .75 | 2.00 |
| ☐ 217 | Dustin Hermanson RL13 | .75 | 2.00 |
| ☐ 218 | Todd Walker RL13 | .75 | 2.00 |
| ☐ 219 | Matt Morris RL13 | .75 | 2.00 |
| ☐ 220 | Darin Erstad RL13 | .75 | 2.00 |
| ☐ 221 | Todd Helton RL13 | 1.25 | 3.00 |
| ☐ 222 | Geoff Jenkins RL13 | .75 | 2.00 |
| ☐ 223 | Eric Chavez RL13 | .75 | 2.00 |
| ☐ 224 | Kris Benson RL13 | .75 | 2.00 |
| ☐ 225 | Jon Garland RL13 | .75 | 2.00 |
| ☐ 226 | Troy Glaus RL13 | .75 | 2.00 |
| ☐ 227 | Vernon Wells RL13 | .75 | 2.00 |
| ☐ 228 | Michael Cuddyer RL13 | .75 | 2.00 |
| ☐ 229 | Justin Verlander RL13 | 3.00 | 8.00 |
| ☐ 230 | Pat Burrell RL13 | .75 | 2.00 |
| ☐ 231 | Mark Mulder RL13 | .75 | 2.00 |
| ☐ 232 | Corey Patterson RL13 | .75 | 2.00 |
| ☐ 233 | J.D. Drew RL13 | .75 | 2.00 |
| ☐ 234 | Austin Kearns RL13 | .60 | 1.50 |
| ☐ 235 | Felipe Lopez RL13 | .75 | 2.00 |
| ☐ 236 | Sean Burroughs RL13 | .75 | 2.00 |
| ☐ 237 | Ben Sheets RL13 | .75 | 2.00 |
| ☐ 238 | Brett Myers RL13 | .75 | 2.00 |
| ☐ 239 | Josh Beckett RL13 | .75 | 2.00 |
| ☐ 240 | Barry Zito RL13 | .75 | 2.00 |
| ☐ 241 | Adrian Gonzalez RL13 | .75 | 2.00 |
| ☐ 242 | Rocco Baldelli RL13 | .75 | 2.00 |
| ☐ 243 | Chris Burke RL13 | .75 | 2.00 |
| ☐ 244 | Joe Mauer RL13 | 2.00 | 5.00 |
| ☐ 245 | Mark Prior RL13 | 1.25 | 3.00 |
| ☐ 246 | Mark Teixeira RL13 | 1.25 | 3.00 |
| ☐ 247 | Khalil Greene RL13 | 1.25 | 3.00 |
| ☐ 248 | Zack Greinke RL13 | .75 | 2.00 |
| ☐ 249 | Prince Fielder RL13 | 3.00 | 8.00 |
| ☐ 250 | Rickie Weeks RL13 | .75 | 2.00 |
| ☐ 251 | Kenji Johjima | 6.00 | 15.00 |

## 2007 Ultra

| | | | |
|---|--------|---|---|
| ☐ | COMP.SET w/o RC's (200) | 20.00 | 50.00 |
| ☐ | COMMON CARD | .20 | .50 |
| ☐ | COMMON ROOKIE | 1.00 | 2.50 |
| ☐ | COMMON L13 | 1.00 | 2.50 |
| ☐ | PRINTING PLATE ODDS 1:1252 HOB/RET | | |
| ☐ | PLATE PRINT RUN 1 SET PER COLOR | | |
| ☐ | BLACK-CYAN-MAGENTA-YELLOW ISSUED | | |
| ☐ | NO PLATE PRICING DUE TO SCARCITY | | |
| ☐ 1 | Brandon Webb | .20 | .50 |
| ☐ 2 | Randy Johnson | .50 | 1.25 |
| ☐ 3 | Conor Jackson | .20 | .50 |
| ☐ 4 | Stephen Drew | .30 | .75 |
| ☐ 5 | Eric Byrnes | .20 | .50 |
| ☐ 6 | Carlos Quentin | .20 | .50 |
| ☐ 7 | Andruw Jones | .30 | .75 |
| ☐ 8 | Chipper Jones | .50 | 1.25 |
| ☐ 9 | Jeff Francoeur | .50 | 1.25 |
| ☐ 10 | Tim Hudson | .20 | .50 |
| ☐ 11 | John Smoltz | .30 | .75 |
| ☐ 12 | Edgar Renteria | .20 | .50 |
| ☐ 13 | Erik Bedard | .20 | .50 |
| ☐ 14 | Kris Benson | .20 | .50 |
| ☐ 15 | Miguel Tejada | .20 | .50 |
| ☐ 16 | Nick Markakis | .30 | .75 |
| ☐ 17 | Brian Roberts | .20 | .50 |
| ☐ 18 | Melvin Mora | .20 | .50 |
| ☐ 19 | Aubrey Huff | .20 | .50 |
| ☐ 20 | Curt Schilling | .30 | .75 |
| ☐ 21 | Jonathan Papelbon | .50 | 1.25 |
| ☐ 22 | Josh Beckett | .30 | .75 |
| ☐ 23 | Jason Varitek | .50 | 1.25 |
| ☐ 24 | David Ortiz | .30 | .75 |
| ☐ 25 | Manny Ramirez | .30 | .75 |
| ☐ 26 | J.D. Drew | .20 | .50 |
| ☐ 27 | Carlos Zambrano | .20 | .50 |
| ☐ 28 | Derrek Lee | .20 | .50 |
| ☐ 29 | Aramis Ramirez | .20 | .50 |
| ☐ 30 | Alfonso Soriano | .20 | .50 |
| ☐ 31 | Rich Hill | .20 | .50 |
| ☐ 32 | Jacque Jones | .20 | .50 |
| ☐ 33 | A.J. Pierzynski | .20 | .50 |
| ☐ 34 | Jermaine Dye | .20 | .50 |
| ☐ 35 | Paul Konerko | .20 | .50 |
| ☐ 36 | Bobby Jenks | .20 | .50 |
| ☐ 37 | Jon Garland | .20 | .50 |
| ☐ 38 | Mark Buehrle | .20 | .50 |
| ☐ 39 | Tadahito Iguchi | .20 | .50 |
| ☐ 40 | Adam Dunn | .20 | .50 |
| ☐ 41 | Ken Griffey Jr. | .75 | 2.00 |
| ☐ 42 | Aaron Harang | .20 | .50 |
| ☐ 43 | Bronson Arroyo | .20 | .50 |
| ☐ 44 | Ryan Freel | .20 | .50 |
| ☐ 45 | Brandon Phillips | .20 | .50 |
| ☐ 46 | Grady Sizemore | .30 | .75 |
| ☐ 47 | Travis Hafner | .20 | .50 |
| ☐ 48 | Victor Martinez | .20 | .50 |
| ☐ 49 | Jhonny Peralta | .20 | .50 |
| ☐ 50 | C.C. Sabathia | .20 | .50 |
| ☐ 51 | Jeremy Sowers | .20 | .50 |
| ☐ 52 | Ryan Garko | .20 | .50 |
| ☐ 53 | Garrett Atkins | .20 | .50 |
| ☐ 54 | Willy Taveras | .20 | .50 |
| ☐ 55 | Todd Helton | .30 | .75 |
| ☐ 56 | Jeff Francis | .20 | .50 |
| ☐ 57 | Brad Hawpe | .20 | .50 |
| ☐ 58 | Matt Holliday | .50 | 1.25 |
| ☐ 59 | Justin Verlander | .50 | 1.25 |
| ☐ 60 | Jeremy Bonderman | .20 | .50 |
| ☐ 61 | Maggio Ordonez | .30 | .75 |
| ☐ 62 | Ivan Rodriguez | .30 | .75 |
| ☐ 63 | Gary Sheffield | .20 | .50 |
| ☐ 64 | Kenny Rogers | .20 | .50 |

| | | |
|---|---|---|
| ❑ 65 Brandon Inge | .20 | .50 |
| ❑ 66 Anibal Sanchez | .20 | .50 |
| ❑ 67 Scott Olsen | .20 | .50 |
| ❑ 68 Dontrelle Willis | .20 | .50 |
| ❑ 69 Dan Uggla | .30 | .75 |
| ❑ 70 Hanley Ramirez | .30 | .75 |
| ❑ 71 Miguel Cabrera | .30 | .75 |
| ❑ 72 Jeremy Hermida | .20 | .50 |
| ❑ 73 Roy Oswalt | .20 | .50 |
| ❑ 74 Brad Lidge | .20 | .50 |
| ❑ 75 Lance Berkman | .20 | .50 |
| ❑ 76 Carlos Lee | .20 | .50 |
| ❑ 77 Morgan Ensberg | .20 | .50 |
| ❑ 78 Craig Biggio | .30 | .75 |
| ❑ 79 Reggie Sanders | .20 | .50 |
| ❑ 80 Mike Sweeney | .20 | .50 |
| ❑ 81 Mark Teahen | .20 | .50 |
| ❑ 82 John Buck | .20 | .50 |
| ❑ 83 Mark Grudzielanek | .20 | .50 |
| ❑ 84 Gary Matthews | .20 | .50 |
| ❑ 85 Vladimir Guerrero | .50 | 1.25 |
| ❑ 86 Garret Anderson | .20 | .50 |
| ❑ 87 Howie Kendrick | .30 | .75 |
| ❑ 88 Jered Weaver | .20 | .50 |
| ❑ 89 Chone Figgins | .20 | .50 |
| ❑ 90 Bartolo Colon | .20 | .50 |
| ❑ 91 Francisco Rodriguez | .20 | .50 |
| ❑ 92 Nomar Garciaparra | .50 | 1.25 |
| ❑ 93 Andre Ethier | .30 | .75 |
| ❑ 94 Rafael Furcal | .20 | .50 |
| ❑ 95 Jeff Kent | .20 | .50 |
| ❑ 96 Derek Lowe | .20 | .50 |
| ❑ 97 Jason Schmidt | .20 | .50 |
| ❑ 98 Takashi Saito | .20 | .50 |
| ❑ 99 Ben Sheets | .20 | .50 |
| ❑ 100 Prince Fielder | .50 | 1.25 |
| ❑ 101 Bill Hall | .20 | .50 |
| ❑ 102 Rickie Weeks | .20 | .50 |
| ❑ 103 Francisco Cordero | .20 | .50 |
| ❑ 104 J.J. Hardy | .20 | .50 |
| ❑ 105 Johan Santana | .30 | .75 |
| ❑ 106 Justin Morneau | .20 | .50 |
| ❑ 107 Joe Mauer | .50 | 1.25 |
| ❑ 108 Joe Nathan | .20 | .50 |
| ❑ 109 Torii Hunter | .20 | .50 |
| ❑ 110 Michael Cuddyer | .20 | .50 |
| ❑ 111 Boof Bonser | .20 | .50 |
| ❑ 112 Tom Glavine | .30 | .75 |
| ❑ 113 Pedro Martinez | .30 | .75 |
| ❑ 114 Billy Wagner | .20 | .50 |
| ❑ 115 Jose Reyes | .50 | 1.25 |
| ❑ 116 David Wright | .75 | 2.00 |
| ❑ 117 Carlos Delgado | .20 | .50 |
| ❑ 118 Carlos Beltran | .20 | .50 |
| ❑ 119 Alex Rodriguez | .75 | 2.00 |
| ❑ 120 Chien-Ming Wang | .50 | 1.25 |
| ❑ 121 Mariano Rivera | .50 | 1.25 |
| ❑ 122 Bobby Abreu | .20 | .50 |
| ❑ 123 Hideki Matsui | .50 | 1.25 |
| ❑ 124 Johnny Damon | .30 | .75 |
| ❑ 125 Robinson Cano | .30 | .75 |
| ❑ 126 Derek Jeter | 1.25 | 3.00 |
| ❑ 127 Nick Swisher | .20 | .50 |
| ❑ 128 Eric Chavez | .20 | .50 |
| ❑ 129 Jason Kendall | .20 | .50 |
| ❑ 130 Bobby Crosby | .20 | .50 |
| ❑ 131 Huston Street | .20 | .50 |
| ❑ 132 Dan Haren | .20 | .50 |
| ❑ 133 Rich Harden | .20 | .50 |
| ❑ 134 Mike Piazza | .50 | 1.25 |
| ❑ 135 Chase Utley | .50 | 1.25 |
| ❑ 136 Jimmy Rollins | .20 | .50 |
| ❑ 137 Aaron Rowand | .20 | .50 |
| ❑ 138 Jamie Moyer | .20 | .50 |
| ❑ 139 Cole Hamels | .50 | 1.25 |
| ❑ 140 Pat Burrell | .20 | .50 |
| ❑ 141 Ryan Howard | .75 | 2.00 |
| ❑ 142 Freddy Sanchez | .20 | .50 |
| ❑ 143 Zach Duke | .20 | .50 |
| ❑ 144 Ian Snell | .20 | .50 |
| ❑ 145 Jack Wilson | .20 | .50 |
| ❑ 146 Jason Bay | .30 | .75 |
| ❑ 147 Albert Pujols | 1.00 | 2.50 |
| ❑ 148 Scott Rolen | .20 | .50 |
| ❑ 149 Jim Edmonds | .30 | .75 |
| ❑ 150 Chris Carpenter | .20 | .50 |
| ❑ 151 Yadier Molina | .20 | .50 |
| ❑ 152 Adam Wainwright | .30 | .75 |

| | | |
|---|---|---|
| ❑ 153 David Eckstein | .20 | .50 |
| ❑ 154 Trevor Hoffman | .20 | .50 |
| ❑ 155 Brian Giles | .20 | .50 |
| ❑ 156 Adrian Gonzalez | .20 | .50 |
| ❑ 157 Jake Peavy | .20 | .50 |
| ❑ 158 Khalil Greene | .30 | .75 |
| ❑ 159 Chris Young | .20 | .50 |
| ❑ 160 Greg Maddux | .75 | 2.00 |
| ❑ 161 Mike Cameron | .20 | .50 |
| ❑ 162 Matt Cain | .30 | .75 |
| ❑ 163 Matt Morris | .20 | .50 |
| ❑ 164 Pedro Feliz | .20 | .50 |
| ❑ 165 Omar Vizquel | .30 | .75 |
| ❑ 166 Randy Winn | .20 | .50 |
| ❑ 167 Barry Zito | .20 | .50 |
| ❑ 168 Adrian Beltre | .20 | .50 |
| ❑ 169 Yuniesky Betancourt | .20 | .50 |
| ❑ 170 Richie Sexson | .20 | .50 |
| ❑ 171 Raul Ibanez | .30 | .75 |
| ❑ 172 Kenji Johjima | .50 | 1.25 |
| ❑ 173 Ichiro Suzuki | .75 | 2.00 |
| ❑ 174 Felix Hernandez | .30 | .75 |
| ❑ 175 Scott Kazmir | .30 | .75 |
| ❑ 176 Carl Crawford | .20 | .50 |
| ❑ 177 B.J. Upton | .20 | .50 |
| ❑ 178 James Shields | .20 | .50 |
| ❑ 179 Rocco Baldelli | .20 | .50 |
| ❑ 180 Jorge Cantu | .20 | .50 |
| ❑ 181 Ty Wigginton | .20 | .50 |
| ❑ 182 Mark Teixeira | .30 | .75 |
| ❑ 183 Hank Blalock | .20 | .50 |
| ❑ 184 Ian Kinsler | .20 | .50 |
| ❑ 185 Michael Young | .20 | .50 |
| ❑ 186 Vicente Padilla | .20 | .50 |
| ❑ 187 Akinori Otsuka | .20 | .50 |
| ❑ 188 Kenny Lofton | .20 | .50 |
| ❑ 189 A.J. Burnett | .20 | .50 |
| ❑ 190 Roy Halladay | .20 | .50 |
| ❑ 191 B.J. Ryan | .20 | .50 |
| ❑ 192 Vernon Wells | .20 | .50 |
| ❑ 193 Alex Rios | .20 | .50 |
| ❑ 194 Troy Glaus | .20 | .50 |
| ❑ 195 Frank Thomas | .50 | 1.25 |
| ❑ 196 Ryan Zimmerman | .50 | 1.25 |
| ❑ 197 Michael O'Connor | .20 | .50 |
| ❑ 198 Chad Cordero | .20 | .50 |
| ❑ 199 Nick Johnson | .20 | .50 |
| ❑ 200 Felipe Lopez | .20 | .50 |
| ❑ 201 Miguel Montero (RC) | 1.00 | 2.50 |
| ❑ 202 Doug Slaten RC | 1.00 | 2.50 |
| ❑ 203 Joseph Bisenius RC | 1.00 | 2.50 |
| ❑ 204 Jared Burton RC | 1.00 | 2.50 |
| ❑ 205 Kevin Cameron RC | 1.00 | 2.50 |
| ❑ 206 Matt Chico (RC) | 1.00 | 2.50 |
| ❑ 207 Chris Stewart RC | 1.00 | 2.50 |
| ❑ 208 Joe Smith RC | 1.00 | 2.50 |
| ❑ 209 Zack Segovia RC | 1.00 | 2.50 |
| ❑ 210 John Danks RC | 1.00 | 2.50 |
| ❑ 211 Lee Gardner (RC) | 1.00 | 2.50 |
| ❑ 212 Jeff Baker (RC) | 1.00 | 2.50 |
| ❑ 213 Jamie Burke (RC) | 1.00 | 2.50 |
| ❑ 214 Phil Hughes (RC) | 5.00 | 12.00 |
| ❑ 215 Mike Rabelo RC | 1.00 | 2.50 |
| ❑ 216 Jose Garcia RC | 1.00 | 2.50 |
| ❑ 217 Hector Gimenez (RC) | 1.00 | 2.50 |
| ❑ 218 Jesus Flores RC | 1.00 | 2.50 |
| ❑ 219 Brandon Morrow RC | 2.50 | 6.00 |
| ❑ 220 Hideki Okajima RC | 5.00 | 12.00 |
| ❑ 221 Jay Marshall RC | 1.00 | 2.50 |
| ❑ 222 Matt Lindstrom (RC) | 1.00 | 2.50 |
| ❑ 223 Juan Salas (RC) | 1.00 | 2.50 |
| ❑ 224 Juan Perez RC | 1.00 | 2.50 |
| ❑ 225 Sean Henn (RC) | 1.00 | 2.50 |
| ❑ 226 Travis Buck (RC) | 1.00 | 2.50 |
| ❑ 227 Gustavo Molina RC | 1.00 | 2.50 |
| ❑ 228 Hunter Pence (RC) | 5.00 | 12.00 |
| ❑ 229 Michael Bourn (RC) | 1.00 | 2.50 |
| ❑ 230 Brian Barden RC | 1.00 | 2.50 |
| ❑ 231 Don Kelly (RC) | 1.00 | 2.50 |
| ❑ 232 Joakim Soria RC | 1.00 | 2.50 |
| ❑ 233 Cesar Jimenez RC | 1.00 | 2.50 |
| ❑ 234 Levale Speigner RC | 1.00 | 2.50 |
| ❑ 235 Micah Owings (RC) | 1.00 | 2.50 |
| ❑ 236 Brian Stokes (RC) | 1.00 | 2.50 |
| ❑ 237 Joaquin Arias (RC) | 1.00 | 2.50 |
| ❑ 238 Josh Hamilton L13 (RC) | 2.50 | 6.00 |
| ❑ 239 Daisuke Matsuzaka L13 RC | 6.00 | 15.00 |
| ❑ 240 Alejandro De Aza L13 RC | 1.50 | 4.00 |

| | | |
|---|---|---|
| ❑ 241 Kory Casto L13 (RC) | 1.00 | 2.50 |
| ❑ 242 Troy Tulowitzki L13 (RC) | 2.50 | 6.00 |
| ❑ 243 Akinori Iwamura L13 RC | 2.50 | 6.00 |
| ❑ 244 Angel Sanchez L13 RC | 1.00 | 2.50 |
| ❑ 245 Ryan Braun L13 (RC) | 6.00 | 15.00 |
| ❑ 246 Alex Gordon L13 RC | 4.00 | 10.00 |
| ❑ 247 Elijah Dukes L13 RC | 1.50 | 4.00 |
| ❑ 248 Kei Igawa L13 RC | 2.50 | 6.00 |
| ❑ 249 Kevin Kouzmanoff L13 (RC) | 1.00 | 2.50 |
| ❑ 250 Delmon Young L13 (RC) | 1.50 | 4.00 |

## 1989 Upper Deck

Orel Hershiser

| | | |
|---|---|---|
| ❑ COMPLETE SET (800) | 40.00 | 80.00 |
| ❑ COMP.FACT.SET (800) | 50.00 | 100.00 |
| ❑ COMP.HI FACT.SET (100) | 4.00 | 10.00 |
| ❑ 1 Ken Griffey Jr. RC | 15.00 | 40.00 |
| ❑ 2 Luis Medina RC | .08 | .25 |
| ❑ 3 Tony Chance RC | .08 | .25 |
| ❑ 4 Dave Otto | .08 | .25 |
| ❑ 5 Sandy Alomar Jr. RC | .40 | 1.00 |
| ❑ 6 Rolando Roomes RC | .08 | .25 |
| ❑ 7 Dave West RC | .08 | .25 |
| ❑ 8 Cris Carpenter RC * | .08 | .25 |
| ❑ 9 Gregg Jefferies | .08 | .25 |
| ❑ 10 Doug Dascenzo RC | .08 | .25 |
| ❑ 11 Ron Jones RC | .08 | .25 |
| ❑ 12 Luis DeLosSantos RC | .08 | .25 |
| ❑ 13 Gary Sheffield RC | 2.00 | 5.00 |
| ❑ 13A Gary Sheffield ERR | 2.00 | 5.00 |
| ❑ 14 Mike Harkey RC | .08 | .25 |
| ❑ 15 Lance Blankenship RC | .08 | .25 |
| ❑ 16 William Brennan RC | .08 | .25 |
| ❑ 17 John Smoltz RC | 2.00 | 5.00 |
| ❑ 18 Ramon Martinez RC | .20 | .50 |
| ❑ 19 Mark Lemke RC | .40 | 1.00 |
| ❑ 20 Juan Bell RC | .08 | .25 |
| ❑ 21 Rey Palacios RC | .08 | .25 |
| ❑ 22 Felix Jose RC | .08 | .25 |
| ❑ 23 Van Snider RC | .08 | .25 |
| ❑ 24 Dante Bichette RC | .40 | 1.00 |
| ❑ 25 Randy Johnson RC | 3.00 | 8.00 |
| ❑ 26 Carlos Quintana RC | .08 | .25 |
| ❑ 27 Star Rookie CL | .08 | .25 |
| ❑ 28 Mike Schooler | .08 | .25 |
| ❑ 29 Randy St.Claire | .08 | .25 |
| ❑ 30 Jerald Clark RC | .08 | .25 |
| ❑ 31 Kevin Gross | .08 | .25 |
| ❑ 32 Dan Firova | .08 | .25 |
| ❑ 33 Jeff Calhoun | .08 | .25 |
| ❑ 34 Tommy Hinzo | .08 | .25 |
| ❑ 35 Ricky Jordan RC * | .20 | .50 |
| ❑ 36 Larry Parrish | .08 | .25 |
| ❑ 37 Bret Saberhagen UER | .15 | .40 |
| ❑ 38 Mike Smithson | .08 | .25 |
| ❑ 39 Dave Dravecky | .08 | .25 |
| ❑ 40 Ed Romero | .08 | .25 |
| ❑ 41 Jeff Musselman | .08 | .25 |
| ❑ 42 Ed Hearn | .08 | .25 |
| ❑ 43 Rance Mulliniks | .08 | .25 |
| ❑ 44 Jim Eisenreich | .08 | .25 |
| ❑ 45 Sil Campusano | .08 | .25 |
| ❑ 46 Mike Krukow | .08 | .25 |
| ❑ 47 Paul Gibson | .08 | .25 |
| ❑ 48 Mike LaCoss | .08 | .25 |
| ❑ 49 Larry Herndon | .08 | .25 |
| ❑ 50 Scott Garrelts | .08 | .25 |
| ❑ 51 Dwayne Henry | .08 | .25 |
| ❑ 52 Jim Acker | .08 | .25 |
| ❑ 53 Steve Sax | .08 | .25 |
| ❑ 54 Pete O'Brien | .08 | .25 |
| ❑ 55 Paul Runge | .08 | .25 |
| ❑ 56 Rick Rhoden | .08 | .25 |
| ❑ 57 John Dopson | .08 | .25 |
| ❑ 58 Casey Candaele UER | .08 | .25 |

| | | |
|---|---|---|
| (No stats for Astros for '88 | | |
| ☐ 59 Dave Righetti | .08 | .25 |
| ☐ 60 Joe Hesketh | .08 | .25 |
| ☐ 61 Frank DiPino | .08 | .25 |
| ☐ 62 Tim Laudner | .08 | .25 |
| ☐ 63 Jamie Moyer | .15 | .40 |
| ☐ 64 Fred Toliver | .08 | .25 |
| ☐ 65 Mitch Webster | .08 | .25 |
| ☐ 66 John Tudor | .15 | .40 |
| ☐ 67 John Cangelosi | .08 | .25 |
| ☐ 68 Mike Devereaux | .25 | .60 |
| ☐ 69 Brian Fisher | .08 | .25 |
| ☐ 70 Mike Marshall | .08 | .25 |
| ☐ 71 Zane Smith | .08 | .25 |
| ☐ 72A Brian Holton ERR | .40 | 1.00 |
| ☐ 72B Brian Holton COR | .15 | .40 |
| ☐ 73 Jose Guzman | .08 | .25 |
| ☐ 74 Rick Mahler | .08 | .25 |
| ☐ 75 John Shelby | .08 | .25 |
| ☐ 76 Jim Deshaies | .08 | .25 |
| ☐ 77 Bobby Meacham | .08 | .25 |
| ☐ 78 Bryn Smith | .08 | .25 |
| ☐ 79 Joaquin Andujar | .15 | .40 |
| ☐ 80 Richard Dotson | .08 | .25 |
| ☐ 81 Charlie Lea | .08 | .25 |
| ☐ 82 Calvin Schiraldi | .08 | .25 |
| ☐ 83 Les Straker | .08 | .25 |
| ☐ 84 Les Lancaster | .08 | .25 |
| ☐ 85 Allan Anderson | .08 | .25 |
| ☐ 86 Junior Ortiz | .08 | .25 |
| ☐ 87 Jesse Orosco | .08 | .25 |
| ☐ 88 Felix Fermin | .08 | .25 |
| ☐ 89 Dave Anderson | .08 | .25 |
| ☐ 90 Rafael Belliard UER (Born '61& not '51) | | |
| ☐ 91 Franklin Stubbs | .08 | .25 |
| ☐ 92 Cecil Espy | .08 | .25 |
| ☐ 93 Albert Hall | .08 | .25 |
| ☐ 94 Tim Leary | .08 | .25 |
| ☐ 95 Mitch Williams | .15 | .40 |
| ☐ 96 Tracy Jones | .08 | .25 |
| ☐ 97 Danny Darwin | .08 | .25 |
| ☐ 98 Gary Ward | .08 | .25 |
| ☐ 99 Neal Heaton | .08 | .25 |
| ☐ 100 Jim Pankovits | .08 | .25 |
| ☐ 101 Bill Doran | .08 | .25 |
| ☐ 102 Tim Wallach | .08 | .25 |
| ☐ 103 Joe Magrane | .08 | .25 |
| ☐ 104 Ozzie Virgil | .08 | .25 |
| ☐ 105 Alvin Davis | .08 | .25 |
| ☐ 106 Tom Brookens | .08 | .25 |
| ☐ 107 Shawon Dunston | .15 | .40 |
| ☐ 108 Tracy Woodson | .08 | .25 |
| ☐ 109 Nelson Liriano | .08 | .25 |
| ☐ 110 Devon White | .15 | .40 |
| ☐ 111 Steve Balboni | .08 | .25 |
| ☐ 112 Buddy Bell | .15 | .40 |
| ☐ 113 German Jimenez | .08 | .25 |
| ☐ 114 Ken Dayley | .08 | .25 |
| ☐ 115 Andres Galarraga | .15 | .40 |
| ☐ 116 Mike Scioscia | .15 | .40 |
| ☐ 117 Gary Pettis | .08 | .25 |
| ☐ 118 Ernie Whitt | .08 | .25 |
| ☐ 119 Bob Boone | .15 | .40 |
| ☐ 120 Ryne Sandberg | .60 | 1.50 |
| ☐ 121 Bruce Benedict | .08 | .25 |
| ☐ 122 Hubie Brooks | .08 | .25 |
| ☐ 123 Mike Moore | .08 | .25 |
| ☐ 124 Wallace Johnson | .08 | .25 |
| ☐ 125 Bob Horner | .15 | .40 |
| ☐ 126 Chili Davis | .15 | .40 |
| ☐ 127 Manny Trillo | .08 | .25 |
| ☐ 128 Chet Lemon | .15 | .40 |
| ☐ 129 John Cerutti | .08 | .25 |
| ☐ 130 Orel Hershiser | .15 | .40 |
| ☐ 131 Terry Pendleton | .15 | .40 |
| ☐ 132 Jeff Blauser | .08 | .25 |
| ☐ 133 Mike Fitzgerald | .08 | .25 |
| ☐ 134 Henry Cotto | .08 | .25 |
| ☐ 135 Gerald Young | .08 | .25 |
| ☐ 136 Luis Salazar | .08 | .25 |
| ☐ 137 Alejandro Pena | .08 | .25 |
| ☐ 138 Jack Howell | .08 | .25 |
| ☐ 139 Tony Fernandez | .08 | .25 |
| ☐ 140 Mark Grace | .40 | 1.00 |
| ☐ 141 Ken Caminiti | .25 | .60 |
| ☐ 142 Mike Jackson | .08 | .25 |
| ☐ 143 Larry McWilliams | .08 | .25 |
| ☐ 144 Andres Thomas | .08 | .25 |
| ☐ 145 Nolan Ryan 3X | 1.50 | 4.00 |
| ☐ 146 Mike Davis | .08 | .25 |
| ☐ 147 DeWayne Buice | .08 | .25 |
| ☐ 148 Jody Davis | .08 | .25 |
| ☐ 149 Jesse Barfield | .15 | .40 |
| ☐ 150 Matt Nokes | .08 | .25 |
| ☐ 151 Jerry Reuss | .08 | .25 |
| ☐ 152 Rick Cerone | .08 | .25 |
| ☐ 153 Storm Davis | .08 | .25 |
| ☐ 154 Marvell Wynne | .08 | .25 |
| ☐ 155 Will Clark | .25 | .60 |
| ☐ 156 Luis Aguayo | .08 | .25 |
| ☐ 157 Willie Upshaw | .08 | .25 |
| ☐ 158 Randy Bush | .08 | .25 |
| ☐ 159 Ron Darling | .15 | .40 |
| ☐ 160 Kal Daniels | .08 | .25 |
| ☐ 161 Spike Owen | .08 | .25 |
| ☐ 162 Luis Polonia | .08 | .25 |
| ☐ 163 Kevin Mitchell UER | .15 | .40 |
| ☐ 164 Dave Gallagher | .08 | .25 |
| ☐ 165 Benito Santiago | .15 | .40 |
| ☐ 166 Greg Gagne | .08 | .25 |
| ☐ 167 Ken Phelps | .08 | .25 |
| ☐ 168 Sid Fernandez | .08 | .25 |
| ☐ 169 Bo Diaz | .08 | .25 |
| ☐ 170 Cory Snyder | .08 | .25 |
| ☐ 171 Eric Show | .08 | .25 |
| ☐ 172 Robby Thompson | .08 | .25 |
| ☐ 173 Marty Barrett | .08 | .25 |
| ☐ 174 Dave Henderson | .08 | .25 |
| ☐ 175 Ozzie Guillen | .15 | .40 |
| ☐ 176 Barry Lyons | .08 | .25 |
| ☐ 177 Kelvin Torve | .08 | .25 |
| ☐ 178 Don Slaught | .08 | .25 |
| ☐ 179 Steve Lombardozzi | .08 | .25 |
| ☐ 180 Chris Sabo RC * | .40 | 1.00 |
| ☐ 181 Jose Uribe | .08 | .25 |
| ☐ 182 Shane Mack | .08 | .25 |
| ☐ 183 Ron Karkovice | .08 | .25 |
| ☐ 184 Todd Benzinger | .08 | .25 |
| ☐ 185 Dave Stewart | .15 | .40 |
| ☐ 186 Julio Franco | .15 | .40 |
| ☐ 187 Ron Robinson | .08 | .25 |
| ☐ 188 Wally Backman | .08 | .25 |
| ☐ 189 Randy Velarde | .08 | .25 |
| ☐ 190 Joe Carter | .15 | .40 |
| ☐ 191 Bob Welch | .15 | .40 |
| ☐ 192 Kelly Paris | .08 | .25 |
| ☐ 193 Chris Brown | .08 | .25 |
| ☐ 194 Rick Reuschel | .15 | .40 |
| ☐ 195 Roger Clemens | .75 | 2.00 |
| ☐ 196 Dave Concepcion | .08 | .25 |
| ☐ 197 Al Newman | .08 | .25 |
| ☐ 198 Brook Jacoby | .08 | .25 |
| ☐ 199 Mookie Wilson | .15 | .40 |
| ☐ 200 Don Mattingly | 1.00 | 2.50 |
| ☐ 201 Dick Schofield | .08 | .25 |
| ☐ 202 Mark Gubicza | .08 | .25 |
| ☐ 203 Gary Gaetti | .08 | .25 |
| ☐ 204 Dan Pasqua | .08 | .25 |
| ☐ 205 Andre Dawson | .25 | .60 |
| ☐ 206 Chris Speier | .08 | .25 |
| ☐ 207 Kent Tekulve | .08 | .25 |
| ☐ 208 Rod Scurry | .08 | .25 |
| ☐ 209 Scott Bailes | .08 | .25 |
| ☐ 210 Rickey Henderson | .40 | 1.00 |
| ☐ 211 Harold Baines | .15 | .40 |
| ☐ 212 Tony Armas | .15 | .40 |
| ☐ 213 Kent Hrbek | .15 | .40 |
| ☐ 214 Darrin Jackson | .15 | .40 |
| ☐ 215 George Brett | 1.00 | 2.50 |
| ☐ 216 Rafael Santana | .08 | .25 |
| ☐ 217 Andy Allanson | .08 | .25 |
| ☐ 218 Brett Butler | .15 | .40 |
| ☐ 219 Steve Jeltz | .08 | .25 |
| ☐ 220 Jay Buhner | .15 | .40 |
| ☐ 221 Bo Jackson | .40 | 1.00 |
| ☐ 222 Angel Salazar | .08 | .25 |
| ☐ 223 Kirk McCaskill | .08 | .25 |
| ☐ 224 Steve Lyons | .08 | .25 |
| ☐ 225 Bert Blyleven | .15 | .40 |
| ☐ 226 Scott Bradley | .08 | .25 |
| ☐ 227 Bob Melvin | .08 | .25 |
| ☐ 228 Ron Kittle | .08 | .25 |
| ☐ 229 Phil Bradley | .08 | .25 |
| ☐ 230 Tommy John | .15 | .40 |
| ☐ 231 Greg Walker | .08 | .25 |
| ☐ 232 Juan Berenguer | .08 | .25 |
| ☐ 233 Pat Tabler | .08 | .25 |
| ☐ 234 Terry Clark | .08 | .25 |
| ☐ 235 Rafael Palmeiro | .40 | 1.00 |
| ☐ 236 Paul Zuvella | .08 | .25 |
| ☐ 237 Willie Randolph | .15 | .40 |
| ☐ 238 Bruce Fields | .08 | .25 |
| ☐ 239 Mike Aldrete | .08 | .25 |
| ☐ 240 Lance Parrish | .15 | .40 |
| ☐ 241 Greg Maddux | 1.00 | 2.50 |
| ☐ 242 John Moses | .08 | .25 |
| ☐ 243 Melido Perez | .08 | .25 |
| ☐ 244 Willie Wilson | .15 | .40 |
| ☐ 245 Mark McLemore | .08 | .25 |
| ☐ 246 Von Hayes | .08 | .25 |
| ☐ 247 Matt Williams | .40 | 1.00 |
| ☐ 248 John Candelaria UER (Listed as Yankee for part o | .08 | .25 |
| ☐ 249 Harold Reynolds | .15 | .40 |
| ☐ 250 Greg Swindell | .08 | .25 |
| ☐ 251 Juan Agosto | .08 | .25 |
| ☐ 252 Mike Felder | .08 | .25 |
| ☐ 253 Vince Coleman | .08 | .25 |
| ☐ 254 Larry Sheets | .08 | .25 |
| ☐ 255 George Bell | .15 | .40 |
| ☐ 256 Terry Steinbach | .15 | .40 |
| ☐ 257 Jack Armstrong RC * | .20 | .50 |
| ☐ 258 Dickie Thon | .08 | .25 |
| ☐ 259 Ray Knight | .15 | .40 |
| ☐ 260 Darryl Strawberry | .15 | .40 |
| ☐ 261 Doug Sisk | .08 | .25 |
| ☐ 262 Alex Trevino | .08 | .25 |
| ☐ 263 Jeffrey Leonard | .08 | .25 |
| ☐ 264 Tom Henke | .08 | .25 |
| ☐ 265 Ozzie Smith | .60 | 1.50 |
| ☐ 266 Dave Bergman | .08 | .25 |
| ☐ 267 Tony Phillips | .08 | .25 |
| ☐ 268 Mark Davis | .08 | .25 |
| ☐ 269 Kevin Elster | .08 | .25 |
| ☐ 270 Barry Larkin | .25 | .60 |
| ☐ 271 Manny Lee | .08 | .25 |
| ☐ 272 Tom Brunansky | .08 | .25 |
| ☐ 273 Craig Biggio RC | 2.50 | 6.00 |
| ☐ 274 Jim Gantner | .08 | .25 |
| ☐ 275 Eddie Murray | .40 | 1.00 |
| ☐ 276 Jeff Reed | .08 | .25 |
| ☐ 277 Tim Teufel | .08 | .25 |
| ☐ 278 Rick Honeycutt | .08 | .25 |
| ☐ 279 Guillermo Hernandez | .08 | .25 |
| ☐ 280 John Kruk | .15 | .40 |
| ☐ 281 Luis Alicea RC * | .20 | .50 |
| ☐ 282 Jim Clancy | .08 | .25 |
| ☐ 283 Billy Ripken | .08 | .25 |
| ☐ 284 Craig Reynolds | .08 | .25 |
| ☐ 285 Robin Yount | .60 | 1.50 |
| ☐ 286 Jimmy Jones | .08 | .25 |
| ☐ 287 Ron Oester | .08 | .25 |
| ☐ 288 Terry Leach | .08 | .25 |
| ☐ 289 Dennis Eckersley | .25 | .60 |
| ☐ 290 Alan Trammell | .15 | .40 |
| ☐ 291 Jimmy Key | .15 | .40 |
| ☐ 292 Chris Bosio | .08 | .25 |
| ☐ 293 Jose DeLeon | .08 | .25 |
| ☐ 294 Jim Traber | .08 | .25 |
| ☐ 295 Mike Scott | .15 | .40 |
| ☐ 296 Roger McDowell | .08 | .25 |
| ☐ 297 Garry Templeton | .15 | .40 |
| ☐ 298 Doyle Alexander | .08 | .25 |
| ☐ 299 Nick Esasky | .08 | .25 |
| ☐ 300 Mark McGwire | 2.00 | 5.00 |
| ☐ 301 Darryl Hamilton RC * | .20 | .50 |
| ☐ 302 Dave Smith | .08 | .25 |
| ☐ 303 Rick Sutcliffe | .15 | .40 |
| ☐ 304 Dave Stapleton | .08 | .25 |
| ☐ 305 Alan Ashby | .08 | .25 |
| ☐ 306 Pedro Guerrero | .15 | .40 |
| ☐ 307 Ron Guidry | .15 | .40 |
| ☐ 308 Steve Farr | .08 | .25 |
| ☐ 309 Curt Ford | .08 | .25 |
| ☐ 310 Claudell Washington | .08 | .25 |
| ☐ 311 Tom Prince | .08 | .25 |
| ☐ 312 Chad Kreuter RC | .20 | .50 |
| ☐ 313 Ken Oberkfell | .08 | .25 |
| ☐ 314 Jerry Browne | .08 | .25 |
| ☐ 315 R.J. Reynolds | .08 | .25 |
| ☐ 316 Scott Bankhead | .08 | .25 |

|  |  | | |
|---|---|---|---|
| ☐ 317 | Milt Thompson | .08 | .25 |
| ☐ 318 | Mario Diaz | .06 | .25 |
| ☐ 319 | Bruce Ruffin | .06 | .25 |
| ☐ 320 | Dave Valle | .08 | .25 |
| ☐ 321A | Gary Varsho ERR | .75 | 2.00 |
| ☐ 321B | Gary Varsho COR | | |
| | (In road uniform) | .08 | .25 |
| ☐ 322 | Paul Mirabella | .08 | .25 |
| ☐ 323 | Chuck Jackson | .08 | .25 |
| ☐ 324 | Drew Hall | .08 | .25 |
| ☐ 325 | Don August | .08 | .25 |
| ☐ 326 | Israel Sanchez | .08 | .25 |
| ☐ 327 | Denny Walling | .08 | .25 |
| ☐ 328 | Joel Skinner | .08 | .25 |
| ☐ 329 | Danny Tartabull | .08 | .25 |
| ☐ 330 | Tony Pena | .08 | .25 |
| ☐ 331 | Jim Sundberg | .15 | .40 |
| ☐ 332 | Jeff D. Robinson | .06 | .25 |
| ☐ 333 | Oddibe McDowell | .06 | .25 |
| ☐ 334 | Jose Lind | .08 | .25 |
| ☐ 335 | Paul Kilgus | .08 | .25 |
| ☐ 336 | Juan Samuel | .08 | .25 |
| ☐ 337 | Mike Campbell | .08 | .25 |
| ☐ 338 | Mike Maddux | .08 | .25 |
| ☐ 339 | Darnell Coles | .08 | .25 |
| ☐ 340 | Bob Dernier | .08 | .25 |
| ☐ 341 | Rafael Ramirez | .08 | .25 |
| ☐ 342 | Scott Sanderson | .08 | .25 |
| ☐ 343 | B.J. Surhoff | .15 | .40 |
| ☐ 344 | Billy Hatcher | .08 | .25 |
| ☐ 345 | Pat Perry | .08 | .25 |
| ☐ 346 | Jack Clark | .15 | .40 |
| ☐ 347 | Gary Thurman | .08 | .25 |
| ☐ 348 | Tim Jones | .08 | .25 |
| ☐ 349 | Dave Winfield | .15 | .40 |
| ☐ 350 | Frank White | .15 | .40 |
| ☐ 351 | Dave Collins | .08 | .25 |
| ☐ 352 | Jack Morris | .15 | .40 |
| ☐ 353 | Eric Plunk | .08 | .25 |
| ☐ 354 | Leon Durham | .08 | .25 |
| ☐ 355 | Ivan DeJesus | .08 | .25 |
| ☐ 356 | Brian Holman RC * | .08 | .25 |
| ☐ 357A | Dale Murphy RevNeg | 12.50 | 30.00 |
| ☐ 357B | Dale Murphy COR | .25 | .60 |
| ☐ 358 | Mark Portugal | .08 | .25 |
| ☐ 359 | Andy McGaffigan | .08 | .25 |
| ☐ 360 | Tom Glavine | .40 | 1.00 |
| ☐ 361 | Keith Moreland | .08 | .25 |
| ☐ 362 | Todd Stottlemyre | .08 | .25 |
| ☐ 363 | Dave Leiper | .08 | .25 |
| ☐ 364 | Cecil Fielder | .15 | .40 |
| ☐ 365 | Carmelo Martinez | .08 | .25 |
| ☐ 366 | Dwight Evans | .25 | .60 |
| ☐ 367 | Kevin McReynolds | .08 | .25 |
| ☐ 368 | Rich Gedman | .08 | .25 |
| ☐ 369 | Len Dykstra | .15 | .40 |
| ☐ 370 | Jody Reed | .08 | .25 |
| ☐ 371 | Jose Canseco | .40 | 1.00 |
| ☐ 372 | Rob Murphy | .08 | .25 |
| ☐ 373 | Mike Henneman | .08 | .25 |
| ☐ 374 | Walt Weiss | .08 | .25 |
| ☐ 375 | Rob Dibble RC | .40 | 1.00 |
| ☐ 376 | Kirby Puckett | .40 | 1.00 |
| ☐ 377 | Dennis Martinez | .15 | .40 |
| ☐ 378 | Ron Gant | .15 | .40 |
| ☐ 379 | Brian Harper | .08 | .25 |
| ☐ 380 | Nelson Santovenia | .08 | .25 |
| ☐ 381 | Lloyd Moseby | .08 | .25 |
| ☐ 382 | Lance McCullers | .08 | .25 |
| ☐ 383 | Dave Stieb | .15 | .40 |
| ☐ 384 | Tony Gwynn | .50 | 1.25 |
| ☐ 385 | Mike Flanagan | .08 | .25 |
| ☐ 386 | Bob Ojeda | .08 | .25 |
| ☐ 387 | Bruce Hurst | .08 | .25 |
| ☐ 388 | Dave Magadan | .08 | .25 |
| ☐ 389 | Wade Boggs | .25 | .60 |
| ☐ 390 | Gary Carter | .15 | .40 |
| ☐ 391 | Frank Tanana | .15 | .40 |
| ☐ 392 | Curt Young | .08 | .25 |
| ☐ 393 | Jeff Treadway | .08 | .25 |
| ☐ 394 | Darrell Evans | .15 | .40 |
| ☐ 395 | Glenn Hubbard | .08 | .25 |
| ☐ 396 | Chuck Cary | .08 | .25 |
| ☐ 397 | Frank Viola | .15 | .40 |
| ☐ 398 | Jeff Parrett | .08 | .25 |
| ☐ 399 | Terry Blocker | .08 | .25 |
| ☐ 400 | Dan Gladden | .08 | .25 |
| ☐ 401 | Louie Meadows | .08 | .25 |
| ☐ 402 | Tim Raines | .15 | .40 |
| ☐ 403 | Joey Meyer | .08 | .25 |
| ☐ 404 | Larry Andersen | .08 | .25 |
| ☐ 405 | Rex Hudler | .08 | .25 |
| ☐ 406 | Mike Schmidt | .75 | 2.00 |
| ☐ 407 | John Franco | .15 | .40 |
| ☐ 408 | Brady Anderson RC | .40 | 1.00 |
| ☐ 409 | Don Carman | .08 | .25 |
| ☐ 410 | Eric Davis | .15 | .40 |
| ☐ 411 | Bob Stanley | .08 | .25 |
| ☐ 412 | Pete Smith | .08 | .25 |
| ☐ 413 | Jim Rice | .15 | .40 |
| ☐ 414 | Bruce Sutter | .15 | .40 |
| ☐ 415 | Oil Can Boyd | .08 | .25 |
| ☐ 416 | Ruben Sierra | .15 | .40 |
| ☐ 417 | Mike LaValliere | .08 | .25 |
| ☐ 418 | Steve Buechele | .08 | .25 |
| ☐ 419 | Gary Redus | .08 | .25 |
| ☐ 420 | Scott Fletcher | .08 | .25 |
| ☐ 421 | Dale Sveum | .08 | .25 |
| ☐ 422 | Bob Knepper | .08 | .25 |
| ☐ 423 | Luis Rivera | .08 | .25 |
| ☐ 424 | Ted Higuera | .08 | .25 |
| ☐ 425 | Kevin Bass | .08 | .25 |
| ☐ 426 | Ken Gerhart | .08 | .25 |
| ☐ 427 | Shane Rawley | .08 | .25 |
| ☐ 428 | Paul O'Neill | .25 | .60 |
| ☐ 429 | Joe Orsulak | .08 | .25 |
| ☐ 430 | Jackie Gutierrez | .08 | .25 |
| ☐ 431 | Gerald Perry | .08 | .25 |
| ☐ 432 | Mike Greenwell | .25 | .60 |
| ☐ 433 | Jerry Royster | .08 | .25 |
| ☐ 434 | Ellis Burks | .15 | .40 |
| ☐ 435 | Ed Olwine | .08 | .25 |
| ☐ 436 | Dave Rucker | .08 | .25 |
| ☐ 437 | Charlie Hough | .15 | .40 |
| ☐ 438 | Bob Walk | .08 | .25 |
| ☐ 439 | Bob Brower | .08 | .25 |
| ☐ 440 | Barry Bonds | 2.00 | 5.00 |
| ☐ 441 | Tom Foley | .08 | .25 |
| ☐ 442 | Rob Deer | .08 | .25 |
| ☐ 443 | Glenn Davis | .08 | .25 |
| ☐ 444 | Dave Martinez | .08 | .25 |
| ☐ 445 | Bill Wegman | .08 | .25 |
| ☐ 446 | Lloyd McClendon | .08 | .25 |
| ☐ 447 | Dave Schmidt | .08 | .25 |
| ☐ 448 | Darren Daulton | .15 | .40 |
| ☐ 449 | Frank Williams | .08 | .25 |
| ☐ 450 | Don Aase | .08 | .25 |
| ☐ 451 | Lou Whitaker | .15 | .40 |
| ☐ 452 | Rich Gossage | .15 | .40 |
| ☐ 453 | Ed Whitson | .08 | .25 |
| ☐ 454 | Jim Walewander | .08 | .25 |
| ☐ 455 | Damon Berryhill | .08 | .25 |
| ☐ 456 | Tim Burke | .08 | .25 |
| ☐ 457 | Barry Jones | .08 | .25 |
| ☐ 458 | Joel Youngblood | .08 | .25 |
| ☐ 459 | Floyd Youmans | .08 | .25 |
| ☐ 460 | Mark Salas | .08 | .25 |
| ☐ 461 | Jeff Russell | .08 | .25 |
| ☐ 462 | Darrell Miller | .08 | .25 |
| ☐ 463 | Jeff Kunkel | .08 | .25 |
| ☐ 464 | Sherman Corbett | .08 | .25 |
| ☐ 465 | Curtis Wilkerson | .08 | .25 |
| ☐ 466 | Bud Black | .08 | .25 |
| ☐ 467 | Cal Ripken | 1.25 | 3.00 |
| ☐ 468 | John Farrell | .08 | .25 |
| ☐ 469 | Terry Kennedy | .08 | .25 |
| ☐ 470 | Tom Candiotti | .08 | .25 |
| ☐ 471 | Roberto Alomar | .40 | 1.00 |
| ☐ 472 | Jeff M. Robinson | .08 | .25 |
| ☐ 473 | Vance Law | .08 | .25 |
| ☐ 474 | Randy Ready UER | .08 | .25 |
| ☐ 475 | Walt Terrell | .08 | .25 |
| ☐ 476 | Kelly Downs | .08 | .25 |
| ☐ 477 | Johnny Paredes | .08 | .25 |
| ☐ 478 | Shawn Hillegas | .08 | .25 |
| ☐ 479 | Bob Brenly | .08 | .25 |
| ☐ 480 | Otis Nixon | .15 | .40 |
| ☐ 481 | Johnny Ray | .08 | .25 |
| ☐ 482 | Geno Petralli | .08 | .25 |
| ☐ 483 | Stu Cliburn | .08 | .25 |
| ☐ 484 | Pete Incaviglia | .08 | .25 |
| ☐ 485 | Brian Downing | .15 | .40 |
| ☐ 486 | Jeff Stone | .08 | .25 |
| ☐ 487 | Carmen Castillo | .08 | .25 |
| ☐ 488 | Tom Niedenfuer | .08 | .25 |
| ☐ 489 | Jay Bell | .15 | .40 |
| ☐ 490 | Rick Schu | .08 | .25 |
| ☐ 491 | Jeff Pico | .08 | .25 |
| ☐ 492 | Mark Parent | .08 | .25 |
| ☐ 493 | Eric King | .08 | .25 |
| ☐ 494 | Al Nipper | .08 | .25 |
| ☐ 495 | Andy Hawkins | .08 | .25 |
| ☐ 496 | Daryl Boston | .08 | .25 |
| ☐ 497 | Ernie Riles | .08 | .25 |
| ☐ 498 | Pascual Perez | .08 | .25 |
| ☐ 499 | Bill Long UER | | |
| | (Games started total | | |
| | 70% should be | | |
| | 708 should be | .08 | .25 |
| ☐ 500 | Kirt Manwaring | .08 | .25 |
| ☐ 501 | Chuck Crim | .08 | .25 |
| ☐ 502 | Candy Maldonado | .08 | .25 |
| ☐ 503 | Dennis Lamp | .08 | .25 |
| ☐ 504 | Glenn Braggs | .08 | .25 |
| ☐ 505 | Joe Price | .08 | .25 |
| ☐ 506 | Ken Williams | .08 | .25 |
| ☐ 507 | Bill Pecota | .08 | .25 |
| ☐ 508 | Rey Quinones | .08 | .25 |
| ☐ 509 | Jeff Bittiger | .08 | .25 |
| ☐ 510 | Kevin Seitzer | .08 | .25 |
| ☐ 511 | Steve Bedrosian | .08 | .25 |
| ☐ 512 | Todd Worrell | .08 | .25 |
| ☐ 513 | Chris James | .08 | .25 |
| ☐ 514 | Jose Oquendo | .08 | .25 |
| ☐ 515 | David Palmer | .08 | .25 |
| ☐ 516 | John Smiley | .08 | .25 |
| ☐ 517 | Dave Clark | .08 | .25 |
| ☐ 518 | Mike Dunne | .08 | .25 |
| ☐ 519 | Ron Washington | .08 | .25 |
| ☐ 520 | Bob Kipper | .08 | .25 |
| ☐ 521 | Lee Smith | .15 | .40 |
| ☐ 522 | Juan Castillo | .08 | .25 |
| ☐ 523 | Don Robinson | .08 | .25 |
| ☐ 524 | Kevin Romine | .08 | .25 |
| ☐ 525 | Paul Molitor | .15 | .40 |
| ☐ 526 | Mark Langston | .08 | .25 |
| ☐ 527 | Donnie Hill | .08 | .25 |
| ☐ 528 | Larry Owen | .08 | .25 |
| ☐ 529 | Jerry Reed | .08 | .25 |
| ☐ 530 | Jack McDowell | .15 | .40 |
| ☐ 531 | Greg Mathews | .08 | .25 |
| ☐ 532 | John Russell | .08 | .25 |
| ☐ 533 | Dan Quisenberry | .08 | .25 |
| ☐ 534 | Greg Gross | .08 | .25 |
| ☐ 535 | Danny Cox | .08 | .25 |
| ☐ 536 | Terry Francona | .15 | .40 |
| ☐ 537 | Andy Van Slyke | .25 | .60 |
| ☐ 538 | Mel Hall | .08 | .25 |
| ☐ 539 | Jim Gott | .08 | .25 |
| ☐ 540 | Doug Jones | .08 | .25 |
| ☐ 541 | Craig Lefferts | .08 | .25 |
| ☐ 542 | Mike Boddicker | .08 | .25 |
| ☐ 543 | Greg Brock | .08 | .25 |
| ☐ 544 | Atlee Hammaker | .08 | .25 |
| ☐ 545 | Tom Bolton | .08 | .25 |
| ☐ 546 | Mike Macfarlane RC * | .20 | .50 |
| ☐ 547 | Rich Renteria | .08 | .25 |
| ☐ 548 | John Davis | .08 | .25 |
| ☐ 549 | Floyd Bannister | .08 | .25 |
| ☐ 550 | Mickey Brantley | .08 | .25 |
| ☐ 551 | Duane Ward | .08 | .25 |
| ☐ 552 | Dan Petry | .08 | .25 |
| ☐ 553 | Mickey Tettleton | .25 | .60 |
| ☐ 554 | Rick Leach | .08 | .25 |
| ☐ 555 | Mike Witt | .08 | .25 |
| ☐ 556 | Sid Bream | .08 | .25 |
| ☐ 557 | Bobby Witt | .15 | .40 |
| ☐ 558 | Tommy Herr | .08 | .25 |
| ☐ 559 | Randy Milligan | .08 | .25 |
| ☐ 560 | Jose Cecena | .08 | .25 |
| ☐ 561 | Mackey Sasser | .08 | .25 |
| ☐ 562 | Carney Lansford | .15 | .40 |
| ☐ 563 | Rick Aguilera | .15 | .40 |
| ☐ 564 | Ron Hassey | .08 | .25 |
| ☐ 565 | Dwight Gooden | .15 | .40 |
| ☐ 566 | Paul Assenmacher | .08 | .25 |
| ☐ 567 | Neil Allen | .08 | .25 |
| ☐ 568 | Jim Morrison | .08 | .25 |
| ☐ 569 | Mike Pagliarulo | .08 | .25 |
| ☐ 570 | Ted Simmons | .15 | .40 |
| ☐ 571 | Mark Thurmond | .08 | .25 |
| ☐ 572 | Fred McGriff | .25 | .60 |
| ☐ 573 | Wally Joyner | .15 | .40 |
| ☐ 574 | Jose Bautista RC | .08 | .25 |
| ☐ 575 | Kelly Gruber | .08 | .25 |

|  |  | | |
|---|---|---|---|
| ❏ 576 | Cecilio Guante | .08 | .25 |
| ❏ 577 | Mark Davidson | .08 | .25 |
| ❏ 578 | Bobby Bonilla UER | .15 | .40 |
| ❏ 579 | Mike Stanley | .08 | .25 |
| ❏ 580 | Gene Larkin | .08 | .25 |
| ❏ 581 | Stan Javier | .08 | .25 |
| ❏ 582 | Howard Johnson | .15 | .40 |
| ❏ 583A | Mike Gallego Rev Ng | .40 | 1.00 |
| ❏ 583B | Mike Gallego COR | .40 | 1.00 |
| ❏ 584 | David Cone | .15 | .40 |
| ❏ 585 | Doug Jennings | .08 | .25 |
| ❏ 586 | Charles Hudson | .08 | .25 |
| ❏ 587 | Dion James | .08 | .25 |
| ❏ 588 | Al Leiter | .40 | 1.00 |
| ❏ 589 | Charlie Puleo | .08 | .25 |
| ❏ 590 | Roberto Kelly | .08 | .25 |
| ❏ 591 | Thad Bosley | .08 | .25 |
| ❏ 592 | Pete Stanicek | .08 | .25 |
| ❏ 593 | Pat Borders RC * | .20 | .50 |
| ❏ 594 | Bryan Harvey RC * | .20 | .50 |
| ❏ 595 | Jeff Ballard | .08 | .25 |
| ❏ 596 | Jeff Reardon | .15 | .40 |
| ❏ 597 | Doug Drabek | .08 | .25 |
| ❏ 598 | Edwin Correa | .08 | .25 |
| ❏ 599 | Keith Atherton | .08 | .25 |
| ❏ 600 | Dave LaPoint | .08 | .25 |
| ❏ 601 | Don Baylor | .15 | .40 |
| ❏ 602 | Tom Pagnozzi | .08 | .25 |
| ❏ 603 | Tim Flannery | .08 | .25 |
| ❏ 604 | Gene Walter | .08 | .25 |
| ❏ 605 | Dave Parker | .15 | .40 |
| ❏ 606 | Mike Diaz | .08 | .25 |
| ❏ 607 | Chris Gwynn | .08 | .25 |
| ❏ 608 | Odell Jones | .08 | .25 |
| ❏ 609 | Carlton Fisk | .25 | .60 |
| ❏ 610 | Jay Howell | .08 | .25 |
| ❏ 611 | Tim Crews | .08 | .25 |
| ❏ 612 | Keith Hernandez | .15 | .40 |
| ❏ 613 | Willie Fraser | .08 | .25 |
| ❏ 614 | Jim Eppard | .08 | .25 |
| ❏ 615 | Jeff Hamilton | .08 | .25 |
| ❏ 616 | Kurt Stillwell | .08 | .25 |
| ❏ 617 | Tom Browning | .08 | .25 |
| ❏ 618 | Jeff Montgomery | .08 | .25 |
| ❏ 619 | Jose Rijo | .15 | .40 |
| ❏ 620 | Jamie Quirk | .08 | .25 |
| ❏ 621 | Willie McGee | .15 | .40 |
| ❏ 622 | Mark Grant UER (Glove on wrong hand) | .08 | .25 |
| ❏ 623 | Bill Swift | .08 | .25 |
| ❏ 624 | Orlando Mercado | .08 | .25 |
| ❏ 625 | John Costello | .08 | .25 |
| ❏ 626 | Jose Gonzalez | .08 | .25 |
| ❏ 627A | Bill Schroeder ERR | .25 | .60 |
| ❏ 627B | Bill Schroeder COR | .25 | .60 |
| ❏ 628A | Fred Manrique ERR Guillen | .25 | .60 |
| ❏ 628B | Fred Manrique COR (Swinging bat on back) | .08 | .25 |
| ❏ 629 | Ricky Horton | .08 | .25 |
| ❏ 630 | Dan Plesac | .08 | .25 |
| ❏ 631 | Alfredo Griffin | .08 | .25 |
| ❏ 632 | Chuck Finley | .15 | .40 |
| ❏ 633 | Kirk Gibson | .15 | .40 |
| ❏ 634 | Randy Myers | .15 | .40 |
| ❏ 635 | Greg Minton | .08 | .25 |
| ❏ 636A | Herm Winningham ERR (W/nningham on back) | .40 | 1.00 |
| ❏ 636B | Herm Winningham COR | .40 | 1.00 |
| ❏ 637 | Charlie Leibrandt | .08 | .25 |
| ❏ 638 | Tim Birtsas | .08 | .25 |
| ❏ 639 | Bill Buckner | .15 | .40 |
| ❏ 640 | Danny Jackson | .08 | .25 |
| ❏ 641 | Greg Booker | .08 | .25 |
| ❏ 642 | Jim Presley | .08 | .25 |
| ❏ 643 | Gene Nelson | .08 | .25 |
| ❏ 644 | Rod Booker | .08 | .25 |
| ❏ 645 | Dennis Rasmussen | .08 | .25 |
| ❏ 646 | Juan Nieves | .08 | .25 |
| ❏ 647 | Bobby Thigpen | .08 | .25 |
| ❏ 648 | Tim Belcher | .08 | .25 |
| ❏ 649 | Mike Young | .08 | .25 |
| ❏ 650 | Ivan Calderon | .08 | .25 |
| ❏ 651 | Oswald Peraza | .08 | .25 |
| ❏ 652A | Pat Sheridan ERR NPO | 6.00 | 15.00 |
| ❏ 652B | Pat Sheridan COR | .08 | .25 |
| ❏ 653 | Mike Morgan | .08 | .25 |
| ❏ 654 | Mike Heath | .08 | .25 |
| ❏ 655 | Jay Tibbs | .08 | .25 |
| ❏ 656 | Fernando Valenzuela | .15 | .40 |
| ❏ 657 | Lee Mazzilli | .15 | .40 |
| ❏ 658 | Frank Viola AL CY | .08 | .25 |
| ❏ 659A | Jose Canseco MVP | .25 | .60 |
| ❏ 659B | Jose Canseco MVP | .25 | .60 |
| ❏ 660 | Walt Weiss AL ROY | .08 | .25 |
| ❏ 661 | Orel Hershiser NL CY | .08 | .25 |
| ❏ 662 | Kirk Gibson NL MVP | .15 | .40 |
| ❏ 663 | Chris Sabo NL ROY | .15 | .40 |
| ❏ 664 | D.Eckersley ALCS MVP | .15 | .40 |
| ❏ 665 | O.Hershiser NLCS MVP | .15 | .40 |
| ❏ 666 | Kirk Gibson WS | .40 | 1.00 |
| ❏ 667 | Orel Hershiser WS MVP | .08 | .25 |
| ❏ 668 | Wally Joyner TC | | |
| | California Angels | .08 | .25 |
| ❏ 669 | Nolan Ryan TC | .50 | 1.25 |
| ❏ 670 | Jose Canseco TC | .25 | .60 |
| ❏ 671 | Fred McGriff TC | .15 | .40 |
| ❏ 672 | Dale Murphy TC | | |
| | Atlanta Braves | .15 | .40 |
| ❏ 673 | Paul Molitor TC | .15 | .40 |
| ❏ 674 | Ozzie Smith TC | .40 | 1.00 |
| ❏ 675 | Ryne Sandberg TC | .40 | 1.00 |
| ❏ 676 | Kirk Gibson TC | .15 | .40 |
| ❏ 677 | Andres Galarraga TC | .08 | .25 |
| ❏ 678 | Will Clark TC | .15 | .40 |
| ❏ 679 | Cory Snyder TC | | |
| | Cleveland Indians | .08 | .25 |
| ❏ 680 | Alvin Davis TC | | |
| | Seattle Mariners | .08 | .25 |
| ❏ 681 | Darryl Strawberry TC | | |
| | New York Mets | .08 | .25 |
| ❏ 682 | Cal Ripken TC | .40 | 1.00 |
| ❏ 683 | Tony Gwynn TC | .25 | .60 |
| ❏ 684 | Mike Schmidt TC | .40 | 1.00 |
| ❏ 685 | Andy Van Slyke TC | | |
| | Pittsburgh Pirates UER (06 Jun | .15 | .40 |
| ❏ 686 | Ruben Sierra TC | .08 | .25 |
| ❏ 687 | Wade Boggs TC | .15 | .40 |
| ❏ 688 | Eric Davis TC | | |
| | Cincinnati Reds | .08 | .25 |
| ❏ 689 | George Brett TC | .40 | 1.00 |
| ❏ 690 | Alan Trammell TC | | |
| | Detroit Tigers | .08 | .25 |
| ❏ 691 | Frank Viola TC | | |
| | Minnesota Twins | .08 | .25 |
| ❏ 692 | Harold Baines TC | | |
| | Chicago White Sox | .08 | .25 |
| ❏ 693 | Don Mattingly TC | .40 | 1.00 |
| ❏ 694 | Checklist 1-100 | .08 | .25 |
| ❏ 695 | Checklist 101-200 | .08 | .25 |
| ❏ 696 | Checklist 201-300 | .08 | .25 |
| ❏ 697 | Checklist 301-400 | .08 | .25 |
| ❏ 698 | Checklist UER | .08 | .25 |
| ❏ 699 | Checklist 501-600 UER (543 Greg Booker) | .08 | .25 |
| ❏ 700 | Checklist 601-700 | .08 | .25 |
| ❏ 701 | Checklist 701-800 | .08 | .25 |
| ❏ 702 | Jesse Barfield | .15 | .40 |
| ❏ 703 | Walt Terrell | .08 | .25 |
| ❏ 704 | Dickie Thon | .08 | .25 |
| ❏ 705 | Al Leiter | .40 | 1.00 |
| ❏ 706 | Dave LaPoint | .08 | .25 |
| ❏ 707 | Charlie Hayes RC | .20 | .50 |
| ❏ 708 | Andy Hawkins | .08 | .25 |
| ❏ 709 | Mickey Hatcher | .08 | .25 |
| ❏ 710 | Lance McCullers | .08 | .25 |
| ❏ 711 | Ron Kittle | .08 | .25 |
| ❏ 712 | Bert Blyleven | .15 | .40 |
| ❏ 713 | Rick Dempsey | .08 | .25 |
| ❏ 714 | Ken Williams | .08 | .25 |
| ❏ 715 | Steve Rosenberg | .08 | .25 |
| ❏ 716 | Joe Skalski | .08 | .25 |
| ❏ 717 | Spike Owen | .08 | .25 |
| ❏ 718 | Todd Burns | .08 | .25 |
| ❏ 719 | Kevin Gross | .08 | .25 |
| ❏ 720 | Tommy Herr | .08 | .25 |
| ❏ 721 | Rob Ducey | .08 | .25 |
| ❏ 722 | Gary Green | .08 | .25 |
| ❏ 723 | Gregg Olson RC | .20 | .50 |
| ❏ 724 | Greg W.Harris RC | .08 | .25 |
| ❏ 725 | Craig Worthington | .08 | .25 |
| ❏ 726 | Thomas Howard RC | .08 | .25 |
| ❏ 727 | Dale Mohorcic | .08 | .25 |
| ❏ 728 | Rich Yett | .08 | .25 |
| ❏ 729 | Mel Hall | .08 | .25 |
| ❏ 730 | Floyd Youmans | .08 | .25 |
| ❏ 731 | Lonnie Smith | .08 | .25 |
| ❏ 732 | Wally Backman | .08 | .25 |
| ❏ 733 | Trevor Wilson RC | .08 | .25 |
| ❏ 734 | Jose Alvarez RC | .08 | .25 |
| ❏ 735 | Bob Milacki | .08 | .25 |
| ❏ 736 | Tom Gordon RC | .60 | 1.50 |
| ❏ 737 | Wally Whitehurst RC | .08 | .25 |
| ❏ 738 | Mike Aldrete | .08 | .25 |
| ❏ 739 | Keith Miller | .08 | .25 |
| ❏ 740 | Randy Milligan | .08 | .25 |
| ❏ 741 | Jeff Parrett | .08 | .25 |
| ❏ 742 | Steve Finley RC | .75 | 2.00 |
| ❏ 743 | Junior Felix RC | .08 | .25 |
| ❏ 744 | Pete Harnisch RC | .20 | .50 |
| ❏ 745 | Billy Spiers RC | .20 | .50 |
| ❏ 746 | Hensley Meulens RC | .08 | .25 |
| ❏ 747 | Juan Bell RC | .08 | .25 |
| ❏ 748 | Steve Sax | .08 | .25 |
| ❏ 749 | Phil Bradley | .08 | .25 |
| ❏ 750 | Rey Quinones | .08 | .25 |
| ❏ 751 | Tommy Gregg | .08 | .25 |
| ❏ 752 | Kevin Brown | .40 | 1.00 |
| ❏ 753 | Derek Lilliquist RC | .08 | .25 |
| ❏ 754 | Todd Zeile RC | .40 | 1.00 |
| ❏ 755 | Jim Abbott RC | .75 | 2.00 |
| ❏ 756 | Ozzie Canseco | .08 | .25 |
| ❏ 757 | Nick Esasky | .08 | .25 |
| ❏ 758 | Mike Moore | .06 | .25 |
| ❏ 759 | Rob Murphy | .08 | .25 |
| ❏ 760 | Rick Mahler | .08 | .25 |
| ❏ 761 | Fred Lynn | .15 | .40 |
| ❏ 762 | Kevin Blankenship | .08 | .25 |
| ❏ 763 | Eddie Murray | .40 | 1.00 |
| ❏ 764 | Steve Searcy | .08 | .25 |
| ❏ 765 | Jerome Walton RC | .20 | .50 |
| ❏ 766 | Erik Hanson RC | .20 | .50 |
| ❏ 767 | Bob Boone | .15 | .40 |
| ❏ 768 | Edgar Martinez RC | .40 | 1.00 |
| ❏ 769 | Jose DeJesus | .08 | .25 |
| ❏ 770 | Greg Briley | .08 | .25 |
| ❏ 771 | Steve Peters | .08 | .25 |
| ❏ 772 | Rafael Palmeiro | .40 | 1.00 |
| ❏ 773 | Jack Clark | .15 | .40 |
| ❏ 774 | Nolan Ryan w/FB | 1.50 | 4.00 |
| ❏ 775 | Lance Parrish | .15 | .40 |
| ❏ 776 | Joe Girardi RC | .40 | 1.00 |
| ❏ 777 | Willie Randolph | .15 | .40 |
| ❏ 778 | Mitch Williams | .08 | .25 |
| ❏ 779 | Dennis Cook RC | .20 | .50 |
| ❏ 780 | Dwight Smith RC | .08 | .25 |
| ❏ 781 | Lenny Harris RC | .20 | .50 |
| ❏ 782 | Torey Lovullo RC | .08 | .25 |
| ❏ 783 | Norm Charlton RC | .20 | .50 |
| ❏ 784 | Chris Brown | .08 | .25 |
| ❏ 785 | Todd Benzinger | .08 | .25 |
| ❏ 786 | Shane Rawley | .08 | .25 |
| ❏ 787 | Omar Vizquel RC | 1.25 | 3.00 |
| ❏ 788 | LaVel Freeman | .08 | .25 |
| ❏ 789 | Jeffrey Leonard | .08 | .25 |
| ❏ 790 | Eddie Williams | .08 | .25 |
| ❏ 791 | Jamie Moyer | .15 | .40 |
| ❏ 792 | Bruce Hurst UER (World Series) | .08 | .25 |
| ❏ 793 | Julio Franco | .15 | .40 |
| ❏ 794 | Claudell Washington | .08 | .25 |
| ❏ 795 | Jody Davis | .08 | .25 |
| ❏ 796 | Oddibe McDowell | .08 | .25 |
| ❏ 797 | Paul Kilgus | .08 | .25 |
| ❏ 798 | Tracy Jones | .08 | .25 |
| ❏ 799 | Steve Wilson | .08 | .25 |
| ❏ 800 | Pete O'Brien | .08 | .25 |

## 1990 Upper Deck

|  | | |
|---|---|---|
| ☐ COMPLETE SET (800) | 10.00 | 25.00 |
| ☐ COMP.FACT.SET (800) | 10.00 | 25.00 |
| ☐ COMPLETE LO SET (700) | 15.00 | 25.00 |
| ☐ COMPLETE HI SET (100) | 2.00 | 5.00 |
| ☐ COMP.LO FACT.SET (100) | 2.00 | 4.00 |
| ☐ COMP.HI FACT.SET (100) | 2.00 | 4.00 |
| ☐ 1 Star Rookie Checklist | .02 | .10 |
| ☐ 2 Randy Nosek RC | .02 | .10 |
| ☐ 3 Tom Drees RC | .02 | .10 |
| ☐ 4 Curt Young | .02 | .10 |
| ☐ 5 Devon White TC | .02 | .10 |
| ☐ 6 Luis Salazar | .02 | .10 |
| ☐ 7 Von Hayes TC | .02 | .10 |
| ☐ 8 Jose Bautista | .02 | .10 |
| ☐ 9 Marquis Grissom RC | .20 | .50 |
| ☐ 10 Orel Hershiser TC | .02 | .10 |
| ☐ 11 Rick Aguilera | .07 | .20 |
| ☐ 12 Benito Santiago TC | .02 | .10 |
| ☐ 13 Deion Sanders | .20 | .50 |
| ☐ 14 Marvell Wynne | .02 | .10 |
| ☐ 15 Dave West | .02 | .10 |
| ☐ 16 Bobby Bonilla TC | .02 | .10 |
| ☐ 17 Sammy Sosa RC | 1.25 | 3.00 |
| ☐ 18 Steve Sax TC | .02 | .10 |
| ☐ 19 Jack Howell | .02 | .10 |
| ☐ 20 Mike Schmidt SPEC | .40 | 1.00 |
| ☐ 21 Robin Ventura | .20 | .50 |
| ☐ 22 Brian Meyer | .02 | .10 |
| ☐ 23 Blaine Beatty RC | .07 | .20 |
| ☐ 24 Ken Griffey Jr. TC | .25 | .60 |
| ☐ 25 Greg Vaughn | .02 | .10 |
| ☐ 26 Xavier Hernandez RC | .02 | .10 |
| ☐ 27 Jason Grimsley RC | .02 | .10 |
| ☐ 28 Eric Anthony RC | .02 | .10 |
| ☐ 29 Tim Raines TC UER | .02 | .10 |
| ☐ 30 David Wells | .07 | .20 |
| ☐ 31 Hal Morris | .02 | .10 |
| ☐ 32 Bo Jackson TC | .10 | .30 |
| ☐ 33 Kelly Mann RC | .02 | .10 |
| ☐ 34 Nolan Ryan SPEC | .40 | 1.00 |
| ☐ 35 Scott Service UER | | |
| (Born Cincinnati on | | |
| 7/27/67 & s | .02 | .10 |
| ☐ 36 Mark McGwire TC | .30 | .75 |
| ☐ 37 Tino Martinez | .40 | 1.00 |
| ☐ 38 Chili Davis | .07 | .20 |
| ☐ 39 Scott Sanderson | .02 | .10 |
| ☐ 40 Kevin Mitchell TC | .02 | .10 |
| ☐ 41 Lou Whitaker TC | .02 | .10 |
| ☐ 42 Scott Coolbaugh RC | .02 | .10 |
| ☐ 43 Jose Cano RC | .02 | .10 |
| ☐ 44 Jose Vizcaino RC | .08 | .25 |
| ☐ 45 Bob Hamelin RC | .08 | .25 |
| ☐ 46 Jose Offerman RC | .08 | .25 |
| ☐ 47 Kevin Blankenship | .02 | .10 |
| ☐ 48 Kirby Puckett TC | .10 | .30 |
| ☐ 49 Tommy Greene UER RC | .07 | .20 |
| ☐ 50 Will Clark SPEC | .07 | .20 |
| ☐ 51 Rob Nelson | .02 | .10 |
| ☐ 52 Chris Hammond UER RC | .02 | .10 |
| ☐ 53 Joe Carter TC | .02 | .10 |
| ☐ 54A Ben McDonald ERR | .75 | 2.00 |
| ☐ 54B Ben McDonald COR RC | .08 | .25 |
| ☐ 55 Andy Benes UER | .07 | .20 |
| ☐ 56 John Olerud RC | .30 | .75 |
| ☐ 57 Roger Clemens TC | .30 | .75 |
| ☐ 58 Tony Armas | .02 | .10 |
| ☐ 59 George Canale RC | .02 | .10 |
| ☐ 60A Mickey Tettleton TC ERR | .75 | 2.00 |
| ☐ 60B Mickey Tettleton TC COR | .08 | .25 |
| ☐ 61 Mike Stanton RC | .08 | .25 |
| ☐ 62 Dwight Gooden TC | .02 | .10 |
| ☐ 63 Kent Mercker RC | .08 | .25 |
| ☐ 64 Francisco Cabrera RC | .02 | .10 |
| ☐ 65 Steve Avery | .02 | .10 |
| ☐ 66 Jose Canseco | .10 | .30 |
| ☐ 67 Matt Merullo | .02 | .10 |
| ☐ 68 Vince Coleman TC UER | .02 | .10 |
| ☐ 69 Ron Karkovice | .02 | .10 |
| ☐ 70 Kevin Maas RC | .08 | .25 |
| ☐ 71 Dennis Cook UER | | |
| (Shown with righty | | |
| glove on card) | .02 | .10 |
| ☐ 72 Juan Gonzalez RC | .60 | 1.50 |
| ☐ 73 Andre Dawson TC | .02 | .10 |
| ☐ 74 Dean Palmer RC | .08 | .25 |
| ☐ 75 Bo Jackson SPEC | .07 | .20 |
| ☐ 76 Rob Richie RC | .02 | .10 |
| ☐ 77 Bobby Rose UER | | |
| (Pickin & should | | |
| be pick in | .02 | .10 |
| ☐ 78 Brian DuBois UER RC | .02 | .10 |
| ☐ 79 Ozzie Guillen TC | .02 | .10 |
| ☐ 80 Gene Nelson | .02 | .10 |
| ☐ 81 Bob McClure | .02 | .10 |
| ☐ 82 Julio Franco TC | .02 | .10 |
| ☐ 83 Greg Minton | .02 | .10 |
| ☐ 84 John Smoltz TC UER | .10 | .30 |
| ☐ 85 Willie Fraser | .02 | .10 |
| ☐ 86 Neal Heaton | .02 | .10 |
| ☐ 87 Kevin Tapani RC | .08 | .25 |
| ☐ 88 Mike Scott TC | .02 | .10 |
| ☐ 89A Jim Gott ERR | .75 | 2.00 |
| ☐ 89B Jim Gott COR | .02 | .10 |
| ☐ 90 Lance Johnson | .02 | .10 |
| ☐ 91 Robin Yount TC UER | .20 | .50 |
| ☐ 92 Jeff Parrett | .02 | .10 |
| ☐ 93 Julio Machado RC | .02 | .10 |
| ☐ 94 Ron Jones | .02 | .10 |
| ☐ 95 George Bell TC | .02 | .10 |
| ☐ 96 Jerry Reuss | .02 | .10 |
| ☐ 97 Brian Fisher | .02 | .10 |
| ☐ 98 Kevin Ritz RC | .02 | .10 |
| ☐ 99 Barry Larkin TC | .07 | .20 |
| ☐ 100 Checklist 1-100 | .02 | .10 |
| ☐ 101 Gerald Perry | .02 | .10 |
| ☐ 102 Kevin Appier | .07 | .20 |
| ☐ 103 Julio Franco | .07 | .20 |
| ☐ 104 Craig Biggio | .20 | .50 |
| ☐ 105 Bo Jackson UER | .20 | .50 |
| ☐ 106 Junior Felix | .02 | .10 |
| ☐ 107 Mike Harkey | .02 | .10 |
| ☐ 108 Fred McGriff | .20 | .50 |
| ☐ 109 Rick Sutcliffe | .07 | .20 |
| ☐ 110 Pete O'Brien | .02 | .10 |
| ☐ 111 Kelly Gruber | .02 | .10 |
| ☐ 112 Dwight Evans | .10 | .30 |
| ☐ 113 Pat Borders | .02 | .10 |
| ☐ 114 Dwight Gooden | .07 | .20 |
| ☐ 115 Kevin Batiste RC | .02 | .10 |
| ☐ 116 Eric Davis | .07 | .20 |
| ☐ 117 Kevin Mitchell UER | | |
| (Career HR total 99 & | | |
| should b | .02 | .10 |
| ☐ 118 Ron Oester | .02 | .10 |
| ☐ 119 Brett Butler | .07 | .20 |
| ☐ 120 Danny Jackson | .02 | .10 |
| ☐ 121 Tommy Gregg | .02 | .10 |
| ☐ 122 Ken Caminiti | .07 | .20 |
| ☐ 123 Kevin Brown | .07 | .20 |
| ☐ 124 George Brett | .50 | 1.25 |
| ☐ 125 Mike Scott | .02 | .10 |
| ☐ 126 Cory Snyder | .02 | .10 |
| ☐ 127 George Bell | .10 | .30 |
| ☐ 128 Mark Grace | .10 | .30 |
| ☐ 129 Devon White | .07 | .20 |
| ☐ 130 Tony Fernandez | .02 | .10 |
| ☐ 131 Don Aase | .02 | .10 |
| ☐ 132 Rance Mulliniks | .02 | .10 |
| ☐ 133 Marty Barrett | .02 | .10 |
| ☐ 134 Nelson Liriano | .02 | .10 |
| ☐ 135 Mark Carreon | .02 | .10 |
| ☐ 136 Candy Maldonado | .02 | .10 |
| ☐ 137 Tim Birtsas | .02 | .10 |
| ☐ 138 Tom Brookens | .02 | .10 |
| ☐ 139 John Franco | .07 | .20 |
| ☐ 140 Mike LaCoss | .02 | .10 |
| ☐ 141 Jeff Treadway | .02 | .10 |
| ☐ 142 Pat Tabler | .02 | .10 |
| ☐ 143 Darrell Evans | .07 | .20 |
| ☐ 144 Rafael Ramirez | .02 | .10 |
| ☐ 145 Oddibe McDowell UER | | |
| (Misspelled Oddibe) | .02 | .10 |
| ☐ 146 Brian Downing | .02 | .10 |
| ☐ 147 Curt Wilkerson | .02 | .10 |
| ☐ 148 Ernie Whitt | .02 | .10 |
| ☐ 149 Bill Schroeder | .02 | .10 |
| ☐ 150 Domingo Ramos UER | | |
| (Says throws right & | | |
| but shows | .02 | .10 |
| ☐ 151 Rick Honeycutt | .02 | .10 |
| ☐ 152 Don Slaught | .02 | .10 |
| ☐ 153 Mitch Webster | .02 | .10 |
| ☐ 154 Tony Phillips | .02 | .10 |
| ☐ 155 Paul Kilgus | .02 | .10 |
| ☐ 156 Ken Griffey Jr. | .60 | 1.50 |
| ☐ 157 Gary Sheffield | .20 | .50 |
| ☐ 158 Wally Backman | .02 | .10 |
| ☐ 159 B.J. Surhoff | .07 | .20 |
| ☐ 160 Louie Meadows | .02 | .10 |
| ☐ 161 Paul O'Neill | .10 | .30 |
| ☐ 162 Jeff McKnight RC | .02 | .10 |
| ☐ 163 Alvaro Espinoza | .02 | .10 |
| ☐ 164 Scott Scudder | .02 | .10 |
| ☐ 165 Jeff Reed | .02 | .10 |
| ☐ 166 Gregg Jefferies | .07 | .20 |
| ☐ 167 Barry Larkin | .10 | .30 |
| ☐ 168 Gary Carter | .07 | .20 |
| ☐ 169 Robby Thompson | .02 | .10 |
| ☐ 170 Rolando Roomes | .02 | .10 |
| ☐ 171 Mark McGwire | .60 | 1.50 |
| ☐ 172 Steve Sax | .02 | .10 |
| ☐ 173 Mark Williamson | .02 | .10 |
| ☐ 174 Mitch Williams | .02 | .10 |
| ☐ 175 Brian Holton | .02 | .10 |
| ☐ 176 Rob Deer | .07 | .20 |
| ☐ 177 Tim Raines | .07 | .20 |
| ☐ 178 Mike Felder | .02 | .10 |
| ☐ 179 Harold Reynolds | .02 | .10 |
| ☐ 180 Terry Francona | .07 | .20 |
| ☐ 181 Chris Sabo | .07 | .20 |
| ☐ 182 Darryl Strawberry | .07 | .20 |
| ☐ 183 Willie Randolph | .07 | .20 |
| ☐ 184 Bill Ripken | .02 | .10 |
| ☐ 185 Mackey Sasser | .02 | .10 |
| ☐ 186 Todd Benzinger | .02 | .10 |
| ☐ 187 Kevin Elster UER | | |
| (16 homers in 1989 & | | |
| should be 1 | .02 | .10 |
| ☐ 188 Jose Uribe | .02 | .10 |
| ☐ 189 Tom Browning | .02 | .10 |
| ☐ 190 Keith Miller | .02 | .10 |
| ☐ 191 Don Mattingly | .50 | 1.25 |
| ☐ 192 Dave Parker | .07 | .20 |
| ☐ 193 Roberto Kelly UER | .02 | .10 |
| ☐ 194 Phil Bradley | .02 | .10 |
| ☐ 195 Ron Hassey | .02 | .10 |
| ☐ 196 Gerald Young | .02 | .10 |
| ☐ 197 Hubie Brooks | .02 | .10 |
| ☐ 198 Bill Doran | .02 | .10 |
| ☐ 199 Al Newman | .02 | .10 |
| ☐ 200 Checklist 101-200 | .02 | .10 |
| ☐ 201 Terry Puhl | .02 | .10 |
| ☐ 202 Frank DiPino | .02 | .10 |
| ☐ 203 Jim Clancy | .02 | .10 |
| ☐ 204 Bob Ojeda | .02 | .10 |
| ☐ 205 Alex Trevino | .02 | .10 |
| ☐ 206 Dave Henderson | .02 | .10 |
| ☐ 207 Henry Cotto | .02 | .10 |
| ☐ 208 Rafael Belliard UER | | |
| (Born 1961 & not 1951) | .02 | .10 |
| ☐ 209 Stan Javier | .02 | .10 |
| ☐ 210 Jerry Reed | .02 | .10 |
| ☐ 211 Doug Dascenzo | .02 | .10 |
| ☐ 212 Andres Thomas | .02 | .10 |
| ☐ 213 Greg Maddux | .30 | .75 |
| ☐ 214 Mike Schooler | .02 | .10 |
| ☐ 215 Lonnie Smith | .02 | .10 |
| ☐ 216 Jose Rijo | .02 | .10 |
| ☐ 217 Greg Gagne | .02 | .10 |
| ☐ 218 Jim Gantner | .02 | .10 |
| ☐ 219 Allan Anderson | .02 | .10 |
| ☐ 220 Rick Mahler | .02 | .10 |
| ☐ 221 Jim Deshaies | .02 | .10 |
| ☐ 222 Keith Hernandez | .07 | .20 |
| ☐ 223 Vince Coleman | .02 | .10 |
| ☐ 224 David Cone | .07 | .20 |
| ☐ 225 Ozzie Smith | .30 | .75 |
| ☐ 226 Matt Nokes | .02 | .10 |
| ☐ 227 Barry Bonds | .60 | 1.50 |
| ☐ 228 Felix Jose | .07 | .20 |
| ☐ 229 Dennis Powell | .02 | .10 |
| ☐ 230 Mike Gallego | .02 | .10 |
| ☐ 231 Shawon Dunston UER | | |
| ('89 stats are | | |
| Andre Dawson's | .02 | .10 |
| ☐ 232 Ron Gant | .07 | .20 |
| ☐ 233 Omar Vizquel | .20 | .50 |
| ☐ 234 Derek Lilliquist | .02 | .10 |
| ☐ 235 Erik Hanson | .02 | .10 |
| ☐ 236 Kirby Puckett | .20 | .50 |
| ☐ 237 Bill Spiers | .02 | .10 |
| ☐ 238 Dan Gladden | .02 | .10 |
| ☐ 239 Bryan Clutterbuck | .02 | .10 |
| ☐ 240 John Moses | .02 | .10 |

|  |  | | |
|---|---|---|---|
| 241 | Ron Darling | .02 | .10 |
| 242 | Joe Magrane | .02 | .10 |
| 243 | Dave Magadan | .02 | .10 |
| 244 | Pedro Guerrero UER (Misspelled Guerrero) | .02 | .10 |
| 245 | Glenn Davis | .02 | .10 |
| 246 | Terry Steinbach | .02 | .10 |
| 247 | Fred Lynn | .02 | .10 |
| 248 | Gary Redus | .02 | .10 |
| 249 | Ken Williams | .02 | .10 |
| 250 | Sid Bream | .02 | .10 |
| 251 | Bob Welch UER (2587 career strike-outs& should | .02 | .10 |
| 252 | Bill Buckner | .02 | .10 |
| 253 | Carney Lansford | .07 | .20 |
| 254 | Paul Molitor | .07 | .20 |
| 255 | Jose DeJesus | .02 | .10 |
| 256 | Orel Hershiser | .07 | .20 |
| 257 | Tom Brunansky | .02 | .10 |
| 258 | Mike Davis | .02 | .10 |
| 259 | Jeff Ballard | .02 | .10 |
| 260 | Scott Terry | .02 | .10 |
| 261 | Sid Fernandez | .02 | .10 |
| 262 | Mike Marshall | .02 | .10 |
| 263 | Howard Johnson UER (192 SO& should be 592) | .02 | .10 |
| 264 | Kirk Gibson | .07 | .20 |
| 265 | Kevin McReynolds | .02 | .10 |
| 266 | Cal Ripken | .60 | 1.50 |
| 267 | Ozzie Guillen UER | .07 | .20 |
| 268 | Jim Traber | .02 | .10 |
| 269 | Bobby Thigpen UER (31 saves in 1989& should be 3 | .02 | .10 |
| 270 | Joe Orsulak | .02 | .10 |
| 271 | Bob Boone | .07 | .20 |
| 272 | Dave Stewart UER | .07 | .20 |
| 273 | Tim Wallach | .02 | .10 |
| 274 | Luis Aquino UER (Says throws lefty& but shows hi | .02 | .10 |
| 275 | Mike Moore | .02 | .10 |
| 276 | Tony Pena | .02 | .10 |
| 277 | Eddie Murray | .20 | .50 |
| 278 | Milt Thompson | .02 | .10 |
| 279 | Alejandro Pena | .02 | .10 |
| 280 | Ken Dayley | .02 | .10 |
| 281 | Carmelo Castillo | .02 | .10 |
| 282 | Tom Henke | .02 | .10 |
| 283 | Mickey Hatcher | .02 | .10 |
| 284 | Roy Smith | .02 | .10 |
| 285 | Manny Lee | .02 | .10 |
| 286 | Dan Pasqua | .02 | .10 |
| 287 | Larry Sheets | .02 | .10 |
| 288 | Garry Templeton | .02 | .10 |
| 289 | Eddie Williams | .02 | .10 |
| 290 | Brady Anderson | .07 | .20 |
| 291 | Spike Owen | .02 | .10 |
| 292 | Storm Davis | .02 | .10 |
| 293 | Chris Bosio | .02 | .10 |
| 294 | Jim Eisenreich | .02 | .10 |
| 295 | Don August | .02 | .10 |
| 296 | Jeff Hamilton | .02 | .10 |
| 297 | Mickey Tettleton | .02 | .10 |
| 298 | Mike Scioscia | .02 | .10 |
| 299 | Kevin Hickey | .02 | .10 |
| 300 | Checklist 201-300 | .02 | .10 |
| 301 | Shawn Abner | .02 | .10 |
| 302 | Kevin Bass | .02 | .10 |
| 303 | Bip Roberts | .02 | .10 |
| 304 | Joe Girardi | .10 | .30 |
| 305 | Danny Darwin | .02 | .10 |
| 306 | Mike Heath | .02 | .10 |
| 307 | Mike Macfarlane | .02 | .10 |
| 308 | Ed Whitson | .02 | .10 |
| 309 | Tracy Jones | .02 | .10 |
| 310 | Scott Fletcher | .02 | .10 |
| 311 | Darnell Coles | .02 | .10 |
| 312 | Mike Brumley | .02 | .10 |
| 313 | Bill Swift | .02 | .10 |
| 314 | Charlie Hough | .07 | .20 |
| 315 | Jim Presley | .02 | .10 |
| 316 | Luis Polonia | .07 | .20 |
| 317 | Mike Morgan | .02 | .10 |
| 318 | Lee Guetterman | .02 | .10 |
| 319 | Jose Oquendo | .02 | .10 |
| 320 | Wayne Tolleson | .02 | .10 |
| 321 | Jody Reed | .02 | .10 |
| 322 | Damon Berryhill | .02 | .10 |
| 323 | Roger Clemens | .60 | 1.50 |
| 324 | Ryne Sandberg | .30 | .75 |
| 325 | Benito Santiago UER | .07 | .20 |
| 326 | Bret Saberhagen UER (1140 hits& should be 1240; | .07 | .20 |
| 327 | Lou Whitaker | .07 | .20 |
| 328 | Dave Gallagher | .02 | .10 |
| 329 | Mike Pagliarulo | .02 | .10 |
| 330 | Doyle Alexander | .02 | .10 |
| 331 | Jeffrey Leonard | .02 | .10 |
| 332 | Torey Lovullo | .02 | .10 |
| 333 | Pete Incaviglia | .02 | .10 |
| 334 | Rickey Henderson | .20 | .50 |
| 335 | Rafael Palmeiro | .10 | .30 |
| 336 | Ken Hill | .07 | .20 |
| 337 | Dave Winfield UER | .07 | .20 |
| 338 | Alfredo Griffin | .02 | .10 |
| 339 | Andy Hawkins | .02 | .10 |
| 340 | Ted Power | .02 | .10 |
| 341 | Steve Wilson | .02 | .10 |
| 342 | Jack Clark UER (916 BB& should be 1006; 1142 SO& | .07 | .20 |
| 343 | Ellis Burks | .10 | .30 |
| 344 | Tony Gwynn | .25 | .60 |
| 345 | Jerome Walton UER (Total At Bats 476& should be | .02 | .10 |
| 346 | Roberto Alomar | .10 | .30 |
| 347 | Carlos Martinez UER (Born 8/11/64& should be 8/1 | .02 | .10 |
| 348 | Chet Lemon | .02 | .10 |
| 349 | Willie Wilson | .02 | .10 |
| 350 | Greg Walker | .02 | .10 |
| 351 | Tom Bolton | .02 | .10 |
| 352 | German Gonzalez | .02 | .10 |
| 353 | Harold Baines | .07 | .20 |
| 354 | Mike Greenwell | .07 | .20 |
| 355 | Ruben Sierra | .20 | .50 |
| 356 | Andres Galarraga | .07 | .20 |
| 357 | Andre Dawson | .07 | .20 |
| 358 | Jeff Brantley | .02 | .10 |
| 359 | Mike Bielecki | .02 | .10 |
| 360 | Ken Oberkfell | .02 | .10 |
| 361 | Kurt Stillwell | .02 | .10 |
| 362 | Brian Holman | .02 | .10 |
| 363 | Kevin Seitzer UER (Career triples total does not | .02 | .10 |
| 364 | Alvin Davis | .02 | .10 |
| 365 | Tom Gordon | .07 | .20 |
| 366 | Bobby Bonilla UER (Two steals in 1987& should be | .07 | .20 |
| 367 | Carlton Fisk | .10 | .30 |
| 368 | Steve Carter UER (Charlottesville) | .02 | .10 |
| 369 | Joel Skinner | .02 | .10 |
| 370 | John Cangelosi | .02 | .10 |
| 371 | Cecil Espy | .02 | .10 |
| 372 | Gary Wayne | .02 | .10 |
| 373 | Jim Rice | .07 | .20 |
| 374 | Mike Dyer RC | .02 | .10 |
| 375 | Joe Carter | .07 | .20 |
| 376 | Dwight Smith | .02 | .10 |
| 377 | John Wetteland | .20 | .50 |
| 378 | Earnie Riles | .02 | .10 |
| 379 | Otis Nixon | .07 | .20 |
| 380 | Vance Law | .02 | .10 |
| 381 | Dave Bergman | .02 | .10 |
| 382 | Frank White | .02 | .10 |
| 383 | Scott Bradley | .02 | .10 |
| 384 | Israel Sanchez UER (Totals don't include '89 s | .02 | .10 |
| 385 | Gary Pettis | .02 | .10 |
| 386 | Donn Pall | .02 | .10 |
| 387 | John Smiley | .07 | .20 |
| 388 | Tom Candiotti | .02 | .10 |
| 389 | Junior Ortiz | .02 | .10 |
| 390 | Steve Lyons | .02 | .10 |
| 391 | Brian Harper | .02 | .10 |
| 392 | Fred Manrique | .02 | .10 |
| 393 | Lee Smith | .07 | .20 |
| 394 | Jeff Kunkel | .02 | .10 |
| 395 | Claudell Washington | .02 | .10 |
| 396 | John Tudor | .02 | .10 |
| 397 | Terry Kennedy UER (Career totals at wrong) | .02 | .10 |
| 398 | Lloyd McClendon | .02 | .10 |
| 399 | Craig Lefferts | .02 | .10 |
| 400 | Checklist 301-400 | .02 | .10 |
| 401 | Keith Moreland | .02 | .10 |
| 402 | Rich Gedman | .02 | .10 |
| 403 | Jeff D. Robinson | .02 | .10 |
| 404 | Randy Ready | .02 | .10 |
| 405 | Rick Cerone | .02 | .10 |
| 406 | Jeff Blauser | .02 | .10 |
| 407 | Larry Andersen | .02 | .10 |
| 408 | Joe Boever | .02 | .10 |
| 409 | Felix Fermin | .02 | .10 |
| 410 | Glenn Wilson | .02 | .10 |
| 411 | Rex Hudler | .02 | .10 |
| 412 | Mark Grant | .02 | .10 |
| 413 | Dennis Martinez | .07 | .20 |
| 414 | Darrin Jackson | .07 | .20 |
| 415 | Mike Aldrete | .02 | .10 |
| 416 | Roger McDowell | .02 | .10 |
| 417 | Jeff Reardon | .07 | .20 |
| 418 | Darren Daulton | .07 | .20 |
| 419 | Tim Laudner | .02 | .10 |
| 420 | Don Carman | .02 | .10 |
| 421 | Lloyd Moseby | .02 | .10 |
| 422 | Doug Drabek | .07 | .20 |
| 423 | Lenny Harris UER (Walks 2 in 1898& should be 20) | .02 | .10 |
| 424 | Jose Lind | .02 | .10 |
| 425 | Dave Wayne Johnson RC | .02 | .10 |
| 426 | Jerry Browne | .02 | .10 |
| 427 | Eric Yelding RC | .02 | .10 |
| 428 | Brad Komminsk | .02 | .10 |
| 429 | Jody Davis | .02 | .10 |
| 430 | Mariano Duncan | .02 | .10 |
| 431 | Mark Davis | .02 | .10 |
| 432 | Nelson Santovenia | .02 | .10 |
| 433 | Bruce Hurst | .07 | .20 |
| 434 | Jeff Huson RC | .07 | .20 |
| 435 | Chris James | .02 | .10 |
| 436 | Mark Guthrie RC | .02 | .10 |
| 437 | Charlie Hayes | .02 | .10 |
| 438 | Shane Rawley | .02 | .10 |
| 439 | Dickie Thon | .02 | .10 |
| 440 | Juan Berenguer | .02 | .10 |
| 441 | Kevin Romine | .02 | .10 |
| 442 | Bill Landrum | .02 | .10 |
| 443 | Todd Frohwirth | .02 | .10 |
| 444 | Craig Worthington | .02 | .10 |
| 445 | Fernando Valenzuela | .07 | .20 |
| 446 | Albert Belle | .20 | .50 |
| 447 | Ed Whited UER RC | .02 | .10 |
| 448 | Dave Smith | .02 | .10 |
| 449 | Dave Clark | .02 | .10 |
| 450 | Juan Agosto | .02 | .10 |
| 451 | Dave Valle | .02 | .10 |
| 452 | Kent Hrbek | .07 | .20 |
| 453 | Von Hayes | .02 | .10 |
| 454 | Gary Gaetti | .07 | .20 |
| 455 | Greg Briley | .02 | .10 |
| 456 | Glenn Braggs | .02 | .10 |
| 457 | Kirt Manwaring | .02 | .10 |
| 458 | Mel Hall | .02 | .10 |
| 459 | Brook Jacoby | .02 | .10 |
| 460 | Pat Sheridan | .02 | .10 |
| 461 | Rob Murphy | .02 | .10 |
| 462 | Jimmy Key | .07 | .20 |
| 463 | Nick Esasky | .02 | .10 |
| 464 | Rob Ducey | .02 | .10 |
| 465 | Carlos Quintana UER (International) | .02 | .10 |
| 466 | Larry Walker RC | .60 | 1.50 |
| 467 | Todd Worrell | .02 | .10 |
| 468 | Kevin Gross | .02 | .10 |
| 469 | Terry Pendleton | .07 | .20 |
| 470 | Dave Martinez | .02 | .10 |
| 471 | Gene Larkin | .02 | .10 |
| 472 | Len Dykstra UER | .07 | .20 |
| 473 | Barry Lyons | .02 | .10 |
| 474 | Terry Mulholland | .02 | .10 |
| 475 | Chip Hale RC | .02 | .10 |
| 476 | Jesse Barfield | .02 | .10 |

|  |  | | |
|---|---|---|---|
| 477 | Dan Plesac | .02 | .10 |
| 478A | Scott Garretts ERR | .75 | 2.00 |
| 478B | Scott Garretts COR | .02 | .10 |
| 479 | Dave Righetti | .02 | .10 |
| 480 | Gus Polidor UER (Wearing 14 on front& but 10 on | .02 | .10 |
| 481 | Mookie Wilson | .07 | .20 |
| 482 | Luis Rivera | .02 | .10 |
| 483 | Mike Flanagan | .02 | .10 |
| 484 | Dennis Boyd | .02 | .10 |
| 485 | John Cerutti | .02 | .10 |
| 486 | John Costello | .02 | .10 |
| 487 | Pascual Perez | .02 | .10 |
| 488 | Tommy Herr | .02 | .10 |
| 489 | Tom Foley | .02 | .10 |
| 490 | Curt Ford | .02 | .10 |
| 491 | Steve Lake | .02 | .10 |
| 492 | Tim Teufel | .02 | .10 |
| 493 | Randy Bush | .02 | .10 |
| 494 | Mike Jackson | .02 | .10 |
| 495 | Steve Jeltz | .02 | .10 |
| 496 | Paul Gibson | .02 | .10 |
| 497 | Steve Balboni | .02 | .10 |
| 498 | Bud Black | .02 | .10 |
| 499 | Dale Sveum | .02 | .10 |
| 500 | Checklist 401-500 | .02 | .10 |
| 501 | Tim Jones | .02 | .10 |
| 502 | Mark Portugal | .02 | .10 |
| 503 | Ivan Calderon | .02 | .10 |
| 504 | Rick Rhoden | .02 | .10 |
| 505 | Willie McGee | .07 | .20 |
| 506 | Kirk McCaskill | .02 | .10 |
| 507 | Dave LaPoint | .02 | .10 |
| 508 | Jay Howell | .02 | .10 |
| 509 | Johnny Ray | .02 | .10 |
| 510 | Dave Anderson | .02 | .10 |
| 511 | Chuck Crim | .02 | .10 |
| 512 | Joe Hesketh | .02 | .10 |
| 513 | Dennis Eckersley | .07 | .20 |
| 514 | Greg Brock | .02 | .10 |
| 515 | Tim Burke | .02 | .10 |
| 516 | Frank Tanana | .02 | .10 |
| 517 | Jay Bell | .07 | .20 |
| 518 | Guillermo Hernandez | .02 | .10 |
| 519 | Randy Kramer UER (Codiroll misspelled as Codorol) | .02 | .10 |
| 520 | Charles Hudson | .02 | .10 |
| 521 | Jim Corsi | .02 | .10 |
| 522 | Steve Rosenberg | .02 | .10 |
| 523 | Cris Carpenter | .02 | .10 |
| 524 | Matt Winters RC | .02 | .10 |
| 525 | Melido Perez | .02 | .10 |
| 526 | Chris Gwynn UER (Albequerque) | .02 | .10 |
| 527 | Bert Blyleven UER | .07 | .20 |
| 528 | Chuck Cary | .02 | .10 |
| 529 | Daryl Boston | .02 | .10 |
| 530 | Dale Mohorcic | .02 | .10 |
| 531 | Geronimo Berroa | .02 | .10 |
| 532 | Edgar Martinez | .10 | .30 |
| 533 | Dale Murphy | .10 | .30 |
| 534 | Jay Buhner | .10 | .30 |
| 535 | John Smoltz | .20 | .50 |
| 536 | Andy Van Slyke | .10 | .30 |
| 537 | Mike Henneman | .02 | .10 |
| 538 | Miguel Garcia | .02 | .10 |
| 539 | Frank Williams | .02 | .10 |
| 540 | R.J. Reynolds | .02 | .10 |
| 541 | Shawn Hillegas | .02 | .10 |
| 542 | Walt Weiss | .02 | .10 |
| 543 | Greg Hibbard RC | .02 | .10 |
| 544 | Nolan Ryan | .75 | 2.00 |
| 545 | Todd Zeile | .07 | .20 |
| 546 | Hensley Meulens | .02 | .10 |
| 547 | Tim Belcher | .02 | .10 |
| 548 | Mike Witt | .02 | .10 |
| 549 | Greg Cadaret UER (Aquirings should be Acquiring) | .02 | .10 |
| 550 | Franklin Stubbs | .02 | .10 |
| 551 | Tony Castillo | .02 | .10 |
| 552 | Jeff M. Robinson | .02 | .10 |
| 553 | Steve Olin RC | .08 | .25 |
| 554 | Alan Trammell | .07 | .20 |
| 555 | Wade Boggs 4X | .10 | .30 |
| 556 | Will Clark | .10 | .30 |
| 557 | Jeff King | .02 | .10 |
| 558 | Mike Fitzgerald | .02 | .10 |
| 559 | Ken Howell | .02 | .10 |
| 560 | Bob Kipper | .02 | .10 |
| 561 | Scott Bankhead | .02 | .10 |
| 562A | Jeff Innis ERR | .75 | 2.00 |
| 562B | Jeff Innis COR RC | .02 | .10 |
| 563 | Randy Johnson | .40 | 1.00 |
| 564 | Wally Whitehurst | .02 | .10 |
| 565 | Gene Harris | .02 | .10 |
| 566 | Norm Charlton | .10 | .30 |
| 567 | Robin Yount UER | .30 | .75 |
| 568 | Joe Oliver | .02 | .10 |
| 569 | Mark Parent | .02 | .10 |
| 570 | John Farrell UER (Loss total added wrong) | .02 | .10 |
| 571 | Tom Glavine | .10 | .30 |
| 572 | Rod Nichols | .02 | .10 |
| 573 | Jack Morris | .07 | .20 |
| 574 | Greg Swindell | .02 | .10 |
| 575 | Steve Searcy | .02 | .10 |
| 576 | Ricky Jordan | .02 | .10 |
| 577 | Matt Williams | .07 | .20 |
| 578 | Mike LaValliere | .02 | .10 |
| 579 | Bryn Smith | .02 | .10 |
| 580 | Bruce Ruffin | .02 | .10 |
| 581 | Randy Myers | .07 | .20 |
| 582 | Rick Wrona | .02 | .10 |
| 583 | Juan Samuel | .02 | .10 |
| 584 | Les Lancaster | .02 | .10 |
| 585 | Jeff Musselman | .02 | .10 |
| 586 | Rob Dibble | .07 | .20 |
| 587 | Eric Show | .02 | .10 |
| 588 | Jesse Orosco | .02 | .10 |
| 589 | Herm Winningham | .02 | .10 |
| 590 | Andy Allanson | .02 | .10 |
| 591 | Dion James | .02 | .10 |
| 592 | Carmelo Martinez | .02 | .10 |
| 593 | Luis Quinones | .02 | .10 |
| 594 | Dennis Rasmussen | .02 | .10 |
| 595 | Rich Yett | .02 | .10 |
| 596 | Bob Walk | .02 | .10 |
| 597A | Andy McGaffigan ERR (Photo actually Rich Thompso) | .75 | 2.00 |
| 597B | Andy McGaffigan COR | .02 | .10 |
| 598 | Billy Hatcher | .02 | .10 |
| 599 | Bob Knepper | .02 | .10 |
| 600 | Checklist 501-600 UER (599 Bob Kneppers) | .02 | .10 |
| 601 | Joey Cora | .07 | .20 |
| 602 | Steve Finley | .07 | .20 |
| 603 | Kal Daniels UER (12 hits in .978 should be 12) | .02 | .10 |
| 604 | Gregg Olson | .07 | .20 |
| 605 | Dave Stieb | .07 | .20 |
| 606 | Kenny Rogers | .07 | .20 |
| 607 | Zane Smith | .02 | .10 |
| 608 | Bob Geren UER (Originally) | .02 | .10 |
| 609 | Chad Kreuter | .02 | .10 |
| 610 | Mike Smithson | .02 | .10 |
| 611 | Jeff Wetherby RC | .02 | .10 |
| 612 | Gary Mielke RC | .02 | .10 |
| 613 | Pete Smith | .02 | .10 |
| 614 | Jack Daugherty RC | .02 | .10 |
| 615 | Lance McCullers | .02 | .10 |
| 616 | Don Robinson | .02 | .10 |
| 617 | Jose Guzman | .02 | .10 |
| 618 | Steve Bedrosian | .02 | .10 |
| 619 | Jamie Moyer | .02 | .10 |
| 620 | Atlee Hammaker | .02 | .10 |
| 621 | Rick Luecken RC | .02 | .10 |
| 622 | Greg W. Harris | .02 | .10 |
| 623 | Pete Harnisch | .02 | .10 |
| 624 | Jerrald Clark | .02 | .10 |
| 625 | Jack McDowell | .07 | .20 |
| 626 | Frank Viola | .02 | .10 |
| 627 | Teddy Higuera | .02 | .10 |
| 628 | Marty Pevey RC | .02 | .10 |
| 629 | Bill Wegman | .02 | .10 |
| 630 | Eric Plunk | .02 | .10 |
| 631 | Drew Hall | .02 | .10 |
| 632 | Doug Jones | .02 | .10 |
| 633 | Geno Petralli UER (Sacramento) | .02 | .10 |
| 634 | Jose Alvarez | .02 | .10 |
| 635 | Bob Milacki | .02 | .10 |
| 636 | Bobby Witt | .02 | .10 |
| 637 | Trevor Wilson | .02 | .10 |
| 638 | Jeff Russell UER (Shutout stats wrong) | .02 | .10 |
| 639 | Mike Krukow | .02 | .10 |
| 640 | Rick Leach | .02 | .10 |
| 641 | Dave Schmidt | .02 | .10 |
| 642 | Terry Leach | .02 | .10 |
| 643 | Calvin Schiraldi | .02 | .10 |
| 644 | Bob Melvin | .02 | .10 |
| 645 | Jim Abbott | .10 | .30 |
| 646 | Jaime Navarro | .02 | .10 |
| 647 | Mark Langston UER (Several errors in stats total | .02 | .10 |
| 648 | Juan Nieves | .02 | .10 |
| 649 | Damaso Garcia | .02 | .10 |
| 650 | Charlie O'Brien | .02 | .10 |
| 651 | Eric King | .02 | .10 |
| 652 | Mike Boddicker | .02 | .10 |
| 653 | Duane Ward | .02 | .10 |
| 654 | Bob Stanley | .02 | .10 |
| 655 | Sandy Alomar Jr. | .07 | .20 |
| 656 | Danny Tartabull UER | .07 | .20 |
| 657 | Randy McCament RC | .02 | .10 |
| 658 | Charlie Leibrandt | .02 | .10 |
| 659 | Dan Quisenberry | .02 | .10 |
| 660 | Paul Assenmacher | .02 | .10 |
| 661 | Walt Terrell | .02 | .10 |
| 662 | Tim Leary | .02 | .10 |
| 663 | Randy Milligan | .02 | .10 |
| 664 | Bo Diaz | .02 | .10 |
| 665 | Mark Lemke UER (Richmond misspelled as Richomond) | .02 | .10 |
| 666 | Jose Gonzalez | .02 | .10 |
| 667 | Chuck Finley UER (Born 11/16/62& should be 11/26) | .07 | .20 |
| 668 | John Kruk | .07 | .20 |
| 669 | Dick Schofield | .02 | .10 |
| 670 | Tim Crews | .02 | .10 |
| 671 | John Dopson | .02 | .10 |
| 672 | John Orton RC | .02 | .10 |
| 673 | Eric Hetzel | .02 | .10 |
| 674 | Lance Parrish | .02 | .10 |
| 675 | Ramon Martinez | .02 | .10 |
| 676 | Mark Gubicza | .02 | .10 |
| 677 | Greg Litton | .02 | .10 |
| 678 | Greg Mathews | .02 | .10 |
| 679 | Dave Dravecky | .07 | .20 |
| 680 | Steve Farr | .02 | .10 |
| 681 | Mike Devereaux | .02 | .10 |
| 682 | Ken Griffey Sr. | .07 | .20 |
| 683A | Jamie Weston ERR | .75 | 2.00 |
| 683B | Mickey Weston COR RC | .02 | .10 |
| 684 | Jack Armstrong | .02 | .10 |
| 685 | Steve Buechele | .02 | .10 |
| 686 | Bryan Harvey | .02 | .10 |
| 687 | Lance Blankenship | .02 | .10 |
| 688 | Dante Bichette | .07 | .20 |
| 689 | Todd Burns | .02 | .10 |
| 690 | Dan Petry | .02 | .10 |
| 691 | Kent Anderson | .02 | .10 |
| 692 | Todd Stottlemyre | .07 | .20 |
| 693 | Wally Joyner UER (Several stats errors) | .07 | .20 |
| 694 | Mike Rochford | .02 | .10 |
| 695 | Floyd Bannister | .02 | .10 |
| 696 | Rick Reuschel | .02 | .10 |
| 697 | Jose DeLeon | .02 | .10 |
| 698 | Jeff Montgomery | .07 | .20 |
| 699 | Kelly Downs | .02 | .10 |
| 700A | CL 601-700 ERR | .75 | 2.00 |
| 700B | Checklist 601-700 (683 Mickey Weston) | .02 | .10 |
| 701 | Jim Gott | .02 | .10 |
| 702 | L.Walker/Grissom/DeSh | .20 | .50 |
| 702A | Mike Witt Black | 4.00 | 10.00 |
| 703 | Alejandro Pena | .02 | .10 |
| 704 | Willie Randolph | .07 | .20 |
| 705 | Tim Leary | .02 | .10 |
| 706 | Chuck McElroy RC | .02 | .10 |
| 707 | Gerald Perry | .02 | .10 |
| 708 | Tom Brunansky | .07 | .20 |
| 709 | John Franco | .07 | .20 |
| 710 | Mark Davis | .02 | .10 |

|  |  | | |
|---|---|---|---|
| 711 | David Justice RC | .30 | .75 |
| 712 | Storm Davis | .02 | .10 |
| 713 | Scott Ruskin RC | .02 | .10 |
| 714 | Glenn Braggs | .02 | .10 |
| 715 | Kevin Bearse RC | .02 | .10 |
| 716 | Jose Nunez | .02 | .10 |
| 717 | Tim Layana RC | .02 | .10 |
| 718 | Greg Myers | .02 | .10 |
| 719 | Pete O'Brien | .02 | .10 |
| 720 | John Candelaria | .02 | .10 |
| 721 | Craig Grebeck RC | .02 | .10 |
| 722 | Shawn Boskie RC | .02 | .10 |
| 723 | Jim Leyritz RC | .08 | .25 |
| 724 | Bill Sampen RC | .02 | .10 |
| 725 | Scott Radinsky RC | .02 | .10 |
| 726 | Todd Hundley RC | .08 | .25 |
| 727 | Scott Hemond RC | .02 | .10 |
| 728 | Lenny Webster RC | .02 | .10 |
| 729 | Jeff Reardon | .07 | .20 |
| 730 | Mitch Webster | .02 | .10 |
| 731 | Brian Bohanon RC | .02 | .10 |
| 732 | Rick Parker RC | .02 | .10 |
| 733 | Terry Shumpert RC | .02 | .10 |
| 734A | Nolan Ryan 6th | 1.25 | 3.00 |
| 734B | Nolan Ryan 6th/300 | .40 | 1.00 |
| 735 | John Burkett | .02 | .10 |
| 736 | Derrick May RC | .02 | .10 |
| 737 | Carlos Baerga RC | .08 | .25 |
| 738 | Greg Smith RC | .02 | .10 |
| 739 | Scott Sanderson | .02 | .10 |
| 740 | Joe Kraemer RC | .02 | .10 |
| 741 | Hector Villanueva RC | .02 | .10 |
| 742 | Mike Fetters RC | .08 | .25 |
| 743 | Mark Gardner RC | .02 | .10 |
| 744 | Matt Nokes | .02 | .10 |
| 745 | Dave Winfield | .07 | .20 |
| 746 | Delino DeShields RC | .08 | .25 |
| 747 | Dann Howitt RC | .02 | .10 |
| 748 | Tony Pena | .02 | .10 |
| 749 | Oil Can Boyd | .02 | .10 |
| 750 | Mike Benjamin RC | .02 | .10 |
| 751 | Alex Cole RC | .02 | .10 |
| 752 | Eric Gunderson RC | .02 | .10 |
| 753 | Howard Farmer RC | .02 | .10 |
| 754 | Joe Carter | .07 | .20 |
| 755 | Ray Lankford RC | .20 | .50 |
| 756 | Sandy Alomar Jr. | .02 | .10 |
| 757 | Alex Sanchez | .02 | .10 |
| 758 | Nick Esasky | .02 | .10 |
| 759 | Stan Belinda RC | .02 | .10 |
| 760 | Jim Presley | .02 | .10 |
| 761 | Gary DiSarcina RC | .08 | .25 |
| 762 | Wayne Edwards RC | .02 | .10 |
| 763 | Pat Combs | .02 | .10 |
| 764 | Mickey Pina RC | .02 | .10 |
| 765 | Wilson Alvarez RC | .08 | .25 |
| 766 | Dave Parker | .07 | .20 |
| 767 | Mike Blowers RC | .02 | .10 |
| 768 | Tony Phillips | .02 | .10 |
| 769 | Pascual Perez | .02 | .10 |
| 770 | Gary Pettis | .02 | .10 |
| 771 | Fred Lynn | .02 | .10 |
| 772 | Mel Rojas RC | .02 | .10 |
| 773 | David Segui RC | .20 | .50 |
| 774 | Gary Carter | .07 | .20 |
| 775 | Rafael Valdez RC | .02 | .10 |
| 776 | Gienallen Hill | .02 | .10 |
| 777 | Keith Hernandez | .07 | .20 |
| 778 | Billy Hatcher | .02 | .10 |
| 779 | Marty Clary | .02 | .10 |
| 780 | Candy Maldonado | .02 | .10 |
| 781 | Mike Marshall | .02 | .10 |
| 782 | Billy Joe Robidoux | .02 | .10 |
| 783 | Mark Langston | .02 | .10 |
| 784 | Paul Sorrento RC | .08 | .25 |
| 785 | Dave Hollins RC | .08 | .25 |
| 786 | Cecil Fielder | .07 | .20 |
| 787 | Matt Young | .02 | .10 |
| 788 | Jeff Huson | .02 | .10 |
| 789 | Lloyd Moseby | .02 | .10 |
| 790 | Ron Kittle | .02 | .10 |
| 791 | Hubie Brooks | .02 | .10 |
| 792 | Craig Lefferts | .02 | .10 |
| 793 | Kevin Bass | .02 | .10 |
| 794 | Bryn Smith | .02 | .10 |
| 795 | Juan Samuel | .02 | .10 |
| 796 | Sam Horn | .02 | .10 |
| 797 | Randy Myers | .07 | .20 |

|  |  | | |
|---|---|---|---|
| 798 | Chris James | .02 | .10 |
| 799 | Bill Gullickson | .02 | .10 |
| 800 | Checklist 701-800 | .02 | .10 |

### 1991 Upper Deck

| | | |
|---|---|---|
| COMPLETE SET (800) | 6.00 | 15.00 |
| COMP.FACT.SET (800) | 8.00 | 20.00 |
| COMPLETE LO SET (700) | 6.00 | 15.00 |
| COMPLETE HI SET (100) | 2.00 | 5.00 |

|  |  | | |
|---|---|---|---|
| 1 | Star Rookie Checklist | .01 | .05 |
| 2 | Phil Plantier RC | .02 | .10 |
| 3 | D.J. Dozier | .01 | .05 |
| 4 | Dave Hansen | .01 | .05 |
| 5 | Mo Vaughn | .02 | .10 |
| 6 | Leo Gomez | .01 | .05 |
| 7 | Scott Aldred | .01 | .05 |
| 8 | Scott Chiamparino | .01 | .05 |
| 9 | Lance Dickson RC | .02 | .10 |
| 10 | Sean Berry RC | .02 | .10 |
| 11 | Bernie Williams | .08 | .25 |
| 12 | Brian Barnes UER RC | .01 | .05 |
| 13 | Narciso Elvira | .01 | .05 |
| 14 | Mike Gardiner RC | .01 | .05 |
| 15 | Greg Colbrunn RC | .08 | .25 |
| 16 | Bernard Gilkey | .01 | .05 |
| 17 | Mark Lewis | .01 | .05 |
| 18 | Mickey Morandini | .01 | .05 |
| 19 | Charles Nagy | .08 | .25 |
| 20 | Geronimo Pena | .01 | .05 |
| 21 | Henry Rodriguez RC | .08 | .25 |
| 22 | Scott Cooper FUDC | .01 | .05 |
| 23 | Andujar Cedeno UER | .01 | .05 |
| 24 | Eric Karros RC | .30 | .75 |
| 25 | Steve Decker UER RC | .01 | .05 |
| 26 | Kevin Belcher RC | .01 | .05 |
| 27 | Jeff Conine RC | .20 | .50 |
| 28 | Dave Stewart TC | .01 | .05 |
| 29 | Carlton Fisk TC | .02 | .10 |
| 30 | Rafael Palmeiro TC | .02 | .10 |
| 31 | Chuck Finley TC | .01 | .05 |
| 32 | Harold Reynolds TC | .01 | .05 |
| 33 | Bret Saberhagen TC | .01 | .05 |
| 34 | Gary Gaetti TC | .01 | .05 |
| 35 | Scott Leius | .01 | .05 |
| 36 | Neal Heaton | .01 | .05 |
| 37 | Terry Lee RC | .01 | .05 |
| 38 | Gary Redus | .01 | .05 |
| 39 | Barry Jones | .01 | .05 |
| 40 | Chuck Knoblauch | .02 | .10 |
| 41 | Larry Andersen | .01 | .05 |
| 42 | Darryl Hamilton | .01 | .05 |
| 43 | Mike Greenwell TC | .01 | .05 |
| 44 | Kelly Gruber TC | .01 | .05 |
| 45 | Jack Morris TC | .01 | .05 |
| 46 | Sandy Alomar Jr. TC | .01 | .05 |
| 47 | Gregg Olson TC | .01 | .05 |
| 48 | Dave Parker TC | .01 | .05 |
| 49 | Roberto Kelly TC | .01 | .05 |
| 50 | Top Prospect Checklist | .01 | .05 |
| 51 | Kyle Abbott | .01 | .05 |
| 52 | Jeff Juden | .01 | .05 |
| 53 | Todd Van Poppel UER RC | .08 | .25 |
| 54 | Steve Karsay RC | .08 | .25 |
| 55 | Chipper Jones RC | 1.50 | 4.00 |
| 56 | Chris Johnson UER RC | .02 | .10 |
| 57 | John Ericks | .01 | .05 |
| 58 | Gary Scott RC | .01 | .05 |
| 59 | Kiki Jones | .01 | .05 |
| 60 | Wil Cordero RC | .02 | .10 |
| 61 | Royce Clayton | .01 | .05 |
| 62 | Tim Costo RC | .02 | .10 |
| 63 | Roger Salkeld FUDC | .01 | .05 |
| 64 | Brook Fordyce RC | .08 | .25 |
| 65 | Mike Mussina RC | .75 | 2.00 |

|  |  | | |
|---|---|---|---|
| 66 | Dave Staton RC | .02 | .10 |
| 67 | Mike Lieberthal RC | .20 | .50 |
| 68 | Kurt Miller RC | .01 | .05 |
| 69 | Dan Peltier RC | .02 | .10 |
| 70 | Greg Blosser FUDC | .01 | .05 |
| 71 | Reggie Sanders RC | .30 | .75 |
| 72 | Brent Mayne | .01 | .05 |
| 73 | Rico Brogna | .01 | .05 |
| 74 | Willie Banks | .01 | .05 |
| 75 | Len Brutcher RC | .01 | .05 |
| 76 | Pat Kelly RC | .02 | .10 |
| 77 | Chris Sabo TC | .01 | .05 |
| 78 | Ramon Martinez TC | .01 | .05n |
| 79 | Matt Williams TC | .01 | .05 |
| 80 | Roberto Alomar TC | .02 | .10 |
| 81 | Glenn Davis TC | .01 | .05 |
| 82 | Ron Gant TC | .01 | .05 |
| 83 | Cecil Fielder's Feat | .01 | .05 |
| 84 | Orlando Merced RC | .01 | .05 |
| 85 | Domingo Ramos | .01 | .05 |
| 86 | Tom Bolton | .01 | .05 |
| 87 | Andres Santana | .01 | .05 |
| 88 | John Dopson | .01 | .05 |
| 89 | Kenny Williams | .01 | .05 |
| 90 | Marty Barrett | .01 | .05 |
| 91 | Tom Pagnozzi | .01 | .05 |
| 92 | Carmelo Martinez | .01 | .05 |
| 93 | Bobby Thigpen SAVE | .01 | .05 |
| 94 | Barry Bonds TC | .20 | .50 |
| 95 | Gregg Jefferies TC | .01 | .05 |
| 96 | Tim Wallach TC | .01 | .05 |
| 97 | Len Dykstra TC | .01 | .05 |
| 98 | Pedro Guerrero TC | .01 | .05 |
| 99 | Mark Grace TC | .01 | .05 |
| 100 | Checklist 1-100 | .01 | .05 |
| 101 | Kevin Elster | .01 | .05 |
| 102 | Tom Brookens | .01 | .05 |
| 103 | Mackey Sasser | .01 | .05 |
| 104 | Felix Fermin | .01 | .05 |
| 105 | Kevin McReynolds | .01 | .05 |
| 106 | Dave Stieb | .01 | .05 |
| 107 | Jeffrey Leonard | .01 | .05 |
| 108 | Dave Henderson | .01 | .05 |
| 109 | Sid Bream | .01 | .05 |
| 110 | Henry Cotto | .01 | .05 |
| 111 | Shawon Dunston | .01 | .05 |
| 112 | Mariano Duncan | .01 | .05 |
| 113 | Joe Girardi | .01 | .05 |
| 114 | Billy Hatcher | .01 | .05 |
| 115 | Greg Maddux | .15 | .40 |
| 116 | Jerry Browne | .01 | .05 |
| 117 | Juan Samuel | .01 | .05 |
| 118 | Steve Olin | .01 | .05 |
| 119 | Alfredo Griffin | .01 | .05 |
| 120 | Mitch Webster | .01 | .05 |
| 121 | Joel Skinner | .01 | .05 |
| 122 | Frank Viola | .02 | .10 |
| 123 | Cory Snyder | .01 | .05 |
| 124 | Howard Johnson | .02 | .10 |
| 125 | Carlos Baerga | .05 | .15 |
| 126 | Tony Fernandez | .01 | .05 |
| 127 | Dave Stewart | .02 | .10 |
| 128 | Jay Buhner | .01 | .05 |
| 129 | Mike LaValliere | .01 | .05 |
| 130 | Scott Bradley | .01 | .05 |
| 131 | Tony Phillips | .01 | .05 |
| 132 | Ryne Sandberg | .15 | .40 |
| 133 | Paul O'Neill | .05 | .15 |
| 134 | Mark Grace | .05 | .15 |
| 135 | Chris Sabo | .01 | .05 |
| 136 | Ramon Martinez | .01 | .05 |
| 137 | Brook Jacoby | .01 | .05 |
| 138 | Candy Maldonado | .01 | .05 |
| 139 | Mike Scioscia | .01 | .05 |
| 140 | Chris James | .01 | .05 |
| 141 | Craig Worthington | .01 | .05 |
| 142 | Manny Lee | .01 | .05 |
| 143 | Tim Raines | .02 | .10 |
| 144 | Sandy Alomar Jr. | .01 | .05 |
| 145 | John Olerud | .01 | .05 |
| 146 | Ozzie Canseco w/Jose | .02 | .10 |
| 147 | Pat Borders | .01 | .05 |
| 148 | Harold Reynolds | .01 | .05 |
| 149 | Tom Henke | .01 | .05 |
| 150 | R.J. Reynolds | .01 | .05 |
| 151 | Mike Gallego | .01 | .05 |
| 152 | Bobby Bonilla | .05 | .15 |
| 153 | Terry Steinbach | .01 | .05 |

|  |  | | |
|---|---|---|---|
| 154 | Barry Bonds | .40 | 1.00 |
| 155 | Jose Canseco | .05 | .15 |
| 156 | Gregg Jefferies | .01 | .05 |
| 157 | Matt Williams | .02 | .10 |
| 158 | Craig Biggio | .05 | .15 |
| 159 | Daryl Boston | .01 | .05 |
| 160 | Ricky Jordan | .01 | .05 |
| 161 | Stan Belinda | .01 | .05 |
| 162 | Ozzie Smith | .15 | .40 |
| 163 | Tom Brunansky | .01 | .05 |
| 164 | Todd Zeile | .01 | .05 |
| 165 | Mike Greenwell | .01 | .05 |
| 166 | Kal Daniels | .01 | .05 |
| 167 | Kent Hrbek | .02 | .10 |
| 168 | Franklin Stubbs | .01 | .05 |
| 169 | Dick Schofield | .01 | .05 |
| 170 | Junior Ortiz | .01 | .05 |
| 171 | Hector Villanueva | .01 | .05 |
| 172 | Dennis Eckersley | .02 | .10 |
| 173 | Mitch Williams | .01 | .05 |
| 174 | Mark McGwire | .30 | .75 |
| 175 | Fernando Valenzuela 3X | .01 | .05 |
| 176 | Gary Carter | .02 | .10 |
| 177 | Dave Magadan | .01 | .05 |
| 178 | Robby Thompson | .01 | .05 |
| 179 | Bob Ojeda | .01 | .05 |
| 180 | Ken Caminiti | .02 | .10 |
| 181 | Don Slaught | .01 | .05 |
| 182 | Luis Rivera | .01 | .05 |
| 183 | Jay Bell | .02 | .10 |
| 184 | Jody Reed | .01 | .05 |
| 185 | Wally Backman | .01 | .05 |
| 186 | Dave Martinez | .01 | .05 |
| 187 | Luis Polonia | .01 | .05 |
| 188 | Shane Mack | .01 | .05 |
| 189 | Spike Owen | .01 | .05 |
| 190 | Scott Bailes | .01 | .05 |
| 191 | John Russell | .01 | .05 |
| 192 | Walt Weiss | .01 | .05 |
| 193 | Jose Oquendo | .01 | .05 |
| 194 | Carney Lansford | .02 | .10 |
| 195 | Jeff Huson | .01 | .05 |
| 196 | Keith Miller | .01 | .05 |
| 197 | Eric Yelding | .01 | .05 |
| 198 | Ron Darling | .01 | .05 |
| 199 | John Kruk | .02 | .10 |
| 200 | Checklist 101-200 | .01 | .05 |
| 201 | John Shelby | .01 | .05 |
| 202 | Bob Geren | .01 | .05 |
| 203 | Lance McCullers | .01 | .05 |
| 204 | Alvaro Espinoza | .01 | .05 |
| 205 | Mark Salas | .01 | .05 |
| 206 | Mike Pagliarulo | .01 | .05 |
| 207 | Jose Uribe | .01 | .05 |
| 208 | Jim Deshaies | .01 | .05 |
| 209 | Ron Karkovice | .01 | .05 |
| 210 | Rafael Ramirez | .01 | .05 |
| 211 | Donnie Hill | .01 | .05 |
| 212 | Brian Harper | .01 | .05 |
| 213 | Jack Howell | .01 | .05 |
| 214 | Wes Gardner | .01 | .05 |
| 215 | Tim Burke | .01 | .05 |
| 216 | Doug Jones | .01 | .05 |
| 217 | Hubie Brooks | .01 | .05 |
| 218 | Tom Candiotti | .01 | .05 |
| 219 | Gerald Perry | .01 | .05 |
| 220 | Jose DeLeon | .01 | .05 |
| 221 | Wally Whitehurst | .01 | .05 |
| 222 | Alan Mills | .01 | .05 |
| 223 | Alan Trammell | .02 | .10 |
| 224 | Dwight Gooden | .02 | .10 |
| 225 | Travis Fryman | .05 | .15 |
| 226 | Joe Carter | .02 | .10 |
| 227 | Julio Franco | .02 | .10 |
| 228 | Craig Lefferts | .01 | .05 |
| 229 | Gary Pettis | .01 | .05 |
| 230 | Dennis Rasmussen | .01 | .05 |
| 231A | Brian Downing ERR | .01 | .05 |
| 231B | Brian Downing COR | .08 | .25 |
| 232 | Carlos Quintana | .01 | .05 |
| 233 | Gary Gaetti | .02 | .10 |
| 234 | Mark Langston | .01 | .05 |
| 235 | Tim Wallach | .01 | .05 |
| 236 | Greg Swindell | .01 | .05 |
| 237 | Eddie Murray | .08 | .25 |
| 238 | Jeff Manto | .01 | .05 |
| 239 | Lenny Harris | .01 | .05 |
| 240 | Jesse Orosco | .01 | .05 |
| 241 | Scott Lusader | .01 | .05 |
| 242 | Sid Fernandez | .01 | .05 |
| 243 | Jim Leyritz | .01 | .05 |
| 244 | Cecil Fielder | .02 | .10 |
| 245 | Darryl Strawberry | .02 | .10 |
| 246 | Frank Thomas | .08 | .25 |
| 247 | Kevin Mitchell | .01 | .05 |
| 248 | Lance Johnson | .01 | .05 |
| 249 | Rick Reuschel | .01 | .05 |
| 250 | Mark Portugal | .01 | .05 |
| 251 | Derek Lilliquist | .01 | .05 |
| 252 | Brian Holman | .01 | .05 |
| 253 | Rafael Valdez UER | .01 | .05 |
| 254 | B.J. Surhoff | .02 | .10 |
| 255 | Tony Gwynn | .10 | .30 |
| 256 | Andy Van Slyke | .05 | .15 |
| 257 | Todd Stottlemyre | .01 | .05 |
| 258 | Jose Lind | .01 | .05 |
| 259 | Greg Myers | .01 | .05 |
| 260 | Jeff Ballard | .01 | .05 |
| 261 | Bobby Thigpen | .01 | .05 |
| 262 | Jimmy Kremers | .01 | .05 |
| 263 | Robin Ventura | .02 | .10 |
| 264 | John Smoltz | .05 | .15 |
| 265 | Sammy Sosa | .08 | .25 |
| 266 | Gary Sheffield | .02 | .10 |
| 267 | Len Dykstra | .02 | .10 |
| 268 | Bill Spiers | .01 | .05 |
| 269 | Charlie Hayes | .01 | .05 |
| 270 | Brett Butler | .02 | .10 |
| 271 | Bip Roberts | .01 | .05 |
| 272 | Rob Deer | .01 | .05 |
| 273 | Fred Lynn | .01 | .05 |
| 274 | Dave Parker | .02 | .10 |
| 275 | Andy Benes | .01 | .05 |
| 276 | Glenallen Hill | .01 | .05 |
| 277 | Steve Howard | .01 | .05 |
| 278 | Doug Drabek | .01 | .05 |
| 279 | Joe Oliver | .01 | .05 |
| 280 | Todd Benzinger | .01 | .05 |
| 281 | Eric King | .01 | .05 |
| 282 | Jim Presley | .01 | .05 |
| 283 | Ken Patterson | .01 | .05 |
| 284 | Jack Daugherty | .01 | .05 |
| 285 | Ivan Calderon | .01 | .05 |
| 286 | Edgar Diaz | .01 | .05 |
| 287 | Kevin Bass | .01 | .05 |
| 288 | Don Carman | .01 | .05 |
| 289 | Greg Brock | .01 | .05 |
| 290 | John Franco | .02 | .10 |
| 291 | Joey Cora | .01 | .05 |
| 292 | Bill Wegman | .01 | .05 |
| 293 | Eric Show | .01 | .05 |
| 294 | Scott Bankhead | .01 | .05 |
| 295 | Garry Templeton | .01 | .05 |
| 296 | Mickey Tettleton | .01 | .05 |
| 297 | Luis Sojo | .01 | .05 |
| 298 | Jose Rijo | .01 | .05 |
| 299 | Dave Johnson | .01 | .05 |
| 300 | Checklist 201-300 | .01 | .05 |
| 301 | Mark Grant | .01 | .05 |
| 302 | Pete Harnisch | .01 | .05 |
| 303 | Greg Olson | .01 | .05 |
| 304 | Anthony Telford RC | .01 | .05 |
| 305 | Lonnie Smith | .01 | .05 |
| 306 | Chris Hoiles FUDC | .01 | .05 |
| 307 | Bryn Smith | .01 | .05 |
| 308 | Mike Devereaux | .01 | .05 |
| 309A | Milt Thompson ERR | .08 | .25 |
| 309B | Milt Thompson COR | .01 | .05 |
| 310 | Bob Melvin | .01 | .05 |
| 311 | Luis Salazar | .01 | .05 |
| 312 | Ed Whitson | .01 | .05 |
| 313 | Charlie Hough | .02 | .10 |
| 314 | Dave Clark | .01 | .05 |
| 315 | Eric Gunderson | .01 | .05 |
| 316 | Dan Petry | .01 | .05 |
| 317 | Dante Bichette | .02 | .10 |
| 318 | Mike Heath | .01 | .05 |
| 319 | Damon Berryhill | .01 | .05 |
| 320 | Walt Terrell | .01 | .05 |
| 321 | Scott Fletcher | .01 | .05 |
| 322 | Dan Plesac | .01 | .05 |
| 323 | Jack McDowell | .01 | .05 |
| 324 | Paul Molitor | .02 | .10 |
| 325 | Ozzie Guillen | .02 | .10 |
| 326 | Gregg Olson | .01 | .05 |
| 327 | Pedro Guerrero | .02 | .10 |
| 328 | Bob Milacki | .01 | .05 |
| 329 | John Tudor UER | .01 | .05 |
| 330 | Steve Finley UER | .02 | .10 |
| 331 | Jack Clark | .02 | .10 |
| 332 | Jerome Walton | .01 | .05 |
| 333 | Andy Hawkins | .01 | .05 |
| 334 | Derrick May | .01 | .05 |
| 335 | Roberto Alomar | .05 | .15 |
| 336 | Jack Morris | .02 | .10 |
| 337 | Dave Winfield | .02 | .10 |
| 338 | Steve Searcy | .01 | .05 |
| 339 | Chili Davis | .02 | .10 |
| 340 | Larry Sheets | .01 | .05 |
| 341 | Ted Higuera | .01 | .05 |
| 342 | David Segui | .01 | .05 |
| 343 | Greg Cadaret | .01 | .05 |
| 344 | Robin Yount | .15 | .40 |
| 345 | Nolan Ryan | .40 | 1.00 |
| 346 | Ray Lankford | .02 | .10 |
| 347 | Cal Ripken | .30 | .75 |
| 348 | Lee Smith | .01 | .05 |
| 349 | Brady Anderson | .02 | .10 |
| 350 | Frank DiPino | .01 | .05 |
| 351 | Hal Morris | .01 | .05 |
| 352 | Deion Sanders | .05 | .15 |
| 353 | Barry Larkin | .05 | .15 |
| 354 | Don Mattingly | .25 | .60 |
| 355 | Eric Davis | .02 | .10 |
| 356 | Jose Offerman | .01 | .05 |
| 357 | Mel Rojas | .01 | .05 |
| 358 | Rudy Seanez | .01 | .05 |
| 359 | Oil Can Boyd | .01 | .05 |
| 360 | Nelson Liriano | .01 | .05 |
| 361 | Ron Gant | .02 | .10 |
| 362 | Howard Farmer | .01 | .05 |
| 363 | David Justice | .05 | .15 |
| 364 | Delino DeShields | .02 | .10 |
| 365 | Steve Avery | .05 | .15 |
| 366 | David Cone | .02 | .10 |
| 367 | Lou Whitaker | .02 | .10 |
| 368 | Von Hayes | .01 | .05 |
| 369 | Frank Tanana | .01 | .05 |
| 370 | Tim Teufel | .01 | .05 |
| 371 | Randy Myers | .01 | .05 |
| 372 | Roberto Kelly | .01 | .05 |
| 373 | Jack Armstrong | .01 | .05 |
| 374 | Kelly Gruber | .01 | .05 |
| 375 | Kevin Maas | .01 | .05 |
| 376 | Randy Johnson | .10 | .30 |
| 377 | David West | .01 | .05 |
| 378 | Brent Knackert | .01 | .05 |
| 379 | Rick Honeycutt | .01 | .05 |
| 380 | Kevin Gross | .01 | .05 |
| 381 | Tom Foley | .01 | .05 |
| 382 | Jeff Blauser | .01 | .05 |
| 383 | Scott Ruskin | .01 | .05 |
| 384 | Andres Thomas | .01 | .05 |
| 385 | Dennis Martinez | .02 | .10 |
| 386 | Mike Henneman | .01 | .05 |
| 387 | Felix Jose | .01 | .05 |
| 388 | Alejandro Pena | .01 | .05 |
| 389 | Chet Lemon | .01 | .05 |
| 390 | Craig Wilson RC | .01 | .05 |
| 391 | Chuck Crim | .01 | .05 |
| 392 | Mel Hall | .01 | .05 |
| 393 | Mark Knudson | .01 | .05 |
| 394 | Norm Charlton | .01 | .05 |
| 395 | Mike Felder | .01 | .05 |
| 396 | Tim Layana | .01 | .05 |
| 397 | Steve Frey | .01 | .05 |
| 398 | Bill Doran | .01 | .05 |
| 399 | Dion James | .01 | .05 |
| 400 | Checklist 301-400 | .01 | .05 |
| 401 | Ron Hassey | .01 | .05 |
| 402 | Don Robinson | .01 | .05 |
| 403 | Gene Nelson | .01 | .05 |
| 404 | Terry Kennedy | .01 | .05 |
| 405 | Todd Burns | .01 | .05 |
| 406 | Roger McDowell | .01 | .05 |
| 407 | Bob Kipper | .01 | .05 |
| 408 | Darren Daulton | .02 | .10 |
| 409 | Chuck Cary | .01 | .05 |
| 410 | Bruce Ruffin | .01 | .05 |
| 411 | Juan Berenguer | .01 | .05 |
| 412 | Gary Ward | .01 | .05 |
| 413 | Al Newman | .01 | .05 |
| 414 | Danny Jackson | .01 | .05 |
| 415 | Greg Gagne | .01 | .05 |

|  |  | | |
|---|--------|---|---|
| ❏ 416 | Tom Herr | .01 | .05 |
| ❏ 417 | Jeff Parrett | .01 | .05 |
| ❏ 418 | Jeff Reardon | .02 | .10 |
| ❏ 419 | Mark Lemke | .01 | .05 |
| ❏ 420 | Charlie O'Brien | .01 | .05 |
| ❏ 421 | Willie Randolph | .02 | .10 |
| ❏ 422 | Steve Bedrosian | .01 | .05 |
| ❏ 423 | Mike Moore | .01 | .05 |
| ❏ 424 | Jeff Brantley | .01 | .05 |
| ❏ 425 | Bob Welch | .01 | .05 |
| ❏ 426 | Terry Mulholland | .01 | .05 |
| ❏ 427 | Willie Blair | .01 | .05 |
| ❏ 428 | Darrin Fletcher | .01 | .05 |
| ❏ 429 | Mike Witt | .01 | .05 |
| ❏ 430 | Joe Boever | .01 | .05 |
| ❏ 431 | Tom Gordon | .01 | .05 |
| ❏ 432 | Pedro Munoz RC | .02 | .10 |
| ❏ 433 | Kevin Seitzer | .01 | .05 |
| ❏ 434 | Kevin Tapani | .01 | .05 |
| ❏ 435 | Bret Saberhagen | .02 | .10 |
| ❏ 436 | Ellis Burks | .02 | .10 |
| ❏ 437 | Chuck Finley | .02 | .10 |
| ❏ 438 | Mike Boddicker | .01 | .05 |
| ❏ 439 | Francisco Cabrera | .01 | .05 |
| ❏ 440 | Todd Hundley | .01 | .05 |
| ❏ 441 | Kelly Downs | .01 | .05 |
| ❏ 442 | Dann Howitt | .01 | .05 |
| ❏ 443 | Scott Garrelts | .01 | .05 |
| ❏ 444 | Rickey Henderson | .08 | .25 |
| ❏ 445 | Will Clark | .05 | .15 |
| ❏ 446 | Ben McDonald | .01 | .05 |
| ❏ 447 | Dale Murphy | .05 | .15 |
| ❏ 448 | Dave Righetti | .02 | .10 |
| ❏ 449 | Dickie Thon | .01 | .05 |
| ❏ 450 | Ted Power | .01 | .05 |
| ❏ 451 | Scott Coolbaugh | .01 | .05 |
| ❏ 452 | Dwight Smith | .01 | .05 |
| ❏ 453 | Pete Incaviglia | .01 | .05 |
| ❏ 454 | Andre Dawson | .02 | .10 |
| ❏ 455 | Ruben Sierra | .02 | .10 |
| ❏ 456 | Andres Galarraga | .02 | .10 |
| ❏ 457 | Alvin Davis | .01 | .05 |
| ❏ 458 | Tony Castillo | .01 | .05 |
| ❏ 459 | Pete O'Brien | .01 | .05 |
| ❏ 460 | Charlie Leibrandt | .01 | .05 |
| ❏ 461 | Vince Coleman | .01 | .05 |
| ❏ 462 | Steve Sax | .01 | .05 |
| ❏ 463 | Omar Olivares RC | .02 | .10 |
| ❏ 464 | Oscar Azocar | .01 | .05 |
| ❏ 465 | Joe Magrane | .01 | .05 |
| ❏ 466 | Karl Rhodes | .01 | .05 |
| ❏ 467 | Benito Santiago | .02 | .10 |
| ❏ 468 | Joe Klink | .01 | .05 |
| ❏ 469 | Sil Campusano | .01 | .05 |
| ❏ 470 | Mark Parent | .01 | .05 |
| ❏ 471 | Shawn Boskie UER | .01 | .05 |
| ❏ 472 | Kevin Brown | .02 | .10 |
| ❏ 473 | Rick Sutcliffe | .02 | .10 |
| ❏ 474 | Rafael Palmeiro | .05 | .15 |
| ❏ 475 | Mike Harkey | .01 | .05 |
| ❏ 476 | Jaime Navarro | .01 | .05 |
| ❏ 477 | Marquis Grissom | .02 | .10 |
| ❏ 478 | Marty Clary | .01 | .05 |
| ❏ 479 | Greg Briley | .01 | .05 |
| ❏ 480 | Tom Glavine | .05 | .15 |
| ❏ 481 | Lee Guetterman | .01 | .05 |
| ❏ 482 | Rex Hudler | .01 | .05 |
| ❏ 483 | Dave LaPoint | .01 | .05 |
| ❏ 484 | Terry Pendleton | .02 | .10 |
| ❏ 485 | Jesse Barfield | .01 | .05 |
| ❏ 486 | Jose DeJesus | .01 | .05 |
| ❏ 487 | Paul Abbott RC | .02 | .10 |
| ❏ 488 | Ken Howell | .01 | .05 |
| ❏ 489 | Greg W. Harris | .01 | .05 |
| ❏ 490 | Roy Smith | .01 | .05 |
| ❏ 491 | Paul Assenmacher | .01 | .05 |
| ❏ 492 | Geno Petralli | .01 | .05 |
| ❏ 493 | Steve Wilson | .01 | .05 |
| ❏ 494 | Kevin Reimer | .01 | .05 |
| ❏ 495 | Bill Long | .01 | .05 |
| ❏ 496 | Mike Jackson | .01 | .05 |
| ❏ 497 | Oddibe McDowell | .01 | .05 |
| ❏ 498 | Bill Swift | .01 | .05 |
| ❏ 499 | Jeff Treadway | .01 | .05 |
| ❏ 500 | Checklist 401-500 | .01 | .05 |
| ❏ 501 | Gene Larkin | .01 | .05 |
| ❏ 502 | Bob Boone | .02 | .10 |
| ❏ 503 | Allan Anderson | .01 | .05 |
| ❏ 504 | Luis Aquino | .01 | .05 |
| ❏ 505 | Mark Guthrie | .01 | .05 |
| ❏ 506 | Joe Orsulak | .01 | .05 |
| ❏ 507 | Dana Kiecker | .01 | .05 |
| ❏ 508 | Dave Gallagher | .01 | .05 |
| ❏ 509 | Greg A. Harris | .01 | .05 |
| ❏ 510 | Mark Williamson | .01 | .05 |
| ❏ 511 | Casey Candaele | .01 | .05 |
| ❏ 512 | Mookie Wilson | .02 | .10 |
| ❏ 513 | Dave Smith | .01 | .05 |
| ❏ 514 | Chuck Carr FUDC | .01 | .05 |
| ❏ 515 | Glenn Wilson | .01 | .05 |
| ❏ 516 | Mike Fitzgerald | .01 | .05 |
| ❏ 517 | Devon White | .02 | .10 |
| ❏ 518 | Dave Hollins | .01 | .05 |
| ❏ 519 | Mark Eichhorn | .01 | .05 |
| ❏ 520 | Otis Nixon | .01 | .05 |
| ❏ 521 | Terry Shumpert | .01 | .05 |
| ❏ 522 | Scott Erickson | .01 | .05 |
| ❏ 523 | Danny Tartabull | .01 | .05 |
| ❏ 524 | Orel Hershiser | .02 | .10 |
| ❏ 525 | George Brett | .25 | .60 |
| ❏ 526 | Greg Vaughn | .01 | .05 |
| ❏ 527 | Tim Naehring FUDC | .01 | .05 |
| ❏ 528 | Curt Schilling | .08 | .25 |
| ❏ 529 | Chris Bosio | .01 | .05 |
| ❏ 530 | Sam Horn | .01 | .05 |
| ❏ 531 | Mike Scott | .01 | .05 |
| ❏ 532 | George Bell | .01 | .05 |
| ❏ 533 | Eric Anthony | .01 | .05 |
| ❏ 534 | Julio Valera | .01 | .05 |
| ❏ 535 | Glenn Davis | .01 | .05 |
| ❏ 536 | Larry Walker | .08 | .25 |
| ❏ 537 | Pat Combs | .01 | .05 |
| ❏ 538 | Chris Nabholz | .01 | .05 |
| ❏ 539 | Kirk McCaskill | .01 | .05 |
| ❏ 540 | Randy Ready | .01 | .05 |
| ❏ 541 | Mark Gubicza | .01 | .05 |
| ❏ 542 | Rick Aguilera | .02 | .10 |
| ❏ 543 | Brian McRae RC | .08 | .25 |
| ❏ 544 | Kirby Puckett | .25 | .60 |
| ❏ 545 | Bo Jackson | .08 | .25 |
| ❏ 546 | Wade Boggs | .05 | .15 |
| ❏ 547 | Tim McIntosh | .01 | .05 |
| ❏ 548 | Randy Milligan | .01 | .05 |
| ❏ 549 | Dwight Evans | .05 | .15 |
| ❏ 550 | Billy Ripken | .01 | .05 |
| ❏ 551 | Erik Hanson | .01 | .05 |
| ❏ 552 | Lance Parrish | .02 | .10 |
| ❏ 553 | Tino Martinez | .08 | .25 |
| ❏ 554 | Jim Abbott | .05 | .15 |
| ❏ 555 | Ken Griffey Sr. | .20 | .50 |
| ❏ 556 | Milt Cuyler | .01 | .05 |
| ❏ 557 | Mark Leonard RC | .01 | .05 |
| ❏ 558 | Jay Howell | .01 | .05 |
| ❏ 559 | Lloyd Moseby | .01 | .05 |
| ❏ 560 | Chris Gwynn | .01 | .05 |
| ❏ 561 | Mark Whiten FUDC | .01 | .05 |
| ❏ 562 | Harold Baines | .02 | .10 |
| ❏ 563 | Junior Felix | .01 | .05 |
| ❏ 564 | Darren Lewis FUDC | .01 | .05 |
| ❏ 565 | Fred McGriff | .05 | .15 |
| ❏ 566 | Kevin Appier | .02 | .10 |
| ❏ 567 | Luis Gonzalez RC | .30 | .75 |
| ❏ 568 | Frank White | .01 | .05 |
| ❏ 569 | Juan Agosto | .01 | .05 |
| ❏ 570 | Mike Macfarlane | .01 | .05 |
| ❏ 571 | Bert Blyleven | .02 | .10 |
| ❏ 572 | Ken Griffey Sr./Jr. | .08 | .25 |
| ❏ 573 | Lee Stevens | .01 | .05 |
| ❏ 574 | Edgar Martinez | .05 | .15 |
| ❏ 575 | Wally Joyner | .02 | .10 |
| ❏ 576 | Tim Belcher | .01 | .05 |
| ❏ 577 | John Burkett | .01 | .05 |
| ❏ 578 | Mike Morgan | .01 | .05 |
| ❏ 579 | Paul Gibson | .01 | .05 |
| ❏ 580 | Jose Vizcaino | .01 | .05 |
| ❏ 581 | Duane Ward | .01 | .05 |
| ❏ 582 | Scott Sanderson | .01 | .05 |
| ❏ 583 | David Wells | .02 | .10 |
| ❏ 584 | Willie McGee | .02 | .10 |
| ❏ 585 | John Cerutti | .01 | .05 |
| ❏ 586 | Danny Darwin | .01 | .05 |
| ❏ 587 | Kurt Stillwell | .01 | .05 |
| ❏ 588 | Rich Gedman | .01 | .05 |
| ❏ 589 | Mark Davis | .01 | .05 |
| ❏ 590 | Bill Gullickson | .01 | .05 |
| ❏ 591 | Matt Young | .01 | .05 |
| ❏ 592 | Bryan Harvey | .01 | .05 |
| ❏ 593 | Omar Vizquel | .05 | .15 |
| ❏ 594 | Scott Lewis RC | .02 | .10 |
| ❏ 595 | Dave Valle | .01 | .05 |
| ❏ 596 | Tim Crews | .01 | .05 |
| ❏ 597 | Mike Bielecki | .01 | .05 |
| ❏ 598 | Mike Sharperson | .01 | .05 |
| ❏ 599 | Dave Bergman | .01 | .05 |
| ❏ 600 | Checklist 501-600 | .01 | .05 |
| ❏ 601 | Steve Lyons | .01 | .05 |
| ❏ 602 | Bruce Hurst | .01 | .05 |
| ❏ 603 | Donn Pall | .01 | .05 |
| ❏ 604 | Jim Vatcher RC | .01 | .05 |
| ❏ 605 | Dan Pasqua | .01 | .05 |
| ❏ 606 | Kenny Rogers | .02 | .10 |
| ❏ 607 | Jeff Schulz RC | .01 | .05 |
| ❏ 608 | Brad Arnsberg | .01 | .05 |
| ❏ 609 | Willie Wilson | .01 | .05 |
| ❏ 610 | Jamie Moyer | .02 | .10 |
| ❏ 611 | Ron Oester | .01 | .05 |
| ❏ 612 | Dennis Cook | .01 | .05 |
| ❏ 613 | Rick Mahler | .01 | .05 |
| ❏ 614 | Bill Landrum | .01 | .05 |
| ❏ 615 | Scott Scudder | .01 | .05 |
| ❏ 616 | Tom Edens RC | .01 | .05 |
| ❏ 617 | 1917 Revisited | .02 | .10 |
| ❏ 618 | Jim Gantner | .01 | .05 |
| ❏ 619 | Darrel Akerfelds | .01 | .05 |
| ❏ 620 | Ron Robinson | .01 | .05 |
| ❏ 621 | Scott Radinsky | .01 | .05 |
| ❏ 622 | Pete Smith | .01 | .05 |
| ❏ 623 | Melido Perez | .01 | .05 |
| ❏ 624 | Jerald Clark | .01 | .05 |
| ❏ 625 | Carlos Martinez | .01 | .05 |
| ❏ 626 | Wes Chamberlain RC | .08 | .25 |
| ❏ 627 | Bobby Witt | .01 | .05 |
| ❏ 628 | Ken Dayley | .01 | .05 |
| ❏ 629 | John Barfield | .01 | .05 |
| ❏ 630 | Bob Tewksbury | .01 | .05 |
| ❏ 631 | Glenn Braggs | .01 | .05 |
| ❏ 632 | Jim Neidlinger RC | .01 | .05 |
| ❏ 633 | Tom Browning | .01 | .05 |
| ❏ 634 | Kirk Gibson | .02 | .10 |
| ❏ 635 | Rob Dibble | .02 | .10 |
| ❏ 636 | R.Henderson/L.Brock | .08 | .25 |
| ❏ 636A | R.Henderson/L.Brock | .08 | .25 |
| ❏ 637 | Jeff Montgomery | .01 | .05 |
| ❏ 638 | Mike Schooler | .01 | .05 |
| ❏ 639 | Storm Davis | .01 | .05 |
| ❏ 640 | Rich Rodriguez RC | .01 | .05 |
| ❏ 641 | Phil Bradley | .01 | .05 |
| ❏ 642 | Kent Mercker | .01 | .05 |
| ❏ 643 | Carlton Fisk | .05 | .15 |
| ❏ 644 | Mike Bell RC | .01 | .05 |
| ❏ 645 | Alex Fernandez | .01 | .05 |
| ❏ 646 | Juan Gonzalez | .08 | .25 |
| ❏ 647 | Ken Hill | .01 | .05 |
| ❏ 648 | Jeff Russell | .01 | .05 |
| ❏ 649 | Chuck Malone | .01 | .05 |
| ❏ 650 | Steve Buechele | .01 | .05 |
| ❏ 651 | Mike Benjamin | .01 | .05 |
| ❏ 652 | Tony Pena | .01 | .05 |
| ❏ 653 | Trevor Wilson | .01 | .05 |
| ❏ 654 | Alex Cole | .01 | .05 |
| ❏ 655 | Roger Clemens | .30 | .75 |
| ❏ 656 | Mark McGwire BASH | .15 | .40 |
| ❏ 657 | Joe Grahe RC | .02 | .10 |
| ❏ 658 | Jim Eisenreich | .01 | .05 |
| ❏ 659 | Dan Gladden | .01 | .05 |
| ❏ 660 | Steve Farr | .01 | .05 |
| ❏ 661 | Bill Sampen | .01 | .05 |
| ❏ 662 | Dave Rohde | .01 | .05 |
| ❏ 663 | Mark Gardner | .01 | .05 |
| ❏ 664 | Mike Simms RC | .01 | .05 |
| ❏ 665 | Moises Alou | .02 | .10 |
| ❏ 666 | Mickey Hatcher | .01 | .05 |
| ❏ 667 | Jimmy Key | .02 | .10 |
| ❏ 668 | John Wetteland | .02 | .10 |
| ❏ 669 | John Smiley | .01 | .05 |
| ❏ 670 | Jim Acker | .01 | .05 |
| ❏ 671 | Pascual Perez | .01 | .05 |
| ❏ 672 | Reggie Harris UER | .01 | .05 |
| ❏ 673 | Matt Nokes | .01 | .05 |
| ❏ 674 | Rafael Novoa RC | .01 | .05 |
| ❏ 675 | Hensley Meulens | .01 | .05 |
| ❏ 676 | Jeff M. Robinson | .01 | .05 |
| ❏ 677 | C.Fisk/R.Ventura | .02 | .10 |
| ❏ 678 | Johnny Ray | .01 | .05 |

| | | |
|---|---|---|
| ☐ 679 Greg Hibbard | .01 | .05 |
| ☐ 680 Paul Sorrento | .01 | .05 |
| ☐ 681 Mike Marshall | .01 | .05 |
| ☐ 682 Jim Clancy | .01 | .05 |
| ☐ 683 Rob Murphy | .01 | .05 |
| ☐ 684 Dave Schmidt | .01 | .05 |
| ☐ 685 Jeff Gray RC | .01 | .05 |
| ☐ 686 Mike Hartley | .01 | .05 |
| ☐ 687 Jeff King | .01 | .05 |
| ☐ 688 Stan Javier | .01 | .05 |
| ☐ 689 Bob Walk | .01 | .05 |
| ☐ 690 Jim Gott | .01 | .05 |
| ☐ 691 Mike LaCoss | .01 | .05 |
| ☐ 692 John Farrell | .01 | .05 |
| ☐ 693 Tim Leary | .01 | .05 |
| ☐ 694 Mike Walker | .01 | .05 |
| ☐ 695 Eric Plunk | .01 | .05 |
| ☐ 696 Mike Fetters | .01 | .05 |
| ☐ 697 Wayne Edwards | .01 | .05 |
| ☐ 698 Tim Drummond | .01 | .05 |
| ☐ 699 Willie Fraser | .01 | .05 |
| ☐ 700 Checklist 601-700 | .01 | .05 |
| ☐ 701 Mike Heath | .01 | .05 |
| ☐ 702 J.Bagwell/L.Gonz/K.Rhodes | .40 | 1.00 |
| ☐ 703 Jose Mesa | .01 | .05 |
| ☐ 704 Dave Smith | .01 | .05 |
| ☐ 705 Danny Darwin | .01 | .05 |
| ☐ 706 Rafael Belliard | .01 | .05 |
| ☐ 707 Rob Murphy | .01 | .05 |
| ☐ 708 Terry Pendleton | .02 | .10 |
| ☐ 709 Mike Pagliarulo | .01 | .05 |
| ☐ 710 Sid Bream | .01 | .05 |
| ☐ 711 Junior Felix | .01 | .05 |
| ☐ 712 Dante Bichette | .02 | .10 |
| ☐ 713 Kevin Gross | .01 | .05 |
| ☐ 714 Luis Sojo | .01 | .05 |
| ☐ 715 Bob Ojeda | .01 | .05 |
| ☐ 716 Julio Machado | .01 | .05 |
| ☐ 717 Steve Farr | .01 | .05 |
| ☐ 718 Franklin Stubbs | .01 | .05 |
| ☐ 719 Mike Boddicker | .01 | .05 |
| ☐ 720 Willie Randolph | .02 | .10 |
| ☐ 721 Willie McGee | .02 | .10 |
| ☐ 722 Chili Davis | .02 | .10 |
| ☐ 723 Danny Jackson | .01 | .05 |
| ☐ 724 Cory Snyder | .01 | .05 |
| ☐ 725 Dawson/Bell/Sandberg | .08 | .25 |
| ☐ 726 Rob Deer | .02 | .10 |
| ☐ 727 Rich DeLucia RC | .01 | .05 |
| ☐ 728 Mike Perez RC | .02 | .10 |
| ☐ 729 Mickey Tettleton | .01 | .05 |
| ☐ 730 Mike Blowers | .01 | .05 |
| ☐ 731 Gary Gaetti | .01 | .05 |
| ☐ 732 Brett Butler | .02 | .10 |
| ☐ 733 Dave Parker | .02 | .10 |
| ☐ 734 Eddie Zosky | .01 | .05 |
| ☐ 735 Jack Clark | .02 | .10 |
| ☐ 736 Jack Morris | .02 | .10 |
| ☐ 737 Kirk Gibson | .02 | .10 |
| ☐ 738 Steve Bedrosian | .01 | .05 |
| ☐ 739 Candy Maldonado | .01 | .05 |
| ☐ 740 Matt Young | .01 | .05 |
| ☐ 741 Rich Garces RC | .02 | .10 |
| ☐ 742 George Bell | .01 | .05 |
| ☐ 743 Deion Sanders | .05 | .15 |
| ☐ 744 Bo Jackson | .08 | .25 |
| ☐ 745 Luis Mercedes RC | .01 | .05 |
| ☐ 746 Reggie Jefferson | .02 | .10 |
| ☐ 747 Pete Incaviglia | .01 | .05 |
| ☐ 748 Chris Hammond | .01 | .05 |
| ☐ 749 Mike Stanton | .01 | .05 |
| ☐ 750 Scott Sanderson | .01 | .05 |
| ☐ 751 Paul Faries RC | .01 | .05 |
| ☐ 752 Al Osuna RC | .01 | .05 |
| ☐ 753 Steve Chitren RC | .01 | .05 |
| ☐ 754 Tony Fernandez | .02 | .10 |
| ☐ 755 Jeff Bagwell UER RC | .60 | 1.50 |
| ☐ 756 Kirk Dressendorfer RC | .02 | .10 |
| ☐ 757 Glenn Davis | .02 | .10 |
| ☐ 758 Gary Carter | .02 | .10 |
| ☐ 759 Zane Smith | .01 | .05 |
| ☐ 760 Vance Law | .01 | .05 |
| ☐ 761 Denis Boucher RC | .02 | .10 |
| ☐ 762 Turner Ward RC | .02 | .10 |
| ☐ 763 Roberto Alomar | .05 | .15 |
| ☐ 764 Albert Belle | .05 | .15 |
| ☐ 765 Joe Carter | .02 | .10 |
| ☐ 766 Pete Schourek RC | .02 | .10 |

| | | |
|---|---|---|
| ☐ 767 Heathcliff Slocumb RC | .02 | .10 |
| ☐ 768 Vince Coleman | .01 | .05 |
| ☐ 769 Mitch Williams | .01 | .05 |
| ☐ 770 Brian Downing | .01 | .05 |
| ☐ 771 Dana Allison RC | .01 | .05 |
| ☐ 772 Pete Harnisch | .01 | .05 |
| ☐ 773 Tim Raines | .02 | .10 |
| ☐ 774 Darryl Kile | .02 | .10 |
| ☐ 775 Fred McGriff | .05 | .15 |
| ☐ 776 Dwight Evans | .05 | .15 |
| ☐ 777 Joe Slusarski RC | .01 | .05 |
| ☐ 778 Dave Righetti | .01 | .05 |
| ☐ 779 Jeff Hamilton | .01 | .05 |
| ☐ 780 Ernest Riles | .01 | .05 |
| ☐ 781 Ken Dayley | .01 | .05 |
| ☐ 782 Eric King | .01 | .05 |
| ☐ 783 Devon White | .02 | .10 |
| ☐ 784 Beau Allred | .01 | .05 |
| ☐ 785 Mike Timlin RC | .08 | .25 |
| ☐ 786 Ivan Calderon | .01 | .05 |
| ☐ 787 Hubie Brooks | .01 | .05 |
| ☐ 788 Juan Agosto | .01 | .05 |
| ☐ 789 Barry Jones | .01 | .05 |
| ☐ 790 Wally Backman | .01 | .05 |
| ☐ 791 Jim Presley | .01 | .05 |
| ☐ 792 Charlie Hough | .02 | .10 |
| ☐ 793 Larry Andersen | .01 | .05 |
| ☐ 794 Steve Finley | .02 | .10 |
| ☐ 795 Shawn Abner | .01 | .05 |
| ☐ 796 Jeff M. Robinson | .01 | .05 |
| ☐ 797 Joe Bitker RC | .01 | .05 |
| ☐ 798 Eric Show | .01 | .05 |
| ☐ 799 Bud Black | .01 | .05 |
| ☐ 800 Checklist 701-800 | .01 | .05 |
| ☐ HH1 Hank Aaron Hologram | .60 | 1.50 |
| ☐ SP1 Michael Jordan | 3.00 | 8.00 |
| ☐ SP2 N.Ryan/R.Henderson | .75 | 2.00 |

## 1992 Upper Deck

| | | |
|---|---|---|
| ☐ COMPLETE SET (800) | 10.00 | 25.00 |
| ☐ COMPLETE LO SET (700) | 8.00 | 20.00 |
| ☐ COMPLETE HI SET (100) | 2.00 | 5.00 |
| ☐ 1 J.Thome/R.Klesko CL | .08 | .25 |
| ☐ 2 Royce Clayton SR | .01 | .05 |
| ☐ 3 Brian Jordan SR | .20 | .50 |
| ☐ 4 Dave Fleming | .01 | .05 |
| ☐ 5 Jim Thome | .08 | .25 |
| ☐ 6 Jeff Juden SR | .01 | .05 |
| ☐ 7 Roberto Hernandez SR | .01 | .05 |
| ☐ 8 Kyle Abbott SR | .01 | .05 |
| ☐ 9 Chris George SR | .01 | .05 |
| ☐ 10 Rob Maurer SR | .01 | .05 |
| ☐ 11 Donald Harris SR | .01 | .05 |
| ☐ 12 Ted Wood SR | .01 | .05 |
| ☐ 13 Patrick Lennon SR | .01 | .05 |
| ☐ 14 Willie Banks SR | .01 | .05 |
| ☐ 15 Roger Salkeld SR UER | .01 | .05 |
| (Bill was his grand- | | |
| father | .01 | .05 |
| ☐ 16 Wil Cordero SR | .01 | .05 |
| ☐ 17 Arthur Rhodes SR | .05 | .15 |
| ☐ 18 Pedro Martinez | .40 | 1.00 |
| ☐ 19 Andy Ashby SR | .01 | .05 |
| ☐ 20 Tom Goodwin SR | .01 | .05 |
| ☐ 21 Braulio Castillo SR | .01 | .05 |
| ☐ 22 Todd Van Poppel | .01 | .05 |
| ☐ 23 Brian Williams RC | .01 | .05 |
| ☐ 24 Ryan Klesko | .02 | .10 |
| ☐ 25 Kenny Lofton | .05 | .15 |
| ☐ 26 Derek Bell | .02 | .10 |
| ☐ 27 Reggie Sanders | .02 | .10 |
| ☐ 28 Dave Winfield's 400th | .01 | .05 |
| ☐ 29 David Justice TC | .01 | .05 |
| ☐ 30 Rob Dibble TC | .01 | .05 |

| | | |
|---|---|---|
| Cincinnati Reds | .01 | .05 |
| ☐ 31 Craig Biggio TC | .02 | .10 |
| ☐ 32 Eddie Murray TC | .05 | .15 |
| ☐ 33 Fred McGriff TC | .02 | .10 |
| ☐ 34 Willie McGee TC | | |
| San Francisco Giants | .01 | .05 |
| ☐ 35 Shawon Dunston TC | | |
| Chicago Cubs | .01 | .05 |
| ☐ 36 Delino DeShields TC | .01 | .05 |
| ☐ 37 Howard Johnson TC | | |
| New York Mets | .01 | .05 |
| ☐ 38 John Kruk TC | .01 | .05 |
| ☐ 39 Doug Drabek TC | | |
| Pittsburgh Pirates | .01 | .05 |
| ☐ 40 Todd Zeile TC | .01 | .05 |
| ☐ 41 Steve Avery Playoff | .01 | .05 |
| ☐ 42 Jeremy Hernandez RC | .01 | .05 |
| ☐ 43 Doug Henry RC | .02 | .10 |
| ☐ 44 Chris Donnels | .01 | .05 |
| ☐ 45 Mo Sanford | .01 | .05 |
| ☐ 46 Scott Kamieniecki | .01 | .05 |
| ☐ 47 Mark Lemke | .01 | .05 |
| ☐ 48 Steve Farr | .01 | .05 |
| ☐ 49 Francisco Oliveras | .01 | .05 |
| ☐ 50 Ced Landrum | .01 | .05 |
| ☐ 51 R.White/M.Newfield CL | .02 | .10 |
| ☐ 52 Eduardo Perez RC | .08 | .25 |
| ☐ 53 Tom Nevers TP | .01 | .05 |
| ☐ 54 David Zancanaro TP | .01 | .05 |
| ☐ 55 Shawn Green RC | .40 | 1.00 |
| ☐ 56 Mark Wohlers TP | .01 | .05 |
| ☐ 57 Dave Nilsson | .01 | .05 |
| ☐ 58 Dmitri Young | .02 | .10 |
| ☐ 59 Ryan Hawblitzel RC | .02 | .10 |
| ☐ 60 Raul Mondesi | .02 | .10 |
| ☐ 61 Rondell White | .02 | .10 |
| ☐ 62 Steve Hosey | .01 | .05 |
| ☐ 63 Manny Ramirez RC | 1.50 | 4.00 |
| ☐ 64 Marc Newfield | .01 | .05 |
| ☐ 65 Jeromy Burnitz | .02 | .10 |
| ☐ 66 Mark Smith RC | .02 | .10 |
| ☐ 67 Joey Hamilton RC | .02 | .10 |
| ☐ 68 Tyler Green RC | .02 | .10 |
| ☐ 69 Jon Farrell RC | .02 | .10 |
| ☐ 70 Kurt Miller TP | .01 | .05 |
| ☐ 71 Jeff Plympton TP | .01 | .05 |
| ☐ 72 Dan Wilson TP | .01 | .05 |
| ☐ 73 Joe Vitiello RC | .02 | .10 |
| ☐ 74 Rico Brogna TP | .01 | .05 |
| ☐ 75 David McCarty RC | .08 | .25 |
| ☐ 76 Bob Wickman | .08 | .25 |
| ☐ 77 Carlos Rodriguez TP | .01 | .05 |
| ☐ 78 Jim Abbott | | |
| Stay in Tune | .02 | .10 |
| ☐ 79 P.Martinez/R.Martinez | .08 | .25 |
| ☐ 80 Kevin Mitchell | | |
| Keith Mitchell | .01 | .05 |
| ☐ 81 Sandy/Roberto Alomar | .02 | .10 |
| ☐ 82 Ripken Brothers | .20 | .50 |
| ☐ 83 Tony/Chris Gwynn | .05 | .15 |
| ☐ 84 D.Gooden/G.Sheffield | .08 | .25 |
| ☐ 85 K.Griffey Jr. w/Family | | |
| ☐ 86 Jim Abbott TC | | |
| California Angels | .02 | .10 |
| ☐ 87 Frank Thomas TC | .05 | .15 |
| ☐ 88 Danny Tartabull TC | | |
| Kansas City Royals | .01 | .05 |
| ☐ 89 Scott Erickson TC | | |
| Minnesota Twins | .01 | .05 |
| ☐ 90 Rickey Henderson TC | .05 | .15 |
| ☐ 91 Edgar Martinez TC | .02 | .10 |
| ☐ 92 Nolan Ryan TC | .20 | .50 |
| ☐ 93 Ben McDonald TC | | |
| Baltimore Orioles | .01 | .05 |
| ☐ 94 Ellis Burks TC | | |
| Boston Red Sox | .01 | .05 |
| ☐ 95 Greg Swindell TC | | |
| Cleveland Indians | .01 | .05 |
| ☐ 96 Cecil Fielder TC | .01 | .05 |
| ☐ 97 Greg Vaughn TC | .01 | .05 |
| ☐ 98 Kevin Maas TC | | |
| New York Yankees | .01 | .05 |
| ☐ 99 Dave Stieb TC | | |
| Toronto Blue Jays | .01 | .05 |
| ☐ 100 Checklist 1-100 | .01 | .05 |
| ☐ 101 Joe Oliver | .01 | .05 |
| ☐ 102 Hector Villanueva | .01 | .05 |
| ☐ 103 Ed Whitson | .01 | .05 |

|  |  | | |
|---|---|---|---|
| 104 | Danny Jackson | .01 | .05 |
| 105 | Chris Hammond | .01 | .05 |
| 106 | Ricky Jordan | .01 | .05 |
| 107 | Kevin Bass | .01 | .05 |
| 108 | Darrin Fletcher | .01 | .05 |
| 109 | Junior Ortiz | .01 | .05 |
| 110 | Tom Bolton | .01 | .05 |
| 111 | Jeff King | .01 | .05 |
| 112 | Dave Magadan | .01 | .05 |
| 113 | Mike LaValliere | .01 | .05 |
| 114 | Hubie Brooks | .01 | .05 |
| 115 | Jay Bell | .02 | .10 |
| 116 | David Wells | .02 | .10 |
| 117 | Jim Leyritz | .01 | .05 |
| 118 | Manuel Lee | .01 | .05 |
| 119 | Alvaro Espinoza | .01 | .05 |
| 120 | B.J. Surhoff | .02 | .10 |
| 121 | Hal Morris | .01 | .05 |
| 122 | Shawon Dawson | .01 | .05 |
| 123 | Chris Sabo | .01 | .05 |
| 124 | Andre Dawson | .02 | .10 |
| 125 | Eric Davis | .02 | .10 |
| 126 | Chili Davis | .02 | .10 |
| 127 | Dale Murphy | .05 | .15 |
| 128 | Kirk McCaskill | .01 | .05 |
| 129 | Terry Mulholland | .01 | .05 |
| 130 | Rick Aguilera | .02 | .10 |
| 131 | Vince Coleman | .01 | .05 |
| 132 | Andy Van Slyke | .05 | .15 |
| 133 | Gregg Jefferies | .01 | .05 |
| 134 | Barry Bonds | .40 | 1.00 |
| 135 | Dwight Gooden | .02 | .10 |
| 136 | Dave Stieb | .01 | .05 |
| 137 | Albert Belle | .05 | .15 |
| 138 | Teddy Higuera | .01 | .05 |
| 139 | Jesse Barfield | .01 | .05 |
| 140 | Pat Borders | .01 | .05 |
| 141 | Bip Roberts | .01 | .05 |
| 142 | Rob Dibble | .02 | .10 |
| 143 | Mark Grace | .05 | .15 |
| 144 | Barry Larkin | .05 | .15 |
| 145 | Ryne Sandberg | .15 | .40 |
| 146 | Scott Erickson | .01 | .05 |
| 147 | Luis Polonia | .01 | .05 |
| 148 | John Burkett | .01 | .05 |
| 149 | Luis Sojo | .01 | .05 |
| 150 | Dickie Thon | .01 | .05 |
| 151 | Walt Weiss | .01 | .05 |
| 152 | Mike Scioscia | .01 | .05 |
| 153 | Mark McGwire | .25 | .60 |
| 154 | Matt Williams | .02 | .10 |
| 155 | Rickey Henderson | .08 | .25 |
| 156 | Sandy Alomar Jr. | .01 | .05 |
| 157 | Brian McRae | .01 | .05 |
| 158 | Harold Baines | .02 | .10 |
| 159 | Kevin Appier | .02 | .10 |
| 160 | Felix Fermin | .01 | .05 |
| 161 | Leo Gomez | .01 | .05 |
| 162 | Craig Biggio | .05 | .15 |
| 163 | Ben McDonald | .01 | .05 |
| 164 | Randy Johnson | .08 | .25 |
| 165 | Cal Ripken | .30 | .75 |
| 166 | Frank Thomas | .08 | .25 |
| 167 | Delino DeShields | .01 | .05 |
| 168 | Greg Gagne | .01 | .05 |
| 169 | Ron Karkovice | .01 | .05 |
| 170 | Charlie Leibrandt | .01 | .05 |
| 171 | Dave Righetti | .02 | .10 |
| 172 | Dave Henderson | .01 | .05 |
| 173 | Steve Decker | .01 | .05 |
| 174 | Darryl Strawberry | .02 | .10 |
| 175 | Will Clark | .05 | .15 |
| 176 | Ruben Sierra | .02 | .10 |
| 177 | Ozzie Smith | .15 | .40 |
| 178 | Charles Nagy | .01 | .05 |
| 179 | Gary Pettis | .01 | .05 |
| 180 | Kirk Gibson | .02 | .10 |
| 181 | Randy Milligan | .01 | .05 |
| 182 | Dave Valle | .01 | .05 |
| 183 | Chris Hoiles | .01 | .05 |
| 184 | Tony Phillips | .01 | .05 |
| 185 | Brady Anderson | .02 | .10 |
| 186 | Scott Fletcher | .01 | .05 |
| 187 | Gene Larkin | .01 | .05 |
| 188 | Lance Johnson | .01 | .05 |
| 189 | Greg Olson | .01 | .05 |
| 190 | Melido Perez | .01 | .05 |
| 191 | Lenny Harris | .01 | .05 |
| 192 | Terry Kennedy | .01 | .05 |
| 193 | Mike Gallego | .01 | .05 |
| 194 | Willie McGee | .01 | .05 |
| 195 | Juan Samuel | .01 | .05 |
| 196 | Jeff Huson | .02 | .10 |
| 197 | Alex Cole | .01 | .05 |
| 198 | Ron Robinson | .01 | .05 |
| 199 | Joel Skinner | .01 | .05 |
| 200 | Checklist 101-200 | .01 | .05 |
| 201 | Kevin Reimer | .01 | .05 |
| 202 | Stan Belinda | .01 | .05 |
| 203 | Pat Tabler | .01 | .05 |
| 204 | Jose Guzman | .01 | .05 |
| 205 | Jose Lind | .01 | .05 |
| 206 | Spike Owen | .01 | .05 |
| 207 | Joe Orsulak | .01 | .05 |
| 208 | Charlie Hayes | .01 | .05 |
| 209 | Mike Devereaux | .01 | .05 |
| 210 | Mike Fitzgerald | .01 | .05 |
| 211 | Willie Randolph | .02 | .10 |
| 212 | Rod Nichols | .01 | .05 |
| 213 | Mike Boddicker | .01 | .05 |
| 214 | Bill Spiers | .01 | .05 |
| 215 | Steve Olin | .01 | .05 |
| 216 | David Howard | .01 | .05 |
| 217 | Gary Varsho | .01 | .05 |
| 218 | Mike Harkey | .01 | .05 |
| 219 | Luis Aquino | .01 | .05 |
| 220 | Chuck McElroy | .01 | .05 |
| 221 | Doug Drabek | .01 | .05 |
| 222 | Dave Winfield | .05 | .15 |
| 223 | Rafael Palmeiro | .05 | .15 |
| 224 | Joe Carter | .02 | .10 |
| 225 | Bobby Bonilla | .02 | .10 |
| 226 | Ivan Calderon | .01 | .05 |
| 227 | Gregg Olson | .01 | .05 |
| 228 | Tim Wallach | .01 | .05 |
| 229 | Terry Pendleton | .02 | .10 |
| 230 | Gilberto Reyes | .01 | .05 |
| 231 | Carlos Baerga | .01 | .05 |
| 232 | Greg Vaughn | .01 | .05 |
| 233 | Bret Saberhagen | .02 | .10 |
| 234 | Gary Sheffield | .02 | .10 |
| 235 | Mark Lewis | .01 | .05 |
| 236 | George Bell | .01 | .05 |
| 237 | Danny Tartabull | .01 | .05 |
| 238 | Willie Wilson | .01 | .05 |
| 239 | Doug Dascenzo | .01 | .05 |
| 240 | Bill Pecota | .01 | .05 |
| 241 | Julio Franco | .02 | .10 |
| 242 | Ed Sprague | .01 | .05 |
| 243 | Juan Gonzalez | .05 | .15 |
| 244 | Chuck Finley | .02 | .10 |
| 245 | Ivan Rodriguez | .08 | .25 |
| 246 | Len Dykstra | .02 | .10 |
| 247 | Deion Sanders | .05 | .15 |
| 248 | Dwight Evans | .05 | .15 |
| 249 | Larry Walker | .05 | .15 |
| 250 | Billy Ripken | .01 | .05 |
| 251 | Mickey Tettleton | .01 | .05 |
| 252 | Tony Pena | .01 | .05 |
| 253 | Benito Santiago | .02 | .10 |
| 254 | Kirby Puckett | .08 | .25 |
| 255 | Cecil Fielder | .02 | .10 |
| 256 | Howard Johnson | .01 | .05 |
| 257 | Andujar Cedeno | .01 | .05 |
| 258 | Jose Rijo | .01 | .05 |
| 259 | Al Osuna | .01 | .05 |
| 260 | Todd Hundley | .01 | .05 |
| 261 | Orel Hershiser | .02 | .10 |
| 262 | Ray Lankford | .02 | .10 |
| 263 | Robin Ventura | .02 | .10 |
| 264 | Felix Jose | .01 | .05 |
| 265 | Eddie Murray | .08 | .25 |
| 266 | Kevin Mitchell | .01 | .05 |
| 267 | Gary Carter | .02 | .10 |
| 268 | Mike Benjamin | .01 | .05 |
| 269 | Dick Schofield | .01 | .05 |
| 270 | Jose Uribe | .01 | .05 |
| 271 | Pete Incaviglia | .01 | .05 |
| 272 | Tony Fernandez | .01 | .05 |
| 273 | Alan Trammell | .02 | .10 |
| 274 | Tony Gwynn | .10 | .30 |
| 275 | Mike Greenwell | .01 | .05 |
| 276 | Jeff Bagwell | .08 | .25 |
| 277 | Frank Viola | .02 | .10 |
| 278 | Randy Myers | .01 | .05 |
| 279 | Ken Caminiti | .02 | .10 |
| 280 | Bill Doran | .01 | .05 |
| 281 | Dan Pasqua | .01 | .05 |
| 282 | Alfredo Griffin | .01 | .05 |
| 283 | Jose Oquendo | .01 | .05 |
| 284 | Kal Daniels | .01 | .05 |
| 285 | Bobby Thigpen | .01 | .05 |
| 286 | Robby Thompson | .01 | .05 |
| 287 | Mark Eichhorn | .01 | .05 |
| 288 | Mike Felder | .01 | .05 |
| 289 | Dave Gallagher | .01 | .05 |
| 290 | Dave Anderson | .01 | .05 |
| 291 | Mel Hall | .01 | .05 |
| 292 | Jerald Clark | .01 | .05 |
| 293 | Al Newman | .01 | .05 |
| 294 | Rob Deer | .01 | .05 |
| 295 | Matt Nokes | .01 | .05 |
| 296 | Jack Armstrong | .01 | .05 |
| 297 | Jim Deshaies | .01 | .05 |
| 298 | Jeff Innis | .01 | .05 |
| 299 | Jeff Reed | .01 | .05 |
| 300 | Checklist 201-300 | .01 | .05 |
| 301 | Lonnie Smith | .01 | .05 |
| 302 | Jimmy Key | .02 | .10 |
| 303 | Junior Felix | .01 | .05 |
| 304 | Mike Heath | .01 | .05 |
| 305 | Mark Langston | .01 | .05 |
| 306 | Greg W. Harris | .01 | .05 |
| 307 | Brett Butler | .02 | .10 |
| 308 | Luis Rivera | .01 | .05 |
| 309 | Bruce Ruffin | .01 | .05 |
| 310 | Paul Faries | .01 | .05 |
| 311 | Terry Leach | .01 | .05 |
| 312 | Scott Brosius RC | .20 | .50 |
| 313 | Scott Leius | .01 | .05 |
| 314 | Harold Reynolds | .02 | .10 |
| 315 | Jack Morris | .02 | .10 |
| 316 | David Segui | .01 | .05 |
| 317 | Bill Gullickson | .01 | .05 |
| 318 | Todd Frohwirth | .01 | .05 |
| 319 | Mark Leiter | .01 | .05 |
| 320 | Jeff M. Robinson | .01 | .05 |
| 321 | Gary Gaetti | .02 | .10 |
| 322 | John Smoltz | .05 | .15 |
| 323 | Andy Benes | .01 | .05 |
| 324 | Kelly Gruber | .01 | .05 |
| 325 | Jim Abbott | .05 | .15 |
| 326 | John Kruk | .02 | .10 |
| 327 | Kevin Seitzer | .01 | .05 |
| 328 | Darrin Jackson | .01 | .05 |
| 329 | Kurt Stillwell | .01 | .05 |
| 330 | Mike Maddux | .01 | .05 |
| 331 | Dennis Eckersley | .02 | .10 |
| 332 | Dan Gladden | .01 | .05 |
| 333 | Jose Canseco | .05 | .15 |
| 334 | Kent Hrbek | .02 | .10 |
| 335 | Ken Griffey Sr. | .01 | .05 |
| 336 | Greg Swindell | .01 | .05 |
| 337 | Trevor Wilson | .01 | .05 |
| 338 | Sam Horn | .01 | .05 |
| 339 | Mike Henneman | .01 | .05 |
| 340 | Jerry Browne | .01 | .05 |
| 341 | Glenn Braggs | .01 | .05 |
| 342 | Tom Glavine | .05 | .15 |
| 343 | Wally Joyner | .02 | .10 |
| 344 | Fred McGriff | .05 | .15 |
| 345 | Ron Gant | .02 | .10 |
| 346 | Ramon Martinez | .01 | .05 |
| 347 | Wes Chamberlain | .01 | .05 |
| 348 | Terry Shumpert | .01 | .05 |
| 349 | Tim Teufel | .01 | .05 |
| 350 | Wally Backman | .01 | .05 |
| 351 | Joe Girard | .01 | .05 |
| 352 | Devon White | .02 | .10 |
| 353 | Greg Maddux | .15 | .40 |
| 354 | Ryan Bowen | .01 | .05 |
| 355 | Roberto Alomar | .05 | .15 |
| 356 | Don Mattingly | .25 | .60 |
| 357 | Pedro Guerrero | .02 | .10 |
| 358 | Steve Sax | .01 | .05 |
| 359 | Joey Cora | .01 | .05 |
| 360 | Jim Gantner | .01 | .05 |
| 361 | Brian Barnes | .01 | .05 |
| 362 | Kevin McReynolds | .01 | .05 |
| 363 | Bret Barberie | .01 | .05 |
| 364 | Lance Dickson | .02 | .10 |
| 365 | Dennis Martinez | .02 | .10 |
| 366 | Brian Hunter | .01 | .05 |
| 367 | Edgar Martinez | .05 | .15 |

|  |  | | |
|---|---|---|---|
| 368 | Steve Finley | .02 | .10 |
| 369 | Greg Briley | .01 | .05 |
| 370 | Jeff Blauser | .01 | .05 |
| 371 | Todd Stottlemyre | .01 | .05 |
| 372 | Luis Gonzalez | .02 | .10 |
| 373 | Rick Wilkins | .01 | .05 |
| 374 | Darryl Kile | .02 | .10 |
| 375 | John Olerud | .02 | .10 |
| 376 | Lee Smith | .02 | .10 |
| 377 | Kevin Maas | .01 | .05 |
| 378 | Dante Bichette | .02 | .10 |
| 379 | Tom Pagnozzi | .01 | .05 |
| 380 | Mike Flanagan | .01 | .05 |
| 381 | Charlie O'Brien | .01 | .05 |
| 382 | Dave Martinez | .01 | .05 |
| 383 | Keith Miller | .01 | .05 |
| 384 | Scott Ruskin | .01 | .05 |
| 385 | Kevin Elster | .01 | .05 |
| 386 | Alvin Davis | .01 | .05 |
| 387 | Casey Candaele | .01 | .05 |
| 388 | Pete O'Brien | .01 | .05 |
| 389 | Jeff Treadway | .01 | .05 |
| 390 | Scott Bradley | .01 | .05 |
| 391 | Mookie Wilson | .02 | .10 |
| 392 | Jimmy Jones | .01 | .05 |
| 393 | Candy Maldonado | .01 | .05 |
| 394 | Eric Yelding | .01 | .05 |
| 395 | Tom Henke | .01 | .05 |
| 396 | Franklin Stubbs | .01 | .05 |
| 397 | Milt Thompson | .01 | .05 |
| 398 | Mark Carreon | .01 | .05 |
| 399 | Randy Velarde | .01 | .05 |
| 400 | Checklist 301-400 | .01 | .05 |
| 401 | Omar Vizquel | .05 | .15 |
| 402 | Joe Boever | .01 | .05 |
| 403 | Bill Krueger | .01 | .05 |
| 404 | Jody Reed | .01 | .05 |
| 405 | Mike Schooler | .01 | .05 |
| 406 | Jason Grimsley | .01 | .05 |
| 407 | Greg Myers | .01 | .05 |
| 408 | Randy Ready | .01 | .05 |
| 409 | Mike Timlin | .01 | .05 |
| 410 | Mitch Williams | .01 | .05 |
| 411 | Garry Templeton | .01 | .05 |
| 412 | Greg Cadaret | .01 | .05 |
| 413 | Donnie Hill | .01 | .05 |
| 414 | Wally Whitehurst | .01 | .05 |
| 415 | Scott Sanderson | .01 | .05 |
| 416 | Thomas Howard | .01 | .05 |
| 417 | Neal Heaton | .01 | .05 |
| 418 | Charlie Hough | .02 | .10 |
| 419 | Jack Howell | .01 | .05 |
| 420 | Greg Hibbard | .01 | .05 |
| 421 | Carlos Quintana | .01 | .05 |
| 422 | Kim Batiste | .01 | .05 |
| 423 | Paul Molitor | .02 | .10 |
| 424 | Ken Griffey Jr. | .15 | .40 |
| 425 | Phil Plantier | .01 | .05 |
| 426 | Denny Neagle | .02 | .10 |
| 427 | Von Hayes | .01 | .05 |
| 428 | Shane Mack | .01 | .05 |
| 429 | Darren Daulton | .02 | .10 |
| 430 | Dwayne Henry | .01 | .05 |
| 431 | Lance Parrish | .02 | .10 |
| 432 | Mike Humphreys | .01 | .05 |
| 433 | Tim Burke | .01 | .05 |
| 434 | Bryan Harvey | .01 | .05 |
| 435 | Pat Kelly | .01 | .05 |
| 436 | Ozzie Guillen | .02 | .10 |
| 437 | Bruce Hurst | .01 | .05 |
| 438 | Sammy Sosa | .08 | .25 |
| 439 | Dennis Rasmussen | .01 | .05 |
| 440 | Ken Patterson | .01 | .05 |
| 441 | Jay Buhner | .02 | .10 |
| 442 | Pat Combs | .01 | .05 |
| 443 | Wade Boggs | .05 | .15 |
| 444 | George Brett | .25 | .60 |
| 445 | Mo Vaughn | .02 | .10 |
| 446 | Chuck Knoblauch | .02 | .10 |
| 447 | Tom Candiotti | .01 | .05 |
| 448 | Mark Portugal | .01 | .05 |
| 449 | Mickey Morandini | .01 | .05 |
| 450 | Duane Ward | .01 | .05 |
| 451 | Otis Nixon | .01 | .05 |
| 452 | Bob Welch | .01 | .05 |
| 453 | Rusty Meacham | .01 | .05 |
| 454 | Keith Mitchell | .01 | .05 |
| 455 | Marquis Grissom | .02 | .10 |
| 456 | Robin Yount | .15 | .40 |
| 457 | Harvey Pulliam | .01 | .05 |
| 458 | Jose DeLeon | .01 | .05 |
| 459 | Mark Gubicza | .01 | .05 |
| 460 | Darryl Hamilton | .01 | .05 |
| 461 | Tom Browning | .01 | .05 |
| 462 | Monty Fariss | .01 | .05 |
| 463 | Jerome Walton | .01 | .05 |
| 464 | Paul O'Neill | .05 | .15 |
| 465 | Dean Palmer | .02 | .10 |
| 466 | Travis Fryman | .02 | .10 |
| 467 | John Smiley | .01 | .05 |
| 468 | Lloyd Moseby | .01 | .05 |
| 469 | John Wehner | .01 | .05 |
| 470 | Skeeter Barnes | .01 | .05 |
| 471 | Steve Chitren | .01 | .05 |
| 472 | Kent Mercker | .01 | .05 |
| 473 | Terry Steinbach | .01 | .05 |
| 474 | Andres Galarraga | .02 | .10 |
| 475 | Steve Avery | .01 | .05 |
| 476 | Tom Gordon | .01 | .05 |
| 477 | Cal Eldred | .01 | .05 |
| 478 | Omar Olivares | .01 | .05 |
| 479 | Julio Machado | .01 | .05 |
| 480 | Bob Milacki | .01 | .05 |
| 481 | Les Lancaster | .01 | .05 |
| 482 | John Candelaria | .01 | .05 |
| 483 | Brian Downing | .01 | .05 |
| 484 | Roger McDowell | .01 | .05 |
| 485 | Scott Scudder | .01 | .05 |
| 486 | Zane Smith | .01 | .05 |
| 487 | John Cerutti | .01 | .05 |
| 488 | Steve Buechele | .01 | .05 |
| 489 | Paul Gibson | .01 | .05 |
| 490 | Curtis Wilkerson | .01 | .05 |
| 491 | Marvin Freeman | .01 | .05 |
| 492 | Tom Foley | .01 | .05 |
| 493 | Juan Berenguer | .01 | .05 |
| 494 | Ernest Riles | .01 | .05 |
| 495 | Sid Bream | .01 | .05 |
| 496 | Chuck Crim | .01 | .05 |
| 497 | Mike Macfarlane | .01 | .05 |
| 498 | Dale Sveum | .01 | .05 |
| 499 | Storm Davis | .01 | .05 |
| 500 | Checklist 401-500 | .02 | .10 |
| 501 | Jeff Reardon | .02 | .10 |
| 502 | Shawn Abner | .01 | .05 |
| 503 | Tony Fossas | .01 | .05 |
| 504 | Cory Snyder | .01 | .05 |
| 505 | Matt Young | .01 | .05 |
| 506 | Allan Anderson | .01 | .05 |
| 507 | Mark Lee | .01 | .05 |
| 508 | Gene Nelson | .01 | .05 |
| 509 | Mike Pagliarulo | .01 | .05 |
| 510 | Rafael Belliard | .01 | .05 |
| 511 | Jay Howell | .01 | .05 |
| 512 | Bob Tewksbury | .01 | .05 |
| 513 | Mike Morgan | .01 | .05 |
| 514 | John Franco | .02 | .10 |
| 515 | Kevin Gross | .01 | .05 |
| 516 | Lou Whitaker | .02 | .10 |
| 517 | Orlando Merced | .01 | .05 |
| 518 | Todd Benzinger | .01 | .05 |
| 519 | Gary Redus | .01 | .05 |
| 520 | Walt Terrell | .01 | .05 |
| 521 | Jack Clark | .02 | .10 |
| 522 | Dave Parker | .02 | .10 |
| 523 | Tim Naehring | .01 | .05 |
| 524 | Mark Whiten | .01 | .05 |
| 525 | Ellis Burks | .02 | .10 |
| 526 | Frank Castillo | .01 | .05 |
| 527 | Brian Harper | .01 | .05 |
| 528 | Brook Jacoby | .01 | .05 |
| 529 | Rick Sutcliffe | .02 | .10 |
| 530 | Joe Klink | .01 | .05 |
| 531 | Terry Bross | .01 | .05 |
| 532 | Jose Offerman | .01 | .05 |
| 533 | Todd Zeile | .01 | .05 |
| 534 | Eric Karros | .02 | .10 |
| 535 | Anthony Young | .01 | .05 |
| 536 | Milt Cuyler | .01 | .05 |
| 537 | Randy Tomlin | .01 | .05 |
| 538 | Scott Livingstone | .01 | .05 |
| 539 | Jim Eisenreich | .01 | .05 |
| 540 | Don Slaught | .01 | .05 |
| 541 | Scott Cooper | .01 | .05 |
| 542 | Joe Grahe | .01 | .05 |
| 543 | Tom Brunansky | .01 | .05 |
| 544 | Eddie Zosky | .01 | .05 |
| 545 | Roger Clemens | .20 | .50 |
| 546 | David Justice | .02 | .10 |
| 547 | Dave Stewart | .02 | .10 |
| 548 | David West | .01 | .05 |
| 549 | Dave Smith | .01 | .05 |
| 550 | Dan Plesac | .01 | .05 |
| 551 | Alex Fernandez | .01 | .05 |
| 552 | Bernard Gilkey | .01 | .05 |
| 553 | Jack McDowell | .01 | .05 |
| 554 | Tino Martinez | .05 | .15 |
| 555 | Bo Jackson | .08 | .25 |
| 556 | Bernie Williams | .05 | .15 |
| 557 | Mark Gardner | .01 | .05 |
| 558 | Glenallen Hill | .01 | .05 |
| 559 | Oil Can Boyd | .01 | .05 |
| 560 | Chris James | .01 | .05 |
| 561 | Scott Servais | .01 | .05 |
| 562 | Rey Sanchez RC | .08 | .25 |
| 563 | Paul McClellan | .01 | .05 |
| 564 | Andy Mota | .01 | .05 |
| 565 | Darren Lewis | .01 | .05 |
| 566 | Jose Melendez | .01 | .05 |
| 567 | Tommy Greene | .01 | .05 |
| 568 | Rich Rodriguez | .01 | .05 |
| 569 | Heathcliff Slocumb | .01 | .05 |
| 570 | Joe Hesketh | .01 | .05 |
| 571 | Carlton Fisk | .05 | .15 |
| 572 | Erik Hanson | .01 | .05 |
| 573 | Wilson Alvarez | .01 | .05 |
| 574 | Rheal Cormier | .01 | .05 |
| 575 | Tim Raines | .02 | .10 |
| 576 | Bobby Witt | .01 | .05 |
| 577 | Roberto Kelly | .01 | .05 |
| 578 | Kevin Brown | .02 | .10 |
| 579 | Chris Nabholz | .01 | .05 |
| 580 | Jesse Orosco | .01 | .05 |
| 581 | Jeff Brantley | .01 | .05 |
| 582 | Rafael Ramirez | .01 | .05 |
| 583 | Kelly Downs | .01 | .05 |
| 584 | Mike Simms | .01 | .05 |
| 585 | Mike Remlinger | .01 | .05 |
| 586 | Dave Hollins | .01 | .05 |
| 587 | Larry Andersen | .01 | .05 |
| 588 | Mike Gardiner | .01 | .05 |
| 589 | Craig Lefferts | .01 | .05 |
| 590 | Paul Assenmacher | .01 | .05 |
| 591 | Bryn Smith | .01 | .05 |
| 592 | Donn Pall | .01 | .05 |
| 593 | Mike Jackson | .01 | .05 |
| 594 | Scott Radinsky | .01 | .05 |
| 595 | Brian Holman | .01 | .05 |
| 596 | Geronimo Pena | .01 | .05 |
| 597 | Mike Jeffcoat | .01 | .05 |
| 598 | Carlos Martinez | .01 | .05 |
| 599 | Geno Petralli | .01 | .05 |
| 600 | Checklist 501-600 | .01 | .05 |
| 601 | Jerry Don Gleaton | .01 | .05 |
| 602 | Adam Peterson | .01 | .05 |
| 603 | Craig Grebeck | .01 | .05 |
| 604 | Mark Guthrie | .01 | .05 |
| 605 | Frank Tanana | .01 | .05 |
| 606 | Hensley Meulens | .01 | .05 |
| 607 | Mark Davis | .01 | .05 |
| 608 | Eric Plunk | .01 | .05 |
| 609 | Mark Williamson | .01 | .05 |
| 610 | Lee Guetterman | .01 | .05 |
| 611 | Bobby Rose | .01 | .05 |
| 612 | Bill Wegman | .01 | .05 |
| 613 | Mike Hartley | .01 | .05 |
| 614 | Chris Beasley | .01 | .05 |
| 615 | Chris Bosio | .01 | .05 |
| 616 | Henry Cotto | .01 | .05 |
| 617 | Chico Walker | .01 | .05 |
| 618 | Russ Swan | .01 | .05 |
| 619 | Bob Walk | .01 | .05 |
| 620 | Bill Swift | .01 | .05 |
| 621 | Warren Newson | .01 | .05 |
| 622 | Steve Bedrosian | .01 | .05 |
| 623 | Ricky Bones | .01 | .05 |
| 624 | Kevin Tapani | .01 | .05 |
| 625 | Juan Guzman | .01 | .05 |
| 626 | Jeff Johnson | .01 | .05 |
| 627 | Jeff Montgomery | .01 | .05 |
| 628 | Ken Hill | .01 | .05 |
| 629 | Gary Thurman | .01 | .05 |
| 630 | Steve Howe | .01 | .05 |
| 631 | Jose DeJesus | .01 | .05 |

|  |  | | |
|------|--------|------|------|
| 632 | Kirk Dressendorfer | .01 | .05 |
| 633 | Jaime Navarro | .01 | .05 |
| 634 | Lee Stevens | .01 | .05 |
| 635 | Pete Harnisch | .01 | .05 |
| 636 | Bill Landrum | .01 | .05 |
| 637 | Rich DeLucia | .01 | .05 |
| 638 | Luis Salazar | .01 | .05 |
| 639 | Rob Murphy | .01 | .05 |
| 640 | J.Canseco/R.Henderson CL | .05 | .15 |
| 641 | Roger Clemens DS | .08 | .25 |
| 642 | Jim Abbott DS | .02 | .10 |
| 643 | Travis Fryman DS | .01 | .05 |
| 644 | Jesse Barfield DS | .01 | .05 |
| 645 | Cal Ripken DS | .15 | .40 |
| 646 | Wade Boggs DS | .02 | .10 |
| 647 | Cecil Fielder DS | .01 | .05 |
| 648 | Rickey Henderson DS | .05 | .15 |
| 649 | Jose Canseco DS | .02 | .10 |
| 650 | Ken Griffey Jr. DS | .08 | .25 |
| 651 | Kenny Rogers | .02 | .10 |
| 652 | Luis Mercedes | .01 | .05 |
| 653 | Mike Stanton | .01 | .05 |
| 654 | Glenn Davis | .01 | .05 |
| 655 | Nolan Ryan | .40 | 1.00 |
| 656 | Reggie Jefferson | .01 | .05 |
| 657 | Javier Ortiz | .01 | .05 |
| 658 | Greg A. Harris | .01 | .05 |
| 659 | Mariano Duncan | .01 | .05 |
| 660 | Jeff Shaw | .01 | .05 |
| 661 | Mike Moore | .01 | .05 |
| 662 | Chris Haney | .01 | .05 |
| 663 | Joe Slusarski | .01 | .05 |
| 664 | Wayne Housie | .01 | .05 |
| 665 | Carlos Garcia | .01 | .05 |
| 666 | Bob Ojeda | .01 | .05 |
| 667 | Bryan Hickerson RC | .02 | .10 |
| 668 | Tim Belcher | .01 | .05 |
| 669 | Ron Darling | .01 | .05 |
| 670 | Rex Hudler | .01 | .05 |
| 671 | Sid Fernandez | .01 | .05 |
| 672 | Chito Martinez | .01 | .05 |
| 673 | Pete Schourek | .01 | .05 |
| 674 | Armando Reynoso RC | .08 | .25 |
| 675 | Mike Mussina | .08 | .25 |
| 676 | Kevin Morton | .01 | .05 |
| 677 | Norm Charlton | .01 | .05 |
| 678 | Danny Darwin | .01 | .05 |
| 679 | Eric King | .01 | .05 |
| 680 | Ted Power | .01 | .05 |
| 681 | Barry Jones | .01 | .05 |
| 682 | Carney Lansford | .02 | .10 |
| 683 | Mel Rojas | .01 | .05 |
| 684 | Rick Honeycutt | .01 | .05 |
| 685 | Jeff Fassero | .01 | .05 |
| 686 | Cris Carpenter | .01 | .05 |
| 687 | Tim Crews | .01 | .05 |
| 688 | Scott Terry | .01 | .05 |
| 689 | Chris Gwynn | .01 | .05 |
| 690 | Gerald Perry | .01 | .05 |
| 691 | John Barfield | .01 | .05 |
| 692 | Bob Melvin | .01 | .05 |
| 693 | Juan Agosto | .01 | .05 |
| 694 | Alejandro Pena | .01 | .05 |
| 695 | Jeff Russell | .01 | .05 |
| 696 | Carmelo Martinez | .01 | .05 |
| 697 | Bud Black | .01 | .05 |
| 698 | Dave Otto | .01 | .05 |
| 699 | Billy Hatcher | .01 | .05 |
| 700 | Checklist 601-700 | .01 | .05 |
| 701 | Clemente Nunez RC | .01 | .05 |
| 702 | M.Clark/Osborne/Jordan | .01 | .05 |
| 703 | Mike Morgan | .01 | .05 |
| 704 | Keith Miller | .01 | .05 |
| 705 | Kurt Stillwell | .01 | .05 |
| 706 | Damon Berryhill | .01 | .05 |
| 707 | Von Hayes | .01 | .05 |
| 708 | Rick Sutcliffe | .02 | .10 |
| 709 | Hubie Brooks | .01 | .05 |
| 710 | Ryan Turner RC | .02 | .10 |
| 711 | B.Bonds/A.Van Slyke CL | .20 | .50 |
| 712 | Jose Rijo DS | .01 | .05 |
| 713 | Tom Glavine DS | .02 | .10 |
| 714 | Shawon Dunston DS | .01 | .05 |
| 715 | Andy Van Slyke DS | .02 | .10 |
| 716 | Ozzie Smith DS | .08 | .25 |
| 717 | Tony Gwynn DS | .05 | .15 |
| 718 | Will Clark DS | .02 | .10 |
| 719 | Marquis Grissom DS | .01 | .05 |
| 720 | Howard Johnson DS | .01 | .05 |
| 721 | Barry Bonds DS | .20 | .50 |
| 722 | Kirk McCaskill | .01 | .05 |
| 723 | Sammy Sosa Cubs | .30 | .75 |
| 724 | George Bell | .01 | .05 |
| 725 | Gregg Jefferies | .01 | .05 |
| 726 | Gary DiSarcina | .01 | .05 |
| 727 | Mike Bordick | .01 | .05 |
| 728 | Eddie Murray 400 HR | .05 | .15 |
| 729 | Rene Gonzales | .01 | .05 |
| 730 | Mike Bielecki | .01 | .05 |
| 731 | Calvin Jones | .01 | .05 |
| 732 | Jack Morris | .02 | .10 |
| 733 | Frank Viola | .02 | .10 |
| 734 | Dave Winfield | .02 | .10 |
| 735 | Kevin Mitchell | .01 | .05 |
| 736 | Bill Swift | .01 | .05 |
| 737 | Dan Gladden | .01 | .05 |
| 738 | Mike Jackson | .01 | .05 |
| 739 | Mark Carreon | .01 | .05 |
| 740 | Kirt Manwaring | .01 | .05 |
| 741 | Randy Myers | .01 | .05 |
| 742 | Kevin McReynolds | .01 | .05 |
| 743 | Steve Sax | .01 | .05 |
| 744 | Wally Joyner | .02 | .10 |
| 745 | Gary Sheffield | .02 | .10 |
| 746 | Danny Tartabull | .02 | .10 |
| 747 | Julio Valera | .01 | .05 |
| 748 | Denny Neagle | .02 | .10 |
| 749 | Lance Blankenship | .01 | .05 |
| 750 | Mike Gallego | .01 | .05 |
| 751 | Bret Saberhagen | .02 | .10 |
| 752 | Ruben Amaro | .01 | .05 |
| 753 | Eddie Murray | .08 | .25 |
| 754 | Kyle Abbott | .01 | .05 |
| 755 | Bobby Bonilla | .02 | .10 |
| 756 | Eric Davis | .02 | .10 |
| 757 | Eddie Taubensee RC | .08 | .25 |
| 758 | Andres Galarraga | .02 | .10 |
| 759 | Pete Incaviglia | .01 | .05 |
| 760 | Tom Candiotti | .01 | .05 |
| 761 | Tim Belcher | .01 | .05 |
| 762 | Ricky Bones | .01 | .05 |
| 763 | Bip Roberts | .01 | .05 |
| 764 | Pedro Munoz | .01 | .05 |
| 765 | Greg Swindell | .01 | .05 |
| 766 | Kenny Lofton | .05 | .15 |
| 767 | Gary Carter | .02 | .10 |
| 768 | Charlie Hayes | .01 | .05 |
| 769 | Dickie Thon | .01 | .05 |
| 770 | Donovan Osborne DD CL | .01 | .05 |
| 771 | Bret Boone | .05 | .15 |
| 772 | Archi Cianfrocco RC | .02 | .10 |
| 773 | Mark Clark RC | .02 | .10 |
| 774 | Chad Curtis RC | .08 | .25 |
| 775 | Pat Listach RC | .08 | .25 |
| 776 | Pat Mahomes RC | .08 | .25 |
| 777 | Donovan Osborne | .01 | .05 |
| 778 | John Patterson RC | .02 | .10 |
| 779 | Andy Stankiewicz DD | .01 | .05 |
| 780 | Turk Wendell RC | .08 | .25 |
| 781 | Bill Krueger | .01 | .05 |
| 782 | Rickey Henderson 1000 | .05 | .15 |
| 783 | Kevin Seitzer | .01 | .05 |
| 784 | Dave Martinez | .01 | .05 |
| 785 | John Smiley | .01 | .05 |
| 786 | Matt Stairs RC | .08 | .25 |
| 787 | Scott Scudder | .01 | .05 |
| 788 | John Wetteland | .02 | .10 |
| 789 | Jack Armstrong | .01 | .05 |
| 790 | Ken Hill | .01 | .05 |
| 791 | Dick Schofield | .01 | .05 |
| 792 | Mariano Duncan | .01 | .05 |
| 793 | Bill Pecota | .01 | .05 |
| 794 | Mike Kelly RC | .02 | .10 |
| 795 | Willie Randolph | .02 | .10 |
| 796 | Butch Henry | .01 | .05 |
| 797 | Carlos Hernandez | .01 | .05 |
| 798 | Doug Jones | .01 | .05 |
| 799 | Melido Perez | .01 | .05 |
| 800 | Checklist 701-800 | .01 | .05 |
| HH2 | Ted Williams Holo | .75 | 2.00 |
| SP3 | Deion Sanders FB/BB | .40 | 1.00 |
| SP4 | F.Thomas/T.Selleck | .40 | 1.00 |

## 1993 Upper Deck

| | | | |
|---|---|---|---|
| | COMPLETE SET (840) | 15.00 | 40.00 |
| | COMP.FACT.SET (840) | 20.00 | 50.00 |
| | COMPLETE SERIES 1 (420) | 6.00 | 15.00 |
| | COMPLETE SERIES 2 (420) | 10.00 | 25.00 |
| 1 | Tim Salmon DS | .07 | .20 |
| 2 | Mike Piazza | 1.25 | 3.00 |
| 3 | Rene Arocha RC | .20 | .50 |
| 4 | Willie Greene | .02 | .10 |
| 5 | Manny Alexander | .02 | .10 |
| 6 | Dan Wilson | .07 | .20 |
| 7 | Dan Smith | .02 | .10 |
| 8 | Kevin Rogers | .02 | .10 |
| 9 | Nigel Wilson | .02 | .10 |
| 10 | Joe Vitko | .02 | .10 |
| 11 | Tim Costo | .02 | .10 |
| 12 | Alan Embree | .02 | .10 |
| 13 | Jim Tatum RC | .05 | .15 |
| 14 | Cris Colon | .02 | .10 |
| 15 | Steve Hosey | .02 | .10 |
| 16 | Sterling Hitchcock RC | .20 | .50 |
| 17 | Dave Mlicki | .02 | .10 |
| 18 | Jessie Hollins | .02 | .10 |
| 19 | Bobby Jones | .07 | .20 |
| 20 | Kurt Miller | .02 | .10 |
| 21 | Melvin Nieves | .02 | .10 |
| 22 | Billy Ashley | .02 | .10 |
| 23 | J.T.Snow RC | .30 | .75 |
| 24 | Chipper Jones | .20 | .50 |
| 25 | Tim Salmon | .10 | .30 |
| 26 | Tim Pugh RC | .05 | .15 |
| 27 | David Nied | .02 | .10 |
| 28 | Mike Trombley | .02 | .10 |
| 29 | Javier Lopez | .10 | .30 |
| 30 | Jim Abbott CH CL | .07 | .20 |
| 31 | Jim Abbott CH | .02 | .10 |
| 32 | Dale Murphy CH | .10 | .30 |
| 33 | Tony Pena CH | .02 | .10 |
| 34 | Kirby Puckett CH | .10 | .30 |
| 35 | Harold Reynolds CH | .02 | .10 |
| 36 | Cal Ripken CH | .30 | .75 |
| 37 | Nolan Ryan CH | .40 | 1.00 |
| 38 | Ryne Sandberg CH | .20 | .50 |
| 39 | Dave Stewart CH | .02 | .10 |
| 40 | Dave Winfield CH | .10 | .30 |
| 41 | M.McGwire/J.Carter CL | .20 | .50 |
| 42 | R.Alomar/J.Carter | .20 | .50 |
| 43 | Molitor/Listach/Yount | .20 | .50 |
| 44 | C.Ripken/B.Anderson | .20 | .50 |
| 45 | Belle/Baerga/Thome/Lofton | .27 | .70 |
| 46 | C.Fielder/M.Tettleton | .25 | .60 |
| 47 | R.Kelly/D.Mattingly | .20 | .50 |
| 48 | R.Clemens/F.Viola | .20 | .50 |
| 49 | R.Sierra/M.McGwire | .20 | .50 |
| 50 | K.Puckett/K.Hrbek | .10 | .30 |
| 51 | F.Thomas/R.Ventura | .10 | .30 |
| 52 | Cans/Rod/Gonz/Palmeiro | .10 | .30 |
| 53 | Lethal Lefties | | |
| | Mark Langston | | |
| | Jim Abbott | | |
| | Chuck F | | |
| 54 | Joyner/Jefferies/Brett | .20 | .50 |
| 55 | K.Griffey/Buhner/Mitchell | .20 | .50 |
| 56 | George Brett | .50 | 1.25 |
| 57 | Scott Cooper | .02 | .10 |
| 58 | Mike Maddux | .02 | .10 |
| 59 | Rusty Meacham | .02 | .10 |
| 60 | Wil Cordero | .02 | .10 |
| 61 | Tim Teufel | .02 | .10 |
| 62 | Jeff Montgomery | .02 | .10 |
| 63 | Scott Livingstone | .02 | .10 |
| 64 | Doug Dascenzo | .02 | .10 |
| 65 | Bret Boone | .07 | .20 |

|  |  | | |
|---|---|---|---|
| 66 | Tim Wakefield | .20 | .50 |
| 67 | Curt Schilling | .07 | .20 |
| 68 | Frank Tanana | .02 | .10 |
| 69 | Len Dykstra | .07 | .20 |
| 70 | Derek Lilliquist | .02 | .10 |
| 71 | Anthony Young | .02 | .10 |
| 72 | Hipolito Pichardo | .02 | .10 |
| 73 | Rod Beck | .02 | .10 |
| 74 | Kent Hrbek | .07 | .20 |
| 75 | Tom Glavine | .10 | .30 |
| 76 | Kevin Brown | .07 | .20 |
| 77 | Chuck Finley | .07 | .20 |
| 78 | Bob Walk | .02 | .10 |
| 79 | Rheal Cormier UER | .02 | .10 |
| 80 | Rick Sutcliffe | .07 | .20 |
| 81 | Harold Baines | .07 | .20 |
| 82 | Lee Smith | .07 | .20 |
| 83 | Geno Petralli | .02 | .10 |
| 84 | Jose Oquendo | .02 | .10 |
| 85 | Mark Gubicza | .02 | .10 |
| 86 | Mickey Tettleton | .07 | .20 |
| 87 | Bobby Witt | .02 | .10 |
| 88 | Mark Lewis | .02 | .10 |
| 89 | Kevin Appier | .07 | .20 |
| 90 | Mike Stanton | .02 | .10 |
| 91 | Rafael Belliard | .02 | .10 |
| 92 | Kenny Rogers | .07 | .20 |
| 93 | Randy Velarde | .02 | .10 |
| 94 | Luis Sojo | .02 | .10 |
| 95 | Mark Leiter | .02 | .10 |
| 96 | Jody Reed | .02 | .10 |
| 97 | Pete Harnisch | .02 | .10 |
| 98 | Tom Candiotti | .02 | .10 |
| 99 | Mark Portugal | .02 | .10 |
| 100 | Dave Valle | .02 | .10 |
| 101 | Shawon Dunston | .07 | .20 |
| 102 | B.J. Surhoff | .07 | .20 |
| 103 | Jay Bell | .07 | .20 |
| 104 | Sid Bream | .02 | .10 |
| 105 | Frank Thomas CL | .10 | .30 |
| 106 | Mike Morgan | .02 | .10 |
| 107 | Bill Doran | .02 | .10 |
| 108 | Lance Blankenship | .02 | .10 |
| 109 | Mark Lemke | .02 | .10 |
| 110 | Brian Harper | .02 | .10 |
| 111 | Brady Anderson | .07 | .20 |
| 112 | Bip Roberts | .02 | .10 |
| 113 | Mitch Williams | .02 | .10 |
| 114 | Craig Biggio | .10 | .30 |
| 115 | Eddie Murray | .20 | .50 |
| 116 | Matt Nokes | .02 | .10 |
| 117 | Lance Parrish | .07 | .20 |
| 118 | Bill Swift | .02 | .10 |
| 119 | Jeff Innis | .02 | .10 |
| 120 | Mike LaValliere | .02 | .10 |
| 121 | Hal Morris | .02 | .10 |
| 122 | Walt Weiss | .02 | .10 |
| 123 | Ivan Rodriguez | .10 | .30 |
| 124 | Andy Van Slyke | .10 | .30 |
| 125 | Roberto Alomar | .10 | .30 |
| 126 | Robby Thompson | .02 | .10 |
| 127 | Sammy Sosa | .20 | .50 |
| 128 | Mark Langston | .07 | .20 |
| 129 | Jerry Browne | .02 | .10 |
| 130 | Chuck McElroy | .02 | .10 |
| 131 | Frank Viola | .07 | .20 |
| 132 | Leo Gomez | .02 | .10 |
| 133 | Ramon Martinez | .07 | .20 |
| 134 | Don Mattingly | .50 | 1.25 |
| 135 | Roger Clemens | .40 | 1.00 |
| 136 | Rickey Henderson | .20 | .50 |
| 137 | Darren Daulton | .07 | .20 |
| 138 | Ken Hill | .02 | .10 |
| 139 | Ozzie Guillen | .07 | .20 |
| 140 | Jerald Clark | .02 | .10 |
| 141 | Dave Fleming | .02 | .10 |
| 142 | Delino DeShields | .07 | .20 |
| 143 | Matt Williams | .07 | .20 |
| 144 | Larry Walker | .07 | .20 |
| 145 | Ruben Sierra | .07 | .20 |
| 146 | Ozzie Smith | .30 | .75 |
| 147 | Chris Sabo | .02 | .10 |
| 148 | Carlos Hernandez | .02 | .10 |
| 149 | Pat Borders | .02 | .10 |
| 150 | Orlando Merced | .02 | .10 |
| 151 | Royce Clayton | .07 | .20 |
| 152 | Kurt Stillwell | .02 | .10 |
| 153 | Dave Hollins | .07 | .20 |
| 154 | Mike Greenwell | .02 | .10 |
| 155 | Nolan Ryan | .75 | 2.00 |
| 156 | Felix Jose | .02 | .10 |
| 157 | Junior Felix | .02 | .10 |
| 158 | Derek Bell | .07 | .20 |
| 159 | Steve Buechele | .02 | .10 |
| 160 | John Burkett | .02 | .10 |
| 161 | Pat Howell | .02 | .10 |
| 162 | Milt Cuyler | .02 | .10 |
| 163 | Terry Pendleton | .07 | .20 |
| 164 | Jack Morris | .07 | .20 |
| 165 | Tony Gwynn | .25 | .60 |
| 166 | Deion Sanders | .10 | .30 |
| 167 | Mike Devereaux | .02 | .10 |
| 168 | Ron Darling | .02 | .10 |
| 169 | Orel Hershiser | .07 | .20 |
| 170 | Mike Jackson | .02 | .10 |
| 171 | Doug Jones | .02 | .10 |
| 172 | Dan Walters | .02 | .10 |
| 173 | Darren Lewis | .02 | .10 |
| 174 | Carlos Baerga | .07 | .20 |
| 175 | Ryne Sandberg | .30 | .75 |
| 176 | Gregg Jefferies | .02 | .10 |
| 177 | John Jaha | .07 | .20 |
| 178 | Luis Polonia | .02 | .10 |
| 179 | Kirt Manwaring | .02 | .10 |
| 180 | Mike Magnante | .02 | .10 |
| 181 | Billy Ripken | .02 | .10 |
| 182 | Mike Moore | .02 | .10 |
| 183 | Eric Anthony | .02 | .10 |
| 184 | Lenny Harris | .02 | .10 |
| 185 | Tony Pena | .02 | .10 |
| 186 | Mike Felder | .02 | .10 |
| 187 | Greg Olson | .02 | .10 |
| 188 | Rene Gonzales | .02 | .10 |
| 189 | Mike Bordick | .02 | .10 |
| 190 | Mel Rojas | .02 | .10 |
| 191 | Todd Frohwirth | .02 | .10 |
| 192 | Darryl Hamilton | .02 | .10 |
| 193 | Mike Fetters | .02 | .10 |
| 194 | Omar Olivares | .02 | .10 |
| 195 | Tony Phillips | .02 | .10 |
| 196 | Paul Sorrento | .02 | .10 |
| 197 | Trevor Wilson | .02 | .10 |
| 198 | Kevin Gross | .02 | .10 |
| 199 | Ron Karkovice | .02 | .10 |
| 200 | Brook Jacoby | .02 | .10 |
| 201 | Mariano Duncan | .02 | .10 |
| 202 | Dennis Cook | .02 | .10 |
| 203 | Daryl Boston | .02 | .10 |
| 204 | Mike Perez | .02 | .10 |
| 205 | Manuel Lee | .02 | .10 |
| 206 | Steve Olin | .02 | .10 |
| 207 | Charlie Hough | .07 | .20 |
| 208 | Scott Scudder | .02 | .10 |
| 209 | Charlie O'Brien | .02 | .10 |
| 210 | Barry Bonds CL | .30 | .75 |
| 211 | Jose Vizcaino | .02 | .10 |
| 212 | Scott Leius | .02 | .10 |
| 213 | Kevin Mitchell | .07 | .20 |
| 214 | Brian Barnes | .02 | .10 |
| 215 | Pat Kelly | .02 | .10 |
| 216 | Chris Hammond | .02 | .10 |
| 217 | Rob Deer | .02 | .10 |
| 218 | Cory Snyder | .02 | .10 |
| 219 | Gary Carter | .07 | .20 |
| 220 | Danny Darwin | .02 | .10 |
| 221 | Tom Gordon | .02 | .10 |
| 222 | Gary Sheffield 2X | .07 | .20 |
| 223 | Joe Carter | .07 | .20 |
| 224 | Jay Buhner | .07 | .20 |
| 225 | Jose Offerman | .02 | .10 |
| 226 | Jose Rijo | .02 | .10 |
| 227 | Mark Whiten | .02 | .10 |
| 228 | Randy Milligan | .02 | .10 |
| 229 | Bud Black | .02 | .10 |
| 230 | Gary DiSarcina | .02 | .10 |
| 231 | Steve Finley | .07 | .20 |
| 232 | Dennis Martinez | .07 | .20 |
| 233 | Mike Mussina | .10 | .30 |
| 234 | Joe Oliver | .02 | .10 |
| 235 | Chad Curtis | .07 | .20 |
| 236 | Shane Mack | .07 | .20 |
| 237 | Jaime Navarro | .02 | .10 |
| 238 | Brian McRae | .02 | .10 |
| 239 | Chili Davis | .07 | .20 |
| 240 | Jeff King | .02 | .10 |
| 241 | Dean Palmer | .07 | .20 |
| 242 | Danny Tartabull | .02 | .10 |
| 243 | Charles Nagy | .07 | .20 |
| 244 | Ray Lankford | .07 | .20 |
| 245 | Barry Larkin | .10 | .30 |
| 246 | Steve Avery | .02 | .10 |
| 247 | John Kruk | .07 | .20 |
| 248 | Derrick May | .02 | .10 |
| 249 | Stan Javier | .02 | .10 |
| 250 | Roger McDowell | .02 | .10 |
| 251 | Dan Gladden | .02 | .10 |
| 252 | Wally Joyner | .07 | .20 |
| 253 | Pat Listach | .02 | .10 |
| 254 | Chuck Knoblauch | .07 | .20 |
| 255 | Sandy Alomar Jr. | .02 | .10 |
| 256 | Jeff Bagwell | .10 | .30 |
| 257 | Andy Stankiewicz | .02 | .10 |
| 258 | Darrin Jackson | .02 | .10 |
| 259 | Brett Butler | .02 | .10 |
| 260 | Joe Orsulak | .02 | .10 |
| 261 | Andy Benes | .07 | .20 |
| 262 | Kenny Lofton | .07 | .20 |
| 263 | Robin Ventura | .07 | .20 |
| 264 | Ron Gant | .07 | .20 |
| 265 | Ellis Burks | .02 | .10 |
| 266 | Juan Guzman | .07 | .20 |
| 267 | Wes Chamberlain | .02 | .10 |
| 268 | John Smiley | .02 | .10 |
| 269 | Franklin Stubbs | .02 | .10 |
| 270 | Tom Browning | .02 | .10 |
| 271 | Dennis Eckersley | .07 | .20 |
| 272 | Carlton Fisk | .10 | .30 |
| 273 | Lou Whitaker | .07 | .20 |
| 274 | Phil Plantier | .07 | .20 |
| 275 | Bobby Bonilla | .07 | .20 |
| 276 | Ben McDonald | .02 | .10 |
| 277 | Bob Zupcic | .02 | .10 |
| 278 | Terry Steinbach | .02 | .10 |
| 279 | Terry Mulholland | .02 | .10 |
| 280 | Lance Johnson | .02 | .10 |
| 281 | Willie McGee | .07 | .20 |
| 282 | Bret Saberhagen | .07 | .20 |
| 283 | Randy Myers | .02 | .10 |
| 284 | Randy Tomlin | .02 | .10 |
| 285 | Mickey Morandini | .02 | .10 |
| 286 | Brian Williams | .02 | .10 |
| 267 | Tino Martinez | .10 | .30 |
| 288 | Jose Melendez | .02 | .10 |
| 289 | Jeff Huson | .02 | .10 |
| 290 | Joe Grahe | .02 | .10 |
| 291 | Mel Hall | .02 | .10 |
| 292 | Otis Nixon | .07 | .20 |
| 293 | Todd Hundley | .02 | .10 |
| 294 | Casey Candaele | .02 | .10 |
| 295 | Kevin Seitzer | .02 | .10 |
| 296 | Eddie Taubensee | .02 | .10 |
| 297 | Moises Alou | .07 | .20 |
| 298 | Scott Radinsky | .02 | .10 |
| 299 | Thomas Howard | .02 | .10 |
| 300 | Kyle Abbott | .02 | .10 |
| 301 | Omar Vizquel | .10 | .30 |
| 302 | Keith Miller | .02 | .10 |
| 303 | Rick Aguilera | .02 | .10 |
| 304 | Bruce Hurst | .07 | .20 |
| 305 | Ken Caminiti | .07 | .20 |
| 306 | Mike Pagliarulo | .02 | .10 |
| 307 | Frank Seminara | .02 | .10 |
| 308 | Andre Dawson | .07 | .20 |
| 309 | Jose Lind | .02 | .10 |
| 310 | Joe Boever | .02 | .10 |
| 311 | Jeff Parrett | .02 | .10 |
| 312 | Alan Mills | .02 | .10 |
| 313 | Kevin Tapani | .07 | .20 |
| 314 | Darryl Kile | .07 | .20 |
| 315 | Checklist 211-315 Will Clark | .07 | .20 |
| 316 | Mike Sharperson | .02 | .10 |
| 317 | John Orton | .02 | .10 |
| 318 | Bob Tewksbury | .02 | .10 |
| 319 | Xavier Hernandez | .02 | .10 |
| 320 | Paul Assenmacher | .02 | .10 |
| 321 | John Franco | .02 | .10 |
| 322 | Mike Timlin | .02 | .10 |
| 323 | Jose Guzman | .02 | .10 |
| 324 | Pedro Martinez | .40 | 1.00 |
| 325 | Bill Spiers | .02 | .10 |
| 326 | Melido Perez | .02 | .10 |
| 327 | Mike Macfarlane | .02 | .10 |
| 328 | Ricky Bones | .02 | .10 |

|  |  | | |
|---|---|---|---|
| ❑ 329 | Scott Bankhead | .02 | .10 |
| ❑ 330 | Rich Rodriguez | .02 | .10 |
| ❑ 331 | Geronimo Pena | .02 | .10 |
| ❑ 332 | Bernie Williams | .10 | .30 |
| ❑ 333 | Paul Molitor | .07 | .20 |
| ❑ 334 | Carlos Garcia | .02 | .10 |
| ❑ 335 | David Cone | .07 | .20 |
| ❑ 336 | Randy Johnson | .20 | .50 |
| ❑ 337 | Pat Mahomes | .02 | .10 |
| ❑ 338 | Erik Hanson | .02 | .10 |
| ❑ 339 | Duane Ward | .02 | .10 |
| ❑ 340 | Al Martin | .02 | .10 |
| ❑ 341 | Pedro Munoz | .02 | .10 |
| ❑ 342 | Greg Colbrunn | .02 | .10 |
| ❑ 343 | Julio Valera | .02 | .10 |
| ❑ 344 | John Olerud | .07 | .20 |
| ❑ 345 | George Bell | .02 | .10 |
| ❑ 346 | Devon White | .07 | .20 |
| ❑ 347 | Donovan Osborne | .02 | .10 |
| ❑ 348 | Mark Gardner | .02 | .10 |
| ❑ 349 | Zane Smith | .02 | .10 |
| ❑ 350 | Wilson Alvarez | .02 | .10 |
| ❑ 351 | Kevin Koslofski | .02 | .10 |
| ❑ 352 | Roberto Hernandez | .02 | .10 |
| ❑ 353 | Glenn Davis | .02 | .10 |
| ❑ 354 | Reggie Sanders | .07 | .20 |
| ❑ 355 | Ken Griffey Jr. | .30 | .75 |
| ❑ 356 | Marquis Grissom | .07 | .20 |
| ❑ 357 | Jack McDowell | .02 | .10 |
| ❑ 358 | Jimmy Key | .07 | .20 |
| ❑ 359 | Stan Belinda | .02 | .10 |
| ❑ 360 | Gerald Williams | .02 | .10 |
| ❑ 361 | Sid Fernandez | .02 | .10 |
| ❑ 362 | Alex Fernandez | .02 | .10 |
| ❑ 363 | John Smoltz | .10 | .30 |
| ❑ 364 | Travis Fryman | .07 | .20 |
| ❑ 365 | Jose Canseco | .10 | .30 |
| ❑ 366 | David Justice | .07 | .20 |
| ❑ 367 | Pedro Astacio | .02 | .10 |
| ❑ 368 | Tim Belcher | .02 | .10 |
| ❑ 369 | Steve Sax | .02 | .10 |
| ❑ 370 | Gary Gaetti | .07 | .20 |
| ❑ 371 | Jeff Frye | .02 | .10 |
| ❑ 372 | Bob Wickman | .02 | .10 |
| ❑ 373 | Ryan Thompson | .02 | .10 |
| ❑ 374 | David Hulse RC | .05 | .15 |
| ❑ 375 | Cal Eldred | .07 | .20 |
| ❑ 376 | Ryan Klesko | .07 | .20 |
| ❑ 377 | Damion Easley | .02 | .10 |
| ❑ 378 | John Kiely | .02 | .10 |
| ❑ 379 | Jim Bullinger | .02 | .10 |
| ❑ 380 | Brian Bohanon | .02 | .10 |
| ❑ 381 | Rod Brewer | .02 | .10 |
| ❑ 382 | Fernando Ramsey RC | .05 | .15 |
| ❑ 383 | Sam Militello | .02 | .10 |
| ❑ 384 | Arthur Rhodes | .07 | .20 |
| ❑ 385 | Eric Karros | .07 | .20 |
| ❑ 386 | Rico Brogna | .02 | .10 |
| ❑ 387 | John Valentin | .02 | .10 |
| ❑ 388 | Kerry Woodson | .02 | .10 |
| ❑ 389 | Ben Rivera | .02 | .10 |
| ❑ 390 | Matt Whiteside RC | .05 | .15 |
| ❑ 391 | Henry Rodriguez | .02 | .10 |
| ❑ 392 | John Wetteland | .07 | .20 |
| ❑ 393 | Kent Mercker | .02 | .10 |
| ❑ 394 | Bernard Gilkey | .07 | .20 |
| ❑ 395 | Doug Henry | .02 | .10 |
| ❑ 396 | Mo Vaughn | .07 | .20 |
| ❑ 397 | Scott Erickson | .02 | .10 |
| ❑ 398 | Bill Gullickson | .02 | .10 |
| ❑ 399 | Mark Guthrie | .02 | .10 |
| ❑ 400 | Dave Martinez | .02 | .10 |
| ❑ 401 | Jeff Kent | .20 | .50 |
| ❑ 402 | Chris Hoiles | .07 | .20 |
| ❑ 403 | Mike Henneman | .02 | .10 |
| ❑ 404 | Chris Nabholz | .02 | .10 |
| ❑ 405 | Tom Pagnozzi | .02 | .10 |
| ❑ 406 | Kelly Gruber | .02 | .10 |
| ❑ 407 | Bob Welch | .02 | .10 |
| ❑ 408 | Frank Castillo | .02 | .10 |
| ❑ 409 | John Dopson | .02 | .10 |
| ❑ 410 | Steve Farr | .02 | .10 |
| ❑ 411 | Henry Cotto | .02 | .10 |
| ❑ 412 | Bob Patterson | .02 | .10 |
| ❑ 413 | Todd Stottlemyre | .02 | .10 |
| ❑ 414 | Greg A. Harris | .02 | .10 |
| ❑ 415 | Denny Neagle | .07 | .20 |
| ❑ 416 | Bill Wegman | .02 | .10 |
| ❑ 417 | Willie Wilson | .02 | .10 |
| ❑ 418 | Terry Leach | .02 | .10 |
| ❑ 419 | Willie Randolph | .07 | .20 |
| ❑ 420 | Checklist 316-420 McGwire | .10 | .10 |
| ❑ 421 | Calvin Murray CL | .02 | .10 |
| ❑ 422 | Pete Janicki RC | .05 | .15 |
| ❑ 423 | Todd Jones TP | .07 | .20 |
| ❑ 424 | Mike Neill | .07 | .20 |
| ❑ 425 | Carlos Delgado | .20 | .50 |
| ❑ 426 | Jose Oliva | .02 | .10 |
| ❑ 427 | Tyrone Hill | .02 | .10 |
| ❑ 428 | Dmitri Young | .07 | .20 |
| ❑ 429 | Derek Wallace RC | .05 | .15 |
| ❑ 430 | Michael Moore RC | .05 | .15 |
| ❑ 431 | Cliff Floyd | .07 | .20 |
| ❑ 432 | Calvin Murray | .02 | .10 |
| ❑ 433 | Manny Ramirez | .30 | .75 |
| ❑ 434 | Marc Newfield | .07 | .20 |
| ❑ 435 | Charles Johnson | .07 | .20 |
| ❑ 436 | Butch Huskey | .02 | .10 |
| ❑ 437 | Brad Pennington TP | .02 | .10 |
| ❑ 438 | Ray McDavid RC | .05 | .15 |
| ❑ 439 | Chad McConnell | .02 | .10 |
| ❑ 440 | Midre Cummings RC | .05 | .15 |
| ❑ 441 | Benji Gil | .02 | .10 |
| ❑ 442 | Frankie Rodriguez | .02 | .10 |
| ❑ 443 | Chad Mottola RC | .05 | .15 |
| ❑ 444 | John Burke RC | .02 | .10 |
| ❑ 445 | Michael Tucker | .07 | .20 |
| ❑ 446 | Rick Greene | .02 | .10 |
| ❑ 447 | Rich Becker | .02 | .10 |
| ❑ 448 | Mike Robertson TP | .02 | .10 |
| ❑ 449 | Derek Jeter RC ! | 4.00 | 10.00 |
| ❑ 450 | I.Rodriguez/D.McCarty CL | .10 | .30 |
| ❑ 451 | Jim Abbott IN | .07 | .20 |
| ❑ 452 | Jeff Bagwell IN | .07 | .20 |
| ❑ 453 | Jason Bere IN | .02 | .10 |
| ❑ 454 | Delino DeShields IN | .02 | .10 |
| ❑ 455 | Travis Fryman IN | .02 | .10 |
| ❑ 456 | Alex Gonzalez IN | .02 | .10 |
| ❑ 457 | Phil Hiatt IN | .02 | .10 |
| ❑ 458 | Dave Hollins IN | .02 | .10 |
| ❑ 459 | Chipper Jones IN | .10 | .30 |
| ❑ 460 | David Justice IN | .02 | .10 |
| ❑ 461 | Ray Lankford IN | .02 | .10 |
| ❑ 462 | David McCarty IN | .02 | .10 |
| ❑ 463 | Mike Mussina IN | .07 | .20 |
| ❑ 464 | Jose Offerman IN | .02 | .10 |
| ❑ 465 | Dean Palmer IN | .02 | .10 |
| ❑ 466 | Geronimo Pena IN | .02 | .10 |
| ❑ 467 | Eduardo Perez IN | .02 | .10 |
| ❑ 468 | Ivan Rodriguez IN | .07 | .20 |
| ❑ 469 | Reggie Sanders IN | .02 | .10 |
| ❑ 470 | Bernie Williams IN | .07 | .20 |
| ❑ 471 | Bonds/Williams/Clark CL | .30 | .75 |
| ❑ 472 | Madd/Avery/Smolt/Glav | .20 | .50 |
| ❑ 473 | Red October | | |
| | Jose Rijo | | |
| | Rob Dibble | | |
| | Roberto Kelly# | | |
| ❑ 474 | Sheff/Plant/Gwynn/McGrif | .07 | .20 |
| ❑ 475 | Biggio/Drabek/Bagwell | .07 | .20 |
| ❑ 476 | Clark/Bonds/Williams | .30 | .75 |
| ❑ 477 | Eric Davis | | |
| | Darryl Strawberry | .07 | .20 |
| ❑ 478 | Bich/Nied/Galarraga | .07 | .20 |
| ❑ 479 | Maga/Destr/Barbe/Conine | .02 | .10 |
| ❑ 480 | Wakefield/Van Slyke/Bell | .07 | .20 |
| ❑ 481 | Griss/DeSh/Marl/Walker | .10 | .30 |
| ❑ 482 | O.Smith/Redbirds | .20 | .50 |
| ❑ 483 | Myers/Sandberg/Grace | .20 | .50 |
| ❑ 484 | Big Apple Power Switch | .10 | .30 |
| ❑ 485 | Kruk/Holl/Daul/Dyks | .02 | .10 |
| ❑ 486 | Barry Bonds AW | .30 | .75 |
| ❑ 487 | Dennis Eckersley AW | .07 | .20 |
| ❑ 488 | Greg Maddux AW | .20 | .50 |
| ❑ 489 | Dennis Eckersley AW | .07 | .20 |
| ❑ 490 | Eric Karros AW | .02 | .10 |
| ❑ 491 | Pat Listach AW | .02 | .10 |
| ❑ 492 | Gary Sheffield AW | .02 | .10 |
| ❑ 493 | Mark McGwire AW | .25 | .60 |
| ❑ 494 | Gary Sheffield AW | .02 | .10 |
| ❑ 495 | Edgar Martinez AW | .02 | .10 |
| ❑ 496 | Fred McGriff AW | .07 | .20 |
| ❑ 497 | Juan Gonzalez AW | .20 | .50 |
| ❑ 498 | Darren Daulton AW | .02 | .10 |
| ❑ 499 | Cecil Fielder AW | .02 | .10 |
| ❑ 500 | Brent Gates CL | .02 | .10 |
| ❑ 501 | Tavo Alvarez | .02 | .10 |
| ❑ 502 | Rod Bolton | .02 | .10 |
| ❑ 503 | John Cummings RC | .05 | .15 |
| ❑ 504 | Brent Gates | .02 | .10 |
| ❑ 505 | Tyler Green | .02 | .10 |
| ❑ 506 | Jose Martinez RC | .05 | .15 |
| ❑ 507 | Troy Percival | .10 | .30 |
| ❑ 508 | Kevin Stocker | .02 | .10 |
| ❑ 509 | Matt Walbeck RC | .05 | .15 |
| ❑ 510 | Rondell White | .20 | .50 |
| ❑ 511 | Billy Ripken | .02 | .10 |
| ❑ 512 | Mike Moore | .02 | .10 |
| ❑ 513 | Jose Lind | .02 | .10 |
| ❑ 514 | Chito Martinez | .02 | .10 |
| ❑ 515 | Jose Guzman | .02 | .10 |
| ❑ 516 | Kim Batiste | .02 | .10 |
| ❑ 517 | Jeff Tackett | .02 | .10 |
| ❑ 518 | Charlie Hough | .07 | .20 |
| ❑ 519 | Marvin Freeman | .02 | .10 |
| ❑ 520 | Carlos Martinez | .02 | .10 |
| ❑ 521 | Eric Young | .07 | .20 |
| ❑ 522 | Pete Incaviglia | .02 | .10 |
| ❑ 523 | Scott Fletcher | .02 | .10 |
| ❑ 524 | Orestes Destrade | .02 | .10 |
| ❑ 525 | Ken Griffey Sr. CL | .20 | .50 |
| ❑ 526 | Ellis Burks | .07 | .20 |
| ❑ 527 | Juan Samuel | .02 | .10 |
| ❑ 528 | Dave Magadan | .02 | .10 |
| ❑ 529 | Jeff Parrett | .02 | .10 |
| ❑ 530 | Bill Krueger | .02 | .10 |
| ❑ 531 | Frank Bolick | .02 | .10 |
| ❑ 532 | Alan Trammell | .07 | .20 |
| ❑ 533 | Walt Weiss | .02 | .10 |
| ❑ 534 | David Cone | .07 | .20 |
| ❑ 535 | Greg Maddux | .30 | .75 |
| ❑ 536 | Kevin Young | .07 | .20 |
| ❑ 537 | Dave Hansen | .02 | .10 |
| ❑ 538 | Alex Cole | .02 | .10 |
| ❑ 539 | Greg Hibbard | .02 | .10 |
| ❑ 540 | Gene Larkin | .02 | .10 |
| ❑ 541 | Jeff Reardon | .07 | .20 |
| ❑ 542 | Felix Jose | .02 | .10 |
| ❑ 543 | Jimmy Key | .07 | .20 |
| ❑ 544 | Reggie Jefferson | .02 | .10 |
| ❑ 545 | Gregg Jefferies | .02 | .10 |
| ❑ 546 | Dave Stewart | .07 | .20 |
| ❑ 547 | Tim Wallach | .02 | .10 |
| ❑ 548 | Spike Owen | .02 | .10 |
| ❑ 549 | Tommy Greene | .02 | .10 |
| ❑ 550 | Fernando Valenzuela | .07 | .20 |
| ❑ 551 | Rich Amaral | .02 | .10 |
| ❑ 552 | Bret Barberie | .02 | .10 |
| ❑ 553 | Edgar Martinez | .10 | .30 |
| ❑ 554 | Jim Abbott | .20 | .50 |
| ❑ 555 | Frank Thomas | .20 | .50 |
| ❑ 556 | Wade Boggs | .20 | .50 |
| ❑ 557 | Tom Henke | .02 | .10 |
| ❑ 558 | Milt Thompson | .02 | .10 |
| ❑ 559 | Lloyd McClendon | .02 | .10 |
| ❑ 560 | Vinny Castilla | .20 | .50 |
| ❑ 561 | Ricky Jordan | .02 | .10 |
| ❑ 562 | Andujar Cedeno | .02 | .10 |
| ❑ 563 | Greg Vaughn | .02 | .10 |
| ❑ 564 | Cecil Fielder | .07 | .20 |
| ❑ 565 | Kirby Puckett | .20 | .50 |
| ❑ 566 | Mark McGwire | .50 | 1.25 |
| ❑ 567 | Barry Bonds | .60 | 1.50 |
| ❑ 568 | Jody Reed | .02 | .10 |
| ❑ 569 | Todd Zeile | .02 | .10 |
| ❑ 570 | Mark Carreon | .02 | .10 |
| ❑ 571 | Joe Girardi | .02 | .10 |
| ❑ 572 | Luis Gonzalez | .07 | .20 |
| ❑ 573 | Mark Grace | .10 | .30 |
| ❑ 574 | Rafael Palmeiro | .10 | .30 |
| ❑ 575 | Darryl Strawberry | .10 | .30 |
| ❑ 576 | Will Clark | .10 | .30 |
| ❑ 577 | Fred McGriff | .10 | .30 |
| ❑ 578 | Kevin Reimer | .02 | .10 |
| ❑ 579 | Dave Righetti | .07 | .20 |
| ❑ 580 | Juan Bell | .02 | .10 |
| ❑ 581 | Jeff Brantley | .02 | .10 |
| ❑ 582 | Brian Hunter | .02 | .10 |
| ❑ 583 | Tim Naehring | .02 | .10 |
| ❑ 584 | Glenallen Hill | .02 | .10 |
| ❑ 585 | Cal Ripken | .60 | 1.50 |
| ❑ 586 | Albert Belle | .07 | .20 |
| ❑ 587 | Robin Yount | .30 | .75 |
| ❑ 588 | Chris Bosio | .02 | .10 |

|  |  | | |
|---|---|---|---|
| ☐ 589 | Pete Smith | .02 | .10 |
| ☐ 590 | Chuck Carr | .02 | .10 |
| ☐ 591 | Jeff Blauser | .02 | .10 |
| ☐ 592 | Kevin McReynolds | .02 | .10 |
| ☐ 593 | Andres Galarraga | .07 | .20 |
| ☐ 594 | Kevin Maas | .02 | .10 |
| ☐ 595 | Eric Davis | .07 | .20 |
| ☐ 596 | Brian Jordan | .07 | .20 |
| ☐ 597 | Tim Raines | .07 | .20 |
| ☐ 598 | Rick Wilkins | .02 | .10 |
| ☐ 599 | Steve Cooke | .02 | .10 |
| ☐ 600 | Mike Gallego | .02 | .10 |
| ☐ 601 | Mike Munoz | .02 | .10 |
| ☐ 602 | Luis Rivera | .02 | .10 |
| ☐ 603 | Junior Ortiz | .02 | .10 |
| ☐ 604 | Brent Mayne | .02 | .10 |
| ☐ 605 | Luis Alicea | .02 | .10 |
| ☐ 606 | Damon Berryhill | .02 | .10 |
| ☐ 607 | Dave Henderson | .02 | .10 |
| ☐ 608 | Kirk McCaskill | .02 | .10 |
| ☐ 609 | Jeff Fassero | .02 | .10 |
| ☐ 610 | Mike Harkey | .02 | .10 |
| ☐ 611 | Francisco Cabrera | .02 | .10 |
| ☐ 612 | Rey Sanchez | .02 | .10 |
| ☐ 613 | Scott Servais | .02 | .10 |
| ☐ 614 | Darrin Fletcher | .02 | .10 |
| ☐ 615 | Felix Fermin | .02 | .10 |
| ☐ 616 | Kevin Seitzer | .02 | .10 |
| ☐ 617 | Bob Scanlan | .02 | .10 |
| ☐ 618 | Billy Hatcher | .02 | .10 |
| ☐ 619 | John Vander Wal | .02 | .10 |
| ☐ 620 | Joe Hesketh | .02 | .10 |
| ☐ 621 | Hector Villanueva | .02 | .10 |
| ☐ 622 | Randy Milligan | .02 | .10 |
| ☐ 623 | Tony Tarasco RC | .05 | .15 |
| ☐ 624 | Russ Swan | .02 | .10 |
| ☐ 625 | Willie Wilson | .02 | .10 |
| ☐ 626 | Frank Tanana | .02 | .10 |
| ☐ 627 | Pete O'Brien | .02 | .10 |
| ☐ 628 | Lenny Webster | .02 | .10 |
| ☐ 629 | Mark Clark | .02 | .10 |
| ☐ 630 | Roger Clemens CL | .20 | .50 |
| ☐ 631 | Alex Arias | .02 | .10 |
| ☐ 632 | Chris Gwynn | .02 | .10 |
| ☐ 633 | Tom Bolton | .02 | .10 |
| ☐ 634 | Greg Briley | .02 | .10 |
| ☐ 635 | Kent Bottenfield | .02 | .10 |
| ☐ 636 | Kelly Downs | .02 | .10 |
| ☐ 637 | Manuel Lee | .02 | .10 |
| ☐ 638 | Al Leiter | .07 | .20 |
| ☐ 639 | Jeff Gardner | .02 | .10 |
| ☐ 640 | Mike Gardiner | .02 | .10 |
| ☐ 641 | Mark Gardner | .02 | .10 |
| ☐ 642 | Jeff Branson | .02 | .10 |
| ☐ 643 | Paul Wagner | .02 | .10 |
| ☐ 644 | Sean Berry | .02 | .10 |
| ☐ 645 | Phil Hiatt | .02 | .10 |
| ☐ 646 | Kevin Mitchell | .02 | .10 |
| ☐ 647 | Charlie Hayes | .02 | .10 |
| ☐ 648 | Jim Deshaies | .02 | .10 |
| ☐ 649 | Dan Pasqua | .02 | .10 |
| ☐ 650 | Mike Maddux | .02 | .10 |
| ☐ 651 | Domingo Martinez RC | .05 | .15 |
| ☐ 652 | Greg McMichael RC | .05 | .15 |
| ☐ 653 | Eric Wedge RC | .20 | .50 |
| ☐ 654 | Mark Whiten | .02 | .10 |
| ☐ 655 | Roberto Kelly | .02 | .10 |
| ☐ 656 | Julio Franco | .07 | .20 |
| ☐ 657 | Gene Harris | .02 | .10 |
| ☐ 658 | Pete Schourek | .02 | .10 |
| ☐ 659 | Mike Bielecki | .02 | .10 |
| ☐ 660 | Ricky Gutierrez | .02 | .10 |
| ☐ 661 | Chris Hammond | .02 | .10 |
| ☐ 662 | Tim Scott | .02 | .10 |
| ☐ 663 | Norm Charlton | .02 | .10 |
| ☐ 664 | Doug Drabek | .02 | .10 |
| ☐ 665 | Dwight Gooden | .07 | .20 |
| ☐ 666 | Jim Gott | .02 | .10 |
| ☐ 667 | Randy Myers | .02 | .10 |
| ☐ 668 | Darren Holmes | .02 | .10 |
| ☐ 669 | Tim Spehr | .02 | .10 |
| ☐ 670 | Bruce Ruffin | .02 | .10 |
| ☐ 671 | Bobby Thigpen | .02 | .10 |
| ☐ 672 | Tony Fernandez | .02 | .10 |
| ☐ 673 | Darrin Jackson | .02 | .10 |
| ☐ 674 | Gregg Olson | .02 | .10 |
| ☐ 675 | Rob Dibble | .07 | .20 |
| ☐ 676 | Howard Johnson | .02 | .10 |
| ☐ 677 | Mike Lansing RC | .20 | .50 |
| ☐ 678 | Charlie Leibrandt | .02 | .10 |
| ☐ 679 | Kevin Bass | .02 | .10 |
| ☐ 680 | Hubie Brooks | .02 | .10 |
| ☐ 681 | Scott Brosius | .07 | .20 |
| ☐ 682 | Randy Knorr | .02 | .10 |
| ☐ 683 | Dante Bichette | .07 | .20 |
| ☐ 684 | Bryan Harvey | .02 | .10 |
| ☐ 685 | Greg Gohr | .02 | .10 |
| ☐ 686 | Willie Banks | .02 | .10 |
| ☐ 687 | Robb Nen | .07 | .20 |
| ☐ 688 | Mike Scioscia | .02 | .10 |
| ☐ 689 | John Farrell | .02 | .10 |
| ☐ 690 | John Candelaria | .02 | .10 |
| ☐ 691 | Damon Buford | .02 | .10 |
| ☐ 692 | Todd Worrell | .02 | .10 |
| ☐ 693 | Pat Hentgen | .02 | .10 |
| ☐ 694 | John Smiley | .02 | .10 |
| ☐ 695 | Greg Swindell | .02 | .10 |
| ☐ 696 | Derek Bell | .02 | .10 |
| ☐ 697 | Terry Jorgensen | .02 | .10 |
| ☐ 698 | Jimmy Jones | .02 | .10 |
| ☐ 699 | David Wells | .07 | .20 |
| ☐ 700 | Dave Martinez | .02 | .10 |
| ☐ 701 | Steve Bedrosian | .02 | .10 |
| ☐ 702 | Jeff Russell | .02 | .10 |
| ☐ 703 | Joe Magrane | .02 | .10 |
| ☐ 704 | Matt Mieske | .02 | .10 |
| ☐ 705 | Paul Molitor | .07 | .20 |
| ☐ 706 | Dale Murphy | .10 | .30 |
| ☐ 707 | Steve Howe | .02 | .10 |
| ☐ 708 | Greg Gagne | .02 | .10 |
| ☐ 709 | Dave Eiland | .02 | .10 |
| ☐ 710 | David West | .02 | .10 |
| ☐ 711 | Luis Aquino | .02 | .10 |
| ☐ 712 | Joe Orsulak | .02 | .10 |
| ☐ 713 | Eric Plunk | .02 | .10 |
| ☐ 714 | Mike Felder | .02 | .10 |
| ☐ 715 | Joe Klink | .02 | .10 |
| ☐ 716 | Lonnie Smith | .02 | .10 |
| ☐ 717 | Monty Fariss | .02 | .10 |
| ☐ 718 | Craig Lefferts | .02 | .10 |
| ☐ 719 | John Habyan | .02 | .10 |
| ☐ 720 | Willie Blair | .02 | .10 |
| ☐ 721 | Darnell Coles | .02 | .10 |
| ☐ 722 | Mark Williamson | .02 | .10 |
| ☐ 723 | Bryn Smith | .02 | .10 |
| ☐ 724 | Greg W. Harris | .02 | .10 |
| ☐ 725 | Graeme Lloyd RC | .20 | .50 |
| ☐ 726 | Cris Carpenter | .02 | .10 |
| ☐ 727 | Chico Walker | .02 | .10 |
| ☐ 728 | Tracy Woodson | .02 | .10 |
| ☐ 729 | Jose Uribe | .02 | .10 |
| ☐ 730 | Stan Javier | .02 | .10 |
| ☐ 731 | Jay Howell | .02 | .10 |
| ☐ 732 | Freddie Benavides | .02 | .10 |
| ☐ 733 | Jeff Reboulet | .02 | .10 |
| ☐ 734 | Scott Sanderson | .02 | .10 |
| ☐ 735 | Ryne Sandberg CL | .20 | .50 |
| ☐ 736 | Archi Cianfrocco | .02 | .10 |
| ☐ 737 | Daryl Boston | .02 | .10 |
| ☐ 738 | Craig Grebeck | .02 | .10 |
| ☐ 739 | Doug Dascenzo | .02 | .10 |
| ☐ 740 | Gerald Young | .02 | .10 |
| ☐ 741 | Candy Maldonado | .02 | .10 |
| ☐ 742 | Joey Cora | .02 | .10 |
| ☐ 743 | Don Slaught | .02 | .10 |
| ☐ 744 | Steve Decker | .02 | .10 |
| ☐ 745 | Blas Minor | .02 | .10 |
| ☐ 746 | Storm Davis | .02 | .10 |
| ☐ 747 | Carlos Quintana | .02 | .10 |
| ☐ 748 | Vince Coleman | .02 | .10 |
| ☐ 749 | Todd Burns | .02 | .10 |
| ☐ 750 | Steve Frey | .02 | .10 |
| ☐ 751 | Ivan Calderon | .02 | .10 |
| ☐ 752 | Steve Reed RC | .05 | .15 |
| ☐ 753 | Danny Jackson | .02 | .10 |
| ☐ 754 | Jeff Conine | .07 | .20 |
| ☐ 755 | Juan Gonzalez | .07 | .20 |
| ☐ 756 | Mike Kelly | .02 | .10 |
| ☐ 757 | John Doherty | .02 | .10 |
| ☐ 758 | Jack Armstrong | .02 | .10 |
| ☐ 759 | John Wehner | .02 | .10 |
| ☐ 760 | Scott Bankhead | .02 | .10 |
| ☐ 761 | Jim Tatum | .02 | .10 |
| ☐ 762 | Scott Pose RC | .05 | .15 |
| ☐ 763 | Andy Ashby | .02 | .10 |
| ☐ 764 | Ed Sprague | .02 | .10 |
| ☐ 765 | Harold Baines | .07 | .20 |
| ☐ 766 | Kirk Gibson | .07 | .20 |
| ☐ 767 | Troy Neel | .02 | .10 |
| ☐ 768 | Dick Schofield | .02 | .10 |
| ☐ 769 | Dickie Thon | .02 | .10 |
| ☐ 770 | Butch Henry | .02 | .10 |
| ☐ 771 | Junior Felix | .02 | .10 |
| ☐ 772 | Ken Ryan RC | .05 | .15 |
| ☐ 773 | Trevor Hoffman | .20 | .50 |
| ☐ 774 | Phil Plantier | .02 | .10 |
| ☐ 775 | Bo Jackson | .20 | .50 |
| ☐ 776 | Benito Santiago | .07 | .20 |
| ☐ 777 | Andre Dawson | .07 | .20 |
| ☐ 778 | Bryan Hickerson | .02 | .10 |
| ☐ 779 | Dennis Moeller | .02 | .10 |
| ☐ 780 | Ryan Bowen | .02 | .10 |
| ☐ 781 | Eric Fox | .02 | .10 |
| ☐ 782 | Joe Kmak | .02 | .10 |
| ☐ 783 | Mike Hampton | .07 | .20 |
| ☐ 784 | Darrell Sherman RC | .05 | .15 |
| ☐ 785 | J.T.Snow | .10 | .30 |
| ☐ 786 | Dave Winfield | .07 | .20 |
| ☐ 787 | Jim Austin | .02 | .10 |
| ☐ 788 | Craig Shipley | .02 | .10 |
| ☐ 789 | Greg Myers | .02 | .10 |
| ☐ 790 | Todd Benzinger | .02 | .10 |
| ☐ 791 | Cory Snyder | .02 | .10 |
| ☐ 792 | David Segui | .02 | .10 |
| ☐ 793 | Armando Reynoso | .02 | .10 |
| ☐ 794 | Chili Davis | .07 | .20 |
| ☐ 795 | Dave Nilsson | .02 | .10 |
| ☐ 796 | Paul O'Neill | .10 | .30 |
| ☐ 797 | Jerald Clark | .02 | .10 |
| ☐ 798 | Jose Mesa | .02 | .10 |
| ☐ 799 | Brain Holman | .02 | .10 |
| ☐ 800 | Jim Eisenreich | .02 | .10 |
| ☐ 801 | Mark McLemore | .02 | .10 |
| ☐ 802 | Luis Sojo | .02 | .10 |
| ☐ 803 | Harold Reynolds | .07 | .20 |
| ☐ 804 | Dan Plesac | .02 | .10 |
| ☐ 805 | Dave Stieb | .02 | .10 |
| ☐ 806 | Tom Brunansky | .02 | .10 |
| ☐ 807 | Kelly Gruber | .02 | .10 |
| ☐ 808 | Bob Ojeda | .02 | .10 |
| ☐ 809 | Dave Burba | .02 | .10 |
| ☐ 810 | Joe Boever | .02 | .10 |
| ☐ 811 | Jeremy Hernandez | .02 | .10 |
| ☐ 812 | Tim Salmon TC | .07 | .20 |
| ☐ 813 | Jeff Bagwell TC | .07 | .20 |
| ☐ 814 | Dennis Eckersley TC | .07 | .20 |
| ☐ 815 | Roberto Alomar TC | .07 | .20 |
| ☐ 816 | Steve Avery TC | .02 | .10 |
| ☐ 817 | Pat Listach TC | .02 | .10 |
| ☐ 818 | Gregg Jefferies TC | .02 | .10 |
| ☐ 819 | Sammy Sosa TC | .20 | .50 |
| ☐ 820 | Darryl Strawberry TC | .02 | .10 |
| ☐ 821 | Dennis Martinez TC | .02 | .10 |
| ☐ 822 | Robby Thompson TC | .02 | .10 |
| ☐ 823 | Albert Belle TC | .07 | .20 |
| ☐ 824 | Randy Johnson TC | .10 | .30 |
| ☐ 825 | Nigel Wilson TC | .02 | .10 |
| ☐ 826 | Bobby Bonilla TC | .02 | .10 |
| ☐ 827 | Glenn Davis TC | .02 | .10 |
| ☐ 828 | Gary Sheffield TC | .02 | .10 |
| ☐ 829 | Darren Daulton TC | .02 | .10 |
| ☐ 830 | Jay Bell TC | .02 | .10 |
| ☐ 831 | Juan Gonzalez TC | .07 | .20 |
| ☐ 832 | Andre Dawson TC | .02 | .10 |
| ☐ 833 | Hal Morris TC | .02 | .10 |
| ☐ 834 | David Nied TC | .02 | .10 |
| ☐ 835 | Felix Jose TC | .02 | .10 |
| ☐ 836 | Travis Fryman TC | .07 | .20 |
| ☐ 837 | Shane Mack TC | .02 | .10 |
| ☐ 838 | Robin Ventura TC | .02 | .10 |
| ☐ 839 | Danny Tartabull TC | .02 | .10 |
| ☐ 840 | Roberto Alomar CL | .07 | .20 |
| ☐ SP5 | G.Brett/R.Yount | .40 | 1.00 |
| ☐ SP6 | Nolan Ryan | .75 | 2.00 |

# 1994 Upper Deck

| | | |
|---|---|---|
| COMPLETE SET (550) | 15.00 | 40.00 |
| COMPLETE SERIES 1 (280) | 12.50 | 25.00 |
| COMPLETE SERIES 2 (270) | 7.50 | 15.00 |
| 1 Brian Anderson RC | .15 | .40 |
| 2 Shane Andrews | .05 | .15 |
| 3 James Baldwin | .05 | .15 |
| 4 Rich Becker | .05 | .15 |
| 5 Greg Blosser | .05 | .15 |
| 6 Ricky Bottalico RC | .05 | .15 |
| 7 Midre Cummings | .05 | .15 |
| 8 Carlos Delgado | .20 | .50 |
| 9 Steve Dreyer RC | .05 | .15 |
| 10 Joey Eischen | .05 | .15 |
| 11 Carl Everett | .10 | .30 |
| 12 Cliff Floyd | .10 | .30 |
| 13 Alex Gonzalez | .05 | .15 |
| 14 Jeff Granger | .05 | .15 |
| 15 Shawn Green | .30 | .75 |
| 16 Brian L. Hunter | .05 | .15 |
| 17 Butch Huskey | .05 | .15 |
| 18 Mark Hutton | .05 | .15 |
| 19 Michael Jordan RC | 3.00 | 8.00 |
| 20 Steve Karsay | .05 | .15 |
| 21 Jeff McNeely | .05 | .15 |
| 22 Marc Newfield | .05 | .15 |
| 23 Manny Ramirez | .30 | .75 |
| 24 Alex Rodriguez RC | 6.00 | 15.00 |
| 25 Scott Ruffcorn UER | .05 | .15 |
| 26 Paul Spoljaric UER | .05 | .15 |
| 27 Salomon Torres | .05 | .15 |
| 28 Steve Trachsel | .05 | .15 |
| 29 Chris Turner | .05 | .15 |
| 30 Gabe White | .05 | .15 |
| 31 Randy Johnson FT | .20 | .50 |
| 32 John Wetteland FT | .05 | .15 |
| 33 Mike Piazza FT | .30 | .75 |
| 34 Rafael Palmeiro FT | .10 | .30 |
| 35 Roberto Alomar FT | .10 | .30 |
| 36 Matt Williams FT | .05 | .15 |
| 37 Travis Fryman FT | .05 | .15 |
| 38 Barry Bonds FT | .40 | 1.00 |
| 39 Marquis Grissom FT | .05 | .15 |
| 40 Albert Belle FT | .10 | .30 |
| 41 Steve Avery FUT | .05 | .15 |
| 42 Jason Bere FUT | .05 | .15 |
| 43 Alex Fernandez FUT | .05 | .15 |
| 44 Mike Mussina FUT | .10 | .30 |
| 45 Aaron Sele FUT | .05 | .15 |
| 46 Rod Beck FUT | .05 | .15 |
| 47 Mike Piazza FUT | .30 | .75 |
| 48 John Olerud FUT | .05 | .15 |
| 49 Carlos Baerga FUT | .05 | .15 |
| 50 Gary Sheffield FUT | .05 | .15 |
| 51 Travis Fryman FUT | .05 | .15 |
| 52 Juan Gonzalez FUT | .20 | .50 |
| 53 Ken Griffey Jr. FUT | .30 | .75 |
| 54 Tim Salmon FUT | .10 | .30 |
| 55 Frank Thomas FUT | .20 | .50 |
| 56 Tony Phillips | .05 | .15 |
| 57 Julio Franco | .10 | .30 |
| 58 Kevin Mitchell | .10 | .30 |
| 59 Raul Mondesi | .30 | .75 |
| 60 Rickey Henderson | .30 | .75 |
| 61 Jay Buhner | .10 | .30 |
| 62 Bill Swift | .05 | .15 |
| 63 Brady Anderson | .10 | .30 |
| 64 Ryan Klesko | .10 | .30 |
| 65 Darren Daulton | .05 | .15 |
| 66 Damion Easley | .05 | .15 |
| 67 Mark McGwire | .75 | 2.00 |
| 68 John Roper | .05 | .15 |
| 69 Dave Telgheder | .05 | .15 |
| 70 David Nied | .05 | .15 |
| 71 Mo Vaughn | .10 | .30 |
| 72 Tyler Green | .05 | .15 |
| 73 Dave Magadan | .05 | .15 |
| 74 Chili Davis | .10 | .30 |
| 75 Archi Cianfrocco | .05 | .15 |
| 76 Joe Girardi | .05 | .15 |
| 77 Chris Hoiles | .05 | .15 |
| 78 Ryan Bowen | .05 | .15 |
| 79 Greg Gagne | .05 | .15 |
| 80 Aaron Sele | .05 | .15 |
| 81 Dave Winfield | .10 | .30 |
| 82 Chad Curtis | .05 | .15 |
| 83 Andy Van Slyke | .20 | .50 |
| 84 Kevin Stocker | .05 | .15 |
| 85 Deion Sanders | .20 | .50 |
| 86 Bernie Williams | .20 | .50 |
| 87 John Smoltz | .20 | .50 |
| 88 Ruben Santana | .05 | .15 |
| 89 Dave Stewart | .10 | .30 |
| 90 Don Mattingly | .75 | 2.00 |
| 91 Joe Carter | .10 | .30 |
| 92 Ryne Sandberg | .50 | 1.25 |
| 93 Chris Gomez | .05 | .15 |
| 94 Tino Martinez | .20 | .50 |
| 95 Terry Pendleton | .10 | .30 |
| 96 Andre Dawson | .10 | .30 |
| 97 Wil Cordero | .05 | .15 |
| 98 Kent Hrbek | .10 | .30 |
| 99 John Olerud | .10 | .30 |
| 100 Kirt Manwaring | .05 | .15 |
| 101 Tim Bogar | .05 | .15 |
| 102 Mike Mussina | .20 | .50 |
| 103 Nigel Wilson | .05 | .15 |
| 104 Ricky Gutierrez | .05 | .15 |
| 105 Roberto Mejia | .05 | .15 |
| 106 Tom Pagnozzi | .05 | .15 |
| 107 Mike Macfarlane | .05 | .15 |
| 108 Jose Bautista | .05 | .15 |
| 109 Luis Ortiz | .05 | .15 |
| 110 Brent Gates | .20 | .50 |
| 111 Tim Salmon | .20 | .50 |
| 112 Wade Boggs | .20 | .50 |
| 113 Tripp Cromer | .05 | .15 |
| 114 Denny Hocking | .05 | .15 |
| 115 Carlos Baerga | .05 | .15 |
| 116 J.R. Phillips | .05 | .15 |
| 117 Bo Jackson | .30 | .75 |
| 118 Lance Johnson | .05 | .15 |
| 119 Bobby Jones | .05 | .15 |
| 120 Bobby Witt | .05 | .15 |
| 121 Ron Karkovice | .05 | .15 |
| 122 Jose Vizcaino | .05 | .15 |
| 123 Danny Darwin | .05 | .15 |
| 124 Eduardo Perez | .05 | .15 |
| 125 Brian Looney RC | .05 | .15 |
| 126 Pat Hentgen | .05 | .15 |
| 127 Frank Viola | .10 | .30 |
| 128 Darren Holmes | .05 | .15 |
| 129 Wally Whitehurst | .05 | .15 |
| 130 Matt Walbeck | .05 | .15 |
| 131 Albert Belle | .30 | .75 |
| 132 Steve Cooke | .05 | .15 |
| 133 Kevin Appier | .10 | .30 |
| 134 Joe Oliver | .05 | .15 |
| 135 Benji Gil | .05 | .15 |
| 136 Steve Buechele | .05 | .15 |
| 137 Devon White | .10 | .30 |
| 138 Sterling Hitchcock UER | .05 | .15 |
| 139 Phil Leftwich RC | .05 | .15 |
| 140 Jose Canseco | .20 | .50 |
| 141 Rick Aguilera | .05 | .15 |
| 142 Rod Beck | .05 | .15 |
| 143 Jose Rijo | .10 | .30 |
| 144 Tom Glavine | .20 | .50 |
| 145 Phil Plantier | .10 | .30 |
| 146 Jason Bere | .05 | .15 |
| 147 Jamie Moyer | .10 | .30 |
| 148 Wes Chamberlain | .05 | .15 |
| 149 Glenallen Hill | .05 | .15 |
| 150 Mark Whiten | .05 | .15 |
| 151 Bret Barberie | .05 | .15 |
| 152 Chuck Knoblauch | .10 | .30 |
| 153 Trevor Hoffman | .20 | .50 |
| 154 Rick Wilkins | .05 | .15 |
| 155 Juan Gonzalez | .30 | .75 |
| 156 Ozzie Guillen | .10 | .30 |
| 157 Jim Eisenreich | .05 | .15 |
| 158 Pedro Astacio | .05 | .15 |
| 159 Joe Magrane | .05 | .15 |
| 160 Ryan Thompson | .05 | .15 |
| 161 Jose Lind | .05 | .15 |
| 162 Jeff Conine | .10 | .30 |
| 163 Todd Benzinger | .05 | .15 |
| 164 Roger Salkeld | .05 | .15 |
| 165 Gary DiSarcina | .05 | .15 |
| 166 Kevin Gross | .05 | .15 |
| 167 Charlie Hayes | .05 | .15 |
| 168 Tim Costo | .05 | .15 |
| 169 Wally Joyner | .10 | .30 |
| 170 Johnny Ruffin | .05 | .15 |
| 171 Kirk Rueter | .05 | .15 |
| 172 Lenny Dykstra | .10 | .30 |
| 173 Ken Hill | .05 | .15 |
| 174 Mike Bordick | .05 | .15 |
| 175 Billy Hall | .05 | .15 |
| 176 Rob Butler | .05 | .15 |
| 177 Jay Bell | .10 | .30 |
| 178 Jeff Kent | .20 | .50 |
| 179 David Wells | .10 | .30 |
| 180 Dean Palmer | .10 | .30 |
| 181 Mariano Duncan | .05 | .15 |
| 182 Orlando Merced | .05 | .15 |
| 183 Brett Butler | .10 | .30 |
| 184 Milt Thompson | .05 | .15 |
| 185 Chipper Jones | .30 | .75 |
| 186 Paul O'Neill | .20 | .50 |
| 187 Mike Greenwell | .05 | .15 |
| 188 Harold Baines | .10 | .30 |
| 189 Todd Stottlemyre | .05 | .15 |
| 190 Jeromy Burnitz | .05 | .15 |
| 191 Rene Arocha | .05 | .15 |
| 192 Jeff Fassero | .05 | .15 |
| 193 Robby Thompson | .05 | .15 |
| 194 Greg W. Harris | .05 | .15 |
| 195 Todd Van Poppel | .05 | .15 |
| 196 Jose Guzman | .05 | .15 |
| 197 Shane Mack | .05 | .15 |
| 198 Carlos Garcia | .05 | .15 |
| 199 Kevin Roberson | .05 | .15 |
| 200 David McCarty | .10 | .30 |
| 201 Alan Trammell | .10 | .30 |
| 202 Chuck Carr | .05 | .15 |
| 203 Tommy Greene | .05 | .15 |
| 204 Wilson Alvarez | .05 | .15 |
| 205 Dwight Gooden | .10 | .30 |
| 206 Tony Tarasco | .05 | .15 |
| 207 Darren Lewis | .05 | .15 |
| 208 Eric Karros | .10 | .30 |
| 209 Chris Hammond | .05 | .15 |
| 210 Jeffrey Hammonds | .05 | .15 |
| 211 Rich Amaral | .05 | .15 |
| 212 Danny Tartabull | .10 | .30 |
| 213 Jeff Russell | .05 | .15 |
| 214 Dave Staton | .05 | .15 |
| 215 Kenny Lofton | .10 | .30 |
| 216 Manuel Lee | .05 | .15 |
| 217 Brian Koelling | .05 | .15 |
| 218 Scott Lydy | .05 | .15 |
| 219 Tony Gwynn | .40 | 1.00 |
| 220 Cecil Fielder | .10 | .30 |
| 221 Royce Clayton | .05 | .15 |
| 222 Reggie Sanders | .10 | .30 |
| 223 Brian Jordan | .10 | .30 |
| 224 Ken Griffey Jr. | .50 | 1.25 |
| 225 Fred McGriff | .20 | .50 |
| 226 Felix Jose | .05 | .15 |
| 227 Brad Pennington | .05 | .15 |
| 228 Chris Bosio | .05 | .15 |
| 229 Mike Stanley | .05 | .15 |
| 230 Willie Greene | .05 | .15 |
| 231 Alex Fernandez | .05 | .15 |
| 232 Brad Ausmus | .10 | .30 |
| 233 Darrell Whitmore | .05 | .15 |
| 234 Marcus Moore | .05 | .15 |
| 235 Allen Watson | .05 | .15 |
| 236 Jose Offerman | .05 | .15 |
| 237 Rondell White | .10 | .30 |
| 238 Jeff King | .05 | .15 |
| 239 Luis Alicea | .05 | .15 |
| 240 Dan Wilson | .05 | .15 |
| 241 Ed Sprague | .05 | .15 |
| 242 Todd Hundley | .05 | .15 |
| 243 Al Martin | .05 | .15 |
| 244 Mike Lansing | .05 | .15 |
| 245 Ivan Rodriguez | .20 | .50 |

|  |  | | |
|---|--------|---|---|
| ❑ 246 Dave Fleming | .05 | .15 |
| ❑ 247 John Doherty | .05 | .15 |
| ❑ 248 Mark McLemore | .05 | .15 |
| ❑ 249 Bob Hamelin | .05 | .15 |
| ❑ 250 Curtis Pride RC | .15 | .40 |
| ❑ 251 Zane Smith | .05 | .15 |
| ❑ 252 Eric Young | .05 | .15 |
| ❑ 253 Brian McRae | .05 | .15 |
| ❑ 254 Tim Raines | .10 | .30 |
| ❑ 255 Javier Lopez | .10 | .30 |
| ❑ 256 Melvin Nieves | .05 | .15 |
| ❑ 257 Randy Myers | .05 | .15 |
| ❑ 258 Willie McGee | .10 | .30 |
| ❑ 259 Jimmy Key UER | .10 | .30 |
| ❑ 260 Tom Candiotti | .05 | .15 |
| ❑ 261 Eric Davis | .10 | .30 |
| ❑ 262 Craig Paquette | .05 | .15 |
| ❑ 263 Robin Ventura | .10 | .30 |
| ❑ 264 Pat Kelly | .05 | .15 |
| ❑ 265 Gregg Jefferies | .05 | .15 |
| ❑ 266 Cory Snyder | .05 | .15 |
| ❑ 267 David Justice HFA | .30 | .75 |
| ❑ 268 Sammy Sosa HFA | .30 | .75 |
| ❑ 269 Barry Larkin HFA | .10 | .30 |
| ❑ 270 Andres Galarraga HFA | .05 | .15 |
| ❑ 271 Gary Sheffield HFA | .05 | .15 |
| ❑ 272 Jeff Bagwell HFA | .10 | .30 |
| ❑ 273 Mike Piazza HFA | .30 | .75 |
| ❑ 274 Larry Walker HFA | .05 | .15 |
| ❑ 275 Bobby Bonilla HFA | .05 | .15 |
| ❑ 276 John Kruk HFA | .05 | .15 |
| ❑ 277 Jay Bell HFA | .05 | .15 |
| ❑ 278 Ozzie Smith HFA | .30 | .75 |
| ❑ 279 Tony Gwynn HFA | .20 | .50 |
| ❑ 280 Barry Bonds HFA | .40 | 1.00 |
| ❑ 281 Cal Ripken HFA | .50 | 1.25 |
| ❑ 282 Mo Vaughn HFA | .05 | .15 |
| ❑ 283 Tim Salmon HFA | .10 | .30 |
| ❑ 284 Frank Thomas HFA | .20 | .50 |
| ❑ 285 Albert Belle HFA | .10 | .30 |
| ❑ 286 Cecil Fielder HFA | .05 | .15 |
| ❑ 287 Wally Joyner HFA | .05 | .15 |
| ❑ 288 Greg Vaughn HFA | .05 | .15 |
| ❑ 289 Kirby Puckett HFA | .20 | .50 |
| ❑ 290 Don Mattingly HFA | .40 | 1.00 |
| ❑ 291 Terry Steinbach HFA | .05 | .15 |
| ❑ 292 Ken Griffey Jr. HFA | .30 | .75 |
| ❑ 293 Juan Gonzalez HFA | .05 | .15 |
| ❑ 294 Paul Molitor HFA | .05 | .15 |
| ❑ 295 Tavo Alvarez UDCA | .05 | .15 |
| ❑ 296 Matt Brunson UDCA | .05 | .15 |
| ❑ 297 Shawn Green UDCA | .10 | .30 |
| ❑ 298 Alex Rodriguez UDCA | 2.00 | 5.00 |
| ❑ 299 Shannon Stewart UDCA | .30 | .75 |
| ❑ 300 Frank Thomas | .30 | .75 |
| ❑ 301 Mickey Tettleton | .05 | .15 |
| ❑ 302 Pedro Munoz | .05 | .15 |
| ❑ 303 Jose Valentin | .05 | .15 |
| ❑ 304 Orestes Destrade | .05 | .15 |
| ❑ 305 Pat Listach | .05 | .15 |
| ❑ 306 Scott Brosius | .10 | .30 |
| ❑ 307 Kurt Miller | .05 | .15 |
| ❑ 308 Rob Dibble | .10 | .30 |
| ❑ 309 Mike Blowers | .05 | .15 |
| ❑ 310 Jim Abbott | .20 | .50 |
| ❑ 311 Mike Jackson | .05 | .15 |
| ❑ 312 Craig Biggio | .20 | .50 |
| ❑ 313 Kurt Abbott RC | .05 | .15 |
| ❑ 314 Chuck Finley | .10 | .30 |
| ❑ 315 Andres Galarraga | .10 | .30 |
| ❑ 316 Mike Moore | .05 | .15 |
| ❑ 317 Doug Strange | .05 | .15 |
| ❑ 318 Pedro Martinez | .30 | .75 |
| ❑ 319 Kevin McReynolds | .05 | .15 |
| ❑ 320 Greg Maddux | .50 | 1.25 |
| ❑ 321 Mike Henneman | .05 | .15 |
| ❑ 322 Scott Leius | .05 | .15 |
| ❑ 323 John Franco | .10 | .30 |
| ❑ 324 Jeff Blauser | .05 | .15 |
| ❑ 325 Kirby Puckett | .30 | .75 |
| ❑ 326 Darryl Hamilton | .05 | .15 |
| ❑ 327 John Smiley | .05 | .15 |
| ❑ 328 Derrick May | .05 | .15 |
| ❑ 329 Jose Vizcaino | .05 | .15 |
| ❑ 330 Randy Johnson | .30 | .75 |
| ❑ 331 Jack Morris | .10 | .30 |
| ❑ 332 Graeme Lloyd | .05 | .15 |
| ❑ 333 Dave Valle | .05 | .15 |

|  |  | | |
|---|--------|---|---|
| ❑ 334 Greg Myers | .05 | .15 |
| ❑ 335 John Wetteland | .10 | .30 |
| ❑ 336 Jim Gott | .05 | .15 |
| ❑ 337 Tim Naehring | .05 | .15 |
| ❑ 338 Mike Kelly | .05 | .15 |
| ❑ 339 Jeff Montgomery | .05 | .15 |
| ❑ 340 Rafael Palmeiro | .20 | .50 |
| ❑ 341 Eddie Murray | .30 | .75 |
| ❑ 342 Xavier Hernandez | .05 | .15 |
| ❑ 343 Bobby Munoz | .05 | .15 |
| ❑ 344 Bobby Bonilla | .10 | .30 |
| ❑ 345 Travis Fryman | .10 | .30 |
| ❑ 346 Steve Finley | .10 | .30 |
| ❑ 347 Chris Sabo | .05 | .15 |
| ❑ 348 Armando Reynoso | .05 | .15 |
| ❑ 349 Ramon Martinez | .05 | .15 |
| ❑ 350 Will Clark | .20 | .50 |
| ❑ 351 Moises Alou | .10 | .30 |
| ❑ 352 Jim Thome | .20 | .50 |
| ❑ 353 Bob Tewksbury | .05 | .15 |
| ❑ 354 Andujar Cedeno | .05 | .15 |
| ❑ 355 Orel Hershiser | .10 | .30 |
| ❑ 356 Mike Devereaux | .05 | .15 |
| ❑ 357 Mike Perez | .05 | .15 |
| ❑ 358 Dennis Martinez | .10 | .30 |
| ❑ 359 Dave Nilsson | .05 | .15 |
| ❑ 360 Ozzie Smith | .50 | 1.25 |
| ❑ 361 Eric Anthony | .05 | .15 |
| ❑ 362 Scott Sanders | .05 | .15 |
| ❑ 363 Paul Sorrento | .05 | .15 |
| ❑ 364 Tim Belcher | .05 | .15 |
| ❑ 365 Dennis Eckersley | .10 | .30 |
| ❑ 366 Mel Rojas | .05 | .15 |
| ❑ 367 Tom Henke | .05 | .15 |
| ❑ 368 Randy Tomlin | .05 | .15 |
| ❑ 369 B.J. Surhoff | .10 | .30 |
| ❑ 370 Larry Walker | .10 | .30 |
| ❑ 371 Joey Cora | .05 | .15 |
| ❑ 372 Mike Harkey | .05 | .15 |
| ❑ 373 John Valentin | .05 | .15 |
| ❑ 374 Doug Jones | .05 | .15 |
| ❑ 375 David Justice | .10 | .30 |
| ❑ 376 Vince Coleman | .05 | .15 |
| ❑ 377 David Hulse | .05 | .15 |
| ❑ 378 Kevin Seitzer | .05 | .15 |
| ❑ 379 Pete Harnisch | .05 | .15 |
| ❑ 380 Ruben Sierra | .10 | .30 |
| ❑ 381 Mark Lewis | .05 | .15 |
| ❑ 382 Bip Roberts | .05 | .15 |
| ❑ 383 Paul Wagner | .05 | .15 |
| ❑ 384 Stan Javier | .05 | .15 |
| ❑ 385 Barry Larkin | .20 | .50 |
| ❑ 386 Mark Portugal | .05 | .15 |
| ❑ 387 Roberto Kelly | .10 | .30 |
| ❑ 388 Andy Benes | .05 | .15 |
| ❑ 389 Felix Fermin | .05 | .15 |
| ❑ 390 Marquis Grissom | .10 | .30 |
| ❑ 391 Troy Neel | .05 | .15 |
| ❑ 392 Chad Kreuter | .05 | .15 |
| ❑ 393 Gregg Olson | .05 | .15 |
| ❑ 394 Charles Nagy | .05 | .15 |
| ❑ 395 Jack McDowell | .05 | .15 |
| ❑ 396 Luis Gonzalez | .10 | .30 |
| ❑ 397 Benito Santiago | .05 | .15 |
| ❑ 398 Chris James | .05 | .15 |
| ❑ 399 Terry Mulholland | .05 | .15 |
| ❑ 400 Barry Bonds | .75 | 2.00 |
| ❑ 401 Joe Grahe | .05 | .15 |
| ❑ 402 Duane Ward | .05 | .15 |
| ❑ 403 John Burkett | .05 | .15 |
| ❑ 404 Scott Servais | .05 | .15 |
| ❑ 405 Bryan Harvey | .05 | .15 |
| ❑ 406 Bernard Gilkey | .05 | .15 |
| ❑ 407 Greg McMichael | .05 | .15 |
| ❑ 408 Tim Wallach | .05 | .15 |
| ❑ 409 Ken Caminiti | .10 | .30 |
| ❑ 410 John Kruk | .10 | .30 |
| ❑ 411 Darrin Jackson | .05 | .15 |
| ❑ 412 Mike Gallego | .05 | .15 |
| ❑ 413 David Cone | .10 | .30 |
| ❑ 414 Lou Whitaker | .10 | .30 |
| ❑ 415 Sandy Alomar Jr. | .05 | .15 |
| ❑ 416 Bill Wegman | .05 | .15 |
| ❑ 417 Pat Borders | .05 | .15 |
| ❑ 418 Roger Pavlik | .05 | .15 |
| ❑ 419 Pete Smith | .05 | .15 |
| ❑ 420 Steve Avery | .05 | .15 |
| ❑ 421 David Segui | .05 | .15 |

|  |  | | |
|---|--------|---|---|
| ❑ 422 Rheal Cormier | .05 | .15 |
| ❑ 423 Harold Reynolds | .10 | .30 |
| ❑ 424 Edgar Martinez | .20 | .50 |
| ❑ 425 Cal Ripken | 1.00 | 2.50 |
| ❑ 426 Jaime Navarro | .05 | .15 |
| ❑ 427 Sean Berry | .05 | .15 |
| ❑ 428 Bret Saberhagen | .10 | .30 |
| ❑ 429 Bob Welch | .05 | .15 |
| ❑ 430 Juan Guzman | .05 | .15 |
| ❑ 431 Cal Eldred | .05 | .15 |
| ❑ 432 Dave Hollins | .05 | .15 |
| ❑ 433 Sid Fernandez | .05 | .15 |
| ❑ 434 Willie Banks | .05 | .15 |
| ❑ 435 Darryl Kile | .10 | .30 |
| ❑ 436 Henry Rodriguez | .05 | .15 |
| ❑ 437 Tony Fernandez | .05 | .15 |
| ❑ 438 Walt Weiss | .05 | .15 |
| ❑ 439 Kevin Tapani | .05 | .15 |
| ❑ 440 Mark Grace | .20 | .50 |
| ❑ 441 Brian Harper | .05 | .15 |
| ❑ 442 Kent Mercker | .05 | .15 |
| ❑ 443 Anthony Young | .05 | .15 |
| ❑ 444 Todd Zeile | .05 | .15 |
| ❑ 445 Greg Vaughn | .05 | .15 |
| ❑ 446 Ray Lankford | .10 | .30 |
| ❑ 447 Dave Weathers | .05 | .15 |
| ❑ 448 Bret Boone | .10 | .30 |
| ❑ 449 Charlie Hough | .10 | .30 |
| ❑ 450 Roger Clemens | .60 | 1.50 |
| ❑ 451 Mike Morgan | .05 | .15 |
| ❑ 452 Doug Drabek | .05 | .15 |
| ❑ 453 Danny Jackson | .05 | .15 |
| ❑ 454 Dante Bichette | .10 | .30 |
| ❑ 455 Roberto Alomar | .20 | .50 |
| ❑ 456 Ben McDonald | .05 | .15 |
| ❑ 457 Kenny Rogers | .10 | .30 |
| ❑ 458 Bill Gullickson | .05 | .15 |
| ❑ 459 Darrin Fletcher | .05 | .15 |
| ❑ 460 Curt Schilling | .10 | .30 |
| ❑ 461 Billy Hatcher | .05 | .15 |
| ❑ 462 Howard Johnson | .05 | .15 |
| ❑ 463 Mickey Morandini | .05 | .15 |
| ❑ 464 Frank Castillo | .05 | .15 |
| ❑ 465 Delino DeShields | .05 | .15 |
| ❑ 466 Gary Gaetti | .10 | .30 |
| ❑ 467 Steve Farr | .05 | .15 |
| ❑ 468 Roberto Hernandez | .05 | .15 |
| ❑ 469 Jack Armstrong | .05 | .15 |
| ❑ 470 Paul Molitor | .10 | .30 |
| ❑ 471 Melido Perez | .05 | .15 |
| ❑ 472 Greg Hibbard | .05 | .15 |
| ❑ 473 Jody Reed | .05 | .15 |
| ❑ 474 Tom Gordon | .05 | .15 |
| ❑ 475 Gary Sheffield | .10 | .30 |
| ❑ 476 John Jaha | .05 | .15 |
| ❑ 477 Shawon Dunston | .05 | .15 |
| ❑ 478 Reggie Jefferson | .05 | .15 |
| ❑ 479 Don Slaught | .05 | .15 |
| ❑ 480 Jeff Bagwell | .20 | .50 |
| ❑ 481 Tim Pugh | .05 | .15 |
| ❑ 482 Kevin Young | .05 | .15 |
| ❑ 483 Ellis Burks | .10 | .30 |
| ❑ 484 Greg Swindell | .05 | .15 |
| ❑ 485 Mark Langston | .05 | .15 |
| ❑ 486 Omar Vizquel | .20 | .50 |
| ❑ 487 Kevin Brown | .10 | .30 |
| ❑ 488 Terry Steinbach | .05 | .15 |
| ❑ 489 Mark Lemke | .05 | .15 |
| ❑ 490 Matt Williams | .10 | .30 |
| ❑ 491 Pete Incaviglia | .05 | .15 |
| ❑ 492 Karl Rhodes | .05 | .15 |
| ❑ 493 Shawn Green | .30 | .75 |
| ❑ 494 Hal Morris | .05 | .15 |
| ❑ 495 Derek Bell | .05 | .15 |
| ❑ 496 Luis Polonia | .05 | .15 |
| ❑ 497 Otis Nixon | .05 | .15 |
| ❑ 498 Ron Darling | .05 | .15 |
| ❑ 499 Mitch Williams | .05 | .15 |
| ❑ 500 Mike Piazza | .60 | 1.50 |
| ❑ 501 Pat Meares | .05 | .15 |
| ❑ 502 Scott Cooper | .05 | .15 |
| ❑ 503 Scott Erickson | .05 | .15 |
| ❑ 504 Jeff Juden | .05 | .15 |
| ❑ 505 Lee Smith | .10 | .30 |
| ❑ 506 Bobby Ayala | .05 | .15 |
| ❑ 507 Dave Henderson | .05 | .15 |
| ❑ 508 Erik Hanson | .05 | .15 |
| ❑ 509 Bob Wickman | .05 | .15 |

| Card | Lo | Hi |
|---|---|---|
| 510 Sammy Sosa | .30 | .75 |
| 511 Hector Carrasco | .05 | .15 |
| 512 Tim Davis | .05 | .15 |
| 513 Joey Hamilton | .05 | .15 |
| 514 Robert Eenhoom | .05 | .15 |
| 515 Jorge Fabregas | .05 | .15 |
| 516 Tim Hyers RC | .05 | .15 |
| 517 John Hudek RC | .05 | .15 |
| 518 James Mouton | .05 | .15 |
| 519 Herbert Perry RC | .05 | .15 |
| 520 Chan Ho Park RC | .30 | .75 |
| 521 W.VanLandingham RC | .05 | .15 |
| 522 Paul Shuey DD | .05 | .15 |
| 523 Ryan Hancock RC | .05 | .15 |
| 524 Billy Wagner RC | .75 | 2.00 |
| 525 Jason Giambi | .30 | .75 |
| 526 Jose Silva RC | .05 | .15 |
| 527 Terrell Wade RC | .05 | .15 |
| 528 Todd Dunn | .05 | .15 |
| 529 Alan Benes RC | .15 | .40 |
| 530 Brooks Kieschnick RC | .05 | .15 |
| 531 Todd Hollandsworth | .05 | .15 |
| 532 Brad Fullmer RC | .15 | .40 |
| 533 Steve Soderstrom RC | .05 | .15 |
| 534 Daron Kirkreit | .05 | .15 |
| 535 Arquimedez Pozo RC | .05 | .15 |
| 536 Charles Johnson | .10 | .30 |
| 537 Preston Wilson | .10 | .30 |
| 538 Alex Ochoa | .05 | .15 |
| 539 Derek Lee RC | 1.50 | 4.00 |
| 540 Wayne Gomes RC | .05 | .15 |
| 541 Jermaine Allensworth RC | .05 | .15 |
| 542 Mike Bell RC | .05 | .15 |
| 543 Trot Nixon RC | .75 | 2.00 |
| 544 Pokey Reese | .05 | .15 |
| 545 Neifi Perez RC | .15 | .40 |
| 546 Johnny Damon | .30 | .75 |
| 547 Matt Brunson RC | .05 | .15 |
| 548 LaTroy Hawkins RC | .15 | .40 |
| 549 Eddie Pearson RC | .05 | .15 |
| 550 Derek Jeter | 1.00 | 2.50 |
| A298 Alex Rodriguez AU | 200.00 | 400.00 |
| P224 Ken Griffey Jr. Promo | .75 | 2.00 |
| GM1 Griffey AU/Mantle AU/1000 | 700.00 | 900.00 |
| KG1 K.Griffey Jr. AU/1000 | 125.00 | 300.00 |
| MM1 M.Mantle AU/1000 | 300.00 | 600.00 |

## 1995 Upper Deck

| | Lo | Hi |
|---|---|---|
| COMP. MASTER SET (495) | 55.00 | 110.00 |
| COMPLETE SET (450) | 20.00 | 50.00 |
| COMPLETE SERIES 1 (225) | 10.00 | 25.00 |
| COMPLETE SERIES 2 (225) | 10.00 | 25.00 |
| COMMON CARD (1-450) | .05 | .15 |
| COMP.TRADE SET (45) | 30.00 | 60.00 |
| COMMON TRADE (451T-495T) | .40 | 1.00 |
| 1 Ruben Rivera | .05 | .15 |
| 2 Bill Pulsipher | .05 | .15 |
| 3 Ben Grieve | .15 | .40 |
| 4 Curtis Goodwin | .05 | .15 |
| 5 Damon Hollins | .05 | .15 |
| 6 Todd Greene | .05 | .15 |
| 7 Glenn Williams | .05 | .15 |
| 8 Bret Wagner | .05 | .15 |
| 9 Karim Garcia RC | .05 | .15 |
| 10 Nomar Garciaparra RC | .75 | 2.00 |
| 11 Raul Casanova RC | .05 | .15 |
| 12 Matt Smith | .05 | .15 |
| 13 Paul Wilson | .05 | .15 |
| 14 Jason Isringhausen | .10 | .30 |
| 15 Reid Ryan | .10 | .30 |
| 16 Lee Smith | .10 | .30 |
| 17 Chili Davis | .05 | .15 |
| 18 Brian Anderson | .05 | .15 |
| 19 Gary DiSarcina | .05 | .15 |
| 20 Bo Jackson | .30 | .75 |
| 21 Chuck Finley | .10 | .30 |
| 22 Darryl Kile | .10 | .30 |
| 23 Shane Reynolds | .05 | .15 |
| 24 Tony Eusebio | .05 | .15 |
| 25 Craig Biggio | .20 | .50 |
| 26 Doug Drabek | .05 | .15 |
| 27 Brian L.Hunter | .05 | .15 |
| 28 James Mouton | .05 | .15 |
| 29 Geronimo Berroa | .05 | .15 |
| 30 Rickey Henderson | .30 | .75 |
| 31 Steve Karsay | .05 | .15 |
| 32 Steve Ontiveros | .05 | .15 |
| 33 Ernie Young | .05 | .15 |
| 34 Dennis Eckersley | .10 | .30 |
| 35 Mark McGwire | .75 | 2.00 |
| 36 Dave Stewart | .10 | .30 |
| 37 Pat Hentgen | .05 | .15 |
| 38 Carlos Delgado | .10 | .30 |
| 39 Joe Carter | .10 | .30 |
| 40 Roberto Alomar | .20 | .50 |
| 41 John Olerud | .10 | .30 |
| 42 Devon White | .10 | .30 |
| 43 Roberto Kelly | .05 | .15 |
| 44 Jeff Blauser | .05 | .15 |
| 45 Fred McGriff | .20 | .50 |
| 46 Tom Glavine | .20 | .50 |
| 47 Mike Kelly | .05 | .15 |
| 48 Javier Lopez | .10 | .30 |
| 49 Greg Maddux | .50 | 1.25 |
| 50 Matt Mieske | .05 | .15 |
| 51 Troy O'Leary | .05 | .15 |
| 52 Jeff Cirillo | .05 | .15 |
| 53 Cal Eldred | .05 | .15 |
| 54 Pat Listach | .05 | .15 |
| 55 Jose Valentin | .05 | .15 |
| 56 John Mabry | .05 | .15 |
| 57 Bob Tewksbury | .05 | .15 |
| 58 Brian Jordan | .10 | .30 |
| 59 Gregg Jefferies | .05 | .15 |
| 60 Ozzie Smith | .50 | 1.25 |
| 61 Geronimo Pena | .05 | .15 |
| 62 Mark Whiten | .05 | .15 |
| 63 Rey Sanchez | .05 | .15 |
| 64 Willie Banks | .05 | .15 |
| 65 Mark Grace | .20 | .50 |
| 66 Randy Myers | .05 | .15 |
| 67 Steve Trachsel | .05 | .15 |
| 68 Derrick May | .05 | .15 |
| 69 Brett Butler | .10 | .30 |
| 70 Eric Karros | .10 | .30 |
| 71 Tim Wallach | .05 | .15 |
| 72 Delino DeShields | .05 | .15 |
| 73 Darren Dreifort | .05 | .15 |
| 74 Orel Hershiser | .10 | .30 |
| 75 Billy Ashley | .05 | .15 |
| 76 Sean Berry | .05 | .15 |
| 77 Ken Hill | .05 | .15 |
| 78 John Wetteland | .10 | .30 |
| 79 Moises Alou | .10 | .30 |
| 80 Cliff Floyd | .10 | .30 |
| 81 Marquis Grissom | .10 | .30 |
| 82 Larry Walker | .20 | .50 |
| 83 Rondell White | .10 | .30 |
| 84 William VanLandingham | .05 | .15 |
| 85 Matt Williams | .10 | .30 |
| 86 Rod Beck | .05 | .15 |
| 87 Darren Lewis | .05 | .15 |
| 88 Robby Thompson | .05 | .15 |
| 89 Darryl Strawberry | .10 | .30 |
| 90 Kenny Lofton | .20 | .50 |
| 91 Charles Nagy | .05 | .15 |
| 92 Sandy Alomar Jr. | .05 | .15 |
| 93 Mark Clark | .05 | .15 |
| 94 Dennis Martinez | .05 | .15 |
| 95 Dave Winfield | .10 | .30 |
| 96 Jim Thome | .20 | .50 |
| 97 Manny Ramirez | .20 | .50 |
| 98 Goose Gossage | .10 | .30 |
| 99 Tino Martinez | .10 | .30 |
| 100 Ken Griffey Jr. | .50 | 1.25 |
| 101 Greg Maddux ANA | .30 | .75 |
| 102 Randy Johnson ANA | .20 | .50 |
| 103 Barry Bonds ANA | .40 | 1.00 |
| 104 Juan Gonzalez ANA | .05 | .15 |
| 105 Frank Thomas ANA | .05 | .15 |
| 106 Matt Williams ANA | .05 | .15 |
| 107 Paul Molitor ANA | .05 | .15 |
| 108 Fred McGriff ANA | .10 | .30 |
| 109 Carlos Baerga ANA | .05 | .15 |
| 110 Ken Griffey Jr. ANA | .30 | .75 |
| 111 Reggie Jefferson | .05 | .15 |
| 112 Randy Johnson | .30 | .75 |
| 113 Marc Newfield | .05 | .15 |
| 114 Robb Nen | .10 | .30 |
| 115 Jeff Conine | .10 | .30 |
| 116 Kurt Abbott | .05 | .15 |
| 117 Charlie Hough | .10 | .30 |
| 118 Dave Weathers | .05 | .15 |
| 119 Juan Castillo | .05 | .15 |
| 120 Bret Saberhagen | .05 | .15 |
| 121 Rico Brogna | .05 | .15 |
| 122 John Franco | .10 | .30 |
| 123 Todd Hundley | .05 | .15 |
| 124 Jason Jacome | .05 | .15 |
| 125 Bobby Jones | .05 | .15 |
| 126 Bret Barberie | .05 | .15 |
| 127 Ben McDonald | .10 | .30 |
| 128 Harold Baines | .10 | .30 |
| 129 Jeffrey Hammonds | .05 | .15 |
| 130 Mike Mussina | .20 | .50 |
| 131 Chris Hoiles | .05 | .15 |
| 132 Brady Anderson | .10 | .30 |
| 133 Eddie Williams | .05 | .15 |
| 134 Andy Benes | .05 | .15 |
| 135 Tony Gwynn | .40 | 1.00 |
| 136 Bip Roberts | .05 | .15 |
| 137 Joey Hamilton | .05 | .15 |
| 138 Luis Lopez | .05 | .15 |
| 139 Ray McDavid | .05 | .15 |
| 140 Lenny Dykstra | .10 | .30 |
| 141 Mariano Duncan | .05 | .15 |
| 142 Fernando Valenzuela | .10 | .30 |
| 143 Bobby Munoz | .05 | .15 |
| 144 Kevin Stocker | .05 | .15 |
| 145 John Kruk | .10 | .30 |
| 146 Jon Leiber | .05 | .15 |
| 147 Zane Smith | .05 | .15 |
| 148 Steve Cooke | .05 | .15 |
| 149 Andy Van Slyke | .20 | .50 |
| 150 Jay Bell | .10 | .30 |
| 151 Carlos Garcia | .05 | .15 |
| 152 John Dettmer | .05 | .15 |
| 153 Darren Oliver | .05 | .15 |
| 154 Dean Palmer | .10 | .30 |
| 155 Otis Nixon | .05 | .15 |
| 156 Rusty Greer | .05 | .15 |
| 157 Rick Helling | .05 | .15 |
| 158 Jose Canseco | .20 | .50 |
| 159 Roger Clemens | .60 | 1.50 |
| 160 Andre Dawson | .10 | .30 |
| 161 Mo Vaughn | .10 | .30 |
| 162 Aaron Sele | .05 | .15 |
| 163 John Valentin | .05 | .15 |
| 164 Brian R. Hunter | .05 | .15 |
| 165 Bret Boone | .10 | .30 |
| 166 Hector Carrasco | .05 | .15 |
| 167 Pete Schourek | .05 | .15 |
| 168 Willie Greene | .05 | .15 |
| 169 Kevin Mitchell | .05 | .15 |
| 170 Deion Sanders | .20 | .50 |
| 171 John Roper | .05 | .15 |
| 172 Charlie Hayes | .05 | .15 |
| 173 David Nied | .05 | .15 |
| 174 Ellis Burks | .10 | .30 |
| 175 Dante Bichette | .10 | .30 |
| 176 Marvin Freeman | .05 | .15 |
| 177 Eric Young | .05 | .15 |
| 178 David Cone | .10 | .30 |
| 179 Greg Gagne | .05 | .15 |
| 180 Bob Hamelin | .05 | .15 |
| 181 Wally Joyner | .05 | .15 |
| 182 Jeff Montgomery | .05 | .15 |
| 183 Jose Lind | .05 | .15 |
| 184 Chris Gomez | .05 | .15 |
| 185 Travis Fryman | .10 | .30 |
| 186 Kirk Gibson | .10 | .30 |
| 187 Mike Moore | .05 | .15 |
| 188 Lou Whitaker | .10 | .30 |
| 189 Sean Bergman | .05 | .15 |
| 190 Shane Mack | .05 | .15 |
| 191 Rick Aguilera | .05 | .15 |
| 192 Denny Hocking | .05 | .15 |
| 193 Chuck Knoblauch | .10 | .30 |
| 194 Kevin Tapani | .05 | .15 |
| 195 Kent Hrbek | .10 | .30 |

|  |  | | |
|---|--------|---|---|
| ❑ 196 | Ozzie Guillen | .10 | .30 |
| ❑ 197 | Wilson Alvarez | .05 | .15 |
| ❑ 198 | Tim Raines | .10 | .30 |
| ❑ 199 | Scott Ruffcorn | .05 | .15 |
| ❑ 200 | Michael Jordan | 1.00 | 2.50 |
| ❑ 201 | Robin Ventura | .10 | .30 |
| ❑ 202 | Jason Bere | .05 | .15 |
| ❑ 203 | Darrin Jackson | .05 | .15 |
| ❑ 204 | Russ Davis | .05 | .15 |
| ❑ 205 | Jimmy Key | .10 | .30 |
| ❑ 206 | Jack McDowell | .05 | .15 |
| ❑ 207 | Jim Abbott | .20 | .50 |
| ❑ 208 | Paul O'Neill | .20 | .50 |
| ❑ 209 | Bernie Williams | .20 | .50 |
| ❑ 210 | Don Mattingly | .75 | 2.00 |
| ❑ 211 | Orlando Miller | .05 | .15 |
| ❑ 212 | Alex Gonzalez | .05 | .15 |
| ❑ 213 | Terrell Wade | .05 | .15 |
| ❑ 214 | Jose Oliva | .05 | .15 |
| ❑ 215 | Alex Rodriguez | .75 | 2.00 |
| ❑ 216 | Garret Anderson | .10 | .30 |
| ❑ 217 | Alan Benes | .05 | .15 |
| ❑ 218 | Armando Benitez | .05 | .15 |
| ❑ 219 | Dustin Hermanson | .05 | .15 |
| ❑ 220 | Charles Johnson | .10 | .30 |
| ❑ 221 | Julian Tavarez | .05 | .15 |
| ❑ 222 | Jason Giambi | .20 | .50 |
| ❑ 223 | LaTroy Hawkins | .05 | .15 |
| ❑ 224 | Todd Hollandsworth | .05 | .15 |
| ❑ 225 | Derek Jeter | .75 | 2.00 |
| ❑ 226 | Hideo Nomo RC | 1.00 | 2.50 |
| ❑ 227 | Tony Clark | .05 | .15 |
| ❑ 228 | Roger Cedeno | .05 | .15 |
| ❑ 229 | Scott Stahoviak | .05 | .15 |
| ❑ 230 | Michael Tucker | .05 | .15 |
| ❑ 231 | Joe Rosselli | .05 | .15 |
| ❑ 232 | Antonio Osuna | .05 | .15 |
| ❑ 233 | Bob Higginson RC | .30 | .75 |
| ❑ 234 | Mark Grudzielanek RC | .30 | .75 |
| ❑ 235 | Ray Durham | .10 | .30 |
| ❑ 236 | Frank Rodriguez | .05 | .15 |
| ❑ 237 | Quilvio Veras | .05 | .15 |
| ❑ 238 | Darren Bragg | .05 | .15 |
| ❑ 239 | Ugueth Urbina | .05 | .15 |
| ❑ 240 | Jason Bates | .05 | .15 |
| ❑ 241 | David Bell | .05 | .15 |
| ❑ 242 | Ron Villone | .05 | .15 |
| ❑ 243 | Joe Randa | .10 | .30 |
| ❑ 244 | Carlos Perez RC | .15 | .40 |
| ❑ 245 | Brad Clontz | .05 | .15 |
| ❑ 246 | Steve Rodriguez | .05 | .15 |
| ❑ 247 | Joe Vitiello | .05 | .15 |
| ❑ 248 | Ozzie Timmons | .05 | .15 |
| ❑ 249 | Rudy Pemberton | .05 | .15 |
| ❑ 250 | Marty Cordova | .15 | .40 |
| ❑ 251 | Tony Graffanino | .15 | .40 |
| ❑ 252 | Mark Johnson RC | .15 | .40 |
| ❑ 253 | Tomas Perez RC | .15 | .40 |
| ❑ 254 | Jimmy Hurst | .05 | .15 |
| ❑ 255 | Edgardo Alfonzo | .05 | .15 |
| ❑ 256 | Jose Malave | .05 | .15 |
| ❑ 257 | Brad Radke RC | .30 | .75 |
| ❑ 258 | Jon Nunnally | .05 | .15 |
| ❑ 259 | Dilson Torres RC | .05 | .15 |
| ❑ 260 | Esteban Loaiza | .05 | .15 |
| ❑ 261 | Freddy Adrian Garcia RC | .05 | .15 |
| ❑ 262 | Don Wengert | .05 | .15 |
| ❑ 263 | Robert Person RC | .15 | .40 |
| ❑ 264 | Tim Unroe RC | .15 | .40 |
| ❑ 265 | Juan Acevedo RC | .15 | .40 |
| ❑ 266 | Eduardo Perez | .05 | .15 |
| ❑ 267 | Tony Phillips | .20 | .50 |
| ❑ 268 | Jim Edmonds | .20 | .50 |
| ❑ 269 | Jorge Fabregas | .05 | .15 |
| ❑ 270 | Tim Salmon | .20 | .50 |
| ❑ 271 | Mark Langston | .05 | .15 |
| ❑ 272 | J.T. Snow | .10 | .30 |
| ❑ 273 | Phil Plantier | .05 | .15 |
| ❑ 274 | Derek Bell | .05 | .15 |
| ❑ 275 | Jeff Bagwell | .20 | .50 |
| ❑ 276 | Luis Gonzalez | .10 | .30 |
| ❑ 277 | John Hudek | .05 | .15 |
| ❑ 278 | Todd Stottlemyre | .05 | .15 |
| ❑ 279 | Mark Acre | .05 | .15 |
| ❑ 280 | Ruben Sierra | .10 | .30 |
| ❑ 281 | Mike Bordick | .05 | .15 |
| ❑ 282 | Ron Darling | .05 | .15 |
| ❑ 283 | Brent Gates | .05 | .15 |
| ❑ 284 | Todd Van Poppel | .05 | .15 |
| ❑ 285 | Paul Molitor | .10 | .30 |
| ❑ 286 | Ed Sprague | .05 | .15 |
| ❑ 287 | Juan Guzman | .05 | .15 |
| ❑ 288 | David Cone | .10 | .30 |
| ❑ 289 | Shawn Green | .10 | .30 |
| ❑ 290 | Marquis Grissom | .10 | .30 |
| ❑ 291 | Kent Mercker | .05 | .15 |
| ❑ 292 | Steve Avery | .05 | .15 |
| ❑ 293 | Chipper Jones | .30 | .75 |
| ❑ 294 | John Smoltz | .20 | .50 |
| ❑ 295 | David Justice | .10 | .30 |
| ❑ 296 | Ryan Klesko | .10 | .30 |
| ❑ 297 | Joe Oliver | .05 | .15 |
| ❑ 298 | Ricky Bones | .05 | .15 |
| ❑ 299 | John Jaha | .05 | .15 |
| ❑ 300 | Greg Vaughn | .05 | .15 |
| ❑ 301 | Dave Nilsson | .05 | .15 |
| ❑ 302 | Kevin Seitzer | .05 | .15 |
| ❑ 303 | Bernard Gilkey | .05 | .15 |
| ❑ 304 | Allen Battle | .05 | .15 |
| ❑ 305 | Ray Lankford | .10 | .30 |
| ❑ 306 | Tom Pagnozzi | .05 | .15 |
| ❑ 307 | Allen Watson | .05 | .15 |
| ❑ 308 | Danny Jackson | .05 | .15 |
| ❑ 309 | Ken Hill | .05 | .15 |
| ❑ 310 | Todd Zeile | .05 | .15 |
| ❑ 311 | Kevin Roberson | .05 | .15 |
| ❑ 312 | Steve Buechele | .05 | .15 |
| ❑ 313 | Rick Wilkins | .05 | .15 |
| ❑ 314 | Kevin Foster | .05 | .15 |
| ❑ 315 | Sammy Sosa | .30 | .75 |
| ❑ 316 | Howard Johnson | .05 | .15 |
| ❑ 317 | Greg Hansell | .05 | .15 |
| ❑ 318 | Pedro Astacio | .05 | .15 |
| ❑ 319 | Rafael Bournigal | .05 | .15 |
| ❑ 320 | Mike Piazza | .50 | 1.25 |
| ❑ 321 | Ramon Martinez | .05 | .15 |
| ❑ 322 | Raul Mondesi | .10 | .30 |
| ❑ 323 | Ismael Valdes | .05 | .15 |
| ❑ 324 | Wil Cordero | .05 | .15 |
| ❑ 325 | Tony Tarasco | .05 | .15 |
| ❑ 326 | Roberto Kelly | .05 | .15 |
| ❑ 327 | Jeff Fassero | .05 | .15 |
| ❑ 328 | Mike Lansing | .05 | .15 |
| ❑ 329 | Pedro Martinez | .20 | .50 |
| ❑ 330 | Kirk Rueter | .05 | .15 |
| ❑ 331 | Glenallen Hill | .05 | .15 |
| ❑ 332 | Kirt Manwaring | .05 | .15 |
| ❑ 333 | Royce Clayton | .05 | .15 |
| ❑ 334 | J.R. Phillips | .05 | .15 |
| ❑ 335 | Barry Bonds | .75 | 2.00 |
| ❑ 336 | Mark Portugal | .05 | .15 |
| ❑ 337 | Terry Mulholland | .05 | .15 |
| ❑ 338 | Omar Vizquel | .20 | .50 |
| ❑ 339 | Carlos Baerga | .20 | .50 |
| ❑ 340 | Albert Belle | .10 | .30 |
| ❑ 341 | Eddie Murray | .30 | .75 |
| ❑ 342 | Wayne Kirby | .05 | .15 |
| ❑ 343 | Chad Ogea | .05 | .15 |
| ❑ 344 | Tim Davis | .05 | .15 |
| ❑ 345 | Jay Buhner | .10 | .30 |
| ❑ 346 | Bobby Ayala | .05 | .15 |
| ❑ 347 | Mike Blowers | .05 | .15 |
| ❑ 348 | Dave Fleming | .05 | .15 |
| ❑ 349 | Edgar Martinez | .20 | .50 |
| ❑ 350 | Andre Dawson | .10 | .30 |
| ❑ 351 | Darrell Whitmore | .05 | .15 |
| ❑ 352 | Chuck Carr | .05 | .15 |
| ❑ 353 | John Burkett | .05 | .15 |
| ❑ 354 | Chris Hammond | .05 | .15 |
| ❑ 355 | Gary Sheffield | .10 | .30 |
| ❑ 356 | Pat Rapp | .05 | .15 |
| ❑ 357 | Greg Colbrunn | .05 | .15 |
| ❑ 358 | David Segui | .05 | .15 |
| ❑ 359 | Jeff Kent | .10 | .30 |
| ❑ 360 | Bobby Bonilla | .10 | .30 |
| ❑ 361 | Pete Harnisch | .05 | .15 |
| ❑ 362 | Ryan Thompson | .05 | .15 |
| ❑ 363 | Jose Vizcaino | .05 | .15 |
| ❑ 364 | Brett Butler | .05 | .15 |
| ❑ 365 | Cal Ripken | 1.00 | 2.50 |
| ❑ 366 | Rafael Palmeiro | .20 | .50 |
| ❑ 367 | Leo Gomez | .05 | .15 |
| ❑ 368 | Andy Van Slyke | .05 | .15 |
| ❑ 369 | Arthur Rhodes | .05 | .15 |
| ❑ 370 | Ken Caminiti | .10 | .30 |
| ❑ 371 | Steve Finley | .10 | .30 |
| ❑ 372 | Melvin Nieves | .05 | .15 |
| ❑ 373 | Andujar Cedeno | .05 | .15 |
| ❑ 374 | Trevor Hoffman | .10 | .30 |
| ❑ 375 | Fernando Valenzuela | .10 | .30 |
| ❑ 376 | Ricky Bottalico | .05 | .15 |
| ❑ 377 | Dave Hollins | .05 | .15 |
| ❑ 378 | Charlie Hayes | .05 | .15 |
| ❑ 379 | Tommy Greene | .05 | .15 |
| ❑ 380 | Darren Daulton | .10 | .30 |
| ❑ 381 | Curt Schilling | .10 | .30 |
| ❑ 382 | Midre Cummings | .05 | .15 |
| ❑ 383 | Al Martin | .05 | .15 |
| ❑ 384 | Jeff King | .05 | .15 |
| ❑ 385 | Orlando Merced | .05 | .15 |
| ❑ 386 | Denny Neagle | .10 | .30 |
| ❑ 387 | Don Slaught | .05 | .15 |
| ❑ 388 | Dave Clark | .05 | .15 |
| ❑ 389 | Kevin Gross | .05 | .15 |
| ❑ 390 | Will Clark | .20 | .50 |
| ❑ 391 | Ivan Rodriguez | .20 | .50 |
| ❑ 392 | Benji Gil | .05 | .15 |
| ❑ 393 | Jeff Frye | .05 | .15 |
| ❑ 394 | Kenny Rogers | .10 | .30 |
| ❑ 395 | Juan Gonzalez | .10 | .30 |
| ❑ 396 | Mike Macfarlane | .05 | .15 |
| ❑ 397 | Lee Tinsley | .05 | .15 |
| ❑ 398 | Tim Naehring | .05 | .15 |
| ❑ 399 | Tim Vanegmond | .05 | .15 |
| ❑ 400 | Mike Greenwell | .05 | .15 |
| ❑ 401 | Ken Ryan | .05 | .15 |
| ❑ 402 | John Smiley | .05 | .15 |
| ❑ 403 | Tim Pugh | .05 | .15 |
| ❑ 404 | Reggie Sanders | .10 | .30 |
| ❑ 405 | Barry Larkin | .20 | .50 |
| ❑ 406 | Hal Morris | .05 | .15 |
| ❑ 407 | Jose Rijo | .05 | .15 |
| ❑ 408 | Lance Painter | .05 | .15 |
| ❑ 409 | Joe Girardi | .05 | .15 |
| ❑ 410 | Andres Galarraga | .10 | .30 |
| ❑ 411 | Mike Kingery | .05 | .15 |
| ❑ 412 | Roberto Mejia | .05 | .15 |
| ❑ 413 | Walt Weiss | .05 | .15 |
| ❑ 414 | Bill Swift | .05 | .15 |
| ❑ 415 | Larry Walker | .10 | .30 |
| ❑ 416 | Billy Brewer | .05 | .15 |
| ❑ 417 | Pat Borders | .05 | .15 |
| ❑ 418 | Tom Gordon | .05 | .15 |
| ❑ 419 | Kevin Appier | .10 | .30 |
| ❑ 420 | Gary Gaetti | .10 | .30 |
| ❑ 421 | Greg Gohr | .05 | .15 |
| ❑ 422 | Felipe Lira | .05 | .15 |
| ❑ 423 | John Doherty | .05 | .15 |
| ❑ 424 | Chad Curtis | .05 | .15 |
| ❑ 425 | Cecil Fielder | .10 | .30 |
| ❑ 426 | Alan Trammell | .10 | .30 |
| ❑ 427 | David McCarty | .05 | .15 |
| ❑ 428 | Scott Erickson | .05 | .15 |
| ❑ 429 | Pat Mahomes | .05 | .15 |
| ❑ 430 | Kirby Puckett | .30 | .75 |
| ❑ 431 | Dave Stevens | .05 | .15 |
| ❑ 432 | Pedro Munoz | .05 | .15 |
| ❑ 433 | Chris Sabo | .05 | .15 |
| ❑ 434 | Alex Fernandez | .05 | .15 |
| ❑ 435 | Frank Thomas | .30 | .75 |
| ❑ 436 | Roberto Hernandez | .05 | .15 |
| ❑ 437 | Lance Johnson | .05 | .15 |
| ❑ 438 | Jim Abbott | .20 | .50 |
| ❑ 439 | John Wetteland | .10 | .30 |
| ❑ 440 | Melido Perez | .05 | .15 |
| ❑ 441 | Tony Fernandez | .05 | .15 |
| ❑ 442 | Pat Kelly | .05 | .15 |
| ❑ 443 | Mike Stanley | .05 | .15 |
| ❑ 444 | Danny Tartabull | .05 | .15 |
| ❑ 445 | Wade Boggs | .20 | .50 |
| ❑ 446 | Robin Yount TRIB | .50 | 1.25 |
| ❑ 447 | Ryne Sandberg TRIB | .50 | 1.25 |
| ❑ 448 | Nolan Ryan TRIB | 1.25 | 3.00 |
| ❑ 449 | George Brett TRIB | .75 | 2.00 |
| ❑ 450 | Mike Schmidt TRIB | .50 | 1.25 |
| ❑ 451 | Jim Abbott TRADE | .75 | 2.00 |
| ❑ 452 | Danny Tartabull TRADE | .40 | 1.00 |
| ❑ 453 | Ariel Prieto TRADE | .40 | 1.00 |
| ❑ 454 | Scott Cooper TRADE | .40 | 1.00 |
| ❑ 455 | Tom Henke TRADE | .40 | 1.00 |
| ❑ 456 | Todd Zeile TRADE | .40 | 1.00 |
| ❑ 457 | Brian McRae TRADE | .40 | 1.00 |
| ❑ 458 | Luis Gonzalez TRADE | .60 | 1.50 |
| ❑ 459 | Jaime Navarro TRADE | .40 | 1.00 |

| | | |
|---|---|---|
| 460 Todd Worrell TRADE | .40 | 1.00 |
| 461 Roberto Kelly TRADE | .40 | 1.00 |
| 462 Chad Fonville TRADE | .40 | 1.00 |
| 463 Shane Andrews TRADE | .40 | 1.00 |
| 464 David Segui TRADE | .40 | 1.00 |
| 465 Deion Sanders TRADE | .75 | 2.00 |
| 466 Orel Hershiser TRADE | .60 | 1.50 |
| 467 Ken Hill TRADE | .40 | 1.00 |
| 468 Andy Benes TRADE | .40 | 1.00 |
| 469 Terry Pendleton TRADE | .60 | 1.50 |
| 470 Bobby Bonilla TRADE | .60 | 1.50 |
| 471 Scott Erickson TRADE | .40 | 1.00 |
| 472 Kevin Brown TRADE | .60 | 1.50 |
| 473 Glenn Dishman TRADE | .40 | 1.00 |
| 474 Phil Plantier TRADE | .40 | 1.00 |
| 475 Gregg Jefferies TRADE | .40 | 1.00 |
| 476 Tyler Green TRADE | .40 | 1.00 |
| 477 Heathcliff Slocumb TRADE | .40 | 1.00 |
| 478 Mark Whiten TRADE | .40 | 1.00 |
| 479 Mickey Tettleton TRADE | .40 | 1.00 |
| 480 Tim Wakefield TRADE | .60 | 1.50 |
| 481 Vaughn Eshelman TRADE | .40 | 1.00 |
| 482 Rick Aguilera TRADE | .40 | 1.00 |
| 483 Erik Hanson TRADE | .40 | 1.00 |
| 484 Willie McGee TRADE | .60 | 1.50 |
| 485 Troy O'Leary TRADE | .40 | 1.00 |
| 486 Benito Santiago TRADE | .60 | 1.50 |
| 487 Darren Lewis TRADE | .40 | 1.00 |
| 488 Dave Burba TRADE | .40 | 1.00 |
| 489 Ron Gant TRADE | .60 | 1.50 |
| 490 Bret Saberhagen TRADE | .60 | 1.50 |
| 491 Vinny Castilla TRADE | .60 | 1.50 |
| 492 Frank Rodriguez TRADE | .40 | 1.00 |
| 493 Andy Pettitte TRADE | .75 | 2.00 |
| 494 Ruben Sierra TRADE | .60 | 1.50 |
| 495 David Cone TRADE | .60 | 1.50 |
| J159 R.Clemens Jumbo AU | 40.00 | 80.00 |
| J215 A.Rodriguez Jumbo AU | 60.00 | 120.00 |
| P100 Ken Griffey Jr. Promo | .75 | 2.00 |

## 1996 Upper Deck

| | | |
|---|---|---|
| COMPLETE SET (480) | 20.00 | 50.00 |
| COMP.FACT.SET (510) | 50.00 | 100.00 |
| COMPLETE SERIES 1 (240) | 10.00 | 25.00 |
| COMPLETE SERIES 2 (240) | 10.00 | 25.00 |
| COMMON CARD (1-480) | .10 | .30 |
| COMP.UPDATE SET (30) | 10.00 | 20.00 |
| COMMON UPDATE (481U-510U) | .20 | .50 |
| 1 Cal Ripken 2131 | 1.50 | 4.00 |
| 2 Eddie Murray 3000 Hits | .20 | .50 |
| 3 Mark Wohlers | .10 | .30 |
| 4 David Justice | .10 | .30 |
| 5 Chipper Jones | .30 | .75 |
| 6 Javier Lopez | .10 | .30 |
| 7 Mark Lemke | .10 | .30 |
| 8 Marquis Grissom | .10 | .30 |
| 9 Tom Glavine | .20 | .50 |
| 10 Greg Maddux | .50 | 1.25 |
| 11 Manny Alexander | .10 | .30 |
| 12 Curtis Goodwin | .10 | .30 |
| 13 Scott Erickson | .10 | .30 |
| 14 Chris Hoiles | .10 | .30 |
| 15 Rafael Palmeiro | .20 | .50 |
| 16 Rick Krivda | .10 | .30 |
| 17 Jeff Manto | .10 | .30 |
| 18 Mo Vaughn | .10 | .30 |
| 19 Tim Wakefield | .10 | .30 |
| 20 Roger Clemens | .60 | 1.50 |
| 21 Tim Naehring | .10 | .30 |
| 22 Troy O'Leary | .10 | .30 |
| 23 Mike Greenwell | .10 | .30 |
| 24 Stan Belinda | .10 | .30 |
| 25 John Valentin | .10 | .30 |
| 26 J.T. Snow | .10 | .30 |
| 27 Gary DiSarcina | .10 | .30 |
| 28 Mark Langston | .10 | .30 |
| 29 Brian Anderson | .10 | .30 |
| 30 Jim Edmonds | .10 | .30 |
| 31 Garret Anderson | .10 | .30 |
| 32 Orlando Palmeiro | .10 | .30 |
| 33 Brian McRae | .10 | .30 |
| 34 Kevin Foster | .10 | .30 |
| 35 Sammy Sosa | .30 | .75 |
| 36 Todd Zeile | .10 | .30 |
| 37 Jim Bullinger | .10 | .30 |
| 38 Luis Gonzalez | .10 | .30 |
| 39 Lyle Mouton | .10 | .30 |
| 40 Ray Durham | .10 | .30 |
| 41 Ozzie Guillen | .10 | .30 |
| 42 Alex Fernandez | .10 | .30 |
| 43 Brian Keyser | .10 | .30 |
| 44 Robin Ventura | .10 | .30 |
| 45 Reggie Sanders | .10 | .30 |
| 46 Pete Schourek | .10 | .30 |
| 47 John Smiley | .10 | .30 |
| 48 Jeff Brantley | .10 | .30 |
| 49 Thomas Howard | .10 | .30 |
| 50 Bret Boone | .10 | .30 |
| 51 Kevin Jarvis | .10 | .30 |
| 52 Jeff Branson | .10 | .30 |
| 53 Carlos Baerga | .20 | .50 |
| 54 Jim Thome | .20 | .50 |
| 55 Manny Ramirez | .20 | .50 |
| 56 Omar Vizquel | .10 | .30 |
| 57 Jose Mesa | .10 | .30 |
| 58 Julian Tavarez UER | .10 | .30 |
| 59 Orel Hershiser | .10 | .30 |
| 60 Larry Walker | .10 | .30 |
| 61 Bret Saberhagen | .10 | .30 |
| 62 Vinny Castilla | .10 | .30 |
| 63 Eric Young | .10 | .30 |
| 64 Bryan Rekar | .10 | .30 |
| 65 Andres Galarraga | .10 | .30 |
| 66 Steve Reed | .10 | .30 |
| 67 Chad Curtis | .10 | .30 |
| 68 Bobby Higginson | .10 | .30 |
| 69 Phil Nevin | .10 | .30 |
| 70 Cecil Fielder | .10 | .30 |
| 71 Felipe Lira | .10 | .30 |
| 72 Chris Gomez | .10 | .30 |
| 73 Charles Johnson | .10 | .30 |
| 74 Quilvio Veras | .10 | .30 |
| 75 Jeff Conine | .10 | .30 |
| 76 John Burkett | .10 | .30 |
| 77 Greg Colbrunn | .10 | .30 |
| 78 Terry Pendleton | .10 | .30 |
| 79 Shane Reynolds | .10 | .30 |
| 80 Jeff Bagwell | .20 | .50 |
| 81 Orlando Miller | .10 | .30 |
| 82 Mike Hampton | .10 | .30 |
| 83 James Mouton | .10 | .30 |
| 84 Brian L. Hunter | .10 | .30 |
| 85 Derek Bell | .10 | .30 |
| 86 Kevin Appier | .10 | .30 |
| 87 Joe Vitiello | .10 | .30 |
| 88 Wally Joyner | .10 | .30 |
| 89 Michael Tucker | .10 | .30 |
| 90 Johnny Damon | .20 | .50 |
| 91 Jon Nunnally | .10 | .30 |
| 92 Jason Jacome | .10 | .30 |
| 93 Chad Fonville | .10 | .30 |
| 94 Chan Ho Park | .30 | .75 |
| 95 Hideo Nomo | .30 | .75 |
| 96 Ismael Valdes | .10 | .30 |
| 97 Greg Gagne | .10 | .30 |
| 98 Diamondbacks-Devil Rays | .30 | .75 |
| 99 Raul Mondesi | .30 | .75 |
| 100 Dave Winfield YH | .10 | .30 |
| 101 Dennis Eckersley YH | .10 | .30 |
| 102 Andre Dawson YH | .10 | .30 |
| 103 Dennis Martinez YH | .10 | .30 |
| 104 Lance Parrish YH | .10 | .30 |
| 105 Eddie Murray YH | .20 | .50 |
| 106 Alan Trammell YH | .10 | .30 |
| 107 Lou Whitaker YH | .10 | .30 |
| 108 Ozzie Smith YH | .30 | .75 |
| 109 Paul Molitor YH | .10 | .30 |
| 110 Rickey Henderson YH | .20 | .50 |
| 111 Tim Raines YH | .10 | .30 |
| 112 Harold Baines YH | .10 | .30 |
| 113 Lee Smith YH | .10 | .30 |
| 114 Fernando Valenzuela YH | .10 | .30 |
| 115 Cal Ripken YH | .50 | 1.25 |
| 116 Tony Gwynn YH | .20 | .50 |
| 117 Wade Boggs | .20 | .50 |
| 118 Todd Hollandsworth | .10 | .30 |
| 119 Dave Nilsson | .10 | .30 |
| 120 Jose Valentin | .10 | .30 |
| 121 Steve Sparks | .10 | .30 |
| 122 Chuck Carr | .10 | .30 |
| 123 John Jaha | .10 | .30 |
| 124 Scott Karl | .10 | .30 |
| 125 Chuck Knoblauch | .10 | .30 |
| 126 Brad Radke | .10 | .30 |
| 127 Pat Meares | .10 | .30 |
| 128 Ron Coomer | .10 | .30 |
| 129 Pedro Munoz | .10 | .30 |
| 130 Kirby Puckett | .30 | .75 |
| 131 David Segui | .10 | .30 |
| 132 Mark Grudzielanek | .10 | .30 |
| 133 Mike Lansing | .10 | .30 |
| 134 Sean Berry | .10 | .30 |
| 135 Rondell White | .10 | .30 |
| 136 Pedro Martinez | .20 | .50 |
| 137 Carl Everett | .10 | .30 |
| 138 Dave Mlicki | .10 | .30 |
| 139 Bill Pulsipher | .10 | .30 |
| 140 Jason Isringhausen | .10 | .30 |
| 141 Rico Brogna | .10 | .30 |
| 142 Edgardo Alfonzo | .10 | .30 |
| 143 Jeff Kent | .10 | .30 |
| 144 Andy Pettitte | .20 | .50 |
| 145 Mike Piazza BO | .30 | .75 |
| 146 Cliff Floyd BO | .10 | .30 |
| 147 Jason Isringhausen BO | .10 | .30 |
| 148 Tim Wakefield BO | .10 | .30 |
| 149 Chipper Jones BO | .20 | .50 |
| 150 Hideo Nomo BO | .20 | .50 |
| 151 Mark McGwire BO | .40 | 1.00 |
| 152 Ron Gant BO | .10 | .30 |
| 153 Gary Gaetti BO | .10 | .30 |
| 154 Don Mattingly | .75 | 2.00 |
| 155 Paul O'Neill | .10 | .30 |
| 156 Derek Jeter | .75 | 2.00 |
| 157 Joe Girardi | .10 | .30 |
| 158 Ruben Sierra | .10 | .30 |
| 159 Jorge Posada | .20 | .50 |
| 160 Geronimo Berroa | .10 | .30 |
| 161 Steve Ontiveros | .10 | .30 |
| 162 George Williams | .10 | .30 |
| 163 Doug Johns | .10 | .30 |
| 164 Ariel Prieto | .10 | .30 |
| 165 Scott Brosius | .10 | .30 |
| 166 Mike Bordick | .10 | .30 |
| 167 Tyler Green | .10 | .30 |
| 168 Mickey Morandini | .10 | .30 |
| 169 Darren Daulton | .10 | .30 |
| 170 Gregg Jefferies | .10 | .30 |
| 171 Jim Eisenreich | .10 | .30 |
| 172 Heathcliff Slocumb | .10 | .30 |
| 173 Kevin Stocker | .10 | .30 |
| 174 Esteban Loaiza | .10 | .30 |
| 175 Jeff King | .10 | .30 |
| 176 Mark Johnson | .10 | .30 |
| 177 Denny Neagle | .10 | .30 |
| 178 Orlando Merced | .10 | .30 |
| 179 Carlos Garcia | .10 | .30 |
| 180 Brian Jordan | .10 | .30 |
| 181 Mike Morgan | .10 | .30 |
| 182 Mark Petkovsek | .10 | .30 |
| 183 Bernard Gilkey | .10 | .30 |
| 184 John Mabry | .10 | .30 |
| 185 Tom Henke | .10 | .30 |
| 186 Glenn Dishman | .10 | .30 |
| 187 Andy Ashby | .10 | .30 |
| 188 Bip Roberts | .10 | .30 |
| 189 Melvin Nieves | .10 | .30 |
| 190 Ken Caminiti | .10 | .30 |
| 191 Brad Ausmus | .10 | .30 |
| 192 Deion Sanders | .20 | .50 |
| 193 Jamie Brewington RC | .10 | .30 |
| 194 Glenallen Hill | .10 | .30 |
| 195 Barry Bonds | .75 | 2.00 |
| 196 Wm. Van Landingham | .10 | .30 |
| 197 Mark Carreon | .10 | .30 |
| 198 Royce Clayton | .10 | .30 |
| 199 Joey Cora | .10 | .30 |
| 200 Ken Griffey Jr. | .50 | 1.25 |
| 201 Jay Buhner | .10 | .30 |
| 202 Alex Rodriguez | .60 | 1.50 |

|  |  | | |
|---|---|---|---|
| ☐ 203 | Norm Charlton | .10 | .30 |
| ☐ 204 | Andy Benes | .10 | .30 |
| ☐ 205 | Edgar Martinez | .20 | .50 |
| ☐ 206 | Juan Gonzalez | .50 | 1.25 |
| ☐ 207 | Will Clark | .20 | .50 |
| ☐ 208 | Kevin Gross | .10 | .30 |
| ☐ 209 | Roger Pavlik | .10 | .30 |
| ☐ 210 | Ivan Rodriguez | .20 | .50 |
| ☐ 211 | Rusty Greer | .10 | .30 |
| ☐ 212 | Angel Martinez | .10 | .30 |
| ☐ 213 | Tomas Perez | .10 | .30 |
| ☐ 214 | Alex Gonzalez | .10 | .30 |
| ☐ 215 | Joe Carter | .10 | .30 |
| ☐ 216 | Shawn Green | .10 | .30 |
| ☐ 217 | Edwin Hurtado | .10 | .30 |
| ☐ 218 | E.Martinez/T.Pena CL | .10 | .30 |
| ☐ 219 | C.Jones/B.Larkin CL | .20 | .50 |
| ☐ 220 | Orel Hershiser CL | .10 | .30 |
| ☐ 221 | Mike Devereaux CL | .10 | .30 |
| ☐ 222 | Tom Glavine CL | .10 | .30 |
| ☐ 223 | Karim Garcia | .10 | .30 |
| ☐ 224 | Arquimedez Pozo | .10 | .30 |
| ☐ 225 | Billy Wagner | .10 | .30 |
| ☐ 226 | John Wasdin | .10 | .30 |
| ☐ 227 | Jeff Suppan | .10 | .30 |
| ☐ 228 | Steve Gibralter | .10 | .30 |
| ☐ 229 | Jimmy Haynes | .10 | .30 |
| ☐ 230 | Ruben Rivera | .10 | .30 |
| ☐ 231 | Chris Snopek | .10 | .30 |
| ☐ 232 | Alex Ochoa | .10 | .30 |
| ☐ 233 | Shannon Stewart | .10 | .30 |
| ☐ 234 | Quinton McCracken | .10 | .30 |
| ☐ 235 | Trey Beamon | .10 | .30 |
| ☐ 236 | Billy McMillon | .10 | .30 |
| ☐ 237 | Steve Cox | .10 | .30 |
| ☐ 238 | George Arias | .10 | .30 |
| ☐ 239 | Yamil Benitez | .10 | .30 |
| ☐ 240 | Todd Greene | .10 | .30 |
| ☐ 241 | Jason Kendall | .10 | .30 |
| ☐ 242 | Brooks Kieschnick | .10 | .30 |
| ☐ 243 | Osvaldo Fernandez RC | .10 | .30 |
| ☐ 244 | Livan Hernandez RC | .40 | 1.00 |
| ☐ 245 | Rey Ordonez | .10 | .30 |
| ☐ 246 | Mike Grace RC | .10 | .30 |
| ☐ 247 | Jay Canizaro | .10 | .30 |
| ☐ 248 | Bob Wolcott | .10 | .30 |
| ☐ 249 | Jermaine Dye | .10 | .30 |
| ☐ 250 | Jason Schmidt | .20 | .50 |
| ☐ 251 | Mike Sweeney RC | .40 | 1.00 |
| ☐ 252 | Marcus Jensen | .10 | .30 |
| ☐ 253 | Mendy Lopez | .10 | .30 |
| ☐ 254 | Wilton Guerrero RC | .10 | .30 |
| ☐ 255 | Paul Wilson | .10 | .30 |
| ☐ 256 | Edgar Renteria | .10 | .30 |
| ☐ 257 | Richard Hidalgo | .10 | .30 |
| ☐ 258 | Bob Abreu | .30 | .75 |
| ☐ 259 | Robert Smith RC | .10 | .30 |
| ☐ 260 | Sal Fasano | .10 | .30 |
| ☐ 261 | Enrique Wilson | .10 | .30 |
| ☐ 262 | Rich Hunter RC | .10 | .30 |
| ☐ 263 | Sergio Nunez | .10 | .30 |
| ☐ 264 | Dan Serafini | .10 | .30 |
| ☐ 265 | David Doster | .10 | .30 |
| ☐ 266 | Ryan McGuire | .10 | .30 |
| ☐ 267 | Scott Spiezio | .10 | .30 |
| ☐ 268 | Rafael Orellano | .10 | .30 |
| ☐ 269 | Steve Avery | .10 | .30 |
| ☐ 270 | Fred McGriff | .20 | .50 |
| ☐ 271 | John Smoltz | .20 | .50 |
| ☐ 272 | Ryan Klesko | .50 | 1.25 |
| ☐ 273 | Jeff Blauser | .10 | .30 |
| ☐ 274 | Brad Clontz | .10 | .30 |
| ☐ 275 | Roberto Alomar | .20 | .50 |
| ☐ 276 | B.J. Surhoff | .10 | .30 |
| ☐ 277 | Jeffrey Hammonds | .10 | .30 |
| ☐ 278 | Brady Anderson | .10 | .30 |
| ☐ 279 | Bobby Bonilla | .10 | .30 |
| ☐ 280 | Cal Ripken | 1.00 | 2.50 |
| ☐ 281 | Mike Mussina | .20 | .50 |
| ☐ 282 | Will Cordero | .10 | .30 |
| ☐ 283 | Mike Stanley | .10 | .30 |
| ☐ 284 | Aaron Sele | .10 | .30 |
| ☐ 285 | Jose Canseco | .20 | .50 |
| ☐ 286 | Tom Gordon | .10 | .30 |
| ☐ 287 | Heathcliff Slocumb | .10 | .30 |
| ☐ 288 | Lee Smith | .10 | .30 |
| ☐ 289 | Troy Percival | .10 | .30 |
| ☐ 290 | Tim Salmon | .20 | .50 |
| ☐ 291 | Chuck Finley | .10 | .30 |
| ☐ 292 | Jim Abbott | .20 | .50 |
| ☐ 293 | Chili Davis | .10 | .30 |
| ☐ 294 | Steve Trachsel | .10 | .30 |
| ☐ 295 | Mark Grace | .20 | .50 |
| ☐ 296 | Rey Sanchez | .10 | .30 |
| ☐ 297 | Scott Servais | .10 | .30 |
| ☐ 298 | Jaime Navarro | .10 | .30 |
| ☐ 299 | Frank Castillo | .10 | .30 |
| ☐ 300 | Frank Thomas | .30 | .75 |
| ☐ 301 | Jason Bere | .10 | .30 |
| ☐ 302 | Danny Tartabull | .10 | .30 |
| ☐ 303 | Darren Lewis | .10 | .30 |
| ☐ 304 | Roberto Hernandez | .10 | .30 |
| ☐ 305 | Tony Phillips | .10 | .30 |
| ☐ 306 | Wilson Alvarez | .10 | .30 |
| ☐ 307 | Jose Rijo | .10 | .30 |
| ☐ 308 | Hal Morris | .10 | .30 |
| ☐ 309 | Mark Portugal | .10 | .30 |
| ☐ 310 | Barry Larkin | .20 | .50 |
| ☐ 311 | Dave Burba | .10 | .30 |
| ☐ 312 | Eddie Taubensee | .10 | .30 |
| ☐ 313 | Sandy Alomar Jr. | .10 | .30 |
| ☐ 314 | Dennis Martinez | .10 | .30 |
| ☐ 315 | Albert Belle | .10 | .30 |
| ☐ 316 | Eddie Murray | .30 | .75 |
| ☐ 317 | Charles Nagy | .10 | .30 |
| ☐ 318 | Chad Ogea | .10 | .30 |
| ☐ 319 | Kenny Lofton | .30 | .75 |
| ☐ 320 | Dante Bichette | .10 | .30 |
| ☐ 321 | Armando Reynoso | .10 | .30 |
| ☐ 322 | Walt Weiss | .10 | .30 |
| ☐ 323 | Ellis Burks | .10 | .30 |
| ☐ 324 | Kevin Ritz | .10 | .30 |
| ☐ 325 | Bill Swift | .10 | .30 |
| ☐ 326 | Jason Bates | .10 | .30 |
| ☐ 327 | Tony Clark | .10 | .30 |
| ☐ 328 | Travis Fryman | .10 | .30 |
| ☐ 329 | Mark Parent | .10 | .30 |
| ☐ 330 | Alan Trammell | .10 | .30 |
| ☐ 331 | C.J. Nitkowski | .10 | .30 |
| ☐ 332 | Jose Lima | .10 | .30 |
| ☐ 333 | Phil Plantier | .10 | .30 |
| ☐ 334 | Kurt Abbott | .10 | .30 |
| ☐ 335 | Andre Dawson | .10 | .30 |
| ☐ 336 | Chris Hammond | .10 | .30 |
| ☐ 337 | Robb Nen | .10 | .30 |
| ☐ 338 | Pat Rapp | .10 | .30 |
| ☐ 339 | Al Leiter | .10 | .30 |
| ☐ 340 | Gary Sheffield | .10 | .30 |
| ☐ 341 | Todd Jones | .10 | .30 |
| ☐ 342 | Doug Drabek | .10 | .30 |
| ☐ 343 | Greg Swindell | .10 | .30 |
| ☐ 344 | Tony Eusebio | .10 | .30 |
| ☐ 345 | Craig Biggio | .20 | .50 |
| ☐ 346 | Darryl Kile | .10 | .30 |
| ☐ 347 | Mike Macfarlane | .10 | .30 |
| ☐ 348 | Jeff Montgomery | .10 | .30 |
| ☐ 349 | Chris Haney | .10 | .30 |
| ☐ 350 | Bip Roberts | .10 | .30 |
| ☐ 351 | Tom Goodwin | .10 | .30 |
| ☐ 352 | Mark Gubicza | .10 | .30 |
| ☐ 353 | Joe Randa | .10 | .30 |
| ☐ 354 | Ramon Martinez | .10 | .30 |
| ☐ 355 | Eric Karros | .10 | .30 |
| ☐ 356 | Delino DeShields | .10 | .30 |
| ☐ 357 | Brett Butler | .10 | .30 |
| ☐ 358 | Todd Worrell | .10 | .30 |
| ☐ 359 | Mike Blowers | .10 | .30 |
| ☐ 360 | Mike Piazza | .50 | 1.25 |
| ☐ 361 | Ben McDonald | .10 | .30 |
| ☐ 362 | Ricky Bones | .10 | .30 |
| ☐ 363 | Greg Vaughn | .10 | .30 |
| ☐ 364 | Matt Mieske | .10 | .30 |
| ☐ 365 | Kevin Seitzer | .10 | .30 |
| ☐ 366 | Jeff Cirillo | .10 | .30 |
| ☐ 367 | LaTroy Hawkins | .10 | .30 |
| ☐ 368 | Frank Rodriguez | .10 | .30 |
| ☐ 369 | Rick Aguilera | .10 | .30 |
| ☐ 370 | Roberto Alomar BG | .10 | .30 |
| ☐ 371 | Albert Belle BG | .10 | .30 |
| ☐ 372 | Wade Boggs BG | .10 | .30 |
| ☐ 373 | Barry Bonds BG | .40 | 1.00 |
| ☐ 374 | Roger Clemens BG | .30 | .75 |
| ☐ 375 | Dennis Eckersley BG | .10 | .30 |
| ☐ 376 | Ken Griffey Jr. BG | .30 | .75 |
| ☐ 377 | Tony Gwynn BG | .20 | .50 |
| ☐ 378 | Rickey Henderson BG | .20 | .50 |
| ☐ 379 | Greg Maddux BG | .30 | .75 |
| ☐ 380 | Fred McGriff BG | .10 | .30 |
| ☐ 381 | Paul Molitor BG | .10 | .30 |
| ☐ 382 | Eddie Murray BG | .20 | .50 |
| ☐ 383 | Mike Piazza BG | .30 | .75 |
| ☐ 384 | Kirby Puckett BG | .20 | .50 |
| ☐ 385 | Cal Ripken BG | .50 | 1.25 |
| ☐ 386 | Ozzie Smith BG | .30 | .75 |
| ☐ 387 | Frank Thomas BG | .20 | .50 |
| ☐ 388 | Matt Walbeck | .10 | .30 |
| ☐ 389 | Dave Stevens | .10 | .30 |
| ☐ 390 | Marty Cordova | .10 | .30 |
| ☐ 391 | Darrin Fletcher | .10 | .30 |
| ☐ 392 | Cliff Floyd | .10 | .30 |
| ☐ 393 | Mel Rojas | .10 | .30 |
| ☐ 394 | Shane Andrews | .10 | .30 |
| ☐ 395 | Moises Alou | .10 | .30 |
| ☐ 396 | Carlos Perez | .10 | .30 |
| ☐ 397 | Jeff Fassero | .10 | .30 |
| ☐ 398 | Bobby Jones | .10 | .30 |
| ☐ 399 | Todd Hundley | .10 | .30 |
| ☐ 400 | John Franco | .10 | .30 |
| ☐ 401 | Jose Vizcaino | .10 | .30 |
| ☐ 402 | Bernard Gilkey | .10 | .30 |
| ☐ 403 | Pete Harnisch | .10 | .30 |
| ☐ 404 | Paul Kelly | .10 | .30 |
| ☐ 405 | David Cone | .10 | .30 |
| ☐ 406 | Bernie Williams | .20 | .50 |
| ☐ 407 | John Wetteland | .10 | .30 |
| ☐ 408 | Scott Kamieniecki | .10 | .30 |
| ☐ 409 | Tim Raines | .10 | .30 |
| ☐ 410 | Wade Boggs | .20 | .50 |
| ☐ 411 | Terry Steinbach | .10 | .30 |
| ☐ 412 | Jason Giambi | .10 | .30 |
| ☐ 413 | Todd Van Poppel | .10 | .30 |
| ☐ 414 | Pedro Munoz | .10 | .30 |
| ☐ 415 | Eddie Murray SBT | .20 | .50 |
| ☐ 416 | Dennis Eckersley SBT | .10 | .30 |
| ☐ 417 | Bip Roberts SBT | .10 | .30 |
| ☐ 418 | Glenallen Hill SBT | .10 | .30 |
| ☐ 419 | John Hudek SBT | .10 | .30 |
| ☐ 420 | Derek Bell SBT | .10 | .30 |
| ☐ 421 | Larry Walker SBT | .10 | .30 |
| ☐ 422 | Greg Maddux SBT | .30 | .75 |
| ☐ 423 | Ken Caminiti SBT | .10 | .30 |
| ☐ 424 | Brent Gates | .10 | .30 |
| ☐ 425 | Mark McGwire | .75 | 2.00 |
| ☐ 426 | Mark Whiten | .10 | .30 |
| ☐ 427 | Sid Fernandez | .10 | .30 |
| ☐ 428 | Ricky Bottalico | .10 | .30 |
| ☐ 429 | Mike Mimbs | .10 | .30 |
| ☐ 430 | Lenny Dykstra | .10 | .30 |
| ☐ 431 | Todd Zeile | .10 | .30 |
| ☐ 432 | Benito Santiago | .10 | .30 |
| ☐ 433 | Danny Miceli | .10 | .30 |
| ☐ 434 | Al Martin | .10 | .30 |
| ☐ 435 | Jay Bell | .10 | .30 |
| ☐ 436 | Charlie Hayes | .10 | .30 |
| ☐ 437 | Mike Kingery | .10 | .30 |
| ☐ 438 | Paul Wagner | .10 | .30 |
| ☐ 439 | Tom Pagnozzi | .10 | .30 |
| ☐ 440 | Ozzie Smith | .50 | 1.25 |
| ☐ 441 | Ray Lankford | .10 | .30 |
| ☐ 442 | Dennis Eckersley | .10 | .30 |
| ☐ 443 | Ron Gant | .10 | .30 |
| ☐ 444 | Alan Benes | .10 | .30 |
| ☐ 445 | Rickey Henderson | .30 | .75 |
| ☐ 446 | Jody Reed | .10 | .30 |
| ☐ 447 | Trevor Hoffman | .10 | .30 |
| ☐ 448 | Andujar Cedeno | .10 | .30 |
| ☐ 449 | Steve Finley | .10 | .30 |
| ☐ 450 | Tony Gwynn | .40 | 1.00 |
| ☐ 451 | Joey Hamilton | .10 | .30 |
| ☐ 452 | Mark Leiter | .10 | .30 |
| ☐ 453 | Rod Beck | .10 | .30 |
| ☐ 454 | Kirt Manwaring | .10 | .30 |
| ☐ 455 | Matt Williams | .10 | .30 |
| ☐ 456 | Robby Thompson | .10 | .30 |
| ☐ 457 | Shawon Dunston | .10 | .30 |
| ☐ 458 | Russ Davis | .10 | .30 |
| ☐ 459 | Paul Sorrento | .10 | .30 |
| ☐ 460 | Randy Johnson | .30 | .75 |
| ☐ 461 | Chris Bosio | .10 | .30 |
| ☐ 462 | Luis Sojo | .10 | .30 |
| ☐ 463 | Sterling Hitchcock | .10 | .30 |
| ☐ 464 | Benji Gil | .10 | .30 |
| ☐ 465 | Mickey Tettleton | .10 | .30 |
| ☐ 466 | Mark McLemore | .10 | .30 |

|  |  | | |
|---|---|---|---|
| 467 | Darryl Hamilton | .10 | .30 |
| 468 | Ken Hill | .10 | .30 |
| 469 | Dean Palmer | .10 | .30 |
| 470 | Carlos Delgado | .10 | .30 |
| 471 | Ed Sprague | .10 | .30 |
| 472 | Otis Nixon | .10 | .30 |
| 473 | Pat Hentgen | .10 | .30 |
| 474 | Juan Guzman | .10 | .30 |
| 475 | John Olerud | .10 | .30 |
| 476 | Buck Showalter CL | .10 | .30 |
| 477 | Bobby Cox CL | .10 | .30 |
| 478 | Tommy Lasorda CL | .10 | .30 |
| 479 | Buck Showalter CL | .10 | .30 |
| 480 | Sparky Anderson CL | .10 | .30 |
| 481U | Randy Myers | .20 | .50 |
| 482U | Kent Mercker | .20 | .50 |
| 483U | David Wells | .30 | .75 |
| 484U | Kevin Mitchell | .20 | .50 |
| 485U | Randy Velarde | .20 | .50 |
| 486U | Ryne Sandberg | 1.50 | 4.00 |
| 487U | Doug Jones | .20 | .50 |
| 488U | Terry Adams | .20 | .50 |
| 489U | Kevin Tapani | .20 | .50 |
| 490U | Harold Baines | .30 | .75 |
| 491U | Eric Davis | .30 | .75 |
| 492U | Julio Franco | .30 | .75 |
| 493U | Jack McDowell | .20 | .50 |
| 494U | Devon White | .30 | .75 |
| 495U | Kevin Brown | .30 | .75 |
| 496U | Rick Wilkins | .20 | .50 |
| 497U | Sean Berry | .20 | .50 |
| 498U | Keith Lockhart | .20 | .50 |
| 499U | Mark Loretta | .20 | .50 |
| 500U | Paul Molitor | .30 | .75 |
| 501U | Roberto Kelly | .20 | .50 |
| 502U | Lance Johnson | .20 | .50 |
| 503U | Tino Martinez | .50 | 1.25 |
| 504U | Kenny Rogers | .20 | .50 |
| 505U | Todd Stottlemyre | .20 | .50 |
| 506U | Gary Gaetti | .30 | .75 |
| 507U | Royce Clayton | .20 | .50 |
| 508U | Andy Benes | .20 | .50 |
| 509U | Wally Joyner | .30 | .75 |
| 510U | Erik Hanson | .20 | .50 |
| P100 | Ken Griffey Jr Promo | 1.25 | 3.00 |

## 1997 Upper Deck

| | | | |
|---|---|---|---|
| COMP.MASTER SET (550) | 80.00 | 200.00 |
| COMPLETE SET (490) | 50.00 | 100.00 |
| COMPLETE SERIES 1 (240) | 20.00 | 40.00 |
| COMPLETE SERIES 2 (250) | 30.00 | 60.00 |
| COMP.SER.2 w/o GHL (240) | 10.00 | 25.00 |
| COMMON (1-240/271-520) | .10 | .30 |
| COMP.UPDATE SET (30) | 40.00 | 80.00 |
| COMMON UPDATE (241-270) | .40 | 1.00 |
| 1 UPD.SET VIA MAIL PER 10 SER.1 WRAPS | | |
| COMMON GHL (415-424) | .60 | 1.50 |
| COMP.TRADE SET (30) | 8.00 | 20.00 |
| COMMON TRADE (521-550) | .20 | .50 |

|  |  | | |
|---|---|---|---|
| 1 | Jackie Robinson | .20 | .50 |
| 2 | Jackie Robinson | .20 | .50 |
| 3 | Jackie Robinson | .20 | .50 |
| 4 | Jackie Robinson | .20 | .50 |
| 5 | Jackie Robinson | .20 | .50 |
| 6 | Jackie Robinson | .20 | .50 |
| 7 | Jackie Robinson | .20 | .50 |
| 8 | Jackie Robinson | .20 | .50 |
| 9 | Jackie Robinson | .20 | .50 |
| 10 | Chipper Jones | .30 | .75 |
| 11 | Marquis Grissom | .10 | .30 |
| 12 | Jermaine Dye | .10 | .30 |
| 13 | Mark Lemke | .10 | .30 |
| 14 | Terrell Wade | .10 | .30 |
| 15 | Fred McGriff | .20 | .50 |
| 16 | Tom Glavine | .20 | .50 |
| 17 | Mark Wohlers | .10 | .30 |
| 18 | Randy Myers | .10 | .30 |
| 19 | Roberto Alomar | .20 | .50 |
| 20 | Cal Ripken | 1.00 | 2.50 |
| 21 | Rafael Palmeiro | .20 | .50 |
| 22 | Mike Mussina | .20 | .50 |
| 23 | Brady Anderson | .10 | .30 |
| 24 | Jose Canseco | .20 | .50 |
| 25 | Mo Vaughn | .10 | .30 |
| 26 | Roger Clemens | .60 | 1.50 |
| 27 | Tim Naehring | .10 | .30 |
| 28 | Jeff Suppan | .10 | .30 |
| 29 | Troy Percival | .10 | .30 |
| 30 | Sammy Sosa | .30 | .75 |
| 31 | Amaury Telemaco | .10 | .30 |
| 32 | Rey Sanchez | .10 | .30 |
| 33 | Scott Servais | .10 | .30 |
| 34 | Steve Trachsel | .10 | .30 |
| 35 | Mark Grace | .20 | .50 |
| 36 | Wilson Alvarez | .10 | .30 |
| 37 | Harold Baines | .10 | .30 |
| 38 | Tony Phillips | .10 | .30 |
| 39 | James Baldwin | .10 | .30 |
| 40 | Frank Thomas UER | .30 | .75 |
| 41 | Lyle Mouton | .10 | .30 |
| 42 | Chris Snopek | .10 | .30 |
| 43 | Hal Morris | .10 | .30 |
| 44 | Eric Davis | .10 | .30 |
| 45 | Barry Larkin | .20 | .50 |
| 46 | Reggie Sanders | .10 | .30 |
| 47 | Pete Schourek | .10 | .30 |
| 48 | Lee Smith | .10 | .30 |
| 49 | Charles Nagy | .10 | .30 |
| 50 | Albert Belle | .30 | .75 |
| 51 | Julio Franco | .10 | .30 |
| 52 | Kenny Lofton | .10 | .30 |
| 53 | Orel Hershiser | .10 | .30 |
| 54 | Omar Vizquel | .20 | .50 |
| 55 | Eric Young | .10 | .30 |
| 56 | Curtis Leskanic | .10 | .30 |
| 57 | Quinton McCracken | .10 | .30 |
| 58 | Kevin Ritz | .10 | .30 |
| 59 | Walt Weiss | .10 | .30 |
| 60 | Dante Bichette | .10 | .30 |
| 61 | Mark Lewis | .10 | .30 |
| 62 | Tony Clark | .10 | .30 |
| 63 | Travis Fryman | .10 | .30 |
| 64 | John Smoltz | .10 | .30 |
| 65 | Greg Maddux SF | .30 | .75 |
| 66 | Tom Glavine SF | .10 | .30 |
| 67 | Mike Mussina SF | .10 | .30 |
| 68 | Andy Pettitte SF | .10 | .30 |
| 69 | Mariano Rivera SF | .20 | .50 |
| 70 | Hideo Nomo SF | .10 | .30 |
| 71 | Kevin Brown SF | .10 | .30 |
| 72 | Randy Johnson SF | .20 | .50 |
| 73 | Felipe Lira | .10 | .30 |
| 74 | Kimera Bartee | .10 | .30 |
| 75 | Alan Trammell | .10 | .30 |
| 76 | Kevin Brown | .10 | .30 |
| 77 | Edgar Renteria | .10 | .30 |
| 78 | Al Leiter | .10 | .30 |
| 79 | Charles Johnson | .10 | .30 |
| 80 | Andre Dawson | .20 | .50 |
| 81 | Billy Wagner | .10 | .30 |
| 82 | Donne Wall | .10 | .30 |
| 83 | Jeff Bagwell | .20 | .50 |
| 84 | Keith Lockhart | .10 | .30 |
| 85 | Jeff Montgomery | .10 | .30 |
| 86 | Tom Goodwin | .10 | .30 |
| 87 | Tim Belcher | .10 | .30 |
| 88 | Mike Macfarlane | .10 | .30 |
| 89 | Joe Randa | .10 | .30 |
| 90 | Brett Butler | .10 | .30 |
| 91 | Todd Worrell | .10 | .30 |
| 92 | Todd Hollandsworth | .10 | .30 |
| 93 | Ismael Valdes | .10 | .30 |
| 94 | Hideo Nomo | .50 | 1.25 |
| 95 | Mike Piazza | .50 | 1.25 |
| 96 | Jeff Cirillo | .10 | .30 |
| 97 | Ricky Bones | .10 | .30 |
| 98 | Fernando Vina | .10 | .30 |
| 99 | Ben McDonald | .10 | .30 |
| 100 | John Jaha | .10 | .30 |
| 101 | Mark Loretta | .10 | .30 |
| 102 | Paul Molitor | .10 | .30 |
| 103 | Rick Aguilera | .10 | .30 |
| 104 | Marty Cordova | .10 | .30 |
| 105 | Kirby Puckett | .30 | .75 |
| 106 | Dan Naulty | .10 | .30 |
| 107 | Frank Rodriguez | .10 | .30 |
| 108 | Shane Andrews | .10 | .30 |
| 109 | Henry Rodriguez | .10 | .30 |
| 110 | Mark Grudzielanek | .10 | .30 |
| 111 | Pedro Martinez | .20 | .50 |
| 112 | Ugueth Urbina | .10 | .30 |
| 113 | David Segui | .10 | .30 |
| 114 | Rey Ordonez | .10 | .30 |
| 115 | Bernard Gilkey | .10 | .30 |
| 116 | Butch Huskey | .10 | .30 |
| 117 | Paul Wilson | .10 | .30 |
| 118 | Alex Ochoa | .10 | .30 |
| 119 | John Franco | .10 | .30 |
| 120 | Dwight Gooden | .10 | .30 |
| 121 | Ruben Rivera | .10 | .30 |
| 122 | Andy Pettitte | .20 | .50 |
| 123 | Tino Martinez | .20 | .50 |
| 124 | Bernie Williams | .20 | .50 |
| 125 | Wade Boggs | .20 | .50 |
| 126 | Paul O'Neill | .20 | .50 |
| 127 | Scott Brosius | .10 | .30 |
| 128 | Ernie Young | .10 | .30 |
| 129 | Doug Johns | .10 | .30 |
| 130 | Geronimo Berroa | .10 | .30 |
| 131 | Jason Giambi | .10 | .30 |
| 132 | John Wasdin | .10 | .30 |
| 133 | Jim Eisenreich | .10 | .30 |
| 134 | Ricky Otero | .10 | .30 |
| 135 | Ricky Bottalico | .10 | .30 |
| 136 | Mark Langston DG | .10 | .30 |
| 137 | Greg Maddux DG | .30 | .75 |
| 138 | Ivan Rodriguez DG | .10 | .30 |
| 139 | Charles Johnson DG | .10 | .30 |
| 140 | J.T. Snow DG | .10 | .30 |
| 141 | Mark Grace DG | .10 | .30 |
| 142 | Roberto Alomar DG | .10 | .30 |
| 143 | Craig Biggio DG | .10 | .30 |
| 144 | Ken Caminiti DG | .10 | .30 |
| 145 | Matt Williams DG | .10 | .30 |
| 146 | Omar Vizquel DG | .10 | .30 |
| 147 | Cal Ripken DG | .50 | 1.25 |
| 148 | Ozzie Smith DG | .30 | .75 |
| 149 | Rey Ordonez DG | .10 | .30 |
| 150 | Ken Griffey Jr. DG | .30 | .75 |
| 151 | Devon White DG | .10 | .30 |
| 152 | Barry Bonds | .40 | 1.00 |
| 153 | Kenny Lofton DG | .10 | .30 |
| 154 | Mickey Morandini | .10 | .30 |
| 155 | Gregg Jefferies | .10 | .30 |
| 156 | Curt Schilling | .10 | .30 |
| 157 | Jason Kendall | .10 | .30 |
| 158 | Francisco Cordova | .10 | .30 |
| 159 | Dennis Eckersley | .10 | .30 |
| 160 | Ron Gant | .10 | .30 |
| 161 | Ozzie Smith | .50 | 1.25 |
| 162 | Brian Jordan | .10 | .30 |
| 163 | John Mabry | .10 | .30 |
| 164 | Andy Ashby | .10 | .30 |
| 165 | Steve Finley | .10 | .30 |
| 166 | Fernando Valenzuela | .10 | .30 |
| 167 | Archi Cianfrocco | .10 | .30 |
| 168 | Wally Joyner | .10 | .30 |
| 169 | Greg Vaughn | .10 | .30 |
| 170 | Barry Bonds | .75 | 2.00 |
| 171 | William VanLandingham | .10 | .30 |
| 172 | Marvin Benard | .10 | .30 |
| 173 | Rich Aurilia | .10 | .30 |
| 174 | Jay Canizaro | .10 | .30 |
| 175 | Ken Griffey Jr. | .50 | 1.25 |
| 176 | Bob Wells | .10 | .30 |
| 177 | Billy Buhner | .10 | .30 |
| 178 | Sterling Hitchcock | .10 | .30 |
| 179 | Edgar Martinez | .20 | .50 |
| 180 | Rusty Greer | .10 | .30 |
| 181 | Dave Nilsson GI | .10 | .30 |
| 182 | Larry Walker GI | .10 | .30 |
| 183 | Edgar Renteria GI | .10 | .30 |
| 184 | Rey Ordonez GI | .10 | .30 |
| 185 | Rafael Palmeiro GI | .10 | .30 |
| 186 | Osvaldo Fernandez GI | .10 | .30 |
| 187 | Raul Mondesi GI | .10 | .30 |
| 188 | Manny Ramirez GI | .10 | .30 |
| 189 | Sammy Sosa GI | .20 | .50 |
| 190 | Robert Eenhoorn GI | .10 | .30 |
| 191 | Devon White GI | .10 | .30 |

|  |  | | |
|---|---|---|---|
| ❑ 192 | Hideo Nomo GI | .10 | .30 |
| ❑ 193 | Mac Suzuki GI | .10 | .30 |
| ❑ 194 | Chan Ho Park GI | .10 | .30 |
| ❑ 195 | Fernando Valenzuela GI | .10 | .30 |
| ❑ 196 | Andruw Jones GI | .10 | .30 |
| ❑ 197 | Vinny Castilla GI | .10 | .30 |
| ❑ 198 | Dennis Martinez GI | .10 | .30 |
| ❑ 199 | Ruben Rivera GI | .10 | .30 |
| ❑ 200 | Juan Gonzalez GI | .10 | .30 |
| ❑ 201 | Roberto Alomar GI | .10 | .30 |
| ❑ 202 | Edgar Martinez GI | .10 | .30 |
| ❑ 203 | Ivan Rodriguez GI | .10 | .30 |
| ❑ 204 | Carlos Delgado GI | .10 | .30 |
| ❑ 205 | Andres Galarraga GI | .10 | .30 |
| ❑ 206 | Ozzie Guillen GI | .10 | .30 |
| ❑ 207 | Midre Cummings GI | .10 | .30 |
| ❑ 208 | Roger Pavlik | .10 | .30 |
| ❑ 209 | Darren Oliver | .10 | .30 |
| ❑ 210 | Dean Palmer | .10 | .30 |
| ❑ 211 | Ivan Rodriguez | .20 | .50 |
| ❑ 212 | Otis Nixon | .10 | .30 |
| ❑ 213 | Pat Hentgen | .10 | .30 |
| ❑ 214 | Ozzie/Dawson/Puckett HI.CL | .20 | .50 |
| ❑ 215 | Bonds/Sheff/Brady HI.CL | .40 | 1.00 |
| ❑ 216 | Ken Caminiti SH CL | .10 | .30 |
| ❑ 217 | John Smoltz SH CL | .10 | .30 |
| ❑ 218 | Eric Young SH CL | .10 | .30 |
| ❑ 219 | Juan Gonzalez SH CL | .10 | .30 |
| ❑ 220 | Eddie Murray SH CL | .20 | .50 |
| ❑ 221 | Tommy Lasorda SH CL | .10 | .30 |
| ❑ 222 | Paul Molitor SH CL | .10 | .30 |
| ❑ 223 | Luis Castillo | .10 | .30 |
| ❑ 224 | Justin Thompson | .10 | .30 |
| ❑ 225 | Rocky Coppinger | .10 | .30 |
| ❑ 226 | Jermaine Allensworth | .10 | .30 |
| ❑ 227 | Jeff D'Amico | .10 | .30 |
| ❑ 228 | Jamey Wright | .10 | .30 |
| ❑ 229 | Scott Rolen | .20 | .50 |
| ❑ 230 | Darin Erstad | .10 | .30 |
| ❑ 231 | Marty Janzen | .10 | .30 |
| ❑ 232 | Jacob Cruz | .10 | .30 |
| ❑ 233 | Raul Ibanez | .10 | .30 |
| ❑ 234 | Nomar Garciaparra | .50 | 1.25 |
| ❑ 235 | Todd Walker | .10 | .30 |
| ❑ 236 | Brian Giles RC | .60 | 1.50 |
| ❑ 237 | Matt Beech | .10 | .30 |
| ❑ 238 | Mike Cameron | .10 | .30 |
| ❑ 239 | Jose Paniagua | .10 | .30 |
| ❑ 240 | Andruw Jones | .20 | .50 |
| ❑ 241 | Brant Brown UPD | .40 | 1.00 |
| ❑ 242 | Robin Jennings UPD | .40 | 1.00 |
| ❑ 243 | Willie Adams UPD | .40 | 1.00 |
| ❑ 244 | Ken Caminiti UPD | .60 | 1.50 |
| ❑ 245 | Brian Jordan UPD | .60 | 1.50 |
| ❑ 246 | Chipper Jones UPD | 1.50 | 4.00 |
| ❑ 247 | Juan Gonzalez UPD | .60 | 1.50 |
| ❑ 248 | Bernie Williams UPD | 1.00 | 2.50 |
| ❑ 249 | Roberto Alomar UPD | 1.00 | 2.50 |
| ❑ 250 | Bernie Williams UPD | 1.00 | 2.50 |
| ❑ 251 | David Wells UPD | .50 | 1.50 |
| ❑ 252 | Cecil Fielder UPD | .50 | 1.50 |
| ❑ 253 | Darryl Strawberry UPD | .50 | 1.50 |
| ❑ 254 | Andy Pettitte UPD | 1.00 | 2.50 |
| ❑ 255 | Javier Lopez UPD | .50 | 1.50 |
| ❑ 256 | Gary Gaetti UPD | .50 | 1.50 |
| ❑ 257 | Ron Gant UPD | .50 | 1.50 |
| ❑ 258 | Brian Jordan UPD | .60 | 1.50 |
| ❑ 259 | John Smoltz UPD | 1.00 | 2.50 |
| ❑ 260 | Greg Maddux UPD | 3.00 | 8.00 |
| ❑ 261 | Tom Glavine UPD | 1.00 | 2.50 |
| ❑ 262 | Andruw Jones UPD | 1.00 | 2.50 |
| ❑ 263 | Greg Maddux UPD | 3.00 | 8.00 |
| ❑ 264 | David Cone UPD | .60 | 1.50 |
| ❑ 265 | Jim Leyritz UPD | .40 | 1.00 |
| ❑ 266 | Andy Pettitte UPD | 1.00 | 2.50 |
| ❑ 267 | John Wetteland UPD | .60 | 1.50 |
| ❑ 268 | Dario Veras UPD | .40 | 1.00 |
| ❑ 269 | Neifi Perez UPD | .40 | 1.00 |
| ❑ 270 | Bill Mueller UPD | 1.50 | 4.00 |
| ❑ 271 | Vladimir Guerrero | .30 | .75 |
| ❑ 272 | Dmitri Young | .10 | .30 |
| ❑ 273 | Nerio Rodriguez RC | .10 | .30 |
| ❑ 274 | Kevin Orie | .10 | .30 |
| ❑ 275 | Felipe Crespo | .10 | .30 |
| ❑ 276 | Danny Graves | .10 | .30 |
| ❑ 277 | Rod Myers | .10 | .30 |
| ❑ 278 | Felix Heredia RC | .10 | .30 |
| ❑ 279 | Ralph Milliard | .10 | .30 |
| ❑ 280 | Greg Norton | .10 | .30 |
| ❑ 281 | Derek Wallace | .10 | .30 |
| ❑ 282 | Trot Nixon | .10 | .30 |
| ❑ 283 | Bobby Chouinard | .10 | .30 |
| ❑ 284 | Jay Witasick | .10 | .30 |
| ❑ 285 | Travis Miller | .10 | .30 |
| ❑ 286 | Brian Bevil | .10 | .30 |
| ❑ 287 | Bobby Estalella | .10 | .30 |
| ❑ 288 | Steve Soderstrom | .10 | .30 |
| ❑ 289 | Mark Langston | .10 | .30 |
| ❑ 290 | Tim Salmon | .20 | .50 |
| ❑ 291 | Jim Edmonds | .10 | .30 |
| ❑ 292 | Garret Anderson | .10 | .30 |
| ❑ 293 | George Arias | .10 | .30 |
| ❑ 294 | Gary DiSarcina | .10 | .30 |
| ❑ 295 | Chuck Finley | .10 | .30 |
| ❑ 296 | Todd Greene | .10 | .30 |
| ❑ 297 | Randy Velarde | .10 | .30 |
| ❑ 298 | David Justice | .10 | .30 |
| ❑ 299 | Ryan Klesko | .10 | .30 |
| ❑ 300 | John Smoltz | .20 | .50 |
| ❑ 301 | Javier Lopez | .10 | .30 |
| ❑ 302 | Greg Maddux | .50 | 1.25 |
| ❑ 303 | Denny Neagle | .10 | .30 |
| ❑ 304 | B.J. Surhoff | .10 | .30 |
| ❑ 305 | Chris Hoiles | .10 | .30 |
| ❑ 306 | Eric Davis | .10 | .30 |
| ❑ 307 | Scott Erickson | .10 | .30 |
| ❑ 308 | Mike Bordick | .10 | .30 |
| ❑ 309 | John Valentin | .10 | .30 |
| ❑ 310 | Heathcliff Slocumb | .10 | .30 |
| ❑ 311 | Tom Gordon | .10 | .30 |
| ❑ 312 | Mike Stanley | .10 | .30 |
| ❑ 313 | Reggie Jefferson | .10 | .30 |
| ❑ 314 | Darren Bragg | .10 | .30 |
| ❑ 315 | Troy O'Leary | .10 | .30 |
| ❑ 316 | John Mabry SH CL | .10 | .30 |
| ❑ 317 | Mark Whiten SH CL | .10 | .30 |
| ❑ 318 | Edgar Martinez SH CL | .10 | .30 |
| ❑ 319 | Alex Rodriguez SH CL | .30 | .75 |
| ❑ 320 | Mark McGwire SH CL | .40 | 1.00 |
| ❑ 321 | Hideo Nomo SH CL | .10 | .30 |
| ❑ 322 | Todd Hundley SH CL | .10 | .30 |
| ❑ 323 | Barry Bonds SH CL | .40 | 1.00 |
| ❑ 324 | Andruw Jones SH CL | .10 | .30 |
| ❑ 325 | Ryne Sandberg | .50 | 1.25 |
| ❑ 326 | Brian McRae | .10 | .30 |
| ❑ 327 | Frank Castillo | .10 | .30 |
| ❑ 328 | Shawon Dunston | .10 | .30 |
| ❑ 329 | Ray Durham | .10 | .30 |
| ❑ 330 | Robin Ventura | .10 | .30 |
| ❑ 331 | Ozzie Guillen | .10 | .30 |
| ❑ 332 | Roberto Hernandez | .10 | .30 |
| ❑ 333 | Albert Belle | .30 | .75 |
| ❑ 334 | Dave Martinez | .10 | .30 |
| ❑ 335 | Willie Greene | .10 | .30 |
| ❑ 336 | Jeff Brantley | .10 | .30 |
| ❑ 337 | Kevin Jarvis | .10 | .30 |
| ❑ 338 | John Smiley | .10 | .30 |
| ❑ 339 | Eddie Taubensee | .10 | .30 |
| ❑ 340 | Bret Boone | .10 | .30 |
| ❑ 341 | Kevin Seitzer | .10 | .30 |
| ❑ 342 | Jack McDowell | .10 | .30 |
| ❑ 343 | Sandy Alomar Jr. | .10 | .30 |
| ❑ 344 | Chad Curtis | .10 | .30 |
| ❑ 345 | Manny Ramirez | .20 | .50 |
| ❑ 346 | Chad Ogea | .10 | .30 |
| ❑ 347 | Jim Thome | .20 | .50 |
| ❑ 348 | Mark Thompson | .10 | .30 |
| ❑ 349 | Ellis Burks | .10 | .30 |
| ❑ 350 | Andres Galarraga | .10 | .30 |
| ❑ 351 | Vinny Castilla | .10 | .30 |
| ❑ 352 | Kirt Manwaring | .10 | .30 |
| ❑ 353 | Larry Walker | .10 | .30 |
| ❑ 354 | Omar Olivares | .10 | .30 |
| ❑ 355 | Bobby Higginson | .10 | .30 |
| ❑ 356 | Melvin Nieves | .10 | .30 |
| ❑ 357 | Brian Johnson | .10 | .30 |
| ❑ 358 | Devon White | .10 | .30 |
| ❑ 359 | Jeff Conine | .10 | .30 |
| ❑ 360 | Gary Sheffield | .10 | .30 |
| ❑ 361 | Robb Nen | .10 | .30 |
| ❑ 362 | Mike Hampton | .10 | .30 |
| ❑ 363 | Bob Abreu | .20 | .50 |
| ❑ 364 | Luis Gonzalez | .10 | .30 |
| ❑ 365 | Derek Bell | .10 | .30 |
| ❑ 366 | Sean Berry | .10 | .30 |
| ❑ 367 | Craig Biggio | .20 | .50 |
| ❑ 368 | Darryl Kile | .10 | .30 |
| ❑ 369 | Shane Reynolds | .10 | .30 |
| ❑ 370 | Jeff Bagwell CF | .10 | .30 |
| ❑ 371 | Ron Gant CF | .10 | .30 |
| ❑ 372 | Andy Benes CF | .10 | .30 |
| ❑ 373 | Gary Gaetti CF | .10 | .30 |
| ❑ 374 | Ramon Martinez CF | .10 | .30 |
| ❑ 375 | Raul Mondesi CF | .10 | .30 |
| ❑ 376 | Steve Finley CF | .10 | .30 |
| ❑ 377 | Ken Caminiti CF | .10 | .30 |
| ❑ 378 | Tony Gwynn CF | .20 | .50 |
| ❑ 379 | Dario Veras RC | .10 | .30 |
| ❑ 380 | Andy Pettitte CF | .10 | .30 |
| ❑ 381 | Ruben Rivera CF | .10 | .30 |
| ❑ 382 | David Cone CF | .10 | .30 |
| ❑ 383 | Roberto Alomar CF | .10 | .30 |
| ❑ 384 | Edgar Martinez CF | .10 | .30 |
| ❑ 385 | Ken Griffey Jr. CF | .30 | .75 |
| ❑ 386 | Mark McGwire CF | .40 | 1.00 |
| ❑ 387 | Rusty Greer CF | .10 | .30 |
| ❑ 388 | Jose Rosado | .10 | .30 |
| ❑ 389 | Kevin Appier | .10 | .30 |
| ❑ 390 | Johnny Damon | .20 | .50 |
| ❑ 391 | Jose Offerman | .10 | .30 |
| ❑ 392 | Michael Tucker | .10 | .30 |
| ❑ 393 | Craig Paquette | .10 | .30 |
| ❑ 394 | Bip Roberts | .10 | .30 |
| ❑ 395 | Ramon Martinez | .10 | .30 |
| ❑ 396 | Greg Gagne | .10 | .30 |
| ❑ 397 | Chan Ho Park | .10 | .30 |
| ❑ 398 | Karim Garcia | .10 | .30 |
| ❑ 399 | Wilton Guerrero | .10 | .30 |
| ❑ 400 | Eric Karros | .10 | .30 |
| ❑ 401 | Raul Mondesi | .10 | .30 |
| ❑ 402 | Matt Mieske | .10 | .30 |
| ❑ 403 | Mike Fetters | .10 | .30 |
| ❑ 404 | Dave Nilsson | .10 | .30 |
| ❑ 405 | Jose Valentin | .10 | .30 |
| ❑ 406 | Scott Karl | .10 | .30 |
| ❑ 407 | Marc Newfield | .10 | .30 |
| ❑ 408 | Cal Eldred | .10 | .30 |
| ❑ 409 | Rich Becker | .10 | .30 |
| ❑ 410 | Terry Steinbach | .10 | .30 |
| ❑ 411 | Chuck Knoblauch | .10 | .30 |
| ❑ 412 | Pat Meares | .10 | .30 |
| ❑ 413 | Brad Radke | .10 | .30 |
| ❑ 414 | Kirby Puckett UER | .30 | .75 |
| ❑ 415 | Andruw Jones GHL SP | .60 | 1.50 |
| ❑ 416 | Chipper Jones GHL SP | 1.00 | 2.50 |
| ❑ 417 | Mo Vaughn GHL SP | .60 | 1.50 |
| ❑ 418 | Frank Thomas GHL SP | 1.00 | 2.50 |
| ❑ 419 | Albert Belle GHL SP | .60 | 1.50 |
| ❑ 420 | Mark McGwire GHL SP | 3.00 | 8.00 |
| ❑ 421 | Derek Jeter GHL SP | 3.00 | 8.00 |
| ❑ 422 | Alex Rodriguez GHL SP | 2.00 | 5.00 |
| ❑ 423 | Juan Gonzalez GHL SP | .60 | 1.50 |
| ❑ 424 | Ken Griffey Jr. GHL SP | 2.00 | 5.00 |
| ❑ 425 | Rondell White | .10 | .30 |
| ❑ 426 | Darrin Fletcher | .10 | .30 |
| ❑ 427 | Cliff Floyd | .10 | .30 |
| ❑ 428 | Mike Lansing | .10 | .30 |
| ❑ 429 | F.P. Santangelo | .10 | .30 |
| ❑ 430 | Todd Hundley | .10 | .30 |
| ❑ 431 | Mark Clark | .10 | .30 |
| ❑ 432 | Pete Harnisch | .10 | .30 |
| ❑ 433 | Jason Isringhausen | .10 | .30 |
| ❑ 434 | Bobby Jones | .10 | .30 |
| ❑ 435 | Lance Johnson | .10 | .30 |
| ❑ 436 | Carlos Baerga | .10 | .30 |
| ❑ 437 | Mariano Duncan | .10 | .30 |
| ❑ 438 | David Cone | .10 | .30 |
| ❑ 439 | Mariano Rivera | .30 | .75 |
| ❑ 440 | Derek Jeter | .75 | 2.00 |
| ❑ 441 | Joe Girardi | .10 | .30 |
| ❑ 442 | Charlie Hayes | .10 | .30 |
| ❑ 443 | Tim Raines | .10 | .30 |
| ❑ 444 | Darryl Strawberry | .10 | .30 |
| ❑ 445 | Cecil Fielder | .10 | .30 |
| ❑ 446 | Ariel Prieto | .10 | .30 |
| ❑ 447 | Tony Batista | .10 | .30 |
| ❑ 448 | Brent Gates | .10 | .30 |
| ❑ 449 | Scott Spiezio | .10 | .30 |
| ❑ 450 | Mark McGwire | .75 | 2.00 |
| ❑ 451 | Don Wengert | .10 | .30 |
| ❑ 452 | Mike Lieberthal | .10 | .30 |
| ❑ 453 | Lenny Dykstra | .10 | .30 |
| ❑ 454 | Rex Hudler | .10 | .30 |
| ❑ 455 | Darren Daulton | .20 | .50 |

|  |  | | |
|---|------|---|---|
| ❑ 456 | Kevin Stocker | .10 | .30 |
| ❑ 457 | Trey Beamon | .10 | .30 |
| ❑ 458 | Midre Cummings | .10 | .30 |
| ❑ 459 | Mark Johnson | .10 | .30 |
| ❑ 460 | Al Martin | .10 | .30 |
| ❑ 461 | Kevin Elster | .10 | .30 |
| ❑ 462 | Jon Lieber | .10 | .30 |
| ❑ 463 | Jason Schmidt | .10 | .30 |
| ❑ 464 | Paul Wagner | .10 | .30 |
| ❑ 465 | Andy Benes | .10 | .30 |
| ❑ 466 | Alan Benes | .10 | .30 |
| ❑ 467 | Royce Clayton | .10 | .30 |
| ❑ 468 | Gary Gaetti | .10 | .30 |
| ❑ 469 | Curt Lyons RC | .10 | .30 |
| ❑ 470 | Eugene Kingsale DD | .10 | .30 |
| ❑ 471 | Damian Jackson DD | .10 | .30 |
| ❑ 472 | Wendell Magee DD | .10 | .30 |
| ❑ 473 | Kevin L. Brown DD | .10 | .30 |
| ❑ 474 | Raul Casanova DD | .10 | .30 |
| ❑ 475 | Ramiro Mendoza RC | .10 | .30 |
| ❑ 476 | Todd Dunn DD | .10 | .30 |
| ❑ 477 | Chad Mottola DD | .10 | .30 |
| ❑ 478 | Andy Larkin DD | .10 | .30 |
| ❑ 479 | Jaime Bluma DD | .10 | .30 |
| ❑ 480 | Mac Suzuki DD | .10 | .30 |
| ❑ 481 | Brian Banks DD | .10 | .30 |
| ❑ 482 | Desi Wilson DD | .10 | .30 |
| ❑ 483 | Einar Diaz DD | .10 | .30 |
| ❑ 484 | Tom Pagnozzi | .10 | .30 |
| ❑ 485 | Ray Lankford | .10 | .30 |
| ❑ 486 | Todd Stottlemyre | .10 | .30 |
| ❑ 487 | Donovan Osborne | .10 | .30 |
| ❑ 488 | Trevor Hoffman | .10 | .30 |
| ❑ 489 | Chris Gomez | .10 | .30 |
| ❑ 490 | Ken Caminiti | .10 | .30 |
| ❑ 491 | John Flaherty | .10 | .30 |
| ❑ 492 | Tony Gwynn | .40 | 1.00 |
| ❑ 493 | Joey Hamilton | .10 | .30 |
| ❑ 494 | Rickey Henderson | .30 | .75 |
| ❑ 495 | Glenallen Hill | .10 | .30 |
| ❑ 496 | Rod Beck | .10 | .30 |
| ❑ 497 | Osvaldo Fernandez | .10 | .30 |
| ❑ 498 | Rick Wilkins | .10 | .30 |
| ❑ 499 | Joey Cora | .10 | .30 |
| ❑ 500 | Alex Gonzalez | .50 | 1.25 |
| ❑ 501 | Randy Johnson | .30 | .75 |
| ❑ 502 | Paul Sorrento | .10 | .30 |
| ❑ 503 | Dan Wilson | .10 | .30 |
| ❑ 504 | Jamie Moyer | .10 | .30 |
| ❑ 505 | Will Clark | .20 | .50 |
| ❑ 506 | Mickey Tettleton | .10 | .30 |
| ❑ 507 | John Burkett | .10 | .30 |
| ❑ 508 | Ken Hill | .10 | .30 |
| ❑ 509 | Mark McLemore | .10 | .30 |
| ❑ 510 | Juan Gonzalez | .30 | .75 |
| ❑ 511 | Bobby Witt | .10 | .30 |
| ❑ 512 | Carlos Delgado | .10 | .30 |
| ❑ 513 | Alex Gonzalez | .10 | .30 |
| ❑ 514 | Shawn Green | .10 | .30 |
| ❑ 515 | Joe Carter | .10 | .30 |
| ❑ 516 | Juan Guzman | .10 | .30 |
| ❑ 517 | Charlie O'Brien | .10 | .30 |
| ❑ 518 | Ed Sprague | .10 | .30 |
| ❑ 519 | Mike Timlin | .10 | .30 |
| ❑ 520 | Roger Clemens | .60 | 1.50 |
| ❑ 521 | Eddie Murray TRADE | .75 | 2.00 |
| ❑ 522 | Jason Dickson TRADE | .20 | .50 |
| ❑ 523 | Jim Leyritz TRADE | .20 | .50 |
| ❑ 524 | Michael Tucker TRADE | .20 | .50 |
| ❑ 525 | Kenny Lofton TRADE | .30 | .75 |
| ❑ 526 | Jimmy Key TRADE | .20 | .50 |
| ❑ 527 | Mel Rojas TRADE | .20 | .50 |
| ❑ 528 | Deion Sanders TRADE | .50 | 1.25 |
| ❑ 529 | Bartolo Colon TRADE | .30 | .75 |
| ❑ 530 | Matt Williams TRADE | .30 | .75 |
| ❑ 531 | Marquis Grissom TRADE | .30 | .75 |
| ❑ 532 | David Justice TRADE | .30 | .75 |
| ❑ 533 | Bubba Trammell TRADE | .30 | .75 |
| ❑ 534 | Moises Alou TRADE | .30 | .75 |
| ❑ 535 | Bobby Bonilla TRADE | .30 | .75 |
| ❑ 536 | Alex Fernandez TRADE | .20 | .50 |
| ❑ 537 | Jay Bell TRADE | .30 | .75 |
| ❑ 538 | Chili Davis TRADE | .30 | .75 |
| ❑ 539 | Jeff King TRADE | .20 | .50 |
| ❑ 540 | Todd Zeile TRADE | .20 | .50 |
| ❑ 541 | John Olerud TRADE | .30 | .75 |
| ❑ 542 | Jose Guillen TRADE | .30 | .75 |
| ❑ 543 | Derrek Lee TRADE | .50 | 1.25 |
| ❑ 544 | Dante Powell TRADE | .20 | .50 |
| ❑ 545 | J.T. Snow TRADE | .30 | .75 |
| ❑ 546 | Jeff Kent TRADE | .30 | .75 |
| ❑ 547 | Jose Cruz Jr. TRADE | .30 | .75 |
| ❑ 548 | John Wetteland TRADE | .30 | .75 |
| ❑ 549 | Orlando Merced TRADE | .20 | .50 |
| ❑ 550 | Hideki Irabu TRADE | .30 | .75 |

**1998 Upper Deck**

| | | |
|---|---|---|
| ❑ COMPLETE SET (751) | 80.00 | 200.00 |
| ❑ COMPLETE SERIES 1 (270) | 15.00 | 40.00 |
| ❑ COMPLETE SERIES 2 (270) | 15.00 | 40.00 |
| ❑ COMPLETE SERIES 3 (211) | 50.00 | 120.00 |
| ❑ COMMON (1-600/631-750) | .10 | .30 |
| ❑ COMMON EP (601-630) | .75 | 2.00 |
| ❑ EP SER.2 ODDS APPROXIMATELY 1:4 | | |

|  |  | | |
|---|------|---|---|
| ❑ 1 | Tino Martinez HIST | .10 | .30 |
| ❑ 2 | Jimmy Key HIST | .10 | .30 |
| ❑ 3 | Jay Buhner HIST | .10 | .30 |
| ❑ 4 | Mark Gardner HIST | .10 | .30 |
| ❑ 5 | Greg Maddux HIST | .30 | .75 |
| ❑ 6 | Pedro Martinez HIST | .20 | .50 |
| ❑ 7 | Hideo Nomo HIST | .20 | .50 |
| ❑ 8 | Sammy Sosa HIST | .40 | 1.00 |
| ❑ 9 | Mark McGwire GHL | .40 | 1.00 |
| ❑ 10 | Ken Griffey Jr. GHL | .50 | 1.25 |
| ❑ 11 | Larry Walker GHL | .10 | .30 |
| ❑ 12 | Tino Martinez GHL | .10 | .30 |
| ❑ 13 | Mike Piazza GHL | .30 | .75 |
| ❑ 14 | Jose Cruz Jr. GHL | .10 | .30 |
| ❑ 15 | Tony Gwynn GHL | .30 | .75 |
| ❑ 16 | Greg Maddux GHL | .30 | .75 |
| ❑ 17 | Roger Clemens GHL | .30 | .75 |
| ❑ 18 | Alex Rodriguez GHL | .30 | .75 |
| ❑ 19 | Shigetoshi Hasegawa | .10 | .30 |
| ❑ 20 | Eddie Murray | .30 | .75 |
| ❑ 21 | Jason Dickson | .10 | .30 |
| ❑ 22 | Darin Erstad | .10 | .30 |
| ❑ 23 | Chuck Finley | .10 | .30 |
| ❑ 24 | Dave Hollins | .10 | .30 |
| ❑ 25 | Garret Anderson | .10 | .30 |
| ❑ 26 | Michael Tucker | .10 | .30 |
| ❑ 27 | Kenny Lofton | .20 | .50 |
| ❑ 28 | Javier Lopez | .10 | .30 |
| ❑ 29 | Fred McGriff | .20 | .50 |
| ❑ 30 | Greg Maddux | .50 | 1.25 |
| ❑ 31 | Jeff Blauser | .10 | .30 |
| ❑ 32 | John Smoltz | .20 | .50 |
| ❑ 33 | Mark Wohlers | .10 | .30 |
| ❑ 34 | Scott Erickson | .10 | .30 |
| ❑ 35 | Jimmy Key | .10 | .30 |
| ❑ 36 | Harold Baines | .10 | .30 |
| ❑ 37 | Randy Myers | .10 | .30 |
| ❑ 38 | B.J. Surhoff | .10 | .30 |
| ❑ 39 | Eric Davis | .10 | .30 |
| ❑ 40 | Rafael Palmeiro | .20 | .50 |
| ❑ 41 | Jeffrey Hammonds | .10 | .30 |
| ❑ 42 | Mo Vaughn | .20 | .50 |
| ❑ 43 | Tom Gordon | .10 | .30 |
| ❑ 44 | Tim Naehring | .10 | .30 |
| ❑ 45 | Darren Bragg | .10 | .30 |
| ❑ 46 | Aaron Sele | .10 | .30 |
| ❑ 47 | Troy O'Leary | .10 | .30 |
| ❑ 48 | John Valentin | .10 | .30 |
| ❑ 49 | Doug Glanville | .10 | .30 |
| ❑ 50 | Ryne Sandberg | .50 | 1.25 |
| ❑ 51 | Steve Trachsel | .10 | .30 |
| ❑ 52 | Mark Grace | .20 | .50 |
| ❑ 53 | Kevin Foster | .10 | .30 |
| ❑ 54 | Kevin Tapani | .10 | .30 |
| ❑ 55 | Kevin Orie | .10 | .30 |
| ❑ 56 | Lyle Mouton | .10 | .30 |
| ❑ 57 | Ray Durham | .10 | .30 |
| ❑ 58 | Jaime Navarro | .10 | .30 |
| ❑ 59 | Mike Cameron | .10 | .30 |
| ❑ 60 | Albert Belle | .10 | .30 |
| ❑ 61 | Doug Drabek | .10 | .30 |
| ❑ 62 | Chris Snopek | .10 | .30 |
| ❑ 63 | Eddie Taubensee | .10 | .30 |
| ❑ 64 | Terry Pendleton | .10 | .30 |
| ❑ 65 | Barry Larkin | .20 | .50 |
| ❑ 66 | Willie Greene | .10 | .30 |
| ❑ 67 | Deion Sanders | .20 | .50 |
| ❑ 68 | Pokey Reese | .10 | .30 |
| ❑ 69 | Jeff Shaw | .10 | .30 |
| ❑ 70 | Jim Thome | .20 | .50 |
| ❑ 71 | Orel Hershiser | .10 | .30 |
| ❑ 72 | Omar Vizquel | .20 | .50 |
| ❑ 73 | Brian Giles | .10 | .30 |
| ❑ 74 | David Justice | .10 | .30 |
| ❑ 75 | Bartolo Colon | .10 | .30 |
| ❑ 76 | Sandy Alomar Jr. | .10 | .30 |
| ❑ 77 | Nefi Perez | .10 | .30 |
| ❑ 78 | Dante Bichette | .10 | .30 |
| ❑ 79 | Vinny Castilla | .10 | .30 |
| ❑ 80 | Eric Young | .10 | .30 |
| ❑ 81 | Quinton McCracken | .10 | .30 |
| ❑ 82 | Jamey Wright | .10 | .30 |
| ❑ 83 | John Thomson | .10 | .30 |
| ❑ 84 | Damion Easley | .10 | .30 |
| ❑ 85 | Justin Thompson | .10 | .30 |
| ❑ 86 | Willie Blair | .10 | .30 |
| ❑ 87 | Raul Casanova | .10 | .30 |
| ❑ 88 | Bobby Higginson | .10 | .30 |
| ❑ 89 | Bubba Trammell | .10 | .30 |
| ❑ 90 | Tony Clark | .10 | .30 |
| ❑ 91 | Livan Hernandez | .10 | .30 |
| ❑ 92 | Charles Johnson | .10 | .30 |
| ❑ 93 | Edgar Renteria | .10 | .30 |
| ❑ 94 | Alex Fernandez | .10 | .30 |
| ❑ 95 | Gary Sheffield | .10 | .30 |
| ❑ 96 | Moises Alou | .10 | .30 |
| ❑ 97 | Tony Saunders | .10 | .30 |
| ❑ 98 | Robb Nen | .10 | .30 |
| ❑ 99 | Darryl Kile | .10 | .30 |
| ❑ 100 | Craig Biggio | .20 | .50 |
| ❑ 101 | Chris Holt | .10 | .30 |
| ❑ 102 | Bob Abreu | .10 | .30 |
| ❑ 103 | Luis Gonzalez | .10 | .30 |
| ❑ 104 | Billy Wagner | .10 | .30 |
| ❑ 105 | Brad Ausmus | .10 | .30 |
| ❑ 106 | Chili Davis | .10 | .30 |
| ❑ 107 | Tim Belcher | .10 | .30 |
| ❑ 108 | Dean Palmer | .10 | .30 |
| ❑ 109 | Jeff King | .10 | .30 |
| ❑ 110 | Jose Rosado | .10 | .30 |
| ❑ 111 | Mike Macfarlane | .10 | .30 |
| ❑ 112 | Jay Bell | .10 | .30 |
| ❑ 113 | Todd Worrell | .10 | .30 |
| ❑ 114 | Chan Ho Park | .10 | .30 |
| ❑ 115 | Raul Mondesi | .10 | .30 |
| ❑ 116 | Brett Butler | .10 | .30 |
| ❑ 117 | Greg Gagne | .10 | .30 |
| ❑ 118 | Hideo Nomo | .30 | .75 |
| ❑ 119 | Todd Zeile | .10 | .30 |
| ❑ 120 | Eric Karros | .10 | .30 |
| ❑ 121 | Cal Eldred | .10 | .30 |
| ❑ 122 | Jeff D'Amico | .10 | .30 |
| ❑ 123 | Antone Williamson | .10 | .30 |
| ❑ 124 | Doug Jones | .10 | .30 |
| ❑ 125 | Dave Nilsson | .10 | .30 |
| ❑ 126 | Gerald Williams | .10 | .30 |
| ❑ 127 | Fernando Vina | .10 | .30 |
| ❑ 128 | Ron Coomer | .10 | .30 |
| ❑ 129 | Matt Lawton | .10 | .30 |
| ❑ 130 | Paul Molitor | .10 | .30 |
| ❑ 131 | Todd Walker | .10 | .30 |
| ❑ 132 | Rick Aguilera | .10 | .30 |
| ❑ 133 | Brad Radke | .10 | .30 |
| ❑ 134 | Bob Tewksbury | .10 | .30 |
| ❑ 135 | Vladimir Guerrero | .30 | .75 |
| ❑ 136 | Tony Gwynn DG | .20 | .50 |
| ❑ 137 | Roger Clemens DG | .30 | .75 |
| ❑ 138 | Dennis Eckersley DG | .10 | .30 |
| ❑ 139 | Brady Anderson DG | .10 | .30 |
| ❑ 140 | Ken Griffey Jr. DG | .30 | .75 |
| ❑ 141 | Derek Jeter DG | .40 | 1.00 |
| ❑ 142 | Ken Caminiti DG | .10 | .30 |
| ❑ 143 | Frank Thomas DG | .20 | .50 |
| ❑ 144 | Barry Bonds DG | .40 | 1.00 |
| ❑ 145 | Cal Ripken DG | .50 | 1.25 |
| ❑ 146 | Alex Rodriguez DG | .30 | .75 |

| | | |
|---|---|---|
| ❑ 147 Greg Maddux DG | .30 | .75 |
| ❑ 148 Kenny Lofton DG | .10 | .30 |
| ❑ 149 Mike Piazza DG | .30 | .75 |
| ❑ 150 Mark McGwire DG | .40 | 1.00 |
| ❑ 151 Andruw Jones DG | .10 | .30 |
| ❑ 152 Rusty Greer DG | .10 | .30 |
| ❑ 153 F.P. Santangelo DG | .10 | .30 |
| ❑ 154 Mike Lansing | .10 | .30 |
| ❑ 155 Lee Smith | .10 | .30 |
| ❑ 156 Carlos Perez | .10 | .30 |
| ❑ 157 Pedro Martinez | .20 | .50 |
| ❑ 158 Ryan McGuire | .10 | .30 |
| ❑ 159 F.P. Santangelo | .10 | .30 |
| ❑ 160 Rondell White | .10 | .30 |
| ❑ 161 Takashi Kashiwada RC | .15 | .40 |
| ❑ 162 Butch Huskey | .10 | .30 |
| ❑ 163 Edgardo Alfonzo | .10 | .30 |
| ❑ 164 John Franco | .10 | .30 |
| ❑ 165 Todd Hundley | .10 | .30 |
| ❑ 166 Rey Ordonez | .10 | .30 |
| ❑ 167 Armando Reynoso | .10 | .30 |
| ❑ 168 John Olerud | .10 | .30 |
| ❑ 169 Bernie Williams | .20 | .50 |
| ❑ 170 Andy Pettitte | .20 | .50 |
| ❑ 171 Wade Boggs | .20 | .50 |
| ❑ 172 Paul O'Neill | .20 | .50 |
| ❑ 173 Cecil Fielder | .10 | .30 |
| ❑ 174 Charlie Hayes | .10 | .30 |
| ❑ 175 David Cone | .10 | .30 |
| ❑ 176 Hideki Irabu | .10 | .30 |
| ❑ 177 Mark Bellhorn | .10 | .30 |
| ❑ 178 Steve Karsay | .10 | .30 |
| ❑ 179 Damon Mashore | .10 | .30 |
| ❑ 180 Jason McDonald | .10 | .30 |
| ❑ 181 Scott Spiezio | .10 | .30 |
| ❑ 182 Ariel Prieto | .10 | .30 |
| ❑ 183 Jason Giambi | .10 | .30 |
| ❑ 184 Wendell Magee | .10 | .30 |
| ❑ 185 Rico Brogna | .10 | .30 |
| ❑ 186 Garrett Stephenson | .10 | .30 |
| ❑ 187 Wayne Gomes | .10 | .30 |
| ❑ 188 Ricky Bottalico | .10 | .30 |
| ❑ 189 Mickey Morandini | .10 | .30 |
| ❑ 190 Mike Lieberthal | .10 | .30 |
| ❑ 191 Kevin Polcovich | .10 | .30 |
| ❑ 192 Francisco Cordova | .10 | .30 |
| ❑ 193 Kevin Young | .10 | .30 |
| ❑ 194 Jon Lieber | .10 | .30 |
| ❑ 195 Kevin Elster | .10 | .30 |
| ❑ 196 Tony Womack | .10 | .30 |
| ❑ 197 Lou Collier | .10 | .30 |
| ❑ 198 Mike Difelice RC | .15 | .40 |
| ❑ 199 Gary Gaetti | .10 | .30 |
| ❑ 200 Dennis Eckersley | .10 | .30 |
| ❑ 201 Alan Benes | .10 | .30 |
| ❑ 202 Willie McGee | .10 | .30 |
| ❑ 203 Ron Gant | .10 | .30 |
| ❑ 204 Fernando Valenzuela | .10 | .30 |
| ❑ 205 Mark McGwire | .75 | 2.00 |
| ❑ 206 Archi Cianfrocco | .10 | .30 |
| ❑ 207 Andy Ashby | .10 | .30 |
| ❑ 208 Steve Finley | .10 | .30 |
| ❑ 209 Quilvio Veras | .10 | .30 |
| ❑ 210 Ken Caminiti | .10 | .30 |
| ❑ 211 Rickey Henderson | .30 | .75 |
| ❑ 212 Joey Hamilton | .10 | .30 |
| ❑ 213 Derek Lee | .20 | .50 |
| ❑ 214 Bill Mueller | .10 | .30 |
| ❑ 215 Shawn Estes | .10 | .30 |
| ❑ 216 J.T. Snow | .10 | .30 |
| ❑ 217 Mark Gardner | .10 | .30 |
| ❑ 218 Terry Mulholland | .10 | .30 |
| ❑ 219 Dante Powell | .10 | .30 |
| ❑ 220 Jeff Kent | .10 | .30 |
| ❑ 221 Jamie Moyer | .10 | .30 |
| ❑ 222 Joey Cora | .10 | .30 |
| ❑ 223 Jeff Fassero | .10 | .30 |
| ❑ 224 Dennis Martinez | .10 | .30 |
| ❑ 225 Ken Griffey Jr. | .50 | 1.25 |
| ❑ 226 Edgar Martinez | .20 | .50 |
| ❑ 227 Russ Davis | .10 | .30 |
| ❑ 228 Dan Wilson | .10 | .30 |
| ❑ 229 Will Clark | .20 | .50 |
| ❑ 230 Ivan Rodriguez | .20 | .50 |
| ❑ 231 Benji Gil | .10 | .30 |
| ❑ 232 Lee Stevens | .10 | .30 |
| ❑ 233 Mickey Tettleton | .10 | .30 |
| ❑ 234 Julio Santana | .10 | .30 |

| | | |
|---|---|---|
| ❑ 235 Rusty Greer | .10 | .30 |
| ❑ 236 Bobby Witt | .10 | .30 |
| ❑ 237 Ed Sprague | .10 | .30 |
| ❑ 238 Pat Hentgen | .10 | .30 |
| ❑ 239 Kelvim Escobar | .10 | .30 |
| ❑ 240 Joe Carter | .10 | .30 |
| ❑ 241 Carlos Delgado | .10 | .30 |
| ❑ 242 Shannon Stewart | .10 | .30 |
| ❑ 243 Benito Santiago | .10 | .30 |
| ❑ 244 Tino Martinez SH | .10 | .30 |
| ❑ 245 Ken Griffey Jr. SH | .30 | .75 |
| ❑ 246 Kevin Brown SH | .10 | .30 |
| ❑ 247 Ryne Sandberg SH | .20 | .50 |
| ❑ 248 Mo Vaughn SH | .10 | .30 |
| ❑ 249 Darryl Hamilton SH | .10 | .30 |
| ❑ 250 Randy Johnson SH | .20 | .50 |
| ❑ 251 Steve Finley SH | .10 | .30 |
| ❑ 252 Bobby Higginson SH | .10 | .30 |
| ❑ 253 Brett Tomko | .10 | .30 |
| ❑ 254 Mark Kotsay | .10 | .30 |
| ❑ 255 Jose Guillen | .10 | .30 |
| ❑ 256 Eli Marrero | .10 | .30 |
| ❑ 257 Dennis Reyes | .10 | .30 |
| ❑ 258 Richie Sexson | .10 | .30 |
| ❑ 259 Pat Cline | .10 | .30 |
| ❑ 260 Todd Helton | .20 | .50 |
| ❑ 261 Juan Melo | .10 | .30 |
| ❑ 262 Matt Morris | .10 | .30 |
| ❑ 263 Jeremi Gonzalez | .10 | .30 |
| ❑ 264 Jeff Abbott | .10 | .30 |
| ❑ 265 Aaron Boone | .10 | .30 |
| ❑ 266 Todd Dunwoody | .10 | .30 |
| ❑ 267 Jaret Wright | .10 | .30 |
| ❑ 268 Derrick Gibson | .10 | .30 |
| ❑ 269 Mario Valdez | .10 | .30 |
| ❑ 270 Fernando Tatis | .10 | .30 |
| ❑ 271 Craig Counsell | .10 | .30 |
| ❑ 272 Brad Rigby | .10 | .30 |
| ❑ 273 Danny Clyburn | .10 | .30 |
| ❑ 274 Brian Rose | .10 | .30 |
| ❑ 275 Miguel Tejada | .30 | .75 |
| ❑ 276 Jason Varitek | .30 | .75 |
| ❑ 277 Dave Dellucci RC | .25 | .60 |
| ❑ 278 Michael Coleman | .10 | .30 |
| ❑ 279 Adam Riggs | .10 | .30 |
| ❑ 280 Ben Grieve | .10 | .30 |
| ❑ 281 Brad Fullmer | .10 | .30 |
| ❑ 282 Ken Cloude | .10 | .30 |
| ❑ 283 Tom Evans | .10 | .30 |
| ❑ 284 Kevin Millwood RC | .40 | 1.00 |
| ❑ 285 Paul Konerko | .10 | .30 |
| ❑ 286 Juan Encarnacion | .10 | .30 |
| ❑ 287 Chris Carpenter | .10 | .30 |
| ❑ 288 Tom Fordham | .10 | .30 |
| ❑ 289 Gary DiSarcina | .10 | .30 |
| ❑ 290 Tim Salmon | .20 | .50 |
| ❑ 291 Troy Percival | .10 | .30 |
| ❑ 292 Todd Greene | .10 | .30 |
| ❑ 293 Ken Hill | .10 | .30 |
| ❑ 294 Dennis Springer | .10 | .30 |
| ❑ 295 Jim Edmonds | .10 | .30 |
| ❑ 296 Allen Watson | .10 | .30 |
| ❑ 297 Brian Anderson | .10 | .30 |
| ❑ 298 Keith Lockhart | .10 | .30 |
| ❑ 299 Tom Glavine | .20 | .50 |
| ❑ 300 Chipper Jones | .30 | .75 |
| ❑ 301 Randall Simon | .10 | .30 |
| ❑ 302 Mark Lemke | .10 | .30 |
| ❑ 303 Ryan Klesko | .10 | .30 |
| ❑ 304 Denny Neagle | .10 | .30 |
| ❑ 305 Andruw Jones | .20 | .50 |
| ❑ 306 Mike Mussina | .20 | .50 |
| ❑ 307 Brady Anderson | .10 | .30 |
| ❑ 308 Chris Hoiles | .10 | .30 |
| ❑ 309 Mike Bordick | .10 | .30 |
| ❑ 310 Cal Ripken | 1.00 | 2.50 |
| ❑ 311 Geronimo Berroa | .10 | .30 |
| ❑ 312 Armando Benitez | .10 | .30 |
| ❑ 313 Roberto Alomar | .20 | .50 |
| ❑ 314 Tim Wakefield | .10 | .30 |
| ❑ 315 Reggie Jefferson | .10 | .30 |
| ❑ 316 Jeff Frye | .10 | .30 |
| ❑ 317 Scott Hatteberg | .10 | .30 |
| ❑ 318 Steve Avery | .10 | .30 |
| ❑ 319 Robinson Checo | .10 | .30 |
| ❑ 320 Nomar Garciaparra | .50 | 1.25 |
| ❑ 321 Lance Johnson | .10 | .30 |
| ❑ 322 Tyler Houston | .10 | .30 |

| | | |
|---|---|---|
| ❑ 323 Mark Clark | .10 | .30 |
| ❑ 324 Terry Adams | .10 | .30 |
| ❑ 325 Sammy Sosa | .30 | .75 |
| ❑ 326 Scott Servais | .10 | .30 |
| ❑ 327 Manny Alexander | .10 | .30 |
| ❑ 328 Norberto Martin | .10 | .30 |
| ❑ 329 Scott Eyre | .10 | .30 |
| ❑ 330 Frank Thomas | .30 | .75 |
| ❑ 331 Robin Ventura | .10 | .30 |
| ❑ 332 Matt Karchner | .10 | .30 |
| ❑ 333 Keith Foulke | .10 | .30 |
| ❑ 334 James Baldwin | .10 | .30 |
| ❑ 335 Chris Snopes | .10 | .30 |
| ❑ 336 Bret Boone | .10 | .30 |
| ❑ 337 Jon Nunnally | .10 | .30 |
| ❑ 338 Dave Burba | .10 | .30 |
| ❑ 339 Eduardo Perez | .10 | .30 |
| ❑ 340 Reggie Sanders | .10 | .30 |
| ❑ 341 Mike Remlinger | .10 | .30 |
| ❑ 342 Pat Watkins | .10 | .30 |
| ❑ 343 Chad Ogea | .10 | .30 |
| ❑ 344 John Smiley | .10 | .30 |
| ❑ 345 Kenny Lofton | .10 | .30 |
| ❑ 346 Jose Mesa | .10 | .30 |
| ❑ 347 Charles Nagy | .10 | .30 |
| ❑ 348 Enrique Wilson | .10 | .30 |
| ❑ 349 Bruce Aven | .10 | .30 |
| ❑ 350 Manny Ramirez | .20 | .50 |
| ❑ 351 Jerry DiPoto | .10 | .30 |
| ❑ 352 Ellis Burks | .10 | .30 |
| ❑ 353 Kirt Manwaring | .10 | .30 |
| ❑ 354 Vinny Castilla | .10 | .30 |
| ❑ 355 Larry Walker | .10 | .30 |
| ❑ 356 Kevin Ritz | .10 | .30 |
| ❑ 357 Pedro Astacio | .10 | .30 |
| ❑ 358 Scott Sanders | .10 | .30 |
| ❑ 359 Deivi Cruz | .10 | .30 |
| ❑ 360 Brian L. Hunter | .10 | .30 |
| ❑ 361 Pedro Martinez HM | .20 | .50 |
| ❑ 362 Tom Glavine HM | .10 | .30 |
| ❑ 363 Willie McGee HM | .10 | .30 |
| ❑ 364 J.T. Snow HM | .10 | .30 |
| ❑ 365 Rusty Greer HM | .10 | .30 |
| ❑ 366 Mike Grace HM | .10 | .30 |
| ❑ 367 Tony Clark HM | .10 | .30 |
| ❑ 368 Ben Grieve HM | .10 | .30 |
| ❑ 369 Gary Sheffield HM | .10 | .30 |
| ❑ 370 Joe Oliver | .10 | .30 |
| ❑ 371 Todd Jones | .10 | .30 |
| ❑ 372 Frank Catalanotto RC | .25 | .60 |
| ❑ 373 Brian Moehler | .10 | .30 |
| ❑ 374 Cliff Floyd | .10 | .30 |
| ❑ 375 Bobby Bonilla | .10 | .30 |
| ❑ 376 Al Leiter | .10 | .30 |
| ❑ 377 Josh Booty | .10 | .30 |
| ❑ 378 Darren Daulton | .10 | .30 |
| ❑ 379 Jay Powell | .10 | .30 |
| ❑ 380 Felix Heredia | .10 | .30 |
| ❑ 381 Jim Eisenreich | .10 | .30 |
| ❑ 382 Richard Hidalgo | .10 | .30 |
| ❑ 383 Mike Hampton | .10 | .30 |
| ❑ 384 Shane Reynolds | .10 | .30 |
| ❑ 385 Jeff Bagwell | .20 | .50 |
| ❑ 386 Derek Bell | .10 | .30 |
| ❑ 387 Ricky Gutierrez | .10 | .30 |
| ❑ 388 Bill Spiers | .10 | .30 |
| ❑ 389 Jose Offerman | .10 | .30 |
| ❑ 390 Johnny Damon | .20 | .50 |
| ❑ 391 Jermaine Dye | .10 | .30 |
| ❑ 392 Jeff Montgomery | .10 | .30 |
| ❑ 393 Glendon Rusch | .10 | .30 |
| ❑ 394 Mike Sweeney | .10 | .30 |
| ❑ 395 Kevin Appier | .10 | .30 |
| ❑ 396 Joe Vitiello | .10 | .30 |
| ❑ 397 Ramon Martinez | .10 | .30 |
| ❑ 398 Darren Dreifort | .10 | .30 |
| ❑ 399 Wilton Guerrero | .10 | .30 |
| ❑ 400 Mike Piazza | .50 | 1.25 |
| ❑ 401 Eddie Murray | .30 | .75 |
| ❑ 402 Ismael Valdes | .10 | .30 |
| ❑ 403 Todd Hollandsworth | .10 | .30 |
| ❑ 404 Mark Loretta | .10 | .30 |
| ❑ 405 Jeromy Burnitz | .10 | .30 |
| ❑ 406 Jeff Cirillo | .10 | .30 |
| ❑ 407 Scott Karl | .10 | .30 |
| ❑ 408 Mike Matheny | .10 | .30 |
| ❑ 409 Jose Valentin | .10 | .30 |
| ❑ 410 John Jaha | .10 | .30 |

|  |  | | |
|---|---|---|---|
| 411 | Terry Steinbach | .10 | .30 |
| 412 | Torii Hunter | .10 | .30 |
| 413 | Pat Meares | .10 | .30 |
| 414 | Marty Cordova | .10 | .30 |
| 415 | Jaret Wright PH | .10 | .30 |
| 416 | Mike Mussina PH | .10 | .30 |
| 417 | John Smoltz PH | .10 | .30 |
| 418 | Devon White PH | .10 | .30 |
| 419 | Denny Neagle PH | .10 | .30 |
| 420 | Livan Hernandez PH | .10 | .30 |
| 421 | Kevin Brown PH | .10 | .30 |
| 422 | Marquis Grissom PH | .10 | .30 |
| 423 | Mike Mussina PH | .10 | .30 |
| 424 | Eric Davis PH | .10 | .30 |
| 425 | Tony Fernandez PH | .10 | .30 |
| 426 | Moises Alou PH | .10 | .30 |
| 427 | Sandy Alomar Jr. PH | .10 | .30 |
| 428 | Gary Sheffield PH | .10 | .30 |
| 429 | Jaret Wright PH | .10 | .30 |
| 430 | Livan Hernandez PH | .10 | .30 |
| 431 | Chad Ogea PH | .10 | .30 |
| 432 | Edgar Renteria PH | .10 | .30 |
| 433 | LaTroy Hawkins | .10 | .30 |
| 434 | Rich Robertson | .10 | .30 |
| 435 | Chuck Knoblauch | .10 | .30 |
| 436 | Jose Vidro | .10 | .30 |
| 437 | Dustin Hermanson | .10 | .30 |
| 438 | Jim Bullinger | .10 | .30 |
| 439 | Orlando Cabrera | .10 | .30 |
| 440 | Vladimir Guerrero | .30 | .75 |
| 441 | Ugueth Urbina | .30 | .75 |
| 442 | Brian McRae | .10 | .30 |
| 443 | Matt Franco | .10 | .30 |
| 444 | Bobby Jones | .10 | .30 |
| 445 | Bernard Gilkey | .10 | .30 |
| 446 | Dave Mlicki | .10 | .30 |
| 447 | Brian Bohanon | .10 | .30 |
| 448 | Mel Rojas | .10 | .30 |
| 449 | Tim Raines | .10 | .30 |
| 450 | Derek Jeter | .75 | 2.00 |
| 451 | Roger Clemens UE | .30 | .75 |
| 452 | Nomar Garciaparra UE | .30 | .75 |
| 453 | Mike Piazza UE | .30 | .75 |
| 454 | Mark McGwire UE | .40 | 1.00 |
| 455 | Ken Griffey Jr. UE | .30 | .75 |
| 456 | Larry Walker UE | .10 | .30 |
| 457 | Alex Rodriguez UE | .30 | .75 |
| 458 | Tony Gwynn UE | .20 | .50 |
| 459 | Frank Thomas UE | .20 | .50 |
| 460 | Tino Martinez UE | .20 | .50 |
| 461 | Chad Curtis | .10 | .30 |
| 462 | Ramiro Mendoza | .10 | .30 |
| 463 | Joe Girardi | .10 | .30 |
| 464 | David Wells | .10 | .30 |
| 465 | Mariano Rivera | .30 | .75 |
| 466 | Willie Adams | .10 | .30 |
| 467 | George Williams | .10 | .30 |
| 468 | Dave Telgheder | .10 | .30 |
| 469 | Dave Magadan | .10 | .30 |
| 470 | Matt Stairs | .10 | .30 |
| 471 | Bill Taylor | .10 | .30 |
| 472 | Jimmy Haynes | .10 | .30 |
| 473 | Gregg Jefferies | .10 | .30 |
| 474 | Midre Cummings | .10 | .30 |
| 475 | Curt Schilling | .10 | .30 |
| 476 | Mike Grace | .10 | .30 |
| 477 | Mark Leiter | .10 | .30 |
| 478 | Matt Beech | .10 | .30 |
| 479 | Scott Rolen | .20 | .50 |
| 480 | Jason Kendall | .10 | .30 |
| 481 | Esteban Loaiza | .10 | .30 |
| 482 | Jermaine Allensworth | .10 | .30 |
| 483 | Mark Smith | .10 | .30 |
| 484 | Jason Schmidt | .10 | .30 |
| 485 | Jose Guillen | .10 | .30 |
| 486 | Al Martin | .10 | .30 |
| 487 | Delino DeShields | .10 | .30 |
| 488 | Todd Stottlemyre | .10 | .30 |
| 489 | Brian Jordan | .10 | .30 |
| 490 | Ray Lankford | .10 | .30 |
| 491 | Matt Morris | .10 | .30 |
| 492 | Royce Clayton | .10 | .30 |
| 493 | John Mabry | .10 | .30 |
| 494 | Wally Joyner | .10 | .30 |
| 495 | Trevor Hoffman | .10 | .30 |
| 496 | Chris Gomez | .10 | .30 |
| 497 | Sterling Hitchcock | .10 | .30 |
| 498 | Pete Smith | .10 | .30 |
| 499 | Greg Vaughn | .10 | .30 |
| 500 | Tony Gwynn | .40 | 1.00 |
| 501 | Will Cunnane | .10 | .30 |
| 502 | Darryl Hamilton | .10 | .30 |
| 503 | Brian Johnson | .10 | .30 |
| 504 | Kirk Rueter | .10 | .30 |
| 505 | Barry Bonds | .75 | 2.00 |
| 506 | Osvaldo Fernandez | .10 | .30 |
| 507 | Stan Javier | .10 | .30 |
| 508 | Julian Tavarez | .10 | .30 |
| 509 | Rich Aurilia | .10 | .30 |
| 510 | Alex Rodriguez | .50 | 1.25 |
| 511 | David Segui | .10 | .30 |
| 512 | Rich Amaral | .10 | .30 |
| 513 | Raul Ibanez | .10 | .30 |
| 514 | Jay Buhner | .10 | .30 |
| 515 | Randy Johnson | .30 | .75 |
| 516 | Heathcliff Slocumb | .10 | .30 |
| 517 | Tony Saunders | .10 | .30 |
| 518 | Kevin Elster | .10 | .30 |
| 519 | John Burkett | .10 | .30 |
| 520 | Juan Gonzalez | .30 | .75 |
| 521 | John Wetteland | .10 | .30 |
| 522 | Domingo Cedeno | .10 | .30 |
| 523 | Darren Oliver | .10 | .30 |
| 524 | Roger Pavlik | .10 | .30 |
| 525 | Jose Cruz Jr. | .30 | .75 |
| 526 | Woody Williams | .10 | .30 |
| 527 | Alex Gonzalez | .10 | .30 |
| 528 | Robert Person | .10 | .30 |
| 529 | Juan Guzman | .10 | .30 |
| 530 | Roger Clemens | .60 | 1.50 |
| 531 | Shawn Green | .30 | .75 |
| 532 | F.Cordova/R.Rincon/M.Smith SH | .10 | .30 |
| 533 | Nomar Garciaparra SH | .30 | .75 |
| 534 | Roger Clemens SH | .30 | .75 |
| 535 | Mark McGwire SH | .40 | 1.00 |
| 536 | Larry Walker SH | .10 | .30 |
| 537 | Mike Piazza SH | .30 | .75 |
| 538 | Curt Schilling SH | .10 | .30 |
| 539 | Tony Gwynn SH | .20 | .50 |
| 540 | Ken Griffey Jr. SH | .30 | .75 |
| 541 | Carl Pavano | .10 | .30 |
| 542 | Shane Monahan | .10 | .30 |
| 543 | Gabe Kapler RC | .25 | .60 |
| 544 | Eric Milton | .10 | .30 |
| 545 | Gary Matthews Jr. RC | .25 | .60 |
| 546 | Mike Kinkade RC | .10 | .30 |
| 547 | Ryan Christenson RC | .10 | .30 |
| 548 | Corey Koskie RC | .25 | .60 |
| 549 | Norm Hutchins | .10 | .30 |
| 550 | Russell Branyan | .10 | .30 |
| 551 | Masato Yoshii RC | .15 | .40 |
| 552 | Jesus Sanchez RC | .10 | .30 |
| 553 | Anthony Sanders | .10 | .30 |
| 554 | Edwin Diaz | .10 | .30 |
| 555 | Gabe Alvarez | .10 | .30 |
| 556 | Carlos Lee RC | .75 | 2.00 |
| 557 | Mike Darr | .10 | .30 |
| 558 | Kerry Wood | .15 | .40 |
| 559 | Carlos Guillen | .10 | .30 |
| 560 | Sean Casey | .10 | .30 |
| 561 | Manny Aybar RC | .10 | .30 |
| 562 | Octavio Dotel | .10 | .30 |
| 563 | Jarrod Washburn | .10 | .30 |
| 564 | Mark L. Johnson | .10 | .30 |
| 565 | Ramon Hernandez | .10 | .30 |
| 566 | Rich Butler RC | .10 | .30 |
| 567 | Mike Caruso | .10 | .30 |
| 568 | Cliff Politte | .10 | .30 |
| 569 | Scott Elarton | .10 | .30 |
| 570 | Magglio Ordonez RC | 1.25 | 3.00 |
| 571 | Adam Butler RC | .10 | .30 |
| 572 | Marlon Anderson | .10 | .30 |
| 573 | Julio Ramirez RC | .10 | .30 |
| 574 | Damon Ingram RC | .10 | .30 |
| 575 | Bruce Chen | .10 | .30 |
| 576 | Steve Woodard | .10 | .30 |
| 577 | Hiram Bocachica | .10 | .30 |
| 578 | Kevin Witt | .10 | .30 |
| 579 | Javier Vazquez | .10 | .30 |
| 580 | Alex Gonzalez | .10 | .30 |
| 581 | Brian Powell | .10 | .30 |
| 582 | Wes Helms | .10 | .30 |
| 583 | Ron Wright | .10 | .30 |
| 584 | Rafael Medina | .10 | .30 |
| 585 | Daryle Ward | .10 | .30 |
| 586 | Geoff Jenkins | .10 | .30 |
| 587 | Preston Wilson | .10 | .30 |
| 588 | Jim Chamblee RC | .10 | .30 |
| 589 | Mike Lowell RC | .60 | 1.50 |
| 590 | A.J. Hinch | .10 | .30 |
| 591 | Francisco Cordero RC | .25 | .60 |
| 592 | Rolando Arrojo RC | .15 | .40 |
| 593 | Braden Looper | .10 | .30 |
| 594 | Sidney Ponson | .10 | .30 |
| 595 | Matt Clement | .10 | .30 |
| 596 | Carlton Loewer | .10 | .30 |
| 597 | Brian Meadows | .10 | .30 |
| 598 | Danny Klassen | .10 | .30 |
| 599 | Larry Sutton | .10 | .30 |
| 600 | Travis Lee | .10 | .30 |
| 601 | Randy Johnson EP | 1.00 | 2.50 |
| 602 | Greg Maddux EP | 1.50 | 4.00 |
| 603 | Roger Clemens EP | 2.00 | 5.00 |
| 604 | Jaret Wright EP | .75 | 2.00 |
| 605 | Mike Piazza EP | 1.50 | 4.00 |
| 606 | Tino Martinez EP | .75 | 2.00 |
| 607 | Frank Thomas EP | 1.00 | 2.50 |
| 608 | Mo Vaughn EP | .75 | 2.00 |
| 609 | Todd Helton EP | .75 | 2.00 |
| 610 | Mark McGwire EP | 2.50 | 6.00 |
| 611 | Jeff Bagwell EP | .75 | 2.00 |
| 612 | Travis Lee EP | .75 | 2.00 |
| 613 | Scott Rolen EP | .75 | 2.00 |
| 614 | Cal Ripken EP | 3.00 | 8.00 |
| 615 | Chipper Jones EP | 1.00 | 2.50 |
| 616 | Nomar Garciaparra EP | 1.50 | 4.00 |
| 617 | Alex Rodriguez EP | 1.50 | 4.00 |
| 618 | Derek Jeter EP | 2.50 | 6.00 |
| 619 | Tony Gwynn EP | 1.25 | 3.00 |
| 620 | Ken Griffey Jr. EP | 1.50 | 4.00 |
| 621 | Kenny Lofton EP | .75 | 2.00 |
| 622 | Juan Gonzalez EP | .75 | 2.00 |
| 623 | Jose Cruz Jr. EP | .75 | 2.00 |
| 624 | Larry Walker EP | .75 | 2.00 |
| 625 | Barry Bonds EP | 2.50 | 6.00 |
| 626 | Ben Grieve EP | .75 | 2.00 |
| 627 | Andruw Jones EP | .75 | 2.00 |
| 628 | Vladimir Guerrero EP | 1.00 | 2.50 |
| 629 | Paul Konerko EP | .75 | 2.00 |
| 630 | Paul Molitor EP | .75 | 2.00 |
| 631 | Cecil Fielder | .10 | .30 |
| 632 | Jack McDowell | .10 | .30 |
| 633 | Mike James | .10 | .30 |
| 634 | Brian Anderson | .10 | .30 |
| 635 | Jay Bell | .10 | .30 |
| 636 | Devon White | .10 | .30 |
| 637 | Andy Stankiewicz | .10 | .30 |
| 638 | Tony Batista | .10 | .30 |
| 639 | Omar Daal | .10 | .30 |
| 640 | Matt Williams | .10 | .30 |
| 641 | Brent Brede | .10 | .30 |
| 642 | Jorge Fabregas | .10 | .30 |
| 643 | Karim Garcia | .10 | .30 |
| 644 | Felix Rodriguez | .10 | .30 |
| 645 | Andy Benes | .10 | .30 |
| 646 | Willie Blair | .10 | .30 |
| 647 | Jeff Suppan | .10 | .30 |
| 648 | Yamil Benitez | .10 | .30 |
| 649 | Walt Weiss | .10 | .30 |
| 650 | Andres Galarraga | .10 | .30 |
| 651 | Doug Drabek | .10 | .30 |
| 652 | Ozzie Guillen | .10 | .30 |
| 653 | Joe Carter | .10 | .30 |
| 654 | Dennis Eckersley | .10 | .30 |
| 655 | Pedro Martinez | .20 | .50 |
| 656 | Jim Leyritz | .10 | .30 |
| 657 | Henry Rodriguez | .10 | .30 |
| 658 | Rod Beck | .10 | .30 |
| 659 | Mickey Morandini | .10 | .30 |
| 660 | Jeff Blauser | .10 | .30 |
| 661 | Ruben Sierra | .10 | .30 |
| 662 | Mike Sirotka | .10 | .30 |
| 663 | Pete Harnisch | .10 | .30 |
| 664 | Damian Jackson | .10 | .30 |
| 665 | Dmitri Young | .10 | .30 |
| 666 | Steve Cooke | .10 | .30 |
| 667 | Geronimo Berroa | .10 | .30 |
| 668 | Shawon Dunston | .10 | .30 |
| 669 | Mike Jackson | .10 | .30 |
| 670 | Travis Fryman | .10 | .30 |
| 671 | Dwight Gooden | .10 | .30 |
| 672 | Paul Assenmacher | .10 | .30 |
| 673 | Eric Plunk | .10 | .30 |
| 674 | Mike Lansing | .10 | .30 |

| | | |
|---|---|---|
| ❏ 675 Darryl Kile | .10 | .30 |
| ❏ 676 Luis Gonzalez | .10 | .30 |
| ❏ 677 Frank Castillo | .10 | .30 |
| ❏ 678 Joe Randa | .10 | .30 |
| ❏ 679 Bip Roberts | .10 | .30 |
| ❏ 680 Derrek Lee | .20 | .50 |
| ❏ 681 M.Piazza Mets SP | 1.25 | 3.00 |
| ❏ 681A M.Piazza Marlins SP | 1.25 | 3.00 |
| ❏ 682 Sean Berry | .10 | .30 |
| ❏ 683 Ramon Garcia | .10 | .30 |
| ❏ 684 Carl Everett | .10 | .30 |
| ❏ 685 Moises Alou | .10 | .30 |
| ❏ 686 Hal Morris | .10 | .30 |
| ❏ 687 Jeff Conine | .10 | .30 |
| ❏ 688 Gary Sheffield | .10 | .30 |
| ❏ 689 Jose Vizcaino | .10 | .30 |
| ❏ 690 Charles Johnson | .10 | .30 |
| ❏ 691 Bobby Bonilla | .10 | .30 |
| ❏ 692 Marquis Grissom | .10 | .30 |
| ❏ 693 Alex Ochoa | .10 | .30 |
| ❏ 694 Mike Morgan | .10 | .30 |
| ❏ 695 Orlando Merced | .10 | .30 |
| ❏ 696 David Ortiz | .40 | 1.00 |
| ❏ 697 Brent Gates | .10 | .30 |
| ❏ 698 Otis Nixon | .10 | .30 |
| ❏ 699 Trey Moore | .10 | .30 |
| ❏ 700 Derrick May | .10 | .30 |
| ❏ 701 Rich Becker | .10 | .30 |
| ❏ 702 Al Leiter | .10 | .30 |
| ❏ 703 Chili Davis | .10 | .30 |
| ❏ 704 Scott Brosius | .10 | .30 |
| ❏ 705 Chuck Knoblauch | .10 | .30 |
| ❏ 706 Kenny Rogers | .10 | .30 |
| ❏ 707 Mike Blowers | .10 | .30 |
| ❏ 708 Mike Fetters | .10 | .30 |
| ❏ 709 Tom Candiotti | .10 | .30 |
| ❏ 710 Rickey Henderson | .30 | .75 |
| ❏ 711 Bob Abreu | .10 | .30 |
| ❏ 712 Mark Lewis | .10 | .30 |
| ❏ 713 Doug Glanville | .10 | .30 |
| ❏ 714 Desi Relaford | .10 | .30 |
| ❏ 715 Kent Mercker | .10 | .30 |
| ❏ 716 Kevin Brown | .20 | .50 |
| ❏ 717 James Mouton | .10 | .30 |
| ❏ 718 Mark Langston | .10 | .30 |
| ❏ 719 Greg Myers | .10 | .30 |
| ❏ 720 Orel Hershiser | .10 | .30 |
| ❏ 721 Charlie Hayes | .10 | .30 |
| ❏ 722 Robb Nen | .10 | .30 |
| ❏ 723 Glenallen Hill | .10 | .30 |
| ❏ 724 Tony Saunders | .10 | .30 |
| ❏ 725 Wade Boggs | .20 | .50 |
| ❏ 726 Kevin Stocker | .10 | .30 |
| ❏ 727 Wilson Alvarez | .10 | .30 |
| ❏ 728 Albie Lopez | .10 | .30 |
| ❏ 729 Dave Martinez | .10 | .30 |
| ❏ 730 Fred McGriff | .20 | .50 |
| ❏ 731 Quinton McCracken | .10 | .30 |
| ❏ 732 Bryan Rekar | .10 | .30 |
| ❏ 733 Paul Sorrento | .10 | .30 |
| ❏ 734 Roberto Hernandez | .10 | .30 |
| ❏ 735 Bubba Trammell | .10 | .30 |
| ❏ 736 Miguel Cairo | .10 | .30 |
| ❏ 737 John Flaherty | .10 | .30 |
| ❏ 738 Terrell Wade | .10 | .30 |
| ❏ 739 Roberto Kelly | .10 | .30 |
| ❏ 740 Mark McLemore | .10 | .30 |
| ❏ 741 Danny Patterson | .10 | .30 |
| ❏ 742 Aaron Sele | .10 | .30 |
| ❏ 743 Tony Fernandez | .10 | .30 |
| ❏ 744 Randy Myers | .10 | .30 |
| ❏ 745 Jose Canseco | .20 | .50 |
| ❏ 746 Darrin Fletcher | .10 | .30 |
| ❏ 747 Mike Stanley | .10 | .30 |
| ❏ 748 Marquis Grissom SH CL | .10 | .30 |
| ❏ 749 Fred McGriff SH CL | .10 | .30 |
| ❏ 750 Travis Lee SH CL | .10 | .30 |

# 1999 Upper Deck

| | | |
|---|---|---|
| ❏ COMPLETE SET (525) | 50.00 | 100.00 |
| ❏ COMPLETE SERIES 1 (255) | 30.00 | 60.00 |
| ❏ COMPLETE SERIES 2 (270) | 20.00 | 40.00 |
| ❏ COMMON (19-255/293-535) | .10 | .30 |
| ❏ COMMON SER.1 SR (1-18) | .20 | .50 |
| ❏ COMMON SER.2 SR (266-292) | .20 | .50 |
| ❏ 1 Troy Glaus SR | .40 | 1.00 |
| ❏ 2 Adrian Beltre SR | .25 | .60 |
| ❏ 3 Matt Anderson SR | .20 | .50 |
| ❏ 4 Eric Chavez SR | .25 | .60 |
| ❏ 5 Jin Ho Cho SR | .20 | .50 |
| ❏ 6 Robert Smith SR | .20 | .50 |
| ❏ 7 George Lombard SR | .20 | .50 |
| ❏ 8 Mike Kinkade SR | .20 | .50 |
| ❏ 9 Seth Greisinger SR | .20 | .50 |
| ❏ 10 J.D. Drew SR | .25 | .60 |
| ❏ 11 Aramis Ramirez SR | .25 | .60 |
| ❏ 12 Carlos Guillen SR | .25 | .60 |
| ❏ 13 Justin Baughman SR | .20 | .50 |
| ❏ 14 Jim Parque SR | .20 | .50 |
| ❏ 15 Ryan Jackson SR | .20 | .50 |
| ❏ 16 Ramon E.Martinez SR RC | .20 | .50 |
| ❏ 17 Orlando Hernandez SR | .25 | .60 |
| ❏ 18 Jeremy Giambi SR | .20 | .50 |
| ❏ 19 Gary DiSarcina | .10 | .30 |
| ❏ 20 Darin Erstad | .10 | .30 |
| ❏ 21 Troy Glaus | .20 | .50 |
| ❏ 22 Chuck Finley | .10 | .30 |
| ❏ 23 Dave Hollins | .10 | .30 |
| ❏ 24 Troy Percival | .10 | .30 |
| ❏ 25 Tim Salmon | .20 | .50 |
| ❏ 26 Brian Anderson | .10 | .30 |
| ❏ 27 Jay Bell | .10 | .30 |
| ❏ 28 Andy Benes | .10 | .30 |
| ❏ 29 Brent Brede | .10 | .30 |
| ❏ 30 David Dellucci | .10 | .30 |
| ❏ 31 Karim Garcia | .10 | .30 |
| ❏ 32 Travis Lee | .10 | .30 |
| ❏ 33 Andres Galarraga | .10 | .30 |
| ❏ 34 Ryan Klesko | .10 | .30 |
| ❏ 35 Keith Lockhart | .10 | .30 |
| ❏ 36 Kevin Millwood | .10 | .30 |
| ❏ 37 Denny Neagle | .10 | .30 |
| ❏ 38 John Smoltz | .20 | .50 |
| ❏ 39 Michael Tucker | .10 | .30 |
| ❏ 40 Walt Weiss | .10 | .30 |
| ❏ 41 Dennis Martinez | .10 | .30 |
| ❏ 42 Javy Lopez | .10 | .30 |
| ❏ 43 Brady Anderson | .10 | .30 |
| ❏ 44 Harold Baines | .10 | .30 |
| ❏ 45 Mike Bordick | .10 | .30 |
| ❏ 46 Roberto Alomar | .20 | .50 |
| ❏ 47 Scott Erickson | .10 | .30 |
| ❏ 48 Mike Mussina | .20 | .50 |
| ❏ 49 Cal Ripken | 1.00 | 2.50 |
| ❏ 50 Darren Bragg | .10 | .30 |
| ❏ 51 Dennis Eckersley | .10 | .30 |
| ❏ 52 Nomar Garciaparra | .50 | 1.25 |
| ❏ 53 Scott Hatteberg | .10 | .30 |
| ❏ 54 Troy O'Leary | .10 | .30 |
| ❏ 55 Bret Saberhagen | .10 | .30 |
| ❏ 56 John Valentin | .10 | .30 |
| ❏ 57 Rod Beck | .10 | .30 |
| ❏ 58 Jeff Blauser | .10 | .30 |
| ❏ 59 Brant Brown | .10 | .30 |
| ❏ 60 Mark Clark | .10 | .30 |
| ❏ 61 Mark Grace | .20 | .50 |
| ❏ 62 Kevin Tapani | .10 | .30 |
| ❏ 63 Henry Rodriguez | .10 | .30 |
| ❏ 64 Mike Cameron | .10 | .30 |
| ❏ 65 Mike Caruso | .10 | .30 |
| ❏ 66 Ray Durham | .10 | .30 |

| | | |
|---|---|---|
| ❏ 67 Jaime Navarro | .10 | .30 |
| ❏ 68 Magglio Ordonez | .10 | .30 |
| ❏ 69 Mike Sirotka | .10 | .30 |
| ❏ 70 Sean Casey | .10 | .30 |
| ❏ 71 Barry Larkin | .20 | .50 |
| ❏ 72 Jon Nunnally | .10 | .30 |
| ❏ 73 Paul Konerko | .10 | .30 |
| ❏ 74 Chris Stynes | .10 | .30 |
| ❏ 75 Brett Tomko | .10 | .30 |
| ❏ 76 Dmitri Young | .10 | .30 |
| ❏ 77 Sandy Alomar Jr. | .10 | .30 |
| ❏ 78 Bartolo Colon | .10 | .30 |
| ❏ 79 Travis Fryman | .10 | .30 |
| ❏ 80 Brian Giles | .10 | .30 |
| ❏ 81 David Justice | .10 | .30 |
| ❏ 82 Omar Vizquel | .20 | .50 |
| ❏ 83 Jaret Wright | .10 | .30 |
| ❏ 84 Jim Thome | .20 | .50 |
| ❏ 85 Charles Nagy | .10 | .30 |
| ❏ 86 Pedro Astacio | .10 | .30 |
| ❏ 87 Todd Helton | .20 | .50 |
| ❏ 88 Darryl Kile | .10 | .30 |
| ❏ 89 Mike Lansing | .10 | .30 |
| ❏ 90 Neifi Perez | .10 | .30 |
| ❏ 91 John Thomson | .10 | .30 |
| ❏ 92 Larry Walker | .10 | .30 |
| ❏ 93 Tony Clark | .10 | .30 |
| ❏ 94 Deivi Cruz | .10 | .30 |
| ❏ 95 Damion Easley | .10 | .30 |
| ❏ 96 Brian L.Hunter | .10 | .30 |
| ❏ 97 Todd Jones | .10 | .30 |
| ❏ 98 Brian Moehler | .10 | .30 |
| ❏ 99 Gabe Alvarez | .10 | .30 |
| ❏ 100 Craig Counsell | .10 | .30 |
| ❏ 101 Cliff Floyd | .10 | .30 |
| ❏ 102 Livan Hernandez | .10 | .30 |
| ❏ 103 Andy Larkin | .10 | .30 |
| ❏ 104 Derrek Lee | .20 | .50 |
| ❏ 105 Brian Meadows | .10 | .30 |
| ❏ 106 Moises Alou | .10 | .30 |
| ❏ 107 Sean Berry | .10 | .30 |
| ❏ 108 Craig Biggio | .20 | .50 |
| ❏ 109 Ricky Gutierrez | .10 | .30 |
| ❏ 110 Mike Hampton | .10 | .30 |
| ❏ 111 Jose Lima | .10 | .30 |
| ❏ 112 Billy Wagner | .10 | .30 |
| ❏ 113 Hal Morris | .10 | .30 |
| ❏ 114 Johnny Damon | .20 | .50 |
| ❏ 115 Jeff King | .10 | .30 |
| ❏ 116 Jeff Montgomery | .10 | .30 |
| ❏ 117 Glendon Rusch | .10 | .30 |
| ❏ 118 Larry Sutton | .10 | .30 |
| ❏ 119 Bobby Bonilla | .10 | .30 |
| ❏ 120 Jim Eisenreich | .10 | .30 |
| ❏ 121 Eric Karros | .10 | .30 |
| ❏ 122 Matt Luke | .10 | .30 |
| ❏ 123 Ramon Martinez | .10 | .30 |
| ❏ 124 Gary Sheffield | .10 | .30 |
| ❏ 125 Eric Young | .10 | .30 |
| ❏ 126 Charles Johnson | .10 | .30 |
| ❏ 127 Jeff Cirillo | .10 | .30 |
| ❏ 128 Marquis Grissom | .10 | .30 |
| ❏ 129 Jeromy Burnitz | .10 | .30 |
| ❏ 130 Bob Wickman | .10 | .30 |
| ❏ 131 Scott Karl | .10 | .30 |
| ❏ 132 Mark Loretta | .10 | .30 |
| ❏ 133 Fernando Vina | .10 | .30 |
| ❏ 134 Matt Lawton | .10 | .30 |
| ❏ 135 Pat Meares | .10 | .30 |
| ❏ 136 Eric Milton | .10 | .30 |
| ❏ 137 Paul Molitor | .30 | .75 |
| ❏ 138 David Ortiz | .30 | .75 |
| ❏ 139 Todd Walker | .10 | .30 |
| ❏ 140 Shane Andrews | .10 | .30 |
| ❏ 141 Brad Fullmer | .10 | .30 |
| ❏ 142 Vladimir Guerrero | .30 | .75 |
| ❏ 143 Dustin Hermanson | .10 | .30 |
| ❏ 144 Ryan McGuire | .10 | .30 |
| ❏ 145 Ugueth Urbina | .10 | .30 |
| ❏ 146 John Franco | .10 | .30 |
| ❏ 147 Butch Huskey | .10 | .30 |
| ❏ 148 Bobby Jones | .10 | .30 |
| ❏ 149 John Olerud | .10 | .30 |
| ❏ 150 Rey Ordonez | .10 | .30 |
| ❏ 151 Mike Piazza | .50 | 1.25 |
| ❏ 152 Hideo Nomo | .30 | .75 |
| ❏ 153 Masato Yoshii | .10 | .30 |
| ❏ 154 Derek Jeter | .75 | 2.00 |

|  |  | | |
|---|---|---|---|
| 155 | Chuck Knoblauch | .10 | .30 |
| 156 | Paul O'Neill | .20 | .50 |
| 157 | Andy Pettitte | .20 | .50 |
| 158 | Mariano Rivera | .30 | .75 |
| 159 | Darryl Strawberry | .10 | .30 |
| 160 | David Wells | .10 | .30 |
| 161 | Jorge Posada | .20 | .50 |
| 162 | Ramiro Mendoza | .10 | .30 |
| 163 | Miguel Tejada | .10 | .30 |
| 164 | Ryan Christenson | .10 | .30 |
| 165 | Rickey Henderson | .30 | .75 |
| 166 | A.J. Hinch | .10 | .30 |
| 167 | Ben Grieve | .10 | .30 |
| 168 | Kenny Rogers | .10 | .30 |
| 169 | Matt Stairs | .10 | .30 |
| 170 | Bob Abreu | .10 | .30 |
| 171 | Rico Brogna | .10 | .30 |
| 172 | Doug Glanville | .10 | .30 |
| 173 | Mike Grace | .10 | .30 |
| 174 | Desi Relaford | .10 | .30 |
| 175 | Scott Rolen | .20 | .50 |
| 176 | Jose Guillen | .10 | .30 |
| 177 | Francisco Cordova | .10 | .30 |
| 178 | Al Martin | .10 | .30 |
| 179 | Jason Schmidt | .10 | .30 |
| 180 | Turner Ward | .10 | .30 |
| 181 | Kevin Young | .10 | .30 |
| 182 | Mark McGwire | .75 | 2.00 |
| 183 | Delino DeShields | .10 | .30 |
| 184 | Eli Marrero | .10 | .30 |
| 185 | Tom Lampkin | .10 | .30 |
| 186 | Ray Lankford | .10 | .30 |
| 187 | Willie McGee | .10 | .30 |
| 188 | Matt Morris | .10 | .30 |
| 189 | Andy Ashby | .10 | .30 |
| 190 | Kevin Brown | .20 | .50 |
| 191 | Ken Caminiti | .10 | .30 |
| 192 | Trevor Hoffman | .10 | .30 |
| 193 | Wally Joyner | .10 | .30 |
| 194 | Greg Vaughn | .10 | .30 |
| 195 | Danny Darwin | .10 | .30 |
| 196 | Shawn Estes | .10 | .30 |
| 197 | Orel Hershiser | .10 | .30 |
| 198 | Jeff Kent | .10 | .30 |
| 199 | Bill Mueller | .10 | .30 |
| 200 | Robb Nen | .10 | .30 |
| 201 | J.T. Snow | .10 | .30 |
| 202 | Ken Cloude | .10 | .30 |
| 203 | Russ Davis | .10 | .30 |
| 204 | Jeff Fassero | .10 | .30 |
| 205 | Ken Griffey Jr. | .50 | 1.25 |
| 206 | Shane Monahan | .10 | .30 |
| 207 | David Segui | .10 | .30 |
| 208 | Dan Wilson | .10 | .30 |
| 209 | Wilson Alvarez | .10 | .30 |
| 210 | Wade Boggs | .20 | .50 |
| 211 | Miguel Cairo | .10 | .30 |
| 212 | Bubba Trammell | .10 | .30 |
| 213 | Quinton McCracken | .10 | .30 |
| 214 | Paul Sorrento | .10 | .30 |
| 215 | Kevin Stocker | .10 | .30 |
| 216 | Will Clark | .20 | .50 |
| 217 | Rusty Greer | .10 | .30 |
| 218 | Rick Helling | .10 | .30 |
| 219 | Mark McLemore | .10 | .30 |
| 220 | Ivan Rodriguez | .20 | .50 |
| 221 | John Wetteland | .10 | .30 |
| 222 | Jose Canseco | .20 | .50 |
| 223 | Roger Clemens | .60 | 1.50 |
| 224 | Carlos Delgado | .10 | .30 |
| 225 | Darrin Fletcher | .10 | .30 |
| 226 | Alex Gonzalez | .10 | .30 |
| 227 | Jose Cruz Jr. | .10 | .30 |
| 228 | Shannon Stewart | .10 | .30 |
| 229 | Rolando Arrojo FF | .10 | .30 |
| 230 | Livan Hernandez FF | .10 | .30 |
| 231 | Orlando Hernandez FF | .20 | .50 |
| 232 | Raul Mondesi FF | .10 | .30 |
| 233 | Moises Alou FF | .10 | .30 |
| 234 | Pedro Martinez FF | .20 | .50 |
| 235 | Sammy Sosa FF | .20 | .50 |
| 236 | Vladimir Guerrero FF | .30 | .75 |
| 237 | Bartolo Colon FF | .10 | .30 |
| 238 | Miguel Tejada FF | .10 | .30 |
| 239 | Ismael Valdes FF | .10 | .30 |
| 240 | Mariano Rivera FF | .20 | .50 |
| 241 | Jose Cruz Jr. FF | .10 | .30 |
| 242 | Juan Gonzalez FF | .10 | .30 |
| 243 | Ivan Rodriguez FF | .20 | .50 |
| 244 | Sandy Alomar Jr. FF | .10 | .30 |
| 245 | Roberto Alomar FF | .20 | .50 |
| 246 | Magglio Ordonez FF | .10 | .30 |
| 247 | Kerry Wood SH CL | .10 | .30 |
| 248 | Mark McGwire SH CL | .75 | 2.00 |
| 249 | David Wells SH CL | .10 | .30 |
| 250 | Rolando Arrojo SH CL | .10 | .30 |
| 251 | Ken Griffey Jr. SH CL | .50 | 1.25 |
| 252 | Trevor Hoffman SH CL | .10 | .30 |
| 253 | Travis Lee SH CL | .10 | .30 |
| 254 | Roberto Alomar SH CL | .10 | .30 |
| 255 | Sammy Sosa SH CL | .20 | .50 |
| 266 | Pat Burrell SR RC | 1.25 | 3.00 |
| 267 | Shea Hillenbrand SR RC | .60 | 1.50 |
| 268 | Robert Fick SR | .20 | .50 |
| 269 | Roy Halladay SR | .25 | .60 |
| 270 | Ruben Mateo SR | .20 | .50 |
| 271 | Bruce Chen SR | .20 | .50 |
| 272 | Angel Pena SR | .20 | .50 |
| 273 | Michael Barrett SR | .20 | .50 |
| 274 | Kevin Witt SR | .20 | .50 |
| 275 | Damon Minor SR | .20 | .50 |
| 276 | Ryan Minor SR | .20 | .50 |
| 277 | A.J. Pierzynski SR | .25 | .60 |
| 278 | A.J. Burnett SR RC | .60 | 1.50 |
| 279 | Dermal Brown SR | .20 | .50 |
| 280 | Joe Lawrence SR | .20 | .50 |
| 281 | Carlos Febles SR | .20 | .50 |
| 282 | Chris Haas SR | .20 | .50 |
| 283 | Cesar King SR | .20 | .50 |
| 284 | Calvin Pickering SR | .20 | .50 |
| 285 | Mitch Meluskey SR | .20 | .50 |
| 286 | Carlos Beltran SR | .40 | 1.00 |
| 287 | Ron Belliard SR | .20 | .50 |
| 288 | Jerry Hairston Jr. SR | .20 | .50 |
| 289 | Fernando Seguignol SR | .20 | .50 |
| 290 | Kris Benson SR | .20 | .50 |
| 292 | Chad Hutchinson SR RC | .25 | .60 |
| 293 | Jarrod Washburn | .10 | .30 |
| 294 | Jason Dickson | .10 | .30 |
| 295 | Mo Vaughn | .30 | .75 |
| 296 | Garret Anderson | .10 | .30 |
| 297 | Jim Edmonds | .10 | .30 |
| 298 | Ken Hill | .10 | .30 |
| 299 | Shigetoshi Hasegawa | .10 | .30 |
| 300 | Todd Stottlemyre | .10 | .30 |
| 301 | Randy Johnson | .30 | .75 |
| 302 | Omar Daal | .10 | .30 |
| 303 | Steve Finley | .10 | .30 |
| 304 | Matt Williams | .10 | .30 |
| 305 | Danny Klassen | .10 | .30 |
| 306 | Tony Batista | .10 | .30 |
| 307 | Brian Jordan | .10 | .30 |
| 308 | Greg Maddux | .50 | 1.25 |
| 309 | Chipper Jones | .30 | .75 |
| 310 | Bret Boone | .10 | .30 |
| 311 | Ozzie Guillen | .10 | .30 |
| 312 | John Rocker | .10 | .30 |
| 313 | Tom Glavine | .20 | .50 |
| 314 | Andruw Jones | .20 | .50 |
| 315 | Albert Belle | .10 | .30 |
| 316 | Charles Johnson | .10 | .30 |
| 317 | Will Clark | .20 | .50 |
| 318 | B.J. Surhoff | .10 | .30 |
| 319 | Delino DeShields | .10 | .30 |
| 320 | Heathcliff Slocumb | .10 | .30 |
| 321 | Sidney Ponson | .10 | .30 |
| 322 | Juan Guzman | .10 | .30 |
| 323 | Reggie Jefferson | .10 | .30 |
| 324 | Mark Portugal | .10 | .30 |
| 325 | Tim Wakefield | .10 | .30 |
| 326 | Jason Varitek | .30 | .75 |
| 327 | Jose Offerman | .10 | .30 |
| 328 | Pedro Martinez | .20 | .50 |
| 329 | Trot Nixon | .10 | .30 |
| 330 | Kerry Wood | .10 | .30 |
| 331 | Sammy Sosa | .30 | .75 |
| 332 | Glenallen Hill | .10 | .30 |
| 333 | Gary Gaetti | .10 | .30 |
| 334 | Mickey Morandini | .10 | .30 |
| 335 | Benito Santiago | .10 | .30 |
| 336 | Jeff Blauser | .10 | .30 |
| 337 | Frank Thomas | .30 | .75 |
| 338 | Paul Konerko | .20 | .50 |
| 339 | Jaime Navarro | .10 | .30 |
| 340 | Carlos Lee | .10 | .30 |
| 341 | Brian Simmons | .10 | .30 |
| 342 | Mark Johnson | .10 | .30 |
| 343 | Jeff Abbott | .10 | .30 |
| 344 | Steve Avery | .10 | .30 |
| 345 | Mike Cameron | .10 | .30 |
| 346 | Michael Tucker | .10 | .30 |
| 347 | Greg Vaughn | .10 | .30 |
| 348 | Hal Morris | .10 | .30 |
| 349 | Pete Harnisch | .10 | .30 |
| 350 | Denny Neagle | .10 | .30 |
| 351 | Manny Ramirez | .20 | .50 |
| 352 | Roberto Alomar | .20 | .50 |
| 353 | Dwight Gooden | .10 | .30 |
| 354 | Kenny Lofton | .10 | .30 |
| 355 | Mike Jackson | .10 | .30 |
| 356 | Charles Nagy | .10 | .30 |
| 357 | Enrique Wilson | .10 | .30 |
| 358 | Russ Branyan | .10 | .30 |
| 359 | Richie Sexson | .10 | .30 |
| 360 | Vinny Castilla | .10 | .30 |
| 361 | Dante Bichette | .10 | .30 |
| 362 | Kirt Manwaring | .10 | .30 |
| 363 | Darryl Hamilton | .10 | .30 |
| 364 | Jamey Wright | .10 | .30 |
| 365 | Curtis Leskanic | .10 | .30 |
| 366 | Jeff Reed | .10 | .30 |
| 367 | Bobby Higginson | .10 | .30 |
| 368 | Justin Thompson | .10 | .30 |
| 369 | Brad Ausmus | .10 | .30 |
| 370 | Dean Palmer | .10 | .30 |
| 371 | Gabe Kapler | .10 | .30 |
| 372 | Juan Encarnacion | .10 | .30 |
| 373 | Karim Garcia | .10 | .30 |
| 374 | Alex Gonzalez | .10 | .30 |
| 375 | Braden Looper | .10 | .30 |
| 376 | Preston Wilson | .10 | .30 |
| 377 | Todd Dunwoody | .10 | .30 |
| 378 | Alex Fernandez | .10 | .30 |
| 379 | Mark Kotsay | .10 | .30 |
| 380 | Matt Mantei | .10 | .30 |
| 381 | Ken Caminiti | .10 | .30 |
| 382 | Scott Elarton | .10 | .30 |
| 383 | Jeff Bagwell | .20 | .50 |
| 384 | Derek Bell | .10 | .30 |
| 385 | Ricky Gutierrez | .10 | .30 |
| 386 | Richard Hidalgo | .10 | .30 |
| 387 | Shane Reynolds | .10 | .30 |
| 388 | Carl Everett | .10 | .30 |
| 389 | Scott Service | .10 | .30 |
| 390 | Jeff Suppan | .10 | .30 |
| 391 | Joe Randa | .10 | .30 |
| 392 | Kevin Appier | .10 | .30 |
| 393 | Shane Halter | .10 | .30 |
| 394 | Chad Kreuter | .10 | .30 |
| 395 | Mike Sweeney | .10 | .30 |
| 396 | Kevin Brown | .20 | .50 |
| 397 | Devon White | .10 | .30 |
| 398 | Todd Hollandsworth | .10 | .30 |
| 399 | Todd Hundley | .10 | .30 |
| 400 | Chan Ho Park | .10 | .30 |
| 401 | Mark Grudzielanek | .10 | .30 |
| 402 | Raul Mondesi | .10 | .30 |
| 403 | Ismael Valdes | .10 | .30 |
| 404 | Rafael Roque RC | .10 | .30 |
| 405 | Sean Berry | .10 | .30 |
| 406 | Kevin Barker | .10 | .30 |
| 407 | Dave Nilsson | .10 | .30 |
| 408 | Geoff Jenkins | .10 | .30 |
| 409 | Jim Abbott | .20 | .50 |
| 410 | Bobby Hughes | .10 | .30 |
| 411 | Corey Koskie | .10 | .30 |
| 412 | Rick Aguilera | .10 | .30 |
| 413 | LaTroy Hawkins | .10 | .30 |
| 414 | Ron Coomer | .10 | .30 |
| 415 | Denny Hocking | .10 | .30 |
| 416 | Marty Cordova | .10 | .30 |
| 417 | Terry Steinbach | .10 | .30 |
| 418 | Rondell White | .10 | .30 |
| 419 | Wilton Guerrero | .10 | .30 |
| 420 | Shane Andrews | .10 | .30 |
| 421 | Orlando Cabrera | .10 | .30 |
| 422 | Carl Pavano | .10 | .30 |
| 423 | Javier Vazquez | .10 | .30 |
| 424 | Chris Widger | .10 | .30 |
| 425 | Robin Ventura | .10 | .30 |
| 426 | Rickey Henderson | .30 | .75 |
| 427 | Al Leiter | .10 | .30 |
| 428 | Bobby Jones | .10 | .30 |

|  |  | | |
|---|--------|------|------|
| 429 | Brian McRae | .10 | .30 |
| 430 | Roger Cedeno | .10 | .30 |
| 431 | Bobby Bonilla | .10 | .30 |
| 432 | Edgardo Alfonzo | .10 | .30 |
| 433 | Bernie Williams | .20 | .50 |
| 434 | Ricky Ledee | .10 | .30 |
| 435 | Chili Davis | .10 | .30 |
| 436 | Tino Martinez | .20 | .50 |
| 437 | Scott Brosius | .10 | .30 |
| 438 | David Cone | .10 | .30 |
| 439 | Joe Girardi | .10 | .30 |
| 440 | Roger Clemens | .60 | 1.50 |
| 441 | Chad Curtis | .10 | .30 |
| 442 | Hideki Irabu | .10 | .30 |
| 443 | Jason Giambi | .10 | .30 |
| 444 | Scott Spiezio | .10 | .30 |
| 445 | Tony Phillips | .10 | .30 |
| 446 | Ramon Hernandez | .10 | .30 |
| 447 | Mike Macfarlane | .10 | .30 |
| 448 | Tom Candiotti | .10 | .30 |
| 449 | Billy Taylor | .10 | .30 |
| 450 | Bobby Estalella | .10 | .30 |
| 451 | Curt Schilling | .10 | .30 |
| 452 | Carlton Loewer | .10 | .30 |
| 453 | Marlon Anderson | .10 | .30 |
| 454 | Kevin Jordan | .10 | .30 |
| 455 | Ron Gant | .10 | .30 |
| 456 | Chad Ogea | .10 | .30 |
| 457 | Abraham Nunez | .10 | .30 |
| 458 | Jason Kendall | .10 | .30 |
| 459 | Pat Meares | .10 | .30 |
| 460 | Brant Brown | .10 | .30 |
| 461 | Brian Giles | .10 | .30 |
| 462 | Chad Hermansen | .10 | .30 |
| 463 | Freddy Adrian Garcia | .10 | .30 |
| 464 | Edgar Renteria | .10 | .30 |
| 465 | Fernando Tatis | .10 | .30 |
| 466 | Eric Davis | .10 | .30 |
| 467 | Darren Bragg | .10 | .30 |
| 468 | Donovan Osborne | .10 | .30 |
| 469 | Manny Aybar | .10 | .30 |
| 470 | Jose Jimenez | .10 | .30 |
| 471 | Kent Mercker | .10 | .30 |
| 472 | Reggie Sanders | .10 | .30 |
| 473 | Ruben Rivera | .10 | .30 |
| 474 | Tony Gwynn | .40 | 1.00 |
| 475 | Jim Leyritz | .10 | .30 |
| 476 | Chris Gomez | .10 | .30 |
| 477 | Matt Clement | .10 | .30 |
| 478 | Carlos Hernandez | .10 | .30 |
| 479 | Sterling Hitchcock | .10 | .30 |
| 480 | Ellis Burks | .10 | .30 |
| 481 | Barry Bonds | .75 | 2.00 |
| 482 | Marvin Benard | .10 | .30 |
| 483 | Kirk Rueter | .10 | .30 |
| 484 | F.P. Santangelo | .10 | .30 |
| 485 | Stan Javier | .10 | .30 |
| 486 | Jeff Kent | .10 | .30 |
| 487 | Alex Rodriguez | .50 | 1.25 |
| 488 | Tom Lampkin | .10 | .30 |
| 489 | Jose Mesa | .10 | .30 |
| 490 | Jay Buhner | .10 | .30 |
| 491 | Edgar Martinez | .20 | .50 |
| 492 | Butch Huskey | .10 | .30 |
| 493 | John Mabry | .10 | .30 |
| 494 | Jamie Moyer | .10 | .30 |
| 495 | Roberto Hernandez | .10 | .30 |
| 496 | Tony Saunders | .10 | .30 |
| 497 | Fred McGriff | .20 | .50 |
| 498 | Dave Martinez | .10 | .30 |
| 499 | Jose Canseco | .20 | .50 |
| 500 | Rolando Arrojo | .10 | .30 |
| 501 | Esteban Yan | .10 | .30 |
| 502 | Juan Gonzalez | .20 | .50 |
| 503 | Rafael Palmeiro | .20 | .50 |
| 504 | Aaron Sele | .10 | .30 |
| 505 | Royce Clayton | .10 | .30 |
| 506 | Todd Zeile | .10 | .30 |
| 507 | Tom Goodwin | .10 | .30 |
| 508 | Lee Stevens | .10 | .30 |
| 509 | Esteban Loaiza | .10 | .30 |
| 510 | Joey Hamilton | .10 | .30 |
| 511 | Homer Bush | .10 | .30 |
| 512 | Willie Greene | .10 | .30 |
| 513 | Shawn Green | .10 | .30 |
| 514 | David Wells | .10 | .30 |
| 515 | Kelvim Escobar | .10 | .30 |
| 516 | Tony Fernandez | .10 | .30 |
| 517 | Pat Hentgen | .10 | .30 |
| 518 | Mark McGwire AR | .40 | 1.00 |
| 519 | Ken Griffey AR | .30 | .75 |
| 520 | Sammy Sosa AR | .20 | .50 |
| 521 | Juan Gonzalez AR | .10 | .30 |
| 522 | J.D. Drew AR | .10 | .30 |
| 523 | Chipper Jones AR | .20 | .50 |
| 524 | Alex Rodriguez AR | .30 | .75 |
| 525 | Mike Piazza AR | .30 | .75 |
| 526 | Nomar Garciaparra AR | .30 | .75 |
| 527 | Mark McGwire SH CL | .40 | 1.00 |
| 528 | Sammy Sosa SH CL | .20 | .50 |
| 529 | Scott Brosius SH CL | .10 | .30 |
| 530 | Cal Ripken SH CL | .50 | 1.25 |
| 531 | Barry Bonds SH CL | .40 | 1.00 |
| 532 | Roger Clemens SH CL | .30 | .75 |
| 533 | Ken Griffey Jr. SH CL | .30 | .75 |
| 534 | Alex Rodriguez SH CL | .30 | .75 |
| 535 | Curt Schilling SH CL | .10 | .30 |
| NNO | K.Griffey Jr. '89 AU/100 | 1000.00 | 1250.00 |

**2000 Upper Deck**

| | | | |
|---|---|---|---|
| | COMPLETE SET (540) | 40.00 | 100.00 |
| | COMPLETE SERIES 1 (270) | 20.00 | 50.00 |
| | COMPLETE SERIES 2 (270) | 20.00 | 50.00 |
| | COMMON CARD (1-540) | .10 | .30 |
| | COMMON SR (1-28/271-297) | .20 | .50 |
| 1 | Rick Ankiel SR | .20 | .50 |
| 2 | Vernon Wells SR | .30 | .75 |
| 3 | Ryan Anderson SR | .20 | .50 |
| 4 | Ed Yarnall SR | .20 | .50 |
| 5 | Brian McNichol SR | .20 | .50 |
| 6 | Ben Petrick SR | .20 | .50 |
| 7 | Kip Wells SR | .20 | .50 |
| 8 | Eric Munson SR | .20 | .50 |
| 9 | Matt Riley SR | .20 | .50 |
| 10 | Peter Bergeron SR | .20 | .50 |
| 11 | Eric Gagne SR | .75 | 2.00 |
| 12 | Ramon Ortiz SR | .20 | .50 |
| 13 | Josh Beckett SR | .75 | 2.00 |
| 14 | Alfonso Soriano SR | .75 | 2.00 |
| 15 | Jorge Toca SR | .20 | .50 |
| 16 | Buddy Carlyle SR | .20 | .50 |
| 17 | Chad Hermansen SR | .20 | .50 |
| 18 | Matt Perisho SR | .20 | .50 |
| 19 | Tomokazu Ohka SR RC | .30 | .75 |
| 20 | Jacque Jones SR | .30 | .75 |
| 21 | Josh Paul SR | .20 | .50 |
| 22 | Dernal Brown SR | .20 | .50 |
| 23 | Adam Kennedy SR | .20 | .50 |
| 24 | Chad Harville SR | .20 | .50 |
| 25 | Calvin Murray SR | .20 | .50 |
| 26 | Chad Meyers SR | .20 | .50 |
| 27 | Brian Cooper SR | .20 | .50 |
| 28 | Troy Glaus SR | .10 | .30 |
| 29 | Ben Molina | .10 | .30 |
| 30 | Troy Percival | .10 | .30 |
| 31 | Ken Hill | .10 | .30 |
| 32 | Chuck Finley | .10 | .30 |
| 33 | Todd Greene | .10 | .30 |
| 34 | Tim Salmon | .20 | .50 |
| 35 | Gary DiSarcina | .10 | .30 |
| 36 | Luis Gonzalez | .10 | .30 |
| 37 | Tony Womack | .10 | .30 |
| 38 | Omar Daal | .10 | .30 |
| 39 | Randy Johnson | .30 | .75 |
| 40 | Erubiel Durazo | .10 | .30 |
| 41 | Jay Bell | .10 | .30 |
| 42 | Steve Finley | .10 | .30 |
| 43 | Travis Lee | .10 | .30 |
| 44 | Greg Maddux | .50 | 1.25 |
| 45 | Bret Boone | .10 | .30 |
| 46 | Brian Jordan | .10 | .30 |
| 47 | Kevin Millwood | .10 | .30 |
| 48 | Odalis Perez | .10 | .30 |
| 49 | Javy Lopez | .10 | .30 |
| 50 | John Smoltz | .20 | .50 |
| 51 | Bruce Chen | .10 | .30 |
| 52 | Albert Belle | .10 | .30 |
| 53 | Jerry Hairston Jr. | .10 | .30 |
| 54 | Will Clark | .20 | .50 |
| 55 | Sidney Ponson | .10 | .30 |
| 56 | Charles Johnson | .10 | .30 |
| 57 | Cal Ripken | 1.00 | 2.50 |
| 58 | Ryan Minor | .10 | .30 |
| 59 | Mike Mussina | .20 | .50 |
| 60 | Tom Gordon | .10 | .30 |
| 61 | Jose Offerman | .10 | .30 |
| 62 | Trot Nixon | .10 | .30 |
| 63 | Pedro Martinez | .20 | .50 |
| 64 | John Valentin | .10 | .30 |
| 65 | Jason Varitek | .30 | .75 |
| 66 | Juan Pena | .10 | .30 |
| 67 | Troy O'Leary | .10 | .30 |
| 68 | Sammy Sosa | .30 | .75 |
| 69 | Henry Rodriguez | .10 | .30 |
| 70 | Kyle Farnsworth | .10 | .30 |
| 71 | Glenallen Hill | .10 | .30 |
| 72 | Lance Johnson | .10 | .30 |
| 73 | Mickey Morandini | .10 | .30 |
| 74 | Jon Lieber | .10 | .30 |
| 75 | Kevin Tapani | .10 | .30 |
| 76 | Carlos Lee | .10 | .30 |
| 77 | Ray Durham | .10 | .30 |
| 78 | Jim Parque | .10 | .30 |
| 79 | Bob Howry | .10 | .30 |
| 80 | Magglio Ordonez | .10 | .30 |
| 81 | Paul Konerko | .10 | .30 |
| 82 | Mike Caruso | .10 | .30 |
| 83 | Chris Singleton | .10 | .30 |
| 84 | Sean Casey | .10 | .30 |
| 85 | Barry Larkin | .20 | .50 |
| 86 | Pokey Reese | .10 | .30 |
| 87 | Eddie Taubensee | .10 | .30 |
| 88 | Scott Williamson | .10 | .30 |
| 89 | Jason LaRue | .10 | .30 |
| 90 | Aaron Boone | .10 | .30 |
| 91 | Jeffrey Hammonds | .10 | .30 |
| 92 | Omar Vizquel | .20 | .50 |
| 93 | Manny Ramirez | .30 | .75 |
| 94 | Kenny Lofton | .10 | .30 |
| 95 | Jaret Wright | .10 | .30 |
| 96 | Einar Diaz | .10 | .30 |
| 97 | Charles Nagy | .10 | .30 |
| 98 | David Justice | .10 | .30 |
| 99 | Richie Sexson | .10 | .30 |
| 100 | Steve Karsay | .10 | .30 |
| 101 | Todd Helton | .20 | .50 |
| 102 | Dante Bichette | .10 | .30 |
| 103 | Larry Walker | .20 | .50 |
| 104 | Pedro Astacio | .10 | .30 |
| 105 | Neifi Perez | .10 | .30 |
| 106 | Brian Bohanon | .10 | .30 |
| 107 | Edgard Clemente | .10 | .30 |
| 108 | Dave Veres | .10 | .30 |
| 109 | Gabe Kapler | .10 | .30 |
| 110 | Juan Encarnacion | .10 | .30 |
| 111 | Jeff Weaver | .10 | .30 |
| 112 | Damion Easley | .10 | .30 |
| 113 | Justin Thompson | .10 | .30 |
| 114 | Brad Ausmus | .10 | .30 |
| 115 | Frank Catalanotto | .10 | .30 |
| 116 | Todd Jones | .10 | .30 |
| 117 | Preston Wilson | .10 | .30 |
| 118 | Cliff Floyd | .10 | .30 |
| 119 | Mike Lowell | .10 | .30 |
| 120 | Antonio Alfonseca | .10 | .30 |
| 121 | Alex Gonzalez | .10 | .30 |
| 122 | Braden Looper | .10 | .30 |
| 123 | Bruce Aven | .10 | .30 |
| 124 | Richard Hidalgo | .10 | .30 |
| 125 | Mitch Meluskey | .10 | .30 |
| 126 | Jeff Bagwell | .20 | .50 |
| 127 | Jose Lima | .10 | .30 |
| 128 | Derek Bell | .10 | .30 |
| 129 | Billy Wagner | .10 | .30 |
| 130 | Shane Reynolds | .10 | .30 |
| 131 | Moises Alou | .10 | .30 |
| 132 | Carlos Beltran | .10 | .30 |
| 133 | Carlos Febles | .10 | .30 |
| 134 | Jermaine Dye | .10 | .30 |
| 135 | Jeremy Giambi | .10 | .30 |

|  |  | | |
|---|---|---|---|
| 136 | Joe Randa | .10 | .30 |
| 137 | Jose Rosado | .10 | .30 |
| 138 | Chad Kreuter | .10 | .30 |
| 139 | Jose Vizcaino | .10 | .30 |
| 140 | Adrian Beltre | .10 | .30 |
| 141 | Kevin Brown | .20 | .50 |
| 142 | Ismael Valdes | .10 | .30 |
| 143 | Angel Pena | .10 | .30 |
| 144 | Chan Ho Park | .10 | .30 |
| 145 | Mark Grudzielanek | .10 | .30 |
| 146 | Jeff Shaw | .10 | .30 |
| 147 | Geoff Jenkins | .10 | .30 |
| 148 | Jeromy Burnitz | .10 | .30 |
| 149 | Hideo Nomo | .30 | .75 |
| 150 | Ron Belliard | .10 | .30 |
| 151 | Sean Berry | .10 | .30 |
| 152 | Mark Loretta | .10 | .30 |
| 153 | Steve Woodard | .10 | .30 |
| 154 | Joe Mays | .10 | .30 |
| 155 | Eric Milton | .10 | .30 |
| 156 | Corey Koskie | .10 | .30 |
| 157 | Ron Coomer | .10 | .30 |
| 158 | Brad Radke | .10 | .30 |
| 159 | Terry Steinbach | .10 | .30 |
| 160 | Cristian Guzman | .10 | .30 |
| 161 | Vladimir Guerrero | .30 | .75 |
| 162 | Wilton Guerrero | .10 | .30 |
| 163 | Michael Barrett | .10 | .30 |
| 164 | Chris Widger | .10 | .30 |
| 165 | Fernando Seguignol | .10 | .30 |
| 166 | Ugueth Urbina | .10 | .30 |
| 167 | Dustin Hermanson | .10 | .30 |
| 168 | Kenny Rogers | .10 | .30 |
| 169 | Edgardo Alfonzo | .10 | .30 |
| 170 | Orel Hershiser | .10 | .30 |
| 171 | Robin Ventura | .10 | .30 |
| 172 | Octavio Dotel | .10 | .30 |
| 173 | Rickey Henderson | .30 | .75 |
| 174 | Roger Cedeno | .10 | .30 |
| 175 | John Olerud | .10 | .30 |
| 176 | Derek Jeter | .75 | 2.00 |
| 177 | Tino Martinez | .20 | .50 |
| 178 | Orlando Hernandez | .30 | .75 |
| 179 | Chuck Knoblauch | .10 | .30 |
| 180 | Bernie Williams | .20 | .50 |
| 181 | Chili Davis | .10 | .30 |
| 182 | David Cone | .10 | .30 |
| 183 | Ricky Ledee | .10 | .30 |
| 184 | Paul O'Neill | .20 | .50 |
| 185 | Jason Giambi | .10 | .30 |
| 186 | Eric Chavez | .10 | .30 |
| 187 | Matt Stairs | .10 | .30 |
| 188 | Miguel Tejada | .10 | .30 |
| 189 | Olmedo Saenz | .10 | .30 |
| 190 | Tim Hudson | .10 | .30 |
| 191 | John Jaha | .10 | .30 |
| 192 | Randy Velarde | .10 | .30 |
| 193 | Rico Brogna | .10 | .30 |
| 194 | Mike Lieberthal | .10 | .30 |
| 195 | Marlon Anderson | .10 | .30 |
| 196 | Bob Abreu | .10 | .30 |
| 197 | Ron Gant | .10 | .30 |
| 198 | Randy Wolf | .10 | .30 |
| 199 | Desi Relaford | .10 | .30 |
| 200 | Doug Glanville | .10 | .30 |
| 201 | Warren Morris | .10 | .30 |
| 202 | Kris Benson | .10 | .30 |
| 203 | Kevin Young | .10 | .30 |
| 204 | Brian Giles | .20 | .50 |
| 205 | Jason Schmidt | .10 | .30 |
| 206 | Ed Sprague | .10 | .30 |
| 207 | Francisco Cordova | .10 | .30 |
| 208 | Mark McGwire | .75 | 2.00 |
| 209 | Jose Jimenez | .10 | .30 |
| 210 | Fernando Tatis | .10 | .30 |
| 211 | Kent Bottenfield | .10 | .30 |
| 212 | Eli Marrero | .10 | .30 |
| 213 | Edgar Renteria | .10 | .30 |
| 214 | Joe McEwing | .10 | .30 |
| 215 | J.D. Drew | .10 | .30 |
| 216 | Tony Gwynn | .40 | 1.00 |
| 217 | Gary Matthews Jr. | .10 | .30 |
| 218 | Eric Owens | .10 | .30 |
| 219 | Damian Jackson | .10 | .30 |
| 220 | Reggie Sanders | .10 | .30 |
| 221 | Trevor Hoffman | .10 | .30 |
| 222 | Ben Davis | .10 | .30 |
| 223 | Shawn Estes | .10 | .30 |
| 224 | F.P. Santangelo | .10 | .30 |
| 225 | Livan Hernandez | .10 | .30 |
| 226 | Ellis Burks | .10 | .30 |
| 227 | J.T. Snow | .10 | .30 |
| 228 | Jeff Kent | .10 | .30 |
| 229 | Robb Nen | .10 | .30 |
| 230 | Marvin Benard | .10 | .30 |
| 231 | Ken Griffey Jr. | .50 | 1.25 |
| 232 | John Halama | .10 | .30 |
| 233 | Gil Meche | .10 | .30 |
| 234 | David Bell | .10 | .30 |
| 235 | Brian Hunter | .10 | .30 |
| 236 | Jay Buhner | .10 | .30 |
| 237 | Edgar Martinez | .20 | .50 |
| 238 | Jose Mesa | .10 | .30 |
| 239 | Wilson Alvarez | .10 | .30 |
| 240 | Wade Boggs | .20 | .50 |
| 241 | Fred McGriff | .20 | .50 |
| 242 | Jose Canseco | .20 | .50 |
| 243 | Kevin Stocker | .10 | .30 |
| 244 | Roberto Hernandez | .10 | .30 |
| 245 | Bubba Trammell | .10 | .30 |
| 246 | John Flaherty | .10 | .30 |
| 247 | Ivan Rodriguez | .20 | .50 |
| 248 | Rusty Greer | .10 | .30 |
| 249 | Rafael Palmeiro | .20 | .50 |
| 250 | Jeff Zimmerman | .10 | .30 |
| 251 | Royce Clayton | .10 | .30 |
| 252 | Todd Zeile | .10 | .30 |
| 253 | John Wetteland | .10 | .30 |
| 254 | Ruben Mateo | .10 | .30 |
| 255 | Kelvim Escobar | .10 | .30 |
| 256 | David Wells | .10 | .30 |
| 257 | Shawn Green | .20 | .50 |
| 258 | Homer Bush | .10 | .30 |
| 259 | Shannon Stewart | .10 | .30 |
| 260 | Carlos Delgado | .20 | .50 |
| 261 | Roy Halladay | .10 | .30 |
| 262 | Fernando Tatis SH CL | .10 | .30 |
| 263 | Jose Jimenez SH CL | .10 | .30 |
| 264 | Tony Gwynn SH CL | .20 | .50 |
| 265 | Wade Boggs SH CL | .20 | .50 |
| 266 | Cal Ripken SH CL | .50 | 1.25 |
| 267 | David Cone SH CL | .10 | .30 |
| 268 | Mark McGwire SH CL | .50 | 1.25 |
| 269 | Pedro Martinez SH CL | .20 | .50 |
| 270 | Nomar Garciaparra SH CL | .30 | .75 |
| 271 | Nick Johnson SR | .30 | .75 |
| 272 | Mark Quinn SR | .20 | .50 |
| 273 | Roosevelt Brown SR | .20 | .50 |
| 274 | Terrence Long SR | .20 | .50 |
| 275 | Jason Marquis SR | .20 | .50 |
| 276 | Kazuhiro Sasaki SR RC | .50 | 1.25 |
| 277 | Aaron Myette SR | .10 | .30 |
| 278 | Danys Baez SR RC | .30 | .75 |
| 279 | Travis Dawkins SR | .20 | .50 |
| 280 | Mark Mulder SR | .30 | .75 |
| 281 | Chris Haas SR | .20 | .50 |
| 282 | Milton Bradley SR | .30 | .75 |
| 283 | Brad Penny SR | .20 | .50 |
| 284 | Rafael Furcal SR | .30 | .75 |
| 285 | Luis Matos SR RC | .30 | .75 |
| 286 | Victor Santos SR RC | .10 | .30 |
| 287 | Rico Washington SR RC | .20 | .50 |
| 288 | Rob Bell SR | .20 | .50 |
| 289 | Joe Crede SR | 1.00 | 2.50 |
| 290 | Pablo Ozuna SR | .20 | .50 |
| 291 | Wascar Serrano SR RC | .20 | .50 |
| 292 | Sang-Hoon Lee SR RC | .20 | .50 |
| 293 | Chris Wakeland SR RC | .20 | .50 |
| 294 | Luis Rivera SR RC | .20 | .50 |
| 295 | Mike Lamb SR RC | .50 | 1.25 |
| 296 | Wily Mo Pena SR | .30 | .75 |
| 297 | Mike Meyers SR RC | .30 | .75 |
| 298 | Mo Vaughn | .10 | .30 |
| 299 | Darin Erstad | .20 | .50 |
| 300 | Garret Anderson | .10 | .30 |
| 301 | Tim Belcher | .10 | .30 |
| 302 | Scott Spiezio | .10 | .30 |
| 303 | Kent Bottenfield | .10 | .30 |
| 304 | Orlando Palmeiro | .10 | .30 |
| 305 | Jason Dickson | .10 | .30 |
| 306 | Matt Williams | .10 | .30 |
| 307 | Brian Anderson | .10 | .30 |
| 308 | Hanley Frias | .10 | .30 |
| 309 | Todd Stottlemyre | .10 | .30 |
| 310 | Matt Mantei | .10 | .30 |
| 311 | David Dellucci | .10 | .30 |
| 312 | Armando Reynoso | .10 | .30 |
| 313 | Bernard Gilkey | .10 | .30 |
| 314 | Chipper Jones | .30 | .75 |
| 315 | Tom Glavine | .20 | .50 |
| 316 | Quilvio Veras | .10 | .30 |
| 317 | Andruw Jones | .30 | .75 |
| 318 | Bobby Bonilla | .10 | .30 |
| 319 | Reggie Sanders | .10 | .30 |
| 320 | Andres Galarraga | .20 | .50 |
| 321 | George Lombard | .10 | .30 |
| 322 | John Rocker | .10 | .30 |
| 323 | Wally Joyner | .10 | .30 |
| 324 | B.J. Surhoff | .10 | .30 |
| 325 | Scott Erickson | .10 | .30 |
| 326 | Delino DeShields | .10 | .30 |
| 327 | Jeff Conine | .10 | .30 |
| 328 | Mike Timlin | .10 | .30 |
| 329 | Brady Anderson | .10 | .30 |
| 330 | Mike Bordick | .10 | .30 |
| 331 | Harold Baines | .10 | .30 |
| 332 | Nomar Garciaparra | .50 | 1.25 |
| 333 | Bret Saberhagen | .10 | .30 |
| 334 | Ramon Martinez | .10 | .30 |
| 335 | Donnie Sadler | .10 | .30 |
| 336 | Wilton Veras | .10 | .30 |
| 337 | Mike Stanley | .10 | .30 |
| 338 | Brian Rose | .10 | .30 |
| 339 | Carl Everett | .10 | .30 |
| 340 | Tim Wakefield | .10 | .30 |
| 341 | Mark Grace | .20 | .50 |
| 342 | Kerry Wood | .10 | .30 |
| 343 | Eric Young | .10 | .30 |
| 344 | Jose Nieves | .10 | .30 |
| 345 | Ismael Valdes | .10 | .30 |
| 346 | Joe Girardi | .10 | .30 |
| 347 | Damon Buford | .10 | .30 |
| 348 | Ricky Gutierrez | .10 | .30 |
| 349 | Frank Thomas | .30 | .75 |
| 350 | Brian Simmons | .10 | .30 |
| 351 | James Baldwin | .10 | .30 |
| 352 | Brook Fordyce | .10 | .30 |
| 353 | Jose Valentin | .10 | .30 |
| 354 | Mike Sirotka | .10 | .30 |
| 355 | Greg Norton | .10 | .30 |
| 356 | Dante Bichette | .10 | .30 |
| 357 | Deion Sanders | .20 | .50 |
| 358 | Ken Griffey Jr. | .50 | 1.25 |
| 359 | Denny Neagle | .10 | .30 |
| 360 | Dmitri Young | .10 | .30 |
| 361 | Pete Harnisch | .10 | .30 |
| 362 | Michael Tucker | .10 | .30 |
| 363 | Roberto Alomar | .20 | .50 |
| 364 | Dave Roberts | .10 | .30 |
| 365 | Jim Thome | .20 | .50 |
| 366 | Bartolo Colon | .10 | .30 |
| 367 | Travis Fryman | .10 | .30 |
| 368 | Chuck Finley | .10 | .30 |
| 369 | Russell Branyan | .10 | .30 |
| 370 | Alex Ramirez | .10 | .30 |
| 371 | Jeff Cirillo | .10 | .30 |
| 372 | Jeffrey Hammonds | .10 | .30 |
| 373 | Scott Karl | .10 | .30 |
| 374 | Brent Mayne | .10 | .30 |
| 375 | Tom Goodwin | .10 | .30 |
| 376 | Jose Jimenez | .10 | .30 |
| 377 | Rolando Arrojo | .10 | .30 |
| 378 | Terry Shumpert | .10 | .30 |
| 379 | Juan Gonzalez | .20 | .50 |
| 380 | Bobby Higginson | .10 | .30 |
| 381 | Tony Clark | .10 | .30 |
| 382 | Dave Mlicki | .10 | .30 |
| 383 | Deivi Cruz | .10 | .30 |
| 384 | Brian Moehler | .10 | .30 |
| 385 | Dean Palmer | .10 | .30 |
| 386 | Luis Castillo | .10 | .30 |
| 387 | Mike Redmond | .10 | .30 |
| 388 | Alex Fernandez | .10 | .30 |
| 389 | Brant Brown | .10 | .30 |
| 390 | Dave Berg | .10 | .30 |
| 391 | A.J. Burnett | .10 | .30 |
| 392 | Mark Kotsay | .10 | .30 |
| 393 | Craig Biggio | .20 | .50 |
| 394 | Daryle Ward | .10 | .30 |
| 395 | Lance Berkman | .10 | .30 |
| 396 | Roger Cedeno | .10 | .30 |
| 397 | Scott Elarton | .10 | .30 |
| 398 | Octavio Dotel | .10 | .30 |
| 399 | Ken Caminiti | .10 | .30 |

| | | |
|---|---|---|
| ☐ 400 Johnny Damon | .20 | .50 |
| ☐ 401 Mike Sweeney | .10 | .30 |
| ☐ 402 Jeff Suppan | .10 | .30 |
| ☐ 403 Rey Sanchez | .10 | .30 |
| ☐ 404 Blake Stein | .10 | .30 |
| ☐ 405 Ricky Bottalico | .10 | .30 |
| ☐ 406 Jay Witasick | .10 | .30 |
| ☐ 407 Shawn Green | .10 | .30 |
| ☐ 408 Orel Hershiser | .10 | .30 |
| ☐ 409 Gary Sheffield | .10 | .30 |
| ☐ 410 Todd Hollandsworth | .10 | .30 |
| ☐ 411 Terry Adams | .10 | .30 |
| ☐ 412 Todd Hundley | .10 | .30 |
| ☐ 413 Eric Karros | .10 | .30 |
| ☐ 414 F.P. Santangelo | .10 | .30 |
| ☐ 415 Alex Cora | .10 | .30 |
| ☐ 416 Marquis Grissom | .10 | .30 |
| ☐ 417 Henry Blanco | .10 | .30 |
| ☐ 418 Jose Hernandez | .10 | .30 |
| ☐ 419 Kyle Peterson | .10 | .30 |
| ☐ 420 John Snyder RC | .10 | .30 |
| ☐ 421 Bob Wickman | .10 | .30 |
| ☐ 422 Jamey Wright | .10 | .30 |
| ☐ 423 Chad Allen | .10 | .30 |
| ☐ 424 Todd Walker | .10 | .30 |
| ☐ 425 J.C. Romero RC | .10 | .30 |
| ☐ 426 Butch Huskey | .10 | .30 |
| ☐ 427 Jacque Jones | .10 | .30 |
| ☐ 428 Matt Lawton | .10 | .30 |
| ☐ 429 Rondell White | .10 | .30 |
| ☐ 430 Jose Vidro | .10 | .30 |
| ☐ 431 Hideki Irabu | .10 | .30 |
| ☐ 432 Javier Vazquez | .10 | .30 |
| ☐ 433 Lee Stevens | .10 | .30 |
| ☐ 434 Mike Thurman | .10 | .30 |
| ☐ 435 Geoff Blum | .10 | .30 |
| ☐ 436 Mike Hampton | .10 | .30 |
| ☐ 437 Mike Piazza | .50 | 1.25 |
| ☐ 438 Al Leiter | .10 | .30 |
| ☐ 439 Derek Bell | .10 | .30 |
| ☐ 440 Armando Benitez | .10 | .30 |
| ☐ 441 Rey Ordonez | .10 | .30 |
| ☐ 442 Todd Zeile | .10 | .30 |
| ☐ 443 Roger Clemens | .60 | 1.50 |
| ☐ 444 Ramiro Mendoza | .10 | .30 |
| ☐ 445 Andy Pettitte | .20 | .50 |
| ☐ 446 Scott Brosius | .10 | .30 |
| ☐ 447 Mariano Rivera | .30 | .75 |
| ☐ 448 Jim Leyritz | .10 | .30 |
| ☐ 449 Jorge Posada | .20 | .50 |
| ☐ 450 Omar Olivares | .10 | .30 |
| ☐ 451 Ben Grieve | .10 | .30 |
| ☐ 452 A.J. Hinch | .10 | .30 |
| ☐ 453 Gil Heredia | .10 | .30 |
| ☐ 454 Kevin Appier | .10 | .30 |
| ☐ 455 Ryan Christenson | .10 | .30 |
| ☐ 456 Ramon Hernandez | .10 | .30 |
| ☐ 457 Scott Rolen | .20 | .50 |
| ☐ 458 Alex Arias | .10 | .30 |
| ☐ 459 Andy Ashby | .10 | .30 |
| ☐ 460 Kevin Jordan UER 474 | .10 | .30 |
| ☐ 461 Robert Person | .10 | .30 |
| ☐ 462 Paul Byrd | .10 | .30 |
| ☐ 463 Curt Schilling | .10 | .30 |
| ☐ 464 Mike Jackson | .10 | .30 |
| ☐ 465 Jason Kendall | .10 | .30 |
| ☐ 466 Pat Meares | .10 | .30 |
| ☐ 467 Bruce Aven | .10 | .30 |
| ☐ 468 Todd Ritchie | .10 | .30 |
| ☐ 469 Wil Cordero | .10 | .30 |
| ☐ 470 Aramis Ramirez | .10 | .30 |
| ☐ 471 Andy Benes | .10 | .30 |
| ☐ 472 Ray Lankford | .10 | .30 |
| ☐ 473 Fernando Vina | .10 | .30 |
| ☐ 474 Jim Edmonds | .10 | .30 |
| ☐ 475 Craig Paquette | .10 | .30 |
| ☐ 476 Pat Hentgen | .10 | .30 |
| ☐ 477 Darryl Kile | .10 | .30 |
| ☐ 478 Sterling Hitchcock | .10 | .30 |
| ☐ 479 Ruben Rivera | .10 | .30 |
| ☐ 480 Ryan Klesko | .10 | .30 |
| ☐ 481 Phil Nevin | .10 | .30 |
| ☐ 482 Woody Williams | .10 | .30 |
| ☐ 483 Carlos Hernandez | .10 | .30 |
| ☐ 484 Brian Meadows | .10 | .30 |
| ☐ 485 Bret Boone | .10 | .30 |
| ☐ 486 Barry Bonds | .75 | 2.00 |
| ☐ 487 Russ Ortiz | .10 | .30 |

| | | |
|---|---|---|
| ☐ 488 Bobby Estalella | .10 | .30 |
| ☐ 489 Rich Aurilia | .10 | .30 |
| ☐ 490 Bill Mueller | .10 | .30 |
| ☐ 491 Joe Nathan | .10 | .30 |
| ☐ 492 Russ Davis | .10 | .30 |
| ☐ 493 John Olerud | .10 | .30 |
| ☐ 494 Alex Rodriguez | .50 | 1.25 |
| ☐ 495 Freddy Garcia | .10 | .30 |
| ☐ 496 Carlos Guillen | .10 | .30 |
| ☐ 497 Aaron Sele | .10 | .30 |
| ☐ 498 Brett Tomko | .10 | .30 |
| ☐ 499 Jamie Moyer | .10 | .30 |
| ☐ 500 Mike Cameron | .10 | .30 |
| ☐ 501 Vinny Castilla | .10 | .30 |
| ☐ 502 Gerald Williams | .10 | .30 |
| ☐ 503 Mike DiFelice | .10 | .30 |
| ☐ 504 Ryan Rupe | .10 | .30 |
| ☐ 505 Greg Vaughn | .10 | .30 |
| ☐ 506 Miguel Cairo | .10 | .30 |
| ☐ 507 Juan Guzman | .10 | .30 |
| ☐ 508 Jose Guillen | .10 | .30 |
| ☐ 509 Gabe Kapler | .10 | .30 |
| ☐ 510 Rick Helling | .10 | .30 |
| ☐ 511 David Segui | .10 | .30 |
| ☐ 512 Doug Davis | .10 | .30 |
| ☐ 513 Justin Thompson | .10 | .30 |
| ☐ 514 Chad Curtis | .10 | .30 |
| ☐ 515 Tony Batista | .10 | .30 |
| ☐ 516 Billy Koch | .10 | .30 |
| ☐ 517 Raul Mondesi | .10 | .30 |
| ☐ 518 Joey Hamilton | .10 | .30 |
| ☐ 519 Darrin Fletcher | .10 | .30 |
| ☐ 520 Brad Fullmer | .10 | .30 |
| ☐ 521 Jose Cruz Jr. | .10 | .30 |
| ☐ 522 Kevin Witt | .10 | .30 |
| ☐ 523 Mark McGwire AUT | .40 | 1.00 |
| ☐ 524 Roberto Alomar AUT | .10 | .30 |
| ☐ 525 Chipper Jones AUT | .20 | .50 |
| ☐ 526 Derek Jeter AUT | .40 | 1.00 |
| ☐ 527 Ken Griffey Jr. AUT | .30 | .75 |
| ☐ 528 Sammy Sosa AUT | .20 | .50 |
| ☐ 529 Manny Ramirez AUT | .20 | .50 |
| ☐ 530 Ivan Rodriguez AUT | .10 | .30 |
| ☐ 531 Pedro Martinez AUT | .20 | .50 |
| ☐ 532 Mariano Rivera CL | .20 | .50 |
| ☐ 533 Sammy Sosa CL | .20 | .50 |
| ☐ 534 Cal Ripken CL | .50 | 1.25 |
| ☐ 535 Vladimir Guerrero CL | .20 | .50 |
| ☐ 536 Tony Gwynn CL | .20 | .50 |
| ☐ 537 Mark McGwire CL | .40 | 1.00 |
| ☐ 538 Bernie Williams CL | .10 | .30 |
| ☐ 539 Pedro Martinez CL | .20 | .50 |
| ☐ 540 Ken Griffey Jr. CL | .30 | .75 |

**2001 Upper Deck**

| | | |
|---|---|---|
| ☐ COMPLETE SET (450) | 90.00 | 150.00 |
| ☐ COMPLETE SERIES 1 (270) | 20.00 | 40.00 |
| ☐ COMPLETE SERIES 2 (180) | 60.00 | 100.00 |
| ☐ COMMON (46-270/300-450) | .10 | .30 |
| ☐ COMMON SR (1-45/271-300) | .20 | .50 |
| ☐ 1 Jeff DaVanon SR | .20 | .50 |
| ☐ 2 Aubrey Huff SR | .20 | .50 |
| ☐ 3 Pasqual Coco SR | .20 | .50 |
| ☐ 4 Barry Zito SR | .25 | .60 |
| ☐ 5 Augie Ojeda SR | .20 | .50 |
| ☐ 6 Chris Richard SR | .20 | .50 |
| ☐ 7 Josh Phelps SR | .20 | .50 |
| ☐ 8 Kevin Nicholson SR | .20 | .50 |
| ☐ 9 Juan Guzman SR | .20 | .50 |
| ☐ 10 Brandon Kolb SR | .20 | .50 |
| ☐ 11 Johan Santana SR | 2.50 | 6.00 |
| ☐ 12 Josh Kalinowski SR | .20 | .50 |
| ☐ 13 Tike Redman SR | .20 | .50 |
| ☐ 14 Ivanon Coffie SR | .20 | .50 |

| | | |
|---|---|---|
| ☐ 15 Chad Durbin SR | .20 | .50 |
| ☐ 16 Derrick Turnbow SR | .20 | .50 |
| ☐ 17 Scott Downs SR | .20 | .50 |
| ☐ 18 Jason Grilli SR | .20 | .50 |
| ☐ 19 Mark Buehrle SR | .25 | .60 |
| ☐ 20 Paxton Crawford SR | .20 | .50 |
| ☐ 21 Bronson Arroyo SR | .40 | 1.00 |
| ☐ 22 Tomas De la Rosa SR | .20 | .50 |
| ☐ 23 Paul Rigdon SR | .20 | .50 |
| ☐ 24 Rob Ramsay SR | .20 | .50 |
| ☐ 25 Damian Rolls SR | .20 | .50 |
| ☐ 26 Jason Conti SR | .20 | .50 |
| ☐ 27 John Parrish SR | .20 | .50 |
| ☐ 28 Geraldo Guzman SR | .20 | .50 |
| ☐ 29 Tony Mota SR | .20 | .50 |
| ☐ 30 Luis Rivas SR | .20 | .50 |
| ☐ 31 Brian Tollberg SR | .20 | .50 |
| ☐ 32 Adam Bernero SR | .20 | .50 |
| ☐ 33 Michael Cuddyer SR | .20 | .50 |
| ☐ 34 Josue Espada SR | .20 | .50 |
| ☐ 35 Joe Lawrence SR | .20 | .50 |
| ☐ 36 Chad Moeller SR | .20 | .50 |
| ☐ 37 Nick Bierbrodt SR | .20 | .50 |
| ☐ 38 DeWayne Wise SR | .20 | .50 |
| ☐ 39 Javier Cardona SR | .20 | .50 |
| ☐ 40 Hiram Bocachica SR | .20 | .50 |
| ☐ 41 Giuseppe Chiaramonte SR | .20 | .50 |
| ☐ 42 Alex Cabrera SR | .20 | .50 |
| ☐ 43 Jimmy Rollins SR | .20 | .50 |
| ☐ 44 Pat Flury SR RC | .20 | .50 |
| ☐ 45 Leo Estrella SR | .20 | .50 |
| ☐ 46 Darin Erstad | .10 | .30 |
| ☐ 47 Seth Etherton | .10 | .30 |
| ☐ 48 Troy Glaus | .10 | .30 |
| ☐ 49 Brian Cooper | .10 | .30 |
| ☐ 50 Tim Salmon | .20 | .50 |
| ☐ 51 Adam Kennedy | .10 | .30 |
| ☐ 52 Bengie Molina | .10 | .30 |
| ☐ 53 Jason Giambi | .10 | .30 |
| ☐ 54 Miguel Tejada | .10 | .30 |
| ☐ 55 Tim Hudson | .10 | .30 |
| ☐ 56 Eric Chavez | .10 | .30 |
| ☐ 57 Terrence Long | .10 | .30 |
| ☐ 58 Jason Isringhausen | .10 | .30 |
| ☐ 59 Ramon Hernandez | .10 | .30 |
| ☐ 60 Raul Mondesi | .10 | .30 |
| ☐ 61 David Wells | .10 | .30 |
| ☐ 62 Shannon Stewart | .10 | .30 |
| ☐ 63 Tony Batista | .10 | .30 |
| ☐ 64 Brad Fullmer | .10 | .30 |
| ☐ 65 Chris Carpenter | .10 | .30 |
| ☐ 66 Homer Bush | .10 | .30 |
| ☐ 67 Gerald Williams | .10 | .30 |
| ☐ 68 Miguel Cairo | .10 | .30 |
| ☐ 69 Ryan Rupe | .10 | .30 |
| ☐ 70 Greg Vaughn | .10 | .30 |
| ☐ 71 John Flaherty | .10 | .30 |
| ☐ 72 Dan Wheeler | .10 | .30 |
| ☐ 73 Fred McGriff | .20 | .50 |
| ☐ 74 Roberto Alomar | .20 | .50 |
| ☐ 75 Bartolo Colon | .10 | .30 |
| ☐ 76 Kenny Lofton | .10 | .30 |
| ☐ 77 David Segui | .10 | .30 |
| ☐ 78 Omar Vizquel | .20 | .50 |
| ☐ 79 Russ Branyan | .10 | .30 |
| ☐ 80 Chuck Finley | .10 | .30 |
| ☐ 81 Manny Ramirez UER | .20 | .50 |
| ☐ 82 Alex Rodriguez | .50 | 1.25 |
| ☐ 83 John Halama | .10 | .30 |
| ☐ 84 Mike Cameron | .10 | .30 |
| ☐ 85 David Bell | .10 | .30 |
| ☐ 86 Jay Buhner | .10 | .30 |
| ☐ 87 Aaron Sele | .10 | .30 |
| ☐ 88 Rickey Henderson | .30 | .75 |
| ☐ 89 Brook Fordyce | .10 | .30 |
| ☐ 90 Cal Ripken | 1.00 | 2.50 |
| ☐ 91 Mike Mussina | .20 | .50 |
| ☐ 92 Delino DeShields | .10 | .30 |
| ☐ 93 Melvin Mora | .10 | .30 |
| ☐ 94 Sidney Ponson | .10 | .30 |
| ☐ 95 Brady Anderson | .10 | .30 |
| ☐ 96 Ivan Rodriguez | .20 | .50 |
| ☐ 97 Ricky Ledee | .10 | .30 |
| ☐ 98 Rick Helling | .10 | .30 |
| ☐ 99 Ruben Mateo | .10 | .30 |
| ☐ 100 Luis Alicea | .10 | .30 |
| ☐ 101 John Wetteland | .10 | .30 |
| ☐ 102 Mike Lamb | .10 | .30 |

|  |  | | |  |  | | |  |  | | |
|---|---|---|---|---|---|---|---|---|---|---|---|
| 103 | Carl Everett | .10 | .30 | 191 | Chan Ho Park | .10 | .30 | 279 | Rafael Soriano SR RC | .20 | .50 |
| 104 | Troy O'Leary | .10 | .30 | 192 | Adrian Beltre | .10 | .30 | 280 | Juan Diaz SR RC | .20 | .50 |
| 105 | Wilton Veras | .10 | .30 | 193 | Mark Grudzielanek | .10 | .30 | 281 | Horacio Ramirez SR RC | .25 | .60 |
| 106 | Pedro Martinez | .20 | .50 | 194 | Gary Sheffield | .10 | .30 | 282 | Tsuyoshi Shinjo SR | .25 | .60 |
| 107 | Rolando Arrojo | .10 | .30 | 195 | Tom Goodwin | .10 | .30 | 283 | Keith Ginter SR | .20 | .50 |
| 108 | Scott Hatteberg | .10 | .30 | 196 | Lee Stevens | .10 | .30 | 284 | Esix Snead SR | .20 | .50 |
| 109 | Jason Varitek | .30 | .75 | 197 | Javier Vazquez | .10 | .30 | 285 | Erick Almonte SR RC | .20 | .50 |
| 110 | Jose Offerman | .10 | .30 | 198 | Milton Bradley | .10 | .30 | 286 | Travis Hafner SR RC | 2.00 | 5.00 |
| 111 | Carlos Beltran | .10 | .30 | 199 | Vladimir Guerrero | .30 | .75 | 287 | Jason Smith SR RC | .20 | .50 |
| 112 | Johnny Damon | .20 | .50 | 200 | Carl Pavano | .10 | .30 | 288 | Jackson Melian SR RC | .20 | .50 |
| 113 | Mark Quinn | .10 | .30 | 201 | Orlando Cabrera | .10 | .30 | 289 | Tyler Walker SR RC | .20 | .50 |
| 114 | Rey Sanchez | .10 | .30 | 202 | Tony Armas Jr. | .10 | .30 | 290 | Jason Standridge SR | .20 | .50 |
| 115 | Mac Suzuki | .10 | .30 | 203 | Jeff Kent | .10 | .30 | 291 | Juan Uribe SR RC | .25 | .60 |
| 116 | Jermaine Dye | .10 | .30 | 204 | Calvin Murray | .10 | .30 | 292 | Adrian Hernandez SR | .20 | .50 |
| 117 | Chris Fussell | .10 | .30 | 205 | Ellis Burks | .10 | .30 | 293 | Jason Michaels SR RC | .20 | .50 |
| 118 | Jeff Weaver | .10 | .30 | 206 | Barry Bonds | .75 | 2.00 | 294 | Jason Hart SR | .20 | .50 |
| 119 | Dean Palmer | .10 | .30 | 207 | Russ Ortiz | .10 | .30 | 295 | Albert Pujols SR RC | 30.00 | 60.00 |
| 120 | Robert Fick | .10 | .30 | 208 | Marvin Benard | .10 | .30 | 296 | Morgan Ensberg SR RC | .75 | 2.00 |
| 121 | Brian Moehler | .10 | .30 | 209 | Joe Nathan | .10 | .30 | 297 | Brandon Inge SR | .20 | .50 |
| 122 | Damion Easley | .10 | .30 | 210 | Preston Wilson | .10 | .30 | 298 | Jesus Colome SR | .20 | .50 |
| 123 | Juan Encarnacion | .10 | .30 | 211 | Cliff Floyd | .10 | .30 | 299 | Kyle Kessel SR RC | .20 | .50 |
| 124 | Tony Clark | .10 | .30 | 212 | Mike Lowell | .10 | .30 | 300 | Timo Perez SR | .20 | .50 |
| 125 | Cristian Guzman | .10 | .30 | 213 | Ryan Dempster | .10 | .30 | 301 | Mo Vaughn | .10 | .30 |
| 126 | Matt LeCroy | .10 | .30 | 214 | Brad Penny | .10 | .30 | 302 | Ismael Valdes | .10 | .30 |
| 127 | Eric Milton | .10 | .30 | 215 | Mike Redmond | .10 | .30 | 303 | Glenallen Hill | .10 | .30 |
| 128 | Jay Canizaro | .10 | .30 | 216 | Luis Castillo | .10 | .30 | 304 | Garret Anderson | .10 | .30 |
| 129 | David Ortiz | .30 | .75 | 217 | Derek Bell | .10 | .30 | 305 | Johnny Damon | .20 | .50 |
| 130 | Brad Radke | .10 | .30 | 218 | Mike Hampton | .10 | .30 | 306 | Jose Ortiz | .10 | .30 |
| 131 | Jacque Jones | .10 | .30 | 219 | Todd Zeile | .10 | .30 | 307 | Mark Mulder | .10 | .30 |
| 132 | Magglio Ordonez | .10 | .30 | 220 | Robin Ventura | .10 | .30 | 308 | Adam Piatt | .10 | .30 |
| 133 | Carlos Lee | .10 | .30 | 221 | Mike Piazza | .50 | 1.25 | 309 | Gil Heredia | .10 | .30 |
| 134 | Mike Sirotka | .10 | .30 | 222 | Al Leiter | .10 | .30 | 310 | Mike Sirotka | .10 | .30 |
| 135 | Ray Durham | .10 | .30 | 223 | Edgardo Alfonzo | .10 | .30 | 311 | Carlos Delgado | .20 | .50 |
| 136 | Paul Konerko | .10 | .30 | 224 | Mike Bordick | .10 | .30 | 312 | Alex Gonzalez | .10 | .30 |
| 137 | Charles Johnson | .10 | .30 | 225 | Phil Nevin | .10 | .30 | 313 | Jose Cruz Jr. | .10 | .30 |
| 138 | James Baldwin | .10 | .30 | 226 | Ryan Klesko | .10 | .30 | 314 | Darrin Fletcher | .10 | .30 |
| 139 | Jeff Abbott | .10 | .30 | 227 | Adam Eaton | .10 | .30 | 315 | Ben Grieve | .10 | .30 |
| 140 | Roger Clemens | .60 | 1.50 | 228 | Eric Owens | .10 | .30 | 316 | Vinny Castilla | .10 | .30 |
| 141 | Derek Jeter | .75 | 2.00 | 229 | Tony Gwynn | .40 | 1.00 | 317 | Wilson Alvarez | .10 | .30 |
| 142 | David Justice | .10 | .30 | 230 | Matt Clement | .10 | .30 | 318 | Brent Abernathy | .10 | .30 |
| 143 | Ramiro Mendoza | .10 | .30 | 231 | Wiki Gonzalez | .10 | .30 | 319 | Ellis Burks | .10 | .30 |
| 144 | Chuck Knoblauch | .10 | .30 | 232 | Robert Person | .10 | .30 | 320 | Jim Thome | .20 | .50 |
| 145 | Orlando Hernandez | .10 | .30 | 233 | Doug Glanville | .10 | .30 | 321 | Juan Gonzalez | .20 | .50 |
| 146 | Alfonso Soriano | .20 | .50 | 234 | Scott Rolen | .20 | .50 | 322 | Ed Taubensee | .10 | .30 |
| 147 | Jeff Bagwell | .20 | .50 | 235 | Mike Lieberthal | .10 | .30 | 323 | Travis Fryman | .10 | .30 |
| 148 | Julio Lugo | .10 | .30 | 236 | Randy Wolf | .10 | .30 | 324 | John Olerud | .10 | .30 |
| 149 | Mitch Meluskey | .10 | .30 | 237 | Bob Abreu | .10 | .30 | 325 | Edgar Martinez | .20 | .50 |
| 150 | Jose Lima | .10 | .30 | 238 | Pat Burrell | .10 | .30 | 326 | Freddy Garcia | .10 | .30 |
| 151 | Richard Hidalgo | .10 | .30 | 239 | Bruce Chen | .10 | .30 | 327 | Bret Boone | .10 | .30 |
| 152 | Moises Alou | .10 | .30 | 240 | Kevin Young | .10 | .30 | 328 | Kazuhiro Sasaki | .10 | .30 |
| 153 | Scott Elarton | .10 | .30 | 241 | Todd Ritchie | .10 | .30 | 329 | Albert Belle | .10 | .30 |
| 154 | Andruw Jones | .20 | .50 | 242 | Adrian Brown | .10 | .30 | 330 | Mike Bordick | .10 | .30 |
| 155 | Quivio Veras | .10 | .30 | 243 | Chad Hermansen | .10 | .30 | 331 | David Segui | .10 | .30 |
| 156 | Greg Maddux | .50 | 1.25 | 244 | Warren Morris | .10 | .30 | 332 | Pat Hentgen | .10 | .30 |
| 157 | Brian Jordan | .10 | .30 | 245 | Kris Benson | .10 | .30 | 333 | Alex Rodriguez | .50 | 1.25 |
| 158 | Andres Galarraga | .10 | .30 | 246 | Jason Kendall | .10 | .30 | 334 | Andres Galarraga | .10 | .30 |
| 159 | Kevin Millwood | .10 | .30 | 247 | Pokey Reese | .10 | .30 | 335 | Gabe Kapler | .10 | .30 |
| 160 | Rafael Furcal | .10 | .30 | 248 | Rob Bell | .10 | .30 | 336 | Ken Caminiti | .10 | .30 |
| 161 | Jeromy Burnitz | .10 | .30 | 249 | Ken Griffey Jr. | .50 | 1.25 | 337 | Rafael Palmeiro | .20 | .50 |
| 162 | Jimmy Haynes | .10 | .30 | 250 | Sean Casey | .10 | .30 | 338 | Manny Ramirez Sox | .20 | .50 |
| 163 | Mark Loretta | .10 | .30 | 251 | Aaron Boone | .10 | .30 | 339 | David Cone | .10 | .30 |
| 164 | Ron Belliard | .10 | .30 | 252 | Pete Harnisch | .10 | .30 | 340 | Nomar Garciaparra | .50 | 1.25 |
| 165 | Richie Sexson | .10 | .30 | 253 | Barry Larkin | .20 | .50 | 341 | Trot Nixon | .10 | .30 |
| 166 | Kevin Barker | .10 | .30 | 254 | Dmitri Young | .10 | .30 | 342 | Derek Lowe | .10 | .30 |
| 167 | Jeff D'Amico | .10 | .30 | 255 | Todd Hollandsworth | .10 | .30 | 343 | Roberto Hernandez | .10 | .30 |
| 168 | Rick Ankiel | .10 | .30 | 256 | Pedro Astacio | .10 | .30 | 344 | Mike Sweeney | .10 | .30 |
| 169 | Mark McGwire | .75 | 2.00 | 257 | Todd Helton | .20 | .50 | 345 | Carlos Febles | .10 | .30 |
| 170 | J.D. Drew | .10 | .30 | 258 | Terry Shumpert | .10 | .30 | 346 | Jeff Suppan | .10 | .30 |
| 171 | Eli Marrero | .10 | .30 | 259 | Neifi Perez | .10 | .30 | 347 | Roger Cedeno | .10 | .30 |
| 172 | Darryl Kile | .10 | .30 | 260 | Jeffrey Hammonds | .10 | .30 | 348 | Bobby Higginson | .10 | .30 |
| 173 | Edgar Renteria | .10 | .30 | 261 | Ben Petrick | .10 | .30 | 349 | Deivi Cruz | .10 | .30 |
| 174 | Will Clark | .20 | .50 | 262 | Mark McGwire SH | .40 | 1.00 | 350 | Mitch Meluskey | .10 | .30 |
| 175 | Eric Young | .10 | .30 | 263 | Derek Jeter SH | .40 | 1.00 | 351 | Matt Lawton | .10 | .30 |
| 176 | Mark Grace | .20 | .50 | 264 | Sammy Sosa SH | .20 | .50 | 352 | Mark Redman | .10 | .30 |
| 177 | Jon Lieber | .10 | .30 | 265 | Cal Ripken SH | .50 | 1.25 | 353 | Jay Canizaro | .10 | .30 |
| 178 | Damon Buford | .10 | .30 | 266 | Pedro Martinez SH | .10 | .30 | 354 | Corey Koskie | .10 | .30 |
| 179 | Kerry Wood | .10 | .30 | 267 | Barry Bonds SH | .40 | 1.00 | 355 | Matt Kinney | .10 | .30 |
| 180 | Rondell White | .10 | .30 | 268 | Fred McGriff SH | .10 | .30 | 356 | Frank Thomas | .30 | .75 |
| 181 | Joe Girardi | .10 | .30 | 269 | Randy Johnson SH | .20 | .50 | 357 | Sandy Alomar Jr. | .10 | .30 |
| 182 | Curt Schilling | .10 | .30 | 270 | Darin Erstad SH | .10 | .30 | 358 | David Wells | .10 | .30 |
| 183 | Randy Johnson | .30 | .75 | 271 | Ichiro Suzuki SR RC | 5.00 | 12.00 | 359 | Jim Parque | .10 | .30 |
| 184 | Steve Finley | .10 | .30 | 272 | Wilson Betemit SR RC | .75 | 2.00 | 360 | Chris Singleton | .10 | .30 |
| 185 | Kelly Stinnett | .10 | .30 | 273 | Corey Patterson SR | .20 | .50 | 361 | Tino Martinez | .20 | .50 |
| 186 | Jay Bell | .10 | .30 | 274 | Sean Douglass SR RC | .20 | .50 | 362 | Paul O'Neill | .20 | .50 |
| 187 | Matt Mantei | .10 | .30 | 275 | Mike Penney SR RC | .20 | .50 | 363 | Mike Mussina | .20 | .50 |
| 188 | Luis Gonzalez | .10 | .30 | 276 | Nate Teut SR RC | .20 | .50 | 364 | Bernie Williams | .20 | .50 |
| 189 | Shawn Green | .10 | .30 | 277 | Ricardo Rodriguez SR RC | .20 | .50 | 365 | Andy Pettite | .20 | .50 |
| 190 | Todd Hundley | .10 | .30 | 278 | Brandon Duckworth SR RC | .20 | .50 | 366 | Mariano Rivera | .30 | .75 |

|  |  | | |
|---|---|---|---|
| ❑ 367 | Brad Ausmus | .10 | .30 |
| ❑ 368 | Craig Biggio | .20 | .50 |
| ❑ 369 | Lance Berkman | .10 | .30 |
| ❑ 370 | Shane Reynolds | .10 | .30 |
| ❑ 371 | Chipper Jones | .30 | .75 |
| ❑ 372 | Tom Glavine | .20 | .50 |
| ❑ 373 | B.J. Surhoff | .10 | .30 |
| ❑ 374 | John Smoltz | .20 | .50 |
| ❑ 375 | Rico Brogna | .10 | .30 |
| ❑ 376 | Geoff Jenkins | .10 | .30 |
| ❑ 377 | Jose Hernandez | .10 | .30 |
| ❑ 378 | Tyler Houston | .10 | .30 |
| ❑ 379 | Henry Blanco | .10 | .30 |
| ❑ 380 | Jeffrey Hammonds | .10 | .30 |
| ❑ 381 | Jim Edmonds | .10 | .30 |
| ❑ 382 | Fernando Vina | .10 | .30 |
| ❑ 383 | Andy Benes | .10 | .30 |
| ❑ 384 | Ray Lankford | .10 | .30 |
| ❑ 385 | Dustin Hermanson | .10 | .30 |
| ❑ 386 | Todd Hundley | .10 | .30 |
| ❑ 387 | Sammy Sosa | .30 | .75 |
| ❑ 388 | Tom Gordon | .10 | .30 |
| ❑ 389 | Bill Mueller | .10 | .30 |
| ❑ 390 | Ron Coomer | .10 | .30 |
| ❑ 391 | Matt Stairs | .10 | .30 |
| ❑ 392 | Mark Grace | .20 | .50 |
| ❑ 393 | Matt Williams | .10 | .30 |
| ❑ 394 | Todd Stottlemyre | .10 | .30 |
| ❑ 395 | Tony Womack | .10 | .30 |
| ❑ 396 | Erubiel Durazo | .10 | .30 |
| ❑ 397 | Reggie Sanders | .10 | .30 |
| ❑ 398 | Andy Ashby | .10 | .30 |
| ❑ 399 | Eric Karros | .10 | .30 |
| ❑ 400 | Kevin Brown | .10 | .30 |
| ❑ 401 | Darren Dreifort | .10 | .30 |
| ❑ 402 | Fernando Tatis | .10 | .30 |
| ❑ 403 | Jose Vidro | .10 | .30 |
| ❑ 404 | Peter Bergeron | .10 | .30 |
| ❑ 405 | Geoff Blum | .10 | .30 |
| ❑ 406 | J.T. Snow | .10 | .30 |
| ❑ 407 | Livan Hernandez | .10 | .30 |
| ❑ 408 | Robb Nen | .10 | .30 |
| ❑ 409 | Bobby Estalella | .10 | .30 |
| ❑ 410 | Rich Aurilia | .10 | .30 |
| ❑ 411 | Eric Davis | .10 | .30 |
| ❑ 412 | Charles Johnson | .10 | .30 |
| ❑ 413 | Alex Gonzalez | .10 | .30 |
| ❑ 414 | A.J. Burnett | .10 | .30 |
| ❑ 415 | Antonio Alfonseca | .10 | .30 |
| ❑ 416 | Derrek Lee | .20 | .50 |
| ❑ 417 | Jay Payton | .10 | .30 |
| ❑ 418 | Kevin Appier | .10 | .30 |
| ❑ 419 | Steve Trachsel | .10 | .30 |
| ❑ 420 | Rey Ordonez | .10 | .30 |
| ❑ 421 | Darryl Hamilton | .10 | .30 |
| ❑ 422 | Ben Davis | .10 | .30 |
| ❑ 423 | Damian Jackson | .10 | .30 |
| ❑ 424 | Mark Kotsay | .10 | .30 |
| ❑ 425 | Trevor Hoffman | .10 | .30 |
| ❑ 426 | Travis Lee | .10 | .30 |
| ❑ 427 | Omar Daal | .10 | .30 |
| ❑ 428 | Paul Byrd | .10 | .30 |
| ❑ 429 | Reggie Taylor | .10 | .30 |
| ❑ 430 | Brian Giles | .10 | .30 |
| ❑ 431 | Derek Bell | .10 | .30 |
| ❑ 432 | Francisco Cordova | .10 | .30 |
| ❑ 433 | Pat Meares | .10 | .30 |
| ❑ 434 | Scott Williamson | .10 | .30 |
| ❑ 435 | Jason LaRue | .10 | .30 |
| ❑ 436 | Michael Tucker | .10 | .30 |
| ❑ 437 | Wilton Guerrero | .10 | .30 |
| ❑ 438 | Mike Hampton | .10 | .30 |
| ❑ 439 | Ron Gant | .10 | .30 |
| ❑ 440 | Jeff Cirillo | .10 | .30 |
| ❑ 441 | Denny Neagle | .10 | .30 |
| ❑ 442 | Larry Walker | .10 | .30 |
| ❑ 443 | Juan Pierre | .10 | .30 |
| ❑ 444 | Todd Walker | .10 | .30 |
| ❑ 445 | Jason Giambi SH CL | .10 | .30 |
| ❑ 446 | Jeff Kent SH CL | .10 | .30 |
| ❑ 447 | Mariano Rivera SH CL | .20 | .50 |
| ❑ 448 | Edgar Martinez SH CL | .10 | .30 |
| ❑ 449 | Troy Glaus SH CL | .10 | .30 |
| ❑ 450 | Alex Rodriguez SH CL | .30 | .75 |

# 2002 Upper Deck

|  |  | | |
|---|---|---|---|
| ❑ | COMPLETE SET (745) | 85.00 | 160.00 |
| ❑ | COMPLETE SERIES 1 (500) | 60.00 | 110.00 |
| ❑ | COMPLETE SERIES 2 (245) | 25.00 | 50.00 |
| ❑ | COMMON (51-500/546-745) | .10 | .30 |
| ❑ | COMMON SR (1-50/501-545) | .40 | 1.00 |
| ❑ 1 | Mark Prior SR | .75 | 2.00 |
| ❑ 2 | Mark Teixeira SR | 2.00 | 5.00 |
| ❑ 3 | Brian Roberts SR | .75 | 2.00 |
| ❑ 4 | Jason Romano SR | .40 | 1.00 |
| ❑ 5 | Dennis Stark SR | .40 | 1.00 |
| ❑ 6 | Oscar Salazar SR | .40 | 1.00 |
| ❑ 7 | John Patterson SR | .40 | 1.00 |
| ❑ 8 | Shane Loux SR | .40 | 1.00 |
| ❑ 9 | Marcus Giles SR | .40 | 1.00 |
| ❑ 10 | Juan Cruz SR | .40 | 1.00 |
| ❑ 11 | Jorge Julio SR | .40 | 1.00 |
| ❑ 12 | Adam Dunn SR | .40 | 1.00 |
| ❑ 13 | Delvin James SR | .40 | 1.00 |
| ❑ 14 | Jeremy Affeldt SR | .40 | 1.00 |
| ❑ 15 | Tim Raines Jr. SR | .40 | 1.00 |
| ❑ 16 | Luke Hudson SR | .40 | 1.00 |
| ❑ 17 | Todd Sears SR | .40 | 1.00 |
| ❑ 18 | George Perez SR | .40 | 1.00 |
| ❑ 19 | Wilmy Caceres SR | .40 | 1.00 |
| ❑ 20 | Abraham Nunez SR | .40 | 1.00 |
| ❑ 21 | Mike Amrhein SR RC | .40 | 1.00 |
| ❑ 22 | Carlos Hernandez SR | .40 | 1.00 |
| ❑ 23 | Scott Hodges SR | .40 | 1.00 |
| ❑ 24 | Brandon Knight SR | .40 | 1.00 |
| ❑ 25 | Geoff Goetz SR | .40 | 1.00 |
| ❑ 26 | Carlos Garcia SR | .40 | 1.00 |
| ❑ 27 | Luis Pineda SR | .40 | 1.00 |
| ❑ 28 | Chris Gissell SR | .40 | 1.00 |
| ❑ 29 | Jae Weong Seo SR | .40 | 1.00 |
| ❑ 30 | Paul Phillips SR | .40 | 1.00 |
| ❑ 31 | Cory Aldridge SR | .40 | 1.00 |
| ❑ 32 | Aaron Cook SR RC | .40 | 1.00 |
| ❑ 33 | Randy Espina SR RC | .40 | 1.00 |
| ❑ 34 | Jason Phillips SR | .40 | 1.00 |
| ❑ 35 | Carlos Silva SR | .40 | 1.00 |
| ❑ 36 | Ryan Mills SR | .40 | 1.00 |
| ❑ 37 | Pedro Santana SR | .40 | 1.00 |
| ❑ 38 | John Grabow SR | .40 | 1.00 |
| ❑ 39 | Cody Ransom SR | .40 | 1.00 |
| ❑ 40 | Orlando Woodards SR | .40 | 1.00 |
| ❑ 41 | Bud Smith SR | .40 | 1.00 |
| ❑ 42 | Junior Guerrero SR | .40 | 1.00 |
| ❑ 43 | David Brous SR | .40 | 1.00 |
| ❑ 44 | Steve Green SR | .40 | 1.00 |
| ❑ 45 | Brian Rogers SR | .40 | 1.00 |
| ❑ 46 | Juan Figueroa SR RC | .40 | 1.00 |
| ❑ 47 | Nick Punto SR | .40 | 1.00 |
| ❑ 48 | Junior Herndon SR | .40 | 1.00 |
| ❑ 49 | Justin Kaye SR | .40 | 1.00 |
| ❑ 50 | Jason Kamuth SR | .40 | 1.00 |
| ❑ 51 | Troy Glaus | .10 | .30 |
| ❑ 52 | Bengie Molina | .10 | .30 |
| ❑ 53 | Ramon Ortiz | .10 | .30 |
| ❑ 54 | Adam Kennedy | .10 | .30 |
| ❑ 55 | Jarrod Washburn | .10 | .30 |
| ❑ 56 | Troy Percival | .10 | .30 |
| ❑ 57 | David Eckstein | .10 | .30 |
| ❑ 58 | Ben Weber | .10 | .30 |
| ❑ 59 | Larry Barnes | .10 | .30 |
| ❑ 60 | Ismael Valdes | .10 | .30 |
| ❑ 61 | Benji Gil | .10 | .30 |
| ❑ 62 | Scott Schoenewels | .10 | .30 |
| ❑ 63 | Pat Rapp | .10 | .30 |
| ❑ 64 | Jason Giambi | .10 | .30 |
| ❑ 65 | Mark Mulder | .10 | .30 |
| ❑ 66 | Ron Gant | .10 | .30 |
| ❑ 67 | Johnny Damon | .20 | .50 |

|  |  | | |
|---|---|---|---|
| ❑ 68 | Adam Piatt | .10 | .30 |
| ❑ 69 | Jermaine Dye | .10 | .30 |
| ❑ 70 | Jason Hart | .10 | .30 |
| ❑ 71 | Eric Chavez | .10 | .30 |
| ❑ 72 | Jim Mecir | .10 | .30 |
| ❑ 73 | Barry Zito | .10 | .30 |
| ❑ 74 | Jason Isringhausen | .10 | .30 |
| ❑ 75 | Jeremy Giambi | .10 | .30 |
| ❑ 76 | Olmedo Saenz | .10 | .30 |
| ❑ 77 | Terrence Long | .10 | .30 |
| ❑ 78 | Ramon Hernandez | .10 | .30 |
| ❑ 79 | Chris Carpenter | .10 | .30 |
| ❑ 80 | Raul Mondesi | .10 | .30 |
| ❑ 81 | Carlos Delgado | .10 | .30 |
| ❑ 82 | Billy Koch | .10 | .30 |
| ❑ 83 | Vernon Wells | .10 | .30 |
| ❑ 84 | Darrin Fletcher | .10 | .30 |
| ❑ 85 | Homer Bush | .10 | .30 |
| ❑ 86 | Pasqual Coco | .10 | .30 |
| ❑ 87 | Shannon Stewart | .10 | .30 |
| ❑ 88 | Chris Woodward | .10 | .30 |
| ❑ 89 | Joe Lawrence | .10 | .30 |
| ❑ 90 | Esteban Loaiza | .10 | .30 |
| ❑ 91 | Cesar Izturis | .10 | .30 |
| ❑ 92 | Kelvim Escobar | .10 | .30 |
| ❑ 93 | Greg Vaughn | .10 | .30 |
| ❑ 94 | Brent Abernathy | .10 | .30 |
| ❑ 95 | Tanyon Sturtze | .10 | .30 |
| ❑ 96 | Steve Cox | .10 | .30 |
| ❑ 97 | Aubrey Huff | .10 | .30 |
| ❑ 98 | Jesus Colome | .10 | .30 |
| ❑ 99 | Ben Grieve | .10 | .30 |
| ❑ 100 | Esteban Yan | .10 | .30 |
| ❑ 101 | Joe Kennedy | .10 | .30 |
| ❑ 102 | Felix Martinez | .10 | .30 |
| ❑ 103 | Nick Bierbrodt | .10 | .30 |
| ❑ 104 | Damian Rolls | .10 | .30 |
| ❑ 105 | Russ Johnson | .10 | .30 |
| ❑ 106 | Toby Hall | .10 | .30 |
| ❑ 107 | Roberto Alomar | .20 | .50 |
| ❑ 108 | Bartolo Colon | .10 | .30 |
| ❑ 109 | John Rocker | .10 | .30 |
| ❑ 110 | Juan Gonzalez | .10 | .30 |
| ❑ 111 | Einar Diaz | .10 | .30 |
| ❑ 112 | Chuck Finley | .10 | .30 |
| ❑ 113 | Kenny Lofton | .10 | .30 |
| ❑ 114 | Danny Baez | .10 | .30 |
| ❑ 115 | Travis Fryman | .10 | .30 |
| ❑ 116 | C.C. Sabathia | .10 | .30 |
| ❑ 117 | Paul Shuey | .10 | .30 |
| ❑ 118 | Marty Cordova | .10 | .30 |
| ❑ 119 | Ellis Burks | .10 | .30 |
| ❑ 120 | Bob Wickman | .10 | .30 |
| ❑ 121 | Edgar Martinez | .20 | .50 |
| ❑ 122 | Freddy Garcia | .10 | .30 |
| ❑ 123 | Ichiro Suzuki | .60 | 1.50 |
| ❑ 124 | John Olerud | .10 | .30 |
| ❑ 125 | Gil Meche | .10 | .30 |
| ❑ 126 | Dan Wilson | .10 | .30 |
| ❑ 127 | Aaron Sele | .10 | .30 |
| ❑ 128 | Kazuhiro Sasaki | .10 | .30 |
| ❑ 129 | Mark McLemore | .10 | .30 |
| ❑ 130 | Carlos Guillen | .10 | .30 |
| ❑ 131 | Al Martin | .10 | .30 |
| ❑ 132 | David Bell | .10 | .30 |
| ❑ 133 | Jay Buhner | .10 | .30 |
| ❑ 134 | Stan Javier | .10 | .30 |
| ❑ 135 | Tony Batista | .10 | .30 |
| ❑ 136 | Jason Johnson | .10 | .30 |
| ❑ 137 | Brook Fordyce | .10 | .30 |
| ❑ 138 | Mike Kinkade | .10 | .30 |
| ❑ 139 | Willis Roberts | .10 | .30 |
| ❑ 140 | David Segui | .10 | .30 |
| ❑ 141 | Josh Towers | .10 | .30 |
| ❑ 142 | Jeff Conine | .10 | .30 |
| ❑ 143 | Chris Richard | .10 | .30 |
| ❑ 144 | Pat Hentgen | .10 | .30 |
| ❑ 145 | Melvin Mora | .10 | .30 |
| ❑ 146 | Jerry Hairston Jr. | .10 | .30 |
| ❑ 147 | Calvin Maduro | .10 | .30 |
| ❑ 148 | Brady Anderson | .10 | .30 |
| ❑ 149 | Alex Rodriguez | .50 | 1.25 |
| ❑ 150 | Kenny Rogers | .10 | .30 |
| ❑ 151 | Chad Curtis | .10 | .30 |
| ❑ 152 | Ricky Ledee | .10 | .30 |
| ❑ 153 | Rafael Palmeiro | .20 | .50 |
| ❑ 154 | Rob Bell | .10 | .30 |
| ❑ 155 | Rick Helling | .10 | .30 |

|  |  | | |
|---|---|---|---|
| ☐ 156 | Doug Davis | .10 | .30 |
| ☐ 157 | Mike Lamb | .10 | .30 |
| ☐ 158 | Gabe Kapler | .10 | .30 |
| ☐ 159 | Jeff Zimmerman | .10 | .30 |
| ☐ 160 | Bill Haselman | .10 | .30 |
| ☐ 161 | Tim Crabtree | .10 | .30 |
| ☐ 162 | Carlos Pena | .20 | .50 |
| ☐ 163 | Nomar Garciaparra | .50 | 1.25 |
| ☐ 164 | Shea Hillenbrand | .10 | .30 |
| ☐ 165 | Hideo Nomo | .30 | .75 |
| ☐ 166 | Manny Ramirez | .20 | .50 |
| ☐ 167 | Jose Offerman | .10 | .30 |
| ☐ 168 | Scott Hatteberg | .10 | .30 |
| ☐ 169 | Trot Nixon | .10 | .30 |
| ☐ 170 | Darren Lewis | .10 | .30 |
| ☐ 171 | Derek Lowe | .10 | .30 |
| ☐ 172 | Troy O'Leary | .10 | .30 |
| ☐ 173 | Tim Wakefield | .10 | .30 |
| ☐ 174 | Chris Stynes | .10 | .30 |
| ☐ 175 | John Valentin | .10 | .30 |
| ☐ 176 | David Cone | .10 | .30 |
| ☐ 177 | Neifi Perez | .10 | .30 |
| ☐ 178 | Brent Mayne | .10 | .30 |
| ☐ 179 | Dan Reichert | .10 | .30 |
| ☐ 180 | A.J. Hinch | .10 | .30 |
| ☐ 181 | Chris George | .10 | .30 |
| ☐ 182 | Mike Sweeney | .10 | .30 |
| ☐ 183 | Jeff Suppan | .10 | .30 |
| ☐ 184 | Roberto Hernandez | .10 | .30 |
| ☐ 185 | Joe Randa | .10 | .30 |
| ☐ 186 | Paul Byrd | .10 | .30 |
| ☐ 187 | Luis Ordaz | .10 | .30 |
| ☐ 188 | Kris Wilson | .10 | .30 |
| ☐ 189 | Dee Brown | .10 | .30 |
| ☐ 190 | Tony Clark | .10 | .30 |
| ☐ 191 | Matt Anderson | .10 | .30 |
| ☐ 192 | Robert Fick | .10 | .30 |
| ☐ 193 | Juan Encarnacion | .10 | .30 |
| ☐ 194 | Dean Palmer | .10 | .30 |
| ☐ 195 | Victor Santos | .10 | .30 |
| ☐ 196 | Damion Easley | .10 | .30 |
| ☐ 197 | Jose Lima | .10 | .30 |
| ☐ 198 | Deivi Cruz | .10 | .30 |
| ☐ 199 | Roger Cedeno | .10 | .30 |
| ☐ 200 | Jose Macias | .10 | .30 |
| ☐ 201 | Jeff Weaver | .10 | .30 |
| ☐ 202 | Brandon Inge | .10 | .30 |
| ☐ 203 | Brian Moehler | .10 | .30 |
| ☐ 204 | Brad Radke | .10 | .30 |
| ☐ 205 | Doug Mientkiewicz | .10 | .30 |
| ☐ 206 | Cristian Guzman | .10 | .30 |
| ☐ 207 | Corey Koskie | .10 | .30 |
| ☐ 208 | LaTroy Hawkins | .10 | .30 |
| ☐ 209 | J.C. Romero | .10 | .30 |
| ☐ 210 | Chad Allen | .10 | .30 |
| ☐ 211 | Torii Hunter | .10 | .30 |
| ☐ 212 | Travis Miller | .10 | .30 |
| ☐ 213 | Joe Mays | .10 | .30 |
| ☐ 214 | Todd Jones | .10 | .30 |
| ☐ 215 | David Ortiz | .30 | .75 |
| ☐ 216 | Brian Buchanan | .10 | .30 |
| ☐ 217 | A.J. Pierzynski | .10 | .30 |
| ☐ 218 | Carlos Lee | .10 | .30 |
| ☐ 219 | Gary Glover | .10 | .30 |
| ☐ 220 | Jose Valentin | .10 | .30 |
| ☐ 221 | Aaron Rowand | .10 | .30 |
| ☐ 222 | Sandy Alomar Jr. | .10 | .30 |
| ☐ 223 | Herbert Perry | .10 | .30 |
| ☐ 224 | Jon Garland | .10 | .30 |
| ☐ 225 | Mark Buehrle | .10 | .30 |
| ☐ 226 | Chris Singleton | .10 | .30 |
| ☐ 227 | Kip Wells | .10 | .30 |
| ☐ 228 | Ray Durham | .10 | .30 |
| ☐ 229 | Joe Crede | .10 | .30 |
| ☐ 230 | Keith Foulke | .10 | .30 |
| ☐ 231 | Royce Clayton | .10 | .30 |
| ☐ 232 | Andy Pettitte | .20 | .50 |
| ☐ 233 | Derek Jeter | .75 | 2.00 |
| ☐ 234 | Jorge Posada | .20 | .50 |
| ☐ 235 | Roger Clemens | .60 | 1.50 |
| ☐ 236 | Paul O'Neill | .20 | .50 |
| ☐ 237 | Nick Johnson | .10 | .30 |
| ☐ 238 | Gerald Williams | .10 | .30 |
| ☐ 239 | Mariano Rivera | .30 | .75 |
| ☐ 240 | Alfonso Soriano | .30 | .75 |
| ☐ 241 | Ramiro Mendoza | .10 | .30 |
| ☐ 242 | Mike Mussina | .20 | .50 |
| ☐ 243 | Luis Sojo | .10 | .30 |
| ☐ 244 | Scott Brosius | .10 | .30 |
| ☐ 245 | David Justice | .10 | .30 |
| ☐ 246 | Wade Miller | .10 | .30 |
| ☐ 247 | Brad Ausmus | .10 | .30 |
| ☐ 248 | Jeff Bagwell | .20 | .50 |
| ☐ 249 | Daryle Ward | .10 | .30 |
| ☐ 250 | Shane Reynolds | .10 | .30 |
| ☐ 251 | Chris Truby | .10 | .30 |
| ☐ 252 | Billy Wagner | .10 | .30 |
| ☐ 253 | Craig Biggio | .20 | .50 |
| ☐ 254 | Moises Alou | .10 | .30 |
| ☐ 255 | Vinny Castilla | .10 | .30 |
| ☐ 256 | Tim Redding | .10 | .30 |
| ☐ 257 | Roy Oswalt | .10 | .30 |
| ☐ 258 | Julio Lugo | .10 | .30 |
| ☐ 259 | Chipper Jones | .30 | .75 |
| ☐ 260 | Greg Maddux | .50 | 1.25 |
| ☐ 261 | Ken Caminiti | .10 | .30 |
| ☐ 262 | Kevin Millwood | .10 | .30 |
| ☐ 263 | Keith Lockhart | .10 | .30 |
| ☐ 264 | Rey Sanchez | .10 | .30 |
| ☐ 265 | Jason Marquis | .10 | .30 |
| ☐ 266 | Brian Jordan | .10 | .30 |
| ☐ 267 | Steve Karsay | .10 | .30 |
| ☐ 268 | Wes Helms | .10 | .30 |
| ☐ 269 | B.J. Surhoff | .10 | .30 |
| ☐ 270 | Wilson Betemit | .10 | .30 |
| ☐ 271 | John Smoltz | .20 | .50 |
| ☐ 272 | Rafael Furcal | .10 | .30 |
| ☐ 273 | Jeromy Burnitz | .10 | .30 |
| ☐ 274 | Jimmy Haynes | .10 | .30 |
| ☐ 275 | Mark Loretta | .10 | .30 |
| ☐ 276 | Jose Hernandez | .10 | .30 |
| ☐ 277 | Paul Rigdon | .10 | .30 |
| ☐ 278 | Alex Sanchez | .10 | .30 |
| ☐ 279 | Chad Fox | .10 | .30 |
| ☐ 280 | Devon White | .10 | .30 |
| ☐ 281 | Tyler Houston | .10 | .30 |
| ☐ 282 | Ronnie Belliard | .10 | .30 |
| ☐ 283 | Luis Lopez | .10 | .30 |
| ☐ 284 | Ben Sheets | .10 | .30 |
| ☐ 285 | Curtis Leskanic | .10 | .30 |
| ☐ 286 | Henry Blanco | .10 | .30 |
| ☐ 287 | Mark McGwire | .75 | 2.00 |
| ☐ 288 | Edgar Renteria | .10 | .30 |
| ☐ 289 | Matt Morris | .10 | .30 |
| ☐ 290 | Gene Stechschulte | .10 | .30 |
| ☐ 291 | Dustin Hermanson | .10 | .30 |
| ☐ 292 | Eli Marrero | .10 | .30 |
| ☐ 293 | Albert Pujols | .60 | 1.50 |
| ☐ 294 | Luis Saturria | .10 | .30 |
| ☐ 295 | Bobby Bonilla | .10 | .30 |
| ☐ 296 | Garrett Stephenson | .10 | .30 |
| ☐ 297 | Jim Edmonds | .10 | .30 |
| ☐ 298 | Rick Ankiel | .10 | .30 |
| ☐ 299 | Placido Polanco | .10 | .30 |
| ☐ 300 | Dave Veres | .10 | .30 |
| ☐ 301 | Sammy Sosa | .30 | .75 |
| ☐ 302 | Eric Young | .10 | .30 |
| ☐ 303 | Kerry Wood | .10 | .30 |
| ☐ 304 | Jon Lieber | .10 | .30 |
| ☐ 305 | Joe Girardi | .10 | .30 |
| ☐ 306 | Fred McGriff | .20 | .50 |
| ☐ 307 | Jeff Fassero | .10 | .30 |
| ☐ 308 | Julio Zuleta | .10 | .30 |
| ☐ 309 | Kevin Tapani | .10 | .30 |
| ☐ 310 | Rondell White | .10 | .30 |
| ☐ 311 | Julian Tavarez | .10 | .30 |
| ☐ 312 | Tom Gordon | .10 | .30 |
| ☐ 313 | Corey Patterson | .10 | .30 |
| ☐ 314 | Bill Mueller | .10 | .30 |
| ☐ 315 | Randy Johnson | .30 | .75 |
| ☐ 316 | Chad Moeller | .10 | .30 |
| ☐ 317 | Tony Womack | .10 | .30 |
| ☐ 318 | Enubiel Durazo | .10 | .30 |
| ☐ 319 | Luis Gonzalez | .10 | .30 |
| ☐ 320 | Brian Anderson | .10 | .30 |
| ☐ 321 | Reggie Sanders | .10 | .30 |
| ☐ 322 | Greg Colbrunn | .10 | .30 |
| ☐ 323 | Robert Ellis | .10 | .30 |
| ☐ 324 | Jack Cust | .10 | .30 |
| ☐ 325 | Bret Prinz | .10 | .30 |
| ☐ 326 | Steve Finley | .10 | .30 |
| ☐ 327 | Byung-Hyun Kim | .10 | .30 |
| ☐ 328 | Albie Lopez | .10 | .30 |
| ☐ 329 | Gary Sheffield | .10 | .30 |
| ☐ 330 | Mark Grudzielanek | .10 | .30 |
| ☐ 331 | Paul LoDuca | .10 | .30 |
| ☐ 332 | Tom Goodwin | .10 | .30 |
| ☐ 333 | Andy Ashby | .10 | .30 |
| ☐ 334 | Hiram Bocachica | .10 | .30 |
| ☐ 335 | Dave Hansen | .10 | .30 |
| ☐ 336 | Kevin Brown | .10 | .30 |
| ☐ 337 | Marquis Grissom | .10 | .30 |
| ☐ 338 | Terry Adams | .10 | .30 |
| ☐ 339 | Chan Ho Park | .10 | .30 |
| ☐ 340 | Adrian Beltre | .10 | .30 |
| ☐ 341 | Luke Prokopec | .10 | .30 |
| ☐ 342 | Jeff Shaw | .10 | .30 |
| ☐ 343 | Vladimir Guerrero | .30 | .75 |
| ☐ 344 | Orlando Cabrera | .10 | .30 |
| ☐ 345 | Tony Armas Jr. | .10 | .30 |
| ☐ 346 | Michael Barrett | .10 | .30 |
| ☐ 347 | Geoff Blum | .10 | .30 |
| ☐ 348 | Ryan Minor | .10 | .30 |
| ☐ 349 | Peter Bergeron | .10 | .30 |
| ☐ 350 | Graeme Lloyd | .10 | .30 |
| ☐ 351 | Jose Vidro | .10 | .30 |
| ☐ 352 | Javier Vazquez | .10 | .30 |
| ☐ 353 | Matt Blank | .10 | .30 |
| ☐ 354 | Masato Yoshii | .10 | .30 |
| ☐ 355 | Carl Pavano | .10 | .30 |
| ☐ 356 | Barry Bonds | .75 | 2.00 |
| ☐ 357 | Shawon Dunston | .10 | .30 |
| ☐ 358 | Livan Hernandez | .10 | .30 |
| ☐ 359 | Felix Rodriguez | .10 | .30 |
| ☐ 360 | Pedro Feliz | .10 | .30 |
| ☐ 361 | Calvin Murray | .10 | .30 |
| ☐ 362 | Robb Nen | .10 | .30 |
| ☐ 363 | Marvin Benard | .10 | .30 |
| ☐ 364 | Russ Ortiz | .10 | .30 |
| ☐ 365 | Jason Schmidt | .10 | .30 |
| ☐ 366 | Rich Aurilia | .10 | .30 |
| ☐ 367 | John Vander Wal | .10 | .30 |
| ☐ 368 | Benito Santiago | .10 | .30 |
| ☐ 369 | Ryan Dempster | .10 | .30 |
| ☐ 370 | Charles Johnson | .10 | .30 |
| ☐ 371 | Alex Gonzalez | .10 | .30 |
| ☐ 372 | Luis Castillo | .10 | .30 |
| ☐ 373 | Mike Lowell | .10 | .30 |
| ☐ 374 | Antonio Alfonseca | .10 | .30 |
| ☐ 375 | A.J. Burnett | .10 | .30 |
| ☐ 376 | Brad Penny | .10 | .30 |
| ☐ 377 | Jason Grilli | .10 | .30 |
| ☐ 378 | Derrek Lee | .20 | .50 |
| ☐ 379 | Matt Clement | .10 | .30 |
| ☐ 380 | Eric Owens | .10 | .30 |
| ☐ 381 | Vladimir Nunez | .10 | .30 |
| ☐ 382 | Cliff Floyd | .10 | .30 |
| ☐ 383 | Mike Piazza | .50 | 1.25 |
| ☐ 384 | Lenny Harris | .10 | .30 |
| ☐ 385 | Glendon Rusch | .10 | .30 |
| ☐ 386 | Todd Zeile | .10 | .30 |
| ☐ 387 | Al Leiter | .10 | .30 |
| ☐ 388 | Armando Benitez | .10 | .30 |
| ☐ 389 | Alex Escobar | .10 | .30 |
| ☐ 390 | Kevin Appier | .10 | .30 |
| ☐ 391 | Matt Lawton | .10 | .30 |
| ☐ 392 | Bruce Chen | .10 | .30 |
| ☐ 393 | John Franco | .10 | .30 |
| ☐ 394 | Tsuyoshi Shinjo | .10 | .30 |
| ☐ 395 | Rey Ordonez | .10 | .30 |
| ☐ 396 | Joe McEwing | .10 | .30 |
| ☐ 397 | Ryan Klesko | .10 | .30 |
| ☐ 398 | Brian Lawrence | .10 | .30 |
| ☐ 399 | Kevin Walker | .10 | .30 |
| ☐ 400 | Phil Nevin | .10 | .30 |
| ☐ 401 | Bubba Trammell | .10 | .30 |
| ☐ 402 | Wiki Gonzalez | .10 | .30 |
| ☐ 403 | D'Angelo Jimenez | .10 | .30 |
| ☐ 404 | Rickey Henderson | .30 | .75 |
| ☐ 405 | Mike Darr | .10 | .30 |
| ☐ 406 | Trevor Hoffman | .10 | .30 |
| ☐ 407 | Damian Jackson | .10 | .30 |
| ☐ 408 | Santiago Perez | .10 | .30 |
| ☐ 409 | Cesar Crespo | .10 | .30 |
| ☐ 410 | Robert Person | .10 | .30 |
| ☐ 411 | Travis Lee | .10 | .30 |
| ☐ 412 | Scott Rolen | .20 | .50 |
| ☐ 413 | Turk Wendell | .10 | .30 |
| ☐ 414 | Randy Wolf | .10 | .30 |
| ☐ 415 | Kevin Jordan | .10 | .30 |
| ☐ 416 | Jose Mesa | .10 | .30 |
| ☐ 417 | Mike Lieberthal | .10 | .30 |
| ☐ 418 | Bobby Abreu | .10 | .30 |
| ☐ 419 | Tomas Perez | .10 | .30 |

|  |  | | |
|---|---|---|---|
| 420 | Doug Glanville | .10 | .30 |
| 421 | Reggie Taylor | .10 | .30 |
| 422 | Jimmy Rollins | .10 | .30 |
| 423 | Brian Giles | .10 | .30 |
| 424 | Rob Mackowiak | .10 | .30 |
| 425 | Bronson Arroyo | .10 | .30 |
| 426 | Kevin Young | .10 | .30 |
| 427 | Jack Wilson | .10 | .30 |
| 428 | Adrian Brown | .10 | .30 |
| 429 | Chad Hermansen | .10 | .30 |
| 430 | Jimmy Anderson | .10 | .30 |
| 431 | Aramis Ramirez | .10 | .30 |
| 432 | Todd Ritchie | .10 | .30 |
| 433 | Pat Meares | .10 | .30 |
| 434 | Warren Morris | .10 | .30 |
| 435 | Derek Bell | .10 | .30 |
| 436 | Ken Griffey Jr. | .50 | 1.25 |
| 437 | Elmer Dessens | .10 | .30 |
| 438 | Ruben Rivera | .10 | .30 |
| 439 | Jason LaRue | .10 | .30 |
| 440 | Sean Casey | .10 | .30 |
| 441 | Pete Harnisch | .10 | .30 |
| 442 | Danny Graves | .10 | .30 |
| 443 | Aaron Boone | .10 | .30 |
| 444 | Dmitri Young | .10 | .30 |
| 445 | Brandon Larson | .10 | .30 |
| 446 | Pokey Reese | .10 | .30 |
| 447 | Todd Walker | .10 | .30 |
| 448 | Juan Castro | .10 | .30 |
| 449 | Todd Helton | .20 | .50 |
| 450 | Ben Petrick | .10 | .30 |
| 451 | Juan Pierre | .10 | .30 |
| 452 | Jeff Cirillo | .10 | .30 |
| 453 | Juan Uribe | .10 | .30 |
| 454 | Brian Bohanon | .10 | .30 |
| 455 | Terry Shumpert | .10 | .30 |
| 456 | Mike Hampton | .10 | .30 |
| 457 | Shawn Chacon | .10 | .30 |
| 458 | Adam Melhuse | .10 | .30 |
| 459 | Greg Norton | .10 | .30 |
| 460 | Gabe White | .10 | .30 |
| 461 | Ichiro Suzuki WS | .30 | .75 |
| 462 | Carlos Delgado WS | .10 | .30 |
| 463 | Manny Ramirez WS | .20 | .50 |
| 464 | Miguel Tejada WS | .10 | .30 |
| 465 | Tsuyoshi Shinjo WS | .10 | .30 |
| 466 | Bernie Williams WS | .10 | .30 |
| 467 | Juan Gonzalez WS | .10 | .30 |
| 468 | Andruw Jones WS | .10 | .30 |
| 469 | Ivan Rodriguez WS | .10 | .30 |
| 470 | Larry Walker WS | .10 | .30 |
| 471 | Hideo Nomo WS | .10 | .30 |
| 472 | Albert Pujols WS | .30 | .75 |
| 473 | Pedro Martinez WS | .20 | .50 |
| 474 | Vladimir Guerrero WS | .20 | .50 |
| 475 | Tony Batista WS | .10 | .30 |
| 476 | Kazuhiro Sasaki WS | .10 | .30 |
| 477 | Richard Hidalgo WS | .10 | .30 |
| 478 | Carlos Lee WS | .10 | .30 |
| 479 | Roberto Alomar WS | .10 | .30 |
| 480 | Rafael Palmeiro WS | .10 | .30 |
| 481 | Ken Griffey Jr. GG | .30 | .75 |
| 482 | Ken Griffey Jr. GG | .30 | .75 |
| 483 | Ken Griffey Jr. GG | .30 | .75 |
| 484 | Ken Griffey Jr. GG | .30 | .75 |
| 485 | Ken Griffey Jr. GG | .30 | .75 |
| 486 | Ken Griffey Jr. GG | .30 | .75 |
| 487 | Ken Griffey Jr. GG | .30 | .75 |
| 488 | Ken Griffey Jr. GG | .30 | .75 |
| 489 | Ken Griffey Jr. GG | .30 | .75 |
| 490 | Ken Griffey Jr. GG | .30 | .75 |
| 491 | Barry Bonds CL | .40 | 1.00 |
| 492 | Hideo Nomo CL | .10 | .30 |
| 493 | Ichiro Suzuki CL | .30 | .75 |
| 494 | Cal Ripken CL | .50 | 1.25 |
| 495 | Tony Gwynn CL | .20 | .50 |
| 496 | Randy Johnson CL | .20 | .50 |
| 497 | A.J. Burnett CL | .10 | .30 |
| 498 | Rickey Henderson CL | .20 | .50 |
| 499 | Albert Pujols CL | .30 | .75 |
| 500 | Luis Gonzalez CL | .10 | .30 |
| 501 | Brandon Puffer SR RC | .40 | 1.00 |
| 502 | Rodrigo Rosario SR RC | .40 | 1.00 |
| 503 | Tom Sheam SR RC | .40 | 1.00 |
| 504 | Reed Johnson SR RC | .60 | 1.50 |
| 505 | Chris Baker SR RC | .40 | 1.00 |
| 506 | John Ennis SR RC | .40 | 1.00 |
| 507 | Luis Martinez SR RC | .40 | 1.00 |
| 508 | So Taguchi SR RC | .60 | 1.50 |
| 509 | Scotty Layfield SR RC | .40 | 1.00 |
| 510 | Francis Beltran SR RC | .40 | 1.00 |
| 511 | Brandon Backe SR RC | .60 | 1.50 |
| 512 | Doug Devore SR RC | .40 | 1.00 |
| 513 | Jeremy Ward SR RC | .40 | 1.00 |
| 514 | Jose Valverde SR RC | .40 | 1.00 |
| 515 | P.J. Bevis SR RC | .40 | 1.00 |
| 516 | Victor Alvarez SR RC | .40 | 1.00 |
| 517 | Kazuhisa Ishii SR RC | .60 | 1.50 |
| 518 | Jorge Nunez SR RC | .40 | 1.00 |
| 519 | Eric Good SR RC | .40 | 1.00 |
| 520 | Ron Calloway SR RC | .40 | 1.00 |
| 521 | Val Pascucci SR RC | .40 | 1.00 |
| 522 | Nelson Castro SR RC | .40 | 1.00 |
| 523 | Deivis Santos SR | .40 | 1.00 |
| 524 | Luis Ugueto SR RC | .40 | 1.00 |
| 525 | Matt Thornton SR RC | .40 | 1.00 |
| 526 | Hansel Izquierdo SR RC | .40 | 1.00 |
| 527 | Tyler Yates SR RC | .40 | 1.00 |
| 528 | Mark Corey SR RC | .40 | 1.00 |
| 529 | Jaime Cerda SR RC | .40 | 1.00 |
| 530 | Satoru Komiyama SR RC | .40 | 1.00 |
| 531 | Steve Bechler SR RC | .40 | 1.00 |
| 532 | Ben Howard SR RC | .40 | 1.00 |
| 533 | Anderson Machado SR RC | .40 | 1.00 |
| 534 | Jorge Padilla SR RC | .40 | 1.00 |
| 535 | Eric Junge SR RC | .40 | 1.00 |
| 536 | Adrian Burnside SR RC | .40 | 1.00 |
| 537 | Mike Gonzalez SR RC | .40 | 1.00 |
| 538 | Josh Hancock SR RC | .50 | 1.25 |
| 539 | Colin Young SR RC | .40 | 1.00 |
| 540 | Rene Reyes SR RC | .40 | 1.00 |
| 541 | Cam Esslinger SR RC | .40 | 1.00 |
| 542 | Tim Kalita SR RC | .40 | 1.00 |
| 543 | Kevin Frederick SR RC | .40 | 1.00 |
| 544 | Kyle Kane SR RC | .40 | 1.00 |
| 545 | Edwin Almonte SR RC | .40 | 1.00 |
| 546 | Aaron Sele | .10 | .30 |
| 547 | Garret Anderson | .10 | .30 |
| 548 | Darin Erstad | .10 | .30 |
| 549 | Brad Fullmer | .10 | .30 |
| 550 | Kevin Appier | .10 | .30 |
| 551 | Tim Salmon | .20 | .50 |
| 552 | David Justice | .10 | .30 |
| 553 | Billy Koch | .10 | .30 |
| 554 | Scott Hatteberg | .10 | .30 |
| 555 | Tim Hudson | .10 | .30 |
| 556 | Miguel Tejada | .10 | .30 |
| 557 | Carlos Pena | .10 | .30 |
| 558 | Mike Sirotka | .10 | .30 |
| 559 | Jose Cruz Jr. | .10 | .30 |
| 560 | Josh Phelps | .10 | .30 |
| 561 | Brandon Lyon | .10 | .30 |
| 562 | Luke Prokopec | .10 | .30 |
| 563 | Felipe Lopez | .10 | .30 |
| 564 | Jason Standridge | .10 | .30 |
| 565 | Chris Gomez | .10 | .30 |
| 566 | John Flaherty | .10 | .30 |
| 567 | Jason Tyner | .10 | .30 |
| 568 | Bobby Smith | .10 | .30 |
| 569 | Wilson Alvarez | .10 | .30 |
| 570 | Matt Lawton | .10 | .30 |
| 571 | Omar Vizquel | .20 | .50 |
| 572 | Jim Thome | .20 | .50 |
| 573 | Brady Anderson | .10 | .30 |
| 574 | Alex Escobar | .10 | .30 |
| 575 | Russell Branyan | .10 | .30 |
| 576 | Bret Boone | .10 | .30 |
| 577 | Ben Davis | .10 | .30 |
| 578 | Mike Cameron | .10 | .30 |
| 579 | Jamie Moyer | .10 | .30 |
| 580 | Ruben Sierra | .10 | .30 |
| 581 | Jeff Cirillo | .10 | .30 |
| 582 | Marty Cordova | .10 | .30 |
| 583 | Mike Bordick | .10 | .30 |
| 584 | Brian Roberts | .10 | .30 |
| 585 | Luis Matos | .10 | .30 |
| 586 | Geronimo Gil | .10 | .30 |
| 587 | Jay Gibbons | .10 | .30 |
| 588 | Carl Everett | .10 | .30 |
| 589 | Ivan Rodriguez | .20 | .50 |
| 590 | Chan Ho Park | .10 | .30 |
| 591 | Juan Gonzalez | .10 | .30 |
| 592 | Hank Blalock | .20 | .50 |
| 593 | Todd Van Poppel | .10 | .30 |
| 594 | Pedro Martinez | .20 | .50 |
| 595 | Jason Varitek | .10 | .30 |
| 596 | Tony Clark | .10 | .30 |
| 597 | Johnny Damon Sox | .20 | .50 |
| 598 | Dustin Hermanson | .10 | .30 |
| 599 | John Burkett | .10 | .30 |
| 600 | Carlos Beltran | .10 | .30 |
| 601 | Mark Quinn | .10 | .30 |
| 602 | Chuck Knoblauch | .10 | .30 |
| 603 | Michael Tucker | .10 | .30 |
| 604 | Carlos Febles | .10 | .30 |
| 605 | Jose Rosado | .10 | .30 |
| 606 | Dmitri Young | .10 | .30 |
| 607 | Bobby Higginson | .10 | .30 |
| 608 | Craig Paquette | .10 | .30 |
| 609 | Mitch Meluskey | .10 | .30 |
| 610 | Wendell Magee | .10 | .30 |
| 611 | Mike Rivera | .10 | .30 |
| 612 | Jacque Jones | .10 | .30 |
| 613 | Luis Rivas | .10 | .30 |
| 614 | Eric Milton | .10 | .30 |
| 615 | Eddie Guardado | .10 | .30 |
| 616 | Matt LaCroy | .10 | .30 |
| 617 | Mike Jackson | .10 | .30 |
| 618 | Magglio Ordonez | .10 | .30 |
| 619 | Frank Thomas | .30 | .75 |
| 620 | Rocky Biddle | .10 | .30 |
| 621 | Paul Konerko | .10 | .30 |
| 622 | Todd Ritchie | .10 | .30 |
| 623 | Jon Rauch | .10 | .30 |
| 624 | John Vander Wal | .10 | .30 |
| 625 | Rondell White | .10 | .30 |
| 626 | Jason Giambi | .10 | .30 |
| 627 | Robin Ventura | .10 | .30 |
| 628 | David Wells | .10 | .30 |
| 629 | Bernie Williams | .20 | .50 |
| 630 | Lance Berkman | .10 | .30 |
| 631 | Richard Hidalgo | .10 | .30 |
| 632 | Greg Zaun | .10 | .30 |
| 633 | Jose Vizcaino | .10 | .30 |
| 634 | Octavio Dotel | .10 | .30 |
| 635 | Morgan Ensberg | .10 | .30 |
| 636 | Andruw Jones | .20 | .50 |
| 637 | Tom Glavine | .10 | .30 |
| 638 | Gary Sheffield | .10 | .30 |
| 639 | Vinny Castilla | .10 | .30 |
| 640 | Javy Lopez | .10 | .30 |
| 641 | Albie Lopez | .10 | .30 |
| 642 | Geoff Jenkins | .10 | .30 |
| 643 | Jeffrey Hammonds | .10 | .30 |
| 644 | Alex Ochoa | .10 | .30 |
| 645 | Richie Sexson | .10 | .30 |
| 646 | Eric Young | .10 | .30 |
| 647 | Glendon Rusch | .10 | .30 |
| 648 | Tino Martinez | .20 | .50 |
| 649 | Fernando Vina | .10 | .30 |
| 650 | J.D. Drew | .10 | .30 |
| 651 | Woody Williams | .10 | .30 |
| 652 | Darryl Kile | .10 | .30 |
| 653 | Jason Isringhausen | .10 | .30 |
| 654 | Moises Alou | .10 | .30 |
| 655 | Alex Gonzalez | .10 | .30 |
| 656 | Delino DeShields | .10 | .30 |
| 657 | Todd Hundley | .10 | .30 |
| 658 | Chris Stynes | .10 | .30 |
| 659 | Jason Bere | .10 | .30 |
| 660 | Curt Schilling | .10 | .30 |
| 661 | Craig Counsell | .10 | .30 |
| 662 | Mark Grace | .20 | .50 |
| 663 | Matt Williams | .10 | .30 |
| 664 | Jay Bell | .10 | .30 |
| 665 | Rick Helling | .10 | .30 |
| 666 | Shawn Green | .10 | .30 |
| 667 | Eric Karros | .10 | .30 |
| 668 | Hideo Nomo | .30 | .75 |
| 669 | Omar Daal | .10 | .30 |
| 670 | Brian Jordan | .10 | .30 |
| 671 | Cesar Izturis | .10 | .30 |
| 672 | Fernando Tatis | .10 | .30 |
| 673 | Lee Stevens | .10 | .30 |
| 674 | Tomo Ohka | .10 | .30 |
| 675 | Brian Schneider | .10 | .30 |
| 676 | Brad Wilkerson | .10 | .30 |
| 677 | Bruce Chen | .10 | .30 |
| 678 | Tsuyoshi Shinjo | .10 | .30 |
| 679 | Jeff Kent | .10 | .30 |
| 680 | Kirk Rueter | .10 | .30 |
| 681 | J.T. Snow | .10 | .30 |
| 682 | David Bell | .10 | .30 |
| 683 | Reggie Sanders | .10 | .30 |

- ☐ 684 Preston Wilson .10 .30
- ☐ 685 Vic Darensbourg .10 .30
- ☐ 686 Josh Beckett .10 .30
- ☐ 687 Pablo Ozuna .10 .30
- ☐ 688 Mike Redmond .10 .30
- ☐ 689 Scott Strickland .10 .30
- ☐ 690 Mo Vaughn .10 .30
- ☐ 691 Roberto Alomar .20 .50
- ☐ 692 Edgardo Alfonzo .10 .30
- ☐ 693 Shawn Estes .10 .30
- ☐ 694 Roger Cedeno .10 .30
- ☐ 695 Jeromy Burnitz .10 .30
- ☐ 696 Ray Lankford .10 .30
- ☐ 697 Mark Kotsay .10 .30
- ☐ 698 Kevin Jarvis .10 .30
- ☐ 699 Bobby Jones .10 .30
- ☐ 700 Sean Burroughs .10 .30
- ☐ 701 Ramon Vazquez .10 .30
- ☐ 702 Pat Burrell .10 .30
- ☐ 703 Marlon Byrd .10 .30
- ☐ 704 Brandon Duckworth .10 .30
- ☐ 705 Marlon Anderson .10 .30
- ☐ 706 Vicente Padilla .10 .30
- ☐ 707 Kip Wells .10 .30
- ☐ 708 Jason Kendall .10 .30
- ☐ 709 Pokey Reese .10 .30
- ☐ 710 Pat Meares .10 .30
- ☐ 711 Kris Benson .10 .30
- ☐ 712 Armando Rios .10 .30
- ☐ 713 Mike Williams .10 .30
- ☐ 714 Barry Larkin .20 .50
- ☐ 715 Adam Dunn .10 .30
- ☐ 716 Juan Encarnacion .10 .30
- ☐ 717 Scott Williamson .10 .30
- ☐ 718 Wilton Guerrero .10 .30
- ☐ 719 Chris Reitsma .10 .30
- ☐ 720 Larry Walker .10 .30
- ☐ 721 Denny Neagle .10 .30
- ☐ 722 Todd Zeile .10 .30
- ☐ 723 Jose Ortiz .10 .30
- ☐ 724 Jason Jennings .10 .30
- ☐ 725 Tony Eusebio .10 .30
- ☐ 726 Ichiro Suzuki YR .30 .75
- ☐ 727 Barry Bonds YR .40 1.00
- ☐ 728 Randy Johnson YR .20 .50
- ☐ 729 Albert Pujols YR .30 .75
- ☐ 730 Roger Clemens YR .30 .75
- ☐ 731 Sammy Sosa YR .30 .75
- ☐ 732 Alex Rodriguez YR .30 .75
- ☐ 733 Chipper Jones YR .20 .50
- ☐ 734 Rickey Henderson YR .20 .50
- ☐ 735 Ichiro Suzuki YR .30 .75
- ☐ 736 Luis Gonzalez SH CL .10 .30
- ☐ 737 Derek Jeter SH CL .40 1.00
- ☐ 738 Ichiro Suzuki SH CL .30 .75
- ☐ 739 Barry Bonds SH CL .40 1.00
- ☐ 740 Curt Schilling SH CL .10 .30
- ☐ 741 Shawn Green SH CL .10 .30
- ☐ 742 Jason Giambi SH CL .10 .30
- ☐ 743 Roberto Alomar SH CL .10 .30
- ☐ 744 Larry Walker SH CL .10 .30
- ☐ 745 Mark McGwire SH CL .40 1.00

**2003 Upper Deck**

- ☐ COMPLETE SERIES 1 (270) 20.00 50.00
- ☐ COMPLETE SERIES 2 (270) 20.00 50.00
- ☐ COMP.UPDATE SET (60) 10.00 20.00
- ☐ COMMON (31-500/531-600) .10 .30
- ☐ COMMON (1-30/501-530) .40 1.00
- ☐ COMMON RC (541-600) .20 .50
- SR 1-30/501-530 ARE NOT SHORT PRINTS
- CARD 19 DOES NOT EXIST
- SCUTARO/NOMAR ARE BOTH CARD 96
- 541-600 ISSUED IN 04 UD1 HOBBY BOXES


- ☐ UPDATE SET EXCH 1:240 '04 UD1 RETAIL
- ☐ UPDATE SET EXCH:DEADLINE 11/10/06
- ☐ 1 John Lackey SR .40 1.00
- ☐ 2 Alex Cintron SR .40 1.00
- ☐ 3 Jose Leon SR .40 1.00
- ☐ 4 Bobby Hill SR .40 1.00
- ☐ 5 Brandon Larson SR .40 1.00
- ☐ 6 Raul Gonzalez SR .40 1.00
- ☐ 7 Ben Broussard SR .40 1.00
- ☐ 8 Earl Snyder SR .40 1.00
- ☐ 9 Ramon Santiago SR .40 1.00
- ☐ 10 Jason Lane SR .40 1.00
- ☐ 11 Keith Ginter SR .40 1.00
- ☐ 12 Kirk Saarloos SR .40 1.00
- ☐ 13 Juan Brito SR .40 1.00
- ☐ 14 Runelvys Hernandez SR .40 1.00
- ☐ 15 Shawn Sedlacek SR .40 1.00
- ☐ 16 Jayson Durocher SR .40 1.00
- ☐ 17 Kevin Frederick SR .40 1.00
- ☐ 18 Zach Day SR .40 1.00
- ☐ 19 Marcos Scutaro SR .40 1.00
- ☐ 20 Marcus Thames SR .40 1.00
- ☐ 21 Esteban German SR .40 1.00
- ☐ 22 Brett Myers SR .40 1.00
- ☐ 23 Oliver Perez SR .40 1.00
- ☐ 24 Dennis Tankersley SR .40 1.00
- ☐ 25 Julius Matos SR .40 1.00
- ☐ 26 Jake Peavy SR .40 1.00
- ☐ 27 Eric Cyr SR .40 1.00
- ☐ 28 Mike Crudale SR .40 1.00
- ☐ 29 Josh Pearce SR .40 1.00
- ☐ 30 Carl Crawford SR .40 1.00
- ☐ 31 Tim Salmon .20 .50
- ☐ 32 Troy Glaus .10 .30
- ☐ 33 Adam Kennedy .10 .30
- ☐ 34 David Eckstein .10 .30
- ☐ 35 Ben Molina .10 .30
- ☐ 36 Jarrod Washburn .10 .30
- ☐ 37 Ramon Ortiz .10 .30
- ☐ 38 Eric Chavez .10 .30
- ☐ 39 Miguel Tejada .10 .30
- ☐ 40 Adam Piatt .10 .30
- ☐ 41 Jermaine Dye .10 .30
- ☐ 42 Olmedo Saenz .10 .30
- ☐ 43 Tim Hudson .10 .30
- ☐ 44 Barry Zito .10 .30
- ☐ 45 Billy Koch .10 .30
- ☐ 46 Brandon Stewart .10 .30
- ☐ 47 Kelvim Escobar .10 .30
- ☐ 48 Jose Cruz Jr. .10 .30
- ☐ 49 Vernon Wells .10 .30
- ☐ 50 Roy Halladay .10 .30
- ☐ 51 Esteban Loaiza .10 .30
- ☐ 52 Eric Hinske .10 .30
- ☐ 53 Steve Cox .10 .30
- ☐ 54 Brent Abernathy .10 .30
- ☐ 55 Ben Grieve .10 .30
- ☐ 56 Aubrey Huff .10 .30
- ☐ 57 Jared Sandberg .10 .30
- ☐ 58 Paul Wilson .10 .30
- ☐ 59 Tanyon Sturtze .10 .30
- ☐ 60 Jim Thome .20 .50
- ☐ 61 Omar Vizquel .20 .50
- ☐ 62 C.C. Sabathia .10 .30
- ☐ 63 Chris Magruder .10 .30
- ☐ 64 Ricky Gutierrez .10 .30
- ☐ 65 Einar Diaz .10 .30
- ☐ 66 Danys Baez .10 .30
- ☐ 67 Ichiro Suzuki .60 1.50
- ☐ 68 Ruben Sierra .10 .30
- ☐ 69 Carlos Guillen .10 .30
- ☐ 70 Mark McLemore .10 .30
- ☐ 71 Dan Wilson .10 .30
- ☐ 72 Jamie Moyer .10 .30
- ☐ 73 Joel Pineiro .10 .30
- ☐ 74 Edgar Martinez .20 .50
- ☐ 75 Tony Batista .10 .30
- ☐ 76 Jay Gibbons .10 .30
- ☐ 77 Chris Singleton .10 .30
- ☐ 78 Melvin Mora .10 .30
- ☐ 79 Geronimo Gil .10 .30
- ☐ 80 Rodrigo Lopez .10 .30
- ☐ 81 Jorge Julio .10 .30
- ☐ 82 Rafael Palmeiro .20 .50
- ☐ 83 Juan Gonzalez .20 .50
- ☐ 84 Mike Young .20 .50
- ☐ 85 Hideki Irabu .10 .30
- ☐ 86 Chan Ho Park .10 .30


- ☐ 87 Kevin Mench .10 .30
- ☐ 88 Doug Davis .10 .30
- ☐ 89 Pedro Martinez .20 .50
- ☐ 90 Shea Hillenbrand .10 .30
- ☐ 91 Derek Lowe .10 .30
- ☐ 92 Jason Varitek .30 .75
- ☐ 93 Tony Clark .10 .30
- ☐ 94 John Burkett .10 .30
- ☐ 95 Frank Castillo .10 .30
- ☐ 96 Nomar Garciaparra .50 1.25
- ☐ 97 Rickey Henderson .30 .75
- ☐ 98 Mike Sweeney .10 .30
- ☐ 99 Carlos Febles .10 .30
- ☐ 100 Mark Quinn .10 .30
- ☐ 101 Raul Ibanez .10 .30
- ☐ 102 A.J. Hinch .10 .30
- ☐ 103 Paul Byrd .10 .30
- ☐ 104 Chuck Knoblauch .10 .30
- ☐ 105 Dmitri Young .10 .30
- ☐ 106 Randall Simon .10 .30
- ☐ 107 Brandon Inge .10 .30
- ☐ 108 Damion Easley .10 .30
- ☐ 109 Carlos Pena .10 .30
- ☐ 110 George Lombard .10 .30
- ☐ 111 Juan Acevedo .10 .30
- ☐ 112 Torii Hunter .10 .30
- ☐ 113 Doug Mientkiewicz .10 .30
- ☐ 114 David Ortiz .20 .50
- ☐ 115 Eric Milton .10 .30
- ☐ 116 Eddie Guardado .10 .30
- ☐ 117 Cristian Guzman .10 .30
- ☐ 118 Corey Koskie .10 .30
- ☐ 119 Magglio Ordonez .10 .30
- ☐ 120 Mark Buehrle .10 .30
- ☐ 121 Todd Ritchie .10 .30
- ☐ 122 Jose Valentin .10 .30
- ☐ 123 Paul Konerko .10 .30
- ☐ 124 Carlos Lee .10 .30
- ☐ 125 Jon Garland .10 .30
- ☐ 126 Jason Giambi .20 .50
- ☐ 127 Derek Jeter .75 2.00
- ☐ 128 Roger Clemens .60 1.50
- ☐ 129 Raul Mondesi .10 .30
- ☐ 130 Jorge Posada .20 .50
- ☐ 131 Rondell White .10 .30
- ☐ 132 Robin Ventura .10 .30
- ☐ 133 Mike Mussina .20 .50
- ☐ 134 Jeff Bagwell .20 .50
- ☐ 135 Craig Biggio .20 .50
- ☐ 136 Morgan Ensberg .10 .30
- ☐ 137 Richard Hidalgo .10 .30
- ☐ 138 Brad Ausmus .10 .30
- ☐ 139 Roy Oswalt .10 .30
- ☐ 140 Carlos Hernandez .10 .30
- ☐ 141 Shane Reynolds .10 .30
- ☐ 142 Gary Sheffield .10 .30
- ☐ 143 Andruw Jones .20 .50
- ☐ 144 Tom Glavine .20 .50
- ☐ 145 Rafael Furcal .10 .30
- ☐ 146 Javy Lopez .10 .30
- ☐ 147 Vinny Castilla .10 .30
- ☐ 148 Marcus Giles .10 .30
- ☐ 149 Kevin Millwood .10 .30
- ☐ 150 Jason Marquis .10 .30
- ☐ 151 Ruben Quevedo .10 .30
- ☐ 152 Ben Sheets .10 .30
- ☐ 153 Geoff Jenkins .10 .30
- ☐ 154 Jesse Hernandez .10 .30
- ☐ 155 Glendon Rusch .10 .30
- ☐ 156 Jeffrey Hammonds .10 .30
- ☐ 157 Alex Sanchez .10 .30
- ☐ 158 Jim Edmonds .10 .30
- ☐ 159 Tino Martinez .20 .50
- ☐ 160 Albert Pujols .60 1.50
- ☐ 161 Eli Marrero .10 .30
- ☐ 162 Woody Williams .10 .30
- ☐ 163 Fernando Vina .10 .30
- ☐ 164 Jason Isringhausen .10 .30
- ☐ 165 Jason Simontacchi .10 .30
- ☐ 166 Kerry Robinson .10 .30
- ☐ 167 Sammy Sosa .30 .75
- ☐ 168 Juan Cruz .10 .30
- ☐ 169 Fred McGriff .20 .50
- ☐ 170 Antonio Alfonseca .10 .30
- ☐ 171 Jon Lieber .10 .30
- ☐ 172 Mark Prior .20 .50
- ☐ 173 Moises Alou .10 .30
- ☐ 174 Matt Clement .10 .30

|  |  | | |
|---|---|---|---|
| ❏ 175 | Mark Bellhorn | .10 | .30 |
| ❏ 176 | Randy Johnson | .30 | .75 |
| ❏ 177 | Luis Gonzalez | .10 | .30 |
| ❏ 178 | Tony Womack | .10 | .30 |
| ❏ 179 | Mark Grace | .20 | .50 |
| ❏ 180 | Junior Spivey | .10 | .30 |
| ❏ 181 | Byung Hyun Kim | .10 | .30 |
| ❏ 182 | Danny Bautista | .10 | .30 |
| ❏ 183 | Brian Anderson | .10 | .30 |
| ❏ 184 | Shawn Green | .10 | .30 |
| ❏ 185 | Brian Jordan | .10 | .30 |
| ❏ 186 | Eric Karros | .10 | .30 |
| ❏ 187 | Andy Ashby | .10 | .30 |
| ❏ 188 | Cesar Izturis | .10 | .30 |
| ❏ 189 | Dave Roberts | .10 | .30 |
| ❏ 190 | Eric Gagne | .10 | .30 |
| ❏ 191 | Kazuhisa Ishii | .10 | .30 |
| ❏ 192 | Adrian Beltre | .10 | .30 |
| ❏ 193 | Vladimir Guerrero | .30 | .75 |
| ❏ 194 | Tony Armas Jr. | .10 | .30 |
| ❏ 195 | Bartolo Colon | .10 | .30 |
| ❏ 196 | Troy O'Leary | .10 | .30 |
| ❏ 197 | Tomo Ohka | .10 | .30 |
| ❏ 198 | Brad Wilkerson | .10 | .30 |
| ❏ 199 | Orlando Cabrera | .10 | .30 |
| ❏ 200 | Barry Bonds | .75 | 2.00 |
| ❏ 201 | David Bell | .10 | .30 |
| ❏ 202 | Tsuyoshi Shinjo | .10 | .30 |
| ❏ 203 | Benito Santiago | .10 | .30 |
| ❏ 204 | Livan Hernandez | .10 | .30 |
| ❏ 205 | Jason Schmidt | .10 | .30 |
| ❏ 206 | Kirk Rueter | .10 | .30 |
| ❏ 207 | Ramon E. Martinez | .10 | .30 |
| ❏ 208 | Mike Lowell | .10 | .30 |
| ❏ 209 | Luis Castillo | .10 | .30 |
| ❏ 210 | Derrek Lee | .20 | .50 |
| ❏ 211 | Andy Fox | .10 | .30 |
| ❏ 212 | Eric Owens | .10 | .30 |
| ❏ 213 | Charles Johnson | .10 | .30 |
| ❏ 214 | Brad Penny | .10 | .30 |
| ❏ 215 | A.J. Burnett | .10 | .30 |
| ❏ 216 | Edgardo Alfonzo | .10 | .30 |
| ❏ 217 | Roberto Alomar | .20 | .50 |
| ❏ 218 | Rey Ordonez | .10 | .30 |
| ❏ 219 | Al Leiter | .10 | .30 |
| ❏ 220 | Roger Cedeno | .10 | .30 |
| ❏ 221 | Timo Perez | .10 | .30 |
| ❏ 222 | Jeromy Burnitz | .10 | .30 |
| ❏ 223 | Pedro Astacio | .10 | .30 |
| ❏ 224 | Joe McEwing | .10 | .30 |
| ❏ 225 | Ryan Klesko | .10 | .30 |
| ❏ 226 | Ramon Vazquez | .10 | .30 |
| ❏ 227 | Mark Kotsay | .10 | .30 |
| ❏ 228 | Bubba Trammell | .10 | .30 |
| ❏ 229 | Wiki Gonzalez | .10 | .30 |
| ❏ 230 | Trevor Hoffman | .10 | .30 |
| ❏ 231 | Ron Gant | .10 | .30 |
| ❏ 232 | Bob Abreu | .10 | .30 |
| ❏ 233 | Marlon Anderson | .10 | .30 |
| ❏ 234 | Jeremy Giambi | .10 | .30 |
| ❏ 235 | Jimmy Rollins | .10 | .30 |
| ❏ 236 | Mike Lieberthal | .10 | .30 |
| ❏ 237 | Vicente Padilla | .10 | .30 |
| ❏ 238 | Randy Wolf | .10 | .30 |
| ❏ 239 | Pokey Reese | .10 | .30 |
| ❏ 240 | Brian Giles | .10 | .30 |
| ❏ 241 | Jack Wilson | .10 | .30 |
| ❏ 242 | Mike Williams | .10 | .30 |
| ❏ 243 | Kip Wells | .10 | .30 |
| ❏ 244 | Rob Mackowiak | .10 | .30 |
| ❏ 245 | Craig Wilson | .10 | .30 |
| ❏ 246 | Adam Dunn | .10 | .30 |
| ❏ 247 | Sean Casey | .10 | .30 |
| ❏ 248 | Todd Walker | .10 | .30 |
| ❏ 249 | Corky Miller | .10 | .30 |
| ❏ 250 | Ryan Dempster | .10 | .30 |
| ❏ 251 | Reggie Taylor | .10 | .30 |
| ❏ 252 | Aaron Boone | .10 | .30 |
| ❏ 253 | Larry Walker | .10 | .30 |
| ❏ 254 | Jose Ortiz | .10 | .30 |
| ❏ 255 | Todd Zeile | .10 | .30 |
| ❏ 256 | Bobby Estalella | .10 | .30 |
| ❏ 257 | Juan Pierre | .10 | .30 |
| ❏ 258 | Terry Shumpert | .10 | .30 |
| ❏ 259 | Mike Hampton | .10 | .30 |
| ❏ 260 | Denny Stark | .10 | .30 |
| ❏ 261 | Shawn Green SH CL | .10 | .30 |
| ❏ 262 | Derek Lowe SH CL | .10 | .30 |
| ❏ 263 | Barry Bonds SH CL | .40 | 1.00 |
| ❏ 264 | Mike Cameron SH CL | .10 | .30 |
| ❏ 265 | Luis Castillo SH CL | .10 | .30 |
| ❏ 266 | Vladimir Guerrero SH CL | .20 | .50 |
| ❏ 267 | Jason Giambi SH CL | .10 | .30 |
| ❏ 268 | Eric Gagne SH CL | .10 | .30 |
| ❏ 269 | Magglio Ordonez SH CL | .10 | .30 |
| ❏ 270 | Jim Thome SH CL | .10 | .30 |
| ❏ 271 | Garret Anderson | .10 | .30 |
| ❏ 272 | Troy Percival | .10 | .30 |
| ❏ 273 | Brad Fullmer | .10 | .30 |
| ❏ 274 | Scott Spiezio | .10 | .30 |
| ❏ 275 | Darin Erstad | .10 | .30 |
| ❏ 276 | Francisco Rodriguez | .10 | .30 |
| ❏ 277 | Kevin Appier | .10 | .30 |
| ❏ 278 | Shawn Wooten | .10 | .30 |
| ❏ 279 | Eric Owens | .10 | .30 |
| ❏ 280 | Scott Hatteberg | .10 | .30 |
| ❏ 281 | Terrence Long | .10 | .30 |
| ❏ 282 | Mark Mulder | .10 | .30 |
| ❏ 283 | Ramon Hernandez | .10 | .30 |
| ❏ 284 | Ted Lilly | .10 | .30 |
| ❏ 285 | Erubiel Durazo | .10 | .30 |
| ❏ 286 | Mark Ellis | .10 | .30 |
| ❏ 287 | Carlos Delgado | .10 | .30 |
| ❏ 288 | Orlando Hudson | .10 | .30 |
| ❏ 289 | Chris Woodward | .10 | .30 |
| ❏ 290 | Mark Hendrickson | .10 | .30 |
| ❏ 291 | Josh Phelps | .10 | .30 |
| ❏ 292 | Ken Huckaby | .10 | .30 |
| ❏ 293 | Justin Miller | .10 | .30 |
| ❏ 294 | Travis Lee | .10 | .30 |
| ❏ 295 | Jorge Sosa | .10 | .30 |
| ❏ 296 | Joe Kennedy | .10 | .30 |
| ❏ 297 | Carl Crawford | .10 | .30 |
| ❏ 298 | Toby Hall | .10 | .30 |
| ❏ 299 | Rey Ordonez | .10 | .30 |
| ❏ 300 | Brandon Phillips | .10 | .30 |
| ❏ 301 | Matt Lawton | .10 | .30 |
| ❏ 302 | Ellis Burks | .10 | .30 |
| ❏ 303 | Bill Selby | .10 | .30 |
| ❏ 304 | Travis Hafner | .10 | .30 |
| ❏ 305 | Milton Bradley | .10 | .30 |
| ❏ 306 | Karim Garcia | .10 | .30 |
| ❏ 307 | Cliff Lee | .10 | .30 |
| ❏ 308 | Jeff Cirillo | .10 | .30 |
| ❏ 309 | John Olerud | .10 | .30 |
| ❏ 310 | Kazuhiro Sasaki | .10 | .30 |
| ❏ 311 | Freddy Garcia | .10 | .30 |
| ❏ 312 | Bret Boone | .10 | .30 |
| ❏ 313 | Mike Cameron | .10 | .30 |
| ❏ 314 | Ben Davis | .10 | .30 |
| ❏ 315 | Randy Winn | .10 | .30 |
| ❏ 316 | Gary Matthews Jr. | .10 | .30 |
| ❏ 317 | Jeff Conine | .10 | .30 |
| ❏ 318 | Sidney Ponson | .10 | .30 |
| ❏ 319 | Jerry Hairston | .10 | .30 |
| ❏ 320 | David Segui | .10 | .30 |
| ❏ 321 | Scott Erickson | .10 | .30 |
| ❏ 322 | Marty Cordova | .10 | .30 |
| ❏ 323 | Hank Blalock | .10 | .30 |
| ❏ 324 | Herbert Perry | .10 | .30 |
| ❏ 325 | Alex Rodriguez | .50 | 1.25 |
| ❏ 326 | Carl Everett | .10 | .30 |
| ❏ 327 | Einar Diaz | .10 | .30 |
| ❏ 328 | Ugueth Urbina | .10 | .30 |
| ❏ 329 | Mark Teixeira | .20 | .50 |
| ❏ 330 | Manny Ramirez | .20 | .50 |
| ❏ 331 | Johnny Damon | .10 | .30 |
| ❏ 332 | Trot Nixon | .10 | .30 |
| ❏ 333 | Tim Wakefield | .10 | .30 |
| ❏ 334 | Casey Fossum | .10 | .30 |
| ❏ 335 | Todd Walker | .10 | .30 |
| ❏ 336 | Jeremy Giambi | .10 | .30 |
| ❏ 337 | Bill Mueller | .10 | .30 |
| ❏ 338 | Ramiro Mendoza | .10 | .30 |
| ❏ 339 | Carlos Beltran | .10 | .30 |
| ❏ 340 | Jason Grimsley | .10 | .30 |
| ❏ 341 | Brent Mayne | .10 | .30 |
| ❏ 342 | Angel Berroa | .10 | .30 |
| ❏ 343 | Albie Lopez | .10 | .30 |
| ❏ 344 | Michael Tucker | .10 | .30 |
| ❏ 345 | Bobby Higginson | .10 | .30 |
| ❏ 346 | Shane Halter | .10 | .30 |
| ❏ 347 | Jeremy Bonderman RC | 1.50 | 4.00 |
| ❏ 348 | Eric Munson | .10 | .30 |
| ❏ 349 | Andy Van Hekken | .10 | .30 |
| ❏ 350 | Matt Anderson | .10 | .30 |
| ❏ 351 | Jacque Jones | .10 | .30 |
| ❏ 352 | A.J. Pierzynski | .10 | .30 |
| ❏ 353 | Joe Mays | .10 | .30 |
| ❏ 354 | Brad Radke | .10 | .30 |
| ❏ 355 | Dustan Mohr | .10 | .30 |
| ❏ 356 | Bobby Kielty | .10 | .30 |
| ❏ 357 | Michael Cuddyer | .10 | .30 |
| ❏ 358 | Luis Rivas | .10 | .30 |
| ❏ 359 | Frank Thomas | .30 | .75 |
| ❏ 360 | Joe Borchard | .10 | .30 |
| ❏ 361 | D'Angelo Jimenez | .10 | .30 |
| ❏ 362 | Bartolo Colon | .10 | .30 |
| ❏ 363 | Joe Crede | .10 | .30 |
| ❏ 364 | Miguel Olivo | .10 | .30 |
| ❏ 365 | Billy Koch | .10 | .30 |
| ❏ 366 | Bernie Williams | .20 | .50 |
| ❏ 367 | Nick Johnson | .10 | .30 |
| ❏ 368 | Andy Pettitte | .20 | .50 |
| ❏ 369 | Mariano Rivera | .30 | .75 |
| ❏ 370 | Alfonso Soriano | .30 | .75 |
| ❏ 371 | David Wells | .10 | .30 |
| ❏ 372 | Drew Henson | .10 | .30 |
| ❏ 373 | Juan Rivera | .10 | .30 |
| ❏ 374 | Steve Karsay | .10 | .30 |
| ❏ 375 | Jeff Kent | .10 | .30 |
| ❏ 376 | Lance Berkman | .10 | .30 |
| ❏ 377 | Octavio Dotel | .10 | .30 |
| ❏ 378 | Julio Lugo | .10 | .30 |
| ❏ 379 | Jason Lane | .10 | .30 |
| ❏ 380 | Wade Miller | .10 | .30 |
| ❏ 381 | Billy Wagner | .10 | .30 |
| ❏ 382 | Brad Ausmus | .10 | .30 |
| ❏ 383 | Mike Hampton | .10 | .30 |
| ❏ 384 | Chipper Jones | .30 | .75 |
| ❏ 385 | John Smoltz | .20 | .50 |
| ❏ 386 | Greg Maddux | .50 | 1.25 |
| ❏ 387 | Javy Lopez | .10 | .30 |
| ❏ 388 | Robert Fick | .10 | .30 |
| ❏ 389 | Mark DeRosa | .10 | .30 |
| ❏ 390 | Russ Ortiz | .10 | .30 |
| ❏ 391 | Julio Franco | .10 | .30 |
| ❏ 392 | Richie Sexson | .10 | .30 |
| ❏ 393 | Eric Young | .10 | .30 |
| ❏ 394 | Robert Machado | .10 | .30 |
| ❏ 395 | Mike DeJean | .10 | .30 |
| ❏ 396 | Todd Ritchie | .10 | .30 |
| ❏ 397 | Royce Clayton | .10 | .30 |
| ❏ 398 | Nick Neugebauer | .10 | .30 |
| ❏ 399 | J.D. Drew | .10 | .30 |
| ❏ 400 | Edgar Renteria | .10 | .30 |
| ❏ 401 | Scott Rolen | .20 | .50 |
| ❏ 402 | Matt Morris | .10 | .30 |
| ❏ 403 | Garrett Stephenson | .10 | .30 |
| ❏ 404 | Eduardo Perez | .10 | .30 |
| ❏ 405 | Mike Matheny | .10 | .30 |
| ❏ 406 | Miguel Cairo | .10 | .30 |
| ❏ 407 | Brett Tomko | .10 | .30 |
| ❏ 408 | Bobby Hill | .10 | .30 |
| ❏ 409 | Troy O'Leary | .10 | .30 |
| ❏ 410 | Corey Patterson | .10 | .30 |
| ❏ 411 | Kerry Wood | .10 | .30 |
| ❏ 412 | Eric Karros | .10 | .30 |
| ❏ 413 | Hee Seop Choi | .10 | .30 |
| ❏ 414 | Alex Gonzalez | .10 | .30 |
| ❏ 415 | Matt Clement | .10 | .30 |
| ❏ 416 | Mark Grudzielanek | .10 | .30 |
| ❏ 417 | Curt Schilling | .10 | .30 |
| ❏ 418 | Steve Finley | .10 | .30 |
| ❏ 419 | Craig Counsell | .10 | .30 |
| ❏ 420 | Matt Williams | .10 | .30 |
| ❏ 421 | Quinton McCracken | .10 | .30 |
| ❏ 422 | Chad Moeller | .10 | .30 |
| ❏ 423 | Lyle Overbay | .10 | .30 |
| ❏ 424 | Miguel Batista | .10 | .30 |
| ❏ 425 | Paul Lo Duca | .10 | .30 |
| ❏ 426 | Kevin Brown | .10 | .30 |
| ❏ 427 | Hideo Nomo | .30 | .75 |
| ❏ 428 | Fred McGriff | .20 | .50 |
| ❏ 429 | Joe Thurston | .10 | .30 |
| ❏ 430 | Odalis Perez | .10 | .30 |
| ❏ 431 | Darren Dreifort | .10 | .30 |
| ❏ 432 | Todd Hundley | .10 | .30 |
| ❏ 433 | Dave Roberts | .10 | .30 |
| ❏ 434 | Jose Vidro | .10 | .30 |
| ❏ 435 | Javier Vazquez | .10 | .30 |
| ❏ 436 | Michael Barrett | .10 | .30 |
| ❏ 437 | Fernando Tatis | .10 | .30 |
| ❏ 438 | Peter Bergeron | .10 | .30 |

|  |  |
|---|---|
| ☐ 439 Endy Chavez | .10 .30 |
| ☐ 440 Orlando Hernandez | .10 .30 |
| ☐ 441 Marvin Benard | .10 .30 |
| ☐ 442 Rich Aurilia | .10 .30 |
| ☐ 443 Pedro Feliz | .10 .30 |
| ☐ 444 Robb Nen | .10 .30 |
| ☐ 445 Ray Durham | .10 .30 |
| ☐ 446 Marquis Grissom | .10 .30 |
| ☐ 447 Damian Moss | .10 .30 |
| ☐ 448 Edgardo Alfonzo | .10 .30 |
| ☐ 449 Juan Pierre | .10 .30 |
| ☐ 450 Braden Looper | .10 .30 |
| ☐ 451 Alex Gonzalez | .10 .30 |
| ☐ 452 Justin Wayne | .10 .30 |
| ☐ 453 Josh Beckett | .10 .30 |
| ☐ 454 Juan Encarnacion | .10 .30 |
| ☐ 455 Ivan Rodriguez | .20 .50 |
| ☐ 456 Todd Hollandsworth | .10 .30 |
| ☐ 457 Cliff Floyd | .10 .30 |
| ☐ 458 Rey Sanchez | .10 .30 |
| ☐ 459 Mike Piazza | .50 1.25 |
| ☐ 460 Mo Vaughn | .10 .30 |
| ☐ 461 Armando Benitez | .10 .30 |
| ☐ 462 Tsuyoshi Shinjo | .10 .30 |
| ☐ 463 Tom Glavine | .20 .50 |
| ☐ 464 David Cone | .10 .30 |
| ☐ 465 Phil Nevin | .10 .30 |
| ☐ 466 Sean Burroughs | .10 .30 |
| ☐ 467 Jake Peavy | .10 .30 |
| ☐ 468 Brian Lawrence | .10 .30 |
| ☐ 469 Mark Loretta | .10 .30 |
| ☐ 470 Dennis Tankersley | .10 .30 |
| ☐ 471 Jesse Orosco | .10 .30 |
| ☐ 472 Jim Thome | .20 .50 |
| ☐ 473 Kevin Millwood | .10 .30 |
| ☐ 474 David Bell | .10 .30 |
| ☐ 475 Pat Burrell | .10 .30 |
| ☐ 476 Brandon Duckworth | .10 .30 |
| ☐ 477 Jose Mesa | .10 .30 |
| ☐ 478 Marlon Byrd | .10 .30 |
| ☐ 479 Reggie Sanders | .10 .30 |
| ☐ 480 Jason Kendall | .10 .30 |
| ☐ 481 Aramis Ramirez | .10 .30 |
| ☐ 482 Kris Benson | .10 .30 |
| ☐ 483 Matt Stairs | .10 .30 |
| ☐ 484 Kevin Young | .10 .30 |
| ☐ 485 Kenny Lofton | .10 .30 |
| ☐ 486 Austin Kearns | .10 .30 |
| ☐ 487 Barry Larkin | .20 .50 |
| ☐ 488 Jason LaRue | .10 .30 |
| ☐ 489 Ken Griffey Jr. | .50 1.25 |
| ☐ 490 Danny Graves | .10 .30 |
| ☐ 491 Russell Branyan | .10 .30 |
| ☐ 492 Reggie Taylor | .10 .30 |
| ☐ 493 Jimmy Haynes | .10 .30 |
| ☐ 494 Charles Johnson | .10 .30 |
| ☐ 495 Todd Helton | .20 .50 |
| ☐ 496 Juan Uribe | .10 .30 |
| ☐ 497 Preston Wilson | .10 .30 |
| ☐ 498 Chris Stynes | .10 .30 |
| ☐ 499 Jason Jennings | .10 .30 |
| ☐ 500 Jay Payton | .10 .30 |
| ☐ 501 Hideki Matsui SR RC | 2.00 5.00 |
| ☐ 502 Jose Contreras SR RC | .60 1.50 |
| ☐ 503 Brandon Webb SR RC | 1.25 3.00 |
| ☐ 504 Robby Hammock SR RC | .40 1.00 |
| ☐ 505 Matt Kata SR RC | .40 1.00 |
| ☐ 506 Tim Olson SR RC | .40 1.00 |
| ☐ 507 Michael Hessman SR RC | .40 1.00 |
| ☐ 508 Jon Leicester SR RC | .40 1.00 |
| ☐ 509 Todd Wellemeyer SR RC | .40 1.00 |
| ☐ 510 David Sanders SR RC | .40 1.00 |
| ☐ 511 Josh Stewart SR RC | .40 1.00 |
| ☐ 512 Luis Ayala SR RC | .40 1.00 |
| ☐ 513 Clint Barmes SR RC | .50 1.25 |
| ☐ 514 Josh Willingham SR RC | .75 2.00 |
| ☐ 515 Alejandro Machado SR RC | .40 1.00 |
| ☐ 516 Felix Sanchez SR RC | .40 1.00 |
| ☐ 517 Willie Eyre SR RC | .40 1.00 |
| ☐ 518 Brent Hoard SR RC | .40 1.00 |
| ☐ 519 Lew Ford SR RC | .60 1.50 |
| ☐ 520 Termel Sledge SR RC | .40 1.00 |
| ☐ 521 Jimmy Griffiths SR RC | .40 1.00 |
| ☐ 522 Phil Seibel SR RC | .40 1.00 |
| ☐ 523 Craig Brazell SR RC | .40 1.00 |
| ☐ 524 Prentice Redman SR RC | .40 1.00 |
| ☐ 525 Jeff Duncan SR RC | .40 1.00 |
| ☐ 526 Shane Bazzell SR RC | .40 1.00 |

|  | |
|---|---|
| ☐ 527 Bernie Castro SR RC | .40 1.00 |
| ☐ 528 Rett Johnson SR RC | .40 1.00 |
| ☐ 529 Bobby Madritsch SR RC | .40 1.00 |
| ☐ 530 Rocco Baldelli SR | .40 1.00 |
| ☐ 531 Alex Rodriguez SH CL | .30 .75 |
| ☐ 532 Eric Chavez SH CL | .10 .30 |
| ☐ 533 Miguel Tejada SH CL | .10 .30 |
| ☐ 534 Ichiro Suzuki SH CL | .30 .75 |
| ☐ 535 Sammy Sosa SH CL | .20 .50 |
| ☐ 536 Barry Zito SH CL | .10 .30 |
| ☐ 537 Darin Erstad SH CL | .10 .30 |
| ☐ 538 Alfonso Soriano SH CL | .10 .30 |
| ☐ 539 Troy Glaus SH CL | .10 .30 |
| ☐ 540 Nomar Garciaparra SH CL | .30 .75 |
| ☐ 541 Bo Hart RC | .20 .50 |
| ☐ 542 Dan Haren RC | .30 .75 |
| ☐ 543 Ryan Wagner RC | .20 .50 |
| ☐ 544 Rich Harden RC | .20 .50 |
| ☐ 545 Dontrelle Willis | .30 .75 |
| ☐ 546 Jerome Williams | .10 .30 |
| ☐ 547 Bobby Crosby | .10 .30 |
| ☐ 548 Greg Jones RC | .20 .50 |
| ☐ 549 Todd Linden | .10 .30 |
| ☐ 550 Byung-Hyun Kim | .10 .30 |
| ☐ 551 Rickie Weeks RC | 1.25 3.00 |
| ☐ 552 Jason Roach RC | .20 .50 |
| ☐ 553 Oscar Villarreal RC | .20 .50 |
| ☐ 554 Justin Duchscherer | .20 .50 |
| ☐ 555 Chris Capuano RC | .60 1.50 |
| ☐ 556 Josh Hall RC | .20 .50 |
| ☐ 557 Luis Matos | .10 .30 |
| ☐ 558 Miguel Ojeda RC | .20 .50 |
| ☐ 559 Kevin Ohme RC | .20 .50 |
| ☐ 560 Julio Manon RC | .20 .50 |
| ☐ 561 Kevin Correia RC | .20 .50 |
| ☐ 562 Delmon Young RC | 2.00 5.00 |
| ☐ 563 Aaron Boone | .10 .30 |
| ☐ 564 Aaron Looper RC | .20 .50 |
| ☐ 565 Mike Neu RC | .20 .50 |
| ☐ 566 Aquilino Lopez RC | .20 .50 |
| ☐ 567 Jhonny Peralta | .30 .75 |
| ☐ 568 Duaner Sanchez | .10 .30 |
| ☐ 569 Stephen Randolph RC | .20 .50 |
| ☐ 570 Nate Bland RC | .20 .50 |
| ☐ 571 Chin-Hui Tsao | .10 .30 |
| ☐ 572 Michel Hernandez RC | .20 .50 |
| ☐ 573 Rocco Baldelli | .20 .50 |
| ☐ 574 Robb Quinlan | .10 .30 |
| ☐ 575 Aaron Heilman | .10 .30 |
| ☐ 576 Jae Weong Seo | .10 .30 |
| ☐ 577 Joe Borowski | .10 .30 |
| ☐ 578 Chris Bootcheck | .10 .30 |
| ☐ 579 Michael Ryan RC | .20 .50 |
| ☐ 580 Mark Malaska RC | .20 .50 |
| ☐ 581 Jose Guillen | .10 .30 |
| ☐ 582 Josh Towers | .10 .30 |
| ☐ 583 Tom Gregorio RC | .20 .50 |
| ☐ 584 Edwin Jackson RC | .20 .50 |
| ☐ 585 Jason Anderson | .10 .30 |
| ☐ 586 Jose Reyes | .30 .75 |
| ☐ 587 Miguel Cabrera | .30 .75 |
| ☐ 588 Nate Bump | .10 .30 |
| ☐ 589 Jeromy Burnitz | .10 .30 |
| ☐ 590 David Ross | .10 .30 |
| ☐ 591 Chase Utley | .30 .75 |
| ☐ 592 Brandon Webb | .60 1.50 |
| ☐ 593 Masao Kida | .10 .30 |
| ☐ 594 Jimmy Journell | .10 .30 |
| ☐ 595 Eric Young | .10 .30 |
| ☐ 596 Tony Womack | .10 .30 |
| ☐ 597 Amaury Telemaco | .10 .30 |
| ☐ 598 Rickey Henderson | .30 .75 |
| ☐ 599 Esteban Loaiza | .10 .30 |
| ☐ 600 Sidney Ponson | .10 .30 |
| ☐ NNO Update Set Exchange Card | |

**2004 Upper Deck**

|  | | |
|---|---|---|
| ☐ COMPLETE SERIES 1 (270) | 20.00 | 50.00 |
| ☐ COMPLETE SERIES 2 (270) | 20.00 | 50.00 |
| ☐ COMP UPDATE SET (50) | 7.50 | 15.00 |
| ☐ COMMON (31-480/541-565) | .40 | 1.00 |
| ☐ COMMON (1-30/481-540) | .40 | 1.00 |
| ☐ COMMON CARD (566-590) | .20 | .50 |
| ☐ 541-590 ONE SET PER '05 UD1 HOBBY BOX | | |
| ☐ UPDATE SET EXCH 1/480 '05 UD1 RETAIL | | |
| ☐ UPDATE SET EXCH.DEADLINE TBD | | |
| ☐ 1 Dontrelle Willis SR | .60 | 1.50 |
| ☐ 2 Edgar Gonzalez SR | .40 | 1.00 |
| ☐ 3 Jose Reyes SR | .40 | 1.00 |
| ☐ 4 Jae Weong Seo SR | .40 | 1.00 |
| ☐ 5 Miguel Cabrera SR | .60 | 1.50 |
| ☐ 6 Jesse Foppert SR | .40 | 1.00 |
| ☐ 7 Mike Neu SR | .40 | 1.00 |
| ☐ 8 Michael Nakamura SR | .40 | 1.00 |
| ☐ 9 Luis Ayala SR | .40 | 1.00 |
| ☐ 10 Jared Sandberg SR | .40 | 1.00 |
| ☐ 11 Jhonny Peralta SR | .40 | 1.00 |
| ☐ 12 Wil Ledezma SR | .40 | 1.00 |
| ☐ 13 Jason Roach SR | .40 | 1.00 |
| ☐ 14 Kirk Saarloos SR | .40 | 1.00 |
| ☐ 15 Cliff Lee SR | .40 | 1.00 |
| ☐ 16 Bobby Hill SR | .40 | 1.00 |
| ☐ 17 Lyle Overbay SR | .40 | 1.00 |
| ☐ 18 Josh Hall SR | .40 | 1.00 |
| ☐ 19 Joe Thurston SR | .40 | 1.00 |
| ☐ 20 Matt Kata SR | .40 | 1.00 |
| ☐ 21 Jeremy Bonderman SR | .40 | 1.00 |
| ☐ 22 Julio Manon SR | .40 | 1.00 |
| ☐ 23 Rodrigo Rosario SR | .40 | 1.00 |
| ☐ 24 Robby Hammock SR | .40 | 1.00 |
| ☐ 25 David Sanders SR | .40 | 1.00 |
| ☐ 26 Miguel Ojeda SR | .40 | 1.00 |
| ☐ 27 Mark Teixeira SR | .60 | 1.50 |
| ☐ 28 Franklyn German SR | .40 | 1.00 |
| ☐ 29 Ken Harvey SR | .40 | 1.00 |
| ☐ 30 Xavier Nady SR | .40 | 1.00 |
| ☐ 31 Tim Salmon | .20 | .50 |
| ☐ 32 Troy Glaus | .10 | .30 |
| ☐ 33 Adam Kennedy | .10 | .30 |
| ☐ 34 David Eckstein | .10 | .30 |
| ☐ 35 Ben Molina | .10 | .30 |
| ☐ 36 Jarrod Washburn | .10 | .30 |
| ☐ 37 Ramon Ortiz | .10 | .30 |
| ☐ 38 Eric Chavez | .10 | .30 |
| ☐ 39 Miguel Tejada | .10 | .30 |
| ☐ 40 Chris Singleton | .10 | .30 |
| ☐ 41 Jermaine Dye | .10 | .30 |
| ☐ 42 John Halama | .10 | .30 |
| ☐ 43 Tim Hudson | .10 | .30 |
| ☐ 44 Barry Zito | .10 | .30 |
| ☐ 45 Ted Lilly | .10 | .30 |
| ☐ 46 Bobby Kielty | .10 | .30 |
| ☐ 47 Kelvim Escobar | .10 | .30 |
| ☐ 48 Josh Phelps | .10 | .30 |
| ☐ 49 Vernon Wells | .10 | .30 |
| ☐ 50 Roy Halladay | .10 | .30 |
| ☐ 51 Orlando Hudson | .10 | .30 |
| ☐ 52 Eric Hinske | .10 | .30 |
| ☐ 53 Brandon Backe | .10 | .30 |
| ☐ 54 Dewon Brazelton | .10 | .30 |
| ☐ 55 Ben Grieve | .10 | .30 |
| ☐ 56 Aubrey Huff | .10 | .30 |
| ☐ 57 Toby Hall | .10 | .30 |
| ☐ 58 Rocco Baldelli | .10 | .30 |
| ☐ 59 Al Martin | .10 | .30 |
| ☐ 60 Brandon Phillips | .10 | .30 |
| ☐ 61 Omar Vizquel | .20 | .50 |
| ☐ 62 C.C. Sabathia | .10 | .30 |
| ☐ 63 Milton Bradley | .10 | .30 |

|  |  | | |  |  | | |  |  | | |
|---|---|---|---|---|---|---|---|---|---|---|---|
| 64 | Ricky Gutierrez | .10 | .30 | 145 | Rafael Furcal | .10 | .30 | 226 | Brian Giles | .10 | .30 |
| 65 | Matt Lawton | .10 | .30 | 146 | Javy Lopez | .10 | .30 | 227 | Mark Kotsay | .10 | .30 |
| 66 | Danys Baez | .10 | .30 | 147 | Shane Reynolds | .10 | .30 | 228 | Brian Lawrence | .10 | .30 |
| 67 | Ichiro Suzuki | .60 | 1.50 | 148 | Horacio Ramirez | .10 | .30 | 229 | Rod Beck | .10 | .30 |
| 68 | Randy Winn | .10 | .30 | 149 | Mike Hampton | .10 | .30 | 230 | Trevor Hoffman | .10 | .30 |
| 69 | Carlos Guillen | .10 | .30 | 150 | Jung Bong | .10 | .30 | 231 | Sean Burroughs | .10 | .30 |
| 70 | Mark McLemore | .10 | .30 | 151 | Ruben Quevedo | .10 | .30 | 232 | Bob Abreu | .10 | .30 |
| 71 | Dan Wilson | .10 | .30 | 152 | Ben Sheets | .10 | .30 | 233 | Jim Thome | .20 | .50 |
| 72 | Jamie Moyer | .10 | .30 | 153 | Geoff Jenkins | .10 | .30 | 234 | David Bell | .10 | .30 |
| 73 | Joel Pineiro | .10 | .30 | 154 | Royce Clayton | .10 | .30 | 235 | Jimmy Rollins | .10 | .30 |
| 74 | Edgar Martinez | .20 | .50 | 155 | Glendon Rusch | .10 | .30 | 236 | Mike Lieberthal | .10 | .30 |
| 75 | Tony Batista | .10 | .30 | 156 | John Vander Wal | .10 | .30 | 237 | Vicente Padilla | .10 | .30 |
| 76 | Jay Gibbons | .10 | .30 | 157 | Scott Podsednik | .10 | .30 | 238 | Randy Wolf | .10 | .30 |
| 77 | Jeff Conine | .10 | .30 | 158 | Jim Edmonds | .10 | .30 | 239 | Reggie Sanders | .10 | .30 |
| 78 | Melvin Mora | .10 | .30 | 159 | Tino Martinez | .20 | .50 | 240 | Jason Kendall | .10 | .30 |
| 79 | Geronimo Gil | .10 | .30 | 160 | Albert Pujols | .60 | 1.50 | 241 | Jack Wilson | .10 | .30 |
| 80 | Rodrigo Lopez | .10 | .30 | 161 | Matt Morris | .10 | .30 | 242 | Jose Hernandez | .10 | .30 |
| 81 | Jorge Julio | .10 | .30 | 162 | Woody Williams | .10 | .30 | 243 | Kip Wells | .10 | .30 |
| 82 | Rafael Palmeiro | .20 | .50 | 163 | Edgar Renteria | .10 | .30 | 244 | Carlos Rivera | .10 | .30 |
| 83 | Juan Gonzalez | .10 | .30 | 164 | Jason Isringhausen | .10 | .30 | 245 | Craig Wilson | .10 | .30 |
| 84 | Mike Young | .10 | .30 | 165 | Jason Simontacchi | .10 | .30 | 246 | Adam Dunn | .10 | .30 |
| 85 | Alex Rodriguez | .50 | 1.25 | 166 | Kerry Robinson | .10 | .30 | 247 | Sean Casey | .10 | .30 |
| 86 | Einar Diaz | .10 | .30 | 167 | Sammy Sosa | .30 | .75 | 248 | Danny Graves | .10 | .30 |
| 87 | Kevin Mench | .10 | .30 | 168 | Joe Borowski | .10 | .30 | 249 | Ryan Dempster | .10 | .30 |
| 88 | Hank Blalock | .10 | .30 | 169 | Tony Womack | .10 | .30 | 250 | Barry Larkin | .20 | .50 |
| 89 | Pedro Martinez | .20 | .50 | 170 | Antonio Alfonseca | .10 | .30 | 251 | Reggie Taylor | .10 | .30 |
| 90 | Byung-Hyun Kim | .10 | .30 | 171 | Corey Patterson | .10 | .30 | 252 | Wily Mo Pena | .10 | .30 |
| 91 | Derek Lowe | .10 | .30 | 172 | Mark Prior | .20 | .50 | 253 | Larry Walker | .10 | .30 |
| 92 | Jason Varitek | .30 | .75 | 173 | Moises Alou | .10 | .30 | 254 | Mark Sweeney | .10 | .30 |
| 93 | Manny Ramirez | .20 | .50 | 174 | Matt Clement | .10 | .30 | 255 | Preston Wilson | .10 | .30 |
| 94 | John Burkett | .10 | .30 | 175 | Randall Simon | .10 | .30 | 256 | Jason Jennings | .10 | .30 |
| 95 | Todd Walker | .10 | .30 | 176 | Randy Johnson | .30 | .75 | 257 | Charles Johnson | .10 | .30 |
| 96 | Nomar Garciaparra | .50 | 1.25 | 177 | Luis Gonzalez | .10 | .30 | 258 | Jay Payton | .10 | .30 |
| 97 | Trot Nixon | .10 | .30 | 178 | Craig Counsell | .10 | .30 | 259 | Chris Stynes | .10 | .30 |
| 98 | Mike Sweeney | .10 | .30 | 179 | Miguel Batista | .10 | .30 | 260 | Juan Uribe | .10 | .30 |
| 99 | Carlos Febles | .10 | .30 | 180 | Steve Finley | .10 | .30 | 261 | Hideki Matsui SH CL | .30 | .75 |
| 100 | Mike MacDougal | .10 | .30 | 181 | Brandon Webb | .10 | .30 | 262 | Barry Bonds SH CL | .40 | 1.00 |
| 101 | Raul Ibanez | .10 | .30 | 182 | Danny Bautista | .10 | .30 | 263 | Dontrelle Willis SH CL | .10 | .30 |
| 102 | Jason Grimsley | .10 | .30 | 183 | Oscar Villarreal | .10 | .30 | 264 | Kevin Millwood SH CL | .10 | .30 |
| 103 | Chris George | .10 | .30 | 184 | Shawn Green | .10 | .30 | 265 | Billy Wagner SH CL | .10 | .30 |
| 104 | Brent Mayne | .10 | .30 | 185 | Brian Jordan | .10 | .30 | 266 | Rocco Baldelli SH CL | .10 | .30 |
| 105 | Dmitri Young | .10 | .30 | 186 | Fred McGriff | .20 | .50 | 267 | Roger Clemens SH CL | .30 | .75 |
| 106 | Eric Munson | .10 | .30 | 187 | Andy Ashby | .10 | .30 | 268 | Rafael Palmeiro SH CL | .10 | .30 |
| 107 | A.J. Hinch | .10 | .30 | 188 | Rickey Henderson | .30 | .75 | 269 | Miguel Cabrera SH CL | .20 | .50 |
| 108 | Andres Torres | .10 | .30 | 189 | Dave Roberts | .10 | .30 | 270 | Jose Contreras SH CL | .10 | .30 |
| 109 | Bobby Higginson | .10 | .30 | 190 | Eric Gagne | .10 | .30 | 271 | Aaron Sele | .10 | .30 |
| 110 | Shane Halter | .10 | .30 | 191 | Kazuhisa Ishii | .10 | .30 | 272 | Bartolo Colon | .10 | .30 |
| 111 | Matt Walbeck | .10 | .30 | 192 | Adrian Beltre | .10 | .30 | 273 | Darin Erstad | .10 | .30 |
| 112 | Torii Hunter | .10 | .30 | 193 | Vladimir Guerrero | .30 | .75 | 274 | Francisco Rodriguez | .10 | .30 |
| 113 | Doug Mientkiewicz | .10 | .30 | 194 | Livan Hernandez | .10 | .30 | 275 | Garret Anderson | .10 | .30 |
| 114 | Lew Ford | .10 | .30 | 195 | Ron Calloway | .10 | .30 | 276 | Jose Guillen | .10 | .30 |
| 115 | Eric Milton | .10 | .30 | 196 | Sun Woo Kim | .10 | .30 | 277 | Troy Percival | .10 | .30 |
| 116 | Eddie Guardado | .10 | .30 | 197 | Wil Cordero | .10 | .30 | 278 | Alex Cintron | .10 | .30 |
| 117 | Cristian Guzman | .10 | .30 | 198 | Brad Wilkerson | .10 | .30 | 279 | Casey Fossum | .10 | .30 |
| 118 | Corey Koskie | .10 | .30 | 199 | Orlando Cabrera | .10 | .30 | 280 | Elmer Dessens | .10 | .30 |
| 119 | Magglio Ordonez | .10 | .30 | 200 | Barry Bonds | .75 | 2.00 | 281 | Jose Valverde | .10 | .30 |
| 120 | Mark Buehrle | .10 | .30 | 201 | Ray Durham | .10 | .30 | 282 | Matt Mantei | .10 | .30 |
| 121 | Billy Koch | .10 | .30 | 202 | Andres Galarraga | .10 | .30 | 283 | Richie Sexson | .10 | .30 |
| 122 | Jose Valentin | .10 | .30 | 203 | Benito Santiago | .10 | .30 | 284 | Roberto Alomar | .20 | .50 |
| 123 | Paul Konerko | .10 | .30 | 204 | Jose Cruz Jr. | .10 | .30 | 285 | Shea Hillenbrand | .10 | .30 |
| 124 | Carlos Lee | .10 | .30 | 205 | Jason Schmidt | .10 | .30 | 286 | Chipper Jones | .30 | .75 |
| 125 | Jon Garland | .10 | .30 | 206 | Kirk Rueter | .10 | .30 | 287 | Greg Maddux | .50 | 1.25 |
| 126 | Jason Giambi | .10 | .30 | 207 | Felix Rodriguez | .10 | .30 | 288 | J.D. Drew | .10 | .30 |
| 127 | Derek Jeter | .60 | 1.50 | 208 | Mike Lowell | .10 | .30 | 289 | Marcus Giles | .10 | .30 |
| 128 | Roger Clemens | .50 | 1.50 | 209 | Luis Castillo | .10 | .30 | 290 | Mike Hessman | .10 | .30 |
| 129 | Andy Pettitte | .20 | .50 | 210 | Derrek Lee | .20 | .50 | 291 | John Thomson | .10 | .30 |
| 130 | Jorge Posada | .20 | .50 | 211 | Andy Fox | .10 | .30 | 292 | Russ Ortiz | .10 | .30 |
| 131 | David Wells | .10 | .30 | 212 | Tommy Phelps | .10 | .30 | 293 | Adam Loewen | .10 | .30 |
| 132 | Hideki Matsui | .50 | 1.25 | 213 | Todd Hollandsworth | .10 | .30 | 294 | Jack Cust | .10 | .30 |
| 133 | Mike Mussina | .20 | .50 | 214 | Brad Penny | .10 | .30 | 295 | Jerry Hairston Jr. | .10 | .30 |
| 134 | Jeff Bagwell | .20 | .50 | 215 | Juan Pierre | .10 | .30 | 296 | Kurt Ainsworth | .10 | .30 |
| 135 | Craig Biggio | .20 | .50 | 216 | Mike Piazza | .50 | 1.25 | 297 | Luis Matos | .10 | .30 |
| 136 | Morgan Ensberg | .10 | .30 | 217 | Jae Weong Seo | .10 | .30 | 298 | Marty Cordova | .10 | .30 |
| 137 | Richard Hidalgo | .10 | .30 | 218 | Ty Wigginton | .10 | .30 | 299 | Sidney Ponson | .10 | .30 |
| 138 | Brad Ausmus | .10 | .30 | 219 | Al Leiter | .10 | .30 | 300 | Bill Mueller | .10 | .30 |
| 139 | Roy Oswalt | .10 | .30 | 220 | Roger Cedeno | .10 | .30 | 301 | Curt Schilling | .10 | .30 |
| 140 | Billy Wagner | .10 | .30 | 221 | Timo Perez | .10 | .30 | 302 | David Ortiz | .20 | .50 |
| 141 | Octavio Dotel | .10 | .30 | 222 | Aaron Heilman | .10 | .30 | 303 | Johnny Damon | .20 | .50 |
| 142 | Gary Sheffield | .10 | .30 | 223 | Pedro Astacio | .10 | .30 | 304 | Keith Foulke Sox | .10 | .30 |
| 143 | Andruw Jones | .20 | .50 | 224 | Joe McEwing | .10 | .30 | 305 | Pokey Reese | .10 | .30 |
| 144 | John Smoltz | .20 | .50 | 225 | Ryan Klesko | .10 | .30 | 306 | Scott Williamson | .10 | .30 |

|  |  | | |
|---|---|---|---|
| 307 | Tim Wakefield | .10 | .30 |
| 308 | Alex S. Gonzalez | .10 | .30 |
| 309 | Aramis Ramirez | .10 | .30 |
| 310 | Carlos Zambrano | .10 | .30 |
| 311 | Juan Cruz | .10 | .30 |
| 312 | Kerry Wood | .10 | .30 |
| 313 | Kyle Farnsworth | .10 | .30 |
| 314 | Aaron Rowand | .10 | .30 |
| 315 | Esteban Loaiza | .10 | .30 |
| 316 | Frank Thomas | .30 | .75 |
| 317 | Joe Borchard | .10 | .30 |
| 318 | Joe Crede | .10 | .30 |
| 319 | Miguel Olivo | .10 | .30 |
| 320 | Willie Harris | .10 | .30 |
| 321 | Aaron Harang | .10 | .30 |
| 322 | Austin Kearns | .10 | .30 |
| 323 | Brandon Claussen | .10 | .30 |
| 324 | Brandon Larson | .10 | .30 |
| 325 | Ryan Freel | .10 | .30 |
| 326 | Ken Griffey Jr. | .50 | 1.25 |
| 327 | Ryan Wagner | .10 | .30 |
| 328 | Alex Escobar | .10 | .30 |
| 329 | Coco Crisp | .10 | .30 |
| 330 | David Riske | .10 | .30 |
| 331 | Jody Gerut | .10 | .30 |
| 332 | Josh Bard | .10 | .30 |
| 333 | Travis Hafner | .10 | .30 |
| 334 | Chin-Hui Tsao | .10 | .30 |
| 335 | Denny Stark | .10 | .30 |
| 336 | Jeromy Burnitz | .10 | .30 |
| 337 | Shawn Chacon | .10 | .30 |
| 338 | Todd Helton | .20 | .50 |
| 339 | Vinny Castilla | .10 | .30 |
| 340 | Alex Sanchez | .10 | .30 |
| 341 | Carlos Pena | .10 | .30 |
| 342 | Fernando Vina | .10 | .30 |
| 343 | Jason Johnson | .10 | .30 |
| 344 | Matt Anderson | .10 | .30 |
| 345 | Mike Maroth | .10 | .30 |
| 346 | Rondell White | .10 | .30 |
| 347 | A.J. Burnett | .10 | .30 |
| 348 | Alex Gonzalez | .10 | .30 |
| 349 | Armando Benitez | .10 | .30 |
| 350 | Carl Pavano | .10 | .30 |
| 351 | Hee Seop Choi | .10 | .30 |
| 352 | Ivan Rodriguez | .20 | .50 |
| 353 | Josh Beckett | .10 | .30 |
| 354 | Josh Willingham | .10 | .30 |
| 355 | Adam Everett | .10 | .30 |
| 356 | Brandon Duckworth | .10 | .30 |
| 357 | Jason Lane | .10 | .30 |
| 358 | Jeff Kent | .10 | .30 |
| 359 | Jeriome Robertson | .10 | .30 |
| 360 | Lance Berkman | .10 | .30 |
| 361 | Wade Miller | .10 | .30 |
| 362 | Aaron Guiel | .10 | .30 |
| 363 | Angel Berroa | .10 | .30 |
| 364 | Carlos Beltran | .10 | .30 |
| 365 | David DeJesus | .10 | .30 |
| 366 | Desi Relaford | .10 | .30 |
| 367 | Joe Randa | .10 | .30 |
| 368 | Runelvys Hernandez | .10 | .30 |
| 369 | Edwin Jackson | .10 | .30 |
| 370 | Hideo Nomo | .30 | .75 |
| 371 | Jeff Weaver | .10 | .30 |
| 372 | Juan Encarnacion | .10 | .30 |
| 373 | Odalis Perez | .10 | .30 |
| 374 | Paul Lo Duca | .10 | .30 |
| 375 | Robin Ventura | .10 | .30 |
| 376 | Bill Hall | .10 | .30 |
| 377 | Chad Moeller | .10 | .30 |
| 378 | Chris Capuano | .10 | .30 |
| 379 | Junior Spivey | .10 | .30 |
| 380 | Rickie Weeks | .10 | .30 |
| 381 | Wes Helms | .10 | .30 |
| 382 | Brad Radke | .10 | .30 |
| 383 | Jacque Jones | .10 | .30 |
| 384 | Joe Mays | .10 | .30 |
| 385 | Joe Nathan | .10 | .30 |
| 386 | Johan Santana | .30 | .75 |
| 387 | Nick Punto | .10 | .30 |
| 388 | Shannon Stewart | .10 | .30 |
| 389 | Carl Everett | .10 | .30 |
| 390 | Claudio Vargas | .10 | .30 |
| 391 | Jose Vidro | .10 | .30 |
| 392 | Nick Johnson | .10 | .30 |
| 393 | Rocky Biddle | .10 | .30 |
| 394 | Tony Armas Jr. | .10 | .30 |
| 395 | Braden Looper | .10 | .30 |
| 396 | Cliff Floyd | .10 | .30 |
| 397 | Jason Phillips | .10 | .30 |
| 398 | Mike Cameron | .10 | .30 |
| 399 | Tom Glavine | .20 | .50 |
| 400 | Kenny Lofton | .10 | .30 |
| 401 | Alfonso Soriano | .20 | .50 |
| 402 | Bernie Williams | .20 | .50 |
| 403 | Javier Vazquez | .10 | .30 |
| 404 | Jon Lieber | .10 | .30 |
| 405 | Jose Contreras | .10 | .30 |
| 406 | Kevin Brown | .10 | .30 |
| 407 | Mariano Rivera | .30 | .75 |
| 408 | Arthur Rhodes | .10 | .30 |
| 409 | Eric Byrnes | .10 | .30 |
| 410 | Erubiel Durazo | .10 | .30 |
| 411 | Graham Koonce | .10 | .30 |
| 412 | Marco Scutaro | .10 | .30 |
| 413 | Mark Mulder | .10 | .30 |
| 414 | Mark Redman | .10 | .30 |
| 415 | Rich Harden | .10 | .30 |
| 416 | Brett Myers | .10 | .30 |
| 417 | Chase Utley | .20 | .50 |
| 418 | Kevin Millwood | .10 | .30 |
| 419 | Marlon Byrd | .10 | .30 |
| 420 | Pat Burrell | .10 | .30 |
| 421 | Placido Polanco | .10 | .30 |
| 422 | Tim Worrell | .10 | .30 |
| 423 | Jason Bay | .10 | .30 |
| 424 | Josh Fogg | .10 | .30 |
| 425 | Kris Benson | .10 | .30 |
| 426 | Mike Gonzalez | .10 | .30 |
| 427 | Oliver Perez | .10 | .30 |
| 428 | Tike Redman | .10 | .30 |
| 429 | Adam Eaton | .10 | .30 |
| 430 | Ismael Valdes | .10 | .30 |
| 431 | Jake Peavy | .10 | .30 |
| 432 | Khalil Greene | .20 | .50 |
| 433 | Mark Loretta | .10 | .30 |
| 434 | Phil Nevin | .10 | .30 |
| 435 | Ramon Hernandez | .10 | .30 |
| 436 | A.J. Pierzynski | .10 | .30 |
| 437 | Edgardo Alfonzo | .10 | .30 |
| 438 | J.T. Snow | .10 | .30 |
| 439 | Jerome Williams | .10 | .30 |
| 440 | Marquis Grissom | .10 | .30 |
| 441 | Robb Nen | .10 | .30 |
| 442 | Bret Boone | .10 | .30 |
| 443 | Freddy Garcia | .10 | .30 |
| 444 | Gil Meche | .10 | .30 |
| 445 | John Olerud | .10 | .30 |
| 446 | Rich Aurilia | .10 | .30 |
| 447 | Shigetoshi Hasegawa | .10 | .30 |
| 448 | Bo Hart | .10 | .30 |
| 449 | Danny Haren | .10 | .30 |
| 450 | Jason Marquis | .10 | .30 |
| 451 | Marlon Anderson | .10 | .30 |
| 452 | Scott Rolen | .20 | .50 |
| 453 | So Taguchi | .10 | .30 |
| 454 | Carl Crawford | .10 | .30 |
| 455 | Delmon Young | .20 | .50 |
| 456 | Geoff Blum | .10 | .30 |
| 457 | Jesus Colome | .10 | .30 |
| 458 | Jonny Gomes | .10 | .30 |
| 459 | Lance Carter | .10 | .30 |
| 460 | Robert Fick | .10 | .30 |
| 461 | Chan Ho Park | .10 | .30 |
| 462 | Francisco Cordero | .10 | .30 |
| 463 | Jeff Nelson | .10 | .30 |
| 464 | Jeff Zimmerman | .10 | .30 |
| 465 | Kenny Rogers | .10 | .30 |
| 466 | Aquilino Lopez | .10 | .30 |
| 467 | Carlos Delgado | .30 | .75 |
| 468 | Frank Catalanotto | .10 | .30 |
| 469 | Reed Johnson | .10 | .30 |
| 470 | Pat Hentgen | .10 | .30 |
| 471 | Curt Schilling SH CL | .10 | .30 |
| 472 | Gary Sheffield SH CL | .10 | .30 |
| 473 | Javier Vazquez SH CL | .20 | .50 |
| 474 | Kazuo Matsui SH CL | .10 | .30 |
| 475 | Kevin Brown SH CL | .10 | .30 |
| 476 | Rafael Palmeiro SH CL | .10 | .30 |
| 477 | Richie Sexson SH CL | .10 | .30 |
| 478 | Roger Clemens SH CL | .30 | .75 |
| 479 | Vladimir Guerrero SH CL | .20 | .50 |
| 480 | Alex Rodriguez SH CL | .30 | .75 |
| 481 | Jake Woods SR RC | .40 | 1.00 |
| 482 | Tim Bittner SR RC | .40 | 1.00 |
| 483 | Brandon Medders SR RC | .40 | 1.00 |
| 484 | Casey Daigle SR RC | .40 | 1.00 |
| 485 | Jerry Gil SR RC | .40 | 1.00 |
| 486 | Mike Gosling SR RC | .40 | 1.00 |
| 487 | Jose Capellan SR RC | .60 | 1.50 |
| 488 | Onil Joseph SR RC | .40 | 1.00 |
| 489 | Roman Colon SR RC | .40 | 1.00 |
| 490 | Dave Crouthers SR RC | .40 | 1.00 |
| 491 | Eddy Rodriguez SR RC | .60 | 1.50 |
| 492 | Franklyn Gracesqui SR RC | .40 | 1.00 |
| 493 | Jamie Brown SR RC | .40 | 1.00 |
| 494 | Jerome Gamble SR RC | .40 | 1.00 |
| 495 | Tim Hamulack SR RC | .40 | 1.00 |
| 496 | Carlos Vasquez SR RC | .60 | 1.50 |
| 497 | Renyel Pinto SR RC | .60 | 1.50 |
| 498 | Ronny Cedeno SR RC | .75 | 2.00 |
| 499 | Enemencio Pacheco SR RC | .40 | 1.00 |
| 500 | Ryan Meaux SR RC | .40 | 1.00 |
| 501 | Ryan Wing SR RC | .40 | 1.00 |
| 502 | Shingo Takatsu SR RC | .60 | 1.50 |
| 503 | William Bergola SR RC | .40 | 1.00 |
| 504 | Ivan Ochoa SR RC | .40 | 1.00 |
| 505 | Mariano Gomez SR RC | .40 | 1.00 |
| 506 | Justin Hampson SR RC | .40 | 1.00 |
| 507 | Justin Huisman SR RC | .40 | 1.00 |
| 508 | Scott Dohmann SR RC | .40 | 1.00 |
| 509 | Donnie Kelly SR RC | .40 | 1.00 |
| 510 | Chris Aguila SR RC | .40 | 1.00 |
| 511 | Lincoln Holdzkom SR RC | .40 | 1.00 |
| 512 | Freddy Guzman SR RC | .40 | 1.00 |
| 513 | Hector Gimenez SR RC | .40 | 1.00 |
| 514 | Jorge Vasquez SR RC | .40 | 1.00 |
| 515 | Jason Frasor SR RC | .40 | 1.00 |
| 516 | Chris Saenz SR RC | .40 | 1.00 |
| 517 | Dennis Sarfate SR RC | .40 | 1.00 |
| 518 | Colby Miller SR RC | .40 | 1.00 |
| 519 | Jason Bartlett SR RC | .60 | 1.50 |
| 520 | Chad Bentz SR RC | .40 | 1.00 |
| 521 | Josh Labandeira SR RC | .40 | 1.00 |
| 522 | Shawn Hill SR RC | .40 | 1.00 |
| 523 | Kazuo Matsui SR RC | .60 | 1.50 |
| 524 | Carlos Hines SR RC | .40 | 1.00 |
| 525 | Mike Vento SR RC | .60 | 1.50 |
| 526 | Scott Proctor SR RC | .60 | 1.50 |
| 527 | Sean Henn SR RC | .40 | 1.00 |
| 528 | David Aardsma SR RC | .60 | 1.50 |
| 529 | Ian Snell SR RC | .75 | 2.00 |
| 530 | Mike Johnston SR RC | .40 | 1.00 |
| 531 | Akinori Otsuka SR RC | .40 | 1.00 |
| 532 | Rusty Tucker SR RC | .60 | 1.50 |
| 533 | Justin Knoedler SR RC | .40 | 1.00 |
| 534 | Merkin Valdez SR RC | .60 | 1.50 |
| 535 | Greg Dobbs SR RC | .40 | 1.00 |
| 536 | Justin Leone SR RC | .60 | 1.50 |
| 537 | Shawn Camp SR RC | .40 | 1.00 |
| 538 | Edwin Moreno SR RC | .40 | 1.00 |
| 539 | Angel Chavez SR RC | .40 | 1.00 |
| 540 | Jesse Harper SR RC | .40 | 1.00 |
| 541 | Alex Rodriguez | .50 | 1.25 |
| 542 | Roger Clemens | .60 | 1.50 |
| 543 | Andy Pettitte | .20 | .50 |
| 544 | Vladimir Guerrero | .30 | .75 |
| 545 | David Wells | .10 | .30 |
| 546 | Derrek Lee | .20 | .50 |
| 547 | Carlos Beltran | .10 | .30 |
| 548 | Orlando Cabrera Sox | .10 | .30 |
| 549 | Paul Lo Duca | .10 | .30 |

| | | |
|---|---|---|
| ☐ 550 Dave Roberts | .10 | .30 |
| ☐ 551 Guillermo Mota | .10 | .30 |
| ☐ 552 Steve Finley | .10 | .30 |
| ☐ 553 Juan Encarnacion | .10 | .30 |
| ☐ 554 Larry Walker | .10 | .30 |
| ☐ 555 Ty Wigginton | .10 | .30 |
| ☐ 556 Doug Mientkiewicz | .10 | .30 |
| ☐ 557 Roberto Alomar | .20 | .50 |
| ☐ 558 B.J. Upton | .20 | .50 |
| ☐ 559 Brad Penny | .10 | .30 |
| ☐ 560 Hee Seop Choi | .10 | .30 |
| ☐ 561 David Wright | 1.25 | 3.00 |
| ☐ 562 Nomar Garciaparra | .50 | 1.25 |
| ☐ 563 Felix Rodriguez | .10 | .30 |
| ☐ 564 Victor Zambrano | .10 | .30 |
| ☐ 565 Kris Benson | .10 | .30 |
| ☐ 566 Aaron Baldiris SR RC | .20 | .50 |
| ☐ 567 Joey Gathright SR RC | .40 | 1.00 |
| ☐ 568 Charles Thomas SR RC | .20 | .50 |
| ☐ 569 Brian Dallimore SR RC | .20 | .50 |
| ☐ 570 Chris Oxspring SR RC | .20 | .50 |
| ☐ 571 Chris Shelton SR RC | .75 | 2.00 |
| ☐ 572 Dioner Navarro SR RC | .50 | 1.25 |
| ☐ 573 Edwardo Sierra SR RC | .20 | .50 |
| ☐ 574 Fernando Nieve SR RC | .30 | .75 |
| ☐ 575 Frank Francisco SR RC | .20 | .50 |
| ☐ 576 Jeff Bennett SR RC | .20 | .50 |
| ☐ 577 Justin Lehr SR RC | .20 | .50 |
| ☐ 578 John Gall SR RC | .20 | .50 |
| ☐ 579 Jorge Sequea SR RC | .20 | .50 |
| ☐ 580 Justin Germano SR RC | .20 | .50 |
| ☐ 581 Kazuhito Tadano SR RC | .20 | .50 |
| ☐ 582 Kevin Cave SR RC | .20 | .50 |
| ☐ 583 Jesse Crain SR RC | .30 | .75 |
| ☐ 584 Luis A. Gonzalez SR RC | .20 | .50 |
| ☐ 585 Michael Wuertz SR RC | .20 | .50 |
| ☐ 586 Orlando Rodriguez SR RC | .20 | .50 |
| ☐ 587 Phil Stockman SR RC | .20 | .50 |
| ☐ 588 Ramon Ramirez SR RC | .20 | .50 |
| ☐ 589 Roberto Novoa SR RC | .20 | .50 |
| ☐ 590 Scott Kazmir SR RC | 1.50 | 4.00 |
| ☐ NNO Update Set Exchange Card | | |

## 2005 Upper Deck

| | | |
|---|---|---|
| ☐ COMPLETE SERIES 1 (300) | 30.00 | 50.00 |
| ☐ COMMON CARD (1-500) | .10 | .30 |
| ☐ COMMON (211-250/426-450) | .40 | 1.00 |
| ☐ OVERALL PLATES SER.1 ODDS 1:1080 H | | |
| ☐ PLATES PRINT RUN 1 #'d SET PER COLOR | | |
| ☐ BLACK-CYAN-MAGENTA-YELLOW ISSUED | | |
| ☐ NO PLATES PRICING DUE TO SCARCITY | | |
| ☐ 1 Casey Kotchman | .10 | .30 |
| ☐ 2 Chone Figgins | .10 | .30 |
| ☐ 3 David Eckstein | .10 | .30 |
| ☐ 4 Jarrod Washburn | .10 | .30 |
| ☐ 5 Robb Quinlan | .10 | .30 |
| ☐ 6 Troy Glaus | .10 | .30 |
| ☐ 7 Vladimir Guerrero | .30 | .75 |
| ☐ 8 Brandon Webb | .10 | .30 |
| ☐ 9 Danny Bautista | .10 | .30 |
| ☐ 10 Luis Gonzalez | .10 | .30 |
| ☐ 11 Matt Kata | .10 | .30 |
| ☐ 12 Randy Johnson | .30 | .75 |
| ☐ 13 Robby Hammock | .10 | .30 |
| ☐ 14 Shea Hillenbrand | .10 | .30 |
| ☐ 15 Adam LaRoche | .10 | .30 |
| ☐ 16 Andruw Jones | .20 | .50 |
| ☐ 17 Horacio Ramirez | .10 | .30 |
| ☐ 18 John Smoltz | .20 | .50 |

| | | |
|---|---|---|
| ☐ 19 Johnny Estrada | .10 | .30 |
| ☐ 20 Mike Hampton | .10 | .30 |
| ☐ 21 Rafael Furcal | .10 | .30 |
| ☐ 22 Brian Roberts | .10 | .30 |
| ☐ 23 Javy Lopez | .10 | .30 |
| ☐ 24 Jay Gibbons | .10 | .30 |
| ☐ 25 Jorge Julio | .10 | .30 |
| ☐ 26 Melvin Mora | .10 | .30 |
| ☐ 27 Miguel Tejada | .10 | .30 |
| ☐ 28 Rafael Palmeiro | .20 | .50 |
| ☐ 29 Derek Lowe | .10 | .30 |
| ☐ 30 Jason Varitek | .30 | .75 |
| ☐ 31 Kevin Youkilis | .10 | .30 |
| ☐ 32 Manny Ramirez | .20 | .50 |
| ☐ 33 Curt Schilling | .20 | .50 |
| ☐ 34 Pedro Martinez | .20 | .50 |
| ☐ 35 Trot Nixon | .10 | .30 |
| ☐ 36 Corey Patterson | .10 | .30 |
| ☐ 37 Derrek Lee | .20 | .50 |
| ☐ 38 LaTroy Hawkins | .10 | .30 |
| ☐ 39 Mark Prior | .20 | .50 |
| ☐ 40 Matt Clement | .10 | .30 |
| ☐ 41 Moises Alou | .10 | .30 |
| ☐ 42 Sammy Sosa | .30 | .75 |
| ☐ 43 Aaron Rowand | .10 | .30 |
| ☐ 44 Carlos Lee | .10 | .30 |
| ☐ 45 Jose Valentin | .10 | .30 |
| ☐ 46 Juan Uribe | .10 | .30 |
| ☐ 47 Magglio Ordonez | .10 | .30 |
| ☐ 48 Mark Buehrle | .10 | .30 |
| ☐ 49 Paul Konerko | .10 | .30 |
| ☐ 50 Adam Dunn | .10 | .30 |
| ☐ 51 Barry Larkin | .20 | .50 |
| ☐ 52 D'Angelo Jimenez | .10 | .30 |
| ☐ 53 Danny Graves | .10 | .30 |
| ☐ 54 Paul Wilson | .10 | .30 |
| ☐ 55 Sean Casey | .10 | .30 |
| ☐ 56 Wily Mo Pena | .10 | .30 |
| ☐ 57 Ben Broussard | .10 | .30 |
| ☐ 58 C.C. Sabathia | .10 | .30 |
| ☐ 59 Casey Blake | .10 | .30 |
| ☐ 60 Cliff Lee | .10 | .30 |
| ☐ 61 Matt Lawton | .10 | .30 |
| ☐ 62 Omar Vizquel | .10 | .30 |
| ☐ 63 Victor Martinez | .10 | .30 |
| ☐ 64 Charles Johnson | .10 | .30 |
| ☐ 65 Joe Kennedy | .10 | .30 |
| ☐ 66 Jeromy Burnitz | .10 | .30 |
| ☐ 67 Matt Holliday | .15 | .40 |
| ☐ 68 Preston Wilson | .10 | .30 |
| ☐ 69 Royce Clayton | .10 | .30 |
| ☐ 70 Shawn Estes | .10 | .30 |
| ☐ 71 Bobby Higginson | .10 | .30 |
| ☐ 72 Brandon Inge | .10 | .30 |
| ☐ 73 Carlos Guillen | .10 | .30 |
| ☐ 74 Dmitri Young | .10 | .30 |
| ☐ 75 Eric Munson | .10 | .30 |
| ☐ 76 Jeremy Bonderman | .10 | .30 |
| ☐ 77 Ugueth Urbina | .10 | .30 |
| ☐ 78 Josh Beckett | .10 | .30 |
| ☐ 79 Dontrelle Willis | .10 | .30 |
| ☐ 80 Jeff Conine | .10 | .30 |
| ☐ 81 Juan Pierre | .10 | .30 |
| ☐ 82 Luis Castillo | .10 | .30 |
| ☐ 83 Miguel Cabrera | .20 | .50 |
| ☐ 84 Mike Lowell | .10 | .30 |
| ☐ 85 Andy Pettitte | .20 | .50 |
| ☐ 86 Brad Lidge | .10 | .30 |
| ☐ 87 Carlos Beltran | .10 | .30 |
| ☐ 88 Craig Biggio | .20 | .50 |
| ☐ 89 Jeff Bagwell | .20 | .50 |
| ☐ 90 Roger Clemens | .50 | 1.25 |
| ☐ 91 Roy Oswalt | .10 | .30 |
| ☐ 92 Benito Santiago | .10 | .30 |
| ☐ 93 Jeremy Affeldt | .10 | .30 |
| ☐ 94 Juan Gonzalez | .10 | .30 |
| ☐ 95 Ken Harvey | .10 | .30 |
| ☐ 96 Mike MacDougal | .10 | .30 |
| ☐ 97 Mike Sweeney | .10 | .30 |
| ☐ 98 Zack Greinke | .10 | .30 |
| ☐ 99 Adrian Beltre | .10 | .30 |

| | | |
|---|---|---|
| ☐ 100 Alex Cora | .10 | .30 |
| ☐ 101 Cesar Izturis | .10 | .30 |
| ☐ 102 Eric Gagne | .10 | .30 |
| ☐ 103 Kazuhisa Ishii | .10 | .30 |
| ☐ 104 Milton Bradley | .10 | .30 |
| ☐ 105 Shawn Green | .10 | .30 |
| ☐ 106 Danny Kolb | .10 | .30 |
| ☐ 107 Ben Sheets | .10 | .30 |
| ☐ 108 Brooks Kieschnick | .10 | .30 |
| ☐ 109 Craig Counsell | .10 | .30 |
| ☐ 110 Geoff Jenkins | .10 | .30 |
| ☐ 111 Lyle Overbay | .10 | .30 |
| ☐ 112 Scott Podsednik | .10 | .30 |
| ☐ 113 Corey Koskie | .10 | .30 |
| ☐ 114 Johan Santana | .30 | .75 |
| ☐ 115 Joe Mauer | .30 | .75 |
| ☐ 116 Justin Morneau | .10 | .30 |
| ☐ 117 Lew Ford | .10 | .30 |
| ☐ 118 Matt LeCroy | .10 | .30 |
| ☐ 119 Torii Hunter | .10 | .30 |
| ☐ 120 Brad Wilkerson | .10 | .30 |
| ☐ 121 Chad Cordero | .10 | .30 |
| ☐ 122 Livan Hernandez | .10 | .30 |
| ☐ 123 Jose Vidro | .10 | .30 |
| ☐ 124 Termel Sledge | .10 | .30 |
| ☐ 125 Tony Batista | .10 | .30 |
| ☐ 126 Zach Day | .10 | .30 |
| ☐ 127 Al Leiter | .10 | .30 |
| ☐ 128 Jae Weong Seo | .10 | .30 |
| ☐ 129 Jose Reyes | .10 | .30 |
| ☐ 130 Kazuo Matsui | .10 | .30 |
| ☐ 131 Mike Piazza | .30 | .75 |
| ☐ 132 Todd Zeile | .10 | .30 |
| ☐ 133 Cliff Floyd | .10 | .30 |
| ☐ 134 Alex Rodriguez | .50 | 1.25 |
| ☐ 135 Derek Jeter | .60 | 1.50 |
| ☐ 136 Gary Sheffield | .10 | .30 |
| ☐ 137 Hideki Matsui | .50 | 1.25 |
| ☐ 138 Jason Giambi | .10 | .30 |
| ☐ 139 Jorge Posada | .20 | .50 |
| ☐ 140 Mike Mussina | .20 | .50 |
| ☐ 141 Barry Zito | .10 | .30 |
| ☐ 142 Bobby Crosby | .10 | .30 |
| ☐ 143 Octavio Dotel | .10 | .30 |
| ☐ 144 Eric Chavez | .10 | .30 |
| ☐ 145 Jermaine Dye | .10 | .30 |
| ☐ 146 Mark Kotsay | .10 | .30 |
| ☐ 147 Tim Hudson | .10 | .30 |
| ☐ 148 Billy Wagner | .10 | .30 |
| ☐ 149 Bobby Abreu | .10 | .30 |
| ☐ 150 David Bell | .10 | .30 |
| ☐ 151 Jim Thome | .20 | .50 |
| ☐ 152 Jimmy Rollins | .10 | .30 |
| ☐ 153 Mike Lieberthal | .10 | .30 |
| ☐ 154 Randy Wolf | .10 | .30 |
| ☐ 155 Craig Wilson | .10 | .30 |
| ☐ 156 Daryle Ward | .10 | .30 |
| ☐ 157 Jack Wilson | .10 | .30 |
| ☐ 158 Jason Kendall | .10 | .30 |
| ☐ 159 Kip Wells | .10 | .30 |
| ☐ 160 Oliver Perez | .10 | .30 |
| ☐ 161 Rob Mackowiak | .10 | .30 |
| ☐ 162 Brian Giles | .10 | .30 |
| ☐ 163 Brian Lawrence | .10 | .30 |
| ☐ 164 David Wells | .10 | .30 |
| ☐ 165 Jay Payton | .10 | .30 |
| ☐ 166 Ryan Klesko | .10 | .30 |
| ☐ 167 Sean Burroughs | .10 | .30 |
| ☐ 168 Trevor Hoffman | .10 | .30 |
| ☐ 169 Brett Tomko | .10 | .30 |
| ☐ 170 J.T. Snow | .10 | .30 |
| ☐ 171 Jason Schmidt | .10 | .30 |
| ☐ 172 Kirk Rueter | .10 | .30 |
| ☐ 173 A.J. Pierzynski | .10 | .30 |
| ☐ 174 Pedro Feliz | .10 | .30 |
| ☐ 175 Ray Durham | .10 | .30 |
| ☐ 176 Eddie Guardado | .10 | .30 |
| ☐ 177 Edgar Martinez | .20 | .50 |
| ☐ 178 Ichiro Suzuki | .60 | 1.50 |
| ☐ 179 Jamie Moyer | .10 | .30 |
| ☐ 180 Joel Pineiro | .10 | .30 |

|  |  | | |
|---|---|---|---|
| 181 | Randy Winn | .10 | .30 |
| 182 | Raul Ibanez | .10 | .30 |
| 183 | Albert Pujols | .60 | 1.50 |
| 184 | Edgar Renteria | .10 | .30 |
| 185 | Jason Isringhausen | .10 | .30 |
| 186 | Jim Edmonds | .10 | .30 |
| 187 | Matt Morris | .10 | .30 |
| 188 | Reggie Sanders | .10 | .30 |
| 189 | Tony Womack | .10 | .30 |
| 190 | Aubrey Huff | .10 | .30 |
| 191 | Danys Baez | .10 | .30 |
| 192 | Carl Crawford | .10 | .30 |
| 193 | Jose Cruz Jr. | .10 | .30 |
| 194 | Rocco Baldelli | .10 | .30 |
| 195 | Tino Martinez | .20 | .50 |
| 196 | Dewon Brazelton | .10 | .30 |
| 197 | Alfonso Soriano | .10 | .30 |
| 198 | Brad Fullmer | .10 | .30 |
| 199 | Gerald Laird | .10 | .30 |
| 200 | Hank Blalock | .10 | .30 |
| 201 | Laynce Nix | .10 | .30 |
| 202 | Mark Teixeira | .20 | .50 |
| 203 | Michael Young | .10 | .30 |
| 204 | Alexis Rios | .10 | .30 |
| 205 | Eric Hinske | .10 | .30 |
| 206 | Miguel Batista | .10 | .30 |
| 207 | Orlando Hudson | .10 | .30 |
| 208 | Roy Halladay | .10 | .30 |
| 209 | Ted Lilly | .10 | .30 |
| 210 | Vernon Wells | .10 | .30 |
| 211 | Aarom Baldiris SR | .40 | 1.00 |
| 212 | B.J. Upton SR | .40 | 1.00 |
| 213 | Dallas McPherson SR | .40 | 1.00 |
| 214 | Brian Dallimore SR | .40 | 1.00 |
| 215 | Chris Oxspring SR | .40 | 1.00 |
| 216 | Chris Shelton SR | .60 | 1.50 |
| 217 | David Wright SR | .75 | 2.00 |
| 218 | Edwardo Sierra SR | .40 | 1.00 |
| 219 | Fernando Nieve SR | .40 | 1.00 |
| 220 | Frank Francisco SR | .40 | 1.00 |
| 221 | Jeff Bennett SR | .40 | 1.00 |
| 222 | Justin Lehr SR | .40 | 1.00 |
| 223 | John Gall SR | .40 | 1.00 |
| 224 | Jorge Sequea SR | .40 | 1.00 |
| 225 | Justin Germano SR | .40 | 1.00 |
| 226 | Kazuhito Tadano SR | .40 | 1.00 |
| 227 | Kevin Cave SR | .40 | 1.00 |
| 228 | Joe Blanton SR | .40 | 1.00 |
| 229 | Luis A. Gonzalez SR | .40 | 1.00 |
| 230 | Michael Wuertz SR | .40 | 1.00 |
| 231 | Mike Rouse SR | .40 | 1.00 |
| 232 | Nick Reglio SR | .40 | 1.00 |
| 233 | Orlando Rodriguez SR | .40 | 1.00 |
| 234 | Phil Stockman SR | .40 | 1.00 |
| 235 | Ramon Ramirez SR | .40 | 1.00 |
| 236 | Roberto Novoa SR | .40 | 1.00 |
| 237 | Dioner Navarro SR | .40 | 1.00 |
| 238 | Tim Bausher SR | .40 | 1.00 |
| 239 | Logan Kensing SR | .40 | 1.00 |
| 240 | Andy Green SR | .40 | 1.00 |
| 241 | Brad Halsey SR | .40 | 1.00 |
| 242 | Charles Thomas SR | .40 | 1.00 |
| 243 | George Sherrill SR | .40 | 1.00 |
| 244 | Jesse Crain SR | .40 | 1.00 |
| 245 | Jimmy Serrano SR | .40 | 1.00 |
| 246 | Joe Horgan SR | .40 | 1.00 |
| 247 | Chris Young SR | .40 | 1.00 |
| 248 | Joey Gathright SR | .40 | 1.00 |
| 249 | Gavin Floyd SR | .40 | 1.00 |
| 250 | Ryan Howard SR | 2.00 | 5.00 |
| 251 | Lance Cormier SR | .40 | 1.00 |
| 252 | Matt Treanor SR | .40 | 1.00 |
| 253 | Jeff Francis SR | .40 | 1.00 |
| 254 | Nick Swisher SR | .40 | 1.00 |
| 255 | Scott Atchison SR | .40 | 1.00 |
| 256 | Travis Blackley SR | .40 | 1.00 |
| 257 | Travis Smith SR | .40 | 1.00 |
| 258 | Yadier Molina SR | .40 | 1.00 |
| 259 | Jeff Keppinger SR | .40 | 1.00 |
| 260 | Scott Kazmir SR | .40 | 1.00 |
| 261 | G.Anderson/V.Guerrero TL | .20 | .50 |
| 262 | L.Gonzalez/R.Johnson TL | .20 | .50 |
| 263 | A.Jones/C.Jones TL | .20 | .50 |
| 264 | M.Tejada/R.Palmeiro TL | .10 | .30 |
| 265 | C.Schilling/M.Ramirez TL | .20 | .50 |
| 266 | M.Prior/S.Sosa TL | .20 | .50 |
| 267 | F.Thomas/M.Ordonez TL | .20 | .50 |
| 268 | B.Larkin/K.Griffey Jr. TL | .30 | .75 |
| 269 | C.Sabathia/V.Martinez TL | .10 | .30 |
| 270 | J.Burnitz/T.Helton TL | .10 | .30 |
| 271 | D.Young/I.Rodriguez TL | .10 | .30 |
| 272 | J.Beckett/M.Cabrera TL | .10 | .30 |
| 273 | J.Bagwell/R.Clemens TL | .30 | .75 |
| 274 | K.Harvey/M.Sweeney TL | .10 | .30 |
| 275 | A.Beltre/E.Gagne TL | .10 | .30 |
| 276 | B.Sheets/G.Jenkins TL | .10 | .30 |
| 277 | J.Mauer/T.Hunter TL | .20 | .50 |
| 278 | J.Vidro/L.Hernandez TL | .10 | .30 |
| 279 | K.Matsui/M.Piazza TL | .20 | .50 |
| 280 | A.Rodriguez/D.Jeter TL | .60 | 1.50 |
| 281 | E.Chavez/T.Hudson TL | .10 | .30 |
| 282 | B.Abreu/J.Thome TL | .10 | .30 |
| 283 | C.Wilson/J.Kendall TL | .10 | .30 |
| 284 | B.Giles/P.Nevin TL | .10 | .30 |
| 285 | A.Pierzynski/J.Schmidt TL | .10 | .30 |
| 286 | B.Boone/I.Suzuki TL | .30 | .75 |
| 287 | A.Pujols/S.Rolen TL | .30 | .75 |
| 288 | A.Huff/T.Martinez TL | .10 | .30 |
| 289 | H.Blalock/M.Teixeira TL | .10 | .30 |
| 290 | C.Delgado/R.Halladay TL | .10 | .30 |
| 291 | Vladimir Guerrero PR | .20 | .50 |
| 292 | Curt Schilling PR | .20 | .50 |
| 293 | Mark Prior PR | .20 | .50 |
| 294 | Josh Beckett PR | .10 | .30 |
| 295 | Roger Clemens PR | .30 | .75 |
| 296 | Derek Jeter PR | .30 | .75 |
| 297 | Eric Chavez PR | .10 | .30 |
| 298 | Jim Thome PR | .10 | .30 |
| 299 | Albert Pujols PR | .30 | .75 |
| 300 | Hank Blalock PR | .10 | .30 |
| 301 | Bartolo Colon | .10 | .30 |
| 302 | Darin Erstad | .10 | .30 |
| 303 | Garret Anderson | .10 | .30 |
| 304 | Orlando Cabrera | .10 | .30 |
| 305 | Steve Finley | .10 | .30 |
| 306 | Javier Vazquez | .10 | .30 |
| 307 | Russ Ortiz | .10 | .30 |
| 308 | Chipper Jones | .30 | .75 |
| 309 | Marcus Giles | .10 | .30 |
| 310 | Raul Mondesi | .10 | .30 |
| 311 | B.J. Ryan | .10 | .30 |
| 312 | Luis Matos | .10 | .30 |
| 313 | Sidney Ponson | .10 | .30 |
| 314 | Bill Mueller | .10 | .30 |
| 315 | David Ortiz | .30 | .75 |
| 316 | Johnny Damon | .20 | .50 |
| 317 | Keith Foulke | .10 | .30 |
| 318 | Mark Bellhorn | .10 | .30 |
| 319 | Wade Miller | .10 | .30 |
| 320 | Aramis Ramirez | .10 | .30 |
| 321 | Carlos Zambrano | .10 | .30 |
| 322 | Greg Maddux | .50 | 1.25 |
| 323 | Kerry Wood | .10 | .30 |
| 324 | Nomar Garciaparra | .30 | .75 |
| 325 | Todd Walker | .10 | .30 |
| 326 | Frank Thomas | .30 | .75 |
| 327 | Freddy Garcia | .10 | .30 |
| 328 | Joe Crede | .10 | .30 |
| 329 | Jose Contreras | .10 | .30 |
| 330 | Orlando Hernandez | .10 | .30 |
| 331 | Shingo Takatsu | .10 | .30 |
| 332 | Austin Kearns | .10 | .30 |
| 333 | Eric Milton | .10 | .30 |
| 334 | Ken Griffey Jr. | .50 | 1.25 |
| 335 | Aaron Boone | .10 | .30 |
| 336 | David Riske | .10 | .30 |
| 337 | Jake Westbrook | .10 | .30 |
| 338 | Kevin Millwood | .10 | .30 |
| 339 | Travis Hafner | .10 | .30 |
| 340 | Aaron Miles | .10 | .30 |
| 341 | Jeff Baker | .10 | .30 |
| 342 | Todd Helton | .20 | .50 |
| 343 | Garrett Atkins | .10 | .30 |
| 344 | Carlos Pena | .10 | .30 |
| 345 | Ivan Rodriguez | .20 | .50 |
| 346 | Rondell White | .10 | .30 |
| 347 | Troy Percival | .10 | .30 |
| 348 | A.J. Burnett | .10 | .30 |
| 349 | Carlos Delgado | .10 | .30 |
| 350 | Guillermo Mota | .10 | .30 |
| 351 | Paul Lo Duca | .10 | .30 |
| 352 | Jason Lane | .10 | .30 |
| 353 | Lance Berkman | .10 | .30 |
| 354 | Angel Berroa | .10 | .30 |
| 355 | David DeJesus | .10 | .30 |
| 356 | Ruben Gotay | .10 | .30 |
| 357 | Jose Lima | .10 | .30 |
| 358 | Brad Penny | .10 | .30 |
| 359 | J.D. Drew | .10 | .30 |
| 360 | Jayson Werth | .10 | .30 |
| 361 | Jeff Kent | .10 | .30 |
| 362 | Odalis Perez | .10 | .30 |
| 363 | Brady Clark | .10 | .30 |
| 364 | Junior Spivey | .10 | .30 |
| 365 | Rickie Weeks | .10 | .30 |
| 366 | Jacque Jones | .10 | .30 |
| 367 | Joe Nathan | .10 | .30 |
| 368 | Nick Punto | .10 | .30 |
| 369 | Shannon Stewart | .10 | .30 |
| 370 | Doug Mientkiewicz | .10 | .30 |
| 371 | Kris Benson | .10 | .30 |
| 372 | Tom Glavine | .20 | .50 |
| 373 | Victor Zambrano | .10 | .30 |
| 374 | Bernie Williams | .20 | .50 |
| 375 | Carl Pavano | .10 | .30 |
| 376 | Jaret Wright | .10 | .30 |
| 377 | Kevin Brown | .10 | .30 |
| 378 | Mariano Rivera | .30 | .75 |
| 379 | Danny Haren | .10 | .30 |
| 380 | Eric Byrnes | .10 | .30 |
| 381 | Erubiel Durazo | .10 | .30 |
| 382 | Rich Harden | .10 | .30 |
| 383 | Brett Myers | .10 | .30 |
| 384 | Chase Utley | .20 | .50 |
| 385 | Marlon Byrd | .10 | .30 |
| 386 | Pat Burrell | .10 | .30 |
| 387 | Placido Polanco | .10 | .30 |
| 388 | Freddy Sanchez | .10 | .30 |
| 389 | Jason Bay | .10 | .30 |
| 390 | Josh Fogg | .10 | .30 |
| 391 | Adam Eaton | .10 | .30 |
| 392 | Jake Peavy | .10 | .30 |
| 393 | Khalil Greene | .20 | .50 |
| 394 | Mark Loretta | .10 | .30 |
| 395 | Phil Nevin | .10 | .30 |
| 396 | Ramon Hernandez | .10 | .30 |
| 397 | Woody Williams | .10 | .30 |
| 398 | Armando Benitez | .10 | .30 |
| 399 | Edgardo Alfonzo | .10 | .30 |
| 400 | Marquis Grissom | .10 | .30 |
| 401 | Mike Matheny | .10 | .30 |
| 402 | Richie Sexson | .10 | .30 |
| 403 | Bret Boone | .10 | .30 |
| 404 | Gil Meche | .10 | .30 |
| 405 | Chris Carpenter | .10 | .30 |
| 406 | Jeff Suppan | .10 | .30 |
| 407 | Larry Walker | .20 | .50 |
| 408 | Mark Grudzielanek | .10 | .30 |
| 409 | Mark Mulder | .10 | .30 |
| 410 | Scott Rolen | .20 | .50 |
| 411 | Josh Phelps | .10 | .30 |
| 412 | Jonny Gomes | .10 | .30 |
| 413 | Francisco Cordero | .10 | .30 |
| 414 | Kenny Rogers | .10 | .30 |
| 415 | Richard Hidalgo | .10 | .30 |
| 416 | Dave Bush | .10 | .30 |
| 417 | Frank Catalanotto | .10 | .30 |
| 418 | Gabe Gross | .10 | .30 |
| 419 | Guillermo Quiroz | .10 | .30 |
| 420 | Reed Johnson | .10 | .30 |
| 421 | Cristian Guzman | .10 | .30 |
| 422 | Esteban Loaiza | .10 | .30 |
| 423 | Jose Guillen | .10 | .30 |

| | | |
|---|---|---|
| 424 Nick Johnson | .10 | .30 |
| 425 Vinny Castilla | .10 | .30 |
| 426 Pete Orr SR RC | .40 | 1.00 |
| 427 Tadahito Iguchi SR RC | 1.00 | 2.50 |
| 428 Jeff Baker SR | .40 | 1.00 |
| 429 Marcos Carvajal SR RC | .40 | 1.00 |
| 430 Justin Verlander SR RC | 2.00 | 5.00 |
| 431 Luke Scott SR RC | 1.25 | 3.00 |
| 432 Willy Taveras SR | .40 | 1.00 |
| 433 Ambiorix Burgos SR RC | .40 | 1.00 |
| 434 Andy Sisco SR | .40 | 1.00 |
| 435 Denny Bautista SR | .40 | 1.00 |
| 436 Mark Teahen SR | .40 | 1.00 |
| 437 Ervin Santana SR | .40 | 1.00 |
| 438 Dennis Houlton SR RC | .40 | 1.00 |
| 439 Philip Humber SR RC | .60 | 1.50 |
| 440 Steve Schmoll SR RC | .40 | 1.00 |
| 441 J.J. Hardy SR | .40 | 1.00 |
| 442 Ambiorix Concepcion SR RC | .40 | 1.00 |
| 443 Chae-Sung Koo SR RC | .40 | 1.00 |
| 444 Andy Phillips SR | .40 | 1.00 |
| 445 Dan Meyer SR | .40 | 1.00 |
| 446 Huston Street SR | .60 | 1.50 |
| 447 Keiichi Yabu SR RC | .40 | 1.00 |
| 448 Jeff Niemann SR RC | .60 | 1.50 |
| 449 Jeremy Reed SR | .40 | 1.00 |
| 450 Tony Blanco SR | .40 | 1.00 |
| 451 Albert Pujols BG | .30 | .75 |
| 452 Alex Rodriguez BG | .30 | .75 |
| 453 Curt Schilling BG | .10 | .30 |
| 454 Derek Jeter BG | .30 | .75 |
| 455 Greg Maddux BG | .30 | .75 |
| 456 Ichiro Suzuki BG | .30 | .75 |
| 457 Ivan Rodriguez BG | .10 | .30 |
| 458 Jeff Bagwell BG | .10 | .30 |
| 459 Jim Thome BG | .10 | .30 |
| 460 Ken Griffey Jr. BG | .30 | .75 |
| 461 Manny Ramirez BG | .20 | .50 |
| 462 Mike Mussina BG | .10 | .30 |
| 463 Mike Piazza BG | .20 | .50 |
| 464 Pedro Martinez BG | .10 | .30 |
| 465 Rafael Palmeiro BG | .10 | .30 |
| 466 Randy Johnson BG | -.20 | .50 |
| 467 Roger Clemens BG | .30 | .75 |
| 468 Sammy Sosa BG | .20 | .50 |
| 469 Todd Helton BG | .10 | .30 |
| 470 Vladimir Guerrero BG | .20 | .50 |
| 471 Vladimir Guerrero BG | .20 | .50 |
| 472 Shawn Green TC | .10 | .30 |
| 473 John Smoltz TC | .10 | .30 |
| 474 Miguel Tejada TC | .10 | .30 |
| 475 Curt Schilling TC | .10 | .30 |
| 476 Mark Prior TC | .10 | .30 |
| 477 Frank Thomas TC | .20 | .50 |
| 478 Ken Griffey Jr. TC | .30 | .75 |
| 479 C.C. Sabathia TC | .10 | .30 |
| 480 Todd Helton TC | .10 | .30 |
| 481 Ivan Rodriguez TC | .10 | .30 |
| 482 Miguel Cabrera TC | .10 | .30 |
| 483 Roger Clemens TC | .30 | .75 |
| 484 Mike Sweeney TC | .10 | .30 |
| 485 Eric Gagne TC | .10 | .30 |
| 486 Ben Sheets TC | .10 | .30 |
| 487 Johan Santana TC | .10 | .30 |
| 488 Mike Piazza TC | .20 | .50 |
| 489 Derek Jeter TC | .30 | .75 |
| 490 Eric Chavez TC | .10 | .30 |
| 491 Jim Thome TC | .10 | .30 |
| 492 Craig Wilson TC | .10 | .30 |
| 493 Jake Peavy TC | .10 | .30 |
| 494 Jason Schmidt TC | .10 | .30 |
| 495 Ichiro Suzuki TC | .30 | .75 |
| 496 Albert Pujols TC | .30 | .75 |
| 497 Carl Crawford TC | .10 | .30 |
| 498 Mark Teixeira TC | .10 | .30 |
| 499 Vernon Wells TC | .10 | .30 |
| 500 Jose Vidro TC | .10 | .30 |

## 2006 Upper Deck

| | | |
|---|---|---|
| COMPLETE SET (1250) | 375.00 | 600.00 |
| COMPLETE SERIES 1 (500) | 125.00 | 200.00 |
| COMPLETE SERIES 2 (500) | 125.00 | 200.00 |
| COMPLETE UPDATE (250) | 125.00 | 200.00 |
| COMP.UPDATE WO SP's (200) | 20.00 | 50.00 |
| COMMON CARD (1-1250) | .15 | .40 |

1-500 ISSUED IN SERIES 1 PACKS
501-1000 ISSUED IN SERIES 2 PACKS
1001-1250 ISSUED IN UPDATE PACKS
BAKER & REPKO BOTH CARD 283
1001-1250 SP STATED ODDS 1:2
SP: 1005/1013/1021/1037/1061/1069
SP: 1077/1093/1101/1117/1125/1133/1149
SP: 1157/1173/1181/1189/1205/1213
SP: 1221-1250
4 MATCHED PLATES 1:2 SER.2 HOBBY CASES
PLATE PRINT RUN 1 SET PER COLOR
BLACK-CYAN-MAGENTA-YELLOW ISSUED
NO PLATE PRICING DUE TO SCARCITY
EXQUISITE EXCH 1 PER SER.2 HOBBY CASE
EXQUISITE EXCH RANDOM IN UPD.CASES
EXQUISITE EXCH DEADLINE 07/27/07

| | | |
|---|---|---|
| 1 Adam Kennedy | .15 | .40 |
| 2 Bartolo Colon | .15 | .40 |
| 3 Bengie Molina | .15 | .40 |
| 4 Casey Kotchman | .15 | .40 |
| 5 Chone Figgins | .15 | .40 |
| 6 Dallas McPherson | .15 | .40 |
| 7 Darin Erstad | .15 | .40 |
| 8 Ervin Santana | .15 | .40 |
| 9 Francisco Rodriguez | .15 | .40 |
| 10 Garret Anderson | .15 | .40 |
| 11 Jarrod Washburn | .15 | .40 |
| 12 John Lackey | .15 | .40 |
| 13 Juan Rivera | .15 | .40 |
| 14 Orlando Cabrera | .15 | .40 |
| 15 Paul Byrd | .15 | .40 |
| 16 Steve Finley | .15 | .40 |
| 17 Vladimir Guerrero | .40 | 1.00 |
| 18 Alex Cintron | .15 | .40 |
| 19 Brandon Lyon | .15 | .40 |
| 20 Brandon Webb | .15 | .40 |
| 21 Chad Tracy | .15 | .40 |
| 22 Chris Snyder | .15 | .40 |
| 23 Claudio Vargas | .15 | .40 |
| 24 Conor Jackson | .25 | .60 |
| 25 Craig Counsell | .15 | .40 |
| 26 Javier Vazquez | .15 | .40 |
| 27 Jose Valverde | .15 | .40 |
| 28 Luis Gonzalez | .15 | .40 |
| 29 Royce Clayton | .15 | .40 |
| 30 Russ Ortiz | .15 | .40 |
| 31 Shawn Green | .15 | .40 |
| 32 Dustin Nippert (RC) | .30 | .75 |
| 33 Tony Clark | .15 | .40 |
| 34 Troy Glaus | .15 | .40 |
| 35 Adam LaRoche | .15 | .40 |
| 36 Andruw Jones | .25 | .60 |
| 37 Craig Hansen RC | 1.25 | 3.00 |
| 38 Chipper Jones | .40 | 1.00 |
| 39 Horacio Ramirez | .15 | .40 |
| 40 Jeff Francoeur | .40 | 1.00 |
| 41 John Smoltz | .25 | .60 |
| 42 Joey Devine RC | .30 | .75 |
| 43 Johnny Estrada | .15 | .40 |
| 44 Anthony Lerew (RC) | .30 | .75 |
| 45 Julio Franco | .15 | .40 |

| | | |
|---|---|---|
| 46 Kyle Farnsworth | .15 | .40 |
| 47 Marcus Giles | .15 | .40 |
| 48 Mike Hampton | .15 | .40 |
| 49 Rafael Furcal | .15 | .40 |
| 50 Chuck James (RC) | .50 | 1.25 |
| 51 Tim Hudson | .15 | .40 |
| 52 B.J. Ryan | .15 | .40 |
| 53 Bernie Castro (RC) | .30 | .75 |
| 54 Brian Roberts | .15 | .40 |
| 55 Walter Young (RC) | .30 | .75 |
| 56 Daniel Cabrera | .15 | .40 |
| 57 Eric Byrnes | .15 | .40 |
| 58 Alejandro Freire RC | .30 | .75 |
| 59 Erik Bedard | .15 | .40 |
| 60 Javy Lopez | .15 | .40 |
| 61 Jay Gibbons | .15 | .40 |
| 62 Jorge Julio | .15 | .40 |
| 63 Luis Matos | .15 | .40 |
| 64 Melvin Mora | .15 | .40 |
| 65 Miguel Tejada | .15 | .40 |
| 66 Rafael Palmeiro | .25 | .60 |
| 67 Rodrigo Lopez | .15 | .40 |
| 68 Sammy Sosa | .40 | 1.00 |
| 69 Alejandro Machado (RC) | .30 | .75 |
| 70 Bill Mueller | .15 | .40 |
| 71 Bronson Arroyo | .15 | .40 |
| 72 Curt Schilling | .25 | .60 |
| 73 David Ortiz | .25 | .60 |
| 74 David Wells | .15 | .40 |
| 75 Edgar Renteria | .15 | .40 |
| 76 Ryan Jorgensen RC | .30 | .75 |
| 77 Jason Varitek | .40 | 1.00 |
| 78 Johnny Damon | .25 | .60 |
| 79 Keith Foulke | .15 | .40 |
| 80 Kevin Youkilis | .15 | .40 |
| 81 Manny Ramirez | .25 | .60 |
| 82 Matt Clement | .15 | .40 |
| 83 Hanley Ramirez (RC) | .75 | 2.00 |
| 84 Tim Wakefield | .15 | .40 |
| 85 Trot Nixon | .15 | .40 |
| 86 Wade Miller | .15 | .40 |
| 87 Aramis Ramirez | .15 | .40 |
| 88 Carlos Zambrano | .15 | .40 |
| 89 Corey Patterson | .15 | .40 |
| 90 Derek Lee | .15 | .40 |
| 91 Geovany Soto (RC) | .75 | 2.00 |
| 92 Greg Maddux | .60 | 1.50 |
| 93 Jeromy Burnitz | .15 | .40 |
| 94 Jerry Hairston | .15 | .40 |
| 95 Kerry Wood | .15 | .40 |
| 96 Mark Prior | .25 | .60 |
| 97 Matt Murton | .15 | .40 |
| 98 Michael Barrett | .15 | .40 |
| 99 Neifi Perez | .15 | .40 |
| 100 Nomar Garciaparra | .40 | 1.00 |
| 101 Rich Hill | .15 | .40 |
| 102 Ryan Dempster | .15 | .40 |
| 103 Todd Walker | .15 | .40 |
| 104 A.J. Pierzynski | .15 | .40 |
| 105 Aaron Rowand | .15 | .40 |
| 106 Bobby Jenks | .15 | .40 |
| 107 Carl Everett | .15 | .40 |
| 108 Dustin Hermanson | .15 | .40 |
| 109 Frank Thomas | .40 | 1.00 |
| 110 Freddy Garcia | .15 | .40 |
| 111 Jermaine Dye | .15 | .40 |
| 112 Joe Crede | .15 | .40 |
| 113 Jon Garland | .15 | .40 |
| 114 Jose Contreras | .15 | .40 |
| 115 Juan Uribe | .15 | .40 |
| 116 Mark Buehrle | .15 | .40 |
| 117 Orlando Hernandez | .15 | .40 |
| 118 Paul Konerko | .25 | .60 |
| 119 Scott Podsednik | .15 | .40 |
| 120 Tadahito Iguchi | .15 | .40 |
| 121 Aaron Harang | .15 | .40 |
| 122 Adam Dunn | .15 | .40 |
| 123 Austin Kearns | .15 | .40 |
| 124 Brandon Claussen | .15 | .40 |
| 125 Chris Denorfia (RC) | .30 | .75 |
| 126 Edwin Encarnacion | .15 | .40 |

|  |  | | |
|---|---|---|---|
| ❏ 127 Miguel Perez (RC) | .30 | .75 |
| ❏ 128 Felipe Lopez | .15 | .40 |
| ❏ 129 Jason LaRue | .15 | .40 |
| ❏ 130 Ken Griffey Jr. | .60 | 1.50 |
| ❏ 131 Chris Booker (RC) | .30 | .75 |
| ❏ 132 Luke Hudson | .15 | .40 |
| ❏ 133 Jason Bergmann RC | .30 | .75 |
| ❏ 134 Ryan Freel | .15 | .40 |
| ❏ 135 Sean Casey | .15 | .40 |
| ❏ 136 Wily Mo Pena | .15 | .40 |
| ❏ 137 Aaron Boone | .15 | .40 |
| ❏ 138 Ben Broussard | .15 | .40 |
| ❏ 139 Ryan Garko (RC) | .30 | .75 |
| ❏ 140 C.C. Sabathia | .15 | .40 |
| ❏ 141 Casey Blake | .15 | .40 |
| ❏ 142 Cliff Lee | .15 | .40 |
| ❏ 143 Coco Crisp | .15 | .40 |
| ❏ 144 David Riske | .15 | .40 |
| ❏ 145 Grady Sizemore | .25 | .50 |
| ❏ 146 Jake Westbrook | .15 | .40 |
| ❏ 147 Jhonny Peralta | .15 | .40 |
| ❏ 148 Josh Bard | .15 | .40 |
| ❏ 149 Kevin Millwood | .15 | .40 |
| ❏ 150 Ronnie Belliard | .15 | .40 |
| ❏ 151 Scott Elarton | .15 | .40 |
| ❏ 152 Travis Hafner | .15 | .40 |
| ❏ 153 Victor Martinez | .15 | .40 |
| ❏ 154 Aaron Cook | .15 | .40 |
| ❏ 155 Aaron Miles | .15 | .40 |
| ❏ 156 Brad Hawpe | .15 | .40 |
| ❏ 157 Mike Esposito (RC) | .30 | .75 |
| ❏ 158 Chin-Hui Tsao | .15 | .40 |
| ❏ 159 Clint Barmes | .15 | .40 |
| ❏ 160 Cory Sullivan | .15 | .40 |
| ❏ 161 Garrett Atkins | .15 | .40 |
| ❏ 162 J.D. Closser | .15 | .40 |
| ❏ 163 Jason Jennings | .15 | .40 |
| ❏ 164 Jeff Baker | .15 | .40 |
| ❏ 165 Jeff Francis | .15 | .40 |
| ❏ 166 Luis A. Gonzalez | .15 | .40 |
| ❏ 167 Matt Holliday | .40 | 1.00 |
| ❏ 168 Todd Helton | .25 | .60 |
| ❏ 169 Brandon Inge | .15 | .40 |
| ❏ 170 Carlos Guillen | .15 | .40 |
| ❏ 171 Carlos Pena | .15 | .40 |
| ❏ 172 Chris Shelton | .15 | .40 |
| ❏ 173 Craig Monroe | .15 | .40 |
| ❏ 174 Curtis Granderson | .15 | .40 |
| ❏ 175 Dmitri Young | .15 | .40 |
| ❏ 176 Ivan Rodriguez | .25 | .60 |
| ❏ 177 Jason Johnson | .15 | .40 |
| ❏ 178 Jeremy Bonderman | .15 | .40 |
| ❏ 179 Magglio Ordonez | .15 | .40 |
| ❏ 180 Mark Woodyard (RC) | .30 | .75 |
| ❏ 181 Nook Logan | .15 | .40 |
| ❏ 182 Omar Infante | .15 | .40 |
| ❏ 183 Placido Polanco | .15 | .40 |
| ❏ 184 Chris Heintz RC | .30 | .75 |
| ❏ 185 A.J. Burnett | .15 | .40 |
| ❏ 186 Alex Gonzalez | .15 | .40 |
| ❏ 187 Josh Johnson (RC) | .30 | .75 |
| ❏ 188 Carlos Delgado | .15 | .40 |
| ❏ 189 Dontrelle Willis | .15 | .40 |
| ❏ 190 Josh Wilson (RC) | .30 | .75 |
| ❏ 191 Jason Vargas | .15 | .40 |
| ❏ 192 Jeff Conine | .15 | .40 |
| ❏ 193 Jeremy Hermida | .15 | .40 |
| ❏ 194 Josh Beckett | .15 | .40 |
| ❏ 195 Juan Encarnacion | .15 | .40 |
| ❏ 196 Juan Pierre | .15 | .40 |
| ❏ 197 Luis Castillo | .15 | .40 |
| ❏ 198 Miguel Cabrera | .25 | .60 |
| ❏ 199 Mike Lowell | .15 | .40 |
| ❏ 200 Paul Lo Duca | .15 | .40 |
| ❏ 201 Todd Jones | .15 | .40 |
| ❏ 202 Adam Everett | .15 | .40 |
| ❏ 203 Andy Pettitte | .25 | .60 |
| ❏ 204 Brad Ausmus | .15 | .40 |
| ❏ 205 Brad Lidge | .15 | .40 |
| ❏ 206 Brandon Backe | .15 | .40 |
| ❏ 207 Charlton Jimerson (RC) | .30 | .75 |
| ❏ 208 Chris Burke | .15 | .40 |
| ❏ 209 Craig Biggio | .25 | .60 |
| ❏ 210 Dan Wheeler | .15 | .40 |
| ❏ 211 Jason Lane | .15 | .40 |
| ❏ 212 Jeff Bagwell | .25 | .60 |
| ❏ 213 Lance Berkman | .15 | .40 |
| ❏ 214 Luke Scott | .15 | .40 |
| ❏ 215 Morgan Ensberg | .15 | .40 |
| ❏ 216 Roger Clemens | .75 | 2.00 |
| ❏ 217 Roy Oswalt | .15 | .40 |
| ❏ 218 Wily Taveras | .15 | .40 |
| ❏ 219 Andres Blanco | .15 | .40 |
| ❏ 220 Angel Berroa | .15 | .40 |
| ❏ 221 Ruben Gotay | .15 | .40 |
| ❏ 222 David DeJesus | .15 | .40 |
| ❏ 223 Emil Brown | .15 | .40 |
| ❏ 224 J.P. Howell | .15 | .40 |
| ❏ 225 Jeremy Affeldt | .15 | .40 |
| ❏ 226 Jimmy Gobble | .15 | .40 |
| ❏ 227 John Buck | .15 | .40 |
| ❏ 228 Jose Lima | .15 | .40 |
| ❏ 229 Mark Teahen | .15 | .40 |
| ❏ 230 Matt Stairs | .15 | .40 |
| ❏ 231 Mike MacDougal | .15 | .40 |
| ❏ 232 Mike Sweeney | .15 | .40 |
| ❏ 233 Runelvys Hernandez | .15 | .40 |
| ❏ 234 Terrence Long | .15 | .40 |
| ❏ 235 Zack Greinke | .15 | .40 |
| ❏ 236 Ron Flores RC | .30 | .75 |
| ❏ 237 Brad Penny | .15 | .40 |
| ❏ 238 Cesar Izturis | .15 | .40 |
| ❏ 239 D.J. Houlton | .15 | .40 |
| ❏ 240 Derek Lowe | .15 | .40 |
| ❏ 241 Eric Gagne | .15 | .40 |
| ❏ 242 Hee Seop Choi | .15 | .40 |
| ❏ 243 J.D. Drew | .15 | .40 |
| ❏ 244 Jason Phillips | .15 | .40 |
| ❏ 245 Jason Repko | .15 | .40 |
| ❏ 246 Jayson Werth | .15 | .40 |
| ❏ 247 Jeff Kent | .15 | .40 |
| ❏ 248 Jeff Weaver | .15 | .40 |
| ❏ 249 Milton Bradley | .15 | .40 |
| ❏ 250 Odalis Perez | .15 | .40 |
| ❏ 251 Hong-Chih Kuo (RC) | .75 | 2.00 |
| ❏ 252 Oscar Robles | .15 | .40 |
| ❏ 253 Ben Sheets | .15 | .40 |
| ❏ 254 Bill Hall | .15 | .40 |
| ❏ 255 Brady Clark | .15 | .40 |
| ❏ 256 Carlos Lee | .15 | .40 |
| ❏ 257 Chris Capuano | .15 | .40 |
| ❏ 258 Nelson Cruz (RC) | .50 | 1.25 |
| ❏ 259 Derrick Turnbow | .15 | .40 |
| ❏ 260 Doug Davis | .15 | .40 |
| ❏ 261 Geoff Jenkins | .15 | .40 |
| ❏ 262 J.J. Hardy | .15 | .40 |
| ❏ 263 Lyle Overbay | .15 | .40 |
| ❏ 264 Prince Fielder | .60 | 1.50 |
| ❏ 265 Rickie Weeks | .15 | .40 |
| ❏ 266 Russell Branyan | .15 | .40 |
| ❏ 267 Tomo Ohka | .15 | .40 |
| ❏ 268 Jonah Bayliss (RC) | .30 | .75 |
| ❏ 269 Brad Radke | .15 | .40 |
| ❏ 270 Carlos Silva | .15 | .40 |
| ❏ 271 Francisco Liriano (RC) | 1.50 | 4.00 |
| ❏ 272 Jacque Jones | .15 | .40 |
| ❏ 273 Joe Mauer | .40 | 1.00 |
| ❏ 274 Travis Bowyer (RC) | .30 | .75 |
| ❏ 275 Joe Nathan | .15 | .40 |
| ❏ 276 Johan Santana | .25 | .60 |
| ❏ 277 Justin Morneau | .15 | .40 |
| ❏ 278 Kyle Lohse | .15 | .40 |
| ❏ 279 Lew Ford | .15 | .40 |
| ❏ 280 Matt LeCroy | .15 | .40 |
| ❏ 281 Michael Cuddyer | .15 | .40 |
| ❏ 282 Nick Punto | .15 | .40 |
| ❏ 283a Scott Baker | .15 | .40 |
| ❏ 283b Jason Repko UER | .15 | .40 |
| ❏ 284 Shannon Stewart | .15 | .40 |
| ❏ 285 Torii Hunter | .15 | .40 |
| ❏ 286 Braden Looper | .15 | .40 |
| ❏ 287 Carlos Beltran | .15 | .40 |
| ❏ 288 Cliff Floyd | .15 | .40 |
| ❏ 289 David Wright | .60 | 1.50 |
| ❏ 290 Doug Mientkiewicz | .15 | .40 |
| ❏ 291 Anderson Hernandez (RC) | .30 | .75 |
| ❏ 292 Jose Reyes | .40 | 1.00 |
| ❏ 293 Kazuo Matsui | .15 | .40 |
| ❏ 294 Kris Benson | .15 | .40 |
| ❏ 295 Miguel Cairo | .15 | .40 |
| ❏ 296 Mike Cameron | .15 | .40 |
| ❏ 297 Robert Andino RC | .30 | .75 |
| ❏ 298 Mike Piazza | .40 | 1.00 |
| ❏ 299 Pedro Martinez | .25 | .60 |
| ❏ 300 Tom Glavine | .25 | .60 |
| ❏ 301 Victor Diaz | .15 | .40 |
| ❏ 302 Tim Hamulack (RC) | .30 | .75 |
| ❏ 303 Alex Rodriguez | .60 | 1.50 |
| ❏ 304 Bernie Williams | .25 | .60 |
| ❏ 305 Carl Pavano | .15 | .40 |
| ❏ 306 Chien-Ming Wang | .40 | 1.00 |
| ❏ 307 Derek Jeter | 1.00 | 2.50 |
| ❏ 308 Gary Sheffield | .15 | .40 |
| ❏ 309 Hideki Matsui | .40 | 1.00 |
| ❏ 310 Jason Giambi | .15 | .40 |
| ❏ 311 Jorge Posada | .25 | .60 |
| ❏ 312 Kevin Brown | .15 | .40 |
| ❏ 313 Mariano Rivera | .40 | 1.00 |
| ❏ 314 Matt Lawton | .15 | .40 |
| ❏ 315 Mike Mussina | .25 | .60 |
| ❏ 316 Randy Johnson | .40 | 1.00 |
| ❏ 317 Robinson Cano | .25 | .60 |
| ❏ 318 Mike Vento (RC) | .30 | .75 |
| ❏ 319 Tino Martinez | .15 | .40 |
| ❏ 320 Tony Womack | .15 | .40 |
| ❏ 321 Barry Zito | .15 | .40 |
| ❏ 322 Bobby Crosby | .15 | .40 |
| ❏ 323 Bobby Kielty | .15 | .40 |
| ❏ 324 Dan Johnson | .15 | .40 |
| ❏ 325 Danny Haren | .15 | .40 |
| ❏ 326 Eric Chavez | .15 | .40 |
| ❏ 327 Enubel Durazo | .15 | .40 |
| ❏ 328 Huston Street | .15 | .40 |
| ❏ 329 Jason Kendall | .15 | .40 |
| ❏ 330 Jay Payton | .15 | .40 |
| ❏ 331 Joe Blanton | .15 | .40 |
| ❏ 332 Joe Kennedy | .15 | .40 |
| ❏ 333 Kirk Saarloos | .15 | .40 |
| ❏ 334 Mark Kotsay | .15 | .40 |
| ❏ 335 Nick Swisher | .15 | .40 |
| ❏ 336 Rich Harden | .15 | .40 |
| ❏ 337 Scott Hatteberg | .15 | .40 |
| ❏ 338 Billy Wagner | .15 | .40 |
| ❏ 339 Bobby Abreu | .15 | .40 |
| ❏ 340 Brett Myers | .15 | .40 |
| ❏ 341 Chase Utley | .40 | 1.00 |
| ❏ 342 Danny Sandoval RC | .30 | .75 |
| ❏ 343 David Bell | .15 | .40 |
| ❏ 344 Gavin Floyd | .15 | .40 |
| ❏ 345 Jim Thome | .25 | .60 |
| ❏ 346 Jimmy Rollins | .15 | .40 |
| ❏ 347 Jon Lieber | .15 | .40 |
| ❏ 348 Kenny Lofton | .15 | .40 |
| ❏ 349 Mike Lieberthal | .15 | .40 |
| ❏ 350 Pat Burrell | .15 | .40 |
| ❏ 351 Randy Wolf | .15 | .40 |
| ❏ 352 Ryan Howard | .60 | 1.50 |
| ❏ 353 Vicente Padilla | .15 | .40 |
| ❏ 354 Bryan Bullington (RC) | .30 | .75 |
| ❏ 355 J.J. Furmaniak (RC) | .30 | .75 |
| ❏ 356 Craig Wilson | .15 | .40 |
| ❏ 357 Matt Capps (RC) | .30 | .75 |
| ❏ 358 Tom Gorzelanny (RC) | .30 | .75 |
| ❏ 359 Jack Wilson | .15 | .40 |
| ❏ 360 Jason Bay | .15 | .40 |
| ❏ 361 Jose Mesa | .15 | .40 |
| ❏ 362 Josh Fogg | .15 | .40 |
| ❏ 363 Kip Wells | .15 | .40 |
| ❏ 364 Steve Stanle RC | .30 | .75 |
| ❏ 365 Oliver Perez | .15 | .40 |
| ❏ 366 Rob Mackowiak | .15 | .40 |
| ❏ 367 Ronny Paulino (RC) | .30 | .75 |
| ❏ 368 Tike Redman | .15 | .40 |

|  |  | | |
|---|---|---|---|
| 369 | Zach Duke | .15 | .40 |
| 370 | Adam Eaton | .15 | .40 |
| 371 | Scott Feldman RC | .50 | 1.25 |
| 372 | Brian Giles | .15 | .40 |
| 373 | Brian Lawrence | .15 | .40 |
| 374 | Damian Jackson | .15 | .40 |
| 375 | Dave Roberts | .15 | .40 |
| 376 | Jake Peavy | .15 | .40 |
| 377 | Joe Randa | .15 | .40 |
| 378 | Khalil Greene | .25 | .60 |
| 379 | Mark Loretta | .15 | .40 |
| 380 | Ramon Hernandez | .15 | .40 |
| 381 | Robert Fick | .15 | .40 |
| 382 | Ryan Klesko | .15 | .40 |
| 383 | Trevor Hoffman | .15 | .40 |
| 384 | Woody Williams | .15 | .40 |
| 385 | Xavier Nady | .15 | .40 |
| 386 | Armando Benitez | .15 | .40 |
| 387 | Brad Hennessey | .15 | .40 |
| 388 | Brian Myrow RC | .30 | .75 |
| 389 | Edgardo Alfonzo | .15 | .40 |
| 390 | J.T. Snow | .15 | .40 |
| 391 | Jeremy Accardo RC | .30 | .75 |
| 392 | Jason Schmidt | .15 | .40 |
| 393 | Lance Niekro | .15 | .40 |
| 394 | Matt Cain | .25 | .60 |
| 395 | Dan Ortmeier (RC) | .30 | .75 |
| 396 | Moises Alou | .15 | .40 |
| 397 | Doug Clark (RC) | .30 | .75 |
| 398 | Omar Vizquel | .25 | .60 |
| 399 | Pedro Feliz | .15 | .40 |
| 400 | Randy Winn | .15 | .40 |
| 401 | Ray Durham | .15 | .40 |
| 402 | Adrian Beltre | .15 | .40 |
| 403 | Eddie Guardado | .15 | .40 |
| 404 | Felix Hernandez | .25 | .60 |
| 405 | Gil Meche | .15 | .40 |
| 406 | Ichiro Suzuki | .60 | 1.50 |
| 407 | Jamie Moyer | .15 | .40 |
| 408 | Jeff Nelson | .15 | .40 |
| 409 | Jeremy Reed | .15 | .40 |
| 410 | Joel Pineiro | .15 | .40 |
| 411 | Jaime Bubela (RC) | .30 | .75 |
| 412 | Raul Ibanez | .25 | .60 |
| 413 | Rickie Sexson | .15 | .40 |
| 414 | Ryan Franklin | .15 | .40 |
| 415 | Willie Bloomquist | .15 | .40 |
| 416 | Yorvit Torrealba | .15 | .40 |
| 417 | Yuniesky Betancourt | .15 | .40 |
| 418 | Jeff Harris RC | .30 | .75 |
| 419 | Albert Pujols | .75 | 2.00 |
| 420 | Chris Carpenter | .15 | .40 |
| 421 | David Eckstein | .15 | .40 |
| 422 | Jason Isringhausen | .15 | .40 |
| 423 | Jason Marquis | .15 | .40 |
| 424 | Adam Wainwright (RC) | .50 | 1.25 |
| 425 | Jim Edmonds | .25 | .60 |
| 426 | Ryan Theriot RC | .30 | .75 |
| 427 | Chris Duncan (RC) | .30 | .75 |
| 428 | Mark Grudzielanek | .15 | .40 |
| 429 | Mark Mulder | .15 | .40 |
| 430 | Matt Morris | .15 | .40 |
| 431 | Reggie Sanders | .15 | .40 |
| 432 | Scott Rolen | .25 | .60 |
| 433 | Tyler Johnson (RC) | .30 | .75 |
| 434 | Yadier Molina | .15 | .40 |
| 435 | Alex S. Gonzalez | .15 | .40 |
| 436 | Aubrey Huff | .15 | .40 |
| 437 | Tim Corcoran RC | .30 | .75 |
| 438 | Carl Crawford | .15 | .40 |
| 439 | Casey Fossum | .15 | .40 |
| 440 | Danys Baez | .15 | .40 |
| 441 | Edwin Jackson | .15 | .40 |
| 442 | Joey Gathright | .15 | .40 |
| 443 | Jonny Gomes | .15 | .40 |
| 444 | Jorge Cantu | .15 | .40 |
| 445 | Julio Lugo | .15 | .40 |
| 446 | Nick Green | .15 | .40 |
| 447 | Rocco Baldelli | .15 | .40 |
| 448 | Scott Kazmir | .25 | .60 |
| 449 | Seth McClung | .15 | .40 |
| 450 | Toby Hall | .15 | .40 |
| 451 | Travis Lee | .15 | .40 |
| 452 | Craig Breslow RC | .30 | .75 |
| 453 | Alfonso Soriano | .15 | .40 |
| 454 | Chris R. Young | .15 | .40 |
| 455 | David Dellucci | .15 | .40 |
| 456 | Francisco Cordero | .15 | .40 |
| 457 | Gary Matthews | .15 | .40 |
| 458 | Hank Blalock | .15 | .40 |
| 459 | Juan Dominguez | .15 | .40 |
| 460 | Josh Rupe (RC) | .30 | .75 |
| 461 | Kenny Rogers | .15 | .40 |
| 462 | Kevin Mench | .15 | .40 |
| 463 | Laynce Nix | .15 | .40 |
| 464 | Mark Teixeira | .25 | .60 |
| 465 | Michael Young | .15 | .40 |
| 466 | Richard Hidalgo | .15 | .40 |
| 467 | Jason Botts (RC) | .30 | .75 |
| 468 | Aaron Hill | .15 | .40 |
| 469 | Alex Rios | .15 | .40 |
| 470 | Corey Koskie | .15 | .40 |
| 471 | Chris Demaria RC | .30 | .75 |
| 472 | Eric Hinske | .15 | .40 |
| 473 | Frank Catalanotto | .15 | .40 |
| 474 | John-Ford Griffin (RC) | .30 | .75 |
| 475 | Gustavo Chacin | .15 | .40 |
| 476 | Josh Towers | .15 | .40 |
| 477 | Miguel Batista | .15 | .40 |
| 478 | Orlando Hudson | .15 | .40 |
| 479 | Reed Johnson | .15 | .40 |
| 480 | Roy Halladay | .15 | .40 |
| 481 | Shaun Marcum (RC) | .30 | .75 |
| 482 | Shea Hillenbrand | .15 | .40 |
| 483 | Ted Lilly | .15 | .40 |
| 484 | Vernon Wells | .15 | .40 |
| 485 | Brad Wilkerson | .15 | .40 |
| 486 | Darrell Rasner (RC) | .30 | .75 |
| 487 | Chad Cordero | .15 | .40 |
| 488 | Cristian Guzman | .15 | .40 |
| 489 | Esteban Loaiza | .15 | .40 |
| 490 | John Patterson | .15 | .40 |
| 491 | Jose Guillen | .15 | .40 |
| 492 | Jose Vidro | .15 | .40 |
| 493 | Livan Hernandez | .15 | .40 |
| 494 | Marlon Byrd | .15 | .40 |
| 495 | Nick Johnson | .15 | .40 |
| 496 | Preston Wilson | .15 | .40 |
| 497 | Ryan Church | .15 | .40 |
| 498 | Ryan Zimmerman (RC) | 1.50 | 4.00 |
| 499 | Tony Armas Jr. | .15 | .40 |
| 500 | Vinny Castilla | .15 | .40 |
| 501 | Andy Green | .15 | .40 |
| 502 | Damion Easley | .15 | .40 |
| 503 | Eric Byrnes | .15 | .40 |
| 504 | Jason Grimsley | .15 | .40 |
| 505 | Jeff DaVanon | .15 | .40 |
| 506 | Johnny Estrada | .15 | .40 |
| 507 | Luis Vizcaino | .15 | .40 |
| 508 | Miguel Batista | .15 | .40 |
| 509 | Orlando Hernandez | .15 | .40 |
| 510 | Orlando Hudson | .15 | .40 |
| 511 | Terry Mulholland | .15 | .40 |
| 512 | Chris Reitsma | .15 | .40 |
| 513 | Edgar Renteria | .15 | .40 |
| 514 | John Thomson | .15 | .40 |
| 515 | Jorge Sosa | .15 | .40 |
| 516 | Oscar Villarreal | .15 | .40 |
| 517 | Pete Orr | .15 | .40 |
| 518 | Ryan Langerhans | .15 | .40 |
| 519 | Todd Pratt | .15 | .40 |
| 520 | Wilson Betemit | .15 | .40 |
| 521 | Brian Jordan | .15 | .40 |
| 522 | Lance Cormier | .15 | .40 |
| 523 | Matt Diaz | .15 | .40 |
| 524 | Mike Remlinger | .15 | .40 |
| 525 | Bruce Chen | .15 | .40 |
| 526 | Chris Gomez | .15 | .40 |
| 527 | Chris Ray | .15 | .40 |
| 528 | Corey Patterson | .15 | .40 |
| 529 | David Newhan | .15 | .40 |
| 530 | Ed Rogers (RC) | .30 | .75 |
| 531 | John Halama | .15 | .40 |
| 532 | Kris Benson | .15 | .40 |
| 533 | LaTroy Hawkins | .15 | .40 |
| 534 | Raul Chavez | .15 | .40 |
| 535 | Alex Cora | .15 | .40 |
| 536 | Alex Gonzalez | .15 | .40 |
| 537 | Coco Crisp | .15 | .40 |
| 538 | David Riske | .15 | .40 |
| 539 | Doug Mirabelli | .15 | .40 |
| 540 | Josh Beckett | .15 | .40 |
| 541 | J.T. Snow | .15 | .40 |
| 542 | Mike Timlin | .15 | .40 |
| 543 | Julian Tavarez | .15 | .40 |
| 544 | Rudy Seanez | .15 | .40 |
| 545 | Wily Mo Pena | .15 | .40 |
| 546 | Bob Howry | .15 | .40 |
| 547 | Glendon Rusch | .15 | .40 |
| 548 | Henry Blanco | .15 | .40 |
| 549 | Jacque Jones | .15 | .40 |
| 550 | Jerome Williams | .15 | .40 |
| 551 | John Mabry | .15 | .40 |
| 552 | Juan Pierre | .15 | .40 |
| 553 | Scott Eyre | .15 | .40 |
| 554 | Scott Williamson | .15 | .40 |
| 555 | Wade Miller | .15 | .40 |
| 556 | Will Ohman | .15 | .40 |
| 557 | Alex Cintron | .15 | .40 |
| 558 | Rob Mackowiak | .15 | .40 |
| 559 | Brandon McCarthy | .15 | .40 |
| 560 | Chris Widger | .15 | .40 |
| 561 | Cliff Politte | .15 | .40 |
| 562 | Javier Vazquez | .15 | .40 |
| 563 | Jim Thome | .25 | .60 |
| 564 | Matt Thornton | .15 | .40 |
| 565 | Neal Cotts | .15 | .40 |
| 566 | Pablo Ozuna | .15 | .40 |
| 567 | Ross Gload | .15 | .40 |
| 568 | Brandon Phillips | .15 | .40 |
| 569 | Bronson Arroyo | .15 | .40 |
| 570 | Dave Williams | .15 | .40 |
| 571 | David Ross | .15 | .40 |
| 572 | David Weathers | .15 | .40 |
| 573 | Eric Milton | .15 | .40 |
| 574 | Javier Valentin | .15 | .40 |
| 575 | Kent Mercker | .15 | .40 |
| 576 | Matt Belisle | .15 | .40 |
| 577 | Paul Wilson | .15 | .40 |
| 578 | Rich Aurilia | .15 | .40 |
| 579 | Rick White | .15 | .40 |
| 580 | Scott Hatteberg | .15 | .40 |
| 581 | Todd Coffey | .15 | .40 |
| 582 | Bob Wickman | .15 | .40 |
| 583 | Danny Graves | .15 | .40 |
| 584 | Eduardo Perez | .15 | .40 |
| 585 | Guillermo Mota | .15 | .40 |
| 586 | Jason Davis | .15 | .40 |
| 587 | Jason Johnson | .15 | .40 |
| 588 | Jason Michaels | .15 | .40 |
| 589 | Rafael Betancourt | .15 | .40 |
| 590 | Ramon Vazquez | .15 | .40 |
| 591 | Scott Sauerbeck | .15 | .40 |
| 592 | Todd Hollandsworth | .15 | .40 |
| 593 | Brian Fuentes | .15 | .40 |
| 594 | Danny Ardoin | .15 | .40 |
| 595 | David Cortes | .15 | .40 |
| 596 | Eli Marrero | .15 | .40 |
| 597 | Jamey Carroll | .15 | .40 |
| 598 | Jason Smith | .15 | .40 |
| 599 | Josh Fogg | .15 | .40 |
| 600 | Miguel Ojeda | .15 | .40 |
| 601 | Mike DeJean | .15 | .40 |
| 602 | Ray King | .15 | .40 |
| 603 | Omar Quintanilla (RC) | .30 | .75 |
| 604 | Zach Day | .15 | .40 |
| 605 | Fernando Rodney | .15 | .40 |
| 606 | Kenny Rogers | .15 | .40 |
| 607 | Mike Maroth | .15 | .40 |
| 608 | Nate Robertson | .15 | .40 |
| 609 | Todd Jones | .15 | .40 |
| 610 | Vance Wilson | .15 | .40 |
| 611 | Bobby Seay | .15 | .40 |

|  |  | | |
|---|--------|---|---|
| ❑ 612 | Chris Spurling | .15 | .40 |
| ❑ 613 | Roman Colon | .15 | .40 |
| ❑ 614 | Jason Grilli | .15 | .40 |
| ❑ 615 | Marcus Thames | .15 | .40 |
| ❑ 616 | Ramon Santiago | .15 | .40 |
| ❑ 617 | Alfredo Amezaga | .15 | .40 |
| ❑ 618 | Brian Moehler | .15 | .40 |
| ❑ 619 | Chris Aguila | .15 | .40 |
| ❑ 620 | Franklyn German | .15 | .40 |
| ❑ 621 | Joe Borowski | .15 | .40 |
| ❑ 622 | Logan Kensing (RC) | .30 | .75 |
| ❑ 623 | Matt Treanor | .15 | .40 |
| ❑ 624 | Miguel Olivo | .15 | .40 |
| ❑ 625 | Sergio Mitre | .15 | .40 |
| ❑ 626 | Todd Wellemeyer | .15 | .40 |
| ❑ 627 | Wes Helms | .15 | .40 |
| ❑ 628 | Chad Qualls | .15 | .40 |
| ❑ 629 | Eric Bruntlett | .15 | .40 |
| ❑ 630 | Mike Gallo | .15 | .40 |
| ❑ 631 | Mike Lamb | .15 | .40 |
| ❑ 632 | Orlando Palmeiro | .15 | .40 |
| ❑ 633 | Russ Springer | .15 | .40 |
| ❑ 634 | Dan Wheeler | .15 | .40 |
| ❑ 635 | Eric Munson | .15 | .40 |
| ❑ 636 | Preston Wilson | .15 | .40 |
| ❑ 637 | Trever Miller | .15 | .40 |
| ❑ 638 | Ambiorix Burgos | .15 | .40 |
| ❑ 639 | Andy Sisco | .15 | .40 |
| ❑ 640 | Denny Bautista | .15 | .40 |
| ❑ 641 | Doug Mientkiewicz | .15 | .40 |
| ❑ 642 | Elmer Dessens | .15 | .40 |
| ❑ 643 | Esteban German | .15 | .40 |
| ❑ 644 | Joe Nelson (RC) | .30 | .75 |
| ❑ 645 | Mark Grudzielanek | .15 | .40 |
| ❑ 646 | Mark Redman | .15 | .40 |
| ❑ 647 | Mike Wood | .15 | .40 |
| ❑ 648 | Paul Bako | .15 | .40 |
| ❑ 649 | Reggie Sanders | .15 | .40 |
| ❑ 650 | Scott Elarton | .15 | .40 |
| ❑ 651 | Shane Costa | .15 | .40 |
| ❑ 652 | Tony Graffanino | .15 | .40 |
| ❑ 653 | Jason Bulger (RC) | .30 | .75 |
| ❑ 654 | Chris Bootcheck (RC) | .30 | .75 |
| ❑ 655 | Esteban Yan | .15 | .40 |
| ❑ 656 | Hector Carrasco | .15 | .40 |
| ❑ 657 | J.C. Romero | .15 | .40 |
| ❑ 658 | Jeff Weaver | .15 | .40 |
| ❑ 659 | Jose Molina | .15 | .40 |
| ❑ 660 | Kelvim Escobar | .15 | .40 |
| ❑ 661 | Maicer Izturis | .15 | .40 |
| ❑ 662 | Robb Quinlan | .15 | .40 |
| ❑ 663 | Scot Shields | .15 | .40 |
| ❑ 664 | Tim Salmon | .15 | .40 |
| ❑ 665 | Bill Mueller | .15 | .40 |
| ❑ 666 | Brett Tomko | .15 | .40 |
| ❑ 667 | Dioner Navarro | .15 | .40 |
| ❑ 668 | Jae Seo | .15 | .40 |
| ❑ 669 | Jose Cruz Jr. | .15 | .40 |
| ❑ 670 | Kenny Lofton | .15 | .40 |
| ❑ 671 | Lance Carter | .15 | .40 |
| ❑ 672 | Nomar Garciaparra | .40 | 1.00 |
| ❑ 673 | Olmedo Saenz | .15 | .40 |
| ❑ 674 | Rafael Furcal | .15 | .40 |
| ❑ 675 | Ramon Martinez | .15 | .40 |
| ❑ 676 | Ricky Ledee | .15 | .40 |
| ❑ 677 | Sandy Alomar Jr. | .15 | .40 |
| ❑ 678 | Yhency Brazoban | .15 | .40 |
| ❑ 679 | Corey Koskie | .15 | .40 |
| ❑ 680 | Dan Kolb | .15 | .40 |
| ❑ 681 | Gabe Gross | .15 | .40 |
| ❑ 682 | Jeff Cirillo | .15 | .40 |
| ❑ 683 | Matt Wise | .15 | .40 |
| ❑ 684 | Rick Helling | .15 | .40 |
| ❑ 685 | Chad Moeller | .15 | .40 |
| ❑ 686 | Dave Bush | .15 | .40 |
| ❑ 687 | Jorge De La Rosa | .15 | .40 |
| ❑ 688 | Justin Lehr | .15 | .40 |
| ❑ 689 | Jason Bartlett | .15 | .40 |
| ❑ 690 | Jesse Crain | .15 | .40 |
| ❑ 691 | Juan Rincon | .15 | .40 |
| ❑ 692 | Luis Castillo | .15 | .40 |
| ❑ 693 | Mike Redmond | .15 | .40 |
| ❑ 694 | Rondell White | .15 | .40 |
| ❑ 695 | Tony Batista | .15 | .40 |
| ❑ 696 | Juan Castro | .15 | .40 |
| ❑ 697 | Luis Rodriguez | .15 | .40 |
| ❑ 698 | Matt Guerrier | .15 | .40 |
| ❑ 699 | Willie Eyre (RC) | .30 | .75 |
| ❑ 700 | Aaron Heilman | .15 | .40 |
| ❑ 701 | Billy Wagner | .15 | .40 |
| ❑ 702 | Carlos Delgado | .15 | .40 |
| ❑ 703 | Chad Bradford | .15 | .40 |
| ❑ 704 | Chris Woodward | .15 | .40 |
| ❑ 705 | Darren Oliver | .15 | .40 |
| ❑ 706 | Duaner Sanchez | .15 | .40 |
| ❑ 707 | Endy Chavez | .15 | .40 |
| ❑ 708 | Jorge Julio | .15 | .40 |
| ❑ 709 | Jose Valentin | .15 | .40 |
| ❑ 710 | Julio Franco | .15 | .40 |
| ❑ 711 | Paul Lo Duca | .15 | .40 |
| ❑ 712 | Ramon Castro | .15 | .40 |
| ❑ 713 | Steve Trachsel | .15 | .40 |
| ❑ 714 | Victor Zambrano | .15 | .40 |
| ❑ 715 | Xavier Nady | .15 | .40 |
| ❑ 716 | Andy Phillips | .15 | .40 |
| ❑ 717 | Bubba Crosby | .15 | .40 |
| ❑ 718 | Jaret Wright | .15 | .40 |
| ❑ 719 | Kelly Stinnett | .15 | .40 |
| ❑ 720 | Kyle Farnsworth | .15 | .40 |
| ❑ 721 | Mike Myers | .15 | .40 |
| ❑ 722 | Octavio Dotel | .15 | .40 |
| ❑ 723 | Ron Villone | .15 | .40 |
| ❑ 724 | Scott Proctor | .15 | .40 |
| ❑ 725 | Shawn Chacon | .15 | .40 |
| ❑ 726 | Tanyon Sturtze | .15 | .40 |
| ❑ 727 | Adam Melhuse | .15 | .40 |
| ❑ 728 | Brad Halsey | .15 | .40 |
| ❑ 729 | Esteban Loaiza | .15 | .40 |
| ❑ 730 | Frank Thomas | .40 | 1.00 |
| ❑ 731 | Jay Witasick | .15 | .40 |
| ❑ 732 | Justin Duchscherer | .15 | .40 |
| ❑ 733 | Kiko Calero | .15 | .40 |
| ❑ 734 | Marco Scutaro | .15 | .40 |
| ❑ 735 | Mark Ellis | .15 | .40 |
| ❑ 736 | Milton Bradley | .15 | .40 |
| ❑ 737 | Aaron Fultz | .15 | .40 |
| ❑ 738 | Aaron Rowand | .15 | .40 |
| ❑ 739 | Geoff Geary | .15 | .40 |
| ❑ 740 | Arthur Rhodes | .15 | .40 |
| ❑ 741 | Chris Coste RC | .30 | .75 |
| ❑ 742 | Rheal Cormier | .15 | .40 |
| ❑ 743 | Ryan Franklin | .15 | .40 |
| ❑ 744 | Ryan Madson | .15 | .40 |
| ❑ 745 | Sal Fasano | .15 | .40 |
| ❑ 746 | Tom Gordon | .15 | .40 |
| ❑ 747 | Abraham Nunez | .15 | .40 |
| ❑ 748 | David Dellucci | .15 | .40 |
| ❑ 749 | Julio Santana | .15 | .40 |
| ❑ 750 | Shane Victorino | .15 | .40 |
| ❑ 751 | Damaso Marte | .15 | .40 |
| ❑ 752 | Freddy Sanchez | .15 | .40 |
| ❑ 753 | Humberto Cota | .15 | .40 |
| ❑ 754 | Jeromy Burnitz | .15 | .40 |
| ❑ 755 | Joe Randa | .15 | .40 |
| ❑ 756 | Jose Castillo | .15 | .40 |
| ❑ 757 | Mike Gonzalez | .15 | .40 |
| ❑ 758 | Ryan Doumit | .15 | .40 |
| ❑ 759 | Sean Burnett | .15 | .40 |
| ❑ 760 | Sean Casey | .15 | .40 |
| ❑ 761 | Ian Snell | .15 | .40 |
| ❑ 762 | John Grabow | .15 | .40 |
| ❑ 763 | Jose Hernandez | .15 | .40 |
| ❑ 764 | Roberto Hernandez | .15 | .40 |
| ❑ 765 | Ryan Vogelsong | .15 | .40 |
| ❑ 766 | Victor Santos | .15 | .40 |
| ❑ 767 | Adrian Gonzalez | .15 | .40 |
| ❑ 768 | Alan Embree | .15 | .40 |
| ❑ 769 | Brian Sweeney (RC) | .30 | .75 |
| ❑ 770 | Chan Ho Park | .15 | .40 |
| ❑ 771 | Clay Hensley | .15 | .40 |
| ❑ 772 | Dewon Brazelton | .15 | .40 |
| ❑ 773 | Doug Brocail | .15 | .40 |
| ❑ 774 | Eric Young | .15 | .40 |
| ❑ 775 | Geoff Blum | .15 | .40 |
| ❑ 776 | Josh Bard | .15 | .40 |
| ❑ 777 | Mark Bellhorn | .15 | .40 |
| ❑ 778 | Mike Cameron | .15 | .40 |
| ❑ 779 | Mike Piazza | .40 | 1.00 |
| ❑ 780 | Rob Bowen | .15 | .40 |
| ❑ 781 | Scott Cassidy | .15 | .40 |
| ❑ 782 | Scott Linebrink | .15 | .40 |
| ❑ 783 | Shawn Estes | .15 | .40 |
| ❑ 784 | Termel Sledge | .15 | .40 |
| ❑ 785 | Vinny Castilla | .15 | .40 |
| ❑ 786 | Jeff Fassero | .15 | .40 |
| ❑ 787 | Jose Vizcaino | .15 | .40 |
| ❑ 788 | Mark Sweeney | .15 | .40 |
| ❑ 789 | Matt Morris | .15 | .40 |
| ❑ 790 | Steve Finley | .15 | .40 |
| ❑ 791 | Tim Worrell | .15 | .40 |
| ❑ 792 | Jamey Wright | .15 | .40 |
| ❑ 793 | Jason Ellison | .15 | .40 |
| ❑ 794 | Noah Lowry | .15 | .40 |
| ❑ 795 | Steve Kline | .15 | .40 |
| ❑ 796 | Todd Greene | .15 | .40 |
| ❑ 797 | Carl Everett | .15 | .40 |
| ❑ 798 | George Sherrill | .15 | .40 |
| ❑ 799 | J.J. Putz | .15 | .40 |
| ❑ 800 | Jake Woods | .15 | .40 |
| ❑ 801 | Jose Lopez | .15 | .40 |
| ❑ 802 | Julio Mateo | .15 | .40 |
| ❑ 803 | Mike Morse | .15 | .40 |
| ❑ 804 | Rafael Soriano | .15 | .40 |
| ❑ 805 | Roberto Petagine | .15 | .40 |
| ❑ 806 | Aaron Miles | .15 | .40 |
| ❑ 807 | Braden Looper | .15 | .40 |
| ❑ 808 | Gary Bennett | .15 | .40 |
| ❑ 809 | Hector Luna | .15 | .40 |
| ❑ 810 | Jeff Suppan | .15 | .40 |
| ❑ 811 | John Rodriguez | .15 | .40 |
| ❑ 812 | Josh Hancock | .15 | .40 |
| ❑ 813 | Juan Encarnacion | .15 | .40 |
| ❑ 814 | Larry Bigbie | .15 | .40 |
| ❑ 815 | Scott Spiezio | .15 | .40 |
| ❑ 816 | Sidney Ponson | .15 | .40 |
| ❑ 817 | So Taguchi | .15 | .40 |
| ❑ 818 | Brian Meadows | .15 | .40 |
| ❑ 819 | Damon Hollins | .15 | .40 |
| ❑ 820 | Dan Miceli | .15 | .40 |
| ❑ 821 | Doug Waechter | .15 | .40 |
| ❑ 822 | Jason Childers RC | .30 | .75 |
| ❑ 823 | Josh Paul | .15 | .40 |
| ❑ 824 | Julio Lugo | .15 | .40 |
| ❑ 825 | Mark Hendrickson | .15 | .40 |
| ❑ 826 | Sean Burroughs | .15 | .40 |
| ❑ 827 | Shawn Camp | .15 | .40 |
| ❑ 828 | Travis Harper | .15 | .40 |
| ❑ 829 | Ty Wigginton | .15 | .40 |
| ❑ 830 | Adam Eaton | .15 | .40 |
| ❑ 831 | Adrian Brown | .15 | .40 |
| ❑ 832 | Akinori Otsuka | .15 | .40 |
| ❑ 833 | Antonio Alfonseca | .15 | .40 |
| ❑ 834 | Brad Wilkerson | .15 | .40 |
| ❑ 835 | D'Angelo Jimenez | .15 | .40 |
| ❑ 836 | Gerald Laird | .15 | .40 |
| ❑ 837 | Joaquin Benoit | .15 | .40 |
| ❑ 838 | Kameron Loe | .15 | .40 |
| ❑ 839 | Kevin Millwood | .15 | .40 |
| ❑ 840 | Mark DeRosa | .15 | .40 |
| ❑ 841 | Phil Nevin | .15 | .40 |
| ❑ 842 | Rod Barajas | .15 | .40 |
| ❑ 843 | Vicente Padilla | .15 | .40 |
| ❑ 844 | A.J. Burnett | .15 | .40 |
| ❑ 845 | Bengie Molina | .15 | .40 |
| ❑ 846 | Gregg Zaun | .15 | .40 |
| ❑ 847 | John McDonald | .15 | .40 |
| ❑ 848 | Lyle Overbay | .15 | .40 |
| ❑ 849 | Russ Adams | .15 | .40 |
| ❑ 850 | Troy Glaus | .15 | .40 |
| ❑ 851 | Vinny Chulk | .15 | .40 |
| ❑ 852 | B.J. Ryan | .15 | .40 |
| ❑ 853 | Justin Speier | .15 | .40 |
| ❑ 854 | Pete Walker | .15 | .40 |

|  |  | | |  |  | | |  |  | | |
|---|---|---|---|---|---|---|---|---|---|---|---|
| ❑ 855 | Scott Downs | .15 | .40 | ❑ 936 | Cody Ross (RC) | .30 | .75 | ❑ 1016 | Phil Stockman (RC) | .30 | .75 |
| ❑ 856 | Scott Schoeneweis | .15 | .40 | ❑ 937 | James Loney (RC) | .50 | 1.25 | ❑ 1017 | Brayan Pena (RC) | .30 | .75 |
| ❑ 857 | Alfonso Soriano | .15 | .40 | ❑ 938 | Takashi Saito RC | .50 | 1.25 | ❑ 1018 | Adam Loewen (RC) | .50 | 1.25 |
| ❑ 858 | Brian Schneider | .15 | .40 | ❑ 939 | Tim Hamulack (RC) | .30 | .75 | ❑ 1019 | Brandon Fahey RC | .30 | .75 |
| ❑ 859 | Daryle Ward | .15 | .40 | ❑ 940 | Chris Demaria RC | .30 | .75 | ❑ 1020 | Jim Hoey RC | .30 | .75 |
| ❑ 860 | Felix Rodriguez | .15 | .40 | ❑ 941 | Jose Capellan (RC) | .30 | .75 | ❑ 1021 | Kurt Birkins SP RC | 3.00 | 8.00 |
| ❑ 861 | Gary Majewski | .15 | .40 | ❑ 942 | David Gassner (RC) | .30 | .75 | ❑ 1022 | Jim Johnson RC | .30 | .75 |
| ❑ 862 | Joey Eischen | .15 | .40 | ❑ 943 | Jason Kubel (RC) | .30 | .75 | ❑ 1023 | Sam Perlozzo MG | .15 | .40 |
| ❑ 863 | Jon Rauch | .15 | .40 | ❑ 944 | Brian Bannister (RC) | .30 | .75 | ❑ 1024 | Cory Morris RC | .30 | .75 |
| ❑ 864 | Marlon Anderson | .15 | .40 | ❑ 945 | Mike Thompson RC | .30 | .75 | ❑ 1025 | Hayden Penn (RC) | .30 | .75 |
| ❑ 865 | Matt LeCroy | .15 | .40 | ❑ 946 | Cole Hamels (RC) | 1.25 | 3.00 | ❑ 1026 | Javy Lopez | .15 | .40 |
| ❑ 866 | Mike Stanton | .15 | .40 | ❑ 947 | Paul Maholm (RC) | .30 | .75 | ❑ 1027 | Dustin Pedroia (RC) | 5.00 | 12.00 |
| ❑ 867 | Ramon Ortiz | .15 | .40 | ❑ 948 | John Van Benschoten (RC) | .30 | .75 | ❑ 1028 | Kason Gabbard (RC) | .30 | .75 |
| ❑ 868 | Robert Fick | .15 | .40 | ❑ 949 | Nate McLouth (RC) | .30 | .75 | ❑ 1029 | David Pauley RC | .30 | .75 |
| ❑ 869 | Royce Clayton | .15 | .40 | ❑ 950 | Ben Johnson (RC) | .30 | .75 | ❑ 1030 | Kyle Snyder | .15 | .40 |
| ❑ 870 | Ryan Drese | .15 | .40 | ❑ 951 | Josh Barfield (RC) | .30 | .75 | ❑ 1031 | Terry Francona MG | .30 | .75 |
| ❑ 871 | Vladimir Guerrero CL | .40 | 1.00 | ❑ 952 | Travis Ishikawa (RC) | .30 | .75 | ❑ 1032 | Craig Breslow RC | .30 | .75 |
| ❑ 872 | Craig Biggio CL | .25 | .60 | ❑ 953 | Jack Taschner (RC) | .30 | .75 | ❑ 1033 | Bryan Corey (RC) | .30 | .75 |
| ❑ 873 | Barry Zito CL | .15 | .40 | ❑ 954 | Kenji Johjima RC | 1.50 | 4.00 | ❑ 1034 | Manny Delcarmen (RC) | .30 | .75 |
| ❑ 874 | Vernon Wells CL | .15 | .40 | ❑ 955 | Skip Schumaker (RC) | .30 | .75 | ❑ 1035 | Carlos Marmol RC | .30 | .75 |
| ❑ 875 | Chipper Jones CL | .40 | 1.00 | ❑ 956 | Ruddy Lugo (RC) | .30 | .75 | ❑ 1036 | Buck Coats (RC) | .30 | .75 |
| ❑ 876 | Prince Fielder CL | .60 | 1.50 | ❑ 957 | Jason Hammel (RC) | .30 | .75 | ❑ 1037 | Ryan O'Malley SP RC | 3.00 | 8.00 |
| ❑ 877 | Albert Pujols CL | .75 | 2.00 | ❑ 958 | Chris Roberson (RC) | .30 | .75 | ❑ 1038 | Angel Guzman (RC) | .30 | .75 |
| ❑ 878 | Greg Maddux CL | .60 | 1.50 | ❑ 959 | Fabio Castro RC | .30 | .75 | ❑ 1039 | Ronny Cedeno | .15 | .40 |
| ❑ 879 | Carl Crawford CL | .15 | .40 | ❑ 960 | Ian Kinsler (RC) | 1.00 | 2.50 | ❑ 1040 | Juan Mateo RC | .30 | .75 |
| ❑ 880 | Brandon Webb CL | .15 | .40 | ❑ 961 | John Koronka (RC) | .30 | .75 | ❑ 1041 | Cesar Izturis | .15 | .40 |
| ❑ 881 | J.D. Drew CL | .15 | .40 | ❑ 962 | Brandon Watson (RC) | .30 | .75 | ❑ 1042 | Les Walrond (RC) | .30 | .75 |
| ❑ 882 | Jason Schmidt CL | .15 | .40 | ❑ 963 | Jon Lester RC | 2.00 | 5.00 | ❑ 1043 | Geovany Soto (RC) | .75 | 2.00 |
| ❑ 883 | Victor Martinez CL | .15 | .40 | ❑ 964 | Ben Hendrickson (RC) | .30 | .75 | ❑ 1044 | Sean Tracey (RC) | .30 | .75 |
| ❑ 884 | Ichiro Suzuki CL | .60 | 1.50 | ❑ 965 | Martin Prado (RC) | .30 | .75 | ❑ 1045 | Ozzie Guillen MG SP | 3.00 | 8.00 |
| ❑ 885 | Miguel Cabrera CL | .25 | .60 | ❑ 966 | Erick Aybar (RC) | .30 | .75 | ❑ 1046 | Royce Clayton | .15 | .40 |
| ❑ 886 | David Wright CL | .60 | 1.50 | ❑ 967 | Bobby Livingston (RC) | .30 | .75 | ❑ 1047 | Norris Hopper RC | .30 | .75 |
| ❑ 887 | Alfonso Soriano CL | .15 | .40 | ❑ 968 | Ryan Spilborghs (RC) | .50 | 1.25 | ❑ 1048 | Bill Bray (RC) | .30 | .75 |
| ❑ 888 | Miguel Tejada CL | .15 | .40 | ❑ 969 | Tommy Murphy (RC) | .30 | .75 | ❑ 1049 | Jerry Narron MG | .15 | .40 |
| ❑ 889 | Khalil Greene CL | .25 | .60 | ❑ 970 | Howie Kendrick (RC) | 1.50 | 4.00 | ❑ 1050 | Brendan Harris (RC) | .30 | .75 |
| ❑ 890 | Ryan Howard CL | .60 | 1.50 | ❑ 971 | Casey Janssen RC | .30 | .75 | ❑ 1051 | Brian Shackelford | .15 | .40 |
| ❑ 891 | Jason Bay CL | .15 | .40 | ❑ 972 | Michael O'Connor RC | .30 | .75 | ❑ 1052 | Jeremy Sowers (RC) | .30 | .75 |
| ❑ 892 | Mark Teixeira CL | .25 | .60 | ❑ 973 | Conor Jackson (RC) | .50 | 1.25 | ❑ 1053 | Joe Inglett RC | .30 | .75 |
| ❑ 893 | Manny Ramirez CL | .25 | .60 | ❑ 974 | Jeremy Hermida (RC) | .30 | .75 | ❑ 1054 | Brian Slocum (RC) | .30 | .75 |
| ❑ 894 | Ken Griffey Jr. CL | .60 | 1.50 | ❑ 975 | Renyel Pinto (RC) | .30 | .75 | ❑ 1055 | Andrew Brown (RC) | .30 | .75 |
| ❑ 895 | Todd Helton CL | .25 | .60 | ❑ 976 | Prince Fielder (RC) | 1.25 | 3.00 | ❑ 1056 | Rafael Perez RC | .30 | .75 |
| ❑ 896 | Angel Berroa CL | .15 | .40 | ❑ 977 | Kevin Frandsen (RC) | .50 | 1.25 | ❑ 1057 | Edward Mujica RC | .30 | .75 |
| ❑ 897 | Ivan Rodriguez CL | .25 | .60 | ❑ 978 | Ty Taubenheim RC | .50 | 1.25 | ❑ 1058 | Andy Marte (RC) | .30 | .75 |
| ❑ 898 | Johan Santana CL | .25 | .60 | ❑ 979 | Rich Hill (RC) | .30 | .75 | ❑ 1059 | Shin-Soo Choo (RC) | .30 | .75 |
| ❑ 899 | Paul Konerko CL | .15 | .40 | ❑ 980 | Jonathan Broxton (RC) | .30 | .75 | ❑ 1060 | Jeremy Guthrie (RC) | .30 | .75 |
| ❑ 900 | Derek Jeter CL | 1.00 | 2.50 | ❑ 981 | Jamie Shields RC | .30 | .75 | ❑ 1061 | Franklin Gutierrez SP (RC) | 3.00 | 8.00 |
| ❑ 901 | Macay McBride (RC) | .30 | .75 | ❑ 982 | Carlos Villanueva RC | .30 | .75 | ❑ 1062 | Kazuo Matsui | .15 | .40 |
| ❑ 902 | Tony Pena (RC) | .30 | .75 | ❑ 983 | Boone Logan RC | .30 | .75 | ❑ 1063 | Chris Iannetta RC | .30 | .75 |
| ❑ 903 | Peter Moylan RC | .30 | .75 | ❑ 984 | Brian Wilson RC | .30 | .75 | ❑ 1064 | Manny Corpas RC | .30 | .75 |
| ❑ 904 | Aaron Rakers (RC) | .30 | .75 | ❑ 985 | Andre Ethier (RC) | .75 | 2.00 | ❑ 1065 | Clint Hurdle MG | .15 | .40 |
| ❑ 905 | Chris Britton RC | .30 | .75 | ❑ 986 | Mike Napoli RC | .75 | 2.00 | ❑ 1066 | Ramon Ramirez (RC) | .30 | .75 |
| ❑ 906 | Nick Markakis (RC) | .50 | 1.25 | ❑ 987 | Agustin Montero (RC) | .30 | .75 | ❑ 1067 | Sean Casey | .15 | .40 |
| ❑ 907 | Sendy Rleal RC | .30 | .75 | ❑ 988 | Jack Hannahan RC | .30 | .75 | ❑ 1068 | Zach Miner (RC) | .30 | .75 |
| ❑ 908 | Val Majewski (RC) | .30 | .75 | ❑ 989 | Boof Bonser (RC) | .30 | .75 | ❑ 1069 | Brent Clevlen SP (RC) | 3.00 | 8.00 |
| ❑ 909 | Jermaine Van Buren (RC) | .30 | .75 | ❑ 990 | Carlos Ruiz (RC) | .30 | .75 | ❑ 1070 | Bob Wickman | .15 | .40 |
| ❑ 910 | Jonathan Papelbon (RC) | 1.50 | 4.00 | ❑ 991 | Jason Botts (RC) | .30 | .75 | ❑ 1071 | Jim Leyland MG | .15 | .40 |
| ❑ 911 | Angel Pagan (RC) | .30 | .75 | ❑ 992 | Kendry Morales (RC) | .75 | 2.00 | ❑ 1072 | Alexis Gomez (RC) | .30 | .75 |
| ❑ 912 | David Aardsma (RC) | .30 | .75 | ❑ 993 | Alay Soler RC | .30 | .75 | ❑ 1073 | Anibal Sanchez (RC) | .50 | 1.25 |
| ❑ 913 | Sean Marshall (RC) | .30 | .75 | ❑ 994 | Santiago Ramirez (RC) | .30 | .75 | ❑ 1074 | Taylor Tankersley (RC) | .30 | .75 |
| ❑ 914 | Brian Anderson (RC) | .30 | .75 | ❑ 995 | Saul Rivera (RC) | .30 | .75 | ❑ 1075 | Eric Wedge MG | .15 | .40 |
| ❑ 915 | Freddie Bynum (RC) | .30 | .75 | ❑ 996 | Anthony Reyes (RC) | .30 | .75 | ❑ 1076 | Jonah Bayliss RC | .30 | .75 |
| ❑ 916 | Fausto Carmona (RC) | .30 | .75 | ❑ 997 | Matt Kemp (RC) | .75 | 2.00 | ❑ 1077 | Paul Hoover SP (RC) | 3.00 | 8.00 |
| ❑ 917 | Kelly Shoppach (RC) | .30 | .75 | ❑ 998 | Jae Kuk Ryu RC | .30 | .75 | ❑ 1078 | Eddie Guardado | .15 | .40 |
| ❑ 918 | Choo Freeman (RC) | .30 | .75 | ❑ 999 | Lastings Milledge (RC) | .50 | 1.25 | ❑ 1079 | Cody Ross (RC) | .30 | .75 |
| ❑ 919 | Ryan Shealy (RC) | .30 | .75 | ❑ NNO | Exquisite Redemption | | | ❑ 1080 | Aubrey Huff | .15 | .40 |
| ❑ 920 | Joel Zumaya (RC) | .75 | 2.00 | ❑ 1000 | Jered Weaver (RC) | 1.50 | 4.00 | ❑ 1081 | Jason Hirsh (RC) | .30 | .75 |
| ❑ 921 | Jordan Tata RC | .30 | .75 | ❑ 1001 | Stephen Drew (RC) | .75 | 2.00 | ❑ 1082 | Brandon League | .15 | .40 |
| ❑ 922 | Justin Verlander (RC) | 1.25 | 3.00 | ❑ 1002 | Carlos Quentin (RC) | .50 | 1.25 | ❑ 1083 | Matt Albers (RC) | .30 | .75 |
| ❑ 923 | Carlos Martinez (RC) | .30 | .75 | ❑ 1003 | Livan Hernandez | .15 | .40 | ❑ 1084 | Chris Sampson RC | .30 | .75 |
| ❑ 924 | Chris Resop (RC) | .30 | .75 | ❑ 1004 | Chris B. Young (RC) | .30 | .75 | ❑ 1085 | Phil Garner MG | .15 | .40 |
| ❑ 925 | Dan Uggla (RC) | .75 | 2.00 | ❑ 1005 | Alberto Callaspo SP (RC) | 3.00 | 8.00 | ❑ 1086 | J.R. House (RC) | .30 | .75 |
| ❑ 926 | Eric Reed (RC) | .30 | .75 | ❑ 1006 | Enrique Gonzalez (RC) | .30 | .75 | ❑ 1087 | Ryan Shealy (RC) | .30 | .75 |
| ❑ 927 | Hanley Ramirez (RC) | .75 | 2.00 | ❑ 1007 | Tony Pena (RC) | .30 | .75 | ❑ 1088 | Stephen Andrade (RC) | .30 | .75 |
| ❑ 928 | Yusmeiro Petit (RC) | .30 | .75 | ❑ 1008 | Bob Melvin MG | .15 | .40 | ❑ 1089 | Bob Keppel (RC) | .30 | .75 |
| ❑ 929 | Josh Willingham (RC) | .30 | .75 | ❑ 1009 | Fernando Tatis | .15 | .40 | ❑ 1090 | Buddy Bell MG | .15 | .40 |
| ❑ 930 | Mike Jacobs (RC) | .30 | .75 | ❑ 1010 | Willy Aybar (RC) | .30 | .75 | ❑ 1091 | Justin Huber (RC) | .30 | .75 |
| ❑ 931 | Reggie Abercrombie (RC) | .30 | .75 | ❑ 1011 | Ken Ray (RC) | .30 | .75 | ❑ 1092 | Paul Phillips (RC) | .30 | .75 |
| ❑ 932 | Ricky Nolasco (RC) | .30 | .75 | ❑ 1012 | Scott Thorman (RC) | .30 | .75 | ❑ 1093 | Greg Jones SP (RC) | 3.00 | 8.00 |
| ❑ 933 | Scott Olsen (RC) | .30 | .75 | ❑ 1013 | Eric Hinske SP | 3.00 | 8.00 | ❑ 1094 | Jeff Mathis (RC) | .30 | .75 |
| ❑ 934 | Fernando Nieve (RC) | .30 | .75 | ❑ 1014 | Kevin Barry (RC) | .30 | .75 | ❑ 1095 | Dustin Moseley (RC) | .30 | .75 |
| ❑ 935 | Taylor Buchholz (RC) | .50 | 1.25 | ❑ 1015 | Bobby Cox MG | .15 | .40 | ❑ 1096 | Joe Saunders (RC) | .30 | .75 |

| | | |
|---|---|---|
| ☐ 1097 Reggie Willits RC | .50 | 1.25 |
| ☐ 1098 Mike Scioscia MG | .15 | .40 |
| ☐ 1099 Greg Maddux | .60 | 1.50 |
| ☐ 1100 Wilson Betemit | .15 | .40 |
| ☐ 1101 Chad Billingsley SP (RC) | 3.00 | 8.00 |
| ☐ 1102 Russell Martin (RC) | .50 | 1.25 |
| ☐ 1103 Grady Little MG | .15 | .40 |
| ☐ 1104 David Bell | .15 | .40 |
| ☐ 1105 Kevin Mench | .15 | .40 |
| ☐ 1106 Laynce Nix | .15 | .40 |
| ☐ 1107 Chris Barnwell RC | .30 | .75 |
| ☐ 1108 Tony Gwynn Jr. (RC) | .30 | .75 |
| ☐ 1109 Corey Hart (RC) | .30 | .75 |
| ☐ 1110 Zach Jackson (RC) | .30 | .75 |
| ☐ 1111 Francisco Cordero | .15 | .40 |
| ☐ 1112 Joe Winkelsas (RC) | .30 | .75 |
| ☐ 1113 Ned Yost MG | .15 | .40 |
| ☐ 1114 Matt Garza (RC) | .30 | .75 |
| ☐ 1115 Chris Heintz | .15 | .40 |
| ☐ 1116 Pat Neshek RC | 3.00 | 8.00 |
| ☐ 1117 Josh Rabe SP RC | 8.00 | 20.00 |
| ☐ 1118 Mike Rivera | .15 | .40 |
| ☐ 1119 Ron Gardenhire MG | .15 | .40 |
| ☐ 1120 Shawn Green | .15 | .40 |
| ☐ 1121 Oliver Perez | .15 | .40 |
| ☐ 1122 Heath Bell | .15 | .40 |
| ☐ 1123 Bartolome Fortunato (RC) | .30 | .75 |
| ☐ 1124 Anderson Garcia RC | .30 | .75 |
| ☐ 1125 John Maine SP (RC) | 3.00 | 8.00 |
| ☐ 1126 Henry Owens RC | .50 | 1.25 |
| ☐ 1127 Mike Pelfrey RC | 1.25 | 3.00 |
| ☐ 1128 Royce Ring (RC) | .30 | .75 |
| ☐ 1129 Willie Randolph MG | .15 | .40 |
| ☐ 1130 Bobby Abreu | .15 | .40 |
| ☐ 1131 Craig Wilson | .15 | .40 |
| ☐ 1132 T.J. Beam (RC) | .30 | .75 |
| ☐ 1133 Colter Bean SP (RC) | 3.00 | 8.00 |
| ☐ 1134 Melky Cabrera (RC) | .50 | 1.25 |
| ☐ 1135 Mitch Jones (RC) | .30 | .75 |
| ☐ 1136 Jeffrey Karstens RC | .75 | 2.00 |
| ☐ 1137 Wil Nieves (RC) | .30 | .75 |
| ☐ 1138 Kevin Reese (RC) | .50 | 1.25 |
| ☐ 1139 Kevin Thompson (RC) | .30 | .75 |
| ☐ 1140 Jose Veras (RC) | .30 | .75 |
| ☐ 1141 Joe Torre MG | .25 | .60 |
| ☐ 1142 Jeremy Brown (RC) | .30 | .75 |
| ☐ 1143 Santiago Casilla (RC) | .30 | .75 |
| ☐ 1144 Shane Komine (RC) | .50 | 1.25 |
| ☐ 1145 Mike Rouse (RC) | .30 | .75 |
| ☐ 1146 Jason Windsor (RC) | .30 | .75 |
| ☐ 1147 Ken Macha MG | .15 | .40 |
| ☐ 1148 Jamie Moyer | .15 | .40 |
| ☐ 1149 Phil Nevin SP | 3.00 | 8.00 |
| ☐ 1150 Eude Brito (RC) | .30 | .75 |
| ☐ 1151 Fabio Castro | .15 | .40 |
| ☐ 1152 Jeff Conine | .15 | .40 |
| ☐ 1153 Scott Mathieson (RC) | .30 | .75 |
| ☐ 1154 Brian Sanches (RC) | .30 | .75 |
| ☐ 1155 Matt Smith RC | .30 | .75 |
| ☐ 1156 Joe Thurston (RC) | .30 | .75 |
| ☐ 1157 Marlon Anderson SP | 3.00 | 8.00 |
| ☐ 1158 Xavier Nady | .15 | .40 |
| ☐ 1159 Shawn Chacon | .15 | .40 |
| ☐ 1160 Rajai Davis (RC) | .30 | .75 |
| ☐ 1161 Yurendell DeCaster (RC) | .30 | .75 |
| ☐ 1162 Marty McLeary (RC) | .30 | .75 |
| ☐ 1163 Chris Duffy | .15 | .40 |
| ☐ 1164 Josh Sharpless RC | .30 | .75 |
| ☐ 1165 Jim Tracy MG | .15 | .40 |
| ☐ 1166 David Wells | .15 | .40 |
| ☐ 1167 Russell Branyan | .15 | .40 |
| ☐ 1168 Todd Walker | .15 | .40 |
| ☐ 1169 Paul McAnulty (RC) | .30 | .75 |
| ☐ 1170 Bruce Bochy MG | .15 | .40 |
| ☐ 1171 Shea Hillenbrand | .15 | .40 |
| ☐ 1172 Eliezer Alfonzo RC | .30 | .75 |
| ☐ 1173 Justin Knoedler SP (RC) | 3.00 | 8.00 |
| ☐ 1174 Jonathan Sanchez (RC) | .75 | 2.00 |
| ☐ 1175 Travis Smith (RC) | .30 | .75 |
| ☐ 1176 Cha-Seung Baek | .15 | .40 |
| ☐ 1177 T.J. Bohn (RC) | .30 | .75 |

| | | |
|---|---|---|
| ☐ 1178 Emiliano Fruto RC | .30 | .75 |
| ☐ 1179 Sean Green RC | .30 | .75 |
| ☐ 1180 Jon Huber RC | .30 | .75 |
| ☐ 1181 Mark Lowe (RC) | .30 | .75 |
| ☐ 1182 Eric O'Flaherty RC | .30 | .75 |
| ☐ 1183 Preston Wilson | .15 | .40 |
| ☐ 1184 Mike Hargrove MG | .15 | .40 |
| ☐ 1185 Jeff Weaver | .15 | .40 |
| ☐ 1186 Ronnie Belliard | .15 | .40 |
| ☐ 1187 John Gall (RC) | .30 | .75 |
| ☐ 1188 Josh Kinney SP RC | 3.00 | 8.00 |
| ☐ 1189 Tony LaRussa MG | .15 | .40 |
| ☐ 1190 Scott Dunn (RC) | .30 | .75 |
| ☐ 1191 B.J. Upton | .15 | .40 |
| ☐ 1192 Jon Switzer (RC) | .30 | .75 |
| ☐ 1193 Ben Zobrist (RC) | .75 | 2.00 |
| ☐ 1194 Joe Maddon | .15 | .40 |
| ☐ 1195 Carlos Lee | .15 | .40 |
| ☐ 1196 Matt Stairs | .15 | .40 |
| ☐ 1197 Nick Masset (RC) | .30 | .75 |
| ☐ 1198 Nelson Cruz (RC) | .50 | 1.25 |
| ☐ 1199 Francisco Rosario (RC) | .30 | .75 |
| ☐ 1200 Wes Littleton (RC) | .30 | .75 |
| ☐ 1201 Drew Meyer (RC) | .30 | .75 |
| ☐ 1202 John Rheineicker (RC) | .30 | .75 |
| ☐ 1203 Robinson Tejeda | .15 | .40 |
| ☐ 1204 Jeremy Accardo SP | 3.00 | 8.00 |
| ☐ 1205 Luis Figueroa RC | .30 | .75 |
| ☐ 1206 Jon Hattig (RC) | .30 | .75 |
| ☐ 1207 Dustin McGowan (RC) | .30 | .75 |
| ☐ 1208 Ryan Roberts RC | .30 | .75 |
| ☐ 1209 Davis Romero (RC) | .30 | .75 |
| ☐ 1210 Ty Taubenheim | .50 | 1.25 |
| ☐ 1211 John Gibbons MG | .15 | .40 |
| ☐ 1212 Shawn Hill SP (RC) | 3.00 | 8.00 |
| ☐ 1213 Brandon Harper RC | .30 | .75 |
| ☐ 1214 Travis Hughes (RC) | .30 | .75 |
| ☐ 1215 Chris Schroder (RC) | .30 | .75 |
| ☐ 1216 Austin Kearns | .15 | .40 |
| ☐ 1217 Felipe Lopez | .15 | .40 |
| ☐ 1218 Roy Corcoran RC | .30 | .75 |
| ☐ 1219 Melvin Dorta RC | .30 | .75 |
| ☐ 1220 Brandon Webb CL SP | 2.00 | 5.00 |
| ☐ 1221 Andruw Jones CL SP | 2.00 | 5.00 |
| ☐ 1222 Miguel Tejada CL SP | 2.00 | 5.00 |
| ☐ 1223 David Ortiz CL SP | 2.00 | 5.00 |
| ☐ 1224 Derrek Lee CL SP | 2.00 | 5.00 |
| ☐ 1225 Jim Thome CL SP | 2.00 | 5.00 |
| ☐ 1226 Ken Griffey Jr. CL SP | 3.00 | 8.00 |
| ☐ 1227 Travis Hafner CL SP | 2.00 | 5.00 |
| ☐ 1228 Todd Helton CL SP | 2.00 | 5.00 |
| ☐ 1229 Magglio Ordonez CL SP | 2.00 | 5.00 |
| ☐ 1230 Miguel Cabrera CL SP | 2.00 | 5.00 |
| ☐ 1231 Lance Berkman CL SP | 2.00 | 5.00 |
| ☐ 1232 Mike Sweeney CL SP | 2.00 | 5.00 |
| ☐ 1233 Vladimir Guerrero CL SP | 2.00 | 5.00 |
| ☐ 1234 Nomar Garciaparra CL SP | 2.00 | 5.00 |
| ☐ 1235 Prince Fielder CL SP | 2.00 | 5.00 |
| ☐ 1236 Johan Santana CL SP | 2.00 | 5.00 |
| ☐ 1237 Pedro Martinez CL SP | 2.00 | 5.00 |
| ☐ 1238 Derek Jeter CL SP | 4.00 | 10.00 |
| ☐ 1239 Barry Zito CL SP | 2.00 | 5.00 |
| ☐ 1240 Ryan Howard CL SP | 3.00 | 8.00 |
| ☐ 1241 Jason Bay CL SP | 2.00 | 5.00 |
| ☐ 1242 Trevor Hoffman CL SP | 2.00 | 5.00 |
| ☐ 1243 Adam Schmidt CL SP | 2.00 | 5.00 |
| ☐ 1244 Ichiro Suzuki CL SP | 3.00 | 8.00 |
| ☐ 1245 Albert Pujols CL SP | 3.00 | 8.00 |
| ☐ 1246 Carl Crawford CL SP | 2.00 | 5.00 |
| ☐ 1247 Mark Teixeira CL SP | 2.00 | 5.00 |
| ☐ 1248 Vernon Wells CL SP | 2.00 | 5.00 |
| ☐ 1249 Alfonso Soriano CL SP | 2.00 | 5.00 |

## 2007 Upper Deck

| | | |
|---|---|---|
| ☐ COMPLETE SET (1020) | 200.00 | 300.00 |
| ☐ COMP.SET w/o RC EXCH (1000) | 120.00 | 200.00 * |
| ☐ COMP.SER.1 w/o RC EXCH (500) | 40.00 | 80.00 |
| ☐ COMP.SER.2 w/o RC EXCH (500) | 80.00 | 120.00 |
| ☐ COMMON CARD (1-1020) | .15 | .40 |
| ☐ COMMON ROOKIE | .30 | .75 |
| ☐ COMMON ROOKIE (501-520) | 1.00 | 2.50 |
| ☐ 1-500 ISSUED IN SERIES 1 PACKS | | |
| ☐ 501-1020 ISSUED IN SERIES 2 PACKS | | |
| ☐ MATSUZAKA JSY RANDOMLY INSERTED | | |
| ☐ NO MATSUZAKA JSY PRICING AVAILABLE | | |
| ☐ OVERALL PLATE SER.1 ODDS 1:192 H | | |
| ☐ OVERALL PLATE SER.2 ODDS 1:96 H | | |
| ☐ PLATE PRINT RUN 1 SET PER COLOR | | |
| ☐ BLACK-CYAN-MAGENTA-YELLOW ISSUED | | |
| ☐ NO PLATE PRICING DUE TO SCARCITY | | |
| ☐ ROOKIE EXCH APPX. 1-2 PER CASE | | |
| ☐ ROOKIE EXCH DEADLINE 02/27/2010 | | |
| ☐ 1 Doug Slaten RC | .30 | .75 |
| ☐ 2 Miguel Montero (RC) | .30 | .75 |
| ☐ 3 Brian Burres (RC) | .30 | .75 |
| ☐ 4 Devern Hansack RC | .30 | .75 |
| ☐ 5 David Murphy (RC) | .30 | .75 |
| ☐ 6 Jose Reyes RC | .30 | .75 |
| ☐ 7 Scott Moore (RC) | .30 | .75 |
| ☐ 8 Josh Fields (RC) | .30 | .75 |
| ☐ 9 Chris Stewart RC | .30 | .75 |
| ☐ 10 Jerry Owens (RC) | .30 | .75 |
| ☐ 11 Ryan Sweeney (RC) | .30 | .75 |
| ☐ 12 Kevin Kouzmanoff (RC) | .30 | .75 |
| ☐ 13 Jeff Baker (RC) | .30 | .75 |
| ☐ 14 Justin Hampson (RC) | .30 | .75 |
| ☐ 15 Jeff Salazar (RC) | .30 | .75 |
| ☐ 16 Alvin Colina RC | .75 | 2.00 |
| ☐ 17 Troy Tulowitzki (RC) | .75 | 2.00 |
| ☐ 18 Andrew Miller RC | 2.00 | 5.00 |
| ☐ 19 Mike Rabelo RC | .30 | .75 |
| ☐ 20 Jose Diaz (RC) | .30 | .75 |
| ☐ 21 Angel Sanchez RC | .30 | .75 |
| ☐ 22 Ryan Braun RC | .30 | .75 |
| ☐ 23 DeWayne Young (RC) | .30 | .75 |
| ☐ 24 Drew Anderson RC | .30 | .75 |
| ☐ 25 Dennis Sarfate (RC) | .30 | .75 |
| ☐ 26 Vinny Rottino (RC) | .30 | .75 |
| ☐ 27 Glen Perkins (RC) | .30 | .75 |
| ☐ 28 Alexi Casilla RC | .50 | 1.25 |
| ☐ 29 Philip Humber (RC) | .30 | .75 |
| ☐ 30 Andy Cannizaro RC | .30 | .75 |
| ☐ 31 Jeremy Brown | .15 | .40 |
| ☐ 32 Sean Henn (RC) | .30 | .75 |
| ☐ 33 Brian Rogers | .15 | .40 |
| ☐ 34 Carlos Maldonado (RC) | .30 | .75 |
| ☐ 35 Juan Morillo (RC) | .30 | .75 |
| ☐ 36 Fred Lewis (RC) | .50 | 1.25 |
| ☐ 37 Patrick Misch (RC) | .30 | .75 |
| ☐ 38 Billy Sadler (RC) | .30 | .75 |
| ☐ 39 Ryan Feierabend (RC) | .30 | .75 |
| ☐ 40 Cesar Jimenez RC | .30 | .75 |
| ☐ 41 Oswaldo Navarro RC | .30 | .75 |
| ☐ 42 Travis Chick (RC) | .30 | .75 |
| ☐ 43 Delmon Young (RC) | .75 | 2.00 |
| ☐ 44 Shawn Riggans (RC) | .30 | .75 |
| ☐ 45 Brian Stokes (RC) | .30 | .75 |
| ☐ 46 Juan Salas (RC) | .30 | .75 |
| ☐ 47 Joaquin Arias (RC) | .30 | .75 |
| ☐ 48 Adam Lind (RC) | .30 | .75 |
| ☐ 49 Beltran Perez (RC) | .30 | .75 |

|  |  | | |
|---|---|---|---|
| 50 | Brett Campbell RC | .30 | .75 |
| 51 | Brian Roberts | .15 | .40 |
| 52 | Miguel Tejada | .15 | .40 |
| 53 | Brandon Fahey | .15 | .40 |
| 54 | Jay Gibbons | .15 | .40 |
| 55 | Corey Patterson | .15 | .40 |
| 56 | Nick Markakis | .25 | .60 |
| 57 | Ramon Hernandez | .15 | .40 |
| 58 | Kris Benson | .15 | .40 |
| 59 | Adam Loewen | .15 | .40 |
| 60 | Erik Bedard | .15 | .40 |
| 61 | Chris Ray | .15 | .40 |
| 62 | Chris Britton | .15 | .40 |
| 63 | Daniel Cabrera | .15 | .40 |
| 64 | Sendy Rleal | .15 | .40 |
| 65 | Manny Ramirez | .25 | .60 |
| 66 | David Ortiz | .25 | .60 |
| 67 | Gabe Kapler | .15 | .40 |
| 68 | Alex Cora | .15 | .40 |
| 69 | Dustin Pedroia | .50 | 1.25 |
| 70 | Trot Nixon | .15 | .40 |
| 71 | Doug Mirabelli | .15 | .40 |
| 72 | Mark Loretta | .15 | .40 |
| 73 | Curt Schilling | .25 | .60 |
| 74 | Jonathan Papelbon | .40 | 1.00 |
| 75 | Tim Wakefield | .15 | .40 |
| 76 | Jon Lester | .25 | .60 |
| 77 | Craig Hansen | .15 | .40 |
| 78 | Keith Foulke | .15 | .40 |
| 79 | Jermaine Dye | .15 | .40 |
| 80 | Jim Thome | .25 | .60 |
| 81 | Tadahito Iguchi | .15 | .40 |
| 82 | Rob Mackowiak | .15 | .40 |
| 83 | Brian Anderson | .15 | .40 |
| 84 | Juan Uribe | .15 | .40 |
| 85 | A.J. Pierzynski | .15 | .40 |
| 86 | Alex Cintron | .15 | .40 |
| 87 | Jon Garland | .15 | .40 |
| 88 | Jose Contreras | .15 | .40 |
| 89 | Neal Cotts | .15 | .40 |
| 90 | Bobby Jenks | .15 | .40 |
| 91 | Mike MacDougal | .15 | .40 |
| 92 | Javier Vazquez | .15 | .40 |
| 93 | Travis Hafner | .15 | .40 |
| 94 | Jhonny Peralta | .15 | .40 |
| 95 | Ryan Garko | .15 | .40 |
| 96 | Victor Martinez | .15 | .40 |
| 97 | Hector Luna | .15 | .40 |
| 98 | Casey Blake | .15 | .40 |
| 99 | Jason Michaels | .15 | .40 |
| 100 | Shin-Soo Choo | .25 | .60 |
| 101 | C.C. Sabathia | .15 | .40 |
| 102 | Paul Byrd | .15 | .40 |
| 103 | Jeremy Sowers | .15 | .40 |
| 104 | Cliff Lee | .15 | .40 |
| 105 | Rafael Betancourt | .15 | .40 |
| 106 | Francisco Cruceta | .15 | .40 |
| 107 | Sean Casey | .15 | .40 |
| 108 | Brandon Inge | .15 | .40 |
| 109 | Placido Polanco | .15 | .40 |
| 110 | Omar Infante | .15 | .40 |
| 111 | Ivan Rodriguez | .25 | .60 |
| 112 | Magglio Ordonez | .15 | .40 |
| 113 | Craig Monroe | .15 | .40 |
| 114 | Marcus Thames | .15 | .40 |
| 115 | Justin Verlander | .40 | 1.00 |
| 116 | Todd Jones | .15 | .40 |
| 117 | Kenny Rogers | .15 | .40 |
| 118 | Joel Zumaya | .25 | .60 |
| 119 | Jeremy Bonderman | .15 | .40 |
| 120 | Nate Robertson | .15 | .40 |
| 121 | Mark Teahen | .15 | .40 |
| 122 | Ryan Shealy | .15 | .40 |
| 123 | Mitch Maier RC | .30 | .75 |
| 124 | Doug Mientkiewicz | .15 | .40 |
| 125 | Mark Grudzielanek | .15 | .40 |
| 126 | Shane Costa | .15 | .40 |
| 127 | John Buck | .15 | .40 |
| 128 | Reggie Sanders | .15 | .40 |
| 129 | Mike Sweeney | .15 | .40 |
| 130 | Mark Redman | .15 | .40 |
| 131 | Todd Wellemeyer | .15 | .40 |
| 132 | Scott Elarton | .15 | .40 |
| 133 | Ambiorix Burgos | .15 | .40 |
| 134 | Joe Nelson | .15 | .40 |
| 135 | Howie Kendrick | .15 | .40 |
| 136 | Chone Figgins | .15 | .40 |
| 137 | Orlando Cabrera | .15 | .40 |
| 138 | Maicer Izturis | .15 | .40 |
| 139 | Jose Molina | .15 | .40 |
| 140 | Vladimir Guerrero | .40 | 1.00 |
| 141 | Darin Erstad | .15 | .40 |
| 142 | Juan Rivera | .15 | .40 |
| 143 | Jered Weaver | .25 | .60 |
| 144 | John Lackey | .15 | .40 |
| 145 | Joe Saunders | .15 | .40 |
| 146 | Bartolo Colon | .15 | .40 |
| 147 | Scot Shields | .15 | .40 |
| 148 | Francisco Rodriguez | .15 | .40 |
| 149 | Justin Morneau | .15 | .40 |
| 150 | Jason Bartlett | .15 | .40 |
| 151 | Luis Castillo | .15 | .40 |
| 152 | Nick Punto | .15 | .40 |
| 153 | Shannon Stewart | .15 | .40 |
| 154 | Michael Cuddyer | .15 | .40 |
| 155 | Jason Kubel | .15 | .40 |
| 156 | Joe Mauer | .40 | 1.00 |
| 157 | Francisco Liriano | .40 | 1.00 |
| 158 | Joe Nathan | .15 | .40 |
| 159 | Dennys Reyes | .15 | .40 |
| 160 | Brad Radke | .15 | .40 |
| 161 | Boof Bonser | .15 | .40 |
| 162 | Juan Rincon | .15 | .40 |
| 163 | Derek Jeter | 1.00 | 2.50 |
| 164 | Jason Giambi | .15 | .40 |
| 165 | Robinson Cano | .25 | .60 |
| 166 | Andy Phillips | .15 | .40 |
| 167 | Bobby Abreu | .15 | .40 |
| 168 | Gary Sheffield | .15 | .40 |
| 169 | Bernie Williams | .25 | .60 |
| 170 | Melky Cabrera | .15 | .40 |
| 171 | Mike Mussina | .25 | .60 |
| 172 | Chien-Ming Wang | .40 | 1.00 |
| 173 | Mariano Rivera | .40 | 1.00 |
| 174 | Scott Proctor | .15 | .40 |
| 175 | Jaret Wright | .15 | .40 |
| 176 | Kyle Farnsworth | .15 | .40 |
| 177 | Eric Chavez | .15 | .40 |
| 178 | Bobby Crosby | .15 | .40 |
| 179 | Frank Thomas | .40 | 1.00 |
| 180 | Dan Johnson | .15 | .40 |
| 181 | Marco Scutaro | .15 | .40 |
| 182 | Nick Swisher | .15 | .40 |
| 183 | Milton Bradley | .15 | .40 |
| 184 | Jay Payton | .15 | .40 |
| 185 | Joe Blanton | .15 | .40 |
| 186 | Barry Zito | .15 | .40 |
| 187 | Rich Harden | .15 | .40 |
| 188 | Esteban Loaiza | .15 | .40 |
| 189 | Huston Street | .15 | .40 |
| 190 | Chad Gaudin | .15 | .40 |
| 191 | Richie Sexson | .15 | .40 |
| 192 | Yuniesky Betancourt | .15 | .40 |
| 193 | Willie Bloomquist | .15 | .40 |
| 194 | Ben Broussard | .15 | .40 |
| 195 | Kenji Johjima | .40 | 1.00 |
| 196 | Ichiro Suzuki | .60 | 1.50 |
| 197 | Raul Ibanez | .25 | .60 |
| 198 | Chris Snelling | .15 | .40 |
| 199 | Felix Hernandez | .25 | .60 |
| 200 | Cha-Seung Baek | .15 | .40 |
| 201 | Joel Pineiro | .15 | .40 |
| 202 | Julio Mateo | .15 | .40 |
| 203 | J.J. Putz | .15 | .40 |
| 204 | Rafael Soriano | .15 | .40 |
| 205 | Jorge Cantu | .15 | .40 |
| 206 | B.J. Upton | .15 | .40 |
| 207 | Ty Wigginton | .15 | .40 |
| 208 | Greg Norton | .15 | .40 |
| 209 | Dioner Navarro | .15 | .40 |
| 210 | Carl Crawford | .15 | .40 |
| 211 | Jonny Gomes | .15 | .40 |
| 212 | Damon Hollins | .15 | .40 |
| 213 | Scott Kazmir | .25 | .60 |
| 214 | Casey Fossum | .15 | .40 |
| 215 | Ruddy Lugo | .15 | .40 |
| 216 | James Shields | .15 | .40 |
| 217 | Tyler Walker | .15 | .40 |
| 218 | Shawn Camp | .15 | .40 |
| 219 | Mark Teixeira | .25 | .60 |
| 220 | Hank Blalock | .15 | .40 |
| 221 | Ian Kinsler | .15 | .40 |
| 222 | Jerry Hairston Jr. | .15 | .40 |
| 223 | Gerald Laird | .15 | .40 |
| 224 | Carlos Lee | .15 | .40 |
| 225 | Gary Matthews | .15 | .40 |
| 226 | Mark DeRosa | .15 | .40 |
| 227 | Kip Wells | .15 | .40 |
| 228 | Akinori Otsuka | .15 | .40 |
| 229 | Vicente Padilla | .15 | .40 |
| 230 | John Koronka | .15 | .40 |
| 231 | Kevin Millwood | .15 | .40 |
| 232 | Wes Littleton | .15 | .40 |
| 233 | Troy Glaus | .15 | .40 |
| 234 | Lyle Overbay | .15 | .40 |
| 235 | Aaron Hill | .15 | .40 |
| 236 | John McDonald | .15 | .40 |
| 237 | Bengie Molina | .15 | .40 |
| 238 | Vernon Wells | .15 | .40 |
| 239 | Reed Johnson | .15 | .40 |
| 240 | Frank Catalanotto | .15 | .40 |
| 241 | Roy Halladay | .15 | .40 |
| 242 | B.J. Ryan | .15 | .40 |
| 243 | Gustavo Chacin | .15 | .40 |
| 244 | Scott Downs | .15 | .40 |
| 245 | Casey Janssen | .15 | .40 |
| 246 | Justin Speier | .15 | .40 |
| 247 | Stephen Drew | .25 | .60 |
| 248 | Conor Jackson | .15 | .40 |
| 249 | Orlando Hudson | .15 | .40 |
| 250 | Chad Tracy | .15 | .40 |
| 251 | Johnny Estrada | .15 | .40 |
| 252 | Luis Gonzalez | .15 | .40 |
| 253 | Eric Byrnes | .15 | .40 |
| 254 | Carlos Quentin | .15 | .40 |
| 255 | Brandon Webb | .15 | .40 |
| 256 | Claudio Vargas | .15 | .40 |
| 257 | Juan Cruz | .15 | .40 |
| 258 | Jorge Julio | .15 | .40 |
| 259 | Luis Vizcaino | .15 | .40 |
| 260 | Livan Hernandez | .15 | .40 |
| 261 | Chipper Jones | .40 | 1.00 |
| 262 | Edgar Renteria | .15 | .40 |
| 263 | Adam LaRoche | .15 | .40 |
| 264 | Willy Aybar | .15 | .40 |
| 265 | Brian McCann | .15 | .40 |
| 266 | Ryan Langerhans | .15 | .40 |
| 267 | Jeff Francoeur | .40 | 1.00 |
| 268 | Matt Diaz | .15 | .40 |
| 269 | Tim Hudson | .15 | .40 |
| 270 | John Smoltz | .25 | .60 |
| 271 | Oscar Villarreal | .15 | .40 |
| 272 | Horacio Ramirez | .15 | .40 |
| 273 | Bob Wickman | .15 | .40 |
| 274 | Chad Paronto | .15 | .40 |
| 275 | Derrek Lee | .15 | .40 |
| 276 | Ryan Theriot | .15 | .40 |
| 277 | Cesar Izturis | .15 | .40 |
| 278 | Ronny Cedeno | .15 | .40 |
| 279 | Michael Barrett | .15 | .40 |
| 280 | Juan Pierre | .15 | .40 |
| 281 | Jacque Jones | .15 | .40 |
| 282 | Matt Murton | .15 | .40 |
| 283 | Carlos Zambrano | .15 | .40 |
| 284 | Mark Prior | .25 | .60 |
| 285 | Rich Hill | .15 | .40 |
| 286 | Sean Marshall | .15 | .40 |
| 287 | Ryan Dempster | .15 | .40 |
| 288 | Ryan O'Malley | .15 | .40 |
| 289 | Scott Hatteberg | .15 | .40 |
| 290 | Brandon Phillips | .15 | .40 |
| 291 | Edwin Encarnacion | .15 | .40 |
| 292 | Rich Aurilia | .15 | .40 |

|  |  | | |
|---|---|---|---|
| 293 | David Ross | .15 | .40 |
| 294 | Ken Griffey Jr. | .60 | 1.50 |
| 295 | Ryan Freel | .15 | .40 |
| 296 | Chris Denorfia | .15 | .40 |
| 297 | Bronson Arroyo | .15 | .40 |
| 298 | Aaron Harang | .15 | .40 |
| 299 | Brandon Claussen | .15 | .40 |
| 300 | Todd Coffey | .15 | .40 |
| 301 | David Weathers | .15 | .40 |
| 302 | Eric Milton | .15 | .40 |
| 303 | Todd Helton | .25 | .60 |
| 304 | Clint Barmes | .15 | .40 |
| 305 | Kazuo Matsui | .15 | .40 |
| 306 | Jamey Carroll | .15 | .40 |
| 307 | Yorvit Torrealba | .15 | .40 |
| 308 | Matt Holliday | .40 | 1.00 |
| 309 | Choo Freeman | .15 | .40 |
| 310 | Brad Hawpe | .15 | .40 |
| 311 | Jason Jennings | .15 | .40 |
| 312 | Jeff Francis | .15 | .40 |
| 313 | Josh Fogg | .15 | .40 |
| 314 | Aaron Cook | .15 | .40 |
| 315 | Ubaldo Jimenez (RC) | .30 | .75 |
| 316 | Manny Corpas | .15 | .40 |
| 317 | Miguel Cabrera | .25 | .60 |
| 318 | Dan Uggla | .25 | .60 |
| 319 | Hanley Ramirez | .25 | .60 |
| 320 | Wes Helms | .15 | .40 |
| 321 | Miguel Olivo | .15 | .40 |
| 322 | Jeremy Hermida | .15 | .40 |
| 323 | Cody Ross | .15 | .40 |
| 324 | Josh Willingham | .15 | .40 |
| 325 | Dontrelle Willis | .15 | .40 |
| 326 | Anibal Sanchez | .15 | .40 |
| 327 | Josh Johnson | .15 | .40 |
| 328 | Jose Garcia RC | .30 | .75 |
| 329 | Joe Borowski | .15 | .40 |
| 330 | Taylor Tankersley | .15 | .40 |
| 331 | Lance Berkman | .15 | .40 |
| 332 | Craig Biggio | .25 | .60 |
| 333 | Aubrey Huff | .15 | .40 |
| 334 | Adam Everett | .15 | .40 |
| 335 | Brad Ausmus | .15 | .40 |
| 336 | Willy Taveras | .15 | .40 |
| 337 | Luke Scott | .15 | .40 |
| 338 | Chris Burke | .15 | .40 |
| 339 | Roger Clemens | .60 | 1.50 |
| 340 | Andy Pettitte | .25 | .60 |
| 341 | Brandon Backe | .15 | .40 |
| 342 | Hector Gimenez (RC) | .30 | .75 |
| 343 | Brad Lidge | .15 | .40 |
| 344 | Dan Wheeler | .15 | .40 |
| 345 | Nomar Garciaparra | .40 | 1.00 |
| 346 | Rafael Furcal | .15 | .40 |
| 347 | Wilson Betemit | .15 | .40 |
| 348 | Julio Lugo | .15 | .40 |
| 349 | Russell Martin | .15 | .40 |
| 350 | Andre Ethier | .25 | .60 |
| 351 | Matt Kemp | .40 | 1.00 |
| 352 | Kenny Lofton | .15 | .40 |
| 353 | Brad Penny | .15 | .40 |
| 354 | Derek Lowe | .15 | .40 |
| 355 | Chad Billingsley | .15 | .40 |
| 356 | Greg Maddux | .60 | 1.50 |
| 357 | Takashi Saito | .15 | .40 |
| 358 | Jonathan Broxton | .15 | .40 |
| 359 | Prince Fielder | .40 | 1.00 |
| 360 | Rickie Weeks | .15 | .40 |
| 361 | Bill Hall | .15 | .40 |
| 362 | J.J. Hardy | .15 | .40 |
| 363 | Jeff Cirillo | .15 | .40 |
| 364 | Tony Gwynn Jr. | .15 | .40 |
| 365 | Corey Hart | .15 | .40 |
| 366 | Laynce Nix | .15 | .40 |
| 367 | Doug Davis | .15 | .40 |
| 368 | Ben Sheets | .15 | .40 |
| 369 | Chris Capuano | .15 | .40 |
| 370 | Dave Bush | .15 | .40 |
| 371 | Derrick Turnbow | .15 | .40 |
| 372 | Francisco Cordero | .15 | .40 |
| 373 | Jose Reyes | .15 | .40 |
| 374 | Carlos Delgado | .15 | .40 |
| 375 | Julio Franco | .15 | .40 |
| 376 | Jose Valentin | .15 | .40 |
| 377 | Paul LoDuca | .15 | .40 |
| 378 | Carlos Beltran | .15 | .40 |
| 379 | Shawn Green | .15 | .40 |
| 380 | Lastings Milledge | .25 | .60 |
| 381 | Endy Chavez | .15 | .40 |
| 382 | Pedro Martinez | .25 | .60 |
| 383 | John Maine | .15 | .40 |
| 384 | Orlando Hernandez | .15 | .40 |
| 385 | Steve Trachsel | .15 | .40 |
| 386 | Billy Wagner | .15 | .40 |
| 387 | Ryan Howard | .60 | 1.50 |
| 388 | Chase Utley | .40 | 1.00 |
| 389 | Jimmy Rollins | .15 | .40 |
| 390 | Chris Coste | .15 | .40 |
| 391 | Jeff Conine | .15 | .40 |
| 392 | Aaron Rowand | .15 | .40 |
| 393 | Shane Victorino | .15 | .40 |
| 394 | David Dellucci | .15 | .40 |
| 395 | Cole Hamels | .40 | 1.00 |
| 396 | Jamie Moyer | .15 | .40 |
| 397 | Ryan Madson | .15 | .40 |
| 398 | Brett Myers | .15 | .40 |
| 399 | Tom Gordon | .15 | .40 |
| 400 | Geoff Geary | .15 | .40 |
| 401 | Freddy Sanchez | .15 | .40 |
| 402 | Xavier Nady | .15 | .40 |
| 403 | Jose Castillo | .15 | .40 |
| 404 | Joe Randa | .15 | .40 |
| 405 | Jason Bay | .25 | .60 |
| 406 | Chris Duffy | .15 | .40 |
| 407 | Jose Bautista | .15 | .40 |
| 408 | Ronny Paulino | .15 | .40 |
| 409 | Ian Snell | .15 | .40 |
| 410 | Zach Duke | .15 | .40 |
| 411 | Tom Gorzelanny | .15 | .40 |
| 412 | Shane Youman RC | .30 | .75 |
| 413 | Mike Gonzalez | .15 | .40 |
| 414 | Matt Capps | .15 | .40 |
| 415 | Adrian Gonzalez | .15 | .40 |
| 416 | Josh Barfield | .15 | .40 |
| 417 | Todd Walker | .15 | .40 |
| 418 | Khalil Greene | .25 | .60 |
| 419 | Mike Piazza | .40 | 1.00 |
| 420 | Dave Roberts | .15 | .40 |
| 421 | Mike Cameron | .15 | .40 |
| 422 | Geoff Blum | .15 | .40 |
| 423 | Jake Peavy | .15 | .40 |
| 424 | Chris R. Young | .15 | .40 |
| 425 | Woody Williams | .15 | .40 |
| 426 | Clay Hensley | .15 | .40 |
| 427 | Cla Meredith | .15 | .40 |
| 428 | Trevor Hoffman | .15 | .40 |
| 429 | Shea Hillenbrand | .15 | .40 |
| 430 | Pedro Feliz | .15 | .40 |
| 431 | Ray Durham | .15 | .40 |
| 432 | Mark Sweeney | .15 | .40 |
| 433 | Eliezer Alfonzo | .15 | .40 |
| 434 | Moises Alou | .15 | .40 |
| 435 | Steve Finley | .15 | .40 |
| 436 | Todd Linden | .15 | .40 |
| 437 | Jason Schmidt | .15 | .40 |
| 438 | Matt Cain | .25 | .60 |
| 439 | Noah Lowry | .15 | .40 |
| 440 | Brad Hennessey | .15 | .40 |
| 441 | Armando Benitez | .15 | .40 |
| 442 | Jonathan Sanchez | .15 | .40 |
| 443 | Albert Pujols | .75 | 2.00 |
| 444 | Ronnie Belliard | .15 | .40 |
| 445 | David Eckstein | .15 | .40 |
| 446 | Aaron Miles | .15 | .40 |
| 447 | Yadier Molina | .15 | .40 |
| 448 | Jim Edmonds | .25 | .60 |
| 449 | Chris Duncan | .15 | .40 |
| 450 | Juan Encarnacion | .15 | .40 |
| 451 | Chris Carpenter | .15 | .40 |
| 452 | Jeff Suppan | .15 | .40 |
| 453 | Jason Marquis | .15 | .40 |
| 454 | Jeff Weaver | .15 | .40 |
| 455 | Jason Isringhausen | .15 | .40 |
| 456 | Braden Looper | .15 | .40 |
| 457 | Ryan Zimmerman | .40 | 1.00 |
| 458 | Nick Johnson | .15 | .40 |
| 459 | Felipe Lopez | .15 | .40 |
| 460 | Brian Schneider | .15 | .40 |
| 461 | Alfonso Soriano | .15 | .40 |
| 462 | Austin Kearns | .15 | .40 |
| 463 | Ryan Church | .15 | .40 |
| 464 | Alex Escobar | .15 | .40 |
| 465 | Ramon Ortiz | .15 | .40 |
| 466 | Tony Armas | .15 | .40 |
| 467 | Michael O'Connor | .15 | .40 |
| 468 | Chad Cordero | .15 | .40 |
| 469 | Jon Rauch | .15 | .40 |
| 470 | Pedro Astacio | .15 | .40 |
| 471 | Miguel Tejada CL | .15 | .40 |
| 472 | David Ortiz CL | .25 | .60 |
| 473 | Jermaine Dye CL | .15 | .40 |
| 474 | Travis Hafner CL | .15 | .40 |
| 475 | Magglio Ordonez CL | .15 | .40 |
| 476 | Mark Teahen CL | .15 | .40 |
| 477 | Vladimir Guerrero CL | .40 | 1.00 |
| 478 | Justin Morneau CL | .15 | .40 |
| 479 | Derek Jeter CL | 1.00 | 2.50 |
| 480 | Nick Swisher CL | .15 | .40 |
| 481 | Ichiro Suzuki CL | .60 | 1.50 |
| 482 | Scott Kazmir CL | .25 | .60 |
| 483 | Mark Teixeira CL | .25 | .60 |
| 484 | Vernon Wells CL | .15 | .40 |
| 485 | Brandon Webb CL | .15 | .40 |
| 486 | Andruw Jones CL | .25 | .60 |
| 487 | Carlos Zambrano CL | .15 | .40 |
| 488 | Adam Dunn CL | .15 | .40 |
| 489 | Matt Holliday CL | .40 | 1.00 |
| 490 | Miguel Cabrera CL | .25 | .60 |
| 491 | Lance Berkman CL | .15 | .40 |
| 492 | Nomar Garciaparra CL | .40 | 1.00 |
| 493 | Prince Fielder CL | .40 | 1.00 |
| 494 | Carlos Beltran CL | .15 | .40 |
| 495 | Ryan Howard CL | .60 | 1.50 |
| 496 | Jason Bay CL | .25 | .60 |
| 497 | Adrian Gonzalez CL | .15 | .40 |
| 498 | Matt Cain CL | .25 | .60 |
| 499 | Albert Pujols CL | .75 | 2.00 |
| 500 | Ryan Zimmerman CL | .40 | 1.00 |
| 501a | D.Matsuzaka Suit RC | 20.00 | 50.00 |
| 501b | D.Matsuzaka Throwing RC | 6.00 | 15.00 |
| 501c | Daisuke Matsuzaka Jsy/100 | | |
| 501d | Daisuke Matsuzaka Ball/150 | | |
| 502 | Kei Igawa RC | 1.50 | 4.00 |
| 503 | Akinori Iwamura RC | 2.50 | 6.00 |
| 504 | Alex Gordon RC | 6.00 | 15.00 |
| 505 | Matt Chico (RC) | 1.00 | 2.50 |
| 506 | John Danks RC | 1.00 | 2.50 |
| 507 | Elijah Dukes RC | 1.00 | 2.50 |
| 508 | Gustavo Molina RC | 1.00 | 2.50 |
| 509 | Joakim Soria RC | 2.50 | 6.00 |
| 510 | Jay Marshall RC | 2.50 | 6.00 |
| 511 | Travis Buck (RC) | 1.00 | 2.50 |
| 512 | Brandon Wood (RC) | 1.00 | 2.50 |
| 513 | Kevin Cameron RC | 1.00 | 2.50 |
| 514 | Jared Burton RC | 2.50 | 6.00 |
| 515 | Kory Casto (RC) | 1.00 | 2.50 |
| 516 | Jose Smith RC | 1.00 | 2.50 |
| 517 | Jose Garcia RC | 1.00 | 2.50 |
| 518 | Hunter Pence (RC) | 6.00 | 15.00 |
| 519 | Felix Pie (RC) | 1.00 | 2.50 |
| 520 | Zach Segovia (RC) | 1.00 | 2.50 |
| 521 | Randy Johnson | .40 | 1.00 |
| 522 | Brandon Lyon | .15 | .40 |
| 523 | Robby Hammock | .15 | .40 |
| 524 | Micah Owings (RC) | .30 | .75 |
| 525 | Doug Davis | .15 | .40 |
| 526 | Brian Barden RC | .30 | .75 |
| 527 | Alberto Callaspo | .15 | .40 |
| 528 | Stephen Drew | .25 | .60 |
| 529 | Chris Young | .15 | .40 |
| 530 | Edgar Gonzalez | .15 | .40 |
| 531 | Brandon Medders | .15 | .40 |
| 532 | Tony Pena | .15 | .40 |

|  |  | | |
|---|---|---|---|
| 533 | Jose Valverde | .15 | .40 |
| 534 | Chris Snyder | .15 | .40 |
| 535 | Tony Clark | .15 | .40 |
| 536 | Scott Hairston | .15 | .40 |
| 537 | Jeff DaVanon | .15 | .40 |
| 538 | Randy Johnson CL | .40 | 1.00 |
| 539 | Mark Redman | .15 | .40 |
| 540 | Andruw Jones | .25 | .60 |
| 541 | Rafael Soriano | .15 | .40 |
| 542 | Scott Thorman | .15 | .40 |
| 543 | Chipper Jones | .40 | 1.00 |
| 544 | Mike Gonzalez | .15 | .40 |
| 545 | Lance Cormier | .15 | .40 |
| 546 | Kyle Davies | .15 | .40 |
| 547 | Mike Hampton | .15 | .40 |
| 548 | Chuck James | .15 | .40 |
| 549 | Macay McBride | .15 | .40 |
| 550 | Tanyon Sturtze | .15 | .40 |
| 551 | Tyler Yates | .15 | .40 |
| 552 | Pete Orr | .15 | .40 |
| 553 | Craig Wilson | .15 | .40 |
| 554 | Chris Woodward | .15 | .40 |
| 555 | Kelly Johnson | .15 | .40 |
| 556 | Chipper Jones CL | .40 | 1.00 |
| 557 | Chad Bradford | .15 | .40 |
| 558 | John Parrish | .15 | .40 |
| 559 | Jeremy Guthrie | .15 | .40 |
| 560 | Steve Trachsel | .15 | .40 |
| 561 | Scott Williamson | .15 | .40 |
| 562 | Jaret Wright | .15 | .40 |
| 563 | Paul Bako | .15 | .40 |
| 564 | Chris Gomez | .15 | .40 |
| 565 | Melvin Mora | .15 | .40 |
| 566 | Freddie Bynum | .15 | .40 |
| 567 | Aubrey Huff | .15 | .40 |
| 568 | Jay Payton | .15 | .40 |
| 569 | Miguel Tejada | .15 | .40 |
| 570 | Kurt Birkins | .15 | .40 |
| 571 | Danys Baez | .15 | .40 |
| 572 | Brian Roberts CL | .15 | .40 |
| 573 | Josh Beckett | .25 | .60 |
| 574 | Matt Clement | .15 | .40 |
| 575 | Hideki Okajima RC | 2.00 | 5.00 |
| 576 | Javier Lopez | .15 | .40 |
| 577 | Joel Pineiro | .15 | .40 |
| 578 | J.C. Romero | .15 | .40 |
| 579 | Kyle Snyder | .15 | .40 |
| 580 | Julian Tavarez | .15 | .40 |
| 581 | Mike Timlin | .15 | .40 |
| 582 | Jason Varitek | .40 | 1.00 |
| 583 | Mike Lowell | .15 | .40 |
| 584 | Kevin Youkilis | .15 | .40 |
| 585 | Coco Crisp | .15 | .40 |
| 586 | J.D. Drew | .15 | .40 |
| 587 | Eric Hinske | .15 | .40 |
| 588 | Wily Mo Pena | .15 | .40 |
| 589 | Julio Lugo | .15 | .40 |
| 590 | David Ortiz | .25 | .60 |
| 591 | Manny Ramirez | .25 | .60 |
| 592 | Daisuke Matsuzaka CL | 1.50 | 4.00 |
| 593 | Scott Eyre | .15 | .40 |
| 594 | Angel Guzman | .15 | .40 |
| 595 | Bob Howry | .15 | .40 |
| 596 | Ted Lilly | .15 | .40 |
| 597 | Juan Mateo | .15 | .40 |
| 598 | Wade Miller | .15 | .40 |
| 599 | Carlos Zambrano | .15 | .40 |
| 600 | Will Ohman | .15 | .40 |
| 601 | Michael Wuertz | .15 | .40 |
| 602 | Henry Blanco | .15 | .40 |
| 603 | Aramis Ramirez | .15 | .40 |
| 604 | Cliff Floyd | .15 | .40 |
| 605 | Kerry Wood | .15 | .40 |
| 606 | Alfonso Soriano | .15 | .40 |
| 607 | Daryle Ward | .15 | .40 |
| 608 | Jason Marquis | .15 | .40 |
| 609 | Mark DeRosa | .15 | .40 |
| 610 | Neal Cotts | .15 | .40 |
| 611 | Derrek Lee | .15 | .40 |
| 612 | Aramis Ramirez CL | .15 | .40 |
| 613 | David Aardsma | .15 | .40 |
| 614 | Mark Buehrle | .15 | .40 |
| 615 | Nick Masset | .15 | .40 |
| 616 | Andrew Sisco | .15 | .40 |
| 617 | Matt Thornton | .15 | .40 |
| 618 | Toby Hall | .15 | .40 |
| 619 | Joe Crede | .15 | .40 |
| 620 | Paul Konerko | .15 | .40 |
| 621 | Darin Erstad | .15 | .40 |
| 622 | Pablo Ozuna | .15 | .40 |
| 623 | Scott Podsednik | .15 | .40 |
| 624 | Jim Thome | .25 | .60 |
| 625 | Jermaine Dye | .15 | .40 |
| 626 | Jim Thome CL | .25 | .60 |
| 627 | Adam Dunn | .15 | .40 |
| 628 | Bill Bray | * .15 | .40 |
| 629 | Alex Gonzalez | .15 | .40 |
| 630 | Josh Hamilton (RC) | 4.00 | 10.00 |
| 631 | Matt Belisle | .15 | .40 |
| 632 | Rheal Cormier | .15 | .40 |
| 633 | Kyle Lohse | .15 | .40 |
| 634 | Eric Milton | .15 | .40 |
| 635 | Kirk Saarloos | .15 | .40 |
| 636 | Mike Stanton | .15 | .40 |
| 637 | Javier Valentin | .15 | .40 |
| 638 | Juan Castro | .15 | .40 |
| 639 | Jeff Conine | .15 | .40 |
| 640 | Jon Coutlangus (RC) | .30 | .75 |
| 641 | Ken Griffey Jr. | .60 | 1.50 |
| 642 | Ken Griffey Jr. CL | .60 | 1.50 |
| 643 | Fernando Cabrera | .15 | .40 |
| 644 | Fausto Carmona | .15 | .40 |
| 645 | Jason Davis | .15 | .40 |
| 646 | Aaron Fultz | .15 | .40 |
| 647 | Roberto Hernandez | .15 | .40 |
| 648 | Jake Westbrook | .15 | .40 |
| 649 | Kelly Shoppach | .15 | .40 |
| 650 | Josh Barfield | .15 | .40 |
| 651 | Andy Marte | .15 | .40 |
| 652 | Joe Inglett | .15 | .40 |
| 653 | David Dellucci | .15 | .40 |
| 654 | Joe Borowski | .15 | .40 |
| 655 | Franklin Gutierrez | .15 | .40 |
| 656 | Trot Nixon | .15 | .40 |
| 657 | Grady Sizemore | .25 | .60 |
| 658 | Mike Rouse | .15 | .40 |
| 659 | Travis Hafner | .15 | .40 |
| 660 | Victor Martinez | .15 | .40 |
| 661 | C.C. Sabathia | .15 | .40 |
| 662 | Grady Sizemore CL | .25 | .60 |
| 663 | Jeremy Affeldt | .15 | .40 |
| 664 | Taylor Buchholz | .15 | .40 |
| 665 | Brian Fuentes | .15 | .40 |
| 666 | Latroy Hawkins | .15 | .40 |
| 667 | Byung-Hyun Kim | .15 | .40 |
| 668 | Brian Lawrence | .15 | .40 |
| 669 | Rodrigo Lopez | .15 | .40 |
| 670 | Jeff Francis | .15 | .40 |
| 671 | Chris Ianetta | .15 | .40 |
| 672 | Garrett Atkins | .15 | .40 |
| 673 | Todd Helton | .25 | .60 |
| 674 | Steve Finley | .15 | .40 |
| 675 | John Mabry | .15 | .40 |
| 676 | Willy Taveras | .15 | .40 |
| 677 | Jason Hirsh | .15 | .40 |
| 678 | Ramon Ramirez | .15 | .40 |
| 679 | Matt Holliday | .40 | 1.00 |
| 680 | Todd Helton CL | .25 | .60 |
| 681 | Roman Colon | .15 | .40 |
| 682 | Chad Durbin | .15 | .40 |
| 683 | Jason Grilli | .15 | .40 |
| 684 | Wilfredo Ledezma | .15 | .40 |
| 685 | Mike Maroth | .15 | .40 |
| 686 | Jose Mesa | .15 | .40 |
| 687 | Justin Verlander | .40 | 1.00 |
| 688 | Fernando Rodney | .15 | .40 |
| 689 | Vance Wilson | .15 | .40 |
| 690 | Carlos Guillen | .15 | .40 |
| 691 | Neifi Perez | .15 | .40 |
| 692 | Curtis Granderson | .15 | .40 |
| 693 | Gary Sheffield | .15 | .40 |
| 694 | Justin Verlander CL | .40 | 1.00 |
| 695 | Kevin Gregg | .15 | .40 |
| 696 | Logan Kensing | .15 | .40 |
| 697 | Randy Messenger | .15 | .40 |
| 698 | Sergio Mitre | .15 | .40 |
| 699 | Ricky Nolasco | .15 | .40 |
| 700 | Scott Olsen | .15 | .40 |
| 701 | Renyel Pinto | .15 | .40 |
| 702 | Matt Treanor | .15 | .40 |
| 703 | Alfredo Amezaga | .15 | .40 |
| 704 | Aaron Boone | .15 | .40 |
| 705 | Mike Jacobs | .15 | .40 |
| 706 | Miguel Cabrera | .25 | .60 |
| 707 | Joe Borchard | .15 | .40 |
| 708 | Jorge Julio | .15 | .40 |
| 709 | Rick Vanden Hurk RC | .50 | 1.25 |
| 710 | Lee Gardner (RC) | .30 | .75 |
| 711 | Matt Lindstrom (RC) | .30 | .75 |
| 712 | Henry Owens | .15 | .40 |
| 713 | Hanley Ramirez | .25 | .60 |
| 714 | Alejandro De Aza RC | .50 | 1.25 |
| 715 | Hanley Ramirez CL | .25 | .60 |
| 716 | Dave Borkowski | .15 | .40 |
| 717 | Jason Jennings | .15 | .40 |
| 718 | Trever Miller | .15 | .40 |
| 719 | Roy Oswalt | .15 | .40 |
| 720 | Wandy Rodriguez | .15 | .40 |
| 721 | Humberto Quintero | .15 | .40 |
| 722 | Morgan Ensberg | .15 | .40 |
| 723 | Mike Lamb | .15 | .40 |
| 724 | Mark Loretta | .15 | .40 |
| 725 | Jason Lane | .15 | .40 |
| 726 | Carlos Lee | .15 | .40 |
| 727 | Orlando Palmeiro | .15 | .40 |
| 728 | Woody Williams | .15 | .40 |
| 729 | Chad Qualls | .15 | .40 |
| 730 | Lance Berkman | .15 | .40 |
| 731 | Rick White | .15 | .40 |
| 732 | Chris Sampson | .15 | .40 |
| 733 | Carlos Lee CL | .15 | .40 |
| 734 | Jorge De La Rosa | .15 | .40 |
| 735 | Octavio Dotel | .15 | .40 |
| 736 | Jimmy Gobble | .15 | .40 |
| 737 | Zack Greinke | .15 | .40 |
| 738 | Luke Hudson | .15 | .40 |
| 739 | Gil Meche | .15 | .40 |
| 740 | Joel Peralta | .15 | .40 |
| 741 | Odalis Perez | .15 | .40 |
| 742 | David Riske | .15 | .40 |
| 743 | Jason LaRue | .15 | .40 |
| 744 | Tony Pena | .15 | .40 |
| 745 | Esteban German | .15 | .40 |
| 746 | Ross Gload | .15 | .40 |
| 747 | Emil Brown | .15 | .40 |
| 748 | David DeJesus | .15 | .40 |
| 749 | Brandon Duckworth | .15 | .40 |
| 750 | Alex Gordon CL | .60 | 1.50 |
| 751 | Jered Weaver | .25 | .60 |
| 752 | Vladimir Guerrero | .40 | 1.00 |
| 753 | Hector Carrasco | .15 | .40 |
| 754 | Kelvim Escobar | .15 | .40 |
| 755 | Darren Oliver | .15 | .40 |
| 756 | Dustin Moseley | .15 | .40 |
| 757 | Ervin Santana | .15 | .40 |
| 758 | Mike Napoli | .15 | .40 |
| 759 | Shea Hillenbrand | .15 | .40 |
| 760 | Casey Kotchman | .15 | .40 |
| 761 | Reggie Willits | .25 | .60 |
| 762 | Robb Quinlan | .15 | .40 |
| 763 | Garret Anderson | .15 | .40 |
| 764 | Gary Matthews | .15 | .40 |
| 765 | Justin Speier | .15 | .40 |
| 766 | Jered Weaver CL | .25 | .60 |
| 767 | Joe Beimel | .15 | .40 |
| 768 | Yhency Brazoban | .15 | .40 |
| 769 | Elmer Dessens | .15 | .40 |
| 770 | Mark Hendrickson | .15 | .40 |
| 771 | Hong-Chih Kuo | .15 | .40 |
| 772 | Jason Schmidt | .15 | .40 |
| 773 | Brett Tomko | .15 | .40 |
| 774 | Randy Wolf | .15 | .40 |
| 775 | Mike Liberthal | .15 | .40 |

| # | Card | Price 1 | Price 2 |
|---|------|--------|--------|
| 776 | Marlon Anderson | .15 | .40 |
| 777 | Jeff Kent | .15 | .40 |
| 778 | Ramon Martinez | .15 | .40 |
| 779 | Olmedo Saenz | .15 | .40 |
| 780 | Luis Gonzalez | .15 | .40 |
| 781 | Juan Pierre | .15 | .40 |
| 782 | Jason Repko | .15 | .40 |
| 783 | Nomar Garciaparra | .40 | 1.00 |
| 784 | Wilson Valdez | .15 | .40 |
| 785 | Jason Schmidt CL | .15 | .40 |
| 786 | Greg Aquino | .15 | .40 |
| 787 | Brian Shouse | .15 | .40 |
| 788 | Jeff Suppan | .15 | .40 |
| 789 | Carlos Villanueva | .15 | .40 |
| 790 | Matt Wise | .15 | .40 |
| 791 | Johnny Estrada | .15 | .40 |
| 792 | Craig Counsell | .15 | .40 |
| 793 | Tony Graffanino | .15 | .40 |
| 794 | Corey Koskie | .15 | .40 |
| 795 | Claudio Vargas | .15 | .40 |
| 796 | Brady Clark | .15 | .40 |
| 797 | Gabe Gross | .15 | .40 |
| 798 | Geoff Jenkins | .15 | .40 |
| 799 | Kevin Mench | .15 | .40 |
| 800 | Bill Hall CL | .15 | .40 |
| 801 | Sidney Ponson | .15 | .40 |
| 802 | Jesse Crain | .15 | .40 |
| 803 | Matt Guerrier | .15 | .40 |
| 804 | Pat Neshek | .25 | .60 |
| 805 | Ramon Ortiz | .15 | .40 |
| 806 | Johan Santana | .25 | .60 |
| 807 | Carlos Silva | .15 | .40 |
| 808 | Mike Redmond | .15 | .40 |
| 809 | Jeff Cirillo | .15 | .40 |
| 810 | Luis Rodriguez | .15 | .40 |
| 811 | Lew Ford | .15 | .40 |
| 812 | Torii Hunter | .15 | .40 |
| 813 | Jason Tyner | .15 | .40 |
| 814 | Rondell White | .15 | .40 |
| 815 | Justin Morneau | .15 | .40 |
| 816 | Joe Mauer | .40 | 1.00 |
| 817 | Johan Santana CL | .25 | .60 |
| 818 | David Newhan | .15 | .40 |
| 819 | Aaron Sele | .15 | .40 |
| 820 | Ambiorix Burgos | .15 | .40 |
| 821 | Pedro Feliciano | .15 | .40 |
| 822 | Tom Glavine | .25 | .60 |
| 823 | Aaron Heilman | .15 | .40 |
| 824 | Guillermo Mota | .15 | .40 |
| 825 | Jose Reyes | .40 | 1.00 |
| 826 | Oliver Perez | .15 | .40 |
| 827 | Duaner Sanchez | .15 | .40 |
| 828 | Scott Schoeneweis | .15 | .40 |
| 829 | Ramon Castro | .15 | .40 |
| 830 | Damion Easley | .15 | .40 |
| 831 | David Wright | .60 | 1.50 |
| 832 | Moises Alou | .15 | .40 |
| 833 | Carlos Beltran | .15 | .40 |
| 834 | Dave Williams | .15 | .40 |
| 835 | David Wright CL | .60 | 1.50 |
| 836 | Brian Bruney | .15 | .40 |
| 837 | Mike Myers | .15 | .40 |
| 838 | Carl Pavano | .15 | .40 |
| 839 | Andy Pettitte | .25 | .60 |
| 840 | Luis Vizcaino | .15 | .40 |
| 841 | Jorge Posada | .25 | .60 |
| 842 | Miguel Cairo | .15 | .40 |
| 843 | Doug Mientkiewicz | .15 | .40 |
| 844 | Derek Jeter | 1.00 | 2.50 |
| 845 | Alex Rodriguez | .60 | 1.50 |
| 846 | Johnny Damon | .25 | .60 |
| 847 | Hideki Matsui | .40 | 1.00 |
| 848 | Josh Phelps | .15 | .40 |
| 849 | Phil Hughes (RC) | 1.50 | 4.00 |
| 850 | Roger Clemens | .60 | 1.50 |
| 851 | Jason Giambi CL | .15 | .40 |
| 852 | Kiko Calero | .15 | .40 |
| 853 | Justin Duchscherer | .15 | .40 |
| 854 | Alan Embree | .15 | .40 |
| 855 | Todd Walker | .15 | .40 |
| 856 | Rich Harden | .15 | .40 |
| 857 | Dan Haren | .15 | .40 |
| 858 | Joe Kennedy | .15 | .40 |
| 859 | Jason Kendall | .15 | .40 |
| 860 | Adam Melhuse | .15 | .40 |
| 861 | Mark Ellis | .15 | .40 |
| 862 | Bobby Kielty | .15 | .40 |
| 863 | Mark Kotsay | .15 | .40 |
| 864 | Shannon Stewart | .15 | .40 |
| 865 | Mike Piazza | .40 | 1.00 |
| 866 | Mike Piazza CL | .40 | 1.00 |
| 867 | Antonio Alfonseca | .15 | .40 |
| 868 | Carlos Ruiz | .15 | .40 |
| 869 | Adam Eaton | .15 | .40 |
| 870 | Freddy Garcia | .15 | .40 |
| 871 | Jon Lieber | .15 | .40 |
| 872 | Matt Smith | .15 | .40 |
| 873 | Rod Barajas | .15 | .40 |
| 874 | Wes Helms | .15 | .40 |
| 875 | Abraham Nunez | .15 | .40 |
| 876 | Pat Burrell | .15 | .40 |
| 877 | Jayson Werth | .15 | .40 |
| 878 | Greg Dobbs | .15 | .40 |
| 879 | Joseph Bisenius RC | .30 | .75 |
| 880 | Michael Bourn (RC) | .30 | .75 |
| 881 | Chase Utley | .40 | 1.00 |
| 882 | Ryan Howard | .60 | 1.50 |
| 883 | Chase Utley CL | .40 | 1.00 |
| 884 | Tony Armas | .15 | .40 |
| 885 | Shawn Chacon | .15 | .40 |
| 886 | John Grabow | .15 | .40 |
| 887 | Paul Maholm | .15 | .40 |
| 888 | Damaso Marte | .15 | .40 |
| 889 | Salomon Torres | .15 | .40 |
| 890 | Humberto Cota | .15 | .40 |
| 891 | Ryan Doumit | .15 | .40 |
| 892 | Adam LaRoche | .15 | .40 |
| 893 | Jack Wilson | .15 | .40 |
| 894 | Nate McLouth | .15 | .40 |
| 895 | Brad Eldred | .15 | .40 |
| 896 | Jonah Bayliss | .15 | .40 |
| 897 | Juan Perez RC | .30 | .75 |
| 898 | Jason Bay | .25 | .60 |
| 899 | Adam LaRoche CL | .15 | .40 |
| 900 | Doug Brocail | .15 | .40 |
| 901 | Scott Cassidy | .15 | .40 |
| 902 | Scott Linebrink | .15 | .40 |
| 903 | Greg Maddux | .60 | 1.50 |
| 904 | Jake Peavy | .15 | .40 |
| 905 | Mike Thompson | .15 | .40 |
| 906 | David Wells | .15 | .40 |
| 907 | Josh Bard | .15 | .40 |
| 908 | Rob Bowen | .15 | .40 |
| 909 | Marcus Giles | .15 | .40 |
| 910 | Russell Branyan | .15 | .40 |
| 911 | Jose Cruz | .15 | .40 |
| 912 | Termel Sledge | .15 | .40 |
| 913 | Trevor Hoffman | .15 | .40 |
| 914 | Brian Giles | .15 | .40 |
| 915 | Trevor Hoffman CL | .15 | .40 |
| 916 | Vinnie Chulk | .15 | .40 |
| 917 | Kevin Correia | .15 | .40 |
| 918 | Tim Lincecum RC | 6.00 | 15.00 |
| 919 | Matt Morris | .15 | .40 |
| 920 | Russ Ortiz | .15 | .40 |
| 921 | Barry Zito | .15 | .40 |
| 922 | Bengie Molina | .15 | .40 |
| 923 | Rich Aurilia | .15 | .40 |
| 924 | Omar Vizquel | .25 | .60 |
| 925 | Jason Ellison | .15 | .40 |
| 926 | Ryan Klesko | .15 | .40 |
| 927 | Dave Roberts | .15 | .40 |
| 928 | Randy Winn | .15 | .40 |
| 929 | Barry Zito CL | .15 | .40 |
| 930 | Miguel Batista | .15 | .40 |
| 931 | Horacio Ramirez | .15 | .40 |
| 932 | Chris Reitsma | .15 | .40 |
| 933 | George Sherrill | .15 | .40 |
| 934 | Jarrod Washburn | .15 | .40 |
| 935 | Jeff Weaver | .15 | .40 |
| 936 | Jake Woods | .15 | .40 |
| 937 | Adrian Beltre | .15 | .40 |
| 938 | Jose Lopez | .15 | .40 |
| 939 | Ichiro Suzuki | .60 | 1.50 |
| 940 | Jose Vidro | .15 | .40 |
| 941 | Jose Guillen | .15 | .40 |
| 942 | Sean White RC | .30 | .75 |
| 943 | Brandon Morrow RC | .75 | 2.00 |
| 944 | Felix Hernandez | .25 | .60 |
| 945 | Felix Hernandez CL | .25 | .60 |
| 946 | Randy Flores | .15 | .40 |
| 947 | Ryan Franklin | .15 | .40 |
| 948 | Kelvin Jimenez RC | .30 | .75 |
| 949 | Tyler Johnson | .15 | .40 |
| 950 | Mark Mulder | .15 | .40 |
| 951 | Anthony Reyes | .15 | .40 |
| 952 | Russ Springer | .15 | .40 |
| 953 | Brad Thompson | .15 | .40 |
| 954 | Adam Wainwright | .25 | .60 |
| 955 | Kip Wells | .15 | .40 |
| 956 | Gary Bennett | .15 | .40 |
| 957 | Adam Kennedy | .15 | .40 |
| 958 | Scott Rolen | .25 | .60 |
| 959 | Scott Spiezio | .15 | .40 |
| 960 | So Taguchi | .15 | .40 |
| 961 | Preston Wilson | .15 | .40 |
| 962 | Skip Schumaker | .15 | .40 |
| 963 | Albert Pujols | .75 | 2.00 |
| 964 | Chris Carpenter | .15 | .40 |
| 965 | Chris Carpenter CL | .15 | .40 |
| 966 | Edwin Jackson | .15 | .40 |
| 967 | Jae Kuk Ryu | .15 | .40 |
| 968 | Jae Seo | .15 | .40 |
| 969 | Jon Switzer | .15 | .40 |
| 970 | Josh Paul | .15 | .40 |
| 971 | Ben Zobrist | .15 | .40 |
| 972 | Rocco Baldelli | .15 | .40 |
| 973 | Scott Kazmir | .25 | .60 |
| 974 | Carl Crawford | .15 | .40 |
| 975 | Delmon Young CL | .25 | .60 |
| 976 | Bruce Chen | .15 | .40 |
| 977 | Joaquin Benoit | .15 | .40 |
| 978 | Scott Feldman | .25 | .60 |
| 979 | Eric Gagne | .15 | .40 |
| 980 | Kameron Loe | .15 | .40 |
| 981 | Brandon McCarthy | .15 | .40 |
| 982 | Robinson Tejeda | .15 | .40 |
| 983 | C.J. Wilson | .15 | .40 |
| 984 | Mark Teixeira | .25 | .60 |
| 985 | Michael Young | .15 | .40 |
| 986 | Kenny Lofton | .15 | .40 |
| 987 | Brad Wilkerson | .15 | .40 |
| 988 | Nelson Cruz | .15 | .40 |
| 989 | Sammy Sosa | .40 | 1.00 |
| 990 | Michael Young CL | .15 | .40 |
| 991 | Vernon Wells | .15 | .40 |
| 992 | Matt Stairs | .15 | .40 |
| 993 | Jeremy Accardo | .15 | .40 |
| 994 | A.J. Burnett | .15 | .40 |
| 995 | Jason Frasor | .15 | .40 |
| 996 | Roy Halladay | .15 | .40 |
| 997 | Shaun Marcum | .15 | .40 |
| 998 | Tomo Ohka | .15 | .40 |
| 999 | Josh Towers | .15 | .40 |
| 1000 | Gregg Zaun | .15 | .40 |
| 1001 | Royce Clayton | .15 | .40 |
| 1002 | Jason Smith | .15 | .40 |
| 1003 | Alex Rios | .15 | .40 |
| 1004 | Frank Thomas | .40 | 1.00 |
| 1005 | Roy Halladay CL | .15 | .40 |
| 1006 | Jesus Flores RC | .30 | .75 |
| 1007 | Dmitri Young | .15 | .40 |
| 1008 | Ray King | .15 | .40 |
| 1009 | Micah Bowie | .15 | .40 |
| 1010 | Shawn Hill | .15 | .40 |
| 1011 | John Patterson | .15 | .40 |
| 1012 | Levale Speigner RC | .30 | .75 |
| 1013 | Ryan Wagner | .15 | .40 |
| 1014 | Jerome Williams | .15 | .40 |
| 1015 | Ryan Zimmerman | .40 | 1.00 |
| 1016 | Cristian Guzman | .15 | .40 |
| 1017 | Nook Logan | .15 | .40 |
| 1018 | Chris Snelling | .15 | .40 |

|  |  | | |
|---|---|---|---|
| ☐ 1019 | Ronnie Belliard | .15 | .40 |
| ☐ 1020 | Nick Johnson CL | .15 | .40 |
| ☐ NNO | Rookie EXCH | 30.00 | 60.00 |

## 2008 Upper Deck

| | | | |
|---|---|---|---|
| ☐ COMPLETE SET (799) | | 50.00 | 100.00 |
| ☐ COMP.SER.1 (1-400) | | 20.00 | 50.00 |
| ☐ COMP.SER.2 (401-799) | | 20.00 | 50.00 |
| ☐ COMMON CARD (1-799) | | .15 | .40 |
| ☐ COMMON ROOKIE (1-799) | | .40 | 1.00 |
| ☐ 1 | Joe Saunders | .15 | .40 |
| ☐ 2 | Kelvim Escobar | .15 | .40 |
| ☐ 3 | Jered Weaver | .15 | .40 |
| ☐ 4 | Justin Speier | .15 | .40 |
| ☐ 5 | Scot Shields | .15 | .40 |
| ☐ 6 | Mike Napoli | .15 | .40 |
| ☐ 7 | Orlando Cabrera | .15 | .40 |
| ☐ 8 | Casey Kotchman | .15 | .40 |
| ☐ 9 | Vladimir Guerrero | .40 | 1.00 |
| ☐ 10 | Garret Anderson | .15 | .40 |
| ☐ 11 | Roy Oswalt | .15 | .40 |
| ☐ 12 | Wandy Rodriguez | .15 | .40 |
| ☐ 13 | Woody Williams | .15 | .40 |
| ☐ 14 | Chad Qualls | .15 | .40 |
| ☐ 15 | Brian Moehler | .15 | .40 |
| ☐ 16 | Mark Loretta | .15 | .40 |
| ☐ 17 | Brad Ausmus | .15 | .40 |
| ☐ 18 | Ty Wigginton | .15 | .40 |
| ☐ 19 | Carlos Lee | .15 | .40 |
| ☐ 20 | Hunter Pence | .40 | 1.00 |
| ☐ 21 | Dan Haren | .15 | .40 |
| ☐ 22 | Lenny DiNardo | .15 | .40 |
| ☐ 23 | Chad Gaudin | .15 | .40 |
| ☐ 24 | Huston Street | .15 | .40 |
| ☐ 25 | Andrew Brown | .15 | .40 |
| ☐ 26 | Mike Piazza | .40 | 1.00 |
| ☐ 27 | Jack Cust | .15 | .40 |
| ☐ 28 | Mark Ellis | .15 | .40 |
| ☐ 29 | Shannon Stewart | .15 | .40 |
| ☐ 30 | Travis Buck | .15 | .40 |
| ☐ 31 | Shaun Marcum | .15 | .40 |
| ☐ 32 | A.J. Burnett | .15 | .40 |
| ☐ 33 | Jesse Litsch | .15 | .40 |
| ☐ 34 | Casey Janssen | .15 | .40 |
| ☐ 35 | Jeremy Accardo | .15 | .40 |
| ☐ 36 | Gregg Zaun | .15 | .40 |
| ☐ 37 | Aaron Hill | .15 | .40 |
| ☐ 38 | Frank Thomas | .40 | 1.00 |
| ☐ 39 | Matt Stairs | .15 | .40 |
| ☐ 40 | Vernon Wells | .15 | .40 |
| ☐ 41 | Tim Hudson | .15 | .40 |
| ☐ 42 | Chuck James | .15 | .40 |
| ☐ 43 | Buddy Carlyle | .15 | .40 |
| ☐ 44 | Rafael Soriano | .15 | .40 |
| ☐ 45 | Peter Moylan | .15 | .40 |
| ☐ 46 | Brian McCann | .25 | .60 |
| ☐ 47 | Edgar Renteria | .25 | .60 |
| ☐ 48 | Mark Teixeira | .25 | .60 |
| ☐ 49 | Willie Harris | .15 | .40 |
| ☐ 50 | Andruw Jones | .15 | .40 |
| ☐ 51 | Ben Sheets | .25 | .60 |
| ☐ 52 | Dave Bush | .15 | .40 |
| ☐ 53 | Yovani Gallardo | .15 | .40 |
| ☐ 54 | Francisco Cordero | .15 | .40 |
| ☐ 55 | Matt Wise | .15 | .40 |
| ☐ 56 | Johnny Estrada | .15 | .40 |
| ☐ 57 | Prince Fielder | .40 | 1.00 |
| ☐ 58 | J.J. Hardy | .15 | .40 |
| ☐ 59 | Corey Hart | .15 | .40 |
| ☐ 60 | Geoff Jenkins | .15 | .40 |
| ☐ 61 | Adam Wainwright | .25 | .60 |
| ☐ 62 | Joel Pineiro | .15 | .40 |
| ☐ 63 | Brad Thompson | .15 | .40 |
| ☐ 64 | Jason Isringhausen | .15 | .40 |
| ☐ 65 | Troy Percival | .15 | .40 |
| ☐ 66 | Yadier Molina | .25 | .60 |
| ☐ 67 | Albert Pujols | .75 | 2.00 |
| ☐ 68 | David Eckstein | .15 | .40 |
| ☐ 69 | Jim Edmonds | .25 | .60 |
| ☐ 70 | Rick Ankiel | .15 | .40 |
| ☐ 71 | Ted Lilly | .15 | .40 |
| ☐ 72 | Rich Hill | .15 | .40 |
| ☐ 73 | Jason Marquis | .15 | .40 |
| ☐ 74 | Carlos Marmol | .15 | .40 |
| ☐ 75 | Ryan Dempster | .15 | .40 |
| ☐ 76 | Jason Kendall | .15 | .40 |
| ☐ 77 | Aramis Ramirez | .15 | .40 |
| ☐ 78 | Ryan Theriot | .15 | .40 |
| ☐ 79 | Alfonso Soriano | .25 | .60 |
| ☐ 80 | Jacque Jones | .15 | .40 |
| ☐ 81 | James Shields | .15 | .40 |
| ☐ 82 | Andy Sonnanstine | .15 | .40 |
| ☐ 83 | Scott Dohmann | .15 | .40 |
| ☐ 84 | Al Reyes | .15 | .40 |
| ☐ 85 | Dioner Navarro | .15 | .40 |
| ☐ 86 | B.J. Upton | .25 | .60 |
| ☐ 87 | Carlos Pena | .40 | 1.00 |
| ☐ 88 | Brendan Harris | .15 | .40 |
| ☐ 89 | Josh Wilson | .15 | .40 |
| ☐ 90 | Jonny Gomes | .15 | .40 |
| ☐ 91 | Brandon Webb | .25 | .60 |
| ☐ 92 | Micah Owings | .15 | .40 |
| ☐ 93 | Livan Hernandez | .15 | .40 |
| ☐ 94 | Doug Slaten | .15 | .40 |
| ☐ 95 | Brandon Lyon | .15 | .40 |
| ☐ 96 | Miguel Montero | .15 | .40 |
| ☐ 97 | Stephen Drew | .15 | .40 |
| ☐ 98 | Mark Reynolds | .15 | .40 |
| ☐ 99 | Conor Jackson | .15 | .40 |
| ☐ 100 | Chris B. Young | .15 | .40 |
| ☐ 101 | Chad Billingsley | .15 | .40 |
| ☐ 102 | Derek Lowe | .15 | .40 |
| ☐ 103 | Mark Hendrickson | .15 | .40 |
| ☐ 104 | Takashi Saito | .15 | .40 |
| ☐ 105 | Rudy Seanez | .15 | .40 |
| ☐ 106 | Russell Martin | .15 | .40 |
| ☐ 107 | Jeff Kent | .15 | .40 |
| ☐ 108 | Nomar Garciaparra | .40 | 1.00 |
| ☐ 109 | Matt Kemp | .40 | 1.00 |
| ☐ 110 | Juan Pierre | .15 | .40 |
| ☐ 111 | Matt Cain | .15 | .40 |
| ☐ 112 | Barry Zito | .15 | .40 |
| ☐ 113 | Kevin Correia | .15 | .40 |
| ☐ 114 | Brad Hennessey | .15 | .40 |
| ☐ 115 | Jack Taschner | .15 | .40 |
| ☐ 116 | Bengie Molina | .15 | .40 |
| ☐ 117 | Ryan Klesko | .15 | .40 |
| ☐ 118 | Omar Vizquel | .15 | .40 |
| ☐ 119 | Dave Roberts | .15 | .40 |
| ☐ 120 | Rajai Davis | .15 | .40 |
| ☐ 121 | Fausto Carmona | .15 | .40 |
| ☐ 122 | Jake Westbrook | .15 | .40 |
| ☐ 123 | Cliff Lee | .15 | .40 |
| ☐ 124 | Rafael Betancourt | .15 | .40 |
| ☐ 125 | Joe Borowski | .15 | .40 |
| ☐ 126 | Victor Martinez | .25 | .60 |
| ☐ 127 | Travis Hafner | .15 | .40 |
| ☐ 128 | Ryan Garko | .15 | .40 |
| ☐ 129 | Kenny Lofton | .15 | .40 |
| ☐ 130 | Franklin Gutierrez | .15 | .40 |
| ☐ 131 | Felix Hernandez | .25 | .60 |
| ☐ 132 | Jeff Weaver | .15 | .40 |
| ☐ 133 | J.J. Putz | .15 | .40 |
| ☐ 134 | Brandon Morrow | .15 | .40 |
| ☐ 135 | Sean Green | .15 | .40 |
| ☐ 136 | Kenji Johjima | .15 | .40 |
| ☐ 137 | Jose Vidro | .15 | .40 |
| ☐ 138 | Richie Sexson | .15 | .40 |
| ☐ 139 | Ichiro Suzuki | .60 | 1.50 |
| ☐ 140 | Ben Broussard | .15 | .40 |
| ☐ 141 | Sergio Mitre | .15 | .40 |
| ☐ 142 | Scott Olsen | .15 | .40 |
| ☐ 143 | Rick Vanden Hurk | .15 | .40 |
| ☐ 144 | Justin Miller | .15 | .40 |
| ☐ 145 | Lee Gardner | .15 | .40 |
| ☐ 146 | Miguel Olivo | .15 | .40 |
| ☐ 147 | Hanley Ramirez | .40 | 1.00 |
| ☐ 148 | Mike Jacobs | .15 | .40 |
| ☐ 149 | Josh Willingham | .15 | .40 |
| ☐ 150 | Alfredo Amezaga | .15 | .40 |
| ☐ 151 | John Maine | .15 | .40 |
| ☐ 152 | Tom Glavine | .25 | .60 |
| ☐ 153 | Orlando Hernandez | .15 | .40 |
| ☐ 154 | Billy Wagner | .15 | .40 |
| ☐ 155 | Aaron Heilman | .15 | .40 |
| ☐ 156 | David Wright | .50 | 1.25 |
| ☐ 157 | Luis Castillo | .15 | .40 |
| ☐ 158 | Shawn Green | .15 | .40 |
| ☐ 159 | Damion Easley | .15 | .40 |
| ☐ 160 | Carlos Delgado | .15 | .40 |
| ☐ 161 | Shawn Hill | .15 | .40 |
| ☐ 162 | Mike Bacsik | .15 | .40 |
| ☐ 163 | John Lannan | .15 | .40 |
| ☐ 164 | Chad Cordero | .15 | .40 |
| ☐ 165 | Jon Rauch | .15 | .40 |
| ☐ 166 | Jesus Flores | .15 | .40 |
| ☐ 167 | Dmitri Young | .15 | .40 |
| ☐ 168 | Cristian Guzman | .15 | .40 |
| ☐ 169 | Austin Kearns | .15 | .40 |
| ☐ 170 | Nook Logan | .15 | .40 |
| ☐ 171 | Erik Bedard | .15 | .40 |
| ☐ 172 | Daniel Cabrera | .15 | .40 |
| ☐ 173 | Chris Ray | .15 | .40 |
| ☐ 174 | Danys Baez | .15 | .40 |
| ☐ 175 | Chad Bradford | .15 | .40 |
| ☐ 176 | Ramon Hernandez | .15 | .40 |
| ☐ 177 | Miguel Tejada | .15 | .40 |
| ☐ 178 | Freddie Bynum | .15 | .40 |
| ☐ 179 | Corey Patterson | .15 | .40 |
| ☐ 180 | Aubrey Huff | .15 | .40 |
| ☐ 181 | Chris Young | .15 | .40 |
| ☐ 182 | Greg Maddux | .50 | 1.25 |
| ☐ 183 | Clay Hensley | .15 | .40 |
| ☐ 184 | Kevin Cameron | .15 | .40 |
| ☐ 185 | Doug Brocail | .15 | .40 |
| ☐ 186 | Josh Bard | .15 | .40 |
| ☐ 187 | Kevin Kouzmanoff | .15 | .40 |
| ☐ 188 | Geoff Blum | .15 | .40 |
| ☐ 189 | Milton Bradley | .15 | .40 |
| ☐ 190 | Brian Giles | .15 | .40 |
| ☐ 191 | Jamie Moyer | .15 | .40 |
| ☐ 192 | Kyle Kendrick | .15 | .40 |
| ☐ 193 | Kyle Lohse | .15 | .40 |
| ☐ 194 | Antonio Alfonseca | .15 | .40 |
| ☐ 195 | Ryan Madson | .15 | .40 |
| ☐ 196 | Chris Coste | .15 | .40 |
| ☐ 197 | Chase Utley | .40 | 1.00 |
| ☐ 198 | Tadahito Iguchi | .15 | .40 |
| ☐ 199 | Aaron Rowand | .15 | .40 |
| ☐ 200 | Shane Victorino | .15 | .40 |
| ☐ 201 | Paul Maholm | .15 | .40 |
| ☐ 202 | Ian Snell | .15 | .40 |
| ☐ 203 | Shane Youman | .15 | .40 |
| ☐ 204 | Damaso Marte | .15 | .40 |
| ☐ 205 | Shawn Chacon | .15 | .40 |
| ☐ 206 | Ronny Paulino | .15 | .40 |
| ☐ 207 | Jack Wilson | .15 | .40 |
| ☐ 208 | Adam LaRoche | .15 | .40 |
| ☐ 209 | Ryan Doumit | .15 | .40 |
| ☐ 210 | Xavier Nady | .15 | .40 |
| ☐ 211 | Kevin Millwood | .15 | .40 |
| ☐ 212 | Brandon McCarthy | .15 | .40 |
| ☐ 213 | Joaquin Benoit | .15 | .40 |
| ☐ 214 | Wes Littleton | .15 | .40 |
| ☐ 215 | Mike Wood | .15 | .40 |
| ☐ 216 | Gerald Laird | .15 | .40 |
| ☐ 217 | Hank Blalock | .15 | .40 |
| ☐ 218 | Ian Kinsler | .25 | .60 |
| ☐ 219 | Marlon Byrd | .15 | .40 |
| ☐ 220 | Brad Wilkerson | .15 | .40 |
| ☐ 221 | Tim Wakefield | .15 | .40 |

|  |  | | |
|---|---|---|---|
| 222 | Daisuke Matsuzaka | .50 | 1.25 |
| 223 | Julian Tavarez | .15 | .40 |
| 224 | Hideki Okajima | .15 | .40 |
| 225 | Manny Delcarmen | .15 | .40 |
| 226 | Doug Mirabelli | .15 | .40 |
| 227 | Dustin Pedroia | .50 | 1.25 |
| 228 | Mike Lowell . | .15 | .40 |
| 229 | Manny Ramirez | .40 | 1.00 |
| 230 | Coco Crisp | .15 | .40 |
| 231 | Bronson Arroyo | .15 | .40 |
| 232 | Matt Belisle | .15 | .40 |
| 233 | Jared Burton | .15 | .40 |
| 234 | David Weathers | .15 | .40 |
| 235 | Mike Gosling | .15 | .40 |
| 236 | David Ross | .15 | .40 |
| 237 | Jeff Keppinger | .15 | .40 |
| 238 | Edwin Encarnacion | .15 | .40 |
| 239 | Ken Griffey Jr. | .60 | 1.50 |
| 240 | Adam Dunn | .15 | .40 |
| 241 | Jeff Francis | .15 | .40 |
| 242 | Jason Hirsh | .15 | .40 |
| 243 | Josh Fogg | .15 | .40 |
| 244 | Manny Corpas | .15 | .40 |
| 245 | Jeremy Affeldt | .15 | .40 |
| 246 | Yorvit Torrealba | .15 | .40 |
| 247 | Todd Helton | .25 | .60 |
| 248 | Kazuo Matsui | .15 | .40 |
| 249 | Brad Hawpe | .15 | .40 |
| 250 | Willy Taveras | .15 | .40 |
| 251 | Brian Bannister | .15 | .40 |
| 252 | Zack Greinke | .15 | .40 |
| 253 | Kyle Davies | .15 | .40 |
| 254 | David Riske | .15 | .40 |
| 255 | Joel Peralta | .15 | .40 |
| 256 | John Buck | .15 | .40 |
| 257 | Mark Grudzielanek | .15 | .40 |
| 258 | Ross Gload | .15 | .40 |
| 259 | Billy Butler | .15 | .40 |
| 260 | David DeJesus | .15 | .40 |
| 261 | Jeremy Bonderman | .15 | .40 |
| 262 | Chad Durbin | .15 | .40 |
| 263 | Andrew Miller | .25 | .60 |
| 264 | Bobby Seay | .15 | .40 |
| 265 | Todd Jones | .15 | .40 |
| 266 | Brandon Inge | .15 | .40 |
| 267 | Sean Casey | .15 | .40 |
| 268 | Placido Polanco | .15 | .40 |
| 269 | Gary Sheffield | .15 | .40 |
| 270 | Magglio Ordonez | .25 | .60 |
| 271 | Matt Garza | .15 | .40 |
| 272 | Boof Bonser | .15 | .40 |
| 273 | Scott Baker | .15 | .40 |
| 274 | Joe Nathan | .15 | .40 |
| 275 | Dennys Reyes | .15 | .40 |
| 276 | Joe Mauer | .40 | 1.00 |
| 277 | Michael Cuddyer | .15 | .40 |
| 278 | Jason Bartlett | .15 | .40 |
| 279 | Torii Hunter | .15 | .40 |
| 280 | Jason Tyner | .15 | .40 |
| 281 | Mark Buehrle | .15 | .40 |
| 282 | Jon Garland | .15 | .40 |
| 283 | Jose Contreras | .15 | .40 |
| 284 | Matt Thornton | .15 | .40 |
| 285 | Ryan Bukvich | .15 | .40 |
| 286 | Juan Uribe | .15 | .40 |
| 287 | Jim Thome | .25 | .60 |
| 288 | Scott Podsednik | .15 | .40 |
| 289 | Jerry Owens | .15 | .40 |
| 290 | Jermaine Dye | .15 | .40 |
| 291 | Andy Pettitte | .25 | .60 |
| 292 | Phil Hughes | .40 | 1.00 |
| 293 | Mike Mussina | .15 | .40 |
| 294 | Joba Chamberlain | .50 | 1.25 |
| 295 | Brian Bruney | .15 | .40 |
| 296 | Jorge Posada | .25 | .60 |
| 297 | Derek Jeter | 1.00 | 2.50 |
| 298 | Jason Giambi | .25 | .60 |
| 299 | Johnny Damon | .25 | .60 |
| 300 | Melky Cabrera | .15 | .40 |
| 301 | Jonathan Albaladejo RC | .60 | 1.50 |
| 302 | Josh Anderson (RC) | .40 | 1.00 |
| 303 | Wladimir Balentien (RC) | .40 | 1.00 |
| 304 | Josh Banks (RC) | .40 | 1.00 |
| 305 | Daric Barton (RC) | .40 | 1.00 |
| 306 | Jerry Blevins RC | .60 | 1.50 |
| 307 | Emilio Bonifacio RC | 1.00 | 2.50 |
| 308 | Lance Broadway (RC) | .40 | 1.00 |
| 309 | Clay Buchholz (RC) | 1.00 | 2.50 |
| 310 | Billy Buckner (RC) | .40 | 1.00 |
| 311 | Jeff Clement (RC) | .60 | 1.50 |
| 312 | Willie Collazo RC | .60 | 1.50 |
| 313 | Ross Detwiler RC | 1.00 | 2.50 |
| 314 | Sam Fuld RC | .40 | 1.00 |
| 315 | Harvey Garcia (RC) | .40 | 1.00 |
| 316 | Alberto Gonzalez (RC) | .60 | 1.50 |
| 317 | Ryan Hanigan RC | .60 | 1.50 |
| 318 | Kevin Hart (RC) | .40 | 1.00 |
| 319 | Luke Hochevar RC | .60 | 1.50 |
| 320 | Chin-Lung Hu (RC) | .60 | 1.50 |
| 321 | Rob Johnson (RC) | .40 | 1.00 |
| 322 | Radhames Liz RC | .60 | 1.50 |
| 323 | Ian Kennedy RC | 1.00 | 2.50 |
| 324 | Joe Koshansky RC | .40 | 1.00 |
| 325 | Donny Lucy (RC) | .40 | 1.00 |
| 326 | Justin Maxwell RC | .60 | 1.50 |
| 327 | Jonathan Meloan RC | .60 | 1.50 |
| 328 | Luis Mendoza (RC) | .40 | 1.00 |
| 329 | Jose Morales (RC) | .40 | 1.00 |
| 330 | Nyjer Morgan (RC) | .40 | 1.00 |
| 331 | Carlos Muniz RC | .60 | 1.50 |
| 332 | Bill Murphy (RC) | .40 | 1.00 |
| 333 | Josh Newman RC | .60 | 1.50 |
| 334 | Ross Ohlendorf RC | .60 | 1.50 |
| 335 | Troy Patton (RC) | .60 | 1.50 |
| 336 | Felipe Paulino RC | .60 | 1.50 |
| 337 | Steve Pearce RC | .60 | 1.50 |
| 338 | Heath Phillips RC | .60 | 1.50 |
| 339 | Justin Ruggiano RC | .60 | 1.50 |
| 340 | Clint Sammons (RC) | .40 | 1.00 |
| 341 | Bronson Sardinha (RC) | .40 | 1.00 |
| 342 | Chris Seddon (RC) | .40 | 1.00 |
| 343 | Seth Smith (RC) | .40 | 1.00 |
| 344 | Mitch Stetter RC | .60 | 1.50 |
| 345 | Dave Davidson RC | .60 | 1.50 |
| 346 | Rich Thompson RC | .60 | 1.50 |
| 347 | J.R. Towles RC | .60 | 1.50 |
| 348 | Eugenio Velez RC | .40 | 1.00 |
| 349 | Joey Votto (RC) | 1.00 | 2.50 |
| 350 | Bill White RC | .40 | 1.00 |
| 351 | Vladimir Guerrero CL | .40 | 1.00 |
| 352 | Lance Berkman CL | .25 | .60 |
| 353 | Dan Haren CL | .15 | .40 |
| 354 | Frank Thomas CL | .40 | 1.00 |
| 355 | Chipper Jones CL | .50 | 1.25 |
| 356 | Prince Fielder CL | .40 | 1.00 |
| 357 | Albert Pujols CL | .75 | 2.00 |
| 358 | Alfonso Soriano CL | .25 | .60 |
| 359 | B.J. Upton CL | .25 | .60 |
| 360 | Eric Byrnes CL | .15 | .40 |
| 361 | Russell Martin CL | .15 | .40 |
| 362 | Tim Lincecum CL | .50 | 1.25 |
| 363 | Grady Sizemore CL | .25 | .60 |
| 364 | Ichiro Suzuki CL | .60 | 1.50 |
| 365 | Hanley Ramirez CL | .40 | 1.00 |
| 366 | David Wright CL | .50 | 1.25 |
| 367 | Ryan Zimmerman CL | .25 | .60 |
| 368 | Nick Markakis CL | .25 | .60 |
| 369 | Jake Peavy CL | .25 | .60 |
| 370 | Ryan Howard CL | .50 | 1.25 |
| 371 | Freddy Sanchez CL | .15 | .40 |
| 372 | Michael Young CL | .25 | .60 |
| 373 | David Ortiz CL | .25 | .60 |
| 374 | Ken Griffey Jr. CL | .60 | 1.50 |
| 375 | Matt Holliday CL | .25 | .60 |
| 376 | Brian Bannister CL | .15 | .40 |
| 377 | Magglio Ordonez CL | .25 | .60 |
| 378 | Johan Santana CL | .25 | .60 |
| 379 | Jim Thome CL | .25 | .60 |
| 380 | Alex Rodriguez CL | .60 | 1.50 |
| 381 | Alex Rodriguez HL | .60 | 1.50 |
| 382 | Brandon Webb HL | .25 | .60 |
| 383 | Chone Figgins HL | .15 | .40 |
| 384 | Clay Buchholz HL | .40 | 1.00 |
| 385 | Curtis Granderson HL | .15 | .40 |
| 386 | Frank Thomas HL | .40 | 1.00 |
| 387 | Fred Lewis HL | .15 | .40 |
| 388 | Garret Anderson HL | .15 | .40 |
| 389 | J.R. Towles HL | .25 | .60 |
| 390 | Jake Peavy HL | .25 | .60 |
| 391 | Jim Thome HL | .25 | .60 |
| 392 | Jimmy Rollins HL | .25 | .60 |
| 393 | Johan Santana HL | .25 | .60 |
| 394 | Justin Verlander HL | .25 | .60 |
| 395 | Mark Buehrle HL | .15 | .40 |
| 396 | Matt Holliday HL | .25 | .60 |
| 397 | Jarrod Saltalamacchia HL | .15 | .40 |
| 398 | Sammy Sosa HL | .25 | .60 |
| 399 | Tom Glavine HL | .25 | .60 |
| 400 | Trevor Hoffman HL | .15 | .40 |
| 401 | Dan Haren | .15 | .40 |
| 402 | Randy Johnson | .40 | 1.00 |
| 403 | Chris Burke | .15 | .40 |
| 404 | Orlando Hudson | .15 | .40 |
| 405 | Justin Upton | .40 | 1.00 |
| 406 | Eric Byrnes | .15 | .40 |
| 407 | Doug Davis | .15 | .40 |
| 408 | Chad Tracy | .15 | .40 |
| 409 | Tom Glavine | .25 | .60 |
| 410 | Kelly Johnson | .15 | .40 |
| 411 | Chipper Jones | .50 | 1.25 |
| 412 | Matt Diaz | .15 | .40 |
| 413 | Jeff Francoeur | .25 | .60 |
| 414 | Mark Kotsay | .15 | .40 |
| 415 | John Smoltz | .40 | 1.00 |
| 416 | Tyler Yates | .15 | .40 |
| 417 | Yunel Escobar | .15 | .40 |
| 418 | Mike Hampton | .15 | .40 |
| 419 | Luke Scott | .15 | .40 |
| 420 | Adam Jones | .15 | .40 |
| 421 | Jeremy Guthrie | .15 | .40 |
| 422 | Nick Markakis | .25 | .60 |
| 423 | Jay Payton | .15 | .40 |
| 424 | Brian Roberts | .25 | .60 |
| 425 | Melvin Mora | .15 | .40 |
| 426 | Adam Loewen | .15 | .40 |
| 427 | Luis Hernandez | .15 | .40 |
| 428 | Steve Trachsel | .15 | .40 |
| 429 | Josh Beckett | .25 | .60 |
| 430 | Jon Lester | .25 | .60 |
| 431 | Curt Schilling | .25 | .60 |
| 432 | Jonathan Papelbon | .25 | .60 |
| 433 | Jason Varitek | .40 | 1.00 |
| 434 | David Ortiz | .25 | .60 |
| 435 | Jacoby Ellsbury | .60 | 1.50 |
| 436 | Julio Lugo | .15 | .40 |
| 437 | Sean Casey | .15 | .40 |
| 438 | Kevin Youkilis | .25 | .60 |
| 439 | J.D. Drew | .15 | .40 |
| 440 | Alex Cora | .15 | .40 |
| 441 | Derrek Lee | .25 | .60 |
| 442 | Carlos Zambrano | .15 | .40 |
| 443 | Sean Marshall | .15 | .40 |
| 444 | Matt Murton | .15 | .40 |
| 445 | Kerry Wood | .15 | .40 |
| 446 | Felix Pie | .15 | .40 |
| 447 | Mark DeRosa | .15 | .40 |
| 448 | Ronny Cedeno | .15 | .40 |
| 449 | Jon Lieber | .15 | .40 |
| 450 | Geovany Soto | .40 | 1.00 |
| 451 | Gavin Floyd | .15 | .40 |
| 452 | Bobby Jenks | .15 | .40 |
| 453 | Scott Linebrink | .15 | .40 |
| 454 | Javier Vazquez | .15 | .40 |
| 455 | A.J. Pierzynski | .15 | .40 |
| 456 | Orlando Cabrera | .15 | .40 |
| 457 | Joe Crede | .15 | .40 |
| 458 | Josh Fields | .15 | .40 |
| 459 | Paul Konerko | .15 | .40 |
| 460 | Brian Anderson | .15 | .40 |
| 461 | Nick Swisher | .25 | .60 |
| 462 | Carlos Quentin | .15 | .40 |
| 463 | Homer Bailey | .25 | .60 |
| 464 | Francisco Cordero | .15 | .40 |

|  |  | | |
|---|---|---|---|
| 465 | Aaron Harang | .15 | .40 |
| 466 | Alex Gonzalez | .15 | .40 |
| 467 | Brandon Phillips | .15 | .40 |
| 468 | Ryan Freel | .15 | .40 |
| 469 | Scott Hatteberg | .15 | .40 |
| 470 | Juan Castro | .15 | .40 |
| 471 | Norris Hopper | .15 | .40 |
| 472 | Josh Barfield | .15 | .40 |
| 473 | Casey Blake | .15 | .40 |
| 474 | Paul Byrd | .15 | .40 |
| 475 | Grady Sizemore | .25 | .60 |
| 476 | Jason Michaels | .15 | .40 |
| 477 | Jhonny Peralta | .15 | .40 |
| 478 | Asdrubal Cabrera | .15 | .40 |
| 479 | David Dellucci | .15 | .40 |
| 480 | C.C. Sabathia | .15 | .40 |
| 481 | Andy Marte | .15 | .40 |
| 482 | Troy Tulowitzki | .25 | .60 |
| 483 | Matt Holliday | .25 | .60 |
| 484 | Garrett Atkins | .15 | .40 |
| 485 | Aaron Cook | .15 | .40 |
| 486 | Brian Fuentes | .15 | .40 |
| 487 | Ryan Spilborghs | .15 | .40 |
| 488 | Ubaldo Jimenez | .15 | .40 |
| 489 | Jayson Nix | .15 | .40 |
| 490 | Nate Robertson | .15 | .40 |
| 491 | Kenny Rogers | .15 | .40 |
| 492 | Justin Verlander | .25 | .60 |
| 493 | Dontrelle Willis | .15 | .40 |
| 494 | Joel Zumaya | .15 | .40 |
| 495 | Ivan Rodriguez | .25 | .60 |
| 496 | Miguel Cabrera | .25 | .60 |
| 497 | Carlos Guillen | .15 | .40 |
| 498 | Edgar Renteria | .15 | .40 |
| 499 | Curtis Granderson | .15 | .40 |
| 500 | Jacque Jones | .15 | .40 |
| 501 | Marcus Thames | .15 | .40 |
| 502 | Josh Johnson | .15 | .40 |
| 503 | Jeremy Hermida | .15 | .40 |
| 504 | Dan Uggla | .25 | .60 |
| 505 | Mark Hendrickson | .15 | .40 |
| 506 | Luis Gonzalez | .15 | .40 |
| 507 | Dallas McPherson | .15 | .40 |
| 508 | Cody Ross | .15 | .40 |
| 509 | Matt Treanor | .15 | .40 |
| 510 | Andrew Miller | .25 | .60 |
| 511 | Jorge Cantu | .15 | .40 |
| 512 | Kazuo Matsui | .15 | .40 |
| 513 | Lance Berkman | .25 | .60 |
| 514 | Darin Erstad | .15 | .40 |
| 515 | Miguel Tejada | .15 | .40 |
| 516 | Jose Valverde | .15 | .40 |
| 517 | Geoff Blum | .15 | .40 |
| 518 | Reggie Abercrombie | .15 | .40 |
| 519 | Brandon Backe | .15 | .40 |
| 520 | Michael Bourn | .15 | .40 |
| 521 | Gil Meche | .15 | .40 |
| 522 | Brett Tomko | .15 | .40 |
| 523 | Miguel Olivo | .15 | .40 |
| 524 | Shane Costa | .15 | .40 |
| 525 | Joey Gathright | .15 | .40 |
| 526 | Mark Teahen | .15 | .40 |
| 527 | Alex Gordon | .25 | .60 |
| 528 | Tony Pena | .15 | .40 |
| 529 | Jose Guillen | .15 | .40 |
| 530 | Torii Hunter | .15 | .40 |
| 531 | Ervin Santana | .15 | .40 |
| 532 | Francisco Rodriguez | .15 | .40 |
| 533 | Howie Kendrick | .15 | .40 |
| 534 | Reggie Willits | .15 | .40 |
| 535 | John Lackey | .15 | .40 |
| 536 | Gary Matthews | .15 | .40 |
| 537 | Jon Garland | .15 | .40 |
| 538 | Kendry Morales | .15 | .40 |
| 539 | Chone Figgins | .15 | .40 |
| 540 | Andruw Jones | .15 | .40 |
| 541 | Jason Schmidt | .15 | .40 |
| 542 | James Loney | .25 | .60 |
| 543 | Andre Ethier | .25 | .60 |
| 544 | Rafael Furcal | .15 | .40 |
| 545 | Brad Penny | .15 | .40 |
| 546 | Hong-Chih Kuo | .15 | .40 |
| 547 | Jonathan Broxton | .15 | .40 |
| 548 | Esteban Loaiza | .15 | .40 |
| 549 | Delwyn Young | .15 | .40 |
| 550 | Mike Cameron | .15 | .40 |
| 551 | Ryan Braun | .50 | 1.25 |
| 552 | Rickie Weeks | .15 | .40 |
| 553 | Bill Hall | .15 | .40 |
| 554 | Tony Gwynn Jr. | .15 | .40 |
| 555 | Eric Gagne | .15 | .40 |
| 556 | Jeff Suppan | .15 | .40 |
| 557 | Chris Capuano | .15 | .40 |
| 558 | Derrick Turnbow | .15 | .40 |
| 559 | Jason Kendall | .15 | .40 |
| 560 | Livan Hernandez | .15 | .40 |
| 561 | Philip Humber | .15 | .40 |
| 562 | Francisco Liriano | .25 | .60 |
| 563 | Pat Neshek | .15 | .40 |
| 564 | Adam Everett | .15 | .40 |
| 565 | Brendan Harris | .15 | .40 |
| 566 | Justin Morneau | .25 | .60 |
| 567 | Craig Monroe | .15 | .40 |
| 568 | Carlos Gomez | .15 | .40 |
| 569 | Delmon Young | .25 | .60 |
| 570 | Mike Lamb | .15 | .40 |
| 571 | Oliver Perez | .15 | .40 |
| 572 | Jose Reyes | .25 | .60 |
| 573 | Moises Alou | .15 | .40 |
| 574 | Carlos Beltran | .15 | .40 |
| 575 | Endy Chavez | .15 | .40 |
| 576 | Ryan Church | .15 | .40 |
| 577 | Pedro Martinez | .25 | .60 |
| 578 | Johan Santana | .25 | .60 |
| 579 | Mike Pelfrey | .15 | .40 |
| 580 | Brian Schneider | .15 | .40 |
| 581 | Joe Smith | .15 | .40 |
| 582 | Matt Wise | .15 | .40 |
| 583 | Duaner Sanchez | .15 | .40 |
| 584 | Ramon Castro | .15 | .40 |
| 585 | Kei Igawa | .15 | .40 |
| 586 | Mariano Rivera | .40 | 1.00 |
| 587 | Chien-Ming Wang | .40 | 1.00 |
| 588 | Wilson Betemit | .15 | .40 |
| 589 | Robinson Cano | .25 | .60 |
| 590 | Alex Rodriguez | .60 | 1.50 |
| 591 | Bobby Abreu | .15 | .40 |
| 592 | Shelley Duncan | .15 | .40 |
| 593 | Hideki Matsui | .40 | 1.00 |
| 594 | Kyle Farnsworth | .15 | .40 |
| 595 | Joe Blanton | .15 | .40 |
| 596 | Bobby Crosby | .15 | .40 |
| 597 | Eric Chavez | .15 | .40 |
| 598 | Dan Johnson | .15 | .40 |
| 599 | Rich Harden | .15 | .40 |
| 600 | Justin Duchscherer | .15 | .40 |
| 601 | Kurt Suzuki | .15 | .40 |
| 602 | Chris Denorfia | .15 | .40 |
| 603 | Emil Brown | .15 | .40 |
| 604 | Ryan Howard | .50 | 1.25 |
| 605 | Jimmy Rollins | .25 | .60 |
| 606 | Pedro Feliz | .15 | .40 |
| 607 | Adam Eaton | .15 | .40 |
| 608 | Brad Lidge | .15 | .40 |
| 609 | Brett Myers | .15 | .40 |
| 610 | Pat Burrell | .15 | .40 |
| 611 | So Taguchi | .15 | .40 |
| 612 | Geoff Jenkins | .15 | .40 |
| 613 | Tom Gordon | .15 | .40 |
| 614 | Zach Duke | .15 | .40 |
| 615 | Matt Morris | .15 | .40 |
| 616 | Tom Gorzelanny | .15 | .40 |
| 617 | Jason Bay | .25 | .60 |
| 618 | Chris Duffy | .15 | .40 |
| 619 | Freddy Sanchez | .15 | .40 |
| 620 | Jose Bautista | .15 | .40 |
| 621 | Nyjer Morgan | .15 | .40 |
| 622 | Matt Capps | .15 | .40 |
| 623 | Paul Maholm | .15 | .40 |
| 624 | Tadahito Iguchi | .15 | .40 |
| 625 | Adrian Gonzalez | .25 | .60 |
| 626 | Jim Edmonds | .25 | .60 |
| 627 | Jake Peavy | .25 | .60 |
| 628 | Khalil Greene | .25 | .60 |
| 629 | Trevor Hoffman | .15 | .40 |
| 630 | Mark Prior | .25 | .60 |
| 631 | Randy Wolf | .15 | .40 |
| 632 | Michael Barrett | .15 | .40 |
| 633 | Scott Hairston | .15 | .40 |
| 634 | Tim Lincecum | .50 | 1.25 |
| 635 | Noah Lowry | .15 | .40 |
| 636 | Rich Aurilia | .15 | .40 |
| 637 | Aaron Rowand | .15 | .40 |
| 638 | Randy Winn | .15 | .40 |
| 639 | Daniel Ortmeier | .15 | .40 |
| 640 | Ray Durham | .15 | .40 |
| 641 | Brian Wilson | .15 | .40 |
| 642 | Adrian Beltre | .15 | .40 |
| 643 | Jeremy Reed | .15 | .40 |
| 644 | Jarrod Washburn | .15 | .40 |
| 645 | Yuniesky Betancourt | .15 | .40 |
| 646 | Jose Lopez | .15 | .40 |
| 647 | Raul Ibanez | .25 | .60 |
| 648 | Mike Morse | .15 | .40 |
| 649 | Erik Bedard | .15 | .40 |
| 650 | Brad Wilkerson | .15 | .40 |
| 651 | Chris Carpenter | .15 | .40 |
| 652 | Mark Mulder | .15 | .40 |
| 653 | Juan Encarnacion | .15 | .40 |
| 654 | Skip Schumaker | .15 | .40 |
| 655 | Troy Glaus | .25 | .60 |
| 656 | Anthony Reyes | .15 | .40 |
| 657 | Cesar Izturis | .15 | .40 |
| 658 | Adam Kennedy | .15 | .40 |
| 659 | Chris Duncan | .15 | .40 |
| 660 | Matt Clement | .15 | .40 |
| 661 | Scott Kazmir | .25 | .60 |
| 662 | Troy Percival | .15 | .40 |
| 663 | Akinori Iwamura | .15 | .40 |
| 664 | Carl Crawford | .15 | .40 |
| 665 | Cliff Floyd | .15 | .40 |
| 666 | Jason Bartlett | .15 | .40 |
| 667 | Rocco Baldelli | .15 | .40 |
| 668 | Matt Garza | .15 | .40 |
| 669 | Edwin Jackson | .15 | .40 |
| 670 | Vicente Padilla | .15 | .40 |
| 671 | Josh Hamilton | .50 | 1.25 |
| 672 | Jason Botts | .15 | .40 |
| 673 | Milton Bradley | .15 | .40 |
| 674 | Michael Young | .15 | .40 |
| 675 | Eddie Guardado | .15 | .40 |
| 676 | David Murphy | .15 | .40 |
| 677 | Ramon Vazquez | .15 | .40 |
| 678 | Ben Broussard | .15 | .40 |
| 679 | C.J. Wilson | .15 | .40 |
| 680 | Jason Jennings | .15 | .40 |
| 681 | Gustavo Chacin | .15 | .40 |
| 682 | BJ Ryan | .15 | .40 |
| 683 | David Eckstein | .15 | .40 |
| 684 | Alex Rios | .15 | .40 |
| 685 | John McDonald | .15 | .40 |
| 686 | Rod Barajas | .15 | .40 |
| 687 | Lyle Overbay | .15 | .40 |
| 688 | Scott Rolen | .25 | .60 |
| 689 | Reed Johnson | .15 | .40 |
| 690 | Marco Scutaro | .15 | .40 |
| 691 | Lastings Milledge | .15 | .40 |
| 692 | Johnny Estrada | .15 | .40 |
| 693 | Paul Lo Duca | .15 | .40 |
| 694 | Ryan Zimmerman | .25 | .60 |
| 695 | Odalis Perez | .15 | .40 |
| 696 | Wily Mo Pena | .15 | .40 |
| 697 | Elijah Dukes | .15 | .40 |
| 698 | Aaron Boone | .15 | .40 |
| 699 | Ronnie Belliard | .15 | .40 |
| 700 | Nick Johnson | .15 | .40 |
| 701 | Randor Bierd RC | .40 | 1.00 |
| 702 | Brian Barton RC | .60 | 1.50 |
| 703 | Brian Bass (RC) | .40 | 1.00 |
| 704 | Brian Bocock RC | .40 | 1.00 |
| 705 | Gregor Blanco (RC) | .40 | 1.00 |
| 706 | Callix Crabbe (RC) | .40 | 1.00 |
| 707 | Johnny Cueto RC | .60 | 1.50 |

|  | | |
|---|---|---|
| 708 Kosuke Fukudome RC | 4.00 | 10.00 |
| 708b K.Fukudome Japanese | 40.00 | 80.00 |
| 709 Scott Kazmir SH | .25 | .60 |
| 710 Steve Holm RC | .40 | 1.00 |
| 711 Fernando Hernandez RC | .40 | 1.00 |
| 712 Elliot Johnson (RC) | .40 | 1.00 |
| 713 Masahide Kobayashi RC | .60 | 1.50 |
| 714 Hiroki Kuroda RC | .60 | 1.50 |
| 715 Blake DeWitt (RC) | 1.00 | 2.50 |
| 716 Kyle McClellan RC | .40 | 1.00 |
| 717 Evan Meek RC | .40 | 1.00 |
| 718 Denard Span (RC) | .60 | 1.50 |
| 719 Darren O'Day RC | .40 | 1.00 |
| 720 Alexei Ramirez RC | 1.50 | 4.00 |
| 721 Alex Romero RC | .60 | 1.50 |
| 722 Clete Thomas RC | .60 | 1.50 |
| 723 Matt Tolbert RC | .60 | 1.50 |
| 724 Ramon Troncoso RC | .40 | 1.00 |
| 725 Matt Tupman RC | .40 | 1.00 |
| 726 Rico Washington (RC) | .40 | 1.00 |
| 727 Randy Wells RC | .60 | 1.50 |
| 728 Wesley Wright RC | .40 | 1.00 |
| 729 Yasuhiko Yabuta RC | .60 | 1.50 |
| 730 Alex Rodriguez SH | .60 | 1.50 |
| 731 Andruw Jones SH | .15 | .40 |
| 732 C.C. Sabathia SH | .15 | .40 |
| 733 Carlos Beltran SH | .15 | .40 |
| 734 David Wright SH | .50 | 1.25 |
| 735 Derrek Lee SH | .25 | .60 |
| 736 Dustin Pedroia SH | .50 | 1.25 |
| 737 Grady Sizemore SH | .25 | .60 |
| 738 Greg Maddux SH | .50 | 1.25 |
| 739 Ichiro Suzuki SH | .60 | 1.50 |
| 740 Ivan Rodriguez SH | .25 | .60 |
| 741 Jake Peavy SH | .25 | .60 |
| 742 Jimmy Rollins SH | .25 | .60 |
| 743 Johan Santana SH | .25 | .60 |
| 744 Josh Beckett SH | .25 | .60 |
| 745 Kevin Youkilis SH | .25 | .60 |
| 746 Matt Holliday SH | .25 | .60 |
| 747 Mike Lowell SH | .15 | .40 |
| 748 Ryan Braun SH | .50 | 1.25 |
| 749 Torii Hunter SH | .15 | .40 |
| 750 Alex Rodriguez SH | .60 | 1.50 |
| 751 Torii Hunter CL | .15 | .40 |
| 752 Miguel Tejada CL | .15 | .40 |
| 753 Huston Street CL | .15 | .40 |
| 754 Scott Rolen CL | .25 | .60 |
| 755 Tom Glavine CL | .25 | .60 |
| 756 Ryan Braun CL | .50 | 1.25 |
| 757 Troy Glaus CL | .25 | .60 |
| 758 Carlos Zambrano CL | .15 | .40 |
| 759 Carl Crawford CL | .15 | .40 |
| 760 Dan Haren CL | .15 | .40 |
| 761 Andruw Jones CL | .15 | .40 |
| 762 Barry Zito CL | .15 | .40 |
| 763 Victor Martinez CL | .15 | .40 |
| 764 Erik Bedard CL | .15 | .40 |
| 765 Josh Willingham CL | .15 | .40 |
| 766 Johan Santana CL | .25 | .60 |
| 767 Dmitri Young CL | .15 | .40 |
| 768 Brian Roberts CL | .25 | .60 |
| 769 Jim Edmonds CL | .25 | .60 |
| 770 Jimmy Rollins CL | .25 | .60 |
| 771 Jason Bay CL | .25 | .60 |
| 772 Josh Hamilton CL | .50 | 1.25 |
| 773 Josh Beckett CL | .25 | .60 |
| 774 Aaron Harang CL | .15 | .40 |
| 775 Troy Tulowitzki CL | .25 | .60 |
| 776 Jose Guillen CL | .15 | .40 |
| 777 Miguel Cabrera CL | .25 | .60 |
| 778 Joe Mauer CL | .40 | 1.00 |
| 779 Nick Swisher CL | .15 | .40 |
| 780 Derek Jeter CL | 1.00 | 2.50 |
| 781 Brandon Webb SH | .25 | .60 |
| 782 Brian Roberts SH | .15 | .40 |
| 783 C.C. Sabathia SH | .15 | .40 |
| 784 Carl Crawford SH | .15 | .40 |
| 785 Curtis Granderson SH | .15 | .40 |
| 786 David Ortiz SH | .25 | .60 |
| 787 Ichiro Suzuki SH | .60 | 1.50 |
| 788 Jake Peavy SH | .25 | .60 |
| 789 Jimmy Rollins SH | .25 | .60 |
| 790 Joe Borowski SH | .15 | .40 |
| 791 Johan Santana SH | .25 | .60 |
| 792 John Lackey SH | .15 | .40 |
| 793 Jose Reyes SH | .25 | .60 |
| 794 Jose Valverde SH | .15 | .40 |
| 795 Josh Beckett SH | .25 | .60 |
| 796 Juan Pierre SH | .15 | .40 |
| 797 Magglio Ordonez SH | .25 | .60 |
| 798 Matt Holliday SH | .25 | .60 |
| 799 Prince Fielder SH | .40 | 1.00 |

## 2009 Upper Deck

| | | |
|---|---|---|
| COMP.SER 1 SET w/o #0 (500) | 40.00 | 80.00 |
| COMP.SER 2 SET w/SP RC (506) | 75.00 | 150.00 |
| COMP.SER 2 SET w/o SP RC (500) | 50.00 | 100.00 |
| COMMON CARD (1-1000) | .15 | .40 |
| COMMON RC (1-1000) | .40 | 1.00 |
| COMMON RC (1001-1006) | 1.25 | 3.00 |
| 0 Joe DiMaggio SP | 40.00 | 80.00 |
| 1 Randy Johnson | .40 | 1.00 |
| 2 Conor Jackson | .15 | .40 |
| 3 Brandon Webb | .25 | .60 |
| 4 Dan Haren | .15 | .40 |
| 5 Orlando Hudson | .15 | .40 |
| 6 Stephen Drew | .15 | .40 |
| 7 Mark Reynolds | .15 | .40 |
| 8 Eric Byrnes | .15 | .40 |
| 9 Justin Upton | .25 | .60 |
| 10 Chris B. Young | .15 | .40 |
| 11 Max Scherzer | .25 | .60 |
| 12 Alex Romero | .15 | .40 |
| 13 Chad Tracy | .15 | .40 |
| 14 Brandon Lyon | .15 | .40 |
| 15 Adam Dunn | .25 | .60 |
| 16 David Eckstein | .15 | .40 |
| 17 Jair Jurrjens | .25 | .60 |
| 18 Mike Hampton | .15 | .40 |
| 19 Brandon Jones | .15 | .40 |
| 20 Tom Glavine | .25 | .60 |
| 21 John Smoltz | .40 | 1.00 |
| 22 Chipper Jones | .40 | 1.00 |
| 23 Yunel Escobar | .15 | .40 |
| 24 Kelly Johnson | .15 | .40 |
| 25 Brian McCann | .25 | .60 |
| 26 Jeff Francoeur | .25 | .60 |
| 27 Tim Hudson | .15 | .40 |
| 28 Casey Kotchman | .15 | .40 |
| 29 Nick Markakis | .25 | .60 |
| 30 Brian Roberts | .15 | .40 |
| 31 Jeremy Guthrie | .15 | .40 |
| 32 Ramon Hernandez | .15 | .40 |
| 33 Adam Jones | .25 | .60 |
| 34 Luke Scott | .15 | .40 |
| 35 Aubrey Huff | .15 | .40 |
| 36 Daniel Cabrera | .15 | .40 |
| 37 George Sherrill | .15 | .40 |
| 38 Melvin Mora | .15 | .40 |
| 39 Jay Payton | .15 | .40 |
| 40 Mark Kotsay | .15 | .40 |
| 41 David Ortiz | .25 | .60 |
| 42 Jacoby Ellsbury | .40 | 1.00 |
| 43 Coco Crisp | .15 | .40 |
| 44 J.D. Drew | .15 | .40 |
| 45 Daisuke Matsuzaka | .60 | 1.50 |
| 46 Josh Beckett | .25 | .60 |
| 47 Curt Schilling | .25 | .60 |
| 48 Clay Buchholz | .25 | .60 |

| | | |
|---|---|---|
| 49 Dustin Pedroia | .50 | 1.25 |
| 50 Julio Lugo | .15 | .40 |
| 51 Mike Lowell | .15 | .40 |
| 52 Jonathan Papelbon | .25 | .60 |
| 53 Jason Varitek | .25 | .60 |
| 54 Hideki Okajima | .15 | .40 |
| 55 Jon Lester | .25 | .60 |
| 56 Tim Wakefield | .15 | .40 |
| 57 Kevin Youkilis | .25 | .60 |
| 58 Jason Bay | .25 | .60 |
| 59 Justin Masterson | .25 | .60 |
| 60 Jeff Samardzija | .25 | .60 |
| 61 Alfonso Soriano | .25 | .60 |
| 62 Derrek Lee | .25 | .60 |
| 63 Aramis Ramirez | .15 | .40 |
| 64 Kerry Wood | .15 | .40 |
| 65 Jim Edmonds | .25 | .60 |
| 66 Kosuke Fukudome | .40 | 1.00 |
| 67 Geovany Soto | .25 | .60 |
| 68 Ted Lilly | .15 | .40 |
| 69 Carlos Zambrano | .15 | .40 |
| 70 Ryan Theriot | .15 | .40 |
| 71 Mark DeRosa | .15 | .40 |
| 72 Ronny Cedeno | .15 | .40 |
| 73 Ryan Dempster | .15 | .40 |
| 74 Jon Lieber | .15 | .40 |
| 75 Rich Hill | .15 | .40 |
| 76 Rich Harden | .15 | .40 |
| 77 Alexei Ramirez | .25 | .60 |
| 78 Nick Swisher | .15 | .40 |
| 79 Carlos Quentin | .15 | .40 |
| 80 Jermaine Dye | .15 | .40 |
| 81 Paul Konerko | .15 | .40 |
| 82 Orlando Cabrera | .15 | .40 |
| 83 Joe Crede | .15 | .40 |
| 84 Jim Thome | .25 | .60 |
| 85 Gavin Floyd | .15 | .40 |
| 86 Javier Vazquez | .15 | .40 |
| 87 Mark Buehrle | .15 | .40 |
| 88 Bobby Jenks | .15 | .40 |
| 89 Brian Anderson | .15 | .40 |
| 90 A.J. Pierzynski | .15 | .40 |
| 91 Jose Contreras | .15 | .40 |
| 92 Juan Uribe | .15 | .40 |
| 93a Ken Griffey Jr. | .60 | 1.50 |
| 93b K.Griffey Jr. SEA | 50.00 | 100.00 |
| 94 Chris Dickerson | .15 | .40 |
| 95 Brandon Phillips | .15 | .40 |
| 96 Aaron Harang | .15 | .40 |
| 97 Bronson Arroyo | .15 | .40 |
| 98 Edinson Volquez | .15 | .40 |
| 99 Johnny Cueto | .15 | .40 |
| 100 Edwin Encarnacion | .15 | .40 |
| 101 Jeff Keppinger | .15 | .40 |
| 102 Joey Votto | .25 | .60 |
| 103 Jay Bruce | .40 | 1.00 |
| 104 Ryan Freel | .15 | .40 |
| 105 Travis Hafner | .15 | .40 |
| 106 Victor Martinez | .15 | .40 |
| 107 Grady Sizemore | .25 | .60 |
| 108 Cliff Lee | .25 | .60 |
| 109 Ryan Garko | .15 | .40 |
| 110 Jhonny Peralta | .15 | .40 |
| 111 Franklin Gutierrez | .15 | .40 |
| 112 Fausto Carmona | .15 | .40 |
| 113 Jeff Baker | .15 | .40 |
| 114 Troy Tulowitzki | .25 | .60 |
| 115 Matt Holliday | .25 | .60 |
| 116 Todd Helton | .25 | .60 |
| 117 Ubaldo Jimenez | .15 | .40 |
| 118 Brian Fuentes | .15 | .40 |
| 119 Willy Taveras | .15 | .40 |
| 120 Aaron Cook | .15 | .40 |
| 121 Jason Grilli | .15 | .40 |
| 122 Garrett Atkins | .15 | .40 |
| 123 Jeff Francis | .15 | .40 |
| 124 Ryan Spilborghs | .15 | .40 |
| 125 Armando Galarraga | .15 | .40 |
| 126 Miguel Cabrera | .25 | .60 |
| 127 Placido Polanco | .15 | .40 |
| 128 Edgar Renteria | .15 | .40 |

|  |  | | |
|---|---|---|---|
| 129 | Carlos Guillen | .15 | .40 |
| 130 | Gary Sheffield | .15 | .40 |
| 131 | Curtis Granderson | .40 | 1.00 |
| 132 | Marcus Thames | .15 | .40 |
| 133 | Magglio Ordonez | .25 | .60 |
| 134 | Jeremy Bonderman | .15 | .40 |
| 135 | Dontrelle Willis | .15 | .40 |
| 136 | Kenny Rogers | .15 | .40 |
| 137 | Justin Verlander | .25 | .60 |
| 138 | Nate Robertson | .15 | .40 |
| 139 | Todd Jones | .15 | .40 |
| 140 | Joel Zumaya | .15 | .40 |
| 141 | Hanley Ramirez | .40 | 1.00 |
| 142 | Jeremy Hermida | .15 | .40 |
| 143 | Mike Jacobs | .15 | .40 |
| 144 | Andrew Miller | .15 | .40 |
| 145 | Josh Willingham | .15 | .40 |
| 146 | Luis Gonzalez | .15 | .40 |
| 147 | Dan Uggla | .25 | .60 |
| 148 | Scott Olsen | .15 | .40 |
| 149 | Josh Johnson | .15 | .40 |
| 150 | Darin Erstad | .15 | .40 |
| 151 | Hunter Pence | .25 | .60 |
| 152 | Roy Oswalt | .25 | .60 |
| 153 | Lance Berkman | .25 | .60 |
| 154 | Carlos Lee | .15 | .40 |
| 155 | Michael Bourn | .15 | .40 |
| 156 | Kazuo Matsui | .15 | .40 |
| 157 | Miguel Tejada | .25 | .60 |
| 158 | Ty Wigginton | .15 | .40 |
| 159 | Jose Valverde | .15 | .40 |
| 160 | J.R. Towles | .15 | .40 |
| 161 | Brandon Backe | .15 | .40 |
| 162 | Randy Wolf | .15 | .40 |
| 163 | Mike Aviles | .15 | .40 |
| 164 | Brian Bannister | .15 | .40 |
| 165 | Zack Greinke | .25 | .60 |
| 166 | Gil Meche | .15 | .40 |
| 167 | Alex Gordon | .25 | .60 |
| 168 | Tony Pena | .15 | .40 |
| 169 | Luke Hochevar | .15 | .40 |
| 170 | Mark Grudzielanek | .15 | .40 |
| 171 | Jose Guillen | .15 | .40 |
| 172 | Billy Butler | .15 | .40 |
| 173 | David DeJesus | .15 | .40 |
| 174 | Joey Gathright | .15 | .40 |
| 175 | Mark Teahen | .15 | .40 |
| 176 | Joakim Soria | .15 | .40 |
| 177 | Mark Teixeira | .40 | 1.00 |
| 178 | Vladimir Guerrero | .40 | 1.00 |
| 179 | Torii Hunter | .15 | .40 |
| 180 | Jered Weaver | .15 | .40 |
| 181 | Chone Figgins | .15 | .40 |
| 182 | Francisco Rodriguez | .25 | .60 |
| 183 | Garret Anderson | .15 | .40 |
| 184 | Howie Kendrick | .15 | .40 |
| 185 | John Lackey | .15 | .40 |
| 186 | Ervin Santana | .15 | .40 |
| 187 | Joe Saunders | .15 | .40 |
| 188 | Gary Matthews | .15 | .40 |
| 189 | Jon Garland | .15 | .40 |
| 190 | Nick Adenhart | .15 | .40 |
| 191 | Manny Ramirez | .40 | 1.00 |
| 192 | Casey Blake | .15 | .40 |
| 193 | Chad Billingsley | .15 | .40 |
| 194 | Russell Martin | .25 | .60 |
| 195 | Matt Kemp | .40 | 1.00 |
| 196 | James Loney | .25 | .60 |
| 197 | Jeff Kent | .15 | .40 |
| 198 | Nomar Garciaparra | .25 | .60 |
| 199 | Rafael Furcal | .15 | .40 |
| 200 | Andruw Jones | .15 | .40 |
| 201 | Andre Ethier | .25 | .60 |
| 202 | Takashi Saito | .15 | .40 |
| 203 | Brad Penny | .15 | .40 |
| 204 | Hiroki Kuroda | .15 | .40 |
| 205 | Jonathan Broxton | .15 | .40 |
| 206 | Chin-Lung Hu | .15 | .40 |
| 207 | Juan Pierre | .15 | .40 |
| 208 | Blake DeWitt | .25 | .60 |
| 209 | Derek Lowe | .15 | .40 |
| 210 | Clayton Kershaw | .40 | 1.00 |
| 211 | Greg Maddux | .50 | 1.25 |
| 212 | CC Sabathia | .25 | .60 |
| 213 | Yovani Gallardo | .15 | .40 |
| 214 | Ryan Braun | .50 | 1.25 |
| 215 | Prince Fielder | .40 | 1.00 |
| 216 | Corey Hart | .15 | .40 |
| 217 | Bill Hall | .15 | .40 |
| 218 | Rickie Weeks | .15 | .40 |
| 219 | Mike Cameron | .15 | .40 |
| 220 | Ben Sheets | .15 | .40 |
| 221 | Jason Kendall | .15 | .40 |
| 222 | J.J. Hardy | .15 | .40 |
| 223 | Jeff Suppan | .15 | .40 |
| 224 | Ray Durham | .15 | .40 |
| 225 | Denard Span | .25 | .60 |
| 226 | Carlos Gomez | .15 | .40 |
| 227 | Joe Mauer | .40 | 1.00 |
| 228 | Justin Morneau | .25 | .60 |
| 229 | Michael Cuddyer | .15 | .40 |
| 230 | Joe Nathan | .15 | .40 |
| 231 | Kevin Slowey | .15 | .40 |
| 232 | Delmon Young | .25 | .60 |
| 233 | Jason Kubel | .15 | .40 |
| 234 | Craig Monroe | .15 | .40 |
| 235 | Livan Hernandez | .15 | .40 |
| 236 | Francisco Liriano | .15 | .40 |
| 237 | Pat Neshek | .25 | .60 |
| 238 | Boof Bonser | .15 | .40 |
| 239 | Nick Blackburn | .15 | .40 |
| 240 | Daniel Murphy RC | 1.00 | 2.50 |
| 241 | Nick Evans | .15 | .40 |
| 242 | Jose Reyes | .40 | 1.00 |
| 243 | David Wright | .50 | 1.25 |
| 244 | Carlos Delgado | .15 | .40 |
| 245 | Luis Castillo | .15 | .40 |
| 246 | Ryan Church | .15 | .40 |
| 247 | Carlos Beltran | .15 | .40 |
| 248 | Moises Alou | .15 | .40 |
| 249 | Pedro Martinez | .25 | .60 |
| 250 | Johan Santana | .15 | .40 |
| 251 | John Maine | .15 | .40 |
| 252 | Endy Chavez | .15 | .40 |
| 253 | Oliver Perez | .15 | .40 |
| 254 | Brian Schneider | .15 | .40 |
| 255 | Fernando Tatis | .15 | .40 |
| 256 | Mike Pelfrey | .15 | .40 |
| 257 | Billy Wagner | .15 | .40 |
| 258 | Ramon Castro | .15 | .40 |
| 259 | Ivan Rodriguez | .25 | .60 |
| 260 | Alex Rodriguez | .60 | 1.50 |
| 261 | Derek Jeter | 1.00 | 2.50 |
| 262 | Robinson Cano | .25 | .60 |
| 263 | Jason Giambi | .15 | .40 |
| 264 | Bobby Abreu | .25 | .60 |
| 265 | Johnny Damon | .25 | .60 |
| 266 | Melky Cabrera | .15 | .40 |
| 267 | Hideki Matsui | .40 | 1.00 |
| 268 | Jorge Posada | .25 | .60 |
| 269 | Joba Chamberlain | .50 | 1.25 |
| 270 | Ian Kennedy | .25 | .60 |
| 271 | Mike Mussina | .25 | .60 |
| 272 | Andy Pettitte | .25 | .60 |
| 273 | Mariano Rivera | .25 | .60 |
| 274 | Chien-Ming Wang | .40 | 1.00 |
| 275 | Phil Hughes | .25 | .60 |
| 276 | Xavier Nady | .15 | .40 |
| 277 | Richie Sexson | .15 | .40 |
| 278 | Brad Ziegler | .15 | .40 |
| 279 | Justin Duchscherer | .15 | .40 |
| 280 | Eric Chavez | .15 | .40 |
| 281 | Bobby Crosby | .15 | .40 |
| 282 | Mark Ellis | .15 | .40 |
| 283 | Daric Barton | .15 | .40 |
| 284 | Frank Thomas | .40 | 1.00 |
| 285 | Emil Brown | .15 | .40 |
| 286 | Huston Street | .15 | .40 |
| 287 | Jack Cust | .15 | .40 |
| 288 | Kurt Suzuki | .15 | .40 |
| 289 | Joe Blanton | .15 | .40 |
| 290 | Ryan Howard | .50 | 1.25 |
| 291 | Chase Utley | .40 | 1.00 |
| 292 | Jimmy Rollins | .25 | .60 |
| 293 | Pedro Feliz | .15 | .40 |
| 294 | Pat Burrell | .25 | .60 |
| 295 | Geoff Jenkins | .15 | .40 |
| 296 | Shane Victorino | .15 | .40 |
| 297 | Brett Myers | .15 | .40 |
| 298 | Brad Lidge | .15 | .40 |
| 299 | Cole Hamels | .40 | 1.00 |
| 300 | Jamie Moyer | .15 | .40 |
| 301 | Adam Eaton | .15 | .40 |
| 302 | Matt Stairs | .15 | .40 |
| 303 | Nate McLouth | .15 | .40 |
| 304 | Ian Snell | .15 | .40 |
| 305 | Matt Capps | .15 | .40 |
| 306 | Freddy Sanchez | .15 | .40 |
| 307 | Ryan Doumit | .15 | .40 |
| 308 | Adam LaRoche | .15 | .40 |
| 309 | Jack Wilson | .15 | .40 |
| 310 | Tom Gorzelanny | .15 | .40 |
| 311 | Jody Gerut | .15 | .40 |
| 312 | Jake Peavy | .25 | .60 |
| 313 | Chris Young | .15 | .40 |
| 314 | Trevor Hoffman | .15 | .40 |
| 315 | Adrian Gonzalez | .25 | .60 |
| 316 | Chase Headley | .15 | .40 |
| 317 | Khalil Greene | .15 | .40 |
| 318 | Kevin Kouzmanoff | .15 | .40 |
| 319 | Brian Giles | .15 | .40 |
| 320 | Josh Bard | .15 | .40 |
| 321 | Scott Hairston | .15 | .40 |
| 322 | Barry Zito | .15 | .40 |
| 323 | Tim Lincecum | .50 | 1.25 |
| 324 | Matt Cain | .15 | .40 |
| 325 | Brian Wilson | .15 | .40 |
| 326 | Aaron Rowand | .15 | .40 |
| 327 | Randy Winn | .15 | .40 |
| 328 | Omar Vizquel | .15 | .40 |
| 329 | Bengie Molina | .15 | .40 |
| 330 | Fred Lewis | .15 | .40 |
| 331 | Erik Bedard | .15 | .40 |
| 332 | Felix Hernandez | .25 | .60 |
| 333 | Ichiro Suzuki | .60 | 1.50 |
| 334 | J.J. Putz | .15 | .40 |
| 335 | Raul Ibanez | .25 | .60 |
| 336 | Adrian Beltre | .15 | .40 |
| 337 | Jose Vidro | .15 | .40 |
| 338 | Jeff Clement | .15 | .40 |
| 339 | Kenji Johjima | .25 | .60 |
| 340 | Wladimir Balentien | .15 | .40 |
| 341 | Jose Lopez | .15 | .40 |
| 342 | Kyle Lohse | .15 | .40 |
| 343 | Albert Pujols | 1.00 | 2.50 |
| 344 | Troy Glaus | .15 | .40 |
| 345 | Chris Carpenter | .25 | .60 |
| 346 | Adam Kennedy | .15 | .40 |
| 347 | Rick Ankiel | .25 | .60 |
| 348 | Adam Wainwright | .25 | .60 |
| 349 | Jason Isringhausen | .15 | .40 |
| 350 | Chris Duncan | .15 | .40 |
| 351 | Skip Schumaker | .15 | .40 |
| 352 | Mark Mulder | .15 | .40 |
| 353 | Todd Wellemeyer | .15 | .40 |
| 354 | Cesar Izturis | .15 | .40 |
| 355 | Ryan Ludwick | .25 | .60 |
| 356 | Yadier Molina | .25 | .60 |
| 357 | Braden Looper | .15 | .40 |
| 358 | B.J. Upton | .25 | .60 |
| 359 | Carl Crawford | .25 | .60 |
| 360 | Evan Longoria | .60 | 1.50 |
| 361 | James Shields | .15 | .40 |
| 362 | Scott Kazmir | .25 | .60 |
| 363 | Carlos Pena | .25 | .60 |
| 364 | Akinori Iwamura | .15 | .40 |
| 365 | Jonny Gomes | .15 | .40 |
| 366 | Cliff Floyd | .15 | .40 |
| 367 | Troy Percival | .15 | .40 |
| 368 | Edwin Jackson | .15 | .40 |
| 369 | Matt Garza | .15 | .40 |
| 370 | Eric Hinske | .15 | .40 |
| 371 | Rocco Baldelli | .15 | .40 |

|  |  | | |
|---|---|---|---|
| ☐ 372 | Chris Davis | .15 | .40 |
| ☐ 373 | Marlon Byrd | .15 | .40 |
| ☐ 374 | Michael Young | .25 | .60 |
| ☐ 375 | Ian Kinsler | .25 | .60 |
| ☐ 376 | Josh Hamilton | .40 | 1.00 |
| ☐ 377 | Hank Blalock | .15 | .40 |
| ☐ 378 | Milton Bradley | .15 | .40 |
| ☐ 379 | Kevin Millwood | .15 | .40 |
| ☐ 380 | Vicente Padilla | .15 | .40 |
| ☐ 381 | Jarrod Saltalamacchia | .15 | .40 |
| ☐ 382 | Jesse Litsch | .15 | .40 |
| ☐ 383 | Roy Halladay | .25 | .60 |
| ☐ 384 | A.J. Burnett | .25 | .60 |
| ☐ 385 | Dustin McGowan | .15 | .40 |
| ☐ 386 | Scott Rolen | .40 | 1.00 |
| ☐ 387 | Alex Rios | .15 | .40 |
| ☐ 388 | Vernon Wells | .15 | .40 |
| ☐ 389 | Shannon Stewart | .15 | .40 |
| ☐ 390 | B.J. Ryan | .15 | .40 |
| ☐ 391 | Lyle Overbay | .15 | .40 |
| ☐ 392 | Elijah Dukes | .15 | .40 |
| ☐ 393 | Lastings Milledge | .15 | .40 |
| ☐ 394 | Chad Cordero | .15 | .40 |
| ☐ 395 | Ryan Zimmerman | .25 | .60 |
| ☐ 396 | Austin Kearns | .15 | .40 |
| ☐ 397 | Wily Mo Pena | .15 | .40 |
| ☐ 398 | Ronnie Belliard | .15 | .40 |
| ☐ 399 | Cristian Guzman | .15 | .40 |
| ☐ 400 | Jesus Flores | .15 | .40 |
| ☐ 401a | David Price RC | 1.25 | 3.00 |
| ☐ 401b | David Price White Uni SP | 50.00 | 100.00 |
| ☐ 402 | Matt Antonelli RC | .60 | 1.50 |
| ☐ 403 | Jonathon Niese RC | .60 | 1.50 |
| ☐ 404 | Phil Coke RC | .60 | 1.50 |
| ☐ 405 | Jason Pridie (RC) | .40 | 1.00 |
| ☐ 406 | Mark Saccomanno RC | .40 | 1.00 |
| ☐ 407 | Freddy Sandoval (RC) | .40 | 1.00 |
| ☐ 408 | Travis Snider RC | 1.00 | 2.50 |
| ☐ 409 | Matt Tuiasosopo (RC) | .40 | 1.00 |
| ☐ 410 | Will Venable RC | .40 | 1.00 |
| ☐ 411 | Brad Nelson RC | .40 | 1.00 |
| ☐ 412 | Aaron Cunningham RC | .40 | 1.00 |
| ☐ 413 | Wilkin Castillo RC | .60 | 1.50 |
| ☐ 414 | Robert Parnell RC | .60 | 1.50 |
| ☐ 415 | Connor Gillaspie RC | 1.00 | 2.50 |
| ☐ 416 | Dexter Fowler (RC) | .60 | 1.50 |
| ☐ 417 | George Kottaras (RC) | .40 | 1.00 |
| ☐ 418 | Josh Roenicke RC | .40 | 1.00 |
| ☐ 419 | Luis Valbuena RC | .60 | 1.50 |
| ☐ 420 | Casey McGehee (RC) | .40 | 1.00 |
| ☐ 421 | Mat Gamel RC | 1.00 | 2.50 |
| ☐ 422 | Greg Golson (RC) | .40 | 1.00 |
| ☐ 423 | Alfredo Aceves RC | .60 | 1.50 |
| ☐ 424 | Michael Bowden (RC) | .60 | 1.50 |
| ☐ 425 | Kila Kaaihue (RC) | .60 | 1.50 |
| ☐ 426 | Josh Geer (RC) | .40 | 1.00 |
| ☐ 427 | James Parr (RC) | .40 | 1.00 |
| ☐ 428 | Chris Lambert (RC) | .40 | 1.00 |
| ☐ 429 | Fernando Perez (RC) | .40 | 1.00 |
| ☐ 430 | Josh Whitesell RC | .60 | 1.50 |
| ☐ 431 | Pedroia/Dice-K/Beckett TL | .60 | 1.50 |
| ☐ 432 | Howard/Hamels/Rollins TL | .50 | 1.25 |
| ☐ 433 | Reyes/Wright/Delgado TL | .50 | 1.25 |
| ☐ 434 | Rodriguez/Jeter/Mussina TL | 1.00 | 2.50 |
| ☐ 435 | Carlos Quentin/Gavin Floyd /Javier Vazquez TL | .15 | .40 |
| ☐ 436 | Ludwick/Pujols/Wellem TL | 1.00 | 2.50 |
| ☐ 437 | Miguel Cabrera/Curtis Granderson /Justin Verlander TL | .40 | 1.00 |
| ☐ 438 | Adrian Gonzalez/Jake Peavy/Brian Giles TL | .25 | .60 |
| ☐ 439 | Braun/Fielder/Sheets TL | .50 | 1.25 |
| ☐ 440 | Cliff Lee/Grady Sizemore/Jhonny Peralta TL | .25 | .60 |
| ☐ 441 | Josh Hamilton/Ian Kinsler/Vicente Padilla TL | .40 | 1.00 |
| ☐ 442 | Jorge Cantu/Hanley Ramirez /Ricky Nolasco TL | .40 | 1.00 |
| ☐ 443 | Carlos Pena/Akinori Iwamura/B.J. Upton TL | .25 | .60 |
| ☐ 444 | Jack Cust/Dana Eveland/Kurt Suzuki TL | .15 | .40 |
| ☐ 445 | Alfonso Soriano/Ryan Dempster /Aramis Ramirez TL | .25 | .60 |
| ☐ 446 | Lance Berkman/Roy Oswalt /Miguel Tejada TL | .25 | .60 |
| ☐ 447 | Matt Holliday/Aaron Cook /Willy Taveras TL | .25 | .60 |
| ☐ 448 | Nate McLouth /Adam LaRoche /Paul Maholm TL | .15 | .40 |
| ☐ 449 | Brian Roberts/Aubrey Huff /Jeremy Guthrie TL | .15 | .40 |
| ☐ 450 | Justin Morneau/Joe Mauer /Carlos Gomez TL | .40 | 1.00 |
| ☐ 451 | Ibanez/Ichiro/King Felix TL | .60 | 1.50 |
| ☐ 452 | Chipper Jones/Jair Jurrjens /Brian McCann TL | .40 | 1.00 |
| ☐ 453 | Brandon Webb/Dan Haren /Stephen Drew TL | .25 | .60 |
| ☐ 454 | Lincecum/Winn/Molina TL | .50 | 1.25 |
| ☐ 455 | Roy Halladay/A.J. Burnett/Alex Rios TL | .25 | .60 |
| ☐ 456 | Edinson Volquez/Brandon Phillips /Edwin Encarnacion TL | .15 | .40 |
| ☐ 457 | Chad Billingsley/Matt Kemp /James Loney TL | .40 | 1.00 |
| ☐ 458 | Ervin Santana/Vladimir Guerrero /Francisco Rodriguez TL | .40 | 1.00 |
| ☐ 459 | Zack Greinke/Gil Meche/David DeJesus TL | .25 | .60 |
| ☐ 460 | Tim Redding/Cristian Guzman /Lastings Milledge TL | .15 | .40 |
| ☐ 461 | Carlos Zambrano HL | .15 | .40 |
| ☐ 462 | Jon Lester HL | .25 | .60 |
| ☐ 463 | Jim Thome HL | .25 | .60 |
| ☐ 464 | Ken Griffey Jr. HL | .60 | 1.50 |
| ☐ 465 | Manny Ramirez HL | .40 | 1.00 |
| ☐ 466 | Derek Jeter HL | 1.00 | 2.50 |
| ☐ 467 | Josh Hamilton HL | .40 | 1.00 |
| ☐ 468 | Francisco Rodriguez HL | .25 | .60 |
| ☐ 469 | Alex Rodriguez HL | .60 | 1.50 |
| ☐ 470 | J.D. Drew HL | .15 | .40 |
| ☐ 471 | David Wright CL | .50 | 1.25 |
| ☐ 472 | Chase Utley CL | .40 | 1.00 |
| ☐ 473 | Chipper Jones CL | .40 | 1.00 |
| ☐ 474 | Cristian Guzman CL | .15 | .40 |
| ☐ 475 | Hanley Ramirez CL | .40 | 1.00 |
| ☐ 476 | CC Sabathia CL | .25 | .60 |
| ☐ 477 | Lance Berkman CL | .25 | .60 |
| ☐ 478 | Alfonso Soriano CL | .25 | .60 |
| ☐ 479 | Albert Pujols CL | 1.00 | 2.50 |
| ☐ 480 | Nate McLouth CL | .15 | .40 |
| ☐ 481 | Brandon Phillips CL | .15 | .40 |
| ☐ 482 | Adrian Gonzalez CL | .25 | .60 |
| ☐ 483 | Brandon Webb CL | .25 | .60 |
| ☐ 484 | Manny Ramirez CL | .40 | 1.00 |
| ☐ 485 | Tim Lincecum CL | .50 | 1.25 |
| ☐ 486 | Matt Holliday CL | .25 | .60 |
| ☐ 487 | Dustin Pedroia CL | .50 | 1.25 |
| ☐ 488 | Alex Rodriguez CL | .50 | 1.50 |
| ☐ 489 | Evan Longoria CL | .60 | 1.50 |
| ☐ 490 | Roy Halladay CL | .25 | .60 |
| ☐ 491 | Nick Markakis CL | .25 | .60 |
| ☐ 492 | Grady Sizemore CL | .25 | .60 |
| ☐ 493 | Carlos Quentin CL | .15 | .40 |
| ☐ 494 | Joakim Soria CL | .15 | .40 |
| ☐ 495 | Miguel Cabrera CL | .25 | .60 |
| ☐ 496 | Joe Mauer CL | .40 | 1.00 |
| ☐ 497 | Francisco Rodriguez CL | .25 | .60 |
| ☐ 498 | Jack Cust CL | .15 | .40 |
| ☐ 499 | Ichiro Suzuki CL | .60 | 1.50 |
| ☐ 500 | Josh Hamilton CL | .40 | 1.00 |
| ☐ 501 | Brandon Webb | .25 | .60 |
| ☐ 502 | Miguel Montero | .15 | .40 |
| ☐ 503 | Tony Pena | .15 | .40 |
| ☐ 504 | Jon Rauch | .15 | .40 |
| ☐ 505 | Augie Ojeda | .15 | .40 |
| ☐ 506 | Yusmeiro Petit | .15 | .40 |
| ☐ 507 | Chris Snyder | .15 | .40 |
| ☐ 508 | Chris B. Young | .15 | .40 |
| ☐ 509 | Doug Slaten | .15 | .40 |
| ☐ 510 | Tony Clark | .15 | .40 |
| ☐ 511 | Justin Upton | .25 | .60 |
| ☐ 512 | Chad Qualls | .15 | .40 |
| ☐ 513 | Doug Davis | .15 | .40 |
| ☐ 514 | Eric Byrnes | .15 | .40 |
| ☐ 515 | Conor Jackson | .15 | .40 |
| ☐ 516 | Mike Gonzalez | .15 | .40 |
| ☐ 517 | Josh Anderson | .15 | .40 |
| ☐ 518 | Tom Glavine | .25 | .60 |
| ☐ 519 | Clint Sammons | .15 | .40 |
| ☐ 520 | Martin Prado | .15 | .40 |
| ☐ 521 | Jorge Campillo | .15 | .40 |
| ☐ 522 | Omar Infante | .15 | .40 |
| ☐ 523 | Javier Vazquez | .15 | .40 |
| ☐ 524 | Jo Jo Reyes | .15 | .40 |
| ☐ 525 | Gregor Blanco | .15 | .40 |
| ☐ 526 | Rafael Soriano | .15 | .40 |
| ☐ 527 | Manny Acosta | .15 | .40 |
| ☐ 528 | Chipper Jones | .40 | 1.00 |
| ☐ 529 | Buddy Carlyle | .15 | .40 |
| ☐ 530 | Radhames Liz | .15 | .40 |
| ☐ 531 | Scott Moore | .15 | .40 |
| ☐ 532 | Jim Johnson | .15 | .40 |
| ☐ 533 | Oscar Salazar | .15 | .40 |
| ☐ 534 | Nick Markakis | .25 | .60 |
| ☐ 535 | Brian Roberts | .15 | .40 |
| ☐ 536 | Jeremy Guthrie | .15 | .40 |
| ☐ 537 | Adam Jones | .25 | .60 |
| ☐ 538 | Chris Ray | .15 | .40 |
| ☐ 539 | Aubrey Huff | .15 | .40 |
| ☐ 540 | Ty Wigginton | .15 | .40 |
| ☐ 541 | Dennis Sarfate | .15 | .40 |
| ☐ 542 | Melvin Mora | .15 | .40 |
| ☐ 543 | Chris Waters | .15 | .40 |
| ☐ 544 | John Smoltz | .40 | 1.00 |
| ☐ 545 | Brad Penny | .15 | .40 |
| ☐ 546 | Josh Bard | .15 | .40 |
| ☐ 547 | Takashi Saito | .15 | .40 |
| ☐ 548 | Jacoby Ellsbury | .40 | 1.00 |
| ☐ 549 | Jeff Bailey | .15 | .40 |
| ☐ 550 | Ramon Ramirez | .15 | .40 |
| ☐ 551 | Daisuke Matsuzaka | .60 | 1.50 |
| ☐ 552 | Josh Beckett | .25 | .60 |
| ☐ 553 | Jed Lowrie | .25 | .60 |
| ☐ 554 | Dustin Pedroia | .50 | 1.25 |
| ☐ 555 | David Ortiz | .25 | .60 |
| ☐ 556 | Jonathan Van Every | .15 | .40 |
| ☐ 557 | Jonathan Papelbon | .25 | .60 |
| ☐ 558 | Manny Delcarmen | .15 | .40 |
| ☐ 559 | Hideki Okajima | .15 | .40 |
| ☐ 560 | Jon Lester | .25 | .60 |
| ☐ 561 | Javier Lopez | .15 | .40 |
| ☐ 562 | Kevin Youkilis | .25 | .60 |
| ☐ 563 | Jason Varitek | .25 | .60 |
| ☐ 564 | Milton Bradley | .15 | .40 |
| ☐ 565 | Mike Fontenot | .15 | .40 |
| ☐ 566 | Micah Hoffpauir | .15 | .40 |
| ☐ 567 | Sean Marshall | .15 | .40 |
| ☐ 568 | Alfonso Soriano | .25 | .60 |
| ☐ 569 | Neal Cotts | .15 | .40 |
| ☐ 570 | Kosuke Fukudome | .40 | 1.00 |
| ☐ 571 | Reed Johnson | .15 | .40 |
| ☐ 572 | Carlos Marmol | .15 | .40 |
| ☐ 573 | Chad Gaudin | .15 | .40 |
| ☐ 574 | Rich Harden | .15 | .40 |
| ☐ 575 | Ted Lilly | .15 | .40 |
| ☐ 576 | Carlos Zambrano | .15 | .40 |
| ☐ 577 | Ryan Theriot | .15 | .40 |
| ☐ 578 | Ryan Dempster | .15 | .40 |
| ☐ 579 | Matt Thornton | .15 | .40 |
| ☐ 580 | Jerry Owens | .15 | .40 |
| ☐ 581 | Alexei Ramirez | .25 | .60 |
| ☐ 582 | John Denks | .15 | .40 |
| ☐ 583 | Carlos Quentin | .15 | .40 |
| ☐ 584 | D.J. Carrasco | .15 | .40 |
| ☐ 585 | Dewayne Wise | .15 | .40 |
| ☐ 586 | Clayton Richard | .15 | .40 |
| ☐ 587 | Brent Lillibridge | .15 | .40 |
| ☐ 588 | Jim Thome | .25 | .60 |
| ☐ 589 | Chris Getz | .15 | .40 |
| ☐ 590 | Octavio Dotel | .15 | .40 |
| ☐ 591 | Mark Buehrle | .15 | .40 |
| ☐ 592 | Bobby Jenks | .15 | .40 |
| ☐ 593 | Joey Votto | .25 | .60 |
| ☐ 594 | Jay Bruce | .40 | 1.00 |
| ☐ 595 | David Weathers | .15 | .40 |
| ☐ 596 | Bill Bray | .15 | .40 |
| ☐ 597 | Mike Lincoln | .15 | .40 |

|  |  | | |  |  | | |  |  | | |
|---|---|---|---|---|---|---|---|---|---|---|---|
| 598 | Norris Hopper | .15 | .40 | 679 | John Bale | .15 | .40 | 760 | Daniel Murphy | .40 | 1.00 |
| 599 | Alex Gonzalez | .15 | .40 | 680 | Alex Gordon | .25 | .60 | 761 | Johan Santana | .40 | 1.00 |
| 600 | Jerry Hairston Jr. | .15 | .40 | 681 | Coco Crisp | .15 | .40 | 762 | Jose Reyes | .40 | 1.00 |
| 601 | Brandon Phillips | .15 | .40 | 682 | Miguel Olivo | .15 | .40 | 763 | David Wright | .50 | 1.25 |
| 602 | Aaron Harang | .15 | .40 | 683 | Alberto Callaspo | .15 | .40 | 764 | Carlos Delgado | .15 | .40 |
| 603 | Bronson Arroyo | .15 | .40 | 684 | Kyle Davies | .15 | .40 | 765 | Pedro Feliciano | .15 | .40 |
| 604 | Edinson Volquez | .15 | .40 | 685 | Brandon Wood | .15 | .40 | 766 | Derek Jeter | 1.00 | 2.50 |
| 605 | Ryan Hanigan | .15 | .40 | 686 | Erick Aybar | .15 | .40 | 767 | Brian Bruney | .15 | .40 |
| 606 | Jared Burton | .15 | .40 | 687 | Robb Quinlan | .15 | .40 | 768 | A.J. Burnett | .25 | .60 |
| 607 | Aaron Laffey | .15 | .40 | 688 | Bobby Abreu | .15 | .40 | 769 | Andy Pettitte | .25 | .60 |
| 608 | Kerry Wood | .15 | .40 | 689 | Jose Arredondo | .15 | .40 | 770 | Nick Swisher | .15 | .40 |
| 609 | Shin-Soo Choo | .15 | .40 | 690 | Juan Rivera | .15 | .40 | 771 | Damaso Marte | .15 | .40 |
| 610 | David Dellucci | .15 | .40 | 691 | Kendry Morales | .15 | .40 | 772 | Edwar Ramirez | .15 | .40 |
| 611 | Mark DeRosa | .15 | .40 | 692 | Vladimir Guerrero | .40 | 1.00 | 773 | CC Sabathia | .25 | .60 |
| 612 | Masahide Kobayashi | .15 | .40 | 693 | Darren Oliver | .15 | .40 | 774 | Chien-Ming Wang | .40 | 1.00 |
| 613 | Rafael Perez | .15 | .40 | 694 | Jeff Mathis | .15 | .40 | 775 | Mariano Rivera | .25 | .60 |
| 614 | Grady Sizemore | .25 | .60 | 695 | Maicer Izturis | .15 | .40 | 776 | Mark Teixeira | .40 | 1.00 |
| 615 | Cliff Lee | .25 | .60 | 696 | Mike Napoli | .15 | .40 | 777 | Joba Chamberlain | .50 | 1.25 |
| 616 | Ben Francisco | .15 | .40 | 697 | Reggie Willits | .15 | .40 | 778 | Jose Veras | .15 | .40 |
| 617 | Jensen Lewis | .15 | .40 | 698 | Scot Shields | .15 | .40 | 779 | Hideki Matsui | .40 | 1.00 |
| 618 | Joe Smith | .15 | .40 | 699 | John Lackey | .15 | .40 | 780 | Jose Molina | .15 | .40 |
| 619 | Asdrubal Cabrera | .15 | .40 | 700 | Manny Ramirez | .40 | 1.00 | 781 | Alex Rodriguez | .60 | 1.50 |
| 620 | Brad Hawpe | .15 | .40 | 701 | Danny Ardoin | .15 | .40 | 782 | Michael Wuertz | .15 | .40 |
| 621 | Chris Iannetta | .15 | .40 | 702 | Orlando Hudson | .15 | .40 | 783 | Orlando Cabrera | .15 | .40 |
| 622 | Clint Barmes | .15 | .40 | 703 | Hong-Chih Kuo | .15 | .40 | 784 | Sean Gallagher | .15 | .40 |
| 623 | Seth Smith | .15 | .40 | 704 | Mark Loretta | .15 | .40 | 785 | Dallas Braden | .15 | .40 |
| 624 | Aaron Cook | .15 | .40 | 705 | Cory Wade | .15 | .40 | 786 | Gio Gonzalez | .15 | .40 |
| 625 | Troy Tulowitzki | .25 | .60 | 706 | Casey Blake | .15 | .40 | 787 | Rajai Davis | .15 | .40 |
| 626 | Todd Helton | .25 | .60 | 707 | Eric Stults | .15 | .40 | 788 | Brad Ziegler | .15 | .40 |
| 627 | Taylor Buchholz | .15 | .40 | 708 | Jason Schmidt | .15 | .40 | 789 | Matt Holliday | .25 | .60 |
| 628 | Jason Marquis | .15 | .40 | 709 | Chad Billingsley | .15 | .40 | 790 | Jack Cust | .15 | .40 |
| 629 | Ian Stewart | .15 | .40 | 710 | Russell Martin | .25 | .60 | 791 | Santiago Casilla | .15 | .40 |
| 630 | Ryan Speier | .15 | .40 | 711 | Matt Kemp | .40 | 1.00 | 792 | Jason Giambi | .15 | .40 |
| 631 | Manny Corpas | .15 | .40 | 712 | James Loney | .25 | .60 | 793 | Joey Devine | .15 | .40 |
| 632 | Yorvit Torrealba | .15 | .40 | 713 | Rafael Furcal | .15 | .40 | 794 | Travis Buck | .15 | .40 |
| 633 | Fernando Rodney | .15 | .40 | 714 | Ramon Troncoso | .15 | .40 | 795 | Justin Duchscherer | .15 | .40 |
| 634 | Justin Verlander | .25 | .60 | 715 | Jonathan Broxton | .15 | .40 | 796 | Rob Bowen | .15 | .40 |
| 635 | Bobby Seay | .15 | .40 | 716 | Hiroki Kuroda | .15 | .40 | 797 | Andrew Brown | .15 | .40 |
| 636 | Clete Thomas | .15 | .40 | 717 | Andre Ethier | .25 | .60 | 798 | Ryan Sweeney | .15 | .40 |
| 637 | Placido Polanco | .15 | .40 | 718 | Corey Hart | .15 | .40 | 799 | Jimmy Rollins | .25 | .60 |
| 638 | Ramon Santiago | .15 | .40 | 719 | Mitch Stetter | .15 | .40 | 800 | Chad Durbin | .15 | .40 |
| 639 | Adam Everett | .15 | .40 | 720 | Manny Parra | .15 | .40 | 801 | Clay Condrey | .15 | .40 |
| 640 | Gary Sheffield | .15 | .40 | 721 | Dave Bush | .15 | .40 | 802 | Chris Coste | .15 | .40 |
| 641 | Curtis Granderson | .40 | 1.00 | 722 | Trevor Hoffman | .15 | .40 | 803 | Ryan Madson | .15 | .40 |
| 642 | Freddy Dolis | .15 | .40 | 723 | Tony Gwynn | .15 | .40 | 804 | Chan Ho Park | .15 | .40 |
| 643 | Magglio Ordonez | .25 | .60 | 724 | Chris Duffy | .15 | .40 | 805 | Carlos Ruiz | .15 | .40 |
| 644 | Zach Miner | .15 | .40 | 725 | Seth McClung | .15 | .40 | 806 | Kyle Kendrick | .15 | .40 |
| 645 | Brandon Inge | .15 | .40 | 726 | J.J. Hardy | .15 | .40 | 807 | Jayson Werth | .15 | .40 |
| 646 | Dallas McPherson | .15 | .40 | 727 | David Riske | .15 | .40 | 808 | Cole Hamels | .40 | 1.00 |
| 647 | Anibal Sanchez | .15 | .40 | 728 | Todd Coffey | .15 | .40 | 809 | Brad Lidge | .15 | .40 |
| 648 | Jorge Cantu | .15 | .40 | 729 | Rickie Weeks | .15 | .40 | 810 | Greg Dobbs | .15 | .40 |
| 649 | John Baker | .15 | .40 | 730 | Mike Rivera | .15 | .40 | 811 | Scott Eyre | .15 | .40 |
| 650 | Wes Helms | .15 | .40 | 731 | Carlos Villanueva | .15 | .40 | 812 | Eric Bruntlett | .15 | .40 |
| 651 | Ricky Nolasco | .15 | .40 | 732 | Ryan Braun | .50 | 1.25 | 813 | Ryan Howard | .50 | 1.25 |
| 652 | Chris Volstad | .15 | .40 | 733 | Nick Punto | .15 | .40 | 814 | Chase Utley | .40 | 1.00 |
| 653 | Renyel Pinto | .15 | .40 | 734 | Francisco Liriano | .15 | .40 | 815 | Paul Maholm | .15 | .40 |
| 654 | Alfredo Amezaga | .15 | .40 | 735 | Craig Breslow | .15 | .40 | 816 | Andy LaRoche | .15 | .40 |
| 655 | Cameron Maybin | .25 | .60 | 736 | Matt Macri | .15 | .40 | 817 | Brandon Moss | .15 | .40 |
| 656 | Matt Lindstrom | .15 | .40 | 737 | Scott Baker | .15 | .40 | 818 | Nyjer Morgan | .15 | .40 |
| 657 | Cody Ross | .15 | .40 | 738 | Jesse Crain | .15 | .40 | 819 | John Grabow | .15 | .40 |
| 658 | Logan Kensing | .15 | .40 | 739 | Brendan Harris | .15 | .40 | 820 | Tom Gorzelanny | .15 | .40 |
| 659 | Tim Byrdak | .15 | .40 | 740 | Alexi Casilla | .15 | .40 | 821 | Steve Pearce | .15 | .40 |
| 660 | Reggie Abercrombie | .15 | .40 | 741 | Nick Blackburn | .15 | .40 | 822 | Sean Burnett | .15 | .40 |
| 661 | Geoff Blum | .15 | .40 | 742 | Brian Buscher | .15 | .40 | 823 | Tyler Yates | .15 | .40 |
| 662 | Humberto Quintero | .15 | .40 | 743 | Denard Span | .25 | .60 | 824 | Zach Duke | .15 | .40 |
| 663 | Doug Brocail | .15 | .40 | 744 | Mike Redmond | .15 | .40 | 825 | Matt Capps | .15 | .40 |
| 664 | Roy Oswalt | .25 | .60 | 745 | Joe Mauer | .40 | 1.00 | 826 | Ross Ohlendorf | .15 | .40 |
| 665 | Lance Berkman | .25 | .60 | 746 | Carlos Gomez | .15 | .40 | 827 | Nate McLouth | .15 | .40 |
| 666 | Carlos Lee | .15 | .40 | 747 | Matt Guerrier | .15 | .40 | 828 | Adrian Gonzalez | .25 | .60 |
| 667 | Latroy Hawkins | .15 | .40 | 748 | Joe Nathan | .15 | .40 | 829 | Heath Bell | .15 | .40 |
| 668 | Geoff Geary | .15 | .40 | 749 | Livan Hernandez | .15 | .40 | 830 | Luis Rodriguez | .15 | .40 |
| 669 | Brian Moehler | .15 | .40 | 750 | Ryan Church | .15 | .40 | 831 | Kevin Kouzmanoff | .15 | .40 |
| 670 | Wandy Rodriguez | .15 | .40 | 751 | Carlos Beltran | .15 | .40 | 832 | Edgar Gonzalez | .15 | .40 |
| 671 | Esteban German | .15 | .40 | 752 | Jeremy Reed | .15 | .40 | 833 | Cha-Seung Baek | .15 | .40 |
| 672 | Ross Gload | .15 | .40 | 753 | Oliver Perez | .15 | .40 | 834 | Cla Meredith | .15 | .40 |
| 673 | Joakim Soria | .15 | .40 | 754 | Duaner Sanchez | .15 | .40 | 835 | Justin Hampson | .15 | .40 |
| 674 | Kyle Farnsworth | .15 | .40 | 755 | J.J. Putz | .15 | .40 | 836 | Nick Hundley | .15 | .40 |
| 675 | Ryan Shealy | .15 | .40 | 756 | Mike Pelfrey | .15 | .40 | 837 | Mike Adams | .15 | .40 |
| 676 | Mike Aviles | .15 | .40 | 757 | Brian Schneider | .15 | .40 | 838 | Jake Peavy | .25 | .60 |
| 677 | John Buck | .15 | .40 | 758 | Francisco Rodriguez | .25 | .60 | 839 | Chris Young | .15 | .40 |
| 678 | Zack Greinke | .25 | .60 | 759 | John Maine | .15 | .40 | 840 | Brian Giles | .15 | .40 |

|  |  | | |
|---|------|---|---|
| 841 | Steve Holm | .15 | .40 |
| 842 | Dave Roberts | .15 | .40 |
| 843 | Travis Ishikawa | .15 | .40 |
| 844 | Pablo Sandoval | .50 | 1.25 |
| 845 | Emmanuel Burriss | .15 | .40 |
| 846 | Nate Schierholtz | .15 | .40 |
| 847 | Randy Johnson | .40 | 1.00 |
| 848 | Kevin Frandsen | .15 | .40 |
| 849 | Edgar Renteria | .15 | .40 |
| 850 | Jack Taschner | .15 | .40 |
| 851 | Tim Lincecum | .50 | 1.25 |
| 852 | Alex Hinshaw | .15 | .40 |
| 853 | Jonathan Sanchez | .15 | .40 |
| 854 | Eugenio Velez | .15 | .40 |
| 855a | K.Griffey Jr. 09 SEA | .60 | 1.50 |
| 855b | K.Griffey Jr. 89 SEA | 30.00 | 60.00 |
| 855c | K.Griffey Jr. 90 SEA | 30.00 | 60.00 |
| 855d | K.Griffey Jr. 91 SEA | 30.00 | 60.00 |
| 855e | K.Griffey Jr. 92 SEA | 30.00 | 60.00 |
| 855f | K.Griffey Jr. 93 SEA | 30.00 | 60.00 |
| 855g | K.Griffey Jr. 94 SEA | 30.00 | 60.00 |
| 855h | K.Griffey Jr. 95 SEA | 30.00 | 60.00 |
| 855i | K.Griffey Jr. 96 SEA | 30.00 | 60.00 |
| 855j | K.Griffey Jr. 97 SEA | 30.00 | 60.00 |
| 855k | K.Griffey Jr. 98 SEA | 30.00 | 60.00 |
| 855l | K.Griffey Jr. 99 SEA | 30.00 | 60.00 |
| 855m | K.Griffey Jr. 00 CIN | 30.00 | 60.00 |
| 855n | K.Griffey Jr. 01 CIN | 30.00 | 60.00 |
| 855o | K.Griffey Jr. 02 CIN | 30.00 | 60.00 |
| 855p | K.Griffey Jr. 03 CIN | 30.00 | 60.00 |
| 855q | K.Griffey Jr. 04 CIN | 30.00 | 60.00 |
| 855r | K.Griffey Jr. 05 CIN | 30.00 | 60.00 |
| 855s | K.Griffey Jr. 06 CIN | 30.00 | 60.00 |
| 855t | K.Griffey Jr. 07 CIN | 30.00 | 60.00 |
| 855u | K.Griffey Jr. 08 CHI | 30.00 | 60.00 |
| 856 | Garrett Olson | .15 | .40 |
| 857 | Cesar Jimenez | .15 | .40 |
| 858 | Bryan LaHair | .15 | .40 |
| 859 | Franklin Gutierrez | .15 | .40 |
| 860 | Brandon Morrow | .15 | .40 |
| 861 | Roy Corcoran | .15 | .40 |
| 862 | Carlos Silva | .15 | .40 |
| 863 | Kenji Johjima | .25 | .60 |
| 864 | Jarrod Washburn | .15 | .40 |
| 865 | Felix Hernandez | .25 | .60 |
| 866 | Ichiro Suzuki | .60 | 1.50 |
| 867 | Miguel Batista | .15 | .40 |
| 868 | Yuniesky Betancourt | .15 | .40 |
| 869 | Adrian Beltre | .15 | .40 |
| 870 | Ryan Rowland-Smith | .15 | .40 |
| 871 | Khalil Greene | .15 | .40 |
| 872 | Kyle McClellan | .15 | .40 |
| 873 | Ryan Franklin | .15 | .40 |
| 874 | Brian Barton | .15 | .40 |
| 875 | Josh Kinney | .15 | .40 |
| 876 | Ryan Ludwick | .25 | .60 |
| 877 | Brendan Ryan | .15 | .40 |
| 878 | Albert Pujols | 1.00 | 2.50 |
| 879 | Troy Glaus | .15 | .40 |
| 880 | Joel Pineiro | .15 | .40 |
| 881 | Jason LaRue | .15 | .40 |
| 882 | Yadier Molina | .25 | .60 |
| 883 | Adam Wainwright | .25 | .60 |
| 884 | Chris Perez | .15 | .40 |
| 885 | Adam Kennedy | .15 | .40 |
| 886 | Akinori Iwamura | .25 | .60 |
| 887 | J.P. Howell | .15 | .40 |
| 888 | Ben Zobrist | .15 | .40 |
| 889 | Gabe Gross | .15 | .40 |
| 890 | Matt Joyce | .15 | .40 |
| 891 | Dan Wheeler | .15 | .40 |
| 892 | Willie Aybar | .15 | .40 |
| 893 | Jason Bartlett | .15 | .40 |
| 894 | Dioner Navarro | .15 | .40 |
| 895 | Andy Sonnanstine | .15 | .40 |
| 896 | B.J. Upton | .25 | .60 |
| 897 | Chad Bradford | .15 | .40 |
| 898 | Evan Longoria | .60 | 1.50 |
| 899 | Shawn Riggans | .15 | .40 |
| 900 | Scott Kazmir | .25 | .60 |
| 901 | Grant Balfour | .15 | .40 |
| 902 | Josh Hamilton | .40 | 1.00 |
| 903 | Frank Francisco | .15 | .40 |
| 904 | Frank Catalanotto | .15 | .40 |
| 905 | German Duran | .15 | .40 |
| 906 | Brandon Boggs | .15 | .40 |
| 907 | Matt Harrison | .15 | .40 |
| 908 | David Murphy | .15 | .40 |
| 909 | Nelson Cruz | .15 | .40 |
| 910 | Joaquin Benoit | .15 | .40 |
| 911 | Taylor Teagarden | .25 | .60 |
| 912 | Joaquin Arias | .15 | .40 |
| 913 | Kevin Millwood | .15 | .40 |
| 914 | Ian Kinsler | .25 | .60 |
| 915 | T.J. Beam | .15 | .40 |
| 916 | Marco Scutaro | .15 | .40 |
| 917 | Adam Lind | .15 | .40 |
| 918 | John McDonald | .15 | .40 |
| 919 | Scott Downs | .15 | .40 |
| 920 | Rod Barajas | .15 | .40 |
| 921 | Joe Inglett | .15 | .40 |
| 922 | Alex Rios | .15 | .40 |
| 923 | David Purcey | .15 | .40 |
| 924 | Roy Halladay | .25 | .60 |
| 925 | Jason Frasor | .15 | .40 |
| 926 | Shaun Marcum | .15 | .40 |
| 927 | Aaron Hill | .15 | .40 |
| 928 | Adam Dunn | .25 | .60 |
| 929 | Shawn Hill | .15 | .40 |
| 930 | Steven Shell | .15 | .40 |
| 931 | Saul Rivera | .15 | .40 |
| 932 | Josh Willingham | .15 | .40 |
| 933 | John Lannan | .15 | .40 |
| 934 | Joel Hanrahan | .15 | .40 |
| 935 | Daniel Cabrera | .15 | .40 |
| 936 | Willie Harris | .15 | .40 |
| 937 | Wil Nieves | .15 | .40 |
| 938 | Nick Johnson | .15 | .40 |
| 939 | Garrett Mock | .15 | .40 |
| 940 | Anderson Hernandez | .15 | .40 |
| 941 | Koji Uehara RC | 1.00 | 2.50 |
| 942 | Kenshin Kawakami RC | 1.00 | 2.50 |
| 943 | Jason Motte (RC) | .40 | 1.00 |
| 944 | Elvis Andrus RC | 1.00 | 2.50 |
| 945 | Rick Porcello RC | 1.50 | 4.00 |
| 946 | Colby Rasmus (RC) | .60 | 1.50 |
| 947 | Shairon Martis RC | .60 | 1.50 |
| 948 | Ricky Romero (RC) | .40 | 1.00 |
| 949 | Kevin Jepsen (RC) | .40 | 1.00 |
| 950 | James McDonald RC | .60 | 1.50 |
| 951 | Joe Mauer AW | .40 | 1.00 |
| 952 | Carlos Pena AW | .25 | .60 |
| 953 | Dustin Pedroia AW | .50 | 1.25 |
| 954 | Adrian Beltre AW | .15 | .40 |
| 955 | Michael Young AW | .25 | .60 |
| 956 | Torii Hunter AW | .15 | .40 |
| 957 | Grady Sizemore AW | .25 | .60 |
| 958 | Ichiro Suzuki AW | .60 | 1.50 |
| 959 | Yadier Molina AW | .25 | .60 |
| 960 | Adrian Gonzalez AW | .15 | .40 |
| 961 | Brandon Phillips AW | .15 | .40 |
| 962 | David Wright AW | .50 | 1.25 |
| 963 | Jimmy Rollins AW | .25 | .60 |
| 964 | Nate McLouth AW | .15 | .40 |
| 965 | Carlos Beltran AW | .15 | .40 |
| 966 | Shane Victorino AW | .15 | .40 |
| 967 | Cliff Lee AW | .25 | .60 |
| 968 | Brad Lidge AW | .15 | .40 |
| 969 | Evan Longoria AW | .60 | 1.50 |
| 970 | Geovany Soto AW | .25 | .60 |
| 971 | Francisco Rodriguez CL | .25 | .60 |
| 972 | Raul Ibanez CL | .25 | .60 |
| 973 | Derek Lowe CL | .15 | .40 |
| 974 | Scott Olsen CL | .15 | .40 |
| 975 | Josh Johnson CL | .15 | .40 |
| 976 | Prince Fielder CL | .40 | 1.00 |
| 977 | Mike Hampton CL | .15 | .40 |
| 978 | Kevin Gregg CL | .15 | .40 |
| 979 | Rick Ankiel CL | .25 | .60 |
| 980 | Nate McLouth CL | .15 | .40 |
| 981 | Ramon Hernandez CL | .15 | .40 |
| 982 | David Eckstein CL | .15 | .40 |
| 983 | Felipe Lopez CL | .15 | .40 |
| 984 | Clayton Kershaw CL | .40 | 1.00 |
| 985 | Randy Johnson CL | .40 | 1.00 |
| 986 | Huston Street CL | .15 | .40 |
| 987 | Rocco Baldelli CL | .15 | .40 |
| 988 | Mark Teixeira CL | .40 | 1.00 |
| 989 | Pat Burrell CL | .25 | .60 |
| 990 | Vernon Wells CL | .15 | .40 |
| 991 | Cesar Izturis CL | .15 | .40 |
| 992 | Kerry Wood CL | .15 | .40 |
| 993 | Wilson Betemit CL | .15 | .40 |
| 994 | Mike Jacobs CL | .15 | .40 |
| 995 | Gerald Laird CL | .15 | .40 |
| 996 | Justin Morneau CL | .25 | .60 |
| 997 | Brian Fuentes CL | .15 | .40 |
| 998 | Jason Giambi CL | .15 | .40 |
| 999 | Greg Chavez CL | .15 | .40 |
| 1000 | Michael Young CL | .25 | .60 |
| 1001 | Brett Anderson SP RC | 2.00 | 5.00 |
| 1002 | Trevor Cahill SP RC | 2.00 | 5.00 |
| 1003 | Jordan Schafer SP (RC) | 2.00 | 5.00 |
| 1004 | Trevor Crowe SP RC | 2.00 | 5.00 |
| 1005 | Everth Cabrera SP RC | 2.00 | 5.00 |
| 1006 | Ryan Perry SP RC | 3.00 | 8.00 |

## 2007 Upper Deck First Edition

| | | |
|---|---|---|
| COMPLETE SET (300) | 20.00 | 50.00 |
| COMMON CARD (1-300) | .12 | .30 |
| COMMON ROOKIE (1-300) | .15 | .40 |
| PRINTING PLATE ODDS 1 PER CASE | | |
| PLATE PRINT RUN 1 SET PER COLOR | | |
| BLACK-CYAN-MAGENTA-YELLOW ISSUED | | |
| NO PLATE PRICING DUE TO SCARCITY | | |
| 1 | Doug Slaten RC | .15 | .40 |
| 2 | Miguel Montero (RC) | .15 | .40 |
| 3 | Brian Burres (RC) | .15 | .40 |
| 4 | Devern Hansack RC | .15 | .40 |
| 5 | David Murphy (RC) | .15 | .40 |
| 6 | Jose Reyes RC | .15 | .40 |
| 7 | Scott Moore (RC) | .15 | .40 |
| 8 | Josh Fields (RC) | .15 | .40 |
| 9 | Chris Stewart RC | .15 | .40 |
| 10 | Jerry Owens (RC) | .15 | .40 |
| 11 | Ryan Sweeney (RC) | .15 | .40 |
| 12 | Kevin Kouzmanoff (RC) | .15 | .40 |
| 13 | Jeff Baker (RC) | .15 | .40 |
| 14 | Justin Hampson (RC) | .15 | .40 |
| 15 | Jeff Salazar (RC) | .15 | .40 |
| 16 | Alvin Colina RC | .40 | 1.00 |
| 17 | Troy Tulowitzki (RC) | .40 | 1.00 |
| 18 | Andrew Miller RC | 1.00 | 2.50 |
| 19 | Mike Rabelo RC | .15 | .40 |
| 20 | Jose Diaz (RC) | .15 | .40 |
| 21 | Angel Sanchez RC | .15 | .40 |
| 22 | Ryan Braun RC | .15 | .40 |
| 23 | Delwyn Young (RC) | .15 | .40 |
| 24 | Drew Anderson RC | .15 | .40 |
| 25 | Dennis Sarfate (RC) | .15 | .40 |
| 26 | Vinny Rottino (RC) | .15 | .40 |
| 27 | Glen Perkins (RC) | .15 | .40 |
| 28 | Alexi Casilla RC | .25 | .60 |
| 29 | Phillip Humber (RC) | .25 | .60 |
| 30 | Andy Cannizaro RC | .15 | .40 |
| 31 | Jeremy Brown | .12 | .30 |
| 32 | Sean Henn (RC) | .15 | .40 |
| 33 | Brian Rogers (RC) | .15 | .40 |
| 34 | Carlos Maldonado (RC) | .15 | .40 |

|  |  | | |
|---|---|---|---|
| 35 | Juan Morillo (RC) | .15 | .40 |
| 36 | Fred Lewis (RC) | .15 | .40 |
| 37 | Patrick Misch (RC) | .15 | .40 |
| 38 | Billy Sadler (RC) | .15 | .40 |
| 39 | Ryan Feierabend (RC) | .15 | .40 |
| 40 | Cesar Jimenez RC | .15 | .40 |
| 41 | Oswaldo Navarro RC | .15 | .40 |
| 42 | Travis Chick (RC) | .15 | .40 |
| 43 | Delmon Young (RC) | .40 | 1.00 |
| 44 | Shawn Riggans (RC) | .15 | .40 |
| 45 | Brian Stokes (RC) | .15 | .40 |
| 46 | Juan Salas (RC) | .15 | .40 |
| 47 | Joaquin Arias (RC) | .15 | .40 |
| 48 | Adam Lind (RC) | .15 | .40 |
| 49 | Beltran Perez (RC) | .15 | .40 |
| 50 | Brett Campbell RC | .15 | .40 |
| 51 | Miguel Tejada | .12 | .30 |
| 52 | Brandon Fahey | .12 | .30 |
| 53 | Jay Gibbons | .12 | .30 |
| 54 | Nick Markakis | .20 | .50 |
| 55 | Kris Benson | .12 | .30 |
| 56 | Erik Bedard | .12 | .30 |
| 57 | Chris Ray | .12 | .30 |
| 58 | Chris Britton | .12 | .30 |
| 59 | Manny Ramirez | .20 | .50 |
| 60 | David Ortiz | .20 | .50 |
| 61 | Alex Cora | .12 | .30 |
| 62 | Trot Nixon | .12 | .30 |
| 63 | Doug Mirabelli | .12 | .30 |
| 64 | Curt Schilling | .20 | .50 |
| 65 | Jonathan Papelbon | .30 | .75 |
| 66 | Craig Hansen | .12 | .30 |
| 67 | Jermaine Dye | .12 | .30 |
| 68 | Jim Thome | .20 | .50 |
| 69 | Rob Mackowiak | .12 | .30 |
| 70 | Brian Anderson | .12 | .30 |
| 71 | A.J. Pierzynski | .12 | .30 |
| 72 | Alex Cintron | .12 | .30 |
| 73 | Jose Contreras | .12 | .30 |
| 74 | Bobby Jenks | .12 | .30 |
| 75 | Mike MacDougal | .12 | .30 |
| 76 | Travis Hafner | .12 | .30 |
| 77 | Ryan Garko | .12 | .30 |
| 78 | Victor Martinez | .12 | .30 |
| 79 | Casey Blake | .12 | .30 |
| 80 | Shin-Soo Choo | .20 | .50 |
| 81 | Paul Byrd | .12 | .30 |
| 82 | Jeremy Sowers | .12 | .30 |
| 83 | Cliff Lee | .12 | .30 |
| 84 | Sean Casey | .12 | .30 |
| 85 | Brandon Inge | .12 | .30 |
| 86 | Omar Infante | .12 | .30 |
| 87 | Magglio Ordonez | .12 | .30 |
| 88 | Marcus Thames | .12 | .30 |
| 89 | Justin Verlander | .30 | .75 |
| 90 | Todd Jones | .12 | .30 |
| 91 | Joel Zumaya | .20 | .50 |
| 92 | Nate Robertson | .12 | .30 |
| 93 | Mark Teahen | .12 | .30 |
| 94 | Ryan Shealy | .12 | .30 |
| 95 | Mark Grudzielanek | .12 | .30 |
| 96 | Shane Costa | .12 | .30 |
| 97 | Reggie Sanders | .12 | .30 |
| 98 | Mark Redman | .12 | .30 |
| 99 | Todd Wellemeyer | .12 | .30 |
| 100 | Ambiorix Burgos | .12 | .30 |
| 101 | Joe Nelson | .12 | .30 |
| 102 | Orlando Cabrera | .12 | .30 |
| 103 | Maicer Izturis | .12 | .30 |
| 104 | Vladimir Guerrero | .30 | .75 |
| 105 | Juan Rivera | .12 | .30 |
| 106 | Jered Weaver | .20 | .50 |
| 107 | Joe Saunders | .12 | .30 |
| 108 | Bartolo Colon | .12 | .30 |
| 109 | Francisco Rodriguez | .12 | .30 |
| 110 | Justin Morneau | .12 | .30 |
| 111 | Luis Castillo | .12 | .30 |
| 112 | Michael Cuddyer | .12 | .30 |
| 113 | Joe Mauer | .30 | .75 |
| 114 | Francisco Liriano | .30 | .75 |
| 115 | Joe Nathan | .12 | .30 |
| 116 | Brad Radke | .12 | .30 |
| 117 | Juan Rincon | .12 | .30 |
| 118 | Derek Jeter | .75 | 2.00 |
| 119 | Jason Giambi | .12 | .30 |
| 120 | Bobby Abreu | .12 | .30 |
| 121 | Gary Sheffield | .12 | .30 |
| 122 | Melky Cabrera | .12 | .30 |
| 123 | Chien-Ming Wang | .30 | .75 |
| 124 | Mariano Rivera | .30 | .75 |
| 125 | Jaret Wright | .12 | .30 |
| 126 | Kyle Farnsworth | .12 | .30 |
| 127 | Frank Thomas | .30 | .75 |
| 128 | Dan Johnson | .12 | .30 |
| 129 | Marco Scutaro | .12 | .30 |
| 130 | Jay Payton | .12 | .30 |
| 131 | Joe Blanton | .12 | .30 |
| 132 | Rich Harden | .12 | .30 |
| 133 | Esteban Loaiza | .12 | .30 |
| 134 | Chad Gaudin | .12 | .30 |
| 135 | Yuniesky Betancourt | .12 | .30 |
| 136 | Willie Bloomquist | .12 | .30 |
| 137 | Ichiro Suzuki | .50 | 1.25 |
| 138 | Raul Ibanez | .20 | .50 |
| 139 | Chris Snelling | .12 | .30 |
| 140 | Cha-Seung Baek | .12 | .30 |
| 141 | Julio Mateo | .12 | .30 |
| 142 | Rafael Soriano | .12 | .30 |
| 143 | Jorge Cantu | .12 | .30 |
| 144 | B.J. Upton | .12 | .30 |
| 145 | Dioner Navarro | .12 | .30 |
| 146 | Carl Crawford | .12 | .30 |
| 147 | Damon Hollins | .12 | .30 |
| 148 | Casey Fossum | .12 | .30 |
| 149 | Ruddy Lugo | .12 | .30 |
| 150 | Tyler Walker | .12 | .30 |
| 151 | Shawn Camp | .12 | .30 |
| 152 | Ian Kinsler | .12 | .30 |
| 153 | Jerry Hairston Jr. | .12 | .30 |
| 154 | Gerald Laird | .12 | .30 |
| 155 | Mark DeRosa | .12 | .30 |
| 156 | Kip Wells | .12 | .30 |
| 157 | Vicente Padilla | .12 | .30 |
| 158 | John Koronka | .12 | .30 |
| 159 | Wes Littleton | .12 | .30 |
| 160 | Lyle Overbay | .12 | .30 |
| 161 | Aaron Hill | .12 | .30 |
| 162 | John McDonald | .12 | .30 |
| 163 | Vernon Wells | .12 | .30 |
| 164 | Frank Catalanotto | .12 | .30 |
| 165 | Roy Halladay | .12 | .30 |
| 166 | B.J. Ryan | .12 | .30 |
| 167 | Casey Janssen | .12 | .30 |
| 168 | Stephen Drew | .20 | .50 |
| 169 | Conor Jackson | .12 | .30 |
| 170 | Chad Tracy | .12 | .30 |
| 171 | Johnny Estrada | .12 | .30 |
| 172 | Eric Byrnes | .12 | .30 |
| 173 | Carlos Quentin | .12 | .30 |
| 174 | Brandon Webb | .12 | .30 |
| 175 | Jorge Julio | .12 | .30 |
| 176 | Luis Vizcaino | .12 | .30 |
| 177 | Chipper Jones | .30 | .75 |
| 178 | Adam LaRoche | .12 | .30 |
| 179 | Brian McCann | .12 | .30 |
| 180 | Ryan Langerhans | .12 | .30 |
| 181 | Matt Diaz | .12 | .30 |
| 182 | John Smoltz | .20 | .50 |
| 183 | Oscar Villarreal | .12 | .30 |
| 184 | Chad Paronto | .12 | .30 |
| 185 | Derrek Lee | .12 | .30 |
| 186 | Ryan Theriot | .12 | .30 |
| 187 | Ronny Cedeno | .12 | .30 |
| 188 | Juan Pierre | .12 | .30 |
| 189 | Matt Murton | .12 | .30 |
| 190 | Carlos Zambrano | .12 | .30 |
| 191 | Mark Prior | .20 | .50 |
| 192 | Ryan Dempster | .12 | .30 |
| 193 | Ryan O'Malley | .12 | .30 |
| 194 | Brandon Phillips | .12 | .30 |
| 195 | Rich Aurilia | .12 | .30 |
| 196 | Ken Griffey Jr. | .50 | 1.25 |
| 197 | Ryan Freel | .12 | .30 |
| 198 | Aaron Harang | .12 | .30 |
| 199 | Brandon Claussen | .12 | .30 |
| 200 | David Weathers | .12 | .30 |
| 201 | Eric Milton | .12 | .30 |
| 202 | Kazuo Matsui | .12 | .30 |
| 203 | Jamey Carroll | .12 | .30 |
| 204 | Matt Holliday | .30 | .75 |
| 205 | Brad Hawpe | .12 | .30 |
| 206 | Jason Jennings | .12 | .30 |
| 207 | Josh Fogg | .12 | .30 |
| 208 | Aaron Cook | .12 | .30 |
| 209 | Miguel Cabrera | .20 | .50 |
| 210 | Dan Uggla | .20 | .50 |
| 211 | Hanley Ramirez | .20 | .50 |
| 212 | Jeremy Hermida | .12 | .30 |
| 213 | Cody Ross | .12 | .30 |
| 214 | Josh Willingham | .12 | .30 |
| 215 | Anibal Sanchez | .12 | .30 |
| 216 | Jose Garcia RC | .15 | .40 |
| 217 | Taylor Tankersley | .12 | .30 |
| 218 | Lance Berkman | .12 | .30 |
| 219 | Craig Biggio | .20 | .50 |
| 220 | Brad Ausmus | .12 | .30 |
| 221 | Willy Taveras | .12 | .30 |
| 222 | Chris Burke | .12 | .30 |
| 223 | Roger Clemens | .50 | 1.25 |
| 224 | Brandon Backe | .12 | .30 |
| 225 | Brad Lidge | .12 | .30 |
| 226 | Dan Wheeler | .12 | .30 |
| 227 | Wilson Betemit | .12 | .30 |
| 228 | Julio Lugo | .12 | .30 |
| 229 | Russell Martin | .12 | .30 |
| 230 | Kenny Lofton | .12 | .30 |
| 231 | Brad Penny | .12 | .30 |
| 232 | Chad Billingsley | .12 | .30 |
| 233 | Greg Maddux | .50 | 1.25 |
| 234 | Jonathan Broxton | .12 | .30 |
| 235 | Rickie Weeks | .12 | .30 |
| 236 | Bill Hall | .12 | .30 |
| 237 | Tony Gwynn Jr. | .12 | .30 |
| 238 | Corey Hart | .12 | .30 |
| 239 | Laynce Nix | .12 | .30 |
| 240 | Ben Sheets | .12 | .30 |
| 241 | Dave Bush | .12 | .30 |
| 242 | Francisco Cordero | .12 | .30 |
| 243 | Jose Reyes | .12 | .30 |
| 244 | Carlos Delgado | .12 | .30 |
| 245 | Paul Lo Duca | .12 | .30 |
| 246 | Carlos Beltran | .12 | .30 |
| 247 | Lastings Milledge | .20 | .50 |
| 248 | Pedro Martinez | .20 | .50 |
| 249 | John Maine | .12 | .30 |
| 250 | Steve Trachsel | .12 | .30 |
| 251 | Ryan Howard | .50 | 1.25 |
| 252 | Jimmy Rollins | .12 | .30 |
| 253 | Chris Coste | .12 | .30 |
| 254 | Jeff Conine | .12 | .30 |
| 255 | David Dellucci | .12 | .30 |
| 256 | Cole Hamels | .30 | .75 |
| 257 | Ryan Madson | .12 | .30 |
| 258 | Brett Myers | .12 | .30 |
| 259 | Freddy Sanchez | .12 | .30 |
| 260 | Xavier Nady | .12 | .30 |
| 261 | Jose Castillo | .12 | .30 |
| 262 | Jason Bay | .20 | .50 |
| 263 | Jose Bautista | .12 | .30 |
| 264 | Ronny Paulino | .12 | .30 |
| 265 | Zach Duke | .12 | .30 |
| 266 | Shane Youman RC | .15 | .40 |
| 267 | Matt Capps | .12 | .30 |
| 268 | Adrian Gonzalez | .12 | .30 |
| 269 | Josh Barfield | .12 | .30 |
| 270 | Mike Piazza | .30 | .75 |
| 271 | Dave Roberts | .12 | .30 |
| 272 | Geoff Blum | .12 | .30 |
| 273 | Chris Young | .12 | .30 |
| 274 | Woody Williams | .12 | .30 |
| 275 | Cla Meredith | .12 | .30 |
| 276 | Trevor Hoffman | .12 | .30 |
| 277 | Ray Durham | .12 | .30 |

|  |  | | |
|---|---|---|---|
| 278 | Mark Sweeney | .12 | .30 |
| 279 | Eliezer Alfonzo | .12 | .30 |
| 280 | Todd Linden | .12 | .30 |
| 281 | Jason Schmidt | .12 | .30 |
| 282 | Noah Lowry | .12 | .30 |
| 283 | Brad Hennessey | .12 | .30 |
| 284 | Jonathan Sanchez | .12 | .30 |
| 285 | Albert Pujols | .60 | 1.50 |
| 286 | David Eckstein | .12 | .30 |
| 287 | Jim Edmonds | .20 | .50 |
| 288 | Chris Duncan | .12 | .30 |
| 289 | Juan Encarnacion | .12 | .30 |
| 290 | Jeff Suppan | .12 | .30 |
| 291 | Jeff Weaver | .12 | .30 |
| 292 | Braden Looper | .12 | .30 |
| 293 | Ryan Zimmerman | .30 | .75 |
| 294 | Nick Johnson | .12 | .30 |
| 295 | Alfonso Soriano | .12 | .30 |
| 296 | Austin Kearns | .12 | .30 |
| 297 | Alex Escobar | .12 | .30 |
| 298 | Tony Armas | .12 | .30 |
| 299 | Chad Cordero | .12 | .30 |
| 300 | Jon Rauch | .12 | .30 |

## 2008 Upper Deck First Edition

| | | | |
|---|---|---|---|
| COMPLETE SET (1-300) | | 10.00 | 25.00 |
| COMP.UPD.SET (301-500) | | 10.00 | 25.00 |
| COMMON CARD (1-250/301-500) | | .12 | .30 |
| COMMON RC (250/300/329/390) | | .20 | .50 |
| 1 | Joe Saunders | .12 | .30 |
| 2 | Kelvim Escobar | .12 | .30 |
| 3 | Jered Weaver | .12 | .30 |
| 4 | Justin Speier | .12 | .30 |
| 5 | Scot Shields | .12 | .30 |
| 6 | Orlando Cabrera | .12 | .30 |
| 7 | Casey Kotchman | .12 | .30 |
| 8 | Vladimir Guerrero | .30 | .75 |
| 9 | Garret Anderson | .12 | .30 |
| 10 | Roy Oswalt | .12 | .30 |
| 11 | Wandy Rodriguez | .12 | .30 |
| 12 | Woody Williams | .12 | .30 |
| 13 | Chad Qualls | .12 | .30 |
| 14 | Mark Loretta | .12 | .30 |
| 15 | Brad Ausmus | .12 | .30 |
| 16 | Carlos Lee | .12 | .30 |
| 17 | Hunter Pence | .30 | .75 |
| 18 | Dan Haren | .12 | .30 |
| 19 | Lenny DiNardo | .12 | .30 |
| 20 | Chad Gaudin | .12 | .30 |
| 21 | Huston Street | .12 | .30 |
| 22 | Andrew Brown | .12 | .30 |
| 23 | Mike Piazza | .30 | .75 |
| 24 | Mark Ellis | .12 | .30 |
| 25 | Shannon Stewart | .12 | .30 |
| 26 | Shaun Marcum | .12 | .30 |
| 27 | A.J. Burnett | .12 | .30 |
| 28 | Casey Janssen | .12 | .30 |
| 29 | Jeremy Accardo | .12 | .30 |
| 30 | Aaron Hill | .12 | .30 |
| 31 | Frank Thomas | .30 | .75 |
| 32 | Matt Stairs | .12 | .30 |
| 33 | Vernon Wells | .12 | .30 |
| 34 | Tim Hudson | .12 | .30 |
| 35 | Buddy Carlyle | .12 | .30 |
| 36 | Rafael Soriano | .12 | .30 |
| 37 | Brian McCann | .20 | .50 |
| 38 | Edgar Renteria | .12 | .30 |
| 39 | Mark Teixeira | .20 | .50 |
| 40 | Willie Harris | .12 | .30 |
| 41 | Andruw Jones | .12 | .30 |
| 42 | Ben Sheets | .20 | .50 |
| 43 | Dave Bush | .12 | .30 |
| 44 | Yovani Gallardo | .12 | .30 |
| 45 | Matt Wise | .12 | .30 |
| 46 | Johnny Estrada | .12 | .30 |
| 47 | Prince Fielder | .30 | .75 |
| 48 | J.J. Hardy | .12 | .30 |
| 49 | Corey Hart | .12 | .30 |
| 50 | Adam Wainwright | .20 | .50 |
| 51 | Joel Pineiro | .12 | .30 |
| 52 | Jason Isringhausen | .12 | .30 |
| 53 | Troy Percival | .12 | .30 |
| 54 | Albert Pujols | .60 | 1.50 |
| 55 | David Eckstein | .12 | .30 |
| 56 | Jim Edmonds | .20 | .50 |
| 57 | Rick Ankiel | .12 | .30 |
| 58 | Ted Lilly | .12 | .30 |
| 59 | Rich Hill | .12 | .30 |
| 60 | Jason Marquis | .12 | .30 |
| 61 | Carlos Marmol | .12 | .30 |
| 62 | Jason Kendall | .12 | .30 |
| 63 | Aramis Ramirez | .12 | .30 |
| 64 | Ryan Theriot | .12 | .30 |
| 65 | Alfonso Soriano | .20 | .50 |
| 66 | Jacque Jones | .12 | .30 |
| 67 | James Shields | .12 | .30 |
| 68 | Andy Sonnanstine | .12 | .30 |
| 69 | Scott Dohmann | .12 | .30 |
| 70 | Dioner Navarro | .12 | .30 |
| 71 | B.J. Upton | .20 | .50 |
| 72 | Carlos Pena | .30 | .75 |
| 73 | Brendan Harris | .12 | .30 |
| 74 | Josh Wilson | .12 | .30 |
| 75 | Brandon Webb | .20 | .50 |
| 76 | Micah Owings | .12 | .30 |
| 77 | Doug Slaten | .12 | .30 |
| 78 | Brandon Lyon | .12 | .30 |
| 79 | Miguel Montero | .12 | .30 |
| 80 | Stephen Drew | .12 | .30 |
| 81 | Mark Reynolds | .12 | .30 |
| 82 | Chris B. Young | .12 | .30 |
| 83 | Chad Billingsley | .12 | .30 |
| 84 | Derek Lowe | .12 | .30 |
| 85 | Mark Hendrickson | .12 | .30 |
| 86 | Takashi Saito | .12 | .30 |
| 87 | Russell Martin | .12 | .30 |
| 88 | Jeff Kent | .12 | .30 |
| 89 | Matt Kemp | .30 | .75 |
| 90 | Juan Pierre | .12 | .30 |
| 91 | Matt Cain | .12 | .30 |
| 92 | Barry Zito | .12 | .30 |
| 93 | Kevin Correia | .12 | .30 |
| 94 | Jack Taschner | .12 | .30 |
| 95 | Bengie Molina | .12 | .30 |
| 96 | Omar Vizquel | .12 | .30 |
| 97 | Dave Roberts | .12 | .30 |
| 98 | Rajai Davis | .12 | .30 |
| 99 | Fausto Carmona | .12 | .30 |
| 100 | Jake Westbrook | .12 | .30 |
| 101 | Rafael Betancourt | .12 | .30 |
| 102 | Joe Borowski | .12 | .30 |
| 103 | Victor Martinez | .12 | .30 |
| 104 | Travis Hafner | .12 | .30 |
| 105 | Ryan Garko | .12 | .30 |
| 106 | Kenny Lofton | .12 | .30 |
| 107 | Franklin Gutierrez | .12 | .30 |
| 108 | Felix Hernandez | .20 | .50 |
| 109 | J.J. Putz | .12 | .30 |
| 110 | Brandon Morrow | .12 | .30 |
| 111 | Kenji Johjima | .12 | .30 |
| 112 | Jose Vidro | .12 | .30 |
| 113 | Richie Sexson | .12 | .30 |
| 114 | Ichiro Suzuki | .50 | 1.25 |
| 115 | Ben Broussard | .12 | .30 |
| 116 | Sergio Mitre | .12 | .30 |
| 117 | Scott Olsen | .12 | .30 |
| 118 | Rick Vanden Hurk | .12 | .30 |
| 119 | Lee Gardner | .12 | .30 |
| 120 | Miguel Olivo | .12 | .30 |
| 121 | Hanley Ramirez | .30 | .75 |
| 122 | Mike Jacobs | .12 | .30 |
| 123 | Josh Willingham | .12 | .30 |
| 124 | John Maine | .12 | .30 |
| 125 | Tom Glavine | .20 | .50 |
| 126 | Billy Wagner | .12 | .30 |
| 127 | Aaron Heilman | .12 | .30 |
| 128 | David Wright | .40 | 1.00 |
| 129 | Luis Castillo | .12 | .30 |
| 130 | Shawn Green | .12 | .30 |
| 131 | Damion Easley | .12 | .30 |
| 132 | Carlos Delgado | .12 | .30 |
| 133 | Shawn Hill | .12 | .30 |
| 134 | John Lannan | .12 | .30 |
| 135 | Chad Cordero | .12 | .30 |
| 136 | Jon Rauch | .12 | .30 |
| 137 | Jesus Flores | .12 | .30 |
| 138 | Dmitri Young | .12 | .30 |
| 139 | Cristian Guzman | .12 | .30 |
| 140 | Austin Kearns | .12 | .30 |
| 141 | Nook Logan | .12 | .30 |
| 142 | Erik Bedard | .12 | .30 |
| 143 | Daniel Cabrera | .12 | .30 |
| 144 | Chris Ray | .12 | .30 |
| 145 | Chad Bradford | .12 | .30 |
| 146 | Ramon Hernandez | .12 | .30 |
| 147 | Miguel Tejada | .12 | .30 |
| 148 | Freddie Bynum | .12 | .30 |
| 149 | Corey Patterson | .12 | .30 |
| 150 | Chris Young | .12 | .30 |
| 151 | Greg Maddux | .40 | 1.00 |
| 152 | Kevin Cameron | .12 | .30 |
| 153 | Doug Brocail | .12 | .30 |
| 154 | Kevin Kouzmanoff | .12 | .30 |
| 155 | Geoff Blum | .12 | .30 |
| 156 | Milton Bradley | .12 | .30 |
| 157 | Brian Giles | .12 | .30 |
| 158 | Jamie Moyer | .12 | .30 |
| 159 | Kyle Kendrick | .12 | .30 |
| 160 | Kyle Lohse | .12 | .30 |
| 161 | Antonio Alfonseca | .12 | .30 |
| 162 | Chris Coste | .12 | .30 |
| 163 | Chase Utley | .30 | .75 |
| 164 | Tadahito Iguchi | .12 | .30 |
| 165 | Aaron Rowand | .12 | .30 |
| 166 | Shane Victorino | .12 | .30 |
| 167 | Ian Snell | .12 | .30 |
| 168 | Shane Youman | .12 | .30 |
| 169 | Shawn Chacon | .12 | .30 |
| 170 | Ronny Paulino | .12 | .30 |
| 171 | Jack Wilson | .12 | .30 |
| 172 | Adam LaRoche | .12 | .30 |
| 173 | Ryan Doumit | .12 | .30 |
| 174 | Xavier Nady | .12 | .30 |
| 175 | Kevin Millwood | .12 | .30 |
| 176 | Brandon McCarthy | .12 | .30 |
| 177 | Wes Littleton | .12 | .30 |
| 178 | Mike Wood | .12 | .30 |
| 179 | Hank Blalock | .12 | .30 |
| 180 | Ian Kinsler | .20 | .50 |
| 181 | Marlon Byrd | .12 | .30 |
| 182 | Brad Wilkerson | .12 | .30 |
| 183 | Tim Wakefield | .12 | .30 |
| 184 | Daisuke Matsuzaka | .40 | 1.00 |
| 185 | Julian Tavarez | .12 | .30 |
| 186 | Hideki Okajima | .12 | .30 |
| 187 | Doug Mirabelli | .12 | .30 |
| 188 | Dustin Pedroia | .40 | 1.00 |
| 189 | Mike Lowell | .12 | .30 |
| 190 | Manny Ramirez | .30 | .75 |
| 191 | Coco Crisp | .12 | .30 |
| 192 | Bronson Arroyo | .12 | .30 |
| 193 | Matt Belisle | .12 | .30 |
| 194 | Jared Burton | .12 | .30 |
| 195 | Mike Gosling | .12 | .30 |
| 196 | David Ross | .12 | .30 |
| 197 | Edwin Encarnacion | .12 | .30 |
| 198 | Ken Griffey Jr. | .50 | 1.25 |
| 199 | Adam Dunn | .12 | .30 |
| 200 | Jeff Francis | .12 | .30 |

|  |  | | |
|---|---|---|---|
| ❑ 201 | Jason Hirsh | .12 | .30 |
| ❑ 202 | Manny Corpas | .12 | .30 |
| ❑ 203 | Jeremy Affeldt | .12 | .30 |
| ❑ 204 | Yorvit Torrealba | .12 | .30 |
| ❑ 205 | Todd Helton | .20 | .50 |
| ❑ 206 | Kazuo Matsui | .12 | .30 |
| ❑ 207 | Brad Hawpe | .12 | .30 |
| ❑ 208 | Willy Taveras | .12 | .30 |
| ❑ 209 | Brian Barnister | .12 | .30 |
| ❑ 210 | Zack Greinke | .12 | .30 |
| ❑ 211 | Kyle Davies | .12 | .30 |
| ❑ 212 | David Riske | .12 | .30 |
| ❑ 213 | John Buck | .12 | .30 |
| ❑ 214 | Mark Grudzielanek | .12 | .30 |
| ❑ 215 | Billy Butler | .12 | .30 |
| ❑ 216 | David DeJesus | .12 | .30 |
| ❑ 217 | Jeremy Bonderman | .12 | .30 |
| ❑ 218 | Chad Durbin | .12 | .30 |
| ❑ 219 | Andrew Miller | .20 | .50 |
| ❑ 220 | Todd Jones | .12 | .30 |
| ❑ 221 | Brandon Inge | .12 | .30 |
| ❑ 222 | Placido Polanco | .12 | .30 |
| ❑ 223 | Gary Sheffield | .12 | .30 |
| ❑ 224 | Magglio Ordonez | .20 | .50 |
| ❑ 225 | Matt Garza | .12 | .30 |
| ❑ 226 | Boof Bonser | .12 | .30 |
| ❑ 227 | Joe Nathan | .12 | .30 |
| ❑ 228 | Dennys Reyes | .12 | .30 |
| ❑ 229 | Joe Mauer | .30 | .75 |
| ❑ 230 | Michael Cuddyer | .12 | .30 |
| ❑ 231 | Jason Bartlett | .12 | .30 |
| ❑ 232 | Torii Hunter | .12 | .30 |
| ❑ 233 | Jason Tyner | .12 | .30 |
| ❑ 234 | Mark Buehrle | .12 | .30 |
| ❑ 235 | Jon Garland | .12 | .30 |
| ❑ 236 | Jose Contreras | .12 | .30 |
| ❑ 237 | Matt Thornton | .12 | .30 |
| ❑ 238 | Juan Uribe | .12 | .30 |
| ❑ 239 | Jim Thome | .20 | .50 |
| ❑ 240 | Jerry Owens | .12 | .30 |
| ❑ 241 | Jermaine Dye | .12 | .30 |
| ❑ 242 | Andy Pettitte | .20 | .50 |
| ❑ 243 | Phil Hughes | .30 | .75 |
| ❑ 244 | Mike Mussina | .12 | .30 |
| ❑ 245 | Joba Chamberlain | .40 | 1.00 |
| ❑ 246 | Brian Bruney | .12 | .30 |
| ❑ 247 | Jorge Posada | .20 | .50 |
| ❑ 248 | Derek Jeter | .75 | 2.00 |
| ❑ 249 | Jason Giambi | .20 | .50 |
| ❑ 250 | Johnny Damon | .20 | .50 |
| ❑ 251 | Jonathan Albaladejo RC | .30 | .75 |
| ❑ 252 | Josh Anderson (RC) | .20 | .50 |
| ❑ 253 | Wladimir Balentien (RC) | .20 | .50 |
| ❑ 254 | Josh Banks (RC) | .20 | .50 |
| ❑ 255 | Daric Barton (RC) | .20 | .50 |
| ❑ 256 | Jerry Blevins RC | .30 | .75 |
| ❑ 257 | Emilio Bonifacio RC | .50 | 1.25 |
| ❑ 258 | Lance Broadway (RC) | .20 | .50 |
| ❑ 259 | Clay Buchholz (RC) | .50 | 1.25 |
| ❑ 260 | Billy Buckner (RC) | .20 | .50 |
| ❑ 261 | Jeff Clement (RC) | .30 | .75 |
| ❑ 262 | Willie Collazo RC | .12 | .30 |
| ❑ 263 | Ross Detwiler RC | .50 | 1.25 |
| ❑ 264 | Sam Fuld RC | .20 | .50 |
| ❑ 265 | Harvey Garcia (RC) | .20 | .50 |
| ❑ 266 | Alberto Gonzalez (RC) | .20 | .50 |
| ❑ 267 | Ryan Hanigan RC | .30 | .75 |
| ❑ 268 | Kevin Hart (RC) | .12 | .30 |
| ❑ 269 | Luke Hochevar RC | .30 | .75 |
| ❑ 270 | Chin-Lung Hu (RC) | .30 | .75 |
| ❑ 271 | Rob Johnson (RC) | .20 | .50 |
| ❑ 272 | Radhames Liz RC | .30 | .75 |
| ❑ 273 | Ian Kennedy RC | .50 | 1.25 |
| ❑ 274 | Joe Koshansky (RC) | .20 | .50 |
| ❑ 275 | Donny Lucy (RC) | .20 | .50 |
| ❑ 276 | Justin Maxwell RC | .30 | .75 |
| ❑ 277 | Jonathan Meloan RC | .30 | .75 |
| ❑ 278 | Luis Mendoza (RC) | .20 | .50 |
| ❑ 279 | Jose Morales (RC) | .20 | .50 |
| ❑ 280 | Nyjer Morgan (RC) | .20 | .50 |
| ❑ 281 | Carlos Muniz RC | .30 | .75 |
| ❑ 282 | Bill Murphy (RC) | .20 | .50 |
| ❑ 283 | Josh Newman RC | .30 | .75 |
| ❑ 284 | Ross Ohlendorf RC | .30 | .75 |
| ❑ 285 | Troy Patton (RC) | .20 | .50 |
| ❑ 286 | Felipe Paulino RC | .30 | .75 |
| ❑ 287 | Steve Pearce RC | .30 | .75 |
| ❑ 288 | Heath Phillips RC | .30 | .75 |
| ❑ 289 | Justin Ruggiano RC | .30 | .75 |
| ❑ 290 | Clint Sammons (RC) | .20 | .50 |
| ❑ 291 | Bronson Sardinha (RC) | .20 | .50 |
| ❑ 292 | Chris Seddon (RC) | .20 | .50 |
| ❑ 293 | Seth Smith (RC) | .20 | .50 |
| ❑ 294 | Mitch Stetter RC | .30 | .75 |
| ❑ 295 | Dave Davidson RC | .30 | .75 |
| ❑ 296 | Rich Thompson RC | .20 | .50 |
| ❑ 297 | J.R. Towles RC | .30 | .75 |
| ❑ 298 | Eugenio Velez RC | .30 | .75 |
| ❑ 299 | Joey Votto (RC) | .50 | 1.25 |
| ❑ 300 | Bill White RC | .20 | .50 |
| ❑ 301 | Dan Haren | .12 | .30 |
| ❑ 302 | Randy Johnson | .30 | .75 |
| ❑ 303 | Justin Upton | .30 | .75 |
| ❑ 304 | Tom Glavine | .20 | .50 |
| ❑ 305 | Chipper Jones | .40 | 1.00 |
| ❑ 306 | Jeff Francoeur | .20 | .50 |
| ❑ 307 | John Smoltz | .30 | .75 |
| ❑ 308 | Yunel Escobar | .12 | .30 |
| ❑ 309 | Adam Jones | .12 | .30 |
| ❑ 310 | Jeremy Guthrie | .12 | .30 |
| ❑ 311 | Nick Markakis | .20 | .50 |
| ❑ 312 | Brian Roberts | .20 | .50 |
| ❑ 313 | Melvin Mora | .12 | .30 |
| ❑ 314 | Josh Beckett | .20 | .50 |
| ❑ 315 | Jon Lester | .20 | .50 |
| ❑ 316 | Curt Schilling | .20 | .50 |
| ❑ 317 | Jonathan Papelbon | .20 | .50 |
| ❑ 318 | Jason Varitek | .30 | .75 |
| ❑ 319 | David Ortiz | .20 | .50 |
| ❑ 320 | Jacoby Ellsbury | .50 | 1.25 |
| ❑ 321 | Julio Lugo | .12 | .30 |
| ❑ 322 | Sean Casey | .12 | .30 |
| ❑ 323 | Kevin Youkilis | .20 | .50 |
| ❑ 324 | J.D. Drew | .12 | .30 |
| ❑ 325 | Derrek Lee | .20 | .50 |
| ❑ 326 | Carlos Zambrano | .12 | .30 |
| ❑ 327 | Kerry Wood | .20 | .50 |
| ❑ 328 | Geovany Soto | .30 | .75 |
| ❑ 329 | Kosuke Fukudome RC | .60 | 1.50 |
| ❑ 330 | Gavin Floyd | .12 | .30 |
| ❑ 331 | Bobby Jenks | .12 | .30 |
| ❑ 332 | Javier Vazquez | .12 | .30 |
| ❑ 333 | A.J. Pierzynski | .12 | .30 |
| ❑ 334 | Orlando Cabrera | .12 | .30 |
| ❑ 335 | Joe Crede | .12 | .30 |
| ❑ 336 | Paul Konerko | .20 | .50 |
| ❑ 337 | Nick Swisher | .12 | .30 |
| ❑ 338 | Carlos Quentin | .20 | .50 |
| ❑ 339 | Alexei Ramirez | .50 | 1.25 |
| ❑ 340 | Johnny Cueto | .20 | .50 |
| ❑ 341 | Aaron Harang | .12 | .30 |
| ❑ 342 | Brandon Phillips | .12 | .30 |
| ❑ 343 | Paul Byrd | .12 | .30 |
| ❑ 344 | Grady Sizemore | .20 | .50 |
| ❑ 345 | Jhonny Peralta | .12 | .30 |
| ❑ 346 | Asdrubal Cabrera | .20 | .50 |
| ❑ 347 | C.C. Sabathia | .12 | .30 |
| ❑ 348 | Troy Tulowitzki | .40 | 1.00 |
| ❑ 349 | Matt Holliday | .20 | .50 |
| ❑ 350 | Garrett Atkins | .12 | .30 |
| ❑ 351 | Ubaldo Jimenez | .12 | .30 |
| ❑ 352 | Kenny Rogers | .12 | .30 |
| ❑ 353 | Justin Verlander | .20 | .50 |
| ❑ 354 | Dontrelle Willis | .12 | .30 |
| ❑ 355 | Joel Zumaya | .12 | .30 |
| ❑ 356 | Ivan Rodriguez | .20 | .50 |
| ❑ 357 | Miguel Cabrera | .20 | .50 |
| ❑ 358 | Carlos Guillen | .12 | .30 |
| ❑ 359 | Edgar Renteria | .12 | .30 |
| ❑ 360 | Curtis Granderson | .12 | .30 |
| ❑ 361 | Jeremy Hermida | .12 | .30 |
| ❑ 362 | Dan Uggla | .20 | .50 |
| ❑ 363 | Luis Gonzalez | .12 | .30 |
| ❑ 364 | Andrew Miller | .20 | .50 |
| ❑ 365 | Jorge Cantu | .12 | .30 |
| ❑ 366 | Kazuo Matsui | .12 | .30 |
| ❑ 367 | Lance Berkman | .20 | .50 |
| ❑ 368 | Miguel Tejada | .12 | .30 |
| ❑ 369 | Jose Valverde | .12 | .30 |
| ❑ 370 | Michael Bourn | .12 | .30 |
| ❑ 371 | Gil Meche | .12 | .30 |
| ❑ 372 | Joey Gathright | .12 | .30 |
| ❑ 373 | Mark Teahen | .12 | .30 |
| ❑ 374 | Alex Gordon | .20 | .50 |
| ❑ 375 | Tony Pena | .12 | .30 |
| ❑ 376 | Jose Guillen | .12 | .30 |
| ❑ 377 | Torii Hunter | .12 | .30 |
| ❑ 378 | Ervin Santana | .12 | .30 |
| ❑ 379 | Francisco Rodriguez | .12 | .30 |
| ❑ 380 | Howie Kendrick | .12 | .30 |
| ❑ 381 | John Lackey | .12 | .30 |
| ❑ 382 | Gary Matthews | .12 | .30 |
| ❑ 383 | Jon Garland | .12 | .30 |
| ❑ 384 | Chone Figgins | .12 | .30 |
| ❑ 385 | Andruw Jones | .12 | .30 |
| ❑ 386 | James Loney | .20 | .50 |
| ❑ 387 | Andre Ethier | .20 | .50 |
| ❑ 388 | Rafael Furcal | .12 | .30 |
| ❑ 389 | Brad Penny | .12 | .30 |
| ❑ 390 | Hiroki Kuroda RC | .30 | .75 |
| ❑ 391 | Blake DeWitt | .30 | .75 |
| ❑ 392 | Mike Cameron | .12 | .30 |
| ❑ 393 | Ryan Braun | .40 | 1.00 |
| ❑ 394 | Rickie Weeks | .12 | .30 |
| ❑ 395 | Bill Hall | .12 | .30 |
| ❑ 396 | Tony Gwynn | .12 | .30 |
| ❑ 397 | Eric Gagne | .12 | .30 |
| ❑ 398 | Jeff Suppan | .12 | .30 |
| ❑ 399 | Jason Kendall | .12 | .30 |
| ❑ 400 | Livan Hernandez | .12 | .30 |
| ❑ 401 | Francisco Liriano | .20 | .50 |
| ❑ 402 | Pat Neshek | .12 | .30 |
| ❑ 403 | Adam Everett | .12 | .30 |
| ❑ 404 | Justin Morneau | .20 | .50 |
| ❑ 405 | Craig Monroe | .12 | .30 |
| ❑ 406 | Carlos Gomez | .12 | .30 |
| ❑ 407 | Delmon Young | .20 | .50 |
| ❑ 408 | Oliver Perez | .12 | .30 |
| ❑ 409 | Jose Reyes | .20 | .50 |
| ❑ 410 | Moises Alou | .12 | .30 |
| ❑ 411 | Carlos Beltran | .20 | .50 |
| ❑ 412 | Endy Chavez | .12 | .30 |
| ❑ 413 | Ryan Church | .12 | .30 |
| ❑ 414 | Pedro Martinez | .20 | .50 |
| ❑ 415 | Johan Santana | .20 | .50 |
| ❑ 416 | Mike Pelfrey | .12 | .30 |
| ❑ 417 | Brian Schneider | .12 | .30 |
| ❑ 418 | Ramon Castro | .12 | .30 |
| ❑ 419 | Kei Igawa | .12 | .30 |
| ❑ 420 | Mariano Rivera | .30 | .75 |
| ❑ 421 | Chien-Ming Wang | .30 | .75 |
| ❑ 422 | Wilson Betemit | .12 | .30 |
| ❑ 423 | Robinson Cano | .20 | .50 |
| ❑ 424 | Alex Rodriguez | .50 | 1.25 |
| ❑ 425 | Bobby Abreu | .12 | .30 |
| ❑ 426 | Shelley Duncan | .12 | .30 |
| ❑ 427 | Hideki Matsui | .30 | .75 |
| ❑ 428 | Joe Blanton | .12 | .30 |
| ❑ 429 | Bobby Crosby | .12 | .30 |
| ❑ 430 | Eric Chavez | .12 | .30 |
| ❑ 431 | Dan Johnson | .12 | .30 |
| ❑ 432 | Rich Harden | .12 | .30 |
| ❑ 433 | Kurt Suzuki | .12 | .30 |
| ❑ 434 | Ryan Howard | .40 | 1.00 |
| ❑ 435 | Jimmy Rollins | .20 | .50 |
| ❑ 436 | Pedro Feliz | .12 | .30 |
| ❑ 437 | Adam Eaton | .12 | .30 |
| ❑ 438 | Brad Lidge | .12 | .30 |
| ❑ 439 | Brett Myers | .12 | .30 |
| ❑ 440 | Pat Burrell | .12 | .30 |
| ❑ 441 | Geoff Jenkins | .12 | .30 |
| ❑ 442 | Zach Duke | .12 | .30 |
| ❑ 443 | Matt Morris | .12 | .30 |

|  |  | | |
|---|------|------|------|
| 444 | Tom Gorzelanny | .12 | .30 |
| 445 | Jason Bay | .20 | .50 |
| 446 | Freddy Sanchez | .12 | .30 |
| 447 | Matt Capps | .12 | .30 |
| 448 | Tadahito Iguchi | .12 | .30 |
| 449 | Adrian Gonzalez | .20 | .50 |
| 450 | Jim Edmonds | .20 | .50 |
| 451 | Jake Peavy | .20 | .50 |
| 452 | Khalil Greene | .20 | .50 |
| 453 | Trevor Hoffman | .12 | .30 |
| 454 | Mark Prior | .20 | .50 |
| 455 | Randy Wolf | .12 | .30 |
| 456 | Scott Hairston | .12 | .30 |
| 457 | Tim Lincecum | .40 | 1.00 |
| 458 | Noah Lowry | .12 | .30 |
| 459 | Aaron Rowand | .12 | .30 |
| 460 | Randy Winn | .12 | .30 |
| 461 | Ray Durham | .12 | .30 |
| 462 | Brian Wilson | .12 | .30 |
| 463 | Adrian Beltre | .12 | .30 |
| 464 | Jarrod Washburn | .12 | .30 |
| 465 | Yuniesky Betancourt | .12 | .30 |
| 466 | Jose Lopez | .12 | .30 |
| 467 | Raul Ibanez | .20 | .50 |
| 468 | Erik Bedard | .12 | .30 |
| 469 | Brad Wilkerson | .12 | .30 |
| 470 | Chris Carpenter | .12 | .30 |
| 471 | Mark Mulder | .12 | .30 |
| 472 | Skip Schumaker | .12 | .30 |
| 473 | Troy Glaus | .20 | .50 |
| 474 | Chris Duncan | .12 | .30 |
| 475 | Scott Kazmir | .20 | .50 |
| 476 | Troy Percival | .12 | .30 |
| 477 | Akinori Iwamura | .12 | .30 |
| 478 | Carl Crawford | .12 | .30 |
| 479 | Cliff Floyd | .12 | .30 |
| 480 | Matt Garza | .12 | .30 |
| 481 | Edwin Jackson | .12 | .30 |
| 482 | Vicente Padilla | .12 | .30 |
| 483 | Josh Hamilton | .40 | 1.00 |
| 484 | Milton Bradley | .12 | .30 |
| 485 | Michael Young | .12 | .30 |
| 486 | David Murphy | .12 | .30 |
| 487 | Ben Broussard | .12 | .30 |
| 488 | B.J. Ryan | .12 | .30 |
| 489 | David Eckstein | .12 | .30 |
| 490 | Alex Rios | .12 | .30 |
| 491 | Lyle Overbay | .12 | .30 |
| 492 | Scott Rolen | .20 | .50 |
| 493 | Lastings Milledge | .12 | .30 |
| 494 | Paul Lo Duca | .12 | .30 |
| 495 | Ryan Zimmerman | .20 | .50 |
| 496 | Odalis Perez | .12 | .30 |
| 497 | Wily Mo Pena | .12 | .30 |
| 498 | Elijah Dukes | .12 | .30 |
| 499 | Ronnie Belliard | .12 | .30 |
| 500 | Nick Johnson | .12 | .30 |

## 2009 Upper Deck First Edition

| | | |
|------|------|------|
| COMP.FACT.SET (400) | 20.00 | 50.00 |
| COMPLETE SET (300) | 15.00 | 40.00 |
| COMMON CARD (1-300) | .12 | .30 |
| COMMON ROOKIE (1-300) | .20 | .50 |
| COMMON CARD (301-384) | .12 | .30 |
| COMMON RC (385-400) | .20 | .50 |
| 300-400 ISSUED IN FACT.SET ONLY | | |

|  |  | | |
|---|------|------|------|
| 1 | Randy Johnson | .30 | .75 |
| 2 | Conor Jackson | .12 | .30 |
| 3 | Brandon Webb | .20 | .50 |
| 4 | Dan Haren | .20 | .50 |
| 5 | Stephen Drew | .12 | .30 |
| 6 | Mark Reynolds | .12 | .30 |
| 7 | Eric Byrnes | .12 | .30 |
| 8 | Justin Upton | .20 | .50 |
| 9 | Chris B. Young | .20 | .50 |
| 10 | Max Scherzer | .20 | .50 |
| 11 | Adam Dunn | .20 | .50 |
| 12 | David Eckstein | .12 | .30 |
| 13 | Jair Jurrjens | .20 | .50 |
| 14 | Brandon Jones | .12 | .30 |
| 15 | Tom Glavine | .20 | .50 |
| 16 | John Smoltz | .30 | .75 |
| 17 | Chipper Jones | .30 | .75 |
| 18 | Yunel Escobar | .12 | .30 |
| 19 | Kelly Johnson | .12 | .30 |
| 20 | Brian McCann | .20 | .50 |
| 21 | Jeff Francoeur | .20 | .50 |
| 22 | Tim Hudson | .12 | .30 |
| 23 | Casey Kotchman | .12 | .30 |
| 24 | James Parr (RC) | .20 | .50 |
| 25 | Nick Markakis | .20 | .50 |
| 26 | Brian Roberts | .12 | .30 |
| 27 | Jeremy Guthrie | .12 | .30 |
| 28 | Adam Jones | .20 | .50 |
| 29 | Luke Scott | .12 | .30 |
| 30 | Aubrey Huff | .12 | .30 |
| 31 | Daniel Cabrera | .12 | .30 |
| 32 | George Sherrill | .12 | .30 |
| 33 | Melvin Mora | .12 | .30 |
| 34 | David Ortiz | .20 | .50 |
| 35 | Jacoby Ellsbury | .30 | .75 |
| 36 | Coco Crisp | .12 | .30 |
| 37 | J.D. Drew | .12 | .30 |
| 38 | Daisuke Matsuzaka | .50 | 1.25 |
| 39 | Josh Beckett | .20 | .50 |
| 40 | Curt Schilling | .20 | .50 |
| 41 | Clay Buchholz | .20 | .50 |
| 42 | Dustin Pedroia | .40 | 1.00 |
| 43 | Julio Lugo | .12 | .30 |
| 44 | Mike Lowell | .12 | .30 |
| 45 | Jonathan Papelbon | .20 | .50 |
| 46 | Jason Varitek | .20 | .50 |
| 47 | Hideki Okajima | .12 | .30 |
| 48 | Jon Lester | .20 | .50 |
| 49 | Tim Wakefield | .12 | .30 |
| 50 | Kevin Youkilis | .20 | .50 |
| 51 | Jason Bay | .20 | .50 |
| 52 | Justin Masterson | .20 | .50 |
| 53 | Jeff Samardzija | .20 | .50 |
| 54 | Alfonso Soriano | .20 | .50 |
| 55 | Derrek Lee | .20 | .50 |
| 56 | Aramis Ramirez | .12 | .30 |
| 57 | Kerry Wood | .12 | .30 |
| 58 | Jim Edmonds | .12 | .30 |
| 59 | Kosuke Fukudome | .30 | .75 |
| 60 | Geovany Soto | .20 | .50 |
| 61 | Ted Lilly | .12 | .30 |
| 62 | Carlos Zambrano | .12 | .30 |
| 63 | Ryan Theriot | .12 | .30 |
| 64 | Mark DeRosa | .12 | .30 |
| 65 | Ryan Dempster | .12 | .30 |
| 66 | Rich Harden | .12 | .30 |
| 67 | Alexei Ramirez | .20 | .50 |
| 68 | Nick Swisher | .12 | .30 |
| 69 | Carlos Quentin | .12 | .30 |
| 70 | Jermaine Dye | .12 | .30 |
| 71 | Paul Konerko | .12 | .30 |
| 72 | Joe Crede | .12 | .30 |
| 73 | Jim Thome | .20 | .50 |
| 74 | Gavin Floyd | .12 | .30 |
| 75 | Javier Vazquez | .12 | .30 |
| 76 | Mark Buehrle | .12 | .30 |
| 77 | Bobby Jenks | .12 | .30 |
| 78 | Ken Griffey Jr. | .50 | 1.25 |
| 79 | Brandon Phillips | .12 | .30 |
| 80 | Aaron Harang | .12 | .30 |
| 81 | Edinson Volquez | .12 | .30 |
| 82 | Johnny Cueto | .12 | .30 |
| 83 | Edwin Encarnacion | .12 | .30 |
| 84 | Joey Votto | .20 | .50 |
| 85 | Jay Bruce | .30 | .75 |
| 86 | Travis Hafner | .12 | .30 |
| 87 | Victor Martinez | .20 | .50 |
| 88 | Grady Sizemore | .20 | .50 |
| 89 | Cliff Lee | .20 | .50 |
| 90 | Ryan Garko | .12 | .30 |
| 91 | Jhonny Peralta | .12 | .30 |
| 92 | Fausto Carmona | .12 | .30 |
| 93 | Troy Tulowitzki | .20 | .50 |
| 94 | Matt Holliday | .20 | .50 |
| 95 | Todd Helton | .20 | .50 |
| 96 | Ubaldo Jimenez | .12 | .30 |
| 97 | Brian Fuentes | .12 | .30 |
| 98 | Willy Taveras | .12 | .30 |
| 99 | Aaron Cook | .12 | .30 |
| 100 | Garrett Atkins | .12 | .30 |
| 101 | Jeff Francis | .12 | .30 |
| 102 | Dexter Fowler (RC) | .30 | .75 |
| 103 | Armando Galarraga | .12 | .30 |
| 104 | Miguel Cabrera | .20 | .50 |
| 105 | Carlos Guillen | .12 | .30 |
| 106 | Gary Sheffield | .12 | .30 |
| 107 | Curtis Granderson | .30 | .75 |
| 108 | Magglio Ordonez | .20 | .50 |
| 109 | Dontrelle Willis | .12 | .30 |
| 110 | Kenny Rogers | .12 | .30 |
| 111 | Justin Verlander | .20 | .50 |
| 112 | Hanley Ramirez | .30 | .75 |
| 113 | Jeremy Hermida | .12 | .30 |
| 114 | Mike Jacobs | .12 | .30 |
| 115 | Andrew Miller | .20 | .50 |
| 116 | Josh Willingham | .12 | .30 |
| 117 | Dan Uggla | .12 | .30 |
| 118 | Josh Johnson | .12 | .30 |
| 119 | Hunter Pence | .20 | .50 |
| 120 | Roy Oswalt | .20 | .50 |
| 121 | Lance Berkman | .20 | .50 |
| 122 | Carlos Lee | .12 | .30 |
| 123 | Michael Bourn | .20 | .50 |
| 124 | Miguel Tejada | .20 | .50 |
| 125 | Jose Valverde | .12 | .30 |
| 126 | Mike Aviles | .12 | .30 |
| 127 | Zack Greinke | .20 | .50 |
| 128 | Gil Meche | .12 | .30 |
| 129 | Alex Gordon | .20 | .50 |
| 130 | Luke Hochevar | .12 | .30 |
| 131 | Jose Guillen | .12 | .30 |
| 132 | Billy Butler | .12 | .30 |
| 133 | David DeJesus | .12 | .30 |
| 134 | Mark Teahen | .12 | .30 |
| 135 | Joakim Soria | .12 | .30 |
| 136 | Mark Teixeira | .30 | .75 |
| 137 | Vladimir Guerrero | .30 | .75 |
| 138 | Torii Hunter | .12 | .30 |
| 139 | Jered Weaver | .12 | .30 |
| 140 | Chone Figgins | .12 | .30 |
| 141 | Francisco Rodriguez | .20 | .50 |
| 142 | Garret Anderson | .12 | .30 |
| 143 | Howie Kendrick | .12 | .30 |
| 144 | John Lackey | .12 | .30 |
| 145 | Ervin Santana | .12 | .30 |
| 146 | Joe Saunders | .12 | .30 |
| 147 | Manny Ramirez | .30 | .75 |
| 148 | Casey Blake | .12 | .30 |
| 149 | Chad Billingsley | .12 | .30 |
| 150 | Russell Martin | .20 | .50 |
| 151 | Matt Kemp | .30 | .75 |
| 152 | James Loney | .20 | .50 |
| 153 | Jeff Kent | .12 | .30 |
| 154 | Nomar Garciaparra | .20 | .50 |
| 155 | Rafael Furcal | .12 | .30 |
| 156 | Andruw Jones | .12 | .30 |
| 157 | Andre Ethier | .12 | .30 |
| 158 | Takashi Saito | .12 | .30 |
| 159 | Brad Penny | .12 | .30 |
| 160 | Hiroki Kuroda | .12 | .30 |
| 161 | Jonathan Broxton | .12 | .30 |
| 162 | Chin-Lung Hu | .12 | .30 |
| 163 | Derek Lowe | .12 | .30 |

|  |  | | |
|---|---|---|---|
| 164 | Clayton Kershaw | .30 | .75 |
| 165 | Greg Maddux | .40 | 1.00 |
| 166 | CC Sabathia | .20 | .50 |
| 167 | Yovani Gallardo | .12 | .30 |
| 168 | Ryan Braun | .40 | 1.00 |
| 169 | Prince Fielder | .30 | .75 |
| 170 | Corey Hart | .12 | .30 |
| 171 | Bill Hall | .12 | .30 |
| 172 | Rickie Weeks | .12 | .30 |
| 173 | Mike Cameron | .12 | .30 |
| 174 | Ben Sheets | .12 | .30 |
| 175 | J.J. Hardy | .12 | .30 |
| 176 | Mat Gamel RC | .50 | 1.25 |
| 177 | Denard Span | .20 | .50 |
| 178 | Carlos Gomez | .12 | .30 |
| 179 | Joe Mauer | .30 | .75 |
| 180 | Justin Morneau | .20 | .50 |
| 181 | Joe Nathan | .12 | .30 |
| 182 | Delmon Young | .20 | .50 |
| 183 | Francisco Liriano | .12 | .30 |
| 184 | Nick Blackburn | .12 | .30 |
| 185 | Daniel Murphy RC | .30 | .75 |
| 186 | Nick Evans | .12 | .30 |
| 187 | Jose Reyes | .30 | .75 |
| 188 | David Wright | .40 | 1.00 |
| 189 | Carlos Delgado | .12 | .30 |
| 190 | Ryan Church | .12 | .30 |
| 191 | Carlos Beltran | .20 | .50 |
| 192 | Pedro Martinez | .30 | .75 |
| 193 | Johan Santana | .30 | .75 |
| 194 | John Maine | .12 | .30 |
| 195 | Endy Chavez | .12 | .30 |
| 196 | Oliver Perez | .12 | .30 |
| 197 | Mike Pelfrey | .12 | .30 |
| 198 | Jonathon Niese RC | .30 | .75 |
| 199 | Ivan Rodriguez | .20 | .50 |
| 200 | Alex Rodriguez | .50 | 1.25 |
| 201 | Derek Jeter | .75 | 2.00 |
| 202 | Robinson Cano | .20 | .50 |
| 203 | Jason Giambi | .12 | .30 |
| 204 | Bobby Abreu | .12 | .30 |
| 205 | Johnny Damon | .20 | .50 |
| 206 | Hideki Matsui | .30 | .75 |
| 207 | Jorge Posada | .20 | .50 |
| 208 | Joba Chamberlain | .40 | 1.00 |
| 209 | Ian Kennedy | .20 | .50 |
| 210 | Mike Mussina | .20 | .50 |
| 211 | Andy Pettitte | .20 | .50 |
| 212 | Mariano Rivera | .20 | .50 |
| 213 | Chien-Ming Wang | .30 | .75 |
| 214 | Phil Hughes | .20 | .50 |
| 215 | Xavier Nady | .12 | .30 |
| 216 | Justin Duchscherer | .12 | .30 |
| 217 | Eric Chavez | .12 | .30 |
| 218 | Bobby Crosby | .12 | .30 |
| 219 | Mark Ellis | .12 | .30 |
| 220 | Daric Barton | .12 | .30 |
| 221 | Frank Thomas | .30 | .75 |
| 222 | Huston Street | .12 | .30 |
| 223 | Jack Cust | .12 | .30 |
| 224 | Greg Golson (RC) | .20 | .50 |
| 225 | Joe Blanton | .12 | .30 |
| 226 | Ryan Howard | .40 | 1.00 |
| 227 | Chase Utley | .30 | .75 |
| 228 | Jimmy Rollins | .20 | .50 |
| 229 | Pat Burrell | .20 | .50 |
| 230 | Shane Victorino | .12 | .30 |
| 231 | Brett Myers | .12 | .30 |
| 232 | Brad Lidge | .12 | .30 |
| 233 | Cole Hamels | .30 | .75 |
| 234 | Nate McLouth | .12 | .30 |
| 235 | Ian Snell | .12 | .30 |
| 236 | Ryan Doumit | .12 | .30 |
| 237 | Matt Antonelli RC | .30 | .75 |
| 238 | Will Venable RC | .20 | .50 |
| 239 | Jake Peavy | .20 | .50 |
| 240 | Chris Young | .12 | .30 |
| 241 | Trevor Hoffman | .12 | .30 |
| 242 | Adrian Gonzalez | .20 | .50 |
| 243 | Chase Headley | .12 | .30 |
| 244 | Khalil Greene | .12 | .30 |
| 245 | Kevin Kouzmanoff | .12 | .30 |
| 246 | Brian Giles | .12 | .30 |
| 247 | Barry Zito | .12 | .30 |
| 248 | Tim Lincecum | .40 | 1.00 |
| 249 | Matt Cain | .12 | .30 |
| 250 | Brian Wilson | .12 | .30 |
| 251 | Aaron Rowand | .12 | .30 |
| 252 | Conor Gillaspie RC | .50 | 1.25 |
| 253 | Omar Vizquel | .12 | .30 |
| 254 | Bengie Molina | .12 | .30 |
| 255 | Erik Bedard | .12 | .30 |
| 256 | Felix Hernandez | .20 | .50 |
| 257 | Ichiro Suzuki | .50 | 1.25 |
| 258 | J.J. Putz | .12 | .30 |
| 259 | Raul Ibanez | .12 | .30 |
| 260 | Adrian Beltre | .12 | .30 |
| 261 | Jeff Clement | .12 | .30 |
| 262 | Kenji Johjima | .20 | .50 |
| 263 | Jose Lopez | .12 | .30 |
| 264 | Albert Pujols | .75 | 2.00 |
| 265 | Troy Glaus | .20 | .50 |
| 266 | Chris Carpenter | .20 | .50 |
| 267 | Rick Ankiel | .20 | .50 |
| 268 | Adam Wainwright | .20 | .50 |
| 269 | Chris Duncan | .12 | .30 |
| 270 | Todd Wellemeyer | .12 | .30 |
| 271 | Ryan Ludwick | .20 | .50 |
| 272 | Yadier Molina | .20 | .50 |
| 273 | B.J. Upton | .20 | .50 |
| 274 | Carl Crawford | .20 | .50 |
| 275 | Evan Longoria | .50 | 1.25 |
| 276 | James Shields | .20 | .50 |
| 277 | Scott Kazmir | .20 | .50 |
| 278 | Carlos Pena | .20 | .50 |
| 279 | Akinori Iwamura | .20 | .50 |
| 280 | David Price RC | .60 | 1.50 |
| 281 | Matt Garza | .12 | .30 |
| 282 | Rocco Baldelli | .12 | .30 |
| 283 | Michael Young | .20 | .50 |
| 284 | Ian Kinsler | .20 | .50 |
| 285 | Josh Hamilton | .30 | .75 |
| 286 | Hank Blalock | .12 | .30 |
| 287 | Milton Bradley | .12 | .30 |
| 288 | Jarrod Saltalamacchia | .12 | .30 |
| 289 | Roy Halladay | .20 | .50 |
| 290 | A.J. Burnett | .20 | .50 |
| 291 | Dustin McGowan | .12 | .30 |
| 292 | Scott Rolen | .30 | .75 |
| 293 | Alex Rios | .12 | .30 |
| 294 | Vernon Wells | .12 | .30 |
| 295 | B.J. Ryan | .12 | .30 |
| 296 | Elijah Dukes | .12 | .30 |
| 297 | Lastings Milledge | .12 | .30 |
| 298 | Chad Cordero | .12 | .30 |
| 299 | Ryan Zimmerman | .20 | .50 |
| 300 | Cristian Guzman | .12 | .30 |
| 301 | Brandon Webb | .20 | .50 |
| 302 | Chris B. Young | .12 | .30 |
| 303 | Justin Upton | .20 | .50 |
| 304 | Conor Jackson | .12 | .30 |
| 305 | Tom Glavine | .20 | .50 |
| 306 | Javier Vazquez | .12 | .30 |
| 307 | Chipper Jones | .30 | .75 |
| 308 | Nick Markakis | .20 | .50 |
| 309 | Brian Roberts | .12 | .30 |
| 310 | Adam Jones | .20 | .50 |
| 311 | Ty Wigginton | .12 | .30 |
| 312 | John Smoltz | .30 | .75 |
| 313 | Brad Penny | .12 | .30 |
| 314 | Takashi Saito | .12 | .30 |
| 315 | Josh Beckett | .20 | .50 |
| 316 | Dustin Pedroia | .40 | 1.00 |
| 317 | David Ortiz | .20 | .50 |
| 318 | Jason Varitek | .12 | .30 |
| 319 | Milton Bradley | .12 | .30 |
| 320 | Alfonso Soriano | .20 | .50 |
| 321 | Kosuke Fukudome | .30 | .75 |
| 322 | Carlos Zambrano | .12 | .30 |
| 323 | Jim Thome | .20 | .50 |
| 324 | Chris Getz | .12 | .30 |
| 325 | Octavio Dotel | .12 | .30 |
| 326 | Joey Votto | .20 | .50 |
| 327 | Jay Bruce | .30 | .75 |
| 328 | Kerry Wood | .12 | .30 |
| 329 | Mark DeRosa | .12 | .30 |
| 330 | Grady Sizemore | .20 | .50 |
| 331 | Troy Tulowitzki | .20 | .50 |
| 332 | Todd Helton | .20 | .50 |
| 333 | Adam Everett | .12 | .30 |
| 334 | Cameron Maybin | .20 | .50 |
| 335 | Roy Oswalt | .20 | .50 |
| 336 | Lance Berkman | .20 | .50 |
| 337 | Joakim Soria | .12 | .30 |
| 338 | Alex Gordon | .20 | .50 |
| 339 | Bobby Abreu | .12 | .30 |
| 340 | Vladimir Guerrero | .30 | .75 |
| 341 | Manny Ramirez | .30 | .75 |
| 342 | Orlando Hudson | .12 | .30 |
| 343 | Mark Loretta | .12 | .30 |
| 344 | Russell Martin | .20 | .50 |
| 345 | Trevor Hoffman | .12 | .30 |
| 346 | Ryan Braun | .40 | 1.00 |
| 347 | Francisco Liriano | .12 | .30 |
| 348 | Joe Mauer | .30 | .75 |
| 349 | Livan Hernandez | .12 | .30 |
| 350 | Jeremy Reed | .12 | .30 |
| 351 | J.J. Putz | .12 | .30 |
| 352 | Francisco Rodriguez | .20 | .50 |
| 353 | Johan Santana | .30 | .75 |
| 354 | Jose Reyes | .30 | .75 |
| 355 | David Wright | .40 | 1.00 |
| 356 | Derek Jeter | .75 | 2.00 |
| 357 | A.J. Burnett | .20 | .50 |
| 358 | Nick Swisher | .12 | .30 |
| 359 | CC Sabathia | .20 | .50 |
| 360 | Chien-Ming Wang | .30 | .75 |
| 361 | Mark Teixeira | .30 | .75 |
| 362 | Joba Chamberlain | .40 | 1.00 |
| 363 | Alex Rodriguez | .50 | 1.25 |
| 364 | Orlando Cabrera | .12 | .30 |
| 365 | Matt Holliday | .20 | .50 |
| 366 | Jason Giambi | .12 | .30 |
| 367 | Chan Ho Park | .12 | .30 |
| 368 | Cole Hamels | .30 | .75 |
| 369 | Ryan Howard | .40 | 1.00 |
| 370 | Chase Utley | .30 | .75 |
| 371 | Randy Johnson | .30 | .75 |
| 372 | Edgar Renteria | .12 | .30 |
| 373 | Ken Griffey Jr. | .50 | 1.25 |
| 374 | Ichiro Suzuki | .50 | 1.25 |
| 375 | Khalil Greene | .12 | .30 |
| 376 | Albert Pujols | .75 | 2.00 |
| 377 | Akinori Iwamura | .20 | .50 |
| 378 | B.J. Upton | .20 | .50 |
| 379 | Evan Longoria | .50 | 1.25 |
| 380 | Josh Hamilton | .30 | .75 |
| 381 | Nelson Cruz | .12 | .30 |
| 382 | Adam Dunn | .20 | .50 |
| 383 | Josh Willingham | .12 | .30 |
| 384 | Daniel Cabrera | .12 | .30 |
| 385 | Koji Uehara RC | .50 | 1.25 |
| 386 | Kenshin Kawakami RC | .50 | 1.25 |
| 387 | Jason Motte (RC) | .20 | .50 |
| 388 | Elvis Andrus RC | .50 | 1.25 |
| 389 | Rick Porcello RC | .75 | 2.00 |
| 390 | Colby Rasmus (RC) | .30 | .75 |
| 391 | Shairon Martis RC | .30 | .75 |
| 392 | Ricky Romero (RC) | .20 | .50 |
| 393 | Kevin Jepsen (RC) | .20 | .50 |
| 394 | James McDonald RC | .50 | 1.25 |
| 395 | Brett Anderson RC | .30 | .75 |
| 396 | Trevor Cahill RC | .30 | .75 |
| 397 | Jordan Schafer RC | .30 | .75 |
| 398 | Trevor Crowe RC | .30 | .75 |
| 399 | Everth Cabrera RC | .30 | .75 |
| 400 | Ryan Perry RC | .50 | 1.25 |

## 2006 Upper Deck Future Stars

| | | |
|---|---|---|
| ☐ COMP.SET w/o AU's (75) | 10.00 | 25.00 |
| ☐ COMMON CARD (1-75) | .15 | .40 |
| ☐ COMMON AU RC (76-159) | 3.00 | 8.00 |
| ☐ FIVE AU PER BOX ON AVERAGE | | |
| ☐ NO SP PRICING DUE TO SCARCITY | | |
| ☐ PRINTING PLATE ODDS 1:2 CASES | | |
| ☐ PLATE PRINT RUN 1 SET PER COLOR | | |
| ☐ BLACK-CYAN-MAGENTA-YELLOW ISSUED | | |
| ☐ NO PLATE PRICING DUE TO SCARCITY | | |
| ☐ 1 Miguel Tejada | .15 | .40 |
| ☐ 2 Brian Roberts | .15 | .40 |
| ☐ 3 Brandon Webb | .15 | .40 |
| ☐ 4 Luis Gonzalez | .15 | .40 |
| ☐ 5 Andruw Jones | .25 | .60 |
| ☐ 6 Chipper Jones | .40 | 1.00 |
| ☐ 7 John Smoltz | .25 | .60 |
| ☐ 8 Curt Schilling | .25 | .60 |
| ☐ 9 Josh Beckett | .15 | .40 |
| ☐ 10 David Ortiz | .25 | .60 |
| ☐ 11 Manny Ramirez | .25 | .60 |
| ☐ 12 Jim Thome | .25 | .60 |
| ☐ 13 Paul Konerko | .15 | .40 |
| ☐ 14 Jermaine Dye | .15 | .40 |
| ☐ 15 Derrek Lee | .15 | .40 |
| ☐ 16 Greg Maddux | .60 | 1.50 |
| ☐ 17 Ken Griffey Jr. | .60 | 1.50 |
| ☐ 18 Adam Dunn | .15 | .40 |
| ☐ 19 Felipe Lopez | .15 | .40 |
| ☐ 20 Travis Hafner | .15 | .40 |
| ☐ 21 Victor Martinez | .15 | .40 |
| ☐ 22 Grady Sizemore | .25 | .60 |
| ☐ 23 Todd Helton | .25 | .60 |
| ☐ 24 Matt Holliday | .40 | 1.00 |
| ☐ 25 Jeremy Bonderman | .15 | .40 |
| ☐ 26 Ivan Rodriguez | .25 | .60 |
| ☐ 27 Miguel Cabrera | .25 | .60 |
| ☐ 28 Dontrelle Willis | .15 | .40 |
| ☐ 29 Roger Clemens | .75 | 2.00 |
| ☐ 30 Roy Oswalt | .15 | .40 |
| ☐ 31 Lance Berkman | .15 | .40 |
| ☐ 32 Reggie Sanders | .15 | .40 |
| ☐ 33 Vladimir Guerrero | .40 | 1.00 |
| ☐ 34 Chone Figgins | .15 | .40 |
| ☐ 35 Jeff Kent | .15 | .40 |
| ☐ 36 Eric Gagne | .15 | .40 |
| ☐ 37 Carlos Lee | .15 | .40 |
| ☐ 38 Rickie Weeks | .15 | .40 |
| ☐ 39 Johan Santana | .25 | .60 |
| ☐ 40 Torii Hunter | .15 | .40 |
| ☐ 41 Alex Rodriguez | .60 | 1.50 |
| ☐ 42 Derek Jeter | 1.00 | 2.50 |
| ☐ 43 Randy Johnson | .40 | 1.00 |
| ☐ 44 Hideki Matsui | .40 | 1.00 |
| ☐ 45 Johnny Damon | .25 | .60 |
| ☐ 46 Pedro Martinez | .25 | .60 |
| ☐ 47 David Wright | .60 | 1.50 |
| ☐ 48 Carlos Beltran | .15 | .40 |
| ☐ 49 Rich Harden | .15 | .40 |
| ☐ 50 Eric Chavez | .15 | .40 |
| ☐ 51 Huston Street | .15 | .40 |
| ☐ 52 Ryan Howard | .60 | 1.50 |
| ☐ 53 Bobby Abreu | .15 | .40 |
| ☐ 54 Chase Utley | .40 | 1.00 |
| ☐ 55 Jason Bay | .15 | .40 |
| ☐ 56 Jake Peavy | .15 | .40 |

| | | |
|---|---|---|
| ☐ 57 Brian Giles | .15 | .40 |
| ☐ 58 Trevor Hoffman | .15 | .40 |
| ☐ 59 Jason Schmidt | .15 | .40 |
| ☐ 60 Randy Winn | .15 | .40 |
| ☐ 61 Kenji Johjima RC | .75 | 2.00 |
| ☐ 62 Ichiro Suzuki | .60 | 1.50 |
| ☐ 63 Felix Hernandez | .25 | .60 |
| ☐ 64 Albert Pujols | .75 | 2.00 |
| ☐ 65 Chris Carpenter | .15 | .40 |
| ☐ 66 Jim Edmonds | .25 | .50 |
| ☐ 67 Carl Crawford | .15 | .40 |
| ☐ 68 Scott Kazmir | .25 | .60 |
| ☐ 69 Jonny Gomes | .15 | .40 |
| ☐ 70 Mark Teixeira | .25 | .60 |
| ☐ 71 Michael Young | .15 | .40 |
| ☐ 72 Vernon Wells | .15 | .40 |
| ☐ 73 Roy Halladay | .15 | .40 |
| ☐ 74 Nick Johnson | .15 | .40 |
| ☐ 75 Alfonso Soriano | .15 | .40 |
| ☐ 76 A.Wainwright AU (RC) | 8.00 | 20.00 |
| ☐ 77 A.Hernandez AU (RC) | 3.00 | 8.00 |
| ☐ 78 A.Ethier AU SP (RC) | 10.00 | 25.00 |
| ☐ 79 Colter Bean AU SP (RC) | 4.00 | 10.00 |
| ☐ 80 Ben Johnson AU (RC) | 3.00 | 8.00 |
| ☐ 81 Boof Bonser AU SP (RC) | 5.00 | 12.00 |
| ☐ 82 Boone Logan AU (RC) | 3.00 | 8.00 |
| ☐ 83 Brian Anderson AU (RC) | 3.00 | 8.00 |
| ☐ 84 B.Bannister AU (RC) | 4.00 | 10.00 |
| ☐ 85 C.Denorfia AU SP (RC) | 4.00 | 10.00 |
| ☐ 86 C.Billingsley AU SP (RC) | 8.00 | 20.00 |
| ☐ 87 Cody Ross AU (RC) | 3.00 | 8.00 |
| ☐ 88 Cole Hamels AU SP (RC) | 30.00 | 60.00 |
| ☐ 89 Conor Jackson AU (RC) | 5.00 | 12.00 |
| ☐ 90 Dan Uggla AU SP (RC) | | |
| ☐ 91 D.Gassner AU SP (RC) | 3.00 | 8.00 |
| ☐ 92 Jordan Tata AU RC | 3.00 | 8.00 |
| ☐ 93 Eric Reed AU (RC) | 3.00 | 8.00 |
| ☐ 94 Fausto Carmona AU (RC) | 5.00 | 12.00 |
| ☐ 95 Luis Figueroa AU SP RC | | |
| ☐ 96 F.Liriano AU SP (RC) | 10.00 | 25.00 |
| ☐ 97 Freddie Bynum AU (RC) | 3.00 | 8.00 |
| ☐ 98 H.Ramirez AU SP (RC) | 8.00 | 20.00 |
| ☐ 99 H.Kuo AU SP (RC) | 30.00 | 60.00 |
| ☐ 100 Ian Kinsler AU (RC) | 6.00 | 15.00 |
| ☐ 101 N.Cruz AU SP (RC) | 5.00 | 12.00 |
| ☐ 102 Ruddy Lugo AU (RC) | 3.00 | 8.00 |
| ☐ 103 J.Kubel AU SP (RC) | 3.00 | 8.00 |
| ☐ 104 Jeff Harris AU RC | 3.00 | 8.00 |
| ☐ 105 S.Ramirez AU (RC) | 3.00 | 8.00 |
| ☐ 106 Jer.Weaver AU SP (RC) | 20.00 | 50.00 |
| ☐ 107 J.Accardo AU SP RC | 6.00 | 15.00 |
| ☐ 108 J.Willingham AU SP (RC) | 3.00 | 8.00 |
| ☐ 109 J.Zumaya AU SP (RC) | 10.00 | 25.00 |
| ☐ 110 Joey Devine AU RC | 3.00 | 8.00 |
| ☐ 111 John Koronka AU (RC) | 3.00 | 8.00 |
| ☐ 112 J.Papelbon AU (RC) | 15.00 | 40.00 |
| ☐ 113 Jose Capellan AU (RC) | 3.00 | 8.00 |
| ☐ 114 Josh Johnson AU (RC) | 5.00 | 12.00 |
| ☐ 115 Josh Rupe AU SP (RC) | 3.00 | 8.00 |
| ☐ 116 J.Hermida AU SP (RC) | 3.00 | 8.00 |
| ☐ 117 Josh Wilson AU (RC) | 3.00 | 8.00 |
| ☐ 118 J.Verlander AU SP (RC) | | |
| ☐ 119 K.Shoppach AU (RC) | | |
| ☐ 120 K.Morales AU (RC) | 3.00 | 8.00 |
| ☐ 121 Sean Tracey AU (RC) | 5.00 | 12.00 |
| ☐ 122 Macay McBride AU (RC) | 3.00 | 8.00 |
| ☐ 123 M.Prado AU SP (RC) | | |
| ☐ 124 Matt Cain AU (RC) | 5.00 | 12.00 |
| ☐ 125 R.Martin AU (RC) | 5.00 | 12.00 |
| ☐ 126 T.Hamulack AU SP (RC) | 3.00 | 8.00 |
| ☐ 127 M.Jacobs AU (RC) | 5.00 | 12.00 |
| ☐ 128 B.Hendrickson AU (RC) | 3.00 | 8.00 |
| ☐ 129 Jack Taschner AU (RC) | 3.00 | 8.00 |
| ☐ 130 N.McLouth AU (RC) | 6.00 | 15.00 |
| ☐ 131 J.Sowers AU SP (RC) | 8.00 | 20.00 |
| ☐ 132 Paul Maholm AU (RC) | 3.00 | 8.00 |
| ☐ 133 S.Drew AU SP (RC) | | |
| ☐ 134 Jason Bergmann AU (RC) | 3.00 | 8.00 |
| ☐ 135 Rich Hill AU SP (RC) | 12.50 | 30.00 |
| ☐ 136 M.Cabrera AU SP (RC) | | |
| ☐ 137 Scott Dunn AU (RC) | 3.00 | 8.00 |

| | | |
|---|---|---|
| ☐ 138 R.Zimmerman AU (RC) | 20.00 | 50.00 |
| ☐ 139 A.Sanchez AU (RC) | 5.00 | 12.00 |
| ☐ 140 Sean Marshall AU (RC) | 5.00 | 12.00 |
| ☐ 141 T.Saito AU SP RC | | |
| ☐ 142 T.Buchholz AU (RC) | 3.00 | 8.00 |
| ☐ 143 C.Quentin AU SP (RC) | 4.00 | 10.00 |
| ☐ 144 Matt Garza AU (RC) | 8.00 | 20.00 |
| ☐ 145 Wil Nieves AU (RC) | 3.00 | 8.00 |
| ☐ 146 Jamie Shields AU RC | 10.00 | 25.00 |
| ☐ 147 Jon Lester AU SP RC | 15.00 | 40.00 |
| ☐ 148 Craig Hansen AU SP RC | | |
| ☐ 149 Aaron Rakers AU (RC) | 3.00 | 8.00 |
| ☐ 150 B.Livingston AU (RC) | 3.00 | 8.00 |
| ☐ 151 B.Harris AU (RC) | 3.00 | 8.00 |
| ☐ 152 Alay Soler AU SP RC | 3.00 | 8.00 |
| ☐ 153 Chris Britton AU RC | 3.00 | 8.00 |
| ☐ 154 H.Kendrick AU SP (RC) | 15.00 | 40.00 |
| ☐ 155 J.Van Buren AU (RC) | 3.00 | 8.00 |
| ☐ 156 C.Freeman AU SP (RC) | 3.00 | 8.00 |
| ☐ 157 Matt Capps AU (RC) | 3.00 | 8.00 |
| ☐ 158 Peter Moylan AU RC | 3.00 | 8.00 |
| ☐ 159 Ty Taubenheim AU RC | 5.00 | 12.00 |

## 2007 Upper Deck Future Stars

| | | |
|---|---|---|
| ☐ COMP.SET w/o AU's (100) | 10.00 | 25.00 |
| ☐ COMMON CARD (1-100) | .15 | .40 |
| ☐ COMMON AU RC (101-190) | 3.00 | 8.00 |
| ☐ 101-190 ODDS 1:6 HOB, 1:24 RET, 1:350 WALMART | | |
| ☐ EXCHANGE DEADLINE 9/5/2009 | | |
| ☐ 1 Brandon Webb | .15 | .40 |
| ☐ 2 Conor Jackson | .15 | .40 |
| ☐ 3 Stephen Drew | .25 | .60 |
| ☐ 4 Chipper Jones | .40 | 1.00 |
| ☐ 5 Andruw Jones | .25 | .60 |
| ☐ 6 Jeff Francoeur | .40 | 1.00 |
| ☐ 7 John Smoltz | .25 | .60 |
| ☐ 8 Miguel Tejada | .15 | .40 |
| ☐ 9 Nick Markakis | .25 | .60 |
| ☐ 10 Brian Roberts | .15 | .40 |
| ☐ 11 David Ortiz | .40 | 1.00 |
| ☐ 12 Manny Ramirez | .25 | .60 |
| ☐ 13 Josh Beckett | .15 | .40 |
| ☐ 14 Curt Schilling | .15 | .40 |
| ☐ 15 Derrek Lee | .15 | .40 |
| ☐ 16 Aramis Ramirez | .15 | .40 |
| ☐ 17 Carlos Zambrano | .15 | .40 |
| ☐ 18 Alfonso Soriano | .15 | .40 |
| ☐ 19 Jim Thome | .25 | .60 |
| ☐ 20 Paul Konerko | .15 | .40 |
| ☐ 21 Jon Garland | .15 | .40 |
| ☐ 22 Ken Griffey Jr. | .60 | 1.50 |
| ☐ 23 Adam Dunn | .15 | .40 |
| ☐ 24 Aaron Harang | .15 | .40 |
| ☐ 25 Travis Hafner | .15 | .40 |
| ☐ 26 Victor Martinez | .15 | .40 |
| ☐ 27 Grady Sizemore | .25 | .60 |
| ☐ 28 C.C. Sabathia | .15 | .40 |
| ☐ 29 Todd Helton | .25 | .60 |
| ☐ 30 Matt Holliday | .20 | .50 |
| ☐ 31 Garrett Atkins | .15 | .40 |
| ☐ 32 Ivan Rodriguez | .25 | .60 |
| ☐ 33 Magglio Ordonez | .15 | .40 |
| ☐ 34 Gary Sheffield | .15 | .40 |
| ☐ 35 Justin Verlander | .40 | 1.00 |
| ☐ 36 Miguel Cabrera | .25 | .60 |
| ☐ 37 Hanley Ramirez | .25 | .60 |
| ☐ 38 Dontrelle Willis | .15 | .40 |

|  | | |
|---|---|---|
| 39 Lance Berkman | .15 | .40 |
| 40 Roy Oswalt | .15 | .40 |
| 41 Carlos Lee | .15 | .40 |
| 42 Gil Meche | .15 | .40 |
| 43 Emil Brown | .15 | .40 |
| 44 Mark Teahen | .15 | .40 |
| 45 Vladimir Guerrero | .40 | 1.00 |
| 46 Jered Weaver | .25 | .60 |
| 47 Howie Kendrick | .15 | .40 |
| 48 Juan Pierre | .15 | .40 |
| 49 Nomar Garciaparra | .40 | 1.00 |
| 50 Rafael Furcal | .15 | .40 |
| 51 Jeff Kent | .15 | .40 |
| 52 Prince Fielder | .40 | 1.00 |
| 53 Ben Sheets | .15 | .40 |
| 54 Rickie Weeks | .15 | .40 |
| 55 Justin Morneau | .15 | .40 |
| 56 Joe Mauer | .25 | .60 |
| 57 Torii Hunter | .15 | .40 |
| 58 Johan Santana | .25 | .60 |
| 59 Jose Reyes | .40 | 1.00 |
| 60 David Wright | .50 | 1.50 |
| 61 Carlos Delgado | .15 | .40 |
| 62 Carlos Beltran | .15 | .40 |
| 63 Derek Jeter | 1.00 | 2.50 |
| 64 Alex Rodriguez | .60 | 1.50 |
| 65 Johnny Damon | .25 | .60 |
| 66 Jason Giambi | .15 | .40 |
| 67 Bobby Abreu | .15 | .40 |
| 68 Mike Piazza | .40 | 1.00 |
| 69 Nick Swisher | .15 | .40 |
| 70 Eric Chavez | .15 | .40 |
| 71 Ryan Howard | .60 | 1.50 |
| 72 Chase Utley | .40 | 1.00 |
| 73 Jimmy Rollins | .15 | .40 |
| 74 Jason Bay | .15 | .40 |
| 75 Freddy Sanchez | .15 | .40 |
| 76 Zach Duke | .15 | .40 |
| 77 Greg Maddux | .60 | 1.50 |
| 78 Adrian Gonzalez | .15 | .40 |
| 79 Jake Peavy | .15 | .40 |
| 80 Ray Durham | .15 | .40 |
| 81 Barry Zito | .15 | .40 |
| 82 Matt Cain | .15 | .40 |
| 83 Ichiro Suzuki | .60 | 1.50 |
| 84 Felix Hernandez | .25 | .60 |
| 85 Richie Sexson | .15 | .40 |
| 86 Albert Pujols | .75 | 2.00 |
| 87 Scott Rolen | .25 | .60 |
| 88 Chris Carpenter | .15 | .40 |
| 89 Chris Duncan | .15 | .40 |
| 90 Carl Crawford | .15 | .40 |
| 91 Rocco Baldelli | .15 | .40 |
| 92 Scott Kazmir | .25 | .60 |
| 93 Michael Young | .25 | .60 |
| 94 Mark Teixeira | .25 | .60 |
| 95 Ian Kinsler | .15 | .40 |
| 96 Troy Glaus | .15 | .40 |
| 97 Vernon Wells | .15 | .40 |
| 98 Roy Halladay | .15 | .40 |
| 99 Ryan Zimmerman | .40 | 1.00 |
| 100 Nick Johnson | .15 | .40 |
| 101 Zack Segovia AU (RC) | 3.00 | 8.00 |
| 102 Joaquin Arias AU (RC) | 3.00 | 8.00 |
| 103 T.Tulowitzki AU SP (RC) | | |
| 104 Travis Buck AU (RC) | 4.00 | 10.00 |
| 105 Mike Schultz AU RC | 3.00 | 8.00 |
| 106 Sean White AU SP RC | | |
| 107 Sean Henn AU (RC) | 3.00 | 8.00 |
| 108 Ryan Z. Braun AU RC | 6.00 | 15.00 |
| 109 Rick Vanden Hurk AU RC | 3.00 | 8.00 |
| 110 Carlos Gomez AU SP RC | | |
| 111 Mike Rabelo AU RC | 4.00 | 10.00 |
| 112 Felix Pie AU (RC) | 4.00 | 10.00 |
| 113 Miguel Montero AU (RC) | 4.00 | 10.00 |
| 114 Michael Bourn AU (RC) | 4.00 | 10.00 |
| 115 M.Owings AU SP (RC) EXCH | | |
| 116 Matt Lindstrom AU (RC) | 3.00 | 8.00 |
| 117 Matt Chico AU (RC) | 3.00 | 8.00 |
| 118 Levale Speigner AU RC | 3.00 | 8.00 |
| 119 Lee Gardner AU (RC) | 3.00 | 8.00 |
| 120 Kory Casto AU (RC) | 4.00 | 10.00 |
| 121 Kevin Kouzmanoff AU (RC) | 4.00 | 10.00 |
| 122 Kevin Cameron AU RC | 3.00 | 8.00 |
| 123 Kei Igawa AU SP RC | | |
| 124 Tyler Clippard AU (RC) | 6.00 | 15.00 |
| 125 Juan Perez AU RC | 3.00 | 8.00 |
| 126 Josh Hamilton AU SP (RC) | 15.00 | 40.00 |
| 127 Joseph Bisenius AU RC | | |
| 128 Jose Luis Garcia AU RC | 3.00 | 8.00 |
| 129 Jon Knott AU RC | 3.00 | 8.00 |
| 130 Jon Coutlangus AU (RC) | 4.00 | 10.00 |
| 131 John Danks AU RC | 4.00 | 10.00 |
| 132 Joe Smith AU RC | 3.00 | 8.00 |
| 133 Matt Brown AU RC | 3.00 | 8.00 |
| 134 Joakim Soria AU RC | 6.00 | 10.00 |
| 135 Jesus Flores AU RC | 6.00 | 15.00 |
| 136 Jeff Baker AU (RC) | 3.00 | 8.00 |
| 137 Jay Marshall AU RC | 3.00 | 8.00 |
| 138 Jared Burton AU RC | 4.00 | 10.00 |
| 139 Jamie Vermilyea AU RC | 4.00 | 10.00 |
| 140 Jamie Burke AU (RC) | 4.00 | 10.00 |
| 141 Ryan Rowland-Smith AU RC | 4.00 | 10.00 |
| 142 Connor Robertson AU RC | 3.00 | 8.00 |
| 143 Hector Gimenez AU (RC) | 3.00 | 8.00 |
| 144 Gustavo Molina AU RC | 4.00 | 10.00 |
| 145 Glen Perkins AU (RC) | 3.00 | 8.00 |
| 146 J.Chamberlain AU SP RC EXCH | 150.00 | 200.00 |
| 147 Doug Slaten AU RC | 3.00 | 8.00 |
| 148 Ryan Braun AU (RC) | 20.00 | 50.00 |
| 149 Delmon Young AU SP (RC) | | |
| 150 Garrett Jones AU (RC) | 8.00 | 20.00 |
| 151 Chris Stewart AU SP RC | | |
| 152 Cesar Jimenez AU RC | 4.00 | 10.00 |
| 153 Brian Stokes AU (RC) | 3.00 | 8.00 |
| 154 Brian Burres AU (RC) | 4.00 | 10.00 |
| 155 Brian Barden AU SP RC | | |
| 156 Kyle Kendrick AU RC | 12.50 | 30.00 |
| 157 Andrew Miller AU RC | 8.00 | 20.00 |
| 158 Alexi Casilla AU (RC) | 3.00 | 8.00 |
| 159 Alex Gordon AU SP RC | 15.00 | 40.00 |
| 160 A.J. Murray AU RC | 4.00 | 10.00 |
| 161 A.Iwamura AU SP RC | | |
| 162 Adam Lind AU (RC) | 4.00 | 10.00 |
| 163 Chase Wright AU RC | 5.00 | 12.00 |
| 164 Dallas Braden AU (RC) | 3.00 | 8.00 |
| 165 Rocky Cherry AU RC | 5.00 | 12.00 |
| 166 Andy Gonzalez AU RC | 3.00 | 8.00 |
| 167 Neal Musser AU RC | 3.00 | 8.00 |
| 168 Mark Reynolds AU RC | 30.00 | 60.00 |
| 169 Dennis Dove AU (RC) | 3.00 | 8.00 |
| 170 Justin Hampson AU (RC) | 4.00 | 10.00 |
| 171 Phil Hughes AU SP (RC) | | |
| 172 Kelvin Jimenez AU RC | 3.00 | 8.00 |
| 173 Hunter Pence AU SP (RC) | | |
| 174 Brad Salmon AU RC | 6.00 | 15.00 |
| 175 Ryan Sweeney AU (RC) | 3.00 | 8.00 |
| 176 Brandon Wood AU (RC) | 6.00 | 15.00 |
| 177 Billy Butler AU SP (RC) | | |
| 178 Ben Francisco AU (RC) | 3.00 | 8.00 |
| 179 Devern Hansack AU SP RC | | |
| 180 Yoel Hernandez AU RC | 3.00 | 8.00 |
| 181 Tim Lincecum AU SP RC | 50.00 | 100.00 |
| 182 Danny Putnam AU (RC) | 5.00 | 12.00 |
| 183 J.Salta AU SP (RC) | 6.00 | 15.00 |
| 184 Andy LaRoche AU SP (RC) | | |
| 185 Matt DeSalvo AU RC | 5.00 | 12.00 |
| 186 Fred Lewis AU (RC) | 3.00 | 8.00 |
| 187 Anthony Lerew AU (RC) | 3.00 | 8.00 |
| 188 Jesse Litsch AU RC | 4.00 | 10.00 |
| 189a Daisuke Matsuzaka RC | | |
| 189b Daisuke Matsuzaka AU RC | 250.00 | 300.00 |

## 2009 Upper Deck Goodwin Champions

| | | |
|---|---|---|
| COMMON CARD (1-150) | .15 | .40 |
| COMMON NIGHT | 5.00 | 12.00 |
| COMMON SP (151-190) | 1.25 | 3.00 |
| COMMON SUPER SP (191-210) | 1.50 | 4.00 |
| PLATES RANDOMLY INSERTED | | |
| PLATE PRINT RUN 1 SET PER COLOR | | |
| BLACK-CYAN-MAGENTA-YELLOW ISSUED | | |
| NO PLATE PRICING DUE TO SCARCITY | | |
| 1a K.Griffey Jr. Day | .60 | 1.50 |
| 1b K.Griffey Jr. Night SP | 8.00 | 20.00 |
| 2 Derek Jeter | 1.00 | 2.50 |
| 3 Jon Lester | .25 | .60 |
| 4 Jorge Posada | .25 | .60 |
| 5 Albert Pujols | 1.00 | 2.50 |
| 6 Chipper Jones | .40 | 1.00 |
| 7a R.Sandberg Day | .75 | 2.00 |
| 7b R.Sandberg Night SP | 6.00 | 15.00 |
| 8 Johnny Damon | .25 | .60 |
| 9 Carlos Delgado | .15 | .40 |
| 10 Vladimir Guerrero | .40 | 1.00 |
| 11 Johnny Bench | .40 | 1.00 |
| 12 Matt Cain | .15 | .40 |
| 13 Bill Skowron CL | .15 | .40 |
| 14 Donovan Bailey | .15 | .40 |
| 15 Dick Allen CL | .15 | .40 |
| 16 Abraham Lincoln | .25 | .60 |
| 17 Rollie Fingers | .25 | .60 |
| 18 Bo Jackson CL | .40 | 1.00 |
| 19 Scott Kazmir | .25 | .60 |
| 20a Grady Sizemore Day | .25 | .60 |
| 20b G.Sizemore Night SP | 5.00 | 12.00 |
| 21 Ian Kinsler | .15 | .40 |
| 22 Jim Palmer | .15 | .40 |
| 23 Kevin Youkilis | .25 | .60 |
| 24 O.J. Mayo | .40 | 1.00 |
| 25 Hunter Pence | .25 | .60 |
| 26 Hiroki Kuroda | .15 | .40 |
| 27 Derek Lee | .25 | .60 |
| 28 Brian McCann | .25 | .60 |
| 29 Carlos Quentin | .15 | .40 |
| 30 Al Kaline | .40 | 1.00 |
| 31 Hanley Ramirez | .40 | 1.00 |
| 32 Josh Hamilton | .40 | 1.00 |
| 33 Jeff Samardzija | .25 | .60 |
| 34 Alexander Ovechkin | .75 | 2.00 |
| 35 Clayton Kershaw | .40 | 1.00 |
| 36 Lyndon Johnson | .15 | .40 |
| 37 Whitey Ford | .25 | .60 |
| 38 Carey Price | .60 | 1.50 |
| 39 Jay Bruce | .40 | 1.00 |
| 40 Phil Niekro | .25 | .60 |
| 41 Ted Williams | 1.00 | 2.50 |
| 42 Justin Upton | .25 | .60 |
| 43 Cole Hamels | .40 | 1.00 |
| 44a B.Obama Day | .40 | 1.00 |
| 44b B.Obama Night SP | 8.00 | 20.00 |
| 45 Peyton Manning | .50 | 1.25 |
| 46 Jim Thome | .25 | .60 |
| 47 Nick Markakis | .25 | .60 |
| 48 Joe Carter CL | .15 | .40 |
| 49 Ryan Braun | .50 | 1.25 |
| 50 Mike Schmidt | .60 | 1.50 |
| 51 Carlos Beltran | .15 | .40 |
| 52 Nolan Ryan | 1.25 | 3.00 |
| 53 Anderson Silva | .50 | 1.25 |
| 54 Kosuke Fukudome | .40 | 1.00 |
| 55 Chad Reed | .15 | .40 |
| 56a O.Smith Day | .60 | 1.50 |
| 56b O.Smith Night SP | 8.00 | 20.00 |
| 57 Eli Manning | .40 | 1.00 |
| 58 CC Sabathia | .25 | .60 |
| 59 Evan Longoria | .60 | 1.50 |
| 60 Matt Garza | .15 | .40 |
| 61 Michael Beasley | .40 | 1.00 |
| 62 Yogi Berra | .40 | 1.00 |
| 63 Brian Roberts | .15 | .40 |
| 64 Alex Rodriguez | .60 | 1.50 |
| 65a T.Woods Day | 1.50 | 4.00 |
| 65b T.Woods Night SP | 12.50 | 30.00 |
| 66 Buffalo Bill Cody | .15 | .40 |
| 67 Josh Beckett | .25 | .60 |
| 68 Matt Ryan | .40 | 1.00 |
| 69a I.Suzuki Day | .60 | 1.50 |
| 69b I.Suzuki Night SP | 8.00 | 20.00 |
| 70 Chuck Liddell | .50 | 1.25 |
| 71 Adrian Gonzalez | .25 | .60 |
| 72 David Wright | .50 | 1.25 |
| 73 LeBron James | 1.50 | 4.00 |

| | | |
|---|---|---|
| ☐ 74a G.Lopez Day | .15 | .40 |
| ☐ 74b G.Lopez Night SP | 5.00 | 12.00 |
| ☐ 75 Carlton Fisk | .25 | .60 |
| ☐ 76 Joe Mauer | .40 | 1.00 |
| ☐ 77 Manny Ramirez | .40 | 1.00 |
| ☐ 78 Jason Varitek | .25 | .60 |
| ☐ 79 John Lackey | .15 | .40 |
| ☐ 80 Ivan Rodriguez | .25 | .60 |
| ☐ 81 Wayne Gretzky | 1.50 | 4.00 |
| ☐ 82 Justin Morneau | .25 | .60 |
| ☐ 83 Akinori Iwamura | .25 | .60 |
| ☐ 84 Joe Lewis | .40 | 1.00 |
| ☐ 85 Lance Berkman | .25 | .60 |
| ☐ 86 Brooks Robinson | .25 | .60 |
| ☐ 87a A.Pettitte Day | .25 | .60 |
| ☐ 87b A.Pettitte Night SP | 5.00 | 12.00 |
| ☐ 88 Peggy Fleming | .15 | .40 |
| ☐ 89 Joe DiMaggio | 1.00 | 2.50 |
| ☐ 90 Jonathan Toews | .60 | 1.50 |
| ☐ 91 Todd Helton | .25 | .60 |
| ☐ 92 Dennis Eckersley | .15 | .40 |
| ☐ 93 Daisuke Matsuzaka | .60 | 1.50 |
| ☐ 94 Adrian Peterson | .60 | 1.50 |
| ☐ 95 Alfonso Soriano | .25 | .60 |
| ☐ 96 Paul Molitor | .40 | 1.00 |
| ☐ 97 Johan Santana | .40 | 1.00 |
| ☐ 98 Jason Giambi | .15 | .40 |
| ☐ 99 Ben Roethlisberger | .50 | 1.25 |
| ☐ 100 Chase Utley | .40 | 1.00 |
| ☐ 101a C.Ripken Jr. Day | 1.50 | 4.00 |
| ☐ 101b C.Ripken Jr. Night SP | 10.00 | 25.00 |
| ☐ 102 Curtis Granderson | .40 | 1.00 |
| ☐ 103 James Shields | .15 | .40 |
| ☐ 104 Nate McLouth | .15 | .40 |
| ☐ 105 Evelyn Ng | .40 | 1.00 |
| ☐ 106a R.Howard Day | .50 | 1.25 |
| ☐ 106b R.Howard Night SP | 6.00 | 15.00 |
| ☐ 107 Joe Nathan | .15 | .40 |
| ☐ 108 Tim Lincecum | .50 | 1.25 |
| ☐ 109 Chad Billingsley | .15 | .40 |
| ☐ 110 Matt Holliday | .25 | .60 |
| ☐ 111 Kevin Garnett | .60 | 1.50 |
| ☐ 112 Robin Roberts | .15 | .40 |
| ☐ 113 Jose Reyes | .40 | 1.00 |
| ☐ 114 Michael Jordan | 1.00 | 2.50 |
| ☐ 115a S.Jones Day | .40 | 1.00 |
| ☐ 115b S.Jones Night SP | 5.00 | 12.00 |
| ☐ 116 Kristi Yamaguchi | .25 | .60 |
| ☐ 117 Carlos Zambrano | .15 | .40 |
| ☐ 118 Bucky Dent CL | .15 | .40 |
| ☐ 119 Carl Yastrzemski | .60 | 1.50 |
| ☐ 120 Stephen Drew | .15 | .40 |
| ☐ 121 Dustin Pedroia | .50 | 1.25 |
| ☐ 122 Jonathan Papelbon | .25 | .60 |
| ☐ 123 B.J. Upton | .25 | .60 |
| ☐ 124 Steve Carlton | .15 | .40 |
| ☐ 125 Chris Johnson | .40 | 1.00 |
| ☐ 126a T.Tulowitzki Day | .25 | .50 |
| ☐ 126b T.Tulowitzki Night SP | 5.00 | 12.00 |
| ☐ 127 Francisco Liriano | .15 | .40 |
| ☐ 128 Bill Rodgers | .15 | .40 |
| ☐ 129 Laird Hamilton | .15 | .40 |
| ☐ 130 Brandon Webb | .25 | .60 |
| ☐ 131 Miguel Cabrera | .25 | .60 |
| ☐ 132a C.Wang Day | .40 | 1.00 |
| ☐ 132b C.Wang Night SP | 5.00 | 12.00 |
| ☐ 133 Joba Chamberlain | .50 | 1.25 |
| ☐ 134 Felix Hernandez | .25 | .60 |
| ☐ 135 Tony Gwynn | .40 | 1.00 |
| ☐ 136 Roy Oswalt | .25 | .60 |
| ☐ 137 Prince Fielder | .40 | 1.00 |
| ☐ 138 Gary Sheffield | .15 | .40 |
| ☐ 139 Koji Uehara RC | .40 | 1.00 |
| ☐ 140a G.Howe Day | 1.25 | 3.00 |
| ☐ 140b G.Howe Night SP | 5.00 | 12.00 |
| ☐ 141 Bobby Orr | 1.00 | 2.50 |
| ☐ 142 Zack Greinke | .25 | .60 |
| ☐ 143 Derrick Rose | .60 | 1.50 |
| ☐ 144 Cliff Lee | .25 | .60 |
| ☐ 145 Joey Votto | .25 | .60 |
| ☐ 146 Phil Hellmuth | .40 | 1.00 |

| | | |
|---|---|---|
| ☐ 147 Mark Teixeira | .40 | 1.00 |
| ☐ 148 David Price RC | .50 | 1.25 |
| ☐ 149 Ryan Ludwick | .25 | .60 |
| ☐ 150 David Ortiz | .25 | .60 |
| ☐ 151 Cory Wade SP | 1.25 | 3.00 |
| ☐ 152 Roy White SP | 1.25 | 3.00 |
| ☐ 153 Jed Lowrie SP | 1.25 | 3.00 |
| ☐ 154 Gavin Floyd SP | 1.25 | 3.00 |
| ☐ 155 Justin Masterson SP | 1.25 | 3.00 |
| ☐ 156 Travis Hafner SP | 1.25 | 3.00 |
| ☐ 157 Kelly Shoppach SP | 1.25 | 3.00 |
| ☐ 158 David Purcey SP | 1.25 | 3.00 |
| ☐ 159 Howie Kendrick SP | 1.25 | 3.00 |
| ☐ 160 Mike Parsons SP | 1.25 | 3.00 |
| ☐ 161 Jeremy Bloom SP | 1.25 | 3.00 |
| ☐ 162 Dave Scott SP | 1.25 | 3.00 |
| ☐ 163 Nyjer Morgan SP | 1.25 | 3.00 |
| ☐ 164 Chris Volstad SP | 1.25 | 3.00 |
| ☐ 165 Barry Zito SP | 1.25 | 3.00 |
| ☐ 166 Adrian Beltre SP | 1.25 | 3.00 |
| ☐ 167 Mark Zupan SP | 1.25 | 3.00 |
| ☐ 168 Victor Martinez SP | 1.25 | 3.00 |
| ☐ 169 Eric Chavez SP | 1.25 | 3.00 |
| ☐ 170 Chris Perez SP | 1.25 | 3.00 |
| ☐ 171 Jered Weaver SP | 1.25 | 3.00 |
| ☐ 172 Justin Verlander SP | 1.25 | 3.00 |
| ☐ 173 Adam Lind SP | 1.25 | 3.00 |
| ☐ 174 Corky Carroll SP | 1.25 | 3.00 |
| ☐ 175 Ryan Zimmerman SP | 1.25 | 3.00 |
| ☐ 176 Josh Willingham SP | 1.25 | 3.00 |
| ☐ 177 Graig Nettles SP | 1.25 | 3.00 |
| ☐ 178 Jonathan Albaladejo SP | 1.25 | 3.00 |
| ☐ 179 Ted Martin SP | 1.25 | 3.00 |
| ☐ 180 Bill Hall SP | 1.25 | 3.00 |
| ☐ 181 Brad Hawpe SP | 1.25 | 3.00 |
| ☐ 182 John Maine SP | 1.25 | 3.00 |
| ☐ 183 Tom Curren SP | 1.25 | 3.00 |
| ☐ 184 Ken Griffey Sr. CL SP | 1.25 | 3.00 |
| ☐ 185 Josh Johnson SP | 1.25 | 3.00 |
| ☐ 186 Phil Hughes SP | 1.25 | 3.00 |
| ☐ 187 Joe Alexander SP | 1.25 | 3.00 |
| ☐ 188 Fausto Carmona SP | 1.25 | 3.00 |
| ☐ 189 Daniel Murphy SP RC | 1.25 | 3.00 |
| ☐ 190 Alex Hinshaw SP | 1.25 | 3.00 |
| ☐ 191 Clayton Richard SP | 1.50 | 4.00 |
| ☐ 192 Sparky Lyle CL SP | 1.50 | 4.00 |
| ☐ 193 Don Gay SP | 1.50 | 4.00 |
| ☐ 194 Aramis Ramirez SP | 1.50 | 4.00 |
| ☐ 195 Gaylord Perry CL SP | 1.50 | 4.00 |
| ☐ 196 Carlos Lee SP | 1.50 | 4.00 |
| ☐ 197 Paul Konerko SP | 1.50 | 4.00 |
| ☐ 198 Kent Hrbek CL SP | 1.50 | 4.00 |
| ☐ 199 Chris B. Young SP | 1.50 | 4.00 |
| ☐ 200 Roy Halladay SP | 1.50 | 4.00 |
| ☐ 201 Geovany Soto SP | 1.50 | 4.00 |
| ☐ 202 Chone Figgins SP | 1.50 | 4.00 |
| ☐ 203 Joe Pepitone CL SP | 1.50 | 4.00 |
| ☐ 204 Mark Allen SP | 1.50 | 4.00 |
| ☐ 205 Garrett Atkins SP | 1.50 | 4.00 |
| ☐ 206 Ken Shamrock SP | 1.50 | 4.00 |
| ☐ 207 Jermaine Dye SP | 1.50 | 4.00 |
| ☐ 208 Don Newcombe CL SP | 1.50 | 4.00 |
| ☐ 209 Rick Cerone CL SP | 1.50 | 4.00 |
| ☐ 210 Adam Jones SP | 1.50 | 4.00 |

### 2007 Upper Deck Goudey

| | | |
|---|---|---|
| ☐ COMP.SET w/o SPs (200) | 20.00 | 50.00 |
| ☐ COMMON CARD (1-200) | .20 | .50 |

| | | |
|---|---|---|
| ☐ COMMON ROOKIE (1-200) | .30 | .75 |
| ☐ COMMON SP (201-240) | 2.00 | 5.00 |
| ☐ SP ODDS 1:6 HOBBY, 1:6 RETAIL | | |
| ☐ 1933 ORIGINALS ODDS TWO PER CASE | | |
| ☐ SEE 1933 GOUDEY PRICING FOR ORIGINALS | | |
| ☐ 1 A.J. Burnett | .20 | .50 |
| ☐ 2 Aaron Boone | .20 | .50 |
| ☐ 3 Aaron Rowand | .20 | .50 |
| ☐ 4 Adam Dunn | .20 | .50 |
| ☐ 5 Adrian Beltre | .20 | .50 |
| ☐ 6 Albert Pujols | 1.00 | 2.50 |
| ☐ 7 Ivan Rodriguez | .30 | .75 |
| ☐ 8 Alfonso Soriano | .20 | .50 |
| ☐ 9 Andruw Jones | .30 | .75 |
| ☐ 10 Andy Pettitte | .30 | .75 |
| ☐ 11 Aramis Ramirez | .20 | .50 |
| ☐ 12 B.J. Upton | .20 | .50 |
| ☐ 13 Barry Zito | .20 | .50 |
| ☐ 14 Bartolo Colon | .20 | .50 |
| ☐ 15 Ben Sheets | .20 | .50 |
| ☐ 16 Bobby Abreu | .20 | .50 |
| ☐ 17 Bobby Crosby | .20 | .50 |
| ☐ 18 Brian Giles | .20 | .50 |
| ☐ 19 Brian Roberts | .20 | .50 |
| ☐ 20 C.C. Sabathia | .20 | .50 |
| ☐ 21 Carlos Beltran | .20 | .50 |
| ☐ 22 Carlos Delgado | .20 | .50 |
| ☐ 23 Carlos Lee | .20 | .50 |
| ☐ 24 Carlos Zambrano | .20 | .50 |
| ☐ 25 Chad Cordero | .20 | .50 |
| ☐ 26 Chad Tracy | .20 | .50 |
| ☐ 27 Chipper Jones | .50 | 1.25 |
| ☐ 28 Craig Biggio | .30 | .75 |
| ☐ 29 Curt Schilling | .30 | .75 |
| ☐ 30 Danny Haren | .20 | .50 |
| ☐ 31 Darin Erstad | .20 | .50 |
| ☐ 32 David Ortiz | .30 | .75 |
| ☐ 33 Billy Wagner | .20 | .50 |
| ☐ 34 Derek Jeter | 1.25 | 3.00 |
| ☐ 35 Derek Lee | .20 | .50 |
| ☐ 36 Dontrelle Willis | .20 | .50 |
| ☐ 37 Edgar Renteria | .20 | .50 |
| ☐ 38 Eric Chavez | .20 | .50 |
| ☐ 39 Felix Hernandez | .30 | .75 |
| ☐ 40 Garret Anderson | .20 | .50 |
| ☐ 41 Garrett Atkins | .20 | .50 |
| ☐ 42 Gary Sheffield | .20 | .50 |
| ☐ 43 Grady Sizemore | .30 | .75 |
| ☐ 44 Greg Maddux | .75 | 2.00 |
| ☐ 45 Hank Blalock | .20 | .50 |
| ☐ 46 Hanley Ramirez | .30 | .75 |
| ☐ 47 J.D. Drew | .20 | .50 |
| ☐ 48 Jacque Jones | .20 | .50 |
| ☐ 49 Jake Peavy | .20 | .50 |
| ☐ 50 Jake Westbrook | .20 | .50 |
| ☐ 51 Jason Bay | .30 | .75 |
| ☐ 52 Jason Giambi | .20 | .50 |
| ☐ 53 Jason Schmidt | .20 | .50 |
| ☐ 54 Jason Varitek | .50 | 1.25 |
| ☐ 55 Troy Tulowitzki (RC) | .75 | 2.00 |
| ☐ 56 Jeff Francoeur | .50 | 1.25 |
| ☐ 57 Jeff Kent | .20 | .50 |
| ☐ 58 Jeremy Bonderman | .20 | .50 |
| ☐ 59 Jim Edmonds | .30 | .75 |
| ☐ 60 Jim Thome | .30 | .75 |
| ☐ 61 Jimmy Rollins | .20 | .50 |
| ☐ 62 Joe Mauer | .50 | 1.25 |
| ☐ 63 Johan Santana | .30 | .75 |
| ☐ 64 John Smoltz | .30 | .75 |
| ☐ 65 Johnny Damon | .30 | .75 |
| ☐ 66 Jose Reyes | .50 | 1.25 |
| ☐ 67 Josh Beckett | .30 | .75 |
| ☐ 68 Justin Morneau | .20 | .50 |
| ☐ 69 Ken Griffey Jr. | .75 | 2.00 |
| ☐ 70 Kerry Wood | .20 | .50 |
| ☐ 71 Khalil Greene | .30 | .75 |
| ☐ 72 Lance Berkman | .20 | .50 |
| ☐ 73 Livan Hernandez | .20 | .50 |
| ☐ 74 Manny Ramirez | .30 | .75 |
| ☐ 75 Mark Mulder | .20 | .50 |
| ☐ 76 Chase Utley | .50 | 1.25 |
| ☐ 77 Mark Teixeira | .30 | .75 |

| | | |
|---|---|---|
| 78 Miguel Tejada | .20 | .50 |
| 79 Miguel Cabrera | .30 | .75 |
| 80 Mike Piazza | .50 | 1.25 |
| 81 Pat Burrell | .20 | .50 |
| 82 Paul LoDuca | .20 | .50 |
| 83 Pedro Martinez | .30 | .75 |
| 84 Prince Fielder | .50 | 1.25 |
| 85 Rafael Furcal | .20 | .50 |
| 86 Randy Johnson | .50 | 1.25 |
| 87 Richie Sexson | .20 | .50 |
| 88 Robinson Cano | .30 | .75 |
| 89 Roy Halladay | .20 | .50 |
| 90 Roy Oswalt | .20 | .50 |
| 91 Scott Rolen | .30 | .75 |
| 92 Tim Hudson | .20 | .50 |
| 93 Todd Helton | .30 | .75 |
| 94 Tom Glavine | .30 | .75 |
| 95 Torii Hunter | .20 | .50 |
| 96 Travis Hafner | .20 | .50 |
| 97 Trevor Hoffman | .20 | .50 |
| 98 Vernon Wells | .20 | .50 |
| 99 Vladimir Guerrero | .50 | 1.25 |
| 100 Zach Duke | .20 | .50 |
| 101 Alex Rodriguez | .75 | 2.00 |
| 102 Ryan Howard | .75 | 2.00 |
| 103 Michael Barrett | .20 | .50 |
| 104 Ichiro Suzuki | .75 | 2.00 |
| 105 Hideki Matsui | .50 | 1.25 |
| 106 Jered Weaver | .30 | .75 |
| 107 Dan Uggla | .20 | .50 |
| 108 Ryan Freel | .20 | .50 |
| 109 Bill Hall | .20 | * .50 |
| 110 Ray Durham | .20 | .50 |
| 111 Morgan Ensberg | .20 | .50 |
| 112 Shawn Green | .20 | .50 |
| 113 Brandon Webb | .30 | .75 |
| 114 Frank Thomas | .50 | 1.25 |
| 115 Corey Patterson | .20 | .50 |
| 116 Edwin Encarnacion | .20 | .50 |
| 117 Mike Cameron | .20 | .50 |
| 118 Matt Holliday | .50 | 1.25 |
| 119 Jhonny Peralta | .20 | .50 |
| 120 Nick Swisher | .20 | .50 |
| 121 Brad Penny | .20 | .50 |
| 122 Kenji Johjima | .50 | 1.25 |
| 123 Francisco Rodriguez | .20 | .50 |
| 124 Mark Teahan | .20 | .50 |
| 125 Jonathan Papelbon | .50 | 1.25 |
| 126 Carlos Guillen | .20 | .50 |
| 127 Freddy Sanchez | .20 | .50 |
| 128 Chien-Ming Wang | .50 | 1.25 |
| 129 Andre Ethier | .30 | .75 |
| 130 Matt Cain | .20 | .50 |
| 131 Austin Kearns | .20 | .50 |
| 132 Ramon Hernandez | .20 | .50 |
| 133 Chris Carpenter | .20 | .50 |
| 134 Michael Cuddyer | .20 | .50 |
| 135 Stephen Drew | .30 | .75 |
| 136 David Wright | .75 | 2.00 |
| 137 David DeJesus | .20 | .50 |
| 138 Gary Matthews | .20 | .50 |
| 139 Brandon Phillips | .20 | .50 |
| 140 Josh Barfield | .20 | .50 |
| 141 Alex Gordon RC | 1.25 | 3.00 |
| 142 Scott Kazmir | .30 | .75 |
| 143 Luis Gonzalez | .20 | .50 |
| 144 Mike Sweeney | .20 | .50 |
| 145 Luis Castillo | .20 | .50 |
| 146 Huston Street | .20 | .50 |
| 147 Phil Hughes (RC) | 1.50 | 4.00 |
| 148 Adrian Gonzalez | .20 | .50 |
| 149 Raul Ibanez | .30 | .75 |
| 150 Joe Crede | .20 | .50 |
| 151 Mark Loretta | .20 | .50 |
| 152 Adam LaRoche (RC) | .30 | .75 |
| 153 Troy Glaus | .20 | .50 |
| 154 Conor Jackson | .20 | .50 |
| 155 Michael Young | .20 | .50 |
| 156 Scott Podsednik | .20 | .50 |
| 157 David Eckstein | .20 | .50 |
| 158 Mike Jacobs | .20 | .50 |

| | | |
|---|---|---|
| 159 Nomar Garciaparra | .50 | 1.25 |
| 160 Mariano Rivera | .50 | 1.25 |
| 161 Pedro Feliz | .20 | .50 |
| 162 Josh Hamilton (RC) | .75 | 2.00 |
| 163 Ryan Langerhans | .20 | .50 |
| 164 Willy Taveras | .20 | .50 |
| 165 Carl Crawford | .20 | .50 |
| 166 Melvin Mora | .20 | .50 |
| 167 Francisco Liriano | .50 | 1.25 |
| 168 Orlando Cabrera | .20 | .50 |
| 169 Chris Duncan | .20 | .50 |
| 170 Johnny Estrada | .20 | .50 |
| 171 Ryan Zimmerman | .50 | 1.25 |
| 172 Rickie Weeks | .20 | .50 |
| 173 Paul Konerko | .20 | .50 |
| 174 Jack Wilson | .20 | .50 |
| 175 Jorge Posada | .30 | .75 |
| 176 Magglio Ordonez | .20 | .50 |
| 177 Nick Johnson | .20 | .50 |
| 178 Geoff Jenkins | .20 | .50 |
| 179 Reggie Sanders | .20 | .50 |
| 180 Moises Alou | .20 | .50 |
| 181 Glen Perkins (RC) | .30 | .75 |
| 182 Brad Lidge | .20 | .50 |
| 183 Kevin Kouzmanoff (RC) | .30 | .75 |
| 184 Jorge Cantu | .20 | .50 |
| 185 Carlos Quentin | .20 | .50 |
| 186 Rich Harden | .20 | .50 |
| 187 Jose Vidro | .20 | .50 |
| 188 Aaron Harang | .20 | .50 |
| 189 Noah Lowry | .20 | .50 |
| 190 Jermaine Dye | .20 | .50 |
| 191 Victor Martinez | .20 | .50 |
| 192 Chone Figgins | .20 | .50 |
| 193 Aubrey Huff | .20 | .50 |
| 194 Jason Isringhausen | .20 | .50 |
| 195 Brian McCann | .20 | .50 |
| 196 Juan Pierre | .20 | .50 |
| 197 Delmon Young (RC) | .50 | 1.25 |
| 198 Felipe Lopez | .20 | .50 |
| 199 Brad Hawpe | .20 | .50 |
| 200 Justin Verlander | .50 | 1.25 |
| 201 Mike Schmidt SP | 4.00 | 10.00 |
| 202 Nolan Ryan SP | 5.00 | 12.00 |
| 203 Cal Ripken Jr. SP | 4.00 | 10.00 |
| 204 Harmon Killebrew SP | 2.50 | 6.00 |
| 205 Reggie Jackson SP | 2.50 | 6.00 |
| 206 Johnny Bench SP | 2.50 | 6.00 |
| 207 Carlton Fisk SP | 2.50 | 6.00 |
| 208 Yogi Berra SP | 2.50 | 6.00 |
| 209 Al Kaline SP | 2.50 | 6.00 |
| 210 Alan Trammell SP | 2.00 | 5.00 |
| 211 Bill Mazeroski SP | 2.50 | 6.00 |
| 212 Bob Gibson SP | 2.50 | 6.00 |
| 213 Brooks Robinson SP | 2.50 | 6.00 |
| 214 Carl Yastrzemski SP | 3.00 | 8.00 |
| 215 Don Mattingly SP | 5.00 | 12.00 |
| 216 Fergie Jenkins SP | 2.00 | 5.00 |
| 217 Jim Rice SP | 2.00 | 5.00 |
| 218 Lou Brock SP | 2.50 | 6.00 |
| 219 Rod Carew SP | 2.50 | 6.00 |
| 220 Stan Musial SP | 3.00 | 8.00 |
| 221 Tom Seaver SP | 2.50 | 6.00 |
| 222 Tony Gwynn SP | 2.50 | 6.00 |
| 223 Wade Boggs SP | 2.50 | 6.00 |
| 224 Alex Rodriguez SP | 3.00 | 8.00 |
| 225 David Wright SP | 3.00 | 8.00 |
| 226 Ryan Howard SP | 3.00 | 8.00 |
| 227 Ichiro Suzuki SP | 3.00 | 8.00 |
| 228 Ken Griffey Jr. SP | 3.00 | 8.00 |
| 229 Daisuke Matsuzaka SP RC | 4.00 | 10.00 |
| 230 Kei Igawa SP RC | 2.50 | 6.00 |
| 231 Akinori Iwamura SP RC | 3.00 | 8.00 |
| 232 Derek Jeter SP | 4.00 | 10.00 |
| 233 Albert Pujols SP | 4.00 | 10.00 |
| 234 Greg Maddux SP | 3.00 | 8.00 |
| 235 David Ortiz SP | 2.50 | 6.00 |
| 236 Manny Ramirez SP | 2.50 | 6.00 |
| 237 Johan Santana SP | 2.50 | 6.00 |
| 238 Pedro Martinez SP | 2.50 | 6.00 |

| | | |
|---|---|---|
| 239 Roger Clemens SP | 4.00 | 10.00 |
| 240 Vladimir Guerrero SP | 2.50 | 6.00 |

## 2008 Upper Deck Goudey

| | | |
|---|---|---|
| COMP SET w/o HIGH #s (200) | 20.00 | 50.00 |
| COMMON CARD (1-200) | .20 | .50 |
| COMMON ROOKIE (1-200) | .30 | .75 |
| COMMON SP (201-230) | 2.00 | 5.00 |
| COMMON SP (231-250) | 1.50 | 4.00 |
| COMMON CARD (251-270) | 2.00 | 5.00 |
| COMMON CARD (271-300) | 2.00 | 5.00 |
| COMMON CARD (301-330) | 3.00 | 8.00 |
| 1 Eric Byrnes | .20 | .50 |
| 2 Randy Johnson | .50 | 1.25 |
| 3 Brandon Webb | .30 | .75 |
| 4 Dan Haren | .20 | .50 |
| 5 Chris B. Young | .20 | .50 |
| 6 Max Scherzer RC | .75 | 2.00 |
| 7 Mark Teixeira | .30 | .75 |
| 8 John Smoltz | .50 | 1.25 |
| 9 Jeff Francoeur | .30 | .75 |
| 10 Phil Niekro | .20 | .50 |
| 11 Chipper Jones | .60 | 1.50 |
| 12 Kelly Johnson | .20 | .50 |
| 13 Tom Glavine | .20 | .50 |
| 14 Yunel Escobar | .20 | .50 |
| 15 Erik Bedard | .20 | .50 |
| 16 Melvin Mora | .20 | .50 |
| 17 Brian Roberts | .30 | .75 |
| 18 Eddie Murray | .50 | 1.25 |
| 19 Jim Palmer | .20 | .50 |
| 20 Jeremy Guthrie | .20 | .50 |
| 21 Nick Markakis | .30 | .75 |
| 22 David Ortiz | .30 | .75 |
| 23 Manny Ramirez | .50 | 1.25 |
| 24 Josh Beckett | .30 | .75 |
| 25 Dustin Pedroia | .60 | 1.50 |
| 26 Bobby Doerr | .20 | .50 |
| 27 Clay Buchholz (RC) | .75 | 2.00 |
| 28 Daisuke Matsuzaka | .60 | 1.50 |
| 29 Jonathan Papelbon | .30 | .75 |
| 30 Kevin Youkilis | .30 | .75 |
| 31 Pee Wee Reese | .30 | .75 |
| 32 Billy Williams | .20 | .50 |
| 33 Alfonso Soriano | .30 | .75 |
| 34 Derrek Lee | .30 | .75 |
| 35 Rich Hill | .20 | .50 |
| 36 Kosuke Fukudome RC | 1.00 | 2.50 |
| 37 Aramis Ramirez | .20 | .50 |
| 38 Carlos Zambrano | .20 | .50 |
| 39 Luis Aparicio | .20 | .50 |
| 40 Mark Buehrle | .20 | .50 |
| 41 Orlando Cabrera | .20 | .50 |
| 42 Paul Konerko | .20 | .50 |
| 43 Jermaine Dye | .20 | .50 |
| 44 Jim Thome | .30 | .75 |
| 45 Nick Swisher | .20 | .50 |
| 46 Sparky Anderson | .20 | .50 |
| 47 Johnny Bench | .50 | 1.25 |
| 48 Joe Morgan | .20 | .50 |
| 49 Tony Perez | .20 | .50 |
| 50 Adam Dunn | .20 | .50 |
| 51 Aaron Harang | .20 | .50 |
| 52 Brandon Phillips | .20 | .50 |
| 53 Edwin Encarnacion | .20 | .50 |
| 54 Ken Griffey Jr. | .75 | 2.00 |
| 55 Larry Doby | .20 | .50 |

|  |  | | |
|---|---|---|---|
| 56 | Bob Feller | .20 | .50 |
| 57 | C.C. Sabathia | .20 | .50 |
| 58 | Travis Hafner | .20 | .50 |
| 59 | Grady Sizemore | .30 | .75 |
| 60 | Fausto Carmona | .20 | .50 |
| 61 | Victor Martinez | .20 | .50 |
| 62 | Brad Hawpe | .20 | .50 |
| 63 | Todd Helton | .30 | .75 |
| 64 | Garrett Atkins | .20 | .50 |
| 65 | Troy Tulowitzki | .30 | .75 |
| 66 | Matt Holliday | .30 | .75 |
| 67 | Jeff Francis | .20 | .50 |
| 68 | Justin Verlander | .30 | .75 |
| 69 | Curtis Granderson | .30 | .75 |
| 70 | Miguel Cabrera | .30 | .75 |
| 71 | Gary Sheffield | .20 | .50 |
| 72 | Magglio Ordonez | .30 | .75 |
| 73 | Jack Morris | .30 | .75 |
| 74 | Andrew Miller | .30 | .75 |
| 75 | Clayton Kershaw RC | 1.50 | 4.00 |
| 76 | Dan Uggla | .30 | .75 |
| 77 | Hanley Ramirez | .50 | 1.25 |
| 78 | Jeremy Hermida | .20 | .50 |
| 79 | Josh Willingham | .20 | .50 |
| 80 | Lance Berkman | .30 | .75 |
| 81 | Roy Oswalt | .20 | .50 |
| 82 | Miguel Tejada | .20 | .50 |
| 83 | Hunter Pence | .50 | 1.25 |
| 84 | Carlos Lee | .20 | .50 |
| 85 | J.R. Towles RC | .50 | 1.25 |
| 86 | Brian Bannister | .20 | .50 |
| 87 | Luke Hochevar RC | .50 | 1.25 |
| 88 | Billy Butler | .20 | .50 |
| 89 | Alex Gordon | .30 | .75 |
| 90 | Kelvim Escobar | .20 | .50 |
| 91 | John Lackey | .20 | .50 |
| 92 | Chone Figgins | .20 | .50 |
| 93 | Jered Weaver | .20 | .50 |
| 94 | Torii Hunter | .30 | .75 |
| 95 | Vladimir Guerrero | .50 | 1.25 |
| 96 | Brad Penny | .20 | .50 |
| 97 | James Loney | .30 | .75 |
| 98 | Andruw Jones | .20 | .50 |
| 99 | Chad Billingsley | .20 | .50 |
| 100 | Chin-Lung Hu (RC) | .50 | 1.25 |
| 101 | Russell Martin | .30 | .75 |
| 102 | Eddie Mathews | .50 | 1.25 |
| 103 | Warren Spahn | .30 | .75 |
| 104 | Prince Fielder | .50 | 1.25 |
| 105 | Ryan Braun | .60 | 1.50 |
| 106 | J.J. Hardy | .20 | .50 |
| 107 | Ben Sheets | .30 | .75 |
| 108 | Corey Hart | .20 | .50 |
| 109 | Yovani Gallardo | .20 | .50 |
| 110 | Joe Mauer | .50 | 1.25 |
| 111 | Delmon Young | .30 | .75 |
| 112 | Johan Santana | .30 | .75 |
| 113 | Glen Perkins | .20 | .50 |
| 114 | Justin Morneau | .30 | .75 |
| 115 | Carlos Beltran | .30 | .75 |
| 116 | Jose Reyes | .30 | .75 |
| 117 | David Wright | .60 | 1.50 |
| 118 | Pedro Martinez | .30 | .75 |
| 119 | Tom Seaver | .30 | .75 |
| 120 | Billy Wagner | .20 | .50 |
| 121 | John Maine | .20 | .50 |
| 122 | Alex Rodriguez | .75 | 2.00 |
| 123 | Chien-Ming Wang | .50 | 1.25 |
| 124 | Hideki Matsui | .50 | 1.25 |
| 125 | Jorge Posada | .30 | .75 |
| 126 | Mariano Rivera | .50 | 1.25 |
| 127 | Phil Rizzuto | .30 | .75 |
| 128 | Bucky Dent | .20 | .50 |
| 129 | Derek Jeter | 1.25 | 3.00 |
| 130 | Graig Nettles | .20 | .50 |
| 131 | Ian Kennedy RC | .75 | 2.00 |
| 132 | Don Larsen | .20 | .50 |
| 133 | Joe Mauer | .20 | .50 |
| 134 | Mark Ellis | .20 | .50 |
| 135 | Dennis Eckersley | .20 | .50 |
| 136 | Rollie Fingers | .20 | .50 |
| 137 | Catfish Hunter | .20 | .50 |
| 138 | Daric Barton (RC) | .30 | .75 |
| 139 | Jack Cust | .20 | .50 |
| 140 | Ryan Howard | .60 | 1.50 |
| 141 | Jimmy Rollins | .30 | .75 |
| 142 | Chase Utley | .50 | 1.25 |
| 143 | Shane Victorino | .20 | .50 |
| 144 | Cole Hamels | .50 | 1.25 |
| 145 | Richie Ashburn | .30 | .75 |
| 146 | Jason Bay | .30 | .75 |
| 147 | Freddy Sanchez | .20 | .50 |
| 148 | Adam LaRoche | .20 | .50 |
| 149 | Jack Wilson | .20 | .50 |
| 150 | Ralph Kiner | .30 | .75 |
| 151 | Bill Mazeroski | .30 | .75 |
| 152 | Tom Gorzelanny | .20 | .50 |
| 153 | Jay Bruce (RC) | 1.25 | 3.00 |
| 154 | Jake Peavy | .30 | .75 |
| 155 | Chris Young | .20 | .50 |
| 156 | Trevor Hoffman | .20 | .50 |
| 157 | Khalil Greene | .30 | .75 |
| 158 | Adrian Gonzalez | .30 | .75 |
| 159 | Tim Lincecum | .60 | 1.50 |
| 160 | Matt Cain | .20 | .50 |
| 161 | Aaron Rowand | .20 | .50 |
| 162 | Orlando Cepeda | .30 | .75 |
| 163 | Juan Marichal | .20 | .50 |
| 164 | Noah Lowry | .20 | .50 |
| 165 | Ichiro Suzuki | .75 | 2.00 |
| 166 | Felix Hernandez | .30 | .75 |
| 167 | J.J. Putz | .20 | .50 |
| 168 | Jose Vidro | .20 | .50 |
| 169 | Raul Ibanez | .30 | .75 |
| 170 | Wladimir Balentien | .20 | .50 |
| 171 | Albert Pujols | 1.00 | 2.50 |
| 172 | Scott Rolen | .30 | .75 |
| 173 | Lou Brock | .30 | .75 |
| 174 | Chris Duncan | .20 | .50 |
| 175 | Vince Coleman | .20 | .50 |
| 176 | B.J. Upton | .30 | .75 |
| 177 | Carl Crawford | .20 | .50 |
| 178 | Carlos Pena | .50 | 1.25 |
| 179 | Scott Kazmir | .30 | .75 |
| 180 | Akinori Iwamura | .20 | .50 |
| 181 | James Shields | .20 | .50 |
| 182 | Michael Young | .20 | .50 |
| 183 | Jarrod Saltalamacchia | .20 | .50 |
| 184 | Hank Blalock | .20 | .50 |
| 185 | Ian Kinsler | .30 | .75 |
| 186 | Josh Hamilton | .60 | 1.50 |
| 187 | Marlon Byrd | .20 | .50 |
| 188 | David Murphy | .20 | .50 |
| 189 | Vernon Wells | .20 | .50 |
| 190 | Roy Halladay | .20 | .50 |
| 191 | Frank Thomas | .50 | 1.25 |
| 192 | Alex Rios | .20 | .50 |
| 193 | Troy Glaus | .30 | .75 |
| 194 | David Eckstein | .20 | .50 |
| 195 | Ryan Zimmerman | .30 | .75 |
| 196 | Dmitri Young | .20 | .50 |
| 197 | Austin Kearns | .20 | .50 |
| 198 | Chad Cordero | .20 | .50 |
| 199 | Ryan Church | .20 | .50 |
| 200 | Evan Longoria RC | 3.00 | 8.00 |
| 201 | Brooks Robinson SP | 2.00 | 5.00 |
| 202 | Cal Ripken Jr. SP | 5.00 | 12.00 |
| 203 | Frank Robinson SP | 2.00 | 5.00 |
| 204 | Carl Yastrzemski SP | 3.00 | 8.00 |
| 205 | Carlton Fisk SP | 2.00 | 5.00 |
| 206 | Fred Lynn SP | 2.00 | 5.00 |
| 207 | Wade Boggs SP | 2.50 | 6.00 |
| 208 | Nolan Ryan SP | 5.00 | 12.00 |
| 209 | Ernie Banks SP | 2.50 | 6.00 |
| 210 | Ryne Sandberg SP | 4.00 | 10.00 |
| 211 | Al Kaline SP | 2.50 | 6.00 |
| 212 | Bo Jackson SP | 2.50 | 6.00 |
| 213 | Paul Molitor SP | 2.50 | 6.00 |
| 214 | Robin Yount SP | 2.50 | 6.00 |
| 215 | Harmon Killebrew SP | 2.50 | 6.00 |
| 216 | Rod Carew SP | 2.00 | 5.00 |
| 217 | Bobby Thomson SP | 2.00 | 5.00 |
| 218 | Gaylord Perry SP | 2.00 | 5.00 |
| 219 | Dave Winfield SP | 2.00 | 5.00 |
| 220 | Don Mattingly SP | 3.00 | 8.00 |
| 221 | Reggie Jackson SP | 2.00 | 5.00 |
| 222 | Roger Clemens SP | 3.00 | 8.00 |
| 223 | Whitey Ford SP | 2.00 | 5.00 |
| 224 | Mike Schmidt SP | 3.00 | 8.00 |
| 225 | Steve Carlton SP | 2.00 | 5.00 |
| 226 | Tony Gwynn SP | 2.00 | 5.00 |
| 227 | Willie McCovey SP | 2.00 | 5.00 |
| 228 | Bob Gibson SP | 2.00 | 5.00 |
| 229 | Ozzie Smith SP | 3.00 | 8.00 |
| 230 | Stan Musial SP | 3.00 | 8.00 |
| 231 | George Washington SP | 2.00 | 5.00 |
| 232 | Thomas Jefferson SP | 2.00 | 5.00 |
| 233 | James Madison SP | 1.50 | 4.00 |
| 234 | James Monroe SP | 1.50 | 4.00 |
| 235 | Andrew Jackson SP | 1.50 | 4.00 |
| 236 | John Tyler SP | 1.50 | 4.00 |
| 237 | Abraham Lincoln SP | 2.00 | 5.00 |
| 238 | Ulysses S. Grant SP | 1.50 | 4.00 |
| 239 | Grover Cleveland SP | 1.50 | 4.00 |
| 240 | Theodore Roosevelt SP | 1.50 | 4.00 |
| 241 | Calvin Coolidge SP | 1.50 | 4.00 |
| 242 | John Adams SP | 1.50 | 4.00 |
| 243 | Martin Van Buren SP | 1.50 | 4.00 |
| 244 | William McKinley SP | 1.50 | 4.00 |
| 245 | Woodrow Wilson SP | 1.50 | 4.00 |
| 246 | James K. Polk SP | 1.50 | 4.00 |
| 247 | Rutherford B. Hayes SP | 1.50 | 4.00 |
| 248 | William H. Taft SP | 1.50 | 4.00 |
| 249 | Andrew Johnson SP | 1.50 | 4.00 |
| 250 | James Buchanan SP | 1.50 | 4.00 |
| 251 | A.Pujols 36 BW SP | 3.00 | 8.00 |
| 252 | A.Rodriguez 36 BW SP | 3.00 | 8.00 |
| 253 | Alfonso Soriano 36 BW SP | 2.50 | 6.00 |
| 254 | C.C. Sabathia 36 BW SP | 2.00 | 5.00 |
| 255 | Chase Utley 36 BW SP | 2.50 | 6.00 |
| 256 | David Ortiz 36 BW SP | 2.50 | 6.00 |
| 257 | D.Wright 36 BW SP | 2.50 | 6.00 |
| 258 | D.Jeter 36 BW SP | 4.00 | 10.00 |
| 259 | Hanley Ramirez 36 BW SP | 2.50 | 6.00 |
| 260 | I.Suzuki 36 BW SP | 3.00 | 8.00 |
| 261 | Jake Peavy 36 BW SP | 2.50 | 6.00 |
| 262 | Johan Santana 36 BW SP | 2.50 | 6.00 |
| 263 | Jose Reyes 36 BW SP | 2.50 | 6.00 |
| 264 | K.Griffey Jr. 36 BW SP | 3.00 | 8.00 |
| 265 | Magglio Ordonez 36 BW SP | 2.50 | 6.00 |
| 266 | Matt Holliday 36 BW SP | 2.50 | 6.00 |
| 267 | Prince Fielder 36 BW SP | 2.50 | 6.00 |
| 268 | R.Braun 36 BW SP | 2.50 | 6.00 |
| 269 | R.Howard 36 BW SP | 2.50 | 6.00 |
| 270 | Vladimir Guerrero 36 BW SP | 2.50 | 6.00 |
| 271 | Carl Yastrzemski SP | 2.50 | 6.00 |
| 272 | Albert Pujols SR SP | 3.00 | 8.00 |
| 273 | Amy Van Dyken SR SP | 2.00 | 5.00 |
| 274 | Tom Seaver SR SP | 2.50 | 6.00 |
| 275 | Brett Favre SR SP | 4.00 | 10.00 |
| 276 | Bruce Jenner SR SP | 2.00 | 5.00 |
| 277 | Bill Russell SR SP | 2.00 | 5.00 |
| 278 | Barry Sanders SR SP | 3.00 | 8.00 |
| 279 | Cynthia Cooper SR SP | 2.00 | 5.00 |
| 280 | Mike Schmidt SR SP | 2.50 | 6.00 |
| 281 | Chipper Jones SR SP | 2.50 | 6.00 |
| 282 | Cal Ripken Jr. SR SP | 4.00 | 10.00 |
| 283 | Cael Sanderson SR SP | 2.00 | 5.00 |
| 284 | Dan Gable SR SP | 2.00 | 5.00 |
| 285 | Derek Jeter SR SP | 4.00 | 10.00 |
| 286 | Andre Dawson SR SP | 2.00 | 5.00 |
| 287 | Dan O'Brien SR SP | 2.00 | 5.00 |
| 288 | Julius Erving SR SP | 2.50 | 6.00 |
| 289 | Emmitt Smith SR SP | 3.00 | 8.00 |
| 290 | Janet Evans SR SP | 2.00 | 5.00 |
| 291 | Chase Utley SR SP | 2.00 | 5.00 |
| 292 | Gary Hall Jr. SR SP | 2.00 | 5.00 |
| 293 | Gordie Howe SR SP | 3.00 | 8.00 |
| 294 | Josh Beckett SR SP | 2.00 | 5.00 |
| 295 | John Elway SR SP | 3.00 | 8.00 |
| 296 | Julie Foudy SR SP | 2.00 | 5.00 |
| 297 | Jackie Joyner-Kersee SR SP | 2.00 | 5.00 |
| 298 | Jack Nicklaus SR SP | 4.00 | 10.00 |

| | | |
|---|---|---|
| ❏ 299 Magic Johnson SR SP | 3.00 | 8.00 |
| ❏ 300 Michael Jordan SR SP | 3.00 | 8.00 |
| ❏ 301 Bo Jackson SR SP | 4.00 | 10.00 |
| ❏ 302 Tom Brady SR SP | 6.00 | 15.00 |
| ❏ 303 Wade Boggs SR SP | 4.00 | 10.00 |
| ❏ 304 Dan Marino SR SP | 6.00 | 15.00 |
| ❏ 305 Dave Winfield SR SP | 3.00 | 8.00 |
| ❏ 306 Jenny Thompson SR SP | 3.00 | 8.00 |
| ❏ 307 Kobe Bryant SR SP | 5.00 | 12.00 |
| ❏ 308 Kevin Durant SR SP | 5.00 | 12.00 |
| ❏ 309 Ken Griffey Jr. SR SP | 5.00 | 12.00 |
| ❏ 310 Kerri Strug SR SP | 4.00 | 10.00 |
| ❏ 311 Kerri Walsh SR SP | 4.00 | 10.00 |
| ❏ 312 Larry Bird SR SP | 6.00 | 15.00 |
| ❏ 313 LeBron James SR SP | 6.00 | 15.00 |
| ❏ 314 Matt Biondi SR SP | 3.00 | 8.00 |
| ❏ 315 Mark Messier SR SP | 4.00 | 10.00 |
| ❏ 316 Michael Johnson SR SP | 3.00 | 8.00 |
| ❏ 317 Misty May-Treanor SR SP | 8.00 | 20.00 |
| ❏ 318 Bob Gibson SR SP | 6.00 | 15.00 |
| ❏ 319 Nolan Ryan SR SP | 6.00 | 15.00 |
| ❏ 320 Ozzie Smith SR SP | 5.00 | 12.00 |
| ❏ 321 Prince Fielder SR SP | 4.00 | 10.00 |
| ❏ 322 Rulon Gardner SR SP | 3.00 | 8.00 |
| ❏ 323 Reggie Jackson SR SP | 4.00 | 10.00 |
| ❏ 324 Ernie Banks SR SP | 5.00 | 12.00 |
| ❏ 325 Sidney Crosby SR SP | 10.00 | 25.00 |
| ❏ 326 Sanya Richards SR SP | 3.00 | 8.00 |
| ❏ 327 Terry Bradshaw SR SP | 4.00 | 10.00 |
| ❏ 328 Tony Gwynn SR SP | 4.00 | 10.00 |
| ❏ 329 Stan Musial SR SP | 6.00 | 15.00 |
| ❏ 330 Tiger Woods SR SP | 30.00 | 60.00 |

## 2009 Upper Deck Goudey

| | | |
|---|---|---|
| ❏ COMPLETE SET (300) | 200.00 | 300.00 |
| ❏ COMP.SET w/o SP's (200) | 20.00 | 50.00 |
| ❏ COMMON CARD (1-200) | .20 | .50 |
| ❏ COMMON RC (1-200) | .40 | 1.00 |
| ❏ COMMON SP (201-300) | 2.00 | 5.00 |
| ❏ APPX.SP ODDS 201-220 1:9 HOBBY | | |
| ❏ APPX.SP ODDS 201-260 1:6 HOBBY | | |
| ❏ APPX.SP ODDS 261-300 1:6 HOBBY | | |
| ❏ 1 Adam Dunn | .30 | .75 |
| ❏ 2 Max Scherzer | .20 | .50 |
| ❏ 3 Stephen Drew | .20 | .50 |
| ❏ 4 Randy Johnson | .50 | 1.25 |
| ❏ 5 Brandon Webb | .30 | .75 |
| ❏ 6 Dan Haren | .20 | .50 |
| ❏ 7 Chris B. Young | .20 | .50 |
| ❏ 8 Brian McCann | .30 | .75 |
| ❏ 9 Jeff Francoeur | .30 | .75 |
| ❏ 10 James Parr (RC) | .40 | 1.00 |
| ❏ 11 Tom Glavine | .30 | .75 |
| ❏ 12 Tim Hudson | .20 | .50 |
| ❏ 13 Chipper Jones | .50 | 1.25 |
| ❏ 14 Kelly Johnson | .20 | .50 |
| ❏ 15 Adam Jones | .30 | .75 |
| ❏ 16 Jeremy Guthrie | .20 | .50 |
| ❏ 17 Brian Roberts | .30 | .75 |
| ❏ 18 Nick Markakis | .30 | .75 |
| ❏ 19 Jed Lowrie | .30 | .75 |
| ❏ 20 Cal Ripken Jr. | 2.00 | 5.00 |
| ❏ 21 Melvin Mora | .20 | .50 |
| ❏ 22 Jason Bay | .30 | .75 |
| ❏ 23 Josh Beckett | .30 | .75 |
| ❏ 24 Justin Masterson | .30 | .75 |
| ❏ 25 Kevin Youkilis | .30 | .75 |
| ❏ 26 Michael Bowden (RC) | .60 | 1.50 |
| ❏ 27 Dustin Pedroia | .60 | 1.50 |
| ❏ 28 Jacoby Ellsbury | .50 | 1.25 |
| ❏ 29 Jason Varitek | .30 | .75 |
| ❏ 30 Jonathan Papelbon | .30 | .75 |
| ❏ 31 David Ortiz | .75 | 2.00 |
| ❏ 32 Daisuke Matsuzaka | .75 | 2.00 |
| ❏ 33 J.D. Drew | .20 | .50 |
| ❏ 34 Curt Schilling | .30 | .75 |
| ❏ 35 Clay Buchholz | .30 | .75 |
| ❏ 36 Wilkin Castillo RC | .60 | 1.50 |
| ❏ 37 Derrek Lee | .30 | .75 |
| ❏ 38 Kosuke Fukudome | .50 | 1.25 |

| | | |
|---|---|---|
| ❏ 39 Aramis Ramirez | .20 | .50 |
| ❏ 40 Alfonso Soriano | .30 | .75 |
| ❏ 41 Kerry Wood | .20 | .50 |
| ❏ 42 Carlos Zambrano | .20 | .50 |
| ❏ 43 Rich Harden | .20 | .50 |
| ❏ 44 Geovany Soto | .30 | .75 |
| ❏ 45 Gavin Floyd | .20 | .50 |
| ❏ 46 Ken Griffey Jr. | .75 | 2.00 |
| ❏ 47 Nick Swisher | .20 | .50 |
| ❏ 48 Jim Thome | .30 | .75 |
| ❏ 49 Jermaine Dye | .20 | .50 |
| ❏ 50 Alexei Ramirez | .30 | .75 |
| ❏ 51 Carlos Quentin | .20 | .50 |
| ❏ 52 Brandon Phillips | .20 | .50 |
| ❏ 53 Johnny Cueto | .20 | .50 |
| ❏ 54 Jay Bruce | .50 | 1.25 |
| ❏ 55 Dave Concepcion | .30 | .75 |
| ❏ 56 Joey Votto | .30 | .75 |
| ❏ 57 Aaron Harang | .20 | .50 |
| ❏ 58 Edinson Volquez | .20 | .50 |
| ❏ 59 Kelly Shoppach | .20 | .50 |
| ❏ 60 Fausto Carmona | .20 | .50 |
| ❏ 61 Grady Sizemore | .30 | .75 |
| ❏ 62 Travis Hafner | .20 | .50 |
| ❏ 63 Victor Martinez | .30 | .75 |
| ❏ 64 Cliff Lee | .50 | 1.25 |
| ❏ 65 Dexter Fowler (RC) | .60 | 1.50 |
| ❏ 66 Garrett Atkins | .20 | .50 |
| ❏ 67 Troy Tulowitzki | .30 | .75 |
| ❏ 68 Matt Holliday | .30 | .75 |
| ❏ 69 Curtis Granderson | .50 | 1.25 |
| ❏ 70 Carlos Guillen | .20 | .50 |
| ❏ 71 Gary Sheffield | .20 | .50 |
| ❏ 72 Miguel Cabrera | .30 | .75 |
| ❏ 73 Magglio Ordonez | .30 | .75 |
| ❏ 74 Justin Verlander | .30 | .75 |
| ❏ 75 Hanley Ramirez | .50 | 1.25 |
| ❏ 76 Josh Willingham | .20 | .50 |
| ❏ 77 Dan Uggla | .20 | .50 |
| ❏ 78 Josh Johnson | .20 | .50 |
| ❏ 79 Carlos Lee | .20 | .50 |
| ❏ 80 Roy Oswalt | .30 | .75 |
| ❏ 81 Miguel Tejada | .30 | .75 |
| ❏ 82 Lance Berkman | .30 | .75 |
| ❏ 83 Klia Ka'aihue (RC) | .60 | 1.50 |
| ❏ 84 Joakim Soria | .20 | .50 |
| ❏ 85 Alex Gordon | .30 | .75 |
| ❏ 86 Chone Figgins | .20 | .50 |
| ❏ 87 John Lackey | .20 | .50 |
| ❏ 88 Jered Weaver | .20 | .50 |
| ❏ 89 Vladimir Guerrero | .50 | 1.25 |
| ❏ 90 Mark Teixeira | .50 | 1.25 |
| ❏ 91 Garret Anderson | .20 | .50 |
| ❏ 92 Torii Hunter | .20 | .50 |
| ❏ 93 Howie Kendrick | .20 | .50 |
| ❏ 94 Clayton Kershaw | .50 | 1.25 |
| ❏ 95 Cory Wade | .20 | .50 |
| ❏ 96 Matt Kemp | .50 | 1.25 |
| ❏ 97 Russell Martin | .30 | .75 |
| ❏ 98 Scott Elbert (RC) | .40 | 1.00 |
| ❏ 99 Manny Ramirez | .50 | 1.25 |
| ❏ 100 Andre Ethier | .30 | .75 |
| ❏ 101 Rafael Furcal | .20 | .50 |
| ❏ 102 Brad Penny | .20 | .50 |
| ❏ 103 Takashi Saito | .20 | .50 |
| ❏ 104 Kirk Gibson | .30 | .75 |
| ❏ 105 Alcides Escobar RC | .60 | 1.50 |
| ❏ 106 Bill Hall | .20 | .50 |
| ❏ 107 Mat Gamel RC | 1.00 | 2.50 |
| ❏ 108 Prince Fielder | .50 | 1.25 |
| ❏ 109 Miguel Montero | .20 | .50 |
| ❏ 110 Yovani Gallardo | .30 | .75 |
| ❏ 111 Ben Sheets | .20 | .50 |
| ❏ 112 CC Sabathia | .50 | 1.25 |
| ❏ 113 Ryan Braun | .60 | 1.50 |
| ❏ 114 J.J. Hardy | .20 | .50 |
| ❏ 115 Denard Span | .30 | .75 |
| ❏ 116 Joe Nathan | .20 | .50 |
| ❏ 117 Nick Blackburn | .20 | .50 |
| ❏ 118 Joe Mauer | .50 | 1.25 |
| ❏ 119 Justin Morneau | .30 | .75 |

| | | |
|---|---|---|
| ❏ 120 Francisco Liriano | .20 | .50 |
| ❏ 121 Kevin Slowey | .30 | .75 |
| ❏ 122 Delmon Young | .20 | .50 |
| ❏ 123 John Maine | .20 | .50 |
| ❏ 124 Jonathon Niese RC | .60 | 1.50 |
| ❏ 125 David Wright | .60 | 1.50 |
| ❏ 126 Jose Reyes | .50 | 1.25 |
| ❏ 127 Carlos Beltran | .20 | .50 |
| ❏ 128 Johan Santana | .50 | 1.25 |
| ❏ 129 A.J. Burnett | .30 | .75 |
| ❏ 130 Derek Jeter | 1.25 | 3.00 |
| ❏ 131 Francisco Cervelli RC | 1.00 | 2.50 |
| ❏ 132 Ian Kennedy | .30 | .75 |
| ❏ 133 Phil Coke RC | .60 | 1.50 |
| ❏ 134 Phil Hughes | .30 | .75 |
| ❏ 135 Alex Rodriguez | .75 | 2.00 |
| ❏ 136 Chien-Ming Wang | .50 | 1.25 |
| ❏ 137 Mariano Rivera | .30 | .75 |
| ❏ 138 Joba Chamberlain | .60 | 1.50 |
| ❏ 139 Jason Giambi | .20 | .50 |
| ❏ 140 Andy Pettitte | .30 | .75 |
| ❏ 141 Greg Smith | .20 | .50 |
| ❏ 142 Marlon Byrd | .20 | .50 |
| ❏ 143 Johnny Damon | .30 | .75 |
| ❏ 144 Frank Thomas | .50 | 1.25 |
| ❏ 145 Carlos Gonzalez | .20 | .50 |
| ❏ 146 Jeff Baisley RC | .40 | 1.00 |
| ❏ 147 Mark Teahen | .20 | .50 |
| ❏ 148 Jack Cust | .20 | .50 |
| ❏ 149 Kurt Suzuki | .20 | .50 |
| ❏ 150 Bobby Crosby | .20 | .50 |
| ❏ 151 Chase Utley | .50 | 1.25 |
| ❏ 152 Lou Marson (RC) | .40 | 1.00 |
| ❏ 153 Jimmy Rollins | .30 | .75 |
| ❏ 154 Chase Utley | .50 | 1.25 |
| ❏ 155 Ryan Howard | .60 | 1.50 |
| ❏ 156 Greg Golson (RC) | .40 | 1.00 |
| ❏ 157 Pat Burrell | .30 | .75 |
| ❏ 158 Shane Victorino | .20 | .50 |
| ❏ 159 Brad Lidge | .20 | .50 |
| ❏ 160 Edwin Encarnacion | .20 | .50 |
| ❏ 161 Nate McLouth | .20 | .50 |
| ❏ 162 Ryan Doumit | .20 | .50 |
| ❏ 163 Adrian Gonzalez | .30 | .75 |
| ❏ 164 Matt Antonelli RC | .60 | 1.50 |
| ❏ 165 Jake Peavy | .30 | .75 |
| ❏ 166 Kevin Kouzmanoff | .20 | .50 |
| ❏ 167 Chris Young | .20 | .50 |
| ❏ 168 Trevor Hoffman | .20 | .50 |
| ❏ 169 Conor Gillaspie RC | 1.00 | 2.50 |
| ❏ 170 Wade LeBlanc RC | .60 | 1.50 |
| ❏ 171 Matt Cain | .30 | .75 |
| ❏ 172 Tim Lincecum | .60 | 1.50 |
| ❏ 173 Matt Tuiasosopo RC | .40 | 1.00 |
| ❏ 174 Ichiro Suzuki | .75 | 2.00 |
| ❏ 175 Felix Hernandez | .30 | .75 |
| ❏ 176 Erik Bedard | .20 | .50 |
| ❏ 177 Ryan Ludwick | .30 | .75 |
| ❏ 178 Albert Pujols | 1.25 | 3.00 |
| ❏ 179 Rick Ankiel | .30 | .75 |
| ❏ 180 Troy Glaus | .20 | .50 |
| ❏ 181 Bob Gibson | .30 | .75 |
| ❏ 182 B.J. Upton | .30 | .75 |
| ❏ 183 David Price RC | 1.25 | 3.00 |
| ❏ 184 Evan Longoria | .75 | 2.00 |
| ❏ 185 Carl Crawford | .30 | .75 |
| ❏ 186 Scott Kazmir | .30 | .75 |
| ❏ 187 Carlos Pena | .30 | .75 |
| ❏ 188 James Shields | .20 | .50 |
| ❏ 189 Josh Hamilton | .50 | 1.25 |
| ❏ 190 Ian Kinsler | .30 | .75 |
| ❏ 191 Michael Young | .30 | .75 |
| ❏ 192 Mike Aviles | .20 | .50 |
| ❏ 193 Roy Halladay | .30 | .75 |
| ❏ 194 Travis Snider RC | 1.00 | 2.50 |
| ❏ 195 Vernon Wells | .20 | .50 |
| ❏ 196 Alex Rios | .20 | .50 |
| ❏ 197 Ryan Zimmerman | .30 | .75 |
| ❏ 198 Shairon Martis RC | .60 | 1.50 |
| ❏ 199 Lastings Milledge | .20 | .50 |
| ❏ 200 Cristian Guzman | .20 | .50 |

| | | |
|---|---|---|
| 201 Brooks Robinson SP | 2.00 | 5.00 |
| 202 Carlton Fisk SP | 2.00 | 5.00 |
| 203 Gaylord Perry SP | 2.00 | 5.00 |
| 204 Jack Morris SP | 2.00 | 5.00 |
| 205 Rollie Fingers SP | 2.00 | 5.00 |
| 206 Ron Santo SP | 2.00 | 5.00 |
| 207 Sparky Lyle SP | 2.00 | 5.00 |
| 208 Nolan Ryan SP | 5.00 | 12.00 |
| 209 Whitey Ford SP | 2.50 | 6.00 |
| 210 Phil Niekro SP | 2.00 | 5.00 |
| 211 Ryne Sandberg SP | 3.00 | 8.00 |
| 212 Jim Palmer SP | 2.50 | 6.00 |
| 213 Joe DiMaggio SP | 5.00 | 12.00 |
| 214 Johnny Bench SP | 3.00 | 8.00 |
| 215 Ted Williams SP | 5.00 | 12.00 |
| 216 Robin Yount SP | 3.00 | 8.00 |
| 217 Ozzie Smith SP | 3.00 | 8.00 |
| 218 Reggie Jackson SP | 2.50 | 6.00 |
| 219 Yogi Berra SP | 3.00 | 8.00 |
| 220 Mike Schmidt SP | 3.00 | 8.00 |
| 221 Cal Ripken Jr. SR SP | 5.00 | 12.00 |
| 222 Ozzie Smith SR SP | 3.00 | 8.00 |
| 223 Tony Gwynn SR SP | 3.00 | 8.00 |
| 224 Don Mattingly SR SP | 3.00 | 8.00 |
| 225 Steve Carlton SR SP | 2.00 | 5.00 |
| 226 Reggie Jackson SR SP | 2.50 | 6.00 |
| 227 Carl Yastrzemski SR SP | 3.00 | 8.00 |
| 228 Johnny Bench SR SP | 3.00 | 8.00 |
| 229 Mike Schmidt SR SP | 3.00 | 8.00 |
| 230 Nolan Ryan SR SP | 5.00 | 12.00 |
| 231 Ernie Banks SR SP | 3.00 | 8.00 |
| 232 Stan Musial SR SP | 4.00 | 10.00 |
| 233 Ryne Sandberg SR SP | 3.00 | 8.00 |
| 234 Bob Gibson SR SP | 3.00 | 8.00 |
| 235 Dennis Eckersley SR SP | 2.00 | 5.00 |
| 236 Felix Hernandez SR SP | 2.50 | 6.00 |
| 237 Jim Rice SR SP | 2.50 | 6.00 |
| 238 Chien-Ming Wang SR SP | 3.00 | 8.00 |
| 239 Jonathan Papelbon SR SP | 2.50 | 6.00 |
| 240 Evan Longoria SR SP | 5.00 | 12.00 |
| 241 Cole Hamels SR SP | 2.50 | 6.00 |
| 242 Ken Griffey Jr. SR SP | 4.00 | 10.00 |
| 243 Tiger Woods SR SP | 15.00 | 40.00 |
| 244 B.J. Upton SR SP | 2.50 | 6.00 |
| 245 Randy Johnson SR SP | 3.00 | 8.00 |
| 246 Guy Lafleur SR SP | 2.50 | 6.00 |
| 247 Nicklas Lidstrom SR SP | 3.00 | 8.00 |
| 248 Mike Bossy SR SP | 2.50 | 6.00 |
| 249 Bobby Orr SR SP | 4.00 | 10.00 |
| 250 Patrick Roy SR SP | 5.00 | 12.00 |
| 251 Adrian Peterson SR SP | 4.00 | 10.00 |
| 252 Juan Marichal SR SP | 2.00 | 5.00 |
| 253 Chipper Jones SR SP | 3.00 | 8.00 |
| 254 Rollie Fingers SR SP | 3.00 | 8.00 |
| 255 Al Kaline SR SP | 3.00 | 8.00 |
| 256 Paul Pierce SR SP | 3.00 | 8.00 |
| 257 Jerry West SR SP | 3.00 | 8.00 |
| 258 Larry Bird SR SP | 3.00 | 8.00 |
| 259 John Havlicek SR SP | 2.50 | 6.00 |
| 260 Michael Jordan SR SP | 5.00 | 12.00 |
| 261 Cal Ripken Jr. HU SP | 5.00 | 12.00 |
| 262 Reggie Jackson HU SP | 3.00 | 8.00 |
| 263 Nolan Ryan HU SP | 5.00 | 12.00 |
| 264 Yogi Berra HU SP | 3.00 | 8.00 |
| 265 Ernie Banks HU SP | 3.00 | 8.00 |
| 266 Dave Winfield HU SP | 2.50 | 6.00 |
| 267 Ozzie Smith HU SP | 3.00 | 8.00 |
| 268 Stan Musial HU SP | 4.00 | 10.00 |
| 269 Ichiro Suzuki HU SP | 4.00 | 10.00 |
| 270 Albert Pujols HU SP | 4.00 | 10.00 |
| 271 Alex Rodriguez HU SP | 4.00 | 10.00 |
| 272 Jose Reyes HU SP | 3.00 | 8.00 |
| 273 David Wright HU SP | 3.00 | 8.00 |
| 274 Johan Santana HU SP | 3.00 | 8.00 |
| 275 Josh Hamilton HU SP | 3.00 | 8.00 |
| 276 David Ortiz HU SP | 3.00 | 8.00 |
| 277 Josh Beckett HU SP | 2.50 | 6.00 |
| 278 Manny Ramirez HU SP | 3.00 | 8.00 |
| 279 Ryan Howard HU SP | 3.00 | 8.00 |
| 280 Chase Utley HU SP | 3.00 | 8.00 |
| 281 Jimmy Rollins HU SP | 3.00 | 8.00 |
| 282 Hanley Ramirez HU SP | 3.00 | 8.00 |
| 283 CC Sabathia HU SP | 3.00 | 8.00 |
| 284 Ryan Braun HU SP | 2.50 | 6.00 |
| 285 Evan Longoria HU SP | 3.00 | 6.00 |
| 286 Grady Sizemore HU SP | 2.50 | 6.00 |
| 287 Dustin Pedroia HU SP | 3.00 | 8.00 |
| 288 Mark Teixeira HU SP | 3.00 | 8.00 |
| 289 Ken Griffey Jr. HU SP | 4.00 | 10.00 |
| 290 Lance Berkman HU SP | 2.50 | 6.00 |
| 291 Alfonso Soriano HU SP | 2.50 | 6.00 |
| 292 Derrek Lee HU SP | 2.50 | 6.00 |
| 293 Brandon Webb HU SP | 2.50 | 6.00 |
| 294 Derek Jeter HU SP | 5.00 | 12.00 |
| 295 Daisuke Matsuzaka HU SP | 3.00 | 8.00 |
| 296 Vladimir Guerrero HU SP | 3.00 | 8.00 |
| 297 Jim Thome HU SP | 2.50 | 6.00 |
| 298 Carlos Zambrano HU SP | 2.00 | 5.00 |
| 299 Justin Morneau HU SP | 2.50 | 6.00 |
| 300 Tim Lincecum HU SP | 3.00 | 8.00 |

## 2008 Upper Deck Heroes

| | | |
|---|---|---|
| COMPLETE SET (200) | 20.00 | 50.00 |
| COMMON CARD (1-200) | .20 | .50 |
| COMMON ROOKIE (1-200) | .40 | 1.00 |
| 1 Brandon Webb | .30 | .75 |
| 2 Dan Haren | .20 | .50 |
| 3 Chris B. Young | .20 | .50 |
| 4 Justin Upton | .50 | 1.25 |
| 5 Randy Johnson | .50 | 1.25 |
| 6 Chipper Jones | .60 | 1.50 |
| 7 John Smoltz | .50 | 1.25 |
| 8 Tom Glavine | .30 | .75 |
| 9 Mark Teixeira | .50 | 1.25 |
| 10 Brian McCann | .30 | .75 |
| 11 Jeff Francoeur | .30 | .75 |
| 12 Josh Hamilton | .60 | 1.50 |
| 13 Tim Hudson | .20 | .50 |
| 14 Nick Markakis | .30 | .75 |
| 15 Brian Roberts | .30 | .75 |
| 16 Cal Ripken Jr. | 2.00 | 5.00 |
| 17 John Maine | .20 | .50 |
| 18 Frank Robinson | .20 | .50 |
| 19 Mike Lowell | .20 | .50 |
| 20 Jason Varitek | .50 | 1.25 |
| 21 David Ortiz | .30 | .75 |
| 22 Manny Ramirez | .50 | 1.25 |
| 23 Jonathan Papelbon | .30 | .75 |
| 24 Jacoby Ellsbury | .75 | 2.00 |
| 25 Kevin Youkilis | .30 | .75 |
| 26 Curt Schilling | .30 | .75 |
| 27 Josh Beckett | .30 | .75 |
| 28 Daisuke Matsuzaka | .60 | 1.50 |
| 29 Clay Buchholz (RC) | 1.00 | 2.50 |
| 30 Dustin Pedroia | .60 | 1.50 |
| 31 Ryan Theriot | .20 | .50 |
| 32 Carlton Fisk | .30 | .75 |
| 33 Carl Yastrzemski | .75 | 2.00 |
| 34 Wade Boggs | .30 | .75 |
| 35 Nolan Ryan | 1.50 | 4.00 |
| 36 Alfonso Soriano | .30 | .75 |
| 37 Kosuke Fukudome RC | 1.25 | 3.00 |
| 38 Derrek Lee | .30 | .75 |
| 39 Carlos Zambrano | .20 | .50 |
| 40 Aramis Ramirez | .20 | .50 |
| 41 Ernie Banks | .50 | 1.25 |
| 42 Jim Thome | .30 | .75 |
| 43 Jermaine Dye | .20 | .50 |
| 44 Paul Konerko | .20 | .50 |
| 45 Nick Swisher | .20 | .50 |
| 46 Corey Hart | .20 | .50 |
| 47 Ken Griffey Jr. | .75 | 2.00 |
| 48 Adam Dunn | .20 | .50 |
| 49 Aaron Harang | .20 | .50 |
| 50 Johnny Bench | .50 | 1.25 |
| 51 Grady Sizemore | .30 | .75 |
| 52 Victor Martinez | .20 | .50 |
| 53 C.C. Sabathia | .20 | .50 |
| 54 Travis Hafner | .20 | .50 |
| 55 Jeff Francis | .20 | .50 |
| 56 Matt Holliday | .30 | .75 |
| 57 Troy Tulowitzki | .30 | .75 |
| 58 Garrett Atkins | .20 | .50 |
| 59 Todd Helton | .30 | .75 |
| 60 Curtis Granderson | .30 | .75 |
| 61 Dontrelle Willis | .20 | .50 |
| 62 Magglio Ordonez | .30 | .75 |
| 63 Gary Sheffield | .20 | .50 |
| 64 Miguel Cabrera | .30 | .75 |
| 65 Justin Verlander | .30 | .75 |
| 66 Ivan Rodriguez | .30 | .75 |
| 67 Al Kaline | .50 | 1.25 |
| 68 Hanley Ramirez | .50 | 1.25 |
| 69 Edinson Volquez | .20 | .50 |
| 70 Dan Uggla | .30 | .75 |
| 71 Andrew Miller | .30 | .75 |
| 72 Josh Willingham | .20 | .50 |
| 73 J.R. Towles RC | .60 | 1.50 |
| 74 Lance Berkman | .30 | .75 |
| 75 Carlos Lee | .20 | .50 |
| 76 Roy Oswalt | .20 | .50 |
| 77 Hunter Pence | .50 | 1.25 |
| 78 Luke Hochevar RC | .60 | 1.50 |
| 79 Alex Gordon | .30 | .75 |
| 80 Matt Cain | .20 | .50 |
| 81 Bo Jackson | .50 | 1.25 |
| 82 Vladimir Guerrero | .50 | 1.25 |
| 83 Torii Hunter | .20 | .50 |
| 84 Howie Kendrick | .20 | .50 |
| 85 John Lackey | .20 | .50 |
| 86 Chone Figgins | .20 | .50 |
| 87 Andruw Jones | .20 | .50 |
| 88 Brad Penny | .20 | .50 |
| 89 James Loney | .30 | .75 |
| 90 Matt Kemp | .50 | 1.25 |
| 91 Nomar Garciaparra | .50 | 1.25 |
| 92 Jon Lester | .30 | .75 |
| 93 Chin-Lung Hu (RC) | .60 | 1.50 |
| 94 Chad Billingsley | .20 | .50 |
| 95 Kelly Johnson | .20 | .50 |
| 96 Prince Fielder | .50 | 1.25 |
| 97 Ryan Braun | .60 | 1.50 |
| 98 Ben Sheets | .30 | .75 |
| 99 Robin Yount | .50 | 1.25 |
| 100 Justin Morneau | .30 | .75 |
| 101 Joe Mauer | .50 | 1.25 |
| 102 Delmon Young | .30 | .75 |
| 103 Rod Carew | .30 | .75 |
| 104 Carlos Beltran | .20 | .50 |
| 105 Jose Reyes | .30 | .75 |
| 106 Pedro Martinez | .30 | .75 |
| 107 David Wright | .60 | 1.50 |
| 108 Johan Santana | .50 | 1.25 |
| 109 Billy Wagner | .20 | .50 |
| 110 Carlos Delgado | .20 | .50 |
| 111 Mariano Rivera | .50 | 1.25 |
| 112 Chien-Ming Wang | .50 | 1.25 |
| 113 Phil Hughes | .50 | 1.25 |
| 114 Derek Jeter | 1.25 | 3.00 |
| 115 Alex Rodriguez | .75 | 2.00 |
| 116 Robinson Cano | .30 | .75 |
| 117 Jorge Posada | .30 | .75 |
| 118 Hideki Matsui | .50 | 1.25 |
| 119 Joba Chamberlain | .60 | 1.50 |
| 120 Ian Kennedy RC | 1.00 | 2.50 |
| 121 Yogi Berra | .50 | 1.25 |
| 122 Reggie Jackson | .30 | .75 |
| 123 Roger Clemens | .60 | 1.50 |
| 124 Ozzie Smith | .75 | 2.00 |
| 125 Don Mattingly | 1.00 | 2.50 |
| 126 Dave Winfield | .20 | .50 |

|  |  | | |
|---|---|---|---|
| 127 | Joe DiMaggio | 1.25 | 3.00 |
| 128 | Eric Chavez | .20 | .50 |
| 129 | Bill Hall | .20 | .50 |
| 130 | Rich Harden | .20 | .50 |
| 131 | Andre Ethier | .30 | .75 |
| 132 | Daric Barton (RC) | .40 | 1.00 |
| 133 | Ryan Howard | .60 | 1.50 |
| 134 | Jimmy Rollins | .30 | .75 |
| 135 | Chase Utley | .50 | 1.25 |
| 136 | Cole Hamels | .50 | 1.25 |
| 137 | Pat Burrell | .20 | .50 |
| 138 | Mike Schmidt | .75 | 2.00 |
| 139 | Steve Carlton | .20 | .50 |
| 140 | Freddy Sanchez | .20 | .50 |
| 141 | Joe Blanton | .20 | .50 |
| 142 | Felix Pie | .20 | .50 |
| 143 | Roberto Clemente | 1.00 | 2.50 |
| 144 | Jake Peavy | .30 | .75 |
| 145 | Greg Maddux | .60 | 1.50 |
| 146 | Tom Gorzelanny | .20 | .50 |
| 147 | Tony Gwynn | .60 | 1.50 |
| 148 | Barry Zito | .20 | .50 |
| 149 | Tim Lincecum | .60 | 1.50 |
| 150 | Rich Hill | .20 | .50 |
| 151 | Omar Vizquel | .20 | .50 |
| 152 | Ichiro Suzuki | .75 | 2.00 |
| 153 | Felix Hernandez | .30 | .75 |
| 154 | Kenji Johjima | .20 | .50 |
| 155 | Erik Bedard | .20 | .50 |
| 156 | Albert Pujols | 1.00 | 2.50 |
| 157 | Troy Glaus | .30 | .75 |
| 158 | Chris Carpenter | .20 | .50 |
| 159 | Chris Duncan | .20 | .50 |
| 160 | Mark Mulder | .20 | .50 |
| 161 | Scott Rolen | .30 | .75 |
| 162 | Stan Musial | .75 | 2.00 |
| 163 | Bob Gibson | .30 | .75 |
| 164 | B.J. Upton | .30 | .75 |
| 165 | Carl Crawford | .20 | .50 |
| 166 | Scott Kazmir | .20 | .50 |
| 167 | Michael Young | .20 | .50 |
| 168 | Luke Scott | .20 | .50 |
| 169 | Roy Halladay | .20 | .50 |
| 170 | Vernon Wells | .20 | .50 |
| 171 | Kevin Kouzmanoff | .20 | .50 |
| 172 | Frank Thomas | .50 | 1.25 |
| 173 | Ryan Zimmerman | .30 | .75 |
| 174 | Lastings Milledge | .20 | .50 |
| 175 | Ian Kinsler | .30 | .75 |
| 176 | D.Mattingly/W.Boggs | 1.00 | 2.50 |
| 177 | C.Fisk/C.Yastrzemski | .75 | 2.00 |
| 178 | A.Pujols/S.Musial | 1.00 | 2.50 |
| 179 | J.Reyes/D.Jeter | 1.25 | 3.00 |
| 180 | C.Ripken/T.Gwynn | 2.00 | 5.00 |
| 181 | Eddie Murray/Prince Fielder | .50 | 1.25 |
| 182 | I.Suzuki/K.Fukudome | .75 | 2.00 |
| 183 | Steve Carlton/Johan Santana | .30 | .75 |
| 184 | Bob Gibson/Jake Peavy | .30 | .75 |
| 185 | Johnny Bench/Ivan Rodriguez | .50 | 1.25 |
| 186 | Vlad/Ichiro/Manny | .75 | 2.00 |
| 187 | Yaz/Fisk/Boggs | .75 | 2.00 |
| 188 | ARod/Jeter/Cano | 1.25 | 3.00 |
| 189 | Chipper/Braun/Mig.Cabrera | .60 | 1.50 |
| 190 | Mattingly/Winfield/Reggie | 1.00 | 2.50 |
| 191 | Utley/Howard/Rollins | .60 | 1.50 |
| 192 | Joe Mauer/Hanley Ramirez /Troy Tulowitzki | .50 | 1.25 |
| 193 | Ryan/Maddux/Unit | 1.50 | 4.00 |
| 194 | Brandon Webb/Justin Verlander /Felix Hernandez | .30 | .75 |
| 195 | Schmidt/Banks/F.Robinson | .75 | 2.00 |
| 196 | Jeter/Griffey/Ripken/Ichiro | 2.00 | 5.00 |
| 197 | Yogi/Reggie/Joe D/Jeter | 1.25 | 3.00 |
| 198 | Jonathan Papelbon/Manny Ramirez /Jason Varitek/David Ortiz | .30 | .75 |
| 199 | Griffey/Clemente/Vlad/Joe D | .75 | 2.00 |
| 200 | Pujols/Jeter/Prince/Papi | .20 | .50 |

## 2009 Upper Deck Icons

| | | | |
|---|---|---|---|
| COMP.SET w/o RC's (100) | | 12.50 | 30.00 |
| COMMON CARD (1-100) | | .15 | .40 |
| COMMON RC (101-130) | | .75 | 2.00 |

|  |  | | |
|---|---|---|---|
| | RC 101-130 PRINT RUN 999 SER.#d SETS | | |
| | COMMON AU RC (131-160) | 3.00 | 8.00 |
| | AU RC PRINT RUN B/WN 50-600 PER | | |
| | OVERALL AU ODDS 1:10 HOBBY | | |
| | EXCHANGE DEADLINE 6/11/2011 | | |
| 1 | A.J. Burnett | .25 | .60 |
| 2 | Adam Dunn | .25 | .60 |
| 3 | Adrian Gonzalez | .25 | .60 |
| 4 | Akinori Iwamura | .25 | .60 |
| 5 | Albert Pujols | 1.00 | 2.50 |
| 6 | Alex Rodriguez | .60 | 1.50 |
| 7 | Alfonso Soriano | .25 | .60 |
| 8 | Aramis Ramirez | .15 | .40 |
| 9 | B.J. Upton | .25 | .60 |
| 10 | Brandon Webb | .25 | .60 |
| 11 | Brian Giles | .15 | .40 |
| 12 | Brian McCann | .25 | .60 |
| 13 | Brian Roberts | .15 | .40 |
| 14 | Carlos Beltran | .15 | .40 |
| 15 | Carlos Lee | .15 | .40 |
| 16 | Carlos Quentin | .15 | .40 |
| 17 | Carlos Zambrano | .15 | .40 |
| 18 | CC Sabathia | .25 | .60 |
| 19 | Chad Billingsley | .15 | .40 |
| 20 | Chase Utley | .40 | 1.00 |
| 21 | Chien-Ming Wang | .40 | 1.00 |
| 22 | Chipper Jones | .40 | 1.00 |
| 23 | Chris B. Young | .15 | .40 |
| 24 | Clayton Kershaw | .40 | 1.00 |
| 25 | Cliff Lee | .25 | .60 |
| 26 | Cole Hamels | .40 | 1.00 |
| 27 | Curtis Granderson | .40 | 1.00 |
| 28 | Daisuke Matsuzaka | .60 | 1.50 |
| 29 | Dan Haren | .15 | .40 |
| 30 | Dan Uggla | .15 | .40 |
| 31 | David Ortiz | .25 | .60 |
| 32 | David Wright | .50 | 1.25 |
| 33 | Derek Jeter | 1.00 | 2.50 |
| 34 | Derrek Lee | .25 | .60 |
| 35 | Dustin Pedroia | .50 | 1.25 |
| 36 | Edinson Volquez | .15 | .40 |
| 37 | Ervin Santana | .15 | .40 |
| 38 | Evan Longoria | .60 | 1.50 |
| 39 | Felix Hernandez | .25 | .60 |
| 40 | Francisco Rodriguez | .25 | .60 |
| 41 | Garrett Atkins | .15 | .40 |
| 42 | Grady Sizemore | .25 | .60 |
| 43 | Hanley Ramirez | .40 | 1.00 |
| 44 | Ian Kinsler | .25 | .60 |
| 45 | Freddy Sanchez | .15 | .40 |
| 46 | Ichiro Suzuki | .60 | 1.50 |
| 47 | Jason Varitek | .25 | .60 |
| 48 | Jake Peavy | .25 | .60 |
| 49 | James Shields | .15 | .40 |
| 50 | Jason Giambi | .15 | .40 |
| 51 | Javier Vazquez | .15 | .40 |
| 52 | Jay Bruce | .40 | 1.00 |
| 53 | Jim Thome | .25 | .60 |
| 54 | Jimmy Rollins | .25 | .60 |
| 55 | Joakim Soria | .15 | .40 |
| 56 | Joba Chamberlain | .50 | 1.25 |
| 57 | Joe Mauer | .40 | 1.00 |
| 58 | Joey Votto | .25 | .60 |
| 59 | Johan Santana | .40 | 1.00 |
| 60 | John Lackey | .25 | .60 |
| 61 | Jon Lester | .25 | .60 |
| 62 | Jonathan Papelbon | .25 | .60 |
| 63 | Jose Reyes | .40 | 1.00 |
| 64 | Josh Beckett | .25 | .60 |
| 65 | Josh Hamilton | .40 | 1.00 |
| 66 | Justin Morneau | .25 | .60 |
| 67 | Justin Verlander | .25 | .60 |
| 68 | Ken Griffey Jr. | .60 | 1.50 |
| 69 | Kerry Wood | .15 | .40 |
| 70 | Kevin Youkilis | .25 | .60 |
| 71 | Kosuke Fukudome | .40 | 1.00 |
| 72 | Lance Berkman | .25 | .60 |
| 73 | Magglio Ordonez | .25 | .60 |
| 74 | Manny Ramirez | .40 | 1.00 |
| 75 | Mariano Rivera | .40 | 1.00 |
| 76 | Mark Teixeira | .40 | 1.00 |

|  |  | | |
|---|---|---|---|
| 77 | Matt Holliday | .25 | .60 |
| 78 | Matt Kemp | .40 | 1.00 |
| 79 | Michael Young | .25 | .60 |
| 80 | Miguel Cabrera | .25 | .60 |
| 81 | Nate McLouth | .15 | .40 |
| 82 | Nick Markakis | .25 | .60 |
| 83 | Prince Fielder | .40 | 1.00 |
| 84 | Randy Johnson | .40 | 1.00 |
| 85 | Rick Ankiel | .25 | .60 |
| 86 | Roy Halladay | .25 | .60 |
| 87 | Roy Oswalt | .25 | .60 |
| 88 | Russell Martin | .25 | .60 |
| 89 | Ryan Braun | .50 | 1.25 |
| 90 | Ryan Dempster | .15 | .40 |
| 91 | Ryan Howard | .50 | 1.25 |
| 92 | Ryan Ludwick | .15 | .40 |
| 93 | Ryan Zimmerman | .25 | .60 |
| 94 | Scott Kazmir | .25 | .60 |
| 95 | Stephen Drew | .15 | .40 |
| 96 | Tim Hudson | .15 | .40 |
| 97 | Tim Lincecum | .50 | 1.25 |
| 98 | Troy Tulowitzki | .25 | .60 |
| 99 | Vernon Wells | .15 | .40 |
| 100 | Vladimir Guerrero | .40 | 1.00 |
| 101 | Koji Uehara RC | 2.00 | 5.00 |
| 102 | Rick Porcello RC | 3.00 | 8.00 |
| 103 | Jason Motte RC | .75 | 2.00 |
| 104 | Colby Rasmus RC | 1.25 | 3.00 |
| 105 | Brett Anderson RC | 1.25 | 3.00 |
| 106 | George Kottaras RC | .75 | 2.00 |
| 107 | Josh Outman RC | 1.25 | 3.00 |
| 108 | Travis Snider RC | 2.00 | 5.00 |
| 109 | Matt Tuiasosopo RC | .75 | 2.00 |
| 110 | Kevin Jepsen RC | .75 | 2.00 |
| 111 | Trevor Cahill RC | 1.25 | 3.00 |
| 112 | Elvis Andrus RC | 2.00 | 5.00 |
| 113 | Jordan Schafer RC | 1.25 | 3.00 |
| 114 | Matt LaPorta RC | 2.00 | 5.00 |
| 115 | Shairon Martis RC | 1.25 | 3.00 |
| 116 | Dexter Fowler RC | 1.25 | 3.00 |
| 117 | Scott Lewis RC | .75 | 2.00 |
| 118 | Everth Cabrera RC | 1.25 | 3.00 |
| 119 | James McDonald RC | 1.25 | 3.00 |
| 120 | David Freese RC | 2.00 | 5.00 |
| 121 | David Patton RC | 1.25 | 3.00 |
| 122 | Kenshin Kawakami RC | 2.00 | 5.00 |
| 123 | David Price RC | 2.50 | 6.00 |
| 124 | Phil Coke RC | .75 | 2.00 |
| 125 | Matt Wieters RC | 15.00 | 40.00 |
| 126 | Mike Hinckley RC | .75 | 2.00 |
| 127 | Ramiro Pena RC | 1.25 | 3.00 |
| 128 | Bobby Parnell RC | 1.25 | 3.00 |
| 129 | Ryan Perry RC | 2.00 | 5.00 |
| 130 | Ricky Romero RC | .75 | 2.00 |
| 131a | Uehara AU/90 * English (RC) | 50.00 | 100.00 |
| 131b | Uehara AU/10 * Kanji (RC) | | |
| 132 | T.Snider AU/100 (RC) | 15.00 | 40.00 |
| 133 | D.Fowler AU/400 (RC) | 5.00 | 12.00 |
| 134 | K.Jepsen AU/600 (RC) | 5.00 | 12.00 |
| 135 | D.Freese AU/200 (RC) | 15.00 | 40.00 |
| 136 | J.Schafer AU/400 (RC) | 6.00 | 15.00 |
| 137 | E.Cabrera AU/600 (RC) | 4.00 | 10.00 |
| 138 | McDonald AU/399 (RC) | 4.00 | 10.00 |
| 139 | Shairon Martis AU/600 (RC) | 3.00 | 8.00 |
| 140 | Josh Outman AU/200 (RC) | 3.00 | 8.00 |
| 141 | Tuiasosopo AU/400 (RC) | 3.00 | 8.00 |
| 142 | P.Coke AU/600 (RC) | 3.00 | 8.00 |
| 143 | Wieters AU/100 (RC) EXCH | 60.00 | 120.00 |
| 144 | R.Romero AU/600 (RC) | 3.00 | 8.00 |
| 145 | Kottaras AU/600 (RC) | 4.00 | 10.00 |
| 146 | E.Andrus AU/200 (RC) | 10.00 | 25.00 |
| 147 | D.Patton AU/50 (RC) | 4.00 | 10.00 |
| 148 | Porcello AU/150 (RC) | 5.00 | 12.00 |
| 149 | T.Cahill AU/300 (RC) | 5.00 | 12.00 |
| 150 | T.Crowe AU/600 (RC) | 3.00 | 8.00 |
| 151 | C.Rasmus AU/400 (RC) | 15.00 | 40.00 |
| 152 | Kawakami AU/400 (RC) | 30.00 | 60.00 |
| 153 | D.Price AU/150 (RC) | 20.00 | 50.00 |
| 154 | R.Porcello AU/100 (RC) | 30.00 | 60.00 |
| 155 | B.Gardner AU/600 (RC) | 10.00 | 25.00 |
| 156 | Davis AU/50 (RC) EXCH | 8.00 | 20.00 |

| | | |
|---|---|---|
| ☐ 157 P.Sandoval AU/100 (RC) | 40.00 | 80.00 |
| ☐ 158 B.Parnell AU/600 (RC) | 4.00 | 10.00 |
| ☐ 159 D.Holland AU/100 RC | 10.00 | 25.00 |
| ☐ 160 M.Gamel AU/200 RC | 6.0015.00- | |

### 2001 Upper Deck Prospect Premieres

| | | |
|---|---|---|
| ☐ COMP.SET w/o SP's (90) | 50.00 | 80.00 |
| ☐ COMMON CARD (1-90) | .15 | .40 |
| ☐ COMMON AUTO (91-102) | 6.00 | 15.00 |
| ☐ 1 Jeff Mathis XRC | .20 | .50 |
| ☐ 2 Jake Woods XRC | .20 | .50 |
| ☐ 3 Dallas McPherson XRC | .40 | 1.00 |
| ☐ 4 Steven Shell XRC | .15 | .40 |
| ☐ 5 Ryan Budde XRC | .15 | .40 |
| ☐ 6 Kirk Saarloos XRC | .15 | .40 |
| ☐ 7 Ryan Stegall XRC | .15 | .40 |
| ☐ 8 Bobby Crosby XRC | 1.25 | 3.00 |
| ☐ 9 J.T. Stotts XRC | .15 | .40 |
| ☐ 10 Neal Cotts XRC | .40 | 1.00 |
| ☐ 11 Jeremy Bonderman XRC | 1.50 | 4.00 |
| ☐ 12 Brandon League XRC | .15 | .40 |
| ☐ 13 Tyrell Godwin XRC | .15 | .40 |
| ☐ 14 Gabe Gross XRC | .20 | .50 |
| ☐ 15 Chris Neylan XRC | .15 | .40 |
| ☐ 16 Macay McBride XRC | .30 | .75 |
| ☐ 17 Josh Burrus XRC | .15 | .40 |
| ☐ 18 Adam Stern XRC | .15 | .40 |
| ☐ 19 Richard Lewis XRC | .15 | .40 |
| ☐ 20 Cole Barthel XRC | .15 | .40 |
| ☐ 21 Mike Jones XRC | .20 | .50 |
| ☐ 22 J.J. Hardy XRC | 2.50 | 6.00 |
| ☐ 23 Jon Steitz XRC | .15 | .40 |
| ☐ 24 Brad Nelson XRC | .15 | .40 |
| ☐ 25 Justin Pope XRC | .15 | .40 |
| ☐ 26 Dan Haren XRC | .75 | 2.00 |
| ☐ 27 Andy Sisco XRC | .15 | .40 |
| ☐ 28 Ryan Theriot XRC | 1.25 | 3.00 |
| ☐ 29 Ricky Nolasco XRC | .75 | 2.00 |
| ☐ 30 Jon Switzer XRC | .15 | .40 |
| ☐ 31 Justin Wechsler XRC | .15 | .40 |
| ☐ 32 Mike Gosling XRC | .15 | .40 |
| ☐ 33 Scott Hairston XRC | .20 | .50 |
| ☐ 34 Brian Pilkington XRC | .15 | .40 |
| ☐ 35 Kole Strayhorn XRC | .15 | .40 |
| ☐ 36 David Taylor XRC | .15 | .40 |
| ☐ 37 Donald Levinski XRC | .15 | .40 |
| ☐ 38 Mike Hinckley XRC | .20 | .50 |
| ☐ 39 Nick Long XRC | .15 | .40 |
| ☐ 40 Brad Hennessey XRC | .20 | .50 |
| ☐ 41 Noah Lowry XRC | .75 | 2.00 |
| ☐ 42 Josh Cram XRC | .15 | .40 |
| ☐ 43 Jesse Foppert XRC | .20 | .50 |
| ☐ 44 Julian Benavidez XRC | .15 | .40 |
| ☐ 45 Dan Denham XRC | .15 | .40 |
| ☐ 46 Travis Foley XRC | .15 | .40 |
| ☐ 47 Mike Conroy XRC | .15 | .40 |
| ☐ 48 Jake Dittler XRC | .15 | .40 |
| ☐ 49 Rene Rivera XRC | .15 | .40 |
| ☐ 50 John Cole XRC | .15 | .40 |
| ☐ 51 Lazaro Abreu XRC | .15 | .40 |
| ☐ 52 David Wright XRC | 8.00 | 20.00 |
| ☐ 53 Aaron Heilman XRC | .20 | .50 |
| ☐ 54 Len DiNardo XRC | .15 | .40 |
| ☐ 55 Alhaji Turay XRC | .15 | .40 |
| ☐ 56 Chris Smith XRC | .15 | .40 |
| ☐ 57 Rommie Lewis XRC | .15 | .40 |

| | | |
|---|---|---|
| ☐ 58 Bryan Bass XRC | .15 | .40 |
| ☐ 59 David Crouthers XRC | .15 | .40 |
| ☐ 60 Josh Barfield XRC | 1.25 | 3.00 |
| ☐ 61 Jake Peavy XRC | 2.50 | 6.00 |
| ☐ 62 Ryan Howard XRC | 8.00 | 20.00 |
| ☐ 63 Gavin Floyd XRC | .40 | 1.00 |
| ☐ 64 Michael Floyd XRC | .15 | .40 |
| ☐ 65 Stefan Bailie XRC | .15 | .40 |
| ☐ 66 Jon DeVries XRC | .15 | .40 |
| ☐ 67 Steve Kelly XRC | .15 | .40 |
| ☐ 68 Alan Moye XRC | .15 | .40 |
| ☐ 69 Justin Gillman XRC | .15 | .40 |
| ☐ 70 Jayson Nix XRC | .15 | .40 |
| ☐ 71 John Draper XRC | .15 | .40 |
| ☐ 72 Kenny Baugh XRC | .15 | .40 |
| ☐ 73 Michael Woods XRC | .15 | .40 |
| ☐ 74 Preston Larrison XRC | .20 | .50 |
| ☐ 75 Matt Coenen XRC | .15 | .40 |
| ☐ 76 Scott Tyler XRC | .20 | .50 |
| ☐ 77 Jose Morales XRC | .15 | .40 |
| ☐ 78 Corwin Malone XRC | .15 | .40 |
| ☐ 79 Dennis Ulacia XRC | .15 | .40 |
| ☐ 80 Andy Gonzalez XRC | .15 | .40 |
| ☐ 81 Kris Honel XRC | .15 | .40 |
| ☐ 82 Wyatt Allen XRC | .15 | .40 |
| ☐ 83 Ryan Wing XRC | .15 | .40 |
| ☐ 84 Sean Henn XRC | .15 | .40 |
| ☐ 85 John-Ford Griffin XRC | .15 | .40 |
| ☐ 86 Bronson Sardinha XRC | .15 | .40 |
| ☐ 87 Jon Skaggs XRC | .15 | .40 |
| ☐ 88 Shelley Duncan XRC | 1.50 | 4.00 |
| ☐ 89 Jason Arnold XRC | .15 | .40 |
| ☐ 90 Aaron Rifkin XRC | .15 | .40 |
| ☐ 91 Colt Griffin AU XRC | 6.00 | 15.00 |
| ☐ 92 J.D. Martin AU XRC | 6.00 | 15.00 |
| ☐ 93 Justin Wayne AU XRC | 6.00 | 15.00 |
| ☐ 94 J.VanBenschoten AU XRC | 6.00 | 15.00 |
| ☐ 95 Chris Burke AU XRC | 10.00 | 25.00 |
| ☐ 96 Casey Kotchman AU XRC | 6.00 | 15.00 |
| ☐ 97 Michael Garciaparra AU XRC | 6.00 | 15.00 |
| ☐ 98 Jake Gautreau AU XRC | 6.00 | 15.00 |
| ☐ 99 Jerome Williams AU XRC | 6.00 | 15.00 |
| ☐ 100 Toe Nash AU XRC | 6.00 | 15.00 |
| ☐ 101 Joe Borchard AU XRC | 6.00 | 15.00 |
| ☐ 102 Mark Prior AU XRC | 15.00 | 40.00 |

### 2002 Upper Deck Prospect Premieres

| | | |
|---|---|---|
| ☐ COMP.SET w/o SP's (72) | 25.00 | 40.00 |
| ☐ COMMON CARD (1-60) | .15 | .40 |
| ☐ COMMON CARD (61-85) | 2.00 | 5.00 |
| ☐ COMMON CARD (86-97) | 3.00 | 8.00 |
| ☐ COMMON RIPKEN (98-99) | .75 | 2.00 |
| ☐ COMMON MCGWIRE (100-105) | .75 | 2.00 |
| ☐ COMMON DIMAGGIO (106-109) | .60 | 1.50 |
| ☐ PENDER COR AVAIL VIA MAIL EXCHANGE | | |
| ☐ 1 Josh Rupe XRC | .15 | .40 |
| ☐ 2 Blair Johnson XRC | .15 | .40 |
| ☐ 3 Jason Pridie XRC | .15 | .40 |
| ☐ 4 Tim Gilhooly XRC | .15 | .40 |
| ☐ 5 Kennard Jones XRC | .15 | .40 |
| ☐ 6 Darrell Rasner XRC | .15 | .40 |
| ☐ 7 Adam Donachie XRC | .15 | .40 |
| ☐ 8 Josh Murray XRC | .15 | .40 |
| ☐ 9 Brian Dopirak XRC | .40 | 1.00 |
| ☐ 10 Jason Cooper XRC | .15 | .40 |
| ☐ 11 Zach Hammes XRC | .15 | .40 |
| ☐ 12 Jon Lester XRC | 8.00 | 20.00 |

| | | |
|---|---|---|
| ☐ 13 Kevin Jepsen XRC | .20 | .50 |
| ☐ 14 Curtis Granderson XRC | 1.50 | 4.00 |
| ☐ 15 David Bush XRC | .40 | 1.00 |
| ☐ 16 Joel Guzman | .30 | .75 |
| ☐ 17A M.Pender UER Granderson | .60 | 1.50 |
| ☐ 17B Matt Pender COR | .40 | 1.00 |
| ☐ 18 Derick Grigsby XRC | .15 | .40 |
| ☐ 19 Jeremy Reed XRC | .40 | 1.00 |
| ☐ 20 Jonathan Broxton XRC | .40 | 1.00 |
| ☐ 21 Jesse Crain XRC | .30 | .75 |
| ☐ 22 Justin Jones XRC | .20 | .50 |
| ☐ 23 Brian Slocum XRC | .15 | .40 |
| ☐ 24 Brian McCann XRC | 3.00 | 8.00 |
| ☐ 25 Francisco Liriano XRC | 3.00 | 8.00 |
| ☐ 26 Fred Lewis XRC | .15 | .40 |
| ☐ 27 Steve Stanley XRC | .15 | .40 |
| ☐ 28 Chris Snyder XRC | .20 | .50 |
| ☐ 29 Dan Cevette XRC | .15 | .40 |
| ☐ 30 Kiel Fisher XRC | .20 | .50 |
| ☐ 31 Brandon Weeden XRC | .15 | .40 |
| ☐ 32 Pat Osborn XRC | .15 | .40 |
| ☐ 33 Taber Lee XRC | .15 | .40 |
| ☐ 34 Dan Ortmeier XRC | .20 | .50 |
| ☐ 35 Josh Johnson XRC | 1.50 | 4.00 |
| ☐ 36 Val Majewski XRC | .15 | .40 |
| ☐ 37 Larry Broadway XRC | .15 | .40 |
| ☐ 38 Joey Gomes XRC | .15 | .40 |
| ☐ 39 Eric Thomas XRC | .15 | .40 |
| ☐ 40 James Loney XRC | 2.00 | 5.00 |
| ☐ 41 Charlie Morton XRC | .15 | .40 |
| ☐ 42 Mark McLemore XRC | .15 | .40 |
| ☐ 43 Matt Craig XRC | .20 | .50 |
| ☐ 44 Ryan Rodriguez XRC | .15 | .40 |
| ☐ 45 Rich Hill XRC | 1.25 | 3.00 |
| ☐ 46 Bob Malek XRC | .15 | .40 |
| ☐ 47 Justin Maureau XRC | .15 | .40 |
| ☐ 48 Randy Braun XRC | .15 | .40 |
| ☐ 49 Brian Grant XRC | .15 | .40 |
| ☐ 50 Tyler Davidson XRC | .20 | .50 |
| ☐ 51 Travis Hanson XRC | .20 | .50 |
| ☐ 52 Kyle Boyer XRC | .15 | .40 |
| ☐ 53 James Holcomb XRC | .15 | .40 |
| ☐ 54 Ryan Williams XRC | .15 | .40 |
| ☐ 55 Ben Crockett XRC | .15 | .40 |
| ☐ 56 Adam Greenberg XRC | .30 | .75 |
| ☐ 57 John Baker XRC | .15 | .40 |
| ☐ 58 Matt Carson XRC | .15 | .40 |
| ☐ 59 Jonathan George XRC | .15 | .40 |
| ☐ 60 David Jensen XRC | .15 | .40 |
| ☐ 61 Nick Swisher JSY XRC | 6.00 | 15.00 |
| ☐ 62 Brent Clevlen JSY UER XRC | 5.00 | 12.00 |
| ☐ 63 Royce Ring JSY XRC | 2.00 | 5.00 |
| ☐ 64 Mike Nixon JSY XRC | 2.00 | 5.00 |
| ☐ 65 Ricky Barrett JSY XRC | 2.00 | 5.00 |
| ☐ 66 Russ Adams JSY XRC | 2.00 | 5.00 |
| ☐ 67 Joe Mauer JSY XRC | 10.00 | 25.00 |
| ☐ 68 Jeff Francoeur JSY XRC | 12.50 | 30.00 |
| ☐ 69 Joe Blanton JSY XRC | 3.00 | 8.00 |
| ☐ 70 Micah Schilling JSY XRC | 2.00 | 5.00 |
| ☐ 71 John McCurdy JSY XRC | 2.00 | 5.00 |
| ☐ 72 Sergio Santos JSY XRC | 3.00 | 8.00 |
| ☐ 73 Josh Womack JSY XRC | 2.00 | 5.00 |
| ☐ 74 Jared Doyle JSY XRC | 2.00 | 5.00 |
| ☐ 75 Ben Fritz JSY XRC | 2.00 | 5.00 |
| ☐ 76 Greg Miller JSY XRC | 2.00 | 5.00 |
| ☐ 77 Luke Hagerty JSY XRC | 2.00 | 5.00 |
| ☐ 78 Matt Whitney JSY XRC | 2.00 | 5.00 |
| ☐ 79 Dan Meyer JSY XRC | 3.00 | 8.00 |
| ☐ 80 Bill Murphy JSY XRC | 2.00 | 5.00 |
| ☐ 81 Zach Segovia JSY XRC | 2.00 | 5.00 |
| ☐ 82 Steve Obenchain JSY XRC | 2.00 | 5.00 |
| ☐ 83 Matt Clanton JSY XRC | 2.00 | 5.00 |
| ☐ 84 Mark Teahen JSY XRC | 3.00 | 8.00 |
| ☐ 85 Kyle Pawelczyk JSY XRC | 2.00 | 5.00 |
| ☐ 86 Khalil Greene AU XRC | 5.00 | 12.00 |
| ☐ 87 Joe Saunders AU XRC | 5.00 | 12.00 |
| ☐ 88 Jeremy Hermida AU XRC | 8.00 | 20.00 |
| ☐ 89 Drew Meyer AU XRC | 3.00 | 8.00 |
| ☐ 90 Jeff Francis AU XRC | 12.50 | 30.00 |
| ☐ 91 Scott Moore AU XRC | 3.00 | 8.00 |
| ☐ 92 Prince Fielder AU XRC | 50.00 | 100.00 |

| | | |
|---|---|---|
| ❏ 93 Zack Greinke AU XRC | 30.00 | 60.00 |
| ❏ 94 Chris Gruler AU XRC | 3.00 | 8.00 |
| ❏ 95 Scott Kazmir AU XRC | 30.00 | 60.00 |
| ❏ 96 B.J. Upton AU XRC | 15.00 | 40.00 |
| ❏ 97 Clint Everts AU XRC | 3.00 | 8.00 |
| ❏ 98 Cal Ripken TRIB | .75 | 2.00 |
| ❏ 99 Cal Ripken TRIB | .75 | 2.00 |
| ❏ 100 Mark McGwire TRIB | .75 | 2.00 |
| ❏ 101 Mark McGwire TRIB | .75 | 2.00 |
| ❏ 102 Mark McGwire TRIB | .75 | 2.00 |
| ❏ 103 Mark McGwire TRIB | .75 | 2.00 |
| ❏ 104 Mark McGwire TRIB | .75 | 2.00 |
| ❏ 105 Joe DiMaggio TRIB | .60 | 1.50 |
| ❏ 106 Joe DiMaggio TRIB | .60 | 1.50 |
| ❏ 107 Joe DiMaggio TRIB | .60 | 1.50 |
| ❏ 108 Joe DiMaggio TRIB | .60 | 1.50 |
| ❏ 109 Joe DiMaggio TRIB | .60 | 1.50 |

## 2003 Upper Deck Prospect Premieres

| | | |
|---|---|---|
| ❏ COMPLETE SET (90) | 20.00 | 40.00 |
| ❏ 1 Bryan Opdyke XRC | .15 | .40 |
| ❏ 2 Gabriel Sosa XRC | .15 | .40 |
| ❏ 3 Tila Reynolds XRC | .15 | .40 |
| ❏ 4 Aaron Hill XRC | .60 | 1.50 |
| ❏ 5 Aaron Marsden XRC | .20 | .50 |
| ❏ 6 Abe Alvarez XRC | .20 | .50 |
| ❏ 7 Adam Jones XRC | 3.00 | 8.00 |
| ❏ 8 Adam Miller XRC | 1.25 | 3.00 |
| ❏ 9 Andre Ethier XRC | 1.25 | 3.00 |
| ❏ 10 Anthony Gwynn XRC | .50 | 1.25 |
| ❏ 11 Brad Snyder XRC | .30 | .75 |
| ❏ 12 Brad Sullivan XRC | .20 | .50 |
| ❏ 13 Brian Anderson XRC | .75 | 2.00 |
| ❏ 14 Brian Buscher XRC | .15 | .40 |
| ❏ 15 Brian Snyder XRC | .20 | .50 |
| ❏ 16 Carlos Quentin XRC | 1.25 | 3.00 |
| ❏ 17 Chad Billingsley XRC | 1.50 | 4.00 |
| ❏ 18 Fraser Dizard XRC | .15 | .40 |
| ❏ 19 Chris Durbin XRC | .15 | .40 |
| ❏ 20 Chris Ray XRC | .40 | 1.00 |
| ❏ 21 Conor Jackson XRC | 1.25 | 3.00 |
| ❏ 22 Kory Casto XRC | .20 | .50 |
| ❏ 23 Craig Whitaker XRC | .20 | .50 |
| ❏ 24 Daniel Moore XRC | .15 | .40 |
| ❏ 25 Daric Barton XRC | 1.25 | 3.00 |
| ❏ 26 Darin Downs XRC | .20 | .50 |
| ❏ 27 David Murphy XRC | .30 | .75 |
| ❏ 28 Dustin Majewski XRC | .20 | .50 |
| ❏ 29 Edgardo Baez XRC | .20 | .50 |
| ❏ 30 Jake Fox XRC | .75 | 2.00 |
| ❏ 31 Jake Stevens XRC | .20 | .50 |
| ❏ 32 Jamie D'Antona XRC | .30 | .75 |
| ❏ 33 James Houser XRC | .20 | .50 |
| ❏ 34 Jarrod Saltalamacchia XRC | 2.00 | 5.00 |
| ❏ 35 Jason Hirsh XRC | .75 | 2.00 |
| ❏ 36 Javi Herrera XRC | .20 | .50 |
| ❏ 37 Jeff Allison XRC | .15 | .40 |
| ❏ 38 John Hudgins XRC | .15 | .40 |
| ❏ 39 Jo Jo Reyes XRC | .40 | 1.00 |
| ❏ 40 Justin James XRC | .15 | .40 |
| ❏ 41 Kurt Isenberg XRC | .15 | .40 |
| ❏ 42 Kyle Boyer XRC | .15 | .40 |
| ❏ 43 Lastings Milledge XRC | 2.00 | 5.00 |
| ❏ 44 Luis Atilano XRC | .15 | .40 |
| ❏ 45 Matt Murton XRC | .75 | 2.00 |
| ❏ 46 Matt Moses XRC | .30 | .75 |
| ❏ 47 Matt Harrison XRC | .30 | .75 |

| | | |
|---|---|---|
| ❏ 48 Michael Bourn XRC | .30 | .75 |
| ❏ 49 Miguel Vega XRC | .15 | .40 |
| ❏ 50 Mitch Maier XRC | .20 | .50 |
| ❏ 51 Omar Quintanilla XRC | .20 | .50 |
| ❏ 52 Ryan Sweeney XRC | .75 | 2.00 |
| ❏ 53 Scott Baker XRC | .40 | 1.00 |
| ❏ 54 Sean Rodriguez XRC | .75 | 2.00 |
| ❏ 55 Steve Lerud XRC | .20 | .50 |
| ❏ 56 Thomas Pauly XRC | .15 | .40 |
| ❏ 57 Tom Gorzelanny XRC | .60 | 1.50 |
| ❏ 58 Tim Moss XRC | .15 | .40 |
| ❏ 59 Robbie Wooley XRC | .20 | .50 |
| ❏ 60 Trey Webb XRC | .15 | .40 |
| ❏ 61 Wes Littleton XRC | .20 | .50 |
| ❏ 62 Beau Vaughan XRC | .20 | .50 |
| ❏ 63 Willy Jo Ronda XRC | .20 | .50 |
| ❏ 64 Chris Lubanski XRC | .50 | 1.25 |
| ❏ 65 Ian Stewart XRC | 2.00 | 5.00 |
| ❏ 66 John Danks XRC | 1.25 | 3.00 |
| ❏ 67 Kyle Sleeth XRC | .20 | .50 |
| ❏ 68 Michael Aubrey XRC | .30 | .75 |
| ❏ 69 Kevin Kouzmanoff XRC | 2.00 | 5.00 |
| ❏ 70 Ryan Harvey XRC | .75 | 2.00 |
| ❏ 71 Tim Stauffer XRC | .30 | .75 |
| ❏ 72 Tony Richie XRC | .15 | .40 |
| ❏ 73 Brandon Wood XRC | 3.00 | 8.00 |
| ❏ 74 David Aardsma XRC | .20 | .50 |
| ❏ 75 David Shinskie XRC | .15 | .40 |
| ❏ 76 Dennis Dove XRC | .20 | .50 |
| ❏ 77 Eric Sultemeier XRC | .15 | .40 |
| ❏ 78 Jay Sborz XRC | .15 | .40 |
| ❏ 79 Jimmy Barthmaier XRC | .15 | .40 |
| ❏ 80 Josh Whitesell XRC | .15 | .40 |
| ❏ 81 Josh Anderson XRC | .20 | .50 |
| ❏ 82 Kenny Lewis XRC | .20 | .50 |
| ❏ 83 Mateo Miramontes XRC | .15 | .40 |
| ❏ 84 Nick Markakis XRC | 2.50 | 6.00 |
| ❏ 85 Paul Bacot XRC | .20 | .50 |
| ❏ 86 Peter Stonard XRC | .15 | .40 |
| ❏ 87 Reggie Willits XRC | 1.00 | 2.50 |
| ❏ 88 Shane Costa XRC | .15 | .40 |
| ❏ 89 Billy Sadler XRC | .15 | .40 |
| ❏ 90 Delmon Young XRC | 3.00 | 8.00 |

## 2007 Upper Deck Spectrum

| | | |
|---|---|---|
| ❏ COMP SET w/o RCs (100) | 10.00 | 25.00 |
| ❏ COMMON CARD (1-100) | .15 | .40 |
| ❏ COMMON AU RC (101-150) | 3.00 | 8.00 |
| ❏ AU RC STATED ODDS 1:18 HOBBY | | |
| ❏ COMMON ROOKIE EXCH (151-170) | 10.00 | 25.00 |
| ❏ EXCHANGE DEADLINE 3/19/2010 | | |
| ❏ 1 Miguel Tejada | .15 | .40 |
| ❏ 2 Brian Roberts | .15 | .40 |
| ❏ 3 Melvin Mora | .15 | .40 |
| ❏ 4 David Ortiz | .25 | .60 |
| ❏ 5 Manny Ramirez | .25 | .60 |
| ❏ 6 Jason Varitek | .40 | 1.00 |
| ❏ 7 Curt Schilling | .25 | .60 |
| ❏ 8 Jim Thome | .25 | .60 |
| ❏ 9 Paul Konerko | .15 | .40 |
| ❏ 10 Jermaine Dye | .15 | .40 |
| ❏ 11 Travis Hafner | .15 | .40 |
| ❏ 12 Victor Martinez | .15 | .40 |
| ❏ 13 Grady Sizemore | .25 | .60 |
| ❏ 14 C.C. Sabathia | .25 | .60 |
| ❏ 15 Ivan Rodriguez | .25 | .60 |
| ❏ 16 Maggilo Ordonez | .15 | .40 |

| | | |
|---|---|---|
| ❏ 17 Carlos Guillen | .15 | .40 |
| ❏ 18 Justin Verlander | .40 | 1.00 |
| ❏ 19 Shane Costa | .15 | .40 |
| ❏ 20 Emil Brown | .15 | .40 |
| ❏ 21 Mark Teahen | .15 | .40 |
| ❏ 22 Vladimir Guerrero | .40 | 1.00 |
| ❏ 23 Jered Weaver | .25 | .60 |
| ❏ 24 Juan Rivera | .15 | .40 |
| ❏ 25 Justin Morneau | .15 | .40 |
| ❏ 26 Joe Mauer | .40 | 1.00 |
| ❏ 27 Torii Hunter | .15 | .40 |
| ❏ 28 Johan Santana | .25 | .60 |
| ❏ 29 Derek Jeter | 1.00 | 2.50 |
| ❏ 30 Alex Rodriguez | .60 | 1.50 |
| ❏ 31 Johnny Damon | .25 | .60 |
| ❏ 32 Jason Giambi | .15 | .40 |
| ❏ 33 Frank Thomas | .40 | 1.00 |
| ❏ 34 Nick Swisher | .15 | .40 |
| ❏ 35 Eric Chavez | .15 | .40 |
| ❏ 36 Ichiro Suzuki | .60 | 1.50 |
| ❏ 37 Raul Ibanez | .25 | .60 |
| ❏ 38 Richie Sexson | .15 | .40 |
| ❏ 39 Carl Crawford | .25 | .60 |
| ❏ 40 Rocco Baldelli | .15 | .40 |
| ❏ 41 Scott Kazmir | .25 | .60 |
| ❏ 42 Michael Young | .15 | .40 |
| ❏ 43 Mark Teixeira | .25 | .60 |
| ❏ 44 Carlos Lee | .15 | .40 |
| ❏ 45 Gary Matthews | .15 | .40 |
| ❏ 46 Vernon Wells | .15 | .40 |
| ❏ 47 Roy Halladay | .25 | .60 |
| ❏ 48 Lyle Overbay | .15 | .40 |
| ❏ 49 Brandon Webb | .25 | .60 |
| ❏ 50 Conor Jackson | .15 | .40 |
| ❏ 51 Stephen Drew | .25 | .60 |
| ❏ 52 Chipper Jones | .40 | 1.00 |
| ❏ 53 Andruw Jones | .25 | .60 |
| ❏ 54 Adam LaRoche | .15 | .40 |
| ❏ 55 John Smoltz | .25 | .60 |
| ❏ 56 Derrek Lee | .15 | .40 |
| ❏ 57 Aramis Ramirez | .15 | .40 |
| ❏ 58 Carlos Zambrano | .15 | .40 |
| ❏ 59 Ken Griffey Jr. | .60 | 1.50 |
| ❏ 60 Adam Dunn | .15 | .40 |
| ❏ 61 Aaron Harang | .15 | .40 |
| ❏ 62 Todd Helton | .25 | .60 |
| ❏ 63 Matt Holliday | .40 | 1.00 |
| ❏ 64 Garrett Atkins | .15 | .40 |
| ❏ 65 Miguel Cabrera | .25 | .60 |
| ❏ 66 Hanley Ramirez | .25 | .60 |
| ❏ 67 Dontrelle Willis | .15 | .40 |
| ❏ 68 Lance Berkman | .15 | .40 |
| ❏ 69 Roy Oswalt | .15 | .40 |
| ❏ 70 Roger Clemens | .60 | 1.50 |
| ❏ 71 J.D. Drew | .15 | .40 |
| ❏ 72 Nomar Garciaparra | .40 | 1.00 |
| ❏ 73 Rafael Furcal | .15 | .40 |
| ❏ 74 Jeff Kent | .15 | .40 |
| ❏ 75 Prince Fielder | .40 | 1.00 |
| ❏ 76 Bill Hall | .15 | .40 |
| ❏ 77 Rickie Weeks | .15 | .40 |
| ❏ 78 Jose Reyes | .40 | 1.00 |
| ❏ 79 David Wright | .60 | 1.50 |
| ❏ 80 Carlos Delgado | .15 | .40 |
| ❏ 81 Carlos Beltran | .25 | .60 |
| ❏ 82 Ryan Howard | .60 | 1.50 |
| ❏ 83 Chase Utley | .40 | 1.00 |
| ❏ 84 Jimmy Rollins | .15 | .40 |
| ❏ 85 Jason Bay | .25 | .60 |
| ❏ 86 Freddy Sanchez | .15 | .40 |
| ❏ 87 Zach Duke | .15 | .40 |
| ❏ 88 Trevor Hoffman | .15 | .40 |
| ❏ 89 Adrian Gonzalez | .15 | .40 |
| ❏ 90 Mike Piazza | .40 | 1.00 |
| ❏ 91 Ray Durham | .15 | .40 |
| ❏ 92 Omar Vizquel | .25 | .60 |
| ❏ 93 Jason Schmidt | .15 | .40 |
| ❏ 94 Albert Pujols | .75 | 2.00 |
| ❏ 95 Scott Rolen | .25 | .60 |
| ❏ 96 Jim Edmonds | .25 | .60 |
| ❏ 97 Chris Carpenter | .15 | .40 |

| | | |
|---|---|---|
| 98 Alfonso Soriano | .15 | .40 |
| 99 Ryan Zimmerman | .40 | 1.00 |
| 100 Nick Johnson | .15 | .40 |
| 101 Adam Lind AU (RC) | 4.00 | 10.00 |
| 102 Alexi Casilla AU RC EXCH | 15.00 | 40.00 |
| 103 Andrew Miller AU RC | 15.00 | 40.00 |
| 104 Andy Cannizaro AU RC | 4.00 | 10.00 |
| 105 Angel Sanchez AU RC EXCH | 6.00 | 15.00 |
| 106 Brian Stokes AU RC | 3.00 | 8.00 |
| 107 Carlos Maldonado AU RC EXCH | 3.00 | 8.00 |
| 108 Cesar Jimenez AU RC EXCH | 3.00 | 8.00 |
| 109 Chris Stewart AU RC | 3.00 | 8.00 |
| 111 David Murphy AU (RC) | 3.00 | 8.00 |
| 112 Delmon Young AU (RC) | 12.50 | 30.00 |
| 113 Delwyn Young AU (RC) | 3.00 | 8.00 |
| 114 Dennis Sarfate AU (RC) | 3.00 | 8.00 |
| 116 Drew Anderson AU RC | 3.00 | 8.00 |
| 117 Fred Lewis AU (RC) | 3.00 | 8.00 |
| 118 Glen Perkins AU (RC) | 4.00 | 10.00 |
| 119 Hector Gimenez AU (RC) EXCH | | |
| 120 Jeff Baker AU (RC) | 3.00 | 8.00 |
| 121 Jeff Fiorentino AU (RC) | 3.00 | 8.00 |
| 122 Jeff Salazar AU (RC) | 3.00 | 8.00 |
| 124 Joaquin Arias AU (RC) | 3.00 | 8.00 |
| 125 Jon Knott AU (RC) | 3.00 | 8.00 |
| 128 Juan Morillo AU (RC) | 3.00 | 8.00 |
| 129 Juan Perez AU RC EXCH | 3.00 | 8.00 |
| 130 Juan Salas AU (RC) | 3.00 | 8.00 |
| 131 Justin Hampson AU (RC) | 3.00 | 8.00 |
| 132 Kevin Hooper AU (RC) | 6.00 | 15.00 |
| 133 Kevin Kouzmanoff AU (RC) | 4.00 | 10.00 |
| 134 Michael Bourn AU (RC) | 3.00 | 8.00 |
| 135 Miguel Montero AU (RC) EXCH | 3.00 | 8.00 |
| 136 Mike Rabelo AU RC EXCH | 10.00 | 25.00 |
| 137 Mitch Maier AU RC | 3.00 | 8.00 |
| 138 Oswaldo Navarro AU RC EXCH | 6.00 | 15.00 |
| 139 Patrick Misch AU (RC) | 3.00 | 8.00 |
| 140 Philip Humber AU (RC) | 6.00 | 15.00 |
| 141 Ryan Braun AU RC | 3.00 | 8.00 |
| 143 Ryan Sweeney AU (RC) | 3.00 | 8.00 |
| 144 Scott Moore AU (RC) | 3.00 | 8.00 |
| 145 Sean Henn AU (RC) | 4.00 | 10.00 |
| 146 Shawn Riggans AU (RC) | 3.00 | 8.00 |
| 148 Troy Tulowitzki AU (RC) | 12.50 | 30.00 |
| 149 Ubaldo Jimenez AU (RC) | 3.00 | 8.00 |
| 151 Rookie EXCH | 10.00 | 25.00 |
| 152 Rookie EXCH | 10.00 | 25.00 |
| 153 Rookie EXCH | 10.00 | 25.00 |
| 154 Rookie EXCH | 10.00 | 25.00 |
| 155 Rookie EXCH | 10.00 | 25.00 |
| 156 Rookie EXCH | 10.00 | 25.00 |
| 157 Elijah Dukes RC | 10.00 | 25.00 |
| 158 Rookie EXCH | 10.00 | 25.00 |
| 159 Rookie EXCH | 10.00 | 25.00 |
| 160 Rookie EXCH | 10.00 | 25.00 |
| 161 Rookie EXCH | 10.00 | 25.00 |
| 162 Rookie EXCH | 10.00 | 25.00 |
| 163 Rookie EXCH | 10.00 | 25.00 |
| 164 Rookie EXCH | 10.00 | 25.00 |
| 165 Rookie EXCH | 10.00 | 25.00 |
| 166 Rookie EXCH | 10.00 | 25.00 |
| 167 Rookie EXCH | 10.00 | 25.00 |
| 168 Rookie EXCH | 10.00 | 25.00 |
| 169 Rookie EXCH | 10.00 | 25.00 |
| 170 Rookie EXCH | 10.00 | 25.00 |

## 2008 Upper Deck Spectrum

| | | |
|---|---|---|
| COMP.SET w/o AUs (100) | 10.00 | 25.00 |
| COMMON CARD | .20 | .50 |
| COMMON AU RC | 3.00 | 8.00 |
| OVERALL AUTO ODDS 1:10 | | |
| PRINTING PLATES RANDOMLY INSERTED | | |
| PLATE PRINT RUN 1 SET PER COLOR | | |
| BLACK-CYAN-MAGENTA-YELLOW ISSUED | | |
| NO PLATE PRICING DUE TO SCARCITY | | |
| 1 Chris B. Young | .20 | .50 |
| 2 Brandon Webb | .30 | .75 |
| 3 Eric Byrnes | .20 | .50 |
| 4 John Smoltz | .50 | 1.25 |
| 5 Chipper Jones | .60 | 1.50 |
| 6 Jeff Francoeur | .30 | .75 |
| 7 Mark Teixeira | .30 | .75 |
| 8 Brian Roberts | .20 | .50 |
| 9 Erik Bedard | .20 | .50 |
| 10 Miguel Tejada | .20 | .50 |
| 11 Nick Markakis | .30 | .75 |
| 12 David Ortiz | .75 | 2.00 |
| 13 Daisuke Matsuzaka | .60 | 1.50 |
| 14 Manny Ramirez | .50 | 1.25 |
| 15 Jonathan Papelbon | .30 | .75 |
| 16 Josh Beckett | .30 | .75 |
| 17 Alfonso Soriano | .30 | .75 |
| 18 Carlos Zambrano | .20 | .50 |
| 19 Derrek Lee | .30 | .75 |
| 20 Aramis Ramirez | .20 | .50 |
| 21 Paul Konerko | .20 | .50 |
| 22 Jermaine Dye | .20 | .50 |
| 23 Jim Thome | .30 | .75 |
| 24 Ken Griffey Jr. | .75 | 2.00 |
| 25 Brandon Phillips | .20 | .50 |
| 26 Adam Dunn | .20 | .50 |
| 27 Grady Sizemore | .30 | .75 |
| 28 Fausto Carmona | .20 | .50 |
| 29 Victor Martinez | .20 | .50 |
| 30 Travis Hafner | .20 | .50 |
| 31 Matt Holliday | .30 | .75 |
| 32 Troy Tulowitzki | .30 | .75 |
| 33 Todd Helton | .30 | .75 |
| 34 Magglio Ordonez | .30 | .75 |
| 35 Justin Verlander | .30 | .75 |
| 36 Gary Sheffield | .20 | .50 |
| 37 Miguel Cabrera | .30 | .75 |
| 38 Hanley Ramirez | .50 | 1.25 |
| 39 Dan Uggla | .30 | .75 |
| 40 Carlos Lee | .20 | .50 |
| 41 Roy Oswalt | .20 | .50 |
| 42 Lance Berkman | .30 | .75 |
| 43 Hunter Pence | .50 | 1.25 |
| 44 Alex Gordon | .30 | .75 |
| 45 David DeJesus | .20 | .50 |
| 46 Vladimir Guerrero | .50 | 1.25 |
| 47 Kelvim Escobar | .20 | .50 |
| 48 Chone Figgins | .20 | .50 |
| 49 Brad Penny | .20 | .50 |
| 50 Takashi Saito | .20 | .50 |
| 51 Russell Martin | .20 | .50 |
| 52 Prince Fielder | .50 | 1.25 |
| 53 Ryan Braun | .60 | 1.50 |
| 54 J.J Hardy | .20 | .50 |
| 55 Johan Santana | .30 | .75 |
| 56 Justin Morneau | .20 | .50 |
| 57 Torii Hunter | .20 | .50 |
| 58 Joe Mauer | .50 | 1.25 |
| 59 Carlos Beltran | .20 | .50 |
| 60 David Wright | .60 | 1.50 |
| 61 Carlos Delgado | .20 | .50 |
| 62 Jose Reyes | .50 | 1.25 |
| 63 Derek Jeter | 1.25 | 3.00 |
| 64 Alex Rodriguez | .75 | 2.00 |
| 65 Robinson Cano | .30 | .75 |
| 66 Hideki Matsui | .50 | 1.25 |
| 67 Mariano Rivera | .50 | 1.25 |
| 68 Dan Haren | .20 | .50 |
| 69 Nick Swisher | .20 | .50 |
| 70 Eric Chavez | .20 | .50 |
| 71 Jimmy Rollins | .30 | .75 |
| 72 Ryan Howard | .60 | 1.50 |
| 73 Cole Hamels | .50 | 1.25 |
| 74 Chase Utley | .50 | 1.25 |
| 75 Freddy Sanchez | .20 | .50 |
| 76 Jason Bay | .30 | .75 |
| 77 Ian Snell | .20 | .50 |

| | | |
|---|---|---|
| 78 Greg Maddux | .60 | 1.50 |
| 79 Jake Peavy | .30 | .75 |
| 80 Chris Young | .20 | .50 |
| 81 Barry Zito | .20 | .50 |
| 82 Tim Lincecum | .60 | 1.50 |
| 83 Omar Vizquel | .20 | .50 |
| 84 Felix Hernandez | .30 | .75 |
| 85 Ichiro Suzuki | .75 | 2.00 |
| 86 Richie Sexson | .20 | .50 |
| 87 Albert Pujols | 1.00 | 2.50 |
| 88 Scott Rolen | .30 | .75 |
| 89 Chris Carpenter | .20 | .50 |
| 90 Delmon Young | .30 | .75 |
| 91 Carl Crawford | .30 | .75 |
| 92 B.J. Upton | .30 | .75 |
| 93 Michael Young | .20 | .50 |
| 94 Hank Blalock | .20 | .50 |
| 95 Sammy Sosa | .30 | .75 |
| 96 Roy Halladay | .30 | .75 |
| 97 Alex Rios | .20 | .50 |
| 98 Vernon Wells | .20 | .50 |
| 99 Ryan Zimmerman | .30 | .75 |
| 100 Dmitri Young | .20 | .50 |
| 101 Alberto Gonzalez AU RC | 10.00 | 25.00 |
| 102 Bill Murphy AU (RC) | 3.00 | 8.00 |
| 103 Bill White AU RC | 3.00 | 8.00 |
| 104 Billy Buckner AU (RC) | 3.00 | 8.00 |
| 105 Brandon Jones AU RC | 3.00 | 8.00 |
| 106 Bronson Sardinha AU (RC) | 3.00 | 8.00 |
| 107 Chin-Lung Hu AU (RC) | 10.00 | 25.00 |
| 108 Chris Seddon AU (RC) | 3.00 | 8.00 |
| 109 Clay Buchholz AU (RC) | 10.00 | 25.00 |
| 110 Clint Sammons AU (RC) | 3.00 | 8.00 |
| 111 Daric Barton AU (RC) | 4.00 | 10.00 |
| 112 Dave Davidson AU RC | 4.00 | 10.00 |
| 113 Donny Lucy AU (RC) | 3.00 | 8.00 |
| 114 Emilio Bonifacio AU RC | 4.00 | 10.00 |
| 115 Eugenio Velez AU RC | 4.00 | 10.00 |
| 116 Felipe Paulino AU RC | | |
| 117 Harvey Garcia AU (RC) | 3.00 | 8.00 |
| 118 Ian Kennedy AU (RC) | 15.00 | 40.00 |
| 119 J.R. Towles AU RC | 6.00 | 15.00 |
| 120 Jeff Clement AU (RC) | | |
| 121 Jerry Blevins AU (RC) | 3.00 | 8.00 |
| 122 Joe Koshansky AU (RC) | 3.00 | 8.00 |
| 123 Joey Votto AU (RC) | 6.00 | 15.00 |
| 124 Jonathan Abaladejo AU RC | 4.00 | 10.00 |
| 125 Jonathan Meloan AU RC | 3.00 | 8.00 |
| 126 Jose Morales AU (RC) | 3.00 | 8.00 |
| 127 Josh Anderson AU (RC) | 3.00 | 8.00 |
| 128 Josh Newman AU RC | 3.00 | 8.00 |
| 129 Justin Maxwell AU RC | 4.00 | 10.00 |
| 130 Justin Ruggiano AU RC | 3.00 | 8.00 |
| 131 Kevin Hart AU (RC) | 3.00 | 8.00 |
| 132 Lance Broadway AU (RC) | 3.00 | 8.00 |
| 133 Luis Mendoza AU (RC) | 3.00 | 8.00 |
| 134 Luke Hochevar AU RC | 6.00 | 15.00 |
| 135 Nyjer Morgan AU (RC) | 3.00 | 8.00 |
| 136 Rob Johnson AU (RC) | 3.00 | 8.00 |
| 137 Ross Detwiler AU RC | 3.00 | 8.00 |
| 138 Ross Ohlendorf AU RC | 4.00 | 10.00 |
| 139 Ryan Hanigan AU RC | 3.00 | 8.00 |
| 140 Seth Smith AU (RC) | 3.00 | 8.00 |
| 141 Steve Pearce AU RC | 3.00 | 8.00 |
| 142 Troy Patton AU (RC) | 3.00 | 8.00 |
| 143 Wladimir Balentien AU (RC) | 4.00 | 10.00 |
| 144 Colt Morton AU RC | 3.00 | 8.00 |
| 145 Carlos Muniz AU RC | | |

## 2009 Upper Deck Spectrum

| | | |
|---|---|---|
| COMP.SET w/ AUs (100) | 8.00 | 20.00 |
| COMMON CARD | .15 | .40 |
| COMMON AU RC | 3.00 | 8.00 |
| OVERALL AUTO ODDS 1:7 | | |
| EXCHANGE DEADLINE 1/29/2011 | | |
| PRINTING PLATES RANDOMLY INSERTED | | |
| PLATE PRINT RUN 1 SET PER COLOR | | |
| BLACK-CYAN-MAGENTA-YELLOW ISSUED | | |
| NO PLATE PRICING DUE TO SCARCITY | | |
| 1 Brandon Webb | .25 | .60 |
| 2 Randy Johnson | .40 | 1.00 |
| 3 Chris B. Young | .15 | .40 |
| 4 Dan Haren | .15 | .40 |

|  |  | | |
|---|---|---|---|
| ❏ 5 | Adam Dunn | .25 | .60 |
| ❏ 6 | Chipper Jones | .40 | 1.00 |
| ❏ 7 | Tim Hudson | .15 | .40 |
| ❏ 8 | John Smoltz | .40 | 1.00 |
| ❏ 9 | Brian Roberts | .15 | .40 |
| ❏ 10 | Nick Markakis | .25 | .60 |
| ❏ 11 | Josh Beckett | .25 | .60 |
| ❏ 12 | David Ortiz | .25 | .60 |
| ❏ 13 | Daisuke Matsuzaka | .60 | 1.50 |
| ❏ 14 | J.D. Drew | .15 | .40 |
| ❏ 15 | Jonathan Papelbon | .25 | .60 |
| ❏ 16 | Mike Lowell | .25 | .60 |
| ❏ 17 | Alfonso Soriano | .25 | .60 |
| ❏ 18 | Derrek Lee | .25 | .60 |
| ❏ 19 | Kosuke Fukudome | .40 | 1.00 |
| ❏ 20 | Carlos Zambrano | .15 | .40 |
| ❏ 21 | Aramis Ramirez | .15 | .40 |
| ❏ 22 | Rich Harden | .15 | .40 |
| ❏ 23 | Carlos Quentin | .15 | .40 |
| ❏ 24 | Jim Thome | .25 | .60 |
| ❏ 25 | Ken Griffey Jr. | .60 | 1.50 |
| ❏ 26 | Jay Bruce | .40 | 1.00 |
| ❏ 27 | Edinson Volquez | .15 | .40 |
| ❏ 28 | Brandon Phillips | .15 | .40 |
| ❏ 29 | Victor Martinez | .25 | .60 |
| ❏ 30 | Grady Sizemore | .25 | .60 |
| ❏ 31 | Travis Hafner | .15 | .40 |
| ❏ 32 | Matt Holliday | .25 | .60 |
| ❏ 33 | Troy Tulowitzki | .25 | .60 |
| ❏ 34 | Garrett Atkins | .15 | .40 |
| ❏ 35 | Miguel Cabrera | .25 | .60 |
| ❏ 36 | Magglio Ordonez | .25 | .60 |
| ❏ 37 | Justin Verlander | .40 | 1.00 |
| ❏ 38 | Hanley Ramirez | .40 | 1.00 |
| ❏ 39 | Dan Uggla | .15 | .40 |
| ❏ 40 | Lance Berkman | .25 | .60 |
| ❏ 41 | Carlos Lee | .25 | .40 |
| ❏ 42 | Roy Oswalt | .25 | .60 |
| ❏ 43 | Miguel Tejada | .15 | .40 |
| ❏ 44 | Joakim Soria | .15 | .40 |
| ❏ 45 | Alex Gordon | .25 | .60 |
| ❏ 46 | Mark Teixeira | .40 | 1.00 |
| ❏ 47 | Vladimir Guerrero | .15 | .40 |
| ❏ 48 | Torii Hunter | .15 | .40 |
| ❏ 49 | John Lackey | .25 | .60 |
| ❏ 50 | Manny Ramirez | .40 | 1.00 |
| ❏ 51 | Russell Martin | .25 | .60 |
| ❏ 52 | Matt Kemp | .40 | 1.00 |
| ❏ 53 | Clayton Kershaw | .40 | 1.00 |
| ❏ 54 | CC Sabathia | .25 | .60 |
| ❏ 55 | Prince Fielder | .25 | .60 |
| ❏ 56 | Ryan Braun | .50 | 1.25 |
| ❏ 57 | Joe Mauer | .25 | .60 |
| ❏ 58 | Justin Morneau | .40 | 1.00 |
| ❏ 59 | Jose Reyes | .40 | 1.00 |
| ❏ 60 | David Wright | .50 | 1.25 |
| ❏ 61 | Johan Santana | .40 | 1.00 |
| ❏ 62 | Carlos Beltran | .15 | .40 |
| ❏ 63 | Ivan Rodriguez | .25 | .60 |
| ❏ 64 | Alex Rodriguez | .60 | 1.50 |
| ❏ 65 | Derek Jeter | 1.00 | 2.50 |
| ❏ 66 | Chien-Ming Wang | .40 | 1.00 |
| ❏ 67 | Jason Giambi | .15 | .40 |
| ❏ 68 | Joba Chamberlain | .50 | 1.25 |
| ❏ 69 | Mariano Rivera | .25 | .60 |
| ❏ 70 | Xavier Nady | .15 | .40 |
| ❏ 71 | Frank Thomas | .40 | 1.00 |
| ❏ 72 | Carlos Gonzalez | .15 | .40 |
| ❏ 73 | Chase Utley | .40 | 1.00 |
| ❏ 74 | Ryan Howard | .50 | 1.25 |
| ❏ 75 | Jimmy Rollins | .25 | .60 |
| ❏ 76 | Andy LaRoche | .15 | .40 |
| ❏ 77 | Nate McLouth | .15 | .40 |
| ❏ 78 | Adrian Gonzalez | .25 | .60 |
| ❏ 79 | Greg Maddux | .50 | 1.25 |
| ❏ 80 | Jake Peavy | .25 | .60 |
| ❏ 81 | Trevor Hoffman | .15 | .40 |
| ❏ 82 | Tim Lincecum | .50 | 1.25 |
| ❏ 83 | Aaron Rowand | .15 | .40 |
| ❏ 84 | Felix Hernandez | .25 | .60 |
| ❏ 85 | Ichiro Suzuki | .60 | 1.50 |
| ❏ 86 | Erik Bedard | .15 | .40 |
| ❏ 87 | Albert Pujols | 1.00 | 2.50 |
| ❏ 88 | Troy Glaus | .15 | .40 |
| ❏ 89 | Rick Ankiel | .25 | .60 |
| ❏ 90 | B.J. Upton | .25 | .60 |
| ❏ 91 | Evan Longoria | .60 | 1.50 |
| ❏ 92 | Scott Kazmir | .25 | .60 |
| ❏ 93 | Carl Crawford | .25 | .60 |
| ❏ 94 | Josh Hamilton | .40 | 1.00 |
| ❏ 95 | Ian Kinsler | .25 | .60 |
| ❏ 96 | Michael Young | .25 | .60 |
| ❏ 97 | Roy Halladay | .25 | .60 |
| ❏ 98 | Vernon Wells | .15 | .40 |
| ❏ 99 | Ryan Zimmerman | .25 | .60 |
| ❏ 100 | Lastings Milledge | .15 | .40 |
| ❏ 101 | David Price AU | 30.00 | 60.00 |
| ❏ 102 | Conor Gillaspie RC | 10.00 | 25.00 |
| ❏ 103 | Jeff Baisley AU RC | 5.00 | 12.00 |
| ❏ 104 | Angel Salome AU (RC) | 6.00 | 15.00 |
| ❏ 105 | Aaron Cunningham AU RC | 3.00 | 8.00 |
| ❏ 106 | Lou Marson AU (RC) | 8.00 | 20.00 |
| ❏ 107 | Matt Antonelli AU RC | 3.00 | 8.00 |
| ❏ 108 | M.Bowden AU (RC) | 8.00 | 20.00 |
| ❏ 109 | F.Cervelli AU RC EXCH | 6.00 | 15.00 |
| ❏ 110 | Phil Coke AU RC | 10.00 | 25.00 |
| ❏ 111 | Josh Outman AU RC | 3.00 | 8.00 |
| ❏ 112 | Shairon Martis AU RC | 4.00 | 10.00 |
| ❏ 113 | Mat Gamel AU RC | 10.00 | 25.00 |
| ❏ 114 | Josh Geer AU (RC) | 3.00 | 8.00 |
| ❏ 115 | Greg Golson AU (RC) | 3.00 | 8.00 |
| ❏ 116 | Kila Ka'aihue AU (RC) | 5.00 | 12.00 |
| ❏ 117 | Wade LeBlanc AU RC | 3.00 | 8.00 |
| ❏ 118 | Chris Lambert AU (RC) | 3.00 | 8.00 |
| ❏ 119 | James Parr AU (RC) | 3.00 | 8.00 |
| ❏ 120 | Tuiasosopo AU (RC) | 4.00 | 10.00 |

## 2008 Upper Deck Timeline

|  | | |
|---|---|---|
| ❏ COMMON CARD (1-50) | .15 | .40 |
| ❏ COMMON RC (51-100) | .25 | .60 |
| ❏ COMMON CARD (101-130) | .25 | .60 |
| ❏ COMMON CARD (131-180) | .25 | .60 |
| ❏ COMMON CARD (181-210) | .25 | .60 |
| ❏ COMMON CARD (211-310) | .25 | .60 |
| ❏ COMMON CARD (311-335) | .40 | 1.00 |
| ❏ COMMON CARD (336-360) | .40 | 1.00 |
| ❏ COMMON CARD (361-385) | .75 | 2.00 |
| ❏ 1 Jose Reyes | .50 | 1.25 |
| ❏ 2 David Wright | .50 | 1.25 |
| ❏ 3 Carlos Beltran | .15 | .40 |
| ❏ 4 Pedro Martinez | .25 | .60 |
| ❏ 5 Johan Santana | .25 | .60 |
| ❏ 6 Hanley Ramirez | .40 | 1.00 |
| ❏ 7 John Smoltz | .40 | 1.00 |
| ❏ 8 Chipper Jones | .50 | 1.25 |
| ❏ 9 Mark Teixeira | .25 | .60 |
| ❏ 10 Chase Utley | .40 | 1.00 |
| ❏ 11 Ryan Howard | .50 | 1.25 |
| ❏ 12 Jimmy Rollins | .25 | .60 |
| ❏ 13 Alfonso Soriano | .25 | .60 |
| ❏ 14 Derrek Lee | .25 | .60 |
| ❏ 15 Jason Bay | .25 | .60 |
| ❏ 16 Lance Berkman | .25 | .60 |
| ❏ 17 Ken Griffey Jr. | .60 | 1.50 |
| ❏ 18 Ryan Braun | .50 | 1.25 |
| ❏ 19 Prince Fielder | .40 | 1.00 |
| ❏ 20 Albert Pujols | .75 | 2.00 |
| ❏ 21 Tim Lincecum | .50 | 1.25 |

|  |  | | |
|---|---|---|---|
| ❏ 22 | Jake Peavy | .25 | .60 |
| ❏ 23 | Matt Kemp | .40 | 1.00 |
| ❏ 24 | Matt Holliday | .25 | .60 |
| ❏ 25 | Brandon Webb | .25 | .60 |
| ❏ 26 | Randy Johnson | .40 | 1.00 |
| ❏ 27 | Alex Rodriguez | .60 | 1.50 |
| ❏ 28 | Derek Jeter | 1.00 | 2.50 |
| ❏ 29 | Chien-Ming Wang | .40 | 1.00 |
| ❏ 30 | David Ortiz | .25 | .60 |
| ❏ 31 | Manny Ramirez | .40 | 1.00 |
| ❏ 32 | Daisuke Matsuzaka | .50 | 1.25 |
| ❏ 33 | B.J. Upton | .25 | .60 |
| ❏ 34 | Nick Markakis | .25 | .60 |
| ❏ 35 | Roy Halladay | .15 | .40 |
| ❏ 36 | Jim Thome | .25 | .60 |
| ❏ 37 | Grady Sizemore | .25 | .60 |
| ❏ 38 | Travis Hafner | .15 | .40 |
| ❏ 39 | C.C. Sabathia | .15 | .40 |
| ❏ 40 | Miguel Cabrera | .25 | .60 |
| ❏ 41 | Justin Verlander | .40 | 1.00 |
| ❏ 42 | Joe Mauer | .40 | 1.00 |
| ❏ 43 | Alex Gordon | .25 | .60 |
| ❏ 44 | Frank Thomas | .40 | 1.00 |
| ❏ 45 | Vladimir Guerrero | .40 | 1.00 |
| ❏ 46 | Torii Hunter | .15 | .40 |
| ❏ 47 | Josh Hamilton | .50 | 1.25 |
| ❏ 48 | Ichiro Suzuki | .60 | 1.50 |
| ❏ 49 | Felix Hernandez | .25 | .60 |
| ❏ 50 | Erik Bedard | .15 | .40 |
| ❏ 51 | Daric Barton (RC) | .25 | .60 |
| ❏ 52 | John Bowker (RC) | .25 | .60 |
| ❏ 53 | Clay Buchholz (RC) | .60 | 1.50 |
| ❏ 54 | Jeff Clement (RC) | .40 | 1.00 |
| ❏ 55 | Johnny Cueto RC | .40 | 1.00 |
| ❏ 56 | Blake DeWitt (RC) | .40 | 1.00 |
| ❏ 57 | German Duran RC | .40 | 1.00 |
| ❏ 58 | Kosuke Fukudome RC | .75 | 2.00 |
| ❏ 59 | Alberto Gonzalez RC | .40 | 1.00 |
| ❏ 60 | Luke Hochevar RC | .40 | 1.00 |
| ❏ 61 | Chin-Lung Hu (RC) | .40 | 1.00 |
| ❏ 62 | Ian Kennedy RC | .60 | 1.50 |
| ❏ 63 | Masahide Kobayashi RC | .40 | 1.00 |
| ❏ 64 | Hiroki Kuroda RC | .40 | 1.00 |
| ❏ 65 | Evan Longoria RC | 2.50 | 6.00 |
| ❏ 66 | Jed Lowrie (RC) | .60 | 1.50 |
| ❏ 67 | Justin Masterson RC | 1.25 | 3.00 |
| ❏ 68 | Nick Blackburn RC | .40 | 1.00 |
| ❏ 69 | Micah Hoffpauir RC | .75 | 2.00 |
| ❏ 70 | Jeff Niemann RC | .25 | .60 |
| ❏ 71 | Ross Ohlendorf RC | .40 | 1.00 |
| ❏ 72 | Jonathan Van Every RC | .25 | .60 |
| ❏ 73 | Alexei Ramirez RC | 1.00 | 2.50 |
| ❏ 74 | Justin Ruggiano RC | .40 | 1.00 |
| ❏ 75 | Max Scherzer RC | .60 | 1.50 |
| ❏ 76 | Greg Smith RC | .25 | .60 |
| ❏ 77 | Denard Span RC | .40 | 1.00 |
| ❏ 78 | Clete Thomas RC | .40 | 1.00 |
| ❏ 79 | Josh Banks (RC) | .25 | .60 |
| ❏ 80 | Clay Timpner RC | .25 | .60 |
| ❏ 81 | Matt Tolbert RC | .25 | .60 |
| ❏ 82 | J.R. Towles RC | .40 | 1.00 |
| ❏ 83 | Eugenio Velez RC | .25 | .60 |
| ❏ 84 | Joey Votto (RC) | .60 | 1.50 |
| ❏ 85 | Rico Washington (RC) | .25 | .60 |
| ❏ 86 | Jay Bruce RC | 1.00 | 2.50 |
| ❏ 87 | Wladimir Balentien (RC) | .25 | .60 |
| ❏ 88 | Burke Badenhop RC | .40 | 1.00 |
| ❏ 89 | Brian Barton RC | .40 | 1.00 |
| ❏ 90 | Brian Bocock RC | .25 | .60 |
| ❏ 91 | Brandon Boggs (RC) | .40 | 1.00 |
| ❏ 92 | Robinzon Diaz (RC) | .25 | .60 |
| ❏ 93 | Heman Iribarren (RC) | .25 | .60 |
| ❏ 94 | Brent Lillibridge (RC) | .25 | .60 |
| ❏ 95 | Yasuhiko Yabuta RC | .40 | 1.00 |
| ❏ 96 | Jeff Samardzija RC | .75 | 2.00 |
| ❏ 97 | Carlos Gonzalez RC | .25 | .60 |
| ❏ 98 | Clayton Kershaw RC | 1.25 | 3.00 |
| ❏ 99 | Jonathan Abaladejo RC | .40 | 1.00 |
| ❏ 100 | Nick Adenhart (RC) | .25 | .60 |
| ❏ 101 | Bobby Wilson 92 ML RC | .25 | .60 |
| ❏ 102 | Brandon Phillips 92 ML | .25 | .60 |

|  |  | | |
|---|---|---|---|
| 103 | Chad Billingsley 92 ML | .25 | .60 |
| 104 | Chris Duncan 92 ML | .25 | .60 |
| 105 | Clay Timpner 92 ML (RC) | .25 | .60 |
| 106 | Clete Thomas 92 ML | .40 | 1.00 |
| 107 | Corey Hart 92 ML | .25 | .60 |
| 108 | Craig Breslow 92 ML | .25 | .60 |
| 109 | David Murphy 92 ML | .25 | .60 |
| 110 | Edinson Volquez 92 ML | .25 | .60 |
| 111 | Elijah Dukes 92 ML | .25 | .60 |
| 112 | Emmanuel Burriss 92 ML RC | .40 | 1.00 |
| 113 | Evan Longoria 92 ML RC | 2.50 | 6.00 |
| 114 | Fred Lewis 92 ML | .25 | .60 |
| 115 | Felix Pie 92 ML | .25 | .60 |
| 116 | German Duran 92 ML RC | .40 | 1.00 |
| 117 | Greg Smith 92 ML RC | .40 | 1.00 |
| 118 | Hernan Iribarren 92 ML | .25 | .60 |
| 119 | Joey Votto 92 ML (RC) | .60 | 1.50 |
| 120 | Jonathan Van Every 92 ML RC | .25 | .60 |
| 121 | Kosuke Fukudome 92 ML RC | .75 | 2.00 |
| 122 | Matt Joyce 92 ML RC | .60 | 1.50 |
| 123 | Max Scherzer 92 ML RC | .60 | 1.50 |
| 124 | Nick Swisher 92 ML | .25 | .60 |
| 125 | Paul Janish 92 ML (RC) | .25 | .60 |
| 126 | Reed Johnson 92 ML | .25 | .60 |
| 127 | Rico Washington 92 ML (RC) | .25 | .60 |
| 128 | Russell Martin 92 ML | .25 | .60 |
| 129 | Scott Kazmir 92 ML | .40 | 1.00 |
| 130 | Tyler Clippard 92 ML | .25 | .60 |
| 131 | Randy Johnson 94 ATH | .60 | 1.50 |
| 132 | Frank Thomas 94 ATH | .60 | 1.50 |
| 133 | Greg Maddux 94 ATH | .75 | 2.00 |
| 135 | Ryan Braun 94 ATH | .75 | 2.00 |
| 136 | David Ortiz 94 ATH | .40 | 1.00 |
| 137 | Jake Peavy 94 ATH | .40 | 1.00 |
| 138 | Mark Teixeira 94 ATH | .40 | 1.00 |
| 139 | Jose Reyes 94 ATH | .40 | 1.00 |
| 140 | Chien-Ming Wang 94 ATH | .60 | 1.50 |
| 141 | Prince Fielder 94 ATH | .60 | 1.50 |
| 142 | Albert Pujols 94 ATH | 1.25 | 3.00 |
| 143 | Johan Santana 94 ATH | .40 | 1.00 |
| 144 | Josh Beckett 94 ATH | .40 | 1.00 |
| 145 | Alex Rodriguez 94 ATH | 1.00 | 2.50 |
| 146 | Felix Hernandez 94 ATH | .40 | 1.00 |
| 147 | Brandon Webb 94 ATH | .40 | 1.00 |
| 148 | Chase Utley 94 ATH | .60 | 1.50 |
| 149 | Derek Jeter 94 ATH | 1.50 | 4.00 |
| 150 | Grady Sizemore 94 ATH | .40 | 1.00 |
| 151 | B.J. Upton 94 ATH | .25 | .60 |
| 152 | Carlos Beltran 94 ATH | .25 | .60 |
| 153 | Hanley Ramirez 94 ATH | .60 | 1.50 |
| 154 | Magglio Ordonez 94 ATH | .40 | 1.00 |
| 155 | Carlos Zambrano 94 ATH | .25 | .60 |
| 156 | Manny Ramirez 94 ATH | .60 | 1.50 |
| 157 | Travis Hafner 94 ATH | .25 | .60 |
| 158 | David Wright 94 ATH | .75 | 2.00 |
| 159 | Jimmy Rollins 94 ATH | .40 | 1.00 |
| 160 | Matt Holliday 94 ATH | .40 | 1.00 |
| 161 | Ken Griffey Jr. 94 ATH | 1.00 | 2.50 |
| 162 | C.C. Sabathia 94 ATH | .25 | .60 |
| 163 | Joe Mauer 94 ATH | .60 | 1.50 |
| 164 | Derrek Lee 94 ATH | .40 | 1.00 |
| 165 | Miguel Cabrera 94 ATH | .40 | 1.00 |
| 166 | Alfonso Soriano 94 ATH | .40 | 1.00 |
| 167 | Ichiro Suzuki 94 ATH | 1.00 | 2.50 |
| 168 | Daisuke Matsuzaka 94 ATH | .75 | 2.00 |
| 169 | Lance Berkman 94 ATH | .40 | 1.00 |
| 170 | Ryan Howard 94 ATH | .75 | 2.00 |
| 171 | J.R. Towles 94 ATH RC | .40 | 1.00 |
| 172 | Max Scherzer 94 ATH RC | .60 | 1.50 |
| 173 | Chin-Lung Hu 94 ATH | .40 | 1.00 |
| 174 | Daric Barton 94 ATH | .25 | .60 |
| 175 | Ian Kennedy 94 ATH | .60 | 1.50 |
| 176 | Clay Buchholz 94 ATH | .60 | 1.50 |
| 177 | Joey Votto 94 ATH (RC) | .60 | 1.50 |
| 178 | Kosuke Fukudome 94 ATH RC | .75 | 2.00 |
| 179 | Johnny Cueto 94 ATH | .60 | 1.50 |
| 180 | Evan Longoria 94 ATH | 2.50 | 6.00 |
| 181 | Brandon Boggs 95 STP (RC) | .25 | .60 |
| 182 | Brian Bocock 95 STP RC | .25 | .60 |
| 183 | Burke Badenhop 95 STP RC | .40 | 1.00 |
| 184 | Callix Crabbe 95 STP (RC) | .25 | .60 |
| 185 | Cha-Seung Baek 95 STP | .25 | .60 |
| 186 | Chris Smith 95 STP (RC) | .25 | .60 |
| 187 | Clayton Kershaw 95 STP RC | 1.25 | 3.00 |
| 188 | Felipe Paulino 95 STP RC | .40 | 1.00 |
| 189 | Glen Perkins 95 STP | .25 | .60 |
| 190 | Homer Bailey 95 STP | .40 | 1.00 |
| 191 | James Loney 95 STP | .40 | 1.00 |
| 192 | Jay Bruce 95 STP (RC) | 1.00 | 2.50 |
| 193 | Jeff Baker 95 STP | .25 | .60 |
| 194 | Jeff Keppinger 95 STP | .25 | .60 |
| 195 | Jesus Flores 95 STP | .25 | .60 |
| 196 | Joakim Soria 95 STP | .25 | .60 |
| 197 | Joey Votto 95 STP (RC) | .60 | 1.50 |
| 198 | Josh Hamilton 95 STP | .75 | 2.00 |
| 199 | Kosuke Fukudome 95 STP RC | .75 | 2.00 |
| 200 | Micah Hoffpauir 95 STP RC | .75 | 2.00 |
| 201 | Nick Blackburn 95 STP RC | .40 | 1.00 |
| 202 | Nyjer Morgan 95 STP (RC) | .25 | .60 |
| 203 | Randor Bierd 95 STP RC | .25 | .60 |
| 204 | Rich Hill 95 STP | .25 | .60 |
| 205 | Ross Ohlendorf 95 STP RC | .40 | 1.00 |
| 206 | Russell Martin 95 STP | .25 | .60 |
| 207 | Ryan Garko 95 STP | .25 | .60 |
| 208 | Seth Smith 95 STP | .25 | .60 |
| 209 | Steve Holm 95 STP RC | .25 | .60 |
| 210 | Travis Hafner 95 STP | .25 | .60 |
| 211 | Brandon Webb 04 TT | .40 | 1.00 |
| 212 | Randy Johnson 04 TT | .60 | 1.50 |
| 213 | Max Scherzer 04 TT RC | .60 | 1.50 |
| 214 | Chris B. Young 04 TT | .25 | .60 |
| 215 | Justin Upton 04 TT | .25 | .60 |
| 216 | John Smoltz 04 TT | .60 | 1.50 |
| 217 | Chipper Jones 04 TT | .75 | 2.00 |
| 218 | Mark Teixeira 04 TT | .40 | 1.00 |
| 219 | Jeff Francoeur 04 TT | .40 | 1.00 |
| 220 | Adrian Gonzalez 04 TT | .40 | 1.00 |
| 221 | Nick Markakis 04 TT | .40 | 1.00 |
| 222 | Jacoby Ellsbury 04 TT | 1.00 | 2.50 |
| 223 | David Ortiz 04 TT | .40 | 1.00 |
| 224 | Manny Ramirez 04 TT | .60 | 1.50 |
| 225 | Daisuke Matsuzaka 04 TT | .75 | 2.00 |
| 226 | Clay Buchholz 04 TT (RC) | .60 | 1.50 |
| 227 | Jed Lowrie 04 TT RC | .60 | 1.50 |
| 228 | Justin Masterson 04 TT RC | 1.25 | 3.00 |
| 229 | Geovany Soto 04 TT | .60 | 1.50 |
| 230 | Alfonso Soriano 04 TT | .40 | 1.00 |
| 231 | Derrek Lee 04 TT | .40 | 1.00 |
| 232 | Kosuke Fukudome 04 TT RC | .75 | 2.00 |
| 233 | Jim Thome 04 TT | .40 | 1.00 |
| 234 | Alexei Ramirez 04 TT RC | 1.00 | 2.50 |
| 235 | Ken Griffey Jr. 04 TT | 1.00 | 2.50 |
| 236 | Johnny Cueto 04 TT RC | .60 | 1.50 |
| 237 | Joey Votto 04 TT (RC) | .60 | 1.50 |
| 238 | Brandon Phillips 04 TT | .25 | .60 |
| 239 | Edinson Volquez 04 TT | .25 | .60 |
| 240 | Grady Sizemore 04 TT | .40 | 1.00 |
| 241 | Travis Hafner 04 TT | .25 | .60 |
| 242 | C.C. Sabathia 04 TT | .25 | .60 |
| 243 | Matt Holliday 04 TT | .40 | 1.00 |
| 244 | Troy Tulowitzki 04 TT | .40 | 1.00 |
| 245 | Miguel Cabrera 04 TT | .40 | 1.00 |
| 246 | Justin Verlander 04 TT | .40 | 1.00 |
| 247 | Matt Tolbert 04 TT RC | .40 | 1.00 |
| 248 | Hanley Ramirez 04 TT | .60 | 1.50 |
| 249 | Jeremy Hermida 04 TT | .25 | .60 |
| 250 | Lance Berkman 04 TT | .40 | 1.00 |
| 251 | J.R. Towles 04 TT RC | .40 | 1.00 |
| 252 | Alex Gordon 04 TT | .40 | 1.00 |
| 253 | Luke Hochevar 04 TT RC | .40 | 1.00 |
| 254 | Vladimir Guerrero 04 TT | .60 | 1.50 |
| 255 | Torii Hunter 04 TT | .25 | .60 |
| 256 | Nick Adenhart 04 TT (RC) | .40 | 1.00 |
| 257 | Garrett Atkins 04 TT | .25 | .60 |
| 258 | Blake DeWitt 04 TT (RC) | .60 | 1.50 |
| 259 | Chin-Lung Hu 04 TT (RC) | .40 | 1.00 |
| 260 | Hiroki Kuroda 04 TT | .40 | 1.00 |
| 261 | Matt Kemp 04 TT | .60 | 1.50 |
| 262 | James Loney 04 TT | .25 | .60 |
| 263 | Justin Morneau 04 TT | .40 | 1.00 |
| 264 | Dan Haren 04 TT | .25 | .60 |
| 265 | Ryan Braun 04 TT | .75 | 2.00 |
| 266 | Corey Hart 04 TT | .25 | .60 |
| 267 | Rickie Weeks 04 TT | .25 | .60 |
| 268 | Prince Fielder 04 TT | .60 | 1.50 |
| 269 | Carlos Gomez 04 TT | .25 | .60 |
| 270 | Joe Mauer 04 TT | .60 | 1.50 |
| 271 | Jose Reyes 04 TT | .40 | 1.00 |
| 272 | David Wright 04 TT | .75 | 2.00 |
| 273 | Carlos Beltran 04 TT | .25 | .60 |
| 274 | Pedro Martinez 04 TT | .40 | 1.00 |
| 275 | Hideki Matsui 04 TT | .60 | 1.50 |
| 276 | Alex Rodriguez 04 TT | 1.00 | 2.50 |
| 277 | Derek Jeter 04 TT | 1.50 | 4.00 |
| 278 | Chien-Ming Wang 04 TT | .60 | 1.50 |
| 279 | Ian Kennedy 04 TT | .60 | 1.50 |
| 280 | Phil Hughes 04 TT | .60 | 1.50 |
| 281 | Frank Thomas T | .60 | 1.50 |
| 282 | Dana Eveland 04 TT | .25 | .60 |
| 283 | Greg Smith 04 TT RC | .25 | .60 |
| 284 | Cole Hamels 04 TT | .60 | 1.50 |
| 285 | Chase Utley 04 TT | .60 | 1.50 |
| 286 | Ryan Howard 04 TT | .75 | 2.00 |
| 287 | Jimmy Rollins 04 TT | .40 | 1.00 |
| 288 | Jason Bay 04 TT | .40 | 1.00 |
| 289 | Jake Peavy 04 TT | .40 | 1.00 |
| 290 | Brian McCann 04 TT | .40 | 1.00 |
| 291 | Tim Lincecum 04 TT | .75 | 2.00 |
| 292 | Justin Ruggiano 04 TT RC | .40 | 1.00 |
| 293 | Jay Bruce 04 TT (RC) | 1.00 | 2.50 |
| 294 | Brian Bocock 04 TT RC | .25 | .60 |
| 295 | Ichiro Suzuki 04 TT | 1.00 | 2.50 |
| 296 | Adam Dunn 04 TT | .25 | .60 |
| 297 | Erik Bedard 04 TT | .25 | .60 |
| 298 | Jeff Clement 04 TT RC | .40 | 1.00 |
| 299 | Felix Hernandez 04 TT | .40 | 1.00 |
| 300 | Albert Pujols 04 TT | 1.25 | 3.00 |
| 301 | Rick Ankiel 04 TT | .25 | .60 |
| 302 | B.J. Upton 04 TT | .40 | 1.00 |
| 303 | Evan Longoria 04 TT RC | 2.50 | 6.00 |
| 304 | Clayton Kershaw 04 TT RC | 1.25 | 3.00 |
| 305 | Carl Crawford 04 TT | .25 | .60 |
| 306 | Russell Martin 04 TT | .25 | .60 |
| 307 | Brandon Boggs 04 TT (RC) | .40 | 1.00 |
| 308 | Josh Hamilton 04 TT | .75 | 2.00 |
| 309 | Roy Halladay 04 TT | .25 | .60 |
| 310 | Ryan Zimmerman 04 TT | .40 | 1.00 |
| 311 | Evan Longoria 93 SP (RC) | 4.00 | 10.00 |
| 312 | Johnny Cueto 93 SP (RC) | .60 | 1.50 |
| 313 | Kosuke Fukudome 93 SP (RC) | 1.25 | 3.00 |
| 314 | Joey Votto 93 SP (RC) | 1.00 | 2.50 |
| 315 | Clay Buchholz 93 SP (RC) | 1.00 | 2.50 |
| 316 | Ian Kennedy 93 SP (RC) | 1.00 | 2.50 |
| 317 | Daric Barton 93 SP (RC) | .40 | 1.00 |
| 318 | Chin-Lung Hu 93 SP (RC) | .60 | 1.50 |
| 319 | Max Scherzer 93 SP (RC) | 1.00 | 2.50 |
| 320 | J.R. Towles 93 SP (RC) | .40 | 1.00 |
| 321 | Nick Adenhart 93 SP (RC) | .40 | 1.00 |
| 322 | Wladimir Balentien 93 SP (RC) | .40 | 1.00 |
| 323 | Brian Barton 93 SP | .60 | 1.50 |
| 324 | Brian Bocock 93 SP | .40 | 1.00 |
| 325 | Jonathan Herrera 93 SP RC | .60 | 1.50 |
| 326 | Jesse Carlson 93 SP RC | .60 | 1.50 |
| 327 | Jeff Clement 93 SP (RC) | .60 | 1.50 |
| 328 | Brandon Jones 93 SP RC | 1.00 | 2.50 |
| 329 | German Duran 93 SP (RC) | .60 | 1.50 |
| 330 | Alex Romero 93 SP (RC) | .60 | 1.50 |
| 331 | Jay Bruce 93 SP (RC) | 1.50 | 4.00 |
| 332 | Luke Hochevar 93 SP (RC) | .60 | 1.50 |
| 333 | Clayton Kershaw 93 SP (RC) | 2.00 | 5.00 |
| 334 | Nick Blackburn 93 SP (RC) | .60 | 1.50 |
| 335 | Jed Lowrie 93 SP (RC) | 1.00 | 2.50 |
| 336 | Evan Longoria 94 SP (RC) | 4.00 | 10.00 |
| 337 | Johnny Cueto 94 SP (RC) | .60 | 1.50 |
| 338 | Kosuke Fukudome 94 SP (RC) | 1.25 | 3.00 |
| 339 | Joey Votto 94 SP (RC) | 1.00 | 2.50 |
| 340 | Clay Buchholz 94 SP (RC) | 1.00 | 2.50 |
| 341 | Ian Kennedy 94 SP (RC) | 1.00 | 2.50 |
| 342 | Daric Barton 94 SP (RC) | .40 | 1.00 |
| 343 | Chin-Lung Hu 94 SP (RC) | .60 | 1.50 |
| 344 | Max Scherzer 94 SP (RC) | 1.00 | 2.50 |
| 345 | J.R. Towles 94 SP (RC) | .60 | 1.50 |

|  |  | | |
|---|---|---|---|
| 346 | Justin Masterson 94 SP (RC) | 2.00 | 5.00 |
| 347 | Kyle McClellan 94 SP RC | .40 | 1.00 |
| 348 | Evan Meek 94 SP RC | .40 | 1.00 |
| 349 | Nyjer Morgan 94 SP RC | .40 | 1.00 |
| 350 | Colt Morton 94 SP RC | .60 | 1.50 |
| 351 | Luke Carlin 94 SP RC | .40 | 1.00 |
| 352 | Emmanuel Burriss 94 SP (RC) | .60 | 1.50 |
| 353 | Clint Sammons 94 SP (RC) | .40 | 1.00 |
| 354 | Ross Ohlendorf 94 SP (RC) | .60 | 1.50 |
| 355 | Jay Bruce 94 SP RC | 1.50 | 4.00 |
| 356 | Felipe Paulino 94 SP (RC) | .60 | 1.50 |
| 357 | Alexei Ramirez 94 SP RC | 1.50 | 4.00 |
| 358 | Clayton Kershaw 94 SP (RC) | 2.00 | 5.00 |
| 359 | Cory Wade 94 SP RC | .40 | 1.00 |
| 360 | Greg Smith 94 SP (RC) | .40 | 1.00 |
| 361 | Evan Longoria 95 SP (RC) | 6.00 | 15.00 |
| 362 | Johnny Cueto 95 SP (RC) | 1.25 | 3.00 |
| 363 | Kosuke Fukudome 95 SP (RC) | 2.00 | 5.00 |
| 364 | Joey Votto 95 SP (RC) | 2.00 | 5.00 |
| 365 | Clay Buchholz 95 SP (RC) | 2.00 | 5.00 |
| 366 | Ian Kennedy 95 SP (RC) | 2.00 | 5.00 |
| 367 | Daric Barton 95 SP (RC) | .75 | 2.00 |
| 368 | Chin-Lung Hu 95 SP RC | 1.25 | 3.00 |
| 369 | Max Scherzer 95 SP RC | 2.00 | 5.00 |
| 370 | J.R. Towles 95 SP (RC) | 1.25 | 3.00 |
| 371 | Mitchell Boggs 95 SP (RC) | .75 | 2.00 |
| 372 | Jay Bruce 95 SP (RC) | 3.00 | 8.00 |
| 373 | Alberto Gonzalez 95 SP RC | 1.25 | 3.00 |
| 374 | Rich Thompson 95 SP RC | 1.25 | 3.00 |
| 375 | Robinzon Diaz 95 SP (RC) | .75 | 2.00 |
| 376 | Clay Timpner 95 SP RC | .75 | 2.00 |
| 377 | Eider Torres 95 SP (RC) | 1.25 | 3.00 |
| 378 | Ramon Troncoso 95 SP RC | .75 | 2.00 |
| 379 | Clayton Kershaw 95 SP (RC) | 4.00 | 10.00 |
| 380 | Rico Washington 95 SP RC | .75 | 2.00 |
| 381 | Brandon Jones 95 SP (RC) | 2.00 | 5.00 |
| 382 | Bobby Wilson 95 SP RC | .75 | 2.00 |
| 383 | Wesley Wright 95 SP (RC) | .75 | 2.00 |
| 384 | Mike Parisi 95 SP RC | 1.25 | 3.00 |
| 385 | Jonathan Van Every 95 SP (RC) | .75 | 2.00 |

## 2008 Upper Deck X

| | | | |
|---|---|---|---|
| COMPLETE SET (100) | | 12.50 | 30.00 |
| COMMON CARD (1-100) | | .40 | |
| COMMON ROOKIE (1-100) | | .25 | .60 |
| PRINTING PLATES RANDOMLY INSERTED | | | |
| PLATE PRINT RUN 1 SET PER COLOR | | | |
| BLACK-CYAN-MAGENTA-YELLOW ISSUED | | | |
| NO PLATE PRICING DUE TO SCARCITY | | | |
| 1 | Randy Johnson | .40 | 1.00 |
| 2 | Conor Jackson | .15 | .40 |
| 3 | Brandon Webb | .25 | .60 |
| 4 | Justin Upton | .40 | 1.00 |
| 5 | Dan Haren | .15 | .40 |
| 6 | John Smoltz | .40 | 1.00 |
| 7 | Chipper Jones | .50 | 1.25 |
| 8 | Mark Teixeira | .25 | .60 |
| 9 | Brian Roberts | .25 | .60 |
| 10 | Nick Markakis | .25 | .60 |
| 11 | Daisuke Matsuzaka | .50 | 1.25 |
| 12 | David Ortiz | .25 | .60 |
| 13 | Manny Ramirez | .40 | 1.00 |
| 14 | Jonathan Papelbon | .25 | .60 |
| 15 | Josh Beckett | .25 | .60 |
| 16 | Clay Buchholz (RC) | .60 | 1.50 |
| 17 | Carlos Zambrano | .15 | .40 |
| 18 | Derrek Lee | .25 | .60 |
| 19 | Aramis Ramirez | .15 | .40 |
| 20 | Kerry Wood | .15 | .40 |
| 21 | Alfonso Soriano | .25 | .60 |
| 22 | Kosuke Fukudome RC | .75 | 2.00 |
| 23 | Geovany Soto | .40 | 1.00 |
| 24 | Paul Konerko | .25 | .60 |
| 25 | Jermaine Dye | .15 | .40 |
| 26 | Carlos Quentin | .15 | .40 |
| 27 | Jim Thome | .25 | .60 |
| 28 | Ken Griffey Jr. | .60 | 1.50 |
| 29 | Adam Dunn | .15 | .40 |
| 30 | Brandon Phillips | .15 | .40 |
| 31 | Edinson Volquez | .15 | .40 |
| 32 | Victor Martinez | .15 | .40 |
| 33 | Travis Hafner | .15 | .40 |
| 34 | CC Sabathia | .15 | .40 |
| 35 | Grady Sizemore | .25 | .60 |
| 36 | Garrett Atkins | .15 | .40 |
| 37 | Matt Holliday | .25 | .60 |
| 38 | Troy Tulowitzki | .25 | .60 |
| 39 | Justin Verlander | .25 | .60 |
| 40 | Miguel Cabrera | .25 | .60 |
| 41 | Gary Sheffield | .15 | .40 |
| 42 | Magglio Ordonez | .25 | .60 |
| 43 | Hanley Ramirez | .40 | 1.00 |
| 44 | Jeremy Hermida | .15 | .40 |
| 45 | Carlos Lee | .15 | .40 |
| 46 | Lance Berkman | .25 | .60 |
| 47 | Roy Oswalt | .15 | .40 |
| 48 | Alex Gordon | .25 | .60 |
| 49 | Zack Greinke | .15 | .40 |
| 50 | Howie Kendrick | .15 | .40 |
| 51 | Torii Hunter | .15 | .40 |
| 52 | Vladimir Guerrero | .40 | 1.00 |
| 53 | Matt Kemp | .40 | 1.00 |
| 54 | Russell Martin | .15 | .40 |
| 55 | Rafael Furcal | .15 | .40 |
| 56 | Ryan Braun | .50 | 1.25 |
| 57 | Prince Fielder | .40 | 1.00 |
| 58 | Corey Hart | .15 | .40 |
| 59 | Justin Morneau | .25 | .60 |
| 60 | Joe Mauer | .40 | 1.00 |
| 61 | Jose Reyes | .25 | .60 |
| 62 | David Wright | .50 | 1.25 |
| 63 | Carlos Beltran | .15 | .40 |
| 64 | Johan Santana | .25 | .60 |
| 65 | Pedro Martinez | .25 | .60 |
| 66 | Ian Kennedy RC | .60 | 1.50 |
| 67 | Hideki Matsui | .40 | 1.00 |
| 68 | Alex Rodriguez | .60 | 1.50 |
| 69 | Chien-Ming Wang | .40 | 1.00 |
| 70 | Derek Jeter | 1.00 | 2.50 |
| 71 | Robinson Cano | .25 | .60 |
| 72 | Eric Chavez | .15 | .40 |
| 73 | Frank Thomas | .40 | 1.00 |
| 74 | Cole Hamels | .40 | 1.00 |
| 75 | Jimmy Rollins | .25 | .60 |
| 76 | Ryan Howard | .50 | 1.25 |
| 77 | Chase Utley | .40 | 1.00 |
| 78 | Nate McLouth | .15 | .40 |
| 79 | Jason Bay | .25 | .60 |
| 80 | Adrian Gonzalez | .25 | .60 |
| 81 | Khalil Greene | .15 | .40 |
| 82 | Jake Peavy | .25 | .60 |
| 83 | Greg Maddux | .50 | 1.25 |
| 84 | Trevor Hoffman | .15 | .40 |
| 85 | Aaron Rowand | .15 | .40 |
| 86 | Tim Lincecum | .50 | 1.25 |
| 87 | Ichiro Suzuki | .60 | 1.50 |
| 88 | Felix Hernandez | .25 | .60 |
| 89 | Erik Bedard | .15 | .40 |
| 90 | Rick Ankiel | .15 | .40 |
| 91 | Albert Pujols | .75 | 2.00 |
| 92 | B.J. Upton | .25 | .60 |
| 93 | Carl Crawford | .25 | .60 |
| 94 | Evan Longoria RC | 2.50 | 6.00 |
| 95 | Josh Hamilton | .50 | 1.25 |
| 96 | Michael Young | .15 | .40 |
| 97 | Vernon Wells | .15 | .40 |
| 98 | Alex Rios | .15 | .40 |
| 99 | Ryan Zimmerman | .25 | .60 |
| 100 | Lastings Milledge | .15 | .40 |

## 2009 Upper Deck X

|  |  | | |
|---|---|---|---|
| 1 | Dan Haren | .15 | .40 |
| 2 | Chris B. Young | .15 | .40 |
| 3 | Brandon Webb | .25 | .60 |
| 4 | Chipper Jones | .40 | 1.00 |
| 5 | Brian McCann | .25 | .60 |
| 6 | Nick Markakis | .25 | .60 |
| 7 | Brian Roberts | .15 | .40 |
| 8 | Kevin Youkilis | .25 | .60 |
| 9 | Josh Beckett | .25 | .60 |
| 10 | Jonathan Papelbon | .25 | .60 |
| 11 | Jacoby Ellsbury | .40 | 1.00 |
| 12 | Dustin Pedroia | .50 | 1.25 |
| 13 | David Ortiz | .25 | .60 |
| 14 | Daisuke Matsuzaka | .60 | 1.50 |
| 15 | Rich Harden | .15 | .40 |
| 16 | Alfonso Soriano | .25 | .60 |
| 17 | Derrek Lee | .25 | .60 |
| 18 | Carlos Zambrano | .15 | .40 |
| 19 | Aramis Ramirez | .15 | .40 |
| 20 | Paul Konerko | .15 | .40 |
| 21 | Jermaine Dye | .15 | .40 |
| 22 | Carlos Quentin | .15 | .40 |
| 23 | Jay Bruce | .40 | 1.00 |
| 24 | Edinson Volquez | .15 | .40 |
| 25 | Brandon Phillips | .15 | .40 |
| 26 | Victor Martinez | .15 | .40 |
| 27 | Travis Hafner | .15 | .40 |
| 28 | Kerry Wood | .15 | .40 |
| 29 | Grady Sizemore | .25 | .60 |
| 30 | Cliff Lee | .15 | .40 |
| 31 | Garrett Atkins | .15 | .40 |
| 32 | Miguel Cabrera | .25 | .60 |
| 33 | Magglio Ordonez | .25 | .60 |
| 34 | Carlos Guillen | .15 | .40 |
| 35 | Hanley Ramirez | .40 | 1.00 |
| 36 | Dan Uggla | .15 | .40 |
| 37 | Miguel Tejada | .25 | .60 |
| 38 | Lance Berkman | .25 | .60 |
| 39 | Carlos Lee | .15 | .40 |
| 40 | Jose Guillen | .15 | .40 |
| 41 | Alex Gordon | .15 | .40 |
| 42 | Vladimir Guerrero | .40 | 1.00 |
| 43 | Torii Hunter | .40 | 1.00 |
| 44 | Bobby Abreu | .15 | .40 |
| 45 | Russell Martin | .15 | .40 |
| 46 | Matt Kemp | .40 | 1.00 |
| 47 | Manny Ramirez | .40 | 1.00 |
| 48 | Ryan Braun | .50 | 1.25 |
| 49 | Prince Fielder | .40 | 1.00 |
| 50 | Corey Hart | .15 | .40 |
| 51 | Joe Nathan | .15 | .40 |
| 52 | Justin Morneau | .25 | .60 |
| 53 | Joe Mauer | .25 | .60 |
| 54 | Jose Reyes | .25 | .60 |
| 55 | Johan Santana | .40 | 1.00 |
| 56 | Francisco Rodriguez | .25 | .60 |
| 57 | David Wright | .50 | 1.25 |
| 58 | Carlos Beltran | .15 | .40 |
| 59 | Mark Teixeira | .40 | 1.00 |
| 60 | Andy Pettitte | .25 | .60 |
| 61 | Joba Chamberlain | .50 | 1.25 |
| 62 | Derek Jeter | 1.00 | 2.50 |
| 63 | Chien-Ming Wang | .40 | 1.00 |
| 64 | CC Sabathia | .25 | .60 |
| 65 | Alex Rodriguez | .60 | 1.50 |
| 66 | Matt Holliday | .25 | .60 |
| 67 | Jason Giambi | .15 | .40 |
| 68 | Jack Cust | .15 | .40 |
| 69 | Ryan Howard | .50 | 1.25 |
| 70 | Jimmy Rollins | .25 | .60 |
| 71 | Chase Utley | .40 | 1.00 |
| 72 | Nate McLouth | .15 | .40 |
| 73 | Ryan Doumit | .15 | .40 |
| 74 | Jake Peavy | .25 | .60 |
| 75 | Adrian Gonzalez | .25 | .60 |
| 76 | Tim Lincecum | .50 | 1.25 |
| 77 | Aaron Rowand | .15 | .40 |
| 78 | Randy Johnson | .40 | 1.00 |
| 79 | Ken Griffey Jr. | .60 | 1.50 |
| 80 | Ichiro Suzuki | .60 | 1.50 |
| 81 | Felix Hernandez | .25 | .60 |
| 82 | Ryan Ludwick | .25 | .60 |
| 83 | Rick Ankiel | .25 | .60 |
| 84 | Albert Pujols | 1.00 | 2.50 |
| 85 | Scott Kazmir | .25 | .60 |
| 86 | Evan Longoria | .60 | 1.50 |
| 87 | Carl Crawford | .25 | .60 |
| 88 | B.J. Upton | .25 | .60 |
| 89 | Josh Hamilton | .40 | 1.00 |
| 90 | Ian Kinsler | .25 | .60 |
| 91 | Vernon Wells | .15 | .40 |
| 92 | Roy Halladay | .40 | 1.00 |
| 93 | Alex Rios | .15 | .40 |
| 94 | Adam Dunn | .25 | .60 |
| 95 | Ryan Zimmerman | .25 | .60 |
| 96 | Rick Porcello RC | 1.50 | 4.00 |
| 97 | Colby Rasmus (RC) | .60 | 1.50 |
| 98 | James McDonald RC | .60 | 1.50 |
| 99 | Koji Uehara RC | 1.00 | 2.50 |
| 100 | Derek Holland RC | 1.00 | 2.50 |

Each year we refine the process of developing the most accurate and up-to-date information for this book. I believe this year's Price Guide is our best yet. Thanks again to all the contributors nationwide (listed below) as well as our staff here in Dallas.

Those who have worked closely with us on this and many other books have again proven themselves invaluable: Ed Allan, Frank and Vivian Barning, Levi Bleam and Jim Fleck (707 Sportscards), T. Scott Brandon, Peter Brennan, Ray Bright, Card Collectors Co., Dwight Chapin, Theo Chen, Barry Colla, Bill and Diane Dodge, Brett Domue, Dan Even, David Festberg, Fleer/SkyBox (Josh Perlman), Steve Freedman, Gervise Ford, Larry and Jeff Fritsch, Tony Galovich, Georgia Music and Sports (Dick DeCourcey), Dick Gilkeson, Steve Gold (AU Sports), Bill Goodwin (St. Louis Baseball Cards), Mike and Howard Gordon, George Grauer, Steve Green (STB Sports), John Greenwald, Bill Henderson, Jerry and Etta Hersh, Mike Hersh, Neil Hoppenworth, Hunt Auction, Mike Jaspersen, Jay and Mary Kasper (Jay's Emporium), Jerry Katz, Pete Kennedy, David Kohler (SportsCards Plus), Terry Knouse (Tik and Tik), Tom Leon, Lew Lipset (Four Base Hits), Mike Livingston (U-Trading Cards), Mark Macrae, Bill Madden, Bill Mastro, Dr.William McAvoy, Michael McDonald, Mid-Atlantic Sports Cards (Bill Bossert), Gary Mills, Ernie Montella, Brian Morris, Mike Mosier (Columbia City Collectibles Co.), B.A. Murry, Ralph Nozaki, Mike O'Brien, Oldies and Goodies (Nigel Spill), Oregon Trail Auctions, Pacific Trading Cards (Mike Cramer and Mike Monson), Playoff Trading Cards (Ben Ecklar, Steve Judd, and Tracy Hackler), Jack Pollard, Jeff Prillaman, Pat Quinn, Jerald Reichstein (Fabulous Cardboard), Tom Reid, Gavin Riley, Clifton Rouse, John Rumierz, Pat Blandford, Lonn Passon and Kevin Savage (Sports Gallery), Gary Sawatski and Jim Justus (The Wizards of Odd), Mike Schechter, Bill and Darlene Shafer, Barry Sloate, John E. Spalding, Phil Spector, Murvin Sterling, Ted Taylor, Lee Temanson, Topps (Marty Appel), Treat (Harold Anderson), Ed Twombly, Upper Deck (Justin Kanoya), Wayne Varner, Rob Veres, Bill Vizas, Waukesha Sportscards, Bill Wesslund (Portland Sports Card Co.), Kit Young, Rick Young, Ted Zanidakis, Robert Zanze (Z-Cards and Sports), Bill Zimpleman, and Dean Zindler. Finally we give a special acknowledgment to the late Dennis W. Eckes, "Mr. Sport Americana." The success of the Beckett Price Guides has always been the result of a team effort.

It is very difficult to be "accurate" — one can only do one's best. But this job is especially difficult since we're shooting at a moving target: Prices are fluctuating all the time. Having several full-time pricing experts has definitely proven to be better than just one, and I thank all of them for working together to provide you, our readers, with the most accurate prices possible.

Many people have provided price input, illustrative material, checklist verifications, errata, and/or background information. We should like to individually thank AbD Cards (Dale Wesolewski), Action Card Sales, Jerry Adamic, Johnny and Sandy Adams, Mehdi Ahlei, Alex's MVP Cards & Comics, Doug Allen, Will Allison, Dennis Anderson, Ed Anderson, Shane Anderson, Ellis Anmuth, Alan Applegate, Ric Apter, Clyde Archer, Randy Archer, Burl Armstrong, Neil Armstrong, Carlos Ayala, B and J Sportscards, Jeremy Bachman, Dave Bailey, Ball Four Cards (Frank and Steve Pemper), Bob Bartosz, Bubba Bennett, Carl Berg, Beulah Sports (Jeff Blatt), B.J. Sportscollectables, David Boedicker (The Wild Pitch Inc.), Louis Bollman, Tim Bond, Andrew Bosarge, Terry Boyd, Dan Brandenberry, Jeff Breitenfield, Scott Brockleman, John Broggi, Virgil Burns, Greg Bussineau, David Byer, California Card Co., Capital Cards, Danny Cariseo, Carl Carlson (C.T.S.), Jim Carr, Ira Cetron, Sandy Chan, Ric Chandgie, Ray Cherry, Bigg Wayne Christian, Josh Chidester, Michael and Abe Citron, Dr. Jeffrey Clair, Michael Cohen, Tom Cohoon (Cardboard Dreams), Gary Collett, Rick Cosmen (RC Card Co.), Lou Costanzo (Champion Sports), Mike Coyne, Tony Craig (T.C. Card Co.), Solomon Cramer, Kevin Crane, Taylor Crane, Chad Cripe, Scott Crump, Allen Custer, Dave Dame, Scott Dantio, Dee's Baseball Cards (Dee Robinson), Joe Delgrippo, Mike DeLuca, Ken Dinerman (California Cruizers), Rob DiSalvatore, Cliff Dolgins, Discount Dorothy, Richard Dolloff (Dolloff Coin Center), Joe Donato, Jerry Dong, Pat Dorsey, Double Play Baseball Cards, Joe Drelich, Richard Duglin (Baseball Cards-N-More), The Dugout, Ken Edick (Home Plate of Utah), Brad Englehardt, Doak Ewing, Terry Falkner, Mike and Chris Fanning, Linda Ferrigno and Mark Mezzardi, Jay Finglass, Bob Flitter, Fremont Fong, Paul Franzetti, Ron Frasier, Tom Freeman, Bob Frye, Bill Fusaro, Chris Gala, Richard Galasso, David Garza, David Gaumer, Georgetown Card Exchange, David Giove, Dick Goddard, Jeff Goldstein, Ron Gomez, Rich Gove, Jay and Jan Grinsby, Bob Grissett, Gerry Guenther, Neil Gubitz (What-A-Card), Hall's Nostalgia, Hershell Hanks, Gregg Hara, Todd Harrell, Robert Harrison, Steve Hart, Floyd Haynes (H and H Baseball Cards), Kevin Heffner, Joel Hellman, Hit and Run Cards (Jon, David, and Kirk Peterson), Vinny Ho, Johnny Hustle Card Co., John Inouye, Vern Isenberg, Dale Jackson, Marshall Jackson, Mike Jardina, Paul Jastrzembski, Jeff's Sports Cards, Donn Jennings Cards, George Johnson, Craig Jones, Chuck Juliana, Nick Kardoulias, Scott Kashner, Frank and Rose Katen, Kevin's Kards, Kingdom Collectibles, Inc., John Klassnik, Rich Klein, Steve Kluback, Don Knutsen, Gregg Kohn,

Mike Kohlhas, Bob & Bryan Kornfield, Carl and Maryanne Laron, Howard Lau, Richard S. Lawrence, William Lawrence, Brent Lee, Morley Leeking, Irv Lerner, Larry and Sally Levine, Larry Loeschen (A and J Sportscards), Neil Lopez, Kendall Loyd (Orlando Sportscards South), Steve Lowe, Jim Macie, Peter Maltin, Paul Marchant, Brian Marcy, Scott Martinez, James S. Maxwell Jr., McDag Productions Inc., Bob McDonald, Steve McHenry, Tony McLaughlin, Mendal Mearkle, Carlos Medina, Ken Melanson, William Mendel, Blake Meyer (Lone Star Sportscards), Tim Meyer, Joe Michalowicz, Lee Milazzo, Cary S. Miller, George Miller, Wayne Miller, Dick Millerd, Frank Mineo, Mitchell's Baseball Cards, John Morales, William Munn, Mark Murphy, Robert Nappe, National Sportscard Exchange, Roger Neufeldt, Steve Novella, Bud Obermeyer, John O'Hara, Glenn Olson, Scott Olson, Ron Oser, Luther Owen, Earle Parrish, Clay Pasternack, Michael Perrotta, Tom Pfirrmann, Don Phlong, Loran Pulver, Bob Ragonese, Bryan Rappaport, Don and Tom Ras, Robert M. Ray, Phil Regli, Rob Resnick, Dave Reynolds, Carson Ritchey, Bill Rodman, Craig Roehrig, Mike Sablow, Terry Sack, Thomas Salem, Barry Sanders, Grant Sandground, Jon Sands, Tony Scarpa, John Schad, Dave Schau (Baseball Cards), Masa Shinohara, Eddie Silard, Mike Slepcevic, Sam Sliheet, Art Smith, Lynn and Todd Solt, Jerry Sorice, Don Spagnolo, Sports Card Fan-Attic, The Sport Hobbyist, Norm Stapleton, Bill Steinberg, Lisa Stellato (Never Enough Cards), Rob Stenzel, Jason Stern, Andy Stoltz, Rob Stenzel, Bill Stone, Ted Straka, Tim Strandberg (East Texas Sports Cards), Edward Strauss, Strike Three, Richard Strobino, Kevin Struss, Superior Sport Card, Dr. Richard Swales, George Tahinos, Brent Thorton, Ian Taylor, The The Thirdhand Shoppe, Brent Thornton, Paul Thornton, Jim and Sally Thurtell, Bud Tompkins (Minnesota Connection), Philip J. Tremont, Ralph Triplette, Umpire's Choice Inc., Eric Unglaub, Hoyt Vanderpool, Steven Wagman, T. Wall, Gary A. Walter, Joe and John Weisenburger (The Wise Guys), Brian and Mike Wentz (BMW Sportscards), Richard West, Mike Wheat, Richard Wiercinski, Don Williams (Robin's Nest of Dolls), Jeff Williams, John Williams, Kent and Louise Williams, Craig Williamson, Rich Wojtasick, John Wolf Jr., Jay Wolt (Cavalcade of Sports), Joe Yanello, Peter Yee, Tom Zocco, Mark Zubrensky, and Tim Zwick.

Every year we make active solicitations for expert input. We are particularly appreciative of help (however extensive or cursory) provided for this volume. We receive many inquiries, comments, and questions regarding material within this book. In fact, each and every one is read and digested. Time constraints, however, prevent us from personally replying. But keep sharing your knowledge. Your letters and input are part of the "big picture" of hobby information we can pass along to readers in our books and magazines. Even though we cannot respond to each letter, you are making significant contributions to the hobby through your interest and comments.

The effort to continually refine and improve this book also involves a growing number of people and types of expertise on our home team. Our company boasts a substantial Sports Data Publishing team, which strengthens our ability to provide comprehensive analysis of the marketplace. SDP capably handled numerous technical details and provided able assistance in the preparation of this edition.

Our analysts played a major part in compiling this year's book, traveling thousands of miles during the past year to attend sports card shows and visit card shops around the United States and Canada. The Beckett baseball specialist is Brian Fleischer (Senior Market Analyst). His pricing analysis and careful proofreading were key contributions to the accuracy of this annual.

He was ably assisted by Matthew Brumley, who helped enter new sets and pricing information and handled the ever-growing quantity of cards we need organized for efforts such as this.

The effort was led by Bill Sutherland (Director, Data Publishing) and Dan Hitt (Senior Manager of Sports Data Publishing) and was assisted by the rest of the Price Guide team: Jeff Camay, Bryan Hornbeck, Keith Hower, Aldous Llanos, Arsenio Tan and Tim Trout.

The price gathering and analytical talents of this fine group of hobbyists have helped make our Beckett team stronger, while making this guide and its companion monthly Price Guide more widely recognized as the hobby's most reliable and relied upon sources of pricing information.

Gean Paul Figari and Pete Adauto were responsible for the layout of the book. The reason this book looks as good as it does is due to the hard work and expertise they put into making this volume each year.

A great many talented and hard working individuals have been instrumental in this growth and success. Our whole team is to be congratulated for what we together have accomplished.

The whole Beckett Media team has our thanks for a job well done.

$10 EACH!

# The ALL-TIME Fan Favorite
# GRADING SPECIAL!

## 10-10-10

Submit 10 or more
cards for grading at the
10-day service level and
pay only $10 per card

## Save $40 or more!

*HURRY, this offer expires
March 31, 2011*